Maximum fines for disobedience to court orders and contempt of court:

PCC(S)A 2000, Sch 7, para 2	Breach of requirement of supervision order	£1,000
PCC(S)A 2000, Sch 3, para 4	Breach of requirement of 'old-style' community order	£1,000
PCC(S)A 2000, s 123(3)	Breach of requirement of suspended sentence supervision order	£1,000
MCA 1980, s 63(3)(*a*)	Disobedience of order other than for payment of money	£5,000
MCA 1980, s 97(4)	Refusal to give evidence	£2,500
CCA 1981, ss 12(2) and 14(2)	Contempt of court	£2,500
PCC(S)A 2000, s 131(1)	Maximum amount payable under a **compensation** order	£5,000
PCC(S)A 2000, s 150	Maximum **recognizance from parent** or guardian (or fine for refusal)	£1,000

continued inside back cover

CALENDAR 2007

GREENWICH MEAN TIME THROUGH OUT, TAKEN FOR LONDON

January

M	W	Sun R	S
1	M	8 06	16 02
2	T	8 06	16 03
3	W	8 06	16 04
4	T	8 06	16 05
5	F	8 06	16 07
6	S	8 05	16 08
7	S	8 05	16 09
8	M	8 04	16 10
9	T	8 04	16 12
10	W	8 03	16 13
11	T	8 03	16 14
12	F	8 02	16 16
13	S	8 01	16 17
14	S	8 01	16 19
15	M	8 00	16 20
16	T	7 59	16 22
17	W	7 58	16 24
18	T	7 57	16 25
19	F	7 56	16 27
20	S	7 55	16 28
21	S	7 54	16 30
22	M	7 53	16 32
23	T	7 52	16 34
24	W	7 51	16 35
25	T	7 49	16 37
26	F	7 48	16 39
27	S	7 47	16 41
28	S	7 45	16 42
29	M	7 44	16 44
30	T	7 43	16 46
31	W	7 41	16 48

February

M	W	Sun R	S
1	T	7 40	16 49
2	F	7 38	16 51
3	S	7 37	16 53
4	S	7 35	16 55
5	M	7 33	16 57
6	T	7 32	16 59
7	W	7 30	17 00
8	T	7 28	17 02
9	F	7 26	17 04
10	S	7 25	17 06
11	S	7 23	17 08
12	M	7 21	17 10
13	T	7 19	17 11
14	W	7 17	17 13
15	T	7 15	17 15
16	F	7 13	17 17
17	S	7 12	17 19
18	S	7 10	17 20
19	M	7 08	17 22
20	T	7 06	17 24
21	W	7 04	17 26
22	T	7 02	17 28
23	F	6 59	17 30
24	S	6 57	17 31
25	S	6 55	17 33
26	M	6 53	17 35
27	T	6 51	17 37
28	W	6 49	17 38

March

M	W	Sun R	S
1	T	6 47	17 40
2	F	6 45	17 42
3	S	6 43	17 44
4	S	6 40	17 46
5	M	6 38	17 47
6	T	6 36	17 49
7	W	6 34	17 51
8	T	6 32	17 52
9	F	6 29	17 54
10	S	6 27	17 56
11	S	6 25	17 58
12	M	6 23	17 59
13	T	6 20	18 01
14	W	6 18	18 03
15	T	6 16	18 05
16	F	6 14	18 06
17	S	6 11	18 08
18	S	6 09	18 10
19	M	6 07	18 11
20	T	6 04	18 13
21	W	6 02	18 15
22	T	6 00	18 16
23	F	5 58	18 18
24	S	5 55	18 20
25	S	5 53	18 21
26	M	5 51	18 23
27	T	5 48	18 25
28	W	5 46	19 27
29	T	5 44	19 28
30	F	5 42	19 30
31	S	5 39	19 32

April

M	W	Sun R	S
1	S	6 37	19 33
2	M	6 35	19 35
3	T	6 33	19 37
4	W	6 30	19 38
5	T	6 28	19 40
6	F	6 26	19 42
7	S	6 24	19 43
8	S	6 21	19 45
9	M	6 19	19 47
10	T	6 17	19 48
11	W	6 15	19 50
12	T	6 13	19 52
13	F	6 10	19 53
14	S	6 08	19 55
15	S	6 06	19 57
16	M	6 04	19 58
17	T	6 02	20 00
18	W	6 00	20 02
19	T	5 58	20 03
20	F	5 55	20 05
21	S	5 53	20 07
22	S	5 51	20 08
23	M	5 49	20 10
24	T	5 47	20 12
25	W	5 45	20 13
26	T	5 43	20 15
27	F	5 41	20 17
28	S	5 39	20 18
29	S	5 37	20 20
30	M	5 35	20 22

May

M	W	Sun R	S
1	T	5 33	20 23
2	W	5 32	20 25
3	T	5 30	20 27
4	F	5 28	20 28
5	S	5 26	20 30
6	S	5 24	20 31
7	M	5 23	20 33
8	T	5 21	20 35
9	W	5 19	20 36
10	T	5 17	20 38
11	F	5 16	20 39
12	S	5 14	20 41
13	S	5 13	20 42
14	M	5 11	20 44
15	T	5 10	20 45
16	W	5 08	20 47
17	T	5 07	20 48
18	F	5 05	20 50
19	S	5 04	20 51
20	S	5 02	20 53
21	M	5 01	20 54
22	T	5 00	20 56
23	W	4 59	20 57
24	T	4 58	20 58
25	F	4 56	21 00
26	S	4 55	21 01
27	S	4 54	21 02
28	M	4 53	21 03
29	T	4 52	21 05
30	W	4 51	21 06
31	T	4 50	21 07

June

M	W	Sun R	S
1	F	4 50	21 08
2	S	4 49	21 09
3	S	4 48	21 10
4	M	4 47	21 11
5	T	4 47	21 12
6	W	4 46	21 13
7	T	4 46	21 14
8	F	4 45	21 15
9	S	4 45	21 16
10	S	4 44	21 16
11	M	4 44	21 17
12	T	4 44	21 18
13	W	4 43	21 18
14	T	4 43	21 19
15	F	4 43	21 19
16	S	4 43	21 20
17	S	4 43	21 20
18	M	4 43	21 21
19	T	4 43	21 21
20	W	4 43	21 21
21	T	4 43	21 22
22	F	4 43	21 22
23	S	4 44	21 22
24	S	4 44	21 22
25	M	4 44	21 22
26	T	4 45	21 22
27	W	4 45	21 22
28	T	4 46	21 22
29	F	4 46	21 22
30	S	4 47	21 21

July

M	W	Sun R	S
1	S	4 47	21 21
2	M	4 48	21 21
3	T	4 49	21 20
4	W	4 50	21 20
5	T	4 50	21 20
6	F	4 51	21 19
7	S	4 52	21 18
8	S	4 53	21 18
9	M	4 54	21 17
10	T	4 55	21 16
11	W	4 56	21 16
12	T	4 57	21 15
13	F	4 58	21 14
14	S	4 59	21 13
15	S	5 01	21 12
16	M	5 02	21 11
17	T	5 03	21 10
18	W	5 04	21 09
19	T	5 05	21 08
20	F	5 07	21 06
21	S	5 08	21 05
22	S	5 09	21 04
23	M	5 11	21 03
24	T	5 12	21 01
25	W	5 13	21 00
26	T	5 15	20 59
27	F	5 16	20 57
28	S	5 18	20 56
29	S	5 19	20 54
30	M	5 21	20 53
31	T	5 22	20 51

August

M	W	Sun R	S
1	W	5 24	20 49
2	T	5 25	20 48
3	F	5 27	20 46
4	S	5 28	20 44
5	S	5 30	20 43
6	M	5 31	20 41
7	T	5 33	20 39
8	W	5 34	20 37
9	T	5 36	20 35
10	F	5 37	20 34
11	S	5 39	20 32
12	S	5 41	20 30
13	M	5 42	20 28
14	T	5 44	20 26
15	W	5 45	20 24
16	T	5 47	20 22
17	F	5 49	20 20
18	S	5 50	20 18
19	S	5 52	20 16
20	M	5 53	20 14
21	T	5 55	20 12
22	W	5 57	20 10
23	T	5 58	20 08
24	F	6 00	20 05
25	S	6 01	20 03
26	S	6 03	20 01
27	M	6 04	19 59
28	T	6 06	19 57
29	W	6 08	19 55
30	T	6 09	19 52
31	F	6 11	19 50

September

M	W	Sun R	S
1	S	6 12	19 48
2	S	6 14	19 46
3	M	6 16	19 44
4	T	6 17	19 41
5	W	6 19	19 39
6	T	6 20	19 37
7	F	6 22	19 35
8	S	6 24	19 32
9	S	6 25	19 30
10	M	6 27	19 28
11	T	6 28	19 25
12	W	6 30	19 23
13	T	6 32	19 21
14	F	6 33	19 19
15	S	6 35	19 16
16	S	6 36	19 14
17	M	6 38	19 12
18	T	6 40	19 09
19	W	6 41	19 07
20	T	6 43	19 05
21	F	6 44	19 02
22	S	6 46	19 00
23	S	6 48	18 58
24	M	6 49	18 55
25	T	6 51	18 53
26	W	6 52	18 51
27	T	6 54	18 49
28	F	6 56	18 46
29	S	6 57	18 44
30	S	6 59	18 42

October

M	W	Sun R	S
1	M	7 01	18 39
2	T	7 02	18 37
3	W	7 04	18 35
4	T	7 05	18 33
5	F	7 07	18 30
6	S	7 09	18 28
7	S	7 10	18 26
8	M	7 12	18 24
9	T	7 14	18 21
10	W	7 15	18 19
11	T	7 17	18 17
12	F	7 19	18 15
13	S	7 20	18 13
14	S	7 22	18 11
15	M	7 24	18 08
16	T	7 26	18 06
17	W	7 27	18 04
18	T	7 29	18 02
19	F	7 31	18 00
20	S	7 32	17 58
21	S	7 34	17 56
22	M	7 36	17 54
23	T	7 38	17 52
24	W	7 39	17 50
25	T	7 41	17 48
26	F	7 43	17 46
27	S	7 45	17 44
28	S	7 46	17 42
29	M	7 48	17 40
30	T	7 50	17 38
31	W	7 52	17 36

November

M	W	Sun R	S
1	T	6 53	16 34
2	F	6 55	16 33
3	S	6 57	16 31
4	S	6 59	16 29
5	M	7 00	16 27
6	T	7 02	16 26
7	W	7 04	16 24
8	T	7 06	16 22
9	F	7 07	16 21
10	S	7 09	16 19
11	S	7 11	16 18
12	M	7 13	16 16
13	T	7 14	16 15
14	W	7 16	16 13
15	T	7 18	16 12
16	F	7 20	16 11
17	S	7 21	16 09
18	S	7 23	16 08
19	M	7 24	16 07
20	T	7 26	16 06
21	W	7 28	16 04
22	T	7 30	16 03
23	F	7 31	16 02
24	S	7 33	16 01
25	S	7 34	16 00
26	M	7 36	15 59
27	T	7 37	15 58
28	W	7 39	15 58
29	T	7 40	15 57
30	F	7 42	15 56

December

M	W	Sun R	S
1	S	7 43	15 55
2	S	7 45	15 55
3	M	7 46	15 54
4	T	7 47	15 54
5	W	7 49	15 53
6	T	7 50	15 53
7	F	7 51	15 52
8	S	7 52	15 52
9	S	7 54	15 52
10	M	7 55	15 52
11	T	7 56	15 52
12	W	7 57	15 52
13	T	7 58	15 52
14	F	7 59	15 52
15	S	8 00	15 52
16	S	8 00	15 52
17	M	8 01	15 52
18	T	8 02	15 52
19	W	8 03	15 53
20	T	8 03	15 53
21	F	8 04	15 53
22	S	8 04	15 54
23	S	8 05	15 54
24	M	8 05	15 55
25	T	8 05	15 56
26	W	8 06	15 56
27	T	8 06	15 57
28	F	8 06	15 58
29	S	8 06	15 59
30	S	8 06	16 00
31	M	8 06	16 01

Bank holidays: January 1, April 6, 9, May 7, 28, August 27, December 25, 26

NOTE: These times are in GMT, except between 0100 on Mar 25 and 0100 on Oct 28, when the times are in BST (1 hour in advance of GMT).

Reproduced, with permission, from data supplied by HM Nautical Almanac Office © Council for the Central Laboratory for the Research Councils.

2006

January – April

	January					February					March					April			
Mon.	[2]	9	16	23	30	6	13	20	27		6	13	20	27		3	10	[17]	24
Tues.	3	10	17	24	31	7	14	21	28		7	14	21	28		4	11	18	25
Wed.	4	11	18	25		1	8	15	22		1	8	15	22	29	5	12	19	26
Thur.	5	12	19	26		2	9	16	23		2	9	16	23	30	6	13	20	27
Fri.	6	13	20	27		3	10	17	24		3	10	17	24	31	7	[14]	21	28
Sat.	7	14	21	28		4	11	18	25		4	11	18	25		1	8	15	22	29
Sun.	1	8	15	22	29	5	12	19	26		5	12	19	26		2	9	16	23	30

May – August

	May					June					July					August			
Mon.	[1]	8	15	22	[29]	5	12	19	26		3	10	17	24	31	7	14	21	[28]
Tues.	2	9	16	23	30	6	13	20	27		4	11	18	25		1	8	15	22	29
Wed.	3	10	17	24	31	7	14	21	28		5	12	19	26		2	9	16	23	30
Thur.	4	11	18	25		1	8	15	22	29	6	13	20	27		3	10	17	24	31
Fri.	5	12	19	26		2	9	16	23	30	7	14	21	28		4	11	18	25
Sat.	6	13	20	27		3	10	17	24		1	8	15	22	29	5	12	19	26
Sun.	7	14	21	28		4	11	18	25		2	9	16	23	30	6	13	20	27

September – December

	September					October					November					December			
Mon.	4	11	18	25		2	9	16	23	30	6	13	20	27		4	11	18	[25]
Tues.	5	12	19	26		3	10	17	24	31	7	14	21	28		5	12	19	[26]
Wed.	6	13	20	27		4	11	18	25		1	8	15	22	29	6	13	20	27
Thur.	7	14	21	28		5	12	19	26		2	9	16	23	30	7	14	21	28
Fri.	1	8	15	22	29	6	13	20	27		3	10	17	24		1	8	15	22	29
Sat.	2	9	16	23	30	7	14	21	28		4	11	18	25		2	9	16	23	30
Sun.	3	10	17	24		1	8	15	22	29	5	12	19	26		3	10	17	24	31

2008

January – April

	January					February					March					April			
Mon.	7	14	21	28		4	11	18	25		3	10	17	[24]	31	7	14	21	28
Tues.	[1]	8	15	22	29	5	12	19	26		4	11	18	25		1	8	15	22	29
Wed.	2	9	16	23	30	6	13	20	27		5	12	19	26		2	9	16	23	30
Thur.	3	10	17	24	31	7	14	21	28		6	13	20	27		3	10	17	24
Fri.	4	11	18	25		1	8	15	22	29	7	14	[21]	28		4	11	18	25
Sat.	5	12	19	26		2	9	16	23		1	8	15	22	29	5	12	19	26
Sun.	6	13	20	27		3	10	17	24		2	9	16	23	30	6	13	20	27

May – August

	May					June					July					August			
Mon.	[5]	12	19	[26]		2	9	16	23	30	7	14	21	28		4	11	18	[25]
Tues.	6	13	20	27		3	10	17	24		1	8	15	22	29	5	12	19	26
Wed.	7	14	21	28		4	11	18	25		2	9	16	23	30	6	13	20	27
Thur.	1	8	15	22	29	5	12	19	26		3	10	17	24	31	7	14	21	28
Fri.	2	9	16	23	30	6	13	20	27		4	11	18	25		1	8	15	22	29
Sat.	3	10	17	24	31	7	14	21	28		5	12	19	26		2	9	16	23	30
Sun.	4	11	18	25		1	8	15	22	29	6	13	20	27		3	10	17	24	31

September – December

	September					October					November					December			
Mon.	1	8	15	22	29	6	13	20	27		3	10	17	24		1	8	15	22	29
Tues.	2	9	16	23	30	7	14	21	28		4	11	18	25		2	9	16	23	30
Wed.	3	10	17	24		1	8	15	22	29	5	12	19	26		3	10	17	24	31
Thur.	4	11	18	25		2	9	16	23	30	6	13	20	27		4	11	18	[25]
Fri.	5	12	19	26		3	10	17	24	31	7	14	21	28		5	12	19	[26]
Sat.	6	13	20	27		4	11	18	25		1	8	15	22	29	6	13	20	27
Sun.	7	14	21	28		5	12	19	26		2	9	16	23	30	7	14	21	28

2007

	January								**February**							**March**				
Mon.	1	8	15	22	29	.	.	5	12	19	26	.	.	5	12	19	26	.
Tues.	2	9	16	23	30	.	.	6	13	20	27	.	.	6	13	20	27	.
Wed.	3	10	17	24	31	.	.	7	14	21	28	.	.	7	14	21	28	.
Thur.	4	11	18	25	.	.	1	8	15	22	.	.	1	8	15	22	29	.
Fri.	5	12	19	26	.	.	2	9	16	23	.	.	2	9	16	23	30	.
Sat.	6	13	20	27	.	.	3	10	17	24	.	.	3	10	17	24	31	.
Sun.	7	14	21	28	.	.	4	11	18	25	.	.	4	11	18	25	.	.

	April							**May**						**June**				
Mon.	.	2	9	16	23	30	.	7	14	21	28	.	.	4	11	18	25	.
Tues.	.	3	10	17	24	.	1	8	15	22	29	.	.	5	12	19	26	.
Wed.	.	4	11	18	25	.	2	9	16	23	30	.	.	6	13	20	27	.
Thur.	.	5	12	19	26	.	3	10	17	24	31	.	.	7	14	21	28	.
Fri.	.	6	13	20	27	.	4	11	18	25	.	.	1	8	15	22	29	.
Sat.	.	7	14	21	28	.	5	12	19	26	.	.	2	9	16	23	30	.
Sun.	1	8	15	22	29	.	6	13	20	27	.	.	3	10	17	24	.	.

	July							**August**						**September**				
Mon.	.	2	9	16	23	30	.	6	13	20	27	.	.	3	10	17	24	.
Tues.	.	3	10	17	24	31	.	7	14	21	28	.	.	4	11	18	25	.
Wed.	.	4	11	18	25	.	1	8	15	22	29	.	.	5	12	19	26	.
Thur.	.	5	12	19	26	.	2	9	16	23	30	.	.	6	13	20	27	.
Fri.	.	6	13	20	27	.	3	10	17	24	31	.	.	7	14	21	28	.
Sat.	.	7	14	21	28	.	4	11	18	25	.	.	1	8	15	22	29	.
Sun.	1	8	15	22	29	.	5	12	19	26	.	.	2	9	16	23	30	.

	October							**November**						**December**					
Mon.	1	8	15	22	29	.	.	5	12	19	26	.	.	3	10	17	24	31
Tues.	2	9	16	23	30	.	.	6	13	20	27	.	.	4	11	18	25	.
Wed.	3	10	17	24	31	.	.	7	14	21	28	.	.	5	12	19	26	.
Thur.	4	11	18	25	.	.	1	8	15	22	29	.	.	6	13	20	27	.
Fri.	5	12	19	26	.	.	2	9	16	23	30	.	.	7	14	21	28	.
Sat.	6	13	20	27	.	.	3	10	17	24	.	.	1	8	15	22	29	.
Sun.	7	14	21	28	.	.	4	11	18	25	.	.	2	9	16	23	30	.

2007

	January	February	March
Mon.			
Tues.			
Wed.			
Thur.			
Fri.			
Sat.			
Sun.			

	April	May	June
Mon.			
Tues.			
Wed.			
Thur.			
Fri.			
Sat.			
Sun.			

	July	August	September
Mon.			
Tues.			
Wed.			
Thur.			
Fri.			
Sat.			
Sun.			

	October	November	December
Mon.			
Tues.			
Wed.			
Thur.			
Fri.			
Sat.			
Sun.			

BUTTERWORTHS

STONE'S

JUSTICES' MANUAL

VOLUME 1

Members of the LexisNexis Group worldwide

United Kingdom	LexisNexis Butterworths, a Division of Reed Elsevier (UK) Ltd, Halsbury House, 35 Chancery Lane, London, WC2A 1EL and London House, 20–22 East London Street, Edinburgh EH7 4BQ
Argentina	LexisNexis Argentina, Buenos Aires
Australia	LexisNexis Butterworths, Chatswood, New South Wales
Austria	LexisNexis Verlag ARD Orac GmbH & Co KG, Vienna
Benelux	LexisNexis Benelux, Amsterdam
Canada	LexisNexis Canada, Markham, Ontario
Chile	LexisNexis Chile Ltda, Santiago
China	LexisNexis China, Beijing and Shanghai
France	LexisNexis SA, Paris
Germany	LexisNexis Deutschland GmbH, Munster
Hong Kong	LexisNexis Hong Kong, Hong Kong
India	LexisNexis India, New Delhi
Italy	Giuffrè Editore, Milan
Japan	LexisNexis Japan, Tokyo
Malaysia	Malayan Law Journal Sdn Bhd, Kuala Lumpur
Mexico	LexisNexis Mexico, Mexico
New Zealand	LexisNexis NZ Ltd, Wellington
Poland	Wydawnictwo Prawnicze LexisNexis Sp, Warsaw
Singapore	LexisNexis Singapore, Singapore
South Africa	LexisNexis Butterworths, Durban
USA	LexisNexis, Dayton, Ohio

© Reed Elsevier (UK) Ltd 2007
Published by LexisNexis Butterworths

A CIP Catalogue record for this book is available from the British Library.

ISBN for this volume

ISBN 13: 9781405725248

ISBN 978-1-4057-2524-8

9 781405 725248

ISBN for the complete set of volumes

ISBN 13: 9781405725231

ISBN 978-1-4057-2523-1

9 781405 725231

Typeset by David Lewis XML Associates Limited
Printed and bound in Great Britain by William Clowes Limited, Beccles, Suffolk

Visit LexisNexis Butterworths at www.lexisnexis.co.uk

BUTTERWORTHS

STONE'S
JUSTICES' MANUAL
2007

One Hundred and Thirty-Ninth Edition

edited by

A P CARR

District Judge (Magistrates' Courts)

and

A J TURNER

Barrister, Chambers of Adrian Turner, Eastbourne

Human Rights contributor

Keir Starmer QC

Doughty Street Chambers, visiting lecturer at King's College, London

Licensing contributor

Ian Seeley

Principal Solicitor, Ipswich Borough Council

VOLUME 1

LexisNexis®
Butterworths

EDITORS OF PREVIOUS EDITIONS

PREFACE

Introduction

2006 was a year in which we did not see a Criminal Justice Act (of that name at any rate), but we were all on tenterhooks wondering whether or not we would see the commencement of the remaining – and for magistrates' courts, all important – sentencing provisions of the 2003 Act, ie "custody plus". Certainly, up to the middle of the year at least, the official position was that they would soon come into effect (together with the new, "Auld"-inspired, plea-bargaining-incorporating, allocation scheme). However, not only did that fail to happen, but the government has also put back by two years the extension of the new community sentences to 16 and 17-year-olds.

These delays are no doubt due to pressure on resources, particularly those of the prison and probation services, rather than "second thoughts". That pressure has no doubt come from many directions, but in our view much of it is likely to be attributable to the consequences of longer tariffs for those convicted of murder, the "dangerousness" provisions of the 2003 Act, the increased use of Home Office recall for breach of licence, and the more intensive supervision of many released offenders.

There was, however, one slightly surprising commencement in April 2007. The surcharge provisions of the Domestic Violence, Crime and Victims Act 2004 (ie s 14 which inserts new ss 161A and 161B in the Criminal Justice Act 2003), while by no means forgotten, had ceased to be in the foreground of attention until the decision was made to bring them into effect on 1 April. However, while the commencement order was made and published in good time, problems with the regulations led to last-minute corrections which courts did not receive until the last moment, even though the surcharge (£15) is obligatory in relation to every offender who is fined.

This is not, of course, the first time that a commencement has failed to proceed with the smoothness that one would have liked; but, as we know only too well as the editors of STONE, the pressure of having to prepare and plan for the implementation of so much law in waiting is immense. This work is littered with statutes that are only partly in force, and the task of keeping track of legislative implementation has become a major problem for practitioners, which is made even more difficult, of course, where there are complex transitional provisions to grapple with. In those circumstances, the occasional error is, if not excusable, at least understandable.

Revisions to the narrative

STONE is, of course, a library of materials, but it also includes textbook-style narrative on practice and procedure, evidence, sentencing, road traffic, youth courts, family law and practice, and many other topics. And just as textbooks need to undergo major revision from time to time, to ensure that their style and content remain contemporary, STONE also needs to evolve. In the last issue, we focused our attention on Part I, which contains the largest section of narrative, dealing with all aspects of criminal procedure from offence to conviction. In the current issue, Parts II (Evidence) and III (Sentencing) have been completely re-written; we have also added a number of paragraphs to Part IV (Road Traffic) to summarise and to explain some the most important topics, such as fixed penalties, penalty points and disqualification. We strongly encourage readers to familiarise themselves with the new structure of these narratives. The time spent will be more than repaid in later searches for material.

Criminal Law

Drunkenness and specific intent

The common law rule is that self-induced intoxication is a defence only to offences that require proof of specific intent (see **1–307**). In *R v Heard* (**8–28421C**) the Court of Appeal had to decide whether the offence of sexual assault, contrary to s 3 of the Sexual Offences Act 2003, fell into this category. Police officers were called to the place where the appellant lived. He was found in an emotional state and he had cut himself. He had plainly been drinking heavily. He said that he wanted help and they took him to the hospital at his request. There, in the waiting area, he became abusive and began to sing noisily, so they took him to wait outside. He then began to dance suggestively in front of one of the officers, and put his hand on his own groin. Next, he made to re-enter the hospital and, when discouraged, he became angry. He punched the officer in the stomach. Then he undid his trousers, took his penis in his hand and rubbed it up and down the thigh of the officer. He was arrested.

At the police station, where he was plainly seen to be drunk, he made the remark that: "The only way I can make money is by moving my hips in a sexual way in Soho and I thought I would get away with doing it to you, but I obviously didn't". In interview the next day the appellant said that he could not remember anything that had occurred, but he accepted that when he was ill or in drink he sometimes might "go silly and start stripping". The judge directed the jury that drunkenness was not a defence. Following this, unsurprisingly, the appellant was convicted. He appealed.

The Court noted that before the Sexual Offences Act 2003, indecent assault could only be committed by intentional touching; yet voluntary intoxication was not a defence. Had the position changed in relation to the offence as now constituted? It was held it had not. "Reckless" touching did not suffice. It had to be deliberate, but on the evidence this was plainly the case. The key question of whether or not the offence was one of general or specific intent was then addressed. The court examined the leading authorities, particularly *DPP v Majewski*, in which Lord Simon stated that

> "The best description of 'specific intent' in this sense that I know is contained in the judgment of Fauteux J in *R v George* (1960) 128 Can CC 289, 301, (namely):
> 'In considering the question of *mens rea*, a distinction is to be made between
> (i) intention as applied to acts considered in relation to their purposes and
> (ii) intention as applied to acts apart from their purposes. A general intent attending the commission of an act is, in some cases, the only intent required to constitute the crime while, in others, there must be, in addition to that general intent, a specific intent attending the purpose for the commission of the act.'"

The present offence fell within the general intent category. Accordingly, drunkenness did not afford a defence. Thus, an outcome that the court clearly considered to be highly unattractive was avoided.

Recklessness and awareness of risks

Running into the road without looking and being struck by a vehicle can land you in hospital and also, it seems, in the dock if the car is damaged. That appears to be the consequence of the Administrative Court's decision in *Booth v CPS* (**8–24740**). The appellant, who was tipsy on drink and drugs at the relevant time but still knew what he was doing, ran across a street without first checking that it was safe to do so, and the result was a collision with a car that was being driven with due care and attention which caused damage to the vehicle. He was charged with criminal damage. The justices found that he "would have" appreciated the risk of damage and found him guilty. The appellant contended on appeal by way of case stated that the justices had not applied the right test.

The Administrative Court upheld the conviction. The justices had been entitled to find that although in crossing the road the risk uppermost in someone's mind would be the risk of personal injury, that did not mean that they were not entitled to conclude that whatever other risks the appellant was or was not aware of, he did in fact appreciate the risk to property. If the appellant was conscious of the risk of a collision, inherent in that risk was not only the risk of personal injury but also the risk of damage to property. It was misconceived to argue that the justices' use of the words "would have" rather than "did" clearly indicated that they had employed the wrong test. The justices in fact found that the appellant was aware of the risks associated with running into the road, namely the risk of a collision and the damage to property. So aware, he deliberately put those risks out of his mind and, for reasons of his own, ran out into the path of a car. Having once found that the appellant was aware of the risk of damage to property and closed his mind to it, the justices had employed the correct test of recklessness.

Racially aggravated offences

Part II of the Crime and Disorder Act 1998 created a number of racially (and religiously) aggravated offences in which the normal forms of offences are aggravated by the racial hostility demonstrated to the victim by reason of his membership or presumed membership of a racial group. The meaning of "racial group" has exercised the higher courts on a number of occasions, it being held that "African" denoted membership of such a group, while "South American" did not. Particular debate was occasioned by the use of such general terms as "immigrant" and "foreigner" when coupled with derogatory adjectives. But in general, a broad approach had been taken to interpretation and words such as "immigrant" or "foreigner" could denote a racial group within the terms of Act. The definition in s 28(4) of the 1998 Act is very wide: "racial group" means a group of persons defined by reference to race, colour, nationality (including citizenship) or ethnic or national origins.

In the closing stages of our preparation for this edition, the House of Lords issued its decision in *R v Rogers* (**1–3822**) on whether an offence is racially aggravated for the purposes of s 28(1) of the Crime and Disorder Act 1998. Baroness Hale gave the judgment of the House and set out in clear terms the rationale for such offences.

> "Their essence is the denial of equal respect and dignity to people who are seen as 'other'. This is more deeply hurtful, damaging and disrespectful to the victims than the simple versions of those offences. It is also more damaging to the community as a whole, by denying acceptance to members of certain groups not for their own sake but for the sake of something they can do nothing about."

The facts were straightforward. The defendant was riding a mobility scooter on the pavement as he was incapacitated by arthritis. There was an exchange with three young Spanish women who were walking home after a birthday celebration in a local restaurant. An altercation took place as the defendant tried to get past them, in the course of which he called them "bloody foreigners", telling them to "go back to your own country" and used other threatening conduct. The defendant was subsequently charged and convicted of using racially aggravated abusive or insulting words or behaviour with intent to cause fear or provoke violence, contrary to s 31(1)(*a*) of the Crime and Disorder Act 1998.

The defendant unsuccessfully appealed to the Court of Appeal, and then to the House of Lords. The only question there was whether the words used demonstrated hostility based on the complainants' membership of a racial group as defined in the 1998 Act. For the defendant it was agreed that if he had used the term "bloody Spaniards" that would have demonstrated hostility to a particular racial group, but the words he used were in respect of foreigners as a whole and it was contended that mere xenophobia did not fall within an ordinary person's concept of hostility to a social group.

Baroness Hale noted that the definition in s 28 of the 1998 Act went beyond groups defined by their colour, race or ethnic origin and encompassed both nationality, including citizenship, and national origins. Her Ladyship did not accept the argument that the definition in the 1998 Act required the group to be defined by what it was (eg Spaniards) rather than what it was not (ie non-British – foreigners). Her Ladyship favoured a broad non-technical approach to construction. The victim might be presumed by the offender to be a member of the hated group even when he was not, and the fact that the hostility was based on other factors as well as racism or xenophobia is immaterial. The mischiefs attacked by the aggravated versions of the offences are racism and xenophobia. No particular words are required to be used but although hostility could be demonstrated by wearing of emblems or singing of certain songs, normally it would be by well-known terms of abuse and the law would not go into fine distinctions depending on the particular words used.

Her Ladyship acknowledged that the very width of the meaning of "racial group" for the purposes of s 28(4) did give rise to a danger that the aggravated form of the offence might be brought where vulgar abuse had included racial epithets that did not, in all the circumstances, indicate hostility to the race in question. However, in those circumstances the normal criteria for bringing proceedings would not be met. Whether the conduct of an offender demonstrated hostility to such a group was a question of fact for the decision-maker in the case.

Aiding and Abetting

Criminal liability is not limited to the principal actor but extends to aiders and abettors in accordance with s 8 of the Accessories and Abettors Act 1861 (indictable offences) and s 44 of the Magistrates' Courts Act 1980 (summary and either way offences). What amounts to "aiding and abetting" can give rise to some difficult analysis.

In *R v Webster* (**1–321**) the defendant was charged with aiding and abetting causing death by dangerous driving. The driver, a Mr Westbrook, had been drinking all day when, late in the evening, the appellant gave him and other passengers a lift home in his car. At some point in the journey however, the appellant let Westbrook take over the driving. He then drove erratically and at excessive speed until the vehicle left the road and one of the passengers was thrown from the vehicle and killed.

The prosecution put the case in two ways: the appellant knew it was dangerous to let Westbrook drive because of his state of intoxication; secondly, that during the journey he should have intervened but failed to do so. The Court of Appeal formulated the issue to be decided as "whether it is sufficient, in order to prove the offence of aiding and abetting causing death by dangerous driving to prove knowledge of the intoxicated state of the driver at the time permission is given .... whether a driver can be guilty of dangerous driving when the reason for danger is the state of the driver rather than the manner of the driving".

Their Lordships gave careful consideration to the words of s 2A of the Road Traffic Act, 1988 which defines dangerous driving, and had regard to earlier authorities which had held that evidence of the driver's ingestion of alcohol was admissible in proceedings alleging dangerous driving. In the present case Moses LJ noted that the definition in s 2A(1) referred only to the *manner* of the driving. The definition in sub-s (2) only extended to the dangerous condition of the vehicle and not the dangerous condition of the driver and so the court concluded that it was not sufficient merely to rely on the condition of the driver in order to prove the offence of dangerous driving. The condition of the driver was relevant and admissible but did not determine whether the way in which the defendant drove was dangerous.

As regards the first argument put by the prosecution, liability turned on whether it could prove knowledge of the "essential matters" which constituted the offence of dangerous driving. The prosecution was precluded by the above from arguing that knowledge that Westbrook had been drinking was sufficient, as the drinking was relevant but not conclusive evidence of dangerous driving. The question was whether the appellant foresaw the likelihood that the driver would drive in a dangerous manner. The evidence of the driver's apparent intoxication was not determinative of the issue but evidence to prove the conclusion which a jury had to reach before it convicted the appellant. The more drunk Westbrook appeared to be, the easier it was for the prosecution to prove that the appellant actually foresaw that he was likely to drive dangerously when he permitted him to drive.

As regards the second basis on which the prosecution put its case, there was no issue of foresight but simply knowledge of what was happening at the time. The real issue related to the act of assistance or encouragement. The prosecution had to prove that there was an opportunity to intervene and that his failure to take the opportunity to exercise his right as owner of the car demonstrated the appellant's encouragement or assistance. Here, the court was on more familiar territory having regard to authorities such as *Du Cross v Lambourne* [1907] 1 KB 40.

In the present case, the prosecution had to prove that Westbrook was driving dangerously by virtue of the speed the vehicle was travelling at the time, and that there was an opportunity to intervene. The Court of Appeal then examined the trial judge's directions to the jury. There were errors in the directions relating to the first way in which the prosecution case had been put in that he conflated its being obvious to the appellant that Westbrook would drive dangerously with the conclusion that he did in fact foresee this, and as regards the second basis on which the prosecution case was put, the judge had not left it to the jury to decide whether the appellant had an opportunity to intervene. The Court of Appeal concluded that on the first basis, the conviction could not be sustained, but that on the second basis of liability, the conviction was "inevitable".

Incitement

Incitement is another form of secondary liability and can give rise to problems not so much in determining what amounts to "incitement" but as to where the offence takes place for the purposes of jurisdiction. *R v Tompkins* (**1–383**) reported only briefly in *The Times*, concerned an appeal by the prosecution against a preliminary ruling made in the Crown Court at Stafford that the court had no jurisdiction to try an offence of inciting the distribution of indecent photographs of children. The decision was apparently based on the view that what determined jurisdiction was that the offence being incited was being committed outside the jurisdiction and it was that offence rather than the incitement which determined where the case should be prosecuted. However, on appeal it was conceded that the domestic court had jurisdiction provided that the distribution of the photographs occurred, at least in part, in England and Wales.

Self-defence

The principles of self-defence are by now well established. However, there was an interesting twist revealed in *R v Rashford* (**8–23065**) which concerned an appeal against a conviction for murder on the basis that the summing-up on self-defence was defective.

The appellant had initially been in possession of a knife "for self-protection" and went to the house of the deceased to attack him for a perceived slight earlier that day. An argument then developed into a fight at which stage the appellant produced a knife and began swinging it. The fight continued after a threat by the appellant to stab the deceased who then staggered back and fell to the ground.

The judge gave comprehensive directions to the jury on self-defence but it was alleged that he misdirected the jury by stating that the appellant would not have honestly believed that it was necessary to use force to defend himself because he had gone there for revenge and taken the violence to the deceased. The jury should not have been precluded, in effect, from considering the use of the knife on the spur of the moment for the purpose of self-defence and that the appellant may have contemplated only a physical confrontation and not violence of the magnitude which occurred or the use of a knife.

The Court of Appeal agreed that the mere fact that a defendant goes somewhere in order to exact revenge from the victim does not of itself rule out the possibility that in any violence that ensues, self-defence is necessarily not available as a defence. It must depend on the circumstances. The court approved of the approach of the Scottish courts in *Burns v H M Advocate* [1995] SLT 1090:

> "The question whether self-defence is available depends . . . whether the retaliation is such that the accused is entitled then to defend himself. That depends on whether the violence offered by the victim was so out of proportion to the accused's own actings as to give rise to the reasonable apprehension that he was in an immediate danger from which he had no other means of escape, and whether the violence which he then used was no more than was necessary to preserve his own life or protect himself from serious injury."

In the present case, the Court of Appeal found that the misdirection on self-defence did not, in the circumstances, make the conviction unsafe.

Where self-defence is claimed the defendant is to be judged on the factual situation that he honestly believed to exist, but what if that belief was wrong and arose from self-induced intoxication? It was held in *R v Hatton* (**8–23066**) that a defendant was not entitled to the benefit of what he mistakenly believed to be the situation where that mistaken belief was brought about by the voluntary consumption of alcohol.

Necessity

Medical necessity is not, by reason of art 8 of the ECHR, a defence to possession of cannabis (see *R v Quayle* [2005] EWCA Crim 1415, [2006] 1 All ER 988, [2005] 1 WLR 3642), so a different "Convention route" was tried in *R v Altham* (**1–324**). The appellant had suffered severe injuries in a traffic accident. He had tried all conventional, and some non-conventional, pain relief strategies. In the end he found that only cannabis had any effect. The argument on his behalf before the Court of Appeal ran like this. Article 3 prohibits inhuman or degrading treatment. There are circumstances where severe medical symptoms can amount to such treatment. If the state provides that the only way to avoid those symptoms is to break the criminal law and risk punishment, then the state is subjecting that person to inhuman or degrading treatment. There is therefore a conflict with art 3. This conflict can only be avoided by reading the Misuse of Drugs

Criminal Law   xv

Act 1971 as if it is subject to the defence of medical necessity. Unsurprisingly, the argument, for all its ingenuity, did not find favour with the court. The state had done nothing to cause the appellant's condition or to exacerbate it, and the state did not have a positive obligation to do anything to relieve it. The appellant had turned to cannabis through choice. (Their Lordships also noted that by the date of the appeal he had been prescribed a drug that gave him effective pain relief.)

No defence of preventing crime of "aggression"

In *R v Jones (Margaret)*, *Ayliffe v DPP* and *Swain v DPP* (**8–24907**) the defendants were charged with various counts arising from their disruptive behaviour at operational military airbases. What motivated this was their opposition to the war in Iraq. By way of defence they asserted that the UK's actions in preparing for, declaring and waging war in Iraq were unlawful acts which they were justified in attempting to prevent by the use of reasonable force under s 3 of the Criminal Law Act 1967. At a preparatory hearing the judge ruled: (i) that the issue of the legality of the war was not justiciable in domestic courts since the government was exercising its prerogative powers in relation to foreign policy and the deployment of the armed forces which were issues into which the courts would not inquire; (ii) that section 3 of the 1967 Act was concerned with the prevention of crimes in domestic law; and (iii) that, although under the International Criminal Court Act 2001 certain war crimes were triable in domestic courts, the customary international law crime of aggression was not. On appeal the Court of Appeal affirmed the judge's second and third rulings and dismissed the appeals. The cases then came before the House of Lords.

It was held that the crime of aggression had become established in customary international law, but this did not result in its automatic assimilation into domestic law. It was for Parliament to determine what should be unlawful and, therefore, attract penalties; thus, new offences could only be created by statute. The main purpose of the 1967 Act was to abolish the distinction between felonies and misdemeanours; its focus was entirely domestic and Parliament would not have understood the word "crime" in s 3 as covering crimes recognised under customary international law but not assimilated into domestic law.

Reducing violent crime

There has been a tendency in recent years for legislation which would formerly have been titled "Criminal Justice Act" to be given a variety of different titles reflecting aspects of their contents. At least, with the current volume of criminal justice legislation, this obviates the prospect of the ungainly "Criminal Justice (No 2) Act" etc but on occasion the juxtaposition of different terms can be unfortunate, as with the linking of police and magistrates' courts in the now long repealed "Police and Magistrates' Courts Act 1994". In this edition we include two criminal justice acts manqué: the Police and Justice Act 2006, which we discuss below under "evidence" and the **Violent Crime Relation Act 2006**.

This Act received Royal Assent on 8 November 2006 and is to be brought into force by commencement orders, two of which had been made at the date of going to press. The Act is a collection of disparate measures with the common aim of reducing violent crime. Because of this we have departed from our usual practice of putting the whole of an Act in one Part or under one title. Instead, readers will find its provisions as described below:

– Alcohol-related violence and disorder (ss 1–27) in PART I: MAGISTRATES' COURTS, PROCEDURE (**1–4604** et seq)
– Dangerous weapons, firearms (ss 28–41, 49–51 and Sch 1) in PART VIII: title FIREARMS (**8–10672** et seq)

- Knives etc (ss 42–48) in PART VIII: title OFFENSIVE WEAPONS (**8–22742A** et seq)
- Football (ss 52–53 and Sch 3) in PART VIII: title PUBLIC MEETING AND PUBLIC ORDER (**8–27849G** et seq)
- Sexual offences (ss 54–58 and Sch 4) in PART VIII: title SEXUAL OFFENCES (**8–2842P** et seq)

Among the Act's many provisions we would draw attention to is the introduction, by Chapter 1 (ss 1–14) (when in force), of the "Drinking Banning Order" lasting for between two months and four years where the court considers such an order is necessary to protect persons from criminal and disorderly conduct by the subject of the order. The order must include prohibitions that are thought necessary on the subjects entering licensed premises or club premises. The criteria and procedures are analogous to those currently in force in relation to anti-social behaviour but the penalty for breach is restricted to a criminal offence with a maximum penalty of level 4 on the standard scale.

Other measures to control disorder arising from the misuse of alcohol are contained in Chapter 2 (ss 15–20) which make provision for local authorities to designate alcohol disorder zones and thereby impose charges on licence holders in the area and use the sums raised in this way for purposes to be specified by the Secretary of State. Chapter 3 (ss 21–27) amends the Licensing Act 2003 to allow for a summary review of a premises licence on the application of a senior police officer and a new offence of persistently selling alcohol to children punishable by a fine and suspension of the licence for a period not exceeding 3 months. Further powers are given to the police to give a closure notice prohibiting sales for a period not exceeding 48 hours and s 27 of the 2006 Act provides for a constable to give a direction to a person who represents a risk of disorder to leave the locality and not return for up to 48 hours. The majority of these provisions (except s 27) came into force on 6 April 2007.

The same date also saw the coming into force of other provisions to tighten the law on weapons by making it an offence for a person to use another, eg a child, to look after, hide etc a dangerous weapon for him, and further restrictions will, when s 31 is in force, be placed on air weapons in that those selling such weapons by way of trade must register as firearms dealers. Such sales will have to be face-to-face and the minimum age for acquiring or possessing an air-weapon will be increased by the Act to 18 years. It will also be an offence to fire an air-weapon beyond the boundary of any premises.

As from 12 February 2007 the penalty for possession of a bladed article was increased to 4 years on indictment and when s 43 is in force it will be an offence to sell knives to persons under 18 instead of 16 as formerly. There is also an interesting point of drafting in that the various defences in s 141A of the Criminal Justice Act 1988 formerly contained a provision that the defendant might escape liability if he "proved" one of the specified circumstances. Now the defence is established if he can "show". We await judicial interpretation of the effect, if any, of this change, although the term "show" is used in some other legislation.

This Act also contains the much publicised provision inserting a new s 150AA into the Education Act 1996 providing powers to members of school staff to search pupils for weapons. Similar powers are extended to higher education institutions and attendance centres. Furthermore, the powers of police to search schools under s 139B of the 1988 Act is now based on reasonable grounds for suspicion rather than reasonable grounds for belief as at present. These provisions come into force on 31 May 2007.

As is not uncommon, having regard to the volume of legislation that is being published, there is a need to reflect on what has previously been legislated for, and to correct more obvious errors or omissions. The legislation regarding football banning orders was due to expire on 27 August 2007; the new Act makes provision for the legislation to have indefinite effect. On the other hand those provisions of the Football Spectators Act 1989 making provision for the introduction of a national membership scheme will be repealed without ever coming fully into force.

A significant lacuna when the Sexual Offences act 2003 was brought into force was the lack of provision to deal with the situation where it could not be proved whether the alleged offence was committed pre or post commencement and was therefore to be prosecuted under the Sexual Offences Act 1956 or the 2003 Act. This loophole is now plugged by s 55 of the 2003 Act (in force 12 February 2007) which establishes certain presumptions as to when the offence took place.

A conundrum in civil proceedings for an ASBO has been the six-month limitation period in s 127 of the Magistrates' Courts Act 1980. Section 59 of the 2006 Act will, when in force, disapply this to proceedings under s 1 of the Crime and Disorder Act 1998. The terminology in s 8 of the 1998 Act (parenting orders) is to be updated to reflect that sex offender orders have been replaced by sexual offences prevention orders. No doubt in succeeding months we will receive further commencement orders bringing these and further provisions into effect.

Actual bodily harm

In *R v Dhaliwal* (**8–23116**) the defendant's wife took her own life after enduring, it was alleged, a history of domestic violence, which her diaries related in detail. There was no doubt that the deceased suffered "psychological damage" as a result of the defendant's ill treatment, but it did not amount to recognisable "psychiatric illness" on the medical evidence and, without this, the Court of Appeal agreed with the trial judge that there could be no actual bodily harm. To blur the distinction between psychiatric illness and psychological injury that fell short of it would involve upsetting a well established line of authority and would pose considerable problems for judges and juries.

Anti-social behaviour

Anti-social behaviour has continued to provide a steady stream of cases for the courts, although recent case law has tended to focus more on closure orders rather than ASBOs. Before we move on to closure orders we might note the point raised in *R v Nicholson* (**1–3804**). The defendant was an animal rights campaigner who was made subject to an ASBO which prohibited her from going within 500 metres of five premises identified in the order. Subsequently, she took part in a demonstration within 500 metres of one of those premises. She was prosecuted for breach of the ASBO and pleaded not guilty. She admitted being where she was alleged to be and that she had not carefully checked the terms of the order, in particular the inclusion in it of the said premises. Her basis of plea was that she had a reasonable excuse because she had no recollection of ever having heard before, or at the demonstration, of a reference to those premises.

The matters came for trial and at a preliminary hearing, the judge ruled that such an offence was one of "strict liability" and that the qualification "without reasonable excuse" should be narrowly construed to exclude ignorance or forgetfulness and misunderstanding of the clear terms of an order. In the light of that ruling the defendant pleaded guilty.

In the Court of Appeal it was submitted that the words "reasonable excuse" should bear their ordinary meaning and that ignorance or forgetfulness or misunderstanding of the terms of the ASBO could amount to a reasonable excuse.

Auld LJ noted there was no authority on the meaning of "without reasonable excuse" in this context although there was in connexion with possession of offensive weapons and breach of a restraining order. His Lordship distinguished the more restrictive scope allowed to forgetfulness in cases of offensive weapons and preferred the approach in *R v Evans* [2005] 1 Cr App R 32 in relation to breach of a restraining order as he could see no difference in the statutory context. It seemed artificial to characterise a claim of

reasonable excuse based on ignorance, whether arising from forgetfulness or misunderstanding of the terms of the order, as an impermissible reliance on an error of law
because the order imposes particular legal restrictions on its subject. What is in issue is a
question of fact and then a value judgment as to the reasonableness of the excuse. This
is a matter for (in the Crown Court) a jury. Therefore the judge was in error to make the
preliminary ruling that he did.

The Anti-social Behaviour Act 2003 made provisions for the police to issue a closure
notice under s 1 of the Act in respect of a suspected "crack house". The police must
then apply to a magistrates' court for a closure order within 48 hours and where the
magistrates are satisfied the statutory criteria are met, they may make an order for up to
three months.

The legislation requires the swift resolution of such applications. Section 2 of the Act
limits the maximum period of adjournment of any such application to 14 days. Can this
be limit ever be extended? Fear of recrimination can also make very difficult to persuade
neighbours to come forward and provide evidence. Can hearsay evidence be received
from such persons? If so, what procedures and principles should govern this?

As to the time-limit question, it was held in *R (Turner) v Highbury Corner Magistrates'
Court* (**1–4508**) that the court could exercise its general powers under s 54 of the
Magistrates' Courts 1980 Act to grant an adjournment if it were satisfied as to the need
for such an adjournment, in the interests of justice. This overrode the intention behind
s 2 that the proceedings should be concluded speedily.

In relation to the service of evidence, the use of hearsay and disclosure the following
guidance was given in *R (on the application of Cleary) v Highbury Corner Magistrates'
Court*.

(1) Fairness requires that the police must normally serve written versions of the
evidence they propose to adduce in sufficient time before the hearing to enable
the defendant fairly to deal with it. The statutory intention is that the first
hearing within 48 hours of the service of a closure notice should be an effective
hearing if possible. If the evidence which the police propose to adduce is not
served by the time of the first 48-hour hearing, or if it is not fully served,
fairness requires that it should be served well in advance of the adjourned
hearing.

(2) Credible direct evidence of a defendant in an application for a closure order
may well carry greater weight than uncross-examined hearsay from an
anonymous witness or several anonymous witnesses. Magistrates are more
likely to be satisfied as to the statutory conditions for the making of an order if
the application is supported by direct evidence of witnesses available for cross-
examination, and if there is hearsay evidence, if what is served and adduced is
first hand and complete. If what is relied on is oral statements to a police
officer, the officer should give direct evidence of what was said and the
circumstances in which it was said.

(3) Rule 3(1) of the Magistrates' Courts (Hearsay Evidence in Civil Proceedings)
Rules 1999 provides that a party who desires to give hearsay evidence at a
hearing must serve a hearsay notice not less than 21 days before the date fixed
for the hearing. This fits ill with the timetable for closure applications.
Therefore, if the police intend to rely on hearsay evidence they will have to
make an application for a direction under r 3(2) to reduce the 21-day period.
They will want to make the application at the first hearing and may need to
serve an application to do so with the closure notice. If the court accedes to
the application the period for serving the hearsay notice will need to be
sufficiently in advance of the adjourned hearing to enable the defendant fairly

to deal with it, including making an application under r 4 of the 1999 rules to call and cross-examine the maker of a statement whom it is not proposed to call.

(4)   Standard disclosure under the CPR which requires a party to disclose only the documents on which he relies and documents which adversely affect his own case or support another party's case is a good guide to what is necessary and proportionate in relation to disclosure. The police should disclose documents which clearly and materially affect their case adversely or support the defendant's case.

It was established in *Metropolitan Police Comr v Hooper* that proceedings for a closure order are civil in nature and in *Chief Constable of Merseyside Police v Harrison (Secretary of State for the Home Department intervening)* it was held that the standard of proof to be applied to the matters specified in s 2(3)(*a*) and (*b*) was the civil standard, ie proof on the balance of probabilities.

A number of outstanding issues were clarified in *R (Errington) v Metropolitan Police Comr* (**1–4507**). Firstly, a police officer can only issue a closure notice under s 1 if he has "reasonable grounds for believing" the required circumstances exist. In *Errington* the making of a closure order was challenged on the basis that no such order could be made unless there had been a valid closure notice which, it was alleged, was not so in this case. In the Administrative Court, Collins J reviewed the whole process, remarking initially on the fact that the police had instituted the proceedings under s 2 by way of the laying of a complaint and the issue of a summons as was the customary practice of the Metropolitan Police. His Lordship however considered that this was an error. Sections 1 and 2 in effect provide their own procedure in that when issuing the closure notice the interested persons are notified of the hearing in the magistrates' court, which will be within the next 48 hours. There is no need for a summons and the court will make inquiry at the hearing to satisfy itself that copies of the notice have been properly served. Any defects in the notice will not affect the validity of the proceedings under s 2 although they might give rise to a defence to any criminal prosecution under s 1(6) for a breach of the closure notice.

The defence sought to challenge the closure notice on two bases: it erroneously referred to the officer having "reasonable grounds to suspect" rather than "reasonable grounds to believe" and secondly that the officer had relied on hearsay in forming his belief. This latter point received short shrift as this was an administrative act and the officer could rely on any material which was relevant, whatever its source. Indeed, in considering proceedings under Part I of the 2003 Act, the justices are able themselves to consider any material, whether hearsay or nor, which is relevant to their determination, attaching such weight to it as they consider appropriate.

When considering the "relevant period" of three months, the superintendent must believe that drug use has existed within the relevant period and that that use, and its associated disturbance and nuisance, is continuing, but as regards the magistrates when exercising their jurisdiction under s 2(3), there is no particular period to which evidence of use is restricted. Normally there will be evidence of use within the previous three months since the notice will have been based on such use although there will in any event have to be evidence which satisfied the magistrates that that use exists and is likely to continue unless an order is made. However, a pattern of such use and disturbance over a long period is likely to be material to the issues before the magistrates.

The Anti-social Behaviour Act 2003 also established dispersal orders, and there have been important case-law developments on this topic. Once an authorisation has been given under s 30(1) (**1–4531**), a constable may make certain directions provided he has reasonable grounds for believing the matters specified in subs (3). In *MB v DPP* a senior police officer had designated the Wimbledon Centre Court Shopping Centre, which is close to Wimbledon station, as a dispersal area pursuant to s 30.

Subsequently, MB, who was 17 years of age, was a member of a group of between 15 and 20 black or Asian youths in that area. MB was going home with his friends. The youths, who were in two groups, were not behaving anti-socially. A police officer, on duty on his regular beat, with considerable experience of the area and its problems, formed the view that the presence of the groups of youths was likely to cause harassment, intimidate and alarm or distress members of the public. He gave the groups, including MB, a direction to disperse. The majority dispersed, but MB did not immediately do so.

The officer invited MB to read the notice on a nearby lamp-post giving notice of the dispersal area. When MB said that he would read it in five minutes, the constable explained that MB could be arrested if he did not move away. MB did not leave the area. He was arrested and subsequently convicted of knowingly contravening a direction. He appealed by way of case stated. The thrust of the appeal was that no reasonable magistrates' court could have found that the police officer had reasonable grounds for believing that the presence of the youths was likely to result in members of the public being intimidated, harassed, alarmed or distressed.

The Administrative Court allowed the appeal. The justices had not been entitled on the evidence to convict the appellant. There had been no evidence that any member of the public was harassed, intimidated, alarmed or distressed. Unless there were exceptional circumstances, a reasonable belief for the purposes of s 30(3) normally had to depend, in part at least, on some behaviour of the group which indicated in some way or other, harassment, intimidation, the cause of alarm or the cause of distress. If that were not so, there would be an illegitimate intrusion into the rights of people to go where they pleased in public. In particular, it would interfere with the legitimate activities of young people going home from school by a reasonable route, who were behaving properly as they did so. On the facts, the police officer's actions had not constituted a proper response within the terms of the legislation.

A dispersal direction is not confined, however, to the purposes for which the authorisation was given, and it can be used to disperse protestors. The Court of Appeal so held in *R (on the application of Singh) v Chief Constable of the West Midlands Police.*

The power to remove to his home an unaccompanied person aged under 16, pursuant to s 30(6), had been held to be permissive only, but this decision was reversed by the Court of Appeal in *R (W) v Metropolitan Police Comr.* To "remove" means "take away using reasonable force if necessary". The purpose for which the power was conferred was to protect children under the age of 16 within a designated dispersal area at night from the physical and social risks of anti-social behaviour by others. Another purpose was to prevent children from themselves participating in anti-social behaviour within a designated dispersal area at night. The section did not confer an arbitrary power to remove children who were not involved in, or at risk from exposure to, actual or imminently anticipated anti-social behaviour. Children were free to go to the area without fear of being removed provided that they did not themselves participate in anti-social behaviour and provided they avoided others who were behaving anti-socially. The power had to be exercised reasonably and constables had to have regard to circumstances such as how young the child was; how late at night it was; whether the child was vulnerable or in distress; the child's explanation for his or her conduct and presence in the area; and the nature of the actual or imminently anticipated anti-social behaviour.

Section 31 (**1–4532**) contains supplemental provisions as to authorisations. An authorisation must be in writing and it must state the grounds on which it was given. It was held in *Sierny v DPP* that this requires more than a bald statement that the relevant officer has reasonable grounds for believing the matters specified. The grounds, if only in general terms, must actually be stated.

In *R v W; R v F* (**3–211**) the question that arose was whether hearsay evidence was admissible in the Crown Court on an application for an ASBO having regard to the fact that there are no rules regarding the service and use of such evidence in that jurisdiction. It was held that hearsay was nonetheless admissible under the Civil Evidence Act 1995 and that the principles set out in the Magistrates' Courts Rules 1981 should be followed. The prosecution should identify the particular facts said to constitute anti-social behaviour and, if not accepted, those facts should be proved to the criminal standard before being acted upon by the judge.

Conspiracy

As the law of conspiracy may be encountered in committal proceedings before magistrates, we have included treatment of this subject in PART VIII. Lord Nicholls in *R v Saik* (**8–4328**) has helpfully set out the ingredients of the statutory offence of conspiracy which we reproduce in a footnote to the Criminal Law Act 1977 in the title CONSPIRACY.

Sexual offences

The Sexual Offences Act 2003 introduced a number of new offences and elements into this area of criminal law. In *R v Abdullahi* (**8–28421L**) the Court of Appeal considered the meaning of "for the purpose of sexual gratification" in the offence of causing a child to watch a sexual act, contrary to s 12 of the Act. It was held that there was nothing in the language of section 12 to suggest that the offence could only be committed if the sexual gratification and the display of the images were simultaneous, or contemporaneous, or synchronised. Provided the purpose was the offender's sexual gratification, it might take any of the myriad forms which sexual pleasure or indulgence, or to use a colloquialism, a sexual thrill might take. Indeed, even if the hope is that at a later stage things might go further, the sexual gratification might simply involve, for example, the perpetrator enjoying the sight of the child looking at the images and his or her reactions or responses, whatever those might be. The purpose might involve both short-term and long-term sexual gratification; immediate or deferred, or immediate and deferred gratification.

In *Hulme v DPP* (**8–28422C**) it was the turn of the offence of sexual activity with a person with a mental disorder impeding choice, contrary to s 30 of the Act, to come under scrutiny. It was held that the following evidence was sufficient to make out the offence: when sexually touched the complainant, a vulnerable person of limited mental capacity, did not know what to do or say, and when the defendant placed her hand (where he should not), her mental condition prevented her from communicating that she did not want to.

The rape of a girl under 13, contrary to s 5 of the Act, is an absolute offence and this does not offend art 6 of the ECHR. The Court of Appeal so held in *R v G (Secretary of State for the Home Department intervening)* (**8–28421E**). On its actual meaning, the offence under s 5 was committed even though the defendant reasonably believed the complainant to be 13 or older; but while an absolute offence could subject a blameless defendant to the imposition of sanction that might infringe other Convention rights, the legislation creating the absolute offence would not render any trial under which the legislation is enforced unfair let alone in breach of the presumption of innocence in art 6(2). However, where the offence was committed by a child and arose from consensual sexual intercourse, it might well be that to prosecute under s 5 rather than s 13, or to prosecute at all, would be a breach of art 8 that was not justified under art 8(2).

Outraging public decency

The relevant act must take place in public view, but how many members of the public must see or be capable of seeing it? This is a question that has taken a very long time to be settled authoritatively, but the moment came in *Rose v DPP* (**8–24907**). The facts were somewhat bizarre and, needless to say, rather salacious. Up to a certain date, the general public could gain access to the ATM machines in the foyer of the Lloyds TSB university branch in Glossop Road, Sheffield by using a swipe card. The foyer was well lit and passers-by would be able to see into the foyer, had they chosen to look. The interior of the foyer was the subject of 24-hour CCTV surveillance. It was part of the duties of the branch's manageress, upon attending work, to view the coverage of the foyer provided by the CCTV during the hours between the closing of the branch (save for the foyer) and its re-opening on the next day. In doing so, she observed CCTV footage for the early hours of 2 February 2005. What she saw must have given her quite a shock! She identified as the appellant a man seated in the foyer with his back to the counter. His penis was exposed and erect, and his girlfriend was performing an act of oral sex upon him. At police interview, the appellant admitted the offence claiming that he and his girlfriend [had] "just forgot about the camera". The appellant was tried for an offence of committing an act of outraging public decency. He did not dispute the factual basis of the allegation and chose not to give evidence. It was contended unsuccessfully on his behalf that the act of oral sex had not been witnessed at the material time, and, therefore, a constituent ingredient of the offence had not been made out. However, he was convicted. The Judge subsequently stated a case for the opinion of the High Court, posing the question: "Was I correct in finding that the witnessing of an event captured on CCTV by a person acting in the course of her employment is sufficient to satisfy the requirements of the offence of outraging the public decency?" "No" was the answer of the Divisional Court. On the evidence there was only one person acting in the course of her employment that had viewed the CCTV and had seen the act complained of. According to the 19th-century authorities there had to be a sufficient public element for the offence to be made out. There is no common law offence if persons committed an act of the kind contemplated in the present case but it was not seen by anyone who was not participating in that act. The same principle applied where the act complained of was only witnessed by one, non-participating person. Liability for the offence could not depend on the chance event of whether or not CCTV caught the incident and, if it did, how many persons actually viewed the video footage.

Sending grossly offensive messages

The improper use of public electronics networks is an offence contrary to s 127 of the Communications Act 2003, but what is meant by its "grossly offensive" element? This question went all of the way to the House of Lords in *R v Collins* (**8–30110B**) and received the following answer. The object was to prohibit the use of a service provided and funded by the public for the benefit of the public, for the transmission of communications that contravened the basic standards of society. The proscribed act was the sending of the message of the proscribed character by the defined means, and the offence was complete when the message was sent. It was for the court, applying the standards of an open and just multiracial society and taking account of the context and all relevant circumstances, to determine as a question of fact whether a message was grossly offensive. It was necessary to show that the defendant intended his words to be grossly offensive to those to whom the message related, or that he was aware that they might be taken to be so. Although s 127(1)(*a*) interfered with the right to freedom of expression under art 10 of the ECHR, it went no further than was necessary in a democratic society for achieving the legitimate objective of preventing the use of the public electronic communications network for attacking the reputations and rights of others.

Elements of escape from lawful custody

We turn, now, to another common law offence the boundaries of which required judicial examination. In *R v Dhillon* (**8–9700**) it was held that an escape is where one who is arrested gains his liberty before he is delivered by the due course of law. The common law offence of escape contains four ingredients that the prosecution must prove: (i) that the defendant was in custody; (ii) that the defendant knew that he was in custody (or at least was reckless as to whether he was or not); (iii) that the custody was lawful; and (iv) that the defendant intentionally escaped from that lawful custody.

Practice and procedure

Bias

The question of when a tribunal should recuse itself on the grounds of apparent bias were comprehensively considered in a series of significant decision of the Court of Appeal and the House of Lords culminating in *Porter v McGill* [2002] UKHL 67. The civil case of *Smith v Kvaerner Cementation Foundations Ltd* (**1–119**) provided an illustration of the more robust view taken by courts to issues of apparent bias post *Porter v McGill* and a guide to legal representatives about how to handle such a situation.

The case concerned an action for personal injuries arising out of a road accident. On the morning of the trial the claimant was informed that the recorder who was to hear the case was the head of chambers to which counsel for both parties belonged. Furthermore, the recorder had acted for companies in the same group as the respondent and was involved in litigation which was still ongoing. Before the Court of Appeal it was not argued that the mere fact that the recorder was head of chambers of counsel appearing before him gave rise to apparent bias, but, it was maintained, issues might arise from the financial consequences to counsel of any judicial decision made and the support, or lack of it, by a head of chambers, might have a significant impact on the career of a barrister.

In rejecting this submission the Lord Chief Justice noted that judges frequently had close professional connexions with those who appear before them and this creates no apparent bias. However, there might be an issue where counsel is affected by a conditional fee arrangement although this did not arise in this case. Accordingly, there was no apparent bias arising in this respect.

As regards the recorder's connexion with other litigation involving the respondent's group of companies, it was accepted that there was an issue of apparent bias and the question for the Court of Appeal was whether this had been properly waived by the claimant. The claimant had been informed of the circumstances before the trial began. He claimed however, that in effect he had been "set-up" into agreeing with advice to allow the case to proceed, which he regretted later.

The Court of Appeal cited the principle in *Locabail v Bayfield Properties Ltd* [2000] QB 451 that a "waiver must be clear and unequivocal, and made with full knowledge of all the facts relevant to the decision whether to waive or not". In the present case, the Court of Appeal was concerned that the claimant should have had the options more clearly explained to him by the court including the length of any subsequent adjournment of the proceedings. It is right that counsel should advise his client of all the implications of the situation, the implications of an adjournment and the judicial oath but it is not permissible to expand on the personal integrity of the individual judge as it makes it difficult for the client to opt for an adjournment without appearing to slight the recommendation. It is not in counsel's duty to then seek to influence the decision taken by the lay client, it is proper to inform him of the implications of his choice but not to urge him to waive his objection to the tribunal.

R v Russell (1–133) is perhaps an example of a claim of apparent bias that was always unlikely to find favour. The defendant was charged before the Crown Court with inter alia offences of attempted murder and perverting the course of justice. During the judge's summing-up to the jury, the defendant escaped from the dock, ran in front of the jury and attacked the judge shouting "do you think you're going to stitch me up . . . look at what I have been through . . . I'm an Englishman, I deserve a fair trial." The Court of Appeal was unimpressed with the defendant's argument that the trial should not have continued as it was self evident that no defendant could obtain the termination of his trial by his own actions such as these. No fair-minded observer could have concluded that it was unfair to proceed.

Abuse of process

On 26 July 2006 the House of Lords delivered judgments in *Jones v Whalley* (1–380). This was a matter which had originally been before the justices at St Helens and arose from an allegation of assault by Mr Whalley on Mr Jones. He admitted the offence to the police and he received a caution. Seven months later, Mr Jones, acting as a private prosecutor, laid an information before the justices charging Mr Whalley with assault occasioning actual bodily harm.

At a subsequent hearing it was argued by the defendant that his acceptance of the police caution should preclude a private prosecution. The justices agreed that to proceed would be an abuse of process. The prosecutor appealed to the Divisional Court where his appeal was successful, it being held that there was no abuse of process. So finally, the matter came before the House of Lords.

Lord Bingham reviewed the development of the practice of cautioning. His Lordship noted the previous decision of the House in *R (R) v Durham Constabulary* [2005] UKHL 21 which had confirmed the practice in respect of the statutory scheme for warnings and reprimands of young offenders and the raison d'être behind the scheme. He also noted the scheme for conditional cautioning of adult offenders in ss 22 and 23 of the Criminal Justice Act 2003 gradually being rolled out across the country. However, the scheme applicable in these proceedings was the non-statutory procedure set out in Home Office Circular 18/1994.

The particular point taken by Mr Whalley was that he agreed to be cautioned on the express assurance of a police officer that he would not have to go before a criminal court in connexion with the matter and by analogy with *R v Croydon JJ, ex p Dean* [1993] QB 769, where a promise had been made, it was an abuse to renege on that promise. The situation did however highlight a conflict between this principle and the express right of an individual to bring a prosecution.

For the prosecutor it was argued that *Hayter v L* [1998] 1 WLR 854 had correctly stated the position with regard to the effect of a caution where the form of caution specifically did not rule out the possibility of a subsequent prosecution.

Lord Bingham focussed on the narrow issue whether a private prosecution may or should be regarded as an abuse of process of the magistrates' court where the defendant has agreed to be formally cautioned by the police on the assurance that, if he agrees, he will not have to go before a criminal court. The abuse complained of was not that he could not obtain a fair trial (the fact of the caution could be excluded from evidence) but that it was unfair to try him at all. His Lordship had no doubt that so long as the formal caution stood, any private prosecution would be an abuse.

However, it is where Lord Bingham considers the broader issue that the case report is of most interest. Mr Whalley contended that irrespective of the form of warning of the caution, a resulting prosecution would be an abuse and that *Hayter v L* was wrongly decided. In essence, a responsible official has made a decision to caution and this decision is open to legal challenge but, while it stands, the decision to caution should be respected and should not be circumvented by a private prosecutor. His Lordship could see very considerable force in this argument and the argument that the right to prosecute privately is a factor of little weight in the balance as it is a somewhat anomalous historical survival. Lord Bingham agreed that it is for the state to investigate alleged crimes and decide whether offenders should be prosecuted. The surviving right of private prosecution is of questionable value, and can be exercised in a way damaging to the public interest. However, although he would not reject this argument, his Lordship did not think the House should accept it in these proceedings as, in essence, the matter had not been fully argued and might in any event benefit from legislative attention. There the matter rests for the present.

However, the issue of the value of private prosecutions did raise its head again in a different form in *R (on the application of Charlson) v Guildford Magistrates' Court* (**1–402**), in which the Administrative Court considered the position where the CPS had brought criminal proceedings and a private individual then sought to bring his own prosecution arising from the same facts. The following principles were held to apply. Private prosecutors are not bound by the Code for Crown Prosecutors and, thus, the Code's requirement as to evidential sufficiency does not apply; nor is the requirement that a conviction be more likely than not the test for courts to apply in determining whether or not there is a case to answer.

Where a magistrate is considering whether to accede to issue a summons for a private prosecution, where the Crown Prosecution Service has already brought *and discontinued* a prosecution arising from the same events, the magistrate should not require special circumstances before agreeing to the issue of the summons. The magistrate should ascertain, in deciding whether to issue a summons: (*a*) whether the allegation is an offence known to the law and, if so, whether the ingredients of the offence are prima facie present; (*b*) that the issue of the summons for the offence is not time barred; (*c*) that the court has jurisdiction; (*d*) whether the informant has the necessary authority to prosecute; and (*e*) any other relevant facts. The magistrate should also consider whether the allegation is vexatious. In the different situation where a magistrate is considering whether to accede to an application to issue a summons for a private prosecution, where the Crown Prosecution Service has already brought a prosecution *and this is still proceeding*, the magistrate should in the absence of special circumstances be slow to issue a summons in respect of the same matter.

Their Lordships stated that our previous commentary, based on the decision in *R v Tower Bridge Metropolitan Stipendiary Magistrate, ex part Chaudhry*, that "special circumstances" needed to be found in all cases where the CPS had brought proceedings, was too wide because it failed to take into account that in *Chaudhry* the CPS prosecution was still proceeding. We are grateful for this correction and we have amended the commentary accordingly.

In recent years the number of abuse of process arguments had grown at a very great rate. To a dispassionate observer it was a matter of surprise that a jurisdiction which had had virtually no part to play in proceedings before magistrates' courts, was now indispensable in putting to right all sorts of abuses which had now been discovered for the first time. The advent of the Human Rights Act 1998 added further grist to the mill. Since then, however, there has been a general settling back and the circumstances in which an abuse argument is likely to succeed have been heavily circumscribed. *R v S* (**1–447**) was a case concerning the jurisdiction of the Crown Court to stay proceedings as an abuse of process on the ground of delay. In that case there had been an interval of a number of years between the alleged sexual abuse and the criminal proceedings. The first question for the Court of Appeal was the nature of the abuse proceedings – was the court required to form a conclusion as to fact based on evidence, and if so on whom was the burden of establishing abuse and on what standard? The answer was that any decision whether to grant a stay is an exercise of judicial assessment dependent on judgment and it is wrong to apply to what is an exercise of discretion, the language of burden and standard of proof. Once the issue has been raised it will be for the prosecution to satisfy the court that a fair trial is still possible.

The Court of Appeal helpfully set out a number of principles for a court hearing an application to stay on the ground of delay:

(i) even where delay is unjustifiable, a permanent stay should be the exception rather than the rule;

(ii) where there is no fault on the part of the complainant or the prosecution, it will be very rare for a stay to be granted;

(iii) no stay should be granted in the absence of serious prejudice to the defence so that no fair trial can be held;

(iv) when assessing possible serious prejudice, the judge should bear in mind his or her power to regulate the admissibility of evidence and that the trial process itself should ensure that all relevant factual issues arising from delay will be placed before the jury for their consideration in accordance with appropriate direction from the Judge;

(v) if, having considered all these factors, a judge's assessment is that a fair trial will be possible, a stay should not be granted.

A reminder of the need to careful scrutiny of applications for stay was given in *R v L* (**1–447**) where it had been alleged to be an abuse of process to prosecute the defendant for the death of a child where the court considering care proceedings in respect of a surviving child was unable to decide responsibility for the death of the other child. In the Court of Appeal (Criminal Division) Sir Igor Judge P identified that in proceedings under the Children Act 1989, the issues are different and the focus of the decision was on the criteria in s 31(2) of the 1989 Act. The issue in the family proceedings was whether, in the light of the care which the child would or would be likely to receive if he continued to live at home with his mother, the surviving child would suffer or be likely to suffer significant harm. Although concerns about harm had arisen from the death of the first child, the proceedings had been brought by the local authority as care proceedings for the surviving child and not criminal proceedings in which the ultimate question for decision was whether the defendant had killed the other child. There was no "prosecution" in the earlier care proceedings and no issues of autrefois acquit could arise. The subsequent criminal proceedings were therefore not an abuse of process.

In *DPP v Ayres* (**1–447**) the respondent faced charges of police assault, disorderly conduct and being drunk and disorderly, which he contested. The court made various directions as to disclosure, etc, with which the prosecution failed to comply. The case was then listed for abuse of process argument, and the prosecution was required to file a skeleton argument by a certain date. They failed to do so and, consequently, the justices decided that they would hear argument only on behalf of the respondent. Initially, they were not minded to stay the proceedings because they believed this was possible only on the ground that a fair trial could not take place and not on the basis of the prosecution's culpable default. After hearing further representations on behalf of the respondent, however, the proceedings were stayed. The prosecution appealed by way of case stated. They complained about being denied an opportunity to present oral argument and about the decision to stay.

The Administrative Court upheld the appeal. Mr Justice Gibbs giving the only judgment held:

> "Criminal proceedings are essentially proceedings conducted through oral submissions. A skeleton argument is a useful device, designed to assist the court and to assist the parties as to what the basic outline of a party's case will be; and it seems to me that, however serious a party's default has been in general terms in the course of a case, it is essentially unjust to deprive that party of the opportunity of putting forward an explanation for the default and/or of making submissions on the important issue as to whether criminal proceedings should be stayed for abuse of process."

However, the history of non-compliance with directions by the prosecution was such that the court declined to remit the case for re-consideration.

Case management

We have reminded readers in earlier editions of STONE of the importance of efficient and effective case management. To this end we have included in this manual the *Criminal Case Management Framework* but the foundation for improved processes is of course the *Criminal Procedure Rules*. The Rules, first made in 2005, are now updated twice yearly as the Rules Committee gradually extends the coverage of the rules into areas which were insufficiently treated by the pre-existing rules. The **Criminal Procedure (Amendment No 2) Rules 2006** added a new Part 33 (expert evidence) and new Part 36 (evidence about a complainant's sexual behaviour) in substitution for the former Parts 33 and 36. Other amendments include making provision for the form and service of requisitions and written charges under s 29 of the Criminal Justice Act 2003.

The **Criminal Procedure (Amendment) Rules 2007** substitute a new Part 4 (service of documents). Part 14 replaces the Indictment Rules 1971 and the rules relating to witness summonses are revised and simplified in a new Part 28. The existing Part 31 (restriction on cross-examination by a defendant acting in person) is amended to apply these rules to the magistrates' court as well as the Crown Court. The new rules came into effect on 2 April 2007.

The Criminal Procedure Rules offer the opportunity for imaginative use of case management powers. *R v K* (**1–422**) was an illustration of conducting a hearing expeditiously where in relation to a preliminary hearing in the Crown Court the extensive nature of the court's case management powers was emphasised. These included the powers of the court to deal with matters preliminary to trial exclusively by means of written submissions and even to specify the length of such submissions.

Effect of procedural failure

We refer to the significant case of *R (Robinson) v Sutton Coldfield Magistrates' Court* (**1–423**) both here and in relation to evidence, post. As regards application of the Criminal Procedure Rules, the Administrative Court has indicated that the time limits in the rules must be observed although in exercising its discretion to extend time limits, the discretion of the court is not restricted to exceptional circumstances. The court will nevertheless closely scrutinise any application and will have regard to: the objective of the Rules to deal with all cases efficiently and expeditiously; the furtherance of the overriding objective; the reasons for the failure (which must be explained clearly); and whether the other party was prejudiced by the failure.

In *R v Ashton, R v Draz, R v O'Reilly* (**1–409**) the Administrative Court considered the effect of a procedural irregularity in the processes leading to the appearance of an accused person before the Crown Court. In one of the appeals it had been thought (wrongly) that the consent of the DPP, which had been a prerequisite to bringing proceedings, had not been obtained. The Crown Court judge, relying on s 66 of the Courts Act 2003, had sat as a district judge, determined mode of trial afresh and then committed the defendant, on his guilty plea, to the Crown Court for sentence. In another of the appeals, the defendant had been wrongly sent to Crown Court for trial rather than committed under the Magistrates' Court Act 1980. The Crown Court judge had rectified this by following the procedure set out in para 7 of Sch 3 to the Crime and Disorder Act 1998 and had then ruled that an indictment was not necessary. In the remaining appeal, the indictment had been amended to include a summary only offence that was, by then, time-barred.

After reviewing the authorities, Fulford J stated:

> "The prevailing approach to litigation is to avoid determining cases on technicalities (when they do not result in real prejudice and injustice) but instead to ensure that they are decided fairly on their merits. This approach is reflected in the Criminal Procedure Rules and, in particular, the overriding objective. Accordingly, ... absent a clear indication that Parliament intended jurisdiction automatically to be removed following procedural failure, the decision of the court should be based on a wide assessment of the interests of justice, with particular focus on whether there was a real possibility that the prosecution or the defendant may suffer prejudice. If that risk is present, the court should then decide whether it is just to permit the proceedings to continue."

Applying those principles, the first and second appeals failed; the errors here were procedural only. However, the third appeal succeeded because the error went to the root of jurisdiction. The offence was time-barred, and this could not be cured by recourse to s 66. As to that provision, his Lordship noted the practical problem of no magistrates' courts' officer being available in the Crown Court to make the register entries required by rule 6.1(1) of the Criminal Procedure Rules in the court register.

> "However, in our view, the problem is readily solved by the court associate entering any adjudication (or other relevant matter) in the Crown Court's records; this will ensure the purpose of the rules is complied with, namely that there should be an accurate and accessible record of any decision or other important feature of the proceedings."

Trial in absence

Another means of ensuring that there is no unnecessary delay is, in appropriate cases, to proceed to hear a trial in the absence of the accused where he has demonstrated a deliberate lack of intention to participate. In earlier editions of STONE, we have considered situations where it may be appropriate to proceed in absence and it suffices to indicate that the issue is now subject to the guidance in the *Practice Direction (criminal: consolidated)* (**1–6970**) at para 1.13.17. The attitude of the accused will be more readily apparent if he has been explicitly warned in his presence of the consequences of any failure to attend on the date set aside for his trial and courts were advised that such a warning should be given to accused when they were being bailed to a trial date in *R v O'Hare* (**1–428**).

Adjournments

One of the main manifestations of delay in magistrates' courts is where cases are not heard on the due date. For some time, the higher courts have been striving to reduce delay occasioned by unnecessary adjournments. We have set out in this manual all relevant decisions to assist justices when considering applications to adjourn and in this edition we are able to include the statement of relevant factors as summarised by Jack J in *R v Picton* (**1–463**).

Apart from the legal guidance in *Picton* what will be of interest is the description of the familiar pressure on listing which is experienced by all magistrates' courts. The actual issue in *Picton* was a challenge by the prosecution to the magistrates' decision to refuse to adjourn a trial listed at 10 o'clock to later in the day as the prosecution had wrongly warned its witnesses to attend for a trial at 2 o'clock. The magistrates had to contend with the fact that they were already double booked with a trial scheduled to last all day with a third trial listed for the afternoon. In the event the magistrates had had in mind the relevant considerations and were justified in refusing the application.

However, *S v DPP* (**1–463**) provides a salutary reminder that justice must be done. S had pleaded not guilty to a charge of committing a common assault upon his 16-year-old son, N, claiming that he had only acted in self-defence. N's credibility was critical. At the time of the trial N had no previous convictions, but he was awaiting trial at the Crown Court on a serious allegation of affray. Since this was clearly potentially very significant, at the pre-trial review S had asked the prosecution to supply details of the outstanding case so that he might consider whether to make an application under s 100 of the Criminal Justice Act 2003. The prosecution failed to provide those details. At trial, S initially was willing to proceed even in the absence of this material, but when the court granted the Crown's application to allow N to testify from behind a screen S applied for an adjournment to enable that further information relating to N's outstanding court appearance to be obtained. The prosecution did not oppose S's application. However, while acknowledging that the Crown had an obligation to disclose this information, the justices noted that the allegations were as yet unproven, that S's counsel had initially been disposed to proceed in the absence of the information, that the defence would have asked for the trial to be vacated if they had truly felt so strongly about the matter, that it was undesirable to make a 16-year-old and his 73-year-old grandmother give evidence twice, and that since the offence had taken place three months earlier it was desirable to proceed without delay. Therefore, the trial proceeded and it resulted in a conviction. S challenged by way of judicial review the refusal of the justices to adjourn the trial.

The Administrative Court noted that adjournments were costly in money and in time and should not be granted unless the imperatives of justice so required. But if they did, the case had to be adjourned, however inconvenient and regrettable the consequences might be. The authorities established clearly the principle that if it was necessary to adjourn the case to enable justice to be done following a failure by the prosecution properly to disclose matters which it should have disclosed, then the adjournment had be granted, unless the court was satisfied that no prejudice would be caused to the defendant by proceeding. In this case, it was clear that everything depended on the credibility and reliability of N. The detail of the case pending against him in the Crown Court might well have damaged his credibility. It might well have borne upon his propensity for violence. In this sense it might have undermined the prosecution or assisted the defence. It should have been disclosed. If it had been, then the defence would have argued that the criteria for admissibility under the 2003 Act were fulfilled. Therefore, and not without sympathy for the justices' desire to avoid delays, the court allowed the appeal.

Bail on expiry of custody time limit

This was considered in *R (O) v Crown Court at Harrow* (**1–3530**). The House of Lords held that s 25 was to be read as placing an evidential burden upon a defendant to whom the section applied to adduce material supporting the existence of exceptional circumstances justifying the grant of bail. When the defendant's custody time limit had expired and the court had refused to extend it because of the prosecution's failure to act with all due diligence and expedition within the meaning of s 22(3)(*b*) of the 1985 Act, the defendant's continued detention in custody did not automatically amount to a violation of art 5(3), and a finding of lack of due diligence on the part of the prosecution did not automatically equate to a breach of the right to trial within a reasonable time. Section 25 should be construed essentially as a guide to the proper operation of the Bail Act 1976, and it operated to disapply the ordinary requirement under the 1987 Regulations that bail should be granted automatically to any defendant whose custody time limit had expired, and so applied the section was compatible with art 5(3).

Live links

Rule 3.2(2)(*h*) of the Criminal Procedure Rules imposes a duty on the court to further the overriding objective by actively managing the case. This includes making use of technology. The introduction of modern technology into a system as inherently cautious as the legal system was always going to be an incremental process but new systems are steadily being put in place and most notably the use of video recorded testimony and live links in the case of vulnerable and intimidated witnesses. These developments have rather tended to overshadow the use of live links between magistrates' courts and prison establishments in matters preliminary to trial.

The **Police and Justice Act 2006** (**1–4604**) has given a boost to this resource-efficient measure by recasting and expanding the circumstances in which a live link direction may be made in respect of a person in prison or remanded to local authority secure accommodation. Section 45 of the 2006 Act has introduced new ss 57A to 57E into the Crime and Disorder Act 1998 in substitution of the existing s 57. In "preliminary hearings' ie a hearing held before the start of a trial, the court must give reasons for not conducting the hearing by video link where it has power to do so and those reasons must be recorded in the court register. These powers apply even where the court itself has not remanded the defendant in custody provided he is likely to be held in custody during the hearing. The significant extension is that the court may, with the consent of the defendant, conduct a sentencing hearing by video link where it considers it is in the interests of justice to do so.

Section 47 of the 2006 Act now extends the power of the court to make a special measures direction in relation to a vulnerable accused. Where such a direction is given, the accused may give evidence by means of live link. The new s 33A inserted in the Youth Justice and Criminal Evidence Act 1999 will enable such accused to participate effectively in the proceedings and will meet the doubts expressed by Baroness Hale in *R(D) v Camberwell Green Youth Court* [2005] UKHL 4 casting doubt on the correctness of the decision in *R (S) v Waltham Forest Youth Court* [2004] EWHC 715. Guidance on the use of such powers is to be found in the *Practice Direction (criminal: consolidated)* at paras III.29 (witness supporter) and III.30 (treatment of vulnerable defendants).

Police and Justice Act 2006

The remaining provisions of the Police and Justice Act 2006 are wide-ranging. Of particular note to readers of this manual are those provisions in ss 7–9 which continue the process of extending the powers of Community Support Officers coupled with the delegation of certain police officers' powers and duties to civilians. Persons designated as community support officers will have standard powers and duties with the addition of any further powers conferred on them by a Chief Constable. Part 2 of the Act amends police powers to detain a person pending consideration by the DPP on whether he should be charged (s 11).

One theme of modern criminal justice legislation is to direct more offences away from the standard process into fixed penalties. Section 15 enables chief police officers to give accreditation to trading standards officers to give them powers to issue penalty notices for a range of offences amounting to disorderly behaviour. An alternative approach is the offer of a caution and s 17 extends the scope of conditions that can be attached to

Conditional Cautions to those which have the objective of punishing the offender eg a financial penalty or attendance at a specified place and time and the completion of specified activity. Failure to comply renders the person liable to arrest and prosecution for the original offence.

Part 3 of the Act strengthens central government direction of local crime and disorder strategy groups with provision for national standards and extends the power to make parenting contracts in respect of anti-social behaviour to local authorities and registered social landlords or ultimately apply to a magistrates' court for a parenting order.

In the "miscellaneous" part of the Act, an anomaly in the "custody plus" sentencing scheme is repealed in relation to sentencing for failing to answer bail. Custodial sentences for such offences are removed from the definition of "sentence of imprisonment" for the purposes of the new provisions in the 2003 Act. Whether this will ever have any practical effect will depend of course on whether "custody plus" is ever brought into force. The Act is to be brought into force in accordance with commencement orders. At the date of going to press two such orders had been made. Of the matters referred to above, only the live link provisions (other than live link to a police station) had been brought into force.

Revisiting decisions

A recurring issue is the question when is it appropriate to revisit an earlier decision made by a different bench. Normally the scope for a change of mind is limited: the provisions for re-sentencing or reopening a case where there has been a not guilty plea are prescribed by s 142 of the Magistrates' Courts Act 1980. There are also well known restrictions on the sentencing powers of a bench in circumstances where the previous bench has given an indication as to the seriousness of the offence. One area where there is, however, greater scope for reconsideration is where justices are hearing committal proceedings In *R (R) v Manchester City Youth Court* (**1–2054**) the defendant, 15 years old and of previous good character, was charged with a single offence of dwelling house burglary. At the youth court the magistrates declined jurisdiction, contrary to the representations of the prosecution and defence, and the case was adjourned for committal proceedings. At the adjourned hearing the defence sought to persuade the bench to exercise their power under s 25(5)(*b*) and (7) of the Magistrates' Courts Act 1980 to revert to summary trial but without success.

In the Administrative Court Ouseley J agreed that the starting point for this type of burglary for an adult first offender would be in the range of 12 months. When considering a youth aged 15, the court would regard a substantially shorter sentence of custody, if custody at all, as probably appropriate. His Lordship had no difficulty in quashing the decision to decline jurisdiction as well as the subsequent decision to decline to revert to summary trial. His Lordship then went on to comment on the power in s 25 and whilst he understood justices' reservations about reaching a different decision on mode of trial before they have done anything substantive by way of inquiry into the case as examining justices, the position of examining justices cannot be fettered, once the inquiry has begun, by a previous decision which their own examination shows to be wrong.

Changing of the mind came up again in *A v South Staffordshire Magistrates* (**1–2056**) where another 15-year-old was charged in July 2004 with assault occasioning actual bodily harm contrary to s 47 of the Offences Against the Persons Act 1861. After some adjournments, the defendant pleaded not guilty and the matter was adjourned for trial. After many more adjournments, at the pre-trial review, the prosecution intimated that they were considering preferring a more serious charge under s 18 or more probably, s 20. After vacating the trial and a further adjournment, a charge of unlawful wounding or grievous bodily harm under s 20 was laid against the accused and no evidence was offered on the s 47 charge which was then dismissed. The second trial date was then vacated and the case was not listed for trial until September 2005. After the prosecution witnesses had given evidence, the prosecutor was of the view that the evidence did not establish that the defendant was the perpetrator of the particular injury which had justified the s 20 charge. The prosecution then offered not to proceed on the s 20 charge if the defendant pleaded guilty to the actual bodily harm under s 47, which he then did.

Unfortunately for the prosecution, the s 47 charge had previously been dismissed and in the Divisional Court Scott Baker LJ pointed to s 27 of the Magistrates' Courts Act 1980 "Where on a summary trial of an information the court dismisses the information, the dismissal shall have the same effect as an acquittal on indictment." The prosecution sought to argue that there had been no hearing on the merits as no evidence had been offered. His Lordship responded by reference to *R v G (autrefois acquit)* [2001] 1 WLR 1727; although it had been decided in relation to trial on indictment the same principles apply to summary trial. A plea of not guilty followed by the offering of no evidence and dismissal precluded a subsequent conviction for assault occasioning actual bodily harm in respect of the same injuries. What the prosecution should have done in this case was either to apply to amend the charge under s 47 to one under s 20 "thereby leaving the option to the court to convict on actual bodily harm if it was not satisfied of grievous bodily harm," or alternatively, to have the actual bodily harm allegation adjourned, leaving it undisputed with the effect being the same. We would respectfully suggest that the latter course would be the preferable one, as in magistrates' court, unlike trial on indictment, there is no power, except under certain statutory provisions in road traffic cases, for a bench to acquit of the more serious charge and convict of a lesser alternative charge embraced in the original charge.

A further point referred to by his Lordship should be noted by all practitioners in the youth court: ". . . it is imperative that the prosecution of young offenders is conducted expeditiously. It is difficult to see why an offence alleged to have been committed in July 2004 was not tried until September 2005."– difficult indeed.

Effect of pleading guilty and principles behind withdrawal of guilty pleas

In *Revitt, Borg and Barnes v DPP* (**1–568**) the defendants, who were not at that stage legally represented, pleaded guilty to dangerous driving and other offences. While the bench was in retirement considering sentence, the defendants left the court, having been advised by the bench legal adviser that they were at risk of a custodial sentence and might want legal representation. The defendants then returned to court, accompanied by solicitors, and they applied to withdraw the guilty pleas to dangerous driving, which they said had been entered under a misapprehension as to the nature of the charge. The justices refused this request and adjourned the case for reports. When the case returned to the list the application to change plea was repeated, but with the same result. The defendants challenged these decisions by appeal by way of case stated.

Lord Philips CJ considered, first, whether domestic law was compatible with the requirements of the Convention. His Lordship concluded that where a defendant made an unequivocal plea of guilty which the court accepted, the defendant was thereupon "proved guilty according to law" within the meaning of art 6(2), the presumption of innocence ceased to apply and he could be sentenced on the basis that he had been proved guilty. However, a guilty plea could only found a conviction and bring to an end the presumption of innocence if it was unequivocal. It was for the party seeking to vacate his plea to establish that the interests of justice so required, and courts would be slow to allow this unless there was some obvious reason why it was appropriate. The sole contention here was that the defendants had thought that they were pleading to nuisance (for which they had originally been arrested) rather than dangerous driving. However, given the explanations that had been made of the charge, etc, the justices had not been wrong to conclude that this was not a credible claim. Accordingly, the appeal was dismissed.

Justices' clerks assistants

As in all editions of STONE, we incorporate the usual crop of new and amending statutory instruments. Apart from regulations relating to legal aid, the significant new regulations should have been the **Assistants to Justices' Clerks Regulations 2006** (**1–4923** et seq) which define roles and responsibilities of those appointed to assist justices' clerks. Unfortunately, the drafting of these regulations left much to be desired leaving uncertain the position of clerks qualified otherwise than by being solicitors or barristers in regard to what powers could be delegated to them. Magistrates' courts legal advisers are, of course, vital to efficient administration and the effectiveness of lay justices. As to that role we note in passing and with a touch of sadness the amendment of the **Local Probation Boards (Appointment) Regulations 2000** by SI 2006/2664 to remove the requirement that where practicable four of the persons appointed to a local probation board should be justices of the peace within the area of the board.

Legal aid

Finally in our review of practice and procedure, we note in the appropriate places amendments relating to legal aid to reflect the changes introduced by the Criminal Defence Service Act 2006 which in turn made amendments to the Access to Justice Act 1999. Whilst many of the changes comprise amendments to regulations already reproduced in STONE, we also include in this edition the **Criminal Defence Service (Financial Eligibility) Regulations 2006** (**1–5699**), the **Criminal Defence Service (Representation Orders and Consequential Amendments) Regulations 2006** (**1–5716**) and the **Criminal Defence Service (Representation Orders: Appeals etc) Regulations 2006** (**1–5722**).

Evidence

We include in this edition the revisions made to the Police and Criminal Evidence Act 1984 Code of Practice A and the new Code of Practice C together with its counterpart, the new Code G in respect of persons arrested under s 41 of the Terrorism Act 2000.

Witness anonymity

It is quite understandable that persons who witness very violent crimes are reluctant to testify for fear of recriminations. Special measures are, of course, available, but these may not provide comfort or assurance in extreme cases. Are the courts able to go further and allow witnesses to testify anonymously? Or does this encroach too far on the defendant's right to a fair trial?

These questions arose in *R v Davis; R v Ellis* (**2–169**) and were answered as follows. The Convention rights of witnesses include, where necessary, the preservation of their anonymity. The concealment of the identity of witnesses is not inconsistent with the right to a fair trial, provided that the need for anonymity is clearly established; that cross-examination of the witness by an advocate for the defendant is permitted; and that the trial is fair. A trial will not inevitably be considered unfair, and a conviction unsafe, simply because the evidence of anonymous witnesses may be decisive to the outcome. The potential disadvantages to a defendant require the court to examine the application for witness anonymity with scrupulous care to ensure that it is necessary and that the witness is indeed in genuine and justified fear of serious consequences if his true identity becomes known to the defendant or his associates. The court should be alert to potential or actual disadvantages faced by a defendant in consequence of any anonymity ruling and should ensure that necessary and appropriate precautions are taken to ensure that the trial itself will be fair. Provided that appropriate safeguards are applied, and the judge is satisfied that a fair trial can take place, it can proceed. If not, the judge should not permit anonymity.

Cross-examination of complainant as to sexual history

Section 41 of the Youth Justice and Criminal Evidence Act 1999 imposes restrictions on evidence or questions about a complainant's sexual history. This provision has generated a considerable amount of case law as defendants have sought to explore the limits of, and the circumstances in which, the protection afforded by the section inhibits their scope for presenting their case. *R v Norova* (**2–1541**) provided a different angle on this issue. In this case it was the *prosecution* who adduced evidence that the complainant had previously had sexual intercourse on one occasion. The purpose in so doing was to bolster her evidence that she had deliberately lied when she told her assailant that she was a virgin.

The background was that the complainant had been seeking employment in a hotel in which the defendant had business interests. She had met him at his flat on three occasions. At the first meeting it was alleged the defendant made unwelcome advances but she returned a week later as she was unable to find other work. She was then indecently assaulted but she went back on a third occasion to collect her wages, when she was raped. The defence case was that she had made it clear from the outset that she was prepared to have or was interested in having a sexual relationship and all that took place subsequently was consensual.

Before the Court of Appeal two grounds of appeal were put forward. One related to fresh evidence, a matter which need not detain us here, and the other related to s 41 of the 1999 Act. At the trial it had been agreed that the complainant should be allowed to give evidence of what she had said during the incident, ie that she was a virgin, to demonstrate that she was not consenting to sexual intercourse and that the appellant knew that she was not. It was also agreed that the jury be told that she had had sex on one occasion and the defence were permitted to comment that that was not a matter that the defence accepted. The thrust of the appeal was that s 41 is incompatible with the requirements of art 6 of the European Convention on Human Rights. It was contended that the defence was placed at a disadvantage when compared with the prosecution. It was argued that her statement should have been edited to exclude reference to her previous experience as the prohibitions should embrace the prosecution; since they did not, the process was unbalanced adversely to the defendant.

The short response from the Court of Appeal was that the Crown was not seeking to rely on the complainant's sexual history. It was an integral part of the incident and relevant and admissible, bearing on the issue of consent. The agreed formula had prevented the jury being misled by the Crown and the falsity of the claim that she was a virgin needed to be exposed to the jury. In any event, the answer to any unfairness claim lay in the application of s 78 of the Police and Criminal Evidence Act 1984 and the discretion to exclude unfair evidence.

Evidence of bad character

The provisions of the Criminal Justice Act 2003 have now had time to bed down and, unsurprisingly, they have attracted a large number of appeals. Two, often intertwined topics have featured prominently in this appellate activity: means of proving previous convictions; and purposes for which bad character evidence may be adduced.

The Court of Appeal handed down two significant judgments on successive days in November 2005 (but reported too late for inclusion in the previous edition of STONE) which cover a number of important issues arising from the bad character provisions of the Criminal Justice Act 2003.

In *R v Renda* (**2–200**) the court presided over by Sir Igor Judge, Head of Criminal Justice, heard six appeals. At the outset the court made plain its approach to dealing with such appeals. It recognised that such decisions and rulings represent either the judgment of the trial judge in the specific factual context of the individual case, or the exercise of a judicial discretion. The circumstances in which the appeal court will interfere with the exercise of judicial discretion will be limited, and the same approach will apply to a fact-specific judgment.

Their Lordships considered that citation from a vast body of "authority" was unnecessary and might be counter productive. What is critical is the first instance court's "feel" for the case. Further discouragement for potential appellants was given by the reminder that the Court of Appeal is ultimately concerned with the safety of any subsequent conviction, and even a clearly incorrect ruling or misdirection will not necessarily result in the quashing of a conviction.

Renda involved the defendant giving a false impression about himself. Again the court discouraged the citation of authorities from the 1898 Act – these were merely factual examples of occasions when it had been decided that an appellant had put his character in issue. The appellant in this case, under cross-examination, resiled from some of his assertions about his employment and, in effect, was forced to concede the truth. The defence then argued that as the truth had come out, it was therefore not appropriate to treat him as giving evidence apt to mislead the jury. The Court of Appeal did not agree. There was a difference between a defendant who makes a specific and positive decision to correct a false impression for which he is responsible, or to disassociate himself from false impressions conveyed by the assertions of others, and the defendant who is obliged under cross examination to concede that he has been misleading the jury.

The prosecution was then allowed to bring evidence of the defendant's bad character, in particular that although he had been found unfit to plead on a charge of assault, the jury had found he had committed the act for which he received an absolute discharge. For the appellant it was argued that as he had received an absolute discharge, this did not amount to a conviction so that he had not been guilty of "reprehensible conduct". The Court of Appeal did not agree. The fact that 18 months later he had been found unfit to plead did not entail that at the time of an apparently gratuitous assault, his mental acuity was so altered as to extinguish any element of culpability.

In the second of the cases in the *Renda* appeal the appellant was charged with rape. The prosecution was refused permission to put in evidence of the defendant's bad character on the sole ground that the accused directly alleged the complainant had fabricated her allegation – with which the Court of Appeal agreed. However, the trial judge did allow the reception of bad character evidence on the basis that the accused had made imputations on the complainant's character in his interviews to the police. Unusually, in those interviews the accused considered no doubt that he was making exculpatory remarks – in essence he was denying rape as he asserted the complainant would have intercourse with any man. The trial judge had admitted the evidence of bad character and declined in his discretion to exclude it as it did not have an adverse effect on the fairness of the proceedings. The Court of Appeal agreed that there was an imputation on the character of the complainant and the judge was right to admit cross-examination of the accused on his bad character.

The fourth of the conjoined appeals concerned an allegation of robbery on a pub landlord. The defence was that the allegation was fabricated. The judge at the trial had permitted the appellant to cross-examine the landlord under s 100 on allegations of misconduct by the witness: his management of the premises produced till shortages; the premises were regularly used for after hours drinking with free drinks leading to stock depletion; there was drug use at these after hours sessions; and the landlord himself used drugs.

Permission to cross-examine about the drug taking was refused and this ruling was supported on appeal as it did not meet the test that it was important explanatory evidence. On the other hand, the prosecution was permitted to cross-examine a defence witness about his recent conviction for serious violence who alleged the allegation had been fabricated by the licensee. The Court of Appeal considered this was of substantive probative value in relation to the witness's credibility as to whether the allegation had been fabricated. The recorder's reasons – that the jury were entitled to know about the witness's character – were described as an "over-parsimonious compliance with the duty of the court under s 110(1) of the 2003 Act to give reasons for any rulings under s 100". The safety of the conviction was not in doubt.

The decision in the five conjoined appeals in *R v Weir* (**2–200**) was given by a differently constituted Court of Appeal, the following day. In *Weir* the prosecution sought to adduce evidence of a caution for an offence contrary to s 1 of the Protection of Children Act 1978 in a prosecution for sexual assault contrary to s 7 of the Sexual Offences Act 2003. The offence under the 1978 Act was not within the sexual offences category of those offences prescribed for the purposes of s 103(4)(*b*) of the Criminal Justice Act 2003. The defence argued that evidence of the caution was inadmissible as the offence was not of the same "category" nor of the same description within s 113(2)(*a*). In rejecting this argument, the Court of Appeal approved the view of Professor Spencer that s 103(2) provides that a defendant's propensity to commit offences of the kind with which he is charged can be proved in ways other than by evidence that he has been convicted of an offence of the same description or an offence of the same category. Such a reading also allows the reception of offences taken into consideration, despite the fact that, like a caution, an offence taken into consideration is not a conviction. The value of section 103(2) and offences being of the same description or category is that it makes the case of deciding admissibility easier.

Samanathan, the second of the appeals, laid to rest the argument that evidence to show propensity, an important issue between the prosecution and the defence, must still in effect satisfy the old "similar fact" rule. The Court of Appeal was emphatic that the 2003 Act completely reverses the pre-existing general rule. "Evidence of bad character is now admissible if it satisfies certain criteria . . . and the approach is no longer one of inadmissibility subject to exceptions . . .." The 2003 Act says nothing about "enhanced probative value" and "enhanced relevance." This might be relevant in relation to s 100 which imposes a higher test in respect of the introduction of a non-defendant's bad character. "If the evidence of a defendant's bad character is relevant to an important issue between the prosecution and the defence then unless there is an application to exclude the evidence, it is admissible." The former one-stage test of balancing probative value against prejudicial effect is obsolete. In considering the discretion to exclude evidence, the Court of Appeal was mindful of art 6 of the European Convention on Human Rights and a judge "should if necessary encourage the making of such an application whenever it appears that the admission of the evidence may have such an adverse effect on the fairness of the proceedings that the court ought not to admit it."

Before dispatching the appeal in *Samanathan*, the court went on to note that as regards "gateway" (*f*) – correcting a false impression, a simple denial of the offence cannot be treated for this purpose as a false impression given by the defendant. Although the provision for exclusion of unfair evidence in s 101(3) does not apply to this gateway, their Lordships had no reason to doubt that the provisions of s 78 of the Police and Criminal Evidence Act 1984 would apply in any event. Finally, it was accepted that the appellant had attacked the complainant's character. The defence sought to argue that the opening of this gateway should not render all available evidence of bad character admissible. Having regard to *R v Highton* [2005] EWCA Crim 1985, an attack on the character of the complainant opens the door to all the evidence on which the prosecution seeks to rely subject to the duty not to admit evidence which would have such an adverse effect on the fairness of the proceedings that it should be excluded.

The third of the appeals raised the issue whether s 100, which permits, in prescribed circumstances, the adducing of evidence of bad character of a non-defendant, includes issues of credibility. The provisions of s 100(1) are stated in terms different from those relating to the introduction of a defendant's bad character. Nevertheless, recognising that to hold otherwise would permit a significant lacuna in the legislation, the Court of Appeal declared that s 100(1) did cover matters of credibility (although, on the facts of the case, the judge erred in admitting evidence of a caution as having substantial probative value in relation to the witness's credibility).

The next appeal concerned the complaint of a 13-year-old girl of three indecent assaults by a man aged 39 years. She gave evidence relating to the first and third allegations by way of video recorded interview. She subsequently gave further video recorded interviews in which she revealed more details. There was other forensic evidence to link the defendant with the allegations. The basis of the appeal was that the judge had been wrong to admit in evidence an earlier sexual relationship with a girl of 16 years when he was 34 years of age on the basis of showing propensity to be attracted to young girls. The Court of Appeal agreed with the appellant that although the definition of "misconduct" in s 112(1) is very wide and reprehensible behaviour may be "misconduct" for the purposes of the legislation although not amounting to an offence, there was no evidence in this case of grooming or parental disapproval, nor that the girl in question was emotionally or physically immature for her age. Therefore evidence of the relationship was not "bad character" evidence and the provisions of the 2003 Act did not apply. The evidence was nevertheless admissible at common law as it was relevant to the issue whether the appellant had, as he maintained, only an asexual interest in the complainant.

A further aspect of the meaning of "reprehensible conduct" and therefore "bad character" was illustrated in the final appeal joined with *Weir* which arose from convictions of several accused of public order offences and violence. One of the accused wished to adduce in evidence the fact that two of his co-defendants had previously been the victims of a knife attack but had refused to provide statements for the police, and on another occasion had been arrested on suspicion of committing a serious assault but had been released without charge after the alleged victims refused to provide statements.

The trial judge was held rightly to have refused to admit evidence of either allegation under s 101(1)(e) (substantial probative value). As neither matter was evidence of bad character, the provisions of the 2003 Act did not apply. Nevertheless the judge admitted the evidence under the common law as he considered it relevant to the appellant's defence of self-defence. However, whilst acknowledging the validity of the trial judge's reasoning as to the law, on the facts the conduct of the co-accused could only be relevant to the appellant's defence if it amounted to a propensity to violent conduct and to show such propensity it had to amount to "bad character". Since it did not, and there was no room for relaxing this approach simply because it was a defendant who sought to introduce the evidence, it should not have been admitted.

As we have mentioned above, it is particularly important to clarify at any early stage of any consideration whether to admit evidence of bad character, to be quite sure that the disputed material is in fact bad character evidence within the meaning of s 98 of the 2003 Act. In *R v S* (**2–202**) the issue concerned the admissibility of a caution for indecently assaulting a 12-year-old girl at a trial for rape and indecent assault of an 11-year-old girl. The defence was one of a denial that the events described by the prosecution witnesses had ever taken place. At the appeal, unsurprisingly in the light of the approach in *Renda,* short shrift was given to the argument that a caution was not properly to be categorised as evidence of bad character. The term "misconduct" in s 98 of the 2003 Act is not limited to previous convictions or cautions but can extend to behaviour which may not have given rise to either a conviction or a caution.

Where the issue is the defendant's propensity to commit offences of the kind with which he is charged, the prosecution is not limited to previous acts of similar misconduct; the offence need not pre-date the offence charged in the instant proceedings: *R v Adenusi* (2–213).

R v Machado (2–202) illustrated a different aspect of the definition of bad character. Here, the complainant had been into Peterborough for a friend's birthday. He consumed four or five pints of lager. On his way home he engaged in conversation with the appellant and his two co-defendants. While walking home, the complainant's evidence was that he felt a bump to the head and fell to the ground. As he started to get up, the three defendants walked away, and then he realized he had been robbed. The appellant's case was in essence, that the complainant had collapsed on to the ground after becoming upset. In his interview with the police, the appellant stated that the complainant offered to supply drugs to him and that he had said that he had taken an ecstasy tablet.

During the course of the trial, the prosecution had successfully argued that the appellant could not put such matters to him as it was evidence of the witness's bad character and therefore excluded by s 100 of the 2003 Act. The Court of Appeal noted however, the definition of "bad character" in s 98 excluded evidence which "has to do with the alleged facts of the offence with which the defendant is charged'. Their Lordships were of the view that what the appellant wished to give evidence of was evidence relating to the very circumstances in which the offence occurred. All the matters were in effect contemporaneous to and closely associated with the alleged facts of the offence. Applying the simple English of the provision, the matters were to do with the alleged facts of the offence and were not evidence of bad character.

In *Weir* it had been held that the provisions relating to the introduction of bad character of non-defendants in s 100(1) extended to matters of credibility as well as propensity. In *R v S* (2–230) it was held that such evidence may also be admitted to show the complainant had a propensity to act in the way asserted by the defendant. The case concerned an allegation of indecent assault of the complainant, who was a prostitute and a heroin addict. The defendant engaged in sexual activity with her in a churchyard and his defence was that she had consented to do so in return for £10. After he had finished she asked him for more money and when he refused, she became hysterical and threatened to accuse him of rape if he did not give her more.

The critical issue at the trial was the credibility of the complainant and the defendant. The defendant sought to cross-examine in relation to certain convictions for dishonesty including burglary to which the complainant had pleaded guilty.

At the trial it was unsuccessfully sought to admit the evidence as going to the complainant's credibility. In the Court of Appeal it was noted that a propensity to be untruthful is not the same as a propensity to dishonesty and the trial judge was right to refuse to admit the evidence of previous convictions to attack the complainant's credibility. But their Lordships considered that there was another basis on which the evidence should have been admitted. The convictions had substantive probative value in relation to an important matter in issue ie that she had a propensity to act dishonestly as alleged by the defendant. Although there is no analogue in s 100 to s 103(1)(*a*) in the case of a defendant's propensity to commit offences of the kind charged, the complainant's propensity to act in the way the defendant asserts is part of the "matters in issue" and the evidence of the complainant's misconduct should have been admitted.

In one of the appeals in *Weir* the trial judge had been relaxed about the admission of bad character evidence of a co-accused on the application of one of the defendants. In *R v Edwards* (**2–214**) the Court of Appeal gave general guidance in relation to co-defendant applications to admit bad character evidence. Again their Lordships advised that the first inquiry is whether it is necessary to go through the bad character gateways at all having regard to the definition of bad character in s 98 of the 2003 Act. Then Scott Baker LJ pointed out that the parties needed to give some thought as to the use to which the bad character evidence was proposed to be put as the gateways needed different consideration. Although in the magistrates' court the position is different, it is helpful to note his Lordship's analysis of the division of responsibility between judge and jury in the Crown Court. The decision whether the evidence is admissible under one of the gateways and if so whether it should be excluded under s 78 of the Police and Criminal Evidence Act 1984 or s 101(3) of the Criminal Justice Act 2003 is a matter for the judge. Once admitted, the weight to be given to such evidence is a matter for the jury. But simply because an application is made by a co-defendant to admit evidence of bad character, a judge is not bound to admit it. The gateway in s 101(1)(*e*) must be gone through. However, analysis with a fine toothcomb is unlikely to be helpful as it is the context of the case as a whole that matters.

His Lordship made several other observations, noting that the gateways under s 101(1)(*d*), (*f*) and (*g*) are only open to the prosecution. Furthermore, as we have mentioned above, s 104(1) (admission of evidence relevant to whether a defendant has a propensity to be untruthful) is not exhaustive of the scope of the gateway under s 101(1)(*e*) (important matter between defendant and co-defendant) and whether a defendant's stance amounts to no more than a denial of participation or gives rise to an important matter in issue between a defendant and a co-defendant will inevitably turn on the facts of the individual case.

It was noted in *Edwards* that in *R v Bovell* [2005] EWCA Crim 1091 the court had entertained considerable doubt whether the mere making of an allegation was capable of being evidence within s 100(1) (non-defendant's bad character). However, Scott Baker LJ stated: ". . . we are persuaded that it is so capable, at any rate when considering the effect of s 109 (assumption of truth) in relation to an issue under s 101(1)(*d*) (relevant to an important matter in issue between the defendant and the prosecution). In our respectful view, however, at least two difficulties arise from this approach. First, s 109 applies no less to s 100 than to s 101. Secondly, it refers to "evidence" and it is difficult to see how a mere "allegation" can be so described. The point may be academic, however, since his Lordship proceeded to state, here approving the approach in *Bovell*: "This is an area, however, in which it is important to guard against satellite litigation . . . Further it is appropriate to proceed with caution and due regard to the judge's discretion to exclude evidence." It seems to us that these considerations will require, in practice, something much more substantial than a mere allegation, as was indeed the case in *Edwards*, to meet the test of admissibility.

One of the aspects of the new bad character provisions that has proved more troublesome, has been the means of proving the bad character. Where it is merely sought to rely on the bare fact of a previous conviction, evidence of that is usually submitted in the form of a print out from the Police National Computer. Where the facts underlying the previous conviction are significant, the Court of Appeal in *R v Hanson* [2005] EWCA Crim 824 expected that generally the relevant circumstances would be capable of agreement and would be put in evidence by way of an admission. Whilst this approach has worked for the majority of cases, there are situations where something more is required. Particular difficulties can arise with regard to allegations rather than formal convictions, or where it is disputed that a conviction relates to this defendant.

Where production of a PNC printout is insufficient, a conviction may be proved by production of a memorandum of conviction under ss 73 and 74 of the Police and Criminal Evidence Act 1984. A cautionary warning to those who attempted to prove convictions in accordance with the business records provisions of s 117 of the Criminal Justice Act 2003 was provided by *R v Humphris* [2005] EWCA Crim 2030 noted in the previous edition. If this route is to be followed, the requirements for the admission of hearsay evidence need to be strictly complied with. Where more detail is required, the prosecution must be careful to obtain the necessary evidence, such as obtaining a statement from the complainant in the earlier case.

In *R v Burns* (**2–218**) the prosecution had served notice of its intention to rely on the defendant's bad character. The prosecution had obtained two memoranda of conviction and a statement of a fingerprint expert but these failed to prove the identity of the defendant named on the memorandum. In due course, four memoranda having been produced, the trial judge admitted them in evidence on the basis that the defendant's name and date of birth were proved to be the same. In considering the appeal against conviction, the Court of Appeal referred to *Pattison v DPP* [2005] EWHC 2938 (Admin) which had considered proof of disqualification in a trial of driving whilst disqualified. In the present case, the appellant sought to distinguish *Pattison* and that a name and date of birth were insufficient, there should be at least a third factor, such as a defendant's address, before a prima facie case could be raised. The Court of Appeal rejected such a prescriptive approach. Each case must depend on its own facts. For example, a common name and a date of birth not precisely the same as that of the defendant might not be properly admissible as proving identity. On the other hand a highly unusual name comprising many different component parts might or might not require resort to an identical date of birth in order to provide prima facie evidence.

In *Ainscough* (**2–218**) the issue was a dispute covering the facts of a previous conviction. The court had not followed the procedure set out in *Humphris* and had permitted a police officer who had no personal knowledge of the defendant's previous convictions for offences of violence to give evidence which included details of the offences based entirely on information supplied by the PNC. In allowing the appeal, the court emphasised the need to follow the guidance in *Humphris* but also to avoid satellite issues as to what did or did not happen in some cases many years ago, particularly where there is a relatively short trial on a simple issue.

Hearsay

Again, the new law has now had time to settle and the Court of Appeal has been active in refining the relevant principles. We begin, however, with a case decided under the now superseded provisions of the Criminal Justice Act 1988, though it is our view that the principles would be found to be same under the new law. It concerned the particularly difficult topic of whether or not the evidence of the principal or sole witnesses could be admitted without infringing the defendant's rights under art 6. In *R v Al-Khawaja* (**2–250**) the defendant was a consultant physician in rehabilitative medicine, whose treatments included hypnotherapy. He was charged with two counts of indecent assault on two female patients who had been referred to him for treatment. One of the patients died before the trial, and at a preliminary hearing the judge decided that her statement could be admitted in evidence under the hearsay provisions of the Criminal Justice Act 1988. The defendant was convicted, and he appealed.

It was held that the important factors were that the witness had died, that she was the only witness whose evidence went directly to the commission of an indecent assault upon her, and that it had been possible to attack the accuracy of her statement by exploring the inconsistencies between it and other witnesses and through expert evidence. The relevant sections of the 1988 Act, designed to protect defendants, had been properly considered by the judge before the statement had been admitted in evidence, and the tribunal of fact had been able, by virtue of an appropriate direction, to take proper account of the difficulties which the admission of the statement might have provided for the defendant. Accordingly, the trial had not been unfair, and the appeal would therefore be dismissed.

The new broad approach to the admission of hearsay evidence being taken has been exemplified in a number of cases. In *R v Taylor* (2–260) the issue was the admissibility of a statement made by prosecution witnesses in video recorded evidence in chief relating to an assault. After they had been told his name by someone else, both witnesses named the defendant as a participant in an attack on the victim. At the trial, the defence applied to exclude these references from the recorded interviews as being hearsay. The Crown argued that they should be admitted under s 114(1)(d) in the interest of justice.

In deciding whether this ground applies, a court is required to give consideration to nine factors listed in s 114(2). The trial judge indicated that he was unable to form a clear view on some of the factors, in particular as to the circumstances in which each witness had been informed of the defendant's name, nor could he form a clear view as to the reliability of the informants on the material which he had. Nevertheless, in the light of the opportunity for the defendant to challenge the assertion about him, he considered it was in the interests of justice to admit the evidence. On appeal the defence submitted that as the judge was unable to come to a view on four of the nine factors, it was not right to admit hearsay evidence of this kind. The Crown's response was to rely on the judgment of the court in *R v Xhabri* (2–282) where blessing was given to the admission of apparently reliable hearsay evidence by reason of its confirmation from other sources than the witness who was giving hearsay evidence. Furthermore, in this case there was a considerable body of other evidence, including eye-witness evidence, implicating the defendant.

The crucial point, according to the Court of Appeal, was the meaning in s 114(2) of the words "the court must have regard to the following factors". Their Lordships were satisfied that they did not require the trial court to embark on an investigation, resulting in some cases in the hearing of evidence, in order to reach a conclusion established by reference to each of the nine factors. There is no obligation to reach a conclusion as what is required is an exercise of judgment in the light of the factors identified in the subsection. The court is required to refer only to those identified factors and any other which the court considers relevant. Then the court must assess the significance of the factors both in relation to each other and having regard to such weight they bear individually and in relation to each other. This is what the judge had done in this case and so the appeal was not allowed.

R v Singh (2–260) was a bold attempt to assert that, in spite of the generally held view, the Criminal Justice Act 2003 had not succeeded in reversing the decision in *R v Kearly (No 1)* [1991] 2 AC 228 where evidence of frequent visitors to a premises seeking drugs had been held to be inadmissible as hearsay since the evidence amounted to an implied assertion.

It was argued that there could be a hearsay statement outside the statutory parameters. In *Kearly* an unintentional implied assertion was excluded as hearsay. But, it was said, s 115 (statements and matters asserted) of the 2003 Act was to draw a line between intentional implied assertions still caught by the hearsay rule and unintentional implied assertions no longer treated as hearsay. Accordingly, so the argument went, only intentional implied assertions are within the regime of the 2003 Act; unintentional implied assertions are therefore, as *Kearly* said they were, inadmissible as hearsay. Needless to say this argument did not find favour, especially as s 118 in clear express terms abolishes the common law hearsay rules (save those expressly preserved) and creates a new rule against hearsay, which does not extend to implied assertions, thereby reversing the effect of *Kearly*. Therefore, as regards evidence of the conspiracy in which Singh was alleged to have been involved, the presence of telephone entries relating to calls from his co-conspirators in his telephones were implied assertions and not hearsay evidence.

R v Xhabri (**2–283**) concerned an unpleasant case where a young woman from Latvia had fallen into the hands of Albanians who ran brothels disguised as saunas. The gist of the allegations was that when not working as a prostitute in a sauna, the complainant was effectively subject to false imprisonment. The defendant alleged that in fact he was in a consensual sexual relationship with her and that although he knew that she was acting as a prostitute, that was an occupation of her own choosing and not through any force or influence exerted by him.

Before the trial began the defence sought to exclude certain hearsay evidence in the form of communications between the complainant directly or indirectly, with her mother, her father, a friend who lived in the same building as her father, and the police. The defence did not object to the complainant herself giving evidence of the communications she had made; what was objected to was the relaying by the recipients of what they had been told.

Unfortunately it seems, the grounds argued by the Crown for admission of the evidence were not soundly based. It was argued that evidence of the statements was admissible under ss 114 and 120 of the 2003 Act (other previous statements of witnesses) and that the evidence of what was told to the police by the neighbour was admissible under s 121 (multiple hearsay). The defence also argued that the provisions in the 2003 Act for admitting hearsay evidence were incompatible with the Human Rights Act 1998.

Their Lordships went back a stage earlier and considered on what basis the complainant herself might recite her earlier statements to the witnesses. They acknowledged that prior to the 2003 Act there might have been some debate on what basis this evidence might have been admissible. Now, their Lordships considered the evidence plainly admissible in the interests of justice not only as evidence of how the complainant was reacting to her situation but also as evidence of the truth of the statements that she was making as to her predicament. The jury would obviously wish to know whether she had sought to communicate with the outside world.

As regards the evidence of those who had received the communications, the provisions of s 120(7) were satisfied in that she was giving oral evidence at the trial as a complainant and the other criteria were satisfied. Furthermore, the court would have admitted the evidence in the interests of justice in any event – if it were said she had never made the statements at all or if it were alleged she were lying, the evidence would be relevant and would not prejudice the defendant. As regards the evidence of the two witnesses who had relayed evidence to the police and who were not available for the trial, there was no prejudice to the accused as the complainant herself was available for cross-examination.

Unsurprisingly, the Convention argument met with no success. The discretion to admit evidence granted by s 114 is not restricted to the admission of a hearsay statement the maker of which is not available for cross-examination and to the extent that art 6 would be infringed, the court has a power to exclude the evidence under s 126 and a duty to do so under the 1984 Act. Accordingly, there can be no question of s 114 being incompatible with the Convention. Furthermore the "equality of arms" provision is not infringed as the hearsay provisions of the 2003 Act apply equally to the prosecution and the defence. Nor does art 6 give a defendant an absolute right to examine every witness whose testimony is adduced against him, the question is whether fairness requires this and in the present trial the complainant had been available for cross-examination.

Xhabri might be considered to be an example of the former law on recent complaint. This permitted the admission of evidence of prior statements by a complainant made soon after the event to demonstrate consistency. However, the law on this has now moved on and s 120 of the 2003 Act is more extensive in scope. The new provisions are not restricted to sexual cases and the new statutory tests are framed differently from the former requirement that a complaint be "recent" – the requirement is for the complaint to have been made as soon as could reasonably be expected after the alleged conduct. This will depend of course on the circumstances. Any statement admitted under the new statutory procedure is now admissible to prove the truth of its contents and not merely to demonstrate consistency of the complainant's account.

One of the grounds for admitting hearsay is that the witness is unavailable. In *R v C and K* (**2–261**) the defendants were charged with conspiracy to defraud. P was an important prosecution witness, who was resident in South Africa. He initially indicated that he would be willing to travel to the United Kingdom to give evidence, and he subsequently confirmed that he would attend. However, approximately three weeks before the trial, when P was contacted in order that travel arrangements could be discussed, he directed that all enquires should be made to his lawyer. Two weeks before the trial, the lawyer telephoned an officer in the case to state that P would not fly to the UK, nor would he agree to give evidence via video link. In a preparatory hearing, and on the prosecution application, the judge ruled that the evidence could be read, as P was outside the UK and that it was not reasonably practicable to secure his attendance, pursuant to s 116(2)(c) of the Criminal Justice Act 2003. He refused the defendants' application to exclude the evidence under s 78 of the Police and Criminal Evidence Act 1984. The defendants appealed against the judge's ruling pursuant to s 35 of the Criminal Procedure and Investigations Act 1996.

The Court of Appeal allowed the appeal. Whilst the expression "reasonably practicable" had to judged on the basis of the steps taken, or not taken, by the party seeking to secure the attendance of the witness, that was only the first stage in a ruling upon the admissibility of the statement or statements. The court should also consider whether to exercise its powers under s 126 of the 2003 Act, which conferred a general discretion to exclude evidence in criminal proceedings, or s 78 of the 1984 Act. Whether it was fair to admit the statement or statements depended, in part, on what efforts should reasonably be made to secure the attendance of the witness or, at least, to arrange a procedure whereby the contents of the statements could be clarified and challenged. In the instant case, further enquiries as to why the witness had changed his mind, and had refused to give evidence via video link were reasonably required. Only once the parties had had an opportunity to make them could rulings on the admissibility of the statement properly be made. As the trial fixture had been vacated, orders in the prosecution's favour were premature and the rulings of the judge could not be upheld. What further steps should be taken was for the parties to consider and then for the judge to determine under his case management powers.

Another, commonly invoked ground for seeking to admit hearsay evidence is that the witness will not attend the trial through fear. What evidence is required of this and what is the standard of proof? These questions arose in *R v Doherty* (**2–261**). G had been returning from the Cup Final by train in the company of his brother, N, when he alleged that D assaulted him. The evidence of N, who had witnessed the assault, was important evidence in the case. Prior to the trial N and his wife, who lived in Ireland, had received various telephone calls, which N interpreted as veiled threats against him. In consequence N, having declined police protection and the offer of special measures to testify in person, explained in a fax sent to the police officer in charge of the investigation that he could not take the risk of testifying in person, no matter how small the risk might appear.

The trial judge, applying a subjective test, concluded that N was in fear and permitted his statement to be given in place of his oral testimony.

On appeal, the appellant argued that there had been no cogent evidence of fear. There had been no threat direct or otherwise of physical or financial harm to the witness or any of his family; no independent evidence of anything that N stated in his fax had been produced before the court; and the court ought not to have acted on that statement alone when it would have been possible to produce some form of corroboration of it by records of telephone calls or enquiries made by the Garda in Ireland.

The Court of Appeal rejected these submissions, however. N's statement was perfectly cogent in that it stated that he was in fear, and why, and there was no reason to doubt these claims. The condition laid down in s 116(2)(e) was obviously satisfied. According to s 116(3), the term "fear" was to be widely construed. Firstly, it was necessary to consider the matter subjectively, and then the witness's statement might only be admitted if it also passed the objective test laid down in s 116(4) and the court concluded that the statement ought to be admitted in the interests of justice. The judge had to perform a balancing exercise, weighing the risk of unfairness to the defence because the evidence could not be challenged against the risk of unfairness to the prosecution, which could not put before the jury all the available evidence. This was an evaluative and fact-sensitive exercise, which a trial judge was in the best position to perform, and an appellate court would only interfere if it was satisfied that the judge's conclusion was obviously "perverse or unreasonable". In this case, although it had not been clear that D had made or directly caused the threats made over the telephone, it had been highly probable that they had been made by somebody connected with him. It followed that N's fear could not be characterized as irrational or sufficiently unfounded to make it unfair for the judge to have ruled that his evidence should be read.

Particular evidential difficulties are often encountered in cases involving allegations of domestic violence. Although the complainant may have made an initial complaint and statement to the police, she may then be reluctant actually to attend court to give evidence. In such cases, the prosecution may consider applying for a witness summons in accordance with the revised Part 28 of the Criminal Procedure Rules, which we have mentioned earlier. However, even if she attends, she may be reluctant to be sworn, or being sworn, suffer from sudden memory loss or change her evidence completely. Developments in the admission of hearsay evidence made possible by the new evidential provisions have led to more effective means of dealing with these issues.

R (Robinson) v Sutton Coldfield Magistrates' Court (**2–261**) is more commonly cited in respect of the application of the Criminal Procedure Rules and we have referred to this above. However, the case has significant implications for the conduct of domestic violence cases in particular.

At the pre-trial review hearing following the defendant's plea of not guilty to assault, the prosecution intimated that it would be seeking to rely on hearsay evidence and in due course filed notices seeking to adduce evidence of bad character and to adduce the complainant's statement in evidence. At the trial, the applications were allowed, the prosecution read the complainant's statement and the defendant was found guilty. The admission of the evidence of bad character was challenged on the basis of the prosecution's failure to comply with the rules and is discussed above. The challenge to the admission of the complainant's evidence by way of reading her statement is of particular note.

In her original statement the complainant had given no indication that she was unwilling or reluctant to give evidence but in a further statement shortly before the trial she had said she did not wish to come to court personally through fear of the defendant locating her by her appearance at court. The defence suggested in the Administrative

Court that the magistrates should have given more scrutiny of the extent, nature and the basis for the alleged fear and whether satisfactory measures could have been put in place to assuage the complainant's fears. As in *Xhabri* the defence maintained that the defendant's right under art 6 had been infringed in that he had not had the opportunity to cross-examine the witness who gave the main evidence against him. The Administrative Court therefore considered the European jurisprudence as distilled by Waller LJ in *R v Sellick* [2005] EWCA Crim 651 and noted the comments of Lord Phillips in *Xhabri*. In the present case Owen J highlighted the factors relevant to the determination of the application before the justices to admit the statement:

- there was evidence in the complainant's second statement of her fear;
- the serious nature of the case and that the interests of justice require that serious assaults in which injury is caused are resolved by a trial where it is possible to hold a trial that is fair to both sides;
- there was photographic evidence, the admissibility of which was not challenged;
- the defendant had admitted under caution that he was present at the time and was drunk and was the only other person present;
- he had the opportunity to comment at interview on the prosecution case;
- he admitted the complainant was not a person who would lie;
- he conceded he could not say whether he had committed the offence or not.

Although as yet not, as far as we are aware, the subject of any authority, we also note that the statement of a complainant which has been admitted in evidence either because it has been used as a memory refreshing document on which she has been cross-examined, or where she has admitted making a previous inconsistent statement or has been treated as hostile, will be admissible as to the truth of its contents.

Those setting examinations on evidence are fond of the question based on the relaying of motorcar registration numbers from one witness to another and the contravention of the hearsay rule. An updated version of this was to be found in *Maher v DPP* (**2–284**). The defendant had parked her Mini motorcar in the car park of a supermarket. The complainant and his girlfriend had parked their Vauxhall Astra nearby. A married couple saw the defendant reverse her Mini out of the parking space into the Astra, get out, look at the damage and drive off. The witnesses made a note of the Mini's registration number and left it on the windscreen of the Astra. The complainants, on returning to their car, telephoned the number to the police who recorded it on the Police Incident log. A subsequent DVLA trace led to the defendant who, when questioned, admitted being the driver of the Mini with the relevant registration number and being there at the time, but denied there was a collision. By the time of the trial, the note was no longer in existence or could not be found. Despite objections from the defence, the magistrates admitted evidence from the log.

The Administrative Court had therefore to analyse the basis, if any, for admitting such hearsay evidence. As regards first hand hearsay, the only ground for admitting it would be that in s 114(1)(*d*) the "interests of justice." But the real issue in this case was multiple hearsay as the witnesses had written down the number, the complainant had telephoned the information to the police, and the police had made the record. The magistrates had reasoned that the police incident log was a business record for the purposes of s 117. Unfortunately, a requirement for admissibility of such a record is that "the person who supplied the information (the "relevant person') contained in the statement had personal knowledge of the matters dealt with" and that each person through whom the information was supplied from the relevant person received the information in the course of a trade, business, profession etc. In this case the person who supplied the information, the relevant person, was the witness. This information was then supplied through the complainant to the police. But the complainant was not acting in the course of a trade, business etcetera and the gateway under s 117 was therefore not available and in turn the criteria for the admission of multiple hearsay in s 121 were not met. However, as we have encountered before in this Preface, the other evidence available militated strongly to the admission of this evidence under s 121(1)(c) as the possibility of error was, in the circumstances, remote.

Inferences from silence

Subject to safeguards, an adverse inference may be drawn from the failure of an accused person to mention when interviewed or charged matters later relied on in his defence (**2–315**). What, however, if the accused person refuses to be interviewed at all? It was held in *R v Johnston* that an inference under s 34 of the Criminal Justice and Public Order Act 1994 could not be drawn in these circumstances; the silence must be in the face of questioning.

Sentencing

New format

We reiterate that the narrative of Part 3 has been rewritten to present the topic (we hope) in a more logical, "post CJA 2003" order and structure. There is much new content, of which the following paragraphs provide only some examples.

Relevance of prison overcrowding

This has been something of a "hot" topic in recent months, with the prison estate struggling to accommodate the numbers remanded in or sentenced to custody. To what extent should this be allowed to influence sentencing? This was considered (not for the first time) in *Attorney General's Reference No 11 of 2006 (Thomas Richard Edwin Scarth)* (**3–130**). It was held that prison overcrowding might be a relevant factor where the sentencing decision was on the cusp. Prison overcrowding would also make it all the more important to comply with the requirements of ss 152 and 154 of the Criminal Justice Act 2003. However, the observations on the need to avoid custodial sentences were subject to the exception that courts should not be deterred from imprisoning for appropriate periods those who committed offences involving violence or intimidation or other grave crimes.

Dangerous offenders

The narrative on the dangerousness provisions of the Criminal Justice Act 2003 will now be found in para **3–153**. This includes the further guidance given by the Court of Appeal in *R v Johnson, R v Lawton, R v Hamilton, R v Gordon, Attorney-General's Reference (No 64 of 2006) Practice Note*. It also includes a number of examples, illustrating the application of the relevant principles.

Release on licence, recall to prison and orders for return

We are in a transitional period regarding release on licence, which we explain in para **3–138**, and the courts have had to grapple with various difficulties arising there from. See, in particular, the cases referred to in Note 1 to s 254 of the Criminal Justice Act 2003 (**3–2041**).

In relation to orders for return on the commission of a further offence under the repealed, but with savings, provisions of s 116 of the Powers of Criminal Courts (Sentencing) Act 2000, we set out our understanding of the position in para **3–150**. The repeal of s 116 is of no effect in relation to sentences of less than 12 months (because "custody plus" has yet to be implemented), nor in relation to longer sentences passed before 4 April 2005 (confirmed in *R v Ian Lloyd Howell*).

ASBOs on conviction

Guidance on the making and terms of ASBOs on conviction will now be found in para **3–211**. This is a topic that has continued to exercise the higher courts. Is it permissible to include a term that goes no further than prohibiting what already amounts to a criminal offence? It was held in *Hills v Chief Constable of Essex* that there was no absolute bar on this. It all depends on whether the particular prohibition is really necessary to protect members of the public from anti-social behaviour by the person who is the subject of the order. The prohibition under consideration in *Hills* was on carrying knives and it was permissible because it was intended to cover behaviour not caught by the criminal law, namely carrying penknives that might be less than 3 inches long.

Unduly wide provisions will be susceptible to appeal, but it now seems that until they are overturned they remain valid. In *DPP v T* (**1–3804**), which concerned a provision "not to act in an anti-social manner", it was held, first, that the normal rule in relation to an order of the court was that it had to be treated as valid and be obeyed unless and until it was set aside. Even if the order should not have been made in the first place, a person might be liable for any breach of it committed before it was set aside. Secondly, the person against whom an ASBO was made had a full opportunity to challenge that order on appeal or to apply to vary it. During the intervening period it could not be treated as a nullity and of no legal effect. The policy consideration that the magistrates' court had jurisdiction to determine issues of the validity of a byelaw or an administrative decision was wholly absent when the issue was the validity of the order of the court. Thus, it had not been open to the district judge, as a matter of jurisdiction, to rule that the original order was invalid. He had been entitled, however, to consider whether the provision lacked sufficient clarity to warrant a finding that the respondent's conduct amounted to a breach of the order; whether the lack of clarity provided a reasonable excuse for non-compliance with the order; and whether, if a breach was established, it was appropriate in the circumstances to impose any penalty for the breach.

Recommendations for deportation

The power to recommend deportation on conviction and the relevance to its exercise of Convention rights were considered in *R v Nelson Carmona* (**8–17695**), though the court was reluctant to express a definitive view because, at the time, the Sentencing Advisory Panel was preparing advice on the topic and Directive 2004/38/EC had not yet come into force (it took effect on 30 April 2006). The latter was expected to have a significant effect on the exercise of the power of the court to recommend deportation, since it would not be right to make such a recommendation in circumstances where the Directive precludes actual deportation. Nevertheless, the court felt able to give the following guidance in relation to Convention rights: (*a*) a recommendation for deportation will not of itself infringe art 8, which may be affected only by the eventual decision of the Home Secretary on the recommendation; (*b*) if the sentencing judge is to consider Convention rights at all it would be illogical to restrict that consideration to members of the offender's family to the exclusion of the rights of the offender himself both under art 8 and also under arts 2 and 3; (*c*) there is now a right of appeal against a decision by the Home Secretary to deport an offender (under s 82(1)(*j*) of the Nationality, Immigration and Asylum Act 2002, as amended) to a tribunal equipped to consider conditions in the country of deportation, which will take into account art 8 considerations in relation to the offender and his family; (*d*) moreover, where the court imposes a substantial prison term, conditions may change appreciably before the time to consider actual deportation arises; (*e*) a recommendation for deportation may engage an offender's rights under art 5, though detention that is reasonably necessary with a view to deportation will not infringe art 5 and, even if no non-custodial direction is made under para 2(1) of Sch 3 to the Immigration Act 1971 as amended, the offender may still apply for bail to a chief immigration officer or to the Asylum Immigration Tribunal.

Sentencing guidelines and examples of sentencing for particular offences

These now begin at para **3–260**. We highlight the following.

At **3–264** we set out the SGC's guidelines on domestic violence. New guidance on the making and terms of restraining orders was given in *R v Debnath* (**3–268**).

At **3–308** we set out the definitive guidelines issued by the SGC in relation to breach of restraining and non-molestation orders.

Generally, we have added a number of cases to this section of the narrative, though they were not expressed as laying down general guidelines, where we believe that they may assist magistrates' courts by providing relevant pointers.

Rehabilitation of offenders

"Oh what a tangled web we weave, when first we practise to deceive!" The words of Sir Walter Scott come to mind when delving into the intricacies of the Rehabilitation of Offenders Act 1974 and the Powers of Criminal Courts (Sentencing) Act 2000.

Section 14(1) of the 2000 Act provides that a conviction of an offence for which an order is made conditionally or absolutely discharging the offender, is to be deemed not to be a conviction except for limited purposes in connexion with the proceedings. The Rehabilitation of Offenders Act 1974 provides that in prescribed circumstances a conviction may become "spent" and a person become "rehabilitated". The effect of this is that a person who has become rehabilitated in respect of a conviction "shall be treated for all purposes in law as a person who has not committed or been charged with or prosecuted for or convicted of or sentenced for the offence or offences which were the subject of that conviction". One of the consequences is that any question being asked of a person (other than in judicial proceedings) "shall be treated as not relating to spent convictions . . . and the answer may be framed accordingly." However, in relation to questions being asked of an applicant for a job in certain professions, the effects of the 1974 Act are excluded by the Rehabilitation of Offenders Act 1974 (Exception) Order 1975, SI 1975/1023 as amended.

R v Patel (**3–940**) concerned an applicant for a post in with a police force. Such employment is exempt from the provisions of the Rehabilitation of Offenders Act 1974. She was subsequently indicted for an offence of obtaining a pecuniary advantage by deception contrary to s 16 of the Theft Act 1968. The proceedings arose from a question asked on her application form "Have you ever been convicted of an offence (including motoring but not parking offences) or is any charge or summons at present outstanding against you?" She replied "No." In fact nine years earlier she had been made the subject of a conditional discharge for shoplifting.

Matters were complicated by the fact that s 1(4) of the 1974 Act provides that notwithstanding s 14 of the 2000 Act, a discharge ranks as a conviction for the purposes of rehabilitation. Hughes LJ explained that this provision was necessary because the effect of rehabilitation under the 1974 Act is wider than that of the 2000 Act, which does not allow a person to assert that they have never committed the offence or that they have never been found guilty of it.

The argument therefore pursued before the Court of Appeal was one described as "arcane". It centred on a distinction between "found guilty" and "conviction" and the court agreed that if the question had been "Have you ever been found guilty of an offence?" the defendant's answer would have been a false representation and capable of being a deception. But the question was "Have you ever been convicted?" The argument put forward by the prosecution that there was a distinction that could be drawn between "conviction" (protected by s 14 of the 2000 Act) and "convicted" (not protected) was rejected, the trial judge observing that such an argument "required delicate dancing on a very small pinhead".

The remedy for employers such as the Police is to ask "Have you ever been found guilty of a criminal offence?" or "Have you ever committed a criminal offence" (although we would respectfully observe that such a question seems to raise a number of difficulties). In any event the question as framed in this case would not have elicited a caution. The result was that the judge's preliminary ruling that there was no case to answer was upheld.

Road Traffic

Dangerous driving

We have discussed above under the heading *Criminal Law* the liability of an owner for aiding and abetting dangerous driving and in particular that for a driver to drive when in a dangerous condition is not per se dangerous driving (*R v Webster* (**4–1372**)). But in that case earlier authorities were accepted that evidence of an additional hazard posed by the driver having consumed alcohol was admissible. The question in *DPP v Milton* (**4–1372**) was the mirror image: was evidence of the defendant's particularly excellent driving skills relevant to the "independent bystander" test?

The facts received some publicity in the national press because the defendant was a police Grade 1 advanced driver. He was on duty and decided to practise his driving skills on a vehicle with which he was unfamiliar, as he had been instructed to do in the course of his police training. He drove just under 5,000 metres at average speeds of 148–149 mph. The Crown argued that the District Judge who acquitted the defendant was wrong to find that driving at grossly excessive speeds (described as "eye watering" speeds) when not responding to an emergency or when otherwise engaged in the prevention and detection of crime, does not fall below the required standard. The test in s 2A of the Road Traffic Act 1988 is a purely objective one.

A person is to be regarded as driving dangerously if the way he drives falls far below what would be expected of a competent and prudent driver and it would be obvious to a competent and prudent driver that driving in that way would be dangerous. The prosecution submitted that, assessed objectively, to drive at speeds in excess of twice the speed limit is dangerous whatever the context. Driving at such speed satisfied the bystander test of "By Jove, that's dangerous" as the car flashed by.

The defendant argued that the circumstances which should be taken into account under s 2A(3) included the defendant's driving skills.

Hallett LJ concluded that the District Judge did have the correct objective test in mind but then erred in taking into account in the respondent's favour the respondent's own knowledge of his own driving skills and imported a subjective element into what is a purely objective test. Her Ladyship could form no concluded view as to whether the judge would have been entitled to impute knowledge of the defendant's driving skills to the independent bystander on the arguments before her as this was not the heart of the case as presented to the Divisional Court. The court was of the view that *R v Woodward* [1995] RTR 130 where the court had admitted evidence of the driver's consumption of alcohol on a charge of dangerous driving was a decision which turned on its own facts and a decision based on the presumed intention of Parliament to penalise not only the driving of a vehicle in a dangerously defective state but also the driving of a vehicle by a driver in a dangerously defective state due to drink. But her Ladyship was not prepared to open the floodgates to the admission of evidence as to an accused's driving skills in every case of driving, although the matter did not in fact arise on the case stated and would rest there as far as the court was concerned.

In the event the court found that the judge had taken into account irrelevant matters and the appeal was allowed. But the court did refuse to find that if an accused drives at twice the limit allowed, he must be convicted, as a matter of law, of dangerous driving. To find otherwise would mean that the driver of an emergency vehicle driving at twice the limit, whatever the road conditions, however much warning was given to other road users, would be guilty of dangerous driving per se.

Drink driving

The case of *Woolfe v DPP* is mentioned both at (**4–1655**) and (**4–1680**). The facts were these. The appellant gave two samples of breath on an Intoximeter and the lower reading was 65 ig of alcohol. However, he testified that he had a tendency to reflux; that he had consumed no more alcohol than would, according to the defence expert evidence, have caused a reading of about 10 ig; therefore, the excess was due to repeated reflux. The justices found in favour of the defence on these evidential issues. Did this provide a defence, or special reasons for not imposing the otherwise obligatory disqualification, or neither?

The first question considered by the Administrative Court was whether the regurgitation and reabsorption of alcohol amounted to "a further consumption", thus bringing into play the "hip-flask" defence in s 15(3) of the Road Traffic Act 1988. However, by the time their Lordships had to answer it all the parties agreed that this "ingenious" argument was wrong and had to be rejected. That left the issue of special reasons. Here, the appellant was successful. Where a medical condition gave rise to a tendency to reflux, and the amount of alcohol consumed by the defendant would not have given a reading in excess of the legal limit, special reasons could be found.

Causing danger to road users

Section 22A of the Road Traffic Act 1988 created an offence of intentionally, etc, causing anything to be on or over a road, etc, in such circumstances that it would be obvious to a reasonable person that to do so would be dangerous. In *DPP v D* (**4–1403**) the characteristics and knowledge of the "reasonable man" were considered. D, a youth, placed a metal road sign in the roadway of the carriageway of a public road during the hours of darkness. A car crashed into a tree some distance beyond the position of the sign, killing both its occupants. At D's trial before the youth court the District Judge accepted a submission that the "reasonable person" must be construed in the context of a reasonable road user and that the dangerousness must relate to injury to a person or serious damage to property, and must be a real and significant danger, not simply a fanciful possibility. He concluded that he could not be satisfied that it would have been obvious to a reasonable person that causing the sign to be in the road would be dangerous. The prosecutor appealed by way of case stated.

The appeal succeeded. The reasonable person would have realized that an obstruction of the sort described in this case could play a part in causing an accident, notwithstanding that the primary cause of such an accident might be bad driving on the part of a motorist, whether in the form of excessive speed or a failure to keep a proper lookout or following other traffic too closely or a combination of such factors. The question to consider was whether a reasonable bystander would consider that what had been placed on the road represented an obvious danger, whether that reasonable bystander was a motorist or not. In this case, the reasonable bystander would have been fully aware that not all drivers drive carefully and well.

"Nearest available weighbridge" defence

It is an offence under s 41B of the Rood Traffic Act 1988 to contravene construction and use requirements as to weight, but this is subject to, inter alia, a "nearest available weighbridge" defence in subs (2). It was held that *Operator Services Agency v F & S Gibbs Transport Services* (**4–1423**) that "nearest available" meant precisely what it said and not the "nearest available weighbridge of which the driver was aware".

Appeals to magistrates' courts

Magistrates' courts have a significant appellate jurisdiction from the decisions of administrative bodies. The most well known is perhaps that from decisions of licensing authorities under the Licensing Act 2003, or in the context of Road Traffic, appeals against the decision of the Secretary of State to withhold a driving licence on grounds of physical fitness or disability.

R (Stace) v Milton Keynes Magistrates' Court (**4–1524**) concerned an appeal to a magistrates' court in accordance with s 119 of the Road Traffic Act 1988 against a decision of a Traffic Commissioner revoking the appellant's entitlement to hold a passenger-carrying vehicle driver's licence. The grant of such a licence requires the Commissioner to be satisfied of the applicant's fitness to hold such a licence having regard to his conduct both as a driver of a motor vehicle and in any other respect relevant to his holding a PCV licence.

The issue of the appellant's fitness arose in connexion with his convictions for three offences of assault on his wife. The appellant failed to attend proceedings before the Commissioner and his licence was revoked. He then appealed to the magistrates' court which subsequently dismissed his appeal. The appellant then sought judicial review of that decision. It should be noted that the more appropriate means of appeal would have been case stated in view of the point which the appellant sought to make, namely that the magistrates had taken into account irrelevant considerations. Owing to a misunderstanding by the appellant that appeal to the Crown Court was open to him, the time limit for case stated had elapsed before he discovered his error. However, Keith J permitted the application for judicial review to proceed because the main reason for preferring case stated – the obligation on the magistrates to state their reasons for their decision and thereby reveal what considerations they had taken into account, had been superseded by the justices giving reasons of their own account.

His Lordship then went on to review the magistrates' decision. He concluded that they had taken into account irrelevant considerations in that when assessing his fitness to hold a PCV licence they had considered the fact that a community rehabilitation order was still in place – the order was made because of the prior conduct, and it was the response to the order that was relevant. Secondly, in considering the appellant's state of depression, the magistrates had appeared to conclude that the fact of the depression was sufficient to dismiss the appeal rather than going on to consider what the depression said about the possibility of a repetition of the conduct. His Lordship concluded therefore, that the magistrates' decision was flawed because they took into account irrelevant considerations: the fact that the community rehabilitation order was still in place; they failed to put the appellant's depression in its proper place; and they appeared not to have looked at his conduct in the context of whether conduct of that particular kind might affect his fitness to drive passenger-carrying vehicles.

Finally, his Lordship commented on the role of magistrates hearing such appeals. They must exercise their own judgment. They may take account of any reasons given by the Traffic Commissioner for the decision appealed from, but they should not approach the appeal on the basis that it is to be dismissed unless there was something wrong in principle with the original decision.

Notice to owner

As we write this Preface, it is reported in the newspapers that 1.3 million people are just one motoring offence away from disqualification from driving. The comment was made in connexion with the proliferation of what are described as "speed cameras", "enforcement cameras" or "safety cameras" depending on the point of view of the writer. With statistics such as these (even taking account of the sensible caution which should be applied to all statistics) it is not surprising that there should be litigation in magistrates' courts concerning the imposition of penalty points arising from the use of cameras. Much of this has originated from the "notice to owner" (strictly "notice to keeper') provisions of s 172 of the Road Traffic Act 1988 and we have by now digested the Human Rights implications of the legislation in *Brown v Stott (Prosecutor Fiscal, Dunfermline)* [2003] 1 AC 68. But other challenges have been brought on the basis of the formalities of completing such a notice.

The latest one was *R (Flegg) v Southampton and New Forest Justices* (**4–1598**). Mr Flegg received a notice under s 172(2) of the 1988 Act in respect of a motorcycle registered to him requiring him to give information about the identity of the driver. He was prosecuted for his failure to comply, and convicted. He applied for judicial review to order the justices to state a case. Unusually, when permission was granted to bring judicial review, the justices, supported by the CPS, "stuck to their guns" and did not thereupon state a case and the matter proceeded by way of judicial review.

The form that had been sent to the claimant contained a general part and then a section with two parts. Part 1 was to be completed if the person to whom it was sent was the driver at the time and Part 2 if he was not the driver and provided for him to state who the driver was or, if unable to do so, to state the reason.

The claimant returned the form with that part completed which applied in all cases but he did not complete Parts 1 or 2 but gave his reason in a covering letter that "on the day of the alleged offence, more than one person used the vehicle," and requested the police send video/photographic evidence which might enable him to provide the required information.

Photo evidence was duly sent. Ultimately, he replied that neither he nor a friend who had access to the motorcycle, could recall travelling in the area on the occasion in question and he could not distinguish if either of them might have been the rider. Eventually a summons was issued.

In the Divisional Court it was argued for the first time by the claimant that there was no failure to comply with s 172(2) at all. As he did not know who was the driver he could not fill out Part 1 or Part 2 of the notice and the form did not require him to provide information about who the possible drivers were. Richards LJ was not persuaded by this. The fact remained that the claimant did not give the name of the driver and was therefore clearly in breach of the statutory requirement. Secondly, the form had asked him to provide the driver's details "or give any information in your power which will lead to the driver's identification" and he had failed to give information about the only other possible driver. His Lordship considered the information given was inaccurate and misleading and the provision of such information does not comply with the requirements of the legislation.

On the evidence before the justices it was clear that the claimant did not in fact believe he was the driver and as he knew there was only one other possibility, he must have believed that the other person was the driver. Whether the other person believed he was the driver was beside the point. It was therefore incumbent on him to make good a defence under s 172(4). This provides that a person is not guilty if he shows that "he did not know and could not with reasonable diligence have ascertained who the driver of the vehicle was".

Not surprisingly, in the light of what had been said, his Lordship did not feel that this defence began to get off the ground. His Lordship felt that the justices had been right to refuse to state a case.

Conditional offer of fixed penalty

Where a document contains both a requirement to given information as to the identity of the driver and a conditional offer of fixed penalty but the conditional offer of fixed penalty fails to comply with the requirement under s 75(7)(c) of the Road Traffic Offenders Act 1988 in that it fails to state that proceedings cannot be brought within 28 days or such longer period as may be specified, this does not preclude the commencement of proceedings outside the 28-day period from the date of the offer or render such a prosecution an abuse of process. The Administrative Court so held in *DPP v Holden* (**4–1735**).

Speed detection devices

Detection of speeding offences by automated devices was an issue in *DPP v Thornley* (**4–1659**) in connexion with the admissibility of photographic evidence. The police alleged that the defendant had exceeded a temporary 40mph speed limit on the M6 at Warrington and relied on photographic images produced by the "*Speed Violation Detection Deterrent System*" (SVDD) which is a device prescribed for the purposes of s 20 of the Road Traffic Offenders Act 1988.

Section 20(1) provides that evidence of a fact relevant to proceedings may be given by the production of a record produced by a prescribed device and a certificate certifying the circumstances in which the record was produced. Sub-section (6) further provides that evidence of a measurement by such a device and that it was an approved device, may be given by production of such a signed certificate.

The issue in this case was the effect of sub-s (8) which states that nothing in sub-ss (1) and (6) makes a document admissible in evidence, in essence, unless it has been served at least seven days before the hearing. The photographic evidence in the present case was served less than seven days before the hearing and the defendant successfully submitted there was no case to answer. However, on appeal, Owen J was of the view that the terms of sub-s (8) are permissive; they do not exclude the possibility of evidence of the record being produced by the prescribed device being adduced in another way.

His Lordship drew an analogy with s 16 of the Road Traffic Offenders Act 1988 and the admission of a printout produced by a device for measuring breath alcohol levels, where it had been held that the admissibility of such a document did not just arise through s 16 but was an admissible document and represented real evidence if properly produced. The purpose of the scheme was to enable the printout, together with an appropriate certificate, to be tendered at the hearing without the necessity of anybody being called but s 20 does not preclude such evidence being called in the conventional manner.

In the present case the prosecution had put the printout from the SVDD before the justices and an officer had given evidence as to the circumstances in which it had been obtained. To the objection that this would circumvent the seven day notice provision and possibly inhibit the defence from subjecting the document to careful analysis, the response was that any disadvantaged defendant could seek an adjournment. It would be expected that an adjournment would be granted in such circumstances, possibly with an order for costs thrown away.

Road Safety Act 2006

Major changes to Road Traffic law are to be introduced by the **Road Safety Act 2006** (**4–2014Q** et seq) the majority of whose sections remain to be implemented. Again this is an Act which achieves much of its purpose by inserting provisions in other legislation. In this edition we have included those sections in the Acts into which they will be inserted with an indication as to whether they have been commenced.

It is not practicable to set out here all the new measures, many of which have already been the subject of debate in the national press. Readers of STONE will no doubt be aware of the proposal to introduce a graduated scheme of fixed penalties and in particular graduated penalty points (which might reduce the possibility of the 1.3 million drivers being taken off the road). It is proposed to change the system of endorsements so that endorsements are for legal purposes recorded on a register at DVLA rather than a "counterpart". This means that fixed penalties will be able to be given to those drivers without a counterpart, such as the holders of foreign licences. Drink driving offences are supplemented by amendments to make an endorsement for failure to provide a specimen stay on the record for 11 years and new provisions are inserted to provide for alcohol ignition interlocks. Speed features again in that "speed assessment detection devices" will be prohibited under the construction and use regulations but this will not extend to such equipment as SAT NAV devices which contain information about published camera site locations. One of the issues in *DPP v Milton* was whether the police officer was using the car for police purposes. In the circumstances of the case this did not need to be finally resolved. Under the new s 19 amendments to s 87 of the Road Traffic Regulation Act 1984 will enable the Secretary of State to prescribe by regulations other purposes for which vehicles may be exempt from speed limits.

Perhaps some of the more difficult decisions for courts will arise under the new offences created by ss 20–29 of the Act. That which has attracted most attention is the offence of causing death by careless or inconsiderate driving which will be triable either way with a maximum penalty of five years' imprisonment. The criminal law generally only punishes offences of intent or where there has been subjective reckless. Offences of negligence are confined to minor matters with the exception of manslaughter where the negligence has to be "gross" such that a jury considers it to be worthy of punishment by the criminal law.

Magistrates' courts see many cases of careless driving where there has been "momentary inadvertence" of the kind which happens on a proportion of all car journeys but which has, through ill fortune, caused death. At present such cases attract a fine and possible disqualification and an effort to console grieving relatives. But the culpability is no greater than many other careless driving cases which are resolved by way of a fixed penalty. Now there is the prospect of a term of imprisonment. There will be an acute need for guidance to the courts on how to deal with such wide ranging powers. Will such a defendant be swept up into the higher levels of sentencing, or will the bottom end of the dangerous drivers be charged with the new offence? The nature of the advice given to those charged with this offence will be significant. Will they be advised to seek trial before a jury? This will be the only form of careless driving which carries a right to choose jury trial.

Less troublesome is the new offence of causing death by driving whilst unlicensed, disqualified or uninsured as there is at least in most cases a conscious decision to take a risk of driving in contravention of the law. A further tightening of the law relating to no insurance is provided by s 22 of the 2006 Act which creates a new s 144A of the 1988 Act to require the registration mark or the vehicle's owner to be specified in an insurance policy or security. Also, the registered keeper of a vehicle which is required to be insured will be guilty of an offence. There will be a number of exceptions, such as where a statutory off road notice has been made. As an alternative to a criminal sanction, failure to comply will attract a fixed penalty and regulations may permit the clamping and disposal of vehicles on reasonable suspicion that an offence under s 144A has been committed. Coupled with this will be greater powers for Motor Insurers' Information Centre to provide information to prescribed persons.

Penalties for a number of offences are increased. The one which received most publicity was the imposing of an endorsement on the use of a hand held mobile phone when driving (s 26, in force from 27 February 2006). A second offence of using a vehicle in a dangerous condition within 3 years of a previous conviction for the same offence will attract a mandatory disqualification (s 24). Section 29 will raise the number of penalty points for those who fail to provide information as to the identity of a driver from 3 to 6 points. Section 34 inserts new ss 30A–30 into the Road Traffic Offenders Act 1988 to provide for a scheme whereby, in prescribed circumstances, offenders convicted of careless or inconsiderate driving, disobeying traffic signs, or speeding, may be offered a course which he must pay for and which if duly completed will entail the court ordering that penalty points for the offence will not be taken into account for totting purposes. The restrictions and qualifications in the legislation will certainly be challenging, if only initially, to those who have to implement it. In tandem, s 35 will extend the scope of the present scheme in ss 34A–C of the Road Traffic Offenders Act 1988 to a wider range of offences.

Finally, we include in this edition the **Passenger and Goods Vehicles (Recording Equipment) (Tachograph Card) Regulations 2006, SI 2006/1937 (4–2701Y)** which are aimed at preventing fraudulent applications for, and misuse of, digital tachograph cards.

Family Law

Breach of good practice precepts and infringements of human rights

Non-compliance with precepts concerned with good practice is one thing, but the infringement of human rights is another. This distinction was highlighted in *Re J (a child) (care proceedings: fair trial)* (**6–164A**). The 17-year-old mother had a one-year-old daughter, C. The mother had experienced a chaotic childhood and adolescence, and had spent time in a psychiatric hospital. Following C's birth, the local authority placed her in short-term foster care. Whilst the mother initially attended contact sessions with C reliably, she experienced further problems and subsequently failed to attend for periods of contact with C, or for meetings with other professionals. The local authority applied for a care order for C upon a plan that she should be adopted. Psychiatric and psychological reports were prepared, including a specialist assessment of the mother's parenting capacity. The local authority set up a meeting about 2 months before the substantive hearing to communicate to the mother its plan to place C for adoption without further delay rather than to gather further views via a residential assessment of the mother with C. The meeting was in three stages: first, a meeting between social workers and the local authority's solicitor; secondly, a meeting between all of them and other interested professionals, including the social worker allocated to the mother, SD, and C's guardian; and thirdly, a meeting with the mother and her representatives.

At the meeting, the mother was not told that SD had not withdrawn an earlier suggestion that other options might remain open, or that C's guardian had not expressly agreed with the local authority's plan. The mother was informed of the plan that C should be adopted, she became extremely upset, and the meeting broke up.

At the substantive hearing, the mother criticised the local authority's conduct of the meeting, contending that there had been lamentable failures in its handling of her case which amounted to an infringement of her human rights under arts 6 and 8 of the Convention. The judge recognised that there had been procedural defects in the August 2005 meeting, contrary to the recommended guidelines, in that the mother and her solicitor had been excluded from discussions and so had been unable to hear the experts and to take part. However, he found that even if the mother had participated in the prior discussions, the local authority's care plan would not have been any different. The judge therefore ordered that C be committed to the local authority's care with a plan for adoption.

The mother's appeal was unsuccessful. Judges should be extremely careful about elevating failure to follow good practice into breach of human rights. The mother's rights under arts 6 and 8 had not been infringed. The failure to follow good practice had not been sufficient to infect the fairness of the proceedings, and nothing she could have done or said at the meeting could have changed the content of the decision that the local authority reached. The prospect of a residential assessment leading to a sufficiently confident decision as to the mother's capacity to care for the child had been negligible.

Privacy of proceedings concerning children

In *Clayton v Clayton* (**6–2B** and **6–2236**) the Court of Appeal considered the prohibitions on publicity in s 97(2) of the Children Act 1989 and s 12 of the Administration of Justice Act 1960. The parties were married in 1997. They separated in spring 2000 and thereafter shared the care of their daughter. In September 2002 the mother commenced proceedings for contact and residence orders. During those proceedings, and before they could be resolved at a hearing, the father abducted the child, removing her from the jurisdiction to Portugal, travelling and living there in a camper van and concealing their whereabouts. The case attracted considerable publicity including regional and national television coverage.

After an absence of five and a half weeks, the father was arrested and imprisoned in Portugal where he remained for two months. On his return to England he was remanded in custody and sentenced to nine months' imprisonment on a plea of guilty to child abduction.

Some four months after his release from prison, the father was able to resume contact with the child by order of the court in the proceedings under the Children Act 1989.

In November 2004 the mother received a copy of an e-mail sent by the father to a BBC reporter indicating the intention of the father to publicise and discuss delays in obtaining Legal Aid, criticisms of the services of CAFCASS, etc; and his intention to revisit Portugal in the near future to make a video diary retracing his steps with the child during their time there together ending in his imprisonment. At that time, the Children Act proceedings were part-heard. On the application of the mother, the judge made an order restraining the father until the child's 18th birthday or until further notice: "from discussing or otherwise communicating (otherwise than for ordinary domestic and social purposes) any matter relating to the education, maintenance, financial circumstances or family circumstances (including any proceedings before any court) of . . . ("the child") other than with: (*a*) any legal adviser whom he may consult or instruct; (*b*) the other parties; (*c*) the medical and educational advisers of the child; (*d*) any person to whom information is communicated for the purpose of enabling the person to exercise any function in relation to the child which is authorised by Statute or by a court of competent jurisdiction; and (*e*) any other person the court may permit . . ." Agreement was subsequently reached about the disposal of the Children Act proceedings and the father applied for the injunction to be lifted in its totality. The judge declined to discharge to do so and the father appealed.

Their Lordships noted that the prohibition in s 97(2) is limited to the duration of the proceedings, but the limitations in s 12 of the Administration of Justice Act 1960 of the publication of proceedings in private remain and a judge can in the welfare interests of the child and in order to protect his or her privacy, make an order under ss 1 and 8 of the Children Act 1989 or grant an injunction which prohibits the identification of the child for a period beyond the end of proceedings. The following was then said about the practical consequences this had for courts hearing Children Act cases:

"... henceforth it will be appropriate for every tribunal, when making what it believes to be a final order in proceedings under the Children Act 1989, to consider whether or not there is an outstanding welfare issue which needs to be addressed by a continuing order for anonymity. This will, I think, be a useful discipline for parties, judges, and family practitioners alike. If there is no outstanding welfare issue, then it is likely that the penal consequences of s 97 of the 1989 Act will cease to have any effect, and the parties will be able to put into the public domain any matter relating to themselves and their children which they wish to publish, provided that the publication does not offend against s 12 of the Administration of Justice Act 1960. Our judgments in this case are likely to have an impact, and must not be misunderstood. The fact that the provisions of s 97(2) of the 1989 Act cease to operate after the conclusion of the proceedings does not mean that parents are free at that point to draw their children into an ongoing public debate about their welfare or other wider issues. The court, after the conclusion of the proceedings, retains its welfare jurisdiction and will be able to intervene where a child's welfare is put at risk by inappropriate parental identification for publicity purposes. Quite where the line is to be drawn between s 1 of the Children Act 1989 and the European Convention, arts 8 and 10, in this context remains to be seen, although I venture to think that in practice most parents will recognise it. But let those parents who do not be in no doubt that the court's powers under ss 1 and 8 of the 1989 Act remain, as do its powers to grant injunctions" (per Sir Mark Potter P at paras 77 and 78).

Duty to provide accommodation does not extend to "secure accommodation"

In *R (M) v Gateshead Metropolitan Borough Council* (**6–2130**) M was born in August 1988 and was voluntarily accommodated by the defendant local authority at the request of her mother for periods during 2004 until her 16th birthday, when she discharged herself from the authority's accommodation and began to live in a hostel. In November 2004 she was arrested for alleged wounding with intent and detained at a police station. She was charged with the offence late that night and the police contacted social services in an attempt to find secure accommodation for her overnight until she was produced before the magistrates' court next morning. No secure accommodation was found, so M was detained overnight at the police station, pursuant to s 38(6) of the Police and Criminal Evidence Act 1984. She sought permission to bring judicial review proceedings, challenging the failure of the authority to provide her with secure accommodation when requested to do so by the police on the basis that it was a breach of the duty imposed on the authority by s 21(2)(b) of the Children Act 1989.

It was held that s 38(6) did not limit the police as to the local authority they had to approach for accommodation. It did not have to be the local authority for that police station area. However, the duty under s 21(2)(b) was a duty to provide accommodation, and to develop that into a duty to provide secure accommodation when this was requested would be an unreasonable interpretation given the resource implications this would have for local authorities. It was a matter for the judgment of the local authority, taking full account of the need to avoid having children detained in police cells if at all possible, to decide what arrangements to make to provide secure accommodation when it was requested by the police. The court would strike down as unlawful arrangements that had been made by local authorities only if satisfied that they had been non-existent, or were ones that could not have been made by a reasonable authority mindful of the need to avoid having children detained in police cells if at all possible.

Expert evidence

A notable feature of children's cases in recent years has been the considerable growth in the use of expert evidence. The use of expert witnesses is of course expensive and contributes greatly to delay. Nevertheless, a denial of the opportunity to instruct an expert may unfairly prejudice the case of a party. A reminder of this fact may be found on *Re S* (**6–35A**) which reports a number of appeals from case management decisions. The first of the appeals concerned the refusal of the court to allow the parents unilaterally to instruct four experts in the course of care proceedings arising from suspected non-accidental injury. The local authority preferred the joint instruction of four other experts. The impetus for the appeal was the judgment of Wall LJ in *W v Oldham Metropolitan Borough Council* [2006] 1 FLR 543 which we noted in the previous edition, in which parents were permitted to instruct their own expert where the whole case would otherwise pivot on one doctor. In the present case however, Wilson LJ was at pains to point out that the court did not intend to suggest that it should favour the instruction of two or more experts in the same discipline additional to such experts already destined to give evidence because of their clinical involvement in the child's case. His Lordship could not see the *Oldham* case as authority for what the parents contended. There was nothing objectionable in a carefully crafted joint letter of instruction to an expert. At this stage in the proceedings how could it be said that there was an expert whose evidence was adverse to the parents and pivotal and so justified a second opinion?

Witness summons

In care proceedings, and family proceedings in general, a child does not give evidence before a family proceedings court. In the county court too, it is not normally appropriate for a child to give evidence and in these courts there is provision even in private law proceedings for a child to be separately represented in accordance with Part 9 of the Family Proceedings Rules 1991. *Re M (a child) care proceedings: witness summons)* (**6–37**) was an interesting case concerning the issue of a witness summons in care proceedings before the county court to a 10-year-old child.

It was alleged by the mother that the child had been physically abused by the father when he was drunk. The child had been interviewed on video by the police in which she disclosed allegations of abuse. Later, the mother retracted her allegations against the father but the local authority persevered with care proceedings. Prior to the mother's retraction, the child had repeated her allegations to a social worker, but since then no further steps had been taken to obtain evidence from the child as to the truth or falsity of her earlier evidence.

At the hearing the mother applied for a witness summons for the child to give evidence by video link. The guardian and the local authority opposed the application. A summons was issued which was challenged by an appeal to the Court of Appeal. At the hearing of the appeal, Lady Justice Smith cited the judgment of Butler-Sloss LJ in *R v B County Council* [1991] 1 FLR 470 that a court should be very cautious in requiring the attendance of a child and doing so risked adverse effects on the child concerned, and in *Re P (Witness summons)* [1997] 2 FLR 447 it had been indicated that it would be only in the most unusual circumstances that a witness summons would be appropriate to compel a child to give evidence in care proceedings.

In the present case Her Ladyship confirmed that the correct starting point is that it is undesirable that a child should have to give evidence in care proceedings and that particular justification will be required before that course is taken. It will be rare that it is right to make an order. The court then outlined the factors to be considered. The fact that the child had given a video interview and would be cross-examined by live link did not change the approach as it does not go to the heart of the problem which is the psychological effect on the child of having to talk about the abuse and having the account challenged as untrue.

Emergency protection orders

We welcome the approach taken by Wall LJ when discussing special guardianship in *In re S* (below) in setting out in detail the background to new legislation together with a detailed commentary on the working of the provisions. This approach has been mirrored by MacFarlane J in an area of vital concern to family proceedings courts. In *Re X (Emergency Protection Orders)* (**6–175**) his Lordship set out detailed guidance for considering applications for emergency protection orders, where he drew together earlier advice given by Munby J in *X Council v B (Emergency Protection Orders)* [2004] EWHC 2015 (Fam).

There is a useful reminder to justices that the making of an emergency protection order is a "draconian" and "extremely harsh" measure requiring "exceptional justification" and to be made only where no other less radical form of order will achieve the end of promoting the child's welfare. Imminent danger must be actually established. Because of the importance of this guidance, we set out the judgment *in extenso*. Indeed, the list of 14 factors contained therein is to be regarded as "required reading" for every magistrate and justices' clerk involved in any emergency protection order application and should be copied and be before them on every occasion that an application is made.

Prohibited steps and specific issue orders

In *Re C (children) (parent: purported marriage between two women: artificial insemination by donor)* (**6–150**) two children were born to a "married" couple by AI. At the relevant times, the mother believed that her "husband", J, was a man. However, in fact and in law he was not (though he later obtained a gender certificate and an amended birth certificate). The "marriage" was, thus, annulled. The mother remarried. J then issued proceedings under s 8 of the Children Act 1989 for, inter alia, a prohibited steps order that the children should not be informed of their parentage and the reasons for the breakdown in relationships, and in particular J's gender, save at such times and in a manner advised by Dr E (a consultant psychiatrist) or such other consultant child psychiatrist as might be agreed; and a specific issue order that Mrs C seek the advice of Dr E.

It was held, and upheld on appeal, that J was not a "parent" within the meaning of s 10 of the Children Act 1989. In any event, the court expressed grave concerns about whether there was jurisdiction by means of such s 8 orders to dictate to a parent what she told her children about their origins.

Care plans

A significant issue for courts which emerged once the provisions of the Children Act 1989 had become established, was the scope for the court to influence the local authority once a care order had been made. This gave rise at one time to the "starred milestones" until such concept was quashed by the House of Lords. It is now understood that the limits to the court's jurisdiction is to satisfy itself that the care plan prepared by the authority will satisfactorily promote the welfare of the child.

In *Re R (Care Plan for Adoption: Best Interest)* (**6–165**) adoption was the proposed outcome of the care plan. In such cases, the court must satisfy itself that the local authority is capable of delivering on its care plan. In general the local authority should have had a best interests panel and had its decision ratified. Otherwise the court is unable to satisfy itself that the social worker who puts forward the care plan can deliver on it in the future. The court would expect there to be prospective adopters who will be capable of meeting the child's needs or in some cases the family placement officer will need to provide evidence that an adoptive placement is capable of being effected. The next stage, the actual matching of the child to adopters will be a decision for the local authority in execution of an approved care plan.

Contact and adoption

Re R (a child) (adoption: content) (**6–2109**) was a reminder that contact orders in adoption proceedings are unusual and involved an application for leave to apply for contact made by the sister of the prospective adopted child. Wall LJ reviewed the provisions of s 10(9) of the 1989 Act. In deciding whether to grant leave, the court is entitled to conduct a broad assessment of the merits of a particular application. The authorities only prohibit a determination of the application on the "no reasonable prospects of success" criteria. Although matters have moved on since some of the earlier authorities, and since the advent of the Adoption and Children Act 2002, contact is more common, nevertheless the imposition on prospective adopters of orders for contact with which they are not in agreement, is extremely, and remains extremely, unusual. In the present case, the issue was not the principle of contact but the nature and quantum of contact between the siblings. In the circumstances, having regard to the interests of the child, the application by the sister was unlikely to result in an order and so the appeal against the judge's refusal to grant leave, was dismissed.

Special guardianship

Special guardianship has now begun to attract the attention of the Court of Appeal and in *In re S (a child) (special guardianship order)* (**6–160**) Wall LJ set out a helpful summary of the legislative background to the introduction of special guardianship orders and the case should be read by all those who practise in this area. In a comprehensive judgment his Lordship includes: the historical background including custodianship and the origins of special guardianship; an analysis of the statutory provisions; the application of the general principles under the Children Act 1989; relationship to adoption; and commentary on the application of the statutory provisions to specific issues such as dispensing with parental consent to adoption.

The relationship between applications under the 1989 Act in various proceedings has always given rise to some issues of complexity but as regards a parent applying for a s 8 order in respect of a child subject to a special guardianship order, it has been confirmed that the leave of the court is not required (*A Local Authority v X, Y, Z* (**6–2108**)). However, a person who is not entitled as of right to make an application for special guardianship must obtain the leave of the court. The requirements regarding notice and a report by the local authority were spelled out by Wall LJ in *R (a child) (special guardianship order)* (**6–2113A**). In particular, that a party to care proceedings who had not yet obtained leave could not give notice to the local authority triggering the preparation of a report. Nor should the court compel the authority to do so except in circumstances where the court considers in proceedings that a special guardianship order should be made even though no application has been made.

Restriction on applications

Re S (children) (restriction on applications) (**6–2230**) concerned two appeals against refusals to allow applications for relief to proceed during the period in which a restriction under s 91(14) of the Children Act 1989 was in force. The issues for determination were (1) is it permissible for the court to impose conditions on the order, restricting or otherwise identifying the circumstances in which an application for permission can be made – to which the answer was no; (2) the evidence required for an application for permission to apply and the manner in which such an application needs to be made; (3) the circumstances in which it is appropriate to make a s 91(14) order without limit of time or until the 16th birthday of the child in question.

In the light of the observations of the Court of Appeal, we have taken the opportunity completely to recast the extensive note to s 91.

Child support

Finally, and with some degree of relief, we report the decision of the House of Lords in *Farley v Secretary of State for Work and Pensions* (**6–2945**) which concludes the litigation about the scope of magistrates' jurisdiction when dealing with applications for liability orders under the Child Support legislation. It has been held that justices are precluded from questioning any aspect of a child maintenance assessment; their jurisdiction is limited to checking that the assessment relates to the defendant brought to court and that the payments have become due and have not been paid.

Animals

Causing unnecessary suffering

In *R (on the application of the RSPCA) v C* (**8–811**) C, who was aged 15, was the owner of a cat. She lived with her father who decided that the cat, which had sustained an injury to his tail, should not receive veterinary attention unless its condition appeared to worsen. C did not seek veterinary care herself but did tell her father that the cat should go to the vet. The RSPCA intervened. They charged the father and C with an offence of causing unnecessary suffering to an animal contrary to s 1(1)(*a*) of the Animals Act 1911. The father pleaded guilty, but C denied the offence.

The facts found by the court were: (i) the respondent had concluded that the cat should be taken to the vet and had told her father that; (ii) the father would have had to pay for such treatment; and (iii) the respondent had had to accept that her father, as head of the house, had decided that it was not necessary to seek veterinary attention. The justices were of the opinion that the cat was caused unnecessary suffering by not receiving timely veterinary treatment, but they accepted that it was reasonable for the respondent, being a young person, not to go against her father's decision. Therefore, they acquitted her of the offence. The RSPCA appealed by way of case stated. They submitted that the justices were not entitled to take into account C's age and her position in the family and that the correct test to establish whether she did not act unreasonably was purely objective, namely did she act as a reasonably competent, reasonably caring owner.

The Administrative Court dismissed the appeal. The test to establish whether the respondent had acted unreasonably by permitting unnecessary suffering was not entirely objective. While the suffering of the animal had to be judged objectively, it was for the justices to decide whether any explanation given by the defendant was or was not reasonable by having regard to subjective considerations. The justices were entitled, indeed obliged, to take account of the defence that C was putting forward in determining whether she had not acted unreasonably in the matter.

Animal Welfare Act 2006

The **Animal Welfare Act 2006** (**8–1568**) is the first major, general legislation on this subject for the best part of a century. It makes comprehensive provision for the welfare of animals, defined to include all vertebrates (and possibly, if regulations are so made, invertebrates of any description). In so doing it repeals, inter alia, most of the provisions of the Protection of Animals Act 1911 and the Protection of Animals Act 1934, ss 2 and 3 of the Pet Animals Act 1951, the Cockfighting Act 1952, the Protection of Animals (Anaesthetics) Acts 1954 and 1964, and the Abandonment of Animals Act 1960.

In summary, its contents are as follows. It creates offences concerned with: causing unnecessary suffering; mutilation; docking of dogs' tails; administration of poisons; and animal fighting (ss 4–8). There is a general duty on those permanently or temporarily responsible for animals to ensure that their needs are met to the extent required by good practice; and for the service by an inspector of an improvement notice if he is of the opinion that a person is not complying with that duty (ss 9 and 10). It is an offence to transfer an animal by way of sale or prize to a person under 16 (s 11). There is a system of licensing or registration of activities involving animals (s 13). Codes of practice will be relevant to liability or non-liability for an offence under the Act (ss 14–17). The Act confers powers in relation to animals in distress and the making of orders in relation to protected (ie commonly domesticated) animals taken into protective care (ss 18–21). Enforcement powers enable the seizure of animals involved in fighting (s 22). There are powers of entry and search, and inspection of records of or in connection with licences or registration, etc (ss 23–29). Local authorities are given a general power to prosecute offences under the Act (s 30). It extends time limits for prosecutions (s 31). Post conviction powers include orders of deprivation, disqualification, destruction, forfeiture, cancellation of licences and reimbursement of expenses (ss 32–45). There are a number of powers in relation to the grant of warrants, powers of entry, power to stop and detain vehicles, etc (ss 51–56). Liability for corporate offences is extended to corporate officers (s 57). Finally, it exempts lawful scientific research and things done in the normal course of fishing (ss 58, 59).

The Act will be brought into force in accordance with commencement orders made under s 68. At the date at which this work states the law, no commencement orders had been made.

Armed forces

The **Armed Forces Act 2006** (**8–2379A**) would, in an ordinary legislative year, have been a contender for the longest Act, but, as will be seen, nothing came anywhere near the Companies Act 2006 for length. In summary, these are its theme and contents.

The Act prospectively replaces the separate (though similar to each other) systems of service law that were based in the Army Act 1955, the Air Force Act 1955 and the Naval Discipline Act 1957.

The main object of the 2006 Act is to provide a single, harmonised and updated system governing all members of the armed forces, though the key elements of the discipline system will remain.

The Act creates offences and provides for the investigation of alleged offences, the arrest, detention and charging of accused persons, and for accused persons to be dealt with summarily by their commanding officer or tried by court-martial. More serious cases must be notified to the service police and passed direct to the Director of Service Prosecutions (DSP). In all cases which it is intended should be tried by the new Court Martial, it will be the DSP who decides whether to prosecute and, if so, the nature of the charges.

The Act, as previously mentioned, is not short with its 19 Parts, 386 sections and 17 schedules. Only those provisions that are relevant to the work of magistrates' courts, however, are reproduced in this work. Nearly all of the Act's provisions are to be brought into force in accordance with commencement orders made under s 383. At the date at which this work states the law no commencement orders had been made, and the Act provides in s 382 for the continuation of the Service Disciplinary Acts, with power under s 381 to amend or repeal their provisions (and those of various other Acts) to align current law more closely to that which will be achieved under the 2006 Act.

Charities

Charities also have a new, comprehensive legal framework with the enactment of the **Charities Act 2006** (**8–3109A**). It is arranged in four Parts, which we summarise as follows.

Part 1 deals with the definition of a charity and charitable purposes. Part 2 deals with the registration of charities. It contains 11 chapters. In the first it establishes a body corporate to be known as the Charity Commission for England and Wales, which supersedes the Charity Commissioners for England and Wales. The remaining chapters are concerned, inter alia, with: a tribunal to hear appeals; registration of charities; changes to the rules governing the application of property "cy-pres"; the assistance and supervision of charities; advertising, investment and mortgages; audit and examination; the establishment of "charitable incorporated organisations"; trustees; transfer of property to other charities; and the spending of capital endowment funds.

Part 3 is concerned with fundraising by, and the funding of, charities and other benevolent or philanthropic organisations. It is arranged in three chapters that deal, respectively, with arrangements for the conduct and regulation of collections, statements to be made to donors and consumers, and new powers for Ministers and the National Assembly to give financial assistance to charities and other benevolent organisations. Part 4 contains the final provisions.

Nearly all of the Acts provisions are to be brought into force in accordance with commencement orders made under s 79. We refer readers to that provision for details of orders made. Only the provisions of the Act that relate directly to offences or powers of entry are reproduced in this work.

Civil rights

Equality Act 2006

We suspect that few readers of this work will be unaware of the enactment of the **Equality Act 2006 (8–3119P)**. However, the news media reporting was largely confined to its potential impact on church-run adoption agencies. The Act, as will be seen, extends very much further. We summarise its contents as follows.

Part 1 of this Act establishes the Commission for Equality and Human Rights, which replaces the Equal Opportunities Commission, the Commission for Racial Equality and the Disability Rights Commission. The new Commission has a general duty, inter alia, to encourage and support the development of equality and to protect individual human rights, dignity and worth. The Commission has investigative powers and may issue "unlawful act" (ie acts contrary to specified equality enactments) notices which may require the recipients to prepare "action plans" to avoid repeating or continuing the specified unlawful acts (an appeal procedure is provided). The Commission may also seek injunctions to prevent prospective unlawful acts. The Commission is further empowered to issue "compliance notices" where it thinks a person has failed to comply with certain, specified duties to eliminate discrimination.

Part 2 of the Act is concerned with discrimination on grounds of religion or belief. It prohibits discrimination (as defined) in the provision of goods, facilities and services. It makes it unlawful for listed educational establishments to discriminate against a person in relation to admission as a pupil and other matters. It further makes it unlawful for any public authority (which is broadly defined) to do any act which constitutes discrimination. It also makes it unlawful to operate discriminatory practices, etc. General exceptions to Part 2 are provided for non-commercial organisations and charities concerned with religious practice or belief, faith schools, etc. A civil enforcement jurisdiction is established, and a criminal offence is created of knowingly or recklessly making a false statement that a proposed act is not unlawful.

Part 3 of the Act is concerned with discrimination on the grounds of sexual orientation. Regulations made under this Part may, inter alia, create criminal offences. It consists merely of enabling provisions. (The explanation given in Parliament for this was that this Part was added too late in the Bill's passage for the detail to be included.) The remaining Parts contain various amendments to the Sex Discrimination Act 1975 and general provisions.

With the exception of ss 41, 42 and 86 the Act will be brought into force in accordance with commencement orders made under s 93, and we refer readers to that provision for details of orders made and provisions brought into force.

Identity cards

The **Identity Cards Act 2006** (**8–3120D**) is another statute that will already be widely known. Its purpose, of course, was to make provision for a national scheme of registration of individuals and for the issue of cards capable of being used for identifying registered individuals. The Act makes it an offence for a person to be in possession or control of an identity document to which he is not entitled, or of apparatus, articles or materials for making false identity documents. Additionally, it amends the Consular Fees Act 1980; it makes provision facilitating the verification of information provided with an application for a passport; and it deals with related matters.

With the exception of ss 36 and 38, the Act will be brought into force in accordance with commencement orders made under s 44. In relation to the offence-creating provisions, it was necessary for the Administrative Court in *R (on the application of the CPS) v Bow Street Magistrates' Court* (**8–3120T**) to "re-write" part of the Identity Cards Act 2006 (Commencement No 1) Order 2006, SI 2006/1439 to achieve the intended, seamless transition.

Companies

To borrow some jargon from "the other side of the pond", the **Companies Act 2006** (**8–3931**) is "the mother of all Acts", at least in terms of length. Indeed, it was so long that there was a substantial delay before the printed version became available. Happily, there was still time to include in this work those parts which are relevant to magistrates' courts, namely the many offence-creating sections and the provisions that are ancillary thereto. Unhappily, there are a great many of them!

In summary, the contents of the Act are as follows. The company law provisions of this Act (Parts 1–39) restate almost all of the provisions of the Companies Act 1985, together with the company law provisions of the like-named Act of 1989 and the Companies (Audit, Investigations and Community Enterprise) Act 2004. The only company law provisions that remain in the aforementioned Acts are those on investigations that go wider than companies (Part 14 of the 1985 Act), and the provisions on community interest companies in Part 2 of the 2004 Act. (Various non-company law provisions remain, however, in the three earlier Acts.) The Act also codifies certain aspects of the case law.

In relation to non-company law, the 2006 Act amends other legislation, particularly the Financial Services and Markets Act 2000, and makes new provision of various kinds, principally in relation to: overseas disqualification of company directors; business names (replacing the Business Names Act 1985); statutory auditors (replacing Part 2 of the Companies Act 1989; and transparency obligations (amending Part 6 of the Financial Services and Markets Act 2000).

The Act provides for a single company law regime applying the whole of the UK. Northern Ireland thus ceases to have separate provision (though it can separately repeal or amend provisions if it so desires).

The Act will be brought into force in accordance with commencement orders made under s 1300. At the date at which this work states the law the Companies Act (Commencement No 1, Transitional Provisions and Savings) Order 2006, SI 2006/3428) had been made.

Consumer credit

The **Consumer Credit Act 2006** (8–5169N) principally amends the Consumer Credit Act 1974 by: providing for the regulation of all consumer credit and hire agreements (with certain exceptions); providing for the licensing of providers of consumer credit, hire and ancillary credit facilities, and making provision in relation to the functions and powers of the Office of Fair Trading in relation to licensing; enabling debtors to challenge unfair relationships with creditors; and providing for an Ombudsman scheme to hear complaints.

Note 1 to the title of the Act sets out the state of commencement as at the date at which this work states the law.

Education

There have been two major statutes on this topic. The **Childcare Act 2006** (8–7941) imposes duties on local authorities with regard to the well-being of young children and it makes provision in relation to childcare, including a new regime of regulation and inspection. The **Education and Inspections Act 2006** (8–7941) is a very much larger Act. The Act implements proposals contained in the White Paper *Higher Standards, Better Schools for All* (Cm 6677, published 25 October 2005). It also reduces the number of public service inspectorates, with the aims of enabling better coordination and reducing duplication.

The Act is divided into 10 Parts. Part 1 places new duties on LEAs. Part 2 re-enacts much of the current law relating to school organisation for England and creates a new procedure for schools to acquire a foundation and some minimum establishment and status requirements, and places school organisation decisions with LEAs, abolishing the school organisation committee. Part 3 creates certain requirements as to foundations and places certain duties on governing bodies. This Part also makes some changes to school admissions law, including banning interviewing. Part 4 gives LEAs new powers to tackle failing and underperforming schools more quickly and effectively. Part 5 sets out a new curriculum entitlement in relation to pupils aged 14–19. Part 6 places new duties on LEAs in relation to school travel. It also permits nutritional standards to be applied to food and drink supplied on school premises. Part 7 is concerned with school discipline. It provides a new power for teachers and other school staff, it extends the scope of parenting orders and parenting contracts and it requires parents to take responsibility for excluded pupils in the first five days of their exclusion. Part 8 provides for the establishment of the Office for Standards in Education, Children's Services and Skills and a new office of HM Chief Inspector of Education, Children's Services and Skills. The new arrangements unite various existing remits. The remaining Parts are concerned with miscellaneous matters and provide for a framework power that enables the National Assembly for Wales by regulations to make any provision that could be made by an Act of Parliament about any of the matters set out in s 178, subject to the limitation provided by s 179.

Only the provisions of this Act that create, or appertain very closely to, powers of entry, or offences, or school discipline are reproduced in this work. We refer readers to the note to the title of the Act for details of commencement orders made. Most of the Act's provisions, however, remain prospective.

Elections

The **Electoral Administration Act 2006** (8–8119ZU et seq) contains measures that are concerned with improving access to voting and helping to achieve the highest possible turnout of voters while, at the same time, reducing the risk of fraud. We refer readers to the note to the title of the Act for details of commencement orders made.

Emergency services

One of the shortest Acts to reach the statute books in 2006 was the **Emergency Workers (Obstruction) Act 2006** (**8–8131**), but such is the importance of the work of these services that we have created a new title in PART VIII to accommodate this legislation.

The Act makes it an offence to obstruct or hinder persons who provide emergency services. The Act is now fully in force.

Extradition

The **Extradition Act 2003** established new, comprehensive extradition procedures, but not entirely without controversy. The case of *R (on the application of Bermingham) v Director of the Serious Fraud Office* (**8–10243** and **8–10299ZD**) (the "Enron" case) attracted particular attention and comment. Time will be the judge of its accuracy and fairness. The case involved too many issues to be capable of adequate summary here, so we mention only that the Administrative Court, in upholding the extradition, held that extradition proceedings could be stayed as an abuse of process, but the question whether it was demonstrated had to be asked and answered in the light of the specifics of the statutory scheme. Provided the prosecutor had acted in good faith, no finding of abuse could be justified by the prosecutor's refusal or failure to disclose evidential material beyond what was contained in the extradition request. The prosecutor must, however, have acted in good faith. Thus, if he knew he had no real case, but was pressing the extradition request for some collateral motive and accordingly tailored the choice of documents accompanying the request, there might be a good submission of abuse of process. Their Lordships also held that where a proposed extradition was properly constituted according to the domestic law of the sending state, and its execution was resisted on art 8 grounds, a wholly exceptional case had to be shown to justify a finding that the extradition would on its particular facts be disproportionate to its legitimate aim.

The House of Lords also became involved in the new statutory scheme when it considered Part 1 warrants (ie extradition to category 1 territories) in *Office of the King's Prosecutor, Brussels v Cando Armas* (**8–10244** and **8–10299H**). Again, the facts and issues were too complicated for adequate summary here and we leave readers to turn to these paragraphs for the detail of what was held.

Health and Safety

The **Safeguarding Vulnerable Groups Act 2006** (**8–16001ZW** et seq) replaces existing statutory provisions providing for lists of those barred from working with or having contact with, children and vulnerable adults. The new scheme will provide for an "Independent Barring Board" with responsibility for maintaining lists of those who are barred from "regulated activities" as defined in the Act and making further provisions which we note to s 1 of the Act. The significant provisions of the Act will be brought into force in due course by commencement order and we reproduce those sections relevant to the criminal sanctions which are created by the act.

The introduction of the ban on smoking in public enclosed spaces by the Health Act 2006 is accompanied by a number of regulations. As this is likely to be a matter of considerable interest at least in its initial stages we include in this edition the **Smoke-free (Premises and Enforcement) Regulations 2006** (**10–6A**); **Smoke-free (Vehicle Operators and Penalty Notices) Regulations 2007** (**10–7**); **Smoke-free (Penalties and Discounted Amounts) Regulations 2007** (**10–8**); and the **Smoke-free (Exemptions and Vehicles) Regulations 2007** (**10–9**).

Immigration

Section 31 of the Immigration and Asylum Act 1999 (**8–17918**) provides defences to refugees who are charged with certain offences of fraud and deception (specified in subs(3)). It supersedes, but does not extend as far as, art 31(1) of the United Nations Convention relating to the Status of Refugees, and, in applying the law, the focus of the prosecuting authorities must now be on the domestic provision rather than the article (see *R (Pepushi) v Crown Prosecution Service*). Nevertheless, prosecution policy and practice may be subject to scrutiny.

In *R v Asfaw* the defendant was Ethiopian, and had left Ethiopia to travel to the United States on forged documents to seek asylum. She arrived at Heathrow airport, on a forged passport, and successfully passed through immigration. She was then given another forged passport and an "E-ticket" purchased in London for a passenger of the same name as the passport, for a flight from Heathrow to Washington. She was arrested after presenting her ticket at the check-in desk. She was charged with using a false instrument with intent (count one), contrary to s 3 of the Forgery and Counterfeiting Act 1981, and attempting to obtain services by deception (count two).

She was acquitted by the jury in relation to count one, having raised the statutory defence under s 31. However, that provision did not extend to the offence charged by count two. The defendant unsuccessfully sought a ruling from the judge that she could rely upon art 31 by way of a defence to that count and, consequently, she pleaded guilty to attempting to obtain services by deception. She was sentenced to 9 months' imprisonment on the basis that a deterrent sentence was justified.

She appealed against conviction. She submitted that the prosecution had acted in abuse of process by seeking to avoid the effect of the statutory defence by prosecuting her under count two on the indictment. The prosecution accepted that, on the facts of the instant case, art 31 required that the defendant should have a defence, even if charged with attempting to obtain services by deception, and that the art and s 31 could apply to an asylum-seeker who was seeking to use the United Kingdom as a transit post in a journey to a preferred place of refuge. However, it contended that Parliament, in enacting s 31, had expressly determined the offences to which the defence should apply, and that there was no basis for contending that the defence should apply to other offences. It was the duty of the CPS to enforce the law of the land, and no criticism could be made of it for including the second count.

The court ruled as follows. Whether or not there was merit in the defendant's argument that there had been an abuse of process, the fair course in the instant case was to grant an order of absolute discharge, which would not be deemed as a conviction for any purpose in the future. There were aspects of the case that had caused concern. It was apparently standard practice where an asylum seeker was attempting to leave the UK for another place of refuge using false documents to combine a charge of infringement of the Forgery and Counterfeiting Act with a charge of attempting to obtain air services by deception. It seemed likely that that practice reflected a policy; however, it was also possible that the decisions in previous cases to withdraw the latter charge reflected some policy consideration. In the event, no firm conclusion could be reached as to why, in cases such as the present one, the prosecution combined the two counts. If it was the case that the second count was added in the interests of immigration control to prevent the asylum seeker from invoking the statutory defence that would otherwise be available, there would be strong grounds for contending that that practice constituted an abuse of process. At the same time, there was the possibility that the prosecution were correct to suggest that the CPS was doing no more than seeking to enforce the law in the interests of the airlines that were put at risk by the use of false documents.

When sentencing the defendant, the judge should have had regard to the circumstances and consequences of the dishonesty, namely that she had attempted to fly to Washington in order to seek asylum (conduct which, on the prosecution's concession, should attract no punishment were there to be full compliance with art 31), and there was no suggestion that the defendant's ticket was not properly purchased, nor any evidence that, had she been carried to Washington, that the airline would have in fact been exposed to the risk of any penalty. The judge's reasoning for imposing the custodial sentence was, thus, not merely inappropriate in the light of the offence for which the defendant fell to be sentenced, but also was at odds with the principle reflected by art 31 and s 31, assuming that each had the ambit which the prosecution had accepted.

In this edition we are able to reproduce guidance on the "refugee" defence in s 31 of the Immigration Act 1971 referred to above as the guidance to be given to juries where such a defence is in issue was set out in *R v Makuwa* (**8–17918**).

We referred in the Preface to the previous edition of STONE to the drafting of s 2 of the Asylum and Immigration (Treatment of Claimants etc) Act 2004 which we described as "Delphic in its obscurity". The true meaning of this section came in for a further elucidation in *Soe Thet v DPP* (**8–18029R**) when it was the turn of the Lord Chief Justice to make sense of its provisions. The objective of s 2 is deal with the problem of asylum seekers who have no documents with them to present to immigration control to establish where they travelled from. The complex provisions of the Act create a criminal offence but also various defences where a person is not able to produce a valid immigration document. These are ostensibly framed in a way to limit the circumstances in which a person may not incur criminal liability by limiting each defence to a specific factual situation. These defences include (*a*) proving that he has a reasonable excuse for not being in possession of an "immigration document" or (*b*) to produce a false immigration document that he used for all purposes in connection with his journey to the United Kingdom or (*c*) to prove that he travelled to the United Kingdom without at any stage having possession of an immigration document.

In the present case the appellant entered the United Kingdom on a false passport which, on entry, he handed back to his "facilitator." Therefore at his immigration interview he had no document to produce. At his trial, he relied on the defence of reasonable excuse for not providing a *genuine* document or in the alternative, *that* he had a reasonable excuse for not producing a *false* document. In the view of the court at first instance, the first defence applied only applied where a genuine document had existed, as regards the false document – that had existed and the defence was open to him but on the facts he had no reasonable excuse for not producing it.

In the Administrative Court, the prosecution did not seek to rely on the first limb of the decision on the court below, ie that the first defence did not apply where a document had never existed, but instead argued a different point that the scope of the defence was limited simply to having a reasonable excuse for not producing an immigration document – false or genuine – *within three days* of the immigration interview (ie for exceeding the time limit and not for having no document at all), which the appellant had failed to do. Recourse was to be had to Parliamentary material in accordance with *Pepper v Hart* [1993] 1 AC 593 to resolve the ambiguity.

In his decision, his Lordship questioned the use of *Pepper v Hart* in the context of a criminal prosecution. If a criminal statute is ambiguous, the defendant should have the benefit of such ambiguity.

The answer in his Lordship's view was that s 2(4)(*c*) provides a defence for a claimant who establishes a reasonable excuse why he did not produce a *genuine* document at, or in certain circumstances within three days of, his interview. He recognised that his finding might undermine the object of s 2 but that resulted from the drafting leaving much to be desired.

We also include in this section, at **8–18029ZZJ** et seq, those provisions of the Immigration, Asylum and Nationality Act 2006 that are relevant to the work of magistrates' courts.

Local government

The magistrates' court now has only an appellate role in liquor licensing, but in many ways this has made its task more difficult. What degree of deference should it accord to decisions of the local authority, and what relevance do general planning considerations have?

In *R (on the application of Blackwood) v Birmingham Magistrates and Birmingham City Council, Mitchells and Butler Leisure Retail Ltd (Interested Party)* (**8–19829Q**) the public house at the centre of the appeal, which was situated in a residential district, had applied to renew, and to vary the terms of, its licence under the Licensing Act's transitional provisions.

Prior to the application the public house had received planning permission which included new lighting arrangements, whose permitted hours coincided with its old licensing hours. The public house applied in standard form under the 2003 Act both to convert the existing licence to a premises licence under the new Act, and also simultaneously to vary the premises licence to enable it to stay open later. The council received representations from local residents objecting to the latter. No representation was made by the planning authority.

At the appeal hearing, the justices, who upheld the council's decision to renew and vary the licence, dealt with the appeal on the basis that they could not vary any existing planning permissions, and that more particularly they could not determine any hypothetical planning application that might be made in the future. On appeal to the Divisional Court, the claimant argued, inter alia, that, in view of the Licensing Act 2003, the licensing guidelines and Birmingham Council's own statement of policy, a licensing authority, and, on appeal, a magistrates' court, must take account of relevant planning matters.

It was held that, other than in respect of the protection of children from harm, there was a plain overlap between the objectives of licensing and planning because each of the licensing objectives was also a land use planning objective. Similar considerations to those that arise on licensing applied to a local planning authority in deciding upon the appropriate planning policy framework for licensed premises applications and in determining planning applications. The planning authority was likely to be concerned about the public impact of the use, direct and indirect, particularly the impact of unsociable hours. Planning authorities must consider the design of any proposed development for leisure use and what conditions should be attached to any permission, if the use might have a detrimental impact on local residents. Local development plans might well adopt policies which direct licensable activities to certain parts of a town centre, and the planning authority might have regard to such policies in determining individual planning applications. However, licensing authorities, in pursuing the licensing objectives, might also have to have regard to locational factors, especially where exceptional circumstances had justified the adoption by the licensing authority of a "cumulative effect" policy of restriction, but also where the express grant of planning permission was not required for a licensable activity because, for example, there was a change of use of the premises within the same planning use class.

Whilst it was relatively easy to state as a target that the statement of licensing policy should indicate that "planning, building control and licensing regimes would be properly separated to avoid duplication and inefficiency", it was much harder to formulate any general principle that would assist in demarcating the respective competences of planning and licensing authorities. Nevertheless, the framework and substance of the Licensing Act 2003, and its underlying rationale, strongly suggested that operational matters were intended primarily for regulation by the licensing authorities. Therefore, once planning permission had been granted for licensed premises, an operational matter, such as opening hours, was intended by the Act to be regulated primarily by the licensing authority. Each case had to be considered upon its own particular facts: the planning authority might, in appropriate circumstances, impose conditions on granting planning permission for licensed premises that concerned operational matters. But in many circumstances the planning authority could properly leave such matters to be regulated by the licensing authority. If the planning authority had not dealt with an operational matter, such as opening hours, the licensing authority, having regard to the licensing objectives, had the primary task of determining what conditions should be imposed.

The justices rightly declined to involve themselves in planning matters. It was not for them, in a licensing appeal, to examine whether the proposed variation required planning consent or to speculate whether, if it did, such consent would be forthcoming, that being a planning matter falling exclusively within the competence of the planning authority.

Section 181 of the Licensing Act 2003 enables a magistrates' court to make such order as to the costs of an appeal as it thinks fit. In the narrative on this in the last edition of this work (**8–19829S**), pending authoritative guidance from the Divisional Court, we opined that the principle in *Bradford Metropolitan District Council v Booth* should be followed; namely, costs should not generally be awarded against a public authority that acted honestly, reasonably and properly on sound grounds. We now have two cases directly on the point. Unfortunately, they cannot easily be reconciled.

In *Crawley Borough Council v Attenborough* (**8–19829S**) the Divisional Court emphasised the very wide nature of the justices' discretion. However, in *R (on the application of Cambridge City Council) v Alex Nesting Ltd* (**8–19829S**) it was held that, although the power to award costs was not confined to cases where the local authority acted unreasonably or in bad faith, the fact that the local authority had acted reasonably and in good faith was plainly a most important factor. We respectfully regard the latter decision as more consistent with public law policy.

Pedlars

It might be though rather quaint and outdated that Pedlars should have their own section in this work (beginning at **8–22910**), but there is more to the retail industry than massive, out-of-town, shopping estates. To operate lawfully, of course, pedlars (unlike the supermarket giants) must be certified, and good behaviour is essential because, if they commit an offence, they may (must, if the offence is begging) lose their certificate under s 16 of the Pedlars Act 1871. However, can they be deprived of their certificate under any other power? This question arose in *R (on the application of Jones) v Chief Constable of Cheshire Police* (**8–22925**).

Mr Jones was arrested on suspicion of an offence of dishonesty and his pedlar's certificate was seized by the police. He sought its return, and by the date the matter came before the Administrative Court it was agreed between the parties that the police had not had the power to seize, suspend or revoke the certificate, so the only task left for the court was to make a formal ruling to that effect, which their Lordships duly did.

Police

The offence of wilful obstruction of a police officer came under consideration in *Sekfall, Banamira and Ouham v DPP* (**8–23824**). The three appellants were observed by staff in a department store trying on leather jackets. The staff thought that their behaviour was suspicious. The police were notified and four officers in plain clothes attended at the store and obtained descriptions of the three men.

Shortly afterwards, the appellants were seen in the vicinity. Two of the officers approached them, identified themselves and displayed their warrant cards. One of the officers testified that he wanted to detain the appellants to ask them questions and to see if they matched the descriptions that had been given by staff at the store. The other officer gave similar evidence, though he said nothing about his intentions. The appellants looked at the warrant cards and at that point all three ran away in different directions. One of them was found on apprehension to be in possession of a brown leather jacket that had come from the store in question. He was arrested and, in due course, he pleaded guilty to the theft. Another defendant was apprehended after a struggle and arrested for theft. The third appellant was also apprehended and he was found to be in possession of a pair of pliers. All three were charged with wilfully obstructing a police constable in the execution of his duty.

The primary submission of law advanced before the magistrates and on appeal was that, since the appellants were not under arrest and therefore owed no duty in law to remain and answer questions when asked to do so by police officers, each was entitled to run away and in so doing could not be guilty of having wilfully obstructed the police officers. It was further submitted that since the purpose and intention of the officers, or at least of one of them, was to question or detain the appellants, there being no power to detain a suspect before questioning, the officers, by reason of their intention, were not acting in the execution of their duty.

The Administrative Court dismissed the appeal. A citizen had no legal duty to assist the police. However, rather than simply declining to answer police questions, refusing to accompany a police officer unless arrested or even indicating that they had no intention of answering questions and that in consequence they were intent on going on their way – all of which they might have done without giving rise to a case which would entitle a court to conclude that in departing the scene they intended to impede the police officers and obstruct the police officers in the execution of their duty – the magistrates found that the appellants had run off to avoid apprehension. This created a completely new state of affairs. As it happened, by fleeing, the appellants provided the police officers with grounds to stop and search them, and to arrest them. Their running away being a wilful act, taken so as to obstruct the police, amounted to an act capable of constituting an offence contrary to s 89(2).

Prisons

Is a person "unlawfully at large" within the meaning of s 49 of the Prisons Act 1952 (**8–24315**) if he should have, and would have still have been, in prison but for an error in the drafting of the commitment warrant, which was not rectified until later? "No" was the answer given by the Court of Appeal in *R (Lunn) v Governor of Moorland Prison* (**8–24315**). The governor had to act in accordance with the warrant and release the prisoner in accordance with its terms as drafted.

Public Order

Advance notice of public processions must be given under s 11 of the Public Order Act 1986 (**8–27730**). Various issues as to the proper interpretation of that section arose in *Kay v Metropolitan Police Comr*. At the centre of the case (which was described by the court as a "friendly" action to resolve some difficult issues of mutual interest to the parties) was "Critical Mass", which was not an organisation but the name given to a recurrent event, namely the gathering of cyclists in cities around the world who, once so assembled, would proceed in whatever direction the cyclists at the front chose to take. Unfortunately, in the view of the police, this too often included travelling towards areas of dense vehicular traffic or areas known to be hazardous to cyclists for such choice of direction to be pure coincidence; ie there was suspicion that "Critical Mass" would indulge in "payback".

Critical mass contended, however, that its activities were not caught be s 11 for four reasons: (1) the event had none of the intentions specified in s 11(1); (2) the event was a commonly or customarily held procession to which the exemption in s 11(2) applied; (3) the event had no organiser capable of being identified under s 11(3); and (4) the event had no proposed route capable of being notified under s 11(3). In fact, only the first two questions were held to be apt for answer in the appeal.

Their Lordships held that a procession with no planned route and no organiser might still be subject to the notice requirements of s 11. The intention to which s 11(1) is directed it to the procession itself, and it was plain that the necessary collective intention was there whatever other reasons – eg enjoying some exercise – the cyclists might have. The exemption for cases in which it is not "reasonably practicable" to give notice was designed to accommodate demonstrations in relation to sudden events and it did not apply simply because there was no planned route or organiser.

As to the exemption for procession "commonly or customarily held in the police area", their Lordships held, for three reasons, that it applied in the circumstances of the present case. First, an unbroken succession of over 140 of these collective cycle rides, setting out from a fixed location on a fixed day of the month and time of day and travelling, albeit by varying routes, through the Metropolitan Police area, could not by now sensibly be called anything but common or customary. Secondly, the absence of a planned route for the procession had no legal consequences if notice of the procession was not required. Thirdly, the procession was not prevented from having acquired a common or customary character by the unproven possibility that one or more individuals had failed to give notice under s 11 when the rides had first started some 12 years ago.

Telecommunications and Broadcasting

The Wireless Telegraphy Act 1949 which has long been a stalwart in STONE, was repealed on 8 February 2007 and replaced by the **Wireless Telegraphy Act 2006** (**8–30112**). In fact, the familiar prosecutions for not having a television licence have been brought for some time under the Communications Act 2003 and the 1949 Act was focused more on transmissions. However, we should remark on the resulting repeal of an Act which has some significance to readers of a certain age: the Marine etc Broadcasting (Offences) Act 1967, the legislation which put an end to the activities of the pirate radio stations and led to the creation of the BBC's Radio One.

Theft and fraud

This title supersedes the title "Theft" in acknowledgement of the Fraud Act 2006 (**8–30845**). The following is a summary of the Act's provisions. It provides for a general offence of fraud, which may be committed by: (*a*) false representation; (*b*) failing to disclose information; and (*c*) abuse of position. It also creates new offences of obtaining services dishonestly and of possessing, making and supplying articles for use in fraud. There is also a new offence, which parallels the offence of fraudulent trading in s 458 of the Companies Act 1986 and extends it to non-corporate businesses. Finally, the Act repeals the deception offences contained in ss 15, 15A, 16 and 20(2) of the Theft Act 1968 (and the corresponding provisions in relation to Northern Ireland), and ss 1 and 2 of the Theft Act 1978 (and, again, the corresponding provisions in relation to Northern Ireland).

The Act was brought fully into force with effect from 15 January 2007, but with transitional provisions that mean that offences committed before or "partly before" (as defined) will continue to be prosecuted under the old deception offences.

Town and Country Planning

Section 336 of the Town and Country Planning Act 1990 defines many terms used in the Act. The longest definition is that which deals with "advertisement". This includes a reference to "purposes", which may be purposes of "advertisement, announcement or direction". It was held in *Butler v Derby City Council* (**8–31704**) that these terms were not mutually exclusive and showed that a broad definition of "advertisement" was intended. Thus, a banner on the front elevation of a house stating opposition to a proposed highway scheme and containing the logo, website and telephone number of a local pressure group was an "advertisement" because it advertised the group (though it might be that a banner that merely conveyed a message such as "ban the bomb" would not be caught); and there could be no complaint that the criminal proceedings breached art 10 since, if for no other reasons, there had been no application to the council for, or denial of, consent to display the banner.

Appreciation

Readers will need no reminding of the sheer volume of new legislation and the often complex (and sometimes confusing) commencement provisions. STONE has always recognised that the basis of magistrates' jurisdiction is statutory and that pride of place must always be given to the text of the statutory provisions themselves. In these circumstances we would wish to pay tribute to the in-house staff who work diligently to ensure that readers have the most accurate and up to date text from which to work. We would also wish to express our own appreciation to the in-house editor who painstakingly transforms our manuscript and instructions into the final polished version.

One of the enduring pleasures of editing STONE is receiving feedback from readers, from which we are often encouraged to undertake new lines of research or to include additional material which is felt might be of use to readers in their practice. For their letters (and e-mails, of course) we are extremely grateful. Finally, but not least, we express our appreciation for the patience and fortitude of our wives, especially in the pressured weeks leading to the publication of this indispensable manual of the magistrates' courts.

We endeavour to state the law as it was on the preceding 1st January. In practice we are usually able to include in the main body of the work additional case law and statutory material to within two months of the date of publication, although this cannot be guaranteed. In order to ensure that STONE is as up to date as possible, we also include in Part X miscellaneous statutory material which was received too late to include under its proper Part and title and we have also, wherever practicable, alerted readers to prospective changes.

A P Carr
A J Turner

Magistrates' Courts, South East London and Barristers' Chambers, Eastbourne

Ready Reference

	Statutory provision		Narrative
Search warrants			1–207
Bail	Bail Act 1976	1–1560	1–464
Exceptions to right to bail	Bail Act 1976, Sch 1	1–1570	1–469
Prosecution appeal	Bail (Amend) Act 1993, s 1	1–3447	1–488
Remand	MCA 1980, ss 128–131	1–2211	1–464
Custody time limits	PO (CTL) Regs 1987	1–6220	
Live link at preliminary hearing	CDA 1998, ss 57A–57B	1–3535/A	1–424A
Disclosure			
Advance	CrimPR Pt 21	1–7441	1–425
Public interest immunity			1–605
Initial	CPIA 1996, s 3	1–3583	1–602
Code of Practice		1–7700	
A-G Guidelines		1–7750	
Representation order			
Financial eligibility	CDS (Fncl Elig) R 2006	1–5699	1–883A
Criteria for grant	AJ A 1999, Sch 3 para 5	1–3983	1–884
Application for	CDS (Gen) (No 2) R 2001	1–5691	1–885
Appeal	CDS (Rep Ord: Appeals etc) Regs 2006	1–5722	1–889
Disqualification and Bias			1–119
Abuse of process			1–447
Information			1–386
Time limit	MCA 1980, s 127	1–2210	1–387
Statement of offence	CrimPR Pt 7 r 7.2	1–7427	1–388
Several offences			1–444
Several defendants			1–445

	Statutory provision		Narrative
Information (*ctd*)			
Adults and minors			1–446
Duplicity	CrimPR Pt 7 r 7.3	1–7427	1–389
Amendment	MCA 1980, s 123	1–2206	1–442
Summons			
Form of	CrimPR Pt 7 r 7.7	1–7427	1–404
Issue of			1–401
Service	CrimPR Pt 4 r 4.2	1–7424	1–406
Proof of service	CrimPR Pt 4 r 4.11	1–7424	
Adjournment			1–463
Plea before venue	MCA 1980, ss 17A–17C	1–2041/43	1–503
Mode of trial	MCA 1980, s 18–21	1–2044/50	1–509
Guidelines	PD (Crim Consol) 2002, para V.51	1–6970	1–521
Adults and youths	MCA 1980, s 24	1–2053	5–10/15
Criminal damage	MCA 1980, s 22	1–2051	1–524
Reverting/re-electing	MCA 1980, s 25	1–2054	1–525
Committal for trial	MCA 1980, s 6	1–2028	1–526
Trial			1–588
Proceeding in absence of accused			1–428
Order of speeches	CrimPR Pt 37 r 37.1	1–7457	1–643
Evidence			
Identification	PACE Code D	2–1938	2–310
Exclusion of unfairly obtained	PACE 1984, s 78	2–1359	2–123
Hearsay	CJA 2003, ss 114–134 CrimPR Pt 34	2–1577/ 1597 1–7454	2–250 ff 1–624
Bad character	CJA 2003, ss 98–112 CrimPR Pt 35	2–1561/ 1575 1–7455	2–200 ff 1–625

	Statutory provision		Narrative
Oaths etc	Oaths Act 1978	2–1190	1–645/8
Competence	YJCEA 1999, s 53	2–1553	2–125/6
Compellability	PACE 1984, s 80	2–1361	2–125/126
Hostile	Crim Proc Act 1865, s 3	1–904	1–661
Special measures	YJCEA 1999, Pt II	2–1517	2–143 ff
Protection from cross examination	YJCEA 1999, Pt II, Ch II	2–1534	2–180
Complainant's sexual history	YJCEA 1999, Pt II, Ch III	2–1541	2–181
Refreshing memory	CJA 2003, s 139	2–1602	1–663
Accused – effect of silence of at trial	CJPOA 1994, s 35	2–1495	2–316
Submission of no case			1–668
Burden and standard of proof			1–685/689
Sentencing			
Purposes	CJA 2003, s 142	3–1930	3–10
Sentencing by live link	CDA 1998, ss 57D, 57E	1–3538C/D	3–33
Principles			3–70
Credit for guilty plea			3–74
Available sentences (adults)			3–90
Magistrates' Association Sentencing guidelines			3–3080
Fine enforcement	MCA 1980 ss 75–91	1–2125/53	3–208
Imprisonment			3–133
– restrictions on	CJA 2003, s 152	3–1940	3–130
– consecutive terms	MCA 1980 s 133	1–2217	3–134
– return to			3–138/150
ASBO on conviction	CDA 1998, s 1C	1–3804C	3–210
Sex offenders	SOA 2003 Pt 2	8–28423Z ff	3–230 ff
Examples of sentencing for particular offences			3–260 ff
Costs	Pros of Offences Act 1985, s 16–19A	1–2910/4	1–800 3–177

Ready Reference

	Statutory provision		Narrative
Road traffic			
Highway Code		4–2031	
NIPs	RTOA 1988, s 1, Sch 1	4–1642	4–17
Offences			
– careless driving	RTA 1988, s 3	4–1373	4–9
– alcohol (OPL)	RTA 1988, s 5	4–1376	
– fail provide specimen	RTA 1988, s 7	4–1378	
– no insurance	RTA 1988, s 143	4–1560	
– fail to stop	RTA 1988, s 170	4–1596	
Penalties			
– list of maximum penalties and endorseable offences	RTOA 1988, Sch 2	4–1769	
– codes		4–2019	
Disqualification			
– mandatory/special reasons	RTOA 1988, s 34(1)	4–1680	
– discretionary	RTOA 1988, s 34(2)	4–1680	
– penalty points/mitigating circumstances	RTOA 1988, s 35	4–1684	4–18

CONTENTS

(WITH REFERENCE TO PARAS)

VOLUME 1

VOLUME 2

VOLUME 3

STONE'S
JUSTICES' MANUAL

PART I
MAGISTRATES' COURTS, PROCEDURE

INTRODUCTION AND CONTENTS

–1   PART I of this Manual deals principally with the constitution, jurisdiction, practice and procedure of magistrates' courts in England and Wales. Other fundamental matters of which courts and practitioners must take notice, such as police enquiries and the prosecution process, principles of criminal law, and appeals from magistrates' courts, are also included here. Finally, we set out the text of statutes, statutory instruments and practice directions on procedure, arranged chronologically and annotated.

Our general scheme in the narrative is to provide a basic statement of authority, which is supplemented, as appropriate, with a commentary, statement of secondary principles, illustrations, procedures and exceptions or variations, cross referenced to the relevant material reproduced later in this PART.

Constitution of magistrates' courts

Magistrates' courts

Investigation of offences

Statutory instruments and Practice Directions on procedure

Codes of Practice and Guidelines

Constitution of magistrates' courts
JUDICIARY

1–20　President of magistrates' courts.　The Lord Chief Justice holds the office of President of the Courts of England and Wales and is Head of the Judiciary of England and Wales[1]. As such he is responsible for: (*a*) representing the views of the judiciary of England and Wales to Parliament, to the Lord Chancellor and to Ministers of the Crown generally; (*b*) the maintenance of appropriate arrangements for the welfare, training and guidance of the judiciary of England and Wales within the resources made available by the Lord Chancellor; and (*c*) the maintenance of appropriate arrangements for the deployment of the judiciary of England and Wales and the allocation of work within courts[2].

---

1. Constitutional Reform Act 2005, s 7, in this PART: STATUTES ON PROCEDURE, post.
2. Constitutional Reform Act 2005, s 7, in this PART: STATUTES ON PROCEDURE, post.

1–21　Independence of, and support for, the Judiciary.　The Lord Chancellor, other Ministers of the Crown and all with responsibility for matters relating to the judiciary or otherwise to the administration of justice must uphold the continued independence of the judiciary[1].

The Lord Chancellor must have regard to: (*a*) the need to defend that independence; (*b*) the need for the judiciary to have the support necessary to enable them to exercise their functions; and (*c*) the need for the public interest in regard to matters relating to the judiciary or otherwise to the administration of justice to be properly represented in decisions affecting those matters[2].

---

1. Constitutional Reform Act 2005, s 3(1), in this PART: STATUTES ON PROCEDURE, post.
2. Constitutional Reform Act 2005, s 3(7), in this PART: STATUTES ON PROCEDURE, post.

1–22　The Commission of the Peace and Justices of the Peace.　Part 2 of the Courts Act 2003[1] established a single commission of the peace for England and Wales[2]. England and Wales was divided into named local justice areas to be specified by orders made by the Lord Chancellor[3]. The Lord Chancellor may, by order, alter or rename such areas, subject to consultation[4].

A 'lay justice' is a justice of the peace who is not a District Judge (Magistrates' Courts)[5]. Lay justices are appointed for England and Wales by the Lord Chancellor by instrument on behalf of and in the name of Her Majesty, and are assigned by the Lord Chief Justice (or his judicial nominee) to one or more local justice areas, though they are capable of acting in other areas provided this is in accordance with arrangements made by or on behalf of the Lord Chief Justice (or his judicial nominee). In exercising the aforementioned powers, the Lord Chief Justice (or his judicial nominee) must consult the Lord Chancellor[6].

Rules may make provision about training to be completed before a lay justice may exercise the functions of his position in any proceedings or class of proceedings specified[7].

The Lord Chancellor, with the concurrence of the Lord Chief Justice, may remove a lay justice from office on the grounds of: (*a*) incapacity or misbehaviour; or (*b*) persistent failure to meet such standards of competence as are prescribed by a direction given by the Lord Chancellor, with the concurrence of the Lord Chief Justice[8]. The Lord Chancellor may also remove a lay justice from office if he is declining or neglecting to take a proper part in the exercise of his functions as a justice of the peace[8].

Lay justices must retire from office when they attain the age of 70 and their names must then be entered on the supplemental list[9].

Lay justices are entitled to travelling and subsistence allowances, at rates determined by the Lord Chancellor, to reimburse such expenditure which is necessarily incurred for the purpose of enabling them to perform their duties[10]. Lay justices are also entitled to financial loss allowance, again at rates determined by the Lord Chancellor, in respect of any other expenditure or any loss of earnings or social security benefits incurred or suffered to enable them to perform their duties[10].

The Lord Chancellor, after consulting the Lord Chief Justice (or his judicial nominee), must appoint a person to be keeper of the rolls for each local justice area (one person may keep the rolls for more than one such area). The keeper must be informed of assignments of lay justices to the area, or any changes to any such assignments, and the keeper must ensure that accurate records are maintained of all current assignees[11].

Each local justice area must have a chairman and one or more deputy chairmen chosen by the lay justices assigned to the area from among their own number[12]. Contested elections must be held by secret ballot[12]. Chairmen and deputy chairmen when present at sittings or meetings of lay justices must (unless ineligible under rules, or in youth or family proceedings courts, or at meetings of committees that have their own chairman, or at sittings where a District Judge (Magistrates' Courts) is engaged in administering justice) take the chair unless, in accordance with rules, they ask other lay justices to preside[13].

Rules may make provision as to: the approval and training of lay justices before they may preside in court; the maximum number of lay justices who may sit to deal with a case; etc[13]. Rules may also make provision as to the training, development and appraisal of lay justices; the functions and constitutions of committees; etc[14]. The Lord Chief Justice (or his judicial nominee) must ensure that training and training materials that appear to him, after consulting the Lord Chancellor, to be appropriate are provided to enable lay justices to comply with any training requirements[15].

The Lord Chancellor and the Lord Chief Justice (or the latter's judicial nominee) must take all reasonable and practicable steps to ensure that lay justices are kept informed of matters affecting them in the performance of their duties and for ascertaining their views on such matters[16].

---

1. See this PART: STATUTES ON PROCEDURE, post.
2. Courts Act 2003, s 7, in this PART: STATUTES ON PROCEDURE, post.
3. Courts Act 2003, s 8, in this PART: STATUTES ON PROCEDURE, post. The Local Justice Areas Order 2005 has been made, in this PART, STATUTORY INSTRUMENTS AND PRACTICE DIRECTIONS ON PROCEDURE, post.
4. Courts Act 2003, s 8, in this PART: STATUTES ON PROCEDURE, post.
5. Courts Act 2003, s 9, in this PART: STATUTES ON PROCEDURE, post.
6. Courts Act 2003, s 10, in this PART: STATUTES ON PROCEDURE, post.
7. Courts Act 2003, s 10(4), in this PART: STATUTES ON PROCEDURE, post. The Justices of the Peace (Training and Appraisal) Rules 2005 have been made, in this PART, STATUTORY INSTRUMENTS AND PRACTICE DIRECTIONS ON PROCEDURE, post.
8. Courts Act 2003, s 11, in this PART: STATUTES ON PROCEDURE, post.
9. Courts Act 2003, ss 12, 13, in this PART: STATUTES ON PROCEDURE, post.
10. Courts Act 2003, s 15, in this PART: STATUTES ON PROCEDURE, post.
11. Courts Act 2003, s 16.
12. Courts Act 2003, s 17, in this PART: STATUTES ON PROCEDURE, post. The Justices of the Peace (Size and Chairmanship of Bench) Rules 2005 have been made, in this PART, STATUTORY INSTRUMENTS AND PRACTICE DIRECTIONS ON PROCEDURE, post.
13. Courts Act 2003, s 18, in this PART: STATUTES ON PROCEDURE, post.
14. Courts Act 2003, s 19, in this PART: STATUTES ON PROCEDURE, post. See Justices of the Peace (Training and Appraisal) Rules 2005, in this PART: STATUTORY INSTRUMENTS AND PRACTICE DIRECTIONS ON PROCEDURE, post.
15. Courts Act 2003, s 19(3), in this PART: STATUTES ON PROCEDURE, post.
16. Courts Act 2003, s 21(1), in this PART: STATUTES ON PROCEDURE, post.

1–23 Subject to certain disqualifications[1], any member of the public may apply for appointment as a justice. Applications must be made on a form prescribed[2] by the Secretary of State and Lord Chancellor and supported by three sponsors who recommend the candidate for appointment. Applications should be forwarded to the secretary of the local advisory committee. A District judge (Magistrates' Courts) by virtue of his office is a justice of the peace for England and Wales[3] and shall sit in any local justice area in accordance with arrangements made by the Lord Chief Justice (or his judicial nominee), after consulting the Lord Chancellor[4].

Before a justice may perform any act as a justice, he must take the oath of allegiance and the judicial oath[5]. The oaths may be taken in any of the divisions of the High Court of Justice, in open court at the Crown Court, or before any two justices of the peace for the area for which the new justice will act[6]. The oaths (or affirmations) are administered in conformity with the requirements of the Oaths Act 1978[7], and are as follows—

OATH OF ALLEGIANCE

I .... do swear that I will be faithful and bear true allegiance to Her Majesty Queen Elizabeth the Second, her heirs and successors, according to law. So help me God.

JUDICIAL OATH

I .... do swear that I will well and truly serve our Sovereign Lady Queen Elizabeth the Second in the office of justice of the peace, and I will do right to all manner of people after the laws and usages of this realm, without fear or favour, affection or illwill. So help me God.

The office of justice of the peace is unaffected by the demise of the Crown[8].

A person shall not act as a justice of the peace while he is *sheriff* of a county; any such acts of his would be void[9]. Where a justice of the peace is reported by an election court or election commissioners as guilty of any *corrupt practice at a parliamentary or municipal election*, he will be reported to the Lord Chancellor by the Director of Public Prosecutions[10]. A magistrate convicted of *treason* forfeits his office[11].

A *coroner* is not disqualified from acting as a justice of the peace[12], but there are certain restrictions on the practice of *solicitors* who are justices[13].

In order to sit as a member of a youth court or a family proceedings court, a justice must be a member of the appropriate panel[14].

---

1. Bankruptcy is no longer a disqualification following the repeal of s 65 of the Justices of the Peace Act 1997 by s 265 of the Enterprise Act 2002.
2. The form of Application for Appointment as a Magistrate and the selection procedures are laid down in the Lord Chancellor's Directions for Advisory Committees on Justices of the Peace (July 1998).
3. Courts Act 2003, s 25(1).
4. Courts Act 2003, s 25(2) and (3).
5. As prescribed by the Promissory Oaths Act 1868, ss 2 and 4.
6. Promissory Oaths Act 1871, s 2 and Declaration thereunder signed by the Queen on 8 July 1974 (see Home Office Circular 142/74).
7. In PART II: EVIDENCE, post.
8. Demise of the Crown Act 1901, s 1; see also Home Office Circular 25/1952.
9. Sheriffs Act 1887, s 17, and see *Ex p Colville* (1875) 1 QBD 133.
10. Representation of the People Act 1983, s 161.
11. Forfeiture Act 1870, s 2.
12. *Davis v Pembrokeshire Justices* (1881) 7 QBD 513.
13. See Solicitors Act 1974, s 38 in PART VIII, title SOLICITORS, post.
14. See the Children and Young Persons Act 1933, s 45 and Sch 2, in PART V: YOUTH COURTS, post, and the Magistrates' Courts Act 1980, s 67, in this PART: STATUTES ON PROCEDURE, post.

1–24 District Judges (Magistrates' Courts) and other judges eligible to sit in magistrates' courts. District Judges (Magistrates' Courts) are barristers or solicitors who have a seven-year general qualification, within the meaning of s 71 of the Courts and Legal Services Act 1990[1], and are appointed by Her Majesty on the recommendation of the Lord Chancellor[2]. The Lord Chancellor may also appoint anyone who has a seven-year qualification to be a Deputy District Judge (Magistrates' Courts) for such a period as the Lord Chancellor considers appropriate[3]. A District Judge (Magistrates' Courts) by virtue of his office is a justice of the peace England and Wales[4] and shall sit in any local justice area in accordance with arrangements made by or on behalf of the Lord Chancellor[5].

A District Judge (Magistrates' Courts) has power to do any act and to exercise alone any jurisdiction which can be done or exercised by two justices, including any act or jurisdiction expressly required to be done or exercised by justices sitting or acting in petty sessions, except that his jurisdiction does not extend to the grant or transfer of any licence[6].

If nominated by the Lord Chancellor to do so, a District Judge (Magistrates' Courts) may hear family proceedings, and when sitting in a family proceedings court the District Judge (Magistrates' Courts) shall sit as chairman with one or two lay justices, or if it is not practicable for such a court to be so composed, he may sit alone[7].

Part 6 of the Courts Act 2003[8], pursuant to the Act's aim to achieve greater flexibility in the deployment of judicial resources, makes District Judges (Magistrates' Courts) judges of the Crown Court[9], and confers the powers of District Judges (Magistrates' Courts), including the power to sit in the Youth Court, on High Court judges and deputy judges, Circuit judges and deputy judges, and recorders[10]. This enables, for example, a Circuit judge to deal with a summary offence in the Crown Court without having to remit the matter to a magistrates' court.

---

1. See Part VIII: title SOLICITORS, post.
2. Courts Act 2003, s 22, in this PART: STATUTES ON PROCEDURE, post.
3. Courts Act 2003, s 24, in this PART: STATUTES ON PROCEDURE, post.
4. Courts Act 2003, s 25(1), in this PART: STATUTES ON PROCEDURE, post.
5. Courts Act 2003, s 25(2), in this PART: STATUTES ON PROCEDURE, post.
6. Courts Act 2003, s 26, in this PART: STATUTES ON PROCEDURE, post.
7. Magistrates' Courts Act 1980, ss 66 and 67, in this PART: STATUTES ON PROCEDURE, post, post.
8. See this PART: STATUTES ON PROCEDURE, post.
9. Courts Act 2003, s 65, in this PART: STATUTES ON PROCEDURE, post, post.
10. Courts Act 2003, s 66, in this PART: STATUTES ON PROCEDURE, post, post.

1–25 Justices' clerks. A justices' clerk is a person appointed by the Lord Chancellor[1] and so designated, after consulting the Lord Chief Justice (or his judicial nominee). A person may not be designated as a justices' clerk unless he has a 5 year magistrates' courts qualification within the meaning given by s 71 of the Courts and Legal Services Act 1990[2], is barrister or solicitor who has served for not less than 5 years as an assistant to a justices' clerk, or has previously been a justices' clerk[3].

The Lord Chancellor must, after consulting the Lord Chief Justice (or the latter's judicial nominee), assign each justices' clerk to one or more local justice areas, and he may change an assignment so as to assign the justices' clerk to one or more different local justice areas[4].

The functions and powers of justices' clerks include giving advice to any or all of the Justices of the Peace to whom he is clerk about matters of law, including practice and procedure, on questions arising in connection with the discharge of there functions, whether or not the justices' clerk is personally attending on them at the relevant time[5]. This does not limit the powers and duties of a justices' clerk or the matters on which justices of the peace may obtain assistance from him[6].

1. Under s 2 of the Courts Act 2003 in this PART: STATUTES ON PROCEDURE, post.
2. See PART VIII: title SOLICITORS, post.
3. Courts Act 2003, s 27(2) in this PART: STATUTES ON PROCEDURE, post. For transitional arrangements see Courts Act 2003, para 9 of Sch 9 in this PART: STATUTES ON PROCEDURE, post.
4. Courts Act 2003, s 27(3) in this PART: STATUTES ON PROCEDURE, post. Before changing an assignment of a justices' clerk so that he is no longer assigned to a local justice area, the Lord Chancellor must consult as required by s 27(4B) and the Lord Chief Justice (or his judicial nominee) must agree to that change (s 27(4C)).
5. Courts Act 2003, s 28(4), (5) in this PART: STATUTES ON PROCEDURE, post. As to role of the legal adviser in court, see para **1–29**, post.
6. Courts Act 2003, s 28(7) in this PART: STATUTES ON PROCEDURE, post.

1–26 *Assistant clerks.* An assistant to a justices' clerk is a person appointed by the Lord Chancellor and so designated[1]. The Lord Chancellor may by regulations provide that, subject to such exceptions as the regulations may prescribe, a person may be so designated only if he has a 5 year magistrates' courts qualification within the meaning given by s 71 of the Courts and Legal Services Act 1990[2], or has such qualifications as may be prescribed by, or approved by the Lord Chancellor in accordance with, the regulations[3].

1. Courts Act 2003, s 27(5) in this PART: STATUTES ON PROCEDURE, post.
2. See PART VIII: title SOLICITORS, post.
3. The Assistants to Justices' Clerks Regulations 2006 have been made, in this PART, STATUTORY INSTRUMENTS AND PRACTICE DIRECTIONS ON PROCEDURE, post.

1–27 *Judicial functions of justices' clerks.* Under the Justices' Clerks Rules 2005[1], the justices' clerk is given certain powers of a single justice. He may delegate those which are of a judicial nature only in accordance with the Justices' Clerk's Rules and not otherwise[2], and the justices cannot be required to reconsider one of his decisions[3]. He may give reasons for his decision, but it is neither usual nor obligatory so to do[3].

Where the justices' clerk forms a view that there is something wrong with an order made by the magistrates, he has no power to ignore the order and should approach the particular magistrate who constituted the court or, if he is unable to do that, another bench, to reconsider the matter or arrange for it to be referred to a superior court[4].

Where, during the course of a trial justices have made a considered ruling on law on the advice of the clerk in court, respect should be given to the general principle, to which there will be exceptions, that decisions arrived at by justices should not be reversed. Accordingly, the powers of the justices' clerk in s 28 of the Courts Act 2003 should not make routine the reversing of decisions taken by magistrates on the basis of advice given by the clerk sitting with them. It is therefore wrong of a Crown prosecutor, in relation to a specific case, where a ruling has been made against him and where there is to be a further hearing, to discuss the issue with the clerk to the justices. Although the possibility is not excluded, having regard to the broad powers of the clerk to the justices under s 45(5), that there may be cases where a party is entitled, before a resumed hearing, to bring matters to the attention of the clerk to the justices, if it is to be done it should normally be done in writing and with notice to the other party[5].

1. SI 2005/545, in this PART, STATUTORY INSTRUMENTS AND PRACTICE DIRECTIONS ON PROCEDURE, post.
2. Justices' Clerk's Rules 2005, r 3, ibid. See also *R v Gateshead Justices, ex p Tesco Stores Ltd; R v Birmingham Justices, ex p D W Parkin Construction Ltd* [1981] QB 470, [1981] 1 All ER 1027; *R v Manchester Stipendiary Magistrate, ex p Hill* [1983] 1 AC 328, [1982] 2 All ER 963, 146 JP 348.
3. *R v Worthing Justices, ex p Norvell* [1981] 1 WLR 413. Under art 6(1) of the European Convention on Human Rights it is a requirement of a fair trial in both criminal and civil matters that a court should give reasons for its judgment. The extent of the duty to give reasons may, however, vary according to the nature of the decision: see *Hadjianastassiou v Greece* (1992) 16 EHRR 219; *Van de Hurk v Netherlands* (1994) 18 EHRR 481; *Ruiz Torija v Spain* (1994) 19 EHRR 553; *Hiro Balani v Spain* (1994) 19 EHRR 566; *Georgiadis v Greece* (1997) 24 EHRR 606; and *Helle v Finland* (1997) 26 EHRR 159. For the duty to give reasons both at common law and under the Convention, see *Stefan v General Medical Council* [1999] 1 WLR 1293, PC.
4. *R v Liverpool Magistrates' Court, ex p Abiaka* (1999) 163 JP 497, DC.
5. *R v Sittingbourne Justices, ex p Stickings* (1996) 160 JP 801, DC.

1–28 *Independence of justices' clerks and assistant clerks.* A justices' clerk exercising: (*a*) any function exercisable by one or more justices of the peace; (*b*) advisory functions on matters of law, practice and procedure; or (*c*) a function as a member of the Criminal Procedure Rule Committee or the Family Procedure Rule Committee, is not subject to the direction of the Lord Chancellor or any other person.[1]

An assistant clerk who is exercising any of the above functions is not subject to the direction of any person other than a justices' clerk[2].

---

1. Courts Act 2003, s 29(1), in this PART: STATUTES ON PROCEDURE, post.
2. Courts Act 2003, s 29(2), in this PART: STATUTES ON PROCEDURE, post.

1-29   *Role of the legal adviser in court: Practice Direction (crime: consolidated).*   Paragraph V.55 of the *Practice Direction (criminal: consolidated)*[1] regulates the role of the legal adviser in court as follows:

"V.55.1. A justices' clerk is responsible for: (a) the legal advice tendered to the justices within the area; (b) the performance of any of the functions set out below by any member of his/her staff acting as legal adviser; (c) ensuring that competent advice is available to justices when the justices' clerk is not personally present in court; and (d) the effective delivery of case management and the reduction of unnecessary delay.

V.55.2. Where a person other than the justices' clerk (a 'legal adviser'), who is authorised[2] to do so, performs any of the functions referred to in this direction he will have the same responsibilities as the justices' clerk. The legal adviser may consult the justices' clerk or other person authorised by the justices' clerk for that purpose before tendering advice to the bench. If the justices' clerk or that person gives any advice directly to the bench, he/she should give the parties or their advocates an opportunity of repeating any relevant submissions prior to the advice being given.

V.55.3. It shall be the responsibility of the legal adviser to provide the justices with any advice they require properly to perform their functions whether or not the justices have requested that advice, on: (a) questions of law (including European Court of Human Rights jurisprudence and those matters set out in s 2(1) of the Human Rights Act 1998); (b) questions of mixed law and fact; (c) matters of practice and procedure;(d) the range of penalties available; (e) any relevant decisions of the superior courts or other guidelines; (f) other issues relevant to the matter before the court; and (g) the appropriate decision making structure to be applied in any given case. In addition to advising the justices it shall be the legal adviser's responsibility to assist the court, where appropriate, as to the formulation of reasons and the recording of those reasons.

V.55.4. A justices' clerk or legal adviser must not play any part in making findings of fact but may assist the bench by reminding them of the evidence, using any notes of the proceedings for this purpose.

V.55.5. A justices' clerk or legal adviser may ask questions of witnesses and the parties in order to clarify the evidence and any issues in the case.

V.55.6. A legal adviser has a duty to ensure that every case is conducted fairly.

V.55.7. When advising the justices the justices' clerk or legal adviser, whether or not previously in court, should: (a) ensure that he/she is aware of the relevant facts; and (b) provide the parties with the information necessary to enable the parties to make any representations they wish as to the advice before it is given.

V.55.8. At any time, justices are entitled to receive advice to assist them in discharging their responsibilities. If they are in any doubt as to the evidence which has been given, they should seek the aid of their legal adviser, referring to his notes as appropriate. This should ordinarily be done in open court. Where the justices request their adviser to join them in the retiring room, this request should be made in the presence of the parties in court. Any legal advice given to the justices other than in open court should be clearly stated to be provisional and the adviser should subsequently repeat the substance of the advice in open court and give the parties an opportunity to make any representations they wish on that provisional advice. The legal adviser should then state in open court whether the provisional advice is confirmed or if it is varied the nature of the variation.

V.55.9. The performance of a legal adviser may be appraised by a person authorised by the magistrates' courts committee to do so. For that purpose the appraiser may be present in the justices' retiring room. The content of the appraisal is confidential, but the fact that an appraisal has taken place, and the presence of the appraiser in the retiring room, should be briefly explained in open court.

V.55.10. The legal adviser is under a duty to assist unrepresented parties to present their case, but must do so without appearing to become an advocate for the party concerned.

V.55.11. The role of legal advisers in fine default proceedings or any other proceedings for the enforcement of financial orders, obligations or penalties is to assist the court. They must not act in an adversarial or partisan manner. With the agreement of the justices a legal adviser may ask questions of the defaulter to elicit information which the justices will require to make an adjudication, for example to facilitate his or her explanation for the default. A legal adviser may also advise the justices in the normal way as to the options open to them in dealing with the case. It would be inappropriate for the legal adviser to set out to establish wilful refusal or neglect or any other type of culpable behaviour, to offer an opinion on the facts, or to urge a particular course of action upon the justices. The duty of impartiality is the paramount consideration for the legal adviser at all times, and this takes precedence over any role he or she may have as a collecting officer. The appointment of other staff to 'prosecute' the case for the collecting officer is not essential to ensure compliance with the law, including the 1998 Act. Whether to make such appointments is a matter for the justices' chief executive."

European Convention on Human Rights — Article 6 and the role of the Clerk

In *Clark (Procurator Fiscal, Kirkcaldy) v Kelly*[3], an art 6 challenge was made to the constitution of the district court in Scotland. It was contended that, in trials, decisions were effectively taken by the clerk of the court, who lacked the independence required by art 6. Moreover, the clerk advised in private, which was said to be in breach of the guarantee of a public hearing under art 6.

The Board ruled that there was no basis upon which a fair-minded and informed observer, having considered the facts relating to the terms of the appointment and employment of the clerks of the court, would conclude that there was a real possibility that, by virtue of the clerk's advisory role, district courts lacked the independence and impartiality required by art 6. Moreover, there would be no breach of art 6 even if the clerk advised in private. A balance had to be struck between the rights of the accused and the requirements of the court when it was seeking to administer justice. It was of primary importance that the decision-making justices should understand the clerk's legal advice. If the entire conversation had to take place in public, so that the accused could follow every word being spoken and every question asked on either side, the giving and understanding of the advice would be unduly inhibited. The fact that the conversation took place in private, even in the retiring room if the justices thought that that would be appropriate, was not in itself objectionable. What was objectionable was depriving the accused of his right to know what was going on during the trial; in particular, his right to know what legal advice was being given so that he could have the opportunity of commenting upon it. The Board added that any advice given by the clerk in private on law, practice or procedure should be regarded by the justices as provisional until the substance of the advice had been repeated in open court with an opportunity afforded to the parties to comment on it. The clerk should then state in open court whether he wished to confirm or vary his advice.

It is clearly established that the justices are the judges not only of fact but also of law, though when they are sitting in the Crown Court they must defer to the views of the presiding judge in matters of law[4]. Therefore, there is no legal requirement that they accept and adopt the advice of the justice's clerk on matters of law, though it is accepted practice that they should do so[5].

No sentencing advice should be offered by a legal adviser until after justices have delivered their verdict, heard antecedents and heard from counsel. Nothing should be done or said as to convictions until a verdict has been announced in open court and if called in to advise, the document giving antecedents should be left elsewhere[6].

---

1. *Practice Direction (criminal: consolidated)* [2002] in this PART, STATUTORY INSTRUMENTS AND PRACTICE DIRECTIONS ON PROCEDURE, post.
2. See the Courts Act 2003, s 27, in this PART: STATUTES ON PROCEDURE, post and the Justices' Clerks Rules 2005, in this PART: STATUTORY INSTRUMENTS AND PRACTICE DIRECTIONS ON PROCEDURE, post.
3. [2003] UKPD D1, [2004] 1 AC 681.
4. *R v Orpin* [1975] QB 283, [1974] 2 All ER 1121, 138 JP 651.
5. *Jones v Nicks* [1977] RTR 72.
6. *R (Murchison) v Southend Magistrates' Court* [2006] EWHC 569 (Admin), 170 JP 230.

1–40   *Notes of evidence taken by the justices' clerk.* There is no statutory obligation on a justices' clerk to take a note of the evidence on the summary trial of an information[1], although it would seem to be incumbent on the justices' clerk to ensure that a sufficient note of the evidence is taken to enable the functions specified in the 2002 Practice Direction[2] to be properly performed, or so that it may be referred to at some later time when, for example, the justices are asked to state a case[3] or required to give reasons[4]. However, a note must be taken of any full argument for bail[5]. Furthermore a note of the substance of the oral evidence must be taken in all family proceedings, including proceedings on an application for adoption[6], an application to vary an order for periodical payments[7], proceedings brought under the Magistrates' Courts Act 1980, s 63 post, alleging disobedience of a court order[8], and it would seem in other proceedings in magistrates' courts from which an appeal by way of rehearing lies to the High Court[9].

Where on the summary trial of an information a note of the evidence is taken, no power rests in the High Court to direct the justices' clerk to furnish notes of evidence to the Crown Court for the purposes of an appeal to that court[10]. Nevertheless, the justices' clerk may be summoned to attend the Crown Court and produce the notes of evidence[11]. Moreover, justices' clerks are recommended to send any case notes to the Crown Court when there is an appeal which should include any reasons given by the magistrates for their decision[12] and justices' clerks should view sympathetically requests for notes of evidence from solicitors of defendants who are appealing against conviction to the Crown court where a proper reason is given for such request[13].

The justices' clerk shall, also forward to the Crown Court a copy of any note of evidence taken in the magistrates' court on a committal for sentence[14], including any reasons given by the magistrates for their decision[12] or on a committal for a hospital order with an order restricting discharge[15], or furnish a copy of any such note to another magistrates' court to which an offender is remitted for sentence[16].

On an appeal to the Family Division of the High Court, three copies of the clerk's notes of the evidence (together with other documents) shall be lodged in the principal registry by the appellant[17]. A justices' clerk may be required to produce his note of evidence in a divorce proceeding[18].

In any proceedings in the High Court or in a county court, an order[19] may be made, in accordance with rules of court[20], requiring a justices' clerk to produce any documents in his possession which are relevant to an issue arising out of the claim or a witness summons may be issued[21].

---

1. See article (1978) 142 JP Jo 512.
2. See para **1–29** ante, and *Practice Direction (criminal: consolidated)* [2002], in this PART, post. See also *Lancashire County Council v Clarke* (1984) 148 JP 656.
3. *Lancashire County Council v Clarke* (1984) 148 JP 656.
4. See *Hadjianastassiou v Greece* (1992) 16 EHRR 219, *Van de Hurk v Netherlands* (1994) 18 EHRR 481, *Ruiz Torija v Spain* (1994) 19 EHRR 553, *Hiro Balani v Spain* (1994) 19 EHRR 566, *Georgiadis v Greece* (1997) 24 EHRR 606 and *Helle v Finland* (1997) 26 EHRR 159.
5. Criminal Procedure Rules 2005, Part 19, in this PART, STATUTORY INSTRUMENTS AND PRACTICE DIRECTIONS ON PROCEDURE, post.
6. See the Family Proceedings Courts (Children Act 1989) Rules 1991, r 20, and the Family Proceedings Courts (Matrimonial Proceedings etc) Rules 1991, r 11, in PART VI: FAMILY LAW, post. See also *Re JS (an infant)* [1959] 3 All ER 856, 124 JP 89 (notes of evidence in adoption applications) and *Snow v Snow* [1972] Fam 74, [1971] 3 All ER 833 (notes of evidence in matrimonial proceedings).
7. *Gray v Gray* (1986) 150 JP 587, [1987] 1 FLR 16, [1986] Fam Law 267.
8. *Head v Head* [1982] 3 All ER 14, 146 JP 406; *Tilmouth v Tilmouth* (1984) 148 JP 705, [1985] FLR 239, [1985] Fam Law 92.
9. See observations of Roxburgh J in *Re JS (an infant)* [1959] 3 All ER 856, 124 JP 89.
10. *R v Clerk to the Lancaster Justices, ex p Hill* (1984) 148 JP 65; followed in *R v Clerk to Highbury Corner Justices, ex p Hussein* [1986] 1 WLR 1266, 150 JP 444.
11. See the Criminal Procedure (Attendance of Witnesses) Act 1965, s 2, in this PART, STATUTES ON PROCEDURE, post.
12. *Practice Direction (criminal: consolidated)* [2002] para V.52, in this PART, post.
13. *R v Clerk to the Highbury Corner Justices, ex p Hussein* [1986] 1 WLR 1266, 150 JP 444.
14. Criminal Procedure Rules 2005, Part 43, in this PART, STATUTORY INSTRUMENTS AND PRACTICE DIRECTIONS ON PROCEDURE, post.
15. Criminal Procedure Rules 2005, Part 43, in this PART, STATUTORY INSTRUMENTS AND PRACTICE DIRECTIONS ON PROCEDURE, post.
16. Criminal Procedure Rules 2005, Part 42, in this PART, STATUTORY INSTRUMENTS AND PRACTICE DIRECTIONS ON PROCEDURE, post.
17. Family Proceedings Rules 1991, r 4.22 and r 8.2, in PART VI: FAMILY LAW, post.
18. *McKinley v McKinley* [1960] 1 All ER 476, 124 JP 171.
19. See the Senior Court Act 1981, s 34, and the County Courts Act 1984, s 53.
20. See the Civil Procedure Rules 1998 r 31.17.
21. See the Civil Procedure Rules 1998 r 34.2.

1–41 Protection and indemnification of justices and justices' clerks. A justice when he is sitting as such is acting judicially, and defamatory observations made by him in the course of the proceedings are not actionable[1]. This privilege does not extend to meetings that are not a "court"[2].

No action lies against a justice of the peace in respect of what he does or omits to do in the execution of his duty, or a justices' clerks or assistant clerk in respect of what he does or omits to do when executing any of the functions of a single justice of the peace by virtue of any enactment, unless the act or omission in question relates to a matter not within his jurisdiction and it is proved that he acted in bad faith[3].

Where an action is brought in circumstances in which no action lies by virtue of the above, the proceedings may be struck out on the application of the defendant and, in that event, the judge may order the person bringing the action to pay costs[4].

A court may not order costs against a justice of the peace in any proceedings in respect of anything done or omitted to be done by him in the execution or purported execution of his duty as a justice of the peace; nor may a court order a justices' clerk or assistant clerk to pay costs in any proceedings in respect of anything done or omitted to be done by him when exercising, in the execution or purported execution of his duty, by virtue of any enactment a function of a justice of the peace[5]. This protection from costs, however, does not apply in relation to any proceedings in which a justice of the peace, justices' clerk or assistant clerk is being tried for an offence or is appealing against conviction, or is proved to have acted in bad faith in respect of the matters giving rise to the proceedings[6]. A court prevented by the above from ordering a justice of the peace, justices' clerk or assistant clerk to pay costs may, instead, order the Lord Chancellor to make a payment in respect of the costs of the proceedings[7].

The Lord Chancellor *must* indemnify a justice of the peace, justices' clerk or assistant clerk in respect of:

(a) indemnifiable amounts that relate to criminal matters, unless it is proved in respect of the matters giving rise to the proceedings or claim that he acted in bad faith; and

(b) other indemnifiable amounts if in respect of the matters giving rise to the claim he acted reasonably and in good faith[8].

The Lord Chancellor *may* indemnify a justice of the peace, justices' clerk or assistant clerk in respect of other indemnifiable amounts unless it is proved, in respect of the matters giving rise to the proceedings or claim, that he acted in bad faith[9].

For the above purposes, "Indemnifiable amounts", in relation to a justice of the peace, justices' clerk or assistant clerk, means:

(i) costs which he reasonably incurs in or in connection with proceedings in respect of anything done or omitted to be done in the exercise or purported exercise of his duty as a justice of the peace, justices' clerk or assistant clerk;

(ii) costs he reasonably incurs in taking steps to dispute a claim which might be made in such proceedings;

(iii) damages awarded against him or costs ordered to be paid by him in such proceedings; and

(iv) sums payable by him in connection with a reasonable settlement of such proceedings or such a claim[10].

"Indemnifiable amounts" relate to criminal matters if the duty mentioned in (i) above relates to criminal matters[11].

Any question whether, or to what extent, a person is to be indemnified under the above is to be determined by the Lord Chancellor[12].

In relation to heads (i), (ii) and (iv) above, if the person claiming indemnification so requests, the Lord Chancellor may make a determination with respect to costs or sums before, respectively, the costs are incurred or the settlement under which the sums are payable is made[13], though this determination may be subject to limitations[14].

1. *Law v Llewellyn* [1906] 1 KB 487.
2. *Royal Aquarium and Summer and Winter Garden Society v Parkinson* [1892] 1 QB 431, 56 JP 404; *Attwood v Chapman* [1914] 3 KB 275, 79 JP 65; *Veal v Heard* (1930) 46 TLR 448; cf *Collins v Henry Whiteway & Co Ltd* [1927] 2 KB 378; and *O'Connor v Waldron* [1935] AC 76.
3. Courts Act 2003, ss 31 and 32, in this PART: STATUTES ON PROCEDURE, post.
4. Courts Act 2003, s 33, in this PART: STATUTES ON PROCEDURE, post.
5. Courts Act 2003, s 34(1) and (2), in this PART: STATUTES ON PROCEDURE, post.
6. Courts Act 2003, s 34(3), in this PART: STATUTES ON PROCEDURE, post.
7. Courts Act 2003, s 34(4), in this PART: STATUTES ON PROCEDURE, post.
8. Courts Act 2003, s 35(3), in this PART: STATUTES ON PROCEDURE, post.
9. Courts Act 2003, s 35(4), in this PART: STATUTES ON PROCEDURE, post.
10. Courts Act 2003, s 35(1), in this PART: STATUTES ON PROCEDURE, post.
11. Courts Act 2003, s 35(2), in this PART: STATUTES ON PROCEDURE, post.
12. Courts Act 2003, s 35(5), in this PART: STATUTES ON PROCEDURE, post.
13. Courts Act 2003, s 35(6), in this PART: STATUTES ON PROCEDURE, post
14. Courts Act 2003, s 35(7), in this PART: STATUTES ON PROCEDURE, post.

ADMINISTRATION

1–42 Duty of the Lord Chancellor to maintain the court system. The Lord Chancellor is under a duty to ensure that there is an efficient and effective system to support the carrying on of the business of the Supreme Court, county courts and magistrates' courts, and that appropriate services are provided for those courts[1]. In this context, 'magistrates' courts' includes a committee of justices[2].

1. Courts Act 2003, s 1, in this PART: STATUTES ON PROCEDURE, post.
2. Courts Act 2003, s 1(2), in this PART: STATUTES ON PROCEDURE, post.

1–43 Court staff, services and accommodation. The Lord Chancellor may appoint such officers and other staff as appear to him appropriate for the purpose of discharging his general duty in relation to the courts[1]. The Lord Chancellor may also enter into such contracts with other persons for the provision by them or their sub-contractors of officers, staff or services as appear to him appropriate for the purpose of discharging his general duty in relation to the courts[2].

The Lord Chancellor may provide, equip, maintain and manage such court-house[3], offices or other accommodation as appear to him appropriate for the purpose of discharging his general duty in relation to the courts, or enter into arrangements for such provision[4].

1. Courts Act 2003, s 1, in this PART: STATUTES ON PROCEDURE, post.
2. Courts Act 2003, s 2(4). Such contracts must not, however, include the provision of officers and staff to discharge functions that involve making judicial decisions or exercising any judicial discretion: Courts Act 2003, s 2(5), or the provision of officers and staff to carry out administrative work unless an order made by the Lord Chancellor authorises him to do so: Courts Act 2003, s 2(6). As to prior consultation before making such an order, and the range of matters that may be specified in such an order and the attachment of conditions to it see, respectively, Courts Act 2003, s 2(7) and (8).
3. "Court-house" means any place where a court sits, and includes the precincts of any building in which it sits: Courts Act 2003, s 3(4), in this PART: STATUTES ON PROCEDURE, post.
4. Courts Act 2003, s 3(1), (2), in this PART: STATUTES ON PROCEDURE, post.

1–44 Courts boards. England and Wales is divided into areas, specified by an order[1] made by the Lord Chancellor, each of which has a courts board[2]. Subject to consultation with any affected board, the Lord Chancellor may make orders altering the areas; "altering", in addition to boundary changes, includes combining an area with one or more other areas, dividing it between one or more other areas and re-naming the area[3]. Before exercising the aforementioned powers to make orders the Lord Chancellor must additionally consult the Lord Chief Justice (or his judicial nominee).

The Lord Chancellor must prepare and issue boards with guidance about how to carry out their functions, and such guidance may from time to time be revised[4]. Before preparing and issuing such guidance or revised guidance to court boards the Lord Chancellor must additionally consult the Lord Chief Justice (or his judicial nominee). It is the duty of each courts board, in accordance with such guidance, to scrutinise, review and make recommendations about the way in which the Lord Chancellor is discharging his general duty in relation to the courts with which the board is concerned and for these purposes to consider draft and final business plans relating to those courts[5]. The Lord

Chancellor must give due considerations to any afore-mentioned recommendations made by courts boards[6], and if he rejects such a recommendation as a result of the board's consideration of a final business plan he must given the board in writing his reasons for doing so[7].

---

1. The Courts Boards Areas Order 2004, SI 2004/1303, has been made, in this PART, STATUTORY INSTRUMENTS AND PRACTICE DIRECTIONS ON PROCEDURE, post. For the constitution and procedure of courts boards, see Sch 1 to the Courts Act 2003, this PART, post.
2. Courts Act 2003, s 4(1), in this PART: STATUTES ON PROCEDURE, post. The courts with which a courts board is concerned are the Crown Court, county courts and magistrates' courts in the board's area: Courts Act 2003, s 5(4).
3. Courts Act 2003, s 4(4), (5), in this PART: STATUTES ON PROCEDURE, post.
4. Courts Act 2003, s 5(5), (7), in this PART: STATUTES ON PROCEDURE, post. Such guidance must be laid before both Houses of Parliament: Courts Act 2003, s 5(8).
5. Courts Act 2003, s 5(1), in this PART: STATUTES ON PROCEDURE, post.
6. Courts Act 2003, s 5(2), in this PART: STATUTES ON PROCEDURE, post.
7. Courts Act 2003, s 5(3), in this PART: STATUTES ON PROCEDURE, post.

1–45   Fines officers and designated officers.   A fines officer is a person appointed by the Lord Chancellor[1], or provided under a contract made by the Lord Chancellor with another person[2], who is designated as a fines officer by the Lord Chancellor[3]. Any reference in an enactment to the designated officer, in relation to a magistrates' court[4], justice of the peace or local justice area, is to a person who is appointed by the Lord Chancellor[1] or provided under a contract by the Lord Chancellor with another person[2], and designated by the Lord Chancellor in relation to that court, justice of the peace or area[5].

---

1. In accordance with the Courts Act 2003, s 2(1), in this PART: STATUTES ON PROCEDURE, post.
2. In accordance with s 2(4) of the Courts Act 2003.
3. Courts Act 2003, s 36, in this PART: STATUTES ON PROCEDURE, post.
4. "Magistrates' court" includes a committee of justices and, when exercising a function exercisable by one or more justices of the peace, a justices' clerk and an assistant clerk: Courts Act 2003, s 37(2), in this PART: STATUTES ON PROCEDURE, post.
5. Courts Act 2003, s 37(1), in this PART: STATUTES ON PROCEDURE, post.

1–46   Application of receipts of magistrates' courts.   Subject to the exceptions stated below, the following must be paid to the Lord Chancellor and then paid by him into the Consolidated Fund: fines[1] imposed by magistrates' courts; sums which become payable by virtue of an order of a magistrates' court, and are by an enactment made applicable as fines (or any descriptions of fines) imposed by magistrates' courts; and all other sums received by a designated officer for a magistrates' court, or a designated officer for a local justice area, in his capacity as such[2]. For these purposes, anything done by the Crown Court on appeal from a magistrates' court is to be treated as done by the magistrates' court[3].

The exceptions referred to above are: (*a*) sums paid on conviction for payment of compensation and costs[4]: (*b*) sums which, by or under any enactment, are directed to be paid to the Commissioners for Customs and Excise, or their officers or appointees[5]; and (*c*) certain other sums[6].

The Lord Chancellor may make regulations about payments, accounting and banking by designated officers[7].

---

1. This includes any pecuniary penalty, forfeiture or compensation payable under a conviction: Courts Act 2003, s 38(2), in this PART: STATUTES ON PROCEDURE, post.
2. Courts Act 2003, s 38(1), (4), in this PART: STATUTES ON PROCEDURE, post.
3. Courts Act 2003, s 38(3), in this PART: STATUTES ON PROCEDURE, post.
4. Courts Act 2003, s 39(1), in this PART: STATUTES ON PROCEDURE, post. See the Magistrates' Courts Act 1980, s 139, in this PART: STATUTES ON PROCEDURE, post.
5. Courts Act 2003, s 39(2), in this PART: STATUTES ON PROCEDURE, post.
6. See Courts Act 2003, s 39(3) and (4), in this PART: STATUTES ON PROCEDURE, post.
7. Courts Act 2003, s 40, in this PART: STATUTES ON PROCEDURE, post.

1–47   Court security staff.   A court security officer is a person appointed by the Lord Chancellor[1], or provided under a contract made by the Lord Chancellor with another person[2], who is designated as a security officer by the Lord Chancellor[3]. A security officer who is not readily identifiable as such is not to be regarded as acting in the course of his duty[4].

A security officer acting in the course of his duty has certain powers of search, exclusion, removal or restraint of persons, and powers of seizure and retention of articles[5].

It is an offence to assault a security officer acting in the execution of his duty[6]. It is also an offence to resist or wilfully obstruct a security officer acting in the execution of his duty[7].

---

1. In accordance with the Courts Act 2003, s 2(1), in this PART: STATUTES ON PROCEDURE, post.
2. Courts Act 2003, s 2(4), in this PART: STATUTES ON PROCEDURE, post.
3. In accordance with the Courts Act 2003, s 51, in this PART: STATUTES ON PROCEDURE, post.
4. Courts Act 2003 s 51(3), in this PART: STATUTES ON PROCEDURE, post.
5. Courts Act 2003, ss 52–55, in this PART: STATUTES ON PROCEDURE, post.
6. Courts Act 2003, s 57(1), in this PART: STATUTES ON PROCEDURE, post.
7. C Courts Act 2003, s 57(3), in this PART: STATUTES ON PROCEDURE, post.

1–48   Inspectors of court administration.   The Lord Chancellor may appoint such number of inspectors of court administration as he considers appropriate and they are known collectively as

'Her Majesty's Inspectorate of Court Administration. It is the function of inspectors of court administration to inspect and report to the Lord Chancellor on the system that supports the carrying on of the business of Crown, county and magistrates' courts and the services provided for those courts, to inspect and report to the Lord Chancellor on the performance of CAFCASS, and to discharge any other functions that may be specified in relation to the aforementioned courts, CAFCASS or related functions of any other person[1]. This does not, however, enable inspectors to inspect persons making judicial decisions or exercising any judicial discretion[2]. There are provisions dealing with rights of entry and inspection, and taking copies of records[3].

1. Courts Act 2003, s 59, in this PART: STATUTES ON PROCEDURE, post.
2. Courts Act 2003, s 59(5), in this PART: STATUTES ON PROCEDURE, post.
3. Courts Act 2003, s 61, in this PART: STATUTES ON PROCEDURE, post.

Magistrates' courts

1–110 The expression "magistrates' court" usually means any justice or justices of the peace acting under any enactment or by virtue of his or their commission[1] or under the common law[2].

1. See note to para **1–22**, ante.
2. Magistrates' Courts Act 1980, s 148, in this PART: STATUTES ON PROCEDURE, post.

PLACES, DATES AND TIMES OF SITTINGS

1–111 The Lord Chancellor, after consulting the Lord Chief Justice (or his judicial nominee), may give directions as to the places in England and Wales at which magistrates' courts may sit[1]. In exercising these powers, the Lord Chancellor shall have regard to the need to ensure that court-houses are accessible to persons resident in each local justice area[2].

The Lord Chancellor may, with the concurrence of the Lord Chief Justice, give directions as to the distribution and transfer of the general business of magistrates' courts between the places specified as those in England and Wales at which magistrates' courts sit[3], and such directions may, in particular, contain provision that, where a person is charged with an offence and is being required to appear before a magistrates' court, the place where he is required to appear is one of the places described below[4].

The places referred to above are: (*a*) a place in the local justice area in which the offence is alleged to have been committed; (*b*) a place in the local justice area in which the person charged with the offence resides; (*c*) a place in the local justice area in which the witnesses, or the majority of the witnesses, reside; and (*d*) a place where other cases raising similar issues are being dealt with[5].

'The general business of magistrates' courts' does not include family proceedings[6].

The Lord Chancellor, after consulting the Lord Chief Justice (or his judicial nominee), may give directions as to the days on which and times at which magistrates' courts may sit[7], but, subject to such directions, the business of magistrates' courts may be conducted on any day and at any time[8].

1. Courts Act 2003, s 30(1), in this PART: STATUTES ON PROCEDURE, post.
2. Courts Act 2003, s 30(2), in this PART: STATUTES ON PROCEDURE, post.
3. Courts Act 2003, s 30(3), in this PART: STATUTES ON PROCEDURE, post.
4. Courts Act 2003, s 30(4), in this PART: STATUTES ON PROCEDURE, post.
5. Courts Act 2003, s 30(5), in this PART: STATUTES ON PROCEDURE, post.
6. Courts Act 2003, s 30(6). "Family proceedings" are defined in the Magistrates' Courts Act 1980, s 65, in this PART: STATUTES ON PROCEDURE, post, post.
7. Courts Act 2003, s 30(7), in this PART: STATUTES ON PROCEDURE, post.
8. Courts Act 2003, s 30(8), in this PART: STATUTES ON PROCEDURE, post.

CONSTITUTION OF THE COURT

1–112 A magistrates' court (if not constituted with a district judge or deputy district judge) must not comprise less than 2 lay justices unless the trial or hearing is one that by virtue of any enactment can take place before a single justice[1]; and a magistrates' court must not comprise more than 3 lay justices unless it is sitting as a youth court, a family proceedings court or betting licensing committee[2].

The presiding justice must be an 'approved court chairman'[3], or have completed the chairman training courses and be under the supervision of a justice who is on the list of approved court chairmen[4].

1. Magistrates' Courts Act 1980, s 121, in this PART: STATUTES ON PROCEDURE, post.
2. The Justices of the Peace (Size and Chairmanship of Bench) Rules 2005, in this PART: STATUTORY INSTRUMENTS AND PRACTICE DIRECTIONS ON PROCEDURE: THE JUSTICES, THE JUSTICES' CLERK AND COMMITTEES, post. For the composition of an adult court hearing proceedings in respect of an anti-social behaviour order where the relevant person is under 18 years, see the *Practice Direction (Magistrates' Courts: Anti-Social Behaviour Orders: Composition of Benches)* [2006], in this PART: STATUTORY INSTRUMENTS AND PRACTICE DIRECTIONS ON PROCEDURE, post.
3. Ie be on the list of approved court chairman maintained by his local justice area Bench Training and Development Committee: see the Justice of the Peace (Training and Appraisal) Rules 2005, in this PART: STATUTORY INSTRUMENTS AND PRACTICE DIRECTIONS ON PROCEDURE: THE JUSTICES, THE JUSTICES' CLERK AND COMMITTEES, post.

4. The Justices of the Peace (Size and Chairmanship of Bench) Rules 2005, r 4, in this PART: STATUTORY INSTRUMENTS AND PRACTICE DIRECTIONS ON PROCEDURE: THE JUSTICES, THE JUSTICES' CLERK AND COMMITTEES, post.

OPEN COURT

1–113   As a general rule the English system of administering justice requires that it be done in public[1], and in relation to magistrates' courts, whether sitting in a court-house or an occasional court-house, there is a statutory obligation to sit in open court[2]. The application of the principle of open justice has two aspects: (1) as respects the proceedings in the court itself it requires that they should be held in open court to which the press and the public are admitted and that, in criminal cases particularly, all evidence communicated to the court is communicated publicly; (2) as respects the publication to a wider public of fair and accurate reports of proceedings the principle requires that nothing should be done to discourage this[3].

Nevertheless, a court, including a magistrates' court[4], may in the exercise of its inherent power to control the conduct of proceedings exclude the public where it becomes necessary in order to administer justice[5]. Usually, except for statutory exceptions[6], the court should only exclude the public if the administration of justice would be rendered impracticable by their presence, whether because the case could not be effectively tried, or the parties entitled to justice would be reasonably deterred from seeking it at the hands of the court[1]. There is however an inherent jurisdiction to restrict access in the interests of the administration of justice, and a court is entitled to take into account such matters as security, public order, decency, safety and the protection of minors[7].

Article 6(1) of the European Convention on Human Rights provides a right to a "public hearing" in the determination of criminal proceedings, subject to very limited exceptions. The purpose of this fundamental guarantee is to protect litigants from the "administration of justice in secret with no public scrutiny"[8], and to maintain public confidence in the courts and the administration of justice. Article 6(1) expressly provides that the press and public may be excluded from all or part of the trial in the interests of morals, public order or national security in a democratic society, where the interests of juveniles or the protection of the private life of the parties so require, to the extent strictly necessary in the opinion of the court in special circumstances where publicity would prejudice the interests of justice. A decision to hold a hearing in private must be "strictly required by the circumstances"[9]. Security can only justify departure from the requirement of a public hearing in the most exceptional circumstances[10].

Departure from the principle of open justice is only justified where the court reasonably believes it to be necessary to serve the interests of justice; it is an exceptional step to take and is to be avoided if there is any other way of serving the interests of justice. A distinction must be drawn between what is strictly necessary and what is merely convenient or expedient. Hearing a matter *in camera* is a course of last resort, only to be adopted if proceeding in open court would frustrate the process of justice; the court should first consider alternatives, such as committal for trial or for sentence, or making an order under s 11 of the Contempt of Court Act 1981 protecting a defendant's identity[7]. But there must be exceptional and compelling reasons for making an order under s 11; it is a misuse of s 11 if the order is made merely out of sympathy for the defendant's well being[4]. Where a witness refused to testify because she felt "uncomfortable" doing so in front of the public and she would not testify until the gallery was cleared, it was "strictly necessary" to do so in order to secure that justice was done. The court's ruling did not therefore, breach art 6 of the ECHR[11].

The procedure of taking a deposition from a witness, pursuant to para 4 of Sch 3 to the 1998 Act, is a proceeding in open court, though justices may exceptionally exclude persons from the taking of the deposition or otherwise modify the procedure where that will assist in the reception of the evidence or it is in the interests of justice to do so[12].

Where a *bona fide* application is made for the public to be excluded, the proper course is for the justices to clear the court in order to consider the application, then announce publicly their decision and proceed accordingly. Where confidentiality has to be preserved, it is preferable to do that by remaining in open court and placing the matter before the court in writing. There will be circumstances when that cannot be done, for example where the matter would be challenged by cross-examination, in which case it will be right to close the court[13].

All persons who so desire may be present to hear what is going on, provided there is room for them and they do not interrupt the proceedings or there is no other good reason why they should be excluded[14]. Where it is necessary to show indecent films, the public can be excluded from any showing, but not normally the press[15]. An *ex parte* application such as an application for a summons or a warrant can be heard privately.

Magistrates have an inherent discretion to receive, during the course of a trial, representations in private. This is an unusual step and the discretion must be exercised sparingly and with caution. It will be particularly rare for a lay bench safely to permit such a course. Except in a case of public interest immunity, all parties should know what is taking place and be represented in chambers; the clerk should make a note as carefully and contemporaneously as possible[16]. There is specific power to clear courts while a minor is giving evidence, and the public have only limited access to youth and family proceedings courts[17].

There is no statutory rule entitling justices to anonymity in any circumstances and any attempt to remain anonymous is inimical to the proper administration of justice[18]. Since the principle of open justice requires that nothing shall be done to discourage the fair and accurate reporting of proceedings in court, it does not allow justices, in the exercise of their power to control the proceedings, to seek anonymity. The *bona fide* enquirer is entitled to know the name of a justice who is sitting or who has sat upon a case, save that a clerk to the justices may act with justification in refusing during and after a hearing to give the name of one of the justices to a person who the clerk reasonably believes requires that information solely for a mischievous purpose[18].

A court may visit the scene of matters it is considering, but witnesses who demonstrate what occurred should be recalled for examination when the hearing resumes in court[19].

Sitting in open court also means that the justices must not discuss the case privately out of the presence of the parties with any person other than the clerk. Convictions have been quashed where justices interviewed a police superintendent in their private room[20], interviewed privately a witness "as to character"[21], where they had a social worker with them during their retirement[22]. It is wrong to retire with the *guardian ad litem* in adoption proceedings[23], or to consider papers not produced in open court[24].

1. *Scott v Scott* [1913] AC 417, HL.
2. Magistrates' Courts Act 1980, s 121(4), in this PART: STATUTES ON PROCEDURE, post, and see *McPherson v McPherson* [1936] AC 177, PC.
3. Per LORD DIPLOCK in *A-G v Leveller Magazine Ltd* [1979] AC 440, [1979] 1 All ER 745, 143 JP 260, HL.
4. *R v Malvern Justices, ex p Evans* [1988] QB 540, [1988] 1 All ER 371, 152 JP 74. See also the Contempt of Court Act 1981, s 11, this PART, post.
5. *R v Governor of Lewes Prison, ex p Doyle* [1917] 2 KB 254.
6. See for example, the Children and Young Persons Act 1933, s 37 (power to clear court while child or young person is giving evidence in certain cases) in PART V: YOUTH COURTS, post.
7. *Re L* (1990) 155 JP 273, [1991] Crim LR 633 (deportation of juvenile hearing behind locked doors in juvenile court not invalid).
8. *Preto v Italy* (1983) 6 EHRR 182; *Diennet v France* (1995) 21 EHRR 554.
9. *Helmers v Sweden* (1991) 15 EHRR 285.
10. *Campbell and Fell v United Kingdom* (1984) 7 EHRR 165.
11. *R v Richards* (1998) 163 JP 246, [1999] Crim LR 764, CA.
12. *R (Crown Prosecution Service) v Bolton Magistrates' Court* [2003] EWHC 2697 (Admin), [2004] 1 WLR 835, [2004] Cr App R 33.
13. *A-G v Leveller Magazine Ltd* [1979] AC 440, [1979] 1 All ER 745, 143 JP 260; *R v Ealing Justices, ex p Weafer* (1982) 74 Cr App Rep 204, [1982] Crim LR 182; *R v Reigate Justices, ex p Argus Newspapers Ltd* [1983] Crim LR 564.
14. *R v Denbigh Justices, ex p Williams* [1974] QB 759, [1974] 2 All ER 1052.
15. *R v Waterfield* [1975] 2 All ER 40, [1975] 1 WLR 711, 131 JP 400. See also *R v Uxbridge Justices, ex p Webb* (1993) 162 JP 198, DC.
16. *R v Nottingham Magistrates' Court, ex p Furnell* (1995) 160 JP 201.
17. Children and Young Persons Act 1933, ss 37, 47, in PART V: YOUTH COURTS, post; Magistrates' Courts Act 1980, s 69, in this PART: STATUTES ON PROCEDURE, post.
18. *R v Felixstowe Justices, ex p Leigh* [1987] QB 582, [1987] 1 All ER 551, 151 JP 65.
19. See *Karamat v R* [1956] AC 256, [1956] 1 All ER 415, 120 JP 136.
20. *R v Bucks Justices* (1922) 86 JP Jo 636.
21. *R v Bodmin Justices, ex p McEwen* [1947] KB 321, [1947] 1 All ER 109, 111 JP 47.
22. *R v Aberdare Justices, ex p Jones* [1973] Crim LR 45.
23. *Re B (a minor) (adoption jurisdiction)* [1975] Fam 127, [1975] 2 All ER 449.
24. *Hastings v Ostle* (1930) 94 JP 209; *Hill v Tothill* [1936] WN 126.

1–114 Prohibitions on publication. In family proceedings a newspaper or periodical may publish only the names, addresses and occupations of the parties and witnesses, the grounds of the application, and a concise statement of the charges, defences and counter-charges in support of which evidence has been given, submissions on points of law and the decisions thereon, and the decision and observations of the court[1]; in adoption proceedings only points of law, and the eventual decision of the court and its observations may be reported, and no particulars calculated to lead to the identification of the child[1].

In relation to any proceedings in any court, the court may direct that no newspaper, sound or television reports shall publish any particulars calculated to lead to the identification of any child or young person concerned in the proceedings[2]; in the case of a youth court there is an absolute prohibition on such publication unless the court or the Secretary of State dispenses with the requirement for the purpose of avoiding injustice to a child or young person[3]; a court dealing with the variation or discharge of a supervision order for a seventeen-year-old must specifically order any prohibition[4].

A party to criminal proceedings may apply to the court for a direction (a "reporting direction") in relation to a witness who has attained 18 years to prohibit the publication in his lifetime of material likely to identify him to members of the public as being a witness in those proceedings. Before making such a direction, the court must be satisfied that he is eligible for protection ie that the quality of his evidence and his degree of cooperation is likely to be diminished by fear and distress and that such a direction is likely to improve the quality of his evidence and the level of cooperation given by him in the preparation of the case[5].

Reports of an application for dismissal to a magistrates' court under s 6 of the Magistrates' Courts Act 1980 must be restricted to identifying the people concerned, the offence or offences with which the accused are charged and decisions of the court, until either a successful conclusion of the application for dismissal, or the conclusion of the trial in the Crown Court of the person or persons charged. Nevertheless, the restrictions on reporting may be removed if the magistrates' court, on an application for the purpose with reference to the proceedings, so orders. Where in the case of two or more accused one of them objects to the making of an order removing the restrictions, the magistrates' court shall make the order if, and only if, the court is satisfied, after hearing representations of the accused, that it is in the interests of justice to do so[6].

There are provisions designed to protect the anonymity of complainants in rape cases and certain other sexual offences[7].

Notwithstanding such special provisions, a magistrates' court may, where it appears to be necessary for avoiding a substantial risk of prejudice to the administration of justice in legal proceedings held in public or in any other proceedings pending or imminent, order that the publication of any report of the proceedings or any part of the proceedings, be postponed for such period as the court thinks necessary for that purpose; failure to observe such an order can make a person guilty of contempt of court under the strict liability rule even where the report was a fair and accurate report published contemporaneously and in good faith[8]. Where a court orders a name or other matter to be withheld from the public in proceedings in court, it may give such directions for the purpose as appear necessary[9].

Cases of alleged contempt can be reported to the Director of Public Prosecutions for action, for example criminal investigation by a newspaper which could prejudice a fair trial[10]. Where a court in the exercise of its control over the conduct of proceedings directs that a witness need not disclose his name when giving evidence, an attempt to frustrate the action of the court by publishing the witness's identity may be a contempt of court if it interferes with the due administration of justice; but, in the absence of such interference, merely running counter to a direction of the court is not of itself enough to make the publication a contempt of court. When making such a direction, the court should make clear what restrictions are intended to be imposed on publishing outside the court, and whether breach of the direction would expose the publisher to the risk of proceedings for contempt[11].

---

1. Magistrates' Courts Act 1980, s 71 , in this PART: STATUTES ON PROCEDURE, post.
2. Children and Young Persons Acts 1933, s 39 and 1963, s 57, in PART V: YOUTH COURTS, post.
3. Children and Young Persons Act 1933, s 49, in PART V: YOUTH COURTS, post.
4. Children and Young Persons Act 1969, s 10, in PART V: YOUTH COURTS, post.
5. Youth Justice and Criminal Evidence Act 1999, s 46, in PART II: EVIDENCE, post. For procedure, see the Criminal Procedure Rules 2005, Part 16, in this PART: STATUTES ON PROCEDURE, post.
6. Magistrates' Courts Act 1980, s 8A, in this PART: STATUTES ON PROCEDURE, post.
7. Sexual Offences (Amendment Act) 1992, s 1 in PART VIII: title SEXUAL OFFENCES, post.
8. See Contempt of Court Act 1981, ss 1–7, in this PART: STATUTES ON PROCEDURE, post, and *R v Horsham Justices, ex p Farquharson* [1982] QB 762, [1982] 2 All ER 269.
9. Contempt of Court Act 1981, s 11, in this PART: STATUTES ON PROCEDURE, post.
10. See *R v Parke* [1903] 2 KB 432, 67 JP 421; *R v Davies* [1906] 1 KB 32.
11. *A-G v Leveller Magazine Ltd* [1979] AC 440, [1979] 1 All ER 745, 143 JP 260, and see s 11 of the Contempt of Court Act 1981, post, also *R v Horsham Justices, ex p Farquharson*, supra.

1-115   Tape recorders, photographs, sketches in court.   It is a contempt of court to use in court or bring into court for use any tape recorder or other instrument for recording sound, except with the leave of the court, or to publish a recording or dispose of it with a view to publication, or to use a recording in contravention of any conditions of leave granted[1]. No person shall take or attempt to take any photograph, or with a view to publication make or attempt to make any portrait or sketch, of a justice, a witness in or a party to any proceedings before the court in a court-room, or in a court building or precincts, or while he is entering or leaving them[2].

The penalty for breach of the tape recorder provisions is one month's imprisonment or a fine not exceeding £2,500[3]. The instrument or any recording or both may be forfeited[1]. There is no limit on the discretion to grant, withhold or withdraw leave, but a court ought to consider the existence of any reasonable need for the recording to be made, the risk of a recording being used to brief witnesses out of court, and the possibility of the use of a recorder disturbing the proceedings, or distracting or worrying anyone taking part in the case[4]. Conditions ought to be considered, and when leave is granted, the applicant should be reminded that he may not publish the recording or dispose of it for that purpose[4].

The penalty for breach of the photograph or sketch provisions is a fine not exceeding **level 3** on the standard scale[2].

---

1. Contempt of Court Act 1981, s 9, in this PART: STATUTES ON PROCEDURE, post.
2. Criminal Justice Act 1925, s 41, in this PART: STATUTES ON PROCEDURE, post.
3. Contempt of Court Act 1981, s 14, in this PART: STATUTES ON PROCEDURE, post.
4. *Practice Direction (criminal: consolidated)* [2002] para I.2, in this PART: STATUTORY INSTRUMENTS AND PRACTICE DIRECTIONS ON PROCEDURE, post.

CONTEMPT OF COURT

1-116   Where any person wilfully insults the justice or justices, any witness before or officer of the court or any solicitor or counsel having business in the court, during his or their sitting or attendance in court, or in going to or returning from the court, or wilfully interrupts the proceedings of the court or otherwise misbehaves in court, the court may order any officer of the court or any constable to take the offender into custody and detain him until the rising of the court; and the court may if it thinks fit, commit the offender (if 18 and over[1]) to custody for a specified period not exceeding one month or impose on him a fine not exceeding £2,500, or both[2]. The powers of the court to deal with contempt where the offender is under 18 are very limited[3].

Legal aid may be granted for the purposes of such proceedings[4]. The court may at any time revoke an order of committal and discharge the offender from custody[2].

In addition to this power, the Queen's Bench Divisional Court has jurisdiction to protect an inferior court by attachment for contempt[5].

1. *R v Selby Justices, ex p Frame* [1992] QB 72, [1991] 2 All ER 344, 155 JP 333.
2. Contempt of Court Act 1981, s 12, post.
3. See *R v Byas* (1995) 16 Cr App Rep(s) 869, [1995] Crim LR 439, CA and commentary.
4. Access to Justice Act 1999, s 12(1)(*f*), in this PART, post. Where an individual's liberty is at stake, legal aid will usually be required under Article 6(3)(*c*) of the European Convention on Human Rights. See *Benham v United Kingdom* (1996) 22 EHRR 293.
5. *R v Parke* [1903] 2 KB 432, 67 JP 421; *R v Davies* [1906] 1 KB 32.

1–117   Practice Direction (criminal: consolidated) para V.54.   The following guidance has been given to district judges and magistrates when dealing with a contempt of court in *Practice Direction (criminal: consolidated)* [2002][1]:

"V.54. Contempt in the face of the magistrates' court
General
V.54.1. Section 12 of the Contempt of Court Act 1981 gives magistrates' courts the power to detain until the court rises, someone, whether a defendant or another person present in court, who wilfully insults anyone specified in s 12 or who interrupts proceedings. In any such case, the court may order any officer of the court, or any constable, to take the offender into custody and detain him until the rising of the court; and the court may, if it thinks fit, commit the offender to custody for a specified period not exceeding one month or impose a fine not exceeding level 4 on the standard scale or both. This power can be used to stop disruption of their proceedings. Detention is until the person can be conveniently dealt with without disruption of the proceedings. Prior to the court using the power the offender should be warned to desist or face the prospect of being detained.
V.54.2. Magistrates' courts also have the power to commit to custody any person attending or brought before a magistrates' court who refuses without just cause to be sworn or to give evidence under s 97(4) of the Magistrates' Courts Act 1980, until the expiration of such period not exceeding one month as may be specified in the warrant or until he sooner gives evidence or produces the document or thing, or impose on him a fine not exceeding £2,500, or both.
V.54.3. In the exercise of any of these powers, as soon as is practical, and in any event prior to an offender being proceeded against, an offender should be told of the conduct which it is alleged to constitute his offending in clear terms. When making an order under s 12 the justices should state their findings of fact as to the contempt.
V.54.4. Exceptional situations require exceptional treatment. While this direction deals with the generality of situations, there will be a minority of situations where the application of the direction will not be consistent with achieving justice in the special circumstances of the particular case. Where this is the situation, the compliance with the direction should be modified so far as is necessary so as to accord with the interests of justice.
V.54.5. The power to bind persons over to be of good behaviour in respect of their conduct in court should cease to be exercised.
Contempt consisting of wilfully insulting anyone specified in s 12 or interrupting proceedings
V.54.6. In the case of someone who wilfully insults anyone specified in s 12 of the 1981 Act or interrupts proceedings, if an offender expresses a willingness to apologise for his misconduct, he should be brought back before the court at the earliest convenient moment in order to make the apology and to give undertakings to the court to refrain from further misbehaviour.
V.54.7. In the majority of cases, an apology and a promise as to future conduct should be sufficient for justices to order an offender's release. However, there are likely to be certain cases where the nature and seriousness of the misconduct requires the justices to consider using their powers under s 12(2) of the 1981 Act either to fine or to order the offender's committal to custody.
Where an offender is detained for contempt of court
V.54.8. Anyone detained under either of these provisions in paras 54.1 or 54.2 should be seen by the duty solicitor or another legal representative and be represented in proceedings if they so wish. Public funding should generally be granted to cover representation. The offender must be afforded adequate time and facilities in order to prepare his case. The matter should be resolved the same day if at all possible.
V.54.9. The offender should be brought back before the court before the justices conclude their daily business. The justices should ensure that he understands the nature of the proceedings, including his opportunity to apologise or give evidence and the alternative of them exercising their powers.
V.54.10. Having heard from the offender's solicitor, the justices should decide whether to take further action.
Sentencing of an offender who admits being in contempt
V.54.11. If an offence of contempt is admitted the justices should consider whether they are able to proceed on the day or whether to adjourn to allow further reflection. The matter should be dealt with on the same day if at all possible. If the justices are of the view to adjourn they should generally grant the offender bail unless one or more of the exceptions to the right to bail in the Bail Act 1976 are made out.
V.54.12. When they come to sentence the offender where the offence has been admitted, the justices should first ask the offender if he has any objection to them dealing with the matter. If there is any objection to the justices dealing with the matter a differently-constituted panel should hear the proceedings. If the offender's conduct was directed to the justices, it will not be appropriate for the same bench to deal with the matter.
V.54.13. The justices should consider whether an order for the offender's discharge is appropriate, taking into account any time spent on remand, whether the offence was admitted and the seriousness of the contempt. Any period of committal should be for the shortest time commensurate with the interests of preserving good order in the administration of justice.
Trial of the issue where the contempt is not admitted
V.54.14. Where the contempt is not admitted the justices' powers are limited to making arrangements for a trial to take place. They should not at this stage make findings against the offender.
V.54.15. In the case of a contested contempt the trial should take place at the earliest opportunity and should be before a bench of justices other than those before whom the alleged contempt took place. If a trial of the

issue can take place on the day such arrangements should be made taking into account the offender's rights under art 6 of the European Convention for the Protection of Human Rights and Fundamental Freedoms 1950 (as set out in Sch 1 to the Human Rights Act 1998). If the trial cannot take place that day the justices should again bail the offender unless there are grounds under the 1976 Act to remand him in custody.

V.54.16. The offender is entitled to call and examine witnesses where evidence is relevant. If the offender is found by the court to have committed contempt the court should again consider first whether an order for his discharge from custody is sufficient to bring proceedings to an end. The justices should also allow the offender a further opportunity to apologise for his contempt or to make representations. If the justices are of the view that they must exercise their powers to commit to custody under s 12(2) of the 1981 Act, they must take into account any time spent on remand and the nature and seriousness of the contempt. Any period of committal should be for the shortest period of time commensurate with the interests of preserving good order in the administration of justice."

---

1. In this Part, STATUTORY INSTRUMENTS AND PRACTICE DIRECTIONS ON PROCEDURE, post.

1–118   Disobeying order of the court.   Where any person disobeys an order of a magistrates' court to do anything other than the payment of money, or to abstain from doing anything, the court may order him to pay a sum not exceeding £50 for every day during which he is in default or a sum not exceeding £5,000, or commit him to custody until he has remedied his default or for a period not exceeding 2 months[1].

In proceedings brought for breach of an order for access or custody relating to children, it is essential for notes of the evidence to be taken by the clerk and for the justices to give reasons for their decision[2].

---

1. Magistrates' Courts Act 1980, s 63 (3), post. For monetary orders and fines, see ss 75–96 of the Act, post. For disobedience to bail orders see Bail Act 1976, s 6, post.
2. *Tilmouth v Tilmouth* (1984) 148 JP 705, [1985] FLR 239, [1985] Fam Law 92.

DISQUALIFICATION OF MAGISTRATES

1–119   In a particular case a magistrate must not sit and adjudicate if—

(1)   some statutory disqualification applies to him, or
(2)   he is disqualified because he is a judge in his own cause, ie where the magistrate is himself a party to the cause or has a relevant interest in its subject matter[1]; or
(3)   there is evidence of *actual bias* on his part[2]; or
(4)   the test to be applied in cases of *apparent bias* is satisfied[2].

Article 6(1) of the European Convention provides a right to a fair and public hearing "by an independent and impartial tribunal". Impartiality in this context includes both subjective and objective impartiality[3].

---

1. *R v Rand* (1866) LR 1 QB 230, 30 JP 293; *R v Gough* [1993] 2 All ER 724.
2. *R v Bow Street Metropolitan Stipendiary Magistrate; ex p Pinochet Ugarte (No 2)* [2000] 1 AC 119, [1999] 1 All ER 577, [1999] 2 WLR 272, HL.
3. *Piersack v Belgium* (1982) 5 EHRR 169. See further paras **1–132** and **1–133**.

1–120   Waiver of objection.   Where a magistrate knows there could be an objection to his sitting on the case, he should take the initiative and withdraw, or at all events bring the matter to the attention of the parties[1]. Any objection to his sitting should be made before the merits of the case are gone into; the parties, knowing of a non-pecuniary interest, may however waive it and request him to act, or may acquiesce in his acting. Where the facts exist that raise an appearance of bias on the part of the judge, it is right that counsel should advise his client of all the implications of the situation, including the implications of an adjournment. He can advise about the judicial oath and explain that judges are trained in considering cases objectively and disregarding any personal view that they may hold. But it is not appropriate to expound on counsel's personal knowledge of the integrity of the individual judge. Counsel should not seek to influence the decision to be taken by the lay client as the choice whether to waive any objection is that of the lay client. While it is proper for counsel to inform the client of the implications of the choice, it is not appropriate for counsel to urge the client to waive his right to object to the tribunal[2].

The simple fact of an objection being made to a justice sitting on a case does not of itself require him to withdraw; indeed if he considers that he is in no way biased or prejudiced or interested, it is his duty to sit and hear the case[3]. Justice should not only be done but should manifestly and undoubtedly be seen to be done; it is however more important that justice should in fact be done[4].

A justice who has withdrawn should not appear to form part of the court, nor sit in such a position as might lead one to think he could exert any influence over the decision of the court; thus it would appear wrong for him to speak to the chairman and refer to papers even though he did not take part in the discussion[5], or for him to sit next to the prosecuting solicitor and exchange a note with the Bench[6], or indeed to sit at the end of the row of justices[7].

The parties may not, knowing of an objection to a magistrate sitting, fail to raise it and then seek to appeal on the ground that one of the justices had an interest[7]. Knowledge of any disqualification must be expressly negatived in the affidavit in support of an application for judicial review[8]. It is not the duty of an advocate who suspects a disqualification to put fishing questions thereon to members of the Bench[9].

1. *R v Altrincham Justices, ex p Pennington* [1975] QB 549, [1975] 2 All ER 78.
2. *Smith v Kvaerner Cementation Foundations Ltd* [2006] EWCA Civ 242, [2006] 3 All ER 593, [2007] 1 WLR 370.
3. *R v Tooke* (1884) 48 JP 661.
4. *R v Camborne Justices, ex p Pearce* [1955] 1 QB 41, [1954] 2 All ER 850, 118 JP 488.
5. *R v Suffolk Justices* (1852) 18 QB 416, 16 JP 296.
6. *R v Budden etc Kent Justices* (1896) 60 JP 166.
7. *R v Byles, ex p Hollidge* (1912) 77 JP 40.
8. *R v Swansea Justices* (1913) 49 L Jo 10.
9. *R v Barnsley County Borough Licensing Justices, ex p Barnsley and District Licensed Victuallers Association* [1959] 2 QB 276, [1959] 2 All ER 635, 123 JP 365.

1–130 Statutory disqualification. A lay justice who is a member of a local authority[1] may not act as a member of the Crown Court or a magistrates' court in proceedings brought by or against, or by way of an appeal from a decision of that local authority, or of one of its committees or officers[2], or if it is operating executive arrangements within the mean of Part 2 of the Local Government Act 2000 the executive of that local authority or any person acting on behalf of its executive[3].

No act is invalidated, however, merely because this statutory disqualification applied to the person by whom it was done[4].

1. Defined in the Courts Act 2003, s 41(6), this PART, post.
2. Defined in the Courts Act 2003, s 41(4).
3. Courts Act 2003, s 41(1). Like provision is made in respect of a lay justice who is a member of the Common Council of the City of London: Courts Act 2003, s 41(2). As to joint committees, etc, see Courts Act 2003, s 41(3).
4. Courts Act 2003, s 41(5).

1–131 Disqualification because he is a judge in his own cause. It is a fundamental principle that a man may not be a judge in his own cause[1]. Once it is shown that a magistrate is himself a party to a cause, or that he has a relevant interest in its subject matter, he is disqualified without any investigation into whether there is a likelihood or suspicion of bias[2]. Therefore, a magistrate, who has a direct pecuniary interest, however small, or a proprietary interest in the outcome of the case, is sitting as a judge in his own cause and such interest is sufficient to cause his automatic disqualification[3]. If a magistrate with a pecuniary or other interest is shown to have adjudicated, public confidence in the administration of justice requires that the decision should not stand[4].

1. *Dimes v Proprietors of Grand Junction Canal* (1852) 3 HL Cas 759, 10 ER 301.
2. *R v Bow Street Metropolitan Stipendiary Magistrate, ex p Pinochet Ugarte (No 2)* [2000] 1 AC 119, [1999] 1 All ER 577, HL.
3. *R v Rand* (1866) LR1 QB 230, 30 JP 293; *R v Bow Street Metropolitan Stipendiary Magistrate, ex p Pinochet Ugarte (No 2)* [2000] 1 AC 119, [1999] 1 All ER 577, HL.
4. *R v Gough* [1993] AC 646, [1993] 2 All ER 724, [1993] 2 WLR 883, HL.

1–132 Actual bias. In the rare case where actual bias is shown to exist the magistrate concerned must disqualify himself[1]. If he does not disqualify himself or if actual bias is proved after the case has been heard, the decision will be set aside on appeal. For subjective impartiality to be made out under Article 6(1) of the European Convention on Human Rights, proof of actual bias is needed[2].

1. *R v Gough* [1993] AC 646, [1993] 2 All ER 724.
2. *Hauschildt v Denmark* (1989) 12 EHRR 266.

1–133 Apparent bias. The same test is applicable in all cases of apparent bias, whether concerned with justices or other members of other inferior tribunals, or with jurors, or with arbitrators[1]. The test of objective impartiality under Article 6(1) of the European Convention on Human Rights requires a determination of whether, quite apart from a magistrate's personal conduct, there are "ascertainable facts which may raise doubts as to his impartiality"[2]. While not determinative, the standpoint of the defendant is important in this assessment[3]. In the light of European jurisprudence, the Court of Appeal and the House of Lords has reviewed earlier authorities[4] and the test to be applied is, having ascertained all the circumstances which have a bearing on the suggestion that the judge or justice was biased, would those circumstances lead a fair-minded and informed observer to conclude that there was a *real possibility* that the tribunal was biased[5]. Bias in this sense means that the judge might unfairly regard (or have unfairly regarded) with favour, or disfavour, the case of a party to the issue under consideration by him[1]. If there are legitimate reasons to fear impartiality, a magistrate must withdraw. The Court of Appeal has said that in considering whether there is a real danger of bias on the part of a judge, everything depends on the facts, which may include the nature of the issue to be decided. However, a judge's religion, ethnic or national origin, gender, age, class, means or sexual orientation cannot form a sound basis of an objection. Nor, ordinarily, can an objection be soundly based on the judge's social, educational, service or employment background or that of his family; his previous political associations; his membership of social, sporting or charitable bodies; his Masonic associations; his previous judicial decisions; his extra-curricular utterances; his previous receipt of instructions to act for or against any party, solicitor or advocate engaged in a case before him; or his membership of the same Inn, circuit, local Law Society or chambers[6]. The fair minded and informed observer will be aware that in the ordinary way contacts between the judiciary and the profession should not be regarded as giving rise to a possibility of bias. Judges should be circumspect about declaring the existence of a relationship where nothing is served by doing so and such disclosure may unnecessarily undermine a litigant's confidence in a judge but where a fair minded and informed observer might apprehend bias, it is important that disclosure, and full disclosure, is made. In borderline cases, disclosure should be made to enable the parties to make submissions whether the judge should withdraw[7]. A judge was not disqualified where on occasions he had met the Chief Constable, a prosecution witness, in a professional context at civic dinners, although the judge was right to declare that fact[8].

Where the chairman of the justices, during the cross-examination of a police officer, intervened saying, "*It is not the practice to call police officers liars in this court*", it was held that there was a real danger that the chairman was unfairly, although unconsciously, prejudiced in favour of the police officer and thus against the defendant when it came to resolving the conflict of evidence between them. Since there was a real possibility that there was not a wholly impartial adjudication of the central dispute arising in the case, the conviction was set aside[9]. Where, as a result of an ambiguous but genuine submission, a judge had, when making a preliminary ruling, proceeded to make a ruling of fact as well as law, it was reasonable of him to decline to withdraw from the case, and to agree to reconsider his findings of fact in the light of further argument. However, there would not be the appearance of justice and fairness where he had then expressed a forceful view about the propriety of the submissions[10].

Magistrates should be sensitive to their appearance on the Bench; they should be seen to be giving their undivided attention to the case. Accordingly, where a magistrate closed her eyes and looked down so that a solicitor was convinced she was asleep or unwell, the Divisional Court set aside a conviction, and said she should have withdrawn from the case on objection being made[11]. During a hearing a magistrate retired from the court and returned with some warrants which he had to sign and proceeded to deal with them while the defendant was speaking. On quashing the conviction the Divisional Court stated that the court must give the case its undivided attention which must be actual and apparent[12]. Therefore a conviction was also quashed where the attention of a justice was substantially diverted from listening to defence evidence in a trial in that she was perusing a copy of the Magistrates' Association sentencing guidelines[13]. It is not an essential feature of a fair trial that the tribunal should be looking at the witness all the time but a complaint that a magistrate was looking at something else falls into a different category[13].

A defendant cannot obtain the termination of a trial by his actions. No fair-minded observer would conclude that continuing with a trial was unfair where the defendant escaped from the dock and attacked the judge[14].

---

1. *R v Gough* [1993] AC 646, [1993] 2 All ER 724.
2. *Hauschildt v Denmark* (1989) 12 EHRR 266 at para 47.
3. *Hauschildt v Denmark* (1989) 12 EHRR 266 at para 48.
4. In particular *R v Gough* [1993] AC 646, [1993] 2 All ER 724, HL and *Locabail UK) Ltd v Bayfield Properties Ltd* [2000] 1 All ER 65, CA.
5. *In re Medicaments (No 2)* [2001] 1 WLR 700, CA modified by removal of the "real danger" formulation and approved in *Porter v Magill* [2001] UKHL 67, [2002] 2 AC 357, [2002] 1 All ER 465, [2002] 2 WLR 37.
6. *Locabail (UK) Ltd. v Bayfield Properties Ltd* [2000] 1 All ER 65, CA.
7. *Taylor v Lawrence* [2002] EWCA Civ 90, [2002] 2 All ER 353, [2002] 3 WLR 640.
8. *R v Mason* [2002] EWCA Crim 385, [2002] Crim LR 841.
9. *R v Highgate Justices, ex p Riley* [1996] RTR 150.
10. *R (Parker) v Warrington Magistrates' Court* [2002] EWHC 1294 (Admin), 166 JP 563.
11. *R v Weston-Super-Mare Justices, ex p Taylor* [1981] Crim LR 179.
12. *R v Marylebone Magistrates' Court, ex p Perry* [1992] Crim LR 514.
13. *R v South Worcestershire Justices, ex p Daniels* (1996) 161 JP 121, DC.
14. *R v Russell* [2006] EWCA Crim 470, [2006] Crim LR 862.

1-134 Business or professional interest. Business or professional interest did not prevent a practising solicitor, a member of the Law Society but not of its Council, from trying the case of a pretended solicitor[1], nor did it disqualify members of the Medical Defence Union from taking part in a disciplinary hearing against a doctor[2]. It did however disqualify a licensed pilot from hearing charges under the Merchant Shipping Act against an unqualified pilot[3]. It was wrong for the solicitor chairman of a rent assessment committee to sit on a case involving the landlord of his father whom he had advised in a separate tenancy dispute[4]. Similarly, it was held to be wrong for a magistrate who was a consultant to a firm employed on a fairly substantial basis by a local authority to sit on a prosecution brought by the local authority without first declaring an interest[5] or a recorder who was the head of chambers of both counsel for the claimant and counsel for the defendant[6]. Since the implementation of the Children Act 1989 everybody engaged in family work has been encouraged to become involved in multi-disciplinary training and other activities. It is beneficial for judges to sit on committees, speak at conferences and training events. Although no clear-cut line can be drawn, whilst it might be appropriate for a judge to sit on a steering group of a project to pilot concurrent planning for children removed under a court order in order to discuss issues of general policy, becoming a party to those policy decisions might be more controversial and require the consent of parties to any hearing. Nor should a judge sit in on sessions which discuss potential real-life cases which might come before the courts. Where an organisation in which a judge has any involvement plays any part in the proceedings, the judge should make his involvement and its extent clear to the parities, preferable before or at the beginning of a hearing or when the connexion becomes clear to the judge[7].

1. *R v Burton, ex p Young* [1897] 2 QB 468, 61 JP 727.
2. *Leeson v General Medical Council* (1889) 43 Ch D 366.
3. *R v Huggins* [1895] 1 QB 563, 59 JP 104.
4. *Metropolitan Properties Co Ltd v Lannon* [1969] 1 QB 577, [1968] 3 All ER 304.
5. *R v Cambridge Justices, ex p Yardline Ltd and Bird* [1990] Crim LR 733.
6. *Smith v Kvaerner Cementation Foundations Ltd* [2006] EWCA Civ 242, [2006] 3 All ER 593, [2007] 1 WLR 370.
7. *M v London Borough of Islington* [2002] 1 FLR 95, FD.

1–135 Membership of a body. Membership of a body may disqualify; thus a member of a board of salmon conservators was not to adjudicate in a case where he had authorised prosecution[1], the chairman of a local Board of Health should not have sat as a justice to hear a case of the Board's dispute over sewage nuisance[2], a riparian owner who as a member of a committee had reported earlier on mining pollution from the defendant's premises should not have sat on the resultant case[3], an alderman co-opted on to an Education Committee should not have tried a council prosecution for short-weight deliveries to schools[4]. On the other hand, a member of a local society affiliated with the London Society for the Prevention of Cruelty to Animals was not disqualified from hearing a prosecution by the parent society[5].

1. *R v Pwllheli Justices, ex p Soane* [1948] 2 All ER 815, 112 JP 441.
2. *R v Meyer* (1875) 1 QBD 173, 40 LT 247.
3. *R v Spedding etc, Justices* (1885) 49 JP Jo 804.
4. *R v Altrincham Justices, ex p Pennington* [1975] QB 549, [1975] 2 All ER 78, 139 JP 434.
5. *R v Deal (Corpn and Justices), ex p Curling* (1881) 46 JP 71.

1–136 Involvement or expression of opinion. Involvement or expression of opinion, depending on the circumstances, may disqualify. A wife in a domestic case knew one of the magistrates and said "he would put her husband through it"[1]; in another case there was an improper private interview by one member of the Bench to try and effect reconciliation[2]. A court hearing an appeal is likely to be prejudiced by a sight of the appellant's antecedents and record[3]. It seems hardly appropriate for a doctor to give advice to a patient, then give evidence of injuries in proceedings where he also sat as a magistrate even though the report shows that the evidence was later held to be good evidence[4]. However, a justice convicting a person of destroying fences was not disqualified although he had previously made an affidavit in an action for injunction against the same person, both being commoners of Epping Forest[5]. A prior meeting of justices to discuss the general question of prosecution under a certain byelaw did not disqualify them from hearing a subsequent particular prosecution[6]. A justice's strong views against motor cars were not by themselves a disqualification even if expressed in court when hearing motoring cases[7].

1. *Cottle v Cottle* [1939] 2 All ER 535.
2. *Jones v Jones* (1941) 105 JP 353.
3. *R v Grimsby Recorder, ex p Fuller* [1956] 1 QB 36, [1955] 3 All ER 300, 119 JP 560.
4. *R v Farrant* (1887) 20 QBD 58, 52 JP 116; see also *R v Tooke* (1884) 48 JP 661 and adverse comments in *Mitchell v Croydon Justices* (1914) 78 JP 385.
5. *R v Alcock, ex p Chilton* (1878) 42 JP 311.
6. *R v Powell* (1884) 48 JP 740.
7. *Ex p Wilder* (1902) 66 JP 761.

1–137 Knowledge of previous proceedings concerning the defendant. A judge or magistrate who has heard one case concerning a litigant cannot, without more, thereupon be said to be likely to be biased one way or the other in any subsequent case concerning that litigant[1]. Nevertheless, it is desirable that an accused person should come before a justice who does not have an intimate knowledge of his record, but that desirability cannot be elevated into a proposition of law sufficient to deprive the justice of jurisdiction[2]. But if in the course of hearing evidence upon a plea of not guilty a magistrate becomes aware that the defendant has previous convictions, it is his duty to disclose that fact forthwith even if it means that the trial then has to start again before a fresh bench[3]. Similarly, justices who have heard an application for legal aid, which included information as to the defendant's previous findings of guilt[4], or an application by the local authority for a secure accommodation order should not, if the defendant pleads not guilty, subsequently sit on the trial of the information[4]. Where justices discover that an accused has previous convictions in circumstances where they should not have done, the relevant test in determining whether they should be discharged is whether there is a real danger of bias bearing in mind that lay justices as well as judges are trained to put out of their mind matters that are irrelevant[5].

There can be no objection in principle to justices continuing to hear a case after listening to (though, in the event, not being required to rule upon) an application for a witness to be screened from the defendant, in support of which the prosecution referred to an alleged history of intimidation; this is not the equivalent of putting in antecedents, let alone undermining the presumption of innocence[6].

Disclosure of a pending charge, albeit more serious, is to be distinguished from disclosure of previous convictions shortly before or at the time of trial[7]. Accordingly, disclosure that the accused is awaiting trial on a more serious charge does not lead to a real danger of bias on the part of a magistrate trying a different charge because the magistrate will be well able to bear in mind that the accused has only been charged and not convicted of that more serious offence[8].

There is nothing improper in placing before the justices a court sheet which refers to all outstanding charges against a defendant to be heard on that day but there may be occasions when it would be undesirable for unrelated charges to be listed together; in the event of complaint, the justices will have to determine whether their knowledge of other charges in their list should cause them to disqualify themselves.

Family proceedings may require a somewhat different approach as judicial continuity has, in respect of judges and district judges, been viewed as a positive advantage; the fact that an earlier hearing involved findings against a party did not of itself found a reasonable view that a judge was biased[9].

---

1. See *Re B (TA) (an infant)* [1971] Ch 270, [1970] 3 All ER 705, 135 JP 7; also *Ex p X and Y* (1972) 122 NLJ 82; *R v McLean, ex p Aikens* (1974) 139 JP 261.
2. *R v A Metropolitan Stipendiary Magistrate, ex p Gallagher* (1972) 136 JP Jo 80.
3. *R v Birmingham Magistrates' Court, ex p Robinson* (1985) 150 JP 1.
4. *R v Blyth Valley Juvenile Court, ex p S* (1987) 151 JP 805.
5. *Johnson v Leicestershire Constabulary* (1998) Times, 7 October DC. See also *R v Downham Market Magistrates' Court, ex p Nudd* (1988) 152 JP 511.
6. *KL and LK v DPP* [2001] EWHC Admin 1112, (2002) 166 JP 369.
7. *R v Weston-Super-Mare Justices, ex p Shaw* [1987] QB 640, [1987] 1 All ER 255, 151 JP 193.
8. *R v Hereford Magistrates' Court, ex p Rowlands* [1998] QB 110, [1997] 2 WLR 854, 161 JP 258.
9. *Re M (minors) (Judicial Continuity)* [1993] 1 FLR 903.

REPRESENTATION

1–138　　In this section we describe a person's right to be represented by an advocate on his behalf, the right to be represented by a professionally qualified advocate and the discretion of the court to permit an unqualified person to act as an advocate or as a "McKenzie friend". Finally we refer to the public funding of legal services.

1–139　Appearance by legal representative.　　A party to any proceedings before a magistrates' court may be represented by a legal representative, and an absent party so represented shall be deemed not to be absent, unless some enactment or recognisance expressly requires his presence[1]. The informant or complainant can himself conduct summary proceedings, the right not being affected by a prosecutor himself giving evidence[2], but the court has a discretion to allow someone else to act on behalf of either party[3]. Right of audience is however customarily restricted to the parties, or their legal representative, unless special provision is made otherwise.

If justices proceed with the hearing of a case against an unrepresented defendant who is handicapped there is a risk that the hearing may be contrary to natural justice. A defendant who is totally deaf and has difficulty in communicating orally or in writing should have the assistance of an interpreter or legal representative, or if need be both[4].

On the summary trial of an information against a corporation, a representative[5] may enter a plea of guilty or not guilty, and for the purposes of a plea of guilty in the absence of accused, a director or the secretary of the corporation may likewise give a notification or intimation[6]. A representative[5] may also make an application to dismiss the charge, or consent or object to summary trial, or claim trial by jury[6]. A corporation will generally otherwise appear by counsel or solicitor.

A youth court with an unrepresented minor before it shall allow his parent, guardian, relative or other responsible person to assist him in conducting his defence to a criminal charge[7]. A magistrates' court has a statutory obligation to assist an unrepresented party in family proceedings to conduct examination and cross-examination[8].

"Legal representative" means an authorised advocate or authorised litigator, as defined by section 119(1) of the Courts and Legal Services Act 1990[9].

Persons in police custody, and on remand in Prison Department establishments, have rights of access to a legal adviser or to facilities for their defence[10].

Magistrates seem unable to insist generally on the personal appearance of a defendant who is legally represented[11]. When a defendant voluntarily absents himself from his trial, it is a matter for his legal representatives, and not for the court, to decide according to the professional rules of conduct and etiquette whether they should continue to represent him[12]. Representation may be provided by an EEC lawyer[13]. Representation in the Crown Court may, in some circumstances, be by a solicitor[14].

---

1. Magistrates' Courts Act 1980, s 122, post.
2. See Criminal Procedure Rules 2005, Part 37, this PART, STATUTORY INSTRUMENTS AND PRACTICE DIRECTIONS ON PROCEDURE, post, and *Duncan v Toms* (1887) 56 LJMC 81, 51 JP 631. Contrast trial on indictment (*R v Brice* (1819) 2 B & Ald 606). See also Report of the Departmental Committee on Justices' Clerks 1944 (Cmnd 6501) para 61 and Report of the Royal Commission on the Police 1962 (Cmnd 1728) para 381. As to the hazards of unrepresented prosecution, see *R v Uxbridge Justices, ex p Conlon* [1979] Crim LR 250.
3. *McKenzie v McKenzie* [1971] P 33, [1970] 3 All ER 1034.
4. *R v Kingston-upon-Thames Magistrates' Court, ex p Davey* (1985) 149 JP 744.
5. Defined and limited in scope by s 33(6) of the Criminal Justice Act 1925, post.
6. See Magistrates' Courts Act 1980, s 12(4) and Sch 3, post.
7. Criminal Procedure Rules 2005, Part 38, in this PART, post.
8. Magistrates' Courts Act 1980, s 73, post.
9. Magistrates' Courts Act 1980, s 150(1), post. For the Courts and Legal Services Act 1990, see PART VIII, title SOLICITORS, post.
10. See (C) Code of Practice for the Detention, Treatment and Questioning of Persons by Police Officers and the Prison Rules 1964, rr 37 and 37A in PART II: EVIDENCE—STATUTORY INSTRUMENTS ON EVIDENCE, post.

11. See *R v Montgomery Justices, ex p Long* (1910) 74 JP 110, but note that in s 23 of the Magistrates' Courts Act 1980 (power of court with consent of legally represented accused to proceed in his absence) the court has a discretion whether or not to proceed.

12. *R v Shaw* [1980] 2 All ER 433, 70 Cr App Rep 313.

13. See the European Communities (Services of Lawyers) Order 1978 in PART VIII: SOLICITORS, post.

14. Supreme Court Act 1981, s 83, post.

1–150 Solicitors. Solicitors are subject to professional control by The Law Society, and complaints about misconduct and inadequate professional services may be made to the Office for the Supervision of Solicitors (OSS), the independent complaints handling arm of the Law Society. The OSS may investigate complaints and reprimand a solicitor for professional misconduct. The OSS may refer more serious matters to the Solicitors Disciplinary Tribunal (although applications may be made direct). This Tribunal may also hear and determine any legal aid complaint relating to the conduct of a solicitor in connection with the giving of advice or provision of services under the Legal Aid Act 1988[1]. The Law Society publishes a *Guide to the Professional Conduct of Solicitors*, 8th edition (1999) which reproduces the Law Society's Code for Advocacy. This Code sets out the principles and standards to be observed by all solicitor advocates when acting as such. The solicitor for the defence must do his best for his client but must never deceive or mislead the court, for example by calling a witness whose evidence he knows to be untrue. He is not under any duty to inform his adversary or the court of facts or of a witness which would assist his adversary to his client's prejudice, except when acting for the prosecution.

Where counsel has been instructed, the instructing solicitor is under a duty to attend or arrange for the attendance of a responsible representative throughout the proceedings, save that attendance may be dispensed with in the magistrates' court or in certain categories of Crown Court proceedings where, in either case, the solicitor is satisfied that it is reasonable in the particular circumstances of the case that counsel be unattended. The solicitor will be so satisfied where it is clear that the interests of justice will not be prejudiced by counsel appearing alone[2].

Copies of communications to the court should be sent to the other side. He may interview a witness for the other side but must not tamper with that witness's evidence nor attempt to suborn him into changing his evidence. If he is called to give evidence which is more than purely formal he will rarely be able to continue to act as a solicitor. If his client admits to perjury or having misled the court in any material matter, the solicitor should decline to act further unless the client agrees to disclose fully his conduct to the court. A solicitor must comply with any order of the court which the court can properly make, requiring him or his firm to take or refrain from taking some particular course of action: equally he is bound to honour his undertakings given to the court. He shall not stand bail for his or a partner's client.

A prosecutor must present his evidence dispassionately and with scrupulous fairness, and must disclose any mitigating circumstances or factual evidence contrary to his case and known to him, as well as giving particulars of witnesses he does not intend to call. If a witness can speak of facts which would tend to show the accused to be innocent, the prosecution must call that witness or make his statement available. Both prosecution and defence must reveal all relevant cases and statutory provisions whether they be for or against their case, but the defence advocate has no other duty of disclosure to the court or prosecution. Whilst he must not without instructions disclose facts nor even correct information given by the prosecution if the correction would be to his client's detriment, he must not knowingly himself put forward or let his client put forward false information with intent to mislead the court.

If the client's express instructions do not permit a solicitor to present the case in the manner he considers to be most appropriate, he may withdraw from the case after seeking the court's approval but without disclosing matters protected by the client's privilege. He is bound to put the client's defence to the court but must never fabricate a defence on the facts. In particular if the client admits his guilt but insists on giving evidence in denial of guilt or instructs his solicitor to make a statement asserting his innocence, the solicitor must decline to act. He may however act if the client admits his guilt but pleads not guilty so as to put the prosecution to proof. If it is clear the client is attempting to put forward false evidence, the solicitor should cease to act. If the client insists on pleading guilty but sets forth facts which could lead to an acquittal, the solicitor should continue to act and do the best he can.

Solicitors (and their clients) are advised to decline to comment on the accuracy of lists of previous convictions, to avoid problems which would otherwise arise if the lists are inaccurate; the advice does not cover the situation where an obvious inaccuracy works to the client's detriment, but presumably comment will be appropriate in such circumstances. A solicitor advocate may be criminally liable for slander of justices[3], but words not wholly irrelevant spoken in good faith by an advocate in the course of his defence of a client, however defamatory they may be of the prosecutor, are not actionable[4] It is improper for a solicitor to prosecute a case against a defendant whom he has earlier advised on his defence[5].

A person who has been arrested and is held in custody in a police station or other premises is entitled, if he so requests, to consult a solicitor privately at any time[6]. Where such a request is made, the person must be permitted to consult a solicitor as soon as practicable, except to the extent that delay is permitted by s 58 of the Police and Criminal Evidence Act 1984[7]. Although these provisions will not normally apply to a person held in custody in cells at a court house, such a person has a common law right, on request, to be permitted to consult a solicitor as soon as is practicable[8].

1. Administration of Justice Act 1985, ss 40 and 43, in PART VIII: SOLICITORS, post.
2. Guide to the Professional Conduct of Solicitors, 8th edition, para 20.04.
3. See post, PART VIII: LIBEL, and *R v Watson* (1878) 23 Sol Jo 86.
4. *Munster v Lamb* (1883) 11 QBD 588, 47 JP 805.
5. *R v Dunstable Magistrates Court, ex p Cox* [1986] NLJ Rep 310.
6. Police and Criminal Evidence Act 1984, s 58(1), this PART, post.
7. Police and Criminal Evidence Act 1984, s 58(4), this PART, post.
8. *R v Chief Constable of South Wales, ex p Merrick* [1994] 2 All ER 560, [1994] 1 WLR 663.

1–151   Barristers.   With the exception of legal aid complaints, there is no statutory control over the conduct of barristers, but any complaint received by the Senate or by the Bench of any Inn alleging misconduct by a barrister shall be referred to the Professional Conduct Committee, which may in turn decide that the complaint shall form the subject matter of a charge before a Disciplinary Tribunal, which will hear it and determine the sentence, if any. A Senate Disciplinary Tribunal may also hear and determine, as a charge of professional misconduct, any legal aid complaint relating to the conduct of a barrister in connection with the giving of advice or provision of services under the Legal Aid Act 1988, and referred to the tribunal in accordance with the regulations of the Senate[1]. The Senate of the Inns of Court and the Bar publishes a *Code of Conduct for the Bar in England and Wales.* It advises in detail on counsel's duty to the court and to his client. Save where attendance may be dispensed with in the magistrates' court or in certain categories of Crown Court proceedings, normally the instructing solicitor or his representative should be present in court, but if not then counsel may still and even, exceptionally, interview supporting witnesses and take proofs of evidence himself. Detailed rules provide for the situation where confessions of guilt are made by the client. Where counsel is told something by the defendant which embarrasses his further conduct of the trial, he is under a duty to investigate the matter fully with the defendant, explain the options open to him and, if necessary, seek an adjournment for that purpose[2]. If the prosecution led the court to believe that an accused has no previous convictions, defence counsel is under no duty to disclose facts to the contrary which are known to him. The naming in court of third parties, whose character would thereby be impugned, should if possible be avoided. The barrister's situation in relation to cases appearing before the bench of which he is a member is analogous to that of a solicitor justice[3].

A barrister should not act as both advocate and witness in the same case[4]. We suggest that this is an appropriate rule for solicitors as well. An advocate is probably a competent witness, but the practice is objectionable[5]. A solicitor may not compromise the case without his client's consent[6]. The relationship between client and legal adviser is protected by privilege, but with exceptions[7].

1. Administration of Justice Act 1985, ss 40–42, in PART VIII: SOLICITORS, post.
2. *Sankar v State of Trinidad and Tobago* [1995] 1 All ER 236, [1995] 1 WLR 194, PC.
3. See Solicitors Act 1974, s 38 in PART VIII: SOLICITORS, post.
4. *R v Secretary of State for India, ex p Ezekiel* [1941] 2 KB 169, [1941] 2 All ER 546.
5. *Campbell v Cochrane* 1928 JC 25; *Cobbett v Hudson* (1852) 1 E & B 11, 17 JP 39 (a civil case); compare proceedings on indictment, *R v Brice* (1819) 2 B & Ald 606.
6. *Swinfen v Swinfen* (1857) 24 Beav 549, 21 JP 773.
7. See post PART II: EVIDENCE, para **2–331 Professional privilege**, post.

1–152   Appearance by other persons and "McKenzie friends".   Subject to the discretion of the magistrates, a person may be assisted in proceedings before a magistrates' court (which includes a "family proceedings court" either by a "McKenzie friend"[1] or by representation by a person who does not have a statutory right of audience.

Any person, whether a professional person or not, may attend a trial as a friend of either party, take notes and quietly make suggestions and give advice to that party[2].

There is, however, no right to advise or to receive advice; justices have a discretion to regulate their own proceedings, and when considering an application that a friend assist an unrepresented defendant, they must strive to ensure that if they refuse the application no injustice will be done, and that the proceedings bear the appearance of fairness[3]. A "McKenzie friend" has no right to address the court on behalf of a party or to "agree" to procedural steps in the absence of a party[4].

The Court of Appeal has given guidance, as follows, on the approach which should be adopted to a request for a litigant in person in the family justice system to allow a McKenzie friend to assist him and the extent to which (if at all) it is necessary for an unrepresented litigant to seek the permission of the court to disclose confidential documents and information generated by the court process both to a McKenzie friend and to other third parties:

> "1. The purpose of allowing a litigant in person the assistance of a McKenzie friend is to further the interests of justice by achieving a level playing field and ensuring a fair hearing. We endorse the proposition that the presumption in favour of allowing a litigant in person the assistance of a *McKenzie* friend is very strong, and that such a request should only be refused for compelling reasons. Furthermore, should a judge identify such reasons, (s)he must explain them carefully and fully to both the litigant in person and the would-be McKenzie friend.
>
> 2. Where a litigant in person wishes to have the assistance of a McKenzie friend in private family law proceedings relating to children, the sooner that intention is made known to the court and the sooner the court's agreement for the use of the particular McKenzie friend is obtained, the better. In the same way that judicial continuity is important, the McKenzie friend, if he is to be involved, will be most useful to the litigant in person and to the court if he is in a position to advise the litigant throughout.

3. We do not think it good practice to exclude the proposed McKenzie friend from the courtroom or chambers whilst the application by the litigant in person for his assistance is being made. The litigant who needs the assistance of a McKenzie friend is likely to need the assistance of such a friend to make the application for his appointment in the first place. In any event, it seems to us helpful for the proposed McKenzie friend to be present so that any concerns about him can be ventilated in his presence, and so that the judge can satisfy her/himself that the McKenzie friend fully understands his role (and in particular the fact that disclosure of confidential court documents is made to him for the purposes of the proceedings only—as to which see [132] to [138] below) and that the McKenzie friend will abide by the court's procedural rules.

4. In this context it will always be helpful for the court if the proposed McKenzie friend can produce either a short curriculum vitae or a statement about himself, confirming that he has no personal interest in the case, and that he understands both the role of the McKenzie friend and the court's rules as to confidentiality.

5. We have already stated that any litigant in person who seeks the assistance of a McKenzie friend should be allowed that assistance unless there are compelling reasons for refusing it. The following, of themselves, do not, in our judgment, constitute compelling reasons:

(1)   that the litigant in person appears to the judge to be of sufficient intelligence to be able to conduct the case on his own without the assistance of a McKenzie friend;

(2)   the fact that the litigant appears to the judge to have a sufficient mastery of the facts of the case and of the documentation to enable him to conduct the case on his own without the assistance of a McKenzie friend;

(3)   the fact that the hearing at which the litigant in person seeks the assistance of a McKenzie friend is a directions appointment, or a case management appointment;

(4)   (subject to what we say below) the fact that the proceedings are confidential and that the court papers contain sensitive information relating to the family's affairs."[5]

The court has a discretion to grant a right of audience to any person in any proceedings[6]. This may extend for example to another police officer prosecuting for the informant[7]. Various statutes give specified persons authority to conduct particular prosecutions, although they may not be of counsel or a solicitor[8].

In civil proceedings in the High Court and the county court a *corporation* may be represented at trial by an employee if the employee has been authorised by the company or corporation to appear at trial on its behalf; and the court gives permission[9].

Magistrates possess an inherent power to regulate their procedure in the interests of justice, and in order to secure or promote convenience and expedition and efficiency in the administration of justice[10]. Magistrates are also under a duty to hear the parties before convicting the accused, or dismissing an information[11]. It is our view that they may accordingly allow anyone who appears in answer to a summons to a corporation, to mitigate or to present a defence. It is however utterly essential that they should first be entirely satisfied as to that person's authority to act and speak for the corporation[12].

---

1. The term "McKenzie Friend" received judicial recognition in *Re O (Children) (Hearing in Private: Assistance)* [2005] EWCA Civ 759, [2006] Fam 1, [2005] 2 FCR 563..

2. *McKenzie v McKenzie* [1971] P 33 [1970] 3 All ER 1034, nor excluded by s 69 of the Magistrates' Courts Act 1980 (domestic proceedings).

3. *R v Leicester City Justices, ex p Barrow* [1991] 3 All ER 935, [1991] 3 WLR 368, CA.

4. *R v Teesside Justices, ex p Nilsson* (1990) 155 JP 101.

5. *Re O (Children) (Hearing in Private: Assistance)* [2005] EWCA Civ 759, [2006] Fam 1, [2005] 2 FCR 563 per Wall LJ at para [128]. See also the guidance issued by the Office of the President of the Family Division relating to McKenzie Friends [2005] 35 Fam Law 405. For disclosure of confidential documents to a McKenzie friend and to third parties, see para **6–29 Disclosure**, post.

6. Courts and Legal Services Act 1990, s 27(2)(c) in PART VIII: SOLICITORS, post.

7. See *O'Toole v Scott* [1965] AC 939, [1965] 2 All ER 240 (a decision of the Judicial Committee of the Privy Council but using English authorities).

8. See eg Local Government Act 1972, s 223 (authorised member or officer of Local Authority); Customs and Excise Management Act 1979, s 155 (authorised officer or other person); Health and Safety at Work etc Act 1974, s 39 (inspector); Wages Act 1986, s 20 (authorised officer); Social Security Administration Act 1992, s 116 (authorised officer).

9. Civil Procedure Rules 1998, SI 1998/3132 r 39.6.

10. See *Collier v Hicks* (1831) 2 B & Ad 663; *Simms v Moore* [1970] 2 QB 327, [1970] 3 All ER 1; *O'Toole v Scott* [1965] AC 939, [1965] 2 All ER 240 (a Privy Council case using early English authorities).

11. Magistrates' Courts Act 1980, s 9, this PART, post.

12. See article at 140 JP 582.

1–153   Publicly funded representation.   Here we summarise the arrangements for the provision of publicly funded legal services. A detailed description of the statutory provisions is set out in the Annex[1].

Funding assistance for advice and representation in proceedings before magistrates' courts is the responsibility of the Legal Services Commission[2]. The Commission administers two schemes: the Community Legal Service for civil proceedings[3]; and the Criminal Defence Service[4] which includes in its scope some civil proceedings which are closely connected with criminal proceedings[5]. Application for assistance and funding under the civil scheme is made direct to the Community Legal Service. In criminal proceedings advice and assistance is provided by holders of franchises under the Criminal Defence Service but application for representation in proceedings (except prescribed proceedings) before magistrates is made to the court itself. Key points about the representation scheme are:

— applies to 'criminal proceedings' and additional prescribed 'criminal proceedings which include proceedings in relation to: enforcement, anti-social behaviour, parenting orders, football banning orders, closure orders;

— application for a grant of representation is to the magistrates; court by prescribed form;

— there is no means test but the application must satisfy statutory criteria

— change of representative is only permitted by order of the court where one of four prescribed criteria has been satisfied.

1. See para **1–870**.
2. See para **1–870, Legal services funded by the Legal Services Commission**, post.
3. See para **1–871, Community Legal Service**, post.
4. See para **1–879, Criminal Defence Service**, post.
5. See para **1–881, Additional prescribed "criminal proceedings"**, post.

Investigation of offences
THE POLICE AND OTHER INVESTIGATING AGENCIES

1–200   The principal agencies for investigating crime are police forces established under the provisions of the Police act 1996. There are also a number of other police forces established under various statutory provisions. The jurisdiction of the police is defined in terms of the powers of a constable and specified in the legislation establishing the particular force; the jurisdictions of forces other than those established under the Police Act 1996 are more restrictively defined. In addition, the Serious Organized Crime Agency has specific functions and powers in relation to serious organized crime. Statutory provisions relating to the establishment, organization and jurisdiction of police officers is contained in PART VIII title POLICE, post.

POLICE AND CRIMINAL EVIDENCE ACT 1984 AND CODES OF PRACTICE

1–201   The powers of a constable are principally regulated by the Police and Criminal Evidence Act 1984[1] and the Codes of Practice made thereunder[2] and the legislation has been extended to the Armed Forces and to Her Majesty's Revenue and Customs[3] and to certain investigations by officers of the Secretary of State[4].

1. See this PART, post and (Police and Criminal Evidence Act 1984, ss 73–82 and Sch 3) PART II: STATUTES ON EVIDENCE, post.
2. See PART II: STATUTORY INSTRUMENTS, CODES OF PRACTICE AND PRACTICE DIRECTIONS ON EVIDENCE, post.
3. PACE 1984, ss 113–114 and notes thereto, this PART, post.
4. PACE 1984, s 114A and note thereto, this PART, post.

POWERS TO STOP AND SEARCH PERSONS

1–202   The powers of a constable to stop and search persons and vehicles have been codified in Part I of the Police and Criminal Evidence Act 1984[1]. A constable may always stop and search with a person's consent: otherwise where a constable has reasonable grounds for suspecting that he will find stolen articles, an offensive weapon or an article for use in burglary, theft, taking a motor vehicle or other conveyance without authority, or obtaining property by deception he may detain and search any person or vehicle or anything in or on a vehicle; the power is exercisable in any place to which people have ready access other than a dwelling[2]. The constable has duties to identify himself, explain the search, and to make a record[3]. There is also a duty to record encounters not governed by statutory powers[4].

The power to stop a vehicle is exercisable only by a constable in uniform[5]. Where a serious arrestable offence is being investigated a police officer of the rank of superintendent or above may in certain circumstances authorise a road check[6].

A constable has powers to search a person on arrest at a police station or elsewhere[7].

Reasonable force may be used[8].

1. Post, para **1–2695** et seq.
2. Police and Criminal Evidence Act 1984, s 1, this PART, post: this is only a bare indication of the much more detailed provision made in the Act.
3. PACE 1984, ss 2, 3, this PART, post.
4. See Code of Practice A paras 4.11–4.20 in PART II: STATUTORY INSTRUMENTS ON EVIDENCE, post.
5. PACE 1984, s 2(9), this PART, post.
6. PACE 1984, s 4, this PART, post.
7. PACE 1984, ss 54 and 55 and s 32, this PART, post.
8. PACE 1984, s 117, this PART, post.

1–203   Code of Practice A.   A Code of Practice[1] has been issued for the exercise by police officers of statutory powers of stop and search. It sets out detailed requirements for action and conduct before, during, and after a search, makes special provision for dealing with unattended vehicles, and in Annex A summarises the main stop and search powers to which the Code applies.

1. The Code of Practice A is reproduced in PART II: EVIDENCE—STATUTORY INSTRUMENTS ON EVIDENCE, post.

SCENES OF CRIME CORDON

1–204   Apart from powers in the Terrorism Act 2000[1], when seeking to investigate crime police officers do not have an unfettered right to restrict movements on private land[2] but are entitled to act on the assumption that the owner of any land over which a right of way exists would consent to the police closing off an area for the purposes of preserving the scene of a crime[3] and it is probable that the landowner could not refuse to consent[4].

---

   1. In PART VIII: title OFFENCES AGAINST THE PERSON, *post*.
   2. *R v Waterfield and Lynn* [1964] 1 QB 164.
   3. *DPP v Morrison* [2003] EWHC Admin 683, 167 JP 561, [2003] Crim LR 727.
   4. *DPP v Morrison, supra* and *Ghani v Jones* [1970] 1 QB 693, [1969] 3 All ER 1700, 134 JP 166, CA.

POWERS OF ENTRY TO PREMISES, SEARCH AND SEIZURE

1–205   An entry by a police officer or other person onto private premises without the occupier's permission or other lawful authority, is an actionable trespass[1]. It will also amount to a breach of Article 8 of the European Convention on Human Rights The citizen appears to retain common law powers to enter premises in order to prevent murder, or if an arrestable offence has been committed and the offender has been followed to the house, or if an arrestable offence is about to be committed and would be committed unless prevented; there must be a prior demand and refusal by the occupier to allow entry before doors can be broken to gain entry[2]. No entry on or interference with property shall be unlawful if it is authorised by a warrant issued by the Secretary of State under s 3 of the Security Service Act 1989, subject to the conditions stipulated in that section.

The powers of a constable to enter and search premises are now almost completely contained in Part II of the Police and Criminal Evidence Act 1984[3]. A constable may always enter and search premises with the occupier's consent. His former powers to enter under common law were abolished with the exception of entry to deal with or prevent a breach of the peace[4]. All other powers are statutory.

Statutory powers of entry and search are as follows.

   1. Entry with a warrant issued for a specific purpose. Many statutes authorise the issue of such warrants. Any special directions in the particular statute must be strictly observed. The draft information and warrant should follow closely the wording of the statutory provision so that all the relevant matters are placed before the magistrate and he can duly authorise, and the executing officer be fully aware of, the extent of the available powers.
   2. Entry with a warrant to search for evidence relevant to an indictable offence which has been committed[5]. This power is subject to a number of qualifications not least of which are the exclusions of items subject to legal privilege, and the need to apply to a circuit judge rather than a justice of the peace when access is sought to certain sensitive items such as confidential occupational records, human tissue and tissue fluid and journalistic material.
   3. Entry to execute a warrant of arrest or commitment, to arrest a person for an indictable offence or certain other specified offences, to recapture a person unlawfully at large, or to save life or limb or prevent serious damage to property[6]; these are situations where the constable may enter without a warrant because either one has not been issued or where one has been issued but he does not have it with him[7].
   4. Search of premises in which a person was when arrested or immediately before he was arrested for evidence relating to the offence for which he was arrested[8], or occupied or controlled by a person under arrest for an indictable offence for evidence relating to that offence or some other connected or similar indictable offence[9].
   5. Entry without a warrant for specified purposes, for example for police to enter licensed premises to investigate licensable activities or to investigate offences[10], for an authorised officer of a Council to enter any premises to ascertain whether there has been a contravention of food legislation[11].

All search warrants are subject to detailed procedural requirements as to application for issue and execution[12]. Reasonable force may be used by a constable in the exercise of a power under the Police and Criminal Evidence Act 1984[13].

A constable who is lawfully on premises has a general power of seizure and retention to prevent anything obtained in consequence of the commission of an offence or which is evidence from being concealed, lost, altered or destroyed[14] as well as any other statutory power which he may otherwise possess, but provision is made for access to and copying of such material by people from whom it has been taken[15]. In difficult circumstances, use can be made of the power of the High Court to issue an injunction for the interim detention, custody, or preservation of property[16].

Where a warrant provides for a search of premises and persons therein, police are acting in the exercise of their powers where they detain a person in one room while they search another[17].

The Criminal Justice and Police Act 2001, Part 2[18], provides additional powers of seizure. The provisions were designed to overcome the difficulties faced by the police and other law enforcement agencies where material was found on premises and it was reasonably believed to be or to contain material that could lawfully be seized, but it was not reasonably practicable to make that determination on the premises, or the material that they were entitled to seize was inextricably linked with other material that they could not seize[19]. In these circumstances, the power of seizure is extended by Part

2 to include power to seize so much of the material as it is necessary to remove to make the necessary determination or separation. Like, additional powers of seizure are provided in respect of searches of the person.

These powers are exercisable only where there is an existing power of seizure, which are listed in Sch 1 to the 2001 Act. In addition to those used by the police, they include powers available to the Serious Fraud Office and various other law enforcement agencies.

Under the European Convention on Human Rights any entry, search and seizure will breach Article 8 (the right to respect for private and family life, home and correspondence) unless it is "in accordance with the law" pursues one or more of the legitimate aims referred to in Article 8(2) and is "necessary in a democratic society" to achieve the aim or aims in question[20].

---

1. *Leach v Money* (1765) 19 State Tr 1001; *Entick v Carrington* (1765) 19 State Tr 1029; and see *Chic Fashions (West Wales) Ltd v Jones* [1967] 2 QB 299, [1968] 1 All ER 229, 132 JP 175, CA, and *Ghani v Jones* [1970] 1 QB 693, [1969] 3 All ER 1700, 134 JP 166, CA.
2. *Swales v Cox* [1981] QB 849, [1981] 1 All ER 1115, 72 Cr App Rep 171.
3. Post, para **1–2702** et seq. However, common law powers are not extinguished by statute unless the statute makes that clear by express provision or by plain implication; therefore, the common law power of search exercisable on the execution of a warrant of arrest for an extradition offence remains in being (*R (on the application of Rottman) v Metropolitan Police Comr* [2002] UKHL 20, [2002] AC 692, [2002] 2 All ER 865, [2002] 2 WLR 1315).
4. Police and Criminal Evidence Act 1984, s 17(5) and (6), this PART, post; and see *Thomas v Sawkins* [1935] 2 KB 249, 99 JP 295; *Swales v Cox*, supra. But see *McLeod v United Kingdom* (1998) 27 EHRR 493 for the position under the European Convention on Human Rights.
5. Police and Criminal Evidence Act 1984, ss 8–14, this PART, post.
6. Police and Criminal Evidence Act 1984, s 17, this PART, post.
7. See Magistrates' Courts Act 1980, s 125, this PART, post.
8. Police and Criminal Evidence Act 1984, s 32(2)(*b*), this PART, post.
9. Police and Criminal Evidence Act 1984, s 18(1), this PART, post.
10. Licensing Act 2003, ss 179, 180 in PART VI: LICENSING, post.
11. Food Safety Act 1990, s 32 in PART VIII: FOOD, post.
12. See Police and Criminal Evidence Act 1984, ss 15 and 16, this PART, post.
13. Police and Criminal Evidence Act 1984, s 117, this PART, post.
14. Police and Criminal Evidence Act 1984, ss 19, 20 and 22, this PART, post.
15. Police and Criminal Evidence Act 1984, s 21, this PART, post.
16. See the Civil Procedure Rules 1998, SI 1998/3132, Part 25 – Interim Remedies, and *West Mercia Constabulary v Wagener* [1981] 3 All ER 378, [1982] 1 WLR 127; *Chief Constable of Kent v V* [1983] QB 34, [1982] 3 All ER 36.
17. *DPP v Meaden* [2003] EWHC 3005 (Admin), [2004] 4 All ER 75, [2004] 1 WLR 945, [2004] Crim LR 587 (warrant under s 23 of the Misuse of Drugs Act 1971).
18. See this PART, para **1–4145**, post.
19. It was held in *R v Chesterfield Justices, ex Bramley* [2000] QB 576, [2000] 1 All ER 411, [2000] Cr App Rep 486 that the police were not entitled to seize material under PACE for the purpose of sifting it elsewhere.
20. *McLeod v United Kingdom* (1998) 27 EHRR 493.

1–206 Code of Practice B. A Code of Practice[1] as been issued for the searching of premises by police officers and the seizure of property found by police officers on persons or premises. It contains the following:

1. Introduction
2. General
3. Search warrants and production orders

    (*a*) Before making an application
    (*b*) Making an application

4. Entry without warrant – particular powers

    (*a*) Making an arrest, etc
    (*b*) Search of premises where arrest takes place or the arrested person was immediately before arrest
    (*c*) Search of premises occupied or controlled by the arrested person

5. Search with consent
6. Searching premises: general considerations

    (*a*) Time of searches
    (*b*) Entry other than with consent
    (*c*) Notice of powers and rights
    (*d*) Conduct of searches
    (*e*) Leaving premises
    (*f*) Searches under PACE Schedule 1 or the Terrorism Act 2000, Sch 5

7. Seizure and retention of property

    (*a*) Seizure
    (*b*) Criminal Justice and Police Act 2001: specific procedures for seize and sift powers
    (*c*) Retention
    (*d*) Rights of owners, etc

8. Action after searches
9. Search registers

---

1. The Code of Practice B is reproduced in PART II: EVIDENCE, STATUTORY INSTRUMENTS ON EVIDENCE, post.

1–207 Search warrants[1]. An application for a warrant to enter and search premises must be made ex parte and be supported by an information in writing[2]

Before making the application, the constable must:

— take reasonable steps to check the information he has received is accurate, recent and not provided maliciously or irresponsibly. Corroboration should be sought for anonymous information;
— ascertain as specifically as possible the nature of the articles concerned and their location;
— make reasonable inquiries to establish if anything is known about the likely occupier of and the nature of the premises;
— obtain any other relevant information.
— support the application by a signed written authority from an officer of inspector rank or above (or next most senior officer in urgent cases);
— consult the local police/community liaison officer (urgent cases as soon as practicable thereafter) where there is reason to believe a search might have an adverse effect on relations between the police and the community[3]

The application must specify:

— the enactment under which it is made, ground on which it is made;
— the premises to be searched ("specific premises warrant") or any premises occupied or controlled by a person specified ("all premises warrant")[4]
—that there are no reasonable grounds to believe the material sought consists or includes items subject to legal privilege or special procedure material
— whether the application is for search on more than one occasion (multiple entry warrant) and if so, whether the number of entries sought is unlimited or the maximum number
— if applicable, a request to authorise a person or persons to accompany the officer who executes the warrant[3]

We suggest the justice hearing the application should:

— confirm that the applicant is a constable;
— consider the written information and the written authority of the inspector;
— identify the statutory authority under which the application is made;
— question the officer on oath to ensure the statutory grounds are made out and the correct procedures have been followed (the officer is required to answer such questions[5], but is not required to reveal the identity of his source[6] (but the justice may enquire as to whether the source has proved reliable on previous occasions);

Where a warrant is issued:

— two copies shall be made and clearly marked as copies[7];
— any search must be made within three calendar months[8];
— any search must be at a reasonable time under this might frustrate the purpose of the search[9];
— a warrant will authorise a search on one occasion only (unless it is a "multiple entry warrant");
— the officer must first try to contact any person entitled to grant access to the premises, explain the authority under which entry is sought and ask for entry to be allowed unless there are reasonable grounds to believe that this would frustrate the object of the search or endanger officers or others[10].
— reasonable and proportionate force may be used if necessary to enter premises[10].
— the search must only be to the extent required for the purpose for which the warrant was issued[11].
— leave a notice providing prescribed information about police powers of search and occupiers' rights and the warrant endorsed that this has been done
— provide evidence of identity to the occupier if present and produce the warrant and provide a copy, otherwise leave a copy of the warrant in a prominent place[5].
— the officer in charge must make sure the premises are left secure either by the presence of the occupier or his agent or by other means[10].
— the police must make a record of the search[13].
— the warrant must be endorsed with the time premises were searched; articles seized and if any were those specified in the warrant; names of the executing officers and any other persons who accompanied them; whether a copy of Notice of Powers and Rights was handed to the occupier or left on premises[13].
— the warrant must be returned within three calendar months of issue[14] and be retained by the designated officer of the court for 12 months[15] who must allow the occupier of the relevant premises to inspect it on request[16].

---

1. For further guidance on and forms of application and warrants, see Home Office Circular 56/2005, relevant parts of which are reproduced in PART IX FORMS AND PRECEDENTS, post.
2. Police and Criminal Evidence Act 1984, s 15(3), in this PART, post.
3. Code of Practice B para 3, in PART II: STATUTORY INSTRUMENTS, CODES OF PRACTICE AND PRACTICE DIRECTIONS ON EVIDENCE, post.
4. PACE 1984, s 15(2).
5. PACE 1984, s 15(4).
6. Note for guidance 3A.
7. PACE 1984, s 15(1).

8. PACE 1984, s 16(3).
9. PACE 1984, s 16(4).
10. Code of Practice B para 6.
11. PACE 1984, s 16(8).
12. PACE 1984, s 16(5).
13. Code of Practice B para 8.
14. PACE 1984, s 16(10).
15. PACE 1984, s 16(11).
16. PACE 1984, s 16(12).

1–208 ***Excluded and special procedure material.*** Application by a constable for an order to produce or give access to excluded material or special procedure material for the purposes of a criminal investigation or for a warrant is by way of an application to a circuit judge or district judge (magistrates' courts)[1] in accordance with Schedule 1 to the Police and Criminal Evidence Act 1984[2]. Excluded material includes personal records held in confidence, or human tissue or fluid taken for the purposes of diagnosis or treatment and held in confidence or journalistic material[3]. Special procedure material is material other than items subject to legal privilege or excluded material acquired or created in the cause of any trade business, profession or other occupation or for the purpose of any office which is held subject to an express or implied undertaking to held it in confidence, or journalistic material[4]. Items subject to legal privilege are, in broad terms, communications between a professional legal adviser and his client in connexion with the giving of advice, or in connexion with or in contemplation of legal proceedings[5].

1. Police and Criminal Evidence Act 1984, s 9, in this PART, post.
2. This PART, post.
3. PACE 1984, ss 11–13.
4. PACE 1984, s 14.
5. PACE 1984, s 10.

INTERCEPTION OF COMMUNICATIONS

1–209 It is an offence, subject to certain exceptions, for a person intentionally and without lawful authority to intercept communications by a public postal service or a public or private telecommunication system[1]. The Secretary of State may issue an interception warrant in accordance with s 5 of the Regulation of Investigatory Powers Act 2000 and in compliance with the safeguards prescribed thereunder. Intercept evidence is not to be disclosed in any legal proceedings[2].

1. Regulation of Investigatory Powers Act 2000, s 1 in PART VIII: title TELECOMMUNICATIONS AND BROADCASTING, post.
2. Regulation of Investigatory Powers Act 2000, ss 17–19.

ARREST

1–220 Arrest consists in the seizure or touching of a person's body with a view to his restraint; words may however amount to an arrest if, in the circumstances of the case, they are calculated to bring, and do bring, to a person's notice that he is under compulsion and he thereafter submits to that compulsion[1]. "Arrest" is an ordinary English word. Whether or not a person has been arrested depends not on the legality of the arrest but on whether he has been deprived of his liberty to go where he pleases[2]. While every arrest involves a deprivation of liberty, the converse is not necessarily true. Arrest can only be effected in the exercise of an asserted authority. If a person is put under restraint arbitrarily or for some expedient motive, he is imprisoned[3].

A person must be informed that he is under arrest and the grounds of his arrest as soon after the arrest as is practicable[4]. If he is arrested elsewhere than at a police station (whether by a constable or by somebody else and then handed into the custody of a constable) he must normally be taken to a police station (normally one designated for police detention) as soon as is practicable after the arrest; alternatively, he may be released on unconditional bail to attend a specified police station at a specified time[5].

A constable may use reasonable force to effect an arrest[6].

Powers of arrest are also governed by Article 5 of the European Convention on Human Rights, which sets out three pre-conditions to a lawful arrest. They are—

1. the arrest must be "lawful";
2. the arrest must be "in accordance with a procedure prescribed by law"; and
3. the grounds for arrest must fall within at least one of the paragraphs 5(1)(*a*) to (*f*) of Article 5.

Paragraph 5(1)(*c*) provides for arrest on reasonable suspicion that an offence has been committed. The arrest must be for the purpose of bringing the person concerned before a "competent legal authority" which includes a magistrates' court. The words "reasonable suspicion" in Article 5(1)(*c*) mean the existence of facts or information which would satisfy an objective observer that the person concerned may have committed the offence[7]. Article 5(2) of the Convention requires that an arrested person be provided with the reasons for an arrest. The person concerned must be told "in simple, non-technical language that he can understand, the essential legal and factual grounds for his arrest so as to be able, if he sees fit, to apply to a court to challenge its lawfulness"[8].

1. See *Alderson v Booth* [1969] 2 QB 216, [1969] 2 All ER 271, 133 JP 346.
2. *Per* VISCOUNT DILHORNE in *Spicer v Holt* [1977] AC 987, [1976] 3 All ER 171, 140 JP 545, HL.
3. *R v Brown* (1976) 64 Cr App Rep 231, [1977] RTR 160, CA.
4. Police and Criminal Evidence Act 1984, s 28, this PART, post.
5. Police and Criminal Evidence Act 1984, s 30, this PART, post.
6. Police and Criminal Evidence Act 1984, s 117, this PART, post.
7. *Fox, Campbell and Hartley v United Kingdom* (1990) 13 EHRR 157.
8. *Fox, Campbell and Hartley v United Kingdom* (1990) 13 EHRR 157 at para 40.

1–221   Arrest under warrant.   Arrest may be effected under the authority of a warrant issued pursuant to some statutory provision. It is usually under provisions[1] which stipulate the following—

1. An information is laid by a police officer or any other person before a justice of the peace that a person has, or is suspected of having, committed an offence.
2. The information must be in writing and substantiated on oath; it ought properly to be the form of a deposition stating shortly the facts rather than a formal document in technical language[2].
3. The application is ex parte and the decision whether or not to issue a warrant is a matter for the magistrate's discretion, which is not reviewable.
4. A warrant as opposed to a summons, may be issued only if the offence is an indictable offence or punishable with imprisonment, or the address of the defendant is not sufficiently established for a summons to be served on him[1].
5. If a warrant is issued, the magistrate should also consider whether or not to endorse it for bail[3].
6. The warrant remains in force until executed or withdrawn, may be executed anywhere in England or Wales by any person to whom it is directed or by any constable acting in his police area, and may be executed by a constable notwithstanding that it is not in his possession at the time[4]: warrants issued in England and Wales may be executed by constables appointed for and acting in Scotland or Northern Ireland[5].

1. Magistrates' Courts Act 1980, s 1, this PART, post.
2. *Herniman v Smith* [1938] AC 305, [1938] 1 All ER 1.
3. Magistrates' Courts Act 1980, s 117, this PART, post.
4. Magistrates' Courts Act 1980, s 125, this PART, post.
5. Criminal Justice and Public Order Act 1994, Pt X—Cross-border enforcement—this PART, post. As to the execution of warrants in the Isle of Man and the Channel Islands, see the Indictable Offences Act 1848, s 13, in PART VIII: title EXTRADITION, etc, post.

1–222   Arrest without a warrant.   The powers of arrest without a warrant are now contained in Part III of the Police and Criminal Evidence Act 1984[1]. This stipulates the powers of arrest—

1. of a constable for any offence[2];
2. of a constable under preserved statutory provisions[3];
3. of persons other than a constable for an indictable offence[4];
4. of persons other than a constable under statutory powers[5].

1. See, this PART, post, ss 24–33.
2. Police and Criminal Evidence Act 1984, s 24, this PART, post.
3. PACE 1984, s 26 and Sch 2, this PART, post.
4. PACE 1984, s 24A, this PART, post.
5. Preserved inferentially by s 26: for example under Immigration Act 1971, Sch 2 (immigration officer); Customs and Excise Management Act 1979, s 138 (customs officer, coastguard, etc).

POLICE DETENTION*

1–223   A person attending voluntarily at a police station or any other place where a constable is present may leave at will unless arrested, in which case he must be told at once that he is under arrest[1]. Once arrested, he may be kept in police detention[2], but only in accordance with Part IV of the Police and Criminal Evidence Act 1984[3]. He must be taken generally without delay[4] to, or kept at, a police station, where a police officer (normally one not involved in the investigation) decides whether or not to charge him[5]. If he is not charged, he must be released, unless that officer has reasonable grounds for believing that his detention without being charged is necessary to secure or preserve evidence relating to an offence for which he is under arrest, or to obtain such evidence by questioning him[6].

If he is going to be kept for more than 6 hours[7], he must be taken to a designated police station[8], where the custody officer takes the required decisions[5], and whose responsibility he becomes[9] including regular reviews of his detention at the required intervals[10].

Detention limits are calculated from "the relevant time", usually the time of arrival or arrest at the police station but with special provision for arrest outside England and Wales, transfers between police areas and removal to hospital; a person may not generally be kept for longer than 24 hours unless he is charged[11].

Longer detention may be possible however, where there are reasonable grounds for believing that—

(a) his detention without charge is necessary to secure or preserve evidence relating to an offence for which he is under arrest, or to obtain such evidence by questioning him, and

(b) an offence for which he is under arrest is an arrestable offence[12], and

(c) the investigation is being conducted diligently and expeditiously[13].

In these circumstances, he may be kept for longer than 24 hours if (1) a police officer of the rank of superintendent or above has first authorised continued detention on these grounds[14] (which can enable his detention to continue for up to 36 hours from the "relevant time"), or (2) a magistrates' court[15] has issued a warrant of further detention on these grounds[16], authorising him to be held for further periods, each not exceeding 36 hours, up to a total detention time of 96 hours from the "relevant time". The *detention of a minor* is subject to the same provisions of the 1984 Act as apply in the case of an adult; additionally, however, a parent or guardian or other person responsible for the minor's welfare is to be notified of his arrest and detention[17], and after the enquiry is complete, if the minor is not to be released, he is to be detained by the local authority unless that is impracticable[18].

---

*Section 28 of the Criminal Justice Act 2003 introduces Sch 2 to that Act, which makes significant changes to the charging of offenders by means of amendments to the Police and Criminal Evidence Act 1984. The effect is that where the custody officer is of the opinion that a suspect should be charged or cautioned, and the suspect is a suitable candidate for bail, the suspect will generally be granted bail pending a decision by the Crown Prosecution Service on whether he should be charged or cautioned or not further proceeded against. Only in minor cases will the police make the charging decision. If the offender is not suitable for bail a Duty Inspector may authorise a charge in an emergency but a prosecutor must be informed as soon as possible for authority to proceed with the prosecution. Since, in custody cases, there may not be sufficient time to obtain all the relevant evidence before the charging decision must be taken, a lower threshold test of "reasonable suspicion" of the commission of the offence will be applied.

These changes are prospective. However, the new charging regime has been operating in certain priority areas since 31 October 2004, and will be implemented nationwide by April 2007.

1. Police and Criminal Evidence Act 1984, s 29, this PART, post.
2. Defined by Police and Criminal Evidence Act 1984, s 118(2), this PART, post.
3. Police and Criminal Evidence Act 1984, s 34, this PART, post.
4. Police and Criminal Evidence Act 1984, s 30, this PART, post allows for some delay.
5. Police and Criminal Evidence Act 1984, ss 36, 37, this PART, post.
6. Police and Criminal Evidence Act 1984, s 37(2), and see also s 47(5) (answering to bail at police stations), this PART, post.
7. Police and Criminal Evidence Act 1984, s 30, this PART, post.
8. Defined by Police and Criminal Evidence Act 1984, s 35, this PART, post.
9. Police and Criminal Evidence Act 1984, s 39, this PART, post: see also Code of Practice for the Detention, Treatment and Questioning of Persons by Police Officers (Code of Practice C) in PART II: EVIDENCE: STATUTORY INSTRUMENTS ON EVIDENCE, post.
10. Police and Criminal Evidence Act 1984, s 40, this PART, post.
11. Police and Criminal Evidence Act 1984, s 41, this PART, post.
12. Defined by Police and Criminal Evidence Act 1984, s 116 and Sch 5, this PART, post.
13. Police and Criminal Evidence Act 1984, ss 42(1), 43(4), this PART, post.
14. Police and Criminal Evidence Act 1984, s 42, this PART, post.
15. Defined for this purpose by Police and Criminal Evidence Act 1984, s 45 this PART, post.
16. Police and Criminal Evidence Act 1984, ss 43, 44, this PART, post.
17. See the Children and Young Persons Act 1933, s 34(2)–(11) in PART V: YOUTH COURTS, post.
18. See the provisions of the Police and Criminal Evidence Act 1984, s 38(6) and (6A), this PART, post.

QUESTIONING AND TREATMENT OF DETAINED PERSONS

1–224   Police powers and responsibilities for the questioning and treatment of detained persons have been codified in Part V of the Police and Criminal Evidence Act 1984, supplemented by the Code of Practice for the Detention, Treatment and Questioning of Persons by Police Officers[1]. Statutory provisions govern the searches of detained persons, including intimate searches[2], and reasonable force may be used in the exercise of the powers[3]. Interviewing is subject to detailed requirements set out in Code of Practice C[4].

The Code of Practice for the Detention, Treatment and Questioning by Police Officers of Persons under section 41 of, and Schedule 8 to, the Terrorism Act 2000 (Code of Practice H)[5] makes analogous provision, with necessary drafting amendments, for the exercise of powers of detention and questioning under the provisions of the 2000 Act.

A court may subsequently refuse to allow evidence on which the prosecution proposes to rely to be given if it appears that, having regard to all the circumstances, including the circumstances in which the evidence was obtained, the admission of the evidence would have such an adverse effect on the fairness of the proceedings that the court ought not to admit it[6]. A breach of the provisions of the 1984 Act or of Code C does not automatically rule out a statement made by a defendant after such breach[7]. The prosecution may also be required to prove beyond reasonable doubt that a confession was not obtained by oppression or in consequence of anything said or done which was likely to render it unreliable[8], failing which the court is bound to exclude it. An offer of immunity from prosecution in return for giving evidence will only rarely be justified: the arrested person should be given a full opportunity of discussing it with a solicitor first[9].

A person who has been arrested and is being held in custody in a police station or other premises is entitled if he so requests—

1.   to have one friend or relative or other person who is known to him or who is likely to take an interest in his welfare told as soon as practicable[10];

2.   to consult a solicitor privately at any time[11].

Delay is permitted in affording these rights only—

1.   in the case of a person held for a serious arrestable offence[12], and
2.   if authorised by an officer of at least superintendent rank, and
3.   if the officer has reasonable grounds for believing that the exercise of the right—

    (a)   will lead to interference with or harm to evidence connected with a serious arrestable offence or interference with or physical injury to other person, or

    (b)   will lead to the alerting of other persons suspected of having committed such an offence but not yet arrested for it, or

    (c)   will hinder the recovery of property obtained as a result of such an offence[13].

    (with the reasons being stated to the detained person and recorded).

The law is modified when the "terrorism provisions" apply[14].

1. In Part II: Evidence, Statutory Instruments, Codes of Practice and Practice Directions on Evidence, post.
2. See post following paragraphs: note also **1–227 Identification by witnesses, fingerprints, photographs, body samples**.
3. Police and Criminal Evidence Act 1984, s 117, this Part, post.
4. See Code of Practice C, paras 11.1A to 14.2 in Part II: Evidence—Statutory Instruments on Evidence, post.
5. In Part II: Evidence, Statutory Instruments, Codes of Practice and Practice Directions on Evidence, post.
6. Police and Criminal Evidence Act 1984, s 78 in Part II: Evidence, post.
7. *R v Parris* (1988) 89 Cr App Rep 68, [1989] Crim LR 214, CA.
8. Police and Criminal Evidence Act 1984, s 76 in Part II: Evidence, post.
9. *R v Mathias* [1989] NLJR 1417.
10. Police and Criminal Evidence Act 1984, s 56, this Part, post.
11. Police and Criminal Evidence Act 1984, s 58, this Part, post.
12. Defined by Police and Criminal Evidence Act 1984, s 116, this Part, post.
13. Police and Criminal Evidence Act 1984, ss 56(5) and 58(8), this Part, post.
14. As defined by Police and Criminal Evidence Act 1984, s 65: see ss 53(2) (search), 56(11) (right to have someone informed), 58(12)–(18) (right to consult a solicitor privately), 61(*a*) and 64(7) (fingerprints), this Part, post.

1–225   Code of Practice C.   A Code of Practice[1] has been issued, governing the detention, treatment and questioning of persons by police officers. It contains the following—

1.   General
2.   Custody records
3.   Initial action
    (including special groups and people attending voluntarily)
4.   Detainee's property
5.   Right not to be held incommunicado
6.   Right to legal advice
7.   Citizens of independent Commonwealth countries or foreign nationals
8.   Conditions of detention
9.   Care and treatment of detained persons (including medical treatment)
10. Cautions
11. Interviews: general
12. Interviews in police stations
13. Interpreters (foreign languages, deaf people and people with a speech handicap)
14. Questioning: special restrictions
15. Reviews and extensions of detention
16. Charging of detained persons

ANNEX A	Intimate and strip searches
ANNEX B	Delay in notifying arrest or allowing access to legal advice
ANNEX C	Restrictions on drawing adverse inferences from silence and terms of the caution when thre restriction applies
ANNEX D	Written statements under caution
ANNEX E	Summary of provisions relating to mentally disordered and otherwise mentally vulnerable people
ANNEX F	Countries with which bilateral consular conventions or agreements requiring notification of the arrest and detention of their nationals are in force as at 1 April 2003
ANNEX G	Fitness to be interviewed
ANNEX H	Detained person: Observation list
ANNEX I	Police areas where the power to test persons aged 18 and over for specified class a drugs under section 63B of PACE has been brought into force
ANNEX J	Police areas where the power to test persons aged 14 and over for specified class a drugs under section 63B of PACE (as amended by section 5 of the criminal justice act 2003) has been brought into force

The relevant provisions of the Police and Criminal Evidence Act 1984 and Code of Practice C are restricted to persons under arrest and at a police station or elsewhere in the charge of a constable. Neither is there any obligation under the jurisprudence on the European Convention on Human Rights to inform a suspect that he has a right to *free* legal advice. Accordingly, there was no impropriety where a trading standards officer gave a suspect the opportunity to seek legal advice but did not inform him of the availability of legal aid and advice[2].

1. Code of Practice C (and Code of Practice H in respect of investigations under the Terrorism Act 2000) is reproduced in PART II: EVIDENCE, STATUTORY INSTRUMENTS, CODES OF PRACTICE AND PRACTICE DIRECTIONS ON EVIDENCE, post.
2. *R (Beale) v South East Wiltshire Magistrates* [2002] EWHC Admin 2961, 167 JP 41.

SEARCH OF DETAINED PERSONS

1–226   A constable's power to search a person held in police detention is governed by statute[1] and by Code of Practice C[2]; in particular detailed safeguards apply to intimate searches, that is a search which consists of the physical examination of a person's body orifices[3].

The statutory provisions apply in the absence of the person's consent: an officer may use reasonable force if necessary[4]. Other powers are the power to stop, detain and search[5] and to search upon arrest[6]. Special provisions also exist in the Terrorism Act 2000 and the Immigration Act 1971.

1. Police and Criminal Evidence Act 1984, ss 53–55, this PART, post.
2. See Code of Practice C para 4.1 and Annex A thereto in PART II: EVIDENCE—STATUTORY INSTRUMENTS ON EVIDENCE, post.
3. Defined by Police and Criminal Evidence Act 1984, s 118(1); see s 55, this PART, post.
4. Police and Criminal Evidence Act 1984, s 117, this PART, post.
5. Police and Criminal Evidence Act 1984, s 1(2) (note restriction under s 2(9)), this PART, post.
6. Police and Criminal Evidence Act 1984, s 32, this PART, post.

IDENTIFICATION BY WITNESSES, FINGERPRINTS, PHOTOGRAPHS, BODY SAMPLES

1–227   Detailed provision is made by the Police and Criminal Evidence Act 1984 for fingerprinting, for the taking of intimate and other samples and for the eventual destruction of fingerprints and samples[1]. The Code of Practice for the Identification of Persons by Police Officers[2] makes comprehensive provision for these matters as well as for identification by witnesses including video identification, identification parades and group identifications, confrontation, and the showing of photographs. An officer may use reasonable force if necessary in the exercise of any of these powers[3].

1. Police and Criminal Evidence Act 1984, ss 61–64, this PART, post; as to the taking of non-intimate body samples without consent, see also the Criminal Evidence (Amendment) Act 1997, ss 1 and 2, this PART, post.
2. Code of Practice D in PART II: EVIDENCE, STATUTORY INSTRUMENTS, CODES OF PRACTICE AND PRACTICE DIRECTIONS ON EVIDENCE, post..
3. Police and Criminal Evidence Act 1984, s 117, this PART, post.

1–228   Code of Practice D.   The Code of Practice D for the Identification of Persons by Police Officers[1] contains the following—

1.   Introduction
2.   General
3.   Identification by witnesses
4.   Identification by fingerprints
5.   Examinations to establish identity and the taking of photographs
6.   Identification by body samples and impressions

ANNEX A	Video identification
ANNEX B	Identification parades
ANNEX C	Group identification
ANNEX D	Confrontation by a witness
ANNEX E	Showing of photographs
ANNEX F	Fingerprints and samples – destruction and speculative searches

1. Code of Practice D in PART II: EVIDENCE, STATUTORY INSTRUMENTS, CODES OF PRACTICE AND PRACTICE DIRECTIONS ON EVIDENCE, post..

RESTRAINT OF PRISONERS

1–229   Whether a prisoner should be handcuffed must depend on the particular circumstances, as for instance the nature of the charge and the conduct and temper of the person in custody. Handcuffing should not be resorted to unless there is fair ground for supposing that violence may be used or an escape attempted. Handcuffing cannot be justified unless there are good special reasons for resorting to it[1].

Constables are not justified in using their truncheons to save themselves trouble, or to punish a prisoner for resistance; they are only justified in using them when they have no other means of protecting themselves from injury, or of preventing the prisoner's escape.

---

1. Home Office Consolidated Circular to the Police on Crime and Kindred Matters, quoted at para 54 of the Law and Procedure volume of the Report of the Royal Commission on Criminal Procedure, supra, and based on *Wright v Court* (1825) 4 B & C 596. For the position under the European Convention on Human Rights, see *Raninen v Finland* (1997) 26 EHRR 563.

CHARGING THE ACCUSED

1–240 The *Criminal Case Management Framework* sets out procedural steps for custody officers and crown prosecutors considering diversion from prosecution as an alternative to charging[1] and the preparatory process by crown prosecutors and police to consider the evidence and the appropriate charge[2].

---

1. Pre-charge consideration Part A, in this PART, CODES OF PRACTICE AND GUIDELINES, post.
2. Pre-Court Process, Parts 1-4, in this PART, CODES OF PRACTICE AND GUIDELINES, post.

AFTER THE CHARGE

1–241 After a person has been charged he must be released unless—

1. his name and address cannot be ascertained or the custody officer has reasonable grounds for doubting the name or address given, or
2. the custody officer has reasonable grounds for believing his detention is necessary for his own protection or to prevent him causing physical injury to any other person or loss of or damage to property
3. the custody officer has reasonable grounds for believing he would fail to answer to bail or his detention is necessary to prevent him from interfering with the administration of justice or with the investigation of offences or of a particular offence
4. (in the case of a juvenile) the custody officer has reasonable grounds for believing that he ought to be detained in his own interests[1].

Whilst in detention he remains the responsibility of the custody officer so far as his treatment in accordance with Code of Practice (C)[2] and requirement for periodic reviews are concerned[3].

A person who has been charged and kept in detention must be brought before a magistrates' court at its next sitting after he was charged or after he arrived in the court's area: if no court is due to sit the same day, the police will notify the clerk to the justices who will then arrange a sitting no later than the following day (or the day after if the following day is Christmas Day, Good Friday or a Sunday)[4].

Where a custody officer grants bail to a person subject to a duty to appear before a magistrates' court, he shall appoint for the appearance—

(a) a date which is not later than the first sitting of the court after the person is charged with the offence; or
(b) where he is informed by the clerk to the justices for the relevant petty sessions area that the appearance cannot be accommodated until a later date, that later date[5].

---

*See the introductory note to para 1–223, ante, regarding the changes to charging prospectively made by the Criminal Justice Act 2003.
1. Police and Criminal Evidence Act 1984, s 38, in this PART: STATUTES ON PROCEDURE, post.
2. See the Code of Practice for the Detention, Treatment and Questioning of Persons by Police Officers (Code of Practice D) in PART II: EVIDENCE—STATUTORY INSTRUMENTS ON EVIDENCE, post.
3. See Police and Criminal Evidence Act 1984, ss 39 and 40, in this PART: STATUTES ON PROCEDURE, post.
4. See Police and Criminal Evidence Act 1984, s 46, in this PART: STATUTES ON PROCEDURE, post.
5. Police and Criminal Evidence Act 1984, s 47(3A) in this PART: STATUTES ON PROCEDURE, post (when fully in force).

WITNESSES

1–242 During the course of an investigation, consideration will have to be given to securing testimony which will be admissible and not be otherwise open to objection in the event of court proceedings. See in particular Part II.—*Evidence* post, as regards competence and compellability (**2–320**), privilege (**2–330, 2–331**), competency of parties and their spouses (**2–332, 2–333**) co-defendants and accomplices (**2–334, 2–336**), deceased and dying persons (**2–340**), experts (**2–343**). For vulnerable and intimidated witnesses, see para **2–345A**. Where the police wish to interview a child who is a ward of court, application for leave must be made to a judge except where immediate action is necessary[1].

---

1. *Practice Direction (criminal: consolidated)* [2002] para I.55, in this PART, post.

1–243 Protection of witnesses. The police and certain other law enforcement agencies may make such arrangements as they consider appropriate to protect persons such as witnesses, jurors, judges, justices of the peace and others involved in the criminal process[1]. Public authorities (other than a court or tribunal) are under a duty to provide reasonable cooperation with a protection provider[2]. It is an office subject to certain defences, for a person who knows or suspects that information relates to information about protection arrangements to disclose such information[3].

It is also an offence subject to certain defences, for a person who has assumed a new identity or for another to reveal the assumption of the new identity[4]. No criminal or civil proceedings may be brought against a protected person or a related person where he has provided false information solely for the purpose of preserving the arrangements for the protection programme[5].

In prescribed circumstances, a court may make a restriction order prohibiting the publication of details likely to identify a person in fear and distress as a witness in proceedings during his lifetime[6].

---

1. Serious Organized Crime and Police Act 2005, 82, in this PART: STATUTES ON PROCEDURE, post.
2. Serious Organized Crime and Police Act 2005, 83, in this PART: STATUTES ON PROCEDURE, post.
3. Serious Organized Crime and Police Act 2005, s 86, in this PART: STATUTES ON PROCEDURE, post.
4. Serious Organized Crime and Police Act 2005, s 88, in this PART: STATUTES ON PROCEDURE, post.
5. Serious Organized Crime and Police Act 2005, s 90, in this PART: STATUTES ON PROCEDURE, post.
6. Youth Justice and Criminal Evidence Act 1999, s 46, in PART II: STATUTES ON EVIDENCE, post.

CAUTIONING

1–244 Cautioning provides an important alternative to prosecution in the case of offending by minors and has now been given statutory effect in procedures for reprimands and warnings[1]; it also represents a possible course of action in the case of adults. Home Office Circular No 18/1994[2] contains guidelines on the cautioning of adults, including the circumstances in which a caution should be administered.

A conditional caution can be given by a constable, an investigating officer or a person authorised for this purpose by a relevant prosecutor[3].

A conditional caution is a caution to which conditions are attached to meet either or both of the following objects: (a) to facilitate the rehabilitation of the offender; and (b) to ensure that he makes reparation for the offence[4].

The requirements that must be satisfied before a conditional caution can be given are: (a) there is evidence that the offender committed an offence; (b) a relevant prosecutor decides that there is sufficient evidence to charge the offender with the offence and that a conditional caution should be given; (c) the offender admits the offence; (d) the effect of a conditional caution is explained to the offender and he is warned that non compliance with its conditions may result in him being prosecuted for the offence; and (e) the offender signs a document containing details of the offence, an admission that he committed it, his consent to receiving a conditional caution and details of the conditions[5].

If the offender fails to comply with the conditions he may be prosecuted and the contents of the above document is admissible in evidence against him. When such a prosecution is instituted the conditional caution ceases to have effect[6].

The Secretary must prepare a Code of Practice in relation to conditional cautions[7].

The statutory duties of the National Probation Service are extended to cover offenders who are being considered for, or have been given, conditional cautions[8].

The High Court, on an application for judicial review, may quash a caution if the guidelines in Home Office Circular 18/1994[2] are not complied with[9]. A caution is likely to be set aside if it can be established that there is no evidence of a clear and reliable admission of guilt[3]. Since a caution is predicated on a reliable admission and genuine consent, any admission must not be vitiated by an inducement to admit the offence and avoid a prosecution. Accordingly, in practice there should be an admission of guilt before formal consideration is given to proceeding by way of caution, or there should be a formal interview which will satisfy the test of admissibility in criminal proceedings[10].

Provided it is clear that there has been an admission, it is not necessary, in the context of a caution, for it to be shown that the admission was obtained in circumstances which satisfied the requirements of the Codes of Practice under the Police and Criminal Evidence Act 1984, although it will be wise in many cases for the police to take precautions which will satisfy the requirements of the Codes[11].

---

1. See post para **5–21B Reprimands and warnings** and the Crime and Disorder Act 1998, ss 65 and 66 and in PART V: YOUTH COURTS, post.
2. Home Office Circular No 18/1994, dated 15 March 1994: The Cautioning of Offenders.
3. Section 22(1) of the Criminal Justice Act 2003, this PART, post. The definition of 'relevant prosecutor' is set out in s 27 and embraces public prosecutors and anyone whom the Secretary of State may specify as a relevant prosecutor for this purpose.
4. Criminal Justice Act 2003, s 22(2) and (3), in this PART: STATUTES ON PROCEDURE, post.
5. Criminal Justice Act 2003, s 23, in this PART: STATUTES ON PROCEDURE, post.
6. Criminal Justice Act 2003, s 24, in this PART: STATUTES ON PROCEDURE, post.
7. Criminal Justice Act 2003, s 25, in this PART: STATUTES ON PROCEDURE, post, wherein the matters that may, in particular, be included in the Code and the procedure by which the Code must be published, etc, and brought into force are specified.
8. Criminal Justice Act 2003, s 26, in this PART: STATUTES ON PROCEDURE, post.
9. *R v Metropolitan Police Comr, ex p P* (1995) 160 JP 367. See also *R v Chief Constable of Kent, ex p L* (1991) 155 JP 760, 93 Cr App Rep 416, [1991] Crim LR 841, DC.
10. *R v Metropolitan Police Comr, ex p Thompson* [1997] 2 Cr App Rep 49, DC.
11. *R v Chief Constable of Lancashire, ex p Atkinson* (1998) 162 JP 275.

Criminal law: general

1–300 In this section we set out those principles which apply across the criminal law in general. We therefore include here: mens rea, modes of participation in crime including joint liability, and liability of secondary parties. We also refer to general defences and distinguish these from those offences which apply only to certain offences: self defence, provocation and mistake.

BREACH OF A CONVENTION RIGHT

1–301 Under the Human Rights Act 1998, it is open to a defendant in any criminal proceedings to challenge any substantive provision of the criminal law on any of the following bases—

1.   that the definition or scope of the provision in question is so vague and imprecise that it violates the principle of certainty inherent in the European Convention of Human Rights and specifically required by Article 7[1];
2.   that the act or conduct penalised did not constitute a criminal offence at the time it was committed[2]; or
3.   that the provision in question breaches a Convention right such as the right to respect for private life[3], freedom of religio[4]or freedom of expression[5].

Equally, existing defences may need re-examination where they are too broad[6].

---

1. See, eg, *Sunday Times v United Kingdom* (1979) 2 EHRR 245, *SW and CR v United Kingdom* (1995) 21 EHRR 363 and Article 7.
2. *Welch v United Kingdom* (1995) 20 EHRR 247 and *Taylor v United Kingdom* (1998) EHRLR 90 concerning confiscation orders. See also *Ibbotson v United Kingdom* (1998) 27 EHRR CD 332 concerning registration under the Sex Offenders Act 1997.
3. See, eg, *Dudgeon v United Kingdom* (1981) 4 EHRR 149, *Norris v Ireland* (1988) 13 EHRR 186 and *Sutherland v United Kingdom* (1997) 24 EHRR CD 22.
4. See, eg, *Kokkinakis v Greece* (1993) 17 EHRR 397.
5. See, eg, *Lingens v Austria* (1986) 8 EHRR 407, *Jersild v Denmark* (1994) 19 EHRR 1 and *Hashman and Harrup v United Kingdom* [2000] Crim LR 185, ECtHR.
6. See, eg, in relation to the defence of reasonable chastisement, *A v United Kingdom* (1998) 27 EHRR 611.

GUILTY MIND (MENS REA)

1–302 In the absence of a clear indication in an Act that an offence is intended to be an absolute offence, for the offence to be proved the onus is on the prosecution[1] to show that the defendant had a guilty mind. Where, however, an offence is clearly intended by the relevant enactment to be an offence of strict liability, this does not engage art 6(2) of the Convention; art 6(2) provides a criterion against which the court could scrutinise procedural and evidential matters but not the substantive elements of an offence[2].

At common law, an honest and reasonable belief in the existence of circumstances which, if true, would make the act an innocent one, has always been held to be a good defence[3]. The requirement that the belief should be reasonable, makes it an objective test, but the tendency in recent cases has been towards a subjective test, looking only towards honest belief, and making the mental element either intention or recklessness as to the act constituting the offence[4].

No child under the age of ten years can be guilty of an offence[5].

---

1. *Woolmington v DPP* [1935] AC 462, 25 Cr App Rep 72. See also Article 6 (2) of the European Convention on Human Rights as interpreted in *Salabiaku v France* (1988) 13 EHRR 379. For recent consideration of the effect of Article 6 (1) on domestic law, see *R v DPP, ex p Kebilene* [1999] 4 All ER 801, HL.
2. *Barnfather v Islington Education Authority* [2003] EWHC 418 (Admin), [2003] 1 WLR 2318. See also *R (on the application of Grundy & Co Excavations Ltd & another) v Halton Division Magistrates' Court* [2003] EWHC Admin 272, (2003) 167 JP 387.
3. *R v Tolson* (1889) 23 QBD 168, and see *Bank of New South Wales v Piper* [1897] AC 383, 61 JP 660; *Warner v Metropolitan Police Comr* [1969] 2 AC 256, [1968] 2 All ER 356, 132 JP 378.
4. See *DPP v Morgan* [1976] AC 182, [1975] 2 All ER 347, 61 Cr App Rep 136; *DPP v Majewski* [1977] AC 443, [1976] 2 All ER 142, 140 JP 315; *R v Sheppard* [1981] AC 394, [1980] 3 All ER 899; but see also *Albert v Lavin* (1980) 72 Cr App Rep 178.
5. See Children and Young Persons Act 1933 s 50, in PART V: YOUTH COURTS, post.

1–303 Intent. Some statutes indicate requirements as to the mental element by the use of particular words. "*With intent to*": where intention to produce a particular result is a necessary element of an offence, no distinction is to be drawn in law between the state of mind of one who does an act because he desires to produce that particular result, and the state of mind of one who, when he does the act, is aware that it is likely to produce that result, but is prepared to take the risk that it may do so, in order to achieve some other purpose which provided his motive for doing what he did. It is by now well-settled law that both states of mind constitute "intention", in the sense in which that expression is used in the definition of a crime whether at common law or in a statute[1].

---

1. Note however the need to weigh carefully considerations of probability and foresight as set out in *R v Moloney* [1985] AC 905, [1985] 1 All ER 1025, 149 JP 369, HL, *R v Hancock and R v Shankland* [1985] AC 455, [1986] 1 All ER 641,

and *R v Scalley* [1995] Crim LR 504, CA and explained in *R v Nedrick* [1986] 3 All ER 1, [1986] 1 WLR 1025 and *R v Smith* [1988] Crim LR 616, CA. See also the Criminal Justice Act 1967, s 8 post as to proof of criminal intent.

1–304   Recklessness. *"Recklessly"* was formerly held to connote two mental states – "advertent" recklessness, ie actual awareness or foresight of the risk in issue; and "inadvertent" recklessness, ie failing to have regard to a risk, though its existence would have been obvious to a reasonable man faced with the same circumstances – and it was a matter of construction in relation to the particular offence as to which of these different meanings applied. These different forms of recklessness were commonly referred to as, respectively, "Cunningham" recklessness and "Caldwell" recklessness[1]. In *R v G*[2], however, the House of Lords departed from its earlier decision in *Caldwell* and held that that foresight of consequences remained an essential ingredient of recklessness in the context of the offence of criminal damage. Therefore, it had to be shown that the defendant's state of mind was culpable in that he acted recklessly in respect of a circumstance if he was aware of a risk which did or would exist, or in respect of a result if he was aware of a risk that it would occur, and it was, in the circumstances known to him, unreasonable to take the risk. Accordingly, a defendant could not be convicted of the offence if, due to his age or personal characteristics, he genuinely did not appreciate or foresee the risks involved in his actions.

1. After the names of the leading authorities *R v Cunningham* [1957] 2 QB 396; [1957] 3 WLR 76; [1957] 2 All ER 412, CCA; and *R v Caldwell* [1982] AC 341; [1981] 2 WLR 509; [1981] 1 All ER 961.
2. [2004] 4 All ER 765, [2003] UKHL 50, [2003] 3 WLR 1060, (2003) 167 JP 621.

1–305   Knowingly. *"Knowingly"*: when used in a statute, shows that *mens rea* applies, but this does not mean that *mens rea* does not apply if it is not used. There are three degrees of knowledge: actual knowledge (which may be inferred from the nature of the act that was done); knowledge of the second degree where the defendant shuts his eyes to an obvious means of knowledge i.e. where the defendant deliberately refrained from making inquiries, the results of which he might not care to have; and "constructive knowledge" where he "ought to have known" ie he had the means of knowledge but failed to make reasonable inquiries. The case of shutting the eyes is actual knowledge; the case of neglecting to make inquiries is not actual knowledge but constructive knowledge[1] which is not enough to demonstrate that something has been done knowingly in the context of a criminal statute[2]. Suspicion alone will not amount to relevant knowledge or belief[3]. Where the prosecution case is that the defendant failed to make what it alleges were reasonable inquiries, it is incumbent on the prosecutor to make it plain what they are alleging[4].

1. *Taylor's Central Garages (Exeter) Ltd v Roper* (1951) 115 JP 445, *Atwal v Massey* [1971] 3 All ER 881, 56 Cr App Rep 6; *R v Griffiths* (1974) 60 Cr App Rep 14; *R v Grainge* [1974] 1 All ER 928, [1974] 1 WLR 619, 138 JP 275; *R v Ismail* [1977] Crim LR 557; *R v Stagg* [1978] Crim LR 227; *R v Lincoln* [1980] Crim LR 575.
2. *R v Grainge* [1974] 1 All ER 928, [1974] 1 WLR 619, 138 JP 275; *R v Pethick* [1980] Crim LR 242.
3. *Taylor's Central Garages (Exeter) Ltd v Roper*, supra cited in *Flintshire County Council v Reynolds* [2006] EWHC 195 (Admin), 170 JP 73 (prosecution under the Social Security Administration Act 1992, s 112).
4. *Flintshire County Council v Reynolds*, supra.

1–306   Maliciously. *"Maliciously"* is now settled to mean "intentionally or recklessly" and the latter is used in the *Cunningham* (ie subjective) sense[1]. In relation to the offences under the Offences Against the Person Act 1861, ss 18 and 20, it is sufficient that the accused foresaw that some bodily harm, not necessarily amounting to grievous bodily harm or wounding, might occur[2]; it is not enough, however, that the accused intended to frighten (unless he foresaw that such fright might result in psychiatric injury)[3]. In the case of an accused who has been drinking, the Court must consider what the accused himself would have foreseen if he had not been drinking and not whether the reasonable sober man would have realised that injury might result[4].

1. Smith and Hogan *Criminal Law* (9th edn, 1999) p 430. See *R v Parmenter* and *R v Savage* [1992] AC 699, [1991] 4 All ER 698, HL.
2. Above, note 11 and see also *DPP v A* [2001] Crim LR 140, DC.
3. *Flack v Hunt* (1979) 70 Cr App Rep 51; *R v Sullivan* [1981] Crim LR 46, CA.
4. *R v Richardson* [1999] 1 Cr App Rep 392, [1999] Crim LR 494, CA.

1–307   Influence of drink or drugs. Where drunkenness causes insanity, this is as much a defence as is insanity from disease of the mind[1]. Short of this, however, self-induced intoxication from alcohol or drugs, or both, is a defence only to an offence requiring a specific intent[2].
   The absence of moral fault by a defendant does not suffice by itself to negative the necessary mental element of the offence with which he is charged. Where it is proved that the necessary intent was present when the act required to constitute the offence had been committed by the defendant the defence of involuntary intoxication is not open to him as a means of securing his acquittal[3].

1. *DPP v Beard* [1920] AC 479.
2. See *DPP v Majewski* [1977] AC 443, [1976] 2 All ER 1, 140 JP 315 and cases referred to therein.
3. *R v Kingston* [1994] 3 All ER 353, [1994] 3 WLR 519, 158 JP 717, HL.

1–308   Automatism, insanity, mental malfunction. An element in the guilty mind is voluntariness of an act; where this is missing, then the defence of automatism may be raised. If automatism arises from a disease of the mind, then the question of insanity is raised, and the magistrates' court will not proceed. Insanity is a defence to a criminal charge if, through defect of reason due to disease of the mind, the defendant either did not know the nature and quality of his act or, if he did, then he did not know he was doing wrong[1]. The common law defence of insanity may be raised as a defence to an appropriate charge being tried summarily in a magistrates' court[2], but only where the offence charged is one in which mens rea is an element[3]. The burden of proving insanity is on the defence[4]. In the absence of a defence of insanity or automatism there is no defence on the ground that the defendant's mind was malfunctioning[5].

If automatism does not rise from a disease of the mind, the accused must lay a proper foundation by producing some evidence from which it can be reasonably inferred that he acted in a state of automatism; if there is real doubt whether he did or did not act in a state of automatism, he should be acquitted[6]. Although stress, anxiety and depression may be the result of the operation of external factors, they are not in themselves, separately or together, external factors of the kind capable in law of causing or contributing to a state of automatism[7]. Medical evidence may be appropriate when a defence of sleep-walking—a kind of automatism—is raised[8]. Where the defence of automatism is raised in a driving case, the justices must decide on the evidence whether the defendant was not conscious of what he was doing and that his actions were automatic and involuntary throughout the period of the driving in question[9]. Driving without awareness is not as a matter of law a state capable of founding a defence of automatism[10]. The *mens rea* necessary for an offence of specific intent may be negatived by self-induced automatism in the same way that it may be by the voluntary taking of drugs or alcohol[11]. Automatism resulting from intoxication as a result of a voluntary ingestion of alcohol or dangerous drugs does not negative the *mens rea* necessary for crimes of basic intent because the conduct of the accused is reckless and that is sufficient to constitute the necessary *mens rea*. Self-induced automatism, other than that due to intoxication from alcohol or drugs, may, however, provide a defence to crimes of basic intent unless the prosecution can prove the necessary element of recklessness[12]. An epileptic fit is akin to insanity in law and comes within the McNaghten Rules[13].

In cases of insanity, the standard of proof required of the defence is that of a balance of probabilities; with automatism the onus of proof is on the prosecution to negative automatism beyond reasonable doubt[14].

---

1. *McNaghten's Case* (1843) 10 Cl & Fin 200. See also *R v Sullivan* [1983] 1 All ER 577, [1983] 2 WLR 392; affd [1984] AC 156, [1983] 2 All ER 673, HL (epilepsy).
2. *R v Horseferry Road Magistrates' Court, ex p K* [1996] 3 All ER 719, [1996] 3 WLR 68, 160 JP 441, [1996] 2 Cr App Rep 574.
3. *DPP v H* [1997] 1 WLR 1406, 161 JP 697, [1998] RTR 200.
4. *R v Smith* (1910) 6 Cr App Rep 19.
5. *R v Isitt* (1977) 67 Cr App Rep 44; *R v Sandie Smith* [1982] Crim LR 531 (premenstrual tension): see also 146 JP Jo 476.
6. *Bratty v A-G for Northern Ireland* [1963] AC 386, [1961] 3 All ER 523; *Watmore v Jenkins* [1962] 2 QB 572, [1962] 2 All ER 868, 126 JP 432; *R v Quick* [1973] QB 910, [1973] 3 All ER 347, 137 JP 763 (hypoglycaemia); *R v Stripp* (1978) 69 Cr App Rep 318 (concussion and/or alcohol) and see *R v T* [1990] Crim LR 256 (post-traumatic stress disorder).
7. *R v Hennessy* [1989] 2 All ER 9, [1989] 1 WLR 287, CA.
8. See *R v Smith* [1979] 3 All ER 605, 69 Cr App Rep 378. See also *Wood v DPP* (1988) 153 JP 20 (limitations on admissibility of doctor's evidence of fact and opinion founded on hearsay).
9. *Broome v Perkins* [1987] RTR 321, 85 Cr App Rep 321.
10. *A-G's Reference (No 2 of 1992)* [1993] 4 All ER 683, 97 Cr App Rep 429.
11. See *DPP v Majewski* [1977] AC 443, [1976] 2 All ER 142.
12. *R v Bailey* [1983] 2 All ER 503, [1983] 1 WLR 760.
13. *R v Sullivan* [1984] AC 156, [1983] 1 All ER 577, CA; affd [1984] AC 156, [1983] 2 All ER 673, HL.
14. See *Bratty v A-G for Northern Ireland*, supra and *R v Burns* (1973) 58 Cr App Rep 364.

1–309 Procedure. A defendant showing signs of mental illness, should be remanded for a medical report; if he is remanded in custody, the committal order should be accompanied by a request that he be placed under observation, and a report of the prison medical officer be supplied to the court. Whether the remand is before or after conviction, it would be appropriate to follow the advice of the Secretary of State that the Clerk to the Justices should straight away inform the medical officer of the circumstances of the offence, the prisoner's previous conduct, his medical history, his family, his home circumstances and his demeanour (if it raises doubts as to his mental condition) and with any reasons which may have led the court to suspect that he may be mentally abnormal. Note the powers of the Secretary of State to give a transfer direction removing prisoners serving sentences of imprisonment, or on remand in custody, from prison to hospital[1]. Consideration should be given, to mentally ill defendants being legally represented.

Where, in the case of an indictable offence, it appears that the defendant is unfit to plead, or where insanity is pleaded as a defence, it is a question of fact triable by a jury and the jury may return a verdict in accordance with the provisions of ss 1 or 4 of the Criminal Procedure (Insanity) Act 1964[2]. Nevertheless, neither that or earlier enactments has removed the jurisdiction of justices from entertaining a defence of insanity[3]. However, s 43 of the Mental Health Act 1983 makes no provision for committal to the Crown Court by the magistrates for imposition of a restriction order under s 41 of the 1983 Act upon a person who has been *acquitted* of an offence by reason of insanity. Justices only have such a power to commit to the Crown Court for that purpose in the case of a person *convicted* of an imprisonable offence whether indictable or summary only[4]. In relation to an offence triable only summarily, there is no power to commit to the Crown Court for a jury to decide fitness to plead[5]. Where the mental illness is not, however, severe, and the justices are satisfied that the defendant did the act or made the omission charged, being an offence punishable on summary conviction with imprisonment, they may remand for an inquiry into the physical and mental condition of the defendant[6] before sentencing[7]. If the accused is under such a disability that he cannot, in the case of an offence triable either way, consent to summary trial, or that he cannot be tried, the justices may in certain circumstances make a hospital or guardianship order without convicting him[8].

1. Mental Health Act 1983, s 47 et seq, in PART VIII: title MENTAL HEALTH, post.
2. See the Criminal Procedure (Insanity) Act 1964, ss 1 and 4.
3. *R v Horseferry Road Magistrates' Court, ex p K* [1996] 3 All ER 719, [1996] 3 WLR 68, 160 JP 441, [1996] 2 Cr App Rep 574.
4. Mental Health Act 1983, s 43, in PART VIII: title MENTAL HEALTH, post.
5. *R v Metropolitan Stipendiary Magistrate Tower Bridge, ex p Aniifowosi* (1985) 149 JP 748.
6. Magistrates' Courts Act 1980, s 30, in this PART: STATUTES ON PROCEDURE, post.
7. See post PART III: SENTENCING, **3–480 Available sentences on mentally disordered offenders.**
8. Mental Health Act 1983, s 37(3); *R v Lincolnshire (Kesteven) Justices, ex p O'Connor* [1983] 1 All ER 901, [1983] 1 WLR 335.

PARTICIPATION IN CRIME

1–320   Joint enterprise[1].   Whenever two or more defendants are charged in the same information with any offence which any can help each other to commit, it is sufficient to support a conviction against any and each of them to prove either—

(*a*)   that he himself did a physical act which is an essential ingredient of the offence charged; or

(*b*)   that he helped another defendant to do such an act;

and that in doing the act or helping the other defendant to do it, he himself had the necessary intent[2].

Where an accused withdraws from a joint enterprise, communication of that withdrawal is a necessary condition for disassociation from an offence of pre-planned violence but not from an offence of spontaneous violence by a co-accused[3].

Although in common usage the phrase "jointly charged" normally means two persons named in the same charge or series of charges; nevertheless in motoring cases where only one person can be driving, two persons who have been charged with driving and allowing themselves to be carried in a motor vehicle taken without the owner's consent, are properly to be considered jointly charged[4]. Acquittal of all but one of persons jointly charged is no bar to conviction of that one[5]. A joint defendant may be convicted as a principal where the crime is committed by a co-accused who is an innocent agent[6]. Where the crime is not capable of being committed by an innocent agent, eg rape, or a driving offence, the accused may be liable for procuring the offence[7] but only where the co defendant has committed the *actus reus* of the substantive offence[8].

Liability for the act of another where there is a joint enterprise may be greater in the case of a parent because of the duty to intervene in the ill-treatment of their child by the other parent[9]. However, owing to the difficulty in identifying which of two or more carers may have caused the death of a child or vulnerable person, provision has been made by statute that where it is established that one must have caused the death and the other must have failed to take reasonable steps to prevent it, the prosecution does not have to prove which is which[10].

Where a co-accused joins in an assault or wounding after harm has already been inflicted, the liability of the co-accused will depend on the facts. Where an accused strikes a blow after grievous bodily harm has already been caused it is the totality of the injuries which can amount to grievous bodily harm, not just the initial injury and the accused therefore participates in the offence. In a case of wounding, where a wound has already been inflicted and the co-accused strikes a blow without having previously formed an intention to be a party to the wounding offence and the blow would not cause a wound or affect the wound, he might be guilty of assault but not the wounding[11].

1. As to the intent or foresight that must be proved to make a secondary party guilty of murder or manslaughter on a joint enterprise basis, see *R v Powell and English* [1999] 1 AC 1, and *A-G's reference (No 3 of 2004)* [2005] EWCA Crim 1882, [2006] Crim LR 63.
2. *DPP v Merriman* [1973] AC 584, [1972] 3 All ER 42, 136 JP 659.
3. *R v Mitchell* (1998) 163 JP 75, [1999] Crim LR 496, CA (defendant walked away before fatal assault by a co-accused).
4. *R v Peterborough Magistrates' Court, ex p Allgood* (1994) 159 JP 627, [1996] RTR 26.
5. *Barsted v Jones* (1960) 124 JP 400; *R v Rowlands* [1972] 1 QB 424, [1972] 1 All ER 306, 136 JP 181.
6. *Hale* [1736] 1 PC 555.
7. *R v Millward* [1994] Crim LR 527, CA, and see *R v Wheelhouse* [1994] Crim LR 756, CA and commentary thereto.
8. *R v Loukes* [1996] 1 Cr App Rep 444, [1996] RTR 164, [1996] Crim LR 341, CA.
9. *R v Russell and Russell* (1987) 85 Cr App Rep 388, [1987] Crim LR 494.
10. Domestic Violence, Crime and Victims Act 2004, ss 5 and 6, in PART VI: FAMILY LAW, post.
11. *R v Percival* (2003) Times, 23 May, CA.

1–321   Aid, abet, counsel or procure.   A person who aids, abets, counsels or procures the commission by another person of an offence has the same criminal liability as that person; this applies both to indictable offences[1] and to summary or triable either way offences[2].

An abettor is one who is present assisting or encouraging a principal at the time of the commission of the offence[3]; a counsellor is one who is knowingly involved before the commission of the offence in advising or assisting a principal in relation to it[4]. To make out the offence of counselling it must be proved that the principal offence was committed by the person counselled and that the person counselled was acting within the scope of his authority and not accidentally[5]. The words "aid, abet, counsel *and* procure" do not signify different offences[6], although a defendant cannot be convicted of aiding and abetting alone unless he was present when the offence was committed[7]. It is now usual to use the complete phrase, and convictions may then follow even when the defendant was not physically present[8].

The test is, that the person knows that the acts which constitute an offence are being done, and he gives assistance or encouragement to the perpetrator of the offence[9]. Mere negligence is not enough[10], but a person may be liable for being passive, instead of active, in discharging a duty[11], or deliberately refraining from making enquiries, the result of which he does not care to have[12], or even of being an onlooker if his presence is not accidental and is found as a fact to be an encouragement to the offender[13]. Proof of prior knowledge of the actual crime intended, is not necessary if he contemplated the commission of one of a limited number of crimes by the principal, and intentionally assisted in their commission[14]. For a secondary party to be found guilty of murder it is not necessary for the prosecution to prove that the principal would kill, it is sufficient to prove that he might kill. The secondary party will not be guilty where the lethal act carried out by the primary party is fundamentally different from the acts foreseen or intended by the secondary party[15]. To establish secondary liability for dangerous driving against the owner who was a passenger in a car driven by a driver who had been drinking, the real question as to the appellant's state of mind is whether he foresaw the likelihood that the driver would drive in a dangerous manner. Evidence that the defendant knew that the driver had not only been drinking but appeared to be intoxicated is powerful evidence that he foresaw that he was likely to drive in a dangerous manner at the time he permitted him to drive. But such evidence of apparent intoxication does not determine the issue. It is merely evidence which tends to prove the conclusion which the court has to reach before it convicts him. In short, the more drunk the driver appeared to be, the easier it is for the prosecution to prove that the defendant foresaw that he was likely to drive dangerously if he permitted him to drive[16]. The use of the word "recklessness" is best avoided when considering the *mens rea* required of someone accused of procuring the commission of a substantive offence[17]. A person who counsels an offence, may not be convicted of a graver offence than that in fact which was committed[18]. Surreptitiously "lacing" the drink of a person about to drive, and who subsequently does drive with excess alcohol, may amount to procuring[19].

In general terms, a person is not entitled to be acquitted merely because the offence by the principal has not been proved[20]. In cases of procuring, it is not necessary that the principal should be convicted. The procurer may be convicted on the basis that he acted through an innocent agent[21], or for offences where this is not possible eg rape or driving offences, it is sufficient that there is the *actus reus* of the principal offence even if the principal offender is entitled to be acquitted because of some defence personal to himself[22]. Similarly, where the offence has been committed by a child aged between 10 and 14 years the prosecution does not need to have negatived *doli incapax* on the part of the principal offender in order for the court to find any secondary party guilty of aiding and abetting[23]. Procuring does not involve a common intention between the accessory and the principal, whereas other forms of aiding and abetting generally do[22].

For *procedure* see Magistrates' Courts Act 1980, s 44, post; for definition of term "accomplice" and procedure for receiving evidence of accomplices see post PART II, EVIDENCE, *Accomplices*: for offences of assisting offender, concealing offence or giving false information see PART VIII: COMPOUNDING OFFENCES, post; also PART VIII: PERVERTING JUSTICE, post.

1. Accessories and Abettors Act 1861, s 8.
2. Magistrates' Courts Act 1980, s 44, in this PART: STATUTES ON PROCEDURE, post.
3. *R v Betts and Ridley* (1930) 22 Cr App Rep 148; *Smith v Baker* [1971] RTR 350; *R v Clarkson* [1971] 3 All ER 344, [1971] 1 WLR 1402, 135 JP 533. However, where an alleged aider and abettor drove the principal to a place where the latter could await an opportunity to carry out a murder by shooting, and the shooting occurred some 12 hours later, the former was rightly convicted of aiding and abetting murder; the delay did not of itself negative intention, there was no intervening event to hinder the plan, and it was unnecessary to prove that the acts of assistance occurred at a time when the killer had formed an intention to murder: *R v Bryce* [2004] EWCA Crim 1231, [2004] Crim LR 936.
4. *National Coal Board v Gamble* [1959] 1 QB 11, [1958] 3 All ER 203, 122 JP 453; *R v Bainbridge* [1960] 1 QB 129, [1959] 3 All ER 200, 123 JP 499.
5. *R v Calhaem* [1985] QB 808, [1985] 2 All ER 266.
6. *Stacey v Whitehurst* (1865) 29 JP 136; *Ex p Smith* (1858) 22 JP 450; *Gough v Rees* (1929) 94 JP 53.
7. *Bowker v Premier Drug Co Ltd* [1928] 1 KB 217, 91 JP 118; *Newman v Overington, Harris and Ash Ltd* (1928) 93 JP 46.
8. *Provincial Motor Cab Co Ltd v Dunning* [1909] 2 KB 599, 73 JP 387 (a corporation); *Cook v Stockwell* (1915) 79 JP 394.
9. *Ackroyd's Air Travel Ltd v DPP* [1950] 1 All ER 933, 114 JP 251; *Thomas v Lindop* [1950] 1 All ER 966, 114 JP 290; *National Coal Board v Gamble*, supra; *John Henshall (Quarries) Ltd v Harvey* [1965] 2 QB 233, [1965] 1 All ER 725, 129 JP 224; *Cassady v Morris (Transport) Ltd* [1975] Crim LR 398.
10. *Callow v Tillstone* (1900) 64 JP 823; *Stanton & Sons Ltd v Webber* (1972) 116 Sol Jo 667.
11. *Rubie v Faulkner* [1940] 1 KB 571, [1940] 1 All ER 285, 104 JP 161.
12. *Taylor's Central Garages (Exeter) Ltd v Roper* (1951) 115 JP 445.
13. *R v Coney* (1882) 8 QBD 534, 46 JP 404; *Wilcox v Jeffrey* [1951] 1 All ER 464, 115 JP 151; *R v Clarkson*, supra. See also *Smith v Reynolds* [1986] Crim LR 559 (passengers in van being driven at a police officer).
14. *DPP for Northern Ireland v Maxwell* [1978] 3 All ER 1140, [1978] 1 WLR 1350, 143 JP 63. For alternative verdicts available on indictment, see *R v Wan* [1995] Crim LR 296, CA; *R v Stewart* [1995] 3 All ER 159, [1995] 1 Cr App Rep 441, [1995] Crim LR 420, CA; *R v Reardon* [1999] Crim LR 392, CA (D handed knife to principal for stabbing of unspecified one of two victims, D guilty of subsequent murder of both victims).
15. *R v Powell* [1997] 4 All ER 545, [1997] 3 WLR 959, [1998] 1 Cr App Rep 261, HL and see *R v Uddin* [1998] 2 All ER 744, [1998] 3 WLR 1000, [1999] 1 Cr App Rep 319, CA.
16. *R v Webster* [2006] EWCA Crim 415, [2006] 2 Cr App R 6 (for an alternative basis for liability in such cases, see note to s 2 of the Road Traffic Act 1988, in PART IV: ROAD TRAFFIC, post).

17. *Blakely v DPP* [1991] RTR 405.
16. *R v Richards* [1974] QB 776; [1973] 3 All ER 1088.
19. *Re A-G's Reference (No 1 of 1975)* [1975] QB 773, [1975] 2 All ER 684, 139 JP 569.
20. *R v Humphreys and Turner* [1965] 3 All ER 689, 130 JP 45 but see *Morris v Tolman* [1923] 1 KB 166, 86 JP 221; *Thornton v Mitchell* [1940] 1 All ER 339, 104 JP 108; *Gough v Rees* (1929) 94 JP 53.
21. *Hale* [1736] 1 PC 555.
22. *R v Millward* (1994) 158 JP 1091, [1994] Crim LR 527, CA, and see *R v Loukes* [1996] 1 Cr App Rep 444, [1996] Crim LR 341, CA (offence of dangerous driving where risk not obvious to driver and as no *actus reus* procurer had to be acquitted also).
23. *DPP v K and B* [1997] 1 Cr App Rep 36, [1997] Crim LR 121, DC (rape committed by boy under 14 who was not brought to trial, two female defendants (who therefore could not be charged as principals) rightly convicted as aiders and abetters even though prosecution had not negatived *doli incapax* on the part of the principal).

1–322 Incitement. A person who incites another to commit an offence, is guilty of an offence at common law, even though an offence is not committed[1]. Where the offence has actually been committed, the incitement is merged in the completed offence and the inciters are liable as accessories.

Convictions have been obtained; of attempting to incite a lad to commit a crime by sending him a letter which did not reach him, or which he did not read[2]; for inciting to procure the commission of acts of gross indecency with certain male unknown persons[3]; for inciting another to receive stolen goods, although it was not proved that any goods of the type mentioned existed at the time of the incitement[4]; for inciting people, through an advertisement, to use unlicensed apparatus for wireless telegraphy by buying a device which would detect police radar speed traps[5]. The person incited must be capable of committing the crime alleged[6]. It appears to be irrelevant that the initiative was taken by the incitee and that he was ready, willing and, indeed, keen to commit the offence[7]. A person subscribing to a website providing child pornography incites the distribution of indecent photographs although the process is entirely automated[8]. Incitement to commit an offence cannot be committed where it is impossible to commit the offence alleged to have been incited; accordingly, it is necessary to analyse the evidence to decide the precise offence which the defendant is alleged to have incited and whether it was possible to commit that offence[9]. For the common law offence of incitement to incite, see *R v Sirat* [1986] Crim LR 245, CA. For *procedure* see Magistrates' Courts Act 1980, s 45, post. Incitement to commit an offence triable either way (except certain offences of aiding, abetting, counselling or procuring the commission of an offence, or attempting to commit an offence), is itself triable either way[10].

There are a number of separate statutory offences of incitement. See also PART VIII: title PERVERTING JUSTICE, post.

1. *R v Gregory* (1867) LR 1 CCR 77, 31 JP 453.
2. *R v Banks* (1873) 12 Cox CC 393; *R v Ransford* (1874) 31 LT 488; *R v Krause* (1902) 66 JP 121.
3. *R v Bentley* [1923] 1 KB 403, 87 JP 55.
4. *R v McDonough* (1963) 47 Cr App Rep 37.
5. *Invicta Plastics Ltd v Clare* [1976] RTR 251.
6. *R v Whitehouse* [1977] QB 868, [1977] 3 All ER 737—the law of this case would today be affected by the Sexual Offences Act 2003, s 26 in PART VIII: title SEXUAL OFFENCES, post.
7. *R v Goldman* [2001] Crim LR 822, CA, (held that where a defendant responded to an advertisement for the sale of pornographic videos by writing to request a compilation tape showing very young girls (aged 7–13) he could be guilty in law of inciting or attempting to incite the distribution of indecent photographs of children, contrary to s 1(1) of the Criminal Attempts Act 1981; the fact that the advertiser was willing to supply its wares was nothing to the point).
8. *R (on the application of O) v Coventry Magistrates' Court* [2004] EWHC 905 (Admin), [2004] Crim LR 948.
9. *R v Fitzmaurice* [1983] QB 1083, [1983] 1 All ER 189.
10. Magistrates' Court Act 1980, Sch 1, para 35, in this PART: STATUTES ON PROCEDURE, post.

ATTEMPTS

1–323 Attempting to commit an indictable offence is an offence, defined and governed as to extent, procedure and penalties by the Criminal Attempts Act 1981, this PART, post. Someone charged with an attempt may still be convicted even though the completed offence is proved[1].

1. *Webley v Buxton* [1977] QB 481, [1977] 2 All ER 595.

DEFENCES

1–324 Duress and Necessity. The starting point of the law is that adults of sound mind are ordinarily to be held responsible for the crimes which they commit[1]. However, the law recognises in certain circumstances a defence of Necessity. Terminology is somewhat fluid as the law develops and 'Necessity' may be used as a general term to comprise the two defences of 'duress by human threats' and 'duress of circumstances[2] or it may be used simply to describe the latter defence[1]. Also, the term 'necessity' has been used to describe those cases where medical practitioners may act in the best interests of persons for whose treatment they are medically responsible in circumstances where those persons are not able to decide for themselves[3]. In this case it is dangerous to seek to extract general principles to be applied across the whole are of defences of duress[4]. The defence of marital coercion under s 47 of the Criminal Justice Act 1925[5] perhaps also has an affinity with duress by human threats[1].

The defence of duress is available for all offences except murder and some forms of treason and the threat or danger in question must be of death or serious injury (but not where the defendant believed his act was immediately necessary to avoid serious psychological injury[6] or to avoid serious pain[4]).

The defendant's belief in the threats must be genuine and reasonable.

A reasonable person, of the defendant's age and background, would have been forced and driven to act as the defendant did.

A defence of duress by human threats or duress of circumstances does not ordinarily operate to negative any legal ingredient of the crime nor is it regarded as justifying the conduct of the defendant; it is regarded as a defence which excuses what would otherwise be criminal conduct[7].

The evidential burden is on the defendant to raise the issue of duress, the legal burden is then on the prosecution to establish to the criminal standard that the defendant did not commit the crime with which he is charged under duress[8]. If the defence is that the accused acted under duress, he must first, by cross-examination of the prosecution witnesses or by evidence called on his behalf, place before the court such material as makes duress a live issue fit and proper to be decided upon; the onus is then on the prosecution to destroy the defence in such a manner as to leave in the court's mind no reasonable doubt that the accused cannot be absolved on the grounds of the alleged compulsion[9]. Where justices are asked, as a preliminary issue, to decide whether the defence of duress may be raised they must take care not at that stage of the case to determine the defence of duress on the merits[10].

---

1. *See R v Z* [2005] UKHL 22, [2005] 2 AC 467, *sub nom R v Hasan*[2005] 4 All ER 685, [2006] Crim LR 142.
2. See, for example, *R v Martin* [1989] 1 All ER 652, 153 JP 231, CA and *R v Cole* [1994] Crim LR 582.
3. See, for example, *Re A (children) (conjoined twins: surgical separation)* [2001] 1 FLR 1, [2001] Crim LR 400, CA.
4. *R v Quayle* [2005] EWCA Crim 1415, [2006] 1 All ER 988, [2005] 1 WLR 3642, [2005] 2 Cr App R 34, [2006] Crim LR 148. See also *R v Altham* [2006] EWCA Crim 7, [2006] 2 Cr App R 8
⁵ In this PART: STATUTES ON PROCEDURE, post.
6. *R v Baker and Wilkins* [1997] Crim LR 497.
7. *R v Z*, supra (duress by human threats), *R v Quayle*, supra (duress of circumstances).
8. *R v Z*, supra.
9. *R v Gill* [1963] 2 All ER 688, [1963] 1 WLR 841, 127 JP 429; *R v Bone* [1968] 2 All ER 644, 132 JP 420.
10. *A v DPP* (2000) 164 JP 317, [2000] Crim LR 572, DC.

1-325 ***Duress by human threats.*** There is a limited exception in favour of those who commit crimes because they are forced or compelled to do so against their will by the threats of another, ie they act as they do because they are subject to duress[1].

The following particular considerations apply to the defence of duress by human threats[2]:

— The threat must be directed against the defendant or his immediate family or a person for whom he reasonably feels responsible.
— The defendant's belief in the threats must be genuine and reasonable.
— A reasonable person, of the defendant's age and background, would have been forced and driven to act as the defendant did.
— The criminal conduct which it is sought to excuse must have been directly caused by the threats which are relied on. The execution of a threat must be reasonably believed to have been imminent and immediate and there was no evasive action the defendant could reasonably have been expected to take. Where any threatened retribution is not reasonably expected to follow immediately or almost immediately, there may be little if any room for doubt that evasive action could have been taken.
— The defendant may not rely on duress when as a result of his voluntary association with others engaged in criminal activity he foresaw or ought reasonably to have foreseen the risk of being subjected to any compulsion by threats or violence.

The relevant tests for duress are largely stated objectively, with reference to the reasonableness of the defendant's perceptions and conduct and not with primary reference to his subjective perceptions[2]. Therefore the prosecution must make the magistrates or jury sure that a sober person of reasonable firmness sharing the defendant's characteristics would not have responded to the threat as he had done[2]. The fact that a defendant's will to resist had been eroded by the voluntary consumption of drink or drugs or both is irrelevant [3]. The fact that a defendant has or may have had a low intelligence quotient is not relevant to a defence of duress, since a low IQ, short of mental impairment or mental defectiveness, cannot be said to be a characteristic that makes those who have it less courageous and less able to withstand threats and pressure[4].

In particular in determining whether an ordinary person showing the characteristics of the defendant would be able to resist the threats made to him, the following principles should be applied:

(1) The mere fact that the accused is more pliable, vulnerable, timid or susceptible to threats than a normal person are not characteristics with which it is legitimate to invest the reasonable/ordinary person for the purpose of considering the objective test.

(2) The defendant may be in a category of persons who the justices may think less able to resist pressure than people not within that category. Obvious examples are age, where a young person may well not be so robust as a mature one; possibly sex, though many women would doubtless consider they had as much moral courage to resist pressure as men; pregnancy, where there is added fear for the unborn child; serious physical disability, which may inhibit self protection; recognised mental illness or psychiatric condition, such as post traumatic stress disorder leading to learned helplessness.

(3) Characteristics which may be relevant in considering provocation, because they relate to the nature of the provocation itself, will not necessarily be relevant in cases of duress. Thus homosexuality

may be relevant to provocation if the provocative words or conduct are related to this characteristic; it cannot be relevant in duress, since there is no reason to think that homosexuals are less robust in resisting threats of the kind that are relevant in duress cases.

(4) Characteristics due to self-induced abuse, such as alcohol, drugs or glue-sniffing, cannot be relevant.

(5) Psychiatric evidence may be admissible to show that the accused is suffering from some mental illness, mental impairment or recognised psychiatric condition provided persons generally suffering from such condition may be more susceptible to pressure and threats and thus to assist the justices in deciding whether a reasonable person suffering from such a condition might have been impelled to act as the defendant did. It is not admissible simply to show that in the doctor's opinion an accused, who is not suffering from such illness or condition, is especially timid, suggestible or vulnerable to pressure and threats. Nor is medical opinion admissible to bolster or support the credibility of the accused[4].

1. See *R v Z* [2005] UKHL 22, [2005] 2 AC 467, [2005] 2 WLR 709, sub nom R v Hasan [2005] 4 All ER 685, [2006] Crim LR 142 and for a comprehensive review of the defence of duress, see the speech of Lord Bingham para [17] ff.
2. *R v Z*, supra.
3. *R v Graham* [1982] 1 WLR 294, (1982) 74 Cr App Rep 235; approved in *R v Howe* [1987] AC 417, [1987] 1 All ER 771 but see *DPP v Rogers* [1998] Crim LR 202, DC and commentary thereto.
4. *R v Bowen* [1996] 4 All ER 837, [1997] 1 WLR 372, [1996] 2 Cr App Rep 157, [1996] Crim LR 577, CA.

1–326 *Duress of circumstances*. The court must be satisfied

— that from an objective standpoint, the accused acted reasonably and proportionately in order to avoid an imminent threat of death or serious injury,
— that the accused was, or might have been, impelled to act as he did because, as a result of what he reasonably believed to be the situation, he had good cause to fear that otherwise death or serious physical injury would result and
— a sober person of reasonable firmness, sharing the characteristics of the accused would have responded to that situation by acting as the accused acted.
— the danger must have been extraneous to the offender himself and be capable of being measured and assessed accordingly[1].

The defence is strictly and scrupulously limited to situations which correspond to its rationale and is not available to those who break the legislation on the misuse of drugs for the relief of pain by the use of cannabis[2]. A possible defence of duress might have arisen to the former offence of reckless driving (now dangerous driving) where someone drives a motor car slowly onto the pavement and into a shopping precinct, and out again to avoid a group of fighting youths[3]. It can be raised as a defence to a charge of driving while disqualified by a husband whose suicidal wife had threatened to kill herself otherwise; it is, however, available only if from the objective standpoint the accused could be said to be acting reasonably and proportionately in order to avoid a threat of death or serious injury[4]. It is sufficient for the accused to show that he acted as he did because he reasonably[5] perceived a threat of serious physical injury or death; he is not required to prove that the threat with which he was confronted was an actual or real threat[6]. Where consideration is being given to whether a defendant is guilty of driving without due care and attention, the justices may, in an appropriate case, take account of the reasons for the driving when those reasons do or may amount to grounds which give rise to the defence of duress of circumstances[7].

In order to establish a defence of necessity, the causative feature of the defendant's committing the offence must be extraneous to the defendant himself so that the defence of necessity does not extend to where the subjective thought processes and emotions of the accused operated as duress[8].

1. *R v Pommell* [1995] 2 Cr App Rep 607.
2. *R v Quayle* [2005] EWCA Crim 1415, [2006] 1 All ER 988, [2005] 1 WLR 3642, [2005] 2 Cr App R 34, [2006] Crim LR 148.
3. *R v Willer* [1987] RTR 22, CA. See also *R v Conway* [1989] QB 290, [1988] 3 All ER 1025, [1989] RTR 35, CA (duress of circumstances defence to reckless driving where driving resulted from fear for motorist's life and that of passenger) and *DPP v Bell* [1992] RTR 335, [1992] Crim LR 176 (defence of duress established where defendant drove a motor vehicle with excess alcohol for only "some distance", while in terror of serious personal injury).
4. *R v Martin* [1989] 1 All ER 652, 153 JP 231, CA.
5. The suggestion in *R v Safi* [2003] EWCA Crim 1809, [2004] 1 Cr App R 14, [2003] Crim LR 721 that a genuine belief was sufficient is now to be doubted having regard to *R v Z,[2005] UKHL 22, [2005] 2 AC 467, [2005] 2 WLR 709, sub nom R v Hasan [2005] 4 All ER 685.*
6. *R v Cairns* [1999] 2 Cr App Rep 137, [2000] RTR 15.
7. *R v Backshall* [1998] 1 WLR 1506, CA.
8. *R v Rodger* [1998] 1 Cr App Rep 143, CA (suicidal thoughts of a prisoner no defence to offence of breaking prison).

1–327 Entrapment. No defence of entrapment exists in English law.[1] The case law of the European Court of Human Rights suggests that the right to a fair trial under article 6(1) of the Convention will be breached where law enforcement agencies go beyond "passive" investigation and exercise an influence such as to incite the commission of an offence[2]. However, the European Court of Human Rights has not propounded a fundamental 'fairness' objection of general application that in the case of incitement or instigation by an agent provocateur, the court should not entertain a prosecution at all, regardless of whether the trial as a whole could be procedurally fair[3]. There is no appreciable difference between domestic law and jurisprudence on article 6(1)[4]. In some circumstances the

Crown Court and the High Court may stay proceedings[5] or a court may be invited to consider the exclusion of unfair evidence but the allegation of an element of entrapment cannot of itself lead to such exclusion[6]. Where a crime has been committed which in truth would not have been committed but for the activities of the informer or of the police officer concerned (for example, as *agent provocateur*) it can, if it thinks right to do so, mitigate the penalty[7].

Proceedings may be stayed where a fair trial is not possible or on broader considerations of the integrity of the criminal process. In this case the judge must weigh countervailing considerations of policy and justice[8]. It is unfair and an abuse of process if a person is hired, incited or pressurised into committing a crime which he would not otherwise have committed, but not where a law enforcement officer behaving as an ordinary member of the public, gives a person an unexceptional opportunity to commit a crime of which he freely takes advantage[4]. For the limited circumstances in which a magistrates' court may determine abuse of process see, ante, para **1–447 Abuse of process of the court**, ante.

---

1. *R v Sang* [1980] AC 402, [1979] 2 All ER 1222, 143 JP 606 HL.
2. *Teixeira de Castro v Portugal* (1998) 28 EHRR 101. See also *Ludi v Switzerland* (1992) 15 EHRR 173.
3. *R v Shannon* [2001] 1 WLR 51, [2001] 1 Cr App Rep 168, [2000] Crim LR 1001, CA. See also *Schenk v Switzerland* (1988) 13 EHRR 242.
4. *R v Looseley* [2001] UKHL 53, [2001] 4 All ER 897, [2001] 1 WLR 2060, [2002] 1 Cr App Rep 360.
5. See the Police and Criminal Evidence Act 1984, s 78 in PART II: EVIDENCE, post, and see *DPP v Marshall and Downes* [1988] Crim LR 750 and *R v Chalkley* [1998] QB 848, [1998] 2 All ER 155, CA.
6. *R v Shannon* supra.
7. *R v Sang* [1980] AC 402, [1979] 2 All ER 1222, 143 JP 606, HL; *R v Mackey and Shaw* [1992] Crim LR 602.
8. *R v Latif* [1996] 1 All ER 353, [1996] 1 WLR 104, [1996] 2 Cr App Rep 92, HL; *R v Shannon* [2000] Crim LR 1001, CA.

1–328   Self defence.   A person may use such force as is reasonable in the circumstances in the prevention of crime, or in effecting or assisting in the lawful arrest of offencers[1]. "Self-defence" is a variant of this defence and applies only to assaults, we discuss this and justification, provocation and mistake at para **8–23065 Self-defence, justification, provocation** and para **8–23066 Mistake**, post. Provocation may, depending on the circumstances, be taken into account as mitigation, but is not a defence to assault, but is a partial defence to murder, permitting an alternative conviction of manslaughter[2].

---

1. Criminal Law Act 1967, s 3, in this PART, STATUTES ON PROCEDURE, post.
2. Homicide Act 1957, s 3, in PART VIII: title PERSONS, OFFENCES AGAINST, post.

PROCEEDINGS AGAINST A CORPORATION

1–329   A corporation may be a defendant and be fined[1] or committed to the Crown Court for sentence[2]. Whether the criminal act of an agent, including his state of mind, intention, knowledge or belief, is the act of the company, must depend on the nature of the charge, the relative position of the officer or agent, and the other relevant facts and circumstances[3]. In cases where the law requires a guilty mind as a condition of a criminal offence, the guilty mind of the directors or the managers will render the company itself guilty[4], but not that of a workman who is not a responsible officer of the company[5]. However, where a company is alleged to have "caused" the commission of an offence, such as causing the pollution of controlled water, the company will be criminally liable for an offence which results from the acts or omissions of its employees acting within the course and scope of their employment when the offence occurred, regardless of whether they could be said to be exercising the controlling mind and will of the company[6]. The only exception to this principle will be if the company establishes that some third party acted in such a way as to interrupt the chain of causation[6].

In prosecutions under consumer protection legislation, the ultimate liability of a company may depend on whether the relevant act was that of a person who could properly be described as a directing mind of the company. Even where absolute liability is imposed under the Trade Descriptions Act 1968[7], a company may seek to avail itself of the "due diligence" defence in s 24 and where the defendant is a limited company a failure to exercise due diligence on its part would only occur where the failure was that of a person who could be identified with the controlling mind and will of the company. Where the act or default is that of one of the subordinate managers who is not identifiable with the company, if that act or default consists of a failure on the manager's part properly to exercise supervisory functions over other servants of the company, this would constitute an act or default of "another person" within the terms of s 24[8]. Where the offence requires knowledge or recklessness, such intent must be that of one of the directing minds of the company[9]. The duty of the company is to take reasonable precautions and exercise due diligence to institute an effective system of supervision to avoid the performing of acts by its employees which would otherwise amount to an offence[8].

Accordingly a company was not liable for recklessly making a false statement in a holiday brochure for whose production an operations controller working within set guidelines and procedures was responsible[10] or for the failure of a supermarket manager properly to supervise a sales assistant[8].

Where the health and safety of employees and others are concerned the liability of an employer is more strict. Subject to the defence of reasonable practicability, failure on the part of an employer to ensure the health and safety of employees and not to expose others to risk creates an offence of absolute liability and corporate liability is not avoided on the basis that the acts were not those of the "directing mind" of the company[10].

Criminal proceedings may not be brought against a company after a winding-up order has been made or a provisional liquidator has been appointed except by leave of the court with jurisdiction over the winding up and subject to such terms as that court may impose[11].

---

1. *Pharmaceutical Society v London and Provincial Supply Association* (1880) 5 App Cas 857, 45 JP 20; *St Helens Tramways Co v Wood* (1891) 56 JP 71; *R v Tyler and the International Commercial Co Ltd* [1891] 2 QB 588, 56 JP 118; *Pearks, Gunston and Tee Ltd v Ward* [1902] 2 KB 1, 66 JP 774; *R v Gainsford Justices* (1913) 29 TLR 359; *DPP v Kent and Sussex Contractors Ltd* [1944] KB 146, [1944] 1 All ER 119, 108 JP 1, and on indictment, *R v Tyler*, supra and *R v Ascanio Puck & Co and Paice* (1912) 76 JP 487.
2. See the Magistrates' Courts Act 1980, s 38, this PART, post.
3. *R v ICR Haulage Ltd* [1944] KB 551, [1944] 1 All ER 691, 108 JP 181.
4. Per DENNING LJ in *HL Bolton (Engineering) Co Ltd v TJ Graham & Sons Ltd* [1957] 1 QB 159, [1956] 3 All ER 624.
5. *John Henshall Quarries Ltd v Harvey* [1965] 2 QB 233, [1965] 1 All ER 725, 129 JP 224.
6. *National Rivers Authority v Alfred McAlpine Homes (East) Ltd* [1994] 4 All ER 286, 158 JP 628.
7. In PART VIII: title CONSUMER PROTECTION, post.
8. *Tesco Supermarkets Ltd v Nattrass* [1972] AC 153, [1971] 2 All ER 127, [1971] 2 WLR 1166, HL.
9. *Yugotours v Wadsley* [1988] Crim LR 623, *Airtours plc v Shipley* (1994) 158 JP 835.
10. *R v British Steel plc* [1995] 1 WLR 1356, CA.
11. Insolvency Act 1986, s 130(2), in PART VIII: title INSOLVENCY, post. See also *R v Dickson and R v Wright* (1991) 94 Cr App Rep 7.

Criminal proceedings in magistrates' courts
CRIMINAL PROSECUTIONS

1–380 Where the offence is not an individual grievance[1], but is a matter of public policy and utility, and concerns the public morals, any person has a general power to prosecute, unless the statute creating the offence contains some restriction or regulation limiting the right to some particular person or party[2]. A number of offences require the consent of the Attorney General or the Director of Public Prosecutions before proceedings may be carried on, and others require notification to be given to the Director of Public Prosecutions. A decision by the Director to consent to a prosecution is not amenable to judicial review in the absence of dishonesty, mala fides or an exceptional circumstance[3]. Crown Prosecutors are empowered to give consents and to take steps on the Director's behalf; the Director acting under the superintendence of the Attorney General, is the head of the Crown Prosecution Service, and conducts all police prosecutions and other similar matters, and may take over any prosecutions[4]. It is the duty of the justice or of the justices' clerk, when issuing process, to satisfy himself that any necessary consent or authority has been obtained[5]. While there is no absolute obligation imposed on the Director to give reasons for a decision not to prosecute, in cases involving a death, especially in the case of the death of a person in the state's custody, the Director, in the absence of compelling reasons to the contrary, should give reasons to meet the reasonable expectation of interested parties that either a prosecution would follow or a reasonable explanation for not prosecuting would be given[6].

The Director has no power to give an undertaking that he will not consent to the prosecution of a crime yet to be committed[7].

Examples of restrictions on the right to prosecute: proceedings under the customs and excise Acts require the authority of the Commissioners, and shall be commenced in the name of an officer[8]; proceedings in respect of offences under the Public Health Act 1936 require the consent of the Attorney General, or be taken by the party aggrieved or by a council or body whose function it is to enforce the provisions[9]; proceedings under health and safety at work provisions may be instituted only by an inspector, or by or with the consent of the Director of Public Prosecutions[10]; proceedings for a weights and measures offence shall not be instituted except by or on behalf of a local weights and measures authority, or the chief officer of police for a police area[11]. When a winding-up order has been made, or a provisional liquidator has been appointed, no action or proceeding shall be proceeded with or commenced against a company except by leave of the court, and subject to such terms as the court may impose[12].

Statutory instruments often contain the phrase "the provisions of this Order, except where it is otherwise provided, shall be executed and enforced by the local authority" or similar words. This does not give the right to prosecute exclusively to the local authority, and the right may be exercised by any private person becoming aware of such an offence[13].

Where a statute directs a particular person to lay an information, it may be laid by his duly authorised agent[14]. In some cases a formal appointment to prosecute may be necessary[15].

The Attorney General's consent to proceedings need not be in writing, and does not require great particularity[16]. Any function of the Attorney General may be exercised by the Solicitor General[17]. Where an enactment prohibits the institution of or carrying on of proceedings except with consent of a Law Officer or of the Director or of the offender may still be arrested and remanded, or a warrant issued[18].

The Director of Public Prosecutions, who is head of the Crown Prosecution Service, is appointed by the Attorney General. The Director shall conduct all police prosecutions, other than specified proceedings[19], and other prosecutions where appropriate[20]. Where the police have investigated, arrested and brought the arrested person to the custody officer to be charged, it is not open to a private individual to take over the conduct of the prosecution[21]. Where a customs officer arrests an accused person, drafts a charge and takes the accused to a police station where a police officer formally charges the accused, this does not prevent Customs and Excise prosecuting the case despite s 3(2)(a) of the Prosecution of Offences Act 1985[21]. Moreover, the seeking of police assistance of itself does not necessarily turn what are in truth proceedings brought by a local authority into police proceedings[22]. For the purposes of an action for malicious prosecution where proceedings were instituted by the police in reliance on a false allegation, it will be the complainant who will be responsible although not technically the prosecutor[23].

The Code for Crown Prosecutors[24] is a public declaration of the principles upon which the Crown Prosecution Service will exercise its functions. It has been stated, obiter, that the fact that there is a duty under s 10 of the Prosecution of Offences Act 1985 to issue a code does not necessarily mean that the Director may not ever give guidance as to how prosecutorial discretion will be exercised in regard to particular offences[25].

Chief Officers of Police have been offered guidelines by the Attorney General giving criteria for prosecution[26]. This advice identifies the following factors to be taken into account as part of the decision to prosecute: sufficiency of evidence leading to a reasonable prospect of a conviction; does the public interest require a prosecution, taking account of a probably minimal penalty, staleness of the offence, youth and attitude of the offender, old age and infirmity, any mental illness or stress which is likely to be considerably and permanently worsened by prosecution. In sexual offences regard should be had to willing participation by the victim, his or her age, the relative ages of the parties and whether or not there was any element of seduction or corruption. The complainant's reluctance to continue with the case would usually lead to no prosecution unless a change of heart was actuated by fear or the offence was of some gravity.

If doubt remains after weighing these matters, then consideration should be given to the accused's character, the attitude of the local community, prevalence of the offence. Any residual doubt is resolved by prosecuting and leaving the court to decide.

A decision of the Crown Prosecution Service not to prosecute in a certain matter may be reviewed by the High Court on an application for judicial review if the applicant is able to show that the decision was reached (1) because of some unlawful policy; or (2) because the Director of Public Prosecutions failed to act in accordance with the Code for Crown Prosecutors, or (3) perversely[27].

The preparatory process by crown prosecutors to consider the evidence and the appropriate charge is set out in the *Criminal Case Management Framework*[28].

The right of a person to institute a private prosecution is expressly preserved[29] although it has been stated that the surviving right of private prosecution is of questionable value[30]. Safeguards to prevent of curb the misuse of this right include: the power of justices to refuse to issue a summons[31] and the power of the Director of Public Prosecutions to take over private prosecutions and bring them to an end[32]. In appropriate circumstances justice may stay proceedings as an abuse of process[33].

---

1. *R v Hicks* (1855) 19 JP 515.
2. Per COCKBURN CJ in *Cole v Coulton* (1860) 24 JP 596.
3. *R v DPP, ex p Kebilene* [2002] 2 AC 326, [1999] 4 All ER 801, HL.
4. Prosecution of Offences Act 1985, ss 1–3, in this PART: STATUTES ON PROCEDURE, post.
5. *Price v Humphries* [1958] 2 QB 353, [1958] 2 All ER 725, 122 JP 423.
6. *R v DPP, ex p Manning* [2000] 3 WLR 463, DC.
7. *R (on the application of Pretty) v DPP* [2001] UKHL 61, [2002] 1 AC 800, [2002] 1 All ER 1, [2002] 1 FCR 1).
8. Customs and Excise Management Act 1979, s 145, in PART VIII: title CUSTOMS AND EXCISE, post.
9. Public Health Act 1936, s 298, in PART VIII: title PUBLIC HEALTH, post.
10. Health and Safety at Work, etc Act 1974, ss 38 and 39, in PART VIII: title HEALTH AND SAFETY, post.
11. Weights and Measures Act 1985, s 83, in PART VIII: title WEIGHTS AND MEASURES, post.
12. Insolvency Act 1986, s 130, in PART VIII: title INSOLVENCY, post.
13. *R v Stewart* [1896] 1 QB 300, 60 JP Jo 356, and see also *RSPCA v Woodhouse* [1984] CLY 693.
14. *Foster v Fyfe* [1896] 2 QB 104, 60 JP 423.
15. See *Bob Keats Ltd v Farrant* [1951] 1 All ER 899, 115 JP 304.
16. *R v Cain and R v Schollick* [1976] QB 496, [1975] 2 All ER 900, 139 JP 598, and see as to the Attorney General's discretion *Gouriet v Union of Post Office Workers* [1977] QB 729, [1977] 1 All ER 696, 141 JP 205, CA; revsd [1978] AC 435, [1977] 3 All ER 70, 141 JP 552, HL.
17. Law Officers Act 1997, s 1.
18. Prosecution of Offences Act 1985, s 25(2), in this PART: STATUTES ON PROCEDURE, post.
19. See the Prosecution of Offences Act 1985 (Specified Proceedings) Order 1999, noted in para **1–2901**, post.
20. See Part I of the Prosecution of Offences Act 1985, in this PART, para **1–2900**, et seq, post.
21. *R v Stafford Justices, ex p Customs and Excise Comrs* [1991] 2 All ER 201, [1990] 3 WLR 656, 154 JP 865, DC; followed in *R (Hunt) v Criminal Cases Review Commission* [2001] QB 1108, [2001] 1 WLR 319, [2001] 2 Cr App Rep 76.
22. *R v Croydon Justices, ex p Holmberg* (1992) 157 JP 277, [1992] Crim LR 892.
23. *Martin v Watson* [1996] AC 74, [1995] 3 All ER 559, HL.
24. See this PART: STATUTORY INSTRUMENTS AND PRACTICE DIRECTIONS ON PROCEDURE, post.
25. *R (on the application of Pretty) v DPP* [2001] UKHL 61, [2002] 1 AC 800, [2002] 1 All ER 1, [2002] 1 FCR 1).
26. See Home Office Circular No 26/1983.
27. *R v DPP, ex p C* [1995] 1 Cr App Rep 136, 159 JP 227.
28. Pre-Court Process Parts 1–4, in this PART, CODES OF PRACTICE AND GUIDELINES, post.
29. Prosecution of Offences Act 1985, s 6(1), in this PART: STATUTES ON PROCEDURE, post.
30. *Jones v Whalley* [2006] UKHL 41, [2007] 1 AC 63, [2006] 4 All ER 113, [2007] 1 Cr App R 2, per Lord Bingham at para [16].
31. See para **1–401 Issue of summons or warrant**, post.
32. Prosecution of Offences Act 1985, s 6(2), in this PART: STATUTES ON PROCEDURE, post.
33. See para **1–447 Abuse of the process of the court**, post.

COMMENCEMENT OF PROCEEDINGS: INFORMATION (INCLUDING CHARGE), SUMMONS, WARRANT

1–381 Criminal proceedings in magistrates' courts are started either by arrest, charge and production to court[1] or by the laying of an information followed by summons or warrant. Every information, summons, warrant or other document laid, issued or made for the purposes of, or in connection with, any proceedings before a magistrates' court for an offence, shall be sufficient if it describes the specific offence with which the accused is charged, or of which he is convicted, in ordinary language avoiding as far as possible the use of technical terms, and without necessarily stating all the elements of the offence, and gives such particulars as may be necessary for giving reasonable information of the nature of the charge[2].

Under 6(3)(*a*) of the European Convention on Human Rights everyone charged with a criminal offence has the right to be informed promptly, in a language he understands and in detail, of the nature and cause of the accusation against him. The purpose of this provision is to provide the accused with the information he needs to begin preparing a defence. The information provided must therefore be more specific than the grounds of arrest required under Article 5(2) of the Convention[3].

---

1. See ante para **1–220 Arrest**. As to when proceedings commence, see *R v Manchester Stipendiary Magistrate, ex p Hill* [1983] 1 AC 328, [1982] 2 All ER 963, 146 JP 348 (when an information is laid or a complaint made); *R v St Albans Juvenile Court, ex p Godman* [1981] QB 964, [1981] 2 All ER 311, 145 JP 137, approved by the House of Lords in *R v Islington North Juvenile Court, ex p Daley* [1983] 1 AC 347, [1982] 2 All ER 974, 146 JP 363 (juvenile attaining 18 before mode of trial decision reached has right to elect trial by jury); Contempt of Court Act 1981, s 2 and Sch 1 (the relevant initial step making criminal proceedings active); *R v Whale and Lockton* [1991] Crim LR 692 (proceedings instituted for the purposes of requiring consent of Attorney General when committal hearing started).
2. Criminal Procedure Rules 2005, r 7.1, in this Part, Statutory instruments and practice directions on procedure, post.
3. *GSM v Austria* (1983) 34 DR 119. But see also *Brozicek v Italy* (1990) 12 EHRR 371.

1–382 Jurisdiction. A magistrates' court has jurisdiction: (*a*) to try any summary offence; (*b*) as examining justices over any offence committed by a person who appears or is brought before the court; (*c*) subject to ss 18–22 of the Magistrates' Courts Act 1980[1], to try summarily any offence which is triable either way; and (*d*) in the exercise of its powers under s 24 of the Magistrates' Courts Act 1980 to try summarily an indictable offence[2].

There is power to transfer criminal proceedings between magistrates' courts[3].

Once a person is in lawful custody within the jurisdiction of the magistrates' court, the justices have no power, whether when sitting as examining justices or exercising their summary jurisdiction, to inquire into the circumstances by which that person has been brought within the jurisdiction. However, the High Court in the exercise of its supervisory jurisdiction has power to conduct such an inquiry and if satisfied that a person has been brought within the jurisdiction in disregard of extradition procedures it may stay the prosecution and release the accused. Where a serious question arises as to the deliberate abuse of extradition procedures, the magistrates' court should allow an adjournment so that an application can be made to the Divisional Court[4].

---

1. In this Part: Statutes on Procedure, post.
2. Courts Act 2003, s 44, in this Part: Statutes on Procedure, post.
3. See Magistrates' Courts Act 1980, s 27A, in this Part: Statutes on Procedure, post.
4. *R v Horseferry Road Magistrates' Court, ex p Bennett* [1994] AC 42, [1993] 3 All ER 138, HL and see *R v Staines Magistrates' Court, ex p Westfallen* [1998] 4 All ER 210, [1998] 1 WLR 652, [1998] Crim LR 414, DC.

1–383 *Territorial jurisdiction.* The general principle of territorial jurisdiction is that where a substantial measure of the activities constituting a crime takes place within the jurisdiction, then the courts of England and Wales have jurisdiction unless it can seriously be argued on a reasonable view that these activities should, on the basis of international comity, be dealt with by another country; it is not necessary that the 'final act' or the 'gist' of the offence should occur within the jurisdiction[1]. If a person abroad commits an offence in England through the agency of another, innocent or guilty, he is liable to be indicted in this country[2]. A person in the United Kingdom may be convicted of inciting an offence where the person incited is abroad, provided the offence took effect at least in part in England and Wales[3].

Several provisions extend territorial jurisdiction over indictable offences; for example, to offences committed on foreign ships within twelve miles of the English or Welsh coast[4], to British aircraft abroad[5], to offences on oil exploration platforms in waters adjacent to British shores[6], to terrorist acts committed in certain foreign countries[7], to murder abroad by a British subject[8], to conspiracy and incitement to commit certain sexual acts abroad[9], to certain other sexual offences committed outside the United Kingdom[10].

Where the area within which a court has jurisdiction is situated on the coast of any sea or abuts on or projects into any bay, channel, lake, river or other navigable water, the court has jurisdiction as respects any offence over any vessel being on, or lying or passing off, that coast or being in or near that bay, channel, lake, river or navigable water and over all persons on board that vessel or for the time being belonging to it[11]. Where any person, being a British subject, is charged with having committed any offence on board any British ship on the high seas or in any foreign port or harbour or on board any foreign ship to which he does not belong, or, not being a British subject, is charged with having committed any offence on board any British ship on the high seas, and that person is found within the jurisdiction of any court in Her Majesty's dominions, which would have had cognizance of the offence if it had been committed on board a British ship within the limits of its ordinary jurisdiction, that court shall have jurisdiction to try the offence as if it had been so committed[12]. "High seas" for the purposes of this provision has the same meaning as when used with reference to the Court of Admiralty, that is, all oceans, seas, bays, channels, rivers, creeks and waters below low-water mark and "where great ships can go", except only such parts of such oceans and other waters as lie within the body of some country[13]. English courts have been held to have jurisdiction in the following cases: theft on a British ship in Nassau, Bahamas (a Commonwealth port)[13]; and criminal damage committed by British subjects aboard a Danish ship on the high seas between Denmark and England[14].

1. *R v Smith (Wallace Duncan) (No 4)* [2004] 3 WLR 229, CA
2. See *R v Baxter* [1972] Q.B. 1, 55 Cr App R 214, CA; *DPP v Stonehouse* [1978] A.C. 55, HL.
3. *R v Tompkins* (2006) Times 17 August, CA (incitement to distribute indecent photographs of children, where the distribution occurred, at least in part, in England and Wales).
4. Territorial Waters Jurisdiction Act 1878, amended by Territorial Sea Act 1987.
5. Civil Aviation Act 1982, s 92, in PART VII: title AVIATION, post.
6. Continental Shelf Act 1964 in PART VIII: title HEALTH AND SAFETY, post and Orders thereunder; see notes to Magistrates' Courts Act 1980, s 2. See also the Oil and Gas (Enterprise) Act 1982, s 22, in Part VIII: title HEALTH AND SAFETY, post, and the Criminal Jurisdiction (Offshore Activities) Order 1987 under the same title.
7. Suppression of Terrorism Act 1978, s 4 in PART VIII: title EXTRADITION, FUGITIVE OFFENDERS AND BACKING OF WARRANTS, post.
8. Offences Against the Person Act 1861, s 9.
9. Sexual Offences (Conspiracy and Incitement) Act 1996, ss 1 and 2, in Part VIII: title SEXUAL OFFENCES, post.
10. Sexual Offences Act 2003, s 72, in PART VIII: title SEXUAL OFFENCES, post.
11. Magistrates' Courts Act 1980, s 3A, in this PART: STATUTES ON PROCEDURE, post and the Merchant Shipping Act 1995, s 280, in PART VII: title MERCHANT SHIPPING, post.
12. Magistrates' Courts Act 1980, s 3A, in this PART: STATUTES ON PROCEDURE, post and the Merchant Shipping Act 1995, s 281, in PART VII: title MERCHANT SHIPPING, post.
13. *R v Liverpool Justices, ex p Molyneux* [1972] 2 QB 384, [1972] 2 All ER 471, 136 JP 477.
14. *R v Kelly* [1981] QB 174, [1981] 1 All ER 370.

1–384   Concurrent jurisdiction.   As well as matters of purely territorial jurisdiction, there can arise questions of *exclusive and concurrent jurisdiction*, and also *ouster of jurisdiction*. Once justices are acting in a case, any purported taking of jurisdiction in that matter by another justice is void and renders him liable to indictment[1]. A decision of one court renders the matter *res judicata* in another[2].

1. *R v Cork Justices* [1912] 1 IR 151; *R v Sainsbury* (1791) 4 Term Rep 451; *R v Great Marlow (Inhabitants)* (1802) 2 East 244.
2. *Kingston's (Duchess) Case* (1776) 1 East PC 468; *Routledge v Hislop* (1860) 2 E & E 549, 24 JP 148 and 32 JP 705. See also *Millett v Coleman* (1875) 39 JP 805; *Hindley v Haslam* (1878) 3 QBD 481. But see also *res judicata*, para **1–448**, post.

1–385   Ouster of jurisdiction.   Justices' jurisdiction in an indictable case may be ousted if the act complained of was done in the exercise of a *bona fide* claim or assertion of title, in which event they must proceed as examining justices[1].
   The justices must decide on the evidence before them, and not just the defendant's statement, whether the claim is *bona fide*[2]. Their decision cannot be questioned by *judicial review*[3]. The claim is not waived by the defendant calling evidence on the merits[4]. Where the statute provides that the offence is triable only summarily, jurisdiction is not ousted[5]. The claim of title must be one that can exist at law[6] and must relate to title to real property; thus it did not apply to the ownership of rabbits caught on land[7] nor to the ownership of a stereo deck[8], but it did apply to the right of the lord of the manor and of freeholders of a common to give a licence to play mechanical organs on the common[9].

1. *R v Cridland* (1857) 7 E & B 853, 21 JP 404; *Penwarden v Palmer* (1894) 10 TLR 362; *Burton v Hudson* [1909] 2 KB 564, 73 JP 401; *R v Holsworthy Justices, ex p Edwards* [1952] 1 All ER 411, 116 JP 130.
2. *R v Dodson* (1839) 9 Ad & El 704, 5 JP 404; *R v Wrottesley and Gordon* (1830) 1 B & Ad 648; *R v Richmond, Surrey Justices* (1860) 24 JP 522; *Legg v Pardoe* (1860) 9 CBNS 289, 25 JP 39; *Cornwell v Sanders* (1862) 3 B & S 206, 27 JP 148; *R v Snape* (1863) 27 JP 134; *Ankerson v Webber* (1863) 32 JP 613; *R v Sandford* (1874) 39 JP 118; *Birnie v Marshall* (1876) 41 JP 22.
3. *Ex p Smith* (1890) 7 TLR 42.
4. *R v Towgood* (1871) 35 JP 791.
5. *R v Ogden, ex p Long Ashton RDC* [1963] 1 All ER 574, 127 JP 206.
6. *Hudson v Macrae* (1863) 4 B & S 585, 28 JP 436; *Croydon RDC v Crowley* (1909) 73 JP 205.
7. *White v Fox* (1880) 44 JP 618.
8. *Eagling v Wheatley* (1976) 141 JP 514, [1977] Crim LR 165.
9. *Andrews v Carlton* (1928) 93 JP 65.

1–386   Information.   An information may be laid by the prosecutor in person or by his counsel or solicitor or other person authorised in that behalf and need not be in writing or on oath, unless some statutory provision requires it[2]. It. In the case of a police prosecution, the information should be laid by the officer reporting the offence, the chief constable, or some other member of the force who is authorised to lay an information[2]. The laying of an information must be a deliberate act with a view to commencing a prosecution[3].

1. Criminal Procedure Rules 2005, r 7.1, in this PART, STATUTORY INSTRUMENTS AND PRACTICE DIRECTIONS ON PROCEDURE, post.
2. *Rubin v DPP* [1990] 2 QB 80, [1989] 2 All ER 241, 153 JP 289.
3. See *Schiavo v Anderton* [1987] QB 20, [1986] 3 All ER 10, 150 JP 264.

1–387 Time limits. The general rule is that there is no limitation on the time for taking proceedings for an indictable offence[1], but that a magistrates' court shall not try an information alleging a summary offence unless the information was laid within six months from the time when the offence was committed[2]. Particular statutes may provide otherwise for their own purposes[3]. Time limits may also be set in relation to the completion of preliminary stages of proceedings for an offence[4]. See also para **1–389** Duplicity.

An information in writing is laid when it is received at the office of the clerk to the justices for the relevant area. It is not necessary for the information to be personally received by a justice or by the clerk to the justices. It is enough that it is received by any member of the staff of the clerk to the justices, expressly or impliedly authorised to receive it, for onward transmission to a justice or to the clerk to the justices. It is immaterial whether the information is laid with a view to the issue of a summons or a warrant[5]. An information may be properly laid within the time limit notwithstanding that it is not in the prescribed form[6]. An oral information should as a matter of practice be addressed by the informant to a justice or the clerk to the justices in person[7]. An information may be laid by inputting it into a computer system at a terminal in a police station which is linked to the court, even though it is not printed out at the court end until later[8]. Where a particular "information date" was shown on the summons received by the appellant, but the summons showed a later date as the date when the information was printed, and the latter was four days outside the six months' time limit and the workings of the computer system meant that it would have been possible for the police, as part of the process on the way to "validation" to have added to the data or to have changed it between those two dates, so possibly delaying the date of the laying of the information until after the end of the time limit set out in s 127 of the 1980 Act, the court was entitled to, and should, decline jurisdiction having regard to the requirement to determine the question whether or not the information was laid in time in accordance with the ordinary criminal burden and standard of proof[9].

In computing the limitation period, the day on which the offence was committed or the matter of complaint arose is not to be included[10]. The limitation period for a continuing offence is counted not from the first discovery but from the date of each day charged, as if a separate offence[11]. Where a number of articles have been appropriated over a period of time, the prosecution may charge the appropriation of the aggregate number on a day within that period[12].

Where an offence consists of a course of conduct, and the last incident relied on to complete it occurred within 6 months of the laying of the information, s 127 of the Magistrates' Courts Act 1980 is not violated[13].

1. "Indictable offence" means an offence which, if committed by an adult, is triable on indictment, whether it is exclusively so triable or triable either way (Interpretation Act 1978, Sch 1, in PART II: EVIDENCE, post).
2. Magistrates' Courts Act 1980, s 127, in this PART: STATUTES ON PROCEDURE, post.
3. For example, National Assistance Act 1948, ss 52, 56, Social Security Administration Act 1992 (offences under the Acts); Licensing Act 1964, s 48(3) (alteration in club rules); Health and Safety at Work etc Act 1974, s 34 (proceedings following report or inquest); Customs and Excise Management Act 1979, s 147 (fraudulent evasion of duty, etc); Magistrates' Courts Act 1980, s 96(2) (civil debt); Plant Varieties and Seeds Act 1964, s 28 (six months from sample for offence of false particulars); Game Act 1831, s 41 (various offences regarding game); Companies Act 1985, s 731(2) (summary offences under the Companies Act 1985); Vehicle Excise and Registration Act 1994, ss 47, 50 (offence under that Act, recovery of duty); Merchant Shipping Act 1995, s 274 (time limit for summary offences under the Merchant Shipping Act 1995).
4. See the Prosecution of Offences Act 1985, s 22, in this PART: STATUTES ON PROCEDURE, post, and regulations made thereunder.
5. *R v Enfield Magistrates' Court, ex p Caldwell* (1996) 161 JP 336.
6. *R v Kennet Justices, ex p Humphrey and Wyatt* [1993] Crim LR 787.
7. *R v Manchester Stipendiary Magistrate, ex p Hill* [1983] 1 AC 328, [1982] 2 All ER 963, 146 JP 348.
8. *R v Pontypridd Juvenile Court, ex p B* [1988] Crim LR 842 (the analogy to posting a letter should in our view be ignored as having been made *per incuriam*).
9. *Atkinson v DPP* [2004] EWHC 1457 (Admin), [2004] 3 All ER 971, [2005] 1 WLR 96, 168 JP 472.
10. *Marren v Dawson Bentley & Co Ltd* [1961] 2 QB 135, [1961] 2 All ER 270.
11. *Barrett v Barrow in Furness Corpn* (1887) 51 JP Jo 803. For continuing offences see *LCC v Worley* [1894] 2 QB 826, 59 JP 263 (building erected contrary to the Metropolis Management Act 1862); *Rowley v T A Everton & Sons Ltd* [1941] 1 KB 86, [1940] 4 All ER 435 (machinery not properly fenced); *R v Chertsey Justices, ex p Franks* [1961] 2 QB 152, [1961] 1 All ER 825, 125 JP 305 (failure to comply with planning enforcement notice); *Mitchell v Lepine-Smith* (1976) 141 JP 510 (failure to send certificate by a specified time); *Camden London Borough Council v Marshall* [1996] 1 WLR 1345 (failure to execute works in accordance with notice under s 352 of the Housing Act 1985).
    The following were not continuing offences or matters of complaint, thus time began to run from the happening of the particular event; *Marshall v Smith* (1873) LR 8 CP 416, 29 JP 36 (wall erected contrary to byelaw); *R v Wimbledon Justices, ex p Derwent* [1953] 1 QB 380, [1953] 1 All ER 390, 117 JP 113 (letting exceeding maximum permitted rent); *Vaughan v Biggs* [1960] 2 All ER 473, [1960] 1 WLR 622, 124 JP 341 (depositing and leaving litter); *Gurdev Singh v R* [1974] 1 All ER 26, [1973] 1 WLR 1444, 138 JP 85 (non-patrial remaining unlawfully in the United Kingdom beyond time limit); *British Telecommunications plc v Nottingham County Council* [1999] Crim LR 217, DC (failing to comply with prescribed requirements when reinstating highway, New Roads and Street Works Act 1991, ss 70, 71 and 95(2)); *John Mann International Ltd v Vehicle Inspectorate* [2004] EWHC 1236 (Admin), 169 JP 171 (failure to comply with notice to produce records (without prejudice to service of further notices), Transport Act 1968, s 99.
12. *DPP v McCabe* [1992] Crim LR 885.
13. *DPP v Baker* [2004] EWHC Admin 2792, (2005) 169 JP 140.
14. *R (on the application of Chief Constable of West Mercia Constabulary) v Boorman* [2005] EWHC Admin 2559, (2005) 169 JP 669.

1–388 *Description of offence.* An information should describe the offence in ordinary language avoiding as far as possible the use of technical language and should give such particulars as may be necessary to provide reasonable information about the nature of the charge. It is not necessary to state all the elements of the offence or negative any matter upon which the accused may rely. Where the offence charged is statutory, the description of the offence must contain a reference to the section of the Act, or the rule, order regulation, bylaw or other instrument creating the offence[1]. Where a particular act constitutes the offence, it is enough to describe it in the words of the statute[2], but where particular means to effect the object are essential to the description of the offence, they should be stated; for example the nature of an alleged deception, or unlawful purpose, or document falsified, etc. Where a statutory provision has been substituted by an amending statute, the words "as substituted by" should be used instead of the words "as amended"[3]. The form of information should state the name and address of the party charged and of the person laying the information, and the offence, when and where it was committed, which must be within the court's jurisdiction[4]. If the informant cannot name the precise day, it will be sufficient to allege the offence to have been committed between stated days[5]. Similarly it had been held at a time when justices only had a national jurisdiction where an offence was indictable, that if the place of commission of an indictable offence was unknown and immaterial to the issue, such particulars might be omitted[6].

1. Criminal Procedure Rules 2005, r 7.2, in this PART, STATUTORY INSTRUMENTS AND PRACTICE DIRECTIONS ON PROCEDURE, post.
2. See *Ex p Grant* (1857) 28 LTOS 266, 21 JP 70.
3. *Jones v Thomas* [1987] Crim LR 133.
4. Magistrates' Courts Act 1980, ss 1–3.
5. *Onley v Gee* (1861) 25 JP 342.
6. *R v Wallwork* (1958) 122 JP 299.

1–389 *Duplicity.* Several accused may be joined in the same information if the act alleged allows the participation of several persons. An information must be for one offence only[1], although a single document may contain more than one information and indeed that single document may have a preamble containing particulars common to a number of otherwise separate allegations without infringing the rule[2]. A charge is bad for *duplicity* when it alleges facts constituting two different activities[3], although it is proper to include in a single charge, facts indicating more than one act, provided that they can be collectively described as the components of a single activity. For example, a single charge of taking and killing two red deer without a licence in the same location and virtually at the same time, was held to be descriptive of a single offence[4]; taking, killing and pursuing game without a licence is a charge of one offence[5]; several counts in an indictment each charging theft from different departments of the same store are not bad for duplicity[6], nor is an information which alleges possession of more than one obscene article, since it charges only one criminal activity[7]; driving without due care and attention where a motorist was seen driving erratically by two police officers in separate observations two miles and ten minutes between observations was held to constitute one continuous activity[8] as was the felling, without a licence, of 90 trees over a period of 3 days[9] and the theft of 76 library books over a two-and-a-half year period[10]. However informations under Seeds Regulations in which were named several purchasers were held to be bad for duplicity[11] as was an information which alleged that a motor vehicle had been driven after consuming so much alcohol that the proportion of it in the defendant's "breath/blood/urine" exceeded the prescribed limit[12]. Two or more complainants may be named in one charge under s 1 of the Protection from Harassment Act 1997; and, if the complainants were "a close knit definable group" and the acts complained of constitute pursuing a single course of conduct aimed at the group, there is no unfairness to the defendant and such a charge is not bad for duplicity merely because only one of the complainants was present on a particular occasion[13]. There is no compelling reason why the expression 'offence or offences' in s 1(1) of the Criminal Law Act 1977 should be construed conjunctively; therefore, a count alleging conspiracy as a single agreement to contravene either s 49(2) of the Drug Trafficking Act 1994 or s 93C(2) of the Criminal Justice Act 1988, contrary to s 1 of the 1977 Act is not bad for duplicity[14]. It is not an essential characteristic of a criminal offence that any prohibited act or omission, in order to constitute a single offence, should take place once and for all on a single day. It may take place, whether continuously or intermittently, over a period of time[15]. Accordingly, an information, alleging that the defendant has on and since a specified date permitted land to be used in contravention of an enforcement notice, is not bad for duplicity since it only alleges a single offence[15]; similarly an information which alleges, over a period of time, management of a brothel, charges a single transaction and is not bad for duplicity[16]. The words "aiding, abetting, counselling *and* procuring" constitute but one offence[17]. Special provision is made for the mode of charging offences specified in the First Schedule to the Children and Young Persons Act 1933[18]. In breach proceedings, where two separate kinds of breach are alleged – for example, failing to keep in touch and failing to reside where directed – there is a need to lay separate informations in respect of each of the kinds of breach, though within each kind there is no need to allege each of the instances separately[19].

1. Criminal Procedure Rules 2005, r 7.3, in this PART, STATUTORY INSTRUMENTS AND PRACTICE DIRECTIONS ON PROCEDURE, post.
2. *DPP v Shah* [1984] 2 All ER 528, [1984] 1 WLR 886, 149 JP 169, HL.
3. *R v Ballysingh* (1953) 37 Cr App Rep 28. See also post para **1–440** and notes to Criminal Procedure Rules 2005, Part 7.
4. *Jemmison v Priddle* [1972] 1 QB 489, [1972] 1 All ER 539, 136 JP 230 under s 4 of the Game Licences Act 1860.

5. *Laxton v Jeffries* (1893) 58 JP 318.
6. *R v Wilson* (1979) 69 Cr App Rep 83. See also *Heaton v Costello* (1984) 148 JP 688, [1984] Crim LR 485, and *Barton v DPP* [2001] EWHC Admin 223, 165 JP 779 (where the court found no discernible prejudice or unfairness to the defendant in regarding 94 till thefts over a 12-month period as a continuous offence.
7. *R v Crown Court at Bristol, ex p Willets* (1985) 149 JP 416, [1985] Crim LR 219.
8. *Horrix v Malam* (1984) 148 JP 30, [1984] RTR 112.
9. *Cullen v Jardine* [1985] Crim LR 668.
10. *DPP v McCabe* (1993) 157 JP 443.
11. *Ministry of Agriculture, Fisheries and Food v Nunn Corn (1987) Ltd* [1990] Crim LR 268.
12. *R v Bolton Justices, ex p Khan* [1999] Crim LR 912.
13. *DPP v Dunn* [2001] 1 Cr App Rep 352, 165 JP 130, [2001] Crim LR 130, DC.
14. *R v Hussain* [2002] 2 Cr App Rep (S) 255.
15. *Hodgetts v Chiltern District Council* [1983] 2 AC 120, [1983] 1 All ER 1057, HL, (Town and Country Planning Act 1990, s 179(6)) and see *Camden London Borough Council v Marshall* [1996] 1 WLR 1345 (failure to execute works in accordance with notice under s 352, Housing Act 1985 s 376(1)).
16. *Anderton v Cooper* (1980) 145 JP 128, [1981] Crim LR 177 (Sexual Offences Act 1956, s 33).
17. *Stacey v Whitehurst* (1865) 18 CBNS 344, 29 JP 136; *Re Smith* (1858) 3 H & N 227, 22 JP 450.
18. Children and Young Persons Act 1933, s 14 in PART V: YOUTH COURTS, post.
19. *S v Doncaster Youth Offending Team* [2003] EWHC Admin 1128, (2003) 167 JP 381.

1–400   Death of informant.   In case of death of informer before the hearing, the proceedings do not lapse but may be continued[1].

1. *R v Truelove* (1880) 5 QBD 336, 44 JP 346.

1–401   Issue of summons or warrant.   When an information has been laid[1], a justice or the justices' clerk must apply his mind to the information, and go through the judicial exercise of deciding whether or not a *summons* or a *warrant* ought to be issued by him[2]. His initial concern will be to see that the information discloses an offence known to law, that he has territorial jurisdiction to act[3], that the date of the alleged offence is within any limitation of time[4], and that any necessary consents to prosecution have been obtained[5]. When considering whether to issue a summons, the justice or justices' clerk has jurisdiction to refuse to issue a summons if to issue a summons would be vexatious and improper even if there were evidence of the offence[6]. A warrant is not to be issued initially for a minor offence[7], nor for any offence where a summons would be equally effectual, except in cases of a very serious nature[8]. If a warrant is to be issued, the information must be in writing[9].

1. See *R v Manchester Stipendiary Magistrate, ex p Hill* [1983] 1 AC 328, [1982] 2 All ER 963, 146 JP 348 (information "laid" when delivered to court office).
2. Magistrates' Courts Act 1980, s 1, in this PART: STATUTES ON PROCEDURE, post; see also cases noted thereto.
3. See ante para **1–382**.
4. See ante para **1–387**.
5. See ante para **1–380**.
6. See *R v Belmarsh Magistrates' Court, ex p Watts* [1999] 2 Cr App Rep 188.
7. Magistrates' Courts Act 1980, s 1(4), in this PART: STATUTES ON PROCEDURE, post.
8. *O'Brien v Brabner* (1885) 49 JP Jo 227.
9. Magistrates' Courts Act 1980, s 1, in this PART: STATUTES ON PROCEDURE, post.

1–402   Private prosecution.   It was held in *R (on the application of Charlson) v Guildford Magistrates' Court and the South Western Magistrates' Court and Walsh (interested party)*[1], in relation to applications by private prosecutors for the issue of summonses, that:

"20. Bearing in mind that the Code for Crown Prosecutors does not apply to private prosecutions, the following principles seem . . . to be applicable:
(i) When magistrates are considering whether to accede to issue a summons for private prosecution, where the Crown Prosecution Service has already brought and discontinued a prosecution arising from the same events, the magistrate should not require special circumstances before agreeing to the issue of the summons.
(ii) In (such a case as aforesaid) the magistrates should ascertain, in deciding whether to issue a summons: (a) whether the allegation is an offence known to the law and, if so, whether the ingredients of the offence are prima facie present; (b) that the issue of the summons for the offence . . . is not time barred; (c) that the court has jurisdiction; (d) whether the information has the necessary authority to prosecute; and (e) any other relevant facts.
(iii) In the different situation where magistrates are considering whether to accede to an application to issue a summons for a private prosecution, where the Crown Prosecution Service has already brought a prosecution which is still proceeding, the magistrate should in the absence of special circumstances be slow to issue a summons at the behest of a private prosecutor against a defendant who already had to answer one or more prosecutions by the Crown Prosecution Service in respect of the same matter."

1. [2006] EWHC 2318 (Admin), (2006) 170 JP 739, [2006] RTR 1 (explaining the decision in *R v Tower Bridge Metropolitan Stipendiary Magistrate, ex p Chaudhry* [1994] 1 All ER 44, [1993] 3 WLR 1154, [1994] RTR 113).

1–403   Limited discretion.   The discretion to issue a summons is not unfettered or unlimited. The general principle is that the magistrates ought to issue summonses pursuant to informations properly laid unless there are compelling reasons not to do so, most obviously if an abuse of the process or impropriety is involved. The justice should not adopt the role of the court of trial and refuse summonses on the basis that the charges would be 'overloaded' and should not seek to determine the number of offences that would meet the justice of the case. It is not the function of the magistrates' court at the stage of issue to decide how the matter can thereafter most fairly be tried or dealt with[1].

1. *R (London Borough of Stratford) v Stratford Magistrates' Court* [2004] EWHC 2506 (Admin) 2506, 168 JP 658.

1–404   *Form etc of summons or warrant.* The form of a summons or warrant is prescribed[1]. A single summons may be issued against a person in respect of several informations, provided it sets out the subject matter of each[2]. A series of summonses may be issued by the same justice if the first cannot be served[3]. However, where a summons has been issued based on a fresh information, it is referable only to that information which must be laid within any relevant time limits otherwise the proceedings will be invalid[4]. The justice or justices' clerk may hear a potential defendant, but that defendant has no right to be heard[5]. There is no obligation on the justice or justices' clerk to make inquiries to satisfy himself that it will not be vexatious to issue a summons[6].

1. See Criminal Procedure Rules 2005, Parts 7 and 18, this PART, STATUTORY INSTRUMENTS ON PROCEDURE, post.
2. Criminal Procedure Rules 2005, Part 7, in this PART: STATUTORY INSTRUMENTS ON PROCEDURE, post.
3. *Ex p Fielding* (1861) 25 JP 759.
4. *R v Network Sites Ltd, ex p London Borough of Havering* (1997) 161 JP 513, [1997] Crim LR 595, DC.
5. *R v West London Justices, ex p Klahn* [1979] 2 All ER 221, [1979] 1 WLR 933, 143 JP 390.
6. *R v Clerk to the Bradford Justices, ex p Sykes and Shoesmith* [1999] Crim LR 748, 163 JP 224.

1–405   *Delay.* It is undesirable for the informant to leave the laying of the information until the last possible moment. When considering an information and whether a summons should be issued, the justice or the justices' clerk should raise a question as to date if it appears from the date given that the information is being laid outside any time limit. If the query is not satisfactorily resolved, by amendment or other explanation, then it will be appropriate for him to refuse to issue the summons[1].

The issue of a summons must not be delayed to the prejudice of a defendant[2], and it must be served a reasonable time before the hearing[3]. Justices have a judicial discretion to decline to proceed, when service of a summons is delayed for so long as to be unconscionable, or to produce substantial prejudice to the accused[4].

1. *R v Blackburn Justices, ex p Holmes* (1999) 164 JP 163, [2000] Crim LR 300, DC.
2. *R v Fairford Justices, ex p Brewster* [1976] QB 600, [1975] 2 All ER 757, 139 JP 574.
3. *R v Benn and Church* (1795) 6 Term Rep 198; *R v Stafford Justices* (1835) 5 Nev & MKB 94; *R v Jenkins* (1862) 26 JP 775; *R v North, ex p Oakey* [1927] 1 KB 491.
4. *R v Watford Justices, ex p Outrim* [1982] LS Gaz R 920 (summons served 22 months after issue). See also, ante, para **1–447 Abuse of the process of the court**.

1–406   *Service of summons.* The method of service of a summons is prescribed by Rule, with a number of special provisions under particular Statutes[1]. The court has no power to direct the prosecutor that a particular method of service be employed[2].

1. See Criminal Procedure Rules 2005, Part 4, this PART: STATUTORY INSTRUMENTS ON PROCEDURE, post and notes thereto.
2. *Durham County Council v North Durham Justices* [2004] EWHC 1073 (Admin), 168 JP 269.

1–407   *Defendant outside the jurisdiction.* A summons may be issued requiring a person charged with an offence to appear before a magistrates' court, notwithstanding that the person in question is outside the United Kingdom, and the summons may be served outside the United Kingdom in accordance with arrangements made by the Secretary of State[1]. A summons requiring a person to attend before a court in the United Kingdom for the purpose of giving evidence in criminal proceedings similarly may also be served outside the United Kingdom[1]. There is no comparable provision for a warrant of arrest to be issued for execution outside the United Kingdom. However, an information may be laid and a warrant may be issued and held pending the return of the accused person to this country, or proceedings may be commenced to secure his return[2]. Despite the differences in legal systems, provision is made for the mutual execution throughout the United Kingdom (ie England & Wales, Northern Ireland and Scotland) of warrants of arrest and the service of summonses[3]. As regards the British Islands (ie the Isle of Man and the Channel Islands) the same provisions apply for the service of a summons as apply to other countries outside the United Kingdom ie in accordance with arrangements made by the Secretary of State[4]; provision is also made for the execution of warrants of arrest[4].

1. Criminal Justice (International Co-operation) Act 1990, s 2, in this PART: STATUTES ON PROCEDURE, post.
2. See PART VIII: title EXTRADITION, FUGITIVE OFFENDERS, BACKING OF WARRANTS, post.
3. See post Criminal Law Act 1977, s 39 (service of summons for offence) and the Criminal Justice and Public Order Act 1994, s 136 (execution of warrant of arrest for offence), in this PART: STATUTES ON PROCEDURE, post.
4. See post, Indictable Offences Act 1861, s 13 as extended by the Magistrates' Courts Act 1980, s 126, in this PART: STATUTES ON PROCEDURE, post.

1–408   *Continuing effect of summons or warrant.* A warrant of arrest remains in force until executed or withdrawn[1], but the Queen's Bench Divisional Court may order its withdrawal if it is plain that no criminal offence has been committed by the person against whom the warrant has been issued; *a quashing order* would issue[2].

A warrant or summons issued by a justice of the peace shall not cease to have effect by reason of his death or his ceasing to be a justice[3].

---

1. Magistrates' Courts Act 1980, s 125, in this PART: STATUTES ON PROCEDURE, post.
2. *R v Crossman, ex p Chetwynd* (1908) 72 JP 250.
3. Magistrates' Courts Act 1980, s 124, in this PART: STATUTES ON PROCEDURE, post.

CRIMINAL PROCEDURE RULES AND THE OVERRIDING OBJECTIVE

1–409 Rules of court[1] govern the practice and procedure to be followed in the criminal courts[2]. These rules are made by the Criminal Rules Committee[3] and are supplemented by Practice Directions made by the Lord Chief Justice, which include the *Practice Direction (crime: consolidated)* [2002][4] and the *Practice Direction (Costs: Criminal Proceedings)* [2004][5]. Pre-existing provisions for court forms are replaced by forms to be issued as an Annex to the *Practice Direction (crime: consolidated)* [2002][6].
The overriding objective of the new procedural code is that criminal cases be dealt with justly[7]. This includes: acquitting the innocent and convicting the guilty; dealing with the prosecution and the defence fairly; recognising the rights of a defendant, particularly those under Article 6 of the European convention on Human Rights; respecting the interest of witnesses, victims and jurors and keeping them informed of the progress of the case; dealing with the case efficiently and expeditiously; ensuring that appropriate information is available to the court when bail and sentence are considered; and dealing with the case in ways that take into account the gravity of the offence alleged, the complexity of what is in issue, the severity of the consequences for the defendant and others affected and the needs of other cases[8].
Each participant in a case has a duty to prepare and conduct the case in accordance with the overriding objective, comply with the Criminal Procedure Rules, practice directions and directions made by the court and at once inform the court and all parties of any significant failure to take any procedural step required by the Criminal Procedure Rules[9].
The court must further the overriding objective in particular when exercising any power given to it by legislation, applying any practice direction or interpreting any rule or practice direction[10].

"The prevailing approach to litigation is to avoid determining cases on technicalities (when they do not result in real prejudice and injustice) but instead to ensure that they are decided fairly on their merits. This approach is reflected in the Criminal Procedure Rules and, in particular, the overriding objective. Accordingly, ... absent a clear indication that Parliament intended jurisdiction automatically to be removed following procedural failure, the decision of the court should be based on a wide assessment of the interests of justice, with particular focus on whether there was a real possibility that the prosecution or the defendant may suffer prejudice. If that risk is present, the court should then decide whether it is just to permit the proceedings to continue."[11]

The overriding objective requires that notice be given to a child victim of alleged sexual abuse who was to be a prosecution witness of a defence application for disclosure of her medical and psychiatric records[12].
The former rule-making power for magistrates' courts[13] has been amended[14] so as to repeal those procedural rules formerly applying in magistrates' courts criminal and family proceedings and in effect to restrict the powers in that section to the making of procedural rules in civil proceedings only. Accordingly, those rules contained in pre-existing secondary legislation continue to apply so far as they extend to civil proceedings and the new Criminal Procedure Rules apply to criminal proceedings whether in being or commenced on or after 4 April 2005[15]. For the Criminal Procedure Rules reference should also be made to the website[16].

---

1. Criminal Procedure Rules 2005, in this PART: STATUTORY INSTRUMENTS AND PRACTICE DIRECTIONS ON PROCEDURE, post.
2. Courts Act 2003, s 69(1), in this PART: STATUTORY INSTRUMENTS AND PRACTICE DIRECTIONS ON PROCEDURE, post.
3. Courts Act 2003, s 69(2), in this PART: STATUTORY INSTRUMENTS AND PRACTICE DIRECTIONS ON PROCEDURE post. More information about the Criminal Procedure Rules Committee is on www.dca.gov.uk/dept/rulecomms/criminalprc.htm.
4. Para **1–6970**, post.
5. Para **1–7390**, post.
6. See para I.14 and Annex D in para **1–6970**, post.
7. Criminal Procedure Rules 2005, r 1.1(1), in this PART: STATUTORY INSTRUMENTS AND PRACTICE DIRECTIONS ON PROCEDURE, post.
8. Criminal Procedure Rules 2005, r 1.1(2), in this PART: STATUTORY INSTRUMENTS AND PRACTICE DIRECTIONS ON PROCEDURE, post.
9. Criminal Procedure Rules 2005, r 1.2, in this PART: STATUTORY INSTRUMENTS AND PRACTICE DIRECTIONS ON PROCEDURE, post.
10. Criminal Procedure Rules 2005, r 1.3, in this PART: STATUTORY INSTRUMENTS AND PRACTICE DIRECTIONS ON PROCEDURE, post.
11. *R v Ashton, R v Draz, R v O'Reilly* [2006] EWCA Crim 794, [2007] 1 WLR 181, [2006] Cr App R 15, at para 9 per Fulford J.
12. *R (on the application of B) v Stafford Combined Court* [2006] EWHC 1645 (Admin), [2007] 1 All ER 102.
13. Ie section 144 of the Magistrates' Courts Act 1980, in this PART: STATUTES ON PROCEDURE, post.
14. Schedule 8, para 245(2)(*a*) to the Courts Act 2003.
15. The new rules have the same effect as the former rules.
16. www.hmcourts-service.gov.uk.

1–420   Case management and the Criminal Case Management Framework.   A criminal court is under a duty to further the overriding objective in particular by actively managing the case[1]. This includes: the early identification of the real issues; the early identification of the needs of witnesses; achieving certainty as to what must be done, by whom and when, in particular by the early setting of a timetable for the progress of the case; monitoring the progress of the case and compliance with directions; ensuring that evidence, whether disputed or not, is presented in the shortest and clearest way; discouraging delay, dealing with as many aspects of the case as possible on the same occasion, and avoiding unnecessary hearings; encouraging the participants to co-operate in the progression of the case; and making use of technology[2]. Any directions should be given as early as possible[3]. In turn the parties must actively assist the court in fulfilling its duty without, or if necessary, with a direction and apply for a direction if needed to further the overriding objective[4]. Case management forms must be used where these are prescribed otherwise no specific formality is required[5] and the court must make available to the parties a record of directions given[6]. The Criminal Procedure Rules are complemented by the *Criminal Case Management Framework*[7] whose purpose *"is to provide a clearer understanding of what should be done at each stage of the trial process, so that cases are prepared appropriately and can be brought to a conclusion with efficiency, the minimum of delay and without adjournments"*[8].

---

   1. Criminal Procedure Rules 2005, r 3.2(1), in this Part, Statutory Instruments and Practice Directions on Procedure, post.
   2. Criminal Procedure Rules 2005, r 3.2(2), in this PART, STATUTORY INSTRUMENTS AND PRACTICE DIRECTIONS ON PROCEDURE, post.
   3. Criminal Procedure Rules 2005, r 3.2(3), in this PART, STATUTORY INSTRUMENTS AND PRACTICE DIRECTIONS ON PROCEDURE, post.
   4. Criminal Procedure Rules 2005, r 3.3, in this PART, STATUTORY INSTRUMENTS AND PRACTICE DIRECTIONS ON PROCEDURE, post.
   5. Criminal Procedure Rules 2005, r 3.11(1), in this PART, STATUTORY INSTRUMENTS AND PRACTICE DIRECTIONS ON PROCEDURE, post.
   6. Criminal Procedure Rules 2005, r 3.11(2), in this PART, STATUTORY INSTRUMENTS AND PRACTICE DIRECTIONS ON PROCEDURE, post.
   7. In this PART, CODES OF PRACTICE AND GUIDELINES, post.
   8. Foreword by the Lord Chief Justice to the *Criminal Case Management Framework* (Second edition July 2005).

1–421   *Case progression officers.*   At the beginning of a case (unless the court otherwise directs) each party is required to nominate an individual responsible for progressing the case and give contact details and the court will nominate the case progression officer in the court administration with responsibility for the case whose duties are to monitor compliance with directions; make sure that the court is kept informed of events that may affect the progress of the case; make sure that he can be contacted promptly about the case during ordinary business hours; act promptly and reasonable in response to communications about the case; and if he will be unavailable, appoint a substitute[1].

---

   1. Criminal Procedure Rules 2005, r 3.4, in this PART, STATUTORY INSTRUMENTS AND PRACTICE DIRECTIONS ON PROCEDURE, post.

1–422   *Case management powers of the court.*   The court may give any direction and take any step actively to manage a case unless that direction or step would be inconsistent with legislation and in particular may appoint a judge, magistrate, justices' clerk or assistant to manage the case; give a direction on its own initiative or on application by a party; ask or allow a party to propose a direction; receive applications and representations be letter, telephone or other form of electronic communication and conduct a hearing by such means; give a direction without a hearing; fix, postpone, bring forward, extend or cancel a hearing; shorten or extend a time limit fixed by a direction; require that issues in the case should be determined separately, and decide in what order they will be determined; and specify the consequences of failing to comply with a direction[1]. A magistrates' court may give a direction that will apply in the Crown Court if the case is to continue there and vice versa and the court may vary or revoke a direction[2].

   It has been held in relation to preliminary hearings in the Crown Court in accordance with s 29 of the Criminal Procedure and Investigations Act 1996 that the case management powers of the court are extensive. They include the power to deal with matters preliminary to trial exclusively by means of written submissions and to specify the length of such submissions. Defendants should be provided with copies of the submissions as should representatives of the media present at any hearing. The court is not bound to allow oral submissions and is entitled to put a time limit on them[3].

---

   1. Criminal Procedure Rules 2005, r 3.5(1), in this Part, Statutory Instruments and Practice Directions on Procedure, post.
   2. Criminal Procedure Rules 2005, r 3.5(3), (4), (5), in this PART, STATUTORY INSTRUMENTS AND PRACTICE DIRECTIONS ON PROCEDURE, post.
   3. *R v K (Note)* [2006] EWCA Crim 724, [2006] 2 All ER 552, [2006] Crim LR 1012.

1–423   *Progressing a case.*   At every hearing, if the case cannot be concluded there and then the court must give directions so that it can be concluded at the next hearing or as soon as possible after that[1]. Steps that the court should take where relevant include: if the defendant is absent, the decide whether to proceed in his absence; take the defendant's plea, or ascertain whether he is likely to plead guilty or not guilty; set a timetable for the progress of the case; ensure judicial continuity and, where appropriate and practicable, that of the parties' representatives; identify responsibility for failure to comply with a direction and take appropriate action[2].

As regards trials, each party must: comply with the court's directions; take every reasonable step to ensure the attendance of his witnesses; make appropriate arrangements to present written or other material; and promptly inform the court and other parties of anything that may affect the date or duration of the trial or significantly affect the progress of the case[3]. The court may require a party to give a certificate of readiness[4]. The court may also require a part to identify: the order of his witnesses and which will give oral evidence; whether he requires the compelling of a witness to attend; any arrangements he proposes to facilitate the giving of evidence by a witness and the participation of any other person, including the defendant; the written evidence to be introduced and any other material; whether he intends to raise any points of law; and the timetable he proposes and expects to follow[5].

---

1. Criminal Procedure Rules 2005, r 3.8(1), in this PART: STATUTORY INSTRUMENTS AND PRACTICE DIRECTIONS ON PROCEDURE, post.
2. Criminal Procedure Rules 2005, r 3.8(2), in this PART: STATUTORY INSTRUMENTS AND PRACTICE DIRECTIONS ON PROCEDURE, post.
3. Criminal Procedure Rules 2005, r 3.9(2), in this PART: STATUTORY INSTRUMENTS AND PRACTICE DIRECTIONS ON PROCEDURE, post.
4. Criminal Procedure Rules 2005, r 3.9(3), in this PART: STATUTORY INSTRUMENTS AND PRACTICE DIRECTIONS ON PROCEDURE, post.
5. Criminal Procedure Rules 2005, r 3.10, in this PART: STATUTORY INSTRUMENTS AND PRACTICE DIRECTIONS ON PROCEDURE, post.

1–423A   Time limits.   The Criminal Procedure Rules prescribe that certain procedural steps must be taken within prescribed time limits with the court having a discretionary power to shorten or extend a time limit. In the case of applications to admit evidence of bad character under Part 35 it has been held that time limits must be observed but that the exercise of its discretion by the court is not restricted to exceptional circumstances. In exercising its discretion, the court will closely scrutinise the application and have regard to the following:

–   the objective of the Rules to deal with all cases efficiently and expeditiously;
–   the furtherance of the overriding objective;
–   the reasons for the failure (set out clearly);
–   whether the other party was prejudiced by the failure.

One factor relevant to prejudice caused by short notice arising from a late application is when the party was first made aware that an application would be made eg at an earlier directions hearing. The fact that the court is made aware of the facts of any previous conviction by, for example, reading the details in the application form, does not preclude it from determining whether to grant an extension of time; the court will put those matters out of mind. Whether the details of previous convictions are in any event relevant to an application to extend time limits, remains to be decided[1].

---

1. *R (Robinson) v Sutton Coldfield Magistrates' Court* [2006] EWHC 307 (Admin), [2006] 4 All ER 1029, [2006] 2 Cr App R 13, 170 JP 336.

EARLY FIRST HEARINGS AND EARLY ADMINISTRATIVE HEARINGS

1–424   Where an accused person has been charged with an offence at a police station, the magistrates' court before whom he appears or is brought for the first time in relation to the charge may, unless the accused is to be dealt with under s 51 of the Crime and Disorder Act 1998, consist of a single justice[1]. At an early administrative hearing conducted by a single justice—

(1)   the accused shall be asked whether he wishes to receive legal aid; and
(2)   if he indicates that he does, his eligibility for it shall be determined, and
(3)   if it is determined that he is eligible for it, the necessary arrangements or grant shall be made for him to obtain it[2].

At such a hearing the single justice may exercise, subject to the above requirements, such of his powers as a single justice as he thinks fit and on adjourning the hearing, may remand the accused in custody or on bail[3].

An early administrative hearing may be conducted by a justices' clerk acting as a single justice, save that the justices' clerk shall not remand an accused person in custody or, without the consent of the prosecutor and the accused, remand the accused on bail on conditions other than those, if any, previously imposed[4]. Any requirement under Part I of the Police and Criminal Evidence Act 1984 for a person to be brought before a magistrates' court is satisfied if the person appears or is brought before the justices' clerk at an early administrative hearing[5].

Detailed provision is made in the *Criminal Case Management Framework* for what is expected of a first hearing[6]. The aim of the parties should be to proceed to sentence where appropriate. In particular, in the case of purely summary offences, a plea should be taken, in the case of an either way offence, the plea before venue procedure should be dealt with.

---

1. Crime and Disorder Act 1998, s 50(1), in this PART: STATUTES ON PROCEDURE, post.
2. Crime and Disorder Act 1998, s 50(2), in this PART: STATUTES ON PROCEDURE, post.
3. Crime and Disorder Act 1998, s 50(3), in this PART: STATUTES ON PROCEDURE, post.
4. Crime and Disorder Act 1998, s 50(4), in this PART: STATUTES ON PROCEDURE, post.
5. Police and Criminal Evidence Act 1984, s 47A, in this PART: STATUTES ON PROCEDURE, post.
6. Pre-Court Process Parts 5–8, in this PART: CODES OF PRACTICE AND GUIDELINES, post.

1–424A   Use of live link at preliminary hearings where accused in custody.   Where it appears to the court before which a preliminary hearing is to take place that the accused is likely to be held in custody during the hearing, the court, after giving the parties the opportunity to make representations, may give a live link direction ie a direction requiring the accused to attend through a live link from the place at which he is being held[1]. A "live link" is an arrangement by which a person is able to see and hear, and to be seen and heard by, the court during a hearing[2]. A "preliminary hearing" means any hearing before the start of the trial ie where the trial is to be on indictment when a guilty plea is accepted or the jury is sworn or, in the case of a summary trial, where the court accepts a guilty plea or begins to hear evidence for the prosecution at the trial or considers whether to exercise its powers to make a hospital order without convicting the accused[3]. The court must give a direction where it has the power to do so or give its reasons for not doing so[4]. A live link hearing may be used in prescribed circumstances for a sentencing hearing[5].

1. Crime and Disorder Act 1998, s 57B, in this PART: STATUTES ON PROCEDURE, post.
2. Crime and Disorder Act 1998, s 57A, in this PART: STATUTES ON PROCEDURE, post.
3. Prosecution of Offences Act 1985, s 22(11B), Crime and Disorder Act 1998, s 57A, in this PART: STATUTES ON PROCEDURE, post.
4. Crime and Disorder Act 1998, s 57B(6), in this PART: STATUTES ON PROCEDURE, post.
5. See para **3–33 Sentencing hearing by live link**, post.

1–425   Advance information.   In addition to the provisions on disclosure[1], in the case of an offence triable either way, the prosecution are obliged in prescribed circumstances to supply the accused with *advance information*; this must comprise either copies of those parts of statements on which the prosecutor seeks to rely or a summary of the facts and matters of which the prosecutor proposes to adduce evidence[2]. The procedure for furnishing advance information is prescribed by rules of court[3]. In the light of the obligation under article 6 of the European Convention on Human Rights[4], where advance information has not be made, including proceedings for a purely summary offence, the court must assess the impact of non-disclosure on the fairness of the trial as a whole[5]. It is submitted that there is nothing to prevent a magistrates' court ordering disclosure where fairness dictates that such a step be taken.

1. See para **1–602**, post.
2. Criminal Law Act 1977, s 48 and Criminal Procedure Rules 2005, Part 21, in this PART: STATUTORY INSTRUMENTS AND PRACTICE DIRECTIONS ON PROCEDURE.
3. Criminal Procedure Rules 2005, Part 21, in this PART, MAGISTRATES' COURTS, PROCEDURE, post.
4. See para **1–604 Disclosure by prosecution: position under the European Convention on Human Rights**.
5. *Ex p Imbert* [1999] 2 Cr App R 276.

ABSENCE OF PARTIES

1–426   Where, at the time and place appointed for the trial or adjourned trial of an information, the prosecutor appears but the accused does not, the court may proceed in his absence[1], subject to the requirements of Article 6 (1) of the European Convention on Human Rights[2], or it may adjourn and, if the offence is punishable with imprisonment in the case of a person who has attained the age of 18, issue a warrant for his arrest[3]. If the accused appears but the prosecutor does not, the court may dismiss the information or, if evidence has been received on a previous occasion, proceed in the absence of the prosecutor[4], or it may adjourn[5]. If neither the accused nor the prosecutor appears, the court may dismiss the information, or if evidence has been received on a previous occasion, it may proceed in their absence[6], or may adjourn[5].

1. Magistrates' Courts Act 1980, s 11, in this PART, post, and see also Criminal Procedure Rules 2005, r 4.1 (method of service) and r 4.2 (proof of service), in this PART: STATUTORY INSTRUMENTS AND PRACTICE DIRECTIONS ON PROCEDURE, post and *R v Seisdon Justices, ex p Dougan* [1983] 1 All ER 6, [1982] 1 WLR 1479, 147 JP 177.
2. See *Ekbetani v Sweden* (1988) 13 EHRR 504, *Ensslin v Germany* (1978) 14 DR 64 and *Colozza v Italy* (1985) 7 EHRR 516. In particular, any waiver of the right of the accused to be present must be clear and unequivocal: *Colozza v Italy*, *Poitrimol v France* (1993) 18 EHRR 130, *Lala v Netherlands* (1994) 18 EHRR 586 and *Pelladoah v Netherlands* (1994) 19 EHRR 81.
3. Magistrates' Courts Act 1980, s 13, in this PART: STATUTES ON PROCEDURE, post, note particularly the restrictions on the use of a warrant when s 12 procedure has been employed.
4. Magistrates' Courts Act 1980, s 15, in this PART: STATUTES ON PROCEDURE, post.
5. Magistrates' Courts Act 1980, s 10, in this PART: STATUTES ON PROCEDURE, post.
6. Magistrates' Courts Act 1980, s 16, in this PART: STATUTES ON PROCEDURE, post. See para **1–428 Proceeding in the absence of the accused**, post.

1–427   When accused is deemed to be present.   This basic statement of the law is subject to important qualifications. A party represented by counsel or a solicitor shall be deemed not to be absent, except where any enactment or a condition of a recognisance expressly requires his presence[1].

1. Magistrates' Courts Act 1980, s 122, in this PART: STATUTES ON PROCEDURE, post.

1–428   Proceeding in absence of the accused.   Guidance on proceeding in the absence of a defendant has been given in the *Practice Direction (criminal: consolidated) 2002*[1] at paras I.13.17 ff:

Trials in absence. I.13.17 A defendant has a right, in general, to be present and to be represented at his trial. However, a defendant may choose not to exercise those rights by voluntarily absenting himself and failing to instruct his lawyers adequately so that they can represent him and, in the case of proceedings before the magistrates' court, there is an express statutory power to hear trials in the defendant's absence (s 11 of the Magistrates' Courts Act 1980). In such circumstances, the court has discretion whether the trial should take place in his/her absence.

I.13.18 The court must exercise its discretion to proceed in the absence of the defendant with the utmost care and caution. The overriding concern must be to ensure that such a trial is as fair as circumstances permit and leads to a just outcome.

I.13.19 Due regard should be had to the judgment of Lord Bingham in *R v Jones* [2003] AC 1, [2002] 2 All ER 113 in which Lord Bingham identified circumstances to be taken into account before proceeding, which include: the conduct of the defendant, the disadvantage to the defendant, public interest, the effect of any delay and whether the attendance of the defendant could be secured at a later hearing. Other relevant considerations are the seriousness of the offence and likely outcome if the defendant is found guilty. If the defendant is only likely to be fined for a summary offence this can be relevant since the costs that a defendant might otherwise be ordered to pay as a result of an adjournment could be disproportionate. In the case of summary proceedings the fact that there can be an appeal that is a complete rehearing is also relevant, as is the power to re-open the case under s 142 of the Magistrates' Court Act 1980.

Where a defendant does not voluntarily absent himself from the trial, the threshold of unfairness is a comparatively low one, in particular where the defendant is a juvenile. It is an important consideration that a juvenile may not have the same development and understanding as an adult. A juvenile who is absent but not deliberately absent from his trial will not have the opportunity of responding to prosecution evidence as it is given at his trial and to provide instruction to those who represent him. Therefore a youth court was wrong to proceed in order to accommodate a prosecution witness where the juvenile was absent because he had been arrested and was detained by the police throughout those parts of the day upon which the prosecution case was heard although the case was adjourned to enable him to be present at the resumed hearing when he gave evidence[2].

The decision to proceed in the absence of the accused must be exercised judicially, with proper regard to the principle that a defendant is entitled to a fair trial; that must include a fair opportunity to be present to hear the evidence given against him, and, should he want to do so, to give evidence in his own defence and call witnesses. If a defendant claims to be ill with apparently responsible professional support for his claim, the court should not reject that claim and proceed to hear the case in the defendant's absence without satisfying itself that the claim may properly be rejected and that no unfairness will thereby be done[3]. The principle that the defendant should have a fair opportunity to be present does not amount to an unlimited opportunity or a defendant could indefinitely postpone the proceedings[4].

In *R v Hayward, R v Jones* and *R v Purvis*[5], Lord Justice Rose stated, after reviewing the relevant domestic and ECHR cases: "the principles which should guide the English courts in relation to the trial of a defendant in his absence are these: (1) A defendant has, in general, a right to be present at his trial and a right to be legally represented. (2) Those rights can be waived, separately or together, wholly or in part, by the defendant himself. They may be wholly waived if, knowing, or having the means of knowledge as to, when and where his trial is to take place, he deliberately and voluntarily absents himself and/or withdraws instructions from those representing him. They may be waived in part if, being present and represented at the outset, the defendant, during the course of the trial, behaves in such a way as to obstruct the proper course of the proceedings and/or withdraws his instructions from those representing him. (3) The trial judge has a discretion as to whether a trial should take place or continue in the absence of a defendant and/or his legal representative. (4) That discretion must be exercised with great care and it is only in rare and exceptional cases that it should be exercised in favour of a trial taking place or continuing, particularly if the defendant is unrepresented. (5) In exercising that discretion, fairness to the defence is of prime importance but fairness to the prosecution must also be taken into account. The judge must have regard to all the circumstances of the case including, in particular: (i) the nature and circumstances of the defendant's behaviour in absenting himself from the trial or disrupting it, as the case may be and, in particular, whether his behaviour was deliberate, voluntary and such as plainly waived his right to appear; (ii) whether an adjournment might result in the defendant being caught or attending voluntarily and/or not disrupting the proceedings; (iii) the likely length of such an adjournment; (iv) whether the defendant, though absent, is, or wishes to be legally represented at the trial or has, by his conduct, waived his right to representation; (v) whether an absent defendant's legal representatives are able to receive instructions from him during the trial and the extent to which they are able to present his defence; (vi) the extent of the disadvantage to the defendant in not being able to give his account of events, having regard to the nature of the evidence against him; (vii) the risk of the jury reaching an improper conclusion about the absence of the defendant; (viii) the seriousness of the offence, which affects defendant, victim and public; (ix) the general public interest and the particular interests of victims and witnesses that a trial should take place within a reasonable time of the events to which it relates; (x) the effect of delay on the memories of witnesses; (xi) where there is more than one defendant and not all have absconded, the undesirability of separate trials, and the prospects of a fair trial for the defendants who are present. (6) If the judge decides that a trial should take place or continue in the absence of an unrepresented defendant, he must ensure that the trial is as fair as the circumstances permit. He must, in particular, take reasonable steps, both during the giving of evidence and in the summing up, to expose weaknesses in the prosecution case and to make such points on behalf of the defendant as the evidence permits." While his lordship was, of course, referring to trial on indictment the same principles are relevant to summary proceedings[6].

In the subsequent appeal to House of Lords[7] it was affirmed that the Crown Court could conduct a trial in the absence of the defendant. In relation to the above check-list, Lord Bingham did not consider that the seriousness of the offence (see 5 (viii) above) was a relevant consideration. The overriding concern was that the trial, if conducted in absence, was as fair as the circumstances could permit and led to a just outcome. Those objects were equally important whether the offence was serious or relatively minor. Secondly, it was generally desirable that a defendant be represented even if he had voluntarily absconded.

When bailing an accused to a trial date, it should be made clear that, should he fail to attend, the trial will proceed in his absence and without legal representation. This will provide incontrovertible means of proof of his knowledge of, or indifference to the consequences of his failure to attend[8].

Before the court can proceed in the absence of the accused, it must be satisfied that the summons was served on him a reasonable time before the hearing, or that he had previously appeared in answer to the information[9]. If it decides to proceed, the court will have to receive proper evidence from the prosecution in the form of witnesses, or of written statements conforming to the requirements of s 9 of the Criminal Justice Act 1967, unless use is made of the procedure under s 12 of the Magistrates' Courts Act 1980 described in the next paragraph. An accused writing a letter in acknowledgement of the service of a summons for a summary offence, frequently invites the court to deal with the matter in his absence, but then goes on to present a defence. The case should be adjourned, and the accused notified to attend and plead not guilty. Where however such a letter simply contains mitigating circumstances, we are of opinion that, once a conviction has been announced, it may properly be read out to the court and taken into account by the magistrates, provided the prosecution do not object to matters stated therein.

If the court decides to proceed in the absence of the accused, and on hearing evidence discovers that the accused presented a defence when interviewed by a police officer, it is not open to the justices to dismiss the information because of doubts created by the prosecution evidence, but they should adjourn the case and notify the accused that he should attend and plead not guilty[9].

A rapid means of disposing of uncontested summary cases carrying not more than a maximum three months imprisonment and not being an offence specified in an order made by the Secretary of State, is provided by *s 12 of the Magistrates' Courts Act 1980*. The main features are as follows:

(1)   Summons is served together with the prescribed statement of facts or statements to be admitted under section 9 of the Criminal Justice Act 1967 and prescribed form of explanation enabling the accused to plead guilty and mitigate in his absence.

(2)   Clerk of the court informs the prosecutor of any written plea of guilty or subsequent withdrawal thereof.

(3)   If service has been proved, and a plea of guilty tendered and not withdrawn, the statement of facts and the mitigation will be read out to the court, exactly as written. The prosecutor need not be present.

(4)   If a claim for costs by the prosecutor against the accused has been notified to the accused in writing, that claim shall be brought to the attention of the court by the clerk of the court[10].

(5)   The court may (a) accept the plea and impose sentence, or (b) accept the plea and adjourn to determine the most appropriate method of dealing with the case, or (c) not accept the plea and adjourn for attendance of the accused or proof of the case by some other means.

(6)   Any adjournment, and the reason therefor, must be adequately notified to the accused, but no notice of adjournment is required in relation to an adjournment (a) which is for not more than four weeks; and (b) the purpose of which is to enable the court to proceed to hear and dispose of the case in the absence of the accused.

A court dealing with an accused in his absence, may take into account previous convictions for summary offences contained on a notice to cite which has been served on the accused[11], as well as particulars on a driving licence produced to the court[12]. Where a person is convicted of a summary offence under the Traffic Acts or the Road Traffic (Driver Licensing and Information Systems) Act 1989, the court may, if the accused is not present in person before the court, take account Where a person convicted of a summary offence under the Traffic Acts or the Road Traffic (Driver Licensing and Information Systems) Act 1989, the court may, if the accused is not present in person before the court, take account of any previous conviction or order arising from an offence involving obligatory endorsement which is specified in a statement that is produced to the court under s 13 of the Road Traffic Offenders Act 1988[13]. It may not pass a custodial sentence on an absent defendant, nor impose any disqualification except after an adjournment and notification to the accused[14].

Where an accused has failed to attend and the court instead of proceeding in the absence of the accused adjourns the trial where a summons has been issued the court may not issue a warrant unless the court is satisfied either that the summons was served on him a reasonable time before the trial or adjourned trial or that the adjournment is a second or subsequent adjournment of the trial, the accused was present on the last occasion and on that occasion the date of the hearing was determined. Where the court proposes to issue a warrant the offence must be imprisonable (if the accused has attained 18 years) or the court, having convicted him, proposes to impose a disqualification; that if it has previously received evidence or convicted the accused, the gravity of the offence makes it undesirable to continue the trial in his absence[15].

Where the person has previously been released on bail in the proceedings and is under a duty to surrender to the custody on a court, and fails to do so, the court may issue a warrant without more formalities[16].

Where the accused gives notification in writing that he desires to plead guilty without appearing before the court, but nevertheless does appear, the court may, if he consents, proceed as if he were absent[17].

---

1. In this PART: STATUTORY INSTRUMENTS AND PRACTICE DIRECTIONS ON PROCEDURE, post.
2. *R (R) v Thames Youth Court* [2002] EWHC Admin 1670, 166 JP 613, [2002] Crim LR 977.
3. *R v Bolton Justices, ex p Merna* (1991) 155 JP 612, [1991] Crim LR 848, DC.
4. *R v Ealing Magistrates' Court, ex p Burgess* (2001) 165 JP 82, [2000] Crim LR 855.
5. [2001] EWCA Crim 168, [2001] QB 862, [2001] 3 WLR 125, [2001] 2 Cr App Rep 156.
6. See *R (on the application of Whitehead) v Horseferry Road Magistrates' Court* [2001] EWHC Admin 492.
7. *R v Jones* [2003] AC1, [2002] UKHL 5, [2002] 2 All ER 113, [2002] 2 WLR 524, 166 JP 333.
8. *R v O'Hare* [2006] EWCA Crim 471, [2006] Crim LR 950.
9. *DPP v Gokceli* (1988) 153 JP 109, DC.
10. *R v Coventry Magistrates' Court, ex p DPP* [1990] RTR 193, 154 JP 765.
11. Magistrates' Courts Act 1980, s 104, in this PART: STATUTES ON PROCEDURE, post.
12. Road Traffic Offenders Act 1988, s 31(1), in PART IV: ROAD TRAFFIC, post.
13. See the Road Traffic Offenders Act 1988, s 13(3A) in: PART IV: ROAD TRAFFIC, post.
14. Magistrates' Courts Act 1980, s 11, in this PART: STATUTES ON PROCEDURE, post.
15. Magistrates' Courts Act 1980, s 13, in this PART: STATUTES ON PROCEDURE, post, note particularly the restrictions on the use of a warrant when s 12 procedure has been employed.
16. Bail Act 1976, s 7(1), in this PART: STATUTES ON PROCEDURE, post.
17. Magistrates' Courts Act 1980, s 12A, in this PART: STATUTES ON PROCEDURE, post.

PRELIMINARY ISSUES

1–429　In this section we include consideration of those processes preliminary to summary trial, either by a plea of guilty or the hearing of evidence. In these stages the procedural framework established by the Criminal Procedure Rules 2005[1] and the Criminal Case Management Framework[2] is particularly important.

---

1. In this PART, STATUTORY INSTRUMENTS AND PRACTICE DIRECTIONS ON PROCEDURE, post.
2. Second edition July 2005 in this PART, CODES OF PRACTICE AND GUIDELINES, post

---

1–440　Objection to the information or charge.　No objection shall be allowed to any information or complaint, or to any summons or warrant to procure the presence of the defendant, for any defect in it in substance or form, or for any variance between it and the evidence addressed on behalf of the prosecutor or complainant at the hearing of the information or complaint[1].

In practice the prosecutor may be required to amend the information to remedy an error in certain circumstances[2] and the court has a wide discretion to amend an information which will ordinarily be exercised in favour of an amendment unless that would result in injustice to the defendant[3]. There are three types of error which can occur in an information and in the summons based on it—

(a)　An error so fundamental that it cannot be rescued by any appropriate and reasonable amendment; this will cause the prosecution to fail without more.

(b)　An error substantial enough to require amendment; the court has the power to allow an amendment (the defence may be allowed an adjournment where it is placed at a disadvantage by the amendment).

(c)　An error so trivial that no amendment is required; if the defendant was always aware of the true basis of the information a conviction will be upheld even on an unamended information[4].

The critical issue for a court to determine when considering alleged defects is whether the information as framed created real unfairness. In deciding this the court is entitled to look at relevant extraneous material, such as any advance information which has been served[5].

Information and summons are sufficient in form if they comply respectively with the Criminal Procedure Rules 2005, Part 7[6]. It is the information which is the foundation of the justices' jurisdiction to hear the case and a warrant or summons is merely a process to compel the accused to appear[7]. Nevertheless, the court may not be able to proceed either in the presence of the accused or in his absence unless it is satisfied that process has been served upon him in the correct form[8].

If a defendant considers that the particulars provided in an information are insufficient the court has the power, at any time after the charge has been preferred, to require the prosecution to furnish him with better and more complete particulars. The defendant should raise this in advance of the trial[9].

Where at any stage in the trial it appears the information is duplicitous, the court will call upon the prosecutor to elect on which offence he requires the court to proceed. The court will strike out the offence on which he does not wish to proceed and try the information afresh. Where the prosecutor refuses to make the election, the information will be dismissed[10].

Where the prosecutor fails to amend a bad information it may be dismissed or a conviction quashed on appeal[11]. *Autrefois acquit* may be an answer to a second information[12]. Amendment can take place at any time until the justices are functus officio[13]. If the court finds there is a variance and intend to proceed, albeit changing the basis on which the case has been presented, the defendant must be informed of the change, so that he is given a fair chance to meet the case against him[14]. If it appears that the defendant has been misled by the variance, he may apply for an adjournment which the court must grant[14].

---

1. Magistrates' Courts Act 1980, s 123, this PART, post.
2. *Garfield v Maddocks* [1974] QB 7, [1973] 2 All ER 303, [1973] 2 WLR 888.
3. *DPP v Short* [2001] EWHC Admin 885, 166 JP 474.
4. *Garfield v Maddocks*, supra; *New Southgate Metals Ltd v London Borough of Islington* [1996] Crim LR 334.
5. *Dacre Son & Hartley Ltd v North Yorkshire Trading Standards* [2004] EWHC 2783 (Admin), 169 JP 59.
6. See this PART, STATUTORY INSTRUMENTS AND PRACTICE DIRECTIONS ON PROCEDURE, post, and para **1-381**, ante.
7. *R v Hughes* (1879) 4 QBD 614, 43 JP 556.
8. See Criminal Procedure Rules 2005, Part 4, this PART, STATUTORY INSTRUMENTS AND PRACTICE DIRECTIONS ON PROCEDURE, post.
9. *R v Aylesbury Justices, ex p Wisbey* [1965] 1 All ER 602, 129 JP 175, *Dacre Son & Hartley Ltd v North Yorkshire Trading Standards* [2004] EWHC 2783 (Admin), 169 JP 59.
10. Criminal Procedure Rules 2005, Part 7, this PART, STATUTORY INSTRUMENTS AND PRACTICE DIRECTIONS ON PROCEDURE, post.
11. See *Hunter v Coombs* [1962] 1 All ER 904, [1962] 1 WLR 573, 126 JP 300.
12. *Halsted v Clark* [1944] KB 250, [1941] 1 All ER 279, 108 JP 70.
13. *Allan v Wiseman* [1975] RTR 217, [1975] Crim LR 37. See also *R (on the application of James) v DPP* [2004] EWHC Admin 1663 (2004) 168 JP 596 (charged amended from "supply" to "attempted to supply" controlled drugs after the conclusion of the defence case).
14. *Morriss v Lawrence* [1977] RTR 205, [1977] Crim LR 170.

1-441   *Objection to summons.*   If a person attends voluntarily, that cures the want of process or any irregularity in service[1], but where a person attends before magistrates to bring to their attention an irregularity and then withdraws from the case, that does not constitute an appearance so as to waive irregularity in service[2]. Where the person appears he should be informed of the objection and his right to object because without that knowledge there can be no waiver[3]. Thereafter when the charge has been put to him, and he waives any objection, agrees to any amendment, does not request an adjournment and answers the charge, the case may properly proceed[4].

Where the defendant who is summoned before the court submits that the wrong person has been prosecuted, even where this is accepted by the prosecutor, it is not an objection to the form of process, but a defence to the charge. Accordingly in such circumstances, the information and summons cannot be amended to show the name of a different defendant. Similarly, where it is found that a summons has been addressed and served on the wrong company, it is not permissible to amend the information and summons by substituting the name of another company[5]. Nor may the name of the company be substituted for that of the secretary[6].

---

1. *R v Hughes* (1879) 4 QBD 614, 43 JP 556.
2. *Pearks, Gunston and Tee Ltd v Richardson* [1902] 1 KB 91, 66 JP 119 and see *Dixon v Wells* (1890) 25 QBD 249, 54 JP 725 (conviction quashed where defendant protested against informal summons).
3. *R v Essex Justices, ex p Perkins* [1927] 2 KB 475, 91 JP 94.
4. *Pearks, Gunston and Tee Ltd v Richardson* [1902] 1 KB 91, 66 JP 119 and see *Dixon v Wells* (1890) 25 QBD 249, 54 JP 725 (conviction quashed where defendant protested against informal summons).
5. *R v Greater Manchester Justices, ex p Aldi GmbH and Co KG* (1994) 159 JP 717; *Marco (Croydon) Ltd v Metropolitan Police* [1984] RTR 25, [1983] Crim LR 395.
6. *City of Oxford Tramway Co v Sankey* (1890) 54 JP 564.

1-442   *Amendment of information or summons.*   If the information discloses no offence in law, it is void *ab initio* and may be dismissed[1]. In deciding whether an offence is disclosed the whole information must be considered and the statutory provision cannot be ignored as it may cure, by making plain what might otherwise be ambiguous, what otherwise would be a defect in the information[2]. If a defective information is good enough to identify the alleged misdoing, it can be amended as long as it continues to allege the same misdoing[3]. Under Article 6(3)(a) of the European Convention on Human Rights everyone charged with a criminal offence has the right to be informed promptly, in a language he understands and in detail, of the nature and cause of the accusation against him. The purpose of this provision is to provide the accused with the information he needs to begin preparing a defence. The information provided must therefore be more specific than the grounds of arrest required under Article 5(2) of the Convention[4].

Omission or incorrect citation of Act—The omission of any reference to the section of an Act creating the offence, which would have led the defendant to understand exactly what was charged against him, may be fatal and not curable[5] but not always[6]. Where the words of an information followed precisely the words of the section, so that the defendant could not have been misled, it was held that the justices had properly allowed the information to be amended to include the section and Act to which the offence was contrary[7]. Similarly where the wrong year was cited for an Act but it was clear the defendant knew which Act was referred to[8] and where a repealed statute has been re-enacted[9]. An information alleging management of public entertainment otherwise than under a licence granted in accordance with para 1 of Sch 12 to the local Government Act 1963 contrary to paras 1 and 10(1)(a) of Sch 12 disclosed an offence although there was a failure to aver that it was an entertainment for which a licence was required or that a licence held did not cover the particular form of activity as reference to para 10(1) would resolve the ambiguity[10]. Similarly, an information alleging *use* of a motor vehicle on a road with excess alcohol in the blood contrary to s 5 of the Road Traffic Act 1988 could be amended to 'drove' as reference to s 5 precluded saying that the information did not disclose an offence known to law[11].

Different offence—The conviction of a defendant for a different offence from that stated in the information is wrong[12]. However, an information can be amended after the expiry of the six month period even to allege a different offence provided that (i) the different offence alleges the "same misdoing" as the original offence; and (ii) the amendment can be made in the interests of justice[13]. However, where the variation between the evidence and the information is slight and does no injustice to the defence, the prosecution may be permitted to amend the information even where a different offence is alleged more than six months after its commission[14].

Variation between the evidence and the information—Where the variance between the information and evidence cannot be said to cause any injustice to the defence, it should be disregarded, for example where the defendants moved a bicycle a mile and a half, left it, and then returned later the same day to remove useful spare parts, they could be convicted on an information which alleged theft at the place where the bicycle was first taken[15].

Defects in informations which have been held to be capable of amendment have included—

date of offence—date omitted[16]; wrong date[17].

place—incorrect description of premises[18]; place of offence not accurately expressed[19]; road misnamed[20].

name—defendant wrongly named[21] (but note that a different person may not be substituted[22]).

ownership—incorrect description[23].

vehicle—"trailer" substituted for 'motor lorry'[24].

In deciding whether to permit the amendment of an information to allege a different offence alleging the "same misdoing", the phrase should not be construed too narrowly; it means that the new offence should arise out of the same (or substantially the same) facts as gave rise to the original offence. Accordingly, where the amended charge arose out of the same facts, the defendant was not prejudiced; the evidence to be addressed was no different and the effect of the amendment was to reduce the gravity of the charge, the court acted reasonably in permitting the amendment of an information for an offence of assault occasioning actual bodily harm to one of common assault[25]. In considering whether it is in the interests of justice to allow such an amendment, the result that a defendant would face a significantly more serious charge will weigh heavily and perhaps conclusively against allowing such an amendment after the six-month time limit has expired. Also the necessity for a further adjournment might be a good reason for refusing an application to amend in view of the purpose of the six-month time limit[26]. An information may be amended so as to bring the offence date within the 6 month time limit provided that the evidence against the accused remains the same as for the original charge, that the decision to amend the information does not unduly delay the speed of the trial, and that the amendment was made in the interests of justice[27].Where an information under s 15(1) of the Food Safety Act 1990 failed to make clear which offence was alleged under that subsection, it could not be amended as it would not then refer to the "same wrong doing" and did not provide the offender with the salient facts of the offence of which he was accused[28].

---

1. *Garman v Plaice* [1969] 1 All ER 62, [1969] 1 WLR 19, 133 JP 114.
2. *Karpinski v City of Westminster* [1993] Crim LR 606; *DPP v Short* [2001] EWHC Admin 885, 166 JP 474.
3. *Simpson v Roberts* (1984) Times, 21 December, DC.
4. *GSM v Austria* (1983) 34 DR 119. See also *Brozicek v Italy* (1990) 12 EHRR 371.
5. *Atterton v Brown* [1945] KB 122, 109 JP 25.
6. *R v Doncaster Justices, ex p Doncaster Corpn* [1962] Crim LR 839.
7. *Thornley v Clegg* [1982] RTR 405, [1982] Crim LR 523.
8. *New Southgate Metals Ltd v London Borough of Islington* [1996] Crim LR 334.
9. *Meek v Powell* [1952] 1 KB 164, [1952] 1 All ER 347, 116 JP 116.
10. *Karpinski v City of Westminster* [1993] Crim LR 606.
11. *DPP v Short* [2001] EWHC Admin 885, 166 JP 474.
12. See *Lawrence v Same* [1968] 2 QB 93, [1968] 1 All ER 1191, 132 JP 277.
13. *R v Scunthorpe Justices, ex p McPhee and Gallagher* (1998) 162 JP 635, DC; *Simpson and Roberts*, ante; *R v Newcastle Justices, ex p John Bryce (Contractors) Ltd* [1976] 2 All ER 611, [1976] 1 WLR 517, 140 JP 440.
14. *R v Newcastle upon Tyne Justices, ex p John Bryce (Contractors) Ltd* [1976] 2 All ER 611, [1976] 1 WLR 517, 140 JP 440.
15. *Creek v Peck and Jones* (1983) 147 JP 537.
16. *R v Godstone Justices, ex p Secretary of State for the Environment* [1974] Crim LR 110.
17. *Exeter Corpn v Heaman* (1877) 42 JP 503.
18. *Fowler v St Mary's Abbot's Vestry* (1872) 36 JP 69.
19. *Moulder v Judd* [1974] Crim LR 111.
20. *Darnell v Holliday* [1973] Crim LR 366.
21. *Dring v Mann* (1948) 112 JP 270; *Allan v Wiseman* [1975] RTR 217, [1975] Crim LR 37.
22. See *R v Greater Manchester Justices, ex p Aldi GmbH and Co KG* (1994) 159 JP 717; *Marco (Croydon) Ltd v Metropolitan Police* [1984] RTR 25, [1983] Crim LR 395; *City of Oxford Tramway Co v Sankey* (1890) 54 JP 564.
23. *Ralph v Hurrell* (1875) 40 JP 119.
24. *Turberville v Wyer* [1977] RTR 29.
25. *R v Thames Magistrates' Court, ex p Stevens* (2000) 164 JP 233, DC.
26. *R v Scunthorpe Justices, ex p McPhee and Gallagher* (1998) 162 JP 635, DC (on the facts information for robbery amended to common assault). See also *R (on the application of DPP) v Everest* [2005] EWHC Admin 1124, (2005) 169 JP 345 (amendment to more serious offence held to have been refused rightly in the circumstances).
27. *R v Blackburn Justices, ex p Holmes* (1999) 164 JP 163, [2000] Crim LR 300, DC.
28. *Ward v London Borough of Barking and Dagenham* [1999] Crim LR 920, DC.

1–443 ***Withdrawal, substitution of information or charge.*** Clear authority exists enabling justices to grant an application to withdraw a summons without an adjudication[1].

Where a prosecutor abandons the charge on which the defendant appears before the court, and proposes to proceed on a new charge, a new information should be prepared and, if the defendant wishes it, the case adjourned so he can have time to answer the charge. If, in committal proceedings, the prosecutor offers no evidence on a charge to which the accused has elected trial by jury, and prefers a lesser charge which is triable only summarily, it is not necessarily an abuse of the process of the court[2]. If the defendant elects to continue with the case, he cannot later change his mind and object[3].

The prosecution do not have an unquestionable right to proceed on any charge they wish. It must, however, be shown that the substituted charge is inappropriate, and to justify a charge of abuse of process there must be shown to be bad faith on the prosecutor's part or unfairness or prejudice to the accused. It is the court's duty to enquire into the situation and ensure that its procedure is not being abused[4]. A delay of several weeks before replacing a charge of an either way offence with a summary offence does not necessarily prejudice a defendant and therefore does not amount to an abuse of process[5].

1. *R v Redbridge Justices, ex p Sainty* [1981] RTR 13.
2. *R v Canterbury and St Augustine Justices, ex p Klisiak* [1982] QB 398, [1981] 2 All ER 129, 145 JP 344.
3. *Egginton v Pearl* (1875) 40 JP 56; *Conn v Turnbull* (1925) 89 JP Jo 300; see also *Shepherd v Postmaster-General* (1864) 5 New Rep 80, 29 JP 166, Treat 338; and *Peek v De Rutzen* (1882) 46 JP 313.
4. *R v Liverpool Stipendiary Magistrates, ex p Ellison* [1989] Crim LR 369.
5. *R v Sheffield Justices, ex p DPP* [1993] Crim LR 136.

1–444 **Several offences.** Where two or more offences are charged at the same time, the court should inquire both of the prosecution and of the defence whether either side has any objection to all the informations being heard together. If consent to such a course is not forthcoming, the justices should rule as they think fit in the interests of justice[1].

Where consent to several informations being tried together is not forthcoming, the justices should then consider the rival submissions and, under any necessary advice from their clerk, rule as they think fit in the overall interests of justice. If the defendant is absent, they should seek the views of the prosecution and rule as they think fit. Absence of consent should not be regarded as a bar to hearing more than one information at the same time when in the justices' view the facts are sufficiently closely connected to justify that course and there is no risk of injustice to the defendant by its adoption. The justices should always ask themselves whether it would be fair and just to the defendant to allow a joint trial[1]. There is no objection in principle to hearing alternative charges together, and there will usually be powerful reasons (of convenience and cost) for doing so[2].

It is a matter of discretion for the court as to whether each trial should be before a differently constituted Bench of justices. They should refuse to try a second or subsequent case themselves if there would be real problems over approaching the matter in a proper and impartial manner[3].

Where a summons and a cross-summons arise out of informations founded on the same incident and the same set of facts, justices do not have power, even with the consent of the parties, to permit the hearing of the informations together[4].

1. *Chief Constable of Norfolk v Clayton* [1983] 2 AC 473, [1983] 1 All ER 984, 147 JP 161.
2. *R (on the application of the CPS) v Blaydon Youth Court* [2004] EWHC Admin 2296, (2004) 168 JP 638, [2005] Crim LR 495.
3. *R v Sandwich Justices, ex p Berry* [1982] Crim LR 121.
4. *R v Epsom Justices, ex p Gibbons* [1984] QB 574, [1983] 3 All ER 523, 148 JP 78.

1–445 **Several accused.** Several accused may be joined in the same information, and convicted together with separate penalties[1]. The acquittal of one co-defendant does not prevent the conviction of another co-defendant[2]. Where two or more defendants are charged on separate informations, but the facts are connected, the justices may, if they think fit, hear the informations together[3]. The justices should inquire both of the prosecution and of the defence whether any of the parties has an objection to all the informations being heard together. If consent to such a course is not forthcoming, the justices should rule as they think fit in the overall interests of justice[3]. Once the court has ordered separate trials, it has power to reverse its order only if fresh material arises[4].

Where the accused are jointly charged, it is for the court to decide on application whether they should be separately tried[5]. Accomplices alleged to have committed an offence when engaged in a common enterprise, may properly be tried together; there is no rule of law that there shall be separate trials where the defence of one accused is an attack upon another, but such a defence is a matter to be considered in deciding whether there should be separate trials[6]. Persons charged jointly with assault, are not entitled to sever their defences in order to give evidence for each other, but it is in the discretion of the court to permit them to do so[7]. A charge against a husband and a wife of knowingly making a false representation as to their means, may be made against both defendants in one information as they are charged with the same offence[8].

The practice of putting into the dock together defendants who are not jointly charged and have been arrested on different occasions or at different places is to be discouraged because it may give the impression of "group justice"[9].

Where consent to informations against two or more defendants being tried together is not forthcoming, the justices should have regard to the same considerations as those set out in paragraph

1–444 above in the case of a defendant who is charged on several informations[3]. The same principles apply where the prosecution as well as the defence ask for separate trials. The justices still have a discretion in such a case though they should be slow to exercise their discretion in favour of a joint trial when all the parties want separate trials[10].

Where cases against more than one defendant are heard separately, and some of the prosecution's evidence is common to all the cases, the court is not entitled to rely upon evidence given in an earlier case, not being the case then before them, to which the latter defendant has had no opportunity of directing cross-examination. However, where a number (3) of breathalyser cases raised an issue of admissibility in relation the same machine, the court was entitled to hear them together to avoid repetition of the same expert evidence, though the defendants were not co-accused; further the court was entitled not to allow witnesses of fact to be cross-examined on behalf of other defendants, and not to allow cross examination of expert witnesses on behalf of defendants who had not served a statement of those experts' evidence on the prosecutor or to take the evidence of those experts into account when considering the cases of those defendants[11].

As a matter of practice it is permissible to hold joint committal proceedings without the consent of the accused, if the charges alleged in the informations could properly be the subject matter of counts in one indictment[12].

We consider that where one person is charged as a principal, and another with aiding and abetting, both may be placed on the same information and treated as having been jointly charged. The situation in respect of motor vehicles is distinctive because inevitably only one person can drive a vehicle at a time. Therefore where one person is charged with driving a vehicle taken without the owner's consent and the other with allowing himself to be carried in it, they are properly to be regarded as being jointly charged[13].

It is desirable that the question of separate trials should be decided before any question of admissibility of evidence is considered[14].

1. *R v Lipscombe, ex p Biggins* (1862) 26 JP 244; *Wells v Cheyney* (1871) 36 JP 198.
2. *Barsted v Jones* (1960) 124 JP 400; *R v Andrews Weatherfoil Ltd* [1972] 1 All ER 65, [1972] 1 WLR 118, 136 JP 128; *R v Rowlands* [1972] 1 QB 424, [1972] 1 All ER 306, 136 JP 181.
3. *Chief Constable of Norfolk v Clayton* [1983] 2 AC 473, [1983] 1 All ER 984, 147 JP 161. See also *R v Liverpool Juvenile Court, ex p B* (1986) Times, 13 May.
4. *R v Bingham Justices, ex p Baxter* [1987] Crim LR 771.
5. *R v Cridland* (1857) 21 JP 404.
6. *R v Grondkowski, R v Malinowski* [1946] KB 369, [1946] 1 All ER 559, 110 JP 193.
7. *Paul v Summerhayes* (1878) 4 QBD 9, 43 JP 188, and see *Re Brighton Stipendiary Magistrate* (1893) 9 TLR 522.
8. *Macphail v Jones* [1914] 3 KB 239, 78 JP 367.
9. See *R v Mansfield Justices, ex p Sharkey* [1985] QB 613, [1985] 1 All ER 193, 149 JP 129.
10. *R v Highbury Corner Magistrates' Court, ex p McGinley* (1986) 150 JP 257.
11. *Skinner v DPP* [2004] EWHC 2914 (Admin), [2005] RTR 17.
12. *R v Camberwell Green Stipendiary Magistrates, ex p Christies* [1978] QB 602, [1978] 2 All ER 377, 142 JP 345.
13. *Ex p Allgood* (1994) Times, 25 November.
14. *R v Pervez and Khan* [1983] Crim LR 108.

1–446 Adults and minors jointly charged.   Several statutory provisions provide for special rules to apply to *joint charges against adults and minors*. They are as follows—

(1) A joint charge involving an adult (18+) and a minor (10–17) shall be heard by a magistrates' court that is not a youth court[1]. But if the adult (or a corporation) pleads guilty on summary trial and the minor pleads not guilty, the court may remit the minor to the youth court before any evidence is called. Likewise if the court proceeds to inquire into the information against the adult or corporation as examining justices, but proceeds to the summary trial of the minor who pleads not guilty, the court may remit the minor to the youth court[2].

(2) A charge against a minor may be heard by a magistrates' court that is not a youth court if an adult is charged at the same time, where either is charged with aiding, abetting, causing, procuring, allowing or permitting the other's offence[3]; or where the minor is charged with an offence arising out of circumstances which are the same as, or connected with, those giving rise to an offence with which the adult is charged at the same time[4].

(3) Normally a minor is tried summarily, unless he is charged jointly with an adult and the court considers it necessary in the interests of justice to commit them both for trial[5]. Where a minor and an adult are committed for trial, the court may also commit the minor for trial for any other indictable offence with which he is charged at the same time, if that offence arises out of circumstances which are the same as or connected with those giving rise to the joint offence[5].

(4) An adult court finding a minor guilty of an offence shall remit the case to a youth court to be dealt with, unless it is satisfied it would be undesirable to do so[6] and subject to the requirement that a minor in criminal proceedings must be able to participate effectively in those proceedings[7].

1. Children and Young Persons Act 1933, s 46(1) in PART V: YOUTH COURTS, post.
2. Magistrates' Courts Act 1980, s 29(2), in this PART: STATUTES ON PROCEDURE, post.
3. Children and Young Persons Act 1933, s 46(1); Children and Young Persons Act 1963, s 18 in PART V: YOUTH COURTS, post.
4. Children and Young Persons Act 1963, s 18 in PART V: YOUTH COURTS, post.
5. Magistrates' Courts Act 1980, s 24, in this PART: STATUTES ON PROCEDURE, post.
6. Powers of Criminal Courts (Sentencing) Act 2000, s 8 in PART III: SENTENCING, post and para **5–54 Remittal to Youth Court** in PART V: YOUTH COURTS, post.
7. See *T v United Kingdom* [2000] Crim LR 187, ECtHR.

1–447   Abuse of the process of the court.   The jurisdiction exercised by justices, to protect the court's process from abuse is confined to matters directly affecting the fairness of the trial of the accused, and it does not extend to the wider supervisory jurisdiction for upholding the rule of law which is vested in the High Court[1]. Accordingly, justices can halt a prosecution on the grounds of abuse of process, but the parameters of this power are set quite narrowly; it must not be used to exercise a disciplinary function over the prosecution, for example[2]. Nevertheless, justices have jurisdiction to investigate the *bona fides* of the prosecution, or of whether the prosecution has been instituted oppressively or unfairly. Since a justice has jurisdiction to refuse to issue a summons that is vexatious he also has jurisdiction to stay proceedings on such a summons at a later stage[3]. Under the Human Rights Act 1998 it is unlawful for any public authority, including magistrates' courts and prosecuting authorities, to act in a way which is incompatible with a right under the European Convention on Human Rights[4]. As to the "reasonable time" requirement of art 6 of the ECHR, see infra.

The minimum requirements for a fair hearing at a criminal trial are: (i) the defendant has to understand what he is said to have done wrong; (ii) the court has to be satisfied that the defendant, when he has done wrong by act or omission, has the means of knowing that was wrong; (iii) the defendant has to understand what defences, if any, were available to him; (iv) the defendant has to have a reasonable opportunity to make relevant representations if he wishes; and (v) the defendant has to have the opportunity to consider what representations he wishes to make once he has understood the issues involved. The defendant therefore has to be able to give proper instructions and to participate by way of providing answers to questions and suggesting questions to his lawyers in the circumstances of the case as they arisen.[5]

Delay may be an abuse of the process of the court[6]. The purpose of the six months limitation period is to ensure that summary offences are charged and tried as soon as reasonably possible after their alleged commission, so that the recollection of witnesses may still be reasonably clear, and so that there shall be no unnecessary delay in the disposal by the magistrates' courts of the summary offences brought before them[7]. Justices, or a justices' clerk, before exercising their discretion to issue a summons, are entitled to inquire why there has been delay in laying an information although the statutory time limit for the laying of the information has not passed[8]. However, it is preferable that the question of whether or not there has been an abuse of process in laying the information should be dealt with after the summons has been issued and in open court[8]. In proceedings before the Crown Court, where a defendant proposes to make an application to stay on indictment on the grounds of abuse of process, he must give 14 days' written notice to the prosecutor and any co-accused and lodge skeleton arguments with the court at least five days before the hearing. We would suggest that a similar procedure should apply in summary proceedings[9]. Justices have jurisdiction to investigate and to dismiss a summons on the ground that there has been an abuse of the process of the court[10]. The investigation must be a full one and the court must act on the correct legal principles[11] and the same principles apply to both regulatory offences and criminal offences in general[12]. It is not sufficient for the prosecution to give an explanation of the delay; the defence are entitled to call evidence[13]. The essential elements in granting relief are inordinate delay and prejudice, whether proved or inferred[14]. However, cases where relief can properly be granted in the absence of any fault on the part of the complainant or prosecution will be rare[14].

In considering the jurisdiction of the Crown Court to stay proceedings as an abuse of process, the Court of Appeal has held that the discretionary decision whether to grant a stay is an exercise in judicial assessment dependent on judgment rather than on any conclusion as to fact based on evidence and it is potentially misleading to apply to the exercise of that discretion the language of burden and standard of proof. Once the issue has been raised it is for the Crown to satisfy the court that a fair trial is still possible. Nevertheless, it must be for the defendant to raise the issue and to identify those respects in which he says that a fair trial is not possible. The correct approach when considering an application for a stay for abuse of process on the ground of delay is to bear in mind the following principles:

(1)   Even where delay is unjustifiable, a permanent stay should be the exception rather than the rule;

(2)   Where there is no fault on the part of the complainant or the prosecution, it will be very rare for a stay to be granted;

(3)   No stay should be granted in the absence of serious prejudice to the defence so that no fair trial can be held;

(4)   When assessing possible serious prejudice, the judge should bear in mind his or her power to regulate the admissibility of evidence and that the trial process itself should ensure that all relevant factual issues arising from delay will be placed before the jury for their consideration in accordance with appropriate direction from the judge;

(5)   If, having considered all these factors, a judge's assessment is that a fair trial will be possible, a stay should not be granted[15].

In cases where there is an issue whether the memory of child witnesses in relation to events a number of years before would be reliable, the better course is for the evidence to be heard before consideration of an abuse argument. In general, where the prosecution has given careful consideration to the decision to proceed having reviewed the evidence and interviewed the witnesses, there should not be an abuse argument as, unless the case is exceptional, the argument will fail[16]. Delay due merely to the complexity of the case or contributed to by the actions of the defendant himself should never be the foundation for relief[17]. However, this is subject to the requirement in Article 6(1) of the

European Convention on Human Rights that criminal proceedings be determined "within a reasonable time". This provision is designed to prevent a person charged from remaining "too long in a state of uncertainty about his fate"[18]. This guarantee runs from the moment that an individual is subject to a "charge" until proceedings are finally determined, including any appeal[19]. In view of the need for expedition in the case of juvenile offenders, different considerations may apply between adults and juveniles jointly charged[20].

In the case of summary offences, the police have an obligation, in order to effect service of the proceedings, to make proper efforts to trace the defendant at or through any address known to them, but there is no obligation on the police to be enterprising in their efforts to trace the defendant[21]. Comparison of the facts of allegations with those of decided cases will rarely be of assistance[22].

The above cases on delay must be read subject to the decision of the House of Lords in *A-G's Ref (No 2 of 2001)*[23] that, if through the action or inaction of a public authority, a criminal charge was not determined within a reasonable time there was necessarily a breach of the defendant's rights under article 6(1) of the Convention, and for such a breach there had to be afforded such remedy as was just and appropriate pursuant to s 8(1) of the Human Rights Act 1998.

The appropriate remedy would depend on the nature of the breach and all the circumstances, including particularly the stage of the proceedings at which the breach was established; but it would be appropriate to stay or dismiss the proceedings only if either a fair hearing was no longer possible or it would be, for any compelling reason, unfair to try the defendant. The public interest in the final determination of criminal charges required that such a charge should not be stayed or dismissed if any lesser remedy would be just and proportionate in all the circumstances.

In the absence of such unfairness the prosecutor and the court would not act incompatibly with the defendant's Convention right in prosecuting or entertaining proceedings after a breach had been established as the breach consisted in the delay which had accrued and not in the prospective hearing. If the breach were established retrospectively it would not be appropriate to quash any conviction unless the hearing was unfair or it had been unfair to try the defendant at all.

The category of cases in which it might be unfair to try a defendant included cases of bad faith, unlawfulness and executive manipulation but was not confined to such cases. However, such cases would be exceptional, and a stay would never be an appropriate remedy if any lesser remedy would adequately vindicate the defendant's Convention right.

Their lordships also confirmed that, as a general rule, time would begin to run for the purposes of art 6(1) from the earliest time at which a person was officially alerted to the likelihood of criminal proceedings being brought against him; and that such period would ordinarily begin when a defendant was formally charged or served with a summons rather than when he was arrested or interviewed under caution.

An excessive delay that breaches the defendant's rights under art 6 can be taken into account in deciding whether in all the circumstances there are grounds for mitigating the normal, points-disqualification consequences of the defendant motorist's conviction[24].

Acts done by the police with the intention of eavesdropping upon communications of suspected persons which are subject to legal professional privilege, are unlawful and capable of infecting the proceedings as an abuse of the court's process; while not every misdemeanour by police officers in the course of an investigation justifies a stay on grounds of abuse, and there are cases where prejudice or detriment to the defendant has to be shown, the court will not tolerate or endorse illegal conduct by police or state prosecutors which threatens or undermines the integrity of the justice system and the rule of law[25].

The soliciting by the police of funds from potential victims of fraud or another crime is, in addition to being ultra vires, fraught with all kinds of dangers; but where police officers did this in good faith, advice was taken and no prejudice was demonstrated, the judge was not wrong to refuse to stay the proceedings[26].

It may be an abuse of process if either (*a*) the prosecution have manipulated or misused the process of the court so as to deprive the defendant of a protection provided by the law or to take unfair advantage of a technicality, or (*b*) on the balance of probability the defendant has been, or will be, prejudiced in the preparation or conduct of his defence by delay on the part of the prosecution which is unjustifiable[27]. The prejudice must be serious to the extent that no fair trial can be held[16]. Accordingly, prosecutions have been stopped where a deliberate attempt has been made to gain further time by laying the information and delaying serving the summons[28], or by laying an information which was in the circumstances ambiguous in the sense that it could be read as referring to one or other of two inconsistent offences and failing to give further particulars before expiry of the limitation period[29]; or where there has been an unconscionable delay on the part of the prosecution in bringing the matter to court which leads to prejudice, unfairness and injustice to the defendant[30]; or where a person who has received a promise, undertaking or representation from the police that he will not be prosecuted is subsequently prosecuted[31]; or where the police interviewed a suspect without a solicitor, were minded to offer a caution, but refused a request by the suspect's solicitor for disclosure of the interview made so that he could advise on whether to accept a caution and then charged the suspect[32]; where the prosecutor sought to re-introduce a charge of driving with excess alcohol having earlier applied for it to be withdrawn on the defendant pleading guilty to two other road traffic offences[33];or where a further information was laid against a defendant acquitted of having an unmuzzled pitbull terrier in a public place who was allowed by the police to take the dog unmuzzled from police custody[34]; or where a company was prosecuted by a local authority for displaying advertisements without obtaining the necessary planning consents when the local authority's officers had informed a director of the company that planning consents were not required for the advertisement in question[35]; or where the prosecution took further witness statements between hearings of an adjourned trial and adduced evidence of those witnesses at the adjourned hearing[36]; or where the prosecution called a witness, contrary to a previous indication[37]; or where the prosecution had indicated in open court that at the next hearing they would offer no evidence[38] (aliter where the prosecution changes its mind in the course of proceedings as to which charge to proceed on in the light of comments from the court[39]). It is not an abuse of process to prosecute a person (under consumer protection legislation) where the background evidence is similar to that which was given in earlier proceedings brought by a different trading standards authority before a different court and that court had acquitted the defendant[40]. Local authorities must, however, consider with care the terms of their own prosecuting policy and ensure that all the relevant criteria are satisfied before proceeding[41].

Where a document incorporated both a requirement to provide information as to the identity of the driver, pursuant to s 172 of the Road Traffic Act 1988, and a conditional offer of fixed penalty, but the latter failed to comply with the requirement of s 75(7)(c) of the Road Traffic Offenders Act 1988 to specify a period, that defect did not did not preclude the commencement of proceedings outside the period of 28 days from the date of the offer (the fixed penalty clerk having given notification under s 76(5) of non payment of the fixed penalty following the expiry of that period), or render such a prosecution an abuse of process[42]. It would amount to an abuse of process as going to the fairness of trying an accused at all, for a private prosecution to be instigated against an accused who had been formally cautioned by the police where that caution had been induced by a representation that he would not be prosecuted[43]. The position has been held to be otherwise where the forms signed by the accused indicated in terms that such cautions did not preclude the bringing of proceedings by an aggrieved party[44] but the issue whether, irrespective of what may be said to an accused or stated in a form, it can ever be other than an abuse of process for a court thereafter to entertain a private prosecution against him has been considered by the House of Lords as one which might benefit from legislative attention or for resolving in any future litigation[43]. It is not an abuse where the police, in good faith had destroyed a video which they had viewed and decided that it contained nothing of value and there was nothing to show that the absence of the tape would affect the outcome of the trial[45]. As contempt proceedings and criminal charges have different purposes, there is no abuse in merely pursing criminal proceedings based on the same facts as had been the subject of a contempt hearing[46]. The issues in care proceedings are quite different and are focussed on the future upbringing of a child. Therefore, it is not an abuse of process to prosecute a person for the death of a child where a court considering care proceedings in respect of a surviving child is unable to decide responsibility for the death of the other child[47]. When determining whether or not to stay proceedings as an abuse of process where the basis of the application is the loss of video evidence, a court should approach the matter in the following way:

1. What was the nature and extent of the investigator/prosecutor's duty to obtain and/or retain the evidence? If none before the defence first sought its retention there could be no question of the trial being unfair on that ground.

2. If the evidence was not obtained and/or retained in breach of the obligations set out in the Code of Practice issued pursuant to ss 23 and 25 of the Criminal Procedure and Investigations Act 1996 and/or the Attorney-General's guidelines issued on November 29, 2000, then the following principles should be invoked: (a) the ultimate objective is to ensure that there should be a fair trial according to law; (b) this involves fairness to both the defence and the prosecution; (c) the trial process is equipped to deal with the bulk of complaints and there will only be a few cases in which a court will be able to conclude that a trial would be unfair; (d) it is commonplace in criminal trials for defendants to rely on holes in the prosecution case and if, in such a case, there is sufficient credible evidence, apart from the missing evidence, which, if believed, would justify a safe conviction, then a trial should proceed leaving the defendant to seek to persuade the court not to convict due to the unavailability, through no fault on his part, of the evidence in question; (e) often the absence of a video film is likely to hamper the prosecution as much as the defence.

3. If the behaviour of the prosecution has been so very bad that it would be unfair to put the defendant on trial the proceedings should be stayed. The most useful test is to ask whether there has been bad faith or at least some serious fault on the part of the police or the prosecution.

4. Where the complaint is raised on appeal from a conviction by justices the appellant should not seek a stay but ask the court to quash the conviction on the grounds his original trial was unfair and the nature of the unfairness was such that it cannot be remedied on appeal.

5. Where a lower court orders a stay it should give its reasons, however briefly, and the advocates have a professional duty to note those reasons[48].

Where incompetent storage by the prosecution rendered a sample unfit for scientific testing by the defence, and such testing could well have established a line of defence, it was not enough for the judge to exclude the prosecution's evidence of analysis, the proceedings should have been stayed; although the scientific examination of samples is subject to the same principles as above, this situation is very different from the situation where a videotape is unavailable but witnesses may be able to testify as to the relevant events[49].

Although serious failings in making disclosure caused by the negligence of the police or prosecution may make it unfair to try a person, that will be rare in the absence of serious misconduct. The essential question is whether a fair trial is possible. Late delivery of evidence even in breach of a court order, may cause delay but a fair trial may still be possible. Late notification of potential witnesses may not prejudice an accused if the witnesses are unlikely to be of use to him. Also, the destruction of some exhibits may not have caused any material prejudice to the defendant as a result[50].

Where a submission of abuse of process is founded upon the failure of the prosecution to comply with directions, however serious the default may be in general terms, it is unjust not to allow the prosecution to present an explanation for the default and/or to make submissions on whether the proceedings should be stayed as an abuse of process[51].

It is impermissible to prosecute a charge of indecent assault under s 14(1) of the Sexual Offences Act 1956 (now repealed) in circumstances where the conduct upon which that charge is based is only an act of unlawful sexual intercourse with a girl under the age of 16 in respect of which no prosecution may be commenced under s 6(1) by virtue of s 37(2) of and Sch 2 to the Act (time limit); however, in very many cases, even where the time limit has passed, there will be independent acts other than sexual intercourse itself, or conduct inherent in or forming part of it, on which a prosecution can properly be founded[52].

Where it is alleged that the police undertook illegal surveillance the proper remedy is to apply under s 78 of PACE to exclude the evidence thereby obtained and not to stay the proceedings as an abuse of process[53].

Police officers are entitled to revisit statement-makers, and while it would be quite improper for the police to put inaccurately the evidence to obtain a statement or a change in a statement from a witness, it must be remembered that it is not the statement that matters but the evidence that is ultimately given at the trial: *R v Evans*[54].

The six months' limit does however apply to the information or complaint and not to the issue of a summons thereon, which may be outside the period provided the information or complaint was within it. This will provide a safeguard where the defendant cannot be found for the time being. Where there is doubt whether an information was laid in time, it should be dismissed[55].

It is not appropriate to dismiss an information where the prosecutor was unaware that the defendant was in custody for another offence[56] nor generally for failure to conform to the advance information Rules[57]. It is an abuse of process where the defendant is prejudiced at his trial because the prosecution has prevented defence witnesses being available coupled with non-disclosure of evidence[58]. An information may be dismissed as an abuse even if brought within a statutory time limit; distress caused by needless delay whilst a sentencing factor, does not justify dismissal because it is not prejudicial to the preparation of the defence[59].

Where a person appeared before justices charged with an offence of driving with excess alcohol, and the prosecutor wished the trial of that offence to be disposed of summarily before commencing a prosecution against him for causing death by reckless driving, arising from the same circumstances and in which the prosecution relied on the consumption of excess alcohol as the basis for the allegation of recklessness, it was held that, in view of the reversal of the normal burden of proof with respect to the offences of driving with excess alcohol, it was a manipulation or misuse of the process of the court which would deprive the accused of a protection provided by law. Accordingly, since it would be an abuse of the process of the court to proceed in the manner proposed by the prosecution, prohibition was granted restraining the justices from continuing the summary trial[60].

Where a magistrates' court dismisses an information without having considered the merits of the case because of the failure of the prosecutor to attend court, there is no rule of law to prevent the court from dealing with an identical information subsequently laid against the same defendant, and the laying of a further information in such circumstances is not in itself an abuse of the process of the court[61]. However, where one justice has considered and ruled upon the question of whether a summons should be issued and has come to the conclusion that it should not be issued, if the matter is taken before a different justice it is a requirement that the second justice be informed what the first justice has decided. Any other course of action is a clear abuse of the process of the court[62].

Examining justices may consider whether an initiation of the process of committal is an abuse of process, but may not refuse to give consideration to the proceedings simply because they think a prosecution should not have been brought because it appears mean-minded, petty, or animated by personal hostility[63].

For consideration of the circumstances when a withdrawal or substitution of a charge may be an abuse of the process of the court, see para **1–443 Withdrawal, substitution of charge**.

---

1. *R v Horseferry Road Magistrates' Court, ex p Bennett* [1994] AC 42, [1993] 3 All ER 138, [1993] 3 WLR 90 and see *R v Staines Magistrates' Court, ex p Westfallen* [1998] 4 All ER 210, [1998] 1 WLR 652, [1998] Crim LR 414, DC. However, a magistrates' court has jurisdiction to stay extradition proceedings as an abuse of process and that jurisdiction is in addition to that of the High Court on an application for habeas corpus (however, it does not follow that there has been an abuse of process simply because the requesting state has instituted second proceedings following the failure of the first due to material non-disclosure)*(R (Kashamu) v Governor of Brixton Prison, R (Kashamu) v Bow Street Magistrates' Court, R (Makhlulif) v Bow Street Magistrates' Court* [2001] EWHC Admin 980, [2002] QB 887). The court's duty under s 51 of the Crime and Disorder Act 1998 to send indictable only cases to the Crown Court forthwith does not preclude it from staying the proceedings as an abuse of process, but it will be appropriate to do so only in rare cases where the defence establishes bad faith or serious misconduct; relatively novel or complex points should normally be left for resolution in the Crown Court or High Court (*R (Salubi) v Bow Street Magistrates' Court* [2002] EWHC 919 (Admin), [2002] 1 WLR 3073, [2003] Crim LR 111).

2. See *R v Derby Magistrates' Court, ex p Brooks*, infra, and *R v Merthyr Tydfil Magistrates' Court and Day, ex p DPP* [1989] Crim LR 148.

3. See *R v Belmarsh Magistrates' Court, ex p Watts* [1999] 2 Cr App Rep 188.

4. Human Rights Act 1998, s 6(1), in PART VIII: title HUMAN RIGHTS, post.

5. *R (on the application of Wotton) v Central Devon Magistrates' Court* [2003] EWHC 146 (Admin), [2003] All ER (D) 114 (Feb), [2003] 167 JPN, 102 (where a stroke had rendered the defendant unfit to stand trial).

6. In sexual cases the courts have been indulgent towards the prosecution in cases of even extreme delay in reporting the offence to the authorities, but it was held in *R v B* [2003] EWCA Crim 319, [2003] 2 Cr App R 13, which concerned a 30-year delay, that there remained in the Court of Appeal a residual discretion to set aside a conviction if it was felt to be unsafe and unfair, even where the trial process itself could not be faulted, and that while it was important that justice was done to the prosecution and to the victim, in the final analysis it was even more important that an injustice was not done to a defendant.

7. Per MAY J in *R v Newcastle upon Tyne Justices, ex p John Bryce (Contractors) Ltd* [1976] 2 All ER 611, [1976] 1 WLR 517, 140 JP 440.

8. *R v Clerk to the Medway Justices, ex p Department of Health and Social Security* (1986) 150 JP 401, [1986] Crim LR 686.

9. See further *Practice Direction (criminal: consolidated)* [2002] para IV.36, in this PART: STATUTORY INSTRUMENTS AND PRACTICE DIRECTIONS ON PROCEDURE, post.

10. See *R v Willesden Magistrates' Court, ex p Clemmings* (1987) 152 JP 286 (reinstating dismissed case).

11. *R v West London Stipendiary Magistrate, ex p Anderson* (1984) 148 JP 683, (principles to be applied to determine whether delay an abuse of the process of the court). See also *R v Crawley Justices, ex p DPP* (1991) 155 JP 841.

12. *R v South Tyneside Justices, ex p Mill Garages Ltd* (1995) Times, 17 April.

13. *R v Clerkenwell Stipendiary Magistrate, ex p Bell* (1991) 155 JP 669, DC.

14. *R v Gateshead Justices, ex p Smith* (1985) 149 JP 681; *R v Bow Street Stipendiary Magistrate, ex p DPP* (1989) 154 JP 237, [1990] Crim LR 318. See also *R (on the application of the DPP) v Croydon Youth Court* (2001) 165 JPN 34, where it was held that the re-institution of proceedings under s 22(B) of the Prosecution of Offences Act 1985 following the dismissal of an application to extend the time limit under s 22(A)(3) was not an abuse of process, even though the defence claimed that an independent witness could no longer be traced.

15. *R v S* [2006] EWCA Crim 756, [2006] 2 Cr App R 23, 170 JP 434.

16. *R v Smolinski* [2004] EWCA Crim1270, [2004] 2 Cr App R 40.

17. *A-G's Reference (No 1 of 1990)* [1992] QB 630, [1992] 3 All ER 169, CA.

18. *Stögmüller v Austria* (1969) 1 EHRR 155.

19. *Eckle v Germany* (1982) 5 EHRR 1. It was confirmed in *A-G's Reference (No 2 of 2001)* [2001] EWCA Crim 1568, [2001] 1 WLR 1869 that, for the purposes of art 6(1), the relevant period normally commences when the defendant is charged or served with a summons; if a defendant has been material prejudiced by the actions of the state prior to that, the period could commence earlier, but a police interview, by itself, would not normally amount to charging a suspect.

20. See *R (Knight) v West Dorset Magistrates' Court* [2002] EWHC 2152 (Admin), 166 JP 705.

21. *R v Canterbury and St Augustine's Magistrates' Court, ex p Barrington* (1993) 158 JP 325.

22. *R v Newham Justices, ex p C* [1993] Crim LR 130.

23. UKHL 68, [2004] AC 72, [2004] 1 All ER 1049, [2004] 2 WLR 1.

24. *Miller v DPP* [2004] EWHC 595 (Admin), [2005] RTR 3 (where two and a half years elapsed between the defendant's guilty pleas and sentence, and a further year was wasted over the appeal).

25. *Regina v Grant* [2005] EWCA Crim 1089, [2006] QB 60, [2005] 3 WLR 437, [2005] 2 Cr App R 28 (prosecution stayed where the police deliberately eavesdropped on and tape recorded legally privileged conversations between suspects and their lawyers, even though no actual prejudice had been caused).

26. *R v Hounsham, R v Mayes, R v Blake* [2005] EWCA Crim 1366, [2005] Crim LR 991.

27. *R v Derby Magistrates' Court, ex p Brooks* (1984) 148 JP 609, sub nom *R v Crown Court at Derby, ex p Brooks* (1984) 70 Cr App Rep 164; *R v Sunderland Magistrates' Court, ex p Z* [1989] Crim LR 56 and see *Sherwood and Hart v Ross, Steward, Ross and Raey* [1989] Crim LR 576. See also *R v Bow Street Stipendiary Magistrate, ex p DPP* (1989) 154 JP 237, [1990] Crim LR 318, (delay in service of a notice under reg 7 of the Police (Discipline) Regulations 1985 on a police officer may be a material consideration).

28. *R v Brentford Justices, ex p Wong* [1981] QB 445, [1981] 1 All ER 884.

29. *R v Newcastle-upon-Tyne Justices, ex p Hindle* [1984] 1 All ER 770.

30. *R v Oxford City Justices, ex p Smith* [1982] RTR 201; *R v Watford Justices, ex p Outrim* [1982] LS Gaz R 920.

31. *R v Croydon Justices, ex p Dean* [1993] QB 769, [1993] 3 All ER 129 and see *R v Townsend* [1998] Crim LR 126 and *R v South East Hampshire Magistrates' Court, ex p Crown Prosecution Service* [1998] Crim LR 422, DC (failure to respond to request for indication of likelihood of further proceedings, not a case of promise of no action).

32. *DPP v Ara* [2001] EWHC Admin 493, [2001] 4 All ER 559, [2002] 1 WLR 815, [2002] 1 Cr App Rep 159.

33. *DPP v Edgar* [2000] 164 JP 471.

34. *R v Liverpool Magistrates' Court, ex p Slade* [1998] 1 All ER 60, [1998] 1 WLR 531, [1998] 1 Cr App Rep 147, DC.

35. *Postermobile plc v Brent London Borough Council* (1997) Times, 8 December.

36. *DPP v Jimale* [2001] Crim LR 138, DC.

37. *R v Drury, Clark* [2001] Crim LR 847, CA.

38. *R v Bloomfied* [1997] 1 Cr App R 135.

39. *R v Mulla* [2003] EWCA Crim 1881, [2004] 1 Cr App R 6.

40. *North Yorkshire Trading Standards Service v Coleman* [2001] EWHC Admin 818, (2001) 166 JP 76.

41. *R v Adaway* [2004] EWCA Crim 2831, (2004) 168 JP 645 (Trading Standards had a policy to prosecute only where the individual or organisation had engaged in fraud or had deliberately or persistently breached regulations: as neither applied the prosecution was oppressive and should have been stayed).

42. *DPP v Holden* [2006] EWHC 658 (Admin), [2007] RTR 5.

43. *Jones v Whalley* [2006] UKHL 41, [2007] 1 AC 63, [2006] 4 All ER 113, [2007] 1 Cr App R 2, [2007] Crim LR 74.

44. *Hayter v L* [1998] 1 WLR 854, DC.

45. *R v Medway* [2000] Crim LR 415, CA.

46. *DPP v Tweddell* [2001] EWHC Admin 188, [2002] 1 FCR 438, [2002] 2 FLR 400.

47. *R v L* [2006] EWCA Crim 1902, [2006] 1 WLR 3092, [2007] 1 Cr App R 1, [2006] 2 FCR 723.

48. *R (on the application of Ebrahim) v Feltham Magistrates' Court*; *Mouat v DPP* [2001] EWHC Admin 130, [2001] 1 WLR 1293, [2001] Crim LR 741. (See also *R v Dobson* (2001) 165 JPN 554.)

49. *R v Boyd* [2002] EWCA Crim 2836, [2004] RTR 3.

50. *R v Sadler* [2002] EWCA Crim 1722, 166 JP 481.

51. *DPP v Ayres* [2004] EWHC 2553 (Admin), [2006] Crim LR 62.

52. *R v J* [2004] UKHL 42, [2004] 3 WLR 1019.

53. *R v Hardy* [2002] EWCA Crim 3012, [2003] 1 Cr App R 30.

54. [2001] EWCA Crim 730.

55. *Lloyd v Young* [1963] Crim LR 703.

56. *R v Merthyr Tydfil Magistrates' Court and Day, ex p DPP*, supra.

57. *King v Kucharz* (1989) 153 JP 336, DC.

58. *R v Schlesinger* [1995] Crim LR 137, CA.

59. *Daventry District Council v Olins* (1990) 154 JP 478, [1990] Crim LR 414.
60. *R v Forest of Dean Justices, ex p Farley* [1990] RTR 228, [1990] Crim LR 568.
61. *Holmes v Campbell* (1998) 162 JP 655.
62. *Gleaves v Insall* [1999] 2 Cr App Rep 466.
63. *R v Telford Justices, ex p Badhan* [1991] 2 QB 78, [1991] 2 All ER 854, 155 JP 481; and see *R v Rotherham Justices, ex p Brough* [1991] Crim LR 522, DC—prohibition where the prosecution arranged for an indictable only offence summons to be returnable after the accused attained the age of 17.

1-448   **Res judicata; estoppel; autrefois convict/acquit; functus officio.**   A matter adjudicated (*res judicata*) by a competent court cannot be re-opened (except by way of appeal). A matter will be *res judicata* only where the identical question once decided is again raised between the same parties[1]. If the facts necessary to prove an offence are not the same, a previous hearing does not make the matter *res judicata*. Where justices provisionally arrange for a part heard case to be tried by a fresh bench which could be convened earlier than they themselves could adjourn to, they could resume the hearing themselves[2]; where, however, they order the case to be relisted before a fresh bench as their earliest date might mean they were unable to remember the evidence, it is not open to the fresh bench to adjourn for the original bench to resume the hearing—they would be functus officio[3].

Where justices found no case to answer on a mistaken view as to the admissibility of certain evidence, and all the parties agreed there was an error, the process of adjudication had not been completed and the justices were not functus officio[4]. In contrast, where, having been refused a further adjournment to secure the attendance of the complainant, the prosecution offered no evidence and the information was dismissed, justices could not reopen the proceedings when it was discovered a few minutes later that the witness had arrived as any future hearing would inevitably give rise to a plea of autrefois acquit[5].

Estoppel is a rule of evidence whereby a party is precluded from denying certain facts. The doctrine of estoppel applies to civil but not to criminal proceedings[6].

1. *Leith Harbour and Docks Comrs v Inspector of the Poor* (1866) LR 1 Sc & Div 17; but see *R v Miles* (1890) 24 QBD 423, 54 JP 549; *Masper v Brown* (1876) 1 CPD 97, 40 JP 265; *Woodland v Woodland (otherwise Belin or Barton)* [1928] P 169. See also *Wright v General Omnibus Co* (1877) 2 QBD 271, 41 JP 486; *Dover v Child* (1876) 1 Ex D 172, 40 JP 296; *Ranson v Platt* [1911] 2 KB 291; *Karflex Ltd v Poole* [1933] 2 KB 251, [1933] All ER Rep 46.
2. *R v Telford Magistrates, ex p Cotton* (15 June 1987, unreported).
3. *R v Trafford Metropolitan Magistrates' Court, ex p Stott* [1989] Crim LR 149.
4. *Steward v DPP* [2003] EWHC 2251 (Admin), [2003] 4 All ER 1105, [2004] 1 WLR 592, (2004) 168 JP 146, [2004] RTR 16.
5. *R (O) v Stratford Youth Court* [2004] EWHC 1553 (Admin), 168 JP 469.
6. *DPP v Humphrys* [1976] 2 All ER 497, 140 JP 386, but see *R v Cwmbran Justices, ex p Pope* (1979) 143 JP 638, where it was held that there was an inherent power in the Divisional Court to inhibit any proceeding which might bear the stamp of oppressiveness or unfairness. For estoppel in civil proceedings, see para **1-751A**.

1-460   *Autrefois convict, autrefois acquit.*   A person cannot be tried for an offence if he has previously been acquitted or convicted of the same, or substantially the same, offence.

A plea of *autrefois acquit* or *autrefois convict* being presentable only at trial on indictment, cannot be entered in a magistrates' court[1] but the same principles apply[2]. Evidence must be given of the identity of the two offences[3].

The defendant who pleads *autrefois acquit* or *autrefois convict* must prove that the judgment or conviction has been legally given[4]. Although the plea of double jeopardy is available in civil proceedings, the plea of *autrefois convict* cannot jump the boundary between civil and criminal proceedings[5].

Where there has been an adjudication, whether or not there was a trial on the merits, the decision is binding and the matter cannot be prosecuted again[6]. However, a defendant may rely on the doctrine of autrefois acquit only where he was put in peril of a conviction on the earlier hearing; in proceedings before justices a defendant is not put in peril until he has been formally required to plead to the charge against him[7], and the mere fact that the defendant may have pleaded not guilty to the charge will not, of itself, amount to an adjudication on the merits, nor will it, of itself, amount to circumstances where it can be said that he has been in peril of conviction[8]. Where a magistrate convicted a person of assault, but later had his attention drawn to the fact that a prosecution witness had not been sworn and at once retried the case, it was held that the defendant had not been in peril on the first trial so the principle of *autrefois convict* did not apply[9]. Where a second information is preferred after a first information is dismissed, the issue is whether the defendant was at risk in relation to the first information and whether there had been sufficient adjudication upon it to bring the principle into operation; clearly he would not have been where the first information was sufficiently faulty in form and content. As a matter of procedure, however, the court may prefer not to adjudicate on either until having heard the evidence on the second information, then to make one comprehensive adjudication[10].

The plea is not available in respect of a judgment or conviction that has been reversed as erroneous in point of law[11]: nor in respect of an acquittal before a court having no jurisdiction to try the offence[12]; nor in respect of a conviction by justices, quashed on *certiorari* on the ground that it is bad on its face, the sentence being one that the justices have no jurisdiction to pronounce[13]. The plea of *autrefois convict* is not available where the offence had been dealt with by a domestic tribunal and not a court of competent jurisdiction[14]. A conviction or acquittal by a foreign court of competent jurisdiction could found a plea in bar to a subsequent English prosecution on the same facts, such a plea is not available when the accused has not in fact been before the foreign court and is not subject to a real risk or danger of punishment in consequence of the foreign conviction eg because he could not be extradited[15].

Where an offence is punishable under either of two statutes, a person who is convicted under one may not be subsequently prosecuted under the other[16]. Where a defendant agreed to two offences being tried together, and the facts were substantially the same, he was precluded from objecting to being convicted and punished on both charges as such agreement meant he was content to have one finding covering both charges[17]. However, where 2 charges are founded on the same facts it is inappropriate to convict the defendant of both of them[18].

A certificate of dismissal under s 44 of the Offences Against the Person Act 1861 is a bar to an indictment for unlawful wounding[19].

The plea of *autrefois acquit* or *convict* does not apply when the acquittal or conviction on the first charge does not necessarily involve an acquittal or conviction on the second, eg where the two offences are not substantially the same[20]. Thus, a conviction of wilful neglect of a child[21] who afterwards died, cannot be pleaded to a subsequent indictment for manslaughter[22]; nor is it an answer to a charge of theft that the defendant has already been acquitted of being in unlawful possession[23]. It is no answer to an information correctly charging an offence that the defendant had been acquitted on an information charging the offence as having been committed on a date clearly shown by the evidence not to have been committed on that date[24]. Where a fresh charge is preferred, the test to be applied is whether the acquittal on the first charge would necessarily involve an acquittal on the fresh charge[25].

If the information is dismissed for want of form, or from a mistaken view of jurisdiction, and without any adjudication on the merits, a second information may be laid and the plea of *autrefois acquit* will not avail[26]. So, where a statute required an information to be laid by a peace officer, and an information was laid by a person who was not such an officer, the defendant was rightly convicted under a second information laid by a peace officer[27]. Where a defendant was discharged because he was illegally arrested and not properly before the court, the Divisional Court held that there was an adjudication and refused a *mandamus* to the justices to hear the case again on a summons[28].

The withdrawal of a summons, with the consent of the justices, on a preliminary point or in consequence of an informality in the proceedings, is not equivalent to a dismissal or acquittal, and is therefore not a bar to subsequent proceedings[29]. Although the withdrawal of a summons, on the basis that the defendant was bound over, is not necessarily a bar to the issue of a second summons in respect of the same charge where the defendant has not been put in peril as a result of the first summons, a second summons will be set aside as an abuse of the process of the court if justices have issued it in ignorance of the first summons and its withdrawal[30].

The Crown Court has power to consider a plea in bar notwithstanding that an appellant has pleaded guilty. The rule that no person should be put in peril twice for the same offence is so fundamental that, when after a plea of guilty it is contended that there are grounds on which such a plea might be based, it is incumbent on the court to enquire into the circumstances to see whether such grounds exist[31].

1. The subject of *autrefois acquit* and *autrefois convict* was extensively reviewed by Lord Morris of Borth-y-Guest in *Connelly v DPP* [1964] AC 1254, [1964] 2 All ER 401, 128 JP 418.
2. See the Magistrates' Courts Act 1980, s 27, in this Part: Statutes on Procedure, post and notes thereto.
3. *Iremonger v Vissengo* [1976] Crim LR 524.
4. *R v Marsham, ex p Pethick Lawrence* [1912] 2 KB 362, 76 JP 208; *R v West* [1964] 1 QB 15, [1962] 2 All ER 624, 126 JP 352.
5. *R v Green* (1992) Times, 14 July (finding in civil proceedings of contempt, which involved a finding of assault; held this did not provide an effective plea in bar to criminal proceedings in which same assault was alleged). See also *R v Sherry, R v El Yamani* [1993] Crim LR 536.
6. See commentary in *R v Pressick* [1978] Crim LR 377 (justices refused an adjournment to a prosecutor who had no evidence to put before the court).
7. *Williams v DPP* [1991] 3 All ER 651, [1991] 1 WLR 1160.
8. *Islington Borough Council v Andreas Michaelides* [2001] EWHC Admin 468, [2001] 26 LS Gaz R 46 (summons for failure to comply with an enforcement notice marked withdrawn after not guilty plea had been entered, in contemplation of the imminent grant of a certificate of lawful development; but when that was later revoked due to non-disclosure and misrepresentation the authority was entitled to bring identical, fresh proceedings).
9. *R v Marsham, ex p Pethick Lawrence* (supra); followed in *Davis v Morton* [1913] 2 KB 479, 77 JP 223; cf *Bannister v Clarke* [1920] 3 KB 598, 85 JP 12; *R v Cronin* [1940] 1 All ER 618, 104 JP 216; *R v West* [1964] 1 QB 15, [1962] 2 All ER 624, 126 JP 352.
10. *DPP v Porthouse* (1988) 153 JP 57, [1989] RTR 177, DC.
11. *R v Drury* (1849) 18 LJMC 189.
12. *R v Bitton* (1833) 6 C & P 92; and see *R v Simpson* [1914] 1 KB 66, 78 JP 55.
13. *Conlin v Patterson* [1915] 2 IR 169.
14. *Lewis v Morgan* [1943] 1 KB 376, [1943] 2 All ER 272, 107 JP 156.
15. *R v Keith Thomas* [1985] QB 604, [1984] 3 All ER 34.
16. *Wemyss v Hopkins* (1875) LR 10 QB 378, 39 JP 549; quoted with approval in *Connelly v DPP* [1964] AC 1254, [1964] 2 All ER 401, 128 JP 418. See also s 18 of the Interpretation Act 1978, post.
17. *Williams v Hallam* (1943) 112 LJKB 353.
18. *Isaac v DPP* [2002] All ER (D) 168 (Oct), [2002] JPN 822.
19. *R v Elrington* (1861) 1 B & S 688, 26 JP 117; and see ss 44 and 45 of the Offences Against the Person Act 1861 in Part VII: title Persons, Offences Against, post.
20. *R v King* [1897] 1 QB 214, 61 JP 329; explained and distinguished in *R v Barron* [1914] 2 KB 570, 78 JP 311; *Bannister v Clarke* [1920] 3 KB 598, 85 JP 12; and see *Connelly v DPP* [1964] AC 1254, [1964] 2 All ER 401, 128 JP 418.
21. Under the Children and Young Persons Act 1933, s 1 in Part V: Youth Courts, post.
22. *R v Tonks* [1916] 1 KB 443, 80 JP 165.
23. *Flatman v Light* [1946] KB 414, [1946] 2 All ER 368, 110 JP 273.
24. *R v West* [1964] 1 QB 15, [1962] 2 All ER 624, 126 JP 352.

25. *R v Truro and South Powder Magistrates' Court, ex p McCullagh* (1990) 155 JP 411, [1991] RTR 374 (statutory defence under Road Traffic Acts available for first charge but not for second).

26. See *R v Ridgway* (1822) 5 B & Ald 527; *R v Herrington* (1864) 3 New Rep 468, 28 JP 485. See also *Broadbent v High* (1984) 149 JP 115.

27. *Foster v Hull* (1869) 33 JP 629.

28. *R v Brakenridge* (1884) 48 JP 293; see also *Halsted v Clark* [1944] KB 250, [1944] 1 All ER 270, 108 JP 70.

29. *Davis v Morton* [1913] 2 KB 479, 77 JP 223; *Owens v Minoprio* [1942] 1 KB 193, [1942] 1 All ER 30, 106 JP 53; *R (McDonnell) v Tyrone Justices* [1912] 2 IR 44.

30. *R v Grays Magistrates, ex p Low* [1988] 3 All ER 834, [1989] 2 WLR 948, 152 JP 627, DC.

31. *Cooper v New Forest District Council* [1992] Crim LR 877 (whether plea in bar available for repeated offence in breach of an enforcement notice).

1–461 Double jeopardy. Double jeopardy is, in effect, a discretionary extension of the rules of law defining the defences of autrefois convict and acquit. A second trial involving the same or similar facts may in the discretion of the court be stayed if to proceed would be oppressive or prejudicial and therefore an abuse of the process of the court[1]. Accordingly, whether a person accused of a minor offence is acquitted or convicted, he shall not be charged on the same facts in a more aggravated form[2], although this principle does not apply where the consequences have changed, ie where a person assaulted has died after a conviction for assault or wounding[3]. For the purpose of deciding whether or not a defendant has been placed in jeopardy, two possible situations should be considered. The first is the "temporal" question, namely whether the proceedings had reached such a stage that he was in peril of conviction; the second is "qualitative", whether the imperfections of the proceedings which led to the original decision in the defendant's favour was of such a kind that he would never have been in danger of conviction[4]. Article 4 of Protocol 7 to the European Convention on Human Rights embodies the prohibition on double jeopardy in criminal cases, subject to specific exceptions[5].

Where excess alcohol was the only foundation for a charge of causing death by reckless driving, and there was no dispute about the cause of death, it was held that the accused would be put in double jeopardy and that it would be oppressive and prejudicial if he were to be tried on indictment for causing death by reckless driving following a summary conviction for driving with excess alcohol. A stay restraining the justices from proceeding with the summary trial was accordingly granted[6]. However, where a defendant was charged with driving with excess alcohol and was subsequently but before plea further charged with dangerous driving arising from the same incident, and there was clear evidence of dangerous driving apart from excess alcohol and there was no question of the prosecution adopting to stratagem to obtain evidence for use against the defendant in the trial of the dangerous driving offence, the defendant's guilty plea to excess alcohol in the magistrates' courts did not give rise to double jeopardy or abuse of process in relation to his trial in the Crown Court on the charge of dangerous driving[7]. Where a woman died of carbon monoxide poisoning caused by the use of a defective gas fire and the landlord was convicted before justices of an offence under the Health and Safety at Work etc Act 1974 arising from a breach of duty to ensure that the appliance was properly maintained, it was held that the Crown Court should have ordered a stay on an indictment for manslaughter founded on the same facts. In so holding, the Court of Appeal said that the public interest in a prosecution for manslaughter and the concerns of the victim's family did not amount to special circumstances sufficient to justify a departure from the general rule[8].

Where a charge was dismissed because it was defective, either as a matter of law, or because the evidence was insufficient to sustain a conviction, or as a rationalisation or reorganisation of the prosecution case, it cannot properly be said that the defendant has ever been in jeopardy of a conviction[9].

Under of s 17 of the Criminal Justice Act 1967, where the prosecutor proposes to offer no evidence the court before which the defendant is arraigned may record a verdict of not guilty and that verdict has the same effect as an acquittal by a jury. Therefore, where no evidence was offered on a charge of common assault and the judge entered a verdict of not guilty, autrefois acquit prevented the prosecution from pursuing a charge of assault occasioning actual bodily harm on the same facts, the two offences having the same mens rea and, apart from actual bodily harm, the same actus reus. By virtue of s 27 of the Magistrates' Courts Act 1980 (see this part, post) the same would appear to apply to magistrates' courts[10].

1. See *Connelly v DPP* [1964] AC 1254, [1964] 2 All ER 401, HL.

2. *R v Elrington* (1861) 1 B & S 688, 26 JP 117.

3. See *R v Thomas* [1950] 1 KB 26, [1949] 2 All ER 662, CCA.

4. *Williams v DPP* [1991] 3 All ER 651, [1991] 1 WLR 1160 (where proceedings before magistrates had never reached the stage that the defendant was in peril of conviction on the information which he was called upon to answer because it had been dismissed as being wrongly laid before he was required to plead, it was held the prosecution were not prevented by the rule against double jeopardy from laying a fresh information in the correct form).

5. The UK has not yet ratified Protocol 7, but the government has indicated its intention to do so.

6. *R v Forest of Dean Justices, ex p Farley* [1990] RTR 228, [1990] Crim LR 568.

7. *R v Hartnett* [2003] EWCA Crim 345, [2003] Crim LR 719.

8. *R v Beedie* [1998] QB 356, [1997] 3 WLR 758, CA.

9. *R v Dabhade* [1992] 4 All ER 796, (1992) 157 JP 234. (Defendant charged with obtaining £6,000 cash by deception by falsely representing himself as payee on a cheque to which he consented to summary trial and pleaded not guilty; further charged with theft of £6,000 since the cheque in question was drawn to cash; prosecution offered no evidence on first charge which was dismissed, and defendant was committed for trial to the Crown Court where he took the point that the Crown Court ought not to proceed against him on the indictment because he had been lawfully acquitted of the offence contained therein. Held that since the first charge was so fundamentally incorrectly framed, the defendant was in no real sense ever in jeopardy on that charge; therefore the special plea in bar was rejected.)

10. *R v G (Autrefois Acquit)* [2001] EWCA Crim 1215, [2001] 1 WLR 1727 (not following *R v Brookes* [1995] Crim LR

630, CA), in which no reference was made to s 27, and by implication raising doubts about *DPP v Khan* [1997] RTR 82, DC, in which *Brookes* was followed, where it was held that where a defendant faced charges of inconsiderate and dangerous driving arising from the same incident, and he pleaded not guilty to both charges, and the prosecution offered no evidence on the lesser offence and he was acquitted of that offence, autrefois acquit did not prevent the prosecution from proceeding on the greater offence. However *R v Dabhade* [1993] QB 329, [1992] 4 All ER 796, [1993] 2 WLR 129, CA – autrefois acquit did not apply where a charge of theft was laid after no evidence had been offered on a charge of obtaining by deception, but the latter charge had been so fundamentally incorrectly framed that the defendant could never have been properly convicted of it – which was referred to in *R v G*, appears to remain good law. See also *R v Barking Youth Court, ex p B* (1999) CO/2692/99.)

1–462   Diplomatic immunity and parliamentary privilege. Immunity from jurisdiction within certain limits is accorded by legislation to persons connected with diplomatic missions, consular posts, certain Commonwealth posts, international organisations and international judicial bodies. The most important legislation in this field is the Diplomatic Privileges Act 1964, the Consular Relations Act 1968, the International Organisations Act 1968, the State Immunity Act 1978 (applied to the Isle of Man by SI 1981/1112), and Orders made under or continued in force by those Acts; eg SI 1974 Nos 1251–1261.

Immunity is often restricted in the case of persons who are citizens of the United Kingdom and Colonies or permanently resident in the United Kingdom.

Under this legislation, a certificate may be issued by or under the authority of the Secretary of State, stating any fact relating to the question of entitlement to immunity. The certificate is conclusive evidence of such facts as are stated, but any other facts, and all questions of law, are for the court to determine.

Imprisonment or restraint of members of the House of Lords, of the House of Commons or of the European Parliament must be immediately notified. Failure to do so may constitute a breach of Parliamentary privilege. Information should be given in all cases in which a member is effectively restricted from attending Parliament, for example by imprisonment, a hospital order, or remand in custody[1].

The notification should state the reason why the member is detained, and in the case of imprisonment on conviction, the charge upon which he was convicted, the date of the conviction and the sentence imposed. The addresses to which the notification should be sent and the person who should sign the notification are as follows—

— Members of the House of Commons: Speaker, House of Commons, London SW1A 0AA (one of the justices forming the court concerned)
— Members of the House of Lords: Clerk of the Parliaments, House of Lords, London SW1A 0PW (clerk to the justices)
— Members of the European Parliament: President of the European Parliament, Centre European, PO Box 1601, Luxembourg (clerk to the justices)

There is no bar on a member of the European Parliament being prosecuted by national courts of member states of the Community unless the review by national authorities of his alleged offence constitutes an interference with the internal functioning of the Parliament, which enjoys only autonomy and not sovereignty[2].

1. See Home Office Circular No 103/1982.
2. *R v Crown Court at Manchester, ex p DPP* [1993] 1 All ER 801.

POWER TO ADJOURN

1–463 Justices have jurisdiction to adjourn proceedings by statute[1]. The decision whether to adjourn is a matter of discretion (and one with which the Administrative Court not will lightly interfere)[2]. Factors to which the court will have consideration include:

— the need for expedition in the prosecution of criminal proceedings[3] (summary justice should be speedy justice which is not a matter of administrative convenience although efficient administration and economy are in themselves desirable ends but delays deprive other defendants of the opportunity of speedy trials when recollections are fresh[4]);
— the interests of justice as they affect both sides eg the interest of the defendant in concluding a matter hanging over him and the interest of the prosecution, representing the public, that a charge properly preferred against the defendant should be the subject of proper adjudication[3];
— also the particular interest of those people who may be personally affected by the alleged offence to whom the proper prosecution and, if appropriate, conviction of an offender might be a very significant event[5];
— whether the prosecution has been at fault[3];
— whether the defendant has been denied a full opportunity to present his case (but a defendant is not to be permitted to frustrate a speedy trial without substantial grounds and a defendant who deliberately seeks to postpone a trial without good reason has no cause for complaint if an adjournment is refused)[4].

Justices must fully examine the circumstances leading to applications, the reasons for such applications and the consequences both to the prosecution and the defence[4]. These factors were summarised by Jack J in *DPP v Picton*[6]:

"(a) A decision whether to adjourn is a decision within the discretion of the trial court. An appellate court will interfere only if very clear grounds for doing so are shown.

(b) Magistrates should pay great attention to the need for expedition in the prosecution of criminal proceedings; delays are scandalous; they bring the law into disrepute; summary justice should be speedy justice; an application for an adjournment should be rigorously scrutinized.

(c) Where an adjournment is sought by the prosecution, magistrates must consider both the interest of the defendant in getting the matter dealt with, and the interest of the public that criminal charges should be adjudicated upon, and the guilty convicted as well as the innocent acquitted. With a more serious charge the public interest that there be a trial will carry greater weight.

(d) Where an adjournment is sought by the accused, the magistrates must consider whether, if it is not granted, he will be able fully to present his defence and, if he will not be able to do so, the degree to which his ability to do so is compromised.

(e) In considering the competing interests of the parties the magistrates should examine the likely consequences of the proposed adjournment, in particular its likely length, and the need to decide the facts while recollections are fresh.

(f) The reason that the adjournment is required should be examined and, if it arises through the fault of the party asking for the adjournment, that is a factor against granting the adjournment, carrying weight in accordance with the gravity of the fault. If that party was not at fault, that may favour an adjournment. Likewise if the party opposing the adjournment has been at fault, that will favour an adjournment.

(g) The magistrates should take appropriate account of the history of the case, and whether there have been earlier adjournments and at whose request and why.

(h) Lastly, of course the factors to be considered cannot be comprehensively stated but depend upon the particular circumstances of each case, and they will often overlap. The court's duty is to do justice between the parties in the circumstances as they have arisen."

If it is necessary to adjourn the case to enable justice to be done following a failure by the prosecution to disclose matters which ought to be disclosed, then the adjournment must be granted, unless the court is satisfied that no prejudice would be caused to the defendant by proceeding[7].

Where they have refused an application by the prosecution to adjourn a trial, justices have no power to *dismiss* an information without hearing any evidence, even though they may be of the view that it would be unjust or prejudicial to the defendant to continue[8]. If justices dismiss an information without hearing the evidence which the parties properly wish to lay before them, they act without jurisdiction and a *quashing order* will issue[9].

Accordingly, if the prosecutor is present and has evidence available which he desires to call, the justices must, if they refuse an application for an adjournment, give the prosecutor the opportunity of calling that evidence if he so wishes, hear that evidence and hear the parties and then adjudicate on all the evidence[10]. Nevertheless, justices have jurisdiction, in certain circumstances, to investigate and to dismiss a summons on the ground that there has been an abuse of the process of the court[11].

It is a breach of the rules of natural justice and unlawful for justices to refuse an adjournment of a case and to go on to dismiss informations for want of prosecution where the justices know that the case has been wrongly listed and that the arrival of the prosecutor is imminent[12]. Having considered all the relevant factors, magistrates were correct to refuse the prosecutor an adjournment where the witnesses had been wrongly notified to attend at 2pm, and had considered that any trial would not have been concluded that day owing to the listing of another case for trial in the afternoon and that there would be significant delay if the case were part heard[13].

Where a prosecutor did not have a file in court for a particular case, although the case was on the court agenda which had been supplied to the Crown Prosecution Service the previous day, justices were wrong to dismiss the matter for want of prosecution without enquiring whether a plea could be taken. A prosecutor 'does not appear' for the purposes of s 15(1) of the Magistrates' Courts Act 1980[14] when, though physically present in court, he is unable to proceed with the particular part of the case which is before the court. If there is enough information before the court to allow the plea of the defendant to be taken and the plea is not guilty, the matter will be put off for a trial. If the plea is guilty, the court will have to decide whether it is in a position to proceed to sentence. If it is, it is at the stage of opening the case that the prosecutor will be in difficulties. The appropriate course will then be to adjourn the case and the court may consider an order for costs[5].

On the other hand where a trial had been listed after a pre-trial review but no prosecution witnesses had appeared and the CPS conceded that no attempt to warn the witnesses the justices were wrong to grant an adjournment on the basis of the seriousness of the allegation and that it was the first listing for trial[15].

Where a magistrates' court under section 15 of the Magistrates' Courts Act 1980 dismisses an information without having considered the merits of the case because of the failure of the prosecutor to attend court, there is no rule of law to prevent the court from dealing with an identical information subsequently laid against the same defendant[16].

---

1. Magistrates' Courts Act 1980, s 10(1) (trial of an information).
2. *R v Aberdare Justices, ex p DPP* (1990) 155 JP 324, *R v Hereford Magistrates' Court, ex p Rowlands* [1998] QB 110.
3. *R v Aberdare Justices, ex p DPP* (1990) 155 JP 324.
4. *R v Hereford Magistrates' Court, ex p Rowlands* [1998] QB 110.
5. *DPP v Shuttleworth* [2002] EWHC 621 (Admin), 166 JP 417.
6. [2006] EWHC 1108 (Admin), 170 JP 567.

7. *S v DPP* [2006] EWHC 1207 (Admin), (2006) 170 JP 707 (prosecution failed to disclose details of a Crown Court case of affray pending against the victim in the current proceedings, whose credibility and reliability were critical and those details might well have damaged his credibility).

8. *R v Birmingham Justices, ex p Lamb* [1983] 3 All ER 23, [1983] 1 WLR 339, 147 JP 75.

9. *Re Harrington* [1984] AC 473, [1984] 2 All ER 474, 149 JP 21, HL. See also *R v Dorchester Magistrates' Court, ex p DPP* (1989) 154 JP 211, [1990] Crim LR 421; *R v Watford Justices, ex p DPP* [1990] RTR 374n, and *R v Milton Keynes Justices, ex p DPP* [1991] Crim LR 712.

10. See *Re Harrington*, supra.

11. See para **1–447 Abuse of the process of the court**, ante.

12. *R v Dudley Justices, ex p DPP* (1992) 157 JP 177; *R v Hendon Justices, ex p DPP* [1993] 1 All ER 411, 157 JP 181, [1993] Crim LR 215. See also *R v Sutton Justices, ex p DPP* [1992] 2 All ER 129, 156 JP 707; and *R (on the application of the Crown Prosecution Service Harrow) v Portsmouth Crown Court* [2004] EWHC Admin 1079, [2004] Crim LR 224.

13. *DPP v Picton* [2006] EWHC 1108 (Admin), 170 JP 567.

14. In this PART: STATUTES ON PROCEDURE, post.

15. *R (Walden) v Highbury Corner Magistrates' Court* [2003] EWHC 708 (Admin).

16. *Holmes v Campbell* (1998) 162 JP 655.

REMANDS AND BAIL

1–464   A magistrates' court may adjourn a hearing at any time; if the offence is indictable or triable either way, it must usually remand the accused in custody or on bail[1]. Varying limits are placed on the maximum period of remand at one time, namely—

(a)   3 clear days remand in the custody of a constable before conviction;

(b)   8 clear days remand in custody to a prison department establishment before conviction, unless the offence is triable either way and to be tried summarily and a court cannot be properly constituted in that time;

(c)   3 weeks remand in custody after conviction for inquiries or a report;

(d)   4 weeks remand on bail after conviction for inquiries or a report;

(e)   any period to which prosecution and defence agree for remand on bail before conviction;

(f)   28 clear days, or a lesser period where an earlier date is fixed for the next stage in the proceedings, remand in custody, provided the court has previously remanded the accused in custody, the accused is before the court, and the court has afforded the parties the opportunity of making representations[2];

(g)   28 clear days remand in custody before conviction, of a person who still has at least that to serve as a custodial sentence;

(h)   until appearance at the Crown Court, when committed for trial or sentence[1]

Where several remands are likely, it may be convenient to order that an accused in custody be brought before a magistrates' court nearer the prison for subsequent remands, until the original court is ready to proceed with the case[2].

Subject to the provisions of s 25 of the Criminal Justice and the Public Order Act 1994[3], a person has a fundamental right to bail; he may be refused bail or have conditions imposed on him whilst on bail, only in certain statutorily defined circumstances, and the reasons must be stated by the court, together with notification about that person's right of appeal if he is unrepresented; this applies before conviction, and also after conviction where the remand is to enable enquiries or a report to be made, to assist the court in dealing with the accused[4].

---

1. As to remand generally, see Magistrates' Courts Act 1980, ss 8, 10, 18, 37, 38, 128–131 but see also Children and Young Persons Act 1969, s 23 in PART V: YOUTH COURTS, post (remand of minors); Children and Young Persons Act 1933, ss 34 and 34A in PART V: YOUTH COURTS, post (notification of parent and attendance at court); and Criminal Justice Act 1948, s 27, this PART, post (remand of persons aged 18–20).

2. Magistrates' Courts Act 1980, s 128A, in this PART: STATUTES ON PROCEDURE, post.

3. See this PART, post.

4. See the Bail Act 1976, ss 3(6), 4, 5(3), 5(6) and Sch 1. in this PART: STATUTES ON PROCEDURE, post.

1–465   *Duty to consider bail.*   Subject to the provisions of s 25 of the Criminal Justice and Public Order Act 1994[1], a person who appears or is brought before a magistrates' court charged with an offence or applies for bail in connection with the proceedings shall be granted bail except as provided in Schedule 1 to the Bail Act 1976[2]. The court is, accordingly, under a duty to consider granting bail on each appearance of the accused. Where the court decides not to grant bail to an accused person, it is nevertheless under a duty to consider at each subsequent hearing whether such an accused ought to be granted bail[3].

At the *first* hearing after that at which the court decided not to grant the accused bail, he may support an application for bail with any argument as to fact or law that he desires (whether or not he has advanced that argument previously), but at subsequent hearings the court need not hear arguments as to fact or law which it has heard previously[4]. This is subject to the requirement under Article 5(4) of the European Convention on Human Rights that there be an opportunity to review the lawfulness of pre-trial detention at reasonable intervals[5].

The four-week time limit on the period of remand on bail for reports is directory and not mandatory, and a failure by the court to comply with it will not render any action in dealing with the case a nullity[6].

Where a magistrates' court withholds bail in criminal proceedings from a person who is not represented by counsel or solicitor, the court shall—

(1) if it is committing him for trial to the Crown Court or if it issues a full argument certificate under s 5(6A) of the Bail Act 1976, inform him that he may apply to the High Court or to the Crown Court to be granted bail;

(2) in any other case, inform him that he may apply to the High Court for that purpose[7].

---

1. See this PART: STATUTES ON PROCEDURE, post.
2. Bail Act 1976, s 4, in this PART: STATUTES ON PROCEDURE, post.
3. Bail Act 1976, Sch 1, Pt IIA, para 1, in this PART: STATUTES ON PROCEDURE, post.
4. Bail Act 1976, Sch 1, Pt IIA, paras 2 and 3, in this PART: STATUTES ON PROCEDURE, post.
5. *Bezicheri v Italy* (1989) 12 EHRR 210.
6. *R v Manchester City Justices, ex p Miley and Dynan* (1977) 141 JP Jo 248.
7. As to application to the Crown Court, see the Bail Act 1976, s 5, post, the Senior Court Act 1981, s 81, post, and the Criminal Procedure Rules 2005, Part 19, this PART: STATUTORY INSTRUMENTS AND PRACTICE DIRECTIONS ON PROCEDURE, post; see also *Practice Direction (criminal: consolidated)* [2002] para V.53, in this PART, post. which states that a copy of the full argument certificate must be attached to the bail application form, that application should be made to the court to which the case will or would have been committed for trial; that a purely summary case should be sent to the Crown Court centre which normally receives class 4 work. The hearing will normally be in chambers, existing legal aid will extend to bail applications, allowing for representation by solicitor only, unless the magistrates' court orders otherwise.

1–466   ***Bail in cases of homicide or rape after a previous conviction of such offences.***   A person who in any proceedings has been charged with or convicted of an offence to which s 25 of the Criminal Justice and Public Order Act 1994 applies, in circumstances to which it applies, shall be granted bail in those proceedings only if the court considering the grant of bail is satisfied that there are exceptional circumstances which justify it[5].

The offences to which s 25 of the 1994 Act applies are as follows:

(*a*) murder;
(*b*) attempted murder;
(*c*) manslaughter;
(*d*) rape and other serious sexual offences and attempts.

Section 25 applies to a person charged with or convicted of any of the above offences only if he has been previously convicted by or before a court in any part of the United Kingdom of any such offence or of culpable homicide and, in the case of a previous conviction of manslaughter or of culpable homicide, if he was then sentenced to imprisonment or, if he was then a child or young person, to long-term detention[1].

As to the application of this section upon the expiry of, and refusal to extend, a custody time limit, it was held as follows in *R (O) v Crown Court at Harrow*[2]: s 25 was to be read as placing an evidential burden upon a defendant to whom the section applied to adduce material supporting the existence of exceptional circumstances justifying the grant of bail; that when the defendant's custody time limit had expired and the court had refused to extend it because of the prosecution's failure to act with all due diligence and expedition within the meaning of section 22(3)(b) of the 1985 Act, the defendant's continued detention in custody did not automatically amount to a violation of art 5(3), and a finding of lack of due diligence on the part of the prosecution did not automatically equate to a breach of the right to trial within a reasonable time; s 25 should be construed essentially as a guide to the proper operation of the Bail Act 1976, and it operated to disapply the ordinary requirement under the 1987 Regulations that bail should be granted automatically to any defendant whose custody time limit had expired, and so applied was compatible with art 5(3).

---

1. Criminal Justice and Public Order Act 1994, s 25, in this PART: STATUTES ON PROCEDURE, post.
2. [2006] UKHL 42, [2006] 3 All ER 1157, [2006] 3 WLR 195.

1–467   ***European Convention.***   It is a requirement of Article 5(3) of the European Convention on Human Rights that a person charged with an offence be released pending trial unless the prosecuting authorities can show that there are "relevant and sufficient" reasons to justify his continued detention[1]. The task of any court considering bail is to "examine all the facts arguing for or against the existence of a genuine requirement of public interest justifying ... a departure from the rule of respect for individual liberty and set them out in their decisions on applications for release"[2]. On several occasions, the European Court of Human Rights has emphasised that some "evidence" may be needed before bail is refused, but it has not elaborated on this requirement[3]. Article 5(4) of the Convention may also require some disclosure before the question of bail is finally determined.

---

1. *Letellier v France* (1992) 14 EHRR 83.
2. *Wemhoff v Germany* (1979) 1 EHRR 55.
3. *Lamy v Belgium* (1989) 11 EHRR 529.

1–468   **Conditional bail.**   The Act does appear to discourage the "unnecessary" use of conditions[1]. In deciding whether to impose a particular condition magistrates have a wide discretion to inquire whether the condition is necessary and are entitled to use their knowledge of local events and conditions[2]. Where is defendant is remanded on bail subject to a condition to remain indoors at a particular address between stated times, the justices can impose a further, doorstep 'presenting' condition to buttress the curfew, though it will always remain a question as to whether or not that particular power should be exercised in a particular case to meet the requirements of s 3(6) of the Bail Act 1976[3]. In Scotland it has been held that a condition which prevented an accused leaving his house for more than two hours a day did not constitute an infringement of his right to liberty under article 5 of the European Convention on Human Rights[4]. In all cases, a court may keep an accused in custody until a condition of bail is complied with[5].

The Act allows the following conditions or requirements to be imposed on a person granted bail in criminal proceedings—

1.   a requirement to provide a surety or sureties to secure his surrender to custody[6];
2.   a requirement to give security for his surrender to custody[7];
3.   a requirement to secure that he surrenders to custody[8];
4.   a requirement to secure that he does not commit an offence while on bail[9];
5.   a requirement to secure that he does not interfere with witnesses or otherwise obstruct the course of justice whether in relation to himself or any other person[10];
6.   for his own protection or, if a child or young person, for his won welfare or in his own interests[11];
7.   a requirement to secure that he makes himself available for the purpose of enabling inquiries or a report to be made to assist the court in dealing with him for the offence[12].
8.   a requirement that before the time appointed for him to surrender to custody, he attends an interview with an authorised advocate or authorised litigator[13];
9.   (child or young person) a requirement to comply with requirements imposed for the purpose of securing the electronic monitoring of his compliance with any other requirement imposed on him as a condition of bail[14];

In the case of a person accused of murder the court granting bail shall, unless it considers that satisfactory reports on his mental condition have already been obtained, impose as conditions of bail (a) a requirement that the accused shall undergo examination by two medical practitioners to enable reports to be prepared, and (b) a requirement that he shall attend such an institution or place as is directed, and comply with any other directions which may be given to him for that purpose by either of those practitioners[15].

Where a person is required as a condition of bail to reside in a bail hostel or probation hostel, he may also be required to comply with the rules of the hostel[16].

A person may appeal to the Crown Court against the imposition of bail conditions of certain specified kinds[17]. Where a court has granted bail the court may, on application by the prosecutor or the accused, vary the conditions of bail or impose conditions on bail which had been granted unconditionally[18].

Before taking a recognizance from a surety, serious efforts must be made by the court and others to establish that the sum in which the recognizance is proposed is realistic and that the surety would be able to meet his or her financial undertaking in the event of the recognizance being declared forfeited[19].

---

1. Bail Act 1976, s 3(4)–(7); see Sch 1, Pt I, para 8(1), in this PART: STATUTES ON PROCEDURE, post.
2. *R v Mansfield Justices, ex p Sharkey* [1985] QB 613, [1985] 1 All ER 193, 139 JP 129.
3. *R (on the application of the Crown Prosecution Service) v Chorley Justices* [2002] EWHC 2162 (Admin), (2002) 166 JP 764.
4. *McDonald v Procurator Fiscal, Elgin* (2003) Times, April 17 (High Court of Justiciary).
5. Bail Act 1976, s 3(4), (5), in this PART: STATUTES ON PROCEDURE, post.
6. Bail Act 1976, s 3(4), in this PART: STATUTES ON PROCEDURE, post.
7. Bail Act 1976, s 3(5), in this PART: STATUTES ON PROCEDURE, post.
8. Bail Act 1976, s 3(6)(a), in this PART: STATUTES ON PROCEDURE, post.
9. Bail Act 1976, s 3(6)(b), in this PART: STATUTES ON PROCEDURE, post.
10. Bail Act 1976, s 3(6)(c), in this PART: STATUTES ON PROCEDURE, post.
11. Bail Act 1976, s 3(6)(ca), in this PART: STATUTES ON PROCEDURE, post.
12. Bail Act 1976, s 3(6)(d), in this PART: STATUTES ON PROCEDURE, post.
13. Bail Act 1976, s 3(6)(e), in this PART: STATUTES ON PROCEDURE, post.
14. Bail Act 1976, s 3(6ZAA), in this PART: STATUTES ON PROCEDURE, post.
15. Bail Act 1976, s 3(6A), in this PART: STATUTES ON PROCEDURE, post.
16. Bail Act 1976, s 3(6ZA), in this PART: STATUTES ON PROCEDURE, post.
17. Criminal Justice Act 2003, s 16, in this PART: STATUTES ON PROCEDURE. For procedure on making such an application, see the Criminal Procedure Rules 2005, Part 19, this PART: STATUTORY INSTRUMENTS AND PRACTICE DIRECTIONS ON PROCEDURE, post.
18. Bail Act 1976, s 3(8), in this PART: STATUTES ON PROCEDURE, post.
19. *R v Birmingham Crown Court, ex p Rashid Ali* (1998) 163 JP 145, [1999] Crim LR 504.

1–469   ***Exceptions to the right to bail: imprisonable offences.***   A defendant need not be granted bail if the court is satisfied that there are substantial grounds for believing that the defendant, if released on bail (whether subject to conditions or not) would:

(a)   fail to surrender;
(b)   commit an offence while on bail;
(c)   interfere with witnesses or otherwise obstruct the course of justice, whether in relation to himself or any other person.

In taking this decision the must have regard to such of the following as appear relevant:

(a)   the nature and seriousness of the offence or default (and the probable method of dealing iwth the defendant for it);

    (*b*)   the character, antecedents, associations and community ties of the defendant;
    (*c*)   the defendant's record as respects the fulfilment of his obligations under previous grants of bail in criminal proceedings;
    (*d*)   except in the case of a defendant whose case is adjourned for inquiries or a report, the strength of the evidence of his having committed the offence or having defaulted;

as well as to any other things which appear to be relevant.

Although these exceptions provide the grounds for refusal of bail in almost all cases where bail is withheld, further exceptions to the right to bail are provided in Sch I Part I to the Bail Act 1976[1].

---

    1. See para **1–1570** ff.

1–480 *Exceptions to the right to bail: non-imprisonable offences.* A defendant need not be granted bail if

—   it appears to the court that, having been previously granted bail in criminal proceedings, he has failed to surrender to custody in accordance with his obligations under the grant of bail; and the court believes, in view of that failure, that the defendant, if released on bail (whether subject to conditions or not) would fail to surrender to custody;
—   the court is satisfied that the defendant should be kept in custody for his own protection or, if he is a child or young person, for his own welfare;
—   he is in custody in pursuance of the sentence of a court or of any authority acting under any of the Services Acts;
—   having been released on bail in or in connection with the proceedings for the offence, he has been arrested in pursuance of section 7 of this Act; and the court is satisfied that there are substantial grounds for believing that the defendant, if released on bail (whether subject to conditions or not) would fail to surrender to custody, commit an offence on bail or interfere with witnesses or otherwise obstruct the course of justice (whether in relation to himself or any other person)[1].

---

    1. See para **1–1578**.

1–481 *Associations and community ties.* When considering associations and community ties of a defendant we would suggest that the court will need to have before it the following information—

    (*a*)   name, age, nationality and (if applicable) his length of residence in the UK;
    (*b*)   family circumstances, whether he is married, has dependent children or other personal responsibilities and whether he lives with wife, parents or other relative;
    (*c*)   residence, type of accommodation and recent addresses with length of stay;
    (*d*)   employment, recent employment record including details of present job, place of work and income;
    (*e*)   possible sureties, any relative, friend, employer, etc in court, and
    (*f*)   any other matter the defendant wishes taken into account, for example medical considerations, employment or domestic difficulties if bail refused.

1–482 *Character and antecedents.* When considering character and antecedents, the court will be able to receive the defendant's record. This is not to prompt speculation as to whether the defendant has committed the present offence, but should be used as an indicator of the defendant's reliability, were he to be released on bail. Information of previous convictions should be submitted in writing, rather than read out in open court[1]. It is desirable that if newspapers are reporting the case, they should not include in the report of the case any mention of previous convictions, although such publication would not be, in itself, a ground for quashing a subsequent conviction[2].

---

    1. *R v Dyson* (1943) 107 JP 178.
    2. See *R v Fletcher* (1949) 113 JP 365; *R v Armstrong* [1951] 2 All ER 219 and *R v Wharton* (1955), printed in Home Office Circular No 132/1955.

1–483 **The bail decision – reasons.** Before a court may make the choice between bail and custody, it needs to consider several specific matters: if it grants bail it may need to give consideration to conditions on bail, and give reasons for any it imposes. Where the prosecutor makes representations in favour of withholding bail, the court is required to give reasons for granting bail, to include a note of those reasons in the record of its decision and to supply the prosecutor, if he so requests, with a copy of that record[1]. Where the court refuses bail it must state its grounds and the reasons for those grounds[2]. Relevant and requisite matters are set out below in the form of suggested announcements of decision.

---

    1. Bail Act 1976, s 5(2A), (2B), this PART, post.
    2. Bail Act 1976, s 5(3), (4), this PART, post.

1–484 *Announcement of decision – bail*

    1. This case will be adjourned to (*date*) at (*time*) (*give reasons for adjournment*) You will be released on bail until then.

2.   CONDITIONS In order to ensure you attend at court, *or*

prevent any offence while on bail, *or*
prevent any interference with witnesses, *or*
prevent the course of justice being obstructed,

we are imposing the following conditions on your bail:

We require (number) surety(ies) in the sum of £ (amount) to guarantee your attendance at court. Your surety(ies) will stand to lose that money if you fail to turn up. (*if sureties are not in court, add*) You will be kept in custody until the (each) surety has signed the bail papers; *or* You will provide the following security (*state*)...; *or*

You will live at (*address*) ......(*if a hostel, add*) and obey the rules of the hostel; or
You will report to (*name*) police station on (*days*) at (*time*); *or*
You will be examined by a/two doctor (s) and obey the directions of (*name*) so a report can be prepared; *or*
You will not communicate with or interfere with the prosecution witnesses; *or*
You will keep completely away from (*name and/or address*); *or*
You will remain indoors at (*state place*) between the hours of (*state times*); *or*
You will (*state any other conditions*)

3.   Make sure you return to this court at the time and date of the next hearing. If you are prevented by some emergency, send a message to the court and come to the court yourself as soon as you can. You must also make sure you obey every condition of your bail. If you fail to do all of this you can expect arrest, and may then be kept in custody.

1–485   *Announcement of decision – custody: imprisonable offence*
1.   This case will be adjourned to (*date*) at (*time*) (*state reasons for adjournment*).
2.   Because of the nature and seriousness of the offence (*or* breach of community order) and the probable method of dealing with you for it; *or*
your character/antecedents/associations/community ties; *or*
your previous failure to comply with bail; *or*
the strength of the evidence of your having committed the offence/breach of community order; *or*
any other appropriate and relevant reason;

We believe that there are substantial grounds for believing that you would
fail to surrender to custody; *or*
commit an offence while on bail; *or*
interfere with witnesses; *or*
obstruct the course of justice:
You will therefore be remanded in custody. *Or—*

3.   Because of

the short time since proceedings against you started, it has not been practicable to obtain sufficient information to enable us to take a decision about bail;*or*
the need for your own protection/welfare (child or young person); *or*

a sentence which has already been passed on you (*state date and name of court*) you are already in custody.

You will therefore be remanded in custody. *Or—*

4.   Because of
your being charged with an indictable/triable either way offence and it appears to the court that you were on bail in criminal proceedings on the date of the offence; *or*
your absconding in relation to your present bail; *or*

your failure to comply with a condition in relation to your present bail; *or*
(certain areas):
(*a*)   there is drug test evidence that you had a specified Class A drug in your body;
(*b*)   the offence is a drugs offence associated with a specified Class A drug offence or the court is satisfied that there are substantial grounds for believing that the misuse of a specified Class A drug caused or contributed to that offence or provided its motivation; and
you do not agree to undergo an assessment, or to a follow up to such an assessment, as to Class A drug dependency or propensity to misuse such drugs
and having regard *to*
the nature and seriousness of the (offence) *or* (breach of community order) and the probable method of dealing with you for it; *or*
your character/antecedents/associations/community ties; *or*
your previous failure to comply with bail; *or*
the strength of the evidence of your having committed the offence/breach of community order.

You will therefore be remanded in custody. *Or—*

4. Because your behaviour suggests that you are unlikely to co-operate with enquiries and we think a report cannot be obtained otherwise than by keeping you in custody. You will therefore be remanded in custody.
5. *Unrepresented defendant only* If you wish to make another application to be released on bail, you may apply to a judge of the Crown Court.

1–486   *Announcement of decision – custody: non-imprisonable offence*
1. This case will be adjourned to (*date*) at (*time*) (*give reason for adjournment*).
2. Because of
> the need for your own protection/welfare (child or young person); *or*
> a sentence which has already been passed on you (state date and name of court) you are already in custody; *or*
> your absconding in relation to your present bail; *or*
> your failure to comply with a condition in relation to your present bail; *or*
> Your previous failure to surrender to bail, we believe that if we released you this time you would again fail to return to court

You will therefore be remanded in custody.
3. *Unrepresented defendant only* If you wish to make another application to be released on bail, you may apply to a judge (*if committing for trial or issuing a full bail argument certificate as well*) of the Crown Court.

1–487   Members of HM Forces.   There is no power, in the case of a person who is charged with an offence and who is a member of HM Forces, to remand that person into service custody; if the court decides that there are grounds for withholding bail and remanding him in custody on the charge before the court, the remand must be into civil and not military custody. The position is otherwise where the serviceman before the court is found to be a deserter or absentee, and he is not required to remain in civil custody for any other cause[1]. In certain circumstances it may be possible to grant bail to a member of HM Forces with a condition that the accused resides in specified barracks during the period of remand, but it is suggested that before imposing such a condition of bail reference should be made by the court to the commanding officer or an officer from the unit attending the court with the accused.

---

1. See the Army and Air Force Acts 1955, s 187, and the Naval Discipline Act 1957, s 109, in PART VIII: title ARMED FORCES, post.

1–488   Prosecution right of appeal.   Where a magistrates' court grants bail to a person who is charged with, or convicted of, an offence punishable by imprisonment the prosecution may appeal to a judge of the Crown Court against the granting of bail[1]. Such an appeal may be made only where the prosecution is conducted by the Director of Public Prosecutions or other person falling within a class prescribed by order of the Secretary of State and it may be made only if the prosecution made representations that bail should not be granted, and the representations were made before it was granted[2].

In the event of the prosecution wishing to exercise this right of appeal, oral notice of appeal must be given to the magistrates' court at the conclusion of the proceedings in which bail has been granted and before the release from custody of the person concerned[3]. Written notice of appeal must then be served on the magistrates' court and the person concerned within two hours of the conclusion of the proceedings[4].

The hearing of an appeal against a decision to grant bail must be commenced within 48 hours, excluding weekends and any public holiday (ie Christmas Day, Good Friday or a bank holiday) from the date on which oral notice of appeal is given[5]. The appeal shall be by way of re-hearing and the judge may remand the person concerned in custody or may grant bail subject to such conditions, if any, as he thinks fit[6].

This right of appeal applies to a child or young person as if for the reference above to a remand in custody there were substituted a reference to a remand to local authority accommodation[7].

---

1. Bail (Amendment) Act 1993, s 1(1), in this PART: STATUTES ON PROCEDURE, post.
2. Bail (Amendment) Act 1993, s 1(2), (3), in this PART: STATUTES ON PROCEDURE, post.
3. Bail (Amendment) Act 1993, s 1(4), in this PART: STATUTES ON PROCEDURE, post.
4. Bail (Amendment) Act 1993, s 1(5), in this PART: STATUTES ON PROCEDURE, post.
5. Bail (Amendment) Act 1993, s 1(8), in this PART: STATUTES ON PROCEDURE, post.
6. Bail (Amendment) Act 1993, s 1(9), in this PART: STATUTES ON PROCEDURE, post.
7. Bail (Amendment) Act 1993, s 1(10), in this PART: STATUTES ON PROCEDURE, post.

1–489   Absconding or breaking conditions of bail.   If a person who has been released on bail fails without reasonable cause to surrender to custody he is guilty of the offence of absconding[1]. Similarly, if such a person having a reasonable cause for not surrendering to custody at the appointed time, fails to surrender to custody at the appointed place as soon after the appointed time as is reasonably practicable he is guilty of an offence[2]. Either offence is punishable on summary conviction or in a higher court as if it were a criminal contempt of court[3].

A person who fails to surrender to custody at the time appointed is liable to arrest, as is a person whom a constable has reasonable grounds for believing is not likely to surrender to custody[4]. If a constable has reasonable grounds for believing that a person is likely to break a condition of bail or suspecting that a condition has been broken, he may arrest that person without warrant[5], in which case the person shall be brought before a justice of the peace[6]. However, there is no power to impose a penalty merely for breach of a condition of bail, and even a flagrant breach of bail conditions does not amount to an offence of contempt[7].

---

1. Bail Act 1976, s 6(1), in this PART: STATUTES ON PROCEDURE, post. See for the procedure for initiating proceedings, *Practice Direction (criminal: consolidated)* [2002] para V.56, in this PART: STATUTORY INSTRUMENTS AND PRACTICE DIRECTIONS ON PROCEDURE, post, also *Schiavo v Anderton* [1987] QB 20, [1986] 3 All ER 10, 150 JP 264, and *France v Dewsbury Magistrates' Court* (1987) 152 JP 301, [1988] Crim LR 295. As to time limits for initiating proceedings, see s 6(10)–(14) of the Bail Act 1976.
2. Bail Act 1976, s 6(2), in this PART: STATUTES ON PROCEDURE, post.
3. Bail Act 1976, s 6(5), in this PART: STATUTES ON PROCEDURE, post.
4. Bail Act 1976, s 7(1) and (3), in this PART: STATUTES ON PROCEDURE, post.
5. Bail Act 1976, s 7(3), in this PART: STATUTES ON PROCEDURE, post.
6. Bail Act 1976, s 7(4), in this PART: STATUTES ON PROCEDURE, post.
7. *R v Ashley* [2003] EWCA Crim 2571, [2004] 1 WLR 2057, [2004] Cr App R 23, [2004] Crim LR 297.

OFFENCES WHICH ARE TO BE TRIED AT THE CROWN COURT

1–500   This part deals with those offences which are to be heard before the Crown Court either by way of a guilty plea or after a trial before a judge and jury. Some offences, *purely indictable*, are charged before a magistrates' court but must then be committed, sent or transferred to the Crown Court for trial. Other *indictable* offences are *triable either way* and may be heard by a magistrate's court on an indication of a guilty plea (and may thereafter be committed to the Crown Court for sentence if the magistrates' court considers its powers of punishment are insufficient) or where there is no indication of a guilty plea, the magistrates have determined after mode of trial proceedings that the case is more suitable to be heard before the Crown Court or the accused has elected for trial before a judge and jury.

1–501   **Classification of offences: purely summary, triable either way, purely indictable.**   An *indictable offence* means an offence which, if committed by an adult, is triable on indictment, whether it is exclusively so triable or triable either way; a *summary offence* means an offence which, if committed by an adult, is triable only summarily; an *offence triable either way* means an offence which, if committed by an adult, is triable either on indictment or summarily[1]. Indictable offences of *criminal damage* excluding arson, or *aggravated vehicle-taking* (where only damage is alleged) must proceed to summary trial where the value of the damage appears to be £5,000 or under and the procedure described in para **1–524** will apply.

---

1. Interpretation Act 1978, Sch 1, in PART II, EVIDENCE, post.

1–502   *Procedures: plea before venue (and committal for sentence); committal for trial; sending for trial.*   There are several procedures for determining where an indictable offence is to be tried. In the case of a purely indictable offence, the jurisdiction of justices in limited to an initial decision as to bail or custody before sending the case to the Crown Court. In the case of an offence triable either way, the defendant is invited to give an indication whether he intends to plead guilty. If he does so then a conviction is recorded and the magistrates proceed to sentence (or committal to the Crown Court for sentence if appropriate). Otherwise, the magistrates will conduct mode of trial proceedings to determine whether the case is more suitable for summary trial or trial on indictment. Where summary trial is deemed more appropriate, the defendant is asked whether he consents to summary trial or whether he wishes to exercise his right to elect for trial in the Crown Court. In the case of certain fraud cases or certain cases involving children, the prosecutor may serve a notice on the court transferring the proceedings to the Crown Court.

1–503   **Offences triable either way: plea before venue.**   Where a person who has attained the age of 18 years appears or is brought before a magistrates' court on an information charging him with an offence triable either way, the court shall cause the charge to be written down, if this has not already been done, and read to the accused[2]. The court must then explain to the accused in ordinary language that he may indicate whether, if the offence were to proceed to trial, he would plead guilty or not guilty[3]. The court must further explain to the accused that if he indicates he would plead guilty:

(a)   the court will proceed as if he had pleaded guilty to an information which was being tried summarily; and

(b)   that he may be committed for sentence to the Crown Court if the court is of opinion that greater punishment should be inflicted for the offence than the court has power to impose[3].

The court shall then ask the accused whether (if the offence were to proceed to trial) he would plead guilty or not guilty[4]. If the accused indicates a guilty plea the court will then hear the prosecution case against him, listen to his mitigation and either determine sentence or commit to the Crown Court for sentence[5]. If the accused indicates he would plead not guilty, or if he fails to indicate how he would plead, he shall be taken to indicate he would plead not guilty, and the procedure described in para **1–508** will apply[6].

For cases where the accused is present before the court, it has been suggested[7] that magistrates' courts may wish to use or adapt the following pronouncement for the purpose of explaining to the accused the initial procedure whereby he may indicate his intention as to plea—

(i) *After reading the charge to the accused and checking if he/she understands it, say: "For this charge you may be tried either in the Magistrates' Court or by a jury in the Crown Court (at......). First however this Court must ask you whether, if the case proceeds to a trial, you would plead Guilty or Not Guilty. Before you answer that I want to explain what will happen then. If you say that you would plead Guilty, the Court will hear the prosecution case against you, listen to your mitigation and formally find you Guilty. The Court will then decide what sentence it thinks you should receive. Do you understand?"*

(ii) *If yes, say: "If the Court believes that you deserve greater punishment than this Court can give (or if you have to be sent to the Crown Court to be tried on a related charge) it will send you to the Crown Court to be sentenced. Otherwise you will be sentenced here. If you do not indicate a Guilty plea the Court will decide whether to send you to the Crown Court for trial. Do you understand that or do you want anything to be explained further?"*

(iii) *Unless repeated or further explanation is required, say "Then, if the charge against you was to go to trial, would you plead Guilty or Not Guilty?"*

1. Interpretation Act 1978, Sch 1, in PART II: EVIDENCE, post.
2. Magistrates' Courts Act 1980, s 17A(1)–(3), in this PART: STATUTES ON PROCEDURE, post.
3. Magistrates' Courts Act 1980, s 17A(4) and (6), in this PART: STATUTES ON PROCEDURE, post. For power in these circumstances to commit to the Crown Court for sentence, see the Powers of Criminal Courts (Sentencing) Act 2000, ss 3 and 4, in this PART: STATUTES ON PROCEDURE, post. For consideration generally of the power to commit for sentence, see also para **3–560**.
4. Magistrates' Courts Act 1980, s 17A(5), in this PART: STATUTES ON PROCEDURE, post.
5. Magistrates' Courts Act 1980, s 17A(6), in this PART: STATUTES ON PROCEDURE, post.
6. Magistrates' Courts Act 1980, s 17A(7)–(8), in this PART: STATUTES ON PROCEDURE, post.
7. See Circular letter dated 30 September 1997 to Justices Clerks from the Judicial Studies Board and see *R v Southampton Magistrates' Court, ex p Sansome* [1998] 1 Cr App Rep (S) 112, [1998] Crim LR 595, DC.

1–504 *Proceeding in absence of accused.* Where the accused is represented by a legal representative and the court considers that by reason of the accused's disorderly conduct before the court it is not practicable for the procedure described above to be conducted in his presence the court may proceed in the absence of the accused and ask the representative whether if the offence were to proceed to trial the accused would plead guilty or not guilty[1].

1. Magistrates' Courts Act 1980, s 17B, in this PART: STATUTES ON PROCEDURE, post.

1–505 *Adjournment and remand.* A magistrates' court which is applying the procedure described above may adjourn the proceedings at any time and if the accused is present may remand him, and shall remand him if when he was brought before the court he was in custody or having been released on bail he surrendered to the custody of the court[1].

1. Magistrates' Courts Act 1980, s 17C, in this PART: STATUTES ON PROCEDURE, post.

1–506 *Committal for sentence, bail and credit for early indication of guilt.* A plea of guilty made at the plea before venue stage does not usually alter the position as regards bail or custody. Where the defendant who pleads guilty has been on bail, the usual practice is to continue bail even though it is anticipated that the Crown Court will impose a custodial sentence unless there are good reasons for remanding the defendant in custody. Similarly where the defendant has been in custody it will be unusual to alter the position if the reasons for remanding him in custody remain unchanged[1].

When a defendant pleads guilty before venue at the magistrates' court and is committed to the Crown Court for sentence, the judge at the Crown Court must have regard to the fact that the plea had been made at that early stage. In the usual case a defendant who enters a plea of guilty before venue should be entitled to a greater discount than a person who delayed making the plea until he pleaded to the indictment in respect of the offence at the Crown Court[1].

1. *R v Rafferty* [1999] 1 Cr App Rep 235, [1998] 2 Cr App Rep (S) 449, (1998) 162 JP 353.

1–507 *Change of plea in Crown Court.* If in the Crown Court it is discovered that the decision to commit for sentence was taken on the wrong view of the facts, the proper approach will be to allow the offender to make an application to change his plea, and, if such application is allowed, the Crown Court may then remit the case to the magistrates' court where the matter can be considered on a proper view of the facts for the purposes of s 3 of the Powers of Criminal Courts (Sentencing) Act 2000[1].

1. *R v Crown Court at Isleworth, ex p Buda* [2000] 1 Cr App Rep (S) 538, [2000] Crim LR 111.

1–508 *Guidance on whether to commit for sentence.* Guidance on the procedure to be followed by a magistrates' court following an indication of a plea of guilty and on the considerations relevant to the decision whether or not an accused should be committed to the Crown Court for sentence under the provisions of s 3 of the Powers of Criminal Courts (Sentencing) Act 2000[1] has been given by the Divisional Court in *R v Warley Magistrates' Court, ex p DPP*[2] which is summarised as follows:

Relevance of existing National Mode of Trial Guidelines

Pending revision to allow for the changes in procedure, the National Mode of Trial Guidelines 1995[3] are likely to be of the greatest assistance in relation to the application of [s 3] (committal for sentence on summary trial of an offence triable either way). The Magistrates' Association Sentencing Guidelines may be of assistance in some cases, but in general they proceed upon the basis that the magistrates' court is retaining jurisdiction.

Significance of plea indication

The magistrates' court must have regard to the discount to be granted on a plea of guilty when deciding whether the punishment which it would have power to inflict for any offence would be adequate. Each offence must be considered separately. If, after discount, any offence ought to attract a sentence in excess of six months' imprisonment, the magistrates' court must commit to the Crown Court. Sentences can only be made consecutive if in principle it is right to make them consecutive, not simply to arrive at a total within the 12 month maximum which seems appropriate for the case as a whole.

If the magistrates' court is only able to retain jurisdiction because it has made allowance for the plea of guilty, and for any other relevant mitigating factors, it is helpful for the court to indicate that.

Mitigation and submissions

Where, owing to the gravity of the offence, whatever may be the mitigation, the punishment should be greater than the magistrates' court has power to impose, the court should be prepared to commit the accused to the Crown Court for sentence without seeking any pre-sentence report or hearing in full the accused's mitigation. In such a case the accused should be told what the court has in mind and a brief submission may be allowed in apposition to that course. If the court is persuaded to change its mind, the prosecution should be invited to make a submission in reply.

If after allowance has been made for a plea of guilty it appears that it will or may be possible for the magistrates' court to sentence properly, the court should proceed to hear the case in the normal way, but should be careful to ensure so long as a committal for sentence remains a possibility, that nothing is said or done to indicate to an accused that that option is ruled out, otherwise if the case comes back before a differently constituted bench its hands are tied.

Character and antecedents[4]

All relevant aspects of character and antecedents can be taken into consideration before a decision is taken whether or not to commit for sentence. If the question whether or not to commit remains a live issue at the end of the hearing, then at that stage the court should seek assistance from the prosecution and from the accused in relation to that course.

Disputes as to the facts

If the magistrates' court comes to the conclusion that however any dispute as to the facts relevant to sentence is resolved, it will have adequate powers of sentence, the magistrates will simply proceed with a *Newton*[5] hearing.

Similarly if, whatever the outcome, the magistrates' court is of the opinion that the case will have to be committed to the Crown Court for sentence, it is clearly preferable for the Crown Court to conduct the *Newton* hearing.

But if the decision as to whether or not to commit for sentence turns or may turn, on the outcome of the *Newton* hearing, the magistrates' court should proceed to conduct the *Newton* hearing. If the case is subsequently committed to the Crown Court for sentence, the magistrates' court must record its findings for the benefit of the Crown Court. The accused should not be allowed to challenge those findings in the Crown Court unless he can point to some significant development – such as the discovery of important new evidence – having occurred since the magistrates' court reached its conclusion.

Reasons for committal

The clear words of s [3] do not leave room for a magistrates' court to commit for sentence even though the court might consider its own sentencing powers to be adequate simply because the case is of a type which ought to be dealt with at a higher level. A magistrates' court only has power to commit for sentence if it is of the opinion that the sentence should be greater than it has power to impose. However, it is unnecessary for justices to state their reasons for committing for sentence since the person so committed will have an opportunity to make full representations to the sentencing court[6].

Where the offence is imprisonable, the court is not minded to impose imprisonment but is of the opinion that the offence deserves a greater fine that it can impose, it may commit for sentence[7].

Function of the Divisional Court

The Divisional Court will not lightly intervene in decisions as to venue, only where the decision is "truly astonishing" or where the magistrates' court fails to have regard to a material consideration.

Adjournment for pre-sentence report

In a number of authorities since the decision in *R v Warley Magistrates' Court, ex p DPP*, supra, the Divisional Court has held that where a defendant gives an indication of a guilty plea under the plea before venue procedure and the magistrates' court adjourns for a pre-sentence report indicating in terms sufficiently unqualified to found a legitimate expectation that the defendant will not be committed to the Crown Court for sentence, a bench dealing with the defendant on a later occasion may not commit the defendant for sentence in the absence of new information justifying a departure from the earlier indication. If on the other hand the magistrates' court says nothing to indicate that it is going to sentence the defendant itself and the court keeps all its options open, the court is entitled to reach its decision on committal for sentence at any stage in the proceedings, and to delay making that decision until after the pre-sentence report has been received[8].

If in a case where the hands of the bench are tied, the justices nevertheless commit the defendant to the Crown Court for sentence, the order for committal will be quashed on an application for judicial review[8].

The failure of the defendant to attend for interview with the probation service so that a pre-sentence report is not available is not a justification for the court to depart from the earlier indication because the defendant is to be punished for his criminal offences and not for any cavalier, dismissive or truculent attitude which he may have displayed towards the probation service[8].

1. In this PART: STATUTES ON PROCEDURE, post.
2. *R v Warley Magistrates' Court, ex p DPP* [1998] 2 Cr App Rep 307, 162 JP 559, [1998] Crim LR 684, DC.
3. Now contained in the *Practice Direction (criminal: consolidated)* [2002] para V.51, in this PART, post.
4. At the date of this guidance, committal for sentence was under the provisions of s 38 of the Magistrates' Courts Act 1980 (now repealed) which made explicit provision for magistrates' to consider character and antecedents.
5. *R v Newton* (1983) 77 Cr App Rep 13, 4 Cr App Rep (S) 338, [1983] Crim LR 198; see also for determining the factual base for sentencing, the commentary at para **3–50**, post.
6. *R v Wirral Magistrates' Court, ex p Jermyn* [2001] 1 Cr App Rep (S) 485, [2001] Crim LR 45, DC.
7. *R v North Essex Justices, ex p Lloyd* [2001] 2 Cr App Rep (S) 86, 165 JP 117.
8. See *R v Norwich Magistrates' Court, ex p Elliott* [2000] 1 Cr App Rep (S) 152; *R v Nottingham Magistrates'. Court, ex p Davidson* [2000] 1 Cr App Rep (S) 167; [2000] Crim LR 118; *R v Horseferry Road Magistrates' Court, ex p Rugless* [2000] 1 Cr App Rep (S) 484, 164 JP 311, [2000] Crim LR 119; *R v Salisbury Magistrates' Court, ex p Gray* [2000] 1 Cr App Rep (S) 267, 163 JP 732; *R v Wirral Magistrates' Court, ex p Jermyn* [2001] 1 Cr App Rep (S) 485, [2001] Crim LR 47, DC. [2001] Crim LR 45; *R v Feltham Justices, ex p Rees* [2001] Crim LR 47, DC; *R (on the application of Walton) v Dewsbury Magistrates' Court* (2001) 165 JPN 894, DC.

1–509   Offences triable either way: mode of trial.   Where a person who has attained the age of 18 appears or is brought before a magistrates' court on an information charging him with an offence triable either way and either he or his representative indicates that if the offence were to proceed to trial he would plead not guilty, the following steps[1] should be followed:–

(1) the accused should be asked if he knows that he may ask the prosecutor for a summary or a copy of statements in his case; he should be asked if he wants an adjournment, if he did not know, or if he has not yet made a request, or if he has made a request with which the prosecutor has not yet complied[2];

(2) the prosecutor and the accused are asked in turn which appears more suitable, summary trial or trial on indictment;

(3) the court decides which mode of trial appears more suitable, having regard particularly to the nature of the case, whether the circumstances make the offence one of a serious character, and whether summary powers would be adequate;

(4) if summary trial appears more suitable, the court addresses the accused as follows[3]—

"It appears to this court more suitable for you to be tried here. You may now consent to be tried by this court, but if you wish, you may choose to be tried by a jury instead. If you are tried by this court and are found guilty, this court may still send you to the Crown Court for sentence if it is of the opinion that greater punishment should be inflicted for the offence than it has power to impose. Do you wish to be tried by this court or do you wish to be tried by a jury?"

If the accused consents, the case proceeds to summary trial[4]; if the accused does not consent to summary trial the court will inquire into the information as examining justices[5];

(5) if trial on indictment seems more suitable, the court addresses the accused as follows—
"It appears to this court more suitable for you to be tried by a jury";

and it will then proceed to inquire into the information as examining justices[5].

To help magistrates' courts decide whether or not to assume jurisdiction over triable either way offences, National Mode of Trial Guidelines have been issued and have been commended to justices by the Lord Chief Justice[6]. The object of the guidelines is to provide guidance not direction, and it remains the duty of the justices to consider each case individually and on its own particular facts.

In determining whether an offence triable either way should be tried summarily or on indictment, s 19(3) of the Magistrates' Courts Act 1980 requires justices to apply their minds, *inter alia*, to the question of whether or not their powers of punishment would be adequate if they dealt with the case summarily. While s 38 of the 1980 Act gives justices an unfettered discretion to commit a defendant to the Crown Court for sentence if, having accepted summary trial, they later decide that their powers are inadequate, justices must still apply their minds to s 19(3) of the 1980 Act in deciding to accept jurisdiction in the first place[7].

1. See Magistrates' Courts Act 1980, ss 18–23, in this PART: STATUTES ON PROCEDURE, post and as to a corporation, see Sch 3 thereof.
2. See the Criminal Law Act 1977, s 48, now superseded by the Courts Act 2003, s 69, in this PART: STATUTES ON PROCEDURE, post, and the Criminal Procedure Rules 2005, Part 21, in this PART: STATUTORY INSTRUMENTS AND PRACTICE DIRECTIONS ON PROCEDURE, post.
3. The form of words recommended here was approved in *R v Southampton Magistrates' Court, ex p Sansome* [1999] 1 Cr App Rep (S) 112, [1998] Crim LR 595, DC.
4. See para **1–566**, post.
5. See para **1–526**, post.

6. See the *Practice Direction (criminal: consolidated)* [2002] para V.51: this PART: STATUTORY INSTRUMENTS AND PRACTICE DIRECTIONS ON PROCEDURE, post.
7. *R v Flax Bourton Magistrates' Court, ex p Customs and Excise Comrs* (1996) 160 JP 481, [1996] Crim LR 907.

1–520   *Absence of the accused.* If the *accused is absent*, but represented by counsel or a solicitor, who says that the accused consents to the proceedings for determining how he is to be tried for the offence being conducted in his absence, and the court is satisfied there is good reason for proceeding in the absence of the accused, it may proceed to steps (1) and (2) above[1]. In this situation, however, steps (3) and (4) are modified as follows; if summary trial appears more suitable, the accused's counsel or solicitor will signify his client's consent, following which the court will proceed with the case[2]. If he does not signify consent, or if trial on indictment seems more suitable to the court, then the court will proceed to inquire into the information as examining justices[3].

The court may have regard to any relevant matters, but not the defendant's antecedents when deciding mode of trial[4].

1. Magistrates' Courts Act 1980, s 23, post. See also ante para **1–139 Appearance by legal representative**.
2. See the Criminal Law Act 1977 and the Criminal Procedure Rules 2005, Part 21.
3. See para **1–526**, post.
4. *R v Colchester Justices, ex p North Essex Building Co Ltd* [1977] 3 All ER 567, [1977] 1 WLR 1109.

1–521   *Mode of trial guidelines.* Guidance for magistrates when determining mode of trial is provided in the *Practice Direction (criminal: consolidated)*[1]:

"Part V Further Directions Applying in the Magistrates' Courts
V.51 Mode of trial
V.51.1 The purpose of these guidelines is to help magistrates decide whether or not to commit defendants charged with 'either way' offences for trial in the Crown Court. Their object is to provide guidance not direction. They are not intended to impinge on a magistrate's duty to consider each case individually and on its own particular facts. These guidelines apply to all defendants aged 18 and above.

General mode of trial considerations V.51.2 Section 19 of the Magistrates' Courts Act 1980 requires magistrates to have regard to the following matters in deciding whether an offence is more suitable for summary trial or trial on indictment: (a) the nature of the case; (b) whether the circumstances make the offence one of a serious character; (c) whether the punishment which a magistrates' court would have power to inflict for it would be adequate; (d) any other circumstances which appear to the court to make it more suitable for the offence to be tried in one way rather than the other; (e) any representations made by the prosecution or the defence.

V.51.3 Certain general observations can be made: (f) the court should never make its decision on the grounds of convenience or expedition; (g) the court should assume for the purpose of deciding mode of trial that the prosecution version of the facts is correct; (h) the fact that the offences are alleged to be specimens is a relevant consideration (although, it has to be borne in mind that difficulties can arise in sentencing in relation to specimen counts, see *R v Clark* [1996] 2 Cr App Rep (S) 351 and *R v Kidd, R v Canavan, R v Shaw* [1998] 1 All ER 42, [1998] 1 Cr App Rep (S) 243); the fact that the defendant will be asking for other offences to be taken into consideration, if convicted, is not; (i) where cases involve complex questions of fact or difficult questions of law, including difficult issues of disclosure of sensitive material, the court should consider committal for trial; (j) where two or more defendants are jointly charged with an offence each has an individual right to elect his mode of trial; k) in general, except where otherwise stated, either way offences should be tried summarily unless the court considers that the particular case has one or more of the features set out in paras V.51.4– V.51.18 and that its sentencing powers are insufficient; (l) the court should also consider its power to commit an offender for sentence under ss 3 and 4 of the Powers of Criminal Courts (Sentencing) Act 2000, if information emerges during the course of the hearing which leads it to conclude that the offence is so serious, or the offender such a risk to the public, that its powers to sentence him are inadequate. This means that committal for sentence is no longer determined by reference to the character and antecedents of the offender.

Features relevant to individual offences V.51.4 Where reference is made in these guidelines to property or damage of 'high value' it means a figure equal to at least twice the amount of the limit (currently £5,000) imposed by statute on a magistrates' court when making a compensation order.

Burglary: dwelling house V.51.5 Cases should be tried summarily unless the court considers that one or more of the following features is present in the case *and* that its sentencing powers are insufficient. Magistrates should take account of their powers under ss 3 and 4 of the Powers of Criminal Courts (Sentencing) Act 2000 to commit for sentence, see para V.51.3(g): (m) entry in the daytime when the occupier (or another) is present; (n) entry at night of a house which is normally occupied, whether or not the occupier (or another) is present; (o) the offence is alleged to be one of a series of similar offences; (p) when soiling, ransacking, damage or vandalism occurs; (q) the offence has professional hallmarks; (r) the unrecovered property is of high value: see para V.51.4 for definition of high value; (s) the offence is racially motivated.

Note: attention is drawn to para 28(c) of Sch 1 to the Magistrates' Courts Act 1980 by which offences of burglary in a dwelling cannot be tried summarily if any person in the dwelling was subjected to violence or the threat of violence.

Burglary: non-dwelling V.51.6 Cases should be tried summarily unless the court considers that one or more of the following features is present in the case and that its sentencing powers are insufficient. Magistrates should take account of their powers under ss 3 and 4 of the 2000 Act to commit for sentence, see para V.51.3(g): (t) entry of a pharmacy or doctor's surgery; (u) fear is caused or violence is done to anyone lawfully on the premises (eg night-watchman, security guard); (v) the offence has professional hallmarks; (w) vandalism on a substantial scale; (x) the unrecovered property is of high value: see para V.51.4 for definition of high value; (y) the offence is racially motivated.

Theft and fraud V.51.7 Cases should be tried summarily unless the court considers that one or more of the following features is present in the case *and* that its sentencing powers are insufficient. Magistrates should take account of their powers under ss 3 and 4 of the 2000 Act to commit for sentence, see para V.51.3(z): (a) breach of trust by a person in a position of substantial authority, or in whom a high degree of trust is placed; (aa) theft or fraud which has been committed or disguised in a sophisticated manner; (bb) theft or fraud committed by an organised gang; (cc) the victim is particularly vulnerable to theft or fraud, eg the elderly or infirm; (dd) the unrecovered property is of high value: see para V.51.4 for definition of high value.

Handling V.51.8 Cases should be tried summarily unless the court considers that one or more of the following features is present in the case and that its sentencing powers are insufficient. Magistrates should take account of their powers under ss 3 and 4 of the 2000 Act to commit for sentence, see para V.51.3(g): (ee) dishonest handling of stolen property by a receiver who has commissioned the theft; (ff) the offence has professional hallmarks; (gg) the property is of high value: see para V.51.4 for definition of high value.

Social security frauds V.51.9 Cases should be tried summarily unless the court considers that one or more of the following features is present in the case and that its sentencing powers are insufficient. Magistrates should take account of their powers under ss 3 and 4 of the 2000 Act to commit for sentence, see para V.51.3(g): (hh) organised fraud on a large scale; (ii) the frauds are substantial and carried out over a long period of time.

Violence (ss 20 and 47 of the Offences against the Person Act 1861) V.51.10 Cases should be tried summarily unless the court considers that one or more of the following features is present in the case *and* that its sentencing powers are insufficient. Magistrates should take account of their powers under ss 3 and 4 of the 2000 Act to commit for sentence, see para V.51.3(g): (jj) the use of a weapon of a kind likely to cause serious injury; (kk) a weapon is used and serious injury is caused; (ll) more than minor injury is caused by kicking or head-butting; (mm) serious violence is caused to those whose work has to be done in contact with the public or are likely to face violence in the course of their work; (nn) violence to vulnerable people, eg the elderly and infirm; (oo) the offence has clear racial motivation.

Note: the same considerations apply to cases of domestic violence.

Public Order Act offences V.51.11 Cases should be tried summarily unless the court considers that one or more of the following features is present in the case and that its sentencing powers are insufficient. Magistrates should take account of their powers under ss 3 and 4 of the 2000 Act to commit for sentence, see para V.51.3(g): (pp) cases of violent disorder should generally be committed for trial; (qq) affray; (i) organised violence or use of weapons; (ii) significant injury or substantial damage; (iii) the offence has clear racial motivation; (iv) an attack on police officers, ambulance staff, fire-fighters and the like.

Violence to and neglect of children V.51.12 Cases should be tried summarily unless the court considers that one or more of the following features is present in the case *and* that its sentencing powers are insufficient. Magistrates should take account of their powers under ss 3 and 4 of the 2000 Act to commit for sentence, see para V.51.3(g): (rr) substantial injury; (ss) repeated violence or serious neglect, even if the physical harm is slight; (tt) sadistic violence, eg deliberate burning or scalding.

Indecent assault V.51.13 Cases should be tried summarily unless the court considers that one or more of the following features is present in the case *and* that its sentencing powers are insufficient. Magistrates should take account of their powers under ss 3 and 4 of the 2000 Act to commit for sentence, see para V.51.3(g): (uu) substantial disparity in age between victim and defendant, and a more serious assault; (vv) violence or threats of violence; (www) relationship of trust or responsibility between defendant and victim; (xx) several more serious similar offences; (yy) the victim is particularly vulnerable; (zz) serious nature of the assault.

Unlawful sexual intercourse V.51.14 Cases should be tried summarily unless the court considers that one or more of the following features is present in the case and that its sentencing powers are insufficient. Magistrates should take account of their powers under ss 3 and 4 of the 2000 Act to commit for sentence, see para V.51.3(g): (aaa) wide disparity of age; (bbb) breach of position of trust; (ccc) the victim is particularly vulnerable.

Note: unlawful sexual intercourse with a girl *under 13* is triable only on indictment.

Drugs V.51.15 Class A: (ddd) supply; possession with intent to supply: these cases should be committed for trial; (eee) possession: should be committed for trial unless the amount is consistent only with personal use.

V.51.16 Class B: (fff) supply; possession with intent to supply: should be committed for trial unless there is only small scale supply for no payment; (ggg) possession: should be committed for trial when the quantity is substantial and not consistent only with personal use.

Dangerous driving and aggravated vehicle taking V.51.17 Cases should be tried summarily unless the court considers that one or more of the following features is present in the case *and* that its sentencing powers are insufficient. Magistrates should take account of their powers under ss 3 and 4 of the 2000 Act to commit for sentence, see para V.51.3(g): (hhh) alcohol or drugs contributing to the dangerous driving; (iii) grossly excessive speed; (jjj) racing; (kkk) prolonged course of dangerous driving; (lll) other related offences; (mmm) significant injury or damage sustained.

    Criminal damage V.51.18   Cases should be tried summarily unless the court considers that one or more of the following features is present in the case and that its sentencing powers are insufficient. Magistrates should take account of their powers under ss 3 and 4 of the 2000 Act to commit for sentence, see para V.51.3(g): (nnn) deliberate fire-raising; (ooo) committed by a group; (ppp) damage of a high value; (qqq) the offence has clear racial motivation."

Note: offences set out in Sch 2 to the Magistrates' Courts Act 1980 (which includes offences of criminal damage which do not amount to arson) *must* be tried summarily if the value of the property damaged or destroyed is £5,000 or less.

---

1. In this PART: STATUTORY INSTRUMENTS AND PRACTICE DIRECTIONS ON PROCEDURE, post.

1–522 *Joint defendants.*   Where two or more accused are jointly charged and one consents to summary trial, but a co-accused elects trial on indictment, the court must proceed to try summarily the accused who consents to summary trial, and must inquire into the information as examining justices in respect of the accused who elects trial on indictment[1]. It is not permissible, for the purpose of avoiding separate trials, for justices when considering whether an offence is more suitable for summary trial or trial on indictment to have regard to an indication that one or more of the accused would elect trial by jury[2]. Nor is it permissible simply for the purpose of avoiding separate trials for justices to exercise their power to revert to being examining justices under s 25 of the Magistrates' Courts Act 1980 (see para **1–525 Reverting and re-electing**)[3].

---

1. *Nicholls v Brentwood Justices* [1992] 1 AC 1, [1991] 3 All ER 359, 155 JP 753, HL. See also *R v Wigan Magistrates' Court, ex p Layland* (1995) 160 JP 223, [1995] Crim LR 892.
2. *R v Ipswich Magistrates' Court, ex p Callaghan* (1995) 159 JP 748.
3. *R v Bradford Magistrates' Court, ex p Grant* [1999] Crim LR 324, 163 JP 717.

1–523 *Youths.*   If the *accused is a youth*, he or she would normally be tried in the youth court[1] but if the decision as to place of trial has not been taken before he or she reaches 18, he or she then has a right to elect trial by jury[2].

---

1. Children and Young Persons Act 1933, s 46 and see paras **5–10** to **5–15 Jurisdiction of the magistrates' and Crown Court**, in PART V: YOUTH COURTS, post.
2. *R v Islington North Juvenile Court, ex p Daley* [1983] 1 AC 347, [1982] 2 All ER 974, 146 JP 363; *R v Lewes Juvenile Court, ex p Turner* (1985) 149 JP 186; *R v Nottingham Justices, ex p Taylor* [1992] 1 QB 557, [1991] 4 All ER 860, DC.

1–524 *Offences of criminal damage where the value is small.*   If the offence charged is *criminal damage*, excluding arson, or *aggravated vehicle-taking* (where only damage is alleged), the court will as a preliminary ask the prosecutor and the accused the value of the damage; if it appears to be £5,000 or under, the court will proceed to summary trial. If it is unclear whether the value is £5,000 or under, the court will read the charge to the accused and then say to him—

    "If you consent now to be tried by this court, you will be so tried, and the maximum imprisonment and fine this court will inflict if it finds you guilty will be three months and £2,500 (or 6 months and/or £5,000 in a case of aggravated vehicle-taking); nor will you be liable to be sent to the Crown court for a heavier sentence. Do you consent to be tried by this court?"

If the accused refuses, the court will proceed to the plea before venue procedure described in para **1–502** and, if the accused then indicates a plea of not guilty or gives no indication as to plea, the court will proceed to the mode of trial procedure described in para **1–508**[1].

These provisions relating to such an offence where the value is small create an absolute obligation on the court to deal with the matter as a summary offence and the procedures for plea before venue and mode of trial do not apply[2]. The court's task is to identify the value of the damage itself and it is not concerned with determining what, if any, consequential losses may have been sustained as a result of the damage; thus, where genetically modified crops were damaged, the farmer valued the damage at £750 but there were also wasted research costs making the overall loss somewhere between £3,250 and £14,650, it was impossible to criticise the justices for concluding that the value for mode of trial purposes was clearly less than £5,000[3]. The difficulty of assessing the value in respect of damaged crops is that there is no open market for sale of damaged genetically modified crops grown for research not sale. In the circumstances of the case a court was justified in concluding that, as the crops in question had a value for research purposes, it was more than the market value of ordinary maize, but as there was no realistic way of putting a price on it, it was justified in holding that it was not clear whether the value was above or below £5,000[4].

---

1. Magistrates' Courts Act 1980, s 22.
2. *R v Kelly* [2001] RTR 45, CA.

3. *R v Colchester Magistrates' Court, ex p Abbott* (2001) 165 JP 386, [2001] Crim LR 564, DC.
4. *R (DPP) v Prestatyn Magistrates' Court* [2002] EWHC 1177 (Admin), [2002] Crim LR 924

1–525 *Reverting and re-electing.* A magistrates' court may discontinue the summary trial and revert to inquiring into the information as examining justices, at any time before the conclusion of the evidence for the prosecution on summary trial, but this power is not available where an unequivocal plea of guilty has been accepted[1] even when a dispute then arises as to the facts of the case, such as to quantity of goods stolen[2]. It is not permissible to exercise the power simply to avoid separate trials of co-accused[3]. The power does not arise until the court has "begun to try the information summarily" in the sense of determining the guilt or innocence of the accused[4]. The trial may begin after a not guilty plea has been entered but before evidence has been called; for example where the justices hear submissions on an application for a preliminary ruling of law which has a direct and immediate bearing on the conduct and content of the trial process[5]. At any time during an inquiry as examining justices, a court may, with the accused's consent, revert to summary trial, if that seems after all suitable, having regard to the evidence and the representations, and the nature of the case[6]. The court must have begun its inquiry; if an earlier court declined summary jurisdiction, it is not open to a later court simply to hear representations and then agree summary trial[7].

The justices have power under s 25(2) of the 1980 Act to re-open mode of trial proceedings if they are apprised of a matter which, while not strictly relevant as evidence in the process of determining guilt or innocence would have been an appropriate consideration under s 19(3) of that Act for the purposes of the original decision as to mode of trial. A possible defence of insanity and the available powers of the court to deal with a defendant who has been proved to have committed the act charged are relevant considerations under s 19(3)[5]. The justices have a discretion where the defendant seeks to withdraw his original election of summary trial[8].

There may be many cases in which a defendant, particularly if unrepresented, has elected trial on indictment, but after proper consideration of the prosecution evidence it would be right for his legal representative to ask for him to change his election and proceed with his case summarily; this however is different from demanding trial on indictment as a trick to obtain statements to which the defence are not entitled, such circumstances may be akin to sharp practice and justices may be entitled to refuse to try the case summarily[9].

The test whether an accused should be allowed to re-elect is whether he properly understood the nature and significance of the choice which he made when consenting to summary trial; since an unrepresented accused who intends to plead guilty is unlikely to direct his mind to where he wishes to be tried, he would be unlikely to understand the nature and significance of his choice as to mode of trial[10]. Once the justices conclude that the proper course is to allow a defendant to change his plea from guilty to not guilty, the defendant must be given the right to consider whether he wishes to re-elect[11]. Therefore, if the accused is subsequently advised that he has a defence and should plead not guilty, the central factor to which the justices should pay attention when faced with an application to re-elect is the accused's state of mind at the time he made the election[10]. Moreover, in the case of an unrepresented young offender who did not understand the choice he was asked to make, it was held that the broad justice of the situation required that he be allowed to re-elect[12]. If, on the other hand the justices find that the accused did understand the choice he was asked to make, they are not obliged to investigate the reasons for that choice or the quality of the advice he had received from the duty solicitor[13]. If the justices hearing such an application to re-elect did not sit on the earlier occasion, they should receive evidence as to what occurred from the court clerk who was then present and also the defendant[14].

---

1. *Re Gillard* [1986] AC 442, [1985] 3 All ER 634, 150 JP 45.
2. *R v Telford Magistrates' Court, ex p Darlington* (1987) 152 JP 215. As to a pre-sentence hearing in these circumstances see para **3–50 General considerations**, post.
3. *R v Bradford Magistrates' Court, ex p Grant* [1999] Crim LR 324, 163 JP 717.
4. *R v Birmingham Stipendiary Magistrate, ex p Webb* (1992) 157 JP 89.
5. *R v Horseferry Road Magistrates' Court, ex p K* [1996] 3 All ER 719, [1996] 3 WLR 68, 160 JP 441, [1996] 2 Cr App Rep 574.
6. Magistrates' Courts Act 1980, s 25, in this PART: STATUTES ON PROCEDURE, post.
7. *R v Liverpool Justices, ex p Crown Prosecution Service* (1989) 154 JP 1, 90 Cr App Rep 261.
8. *R v Southampton City Justices, ex p Robins* (1980) 144 JP 288.
9. *R v Warrington Justices, ex p McDonagh* [1981] LS Gaz R 785.
10. *R v Birmingham Justices, ex p Hodgson* [1985] QB 1131, [1985] 2 All ER 193, 149 JP 193 and see *R v West London Stipendiary Magistrate, ex p Keane* (1992) 156 JP 612 (a 1985 case).
11. *R v Bow Street Magistrates' Court, ex p Welcome* (1992) 156 JP 609.
12. *R v Highbury Corner Metropolitan Stipendiary Magistrate, ex p Weekes* [1985] QB 1147, [1985] 2 WLR 643, 149 JP 204.
13. *R v Bourne Justices, ex p Cope* (1988) 153 JP 161, DC.
14. *R v Forest Magistrates' Court, ex p Spicer* (1988) 153 JP 81, [1988] Crim LR 619, DC.

1–526 Committal for Crown Court trial. *The procedures in committal proceedings which are explained in paragraphs 1–526 to 1–540 do not apply in the case of a person aged 18 or over, or a corporation, charged with an indictable-only offence to which s 51 of the Crime and Disorder Act 1998 applies; see paragraph 1–543 below.*

Save in those cases to which s 51 of the Crime and Disorder Act 1998 applies, the function of examining justices (which may be discharged by a single justice) is to inquire into indictable offences, and if, on consideration of the evidence, the court is of opinion that there is sufficient evidence to put the accused on trial by jury, it shall commit him for trial; otherwise it shall discharge him[1]. The function of committal proceedings is to ensure that no one shall stand his trial unless a *prima facie* case has been made out against him[2].

The changes as to the form of committal proceedings do not affect the principle that the prosecution may choose which witnesses to rely upon for the purposes of the committal proceedings. It is enough for the prosecutor to show the examining justices that there is sufficient evidence to put the accused on trial, provided always that, in deciding what evidence to tender, the prosecutor does not mislead the court or take unfair advantage of the accused. The duty to the examining justices is to consider the evidence tendered by the prosecutor in accordance with s 5A of the Magistrates' Court Act 1980[3].

If the court is satisfied that all the evidence tendered by or on behalf of the prosecutor is admissible[4], it may commit the accused for trial for the offence without consideration of the contents of any statements, depositions or other documents, and without consideration of any exhibits which are not documents, provided the accused, or each of the accused, has a legal representative acting for him in the case, and none of the legal representatives for the accused has requested the court to consider a submission that there is insufficient evidence to put that accused on trial by jury for the offence. Otherwise the court will consider the evidence which has been tendered by the prosecutor and hear any submission on behalf of the accused that there is insufficient evidence to put that accused on trial by jury before deciding whether to commit him for trial or discharge him[5]. The court must specify the place of trial having regard to the convenience of the defence, the prosecution and the witnesses, the expediting of the trial, and any direction of the Lord Chief Justice[6]. The statements, depositions or documentary exhibits are forwarded to the court of trial within four days of the committal[7], and the trial in the Crown Court will not ordinarily commence sooner than 14 days after the committal or later than 8 weeks after the committal for trial[8]. The bill of indictment is to be preferred within a period of 28 days commencing with the date of committal unless that period is extended by the Crown Court[9].

---

1. See Magistrates' Courts Act 1980, ss 4–8, in this PART: STATUTES ON PROCEDURE, post and Criminal Procedure Rules 2005, Parts 10 and 19, in this PART: STATUTORY INSTRUMENTS AND PRACTICE DIRECTIONS ON PROCEDURE, post. As to a corporation see Sch 3 of the 1980 Act, in this PART: STATUTES ON PROCEDURE, post.
2. *R v Epping and Harlow Justices, ex p Massaro* [1973] QB 433, 137 JP 373.
3. *Wilkinson v DPP* (1998) 162 JP 591, [1998] Crim LR 743.
4. To be admissible the evidence must fall within the requirements of s 5A(3) of the Magistrates' Courts Act 1980, in this PART: STATUTES ON PROCEDURE, post.
5. Magistrates' Courts Act 1980, s 6(1), (2), in this PART: STATUTES ON PROCEDURE, post.
6. See *Directions of the Lord Chief Justice*, in this PART: STATUTORY INSTRUMENTS AND PRACTICE DIRECTIONS ON PROCEDURE, post.
7. Criminal Procedure Rules 2005, Part 10, in this PART: STATUTORY INSTRUMENTS AND PRACTICE DIRECTIONS ON PROCEDURE, post.
8. Criminal Procedure Rules 2005, Part 39, in this PART: STATUTORY INSTRUMENTS AND PRACTICE DIRECTIONS ON PROCEDURE, post.
9. Criminal Procedure Rules 2005, Part 14, in this PART: STATUTORY INSTRUMENTS AND PRACTICE DIRECTIONS ON PROCEDURE, post.

1–527 The *sequence of events* in committal proceedings depends on whether the court is required to consider the evidence which has been tendered, or whether there is to be a committal for trial without consideration of the evidence[1]. These alternative procedures are considered in the following paragraphs.

Evidence shall be admissible by a magistrates' court inquiring into an offence as examining justices if it is tendered by or on behalf of the prosecutor and it falls within s 5A(3) of the Magistrates' Courts Act 1980. The following evidence falls within s 5A(3)[2]:

(*a*)   written statements complying with s 5B of the 1980 Act;
(*b*)   the documents or other exhibits (if any) referred to in such statements;
(*c*)   depositions complying with section 5C of the 1980 Act;
(*d*)   the documents or other exhibits (if any) referred to in such depositions;
(*e*)   statements complying with section 5D of the 1980 Act;
(*f*)   documents falling within section 5E of the 1980 Act.

For the purposes of the above provisions "document" means anything in which information of any description is recorded[3].

On committing the accused for trial, the court is required forthwith to remind him of his right to object by written notification to the prosecutor and the Crown Court within 14 days of being committed, unless the court in its discretion permits such an objection to be made outside that period, to a statement or deposition being read as evidence at the trial without oral evidence being given by the person who made the statement or deposition, and without the opportunity to cross-examine that person[4].

If plea and directions hearings have been established in the Crown Court at the place to which the case is committed, the magistrates' court must also specify the date on which the accused shall appear in the Crown Court for an initial plea and directions hearing[5].

---

1. In an appropriate case the initial procedure for offences triable either way will have preceded this see ante, para **1–502**. As to the sequence see generally Magistrates' Courts Act 1980, ss 4–8, in this PART: STATUTES ON PROCEDURE,

post and Criminal Procedure Rules 2005, Part 10, in this PART: STATUTORY INSTRUMENTS AND PRACTICE DIRECTIONS ON PROCEDURE, post.

    2. See this PART: STATUTES ON PROCEDURE, post.

    3. Magistrates' Courts Act 1980, s 5A(4), in this PART: STATUTES ON PROCEDURE, post.

    4. Criminal Procedure Rules 2005, Part 10, in this PART: STATUTORY INSTRUMENTS AND PRACTICE DIRECTIONS ON PROCEDURE, post.

    5. *Practice Direction (criminal: consolidated)* [2002] para V.53, in this PART: STATUTORY INSTRUMENTS AND PRACTICE DIRECTIONS ON PROCEDURE, post.

1–528   *Committal for trial s 6(1) MCA 1980—consideration of the evidence*

(1)   The accused is identified and if he is not represented, the nature of the proceedings are explained.

(2)   The accused is told—

"Until the proceedings are entirely finished, any report or broadcast about what happens in this court will be restricted to identifying all the people concerned, the offence or offences being inquired into, and any decisions of this court. You have the right to apply to this court to have these reporting restrictions removed, if you so wish. Do you want to make such an application?"

If there is more than one accused, the court will make an order only if it is satisfied, after hearing representations from the accused, that it is in the interests of justice to make it. Any such order is put in the court register, and repeated at the beginning of any adjourned hearing[1].

(3)   The court, having ascertained—

    (*a*)   that the accused has no legal representative acting for him in the case; or

    (*b*)   that the accused's legal representative has requested the court to consider a submission that there is insufficient evidence to put the accused on trial by jury for the offence with which he is charged, as the case may be,

shall permit the prosecutor to make an opening address to the court, if he so wishes, before any evidence is tendered[2].

(4)   After such opening address, if any, the court shall cause evidence to be tendered[3] by being read out aloud, except where the court otherwise directs or to the extent that it directs that an oral account be given of any of the evidence[4].

(5)   The court may view any exhibits produced before the court and may take possession of them[5].

(6)   After the evidence has been tendered the court shall hear any submission which the accused may wish to make as to whether there is sufficient evidence to put him on trial by jury for any indictable offence[6].

(7)   The court shall permit the prosecutor to make a submission—

    (*a*)   in reply to any submission made by the accused under (6) above; or

    (*b*)   where the accused has not made any such submission but the court is nevertheless minded not to commit him for trial[7].

(8)   After the hearing any submission under (6) and (7) above, the court shall, unless it decides not to commit the accused for trial, cause the charge to be written down, if this has not already been done, and, if the accused is not represented by counsel or a solicitor, shall read the charge to him and explain it in ordinary language. The court will then formally commit the accused for trial[8].

---

    1. Magistrates' Courts Act 1980, s 8, in this PART: STATUTES ON PROCEDURE, post; Criminal Procedure Rules 2005, Part 10, in this PART: STATUTORY INSTRUMENTS AND PRACTICE DIRECTIONS ON PROCEDURE, post.

    2. Criminal Procedure Rules 2005, Part 10, in this PART: STATUTORY INSTRUMENTS AND PRACTICE DIRECTIONS ON PROCEDURE,, post.

    3. Evidence to be tendered is to be in accordance with ss 5B(4), 5C(4), 5D(5) and 5E(3) of the Magistrates' Courts Act 1980, in this PART: STATUTES ON PROCEDURE,, post (Criminal Procedure Rules 2005, Part 10, in this PART: STATUTORY INSTRUMENTS AND PRACTICE DIRECTIONS ON PROCEDURE, post).

    4. Criminal Procedure Rules 2005, Part 10, in this PART: STATUTORY INSTRUMENTS AND PRACTICE DIRECTIONS ON PROCEDURE,, post.

    5. Criminal Procedure Rules 2005, Part 10, in this PART: STATUTORY INSTRUMENTS AND PRACTICE DIRECTIONS ON PROCEDURE,, post.

    6. Criminal Procedure Rules 2005, Part 10, in this PART: STATUTORY INSTRUMENTS AND PRACTICE DIRECTIONS ON PROCEDURE,, post.

    7. Criminal Procedure Rules 2005, Part 10, in this PART: STATUTORY INSTRUMENTS AND PRACTICE DIRECTIONS ON PROCEDURE,, post.

    8. Criminal Procedure Rules 2005, Part 10, in this PART: STATUTORY INSTRUMENTS AND PRACTICE DIRECTIONS ON PROCEDURE,, post.

1–529   *Committal for trial s 6(2) MCA 1980—without consideration of the evidence*

(1)   The accused is identified and the fact that he has a solicitor acting for him in the case is established[1].

(2)   The prosecution informs the court that all the evidence tendered by or on behalf of the prosecutor falls within s 5A(3) of the Magistrates' Courts Act 1980, a copy of such evidence having been given by the prosecutor to the accused before being tendered in evidence[1].

(3)   The charge is written down if this has not already been done and read to the accused[2].

(4)   The court shall ascertain whether the accused submits that there is insufficient evidence to put him on trial by jury for the offence with which he is charged[2].

(5) If the court is satisfied that the accused does not wish to make such a submission, it shall after receiving any written evidence falling within s 5A(3) of the 1980 Act, determine whether or not to commit the accused for trial without consideration of the evidence, and where it determines not to so commit it shall proceed in accordance with para **1–528**, ante[3].

(6) The court invites representations and makes orders on the place of trial, whether the accused shall be in custody or on bail[4] in the meantime and with regard to representation under any legal aid order.

When a copy of evidence tendered in accordance with s 5A of the 1980 Act is given or served on any party to the proceedings, the accused shall be given notice of his right to object to the statement being tendered in evidence[5].

1. Criminal Procedure Rules 2005, Part 10, this PART: STATUTORY INSTRUMENTS AND PRACTICE DIRECTIONS ON PROCEDURE, post.
2. Criminal Procedure Rules 2005, Part 10, in this PART: STATUTORY INSTRUMENTS AND PRACTICE DIRECTIONS ON PROCEDURE, post.
3. Criminal Procedure Rules 2005, Part 10, in this PART: STATUTORY INSTRUMENTS AND PRACTICE DIRECTIONS ON PROCEDURE, post.
4. See Bail Act 1976, s 5, in this PART: STATUTES ON PROCEDURE, post and para **1–464**, ante.
5. Criminal Procedure Rules 2005, Part 27, in this PART: STATUTORY INSTRUMENTS AND PRACTICE DIRECTIONS ON PROCEDURE, post.

1–540 *Committal for trial—general principles.* A committal for trial in respect of an offence triable summarily only, is a nullity and does not prevent a subsequent hearing and conviction summarily[1]. Similarly an acquittal by a magistrates' court on a charge triable only on indictment is a nullity, and a magistrates' court sitting as examining justices may thereafter commit the accused for trial[2]. A committal for trial on a charge which might be said to be duplicitous is not such a defect as would lead to the quashing of the committal[3]. Charges of gravity should not be reduced merely for the purpose of founding jurisdiction in a magistrates' court but should be committed to the Crown Court[4]. But if in committal proceedings the prosecutor offers no evidence, the consent of the examining justices is not required; moreover it is not necessarily an abuse of the process of the court, for the prosecutor to offer no evidence on a charge to which the accused has elected trial by jury, and prefer a lesser charge which is triable only summarily[5]. The fact that the prosecution wish to add to or substitute charges either to ensure the case is tried summarily or in the Crown Court is not a ground for refusing the issue of such process provided that the prosecution proposal is appropriate on the facts before the court[6]. Where the prosecution declines to tender evidence the justices must discharge the accused, even though he has served on the court admissions under s 10 of the Criminal Justice Act 1967[7]. If the justices are evenly divided in opinion, they may adjourn so that the charge may be reheard before a reconstituted bench[8]. Examining justices have jurisdiction to entertain committal proceedings relating to charges on which the accused has previously been discharged under s 6, but repeated use of the procedure whereby it becomes vexatious or an abuse of the process of the court will be prohibited by the High Court[9]. Examining justices may consider whether an initiation of the process of committal is an abuse of process, but may not refuse to embark on their inquiry simply because they think a prosecution should not have been brought because it appears mean-minded, petty, or animated by personal hostility[10].

Where no proceedings have been taken under the Magistrates' Courts Act 1980, or an examining justice has refused to commit for trial, an application may be made to a judge of the High Court for consent to prefer a bill of indictment[11].

It is not a breach of the Act or the Rules, nor of the rules of natural justice, for an examining justice to look at the case papers in advance; indeed it could be a useful practice, but such an examination must not be regarded as a tendering of evidence[12].

As a general rule, evidence should not be excluded on the sole ground that it may be unfairly prejudicial to the accused; this issue should be left to the court of trial[13]. A committal for trial is not invalidated by the fact that inadmissible evidence has been tendered before the examining justice[14]. In proceedings before examining justices, a confession made by an accused person may be given in evidence against him in so far as it is relevant to any matter in issue, but there is no power for the examining justices to conduct an inquiry under s 76(2) of the Police and Criminal Evidence Act 1984[15]. Where in committal proceedings an arguable point of statutory interpretation is raised, the better course is for the justices to commit for trial and leave the point to be argued in the Crown Court[16].

1. *Bannister v Clarke* [1920] 3 KB 598, 85 JP 12.
2. *R v West* [1964] 1 QB 15, [1962] 2 All ER 624, 126 JP 352.
3. See *R v Newcastle-under-Lyme Justices, ex p Hemmings* [1987] Crim LR 416.
4. *R v Weeks* (1928) 20 Cr App Rep 188; *R v Bodmin Justices, ex p McEwen* [1947] KB 321, [1941] 1 All ER 109, 111 JP 47.
5. *R v Canterbury and St Augustine's Justices, ex p Klisiak* [1982] QB 398, [1981] 2 All ER 129, 145 JP 344.
6. *R v Redbridge Justices and Fox, ex p Whitehouse* (1992) 156 JP 293.
7. *R v Horseferry Road Metropolitan Stipendiary Magistrate, ex p O'Regan* (1986) 150 JP 535, [1986] Crim LR 679.
8. *R v Hertfordshire Justices, ex p Larsen* [1926] 1 KB 191, 89 JP 205.
9. *R v Manchester City Stipendiary Magistrate, ex p Snelson* [1978] 2 All ER 62, [1977] 1 WLR 911, 142 JP 274; *R v Horsham Justices, ex p Reeves* [1981] Crim LR 566.
10. *R v Telford Justices, ex p Badhan* [1991] 2 QB 78, [1991] 2 All ER 854, 155 JP 481; and see *R v Rotherham Justices, ex p Brough* [1991] Crim LR 522—prohibition where the prosecution arranged for an indictable only offence summons to

be returnable after the accused attained the age of 17 (the age (now 18) at which the defendant became an adult for the purposes of mode of trial).

11. Administration of Justice (Miscellaneous Provisions) Act 1933, s 2; see para **1–563**, post.
12. *R v Colchester Stipendiary Magistrate, ex p Beck* [1979] QB 674, [1979] 2 All ER 1035.
13. *R v G Weaver, R v J Weaver* [1968] 1 QB 353, [1967] 1 All ER 277, 131 JP 173.
14. *R v Norfolk Quarter Sessions, ex p Brunson* [1953] 1 QB 503, [1953] 1 All ER 346, 117 JP 100.
15. Police and Criminal Evidence Act 1984 s 76(1) and (9) in PART II: EVIDENCE, post.
16. *R v Chichester Justices, ex p Chichester District Council* (1990) 155 JP 6, 88 LGR 707, DC.

1–541   *Exhibits.* The court has a responsibility to preserve and retain any exhibits, or to arrange for their preservation or retention for the purposes of justice. The usual course is for the court to entrust the exhibits to the Director of Public Prosecutions, the police or other prosecutor. Where the court does so entrust exhibits, it can impose such restrictions as it considers proper in all the circumstances. But if the court imposes no restrictions, it is for the recipient of the exhibits to deal with them in whatever way appears best for the purposes of justice[1].

----

1. *R v Lambeth Metropolitan Stipendiary Magistrate, ex p McComb* [1983] QB 551, [1983] 1 All ER 321, 76 Cr App Rep 246.

1–542   *Coroner.* Where a person is charged before a magistrates' court with murder, manslaughter or infanticide, or an offence under s 1 of the Road Traffic Act 1988 (causing death by dangerous driving) or an offence under s 2(1) of the Suicide Act 1961 consisting of aiding, abetting, counselling or procuring the suicide of another, the clerk to the justices shall inform the coroner, who is responsible for holding an inquest into the death, of the making of the charge and of the result of the proceedings before that court[1]. In such cases the coroner is required by s 16 of the Coroners Act 1988 to adjourn the inquest pending the conclusion of the criminal proceedings. In cases where s 16 of the Coroners Act 1988 does not apply, but a prosecution is pending relating to an incident regarding which an inquest has been opened, as a matter of practice, justices ought not to proceed with the case until the inquest has been held[2].

----

1. Coroners Act 1988, s 17, in PART VIII: title CORONERS, post.
2. *Smith v DPP* [2000] RTR 36, 164 JP 96.

1–543   Sending for trial – indictable only offences. Where a person aged 18 or over appears or is brought before a magistrates' court charged with an offence triable only on indictment ("the indictable-only offence"), the court shall send him forthwith to the Crown Court for trial for that offence and for any triable either-way offence or summary offence which fulfils the requisite conditions[1]. An offence fulfils the requisite conditions if—

(1) it appears to the court to be related to the indictable-only offence; and
(2) in the case of a summary offence, it is punishable with imprisonment or involves obligatory or discretionary disqualification from driving[2].

----

1. Crime and Disorder Act 1998, s 51(1), in this PART: STATUTES ON PROCEDURE, post.
2. Crime and Disorder Act 1998, s 51(11), in this PART: STATUTES ON PROCEDURE, post.

1–544   *Related offences triable either way and summary offences.* A triable either-way offence for this purpose is related to an indictable-only offence if the charge for the either-way offence could be joined in the same indictment as the charge for the indictable-only offence[2]. A summary offence is related to an indictable-only offence if it arises out of circumstances which are the same as or connected with those giving rise to the indictable-only offence[2].

Where an accused person who has been sent for trial under these provisions subsequently appears or is brought before a magistrates' court charged with an either-way offence or a summary offence which fulfils the requisite conditions referred to above, the court may send him forthwith to the Crown Court for trial for the either-way or summary offence[4].

Where—

(1) the court sends an adult for trial in accordance with this procedure;
(2) another adult appears or is brought before the court on the same or a subsequent occasion charged jointly with him with an either-way offence; and
(3) that offence appears to the court to be related to the indictable-only offence,

the court *shall* where it is the same occasion, and *may* where it is a subsequent occasion, send the other adult forthwith to the Crown Court for trial for the either-way offence[3]. Where a court sends another adult for trial in these circumstances, it shall at the same time send him to the Crown Court for trial for any either-way or summary offence with which he is charged which fulfils the requisite conditions[4].

----

1. Crime and Disorder Act 1998, s 51(12), in this PART: STATUTES ON PROCEDURE, post.
2. Crime and Disorder Act 1998, s 51(2), in this PART: STATUTES ON PROCEDURE, post.
3. Crime and Disorder Act 1998, s 51(3), in this PART: STATUTES ON PROCEDURE, post.
4. Crime and Disorder Act 1998, s 51(4), in this PART: STATUTES ON PROCEDURE, post.

1–545   *Children or young persons charged with related either way offences.*   Where—

(1)   the court sends an adult for trial (whether as the original adult or another adult) under the above procedure; and

(2)   a child or young person appears or is brought before the court on the same or a subsequent occasion charged jointly with the adult with an indictable offence for which the adult is sent for trial,

the court shall, if it considers it necessary in the interests of justice to do so, send the child or young person forthwith to the Crown Court for trial for the indictable offence[1]. Where a court sends a child or young person for trial under this procedure, it may at the same time send him to the Crown Court for trial for any either-way or summary offence with which he is charged which fulfils the requisite conditions[2].

---

1. Crime and Disorder Act 1998, s 51(5), in this PART: STATUTES ON PROCEDURE, post.
2. Crime and Disorder Act 1998, s 51(6), in this PART: STATUTES ON PROCEDURE, post.

1–546   *Procedure.*   The court must specify in a notice the offence or offences for which a person is sent for trial under s 51 of the Crime and Disorder Act 1998 and the place at which he is to be tried[1]. In a case where there is more than one indictable-only offence and the court includes an either-way or a summary offence in the notice, the court must specify in that notice the indictable-only offence to which the either-way offence or, as the case may be, the summary offence appears to be related[2].

A magistrates' court may send a person for trial under s 51 of the Crime and Disorder Act 1998 in custody or on bail in accordance with the Bail Act 1976[3]. Before taking that decision a magistrates' court may adjourn any proceedings under s 51 and, if it does so, shall remand the accused[4].

The procedures to be followed in the Crown Court with respect to a person who has been sent for trial under s 51 of the Crime and Disorder Act 1998 are set out in Schedule 3 to the Act. Provision is also made for a justice to take evidence as a deposition from a witness who is likely to be able to make, on behalf of the prosecutor, a written statement containing material evidence, or produce a document or other exhibit likely to be material evidence, for the purposes of proceedings for an offence for which a person has been sent for trial under s 51 of that Act and the witness will not voluntarily make the statement or produce the document or other exhibit[5].

Where a magistrates' court has sent a person charged with an offence triable only on indictment to the Crown Court for trial under s 51 of the 1998 Act, the Crown Court has the power to alter the place of trial under s 76 of the Senior Court Act 1981[6].

---

1. Crime and Disorder Act 1998, s 51(7), in this PART: STATUTES ON PROCEDURE, post.
2. Crime and Disorder Act 1998, s 51(8), in this PART: STATUTES ON PROCEDURE, post.
3. Crime and Disorder Act 1998, s 52(1), in this PART: STATUTES ON PROCEDURE, post.
4. Crime and Disorder Act 1998, s 52(5), in this PART: STATUTES ON PROCEDURE, post.
5. Crime and Disorder Act 1998, Sch 3, in this PART: STATUTES ON PROCEDURE, post.
6. *R v Crown Court at Croydon, ex p Britton* (2000) 164 JP 729, DC.

1–547   Transfer of fraud or certain cases involving children to the Crown Court.   The following comments refer to fraud cases. Likewise a person charged with sexual offences and offences involving violence or cruelty concerning children may be transferred to the Crown Court under the provisions of the Criminal Justice Act 1991, s 53 and Sch 6 in PART III: SENTENCING, post.

If a person has been charged with an indictable offence; and in the opinion of the designated authority the evidence of the offence charged (*a*) would be sufficient for the proceedings against the person charged to be transferred for trial, and (*b*) reveals a case of fraud of such seriousness and complexity that it is appropriate that the management of the case should without delay be taken over by the Crown Court; and not later than the time at which the authority would be required to serve a notice of the prosecution case under s 5 of the Magistrates' Courts Act 1980, the designated authority gives the court a notice of transfer certifying that opinion, the functions of the magistrates' court shall, subject to certain exceptions, cease in relation to the case[1].

A notice of transfer shall specify the proposed place of trial and the charge or charges to which it relates, together with such additional matter as may be prescribed by regulations[2]. Serious and complex fraud cases should be heard at specially designated Crown Court centres[3]. Where notice of transfer is given, the person charged may at any time before he is arraigned apply orally or in writing to the Crown Court for the charge to be dismissed on the ground that the evidence which has been disclosed would not be sufficient for a jury properly to convict him of it[4]. In deciding whether to grant such an application the judge shall have regard—(*a*) to the evidence tendered by the prosecution; (*b*) to any written or oral statement tendered by the defence in support of the application; and (*c*) to any oral evidence on behalf of the prosecution or the defence which is given by leave of the judge[5]. A discharge by the judge shall have the same effect as the dismissal of a charge against an accused under s 6 of the Magistrates' Courts Act 1980, except that no further proceedings may thereafter be brought on the charge except by means of the preferment of a voluntary bill of indictment[6].

---

1. Criminal Justice Act 1987, s 4(1), in this PART: STATUTES ON PROCEDURE, post.
2. Criminal Justice Act 1987, s 5(1), (2), in this PART: STATUTES ON PROCEDURE, post.
3. *Practice Note* [1993] 1 All ER 41, CA; noted to s 5 of the Criminal Justice Act 1987 in this PART: STATUTES ON PROCEDURE, post.
4. Criminal Justice Act 1987, s 6(1), in this PART: STATUTES ON PROCEDURE, post.
5. Criminal Justice Act 1987, s 6(6), in this PART: STATUTES ON PROCEDURE, post.
6. Criminal Justice Act 1987, s 6(7), in this PART: STATUTES ON PROCEDURE, post.

1–548   *Designated authorities.*   The designated authorities are—

   (*a*)   the Director of Public Prosecutions;
   (*b*)   the Director of the Serious Fraud Office;
   (*c*)   the Commissioners of Inland Revenue;
   (*d*)   the Commissioners of Customs and Excise; and
   (*e*)   the Secretary of State[1].

The provisions of s 40 of the Criminal Justice Act 1988 (power to join in indictment count for specified summary offences)[2] do not apply where proceedings have been transferred for trial under s 53 of the Criminal Justice Act 1988[3].

---

   1.   Criminal Justice Act 1987, s 4(2), in this PART: STATUTES ON PROCEDURE, post.
   2.   In this PART: STATUTES ON PROCEDURE, post.
   3.   *R v T and K* [2001] 1 Cr App Rep 446, 165 JP 306, [2001] Crim LR 398, CA.

1–549   *Bail.*   After notice of transfer has been given to a magistrates' court that court shall, if it has previously remanded the accused in custody, have power to order that he be safely kept in custody until delivered to the Crown Court, or that he be released on bail in accordance with the Bail Act 1976, either conditionally or unconditionally. Where the magistrates' court would have had power, by virtue of s 128(3A) of the Magistrates' Courts Act 1980, further to remand the accused without appearing before the court, it may still exercise that power if satisfied that the accused has given written consent to the power being exercised, and that when he gave his consent, he knew that the notice of transfer had been issued[1].

---

   1.   Criminal Justice Act 1987, s 5(3)–(5), in this PART: STATUTES ON PROCEDURE, post.

1–550   *Representation.*   Where notice of transfer is given, the magistrates' court to which notice is given, or the Crown Court, may order that the accused shall be granted representation for the purposes of the trial[1].

---

   1.   Criminal Defence Service (General) (No 2) Regulations 2001, reg 9, in this PART: STATUTORY INSTRUMENTS AND PRACTICE DIRECTIONS ON PROCEDURE, post.

1–560   *Witnesses at trial.*   The provisions of the Criminal Procedure (Attendance of Witnesses) Act 1965[1] shall apply to a person whose written statement is tendered in evidence for the purposes of the notice of transfer and that person shall be treated as a person who has been examined by the magistrates' court[2].

---

   1.   See this PART: STATUTES ON PROCEDURE, post.
   2.   Criminal Justice Act 1987, s 5(8), in this PART: STATUTES ON PROCEDURE, post.

1–561   *Preparatory hearing—fraud cases* .   Where it appears to a judge of the Crown Court that the evidence on an indictment reveals a case of fraud of such seriousness and complexity that substantial benefits are likely to accrue from a preparatory hearing before the jury are sworn he may make an order to that effect[1].

---

   1.   Criminal Justice Act 1987, s 7, in this PART: STATUTES ON PROCEDURE, post.

1–562   *Reporting restrictions—fraud cases.*   Reporting restrictions are imposed in relation to both applications to the Crown Court for dismissal of the charge and preparatory hearings[1].

---

   1.   Criminal Justice Act 1987, s 11, in this PART: STATUTES ON PROCEDURE, post.

1–563   **Indictments.**   The Indictments Act 1915 regulates the form of indictments and provides that every indictment shall contain, and shall be sufficient if it contains, a statement of the specific offence or offences with which the accused person is charged, together with such particulars as may be necessary for giving reasonable information as to the nature of the charge[1]. Subject to the provisions of the Act, an indictment shall not be open to objection in respect of its form or contents if it is framed in accordance with the Criminal Procedure Rules[2]. Where, before trial, or at any stage of a trial, it appears to the Crown Court that the indictment is defective, the court shall make such order for the amendment of the indictment as the court thinks necessary to meet the circumstances of the case, unless, having regard to the merits of the case, the required amendments cannot be made without injustice[3].

No bill of indictment charging any person with an indictable offence shall be preferred unless[4] either–

   (*a*)   the person charged has been committed[5] for trial for the offence; or
   (*b*)   the offence is specified in a notice of transfer under s 4 of the Criminal Justice Act 1987 (serious and complex fraud); or
   (*c*)   the offence is specified in a notice under s 53 of the Criminal Justice Act 1991 (violent or sexual offences against children); or

(d)　the person has been sent for trial for the offence under section 51 (no committal proceedings for indictable-only offences) of the Crime and Disorder Act 1998; or

(e)　the bill is preferred by the direction of the criminal division of the Court of Appeal or by the direction or with the consent of a judge of the High Court; or

(f)　the bill is preferred under section 22B(3)(a) of the Prosecution of Offences Act 1985.

Where an indictment is invalid because it has not been drawn according to the Rules, it is open to the Crown Court to grant the prosecution leave to prefer out of time fresh indictments which conform with the Rules[6].

---

1. Indictments Act 1915, s 3.
2. Criminal Procedure Rules 2005, Part 14..
3. Indictments Act 1915, s 5.
4. Administration of Justice (Miscellaneous Provisions) Act 1933, s 2(2).
5. This means lawfully committed, and legally committed for trial: see *R v Gee* [1936] 2 KB 442, [1936] 2 All ER 89, 100 JP 227 and, *R v Phillips, R v Quayle* [1939] 1 KB 63, [1938] 3 All ER 674, 102 JP 467; *R v Grant* [1944] 2 All ER 311; *R v Healy* (1944) 109 JP Jo 39; *R v Norfolk Quarter Sessions, ex p Brunson* [1953] 1 All ER 346, 117 JP 100, and where a common law offence is the same as a statutory offence, *R v Beckley* (1887) 20 QBD 187, 52 JP 120.
6. *R v Follett* [1989] QB 338, [1989] 1 All ER 995, CA.

1–564　*Voluntary bills.* The usual way of bringing a defendant to trial is by methods (a) to (d) in para **1–563**, ante. An application under s 2(2)(b) of the Administration of Justice (Miscellaneous Provisions) Act 1933 for the direction or consent of a judge of the High Court to the preferment of a bill of indictment (known as a "voluntary bill") should be granted only where good reason to depart from the normal procedure is clearly shown and only where the interests of justice, rather than considerations of administrative convenience, require it[1].

On an application for leave to prefer a bill of indictment the defendant has no right to be heard or make representations to the High Court judge[2] but in exceptional circumstances the judge may invite written submissions on behalf of any defendant affected if, in his judgment, the interests of justice so require[1] Probably, only the Court of Appeal has power to review a decision made by a High Court judge on an application for leave to prefer a bill of indictment[1].

The Criminal Procedure Rules 2005[3] provide as to the manner in which and the time at which bills of indictment are to be preferred, and the manner in which application is to be made for the consent of a judge of the High Court for the preferment of a bill of indictment.

Applications for voluntary bills must also be accompanied by:

(a)　a copy of any charges on which the defendant has been committed for trial;

(b)　a copy of any charges on which his committal for trial was refused by the magistrates' court;

(c)　a copy of any existing indictment which has been preferred in consequence of his committal;

(d)　a summary of the evidence or other document which—

　　(i)　identifies the counts in the proposed indictment on which he has been committed for trial (or which are substantially the same as charges on which he has been so committed), and

　　(ii)　in relation to each other count in the proposed indictment, identifies the pages in the accompanying statements and exhibits where the essential evidence said to support the count is to be found;

(e)　marginal markings of the relevant passages on the pages of the statements and exhibits identified under (d)(ii).

This must be complied with in relation to each defendant named in the indictment for which leave is sought, whether or not it is proposed to prefer any new count against him[1].

Where it is proposed to prefer a bill of indictment where no proceedings have been taken under the Magistrates' Courts Act 1980 or the examining justices have refused[4] to commit for trial, the procedure laid down by the Administration of Justice (Miscellaneous Provisions) Act 1933 and the Rules should be carefully observed. It is the duty of any clerk to the justices or other person in possession of any committal documents to give to any person desiring to make an application for leave to prefer a bill of indictment against a person in respect of whom committal proceedings have taken place a reasonable opportunity to inspect the committal documents and, if so required by him, to supply him with copies of the documents or any part thereof[5].

---

1. *Practice Direction (criminal: consolidated)* [2002] para IV.35, in this PART: STATUTORY INSTRUMENTS AND PRACTICE DIRECTIONS ON PROCEDURE, post.
2. *R v Raymond* [1981] QB 910, [1981] 2 All ER 246, CA.
3. See the Criminal Procedure Rules 2005, r 14.1, in this PART: STATUTORY INSTRUMENTS AND PRACTICE DIRECTIONS ON PROCEDURE, post.
4. See the Magistrates' Courts Act 1980, s 6, in this PART: STATUTES ON PROCEDURE, post.
5. See the Criminal Procedure Rules 2005, Part 14, in this PART: STATUTORY INSTRUMENTS AND PRACTICE DIRECTIONS ON PROCEDURE, post.

1–565　*Inclusion of further counts.* The Administration of Justice (Miscellaneous Provisions) Act 1933, s 2(2), provides that further counts can be joined in an indictment in the following cases:

(i)　where the person charged has been committed for trial, the bill of indictment against him may include, either in substitution for or in addition to counts charging the offence for which he was committed, any counts founded on facts or evidence disclosed to the magistrates' court inquiring into that offence as examining justices, being counts which may lawfully be joined in the same indictment;

(ii) in a case to which paragraph (*b*) or (*c*) of para **1–563** applies, the bill of indictment may include, either in substitution for or in addition to any count charging an offence specified in the notice of transfer, any counts founded on material that accompanied the copy of that notice which was given to the person charged, being counts which may lawfully be joined in the same indictment;

(iii) in the case to which paragraph (*d*) of para **1–563** applies, the bill of indictment may include, either in substitution for or in addition to any count charging an offence specified in the notice under section 51(7) of the 1998 Act, any count founded on material which, in pursuance of regulations made under paragraph 1 of Sch 3 to that Act, was served on the person charged, being counts which may be lawfully joined in the same indictment;

(iv) a charge of a previous conviction of an offence may, notwithstanding that it was not included in the committal or in any such direction or consent as aforesaid, be included in any bill of indictment.

Where justices have refused to commit a charge the prosecution may nevertheless include a count for that charge in the indictment. The consent of the court is unnecessary before such added counts are included, but the trial judge must decide, on a motion to quash the indictment (or where he raises the question), whether they should be added[1]. The judge has the power to allow the prosecution to include on the indictment charges which had been stayed by the magistrate on the ground of abuse of process where they are founded by the statements[3]. Another count may be added after committal, even though further evidence may be required at the trial to complete the prosecution's case[3]. The defence should be given notice of any substituted or additional charge[4].

---

1. *R v Morry* [1946] KB 153, [1945] 2 All ER 632, 110 JP 124.
2. *R v Cooper* (1994) Times, 22 November.
3. *R v Thomas* (1947) 32 Cr App Rep 50, CCA.
4. *Practice Direction (criminal: consolidated)* [2002] para IV.34, in this PART, post.

SUMMARY CRIMINAL TRIAL

1–566   This part deals with the procedure for trials before magistrates' courts. The term 'summary trial' includes proceedings where there is a guilty plea and proceedings where evidence is heard following a plea of not guilty. Sometimes, the term 'trial' may be used in a context where it refers to the court beginning to hear evidence.

Detailed provision is made in the *Criminal Case Management Framework* for what is expected where a not guilty plea is to be entered[1]. The aim should be to determine the future timetable of the case, including if appropriate, fixing a trial date.

---

1. Pre-Court Process Parts 15–19, in this PART: CODES OF PRACTICE AND GUIDELINES, post.

1–567   Taking a plea.   On the summary trial of an information the court shall, if the accused appears, state to him the substance of the information and, if he is unrepresented, explain it to him in simple language[1], and ask him if he pleads guilty or not guilty. If the accused pleads guilty, the court may convict him without hearing evidence[2].

The accused should be asked personally to plead even though he is represented by counsel or solicitor[3]. If the defendant is deaf and has difficulty in communicating orally, he should have assistance either from an interpreter or legal representative, or if need be both[4]. Special pleading must not be entertained[5]. When the accused does not attend court but is represented by counsel or solicitor, such advocate may enter a plea on his behalf[6]; if a juvenile defendant is absent, his distinct personal authority is necessary[7].

---

1. Criminal Procedure Rules 2005, Part 37, in this PART: STATUTORY INSTRUMENTS AND PRACTICE DIRECTIONS ON PROCEDURE, post.
2. Magistrates' Courts Act 1980, s 9, in this PART: STATUTES ON PROCEDURE, post. As to the procedure where the defendant, though pleading guilty, disputes the prosecution version of the facts see para **1–508** ante. If the defendant does not appear, see para **1–752**, ante.
3. *R v Wakefield Justices, ex p Butterworth* [1970] 1 All ER 1181, 134 JP 347. See also, generally, para **1–139 Appearance by legal representative**, ante.
4. *R v Kingston-upon-Thames Magistrates' Court, ex p Davey* (1985) 149 JP 744.
5. *Barnes v Norris* (1876) 41 JP 150, per Field J.
6. Note Magistrates' Courts Act 1980, s 122, in this PART: STATUTES ON PROCEDURE, post. See also para **1–139**, ante.
7. *R v Aves* (1871) 35 JP 533.

1–567A   *Corporations.*   On the summary trial of an information against a corporation, a representative[1] may enter a plea of guilty or not guilty, and for the purposes of a plea of guilty in the absence of accused, a director or the secretary of the corporation may likewise give a notification or intimation[2]. A representative[1] may also make an application to dismiss the charge, or consent or object to summary trial, or claim trial by jury[2]. A corporation will generally otherwise appear by counsel or solicitor.

As to guilty pleas, see further para **1–XXX**, post.

---

1. Defined and limited in scope by s 33(6) of the Criminal Justice Act 1925, in this PART: STATUTES ON PROCEDURE, post.
2. See Magistrates' Courts Act 1980, s 12(4) and Sch 3, in this PART: STATUTES ON PROCEDURE, post.

1–568   Withdrawal of a guilty plea.   A magistrates' court may allow a defendant to withdraw his plea of guilty at any time up to sentence being passed[1]. The same principle applies when the defendant is committed to the Crown Court for sentence, and if the Crown Court accedes to the application it will remit the case to the justices on the basis of a plea (or an indicated plea) of not guilty[2]. Justices who have adjourned a case on recommending legal representation because they contemplated a custodial sentence are entitled in their discretion to refuse the withdrawal of an unequivocal plea of guilty[3]. Where a plea of guilty is withdrawn, evidence of that plea as a confession of fact is admissible at the trial; the court should however carefully balance the probative value of such evidence against its prejudicial nature, and will usually not admit it[4].

As to the principles that govern allowing a defendant to withdraw his guilty plea, Lord Phillips CJ in *Revitt, Borg and Barnes v DPP*[5] described as "better general guidance" the following comments of Lord Morris in *R v Recorder of Manchester*, supra, namely: "The duty of any court to clear the innocent must be equal or superior in importance to its duty to convict and punish the guilty. The court will, however, have great concern if any doubt exists as to whether a confession was intended or whether it ought really ever to have been made". The onus lies on a party seeking to vacate his guilty plea to demonstrate that justice requires that this should be permitted[5].

---

1. *R v Campbell, ex p Hoy* [1953] 1 QB 585, [1953] 1 All ER 684, 117 JP 189; *R v McNally* [1954] 2 All ER 372, [1954] 1 WLR 933, 118 JP 399; *S (an infant) v Manchester City Recorder* [1971] AC 481, [1969] 3 All ER 1230.
2. *R v Mutford and Lothingland Justices, ex p Harber* [1971] 2 QB 291, [1971] 1 All ER 81, 135 JP 107; *R v Fareham Justices, ex p Long* [1976] Crim LR 269; *R v Inner London Crown Court, ex p Sloper* (1978) 69 Cr App Rep 1 (decided before the plea before venue procedure was introduced for either way offences).
3. *R v South Tameside Magistrates' Court, ex p Rowland* [1983] 3 All ER 689, 148 JP 202. See also *R v Sheik* [2004] EWCA Crim 492, [2004] 2 Cr App R 13 (Crown Court refused to allow change of plea where defendants had not been warned of possibility of confiscation proceedings).
4. *R v Rimmer* [1972] 1 All ER 604, [1972] 1 WLR 268, 136 JP 242.
5. [2006] EWHC 2266 (Admin), (2006) 170 JP 729.

GUILTY PLEA

1–569   If, having been asked whether he pleads guilty or not guilty, the accused pleads guilty, the court may convict him without hearing evidence[1].

---

1. Magistrates' Courts Act 1980, s 9(3), in this PART: STATUTES ON PROCEDURE, post.

1–580   Credit for guilty plea.   Depending upon the stage in the proceedings at which it is entered, a guilty plea will attract a discount of up to one third on the sentence that would otherwise have been passed[1]. Where the court imposes a less severe sentence as a result of a guilty plea it shall state in open court that it has done so[2].

---

1. See para **3–171**, PART III: SENTENCING, post, and the Criminal Justice Act 2003, s 144, in PART III: SENTENCING, post.
2. Criminal Justice Act 2003, s 174(2)(*d*), in PART III: SENTENCING, post..

1–581   Equivocal plea.   To make a plea of guilty binding and effective it must be unambiguous[1]. If the accused pleads guilty and later makes a statement which, if true, would be a defence to the charge, the court should then enter a plea (or an indicated plea) of not guilty[2]. Indeed a change of plea should be invited where a solicitor's mitigation shows the inappropriateness of a guilty plea to the whole of the charge[3]. If material comes to the attention of the court before sentence, raising a suspicion that the defendant did not really mean to plead guilty, that renders the plea equivocal[4]. A mistake in law does not necessarily make a plea equivocal[5]. The same may apply where a plea of guilty is entered as a result of a mistake made by the defendant's solicitors in understanding his instructions[6].

---

1. *R v Golathan* (1915) 79 JP 270; *R v Ingleson* [1915] 1 KB 512; *R v Emery* (1943) 29 Cr App Rep 47; *R v Field* (1943) 29 Cr App Rep 151; *R v Tottenham Justices, ex p Rubens* [1970] 1 All ER 879, [1970] 1 WLR 300, 134 JP 285.
2. *R v Durham Quarter Sessions, ex p Virgo* [1952] 2 QB 1, [1952] 1 All ER 466; *R v Blandford Justices, ex p G (an infant)* [1967] 1 QB 82, [1966] 1 All ER 1021 and cf *R v West Kent Quarter Sessions Appeal Committee, ex p Files* [1951] 2 All ER 728, 115 JP 522; *R v London County Quarter Sessions Appeal Committee Deputy Chairman, ex p Borg* [1958] 1 QB 43, [1957] 3 All ER 28, 121 JP 562 explaining *Mittlemann v Denman* [1920] 1 KB 519, 84 JP 39 (decided before the plea before venue procedure was introduced for either way offences).
3. *R v South Sefton Justices, ex p Rabaca* (1986) Times, 20 February (theft acknowledged of only 1/28 of the value of the property in the information).
4. *Leahy v Rawlinson* [1978] Crim LR 106.
5. *P Foster (Haulage) Ltd v Roberts* [1978] 2 All ER 751, 142 JP 44.
6. *R v Bristol Justices, ex p Sawyers* (1988) Times, 23 June, DC.

1–582   *Appeal against conviction following an equivocal guilty plea.*   The defendant may appeal against conviction if the magistrates' court treats an equivocal plea as a plea of guilty; the Crown Court must make a proper enquiry as to what happened in the magistrates' court as to plea, before considering remitting the case[1]; it does not have a duty to inquire into the matter unless it is told something which suggests the justices ought to have considered permitting a change of plea[2]. In the rare cases where prima facie evidence of this nature is produced, the Crown Court should obtain further affidavit evidence from the justices' clerk or the chairman of the bench or both with regard to the proceedings which took place in the magistrates' court. If, after obtaining such evidence, the Crown Court remains satisfied that the plea was equivocal, should it remit the case to the justices for rehearing[3]. The Crown Court has jurisdiction to investigate the matter, if it is alleged that the plea of guilty before the justices was entered under duress, for such a plea should be treated either as a nullity or as an equivocal plea[4].

1-583　Procedure where defendant pleads guilty, but disputes the facts advanced by the prosecution(a) The relevant principles. If the defendant wishes to ask the court to pass sentence on any other basis than that disclosed in the Crown case, it is necessary for the defendant to make that quite clear. The initiative rests with the defence. If the Crown does not accept the defence account, and if the discrepancy between the two accounts is such as to have a potentially significant effect on the level of sentence, then consideration must be given to the holding of a *Newton* hearing to resolve the issue[1]. If the defendant wishes to rely on a more favourable account of the offence contained in the pre-sentence report, the defendant should expressly draw the relevant paragraphs to the attention of the court and ask that it be treated as the basis for sentence[1]. Circumstances may sometimes require that the court hear evidence; it should first hear submissions on the propriety of holding such a trial, but whether a trial should be held does not depend on counsel for the defendant[2]. The court is not justified in making an adverse inference which is not supported by evidence[3]. If the court does not hear evidence on the disputed matter, it must accept the defendant's version so far as possible[4], unless the defendant's story is so manifestly false[5] or wholly implausible[6] that the court is entitled to reject it. If the defendant, having pleaded guilty, advances an account of the offence which the prosecution does not, or feels it cannot, challenge, but which the court feels unable to accept, whether because it conflicts with the facts disclosed in the Crown case or because it is inherently incredible and defies common sense, it is desirable that the court should make it clear that it does not accept the defence account and why[1].

If the sentencer says that mitigation is not accepted and indicates his willingness to hold a *Newton* hearing but the defendant declines to call evidence, the sentencer may proceed on the basis of rejecting the mitigation[7]. However, if evidence is to be heard, the court may decide to hear that of the accused on the issue, and then only hear the evidence of the victim if the accused's evidence appears to be in the slightest degree credible[8]. Moreover, the court may remind the defendant that causing the victim to give evidence may largely nullify any discount to be gained from a plea of guilty[9]. The prosecutor should ask appropriate questions to test the defendant's evidence, adopting for this purpose the role of an amicus, exploring matters which the court wishes to be explored[1]. Whilst it may form its own view of the material before it, it should not adopt a graver view of the facts than is put forward by the prosecution unless there is a substantial basis in evidence for doing so[10]. A *Newton* hearing is to be held only where the difference on facts is material to sentence[11]. A *Newton* hearing is not necessary when the offender seeks to put forward extraneous mitigation which does not contradict the prosecution case[12]. But if any matter is left in doubt, the accused must have the benefit of it[13]. The initiative for holding a *Newton* hearing must be with the court, and it is not dependent on the prosecution or defence asking for such an inquiry to be conducted[14]. The prosecution should not lend itself to any agreement with the defence founded on an unreal and untrue set of facts, but where that happens the court is entitled to direct the trial of an issue so it can determine the true factual basis[15].

---

1. *R v Tolera* [1999] 1 Cr App Rep 29, [1999] 1 Cr App Rep (S) 25, [1998] Crim LR 425. See also *R v Anderson* [2002] EWCA Crim 1850, [203] 1 Cr App R (S) 82. See further, *R v Underwood*, infra. For the administrative requirements and expectations where there is to be a *Newton* hearing, see the *Criminal Case Management Framework* Part 7, in this PART: CODES OF PRACTICE AND GUIDELINES, post.
2. *R v Philip Andrew Smith* (1986) 8 Cr App Rep (S) 169, CA.
3. *R v Hearne* [1976] Crim LR 753; *R v Wishart* [1980] Crim LR 113.
4. *R v Newton* (1983) 77 Cr App Rep 13, [1983] Crim LR 198.
5. *R v Hawkins* (1985) 7 Cr App Rep (S) 351, [1986] Crim LR 194 and see *R v Walton* (1987) 9 Cr App Rep (S) 107, [1987] Crim LR 512 and *R v Mudd* (1988) 10 Cr App Rep (S) 22, [1988] Crim LR 326.
6. *R v Palmer* (1993) 15 Cr App Rep (S) 123.
7. *R v Mirza* (1993) 14 Cr App Rep (S) 64, [1992] Crim LR 600.
8. *R v Mackenzie* (1985) 7 Cr App Rep (S) 441, [1986] Crim LR 346.
9. *R v Pearce* (1979) 1 Cr App Rep (S) 317.
10. *R v Guppy and Marsh* [1994] Crim LR 614.
11. *R v Sweeting* (1987) 9 Cr App Rep (S) 372, [1988] Crim LR 131, CA.
12. *R v Jackson* (1987) 9 Cr App Rep (S) 480, [1988] Crim LR 184, CA.
13. *R v Costley* (1989) 11 Cr App Rep (S) 357, [1989] Crim LR 913, CA.
14. *R v Beswick* [1996] 1 Cr App Rep (S) 343, 160 JP 33, [1996] 1 Cr App Rep 427; *R v Myers* [1996] 1 Cr App Rep (S) 187, [1996] Crim LR 62.
15. *R v Cunnah* [1996] 1 Cr App Rep (S) 393, [1996] Crim LR 64; *A-G's References Nos 3 and 4 of 1996 (Healy v Taylor)* (1996) 1 Cr App Rep (S) 29; *R v Oakley* [1997] Crim LR 607.

1-584　(b) The appropriate approach. Comprehensive guidance as to the appropriate approach where the defendant disputes the prosecution's factual basis and pleads guilty on a specified basis was given in *R v Underwood and other appeals*[1]:

(i) the essential principle is that the sentencing judge must do justice and so far as possible the offender should be sentenced on a basis which accurately reflects the facts of the individual case;

(ii) if the resolution of the facts in dispute may matter to the sentencing decision, the responsibility for taking any initiative and alerting the prosecutor to the areas of dispute rests with the defence;

(iii) the Crown should not be taken by surprise and if it is suddenly faced with a proposed basis of a plea of guilty where important facts are disputed, it should, if necessary, take time for proper reflection and consultation to consider its position and the interests of justice; whatever view is formed by the Crown on any proposed basis of plea is deemed to be conditional on the judge's acceptance of it, the Crown may accept and agree the defendant's account of the disputed facts and if so the agreement should be reduced into writing and signed by both advocates;

(iv) the agreement should be made available to the judge before the start of the Crown's opening and if possible before he is invited to approve the acceptance of any plea or pleas, or if the pleas have already been accepted and approved then it should be available before the sentencing hearing begins; if the agreed basis of plea is not signed by the advocates for both sides the judge is entitled to ignore it, or similarly if it is not legible, if the Crown reject the defendant's version the areas of dispute should be identified in writing and the document should focus the court's attention on the precise fact or facts which are in dispute;

(v) the most difficult situation arises when the Crown may lack the evidence positively to dispute the defendant's account and in many cases an issue raised by the defence is outside the knowledge of the prosecution, the prosecution's position might be that they have no evidence to contradict the defence assertions: that does not mean that the truth of matters outside their own knowledge should be agreed; in these circumstances, particularly if the facts relied on by the defendant arise from his personal knowledge and depend on his own account of the facts, the Crown should not normally agree the defendant's account unless it is supported by other material; there is an important distinction between assertions about the facts that the Crown is prepared to agree and its making an agreement to facts about which in truth the prosecution is ignorant; neither the prosecution, nor the judge is bound to agree facts merely because the prosecution cannot gainsay the defendant's account and again the court should be notified at the outset, in writing, of the points at issue and Crown's responses;

(vi) whether or not the basis of plea is agreed, the judge is not bound by any such agreement, and is entitled of his own motion to insist that any evidence relevant to the facts in dispute should be called before him; no doubt in doing so he will examine any agreement reached by the advocates, paying appropriate regard to it, and any reasons which the Crown in particular may advance to justify him proceeding immediately to sentence, the judge is responsible for the sentencing decision and may order a Newton hearing to ascertain the truth about disputed facts;

(vii) the prosecution and defence should call any relevant evidence and where the issue arises from facts which are within the exclusive knowledge of the defendant and the defendant is willing to give evidence in support of his case be prepared to call him, and if he is not, subject to any explanation, the judge may draw such inferences as he thinks fit;

(viii) an adjournment for these purposes is often unnecessary; if the plea is tendered late witnesses for the Crown are likely to be available, the Newton hearing should proceed immediately, and might be sufficient for the judge's purpose to hear the defendant;

(ix) the judge should direct himself on the burden and standard of proof in accordance with ordinary principles;

(x) a Newton hearing has the following limitations:

    (*a*) some issues required a verdict from a jury, for example: intent;

    (*b*) a judge can not make findings of fact and sentence which are inconsistent with the pleas to the counts on the indictment;

    (*c*) where a number of defendants are charged with a joint enterprise the seriousness and context is always relevant;

    (*d*) matters of mitigation are not normally dealt with by a Newton hearing but where a there is no evidence to support a defendant's account other than his contention, the judge is entitled to invite defence counsel to call his client;

    (*e*) where the impact of the dispute on the eventual sentencing decision is minimal a Newton hearing is unnecessary; the judge is rarely likely to be concerned with minute differences about events on the periphery;

    (*f*) the judge is entitled to decline to hear evidence about disputed facts if the case advanced on the defendant's behalf is for good reason to be regarded as absurd or obviously untenable; if so however, he should explain why he has reached his conclusion;

(xi) if issues on a Newton hearing are resolved in the defendant's favour, the credit due to him for a guilty plea should not be reduced; if a the defendant is disbelieved or obliges the prosecution to call evidence from a witness causing unnecessary and inappropriate distress and if the defendant conveyed to the judge that he has no insight into the consequences of his offence, and no genuine remorse for it, these are all matters which may lead the judge to reduce the discount that the defendant would otherwise have received for his guilty plea, particularly if that plea is tendered at a very later stage; there might be an exceptional case in which the normal entitlement to credit for a plea of guilty is wholly dissipated by the Newton hearing and in such a case the judge should explain his reasons.

---

1. [2004] EWCA Crim 2256, [2005] 1 Cr App R 13.

1–585 *Procedure where, following committal for sentence to the Crown Court, the correct factual basis for sentencing is disputed.* Where a defendant who has been committed to the Crown Court for sentence disagrees with the prosecution version of the facts, it is open to the Crown Court to remit the matter to the magistrates for them to find the correct version of the facts. Equally, the Crown Court has power to try the issue itself; and it should normally do so if the issue does not arise until the case is before the Crown Court[1].

---

1. *Munroe v Crown Prosecution Service* [1988] Crim LR 823.

1–586 Change of plea from not guilty to guilty. A defendant may change his plea from not guilty to guilty at any stage before a verdict is returned. While in the Crown Court this requires the leave of the judge, in the magistrates' court it is improper for the court to enquire into the defendant's reasons for the change of plea unless the new plea is equivocal[1].

---

1. *R v Eccles Justices, ex p Fitzpatrick* (1989) 153 JP 470, 89 Cr App Rep 324, [1989] NLJR.

NOT GUILTY PLEA – TRIAL BEFORE THE MAGISTRATES' COURT

1–588 In this part we discuss procedure following a plea of not guilty. The court is required, after hearing the evidence and the parties, to convict the accused or dismiss the information[1]. We particularly emphasise the obligation on the court and the parties to ensure that proper preparations are made for a summary trial which include ensuring that the procedural steps have been taken for the admissibility of certain forms of evidence. We then describe the usual stages of the trial.

---

1. Magistrates' Courts Act 1980, s 9(2), this PART, post.

1–589 Case management. Where a not guilty plea has been entered, the case management duties of the court and of the parties in Part 3 of the Criminal Procedure Rules 2005 must be complied with. In particular as regards trials, each party must: comply with the court's directions; take every reasonable step to ensure the attendance of his witnesses; make appropriate arrangements to present written or other material; and promptly inform the court and other parties of anything that may affect the date or duration of the trial or significantly affect the progress of the case[1]. The court may require a party to give a certificate of readiness[2]. The court may also require a party to identify: the order of his witnesses and which will give oral evidence; whether he requires the compelling of a witness to attend; any arrangements he proposes to facilitate the giving of evidence by a witness and the participation of any other person, including the defendant; the written evidence to be introduced and any other material; whether he intends to raise any points of law; and the timetable he proposes and expects to follow[3].

Although it should not become a routine feature of trial management that time-limits for evidence in chief or cross-examination of witnesses should be imposed, where counsel indulges in prolix and repetitive questioning, courts are fully entitled, and indeed obliged, to impose reasonable time-limits[4].

When bailing an accused to a trial date, the court should remind a defendant of the consequences of his failing to attend at his trial, ie that the trial will proceed in his absence[5].

---

1. Criminal Procedure Rules 2005, r 3.9(2), in this PART: STATUTORY INSTRUMENTS AND PRACTICE DIRECTIONS ON PROCEDURE, post.
2. Criminal Procedure Rules 2005, r 3.9(3), in this PART: STATUTORY INSTRUMENTS AND PRACTICE DIRECTIONS ON PROCEDURE,.
3. Criminal Procedure Rules 2005, r 3.10, in this PART: STATUTORY INSTRUMENTS AND PRACTICE DIRECTIONS ON PROCEDURE, post.
4. *R v Butt* [2005] EWCA Crim 805, [2006] Crim LR 54.
5. See para **1–428 Proceeding in the absence of the accused**, ante.

1–600 Power to make rulings at pre-trial hearings. A pre-trial hearing, for the purposes stated below, means a hearing which relates to an information which is to be tried summarily and to which the accused has pleaded not guilty, and which takes place before the start of the trial[1]. The start of a summary trial occurs when the court begins to hear prosecution evidence, or begins to consider whether to exercise its power to make a hospital order under s 37(3) without convicting the accused[2].

At a pre-trial hearing a magistrates' court may make a ruling, on an application by a party to the case or on its own motion, as to any question of admissibility of evidence or any other question of law relating to the case, provided that: a) the accused, if not legally represented, has been asked whether he wishes to be granted a right to publicly funded representation and, if that was his wish, the court has decided whether or not to grant him that right; b) the court has given the parties an opportunity to be heard; and c) it appears to the court that it is in the interests of justice to make the ruling[3].

A pre-trial ruling has binding effect until the case against the accused, or the last of the accused if more than one, has been disposed of by way of conviction, withdrawal/discontinuance or acquittal[4]. A magistrates' court may, on application by a party to the case provided there has been a material change of circumstances since the ruling or last application to vary it has been made, or of its own motion, discharge, vary or further vary a pre-trial ruling if the conditions set out in (*a*)–(*c*) in the preceding paragraph are met[5].

There are reporting restrictions and offences in connection with reporting pre-trial rulings[6].

---

1. Magistrates' Courts Act 1980, s 8A(1), in this PART: STATUTES ON PROCEDURE, post. The start of a summary trial occurs when the court begins to hear prosecution evidence, or begins to consider whether to exercise its power to make a hospital order under s 37(3) without convicting the accused: Magistrates' Courts Act 1980, s 8A(2).
2. Magistrates' Courts Act 1980, s 8A(2), in this PART: STATUTES ON PROCEDURE, post.
3. Magistrates' Courts Act 1980, s 8A(3)–(6), in this PART: STATUTES ON PROCEDURE, post.
4. Magistrates' Courts Act 1980, s 8B(1)–(2), in this PART: STATUTES ON PROCEDURE, post.
5. Magistrates' Courts Act 1980, s 8B(3)–(5), in this PART: STATUTES ON PROCEDURE, post.
6. Magistrates' Courts Act 1980, ss 8C and 8D, in this PART: STATUTES ON PROCEDURE, post.

1–602 Disclosure by the prosecution. The initial duty[1] of disclosure applies to proceedings in a magistrates' court where—

(*a*) a person is charged with a summary offence in respect of which a court proceeds to summary trial and in respect of which he pleads not guilty,

(*b*) a person who has attained the age of 18 is charged with an offence which is triable either way, in respect of which a court proceeds to summary trial and in respect of which he pleads not guilty, or

(*c*) a person under the age of 18 is charged with an indictable offence in respect of which a court proceeds to summary trial and in respect of which he pleads not guilty[2].

The initial duty of disclosure has no application in proceedings before examining justices, but it does apply in the case of a person who is charged with an indictable offence and he is committed for trial or the proceedings for the trial of the person on the charge concerned are transferred to the Crown Court[3].

The prosecutor must—

(i) disclose to the accused any prosecution material which has not previously been disclosed to the accused and which might reasonably be considered capable of undermining the case for the prosecution against the accused or of assisting the case for the accused, or

(ii) give the accused a written statement that there is no material of a description mentioned in paragraph (i) above[4].

For these purposes prosecution material is material which is in the prosecutor's possession, and came into his possession in connection with the case for the prosecution against the accused, or which, in pursuance of the Code of Practice[5] under Part II of the Criminal Procedure and Investigations Act 1996, he has inspected in connection with the case[6] for the prosecution against the accused[7]. Thus, there is no obligation under s 3 (or s 7) to disclose material that formed part of other criminal proceedings, but that is not an end of the matter; the Crown has a duty to act fairly[8].

Where material consists of information which has been recorded in any form the prosecutor discloses it:

(*a*) by securing that a copy is made of it and that a copy is given to the accused, or

(*b*) if in the prosecutor's opinion that is not practicable or not desirable, by allowing the accused to inspect it at a reasonable time and place or by taking steps to secure that he is allowed to do so;

and a copy may be in such form as the prosecutor thinks fit and need not be in the same form as that in which the information has already been recorded[9]. Where material consists of information which has not been recorded the prosecutor discloses it by securing that it is recorded in such form as he thinks fit and by complying with the requirements in (*a*) and (*b*) above[10]. Where material does not consist of information the prosecutor discloses it by allowing the accused to inspect it at a reasonable time and place or by taking steps to secure that he is allowed to do so[11].

Material must not be disclosed to the extent that the court, on an application by the prosecutor, concludes it is not in the public interest to disclose it and orders accordingly[12]. The rules of common law continue to apply as to whether disclosure is in the public interest[13].

Material must not be disclosed to the extent that it has been intercepted in obedience to a warrant under s 5 of the Regulation of Investigatory Powers Act 2000[14]; or it indicates that such a warrant has been issued or that material has been intercepted in obedience to such a warrant[15].

The prosecutor is under a continuing duty to keep under review (and in particular following the giving of a defence statement) whether there is prosecution material which he must disclose[16].

---

1. For the obligations of the prosecutor generally, see the Attorney General's Guidelines on disclosure, in this PART: CODES OF PRACTICE AND GUIDELINES, post.
2. Criminal Procedure and Investigations Act 1996, s 1(1), in this PART: STATUTES ON PROCEDURE, post.
3. Criminal Procedure and Investigations Act 1996, s 1(2), in this PART: STATUTES ON PROCEDURE, post.
4. Criminal Procedure and Investigations Act 1996, s 3(1), in this PART: STATUTES ON PROCEDURE, post.
5. Criminal Procedure and Investigations Act 1996: Code of Practice under Part II, in this PART: STATUTES ON PROCEDURE, post.
6. For the immunity of persons involved in a criminal suit from an action for defamation, see *Taylor v Serious Fraud Office* [1998] 4 All ER 801, [1998] 3 WLR 1040, HL.
7. Criminal Procedure and Investigations Act 1996, s 3(2), in this PART: STATUTES ON PROCEDURE, post.
8. *R v C* [2001] EWCA Crim 1529.
9. Criminal Procedure and Investigations Act 1996, s 3(3), in this PART: STATUTES ON PROCEDURE, post.

10. Criminal Procedure and Investigations Act 1996, s 3(4), in this PART: STATUTES ON PROCEDURE, post.
11. Criminal Procedure and Investigations Act 1996, s 3(5), in this PART: STATUTES ON PROCEDURE, post.
12. Criminal Procedure and Investigations Act 1996, s 3(6), in this PART: STATUTES ON PROCEDURE, post.
13. Criminal Procedure and Investigations Act 1996, s 20(2), in this PART: STATUTES ON PROCEDURE, post.
14. Formerly s 2 of the Interception of Communications Act 1985, see title TELECOMMUNICATIONS AND BROADCASTING, in PART VIII, post.
15. Criminal Procedure and Investigations Act 1996, s 3(7), in this PART: STATUTES ON PROCEDURE, post.
16. Criminal Procedure and Investigations Act 1996, s 7A, in this PART: STATUTES ON PROCEDURE, post.

1–603 Duty to disclose as soon as reasonably practicable. The prosecutor must act with a view to disclosure of material as soon as reasonably practicable after the accused pleads not guilty, is committed for trial or the proceedings against him are transferred to the Crown Court[1]. The failure of the prosecutor to act as soon as reasonably practicable does not on its own constitute grounds for staying the proceedings for abuse of process unless the delay by the prosecutor denies the accused a fair trial[2].

1. Criminal Procedure and Investigations Act 1996, s 3(8), s 12 and s 13, in this PART: MAGISTRATES' COURTS PROCEDURE, post.
2. Criminal Procedure and Investigations Act 1996, s 10(2)–(3), in this PART: MAGISTRATES' COURTS, PROCEDURE, post..

1–603A Disclosure where offence to be tried in the Crown Court . Although in the case of an indictable offence, the disclosure provisions in Part I of the Criminal Procedure and Investigations Act 1996 do not apply until after the accused has been committed for trial, the obligation on the prosecutor under s 3 of the 1996 Act to give initial disclosure clearly envisages that some disclosure may be required to take place before then. The prosecutor, therefore, must always be alive to the need to make advance disclosure of material of which he is aware and which he, as a responsible prosecutor, recognises should be disclosed at an earlier stage. Examples of such material include (*a*) previous convictions of a complainant or deceased if that information can reasonably be expected to assist the defence when applying for bail; (*b*) material which may enable an accused to make a pre-committal application to stay the proceedings as an abuse of process; (*c*) material which may enable an accused to submit that he should only be committed for trial on a lesser charge, or that he should not be committed for trial at all; (*d*) material which will enable the accused and his legal advisers to make preparations for trial which may be significantly less effective if disclosure is delayed (eg names of eye witnesses who the prosecution do not intend to use). However, any disclosure by the prosecutor prior to committal should not exceed the primary disclosure required after committal by s 3 of the Act[1].

1. *R v DPP, ex p Lee* [1999] 2 All ER 737, 163 JP 569, [1999] 2 Cr App Rep 304.

1–604 Disclosure by prosecution: position under the European Convention on Human Rights. There is a general requirement under Article 6 of the European Convention on Human Rights that "all material evidence for or against the accused" be disclosed before trial[1]. The European Commission of Human Rights has held that the "equality of arms" principle imposed on prosecuting and investigating authorities an obligation to disclose any material in their possession, or to which they could gain access, which may assist the accused in exonerating himself or in obtaining a reduction in sentence[2]. This duty is not absolute as it may sometimes be necessary to withhold evidence in order to safeguard competing rights, such as national security, safety of witnesses and preserving secrecy in police investigations[3]. However restrictions on disclosure must be strictly necessary and must be sufficiently counter-balanced by the procedures followed by judicial authorities. Accordingly, it was a violation of Article 6(1) for the prosecution to make a unilateral decision to withhold material without a hearing before a judicial authority[4]. It would seem that it is sufficient for the prosecution to make an application on notice to the defence and for the court to give the defence as much information regarding the nature of the withheld evidence without revealing what it is, and for the defence to be permitted to outline their case to the court before the court determines on an *ex parte* basis whether the evidence should be withheld after hearing any arguments from the prosecution[5]. Where disclosure is not made, the court must assess the impact of non-disclosure on the fairness of the trial as a whole[6]. But, it is submitted, there is nothing to prevent a magistrates' court ordering disclosure where fairness dictates that such a step be taken.

Article 6 recognises that concerns for the protection of vulnerable prosecution witnesses will deserve consideration when an issue arises as to the fairness of the proceedings. That consideration, requiring a proper investigation of the facts, going to determination of the issue, is best done at the pre-trial stage and/or in the course of the trial. Normally, where the prosecution seeks to rely on copiable exhibits as an important part of its case, the defence is entitled as a matter of fairness to provision of copies of them in good time to prepare its case for trial. However, the provision of copies of copiable exhibits is not an absolute entitlement of the defence and provided a defendant has adequate notice of the case and of the evidence he has to meet; full opportunity to prepare to meet it and unhindered and private access to his legal representatives in doing so, the principle of fairness of trial for the defendant under Article 6 is not infringed. Accordingly, where there are fears for the safety of a prosecution witness, the prosecution may be justified in not providing the defence with copies of audio and video tapes, but instead providing the defence with transcripts of the tapes and confining them to inspection of the tapes under controlled conditions[7].

The "Equality of Arms" principle is not breached where the court uses information received in a public interest immunity investigation to determine whether or not the police had reasonable suspicion that the defendant had committed the offence or had reasonable cause to arrest him[8].

However, where it is claimed that the defendant was the victim of entrapment and material and evidence relevant to this issue has been considered by the court which decided to withhold disclosure on the ground of public interest immunity, the procedure does not comply with the requirements to provide adversarial proceedings and equality of arms[9].

---

1. *Edwards v United Kingdom* (1992) 15 EHRR 417 at para 36.
2. *Jespers v Belgium* (1981) 27 DR 61.
3. For a case involving a conflict between the principles governing disclosure by the prosecution and the narrower principles governing third party disclosure, see *R v Brushett* [2001] Crim LR 471, CA (which concerned disclosure of social services files on prosecution witnesses).
4. *Rowe and Davies v United Kingdom* (2000) 8 BHRC 325, [2000] Crim LR 584, ECtHR. Although the ECHR held in *Rowe and Davies v United Kingdom* (supra) and *Atlan v United Kindgom* 12 June 2001, that the Court of Appeal's review of undisclosed evidence was insufficient in those cases to remedy the unfairness caused by the absence of any scrutiny of the withheld material by the trial judge, there was nothing in those judgments to suggest that an ex parte examination of material by the Court of Appeal was, of itself, unfair; indeed, if that were the position, the Court of Appeal would be unable to quash a conviction without ordering a retrial in a case where none of the material which rendered the conviction unsafe had been seen by the trial judge and PII was still being claimed before the Court of Appeal (*R v Botmeh* [2001] EWCA Crim 2226, [2002] 1 WLR 531, [2002] 1 Cr App Rep 28, [2002] Crim LR 209).
5. *Jasper v United Kingdom* [2000] Crim LR 586, ECtHR.
6. *R v Staffordshire Justices, ex p Imbert* [1997] 2 Cr App Rep 276, 163 JP 693.
7. *R v DPP, ex p J* [2000] 1 WLR 1215, DC.
8. *R v Smith (Joe)* [2001] 1 WLR 1031, [2001] 2 Cr App Rep 1, CA.
9. *Edwards and Lewis v United Kingdom* [2003] Crim LR 891, ECtHR.

1–605   *Public interest immunity.* The law on disclosure, including the use of special counsel to provide an adversarial element where PII is asserted, was comprehensively reviewed by the House of Lords in *R v H; R v C*[1]. The defendants faced charges of conspiring to supply Class A drugs. The prosecution based its case on surveillance evidence. The defendants made far-reaching requests for disclosure, including details of covert human intelligence, and it soon became apparent that the prosecution needed to assert public interest immunity to withhold certain items from the defence. At a preliminary hearing the trial judge, without looking at any of the material, held that it was necessary to appoint special counsel to comply with art 6 since there could otherwise be a perception of unfairness. The prosecution appealed on the basis that it was premature to appoint special counsel. The judge should first have looked at the material and assessed its relevance in relation to the issues in the case. This argument succeeded in the Court of Appeal. The House of Lords affirmed the Court of Appeal decision and ruled as follows. The prosecution had a duty to disclose material in its possession that weakened its own case or strengthened the case of the defence. Where material could not be disclosed without the risk of serious prejudice to an important public interest, some derogation from the normal rule could be justified provided it was kept to the minimum. However, such derogation had never to affect the overall fairness of the trial. Provided that the procedures that were followed to deal with claims of PII followed these general principles, and there was continuing regard to the interests of the defendant, there would be no violation of art 6. Since, in the present case, the judge had not addressed the question of the nature of the material sought to be withheld he had acted prematurely in appointing special counsel.

Their lordships were also invited to consider the position in magistrates' courts. In this context attention was drawn to two authorities: *R v Stipendiary Magistrate for Norfolk, ex p Taylor*[2], and *R (on the application of DPP) v Acton Youth Court*[3]. Lord Bingham, who gave the only judgment, stated as follows (at para 44):

> "The first of these cases must now be read subject to two qualifications: first, that the test for disclosure is now that laid down in the 1996 Act and not the earlier test of relevance on which the judgment was based (see (1997) 161 JP 773 at 777); and secondly that the test of apparent bias laid down in *R v Gough*[4] has now been restated by the House in *Porter v Magill*[5]. In the second case the relevant principles were correctly applied. If PII applications are confined, as they should be, to material which undermines the prosecution case or strengthens that of the defence, the bench will not be alerted to material damaging to the defendant. If it is, the principles which should govern the court's decision whether to recuse itself are the same as in the case of any other tribunal of fact, but the court's duty of continuing review ordinarily militates in favour of continuing the proceedings before the court which determines the PII application. If a case raises complex and contentious PII issues, and the court has discretion to send the case to the crown court for trial, the magistrates' court should carefully consider whether those issues are best resolved in the Crown Court. The occasions on which it will be appropriate to appoint special counsel in the magistrates' court will be even rarer than in the Crown Court."

The procedure for making an application to withhold disclosure on the grounds of public interest immunity is prescribed by rules of court[6].

---

1. [2004] UKHL 3, [2004] 2 AC 134, [2004] 1 All ER 1269, [2004] 2 WLR 335.
2. (1997) 161 JP 773.
3. [2001] EWHC Admin 402, [2001] 1 WLR 1828.
4. [1993] 2 All ER 724, [1993] AC 646.
5. [2001] UKHL 67 at [102]-[103], [2002] 1 All ER 465 at [102]-[103], [2002] 2 AC 357.

6. Criminal Procedure Rules 2005, Part 25, in this PART: STATUTORY INSTRUMENTS AND PRACTICE DIRECTIONS ON PROCEDURE, post.

1–606   **Disclosure by the defence.**   In proceedings before a magistrates' court, disclosure by the defence is not compulsory (except in the case of expert evidence) but the defence may give a defence statement to the prosecution which may result in further disclosure[1].

1. Criminal Procedure and Investigations Act 1996, ss 6A and 6B, in this PART: STATUTES ON PROCEDURE, post.

1–607   **Disclosure of expert evidence.**   Where a magistrates' court is to proceed to summary trial following a plea of not guilty, if any party proposes to adduce expert evidence[1] (whether of fact or opinion) in the proceedings (otherwise than in relation to sentence) he must, as soon as practicable, supply the other party and the court with a written statement of any expert's finding or opinion and on request in writing, a copy (or a reasonable opportunity to examine) any observation, test, calculation or other procedure on which such finding or opinion is based and any document or other thing or substance in respect of which any such procedure has been carried out. These requirements may be waived by notice in writing and any statement may then be given orally[2]. Notice of any disclosure made must be given to the expert witness[2].

A party may decline to comply with the requirements as to notice where he has reasonable grounds for believing that such disclosure might lead to intimidation of a witness or otherwise to the course of justice being interfered with. In this case, he must notify the other party in writing[3].

Where the requirements as to notice have not been complied with, a party may not adduce such expert evidence without the leave of the court[4].

1. For the admissibility of expert evidence, see **2–343 Expert opinion, 2–345 Expert reports**, in PART II: EVIDENCE, post.
2. Criminal Procedure Rules 2005, Part 24, in this PART: STATUTORY INSTRUMENTS AND PRACTICE DIRECTIONS ON PROCEDURE, post.
3. Criminal Procedure Rules 2005, r 24.2, in this PART: STATUTORY INSTRUMENTS AND PRACTICE DIRECTIONS ON PROCEDURE, post.
4. Criminal Procedure Rules 2005, r 24.3, in this PART: STATUTORY INSTRUMENTS AND PRACTICE DIRECTIONS ON PROCEDURE, post.

1–608   **Disclosure – other issues.**   The duty of disclosure is a positive duty independent of Part 24 of the Criminal Procedure Rules 2005[1]. Material such as results from tests or experiments carried out by expert witnesses which cast doubt on an expert's opinion should be disclosed to the instructing solicitor in order that the solicitor might disclose to the other party[2]. If unused material could be material to the case it should be disclosed to the defence and to prosecuting counsel. It does not matter whether or not the material could be admitted in evidence[3]. It is clear that it is the Crown's duty to disclose material which might be unknown to prosecuting counsel but which is known to the prosecuting authority[4]. In a trial on indictment the issue as to whether unused material should be disclosed must be determined by a judge at the Crown Court, and it is inappropriate for such decisions to be taken by examining justices prior to committal[5]. Justices may quite properly decide issues of disclosure. They should not, as an invariable rule, commit to the Crown Court any case where an issue of disclosure is raised or is likely to be raised; it is essentially a matter for the judgment of the justices in each case[6].

Disclosure of whether a witness was an informer or not may be vital to the defence. Accordingly, the need to protect informers must give way to the need to allow the defence to present a tenable case in its best light[7]. In identification cases material photographs and crime reports are disclosable and ought to be forwarded routinely by the police to the Crown Prosecution Service[8].

The tests in s 97 of the Magistrates' Courts Act 1980 for the issue of a witness summons for production of documents by third parties in criminal proceedings remain untouched by other, less stringent, developments in the rules of disclosure in criminal proceedings[9]. As to the obligations of the prosecutor to seek a witness summons in respect of material held by a third party, see the Attorney General's Guidelines on disclosure[10].

1. In this PART: STATUTORY INSTRUMENTS AND PRACTICE DIRECTIONS ON PROCEDURE,, post.
2. *R v Ward* [1993] 2 All ER 643, [1993] 1 WLR 619, 97 Cr App Rep 1,
3. *R v Preston* [1994] 2 AC 130, [1993] 4 All ER 638, 3 WLR 891, 98 Cr App Rep 405, HL.
4. *R v McCarthy* (1993) 158 JP 283, CA.
5. See *R v Crown Prosecution Service, ex p Warby* (1993) 158 JP 190, [1994] Crim LR 281.
6. *R v Stipendiary Magistrate for Norfolk, ex p Taylor* (1997) 161 JP 773, DC following *R v Bromley Magistrates' Court, ex p Smith and Wilkins* [1995] 4 All ER 164, [1995] 1 WLR 944, [1995] 2 Cr App Rep 285. This remains the position after implementation of the Human Rights Act 1998: see *R (DPP) v Acton Youth Court* [2001] EWHC Admin 402, [2001] 1 WLR 1828.
7. *R v Reilly* [1994] Crim LR 279, CA. See also *R v Turner* [1995] 3 All ER 432, [1995] 1 WLR 264, [1995] 2 Cr App Rep 94, CA.
8. *R v F (a juvenile)* (1993) 158 JP 49.
9. *R v Reading Justices, ex p Berkshire County Council* [1996] 1 Cr App Rep 239, [1996] 1 FLR 149, [1996] Crim LR 347.
10. In this PART, CODES OF PRACTICE AND GUIDELINES, post.

1–609   **Application by the defence for further disclosure (section 8).**   Where the accused has served a defence statement and the prosecutor has purported to comply with his duty of disclosure or has given the accused a statement that he is not required to make any disclosure, the accused may make an application to the court for disclosure[1].

---

1. Criminal Procedure and Investigations Act 1996, s 8, in this PART: STATUTES ON PROCEDURE, post.

1-620　Preparation of evidence.　This part is concerned with ensuring that, where a case is adjourned for trial, proper steps have been taken to ensure that all the evidence will be available for the hearing. The substantive law of evidence is discussed in PART II of this manual. The procedural requirements for the admission of evidence are now set out in the Criminal Procedure Rules 2005[1], and include in particular requirements for the admission of hearsay evidence, or of the defendant's or a non-defendant's bad character, or for the use of special measures to enhance the quality of the evidence of vulnerable or intimidated witnesses.

---

1. In this PART: STATUTORY INSTRUMENTS AND PRACTICE DIRECTIONS ON PROCEDURE, post.

1-621　*Witness statements—s 9 Criminal Justice Act 1967.*　Evidence of a witness in the form of a written statement[1] may be admissible in evidence in criminal proceedings in accordance with the provisions of section 9 of the Criminal Justice Act 1967[2]. The statement must be in the prescribed form[3] and meet certain conditions, in particular that it must be served on each of the other parties to the proceedings (and the court[3]) and none of the other parties has within seven days from the service of the copy of the statement served a notice objecting to the admission of the statement in evidence[4]. Nevertheless, the court may of its own motion or on application require a person who has made a s 9 statement to attend court and give evidence[5].

---

1. In this PART: STATUTES ON PROCEDURE, post.
2. See para **2-191 Written statements**, in PART II: EVIDENCE, post.
3. Criminal Procedure Rules 2005, r 27.1, in this PART: STATUTORY INSTRUMENTS AND PRACTICE DIRECTIONS ON PROCEDURE, post.
4. Criminal Justice Act 1967, s 9, in this PART: STATUTES ON PROCEDURE, post.
5. Criminal Justice Act 1967, s 9(4)(b), in this PART: STATUTES ON PROCEDURE, post.

1-622　*Witness summonses and warrants.*　The attendance of witnesses at court and (where appropriate) production by them of any document or thing, is secured by the issue of a summons or warrant where a justice of the peace or the justices' clerk is satisfied that they can provide material evidence and it is in the interests of justice. Similar provision is made to secure the attendance of a person where a justice or the justices' clerk is satisfied that person is likely to be able to make on behalf of the prosecutor a written statement containing material evidence, or produce on behalf of the prosecutor a document or other exhibit likely to be material evidence, for the purposes of proceedings before a magistrates' court inquiring into an offence as examining justices, and it is in the interests of justice[2]. The procedure for making an application for a witness summons or warrant is set out in Part 28 of the Criminal Procedure Rules 2005[3].

---

1. Magistrates' Courts Act 1980, s 97 in this PART: STATUTES ON PROCEDURE, post.
2. Magistrates' Courts Act 1980, s 97A, in this PART: STATUTES ON PROCEDURE, post.
3. In this PART: STATUTORY INSTRUMENTS AND PRACTICE DIRECTIONS ON PROCEDURE, post.

1-623　*Application for special measures directions.*　An application for a special measures direction[1] in respect of a vulnerable or intimidated witness must be made in writing in the prescribed form and sent to the court officer and every other party to the proceedings[2]. In the case of a youth court the application must be received within 28 days of the date on which the defendant first appears or is brought before the court in connection with the offence[3]. Where the application is to a magistrates' court, application must be made within 14 days of the defendant indicating his intention to plead not guilty to any charge brought against him and in relation to which a special measures direction may be sought[4]. Except in the case of a child witness in need of special protection, a party must notify the court and the other parties of any opposition to the application within 14 days[5]. Provision is made by rules of court for an extension of time and for late applications[6].

---

1. For special measures directions, see **2-345A Special Measures Directions in case of vulnerable and intimidated witnesses**, in PART II: EVIDENCE, post and the Criminal Procedure Rules 2005, Part 29, in this PART: STATUTORY INSTRUMENTS AND PRACTICE DIRECTIONS ON PROCEDURE,, post.
2. Criminal Procedure Rules 2005, r 29.1(1), in this PART: STATUTORY INSTRUMENTS AND PRACTICE DIRECTIONS ON PROCEDURE, post.
3. Criminal Procedure Rules 2005, r 29.1(3)(*a*), in this PART: STATUTORY INSTRUMENTS AND PRACTICE DIRECTIONS ON PROCEDURE, post.
4. Criminal Procedure Rules 2005, r 29.1(3)(*b*), in this PART: STATUTORY INSTRUMENTS AND PRACTICE DIRECTIONS ON PROCEDURE, post.
5. Criminal Procedure Rules 2005, r 29.1(5), (6), in this PART: STATUTORY INSTRUMENTS AND PRACTICE DIRECTIONS ON PROCEDURE, post.
6. Criminal Procedure Rules 2005, rr 29.2, 29.3, in this PART: STATUTORY INSTRUMENTS AND PRACTICE DIRECTIONS ON PROCEDURE, post.

1-623A　*Direction prohibiting accused from cross-examining particular witness.*　Application for a direction prohibiting cross-examination of a witness who does not have automatic eligibility for such protection[1] may be made in accordance with Part 31 of the Criminal Procedure Rules[2] by the prosecution or the court of its own motion[3].

1. Ie under the Youth Justice and Criminal Evidence Act 1999, ss 34 and 35 (complainants in proceedings for sexual offences and child complainants and other child witnesses, in PART II: EVIDENCE, post and see para **2–180 Protection of witnesses from cross examination by accused in person**.
2. In this PART: STATUTORY INSTRUMENTS AND PRACTICE DIRECTIONS ON PROCEDURE, post.
3. Youth Justice and Criminal Evidence Act 1999, s 36, in PART II: EVIDENCE, post.

1–623B   *Live link evidence for certain accused persons.*   A court may in criminal proceedings give a direction that the evidence of a vulnerable accused may give evidence by way of live link[1]. Application for the use of a live link is made by the accused[2]. No procedural provision is made in the Criminal Procedure Rules 2005, but the *Practice Direction (crime: consolidated)* [2002][3] requires courts to take account of a defendant's age and maturity, and of his or her ability to understand what is going on, in making arrangements for trial.

1. Youth Justice and Criminal Evidence Act 1999, Part 2, Chapter 1A, in PART II: EVIDENCE, post and see para **2–168 Use of live links for certain accused persons**.
2. Youth Justice and Criminal Evidence Act 1999, s 33A(2), in PART II: EVIDENCE, post.
3. Para III.30 ff at **1–6970**, post.

1–623C   Directions as to expert evidence[1].   Where more than one *party* wants to introduce expert evidence the court may direct the experts to discuss the expert issues in the proceedings; and prepare a statement for the court of the matters on which they agree and disagree, giving their reasons. The content of the discussion must not be referred to without the court's permission. In the event of failure to comply, the expert evidence is inadmissible.

Where more than one *defendant* wants to introduce expert evidence on an issue at trial, the court may direct that the evidence on that issue is to be given by one expert only. Where the selection of the expert is not agreed, the court will resolve the issue. Where the court gives a direction for a single joint expert to be used, each of the co-defendants may give instructions to the expert and the court may give a direction about payment of the expert's fees and expenses (including any limitation on the amount); and any examination, measurement, test or experiment which the expert wishes to carry out. A copy of a co-defendant's instructions to the expert must be sent to the other co-defendant(s). Unless the court otherwise directs, the instructing co-defendants are jointly and severally liable for the payment of the expert's fees and expenses[2].

1. See also the Criminal Procedure Rules 2005, Part 24, in this PART: STATUTORY INSTRUMENTS AND PRACTICE DIRECTIONS ON PROCEDURE, post and para **1–607 Disclosure of expert evidence**, ante and paras **2–103** et seq **Matters on which expert evidence may be called**, **2–105 Expert reports** in PART II: EVIDENCE, post.
2. Criminal Procedure Rules 2000, Part 33, in this PART: STATUTORY INSTRUMENTS AND PRACTICE ON PROCEDURE, post.

1–624   *Application to admit hearsay evidence.*   A party who wants to introduce hearsay evidence[1] in accordance with one or more of the following sections of the Criminal Justice Act 2003: s 114(*d*) (interests of justice), s 116 (witness unavailable to attend), s 117 (evidence contained in a business, or other, document); or s 121 (multiple hearsay)[2] must give notice in the prescribed form to the court and all other parties[3]. The prosecutor must give notice at the same time as he complies with his duty of disclosure under s 3 of the Criminal Procedure and Investigations Act 1996[4]. A defendant must give notice of hearsay evidence of more than 14 days after the prosecutor has complied with his duty of disclosure[5]. An application may be opposed by giving notice to the court and the other parties not more than 14 after receiving the application[6]. Notice may be waived[7] and the court has power to vary notice requirements[8].

1. See para **2–466 Hearsay and the European Convention on Human Rights** and **2–475A Hearsay under the Criminal Justice Act 2003**, in PART II: EVIDENCE, post.
2. In PART II: EVIDENCE, post.
3. Criminal Procedure Rules 2005, r 34.2, in this PART: STATUTORY INSTRUMENTS AND PRACTICE DIRECTIONS ON PROCEDURE, post.
4. Criminal Procedure Rules 2005, r 34.3, in this PART: STATUTORY INSTRUMENTS AND PRACTICE DIRECTIONS ON PROCEDURE, post.
5. Criminal Procedure Rules 2005, r 34.4, in this PART: STATUTORY INSTRUMENTS AND PRACTICE DIRECTIONS ON PROCEDURE, post.
6. Criminal Procedure Rules 2005, r 34.5, in this PART: STATUTORY INSTRUMENTS AND PRACTICE DIRECTIONS ON PROCEDURE, post.
7. Criminal Procedure Rules 2005, r 34.8, in this PART: STATUTORY INSTRUMENTS AND PRACTICE DIRECTIONS ON PROCEDURE, post.
8. Criminal Procedure Rules 2005, r 34.7, in this PART: STATUTORY INSTRUMENTS AND PRACTICE DIRECTIONS ON PROCEDURE, post.

1–625   *Application to admit evidence of bad character.*   A party who wants to introduce evidence of a non-defendant's bad character[1] under s 100 of the Criminal Justice Act 2003 must apply in the prescribed form which must be received by the court officer and the other parties not more than 14 days after the prosecutor has complied with his duty of disclosure under s 3 of the Criminal Procedure and Investigations Act 1996 or has disclosed the previous convictions of that non-defendant, or where the evidence is that of a non-defendant who is to be invited to give or has given evidence for a defendant, as soon as reasonably practicable[2]. An application may be opposed by giving notice to the court and the other parties not more than 14 days after receiving the application[3].

A prosecutor who wants to adduce evidence of a defendant's bad character must give notice in the prescribed form to the court and all other parties at the same time as he complies with the duty of disclosure[4]. Similar requirements apply to a co-defendant who wishes to introduce evidence of the defendant's bad character[5].

A defendant who wishes to exclude evidence of his bad character must make application to do so not more than 14 days after his receipt of the prosecutor's or co-defendant's notice[6].

Where a notice or application is required under the above rules to be given or sent it may, with the consent of the addressee, be instead sent by fax or other electronic means[7].

The court may allow notices or applications to be given in a different form or orally and it may shorten a time limit or extend it even after it has expired[8].

---

1. See para **2–494A Defendant's bad character** and para **2–501 Bad character of non defendants**, in PART II: EVIDENCE, post.
2. Criminal Procedure Rules 2005, r 35.2, in this PART: STATUTORY INSTRUMENTS AND PRACTICE DIRECTIONS ON PROCEDURE, post.
3. Criminal Procedure Rules 2005, r 35.3, in this PART: STATUTORY INSTRUMENTS AND PRACTICE DIRECTIONS ON PROCEDURE, post.
4. Criminal Procedure Rules 2005, r 35.4, in this PART: STATUTORY INSTRUMENTS AND PRACTICE DIRECTIONS ON PROCEDURE, post.
5. Criminal Procedure Rules 2005, r 35.5, in this PART: STATUTORY INSTRUMENTS AND PRACTICE DIRECTIONS ON PROCEDURE, post.
6. Criminal Procedure Rules 2005, r 35.6, in this PART: STATUTORY INSTRUMENTS AND PRACTICE DIRECTIONS ON PROCEDURE, post.
7. Criminal Procedure Rules 2005, r 35.7, in this PART: STATUTORY INSTRUMENTS AND PRACTICE DIRECTIONS ON PROCEDURE, post.
8. Criminal Procedure Rules 2005, r 35.7, in this PART: STATUTORY INSTRUMENTS AND PRACTICE DIRECTIONS ON PROCEDURE, post. Oral application may be allowed during the trial itself, perhaps at a late stage in the prosecution case where the history of the case justifies it and there is no prejudice or none that cannot be avoided by procedural measures such as allowing the recall of a witness: *R v Delay* [2006] EWCA Crim 1110, (2006) 170 JP 581. For effect of a breach of time limits, see para **1–423A Time limits**, ante.

1–625A   Application to introduce evidence of a complainant's sexual behaviour. Where a defendant wants to introduce evidence; or cross-examine a witness about a complainant's sexual behaviour despite the prohibition in s 41 of the Youth Justice and Criminal Evidence Act 1999[1] he must apply for permission to do so in writing, not more than 28 days after the prosecutor has complied or purported to comply initial disclosure of evidence[2].

The application must contain prescribed particulars and be served on the court officer and all other parties[3]. A party may make representations but must do so in writing not more than 14 days after receiving it and must serve those representations on the court officer and all other parties[4]. Where an application is allowed a party may apply not more than 14 days later for a special measures direction or for the variation of an existing special measures direction, and the court may shorten the time for opposing that application[5]. In any event the court may shorten or extend a time limit (even after it has expired)[6].

---

1. In PART II: EVIDENCE, post and see para **2–181 Protection of complainants in proceedings for sexual offences**, post.
2. Criminal Procedure Rules 2005, r 36.1, 36.2, in this PART: STATUTORY INSTRUMENTS AND PRACTICE DIRECTIONS ON PROCEDURE, post.
3. Criminal Procedure Rules 2005, r 36.3, 36.4, in this PART: STATUTORY INSTRUMENTS AND PRACTICE DIRECTIONS ON PROCEDURE, post.
4. Criminal Procedure Rules 2005, r 36.5, in this PART: STATUTORY INSTRUMENTS AND PRACTICE DIRECTIONS ON PROCEDURE, post.
5. Criminal Procedure Rules 2005, r 36.6, in this PART: STATUTORY INSTRUMENTS AND PRACTICE DIRECTIONS ON PROCEDURE, post.
6. Criminal Procedure Rules 2005, r 36.7, in this PART: STATUTORY INSTRUMENTS AND PRACTICE DIRECTIONS ON PROCEDURE, post.

1–626   Where the case is not able to proceed on the day of trial. Where the case is not able to proceed on the day of trial, the justices must conduct a full enquiry as to the reason before deciding whether to grant an adjournment. Furthermore, justices may not dismiss an information without giving the prosecutor the opportunity to adduce such evidence as may be available. The principles on which such decisions are made are stated above[1].

---

¹ See para **1–463 Power to adjourn**, ante.

THE COURSE OF EVIDENCE IN A CRIMINAL TRIAL

1–627   In this part we give an outline of proceedings in a summary trial in the sequence in which evidence is likely to be adduced. First however, we note the role of the court in summary proceedings, and the role of the prosecution.

1–628   The role of the court. The law of evidence lays down the principles as to how facts may be proved in court and what facts may not be proved[1]. It also prescribes standards as to the sufficiency of evidence, whether the court can judge the weight of particular evidence to be insufficient, *prima facie* or conclusive[2], and establishes requirements for certain classes of witnesses[3]. The court has therefore the primary responsibility to satisfy itself as to admissibility of evidence and as to proof of fact which that evidence seeks to achieve.

It is the function of the court at a criminal trial as respects the admission of evidence to see that the accused has a fair trial according to law[4]. The court should not wait for an objection to be taken to the admissibility of the evidence but should stop such questions itself[5]. A court in a criminal trial has a discretion to refuse to admit evidence if in its opinion its prejudicial effect outweighs its probative value. But save with regard to admissions and confessions and generally with regard to evidence obtained from the accused after commission of the offence it has no discretion to refuse to admit relevant admissible evidence on the ground that it was obtained by improper or unfair means, for example as the result of the activities of an *agent provocateur*[6].

The court will concern itself to see that it admits relevant evidence[7] and it will weigh all the relevant admissible evidence before it comes to a conclusion[8]. The fact that the court has once ruled a written statement inadmissible will not prevent that ruling being reversed at a later stage as further evidence emerges[9].

"Where the trial is with a jury, the judge can hear argument and decide whether or not to exercise his discretion in the absence of the jury. In a trial in a magistrates' court that is not possible. When considering the admissibility of any evidence, the magistrates must know what evidence it is proposed to tender. If they decide that it is inadmissible, they will ignore it in reaching their conclusion. In the same way, it falls on them to decide whether, on account of its prejudicial effect outweighing its probative value, certain evidence should not be given. Again they will be informed of the nature of the evidence and if they rule that it should not be admitted, they no doubt will ignore it in reaching their conclusions"[10].

The court should restrain unnecessary cross-examination on matters which are not really in issue[11].

---

1. See post **2–451** et seq. WHAT IS EVIDENCE? for the general principles of admissibility and **2–50** et seq. ORAL TESTIMONY and **2–180** et seq. DOCUMENTS AND MATERIAL OBJECTS for the mechanism of evidence and the way in which particular kinds of evidence may be presented.
2. See post **2–600** et seq. HOW MUCH EVIDENCE IS REQUIRED? with regard to proof.
3. See post **2–320** et seq. WITNESSES which deals with matters of competence and compellability.
4. *R v Sang* [1980] AC 402, [1979] 2 All ER 1222. Since courts and tribunals are public authorities under the Human Rights Act 1998, it is now unlawful for them to act in a way which is incompatible with Convention rights, including the right to a fair trial under Article 6.
5. *R v Ellis* [1910] 2 KB 746, 74 JP 388; *Stirland v DPP* [1944] AC 315, [1944] 2 All ER 13, 190 JP 1.
6. *R v Sang*, supra, and see post **2–471 Evidence obtained by inadmissible confessions or otherwise unlawfully or unfairly.** However, Article 6 of the European Convention on Human Rights is relevant to the admissibility of evidence and there may be circumstances in which evidence obtained in breach of domestic law or a Convention right is inadmissible. See, for example, *Khan v United Kingdom* [1999] Crim LR 666 (the exclusion of improperly obtained evidence) and *Teixeira de Castro v Portugal* (1999) 28 EHRR 101 (entrapment evidence).
7. See post **2–451 Relevance and admissibility**.
8. See post **2–600 Proof**.
9. *R v Watson* [1980] 2 All ER 293, 70 Cr App Rep 273.
10. *R v Sang*, supra.
11. See *R v Kalia* [1975] Crim LR 181 and *R v Maynard* (1979) 69 Cr App Rep 309.

1–629   *Court calling a witness.*   In criminal proceedings the court has a right to call and examine a witness, but the discretion should be exercised with care[1]; the court's permission is necessary before the prosecution or defence can question a witness so called[2]. After the close of the defence case the right of the court to call a witness is usually limited to cases where matters have arisen *ex improviso* which no human ingenuity could foresee[3]. A witness may be recalled in criminal proceedings so the justices can refresh their memory on a part of his evidence[4].

Where in a summary trial, it is shown that the prosecution has acted improperly in not calling a witness, it is open to the justices to invite the prosecution to tender the witness and, if they refuse, to call the witness themselves for cross-examination by the defence[5]. In such circumstances, where the interests of justice require that the witness should give evidence, the justices should exercise their power to call the witness in preference to dismissing the case as an abuse of process[6].

---

1. *R v Wallwork* (1958) 122 JP 299, 42 Cr App Rep 153; *R v Cleghorn* [1967] 2 QB 584, [1967] 1 All ER 996, 131 JP 320 and see *R v Roberts* (1984) 80 Cr App Rep 89.
2. *Coulson v Disborough* [1894] 2 QB 316, 58 JP 784; *R v Cliburn* (1898) 62 JP 232. It is likely that these cases will require re-examination under art 6 of the European Convention on Human Rights.
3. See *R v Cleghorn*, supra.
4. *Phelan v Black* [1972] 1 All ER 901, [1972] 1 WLR 273, 136 JP 298.
5. *R v Wellingborough Magistrates Court, ex p François* (1994) 158 JP 813.
6. *R v Haringey Justices, ex p DPP* [1996] QB 351, [1996] 1 All ER 828, [1996] 2 Cr App Rep 119.

1–640   *Court questioning a witness.*   The court may question any witness at any stage of the proceedings but should be careful not to take an undue part[1], for example by severe cross-examination during examination in chief[2], or make it impossible for the defence advocate to present his case properly or prevent the accused from doing himself justice[3]. Where evidence has gone unchallenged, justices are not bound to accept it[4], and we are of opinion that the court may give the witness an opportunity of clarifying his evidence where the court doubts it in some respect.

Justices have an inherent power to regulate the procedure of their courts in the interests of justice and a fair and expeditious trial, and they can in their discretion permit the clerk to examine witnesses on behalf of an unrepresented party[5] who is not competent to do so himself. Witnesses should not be examined by the clerk, however, if the party is competent and desires to do so himself[6], nor if the party is legally represented[7].

<blockquote>
1. *Yuill v Yuill* [1945] P 15, [1945] 1 All ER 183.
2. *R v Bateman* (1946) 110 JP 133.
3. *R v Hulusi, R v Purvis* (1973) 58 Cr App Rep 378.
4. *O'Connell v Adams* [1973] Crim LR 113.
5. Note the duties placed on the court by the Magistrates' Courts Act 1980, s 73 (family proceedings) and the Criminal Procedure Rules 2005, Part 38, in this PART: STATUTORY INSTRUMENTS AND PRACTICE DIRECTIONS ON PROCEDURE, ante.
6. *Simms v Moore* [1970] 2 QB 327, [1970] 3 All ER 1, 134 JP 573.
7. *Hobby v Hobby* [1954] 2 All ER 395, [1954] 1 WLR 1020, 118 JP 331.
</blockquote>

1–641   Court ordering witnesses to leave court-room.   It is a common practice when the case is called on for hearing, for the court to order witnesses on both sides to leave the court-room. If a witness remains in court in defiance of an order to exclude him, justices have a discretion whether to admit his evidence subsequently[1]. A plaintiff cannot be included in the order to withdraw[2]. In the absence of an order to leave, a witness may stay in court until he is called to give evidence[3].

<blockquote>
1. *Tomlinson v Tomlinson* [1980] 1 All ER 593, [1980] 1 WLR 322 (domestic court).
2. *Selfe v Isaacson* (1858) 1 F & F 194.
3. *R v Briggs* (1930) 22 Cr App Rep 68.
</blockquote>

1–642   Duty of the prosecution – calling witnesses.   The prosecution in a criminal case are to be expected to behave as ministers of justice assisting in its administration rather than as advocates of a cause[1]. The discretion of the prosecution to call witnesses or tender them for cross-examination has to be exercised in a manner which is calculated to further the interests of justice and at the same time be fair to the defence[2]. There is no reason in principle why the prosecution should not call a witness whom it considers to be truthful only in part, since a court or jury is entitled to accept the evidence of a witness in part[3]. However, where the prosecution did not regard a witness as likely to tell the truth and, therefore, did not call her but sought to rely on the evidence of others as to what she said at the time of the alleged offence (under the res gestae exception to the hearsay rule), the evidence was admissible but the judge should have been willing to entertain a defence application to exclude it under s 78 of PACE; as a general principle, it could not be right that the Crown should be permitted to rely only on such part of a victim's evidence as they considered reliable, without being prepared to tender the victim to the defence[4]. A request for a reward by a witness may have a bearing on his motives for coming forward to give evidence; therefore, it must always be disclosed to the defence[5]. The prosecution should inform the defence of any previous convictions which a prosecution witness is known to have[6]. The duty of disclosure also arises in respect of other material which casts doubt upon the testimony of a prosecution witness; the duty is not discharged by disclosing the existence of a document but not its nature[7].

In the magistrates' court the prosecution has an unfettered discretion as to which witness to call, up to the point, in cases which are triable either way, when witness statements are served by way of advance information. In other cases the prosecution retains an unfettered discretion as to which witnesses to call until the case starts and the outline of evidence is given to the court[8].

Although the defence may call a witness not called by the prosecution, it will be unrealistic to require the defence to do so where the witness is a police officer, nor will it be in the interests of justice to do so. Where in the exercise of their unfettered discretion, the prosecution choose not to call a witness and the justices are satisfied that the interests of justice require that witness should give evidence and that it would be unfair to the defence if he did not do so, they should so rule. If the prosecution continue to refuse to call the witness, the justices cannot compel them to do so. However, the justices have the power to call the witness themselves, and should do so in preference to dismissing the case as an abuse of process[9].

The prosecution ought normally to call or offer to call all witnesses who give direct evidence of the primary facts of the case, unless for good reason the prosecutor regards the witness's evidence as unworthy of belief, ie incredible, and not for the reason that the witness's account is at variance with other prosecution witnesses and is less favourable to the prosecution[9].

<blockquote>
1. *R v Puddick* (1865) 4 F & F 497; *R v Banks* [1916] 2 KB 621, 80 JP 432, 12 Cr App Rep 74.
2. *R v Wellingborough Magistrates' Court, ex p François* (1994) 158 JP 813.
3. *R v Cairns, R v Zaidi, R v Chaudhary* [2002] EWCA Crim 2838, [2003] 1 WLR 796, [2003] Cr App R 38, [2003] Crim LR 403.
4. *A-G's Reference (No 1 of 2003)* [2003] 2 Cr App R 29.
5. *R v Rasheed* (1994) 158 JP 941, CA.
6. *R v Collister and R v Warhurst* (1955) 39 Cr App Rep 100; *R v Paraskeva* (1982) 76 Cr App Rep 162, [1983] Crim LR 186.
7. *R v Livingstone* [1993] Crim LR 597, CA.
8. *R v Haringey Justices, ex p DPP* [1996] QB 351, [1996] 1 All ER 828, [1996] 2 Cr App Rep 119.
9. *R v Russell-Jones* [1995] 3 All ER 239, [1995] 1 Cr App Rep 538, [1995] Crim LR 832, CA.
</blockquote>

1–643   Order of speeches.   Rules[1] provide that—
1. On the summary trial of an information, where the accused does not plead guilty, the prosecutor shall call the evidence for the prosecution, and before doing so may address the court.

2. At the conclusion of the evidence for the prosecution, the accused may address the court, whether or not he afterwards calls evidence.

3. At the conclusion of the evidence, if any, for the defence, the prosecution may call evidence to rebut that evidence.

4. At the conclusion of the evidence for the defence and the evidence, if any, in rebuttal, the accused may address the court if he has not already done so.

5. Either party may, with the leave of the court, address the court a second time, but where the court grants leave to one party it shall not refuse leave to the other.

6. Where both parties address the court twice the prosecutor shall address the court for the second time before the accused does so.

---

1. Criminal Procedure Rules 2005, Part 37, in this PART: STATUTORY INSTRUMENTS AND PRACTICE DIRECTIONS ON PROCEDURE, post.

1–644   Where the accused pleads guilty, the prosecutor states the facts of the case after which the accused addresses the court in mitigation, and the court then pronounces judgment.

A submission on a point of law is not a "speech" under the rules: either party may, at an appropriate time, make such a submission and the other party should be allowed to make a submission in reply thereto[1]. The court should not hear argument and then rule on agreed facts as being conclusive of guilt, before plea[2].

Evidence in rebuttal must be confined to a matter which arises unexpectedly in the course of the defence; there must be a very good reason why it was not called earlier[3].

It should be noted that the Rules ensure that the accused has the last word in a trial. There is nothing unfair in the prosecutor being invited to address the court on a second occasion at the beginning of a resumed hearing where the justices wish to be reminded of the evidence which has already been given, provided the defence are allowed to address the court in reply[4].

Where two defendants are jointly charged or summoned and are separately represented, in the absence of agreement as to the order in which they should cross-examine, and address the court, we suggest that the established practice on trial on indictment should be followed, and that they proceed in the order in which the defendants' names appear on the court register[5]. As to calling evidence after the case is closed, see para **1–683**, post.

Where a magistrates' court is inquiring into an offence as examining justices and the accused's legal representative has requested the court to consider a submission that there is insufficient evidence to put the accused on trial by jury, the prosecutor shall be allowed to make an opening address to the court, if he so wishes, before any evidence is tendered. After the evidence has been tendered the court shall hear any submission which the accused may wish to make as to whether there is sufficient evidence to put him on trial by jury. The prosecutor may then make a submission in reply[6].

---

1. See *R v Wandsworth Justices, ex p Read* [1942] 1 KB 281, [1942] 1 All ER 56, 106 JP 50 (denial of natural justice).
2. *R v Vickers* [1975] 2 All ER 945, [1975] 1 WLR 811, 139 JP 623.
3. *R v Day* [1940] 1 All ER 402, 104 JP 181 (need to call handwriting expert in forgery case should have been foreseen); *R v Flynn* (1957) 42 Cr App Rep 15; *R v Scott* (1984) 148 JP 731, 79 Cr App Rep 49, CA (evidence to rebut alibi first raised when accused gave evidence).
4. See *L and B v DPP* [1998] 2 Cr App Rep 69.
5. See *R v Barber* (1844) 1 Car & Kir 434; *R v Richards, Barber Fletcher and Dorey* (1844) 1 Cox CC 62.
6. Criminal Procedure Rules 2005, r 10.3, in this PART: STATUTORY INSTRUMENTS AND PRACTICE DIRECTIONS ON PROCEDURE, post.

1–645   Swearing a witness.   Evidence is given upon oath in the prescribed manner or, in the case of a person who objects to being sworn, by means of a solemn affirmation[1]. Any question whether a witness in criminal proceedings may be sworn for the purpose of giving evidence on oath must be determined by the court except that a witness may not be sworn unless

(a)   he has attained the age of 14, and
(b)   he has a sufficient appreciation of the solemnity of the occasion and of the particular responsibility to tell the truth which is involved in taking the oath[2].

If he is able to give intelligible testimony that is, he is able to understand questions put to him as a witness and give answers which can be understood[3], the witness must be presumed to have a sufficient appreciation of those matters if no evidence tending to show the contrary is adduced (by any party). If such evidence is adduced, it is for the party seeking to have the witness sworn, to satisfy the court on a balance of probabilities, that the witness has attained 14 years and has sufficient appreciation of the required matters. Any questioning of the witness (where the court considers that necessary) must be conducted in the presence of the parties and the court may receive expert evidence on the question[4].

It is generally impermissible to cross-examine a witness who has affirmed as to his reason for not taking the oath, except that the court may exceptionally allow the matter to be sensitively explored where the ground has properly been laid for an expectation that the witness would normally take the oath on a holy book[8].

---

1. Oaths Act 1978, in PART II: EVIDENCE,, post.
2. Youth Justice and Criminal Evidence Act 1999, s 55(1), (2), in PART II: EVIDENCE,, post.
3. Youth Justice and Criminal Evidence Act 1999, s 55(8), in PART II: EVIDENCE,, post.

4. Youth Justice and Criminal Evidence Act 1999, s 55(3)–(7), in PART II: EVIDENCE,, post.
8. *R v Mehrban* [2001] EWCA Crim 2627, [2002] 1 Cr App Rep 40.

1–646 *Oath and affirmation.* The person taking the oath shall hold the New Testament, or in the case of a Jew the Old Testament, in his uplifted hand and shall say or repeat the oath after the officer administering it[1]. The form of oath has not been fully prescribed[2] but is commonly:

I swear by Almighty God that the evidence I shall give shall be the truth, the whole truth and nothing but the truth.

When an oath is administered in a youth court, or is taken by a child or young person in any court, the wording is again only partly prescribed but is commonly:

I promise before Almighty God to tell the truth[3].

The normal practice is to proceed with the administration of the oath unless and until the witness voluntarily objects. He is not required to state the grounds of his objection. Once objection is made, the person must be allowed to affirm as follows:

I do solemnly, sincerely and truly declare and affirm that the evidence I shall give shall be the truth, the whole truth and nothing but the truth;

or

I do solemnly, sincerely and truly declare and affirm that I shall tell the truth[4].

A witness may desire to use the Scottish form of oath[5] according to which, with uplifted hand, he says:

I swear by Almighty God, as I shall answer to God at the Great Day of Judgment, that I will speak the truth, the whole truth and nothing but the truth.

If none of the above forms is appropriate, the witness will be sworn in the particular form and manner binding on his conscience, or affirm, according to the circumstances. Whether the administration of the oath was lawful concerns two matters only; did the oath appear to the court to be binding on the witness's conscience and if so, did the witness himself consider the oath to be so binding. The court is not required to go into what may be the considerable intricacies of the witness's religion[6]. For the purposes of the Perjury Act 1911, the forms and ceremonies used in administering an oath are immaterial, if the oath has been administered in a form and with ceremonies which the person taking the oath has accepted without objection, or has declared to be binding on him[7].

A Muslim is sworn on the Koran. A Sikh may be sworn on the Granth[8] but this is no longer the only possible preliminary to evidence by a Sikh. A Chinese witness has been sworn in the following manner; he knelt in the witness box and broke a saucer on the brass rail, the officer then saying to him "You shall tell the truth and the whole truth; the saucer is cracked and if you do not tell the truth your soul will be cracked like the saucer"[9].

It is not advisable for a person appearing as a witness in a series of trials to be sworn only the once; the position may however be different where the witness does not leave the witness box during formal proof in a succession of cases, for example for the recovery of rates.

1. Oaths Act 1978, s 1, in PART II: EVIDENCE, post.
2. Children and Young Persons Act 1963, s 28 in PART V: YOUTH COURTS, post.
3. Oaths Act 1978, ss 5, 6 in PART II: EVIDENCE, post.
4. Oaths Act 1978, s 3, in PART II: EVIDENCE, post.
5. *R v Kemble* [1990] 3 All ER 116, [1990] 1 WLR 1111, 154 JP 593, CA.
6. Perjury Act 1911, s 15(1) in PART VIII: title PERJURY, post.
7. See *R v Pritam Singh* [1958] 1 All ER 199, [1958] 1 WLR 143, 122 JP 85.
8. *R v Entrehman* (1842) Car & M 248.

1–647 Witnesses who may give evidence unsworn. Where a witness (of any age) is competent to give evidence in criminal proceedings but is not permitted to give evidence on oath, his evidence must be given unsworn and any deposition of his may be taken unsworn[1]. A court in criminal proceedings must accordingly receive in evidence any such evidence given unsworn[2]. A person who gives unsworn evidence in criminal proceedings in pursuance of these provisions and wilfully gives false evidence in such circumstances that, had the evidence been given on oath he would have been guilty of perjury, is guilty of an offence[3].

1. Youth Justice and Criminal Evidence Act 1999, s 56, in PART II: EVIDENCE, post.
2. Youth Justice and Criminal Evidence Act 1999, s 56(4), in PART II: EVIDENCE, post.
3. Youth Justice and Criminal Evidence Act 1999, s 57, in PART II: EVIDENCE, post.

1–648 Witness who refuses to be sworn or give evidence. A person in court is bound to give evidence if called[1]. Evidence is normally to be given from the witness box unless the court otherwise ordered by the court[2]. If any person attending or brought before a magistrates' court, refuses without just excuse to be sworn or given evidence, or to produce any document or thing, the court may commit him to custody until the expiration of such period not exceeding one month as may be specified in the warrant, or until he sooner gives evidence or produces the document or thing, or impose on him a fine not exceeding £2,500 or both[3].

For guidance in relation to refusal to give evidence see *Practice Direction (crime: consolidated)* in para **1–629**, ante. The effect of committal on a witness should be considered eg whether he has antecedents, the separation of a mother from her child and whether there is a need for special deterrence[4].

1. *R v Sadler* (1830) 4 C & P 218.
2. Criminal Evidence Act 1898, s 1(4), in PART II: EVIDENCE, post.

3. Magistrates' Courts Act 1980, s 97, in this PART: STATUTES ON PROCEDURE, post. For the position under the European Convention on Human Rights see *Serves v France* (1998) 28 EHRR 265.

4. *R v Montgomery* [1995] 2 All ER 28, [1995] 2 Cr App Rep 23, 16 Cr App Rep (S) 274, CA.

1–649   Interpreters.   Proceedings in English and Welsh courts are conducted in the English language but provision is made for the use of the Welsh language in court proceedings in Wales and for the provision and employment of interpreters of the Welsh and English languages in Wales[1].

Where a prisoner who is ignorant of the English language is being tried and is unrepresented, the evidence must be translated to him. If he is represented, the evidence should be translated unless he or his advocate wish to dispense with the translation, and the court is of opinion that the accused substantially understands the evidence to be given against him[2]. The onus is however, on the court to ensure that, even where the defendant's advocate is willing to make do with an inadequate interpreter, the defendant is fully able to participate in any important part of the proceedings otherwise his rights under article 6 of the European Convention on Human Rights may be infringed[3].

Article 6(3)(*e*) of the European Convention on Human Rights guarantees to everyone charged with a criminal offence the right "to have the free assistance of an interpreter if he cannot understand or speak the language used in court". This right is unconditional and the European Court of Human Rights has emphasised that the word "free" in Article 6(3)(*e*) is to be given an unqualified meaning: once it is established that a defendant cannot understand or speak the language used in court, the services of an interpreter must be provided free of cost, irrespective of the defendant's financial status[4].

The form of interpreter's oath has not been fully prescribed but is commonly, as follows:

> *I swear by Almighty God that I will well and truly interpret and explanation make to the court and the witness of all such matters and things as shall be required of me to the best of my skill and understanding.*

The provisions of the Oaths Act 1978, for example enabling the alternative use of an affirmation, and the sanctions of the Perjury Act 1911 for breach of the oath, apply to an interpreter equally as to a witness.

It is important to ensure that the interpreter is a person who can be relied on to interpret impartially[5].

Where it is impossible to find an interpreter fluent in both English and the language the defendant is fluent in, provided both interpreters are suitably skilled and wholly impartial, it is permissible to allow the use of double translation[6]. An interpreter is under an equal duty to that of a solicitor to keep confidential what he hears during a conference between solicitor and client. Where an interpreter interpreted the breath test procedure at the police station and also at court interpreted for the defendant and his solicitor, having regard to the duty of confidentiality and that the interpreter's evidence for the prosecution was of a formal nature, there would be no breach of article 6 of the European Convention on Human Rights, nor of s 78 of the Police and Criminal Evidence Act 1984. If an issue about the interpreter's evidence should arise at the trial, it could be dealt with by the discretion to exclude evidence under s 78[7].

---

1. See the Welsh Language Act 1993, s 24, this PART, post.
2. *R v Lee Kun* [1915] 1 KB 337, 80 JP 166, 11 Cr App Rep 293; *Kunnath v The State* [1993] 4 All ER 30.
3. *Cuscani v United Kingdom* [2003] Crim LR 50, ECtHR.
4. See *Luedicke, Belkacem and Koc v Germany* (1978) 2 EHRR 149.
5. *R v Mitchell* [1970] Crim LR 153 (interpreter servant of assault victim).
6. *R v West London Youth Court, ex p N* [2000] 1 All ER 823, [2000] 1 WLR 2368, DC.
7. *R (Boskurt) v Thames Magistrates' Court* [2001] EWHC Admin 400, [2002] RTR 15.

1–660   Examination in chief.   A witness is first questioned by the party calling him (examination in chief), then by the opposite party (cross-examination) then again by the party calling him (re-examination). A party producing a witness is not allowed to impeach the credibility of his own witness. However, where in the opinion of the court he proves adverse, the witness may contradicted by other evidence or, by leave of the court, prove that he has made at other times a statement inconsistent with his present testimony although the witness must first be asked whether or not he has made such a statement[1].

Following charge, the accused will normally be interviewed by the police or other investigating authority in accordance with Code of Practice C: Code of Practice for the Detention, Treatment, and Questioning of Persons by Police Officers[2]. Although the recounting by a police officer of any such statement is hearsay, it is admissible as an exception to the rule against admitting hearsay evidence. As hearsay evidence, the prosecution should be required by Part 34 of the Criminal Procedure Rules 2005 to give notice of its intention to do so but this appears to be an oversight in the rules and is not given in practice[3].

Evidence of the bad character of the accused or a person who is not a party to the proceedings may not be given without the leave of the court[4].

Evidence of good character called by the prosecutor to bolster the testimony of prosecution witnesses has no probative value in relation to any issue in the case and is to be excluded on the ground of collaterality[5]. Nevertheless, in cases where the evidence is essentially limited to the testimony of the parties and is likely to depend on the balance of credibility between them, it would seem that the court may be prepared in sexual cases to admit some evidence to support the complainant's credibility on the basis that in such cases questions going to credit and those going to the issue might amount to the same thing[6].

1. See the Criminal Procedure Act 1865, s 3 in this PART: STATUTES ON PROCEDURE and para **1–661 Hostile witness**, post. Also see para **1–665 Cross examination on previous inconsistent statement**, post.
2. In PART II: EVIDENCE, post.
3. In this PART: STATUTORY INSTRUMENTS AND PRACTICE DIRECTIONS ON PROCEDURE, post.
4. See para **1–625 Application to admit evidence of bad character**, ante and **2–494J**.
5. *R v Hamilton* [1999] 1 Cr App Rep (S) 187, CA, and see *R v Beard* [1998] Crim LR 585.
6. See *R v Tobin* [2003] EWCA Crim 190, [2003] Crim LR 408 and para **1–666 Cross-examination as to credit**.

1–661 Hostile witness. A party producing a witness shall not be allowed to impeach his credit by general evidence of bad character; but he may, in case the witness shall, in the opinion of the judge, prove adverse, contradict him by other evidence or, by leave of the judge, prove that he has made at other times a statement inconsistent with his present testimony; but before such last-mentioned proof can be given, the circumstances of the supposed statement, sufficient to designate the particular occasion, must be mentioned to the witness, and he must be asked whether or not he has made such a statement[1].

The question of allowing a witness to be treated as hostile is entirely for the court to decide[2]. The witness must be shown to be adverse in the sense of actual hostility and not merely in the sense of giving evidence which is unfavourable[3], but what he says does not have to be completely at variance with what he said earlier in order for the hostile witness procedure to be employed[4]. The hostile witness procedure may arise out of cross-examination[5] or indeed at any time during that witness's evidence[6].

Where the hostility comprises a refusal to give evidence, the statutory procedure cannot apply, but the court may still in its discretion allow the party calling the witness to cross-examine him[7].

Where a witness's evidence is shown to be inconsistent with previous statements made by him but he sticks to that evidence, proof of the earlier statement is admissible as evidence of any matter stated of which oral evidence by him would be admissible[8].

1. See Criminal Procedure Act 1865, s 3, in this PART: STATUTES ON PROCEDURE, post.
2. *Rice v Howard* (1886) 16 QBD 681; *Price v Manning* (1889) 42 Ch D 372; *R v Williams* (1913) 77 JP 240.
3. *Greenough v Eccles* (1859) 5 CBNS 786.
4. *Jackson v Thomason* (1861) 31 LJQB 11.
5. *R v Little* (1883) 15 Cox CC 319; cf *Cartwright v W Richardson & Co Ltd* [1955] 1 All ER 742.
6. *R v Powell* [1985] Crim LR 592, CA.
7. *R v Thompson* (1976) 64 Cr App Rep 96, [1977] Crim LR 162 and note Magistrates' Courts Act 1980, s 97(4) in this PART: STATUTES ON PROCEDURE, post(reluctant witness).
8. Criminal Justice Act 2003, s 119, in PART II: EVIDENCE, post. See also paras **1–665 Cross examination on previous inconsistent statement** and **2–282 Previous statements by a witness**, post.

1–662 Leading questions. In examination in chief and re-examination, as a rule, neither leading questions (that is, questions suggesting the desired answer) nor questions disparaging the witness's credit may be put.

The witness may usually be led by direct questions on introductory or undisputed matters[1] or when he is called specifically to contradict what has been said by an earlier witness[2].

1. *R v Robinson* (1897) 61 JP 520.
2. *Courteen v Touse* (1807) 1 Camp 43.

1–663 Refreshing memory. A person given oral evidence may refresh his memory from a document that he made or verified at an earlier time, or from an earlier oral account of which a sound recording was made of which there is a transcript, provided that he states that the document/account represented his recollection at the time and that his recollection is likely to have been significantly better at that time[1].

1. Criminal Justice Act 2003, s 139 in PART II: EVIDENCE, post. This applies to criminal proceedings begun on or after 5 April 2004: see s 141 of the Criminal Justice Act 2003 and the Criminal Justice Act (Commencement No 3 and Transitional Provisions) Order 2004, SI 2004/929.

1–664 Cross-examination. The following restrictions on the right to cross-examine a witness should be noted: eliciting evidence of a complainant's sexual history[1]; limitations on the right of accused to cross-examine certain complainants in person[2] and when fully in force, examination of a witness through an intermediary[3].

In cross-examination the form of questioning should not be such as to put words into the mouth of a witness for him to echo[4], nor to invite argument rather than to obtain answers on matters of fact, nor to state purported fact or opinion[5], nor to invite inference from facts[6]. Any necessary questions may be put to a witness by the court on behalf of an unrepresented accused who has made assertions instead of putting questions by way of cross-examination[7]. Any party may cross-examine a witness he has not called, even when no question has been asked in chief[8], and even when the witness gave no evidence against him[9]. Questions put in cross-examination should be relevant to the issues in the case[10], thus prosecution evidence should not generally be introduced for the first time during cross-examination[11]. If it is intended to contradict the evidence of a witness by later evidence, he should be cross-examined on the disputed matters[12]. Justices are not however bound to accept a witness's evidence merely because it has gone unchallenged[13]. Cross-examination may also test the witness's credibility as a witness, for example his powers of observation, or his detachment or objectivity. Where instructions justify it, it may also test his credit[14].

1. Youth Justice and Criminal Evidence Act 1999, s 41, in PART II: EVIDENCE, post and see para **2–181 Protection of complainants in proceedings for sexual offences**.
2. Youth Justice and Criminal Evidence Act 1999, ss 34–36, in PART II: EVIDENCE, post and see para **2–180 Protection of witnesses from cross examination by accused in person**.
3. Youth Justice and Criminal Evidence Act 1999, s 29, in PART II: EVIDENCE, post and see para **2–166 *Examination of witness through intermediary***.
4. *R v Hardy* (1794) 24 State Tr 199, 414, and see *R v McDonnell (or McDonald)* (1909) 73 JP 490.
5. *R v Baldwin* (1925) 89 JP 116, 18 Cr App Rep 175.
6. *R v Bernard* (1858) 1 F & F 240.
7. Criminal Procedure Rules 2005, Part 37, in this PART: STATUTORY INSTRUMENTS AND PRACTICE DIRECTIONS ON PROCEDURE, post.
8. *Phillips v Eamer* [1795] 1 Esp 355; *Morgan v Brydges* (1818) 2 Stark 314; *R v Brooke* (1819) 2 Stark 472; but not where witness called by mistake—see *Clifford v Hunter* (1827) 3 C & P 16; *Wood v Mackinson* (1840) 2 Mood & R 273.
9. *R v Hilton* [1972] 1 QB 421, [1971] 3 All ER 541, 135 JP 590 (witness co-accused).
10. *R v St George* (1840) 9 C & P 483; *R v Treacy* [1944] 2 All ER 229; *Blaise v Blaise* [1969] P 54, [1969] 2 All ER 1032.
11. *R v Rice* [1963] 1 QB 857, [1963] 1 All ER 832.
12. *Browne v Dunn* (1893) 6 R 67, HL; *R v Hart* (1932) 23 Cr App Rep 202.
13. *O'Connell v Adams* [1973] Crim LR 113.
14. See **1–666 Cross-examination as to credit**, post.

1–665　*Cross-examination on previous inconsistent statement.* *Criminal Procedure Act 1865, s 4:* Where a witness on being cross-examined about a previous statement, which is relevant to the proceedings but inconsistent with his present testimony, does not admit that he has made such a statement, proof may be given that he did in fact make it. However, before such proof can be given the circumstances of the supposed statement, sufficient to identify the particular occasion, must be mentioned to the witness, and he must be asked whether or not he has made such a statement[1].

Criminal Procedure Act 1865, s 5: A witness may be cross-examined as to previous statements made by him in writing, or reduced into writing, relative to the subject matter of the proceedings, without such writing being shown to him. However, if it is intended to contradict such witness by the writing, his attention must, before such contradictory proof can be given, be called to those parts of the writing which are to be used for the purpose of so contradicting[2].

Sections 4 and 5 of the Criminal Procedure Act 1865 do not distinguish between oral and written statements. Although s 5 of the 1865 Act clearly refers only to written statements, s 4 covers both oral and written statements. Section 4 allows proof that a previous inconsistent statement was made if that is not distinctly admitted. Section 5 additionally permits (*a*) cross-examination of a witness as to a previous inconsistent written statement without showing him or her the statement and (*b*) contradiction of the witness's testimony by putting the previous statement to him. If he denies making it, the statement can be proved under s 4. Even if he admits making the statement, but adheres to evidence inconsistent with it, the statement, or such part of it as the judge thinks proper, may be put before the jury under s 5[3].

If a witness gives oral evidence and admits making a previous inconsistent statement or such a statement is proved by virtue of ss 3, 4 or 5 of the Criminal Procedure Act 1865, the statement is admissible as evidence of any matter stated in it of which oral evidence by that person would be admissible[4]. Provision is made for the admissibility of other previous statements of witnesses[5].

1. Criminal Procedure Act 1865, s 4, in this PART: STATUTES ON PROCEDURE, post.
2. Criminal Procedure Act 1865, s 5, in this PART: STATUTES ON PROCEDURE, post.
3. *R v Derby Magistrates' Court, ex p B* [1996] AC 487, [1995] 4 All ER 526, HL.
4. Criminal Justice Act 2003, s 119, in PART II: EVIDENCE, post..
5. Criminal Justice Act 2003, s 120, in PART II: EVIDENCE, post.

1–666　*Cross-examination as to credit.* In cross-examination to the issue, a witness's answers may be contradicted by later evidence, but in cross-examination as to credit, the witness's answers are usually final[1]. In the case of cross-examination designed to adduce evidence of the bad character of an accused or a non party, such evidence is only admissible with the leave of the court in accordance with the provisions of the Criminal Justice Act[2].

In the following exceptional cases, a witness's answers in cross-examination as to credit are not final.

1.　If the witness denies he has been previously convicted, the conviction may be proved by certificate[3].
2.　A further witness may be called to say that a witness has a reputation for untruthfulness and he would not believe him on oath[4]; no reason for the belief may be given in examination in chief but reasons may be asked for in cross-examination, and answers then given cannot be contradicted[5].
3.　If the witness denies he is biased, he may be contradicted by evidence[6].
4.　If the witness does not admit having made a statement inconsistent with his present testimony, proof may be given that he did indeed make it[7].

5. Medical evidence is admissible to show that a witness suffers from some physical or mental disease or abnormality making him not capable of giving a true or reliable account[8].

1. See *A-G v Hitchcock* (1847) 1 Exch 91; cf *R v Phillips* (1936) 101 JP 117, 26 Cr App Rep 17 (foundation of defence).
2. See post para **2–210 Evidence of bad character of the defendant** ff.
3. See para **2–64**, sub-para 8, post but note restrictions imposed by the Rehabilitation of Offenders Act 1974, s 4 in PART III: SENTENCING, post, and that exceptions to its application under s 7 thereto do not apply to all civil proceedings.
4. *R v Bispham* (1830) 4 C & P 392; *R v Brown and Hedley* (1867) LR 1 CCR 70, 36 LJMC 59; *R v Richardson, R v Longman* [1968] 1 QB 299, [1968] 2 All ER 761, 132 JP 371.
5. *R v Gunewardene* [1951] 2 KB 600, [1951] 2 All ER 290, 115 JP 415.
6. *Thomas v David* (1836) 7 C & P 350 (plaintiff's mistress); *Dunn v Aslett* (1838) 2 Mood & R 122; *R v Shaw* (1888) 16 Cox 503 (quarrel with defendant denied); *R v Mendy* (1976) 64 Cr App Rep 4 (note of previous witness's evidence given to later witness).
7. Criminal Procedure Act 1865, s 4, post.
8. *Toohey v Metropolitan Police Comr* [1965] AC 595, [1965] 1 All ER 506, 129 JP 181; see para **2–811 Medical records**, post.

1–667 Re-examination. Re-examination is limited to questions on new matters arising out of the cross-examination, or to explain answers given in cross-examination. The permission of the court must be obtained to go beyond this.

1–668 Submission of no case to answer. Once all the evidence for the prosecution has been heard, the court may dismiss the case either of its own motion or on a submission of no case to answer if it believes it need not hear the evidence for the defence. In criminal proceedings where the justices are provisionally minded to dismiss an information prior to the start of the defence case, they should not do so without calling on the prosecutor to address the court[1].

The fact that two police officers do not agree in relation to one issue of fact would not normally be regarded as a ground for submitting no case to answer unless the issue was crucial in relation to the offence or offences charged and the court could see no way of distinguishing between the evidence of the two officers[2].

1. *R v Barking and Dagenham Justices, ex p DPP* (1994) 159 JP 373, [1995] Crim LR 953.
2. *DPP v Morrison* [2003] EWHC 683 (Admin), 167 JP 577, [2003] Crim LR 727.

1–669 *Test for submission of no case.* *In criminal cases* guidance to magistrates' courts was formerly contained in a *Practice Note* [1962][1]. Following the revocation of the *Practice Note*[2] we would submit that the principles applicable to submissions of no case to answer in the Crown Court as set out in *R v Galbraith* should be followed:

"How then should the judge approach a submission of 'no case'? (1) If there is no evidence that the crime alleged has been committed by the defendant, there is no difficulty. The judge will of course stop the case. (2) The difficulty arises where there is some evidence but it is of a tenuous character, for example because of inherent weakness or vagueness or because it is inconsistent with other evidence. (a) Where the judge comes to the conclusion that the Crown's evidence, taken at its highest, is such that a jury properly directed could not properly convict on it, it is his duty, on a submission being made, to stop the case. (b) Where however the Crown's evidence is such that its strength or weakness depends on the view to be taken of a witness's reliability, or other matters which are generally speaking within the province of the jury and where on one possible view of the facts there *is* evidence on which a jury could properly come to the conclusion that the defendant is guilty, then the judge should allow the matter to be tried by the jury[4]."

Although magistrates are judges of both fact and law, we would suggest that a submission of no case to answer is, having regard to the roles of judge and jury outlined above, a submission of law. Accordingly, magistrates' considering a submission are not at that stage in the proceedings deciding whether they themselves believe the witnesses but only whether they are capable of belief[5]. Accordingly, we would submit that, in a magistrates' court, a submission that there is no case to answer may properly be made and upheld (a) where there is no evidence that the crime alleged has been committed by the defendant; (b) where there is some evidence but it is of a tenuous character, for example because of inherent weakness or vagueness or because it is inconsistent with other evidence and the prosecution's evidence, taken at its highest, is such that magistrates, properly advised, could not properly convict. But, apart from these two situations, magistrates should continue to follow the former advice in the *Practice Note* and should not in general be called on to reach a decision as to conviction or acquittal until the whole of the evidence which either side wishes to tender has been placed before it. If however a submission is made that there is no case to answer, the decision should depend not so much on whether the adjudicating tribunal (if compelled to do so) would at that stage convict or acquit but on whether the evidence is such that a reasonable tribunal might convict. If a reasonable tribunal might convict on the evidence so far laid before it, there is a case to answer. Accordingly, where a defendant had unsuccessfully submitted that there was insufficient evidence to attribute responsibility to the third party defendant firm in a food and drugs prosecution, rejection of the submission did not impute a finding that the prosecutor had satisfied the burden of proof placed on him to establish beyond reasonable doubt that an offence had been committed; it remained for the magistrates, where the defendant subsequently called no evidence, to review the prosecution case before, on the facts, finding that the prosecutor had satisfied the burden of proof[6].

It will normally be clear if the defence is submitting "no case to answer", but if, misunderstanding the submission, the court inadvertently convicts the accused, it may direct that the case be heard again by different justices[7].

     1. [1962] 1 All ER 448.
     2. By the *Practice Direction (criminal: consolidated)* [2002] in this PART: STATUTORY INSTRUMENTS AND PRACTICE DIRECTIONS ON PROCEDURE, post
     3. *R v Galbraith* [1981] 2 All ER 1060, 73 Cr App Rep 124.
     4. *R v Galbraith* [1981] 2 All ER 1060, at p 1062 e–g per Lord Lane CJ.
     5. *R v Barking and Dagenham Justices, ex p DPP* (1994) 159 JP 373, [1995] Crim LR 953.
     6. *Lyons Maid Ltd v John Hardy Burrows* (1974) 138 JPN 701
     7. See Magistrates' Courts Act 1980, s 142 in this PART: STATUTORY INSTRUMENTS AND PRACTICE DIRECTIONS ON PROCEDURE, post.

1–680   The defence case.   The principles about the presentation of evidence that apply to the prosecution case, apply also to the defence case ie general prohibition on leading questions, impeaching own witnesses, and previous inconsistent statements. It is normally inappropriate for a solicitor to take instructions from his client whilst in the middle of his giving evidence. Where he wishes to do so, the onus is on the advocate to make plain that he wishes to adopt this unusual course and to give appropriate assurances as to the extent of the proposed discussion[1].

     1. *R v Reading and West Berkshire Stipendiary Magistrate, ex p Dyas* (1999) 164 JP 117, DC (magistrate under the impression there was to be a discussion on change of plea lawfully refused to allow re-examination where solicitor had obtained leave to retire to speak with his client after cross-examination.

1–681   *Defendant to give evidence first.*   Where the defence intends to call two or more witnesses to the facts of the case and those witnesses include the accused, the accused must be called before the other witness or witnesses unless the court in its discretion otherwise directs[1].

     1. Police and Criminal Evidence Act 1984, s 79, in PART II: EVIDENCE, post.

1–682   *Defendant's evidence to be given from witness box.*   Evidence should be given from the witness box or other place from which witnesses normally give their evidence[1]. Certain vulnerable accused persons may be permitted to give evidence by way of live link[2]. The defendant when giving evidence has the right to give his evidence from the witness box.

In order to ensure that the defendant is given a fair trial and that justice is not only done but seen to be done, there must be no suggestion that a defendant is adversely treated compared to other witnesses by being required to give his evidence from the dock. Accordingly the defendant should not be expected to make a choice between the dock and the witness box. Only in exceptional circumstances, such as misconduct, may justices in criminal proceedings deny the defendant the right he would otherwise have to give evidence from the witness box and order that he gives his evidence from the dock[3].

     1. Criminal Evidence Act 1898, s 1(4), in PART II: EVIDENCE, post.
     2. Youth Justice and Criminal Evidence Act 1999, Part 2, Chapter 1A, in PART II: EVIDENCE post and see para **2–168 Use of live links for certain accused persons**.
     3. *R v Farnham Justices, ex p Gibson* (1991) 155 JP 792, [1991] RTR 309.

1–683   Calling evidence after case closed.   As a rule, once a party has closed his case, he may not call further evidence, except rebuttal evidence such as is provided for in Rules[1]. The court has however a discretion to allow a case to be reopened at any time before final adjudication, but this discretion is a limited one[2]. Before exercising the discretion, the justices should look carefully at the interests of justice overall, and in particular, the risk of any prejudice whatsoever to the defendant[3].

     1. See Criminal Procedure Rules 2005, Part 37, in this PART: STATUTORY INSTRUMENTS AND PRACTICE DIRECTIONS ON PROCEDURE, post.
     2. We are not concerned here with the power to reopen a criminal case to rectify mistakes (Magistrates' Courts Act 1980, s 142 in this PART: STATUTES ON PROCEDURE, post).
     3. *Jolly v DPP* [2000] Crim LR 471, DC. See also *Cook v DPP* [2001] Crim LR, DC where, in a Crown Court appeal against conviction, the prosecution omitted to adduce evidence under s 69 of PACE (since repealed) of the proper functioning of an Intoximeter device and sought leave to do so after the defence had begun its closing speech; held once the judge had decided that the evidence was admissible by way of recall the only lawful way he could exercise his discretion was to grant the application.

1–684   As a general rule, and in the absence of some special circumstances, it is wrong for justices to allow evidence to be called once they have retired[1]. A witness may be recalled to present evidence of a formal nature such as the production of an authority under which the prosecution is brought[2], but not to bring in evidence to mend a deficiency which goes to the merits of the case[3], nor merely because additional evidence would be in the interests of justice; the rule that the prosecution must finish their case before the start of the defence case so that the accused will know the case against him is an important and salutary rule[4]. Nevertheless justices have a discretion whether or not to allow the prosecution to reopen their case, and it is not limited to where what was omitted was merely formal or technical or arising ex improviso but includes matters of substance; the discretion must always be exercised judicially[5]. When a point without merit arises out of an omission or oversight on the part of the prosecutor and is taken in a trial, justices should use their discretion to allow the relevant witness to be recalled to give further evidence, particularly where that evidence will be uncontroversial and any eventual conviction would be unmeritorious[6].

In matrimonial proceedings, justices have a discretion to allow the defendant to reopen his case before they make their final order, even after they have announced their findings on the grounds of the complaint[7].

1. *Webb v Leadbetter* [1966] 2 All ER 114, [1966] 1 WLR 245, 130 JP 277; *French's Dairies (Sevenoaks) Ltd v Davies* [1973] Crim LR 630 (justices returned to court and themselves called witness whose evidence had been tendered by written statement); cf *Phelan v Black* [1972] 1 All ER 901, [1972] 1 WLR 273, 136 JP 298 (refreshing memory of part of evidence).
2. *Hargreaves v Hilliam* (1894) 58 JP 655; *Duffin v Markham* (1918) 82 JP 281; *R v Kakelo* [1923] 2 KB 793, 87 JP 184; *Price v Humphreys* [1958] 2 QB 353, [1958] 2 All ER 725, 122 JP 423; *Royal v Prescott-Clarke* [1966] 2 All ER 366, [1966] 1 WLR 788, 130 JP 274; *Hammond v Wilkinson* (2000) 165 JP 786, [2001] Crim LR 323, DC.
3. *R v Day* [1940] 1 All ER 402, 104 JP 181; but see *Middleton v Rowlett* [1954] 2 All ER 277, [1954] 1 WLR 831, 188 JP 362 (failure to identify driver "borderline"); *R v Tate* [1977] RTR 17 (second analyst called to avoid part of first analyst's evidence being hearsay).
4. *R v Pilcher* (1975) 60 Cr App Rep 1.
5. *Mathews v Morris* (1981) 145 JP 262 (statement under s 9 of the Criminal Justice Act 1967 forgotten but permitted to be put in evidence); *James v South Glamorgan County Council* [1992] RTR 312 (witness arriving late because of transport difficulties and locating the court; prosecution allowed to reopen case); *Cook v DPP* [2001] Crim LR 321, DC (defence did not raise issue of police officer not reading out proforma that evidence of intoximeter reading complied with the (then) requirement for admissibility of computer evidence until closing speech); *Khatibi v DPP* [2004] EWHC Admin 83, (2004) 168 JP 361 (only evidence that specimen of blood came from defendant was from a forensic assistant – prosecution allowed to re-open its case to call that assistant).
6. *Hughes v DPP* [2003] EWHC Admin 2470, (2003) 167 JP 167.
7. *Robbins v Robbins* [1971] P 236, [1970] 2 All ER 742, 134 JP 550; *R v Leeds Justices, ex p T* (1983) Times, 22 April.

1–685   Proof.   Sufficient evidence must be adduced of all relevant facts, although sometimes this rule is modified for example when the law allows judicial notice to be taken of a fact, or for matters otherwise normally in issue to be agreed or admitted.

There are three aspects to proof: the burden of proof, that is to say the responsibility which rests on a party to prove matters in issue; the onus of proof, that is to say which party in the proceedings bears that responsibility at a particular stage of the proceedings; and the standard of proof, that is to say the point to which the evidence must go for the court to declare itself satisfied as to the fact in issue.

The court has the responsibility of weighing the evidence; ". . . . 'weight' of evidence is the degree of probability (both intrinsically and inferentially) which is attached to it by the tribunal of fact once it is established to be relevant and admissible in law (though its relevance may exceptionally . . . be dependent on its evaluation by the tribunal of fact)"[1]. As a result of this exercise, a court may find evidence to be insufficient, *prima facie*, or conclusive.

The court may reject the evidence of a witness even though the other party did not cross-examine that witness; where a defendant was convicted despite the failure of the prosecutor to cross examination her the substantial question was whether the trial had been fair and whether the defendant had been disadvantaged by the course taken by the prosecutor[2].

1. *DPP v Kilbourne* [1973] 1 All ER 440 *per* Lord Simon of Glaisdale.
2. *R (on the application of Wilkinson) v DPP* [2003] EWHC Admin 865, (2003) 167 JP 239 (a prosecutor should, however, make it clear to a defendant while he was in the witness box that his account was disputed).

1–686   *Burden of proof.*   There are three distinct aspects to the burden of proof. There is the burden of adducing enough evidence to raise a particular issue, known as the "evidential burden". There is the burden of establishing the admissibility of evidence. Finally there is the burden of satisfying a court on a particular issue, sometimes called the "legal burden" or the "persuasive burden".

The informant does not necessarily need to prove the whole of the particulars or to the full extent charged in the information: he must however prove so much as will constitute the substantive offence, for example theft of part of the property mentioned in the information[1], or of all the goods where theft of only part is charged[2]. The court should not adopt a practice of hearing argument before plea and ruling on agreed facts as being conclusive of guilt[3].

1. *Machent v Quinn* [1970] 2 All ER 255, 134 JP 501; *R v Parker* [1969] 2 QB 248, [1969] 2 All ER 15.
2. *Pilgram v Rice-Smith* [1977] 2 All ER 658, 141 JP 427.
3. *R v Vickers* [1975] 2 All ER 945, [1975] 1 WLR 811, 139 JP 623, CA.

1–687   *Onus of proof.*   The initial onus of proof rests with the party who asserts the affirmative of the issue: that the court should make an order, that some particular evidence is admissible, that the defendant is guilty of the offence, but it may shift at particular moments, for example to the defence when a *prima facie* case is made out, or to the prosecution where a particular defence is raised[1]. The evidential burden is discharged in criminal proceedings when the prosecution raise a *prima facie* case, but the persuasive burden remains with the prosecution throughout, except where the defence raise insanity, a statutory exception or proviso, or where statute transfers the onus[2]. A similar rule applies in civil proceedings.

Article 6(2) of the European Convention on Human Rights guarantees the right to everyone charged with a criminal offence to be "presumed innocent until proven guilty according to law". It flows from this that the burden of proof in criminal proceedings is on the prosecution[3]. However, this principle is subject to two qualifications. First, where the defendant is seeking to establish a specific defence, the burden of proof may be transferred from prosecution to defence[4]. Second, within limits, rules under which presumptions of law or fact operate against a defendant are not incompatible with the Convention[5].

1. See eg *R v Twyning (Gloucestershire) Inhabitants* (1819) 2 B & Ald 386.
2. *R v Schama* (1914) 79 JP 184; *R v Johnson* [1961] 3 All ER 969, 126 JP 40, and see Magistrates' Courts Act 1980, s 101, in this PART: STATUTES ON PROCEDURE, post.
3. *Austria v Italy* (1963) 6 Yearbook 740; *Barberà, Messegué and Jabardo v Spain* (1988) 11 EHRR 360.
4. *Lingens v Austria* (1981) 26 DR 171.
5. *Salabiaku v France* (1988) 13 EHRR 379.

1–688   Woolmington – the Golden Thread   "Throughout the web of the English criminal law one golden thread is always to be seen, that it is the duty of the prosecution to prove the prisoner's guilt . . . No matter what the charge or where the trial, the principle that the prosecution must prove the guilt of the prisoner is part of the common law of England and no attempt to whittle it down can be entertained"[1].

A statutory exception may be created either expressly or by necessary implication, and the burden of proof may be placed on the accused whether the exception appears in the same clause of the enactment creating the offence or in a subsequent proviso[2].

Where a defendant in summary criminal or civil proceedings relies for his defence on any exception, exemption, proviso, excuse or qualification, the persuasive burden of proving it rests on him[3], for example possession of a driving licence[4] or motor insurance[5] or a motor vehicle test certificate[6] or a prescription for drugs[7] or a licence to sell liquor[8]. This rule is not confined to cases where the excuse, qualification etc is a matter peculiarly within the knowledge of the defendant[8].

This should not be confused with issues such as self-defence where it remains the responsibility of the prosecution *throughout* to satisfy the court that the defendant was not acting in self-defence, and not for the defendant to prove he was indeed acting in self-defence[9]; there ". . . the defence must raise the point, but at the end of the day it will be for the prosecution to show that the story could not be true"[10]. The defence must "raise the point" by evidence[11].

1. *Woolmington v DPP* [1935] AC 462, 25 Cr App Rep 72.
2. *R v Hunt* [1987] AC 352, [1987] 1 All ER 1.
3. Magistrates' Courts Act 1980, s 101 in PART I: MAGISTRATES' COURTS, PROCEDURE, ante.
4. *John v Humphreys* [1955] 1 All ER 793, 119 JP 39; *Tynan v Jones* [1975] RTR 465.
5. *Leathley v Drummond* [1972] RTR 293, [1972] Crim LR 227.
6. *Davey v Towle* [1973] RTR 328, [1973] Crim LR 360.
7. *R v Ewens* [1966] 2 All ER 470.
8. *R v Edwards* [1975] QB 27, [1974] 2 All ER 1085, 138 JP 621.
9. *R v Abraham* (1973) 57 Cr App Rep 799.
10. *Rowlands v Hamilton* [1971] 1 All ER 1089, [1971] 1 WLR 647; and see *R v Newcastle-upon-Tyne Justices, ex p Hindle* [1984] 1 All ER 770.
11. *R v Lobell* [1957] 1 QB 547, [1957] 1 All ER 734.

1–688A   Reverse burdens and the European Convention on Human Rights.   Article 6(2) of the European Convention on Human Rights provides "Everyone charged with a criminal offence shall be presumed innocent until proved guilty according to law"[1]. The issue has arisen as to the compatibility of various statutory defences that must be "proved" by the defendant and whether, having regard to Art 6(2), they should now be regarded as imposing only an evidential or a persuasive burden. The proper approach was stated by Lord Nicholls in *R v Johnstone*[2] and an extensive extract his Lordship's judgment is set out in the notes to article 6[3]. Where the status of a statutory defence has been judicially decided, this is noted to the relevant statutory provision in this manual.

1. See the Human Rights Act 1998, Sch 1, Part I in PART VIII: title HUMAN RIGHTS, post.
2. [2003] UKHL 28, [2003] 3 All ER 884, [2003] 1 WLR 1736, 167 JP 281.
3. See para **8–17631W**, post.

1–689   Standard of proof.   There are two standards of proof: proof beyond reasonable doubt and proof on the balance of probabilities[1]. In a criminal case the prosecutor must prove the defendant's guilt beyond reasonable doubt[2]. Where, either by statute or at common law, the accused bears a burden of proof, the standard applicable is proof on a balance of probabilities[3]. In civil cases the standard of proof applicable is proof on the balance of probabilities[4].

The distinction between these two standards has been explained[1] as follows: as to a reasonable doubt "it need not reach certainty but it must carry a high degree of probability. Proof beyond a reasonable doubt does not mean proof beyond the shadow of a doubt. The law would fail to protect the community if it admitted fanciful possibilities to deflect the course of justice. If the evidence is so strong against a man as to leave only a remote possibility in his favour, which can be dismissed with the sentence 'of course it is possible but not in the least probable' the case is proved beyond reasonable doubt, but nothing short of that will suffice"; and as to balance of probabilities "it must carry a reasonable degree of probability, but not so high as is required in a criminal case. If the evidence is such that the tribunal can say 'we think it more probable than not', the burden is discharged, but if the probabilities are equal it is not". The standard of beyond reasonable doubt has been often explained to a jury as a direction that before they convict they must be "satisfied so that they are sure" of the guilt of the accused[5] and this has some judicial authority, but one must be careful not to use phrases like "pretty certain", or "reasonably sure"[6].

---

1. *Miller v Ministry of Pensions* [1947] 2 All ER 372 (Denning J as he then was).
2. *R v Stoddart* (1909) 73 JP 348; *R v Schama* (1914) 79 JP 184; *Woolmington v DPP* [1935] AC 462, 25 Cr App Rep 72, explained in *Mancini v DPP* [1942] AC 1, [1941] 3 All ER 272; *R v Currell* (1935) 25 Cr App Rep 116; *R v Prince* [1941] 3 All ER 37.
3. *R v Carr-Briant* [1943] KB 607, [1943] 2 All ER 156, 107 JP 167; *Islington London Borough v Panico* [1973] 3 All ER 483, [1973] 1 WLR 1166.
4. For this test, see further **Civil proceedings** para **1–753D Standard of proof**.
5. *R v Summers* (1952) 36 Cr App Rep 14.
6. *R v Law* [1961] Crim LR 52, CA; *R v Woods* [1961] Crim LR 324, CCA; *R v Sweeney* (1983) Times, 22 October, CA.

1–701   Magistrates' conduct in proceedings.   A magistrate must not adjudicate unless he has sat throughout the entire case[1]. The only exception is after an adjournment under s 10 of the Magistrates' Courts Act 1980 after conviction and before sentence, a court differently constituted may sentence or otherwise deal with a defendant[2].

An application for *judicial review* may be made if a *justice refuses to perform any duty*. If justices have refused to hear an application for a summons for an indictable offence, or if after hearing they refuse to grant it from a mistaken view of their duty, *mandatory order* will be granted; but not, it seems, where they have heard and determined the application, and on the merits have declined to grant it[3]. The proper course on a second application is to ask the justice to whom the application was first made to rehear the matter[4].

Justices have power to discontinue a trial and to order a re-trial before a fresh bench of magistrates if it is in the interests of justice to do so[5].

A magistrate has a duty to give the case his *undivided attention*[6]; and any behaviour which might give a contrary impression is inappropriate[7]. Where after re-examination of a witness, magistrates are given the opportunity to ask questions of the witness, such questions should be to clear up uncertainties, fill gaps or to answer queries; they should not be in the nature of a prosecution cross-examination[8].

---

1. *Re Guerin* (1888) 53 JP 468. This rule was applied where a justice was absent for part of the hearing with the consent of the parties (*Whittle v Whittle* [1939] 1 All ER 374), and where another justice came on to the Bench part of the way through a hearing, and appeared to join in the adjudication (*R v Manchester Justices, ex p Burke* (1961) 125 JP 387).
2. Magistrates' Courts Act 1980, s 121, post, but note that the new court must fully acquaint itself of all the facts and circumstances of the case.
3. *Ex p Lewis* (1888) 21 QBD 191, 52 JP 773, nor, it seems will *mandamus* issue even if the discretion was exercised erroneously (*ex p MacMahon* (1883) 48 JP 70; *Ex p Reid* (1885) 49 JP 600. The following cases illustrate the application of *mandamus* in these circumstances: *R v Adamson* (1875) 1 QBD 201, 40 JP 182 (refusal to issue summons was based on extraneous knowledge or belief, *mandamus* issued); *R v Surrey Justices* (1875) 10 LJMC 171 (without proper inquiry, justices refused perjury summons because they inferred spite for circumstances, *mandamus* issued); *R v Evans* (1890) 54 JP 471 (prosecution for libel adjourned until action between parties tried out, *mandamus* issued); *R v Huggins, etc, Justices, and Humphreys* (1891) 60 LJMC 139; (solicitor stated what he was prepared to prove in application to vary maintenance order, justices said they would not vary on such evidence, *mandamus* refused); *R v Bennett and Bond, ex p Bennett* (1908) 72 JP 362 (prosecutor failed to attend hearing on earlier process, magistrate refused further process for that reason, *mandamus* issued); *R v Mead, ex p National Insurance Comrs* (1916) 80 JP 332 (magistrate refused to issue summons against employer unless summonses applied for against employees, *mandamus* issued).
4. *R v Biron* (1884) 14 QBD 474, 49 JP 68.
5. *R v Ripon Liberty Justices, ex p Bugg* (1990) 155 JP 213; followed in *R v Birmingham Magistrates' Court, ex p Shields* (1994) 158 JP 845 (justices ordered a re-trial before a differently constituted bench because the chairman of the court would have retired and would be unable to sit on adjourned date of trial).
6. *R v Marylebone Magistrates' Court, ex p Perry* [1992] Crim LR 514.
7. *R v Marylebone Magistrates' Court, ex p Joseph* [1993] NLJR 655n. See further para **1–133 Apparent bias**, ante.
8. *R v Wiggan* (1999) Times, 22 March, CA.

1–702   Adjudication.   The judgment will be according to the opinion of the *majority of the justices* present at the hearing, and wherever possible an uneven number of justices should sit to adjudicate[1]. If three justices are sitting they are under a duty to come to a decision; if they fail to do so, *mandamus* will lie[2]. The chairman may, of course, vote with the other magistrates, but where this produces an equal division, he has no double or casting vote. Instead, the case will be adjourned for rehearing before a reconstituted court[3]. If there is an equal division on the question of sentence in a criminal case, it may be adjourned under the Magistrates' Courts Act 1980, s 10, post. If a decision which is not in accordance with the opinion of the majority is delivered by the chairman, and recorded with the tacit consent of the other justices, it will be considered as that of the court, and the High Court will not go behind the record or interfere[4].

Under Article 6(1) of the European Convention on Human Rights it is a requirement of a fair trial in both criminal and civil matters that a court should give reasons for its judgment. The extent of the duty to give reasons may, however, vary according to the nature of the decision[5].

If an *adjournment for a long period* amounts to a refusal to adjudicate, *judicial review* will be granted[6]. As a matter of practice, cases are frequently adjourned *sine die* with the consent of the parties, who may apply at any time to resume the hearing[7]. It is suggested that where two charges are preferred arising out of the same incident, and a conviction is recorded in respect of one of them, the other should not be adjourned *sine die* but should be marked "not proceeded with", or "withdrawn"[8]. Where magistrates are conducting separate hearings of "alternative" informations against the same defendant, or of informations against several defendants arising out of the same incident, they should not "reserve judgment" at the end of one case until they have heard the remaining case or cases, but should announce conviction or dismissal[9]. When it comes to fixing a penalty, however, magistrates may defer this with a view to determining the most suitable method of dealing with the case[10].

A *premature note of decision* should not be prepared by the magistrates in advance of the decision itself as the observer might conclude that the trial had not been fair[11].

----

1. *Per* LORD GODDARD CJ in *Barnsley v Marsh* [1947] KB 672, [1947] 1 All ER 874, 111 JP 363.
2. *R v Bridgend Justices, ex p Randall* [1975] Crim LR 287; *R v Bromley Justices, ex p Haymills (Contractors) Ltd* (1984) 148 JP 363, [1984] Crim LR 235.
3. *Jones v Williams and Roberts* (1877) 41 JP 614; *Bagg v Colquhoun* [1904] 1 KB 554, 68 JP 159; *R v Hertfordshire Justices, ex p Larsen* [1926] 1 KB 191, 89 JP 205; *Fussell v Somerset Justices Licensing Committee* [1947] KB 276, [1947] 1 All ER 44, 111 JP 45 (licensing justices); *Barnsley v Marsh* [1947] KB 672, [1947] 1 All ER 874, 111 JP 363 (complaint for affiliation order). In *Barnsley v Marsh*, the practice considered in *ex p Evans* [1894] AC 16, 58 JP 260 of justice retiring or withdrawing his opinion in order to leave the remaining justices in a majority, was disapproved. If, however, instead of adjourning, the justices dismiss the information for the want of a majority in favour of a conviction, this will be an answer to a second information upon the same subject matter (*Kinnis v Graves* (1898) 67 LJQB 583).
4. *Ex p A-G* (1877) 41 JP 118, *R v Middlesex Justices* (1877) 2 QBD 516, 41 JP 629; *R v Thomas, ex p O'Hare* [1914] 1 KB 32, 78 JP 55; and see Treat 77 JP Jo 553.
5. See *Hadjianastassiou v Greece* (1992) 16 EHRR 219, *Van de Hurk v Netherlands* (1994) 18 EHRR 481, *Ruiz Torija v Spain* (1994) 19 EHRR 553, *Hiro Balani v Spain* (1994) 19 EHRR 566, *Georgiadis v Greece* (1997) 24 EHRR 606 and *Helle v Finland* (1997) 26 EHRR 159. For recent consideration of the duty to give reasons both at common law and under the Convention see *Stefan v General Medical Council* [1999] 1 WLR 1293, PC. As to the requirement to give reasoned judgments in civil cases and the need, when considering the extent to which reasons should be given, to have regard to the practical requirements of the appellate system, see *English v Emery Reimbold & Strick Ltd* [2002] EWCA Civ 605, [2002] 3 All ER 385, [2002] 1 WLR 2409. It is unnecessary for justices to state their reasons for committing for sentence since the person so committed will have an opportunity to make full representations to the sentencing court: *R v Wirral Magistrates' Court, ex p Jermyn* [2001] 1 Cr App Rep (S) 485, [2001] Crim LR 45, DC. At the other extreme, in *R (on the application of Howson-Ball) v Crown Court at Canterbury* CO/1148/2000 (which concerned an appeal against conviction) a great deal of expert evidence was called on both sides in a case of alleged statutory nuisance and some analysis, however brief, was required for it to be possible, on review, to decide whether the conclusions reached were rational. See also *McKerry v Teesdale and Wear Valley Justices* (2000) 164 JP 355, [2000] Crim LR 594, CA where it was stated that justices are not obliged to state reasons in the form of a judgment or in any elaborate form, and if an aggrieved person wishes to obtain more detailed reasons from a magistrates' court he can apply to the justices to state a case; followed in *R (on the application of McGowan) v Brent Justices* [2001] EWHC Admin 814, [2002] Crim LR 412, DC where it was held that what was necessary for justices to show that they had applied their minds to the ingredients of the offence and had appreciated the defendant's state of mind, and that the essence of the exercise was to inform the defendant why he had been found guilty and that could be done in a few sentences. Where the Crown Court upholds an appeal against sentence it should give its reasons for its decision on costs (unless they are obvious, such as costs following the event): *Cunningham v Exeter Crown Court* [2003] EWHC Admin 184, (2003) 167 JP 93, [2003] Crim LR 340.
6. *R v Evans* (1890) 54 JP 471, where the purpose of the objectionable adjournment was civil litigation; see also *R v Southampton Justices, ex p Lebern* (1907) 71 JP 332, and *R v Bennett and Bond, ex p Bennett* (1908) 72 JP 362. The Divisional Court would probably not interfere where the adjournment was for a proper reason within the magistrates' discretion, for example to attempt a settlement or reconciliation.
7. A fresh summons may therefore be issued on the original information or complaint. A fresh information may be laid or complaint made if the statutory period of limitation allows.
8. In this way there can be no danger of a matter which has been effectively adjudicated upon, being wrongly resurrected. See, however, *Shuttleworth v Leeds Greyhound Association Ltd* [1933] 1 KB 400, 97 JP 37 where the Divisional Court directed a magistrate to adjudicate on one summons and to adjourn another *sine die*. Where one is dealing with an indictable offence, s 10 of the Magistrates' Courts Act 1980 precludes an adjournment *sine die*.
9. *Hamilton v Walker* [1892] 2 QB 25, 56 JP 583 (two informations under different sections of the same Act); *R v Chambers* (1939) 83 Sol Jo 439 (hearing charges of driving without due care against the two drivers of vehicles involved in a cross-roads collision).
10. *R v Fry etc Justices, and Stoker, ex p Masters* (1898) 62 JP 457, and see also the Magistrates' Courts Act 1980, s 10(3), post. Thus a court may announce a conviction but defer sentence until it has heard subsequent cases.
11. *R v Romsey Justices, ex p Gale and Green* (1992) 156 JP 567, [1992] Crim LR 451.

1-703 Conviction.

The word "conviction" is commonly used with two different meanings; to mean final disposal of a case and to mean a finding of guilt[1].

Where the facts of one offence really merge into a conviction for a graver charge, the two charges arising from one and the same incident, two convictions should not be recorded[2]; the lesser offence should not however be dismissed but marked "not proceeded with". Where following not guilty pleas a defendant is tried on alternative charges and the justices convict on the more serious charge, it is not lawful to dismiss the lesser charge on the ground that it would be oppressive to convict on that also. Instead, the court should either convict on the lesser charge and impose a nominal penalty, or adjourn that charge to see whether there is a successful appeal against the conviction on the more serious charge[3].

A form of summary conviction shall be drawn up if required for an appeal or other legal purpose, and if drawn up shall be in a prescribed form, including (where appropriate) the statement that the accused consented to the summary trial[4].

A conviction without a sentence is still a conviction[5]. It appears that the defendant is entitled to a copy of a conviction[6]. The statement of the offence follows the rules applicable to the information and summons[7]; surplus words in a conviction can be disregarded[8].

More important in practical terms than the form of summary conviction are the various "executive" documents following the conviction. These are prescribed[9] according to their purpose; a warrant of commitment in particular has to comply with precise requirements[10], notwithstanding which, if it is issued in pursuance of a valid conviction, and alleges that the person committed has been convicted, it shall not be held void by reason of any defect in the warrant[10]. On discovery of the defect the court should substitute a fresh warrant for the faulty one[11].

A priest or deacon convicted of an offence and sentenced to imprisonment, either immediate or suspended, is liable to removal from or disqualification for holding a preferment; a certificate of such conviction is to be sent to the bishop of the diocese in which the court sits[12].

1. See *S (an infant) v Manchester City Recorder* [1971] AC 481, [1969] 3 All ER 1230, 134 JP 3.
2. *R v Harris* [1969] 2 All ER 599n, [1969] 1 WLR 745, 133 JP 422, and see *Welton v Taneborne* (1908) 72 JP 419; *R v Burnham Justices, ex p Ansorge* [1959] 3 All ER 505, [1959] 1 WLR 1041, 133 JP 539, but cf *Kite v Brown* [1941] 1 KB 26, [1940] 4 All ER 293, 104 JP 458; *R v Coventry Magistrates' Court, ex p Wilson* [1982] RTR 177.
3. *DPP v Gane* [1991] Crim LR 711, 155 JP 846.
4. Criminal Procedure Rules 2005, Part 6, in this PART: STATUTORY INSTRUMENTS AND PRACTICE DIRECTIONS ON PROCEDURE, post.
5. *R v Sheridan* [1937] 1 KB 223, [1936] 2 All ER 883, 100 JP 3.
6. *R v Midlam* (1765) 3 Burr 1720.
7. See the Criminal Procedure Rules 2005, r 7.2, in this PART: STATUTORY INSTRUMENTS AND PRACTICE DIRECTIONS ON PROCEDURE, post.
8. See *Hollyhomes v Hind* [1944] KB 571, [1944] 2 All ER 8, 108 JP 190.
9. By Annex D to the *Practice Direction (criminal: consolidated)* [2002] in this PART: STATUTORY INSTRUMENTS AND PRACTICE DIRECTIONS ON PROCEDURE, post.
10. See Criminal Procedure Rules 2005, Part 18, in this PART: STATUTORY INSTRUMENTS AND PRACTICE DIRECTIONS ON PROCEDURE, post.
11. See *Ex p Cross* (1857) 21 JP 407.
12. Ecclesiastical Jurisdiction Measures 1963, ss 55(1), 79(3) and 1974 ss 1 and 2. See also Home Office Circular No 112/1983, dated 16 November, 1983.

Civil proceedings

COMMENCEMENT OF PROCEEDINGS; COMPLAINT, SUMMONS

1–750 Civil proceedings in magistrates' courts are started by the making of a complaint, followed by the issue of a summons[1]. Most family proceedings, however, are commenced by filing an application with the justices' clerk[2].

A magistrates' court has jurisdiction to hear any complaint[3], and there is power to transfer civil proceedings (other than family proceedings) between magistrates' courts[4]. A magistrates' court has jurisdiction to entertain proceedings for maintenance notwithstanding that proceedings of a similar nature are concurrent in the Divorce Court, but normally it will adjourn its proceedings until the divorce proceedings have ended[5].

A complaint need not be in writing or on oath[6]. It may be made by the complainant in person, or by his counsel or solicitor, or other person authorised in that behalf[6]. It is not necessary to specify or negative an exception, exemption, proviso, excuse or qualification, whether or not it accompanies the matter of complaint contained in the enactment on which the complaint is founded[6].

The form of complaint is prescribed[7], and stipulates that the name and address of the complainant and defendant shall be set out, and short particulars and statute of the matter or complaint stated. Unlike a criminal information, it may contain several matters[8]. The death of a complainant will cause proceedings to lapse.

1. Magistrates' Courts Act 1980, s 51, in this PART: STATUTES ON PROCEDURE, post.
2. Family Proceedings Courts (Children Act 1989) Rules 1991, r 4; Family Proceedings Courts (Matrimonial Proceedings etc) Rules 1991, r 3, in PART IV: FAMILY LAW, post.
3. Magistrates' Courts Act 1980, s 52, in this PART: STATUTES ON PROCEDURE, post.
4. Magistrates' Courts Act 1980, s 57A, in this PART: STATUTES ON PROCEDURE, post.
5. *Kaye v Kaye* [1965] P 100, [1964] 1 All ER 620, 128 JP 193.
6. Magistrates' Courts Rules 1981, r 4, this PART: STATUTORY INSTRUMENTS AND PRACTICE DIRECTIONS ON PROCEDURE, post.
7. See Magistrates' Courts (Forms) Rules 1981 Form 98 in PART IX: PRECEDENTS AND FORMS, post.
8. *Tyrrell v Tyrrell* (1928) 92 JP 45.

ISSUE OF SUMMONS

1–751 After a complaint is made, a justice or the justices' clerk must apply his mind to the complaint and go through the judicial exercise of deciding whether or not to issue a summons[1]. His initial concern will be to see that the court will have *prima facie* power to make the order asked for, that the matter of complaint is within any limitation of time. A magistrates' court shall not hear a complaint unless the information was laid or the complaint made within six months from the time when the offence was committed, or the matter of complaint arose[2].

The form of summons is prescribed[3]; the one summons may contain the several matters of complaint. Method of service of the summons is also prescribed[4].

1. Magistrates' Courts Act 1980, s 51; *R v Brentford Justices, ex p Catlin* [1975] QB 455, [1975] 2 All ER 201, 139 JP 516; *R v Gateshead Justices, ex p Tesco Stores Ltd* [1981] QB 470, [1981] 1 All ER 1027, 145 JP 200; *R v Dartford Justices, ex p Dhesi; R v Manchester Stipendiary Magistrate, ex p Hill; R v Edmonton Justices, ex p Hughes* [1983] 1 AC 328, [1982] 2 All ER 963, 146 JP 348.

2. Magistrates' Courts Act 1980, s 127, in this PART: STATUTES ON PROCEDURE, post.³Magistrates' Courts (Forms) Rules 1981 Form 99 and see Magistrates' Courts Rules 1981 r 98, in this PART: STATUTORY INSTRUMENTS AND PRACTICE DIRECTIONS ON PROCEDURE, post: note also the forms in Family Proceedings Rules in the Family Proceedings Courts (Matrimonial Proceedings etc) Rules 1991 and the Family Proceedings Courts (Children Act 1989) Rules 1991 in PART IX: PRECEDENTS AND FORMS, post.
4. Magistrates' Courts Rules 1981, r 99, in this PART: STATUTORY INSTRUMENTS AND PRACTICE DIRECTIONS ON PROCEDURE, post.

1–751A   Estoppel.   Estoppel is a rule of evidence whereby a party is precluded from denying certain facts. The doctrine of estoppel applies to civil but not to criminal proceedings¹. Estoppels are of three kinds: by matter or record; by deed; and by matter *in pais* or by conduct. Estoppel by record is an estoppel by judgment. Judgments are of two kinds, namely, a judgment *in rem* and a judgment *inter parties*. A judgment *in rem* declares the status of some particular subject-matter, either relating to a person or thing, eg questions of legitimacy, marriage or divorce, the status of a street¹. It is binding upon all the world, and not only on the tribunals of the country where pronounced, but on the tribunals of other countries provided it was not obtained by fraud, does not carry a manifest error on its face, and is not contrary to natural justice.

> "Every judgment is conclusive proof as against parties and privies of facts directly in issue in the case decided by the court and appearing from the judgment itself to be the ground upon which it is based; unless evidence was admitted in the action in which the judgment was delivered which is excluded in the action in which that judgment is intended to be proved"².

In order to create issue estoppel *per rem judicatam* three requirements have to be satisfied:

1.   The judgment in the earlier action relied on as creating the estoppel must be:

    (*a*)   of a court of competent jurisdiction;
    (*b*)   final and conclusive; and
    (*c*)   on the merits.

2.   The parties or privies in the earlier action relied on as creating the estoppel and those in the later action in which that estoppel is raised must be the same.

3.   The issue in the later action in which the estoppel is raised in bar must be the same issue as that decided by the judgment in the earlier action³.

Fresh evidence may be admissible if it has become available to show the earlier judgment was wrong⁴.

If a decree of divorce gives the wife the custody of a child, the husband is estopped from denying its legitimacy⁵.

In matrimonial proceedings the principle of estoppel binds the parties but will not necessarily bind the court. In particular, the Divorce Court is not bound by the findings of a magistrates' court⁶; and a finding of the Divorce Court in a divorce suit, and in other matrimonial suits, will invalidate any previous decision of justices to the contrary⁷.

However, since the implementation of the Children Act there has been a greater acknowledgment of the findings of justices and the principle of issue estoppel will generally apply in proceedings under the Children Act since the family proceedings court is a court of competent jurisdiction⁸. The application of issue estoppel is subject to the need to place welfare paramount. The court has an overriding duty to the child to get to the truth and, if necessary, to refuse to be bound by a rule of estoppel. The overwhelming justification for setting aside the rule must be to do justice⁸.

In care proceedings the doctrine of *res judicata* will rarely be applicable, since it is a doctrine which belongs to jurisdictions more adversarial in character than those in which the principal concern is the welfare of the child⁹. However, where the issue raised relates to specific acts of abuse on children the subject of care proceedings, the doctrine of issue estoppel may be imported where the perpetration of those acts had been directly relevant in the earlier proceedings, had been fully investigated and had been the subject of an express finding with the appropriate standard of proof¹⁰.

---

1. *DPP v Humphrys* [1976] 2 All ER 497, 140 JP 386, but see *R v Cwmbran Justices, ex p Pope* (1979) 143 JP 638, where it was held that there was an inherent power in the Divisional Court to inhibit any proceeding which might bear the stamp of oppressiveness or unfairness.
2. Stephen's Digest of Evidence, Art 41; approved in *Woodland v Woodland (otherwise Belin or Barton)* [1928] P 169; *Papadopoulos v Papadopoulos* [1930] P 55, 94 JP 39.
3. *DSW Silo-und Verwaltungsgesellschaft mbH v Owners of Sennar, The Sennar (No 2)* [1985] 2 All ER 104, [1985] 1 WLR 490, HL.
4. *Hunter v Chief Constable of West Midlands Police* [1982] AC 529, [1981] 3 All ER 727, HL.
5. *Lindsay v Lindsay* [1934] P 162.
6. See *Hudson v Hudson* [1948] P 292, [1948] 1 All ER 773; *Harriman v Harriman* [1909] P 123, 73 JP 193.
7. *Pratt v Pratt* (1927) 96 LJP 123; *Kendall v Kendall* [1952] 2 All ER 1038n, 117 JP 8; *Sternberg v Sternberg* [1963] 3 All ER 319, [1963] 1 WLR 1036, 127 JP 523.
8. *K v P (Children Act Proceedings: Estoppel)* [1995] 1 FLR 248, [1995] 2 FCR 457.
9. *B v Derbyshire County Council* [1992] 1 FLR 538, [1992] 2 FCR 14 and see *Re S, S and A (Care Proceedings: Issue Estoppel)* [1995] 2 FLR 244 and *Re B (minors) (care proceedings: evidence)* [1997] 2 All ER 29, [1997] 3 WLR 1, [1997] 1 FCR 477, [1997] 1 FLR 285.
10. *Re L (minors) (Care Proceedings: Issue Estoppel)* [1996] 1 FCR 221.

ABSENCE OF PARTIES

1–752   Where at the time and place appointed for the hearing or adjourned hearing of a complaint, the complainant appears but the defendant does not, the court may proceed in his absence, subject to the requirements of Article 6(1) of the European Convention on Human Rights[1], or may adjourn and, if the complaint has been substantiated on oath, issue a warrant for the arrest of the defendant[2]. If the defendant appears but the complainant does not, the court may dismiss the complaint or, if evidence has been received on a previous occasion, may proceed in the absence of the complainant[3], or may adjourn[4]. If neither the defendant nor the complainant appears, the court may dismiss the complaint[5] or adjourn[6].

This basic statement of the law is subject to important qualifications. A party represented by counsel or a solicitor shall be deemed not to be absent except where any enactment or a condition of a recognizance expressly requires his presence[6]. The court shall not begin to hear a complaint in the absence of the defendant, or issue a warrant for his arrest, unless either it is proved to the satisfaction of the court on oath or by certificate[7] that the summons was served on him a reasonable time before the hearing, or the defendant appeared on a previous occasion to answer to the complaint; on an adjourned hearing the court must be satisfied that he had adequate notice of the time and place of the adjourned hearing[1]. On arrest, a defendant will be remanded in custody for up to eight days at a time or on bail with a recognizance, and with or without sureties conditioned for his appearance at the end of the period of remand and at every time and place to which during the course of the proceedings the hearing may be adjourned[8]. Once a defendant has given evidence in the proceedings, a warrant shall not be issued nor may he be remanded or further remanded[2].

---

1. See *X v Sweden* (1959) 2 Yearbook 354, *X v Germany* (1963) 6 Yearbook 520 and *X v Austria* (1983) 31 DR 66.
2. Magistrates' Courts Act 1980, s 55, in this PART: STATUTES ON PROCEDURE, post.
3. Magistrates' Courts Act 1980, s 56, in this PART: STATUTES ON PROCEDURE, post.
4. Magistrates' Courts Act 1980, s 54, in this PART: STATUTES ON PROCEDURE, post.
5. Magistrates' Courts Act 1980, s 57, in this PART: STATUTES ON PROCEDURE, post.
6. Magistrates' Courts Act 1980, s 122, in this PART: STATUTES ON PROCEDURE, post. See also ante para **1–139 Appearance by legal representative**.
7. See Magistrates' Courts Rules 1981, r 67, this PART: STATUTORY INSTRUMENTS AND PRACTICE DIRECTIONS ON PROCEDURE, post.
8. See Magistrates' Courts Act 1980, s 128, in this PART: STATUTES ON PROCEDURE, post; the Bail Act 1976 will not apply.

HEARING OF COMPLAINT

1–753 On the hearing of a complaint, if the defendant appears the court shall state to him the substance of the complaint, then after hearing the evidence and the parties it shall make the order for which the complaint is made or dismiss the complaint[1].

Witnesses, including the party, may be called in whatever sequence is chosen by the party's advocate[2]. In civil cases the court may not call a witness without the consent of the parties[3]. The court must hear such evidence as is necessary to be called to prove the complaint, and such evidence as the defendant desires to call, and hear both parties or such of them who desires to address the court: the court is not required to hear evidence upon admitted facts[4], and indeed in a limited class of cases the court may make the order with the consent of the defendant without hearing evidence[5]. Although jurisdiction cannot be conferred on a court by consent of the parties, the parties can admit facts which, if accepted, form the basis of the court's jurisdiction and entitle the court to make the order applied for without hearing evidence[6]. Justices have the right to stop a case at the close of the complainant's evidence either of their own motion or upon a submission to that effect[7].

If on the hearing of a complaint the justices, for whatever reason, doubt the evidence that a party is giving, particularly if it is unchallenged or if no evidence to the contrary has been or is likely to be given by the other party, it is incumbent upon them in the interests of justice, before dismissing his evidence out of hand, to give him some warning of their doubts and where appropriate to invite some further explanation[8].

The requirement as to translation where a party is unable to follow proceedings applies equally to matrimonial proceedings[9] and would probably be held to apply to other civil proceedings[10].

Under Article 6(1) of the European Convention on Human Rights it is a requirement of a fair trial in both criminal and civil matters that a court should give reasons for its judgment. The extent of the duty to give reasons may, however, vary according to the nature of the decision[11].

---

1. Magistrates' Courts Act 1980, s 53.
2. *Briscoe v Briscoe* [1968] P 501, [1966] 1 All ER 465, 130 JP 12.
3. *Re Enoch and Zaretsky, Bock & Co* [1910] 1 KB 327.
4. *Berkhamsted RDC v Duerdin-Dutton* (1964) 108 Sol Jo 157.
5. Magistrates' Courts Act 1980, s 53, post, and see also the Domestic Proceedings and Magistrates' Courts Act 1978, ss 6 and 7 in PART IV: FAMILY LAW, post.
6. *R v King's Lynn Magistrates' Court, ex p M* [1988] FCR 436, [1988] 2 FLR 79, (admission of defendant in affiliation proceedings that he was the father and that he consented to the making of an affiliation order held gave the court jurisdiction to make the order without hearing evidence).
7. See *Mayes v Mayes* [1971] 2 All ER 397, [1971] 1 WLR 679, 125 JP 487 and para **2–614** in PART II: EVIDENCE, post.
8. See *Comley-Ross v Comley-Ross* [1986] 2 FLR 1, [1986] Fam Law 132.
9. *Kashich v Kashich* (1951) 116 JP 6.
10. For interpreters, see para **1–649 Interpreters**, ante.
11. As to the requirement to give reasoned judgments in civil cases and the need, when considering the extent to which reasons should be given, to have regard to the practical requirements of the appellate system, see *English v Emery Reimbold & Strick Ltd* [2002] EWCA Civ 605, [2002] 3 All ER 385, [2002] 1 WLR 2409. See also *Hadjianastassiou v Greece* (1992)

16 EHRR 219, *Van de Hurk v Netherlands* (1994) 18 EHRR 481, *Ruiz Torija v Spain* (1994) 19 EHRR 553, *Hiro Balani v Spain* (1994) 19 EHRR 566, *Georgiadis v Greece* (1997) 24 EHRR 606 and *Helle v Finland* (1997) 26 EHRR 159, and *Stefan v General Medical Council* [1999] 1 WLR 1293, PC.

1–753A Submission of no case to answer. Once all the evidence for the complainant has been heard[1], the court may dismiss the case either of its own motion or on a submission of no case to answer if it believes it need not hear the evidence for the defence.

In a civil case (but not in a criminal case) the defendant's advocate should be given the choice of making a submission or of calling evidence, but if he is not given the choice, he should then be allowed to call evidence if the submission fails[2]. In any event, the complainant's solicitor must be given the opportunity to address the court before it considers a dismissal[3]. Where a submission fails, the defendant or his advocate is then entitled to address the court on the facts[4].

In family proceedings the concept of "no case to answer" generally has no place[5]. In matrimonial proceedings, where it was necessary for the applicant to make out a ground for relief, it was rare for such a submission to be appropriate[6] and it is quite inapt for proceedings under the Children Act[7].

In other cases: We would suggest that in civil proceedings other than family proceedings, the test for submissions of no case as stated in criminal cases would apply[8].

---

1. *Vye v Vye* [1969] 2 All ER 29, [1969] 1 WLR 588.
2. *Jones v Metcalfe* [1967] 3 All ER 205, 131 JP 494; *Alexander v Rayson* [1936] 1 KB 169; *Muller & Co v Ebbw Vale Steel, Iron and Coal Co Ltd* [1936] 2 All ER 1363; *Parry v Aluminium Corpn Ltd* (1940) 162 LT 236; *Laurie v Ragland Building Co Ltd* [1942] 1 KB 152, [1941] 3 All ER 332; *Wilson v Wilson* [1958] 3 All ER 195, [1958] 1 WLR 1090; *Storey v Storey* [1961] P 63, [1960] 3 All ER 279, 124 JP 485; *Bond v Bond* [1967] P 39, [1964] 3 All ER 346, 128 JP 568.
3. *Mayes v Mayes* [1971] 2 All ER 397, 135 JP 487; applied in *Simmons v Croydon London Borough* [1985] FLR 1092 (application for access order in respect of child in care).
4. *Disher v Disher* [1965] P 31, [1963] 3 All ER 933.
5. *Re S and P (Discharge of Care Order)* [1995] 2 FLR 782, sub nom *P v Bradford Metropolitan Borough Council* [1996] 2 FCR 227.
6. *Bond v Bond* [1967] P 39, [1964] 3 All ER 346, 128 JP 568; *McCartney v McCartney* [1981] Fam 59, [1981] 1 All ER 597.
7. For the practice in Children Act proceedings, see para **6–37 Conduct of proceedings** in PART VI: FAMILY LAW, post.
8. See para **1–669 *Test for submission of no case*,** ante.

1–753B Defendant's evidence. In criminal proceedings, it is provided that evidence should be given from the witness box or other place from which witnesses normally give their evidence[1]. The defendant when giving evidence has the right to give his evidence from the witness box[2].

In order to ensure that the defendant is given a fair trial and that justice is not only done but seen to be done, there must be no suggestion that a defendant is adversely treated compared to other witnesses by being required to give his evidence from the dock[2]. We are of the view that the principles set out above apply equally to defendants giving evidence in civil proceedings, including those defendants giving evidence on an inquiry into their means for non-payment of a sum of money such as a fine.

---

1. Criminal Evidence Act 1898, s 1(4), in PART II: EVIDENCE, post and see para **1–682 *Defendant's evidence to be given from witness box*,** ante.
2. *R v Farnham Justices, ex p Gibson* (1991) 155 JP 792, [1991] RTR 309.

1–753C Calling evidence after case closed. As a rule, once a party has closed his case, he may not call further evidence, except rebuttal evidence such as is provided for in Rules[1]. The court has however a discretion to allow a case to be reopened at any time before final adjudication, but this discretion is a limited one and in criminal proceedings it has been held that the justices should look carefully at the interests of justice overall, and in particular, the risk of any prejudice whatsoever to the defendant[2]. In matrimonial proceedings, justices have a discretion to allow the defendant to reopen his case before they make their final order, even after they have announced their findings on the grounds of the complaint[3].

---

1. See Magistrates' Courts Rules 1981, r 14 in this PART: STATUTORY INSTRUMENTS AND PRACTICE DIRECTIONS ON PROCEDURE, post.
2. See para **1–683 Calling evidence after case closed**, ante.
3. *Robbins v Robbins* [1971] P 236, [1970] 2 All ER 742, 134 JP 550; *R v Leeds Justices, ex p T* (1983) Times, 22 April.

1–753D Standard of proof. We have referred above to the two standards of proof: proof beyond reasonable doubt and proof on the balance of probabilities[1]. In civil cases the standard of proof applicable is proof on the balance of probabilities although its application will vary with the gravity of the issue to be decided.

In *R (N) v Mental Health Tribunal (Northern Region)*[2] Richards LJ summarised the approach to be followed:

"Although there is a single civil standard of proof on the balance of probabilities, it is flexible in its application. In particular, the more serious the allegation or the more serious the consequences if the allegation is proved, the stronger must be the evidence before a court will find the allegation proved on the balance of probabilities. Thus, the flexibility of the standard lies not in any adjustment to the degree of probability required for an allegation to be proved, such that a more serious allegation has to be proved to a higher degree of probability, but in the strength or quality of the evidence that will, in practice, be required for an allegation to be proved on the balance of probabilities."

In child cases, including those where there is an allegation of abuse of children, the standard of proof required is that of a balance of probabilities. There are two stages in the decision making in child cases. First, the court must find facts on events that have occurred in the past on the balance of probabilities. Second, the court must evaluate the evidence adduced both as to facts already in existence and any expert evidence as to the future advantages and risks of possible decision as to the child's future. At the second stage, in exercising its discretion, with the test of the welfare of the child paramount, the court shall assess the risks and, if there is a real possibility that the child will be at risk, the court shall take steps to safeguard the child[3].

In child abuse cases, there may be clear evidence of abuse, but difficulty in identifying which of the child's parents was the perpetrator or whether both were the perpetrators. The same balance of probabilities standard applies to the identification issue as to the proof of abuse[4].

Proceedings for an anti-social behaviour order under s 1(1) of the Crime and Disorder Act 1998[5] are civil, not criminal, both as a matter of domestic law and for the purposes of art but magistrates must, apply, in relation to s 1(1)(*a*), the criminal standard of proof[6].

---

1. See para **1–689** *Standard of proof*, ante and also paras **1– 685 Proof**, **1– 686** *Burden of proof* and **1–687** *Onus of proof*, ante.
2. [2005] EWCA Civ 1605, [2006] 4 All ER 194, [2006] 2 WLR 850 at para [62].
3. *H v H, K v K (Child Abuse: Evidence)* [1990] Fam 86, [1989] 3 All ER 740, [1989] FCR 356, CA; followed in *Re H (minors) (Sexual Abuse: Standard of Proof)* [1996] AC 563, [1996] 1 All ER 1, [1996] 1 FCR 509, HL. See also *Re U (Serious Injury: Standard of Proof); Re B* [2004] EWCA Civ 567, [2004] 2 FLR 263, *Re T (Abuse: Standard of Proof)* [2004] EWCA Civ 558, [2004] 2 FLR 838 and para **6–165 Care and supervision orders: test to be applied**, in PART VI: FAMILY LAW, post.
4. *Re G (a child) (care order: threshold criteria)* [2001] 1 FCR 165, CA.
5. In this PART: STATUTES ON PROCEDURE, post.
6. *R (on the application of McCann) v Crown Court at Manchester, Clingham v Kensington and Chelsea Royal London Borough Council* [2002] UKHL 39, [2003] 1 AC 787, [2002] 4 All ER 593, [2002] 3 WLR 1313).

THE ORDER

1–754   A form of order made on complaint shall be drawn up if required for an appeal or other legal purpose, and if drawn up shall be in such one of the prescribed forms as is appropriate to the case[1].

It is unusual not to draw up an order following civil proceedings. The majority will be covered by the provision[2] that where a magistrates' court makes, revokes, discharges, suspends, revives, alters or varies a magistrates' court maintenance order or order enforceable as a magistrates' court maintenance order or an order regarding lump sums, it must serve a copy on the defendant. The form of most orders is prescribed[3], but if it is not, it should be noted that an order made by justices must state sufficient on the face of it to show jurisdiction to make the order, or from which jurisdiction to make it may be inferred[4].

A minute or memorandum of every adjudication must be entered in the court register, but the written order may be drawn up and signed by the justices on a subsequent day to the hearing, and it will relate back to the time of pronouncing the verbal order[5]. There is no need for the justices to be together when the order is signed. Care must be taken in pronouncing the order and in drawing it up in writing, as it would appear that there is no power to correct any mistake once made[6], unlike the case when dealing with an offender[7], although where an incorrect record of an affiliation order orally pronounced in court was drawn up, a correct record was allowed to be substituted[8]. Appeal would seem to be the only recourse[9] otherwise. If an order is part good part bad, the good part may be implemented[10].

Justices are not *functi officio* until they have discharged all their judicial functions in a case. Accordingly, in affiliation proceedings, where there were three stages: first, consideration of paternity, second, consideration of financial provision, and third, considering how any periodical payments were to be made, it was held that justices were not *functi officio* until they had dealt with the third stage of deciding how the periodical payments were to be made[11]. Similarly, where justices having heard a disputed application for access to a child, announced that they were of opinion that access should be granted to the father, but adjourned the complaint for arrangements to be made for the supervision of access, it was held that the issue as to access remained alive at the adjourned hearing and it was open to the justices in their discretion to permit further evidence to be adduced in regard to it[12].

In proceedings for a liability order to recover non-domestic rates, where justices had made an order unware of an application to adjourn, they had jurisdiction set aside their order. Although there was no express statutory provision, the justices had not exhausted their jurisdiction where they had failed to exercise a judicial discretion whether to proceed or adjourn[13]. Although magistrates of their own motion might correct a clear mistake by the court itself going to the basis of its jurisdiction, or the fairness of the proceedings, they do not have a general power to set aside their own decision merely because of the existence of grounds which might support an application for judicial review. However, it might be sensible, where there had for example been an obvious mistake or where a party had failed to attend through no fault of his own, such as a traffic accident, for all parties to agree to rehear the matter and thereby avoid the expense and delay of judicial review[14].

A priest or deacon having a matrimonial order made against him, is liable to removal from or disqualification from holding a preferment; a certificate of the order is to be sent to the bishop of the diocese in which the court sits[15].

1. Magistrates' Courts Rules 1981, r 16(1), this PART: STATUTORY INSTRUMENTS ON PROCEDURE, post.
2. Magistrates' Courts Rules 1981, r 43.
3. See Magistrates' Courts (Forms) Rules 1981 in PART IX: PRECEDENTS AND FORMS, post.
4. *R v Bradlaugh* (1878) 43 JP 125; *R v Kent County Treasurer* (1889) 22 QBD 603, 53 JP 279.
5. See Magistrates' Courts Rules 1981, r 66, this PART: STATUTORY INSTRUMENTS ON PROCEDURE, post and *R v Huntingdonshire Justices* (1850) 1 LM & P 78, 14 JP Jo 94, 233; *Ratt v Parkinson* (1851) 15 JP 356; *Nutter v Moorhouse* (1903) 68 JP 134.
6. *R v Cheshire Justices* (1833) 5 B & Ad 439; *Pearson v Heys* (1881) 7 QBD 260, 45 JP 730; *Nutter v Moorhouse*, supra. See also *R v Brighton Magistrates' Court, ex p Budd* [1986] 1 FLR 426, [1986] Fam Law 134.
7. Magistrates' Courts Act 1980, s 142 does not apply to civil matters.
8. *R v Lanyon* (1872) 27 LT 355; cf *Cooper v Cooper* [1940] P 204, [1940] 3 All ER 579. See also *R v Chester Justices, ex p Holland* (1984) 148 JP 257.
9. See Supreme Court Act 1981, ss 28–48, post.
10. *R v Maulden Inhabitants* (1828) 8 B & C 78; *R v St Nicholas Leicester, Inhabitants* (1835) 3 Ad & El 79; *R v Winster Inhabitants* (1850) 14 QB 344, 14 JP 304; *Ex p Coley* (1851) 15 JP 420; *R v Fletcher* (1884) 48 JP 407; *Chepstow Electric Light and Power Co v Chepstow Gas and Coke Consumers Co* [1905] 1 KB 198, 69 JP 72.
11. *R v Camberwell Green Magistrates' Court, ex p Brown* (1983) 4 FLR 767, 13 Fam Law 212.
12. *R v Leeds Justices, ex p Thompson* (1983) 147 JP 334, [1983] FLR 773, [1984] Fam Law 20.
13. *Liverpool City Council v Pleroma Distribution Ltd* [2003] 04 LS Gaz R 33.
14. *R (Mathialagan) v Southwark London Borough Council* [2004] EWCA Civ 1689, [2004] All ER (D) 179 (Dec), 169 JPN 26.
15. Ecclesiastical Jurisdiction Measure 1963, ss 55(1), 79(3) and 1974 ss 1 and 2. See also Home Office Circular No 112/1983, dated 16th November 1983.

Costs
CRIMINAL PROCEEDINGS

1–800 In *criminal proceedings* a magistrates' court may make a defendant's costs order for his costs to be paid out of central funds where an information against him is not proceeded with, or it determines not to transfer for trial proceedings for an indictable offence or it dismisses the information[1]. No "right" to costs or expenses can be read into the European convention on Human Rights, but decisions about costs where an information is not proceeded with or a defendant is acquitted can raise issues relating to the presumption of innocence under Article 6(2)[2]. Where it convicts him it may award costs against him[3]. The court may order prosecution costs to be paid out of central funds in proceedings in a magistrates' court for an indictable offence, but not in favour of a public authority or a person acting on behalf of such an authority or as an official of it[4].

Regulations[5] empower courts to make an order against a party in respect of costs incurred as a result of an unnecessary or improper act or omission, or to compensate a witness, interpreter, or medical practitioner for an oral or written report.

In criminal proceedings a magistrates' court may also disallow, or, as the case may be, order[6] the legal or other representative concerned to meet, the whole of any wasted costs or such part of them as may be determined in accordance with Regulations[7]. For this purpose, wasted costs includes any costs incurred by a party as a result of any improper, unreasonable or negligent act or omission on the part of any representative[8]. "Legal or other representative" means a person who is exercising a right of audience, or a right to conduct litigation, on behalf of any party to the proceedings[8].

Comprehensive guidance on the making of orders for costs is given in the *Practice Direction (Costs: Criminal proceedings) 2004*[9].

Costs out of central funds are of such amount as the court considers reasonably sufficient to compensate for expenses properly incurred in the proceedings, but may be less than the full amount if the circumstances make that just and reasonable[10]; the amount will either be specified in the court order if that is appropriate and the person in whose favour the order is made agrees, or else it will be determined in accordance with regulations[11].

1. Prosecution of Offences Act 1985, s 16, in this PART: STATUTES ON PROCEDURE, post. For principles to be applied, see notes thereto. See also *Practice Direction (Costs: Criminal proceedings)* [2004]—reproduced in this PART: STATUTORY INSTRUMENTS AND PRACTICE DIRECTIONS ON PROCEDURE, post.
2. In *Minelli v Switzerland* (1983) 5 EHRR 554 a breach of Article 6(2) was found where a court ordered a defendant to pay part of the prosecutor' costs on the basis that if the case had progressed to trial, he would 'very probably' have been found guilty. See further *Sekanina v Austria* (1993) 17 EHRR 221 and *Byrne v United Kingdom* (1998) EHRLR 626.
3. Prosecution of Offences Act 1985, s 18, in this PART: STATUTES ON PROCEDURE, post. For principles to be applied, see para **3–522**, post. See also *Practice Direction (Costs: Criminal proceedings)* [2004] this PART: STATUTORY INSTRUMENTS AND PRACTICE DIRECTIONS ON PROCEDURE, post.
4. Prosecution of Offences Act 1985, s 17, in this PART: STATUTES ON PROCEDURE, post.
5. See the Costs in Criminal Cases (General) Regulations 1986, reg 3, this PART: STATUTORY INSTRUMENTS AND PRACTICE DIRECTIONS ON PROCEDURE, post.
6. Prosecution of Offences Act 1985, s 19A, in this PART: STATUTES ON PROCEDURE, post.
7. Costs in Criminal Cases (General) Regulations 1986, reg 3A–3D, this PART: STATUTORY INSTRUMENTS AND PRACTICE DIRECTIONS ON PROCEDURE, post.
8. Prosecution of Offences Act 1985, s 19A(3), in this PART: STATUTES ON PROCEDURE, post.
9. See para **1–7390**, post.
10. Prosecution of Offences Act 1985, ss 16(6) and (7), 17(1) and (3), in this PART: STATUTES ON PROCEDURE, post.

See also for guidance on calculating hourly charging rate (*L v L (Legal Aid Taxation)* [1996] 2 FCR 193, [1996] 1 FLR 873, CA, and *Re R (costs: child abduction)* [1996] 2 FCR 324, [1995] 2 FLR 774).

11. Prosecution of Offences Act 1985, ss 16(9) and 17(4), in this PART: STATUTES ON PROCEDURE, post.

1-801   Costs from central funds – prosecution costs order.   A *prosecution costs order* from central funds for a private prosecutor in proceedings in a magistrates' court for an indictable offence[1] should be made except where there is good reason for not doing so, for example where proceedings were instituted or continued without good cause[2]. The amount may be determined by the appropriate officer of the court[1]. The court may direct costs to be disallowed, or to be considered or investigated on taxation if they were or may have been improperly incurred: a proper opportunity must be given for representations to be made[2].

1. Prosecution of Offences Act 1985, s 17, in this PART: STATUTES ON PROCEDURE, post.
2. *R v Birmingham Juvenile Court, ex p H* (1992) 156 JP 445.

1-802   Costs from central funds – defendant's costs order.   A *defendant's costs order* should normally be made unless there are positive reasons for not doing so; examples of such reasons are:

(a) the defendant's own conduct has brought suspicion on himself and[1] has misled the prosecution into thinking that the case against him is stronger than it is;

(b) where the defendant is convicted of some charges but acquitted of others, the order may be for only part of the costs incurred where the court thinks it would be inappropriate for the defendant to recover all the costs[2].

On an application for a defendant's costs order, where the charge has been dismissed or discontinued because of insufficient evidence, it is not necessary for the justices to hear oral evidence before making the order. They may come to a decision that the defendant has brought suspicion on himself and misled the prosecution on the basis of a statement of facts provided by the prosecution. However, the mere assertion that an allegation has been made and withdrawn is not sufficient upon which to conclude that the defendant has brought the proceedings on his own head. The information provided by the prosecution should contain independent evidence to support the truth of the allegation, such as medical evidence or an admission by the defendant[3]. When considering an application for a defendant's costs order, the fact that there is no suggestion that the prosecution was malicious is irrelevant[4].

Where no evidence on the substantive charge has been offered as a result of a caution being accepted, this is not to be equated with a conviction as a positive reason for not making an order in his favour. Nor is there any obligation on the defendant to seek a caution[5].

A legally assisted person's costs do not include, for the purpose of making a defence costs order, the cost of representation funded by him by the Legal Services Commission as part of the Criminal Defence Service[6].

The amount may be determined by the appropriate officer of the court[7]. A defendant has 'properly incurred' costs where he is under a contractual liability to pay his solicitor even though there might be little prospect of any payment being recovered[8]. The court may direct costs to be disallowed, or to be considered or investigated on taxation if they were or may have been improperly incurred: a proper opportunity must be given for representations to be made[4].

1. Note that the two limbs of this provision must be satisfied if the court is not to award costs, see *R v South West Surrey Magistrates' Courts, ex p James* [2000] Crim LR 690, DC and commentary thereto.
2. *Practice Direction (Costs: Criminal proceedings)* [2004] this PART: STATUTORY INSTRUMENTS AND PRACTICE DIRECTIONS ON PROCEDURE, post.
3. *Mooney v Cardiff Magistrates' Court* (1999) 164 JP 220, DC.
4. *R v Birmingham Juvenile Court, ex p H* (1992) 156 JP 445.
5. *R (Stoddart) v Oxford Magistrates' Court* [2005] EWHC 2733 (Admin), 169 JP 683.
6. Prosecution of Offences Act 1985, s 21(4A)(a), in this PART: STATUTES ON PROCEDURE, post.
7. Prosecution of Offences Act 1985, s 16, in this PART: STATUTES ON PROCEDURE, post. For principles to be applied, see notes thereto. See also *Practice Direction (Costs: Criminal proceedings)* [2004]—reproduced in this PART: STATUTORY INSTRUMENTS AND PRACTICE DIRECTIONS ON PROCEDURE, post.
8. *R (on the application of McCormick) v Liverpool City Magistrates' Court* [2001] 2 All ER 705, 165 JP 362, DC.

1-803   Inter partes costs order.   It is inappropriate to order a prosecutor to pay costs to a defendant acquitted of an offence under trade description or consumer protection legislation under a "due diligence" defence where there were serious and important questions of diligence to be considered by the court[1].

1. *Suffolk County Council v Rexmore Wholesale Services Ltd* (1994) 159 JP 390.

1-804   Legal representative costs order – "wasted costs".   *Legal representatives costs order* ("wasted costs")[1] may be made in respect of costs wasted as a result of any improper, unreasonable or negligent act or omission on the part of any representative or his employee or which in the light of any such act or omission occurring after they were incurred, the court considers it unreasonable to expect that party to pay[2]. For this purpose *"improper"* applies to conduct which amounts to any significant breach of a substantial duty imposed by a relevant code of professional conduct and includes conduct so regarded by the consensus of professional (including judicial) opinion. *"Unreasonable"* describes conduct which is vexatious, designed to harass the other side rather than advance the resolution of the case. Conduct cannot be described as unreasonable simply because it leads in the event to an unsuccessful result or because other more cautious legal representatives would have acted differently. The test is whether the conduct permits of a reasonable explanation. *"Negligent"* is to be understood in an untechnical way to denote a failure to act with the competence reasonably to be expected of ordinary members of the profession[3]. An order should only be made where and to the extent that the conduct so characterised has been established as directly causative of wasted costs[3]. Only in the most exceptional circumstances is it appropriate to pass the matter of wasted costs to another judge to determine[4]. The standard of proof to be applied is on the balance of probability and, when assessing probabilities, the court should have in mind, to whatever extent was appropriate in the particular case, that the more serious the allegation the less likely it was that the event had occurred and, therefore, the stronger the evidence should be before the allegation was established to the required standard[4].

It would seem that a wasted costs order may be made in respect of costs incurred by a party served with a witness summons[5]. However, the term "party" is not an open-ended category and is limited to a person who has been served with notice of or has intervened in proceedings by virtue of rules of court or other statutory provision[6].

A court which is intending to make a wasted costs order must formulate clearly and with particularity the complaint and grounds for the order. The court should only make an order after hearing representations from the legal representative concerned in the presence of any defendant whose trial might be affected and any other party to the proceedings if appropriate[7]. A wasted costs order is fatally flawed if the court fails to specify the amount of costs disallowed[7].

It is our view that the wasted costs provisions are primarily intended to relieve parties of the burden of costs incurred because of a legal representative's improper, unreasonable or negligent act or omission; nothing is to be added to that figure to mark the disapproval of the court or by way of deterrence[8].

---

1. See the *Practice Direction (Costs: Criminal proceedings)* [2004], this PART: STATUTORY INSTRUMENTS AND PRACTICE DIRECTIONS ON PROCEDURE, post.
2. See the Prosecution of Offences Act 1985, s 19A, in this PART: STATUTES ON PROCEDURE, post.
3. *Ridehalgh v Horsefield* [1994] 3 All ER 848, [1994] 2 FLR 194.
4. *Re P (a barrister)* [2001] EWCA Crim 1728, [2002] 1 Cr App R 207, sub nom; *Re a Barrister (wasted costs order)* (2001) 165 JPN 594.
5. See *Re a Solicitor (Wasted Costs Order)* [1996] 3 FCR 365, [1996] 1 FLR 40.
6. *R v Camden London Borough Council, ex p Martin* [1997] 1 All ER 307, [1997] 1 WLR 359, [1997] 1 FLR 950.
7. *Re a Barrister (wasted costs order) (No 1 of 1991)* [1993] QB 293, [1992] 3 All ER 429, [1992] 3 WLR 662, CA. See also *In re Harry Jagdev and Co (Wasted Costs Order) (No 2 of 1999)* [1999] 33 LS Gaz R 32, CA.
8. Some guidance is to be found in *Holden & Co v Crown Prosecution Service* [1990] 2 QB 261, [1990] 1 All ER 368, CA, which, together with the *Practice Direction (Costs: Criminal proceedings)* [2004], supra, would appear to govern awards of costs against solicitors under the Supreme Court's inherent jurisdiction which enables the Supreme Court to order a solicitor personally to pay costs thrown away by reason of a serious dereliction on the solicitor's part of his duty to the court. For further guidance, see also *Re a Barrister (wasted costs order) (No 1 of 1991)* [1993] QB 293, [1992] 3 All ER 429, [1992] 3 WLR 662, CA. As to the making of a wasted costs order in care proceedings, see *Re G (care proceedings: wasted costs)* [1999] 4 All ER 371, [1999] 3 FCR 303, [2000] 1 FLR 52.

CIVIL PROCEEDINGS

1–805   In a *civil* case (complaint for an order) costs may be ordered under the power contained in s 64 of the Magistrates' Courts Act 1980[1]. The Divisional Court has held that the proper approach to the award of costs on the hearing of a complaint can be summarised by the following proposition—

1.   Section 64(1) confers a discretion upon a magistrates' court to make such order as to costs as it thinks just and reasonable. That provision applies both to the quantum of the costs (if any) to be paid, but also as to the party (if any) which should pay them.
2.   What the court will think just and reasonable will depend on all the relevant facts and circumstances of the case before the court. The court may think it just and reasonable that costs should follow the event, but need not think so in all cases covered by the subsection.
3.   Where a complainant has successfully challenged before justices an administrative decision made by a police or regulatory authority acting honestly, reasonably, properly and on grounds that reasonably appeared to be sound, in exercise of its public duty, the court should consider, in addition to any other relevant fact or circumstances, both (i) the financial prejudice to the particular complainant in the particular circumstances if an order for costs is not made in his favour; and (ii) the need to encourage public authorities to make and stand by honest, reasonable and apparently sound administrative decisions made in the public interest without fear of exposure to undue financial prejudice if the decision is successfully challenged[2].

Where a party is legally assisted, the condition of his representation is that any sums recovered by virtue of an order or agreement for costs, made in his favour, are paid to the client's solicitor[3]. Conversely, where a court makes an order for costs in favour of the unassisted party, the assisted person generally[4] enjoys 'cost protection' in that the amount of costs which he may be ordered to meet must be such sum as is reasonable for the client to pay having regard to all the circumstances including the financial resources of all the parties to the proceedings and their conduct in connection with the dispute to which the proceedings relate[5]. The unassisted person may apply to the court for an order that the Commission pay the whole or any part of the costs on behalf of an assisted client[6] and the Commission must be allowed to attend and make representations at any hearing which is to decide whether to make such an order[7]. The functions of the court in deciding whether to make an order against the Commission are exercised by a single justice or the justices' clerk and not by the original trial court[8]. An order against the Commission may be made in favour of a body which is financed by public funds[9].

Where any costs of a litigant in person are ordered to be paid by any other party to the proceedings or in any other way, there may be allowed on taxation or other determination of those costs sums in respect of any work done, and any expenses and losses incurred, by the litigant in or in connection with the proceedings to which the order relates[10].

In any civil proceedings, a magistrates' court may disallow, or, as the case may be, order[11] the legal or other representative concerned to meet the whole of any wasted costs or such part of them as may be determined in accordance with rules. Wasted costs include costs incurred by a party as a result of any improper, unreasonable or negligent act or omission on the part of any legal or other representative[12]. "Legal or other representative" means any person who is exercising a right of audience, or a right to conduct litigation, on behalf of any party to the proceedings[13].

---

1. Magistrates' Courts Act 1980, s 64, in this PART: STATUTES ON PROCEDURE, post.
2. *Bradford Metropolitan District Council v Booth* (2000) 164 JP 485, DC. These principles apply equally to awards of costs in liquor licensing appeals under s 181 of the Licensing Act 2003, but two cases decided in relation to s 181 cannot easily be reconciled. In *Crawley Borough Council v Attenborough* [2006] EWHC 1278 (Admin), (2006) 170 JP 593 the Divisional Court emphasised the very wide nature of the justices' discretion. However, in *Cambridge City Council v Alex Nesting Ltd* [2006] EWHC 1374 (Admin), (2006) 170 JP 539, it was held that, although the power to award costs was not confined to cases where the local authority acted unreasonably or in bad faith, the fact that the local authority had acted reasonably and in good faith was plainly a most important factor.
3. Community Legal Service (Costs) Regulations 2000, reg 18, in this PART: STATUTORY INSTRUMENTS AND PRACTICE DIRECTIONS ON PROCEDURE, post.
4. For exceptions, see the Community Legal Service (Cost Protection) Regulations 2000, reg 3, in this PART: STATUTORY INSTRUMENTS AND PRACTICE DIRECTIONS ON PROCEDURE, post.
5. See the Community Legal Service (Costs) Regulations 2000, regs 9–10, in this PART: STATUTORY INSTRUMENTS AND PRACTICE DIRECTIONS ON PROCEDURE, post.
6. Community Legal Service (Cost Protection) Regulations 2000, reg 5, in this PART: STATUTORY INSTRUMENTS AND PRACTICE DIRECTIONS ON PROCEDURE, post. For a detailed description of the procedure, see *R v Secretary of State for the Home Department, ex p Gunn* [2001] EWCA Civ 891 at [29]–[31], [2001] 3 All ER 481.
7. Community Legal Service (Costs) Regulations 2000, reg 13, in this PART: STATUTORY INSTRUMENTS AND PRACTICE DIRECTIONS ON PROCEDURE, post.
8. Community Legal Service (Costs) Regulations 2000, reg 10(10), in this PART: STATUTORY INSTRUMENTS AND PRACTICE DIRECTIONS ON PROCEDURE, post and see *R v Secretary of State for the Home Department, ex p Gunn* [2001] EWCA Civ 891 at [29] – [31], [2001] 3 All ER 481.
9. *R v Secretary of State for the Home Department, ex p Gunn* supra at para [40].
10. Litigants in Person (Costs and Expenses) Act 1975, s 1(1), in this PART: STATUTES ON PROCEDURE, post.
11. Magistrates' Courts Act 1980, s 145A, in this PART: STATUTES ON PROCEDURE, post.
12. Magistrates' Courts Act 1980, s 145A(2), in this PART: STATUTES ON PROCEDURE, post.
13. Magistrates' Courts Act 1980, s 145A(3), in this PART: STATUTES ON PROCEDURE, post.

Appeal and judicial review

AVAILABLE AVENUES OF APPEAL OR JUDICIAL REVIEW

1–820 The following avenues of appeal and judicial review are open in appropriate circumstances in relation to magistrates' courts' proceedings.

1   Appeal to the Crown Court from

    (a)   a conviction or sentence for a criminal offence;
    (b)   a binding over or contempt of court order;
    (c)   a decision relating to betting or gaming licensing.

2   Appeal to the High Court

    (a)   against a decision in adoption or family proceedings[1];
    (b)   by way of case stated on a question of law or jurisdiction;
    (c)   by way of a claim for judicial review.

These are the usual avenues of appeal and review, and are considered in more detail in succeeding paragraphs. There are other ways in which magistrates' court decisions may be challenged or modified, which may be appropriate in particular circumstances.

3   Application for a writ of habeas corpus

This is an easy and quick mode of questioning the deprivation of someone's liberty, although it may also issue when he is on bail[2]. It is not an appropriate means of appealing from a sentence of imprisonment[3], nor for securing the release of a person who has been committed to custody for failing to pay a fine by a warrant which is defective[4]. Procedure is prescribed by Rules of Court[5].

4   Application to the Crown Court for bail

Where a magistrates' court withholds bail, or grants bail subject to conditions in criminal proceedings, either when committing, sending or transferring a case for trial or when remanding a person in custody under ss 4, 8, 10, 18 or 30 of the Magistrates' Courts Act 1980 and issues a full argument certificate under s 5 of the Bail Act 1976, the defendant may make an application for bail to the Crown Court[6].

5   *Application to a High Court judge for leave to prefer a voluntary bill of indictment*

Where no proceedings for the transfer for trial of a charge have taken place or a magistrates' court has dismissed a charge on an application for dismissal, an application may be made to a judge of the High Court for leave to prefer a bill of indictment[7].

6   *Declaration to invalidate proceedings*

If an accused person makes a statutory declaration, at any time during or after the trial of an information, that he did not know of the summons or proceedings until a date specified in the declaration, being a date after the court began to try the information, and serves the declaration on the clerk to the justices within 21 days of that date, the summons and all subsequent proceedings shall be void. A fresh summons may be issued, but the information shall not be tried again by any of the same justices[8].

7   *Power to re-open case to rectify mistakes, etc*

A magistrates' court may vary or rescind a sentence or other order imposed or made by it when dealing with an offender it if appears to the court to be in the interests of justice to do so[9]. Where a person has been convicted by a magistrates' court and it subsequently appears to the court that it would be in the interests of justice that the case should be heard again by different justices, the court may so direct[9].

8   *Applications to alter sentences*

There are several provisions enabling applications to be made to modify sentences; for example to remit a penalty in criminal or quasi-criminal proceedings[10]; to remit a fine and any associated term of imprisonment in default of payment on inquiry into means[11]; to discharge or reduce a compensation order[12]; to remove driving disqualification[14].

9   *Application for a royal pardon to nullify a conviction*

Power exists in the royal prerogative of mercy, for a pardon to be given under the sign manual[15]. This course may be used where all proper form was followed in achieving the conviction and no recourse to appeal or review exists, but where it is abundantly clear that the conviction was wrong, for example from unimpeachable evidence which emerges later. The effect of the pardon is to remove from the subject of the pardon, "all pains penalties and punishments whatsoever that from the said conviction may ensue", but not to eliminate the conviction itself[16].

10   *Petition to the European Commission of Human Rights*

Nothing in the Human Rights Act 1998[17] affects the right of individual petition to Strasbourg under the European Convention on Human Rights[17]. The Convention, which came into force on 3 September 1953, is divided into three sections. Section I describes and defines the rights and freedoms guaranteed under the Convention. Section II establishes the European Court of Human Rights and provides for its operation. Section III deals with miscellaneous provisions such as territorial application, reservations, denunciations, signature and ratification.

Since it was first drafted, the Convention has been amplified by a number of Protocols. One of the most important is Protocol 11, which abolished the European Commission of Human Rights. As a result, the Convention is now administered by two bodies: the European Court of Human Rights and the Committee of Ministers of the Council of Europe.

At the international level, any individual, non-governmental organisation or group of individuals can petition the European Court of Human Rights in Strasbourg alleging a violation of Convention rights. Three judges of the Court sitting in Committee determine whether a petition is "admissible". If so, seven judges of the Court sitting as a Chamber determine the merits of the petition. Cases involving a serious question affecting the interpretation of the Convention are dealt with by a Grand Chamber of eleven judges.

There is extensive case law on the various Articles of the Convention. Most of the judgments of the European Court of Human Rights are found in the series known as the *European Human Rights Reports* (EHRR) and many of the decisions of the (now abolished) European Commission on Human Rights are found in the series known as *Decisions and Reports* (DR) published by the Council of Europe. In addition both the Court and the Commission have websites. For the Court, the website is http://www.dhcour.coe.fr. For the Commission the website is http://www.dhcomm.coe.fr.

Petitions should be addressed to—

Secretary of the Court of Human Rights,
Council of Europe,
F-67075, Strasbourg, Cedex, France.
Tel: 00 33 3 88 41 2000.
The following information will be required—

1.   The applicant's name, age, address, and occupation.
2.   The name, address and occupation of anyone acting as the applicant's representative.
3.   The respondent country.
4.   A clear and concise statement of the facts including exact dates.
5.   The relevant domestic law.
6.   The provisions of the Convention relied upon together with any relevant case law and a summary of alleged violations.
7.   The object of the application (for example, the repeal or amendment of certain legislation or the reversal of a decision and compensation).
8.   The details of all remedies (including any appeal) which have been pursued within the country concerned and, where appropriate, an explanation of why any available remedies have not been pursued.

9.   The judgments, decisions and any other documents relating to the complaint.

Failure to include the content requested may result in the case not being registered with the effect that the case will not be examined.

---

1. For such appeals, see generally para **6–43 Appeals to the High Court in family proceedings**, in PART VI, post.

2. *Re Amand* [1942] 1 KB 445, [1942] 1 All ER 236.

3. *Ex p Corke* [1954] 2 All ER 440, [1954] 1 WLR 899.

4. *R v Oldham Justices, ex p Cawley* [1996] 1 All ER 464, [1996] 2 WLR 681, 160 JP 133.

5. See the Civil Procedure Rules 1998, Part 52, this PART: STATUTORY INSTRUMENTS AND PRACTICE DIRECTIONS ON PROCEDURE, post; also the Administration of Justice Act 1960, ss 14, 15 this PART, post.

6. See the Senior Court Act 1981, s 81, in this PART: STATUTES ON PROCEDURE, post, and Criminal Procedure Rules 2005, Part 19 (Crown Court), in this PART: STATUTORY INSTRUMENTS AND PRACTICE DIRECTIONS ON PROCEDURE, post.

7. See the Administration of Justice (Miscellaneous Provisions) Act 1933, s 2, in this PART STATUTES ON PROCEDURE, para **1–563 Indictments**, ante.

8. Magistrates' Courts Act 1980, s 14, in this PART: STATUTES ON PROCEDURE, post, and see Criminal Procedure Rules 2005, Part 7, this PART: STATUTORY INSTRUMENTS AND PRACTICE DIRECTIONS ON PROCEDURE, post, and Precedent in PART IX: PRECEDENTS AND FORMS, post.

9. Magistrates' Courts Act 1980, s 142, in this PART: STATUTES ON PROCEDURE, post.

10. Remission of Penalties Act 1859, s 1, in this PART: STATUTES ON PROCEDURE, and see *Todd v Robinson* (1884) 12 QBD 530, 48 JP 692.

11. Magistrates' Courts Act 1980, s 85, in this PART: STATUTES ON PROCEDURE, post.

12. Powers of Criminal Courts (Sentencing) Act 2000, s 133 in PART III: SENTENCING, post.

14. Road Traffic Offenders Act 1988, s 42 in PART IV: ROAD TRAFFIC, post.

15. See Criminal Law Act 1967, s 9, in this PART: STATUTES ON PROCEDURE, post.

16. *R v Foster* [1984] QB 115, [1984] 2 All ER 679, 148 JP 747.

17. For the Human Rights Act 1998 and the Convention for the Protection of Human Rights and Fundamental Freedoms, see PART VIII: title HUMAN RIGHTS, post.

APPEAL TO THE CROWN COURT FROM A CONVICTION, SENTENCE OR ORDER OF A MAGISTRATES' COURT

1–821   A person convicted by a magistrates' court may appeal to the Crown Court, if he pleaded guilty, against his sentence; if he did not plead guilty, against the conviction or sentence[1]. This applies additionally to an order for contempt of a magistrates' court[2], an order to enter into a recognizance to keep the peace or to be of good behaviour[3], and a sentence on breach or revocation of community orders[4]. Youth courts are magistrates' courts[5], and these appeal provisions will apply to minors[6].

Notice of appeal must be given within 21 days after the day on which the decision appealed against was given; where conviction and sentence were on different days, the time limit is measured from the date of sentence[7].

The general principle is that once a sentence has been passed it is then in force and enforceable in the absence of specific provisions to the contrary. The fact that the defendant has given notice of appeal to the Crown Court does not prevent the sentence being enforced. The service of a notice of appeal may be a relevant consideration when considering whether the defendant has a reasonable excuse for not complying with an order such as a community order[8].

There is no appeal against sentence where the order in question is an order for payment of costs, an order for the destruction of an animal, or an order made in pursuance of any enactment under which the court has no discretion as to the making of the order or its terms. Even in these cases, there is a right of appeal against conviction where the defendant did not plead guilty or admit the truth of the information. There is no right of appeal against a committal for sentence[9], but there is a right of appeal against the conviction on which the committal for sentence was founded, provided that the accused did not plead guilty. There is no appeal against dismissal or acquittal unless expressly given by statute[10].

Provisions as to notice of appeal, documents to be sent to the Crown Court, entry of appeal and notice of hearing, abandonment of appeal, are specified by Rule[11], and must be observed; they include provision for extension of time for giving notice of appeal. If the appellant dies, his appeal will lapse, but proceedings do not lapse on the death of the informant[12].

Detailed provision for administrative requirements and expectations where there is to be an appeal to the Crown Court is made in the *Criminal Case Management Framework*[13].

---

1. Magistrates' Courts Act 1980, s 108, in this PART: STATUTES ON PROCEDURE, post.

2. Contempt of Court Act 1981, s 12(5), in this PART: STATUTES ON PROCEDURE, post.

3. Magistrates' Courts (Appeals from Binding Over Orders) Act 1956, s 1, in this PART: STATUTES ON PROCEDURE, post.

4. Criminal Justice Act 2003, Sch 8 para 13, in PART III: SENTENCING, post.

5. See Magistrates' Courts Act 1980, ss 148, 152, in this PART: STATUTES ON PROCEDURE, post and Children and Young Persons Act 1933, ss 45, 46 in PART V: YOUTH COURTS, post.

6. See the Powers of Criminal Courts (Sentencing) Act 2000, s 137 in PART III: SENTENCING, post and Magistrates' Courts Act 1980, s 81(6) (orders for parent to pay fine, compensation, costs of minors who are offenders or defaulters).

7. Crown Court Rules 1982, r 7 and the Criminal Procedure Rules 2005, Part 63, in this PART: STATUTORY INSTRUMENTS AND PRACTICE DIRECTIONS ON PROCEDURE, post.

8. *Greater Manchester Probation Committee v Bent* (1996) 160 JP 297.

9. Under s 3 of the Powers of Criminal Courts (Sentencing) Act 2000; *R v London Sessions, ex p Rogers* [1951] 2 KB 74, [1951] 1 All ER 343, 115 JP 108.

10. *R v London County Keepers of the Peace and Justices* (1890) 25 QBD 357, 55 JP 56; *R v Wright, ex p Bradford Corpn*

(1907) 72 JP 23; *Benson v Northern Ireland Road Transport Board* [1942] AC 520, [1942] 1 All ER 465; *R v London County Keepers of the Peace and Justices* [1945] KB 528, [1945] 2 All ER 298, 110 JP 58. For a right of appeal against acquittal see the Customs and Excise Management Act 1979, s 147.

   11. See Crown Court Rules 1982, rr 6–11 and Criminal Procedure Rules 2005, Part 63, this PART: STATUTORY INSTRUMENTS AND PRACTICE DIRECTIONS ON PROCEDURE, post, as to abandonment, see also Magistrates' Courts Act 1980, s 109, in this PART: STATUTES ON PROCEDURE, post, and r 75 of the 1981 Rules.

   12. See *R v Jefferies* [1969] 1 QB 120, [1968] 3 All ER 238 and *R v Truelove* (1880) 5 QBD 336, 44 JP 346.

   13. Crown Court – Appeals from Magistrates' Court Parts 26–27, in this PART: CODES OF PRACTICE AND GUIDELINES, post.

HEARING OF THE APPEAL IN THE CROWN COURT

1–822   On hearing an appeal, the Crown Court will comprise a judge sitting with usually not less than two and not more than four justices[1], who were not concerned with the original case[2]. The appeal is treated as a re-hearing[3], although this apparently does not prevent the Crown Court dealing with a procedural irregularity in the magistrates' court[4]. When the Crown Court has an appeal against sentence, it should go through the sentencing procedure on a rehearing basis without regard to the existing order of the magistrates' court. The court should decide how the appellant ought to be sentenced and then see to what extent, if at all, it differs from the order made in the magistrates' court. If it differs to a significant degree, the appeal should be allowed to that extent[5]. The Crown Court should ask itself not whether the justices' sentence was within their discretion to pass but what was the right sentence[6]. Whether or not an issue should be tried is a matter for the decision of the court. Where there is a sharp divergence on a question of fact, following an admission of an offence, the judge may hear evidence from both sides and come to his own conclusion; or alternatively hear no evidence but listen to the submissions of counsel and come to a conclusion, but here if there is a substantial conflict between the two sides the defendant's version must so far as possible be accepted[7].

   The Crown Court has no power to amend an information on appeal[8] (if appropriate, the Crown Court may nevertheless proceed to deal with an appeal based on a defective information without amendment[9]), or to hear an appeal against an amendment made by the justices[10], nor may the Crown Court having found the appellant not guilty of the full offence laid in the information, substitute a conviction of attempting to commit that offence[11]. The Crown Court may not order the sentence the subject of the appeal to be consecutive to another sentence passed after the magistrates' hearing of the original offence[12]. The Crown Court may in the course of hearing an appeal, correct any error or mistake in the order or judgment incorporating the decision which is the subject of appeal, and on the termination of the hearing may *inter alia* confirm, reverse or vary the decision appealed against, which includes varying sentences not appealed against but delivered at the same time by the justices, for example in order to impose penalty points in driving cases[13]. Similarly, the Crown Court may reverse or vary a determination not to impose a separate penalty in respect of an offence[14]. When the Crown Court dismisses an appeal against a sentence imposed by a magistrates' court, it has power to vary an order made by the magistrates' court requiring the defendant to pay the costs of the prosecutor in relation to the proceedings in the magistrates' court[15].

   The parties are in no way confined to the evidence given in the magistrates' court, the Crown Court sits in place of that court[16]. When dismissing an appeal against conviction by justices, the Crown Court must give sufficient reasons, which do not need to be elaborate, to demonstrate that it has identified the main contentious issues in the case and how it has resolved them[17]. A failure to give reasons will not be fatal to the decision of the Crown Court where, for example, the reasons are obvious, the case is simple or the subject matter of the appeal is unimportant[18]. The court should also give reasons for its decision on the costs of the appeal (unless the reasons are obvious, such as costs following the event), and where an appeal against conviction or sentence succeeds the Crown Court should normally award costs in the appellant's favour[19].

   The Crown Court should award a successful appellant his costs unless there are positive reasons for not doing so[20].

   The justices from whose decision the appeal is being brought, have a right to appear and to call evidence in support of their decision, but in so doing the justices do not make themselves a party to the appeal, and, therefore, do not incur a liability in costs[21]. The person who initiated the proceedings is the proper respondent, and normally the only respondent, to the appeal. Justices, generally, will not wish to be represented on the hearing of an appeal in the Crown Court where the prosecutor is to be represented. However, if the justices know that the original prosecutor will not appear, it is their duty to appear to call evidence to support the conclusion at which they had arrived, or to arrange with some other persons, such as the local police authority to act on their behalf[17]. If no-one appears to sustain the conviction, the Crown Court may quash it[22], but on appeal against sentence only, the conviction itself must not be quashed[23]. Where an appellant persistently fails to appear for the appeal hearing and provides no evidence for the cause of the failure, the Crown Court has a discretion to proceed in his absence where he is represented by counsel and he (the defendant) is under no strict legal obligation to be present in person; the Crown Court may not, however, treat a course of action that is intended to frustrate the course of the proceedings as amounting, in fact, to an abandonment of the appeal[24].

---

   1. Senior Court Act 1981, s 74, in this PART: STATUTES ON PROCEDURE, post although exceptionally justices may be dispensed with: Crown Court Rules 1982, r 4; Criminal Procedure Rules 2005, Part 63, in this PART: STATUTORY INSTRUMENTS AND PRACTICE DIRECTIONS ON PROCEDURE, post.

   2. Crown Court Rules 1982, r 5; Criminal Procedure Rules 2005, Part 63, in this PART: STATUTORY INSTRUMENTS AND PRACTICE DIRECTIONS ON PROCEDURE, post.

3. *R v Newbury Inhabitants* (1791) 4 Term Rep 475; *Paprika Ltd v Board of Trade* [1944] KB 327, [1944] 1 All ER 372, 108 JP 104; *Rugman v Drover* [1951] 1 KB 380, [1950] 2 All ER 572, 114 JP 452.
4. *R v Teeside Magistrates' Court, ex p Bujnowski* (1996) 161 JP 302, [1997] Crim LR 51, DC (on an appeal on the merits against conviction for failing to surrender to bail, the Crown Court had jurisdiction to determine the appeal additionally on the basis that the magistrates' court had acted in clear breach of the *Practice Direction (criminal: consolidated)* [2002] para V.56, in this Part, post).
5. *R v Crown Court at Knutsford, ex p Jones, Gains and Garstang* (1985) 7 Cr App Rep (S) 448.
6. *R v Swindon Crown Court, ex p Murray* (1997) 162 JP 36, DC.
7. *R v Williams* (1983) 148 JP 375; *Bussey v DPP* [1999] 1 Cr App Rep (S) 125.
8. *Garfield v Maddocks* [1974] QB 7, [1973] 2 All ER 303, 137 JP 461; but see *R v Crown Court at Norwich, ex p Russell* [1993] Crim LR 518.
9. *R v Crown Court at Swansea, ex p Stacey* (1990) 154 JP 185, [1990] RTR 183, DC.
10. *Fairgrieve v Newman* (1986) 82 Cr App Rep 60, [1986] Crim LR 47.
11. *R v Crown Court at Manchester, ex p Hill* (1984) 149 JP 257.
12. *R v Crown Court at Portsmouth, ex p Ballard* (1989) 154 JP 109, DC.
13. Senior Court Act 1981, s 48, in this PART: STATUTES ON PROCEDURE, post, and see *Dutta v Westcott* [1987] QB 291, [1986] 3 All ER 381.
14. Senior Court Act 1981, s 48(2)(*a*), in this PART: STATUTES ON PROCEDURE, post.
15. *Hamilton-Johnson v RSPCA* [2000] 2 Cr App Rep (S) 390, 164 JP 345, DC.
16. *R v Hall* (1866) LR 1 QB 632; *Sagnata Investments, Ltd v Norwich Corpn* [1971] 2 QB 614, [1971] 2 All ER 1441.
17. *R v Crown Court at Harrow, ex p Dave* [1994] 1 All ER 315, [1994] 1 WLR 98, 99 Cr App Rep 114, (1993) 158 JP 250; *R v Crown Court at Snaresbrook, ex p Input Management Ltd* (1999) 163 JP 533, DC.
18. *R v Crown Court at Kingston, ex p Bell* (2000) 164 JP 633, DC (failure to give reasons for allowing appeal against decision of the youth court to refuse extension of time limits was fatal to the Crown Court's decision).
19. *Cunningham v Exeter Crown Court* [2003] EWHC Admin 184, (2003) 167 JP 93, [2003] Crim LR 340.
20. *R (on the application of Cunningham) v Exeter Crown Court* [2003] EWHC 184 (Admin), [2003] 2 Cr App R (S) 64).
21. *R v Kent Justices, ex p Metropolitan Police Comr* [1936] 1 KB 547, 100 JP 17, see also as to costs, *R v Davidson, Nanson and Marley* (1871) 35 JP 500; *R v Hants Justices* (1830) 1 B & Ad 654; *R v Goodall* (1874) LR 9 QB 557, 38 JP 616.

APPEAL FROM DECISION OF CROWN COURT ON APPEAL

1-823 Appeal from the decision of the Crown Court on appeal may lie to the Court of Appeal[1] or to the High Court by way of case stated[2].

1. See Criminal Appeal Act 1968, in this PART: STATUTES ON PROCEDURE, post.
2. Senior Court Act 1981, s 28, in this PART: STATUTES ON PROCEDURE, post.

THE HIGH COURT (ADMINISTRATIVE COURT)

1-824 The work of the High Court in hearing appeals by way of case stated or in hearing claims for judicial review is assigned to a specialist court named the 'Administrative Court' with a lead nominated judge with overall responsibility for the speed, efficiency and economy with which the work of the Administrative Court is conducted. The address of the *Administrative Court Office* is:
Administrative Court OfficeRoyal Courts of JusticeStrandLondonWC2A 2LL
Telephone: 020 7947 6517 (Direct Line)020 7947 6491/6655 (General enquiries)(Direct line between 9.00am and 5.00pm)Fax: 020 7947 6802 (General Office)020 7947 6330 (List Office)DX: 44450 StrandMinicom: 020 7947 7594

APPEALS TO THE ADMINISTRATIVE COURT BY CASE STATED

1-825 Except where there is a right of appeal[1] to the High Court, or where some enactment makes the magistrates' decision final, any person who was a party to any proceeding before a magistrates' court, or is aggrieved by the conviction, order, determination or other proceeding of the court, may question the proceeding on the ground that it is wrong in law or is in excess of jurisdiction, by applying to the justices composing the court to state a case for the opinion of the High Court[2] or more particularly by that part of the High Court which is designated as the Administrative Court[3]. However, if the defendant is aggrieved by a decision of justices on matters of fact, the proper remedy is by appeal to the Crown Court[4]. Any challenge made to a sentence imposed by justices should be by way of appeal to the Crown Court, rather than by way of case stated to the High Court[5], in all but the most exceptional case[6].

1. For example under the Domestic Proceedings and Magistrates' Courts Act 1978, s 29 in PART VI: FAMILY LAW, post.
2. Magistrates' Courts Act 1980, s 111, post.
3. See para **1-824 The High Court (Administrative Court)**, ante.
4. *James v Chief Constable of Kent* (1986) Times, 7 June.
5. Appeals by way of case stated against decisions of magistrates other than in family proceedings are generally to the High Court (Administrative Court) (Civil Procedure Rules 1998, Part 52, in this PART, post).
6. *Tucker v DPP* [1992] 4 All ER 901.

1-826 Time limit. An application to state a case must be made within 21 days after the day on which the decision of the magistrates' court was given[1]. The court may refuse to state a case if of opinion that the application is frivolous[1]; the applicant may then make a claim for a mandatory order in judicial review proceedings requiring the justices to state a case and/or to quash the order sought to be appealed[2]. An appellant in an appeal by way of case stated is entitled to withdraw his appeal and the leave of the High Court is not required[3].

1. Magistrates' Courts Act 1980, s 111, post.
2. *Sunworld Ltd v Hammersmith and Fulham London Borough Council* [2000] 2 All ER 837, [2000] Crim LR 593, DC.
3. *Collett v Bromsgrove District Council* (1996) 160 JP 593, [1997] Crim LR 206.

1–827 When appropriate. As to *when a case stated is appropriate*, it should be observed that it may be applied for only on a contention that a proceeding is wrong in law or is in excess of jurisdiction[1]. Justices have no jurisdiction to state a case in criminal proceedings unless and until they have reached a final determination on the matter before them; accordingly, a magistrates' court has no jurisdiction to state an "interlocutory" case during the hearing[2], but the decision to amend an information to substitute one defendant for another may be challenged by judicial review where the case is adjourned for service of a summons on the substituted defendant[3]. Examining justices taking depositions are not exercising a summary jurisdiction and cannot state a case[4], nor are committal proceedings a final determination and thus cannot be reviewed by case stated[5]. In civil proceedings, however, justices have a discretion to state a case at an interlocutory stage, but this discretion should be exercised sparingly and only in exceptional circumstances[6]. It may be applied for by a party *or* a person aggrieved[7], by a prosecutor when a case is dismissed[8], or where a person is aggrieved at the incompleteness of his success[9]. A case cannot be stated to decide a question of jurisdiction, unless there has been a hearing in the magistrates' court[10]; where, for instance, the case was dismissed for want of jurisdiction[11]. Where the defence was given no opportunity of answering the charge, whereby there was a denial of natural justice, the remedy is not by case stated but by proceedings[12]. The manner of exercising a discretion is not a matter of law[13]. It is not perverse, even if it is mistaken, to prefer the evidence of A to that of B where they are in conflict. In the absence of special and unusual circumstances, this gives rise to no error of law challengeable by case stated in the High Court. It gives rise to an error of fact properly to be pursued in the Crown Court[14]. However, if a court comes to a decision to which no reasonable bench of magistrates could come, the High Court can interfere, because the position then is the same as if the justices had come to a decision of fact which there was no evidence to support[15]. The fact that there is an alternative way in which the magistrates' court can be invited to reconsider the matter, such as the power of the court to review under s 18 of the Maintenance Orders Act 1958 a committal order, does not by itself stand in the way of the propriety of asking for a case to be stated[16]. A case may be stated on the grounds that the sentence imposed by the justices on the defendant was harsh and oppressive, or so far outside the normal discretionary limits as to entitle the High Court to say that its imposition must involve an error of law[17]. Even where the decision of a Judge of the Chancery Division has been followed, a case stated may be required, because the Queen's Bench Division is the court of appeal on questions of law in magistrates' courts[18].

1. *Westminster Corpn v Gorden Hotels Ltd* [1908] AC 142, 72 JP 201.
2. *Streames v Copping* [1985] QB 920, [1985] 2 All ER 122, 149 JP 305; followed in *R v Greater Manchester Justices, ex p Aldi GmbH and Co KG* (1994) 159 JP 717.
3. *R v Greater Manchester Justices, ex p Aldi GmbH & Co KG* (1994) 159 JP 717.
4. *Foss v Best* [1906] 2 KB 105.
5. *Card v Salmon* [1953] 1 All ER 324, DC, *Atkinson v United States Government* [1969] 3 All ER 1317, HL and see *Dewing v Cummings* [1971] RTR 295.
6. *R v Chesterfield Justices, ex p Kovacs* [1992] 2 All ER 325, 154 JP 1023.
7. *Drapers' Co v Hadder* (1892) 57 JP 200; *R v Newport (Salop) Justices, ex p Wright* [1929] 2 KB 416, 93 JP 179; normally a public authority is entitled to be treated as a "person aggrieved"; see *Cook v Southend Borough Council* [1990] 2 QB 1, [1990] 1 All ER 243, 154 JP 145, CA.
8. *Davys v Douglas* (1859) 23 JP 135; *R v Newport (Salop) Justices,* supra; *Ruse v Read* [1949] 1 KB 377, [1949] 1 All ER 398.
9. *Burke v Copper* [1962] 2 All ER 14, [1962] 1 WLR 700, 126 JP 319 (some only of a large number of obscene articles forfeited).
10. *Wakefield Local Board v West Riding Rly Co* (1866) 30 JP 628; *Pratt v AA Sites Ltd* [1938] 2 KB 459, [1938] 2 All ER 371, 102 JP 278.
11. *R v Wisbech Justices* (1890) 54 JP 743; *Ex p McLeod* (1861) 25 JP Jo 84; *Muir v Hore* (1877) 41 JP 471.
12. *R v Wandsworth Justices, ex p Read* [1942] 1 KB 281, [1942] 1 All ER 56, 106 JP 50, see also *Rigby v Woodward* [1957] 1 All ER 391, [1957] 1 WLR 250, 121 JP 129.
13. *Diss Urban Sanitary Authority v Aldrich* (1877) 2 QBD 179, 41 JP 549.
14. *R v Mildenhall Magistrates' Court, ex p Forest Heath District Council* (1997) 161 JP 401, CA.
15. *Per* LORD GODDARD CJ in *Bracegirdle v Oxley* [1947] KB 349, [1947] 1 All ER 126, 111 JP 131, followed by *Afford v Pettit* (1949) 113 JP 433 and *Marson v Thompson* (1955) 119 JP Jo 172, and, note Part 64 of the Criminal Procedure Rules 2005, this PART: STATUTORY INSTRUMENTS ON PROCEDURE, post.
16. *R v Horseferry Road Magistrates' Court, ex p Bernstein* (1986) 151 JP 56, [1987] 1 FLR 504, [1987] Fam Law 161.
17. *Universal Salvage Ltd and Robinson v Boothby* (1983) 148 JP 347, [1984] RTR 289. See also *Tucker v DPP* [1992] 4 All ER 901, [1994] RTR 203.
18. *R v Watson, ex p Bretherton* [1945] KB 96, [1944] 2 All ER 562, 109 JP 38, compare *R v Shiel* (1900) 82 LT 587.

1–828 Appeals against sentence. *Appeal against sentence* Appeals against sentence by way of case stated or by way of a claim for judicial review are generally to be deprecated:

'I hope that the fact of this matter coming before the court today will result in a loud and clear signal being received by those who have to advise defendants where they contend that something may have gone wrong in the sentencing process of a lower court. Even if there were not the delays which had occurred in this case, the procedure of coming to this court by way either of judicial review or of case stated is one which created difficulties and problems. Although this court seeks to deal with appeals by case stated and applications for judicial review as promptly as possible, inevitably there are delays....Even if the appeal or application for judicial review is successful, the best that a defendant can hope to achieve is that he will have to be sentenced again. He is therefore either in a position where he remains in custody if a sentence of imprisonment has been imposed..., pending the matter coming before this court, or...he applies for and obtains bail, and then is faced with the danger months later of having to return to prison to complete a sentence, a sentence which may be of short duration.[1]'

1. *Allen v West Yorkshire Probation Service* [2001] EWHC Admin 2, 165 JP 313, DC per Lord Woolf CJ.

1–829   Appeal from the Administrative Court.   *Appeal from the High Court* in a criminal cause or matter lies to the House of Lords; the High Court must first certify that a point of law of general public importance is involved in the decision, and either that court or the House of Lords must give leave to appeal[1]. An application to estreat a recognizance is not included in the definition of "criminal cause or matter"[2]. An appeal lies in a non-criminal matter from the High Court to the Court of Appeal, but the permission of the High Court or of the Court of Appeal is necessary[3].

1. Administration of Justice Act 1960, s 1.
2. *R v Southampton Justices, ex p Green* [1976] QB 11, [1975] 2 All ER 1073, 139 JP 667.
3. See the Senior Court Act 1981, ss 19 and 28.

1–830   Procedure for stating a case.   The procedure for stating a case must be in compliance with Rules[1]. We recommend[2] the following as the normal practice—

1.   On receipt of a proper application, the justices' clerk should prepare a draft case immediately, unless the justices are likely to refuse to state a case[1].
2.   For the purpose of preparing the first draft, the justices' clerk should, if necessary, consult the justices, and may informally discuss the application with either or both parties.
3.   The first draft should be sent to the justices and to the parties within 21 days of the application being received.
4.   When the draft is sent to the parties they should be specifically reminded that they must make representations within 21 days of receiving the draft case.
5.   The justices' clerk may informally discuss the draft case with the parties prior to their making representations.
6.   Immediately after the expiry of the date by which representations should be made by the parties, the justices' clerk should notify the justices of any representations, or provide a revised draft of the case, and agree the final form of the case with them.
7.   The final form of the draft will be signed by any two of the justices' or by the justices' clerk, and sent to the applicant or his solicitor within 21 days of the last date for making representations.

If there has been any delay in complying with the 21 day limits or an extension of time has been agreed, the justices' clerk must attach to the case a statement of the delay and the reasons therefor[3]. As a general rule, the justices' clerk should prepare the first draft of the case, a view expressed by the Lord Chief Justice. Exceptionally it may be appropriate for the applicant to prepare the draft and it may be that the magistrates—and particularly a District Judge (Magistrates' Courts)—will wish to do so themselves. Even in these exceptional circumstances, the justices' clerk remains under a duty to comply with time limits. Where the applicant asked the justices' clerk to delay, so he could obtain permission to enter into the recognizance from the local authority, the High Court later refused to adjudicate on the case stated, because of the delay[4]. It is irrelevant that the decision was by a majority[5]; if justices sign the case, it is not necessary that each of those who sign will have formed part of the majority.

1. See Criminal Procedure Rules 2005, Part 64, this PART: STATUTORY INSTRUMENTS ON PROCEDURE, post. The form of case is prescribed as Form 155 in PART IX: PRECEDENTS AND FORMS. See *Practice Direction* [1972] 1 All ER 286, [1972] 1 WLR 4.
2. This procedure has been judicially approved in *Tesco Stores Ltd v Seabridge* [1988] Crim LR 517; appellants in that case were not allowed to adduce a draft of the case which differed from the case stated for the High Court.
3. Criminal Procedure Rules 2005, Part 64, this PART: STATUTORY INSTRUMENTS ON PROCEDURE, post.
4. *Parsons v F W Woolworth & Co Ltd* [1980] 3 All ER 456, [1980] 1 WLR 1472.
5. *More O'Ferrall Ltd v Harrow UDC* [1947] KB 66, [1946] 2 All ER 489, 110 JP 357.

1–831   *Content of the case.*   The content of the case includes the facts found by the court, and the question or questions of law or jurisdiction on which the opinion of the High Court is sought[1]. It should also state the contentions of the parties, and the opinion or decision of the justices[2]. The question stated should reflect the findings of fact, and be the one, the answer to which is going to resolve whether the conviction or order should be sustained[3]. The question raised by a case stated should be as simple as possible and directed to the crucial question on which the case turns. It is also desirable that the summary of the competing submissions should be reasonably succinct[4]. It is implicit in the procedure that the parties must be frank with the court and that all concerned should attempt to define the question upon which the opinion of the High Court is sought. If a properly framed question is to be fundamentally altered, the party which framed the question ought then to have an opportunity to comment upon it[5]. Where one of the questions is whether there was evidence on which the magistrates' court could come to its decision, the particular finding of fact which, it is claimed, cannot be supported by the evidence, shall be specified in the case[1].

Where a document forms a material part of the case stated, the original document or a photocopy of the whole of the document should be appended to the case[6], similarly with a computer disc where appropriate[7]. Justices must state only facts as found by them, not the evidence upon which their findings is based[8], unless one of the questions is whether there was evidence on which the magistrates' court could come to its decision[1]. The case should never state that the justices' decision was of a majority[2].

On an appeal relating to a criminal charge, the High Court will consider a point of law which might afford a good defence, notwithstanding that the point was a new point and was not taken before the justices[9]. The court will consider a point of law depending on facts stated in the case, but not which depends on further findings of fact[10]. The High Court will rely on the justices and take the case as stated, unless there is a patent defect on the fact of it, notwithstanding that one of the parties disputes by affidavit the facts as stated, and declares that they raise a different question[11], but costs may be awarded against justices who do not fairly state a case[12]. If a party is of opinion that the facts have not been properly stated, he should without delay make an application to the High Court, supported by affidavit, for the case to be sent back for amendment[13].

Inferences properly drawn will not be disturbed[14]. The High Court will decline to hear a case which has been so stated that the judgment will not finally dispose of it[15], and as a rule will refuse to decide an academic question[16] or a case stated in an alternative form[17]. Objections will not be allowed which were not taken before the justices[18], nor can a point be taken upon the facts stated, which was not taken before the justices, except upon a question of law which no evidence could alter[19]. The High Court will not review the issue of the justices' discretion to exclude evidence under s 78 of the Police and Criminal Evidence Act 1984, when that was not raised before the justices[20].

---

1. Criminal Procedure Rules 2005, Part 64, this PART: STATUTORY INSTRUMENTS ON PROCEDURE, post.
2. See *Downsborough v Huddersfield Industrial Society Ltd* [1942] 1 KB 306, [1941] 3 All ER 434, 106 JP 25.
3. *Corcoran v Anderton* (1980) 71 Cr App Rep 104.
4. See *Nottingham City Council v Amin* [2000] 2 All ER 946, [2000] 1 WLR 1071, [2000] 1 Cr App Rep 426, [2000] Crim LR 174.
5. *Waldie v DPP* (1995) 159 JP 514.
6. See *Gaimster v Marlow* [1984] QB 218, [1985] 1 All ER 82, [1984] RTR 49. As to the marking and use of exhibits and bundles of documents generally in the High Court, see Practice Note [1983] 3 All ER 33, [1983] 1 WLR 922.
7. *Kent County Council v Multi Media Marketing (Canterbury) Ltd* (1994) Times, 7 December.
8. *Per* LORD ALVERSTONE CJ in *Betts v Stevens* [1910] 1 KB 1, 73 JP 486; *Mills v Boddy* (1950) 94 Sol Jo 371. See also *Cotgreave and Cotgreave v Cheshire County Council* (1992) 157 JP 85.
9. *Whitehead v Haines* [1965] 1 QB 200, [1964] 2 All ER 530, 128 JP 372.
10. *Ross v Moss* [1965] 2 QB 396, [1965] 3 All ER 145, 129 JP 537.
11. *Musther v Musther* (1894) 58 JP Jo. 53; *Chatham Corpn v Wright* (1929) 94 JP 43.
12. *Edge v Edwards* (1932) 48 TLR 449, see also 80 JPJo 331 and 94 JP Jo 680 (application for *mandamus* to state the case fairly).
13. See Senior Court Act 1981, s 28A, this PART, post.
14. *White v Cubitt* [1930] 1 KB 443, 94 JP 60.
15. *R v Headington Union* (1883) 47 JP Jo 756.
16. *Tindall v Wright* (1922) 86 JP 108.
17. *Sheffield Waterworks Co v Sheffield Union* (1887) 31 Sol Jo 271.
18. *Purkiss v Huxtable* (1859) 23 JP Jo 293; *Motteram v Eastern Counties Rly Co* (1859) 7 CBNS 58, 24 JP 40, but see also *Ex p Markham* (1869) 34 JP 150; *Knight v Halliwell* (1874) LR 9 QB 412, 38 JP 470.
19. *Kates v Jeffrey* [1914] 3 KB 160, 78 JP 310; *LCC v Farren* [1956] 3 All ER 401, 120 JP 542. See also *Kavanagh v Glorney* (1876) IR 10 CL 210 and *London, Edinburgh and Glasgow Assurance Co Ltd v Partington* (1903) 67 JP 255.
20. *Braham v DPP* (1994) 159 JP 527.

1–832   Hearing in the Administrative Court[1].   The case now proceeds to its hearing in the High Court, by means of being lodged within 10 days of its receipt, and a notice of entry of appeal is sent to the respondent within four days thereafter in conformity with Rules[2]. Appeals may be dismissed by consent and unopposed appeals may be allowed on paper[3]. Although the position is not certain beyond doubt, it would appear that the High Court may allow a case to proceed after the death of one of the parties if the executors or successor of the deceased party have an interest in the case[4]. The High Court will simply hear only one counsel on each side[5]. Justices would seem to be unable to appear, unless joined as a party or accused of misconduct; when appearing they may become liable in costs[6]. They may however file affidavits instead which will be considered by the High Court[7]. In an appropriate case the Court may ask the Attorney General to consider appointing an *amicus curiae* to argue matters of relevance which might otherwise not be drawn to the Court's attention; this may be of especial assistance where the matter in issue is a sentencing matter about which the prosecution in an English criminal court has traditionally avoided comment, and where the justices have reasons which they believe should be fully presented but they are not represented. Having heard and determined the question or questions of law, the court may reverse, affirm or amend the determination in respect of which the case has been stated, or remit the matter to the justice or justices with the opinion of the court thereon, or make such other order in relation to the matter as to the court may seem fit[8]. The court has no power to reduce the penalty[9] but on reversing the justices' decision to dismiss an information it may impose what would seem to be the only proper penalty the justices could impose in the circumstances of the case[10], and it may substitute a valid for an invalid sentence[11]. In appropriate circumstances, the court can order a rehearing before the same or a different bench of justices[12]. Where a case is sent back with an opinion that the justices ought to have convicted, the case ought to be reinstated and proceed to conviction, otherwise the justices risk *a* quashing order in judicial review proceedings with costs[13].

Costs between parties are at the discretion of the court[14], but as a general rule will be given to the successful party[15]. Although costs have been refused to a successful appellant against a respondent who did not appear, in more recent times the tendency has been to award costs to him because he set the law in motion to get a point decided, or because the case stated was made necessary by an objection taken by the respondent[16]. In appropriate cases the court may award to a successful appellant costs in respect of his appearance before justices[17]. Where justices are (unusually) made parties to the appeal, then costs may be awarded to or against them[18]. Justices may challenge an order of costs against them by an application to set aside under CPR r 39.3. If justices have not appeared, the normal 7 day time limit will normally be extended to 21 days from receipt of the transcript of the judgment[19]. The principles which the High Court will apply, especially in civil cases, will be similar to those applied in judicial review proceedings—see para **1–854**, **Liability of justices and the Lord Chancellor for costs**.

1. For detailed procedural requirements for proceedings in the High Court including the appellant's notice, service of appellant's notice, documents to be lodged, skeleton arguments and the appeal Court's powers, see generally the Civil Procedure Rules, Part 52 and the *Practice Direction - Appeals* in this PART, post.
2. *Practice Direction–Appeals*, paras 18.4 and 18.6 in this PART, post.
3. See *Practice Direction–Appeals*, paras 12 and 13 in this PART, post.
4. Note *R v Jefferies* [1969] 1 QB 120, [1968] 3 All ER 238, and *Finchley UDC v Blyton* (1913) 77 JP Jo 556, but see *Garnsworthy v Pyne* (1870) 35 JP 21; *Hodgson v Lakeman* [1943] 1 KB 15, 107 JP 27; *R v Rowe* [1955] 1 QB 573, [1955] 2 All ER 234, 119 JP 349; *Richards v Bloxham* (1968) 112 Sol Jo 543; *Hawkins v Bepey* [1980] 1 All ER 797, 144 JP 203.
5. *Howes v Peake* (1876) 33 LT 818 and see the Civil Procedure Rules 1998, r 52.11, in this PART, post.
6. See *R v Camborne Justices, ex p Pearce* [1952] 2 All ER 850; *R v Llanidloes Licensing Justices, ex p Davies* [1957] 2 All ER 610n, [1957] 1 WLR 809n.
7. Review of Justices' Decisions Act 1872, post.
8. See Supreme Court Act 1981, s 28A, this PART, post.
9. *Evans v Hemingway* (1887) 52 JP 134.
10. *Coote v Winfield* [1980] RTR 42.
11. Administration of Justice Act 1960, s 16.
12. *Griffiths v Jenkins* [1992] 2 AC 76, [1992] 1 All ER 65.
13. *R v Haden Corser* (1892) 8 TLR 563.
14. *Chandler v Emerton Justices* [1940] 2 KB 261, [1940] 3 All ER 146, 104 JP 342; *R v East Riding Quarter Sessions, ex p Newton* [1968] 1 QB 43, [1967] 3 All ER 118 and see the Civil Procedure Rules 1998, r 52.10(2)(e), in this PART, post.
15. *Youdon v Crookes* (1858) 22 JP Jo 287; *Moore v Smith* (1859) 23 JP 133 (payment by Crown).
16. See as to refusal of costs, *Lee v Strain* (1859) 28 LJMC 221; *Halse v Alder* (1874) 38 JP 407; *Smith v Butler* (1885) 16 QBD 349, 50 JP 260 and as to grant of costs against respondent, *Shepherd v Folland* (1884) 49 JP 165; *Greenbank v Sanderson* (1884) 49 JP 40; *Gordon v Cann* (1888) 63 JP 324; *Robinson v Gregory* [1905] 1 KB 534, 69 JP 161.
17. *Turner & Son Ltd v Owen* [1956] 1 QB 48, [1955] 3 All ER 565, 120 JP 15.
18. *R v Llanidloes Licensing Justices, ex p Davies* [1957] 2 All ER 610n, [1957] 1 WLR 809n, 121 JP 454.
19. *R v Newcastle under Lyme Magistrates' Court, ex p Massey* [1995] 1 All ER 120, [1994] 1 WLR 1684 (1994) 158 JP 1037.

CLAIMS FOR JUDICIAL REVIEW[1]

1–833   The High Court[2] has jurisdiction to make of quashing orders, mandatory orders and prohibiting orders, the claim for which shall be made in accordance with rules of court, by a procedure known as a claim for judicial review[3]. Judicial review is limited to considering whether the magistrates' court has failed to exercise its jurisdiction properly or whether it has come to some error of law which appears on the face of the record[4]. Judicial review is concerned, not with the decision but with the decision-making process; it is the legality of the process which is under review, not whether it is right or wrong[5]. An application for judicial review may be made notwithstanding that other avenues of appeal have not been exhausted[56], although in the case of a sentence which has been passed such applications should be discouraged[7]. In general, case stated is preferable to judicial review as a means of examining justices' decisions since the latter process is reserved for cases where legislation has provided no alternative remedy[8] and this is particularly so where the case bristles with factual difficulties as the case stated will set out the facts found by the justices[9]. In the absence of a specific definition, judicial review is not excluded by a statutory provision to the effect that a person shall not be liable to any civil proceedings[10]. Judicial review is not appropriate with regard to the grant of bail where bail has been refused, or as to conditions of bail, until all the remedies in the Crown Court and High Court under s 81 of the Supreme Court Act 1981 and s 22 of the Criminal Justice Act 1967 (bail on appeal by case stated) have been exhausted[11]. In general it is inappropriate to intervene at an interlocutory stage[12]. The court must decide all issues whether of fact or law for itself and reach its decision. If the decision is, or is alleged to have been, tainted by any errors of law, a case can be stated or exceptionally judicial review proceeding can then be brought: It is particularly inappropriate to permit judicial review before the final decision in cases where speed, and the continuing protection of the public, are of particular importance[13].

By means of a quashing order, the High Court exercises a supervision over any inferior court which exceeds its jurisdiction, or makes an error of law which appears on the face of the record, or is affected by bias, or contravenes the rules of natural justice, or where the decision was obtained by fraud or collusion; the remedy is however not concerned with a miscarriage of justice arising on evidence, but with jurisdiction and the regularity of the proceedings[14]. If, by a quashing order, the

High Court quashes the decision to which the application relates, it may remit the matter to the court concerned with a direction to reconsider it and reach a decision in accordance with the findings of the High Court[15]; where the case involves a person who has been sentenced and the High Court determines that the court has no power to pass the sentence, it may instead of quashing the conviction, amend it by substituting a sentence which the original court had power to impose[16].

By means of a mandatory order, the High Court requests justices of the peace to do any act relating to the duties of their office, or requires a magistrates' court to state a case for the opinion of the High Court[17], but a mandatory order is not appropriate to control the conduct of a case or the exercise of a discretion[18].

A prohibiting order prevents a court from proceeding further in excess of its jurisdiction or where it is biased, or has an interest in the subject matter of the proceedings or unlawfully purports to alter its adjudication[19] or where it would otherwise proceed in disregard of important principle[20].

Permission of the High Court must first be obtained before a claim for judicial review is made[21]. The claim form must be filed promptly and in any event not later than 3 months after the grounds to make the claim first arose[22]. Where permission is given to proceed, the Court may also give directions which may include a stay of the proceedings to which the claim relates[23].

---

1. Supreme Court Act 1981, ss 29, 31, post; Civil Procedure Rules 1998, Part 54, this PART, post.
2. See para **1–824 The High Court (Administrative Court)**, ante.
3. Civil Procedure Rules 1998, r 54.1(2)(a) in this PART, post.
4. Claims for judicial review of decisions of magistrates' courts are made to the High Court (Administrative Court) (Civil Procedure Rules 1998, Part 54, in this PART, post) and see **1–824 The High Court (Administrative Court)**, ante.
5. Civil Procedure Rules 1998, r 54.1(2)(b)–(d), in this PART, post.
6. *Chief Constable of the North Wales Police v Evans* [1982] 3 All ER 141, [1982] 1 WLR 115, 147 JP 6, HL; *R v Slough Justices, ex p B* [1985] FLR 384, [1985] Fam Law 189.
7. *R v Bristol Magistrates' Court, ex p Rowles* [1994] RTR 40.
8. *R v Ealing Justices, ex p Scrafield* [1994] RTR 195. For the undesirability of challenging a sentencing decision by way of judicial review, see *Allen v West Yorkshire Probation Service* [2001] EWHC Admin 2, 165 JP 313, DC and para **1–825**, ante.
9. *R v Crown Court at Ipswich, ex p Baldwin* [1981] 1 All ER 596; *R v Poole Justices, ex p Benham* (1991) 156 JP 177, [1991] RVR 217.
10. *R v Crown Court at Ipswich, ex p Baldwin*, supra.
11. *Re Waldron* [1986] QB 824, [1985] 3 All ER 775.
12. *R v Rochford Justices, ex p Buck* (1978) 68 Cr App R 114, [1978] Crim LR 492.
13. *R (Errington) v Metropolitan Police Authority* [2006] EWHC 1155 (Admin), 171 JP 89 (wrong for Crown Court to adjourn proceedings for closure order awaiting decision of Administrative Court as to legality of closure notice).
14. *Re Herbage* (1985) Times, 25 October; *R v Guildhall Justices, ex p Prushinowski* (1985) Times, 14 December.
15. *R v West Sussex Quarter Sessions, ex p Albert and Maud Johnson Trusts Ltd* [1974] QB 24, [1973] 3 All ER 289.
16. Supreme Court Act 1981, s 31(5), post.
17. Supreme Court Act 1981, s 43, post.
18. Supreme Court Act 1981, s 29(4); Justices of the Peace Act 1979, s 48(1).
19. *R v Carden* (1879) 5 QBD 1, 44 JP 119, 137, *Ex p Lewis* (1888) 21 QBD 191; *R v Wells Street Stipendiary Magistrate, ex p Seillon* [1978] 3 All ER 257, [1978] 1 WLR 1002, [1978] Crim LR 360; *R v Rochford Justices, ex p Buck* (1978) 68 Cr App R 114, [1978] Crim LR 492; *R v Horsham Justices, ex p Bukhari* (1982) 74 Cr App Rep 291.
20. *R v North, ex p Oakey* [1927] 1 KB 491; *R v Wimbledon Justices, ex p Derwent* [1953] 1 QB 380, [1953] 1 All ER 390; *R v Wilson, ex p Neil* (1953) Times, 18 April; and see *R v Tottenham and District Rent Tribunal, ex p Northfield (Highgate) Ltd* [1957] 1 QB 103, [1956] 2 All ER 863, 120 JP 472.
21. See *R v West London Stipendiary Magistrate, ex p Anderson* (1984) 148 JP 683 (reason for delay and possible prejudice therefrom).
22. Civil Procedure Rules 1998, r 54.4, in this PART, post.
23. Civil Procedure Rules 1998, r 54.5, in this PART, post.

1–834   Discretionary remedy.   Judicial review is not an appeal but is a collateral challenge to the decision making process. It is a discretionary remedy and the principles on which the Divisional Court will exercise that discretion were considered in *R v Peterborough Justices ex p Dowler*[1] and *R v Hereford Magistrates' Court, ex p Rowlands*[2] where the authorities were extensively reviewed. The decision in *Dowler* should not be treated as authority that a party complaining of procedural unfairness or bias in the magistrates' court should be denied leave to move for judicial review and left to whatever rights he may have in the Crown Court[2].

Nevertheless, leave to move should not be granted unless the applicant advances an apparently plausible complaint which, if made good, might arguably be held to vitiate the proceedings in the magistrates' court. Moreover, the decision whether or not to grant relief by way of judicial review is always a discretionary one[3].

In considering the decisions and reasons of lay justices, the court will not intervene just because the reasons given, if strictly construed, may disclose an error of law. The jurisdiction to quash a decision only exists where there has in fact been an error of law and the court will not expect the same degree of accuracy in the use of language which a lawyer may adopt[4]. However, where a decision of justices is announced orally, it is that order, not any other material such as the written register of conviction, which is the proper subject of judicial review. A subsequent written elucidation of these reasons must be distinguished from an ex post facto rationalisation of what has been said[5].

It is only in an exceptional case that the court will exercise its supervisory jurisdiction either to intervene and quash a decision made by justices in the exercise of their discretion not to stay criminal proceedings for abuse of process or to interfere with the Crown Prosecution Service's decision on whether to prosecute[6]. The exercise of discretion to allow relief will depend upon a variety of circumstances including:

(a) the seriousness of criminal charges,

(b) the nature of the evidence in the case and in particular the extent to which its quality may be affected by delay,

(c) the extent, if any, to which the defendant has brought about or contributed to the justices' error,

(d) the extent, if any, the defendant has brought about or contributed to the delay in the hearing of the challenge, and

(e) how far the complainant would feel justifiably aggrieved by the proceedings being halted and the defendant would feel justifiably aggrieved by their being continued[7].

1. Civil Procedure Rules 1998, r 54.10, in this PART, post.
2. *R v Peterborough Justices, ex p Dowler*, [1996] 2 Cr App Rep 561, 160 JP 561, [1997] 2 WLR 843, DC.
3. *R v Hereford Magistrates' Court, ex p Rowlands* [1997] 2 WLR 854, 161 JP 258, [1997] 2 Crim App Rep 340.
4. *R v Newcastle-under-Lyme Magistrates' Court, ex p Cloudside Outdoor Pursuits Ltd* (1995) Times, 7 April.
5. *Customs and Excise Comrs v Shah* (1999) 163 JP 759, DC.
6. *R v Liverpool City Justices, ex p Price* (1998) 162 JP 766, DC.
7. *R v Neath and Port Talbot Magistrates' Court, ex p DPP* [2000] 1 WLR 1376, 164 JP 323, [2000] Crim LR 674, DC.

1–835 Quashing order. A claim for a quashing order should not be made where an application for case stated would be more appropriate or is proceeding[1], nor where the magistrates' courts proceedings could be voided or re-opened[2]; nor where the magistrates' court proceedings are not completed[3]. This is so even where there is an important substantive point which has arisen during a trial as the proper course is to proceed to the end of the trial in the lower court and then test the matter by way of case stated[4]. The High Court may in the exercise of its discretion decline to entertain an application for judicial review of a sentence passed by a magistrates' court if the alternative procedure of appeal to the Crown Court has not been exhausted[5]. Justices have no power to grant bail to a convicted person pending a review of their conviction by *certiorari*[6]; this is a matter for the High Court[7].

Where the justices have acted within their jurisdiction, judicial review cannot be used to inquire into the exercise of their discretion, their findings of fact or of law, or their decision; for example a person's capacity or status in relation to an offence[8]; a decision after a plea of guilty[9]; where the conviction seems regular on the face of it[10]; an acquittal after a trial on the merits[11]; a finding of corroboration in affiliation proceedings, even if erroneous[12]; a decision on the weight of evidence, even if misdirected[13].

A quashing order may be made where there is an error of law on the face of the record, including wrong procedures; for example a period of disqualification beyond what the law allows (but leaving the conviction and a fine intact)[14]; a finding of due service of an affiliation summons[15]; a difference between the charge stated and the offence for which there has been a conviction[16]; an order or sentence not authorised by law[17]; where a sentence is so far outside the normal discretionary limits that its imposition amounts to an error of law[18], or that the sentence was by any acceptable standard truly astonishing[19]; that the mode of trial decision was truly astonishing[20]; where a young offender should clearly have been committed for trial for a grave crime[21]; a witness summons wrongfully issued[22]; an invalid committal for sentence[23]; or a dismissal of an information by justices who act without jurisdiction[24].

A quashing order may be made in respect of a committal for trial by examining justices where there was misreception of inadmissible hearsay evidence by the justices and no other evidence capable of being deemed sufficient to put the accused on trial by jury[25]. However, in these circumstances, relief will not be granted as a matter of course, but only in the case of a really substantial error leading to manifest injustice and irregularity having substantial adverse consequences for the accused[25]. Moreover, where examining justices, contrary to s 76(2) of the Police and Criminal Evidence Act 1984 allow evidence of a confession to be given in evidence without requiring the prosecution to prove beyond reasonable doubt that it was voluntary, that omission may be a ground for granting judicial review of the committal proceedings, although, save in the exceptional case, the High Court will not quash the committal on that ground alone[26]. A procedural error by examining justices may also result in quashing their decision by a quashing order[27].

Where the High Court quashes the committal of a person to prison or detention in default of payment of a sum adjudged to be paid on conviction, or for want of sufficient distress, the High Court may deal with the person for the default, or want of sufficient distress, in any way in which the magistrates' court would have power to deal with him if it were dealing with him at the time the committal is quashed[28].

Natural justice requires the application of certain rules which judicial review can ensure; for example a magistrate's duty to act impartially, without apparent or actual bias[29]; allowing a defendant a reasonable opportunity to prepare his case[30]; grant an adjournment until the time later in the day when prosecution witnesses had mistakenly been notified to attend[31]; grant an adjournment where trial mistakenly fixed for date when prosecution witness could not attend[32]; prosecution to inform the defendant of witnesses from whom statements have been taken but who are not called to give evidence[33]; on a summary trial where prosecution statements are not given to defence, to make defence aware of material differences between a witness's evidence and any earlier statement[34] magistrates not to take evidence or significant information privately[35]; failure of prosecution witness to disclose his bad character which deprived the accused of a valuable plank in his defence[36]; failure of prosecution to carry out its duty to bring before the court all the material evidence[37]; Crown Court to hear appeal on its merits by receiving all admissible evidence desired to be led[38].

Fraud, collusion, perjury may lead to the quashing of an order where for example an appellant obtains the quashing of an order on appeal by means of perjured evidence[39], but not where a witness committed perjury and was not in collusion with a party[40]. Where a Crown Court was induced by fraud to substitute an acquittal for a conviction before magistrates, the decision was quashed[41]. A quashing order will also be granted where the prosecutor so corrupts the process leading to conviction that it gives the defendant no proper opportunity to decide whether to plead guilty or not guilty[42]. This may be so where the conduct of the prosecutor can be fairly categorised as being analogous to fraud even where there is no actual fraud or dishonesty[43].

---

1. *Palmer v Thatcher* (1878) 3 QBD 346.
2. See Magistrates' Courts Act 1980, ss 14 and 142, respectively, post and *R v Brighton Justices, ex p Robinson* [1973] 1 WLR 69 and *R v Wells Street Justices, ex p Collett* [1981] RTR 272.
3. *R v Rochford Justices, ex p Buck* (1978) 68 Cr App R 114, [1978] Crim LR 492.
4. *R (Hoar-Stevens) v Richmond Magistrates' Court* [2003] EWHC 2660 (Admin), [2004] Crim LR 474.
5. *R v Battle Magistrates' Court, ex p Shepherd* (1983) 147 JP 372, 5 Cr App Rep (S) 124; *R v Ealing Justices, ex p Scrafield* [1994] RTR 195.
6. *Ex p Blyth* [1944] KB 532, [1944] 1 All ER 587, and see *Practice Note* [1946] WN 103.
7. See Criminal Justice Act 1948, s 37, and Rules of the Supreme Court 1965, Ord 79, r 9, this PART: STATUTORY INSTRUMENTS ON PROCEDURE, post.
8. *R v Weston-super-Mare Justices, ex p Barkers (Contractors) Ltd* [1944] 1 All ER 747, 108 JP 186.
9. *R v Stafford Justices, ex p Stafford Corpn* [1940] 2 KB 33, 104 JP 266; *R v Campbell, ex p Nomikos* [1956] 2 All ER 280, 120 JP 320.
10. *R v Mahoney* [1910] 2 IR 695; *R v Markham, ex p Marsh* (1923) 67 Sol Jo 518.
11. *R v Simpson* [1914] 1 KB 66.
12. *R v Lincolnshire Justices, ex p Brett* [1926] 2 KB 192, 90 JP 149.
13. *Davies v Price* [1958] 1 All ER 671, [1958] 1 WLR 434.
14. *R v Arundel Justices, ex p Jackson* [1959] 2 QB 89, [1959] 2 All ER 407, 123 JP 346.
15. *R v Farmer* [1892] 1 QB 637, 56 JP 341.
16. *R v Bolton* (1841) 1 QB 66.
17. *R v Highgate Justices, ex p Petrou* [1954] 1 All ER 406, [1954] 1 WLR 485, 118 JP 151; *R v Arundel Justices, ex p Jackson* [1959] 2 QB 89, [1959] 2 All ER 407; *R v Willesden Justices, ex p Utley* [1948] 1 KB 397, [1947] 2 All ER 838; *R v East Grinstead Justices, ex p Doeve* [1969] 1 QB 136, [1968] 3 All ER 666; *R v Birmingham Justices, ex p Wyatt* [1975] 3 All ER 897, [1976] 1 WLR 260. Note Supreme Court Act 1981, s 43 (power to substitute sentence).
18. *R v Crown Court at St Albans, ex p Cinnamond* [1981] QB 480, [1981] 1 All ER 802, 145 JP 277; *R v DPP, ex p McGeary* [1999] Crim LR 430. For the undesirability of challenging a sentencing decision by way of judicial review, see *Allen v West Yorkshire Probation Service* [2001] EWHC Admin 2, 165 JP 313, DC and para **1–825**, ante.
19. *R v Crown Court at Acton, ex p Bewley* (1988) 152 JP 327, 10 Cr App Rep (S) 105.
20. *R v Northampton Magistrates' Court, ex p Customs and Excise Comrs* (1994) 158 JP 1083, [1994] Crim LR 598.
21. *R v North Hampshire Youth Court, ex p DPP* (2000) 164 JP 377, DC.
22. *R v Hove Justices, ex p Donne* [1967] 2 All ER 1253n, 131 JP 460; *R v Cheltenham Justices, ex p Secretary of State for Trade* [1977] 1 All ER 460, [1977] 1 WLR 95.
23. *R v Lymm Justices, ex p Browne* [1973] 1 All ER 716, [1973] 1 WLR 1039, 137 JP 269; *R v Rugby Justices, ex p Prince* [1974] 2 All ER 116, 59 Cr App Rep 31.
24. *Re Harrington* [1984] AC 473, [1984] 2 All ER 474, 149 JP 211.
25. *Williams v Bedwellty Justices* [1996] 3 All ER 737, [1996] 3 WLR 361, 160 JP 549.
26. *R v Oxford City Justices, ex p Berry* [1987] 1 All ER 1244, 151 JP 505.
27. *R v Horseferry Road Stipendiary Magistrate, ex p Adams* [1978] 1 All ER 373, [1977] 1 WLR 1197; see also *R v Ipswich Justices, ex p Edwards* (1979) 143 JP 699.
28. Supreme Court Act 1981, s 43ZA, this PART, post.
29. *R v Altrincham Justices, ex p Pennington* [1975] QB 549, [1975] 2 All ER 78.
30. *R v Thames Magistrates' Court, ex p Polemis* [1974] 2 All ER 1219, [1974] 1 WLR 1371.
31. *R v Parker and Barnet Magistrates' Court, ex p DPP* (1994) 158 JP 1060.
32. *R v Neath and Port Talbot Magistrates' Court, ex p DPP* [2000] 1 WLR 1376, 164 JP 323, [2000] Crim LR 674, DC.
33. *R v Leyland Magistrates, ex p Hawthorn* [1979] QB 283, [1979] 1 All ER 209, 143 JP 181.
34. *R v Halton Justices, ex p Hughes* (1991) 155 JP 837, DC.
35. *R v Bodmin Justices, ex p McEwen* [1947] KB 321, [1947] 1 All ER 109, 111 JP 47; *R v Aberdare Justices, ex p Hones* [1973] Crim LR 45 and see also ante para **1–25** as to the way in which the Justices Clerk should conduct himself.
36. *R v Crown Court at Knightsbridge, ex p Goonatilleke* [1986] QB 1, [1985] 2 All ER 498.
37. *R v Crown Court at Liverpool, ex p Roberts* [1986] Crim LR 622.
38. *Weight v MacKay* [1984] 2 All ER 673, [1984] 1 WLR 980, 148 JP 673, HL.
39. *R v Leicester Recorder, ex p Wood* [1947] KB 726, [1947] 1 All ER 928, 111 JP 355.
40. *R v Ashford (Kent) Justices, ex p Richley* [1956] 1 QB 167, [1955] 3 All ER 604.
41. *R v Crown Court at Wolverhampton, ex p Crofts* [1983] 3 All ER 702, [1983] 1 WLR 204, 76 Cr App Rep 8.
42. *R v Bolton Justices, ex p Scally* [1991] 1 QB 537, [1991] 2 All ER 619, 155 JP 501.
43. *R v Burton upon Trent Justices, ex p Woolley* [1995] RTR 139, [1994] 159 JP 165; followed in *R v Dolgellau Justices, ex p Cartledge* [1996] RTR 207, [1996] Crim LR 337.

1–836 Mandatory order. A mandatory order should not be sought for where some form of appeal would do as well[1], nor when there has been an appeal to the Crown Court[2] as opposed to the mere giving of notice of appeal[3]. Like a quashing order, it is not used to correct justices who have acted within their jurisdiction, albeit wrongly; for example refusal to receive admissible evidence[4]; refusal to issue a summons considered vexatious[5]; refusal to continue proceedings considered futile[6]; exercise of discretion in interpreting statutes[7]; refusal to allow a line of cross-examination[8].

A mandatory order commands the justices to carry out their duties where other remedies are non-existent or not as effective; for example where an information was dismissed on the irrelevant ground that other persons had not been joined as co-defendants[9]; where justices refused to issue a distress warrant for rates because they considered the amount excessive[10]; a refusal of justices to hear a not guilty plea on a remittal from a higher court[11]; a refusal to enforce an affiliation order because the defendant alleged there was no jurisdiction to make the original order[12]; a refusal to grant legal aid for extraneous reasons ("unnecessary" cross-examination)[13]; refusal to withdraw a warrant where there was clearly no offence[14]; a failure to dispose of a case finally by sentence[15]; a refusal to consider each case on its merits[16] a dismissal of informations without jurisdiction amounting to a nullity[17].

---

1. *R v Thomas* [1892] 1 QB 426, 56 JP 151 (Licensing appeal); *R v Lewisham Corpn, ex p Jackson* (1929) 93 JP 171 (appeal to Justices); *R v Slough Justices, ex p B* [1985] FLR 384, [1985] Fam Law 189 (appeal under s 12C of the Child Care Act 1980 to the High Court).
2. *R v Bristol Licensing Justices, R v Gloucestershire Justices* (1893) 57 JP 486.
3. *R v Howard etc Farnham Licensing Justices* [1902] 2 KB 363, 66 JP 57.
4. *R v Yorkshire Justices, ex p Gill* (1885) 49 JP 729.
5. *R v Bros* (1901) 66 JP 54; *R v Kennedy* (1902) 86 LT 753.
6. *R v Rose, ex p Amalgamated Engineering Union* (1943) 107 JP Jo 88.
7. *R v London Justices* [1895] QB 214.
8. *R v Wells Street Stipendiary Magistrate, ex p Seillon* [1978] 3 All ER 257, [1978] 1 WLR 1002.
9. *R v Brown* (1857) 7 E & B 757, 22 JP 54.
10. *R v Essex Justices* (1877) 41 JP 676.
11. *R v Tottenham Justices, ex p Rubens* [1970] 1 All ER 879, [1970] 1 WLR 800.
12. *R v Lancashire Justices, ex p Tyrer* [1925] 1 KB 200.
13. *R v Derby Justices, ex p Kooner* [1971] 1 QB 147, [1970] 3 All ER 399.
14. *R v Crossman, ex p Chetwynd* (1908) 98 LT 760, 72 JP 250.
15. *R v Norfolk Justices, ex p DPP* [1950] 2 KB 558, [1950] 2 All ER 42, 114 JP 312.
16. *R v Oldham Justices, ex p Mellor* (1909) 73 JP 390, 101 LT 430 (certain applications at General Annual Licensing Meeting only).
17. *Re Harrington* [1984] AC 473, [1984] 2 All ER 474, 149 JP 211.

1–837 Prohibiting order. A prohibiting order is appropriate only where the proceedings to be reviewed are incomplete and there is a possibility of correcting the alleged fault[1]. It will not lie when no remedy of a preventive, as distinct from a corrective, nature can result[2]. It may issue where there has been delay and the magistrates have not adequately considered whether it was attributable to prosecution inefficiency and whether the defendant has been prejudiced by it[3]. Accordingly, it has been used where there had been a $3^1/_2$ year delay in bringing a case to court, attributable to the fault of both prosecution and defence and from which prejudice to the defendant could be inferred[3].

---

1. *R v Kent Justices* (1889) 24 QBD 181, 54 JP 453; *R v Farrant* (1887) 20 QBD 58, 52 JP 116, 130.
2. *R v Norfolk Justices, ex p Davidson* (1925) 69 Sol Jo 558.
3. *R v West London Stipendiary Magistrate, ex p Anderson* (1984) 148 JP 683.

1–838 Procedure. Rules about judicial review are contained in Part 54 of the Civil Procedure Rules 1998[1]. A claim for judicial review means a claim to review the lawfulness of an enactment or a decision, action or failure to act in relation to the exercise of a public function[2]. Where a claimant is seeking a mandatory order; a prohibiting order; a quashing order or an injunction under section 30 of the Senior Court Act 1981; or a declaration or injunction in addition to one of these remedies, the claimant must use the judicial review procedure[3], that is, the general claim procedure in Part 8 of the Civil Procedure Rules 1998 as modified by Part 54[4]. A claim for judicial review may include a claim for damages but may not seek damages alone[5].

---

1. In this PART, post.
2. Civil Procedure Rules 1998, r 54.1, in this PART, post.
3. Civil Procedure Rules 1998, r 54.2, in this PART, post.
4. Civil Procedure Rules 1998, r 54.1, in this PART, post.
5. Civil Procedure Rules 1998, r 54.3, in this PART, post.

1–839 *Pre-action protocol and urgent applications.* All claims for judicial review lodged on or after 4 March 2002 must comply with the pre-action protocol[1] for judicial review and claims must indicate that this has been complied with or reasons for non-compliance given on the form 1.

The procedure for dealing with urgent applications has also been prescribed[2].

---

1. Available on the Court Service website.
2. *Practice Statement (Administrative Court – Procedure for urgent applications – Listing Policy)* [2002] 1 All ER 633, [2002] 1 WLR 810.

1–850 *Claim form.* The claimant must complete a claim form setting out the matters referred to in rule 8.2 but in addition the claim form must state the name and address of any person the claimant considers to be an interested party, that he is requesting permission to proceed with a claim for judicial review and any remedy (including any interim remedy) he is claiming[1]. Parties to an application for judicial review are described in the proceedings as being *"The Queen on the application of (name of applicant) - Claimant, versus, the public body against whom the proceedings are brought - Defendant."*[2] The claim form must be filed promptly and in any event not later than 3 months after the grounds to make the claim first arose unless any other enactment specifies a shorter time limit for making the claim for judicial review. This time limit may not be extended by agreement between the parties[3].

The claim form must be served on the defendant and, unless the High Court otherwise directs, any person the claimant considers to be an interested party within 7 days after the date of issue[4].

Any person served with a claim form who wishes to take part in the judicial review must file an acknowledgement of service in the relevant practice form not more than 2 days after service of the claim form on the claimant and subject to any direction of the High Court, on any other person named in the claim form as soon as practicable and, in any event, not later than 7 days after it is filed. These time limits may not be extended by agreement between the parties[5]. The acknowledgement of service form must, where the claim is contested, set out a summary of the grounds for doing so and state the name and address of any person the person filing it considers to be an interested party and may include an application for directions. Failure to acknowledge service precludes the person from taking part in a hearing to decide whether permission should be given to proceed with the claim for judicial review but where permission is granted the person may subsequently participate in the hearing of the judicial review provided he complies subsequently with the requirements for serving a response to the claim[6].

1. Civil Procedure Rules 1998, r 54.6, in this PART, post.
2. *Practice Note (Administrative Court: establishment)* [2000] 4 All ER 1071.
3. Civil Procedure Rules 1998, r 54.5, in this PART, post.
4. Civil Procedure Rules 1998, r 54.7, in this PART, post.
5. Civil Procedure Rules 1998, r 54.8, in this PART, post.
6. Civil Procedure Rules 1998, r 54.9, in this PART, post.

1–851　Permission.　The permission of the High Court is required to proceed with a claim for judicial review[1]. The purpose of requiring the claimant to set out his grounds in the claim form and providing the defendant with the opportunity to set out a summary of his grounds for contesting the claim in his acknowledgement of service is to enable the High Court to exercise greater scrutiny of claims before they are permitted to proceed to a full hearing. The High Court may consider the permission decision without a hearing and where permission is refused or granted subject to conditions or on certain grounds only, the claimant may request the decision to be reconsidered at a hearing. The defendant and any interested parties will be given at least 2 days notice of the hearing date[2]. Neither the defendant nor any other interested party may apply to set aside an order giving permission to proceed[3].

Hearing of judicial review Where permission to proceed is given, the defendant and any other person served with the claim form who wishes to contest the claim or support it on additional grounds must file and serve: detailed grounds for contesting the claim or supporting it on additional grounds and any written evidence within 35 days after service of the order giving permission[4]. The permission of the High Court is required if the claimant seeks to rely on grounds other than those for which he has been given permission to proceed[5]. No written evidence may be relied on unless it has been served in accordance with any rule under Part 54 or the direction of the court or the court gives permission[6]. Provided the application is made promptly, any person may apply for permission to file any evidence or make representations at the hearing for judicial review[7]. Where all parties agree, the court may decide the claim for judicial review without a hearing[8]. *Where the court makes a quashing order* The High Court may:

–　remit the matter to the decision-maker; and
–　direct it to reconsider the matter and reach a decision in accordance with the judgment of the court.

Where the High Court considers that there is no purpose to be served in remitting the matter to the decision-maker, it may, subject to any statutory provision, take the decision itself[9].

1. Civil Procedure Rules 1998, r 54.4, in this PART, post.
2. Civil Procedure Rules 1998, r 54.12, in this PART, post.
3. Civil Procedure Rules 1998, r 54.13, in this PART, post.
4. Civil Procedure Rules 1998, r 54.14, in this PART, post.
5. Civil Procedure Rules 1998, r 54.15, in this PART, post.
6. Civil Procedure Rules 1998, r 54.16, in this PART, post.
7. Civil Procedure Rules 1998, r 54.17, in this PART, post.
8. Civil Procedure Rules 1998, r 54.18, in this PART, post.
9. Civil Procedure Rules 1998, r 54.19, in this PART, post.

1–852　Transfer.　The High Court may order a claim to continue as if it had not been started under Part 54 (judicial review) and where it does so, give directions about the future management of the claim[1].

1. Civil Procedure Rules 1998, r 54.20, in this PART, post.

1–853　Appearance by justices.　The appearance by justices on an application for judicial review is inappropriate unless their character or *bona fides* is questioned, or other special circumstances are present, for example where the High Court wishes it[1]. The function of a court in judicial review proceedings is not, other than in an exceptional case, to contest the proceedings, but to place as much useful evidence as it can before the Administrative or Divisional Court in order to enable the High Court to perform its judicial function. It is desirable that the forms under the new procedures in Part 54 of the Civil Procedure Rules 1998 should be amended so that the lower courts should not be obliged to tick a box stating that they are contesting the claim, part of the claim or not contesting the proceedings. The court should not be obliged to take an adversarial role from the outset when an adversarial role is inappropriate. The court or justices' clerk should not enter into the arena of the judicial review proceedings unless there is an exceptional feature of the case[2]. They may however file a response in accordance with the Civil Procedure Rules 1998, r 54.14[3] or file an affidavit with the Administrative Court Office, Royal Courts of Justice, Strand, London (no fee is payable)[4].

The Secretary of Commissions has indicated (by a letter of 17 June 1981) that if the Administrative Court wishes the justices to be represented, the Master of the Crown Office will so inform the Clerk to the Justices. On receipt of a letter from the Master, or in the following circumstances, the Clerk should notify the HMCS Criminal Justice Delivery Unit (criminal business) or the HMCS Customer Service Unit (civil and family business):

—   where the magistrates' court thinks it may need legal representation at a hearing before the Administrative Court (eg where there is no interested party to respond);
—   where the Administrative Court invites representation by the magistrates' court;
—   where there is an additional claim for damages against the magistrates' court or Department;
—   where the magistrates' court is informed that there is an application for costs against the court, the justices' clerk or the Lord Chancellor under s 34 of the Courts Act 2003;
—   where the claim has wider importance or sensitivity either for magistrates' courts generally or for the Department (e.g. an important point of law or practice)[5].

If the Clerk to the Justices believes the Court might require the justices to be represented, he should contact the Administrative Court Office to ascertain whether this is so. If it is not, he should himself arrange to have an affidavit sworn and filed if this is considered necessary.

1.   *R v Camborne Justices, ex p Pearce* [1955] 1 QB 41, [1954] 2 All ER 850, 118 JP 488; *R v Marlow (Bucks) Justices, ex p Schiller* [1957] 2 QB 508, [1957] 2 All ER 783; *R v Llanidloes Licensing Justices, ex p Davies* [1957] 2 All ER 610n, 121 JP 454; *R v Newcastle-under-Lyme Justices, ex p Massey* [1995] 1 All ER 120, [1994] 1 WLR 1684, 158 JP 1037.
2.   See *R (on the application of Stokes) v Gwent Magistrates' Court* [2001] EWHC Admin 569, (2001) 165 JP 766 at paras [23] and [24] per Brook LJ.
3.   In this PART, post.
4.   See Review of Justices' Decisions Act 1872, in this PART, post and the Practice Direction to the Civil Procedure Rules 1998, Part 32 for the form and content of affidavits.
5.   HMCS Customer Services letter 11 March 2005.

1–854   ***Liability of justices and the Lord Chancellor for costs.***   A Court may not order any justice of the peace or justices' clerk to pay costs in any proceedings in respect of any act or omission of his in the execution or purported execution of his duty as such a justice or as such a clerk exercising, by virtue of any statutory provision, any of the functions of a single justice[1]. Such immunity does not apply in relation to any proceedings in which he is being tried for an offence or is appealing against conviction or any proceedings in which it is proved that he acted in bad faith[2]. Where a court is prevented by these provisions from ordering a justice or justices' clerk to pay costs of a person in the proceedings, the court may instead order the making by the Lord Chancellor of a payment in respect of the costs of a person in the proceedings[3].

The circumstances in which a court may not make an order for payment of costs by the Lord Chancellor and the amount of any such payment are prescribed by regulations[4].

Whilst we would suggest that justices now have general immunity from costs in judicial review proceedings where exceptionally, costs are awarded against them, the following principles which applied to the former jurisdiction to order costs against justices would still seem to have some relevance—

(i)   It is not in every case that a successful litigant can expect to recover his costs against anyone[5].
(ii)   If justices do not appear, an order for costs in relation to the merits of the application or appeal is only likely to be made against them in exceptional circumstances, but justices should first be invited by High Court to appear to explain their apparently unreasonable behaviour[6].
(iii)   No final costs order should be made by the High Court against justices without giving them the opportunity to be heard. The preferable route of challenge to such an order is an application to set aside under Part 39, rather than an appeal to the Court of Appeal under Part 52 of the Civil Procedure Rules 1998. The court may grant the application to set aside only if the applicant (*a*) acted promptly when he found out that the court had exercised its power to strike out or to enter judgment or make an order against him; (*b*) had a good reason for not attending the trial; and (*c*) has a reasonable prospect of success at the trial[7]. Where justices have refused to state a case for the opinion of the High Court on the ground that the application was frivolous and have been informed that a High Court Judge has subsequently granted leave to apply for judicial review, the justices must give proper weight to the decision. If they fail to do so and persist in the view that the application to state a case is frivolous, they may be ordered to pay costs of the substantive application for mandamus[8].

Similarly, justices who failed to make proper inquiry as to whether a show cause notice in respect of a postponed committal for non payment of community charge had been received, having been at fault in a similar respect in a previous case were ordered to pay the costs of the judicial review[9].

1.   Courts Act 2003, s 34(1), (2), this PART, post.
2.   Courts Act 2003, s 34(3), this PART, post.
3.   Courts Act 2003, s 34(4), this PART, post.
4.   Justices and Justices' Clerks (Costs) Regulations 2001, this PART, post.
5.   Per LORD BRIDGE OF HARWICH in *Holden & Co v Crown Prosecution Service (No 2)* [1994] AC 22, 39H, [1993] 2 All ER 769, HL.

6. *R v York City Justices, ex p Farmery* (1988) 153 JP 257.
7. Civil Procedure Rules 1998, SI 1998/3132, r 39(3)(5).
8. *R v Aldershot Justices, ex p Rushmoor Borough Council* (1995) 160 JP 388.
9. *R v Newcastle upon Tyne Justices, ex p Devine* (1998) 162 JP 602, DC.

THE HUMAN RIGHTS ACT 1998

1–855   Under the Human Rights Act 1998, it is unlawful for a public authority (which includes any court or tribunal) to act in any way which is incompatible with a right protected by the European Convention on Human Rights[1]. Any person who claims that a public authority has acted (or proposes to act) in a way which is incompatible with a Convention right may bring proceedings against the authority or rely on the Convention rights or rights concerned in any legal proceedings[2]. However, proceedings in respect of a judicial act may be brought only by exercising a right of appeal[3]. In proceedings under the Act in respect of a judicial act done in good faith, damages may not be awarded otherwise than to compensate a person to the extent required by Article 5(5) of the Convention[4].

1. Human Rights Act 1998, s 6(1), in PART VIII: title HUMAN RIGHTS, post.
2. Human Rights Act 1998, s 7(1), in PART VIII: title HUMAN RIGHTS, post.
3. Human Rights Act 1998, s 9(1), in PART VIII: title HUMAN RIGHTS, post.
4. Human Rights Act 1998, s 9(3), in PART VIII: title HUMAN RIGHTS, post.

1–856   The application of Article 6 in appeal proceedings.   The European Convention on Human Rights does not guarantee a right of appeal as such. This is provided for by Article 2 of Protocol 7 (which has not yet entered force). However, where a right of appeal is provided in domestic law, whether on grounds of fact or law, Article 6 (fair trial) applies. The manner of application will depend on the nature of the hearing and some Article 6 guarantees, such as the right to an oral hearing and the right to be present, are less strictly applied in appeal proceedings, particularly where the only issues raised are points of law[1]. In general, where an appeal involves an assessment of disputed questions of fact, the requirements of fairness are more akin to those of a criminal trial.

1. See *Monnell and Morris v United Kingdom* (1988) 10 EHRR 205, *Ekbatani v Sweden* (1988) 13 EHRR 504, *Andersson v Sweden* (1991) 15 EHRR 218 and *Helmers v Sweden* (1991) 15 EHRR 285.

Annex
Publicly funded legal services
LEGAL SERVICES FUNDED BY THE LEGAL SERVICES COMMISSION

1–870   The provision of publicly funded legal services is the responsibility of the Legal Services Commission ("the Commission") established under Part I of the Access to Justice Act 1999[1]. The Commission is required to establish the Community Legal Service for the provision of legal services in relation to civil matters and the Criminal Defence Service[2].
Foreign law The Commission may not fund as part of the Community Legal Service or Criminal Defence Service services relating to any law other than that of England and Wales, unless any such law is relevant for determining any issue relating to the law of England and Wales[3].
Service providers In order to deliver the Community Legal Service and the Criminal Defence Service, the Commission may enter into contracts with, make payments, grants or loans to persons or bodies, employ its own staff or do anything it considers appropriate to provide services, advice and assistance and representation[4].
The Commission may set and monitor standards in relation to the services it provides and may accredit or authorise others to accredit, persons or bodies providing services and to monitor the services provided by accredited persons and bodies and withdraw accreditation from any who provide services of unsatisfactory quality[5].
A service provider may not take any payment in respect of the services provided by him apart from payment made by way of that funding and any authorised by the Commission to be taken[6].
Legal status of a funded client The fact that services are provided for an individual by the Community Legal Service or the Criminal Defence Service does not affect the relationship between the client and the person providing the service or any privilege arising out of the relationship and any right of the client which he may have to be indemnified in respect of expenses incurred by him by any other person[7]. Nor does the fact that he is funded affect the rights or other liabilities of other parties to the proceedings or the principles on which the discretion of any court or tribunal is normally exercised[8].
Misrepresentation A person who intentionally fails to comply with a requirement to furnish information to the Commission or makes a statement or representation which he knows or believes to be false, commits an offence[9]. A supplier of services has a duty to report any abuse to the Commission immediately[10].
Disclosure of information Information furnished to the Commission or any court, tribunal or other person or body in connexion with the case of an individual seeking or receiving services funded by the Commission may not be disclosed except in prescribed circumstances such as to enable the Commission, the Lord Chancellor or a court to discharge its functions in relation to such services or

in relation to the investigation or prosecution of an offence or where the individual consents to disclosure[11]. Legal privilege is deemed not to apply[12].

1. In this PART, post.
2. Access to Justice Act 1999, ss 1(2), 4 and 12 in this PART, post.
3. Access to Justice Act 1999, s 19, in this PART, post.
4. Access to Justice Act 1999, ss 6(3), 13(2) and 14(2), in this PART, post.
5. Access to Justice Act 1999, ss 4(8) and 12(4), in this PART, post.
6. Access to Justice Act 1999, s 22(2), in this PART, post.
7. Access to Justice Act 1999, s 22 (1), in this PART, post.
8. Access to Justice Act 1999, s 22(4), in this PART, post.
9. Access to Justice Act 1999, s 21, in this PART, post.
10. Criminal Defence Service (General) (No 2) Regulations 2001, reg 24, in this PART, post.
11. Access to Justice Act 1999, s 20, in this PART, post.
12. See the Legal Services Commission (Disclosure of Information) Regulations 2000, SI 2000/442.

COMMUNITY LEGAL SERVICE

1–871   The Commission must establish, maintain and develop the Community Legal Service for the purpose of promoting the availability of the following services to individuals which (within available resources and set priorities) effectively meet their needs[1].

Services which the Commission is required to fund as part of the Criminal Defence Service do not come within these services[2]. Every person who exercises any function relating to the Community Legal Service must have regard to the desirability of exercising it, so far as reasonably practicable, as to promote improvements in the range and quality of services and their accessibility to those who need them; secure that the services are appropriate having regard to the nature and importance of the matter concerned and achieve the swift and fair resolution of disputes without unnecessary or unduly protracted proceedings in court[3]. The Commission must inform itself about the need for, and provision of services by the Community Legal Service and the quality of services provided and plan for the meeting of those needs[4].

1. Access to Justice Act 1999, s 4(1), in this PART, post.
2. Access to Justice Act 1999, s 4(3), in this PART, post.
3. Access to Justice Act 1999, s 4(4), in this PART, post.
4. Access to Justice Act 1999, s 4(6), in this PART, post.

1–872   Funding of services.   The Commission must establish and maintain the Community Legal Service Fund paid to the Commission by the Lord Chancellor from which it funds services as part of the Community Legal Service and in funding these services the Commission must aim to obtain the best possible value for money[1]. The Commission must set priorities in its funding of services as part of the Community Legal Service in accordance with any directions given by the Lord Chancellor, after taking into account the need for services and what services are considered by the Commission to be appropriate[2].

1. Access to Justice Act 1999, s 5, in this PART, post.
2. Access to Justice Act 1999, s 6(1), (2), in this PART, post.

1–873   Community Legal Services: scope.   These include services consisting of the provision of

(a)   general information about the law and legal system and the availability of legal services,
(b)   help by the giving of advice as to how the law applies in particular circumstances,
(c)   help in preventing, or settling or otherwise resolving, disputes about legal rights and duties,
(d)   help in enforcing decisions by which such disputes are resolved,
(e)   help in relation to legal proceedings not relating to disputes[1] and advocacy in certain proceedings in the Higher Courts and specified tribunals and the following proceedings[2]:

Crown Court

(a)   variation or discharge of an order under section 5 of the Protection of Harassment Act 1997;
(b)   which relate to an order under section 10 of the Crime and Disorder Act 1998;
(c)   an application for a restraint order under Part 2 of the Proceeds of Crime Act 2002.

Magistrates' Court

(a)   under section 43 or 47 of the National Assistance Act 1948, section 22 of the Maintenance Orders Act 1950, section 4 of the Maintenance Orders Act 1958 or section 106 of the Social Security Administration Act 1992,
(b)   under Part I of the Maintenance Orders (Reciprocal Enforcement Act 1972 relating to a maintenance order made by a court of a country outside the United Kingdom.
(c)   in relation to an application for leave of the court to remove a child from a person's custody under section 27 or 28 of the Adoption Act 1976 or in which the making of an order under Part II or section 29 or 55 of that Act is apposed by any party to the proceedings,
(d)   for or in relation to an order under Part I of the Domestic Proceedings and Magistrates' Courts Act 1978,

    (i)   under the Children Act 1989,
    (ii) under section 30 of the Human Fertilisation and Embryology Act 1990,
    (iii) under section 20 or 27 of the Child Support Act 1991,
    (iv) under Part IV of the Family Law Act 1996,
    (v) for the variation or discharge of an order made under section 5 of the Protection from Harassment Act 1997,
    (vi) under section 1, 2, 8 or 11 of the Crime and Disorder Act 1998.

---

1. See the Access to Justice Act 1999, s 4(2), in this PART, post.
2. Access to Justice Act 1999, s 6(6) and Sch 2, in this PART, post.

1-874   Community Legal Service: financial eligibility. The Commission may only fund services for an individual as part of the Community Legal Service if his means are such that under the regulations he may be funded[1]. In circumstances prescribed by regulations services may be provided without reference to the person's means[2].

Criteria for the decision whether to fund or continue to fund services for an individual as part of the Community Legal Service are set out in a Code prepared by the Commission[3].

An individual for whom services are funded as part of the Community Legal Service may be required to make payment in respect of the service in accordance with regulations[4]. Payment may include a fee, a fixed or assessed contribution to the cost of the services or a payment as part of a settlement[5]. Payment may be by periodical payments or capital sums or both and interest may be payable, and there is provision for a statutory charge on any property recovered or preserved by the funded individual[6].

Application for funding is generally made to the 'supplier' ie the solicitor, mediator or agency being requested to provide funded services to the client[7].

Services available without reference to the client's financial resources include:

Legal Representation in proceedings under the Children Act 1989 applied for by or on behalf of:

    (a) a child in respect of whom an application is made for an order under:

        (i)   section 31 (care or supervision order);
        (ii) section 43 (child assessment order);
        (iii) section 44 (emergency protection order); or
        (iv) section 45 (extension or discharge of emergency protection order);

    (b) a parent of such a child, or a person with parental responsibility for such a child within the meaning of the Children Act 1989; or
    (c) a child who is brought before a court under section 25 (use of accommodation for restricting liberty) who is not, but wishes to be, legally represented before the court;

Legal Representation in proceedings related to the above proceedings which are being heard together with those proceedings or in which an order is being sought as an alternative to an order in those proceedings;

Legal Representation of a person who:

    (a) appeals to a magistrates' court against the registration of, or the refusal to register, a maintenance order made in a Hague Convention country under the Maintenance Orders (Reciprocal Enforcement) Act 1972; or
    (b) applies for the registration of a judgment under section 4 of the Civil Jurisdiction and Judgments Act 1982.

and who benefited from complete or partial assistance with, or exemption from, costs or expenses in the country in which the maintenance order was made or the judgment was given[8].

In other proceedings it is for the "assessing authority" to determine the client's financial eligibility based on information supplied by the client in accordance with regulations[9] and whether the client is required to pay a contribution from disposable income or capital or both and whether the client is liable to a statutory charge on any property or money recovered or preserved by a client, whether for himself or for any other person[10] subject to exemptions which include any periodical payment of maintenance[11].

---

1. Access to Justice Act 1999, s 7(1) and the Community Legal Service (Financial) Regulations 2000, in this PART, post.
2. Access to Justice Act 1999, s 7(2) and the Community Legal Service (Financial) Regulations 2000, reg 3, in this PART, post.
3. Access to Justice Act 1999, s 8(1) and the Community Legal Service (Financial) Regulations 2000, reg 3, in this PART, post.
4. Access to Justice Act 1999, s 10(1) and the Community Legal Service (Financial) Regulations 2000, and see the Community Legal Services (Costs) Regulations 2000 for payment to the Commission of costs recovered by the client in any proceedings in this PART, post.
5. Access to Justice Act 1999, s 10(2), in this PART, post.
6. Access to Justice Act 1999, s 10(7), in this PART, post.
7. Community Legal Service (Financial) Regulations 2000, regs 2, 4, 5(6), in this PART, post.
8. Community Legal Service (Financial) Regulations 2000, reg 3, in this PART, post.
9. See the Community Legal Service (Financial) Regulations 2000, in this PART, post.
10. Community Legal Service (Financial) Regulations 2000, Part III, in this PART, post.
11. Community Legal Service (Financial) Regulations 2000, reg 44(1)(a), in this PART, post.

1–875   Costs in funded cases.   Provision is made for costs ordered in proceedings involving an individual who is funded by the Commission as part of the Community Legal Service[1]. A court is not required to make a costs order where it would not otherwise have made a costs order nor are the powers of the court to make a wasted costs order against a legal representative affected[2].

---

  1. Access to Justice Act 1999, s 11, Community Legal Service (Costs) Regulations 2000,
  2. Community Legal Service (Cost Protection) Regulations 2000, in this PART, post.

1–876   *Costs ordered against funded individual and against the Commission.*   Costs ordered against a funded individual must not, except in prescribed circumstances, exceed the amount (if any) which is a reasonable one for him to pay having regard to all the circumstances including the financial resources of all the parties and their conduct in connexion with the dispute – a "section 11(1) costs order"[1].

    Cost Protection The limit on costs awarded against a client provided by a section 11(1) costs order – "Cost Protection" applies in circumstances prescribed by regulations ie generally where a client has Legal Representation or Approved Family Help and funding has not been withdrawn by the *revocation* of the client's certificate[2]. Where a funded party has cost protection and an order for costs is made against the client the court[3] may order the Commission to pay the whole or part of the costs of the non-funded party where the following conditions are satisfied:

    (*a*)   a costs order has been made against the client in a sum which is less than the amount of the full costs;

    (*b*)   (unless there is good reason for the delay) the non funded party makes a request within three months of the making of the costs order;

    (*c*)   the proceedings were instituted by the client, the non-funded party is an individual, and the court is satisfied that the non-funded party will suffer financial hardship unless the order is made; and

    (*d*)   in any case, the court is satisfied that it is just and equitable in the circumstances that provision for the costs should be made out of public funds[4].

---

  1. Access to Justice Act 1999, s 11(1), in this PART, post.
  2. Community Legal Service (Cost Protection) Regulations 2000, reg 2 and 3, in this PART, post.
  3. Or a single justice or the justices' clerk Community Legal Service (Cost Protection) Regulations 2000, reg 5(3A), in this PART, post.
  4. Community Legal Service (Cost Protection) Regulations 2000, reg 5, in this PART, post.

1–877   *Procedure for ordering costs against client and the Commission.*   The court must consider whether, but for cost protection, it would have made a costs order against the client and if so, whether it would have specified the amount to be paid under that order[1]. If it would not have specified the amount, the court must, when making a section 11(1) costs order, specify the amount (if any) that the client is to pay under that order but only if it has sufficient information to decide what is a reasonable amount for the client to pay and it is satisfied that if it were to determine the full costs at that time they would exceed the amount of the costs ordered to be paid by the client[2]. Where the court considers that it would have made a costs order against the client and would have specified the amount to be paid under it the court must specify the amount that the client is to pay under a section 11(1) costs order if it has sufficient information as to what is a reasonable amount for the client to pay or may order a sum of costs to be paid on account[3], otherwise it must not specify the amount that the client is to pay but any order must state the full costs[4]. Where the amount to be paid by the client is not specified in the order, the amount will be determined at a costs hearing[5]. The party in whose favour the order for costs was made may within 3 months after the making of the section 11(1) costs order request a hearing to determine the amount of costs payable to him[6]. Where the receiving party requests that the Commission pay the costs, notice must be served on the Regional Director who may appear at any hearing to determine costs or any appeal against the assessment[7].

---

  1. Community Legal Service (Costs) Regulations 2000, reg 9(1), in this PART, post.
  2. Community Legal Service (Costs) Regulations 2000, reg 9(2), in this PART, post.
  3. Community Legal Service (Costs) Regulations 2000, reg 10A, in this PART, post.
  4. Community Legal Service (Costs) Regulations 2000, reg 9(3), (4), in this PART, post.
  5. Community Legal Service (Costs) Regulations 2000, reg 9(5), (6), in this PART, post.
  6. Community Legal Service (Costs) Regulations 2000, reg 10, in this PART, post.
  7. Community Legal Service (Costs) Regulations 2000, reg 10(3), (4), in this PART, post.

1–878   *Costs order in favour of a funded client.*   Where a funded client obtains a costs order against another party the amount of costs to be paid are determined on the same basis as a person who is not receiving funding[1], and the costs recoverable by him are not limited by any rule of law which limits the costs recoverable by a party to proceedings to the amount he is liable to pay his legal representative where the supplier has been authorised by the commission to take payment for the relevant work other than that funded by the Commission[2]. Money recovered by a client is payable to the client's solicitor[3] (who will pay money recovered to the Commission[4]) or, where the client is no longer being represented by a solicitor to the Commission subject to exceptions which include any periodical payment of maintenance[5].

1. Community Legal Service (Costs) Regulations 2000, reg 15(1), in this PART, post.
2. Community Legal Service (Costs) Regulations 2000, reg 15(2), (3), in this PART, post.
3. Community Legal Service (Costs) Regulations 2000, reg 18(1), in this PART, post.
4. Community Legal Service (Costs) Regulations 2000, reg 17(2), in this PART, post.
5. Community Legal Service (Costs) Regulations 2000, reg 18(2), in this PART, post.

CRIMINAL DEFENCE SERVICE

1-879   The Legal Services Commission must establish, maintain and develop a service known as the Criminal Defence Service for the purpose of showing that individuals involved in criminal investigations or criminal proceedings have access to such advice, assistance and representation as the interests of justice require[1].

1. Access to Justice Act 1999, s 12(1), in this PART, post.

1-880   Criminal proceedings.   "Criminal proceedings" are defined as:

(a)   proceedings before any court for dealing with an individual accused of an offence[1],
(b)   proceedings before any court for dealing with an individual convicted of an offence[1] (including proceedings in respect of a sentence or order),
(c)   proceedings for dealing with an individual under the Extradition Act 2003,
(d)   proceedings for binding an individual over to keep the peace or to be of good behaviour under s 115 of the Magistrates' Courts Act 1980 and for dealing with an individual who fails to comply with an order under that section,
(e)   proceedings on an appeal brought by an individual under s 44A of the Criminal Appeal Act 1968,
(f)   proceedings for contempt committed, or alleged to have been committed, by an individual in the face of a court, and
(g)   such other proceedings concerning an individual, before any such court or other body, as may be prescribed[1].

1. Access to Justice Act 1999, s 12(2), in this PART, post.

1-881   *Additional prescribed "criminal proceedings".*   The following proceedings have been prescribed for these purposes:

(a)   civil proceedings in a magistrates' court arising from failure to pay a sum due or to obey an order of that court where such failure carries the risk of imprisonment;
(b)   proceedings under sections 1, 1D and 4 of the Crime and Disorder Act 1998;
(ba)   proceedings under sections 1G and 1H of the 1998 Act relating to intervention orders, in which an application for an anti-social behaviour order has been made;
(c)   proceedings under section 8(1)(b) of the 1998 Act relating to parenting orders made where an anti-social behaviour order or a sex offender order is made in respect of a child;
(d)   proceedings under section 8(1)(c) of the 1998 Act relating to parenting orders made on the conviction of a child;
(e)   proceedings under section 9(5) of the 1998 act to discharge or vary a parenting order made as mentioned in paras (c) or (d);
(f)   proceedings under section 10 of the 1998 Act to appeal against a parenting order made as mentioned in paras (c) or (d);
(g)   proceedings under sections 14B, 14D, 14G, 14H, 21B and 21D of the Football Spectators Act 1989 (banning orders and references to a court);
(h)   proceedings under section 137 of the Financial Services and Markets Act 2000 to appeal against a decision of the Financial Services and Markets Tribunal;
(i)   proceedings under sections 2, 5 and 6 of the Anti-social Behaviour Act 2003 relating to closure orders[1];
(j)   proceedings under sections 20, 22, 26 and 28 of the Anti-Social Behaviour Act 2003 relating to parenting orders in cases of exclusion from school and parenting orders in respect of criminal conduct and anti-social behaviour;
(k)   proceedings under sections 97, 100 and 101 of the Sexual Offences Act 2003 relating to notification orders and interim notification orders;
(l)   proceedings under sections 104, 108, 109 and 110 of the Sexual Offences Act 2003 relating to sexual offences prevention orders and interim sexual offences prevention orders;
(m)   proceedings under sections 114, 118 and 119 of the Sexual Offences Act 2003 relating to foreign travel orders;
(n)   proceedings under sections 123, 125, 126 and 127 of the Sexual Offences Act 2003 relating to risk of sexual harm orders and interim risk of sexual harm orders;
(o)   proceedings under Part 1A of Schedule 1 to the Powers of Criminal Courts (Sentencing) Act 2000 relating to parenting orders for failure to comply with orders under section 20 of that Act; and
(p)   proceedings under section 5A of the Protection from Harassment Act 1997 relating to restraining orders on acquittal.

Proceedings in the Crown court, following committal for sentence by a magistrates' court (but not applications for judicial review or habeas corpus relating to any criminal investigations or proceedings) are to be regarded as incidental to criminal proceedings from which they arise[2].

1. Criminal Defence Service (General) (No 2) Regulations 2001, reg 3(2), in this PART, post.
2. Criminal Defence Service (General) (No 2) Regulations 2001, reg 3(3), in this PART, post.

1–882   Advice and assistance.   The Commission must fund such advice and assistance as it considers appropriate circumstances

(a) for individuals who are arrested and held in custody at a police station or other premises; and
(b) for individuals involved in "criminal investigations" (ie investigations relating to offences or to individuals convicted of an offence) in such other as may be prescribed[1].

For this purpose the Commission has established as part of the Criminal Defence Service the Police Station Duty Solicitor Scheme and the Magistrates' Court Duty Solicitor Scheme to ensure individuals requiring Advice and Assistance at a Police Station or who do not have help from their own solicitor have access to a duty solicitor accredited by the Commission[2].

Such advice and assistance is generally granted for matters connected with criminal proceedings in a police station or before a magistrates' or Crown Court without reference to the financial resources of the individual[3].

1. Access to Justice Act 1999, s 13, for the full range of circumstances in which assistance, including advocacy assistance, may be provided, see the Criminal Defence Service (General) (No 2) Regulations 2001, reg 4, in this PART, post. See also the *Criminal Defence Service Duty Solicitor Arrangement 2001*.
2. See para **1–880**, ante.
3. Criminal Defence Service (General) (No 2) Regulations 2001, reg 5, in this PART, post.

1–883   Representation.   The Commission must fund representation to an individual who has been granted a right of representation[1]. A right of representation may be granted in respect of "criminal proceedings"[2] and also to enable an individual to resist an appeal to the Crown Court otherwise than in an official capacity[3]. The grant of representation includes the right to representation for the purposes of any related bail proceedings and any preliminary or incidental proceedings[4]. A "representation order" means a document granting a right to representation under s 14 of the Access to Justice Act 1999[5]. The date of any representation order is the date on which the application for the grant of such an order is received in accordance with the regulations[6].

A representation order granted to an individual extends to the Crown Court, if the proceedings continue there and any proceedings incidental to the proceedings but does not extend to an appeal[7].

1. Access to Justice Act 1999, s 14 and Sch 3, in this PART: STATUTES ON PROCEDURE, post.
2. Access to Justice Act 1999, Sch 3 para 1(1), and see s 12(2), in this PART: STATUTES ON PROCEDURE, post.
3. Access to Justice Act 1999, Sch 3 para 1(2), in this PART: STATUTES ON PROCEDURE, post.
4. Access to Justice Act 1999, Sch 3 para 2(2), in this PART: STATUTES ON PROCEDURE, post.
5. Criminal Defence Service (Representation Orders and Consequential Amendments) Regulations 2006, regs 2 and 3, in this PART: STATUTES ON PROCEDURE, post.
6. Criminal Defence Service (General) (No 2) Regulations 2001, reg 6(1), in this PART: STATUTORY INSTRUMENTS AND PRACTICE DIRECTIONS ON PROCEDURE, post.
7. Criminal Defence Service (Representation Orders and Consequential Amendments) Regulations 2006, reg 4, in this PART: STATUTORY INSTRUMENTS AND PRACTICE DIRECTIONS ON PROCEDURE, post.

1--883A   *Financial eligibility.*   The power to grant a right to representation may only be exercised in relation to an individual whose financial resources appear to the relevant authority to be such that, under regulations, he is eligible to be granted such a right[1]. Also, such right to representation will be withdrawn if it appears that his financial resources are not such that he is eligible to be granted such a right or that he has failed, in relation to the right, to comply with regulations about the furnishing of information[2].

Detailed provision for the furnishing of evidence and assessment of the applicant's means is prescribed by regulations[3]. The applicant must notify any change in financial circumstances[4]. Provision is made for re-calculation of income where there has been an error or renewal of application where there has been a change of circumstances[5]. There may be an application for review where there has been a miscalculation of income or an administrative error and in particular an application for a review may be made on grounds of hardship[6].

1. Access to Justice Act 1999, Sch 3 para 3B(1), in this PART: STATUTES ON PROCEDURE, post.
2. Access to Justice Act 1999, Sch 3 para 3B(2), in this PART: STATUTES ON PROCEDURE, post and Criminal Defence Service (Financial Eligibility) Regulations 2006, in this PART: STATUTORY INSTRUMENTS AND PRACTICE DIRECTIONS ON PROCEDURE, post.
3. Criminal Defence Service (Financial Eligibility) Regulations 2006, in this PART: STATUTORY INSTRUMENTS AND PRACTICE DIRECTIONS ON PROCEDURE, post.
4. Criminal Defence Service (Financial Eligibility) Regulations 2006, reg 11, in this PART: STATUTORY INSTRUMENTS AND PRACTICE DIRECTIONS ON PROCEDURE, post.
5. Criminal Defence Service (Financial Eligibility) Regulations 2006, regs 12 and 13, in this PART: STATUTORY INSTRUMENTS AND PRACTICE DIRECTIONS ON PROCEDURE, post.
6. Criminal Defence Service (Financial Eligibility) Regulations 2006, reg 14, in this PART: STATUTORY INSTRUMENTS AND PRACTICE DIRECTIONS ON PROCEDURE, post.

1–884 *Criteria for grant of a right to representation.* Any question as to whether a right of representation should be granted must, in addition, be determined according to the interests of justice and in deciding this the following factors must be taken into account[1]:

(a)   whether the individual would, if any matter arising in the proceedings is decided against him, be likely to lose his liberty or livelihood or suffer serious damage to his reputation;

(b)   whether the determination of any matter arising in the proceedings may involve consideration of a substantial question of law;

(c)   whether the individual may be unable to understand the proceedings or to state his own case[2];

(d)   whether the proceedings may involve the tracing, interviewing or expert cross-examination of witnesses on behalf of an individual; and

Whether it is in the interests of another person that the individual be represented.

A right to representation must always be granted in such circumstances as a prescribed by regulations[3].

Loss of liberty, livelihood, damage to reputation A community punishment order is not properly to be regarded as depriving the accused of his liberty[4]. However, the list of factors in what is now Sch 3 para 5 of the 1999 Act and was formerly contained in s 22 of the Legal Aid Act 1988 is not exhaustive and the possibility of a community punishment order may be a factor to be considered when considering whether or not to grant a right of representation[5]. Legal aid should be granted to a serving officer charged with indecent exposure when there is an issue as to identity[6].

Regard must be had to the serious damage to an accused's reputation which would result from a conviction for an offence contrary to s 5 of the Public Order Act 1986[7].

Tracing witness etc "Expert" qualifies the nature of the cross-examination not the witness[8]. Refusal to grant legal aid to a defendant aged 16 who wishes to challenge whether a police constable has acted in the execution of his duty is irrational as the expertise required to cross examine police witnesses and find, select and proof defence witnesses is beyond that of a defendant aged 16[9]. Legal aid should be granted to a defendant who is seeking to establish special reasons on the basis that her drink had been spiked because a scientific expert would be required to give evidence and the assistance of a solicitor would be required to find witnesses of the facts[10].

---

1. Access to Justice Act 1999, Sch 3 para 5, in this PART, post.
2. For an example of a case where this criterion was applicable see *R (on the application of Matara) v Brent Magistrates' Court* [2005] EWHC Admin 1829, (2005) 169 JP 576.
3. Access to Justice Act 1999, Sch 3 para 5(4), in this PART, post.
4. *R v Liverpool City Magistrates' Court, ex p McGhee* (1993) 158 JP 275, [1993] Crim LR 609.
5. *R v Liverpool City Magistrates' Court, ex p McGhee,* supra.
6. *R v Brigg Justices, ex p Lynch* (1984) 148 JP 214.
7. *R v Chester Magistrates' Court, ex p Ball* (1999) 163 JP 757.
8. *R v Liverpool City Magistrates' Court, ex p McGhee,* supra.
9. *R v Scunthorpe Justices, ex p S* (1998) Times, 5 March DC.
10. *R v Gravesend Magistrates' Court, ex p Baker* (1997) 161 JP 765, [1998] RTR 45.

1–885 *Application for grant of right of representation: magistrates' court.* There is no prescribed form of application[1]. Applications in respect of 'relevant proceedings' i.e. those proceedings listed in 1–880 (and para (h) of 1–881)[2] are made in accordance with the Criminal Defence Service (Representation Orders and Consequential Amendments) Regulations 2006[3], and the functions of the Commission have been delegated to the court staff of Her Majesty's Court Service[4]. A representation order may be granted to an individual at any stage of the proceedings[5]. In respect of those proceedings listed in 1–881 *(except proceedings referred to in para (h))* application is to the Commission[6] and may be granted only by the Commission or a person acting on behalf of the Commission where such function has been delegated[7].

The date of any representation order is the date on which the application for the grant of such an order is received in accordance with the regulations[8].

Where the person who requires representation is aged less than 18, the application may be made by his parent or guardian on his behalf[9]. The appropriate officer is required to keep a record of every application to that court for a representation order, and of its outcome and provide returns of information to the Lord Chancellor on request[10].

Where an application is refused, we suggest that in all cases the applicant should be supplied with written reasons for refusal; and details of the appeals process[11].

---

1. The former requirement in the Criminal Defence Service (General) (No 2) Regulations 2001, reg 6(1) that the application be made in a prescribed form, was revoked by the Criminal Defence Service (General) (No 2) (Amendment) Regulations 2006, SI 2006/2490.
2. Criminal Defence Service (Representation Orders and Consequential Amendments) Regulations 2006, reg 2, in this PART: STATUTORY INSTRUMENTS AND PRACTICE DIRECTIONS ON PROCEDURE, post.
3. In this PART: STATUTORY INSTRUMENTS AND PRACTICE DIRECTIONS ON PROCEDURE, post.
4. Access to Justice Act 1999, Sch 3, paras 2A, in this PART: STATUTES ON PROCEDURE, post.
5. Criminal Defence Service (Representation Orders and Consequential Amendments) Regulations 2006, reg 3, in this PART: STATUTORY INSTRUMENTS AND PRACTICE DIRECTIONS ON PROCEDURE, post.
6. Criminal Defence Service (General) (No 2) Regulations 2001, reg 6(3), in this PART: STATUTORY INSTRUMENTS AND PRACTICE DIRECTIONS ON PROCEDURE, post.
7. Access to Justice Access 1999, s 3(4) and Sch 3 para 3, in this PART: STATUTES ON PROCEDURE, post.
8. Criminal Defence Service (General) (No 2) Regulations 2001, reg 6(1), in this PART: STATUTORY INSTRUMENTS AND PRACTICE DIRECTIONS ON PROCEDURE, post.

9. Criminal Defence Service (General) (No 2) Regulations 2001, reg 6(5), in this PART: STATUTORY INSTRUMENTS AND PRACTICE DIRECTIONS ON PROCEDURE, post.
10. Criminal Defence Service (General) (No 2) Regulations 2001, reg 6(6), (7), in this PART: STATUTORY INSTRUMENTS AND PRACTICE DIRECTIONS ON PROCEDURE, post.
11. Criminal Defence Service (General) (No 2) Regulations 2001, reg 6(4), in this Part, post. (Although this provision only applies to proceedings listed in **1–881** as a result of the revocation of reg 8(3) without equivalent provision in the Criminal Defence Service (Representation Orders and Consequential Amendments) Regulations 2006, in this PART: STATUTORY INSTRUMENTS AND PRACTICE DIRECTIONS ON PROCEDURE, post).

1–886   *Proceedings before the Crown Court.*   Where criminal proceedings are committed, sent or transferred for trial, or committed for sentence such proceedings will be included in any representation order granted to an individual for proceedings in the magistrates' court[1]. Where an application for such an order in respect of the proceedings in a magistrates' court has not been made or has been refused, an application for a representation order in respect of the proceedings may be made orally or in writing to the Crown Court; or in writing to the magistrates' court at the conclusion of the proceedings there or in any committal or sending for trial proceedings or any transfers for trial. In the case of an appeal to the Crown Court from a magistrates' court, application may be made to the appropriate officer of the magistrates' court[2].

1. Criminal Defence Service (Representation Orders and Consequential Amendments) Regulations 2006, reg 4, in this PART: STATUTORY INSTRUMENTS AND PRACTICE DIRECTIONS ON PROCEDURE, post.
2. Criminal Defence Service (General) (No 2) Regulations 2001, reg 9(1), in this PART: STATUTORY INSTRUMENTS AND PRACTICE DIRECTIONS ON PROCEDURE, post.

1–887   *Representation in magistrates' court.*   An individual who has been granted a right to representation may select any representative willing to act for him[1] except as follows:

Where advice and assistance has been given Where advice and assistance funded by the Commission has already been given by a person he chose to provide it for him, an individual is taken to have selected that person as his representative[2].

Restriction on representatives Except in proceedings for contempt in the face of the court[3] representatives must be employed by the Commission to provide such representation or authorised to do so under a crime franchise contract which commenced on or after 2 April 2001 and specifies the rate of remuneration for such representation[4]. A representation order for the purpose of proceedings in the magistrates' court may only include representation by an 'advocate' i.e. a barrister or a solicitor who has obtained a higher courts advocacy qualification in accordance with regulations and rules of conduct of the Law Society in the case of:

(a) any indictable offence, including an offence which is triable either way; or
(b) proceedings under section 9 of, or paragraph 6 of Schedule 1 to, the Extradition Act 1989

where the court is of the opinion that, because of circumstances which make the proceedings unusually grave or difficult, representation by both a solicitor and an advocate would be desirable[5].

Co-defendants Where an individual is one of two or more co-defendants whose cases are to be heard together, he must select the same representative as a co-defendant unless there is, or is likely to be, a conflict of interest[6].

Change of representative Application may be made to the court to select a representative in place of the representative previously selected, stating the grounds on which it is made. The court may grant the application where:

(a) the representative considers himself to be professionally embarrassed and provides details of the duty to withdraw;
(b) there is a breakdown in the relationship with the assisted person so that effective representation can no longer be provided and the representative gives details of the breakdown;
(c) the representative is no longer able to represent the assisted person through circumstances beyond his control
(d) some other substantial or compelling reason exists; or the court may refuse the application[7].

Very high costs cases Where representation has been granted in a very high cost case ie where the trial is likely to last for 25 days or more or specified costs are likely to amount to £150,000 or more, the Commission may wish to enter into an individual contract for the provision of funded services in relation to that case where the Commission or the current representatives do not wish to contract with each other, provision is made for the selection of new representatives[8].

1. Access to Justice Act 1999, s 15(1), in this PART, post.
2. Access to Justice Act 1999, s 15(2)(b), in this PART, post.
3. Criminal Defence Service (General) (No 2) Regulations 2001, reg 11(3), in this PART, post.
4. Criminal Defence Service (General) (No 2) Regulations 2001, reg 11(1), in this PART, post.
5. Criminal Defence Service (General) (No 2) Regulations 2001, reg 12, in this PART, post.
6. Criminal Defence Service (General) (No 2) Regulations 2001, reg 16A, in this PART, post.
7. Criminal Defence Service (General) (No 2) Regulations 2001, reg 16, in this PART, post.
8. See the Criminal Defence Service (Choice in Very High Cost Cases) Regulations 2001, in this PART, post.

1–888   Withdrawal of representationWhere any charge or proceedings against an individual are varied, the court or representation authority must:

(a)   consider whether the interests of justice require that he be represented in respect of the varied charge or proceedings; and

(b)   withdraw the representation order if the interests of justice do not so require.

The court or representation authority must consider whether to withdraw the representation order in any of the following circumstances—

(a)   where the individual declines to accept the order in the terms on which it is granted;

(b)   otherwise at the request of the individual; or

(c)   where the representative named in the representation order declines to continue to represent the individual[1].

---

1. Access to Justice Act 1999, Sch 3, paras 2A(1) and 3, in this PART: STATUTES ON PROCEDURE, post and the Criminal Defence Service (Representation Orders and Consequential Amendments) Regulations 2006, reg 5, Criminal Defence Service (General) (No 2) Regulations 2001, reg 17, in this PART: STATUTORY INSTRUMENTS AND PRACTICE DIRECTIONS ON PROCEDURE, post.

1–889   ***Appeal against refusal to grant, or the withdrawal of, a representation order.***   Where an application for a grant of a representation order is refused on the ground that the interests of justice do not require such an order to be granted (but not a decision that the applicant is not financially eligible to be granted such an order[1]), appeal is to the court (which includes a single justice) [2]. An appeal is determined without a hearing unless otherwise directled[3]. Written reasons must be given for any decision on an appeal[3]. The date of any representation order granted on such an appeal is the date on which the original application was received[3].

Where the appeal is resolved in the applicant's favour, he must then apply to the representation authority and satisfy the test for financial eligibility before a representation order will be granted[2].

An individual whose representation order has been withdrawn may apply on one occasion to the person who, or body which, withdrew the order to set aside the withdrawal[4].

---

1. Criminal Defence Service (Representation Orders: Appeals etc) Regulations 2006, reg 5, in this PART: STATUTORY INSTRUMENTS AND PRACTICE DIRECTIONS ON PROCEDURE, post.

2. Access to Justice Act 1999, Sch 3, para 4, in this PART: STATUTES ON PROCEDURE, post and the Criminal Defence Service (Representation Orders: Appeals etc) Regulations 2006, reg 4, in this PART: STATUTORY INSTRUMENTS AND PRACTICE DIRECTIONS ON PROCEDURE, post.

3. Criminal Defence Service (Representation Orders: Appeals etc) Regulations 2006, reg 3, in this PART: STATUTORY INSTRUMENTS AND PRACTICE DIRECTIONS ON PROCEDURE, post.

4. Criminal Defence Service (Representation Orders: Appeals etc) Regulations 2006, reg 9, in this PART: STATUTORY INSTRUMENTS AND PRACTICE DIRECTIONS ON PROCEDURE, post.

Statutes on Procedure

Remission of Penalties Act 1859

(22 Vict c 32)

1–900   **1. Remission of penalties.**   It shall be lawful for Her Majesty to remit in whole or in part any sum of money which under any Act now in force or hereafter to be passed may be imposed as a penalty or forfeiture on a convicted offender, although such money may be in whole or in part payable to some party other than the Crown, and to extend the Royal Mercy to any person who may be imprisoned for non-payment of any sum of money so imposed, although the same may be in whole or in part payable to some party other than the Crown.

[Remission of Penalties Act 1859, s 1.]

Criminal[1] Procedure Act 1865

(28 & 29 Vict c 18)

1–903   **1. Section 2 to apply to all trials for felony or misdemeanour; ss 3 to 8 to all courts and persons authorised to hear evidence.**   The provisions of section two[2] of this Act shall apply to every trial; and the provisions of sections from three to eight, inclusive, of this Act shall apply to all courts of judicature, as well criminal[2] as all others, and to all persons having, by law or by consent of parties, authority to hear, receive, and examine evidence.

[Criminal Procedure Act 1865, s 1 as amended by the Statute Law Revision Act 1893, the Criminal Law Act 1967, s 10(2) and Sch 3.]

---

1. Despite its title, ss 3–8 of this Act apply equally to civil as well as criminal proceedings.

2. Section 2 makes provision for the examining of witnesses and summing-up by parties; it would appear to have been superseded in magistrates' courts by the Criminal Procedure Rules 2005, Part 37.

1–904   3. How far witness may be discredited by the party producing[1]. A party producing a witness shall not be allowed to impeach his credit by general evidence of bad character; but he may, in case the witness shall in the opinion of the judge prove adverse, contradict him by other evidence, or, by leave of the judge, prove that he has made at other times a statement inconsistent with his present testimony; but before such last-mentioned proof can be given the circumstances of the supposed statement, sufficient to designate the particular occasion, must be mentioned to the witness, and he must be asked whether or not he has made such statement.
[Criminal Procedure Act 1865, s 3.]

————————————

1. The application of this section is dealt with in para **1–661** *Hostile witness*, in this PART: MAGISTRATES' COURTS, PROCEDURE, ante.

1–905   4. As to proof of contradictory statements of adverse witness[1]. If a witness, upon cross-examination as to a former statement made by him relative to the subject matter of the indictment or proceeding, and inconsistent with his present testimony, does not distinctly admit that he has made such statement, proof may be given that he did in fact make it; but before such proof can be given the circumstances of the supposed statement, sufficient to designate the particular occasion, must be mentioned to the witness, and he must be asked whether or not he has made such statement.
[Criminal Procedure Act 1865, s 4.]

————————————

1. The application of this section is dealt with ante in para **1–661** *Hostile witness*, in this PART: MAGISTRATES' COURTS, PROCEDURE, ante.

1–906   5. Cross-examinations as to previous statements in writing[1]. A witness may be cross-examined as to previous statements[2] made by him in writing, or reduced into writing, relative to the subject matter of the indictment or proceeding, without such writing being shown to him[3]; but if it is intended to contradict such witness by the writing, his attention must, before such contradictory proof can be given, be called to those parts of the writing which are to be used for the purpose of so contradicting: Provided always, that it shall be competent for the judge, at any time during the trial, to require the production of the writing for his inspection, and he may thereupon make such use of it for the purposes of the trial as he may think fit[4].
[Criminal Procedure Act 1865, s 5.]

————————————

1. The application of this section is dealt with in para **1–661** *Hostile witness*, in this PART: MAGISTRATES' COURTS, PROCEDURE, ante.
2. A defendant who has put his good character in issue cannot be cross-examined about his legal aid application form, an entry in which is alleged to be false (*R v Stubbs* [1982] 1 All ER 424, [1982] 1 WLR 509, CA). The right is subject only to relevancy, but where the cross-examination is about an excluded statement, care should be taken not to allow the excluded statement thereby to become evidence supporting the prosecution case (*Lui Mei Lin v R* [1989] Crim LR 364).
3. The writing must be in court and capable of being produced: it is wrong to suggest it can be produced if it cannot (*R v Anderson* (1929) 142 LT 580).
4. It may be appropriate to allow only those parts of a statement upon which cross-examination on inconsistencies has been based to be placed before the jury; see *R v Beattie* (1989) 89 Cr App Rep 302, CA.

1–907   6. Proof of conviction[1] of witness for felony or misdemeanour may be given.   (1) If, upon a witness being lawfully questioned[2] as to whether he has been convicted of any felony or misdemeanour, he either denies or does not admit the fact, or refuses to answer, it shall be lawful for the cross examining party to prove such conviction[3]; and a certificate containing the substance and effect only (omitting the formal part) of the indictment and conviction for such offence, purporting to be signed by the proper officer of the court where the offender was convicted (for which certificate a fee of 25p and no more shall be demanded or taken,) shall, upon proof of the identity of the person, be sufficient evidence of the said conviction, without proof of the signature or official character of the person appearing to have signed the same.* **

(2) In subsection (1) "proper officer" means—

(*a*) in relation to a magistrates' court in England and Wales, the designated officer for the court; and

(*b*) in relation to any other court, the clerk of the court or other officer having the custody of the records of the court, or the deputy of such clerk or other officer.
[Criminal Procedure Act 1865, s 6, as amended by the Access to Justice Act 1999, Sch 13, the Criminal Justice Act 2003, Sch 36 and the Courts Act 2003, Sch 8.]

————————————

***Sub-section (1) reproduced as amended by the Criminal Justice Act 2003, Sch 36, not yet in force in Northern Ireland.**
****Repealed in relation to criminal proceedings by the Police and Criminal Evidence Act 1984, Sch 7, from a date to be appointed.**
1. Other methods of proof are provided for by the Evidence Act 1951, s 13, the Prevention of Crimes Act 1871, s 18, the Criminal Justice Act 1948, s 39 (fingerprints)and the Criminal Procedure Rules 2005, Part 6.
2. The Rehabilitation of Offenders Act 1974, s 4(1) makes evidence of spent convictions inadmissible, subject to exceptions stated in s 7(2); see Statutes on Sentencing in PART III: SENTENCING, post. As to the restrictions on the admission of evidence of bad character of defendants and non-defendants, see the Criminal Justice Act 2003, Part II, Chapter 1, ss 98–113, in PART II: EVIDENCE, post.
3. As to proof of conviction, see the Police and Criminal Evidence Act 1984, ss 73–75, post, the Criminal Justice Act 1948, s 39 (fingerprints), and the Criminal Procedure Rules 2005, Part 6.

1–908 7. Proof of instrument to validity of which whereof attestation is not necessary. It shall not be necessary to prove by the attesting witness any instrument to the validity of which attestation is not requisite, and such instrument may be proved as if there had been no attesting witness thereto.
[Criminal Procedure Act 1865, s 7.]

1–909 8. Comparison of disputed writing with writing proved to be genuine. Comparison of a disputed writing[1] with any writing proved to the satisfaction of the judge[2] to be genuine shall be permitted to be made by witnesses; and such writings, and the evidence of witnesses respecting the same, may be submitted to the court and jury as evidence of the genuineness or otherwise of the writing in dispute.
[Criminal Procedure Act 1865, s 8.]

---

1. An opinion based upon a facsimile reproduction of disputed writing, such as a photocopy of a lost cheque, could be admitted under this section (*Lockheed–Arabia v Owen* [1993] QB 806, [1993] 3 All ER 641).
2. It would appear that the civil standard of proof on the balance of probabilities applies when this section is used in civil cases, and the criminal standard of proof beyond reasonable doubt applies when this section is used in criminal cases (*R v Ewing* [1983] QB 1039, [1983] 2 All ER 645, CA).

Criminal Law Amendment Act 1867
(30 & 31 Vict c 35)

1–912 10. Removal of prisoner without habeas corpus. Where a person who has been granted bail in criminal proceedings is, while awaiting trial for the offence before the Crown Court, in prison under warrant of commitment or[1] under sentence of some other offence, it shall be lawful for the court, by order in writing, to direct the governor of the said prison to bring up the body of such person in order that he may be arraigned on such indictment without writ of *habeas corpus*, and the said governor shall thereupon obey such order.
[Criminal Law Amendment Act 1867, s 10, as amended by the Bail Act 1976, Sch 2.]

---

1. The Home Secretary issued a circular letter 20 August 1896, upon the hardship occasioned by re-arresting a prisoner at the prison gates at the expiration of a sentence for an offence of a precisely similar nature committed in another jurisdiction, and urged that when a person is to be tried for an offence committed either prior to or in connection with another offence of a similar nature for which he has already suffered punishment, the fact may always be brought to the notice of the court by whom in the event of conviction judgment will be passed, and that any remarks which may have been made by the court before whom the earlier case was tried may also be brought to the notice of the judge who hears the latter case. If an outstanding charge could properly have been tried while a prisoner was serving a term, the Court of Criminal Appeal will not permit the indictment therefore to be prosecuted after his term has expired (*R v Rose* (1923) 87 JP 136).

Review of Justices' Decisions Act 1872
(35 & 36 Vict c 26)

1–930 2. Review of justices' decisions—Justices may file affidavit. Whenever the decision of any justice or justices is called in question in any superior court of common law by a rule[1] to show cause or other process issued upon an *ex parte* application, it shall be lawful for any such justice to make and file in such court an affidavit[2] setting forth the grounds of the decision so brought under review, and any facts which he may consider to have a material bearing upon the question at issue, without being required to pay any fee in respect of filing such affidavit and such affidavit . . . may be forwarded by post to one of the Masters of the Court for the purpose of being so filed.
[Review of Justices' Decisions Act 1872, s 2.]

---

1. This procedure is not appropriate in an adoption appeal; see *Re J S (an infant)* [1959] 3 All ER 856, [1959] 1 WLR 1218, 124 JP 89, nor to an appeal to a Divisional Court in a matrimonial case; *Bond v Bond* [1967] P 39, [1964] 3 All ER 346, 128 JP 568.
2. See Precedent No 8 in PART IX: PRECEDENTS AND FORMS, post. Where there is no allegation of misconduct by the justices, an affidavit should be filed, rather than an appearance by Counsel (see remark by LORD GODDARD CJ, in *R v Camborne Justices, ex p Pearce* [1955] 1 QB 41, [1954] 2 All ER 850, 118 JP 488), otherwise justices making themselves parties to an appeal may become liable in costs (*R v Llanidloes Licensing Justices, ex p Davies* [1957] 2 All ER 610, [1957] 1 WLR 809, 121 JP 454; *R v Marlow (Bucks) Justices, ex p Schiller* [1957] 2 QB 508, [1957] 2 All ER 783, 121 JP 519); *R v Newcastle-under-Lyme Justices, ex p Massey* [1994] 1 WLR 1684, 158 JP 1037. The affidavit must be made by one or more of the justices, and not by the clerk to the justices, or a police constable (*R v Sperling* (1873) 37 JP Jo 87). Justices dissenting from the decision appealed against have no right to appear as partisans and to make and file an affidavit (*R v Waddingham, etc, Gloucestershire Justices and Tustin* (1896) 60 JP Jo 372). Cross-examination on the affidavit is allowed only in very exceptional circumstances (*R v Kent Justices, ex p Smith* [1928] WN 137), such as arose in *R v Stokesley (Yorks) Justices, ex p Bartram* [1956] 1 All ER 563, [1956] 1 WLR 254.

1–931 3. Such affidavit to be taken into consideration. Whenever any such affidavit has been filed as aforesaid, the court shall, before making the rule absolute against the justice or justices, or otherwise determining the matter so as to overrule or set aside the acts or decisions of the justice or

justices to which the application relates, take into consideration the matters set forth in such affidavit, notwithstanding that no counsel appear on behalf of the said justices.
[Review of Justices' Decisions Act 1872, s 3.]

Summary Jurisdiction (Process) Act 1881[1]
(44 & 45 Vict c 24)

1–950   **4. Service of process of English court in Scotland and of Scotch court in England.**
Subject to the provisions of this Act, any process[2] issued under the Summary Jurisdiction Acts[3] may, if issued by a court of summary jurisdiction[4] in England and endorsed by a court of summary jurisdiction in Scotland, or issued by a court of summary jurisdiction[4] in Scotland and endorsed by a court of summary jurisdiction in England, be served and executed within the jurisdiction of the endorsing court in like manner as it may be served and executed in the jurisdiction of the issuing court, and that by an officer either of the issuing or of the endorsing court.
    For the purposes of this Act—

(1) Any process may be issued and endorsed under the hand of any such person as is declared by this Act to be a court of summary jurisdiction, and may be endorsed upon proof alone of the handwriting of the person issuing it, and such proof may be either on oath or by such solemn declaration as is mentioned in section 41[5] of the Summary Jurisdiction Act 1879, or by any like declaration taken in Scotland before a sheriff[6], justice of the peace, or other magistrate having the authority of a justice of the peace. Such endorsement may be in the form contained in the schedule to this Act annexed, or in a form to the like effect;

(2) Where any process requiring the appearance of a person to answer any information or complaint has been served in pursuance of this section, the court, before issuing a warrant for the apprehension of such person for failure so to appear, shall be satisfied on oath that there is sufficient *prima facie* evidence in support of such information or complaint;

(3) If the process is to secure the attendance of a witness, the court issuing the process shall be satisfied on oath of the probability that the evidence of such witness will be material, and that the witness will not appear voluntarily without such process, and the witness shall not be subject to any liability for not obeying the process unless a reasonable amount for his expenses has been paid or tendered to him;

(4) This Act shall not apply to any process requiring the appearance of a person to answer a complaint if issued by an English court of summary jurisdiction for the recovery of a sum of money which is a civil debt within the meaning of the Summary Jurisdiction Act 1879[7], or if issued by a Scotch court in a case which falls within the definition of "civil jurisdiction" contained in the Summary Procedure Act 1864[8].

[Summary Jurisdiction (Process) Act 1881, s 4.]

---

  1. Her Majesty may by Order in Council make rules extending the operation of this Act to all parts of the British Islands (Criminal Justice Administration Act 1914, s 40(2)). The provisions of this Act have been superseded by s 39 of the Criminal Law Act 1977, post, with respect to the service in Scotland of a summons requiring a person charged with an offence to appear before a court in England or Wales. See also the Criminal Procedure Rules 2005, Part 4, this PART: STATUTORY INSTRUMENTS ON PROCEDURE, post.

  2. For definition of "process", see s 8, post. The Scottish Court is bound to endorse, on being satisfied as to the proof of the writing of the person issuing the process (*Murphy v Brooks* 1935 JC 11). As to service of process on a company registered in Scotland which carries on business in England, see Companies Act 1985, s 725(2).
  For execution in Scotland or Northern Ireland of warrants issued in England or Wales, see the Criminal Justice and Public Order Act 1994, s 136, et seq, this PART, post.

  3. Repealed and consolidated in the Magistrates' Courts Act 1952, now the Magistrates' Courts Act 1980. This section also applies to process issued under the provisions of the Criminal Justice Act 1972 in PART III: SENTENCING, post, specified in s 51(3) of that Act; it also applies to process issued by a justices' clerk, see s 51(4) of the 1972 Act; and to process issued under the Powers of Criminal Courts (Sentencing) Act 2000, in PART III: SENTENCING, post, specified in s 159 of the 2000 Act. "Summary Jurisdiction Acts" includes Part IX of the Criminal Procedure (Scotland) Act 1995 (*R v Manchester Stipendiary Magistrate, ex p Granada Television Ltd* [1999] QB 1202, [1999] 2 WLR 460, DC, [1999] Crim LR 162, DC). Indorsement of a warrant under this section to search for material in England which includes or might include excluded or special procedure material is not precluded by s 9(2) of the Police and Criminal Evidence Act 1984 (*R v Manchester Stipendiary Magistrate, ex p Granada Television Ltd* [2001] 1 AC 300, [2000] 1 All ER 135, [2000] 2 WLR 1, HL).

  4. For definition of "court of summary jurisdiction", see s 8, post. Proceedings in connection with maintenance orders are covered by the Maintenance Orders Act 1950, s 15, in PART VI: title FAMILY LAW, post.

  5. This section has been repealed by Magistrates' Courts Act 1952, Sch 6, and replaced by Criminal Procedure Rules 2005, Part 4, this PART: STATUTORY INSTRUMENTS ON PROCEDURE, post.

  6. This expression includes sheriff-substitute (s 8, post).

  7. Repealed and replaced by Magistrates' Courts Act 1980; see now s 58 thereof, post.

  8. As to service or execution of Scottish process outside Scotland, see Summary Jurisdiction (Scotland) Act 1954, s 22.

1–951   **5.** *Repealed.*

1–952   **7. Saving.** This Act shall be in addition to and not in derogation of any power existing under any other Act relating to the execution of any warrant or other process in England and Scotland respectively.
[Summary Jurisdiction (Process) Act 1881, s 7.]

1–953   8. Definitions.   In this Act, unless the context otherwise requires,—

The expression "process" includes any summons or warrant of citation to appear either to answer any information or complaint, or as a witness; also any warrant of commitment, any warrant of imprisonment, any warrant of distress, also any order or minute of a court of summary jurisdiction or copy of such order or minute, also an extract decree, and any other document or process, other than a warrant of arrestment, required for any purpose connected with a court of summary jurisdiction to be served or executed.

The expression "sheriff" shall include sheriff substitute.

The expression "court of summary jurisdiction" means any justice of the peace, also any officer or other magistrate having the authority in England or Scotland of a justice of the peace, also in Scotland the sheriff.

The expression "officer of a court of summary jurisdiction" means the constable, officer, or person to whom any process issued by the court is directed, or who is by law required or authorised to serve or execute any process issued by the court.

[Summary Jurisdiction (Process) Act 1881, s 8 as amended by the Statute Law Revision Act 1894 and the Abolition of Poindings and Warrant Sales Act 2001, s 1.]

Criminal Justice Administration Act 1914
(4 & 5 Geo 5, c 58)

1–970   24. Recognizances of principal and sureties may be taken separately.   For removing doubts it is hereby declared that where as a condition of the release of any person he is required to enter into a recognizance with sureties, the recognizances of the sureties may be taken separately and either before or after the recognizances of the principal, and if so taken the recognizances of the principal and sureties shall be as binding as if they had been taken together and at the same time.

[Criminal Justice Administration Act 1914, s 24.]

1–971   40. Extension of the power to make rules.   (1) *Repealed.*

(2) Her Majesty may, by Order[1] in Council, make rules extending the operation of the Summary Jurisdiction (Process) Act 1881, as amended by any subsequent enactment (which relates to the service and execution in Scotland of process issued by courts of summary jurisdiction in England, and in England of process issued by courts of summary jurisdiction and sheriff courts in Scotland respectively in bastardy proceedings), so as to make the provisions of that Act, subject to the necessary adaptations, applicable as between any one part of the British Islands and any other part of the British Islands in like manner as it applies as between England and Scotland.

This subsection shall extend to the Isle of Man and the Channel Islands, and the Royal Courts of the Channel Islands shall register the same accordingly.

[Criminal Justice Administration Act 1914, s 40 as amended by the Justice of the Peace Act 1949, Sch 7.]

---

1. See the Summary Jurisdiction Process (Isle of Man) Order 1928, SR & O 1928 No 377, [1928] WN (Misc) 161, applying the Summary Jurisdiction (Process) Act 1881, ante, as between England and the Isle of Man, subject to the adaptations set out in the Schedule.

Criminal Justice Act 1925
(15 & 16 Geo 5, c 86)

PART II
JURISDICTION AND PROCEDURE

Indictable offences generally

1–990   11. Venue in indictable offences.   (3) Where a person is charged with an offence . . . under any Act for the time being in force, consisting in the forging or altering of any matter whatsoever, or in offering, uttering, disposing of or putting off any matter whatsoever, knowing the same to be forged or altered, and the offence relates to documents made for the purpose of any Act relating to the suppression of the slave trade, the offence shall for the purposes of jurisdiction and trial be treated as an offence against the Slave Trade Act 1873.

[Criminal Justice Act 1925, s 11, as amended by Courts Act 1971, Sch 11 and the Forgery and Counterfeiting Act 1981, Schedule.]

Miscellaneous

1–992   33. Procedure on charge of offence against a corporation.   (1), (2) *Repealed.*

(3) On arraignment of a corporation, the corporation may enter in writing by its representative a plea of guilt or not guilty, and if either the corporation does not appear by a representative or, though it does so appear, fails to enter as aforesaid any plea, the court shall order a plea of not guilty to be entered and the trial shall proceed as though the corporation had duly entered a plea of not guilty[1].

(4) Provision may be made by rules under the Indictments Act 1915, with respect to the service on any corporation charged with an indictable offence of any documents requiring to be served in

connection with the proceedings, except in so far as such provision may be made by rules under s 144 of the Magistrates' Courts Act 1980.

(5) *Repealed.*

(6) In this section the expression "representative" in relation to a corporation means a person duly appointed by the corporation to represent it for the purpose of doing any act or thing[2] which the representative of a corporation is by this section authorised to do, but a person so appointed shall not, by virtue only of being so appointed, be qualified to act on behalf of the corporation before any court for any other purpose.

A representative for the purposes of this section need not be appointed under the seal of the corporation, and a statement in writing purporting to be signed by a managing director of the corporation, or by any person (by whatever name called) having, or being one of the persons having, the management of the affairs of the corporation, to the effect that the person named in the statement has been appointed as the representative of the corporation for the purposes of this section shall be admissible without further proof as *prima facie* evidence that that person has been so appointed.★

[Criminal Justice Act 1925, s 33, as amended by Magistrates' Courts Act 1952, Sch 6, the Courts Act 1971, Sch 8, and the Magistrates' Courts Act 1980, Sch 7.]

★**Section repealed in relation to the Isle of Man by the Statute Law (Repeals) Act 2004.**
1. For procedure on committal of a corporation for trial, see Magistrates' Courts Act 1980, Sch 3, post.
2. See Magistrates' Courts Act 1980, Sch 3, post.

PART III
AMENDMENTS AS TO OFFENCES

1–993 36. Forgery of passport.   (1) The making by any person of a statement which is to his knowledge untrue for the purpose of procuring a passport, whether for himself or any other person, shall be an offence[1] punishable with imprisonment not exceeding **two years** or a fine or both such imprisonment and fine.

(2) *Repealed.*★

[Criminal Justice Act 1925, s 36, as amended by the Criminal Law Act 1967, s 1, the Criminal Justice Act 1967, s 92, and the Forgery and Counterfeiting Act 1981, Sch.]

★**Section repealed in relation to the Isle of Man by the Statute Law (Repeals) Act 2004.**
1. This offence is triable either way (Magistrates' Courts Act 1980, Sch 1). For procedure, see the Magistrates' Courts Act 1980, ss 18–21, this PART, post.
Where the facts warrant it and there was an obtaining of a passport by a false statement, it will be appropriate to charge the offence of obtaining property by deception, contrary to s 15 of the Theft Act 1968, rather than the making of the application under this section (*R v Ashbee* [1989] 1 WLR 109, 88 Cr App Rep 357, CA). However, where there is no actual obtaining of the passport, it is sufficient and more appropriate to prefer a charge under s 36 of the 1925 Act; see *R v Bunche* [1993] 96 Cr App Rep 274, 157 JP 780 CA.

1–994 37. Unlawful possession of pension documents.   (1) If any person receives, detains or has in his possession any document to which this section applies as a pledge or a security for a debt or with a view to obtaining payment from the person entitled thereto of a debt due either to himself or to any other person, he shall be liable, on summary conviction, to a fine not exceeding **level 3** on the standard scale, or to imprisonment for a term not exceeding **six months**, or to both such fine and imprisonment.

(2) This section applies to certificates or official documents evidencing or issued in connection with the right of persons to pensions or allowances payable out of any grant which may be made out of the Consolidated Fund of the United Kingdom in pursuance of any Act for civil non-effective services.★

[Criminal Justice Act 1925, s 37, as amended by the Criminal Justice Act 1967, s 92 and Sch 3, and the Criminal Justice Act 1982, ss 38 and 46.]

★**Section repealed in relation to the Isle of Man by the Statute Law (Repeals) Act 2004.**

1–995 41. Prohibition on taking photographs, etc, in court.   (1) No person shall—

(a) take or attempt to take in any court any photograph[1], or with a view to publication make or attempt to make in any court any portrait or sketch, of any person, being a judge of the court or a juror or a witness in or a party to any proceedings before the court, whether civil or criminal; or

(b) publish any photograph[1], portrait or sketch taken or made in contravention of the foregoing provisions of this section or any reproduction thereof;

and if any person acts in contravention of this section he shall, on summary conviction, be liable in respect of each offence to a fine not exceeding **level 3** on the standard scale.

(2) For the purposes of this section—

(a) the expression "court" means any court of justice, including the court of a coroner:

(b) the expression "judge" includes . . ., registrar, magistrate, justice and coroner:

(c) a photograph, portrait or sketch shall be deemed to be a photograph, portrait or sketch taken or made in court if it is taken or made in the court-room or in the building or in the precincts of the building in which the court is held, or if it is a photograph, portrait or sketch taken or

made of the person while he is entering or leaving the court-room or any such building or precincts as aforesaid.★
[Criminal Justice Act 1925, s 41 as amended by the Criminal Justice Act 1982, ss 38 and 46.]

★Section repealed in relation to the Isle of Man by the Statute Law (Repeals) Act 2004.
1. This section applies to photographs taken by way of a video recording. Accordingly it was unlawful for the police to video defendants whilst they were at a magistrates' court (*R v Loveridge* [2001] EWCA Crim 973, [2001] 2 Cr App Rep 591).

PART IV
MISCELLANEOUS AND GENERAL

1–996   47. Abolition of presumption of coercion of married women by husband. Any presumption of law that an offence committed by a wife in the presence of her husband is committed under the coercion of the husband is hereby abolished, but on a charge against a wife for any offence other than treason or murder it shall be a good defence to prove that the offence was committed in the presence of, and under the coercion[1] of, the husband[2].
[Criminal Justice Act 1925, s 47.]

★Section repealed in relation to the Isle of Man by the Statute Law (Repeals) Act 2004.
1. The defence of coercion must be distinguished from that of duress. Coercion does not necessarily mean physical force or the threat of physical force, it could be physical, or moral. The defendant has to prove on the balance of probabilities that her will was overborne by her husband (*R v Shortland* [1996] 1 Cr App Rep 116, 160 JP 5, CA).
2. Before a woman can bring herself within the terms of this section it must be shown that she is a wife in the strict sense of the term and that the person who coerced her was her husband. The fact that the woman may have believed, even on reasonable grounds, that she was married when she was not is not sufficient (*R v Kara* [1988] Crim LR 42, CA).

1–997   49. Short title, interpretation, extent. (1) This Act may be cited as the Criminal Justice Act 1925.
  (2) In this Act, unless the context otherwise requires—

The expression "examining justices" means the justices before whom a charge is made against any person for an indictable offence, and references to examining justices include a reference to a single examining justice:

  (3) This Act shall not extend to Scotland or Northern Ireland, and references therein to warrants issued shall not be construed as including warrants issued elsewhere than in England or Wales.★
[Criminal Justice Act 1925, s 49, as amended by the Statute Law Revision Act 1950, and the Courts Act 1971, s 56 and Sch 11.]

★Section repealed in relation to the Isle of Man by the Statute Law (Repeals) Act 2004.

Criminal Justice Act 1948
(11 & 12 Geo 6, c 58)

PART I
POWERS AND PROCEEDINGS OF COURTS
Powers relating to young offenders

1–998   27. Remand of persons aged seventeen to twenty. (1) Where a court remands a person charged with or convicted of an offence or commits him for trial or sentence[1] and he is not less than seventeen but under twenty-one years old and is not released on bail, then, if the court has been notified by the Secretary of State that a remand centre[1] is available for the reception from the court of persons of his class or description, it shall commit him to a remand centre and, if he has not been so notified,★ it shall commit him to a prison.
  (2) Where a person is committed to a remand centre in pursuance of this section, the centre shall be specified in the warrant and he shall be detained there for the period for which he is remanded or until he is delivered thence in due course of law.★
  (3) In this section "court" includes a justice; and nothing in this section affects the provisions of section 128(7) of the Magistrates' Courts Act 1980 (which provides for remands to the custody of a constable).
[Criminal Justice Act 1948, s 27, as substituted by the Children and Young Persons Act 1969, Sch 5, and amended by the Magistrates' Courts Act 1980, Sch 7.]

★Repealed by the Criminal Justice and Court Services Act 2000, Sch 8 from a date to be appointed.
1. For meaning of "sentence", "remand centre", see s 80(1), post.

Miscellaneous provisions relating to procedure, appeals, evidence, etc

1–999   31. Jurisdiction and procedure in respect of certain indictable offences committed in foreign countries. (1) Any British subject employed under Her Majesty's Government in the United Kingdom in the service of the Crown who commits, in a foreign country, when acting or purporting to act in the course of his employment, any offence which, if committed in England,

would be punishable on indictment, shall be guilty of an offence, and subject to the same punishment, as if the offence had been committed in England.
[Criminal Justice Act 1948, s 31, as amended by Criminal Law Act 1967, Sch 3.]

1–1000   37. Bail on appeal, case stated or application for certiorari[1].   (1) Without prejudice to the powers vested before the commencement of this Act in any court to admit or direct the admission of a person to bail—

    (*a*)   Repealed by the Criminal Justice Act 1967, s 103(2), Sch 7, Part I
    (*b*)[2]   the High Court may, subject to section 25 of the Criminal Justice and Public Order Act 1994, grant bail to a person—

        (i)   who, after the decision of his case by the Crown Court, has applied to the Crown Court for the statement of a case for the High Court on that decision, or
        (ii)   who has applied to the High Court for an order of certiorari to remove proceedings in the Crown Court in his case into the High Court, or has applied to the High Court for leave to make such an application.

    (*c*)   Repealed by the Criminal Justice Act 1967, s 103(2), Sch 7, Part I
    (*d*)[2]   the High Court may, subject to section 25 of the Criminal Justice and Public Order Act 1994, grant bail to a person who has been convicted or sentenced by a magistrates' court and has applied to the High Court for an order of *certiorari* to remove the proceedings into the High Court or has applied to the High Court for leave to make such an application.

(1A)   Where the court grants bail to a person under paragraph (*d*) of subsection (1) above—

    (*a*)   the time at which he is to appear in the event of the conviction or sentence not being quashed by the High Court shall be such time within ten days after the judgment of the High Court has been given as may be specified by the High Court; and
    (*b*)   the place at which he is to appear in that event shall be a magistrates' court acting for the same petty sessions area as the court which convicted or sentenced him.

(4)   Criminal Procedure Rules may be made for authorising the recommittal, in such cases and by such courts or justices as may be prescribed by the rules, of persons released from custody under this section.
(5)   *Repealed.*
(6)   The time during which a person is released on bail under paragraph (*b*) or (*d*) of subsection (1) of this section shall not count as part of any term of imprisonment under his sentence; and any sentence of imprisonment imposed by a court of summary jurisdiction, or, on appeal, by the Crown Court, after the imposition of which a person is so released on bail, shall be deemed to begin to run or to be resumed as from the day on which he is received in prison under the sentence; and for the purpose of this subsection the expression "prison" shall be deemed to include a young offender institution and remand home and the expression "imprisonment" shall be construed accordingly.
[Criminal Justice Act 1948, s 37, as amended by Administration of Justice Act 1964, Sch 3, Criminal Justice Act 1967, Sch 7, Justices of the Peace Act 1968, Sch 3, Courts Act 1971, Schs 8 and 11, Bail Act 1976, Schs 2 and 3, the Supreme Court Act 1981, Schs 6 and 7, the Criminal Justice Act 1988, Sch 8, the Criminal Justice and Public Order Act 1994, Sch 10 and the Courts Act 2003, Sch 8.]

    1.   The power of the High Court to grant or vary conditions of bail is extended by the Criminal Justice Act 1967, s 22, in this PART, post; see this section and notes thereto.
    2.   In so far as these paragraphs relate to the powers of the High Court with regard to criminal proceedings before a magistrates' court, further provisions are contained in the Criminal Justice Act 1967, s 22, this PART, post.
    3.   See Rules of the Supreme Court, Ord 79, r 9, this PART, post.

1–1001   39.   *Repealed.*

1–1002   41. Evidence by certificate.   (1) In any criminal proceedings, a certificate purporting to be signed by a constable, or by a person having the prescribed[1] qualifications, and certifying that a plan or drawing exhibited thereto is a plan or drawing made by him of the place or object specified in the certificate, and that the plan or drawing is correctly drawn to scale so specified, shall be evidence[2] of the relative position of the things shown on the plan or drawing.
(2)–(3)   *Repealed.*
(4)   Nothing in this section shall be deemed to make a certificate admissible as evidence in proceedings for an offence except in a case where and to the extent to which oral evidence to the like[3] effect would have been admissible in those proceedings.
(5)   Nothing in this section shall be deemed to make a certificate admissible as evidence in proceedings for any offence—

    (*a*)   unless a copy thereof has, not less than seven days before the hearing or trial, been served in the prescribed[4] manner on the person charged with the offence; or
    (*b*)   if that person, not later than three days before the hearing or trial or within such further time as the court may in special circumstances allow, serves notice in the prescribed[4] form and manner on the prosecutor requiring the attendance at the trial of the person who signed the certificate.

(5A)   Where the proceedings mentioned in subsection (1) above are proceedings before a magistrates' court inquiring into an offence as examining justices this section shall have effect with the omission of—

(*a*) subsection (4), and

(*b*) in subsection (5), paragraph (*b*) and the word "or" immediately preceding it.

(6) In this section the expression "prescribed" means by rules made by the Secretary of State. [Criminal Justice Act 1948, s 41, as amended by the Theft Act 1968 and the Criminal Procedure and Investigations Act 1996, Sch 1.]

1. Prescribed in the Evidence by Certificate Rules 1961, SI 1961/248, as
   (*a*) registration as an architect under the Architects (Registration) Act 1931 to 1938, or
   (*b*) membership of any of the following bodies, that is to say, the Royal Institution of Chartered Surveyors, the Institution of Civil Engineers, the Institution of Municipal Engineers and the Land Agents Society
2. This is subject to the conditions of sub-ss (4) and (5) and is limited to criminal proceedings.
3. The declaration should not contain facts other than those made admissible, eg, a statement of hearsay, etc; *R v Marley* [1958] 2 All ER 359, 122 JP 413, in which a declaration containing inadmissible evidence was criticised.
4. The Evidence by Certificate Rules 1961, SI 1961/248, require service in the following manner:
   (*a*) where the person to be served is a corporation, by addressing it to the corporation and leaving it at, or sending it by registered post or by the recorded delivery service to, the registered office of the corporation or, if there is no such office, its principal office or place at which it conducts its business;
   (*b*) in any other case, by delivering it personally to the person to be served or by addressing it to him and leaving it at, or sending it by registered post or by the recorded delivery service to, his last or usual place of abode or place of business.

1–1003 42. Order of speeches. (1) Notwithstanding anything in section two of the Criminal Procedure Act 1865, as amended by section three of the Criminal Evidence Act 1898, the prosecution shall not be entitled to the right of reply upon the trial of any person or indictment on the ground only that documents have been put in evidence for the defence.

(2) and (3) *Repealed by Magistrates' Courts Act 1952, 6th Sch.*
[Criminal Justice Act 1948, s 42.]

PART II
ADMINISTRATIVE PROVISIONS AND PROVISIONS AS TO TREATMENT OF PRISONERS, ETC

Institutions for offenders

1–1004 49. Remand homes. (1) As from such date as may be specified in an order made by statutory instrument by the Secretary of State, no premises shall be used as a remand home unless a certificate of approval has been issued by the Secretary of State.

(2) The Secretary of State may by rules made under this Act apply to remand homes, with such adaptations and modifications as he thinks fit, the provisions of sections 79 and 106(3) of the Children and Young Persons Act 1933 (which relate to the approval of schools for the purposes of that Act and the evidence of such approval).

(3) No person shall be appointed after the commencement of this Act to be in charge of a remand home established by a county council or a county borough council unless his appointment has been approved by the Secretary of State.

(4) Councils of counties and county boroughs may provide in remand homes provided for their areas facilities for the observation of any person detained therein on whose physical or mental condition a medical report may be desirable for the assistance of the court in determining the most suitable method of dealing with his case, or may, if facilities for observation are available at any other institution or place, arrange for the use of those facilities for the observation of any such person as aforesaid.

(5) *Repealed.*

(6) Any expenses incurred by the council of a county or county borough in giving effect to arrangements made under subsection (4) of this action, and any sums paid by such a council under subsection (4) of the last foregoing section, shall be treated for the purposes of any grant under section 104 of the Children and Young Persons Act 1933, as expenses of the council in respect of remand homes.*
[Criminal Justice Act 1948, s 49, as amended by the Children and Young Persons Act 1969, Sch 6.]

*Repealed by the Children and Young Persons Act 1969, Sch 6, when in force.

Miscellaneous

1–1005 66. Legal custody. Any person required or authorised by or under this Act to be taken to any place or to be kept in custody shall, while being so taken or kept, be deemed to be in legal custody; and a constable, while taking or keeping any such person as aforesaid, shall have all the powers, authorities, protection and privileges of a constable as well beyond his constablewick as within it.
[Criminal Justice Act 1948, s 49, as amended by the Children and Young Persons Act 1969, Sch 6.]

PART III
SUPPLEMENTAL

1–1006 80. Interpretation. (1) In this Act, unless the context otherwise requires, the following expressions have the meaning hereby respectively assigned to them, that is to say:

"Approved school" means a school approved under section seventy-nine of the Children and Young Persons Act 1933;★

"Court" does not include a court-martial;

"Court of summary jurisdiction" includes examining justices within the meaning of the Criminal Justice Act 1925;

"Young offender institution" has the meaning assigned to it by section forty-eight of this Act[1];

"Enactment" includes an enactment contained in a local Act and any order, regulation or other instrument having effect by virtue of an Act;

"England" includes Wales;

"Impose imprisonment" means pass a sentence of imprisonment or commit to prison in default of payment of any sum of money or for failing to do or abstain from doing anything required to be done or left undone;

"Local authority" means, in relation to any probation area, any authority out of whose funds the salary of the clerk to the justices for a petty sessions area or place contained in the probation area is paid;★

"Remand centre" has the meaning assigned to it by section forty-eight of this Act[1];★

"Remand home" means premises established or used by the council of a county or county borough under the provisions of section seventy-seven of the Children and Young Persons Act 1933;★

"Sentence" includes a sentence of detention in a young offender institution, but does not include a committal in default of payment of any sum of money or failing to do or abstain from doing anything required to be done or left undone;

"The statutory restrictions upon the imprisonment of young offenders" has the same meaning as in the Criminal Justice Act 1961.

"Supervision order" has the meaning ascribed to it by section seventy-four of this Act.

(2) Any reference in this Act to a previous sentence of imprisonment shall be construed as including a reference to a previous sentence of penal servitude; any such reference to a previous sentence of detention in a young offender institution shall be construed as including a reference to a previous sentence of detention in a young offender institution; and any such reference to a previous conviction or sentence shall be construed as a reference to a previous conviction by a court in any part of Great Britain and to a previous sentence passed by any such court.

(3) Where the age of any person at any time is material for the purposes of any provision of this Act, or of any Order in Council made thereunder, regulating the powers of a court, his age at the material time shall be deemed to be or to have been that which appears to the court after considering any available evidence to be or to have been his age at that time.

(4) References in this Act to an offence punishable with imprisonment shall be construed, in relation to any offender, without regard to any prohibition or restriction imposed by or under any enactment upon the imprisonment of offenders of his age, but shall not be construed as including an offence for which the court is required to impose a sentence of imprisonment for life.

(5) *Repealed.*

(6) Where any provision of this Act empowers a court on conviction of an offender to pass a sentence or make an order in lieu of dealing with him in any other manner, the said provision shall not be construed as taking away any power of the court to order the offender to pay costs or compensation.

(7) References in this Act to any enactment shall, unless the context otherwise requires, be construed as references to that enactment as amended by any subsequent enactment including this Act.

[Criminal Justice Act 1948, s 80, as amended by the Mental Health Act 1959, Sch 8, Criminal Justice Act 1961, 4th Sch, the Administration of Justice Act 1964, Sch 5, the Children and Young Persons Act 1969, Sch 6, the Criminal Justice Act 1972, Sch 6, the Powers of Criminal Courts Act 1973, Sch 6, the Criminal Justice Act 1982, s 65, the Criminal Justice Act 1988, Sch 8 and the Access to Justice Act 1999, Sch 10.]

★Repealed by the Children and Young Persons Act 1969, Sch 6, Sch 8 when in force.

1. Section 48 of this Act was repealed by the Prison Act 1954, s 54(2) and Sch 4, and replaced by s 43(1) of that Act. For the meanings of "young offender institution" and "remand centre", see s 43(1) of the Prison Act 1952 in PART VIII title PRISONS, post.

Magistrates' Courts (Appeals from Binding over Orders) Act 1956
(4 & 5 Eliz 2, c 44)

1–1020 1. Right of appeal to the Crown Court. (1) Where, under the Justices of the Peace Act 1361, or otherwise[1], a person is ordered by a magistrates' court (as defined in the Magistrates' Courts Act 1980[2]), to enter into a recognizance with or without sureties to keep the peace or to be of good behaviour, he may appeal to the Crown Court.

(2) In the case of an appeal[3] under this section—

(a) the other party[4] to the proceedings which were the occasion of the making of the order shall be the respondent to the appeal;

(b) In relation to an appellant in custody for failure to comply with the order, so much of section 37 of the Criminal Justice Act 1948[5], as relates to the release of convicted persons from custody pending an appeal to the Crown Court shall, with the necessary adaptations, apply as if the appeal were an appeal against a conviction.

(3) Nothing in this section shall apply in relation to any order an appeal from which lies to the Crown Court apart from the provisions of this section[6].

[Magistrates' Courts (Appeals from Binding Over Orders) Act 1956, s 1, as amended by the Criminal Justice Act 1967, Sch 7, the Courts Act 1971, Sch 9 and the Magistrates' Courts Act 1980, Sch 7.]

---

  1. See PART III: SENTENCING, para **3–540**, post.
  2. See s 148 thereof, post.
  3. Representation may be granted to the appellant and the other party, see ss 19 and 21(1) of the Legal Aid Act 1988, this PART, post.
  4. Particular regard should be had to this where a magistrates' court is considering binding over of a witness in proceedings: cf *Sheldon v Bromfield Justices* [1964] 2 QB 573, [1964] 2 All ER 131, 128 JP 303.
  5. See this PART, ante. The ancillary provisions of this section are applied to the extended power of the High Court to grant bail in accordance with s 22 of the Criminal Justice Act 1967. The like power of the magistrates' court is contained in the Magistrates' Courts Act 1980, s 113, post.
  6. See Magistrates' Courts Act 1980, s 108, post.

Administration of Justice Act 1960
(1960 c 65)

Contempt of court, habeas corpus and certiorari

1–1029   12. Publication of information relating to proceedings in private. (1) The publication of information relating to proceedings before any court sitting in private shall not of itself be contempt of court except in the following cases, that is to say—

(a) where the proceedings—

    (i) relate to the exercise of the inherent jurisdiction of the High Court with respect to minors;
    (ii) are brought under the Children Act 1989 or the Adoption and Children Act 2002; or
    (iii) otherwise relate wholly or mainly to the maintenance or upbringing of a minor;

(b) where the proceedings are brought under Part VIII of the Mental Health Act 1959, or under any provision of that* Act authorising an application or reference to be made to a Mental Health Review Tribunal or to a county court;

(c) where the court sits in private for reasons of national security during that part of the proceedings about which the information in question is published;

(d) where the information relates to a secret process, discovery or invention which is in issue in the proceedings;

(e) where the court (having power to do so) expressly prohibits the publication of all information relating to the proceedings or of information of the description which is published.

(2) Without prejudice to the foregoing subsection, the publication of the text or a summary of the whole or part of an order made by a court sitting in private shall not of itself be contempt of court except where the court (having power to do so) expressly prohibits the publication.

(3) In this section references to a court include references to a judge and to a tribunal and to any person exercising the functions of a court, a judge or a tribunal; and references to a court sitting in private include references to a court sitting in camera or in chambers.

(4) Nothing in this section shall be construed as implying that any publication is punishable as contempt of court which would not be so punishable apart from this section (and in particular where the publication is not so punishable by reason of being authorised by rules of court).

[Administration of Justice Act 1960, s 12, as amended by the Children Act 1989, Sch 13, the Adoption and Children Act 2002, s 101 and the Children Act 2004, s 62.]

---

*Words substituted by the Mental Capacity Act 2005, Sch 6 from a date to be appointed.

1–1030   13. Appeal in cases of contempt of court. (1) Subject to the provisions of this section, an appeal shall lie under this section from any order or decision of a court in the exercise of jurisdiction to punish for contempt of court (including criminal contempt); and in relation to any such order or decision the provisions of this section shall have effect in substitution for any other enactment relating to appeals in civil or criminal proceedings.

(2) An appeal under this section shall lie in any case at the instance of the defendant and, in the case of an application for committal or attachment, at the instance of the applicant; and the appeal shall lie—

(a) from an order or decision of any inferior court not referred to in the next following paragraph, to the High Court;

(b) from an order or decision of a county court or any other inferior court from which appeals generally lie to the Court of Appeal, and from an order or decision (other than a decision on an appeal under this section) of a single judge of the High Court, or of any court having the powers of the High Court or of a judge of that court, to the Court of Appeal;

(*bb*) from an order or decision of the Crown Court to the Court of Appeal;
(*c*) from a decision of a single judge of the High Court on an appeal under this section, from an order or decision of a Divisional Court or the Court of Appeal (including a decision of either of those courts on an appeal under this section), and from an order or decision of the Court of Criminal Appeal or the Courts-Martial Appeal Court, to the House of Lords.

(3) The court to which an appeal is brought under this section may reverse or vary the order or decision of the court below, and make such other order as may be just; and without prejudice to the inherent powers of any court referred to in subsection (2) of this section, provision may be made by rules of court for authorising the release on bail of an appellant under this section.

(4) Subsections (2) to (4) of section one and section two of this Act shall apply to an appeal to the House of Lords under this section as they apply to an appeal to that House under the said section one, except that so much of the said subsection (2) as restricts the grant of leave to appeal shall apply only where the decision of the court below is a decision on appeal to that court under this section.

(5) In this section "court" includes any tribunal or person having power to punish for contempt; and references in this section to an order or decision of a court in the exercise of jurisdiction to punish for contempt of court include references—

(*a*) to an order or decision of the High Court, the Crown Court or a county court under any enactment enabling that court to deal with an offence as if it were contempt of court;
(*b*) to an order or decision of a county court, or of any court having the powers of a county court, under section 14, 92 or 118 of the County Courts Act 1984;
(*c*) to an order or decision[1] of a magistrates' court under subsection (3) of section 63 of the Magistrates' Courts Act 1980[2],

but do not include references to orders under section five of the Debtors Act 1869, or under any provision of the Magistrates' Courts Act 1980, or the County Courts Act 1984, except those referred to in paragraphs (*b*) and (*c*) of this subsection and except sections 38 and 142 of the last mentioned Act so far as those sections confer jurisdiction in respect of contempt of court.

(6) This section does not apply to a conviction or sentence in respect of which an appeal lies under Part I of the Criminal Appeal Act 1968, or to a decision of the criminal division of the Court of Appeal under that Part of that Act.
[Administration of Justice Act 1960, s 13, as amended by the Criminal Appeal Act 1968, s 52 and Sch 5, the Courts Act 1971, Schs 8 and 11, the Magistrates' Courts Act 1980, Sch 7, the Supreme Court Act 1981, Sch 7, the County Courts Act 1984, Sch 2 and the Access to Justice Act 1999, s 64 and Sch 15.]

---

1. For procedure on an appeal from an order or decision of a magistrates' court, see the Rules of the Supreme Court 1965, Ord 109, r 2, this PART: STATUTORY INSTRUMENTS ON PROCEDURE, post.
2. See this PART, post.

1–1031   14. Procedure on application for habeas corpus[1]. (1) *Repealed.*
(2) Notwithstanding anything in any enactment or rule of law, where a criminal or civil application for habeas corpus has been made by or in respect of any person, no such application shall again be made by or in respect of that person on the same grounds, whether to the same court or judge or to any other court or judge, unless fresh evidence is adduced in support of the application.
(3) In every case where the person by or in respect of whom an application for habeas corpus is made is restrained as a person liable, or treated by virtue of any enactment as liable, to be detained in pursuance of an order or direction under Part V of the Mental Health Act 1959[2] (otherwise than by virtue of paragraph (*e*) or paragraph (*f*) of subsection (2) of section seventy-three of that Act), the application shall be deemed for the purposes of this section and of any appeal in the proceedings to constitute a criminal cause or matter.
[Administration of Justice Act 1960, s 14, as amended by the Access to Justice Act 1999, s 65 and Sch 15 and the Constitutional Reform Act 2005, Sch 4.]

---

1. See also the Rules of the Supreme Court 1965, Ord 54, this PART: STATUTORY INSTRUMENTS ON PROCEDURE, post.
2. See now Part III of the Mental Health Act 1983.

1–1032   15. Appeal in habeas corpus proceedings[1]. (1) Subject to the provisions of this section, an appeal shall lie, in any proceedings upon application for habeas corpus, whether civil or criminal, against an order for the release of the person restrained as well as against the refusal of such an order.
(2) *Repealed.*
(3) In relation to a decision of the High Court on a criminal application for habeas corpus, section 1 of this Act shall have effect as if so much of subsection (2) as restricts the grant of leave to appeal were omitted.
(4) Except as provided by section 5 of this Act in the case of an appeal against an order of the High Court on a criminal application, an appeal brought by virtue of this section shall not affect the right of the person restrained to be discharged in pursuance of the order under appeal and (unless an order under subsection (1) of that section is in force at the determination of the appeal) to remain at large regardless of the decision on appeal.
[Administration of Justice Act 1960, s 15, as amended by the Access to Justice Act 1999, s 65 and Sch 15.]

1. See also the Rules of the Supreme Court 1965, Ord 54, this PART: STATUTORY INSTRUMENTS ON PROCEDURE, post.

Supplementary

1–1033 17. Interpretation. (1) In this Act any reference to the defendant shall be construed—

(a) in relation to proceedings for an offence, and in relation to an application for an order of mandamus, prohibition or certiorari in connection with such proceedings, as a reference to the person who was or would have been the defendant in those proceedings;

(b) in relation to any proceedings or order for or in respect of contempt of court, as a reference to the person against whom the proceedings were brought or the order was made;

(c) in relation to a criminal application for habeas corpus, as a reference to the person by or in respect of whom that application was made,

and any reference to the prosecutor shall be construed accordingly.

(2) In this Act "application for habeas corpus" means an application for a writ of habeas corpus ad subjiciendum and references to a criminal application or civil application shall be construed according as the application does or does not constitute a criminal cause or matter.

(3) In this Act any reference to the court below shall, in relation to any function of a Divisional Court, be construed as a reference to the Divisional Court or to a judge according as the function is by virtue of rules of court exercisable by the Divisional Court or a judge.

(4) *Appeal under section 1.*

(5) *Repealed.*

(6) Any reference in this Act to any other enactment is a reference thereto as amended by or under any other enactment, including this Act.

[Administration of Justice Act 1960, s 17, as amended by the Criminal Appeal Act 1966, s 10 and Sch 3.]

Criminal Procedure (Attendance of Witnesses) Act 1965

(1965 c 69)

1–1051 2. Issue of witness summons on application to Crown Court. (1) This section applies where the Crown Court is satisfied that—

(a) a person is likely to be able to give evidence likely to be material evidence, or produce any document or thing likely to be material evidence, for the purpose of any criminal proceedings before the Crown Court, and

(b) it is in the interests of justice to issue a summons under this section to secure the attendance of that person to give evidence or to produce the document or thing

(2) In such a case the Crown Court shall, subject to the following provisions of this section, issue a summons (a witness summons) directed to the person concerned and requiring him to—

(a) attend before the Crown Court at the time and place stated in the summons, and

(b) give the evidence or produce the document or thing.

(3) A witness summons may only be issued under this section on an application; and the Crown Court may refuse to issue the summons if any requirement relating to the application is not fulfilled.

(4) Where a person has been committed for trial, or sent for trial under section 51 of the Crime and Disorder Act 1998[1], for any offence to which the proceedings concerned relate, an application must be made as soon as is reasonably practicable after the committal.★

(5) Where the proceedings concerned have been transferred to the Crown Court, an application must be made as soon as is reasonably practicable after the transfer.★

(6) Where the proceedings concerned relate to an offence in relation to which a bill of indictment has been preferred under the authority of section 2(2)(b) of the Administration of Justice (Miscellaneous Provisions) Act 1933 (bill preferred by direction of Court of Appeal, or by direction or with consent of judge) an application must be made as soon as is reasonably practicable after the bill was preferred.

(7) An application must be made in accordance with Criminal Procedure Rules; and different provision may be made for different cases or descriptions of case.

(8) Criminal Procedure Rules—

(a) may, in such cases as the rules may specify, require an application to be made by a party to the case;

(b) may, in such cases as the rules may specify, require the service of notice of an application on the person to whom the witness summons is proposed to be directed;

(c) may, in such cases as the rules may specify, require an application to be supported by an affidavit containing such matters as the rules may stipulate;

(d) may, in such cases as the rules may specify, make provision for enabling the person to whom the witness summons is proposed to be directed to be present or represented at the hearing of the application for the witness summons.

(9) Provision contained in Criminal Procedure Rules by virtue of subsection (8)(c) above may in particular require an affidavit to—

(a) set out any charge on which the proceedings concerned are based;

(*b*) specify any stipulated evidence, document or thing in such a way as to enable the directed person to identify it;

(*c*) specify grounds for believing that the directed person is likely to be able to give any stipulated evidence or produce any stipulated document or thing;

(*d*) specify grounds for believing that any stipulated evidence is likely to be material evidence;

(*e*) specify grounds for believing that any stipulated document or thing is likely to be material evidence.

(10) In subsection (9) above—

(*a*) references to any stipulated evidence, document or thing are to any evidence, document or thing whose giving or production is proposed to be required by the witness summons;

(*b*) references to the directed person are to the person to whom the witness summons is proposed to be directed[2].

[Criminal Procedure (Attendance of Witnesses) Act 1965, s 2, as substituted together with ss 2A–2E by the Criminal Procedure and Investigations Act 1996, s 66 and amended by the Crime and Disorder Act 1998, Sch 8, the Courts Act 2003, Sch 8 and the Serious Organised Crime and Police Act 2005, s 169.]

---

*Sub-section (4) substituted and sub-s (5) repealed by the Criminal Justice Act 2003, Sch 3 from a date to be appointed.

1. Words inserted by the Crime and Disorder Act 1998, s 119 are only in force for the purpose of sending any person for trial under the Crime and Disorder Act 1998, s 51 in relation to certain specified areas: see SI 1998/2327.

2. The new Section 2 has effect in relation to any proceedings for the purpose of which no witness summons has been issued under this section before 1 April 1999: see SI 1999/718.

1–1051A 2A. Power to require advance production. A witness summons which is issued under section 2 above and which requires a person to produce a document or thing as mentioned in section 2(2) above may also require him to produce the document or thing—

(*a*) at a place stated in the summons, and

(*b*) at a time which is so stated and precedes that stated under section 2(2) above,

for inspection by the person applying for the summons[1].

[Criminal Procedure (Attendance of Witnesses) Act 1965, s 2A, as substituted together with ss 2 and 2B–2E by the Criminal Procedure and Investigations Act 1996, s 66.]

---

1. The new section 2A has effect in relation to any proceedings for the purpose of which no witness summons has been issued under this section before 1 April 1999: see SI 1999/718.

1–1051B 2B. Summons no longer needed. (1) If—

(*a*) a document or thing is produced in pursuance of a requirement imposed by a witness summons under section 2A above,

(*b*) the person applying for the summons concludes that a requirement imposed by the summons under section 2(2) above is no longer needed, and

(*c*) he accordingly applies to the Crown Court for a direction that the summons shall be of no further effect,

the court may direct accordingly.

(2) An application under this section must be made in accordance with Criminal Procedure Rules; and different provision may be made for different cases or descriptions of case.

(3) Criminal Procedure Rules may, in such cases as the rules may specify, require the effect of a direction under this section to be notified to the person to whom the summons is directed[1].

[Criminal Procedure (Attendance of Witnesses) Act 1965, s 2B, as substituted together with ss 2, 2A and 2C–2E by the Criminal Procedure and Investigations Act 1996, s 66 and amended by the Courts Act 2003, Sch 8.]

---

1. The new section 2B has effect in relation to any proceedings for the purpose of which no witness summons has been issued under this section before 1 April 1999: see SI 1999/718.

1–1051C 2C. Application to make summons ineffective. (1) If a witness summons issued under section 2 above is directed to a person who—

(*a*) applies to the Crown Court,

(*b*) satisfies the court that he was not served with notice of the application to issue the summons and that he was neither present nor represented at the hearing of the application, and

(*c*) satisfies the court that he cannot give any evidence likely to be material evidence or, as the case may be, produce any document or thing likely to be material evidence,

the court may direct that the summons shall be of no effect.

(2) For the purposes of subsection (1) above it is immaterial—

(*a*) whether or not Criminal Procedure Rules require the person to be served with notice of the application to issue the summons;

(*b*) whether or not Criminal Procedure Rules enable the person to be present or represented at the hearing of the application.

(3) In subsection (1)(*b*) above "served" means—

(*a*) served in accordance with Criminal Procedure Rules, in a case where such rules require the person to be served with notice of the application to issue the summons;

(*b*) served in such way as appears reasonable to the court to which the application is made under this section, in any other case.

(4) The Crown Court may refuse to make a direction under this section if any requirement relating to the application under this section is not fulfilled.

(5) An application under this section must be made in accordance with Criminal Procedure Rules; and different provision may be made for different cases or descriptions of case.

(6) Criminal Procedure Rules may, in such cases as the rules may specify, require the service of notice of an application under this section on the person on whose application the witness summons was issued.

(7) Criminal Procedure Rules may, in such cases as the rules may specify, require that where—

(*a*) a person applying under this section can produce a particular document or thing, but

(*b*) he seeks to satisfy the court that the document or thing is not likely to be material evidence,

he must arrange for the document or thing to be available at the hearing of the application.

(8) Where a direction is made under this section that a witness summons shall be of no effect, the person on whose application the summons was issued may be ordered to pay the whole or any part of the costs of the application under this section.

(9) Any costs payable under an order made under subsection (8) above shall be taxed by the proper officer of the court, and payment of those costs shall be enforceable in the same manner as an order for payment of costs made by the High Court in a civil case or as a sum adjudged summarily to be paid as a civil debt[1].

[Criminal Procedure (Attendance of Witnesses) Act 1965, s 2C, as substituted together with ss 2–2B, 2D and 2E by the Criminal Procedure and Investigations Act 1996, s 66 and amended by the Courts Act 2003, Sch 8.]

---

1. The new section 2C has effect in relation to any proceedings for the purpose of which no witness summons has been issued under this section before 1 April 1999: see SI 1999/718.

1–1051D   **2D. Issue of witness summons of Crown Court's own motion.**   For the purpose of any criminal proceedings before it, the Crown Court may of its own motion issue a summons (a witness summons) directed to a person and requiring him to—

(*a*) attend before the court at the time and place stated in the summons, and

(*b*) give evidence, or produce any document or thing specified in the summons[1].

[Criminal Procedure (Attendance of Witnesses) Act 1965, s 2D, as substituted together with ss 2–2C and 2E by the Criminal Procedure and Investigations Act 1996, s 66.]

---

1. The new section 2D has effect in relation to any proceedings for the purpose of which no witness summons has been issued under this section before 1 April 1999: see SI 1999/718.

1–1051E   **2E. Application to make summons ineffective.**   (1) If a witness summons issued under section 2D above is directed to a person who—

(*a*) applies to the Crown Court, and

(*b*) satisfies the court that he cannot give any evidence likely to be material evidence or, as the case may be, produce any document or thing likely to be material evidence,

the court may direct that the summons shall be of no effect.

(2) The Crown Court may refuse to make a direction under this section if any requirement relating to the application under this section is not fulfilled.

(3) An application under this section must be made in accordance with Criminal Procedure Rules; and different provision may be made for different cases or descriptions of case.

(4) Criminal Procedure Rulesmay, in such cases as the rules may specify, require that where—

(*a*) a person applying under this section can produce a particular document or thing, but

(*b*) he seeks to satisfy the court that the document or thing is not likely to be material evidence,

he must arrange for the document or thing to be available at the hearing of the application[1].

[Criminal Procedure (Attendance of Witnesses) Act 1965, s 2E, as substituted together with ss 2–2D by the Criminal Procedure and Investigations Act 1996, s 66 and amended by the Courts Act 2003, Sch 8.]

---

1. The new section 2E has effect in relation to any proceedings for the purpose of which no witness summons has been issued under this section before 1 April 1999: see SI 1999/718.

1–1052   **3. Punishment for disobedience to witness order or witness summons.**   (1) Any person who without just excuse disobeys a witness summons requiring him to attend before any court shall be guilty of contempt of that court and may be punished summarily by that court as if his contempt had been committed in the face of the court.

(1A) Any person who without just excuse disobeys a requirement made by any court under section 2A above shall be guilty of contempt of that court and may be punished summarily by that court as if his contempt had been committed in the face of the court.

(2) No person shall by reason of any disobedience mentioned in subsection (1) or (1A) above be liable to imprisonment for a period exceeding three months[1].

(3) *Repealed*[2].

[Criminal Procedure (Attendance of Witnesses) Act 1965, s 3, as amended by the Courts Act 1971, Sch 11 and by the Criminal Procedure and Investigations Act 1996, ss 65 and 66.]

---

1. Amendments made by the Criminal Procedure and Investigations Act 1996, s 66 have effect in relation to any proceedings for the purpose of which no witness summons has been issued under s 2 of this Act before 1 April 1999: see SI 1999/718.
2. Although the section makes disobedience of an order punishable only when it occurs "without just excuse" it is otherwise an absolute offence to disobey; forgetfulness has been held not to afford a defence (*R v Lennock* (1993) 157 JP 1068, 97 Cr App Rep 228, CA.

1-1053   4. Further process to secure attendance of witness.   (1) If a judge of the Crown Court is satisfied by evidence on oath that a witness in respect of whom a witness summons is in force is unlikely to comply with the summons, the judge may issue a warrant to arrest the witness and bring him before the court before which he is required to attend:

Provided that a warrant shall not be issued under this subsection unless the judge is satisfied by such evidence as aforesaid that the witness is likely to be able to give evidence likely to be material evidence or produce any document or thing likely to be material evidence in the proceedings[1].

(2) Where a witness who is required to attend before the Crown Court by virtue of a witness summons fails to attend in compliance with the summons, that court may—

(*a*)   in any case, cause to be served on him a notice requiring him to attend the court forthwith or at such time as may be specified in the notice;

(*b*)   if the court is satisfied that there are reasonable grounds for believing that he has failed to attend without just excuse, or if he has failed to comply with a notice under paragraph (*a*) above, issue a warrant to arrest him and bring him before the court.

(3) A witness brought before the court in pursuance of a warrant[2] under this section may be remanded by that court in custody or on bail (with or without sureties) until such time as the court may appoint for receiving his evidence or dealing with him under section 3 of this Act; and where a witness attends a court in pursuance of a notice under this section the court may direct that the notice shall have effect as if it required him to attend at any later time appointed by the court for receiving his evidence or dealing with him as aforesaid.
[Criminal Procedure (Attendance of Witnesses) Act 1965, s 4, as amended by the Courts Act 1971, Sch 8 and the Criminal Procedure and Investigations Act 1996, ss 65–67.]

---

1. Amendments made by the Criminal Procedure and Investigations Act 1996, ss 66 and 67 have effect in relation to any proceedings for the purpose of which no witness summons has been issued under s 2 of this Act before 1 April 1999: see SI 1999/716 and SI 1999/718.
2. A warrant issued under this section is treated as a warrant under ss 80 and 81 of the Supreme Court Act 1981. An application is made *ex parte* and counsel for the defendants can be heard only as *amicus curiae* and has no right of cross-examination. A summons is treated as being in force notwithstanding that it did not become enforceable until the witness's entry into the jurisdiction. It is not necessary to show that the witness was unwilling to attend (*R v Sokolovics, Tajik, Bampton and Clements* [1981] Crim LR 788).

Criminal Law Act 1967[1]
(1967 c 58)

PART I
FELONY AND MISDEMEANOUR

1-1070   1. Abolition of distinction between felony and misdemeanour.   (1) All distinctions between felony and misdemeanour are hereby abolished.

(2) Subject to the provisions of this Act, on all matters on which a distinction has previously been made between felony and misdemeanour, including mode of trial, the law and practice in relation to all offences cognisable under the law of England and Wales (including piracy) shall be the law and practice applicable at the commencement of this Act in relation to misdemeanour.
[Criminal Law Act 1967, s 1.]

---

1. For ss 4 and 5 of this Act (compounding offences) see PART VIII, title COMPOUNDING OFFENCES, *post*.

1-1071   3. Use of force in making arrest, etc[1].   (1) A person may use such force as is reasonable[2] in the circumstances in the prevention of crime[3], or in effecting or assisting in the lawful arrest[4] of offenders or suspected offenders or of persons unlawfully at large.

(2) Subsection (1) above shall replace the rules of the common law on the question when force used for a purpose mentioned in the subsection is justified by that purpose.
[Criminal Law Act 1967, s 3.]

---

1. The Aviation Security Act 1982, s 7, in PART VII: TRANSPORT, title AVIATION, *post*, has effect without prejudice to the operation, in relation to any offence under Part I of that Act (other than s 4), of ss 2 and 3 of this Act.
2. Ie reasonable in the circumstances that the defendant honestly believed them to be (*Palmer v R* (1971) 55 Cr App Rep 223). The burden is on the prosecution to prove the absence of any such belief (*R v Khan* [1995] Crim LR 78, CA).
3. "Crime" here means an offence under domestic law, and the crime "against peace" or "of aggression" is not a domestic crime and does not fall within this provision: *R v Jones (Margaret), Ayliffe v DPP, Swain v DPP* [2006] UKHL 16, [2006] 2 All ER 741, [2006] 2 WLR 772, [2006] 2 Cr App R 9.

4. This section is capable of affording a defence to a charge of reckless driving (*R v Renouf* [1986] 2 All ER 449, [1986] 1 WLR 522). As to arrest, see now the Police and Criminal Evidence Act 1984, ss 24 and 25 post, and note s 117 thereof which enables reasonable force to be used in the exercise of a power under that Act.

1–1072   9. Pardon.   Nothing in this Act shall affect Her Majesty's royal prerogative of mercy, but a pardon in respect of any offence if granted by warrant under Her royal sign manual, countersigned by the Secretary of State, shall be of like effect as a pardon under the great seal.
[Criminal Law Act 1967, s 9.]

1–1073   12. Commencement, savings, and other general provisions.   (4) Where a person has been tried for or convicted of felony before the commencement of this Part of this Act, the trial or conviction may be proved in any manner in which it could have been proved if this Part of this Act had not been passed.

(5) Subject to any express amendment or repeal made by this Act, the following provisions shall have effect in relation to any Act passed before this Act—

(a) any enactment creating an offence by directing it to be felony shall be read as directing it to be an offence, and nothing in this Part of this Act shall affect the operation of any reference to an offence in the enactments specially relating to that offence by reason only of the reference being in terms no longer applicable after the commencement of this Part of this Act;

(b) any enactment referring to felonious stealing shall be read as referring merely to stealing;

(c) nothing in this Part of this Act shall affect the punishment provided for an offence by the enactments specially relating to that offence.
[Criminal Law Act 1967, s 12(4) and (5).]

Criminal Justice Act 1967
(1967 c 80)

PART I
CRIMINAL PROCEDURE, ETC

Miscellaneous provisions as to evidence, procedure and trial

1–1091   8. Proof of criminal intent.   A court or jury, in determining whether a person has committed an offence—

(a) shall not be bound in law to infer that he intended or foresaw a result of his actions by reason only of its being a natural and probable consequence of those actions[1]; but

(b) shall decide whether he did intend or foresee that result by reference to all the evidence[2], drawing such inferences from the evidence as appear proper in the circumstances.
[Criminal Justice Act 1967, s 8.]

---

1. This section abrogates the decision in *DPP v Smith* [1961] AC 290, [1960] 3 All ER 161, 124 JP 473 and was considered in *R v Wallett* [1968] 2 QB 367, [1968] 2 All ER 296, 132 JP 318. The probability of the consequence of the defendant's actions is no more than evidence on which the court is entitled to rely when deciding what was the defendant's intention. The court may draw inferences relevant to the defendant's intent in addition to evidence of the defendant's actions and their consequences to the victim. In a case where the defendant is not proved to have *desired* the act the court is nevertheless entitled to infer that he *intended* it if the court is sure that what occurred was a "virtually certain" result of the defendant's action (baring some unforeseen intervention) and that the defendant had appreciated that fact: *R v Woollin* [1999] AC 82, [1998] 4 All ER 103, [1998] 3 WLR 382. However, the "virtual certainty" test has not yet been elevated into a substantive rule of law rather than a rule of evidence and the fact that the accused foresaw that death was a virtual certainty is a matter from which a jury may conclude that he intended that result rather than they are bound by law to do so: *R v Matthews and Alleyne* [2003] EWCA Crim 192, [2003] 2 Cr App R 30, [2003] Crim LR 553.
2. Ie all the *relevant* evidence; in crimes of basic intent the factor of self-induced intoxication is irrelevant: see *DPP v Majewski* [1977] AC 443, [1976] 2 All ER 142, 140 JP 315.

1–1092   9. Proof by written statement.   (1) In any criminal proceedings, other than committal proceedings, a written statement[1] by any person shall, if such of the conditions mentioned in the next following subsection as are applicable are satisfied, be admissible as evidence to the like extent as oral evidence to the like effect by that person[2].

(2) The said conditions are—

(a) the statement purports to be signed by the person who made it;

(b) the statement contains a declaration[3] by that person to the effect that it is true to the best of his knowledge and belief and that he made the statement knowing that, if it were tendered in evidence, he would be liable to prosecution if he wilfully stated in it anything which he knew to be false or did not believe to be true[4];

(c) before the hearing[5] at which the statement is tendered in evidence, a copy of the statement is served, by or on behalf of the party proposing to tender it, on each of the other parties to the proceedings; and

(d) none of the other parties or their solicitors, within seven days from the service of the copy of the statement[5], serves a notice on the party so proposing objecting to the statement being tendered in evidence under this section:

Provided that the conditions mentioned in paragraphs (c) and (d) of this subsection shall not apply if the parties agree before or during the hearing that the statement shall be so tendered.

(3) The following provisions shall also have effect in relation to any written statement tendered in evidence under this section, that is to say—

(a) if the statement is made by a person under the age of eighteen, it shall give his age;

(b) if it is made by a person who cannot read it, it shall be read to him before he signs it and shall be accompanied by a declaration by the person who so read the statement to the effect that it was so read; and

(c) if it refers to any other document as an exhibit, the copy served on any other party to the proceedings under paragraph (c) of the last foregoing subsection shall be accompanied by a copy of that document or by such information as may be necessary in order to enable the party on whom it is served to inspect that document or a copy thereof.

(3A) In the case of a statement which indicates in pursuance of subsection (3)(a) of this section that the person making it has not attained the age of fourteen, subsection (2)(b) of this section shall have effect as if for the words from "made" onwards there were substituted the words "understands the importance of telling the truth in it".*

(4) Notwithstanding that a written statement made by any person may be admissible as evidence by virtue of this section—

(a) the party by whom or on whose behalf a copy of the statement was served may call that person to give evidence; and

(b) the court may, of its own motion or on the application of any party to the proceedings, require that person to attend before the court and give evidence.

(5) An application under paragraph (b) of the last foregoing subsection to a court other than a magistrates' court may be made before the hearing and on any such application the powers of the court shall be exercisable by a puisne judge of the High Court, a Circuit judge or Recorder sitting alone.

(6) So much of any statement as is admitted in evidence by virtue of this section shall, unless the court otherwise directs, be read aloud at the hearing and where the court so directs an account shall be given orally of so much of any statement as is not read aloud.

(7) Any document or object referred to as an exhibit and identified in a written statement tendered in evidence under this section shall be treated as if it had been produced as an exhibit and identified in court by the maker of the statement.

(8) A document required by this section to be served on any person may be served—

(a) by delivering it to him or to his solicitor; or

(b) by addressing it to him and leaving it at his usual or last known place of abode or place of business or by addressing it to his solicitor and leaving it at his office; or

(c) by sending it in a registered letter or by the recorded delivery service or by first class post addressed to him at his usual or last known place of abode or place of business or addressed to his solicitor at his office; or

(d) in the case of a body corporate, by delivering it to the secretary or clerk of the body at its registered or principal office or sending it in a registered letter or by the recorded delivery service or by first class post addressed to the secretary or clerk of that body at that office; and in paragraph (d) of this subsection references to the secretary, in relation to a limited liability partnership, are to any designated member of the limited liability partnership.

[Criminal Justice Act 1967, s 9 as amended by the Criminal Justice and Public Order Act 1994, Sch 9, the Criminal Procedure and Investigations Act 1996, s 69 and SI 2001/1090.]

---

*Subsection printed as inserted by the Children and Young Persons Act 1969, Sch 5, from a date to be appointed.

1. Statements made in Scotland and Northern Ireland may be admitted under this section: see s 46 of the Criminal Justice Act 1972 in PART III: SENTENCING, post. *Practice Direction (criminal: consolidated)* [2002] para III.24, in this PART, post, gives directions on the preparation of statements. Where editing is thought necessary, copies of the statement will be marked to show parts on which the prosecution will not rely; a photocopy with deleted material obliterated is not permissible. The original signed statement tendered to the court is not to be marked in any way and similarly documents exhibited in committal proceedings should remain in their original state. The Note indicates circumstances where a fresh statement is preferable to edited copies; where other suspects were not charged, where other offences not charged were inquired into, where only a small part of the original is to be used, where the original contains material which the prosecution is entitled to withhold from the defence.

2. The conditions upon which this subsection is dependent are prescribed by subsequent provisions of the section. By sub-s (4), post, the party operating the section may nevertheless call the maker of the statement as a witness and the court, of its own motion, or on the application of either party may require the maker of the statement to attend and give evidence. The words "I know Clive Jones" in a statement under this section should be regarded by the court as, *prima facie*, referring to a defendant of the same name who is present and has answered to his name: see *Ellis v Jones* [1973] 2 All ER 893, 137 JP 581. A statement tendered under s 9 is not deemed to be conclusive evidence but is treated as if the maker of the statement had been called as a witness to give that evidence; the Divisional Court has said that where the prosecution have witnesses essential to the central issue in their case, it is desirable that they should call them to give evidence in person as opposed to providing a statement of evidence under s 9 (*Lister v Quaife* [1983] 2 All ER 29, [1983] 1 WLR 48). See Criminal Procedure Rules 2005, Part 27, this PART: STATUTORY INSTRUMENTS ON PROCEDURE, post, for provisions governing the operation of this section. The requirements of this section and the Rules must be strictly complied with otherwise the statement will be inadmissible; see *Paterson v DPP* [1990] RTR 329, [1990] Crim LR 651.

3. This declaration need not be separately signed (*Chapman v Ingleton* (1973) 57 Cr App Rep 476).

4. For punishment of this offence, see s 89, post.

5. By reason of the time for objection prescribed by para (*d*), the copy statement must be served more than seven days before the hearing unless the parties otherwise agree in accordance with the proviso.

1–1093   10. Proof by formal admission.   (1) Subject to the provisions of this section, any fact of which oral evidence may be given in any criminal proceedings[1] may be admitted for the purpose of those proceedings[2] by or on behalf of the prosecutor or defendant, and the admission by any party of any such fact under this section shall as against that party be conclusive evidence[3] in those proceedings of the fact admitted.

(2) An admission under this section—

(*a*)   may be made before or at the proceedings;

(*b*)   if made otherwise than in court, shall be in writing;

(*c*)   if made in writing by an individual, shall purport to be signed by the person making it and, if so made by a body corporate, shall purport to be signed by a director[4] or manager, or the secretary or clerk, or some other similar officer of the body corporate;

(*d*)   if made on behalf of a defendant who is an individual, shall be made by his counsel or solicitor;

(*e*)   if made at any stage before the trial by a defendant who is an individual, must be approved by his counsel or solicitor (whether at the time it was made or subsequently) before or at the proceedings in question[5].

(3) An admission under this section for the purpose of proceedings relating to any matter shall be treated as an admission for the purpose of any subsequent criminal proceedings relating to that matter (including any appeal or retrial).

(4) An admission under this section may with the leave of the court be withdrawn in the proceedings for the purpose of which it is made or any subsequent criminal proceedings relating to the same matter.

[Criminal Justice Act 1967, s 10.]

---

1. This section is limited to the admission of facts which would be admissible in evidence.

2. Including proceedings on transfer for trial. The Criminal Procedure Rules 2005, Part 37, this PART: STATUTORY INSTRUMENTS ON PROCEDURE, post, requires that the admission shall be written down and signed by or on behalf of the party making it.

3. The admission may be withdrawn with leave of the court: sub-s (4), infra. Permission to withdraw an admission is unlikely to be given unless the court receives evidence from the accused and those advising him that the admissions had been made by a matter of mistake or misunderstanding (*R v Kolton* [2000] Crim LR 761. CA).

4. "Director", in relation to a body corporate which is established by or under any enactment for the purpose of carrying on under national ownership any industry or part of an industry or undertaking and whose affairs are managed by the members thereof, means a member of that body (s 36(1)).

5. This sub-section provides for two distinct circumstances under which an admission may be made—

   A   *Before the trial*, when—

     (i)   it shall be in writing (para (*b*));
     (ii)   it shall be signed (para (*c*));
       and (if made by a *defendant* who is an individual as distinct from a corporate body),
     (iii)   it shall be approved by his counsel or solicitor before or at the hearing (para (*e*)).

   B   *At the trial*, when—

     (i)   it must be written down and signed (para (*c*) and Criminal Procedure Rules 2005, Part 37, this PART: STATUTORY INSTRUMENTS ON PROCEDURE, post),
       and (if made *on behalf of* a *defendant* who is an individual as distinct from a corporate body),
     (ii)   it shall be *made* by his counsel or solicitor (para (*d*)).

An admission made in committal proceedings will be written down, signed by or on behalf of the party making it, and forwarded to the court of trial (Criminal Procedure Rules 2005, Parts 10 and 37).

1–1095   20. Power of magistrates' court to commit on bail for sentence.   Where a magistrates' court has power to commit an offender to the Crown Court under s 5 of the Vagrancy Act 1824[1] (incorrigible rogues), the court may instead of committing him in custody commit him on bail.

[Criminal Justice Act 1967, s 20, as amended by the Courts Act 1971, Sch 8, and the Magistrates' Courts Act 1980, Sch 9.]

---

1. See PART VIII, title VAGRANCY, post.

1–1096   22. Extension of power of High Court to grant, or vary conditions of, bail.

(1) Where a magistrates' court withholds bail in criminal proceedings or imposes conditions in granting bail in criminal proceedings, the High Court may, subject to section 25 of the Criminal Justice and Public Order Act 1994[1], grant bail or vary the conditions.

(2) Where the High Court grants a person bail under this section it may direct him to appear at a time and place which the magistrates' court could have directed and the recognizance of any surety shall be conditioned accordingly.

(3) S 37(4) and (6) of the Criminal Justice Act 1948[2] (ancillary provisions as to persons granted bail by the High Court under that section and the currency of sentence in the case of persons so admitted) shall apply in relation to the powers conferred by this section and persons granted bail in pursuance of those powers as it applies in relation to the powers conferred by that section and persons granted bail in pursuance of those powers, except that the said subsection (6)[3] shall not apply in relation to a person granted bail pending an appeal from a magistrates' court to the Crown Court.

(4) In this section "bail in criminal proceedings" and "vary" have the same meanings as they have in the Bail Act 1976.

(5) The powers conferred on the High Court by this section shall be in substitution for the powers so conferred by paragraphs (*a*), (*b*) and (*c*) of s 37(1) of the Criminal Justice Act 1948[4], but except as aforesaid this section shall not prejudice any powers of the High Court to admit or direct the admission of persons to bail.

[Criminal Justice Act 1967, s 22, as amended by the Courts Act 1971, Schs 8 and 11, the Bail Act 1976, Sch 2, the Criminal Law Act 1977, Sch 12 and the Criminal Justice and Public Order Act 1994, Sch 10.]

1. See this PART, post.
2. See this PART, ante.
3. Sub-section (6) provides that in relation to certain types of appeals, the time during which a person is released on bail pending the hearing of his appeal shall not count as part of his term of imprisonment. The subsection does not apply to appeals from a magistrates' court to the Crown Court and is similarly excluded here. In respect of those appeals the relevant provision is s 110 of the Magistrates' Courts Act 1980, post, by virtue of which the decision of the Crown Court on the appeal is conveyed to the prison governor.
4. Only paragraphs (*a*) and (*c*) of s 37(1) have been repealed by this Act, but in so far as they related to the High Court, the powers conferred by paras (*a*), (*b*) and (*c*) have been replaced by those contained in this section.

The substitution effected by sub-s (5) has the following results—
   (i) Paragraph (*a*) of s 37(1) of the Criminal Justice Act 1948 related to an appeal from a magistrates' court to the Crown Court. In that case, the magistrates' court has power to grant bail under s 113(1) of the Magistrates' Courts Act 1980, post.
   (ii) Paragraph (*b*) relates to an appeal from the Crown Court by way of case stated. It enables the Crown Court to grant bail and, to that extent, is not affected by this section.
   (iii) Paragraph (*c*) related to an appeal from a magistrates' court by way of case stated. In that case, the magistrates' court has power to grant bail under s 113(1) of the Magistrates' Courts Act 1980, post.
   (iv) Paragraph (*d*) which relates to applications for an order of *certiorari* in respect of proceedings in a magistrates' court is retained in the Criminal Justice Act 1948 and enables the High Court to grant bail in such a case.

If, in (i) or (iii) above, the decision of the "inferior court" regarding bail is unacceptable, application may be made to the High Court under this section. The Rules of the Supreme Court, Ord 79, r 9, this PART: STATUTORY INSTRUMENTS ON PROCEDURE, post, will apply.

1–1098 32. Amendments of Costs in Criminal Cases Act 1973[1]. (1) *Repealed by the Courts Act 1971, s 56(4), Sch 11, Part III.*

(2) *Section 33 of the Courts-Martial (Appeals) Act 1968 to apply in relation to a registered medical practitioner making a written report to a Court in pursuance of a request to which this subsection applies.*

(3) The last foregoing subsection applies to a request to a registered medical practitioner to make a written or oral report on the medical condition of an offender or defendant, being a request made by a court—
   (*a*) for the purpose of determining whether or not to include in a community order (within the meaning of Part 12 of the Criminal Justice Act 2003) a mental health requirement under section 207 of that Act or make an order under s 60 of the Mental Health Act 1959[2] (hospital orders and guardianship orders) or otherwise for the purpose of determining the most suitable method of dealing with an offender; or
   (*b*) in exercise of the powers conferred by section 11 of the Powers of Criminal Courts (Sentencing) Act 2000 (remand of a defendant for medical examination and requirement of such an examination on committing a defendant for trial on bail).

(4), (5) *Repealed by the Costs in Criminal Cases Act 1973, s 21, Sch 2; the Criminal Appeal Act 1968, s 54, Sch 7.*

[Criminal Justice Act 1967, s 32, as amended by The Criminal Appeal Act 1968, s 54, Sch 7, the Courts Act 1971, Sch 11, the Costs in Criminal Cases Act 1973, Schs 1 and 2, the Powers of Criminal Courts Act 1973, Sch 5, the Magistrates' Courts Act 1980, Sch 7, the Prosecution of Offences Act 1985, Sch 1, the Powers of Criminal Courts (Sentencing) Act 2000, Sch 9 and the Criminal Justice Act 2003, Sch 32.]

1. The Costs in Criminal Cases Act 1973 has been repealed and replaced by the Prosecution of Offences Act 1985 (Part II); see s 19(3) thereof in this PART, post. As to written medical reports, see also the Costs in Criminal Cases (General) Regulations 1986, reg 25, this PART: STATUTORY INSTRUMENTS ON PROCEDURE, post.
2. See now s 37 of the Mental Health Act 1983, in PART VIII, title MENTAL HEALTH, post.

1–1100 36. Interpretation of Part I. (1) In this Part of this Act—
"committal proceedings" means proceedings before a magistrates' court acting as examining justices;
"director", in relation to a body corporate which is established by or under any enactment for the purpose of carrying on under national ownership any industry or part of an industry or undertaking and whose affairs are managed by the members thereof, means a member of that body.

(2) Expressions used in any provision of this Part of this Act relating to magistrates' courts or proceedings before such courts and also used in the Magistrates' Courts Act 1980 have the same meanings in any such provision as they have in that Act.

[Criminal Justice Act 1967, s 36, as amended by the Magistrates' Courts Act 1980, Schs 7 and 9.]

PART II
POWERS OF COURTS TO DEAL WITH OFFENDERS
Enforcement of payment of fines, etc

1–1101 48. Enforcement in Scotland of fines imposed at assizes or quarter sessions.
(1) The power of a court of summary jurisdiction in Scotland to make a transfer of fine order under

s 44 of the Summary Jurisdiction (Scotland) Act 1954 (transfer of fine orders within and from Scotland)[1] shall be exercisable in relation to a fine imposed on any person or a sum due from any person under a recognizance forfeited by the Crown Court the payment of which is enforceable by the court of summary jurisdiction, notwithstanding that the Crown Court has in pursuance of s 31 of the Powers of Criminal Courts Act 1973 fixed a term of imprisonment which that person is to undergo if the fine or other sum is not duly paid or recovered.
[Criminal Justice Act 1967, s 48 as amended by the Courts Act 1971, Sch 8 and the Powers of Criminal Courts Act 1973, Schs 5 and 6.]

1. See now the Criminal Procedure (Scotland) Act 1975, s 403.

Miscellaneous

1–1102   56. Committal for sentence for offences tried summarily.   *Repealed.*

PART III
TREATMENT OF OFFENDERS
Miscellaneous

1–1108   67. Computation of sentences of imprisonment passed in England and Wales[1].
Repealed.

1–1108A

PART IV
LEGAL AID IN CRIMINAL PROCEEDINGS (SS 73–84)

   Repealed.

1–1108B

PART V
FIREARMS (SS 85–88)

   Repealed.

PART VI
MISCELLANEOUS AND GENERAL
Offences

1–1109   89. False written statements tendered in evidence.   (1) If any person in a written statement tendered in evidence in criminal proceedings by virtue of s 9[1] of this Act or in proceedings before a court-martial by virtue of the said section 9 as extended by section 12 above or by section 99A of the Army Act 1955 or section 99A of the Air Force Act 1955 wilfully makes a statement material in those proceedings which he knows to be false or does not believe to be true, he shall be liable on conviction on indictment to imprisonment for a term not exceeding **two years** or a **fine** or **both**.
   (2) The Perjury Act 1911 shall have effect as if this section were contained in that Act.
[Criminal Justice Act 1967, s 89, as amended by the Armed Forces Act 1976, Sch 9, and the Magistrates' Courts Act 1980, Sch 9.]

1. Section 9, ante, relates to proof by written statement in criminal proceedings generally.

1–1120   91. Drunkenness in a public place[1]

1. This section is printed in full in PART VIII: title PUBLIC MEETING AND PUBLIC ORDER, post.

Fees

1–1122   94. Abolition of fees in criminal proceedings in magistrates' courts.   (1) No fees shall be chargeable by a justices' clerk in respect of any criminal matter[1].
   (2) The foregoing subsection shall not prevent any such clerk from charging a fee for supplying, for use in connection with a matter which is not a criminal matter, a copy of a document prepared for use in connection with a criminal matter.
[Criminal Justice Act 1967, s 94.]

1. For fees chargeable in civil proceedings, see Magistrates' Courts Fees Order 2005, SI 2005/3444, post.

1–1123   104. General provisions as to interpretation.   (1) In this Act, except so far as the context otherwise requires, the following expressions have the meanings hereby respectively assigned to them; that is to say—

"court" does not include a court-martial;

"extended sentence certificate" means a certificate issued under section 28 of the Powers of Criminal Courts Act 1973 stating that an extended term of imprisonment was imposed on an offender under that section;

"prison rules" means rules under s 47 of the Prison Act 1952[1];

"sentence of imprisonment" does not include a committal in default of payment of any sum of money, or for want of sufficient distress to satisfy any sum of money, or for failure to do or abstain from doing anything required to be done or left undone.

(2) *Repealed.*

(3) Any reference in this Act however expressed to a previous conviction or sentence shall be construed as a reference to a previous conviction by a court in any part of Great Britain and to a previous sentence passed by any such court.

(4) Any reference in this Act to an offence punishable with imprisonment shall be construed, in relation to any offender, without regard to any prohibition or restriction imposed by or under any enactment on the imprisonment of offenders of his age.

(5) Any reference in this Act to any other enactment is a reference thereto as amended, and includes a reference thereto as extended or applied, by or under any other enactment, including this Act.

[Criminal Justice Act 1967, s 104 amended by the Statute Law (Repeals) Act 1993, Sch 1, the Crime and Disorder Act 1998, Sch 8, the Powers of Criminal Courts (Sentencing) Act 2000, Sch 9 and the Criminal Justice Act 2003, Sch 32.]

1. See Part VIII, title Prisons, post.

1–1124 106. *Short title, extent and commencement.*

SCHEDULES

Sections 46, 79   SCHEDULE 1

Application of the Maintenance Orders Act 1958 to Attachment of Earnings Orders under Section 46 or 79

1–1125 1. The provisions of Part II of the Maintenance Orders Act 1958[1] and so much of Part III of that Act as relates to the said Part II shall apply in relation to an attachment of earnings order under s 46[2] or 79[3] of this Act as they apply in relation to an attachment of earnings order under s 6(1) of that Act, subject, however, to the exceptions and modifications specified in the following provisions of this Schedule.

2. Sections 6(1) and (2), 7, 8, 9(3) to (5) and 13(1) and (2) of that Act shall not apply in relation to an attachment of earnings order under s 46 or 79 of this Act.

3. Section 6(3) of that Act shall have effect in relation to any such order as if—

(a) it required the order to specify, in addition to the matters required to be specified by that subsection, the amount payment of which is to be secured by means of the order; and

(b) the normal deduction rate required by paragraph (a) of that subsection to be specified in an order under that section were the rate at which the court making or varying the order thinks it reasonable that the earnings to which the order relates should be applied from time to time in order to pay the said amount.

4. Section 9(1) of that Act shall have effect in relation to any such order as if for the reference to a person entitled to receive payments under the related maintenance order there were substituted a reference to the clerk of the court.

5. Section 9(2) of that Act shall have effect in relation to an attachment of earnings order under s 46 or 79[3] of this Act as if for paragraphs (a) to (e) there were substituted the words "upon the payment of the whole of the amount payment of which is to be secured by means of the order or the issue of a warrant committing the offender to prison for default in paying it".

6. In s 10(2) of that Act the reference to attachment of earnings orders shall be construed as including a reference to attachment of earnings orders under s 46 or 79 of this Act.

7. Section 20(5)(i) of that Act shall have effect in relation to an attachment of earnings order under s 46 or 79 of this Act as if for the reference to a sum due under the related maintenance order there were substituted a reference to a sum due to the clerk of the court and as if the subsection required the clerk to give to the person to whom the order is directed notice of any variation determined by a magistrates' court thereunder.

[Criminal Justice Act 1967, Sch 1.]

1. See this Act, in Part VI: title Family Law, post.
2. Section 46 relates to the enforcement of fines by way of an attachment of earnings order.
3. Section 79 has been repealed by the Legal Aid Act 1974.

Criminal Appeal Act 1968
(1968 c 19)

1–1230 Jurisdiction The Criminal Appeal Act 1907 established the Court of Criminal Appeal which ceased to exist when the Act of 1966 created the criminal division of the Court of Appeal to take over the jurisdiction of the former court. For procedure, see the Criminal Procedure Rules 2005 as amended.

1–1231 Right of appeal A person convicted on indictment may appeal to the Court of Appeal (a) against his conviction with the leave of the Court of Appeal, or if the judge of the court of trial grants a certificate that the case is fit for appeal, and (*b*) with the leave of the Court against any sentence[1] (not being a sentence fixed by law) passed on him for the offence of which he was convicted, whether passed on his conviction or in subsequent proceedings; and in specified circumstances, a person convicted of an offence by a magistrates' court and committed to the Crown Court for sentence[2] or to be dealt with may, with the leave of the Court, so appeal [Criminal Appeal Act 1968, ss 1, 9, 10 and 11, amended by the Criminal Justice Act 1988, Sch 15, the Criminal Justice and Public Order Act 1994, Sch 10, the Criminal Appeal Act 1995, s 1, the Crime and Disorder Act 1998, Schs 8 and 10, the Access to Justice Act 1999, s 58, the Football (Offences and Disorder) Act 1999, ss 6 and 7, the Football (Disorder) Act 2000, Schs 2 and 3 and the Powers of Criminal Courts (Sentencing) Act 2000, Sch 9.] The Court of Appeal may, for the purposes of the Act, order the examination of witnesses to be conducted in manner provided by rules of court before any judge of the court or before any officer of the court or other person appointed by the court for the purpose, and allow the admission of any depositions so taken as evidence before the court. [Ibid, s 23, amended by the Criminal Appeal Act 1995, s 4 and Sch 2.] The Court of Appeal may, subject to s 25 of the Criminal Justice and Public Order Act 1994, if they think fit, on the application of the appellant or on a reference by the registrar of criminal appeals, grant the appellant bail[3] pending the determination of his appeal, revoke bail granted to the appellant by the Crown Court or vary the conditions of bail granted to an appellant.

[Criminal Appeal Act 1968, s 19, amended by the Criminal Justice Act 1982, s 29, the Criminal Justice Act 1988, Sch 15 and the Criminal Justice and Public Order Act 1994, Sch 10.]

Where an appeal is allowed by reason only of evidence received or available to be received under s 23, supra, and it appears to the Court of Appeal that the interests of justice so require, the Court may order the appellant to be re-tried, but he shall not receive a sentence of greater severity than that passed on the original conviction.

[Criminal Appeal Act 1968, ss 7 and 8 and Sch 2, amended by the Criminal Justice Act 1988, s 43, the Criminal Justice and Public Order Act 1994, Sch 10 and the Powers of Criminal Courts (Sentencing) Act 2000, Sch 9.]

1. An order for costs under s 4(1) of the Costs in Criminal Cases Act 1973 was a "sentence" but an order for contribution to legal aid costs is not (*R v Hayden* [1975] 2 All ER 558, [1975] 1 WLR 852, 139 JP 564).
2. However, s 10(3) of the Criminal Appeal Act 1968 expressly precludes an appeal to the Court of Appeal against a prison sentence of less than 6 months unless that sentence followed a trial on indictment, though, the Divisional Court has, on occasions, entertained applications for judicial review of such sentences: see *R (on the application of Sogbesan) v Inner London Crown Court* [2002] EWHC 1581, [2002] Crim LR 748 and the commentary thereon.
3. But see *R v Watton* (1978) 68 Cr App Rep 293, [1979] Crim LR 246.

1–1232 30. Restitution of property. (1) The operation of an order for the restitution of property to a person made by the Crown Court shall, unless the Court direct to the contrary in any case in which, in their opinion, the title to the property is not in dispute, be suspended until (disregarding any power of a court to grant leave to appeal out of time) there is no further possibility of an appeal on which the order could be varied or set aside, and provision may be made by rules of court for the custody of any property in the meantime.

(2) The Court of Appeal may by order annul or vary any order made by the court of trial for the restitution of property to any person, although the conviction is not quashed; and the order, if annulled, shall not take effect and, if varied, shall take effect as so varied.

(3) Where the House of Lords restores a conviction, it may make any order for the restitution of property which the court of trial could have made.

[Criminal Appeal Act 1968, s 30, as substituted by the Criminal Justice Act, 1988, Sch 15.]

Justices of the Peace Act 1968
(1968 c 69)

1–1250 1. Appointment of justices, oaths of office, etc. (1)–(6) *Repealed.*

(7) It is hereby declared that any court of record having a criminal jurisdiction has, as ancillary to that jurisdiction, the power to bind over[1] to keep the peace, and power to bind over[1] to be of good behaviour, a person who or whose case is before the court[2], by requiring him to enter into his own recognisances or to find sureties or both, and committing him to prison if he does not comply; but there is hereby abolished any power to commit to prison, or to issue warrants of arrest or search warrants, which may have been exercisable at common law by the Sovereign in person, or by the Privy Council, members of the Privy Council or the Secretary of State, whether on their or his own authority or on the special direction of the Sovereign.

(8) *Repealed.*

[Justices of the Peace Act 1968, s 1, as amended by the Courts Act 1971, Sch 11, the Administration of Justice Act 1973, Sch 5, and the Justices of the Peace Act 1979, Sch 3.]

1. A binding over order under this section should only be made where there is evidence before the court which indicates the likelihood that the peace will not be kept (*R v Crown Court at Swindon, ex p Patwittar Singh* [1984] 1 All ER 941, [1984] 1 WLR 449, 148 JP 221).
2. A person who is present at the Crown Court in the capacity of answering a requirement that he should give evidence as a witness is not a person "whose case is before the court" unless he attains or assumes the role of a witness by being called to give evidence (*R v Crown Court at Swindon, ex p Patwittar Singh* [1984] 1 All ER 941, [1984] 1 WLR 449, 148 JP 221) and see *R v Crown Court at Lincoln, ex p Jones* (1989) Times, 16 June, [1990] COD 15 DC.

Administration of Justice Act 1970
(1970 c 31)

PART II
ENFORCEMENT OF DEBT

Provisions restricting sanction of imprisonment

1–1260   11. Restriction on power of committal under Debtors Act 1869.   The jurisdiction given by section 5 of the Debtors Act 1869 to commit to prison a person who makes default in payment of a debt, or instalment of a debt, due from him in pursuance of an order or judgment shall be exercisable only—

(a)   by the High Court in respect of a High Court maintenance order; and

(b)   by a county court in respect of—

    (i)   a High Court or a county court maintenance order; or

    (ii)   a judgment or order which is enforceable by a court in England and Wales and is for the payment of any of the taxes contributions, premiums or liabilities specified in Schedule 4 to this Act.

[Administration of Justice Act 1970, s 11, as amended by the Social Security Act 1973, Sch 27.]

1–1261   12. *Repealed.*

1–1262   28. Other provisions for interpretation of Part II.   (1) In this Part of this Act, except where the context otherwise requires—

"High Court maintenance order", "county court maintenance order" mean respectively a maintenance order enforceable by the High Court, a county court;

"maintenance order" means any order specified in Schedule 8 to this Act and includes such an order which has been discharged, if any arrears are recoverable thereunder;

[Administration of Justice Act 1970, s 28, as amended by the Attachment of Earnings Act 1971, Sch 6, and the Magistrates' Courts Act 1980, Sch 9.]

PART V
MISCELLANEOUS PROVISIONS

1–1263   40. Punishment for unlawful harassment of debtors.   (1) A person commits an offence if, with the object of coercing another person to pay money claimed from the other as a debt due under a contract[1], he—

(a)   harasses the other with demands for payment which, in respect of their frequency or the manner or occasion of making any such demand, or of any threat or publicity by which any demand is accompanied, are calculated[2] to subject him or members of his family or household to alarm, distress or humiliation;

(b)   falsely represents, in relation to the money claimed, that criminal proceedings lie for failure to pay it;

(c)   falsely represents himself to be authorised in some official capacity to claim or enforce payment; or

(d)   utters a document falsely represented by him to have some official character or purporting to have some official character which he knows it has not.

(2) A person may be guilty of an offence by virtue of subsection (1)(a) above if he concerts with others in the taking of such action as is described in that paragraph, notwithstanding that his own course of conduct does not by itself amount to harassment.

(3) Subsection (1)(a) above does not apply to anything done by a person which is reasonable (and otherwise permissible in law) for the purpose—

(a)   of securing the discharge of an obligation due, or believed by him to be due, to himself or to persons for whom he acts, or protecting himself or them from future loss; or

(b)   of the enforcement of any liability by legal process.

(4) A person guilty of an offence under this section shall be liable on summary conviction to a fine of not more than **level 5** on the standard scale.

[Administration of Justice Act 1970, s 40 as amended by the Criminal Justice Act 1982, ss 35, 38 and 46.]

---

1. A general agreement for the supply of electricity between a tariff customer and a public electricity supplier under the Electricity Act 1989 is not a contract (*Norweb plc v Dixon* [1995] 3 All ER 952, [1995] 1 WLR 636).
2. Means "likely to subject" not "intended to subject" (*Norweb plc v Dixon* [1995] 3 All ER 952, [1995] 1 WLR 636).

1–1264   41. Recovery of costs and compensation awarded by magistrates, Crown Court, etc. (1) In the cases specified in Part I of Schedule 9 to this Act (being cases where, in criminal proceedings, a court makes an order against the accused for the payment of costs, compensation[1], etc) any sum required to be paid by such an order as is there mentioned shall be treated, for the purposes of collection and enforcement, as if it had been adjudged to be paid on a conviction by a magistrates' court, being—

    (*a*) where the order is made by a magistrates' court, that court; and

    (*b*) in any other case, such magistrates' court as may be specified in the order.

(2) In the cases specified in Part II of the said Schedule (being cases where a court makes an order against the prosecutor in criminal proceedings, and certain cases where an order for costs arises out of an appeal to the Crown Court in proceedings which are not criminal) any sum required to be paid by such an order as is there mentioned shall be enforceable as if the order were for the payment of money recoverable summarily as a civil debt[2].

(3) Without prejudice to the foregoing subsections, but subject to subsection (4) below, in the cases specified in Schedule 9 to this Act any sum required to be paid by such an order as is there mentioned shall be enforceable by the High Court or a county court (otherwise than by issue of a writ of *fieri facias* or other process against goods or by imprisonment or attachment of earnings) as if the sum were due in pursuance of a judgment or order of the High Court or county court, as the case may be.

(4)–(4A) *Repealed.*

(5)–(7) *Repealed.*

(8) Subject to subsection (8A) below, where in the case specified in paragraph 10 of Schedule 9 to this Act the Crown Court thinks that the period for which the person subject to the order is liable apart from this subsection to be committed to prison for default under the order is insufficient, it may specify a longer period for that purpose; and then, in the case of default—

    (*a*) the specified period shall be substituted as the maximum for which the person may be imprisoned under section 76 of the Magistrates' Courts Act 1980; and

    (*b*) paragraph 2 of Schedule 4 to that Act shall apply, with any necessary modifications, for the reduction of the specified period where, at the time of the person's imprisonment, he has made part payment under the order.

(8A) The Crown Court may not specify under subsection (8) above a period of imprisonment longer than that which it could order a person to undergo on imposing on him a fine equal in amount to the sum required to be paid by the order.

(9) Where a magistrates' court has power[3] to commit a person to prison for default in paying a sum due under an order enforceable as mentioned in this section, the court shall not exercise the power unless it is satisfied that all other methods of enforcing payment have been tried or considered and either have proved unsuccessful or are likely to do so.

[Administration of Justice Act 1970, s 41, as amended by the Criminal Law Act 1977, Sch 13, the Magistrates' Courts Act 1980, Sch 7, the County Courts Act 1984, Sch 2, the Criminal Justice Act 1988, s 106, the Criminal Justice Act 1991, Sch 13, SI 1991/724 and the Statute Law (Repeals) Act 2004.]

---

1. The Crown Court has no power to fix imprisonment in default of payment of costs and compensation (*R v Komsta and Murphy* (1990) 154 JP 440, CA), unlike fines and forfeited recognizances, for which see the Powers of Criminal Courts Act 1973, s 31, post.

2. Note the restrictions on committal for default in s 92 of the Magistrates' Courts Act 1980, post; by virtue of the provisions of ss 1 and 2 of the Attachment of Earnings Act 1971, post, a county court, but not a magistrates' court, may make an attachment of earnings order in respect of costs falling under this subsection.

3. Maximum periods of imprisonment in default applying to magistrates' courts are contained in the Magistrates' Courts Act 1980, Sch 4. On enforcement by the Crown Court generally, see *R v Bunce* (1977) 66 Cr App Rep 109 and *R v Ramsey* (1987) 9 Cr App Rep (S) 251, [1987] Crim LR 714.

Sections 11, 12 and 14   SCHEDULE 4

(As amended by the Social Security Act 1973, Sch 28, the Social Security (Consequential Provisions) Act 1975, Sch 2, Social Security Pensions Act 1975, Sch 4, the Statute Law (Repeals) Act 1989, Sch 1, the Social Security (Consequential Provisions) Act 1992, Sch 2, the Pension Schemes Act 1993, Sch 8 and the Pensions Act 1995, Sch 5.)

TAXES, SOCIAL INSURANCE CONTRIBUTIONS, ETC SUBJECT TO SPECIAL ENFORCEMENT PROVISIONS IN PART II

1–1265 **1.** Income tax or any other tax or liability recoverable under section 65, 66 or 68 of the Taxes Management Act 1970.

    2. *Repealed.*

    3. Contributions equivalent premiums under Part III of the Pension Schemes Act 1993.

    3A. Class 1, 2 and 4 contributions under Part I of the Social Security Contribution and Benefits Act 1992.

Section 28   SCHEDULE 8

MAINTENANCE ORDERS FOR PURPOSES OF 1958 ACT AND PART II OF THIS ACT

(Printed as amended by the Matrimonial Proceedings and Property Act 1970, Sch 2, the Guardianship of Minors Acts 1971, Sch 1 and 1973, s 9, the Maintenance Orders (Reciprocal Enforcement) Act 1972, Sch, the Matrimonial Causes Act 1973, Sch 2, Children Act 1975, Sch 3, the Supplementary Benefits Act 1976, Sch 7, the Domestic Proceedings and Magistrates' Courts Act 1978, Sch 2, the Child Care Act 1980, Sch 5, the Civil Jurisdiction and Judgments Act 1982, Sch 12, the Matrimonial and Family Proceedings Act 1984, Sch 1, the Social Security Act 1986 Sch 10, the Family Law Reform Act 1987, Schs 2 and 4, the Courts and Legal Services Act 1990, Schs 16 and 20, the Social Security (Consequential Provisions) Act 1992, Sch 2 and SI 2001/3929.)

1–1266 **1.** An order for alimony, maintenance or other payments made, or having effect as if made, under Part II of the Matrimonial Causes Act 1973 financial relief for parties to marriage and children of family.

    2. An order for payments to or in respect of a child being an order made, or having effect as if made, under Part III of the said Act of 1973 (maintenance of children following divorce, etc).

2A. An order for periodical or other payments made, or having effect as if made under Part II of the Matrimonial Causes Act 1973.

3. An order for maintenance or other payments to or in respect of a spouse or child being an order made under Part I of the Domestic Proceedings and Magistrates' Courts Act 1978.

4. An order for periodical or other payments made or having effect as if made under Schedule 1 to the Children Act 1989

5. *Repealed.*

6. An order

(a) made or having effect as if made under paragraph 23 of Schedule 2 to the Children Act 1989; or

(b) made under section 23 of the Ministry of Social Security Act 1966, section 18 of the Supplementary Benefits Act 1976, section 24 of the Social Security Act 1986 or section 106 of the Social Security Administration Act 1992 (various provisions for obtaining contributions from a person whose dependants are assisted or maintained out of public funds).

7. An order under section 43 of the National Assistance Act 1948 (recovery of costs of maintaining assisted person).

8. An order to which section 16 of the Maintenance Orders Act 1950 applies by virtue of subsection (2)(b) or (c) of that section (that is to say an order made by a court in Scotland or Northern Ireland and corresponding to one of those specified in the foregoing paragraphs) and which has been registered in a court in England and Wales under Part II of that Act.

9. A maintenance order within the meaning of the Maintenance Orders (Facilities for Enforcement) Act 1920 (Commonwealth orders enforceable in the United Kingdom) registered in, or confirmed by, a court in England and Wales under that Act.

10. An order for periodical or other payments made under Part I of the Matrimonial Proceedings and Property Act 1970.

11. A maintenance order within the meaning of Part I of the Maintenance Orders (Reciprocal Enforcement) Act 1972 registered in a magistrates' court under the said Part I.

12. *Repealed.*

13. A maintenance order within the meaning of Part I of the Civil Jurisdiction and Judgments Act 1982 which is registered in a magistrates' court under that Part.

13A. A maintenance judgment within the meaning of Council Regulation (EC) No 44/2001 of 22nd December 2000 on jurisdiction and the recognition and enforcement of judgments in civil and commercial matters, which is registered in a magistrates' court under that Regulation.

14. An order for periodical or other payments made under Part III of the Matrimonial and Family Proceedings Act 1984.

Section 41   SCHEDULE 9
                    ENFORCEMENT OF ORDERS FOR COSTS, COMPENSATION, ETC

(As amended by the Courts Act 1971, the Criminal Justice Act 1972, the Costs in Criminal Cases Act 1973, the Criminal Law Act 1977, Sch 13, the Prosecution of Offences Act 1985, Schs 1 and 2 and the Powers of Criminal Courts (Sentencing) Act 2000, Sch 9.)

PART I
CASES WHERE PAYMENT ENFORCEABLE AS ON SUMMARY CONVICTION

Costs awarded by magistrates

1–1267 **1.** Where a magistrates' court, on the summary trial of an information, makes an order as to costs to be paid by the accused to the prosecutor.

1A. Where a magistrates' court makes an order as to costs to be paid by the accused in exercise of any power in that behalf conferred by regulations made under section 19(1) of the Prosecution of Offences Act 1985.

2. Where an appellant to the Crown Court against conviction or sentence by a magistrates' court abandons his appeal and the magistrates' court orders him to pay costs to the other party to the appeal.

Costs awarded by the Crown Court

3. Where a person appeals to the Crown Court against conviction or sentence by a magistrates' court, and the Crown Court makes an order as to costs to be paid by him.

4. Where a person is prosecuted or tried on indictment before the Crown Court and is convicted, and the court makes an order as to costs to be paid by him.

4A. Where the Crown Court makes an order as to costs to be paid by the accused in exercise of any power in that behalf conferred by regulations made under section 19(1) of the Prosecution of Offences Act 1985.

Costs awarded by Court of Appeal (criminal division) or House of Lords

6. Where the criminal division of the Court of Appeal makes an order as to costs to be paid by—

(a) an appellant;

(b) an applicant for leave to appeal to that court; or

(c) in the case of an application for leave to appeal to the House of Lords, an applicant who was the appellant before the criminal division.

Miscellaneous orders for costs, compensation, damages, etc

9. Where a court makes an order by virtue of regulations made under section 19(5) of the Prosecution of Offences Act 1985 for the payment of costs by an offender.

10. Where under s 130 of the Powers of Criminal Courts (Sentencing) Act 2000 a court orders the payment of compensation.

12. Where under section 137 of the Powers of Criminal Courts (Sentencing) Act 2000 a court orders any fine, damages, compensation or costs, or any sum awarded by way of satisfaction or compensation to be paid by the parent or guardian of a child or young person.

PART II
CASES WHERE COSTS ENFORCEABLE SUMMARILY AS CIVIL DEBT

Costs awarded by magistrates

1–1268 **13.** Where a magistrates' court makes an order as to costs to be paid by the prosecutor in exercise of any power in that behalf conferred by regulations made under section 19(1) of the Prosecution of Offences Act 1985.

14. Where an appellant to the Crown Court from a magistrates' court (otherwise than against conviction or sentence) abandons his appeal and the magistrates' court orders him to pay costs to the other party to the appeal.

15. *Repealed.*

Costs awarded by the Crown Court

16. Any order for the payment of costs made by the Crown Court, other than an order falling within Part I above, or an order for costs to be paid out of money provided by Parliament.

Costs awarded by Court of Appeal (criminal division)

16A. Where the criminal division of the Court of Appeal makes an order as to costs to be paid by the respondent or, in the case of an application for leave to appeal to the House of Lords, an applicant who was the respondent before the criminal division, and does so in exercise of any power in that behalf conferred by regulations made under section 19(1) of the Prosecution of Offences Act 1985.

Courts Act 1971
(1971 c 23)

PART VI
MISCELLANEOUS AND SUPPLEMENTAL

Costs

1–1370 **52. Award of costs where information or complaint is not proceeded with.** (1),

(2) *Repealed.*

(3) Where—

(a) *Repealed;*
(b) a complaint is made to a justice of the peace acting for any area but the complaint[1] is not proceeded with,

a magistrates' court for that area may make such order[2] as to costs to be paid by the complainant to the defendant as it thinks just and reasonable.

(4) An order under subsection (3) above shall specify the amount of the costs ordered to be paid.

(5) For the purpose of enforcement an order under subsection (3) above made in relation to a complaint which is not proceeded with shall be treated as if it were an order made under section 64 of the Magistrates' Courts Act 1980 (power to award, and enforcement of, costs in civil proceedings). [Courts Act 1971, s 52, as amended by the Costs in Criminal Cases Act 1973, Sch 2, and the Magistrates' Courts Act 1980, Sch 7.]

---

1. For a similar provision in respect of an information in a criminal case, see s 16 of the Prosecution of Offences Act 1985, post.
2. This power is limited to making an order as to the costs of the proceedings on the complaint in question and does not give authority to award costs which may have been incurred in other proceedings (*R v Magistrates' Court at Dover, ex p Customs and Excise Comrs*) (1995) 160 JP 233). There is no right of appeal to the Crown Court against such an order (*R v Crown Court at Lewes, ex p Rogers* [1974] 1 All ER 589, [1974] 1 WLR 196, 138 JP 249).

Section 28   SCHEDULE 3
PREMISES FORMERLY USED FOR BUSINESS OF ABOLISHED COURTS

(As amended by the Acquisition of Land Act 1981, Sch 4 and SI 2003/1887.)

Right of use for Supreme Court and county courts

1–1371 **1.** (1) This paragraph has effect—

(a) as respects any premises which were, up to the appointed day, being used to any extent for business of the abolished courts, and
(b) as respects the local authority who were providing the accommodation for the abolished courts,

and has effect in particular to ensure that court proceedings, including proceedings in cases in the course of hearing on the appointed day, can be conducted without any interruption or interference in the transition from the jurisdiction of the abolished courts to the jurisdiction conferred by this Act.

(2) On and after the appointed day it shall be the duty of the authority, up to the extent to which the premises were being used for business of the abolished courts, to make the premises available for Supreme Court or county court business, together with all the fittings, and all furniture, office and other equipment and other chattels previously made available for business of the abolished courts.

(3) If the premises, or any larger premises of which they form part, consist of or comprise a courtroom used or available for use as a magistrates' court (whether or not it has also been used for business of the abolished courts), and at any time the Lord Chancellor so directs, it shall be the duty of the authority to make the courtroom available for Supreme Court or county court business to the exclusion of all other business, or to such extent as the Lord Chancellor may direct.

A direction under this sub-paragraph may also apply to all other parts of the building used or available for use for the sitting or other business of the magistrates' court, together with all the fittings, and all furniture, office and other equipment and other chattels, in the courtroom or elsewhere, previously available for business of the magistrates' court.

(4) Before giving a direction under sub-paragraph (3) above the Lord Chancellor shall consult the Secretary of State, the local authority and any magistrates' courts committee concerned.

(5)–(10) *Duty of local authority to maintain premises made available.*

Premises acquired by Secretary of State

1–1372 **2.** (1) Before any premises used for the business of the abolished courts are purchased by the Secretary of State, he shall consult any magistrates' courts committee concerned.

(2) A local authority owning any premises used for the business of the abolished courts shall have power to sell, lease or otherwise dispose of the premises to the Secretary of State, notwithstanding that they are subject to any trust, or have been dedicated to the public.

(3) Sub-paragraph (2) above shall not be construed as authorising the extinction or curtailment of any public right of way over any part of premises so acquired.

(4) It is hereby declared that any responsibility of a local authority to provide a courtroom or other accommodation for any magistrates' court remains unaffected by the acquisition, whether by agreement or compulsorily, by the Secretary of State of any premises used for any such purpose, and accordingly where the Secretary of State acquires any premises the power of the Secretary of State to make the premises available for continued use, to any extent, by a magistrates' court does not affect the local authority's responsibility, or absolve them from the duty to pay a proper rent for the accommodation, on such terms and subject to such conditions as may be agreed.

Supplemental

1–1373 **12.** (1) In this Schedule, unless the context otherwise requires—

the "appropriate Minister" means either the Secretary of State or the Lord Chancellor, and, where a liability to make any payment is imposed on the appropriate Minister, it shall be the liability of either of them, or divided between them, as they may agree with the concurrence of the Treasury.
"business of the abolished courts" means the holding of—

> (*a*) a court of assize or court of quarter sessions, or
> (*b*) any other court abolished by this Act,

and any official business in connection with the work of any such court;

"local authority" has the same meaning as in the Acquisition of Land Act 1981,
"Supreme Court and county court business" includes any official business in connection with the work of any such court.

(2) Any reference in this Schedule to use for business of the abolished courts, or for Supreme Court or county court business, includes use for any purpose ancillary to that business, and includes in particular use of a car park by officials and members of the public when attending in connection with any such business, and in determining the extent of use of any premises, account shall be taken of the periods when use is made of the premises, the degree of use of the premises, and the availability of the premises for other purposes when not so used.

(3) In determining for the purposes of this Schedule what use was made of any premises up to the appointed day, account shall primarily be taken of use in the two years ending with the appointed day, but allowing for the periodical or seasonal nature of the sittings of courts of assize or other courts, and where the degree of use is different in the two years, making an estimate of the average use.

(4) If on the appointed day any building is in course of construction which is designed and intended for use, to any extent, for business of the abolished courts, this Schedule shall, except where the context otherwise requires, apply as if it were a completed building being used up to the appointed day for the purposes for which it is intended.

SCHEDULE 8

(As amended by the Prosecution of Offences Act 1979, Sch 2, the Wildlife and Countryside Act 1981, Sch 17 and the Statute Law (Repeals) Act 1993, Sch 1.)

General rules of construction

1–1374 **2.** (1) In any enactment or other instrument for any reference or expression in the first column of the Table below there shall be substituted the relevant reference or expression in the second column of the Table.

(2) Sub-paragraph (1) above applies to Acts or instruments passed or made before the appointed day or later.

(3) The preceding provisions of this paragraph apply subject to the provisions of this Act, and only except where the context otherwise requires, and in particular do not apply in relation to a sentence imposed, or other thing done, by a court before the appointed day.

TABLE

REFERENCE	SUBSTITUTED REFERENCE
1. Court of gaol delivery or of oyer and terminer.	The Crown Court.
2. Court of assize, or assizes, where the context does not relate to civil jurisdiction.	The Crown Court.
3. Court of assize, or assizes, where the context relates either to criminal or civil jurisdiction, or exclusively to civil jurisdiction.	The Crown Court or the High Court, or as the case may be the High Court and not the Crown Court.
4. Court of quarter sessions, or committee of a court of quarter sessions, except in relation to functions transferred to some authority other than the Crown Court. This paragraph applies to references to courts of quarter sessions, however expressed, and applies in particular to any reference to "the next court of quarter sessions", or to the quarter sessions for any particular area or to any sessions which, by section 13(14) of the Interpretation Act 1889, were included in the expression "court of quarter sessions".	The Crown Court.
5. Judge or commissioner of assize, or judge acting during assizes.	The Crown Court or the High Court, or both, according as the reference is to criminal jurisdiction, or civil jurisdiction, or to both.
6. Chairman or deputy chairman of quarter sessions.	The Crown Court.
7. Recorder, or deputy, assistant or temporary recorder, of a borough (but not the Recorder of London).	(*a*) Where the context implies a reference to jurisdiction of the Crown Court, the Crown Court. (*b*) Where the context implies a reference to any judicial function not related to a court of quarter sessions (or the Crown Court) such Circuit judge or Recorder as the Lord Chancellor may nominate for the purpose. (*c*) In any other case, such local authority, member of a local authority or officer of a local authority as the Lord Chancellor may nominate.
8. County court judge	A judge assigned to a county court district, or acting as a judge so assigned.
9. The judge or chairman of the court where the court is the Crown Court and comprises justices of the peace and the reference was applicable before the appointed day to county quarter sessions and meant the chairman or acting chairman of the bench.	The judge presiding in the Crown Court proceedings.
10. Clerk of assize or other officer whose duties related exclusively to the criminal jurisdiction of courts of assize.	The appropriate officer of the Crown Court.
11. Clerk of the peace or deputy clerk of the peace, except in relation to functions transferred to local authorities or officers of local authorities.	The appropriate officer of the Crown Court.
12. Clerk of the court where the court is the Crown Court.	The appropriate officer of the Crown Court.
13. A borough having a separate court of quarter sessions.	A borough which, immediately before the appointed day, had a separate court of quarter sessions.
14. Any period limited by reference to the next sitting, or the beginning or end of the next sitting, of a court of quarter sessions.	30 days or such other period as the Lord Chancellor may direct.
15. Any right to apply to a court of quarter sessions limited to a specified sitting of the court next after, or in the calendar year of, a 21st or other anniversary of an enclosure award or other event.	A right to apply to the Crown Court within twelve months from the anniversary. The Crown Court may modify or supersede any associated time limit for the giving of notice of the application, or for the confirmation of any decision on the application.
16. Any reference to local funds in the context of a reference to the Costs in Criminal Cases Act 1952.	Central funds, that is to say money provided by Parliament.

Nothing in the Table above shall be taken as affecting any enactment which, as respects any judicial or other office abolished by this Act, provides for—

    (*a*) the appointment, retirement, or removal of the officer, or
    (*b*) the tenure of office and oaths to be taken by any such officer, or
    (*c*) the remuneration, allowances or pensions of any such offices;

and nothing in the Table above shall apply to any reference to records of any court.

---

1. The Act currently in force is the Prosecution of Offences Act 1985, *post.*

Attachment of Earnings Act 1971[1]

(1971 c 32)

Cases in which attachment is available

1–1390 1. Courts with power to attach earnings[2]. (1) The High Court may make an attachment of earnings order to secure payments under a High Court maintenance order.

(2) A county court may make an attachment or earnings order to secure—

(a) payments under a High Court or a county court maintenance order;

(b) the payment of a judgment debt[3] other than a debt of less than £5 or such other sum as may be prescribed by county court rules; or

(c) payments under an administration order.

(3) A magistrates' court may make an attachment of earnings order to secure—

(a) payments under a magistrates' court maintenance order[4]; or

(b) *repealed*

(c) the payment of any sum required to be paid by an order under section 17(2) of the Access to Justice Act 1999 or under regulations under section 17A(1) of that Act.

(4) *Repealed.*

(5) Any power conferred by this Act to make an attachment of earnings order includes a power to make such an order to secure the discharge of liabilities arising before the coming into force of this Act.

[Attachment of Earnings Act 1971, s 1 amended by the Access to Justice Act 1999, Sch 4, SI 2006/1737 and the Criminal Defence Service Act 2006, s 4.]

---

1. For Rules of procedure, jurisdiction, etc see the Magistrates' Courts (Attachment of Earnings) Rules 1971, this PART: STATUTORY INSTRUMENTS ON PROCEDURE, post.
     Guidance on this Act and the Rules is contained in Home Office Circular No 115/1971.
2. "Earnings" is defined in s 24, post.
3. By virtue of the definition in s 2(c), post, this includes any sum recoverable summarily as a civil debt.
4. Defined in s 2(b), post.

1–1390A 1A. Orders to which this Act applies. The following provisions of this Act apply, except where otherwise stated, to attachment of earnings orders made, or to be made, by any court under this Act or under Schedule 5 to the Courts Act 2003, or by a fines officer under that Schedule.
[Attachment of Earnings Act 1971, s 1A as inserted by SI 2006/1737.]

1–1391 2. Principal definitions. In this Act—

(a) "maintenance order" means any order specified in Schedule 1 to this Act and includes such an order which has been discharged if any arrears are recoverable thereunder;

(b) "High Court maintenance order", "county court maintenance order" and "magistrates' court maintenance order" mean respectively a maintenance order enforceable by the High Court, a county court and a magistrates' court;

(c) "judgment debt" means a sum payable under—

(i) a judgment or order enforceable by a court in England and Wales (not being a magistrates' court);

(ii) an order of a magistrates' court for the payment of money recoverable summarily as a civil debt; or

(iii) an order of any court which is enforceable as if it were for the payment of money so recoverable,

but does not include any sum payable under a maintenance order or an administration order;

(d) "the relevant adjudication", in relation to any payment secured or to be secured by an attachment of earnings order, means the conviction, judgment, order or other adjudication from which there arises the liability to make the payment; and

(e) "the debtor", in relation to an attachment of earnings order, or to proceedings on which a court has power to make an attachment of earnings order, or to proceedings arising out of such an order, means the person by whom payment is required by the relevant adjudication to be made.

[Attachment of Earnings Act 1971, s 2.]

1–1392 3. Application for order and conditions of court's power to make it. (A1) This section shall not apply to an attachment of earnings order to be made under Schedule 5 to the Courts Act 2003.

(1) The following persons may apply[1] for an attachment of earnings order—

(a) the person to whom payment under the relevant adjudication is required to be made (whether directly or through an officer of any court);

(b) where the relevant adjudication is an administration order, any one of the creditors scheduled to the order;

(c) without prejudice to paragraph (a) above, where the application is to a magistrates' court for an order to secure maintenance payments[2], and there is in force an order under section 59 of the Magistrates' Courts Act 1980, or section 19(2) of the Maintenance Orders Act 1950, that those payments be made to the a justices' chief executive, that justices' chief executive[3];

(*d*) in the following cases the debtor—

(i) where the application is to a magistrates' court or

(ii) where the application is to the High Court or a county court for an order to secure maintenance payments.

(2) *Repealed.*

(3) Subject to subsection (3A) below, for an attachment of earnings order to be made on the application of any person other than the debtor it must appear to the court that the debtor has failed to make one or more payments required by the relevant adjudication.

(3A) Subsection (3) above shall not apply where the relevant adjudication is a maintenance order.

(3B) *Repealed.*

(3C) *Repealed.*

(4) Where proceedings are brought—

(*a*) in the High Court or a county court for the enforcement of a maintenance order by committal under section 5 of the Debtors Act 1869; or

(*b*) in a magistrates' court for the enforcement of a maintenance order under section 76 of the Magistrates' Courts Act 1980 (distress or committal),

then the court may make an attachment of earnings order to secure payments under the maintenance order, instead of dealing with the case under section 5 of the said Act of 1869 or, as the case may be, section 76 of the said Act of 1980.

(5) *Repealed.*

(6), (7) *County courts.*

[Attachment of Earnings Act 1971, s 3, as amended by the Magistrates' Courts Act 1980, Sch 7, the Maintenance Enforcement Act 1991, Sch 2, the Criminal Procedure and Investigations Act 1996, s 53, the Powers of Criminal Courts (Sentencing) Act 2000, Sch 9, the Access to Justice Act 1999, Sch 13 and SI 2006/1737.]

---

1. Application shall be by complaint, see s 19, post; but note the power in sub-ss (3B) and (3C) to make an attachment of earnings order by consent without an application for recovery of a fine or compensation, and the power in sub-s (4) to make an attachment of earnings order without application in proceedings to enforce a maintenance order. The magistrates' court having jurisdiction to make an attachment of earnings order will be the court enforcing payment: see ss 76, 89 and 90 of the Magistrates' Courts Act 1980 (fines, etc); Legal Aid Act 1988, s 24 and Sch 3 (legal aid contributions); and r 4 of the Magistrates' Courts (Attachment of Earnings) Rules 1971 (maintenance payments).

2. Defined in s 25(1), post.

3. But the justices' chief executive shall not apply for an order unless requested in writing to do so by a person entitled to payments through him, s 18, post.

1–1393   5. *County courts.*

Consequences of attachment order

1–1394   6. Effect and contents of order.   (1) An attachment of earnings order shall be an order directed[1] to a person who appears to the court, or as the case may be the fines officer, making the order to have the debtor in his employment and shall operate as an instruction to that person—

(*a*) to make periodical deductions from the debtor's earnings in accordance with Part I of Schedule 3 to this Act; and

(*b*) at such times as the order may require, or as the court, or where the order is made under Schedule 5 to the Courts Act 2003, as the court or the fines officer as the case may be, may allow, to pay the amounts deducted to the collecting officer[2] of the court, as specified in the order.

(2) For the purposes of this Act, the relationship of employer and employee shall be treated as subsisting between two persons if one of them, as a principal and not as a servant or agent, pays to the other any sums defined as earnings by section 24 of this Act.

(3) An attachment of earnings order shall contain prescribed particulars[3] enabling the debtor to be identified by the employer.

(4) Except where it is made to secure maintenance payments, the order shall specify the whole amount payable under the relevant adjudication (or so much of that amount as remains unpaid), including any relevant costs.

(5) Subject to subsection (5A) below, the order shall specify—

(*a*) the normal deduction rate[4], that is to say, the rate (expressed as a sum of money per week, month or other period) at which the court thinks it reasonable for the debtor's earnings to be applied to meeting his liability under the relevant adjudication; and

(*b*) the protected earnings rate, that is to say the rate (so expressed) below which, having regard to the debtor's resources and needs[5], the court thinks it reasonable that the earnings actually paid to him should not be reduced.

(5A) If the order is made under Schedule 5 to the Courts Act 2003 then it shall specify the percentage deduction rate in accordance with fines collection regulations made under that Schedule.

(6) In the case of an order made to secure payments under a maintenance order (not being an order for the payment of a lump sum), the normal deduction rate—

(a) shall be determined after taking account of any right or liability of the debtor to deduct income tax[6] when making the payments; and

(b) shall not exceed the rate which appears to the court necessary for the purpose of—

　(i) securing payment of the sums falling due from time to time under the maintenance order, and

　(ii) securing payment within a reasonable period of any sums already due and unpaid under the maintenance order.

(7) For the purposes of an attachment of earnings order, the collecting officer of the court shall be (subject to later variation of the order under section 9 of this Act)—

(a) in the case of an order made by the High Court, either—

　(i) the proper officer of the High Court, or

　(ii) the appropriate officer of such county court as the order may specify;

(b) in the case of an order made by a county court, the appropriate officer of that court; and

(c) in the case of an order made by a magistrates' court, the justices' chief executive for that court or for another magistrates' court specified in the order.

(8) In subsection (7) above "appropriate officer" means an officer designated by the Lord Chancellor.

(9) The Lord Chancellor may by order make such provision as he considers expedient (including transitional provision) with a view to providing for the payment of amounts deducted under attachment of earnings orders to be made to such officers as may be designated by the order rather than to collecting officers of the court.★

(10) Any such order may make such amendments in this Act, in relation to functions exercised by or in relation to collecting officers of the court as he considers expedient in consequence of the provision made by virtue of subsection (9) above.★

(11) The power to make such an order shall be exercisable by statutory instrument.★

(12) Any such statutory instrument shall be subject to annulment in pursuance of a resolution of either House of Parliament.★

[Attachment of Earnings Act 1971, s 6, as amended by the Administration of Justice Act 1977, s 19, the Access to Justice Act 1999, Sch 13 and SI 2006/1737.]

★**Section 6(9), (10), (11) and (12) inserted by the Courts and Legal Services Act 1990, Sch 17, when in force.**

1. The form of order is set out in the Schedule to the Magistrates' Courts (Attachment of Earnings) Rules 1971: Form 1 for maintenance payments; Form 2 for the other sums. As to service of the order, see rr 6 and 20 of the 1971 Rules, this PART: STATUTORY INSTRUMENTS ON PROCEDURE, post.

2. "Collecting officer" is defined in sub-s (7), infra.

3. See r 7 of the Magistrates' Courts (Attachment of Earnings) Rules 1971, this PART: STATUTORY INSTRUMENTS ON PROCEDURE, post.

4. The amount fixed as the normal deduction rate when an attachment of earnings order is made is in no way binding in subsequent proceedings for variation of the amount due under the order (*Pepper v Pepper* [1960] 1 All ER 529, [1960] 1 WLR 131, 124 JP 184).

5. The reference to the debtor's needs includes a reference to the needs of any person for whom he must, or reasonably may, provide (s 25(3), post. There is no principle of law prohibiting justices fixing the protected earnings rate below the scale rate of the Supplementary Benefits Commission, although in most cases it would be unreasonable so to do (*Billington v Billington* [1974] Fam 24, [1974] 1 All ER 546, 138 JP 228).

6. Maintenance orders are now paid gross; see PART VIII title TAX AND DUTIES, "Income tax and maintenance orders", post.

1–1395 7. Compliance with order by employer[1]. (1) Where an attachment of earnings order has been made, the employer shall, if he has been served with the order, comply with it; but he shall be under no liability for non-compliance before seven days have elapsed since the service.

(2) Where a person is served with an attachment of earnings order directed to him and he has not the debtor in his employment, or the debtor subsequently ceases to be in his employment, he shall (in either case), within ten days from the date of service or, as the case may be, the cesser, give notice of that fact to the court.

(3) Part II of Schedule 3 to this Act shall have effect with respect to the priority to be accorded as between two or more attachment of earnings orders directed to a person in respect of the same debtor.

(4) On any occasion when the employer makes, in compliance with the order, a deduction from the debtor's earnings—

(a) he shall be entitled to deduct, in addition, five new pence[2] or such other sum as may be prescribed by order made by the Lord Chancellor, towards his clerical and administrative costs; and

(b) he shall give to the debtor a statement in writing of the total amount of the deduction.

(5) An order of the Lord Chancellor under subsection (4)(a) above—

(a) may prescribe different sums in relation to different classes of cases;

(b) may be varied or revoked by a subsequent order made under that paragraph; and

(c) shall be made by statutory instrument subject to annulment by resolution of either House of Parliament.

[Attachment of Earnings Act 1971, s 7.]

1. *Attachment Orders—A Handbook for Employers* (1994) has been published by the Lord Chancellor's Department; it explains an employer's obligations under an attachment of earnings order and how the order should be operated.
2. The authorised deduction is now £1 (SI 1991/356).

1-1396 8. Interrelation with alternative remedies open to creditor. (1) Where an attachment of earnings order has been made to secure maintenance payments, no order or warrant of commitment shall be issued in consequence of any proceedings for the enforcement of the related maintenance order begun before the making of the attachment of earnings order.

(2) Where a county court has made an attachment of earnings order to secure the payment of a judgment debt[1]—

(a) no order or warrant of commitment shall be issued in consequence of any proceedings for the enforcement of the debt begun before the making of the attachment of earnings order; and

(b) so long as the order is in force, no execution for the recovery of the debt shall issue against any property of the debtor without the leave of the county court.

(3) An attachment of earnings order made to secure maintenance payments shall cease to have effect upon the making of an order of commitment or the issue of a warrant of commitment for the enforcement of the related maintenance order, or upon the exercise for that purpose of the power conferred on a magistrates' court by section 77(2) of the Magistrates' Courts Act 1980 to postpone the issue of such a warrant.

(4) An attachment of earnings order made to secure the payment of a judgment debt shall cease to have effect on the making of an order of commitment or the issue of a warrant of commitment for the enforcement of the debt.

(5) An attachment of earnings order made to secure—

(a) any payment mentioned in section 1(3)(c) of this Act; or

(b) the payment of any sum mentioned in paragraph 1 of Schedule 5 to the Courts Act 2003,

shall cease to have effect on the issue of a warrant committing the debtor to prison for default in making that payment.

[Attachment of Earnings Act 1971, s 8, amended by the Magistrates' Courts Act 1980, Sch 7 and SI 2006/1737.]

1. County Court Rules provide for the magistrates' court to be informed of the making or discharge of an attachment of earnings order to secure payment of a sum recoverable summarily as a civil debt by order of that magistrates' court (Home Office Circular No 115/1971).

Subsequent proceedings

1-1397 9. Variation, lapse and discharge of orders. (1) The court[1], or where an attachment of earnings order is made under Schedule 5 to the Courts Act 2003, the court or the fines officer as the case may be, may make an order[2] discharging or varying an attachment of earnings order.

(2) Where an order is varied, the employer shall, if he has been served with notice of the variation, comply with the order as varied; but he shall be under no liability for non-compliance before seven days have elapsed since the service.

(3) Rules of court may make provision—

(a) as to the circumstances in which an attachment of earnings order made under this Act may be varied or discharged by the court of its own motion[3];

(aa) as to the circumstances in which an attachment of earnings order made under Schedule 5 to the Courts Act 2003 may be varied or discharged by the court or the fines officer of its or his own motion;

(b) in the case of an attachment of earnings order made by a magistrates' court, for enabling a single justice, on an application made by the debtor on the ground of a material change in his resources and needs[4] since the order was made or last varied, to vary the order for a period of not more than four weeks by an increase of the protected earnings rate[5].

(4) Where an attachment of earnings order has been made and the person to whom it is directed ceases to have the debtor in his employment, the order shall lapse (except as respects deduction from earnings paid after the cesser and payment to the collecting officer of amounts deducted at any time) and be of no effect unless and until the court, or where the order was made under Schedule 5 to the Courts Act 2003, unless and until the court or the fines officer as the case may be, again directs it[6] to a person (whether the same as before or another) who appears to the court or the fines officer (as the case may be) to have the debtor in his employment.

(5) The lapse of an order under subsection (4) above shall not prevent its being treated as remaining in force for other purposes[7].

[Attachment of Earnings Act 1971, s 9 as amended by SI 2006/1737.]

1. Defined in s 25(1), post. In bankruptcy proceedings, where the court to which those proceedings have been allocated makes an income payments order under s 310 of the Insolvency Act 1986 it may, if it thinks fit, discharge or vary any attachment of earnings order that is for the time being in force (Insolvency Act 1986, s 310(4)).
2. On complaint, see s 19, post: and see rr 6 and 21 of the Magistrates' Courts (Attachment of Earnings) Rules 1971, this PART: STATUTORY INSTRUMENTS ON PROCEDURE, post, for provisions as to service of copies of such orders.
3. See rr 12 and 13 of the Magistrates' Courts (Attachment of Earnings) Rules 1971, this PART: STATUTORY INSTRUMENTS ON PROCEDURE, post.
4. The reference to the debtor's needs includes a reference to the needs of any person for whom he must, or reasonably may, provide: s 25(3), post.

5. By r 14 of the Magistrates' Courts (Attachment of Earnings) Rules 1971 the court or the justices' clerk may temporarily increase the protected earnings rate for a period of not more than 4 weeks (eg, pending an application to vary the order).

6. In the Magistrates' Courts (Attachment of Earnings) Rules 1971, this PART: STATUTORY INSTRUMENTS ON PROCEDURE, post, it is provided that the court or justices' clerk may vary a lapsed order directing it to the new employer (r 12); or may discharge the order if the debtor is unemployed or if the related maintenance order ceases to have effect through re-marriage (r 13).

7. It will, therefore, remain in force for the purpose of s 14(2), post, so the court will have power to order the debtor to give a statement of earnings, etc.

1–1398   **10. Normal deduction rate to be reduced in certain cases.**   (1) The following provisions shall have effect, in the case of an attachment of earnings order made to secure maintenance payments, where it appears to the collecting officer of the court that—

     (a)   the aggregate of the payments made for the purposes of the related maintenance order by the debtor (whether under the attachment of earnings order or otherwise) exceeds the aggregate of the payments required up to that time by the maintenance order; and

     (b)   the normal deduction rate specified by the attachment of earnings order (or, where two or more such orders are in force in relation to the maintenance order, the aggregate of the normal deduction rates specified by those orders) exceeds the rate of payments required by the maintenance order; and

     (c)   no proceedings for the variation or discharge of the attachment of earnings order are pending.

(2) In the case of an order made by the High Court or a county court, the collecting officer shall give the prescribed notice to the person to whom he is required to pay sums received under the attachment of earnings order, and to the debtor; and the court shall make the appropriate variation order, unless the debtor requests it to discharge the attachment of earnings order, or to vary it in some other way, and the court thinks fit to comply with the request.

(3) In the case of an order made by a magistrates' court, the collecting officer shall apply[1] to the court for the appropriate variation order; and the court shall grant the application unless the debtor appears at the hearing and requests the court to discharge the attachment of earnings order, or to vary it in some other way, and the court thinks fit to comply with the request.

(4) In this section "the appropriate variation order" means an order varying the attachment of earnings order in question by reducing the normal deduction rate specified thereby so as to secure that that rate (or, in the case mentioned in subsection (1)(b) above, the aggregate of the rates therein mentioned)—

     (a)   is the same as the rate of payments required by the maintenance order; or

     (b)   is such lower rate as the court thinks fit having regard to the amount of the excess mentioned in subsection (1)(a).

[Attachment of Earnings Act 1971, s 10.]

---

1. The application is by way of complaint, s 19(1), post; it is deemed to be made at the request of the person in whose favour the order was made, s 18(3), post; a summons must be served on the debtor, see s 19(4), post; and a notice of the hearing must be sent to the person entitled to payments, r 8 of the Magistrates' Courts (Attachment of Earnings) Rules 1971, this PART: STATUTORY INSTRUMENTS ON PROCEDURE, post.

1–1399   **11. Attachment order in respect of maintenance payments to cease to have effect on the occurrence of certain events.**   (1) An attachment of earnings order made to secure maintenance payments shall cease to have effect[1]—

     (a)   upon the grant of an application for registration of the related maintenance order under section 2 of the Maintenance Orders Act 1958 (which provides for the registration in a magistrates' court of a High Court or county court maintenance order, and for registration in the High Court of a magistrates' court maintenance order);

     (b)   where the related maintenance order is registered under Part I of the said Act of 1958, upon the giving notice with respect thereto under section 5 of that Act (notice with view to cancellation of registration);

     (c)   subject to subsection (3) below, upon the discharge of the related maintenance order while it is not registered under Part I of the said Act of 1958;

     (d)   upon the related maintenance order ceasing to be registered in a court in England and Wales, or becoming registered in a court in Scotland or Northern Ireland, under Part II of the Maintenance Orders Act 1950.

(2) Subsection (1)(a) above shall have effect, in the case of an application for registration under section 2(1) of the said Act of 1958, notwithstanding that the grant of the application may subsequently become void under subsection (2) of that section.

(3) Where the related maintenance order is discharged as mentioned in subsection (1)(c) above and it appears to the court discharging the order that arrears thereunder will remain to be recovered after the discharge, that court may, if it thinks fit, direct that subsection (1) shall not apply.

[Attachment of Earnings Act 1971, s 11.]

---

1. See also r 13 of the Magistrates' Courts (Attachment of Earnings) Rules 1971, this PART: STATUTORY INSTRUMENTS ON PROCEDURE, post, for power of court to discharge an order on its own motion in the circumstances there specified.

1–1400   12. Termination of employer's liability to make deductions. (1) Where an attachment of earnings ceases to have effect under section 8 or 11 of this Act, the proper officer of the prescribed court[1] shall give notice of the cesser to the person to whom the order was directed.

(2) Where, in the case of an attachment of earnings order made otherwise than to secure maintenance payments, the whole amount payable under the relevant adjudication has been paid, and also any relevant costs, the court shall give notice to the employer that no further compliance with the order is required.

(3) Where an attachment of earnings order—

(*a*) ceases to have effect under section 8 or 11 of this Act; or

(*b*) is discharged under section 9.

the person to whom the order has been directed shall be under no liability in consequence of his treating the order as still in force at any time before the expiration of seven days from the date on which the notice required by subsection (1) above or, as the case may be, a copy of the discharging order is served on him.

[Attachment of Earnings Act 1971, s 12.]

1. In magistrates' courts this will be the justices' clerk for the court prescribed by r 6 of the Magistrates' Courts (Attachment of Earnings) Rules 1971, this PART: STATUTORY INSTRUMENTS ON PROCEDURE, post.

Administrative provisions

1–1401   13. Application of sums received by collecting officer. (1) Subject to subsection (3) below, the collecting officer to whom a person makes payments in compliance with an attachment of earnings order shall, after deducting such court fees, if any, in respect of proceedings for or arising out of the order, as are deductible from those payments, deal with the sums paid in the same way as he would if they had been paid by the debtor to satisfy the relevant adjudication[1].

(2) Any sums paid to the collecting officer under an attachment of earnings order made to secure maintenance payments shall, when paid to the person entitled to receive those payments, be deemed to be payments made by the debtor (with such deductions, if any, in respect of income tax[2] as the debtor is entitled or required to make) so as to discharge—

(*a*) first, any sums for the time being due and unpaid under the related maintenance order (a sum at an earlier date being discharged before a sum due at a later date)[3]; and

(*b*) secondly, any costs incurred in proceedings relating to the related maintenance order which were payable by the debtor when the attachment of earnings order was made or last varied.

(3) Where a county court makes an attachment of earnings order to secure the payment of a judgment debt and also, under section 4(1) of this Act, orders the debtor to furnish to the court a list of all his creditors, sums paid to the collecting officer in compliance with the attachment of earnings order shall not be dealt with by him as mentioned in subsection (1) above, but shall be retained by him pending the decision of the court whether or not to make an administration order and shall then be dealt with by him as the court may direct.

[Attachment of Earnings Act 1971, s 13.]

1. See Magistrates' Courts Act 1980, s 139, post, for disposal of sums ordered on conviction.
2. See note to s 6(6)(*a*), ante, relating to deduction of income tax.
3. This appropriation accords with that which operates when the issue of a warrant of commitment is postponed on condition that the defendant maintains current payments to become due, together with further payments on account of arrears: see *R v Miskin Lower Justices, ex p Young* [1953] 1 QB 533, [1953] 1 All ER 495, 117 JP 166.

1–1402   14. Power of court to obtain statements of earnings, etc. (1) Where in any proceedings a court has power under this Act or under Schedule 5 to the Courts Act 2003, or a fines officer has power under that Schedule, to make an attachment of earnings order, the court or the fines officer, as the case may be, may—

(*a*) order a debtor to give to the court or the fines officer, as the case may be, within a specified period, a statement signed by him of—

(i)   the name and address of any person by whom earnings are paid to him;

(ii) specified particulars as to his earnings and anticipated earnings, and as to his resources and needs[1]; and

(iii) specified particulars for the purpose of enabling the debtor to be identified by any employer of his;

(*b*) order any person appearing to the court or the fines officer, as the case may be, to have the debtor in his employment to give to the court or the fines officer, as the case may be, within a specified period, a statement signed by him or on his behalf of specified particulars of the debtor's earnings and anticipated earnings.

(2) Where an attachment of earnings order has been made, the court or the fines officer, as the case may be, may at any time thereafter while the order is in force

(*a*) make such an order as is described in subsection (1)(*a*) or (*b*) above; and

(*b*) order the debtor to attend before the court on a day and at a time specified in the order to give the information described in subsection (1)(*a*) above.

(3) In the case of an application to a magistrates' court for an attachment of earnings order, or for the variation or discharge of such an order, the power to make an order under subsection (1) or (2) above shall be exercisable also, before the hearing of the application, by a single justice[2].

(4) Without prejudice to subsections (1) to (3) above, rules of court may provide that where notice of an application for an attachment of earnings order is served on the debtor, it shall include a requirement that he shall give to the court, within such period and in such manner as may be prescribed, a statement in writing of the matters specified in subsection (1)(a) above and of any other prescribed matters which are, or may be, relevant under section 6 of this Act to the determination of the normal deduction rate and the protected earnings rate to be specified in any order made on the application.

This subsection does not apply to an attachment of earnings order to be made under Schedule 5 to the Courts Act 2003.

(5) In any proceedings in which a court has power under this Act or under Schedule 5 to the Courts Act 2003, or a fines officer has power under that Schedule, to make an attachment of earnings order, and in any proceedings for the making, variation or discharge of such an order, a document purporting to be a statement given to the court or the fines officer, as the case may be, in compliance with an order under subsection (1)(a) or (b) above, or with any such requirement of a notice of application for an attachment of earnings order as is mentioned in subsection (4) above, shall, in the absence of proof to the contrary, be deemed to be a statement so given and shall be evidence of the facts stated therein.

[Attachment of Earnings Act 1971, s 14 as amended by the Administration of Justice Act 1982, s 53 and SI 2006/1737.]

---

1. The reference to the debtor's needs includes a reference to the needs of any person for whom he must, or reasonably may, provide: s 25(3), post.
2. Or the justices' clerk: r 22 of the Magistrates' Courts (Attachment of Earnings) Rules 1971, this PART: STATUTORY INSTRUMENTS ON PROCEDURE, post.

1–1403   15. Obligation of debtor and his employers to notify changes of employment and earnings. (1) While an attachment of earnings order is in force—

(a) the debtor shall from time to time notify the court in writing of every occasion on which he leaves any employment, or becomes employed or re-employed, not later (in each case) than seven days from the date on which he did so;

(b) the debtor shall, on any occasion when he becomes employed or re-employed, include in his notification under paragraph (a) above particulars of his earnings and anticipated earnings from the relevant employment; and

(c) any person who becomes the debtor's employer and knows that the order is in force and by, or (if the order was made by a fines officer) for, which court it was made shall, within seven days of his becoming the debtor's employer or of acquiring that knowledge (whichever is the later) notify that court in writing that he is the debtor's employer, and include in his notification a statement of the debtor's earnings and anticipated earnings.

(2) In the case of an attachment of earnings order made by a fines officer, the reference to "the court" in subsection (1)(a) above shall mean the court for which that order was made.

[Attachment of Earnings Act 1971, s 15 as amended by SI 2006/1737.]

1–1404   16. Power of court to determine whether particular payments are earnings. (1) Where an attachment of earnings order is in force, the court shall, on the application[1] of a person specified in subsection (2) below, determine whether payments to the debtor of a particular class or description specified by the application are earnings[2] for the purposes of the order, and the employer shall be entitled to give effect to any determination for the time being in force under this section.

(2) The persons referred to in subsection (1) above are—

(a) the employer;

(b) the debtor;

(c) the person to whom payment under the relevant adjudication is required to be made (whether directly or through an officer of any court); and

(d) without prejudice to paragraph (c) above, where the application is in respect of an attachment of earnings order made to secure payments under a magistrates' court maintenance order, the collecting officer.

(3) Where an application under this section is made by the employer, he shall not incur any liability for non-compliance with the order as respects any payments of the class or description specified by the application which are made by him to the debtor while the application, or any appeal[3] in consequence thereof, is pending; but this subsection shall not, unless the court otherwise orders, apply as respects such payments if the employer subsequently withdraws the application or, as the case may be, abandons the appeal.

[Attachment of Earnings Act 1971, s 16.]

---

1. By way of complaint: see s 19(3), post.
2. "Earnings" is defined in s 24, post.
3. An appeal lies by way of case stated (Magistrates' Courts Act 1980, s 111).

1–1405   **17. Consolidated attachment orders.**   (1) The powers of a county court under sections 1 and 3 of this Act shall include power to make an attachment of earnings order to secure the payment of any number of judgment debts; and the powers of a magistrates' court under those sections or under Schedule 5 to the Courts Act 2003, and the powers of a fines officer under that Schedule, shall include power to make an attachment of earnings order to secure the discharge of any number of such liabilities as are specified in section 1(3)[1] of this Act and paragraph 1 of Schedule 5 to the Courts Act 2003.

(2) An attachment of earnings order made by virtue of this section shall be known as a consolidated attachment order.

(3) The power to make a consolidated attachment order shall be exercised subject to and in accordance with rules of court[2], and rules made for the purposes of this section may provide—

  (*a*)   for the transfer from one court to another or (where Schedule 5 to the Courts Act 2003 applies) from a court or a fines officer, as the case may be, acting in one local justice area, to a court or a fines officer, as the case may be, acting in another local justice area—

    (i)   of an attachment of earnings order, or any proceedings for or rising out of such an order; and

    (ii)   of functions relating to the enforcement of any liability capable of being secured by attachment of earnings;

  (*b*)   for enabling a court or a fines officer, as the case may be, to which or to whom any order, proceedings or functions have been transferred under the rules to vary or discharge an attachment of earnings order made by another court or fines officer and to replace it (if the court, or fines officer as the case may be, thinks fit) with a consolidated attachment order;

  (*c*)   for the cases in which any power exercisable under this section or the rules may be exercised by a court or a fines officer, as the case may be, of its or his own motion or on the application of a prescribed person;

  (*d*)   for requiring the officer of a court who receives payments made to him in compliance with an attachment of earnings order, instead of complying with section 13 of this Act, to deal with them as directed by the court or the rules; and

  (*e*)   for modifying or excluding provisions of this Act or Part III of the Magistrates' Courts Act 1980, but only so far as may be necessary or expedient for securing conformity with the operation of rules made by virtue of paragraphs (*a*) to (*d*) of this subsection.

[Attachment of Earnings Act 1971, s 17, as amended by the Magistrates' Courts Act 1980, Sch 7, the Access to Justice Act 1999, Sch 13 and SI 2006/1737.]

---

    1. By r 15(1) of the Magistrates' Courts (Attachment of Earnings) Rules 1971 maintenance payments are excluded and may not, therefore, be made the subject of a consolidated attachment order.

    2. See the Magistrates' Courts (Attachment of Earnings) Rules 1971; a detailed procedure for making a consolidated attachment order is prescribed by rr 15 – 17, this PART: STATUTORY INSTRUMENTS ON PROCEDURE, post.

Special provisions with respect to magistrates' courts

1–1406   **18. Certain action not to be taken by collecting officer except on request.**   (1) A justices' chief executive who is entitled to receive payments under a maintenance order for transmission to another person shall not—

  (*a*)   apply for an attachment of earnings order to secure payments under the maintenance order; or

  (*b*)   except as provided by section 10(3) of this Act, apply for an order discharging or varying such an attachment of earnings order; or

  (*c*)   apply for a determination under section 16 of this Act,

unless he is requested in writing to do so by a person entitled to receive the payments through him.

(2) Where a justices' chief executive is so requested—

  (*a*)   he shall comply with the request unless it appears to him unreasonable in the circumstances to do so; and

  (*b*)   the person by whom the request was made shall have the same liabilities for all the costs properly incurred in or about any proceedings taken in pursuance of the request as if the proceedings had been taken by that person.

(3) For the purposes of subsection (2)(*b*) above, any application made by a justices' chief executive as required by section 10(3) of this Act shall be deemed to be made on the request of the person in whose favour the attachment of earnings order in question was made.★

[Attachment of Earnings Act 1971, s 18 as amended y the Access to Justice Act 1999, Sch 13.]

1–1407   **19. Procedure on applications.**   (1) Subject to rules of court made by virtue of the following subsection, an application to a magistrates' court for an attachment of earnings order, or an order discharging or varying an attachment of earnings order, shall be made by complaint.

(2) Rules of court may make provision excluding subsection (1) in the case of such an application as is referred to in section 9(3)(*b*) of this Act.

(3) An application to a magistrates' court for a determination under section 16 of this Act shall be made by complaint.

(4) For the purposes of section 51 of the Magistrates' Courts Act 1980 (which provides for the

issue of a summons directed to the person against whom an order may be made in pursuance of a complaint)—

(a) the power to make an order in pursuance of a complaint by the debtor for an attachment of earnings order, or the discharge or variation of such an order, shall be deemed to be a power to make an order against the person to whom payment under the relevant adjudication is required to be made (whether directly or through an officer of any court); and

(b) the power to make an attachment of earnings order, or an order discharging or varying an attachment of earnings order, in pursuance of a complaint by any other person (including a complaint in proceedings to which section 3(4) (b) of this Act applies) shall be deemed to be a power to make an order against the debtor.

(5) A complaint for an attachment of earnings order may be heard notwithstanding that it was not made within the six months allowed by section 127(1) of the Magistrates' Courts Act 1980.
[Attachment of Earnings Act 1971, s 19, amended by the Magistrates' Courts Act 1980, Sch 7.]

1–1408   20. Jurisdiction in respect of persons residing outside England and Wales. (1) It is hereby declared that a magistrates' court has jurisdiction to hear a complaint by or against a person residing outside England and Wales for the discharge or variation of an attachment of earnings order made by a magistrates' court to secure maintenance payments; and where such a complaint is made, the following provisions shall have effect.

(2) If the person resides in Scotland or Northern Ireland, section 15 of the Maintenance Orders Act 1950 (which relates to the service of process on persons residing in those countries) shall have effect in relation to the complaint as it has effect in relation to the proceedings therein mentioned.

(3) Subject to the following subsection, if the person resides outside the United Kingdom and does not appear at the time and place appointed for the hearing of the complaint, the court may, if it thinks it reasonable in all the circumstances to do so, proceed to hear and determine the complaint at the time and place appointed for the hearing, or for any adjourned hearing, in like manner as if the person had then appeared.

(4) Subsection (3) above shall apply only if it is proved to the satisfaction of the court, on oath or in such other manner as may be prescribed, that the complainant has taken such steps as may be prescribed[1] to give to the said person notice of the complaint and of the time and place appointed for the hearing of it.
[Attachment of Earnings Act 1971, s 20.]

---

1. The steps prescribed are set out in rr 10 and 11 of the Magistrates' Courts (Attachment of Earnings) Rules 1971, this Part: STATUTORY INSTRUMENTS ON PROCEDURE, post.

1–1409   21. Costs on application under s 16. (1) On making a determination under section 16 of this Act, a magistrates' court may in its discretion make such order as it thinks just and reasonable for payment by any of the persons mentioned in subsection (2) of that section of the whole or any part of the costs of the determination (but subject to section 18(2)(b) of this Act).

(2) Costs ordered to be paid under this section shall—

(a) in the case of costs to be paid by the debtor to the person in whose favour the attachment of earnings order in question was made, be deemed—

(i) if the attachment of earnings order was made to secure maintenance payments, to be a sum due under the related maintenance order, and

(ii) otherwise, to be a sum due to the justices' chief executive for the court; and

(b) in any other case, be enforceable as a civil debt.
[Attachment of Earnings Act 1971, s 21 as amended by the Access to Justice Act 1999, Sch 13.]

Miscellaneous provisions

1–1420   22. Persons employed under the Crown. (1) The fact that an attachment of earnings order is made at the suit of the Crown shall not prevent its operation at any time when the debtor is in the employment of the Crown.

(2) Where a debtor is in the employment of the Crown and an attachment of earnings order is made in respect of him, then for the purposes of this Act—

(a) the chief officer for the time being of the department, office or other body in which the debtor is employed shall be treated as having the debtor in his employment (any transfer of the debtor from one department, office or body to another being treated as a change of employment); and

(b) any earnings paid by the Crown or a Minister of the Crown, or out of the public revenue of the United Kingdom, shall be treated as paid by the said chief officer.

(3) If any question arises, in proceedings for or arising out of an attachment of earnings order, as to what department, office or other body is concerned for the purposes of this section, or as to who for those purposes is the chief officer thereof, the question shall be referred to and determined by the Minister for the Civil Service; but that Minister shall not be under any obligation to consider a reference under this subsection unless it is made by the court.

(4) A document purporting to set out a determination of the said Minister under subsection (3) above and to be signed by an official of the Office of the said Minister shall, in any such proceedings

as are mentioned in that subsection, be admissible in evidence and be deemed to contain an accurate statement of such a determination unless the contrary is shown.

(5) This Act shall have effect notwithstanding any enactment passed before 29th May 1970 and preventing or avoiding the attachment or diversion of sums due to a person in respect of service under the Crown, whether by way of remuneration, pension or otherwise.

[Attachment of Earnings Act 1971, s 22, as amended by the Transfer of Functions (Minister for the Civil Service and Treasury) Order 1981, SI 1981/1670 and SI 1987/2039.]

1–1421   23. Enforcement provisions.   (1) If, after being served with notice of an application to a county court for an attachment of earnings order or for the variation of such an order or with an order made under section 14(2)(*b*) above, the debtor fails to attend on the day and at the time specified for any hearing of the application or specified in the order, the court may adjourn the hearing and order him to attend at a specified time on another day; and if the debtor—

(*a*)   fails to attend at that time on that day; or
(*b*)   attends, but refuses to be sworn or give evidence,

he may be ordered by the judge to be imprisoned for not more than fourteen days.

(1A) In any case where the judge has power to make an order of imprisonment under subsection (1) for failure to attend, he may, in lieu of or in addition to making that order, order the debtor to be arrested and brought before the court either forthwith or at such time as the judge may direct.

(2) Subject to this section, a person commits an offence if—

(*a*)   being required by section 7(1) or 9(2) of this Act to comply with an attachment of earnings order, he fails to do so; or
(*b*)   being required by section 7(2) of this Act to give a notice for the purposes of that subsection, he fails to give it, or fails to give it within the time required by that subsection; or
(*c*)   he fails to comply with an order under section 14(1) of this Act or with any such requirement of a notice of application for an attachment of earnings order as is mentioned in section 14(4), or fails (in either case) to comply within the time required by the order or notice; or
(*d*)   he fails to comply with section 15 of this Act; or
(*e*)   he gives a notice for the purposes of section 7(2) of this Act, or a notification for the purposes of section 15, which he knows to be false in a material particular, or recklessly gives such a notice or notification which is false in a material particular; or
(*f*)   in purported compliance with section 7(2) or 15 of this Act, or with any order under section 14(1), or with any such requirement of a notice of application for an attachment of earnings order as is mentioned in section 14(4), he makes any statement which he knows to be false in a material particular, or recklessly makes any statement which is false in a material particular.

(3) Where a person commits an offence under subsection (2) above in relation to proceedings in, or to an attachment of earnings order made by, the High Court or a county court, he shall be liable on summary conviction to a fine of not more than **level 2** on the standard scale or he may be ordered by a judge of the High Court or the county court judge (as the case may be) to pay a fine of not more than £250 or, in the case of an offence specified in subsection (4) below, to be imprisoned for not more than fourteen days; and where a person commits an offence under subsection (2) otherwise than as mentioned above in this subsection, he shall be liable on summary conviction to a fine of not more than **level 2** on the standard scale.

(4) The offences referred to above in the case of which a judge may impose imprisonment are—

(*a*)   an offence under subsection (2)(*c*) or (*d*), if committed by the debtor; and
(*b*)   an offence under subsection (2)(*e*) or (*f*), whether committed by the debtor or any other person.

(5) It shall be a defence—

(*a*)   for a person charged with an offence under subsection (2)(*a*) above to prove that he took all reasonable steps to comply with the attachment of earnings order in question;
(*b*)   for a person charged with an offence under subsection (2)(*b*) to prove that he did not know, and could not reasonably be expected to know, that the debtor was not in his employment, or (as the case may be) had ceased to be so, and that he gave the required notice as soon as reasonably practicable after the fact came to his knowledge.

(6) Where a person is convicted or dealt with for an offence under subsection (2)(*a*), the court may order him to pay, to whoever is the collecting officer of the court for the purposes of the attachment of earnings order in question, any sums deducted by that person from the debtor's earnings and not already paid to the collecting officer.

(7) Where under this section a person is ordered by a judge of the High Court or a county court judge to be imprisoned, the judge may at any time revoke the order and, if the person is already in custody, order his discharge.

(8) Any fine imposed by a judge of the High Court under subsection (3) above and any sums ordered by the High Court to be paid under subsection (6) above shall be recoverable in the same way as a fine imposed by that court in the exercise of its jurisdiction to punish for contempt of court; section 129 of the County Courts Act 1984 (enforcement of fines) shall apply to payment of a fine imposed by a county court judge under subsection (3) and of any sums ordered by a county court judge to be paid under subsection (6); and any sum ordered by a magistrates' court to be paid under subsection (6) shall be recoverable as a sum adjudged to be paid on a conviction by that court.

(9) For the purposes of section 13 of the Administration of Justice Act 1960 (appeal in cases of contempt of court), subsection (3) above shall be treated as an enactment enabling the High Court or a county court to deal with an offence under subsection (2) above as if it were contempt of court.

(10) In this section reference to proceedings in a court are to proceedings in which that court has power to make an attachment of earnings order or has made such an order.

(11) A district judge, assistant district judge or deputy district judge shall have the same powers under this section as a judge of a county court.

[Attachment of Earnings Act 1971, s 23, as amended by the Contempt of Court Act 1981, Sch 2, the Criminal Justice Act 1982, s 38, 39 and 46, and Sch 4, the Administration of Justice Act 1982, s 53, SI 1984/447, the County Courts Act 1984, Sch 2, the Courts and Legal Services Act 1990, Sch 17 and the Criminal Justices Act 1991, Sch 4.]

1–1422   24. Meaning of "earnings".   (1) For the purposes of this Act, but subject to the following subsection, "earnings" are any sums payable to a person—

(a) by way of wages or salary (including any fees, bonus, commission, overtime pay or other emoluments payable in addition to wages or salary or payable under a contract of service);

(b) by way of pension (including an annuity in respect of past services, whether or not rendered to the person paying the annuity, and including periodical payments by way of compensation for the loss, abolition or relinquishment, or diminution in the emoluments, of any office or employment);

(c) by way of statutory sick pay.

(2) The following shall not be treated as earnings—

(a) sums payable by any public department of the Government of Northern Ireland or of a territory outside the United Kingdom;

(b) pay or allowances payable to the debtor as a member of Her Majesty's forces other than pay or allowances payable by his employer to him as a special member of a reserve force (within the meaning of the Reserve Forces Act 1996);

(ba) a tax credit (within the meaning of the Tax Credits Act 2002;

(c) pension, allowances or benefit payable under any enactment relating to social security;

(d) pension[1] or allowances payable in respect of disablement or disability;

(e) except in relation to a maintenance order, wages payable to a person as a seaman[2], other than wages payable to him as a seaman of a fishing boat;

(f) guaranteed minimum pension within the meaning of the Pension Schemes Act 1993.

(3) In subsection (2)(e) above,

"fishing boat" means a vessel of whatever size, and in whatever way propelled, which is for the time being employed in sea fishing or in the sea-fishing service;

"seaman" includes every person (except masters and pilots) employed or engaged in any capacity on board any ship; and

"wages" includes emoluments.

[Attachment of Earnings Act 1971, s 24, as amended by the Social Security Pensions Act 1975, Sch 4, the Merchant Shipping Act 1979, s 39, the Social Security Act 1985, Sch 4, the Social Security Act 1986, Sch 10, the Pension Schemes Act 1993, Sch 8, the Merchant Shipping Act 1995, Sch 13, SI 1998/3086 and the Tax Credits Act 2002, Sch 3.]

---

1. An "ill-health pension" payable under a pension scheme to a fireman on his premature retirement owing to arthritis was held not to be a pension payable in respect of disablement or disability because its amount depended wholly on length of pensionable service and not on the degree of disablement (*Miles v Miles* [1979] 1 All ER 865, [1979] 1 WLR 371).

2. The General Council of British Shipping may be approached for information on the whereabouts of registered seamen or for the address of their employer; see Home Office Circular No 124/1979, dated 31 July 1979.

1–1423   25. General interpretation.   (1) In this Act, except where the context otherwise requires—

"administration order" means an order made under, and so referred to in, Part VI of the County Courts Act 1984;

"the court" in relation to an attachment of earnings order, means the court which made the order, subject to rules of court as to the venue for, and the transfer of, proceedings in county courts and magistrates' courts;

"debtor" and "relevant adjudication" have the meanings given by section 2 of this Act;

"the employer", in relation to an attachment of earnings order, means the person who is required by the order to make deductions from earnings paid by him to the debtor;

"the fines officer", in relation to a debtor who is subject to a collection order made under Schedule 5 to the Courts Act 2003, means any fines officer working at the fines office specified in that order;

"judgment debt" has the meaning given by section 2 of this Act;

"maintenance order" has the meaning given by section 2 of this Act;

"maintenance payments" mean payments required under a maintenance order;

"prescribed" means prescribed by rules of court.

(2) Any reference in this Act to sums payable under a judgment or order, or to the payment of such sums, includes a reference to costs and the payment of them; and the references in sections 6(4)

and 12(2) to relevant costs are to any costs of the proceedings in which the attachment of earnings order in question was made, being costs which the debtor is liable to pay.

(3) References in section 6(5)(*b*), 9(3)(*b*) and 14(1)(*a*) of this Act to the debtor's needs include references to the needs of any person for whom he must, or reasonably may, provide.

(4) *Repealed.*

(5) Any power to make rules which is conferred by this Act is without prejudice to any other power to make rules of court.

(6) This Act, so far as it relates to magistrates' courts, and Part III of the Magistrates' Courts Act 1980 shall be construed as if this Act were contained in that Part.

(7) References in this Act to any enactment include references to that enactment as amended by or under any other enactment, including this Act.

[Attachment of Earnings Act 1971, s 25, as amended by the Legal Aid Act 1974, Sch 4, the Magistrates' Courts Act 1980, Sch 7, the Legal Aid Act 1982, s 14, the County Courts Act 1984, Sch 2, the Legal Aid Act 1988, Sch 5, the Dock Work Act 1989, Sch 1, the Access to Justice Act 1999, Sch 15, the Courts Act 2003, Sch 8 and SI 2006/1737.]

General

1–1424 26. Transitional provision. (1) As from that appointed day[1], an attachment of earnings order made before that day under Part II of the Maintenance Orders Act 1958 (including an order made under that Part of that Act as applied by section 46 or 79 of the Criminal Justice Act 1967) shall take effect as an attachment of earnings order made under the corresponding power in this Act, and the provisions of this Act shall apply to it accordingly, so far as they are capable of doing so.

(2) Rules of court[2] may make such provision as the rule-making authority considers requisite—

(*a*) for enabling an attachment of earnings order to which subsection (1) above applies to be varied so as to bring it into conformity, as from the appointed day, with the provisions of this Act, or to be replaced by an attachment of earnings order having effect as if made under the corresponding power in this Act;

(*b*) to secure that anything required or authorised by this Act to be done in relation to an attachment of earnings order made thereunder is required or, as the case may be, authorised to be done in relation to an attachment of earnings order to which the said subsection (1) applies.

(3) In this section, "the appointed day" means the day appointed under section 54 of the Administration of Justice Act 1970 for the coming into force of Part II of that Act.

[Attachment of Earnings Act 1971, s 26.]

---

1. The appointed day was August 2nd, 1971: see sub-s (3) below and the Administration of Justice Act 1970 (Commencement No 4) Order 1971, SI 1971/834.

2. See r 24 of the Magistrates' Courts (Attachment of Earnings) Rules 1971, this PART: STATUTORY INSTRUMENTS ON PROCEDURE, post.

SCHEDULE 1
MAINTENANCE ORDERS TO WHICH THIS ACT APPLIES

(*As amended by the Maintenance Orders (Reciprocal Enforcement) Act 1972, Sch, the Guardianship Act 1973, s 9, Children Act 1975, Sch 3, the Supplementary Benefits Act 1976, Sch 7, the Domestic Proceedings and Magistrates' Courts Act 1978, Sch 2, the Child Care Act 1980, Sch 5, the Civil Jurisdiction and Judgments Act 1982, Sch 12, the Social Security Act 1986, Sch 10, the Family Law Act 1987, Schs 2 and 4, the Children Act 1989, Sch 13, the Courts and Legal Services Act 1990, Sch 16, the Social Security (Consequential Provisions) Act 1992, Sch 2 and SI 2001/3929.*)

1–1425 1. An order for alimony, maintenance or other payments made, or having effect as if made, under Part II of the Matrimonial Causes Act [1973] [financial relief for parties to marriage and children of family].

2. An order for payments to or in respect of a child, being an order made, or having effect as if made, under Part III of the said Act of 1965 (maintenance of children following divorce, etc).

3. An order for periodical or other payments made, or having effect as if made, under Part II of the Matrimonial Causes Act 1973.

4. An order for maintenance or other payments to or in respect of a spouse or child, being an order made under Part I of the Domestic Proceedings and Magistrates' Courts Act 1978, Sch 2.

5. An order for periodical or other payments made or having effect as if made under Schedule 1 to the Children Act 1989.

6. *Repealed.*

7. An order under paragraph 23 of Schedule 2 to the Children Act 1989, section 23 of the Ministry of Social Security Act 1966, section 18 of the Supplementary Benefits Act 1976, section 24 of the Social Security Act 1986 or section 106 of the Social Security Administration Act 1992 (various provisions for obtaining contributions from a person whose dependants are assisted or maintained out of public funds).

8. An order under section 43 of the National Assistance Act 1948 (recovery of costs of maintaining assisted person).

9. An order to which section 16 of the Maintenance Orders Act 1950 applies by virtue of subsection (2)(*b*) or (*c*) of that section (that is to say an order made by a court in Scotland or Northern Ireland and corresponding to one of those specified in the foregoing paragraphs) and which has been registered in a court in England and Wales under Part II of that Act.

10. A maintenance order within the meaning of the Maintenance Orders (Facilities for Enforcement) Act 1920 (Commonwealth orders enforceable in the United Kingdom) registered in, or confirmed by, a court in England and Wales under that Act.

11. A maintenance order within the meaning of Part I of the Maintenance Orders (Reciprocal Enforcement) Act 1972 registered in a magistrates' court under the said Part I.

12. An order under section 34(1)(b) of the Children Act 1975 (payments of maintenance in respect of a child to his custodian).

13. A maintenance order within the meaning of Part I of the Civil Jurisdiction and Judgments Act 1982 which is registered in a magistrates' court under that Part.

14. A maintenance judgment within the meaning of Council Regulation (EC) No 44/2001 of 22nd December 2000 on jurisdiction and the recognition and enforcement of judgments in civil and commercial matters, which is registered in a magistrates' court under that Regulation.

SCHEDULE 3
DEDUCTIONS BY EMPLOYER UNDER ATTACHMENT OF EARNINGS ORDER

(As amended by the Social Security (Consequential Provisions) Act 1975, Sch 2, the Wages Councils Act 1979, Sch 6, the Administration of Justice Act 1982, s 54, the Wages Act 1986, Sch 4 and the Employment Rights Act 1996, Sch 1 and SI 2006/1737.)

PART I
SCHEME OF DEDUCTIONS
Preliminary definitions

1-1426 **1.** The following three paragraphs have effect for defining and explaining, for purposes of this Schedule, expressions used therein.

2. "Pay-day", in relation to earnings paid to a debtor, means an occasion on which they are paid.

3. "Attachable earnings", in relation to a pay-day, are the earnings which remain payable to the debtor on that day after deduction by the employer of—

(a) income tax;
(b) *repealed*
(bb) primary Class 1 contributions under Part I of the Social Security Act 1975;
(c) amounts deductible under any enactment, or in pursuance of a request in writing by the debtor, for the purposes of a superannuation scheme, namely any enactment, rules, deed or other instrument providing for the payment of annuities or lump sums—

   (i) to the persons with respect to whom the instrument has effect on their retirement at a specified age or on becoming incapacitated at some earlier age, or
   (ii) to the personal representatives or the widows, relatives or dependants of such persons on their death or otherwise,

whether with or without any further or other benefits.

4. (1) On any pay-day—

(a) "the normal deduction" is arrived at by applying the normal deduction rate (as specified in the relevant attachment of earnings order) with respect to the relevant period; and
(b) "the protected earnings" are arrived at by applying the protected earnings rate (as so specified) with respect to the said relevant period.

(2) For the purposes of this paragraph the relevant period in relation to any pay-day is the period beginning—

(a) if it is the first pay-day of the debtor's employment with the employer, with the first day of the employment; or
(b) if on the last pay-day earnings were paid in respect of a period falling wholly or partly after that payday, with the first day after the end of that period; or
(c) in any other case, with the first day after the last pay-day, and ending—

   (i) where earnings are paid in respect of a period falling wholly or partly after the pay-day, with the last day of that period; or
   (ii) in any other case, with the pay-day.

Employer's deduction (judgment debts and administration orders)

1-1427 **5.** In the case of an attachment of earnings order made to secure the payment of a judgment debt or payments under an administration order, the employer shall on any pay-day—

(a) if the attachable earnings exceed the protected earnings, deduct from the attachable earnings the amount of the excess or the normal deduction, whichever is the less;
(b) make no deduction if the attachable earnings are equal to, or less than, the protected earnings.

Employer's deduction (other cases)

6. (1) The following provision shall have effect in the case of an attachment of earnings order to which paragraph 5 above and paragraph 6A below do not apply.

(2) If on a pay-day the attachable earnings exceed the sum of—

(a) the protected earnings; and
(b) so much of any amount by which the attachable earnings on any previous pay-day fell short of the protected earnings as has not been made good by virtue of this sub-paragraph on another previous pay-day.

then, in so far as the excess allows, the employer shall deduct from the attachable earnings the amount specified in the following sub-paragraph.

(3) The said amount is the sum of—

(a) the normal deduction; and
(b) so much of the normal deduction on any previous pay-day as was not deducted on that day and has not been paid by virtue of this sub-paragraph on any other previous pay-day.

(4) No deduction shall be made on any pay-day when the attachable earnings are equal to, or less than, the protected earnings.

6A. In the case of an attachment of earnings order made under Schedule 5 to the Courts Act 2003, the employer shall make deductions from the debtor's earnings in accordance with fines collection regulations made under that Schedule.

PART II

PRIORITY AS BETWEEN ORDERS

1–1428   7. Where the employer is required to comply with two or more attachment of earnings orders in respect of the same debtor, all or none of which orders are made to secure either the payment or judgment debts or payments under an administration order, then on any pay-day the employer shall, for the purpose of complying with Part I of this Schedule—

    (a) deal with the orders according to the respective dates on which they were made, disregarding any later order until an earlier one has been dealt with;

    (b) deal with any later order as if the earnings to which it relates were the residue of the debtor's earnings after the making of any deduction to comply with any earlier order.

8. Where the employer is required to comply with two or more attachment of earnings orders, and one or more (but not all) of these orders are made to secure either the payment of judgment debts or payments under an administration order, then on any pay-day the employer shall, for the purpose of complying with Part I of this Schedule—

    (a) deal first with any order which is not made to secure the payment of a judgment debt or payments under an administration order (complying with paragraph 7 above if there are two or more such orders); and

    (b) deal thereafter with any order which is made to secure the payment of a judgment debt or payments under an administration order as if the earnings to which it relates were the residue of the debtor's earnings after the making of any deduction to comply with an order having priority by virtue of sub-paragraph (a) above; and

    (c) if there are two or more orders to which sub-paragraph (b) above applies, comply with paragraph 7 above in respect of those orders.

European Communities Act 1972[1]

(1972 c 68)

1–1430   2. General implementation of Treaties.   (1) All such rights, powers, liabilities, obligations and restrictions from time to time created or arising by or under the Treaties[2], and all such remedies and procedures from time to time provided for by or under the Treaties[2], as in accordance with the Treaties are without further enactment[3] to be given legal effect or used in the United Kingdom shall be recognised and available in law, and be enforced, allowed and followed accordingly; and the expression "enforceable Community right" and similar expressions shall be read as referring to one to which this subsection applies.

    (2) Subject to Schedule 2 to this Act, at any time after its passing Her Majesty may by Order in Council, and any designated Minister or department may by regulations[4], make provision—

    (a) for the purpose of implementing any Community obligation of the United Kingdom, or enabling any such obligation to be implemented, or of enabling any rights enjoyed or to be enjoyed by the United Kingdom under or by virtue of the Treaties to be exercised; or

    (b) for the purpose of dealing with matters arising out of or related to any such obligation or rights or the coming into force, or the operation from time to time, of subsection (1) above;

and in the exercise of any statutory power or duty, including any power to give directions or to legislate by means of orders, rules, regulations or other subordinate instrument, the person entrusted with the power or duty may have regard to the objects of the Communities and to any such obligation or rights as aforesaid.

    In this subsection "designated Minister or department" means such Minister of the Crown or government department as may from time to time be designated by Order in Council in relation to any matter or for any purpose, but subject to such restrictions or conditions (if any) as may be specified by the Order in Council.

    (3) *Charges on Consolidated Fund.*

    (4) The provision that may be made under subsection (2) above includes, subject to Schedule 2 to this Act, any such provision (of any such extent) as might be made by Act of Parliament, and any enactment passed or to be passed, other than one contained in this Part of this Act, shall be construed and have effect subject to the foregoing provisions of this section; but, except as may be provided by any Act passed after this Act, Schedule 2 shall have effect in connection with the powers conferred by this and the following sections of this Act to make Orders in Council and regulations.

    (5) and (6) *Northern Ireland, Channel Islands etc.*

[European Communities Act 1972, s 2.]

---

    1. Amended by the European Communities (Amendment) Act 2002 (not reproduced), but without affecting the provisions reproduced in this work.

    The European Communities Act 1972 is a 'constitutional' statute which may only be repealed by specific provision and thus may not be impliedly repealed. Further, as there is generally no inconsistency between a provision conferring a power to amend future legislation and the terms of any such legislation, in the absence of any specific provision to the contrary, regulations made under s 2(2) may repeal a statute enacted subsequently to the 1972 Act (*Thoburn v Sunderland City Council* [2002] EWHC Admin 195 (Admin), [2003] QB 151, [2002] 4 All ER 156, 166 JP 257).

    2. These are the Treaties creating the EEC, together with any ancillary treaties, and the Treaty of Accession whereby the UK became a member of the Community (s 1). They are thus part of UK law. Certain provisions of the Treaty

establishing the European Economic Community which may be referred to in proceedings in magistrates' courts are set out in PART VIII: title EUROPEAN COMMUNITIES, post.

3. EEC Regulations have direct and binding effect as law; Directives and Decisions are generally implemented by Act of Parliament or Statutory Instrument and until then have no force in the UK.

4. Schedule 2 to the Act enables penalty provisions to be included. The Criminal Law Act 1977, s 32 put the maximum daily fine following summary conviction up to £100.

Regulations made under s 2 of this Act, which are relevant to the work of magistrates' courts, are referred to in the preliminary note to each title in PART VIII.

1–1431   3. Decisions on, and proof of, Treaties and Community instruments etc.   (1) For the purposes of all legal proceedings any question as to the meaning or effect of any of the Treaties, or as to the validity, meaning or effect of any Community instrument, shall be treated as a question of law[1] (and, if not referred to the European Court[2], be for determination as such in accordance with the principles laid down by and any relevant decision of the European Court[3] or any court attached thereto).

(2) Judicial notice shall be taken of the Treaties[4], of the Official Journal of the Communities[4] and of any decision of, or expression of opinion by, the European Court or any court attached thereto on any such question as aforesaid; and the Official Journal shall be admissible as evidence of any instrument or other act thereby communicated of any of the Communities or of any Community institution.

(3) Evidence of any instrument issued by a Community institution, including any judgment or order of the European Court or any court attached thereto, or of any document in the custody of a Community institution, or any entry in or extract from such a document, may be given in any legal proceedings by production of a copy certified as a true copy by an official of that institution; and any document purporting to be such a copy shall be received in evidence without proof of the official position or handwriting of the person signing the certificate.

(4) Evidence of any Community instrument may also be given in any legal proceedings—

(a) by production of a copy purporting to be printed by the Queen's Printer;
(b) where the instrument is in the custody of a government department (including a department of the Government of Northern Ireland), by production of a copy certified on behalf of the department to be a true copy by an officer of the department generally or specially authorised so to do;

and any document purporting to be such a copy as is mentioned in paragraph (b) above of an instrument in the custody of a department shall be received in evidence without proof of the official position or handwriting of the person signing the certificate, or of his authority to do so, or the document being in the custody of the department.

[European Communities Act 1972, s 3 as amended by the European Communities (Amendment) Act 1986, s 2.]

---

1. It may not be treated as a matter of fact, and it is accordingly not proper to seek to call expert evidence as would be the case when considering other systems of law.

The issue whether a prohibition on importation imposed by UK legislation is ineffective by virtue of art 30 of the EEC Treaty, in PART VIII: title EUROPEAN COMMUNITIES, post, which prohibits quantitative restrictions on imports between member states of the EEC, or is "justified on grounds of public policy or public security or the protection of life", within art 36 of the treaty, is a question regarding the meaning or effect of the EEC Treaty which, by virtue of s 3(1) is to be treated as a question of law (*R v Goldstein* [1983] 1 All ER 434, [1983] 1 WLR 151, HL).

2. Article 177 of the Treaty of Rome enables the European Court of Justice at Luxembourg to give preliminary rulings concerning interpretation of the Treaty, and validity and interpretation of acts of the institutions of the Community, and the interpretation of the statutes of bodies established by an act of the Council, where those statutes so provide.

Before requesting such a ruling, a magistrates' court ought to be sure; (1) that a decision on the question is necessary to enable it to give judgment; (2) that it cannot interpret the provision clearly, according to the principles and decisions of the European Court; (3) that it is a question of *interpretation* and not *application* of a Community provision, because only the former is referable; (4) that it is indeed a Community provision, because English law originating in Parliament is not referable; (5) that the question could not equally well be resolved by stating a case for the opinion of the High Court.

In reaching a conclusion, the court should put in the balance the expense, delay and hardship to the parties likely to be caused by a reference to Luxembourg (see *H P Bulmer Ltd v J Bollinger SA* [1974] Ch 401, [1974] 2 All ER 1226), and any question of interpretation should be so expressed clearly, and not mixed up with questions of fact in the case. " . . . In a criminal trial upon indictment it can seldom be a proper exercise of the presiding judge's discretion to seek a preliminary ruling before the facts of the alleged offence have been ascertained. . . . It is generally better, as the judge himself put it, that the question be decided by him in the first instance and reviewed hereafter if necessary through the hierarchy of the national courts", *per* LORD DIPLOCK in *R v Henn* [1980] 2 All ER 166. In the ordinary case it would be highly undesirable for justices to decide to refer until all the evidence had been called and until satisfied that the defendant would not be acquitted on the facts; however where there is a submission of no case to answer at the end of the prosecution case a decision on a question of community law might be necessary before the court could rule on such a submission (*R v Plymouth Justices, ex p Rogers* [1982] QB 863, [1982] 2 All ER 175, 75 Cr App Rep 64).

A reference by a magistrates' court to the European Court is a step in the proceedings before the magistrates' court and as such may be covered by a legal aid order under s 28(2) of the Legal Aid 1974, (repealed, but see now s 19(2) of the Legal Aid Act 1988, post), (*R v Marlborough Street Stipendiary Magistrate, ex p Bouchereau* [1977] 3 All ER 365, 142 JP 27).

3. These are variously reported; the most important rule is that in the event of conflict between a Community provision and the law of an individual member state, the Community provision shall prevail.

Section 2   SCHEDULE 2
                          PROVISIONS AS TO SUBORDINATE LEGISLATION

(As amended by the Criminal Law Act 1977, ss 28 and 32, the Customs and Excise Duties (General Reliefs) Act 1979, Sch 2, the Criminal Justice Act 1982, s 46 and the Legislative and Regulatory Reform Act 2006, s 28.)

1–1432   1. (1) The powers conferred by section 2(2) of this Act to make provision for the purposes mentioned in section 2(2)(a) and (b) shall not include power—

(a) to make any provision imposing or increasing taxation; or
(b) to make any provision taking effect from a date earlier than that of the making of the instrument containing the provision; or
(c) to confer any power to legislate by means of orders, rules, regulations or other subordinate instrument, other than rules of procedure for any court or tribunal; or
(d) to create any new criminal offence punishable with imprisonment for more than two years or punishable on summary conviction with imprisonment for more than three months* or with a fine of more than level 5 on the standard scale (if not calculated on a daily basis) or with a fine of more than £100 a day.

(2) Sub-paragraph (1)(c) above shall not be taken to preclude the modification of a power to legislate conferred otherwise than under section 2(2), or the extension of any such power to purposes of the like nature as those for which it was conferred; and a power to give directions as to matters of administration is not to be regarded as a power to legislate within the meaning of sub-paragraph (1)(c).*

1A. (1) Where—

(a) subordinate legislation makes provision for a purpose mentioned in section 2(2) of this Act,
(b) the legislation contains a reference to a Community instrument or any provision of a Community instrument, and
(c) it appears to the person making the legislation that it is necessary or expedient for the reference to be construed as a reference to that instrument or that provision as amended from time to time,

the subordinate legislation may make express provision to that effect.

(2) In this paragraph "subordinate legislation" means any Order in Council, order, rules, regulations, scheme, warrant, byelaws or other instrument made after the coming into force of this paragraph under any Act, Act of the Scottish Parliament or Northern Ireland legislation passed or made before or after the coming into force of this paragraph.

2. (1) Subject to paragraph 3 below, where a provision contained in any section of this Act confers power to make any order, rules, regulations or scheme (otherwise than by modification or extension of an existing power), the power shall be exercisable by statutory instrument.

(2) Any statutory instrument containing an Order in Council or any order, rules, regulations or scheme made in the exercise of a power so conferred, if made without a draft having been approved by resolution of each House of Parliament, shall be subject to annulment in pursuance of a resolution of either House.

2A. (1) This paragraph applies where, pursuant to paragraph 2(2) above, a draft of a statutory instrument containing provision made in exercise of the power conferred by section 2(2) of this Act is laid before Parliament for approval by resolution of each House of Parliament and—

(a) the instrument also contains provision made in exercise of a power conferred by any other enactment; and
(b) apart from this paragraph, any of the conditions in sub-paragraph (2) below applies in relation to the instrument so far as containing that provision.

(2) The conditions referred to in sub-paragraph (1)(b) above are that—

(a) the instrument, so far as containing the provision referred to in sub-paragraph (1)(a) above, is by virtue of any enactment subject to annulment in pursuance of a resolution of either House of Parliament;
(b) the instrument so far as containing that provision is by virtue of any enactment required to be laid before Parliament after being made and to be approved by resolution of each House of Parliament in order to come into or remain in force;
(c) in a case not falling within paragraph (a) or (b) above, the instrument so far as containing that provision is by virtue of any enactment required to be laid before Parliament after being made;
(d) the instrument or a draft of the instrument so far as containing that provision is not by virtue of any enactment required at any time to be laid before Parliament.

(3) Where this paragraph applies in relation to the draft of a statutory instrument—

(a) the instrument, so far as containing the provision referred to in sub-paragraph (1)(a) above, may not be made unless the draft is approved by a resolution of each House of Parliament;
(b) in a case where the condition in sub-paragraph (2)(a) above is satisfied, the instrument so far as containing that provision is not subject to annulment in pursuance of a resolution of either House of Parliament;
(c) in a case where the condition in sub-paragraph (2)(b) above is satisfied, the instrument is not required to be laid before Parliament after being made (and accordingly any requirement that the instrument be approved by each House of Parliament in order for it to come into or remain in force does not apply); and
(d) in a case where the condition in sub-paragraph (2)(c) above is satisfied, the instrument so far as containing that provision is not required to be laid before Parliament after being made.

(4) In this paragraph, references to an enactment are to an enactment passed or made before or after the coming into force of this paragraph.

2B. (1) This paragraph applies where, pursuant to paragraph 2(2) above, a statutory instrument containing provision made in exercise of the power conferred by section 2(2) of this Act is laid before Parliament under section 5 of the Statutory Instruments Act 1946 (instruments subject to annulment) and—

(a) the instrument also contains provision made in exercise of a power conferred by any other enactment; and
(b) apart from this paragraph, either of the conditions in sub-paragraph (2) below applies in relation to the instrument so far as containing that provision.

(2) The conditions referred to in sub-paragraph (1)(b) above are that—

(a) the instrument so far as containing the provision referred to in sub-paragraph (1)(a) above is by virtue of any enactment required to be laid before Parliament after being made but—

(i) is not subject to annulment in pursuance of a resolution of either House of Parliament; and
(ii) is not by virtue of any enactment required to be approved by resolution of each House of Parliament in order to come into or remain in force;

(b) the instrument or a draft of the instrument so far as containing that provision is not by virtue of any enactment required at any time to be laid before Parliament.

(3) Where this paragraph applies in relation to a statutory instrument, the instrument, so far as containing the

provision referred to in sub-paragraph (1)(*a*) above, is subject to annulment in pursuance of a resolution of either House of Parliament.

(4) In this paragraph, references to an enactment are to an enactment passed or made before or after the coming into force of this paragraph.

2C. Paragraphs 2A and 2B above apply to a Scottish statutory instrument containing provision made in the exercise of the power conferred by section 2(2) of this Act (and a draft of any such instrument) as they apply to any other statutory instrument containing such provision (or, as the case may be, any draft of such an instrument), but subject to the following modifications—

(*a*) references to Parliament and to each or either House of Parliament are to be read as references to the Scottish Parliament;

(*b*) references to an enactment include an enactment comprised in, or in an instrument made under, an Act of the Scottish Parliament; and

(*c*) the reference in paragraph 2B(1) to section 5 of the Statutory Instruments Act 1946 is to be read as a reference to article 11 of the Scotland Act 1998 (Transitory and Transitional Provisions) (Statutory Instruments) Order 1999 (SI 1999/1096).

3. *Northern Ireland.*

4. *Power to make orders.*

*Sub-paragraph (1) amended and sup-para (3) inserted by the Criminal Justice Act 2003, Sch 27 from a date to be appointed.

Local Government Act 1972
(1972 c 70)

PART X
JUDICIAL AND RELATED MATTERS

1–1530   216. Adaptation of law relating to old counties. (1) For the purposes of commissions of the peace and the law relating to justices of the peace, magistrates' courts, the custos rotulorum, lieutenants, sheriffs and matters connected with any of those matters, new counties shall, without prejudice to section 179(1) above, be substituted for counties of any other description.

(2) For the purposes of this section and sections 218 and 219 below the Isles of Scilly shall be deemed to form part of the county of Cornwall.
[Local Government Act 1972, s 216, as amended by the Justices of the Peace Act 1979, Sch 3.]

Administration of Justice Act 1973
(1973 c 15)

PART II

1–1540   9. Judicial salaries and pensions. Section 9 provides that judicial salaries (including those of District Judges (Magistrates' Courts)) shall be such as may be determined by the Lord Chancellor, with the consent of the Minister for the Civil Service.
[Administration of Justice Act 1973, s 9, amended by the Criminal Law Act 1977, Sch 12, the Justices of the Peace Act 1979, Sch 2, the Supreme Court Act 1981, Sch 7, the Courts and Legal Services Act 1990, Sch 20, the Justices of the Peace Act 1997, Sch 5, the Access to Justice Act 1999, Sch 11 and prospectively amended by the Justice (Northern Ireland) Act 2002, Sch 12 from a date to be appointed—summarised.]

SCHEDULES

Sections 5 and 20   SCHEDULE 1

(*As amended by the Administration of Justice Act 1977, Schs 2 and 5, the Justices of the Peace Act 1979, Schs 2 and 3, the Judicial Pensions Act 1981, Sch 4, the Local Government Act 1985, Sch 17, the Justices of the Peace Act 1997, Sch 5 and SI 2002/1057.*)

PART II
SUPPLEMENTAL LIST FOR ENGLAND AND WALES

1–1541   4–6. *Repealed.*

7. Any such act as is mentioned in section 9(2)(*a*) to (*c*) of the Justices of the Peace Act 1997, where it may be done by a justice of the peace, may, subject to any express provision made to the contrary by any enactment or instrument relating to that act, be done also by any person who is mayor of a London borough or chairman of a county or district council in England or Wales.

7A. Where the council of a London borough are operating executive arrangements, which involve a mayor and cabinet executive or a mayor and council manager executive, paragraph 7 shall have effect as if for the expression "mayor of a London borough" there were substituted "chairman of a London borough".

7B. In this Part, "executive arrangements", "mayor and cabinet executive" and "mayor and council manager executive" have the same meaning as in Part II of the Local Government Act 2000.

Litigants in Person (Costs and Expenses) Act 1975
(1975 c 47)

1–1542   1. Costs or expenses recoverable. (1) Where, in any proceedings to which this subsection applies, any costs of a litigant in person are ordered to be paid by any other party to the proceedings or in any other way, there may, subject to rules of court[1], be allowed on the taxation or other determination of those costs sums in respect of any work done, and any expenses and losses incurred, by the litigant in or in connection with the proceedings to which the order relates.

This subsection applies to civil proceedings—

(a) in a county court, in the Supreme Court or in the House of Lords on appeal from the High Court or the Court of Appeal,*

(b) before the Lands Tribunal or the Lands Tribunal for Northern Ireland, or

(c) in or before any other court or tribunal specified in an order[2] made under this subsection by the Lord Chancellor.

(2)–(5)
[Litigants in Person (Costs and Expenses) Act 1975, s 1.]

---

*Amended by the Constitutional Reform Act 2005, Sch 11 from a date to be appointed.
1. Ie rules made under s 144 of the Magistrates' Courts Act 1980. See the Magistrates' Courts Rules 1981, this PART, post.
2. Civil proceedings in magistrates' courts are specified for the purposes of this subsection by the Litigants in Person (Costs and Expenses) (Magistrates' Courts) Order 2001, SI 2001/3438

1–1543 **2.** *Short title, commencement and extent*

Bail Act 1976[1]
(1976 c 63)

PRELIMINARY

1–1560 **1. Meaning of "bail in criminal proceedings"[2].** (1) In this Act "bail in criminal proceedings" means—

(a) bail grantable in or in connection with proceedings for an offence to a person who is accused or convicted of the offence, or

(b) bail grantable in connection with an offence to a person who is under arrest for the offence or for whose arrest for the offence a warrant (endorsed for bail) is being issued, or

(c) bail grantable in connection with extradition proceedings in respect of an offence[3].

(2) In this Act "bail" means bail grantable under the law (including common law) for the time being in force.

(3) Except as provided by section 13(3) of this Act, this section does not apply to bail in or in connection with proceedings outside England and Wales.

(4) *Repealed.*

(5) This section applies—

(a) whether the offence was committed in England or Wales or elsewhere, and

(b) whether it is an offence under the law of England and Wales, or of any other country or territory.

(6) Bail in criminal proceedings shall be granted (and in particular shall be granted unconditionally or conditionally) in accordance with this Act.
[Bail Act 1976, s 1 as amended by the Criminal Justice and Public Order Act 1994, Sch 11 and the Extradition Act 2003, s 198(1).]

---

1. Under the Human Rights Act 1998, this Act, so far as it is possible to do so, must be read and given effect in a way which is compatible with the Convention rights; in particular art 5(3) and 5(4) of the Convention. Under art 5(3) a person charged with an offence must be released pending trial unless the prosecuting authorities can show that there are "relevant and sufficient" reasons to justify his continued detention: *Wemhoff v Germany* (1979) 1 EHRR 55. This requires the exercise of judicial discretion: *CC v United Kingdom* (1999) EHRLR 210.

The European Court of Human Rights has identified four grounds upon which pre-trial detention may be justified under the Convention—

1. fear of absconding;
2. interference with the course of justice;
3. the prevention of crime; and
4. the preservation of public order.

In each case something more than generalised assertions is needed and in some cases, supporting evidence must be provided in support of any objection to bail: *Clooth v Belgium* (1991) 14 EHRR 717. Moreover, under art 5(4) of the Convention disclosure of documentation relevant to the question of bail may be required: *Lamy v Belgium* (1989) 11 EHRR 529.

Article 5 generally requires that the accused and his legal representative be present at an oral hearing for the determination of bail: *Keus v Switzerland* (1990) 13 EHRR 700). Article 5(3) requires the court to "examine" all the facts relevant to the question of bail and to give reasons for its decision: *Letellier v France* (1992) 14 EHRR 83. Article 5(3) also requires the court to permit renewed applications at reasonable intervals: *Bezicheri v Italy* (1989) 12 EHRR 210.

Permissible conditions of bail under art 5(3) include a requirement to surrender travel documents (*Stögmüller v Austria* (1969) 1 EHRR 155, *Schmidt v Austria* 44 DR 195); the imposition of a residence requirement (*Schmidt v Austria* above); and the provision of a sum of money as a surety or security (*Wemhoff v Germany* (1979) 1 EHRR 155).

2. This Act applies only to bail in criminal proceedings and has no application to proceedings which do not come within the definition. A full examination of the historical background of bail prior to the passing of this Act may be found in the

Report of the Home Office Working Party entitled "Bail Procedures in Magistrates' Courts" and published by HMSO in 1974.

3. Para 1(*c*) does not apply in relation to extradition requests received and extraditions made on or before 31 December 2003.

1–1561   2. Other definitions.   (1) In this Act, unless the context otherwise requires, "conviction" includes—

    (*a*) a finding of guilt,

    (*b*) a finding that a person is not guilty by reason of insanity,

    (*c*) a finding under section 11(1) the Powers of Criminal Courts (Sentencing) Act 2000 (remand for medical examination) that the person in question did the act or made the omission charged, and

    (*d*) a conviction of an offence for which an order is made placing the offender on probation or discharging him absolutely or conditionally,

and "convicted" shall be construed accordingly.

    (2) In this Act, unless the context otherwise requires—

"bail hostel" means premises for accommodation of persons remanded on bail,

"child" means a person under the age of fourteen,

"court" includes a judge of a court, or a justice of the peace and, in the case of a specified court, includes a judge or (as the case may be) justice having powers to act in connection with proceedings before that court,

"Courts-Martial Appeal rules" means rules made under section 49 of the Courts-Martial (Appeals) Act 1968,

"extradition proceedings" means proceedings under the Extradition Act 2003,[1]

"offence" includes an alleged offence,

"probation hostel" means premises for the accommodation of persons who may be required to reside there by a probation order,

"prosecutor", in relation to extradition proceedings, means the person acting on behalf of the territory to which extradition is sought,[1]

"surrender to custody" means, in relation to a person released on bail, surrendering himself into the custody of the court or of the constable (according to the requirements of the grant of bail) at the time and place for the time being appointed for him to do so[2],

"vary", in relation to bail, means imposing further conditions after bail is granted, or varying or rescinding conditions,

"young person" means a person who has attained the age of fourteen and is under the age of seventeen.

    (3) Where an enactment (whenever passed) which relates to bail in criminal proceedings refers to the person bailed appearing before a court it is to be construed unless the context otherwise requires as referring to his surrendering himself into the custody of the court.

    (4) Any reference in this Act to any other enactment is a reference thereto as amended, and includes a reference thereto as extended or applied, by or under any other enactment, including this Act.

[Bail Act 1976, s 2, as amended by the Criminal Law Act 1977, Schs 12 and 13, the Magistrates' Courts Act 1980, Sch 7, the Criminal Justice Act 1988, Sch 15, the Extradition Act 1989, s 36, the Powers of Criminal Courts (Sentencing) Act 2000, Sch 9, the Extradition Act 2003, s 198(1) and the Courts Act 2003, Sch 8.]

---

    1. Definitions "extradition proceedings" and "prosecutor" do not apply in relation to extradition requests received and extraditions made on or before 31 December 2003.

    2. A surrender to the custody of the court occurs when a defendant on bail and under a duty to surrender is required to attend the court and responds by attending the court and overtly subjecting himself to the direction of the court (*R v Central Criminal Court, ex p Guney* [1995] 2 All ER 577, [1995] 2 Cr App Rep 350, CA); decision of Court of Appeal affirmed by the House of Lords [1996] AC 616, [1996] 2 All ER 705). Where a defendant has reported to a court official deputed for that purpose, he has surrendered to custody; where he is allowed to remain at liberty until his case is called on, he should be clearly instructed not to leave the court building without consent as otherwise there could be problems in issuing a warrant under s 7(2), post (*DPP v Richards* [1988] QB 701, [1988] 3 All ER 406, 152 JP 333). In *E v DPP* [2002] All ER (D) 348 (Feb) a youth was remanded into the care of the local authority, in secure accommodation, and had been brought to court by the persons who were responsible for him. Owing to lack of space he was not detained there in secure accommodation. He absconded before his case was called on. An argument that he was not under the direct control of the youth offending team and thus not in lawful custody was rejected and he was liable for escaping from lawful custody. "Lawful custody" in such cases is a question of fact. Similarly, in *H v DPP* [2003] EWHC Admin 878, 167 JP 486 a youth escaped from lawful custody where, having been remanded to local authority accommodation under s 23 of the Children and Young Persons Act 1969 without any security condition, he absconded whilst being told to wait on the steps outside the youth court as he was under the direct control of a member of the youth offending team following his remand. In *R v Rumble* [2003] EWCA Crim 770, 167 JP 205 the defendant absconded from the dock when a custodial sentence was pronounced, there being no security officers in court. Rejecting an argument based on *E v DPP* supra, that he was not under the direct control of anyone in the court room, once a person has surrendered at the court, the court's right to control him does not depend on the precise nature of the physical constraints imposed on him. For sentence in cases of escape, see para **3–240** in PART III: SENTENCING, ante.

Incidents of bail in criminal proceedings

1–1562   3. General provisions.   (1) A person granted bail in criminal proceedings shall be under a duty to surrender to custody[1], and that duty is enforceable in accordance with section 6 of this Act.

    (2) No recognizance for his surrender to custody shall be taken from him.

(3) Except as provided by this section—

 (a) no security for his surrender to custody shall be taken from him,
 (b) he shall not be required to provide a surety or sureties for his surrender to custody, and
 (c) no other requirement shall be imposed on him as a condition of bail.

(4) He may be required, before release on bail, to provide a surety or sureties[2] to secure his surrender to custody.

(5) He may be required, before release on bail, to give security[3] for his surrender to custody. The security may be given by him or on his behalf.

(6) He may be required[4] to comply, before release on bail or later, with such requirements as appear to the court to be necessary—

 (a) to secure that he surrenders to custody,
 (b) to secure that he does not commit an offence while on bail[5],
 (c) to secure that he does not interfere with witnesses or otherwise obstruct the course of justice whether in relation to himself or any other person,
 (ca) for his own protection or, if he is a child or young person, for his own welfare or in his own interests,
 (d) to secure that he makes himself available for the purpose of enabling inquiries or a report to be made to assist the court in dealing with him for the offence,
 (e) to secure that before the time appointed for him to surrender to custody, he attends an interview with an authorised advocate or authorised litigator, as defined by section 119(1) of the Courts and Legal Services Act 1990,

and, in any Act, "the normal powers to impose conditions of bail" means the powers to impose conditions under paragraph (a), (b), (c) or (ca) above.

(6ZAA) Subject to section 3AA below, if he is a child or young person he may be required to comply with requirements imposed for the purpose of securing the electronic monitoring of his compliance with any other requirement imposed on him as a condition of bail.

(6ZA) Where he is required under subsection (6) above to reside in a bail hostel or probation hostel, he may also be required to comply with the rules of the hostel.

(6A) In the case of a person accused of murder the court granting bail shall, unless it considers that satisfactory reports on his mental condition have already been obtained, impose as conditions of bail—

 (a) a requirement that the accused shall undergo examination by two medical practitioners for the purpose of enabling such reports[6] to be prepared; and
 (b) a requirement that he shall for that purpose attend such an institution or place as the court directs and comply with any other directions which may be given to him for that purpose by either of those practitioners.

(6B) Of the medical practitioners referred to in subsection (6A) above at least one shall be a practitioner approved for the purposes of section 12 of the Mental Health Act 1983.

(6C) Subsection (6D) below applies where—

 (a) the court has been notified[7] by the Secretary of State that arrangements for conducting a relevant assessment or, as the case may be, providing relevant follow-up have been made for the petty sessions area in which it appears to the court that the person referred to in subsection (6D) would reside if granted bail; and
 (b) the notice has not been withdrawn.

(6D) In the case of a person ("P")—

 (a) in relation to whom paragraphs (a) to (c) of paragraph 6B(1) of Part 1 of Schedule 1 to this Act apply;
 (b) who, after analysis of the sample referred to in paragraph (b) of that paragraph, has been offered a relevant assessment or, if a relevant assessment has been carried out, has had relevant follow-up proposed to him; and
 (c) who has agreed to undergo the relevant assessment or, as the case may be, to participate in the relevant follow-up,

the court, if it grants bail, shall impose as a condition of bail that P both undergo the relevant assessment and participate in any relevant follow-up proposed to him or, if a relevant assessment has been carried out, that P participate in the relevant follow-up.

(6E) In subsections (6C) and (6D) above—

 (a) "relevant assessment" means an assessment conducted by a suitably qualified person of whether P is dependent upon or has a propensity to misuse any specified Class A drugs;
 (b) "relevant follow-up" means, in a case where the person who conducted the relevant assessment believes P to have such a dependency or propensity, such further assessment, and such assistance or treatment (or both) in connection with the dependency or propensity, as the person who conducted the relevant assessment (or conducts any later assessment) considers to be appropriate in P's case,

and in paragraph (a) above "Class A drug" and "misuse" have the same meaning as in the Misuse of Drugs Act 1971, and "specified" (in relation to a Class A drug) has the same meaning as in Part 3 of the Criminal Justice and Court Services Act 2000.

(6F) In subsection (6E)(a) above, "suitably qualified person" means a person who has such qualifications or experience as are from time to time specified by the Secretary of State for the purposes of this subsection.

(7) If a parent or guardian of a child or young person consents to be surety[1] for the child or young person for the purposes of this subsection, the parent or guardian may be required to secure that the child or young person complies with any requirement imposed on him by virtue of subsection (6), (6ZAA) or (6A) above, but—

(a) no requirement shall be imposed on the parent or the guardian of a young person by virtue of this subsection where it appears that the young person will attain the age of seventeen before the time to be appointed for him to surrender to custody; and

(b) the parent or guardian shall not be required to secure compliance with any requirement to which his consent does not extend and shall not, in respect of those requirements to which his consent does extend, be bound in a sum greater than £50.

(8) Where a court has granted bail in criminal proceedings that court or, where that court has committed a person on bail to the Crown Court for trial or to be sentenced or otherwise dealt with, that court[8] or the Crown Court may on application—

(a) by or on behalf of the person to whom bail was granted, or

(b) by the prosecutor or a constable,

vary the conditions of bail or impose conditions in respect of bail which has been granted unconditionally[9].

(8A) Where a notice of transfer is given under a relevant transfer provision, subsection (8) above shall have effect in relation to a person in relation to whose case the notice is given as if he had been committed on bail to the Crown Court for trial.

(8B) Subsection (8) above applies where a court has sent a person on bail to the Crown Court for trial under section 51 of the Crime and Disorder Act 1998 as it applies where a court has committed a person on bail to the Crown Court for trial.

(9) This section is subject to subsection (3) of section 11 of the Powers of Criminal Courts (Sentencing) Act 2000 (conditions of bail on remand for medical examination).

(10)[910] In subsection (8A) above "relevant transfer provision" means—

(a) section 4 of the Criminal Justice Act 1987, or

(b) section 53 of the Criminal Justice Act 1991.

(10)[10] This section is subject, in its application to bail granted by a constable, to section 3A of this Act.

[Bail Act 1976, s 3, as amended by the Criminal Law Act 1977, Sch 12, the Magistrates' Courts Act 1980, Sch 7, the Mental Health (Amendment) Act 1982, s 34, the Mental Health Act 1983, Sch 4, the Criminal Justice Act 1987, Sch 2, the Criminal Justice Act 1988, s 131, the Criminal Justice and Public Order Act 1994, s 27 and Schs 9 and 11, the Crime and Disorder Act 1998, s 54 and Schs 8 and 10, the Powers of Criminal Courts (Sentencing) Act 2000, Sch 9, the Criminal Justice and Police Act 2001, s 131 and the Criminal Justice Act 2003, s 41.]

---

1. "Surrender to custody" is defined in s 2(1), supra.

2. For further provisions concerning sureties, see s 8, post.

3. The power to order forfeiture of a security is contained in s 5(7)–(9), post. A security should normally be an asset, which can be readily forfeited on the defendant's non-appearance eg cash or a banker's draft, to avoid problems of valuation, storage or conversion. Where a third party has made an asset available to the defendant as a security, the court is not concerned with the arrangement between them and where forfeiture is contemplated, there is no requirement to serve notice on the third party (*R (Stevens) v Truro Magistrates' Court* [2001] EWHC Admin 558, [2002] 1 WLR 144).

4. Notwithstanding the absence in Part II of Sch 1, post, of a paragraph similar to para 8 of Pt I of that Schedule, conditions may be imposed in cases involving non-imprisonable offences (*R v Bournemouth Magistrates' Court, ex p Cross, Griffin and Pamment* (1988) 153 JP 440, 89 Cr App Rep 90, [1989] Crim LR 207).

5. All that is required of magistrates before they impose this condition is that they perceive a real and not a fanciful risk of the person bailed committing an offence while on bail. In deciding whether to impose a particular condition magistrates have a wide discretion to inquire whether the condition is necessary and are entitled to use their knowledge of local events and conditions (*R v Mansfield Justices, ex p Sharkey* [1985] 1 QB 613, [1985] 1 All ER 193, 149 JP 129). Where is defendant is remanded on bail subject to a condition to remain indoors at a particular address between stated times, the justices can impose a further, doorstep 'presenting' condition to buttress the curfew, though it will always remain a question as to whether or not that particular power should be exercised in a particular case to meet the requirements of s 3(6) of the Bail Act 1976 (*R (on the application of the Crown Prosecution Service) v Chorley Justices* [2002] EWHC 2162 (Admin), (2002) 166 JP 764.

6. The Crown Court may order the payment out of central funds of such sums as appear to it reasonably sufficient to compensate any medical practitioner for the expenses, trouble or loss of time properly incurred by him in preparing and making a report to the court on the mental condition of a person accused of murder (Mental Health (Amendment) Act 1982, s 34(5)).

7. Pilot courts were notified with effect from May 2004 (HOC 22/2004) and further pilot sites were notified with effect from 31 January 2005 and 1 April 2005 (HOC 1/2005).

8. During the period between the committal to the Crown Court and the surrender to the custody of the Crown Court, the magistrates and the Crown Court enjoy a concurrent jurisdiction in relation to applications to vary conditions of bail. Where an accused has surrendered to the custody of the Crown Court and is released on bail, application to vary conditions may thereafter only be made to the Crown Court (*R v Lincoln Magistrates' Court, ex p Mawer* (1995) 160 JP 219, [1995] Crim LR 878).

9. Consideration ought to be given to warning sureties that conditions might be varied, especially if they were concerned about those conditions (*R v Wells Street Magistrates' Court, ex p Albanese* [1982] QB 333, [1981] 3 All ER 769, 146 JP 177).

10. Two subsections (10) have been inserted by the Criminal Justice and Public Order Act 1994; the first was inserted by Sch 9, para 12, the Criminal Justice and Public Order Act 1994, and the second by s 27(2), the Criminal Justice and Public Order Act 1994.

1–1562A   3AA. Electronic monitoring of compliance with bail conditions. (1) A court shall not impose on a child or young person a requirement under section 3(6ZAA) above (an 'electronic monitoring requirement') unless each of the following conditions is satisfied.

(2) The first condition is that the child or young person has attained the age of twelve years.

(3) The second condition is that—

(a) the child or young person is charged with or has been convicted of a violent or sexual offence, or an offence punishable in the case of an adult with imprisonment for a term of fourteen years or more; or

(b) he is charged with or has been convicted of one or more imprisonable offences which, together with any other imprisonable offences of which he has been convicted in any proceedings—

(i) amount, or

(ii) would, if he were convicted of the offences with which he is charged, amount,

to a recent history of repeatedly committing imprisonable offences while remanded on bail or to local authority accommodation.

(4) The third condition is that the court—

(a) has been notified[1] by the Secretary of State that electronic monitoring arrangements are available in each petty sessions area which is a relevant area; and

(b) is satisfied that the necessary provision can be made under those arrangements.

(5) The fourth condition is that a youth offending team has informed the court that in its opinion the imposition of such a requirement will be suitable in the case of the child or young person.

(6) Where a court imposes an electronic monitoring requirement, the requirement shall include provision for making a person responsible for the monitoring; and a person who is made so responsible shall be of a description specified in an order[2] made by the Secretary of State.

(7) The Secretary of State may make rules for regulating—

(a) the electronic monitoring of compliance with requirements imposed on a child or young person as a condition of bail; and

(b) without prejudice to the generality of paragraph (a) above, the functions of persons made responsible for securing the electronic monitoring of compliance with such requirements.

(8) Rules under this section may make different provision for different cases.

(9) Any power of the Secretary of State to make an order or rules under this section shall be exercisable by statutory instrument.

(10) A statutory instrument containing rules made under this section shall be subject to annulment in pursuance of a resolution of either House of Parliament.

(11) In this section 'local authority accommodation' has the same meaning as in the Children and Young Persons Act 1969 (c 54).

(12) For the purposes of this section a petty sessions area is a relevant area in relation to a proposed electronic monitoring requirement if the court considers that it will not be practicable to secure the electronic monitoring in question unless electronic monitoring arrangements are available in that area.

[Bail Act 1976, s 3AA, as inserted by the Criminal Justice and Police Act 2001, s 131(2).]

---

1. These provisions came into effect in respect of courts in the 10 "street crime'" areas: Inner London, Greater Manchester, West Midlands, Thames Valley, Avon and Somerset, Lancashire, West Yorkshire, South Yorkshire, Merseyside and Nottinghamshire, plus Northumbria on 22 April 2002, see Home Office Guidance: *Criminal Justice and Police Act 2001 Electronic Monitoring of 12–16 year olds on Bail and on Remand to Local Authority Accommodation* (17 April 2002) and nationally as from 1 June 2002. Bail tagging for 17 year olds in these areas was implemented in the 11 areas on 8 July 2002 and electronic tagging was extended to 17 year olds nationally as from 5 January 2004 by Home Office Guidance: *Electronic Tagging of 17 year olds on Bail: Extension to England and Wales* (12 December 2003).

2. See the Bail (Electronic Monitoring of Requirements) (Responsible Officer) Order 2002, SI 2002/844 amended by SI 2005/984.

1–1562B   3A. Conditions of bail in case of police bail. (1) Section 3 of this Act applies, in relation to bail granted by a custody officer under Part IV of the Police and Criminal Evidence Act 1984 in cases where the normal powers to impose conditions of bail are available to him, subject to the following modifications.

(2) Subsection (6) does not authorise the imposition of a requirement to reside in a bail hostel or any requirement under paragraph (d) or (e).

(3) Subsections (6ZAA), (6ZA), (6A) and (6B) shall be omitted.

(4) For subsection (8), substitute the following—

"(8) Where a custody officer has granted bail in criminal proceedings he or another custody officer serving at the same police station may, at the request of the person to whom it was granted, vary the conditions of bail; and in doing so he may impose conditions or more onerous conditions.".

(5) Where a constable grants bail to a person no conditions shall be imposed under subsections (4), (5), (6) or (7) of section 3 of this Act unless it appears to the constable that it is necessary to do so—

(a) for the purpose of preventing that person from failing to surrender to custody, or

(b) for the purpose of preventing that person from committing an offence while on bail, or

(c) for the purpose of preventing that person from interfering with witnesses or otherwise obstructing the course of justice, whether in relation to himself or any other person or

(d) for that person's own protection or, if he is a child or young person, for his own welfare or in his own interests.

(6) Subsection (5) above also applies on any request to a custody officer under subsection (8) of section 3 of this Act to vary the conditions of bail.

[Bail Act 1976, s 3A, as inserted by the Criminal Justice and Public Order Act 1994, s 27 and amended by the Crime and Disorder Act 1998, s 54, the Criminal Justice and Police Act 2001, s 131 and the Criminal Justice Act 2003.]

Bail for accused persons and others

1–1563 4. General right to bail of accused persons and others. (1) A person to whom this section applies shall be granted bail except as provided in Schedule 1 to this Act[1].

(2) This section applies to a person who is accused of an offence when—

(a) he appears or is brought before a magistrates' court[2] or the Crown Court in the course of or in connection with proceedings for the offence, or

(b) he applies to a court[3] for bail or for a variation of the condition of bail in connection with the proceedings.

This subsection does not apply as respects proceedings on or after a person's conviction of the offence.

(2A) This section also applies to a person whose extradition is sought in respect of an offence, when—

(a) he appears or is brought before a court in the course of or in connection with extradition proceedings in respect of the offence, or

(b) he applies to a court for bail or for a variation of the conditions of bail in connection with the proceedings.[4]

(2B) But subsection (2A) above does not apply if the person is alleged to be unlawfully at large after conviction.[4]

(3) This section also applies to a person who, having been convicted of an offence, appears or is brought before a magistrates' court to be dealt with under Part II of Schedule 3 to the Powers of Criminal Courts (Sentencing) Act 2000 (breach of certain community orders).

(4) This section also applies to a person who has been convicted of an offence and whose case is adjourned by the court for the purpose of enabling inquiries or a report to be made to assist the court in dealing with him for the offence.

(5) Schedule 1 to this Act also has effect as respects conditions of bail for a person to whom this section applies.

(6) In Schedule 1 to this Act "the defendant" means a person to whom this section applies and any reference to a defendant whose case is adjourned for inquiries or a report is a reference to a person to whom this section applies by virtue of subsection (4) above.

(7) This section is subject to section 41 of the Magistrates' Courts Act 1980 (restriction of bail by magistrates' court in cases of treason).

(8) This section is subject to section 25 of the Criminal Justice and Public Order Act 1994 (exclusion of bail in cases of homicide and rape).

(9) In taking any decisions required by Part I or II of Schedule 1 to this Act, the considerations to which the court is to have regard include, so far as relevant, any misuse of controlled drugs by the defendant ("controlled drugs" and "misuse" having the same meanings as in the Misuse of Drugs Act 1971).

[Bail Act 1976, s 4, as amended by the Magistrates' Courts Act 1980, Sch 7, the Criminal Justice Act 1991, Sch 11, the Criminal Justice and Public Order Act 1994, Sch 10, the Powers of Criminal Courts (Sentencing) Act 2000, Sch 9, the Criminal Justice and Court Services Act 2000, s 58 and the Extradition Act 2003, s 198.]

---

1. As to renewed applications, see ante para **1–465**.
2. This includes a youth court.
3. "Court" includes a justice of the peace (s 2(2), ante).
4. Subsections (2A) and (2B) do not apply in relation to extradition requests received and extraditions made on or before 31 December 2003.

Supplementary

1–1564 5. Supplementary provisions about decisions on bail. (A1) This section applies in any of these cases—

(a) a magistrates' court has granted bail in criminal proceedings in connection with an offence to which this section applies or proceedings for such an offence;

(b) a constable has granted bail in criminal proceedings in connection with proceedings for such an offence;

(c) a magistrates' court or a constable has granted bail in connection with extradition proceedings.

(1) The court[1] or the appropriate court in relation to the constable may, on application by the prosecutor for the decision to be reconsidered—

(a) vary the conditions of bail,

(b)   impose conditions in respect of bail which has been granted unconditionally, or

(c)   withhold bail[2].

(2)   Where bail in criminal proceedings is granted by endorsing a warrant of arrest for bail the constable who releases on bail the person arrested shall make the record required by subsection (1) above instead of the judge or justice who issued the warrant.

(2A)   Where a magistrates' court or the Crown Court grants bail in criminal proceedings to a person to whom section 4 of this Act applies after hearing representations from the prosecutor in favour of withholding bail, then the court shall give reasons for granting bail.

(2B)   A court which is by virtue of subsection (2A) above required to give reasons for its decision shall include a note of those reasons in the record of its decision and, if requested to do so by the prosecutor, shall cause the prosecutor to be given a copy of the record of the decision as soon as practicable after the record is made.

(3)   Where a magistrates' court or the Crown Court—

(a)   withholds bail in criminal proceedings, or

(b)   imposes conditions in granting bail in criminal proceedings, or

(c)   varies any conditions of bail or imposes conditions in respect of bail in criminal proceedings[3],

and does so in relation to a person to whom section 4 of this Act applies, then the court shall, with a view to enabling him to consider making an application in the matter to another court, give reasons for withholding bail or for imposing or varying the conditions.

(4)   A court which is by virtue of subsection (3) above required to give reasons for its decision shall include a note of those reasons in the record of its decision and shall (except in a case where, by virtue of subsection (5) below, this need not be done) give a copy of that note to the person in relation to whom the decision was taken.

(5)   The Crown Court need not give a copy of the note of the reasons for its decision to the person in relation to whom the decision was taken where that person is represented by counsel or a solicitor unless his counsel or solicitor requests the court to do so.

(6)   Where a magistrates' court withholds bail in criminal proceedings from a person who is not represented by counsel or solicitor, the court shall—

(a)   if it is committing him for trial to the Crown Court or if it issues a certificate under subsection (6A) below, inform him that he may apply tto the Crown Court[4] to be granted bail;

(b)   *repealed.*

(6A)   Where in criminal proceedings—

(a)   a magistrates' court remands a person in custody under section 11 of the Powers of Criminal Courts (Sentencing) Act 2000 (remand for medical examination) or any of the following provisions of the Magistrates' Courts Act 1980—

     (i)   section 5 (adjournment of inquiry into offence);

     (ii)   section 10 (adjournment of trial); or

     (iii)   section 18 (initial procedure on information against adult for offence triable either way); or

     (iv)   *repealed,*

     after hearing full argument on an application for bail from him; and

(b)   either—

     (i)   it has not previously heard such argument on an application for bail from him in those proceedings; or

     (ii)   it has previously heard full argument from him on such an application but it is satisfied that there has been a change in his circumstances or that new considerations have been placed before it,

it shall be the duty of the court to issue a certificate in the prescribed form that they heard full argument on his application for bail before they refused the application.

(6B)   Where the court issues a certificate under subsection (6A) above in a case to which paragraph (b)(ii) of that subsection applies, it shall state in the certificate the nature of the change of circumstances or the new considerations which caused it to hear a further fully argued bail application.

(6C)   Where a court issues a certificate under subsection (6A) above it shall cause the person to whom it refuses bail to be given a copy of the certificate.

(7)   Where a person has given security in pursuance of section 3(5) above and a court is satisfied that he failed to surrender to custody then, unless it appears that he had reasonable cause for his failure, the court may order forfeiture of the security.

(8)   If the court orders the forfeiture of a security under subsection (7) above, the court may declare that the forfeiture extends to such amount less than the full value of the security as it thinks fit to order.

(8A)   An order under subsection (7) above shall, unless previously revoked, take effect at the end of twenty-one days beginning with the day on which it is made.

(8B)   A court which has ordered the forfeiture of a security under subsection (7) above may, if satisfied on an application made by or on behalf of the person who gave it that he did after all have reasonable cause for his failure to surrender to custody, by order remit the forfeiture or declare that it extends to such amount less than the full value of the security as it thinks fit to order.

(8C)   An application under subsection (8B) above may be made before or after the order for forfeiture has taken effect, but shall not be entertained unless the court is satisfied that the prosecution was given reasonable notice of the applicant's intention to make it.

(9) A security which has been ordered to be forfeited by a court under subsection (7) above shall, to the extent of the forfeiture—

(a) if it consists of money, be accounted for and paid in the same manner as a fine imposed by that court would be;

(b) if it does not consist of money, be enforced by such magistrates' court[4] as may be specified in the order.

(9A) Where an order is made under subsection (8B) above after the order for forfeiture of the security in question has taken effect, any money which would have fallen to be repaid or paid over to the person who gave the security if the order under subsection (8B) had been made before the order for forfeiture took effect shall be repaid or paid over to him.

(10) In this section "prescribed" means, in relation to the decision of a court or an officer of a court, prescribed by Civil Procedure Rules, Courts-Martial Appeal rules or Criminal Procedure Rules[5], as the case requires or, in relation to a decision of a constable, prescribed by direction of the Secretary of State.

(11) This section is subject, in its application to bail granted by a constable, to section 5A of this Act.

[Bail Act 1976, s 5, as amended by the Criminal Law Act 1977, Sch 12, the Criminal Justice Act 1982, s 60, the Criminal Justice and Public Order Act 1994, Sch 3, the Powers of Criminal Courts (Sentencing) Act 2000, Sch 9 and the Criminal Justice and Police Act 2001, s 129(1), the Extradition Act 2003, s and the Courts Act 2003, Sch 198.]

---

1. "Court" includes a justice of the peace (s 2(2), ante).
2. Subsections (A1) and (1) as substituted do not apply in relation to extradition requests received and extraditions made on or before 31 December 2003.
3. Article 5(3) of the European Convention on Human Rights requires the court to "examine" all the facts relevant to the question of bail and to give reasons for its decision: *Letellier v France* (1992) 14 EHRR 83.
4. For disposal of a non-pecuniary forfeiture, see s 140 of the Magistrates' Courts Act 1980, post.
5. See the Criminal Procedure Rules this PART: STATUTORY INSTRUMENTS ON PROCEDURE, post.

1–1564A 5A. Supplementary provisions in cases of police bail. (1) Section 5 of this Act applies, in relation to bail granted by a custody officer under Part IV of the Police and Criminal Evidence Act 1984 in cases where the normal powers to impose conditions of bail are available to him, subject to the following modifications.

(1A) Subsections (2A) and (2B) shall be omitted.

(2) For subsection (3) substitute the following—

"(3) Where a custody officer, in relation to any person,—

(a) imposes conditions in granting bail in criminal proceedings, or

(b) varies any conditions of bail or imposes conditions in respect of bail, in criminal proceedings,

the custody officer shall, with a view to enabling that person to consider requesting him or another custody officer, or making an application to a magistrates' court, to vary the conditions, give reasons for imposing or varying the conditions.".

(3) For subsection (4) substitute the following—

"(4) A custody officer who is by virtue of subsection (3) above required to give reasons for his decision shall include a note of those reasons in the custody record and shall give a copy of that note to the person in relation to whom the decision was taken".

(4) Subsections (5) and (6) shall be omitted.

[Bail Act 1976, s 5A, as inserted by the Criminal Justice, Public Order Act 1994, Sch 3 and amended by the Criminal Justice and Police Act 2001, s 129(2).]

1–1564B 5B. Reconsideration of decisions granting bail. (A1) This section applies in any of these cases—

(a) a magistrates' court has granted bail in criminal proceedings in connection with an offence to which this section applies or proceedings for such an offence;

(b) a constable has granted bail in criminal proceedings in connection with proceedings for such an offence;(c)a magistrates' court or a constable has granted bail in connection with extradition proceedings.

(1) The court[1] or the appropriate court in relation to the constable may, on application by the prosecutor for the decision to be reconsidered—

(a) vary the conditions of bail,

(b) impose conditions in respect of bail which has been granted unconditionally, or

(c) withhold bail.

(2) The offences to which this section applies are offences triable on indictment and offences triable either way.

(3) No application[1] for the reconsideration of a decision under this section shall be made unless it

is based on information which was not available to the court or constable when the decision was taken.

(4) Whether or not the person to whom the application[1] relates appears before it, the magistrates' court shall take the decision in accordance with section 4(1) (and Schedule 1) of this Act.

(5) Where the decision of the court on a reconsideration under this section is to withhold bail from the person to whom it was originally granted the court shall—

(a) if that person is before the court, remand him in custody, and

(b) if that person is not before the court, order him to surrender himself forthwith into the custody of the court.

(6) Where a person surrenders himself into the custody of the court in compliance with an order under subsection (5) above, the court shall remand him in custody.

(7) A person who has been ordered to surrender to custody under subsection (5) above may be arrested without warrant by a constable if he fails without reasonable cause to surrender to custody in accordance with the order.

(8) A person arrested in pursuance of subsection (7) above shall be brought as soon as practicable, and in any event within 24 hours after his arrest, before a justice of the peace for the petty sessions area in which he was arrested and the justice shall remand him in custody.

In reckoning for the purposes of this subsection any period of 24 hours, no account shall be taken of Christmas Day, Good Friday or any Sunday.

(8A) Where the court, on a reconsideration under this section, refuses to withhold bail from a relevant person after hearing representations from the prosecutor in favour of withholding bail, then the court shall give reasons for refusing to withhold bail.

(8B) In subsection (8A) above, "relevant person" means a person to whom section 4(1) (and Schedule 1) of this Act is applicable in accordance with subsection (4) above.

(8C) A court which is by virtue of subsection (8A) above required to give reasons for its decision shall include a note of those reasons in any record of its decision and, if requested to do so by the prosecutor, shall cause the prosecutor to be given a copy of any such record as soon as practicable after the record is made.

(9) Criminal Procedure Rules shall include provision—

(a) requiring notice of an application under this section and of the grounds for it to be given to the person affected, including notice of the powers available to the court under it;

(b) for securing that any representations made by the person affected (whether in writing or orally) are considered by the court before making its decision; and

(c) designating the court which is the appropriate court in relation to the decision of any constable to grant bail.

[Bail Act 1976, s 5B, as inserted by the Criminal Justice, Public Order Act 1994, s 30 and amended by the Criminal Justice and Police Act 2001, s 129(3) and the Extradition Act 2003, s 198.]

---

1. For the procedure on reconsideration of a decision to grant bail, see Criminal Procedure Rules 2005, Part 19, this PART: STATUTORY INSTRUMENTS ON PROCEDURE, post.

1–1565   6. Offence of absconding by person released on bail.   (1) If a person who has been released on bail in criminal proceedings fails without reasonable cause[1] to surrender to custody he shall be guilty of an offence[2].

(2) If a person who—

(a) has been released on bail in criminal proceedings, and

(b) having reasonable cause therefor, has failed to surrender to custody,

fails to surrender to custody at the appointed place as soon after the appointed time as is reasonably practicable he shall be guilty of an offence[1].

(3) It shall be for the accused to prove[3] that he had reasonable cause for his failure to surrender to custody.

(4) A failure to give a person granted bail in criminal proceedings a copy of the record of the decision shall not constitute a reasonable cause for that person's failure to surrender to custody.

(5) An offence under subsection (1) or (2) above shall be punishable either on summary[4] conviction or as if it were a criminal contempt of court[5].

(6) Where a magistrates' court convicts a person of an offence under subsection (1) or (2) above the court may, if it thinks—

(a) that the circumstances of the offence are such that greater punishment should be inflicted for that offence than the court has power to inflict, or

(b) in a case where it commits that person for trial to the Crown Court for another offence, that it would be appropriate for him to be dealt with for the offence under subsection (1) or (2) above by the court before which he is tried for the other offence,

commit him in custody or on bail to the Crown Court for sentence.

(7) A person who is convicted summarily of an offence under subsection (1) or (2) above and is not committed to the Crown Court for sentence shall be liable to imprisonment for a term not exceeding **3 months** or to a fine not exceeding **level 5** on the standard scale or to both and a person who is so committed for sentence or is dealt with as for such a contempt shall be liable to imprisonment for a term not exceeding **12 months** or to a fine or to both.

(8) In any proceedings for an offence under subsection (1) or (2) above a document purporting to be a copy of the part of the prescribed record which relates to the time and place appointed for the person specified in the record to surrender to custody and to be duly certified to be a true copy of that part of the record shall be evidence of the time and place appointed for that person to surrender to custody.

(9) For the purposes of subsection (8) above—

(a) "the prescribed record" means the record of the decision of the court, officer or constable made in pursuance of section 5(1) of this Act;

(b) the copy of the prescribed record is duly certified if it is certified by the appropriate officer of the court or, as the case may be, by the constable who took the decision or a constable designated for the purpose by the officer in charge of the police station from which the person to whom the record relates was released;

(c) "the appropriate officer" of the court is—

(i) in the case of a magistrates' court, the justices' chief executive;

(ii) in the case of the Crown Court, such officer as may be designated for the purpose in accordance with arrangements made by the Lord Chancellor;

(iii) in the case of the High Court, such officer as may be designated for the purpose in accordance with arrangements made by the Lord Chancellor;

(iv) in the case of the Court of Appeal, the registrar of criminal appeals or such other officer as may be authorised by him to act for the purpose;

(v) in the case of the Courts-Martial Appeal Court, the registrar or other such officer as may be authorised by him to act for the purpose.

(10) Section 127 of the Magistrates' Courts Act 1980 shall not apply in relation to an offence under subsection (1) or (2) above.

(11) Where a person has been released on bail in criminal proceedings and that bail was granted by a constable, a magistrates' court shall not try that person for an offence under subsection (1) or (2) above in relation to that bail (the "relevant offence") unless either or both of subsections (12) and (13) below applies.

(12) This subsection applies if an information is laid for the relevant offence within 6 months from the time of the commission of the relevant offence.

(13) This subsection applies if an information is laid for the relevant offence no later than 3 months from the time of the occurrence of the first of the events mentioned in subsection (14) below to occur after the commission of the relevant offence.

(14) Those events are—

(a) the person surrenders to custody at the appointed place;

(b) the person is arrested, or attends at a police station, in connection with the relevant offence or the offence for which he was granted bail;

(c) the person appears or is brought before a court in connection with the relevant offence or the offence for which he was granted bail.

[Bail Act 1976, s 6 as amended by the Criminal Justice Act 1982, ss 38 and 46, the Access to Justice Act 1999, Sch 13 and the Criminal Justice Act 2003.]

---

1. The fact that a defendant mistakenly formed the opinion he was required to surrender on a later date was held not to amount to a "reasonable cause" (*Laidlaw v Atkinson* (1986) Times, 2 August).

2. The procedure for dealing with an offence arising from a failure to surrender is regulated by the *Practice Direction (criminal: consolidated) 2002* at paras I.13.4 to I.13.16, in this PART, post and see para **1-489 Absconding or breaking conditions of bail**, ante.

3. An accused who raises this defence is not required to establish it beyond reasonable doubt, but on the balance of probabilities; see *R v Carr-Briant* [1943] KB 607, [1943] 2 All ER 156, 107 JP 167.

4. For punishment of failure to attend at the Crown Court, which must be dealt with as a criminal contempt, see *R v Maguire* [1993] RTR 306. Where a person fails to surrender to the court for his trial, that person's criminality, so far as the bail offence is concerned, is not affected by whether or not he is subsequently acquitted or convicted of the principal offence (*R v Clarke* [2000] 1 Cr App Rep (S) 224 – 7 ½ months' imprisonment for failing to surrender to bail in the Crown Court where the defendant was eventually acquitted of the principal offence).

5. See *R v Singh* [1979] QB 319, [1979] 1 All ER 524. A suspended sentence may be activated; *R v Tyson* (1978) 68 Cr App Rep 314, [1979] Crim LR 398.

1–1566 7. Liability to arrest for absconding or breaking conditions of bail[1]. (1) If a person who has been released on bail in criminal proceedings and is under a duty to surrender into the custody of a court fails to surrender to custody[2] at the time appointed for him to do so the court may issue a warrant[3] for his arrest.

(1A) Subsection (1B) applies if—

(a) a person has been released on bail in connection with extradition proceedings,

(b) the person is under a duty to surrender into the custody of a constable, and

(c) the person fails to surrender to custody at the time appointed for him to do so.[4]

(1B) A magistrates' court may issue a warrant for the person's arrest.[4]

(2) If a person who has been released on bail in criminal proceedings absents himself from the court at any time after he has surrendered into the custody[2] of the court and before the court is ready to begin or to resume the hearing of the proceedings, the court may issue a warrant[5] for his arrest; but no warrant shall be issued under this subsection where that person is absent in accordance with leave given to him by or on behalf of the court.

(3) A person who has been released on bail in criminal proceedings and is under a duty to surrender into the custody of a court may be arrested[4] without a warrant by a constable—

(a) if a constable has reasonable grounds for believing that that person is not likely to surrender to custody;

(b) if the constable has reasonable grounds for believing that that person is likely to break any of the conditions of his bail or has reasonable grounds for suspecting that that person has broken any of those conditions; or

(c) in a case where that person was released on bail with one or more surety or sureties, if a surety notifies[6] a constable in writing that that person is unlikely to surrender to custody and that for that reason the surety wishes to be relieved of his obligations as a surety.

(4) A person arrested in pursuance of subsection (3) above—

(a) shall, except where he was arrested within 24 hours of the time appointed for him to surrender to custody, be brought as soon as practicable and in any event within 24 hours[7] after his arrest before a justice of the peace[8] for the petty sessions area in which he was arrested; and

(b) in the said excepted case shall be brought before the court at which he was to have surrendered to custody.

(4A) A person who has been released on bail in connection with extradition proceedings and is under a duty to surrender into the custody of a constable may be arrested without warrant by a constable on any of the grounds set out in paragraphs (a) to (c) of subsection (3).[5]

(4B) A person arrested in pursuance of subsection (4A) above shall be brought as soon as practicable and in any event within 24 hours after his arrest before a justice of the peace for the petty sessions area in which he was arrested.[5]

(5) A justice of the peace before whom a person is brought under subsection (4) above may, subject to subsection (6) below, if of the opinion that that person—

(a) is not likely to surrender to custody, or

(b) has broken or is likely to break any condition of his bail,

remand him in custody[9] or commit him to custody, as the case may require, or alternatively, grant him bail subject to the same or to different conditions, but if not of that opinion shall grant him bail subject to the same conditions (if any) as were originally imposed[10].

(6) Where the person so brought before the justice is a child or young person and the justice does not grant him bail, subsection (5) above shall have effect subject to the provisions of section 23 of the Children and Young Persons Act 1969 (remands to the care of local authorities).

(7) In reckoning for the purposes of this section any period of 24 hours, no account shall be taken of Christmas Day, Good Friday or any Sunday.[5]

[Bail Act 1976, s 7, as amended by the Criminal Law Act 1977, Sch 12 and the Extradition Act 2003, s 198.]

---

1. Section 7 does not create an offence, and a mere failure to comply with bail conditions, without more, does not amount to a contempt of court (*R v Ashley* [2003] EWCA Crim 2571, (2003) 167 JP 548).

2. See definition of "surrender to custody" in s 2(1) supra.

3. See s 125D of the Magistrates' Courts Act 1980, post, for further provisions concerning warrants of arrest. It is arguable (on the wording of s 125(3), the Magistrates' Courts Act 1980) that the constable executing a warrant under s 7(1) or (2) of the Bail Act 1976 should have it in his possession at the time. Accordingly, some courts may prefer to issue a warrant under s 1 of the Magistrates' Courts Act 1980, post, instead.

4. This power of arrest is preserved by the Police and Criminal Evidence Act 1984, s 26 and Sch 2, post.

5. Subsections (1A), (1B), (4A), (4B) and (7) do not apply in relation to extradition requests received and extraditions made on or before 31 December 2003.

6. A surety is not automatically relieved of his duties by going to the police (*R v Crown Court at Ipswich, ex p Reddington* [1981] Crim LR 618). It would seem that a surety may only withdraw from his recognizance if the defendant is before the court and an appropriate application is made, under s 3(8) ante, to vary the conditions of bail; see *R v Crown Court at Wood Green, ex p Howe* [1992] 3 All ER 366, [1992] 1 WLR 702.

7. Unless the provisions of s 7(4) are faithfully complied with, the justices have no jurisdiction to deal with the breach of bail conditions under s 7(5). Accordingly, where a person was brought to the court precincts or cells within the 24 hour period, but not brought before a justice until after the expiry of that period, it was held that the justices had no jurisdiction to deal with the breach of bail conditions (*R v Governor of Glen Parva Young Offender Institution, ex p G (A Minor)* [1998] QB 877, [1998] 3 WLR 13, 162 JP 225, [1998] 2 Cr App Rep 349).

Subject, however, to the hearing starting within 24 hours, and bearing in mind that a defendant should not be kept waiting any longer than is necessary for the court to determine the matter, there is no reason why a breach of bail should not be released by one bench of justices to another: *R (on the application of Hussain) v Derby Magistrates' Court* [2002] 1 Cr App Rep 37, [2001] EWHC Admin 507, [2001] 1 WLR 2454 (hearing put back until the afternoon).

8. A recorder of the Crown Court is not a justice of the peace for the purposes of this section (*Re Marshall* (1994) 159 JP 688 [1994] Crim LR 915).

9. This section provides a simple, expeditious and informal procedure whereby a person who has been arrested under sub-s (3) may be dealt with by a single justice.

In *R v Liverpool City Justices, ex p DPP* [1993] QB 233, the Divisional Court established the following propositions with regard to the application of s 7:

(a) The section contemplates the constable who has arrested the person bailed bringing him before the justice and stating his, namely the constable's, grounds for believing that the defendant has broken or is likely to break a condition of his bail; this may well involve the giving of "hearsay evidence".

(b) In the proceeding before the justice, even where the defendant disputes the ground on which he was arrested, there is no necessity for the giving of evidence on oath or providing an opportunity to the person arrested, or his legal representative, to cross-examine, or give evidence himself. Nevertheless, the justice should give the defendant an opportunity to respond to what the constable alleges.

(c) The justice has no power to adjourn the proceeding, but must consider, on the material before him, whether he is able to form one of the opinions set out in s 7(5), and if he does so, go on to decide whether to remand the defendant in custody or on bail on the same or more stringent conditions.

(*d*) If the justice feels unable to form one of the opinions set out in s 7(5), he must order the person concerned to be released on bail on the same terms as were originally imposed.

(*e*) A proceeding under s 7(5) does not preclude a defendant who is remanded in custody from making an application for bail to the justices, or to the Crown Court or to a judge, as appropriate. The presumption in favour of granting bail under s 4 of the Act will be subject not only to the exceptions to the right to bail in Part I, para 2 of Sch 1 to the Act, but also to the exception in para 6 of that Schedule.

Article 5 of the European Convention on Human Rights does not require any approach different from the propositions laid down in *R v Liverpool City Justices, ex p DPP*, supra. Accordingly, where a justice is forming an opinion as to whether a defendant has breached a condition of his bail, Article 5 does not restrict him to considering only evidence that is admissible in the strict sense, nor does it require that the facts relevant to his decision are proved to the criminal standard of proof. Article 5, however, does require that the justice takes proper account of the quality of material upon which he is asked to adjudicate and give the defendant a full and fair opportunity to comment on and answer that material (*R v Havering Magistrates' Court, ex p DPP; R v Wirral Borough Magistrates' Court, ex p McKeown* [2001] 3 All ER 997, 165 JP 391, DC).

Proceedings under s 7(5) involve a two-stage process. First a decision must be make as to whether or not there has been a breach of a condition. If there has been no breach of a condition then the bailed person is entitled to be admitted to bail on precisely the same conditions. This stage does not involve the justices in an inquiry as to whether the arrested person had a reasonable excuse for being in breach. At the second stage, the justices will have to consider whether to grant bail or remand in custody. At this stage the question of why the bailed person breached his condition will be relevant (*R (Vickers) v West London Magistrates' Court* [2003] EWHC 1809 (Admin), 167 JP 473, [2004] Crim LR 63).

Where a defendant is brought before a justice under s 7(4) for breach of bail conditions, the justice must deal with him in accordance with s 7(5) and decide whether to grant or refuse bail. The defendant may not be committed in custody to the Crown Court so that the Crown Court can deal with bail thereafter; the appropriate course is for the defendant to be committed to the Crown Court until his trial or further order (*R v Teesside Magistrates' Court, ex p Ellison* [2001] EWCA Admin 11, 165 JP 355, DC).

10. Consideration ought to be given to warning sureties that conditions might be varied, especially if they were concerned about those conditions (*R v Wells Street Magistrates' Court, ex p Albanese* [1982] 2 QB 333, [1981] 3 All ER 769, 146 JP 177. The arrest of a person pursuant to s 7 is one of the exceptions to the right to bail, see Sch 1, post.

1–1567 8. Bail with sureties. (1) This section applies where a person is granted bail in criminal proceedings on condition that he provides one or more surety or sureties for the purpose of securing that he surrenders to custody[1].

(2) In considering the suitability[2] for that purpose of a proposed surety, regard may be had (amongst other things) to—

(*a*) the surety's financial resources;

(*b*) his character and any previous convictions of his; and

(*c*) his proximity (whether in point of kinship, place or residence or otherwise) to the person for whom he is to be surety.

(3) Where a court grants a person bail in criminal proceedings on such a condition but is unable to release him because no surety or no suitable surety is available, the court shall fix the amount in which the surety is to be bound and subsections (4) and (5) below, or in a case where the proposed surety resides in Scotland subsection (6) below, shall apply for the purpose of enabling the recognizance of the surety to be entered into subsequently.

(4) Where this subsection applies the recognizance of the surety may be entered into before such of the following persons or descriptions of persons as the court may by order specify or, if it makes no such order, before any of the following persons, that is to say—

(*a*) where the decision is taken by a magistrates' court, before a justice of the peace, a justices' clerk or a police officer who either is of the rank of inspector or above or is in charge of a police station or, if Criminal Procedure Rules so provide, by a person of such other description as is specified in the rules;

(*b*) where the decision is taken by the Crown Court, before any of the persons specified in paragraph (*a*) above or, if Criminal Procedure Rules so provide, by a person of such other description as is specified in the rules;

(*c*) where the decision is taken by the High Court or the Court of Appeal, before any of the persons specified in paragraph (*a*) above or, if Civil Procedure Rules or Criminal Procedure Rules so provide, by a person of such other description as is specified in the rules;

(*d*) where the decision is taken by the Courts-Martial Appeal Court, before any of the persons specified in paragraph (*a*) above or, if Courts-Martial Appeal rules so provide, by a person of such other description as is specified in the rules;

and Civil Procedure Rules, Criminal Procedure Rules or Courts-Martial Appeal rules may also prescribe the manner in which a recognizance which is to be entered into before such a person is to be entered into and the persons by whom and the manner in which the recognizance may be enforced.

(5) Where a surety seeks to enter into his recognizance before any person in accordance with subsection (4) above but that person declines to take his recognizance because he is not satisfied of the surety's suitability, the surety may apply to—

(*a*) the court which fixed the amount of the recognizance in which the surety was to be bound, or

(*b*) a magistrates' court for the petty sessions area in which he resides,

for that court to take his recognizance and that court shall, if satisfied of his suitability, take his recognizance.

(6) Where this subsection applies, the court, if satisfied of the suitability of the proposed surety, may direct that arrangements be made for the recognizance of the surety to be entered into in Scotland before any constable, within the meaning of the Police (Scotland) Act 1967, having charge

at any police office or station in like manner as the recognizance would be entered into in England and Wales.

(7) Where, in pursuance of subsection (4) or (6) above, a recognizance is entered into otherwise than before the court that fixed the amount of the recognizance, the same consequences shall follow as if it had been entered into before that court.

[Bail Act 1976, s 8 as amended by the Courts Act 2003, Sch 8.]

1. If the person granted bail fails to surrender to custody, the court must declare the recogniznace to be forfeited, and issue a summons requiring him to appear before the court to show cause why he should not be adjudged to pay the sum in which he is bound (Magistrates' Courts Act 1980, s 120(1A), in this PART: STATUTES ON PROCEDURE, post).

Before a surety formally accepts obligations, there is a requirement to explain what the obligations involve, ensure they are understood and that, in the light of their understanding, the surety is willing to undertake the obligations and is worth the sum involved after all debts are paid and to warn the surety of the consequences, including possible imprisonment, if the accused fails to appear (*R v Kent Crown Court, ex p Jodka* (1997) 161 JP 638, DC).

Where the recognizance is forfeited, is is for the surety to establish to the satisfaction of the court that there are grounds upon which the court may remit from forfeiture part, or wholly exceptionally, the whole recognizance. The presence or absence of culpability, is not in itself a reason to reduce or set aside the obligation entered into by the surety to pay in the event of a failure to bring the defendant to court (*R v Crown Court at Maidstone, ex p Lever* [1995] 1 WLR 928). Where a surety is unrepresented, the court should explain that the full recognizance should be forfeited unless it appears just and fair that a lesser sum should be forfeited or none at all, and that the burden of satisfying the court that the full sum should not be forfeited rests on the surety and it is for him to lay before the court the evidence of means and want of culpability on which he relies (*R v Uxbridge Justices, ex p Heward-Mills* [1983] 1 All ER 530, [1983] 1 WLR 56, 147 JP 225).

The court must start on the footing that the surety has entered into a serious obligation and ought to pay the amount which he or she has promised unless there are circumstances in the case, either relating to the surety's means or culpability, which make it fair and just to pay a smaller sum (*R v Horseferry Road Magistrates' Court, ex p Pearson* [1976] 2 All ER 264, [1976] 1 WLR 511, 140 JP 382); and the mere fact that every effort has been made to secure the appearance of the accused and there has been no want of due diligence does not mean that the obligation should be remitted entirely (*R v Waltham Forest Justices, ex p Parfrey* (1980) 2 Cr App Rep (S) 208). The courts rely on the moral pressure on the accused to attend his trial rather than subject his surety to suffering on account of his wrongdoing and generally do not place much weight on a plea of lack of culpability when it turns out that the surety's trust in the defendant was misplaced (see *R v Southampton Justices, ex p Corker* (1976) 120 Sol Jo 214). Where a surety has limited means, it does not necessarily follow that his recognizance should not be estreated in whole or at least in substantial part. Relevant matters which the surety is entitled to place before the court include the effect of the estreatment on the surety and others who will be affected, for example members of his family, and where estreatment involves the sale of property in which the surety has a joint interest with another person or a home in which the surety lives with his family. (*R v Crown Court at York, ex p Coleman and How* (1987) 86 Cr App Rep 151, [1987] Crim LR 761). However, the powers of the court in section 120 of the Magistrates' Courts Act 1980 make no reference to a change of circumstances and give the court a wide power to remit the whole or any part of the sum adjudged to be owing, for example where there has been no proper means inquiry (*R v Crown Court at Birmingham, ex p Ali* (1998) 163 JP 145, [1999] Crim LR 504). The means of the offender at the time of the estratment is a relevant factor for the court to consider (*R v Leicestershire Stipendiary Magistrate, ex p Kaur* (1999) 164 JP 127, DC).

The principles relevant to forfeiture of recognizances to secure a defendant's appearance before the court were summarised in *R v Leicestershire Stipendiary Magistrate, ex p Kaur* (1999) 164 JP 127, DC:

1.   Justices have a wide discretion under s. 120 whether to remit in whole or in part.
2.   In exercising that discretion, they must plainly have regard only to the surety's assets. The assets of other persons are not assets which can properly be called upon to satisfy a surety's liability.
3.   Want of culpability by a surety in the accused's failure to appear is not in itself a reason for not forfeiting or for remitting a recognizance. But there may be circumstances, where the amount forfeited may be reduced because a culpable surety has made very considerable efforts to carry out his or her undertaking.
4.   Regard may properly be had to a surety's share in the equity of a matrimonial home when a recognizance is being entered into.
5.   When enforcement of a recognizance is being considered under s.120, the means of the surety at that time is one of the factors to be considered and, at that stage, the impact on both the surety and on others, if the matrimonial home has to be sold to satisfy the recognizance, is a relevant factor when deciding whether to remit a recognizance in whole or in part.

2. Serious efforts must be made by legal representatives who tender anyone as a surety, and those who are authorised to take a recognizance, to ensure that appropriate inquiries are made to establish that the recognizance is realistic and that the surety would be able to meet his or her financial undertaking in the event of the recognizance being declared forfeited (*R v Birmingham Crown Court, ex p Rashid Ali* (1998) 163 JP 145, [1999] Crim LR 504).

Miscellaneous

1–1568 **9. Offence of agreeing to indemnify sureties in criminal proceedings.** (1) If a person agrees with another to indemnify that other against any liability which that other may incur as a surety to secure the surrender to custody of a person accused or convicted of or under arrest for an offence, he and that other person shall be guilty of an offence[1].

(2) An offence under subsection (1) above is committed whether the agreement is made before or after the person to be indemnified becomes a surety and whether or not he becomes a surety and whether the agreement contemplates compensation in money or in money's worth.

(3) Where a magistrates' court convicts a person of an offence under subsection (1) above the court may, if it thinks—

(a)   that the circumstances of the offence are such that greater punishment should be inflicted for that offence than the court has power to inflict, or

(b)   in a case where it commits that person for trial to the Crown Court for another offence, that it would be appropriate for him to be dealt with for the offence under subsection (1) above by the court before which he is tried for the other offence,

commit him in custody or on bail to the Crown Court for sentence.

(4) A person guilty of an offence under subsection (1) above shall be liable—

(a)   on summary conviction, to imprisonment for a term not exceeding **3 months** or to a fine not exceeding **the statutory maximum** or to both; or (*b*) on conviction on indictment or if sentenced by the Crown Court on committal for sentence under subsection (3) above, to imprisonment for a term not exceeding **12 months** or to a fine or to both.

(5) No proceedings for an offence under subsection (1) above shall be instituted except by or with the consent of the Director of Public Prosecutions.

[Bail Act 1976, s 9, as amended by the Criminal Law Act 1977, s 28.]

---

1. This offence is triable either way, see sub-s (4). For procedure in respect of an offence triable either way, see ss 17A–21 of the Magistrates' Courts Act 1980, post.

1–1569 **13.** (1) This Act may be cited as the Bail Act 1976.

(2) This Act (except this section) shall come into force on such day as the Secretary of State may by order in a statutory instrument appoint.

(3) Section 1 of this Act applies to bail grantable by the Courts-Martial Appeal Court when sitting outside England and Wales and accordingly section 6 of this Act applies to a failure outside England and Wales by a person granted bail by that Court to surrender to custody.

(4) Except as provided by subsection (3) above and with the exception of so much of section 8 as relates to entering into recognizances in Scotland and paragraphs 31 and 46 of Schedule 2 to this Act, this Act does not extend beyond England and Wales.

[Bail Act 1976, s 13.]

Section 4

SCHEDULE 1
PERSONS ENTITLED TO BAIL: SUPPLEMENTARY PROVISIONS

(As amended by the Magistrates' Courts Act 1980, Sch 7, the Mental Health (Amendment) Act 1982, s 34, the Criminal Justice Act 1988, ss 131, 153, 154 and 155, the Criminal Justice Act 1991, Sch 11 the Criminal Justice and Public Order Act 1994, s 26 and Sch 10, the Crime and Disorder Act 1998, Sch 8, the Powers of Criminal Courts (Sentencing) Act 2000, Sch 9, the Criminal Justice and Police Act 2001, Sch 7, the Extradition Act 2003, s 198 and the Criminal Justice Act 2003.)

PART I
DEFENDANTS ACCUSED OR CONVICTED OF IMPRISONABLE OFFENCES

Defendants to whom Part I applies

1–1570 **1.** The following provisions of this Part of this Schedule apply to the defendant if—

(*a*) the offence or one of the offences of which he is accused or convicted in the proceedings is punishable with imprisonment, or

(*b*) his extradition is sought in respect of an offence[1].

Exceptions to right to bail

1–1571 **2.** (1) The defendant need not be granted bail if the court is satisfied that there are substantial grounds for believing that the defendant, if released on bail (whether subject to conditions or not) would[2]—

(*a*) fail to surrender to custody[3], or

(*b*) commit an offence while on bail[4], or

(*c*) interfere with witnesses or otherwise obstruct the course of justice, whether in relation to himself or any other person[5].

(2) Where the defendant falls within one or more of paragraphs 2A, 6 and 6B of this Part of this Schedule, this paragraph shall not apply unless—

(*a*) where the defendant falls within paragraph 2A, the court is satisfied as mentioned in sub-paragraph (1) of that paragraph;

(*b*) where the defendant falls within paragraph 6, the court is satisfied as mentioned in sub-paragraph (1) of that paragraph;

(*c*) where the defendant falls within paragraph 6B, the court is satisfied as mentioned in paragraph 6A of this Part of this Schedule or paragraph 6A does not apply by virtue of paragraph 6C of this Part of this Schedule.

2A. *The defendant need not be granted bail if—*

(*a*) *the offence is an indictable offence or an offence triable either way; and*

(*b*) *it appears to the court that he was on bail in criminal proceedings on the date of the offence.*

2A. (1) If the defendant falls within this paragraph he may not be granted bail unless the court is satisfied that there is no significant risk of his committing an offence while on bail (whether subject to conditions or not).

(2) The defendant falls within this paragraph if—

(*a*) he is aged 18 or over, and

(*b*) it appears to the court that he was on bail in criminal proceedings on the date of the offence.*

2B. The defendant need not be granted bail in connection with extradition proceedings if—

(*a*) the conduct constituting the offence would, if carried out by the defendant in England and Wales, constitute an indictable offence or an offence triable either way; and

(*b*) it appears to the court that the defendant was on bail on the date of the offence[1].

---

*This para 2A was substituted for the preceding para 2A by s 14 of the Criminal Justice Act 2003, but it applies only to offences committed on or after 1 January 2007 and which are punishable on conviction with imprisonment/detention/custody for life: see Criminal Justices Act 2003 (Commencement No 14 and Transitional Provision) Order 2006, SI 2006/3217.

3. The defendant need not be granted bail if the court is satisfied that the defendant should be kept in custody for his own protection or, if he is a child or young person, for his own welfare.

4. The defendant need not be granted bail if he is in custody in pursuance of the sentence of a court or of any authority acting under any of the Services Acts.

5. The defendant need not be granted bail where the court is satisfied that it has not been practicable to obtain sufficient information for the purpose of taking the decisions required by this Part of this Schedule for want of time since the institution of the proceedings against him.

6. *The defendant need not be granted bail if, having been released on bail in or in connection with the proceedings for the offence or the extradition proceedings[1], he has been arrested in pursuance of section 7 of this Act.*

6. (1) If the defendant falls within this paragraph, he may not be granted bail unless the court is satisfied that there is no significant risk that, if released on bail (whether subject to conditions or not), he would fail to surrender to custody.

(2) Subject to sub-paragraph (3) below, the defendant falls within this paragraph if—

(a) he is aged 18 or over, and
(b) it appears to the court that, having been released on bail in or in connection with the proceedings for the offence, he failed to surrender to custody.

(3) Where it appears to the court that the defendant had reasonable cause for his failure to surrender to custody, he does not fall within this paragraph unless it also appears to the court that he failed to surrender to custody at the appointed place as soon as reasonably practicable after the appointed time.

(4) For the purposes of sub-paragraph (3) above, a failure to give to the defendant a copy of the record of the decision to grant him bail shall not constitute a reasonable cause for his failure to surrender to custody.*

6A. Exception applicable to drug users in certain areas. Subject to paragraph 6C below, a defendant who falls within paragraph 6B below may not be granted bail unless the court is satisfied that there is no significant risk of his committing an offence while on bail (whether subject to conditions or not).

6B. (1) A defendant falls within this paragraph if—

(a) he is aged 18 or over;
(b) a sample taken—

(i) under section 63B of the Police and Criminal Evidence Act 1984 (testing for presence of Class A drugs) in connection with the offence; or
(ii) under section 161 of the Criminal Justice Act 2003 (drug testing after conviction of an offence but before sentence),

has revealed the presence in his body of a specified Class A drug;

(c) either the offence is one under section 5(2) or (3) of the Misuse of Drugs Act 1971 and relates to a specified Class A drug, or the court is satisfied that there are substantial grounds for believing—

(i) that misuse by him of any specified Class A drug caused or contributed to the offence; or
(ii) (even if it did not) that the offence was motivated wholly or partly by his intended misuse of such a drug; and

(d) the condition set out in sub-paragraph (2) below is satisfied or (if the court is considering on a second or subsequent occasion whether or not to grant bail) has been, and continues to be, satisfied.

(2) The condition referred to is that after the taking and analysis of the sample—

(a) a relevant assessment has been offered to the defendant but he does not agree to undergo it; or
(b) he has undergone a relevant assessment, and relevant follow-up has been proposed to him, but he does not agree to participate in it.

(3) In this paragraph and paragraph 6C below—

(a) "Class A drug" and "misuse" have the same meaning as in the Misuse of Drugs Act 1971;
(b) "relevant assessment" and "relevant follow-up" have the meaning given by section 3(6E) of this Act;
(c) "specified" (in relation to a Class A drug) has the same meaning as in Part 3 of the Criminal Justice and Court Services Act 2000.

6C. Paragraph 6A above does not apply unless—

(a) the court has been notified by the Secretary of State that arrangements for conducting a relevant assessment or, as the case may be, providing relevant follow-up have been made for the petty sessions area in which it appears to the court that the defendant would reside if granted bail; and
(b) the notice has not been withdrawn.

---

*This para 6 was substituted for the preceding para 6 by s 15 of the Criminal Justice Act 2003, but it applies only where the absconding occurred on or after 1 January 2007 and relates to an offence punishable on conviction with imprisonment/detention/custody for life: see Criminal Justices Act 2003 (Commencement No 14 and Transitional Provision) Order 2006, SI 2006/3217.

1. Paragraphs (1), (2B) and words "or the extradition proceedings" do not apply in relation to extradition requests received and extraditions made on or before 31 December 2003.

2. Before the Human Rights Act 1998 came into force, the position under the Bail Act 1976 was that an informal inquiry should be conducted by the court to see whether there was anything to displace the *prima facie* entitlement to every accused person to bail. Accordingly, case law suggested that the strict rules of evidence are inappropriate when a court is considering whether there are substantial grounds for believing something on an application for bail under the Bail Act 1976 (*Re Moles* [1981] Crim LR 170). The position under the European Convention on Human Rights is stricter. Article 5(3) requires the court to "examine" all the facts relevant to the question of bail and to give reasons for its decision: *Letellier v France* (1992) 14 EHRR 83. Case law also suggests that "evidence" must be provided in support of any objection to bail: *Clooth v Belgium* (1991) 14 EHRR 717, and in some circumstances, disclosure of documentation relevant to the question of bail may be required: *Lamy v Belgium* (1989) 11 EHRR 529.

3. Under the European Convention on Human Rights, fear of absconding cannot be gauged solely on the basis of the severity of the sentence risked: at most, this is a factor to be taken into account when assessing whether any of the four valid grounds for refusing bail are made out: *Letellier v France* (1992) 14 EHRR 83. Regard must also be had to the character of the person involved and his background, assets and links with the community: *W v Switzerland*: (1993) 17 EHRR 60. In some cases a general statement that the accused will abscond or engage in the prohibited activity is not enough; supporting evidence must be provided: *Clooth v Belgium* (1991) 14 EHRR 717.

4. Under the European Convention on Human Rights, before pre-trial detention can be authorised on this basis account

must be taken of the background and personal circumstances of the accused: *Clooth v Belgium* (1991) 14 EHRR 717. Previous convictions which are not comparable, either in nature or seriousness, with the charges preferred against an accused, are not sufficient to justify a fear that further offences will be committed within the meaning of art 5(3): *ibid*. Where medical reports suggest that further offences might committed by reason of the accused's psychiatric disposition, pre-trial detention will only be justified under art 5(3) of the Convention if appropriate therapeutic care is provided: *ibid*.

5. Under the European Convention on Human Rights, general and abstract references to the possibility that there might be interference with the course of justice will not satisfy the strict requirements of art 5(3): *Clooth v Belgium* (1991) 14 EHRR 717. Where bail is withheld on this basis, pre-trial detention can only be justified so long as a real risk of such conduct persists: *Kemmache v France* (1991) 14 EHRR 520. Once the risk subsides, release on bail should be ordered.

Exception applicable only to defendant whose case is adjourned for inquiries or a report

1-1572 **7.** Where his case is adjourned for inquiries or a report, the defendant need not be granted bail if it appears to the court that it would be impracticable to complete the inquiries or make the report without keeping the defendant in custody.

Restriction of conditions of bail

1-1573 **8.** (1) Subject to sub-paragraph (3) below, where the defendant is granted bail, no conditions shall be imposed under subsections (4) to (6B) or (7) (except subsection (6)(*d*)) or (*e*) of section 3 of this Act unless it appears[1] to the court that it is necessary to do so—

(*a*) for the purpose of preventing the occurrence of any of the events mentioned in paragraph 2(1) of this Part of this Schedule, or

(*b*) for the defendant's own protection or, if he is a child or young person, for his own welfare or in his own interests.

(1A) No condition shall be imposed under section 3(6)(*d*) of this Act unless it appears to be necessary to do so for the purpose of enabling inquiries or a report to be made.

(2) Sub-paragraphs (1) and (1A) above also apply on any application to the court to vary the conditions of bail or to impose conditions in respect of bail which has been granted unconditionally.

(3) The restriction imposed by sub-paragraph (1A) above shall not apply to the conditions required to be imposed under section 3(6A) of this Act or operate to override the direction in section 11(3) of the Powers of Criminal Courts (Sentencing) Act 2000 to a magistrates' court to impose conditions of bail under section 3(6)(*d*) of this Act of the description specified in the said section 11(3) in the circumstances so specified.

---

1. Although when withholding bail the court is required by para 2, ante, to have "substantial grounds" for believing that he would, for example, commit an offence when on bail, the requirement of having "substantial grounds" does not apply to the grant of conditional bail; see *R v Mansfield Justices, ex p Sharkey* [1985] QB 613, [1985] 1 All ER 193, 149 JP 129. See also s 3(6) and notes thereto, ante.

Decisions under paragraph 2

1-1574 **9.** In taking the decisions required by paragraph 2(1), or in deciding whether it is satisfied as mentioned in paragraph 2A(1), 6(1) or 6A, of this Part of this Schedule, the court shall have regard to such of the following considerations as appear to it to be relevant, that is to say—

(*a*) the nature and seriousness of the offence or default (and the probable method of dealing with the defendant for it),

(*b*) the character, antecedents[1], associations and community ties[2] of the defendant,

(*c*) the defendant's record as respects the fulfilment of his obligations under previous grants of bail in criminal proceedings,

(*d*) except in the case of a defendant whose case is adjourned for inquiries or a report, the strength of the evidence of his having committed the offence or having defaulted,

as well as to any other things[3] which appear to be relevant.

9AA (1) This paragraph applies if—

(*a*) the defendant is under the age of 18, and

(*b*) it appears to the court that he was on bail in criminal proceedings on the date of the offence.

(2) In deciding for the purposes of paragraph 2(1) of this Part of this Schedule whether it is satisfied that there are substantial grounds for believing that the defendant, if released on bail (whether subject to conditions or not), would commit an offence while on bail, the court shall give particular weight to the fact that the defendant was on bail in criminal proceedings on the date of the offence.*

9AB (1) Subject to sub-paragraph (2) below, this paragraph applies if—

(*a*) the defendant is under the age of 18, and

(*b*) it appears to the court that, having been released on bail in or in connection with the proceedings for the offence, he failed to surrender to custody.

(2) Where it appears to the court that the defendant had reasonable cause for his failure to surrender to custody, this paragraph does not apply unless it also appears to the court that he failed to surrender to custody at the appointed place as soon as reasonably practicable after the appointed time.

(3) In deciding for the purposes of paragraph 2(1) of this Part of this Schedule whether it is satisfied that there are substantial grounds for believing that the defendant, if released on bail (whether subject to conditions or not), would fail to surrender to custody, the court shall give particular weight to—

(*a*) where the defendant did not have reasonable cause for his failure to surrender to custody, the fact that he failed to surrender to custody, or

(*b*) where he did have reasonable cause for his failure to surrender to custody, the fact that he failed to surrender to custody at the appointed place as soon as reasonably practicable after the appointed time.

(4) For the purposes of this paragraph, a failure to give to the defendant a copy of the record of the decision to grant him bail shall not constitute a reasonable cause for his failure to surrender to custody.**

*Para 9AA was inserted by s 14 of the Criminal Justice Act 2003, but it applies only to offences committed on or after 1 January 2007 and which are punishable on conviction with imprisonment/detention/custody for life: see Criminal Justices Act 2003 (Commencement No 14 and Transitional Provision) Order 2006, SI 2006/3217.

**Para 9AB was inserted by s 15 of the Criminal Justice Act 2003, but it applies only where the absconding occurred on or after 1 January 2007 and relates to an offence punishable on conviction with imprisonment/ detention/custody for life: see Criminal Justices Act 2003 (Commencement No 14 and Transitional Provision) Order 2006, SI 2006/32.

1. As to information about previous convictions, see ante para **1–482**, ante.

2. The procedure for dealing with bail applications and for applying these provisions is set out ante in paras **1–464** to **1–489**, ante.

3. In *R v Vernege* [1982] 1 All ER 403n, [1982] 1 WLR 293n the Court of Appeal stated that in committal proceedings for murder, a proper consideration for the magistrates to take into account when considering bail is that in his own interests the accused should be examined by a prison doctor so that the various relevant matters affecting his state of mind at the time of the offence may be considered by the doctor, and in particular the possibility of a defence of diminished responsibility.

1–1575   9A. *Repealed.*

Cases under section 128A of Magistrates' Courts Act 1980

1–1576   9B. Where the court is considering exercising the power conferred by section 128A of the Magistrates' Courts Act 1980 (power to remand in custody for more than 8 clear days), it shall have regard to the total length of time which the accused would spend in custody if it were to exercise the power.

PART II
DEFENDANTS ACCUSED OR CONVICTED OF NON-IMPRISONABLE OFFENCES
Defendants to whom Part II applies

1–1577   1. Where the offence or every offence of which the defendant is accused or convicted in the proceedings is one which is not punishable with imprisonment the following provisions of this Part of this Schedule apply.

Exceptions to right to bail

1–1578   2. The defendant need not be granted bail if—

    (*a*)   it appears to the court that, having been previously granted bail in criminal proceedings, he has failed to surrender to custody in accordance with his obligations under the grant of bail; and

    (*b*)   the court believes, in view of that failure, that the defendant, if released on bail (whether subject to conditions or not) would fail to surrender to custody.

3. The defendant need not be granted bail if the court is satisfied that the defendant should be kept in custody for his own protection or, if he is a child or young person, for his own welfare.

4. The defendant need not be granted bail if he is in custody in pursuance of the sentence of a court or of any authority acting under any of the Services Acts.

5. The defendant need not be granted bail if—

    (*a*)   having been released on bail in or in connection with the proceedings for the offence, he has been arrested in pursuance of section 7 of this Act; and

    (*b*)   the court is satisfied that there are substantial grounds for believing that the defendant, if released on bail (whether subject to conditions or not) would fail to surrender to custody, commit an offence on bail or interfere with witnesses or otherwise obstruct the course of justice (whether in relation to himself or any other person).

PART IIA
DECISIONS WHERE BAIL REFUSED ON PREVIOUS HEARING

1–1579   1. If the court decides not to grant the defendant bail, it is the court's duty to consider, at each subsequent hearing while the defendant is a person to whom section 4 above applies and remains in custody, whether he ought to be granted bail.

2. At the first hearing[1] after that at which the court decided not to grant the defendant bail he may support an application for bail with any argument as to fact or law that he desires (whether or not he has advanced that argument previously).

3. At subsequent hearings the court need not hear arguments as to fact or law which it has heard previously.

---

1. An earlier hearing at which the court withheld bail under para 5 of Pt I is to be disregarded for this purpose. Therefore, if on a first appearance bail is refused on the ground contained in para 5, the defendant has the right to make two further unrestricted applications for bail (*R v Calder Justices, ex p Kennedy* (1992) 156 JP 716, [1992] Crim LR 496).

Previous occasions when a defendant has been remanded in custody in his absence with his consent are not "hearings" for the purposes of para 2 (*R v Dover and East Kent Justices, ex p Dean* (1991) 156 JP 357).

This provision may need re-examination under the Human Rights Act 1998. Article 5(3) of the European Convention on Human Rights requires the court to permit renewed applications at reasonable intervals: *Bezicheri v Italy* (1989) 12 EHRR 210.

PART III
INTERPRETATION

1–1590   1. For the purposes of this Schedule the question whether an offence is one which is punishable with imprisonment shall be determined without regard to any enactment prohibiting or restricting the imprisonment of young offenders or first offenders.

2. References in this Schedule to previous grants of bail in criminal proceedings include references to bail granted before the coming into force of this Act; and so as respects the reference to an offence committed by a person on bail in relation to any period before the coming into force of paragraph 2A of Part 1 of this Schedule.

3. References in this Schedule to a defendant's being kept in custody or being in custody include (where the defendant is a child or young person) references to his being kept or being in the care of a local authority in pursuance of a warrant of commitment under section 23(1) of the Children and Young Persons Act 1969.

4. In this Schedule—

"court", in the expression "sentence of a court", includes a service court as defined in section 12(1) of the Visiting Forces Act 1952 and "sentence", in that expression, shall be construed in accordance with that definition;

"default", in relation to the defendant, means the default for which he is to be dealt with under Part II of Schedule 3 to the Powers of Criminal Courts (Sentencing) Act 2000;

"the Services Acts" means the Army Act 1955, the Air Force Act 1955 and the Naval Discipline Act 1957.

Criminal Law Act 1977[1]
(1977 c 45)

PART III[2]
CRIMINAL PROCEDURE, PENALTIES, ETC

Penalties

1–1690   31. Increase of fines for certain summary offences.   (1)–(4) *Maximum fines increased for offences contained in Schedule 6 and for offences under certain byelaws.*

(5) This subsection applies to any pre-1949 enactment (however framed or worded) which—

(a) as regards any summary offence makes a person liable on conviction thereof to a fine of, or not exceeding, a specified amount less than £50 which has not been altered since the end of 1948 (and is not altered by this Act); or

(b) confers power by subordinate instrument to make a person, as regards any summary offence (whether or not created by the instrument), liable on conviction thereof to a fine of, or not exceeding, a specified amount less than £50 which has not been altered since the end of 1948 (and is not altered by this Act).

(6) Every enactment to which subsection (5) above applies shall have effect as if for the specified amount less than £50 there mentioned there were substituted—

(a) **£25** if the specified amount is less than £20; or

(b) **£50** if the specified amount is not less than £20.

(7) *Repealed.*

(8) Subsection (6) above shall not affect so much of any enactment as (in whatever words) makes a person liable on summary conviction to a fine not exceeding a specified amount for each day on which a continuing offence is continued after conviction or the occurrence of any other specified event.

(9) In subsection (5) above "pre-1949 enactment" means an enactment passed before 1st January 1949 or an enactment passed on or after that date which (whether directly or, through successive re-enactments, indirectly) re-enacts with or without modification an enactment passed before that date.

(10) *Amendment of maximum penalty in s 67(6) of the Medicines Act 1968.*

(11) In this section "enactment" does not include an enactment contained in an order, regulation or other instrument made under an Act.

[Criminal Law Act 1977, s 31, as amended by the Criminal Justice Act 1982, Sch 16 and the Weights and Measures Act 1985, Sch 13.]

1. Only the parts of the Act affecting the procedure of courts are printed here. Sections amending other provisions of the law are incorporated with the appropriate provisions throughout this work.
2. Part III comprises ss 14–19.

1–1691   32. Other provisions as to maximum fines.   (1) Where a person convicted on indictment of any offence (whether triable only on indictment or either way) would, apart from this subsection, be liable to a fine not exceeding a specified amount, he shall by virtue of this subsection be liable to a fine of any amount.

(2)–(3) *Miscellaneous provisions as to maximum fines.*

[Criminal Law Act 1977, s 32.]

Cross-border enforcement

1–1692   38A. Execution in different parts of United Kingdom of warrants for imprisonment for non-payment of fine.   (1) Subject to subsection (6) below, a person against whom an extract conviction is issued in Scotland for imprisonment in default of payment of a fine may be arrested—

(a) in England and Wales, by any constable acting within his police area;

(b) in Northern Ireland, by any member of the Police Service of Northern Ireland or the Police Service of Northern Ireland Reserve;

and subsections (4) and (5) of section 159 of the Magistrates' Courts Act (Northern Ireland) 1964 (execution without possession of the warrant and execution on Sunday) shall apply to the execution in Northern Ireland of any such extract conviction as those subsections apply in relation to the execution of a warrant for arrest.

(2) Subject to subsection (6) below, a person against whom there has been issued in England, Wales or Northern Ireland a warrant committing him to prison in default of payment of a sum adjudged to be paid by a conviction may be arrested in Scotland, by any constable appointed for a police area, in like manner as if the warrant were an extract conviction for imprisonment issued in Scotland in default of payment of a fine.

(3) A person arrested by virtue of subsection (1) above under an extract conviction or by virtue of subsection (2) above under a warrant of commitment may be detained under it in any prison in the part of the United Kingdom in which he was arrested; and while so detained he shall be treated for all purposes as if he were detained under a warrant of commitment or extract conviction issued in that part of the United Kingdom.

(4) An extract conviction or a warrant of commitment may be executed by virtue of this section whether or not it has been endorsed under section 4 of the Summary Jurisdiction (Process) Act 1881 or under section 27 of the Petty Sessions (Ireland) Act 1851.

(5) In this section—

"fine" includes any sum treated by any enactment as a fine for the purposes of its enforcement and any sum to be found as caution;

"imprisonment" includes, in the case of a person who is under the age of 21 years, detention;

"part of the United Kingdom" means England and Wales, Scotland or Northern Ireland;

"prison" means—

(i) in the case of a person who is under the age of 21 years arrested in Scotland, a young offenders institution; and

(ia) in the case of a person under that age arrested in England and Wales, any place in which he could be detained under section 108(5) of the Powers of Criminal Courts (Sentencing) Act 2000*;

(ii) in the case of a person under that age arrested in Northern Ireland, a young offenders centre; and

"sum adjudged to be paid by a conviction" has the meaning given by section 150(3) of the Magistrates' Courts Act 1980 or, in Northern Ireland, section 169(2) of the Magistrates' Courts (Northern Ireland) Act 1964.

(6) This section shall not apply to the arrest of persons under the age of 18 years.

[Criminal Law Act 1977, s 38A, as inserted by the Criminal Justice (Scotland) Act 1980, s 51 and amended by the Criminal Justice Act 1982, Sch 14, the Criminal Justice and Public Order Act 1994, Sch 9, the Powers of Criminal Courts (Sentencing) Act 2000, Sch 9 and the Police (Northern Ireland) Act 2000, s 78.]

---

*Paragraph (ia) is prospectively substituted by virtue of the the Criminal Justice and Court Services Act 2000, Sch 7 from a date to be appointed.

1-1693 38B. Further provision for execution of warrants of commitment for non-payment of sum adjudged to be paid by conviction in England and Wales or Northern Ireland.
(1) Subject to subsection (6) below, a person against whom there has been issued in England and Wales a warrant committing him to prison in default of payment of a sum adjudged to be paid by a conviction may be arrested in Northern Ireland by any member of the Police Service of Northern Ireland or the Police Service of Northern Ireland Reservein like manner as if the warrant were a warrant committing him to prison in default of payment of a sum adjudged to be paid by a conviction in Northern Ireland; and Article 158(4) and (5) of the Magistrates' Courts (Northern Ireland) Order 1981 (execution without possession of the warrant and execution on Sunday) shall apply to the execution in Northern Ireland of any such warrant which has been issued in England and Wales as they apply in relation to the execution of a warrant for arrest.

(2) Subject to subsection (6) below, a person against whom there has been issued in Northern Ireland a warrant committing him to prison in default of payment of a sum adjudged to be paid by a conviction may be arrested in England and Wales by any constable acting within his police area in like manner as if the warrant were a warrant committing him to prison in default of payment of a sum adjudged to be paid by a conviction in England and Wales.

(3) A person arrested by virtue of subsection (1) or (2) above under a warrant of commitment may be detained under it in any prison in the part of the United Kingdom in which he was arrested; and while so detained he shall be treated for all purposes as if he were detained under a warrant of commitment issued in that part of the United Kingdom.

(4) A warrant of commitment issued by a court in Northern Ireland may be executed in England and Wales by virtue of this section whether or not it has been endorsed under section 27 of the Petty Sessions (Ireland) Act 1851.

(5) In this section—

"part of the United Kingdom" means England and Wales or Northern Ireland;

"prison" means—

(a) in the case of a person who is under the age of 21 years arrested in England and Wales, any place in which he could be detained under section 108(5) of the Powers of Criminal Courts (Sentencing) Act 2000*

(b) in the case of a person under that age arrested in Northern Ireland, a young offenders centre; and

"sum adjudged to be paid by a conviction" has the meaning given by section 150(3) of the Magistrates' Courts Act 1980 or, in Northern Ireland, Article 2(5) of the Magistrates' Courts (Northern Ireland) Order 1981.

(6) This section shall not apply to the arrest of persons under the age of 18 years.
[Criminal Law Act 1977, s 38B, as inserted by the Criminal Justice Act 1982, s 52 and amended by the Criminal Justice and Public Order Act 1994, Sch 9, the Powers of Criminal Courts (Sentencing) Act 2000, Sch 9 and the Police (Northern Ireland) Act 2000, s 78.]

---

*In the definition of "prison", para (a) is prospectively substituted by virtue of he Criminal Justice and Court Services Act 2000, Sch 7 from a date to be appointed.

1–1694 39. Service of summons and citation throughout United Kingdom. (1) A summons requiring a person charged with an offence to appear before a court in England or Wales may, in such manner as may be prescribed by rules of court, be served on him in Scotland or Northern Ireland.*

(2) A summons requiring a person charged with an offence to appear before a court in Northern Ireland may, in such manner as may be prescribed by rules of court, be served on him in England, Wales or Scotland.

(3) Citation of a person charged with a crime or offence to appear before a court in Scotland may be effected in any other part of the United Kingdom in like manner as it may be done in Scotland, and for this purpose the persons authorised to effect such citation shall include—

(a) in England and Wales and Northern Ireland, constables and prison officers serving in those parts of the United Kingdom,

(b) persons authorised by a chief officer of police in England or Wales to serve summonses there.
[Criminal Law Act 1977, s 39, as amended by the Criminal Justice (Scotland) Act 1980, Sch 7.]

---

*Substituted by the Criminal Justice Act 2003, Sch 36 from a date to be appointed.

Other provisions

1–1695 48. Power to make rules as to furnishing of information by prosecutor in criminal proceedings. (1) Criminal Procedure Rules may make, with respect to proceedings against any person for a prescribed offence or an offence of any prescribed class, provision—

(a) for requiring the prosecutor to do such things as may be prescribed for the purpose of securing that the accused or a person representing him is furnished with, or can obtain, advance information concerning all, or any prescribed class of, the facts and matters of which the prosecutor proposes to adduce evidence; and

(b) for requiring a magistrates' court, if satisfied that any requirement imposed by virtue of paragraph (a) above has not been complied with, to adjourn the proceedings pending compliance with that requirement unless the court is satisfied that the conduct of the case for the accused will not be substantially prejudiced by non-compliance with the requirement.

(2) Rules made by virtue of subsection (1)(a) above—

(a) may require the prosecutor to do as provided in the rules either—

(i) in all cases; or
(ii) only if so requested by or on behalf of the accused;

(b) may exempt facts and matters of any prescribed description from any requirement imposed by the rules, and may make the opinion of the prosecutor material for the purposes of any such exemption; and

(c) may make different provision with respect to different offences or offences of different classes.

(3) It shall not be open to a person convicted of an offence to appeal against the conviction on the ground that a requirement imposed by virtue of subsection (1) above was not complied with by the prosecutor.
[Criminal Law Act 1977, s 48, amended by the Magistrates' Courts Act 1980, Sch 7 and the Courts Act 2003, Sch 8.]

---

1. These powers have been superseded by the Courts Act 2003, s 69.

PART VI
SUPPLEMENTARY

1–1696 64. Meaning of "indictable offence", "summary offence", and "offence triable either way" in England and Wales. (1) In this Act[1]

(a) "indictable offence" means an offence which, if committed by an adult, is triable on indictment, whether it is exclusively so triable or triable either way;

(b) "summary offence" means an offence which, if committed by an adult, is triable only summarily;

(*c*) "offence triable either way" means an offence which, if committed by an adult, is triable either on indictment or summarily;

and the terms "indictable", "summary" and "triable either way", in their application to offences, shall be construed accordingly.

(2) In the definitions in subsection (1) above references to the way or ways in which an offence is triable are to be construed without regard to the effect, if any, of section 22 of the Magistrates' Courts Act 1980 (cases where value involved is small) on the mode of trial.

[Criminal Law Act 1977, s 64, as amended by the Interpretation Act 1978, Sch 3, and the Magistrates' Courts Act 1980, Sch 7.]

1. For other Acts the definition contained in Sch 1 of the Interpretation Act 1978 in Part II: Evidence, post, applied.

1–1699   SCHEDULE 1

Offences Made Triable Only Summarily, and Related Amendments

SCHEDULE 9

Matters Ancillary to Section 47

1–1700   *This schedule is spent.*

Section 65   SCHEDULE 14

Transitional Provisions

(*As amended by the Magistrates' Courts Act 1980, Schs 7 and 9.*)

1–1705   **1.** A provision contained in any of section 15 and 17 above or in Schedule 11 to this Act, and any related amendment or repeal provided for in Schedule 12 or 13 to this Act, shall not apply in relation to proceedings commenced[1] before the coming into force of that provision.

2. *Repealed.*

3. (1) This paragraph applies to any provision of this Act which relates to the punishment by way of fine or imprisonment which may be imposed on summary conviction of offences mentioned in section 30(3) above, in Schedule 1 to this Act or in Schedule 7A to the Criminal Procedure (Scotland) Act 1975.

(2) A provision to which this paragraph applies shall have effect in relation to an offence for which proceedings are commenced after the material time even if that offence was committed before that time; but in the case of an offence committed before the material time, such a provision shall not render a person liable on summary conviction to any punishment greater than that to which he would have been liable on conviction on indictment if at the time of his conviction that provision had not yet come into force.

(3) In relation to a provision to which this paragraph applies "the material time" means the time when that provision comes into force.

4. *Repealed.*

5. Except as provided in paragraph 3 above a provision of this Act which relates to the punishment by way of fine or imprisonment for any offence shall not affect the punishment for an offence committed before that provision comes into force.

1. In *R v Brentwood Justices, ex p Jones* (1979) 143 JP 211, [1979] Crim LR 115 it was held, in relation to a defendant who had been arrested and charged, that the proceedings had commenced when he was charged with the offence at the police station and not when he appeared before the justices.

Magistrates' Courts Act 1980
(1980 c 43)

Part I[1]

Criminal Jurisdiction and Procedure

Jurisdiction to issue process and deal with charges

1–2020   **1. Issue of summons to accused or warrant for his arrest**[2]. (1) On an information being laid[3] before a justice of the peace that a person has, or is suspected of having, committed an offence, the justice may[4] issue—

(*a*) a summons[5] directed to that person requiring him to appear before a magistrates' court to answer the information, or

(*b*) a warrant[6] to arrest that person and bring him before a magistrates' court.

(2) *Repealed.*

(3) No warrant shall be issued under this section* unless the information is in writing[7].

(4) No warrant shall be issued under this section for the arrest of any person who has attained the age of 18 unless—

(*a*) the offence to which the warrant relates is an indictable offence[8] or is punishable with imprisonment[9], or

(*b*) the person's address is not sufficiently established for a summons** to be served on him.

(5) *Repealed.*

(6) Where the offence charged is an indictable offence, a warrant under this section may be issued at any time notwithstanding that a summons has* previously been issued.

(7) A justice of the peace may issue a summons or warrant under this section upon an information being laid before him notwithstanding any enactment requiring the information to be laid before two or more justices.

(8) *Repealed.*

[Magistrates' Courts Act 1980, s 1 as amended by the Criminal Justice Act 1991, Sch 8, the Local Government (Wales) Act 1994, Sch 2, SI 1996/674 and 675, the Criminal Justice Act 2003, Sch 7 and the Courts Act 2003, s 43, Sch 10.]

---

*Words inserted by the Criminal Justice Act 2003, Sch 36, from a date to be appointed.

1. For further commentary, see para **1–401 Issue of summons or warrant**.

2. Part I contains ss 1–50.

3. The Criminal Procedure Rules 2005, this PART: STATUTORY INSTRUMENTS ON PROCEDURE, post provide for the form of information. The application for a summons or warrant is normally made *ex parte* before a justice (or, if for a summons, the Justices' Clerk, see the Justices' Clerks Rules 2005, this PART: STATUTORY INSTRUMENTS ON PROCEDURE, post). An information in writing is laid when it is received at the office of the clerk to the justices for the relevant area. The delivery and receipt of an information is ministerial, and authority to receive an information may be delegated to any member of the staff in the office of the clerk to the justices (*R v Manchester Stipendiary Magistrate, ex p Hill* [1983] 1 AC 328, [1982] 2 All ER 963, 146 JP 348). An oral information should as a matter of practice be addressed by the informant or his authorised agent to a justice or the clerk to the justices in person (*R v Manchester Stipendiary Magistrate, ex p Hill*, supra).

4. A justice, or the justices' clerk, must apply his mind to the information and go through the judicial exercise of deciding whether or not process ought to be issued, see observations of LORD WIDGERY CJ in *R v Brentford Justices, ex p Catlin* [1975] 2 WLR 506 at 512. The function of a justice or of the clerk to the justices in determining whether a summons should be issued is a judicial function which must be performed judicially and cannot be delegated (*R v Manchester Stipendiary Magistrate, ex p Hill* [1983] 1 AC 328, [1982] 2 All ER 963, 146 JP 348). This task can be lightened by batches of informations having similar characteristics being assembled and placed before a single individual; see *R v Gateshead Justices, ex p Tesco Stores Ltd* [1981] QB 470, [1981] 1 All ER 1027, 145 JP 200. There is no question of conducting a preliminary hearing, simply the need to be satisfied that it is a proper case to issue process. A magistrate has power to hear a potential defendant, but that defendant has no right to be heard (*R v West London Justices, ex p Klahn* [1979] 2 All ER 221, [1979] 1 WLR 933). There is no obligation on the justice or justices' clerk to make inquiries to satisfy himself that it will not be vexatious to issue a summons. The protection for a defendant against whom an alleged vexatious summons is issued is to apply to the justices to dismiss it or stay it on the ground that it was an abuse of the process to have issued it at all (*R v Clerk to the Bradford Justices, ex p Sykes and Shoesmith* (1999) 163 JP 224, [1999] Crim LR 748). There is no express provision laying down a period in which the summons must follow the information, but it must not be delayed to the prejudice of the defendant (*R v Fairford Justices, ex p Brewster* [1975] 2 All ER 757, 139 JP 574). *Mandamus* will not be granted if an application for process seems to be a vexatious proceeding (*Ex p Lloyd* (1889) 53 JP 612), but the High Court will grant relief by way of judicial review to quash a summons if it is shown that the issue of the summons was an abuse of the process of the court and that the allegations which the summons made were oppressive and vexatious (*R v Bury Magistrates, ex p Anderton* [1987] NLJ Rep 410).

5. For power to issue a single summons in respect of several informations, see Criminal Procedure Rules 2005, Part 7, this PART: STATUTORY INSTRUMENTS ON PROCEDURE, post.

6. A warrant should not be issued where a summons will be equally effectual except when the charge is of a serious nature (see *O'Brien v Brabner* (1885) 49 JP Jo 227). Where a warrant was issued informally and without oath, it was held that the irregularity in the process of bringing the defendant before the court had no effect on the jurisdiction, and the defendant and a person who committed perjury on the hearing were rightly convicted (*R v Hughes* (1879) 4 QBD 614, 43 JP 556. See also *Gray v Customs Comrs* (1884) 48 JP 343). For power to endorse warrant that on arrest the offender shall be released on bail, see s 117, post. Before issuing a warrant for failure to appear to process served in Scotland, the court must be satisfied on oath that there is sufficient *prima facie* evidence in support of the information or complaint (Summary Jurisdiction (Process) Act 1881, s 4(2)). See PART VIII, title EXTRADITION, FUGITIVE OFFENDERS AND BACKING OF WARRANTS, post, for power to issue warrant for person on his way to the United Kingdom (Extradition Act 1989, s 8 and Sch 1).

7. It is customary to take an information in the form of a deposition, stating shortly the facts; a formal information in the technical language of the warrant was disapproved by the House of Lords in *Herniman v Smith* [1938] AC 305, [1938] 1 All ER 1. The accused is not entitled as of right to a sight of the information on which was issued the warrant by virtue of which he was arrested (*R v Aylesbury Justices, ex p Wisbey* [1965] 1 All ER 602, [1965] 1 WLR 339, 129 JP 175).

8. "Indictable offence" is defined in the Interpretation Act 1978, Sch 1, in PART II: EVIDENCE, post.

9. See s 150(6), post.

1–2021 2. Trial of summary offences.   (1) A magistrates' court has jurisdiction to try any summary offence[1].

(2) A magistrates' court has jurisdiction as examining justices over any offence committed by a person who appears or is brought before the court.

(3) Subject to—

(*a*) sections 18 to 22, and

(*b*) any other enactment (wherever contained) relating to the mode of trial of offences triable either way,

a magistrates' court has jurisdiction to try summarily any offence which is triable either way.

(4) A magistrates' court has jurisdiction, in the exercise of its powers under section 24, to try summarily an indictable offence.

(5) This section does not affect any jurisdiction over offences conferred on a magistrates' court by any enactment[2] not contained in this Act.

[Magistrates' Courts Act 1980, s 2 as substituted by the Courts Act 2003, s 44.]

---

1. "Summary offence" is defined in the Criminal Law Act 1977, s 64, ante.

2. As to proceedings against a person who is in a foreign country, see the Extradition Act 1989 in PART VIII title EXTRADITION, FUGITIVE OFFENDERS AND BACKING OF WARRANTS, post. No British subject can be tried under English law for an offence committed on land abroad, unless there is statutory provision to the contrary, eg in the Offences Against the Person Act 1861, s 9 (murder abroad by a British subject).

English courts will try offences committed within the jurisdiction of the Admiralty, ie on British ships, not only on the high seas, but also in foreign rivers below the bridges where the tide ebbs and flows and where great ships go, even though concurrent jurisdiction may be vested in a foreign state. See *Oteri v R* [1976] 1 WLR 1272, for a case in which two Australian citizens in a fishing boat twenty two miles off the coast of West Australia were convicted under the English Theft Act 1968 of stealing two crayfish pots. English courts have jurisdiction over offences committed on the high seas in a foreign ship under command of a foreigner, within twelve miles of the English coast, by the Territorial Waters Jurisdiction Act 1878 and the Territorial Sea Act 1987. As to proof that a ship is a British ship, see *R v Seberg* (1870) LR 1 CCR 264, 34 JP 468; *R v Armstrong* (1875) 13 Cox CC 184; *R v Allen* (1866) 10 Cox CC 405; *R v Bjornsen* (1865) Le & Ca 545, 29 JP 373. As to the trial of a person subject to military law for certain offences committed on the high seas, see *R v Gordon-Finlayson, ex p an Officer* [1941] 1 KB 171.

Jurisdiction in respect of an offence against English Law, committed on a British aircraft, is conferred by the Civil Aviation Act 1982, s 92, in PART VII: TRANSPORT, title AVIATION, post.

By virtue of the Continental Shelf Act 1964 operations may be conducted on designated parts of the continental shelf adjacent to Britain in relation to the search for and production of oil on the sea-bed. The platforms, etc erected in the sea are described as "installations". Any act or omission thereabouts which would be an offence against the law of the United Kingdom shall be treated as having taken place in the United Kingdom. Proceedings in respect thereof may be taken in any place in this country; see the Criminal Jurisdiction (Offshore Activities) Order 1987, SI 1987/2198 (made under the Oil and Gas Enterprise Act 1982, s 22) in PART VIII, title HEALTH AND SAFETY, post.

1–2022   3. Offences committed on boundaries, etc. (1) Where an offence has been committed on the boundary between two or more areas to which this section applies, or within 500 yards[1] of such a boundary, or in any harbour, river, arm of the sea or other water lying between two or more such areas, the offence may be treated for the purposes of the preceding provisions of this Act as having been committed in any of those areas.

(2) An offence begun in one area to which this section applies and completed[2] in another may be treated for the purposes of the preceding provisions of this Act as having been wholly committed in either.

(3) Where an offence has been committed on any person, or on or in respect of any property, in or on a vehicle[3] or vessel engaged on any journey or voyage through two or more areas to which this section applies, the offence may be treated for the purposes of the preceding provisions of this Act as having been committed in any of those areas; and where the side or any part of a road or any water along which the vehicle or vessel passed in the course of the journey or voyage forms the boundary between two or more areas to which this section applies, the offence may be treated for the purposes of the preceding provisions of this Act as having been committed in any of those areas.

(4) The areas to which this section applies are commission areas.
[Magistrates' Courts Act 1980, s 3 as amended by the Local Government (Wales) Act 1994, Sch 2 and SI 1996/674 and 675.]

1. The distance will be measured in a straight line on a horizontal plane (ie "*as the crow flies*") (Interpretation Act 1978, s 8) (*Stokes v Grissell* (1854) 14 CB 678, 18 JP 378).
2. A railway company forwarding cattle contrary to the Diseases of Animals Act into a prohibited place by another railway was convicted in the district of that other place (*Midland Rly Co v Freeman* (1884) 12 QBD 629, 48 JP 660), but an offence of taking an excessive hackney carriage fare is committed at the place of taking only (*Ely v Godfrey* (1922) 86 JP 82).
3. An offence consisting of the mere unlawful use of a vehicle is not "in or on a vehicle" for the purposes of this subsection (*A F Wardhaugh Ltd v Mace* [1952] 2 All ER 28, 116 JP 369).

1–2022A   3A. Offences committed on ships and abroad. Sections 280, 281 and 282 of the Merchant Shipping Act 1995 (offences on ships and abroad by British citizens and others) apply in relation to other offences under the law of England and Wales as they apply to offences under that Act or instruments under that Act.
[Magistrates' Courts Act 1980, s 3A, inserted by the Merchant Shipping Act 1995, Sch 13.]

1–2022B   3B. Transfer of trials of summary offences. *Repealed.*

Committal proceedings

1–2022C   4. General nature of committal proceedings. (1) The functions of examining justices[1] may be discharged by a single justice.

(2) Examining justices shall sit in open court except where any enactment contains an express provision to the contrary[2] and except where it appears to them as respects the whole or any part of committal proceedings that the ends of justice would not be served by their sitting in open court.

(3) Subject to subsection (4) below, evidence tendered before examining justices shall be tendered in the presence[3] of the accused.

(4) Examining justices may allow evidence to be tendered before them in the absence of the accused if—

(a) they consider that by reason of his disorderly conduct[4] before them it is not practicable for the evidence to be tendered in his presence, or
(b) he cannot be present for reasons of health but is represented by a legal representative and has consented to the evidence being tendered in his absence.
[Magistrates' Courts Act 1980, s 4 as amended by the Courts and Legal Services Act 1990, Sch 18 and the Criminal Procedure and Investigations Act 1996, Sch 1.]

1. As to procedure, see ss 18, 19, 21 and 6, post; and the Criminal Procedure Rules 2005, Parts 10 and 19, this PART: STATUTORY INSTRUMENTS ON PROCEDURE, post. See also para **1–526 Committal for Crown Court trial**.
2. For example, see Official Secrets Act 1920, s 8(4), in PART VIII, title OFFICIAL SECRETS, post.

3. The provisions of s 4 apply both to committals under s 6(1) and (2) and refer to committal proceedings as a whole. Accordingly s 4 is not limited to the tendering of statements under s 6(2) but extends to the consideration of whether the accused should be committed for trial. Further, where an accused is represented in his absence by a solicitor he is deemed not to be absent for the purpose of committal proceedings under s 6(1) and (2) by virtue of s 122 of the Magistrates' Courts Act 1980 (*R v Liverpool City Magistrates' Court, ex p Quantrell* [1999] 2 Cr App Rep 24, 163 JP 408, [1999] Crim LR 734, DC).

4. See also s 18(3) for exclusion of a disorderly accused during initial procedure on information against an adult for an offence triable either way.

1–2022D   5. Adjournment of inquiry.   (1) A magistrates' court may, before beginning to inquire into an offence as examining justices, or at any time during the inquiry, adjourn[1] the hearing, and if it does so shall remand[2] the accused.

(2) The court shall when adjourning fix the time and place at which the hearing is to be resumed; and the time fixed shall be that at which the accused is required to appear or be brought before the court in pursuance of the remand or would be required to be brought before the court but for section 128(3A) below.

[Magistrates' Courts Act 1980, s 5 as amended by the Criminal Justice Act 1982, Sch 9.]

---

1. A defendant cannot claim an adjournment as a matter of right to enable him to obtain professional assistance (*R v Lipscombe, ex p Biggins* (1862) 26 JP 244). *Mandamus* was granted where the hearing had been adjourned for a long period (*R v Evans* (1890) 54 JP 471 distinguished in *R v Southampton Justices, ex p Lebern* (1907) 71 JP 332); see also *R v Bennett and Bond, ex p Bennett* (1908) 72 JP 362.
2. "Remand", in this Act, requires that the accused shall be committed to custody or released on bail; see generally, ss 128, 129, post. Bail shall be granted except as provided by Sch 1 to the Bail Act 1976, ante. See s 130, post, for transfer of remand hearings to a court nearer a prison.

1–2022E   5A. Evidence which is admissible.   (1) Evidence falling within subsection (2) below, and only that evidence, shall be admissible by a magistrates' court inquiring into an offence as examining justices.

(2) Evidence falls within this subsection if it—

(*a*) is tendered by or on behalf of the prosecutor, and
(*b*) falls within subsection (3) below.

(3) The following evidence falls within this subsection—

(*a*) written statements[1] complying with section 5B below;
(*b*) the documents or other exhibits (if any) referred to in such statements;
(*c*) depositions complying with section 5C below;
(*d*) the documents or other exhibits (if any) referred to in such depositions;
(*e*) statements complying with section 5D below;
(*f*) documents falling within section 5E below.

(4) In this section "document" means anything in which information of any description is recorded.

[Magistrates' Courts Act 1980, s 5A, as inserted by the Criminal Procedure and Investigations Act 1996 Sch 1.]

---

1. Any such statement must be that of the witness and where the witness is a foreign language-speaker the statement should contain the witness' account recorded in the foreign language and not be a translation of what the witness said to an interpreter (*R v Raynor* (2000) 165 JP 149, CA).

1–2023   5B. Written statements.   (1) For the purposes of section 5A above a written statement complies with this section if—

(*a*) the conditions falling within subsection (2) below are met, and
(*b*) such of the conditions falling within subsection (3) below as apply are met.

(2) The conditions falling within this subsection are that—

(*a*) the statement purports to be signed by the person who made it;
(*b*) the statement contains a declaration by that person to the effect that it is true to the best of his knowledge and belief and that he made the statement knowing that, if it were tendered in evidence, he would be liable to prosecution if he wilfully stated in it anything which he knew to be false or did not believe to be true;
(*c*) before the statement is tendered in evidence a copy of the statement is given[1], by or on behalf of the prosecutor, to each of the other parties to the proceedings.

(3) The conditions falling within this subsection are that—

(*a*) if the statement is made by a person under 18 years old, it gives his age;
(*b*) if it is made by a person who cannot read it, it is read to him before he signs it and is accompanied by a declaration by the person who so read the statement to the effect that it was so read;
(*c*) if it refers to any other document as an exhibit, the copy given to any other party to the proceedings under subsection (2)(*c*) above is accompanied by a copy of that document or by such information as may be necessary to enable the party to whom it is given[1] to inspect that document or a copy of it.

(4) So much of any statement as is admitted in evidence by virtue of this section shall, unless the court commits the accused for trial by virtue of section 6(2) below or the court otherwise directs, be

read aloud at the hearing; and where the court so directs an account shall be given orally of so much of any statement as is not read aloud.

(5) Any document or other object referred to as an exhibit and identified in a statement admitted in evidence by virtue of this section shall be treated as if it had been produced as an exhibit and identified in court by the maker of the statement.

(6) In this section "document" means anything in which information of any description is recorded.

[Magistrates' Courts Act 1980, s 5B, as inserted by the Criminal Procedure and Investigations Act 1996, Sch 1.]

---

1. In the case of any disclosure in relation to which s 3(1) of the Sexual Offences (Protected Material) Act 1997 applies, this is to be construed as a reference to the document being disclosed in accordance with the procedures under that Act (Sexual Offences (Protected Material) Act 1997, s 9(1), in PART VIII, title SEXUAL OFFENCES, post).

1–2024   5C. Depositions.   (1) For the purposes of section 5A above a deposition complies with this section if—

   (a) a copy of it is sent to the prosecutor under section 97A(9) below,
   (b) the condition falling within subsection (2) below is met, and
   (c) the condition falling within subsection (3) below is met, in a case where it applies.

(2) The condition falling within this subsection is that before the magistrates' court begins to inquire into the offence concerned as examining justices a copy of the deposition is given[1], by or on behalf of the prosecutor, to each of the other parties to the proceedings.

(3) The condition falling within this subsection is that, if the deposition refers to any other document as an exhibit, the copy given to any other party to the proceedings under subsection (2) above is accompanied by a copy of that document or by such information as may be necessary to enable the party to whom it is given[1] to inspect that document or a copy of it.

(4) So much of any deposition as is admitted in evidence by virtue of this section shall, unless the court commits the accused for trial by virtue of section 6(2) below or the court otherwise directs, be read aloud at the hearing; and where the court so directs an account shall be given orally of so much of any deposition as is not read aloud.

(5) Any document or other object referred to as an exhibit and identified in a deposition admitted in evidence by virtue of this section shall be treated as if it had been produced as an exhibit and identified in court by the person whose evidence is taken as the deposition.

(6) In this section "document" means anything in which information of any description is recorded.

[Magistrates' Courts Act 1980, s 5C, as inserted by the Criminal Procedure and Investigations Act 1996, Sch 1.]

---

1. See note 1 to s 5B, ante.

1–2025   5D. Statements.   (1) For the purposes of section 5A above a statement complies with this section if the conditions falling within subsections (2) to (4) below are met.

(2) The condition falling within this subsection is that, before the committal proceedings begin, the prosecutor notifies the magistrates' court and each of the other parties to the proceedings that he believes—

   (a) that the statement might by virtue of section 23 or 24 of the Criminal Justice Act 1988 (statements in certain documents) be admissible as evidence if the case came to trial, and
   (b) that the statement would not be admissible as evidence otherwise than by virtue of section 23 or 24 of that Act if the case came to trial.

(3) The condition falling within this subsection is that—

   (a) the prosecutor's belief is based on information available to him at the time he makes the notification,
   (b) he has reasonable grounds for his belief, and
   (c) he gives the reasons for his belief when he makes the notification.

(4) The condition falling within this subsection is that when the court or a party is notified as mentioned in subsection (2) above a copy of the statement is given[1], by or on behalf of the prosecutor, to the court or the party concerned.

(5) So much of any statement as is in writing and is admitted in evidence by virtue of this section shall, unless the court commits the accused for trial by virtue of section 6(2) below or the court otherwise directs, be read aloud at the hearing; and where the court so directs an account shall be given orally of so much of any statement as is not read aloud.

[Magistrates' Courts Act 1980, s 5D, as inserted by the Criminal Procedure and Investigations Act 1996, Sch 1.]

---

1. See note 1 to s 5B, ante.

1–2026   5E. Other documents.   (1) The following documents fall within this section—

   (a) any document which by virtue of any enactment is evidence in proceedings before a magistrates' court inquiring into an offence as examining justices;
   (b) any document which by virtue of any enactment is admissible, or may be used, or is to be admitted or received, in or as evidence in such proceedings;

(c)　any document which by virtue of any enactment may be considered in such proceedings;

(d)　any document whose production constitutes proof in such proceedings by virtue of any enactment;

(e)　any document by the production of which evidence may be given in such proceedings by virtue of any enactment.

(2)　In subsection (1) above—

(a)　references to evidence include references to prima facie evidence;

(b)　references to any enactment include references to any provision of this Act.

(3)　So much of any document as is admitted in evidence by virtue of this section shall, unless the court commits the accused for trial by virtue of section 6(2) below or the court otherwise directs, be read aloud at the hearing; and where the court so directs an account shall be given orally of so much of any document as is not read aloud.

(4)　In this section "document" means anything in which information of any description is recorded.

[Magistrates' Courts Act 1980, s 5E, as inserted by the Criminal Procedure and Investigations Act 1996, Sch 1.]

1–2027　5F. Proof by production of copy.　(1) Where a statement, deposition or document is admissible in evidence by virtue of section 5B, 5C, 5D or 5E above it may be proved by the production of—

(a)　the statement, deposition or document, or

(b)　a copy of it or the material part of it.

(2)　Subsection (1)(b) above applies whether or not the statement, deposition or document is still in existence.

(3)　It is immaterial for the purposes of this section how many removes there are between a copy and the original.

(4)　In this section "copy", in relation to a statement, deposition or document, means anything onto which information recorded in the statement, deposition or document has been copied, by whatever means and whether directly or indirectly.

[Magistrates' Courts Act 1980, s 5F, as inserted by the Criminal Procedure and Investigations Act 1996, Sch 1.]

1–2028　6. Discharge or committal for trial[1].　(1) A magistrates' court inquiring into an offence as examining justices[2] shall on consideration of the evidence—

(a)　commit the accused for trial if it is of the opinion that there is sufficient evidence to put him on trial by jury for any indictable offence[3];

(b)　discharge[4] him if it is not of that opinion and he is in custody for no other cause than the offence under inquiry;

but the preceding provisions of this subsection have effect subject to the provisions of this and any other Act relating to the summary trial of indictable offences.

(2)　If a magistrates' court inquiring into an offence as examining justices is satisfied that all the evidence tendered by or on behalf of the prosecutor falls within section 5A(3) above, it may commit the accused for trial for the offence without consideration[5] of the contents of any statements, depositions or other documents, and without consideration of any exhibits which are not documents, unless—

(a)　the accused or one of the accused has no legal representative acting for him in the case, or

(b)　a legal representative for the accused or one of the accused, as the case may be, has requested the court to consider a submission that there is insufficient evidence to put that accused on trial by jury for the offence;

and subsection (1) above shall not apply to a committal for trial under this subsection.

(3)　Subject to section 4 of the Bail Act 1976 and section 41 below, the court may commit a person for trial—

(a)　in custody[6], that is to say, by committing him to custody there to be safely kept until delivered in due course of law, or

(b)　on bail[7] in accordance with the Bail Act 1976, that is to say, by directing him to appear before the Crown Court for trial;

and where his release on bail is conditional on his providing one or more surety or sureties and, in accordance with section 8(3) of the Bail Act 1976[8], the court fixes the amount in which the surety is to be bound with a view to his entering into his recognizance subsequently in accordance with subsections (4) and (5) or (6) of that section the court shall in the meantime commit the accused to custody in accordance with paragraph (a) of this subsection.

(4)　Where the court has committed a person to custody in accordance with paragraph (a) of subsection (3) above, then, if that person is in custody for no other cause, the court[9] may, at any time before his first appearance before the Crown Court, grant him bail in accordance with the Bail Act 1976 subject to a duty to appear before the Crown Court for trial.

(5)　Where a magistrates' court acting as examining justices commits any person for trial or determines to discharge him, the justices' chief executive for the court shall, on the day on which the committal proceedings are concluded or the next day, cause to be displayed[10] in a part of the court house to which the public have access a notice—

(a) in either case giving that person's name, address, and age (if known);

(b) in a case where the court so commits him, stating the charge or charges on which he is committed and the court to which he is committed;

(c) in a case where the court determines to discharge him, describing the offence charged and stating that it has so determined;

but this subsection shall have effect subject to section 4 of the Sexual Offences (Amendment) Act 1976 (anonymity of complainant in rape etc cases).

(6) A notice displayed in pursuance of subsection (5) above shall not contain the name or address of any person under the age of 17 unless the justices in question have stated that in their opinion he would be mentioned in the notice apart from the preceding provisions of this subsection and should be mentioned in it for the purpose of avoiding injustice to him.

[Magistrates' Courts Act 1980, s 6 as amended by the Criminal Justice Act 1982, s 61, the Criminal Justice Act 1988, Sch 15, the Courts and Legal Services Act 1990, Sch 18, the Criminal Procedure and Investigations Act 1996, Sch 1, and the Access to Justice Act 1999, Sch 13.]

---

1. Where a person is charged before a magistrates' court with murder, manslaughter or infanticide or an offence under s 1 of the Road Traffic Act 1988 (causing death by reckless driving) or an offence under s 2(1) of the Suicide Act 1961, consisting of aiding, abetting, counselling or procuring the suicide of another, the clerk of the magistrates' court shall inform the coroner, who is responsible for holding an inquest, of the making of the charge and of the result of the proceedings (Coroners Act 1988, s 17, in PART VIII, title CORONERS, post).

2. From the time a mode of trial decision is made justices are examining justices; however, inquiry into the offence begins when the prosecutor opens his case or calls a witness; it is not irregular although it is undesirable for one bench to hear a submission (on abuse of process) and for a separate bench to hear the evidence in support of committal (*R v Worcester Magistrates' Court, ex p Leavesley* (1993) Times, 14 January).

3. "Any indictable offence" contemplates committal for trial either for the offence of which the accused has been formally charged or some other indictable offence as disclosed by the evidence. If a defendant appears before the court charged with an offence triable on indictment only and the examining magistrates find that the evidence only discloses a prima facie case of a lesser offence which is triable either way, the magistrates are nevertheless required by s 6(1) to commit the defendant for trial in the Crown Court and are not entitled to try the lesser offence summarily (*R v Cambridge Justices, ex p Fraser* [1985] 1 All ER 667, [1984] 1 WLR 1391, 148 JP 720). However, if a defendant appears charged with an offence triable either way and the magistrates find that the evidence does not support a prima facie case of that offence but does support some other offence triable either way, it would seem they have jurisdiction under s 25(3), post, to try that other offence summarily; see *R v Cambridge Justices, ex p Fraser*, supra).

If there are lesser alternative charges which are also triable on indictment, the examining justices should hear submissions in relation to all the charges and determine on which of those charges, if any, the accused shall be committed for trial. It is bad practice to invite the examining justices to consider the alternative charges only after a decision not to commit on the substantive charge; see *R v Gloucester Magistrates' Court, ex p Chung* (1988) 153 JP 75.

4. Where the accused is discharged the examining justices may direct payment of expenses properly incurred by him in his defence out of central funds by means of a defence costs order under s 16 of the Prosecution of Offences Act 1985.

5. Despite this provision, it may be necessary to consider the contents of the statements in order to determine the appropriate court of trial, and applications for bail or legal aid. The contents of the statements may also be relevant when the court is required to determine the costs of the prosecution. See Part 10 of the Criminal Procedure Rules 2005, this PART: STATUTORY INSTRUMENTS ON PROCEDURE, post, which governs the application of this section.

6. Note what is then immediately required of the court by s 5 of the Bail Act 1976, ante.

7. Note the requirements of Criminal Procedure Rules 2005, Part 19, this PART: STATUTORY INSTRUMENTS ON PROCEDURE, post, as to notice to prison or remand centre governor. For consideration as to when a magistrate dealing with the question of bail becomes *functus officio*, see *Re Harris* (1984) 148 JP 584, [1984] Crim LR 618. Bail granted by a magistrates' court on committal for trial ceases when the defendant surrenders to the custody of the Crown Court. Accordingly the Crown Court must consider afresh the position of any surety, otherwise the obligations of the surety will cease when the defendant surrenders on that date (*R v Kent Crown Court, ex p Jodka* (1997) 161 JP 638, DC).

8. Power to postpone taking the recognizance of a surety.

9. This may be any court acting for the same petty sessions area, not necessarily the court which, sitting as examining justices, committed the accused for trial (see s 148(2), post).

10. No period of display is prescribed.

1-2029 7. Place of trial on indictment. A magistrates' court committing a person for trial[1] shall specify[2] the place at which he is to be tried, and in selecting that place shall have regard to—

(a) the convenience of the defence, the prosecution and the witnesses,

(b) the expediting of the trial, and

(c) any direction given by or on behalf of the Lord Chief Justice with the concurrence of the Lord Chancellor under section 4(5) of the Courts Act 1971[3].

[Magistrates' Courts Act 1980, s 7.]

---

1. A committal in respect of a summary offence only is a nullity, and the defendant can be tried and convicted summarily later (*Bannister v Clarke* [1920] 3 KB 598, 85 JP 12); similarly, an acquittal by a magistrates' court on a charge triable only on indictment is a nullity, and a magistrates' court, sitting as examining justices, may thereafter commit the accused for trial *(R v West* [1964] 1 QB 15, [1962] 2 All ER 624, 126 JP 352). As to the inclusion in an indictment of offences in respect of which the justices refuse to commit, see *R v Morry* [1946] KB 153, [1945] 2 All ER 632, 110 JP 124.

2. If plea and directions hearings have been established in the Crown Court at the place to which the case is committed, the magistrates' court must also specify the date on which the accused shall appear in the Crown Court for an initial plea and directions hearing; see *Practice Direction (criminal: consolidated)* [2002] para IV.41, in this PART, post.

3. Directions given under s 4(5) of the Act are set out in this PART: STATUTORY INSTRUMENTS ON PROCEDURE, post.

1-2030 8. Restrictions on reports of committal proceedings. (1) Except as provided by subsections (2), (3) and (8) below, it shall not be lawful to publish in Great Britain a written report, or to include in a relevant programme for reception in Great Britain a report, of any committal proceedings in England and Wales containing any matter other than that permitted by subsection (4) below.

(2) Subject to subsection (2A) below a magistrates' court shall, on an application[1] for the purpose made with reference to any committal proceedings by the accused or one of the accused, as the case may be, order[2] that subsection (1) above shall not apply to reports of those proceedings.

(2A) Where in the case of two or more accused one of them objects to the making of an order under subsection (2) above, the court shall make the order if, and only if, it is satisfied, after hearing the representations of the accused, that it is in the interests of justice to do so[3].

(2B) An order under subsection (2) above shall not apply to reports of proceedings under subsection (2A) above, but any decision of the court to make or not to make such an order may be contained in reports published or included in a relevant programme before the time authorised by subsection (3) below.

(3) It shall not be unlawful under this section to publish or include in a relevant programme a report of committal proceedings containing any matter other than that permitted by subsection (4) below—

(a) where the magistrates' court determines not to commit the accused, or determines to commit none of the accused, for trial, after it so determines;

(b) where the court commits the accused or any of the accused for trial, after the conclusion of his trial or, as the case may be, the trial of the last to be tried;

and where at any time during the inquiry the court proceeds to try summarily the case of one or more of the accused under section 25(3) or (7) below, while committing the other accused or one or more of the other accused for trial, it shall not be unlawful under this section to publish or include in a relevant programme as part of a report of the summary trial, after the court determines to proceed as aforesaid, a report of so much of the committal proceedings containing any such matter as takes place before the determination.

(4) The following matters may be contained in a report of committal proceedings published or included in a relevant programme without an order under subsection (2) above before the time authorised by subsection (3) above, that is to say—

(a) the identity of the court and the names of the examining justices;

(b) the names, addresses and occupations of the parties and witnesses and the ages of the accused and witnesses;

(c) the offence or offences, or a summary of them, with which the accused is or are charged;

(d) the names of the legal representatives engaged in the proceedings;

(e) any decision of the court to commit the accused or any of the accused for trial, and any decision of the court on the disposal of the case of any accused not committed;

(f) where the court commits the accused or any of the accused for trial, the charge or charges, or a summary of them, on which he is committed and the court to which he is committed;

(g) where the committal proceedings are adjourned, the date and place to which they are adjourned;

(h) any arrangements as to bail on committal or adjournment;

(i) whether a right to representation funded by the Legal Services Commission as part of the Criminal Defence Service was granted to the accused or any of the accused.

(5) If a report is published, or included in a relevant programme in contravention of this section, the following persons, that is to say—

(a) in the case of a publication of a written report as part of a newspaper or periodical, any proprietor, editor or publisher of the newspaper or periodical;

(b) in the case of a publication of a written report otherwise than as part of a newspaper or periodical, the person who publishes it;

(c) in the case of the inclusion of a report in a relevant programme, any body corporate which provides the service in which the programme is included and any person having functions in relation to the programme corresponding to those of an editor of a newspaper,

shall be liable on summary conviction to a fine not exceeding **level 5** on the standard scale.

(6) Proceedings for an offence under this section shall not, in England and Wales, be instituted otherwise than by or with the consent of the Attorney-General.

(7) Subsection (1) above shall be in addition to, and not in derogation from, the provisions of any other enactment with respect to the publication of reports and proceedings of magistrates' and other courts.

(8) For the purposes of this section committal proceedings shall, in relation to an information charging an indictable offence, be deemed to include any proceedings in the magistrates' court before the court proceeds to inquire into the information as examining justices; but where a magistrates' court which has begun to try an information summarily discontinues the summary trial in pursuance of section 25(2) or (6) below and proceeds to inquire into the information as examining justices, that circumstance shall not make it unlawful under this section for a report of any proceedings on the information which was published, or included in a relevant programme before the court determined to proceed as aforesaid to have been so published, or included in a relevant programme.

(9) *Repealed.*

(10) In this section—

"publish", in relation to a report, means publish the report, either by itself or as part of a newspaper or periodical, for distribution to the public;

"relevant programme" means a programme included in a programme service (within the meaning of the Broadcasting Act 1990).

[Magistrates' Courts Act 1980, s 8, as amended by the Criminal Justice (Amendment) Act 1981, s 1, the Contempt of Court Act 1981, s 4, the Criminal Justice Act 1982, ss 38 and 46, the Cable and Broadcasting Act 1984, Sch 5, the Broadcasting Act 1990, Schs 20 and 21, the Courts and Legal Services Act 1990, Sch 18 and the Access to Justice Act 1999, Sch 13.]

---

1. Criminal Procedure Rules 2005, Part 10, this PART: STATUTORY INSTRUMENTS ON PROCEDURE, post, requires the court to explain his right to apply, to the accused.
2. An order under sub-s (2) may be made before the committal proceedings proper are begun (*R v Bow Street Magistrates, ex p Kray* [1969] 1 QB 473, [1968] 3 All ER 872, 133 JP 54). All accused must be given the opportunity of making representations, and a balance of competing interests struck (*R v Wirral District Magistrates' Court, ex p Meikle* (1990) 154 JP 1035, [1990] Crim LR 801).
3. In such circumstances, a powerful case must be made out that the interests of justice, as affecting the accused, demand the lifting of restrictions (*R v Leeds Justices, ex p Sykes* [1983] 1 All ER 460, [1983] 1 WLR 132, 147 JP 129).

Pre-trial hearings

1–2030A   **8A. Power to make rulings at pre-trial hearing.**   (1) For the purposes of this section a hearing is a pre-trial hearing if—

   (*a*)   it relates to an information—

      (i)   which is to be tried summarily, and
      (ii)   to which the accused has pleaded not guilty, and

   (*b*)   it takes place before the start of the trial.

(2) For the purposes of subsection (1)(*b*), the start of a summary trial occurs when the court begins—

   (*a*)   to hear evidence from the prosecution at the trial, or
   (*b*)   to consider whether to exercise its power under section 37(3) of the Mental Health Act 1983 (power to make hospital order without convicting the accused).

(3) At a pre-trial hearing, a magistrates' court may make a ruling as to any matter mentioned in subsection (4) if—

   (*a*)   the condition in subsection (5) is met,
   (*b*)   the court has given the parties an opportunity to be heard, and
   (*c*)   it appears to the court that it is in the interests of justice to make the ruling.

(4) The matters are—

   (*a*)   any question as to the admissibility of evidence;
   (*b*)   any other question of law relating to the case.

(5) The condition is that, if the accused is not legally represented—

   (*a*)   the court must ask whether he wishes to be granted a right to representation funded by the Legal Services Commission as part of the Criminal Defence Service, and
   (*b*)   if he does, the Legal Services Commission must decide whether or not to grant him that right.

(6) A ruling may be made under this section—

   (*a*)   on an application by a party to the case, or
   (*b*)   of the court's own motion.

(7) For the purposes of this section and section 8B, references to the prosecutor are to any person acting as prosecutor, whether an individual or body.
[Magistrates' Courts Act 1980, s 8A, as inserted by the Courts Act 2003, Sch 3 and amended by SI 2006/2493.]

1–2030B   **8B. Effect of rulings at pre-trial hearing.**   (1) Subject to subsections (3) and (6), a ruling under section 8A has binding effect from the time it is made until the case against the accused or, if there is more than one, against each of them, is disposed of.

(2) The case against an accused is disposed of if—

   (*a*)   he is acquitted or convicted,
   (*b*)   the prosecutor decides not to proceed with the case against him, or
   (*c*)   the information is dismissed.

(3) A magistrates' court may discharge or vary (or further vary) a ruling under section 8A if—

   (*a*)   the condition in section 8A(5) is met,
   (*b*)   the court has given the parties an opportunity to be heard, and
   (*c*)   it appears to the court that it is in the interests of justice to do so.

(4) The court may act under subsection (3)—

   (*a*)   on an application by a party to the case, or
   (*b*)   of its own motion.

(5) No application may be made under subsection (4)(*a*) unless there has been a material change of circumstances since the ruling was made or, if a previous application has been made, since the application (or last application) was made.

(6) A ruling under section 8A is discharged in relation to an accused if—

(a) the magistrates' court commits or sends him to the Crown Court for trial for the offence charged in the information, or

(b) a count charging him with the offence is included in an indictment by virtue of section 40 of the Criminal Justice Act 1988.

[Magistrates' Courts Act 1980, s 8B, as inserted by the Courts Act 2003, Sch 3.]

1–2030C 8C. Restrictions on reporting. (1) Except as provided by this section no report of matters falling within subsection (2) may be published in England and Wales.

(2) The following matters fall within this subsection—

(a) a ruling under section 8A;

(b) proceedings on an application for a ruling under section 8A;

(c) an order under section 8B that a ruling under section 8A be discharged, varied or further varied;

(d) proceedings on an application under section 8B for a ruling under section 8A to be discharged, varied or further varied.

(3) A magistrates' court dealing with any matter falling within subsection (2) may order that subsection (1) does not apply, or does not apply to a specified extent, to a report of the matter.

(4) Where there is only one accused and he objects to the making of an order under subsection (3)—

(a) the court may make the order if (and only if) satisfied after hearing the representations of the accused that it is in the interests of justice to do so, and

(b) if the order is made, it shall not apply to the extent that a report deals with any such objection or representations.

(5) Where there are two or more accused and one or more of them objects to the making of an order under subsection (3)—

(a) the court may make the order if (and only if) satisfied after hearing the representations of each of the accused that it is in the interests of justice to do so, and

(b) if the order is made, it shall not apply to the extent that a report deals with any such objection or representations.

(6) Subsection (1) does not apply to the publication of a report of matters after the case against the accused or, if more than one, against each of them, is disposed of.

(7) Subsection (1) does not apply to a report which contains only one or more of the following matters—

(a) the identity of the court and the names of the justices;

(b) the names, ages, home addresses and occupations of the accused and witnesses;

(c) the offence or offences, or a summary of them, with which the accused or any of the accused are charged;

(d) the names of counsel and solicitors in the proceedings;

(e) where the proceedings are adjourned, the date and place to which they are adjourned;

(f) any arrangements as to bail;

(g) whether a right to representation funded by the Legal Services Commission as part of the Criminal Defence Service was granted to the accused or any of the accused.

(8) The addresses that may be included in a report by virtue of subsection (7) are addresses—

(a) at any relevant time, and

(b) at the time of their inclusion in the publication.

(9) In subsection (8), "relevant time" means a time when events giving rise to the charges to which the proceedings relate are alleged to have occurred.

(10) Nothing in this section affects any prohibition or restriction imposed by virtue of any other enactment on the publication of a report of any matter.

(11) In this section and in section 8D—

(a) references to publication of a report of matters falling within subsection (2)—

(i) include references to inclusion of those matters in any speech, writing, relevant programme or other communication in whatever form which is addressed to the public at large or any section of the public (and for this purpose every relevant programme is to be taken to be so addressed), but

(ii) do not include references to inclusion of those matters in a document prepared for use in particular legal proceedings;

(b) "relevant programme" means a programme included in a programme service, within the meaning of the Broadcasting Act 1990.

[Magistrates' Courts Act 1980, s 8C, as inserted by the Courts Act 2003, Sch 3.]

1–2030D 8D. Offences in connection with reporting. (1) If a report is published in contravention of section 8C each of the following persons is guilty of an offence—

(a) in the case of a publication of a report as part of a newspaper or periodical, any proprietor, editor or publisher of the newspaper or periodical;

    (*b*)   in the case of the inclusion of a report in a relevant programme, any body corporate which is engaged in providing the service in which the programme is included and any person having functions in relation to the programme corresponding to those of an editor of a newspaper;

    (*c*)   in the case of any other publication, any person publishing it.

  (2) If an offence under this section committed by a body corporate is proved—

    (*a*)   to have been committed with the consent or connivance of, or

    (*b*)   to be attributable to any neglect on the part of,

an officer, the officer as well as the body corporate is guilty of the offence and liable to be proceeded against and punished accordingly.

  (3) In subsection (2), "officer" means a director, manager, secretary or other similar officer of the body, or a person purporting to act in any such capacity.

  (4) If the affairs of a body corporate are managed by its members, "director" in subsection (3) means a member of that body.

  (5) A person guilty of an offence under this section is liable on summary conviction to a fine of an amount not exceeding level 5 on the standard scale.

  (6) Proceedings for an offence under this section may not be instituted otherwise than by or with the consent of the Attorney General.

[Magistrates' Courts Act 1980, s 8D, as inserted by the Courts Act 2003, Sch 3.]

Summary trial of information

1–2031 9. Procedure on trial.   (1) On the summary trial[1] of an information, the court shall, if the accused appears, state to him the substance of the information and ask him[2] whether he pleads guilty[3] or not guilty.

  (2) The court, after hearing the evidence[4] and the parties[5], shall convict the accused or dismiss[6] the information[7].

  (3) If the accused pleads guilty, the court may convict him without hearing evidence[8].

[Magistrates' Courts Act 1980, s 9.]

---

  1. For rules relating to summary trial, see Criminal Procedure Rules 2005, Part 37, this Part: Statutory Instruments on Procedure, post. For special procedure enabling the acceptance of a plea of guilty to a summary offence in the absence of the accused, see s 12, post.

  2. In our opinion where the accused does not attend court but is represented by counsel or solicitor, such advocate may enter a plea on behalf of the accused.

  3. For detailed examination of the law as to pleas, including change of plea, mistaken plea, equivocal plea, see ante para **1–566** et seq.

  4. The court must give the prosecution an opportunity of calling such evidence as they have, and not dismiss the case on an application to adjourn because one witness is missing (*R v Milton Keynes Justices, ex p DPP* [1991] Crim LR 712). Once the defendant has appeared and pleaded, evidence that he was charged by the police is unnecessary (*Rees v Barlow* [1974] Crim LR 713).

In accordance with the provision of s 9 of the Criminal Justice Act 1967, ante, evidence may be proffered by way of written statement subject to the conditions which that section prescribes. Furthermore, any fact of which oral evidence may be given in criminal proceedings may be the subject of a formal admission and accepted as conclusive evidence of such fact (ibid, s 10, ante). These sections contain detailed provisions which are pre-requisite to their application. Witnesses for the prosecution may be called in any order. Where the defendant is called as a witness he must be called before the other witnesses for the defence unless the court in its discretion otherwise directs, see the Police and Criminal Evidence Act 1984, s 79 in Part II: Evidence, post. As to conduct of a case by the informant or his representative, see ante para **1–888**.

  5. For rule relating to the order of speeches, see Criminal Procedure Rules 2005, Part 37, this Part: Statutory Instruments on Procedure, post. Where no opportunity is given to the defence to answer a charge whereby there is a denial of natural justice, the remedy is *certiorari* and not appeal by way of case stated (*R v Wandsworth Justices, ex p Read* [1942] 1 KB 281, [1942] 1 All ER 56, 106 JP 50). "Trial on the merits" in this context means not the weighing of evidence but that the accused has been in jeopardy of conviction. Where the prosecution have no witnesses in court but are refused an adjournment, the proper course is not to bring further proceedings but to apply for judicial review (*R v Swansea Justices, ex p Purvis* (1981) 145 JP 252).

  6. Justices cannot dismiss an information until after they have heard the parties and whatever evidence the parties may properly lay before them. If the justices act in breach of this statutory duty, *certiorari* will issue (*Re Harrington* [1984] AC 743, [1984] 2 All ER 474, 149 JP 211, HL). See also *R v Dorchester Magistrates' Court, ex p DPP* (1989) 154 211, [1990] Crim LR 421 and *R v Watford Justices, ex p DPP* [1990] RTR 374n. If the court comprises two magistrates who disagree, they must adjourn the case for trial by a bench of three (*R v Redbridge Justices, ex p Ram* [1992] 1 QB 384, [1992] 1 All ER 652, 156 JP 203).

Where justices are provisionally minded to dismiss an information at the end of the prosecution case, either of their own motion or upon hearing a defence submission to that effect, they should not so rule without first calling upon the prosecution to address the court (*R v Barking and Dagenham Justices, ex p DPP* (1994) 159 JP 373, [1995] Crim LR 953).

  7. Under art 6(1) of the European Convention on Human Rights it is a requirement of a fair trial in both criminal and civil matters that a court should give reasons for its judgment. The extent of the duty to give reasons may, however, vary according to the nature of the decision. See *Hadjianastassiou v Greece* (1992) 16 EHRR 219, *Van de Hurk v Netherlands* (1994) 18 EHRR 481, *Ruiz Torija v Spain* (1994) 19 EHRR 553, *Hiro Balani v Spain* (1994) 19 EHRR 566, *Georgiadis v Greece* (1997) 24 EHRR 606 and *Helle v Finland* (1997) 26 EHRR 159. For recent consideration of the duty to give reasons both at common law and under the Convention see *Stefan v General Medical Council* [1999] 1 WLR 1293, PC. See also *McKerry v Teesdale and Wear Valley Justices* (2000) 164 JP 355, [2000] Crim LR 594, CA where it was stated that justices are not obliged to state reasons in the form of a judgment or in any elaborate form, and if an aggrieved person wishes to obtain more detailed reasons from a magistrates' court he can apply to the justices to state a case; followed in *R (on the application of McGowan) v Brent Justices* [2002] Crim LR 412, DC where it was held that what was necessary was for justices to show that they had applied their minds to the ingredients of the offence and had appreciated the defendant's

state of mind, and that the essence of the exercise was to inform the defendant why he had been found guilty and that could be done in a few sentences.

There is no legal obligation upon justices to give reasons for rejecting a submission of no case to answer (*Moran v DPP* [2002] EWHC 89 (Admin), (2002) 166 JP 467, DC).

8. This does not prevent the court hearing evidence if it so desires; it is often desirable to hear some evidence, particularly where it is part of the prosecution's case that the offence was committed in circumstances of aggravation.

1–2032   10. Adjournment of trial.   (1) A magistrates' court may at any time, whether before or after beginning to try an information, adjourn[1] the trial, and may do so, notwithstanding anything in this Act, when composed of a single justice[2].

(2) The court may when adjourning either[3] fix the time and place at which the trial is to be resumed, or, unless it remands the accused, leave the time and place to be determined later by the court; but the trial shall not be resumed at that time and place unless the court is satisfied that the parties have had adequate notice[4] thereof.

(3) A magistrates' court may[5], for the purpose of enabling inquiries to be made or of determining the most suitable method of dealing with the case, exercise its power to adjourn after convicting the accused and before sentencing[6] him or otherwise dealing with him; but, if it does so, the adjournment shall not be for more than 4 weeks at a time unless the court remands the accused in custody and, where it so remands him, the adjournment shall not be for more than 3 weeks at a time.

(3A) A youth court shall not be required to adjourn any proceedings for an offence at any stage by reason only of the fact—

(a)   that the court commits the accused for trial for another offence; or
(b)   that the accused is charged with another offence.

(4) On adjourning the trial of an information the court may remand[7] the accused and, where the accused has attained the age of 18, shall do so if the offence is triable either way[8] and—

(a)   on the occasion on which the accused first appeared, or was brought before the court to answer to the information he was in custody or, having been released on bail, surrendered to the custody of the court[9]; or
(b)   the accused has been remanded at any time in the course of proceedings on the information[9];

and, where the court remands the accused, the time fixed for the resumption of the trial shall be at which he is required to appear or be brought before the court in pursuance of the remand or would be required to be brought before the court but for section 128(3A) below.

[Magistrates' Courts Act 1980, s 10 as amended by the Criminal Justice Act 1982, Sch 9, the Criminal Justice Act 1991, Sch 8 and the Crime and Disorder Act 1998, s 47.]

---

1. The power to adjourn is unrestricted, and may be exercised in the absence of both parties. For the general principles that apply to the exercise of the power to adjourn, see para **1–483**, this PART, ante. The following is concerned with specific topics under the heading of adjournments of trials.

Double-booked trial courts
Before determining which of 2 trials should proceed first, the court should ascertain the custody time limit in each case: *R v Croydon Youth Court, ex p C* [2001] Crim LR, 40.

Adjourning discontinued trial to a new bench
The wording of s 10 is wide enough to encompass the adjournment of a discontinued trial to a different bench: *R v Ripon Liberty Justices, ex p Bugg* (1990) 155 JP 213); followed in *R v Birmingham Magistrates' Court, ex p Shields* (1994) 158 JP 845 (adjournment for a re-trial before a differently constituted bench because the chairman of the justices was due to retire before hearing of trial could be resumed).

Adjourning part heard
Where one bench of justices has heard the prosecution case in its entirety and has adjourned part-heard (due to lack of time) that decision may subsequently be overturned by a differently constituted bench provided that there are exceptional circumstances, and the latter bench may direct that the matter be heard afresh before a differently constituted court from that which heard the prosecution case: *DPP v Khan* CO/453/2000. Where the court adjourned a trial part-heard to enable the prosecution to call a forensic scientist, the delay of 5 months before the trial was able to be resumed was held not to be in breach of the defendant's right to a fair trial under art 6: *Khatibi v DPP* [2004] EWHC Admin 83, (2004) 168 JP 361.

Relevance of previous indications
Although justices are entitled to have regard to indications given by their colleagues when granting an adjournment on a previous occasion that the case must proceed at the next hearing, it is incumbent upon them to have regard to the situation which actually presents itself on the day of the hearing before them: see *R v Aberdare Justices, ex p DPP* (1990) 155 JP 324.

Defendant prejudiced by late service of evidence, non-disclosure, etc
In *R (on the application of Rashid) v Horseferry Road Magistrates' Court* CO/2951/2000, it was held that an adjournment should have been allowed where legal aid had not been granted and prosecution statements and interview summary had not been served until the morning of the trial, it had been difficult to take instructions from the defendant because of his lack of English and the applicants might have wished to call additional evidence which was not available on the day.

If it is necessary to adjourn the case to enable justice to be done following a failure by the prosecution to disclose matters which ought to be disclosed, then the adjournment must be granted, unless the court is satisfied that no prejudice would be caused to the defendant by proceeding: *S v DPP* [2006] EWHC 1207 (Admin), (2006) 170 JP 707 (prosecution failed to disclose details of a Crown Court case of affray pending against the victim in the current proceedings, whose credibility and reliability were critical and those details might well have damaged his credibility).

Failure of witnesses to attend
In *R v Bristol Magistrates' Court, ex p Rowles* [1994] RTR 40 it was held that the justices' refusal to grant an adjournment, when two witnesses essential to the defence failed to attend, was contrary to natural justice. However, in *R (on the application of Walden) v Highbury Corner Magistrates' Court* and *R (on the application of Stern) v Highbury Corner Magistrates' Court* [2003] All ER (D) 285 (Mar), 167 JPN 222, the justices' decisions to grant adjournments were quashed where prosecution witnesses had failed to attend on the day set for the trial of 2 drink driving cases, the prosecution had given no reason for their absence, the inevitable inference was that the witnesses had not been warned, but in neither case had the prosecution

been sent away to find an explanation). See also *R (on the application of the DPP) v Bridgend Justices* CO/2651/2000, where it was held the justices had been entitled to refuse to adjourn a trial where 2 previous trial dates had been abortive due to the inefficiency of the prosecution, the problem—main prosecution witnesses unavailable due to sitting examinations had been known to the CPS 16 days before the third trial date, but no approach had been made to the court until 2 days before the third trial date).

Order of priority as between trials and coroners' inquests concerning the same incident

Where the information before the court relates to an incident with respect to which an inquest has been opened, as a matter of practice, justices ought not to proceed with the summary trial of the information but should adjourn it until the inquest has been held: *Smith v DPP* [2000] RTR 36, 164 JP 96. In cases to be tried on indictment to which ss 16 and 17 of the Coroners Act 1988 apply, the reverse situation applies and the coroner is required to adjourn the inquest until after the conclusion of the relevant criminal proceedings (Coroners Act 1988, s 16, in PART VIII: title CORONERS, post).

2. A justices' clerk may further adjourn criminal proceedings in the limited circumstances set out in the Schedule to the Justices' Clerks Rules 1999, this PART: STATUTORY INSTRUMENTS ON PROCEDURE, post. Sub-s (1) is restricted to an adjournment before a verdict has been returned; *Per* LORD WIDGERY CJ, *R v Talgarth Justices, ex p Bithell* [1973] 2 All ER 717 at 719.

3. An express power to adjourn *sine die* may only be exercised on a simple adjournment: where there is a remand (in custody or on bail) the time and place of the adjourned hearing must be determined.

4. Where the adjournment is in consequence of the court's decision not to proceed with the case in the absence of the accused in accordance with s 12, post, the notice must also give the reason for the adjournment. A similar provision applies where the court adjourns a case in the absence of the defendant with the intention of imposing a disqualification on him when the hearing is resumed; s 11(4).

5. The power to adjourn after conviction must be exercised judicially, and for a proper purpose, ie, to enable inquiries to be made or to determine the most suitable method of dealing with the case; the practice of postponing sentence and remanding in custody after a finding of guilt is not approved by the Court of Appeal (see remarks of LORD GODDARD, CJ in *R v Easterling* (1946) 175 LT 520).

6. For meaning of "sentence", see s 150, post. At the adjourned hearing the court need not be composed of the same justices, see s 121(7), post. Magistrates considering disqualification must adjourn the whole question of sentencing and deal with it as one matter on the adjourned hearing (*R v Talgarth Justices, ex p Bithell* [1973] 2 All ER 717, [1973] 1 WLR 1327, 137 JP 666). It would be improper for a court to adjourn until the defendant attained 21 in order to pass a sentence of imprisonment (*Arthur v Stringer* (1986) 151 JP 97).

7. The remand may be in custody or on bail, see s 128, post; and for power of further remand, see s 129, post. For power to remand medical examination, see the Powers of Criminal Courts (Sentencing) Act 2000, s 11 in PART III: SENTENCING, post. Where the offence is not punishable on summary conviction by imprisonment, s 30 has no application; nevertheless, the accused may be remanded for a medical report under s 10, ante (*Boaks v Reece* [1957] 1 QB 219, [1956] 3 All ER 986, 121 JP 51). Bail shall be granted except as provided by Schedule 1 to the Bail Act 1976, ante. For rules relating to remand, see Criminal Procedure Rules 2005, Parts 18 and 19, this PART: STATUTORY INSTRUMENTS ON PROCEDURE, post. A justice who, in determining the question of bail, has been informed that the defendant has previous convictions, shall not take part in trying his guilt on the summary trial of the offence, s 42, post. Subject to s 42(2), post, this does not disqualify such a justice from sitting as an examining magistrate in subsequent proceedings.

8. Defined in the Interpretation Act 1978, Sch 1, in PART II: EVIDENCE, post.

9. In either of these circumstances there is an obligation to remand (in custody or on bail). For offences triable either way which do not fall within sub-paras (*a*) or (*b*) and for summary offences the power to remand is discretionary.

1–2033   11. Non-appearance of accused: general provisions.   (1) Subject to the provisions of this Act, where at the time and place appointed for the trial or adjourned trial of an information the prosecutor appears but the accused does not, the court may proceed in his absence[1].

(2) Where a summons has been issued, the court shall not begin to try the information in the absence of the accused unless either it is proved to the satisfaction of the court, on oath or in such other manner as may be prescribed[2], that the summons was served[2] on the accused within what appears to the court to be a reasonable time before the trial or adjourned trial or the accused has appeared on a previous occasion to answer to the information.

(3) A magistrates' court shall not in a person's absence[1] sentence[3] him to imprisonment or detention in a young offender institution or make a detention and training order or an order under section 119 of the Powers of Criminal Courts (Sentencing) Act 2000 that a suspended sentence passed on him shall take effect.

(4) A magistrates' court shall not in a person's absence[1] impose any disqualification[4] on him, except on resumption of the hearing after an adjournment under section 10(3) above; and where a trial is adjourned in pursuance of this subsection the notice required by section 10(2) above shall include notice of the reason for the adjournment.

[Magistrates' Courts Act 1980, s 11 as amended by virtue of the Criminal Justice Act 1988, Sch 8, the Criminal Justice and Public Order Act 1994, Sch 10, the Crime and Disorder Act 1998, Sch 8 and the Powers of Criminal Courts (Sentencing) Act 2000, Sch 9.]

---

1. For detailed commentary on this section see para **1–423**, ante.

Where a defendant has been found guilty in his absence under s 11(1), the court may not rehear the evidence in the case except in accordance with the provisions of s 142, post (*R v Maidstone Justices, ex p Booth* (1980) 144 JP 354). This is now subject to the requirements of art 6(1) of the European Convention on Human Rights.

2. See Criminal Procedure Rules 2005, this PART: STATUTORY INSTRUMENTS ON PROCEDURE, post, as to proof of service and methods of service (Part 4).

3. "Sentence" does not include a committal in default of payment of any sum of money or for want of sufficient distress to satisfy any sum of money, or for failure to do or abstain from doing anything required to be done or left undone; see s 150(1), post.

4. Examples of disqualifications which may be ordered by a magistrates' court are: disqualification for keeping any animal (Protection of Animals (Amendment) Act 1954, s 1); disqualification for keeping a pet shop (Pet Animals Act 1951, s 5); disqualification for holding a licence to drive a motor vehicle (Road Traffic Offenders Act 1988, ss 34–36); disqualification for keeping a boarding establishment for animals (Animal Boarding Establishments Act 1963, s 5). Magistrates considering a driving disqualification and adjourning under this section are under a duty to adjourn the whole question of sentence (*R v Talgarth Justices, ex p Bithell* [1973] 2 All ER 717, [1973] 1 WLR 1327, 137 JP 666).

1–2034 **12. Non-appearance of accused: plea of guilty.** (1) This section shall apply where—

(a) a summons has been issued requiring a person to appear before a magistrates' court, other than a youth court, to answer to an information for a summary offence[1], not being—

  (i) an offence for which the accused is liable to be sentenced to be imprisoned for a term exceeding 3 months; or

  (ii) an offence specified in an order made by the Secretary of State by statutory instrument; and

(b) the justices' chief executive for the court is notified by or on behalf of the prosecutor that the documents mentioned in subsection (3) below have been served upon the accused with the summons.

(2) The reference in subsection (1)(a) above to the issue of a summons requiring a person to appear before a magistrates' court other than a youth court includes a reference to the issue of a summons requiring a person who has attained the age of 16 at the time when it is issued to appear before a youth court.

(3) The documents referred to in subsection (1)(b) above are—

(a) a notice containing such statement of the effect of this section as may be prescribed;

(b) either of the following, namely—

  (i) a concise statement of such facts relating to the charge as will be placed before the court by the prosecutor if the accused pleads guilty without appearing before the court, or

  (ii) a copy of such written statement or statements complying with subsections (2)(a) and (b) and (3) of section 9 of the Criminal Justice Act 1967 (proof by written statement) as will be so placed in those circumstances; and

(c) if any information relating to the accused will or may, in those circumstances, be placed before the court by or on behalf of the prosecutor, a notice containing or describing that information.

(4) Where the justices' chief executive for the court receives[2] a notification in writing purporting to be given by the accused[3] or by a legal representative acting on his behalf that the accused desires to plead guilty[4] without appearing before the court—

(a) the justices' chief executive for the court shall inform the prosecutor of the receipt of the notification; and

(b) the following provisions of this section shall apply.

(5) If at the time and place appointed for the trial or adjourned trial of the information—

(a) the accused does not appear; and

(b) it is proved to the satisfaction of the court, on oath or in such manner as may be prescribed, that the documents mentioned in subsection (3) above have been served[5] upon the accused with the summons,

the court may, subject to section 11(3) and (4) above and subsections (6) to (8) below, proceed to hear and dispose of the case in the absence of the accused, whether or not the prosecutor is also absent, in like manner as if both parties had appeared and the accused had pleaded guilty.

(6) If at any time before the hearing the justices' chief executive for the court receives an indication in writing purporting to be given by or on behalf of the accused that he wishes to withdraw the notification—

(a) the justices' chief executive for the court shall inform the prosecutor of the withdrawal; and

(b) the court shall deal with the information as if the notification had not been given.

(7) Before accepting the plea of guilty and convicting the accused under subsection (5) above, the court shall cause the following to be read out[6] before the court by the clerk of the court, namely—

(a) in a case where a statement of facts as mentioned in subsection (3)(b)(i) above was served on the accused with the summons, that statement;

(aa) in a case where a statement or statements as mentioned in subsection (3)(b)(ii) above was served on the accused with the summons and the court does not otherwise direct, that statement or those statements;

(b) any information contained in a notice so served, and any information described in such a notice and produced by or on behalf of the prosecutor;

(c) the notification under subsection (4) above; and

(d) any submission received with the notification which the accused wishes to be brought to the attention of the court with a view to mitigation of sentence.

(7A) Where the court gives a direction under subsection (7)(aa) above the court shall cause an account to be given orally before the court by the clerk of the court of so much of any statement as is not read aloud.

(7B) Whether or not a direction under paragraph (aa) of subsection (7) above is given in relation to any statement served as mentioned in that paragraph the court need not cause to be read out the declaration required by section 9(2)(b) of the Criminal Justice Act 1967.

(8) If the court proceeds under subsection (5) above to hear and dispose of the case in the absence of the accused, the court shall not permit—

(a) any other statement with respect to any facts relating to the offence charged; or

(b) any other information relating to the accused,

to be made or placed before the court by or on behalf of the prosecutor except on a resumption of the trial after an adjournment under section 10(3) above.

(9) If the court decides not to proceed under subsection (5) above to hear and dispose of the case in the absence of the accused, it shall adjourn or further adjourn the trial for the purpose of dealing with the information as if the notification under subsection (4) above had not been given.

(10) In relation to an adjournment on the occasion of the accused's conviction in his absence under subsection (5) above or to an adjournment required by subsection (9) above, the notice required by section 10(2) above shall include notice of the reason[7] for the adjournment.

(11) No notice shall be required by section 10(2) above in relation to an adjournment—

(a) which is for not more than 4 weeks; and

(b) the purpose of which is to enable the court to proceed under subsection (5) above at a later time.

(12) No order shall be made under subsection (1) above unless a draft of the order has been laid before and approved by resolution of each House of Parliament.

(13) Any such document as is mentioned in subsection (3) above may be served in Scotland with a summons which is so served under the Summary Jurisdiction (Process) Act 1881.

[Magistrates' Courts Act 1980, s 12, as substituted by the Criminal Justice and Public Order Act 1994, Sch 5 and amended by the Magistrates' Courts (Procedure) Act 1998, s 1 and the Access to Justice Act 1999, Sch 13.]

1. For meaning of "summary offence" see the Interpretation Act 1978, Sch 1, in PART II: EVIDENCE, post.

2. The receipt may be at any time before the actual hearing, even if this is by adjournment after the return date mentioned in the summons; see *R v Norham and Islandshire Justices, ex p Sunter Bros Ltd* [1961] 1 All ER 455, [1961] 1 WLR 364, 125 JP 181.

3. In the case of a defendant corporation, notice may be given on its behalf by a director or the secretary and the court may act upon a notification which purports to be so given; see Sch 3 para 4(1), post.

4. It must be clear that the plea of guilty relates to each offence, if more than one is charged (*R v Burnham Justices, ex p Ansorge* [1959] 3 All ER 505, [1959] 1 WLR 1041, 123 JP 539). The accused is required, when submitting a notification that he desires to plead guilty to an offence involving endorsements of driving licence or disqualification, to include in that notification a statement of his date of birth and sex (Road Traffic Offenders Act 1988, s 8, in PART VII, post).

5. See Criminal Procedure Rules 2005, this PART: STATUTORY INSTRUMENTS ON PROCEDURE, post, as to proof of service and methods of service (Part 4).

6. Before magistrates can exercise jurisdiction under this section, they must strictly observe the conditions of the statute. The statement of mitigating circumstances (as well as the notification of plea of guilty and the statement of facts) must be *read out* before the court: it is not sufficient if these documents are passed to the bench for the justices to read for themselves (*R v Oldham Justices, ex p Morrissey* [1958] 3 All ER 559, [1959] 1 WLR 58, 123 JP 38); followed in *R v Epping and Ongar Justices, ex p C Shippam Ltd* (1986) 150 JP 425, [1986] Crim LR 810. In the ordinary case, we suggest that the clerk should first read out the notification that the defendant desires to plead guilty without appearing before the court, followed by the statement of facts served by the prosecutor, and then any submission made with a view to mitigation of sentence.

A claim for costs by the prosecution against the defendant, in a case dealt with under this section, may be notified to the defendant in the same document as contains the statement of facts, but if so notified does not form part of that statement. Where such a claim is so notified, the justices' clerk must bring the claim for costs to the attention of the court so that the justices may properly adjudicate on the application (*R v Coventry Magistrates' Court, ex p DPP* [1990] RTR 193, 154 JP 765).

If the procedure laid down is not strictly observed, but the justices proceed to convict, there may be an application for judicial review; where possible such an application should be made under the consent procedure (*Practice Note (Crown Office List: Consent Orders)* [1997] 2 All ER 799, [1997] 1 WLR 825) to avoid the appearance of counsel before the Divisional Court. There is no power to rectify a procedural defect in proceedings under s 12 by means of s 142 post; see *R v Epping and Ongar Justices, ex p C Shippam Ltd*, supra.

7. Failure to specify the reason for the adjournment to the notice thereof will prohibit the court from imposing a disqualification on the defendant (s 11(4), supra), see *R v Mason* [1965] 2 All ER 308, 129 JP 363.

1–2035   12A. Application of section 12 where accused appears. (1) Where the clerk of the court has received such a notification as is mentioned in subsection (4) of section 12 above but the accused nevertheless appears before the court at the time and place appointed for the trial or adjourned trial, the court may, if he consents, proceed under subsection (5) of that section as if he were absent.

(2) Where the clerk of the court has not received such a notification and the accused appears before the court at that time and place and informs the court that he desires to plead guilty, the court may, if he consents, proceed under section 12(5) above as if he were absent and the clerk had received such a notification.

(3) For the purposes of subsections (1) and (2) above, subsections (6) to (11) of section 12 above shall apply with the modifications mentioned in subsection (4) or, as the case may be, subsection (5) below.

(4) The modifications for the purposes of subsection (1) above are that—

(a) before accepting the plea of guilty and convicting the accused under subsection (5) of section 12 above, the court shall afford the accused an opportunity to make an oral submission with a view to mitigation of sentence; and

(b) where he makes such a submission, subsection (7)(d) of that section shall not apply.

(5) The modifications for the purposes of subsection (2) above are that—

(a) subsection (6) of section 12 above shall apply as if any reference to the notification under subsection (4) of that section were a reference to the consent under subsection (2) above;

(b) subsection (7)(c) and (d) of that section shall not apply; and

(c) before accepting the plea of guilty and convicting the accused under subsection (5) of that section, the court shall afford the accused an opportunity to make an oral submission with a view to mitigation of sentence.

[Magistrates' Courts Act 1980, s 12A, as inserted by the Criminal Justice and Public Order Act 1994, Sch 5.]

1–2036 **13. Non-appearance of accused: issue of warrant.** (1) Subject to the provisions of this section, where the court, instead of proceeding in the absence of the accused, adjourns or further adjourns the trial, the court may issue a warrant[1] for his arrest.

(2) Where a summons has been issued, the court shall not issue a warrant under this section unless the condition in subsection (2A) below or that in subsection (2B) below is fulfilled.

(2A) The condition in this subsection is that it is proved to the satisfaction of the court, on oath or in such other manner as may be prescribed, that the summons was served[2] on the accused within what appears to the court to be a reasonable time before the trial or adjourned trial.

(2B) The condition in this subsection is that—

(a) the adjournment now being made is a second or subsequent adjournment of the trial,
(b) the accused was present on the last (or only) occasion when the trial was adjourned, and
(c) on that occasion the court determined the time for the hearing at which the adjournment is now being made.

(3) A warrant for the arrest of any person who has attained the age of 18 shall not be issued under this section unless—

(a) offence to which the warrant relates is punishable with imprisonment, or
(b) the court, having convicted the accused, proposes to impose a disqualification on him.

(3A) A warrant for the arrest of any person who has not attained the age of 18 shall not be issued under this section unless—

(a) the offence to which the warrant relates is punishable, in the case of a person who has attained the age of 18, with imprisonment, or
(b) the court, having convicted the accused, proposes to impose a disqualification on him.

(4) This section shall not apply to an adjournment on the occasion of the accused's conviction in his absence under subsection (5) of section 12 above or to an adjournment required by subsection (9) of that section.[3]

(5) Where the court adjourns the trial—

(a) after having, either on that or on a previous occasion, received any evidence or convicted the accused without hearing evidence on his pleading guilty under section 9(3) above; or
(b) after having on a previous occasion convicted the accused without hearing evidence on his pleading guilty under section 12(5) above,

the court shall not issue a warrant under this section unless it thinks it undesirable, by reason of the gravity of the offence, to continue the trial in the absence of the accused.

[Magistrates' Courts Act 1980, s 13 as amended by the Criminal Justice Act 1991, Sch 8, the Criminal Justice and Public Order Act 1994, Sch 5, the Criminal Procedure and Investigations Act 1996, s 48, the Magistrates' Courts (Procedure) Act 1998, s 3 and the Criminal Justice Act 2003, s 31 and Sch 37.]

---

1. For execution of a warrant of arrest in Scotland or Northern Ireland, see the Criminal Justice and Public Order Act 1994, this PART, post, and for the execution of a warrant of arrest in the Isle of Man or the Channel Islands, see s 126, post, and the Indictable Offences Act 1848, s 13, in PART VIII: title EXTRADITION, etc, post. Where a defendant has been released on bail in criminal proceedings and fails to surrender into the custody of a court, a warrant may be issued under the Bail Act 1976, s 7(1) or (2), ante.
2. See Criminal Procedure Rules 2005, this PART: STATUTORY INSTRUMENTS ON PROCEDURE, post as to proof of service and methods of service (Part 4).
3. If he still does not appear at the adjourned hearing, a warrant may then be issued, subject to any other restrictions contained in s 13.

1–2037 **14. Proceedings invalid where accused did not know of them.** (1) Where a summons has been issued under section 1 above and a magistrates' court has begun to try the information to which the summons relates, then, if—

(a) the accused, at any time during or after the trial, makes a statutory declaration[1] that he did not know of the summons or the proceedings until a date specified in the declaration, being a date after the court has begun to try the information; and
(b) within 21 days of that date the declaration is served on the justices' chief executive for the court,

without prejudice to the validity of the information[2], the summons and all subsequent proceedings shall be void[3].

(2) For the purposes of subsection (1) above a statutory declaration shall be deemed to be duly served on the justices' chief executive if it is delivered to him, or left at his office, or is sent in a registered letter or by the recorded delivery service addressed to him at his office.

(3) If on the application of the accused it appears to a magistrates' court (which for this purpose may be composed of a single justice[4]) that it was not reasonable to expect the accused to serve such a statutory declaration as is mentioned in subsection (1) above within the period allowed by that subsection, the court may accept service of such a declaration by the accused after that period has expired; and a statutory declaration accepted under this subsection shall be deemed to have been served as required by that subsection.

(4) Where any proceedings have become void by virtue of subsection (1) above, the information shall not be tried again by any of the same justices.

[Magistrates' Courts Act 1980, s 14, as amended by the Access to Justice Act 1999, Sch 13.]

1. See Precedent 10 in PART IX: PRECEDENTS AND FORMS, post. Knowingly and wilfully making a false statement therein will be an offence against s 5 of the Perjury Act 1911, in PART VIII title PERJURY, post.
2. Consequently, a fresh summons may be issued without regard to any limitation of time for summary proceedings.
3. The summons and subsequent proceedings, including any order of the court such as a disqualification from driving, become void from the time when the statutory declaration is served on the clerk to the justices and they are not void *ab initio* (*Singh v DPP* [1999] Crim LR 914, 164 JP 82).
4. Or the justices' clerk (Justices' Clerks Rules 1999, Schedule, para 28).

1–2038   15. Non-appearance of prosecutor.   (1) Where at the time and place appointed for the trial or adjourned trial of an information the accused appears or is brought before the court and the prosecutor does not appear,[1] the court may dismiss[2] the information[3] or, if evidence has been received on a previous occasion, proceed in the absence of the prosecutor.

(2) Where, instead of dismissing the information or proceeding in the absence of the prosecutor, the court adjourns the trial, it shall not remand the accused in custody unless he has been brought from custody or cannot be remanded on bail by reason of his failure to find sureties.
[Magistrates' Courts Act 1980, s 15.]

1. Where the prosecutor is represented by counsel or a solicitor, he shall be deemed not to be absent (s 122, post). A prosecutor 'does not appear' for the purposes of s 15(1) of the Magistrates' Courts Act 1980 when, though physically present in court, he is unable to proceed with the particular part of the case which is before the court. Magistrates were therefore wrong to dismiss a case where, although given advance notice, the prosecutor did not have the file in court but where there was sufficient information to take a plea from the defendant. It was only at the stage of proceeding to sentence after a guilty plea that the prosecutor would have been in difficulties and would have been required to seek an adjournment (*DPP v Shuttleworth* [2002] EWHC 621 (Admin), 166 JP 417).
2. It is a breach of the rules of natural justice and unlawful for justices to dismiss an information for want of prosecution when they know the case has been wrongly listed and the arrival of the prosecutor is imminent (*R v Dudley Justices, ex p DPP* (1992) 157 JP 177). It is wrong to use the power of dismissal under s 15 so as to punish the prosecutor for inefficiency which is merely apparent and which is liable to be dispelled on enquiry (*R v Hendon Justices, ex p DPP* [1993] 1 All ER 411, 157 JP 181, [1993] Crim LR 215). See further the commentary at para **1–463 Power to adjourn.**
3. The court should be cautious over taking these words literally. See *R v Uxbridge Justices, ex p Smith* [1977] RTR 93, where justices were held wrong to allow a change of plea as a device to facilitate an application to strike out for want of prosecution, taking advantage of the informant's late appearance.

1–2039   16. Non-appearance of both parties.   Subject to section 11(3) and (4) and to section 12 above[1], where at the time and place appointed for the trial or adjourned trial of an information neither the prosecutor nor the accused appears, the court may dismiss the information or, if evidence has been received on a previous occasion, proceed in their absence[2].
[Magistrates' Courts Act 1980, s 16.]

1. These sections forbid the passing of a sentence of imprisonment, or detention in a young offender institution, or the making of a dentention and training order, or the implementation of a suspended sentence, or the imposition of disqualification without adjournment, in the absence of the accused. He must also be present for the making of a probation order or order for conditional discharge (Powers of Criminal Courts (Sentencing) Act 2000, ss 12(4) and 41(7)), and to consent to give a recognizance to keep the peace or to be of good behaviour (but see also Criminal Procedure Rules 2005, Part 19, this PART: STATUTORY INSTRUMENTS ON PROCEDURE, post).
2. The proceedings may also be adjourned, of course (s 10, ante). See s 122, post where counsel or a solicitor appears for absent party.

Offences triable on indictment or summarily

1–2040   17. Certain offences triable either way[1].   (1) The offences listed in Schedule 1 to this Act shall be triable either way.

(2) Subsection (1) above is without prejudice to any other enactment by virtue of which any offence is triable either way.
[Magistrates' Courts Act 1980, s 17.]

1. An "offence triable either way" means an offence, other than an offence triable on indictment only by virtue of Part V of the Criminal Justice Act 1988, which, if committed by an adult, is triable either on indictment or summarily (Interpretation Act 1978, Sch 1, in PART II: EVIDENCE, post).
    Where a person is charged with a Class A drug trafficking offence or a burglary committed in respect of a building or a part of a building which is a dwelling, and if convicted such offence would be a third offence for the purposes of ss 110 or 111 of the Powers of Criminal Courts (Sentencing) Act 2000, the offence shall not be triable either way but triable only on indictment; see Powers of Criminal Courts (Sentencing) Act 2000, ss 110 and 111, in PART III: SENTENCING, post.

1–2041   17A. Initial procedure: accused to indicate intention as to plea[1].   (1) This section shall have effect where a person who has attained the age of 18 years appears or is brought before a magistrates' court on an information charging him with an offence triable either way.

(2) Everything that the court is required to do under the following provisions of this section must be done with the accused present in court.

(3) The court shall cause the charge to be written down, if this has not already been done, and to be read to the accused.

(4) The court shall then explain to the accused in ordinary language that he may indicate whether (if the offence were to proceed to trial) he would plead guilty or not guilty, and that if he indicates that he would plead guilty—

(*a*) the court must proceed as mentioned in subsection (6) below; and (b)　he may be committed for sentence[2] to the Crown Court under section 3 of the Powers of Criminal Courts (Sentencing) Act 2000 if the court is of such opinion as is mentioned in subsection (2) of that section.

(5)　The court shall then ask the accused whether (if the offence were to proceed to trial) he would plead guilty or not guilty.

(6)　If the accused indicates that he would plead guilty the court shall proceed as if—

(a)　the proceedings constituted from the beginning the summary trial of the information; and
(b)　section 9(1) above was complied with and he pleaded guilty under it.

(7)　If the accused indicates that he would plead not guilty section 18(1) below shall apply.

(8)　If the accused in fact fails to indicate how he would plead, for the purposes of this section and section 18(1) below he shall be taken to indicate that he would plead not guilty.

(9)　Subject to subsection (6) above, the following shall not for any purpose be taken to constitute the taking of a plea—

(a)　asking the accused under this section whether (if the offence were to proceed to trial) he would plead guilty or not guilty;
(b)　an indication by the accused under this section of how he would plead.

[Magistrates' Courts Act 1980, s 17A, as inserted by the Criminal Procedure and Investigations Act 1996, s 49 and the Powers of Criminal Courts (Sentencing) Act 2000, Sch 9.]

---

1. For detailed guidance on this section and the exercise of the justices' power to commit for sentence under s 3 of the Powers of Criminal Courts (Sentencing) Act 2000 in PART III: SENTENCING, post, see *R v Warley Magistrates' Court, ex p DPP* [1998] 2 Cr App Rep 307, 162 JP 559 [1998] Crim LR 684, DC, and the commentary at para **1–508 Guidance on whether to commit for sentence**.

2. For the decision as to whether the committal is on bail or in custody, see *R v Rafferty* [1999] 1 Cr App Rep 235, [1998] 2 Cr App Rep (S) 449, 162 JP 353 and the Introduction to this PART, para **1–501** et seq, ante.

1–2042   17B. Intention as to plea: absence of accused.   (1) This section shall have effect where—

(a)　a person who has attained the age of 18 years appears or is brought before a magistrates' court on an information charging him with an offence triable either way,
(b)　the accused is represented by a legal representative,
(c)　the court considers that by reason of the accused's disorderly conduct before the court it is not practicable for proceedings under section 17A above to be conducted in his presence, and
(d)　the court considers that it should proceed in the absence of the accused.

(2)　In such a case—

(a)　the court shall cause the charge to be written down, if this has not already been done, and to be read to the representative;
(b)　the court shall ask the representative whether (if the offence were to proceed to trial) the accused would plead guilty or not guilty;
(c)　if the representative indicates that the accused would plead guilty the court shall proceed as if the proceedings constituted from the beginning the summary trial of the information, and as if section 9(1) above was complied with and the accused pleaded guilty under it;
(d)　if the representative indicates that the accused would plead not guilty section 18(1) below shall apply.

(3)　If the representative in fact fails to indicate how the accused would plead, for the purposes of this section and section 18(1) below he shall be taken to indicate that the accused would plead not guilty.

(4)　Subject to subsection (2)(c) above, the following shall not for any purpose be taken to constitute the taking of a plea—

(a)　asking the representative under this section whether (if the offence were to proceed to trial) the accused would plead guilty or not guilty;
(b)　an indication by the representative under this section of how the accused would plead.

[Magistrates' Courts Act 1980, s 17B, as inserted by the Criminal Procedure and Investigations Act 1996, s 49.]

1–2043   17C. Intention as to plea: adjournment.   A magistrates' court proceeding under section 17A or 17B above may adjourn the proceedings at any time, and on doing so on any occasion when the accused is present may remand the accused, and shall remand him if—

(a)　on the occasion on which he first appeared, or was brought, before the court to answer to the information he was in custody or, having been released on bail, surrendered to the custody of the court; or
(b)　he has been remanded at any time in the course of proceedings on the information;

and where the court remands the accused, the time fixed for the resumption of proceedings shall be that at which he is required to appear or be brought before the court in pursuance of the remand or would be required to be brought before the court but for section 128(3A) below.

[Magistrates' Courts Act 1980, s 17C, as inserted by the Criminal Procedure and Investigations Act 1996, s 49.]

1–2044   18. Initial procedure on information against adult for offence triable either way.
(1)　Sections 19 to 23 below shall have effect where a person who has attained the age of 18[1] appears

or is brought before a magistrates' court on an information charging him with an offence triable either way and—

(a) he indicates under section 17A above that (if the offence were to proceed to trial) he would plead not guilty, or

(b) his representative indicates under section 17B above that (if the offence were to proceed to trial) he would plead not guilty.

(2) Without prejudice to section 11(1) above, everything that the court is required[2] to do under sections 19 to 22 below must be done before any evidence is called and, subject to subsection (3) below and section 23 below, with the accused present in court.

(3) The court may proceed in the absence of the accused in accordance with such of the provisions of sections 19 to 22 below as are applicable in the circumstances if the court considers that by reason of his disorderly conduct before the court it is not practicable for the proceedings to be conducted in his presence; and subsections (3) to (5) of section 23 below, so far as applicable, shall have effect in relation to proceedings conducted in the absence of the accused by virtue of this subsection (references in those subsections to the person representing the accused being for this purpose read as references to the person, if any, representing him).

(4) A magistrates' court proceeding under sections 19 to 23 below may adjourn the proceedings at any time, and on doing so on any occasion when the accused is present may remand the accused, and shall remand him if—

(a) on the occasion on which he first appeared, or was brought, before the court to answer to the information he was in custody or, having been released on bail, surrendered to the custody of the court; or

(b) if he has been remanded at any time in the course of proceedings on the information;

and where the court remands the accused, the time fixed for the resumption of the proceedings shall be that at which he is required to appear or be brought before the court in pursuance of the remand or would be required to be brought before the court but for section 128(3A) below.

(5) The functions of a magistrates' court under sections 19 to 23 below may be discharged by a single justice, but the foregoing provision shall not be taken to authorise the summary trial of an information by a magistrates' court composed of less than two justices.

[Magistrates' Courts Act 1980, s 18 as amended by the Criminal Justice Act 1982, Sch 9, the Criminal Justice Act 1991, Sch 8 and the Criminal Procedure and Investigations Act 1996, s 49.]

---

1. See reference under s 24(1), post, to *R v Islington North Juvenile Court, ex p Daley* [1983] 1 AC 347, [1982] 2 All ER 974, 146 JP 363.

2. These provisions are mandatory (*R v Tottenham Justices, ex p Arthur's Transport Services* [1981] Crim LR 180). For a detailed summary of the procedure, see para 1–501 et seq, ante. However, ss 19–22 do not apply if, in an appropriate case, the justices have power to make a hospital order under s 37(3) of the Mental Health Act 1983 without convicting the accused (*R v Lincoln (Kesteven) Justices, ex p O'Connor* [1983] 1 All ER 901, [1983] 1 WLR 335, 147 JP 97).

1–2045　19. Court to begin by considering which mode of trial appears more suitable.
(1) The court shall consider whether, having regard to the matters mentioned in subsection (3) below and any representations made by the prosecutor or the accused[1], the offence appears to the court more suitable for summary trial or for trial on indictment[2].

(2) Before so considering, the court—

(a) *Repealed;*

(b) shall afford first the prosecutor and then the accused an opportunity to make representations as to which mode of trial would be more suitable.

(3) The matters to which the court is to have regard under subsection (1) above are the nature of the case; whether the circumstances make the offence one of serious character; whether the punishment which a magistrates' court would have power to inflict for it would be adequate; and any other circumstances which appear to the court to make it more suitable for the offence to be tried in one way rather than the other[3].

(4) If the prosecution is being carried on by the Attorney General, the Solicitor General or the Director of Public Prosecutions and he applies for the offence to be tried on indictment, the preceding provisions of this section and sections 20 and 21 below shall not apply, and the court shall proceed to inquire into the information as examining justices.

(5) The power of the Director of Public Prosecutions under subsection (4) above to apply for an offence to be tried on indictment shall not be exercised except with the consent of the Attorney General.

[Magistrates' Courts Act 1980, s 19 as amended by the Prosecution of Offences Act 1985, Sch 1 and the Criminal Procedure and Investigations Act 1996, s 49 and Sch 5.]

---

1. Where the accused is a corporation, see Sch 3, post.

2. For the purpose of considering whether the offence appears to the court to be more suitable for summary trial or for trial on indictment, it is not permissible, for the purpose of avoiding separate trials, for the justices to base their decision on the fact that an indication has been given by some of the accused that they would elect trial by jury (*R v Ipswich Magistrates' Court, ex p Callaghan* (1995) 159 JP 748). Once justices have determined, under s 19(1), what the mode of trial shall be it is not permissible for them to reconsider their decision; see *R v Brentwood Justices, ex p Nicholls* [1990] 2 QB 598, [1990] 3 All ER 516, 154 JP 487.

3. When considering such matters, the court should not be given, in any form, information which discloses previous

convictions of the accused; see *R v Colchester Justices, ex p North Essex Building Co Ltd* [1977] 3 All ER 567, [1971] 1 WLR 1109, 141 JP 713.

1–2046   20. Procedure where summary trial appears more suitable. (1) If, where the court has considered as required by section 19(1) above, it appears to the court that the offence is more suitable for summary trial, the following provisions of this section shall apply (unless excluded by section 23 below).

(2) The court shall explain to the accused[1] in ordinary language—

(a) that it appears to the court more suitable for him to be tried summarily for the offence, and that he can either consent to be so tried or, if he wishes, be tried by a jury; and

(b) that if he is tried summarily and is convicted by the court, he may be committed for sentence to the Crown Court under section 3 of the Powers of Criminal Courts (Sentencing) Act 2000 if the convicting court is of such opinion as is mentioned in subsection (2) of that section.

(3) After explaining to the accused[1] as provided by subsection (2) above the court shall ask him whether he consents to be tried summarily or wishes to be tried by a jury, and—

(a) if he consents[2] to be tried summarily, shall proceed to the summary trial of the information;

(b) if he does not so consent, shall proceed to inquire into the information as examining justices.

[Magistrates' Courts Act 1980, s 20 as amended by the Criminal Justice Act 1991, Sch 11 and the Powers of Criminal Courts (Sentencing) Act 2000, Sch 9.]

---

1. Where the accused is a corporation, see Sch 3, post.

This right of election is given to each accused person individually and not to all the accused collectively; accordingly, the election of one accused is not affected by a different election made by any of his co-accused. Therefore, when an accused elects summary trial but another co-accused elects trial on indictment, the court must proceed to try summarily the accused who elects summary trial and inquire into the information as examining justices in respect of the accused who elects trial on indictment (*Nicholls v Brentwood Justices* [1991] 3 All ER 359, [1991] 3 WLR 201, 155 JP 753, HL).

2. Where the accused consents to summary trial and pleads guilty and then applies to elect trial by jury on the grounds that he has a defence, the test whether he should be allowed to re-elect is whether he properly understood the nature and significance of the choice which he made when he consented to summary trial (*R v Birmingham Justices, ex p Hodgson* [1985] QB 1131, [1985] 2 All ER 193, 149 JP 193). See also *R v Highbury Corner Metropolitan Stipendiary Magistrate, ex p Weekes* [1985] QB 1147, [1985] 2 WLR 643, 149 JP 204. If the justices dealing with an application to re-elect did not sit on the earlier occasion, they shall receive evidence as to what occurred from the court clerk who was then present and also the defendant if unrepresented (*R v Forest Magistrates' Court, ex p Spicer* (1988) 153 JP 81, [1988] Crim LR 619).

1–2050   21. Procedure where trial on indictment appears more suitable. If, where the court has considered as required by section 19(1) above, it appears to the court that the offence is more suitable for trial on indictment, the court shall tell the accused that the court has decided that it is more suitable for him to be tried for the offence by a jury, and shall proceed to inquire into the information as examining justices.

[Magistrates' Courts Act 1980, s 21.]

1–2051   22. Certain offences triable either way to be tried summarily if value involved is small. (1) If the offence charged by the information is one of those mentioned in the first column of Schedule 2 to this Act (in this section referred to as "scheduled offences") then, the court shall, before proceeding in accordance with section 19 above, consider whether, having regard to any representations[1] made by the prosecutor or the accused, the value[2] involved (as defined in subsection (10) below) appears to the court to exceed the relevant sum.

For the purposes of this section the relevant sum is £5,000[3].

(2) If, where subsection (1) above applies, it appears to the court clear that, for the offence charged, the value involved does not exceed the relevant sum, the court shall proceed as if the offence were triable only summarily, and sections 19 to 21[4] above shall not apply.

(3) If, where subsection (1) above applies, it appears to the court clear that, for the offence charged, the value involved exceeds the relevant sum, the court shall thereupon proceed in accordance with section 19 above in the ordinary way without further regard to the provisions of this section.

(4) If, where subsection (1) above applies, it appears to the court for any reason not clear whether, for the offence charged, the value involved does or does not exceed the relevant sum, the provisions of subsections (5) and (6) below shall apply.

(5) The court shall cause the charge to be written down, if this has not already been done, and read to the accused, and shall explain to him in ordinary language—

(a) that he can, if he wishes, consent to be tried summarily for the offence and that if he consents to be so tried, he will definitely be tried in that way; and

(b) that if he is tried summarily and is convicted by the court, his liability to imprisonment or a fine will be limited as provided in section 33 below.

(6) After explaining to the accused as provided by subsection (5) above the court shall ask him whether he consents to be tried summarily and—

(a) if he so consents, shall proceed in accordance with subsection (2) above as if that subsection applied;

(b) if he does not so consent, shall proceed in accordance with subsection (3) above as if that subsection applied.

(7) *Repealed.*

(8) Where a person is convicted by a magistrates' court of a scheduled offence, it shall not be open to him to appeal to the Crown Court against the conviction on the ground that the convicting court's decision as to the value involved was mistaken.

(9) If, where subsection (1) above applies, the offence charged is one with which the accused is charged jointly with a person who has not attained the age of 18, the reference in that subsection to any representations made by the accused shall be read as including any representations made by the person under 18.

(10) In this section "the value involved"[2], in relation to any scheduled offence, means the value indicated in the second column of Schedule 2 to this Act, measured as indicated in the third column of that Schedule; and in that Schedule "the material time" means the time of the alleged offence.

(11)[5] Where—

(a) the accused is charged on the same occasion with two or more scheduled offences and it appears to the court that they constitute or form part of a series[6] of two or more offences of the same or a similar[7] character; or

(b) the offence charged consists in incitement to commit two or more scheduled offences,

this section shall have effect as if any reference in it to the value involved were a reference to the aggregate of the values involved.

(12) Subsection (8) of section 12A of the Theft Act 1968 (which determines when a vehicle is recovered) shall apply for the purposes of paragraph 3 of Schedule 2 to this Act as it applies for the purposes of that section.

[Magistrates' Courts Act 1980, s 22 as amended by SI 1984/447, the Criminal Justice Act 1988, s 38 and Sch 16, the Criminal Justice Act 1991, Sch 8, the Aggravated Vehicle-Taking Act 1992, s 2 and the Criminal Justice and Public Order Act 1994, s 46 and Sch 11.]

---

1. The court is required merely to have regard to "representations" as to the value of the damage involved, namely submissions coupled with assertions of fact and sometimes production of documents. The court is not bound to hear evidence as to the value of damage, although it has a discretion to do so (*R v Canterbury and St Augustine's Justices, ex p Klisiak* [1982] QB 398, [1981] 2 All ER 129, 145 JP 344). Where there are problems in establishing the value of property damaged, the prosecution is entitled to set out to prove the minimum amount of damage (*R v Salisbury Justices, ex p Mastin* (1986) 84 Cr App Rep 248—several defendants ruined a crop of beans valued at £5,800; individually charged with amount based on distance each vehicle appeared to have travelled into the field, thus making each offence a summary one).

2. Schedule 2 to the act is directed simply and solely to identifying the value of the damage itself and it is not concerned with determining what, if any, consequential losses may have been sustained as a result of the damage; thus, where genetically modified crops were damaged, the farmer valued the damage at £750 but there were also wasted research costs making the overall loss somewhere between £3,250 and £14,650, it was impossible to criticise the justices for concluding that the value for mode of trial purposes was clearly less than £5,000: *R v Colchester Magistrates' Court, ex p Abbott* [2001] Crim LR 564, 165 JP 386, DC.

3. The relevant sum was raised from £2,000 to £5,000 by the Criminal Justice and Public Order Act 1994, s 46.

4. The requirement that the offence be tried summarily also precludes the plea before venue procedure in ss 17A, see *R v Kelly* [2001] RTR 45, CA and para 1–524, ante.

5. Although similar in some respects to s 22(7) which it replaces, s 22(11) is less restrictive than its predecessor in the application of s 22 when two or more scheduled offences are charged on the same occasion. Subsection (11) shall not, however, apply where any of the offences are charged in respect of acts done before s 38 of the Criminal Justice Act 1988 came into force on 12 October 1988 (Criminal Justice Act 1988, s 38(4)).

6. An original charge and a substituted charge, which covers much the same items of damage, do not constitute part of a series of offences (*R v Canterbury and St Augustine's Justices, ex p Klisiak* [1982] QB 398, [1981] 2 All ER 129, 145 JP 344). In *R v St Helens Justices, ex p McClorie* (1984) 78 Cr App Rep 1, the defendant broke a padlock to enter a yard and then resisted arrest, damaging a wrist watch: the two charges were for damage respectively of £5 and £15; he was entitled to elect trial by jury. But in *R v Braden* (1987) 152 JP 92, CA, where the defendant was charged with damaging two parked vehicles as he attempted to extricate his own vehicle from a parked position, and with damaging an hour later a police station cell, it was held that the charges of damage to the vehicles were remote from that of damage to the police station cell and the three offences did not form part of a series.

7. It would seem that the *eiusdem generis* rule should apply here; the section does *not* say "arising out of the same circumstances". In *Re Prescott* (1979) 70 Cr App Rep 244, criminal damage and obstructing a police officer were held not to be similar offences or part of a series of offences of a similar character; and in *R v Considine* (1979) 70 Cr App Rep 239, criminal damage and burglary were held not to be offences of the same or similar character; nor were common assault and criminal damage in *R v Tottenham Justices, ex p Tibble* (1981) 73 Cr App Rep 55. In *R v Hatfield Justices, ex p Castle* [1980] 3 All ER 509, [1981] 1 WLR 217, 145 JP 265, it was held that, in order for, what was s 22(7)(a), but is now s 22(11)(a) to apply, the offence charged and the other offence or offences (i) must bear a similarity both of fact and law, (ii) must be classified as triable either way, and (iii) must form part of a series of two or more offences. For interpretation of similar words which appear in what is now r 14.2 of the Criminal Procedure Rules 2005, see *Ludlow v Metropolitan Police Comr* [1971] AC 29, [1970] 1 All ER 567.

1–2052   **23. Power of court, with consent of legally represented accused to proceed in his absence.** (1) Where—

(a) the accused is represented by a legal representative who in his absence signifies to the court the accused's consent to the proceedings for determining how he is to be tried for the offence being conducted in his absence; and

(b) the court is satisfied that there is good reason for proceeding in the absence of the accused,

the following provisions of this section shall apply.

(2) Subject to the following provisions of this section, the court may proceed in the absence of the accused in accordance with such of the provisions of sections 19 to 22 above as are applicable in the circumstances.

(3) If, in a case where subsection (1) of section 22 above applies, it appears to the court as

mentioned in subsection (4) of that section, subsections (5) and (6) of that section shall not apply and the court—

(a) if the accused's consent to be tried summarily has been or is signified by the person representing him, shall proceed in accordance with subsection (2) of that section as if that subsection applied; or

(b) if that consent has not been and is not so signified, shall proceed in accordance with subsection (3) of that section as if that subsection applied.

(4) If, where the court has considered as required by section 19(1) above, it appears to the court that the offence is more suitable for summary trial then—

(a) if the accused's consent to be tried summarily has been or is signified by the person representing him, section 20 above shall not apply, and the court shall proceed to the summary trial of the information; or

(b) if that consent has not been and is not so signified, section 20 above shall not apply and the court shall proceed to inquire into the information as examining justices and may adjourn the hearing without remanding the accused.

(5) If, where the court has considered as required by section 19(1) above, it appears to the court that the offence is more suitable for trial on indictment, section 21 above shall not apply, and the court shall proceed to inquire into the information as examining justices and may adjourn the hearing without remanding the accused.

[Magistrates' Courts Act 1980, s 23 as amended by the Courts and Legal Services Act 1990, Sch 18.]

1–2053   24. Summary trial of information against child or young person for indictable offence[1].   (1)   Where a person under the age of 18[2] appears or is brought before a magistrates' court on an information charging him with an indictable offence other than one falling within subsection (1B) below, he shall be tried summarily[3] unless—

(a) the offence is such as is mentioned in subsection (1) or (2) of section 91 of the Powers of Criminal Courts (Sentencing) Act 2000 (under which young persons convicted on indictment of certain grave crimes may be sentenced to be detained for long periods) and the court considers[4] that if he is found guilty of the offence it ought to be possible to sentence him in pursuance of subsection (3) of that section; or

(b) he is charged jointly[5] with a person who has attained the age of 18 and the court considers[6] it necessary in the interests of justice to commit them both for trial;

and accordingly in a case falling within paragraph (a) or (b) of this subsection the court shall commit the accused for trial if either it is of opinion that there is sufficient evidence[7] to put him on trial or it has power under section 6(2) above so to commit him without consideration of the evidence[7].★

(1A)   Where a magistrates' court—

(a) commits a person under the age of 18 for trial for an offence falling within subsection (1B) below; or

(b) in a case falling within subsection (1)(a) above, commits such a person for trial for an offence,

the court may also commit him for trial for any other indictable offence with which he is charged at the same time if the charges for both offences could be joined in the same indictment[8].★

(1B)   An offence falls within this subsection if—

(a) it is an offence of homicide[9]; or

(b) each of the requirements of section 51A(1) of the Firearms Act 1968 would be satisfied with respect to—

(i) the offence; and
(ii) the person charged with it,

if he were convicted of the offence.

(2)   Where, in a case falling within subsection (1)(b) above, a magistrates' court commits a person under the age of 18 for trial for an offence with which he is charged jointly with a person who has attained that age, the court may also commit him for trial for any other indictable offence with which he is charged at the same time (whether jointly with the person who has attained that age or not) if the charges for both offences could be joined in the same indictment.★

(3)   If on trying a person summarily in pursuance of subsection (1) above the court finds him guilty[10], it may impose a fine of an amount not exceeding £1,000 or may exercise the same powers as it could have exercised if he had been found guilty of an offence for which, but for section 89(1) of the said Act of 2000, it could have sentenced him to imprisonment for a term not exceeding—

(a) the maximum term of imprisonment for the offence on conviction on indictment; or
(b) six months,

whichever is the less.

(4)   In relation to a person under the age of 14 subsection (3) above shall have effect as if for the words "£1,000" there were substituted the words "£250".

[Magistrates' Courts Act 1980, s 24 as amended by the Criminal Justice Act 1982, Sch 14, SI 1984/447, the Criminal Justice Act 1991 s 17 and Schs 8 and 13, the Criminal Justice and Public Order Act 1994, Schs 10 and 11, the Crime and Disorder Act 1998, s 47 and Sch 8, the Powers of Criminal Courts (Sentencing) Act 2000, Sch 9 and the Criminal Justice Act 2003, s 42.]

*Subsection (1) substituted, sub-ss (1A) and (2) repealed by the Criminal Justice Act 2003, Sch 3 and new ss 24A–24D inserted, from a date to be appointed.

1. Section 24, in its form as at the date at which this work states the law, namely pending the implementation of para 9 of Sch 3 to the Criminal Justice Act 2003, should be approached in the following manner: (i) the policy of the legislature is that those aged under 18 should, wherever possible, be tried in the youth court; (ii) the guidance given by the Court of Appeal in *R v Lang* [2005] EWCA Crim 2864, [2005] All ER (D) 54 (Nov) particularly in relation to non-serious specified offences, should be borne in mind; (iii) there is a need in relation to those aged under 18 to be particularly rigorous before concluding that there is a significant risk of serious harm occasioned by the commission of further specified offences, and such a conclusion is unlikely to be appropriate in the absence of a pre-sentence report; (iv) in most cases where a non-serious specified offence is charged an assessment of dangerousness will not be appropriate until after conviction, when, if the relevant criteria are met, the defendant can be committed to the Crown Court for sentence; and (v) where a youth is jointly charged with an adult, an exercise of judgment will be called for by the youth court when assessing the competing presumptions in favour of the joint trial of those jointly charged and the trial of youths in the youth court. Matters relevant to the latter judgment will include the age and maturity of the youth, the comparative culpability and criminal records of the defendants and whether the trial can be severed without either injustice of undue inconvenience to witnesses: *R (DPP) v South East Surrey Youth Court* [2005] EWHC 2929 (Admin), [2006] 2 All ER 444, [2006] Crim LR 367, sub nom *CPS v MLG*.

2. If the accused is found to be over 18 during the hearing, the youth court may continue to deal with the case (Children and Young Persons Act 1933, s 48(1); likewise if he attains 18 during the proceedings (Children and Young Persons Act 1963, s 29(1)). As to ascertaining the accused's age see s 150(4), post. The court may not deal with a further charge preferred after the defendant is known to have attained 18 years (*R v Chelsea Justices, ex p DPP* [1963] 3 All ER 657, [1963] 1 WLR 1138, 128 JP 18). The appropriate date at which to determine whether an accused person has attained the age of 18, thus entitling him to elect to be tried by a jury, is the date of his appearance before the court on the occasion when the court makes its decision as to the mode of trial (*R v Islington North Juvenile Court, ex p Daley* [1983] 1 AC 347, [1982] 2 All ER 974, 146 JP 363); it is the date when the charge is put and the proceedings are ready to be commenced (*R v Vale of Glamorgan Juvenile Justices, ex p Beattie* (1984) 149 JP 120). See also *R v Lewes Juvenile Court, ex p Turner* (1984) 149 JP 186, and *R v West London Justices, ex p Siley-Winditt* (2000) 165 JP 112, [2000] Crim LR 926, DC, *R v Nottingham Justices, ex p Taylor* [1992] QB 557, [1991] 4 All ER 860, [1991] 3 WLR 694, DC.

3. Jurisdiction is given by s 2(5), ante. Once a properly constituted bench has considered all the factors placed before the court that are relevant to the exercise of their discretion under s 24(1) and ordered summary trial, a differently constituted bench has no power to re-examine that decision on the same material) (*R v Newham Juvenile Court, ex p F (a minor)* [1986] 3 All ER 17, [1986] 1 WLR 939); but such a review is permissible at any stage up to the beginning of the summary trial if a change of circumstances has occurred or if there are new or additional factors to be brought to the attention of the court (*R v Newham Juvenile Court, ex p F (a minor)* supra, but see *R v Liverpool Justices, ex p Crown Prosecution Service* (1989) 154 JP 1, 90 Cr App Rep 261, [1989] Crim LR 655). Moreover, once the court has begun to try the information summarily, it may, before the conclusion of the evidence for the prosecution, discontinue the summary trial and proceed to inquire into the information as examining justices; see s 25(5)–(6), post. The requirement that a child or young person shall be tried summarily unless one of the exceptions in s 24(1)(*a*) or (*b*) applies, does not prevent the joinder of a count in respect of an indictable offence in an indictment containing other offences transferred for trial, where no plea was formally recorded and conviction entered in the register of the youth court (*R v Stephenson* (1998) 162 JP 495, [1998] Crim LR 576).

4. The proper approach for the magistrates' court is to ask itself whether it would be proper for the Crown Court sentencing the defendant for the offence of which he is charged to exercise its powers under s 91 of the Powers of Criminal Courts (Sentencing) Act 2000 (*R v Inner London Youth Court, ex p DPP* (1996) 161 JP 178, [1996] Crim LR 834. Magistrates should not decline jurisdiction unless the offence and the circumstances surrounding it and the offender are such as to make it "more than a vague or theoretical possibility", a "real possibility" or a "real prospect" that a sentence of at least two years will be imposed (See *R (CPS) v Redbridge Youth Court* [2005] EWHC 1390 (Admin), 169 JP 393). Part of the material which should be available to the youth court when considering mode of trial are the previous convictions of the defendant (*R (Tullet) v Medway Magistrates' Court* [2003] EWHC 2279 (Admin), 167 JP 541).

The Divisional Court has been concerned at the number of inappropriate committals for trial of juveniles who have not attained 15 years and has emphasised that such committals should be rare in *R (on the application of D) v Manchester City Youth Court* [2001] EWHC 2279 (Admin), 166 JP 15 and in a number of authorities cited below. In *R (H, A and O) v Southampton Youth Court* [2004] EWHC 2912 (Admin), 169 JP 37 Leveson J, with the approval of the Vice President of the Court of Appeal (Criminal Division) summarised the position for the assistance of magistrates:

> "[33] 1 The general policy of the legislature is that those who are under 18 years of age and in particular children of under 15 years of age should, wherever possible, be tried in the youth court. It is that court which is best designed to meet their specific needs. A trial in the Crown Court with the inevitably greater formality and greatly increased number of people involved (including a jury and the public) should be reserved for the most serious cases.
>
> [34] 2 It is further policy of the legislature that, generally speaking, first-time offenders aged 12 to 14 and all offenders under 12 should not be detained in custody and decisions as to jurisdiction should have regard to the fact that the exceptional power to detain for grave offences should not be used to water down the general principle. Those under '15 will rarely attract a period of detention and, even more rarely, those who are under 12.
>
> [35] 3 In each case the court should ask itself whether there is a real prospect, having regard to his or her age, that this defendant whose case they are considering might require a sentence of , or in excess of, two years or, alternatively, whether although the sentence might be less than two years, there is some unusual feature of the case which justifies declining jurisdiction, bearing in mind that the absence of a power to impose a detention and training order because the defendant is under 15 is not an unusual feature."

Previous authorities where detention of less than two years was imposed were generally decided before the advent of detention and training orders and should now be read in this light (*R (M) v Waltham Forest Youth Court and the DPP* [2002] EWHC 1252 (Admin), 166 JP 453, [2002] Crim LR 681). See *R (W) v Southampton Youth Court, R (K) v Wirral Borough Magistrates' Court* [2002] EWHC 1640 (Admin), 166 JP 569, [2002] Crim LR 750 (W 14 years no previous convictions 'borderline' case for committal for robbery of a bike using a broken bottle to make threats; K 13 years, should not have been committed for indecent assault on child aged 6). See also *C v Balham Youth Court* [2003] EWHC 1332 (Admin), (2003) 167 JP 525, [2003] Crim LR 636 (Committal for trial of 14-year-old youth charged with robbery who was not a persistent offender quashed); followed in *H v Balham Youth Court* [2003] EWHC Admin 3267, (2004) 168 JP 177. It had been stated that a magistrates' court dealing with a minor charged with rape should *never* accept jurisdiction to deal with the case itself, but should invariably commit the case to the Crown Court for trial to ensure that the power under s 91 of the 2000 Act was available (*R v Billam* [1986] 1 All ER 985, 82 Cr App Rep 347; applied in *R v Fareham Youth Court, ex p M* [1999] Crim LR 325, 163 JP 812). However, at the time of that statement rape could not be committed by a person under the age of 14 years, and there may well be cases where is not appropriate to commit a defendant charged with rape but aged under 14 to the Crown Court (per Smith LJ in *R (on the application of W) v Brent Youth Court and the Crown Prosecution Service (Interested Party), R (on the application of S) v Enfield Youth Court and the Crown Prosecution Service (Interested Party, R (on the application of B) v Richmond-on-Thames Youth Court and the Crown Prosecution Service (Interested Party)* [2006] EWHC Admin 95, (2006) 170 JP 198. *R v North Hampshire Youth Court, ex p DPP* (2000) 164

JP 377, DC (girls aged 15 grievous bodily harm with intent, lack of permanent injury to the aggrieved). For sentencing guidance in respect of robberies on trains, see *A-G's References (Nos 7, 8, 9 and 10 of 2000)* [2001] 1 Cr App Rep (S) 166, (2000) Times, June 15. Courts should think long and hard, however, before sentencing young offenders aged 15-17 to sentences exceeding 24 months' detention, and it was inappropriate to do so where a 17-year-old male, with only one previous conviction (for theft), snatched a mobile phone from a 15-year-old male in the street and no violence was used over and above that which was necessary to extract the telephone (*R v H* [2003] 167 JPN 62 – 30 months reduced to 18 months). (However, a robbery committed at night by a group of youths involving gratuitous violence, including stamping, merits a term substantially in excess of 2 years: see *A-G's ref (No 98 of 2004)* [2004] EWCA Crim 2311, [2005] 1 Cr App R (S) 125, in which a sentence of 30 months' detention was increased to 4 years.) If the conditions expressly laid down by s 24(1)(a) or (b) are satisfied, the court must commit the accused for trial; the suitability of the Crown Court for the trial of a young person is not a separate consideration to take into account by the youth court in making this decision (*R (D) v Sheffield Youth Court* [2003] EWHC 35 (Admin), 167 JP 159 – not following *R (on the application of R) v Balham Youth Court* [2003] All ER (D) 73 (Sep) on this point; see also *R v Devizes Youth Court, ex p A* (2000) 164 JP 330). For a case where the Court of Appeal was critical of the decision to commit a 14-year-old to the Crown Court on charges of indecent assault and gross indecency, see *R v B (child)(mode of trial)* [2001] EWCA Crim 194, [2001] 3 FCR 341. See *R (H, A and O) v Southampton Youth Court* [2004] EWHC 2912 (Admin), 169 JP 37, [2005] 2 Cr App R (S) 30 (committal for trial quashed of three boys under 13 years with no previous convictions for indecent assault on youth of similar age).

The appropriate way to challenge a decision to commit to the Crown Court for trial is to apply for judicial review and not to apply to the Crown to stay the proceedings as an abuse of process: *R v AH* [2002] EWCA Crim 2938, (2003) 167 JP 30.

If the Director of Public Prosecutions is concerned about a decision of a youth court to retain jurisdiction he can either seek judicial review or apply for a voluntary bill of indictment; but the defendant's rights are better safeguarded in judicial review and that is the course which should normally be followed: *R (on the application of DPP) v Camberwell Youth Court* and *R (on the application of H) v Camberwell Youth Court* [2004] EWHC Admin 1805, [2005] 1 All ER 999, [2005] 1 WLR 810, (2005) 169 JP 105 , [2005] Crim LR 165.⁵ The word "jointly" in this section does not acquire a restricted meaning, but shall be given its natural meaning. The phrase "jointly charged" normally means two persons named in the same charge or series of charges; nevertheless in motoring cases where only one person can be driving, two persons who have been charged with driving and allowing themselves to be carried in a motor vehicle taken without the owner's consent, are properly to be considered jointly charged (*R v Peterborough Magistrates' Court, ex p Allgood* (1995) 159 JP 627 [1996] RTR 26).

6. The court has a judicial discretion (*R v Newham Justices, ex p Knight* [1976] Crim LR 323).

7. Where, in ignorance of this provision, a youth court put a charge under s 20 of the Offences Against the Person Act 1861 which was linked with a charge under s 18 that was committed to the Crown Court, it had no power subsequently to set aside that decision; the power to review mode of trial decision is limited to the circumstances specified in s 25 of the Magistrates' Courts Act 1980, post (*R (on the application of C) v Grimsby and Cleethorpes Magistrates' Court* [2004] EWHC Admin 2240, (2004) 168 JP 569).

8. The court is not obliged to consider the evidence but may decide the case is appropriate for trial on indictment after looking at the charges and hearing representations (*R v South Hackney Juvenile Court, ex p RB (a minor) and CB (a minor)* (1983) 77 Cr App Rep 294 (overruled in respect of the entitlement of the court to see the defendant's antecedents when considering mode of trial by *R (Tullet) v Medway Magistrates' Court*, supra)). 'The youth court should take into account any undisputed mitigation put forward on behalf of the accused (eg good character), but contentious mitigation should be ignored (*R (on the application of C and D) v Sheffield Youth Court* and R (on the application of N) v Sheffield Youth Court, supra).

9. In previous editions of this work we have expressed the view that the offence of causing death by dangerous driving (s 1 of the Road Traffic Act 1988) is an offence of homicide requiring committal for trial to the Crown court. However, this opinion may need reconsideration in the light of the inclusion of this offence (and the offence under s 3A of the same Act) in s 91 of the Powers of Criminal Courts (Sentencing) Act 2000.

10. An adult court finding a minor guilty shall, unless satisfied it would be undesirable to do so, remit him to a youth court for his home area.

1–2054   25. Power to change from summary trial to committal proceedings, and vice versa¹.

(1) Subsections (2) to (4) below shall have effect where a person who has attained the age of 18 appears or is brought before a magistrates' court on an information charging him with an offence triable either way.

(2) Where the court has (otherwise than in pursuance of section 22(2) above) begun to try the information summarily, the court may, at any time before the conclusion² of the evidence for the prosecution, discontinue³ the summary trial and proceed to inquire into the information as examining justices and, on doing so, shall adjourn the hearing.

(3) Where the court has begun to inquire into the information as examining justices, then, if at any time during the inquiry it appears to the court, having regard to any representations made in the presence of the accused by the prosecutor, or made by the accused, and to the nature of the case, that the offence is after all more suitable for summary trial, the court may, after doing as provided in subsection (4) below, ask the accused whether he consents to be tried summarily and, if he so consents, may subject to subsection (3A) below proceed to try the information summarily.

(3A) Where the prosecution is being carried on by the Attorney General or the Solicitor General, the court shall not exercise the power conferred by subsection (3) above without his consent and, where the prosecution is being carried on by the Director of Public Prosecutions, shall not exercise that power if the Attorney General directs that it should not be exercised.

(4) Before asking the accused under subsection (3) above whether he consents to be tried summarily, the court shall in ordinary language—

(a) explain to him that it appears to the court more suitable for him to be tried summarily for the offence, but that this can only be done if he consents to be so tried; and

(b) unless it has already done so, explain to him, as provided in section 20(2)(b) above, about the court's power to commit to the Crown Court for sentence.

(5) Where a person under the age of 18 appears or is brought before a magistrates' court on an information charging him with an indictable offence other than homicide, and the court—

(a) has begun to try the information summarily on the footing that the case does not fall within paragraph (a) or (b) of section 24(1) above and must therefore be tried summarily, as required by the said section 24(1); or

(b) has begun to inquire into the case as examining justices on the footing that the case does so fall,

subsection (6) or (7) below, as the case may be, shall have effect.

(6) If, in a case falling within subsection (5)(a) above, it appears to the court at any time before the conclusion of the evidence for the prosecution that the case is after all one which under the said section 24(1) ought not to be tried summarily, the court may discontinue the summary trial and proceed to inquire into the information as examining justices and, on doing so, shall adjourn the hearing.

(7) If, in a case falling within subsection (5)(b) above, it appears to the court at any time during the inquiry that the case is after all one which under the said section 24(1) ought to be tried summarily, the court may proceed to try the information summarily.

(8) If the court adjourns the hearing under subsection (2) or (6) above it may (if it thinks fit) do so without remanding the accused.

[Magistrates' Courts Act 1980, s 25 as amended by the Prosecution of Offences Act 1985, Schs 1 and 2, the Criminal Justice Act 1991, Sch 8 and the Criminal Procedure and Investigations Act 1996, Sch 1.]

---

1. For further consideration of the application of this section, see para **1–525 Reverting, re-electing**, ante.

2. Where justices disagree and the case is put back for rehearing, it cannot be said that the prosecution case has been concluded (*R v Coventry City Justices, ex p Wilson* [1981] Crim LR 787).

3. The power to discontinue the summary trial is not available where the defendant has pleaded guilty and his plea has been accepted (*Re Gillard* [1986] AC 442, [1985] 3 All ER 634, 150 JP 45). *Gillard* was applied in *R (on the application of DPP) v Camberwell Youth Court* [2003] EWHC Admin 3217, (2004) 168 JP 157, where it was held that there was no power in a magistrates' court to reopen the decision as to mode of trial in circumstances other than those provided for in s 25(2), and this decision was followed in *R (on the application of C) v Grimsby and Cleethorpes Magistrates' Court* [2004] EWHC Admin 2240, (2004) 168 JP 569. (See also *H v Balham Youth Court* [2003] EWHC Admin 3267, (2004) 168 JP 177.) A problem arises where, as in *R v Southend Justices, ex p Wood* (1986) 152 JP 97, further indictable offences are brought and the court which has already agreed to summary trial on the earlier matters, now wishes to commit all matters for trial. There is no escape from the technical language of the section and the court must begin to hear evidence on the summary trial before it can discontinue the summary trial (*R v St Helens Magistrates' Court, ex p Critchley* (1987) 152 JP 102, [1988] Crim LR 311). The discretion of examining justices under this provision is not fettered by a previous decision of justices to decline jurisdiction which their own examination shows to be wrong even where nothing is before them other than that which was already before the justices on the earlier occasion (*R (R) v Manchester City Youth Court* [2006] EWHC 564 (Admin), 170 JP 217, [2006] Crim LR 849). Receiving evidence at a preliminary hearing, which was not part of the process of determining the guilt or innocence of the accused was held not to have begun the summary trial (*R v Birmingham Stipendiary Magistrate, ex p Webb* (1992) 157 JP 89). Whilst the justices have discretion as to when to employ sub-s (2) it is not a reasonable exercise of that discretion to circumvent the decision in *R v Brentwood Justices, ex p Nicholls* [1990] 2 QB 598, [1990] 3 All ER 516, so as to prevent trials in separate venues (*R v West Norfolk Justices, ex p McMullen* (1992) 157 JP 461).

1–2055   26. Power to issue summons to accused in certain circumstances.   (1) Where—

(a) in the circumstances mentioned in section 23(1)(a) above the court is not satisfied that there is good reason for proceeding in the absence of the accused; or

(b) subsection (4)(b) or (5) of section 23 or subsection (2) or (6) of section 25 above applies, and the court adjourns the hearing in pursuance of that subsection without remanding the accused,

the justice or any of the justices of which the court is composed may issue a summons directed to the accused requiring his presence before the court.

(2) If the accused is not present at the time and place appointed—

(a) in a case within subsection (1)(a) above, for the proceedings under section 19(1) or 22(1) above, as the case may be; or

(b) in a case within subsection (1)(b) above, for the resumption of the hearing,

the court may issue a warrant for his arrest.

[Magistrates' Courts Act 1980, s 26.]

1–2056   27. Effect of dismissal of information for offence triable either way.   Where on the summary trial of an information for an offence triable either way the court dismisses the information, the dismissal shall have the same effect[1] as an acquittal on indictment[2].

[Magistrates' Courts Act 1980, s 27.]

---

1. Notwithstanding this provision a Divisional Court of the Queen's Bench Division will consider an appeal by way of case stated on the ground that dismissal by a magistrates' court was wrong in law (see eg *Ruse v Read* [1949] 1 KB 377, [1949] 1 All ER 398; *Afford v Pettit* (1949) 113 JP 433; *Russell v Smith* [1958] 1 QB 27, [1957] 2 All ER 796, 121 JP 538).

2. Under s 17 of the Criminal Justice Act 1967, where the prosecutor proposes to offer no evidence the court before which the defendant is arraigned may record a verdict of not guilty and that verdict has the same effect as an acquittal by a jury. Therefore, where no evidence was offered on a charge of common assault and the judge entered a verdict of not guilty, autrefois acquit prevented the prosecution from pursuing a charge of assault occasioning actual bodily harm on the same facts, the two offences having the same mens rea and, apart from actual bodily harm, the same actus reus. By virtue of s 27 of the Magistrates' Courts Act 1980 the same would appear to apply to magistrates' courts. See *R v G (Autrefois Acquit)* [2001] EWCA Crim 1215, [2001] 1 WLR 1727 (not following *R v Brookes* [1995] Crim LR 630, CA, where s 27 was not considered by the court). See also *R (on the application of A) v South Staffordshire Magistrates* [2006] EWCH 1200

(Admin), 171 JP 36 (CPS previously offered no evidence on charge of assault occasioning actual bodily harm, preferring to "upgrade" charge to s 20, could not later offer to accept plea to ABH founded on same facts as original charge).

Transfer of criminal proceedings

1–2056A   27A. Power to transfer criminal proceedings.   (1) Where a person appears or is brought before a magistrates' court—

    (*a*) to be tried by the court for an offence, or
    (*b*) for the court to inquire into the offence as examining justices,

the court may transfer the matter to another magistrates' court.

    (2) The court may transfer the matter before or after beginning the trial or inquiry.

    (3) But if the court transfers the matter after it has begun to hear the evidence and the parties, the court to which the matter is transferred must begin hearing the evidence and the parties again.

    (4) The power of the court under this section to transfer any matter must be exercised in accordance with any directions given under section 30(3) of the Courts Act 2003.

[Magistrates' Courts Act 1980, s 27A as inserted by the Courts Act 2003, s 46.]

Power to remit person under 18 for trial to youth court

1–2058   29. Power of magistrates' court to remit a person under 18 for trial to a youth court in certain circumstances.   (1) Where—

    (*a*) a person under the age of 18 ("the juvenile") appears or is brought before a magistrates' court other than a youth court on an information jointly charging him and one or more other persons with an offence: and
    (*b*) that other person, or any of those other persons, has attained that age,

subsection (2) below shall have effect notwithstanding proviso (*a*) in section 46(1) of the Children and Young Persons Act 1933 (which would otherwise require the charge against the juvenile to be heard by a magistrates' court other than a youth court).

In the following provisions of this section "the older accused" means such one or more of the accused as have attained the age of 18.

    (2) If—

    (*a*) the court proceeds to the summary trial of the information in the case of both or all of the accused, and the older accused or each of the older accused pleads guilty; or
    (*b*) the court—

        (i)   in the case of the older accused or each of the older accused, proceeds to inquire into the information as examining justices and either commits him for trial or discharges him, and
        (ii) in the case of the juvenile, proceeds to the summary trial of the information,

then, if in either situation the juvenile pleads not guilty, the court may before any evidence is called in his case remit[1] him for trial to a youth court acting for the same place as the remitting court or for the place where he habitually resides.

    (3) A person remitted to a youth court under subsection (2) above shall be brought before and tried by a youth court accordingly.

    (4) Where a person is so remitted to a youth court—

    (*a*) he shall have no right of appeal against the order of remission; and
    (*b*) the remitting court may, subject to section 25 of the Criminal Justice and Public Order Act 1994, give such directions as appear to be necessary with respect to his custody or for his release on bail until he can be brought before the youth court.

    (5) The preceding provisions of this section shall apply in relation to a corporation as if it were an individual who has attained the age of 17.

[Magistrates' Courts Act 1980, s 29 as amended by the Criminal Justice Act 1991, Schs 8 and 11 and the Criminal Justice and Public Order Act 1994, Sch 10.]

---

   1. Before taking this course with respect to an indictable offence, the adult court must determine mode of trial under s 24(1)(*a*) ante; there is no power for the adult court to remit the case to the youth court for that court to decide upon mode of trial (*R v Tottenham Youth Court, ex p Fawzy* [1998] 1 All ER 365, [1999] 1 WLR 1350, sub nom; *R v Haringey Justices, ex p Fawzy* [1998] 1 Cr App Rep 411).

Remand for medical examination

1–2059   30. Remand for medical examination.   *Repealed.*

Powers in respect of offenders

1–2060   31. General limit on power of magistrates' court to impose imprisonment.   *Repealed.*

1–2061   32. Penalties on summary conviction for offences triable either way.   (1) On summary conviction of any of the offences triable either way listed in Schedule 1 to this Act a person shall be liable to imprisonment for a term not exceeding **6 months** or to a fine not exceeding the prescribed sum[1] or both, except that—

(a) a magistrates' court shall not have power to impose imprisonment for an offence so listed if the Crown Court would not have that power in the case of an adult convicted of it on indictment;

(b) on summary conviction of an offence consisting in the incitement to commit an offence triable either way a person shall not be liable to any greater penalty than he would be liable to on summary conviction of the last-mentioned offence: and

(c) *Repealed.*

(2) For any offence triable either way which is not listed in Schedule 1 to this Act, being an offence under a relevant enactment, the maximum fine which may be imposed on summary conviction shall by virtue of this subsection be the prescribed sum unless the offence is one for which by virtue of an enactment other than this subsection a larger fine may be imposed on summary conviction.

(3) Where, by virtue of any relevant enactment, a person summarily convicted of an offence triable either way would, apart from this section, be liable to a maximum fine of one amount in the case of a first conviction and of a different amount in the case of a second or subsequent conviction, subsection (2) above shall apply irrespective of whether the conviction is a first, second or subsequent one.

(4) Subsection (2) above shall not affect so much of any enactment as (in whatever words) makes a person liable on summary conviction to a fine not exceeding a specified amount for each day on which a continuing offence is continued after conviction or the occurrence of any other specified event.

(5) Subsection (2) above shall not apply on summary conviction of any of the following offences—

(a) offences under section 5(2) of the Misuse of Drugs Act 1971 (having possession of a controlled drug) where the controlled drug in relation to which the offence was committed was a Class B or Class C drug;

(b) offences under the following provisions of that Act, where the controlled drug in relation to which the offence was committed was a Class C drug, namely—

(i) section 4(2) (production, or being concerned in the production, of a controlled drug);

(ii) section 4(3) (supplying or offering a controlled drug or being concerned in the doing of either activity by another);

(iii) section 5(3) (having possession of a controlled drug with intent to supply it to another);

(iv) section 8 (being the occupier, or concerned in the management, of premises and permitting or suffering certain activities to take place there);

(v) section 12(6) (contravention of direction prohibiting practitioner etc from possessing, supplying etc controlled drugs); or

(vi) section 13(3) (contravention of direction prohibiting practitioner etc from prescribing, supplying etc controlled drugs).

(6) Where, as regards any offence triable either way, there is under any enactment (however framed or worded) a power by subordinate instrument to restrict the amount of the fine which on summary conviction can be imposed in respect of that offence—

(a) subsection (2) above shall not affect that power or override any restriction imposed in exercise of that power; and

(b) the amount to which that fine may be restricted in exercise of that power shall be any amount less than the maximum fine which could be imposed on summary conviction in respect of the offence apart from any restriction so imposed.

(7) *Repealed.*

(8) In subsection (5) above "controlled drug", "Class B drug" and "Class C drug" have the same meaning as in the Misuse of Drugs Act 1971.

(9) In this section—

"fine" includes a pecuniary penalty but does not include a pecuniary forfeiture or pecuniary compensation;

"the prescribed sum"[1] means £5,000 or such sum as is for the time being substituted in this definition by an order in force under section 143(1) below;

"relevant enactment" means an enactment contained in the Criminal Law Act 1977 or in any Act passed before, or in the same Session as, that Act.

[Magistrates' Courts Act 1980, s 32, as amended by the Criminal Attempts Act 1981, Sch, SI 1984/447, the Criminal Justice Act 1988, Sch 16 and the Criminal Justice Act 1991, s 17.]

---

1. The term "the prescribed sum" as used here would appear to be interchangeable with the term "the statutory maximum"; see the Interpretation Act 1978, Sch 1 in PART II: EVIDENCE, post. It is important not to confuse the second of these phrases with the statutory maximum imprisonment under sub-s (1) above; that is reserved to Sch 1 offences.

1–2062 33. Maximum penalties on summary conviction in pursuance of section 22.
(1) Where in pursuance of subsection (2) of section 22 above a magistrates' court proceeds to the summary trial of an information, then, if the accused is summarily convicted of the offence—

(a) subject to subsection (3) below the court shall not have power to impose on him in respect of that offence imprisonment for more than **3 months** or a fine greater than **level 4** on the standard scale; and

(b) section 3 of the Powers of Criminal Courts (Sentencing) Act 2000 (committal to Crown Court for sentence) shall not apply as regards that offence.

(2) In subsection (1) above "fine" includes a pecuniary penalty but does not include a pecuniary forfeiture or pecuniary compensation.

(3) Paragraph (*a*) of subsection (1) above does not apply to an offence under section 12A of the Theft Act 1968 (aggravated vehicle-taking).

[Magistrates' Courts Act 1980, s 33 as amended by SI 1984/447, the Criminal Justice Act 1991, Sch 4, the Aggravated Vehicle-Taking Act 1992, s 2 and the Powers of Criminal Courts (Sentencing) Act 2000, Sch 9.]

1–2063   34. Mitigation of penalties, etc.   (1) Where under any enactment whether passed before or after the commencement of this Act a magistrates' court has power to sentence[1] an offender to imprisonment for a period specified by the enactment, or to a fine of an amount specified by the enactment, then, except where an Act passed after 31st December 1879 expressly provides to the contrary, the court may sentence him to imprisonment for less than that period or, as the case may be, to a fine of less than that amount[2].

(2) Where under any such enactment an offender sentenced on summary conviction to imprisonment or a fine is required to enter into a recognizance with or without sureties to keep the peace or observe any other condition, the court convicting him may dispense with or modify the requirement.

(3) Where under any such enactment a magistrates' court has power to sentence an offender to imprisonment or other detention but not to a fine, then, except where an Act passed after 31st December 1879 expressly provides to the contrary, the court may, instead of sentencing him to imprisonment or other detention, impose a fine which—

(a) for an offence triable either way, shall not exceed the prescribed sum within the meaning of section 32 above; and

(b) for a summary offence, shall—

(i) not exceed **level 3** on the standard scale; and

(ii) not be of such an amount as would subject the offender, in default of payment of the fine, to a longer term of imprisonment or detention than the term to which he is liable[3] on conviction of the offence.

[Magistrates' Courts Act 1980, s 34 as amended by SI 1984/447 and the Criminal Justice Act 1991, Sch 4.]

---

1. Defined in s 150(1), post.
2. Unless Parliament legislates to the contrary in a particular case (*Osborn v Wood Bros* [1897] 1 QB 197, 61 JP 118). This provision would not empower reduction of arrears recoverable as a penalty, eg National Insurance contributions (*Leach v Litchfield* [1960] 3 All ER 739, [1960] 1 WLR 1392, 125 JP 115).
3. Liability to imprisonment in default of payment of a fine will be in accordance with the scale set out in Sch 4, post. An example of the operation of this subsection is to be found in *Lowther v Smith* [1949] 1 All ER 943, 113 JP 297.

1–2065   36. Restriction on fines in respect of young persons.   *Repealed.*

1–2066   37. Committal to Crown Court with a view to a sentence of detention in a young offender institution.   *Repealed.*

1–2067   38. Committal for sentence on summary trial of offence triable either way.   *Repealed.*

1–2068   38A. Committal for sentence on indication of guilty plea to offence triable either way[1].   *Repealed.*

---

1. Please see the Powers of Criminal Courts (Sentencing) Act 2000, s 4, in PART III: SENTENCING, post.

1–2069   39. Cases where magistrates' court may remit offender to another such court for sentence.   *Repealed.*

1–2070   40. Restriction on amount payable under compensation order of magistrates' court.   *Repealed.*

Miscellaneous

1–2079   41. Restriction on grant of bail in treason.   A person charged with treason shall not be granted bail except by order of a judge of the High Court or the Secretary of State.

[Magistrates' Courts Act 1980, s 41.]

1–2080   42. Restriction on justices sitting after dealing with bail.   (1) A justice of the peace shall not take part in trying the issue of an accused's guilt on the summary trial of an information if in the course of the same proceedings the justice has been informed, for the purpose of determining whether the accused shall be granted bail, that he has one or more previous convictions[1].

(2) For the purposes of this section any committal proceedings from which the proceedings on the summary trial arose[2] shall be treated as part of the trial.

[Magistrates' Courts Act 1980, s 42.]

1. For the position under the European Convention on Human Rights see *Hauschildt v Denmark* (1989) 12 EHRR 266.
2. Sub-s (2) applies if committal proceedings are discontinued in favour of summary trial under s 25(3), ante.

1–2081   43. Bail on arrest[1]. (1) Where a person has been granted bail under Part IV of the Police and Criminal Evidence Act 1984 subject to a duty to appear before a magistrates' court, the court before which he is to appear may appoint a later time as the time at which he is to appear and may enlarge the recognizances of any sureties for him at that time.

(2) The recognizance of any surety for any person granted bail subject to a duty to attend at a police station may be enforced as if it were conditioned for his appearance before a magistrates' court for the petty sessions area in which the police station named in the recognizance is situated.
[Magistrates' Courts Act 1980, s 43 as substituted by the Police and Criminal Evidence Act 1984, s 47 and amended by the Criminal Justice and Public Order Act 1994, Sch 10.]

1. Section 47 of the 1984 Act deals with bail after arrest.

1–2082   43A. Functions of magistrates' court where a person in custody is brought before it with a view to his appearance before the Crown Court. (1) Where a person in custody in pursuance of a warrant issued by the Crown Court with a view to his appearance before the Crown Court is brought before a magistrates' court in pursuance of section 81(5) of the Supreme Court Act 1981—

(a)   the magistrates' court shall commit him in custody or release him on bail until he can be brought or appear before the Crown Court at the time and place appointed by the Crown Court;

(b)   if the warrant is endorsed for bail, but the person in custody is unable to satisfy the conditions endorsed, the magistrates' court may vary those conditions, if satisfied that it is proper to do so.

(2) A magistrates' court shall have jurisdiction under subsection (1) whether or not the offence was committed, or the arrest was made, within the court's area.
[Magistrates' Courts Act 1980, s 43A added by the Supreme Court Act 1981, Sch 5.]

1–2083   43B. Power to grant bail where police bail has been granted. (1) Where a custody officer—

(a)   grants bail to any person under Part IV of the Police and Criminal Evidence Act 1984 in criminal proceedings and imposes conditions, or

(b)   varies, in relation to any person, conditions of bail in criminal proceedings under section 3(8) of the Bail Act 1976,

a magistrates' court may, on application[1] by or on behalf of that person, grant bail or vary the conditions.

(2) On an application[1] under subsection (1) the court, if it grants bail and imposes conditions or if it varies the conditions, may impose more onerous conditions.

(3) On determining an application[1] under subsection (1) the court shall remand the applicant, in custody or on bail in accordance with the determination, and, where the court withholds bail or grants bail the grant of bail made by the custody officer shall lapse.

(4) In this section "bail in criminal proceedings" and "vary" have the same meanings as they have in the Bail Act 1976.
[Magistrates' Courts Act 1980, s 43B, as inserted by the Criminal Justice and Public Order Act 1994, Sch 3.]

1. For the procedure on an application for bail following grant of conditional police bail, see Criminal Procedure Rules 2005, Part 19, this PART: STATUTORY INSTRUMENTS ON PROCEDURE, post.

1–2084   44. Aiders and abettors. (1) A person who aids, abets, counsels or procures[1] the commission by another person of a summary offence shall be guilty of the like offence and may be tried[2] (whether or not he is charged as a principal) either[3] by a court having jurisdiction to try that other person or by a court having by virtue of his own offence jurisdiction to try him.

(2) Any offence consisting in aiding, abetting, counselling or procuring the commission of an offence triable either way (other than an offence listed in Schedule 1 to this Act) shall by virtue of this subsection be triable either way.
[Magistrates' Courts Act 1980, s 44.]

1. See ante para **1–321 Aid, abet, counsel or procure**.
2. Subject to the same limit (*Gould & Co v Houghton* [1921] 1 KB 509, 85 JP 93; *Homolka v Osmond* [1939] 1 All ER 154.
3. Concurrent jurisdiction is given in this subsection to the court of the district either in which the aiding, abetting, counselling or procuring was committed, or where the principal offence was committed.

1–2085   45. Incitement. (1) Any offence consisting in the incitement to commit a summary offence shall be triable only summarily.

(2) Subsection (1) above is without prejudice to any other enactment by virtue of which any offence is triable only summarily.

(3) On conviction of an offence consisting in the incitement to commit a summary offence a

person shall be liable to the same penalties as he would be liable to on conviction of the last-mentioned offence.
[Magistrates' Courts Act 1980, s 45.]

1-2086   46. Corporations.   The provisions of Schedule 3 to this Act shall have effect where a corporation is charged[1] with an offence before a magistrates' court.
[Magistrates' Courts Act 1980, s 46.]

---

1. The Criminal Justice Act 1925, s 33 stipulates the procedure on charge of an offence against a corporation. See also para **1-139** as to representation for a corporation. For service on a corporation, see Criminal Procedure Rules 2005, Part 4, this PART: STATUTORY INSTRUMENTS ON PROCEDURE, post.

1-2087   47. Service of summons out of time after failure to prove service by post.   Where any enactment requires, expressly or by implication, that a summons in respect of an offence shall be issued or served within a specified period[1] after the commission of the offence, and service of the summons may under rules of court [2] be effected by post, then, if under the rules service of the summons is not treated as proved, but it is shown that a letter containing the summons was posted at such time as to enable it to be delivered in the ordinary course of post within that period, a second summons may be issued on the same information; and the enactment shall have effect, in relation to that summons, as if the specified period were a period running from the return day of the original summons.
[Magistrates' Courts Act 1980, s 47 as amended by the Courts Act 2003, Sch 8.]

---

1. For example, Road Traffic Offenders Act 1988, s 1.
2. See Criminal Procedure Rules 2005, r 4.1, this PART: STATUTORY INSTRUMENTS AND PRACTICE DIRECTIONS ON PROCEDURE, post.

1-2088   48. Return of property taken from accused[1].   Where a summons or warrant has been issued requiring any person to appear or be brought before a magistrates' court to answer to an information, or where any person has been arrested without a warrant for an offence, and property has been taken from him[2] after the issue of the summons or warrant or, as the case may be, on or after his arrest without a warrant, the police shall report the taking of the property, with particulars of the property, to the magistrates' court which deals with the case; and, if the court, being of the opinion that the whole or any part of the property can be returned to the accused consistently with the interests of justice[3] and the safe custody of the accused, so directs, the property, or such part of it as the court directs, shall be returned to the accused or to such other person as he may require.
[Magistrates' Courts Act 1980, s 48.]

---

1. This section is limited to persons under charge and to the time during which they are under charge (*R v D'Eyncourt* (1888) 21 QBD 109, 52 JP 628). The section applies only to the case of a person from whom property has been taken over after an accusation of a charge of some nature in respect of which he subsequently comes before a magistrates' court (*Arnell v Harris* [1945] KB 60, [1944] 2 All ER 522, 109 JP 14).
2. A court will have no power under this section to return property or documents taken from premises on or after arrest, although they can adjourn and refuse to proceed if satisfied that the documents are necessary for the conduct of the defence (*R v Southampton Magistrates' Court, ex p Newman* [1988] 3 All ER 669, 152 JP 664).
3. Where there is reason to suppose that the property is the proceeds of stolen property the subject of the charge, the court should consider the possibility of the exercise of the powers of restitution under s 148 of the Powers of Criminal Courts (Sentencing) Act 2000 in PART III: SENTENCING, post, whether or not it otherwise defers passing sentence.

1-2089   49. *Repealed.*

1-2090   50. Construction of references to complaint in enactments dealing with offences.
In any enactment conferring power on a magistrates' court to deal with an offence, or to issue a summons or warrant against a person suspected of an offence, on the complaint of any person, for references to a complaint there shall be substituted references to an information[1].
[Magistrates' Courts Act 1980, s 50.]

---

1. Many old statutes used the expressions "information" and "complaint" indiscriminately. Where they are printed in this Manual, alterations have been made so they accord with this section.

PART II[1]
CIVIL JURISDICTION AND PROCEDURE
Jurisdiction to issue summons and deal with complaints

1-2091   51. Issue of summons on complaint.   Where a complaint relating to a person is made[2] to a justice of the peace[3], the justice of the peace may issue a summons[4] to the person requiring him to appear before a magistrates' court to answer to the complaint.
[Magistrates' Courts Act 1980, s 51 as substituted by the Courts Act 2003, s 47.]

---

1. Part II comprises ss 51–74.
2. A justice, or the justices' clerk, must apply his mind to the complaint and go through the judicial exercise of deciding whether or not process ought to be issued; see observations of LORD WIDGERY CJ in *R v Brentford Justices, ex p Catlin* [1975] 2 WLR 506 at 512. The function of a justice or the clerk to the justices in determining whether a summons should

be issued is a judicial function and cannot be delegated (*R v Manchester Stipendiary Magistrate, ex p Hill* [1983] 1 AC 328, [1982] 2 All ER 963, 146 JP 348).

3. A complaint not on oath may be made to a justices' clerk for the appropriate petty sessions area who may issue a summons thereon, Justices' Clerks Rules 2005, this PART: STATUTORY INSTRUMENTS ON PROCEDURE, post.

4. See *Practice Direction* [1973] 1 All ER 61, [1973] 1 WLR 60, for arrangements which have been made to enable a court to obtain addresses from official records in maintenance proceedings; also the Social Security Administration Act 1992, s 133.

1–2092   52. Jurisdiction to deal with complaints.   (1) A magistrates' court has jurisdiction to hear any complaint.

(2) But subsection (1) is subject to provision made by any enactment.

[Magistrates' Courts Act 1980, s 52 as amended by the Justices of the Peace Act 1997, Sch 5 and the Access to Justice Act 1999, Sch 15 as substituted by the Courts Act 2003, s 47.]

Hearing of complaint

1–2093   53. Procedure on hearing.   (1) On the hearing of a complaint[1], the court shall, if the defendant appears, state to him the substance of the complaint.

(2) The court, after hearing the evidence and the parties, shall make the order for which the complaint is made or dismiss the complaint[2].

(3) Where a complaint is for an order for the payment of a sum recoverable summarily as a civil debt, or for the variation of the rate of any periodical payments ordered by a magistrates' court to be made, or for such other matter as may be prescribed, the court may make the order with the consent of the defendant without hearing evidence.

[Magistrates' Courts Act 1980, s 53.]

1. For case-law and commentary on the hearing of a complaint see para **1–753** ff ante.

2. Under art 6(1) of the European Convention on Human Rights it is a requirement of a fair trial in both criminal and civil matters that a court should give reasons for its judgment. The extent of the duty to give reasons may, however, vary according to the nature of the decision. See *Hadjianastassiou v Greece* (1992) 16 EHRR 219, *Van de Hurk v Netherlands* (1994) 18 EHRR 481, *Ruiz Torija v Spain* (1994) 19 EHRR 553, *Hiro Balani v Spain* (1994) 19 EHRR 566, *Georgiadis v Greece* (1997) 24 EHRR 606 and *Helle v Finland* (1997) 26 EHRR 159. For recent consideration of the duty to give reasons both at common law and under the Convention see *Stefan v General Medical Council* [1999] 1 WLR 1293, PC. See also *McKerry v Teesdale and Wear Valley Justices* (2000) 164 JP 355, [2000] Crim LR 594, where it was stated that justices are not obliged to state reasons in the form of a judgment or in any elaborate form, and if an aggrieved person wishes to obtain more detailed reasons from a magistrates' court he can apply to the justices to state a case.

1–2094   54. Adjournment.   (1) A magistrates' court may at any time, whether before or after beginning to hear a complaint, adjourn[1] the hearing, and may do so, notwithstanding anything in this Act, when composed of a single justice[2].

(2) The court may when adjourning either[3] fix the time and place at which the hearing is to be resumed or, unless it remands the defendant under section 55 below, leave the time and place to be determined later by the court; but the hearing shall not be resumed at that time and place unless the court is satisfied that the parties have had adequate notice thereof.

[Magistrates' Courts Act 1980, s 54.]

1. A defendant cannot claim an adjournment as a matter of right to enable him to obtain professional assistance (*R v Lipscombe, ex p Biggins* (1862) 26 JP 244). The Family Division has directed that a notice of an adjourned hearing in a domestic case should be served with the same degree of solemnity as a summons; see *Unitt v Unitt* (1979) 10 Fam Law 119, 124 Sol Jo 80 and Magistrates' Courts Rules 1981, r 99, this PART: STATUTORY INSTRUMENTS AND PRACTICE DIRECTIONS ON PROCEDURE, post.

2. A justices' clerk may adjourn the hearing of a complaint if the parties consent to an adjournment, Justices' Clerks Rules 2005, this PART: STATUTORY INSTRUMENTS AND PRACTICE DIRECTIONS ON PROCEDURE, post.

3. No limit on the period of adjournment is imposed: there is power to adjourn sine die, so assimilating the general law in civil matters to what has hitherto been the rule only in bastardy (see *Barnsley v Marsh* [1947] KB 672, [1947] 1 All ER 874, 111 JP 363).

1–2095   55. Non-appearance of defendant[1].   (1) Where at the time and place appointed for the hearing or adjourned hearing of a complaint the complainant appears but the defendant does not, the court may, subject to subsection (3) below, proceed in his absence[2].

(2) Where the court, instead of proceeding in the absence of the defendant[2], adjourns, or further adjourns, the hearing, the court may, if the complaint has been substantiated on oath, and subject to the following provisions of this section, issue a warrant[3] for his arrest.

(3) The court shall not begin to hear the complaint in the absence of the defendant[2] or issue a warrant under this section unless either it is proved to the satisfaction of the court, on oath or in such other manner as may be prescribed[4], that the summons was served[4] on him within what appears to the court to be a reasonable time[5] before the hearing or adjourned hearing or the defendant has appeared on a previous occasion to answer to the complaint.

(4) Where the defendant fails to appear at an adjourned hearing, the court shall not issue a warrant under this section unless it is satisfied that he has had adequate notice of the time and place of the adjourned hearing.

(5) Where the defendant is arrested under a warrant issued under this section, the court may, on any subsequent adjournment of the hearing, but subject to the provisions of subsection (6) below, remand him.

(6) The court shall not issue a warrant or remand[6] a defendant under this section or further remand him by virtue of section 128(3) below after he has given evidence in the proceedings.

(7) Where the court remands the defendant, the time fixed for the resumption of the hearing shall be that at which he is required to appear or be brought before the court in pursuance of the remand.

(8) A warrant under this section shall not be issued in any proceedings for the recovery or enforcement of a sum recoverable summarily as a civil debt or in proceedings in any matter of bastardy[7].

[Magistrates' Courts Act 1980, s 55.]

1. For the purpose of civil contempt proceedings under s 63(3) of this Act, this section has been modified by the Contempt of Court Act 1981, Sch 3, post.

2. Where a party is represented by counsel or solicitor he shall be deemed not to be absent (s 99, post). See *Smith v Smith* [1957] 2 All ER 397, [1957] 1 WLR 802, 121 JP 391, in which a magistrates' court was held to be wrong in permitting a probation officer to make an admission on behalf of an absent defendant. This is now subject to the requirements of art 6(1) of the European Convention on Human Rights.

3. But note sub-ss (4), (6) and (8), infra, which limit the power to issue a warrant. The justice issuing the warrant may endorse it with a direction that the defendant shall be released on bail (s 117, post). A police officer need not have the warrant with him in order to execute it; see s 125, post.

4. Manner of service is prescribed by r 99 and manner of proving service, is prescribed by r 67 of the Magistrates' Courts Rules 1981, this PART: STATUTORY INSTRUMENTS ON PROCEDURE, post.

5. The justices are the judges of what in the circumstances is a reasonable time (*Ex p Williams* (1851) 15 JP 757).

6. The restrictions in s 55(6) do not apply in binding-over proceedings (s 115(2), post).

7. Section 93(3), post, nevertheless empowers the issue of a warrant for maintenance arrears, and proceedings in the complainant's absence irrespective of whether there has been previous evidence.

1–2096   56. Non-appearance of complainant.   Where at the time and place appointed for the hearing or adjourned hearing of a complaint the defendant appears but the complainant does not, the court may dismiss the complaint or, if evidence has been received on a previous occasion proceed in the absence of the complainant[1].

[Magistrates' Courts Act 1980, s 56.]

1. The court may instead adjourn under s 54, ante. This is now subject to the requirements of art 6(1) of the European Convention on Human Rights.

1–2097   57. Non-appearance of both parties.   Where at the time and place appointed for the hearing or adjourned hearing of a complaint neither the complainant nor the defendant appears, the court may dismiss the complaint[1].

[Magistrates' Courts Act 1980, s 57.]

1. The court may instead adjourn under s 54, ante. This is now subject to the requirements of art 6(1) of the European Convention on Human Rights.

1–2097A
Transfer of civil proceedings (other than family proceedings)

57A. Power to transfer civil proceedings (other than family proceedings).   (1) A magistrates' court may at any time, whether before or after beginning to hear a complaint, transfer the hearing to another magistrates' court.

(2) But if the court transfers the matter after it has begun to hear the evidence and the parties, the court to which the matter is transferred must begin hearing the evidence and the parties again.

(3) This section does not apply to family proceedings.

(4) The power of the court under this section to transfer a hearing must be exercised in accordance with any directions given under section 30(3) of the Courts Act 2003.

[Magistrates' Courts Act 1980, s 57A as inserted by the Courts Act 2003, s 48.]

Civil debt

1–2098   58. Money recoverable summarily as civil debt.   (1) A magistrates' court shall have power[1] to make an order on complaint for the payment of any money recoverable[2] summarily as a civil debt[3].

(2) Any sum payment of which may be ordered by a magistrates' court shall be recoverable summarily as a civil debt except—

(a) a sum recoverable on complaint for a magistrates' courts maintenance order; or

(b) a sum that may be adjudged to be paid by a summary conviction or by an order enforceable as if it were a summary conviction.

[Magistrates' Courts Act 1980, s 58 as amended by the Family Law Reform Act 1987, Sch 2.]

1. Note the protection given by Reserve and Auxiliary Forces (Protection of Civil Interests) Act 1951, to persons affected by that Act.

2. A bankruptcy order under s 264 of the Insolvency Act 1986, or an administration order under s 112 of the County Courts Act 1984, would be sufficient answer to any proceedings taken to enforce payment of a debt provable in bankruptcy. Likewise, a bankruptcy notice (now a statutory demand under s 268 of the Insolvency Act 1986) may be founded on an order made under this section (*Re A Debtor (No 48 of 1952), ex p Ampthill RDC v Debtor* [1952] Ch 335, [1953] 1 All ER 545, 117 JP 174).

3. For restrictions on committal for civil debt, see s 96, post, and Magistrates' Courts Rules 1981, r 53 (notice to

defendant before enforcing order); r 54 (execution of distress warrant); r 58 (judgment summons); this PART: STATUTORY INSTRUMENTS ON PROCEDURE, post. Section 127, post, imposes a six month limitation period from the time the debt became due and payable, but note the twelve month period provided in respect of tax on Sch E as well as the limit of under £1,000 recoverable summarily as a civil debt by Taxes Management Act 1970, s 65, in PART VIII: TAX AND DUTIES, post. For form of order, see Form 106 in PART IX: PRECEDENTS AND FORMS, post.

Orders for periodical payment

1–2099 59. Orders for periodical payment: means of payment. (1) In any case where a magistrates' court orders money to be paid periodically by one person (in this section referred to as "the debtor") to another (in this section referred to as "the creditor"), then—

(a) if the order is a qualifying maintenance order, the court shall at the same time exercise one of its powers under paragraphs (a) to (d) of subsection (3) below;

(b) if the order is not a maintenance order, the court shall at the same time exercise one of its powers under paragraphs (a) and (b) of that subsection.

(2) For the purposes of this section a maintenance order is a "qualifying maintenance order" if, at the time it is made, the debtor is ordinarily resident in England and Wales.

(3) The powers of the court are—

(a) the power to order that payments under the order be made directly by the debtor to the creditor;

(b) the power to order that payments[1] under the order be made to the clerk of the court[2] or to a justices' chief executive;

(c) the power to order that payments under the order be made by the debtor to the creditor by such method of payment falling within subsection (6) below as may be specified;

(cc) the power to order that payments under the order be made in accordance with arrangements made by the Secretary of State for their collection;

(d) the power to make an attachment of earnings order under the Attachment of Earnings Act 1971 to secure payments under the order.

(3A) No order made by a magistrates' court under paragraphs (a) to (d) of subsection (3) above (other than one made under paragraph (cc)) shall have effect at any time when the Secretary of State is arranging for the collection of payments under the qualifying maintenance order concerned.

(4) In any case where—

(a) the court proposes to exercise its power under paragraph (c) of subsection (3) above, and

(b) having given the debtor an opportunity of opening an account from which payments under the order may be made in accordance with the method of payment proposed to be ordered under that paragraph, the court is satisfied that the debtor has failed, without reasonable excuse, to open such an account,

the court in exercising its power under that paragraph may order that the debtor open such an account.

(5) In deciding, in the case of a maintenance order, which of the powers under paragraphs (a) to (d) of subsection (3) above (other than paragraph (cc)) it is to exercise, the court having (if practicable) given them an opportunity to make representations shall have regard to any representations made—

(a) by the debtor,

(b) by the creditor, and

(c) if the person who applied for the maintenance order is a person other than the creditor, by that other person.

(6) The methods of payment referred to in subsection (3)(c) above are the following, that is to say—

(a) payment by standing order; or

(b) payment by any other method which requires one person to give his authority for payments of a specific amount to be made from an account of his to an account of another's on specific dates during the period for which the authority is in force and without the need for any further authority from him.

(7) Where the maintenance order is an order—

(a) under the Guardianship of Minors Acts 1971 and 1973[3],

(b) under Part I of the Domestic Proceedings and Magistrates' Courts Act 1978[3] or Schedule 5 to the Civil Partnership Act 2004, or

(c) under, or having effect as if made under, Schedule 1 to the Children Act 1989[3],

and the court does not propose to exercise its powers under paragraph (c), (cc) or (d) of subsection (3) above, the court shall, unless upon representations expressly made in that behalf by the person who applied for the maintenance order it is satisfied that it is undesirable to do so, exercise its power under paragraph (b) of that subsection.

(8) The Lord Chancellor may by regulations confer on magistrates' courts, in addition to their powers under paragraphs (a) to (d) of subsection (3) above, the power (the "additional power") to order that payments under a qualifying maintenance order be made by the debtor to the creditor or a justices' chief executive (as the regulations may provide) by such method of payment as may be specified in the regulations.

(9) Any reference in any enactment to paragraphs (*a*) to (*d*) of subsection (3) above (but not a reference to any specific paragraph of that subsection) shall be taken to include a reference to the additional power, and the reference in subsection (10) below to the additional power shall be construed accordingly.

(10) Regulations under subsection (8) above may make provision for any enactment concerning, or connected with, payments under maintenance orders to apply, with or without modifications, in relation to the additional power.

(11) The power of the Lord Chancellor to make regulations under subsection (8) above shall be exercisable by statutory instrument and any such statutory instrument shall be subject to annulment in pursuance of a resolution of either House of Parliament.

(12) For the purposes of this section—

(*a*) the reference in subsection (1) above to money paid periodically by one person to another includes, in the case of a maintenance order, a reference to a lump sum paid by instalments by one person to another; and

(*b*) references to arrangements made by the Secretary of State for the collection of payments are to arrangements made by him under section 30 of the Child Support Act 1991 and regulations made under that section.

[Magistrates' Courts Act 1980, s 59 as substituted by the Maintenance Enforcement Act 1991, s 2 and as amended by SI 1992/709, SI 1994/731, the Access to Justice Act 1999, Sch 13 and the Civil Partnership Act 2004, Sch 27.]

1. For restrictions on the amount that can be offered in coin ("legal tender") see the Coinage Act 1971, s 2 in PART VIII, title CURRENCY, post.
2. The justices' chief executive by virtue of his office is collecting officer of the magistrates' court (Justices of the Peace Act 1997, s 41A, ante): he is not the agent of the justices when he receives payment by virtue of an order made under this section (*O'Connor v Isaacs* [1956] 2 QB 288, [1956] 2 All ER 417, 120 JP 325). The justices' chief executive is not permitted to withhold payments pending appeal, see *Board v Board* (1981) 11 Fam Law 210, [1981] LS Gaz R 842. For rules relating to the method of making periodical payments, see Magistrates' Courts Rules 1981, r 39, this PART: STATUTORY INSTRUMENTS AND PRACTICE DIRECTIONS ON PROCEDURE, post.
3. In PART VI: FAMILY LAW, post.

1–2100   59A. Orders for periodical payment: proceedings by designated officer. (1) Where payments under a relevant UK order are required to be made periodically—

(*a*) to or through the designated officer for a magistrates' court, or
(*b*) by any method of payment falling within section 59(6) above,

and any sums payable under the order are in arrear, the relevant designated officer shall, if the person for whose benefit the payments are required to be made so requests in writing, and unless it appears to that designated officer that it is unreasonable in the circumstances to do so, proceed in his own name for the recovery of those sums.

(2) Where payments under a relevant UK order are required to be made periodically to or through the designated officer for a magistrates' court, the person for whose benefit the payments are required to be made may, at any time during the period in which the payments are required to be so made, give authority in writing to the relevant designated officer for him to proceed as mentioned in subsection (3) below.

(3) Where authority under subsection (2) above is given to the relevant designated officer, he shall, unless it appears to him that it is unreasonable in the circumstances to do so, proceed in his own name for the recovery of any sums payable to or through him under the order in question which, on or after the date of the giving of the authority, fall into arrear.

(4) In any case where—

(*a*) authority under subsection (2) above has been given to the relevant designated officer, and
(*b*) the person for whose benefit the payments are required to be made gives notice in writing to the designated officer cancelling the authority,

the authority shall cease to have effect and, accordingly, the relevant designated officer shall not continue any proceedings already commenced by virtue of the authority.

(5) The person for whose benefit the payments are required to be made shall have the same liability for all the costs properly incurred in or about proceedings taken under subsection (1) above at his request or under subsection (3) above by virtue of his authority (including any costs incurred as a result of any proceedings commenced not being continued) as if the proceedings had been taken by him.

(6) Nothing in subsection (1) or (3) above shall affect any right of a person to proceed in his own name for the recovery of sums payable on his behalf under an order of any court.

(7) In this section—

"the relevant designated officer", in relation to an order, means—

(*a*) in a case where payments under the order are required to be made to or through the designated officer for a magistrates' court, the designated officer for that magistrates' court;
(*b*) in a case where such payments are required to be made by any method of payment falling within section 59(6) and the order was made by a magistrates' court, the designated officer for that magistrates' court; and
(*c*) in a case where such payments are required to be made by any method of payment falling within section 59(6) and the order was not made by a magistrates' court, the designated officer for the magistrates' court in which the order is registered;

"relevant UK order" means—

   (a) an order made by a magistrates' court, other than an order made by virtue of Part II of the Maintenance Orders (Reciprocal Enforcement) Act 1972;

   (b) an order made by the High Court or a county court (including an order deemed to be made by the High Court by virtue of section 1(2) of the Maintenance Orders Act 1958) and registered under Part I of that Act of 1958 in a magistrates' court; or

   (c) an order made by a court in Scotland or Northern Ireland and registered under Part II of the Maintenance Orders Act 1950 in a magistrates' court;

and any reference to payments required to be made periodically includes, in the case of a maintenance order, a reference to instalments required to be paid in respect of a lump sum payable by instalment.
[Magistrates' Courts Act 1980, s 59A, as inserted by the Maintenance Enforcement Act 19971, s 3 and amended by the Access to Justice Act 1999, Sch 13 and the Courts Act 2003, Sch 8.]

---

1. For duty of designated officer to notify arrears of weekly payments, see Magistrates' Courts Rules 1981, r 40, this PART: STATUTORY INSTRUMENTS AND PRACTICE DIRECTIONS ON PROCEDURE, post. The mechanics of enforcement proceedings are governed by r 59 which also covers the situation where the defendant lives in another petty sessions area. Note the provisions of s 99 of the Magistrates' Courts Act, 1980, post, enabling proof of non-payment by means of certificate or statutory declaration.
2. The designated officer discretion is absolute, but his refusal to proceed in his own name is no bar to the person entitled to the payments proceeding direct (sub-s (6), infra).

1-2101   59B. Maintenance orders: penalty for breach[1]. (1) In any case where—

   (a) payments under a relevant English maintenance order are required to be made periodically in the manner mentioned in paragraph (a) or (b) of section 59A(1) above, and

   (b) the debtor fails, on or after the date of commencement of this section, to comply with the order in so far as the order relates to the manner of payment concerned,

the person for whose benefit the payments are required to be made may make a complaint to a relevant justice giving details of the failure to comply.

(2) If the relevant justice is satisfied that the nature of the alleged failure to comply may be such as to justify the relevant court in exercising its power under subsection (3) below, he shall issue a summons directed to the debtor requiring him to appear before the relevant court to answer the complaint.

(3) On the hearing of the complaint, the relevant court may order the debtor to pay a sum not exceeding **£1,000**.

(4) Any sum ordered to be paid under subsection (3) above shall for the purposes of this Act be treated as adjudged to be paid by a conviction of a magistrates' court.

(5) In this section—

"debtor" has the same meaning as it has in section 59 above;

"the relevant court" has the same meaning as it has in section 59A above;

"relevant English maintenance order" means—

   (a) a maintenance order made by a magistrates' court, other than an order made by virtue of Part II of the Maintenance Orders (Reciprocal Enforcement) Act 1972; or

   (b) an order made by the High Court or a county court (other than an order deemed to be made by the High Court by virtue of section 1(2) of the Maintenance Orders Act 1958) and registered under Part I of that Act of 1958 in a magistrates' court;

"relevant justice", in relation to a relevant court, means a justice of the peace for the petty sessions area for which the relevant court is acting;

and any reference to payments required to be made periodically includes a reference to instalments required to be paid in respect of a lump sum payable by instalments.
[Magistrates' Courts Act 1980, s 59B as added by the Maintenance Enforcement Act 1991, s 3.]

---

1. In *Santa Cruz Ruiz v United Kingdom* (1998) EHRLR 208 the European Commission of Human Rights treated proceedings for non-payment of maintenance as "criminal" for the purposes of art 6 of the European Convention on Human Rights.

1-2102   60. Revocation, variation, etc of orders for periodical payment. (1) Where a magistrates' court has made an order for money to be paid periodically by one person to another, the court may, by order[1] on complaint[2], revoke[3], revive or vary the order.

(2) The power under subsection (1) above to vary an order shall include power to suspend the operation of any provision of the order temporarily and to revive the operation of any provision so suspended.

(3) Where the order mentioned in subsection (1) above is a maintenance order, the power under that subsection to vary the order shall include power, if the court is satisfied that payment has not been made in accordance with the order, to exercise one of its powers under paragraphs (a) to (d) of section 59(3) above.

(4) In any case where—

   (a) a magistrates' court has made a maintenance order, and

   (b) payments under the order are required to be made by any method of payment falling within section 59(6) above, an interested party may apply in writing to the clerk of the court for the order to be varied as mentioned in subsection (5) below.

(5) Subject to subsection (8) below, where an application has been made under subsection (4) above, the clerk, after giving written notice (by post or otherwise) of the application to any other interested party and allowing that party, within the period of 14 days beginning with the date of the giving of that notice, an opportunity to make written representations, may vary the order to provide that payments under the order shall be made to the justices' chief executive for the court.

(6) The clerk may proceed with an application under subsection (4) above notwithstanding that any such interested party as is referred to in subsection (5) above has not received written notice of the application.

(7) In subsections (4) to (6) above "interested party", in relation to a maintenance order, means—

(a) the debtor;
(b) the creditor; and
(c) if the person who applied for the maintenance order is a person other than the creditor, that other person.

(8) Where an application has been made under subsection (4) above, the clerk may, if he considers it inappropriate to exercise his power under subsection (5) above, refer the matter to the court which may vary the order by exercising one of its powers under paragraphs (a) to (d) of section 59(3) above.

(9) Subsections (4), (5) and (7) of section 59 above shall apply for the purposes of subsections (3) and (8) above as they apply for the purposes of that section.

(10) None of the powers of the court, or of the clerk of the court, conferred by subsections (3) to (9) above shall be exercisable in relation to a maintenance order which is not a qualifying maintenance order (within the meaning of section 59 above).

(11) For the purposes of this section—

(a) "creditor" and "debtor" have the same meaning as they have in section 59 above; and
(b) the reference in subsection (1) above to money paid periodically by one person to another includes, in the case of a maintenance order, a reference to a lump sum paid by instalments by one person to another.

[Magistrates' Courts Act 1980, s 60 as substituted by the Maintenance Enforcement Act 1991, s 4 and amended by the Access to Justice Act 1999, Sch 13.]

1. Procedure is governed by r 41 of the Magistrates' Courts Rules 1981, this PART: STATUTORY INSTRUMENTS ON PROCEDURE, post. See also forms 111–113 in PART IX: PRECEDENTS AND FORMS, post. For costs see s 64, post. Section 60 does not apply to orders made under Part I of the Domestic Proceedings and Magistrates' Courts Act 1978 (s 23 (2)) as they have their own code under ibid, ss 20–24; nor to orders for maintenance of a child made under the Children Act 1989, Sch 1 (see ibid, Sch 1 paras 6, 6A) in PART VI: FAMILY LAW, post. As to the variation of orders by or against persons outside England and Wales, see the Maintenance Orders (Facilities for Enforcement) Act 1920 and the Maintenance Orders (Reciprocal Enforcement) Act 1972. For procedure for variation of High Court or County Court orders registered in a magistrates' court, see Maintenance Orders Act 1958, s 4 in PART VI, title FAMILY LAW, post. Note the provisions of r 106 of the Magistrates' Courts Rules 1981, this PART: STATUTORY INSTRUMENTS ON PROCEDURE, post.

In the case of an affiliation order pursuant to s 5(1) of the Affiliation Proceedings Act 1957, which was made before the amendment of that section by s 51 of the Domestic Proceedings and Magistrates' Courts Act 1978 became effective on 1 February 1981, or a maintenance order made under s 2 of the Matrimonial Proceedings (Magistrates' Courts) Act 1960, where payments were required to be made to a person for the maintenance of a child, there was no power for the court to vary the order so as to provide that payments should be made to the child himself (*Boniface v Harris* (1983) 147 JP 208, 13 Fam Law 117). A similar situation arose in the case of a maintenance order made before 1 February 1981 under s 9(2) of the Guardianship of Minors Act 1971. However, since 12 October 1984, the problem appears to have been resolved by Sch 1, para 27, to the Matrimonial and Family Proceedings Act 1984, which has amended Sch 1 (transitional provisions) to the Domestic Proceedings and Magistrates' Courts Act 1978, in PART VI: FAMILY LAW, post. Paragraph 27(a) of Sch 1 to the 1984 Act amends the transitional provisions by modifying the continued application of the Matrimonial Proceedings (Magistrates' Courts) Act 1960 to include the power to vary orders to direct payment to a child, and para 27(b) provides that changes made by the Domestic Proceedings and Magistrates' Courts Act 1978 to Acts other than the Act of 1960 will now apply to orders made before those changes took effect.

2. Complaint may be made by any person who has the right to recover for his own benefit the amount payable under the order (*Moore v Ball* [1984] Fam 41, [1984] 2 All ER 327, 148 JP 425).

3. A magistrates' court has no power to revoke an adjudication of paternity on which an affiliation order is based (*R v Copestake, ex p Wilkinson* [1927] 1 KB 468, 90 JP 191).

1–2111 61. Periodical payments payable by one person under more than one order.

(1) The power to make rules conferred by section 144 below shall, without prejudice to the generality of subsection (1) of that section, include power to make provision—

(a) for enabling a person to make one complaint for the recovery of payments required to be made to him by another person under more than one periodical payments order; and
(b) for apportioning between two or more periodical payments orders, in such manner as may be prescribed by the rules, any sum paid to a justices' chief executive on any date by the person liable to make payments under the orders which is less than the total sum required to be paid on that date to that justices' chief executive by that person in respect of those orders (being orders one of which requires payments to be made for the benefit of a child to the person with whom the child has his home and one or more of which requires payments to be made to that person either for his own benefit or for the benefit of another child who has his home with him).

(2) In this section—

"child" means a person who has not attained the age of 18;

"periodical payments order" means an order made by a magistrates' court, or registered in a magistrates' court under Part II of the Maintenance Orders Act 1950 or Part I of the Maintenance Orders Act 1958, which requires the making of periodical payments,

and any payments required under a periodical payments order to be made to a child shall for the purposes of subsection (1) above be treated as if they were required to be made to the person with whom the child has his home.

[Magistrates' Courts Act 1980, s 61, as amended by the Access to Justice Act 1999, Sch 13.]

Payments to children

1–2112   62. Provisions as to payments required to be made to a child, etc. (1) Where—

(a) periodical payments are required to be made, or a lump sum is required to be paid, to a child under an order made by a magistrates' court, or

(b) periodical payments are required to be made to a child under an order which is registered in a magistrates' court,

any sum required under the order to be paid to the child may be paid to the person with whom the child has his home, and that person—

(i) may proceed in his own name for the variation, revival or revocation of the order, and

(ii) may either proceed in his own name for the recovery of any sum required to be paid under the order or request or authorises the justices' chief executive for the magistrates' court under subsection (1) or subsection (2) respectively of section 59A above, to proceed for the recovery of that sum.

(2) Where a child has a right under any enactment to apply for the revival of an order made by a magistrates' court which provided for the making of periodical payments to or for the benefit of the child, the person with whom the child has his home may proceed in his own name for the revival of that order.

(3) Where any person by whom periodical payments are required to be paid to a child under an order made by or registered in a magistrates' court makes a complaint for the variation or revocation of that order, the person with whom the child has his home may answer the complaint in his own name.

(4) Nothing in subsections (1) and (2) above shall affect any right of a child to proceed in his own name for the variation, revival or revocation of an order or for the recovery of any sum payable thereunder.

(5) In this section references to the person with whom a child has his home—

(a) in the case of any child who is being looked after by a local authority (within the meaning of section 22 of the Children Act 1989), are references to that local authority; and

(b) in any other case, are references to the person who, disregarding any absence of the child at a hospital or boarding school and any other temporary absence, has care of the child.

(6) In this section any reference to an order registered in a magistrates' court is a reference to an order registered in a magistrates' court under Part II of the Maintenance Orders Act 1950 or Part I of the Maintenance Orders Act 1958.

(7) In this section "child" means a person who has not attained the age of 18.

[Magistrates' Courts Act 1980, s 62 as amended by the Children Act 1989, Sch 13, the Maintenance Enforcement Act 1991, Sch 2 and the Access to Justice Act 1999, Sch 13.]

Orders other than for payment of money

1–2113   63. Orders other than for payment of money[1]. (1) Where under any Act passed after 31st December 1879 a magistrates' court has power to require the doing of anything other than the payment of money, or to prohibit the doing of anything, any order of the court for the purpose of exercising that power may contain such provisions for the manner in which anything is to be done, for the time within which anything is to be done, or during which anything is not to be done, and generally for giving effect to the order, as the court thinks fit.

(2) The court may by order made on complaint suspend or rescind[2] any such order as aforesaid.

(3) Where any person disobeys[3] an order of a magistrates' court made under an Act passed after 31st December 1879 to do anything other than the payment of money or to abstain from doing anything the court may[4]—

(a) order[5] him to pay a sum not exceeding £50 for every day during which he is in default or a sum not exceeding £5,000[6]; or

(b) commit him to custody until he has remedied his default[5] or for a period not exceeding **2 months**[7];

but a person who is ordered to pay a sum for every day during which he is in default or who is committed to custody until he has remedied[7] his default shall not by virtue of this section be ordered to pay more than £1,000 or be committed for more than 2 months in all for doing or abstaining from doing the same thing contrary to the order (without prejudice to the operation of this section in relation to any subsequent default).

(4) Any sum ordered to be paid under subsection (3) above shall for the purposes of this Act be treated as adjudged to be paid by a conviction[8] of a magistrates' court.

(5) The preceding provisions of this section shall not apply to any order for the enforcement of which provision is made by any other enactment.

[Magistrates' Courts Act 1980, s 63 as amended by SI 1984/447 and the Criminal Justice Act 1991, Sch 4.]

---

1. For further provisions on the exercise of the powers under s 63(3) either of the court's own motion or by order on complaint, see the Contempt of Court Act 1981, s 17 and Sch 3, post.

For the enforcement under this section of a contact order under s 8 of the Children Act 1989, see para **6–151 Contact order**.

2. This subsection does not apply to orders made under Part I of the Domestic Proceedings and Magistrates' Courts Act 1978 (s 23(2)).

3. A summons should be issued, reciting the disobedience of the order and requiring the defaulter to appear for the purpose of showing cause why an order requiring him to pay money or be committed to prison should not be made. The summons should state details of the alleged breach with clarity and indicate time, date and place; the section requires deliberate and wilful disobedience rather than unintended default, and applies to orders for child access; see *P v W (Access order: Breach)* [1984] Fam 32, [1984] 1 All ER 866, 148 JP 161. Committal proceedings are a criminal charge for the purposes of art 6(3)(c) of the European Convention on Human Rights and the parent in default is entitled to the benefit of legal representation (although not necessarily entitled to indefinite offers of legal assistance if they behave so unreasonably as to make it impossible for the funders to continue sensibly to provide legal assistance) (*Re K (children: committal proceedings)* [2003] EWCA Civ 1559, [2003] 2 FCR 336, [2003] 1 FLR 277). In *T v T* (1984) Times, 19 July, the Divisional Court counselled caution when dealing with a custodial parent under this section for breach of an access order; the justices should try to discover why access had been prevented and the endeavour to make a variation acceptable to both parents. Appeal against a decision lies to the Divisional Court (*B BPM v B MM* [1969] P 103, [1969] 1 All ER 891, 133 JP 245). A note of the evidence given before the justices should be taken, so that it can be made available in the event of an appeal (*Head v Head* [1982] 3 All ER 14, [1982] 1 WLR 1186, 146 JP 406). Where there are proceedings pending in the County Court relating to access, a magistrates' court should not proceed to hear default proceedings relating to an existing order (*Thomason v Thomason* (1984) 149 JP 21, [1985] FLR 214, [1985] Fam Law 91).

4. In *Hale v Tanner* [2000] 3 FCR 62, [2000] 2 FLR 879, the Court of Appeal in considering an application to commit for breach of a non-molestation order made by the county court gave guidance on the appropriate matters for the court to take into consideration which will, we suggest, be helpful to magistrates exercising their family jurisdiction. Family cases raise different considerations from those elsewhere in the civil law, in particular (*a*) the heightened emotional tensions that arise between family members; and (*b*) the need often for those family members to continue to be in contact with each other because they have children together or the like:

1. Imprisonment is not to be regarded as the automatic consequence of the breach of an order. There is, however, no principle that imprisonment is not to be imposed at the first occasion. But it is usually appropriate to take some other course on the first occasion.
2. Particularly where no actual violence has been used, the court may use a range of alternatives including an adjournment, a fine or it may be that proceedings are taken under the mental health legislation.
3. Any term of imprisonment should be decided without reference to whether it is suspended or not.
4. The length of the term will depend on the objectives of the court: to mark the court's disapproval of the order; to secure compliance.
5. The length of the committal must bear some relationship to the maximum term available.
6. Suspension is more widely available than in criminal cases; the case does not have to be exceptional.
7. The length of suspension requires separate consideration although it is often appropriate for it to be linked to continued compliance with the order.
8. The context must be borne in mind : the break up of an intimate relationship where emotions run high and people behave in silly ways; the context of the parties having had children together - aggravating where there is greater fear engendered or mitigating where there is reason to suppose that once immediate emotions have died down, the molestation and threats will not continue.
9. Concurrent proceedings such as under the Protection from Harassment Act 1997 may have to be taken into account as the court will not wish to punish the defendant twice.
10. The court should explain briefly to the defendant why he or she is being sentenced to imprisonment, why it is of the length it is, (if suspended) why the suspension is as it is.

Where there are concurrent proceedings in the civil and criminal courts, the first court to sentence must not anticipate or allow for a likely future sentence. It is for the second court to sentence to reflect the prior sentence in its judgment in order to ensure that the defendant is not twice punished for the same act. For this purpose it is essential that the second court should be fully informed of the factors and circumstances reflected in the first sentence (*Lomas v Parle* [2003] EWCA Civ 1804, [2004] 1 All ER 1173, [2004] 1 WLR 1642, [2004] 1 FCR 97, [2004 FLR 812). The Court of Appeal (Civil Division) has also given guidance to courts dealing with breach of injunctions. Cases of domestic and other violence associated with harassment and molestation demand more condign deterrent punishment than formerly and sentences in such cases should not be materially divergent from those imposed under the Protection from Harassment Act 1997, *H v O (Contempt of Court: Sentencing)* [2004] EWCA Civ 1691, [2005] 2 FLR 329. However, custody should only be imposed where justified and it is wrong in principle to impose custody where a fine would be appropriate and it is wrong to impose custody (albeit suspended) on the basis that a person lacked means to pay a fine, *Re M (Contact Order)* [2005] EWCA Civ 615, [2005] 2 FLR 1006. The purposes of sentencing set out in s 42 of the Criminal Justice Act 2003 are very relevant even in relation to family cases (*Robinson v Murray* [2005] EWCA Civ 935, [2005] 3 FCR 505, *sub nom Murray v Robinson* [2006] 1 FLR 365).

5. Appeal lies to a Divisional Court of the High Court (Administration of Justice Act 1960, s 13, in this PART, ante). Procedure on such an appeal is governed by the Civil Procedure Rules 1998, Part 52, this PART: STATUTORY INSTRUMENTS ON PROCEDURE, post.

6. The statute does not provide for officially informing the keeper that the default has been remedied; we think the *liberate* should be made upon a certificate of the committing justice. There is no power to suspend the operation of a committal under this section; what is now s 118 of the Powers of Criminal Courts (Sentencing) Act 2000 does not apply (*B BPM v B MM* [1969] P 103, [1969] 1 All ER 891, 133 JP 245) but see the power to suspend for breach of occupation and non-molestation orders under the Family Law Act 1996 and exclusion requirements under the Children Act 1989 in s 50 of the Family Law Act 1996, in PART VI: FAMILY LAW post.

7. There is no power to make consecutive committal orders under this section (*Head v Head* [1982] 3 All ER 14, [1982] 1 WLR 1186, 146 JP 406).

8. For enforcement see s 75 et seq, post.

Costs

1–2114   64.   Power to award costs and enforcement of costs[1].   (1) On the hearing of a complaint, a magistrates' court shall have power in its discretion to make such order as to costs—

    (*a*)   on making the order for which the complaint is made, to be paid by the defendant to the complainant;

    (*b*)   on dismissing the complaint, to be paid by the complainant to the defendant,

as it thinks just and reasonable[2]; but if the complaint is for an order for the periodical payment of money, or for the revocation, revival or variation of such an order, or for the enforcement of such an order, the court may, whatever adjudication it makes, order either party to pay the whole or any part of the other's costs.

    (2)   The amount of any sum ordered to be paid under subsection (1) above shall be specified[3] in the order, or order of dismissal, as the case may be.

    (3)   Subject to subsection (4) below, costs ordered to be paid under this section shall be enforceable as a civil debt[4].

    (4)   Any costs awarded on a complaint for a maintenance order, or for the enforcement, variation, revocation, discharge or revival of such an order, against the person liable to make payments under the order shall be enforceable as a sum ordered to be paid by a magistrates' court maintenance order.

    (5)   The preceding provisions of this section shall have effect subject to any other Act enabling a magistrates' court to order a successful party to pay the other party's costs.

[Magistrates' Courts Act 1980, s 64 as amended by the Family Law Reform Act 1987, Sch 2.]

----

    1.   This section relates to costs in civil cases: for the approach that should be adopted by justices when considering whether or not to make an order for costs, see para **1–644**. For criminal cases see Pt II of the Prosecution of Offences Act 1985, post. For award of costs where the complaint is not proceeded with, see Courts Act 1971, s 52(3), ante. For table of fees to be taken by the court, see the Magistrates' Courts Fees Order 2005, SI 2005/3444, this PART, STATUTORY INSTRUMENTS AND PRACTICE DIRECTIONS ON PROCEDURE, post. Expenses of police officers serving summonses or executing warrants are payable not by the parties, but out of the police fund (see 62 JP Jo 411). It is incumbent upon the parties to have material available upon which the court can make its determination on costs (*R v West London Magistrates' Court, ex p Kyprianou* (1993) Times, 3 May).

    2.   This sum should not be in excess of the proper costs incurred; not a penalty in the guise of costs (see *R v Highgate Justices, ex p Petrou* [1954] 1 All ER 406, [1954] 1 WLR 485, 118 JP 151). It is appropriate, at discretion, to award costs to a successful legally aided party in domestic proceedings; see Home Office Circular, No 154/63, dated 15 July 1963. Where one party is legally aided and the successful party is not, the court may order costs to be paid to the unassisted party by the Legal Aid Board: Legal Aid Act 1988, s 18, this Part, post.

    3.   The amount of the costs must be fixed by the court as part of the adjudication (*R v Pwllheli Justices, ex p Soane* [1948] 2 All ER 815, 112 JP 441); and may include the expenses of the complainant's witnesses, as well as a fee for his solicitor. An order for costs is in two stages since quantification follows the making of the primary decision that an order for costs will be made. In the period between the two decisions, the order for costs is not bad but merely incomplete and thereby for the time being ineffective. Accordingly where a court made an order that costs follow the event but had overlooked a faxed copy of the successful party's costs, it had, on the facts, not made a final decision and could, after considering representations from the unsuccessful party, perfect the order (*Blustarling Ltd v Westminster City Council* (1996) Times, 24 July).

    4.   Defined in s 150(1), post. See also s 58, ante.

Family proceedings

1–2115   65.   Meaning of family proceedings.   (1) In this Act "family proceedings" means proceedings under any of the following enactments, that is to say—

    (*a*)   the Maintenance Orders (Facilities for Enforcement) Act 1920;

    (*b*)   section 43 of the National Assistance Act 1948;

    (*c*)   section 3 of the Marriage Act 1949;

    (*ca*)   Schedule 2 to the Civil Partnership Act 2004;

    (*d*)   *Repealed*;

    (*e*)   *Repealed*;

    (*ee*)   section 35 of the Matrimonial Causes Act 1973;

    (*ef*)   paragraphs 69 to 72 of Schedule 5 to the Civil Partnership Act 2004;

    (*f*)   Part I of the Maintenance Orders (Reciprocal Enforcement) Act 1972;

    (*g*)   *Repealed*;

    (*h*)   the Adoption and Children Act 2002;

    (*i*)   section 18 of the Supplementary Benefits Act 1976;

    (*j*)   Part I of the Domestic Proceedings and Magistrates' Courts Act 1978;

    (*ja*)   Schedule 6 to the Civil Partnership Act 2004;

    (*k*)   *Repealed*;

    (*l*)   section 60 of this Act;

    (*m*)[1] Part I of the Civil Jurisdiction and Judgments Act 1982, so far as that Part relates to the recognition or enforcement of maintenance orders;

    (*mm*) section 55A of the Family Law Act 1986;

    (*n*)   the Children Act 1989;

    (*n*)   section 106 of the Social Security Administration Act 1992;[2]*

    (*na*) section 30 of the Human Fertilisation and Embryology Act 1990;

    (*nb*) section 106 of the Social Security Administration Act 1992;

    (*o*)   section 20 (so far as it provides, by virtue of an order under section 45, for appeals to be made to a court) of the Child Support Act 1991;

(p) Part IV of the Family Law Act 1996;
(q) sections 11 and 12 of the Crime and Disorder Act 1998;
(r) Council Regulation (EC) No 44/2001 of 22nd December 2000 on jurisdiction and the recognition and enforcement of judgments in civil and commercial matters, so far as that Regulation relates to the recognition or enforcement of maintenance orders;
(s) Council Regulation (EC) No 2201/2003 of 27th November 2003 concerning jurisdiction and the recognition and enforcement of judgments in matrimonial matters and matters of parental responsibility, so far as that Regulation relates to jurisdiction, recognition and enforcement in parental responsibility matters;

except that, subject to subsection (2) below, it does not include—

(i)   proceeding for the enforcement of any order made, confirmed or registered under any of those enactments;
(ii) proceedings for the variation of any provision for the periodical payment of money contained in an order made, confirmed or registered under any of those enactments; or
(iii) proceedings on an information in respect of the commission of an offence under any of those enactments.

(2) The court before which there fall to be heard any of the following proceedings, that is to say—

(a) proceedings (whether under this Act or any other enactment) for the enforcement of any order made, confirmed or registered under any of the enactments specified in paragraphs (a) to (k), (m), (n), (p) and (r) of subsection (1) above;
(b) proceedings (whether under this Act or any other enactment) for the variation of any provision for the making of periodical payments contained in an order made, confirmed or registered under any of those enactments;
(c) proceedings for an attachment of earnings order to secure maintenance payments within the meaning of the Attachment of Earnings Act 1971 or for the discharge or variation of such an order; or
(d) proceedings for the enforcement of a maintenance order which is registered in a magistrates' court under Part II of the Maintenance Orders Act 1950 or Part I of the Maintenance Orders Act 1958 or for the variation of the rate of payments specified by such an order,
(e) proceedings under section 20 (so far as it provides, by virtue of an order under section 45, for appeals to be made to a court) of the Child Support Act 1991,

may if it thinks fit order that those proceedings and any other proceedings being heard therewith shall, notwithstanding anything in subsection (1) above, be treated as family proceedings for the purposes of this Act.

(3) Where the same parties are parties—

(a) to proceedings which are family proceedings by virtue of subsection (1) above, and
(b) to proceedings which the court has power to treat as family proceedings by virtue of subsection (2) above,

and the proceedings are heard together by a magistrates' court, the whole of those proceedings shall be treated as family proceedings for the purposes of this Act.

(4) No appeal shall lie from the making of, or refusal to make, an order under subsection (2) above.

(5) *Spent.*
(6) *Spent.*

[Magistrates' Courts Act 1980, s 65 as amended by the Civil Jurisdiction and Judgments Act 1982, Sch 12, the Matrimonial and Family Proceedings Act 1984, s 44, the Social Security Act 1986, Sch 10, the Family Law Reform Act 1987, Schs 2 and 4, the Children Act 1989, Schs 11 and 15, the Courts and Legal Services Act 1990, Schs 16 and 20, the Social Security (Consequential Provisions) Act 1992, Schs 1 and 2, the Family Law Act 1996, Sch 8, SI 1997/1898, the Crime and Disorder Act 1998, Sch 8, the Child Support, Pensions and Social Security Act 2000, Sch 8, SI 2001/3929, the Adoption and Children Act 2002, Sch 3, the Courts Act 2003, Sch 8, the Civil Partnership Act 2004, Sch 27 and SI 2005/265.]

*New para (nza) inserted by the Childcare Act 2006, Sch 2 from a date to be appointed..
1. Three paragraphs (m) have been added to s 65(1). The first paragraph (m) printed here was added by the Civil Jurisdiction and Judgments Act 1982, Sch 12, the second (now repealed) by the Social Security Act 1986, Sch 10, and the third (now repealed) by the Family Law Reform Act 1987, Sch 2.
2. Two paragraphs (n) have been added to s 65(1), the first by the Children Act 1989 and the second by the Social Security (Consequential Provisions) Act 1992, Sch 2, para 60.

1–2116 66. Composition of magistrates' courts for family proceedings: general. (1) A magistrates' court when hearing family proceedings shall be composed of—

(a) two or three lay justices; or
(b) a District Judge (Magistrates' Courts) as chairman and one or two lay justices;

or, if it is not practicable for such a court to be so composed, a District Judge (Magistrates' Courts) sitting alone.

(2) Except where such a court is composed of a District Judge (Magistrates' Courts) sitting alone, it shall, so far as practicable, include both a man and a woman.

(3) In this section and section 67 below "lay justices" means justices of the peace who are not District Judges (Magistrates' Courts).
[Magistrates' Courts Act 1980, s 66, as amended by the Access to Justice Act 1999, Sch 11.]

1–2117   67. Family proceedings courts.   (1) Magistrates' courts—

   (a) constituted in accordance with this section or section 66 of the Courts Act 2003 (judges having powers of District Judges (Magistrates' Courts)), and
   (b) sitting for the purpose of hearing family proceedings,

are to be known as family proceedings courts.

(2) A justice of the peace is not qualified to sit as a member of a family proceedings court to hear family proceedings of any description unless he has an authorisation extending to the proceedings.

(3) He has an authorisation extending to the proceedings only if he has been authorised by the Lord Chief Justice to sit as a member of a family proceedings court to hear—

   (a) proceedings of that description, or
   (b) all family proceedings.

(4) The Lord Chief Justice may, after consulting the Lord Chancellor, by rules make provision about—

   (a) the grant and revocation of authorisations,
   (b) the appointment of chairmen of family proceedings courts, and
   (c) the composition of family proceedings courts.

(5) Rules under subsection (4) may confer powers on the Lord Chief Justice with respect to any of the matters specified in the rules.

(6) Rules under subsection (4) may be made only after consultation with the Family Procedure Rule Committee.

(7) Rules under subsection (4) are to be made by statutory instrument.

(8) A statutory instrument containing rules under subsection (4) is subject to annulment in pursuance of a resolution of either House of Parliament.

(9) The Lord Chief Justice may nominate a judicial office holder (as defined in section 109(4) of the Constitutional Reform Act 2005) to exercise his functions under subsection (3) or (4) or the powers conferred on him by rules under subsection (4).
[Magistrates' Courts Act 1980, s 67 as substituted by the Courts Act 2003, s 49 as amended by the Constitutional Reform Act 2005, s 15(1), Sch 4.]

1–2118   68. Combined family panels.   *Repealed.*

1–2119   69. Sittings of magistrates' courts for family proceedings.   (1) The business of magistrates' courts shall, so far as is consistent with the due dispatch of business, be arranged in such manner as may be requisite for separating the hearing and determination of family proceedings from other business.

(2) In the case of family proceedings in a magistrates' court other than proceedings under the Adoption and Children Act 2002, no person shall be present during the hearing and determination by the court of the proceedings[1] except—

   (a) officers of the court;
   (b) parties to the case before the court, their legal representatives, witnesses and other persons directly concerned in the case;
   (c) representatives of newspapers or news agencies;
   (d) any other person whom the court may in its discretion permit to be present, so, however, that permission shall not be withheld from a person who appears to the court to have adequate grounds for attendance.

(3) In relation to any family proceedings under the Adoption and Children Act 2002, subsection (2) above shall apply with the omission of paragraphs (c) and (d).

(4) When hearing family proceedings, a magistrates' court may, if it thinks it necessary in the interest of the administration of justice or of public decency, direct that any persons, not being officers of the court or parties to the case, the parties' legal representatives, or other persons directly concerned in the case, be excluded during the taking of any indecent evidence.

(5) The powers conferred on a magistrates' court by this section shall be in addition and without prejudice to any other powers of the court to hear proceedings in camera.

(6) Nothing in this section shall affect the exercise by a magistrates' court of the power to direct that witnesses shall be excluded[2] until they are called for examination.

(7) *Spent.*
[Magistrates' Courts Act 1980, s 69 as amended by the Children Act 1989, Sch 11, the Courts and Legal Services Act 1990, Sch 18 and the Adoption and Children Act 2002, Sch 3.]

---

   1. A court hearing an appeal from such a decision may also sit in private; see the Domestic and Appellate Proceedings (Restriction of Publicity) Act 1968.
   2. See *R v Briggs* (1930) 22 Cr App Rep 68. Witnesses should not however be obliged to leave the court unless an order is made excluding them. If an application is made to exclude witnesses, then an order should be made unless the justices think such a step is inappropriate. If a party is unrepresented, and the justices think a witness should be excluded, then they should suggest to the unrepresented party that an application should be made. If a witness remains in court in defiance

of an order excluding him, the justices then have a discretion whether to admit his evidence; otherwise his evidence should be admitted (*Tomlinson v Tomlinson* [1980] 1 All ER 593, [1980] 1 WLR 322).

1–2120 70. Jurisdiction of magistrates' courts in inner London for family proceedings.
(1) A relevant court for an inner London petty sessions area shall, in addition to hearing proceedings which (apart from subsection (2) below) may be heard by a relevant court for that area, have jurisdiction to hear proceedings which could be heard before a relevant court for any other such area, but shall not exercise the jurisdiction conferred by this subsection except in such cases or classes of case as may be determined by the magistrates' courts committee whose area consists of or includes that petty sessions area.

(2) A magistrates' court for an inner London petty sessions area shall not hear any family proceedings if the magistrates' courts committee whose area consists of or includes that petty sessions area so determine.

(3) In this section—

"relevant court" means a magistrates' court when composed for the purpose of exercising jurisdiction to hear family proceedings;

"inner London petty sessions area" means any petty sessions area falling wholly or partly within the area consisting of the inner London boroughs and the City of London.

[Magistrates' Courts Act 1980, s 70 as amended by the Children Act 1989, Sch 11, the Police and Magistrates' Courts Act 1994, Sch 8 and the Access to Justice Act 1999, Sch 10.]

1–2121 71. Newspaper reports of family proceedings. (1) In the case of family proceedings in a magistrates' court it shall not be lawful for a person to whom this subsection applies—

(a) to print or publish, or cause or procure to be printed or published, in a newspaper or periodical, or

(b) to include, or cause or procure to be included, in a programme included in a programme service (within the meaning of the Broadcasting Act 1990) for reception in Great Britain,

any particulars of the proceedings other than such particulars as are mentioned in subsection (1A) below.

(1A) The particulars referred to in subsection (1) above are—

(a) the names, addresses and occupations of the parties and witnesses;

(b) the grounds of the application, and a concise statement of the charges, defences and counter-charges in support of which evidence has been given;

(c) submissions on any point of law arising in the course of the proceedings and the decision of the court on the submissions;

(d) the decision of the court, and any observations made by the court in giving it.

(1B) Subsection (1) above applies—

(a) in relation to paragraphs (a) of that subsection, to the proprietor, editor or publisher of the newspaper or periodical, and

(b) in relation to paragraph (b) of that subsection, to any body corporate which provides the service in which the programme is included and to any person having functions in relation to the programme corresponding to those of an editor of a newspaper.

(2) In the case of family proceedings in a magistrates' court under the Adoption and Children Act 2002, subsection (1A) above shall apply with the omission of paragraphs (a) and (b).

(3) Any person acting in contravention of this section shall be liable on summary conviction to a fine not exceeding **level 4** on the standard scale.

(4) No prosecution for an offence under this section shall be begun without the consent of the Attorney General.

(5) Nothing in this section shall prohibit the printing or publishing of any matter in a newspaper or periodical of a technical character bona fide intended for circulation among members of the legal or medical professions.

(6) *Spent.*

[Magistrates' Courts Act 1980, s 71 as amended by the Criminal Justice Act 1982, s 46, the Children Act 1989, Sch 11, the Broadcasting Act 1990, Sch 20 and the Adoption and Children Act 2002, Sch 3.]

1–2122 72. *Repealed.*

1–2123 73. Examination of witnesses by court. Where in any family proceedings, or in any proceedings for the enforcement or variation of an order made in family proceedings, it appears to a magistrates' court that any party to the proceedings who is not legally represented is unable effectively to examine or cross-examine a witness, the court shall ascertain[1] from that party what are the matters about which the witness may be able to depose or on which the witness ought to be cross-examined, as the case may be, and shall put, or cause to be put, to the witness such questions in the interests of that party as may appear to the court to be proper.

[Magistrates' Courts Act 1980, s 73 as amended by the Children Act 1989, Sch 11.]

---

1. This section should be applied where a defendant writes a letter to the court setting out his answers to the complaint (*Marjoram v Marjoram* [1955] 2 All ER 1, [1955] 1 WLR 520, 119 JP 291). Disregard of this section may result in the case being remitted for rehearing (*Fox v Fox* [1954] 3 All ER 526, [1954] 1 WLR 1472, 119 JP 42). The section does not

however invite indiscriminate and unjustified cross-examination (*Brewster v Brewster* [1971] 2 All ER 993, [1971] 1 WLR 1102, 135 JP 501.) The Court is under no duty to cross-examine on behalf of a legally represented party (*Ratcliff v Ratcliff* [1964] 3 All ER 351, [1964] 1 WLR 1098).

1–2124　74. Reasons for decisions in family proceedings[1].　(1) The power to make rules conferred by section 144 below shall, without prejudice to the generality of subsection (1) of that section, include power to make provision for the recording by a magistrates' court, in such manner as may be prescribed by the rules, of reasons for a decision made in such family proceedings or class of family proceedings as may be so prescribed, and for making available a copy of any record made in accordance with those rules of the reasons for a decision of a magistrates' court to any person who requests a copy thereof for the purposes of an appeal against that decision or for the purpose of deciding whether or not to appeal against that decision.

(2) A copy of any record made by virtue of this section of that reasons for a decision of a magistrates' court shall, if certified by such officer of the court as may be prescribed, be admissible as evidence of those reasons.

[Magistrates' Courts Act 1980, s 74 as amended by the Children Act 1989, Sch 11.]

1. For guidance on the preparation of reasons required by rules made under this section, see *Hutchinson v Hutchinson* (1980) 2 FLR 167. Under art 6(1) of the European Convention on Human Rights it is a requirement of a fair trial in both criminal and civil matters that a court should give reasons for its judgment. The extent of the duty to give reasons may, however, vary according to the nature of the decision. See *Hadjianastassiou v Greece* (1992) 16 EHRR 219, *Van de Hurk v Netherlands* (1994) 18 EHRR 481, *Ruiz Torija v Spain* (1994) 19 EHRR 553, *Hiro Balani v Spain* (1994) 19 EHRR 566, *Georgiadis v Greece* (1997) 24 EHRR 606 and *Helle v Finland* (1997) 26 EHRR 159. For recent consideration of the duty to give reasons both at common law and under the Convention see *Stefan v General Medical Council* [1999] 1 WLR 1293, PC.

PART III[1]

SATISFACTION AND ENFORCEMENT

General provisions

1–2125　75. Power to dispense with immediate payment.　(1) A magistrates' court by whose conviction or order a sum is adjudged to be paid may, instead of requiring immediate payment, allow time for payment, or order payment by instalments[2].

(2) Where a magistrates' court has allowed time for payment, the court[3] may, on application by[4] or on behalf of the person liable to make the payment, allow further time or order payment by instalments.

(2A) An order under this section that a lump sum required to be paid under a maintenance order shall be paid by instalments (a "maintenance instalments order") shall be treated for the purposes of sections 59, 59B and 60 above as a maintenance order.

(2B) Subsections (5) and (7) of section 59 above (including those subsections as they apply for the purposes of section 60 above) shall have effect in relation to a maintenance instalments order—

(*a*)　as if subsection (5), subsection (*c*) and the word "and" immediately preceding it were omitted; and
(*b*)　as if in subsection (7)—

(i)　the reference to the maintenance order were a reference to the maintenance order in respect of which the maintenance instalments order in question is made;
(ii)　for the words "the person who applied for the maintenance order" there were substituted "the debtor".

(2C) Section 60 above shall have effect in relation to a maintenance instalments order as if in subsection (7), paragraph (*c*) and the word "and" immediately preceding it were omitted.

(3) Where a court has ordered payment by instalments[2] and default is made in the payment of any one instalment, proceedings may be taken as if the default had been made in the payment of all the instalments then unpaid.

[Magistrates' Courts Act 1980, s 75 as amended by the Maintenance Enforcement Act 1991, Sch 2.]

1. PART III contains ss 75–96.
2. Where time or further time is allowed for payment or direction for payment by instalments is given, entry must be made in the court register or a separate record kept for the purpose (Magistrates' Courts Rules 1981, rr 62 and the Criminal Procedure Rules 2005, Part 52, this PART: STATUTORY INSTRUMENTS ON PROCEDURE, post). For restriction on the amount that can be offered in coin ("legal tender") see Coinage Act 1971, s 2 in PART VIII, title CURRENCY, post. Under s 86, post, where the offender is in court, the court may fix a day on which, if the payment has not been fully made, the offender must appear before the court. Failure to do so can lead to the issue of a warrant.
3. Or the justices' clerk (Justices' Clerks Rules 1999, this PART: STATUTORY INSTRUMENTS ON PROCEDURE, post).
4. This application, unless the court requires the applicant to attend, may be made in writing (Criminal Procedure Rules 2005, Part 52, this PART: STATUTORY INSTRUMENTS ON PROCEDURE, post).

1–2126　76. Enforcement of sums adjudged to be paid.　(1) Subject to the following provisions of this Part of this Act, and to section 132 below[1], where default is made in paying a sum[2] adjudged to be paid by a conviction[3] or order[4] of a magistrates' court, the court may[5] issue[6] a warrant of distress[7] for the purpose of levying[8] the sum or issue a warrant committing[9] the defaulter to prison.

(2) A warrant of commitment[10] may be issued as aforesaid either—

(*a*) where it appears on the return to a warrant of distress that the money and goods of the defaulter are insufficient to satisfy the sum with the costs and charges of levying the sum; or

(*b*) instead of a warrant of distress.

(3) The period for which a person may be committed to prison under such a warrant as aforesaid shall not, subject to the provisions of any enactment passed after 31st December 1879[11], exceed the period applicable to the case under Schedule 4[12] to this Act.

(4) Where proceedings are brought for the enforcement of a magistrates' court maintenance order under this section, the court may vary the order by exercising one of its powers under paragraphs (*a*) to (*d*) of section 59(3) above.

(5) Subsections (4), (5) and (7) of section 59 above shall apply for the purposes of subsection (4) above as they apply for the purposes of that section.

(6) Subsections (4) and (5) above shall not have effect in relation to a maintenance order which is not a qualifying maintenance order (within the meaning of section 59 above).

[Magistrates' Courts Act 1980, s 76 as amended by the Criminal Justice Act 1982, Sch 16 and the Maintenance Enforcement Act 1991, s 7.]

---

1. Minimum term of imprisonment of five days.

2. Where the fine and costs are not to exceed a fixed sum, the further costs of a distress warrant may be added (*Cook v Plaskett* (1882) 47 JP 265). For restrictions on the amount that can be offered in coin ("legal tender"), see the Coinage Act 1971, s 2 in PART VIII, title CURRENCY, post.

3. A sum adjudged to be paid by a conviction shall include costs, damages or compensation (see s 150(3), post). See Home Office circular No 149/1970 for guidance in respect of fines imposed on members of the Armed Forces.

4. But see s 92, post restricting the power to commit for debt except in respect of the defaults there specified, s 96 as to complaint for non payment of a civil debt, and s 92 for restriction on power of committal for civil debt.

5. It would seem that before exercising their discretion to issue a warrant of commitment under this section justices must have regard to the means of the defaulter and any assets which may be available for distress even in those cases where the court may by virtue of s 82(3)(*a*), post, dispense with the holding of a means inquiry. See *R v Clacton Justices, ex p Customs and Excise Comrs* (1987) 152 JP 129.

The mere fact that a mother who has obtained an affiliation order is outside the jurisdiction and cannot be served with a summons to vary does not prevent enforcement proceedings; if the father showed a *prima facie* case for variation, the justices have power to remit arrears and, in any event, cannot commit for default or make an attachment of earnings order unless there has been wilful refusal or culpable neglect: see *R v Gravesend Justices, ex p Doodney* [1971] 2 All ER 364, [1971] 1 WLR 818, 135 JP 353.

6. It is no defence to *mandamus* that an order made within the justices' jurisdiction and unappealed from was improperly made (*R v Swindon Justices* (1878) 42 JP 407). Upon hearing an application for enforcement of an order previously made, the court has no jurisdiction to consider the validity of the order, and if they refuse to enforce it on the ground that it is invalid an application for *mandamus* is the appropriate remedy, which seemingly will only be refused if it appears on admitted and undisputed evidence that the order should not have been made (*R v Lancashire Justices, ex p Tyrer* [1925] 1 KB 200, 89 JP 17; cf *Selby v Atkins* (1926) 90 JP 117). After a defendant is committed for arrears under an affiliation order made without jurisdiction, he can apply for *habeas corpus* (*Vevers v Mains* (1888) 4 TLR 724).

7. A policy of issuing distress warrants for all fines over £25 not paid within the time specified in a form of final demand sent to the defaulter, where a judicial discretion was exercised in the issue of each warrant, was held to be both lawful and commendable (*R v Hereford and Worcester Magistrates' Court, ex p MacRae* (1998) 163 JP 433).

It is only when considering whether to issue a warrant of commitment that the court is required to conduct a means inquiry, and there is, therefore, no requirement to hold such an inquiry before issuing a distress warrant (*R v Hereford and Worcester Magistrates' Court, ex p MacRae* (1998) 163 JP 433). Nevertheless, when inquiring into the means of a defaulter, justices may require affirmative evidence that the defendant has goods before issuing a distress warrant (*R v German* (1891) 56 JP 358). See also *R v Mortimer* (1906) 70 JP 542. If the evidence reveals that there is a reasonable likelihood that the defaulter has assets available to satisfy the sum he owes, the justices should proceed by way of warrant of distress rather than by way of a warrant of commitment (*R v Birmingham Justices, ex p Bennett* [1983] 1 WLR 114, 147 JP 279). Where justices are conducting a means inquiry in respect of an unrepresented defaulter and the court has it in mind to issue a distress warrant, sufficient notice must be given to the defaulter that the court is considering such a course so that the defaulter may have the opportunity to make representations thereon (*R v Guildford Justices, ex p Rich* (1996) 1 Cr App Rep (S) 49, 160 JP 645). For rule relating to the issue and execution of a distress warrant, see Magistrates' Courts Rules 1981, r 54, Criminal Procedure Rules 2005, Part 52, this PART: STATUTORY INSTRUMENTS ON PROCEDURE, post.

8. Note the protection given by Reserve and Auxiliary Forces (Protection of Civil Interests) Act 1951, to persons affected by that Act.

9. The minimum period of imprisonment is five days (s 132, post). Consecutive terms of imprisonment may be imposed in default of payment of fines imposed on separate offences (see s 133(5), post), but the total period where several sums appear on one warrant must not exceed the maximum stated in Sch 4, post, as being appropriate for the aggregate sum (*R v Southampton Justices, ex p Davies* [1981] 1 All ER 722, [1981] 1 WLR 374, 145 JP 247); followed in *R v Midhurst Justices, ex p Seymour* (1983) 147 JP 266, where the Divisional Court disapproved of a single document which was intended to be construed as a series of warrants, and ruled that when the aggregate of the terms of imprisonment imposed consecutively exceeded the statutory maximum for the total sum outstanding, a separate warrant in respect of each committal must be issued. When deciding whether to make the terms concurrent or consecutive, the court should consider whether the totality of the sentence is appropriate—for example consecutive terms in respect of several offences arising from the same incident would generally be wrong (*R v Southampton Justices, ex p Davies*, supra).

10. A police officer need not have the warrant with him in order to execute it; see s 125, post. For the execution of a warrant of commitment in Scotland or Northern Ireland, see the Criminal Justice and Public Order Act 1994, s 136, this PART, post.

11. That is, subsequent to the Summary Jurisdiction Act 1879.

12. Post. Where it was enacted that a person convicted of an offence against its provisions should be liable to a penalty of not more than forty shillings, or, in the discretion of the magistrate, to be imprisoned for not more than three days, the limit of three days did not apply to imprisonment in default of payment of the penalty (*R v Hopkins* [1893] 1 QB 621, 57 JP 152). This case was followed in *R v Leach, ex p Fritchley* [1913] 3 KB 40, 77 JP 255.

1–2127 **77. Postponement of issue of warrant.** (1) Where a magistrates' court has power to issue a warrant of distress under this Part[1] of this Act, it may, if it thinks it expedient to so do, postpone[2] the issue of the warrant until such time and on such conditions, if any, as the court thinks just.

(2) Where a magistrates' court has power to issue a warrant of commitment under this Part of this Act, it may, if it thinks it expedient to do so, fix a term of imprisonment or detention under section 108 of the Powers of Criminal Courts (Sentencing) Act 2000 (detention of persons aged 18 to 20 for default)★ and postpone the issue of the warrant until such time and on such conditions[3], if any, as the court thinks just.

(3) A magistrates' court shall have power at any time to do either or both of the following—

(a) to direct that the issue of the warrant of commitment shall be postponed until a time different from that to which it was previously postponed;

(b) to vary any of the conditions on which its issue is postponed,

but only if it thinks it just to do so having regard to a change of circumstances since the relevant time.

(4) In this section "the relevant time" means—

(a) where neither of the powers conferred by subsection (3) above has been exercised previously, the date when the issue of the warrant was postponed under subsection (2) above; and

(b) in any other case, the date of the exercise or latest exercise of either or both of the powers.

(5) Without prejudice to the generality of subsection (3) above, if on an application by a person in respect of whom issue of a warrant has been postponed it appears to a justice of the peace acting for the petty sessions area in which the warrant has been or would have been issued that since the relevant time there has been a change of circumstances which would make it just for the court to exercise one or other or both of the powers conferred by that subsection, he shall refer the application to the court.

(6) Where such an application is referred to the court—

(a) the clerk of the court shall fix a time and place for the application to be heard; and

(b) the justices' chief executive for the court shall give the applicant notice of that time and place.

(7) Where such a notice has been given but the applicant does not appear at the time and place specified in the notice, the court may proceed with the consideration of the application in his absence.

(8) If a warrant of commitment in respect of the sum adjudged to be paid has been issued before the hearing of the application, the court shall have power to order that the warrant shall cease to have effect and, if the applicant has been arrested in pursuance of it, to order that he shall be released, but it shall only make an order under this subsection if it is satisfied that the change of circumstances on which the applicant relies was not put before the court when it was determining whether to issue the warrant.

[Magistrates' Courts Act 1980, s 77 as amended by the Criminal Justice Act 1982, Sch 14, and the Criminal Justice Act 1988, s 61, the Powers of Criminal Courts (Sentencing) Act 2000, Sch 9 and SI 2001/618.]

★Repealed by the Criminal Justice and Court Services Act 2000, Sch 7, Sch 8 from a date to be appointed.

1. Warrants of commitment under this Part of the Act (Pt III) may be issued in respect of a sum adjudged to be paid by a conviction or order (s 76), a sum enforceable as a civil debt (s 96) a sum ordered to be paid by a magistrates' court maintenance order (s 93). The provisions of ss 77(1) and 78 of this Act apply to warrants of distress issued under the provisions of the Sea Fisheries Act 1968, s 12, PART VIII: title FISHERIES, post.

2. There is no power for justices to postpone the operation of a distress warrant after the warrant has been issued (*Crossland v Crossland* [1992] 2 FCR 45, [1993] 1 FLR 175), nor is there power for justices to cancel a distress warrant because once the warrant has been issued, the court is *functus officio* (*R v Hereford and Worcester Magistrates' Court, ex p MacRae* (1998) 163 JP 433).

3. If the issue of the commitment warrant is postponed on condition that a defendant maintains the current payments to become due under a maintenance order; together with further payments on account of arrears, all amounts paid by him thereafter should first be appropriated to the arrears in respect of which the committal order was made (*R v Miskin Lower Justices, ex p Young* [1953] 1 QB 533, [1953] 1 All ER 495, 117 JP 166). It is inappropriate for a committal order to be suspended during payment only of an additional amount in relation to the arrears. The preferable practice is for the terms of postponement to require payment of the periodical amount of the order, plus the amount to be paid in respect of the arrears (*Fowler v Fowler* (1979) 2 FLR 141). On failure to fulfil the conditions, the warrant may be issued, but current payments which have accrued since the warrant was granted may not be added to the arrears (*R v Bedford Prison (Governor), ex p Ames* [1953] 1 All ER 1002, 117 JP 237). In the case of arrears under a maintenance order, the committal is subject to review; see Maintenance Orders Act 1958, s 18 PART VI, title FAMILY LAW, post.

1–2128 78. Defect in distress warrant and irregularity in its execution. (1) A warrant of distress issued for the purpose of levying a sum adjudged to be paid by the conviction or order of a magistrates' court shall not, if it states that the sum has been so adjudged to be paid, be held void by reason of any defect in the warrant.

(2) A person acting under a warrant of distress shall not be deemed to be a trespasser from the beginning by reason only of any irregularity in the execution of the warrant[1].

(3) Nothing in this section shall prejudice the claim of any person for special damages in respect of any loss caused by a defect in the warrant or irregularity in its execution.

(4) If any person removes any goods marked in accordance with rules of court [2] as articles impounded in the execution of a warrant of distress, or defaces or removes any such mark, he shall be liable on summary conviction to a fine not exceeding **level 1** on the standard scale.

(5) If any person charged with the execution of a warrant of distress wilfully retains from the proceeds of a sale of the goods on which distress is levied, or otherwise exacts, any greater costs and charges than those properly payable, or makes any improper charge, he shall be liable on summary conviction to a fine not exceeding **level 1** on the standard scale.

[Magistrates' Courts Act 1980, s 78 as amended by the Criminal Justice Act 1982, s 46 and the Courts Act 2003, Sch 8.]

1. Actual entry to seize and impound goods is necessary (*Evans v South Ribble Borough Council* [1992] 2 All ER 695, [1992] 2 WLR 429).
2. See Magistrates' Court Rules 1981, r 54(8), Criminal Procedure Rules 2005, Part 52, this PART: STATUTORY INSTRUMENTS AND PRACTICE DIRECTIONS ON PROCEDURE, post.

1–2129   **79. Release from custody and reduction of detention on payment.**   (1) Where imprisonment or other detention[1] has been imposed on any person by the order of a magistrates' court in default of payment[2] of any sum adjudged to be paid by the conviction or order of a magistrates' court or for want of sufficient distress to satisfy such a sum, then, on the payment of the sum, together with costs and charges, if any, of the commitment and distress, the order shall cease to have effect; and if the person has been committed to custody he shall be released unless he is in custody for some other cause.

(2)[3] Where, after a period of imprisonment or other detention has been imposed on any person in default of payment of any sum adjudged to be paid by the conviction or order of a magistrates' court or for want of sufficient distress to satisfy such a sum, payment is made in accordance with rules of court[4] of part of the sum, the period of detention shall be reduced by such number of days as bears to the total number of days in that period less one day the same proportion as the amount so paid bears to so much of the said sum, and the costs and charges of any distress levied to satisfy that sum, as was due at the time the period of detention was imposed.

(3) In calculating the reduction required under subsection (2) above any fraction of a day shall be left out of account.

[Magistrates' Courts Act 1980, s 79 as amended by the Courts Act 2003, Sch 8.]

1. This section relates to all forms of detention, including detention under ss 135 and 136, post.
2. For restriction on the amount that can be offered in coin ("legal tender") see the Coinage Act 1971, s 2 in PART VIII, title CURRENCY, post.
3. For application of this subsection, see s 151(2) post.
4. For rule relating to payment after imprisonment or detention has been imposed, see Magistrates' Courts Rules 1981, r 55, Criminal Procedure Rules 2005, Part 52, this PART: STATUTORY INSTRUMENTS ON PROCEDURE, post.

1–2140   **80. Application of money found on defaulter to satisfy sum adjudged.**   (1) Where a magistrates' court has adjudged a person to pay a sum by a conviction[1] or has ordered the enforcement of a sum due from a person under a magistrates' court maintenance order[2], the court may order him to be searched.

(2) Any money found on the arrest of a person adjudged to pay such a sum as aforesaid, or on a search as aforesaid, or on his being taken to a prison or other place of detention in default of payment of such a sum or for want of sufficient distress to satisfy such a sum, may, unless the court otherwise directs[3], be applied towards payment of the said sum; and the balance, if any, shall be returned to him.

(3) A magistrates' court shall not allow the application as aforesaid of any money found on a person if it is satisfied that the money does not belong to him or that the loss of the money would be more injurious to his family than would be his detention.

[Magistrates' Courts Act 1980, s 80 as amended by the Family Law Reform Act 1987, Sch 2.]

1. Defined by s 150, post.
2. For a list of orders enforceable as a magistrates' court maintenance order, see footnote to s 93(1), post.
3. Any direction of the court under this subsection must be noted on the warrant of commitment (Magistrates' Courts Rules 1981, r 64, Criminal Procedure Rules 2005, Part 52, this PART: STATUTORY INSTRUMENTS ON PROCEDURE, post). On the grounds specified in sub-s (3) the court is obliged to give this direction: on other grounds the court has a discretion.

Sums adjudged to be paid by a conviction

1–2141   **81. Enforcement of fines imposed on young offenders.**   (1) Where a magistrates' court would, but for section 89 of the Powers of Criminal Courts (Sentencing) Act 2000, have power to commit to prison a person under the age of 18 for a default consisting in failure to pay, or want of sufficient distress to satisfy, a sum adjudged to be paid by a conviction, the court may, subject to the following provisions of this section, make—

(a) an order requiring the defaulter's parent or guardian to enter into a recognizance to ensure that the defaulter pays so much of that sum as remains unpaid; or

(b) an order directing so much of that sum as remains unpaid to be paid by the defaulter's parent or guardian instead of by the defaulter.

(2) An order under subsection (1) above shall not be made in respect of a defaulter—

(a) in pursuance of paragraph (a) of that subsection, unless the parent or guardian in question consents;

(b) in pursuance of paragraph (b) of that subsection, unless the court is satisfied in all the circumstances that it is reasonable to make the order.

(3) None of the following orders, namely—

(a) an order under section 60(1) of the said Act of 2000 for attendance at an attendance centre; or

(b) any order under subsection (1) above,

shall be made by a magistrates' court in consequence of a default of a person under the age of 18 years consisting in failure to pay, or want of sufficient distress to satisfy, a sum adjudged to be paid by a conviction unless the court has since the conviction inquired into the defaulter's means in his presence on at least one occasion.

(4) An order under subsection (1) above shall not be made by a magistrates' court unless the court is satisfied that the defaulter has, or has had since the date on which the sum in question was adjudged to be paid, the means to pay the sum or any instalment of it on which he has defaulted, and refuses or neglects or, as the case may be, has refused or neglected, to pay it.

(5) An order under subsection (1) above may be made in pursuance of paragraph (b) of that subsection against a parent or guardian who, having been required to attend, has failed to do so; but, save as aforesaid, an order under that subsection shall not be made in pursuance of that paragraph without giving the parent or guardian an opportunity of being heard.

(6) A parent of guardian may appeal to the Crown Court against an order under subsection (1) above made in pursuance of paragraph (b) of that subsection.

(7) Any sum ordered under subsection (1)(b) above to be paid by a parent or guardian may be recovered from him in like manner as if the order had been made on the conviction of the parent or guardian of an offence.

(8) In this section—

"guardian"[1], in relation to a person under the age of 18, means a person appointed, according to law, to be his guardian, or by order of a court of competent jurisdiction;

"sum adjudged to be paid by a conviction" means any fine, costs, compensation or other sum adjudged to be paid by an order made on a finding of guilt, including an order made under section 130 of the said Act of 2000 (compensation orders).

[Magistrates' Courts Act 1980, s 81 as amended by the Criminal Justice Act 1982, Schs 14 and 16, the Children Act 1989, Sch 15, the Criminal Justice Act 1991, Schs 8 and 11 and the Powers of Criminal Courts (Sentencing) Act 2000, Sch 9.]

---

1. A local authority to whose care a child has been committed is not a guardian for the purposes of s 81 (*R v Barnet Juvenile Court, ex p Barnet London Borough Council* (1982) 4 Cr App Rep (S) 221, [1982] Crim LR 592).

1-2142 82. Restriction on power to impose imprisonment for default. (1) A magistrates' court shall not on the occasion of convicting an offender of an offence issue a warrant of commitment[1] for a default in paying any sum adjudged to be paid by the conviction unless—

(a) in the case of an offence punishable with imprisonment, he appears to the court to have sufficient means to pay the sum forthwith[2];

(b) it appears to the court that he is unlikely to remain long enough at a place of abode in the United Kingdom to enable payment of the sum to be enforced by other methods; or

(c) on the occasion of that conviction the court sentences him to immediate imprisonment, detention in a young offender institution for that or another offence or he is already serving a sentence of custody for life, or a term of imprisonment, detention in a young offender institution, or detention under section 9 of the Criminal Justice Act 1982*.

(2) A magistrates' court shall not in advance of the issue of a warrant of commitment fix a term of imprisonment which is to be served by an offender in the event of a default in paying a sum adjudged to be paid by a conviction, except where it has power to issue a warrant of commitment forthwith, but postpones issuing the warrant under section 77(2) above.

(3) Where on the occasion of the offender's conviction a magistrates' court does not issue a warrant of commitment for a default in paying any such sum as aforesaid or fix a term of imprisonment[3] under the said section 77(2) which is to be served by him in the event of any such default, it shall not thereafter issue a warrant of commitment for any such default or for want of sufficient distress to satisfy such a sum unless—

(a) he is already serving a sentence[4] of custody for life, or a term of imprisonment, detention in a young offender institution, or detention under section 9 of the Criminal Justice Act 1982[5]*; or

(b) the court has since the conviction inquired[6] into his means in his presence on at least one occasion.

(4) Where a magistrates' court is required by subsection (3) above to inquire into a person's means, the court may not on the occasion of the inquiry or at any time thereafter issue a warrant of commitment for a default in paying any such sum unless—

(a) in the case of an offence punishable with imprisonment, the offender appears to the court to have sufficient means to pay the sum forthwith[2]; or

(b) the court—

(i) is satisfied that the default is due to the offender's wilful refusal or culpable neglect; and

(ii) has considered or tried[7] all other methods[8] of enforcing payment of the sum and it appears to the court that they are inappropriate or unsuccessful.

(4A) The methods of enforcing payment mentioned in subsection (4)(b)(ii) above are—

(a) a warrant of distress under section 76 above;

(b) an application to the High Court or county court for enforcement under section 87 below;

(c) an order under section 88 below;

(d) an attachment of earnings order; and

(e)   if the offender is under the age of 25, an order under section 17 of the Criminal Justice Act 1982★ (attendance centre orders).

(5)   After the occasion of an offender's conviction by a magistrates' court, the court shall not, unless—

(a)   the court has previously fixed a term of imprisonment under section 77(2) above which is to be served by the offender in the event of a default in paying a sum adjudged to be paid by the conviction; or

(b)   the offender is serving a sentence of custody for life, or a term of imprisonment, detention in a young offender institution, or detention under section 9 of the Criminal Justice Act 1982★,

issue a warrant of commitment for a default in paying the sum or fix such a term except at a hearing at which the offender is present.

(5A)   A magistrates' court may not issue a warrant of commitment under subsection (5) above at a hearing[9] at which the offender is not present unless the justices' chief executive for the court has first served on the offender a notice[10] in writing stating that the court intends to hold a hearing to consider whether to issue such a warrant and giving the reason why the court so intends.

(5B)   Where after the occasion of an offender's conviction by a magistrates' court the court holds a hearing for the purpose of considering whether to issue a warrant of commitment for default in paying a sum adjudged to be paid by the conviction, it shall consider such information about the offender's means as is available to it unless it has previously—

(a)   inquired into the offender's means; and

(b)   postponed the issue of the warrant of commitment under section 77(2) above.

(5C)   A notice under subsection (5A) above—

(a)   shall state the time and place appointed for the hearing; and

(b)   shall inform the offender that, if he considers that there are grounds why the warrant should not be issued, he may make representations to the court in person or in writing,

but the court may exercise its powers in relation to the issue of a warrant whether or not he makes representations.

(5D)   Except as mentioned in subsection (5E) below, the time stated in a notice under subsection (5A) above shall not be earlier than 21 days after the issue of the notice.

(5E)   Where a magistrates' court exercises in relation to an offender the power conferred by section 77(2) above and at the same hearing issues a notice under subsection (5A) above in relation to him, the time stated in the notice may be a time on any day following the end of the period for which the issue of the warrant of commitment has been postponed.

(5F)   A notice under subsection (5A) above to be served on any person shall be deemed to be served on that person if it is sent by registered post or the recorded delivery service addressed to him at his last known address, notwithstanding that the notice is returned as undelivered or is for any other reason not received by that person.

(6)   Where a magistrates' court issues a warrant of commitment on the ground that one of the conditions mentioned in subsection (1) or (4) above is satisfied, it shall state that fact, specifying the ground, in the warrant.

[Magistrates' Courts Act 1980, s 82 as amended by the Criminal Justice Act 1982, Sch 14, the Criminal Justice Act 1988, s 61 and Sch 8 and the Crime (Sentences) Act 1997, Sch 4.]

★**Amended by the Criminal Justice and Court Services Act 2000, Sch 7 from a date to be appointed.**

1.   Note with care the provisions of sub-s (5)–(5F) below with respect to the issue of a warrant of commitment after the occasion of an offender's conviction.

2.   For meaning of "forthwith" see PART II: EVIDENCE, para 2–744 Time, post.

3.   Accordingly, if the magistrates' court on the occasion of the offender's conviction has fixed a term of imprisonment in default and postponed the issue of the warrant of commitment under s 77(2), ante, there is no requirement to hold a means inquiry before issuing the warrant of commitment. Similarly, if a term of imprisonment was fixed by the Crown Court under s 139(2) of the Powers of Criminal Courts (Sentencing) Act 2000, that term is to be treated as having been fixed by the magistrates' court and therefore in the event of default there is no requirement to hold a means enquiry before issuing the warrant of commitment (*R v Hastings and Rother Justices, ex p Anscombe* (1998) 162 JP 340).

4.   An offender is "already serving . . . a term of imprisonment" once the sentence is pronounced; therefore, a warrant of commitment may be issued under s 82(3)(a) in the same proceedings as those in which the substantive sentence is passed (*R v Grimsby and Cleethorpes Justices, ex p Walters* [1997] 1 WLR 89, 161 JP 25).

5.   The term in default may be consecutive to this term (s 133(4), post).

Although the court is not required, when subsection (3)(a) applies, to hold a means inquiry, it would appear that the court must, nevertheless, have regard to the means of the defaulter and any assets which may be available for distress before issuing a warrant of commitment; see *R v Clacton Justices, ex p Customs and Excise Comrs* (1987) 152 JP 129. Moreover, a party who has a direct interest in the proceeds of the sum adjudged to be paid should be given notice of the hearing at which a decision whether or not to issue the warrant of commitment is to be taken; see *R v Clacton Justices, ex p Customs and Excise Comrs* (1987) 152 JP 129. Similarly, where the court is enforcing a confiscation order under s 2 of the Drug Trafficking Act 1994, justices should not issue a warrant of commitment under subsection (3)(a) without first considering all other methods of enforcement and without according the prosecutor an opportunity to be heard, otherwise the object of the confiscation order may be frustrated (*R v Harrow Justices, ex p DPP* [1991] 3 All ER 873, [1991] 1 WLR 395, 155 JP 979; *R v Liverpool Magistrates' Court, ex p Ansen* [1998] 1 All ER 692, DC).

6.   There is no objection to the justices' clerk at the express or implied request of the justices asking questions of the offender relevant to his or her means for the purposes of the means inquiry (*R v Corby Justices, ex p Mort* (1998) 162 JP 310).

7.   These words are peremptory. There is no discretion in the court, it must either *consider* or *try* all the other methods of enforcing payment (*R v Norwich Magistrates' Court, ex p Lilly* (1987) 151 JP 689). See also *R v Exeter City Justices, ex p Sugar* (1992) 157 JP 766 as to the duty to consider supervision pending payment.

8. See subsection (4A), post, inserted by the Criminal Justice Act 1988, s 61. See also comments about fine enforcement in para 3–209B in PART III: SENTENCING, post.

9. In relation to fine enforcement proceedings, all relevant information concerning the offender's ability to pay which has been provided by him to the justices' clerk's office should be recorded on the court file so that if the offender is not present at the next hearing the information can be brought to the attention of the court; see *R v Newport Pagnell Justices, ex p Smith* (1988) 152 JP 475.

10. In *R v Doncaster Justices, ex p Hannan* (1998) 163 JP 182, it was held that justices had acted perversely by issuing a warrant of commitment following postponement because the notice of hearing had been returned to the court marked "address inaccessible" and that the justices should have adjourned the question of whether or not a warrant of commitment should be issued until such time as she had been served with notice of the proceedings. However, the attention of the Divisional Court does not appear to have been drawn to s 82(5F) which provides that such a notice shall be deemed to be served on the offender if it is sent by registered post or the recorded delivery service addressed to him at his last-known address, "notwithstanding that the notice is returned as undelivered or is for any other reason not received by that person".

1–2143   83. Process for securing attendance of offender.   (1) A magistrates' court may, for the purpose of enabling inquiry to be made under section 82 above or for securing the attendance of an offender at a hearing required to be held by subsection (5) of that section—

(a) issue a summons requiring the offender to appear before the court at the time and place appointed in the summons; or

(b) issue a warrant to arrest him and bring him before the court.

(2) On the failure of the offender to appear before the court in answer to a summons issued under this section, or by virtue of Schedule 5 to the Courts Act 2003 the court may issue a warrant to arrest him and bring him before the court.

(3) A warrant issued under this section may be executed in like manner, and the like proceedings may be taken with a view to its execution, in any part of the United Kingdom[1], as if it had been issued under section 13 above.

(4) *Repealed.*

[Magistrates' Courts Act 1980, s 83, as amended by the Access to Justice Act 1999, Sch 15 and SI 2006/1737.]

1. It therefore applies to Scotland and Northern Ireland (see s 155, post).

1–2144   84. Power to require statement of means.   (1) A magistrates' court may, either before or on inquiring into a person's means under section 82 above, and a justice of the peace[1] acting for the same petty sessions area as that court may before any such inquiry, order him to furnish to the court within a period specified in the order such a statement of his means as the court may require.

(2) A person who fails to comply with an order under subsection (1) above shall be liable on summary conviction to a fine not exceeding level 3 on the standard scale.

(3) If a person in furnishing any statement in pursuance of an order under subsection (1) above makes a statement which he knows to be false in a material particular or recklessly furnishes a statement which is false in a material particular, or knowingly fails to disclose any material fact, he shall be liable on summary conviction to imprisonment for a term not exceeding 4 months or a fine not exceeding level 3 on the standard scale or both.

(4) Proceedings in respect of an offence under subsection (3) above may, notwithstanding anything in section 127(1) below, be commenced at any time within 2 years from the date of the commission of the offence or within 6 months from its first discovery by the prosecutor, whichever period expires the earlier.

[Magistrates' Courts Act 1980, s 84 as amended by the Criminal Justice Act 1982, ss 38 and 46.]

1. Or justices' clerk, see Justices' Clerks Rules 1999, this PART: STATUTORY INSTRUMENTS ON PROCEDURE, post.

1–2145   85. Power to remit fine.   (1) Where a fine has been imposed on conviction of an offender by a magistrates' court[1], the court may at any time remit[2] the whole or any part of the fine, but only if it thinks it just to do so having regard to a change of circumstances which has occurred—

(a) where the court is considering whether to issue a warrant of commitment after the issue of such a warrant in respect of the fine has been postponed under subsection (2) of section 77 above, since the relevant time as defined in subsection (4) of that section; and

(b) in any other case, since the date of the conviction.

(2) Where the court remits the whole or part of the fine after a term of imprisonment has been fixed, it shall also reduce the term by an amount which bears the same proportion to the whole term as the amount remitted bears to the whole or, as the case may be, shall remit the whole term.

(2A) Where the court remits the whole or part of the fine after an order has been made under section 35(2)(a) or (b) of the Crime (Sentences) Act 1997, it shall also reduce the total number of hours or days to which the order relates by a number which bears the same proportion as the amount remitted bears to the whole sum or, as the case may be, shall revoke the order.

(3) In calculating any reduction required by subsection (2) or (2A) above any fraction of a day or hour shall be left out of account.

(4) Notwithstanding the definition of "fine" in section 150(1) below, references in this section to a fine do not include any other sum adjudged to be paid on conviction, whether as a pecuniary penalty, forfeiture, compensation or otherwise.

[Magistrates' Courts Act 1980, s 85, as substituted by the Criminal Justice Act 1988, s 61 and amended by the Crime (Sentences) Act 1997, Sch 4 and the Crime and Disorder Act 1998, Sch 7.]

1. Remission of a Crown Court fine requires that court's consent; Powers of Criminal Courts (Sentencing) Act 2000, s 140(5) in PART III: SENTENCING, post.
2. See also the Powers of Criminal Courts (Sentencing) Act 2000, s 129 in Part III post which enables the court to remit a fine where it has determined the offender's circumstances under s 128(5) of that Act.

1–2146 85A. Variation of instalments of sum adjudged to be paid by conviction. Where under section 75 above a magistrates' court orders that a sum adjudged to be paid by a conviction shall be paid by instalments, the court, on an application made by the person liable to pay that sum, shall have power to vary that order by varying the number of instalments payable, the amount of any instalment payable, and the date on which any instalment becomes payable.
[Magistrates' Courts Act 1980, s 85A, as inserted by the Criminal Justice Act 1982, s 51.]

1–2147 86. Power of magistrates' court to fix day for appearance of offender at means inquiry, etc. (1) A magistrates' court which has exercised in relation to a sum adjudged to be paid by a conviction either of the powers conferred by section 75(1) above shall have power, either then or later, to fix a day on which, if the relevant condition is satisfied, the offender must appear in person before the court for either or both of the following purposes, namely—

(*a*) to enable an inquiry into his means to be made under section 82 above;
(*b*) to enable a hearing required by subsection (5) of the said section 82 to be held.

(1A) Where the power which the court has exercised is the power to allow time for payment of a sum ("the adjudged sum"), the relevant condition is satisfied if any part of that sum remains unpaid on the day fixed by the court.
(1B) Where the power which the court has exercised is the power to order payment by instalments, the relevant condition is satisfied if an instalment which has fallen due remains unpaid on the day fixed by the court.
(2) Except as provided in subsection (3) below, the power to fix a day under this section shall be exercisable only in the presence of the offender.
(3) Where a day has been fixed under this section, the court may fix a later day in substitution for the day previously fixed, and may do so—

(*a*) when composed of a single justice[1]; and
(*b*) whether the offender is present or not.

(4) Subject to subsection (5) below, if on the day fixed under this section—

(*a*) the relevant condition is satisfied; and
(*b*) the offender fails to appear in person before the court,

the court may issue a warrant to arrest him and bring him before the court; and subsection (3) of section 83 above shall apply in relation to a warrant issued under this section.
(5) Where under subsection (5) above a later day has in the absence of the offender been fixed in substitution for a day previously fixed under this section, the court shall not issue a warrant under this section unless it is proved to the satisfaction of the court, on oath or in such other manner as may be prescribed, that notice in writing of the substituted day was served on the offender not less than what appears to the court to be a reasonable time before that day.
[Magistrates' Courts Act 1980, s 86 as amended by the Criminal Justice Act 1982, s 51 and the Access to Justice Act 1999, s 97.]

1. Or the justices' clerk (Justices' Clerks Rules 1999, Sch, para 34).

1–2148 87. Enforcement of payment of fines by High Court and county court. (1) Subject to the provisions of subsection (2) below, payment of a sum adjudged to be paid by a conviction of a magistrates' court may be enforced by the High Court or a county court[1] (otherwise than by issue of a writ of fieri facias or other process against goods or by imprisonment or attachment of earnings) as if the sum were due to the designated officer for the magistrates' court in pursuance of a judgment[2] or order of the High Court or county court, as the case may be.
(1A) For the purposes of taking the step mentioned in paragraph 38(1)(*e*) of Schedule 5 to the Courts Act 2003, the reference in subsection (1) above to "the designated officer for the magistrates' court" shall be construed as a reference to the fines officer.
(2), (2A) *Repealed.*
(3) The designated officer for the magistrates' court shall not take proceedings by virtue of subsection (1) above to recover any sum adjudged to be paid[3] by a conviction of the court from any person unless there has been an inquiry under section 82 above into that person's means and he appeared to the court to have sufficient means to pay the sum forthwith.
(3A) The fines officer shall not, for the purposes of taking the step mentioned in paragraph 38(1)(*e*) of Schedule 5 to the Courts Act 2003, take proceedings by virtue of subsection (1) above to recover from any person a sum mentioned in paragraph 1 of that Schedule, unless the fines officer has made an inquiry into that person's means and he appeared to the fines officer to have sufficient means to pay the sum forthwith.
(4) *Repealed.*
[Magistrates' Courts Act 1980, s 87 as amended by the Supreme Court Act 1981, Sch 5, the County Courts Act 1984, Sch 2, the High Court and County Courts Jurisdiction Order 1991, SI 1991/724, the Criminal Procedure

and Investigations Act 1996, s 50, the Justices of the Peace Act 1997, Sch 5, the Access to Justice Act 1999, Sch 13, the Courts Act 2003, Sch 8 and SI 2006/1737.]

---

1. The effect of this provision is to apply to sums adjudged to be paid by a conviction methods of recovery which are not available in a magistrates' court, eg—garnishee, equitable execution etc. A county court has jurisdiction under this section whatever the amount involved in the proceedings (High Court and County Courts Jurisdiction Order 1991, SI 1991/724, amended by SI 1993/1407, SI 1995/205, SI 1996/3141 and SI 1999/1014).

2. This means that the offender is deemed to be a judgment debtor and the clerk of the magistrates' court a judgment creditor, both having all the rights of ordinary judgment debtors and creditors including an unrestricted right of appeal; see *Gooch v Ewing (Allied Irish Bank Ltd, garnishee)* [1986] QB 791, [1985] 3 All ER 654, CA.

3. The court has no power to authorise the clerk of the magistrates' court to take proceedings to enforce a compensation order if the operation of that order is suspended by virtue of s 132 of the Powers of Criminal Courts (Sentencing) Act 2000, in PART III: SENTENCING, post; see *Gooch v Ewing (Allied Irish Bank Ltd, garnishee)* [1986] QB 791, [1985] 3 All ER 654, CA.

1-2149 87A. Fines imposed on companies. (1) Where—

(*a*) a magistrates' court has, or is treated by any enactment as having, adjudged a company by a conviction to pay a sum; and

(*b*) the court has issued a warrant of distress under section 76(1) above for the purpose of levying the sum; and

(*c*) it appears on the return to the warrant that the money and goods of the company are insufficient to satisfy the sum with the costs and charges of levying the same,

the designated officer for the court may make an application in relation to the company under section 124 of, or paragraph 12 of Schedule B1 to, the Insolvency Act 1986 (administration or winding up)[1].

(2) *Repealed.*

[Magistrates' Courts Act 1980, s 87A, as inserted by the Criminal Justice Act 1988, s 62 and amended by the Justices of the Peace Act 1997, Sch 5, the Access to Justice Act 1999, Sch 13, the Enterprise Act 2002, Sch 17, the Courts Act 2003, Sch 3.]

---

1. For section 124 of, or paragraph 12 of Schedule B1 to, the Insolvency Act 1986, see PART VIII: title INSOLVENCY, post.

1-2150 88. Supervision pending payment. (1) Where any person is adjudged to pay a sum by a summary conviction[1] and the convicting court does not commit him to prison forthwith in default of payment, the court may, either on the occasion of the conviction or on a subsequent occasion, order[2] him to be placed under the supervision of such person as the court may from time to time appoint.

(2) An order placing a person under supervision in respect of any sum shall remain in force so long as he remains liable to pay the sum or any part of it unless the order ceases to have effect or is discharged under subsection (3) below.

(3) An order under this section shall cease to have effect on the making of a transfer of fine order under section 89 below with respect to the sum adjudged to be paid and may be discharged by the court that made it, without prejudice in either case to the making of a new order.

(4) Where a person under 21 years old[3] has been adjudged to pay a sum by a summary conviction and the convicting court does not commit him to detention under section 108 of the Powers of Criminal Courts (Sentencing) Act 2000[4*] forthwith in default of payment, the court shall not commit him to such detention in default of payment of the sum, or for want of sufficient distress to satisfy the sum, unless he has been placed under supervision in respect of the sum or the court is satisfied that it is undesirable or impracticable to place him under supervision.

(5) Where a court, being satisfied as aforesaid, commits a person under 21 years old to such detention* without an order under this section having been made, the court shall state the grounds on which it is so satisfied in the warrant of commitment.

(6) Where an order placing a person under supervision with respect to a sum is in force, a magistrates' court shall not commit him to prison[5] in default of payment of the sum, or for want of sufficient distress to satisfy the sum, unless the court has before committing him taken such steps as may be reasonably practicable to obtain from the person appointed for his supervision an oral or written report on the offender's conduct and means and has considered any report so obtained, in addition, in a case where an inquiry is required by section 82 above, to that inquiry.

[Magistrates' Courts Act 1980, s 88 as amended by the Criminal Justice Act 1982, Sch 14 and the Powers of Criminal Courts (Sentencing) Act 2000, Sch 9.]

---

*Amended by the Criminal Justice and Court Services Act 2000, Sch 7 from a date to be appointed.

1. Including costs, damages or compensation (s 150(3), post).

2. A supervision order under this section does not require that the offender shall agree: no summons need be issued. If it is not made in the presence of the offender, the clerk must deliver or send to him notice in writing of the order. The duty of the person appointed is to advise and befriend the offender with a view to inducing him to pay and thereby avoid imprisonment, and if required, to report to the court as to his conduct and means (Criminal Procedure Rules 2005, Part 52, this PART: STATUTORY INSTRUMENTS AND PRACTICE DIRECTIONS ON PROCEDURE, post).

3. See s 150(4), post for assumptions as to age.

4. Detention for one day in court house or police station under s 135, post, or committal to custody overnight under s 136, post, may be ordered without reference to this section.

5. Natural justice would require that a defaulter be given an opportunity of making representations before a warrant of commitment was issued; see *Re Wilson* [1985] AC 750, [1985] 2 All ER 97, 149 JP 337, HL).

1–2151   89. Transfer of fine order.   (1) Where a magistrates' court in a local justice area has, or is treated by any enactment as having, adjudged a person by a conviction[1] to pay a sum and it appears to the court,[2] or where that sum is the subject of a collection order, it appears to the court or the fines officer as the case may be, that the person is residing in England and Wales, the court[2] or the fines officer as the case may be, may make a transfer of fine order[3], that is to say, an order making payment enforceable in another local justice areaand that area shall be specified in the order.

(2) As from the date on which a transfer of fine order is made with respect to any sum, all functions under this Part of this Act or under Schedule 5 to the Courts Act 2003 relating to that sum which, if no order had been made, would have been exercisable by any court or person mentioned in column 1 of the Table below shall be exercisable by the court or person mentioned in the corresponding entry in column 2, and not otherwise.

Table

Column 1	Column 2
(A) The court which made the order. (B) A court acting in the same local justice area as was the fines officer who made the order	In either case, a court acting in the local justice area specified in the order.
The designated officer for the court mentioned in the row above.	The designated officer for the court mentioned in the row above.
(A) The fines officer who made the order. (B) A fines officer acting in the same local justice area as was the court which made the order.	In either case, a fines officer acting in the local justice area specified in the order.

(2A) The functions of the court [under this Part of this Act to which subsection (2) above relates shall be deemed to include the court's power to apply to the Secretary of State under any regulations made by him under section 24(1)(*a*) of the Criminal Justice Act 1991 (power to deduct fines etc from income support).

(3) A court or a fines officer, as the case may be, by which or whom functions in relation to any sum are for the time being exercisable by virtue of a transfer of fine order may make a further transfer of fine order with respect to that sum.

(4) In this section and sections 90 and 91 below, references to this part of this Act do not include references to section 81(1) above.

[Magistrates' Courts Act 1980, s 89 as amended by the Criminal Justice and Public Order Act 1994, s 47, the Access to Justice Act 1999, Sch 13, the Courts Act 2003, Sch 3 and SI 2006/1737.]

---

1. Including costs, damages or compensation (s 150(3), post).
2. Or justices' clerk: Justices' Clerks Rules 1999, this PART: STATUTORY INSTRUMENTS AND PRACTICE DIRECTIONS ON PROCEDURE, post.
3. The offender's consent is not required, no summons need be issued. For procedure see Criminal Procedure Rules 2005, Part 52, this PART: STATUTORY INSTRUMENTS AND PRACTICE DIRECTIONS ON PROCEDURE, post.

1–2152   90. Transfer of fines to Scotland or Northern Ireland.   (1) Where a magistrates' court has, or is treated by any enactment as having, adjudged a person by a conviction to pay a sum, and it appears to the court (or where that sum is the subject of a collection order, it appears to the court or the fines officer as the case may be) that he is residing—

(*a*) within the jurisdiction of a court of summary jurisdiction in Scotland, or

(*b*) in any petty sessions district in Northern Ireland,

the court (or the fines officer as the case may be) may order that payment of the sum shall be enforceable by that court of summary jurisdiction or, as the case may be, in that petty sessions district.

(2) An order under this section shall specify the court of summary jurisdiction by which or petty sessions district in which payment of the sum in question is to be enforceable; and if—

(*a*) that sum is more than £100 or is a fine originally imposed by the Crown Court or the sheriff court, and

(*b*) payment is to be enforceable in Scotland,

the court to be so specified shall be the sheriff court.

(3) Where an order is made under this section with respect to any sum, any functions under this Part of this Act relating to that sum which, if no such order had been made, would have been exercisable by the court which made the order or by the justices' chief executive for that court shall cease to be so exercisable.

(3A) The functions of the court which shall cease to be exercisable by virtue of subsection (3) above shall be deemed to include the court's power to apply to the Secretary of State under regulations made by him under section 24(1)(*a*) of the Criminal Justice Act 1991 (power to deduct fines from income support).

[Magistrates' Courts Act 1980, s 90 as amended by the Criminal Justice and Public Order Act 1994, s 47,the Access to Justice Act 1999, Sch 13 and SI 2006/1737.]

1–2153　91. Transfer of fines from Scotland or Northern Ireland. (1) Where a transfer of fine order under section 403[1] of the Criminal Procedure (Scotland) Act 1975 or Article 95 of the Magistrates' Courts (Northern Ireland) Order 1981 provides that payment of a sum shall be enforceable by a magistrates' court in England and Wales, a magistrates' courtcourt in England and Wales, a magistrates' court (or a fines officer as the case may be) acting in the area in which the person subject to the order resides, and the designated officer forfor that court, shall, subject to the provisions of this section, have all the like functions under this part of this Act (or under Schedule 5 to the Courts Act 2003 as the case may be) in respect of the sum (including power to make an order under section 89 or section 90 above) as if the sum were a sum adjudged to be paid by a conviction of that court and as if any order made under the said Act of 1975 or, as the case may be, the said Order of 1981 in respect of the sum before the making of the transfer of fine order had been made by that court.

(2) For the purpose of determining the period of imprisonment which may be imposed under this Act in default of payment of a fine originally imposed by a court in Scotland, Schedule 4 to this Act shall have effect as if for the Table set out in paragraph 1 there were substituted the Table set out in section 407 of the Criminal Procedure (Scotland) Act 1975.

(3) Where a transfer of fine order under section 403 of the Criminal Procedure (Scotland) Act 1975 or Article 95 of the Magistrates' Courts (Northern Ireland) Order 1981 provides for the enforcement by a magistrates' court in England and Wales of a fine originally imposed by the Crown Court, a magistrates' court (or a fines officer as the case may be) acting in the area in which the person subject to the order resides shall have all the like functions under this Part of this Act (or under Schedule 5 to the Courts Act 2003 as the case may be), exercisable subject to the like restrictions, as if it were the magistrates' court by which payment of the fine fell to be enforced by virtue of section 140(1) of the Powers of Criminal Courts (Sentencing) Act 2000 (or as if he were a fines officer acting in the same local justice area as that court as the case may be), and as if any order made under the said Act of 1975 or, as the case may be, the said Order of 1981 in respect of the fine before the making of the transfer of fine order had been made by that court.

[Magistrates' Courts Act 1980, s 91 as amended by the Powers of Criminal Courts (Sentencing) Act 2000, Sch 9, the Access to Justice Act 1999, Sch 13, the Courts Act 2003, Sch 8 and SI 2006/1737.]

---

1. Section 403 has been extended to apply in relation to compensation orders as it applies in relation to fines (Criminal Justice (Scotland) Act 1980, s 66).

Sums adjudged to be paid by an order

1–2154　92. Restriction on power to impose imprisonment for default. (1) A magistrates' court shall not exercise its power under section 76 above to issue a warrant to commit to prison a person who makes default in paying a sum adjudged to be paid by an order of such a court except where the default is under—

(a) a magistrates' court maintenance order;
(b) an order under section 17(2) of the Access to Justice Act 1999 (payment by individual in respect of cost of his defence in a criminal case); or
(c) an order for the payment of any of the taxes, contributions, premiums or liabilities specified in Schedule 4 to the Administration of Justice Act 1970.

(2) This section does not affect the power of a magistrates' court to issue such a warrant as aforesaid in the case of default in paying a sum adjudged to be paid by a conviction, or treated (by any enactment relating to the collection or enforcement of fines, costs, compensation or forfeited recognizances) as so adjudged to be paid.

(3) *Repealed.*

[Magistrates' Courts Act 1980, s 92 as amended by the Legal Aid Act 1982, s 14, the Family Law Reform Act 1987, Sch 4, the Legal Aid Act 1988, Sch 5 and the Access to Justice Act 1999, Sch 4.]

1–2155　93. Complaint for arrears. (1) Where default is made in paying a sum ordered to be paid by a magistrates' court maintenance order[1], the court shall not enforce payment of the sum under section 76 above except by an order made on complaint[2].

(2) A complaint under this section shall be made not earlier than the fifteenth day after the making of the order[3] for the enforcement of which it is made; but subject to this such a complaint may be made at any time notwithstanding anything in this or any other Act.

(3) In relation to complaints under this section, section 55 above shall not apply and section 56 above shall have effect as if the words "if evidence has been received on a previous occasion" were omitted.

(4) Where at the time and place appointed for the hearing or adjourned hearing of a complaint under this section the complainant appears but the defendant does not, the court may proceed in his absence; but the court shall not begin to hear the complaint in the absence of the defendant unless either it is proved to the satisfaction of the court, on oath or in such other manner as may be prescribed[4], that the summons was served on him within what appears to the court to be a reasonable time before the hearing or adjourned hearing or the defendant has appeared on a previous occasion to answer the complaint.

(5) If a complaint under this section is substantiated on oath, any justice of the peace acting for the same petty sessions area as a court having jurisdiction to hear the complaint may issue a warrant[5] for the defendant's arrest, whether or not a summons has been previously issued.

(6) A magistrates' court shall not impose imprisonment in respect of a default to which a complaint under this section relates unless the court has inquired in the presence of the defendant[6] whether the default was due to the defendant's wilful refusal or culpable neglect[7], and shall not impose imprisonment as aforesaid if it is of opinion that the default was not so due[8]; and, without prejudice to the preceding provisions of this subsection, a magistrates' court shall not impose imprisonment as aforesaid—

(*a*) in the absence of the defendant; or

(*b*) in a case where the court has power to do so, if it is of the opinion that it is appropriate—

   (i)   to make an attachment of earnings order[9]; or

   (ii) to order that payments under the order be made by any method of payment falling within section 59(6) above; or

(*c*) where the sum to which the default relates comprises only interest which the defendant has been ordered to pay by virtue of section 94A(1) below.

(7) Notwithstanding anything in section 76(3) above, the period for which a defendant may be committed to prison under a warrant of commitment[10] issued in pursuance of a complaint under this section shall not exceed 6 weeks.

(8) The imprisonment or other detention of a defendant under a warrant of commitment issued as aforesaid shall not operate to discharge[11] the defendant from his liability to pay the sum in respect of which the warrant was issued.

[Magistrates' Courts Act 1980, s 93 as amended by the Family Law Reform Act 1987, Sch 2 and the Maintenance Enforcement Act 1991, Sch 2.]

---

1. Orders under the following provisions are enforceable as a magistrates' court maintenance order: Domestic Proceedings and Magistrates' Courts Act 1978, Pt I; National Assistance Act 1948, s 43 (recovery of cost of assistance); Supplementary Benefits Act 1976, s 18 (recovery of cost of benefit); Social Security Act 1986, s 24; Maintenance Orders Act 1958 (High Court or County Court orders registered in Magistrates' Court); Maintenance Orders Act 1950, Pt II (order made in one part of the United Kingdom registered in another part); Maintenance Orders (Facilities for Enforcement) Act 1920 (registered or confirmed order originating outside the United Kingdom); Maintenance Orders (Reciprocal Enforcement) Act 1972 (order made in reciprocating country and registered in United Kingdom); Children Act 1989, Sch 1; Social Security Administration Act 1992, s 106. By virtue of transitional provisions, orders made under the Affiliation Proceedings Act 1957, the Matrimonial Proceedings (Magistrates' Courts) Act 1960; Guardianship of Minors Act 1971 and 1973 and Child Care Act 1980, s 47 (contribution order) are similarly enforceable.
2. As to the enforcement of contribution orders in respect of the costs of representation granted to a legally assisted person, see the Legal Aid Act 1988, s 24 and Sch 3, this PART, post. Rule 59 of the Magistrates' Courts Rules 1981, this PART: STATUTORY INSTRUMENTS ON PROCEDURE, post applies.
   A financial obligation arising from an order made in domestic proceedings, as defined in s 65, ante, or in proceedings which would be domestic proceedings but for s 65(1)(ii) of this Act (proceedings for variation of order for periodical payments) is not provable in bankruptcy (Insolvency Rules 1986, r 12.3; Insolvency Act 1986, s 281(8)).
   As to the enforcement of an order against members of the Armed Forces, see the Naval Forces (Enforcement of Maintenance Liabilities) Act 1947, Army Act 1955, ss 150 and 151 as amended, Air Force Act 1955, ss 150 and 151 as amended in PART VIII: title ARMED FORCES, post.
3. Nothing expressly requires that a copy of the order shall be served before it may be enforced (unlike civil debt, see Magistrates' Courts Rules 1981, r 53, this PART: STATUTORY INSTRUMENTS AND PRACTICE DIRECTIONS ON PROCEDURE, post). Note however requirement of service by r 36.
4. This is prescribed by Magistrates' Courts Rules 1981, r 67, this PART: STATUTORY INSTRUMENTS AND PRACTICE DIRECTIONS ON PROCEDURE, post.
5. A police officer need not have the warrant with him in order to execute it; see s 125 post.
6. There is no obligation before imposing imprisonment to inform the defendant of the existence of legal aid (*R v Cardiff Justices, ex p Salter* (1985) 149 JP 721, [1986] 1 FLR 162, [1986] Fam Law 53).
7. The fact the defendant is in receipt of payments from the DSS is not conclusive of the question whether default was due to "wilful refusal" or "culpable neglect"; it is only a factor which should be taken into account as a guide to a decision (*R v Cardiff Justices, ex p Salter* (1985) 149 JP 721, [1986] 1 FLR 162, [1986] Fam Law 53). Imprisonment being a sanction of last resort, these words set the blameworthiness at a very high level: improvidence or dilatoriness are not sufficient, something in the nature of a deliberate defiance or reckless disregard of the court's order is required (*R v Luton Magistrates' Court, ex p Sullivan* [1992] 1 FCR 475, [1992] Fam Law 380; it would seem that s 41(9) of the Administration of Justice Act 1970 applies, see also (1992) 156 JP Jo 404). Where magistrates are satisfied that the defaulter has lied about his unemployment they must have full and detailed history of how the arrears had arisen before refusing to remit any arrears and go on to consider the actual means at the date of the hearing before fixing terms for repayment of arrears (*SN v ST (Maintenance Order: Enforcement)* [1995] 1 FLR 868).
8. This section places on the defendant the onus of showing to the satisfaction of the justices that the default was not due to his wilful refusal or culpable neglect (*R v Cardiff Magistrates, ex p Czech* [1999] 1 FCR 721, [1999] 1 FLR 95).
9. See Attachment of Earnings Act 1971, ante.
10. For the execution of a warrant of commitment in Scotland or Northern Ireland, see the Criminal Justice and Public Order Act 1994, s 136, this PART, post.
11. Arrears are discharged where imprisonment has been served under a warrant of commitment issued before 16 February 1959, the date on which the Maintenance Orders Act 1958 came into operation (ibid, s 16(2)). A defaulter may not be imprisoned more than once in respect of the same arrears (Maintenance Orders Act 1958, s 17, post).

1–2156 94. Effect of committal on arrears. Where a person is committed to custody under this Part of this Act for failure to pay a sum due under a magistrates' court maintenance order, then, unless the court that commits him otherwise directs[1], no arrears shall accrue under the order while he is in custody[2].

[Magistrates' Courts Act 1980, s 94 as amended by the Family Law Reform Act 1987, Sch 2.]

---

1. Such a direction may be appropriate where the defendant is contumacious (*per* LORD MERRIMAN P, in *Starkey v Starkey* [1954] P 449 at 454, [1954] 1 All ER 1036 at 1039, and 118 JP 279 at 281).

2. The justices' chief executive will be informed of the dates of reception into custody and discharge (Magistrates' Courts Rules 1981, r 63, this PART: STATUTORY INSTRUMENTS ON PROCEDURE, post).

1–2157 94A. Interest on arrears.   (1) The Lord Chancellor may by order provide that a magistrates' court, on the hearing of a complaint for the enforcement, revocation, revival, variation or discharge of an English maintenance order, may order that interest of an amount calculated at the prescribed rate shall be paid on so much of the sum due under the order as they may determine.

(2) In subsection (1) above "the prescribed rate" means such rate of interest as the Lord Chancellor may by order prescribe.

(3) An order under this section may make provision for the manner in which and the periods by reference to which interest is to be calculated.

(4) Where, by virtue of subsection (1) above, a magistrates' court orders the payment of interest on any sum due under a maintenance order—

(*a*)   then if it orders that the whole or any part of the interest be paid by instalments that order shall be regarded as an instalments order for the purposes of section 95 below and that section shall accordingly apply in relation to it; and

(*b*)   the whole of the interest shall be enforceable as a sum adjudged to be paid by the maintenance order.

(5) In this section—

"English maintenance order" means—

(*a*)   a qualifying maintenance order made by a magistrates' court, other than an order made by virtue of Part II of the Maintenance Orders (Reciprocal Enforcement) Act 1972; or

(*b*)   an order made by the High Court or a county court (other than an order deemed to be made by the High Court by virtue of section 1(2) of the Maintenance Orders Act 1958) and registered under Part I of that Act of 1958 in a magistrates' court;

"qualifying maintenance order" has the same meaning as it has in section 59 above.

(6) *Order provision.*
[Magistrates' Courts Act 1980, s 94A as added by the Maintenance Enforcement Act 1991, s 8 and as amended by SI 1992/709.]

1–2158 95. Remission of arrears and manner in which arrears to be paid.   (1) On the hearing of a complaint for the enforcement, revocation, revival, variation or discharge of a magistrates' court maintenance order, a magistrates' court may remit[1] the whole or any part of the sum due[2] under the order[3].

(2) If, on the hearing of a complaint for the enforcement, revocation, revival, variation or discharge of a magistrates' court maintenance order, a magistrates' court orders that the whole or any part of the sum due under the order be paid by instalments (an "instalments order"), then—

(*a*)   if the maintenance order is an English maintenance order, the court shall at the same time exercise one of its powers under paragraphs (*a*) to (*d*) of section 59(3) above in relation to the instalments order;

(*b*)   if the maintenance order is a non-English maintenance order, the court shall at the same time exercise one of its powers under subsection (3) below in relation to the instalments order.

(3) The powers of the court referred to in subsection (2)(*b*) above are—

(*a*)   the power to order that payments under the order be made directly to a justices' chief executive;

(*b*)   the power to order that payments under the order be made to a justices' chief executive, by such method of payment falling within section 59(6) above as may be specified;

(*c*)   the power to make an attachment of earnings order under the Attachment of Earnings Act 1971 to secure payments under the order.

(4) The court may in the course of any proceedings concerning an instalments order or the magistrates' court maintenance order to which it relates vary the instalments order by exercising—

(*a*)   in respect of an English maintenance order, one of the powers referred to in subsection (2)(*a*) above;

(*b*)   in respect of a non-English maintenance order, one of its powers under subsection (3) above.

(5) In respect of an English maintenance order, subsections (4), (5) and (7) of section 59 above shall apply for the purposes of subsections (2)(*a*) and (4)(*a*) above as they apply for the purposes of that section.

(6) In respect of a non-English maintenance order—

(*a*)   subsection (4) of section 59 above shall apply for the purposes of subsections (2)(*b*) and (4)(*b*) above as it applies for the purposes of that section but as if for paragraph (*a*) there were substituted—

    "(*a*) the court proposes to exercise its power under paragraph (*b*) of section 95(3) below;" and

(b)   in deciding which of the powers under subsection (3) above it is to exercise the court shall have regard to any representations made by the debtor (within the meaning of section 59 above).

(7)   In this section—

"English maintenance order" has the same meaning as it has in section 94A above;
"non-English maintenance order" means—

(a)   a maintenance order registered in, or confirmed by, a magistrates' court—

(i)   under the Maintenance Orders (Facilities for Enforcement) Act 1920;
(ii)   under Part II of the Maintenance Orders Act 1950;
(iii)   under Part I of the Maintenance Orders (Reciprocal Enforcement) Act 1972; or
(iv)   under Part I of the Civil Jurisdiction and Judgments Act 1982; or
(v)   under Council Regulation (EC) No 44/2001 of 22nd December 2000 on jurisdiction and the recognition and enforcement of judgments in civil and commercial matters;

(b)   an order deemed to be made by the High Court by virtue of section 1(2) of the Maintenance Orders Act 1958 and registered under Part I of that Act in a magistrates' court; or

(c)   a maintenance order made by a magistrates' court by virtue of Part II of the Maintenance Orders (Reciprocal Enforcement) Act 1972.

[Magistrates' Courts Act 1980, s 95 as substituted by the Maintenance Enforcement Act 1991, Sch 2 and amended by the Access to Justice Act 1999, Sch 13 and SI 2001/3929.]

---

1. See Magistrates' Courts Rules 1981, r 44, this PART: STATUTORY INSTRUMENTS ON PROCEDURE, for requirement to notify person in whose favour the order is made of intention to remit arrears and to consider representations by that person.

2. This is a comprehensive power to remit arrears in whole or in part in proceedings of any kind brought before the court on complaint in connection with a magistrates' court maintenance order previously made. The general rule is that arrears are not enforced after a year (*Bernstein v O'Neill* [1989] FCR 79, [1989] 2 FLR 1, following a long line of case-law) except in special circumstances (see *C v S (maintenance order: enforcement)* [1997] 3 FCR 423, [1997] 1 FLR 298: enforcement in the magistrates' court delayed by proceedings in the county court and errors made by the magistrates' court administration, also arrears could be paid off in a short period). The proper approach of the court is to decide how it should exercise the discretion to enforce the arrears rather than decide how it should exercise a discretion to remit the arrears (*B v C (enforcement: arrears)* [1995] 1 FLR 467, [1995] 2 FCR 678). Where an order is discharged, money paid to the collecting officer before the date of the complaint to discharge the order may not be remitted (*Fildes (formerly Simkin) v Simkin* [1960] P 70, [1959] 3 All ER 697, 124 JP 13); nor may it be ordered that money paid without knowledge that the divorced wife had remarried shall be refunded (*Young v Young (No 2)* [1962] P 218, [1961] 3 All ER 793). It is wrong to order remission of arrears as a penalty for not allowing access (*R v Halifax Justices, ex p Woolverton* (1979) 2 FLR 369). Justices, who remitted arrears because the husband had paid off some of his wife's debts, were held not to have acted judicially since the arrears were payable to the children and it was wrong to deprive the children of their money to satisfy another person's debt, albeit it was their mother (*Parry v Meugens* (1985) 150 JP 152, [1986] 1 FLR 125, [1986] Fam Law 53).

3. There is no specific provision for any appeal to the High Court against an order to remit or a refusal to remit arrears, and, therefore, the decision can be challenged only by case stated on the ground of error of law or excess of jurisdiction; see *Berry v Berry* [1987] Fam 1, [1986] 2 All ER 948, 150 JP 319, CA; for procedure, see s 111, post; RSC Ord 56, r 5(2), this PART: STATUTORY INSTRUMENTS ON PROCEDURE, post.

1–2159   96. Civil debt: complaint for non-payment.   (1) A magistrates' court shall not commit any person[1] to prison[2] or other detention in default of payment[3] of a sum enforceable as a civil debt[4] or for want of sufficient distress to satisfy such a sum except by an order made on complaint[5] and on proof to the satisfaction of the court that that person has, or has had since the date on which the sum was adjudged to be paid, the means to pay the sum or any instalment of it on which he has defaulted, and refuses or neglects or, as the case may be, has refused or neglected to pay it.

(2)   A complaint under this section may be made at any time notwithstanding anything in this[6] or any other Act.

(3)   Where on any such complaint the defendant is committed to custody[7], such costs incurred by the complainant in proceedings for the enforcement of the sum as the court may direct shall be included in the sum on payment of which the defendant may be released from custody.

[Magistrates' Courts Act 1980, s 96.]

---

1. Note the protection given by Reserve and Auxiliary Forces (Protection of Civil Interests) Act 1951 to persons affected by that Act.

2. The maximum period of detention for non-payment of a civil debt of any amount is six weeks (Sch 4, para 3, post). When time is given for the payment of a civil debt it was held to be necessary, before issuing a warrant of distress or commitment, to summon the defendant to show cause why this should not be done (*Abley v Dale* (1850) 15 JP 147; *Kinning's Case* (1847) 10 QB 730). When any length of time has elapsed from the judgment, we advise a summons to precede further proceedings in all cases. The court may distrain under s 76 ante, but may not make a money payments supervision order under s 88 nor remit the debt under s 95 as neither of these powers applies to civil debt. Costs may be awarded under s 64 ante.

3. For restriction on the amount that can be offered in coin ("legal tender"), see the Coinage Act 1971, s 2 in PART VIII, title CURRENCY, post.

4. For meaning of the expression "sum enforceable as a civil debt", see s 150(1), post, and as to restrictions on magistrates' power of committal for civil debt except in a limited category of cases, see s 92 of the Magistrates' Courts Act 1980, ante.

5. A judgment summons will be issued on this complaint: it must be served on the defendant personally (unless substituted service is allowed) and, unless the defendant appears and consents to an immediate hearing, the court shall not hear the complaint unless the summons was served at least 3 clear days before the hearing (Magistrates' Courts Rules

1981, r 58, this PART: STATUTORY INSTRUMENTS AND PRACTICE DIRECTIONS ON PROCEDURE, post). As proceedings
are by complaint there is power to issue a witness summons under s 97, post.
  6. See for example s 127, post.
  7. Section 126, post applies to execution of warrants outside England and Wales.

1–2160 96A. Application of Part III to persons aged 18 to 20. This Part of this Act shall have
effect in relation to a person aged 18 or over but less than 21 as if any reference to committing a
person to prison, or fixing a term of imprisonment for a default, were a reference to committing the
person to, or, as the case may be, to fixing a term of, detention under section 108 of the Powers of
Criminal Courts (Sentencing) Act 2000; and any reference to warrants of commitment, or to periods
of imprisonment imposed for default, shall be construed accordingly.*
[Magistrates' Courts Act 1980, s 96A, as inserted by the Criminal Justice Act 1982, Sch 14, amended by the
Criminal Justice Act 1991, Sch 8 and the Powers of Criminal Courts (Sentencing) Act 2000, Sch 9.]

---

*Repealed by the Criminal Justice and Court Services Act 2000, Sch 7, Sch 8 from a date to be appointed.

PART IV[1]
WITNESSES AND EVIDENCE
Procuring attendance of witness

1–2169 97. Summons to witness and warrant for his arrest. (1) Where a justice of the peace[2]
is satisfied that—

  (a) any person[3] in England or Wales is likely to be able to give material evidence, or produce any
       document or thing likely to be material evidence[4], at the summary trial of an information or
       hearing of a complaint or of an application under the Adoption and Children Act 2002 (c 38)
       by a magistrates' court, and
  (b) it is in the interests of justice to issue a summons under this subsection to secure the attendance
       of that person to give evidence or produce the document[5] or thing,

the justice shall issue a summons directed[6] to that person requiring him to attend before the court at
the time and place appointed in the summons to give evidence or to produce the document or thing.
  (2) If a justice of the peace is satisfied by evidence on oath of the matters mentioned in subsection
(1) above, and also that it is probable that a summons under that subsection would not procure the
attendance of the person in question, the justice may instead of issuing a summons issue a warrant[7]
to arrest that person and bring him before such a court, as aforesaid at a time and place specified in
the warrant; but a warrant shall not be issued under this subsection where the attendance is required
for the hearing of a complaint or of an application under the Adoption and Children Act 2002 (c 38).
  (2A) A summons may also be issued under subsection (1) above if the justice is satisfied that the
person in question is outside the British Islands but no warrant shall be issued under subsection (2)
above unless the justice is satisfied by evidence on oath that the person in question is in England or
Wales.
  (2B)[8] A justice may refuse to issue a summons under subsection (1) above in relation to the
summary trial of an information if he is not satisfied that an application for the summons was made
by a party to the case as soon as reasonably practicable after the accused pleaded not guilty.
  (2C)[8] In relation to the summary trial of an information, subsection (2) above shall have effect as
if the reference to the matters mentioned in subsection (1) above included a reference to the matter
mentioned in subsection (2B) above.
  (3) On the failure of any person to attend before a magistrates' court in answer to a summons
under this section, if—

  (a) the court is satisfied by evidence on oath that he is likely to be able to give material evidence
       or produce any document or thing likely to be material evidence in the proceedings; and
  (b) it is proved on oath, or in such other manner as may be prescribed, that he has been duly
       served with the summons, and that a reasonable sum has been paid or tendered to him for
       costs and expenses; and
  (c) it appears to the court that there is no just excuse for the failure,

the court may[9] issue a warrant to arrest him and bring him before the court at a time and place
specified in the warrant.
  (4) If any person attending or brought before a magistrates' court refuses without just excuse[10] to
be sworn or give evidence, or to produce any document[11] or thing, the court, may commit him to
custody[12] until the expiration of such period not exceeding one month as may be specified in the
warrant or until he sooner[13] gives evidence or produces the document or thing or impose on him a
fine not exceeding £2,500, or both.
  (5) A fine imposed under subsection (4) above shall be deemed, for the purposes of any
enactment, to be a sum adjudged to be paid by a conviction.
[Magistrates' Courts Act 1980, s 97 as amended by the Contempt of Court Act 1981, Sch 2, SI 1984/447, the
Criminal Justice (International Co-operation) Act 1990, Sch 4, the Criminal Justice Act 1991, Sch 4, the Criminal
Justice Act 1993, Sch 3, SI 1996/674 and 675, the Serious Organised Crime and Police Act 2005, s 169 the
Criminal Procedure and Investigations Act 1996, s 51 and Sch 1, the Adoption and Children Act 2002 and
SI 2005/3275.]

---

  1. PART IV contains ss 97–107. For procedure for making application in criminal proceedings, see the Criminal
Procedure Rules 2005, Part 28, in this PART: STATUTORY INSTRUMENTS AND PRACTICE DIRECTIONS ON PROCEDURE,
post.

2. Or justices' clerk (Justices' Clerks Rules 2005, this PART: STATUTORY INSTRUMENTS AND PRACTICE DIRECTIONS ON PROCEDURE, post).

3. Where the person concerned is a child, it is for the court of trial, and not the justice to whom an application for a witness summons is made, to undertake the balancing act of deciding whether the harm to the party seeking to call the child is outweighed by the interests of the child; see *R v Highbury Corner Magistrates' Court, ex p D* [1997] 2 FCR 569, [1997] 1 FLR 683, [1996] 161 JP 138, [1997] Crim LR 59.

4. On an application for a witness summons, justices should enquire into the nature of the evidence and whether it was material; the applicant should offer some material sufficient to satisfy the court (*R v Peterborough Magistrates' Court, ex p Willis and Amos* (1987) 151 JP 785. The tests in s 97 for the issue of a witness summons remain unaffected by other, less stringent developments in the rules of disclosure in the criminal law. Accordingly, justices had proceeded on the wrong basis in issuing a summons to produce documents including the social services file on the victim of an alleged assault on the ground that such evidence should not be excluded without an opportunity of testing the relevance and importance of the evidence and that there might have been such material contained in the documents (*R v Reading Justices, ex p Berkshire County Council* [1996] 1 Cr App Rep 239, [1996] 1 FLR 149, 160 JP 392. It must be shown that the evidence would be material to the party seeking the summons; this could not be the case where the witness would give hostile evidence (*R v Marylebone Magistrates' Court, ex p Gatting and Emburey* (1990) 154 JP 549, [1990] Crim LR 578 DC). The High Court may set aside a witness summons if it appears that the person summoned is not likely to be able to give material evidence (see *R v Hove Justices, ex p Donne* [1967] 2 All ER 1253, 131 JP 460) or if the summons requires production of a document which is not admissible as evidence in the proceedings (*R v Cheltenham Justices, ex p Secretary of State for Trade* [1977] 1 All ER 460, [1977] 1 WLR 95, 141 JP 175). Accordingly, witness summonses directed to police officers requiring them to produce, in the course of a prosecution for driving a motor vehicle on a road having consumed an excess quantity of alcohol, a log book of the Lion Intoximeter 3000 that had been used were quashed because the log book would have had no probative value in relation to the charge; see *R v Coventry Magistrates' Court, ex p Perks* [1985] RTR 74. A summons to produce the service record and log of a breath-testing machine because it was alleged that police officers had been tinkering with the machine and saying it was not working properly, was quashed. The defence should call evidence at the trial following which the prosecution could then decide whether to call evidence of the machine's reliability; the application for the witness summons was a fishing expedition for evidence (*R v Tower Bridge Magistrates' Court, ex p DPP* [1988] Crim LR 759). Ministers of the Crown have no special privilege exempting them from attending, but process used for improper motives will be set aside (*R v Baines* [1909] 1 KB 258, 72 JP 524, and see *R v Investors Review Ltd, ex p Wheeler* [1928] 2 KB 644. There is no power of discovery in a magistrates' court and this section cannot be used for such purpose; *R v Sheffield Justices, ex p Wrigley* [1985] RTR 78n; see *R v Skegness Magistrates' Court, ex p Cardy* [1985] RTR 49, [1985] LS Gaz R 929. Before requiring the production of a number of documents each one must be considered individually to determine whether it is relevant to the proceedings; if it is established as relevant, it may then be necessary to decide whether it is privileged; see *R v Greenwich Juvenile Court, ex p Greenwich London Borough Council* (1977) 76 LGR 99. In *R v Bournemouth Justices, ex p Grey* (1986) 150 JP 392, [1987] 1 FLR 36, [1986] Fam Law 337, it was held, on the facts of that case, there was no public interest immunity which prevented a witness summons being issued requiring a social worker of an adoption agency to attend the hearing of affiliation proceedings and produce a form which the defendant had signed accepting that he was the father of the child.

A witness summons should not be issued requiring the prosecution to disclose whether a telephone intercept has taken place or to produce recordings or transcripts arising from an alleged intercept, unless the justices are satisfied that the private interests of the defendant should override the public interest. An application of this kind should never be dealt with by justices (*ex p R v Guildhall Justices, and Carson-Selman, ex p DPP* (1983) 148 JP 385, 78 Cr App Rep 269).

A witness summons should not be issued to compel production by a prosecution witness of proofs of evidence and attendance notes giving factual instructions to his solicitor which may contain or record previous inconsistent statements by the witness; and/or which are the subject of legal professional privilege which has not been waived, since the inadmissibility of such evidence by virtue of the privilege means that it is not "likely to be material evidence" for the purposes of s 97 (*R v Derby Magistrates' Court, ex p B* [1995] 4 All ER 526, [1995] 3 WLR 681, HL). It is not a breach of legal privilege to require a solicitor present at the hearing at which a defendant was disqualified from driving to give evidence as to identity and a witness summons may be issued to him to attend and produce his attendance note, although this is a procedure to be adopted by the prosecution where there is no reasonable alternative (*R (Howe) v South Durham Magistrates' Court* [2004] EWHC 362 (Admin) , 168 JP 424). As to the effect of commercial confidentiality on whether a witness summons should be issued to a third party to produce documents (records of Intoximeters UK), see *DPP v Wood* [2006] EWHC 32 (Admin), 170 JP 177. The "document or thing" must itself be likely to be material evidence; a witness summons will not be issued for documents which will not themselves constitute evidence in the case but merely give rise to a line of enquiry which might result in evidence being obtained, still less for documents merely capable of use in cross-examination as to credit (*R v Alibhai* [2004] EWCA Crim 681).

In *R v Barking Justices, ex p Goodspeed* [1985] RTR 70n, an application for a witness summons directed to a court clerk, present during an earlier abortive hearing of the case, to produce his notes of evidence with reference to a point which only went to the credit of the police officer was held to have been properly refused having regard to the Criminal Procedure Act 1865, s 4, in PART II: EVIDENCE, post, and the decision in *R v Hart* (1957) 42 Cr App Rep 47.

5. No process for the production of any document kept by the Registrar of Companies shall issue from any court except with the leave of that court, and any such process if issued shall bear thereon a statement that it is issued with the leave of that court (Companies Act 1985, s 710(1)).

6. A witness summons in civil proceedings may not be served by post (Magistrates' Courts Rules 1981, r 99(6), for criminal proceedings, see the Criminal Procedure Rules 2005, r 4.7, this PART: STATUTORY INSTRUMENTS AND PRACTICE DIRECTIONS ON PROCEDURE, post).

7. A police officer need not have the warrant with him in order to execute it; see s 125, post.

8. Subsections (2B) and (2C) were inserted by the Criminal Procedure and Investigations Act 1996, s 51, and apply in relation to any proceedings for the purpose of which no summons has been issued under s 97(1) and no warrant has been issued under s 97(2) before the appointed day, namely the 1 April 1997 (Criminal Procedure and Investigations Act 1996, s 51 and the Criminal Procedure and Investigations Act 1996 (Appointed Day No 3) Order 1997, SI 1997/682).

9. A warrant should be issued where the evidence sought to be adduced is critical to the proper trial of the defendant (*R v Bradford Justices, ex p Wilkinson* [1990] 2 All ER 833, [1990] 1 WLR 692; applied in *R v Bristol Magistrates' Court, ex p Rowles* [1994] RTR 40). In determining whether to issue a warrant it is irrelevant to take into account the fact that as the defendant was represented by a solicitor, his case would be adequately presented to the court (*R v Nottingham Justices, ex p Fraser* (1995) 159 JP 612).

10. In *R v K* (1983) 148 JP 410, 78 Cr App Rep 82, CA, it was held that duress could be a defence to an allegation of contempt of court where a witness refused to give evidence before the Crown Court.

11. When produced the justice is entitled to open a packet of documents to see whether they are material to the case (*R v Cardiff (Lord Mayor), ex p Lewis* [1922] 2 KB 777, 86 JP 207).

12. The power to commit to custody extends to all recalcitrant witnesses present in court, whether brought before the court by summons or warrant or otherwise under this section or attending voluntarily.

13. This provision seems to be apt only in the case where a court will be sitting for the purpose of receiving the evidence

during the period in which the witness has been committed to custody. For form of commitment, see Form 139 in PART IX: PRECEDENTS AND FORMS, post.

1–2170   97A. Summons or warrant as to committal proceedings.   (1) Subsection (2) below applies where a justice of the peace is satisfied that—

(a) any person in England or Wales is likely to be able to make on behalf of the prosecutor a written statement containing material evidence, or produce on behalf of the prosecutor a document or other exhibit likely to be material evidence, for the purposes of proceedings before a magistrates' court inquiring into an offence as examining justices,

(b) it is in the interests of justice to issue a summons under this section to secure the attendance of that person to give evidence or to produce the document or other exhibit, and

(c) repealed.

(2) In such a case the justice shall issue a summons directed to that person requiring him to attend before a justice at the time and place appointed in the summons to have his evidence taken as a deposition or to produce the document or other exhibit[1].

(3) If a justice of the peace is satisfied by evidence on oath of the matters mentioned in subsection (1) above, and also that it is probable that a summons under subsection (2) above would not procure the result required by it, the justice may instead of issuing a summons issue a warrant to arrest the person concerned and bring him before a justice at the time and place specified in the warrant.

(4) A summons may also be issued under subsection (2) above if the justice is satisfied that the person concerned is outside the British Islands, but no warrant may be issued under subsection (3) above unless the justice is satisfied by evidence on oath that the person concerned is in England or Wales.

(5) If—

(a) a person fails to attend before a justice in answer to a summons under this section,

(b) the justice is satisfied by evidence on oath that he is likely to be able to make a statement or produce a document or other exhibit as mentioned in subsection (1)(a) above,

(c) it is proved on oath, or in such other manner as may be prescribed, that he has been duly served with the summons and that a reasonable sum has been paid or tendered to him for costs and expenses, and

(d) it appears to the justice that there is no just excuse for the failure,

the justice may issue a warrant to arrest him and bring him before a justice at a time and place specified in the warrant.

(6) Where—

(a) a summons is issued under subsection (2) above or a warrant is issued under subsection (3) or (5) above, and

(b) the summons or warrant is issued with a view to securing that a person has his evidence taken as a deposition,

the time appointed in the summons or specified in the warrant shall be such as to enable the evidence to be taken as a deposition before a magistrates' court begins to inquire into the offence concerned as examining justices.

(7) If any person attending or brought before a justice in pursuance of this section refuses without just excuse to have his evidence taken as a deposition, or to produce the document or other exhibit, the justice may do one or both of the following—

(a) commit him to custody until the expiration of such period not exceeding one month as may be specified in the summons or warrant or until he sooner has his evidence taken as a deposition or produces the document or other exhibit;

(b) impose on him a fine not exceeding £2,500.

(8) A fine imposed under subsection (7) above shall be deemed, for the purposes of any enactment, to be a sum adjudged to be paid by a conviction.

(9) If in pursuance of this section a person has his evidence taken as a deposition, the chief executive to the justice concerned shall as soon as is reasonably practicable send a copy of the deposition to the prosecutor.

(10) If in pursuance of this section a person produces an exhibit which is a document, the chief executive to the justice concerned shall as soon as is reasonably practicable send a copy of the document to the prosecutor.

(11) If in pursuance of this section a person produces an exhibit which is not a document, the chief executive to the justice concerned shall as soon as is reasonably practicable inform the prosecutor of the fact and of the nature of the exhibit.*

[Magistrates' Courts Act 1980, s 97A, as inserted by the Criminal Procedure and Investigations Act 1996, Sch 1 and amended by the Access to Justice Act 1999, Sch 13 and the Serious Organised Crime and Police Act 2005, s 169.]

---

*Repealed by the Criminal Justice Act 2003, Sch 3 from a date to be appointed.
1. The procedure of taking a deposition from a witness, pursuant to para 4 of Sch 3 to the 1998 Act, is a proceeding in open court, though justices may exceptionally exclude persons from the taking of the deposition or otherwise modify the procedure where that will assist in the reception of the evidence or it is in the interests of justice to do so: *Regina (Crown Prosecution Service) v Bolton Magistrates' Court* [2003] EWHC 2697 (Admin), [2004] 1 WLR 835, [2004] Cr App R 33.
   The lawyer representing the defendant in the proceedings for which the deposition is sought is entitled to attend the

hearing to take the deposition unless there is some special reason justifying his exclusion; cross-examination, however, should generally be left until the Crown Court trial, though there may be cases where the reluctant witness is likely to be unavailable at the Crown Court, or can perhaps be spared attendance there if one or two questions are asked and in such a situation it would be open to the justice to permit cross-examination: *Regina (Crown Prosecution Service) v Bolton Magistrates' Court*, supra.

Evidence generally

1–2171   98. Evidence on oath.   Subject to the provisions of any enactment[1] or rule of law authorising the reception of unsworn evidence, evidence given before a magistrates' court shall be given on oath[2].
[Magistrates' Courts Act 1980, s 98.]

    1. For instance, Youth Justice and Criminal Evidence Act 1999, ss55(2) in PART II: EVIDENCE, post.
    2. As to objections to taking an oath, see 2–64 et seq Attendance of witnesses and the oath, post, and as to use of the Welsh Language see 2–66 Interpreters, post in PART II: EVIDENCE.

1–2172   99. Proof of non-payment of sum adjudged.   Where a magistrates' court has ordered one person to pay to another any sum of money, and proceedings are taken before that or any other magistrates' court to enforce payment of that sum, then—

    (*a*) if the person to whom the sum is ordered to be paid is a justices' chief executive, a certificate[1] purporting to be signed by the justices' chief executive that the sum has not been paid to him; and

    (*b*) in any other case a document purporting to be a statutory declaration[1] by the person to whom the sum is ordered to be paid that the sum has not been paid to him,

shall be admissible as evidence that the sum has not been paid to him, unless the court requires the justices' chief executive or other person to be called as a witness.
[Magistrates' Courts Act 1980, s 99, as amended by the Access to Justice Act 1999, Sch 13.]

    1. See Forms 146 and 147 in PART IX: PRECEDENTS AND FORMS, post.

1–2173   100. Statements of wages to be evidence.   A statement in writing to the effect that wages of any amount have been paid to a person during any period, purporting to be signed by or on behalf of his employer, shall be evidence of the facts therein stated in any proceedings taken before a magistrates' court—

    (*a*) for enforcing payment by the person to whom the wages are stated to have been paid of a sum adjudged to be paid by a summary conviction or order; or

    (*b*) on any application made by or against that person for the making of a magistrates' court maintenance order, or for the variation, revocation, discharge or revival of such an order.
[Magistrates' Courts Act 1980, s 100 as amended by the Family Law Reform Act 1987, Sch 2.]

1–2174   101. Onus of proving exceptions, etc.   Where the defendant to an information or complaint relies for his defence on any exception, exemption, proviso, excuse or qualification, whether or not it accompanies the description of the offence or matter of complaint in the enactment creating the offence or on which the complaint is founded, the burden of proving the exception, exemption, proviso, excuse or qualification shall be on him[1]; and this notwithstanding that the information or complaint contains[2] an allegation negativing the exception, exemption, proviso, excuse or qualification.
[Magistrates' Courts Act 1980, s 101.]

    1. And not on the prosecution: see *Williams v Russell* (1933) 97 JP 128; *Machin v Ash* [1950] WN 478 (motor insurance); *R v Oliver* [1944] KB 68, [1943] 2 All ER 800, 108 JP 30; *John v Humphreys* [1955] 1 All ER 793, [1955] 1 WLR 325, 119 JP 309; *R v Edwards* [1975] QB 27, [1974] 2 All ER 1085, 138 JP 621 (licence, permit, authority); *Nimmo v Alexander Cowan & Sons Ltd* [1968] AC 107, [1967] 3 All ER 187 (not reasonably practicable to provide and maintain safe means of access, Factories Act 1961, s 29(1)). Courts should consider carefully the issues of fact they have to decide before proceeding to consider the application and effect of this section to any particular statutory offence. There should be a case-specific approach rather than the adoption of a blanket s 101 approach to complex offence-creating statutory provisions involving exceptions and exceptions to exceptions (*Environment Agency v M E Foley Contractors Ltd* [2002] EWHC 258 (Admin), [2002] 1 WLR 1754).
    The standard of proof is that of a balance of probabilities (see *Islington London Borough v Panico* [1973] 3 All ER 485, [1973] 1 WLR 1166).
    A person disqualified from driving until he passes a test who is charged with driving whilst disqualified has the onus of proving that he obtained a provisional licence and was complying with its conditions: *DPP v Barker* [2004] EWHC Admin 2502, (2004) 168 JP 617.
    2. It is not necessary that the information or complaint shall specify or negative the exception, etc (Magistrates' Courts Rules 1981, r 4(3), Criminal Procedure Rules 2005, Part 7, this PART: STATUTORY INSTRUMENTS ON PROCEDURE, post).

Evidence in criminal cases

1–2174A   103. Evidence of persons under 14 in committal proceedings for assault, sexual offences, etc.   (1) In any proceedings before a magistrates' court inquiring as examining justices into an offence to which this section applies, a statement made in writing by or taken in writing from a child shall be admissible[1] in evidence of any matter.
    (2) This section applies—

(a) to an offence which involves an assault, or injury or a threat of injury to, a person;
(b) to an offence under section 1 of the Children and Young Persons Act 1933 (cruelty to persons under 16);
(c) to an offence under the Sexual Offences Act 1956, the Protection of Children Act 1978 or Part 1 of the Sexual Offences Act 2003; and
(d) to an offence which consists of attempting or conspiring to commit, or of aiding, abetting, counselling, procuring or inciting the commission of, an offence falling within paragraph (a), (b) or (c) above.

(3)–(4) *Repealed.*
(5) In this section "child" has the same meaning as in section 53 of the Criminal Justice Act 1991.*
[Magistrates' Courts Act 1980, s 103, as substituted by the Criminal Justice Act 1988, s 33 and amended by the Criminal Justice Act 1991, s 55, the Criminal Procedure and Investigations Act 1996, Schs 1 and 5 and the Sexual Offences Act 2003, Sch 6.]

---

*Repealed by the Criminal Justice Act 2003, Sch 3 from a date to be appointed.
1. A video-tape of a police interview with a child from which a transcript was made, exhibited to the police officer's evidence at committal proceedings, was held to constitute a statement admissible in evidence for the purposes of this section (*R v H* (1990) 155 JP 561, CA).

1–2175 **104. Proof of previous convictions.** Where a person is convicted of a summary offence[1] by a magistrates' court, other than a youth court, and—

(a) it is proved to the satisfaction of the court, on oath or in such other manner as may be prescribed[2], that not less than 7 days previously a notice was served on the accused in the prescribed form and manner specifying any alleged previous conviction of the accused of a summary offence proposed to be brought to the notice of the court in the event of his conviction of the offence charged; and
(b) the accused is not present in person before the court,

the court may take account of any such previous conviction so specified as if the accused had appeared and admitted it.
[Magistrates' Courts Act 1980, s 104 as amended by the Criminal Justice Act 1991, Sch 11.]

---

1. For meaning of "summary offence", see Criminal Law Act 1977, s 64, ante. Note that this section relates only to proof of previous convictions for *summary* offences after conviction of the accused of a *summary* offence. It is not restricted to cases where the accused has pleaded guilty by post.
2. See Criminal Procedure Rules 2005, Part 4, this PART: STATUTORY INSTRUMENTS ON PROCEDURE, post.

Offences

1–2175A **106. False written statements admitted in evidence.** (1) If any person in a written statement admitted in evidence in criminal proceedings by virtue of section 5B above wilfully makes a statement material in those proceedings which he knows to be false or does not believe to be true, he shall be liable on conviction on indictment to imprisonment for a term not exceeding 2 years or a fine or both.

(2) The Perjury Act 1911 shall have effect as if this section were contained in that Act.
[Magistrates' Courts Act 1980, s 106 as amended by the Criminal Procedure and Investigations Act 1996, Sch 1.]

1–2176 **107. False statements in declaration proving service, etc.** If, in any solemn declaration, certificate or other writing made or given for the purpose of its being used in pursuance of rules of court[1] as evidence of the service of any document or the handwriting or seal of any person, a person makes a statement that he knows to be false in a material particular, or recklessly makes any statement that is false in a material particular, he shall be liable on summary conviction[2] to imprisonment for a term not exceeding 6 months or a fine not exceeding level 3 on the standard scale or both.
[Magistrates' Courts Act 1980, s 107 as amended by the Criminal Justice Act 1982, ss 38 and 46 and the Courts Act 2003, Sch 8.]

---

1. See Criminal Procedure Rules 2005, Part 4, this PART: STATUTORY INSTRUMENTS ON PROCEDURE, post.
2. This section does not operate as a bar to proceedings being taken under the Perjury Act 1911, s 5, for s 16(3) of that Act expressly provides that proceedings under that Act may be taken as an alternative to summary proceedings under any other Act.

PART V[1]
APPEAL AND CASE STATED

Appeal

1–2177 **108. Right of appeal to the Crown Court.** (1) A person convicted by a magistrates' court may appeal[2] to the Crown Court—

(a) if he pleaded guilty[3], against his sentence;
(b) if he did not, against the conviction[3] or sentence.

(1A) Section 14 of the Powers of Criminal Courts (Sentencing) Act 2000 (under which a conviction of an offence for which an order for conditional or absolute discharge is made is deemed not to be a conviction except for certain purposes) shall not prevent an appeal under this section, whether against conviction or otherwise.

(2) A person sentenced by a magistrates' court for an offence in respect of which an order for conditional discharge has been previously made may appeal to the Crown Court against the sentence.

(3) In this section "sentence"[4] includes any order made on conviction by a magistrates' court, not being—

(a) Repealed.

(b) an order for the payment of costs;

(c) an order under section 2 of the Protection of Animals Act 1911 (which enables a court to order the destruction of an animal); or

(d) an order made in pursuance of any enactment under which the court has no discretion as to the making of the order or its terms,

and also includes a declaration of relevance under the Football Spectators Act 1989.

[Magistrates' Courts Act 1980, s 108 as amended by the Criminal Justice Act 1982, s 66 and Sch 16, the Football Spectators Act 1989, s 23, the Criminal Justice Act 1991, Sch 13, the Criminal Justice and Public Order Act 1994, Sch 9, the Crime and Disorder Act 1998, Schs 8 and 10 the Football (Offences and Disorder) Act 1999, s 7, the Powers of Criminal Courts (Sentencing) Act 2000, Sch 9 and the Football (Disorder) Act 2000, Sch 3.]

---

1. PART V contains ss 108–114.
2. See requirements as to notice of appeal in Criminal Procedure Rules 2005, Part 63, this PART: STATUTORY INSTRUMENTS ON PROCEDURE, post. As to caselaw and commentary, see ante para 1–821.
3. The extensive case law on equivocal pleas is noted in para 1–581 et seq ante.
4. See also para 1–821 ante.

1–2178 109. Abandonment of appeal[1]. (1) Where notice to abandon an appeal has been duly given by the appellant—

(a) the court against whose decision the appeal was brought may issue process[1] for enforcing that decision, subject to anything already suffered or done under it by the appellant; and

(b) the said court may, on the application of the other party to the appeal, order the appellant to pay to that party such costs[2] as appear to the court to be just and reasonable in respect of expenses properly incurred by that party in connection with the appeal before notice of the abandonment was given to that party.

(2) In this section "appeal" means an appeal from a magistrates' court to the Crown Court, and the reference to a notice to abandon an appeal is a reference to a notice shown to the satisfaction of the magistrates' court to have been given in accordance with rules of court[3].

[Magistrates' Courts Act 1980, s 109 as amended by the Courts Act 2003, Sch 8.]

---

1. For effect of abandonment of an appeal upon a recognizance in a case where the appellant has been released from custody pending his appeal, see Criminal Procedure Rules 2005, Part 63, this PART: STATUTORY INSTRUMENTS AND PRACTICE DIRECTIONS ON PROCEDURE, post.
2. Enforceable in accordance with s 41 of the Administration of Justice Act 1970.
3. See the Criminal Procedure Rules 2005, Part 63, this PART: STATUTORY INSTRUMENTS AND PRACTICE DIRECTIONS ON PROCEDURE, post.

1–2179 110. Enforcement of decision of the Crown Court. After the determination by the Crown Court of an appeal from a magistrates' court the decision appealed against as confirmed or varied[1] by the Crown Court or any decision of the Crown Court substituted for the decision appealed against, may, without prejudice to the powers of the Crown Court to enforce the decision, be enforced—

(a) by the issue by the court by which the decision appealed against was given of any process that it could have issued if it had decided the case as the Crown Court decided it;

(b) so far as the nature of any process already issued to enforce the decision appealed against permits, by that process;

and the decision[2] of the Crown Court shall have effect as if it had been made by the magistrates' court[3] against whose decision the appeal is brought.

[Magistrates' Courts Act 1980, s 110.]

---

1. The power of the Crown Court to vary the sentence will not be reviewed by the High Court by *certiorari* (*R v Leicester Recorder, ex p Gabbitas* [1946] 1 All ER 615, 110 JP 228).
2. Where an appeal against sentence is allowed to proceed on the basis of the evidence in the court below, the appellant cannot thereafter be allowed to say that for that reason alone the sentence cannot be allowed to stand; the same strictness of proof is not required in matters relevant to sentence as in matters relevant to conviction (*Paprika Ltd v Board of Trade* [1944] KB 327, [1944] 1 All ER 372, 108 JP 104).
3. For a similar power in a magistrates' court to enforce a judgment or order of the High Court given or made on an appeal by way of case stated, see s 112, post.

Case stated

1–2180 111. Statement of case by magistrates' court[1]. (1) Any person who was a party to any proceeding before a magistrates' court[2] or is aggrieved by the conviction order, determination or other proceeding of the court may question the proceeding on the ground that it is wrong in law or is in excess of jurisdiction by applying to the justices composing the court to state a case for the opinion of the High Court on the question of law or jurisdiction involved; but a person shall not make an application under this section in respect of a decision against which he has a right of appeal to the High Court[3] or which by virtue of any enactment passed after 31st December 1879 is final.

(2) An application under subsection (1) above shall be made within 21 days after the day on which the decision of the magistrates' court was given.

(3) For the purpose of subsection (2) above, the day on which the decision of the magistrates' court is given shall, where the court has adjourned the trial of an information after conviction, be the day on which the court sentences or otherwise deals with[4] the offender.

(4) On the making of an application under this section in respect of a decision any right of the applicant to appeal against the decision to the Crown Court[5] shall cease.

(5) If the justices are of opinion that an application under this section is frivolous, they may refuse to state a case, and, if the applicant so requires, shall give him a certificate stating that the application has been refused; but the justices shall not refuse to state a case if the application is made by or under the direction of the Attorney General.

(6) Where justices refuse to state a case, the High Court may, on the application of the person who applied for the case to be stated, make an order of mandamus[5] requiring the justices to state a case.

[Magistrates' Courts Act 1980, s 111.]

1. For detailed commentary on case stated see ante para 1–825 et seq.
2. Defined by s 148, post.
3. See eg Domestic Proceedings and Magistrates' Courts Act 1978, s 29, in PART IV: title FAMILY LAW (Matrimonial Proceedings), post; and *Manders v Manders* [1897] 1 QB 474, 61 JP 105; discussed in *Peagram v Peagram* [1926] 2 KB 165, 90 JP 136.
4. This will include the day on which a decision on costs is made where that is the final termination of the proceedings (*Liverpool City Council v Worthington* (1998) Times, 16 June, DC).
5. This applies even when the appeal by way of case stated has been abandoned; once the choice is made, the applicant is bound by it; see *R v Crown Court at Winchester, ex p Lewington* [1982] 1 WLR 1277, [1982] Crim LR 664. However, where an application to state a case is made out of time for the purposes of s 111(2), it would seem that the right of appeal to the Crown Court is not excluded; see *P and M Supplies (Essex) Ltd v Hackney London Borough Council* (1990) 154 JP 814, [1990] Crim LR 569. There may be an appeal by way of case stated from a decision of the Crown Court on an appeal from a magistrates' court; but where the matter does not involve a conviction, the Crown Court has a discretion whether or not to state a case; if they refuse there is no power in the High Court to compel it by *mandamus* to do so (*R v Somerset Justices, ex p Ernest J Cole & Partners Ltd* [1950] 1 KB 519, [1950] 1 All ER 264, 114 JP 133); application for a case to be stated must be made in writing within a reasonable time (see *Chesterton RDC v Ralph Thompson Ltd* [1944] KB 417, [1944] 1 All ER 666, 108 JP 209). Where a party applies for the Crown Court to state a case in respect of a decision on appeal from a magistrates' court, the Crown Court may order that the applicant shall enter into a recognizance (to prosecute the appeal) before an officer of the Crown Court or a justice of the peace (see the Supreme Court Act 1981, ss 28 and 81, post, and the Crown Court Rules 1982, this PART: STATUTORY INSTRUMENTS AND PRACTICE DIRECTIONS ON PROCEDURE, post. Bail may be granted by the Crown Court or the High Court (see the Supreme Court Act 1981, s 81, post and s 37(1)(*b*) of the Criminal Justice Act 1948 as amended by the Courts Act 1971).
6. The Civil Procedure Rules 1998, Part 54 govern claims for judicial review seeking quashing, mandatory or prohibiting orders, in this PART, post.

1–2181   112. Effect of decision of High Court on case stated by magistrates' court.   Any conviction, order, determination, or other proceeding of a magistrates' court varied by the High Court on an appeal by case stated, and any judgment or order of the High Court on such an appeal may be enforced as if it were a decision of the magistrates' court[1] from which the appeal was brought.

[Magistrates' Courts Act 1980, s 112.]

1. For a similar power in a magistrates' court to enforce a decision of the Crown Court given on appeal, see s 110, ante.

Supplemental provisions as to appeal and case stated

1–2182   113. Bail on appeal or case stated.   (1) Where a person has given notice of appeal[1] to the Crown Court against the decision of a magistrates' court or has applied to a magistrates' court to state a case for the opinion of the High Court, then, if he is in custody[2], the magistrates' court may[3], subject to section 25 of the Criminal Justice and Public Order Act 1994, grant him bail.

(2) If a person is granted bail under subsection (1) above, the time and place at which he is to appear (except in the event of the determination in respect of which the case is stated being reversed by the High Court) shall be—

(*a*) if he has given notice of appeal, the Crown Court at the time appointed for the hearing of the appeal;

(*b*) if he has applied for the statement of a case, the magistrates' court at such time within 10 days after the judgment of the High Court has been given as may be specified by the magistrates' court;

and any recognizance[4] that may be taken from him or from any surety for him shall be conditioned accordingly.

(3) Subsection (1) above shall not apply where the accused has been committed to the Crown Court for sentence under section 37 above or section 3 of the Powers of Criminal Courts (Sentencing) Act 2000.

(4) Section 37(6) of the Criminal Justice Act 1948 (which relates to the currency of a sentence while a person is released on bail by the High Court) shall apply to a person released on bail by a

magistrates' court under this section pending the hearing of a case stated as it applies to a person released on bail by the High Court under section 22 of the Criminal Justice Act 1967.
[Magistrates' Courts Act 1980, s 113 as amended by the Criminal Justice and Public Order Act 1994, Sch 10, and the Powers of Criminal Courts (Sentencing) Act 2000, Sch 9.]

----

1. Notice must be given under the Criminal Procedure Rules 2005, Part 63, this PART: STATUTORY INSTRUMENTS AND PRACTICE DIRECTIONS ON PROCEDURE, post. It is submitted that the power to grant bail, relates to an effective notice and not to a notice given out of time where no extension has been granted by the Crown Court.
2. It would appear that a juvenile who is subject to a care order following a finding of guilt is "in custody", and bail may be granted pending appeal; see *R v P* (1979) 144 JP 39.
3. The magistrates' court has a discretion. If the appellant has been committed to custody on conviction for an offence, the provisions of the Bail Act 1976 with respect to bail in criminal proceedings will apply, except that s 4 of that Act (general right to bail of accused persons) will not apply. Accordingly, if bail is withheld, an unrepresented appellant must be informed that he may apply to the High Court for bail (Bail Act 1976, s 5(6), ante). Where the appeal is to the Crown Court we would suggest that the appellant should also be advised of his right to apply to that Court for bail (see Supreme Court Act 1981, s 81, post). If the appellant has been committed to custody for any other reason, and the magistrates' court decides to release him on bail, the appellant may be required to enter into a recognizance with or without sureties. *R v Watton* [1979] Crim LR 246, CA would suggest that bail should be granted pending appeal only in exceptional circumstances. We would expect magistrates who have imposed a custodial sentence to be reluctant to grant bail.
4. See Forms 120 and 121 in PART IX: PRECEDENTS AND FORMS, post.

1–2183 114. Recognizances and fees on case stated. Justices to whom application has been made to state a case for the opinion of the High Court on any proceeding of a magistrates' court shall not be required to state the case until the applicant has entered into a recognizance[1], with or without sureties, before the magistrates' court, conditioned to prosecute the appeal without delay and to submit to the judgment of the High Court and pay such costs as that Court may award; and (except in any criminal matter) the clerk of a magistrates' court shall not be required to deliver the case to the applicant until the applicant has paid the fees payable for the case and for the recognizances to the justices' chief executive for the court.
[Magistrates' Courts Act 1980, s 114, as amended by the Access to Justice Act 1999, Sch 13.]

----

1. See commentary on case stated, ante para 1–825 et seq.
2. Stipulated in Sch 6, post.

PART VI[1]
RECOGNIZANCES

Recognizances to keep the peace or be of good behaviour

1–2184 115. Binding over to keep the peace or be of good behaviour[2]. (1) The power of a magistrates' court on the complaint of any person to adjudge any other person to enter into a recognizance, with or without sureties, to keep the peace or to be of good behaviour towards the complainant shall be exercised by order on complaint[3].
(2) Where a complaint is made under this section, the power of the court to remand the defendant under subsection (5) of section 55 above shall not be subject to the restrictions imposed by subsection (6) of that section[4].
(3) If any person ordered by a magistrates' court under subsection (1) above to enter into a recognizance[5], with or without sureties, to keep the peace or to be of good behaviour fails to comply with the order, the court may commit[6] him to custody for a period not exceeding 6 months or until he sooner complies with the order.
[Magistrates' Courts Act 1980, s 115.]

----

1. For consideration of this power, see para 3–540 et seq—Surety to keep the peace and be of good behaviour, in PART III: SENTENCING, post.
2. PART VI contains ss 115–120. The law and practice for dealing with bind overs may require re-examination in light of the adverse decision of the European Court of Human Rights in *Hashman and Harrup v United Kingdom* [2000] Crim LR 185, ECtHR where the notion of "good behaviour" was found to breach the European Convention on Human Rights because it was too vague and uncertain. But see also *Steel v United Kingdom* (1998) 28 EHRR 603.
3. It does not appear to be necessary for any formal complaint to be made if the party is already before the justices on another charge, eg assault (*per* BLACKBURN J, in *Ex p Davis* (1871) 35 JP 551). Where a defendant has been arrested at common law for breach of the peace, any "charge" sheet or similar document may be treated as a complaint under this section, or if read out to the court, treated as an oral complaint. A failure to refer to s 115 in the "complaint" may be cured by amendment under s 123, post: *DPP v Speede* [1998] 2 Cr App Rep 108, DC. Representation may be granted to the defendant: s 19 of the Legal Aid Act 1988, this PART, post.
Notwithstanding the references to "complaint" and to s 55 of this Act in sub-s (2) below, in *R v Bolton Justices, ex p Graeme* (1986) 150 JP 190, the Court of Appeal expressed the view that, for the purposes of s 18(1) of the Supreme Court Act 1981 (Restrictions on appeals to Court of Appeal), an application relating to a complaint under this section was a criminal cause or matter.
Notwithstanding that for some purposes proceedings under s 115 are treated as criminal proceedings, since the procedure is by way of complaint it is primarily a civil process. The jurisdiction of the justices does not depend on a summons being issued, nor does the absence of a complaint in the form prescribed invalidate the procedure (*R v Coventry Magistrates' Court, ex p Crown Prosecution Service* (1996) 160 JP 741, [1996] Crim LR 723 and see *DPP v Speede*, ante).
Where proceedings under s 115 are conducted by the Crown Prosecution Service by virtue of s 3(2)(c) of the Prosecution of Offences Act 1985 and the complaint is dismissed, there is no power to award defence costs against the Crown Prosecution Service but an order for costs may be made against the complainant (*R v Coventry Magistrates' Court, ex p Crown Prosecution Service* (1996) 160 JP 741, [1996] Crim LR 723).
4. This means the court may remand or further remand a person who has been arrested on a warrant issued in

consequence of that person's failure to appear either in answer to a summons or at an adjourned hearing, and, if the latter, even though he has given evidence in the proceedings.

5. See generally as to recognizances, Magistrates' Courts Rules 1981, rr 82–89, this PART: STATUTORY INSTRUMENTS AND PRACTICE DIRECTIONS ON PROCEDURE, post.

6. This power is not available in the case of a person under 18 (17 before the amendments introduced by the Criminal Justice Act 1991) who refuses to enter into a recognizance (*Veater v G* [1981] 2 All ER 304, 145 JP 158), but in the case of a person aged 18 and under 21 the power to commit to detention under s 9(1)(c) of the Criminal Justice Act 1982, PART III, post may in certain circumstances be available (*Howley v Oxford* (1985) 149 JP 363). In the unusual case that the order was not made in the defendant's presence or the warrant was not issued on that occasion, notice must be given to him before the order may be enforced; see Magistrates' Courts Rules 1981, r 53, this PART: STATUTORY INSTRUMENTS AND PRACTICE DIRECTIONS ON PROCEDURE, post. At any time after the person has been committed, the court may vary or dispense with the requirement as to sureties (see s 94, post). Application in such a case will be by complaint against the person at whose instance the order to find sureties was made (Magistrates' Courts Rules, 1981, r 83, this PART: STATUTORY INSTRUMENTS AND PRACTICE DIRECTIONS ON PROCEDURE, post).

1–2185 116. Discharge of recognizance to keep the peace or be of good behaviour on complaint of surety[1]. (1) On complaint being made to a justice of the peace for any area to which this section applies by a surety to a recognizance to keep the peace or to be of good behaviour entered into before a magistrates' court[2] that the person bound by the recognizance as principal has been, or is about to be, guilty of conduct constituting a breach of the conditions of the recognizance, the justice may, if the complaint alleges that the principal is, or is believed to be, in that area, or if the recognizance was entered into before a magistrates' court for that area, issue a warrant to arrest the principal and bring him before a magistrates' court for that area or a summons requiring the principal to appear before such a court; but the justice shall not issue a warrant unless the complaint is in writing and substantiated on oath.

(2) The magistrates' court before which the principal appears or is brought in pursuance of such a summons or warrant as aforesaid may, unless it adjudges the recognizance to be forfeited[3], order the recognizance to be discharged[4] and order the principal to enter into a new recognizance, with or without sureties, to keep the peace or to be of good behaviour.

(3) The areas to which this section applies are commission areas.
[Magistrates' Courts Act 1980, s 116 as amended by SI 1996/674 and 675.]

1. For the position under the European Convention on Human Rights see para 1–2184 above.
2. Persons who entered into recognizances before the Crown Court should not be dealt with under this section.
3. See s 120 as to forfeiture.
4. Where the recognizance is discharged by a different court from that before which it was entered into, note the duty to notify in Magistrates' Courts Rules 1981, r 82, this PART: STATUTORY INSTRUMENTS AND PRACTICE DIRECTIONS ON PROCEDURE, post.

Other provisions

1–2200 117. Warrant endorsed for bail. (1) A justice of the peace on issuing a warrant for the arrest of any person may grant him bail by endorsing the warrant for bail, that is to say, by endorsing the warrant with a direction in accordance with subsection (2) below.

(2) A direction for bail endorsed on a warrant under subsection (1) above shall—

(a) in the case of bail in criminal proceedings, state that the person arrested is to be released on bail subject to a duty to appear before such magistrates' court and at such time as may be specified in the endorsement;

(b) in the case of bail otherwise than in criminal proceedings, state that the person arrested is to be released on bail on his entering into such a recognizance (with or without sureties) conditioned for his appearance before a magistrates' court as may be specified in the endorsement;

and the endorsement shall fix the amounts in which any sureties and, in a case falling within paragraph (b) above, that person is or are to be bound.

(3) Where a warrant has been endorsed for bail under subsection (1) above—

(a) where the person arrested is to be released on bail on his entering into a recognizance without sureties, it shall not be necessary to take him to a police station, but if he is so taken, he shall be released from custody on his entering into the recognizance; and

(b) where he is to be released on his entering into a recognizance with sureties, he shall be taken to a police station on his arrest, and the custody officer there shall (subject to his approving any surety tendered in compliance with the endorsement) release him from custody as directed in the endorsement.
[Magistrates' Courts Act 1980, s 117 as amended by the Police and Criminal Evidence Act 1984, s 47(8).]

1–2201 118. Varying or dispensing with requirement as to sureties. (1) Subject to subsection (2) below, where a magistrates' court has committed[1] a person to custody in default of finding sureties, the court[2] may, on application[3] by or on behalf of the person committed, and after hearing fresh evidence, reduce the amount in which it is proposed that any surety should be bound or dispense with any of the sureties or otherwise deal with the case as it thinks just.

(2) Subsection (1) above does not apply in relation to a person granted bail in criminal proceedings.
[Magistrates' Courts Act 1980, s 118.]

1. Note that the section relates to any person committed to custody in default of finding sureties; whether on remand or to keep the peace or be of good behaviour. For order to bring up prisoner, see Form 141 in PART IX: PRECEDENTS AND FORMS, post.
2. Not necessarily composed of the same justices as sat when the person was committed to custody (see s 148(2), post).
3. Where the order to find sureties was made at the instance of another person, the application under this section will be by way of complaint against the person at whose instance the order to find sureties was made (Magistrates' Courts Rules 1981, r 83, this PART: STATUTORY INSTRUMENTS AND PRACTICE DIRECTIONS ON PROCEDURE, post).

1–2202 119. Postponement of taking recognizance. (1) Where a magistrates' court has power to take any recognizance, the court may, instead of taking it, fix the amount in which the principal and his sureties, if any, are to be bound; and thereafter the recognizance may be taken by any such person as may be prescribed[1].

(2) Where, in pursuance of this section, a recognizance is entered into otherwise than before the court that fixed the amount of it, the same consequences shall follow as if it had been entered into before that court; and references in this or any other Act to the court before which a recognizance was entered into shall be construed accordingly.

(3) Nothing in this section shall enable a magistrates' court to alter the amount of a recognizance fixed by the High Court or the Crown Court.

[Magistrates' Courts Act 1980, s 119 as amended by the Criminal Justice Act 1982, Sch 14.]

1. They are prescribed by the Criminal Procedure Rules 2005, Part 19, this PART: STATUTORY INSTRUMENTS AND PRACTICE DIRECTIONS ON PROCEDURE, post.

1–2203 120. Forfeiture of recognizance. (1) This section applies where—

(a) a recognizance[1] to keep the peace or to be of good behaviour has been entered into before a magistrates' court; or

(b) any recognizance[1] is conditioned for the appearance of a person before a magistrates' court, or for his doing any other thing[2] connected with a proceeding before a magistrates' court.

(1A) If, in the case of a recognizance[1] which is conditioned for the appearance of an accused before a magistrates' court, the accused fails to appear in accordance with the condition, the court shall—

(a) declare the recognizance to be forfeited[3];

(b) issue a summons directed to each person bound by the recognizance as surety, requiring him to appear before the court on a date specified in the summons to show cause why he should not be adjudged to pay the sum in which he is bound;

and on that date the court may proceed in the absence of any surety if it is satisfied that he has been served with the summons.

(2) If, in any other case falling within subsection (1) above, the recognizance appears[4] to the magistrates' court[5] to be forfeited, the court may—

(a) declare the recognizance to be forfeited[3]; and

(b) adjudge each person bound by it, whether as principal or surety, to pay the sum in which he is bound;

but in a case falling within subsection (1)(a) above, the court shall not declare the recognizance to be forfeited except by order[4] made on complaint.

(3) The court which declares the recognizance to be forfeited may, instead of adjudging any person to pay the whole sum in which he is bound, adjudge him to pay part only of the sum or remit the sum.

(4) Payment of any sum adjudged to be paid under this section, including any costs awarded against the defendant, may be enforced, and any such sum shall be applied, as if it were a fine[6] and as if the adjudication were a summary conviction of an offence not punishable with imprisonment[7] and so much of section 85(1) above as empowers a court to remit fines shall not apply to the sum but so much thereof as relates to remission[8] after a term of imprisonment has been imposed shall so apply; but at any time before the issue of a warrant of commitment to enforce payment of the sum, or before the sale of goods under a warrant of distress to satisfy the sum, the court may remit the whole or any part of the sum either absolutely or on such conditions as the court thinks just.

(5) A recognizance such as is mentioned in this section shall not be enforced otherwise than in accordance with this section, and accordingly shall not be transmitted to the Crown Court nor shall its forfeiture be certified to that court.

[Magistrates' Courts Act 1980, s 120 as amended by the Crime and Disorder Act 1998, s 55.]

1. Generally it will be presumed that a recognizance was properly entered into (*Ex p Jeffreys* (1888) 52 JP 280); *aliter*, if by a person certified to be of unsound mind (*R v Green-Emmot* (1931) 144 LT 671, 22 Cr App Rep 183).
2. Where the principal was committed on bail under s 9(8) of the Extradition Act 1989 to await the Home Secretary's decision as to her return in respect of extradition proceedings, and there was a surety with an obligation to pay if the principal "failed to surrender to custody at a place, time and date notified by the police on behalf of the Secretary of State", but no such notification occurred and the principal, in breach of a bail condition not to leave the country, went to America and then agreed to return to the country seeking her extradition (Switzerland), there could be no breach of the surety's recognisance and s 120 never arose: *R (Hart) v Bow Street Magistrates'* [2001] EWHC Admin 1141, [2002] 1 WLR 1242 (the court added, however, that the departure of the fugitive to a country other than the requesting country did not bring the extradition process to an end and it would have been open to the police to require the principal to attend court at a given place and time and if she had failed to attend the power to forfeit the recognisance would then have arisen.

3. In the case of a recognizance conditioned for the appearance of an accused before the magistrates' court, while forfeiture is automatic the court may, under sub-s (3), instead of adjudging the person to pay the whole sum in which he bound, adjudge him to pay part only of the sum or remit the sum.

In other cases within sub-s (1), forfeiture is not automatic and sub-s (2) should be read with sub-s (3). For the purpose of such cases, it would seem that reported decisions based on the provisions of this section before it was amended by the Crime and Disorder Act 1998, s 55, will continue to apply. Accordingly, in cases to which sub-s (2) applies justices *must* consider the extent to which the person bound is at fault, ie must enquire into the culpability of the person bound: see *R v Southampton Justices, ex p Green* [1976] 1 QB 11, [1975] 2 All ER 1073, 139 JP 667; where the forfeiture of a recognizance was quashed on the ground that the court had not so enquired. See also *R v Horseferry Road Magistrates' Court, ex p Pearson* [1976] 2 All ER 264, 140 JP 382; and *R v Tottenham Magistrates' Court, ex p Riccardi* (1977) 66 Cr App Rep 150 as well as notes to s 8 of the Bail Act 1976, ante. The mere admission of conduct which justifies the making of a further binding over order to keep the peace is not in itself an admission of a breach of the peace (*Jackson v Lilley* (1982) 146 JP 132). The adjudication of forfeiture is not a "conviction", so there is no right of appeal under s 108, ante (see *R v Durham Justices, ex p Laurent* [1945] KB 33, [1944] 2 All ER 530, 109 JP 21); but may be challenged by way of *certiorari* (*R v Southampton Justices, ex p Green*, supra). An order of discharge in bankruptcy does not release the bankrupt from any liability under a recognizance (Insolvency Act 1986, s 281(4), in PART VIII: title INSOLVENCY, post).

4. As these are civil proceedings, the civil standard of proof is to be applied (*R v Marlow Justices, ex p O'Sullivan* [1984] QB 381, [1983] 3 All ER 578, 148 JP 82).

5. We are of the opinion that jurisdiction to order forfeiture of a recognizance to keep the peace or to be of good behaviour is confined to a magistrates' court acting for the same petty sessions area as the court before which the recognizance was entered into.

6. For meaning of "fine" see s 150(1), post. For provisions as to enforcement, see ss 75–89, ante.

7. There is no power to issue a warrant of commitment for default in paying, on the ground that the offender appears to have sufficient means to pay forthwith; s 82(1) and (4), ante.

8. Where a magistrates' court is required to enforce the payment of a forfeiture ordered by a court or other authority, the magistrates' court must not act as an appellate court and should not readily come to a different conclusion as to what sum should be paid. Nevertheless, if for whatever reason, there has been no proper means of inquiry before ordering forfeiture of a recognizance entered into by a surety, it is open to the surety to seek to restrict his liability, the burden being on him, and the court should not hesitate to deploy fully the powers given under this section to consider remission. The court in a normal case should be thinking of a sum not exceeding that which the surety could reasonably be expected to pay in full within two or at most three years; see *R v Birmingham Crown Court, ex p Rashid Ali* (1998) 163 JP 145, [1999] Crim LR 504.

PART VII[1]
MISCELLANEOUS AND SUPPLEMENTARY

Constitution and place of sitting of magistrates' courts

1–2204   **121. Constitution and place of sitting of court.**   (1) A magistrates' court shall not try an information summarily or hear a complaint except when composed of at least 2 justices[2] unless the trial or hearing is one that by virtue of any enactment may take place before a single justice.

(2) A magistrates' court shall not hold an inquiry into the means of an offender for the purposes of section 82 above or determine under that section at a hearing at which the offender is not present whether to issue a warrant of commitment except when composed of at least 2 justices[2].

(3) A magistrates' court shall not—

(a) try summarily an information for an indictable offence or hear a complaint except when sitting in a petty-sessional court-house[3];

(b) try an information for a summary offence or hold an inquiry into the means of an offender for the purposes of section 82 above, or impose imprisonment, except when sitting in a petty-sessional court-house or an occasional court-house[4].

(4) Subject to the provisions of any enactment to the contrary, where a magistrates' court is required by this section to sit in a petty-sessional or occasional court-house, it shall sit in open court[5].

(5) A magistrates' court composed of a single justice, or sitting in an occasional court-house, shall not impose imprisonment for a period exceeding 14 days or order[6] a person to pay more than £1.

(6) Subject to the provisions of subsection (7) below[7], the justices composing the court before which any proceedings take place shall be present during the whole of the proceedings; but, if during the course of the proceedings any justice absents himself, he shall cease to act further therein and, if the remaining justices are enough to satisfy the requirements of the preceding provisions of this section, the proceedings may continue before a court composed of those justices.

(7) Where the trial of an information is adjourned after the accused has been convicted and before he is sentenced or otherwise dealt with, the court which sentences or deals with him need not be composed of the same justices as that which convicted him; but, where among the justices composing the court which sentences or deals with an offender there are any who were not sitting when he was convicted, the court which sentences or deals with the offender shall before doing so make such inquiry into the facts and circumstances of the case as will enable the justices who were not sitting when the offender was convicted to be fully acquainted with those facts and circumstances.

(8) This section shall have effect subject to the provisions[8] of this Act relating to family proceedings.
[Magistrates' Courts Act 1980, s 121, as amended by the Criminal Justice Act 1988, s 61 and the Children Act 1989, Sch 11.]

---

1. PART VII contains ss 121–155.
2. But not more than three (Justices of the Peace (Size and Chairmanship of Bench) Rules 1995, this PART: STATUTORY INSTRUMENTS AND PRACTICE DIRECTIONS ON PROCEDURE, post.
3. For appointment of a petty sessional court house, see Justices of the Peace Act 1979, s 56, ante.
4. For appointment of an occasional court-house, see s 147, post.
5. For detailed commentary on "open court" see para 1–113, ante.
6. Whether by way of fine, costs, compensation or otherwise.

7. See also Domestic Proceedings and Magistrates' Courts Act 1978, s 31 in PART VI: FAMILY LAW, post.
8. See ss 65–70, ante, and note also s 152, post (Saving for youth courts).

Appearance by counsel or solicitor

1–2205   122. Appearance by a legal representative.   (1) A party to any proceedings before a magistrates' court may be represented by a legal representative[1].

(2) Subject to subsection (3) below, and absent party so represented shall be deemed not to be absent[2].

(3) Appearance of a party by a legal representative shall not satisfy any provision of any enactment[3] or any condition of a recognizance expressly requiring his presence.

[Magistrates' Courts Act 1980, s 122 as amended by the Courts and Legal Services Act 1990, Sch 18.]

---

1. See ante para 1–139 Appearance by legal representative.
2. No warrant for his arrest may be issued (see *R v Thompson* [1909] 2 KB 614, 73 JP 403.) Sections 11–16 and 55–57 will not apply. Note s 23, supra (power of court, with consent of legally represented accused, to proceed in his absence).
3. For example, the following provisions require a defendant's personal appearance; s 82(3), ante (means enquiry on defaulter); s 93(6) enquiry into default in paying a magistrates' court maintenance order. Counsel or a solicitor may do all that a representative is empowered to do on behalf of a corporation under Sch 3, post.

Process

1–2206   123. Defect in process[1].   (1) No objection[2] shall be allowed to any information or complaint, or to any summons or warrant to procure the presence of the defendant, for any defect in it in substance or in form, or for any variance between it and the evidence adduced on behalf of the prosecutor or complainant at the hearing of the information or complaint.

(2) If it appears to a magistrates' court that any variance between a summons or warrant and the evidence adduced on behalf of the prosecutor or complainant is such that the defendant has been misled by the variance, the court shall, on the application of the defendant, adjourn the hearing.

[Magistrates' Courts Act 1980, s 123.]

---

1. For the purpose of civil contempt proceedings under s 63(3) of this Act, this section has been modified by the Contempt of Court Act 1981, Sch 3, post.
2. For detailed commentary on this section see para 1–440, ante.

1–2207   124. Process valid notwithstanding death, etc, of justice.   A warrant or summons issued by a justice of the peace shall not cease to have effect by reason of his death or his ceasing to be a justice.

[Magistrates' Courts Act 1980, s 124.]

1–2208   125. Warrants.   (1) A warrant of arrest issued by a justice of the peace shall remain in force until it is executed[1] or withdrawn[2] or it ceases to have effect in accordance with rules of court.

(2) A warrant of arrest, warrant of commitment, warrant of detention, warrant of distress or search warrant issued by a justice of the peace may be executed[1] anywhere in England[3] and Wales by any person to whom it is directed or by any constable acting within his police area.

(3) *Repealed.*

(4) *Repealed.*

[Magistrates' Courts Act 1980, s 125 as amended by the Police and Criminal Evidence Act 1984, s 33, the Criminal Justice Act 1988, s 65, the Courts and Legal Services Act 1990, Sch 17, SI 1997/1898 and the Crime and Disorder Act 1998, Schs 8 and 10, the Youth Justice and Criminal Evidence Act 1999, Sch 4, the Powers of Criminal Courts (Sentencing) Act 2000, Sch 9, the Access to Justice Act 1999, Sch 15 and the Courts Act 2003, Sch 8.]

---

1. Where a person is arrested and detained on suspicion of the commission of a criminal offence, and the police already hold or are aware of the existence of an arrest warrant (in this case issued for fine default) that includes an order to bring the person before the court "immediately" or words to that effect, the police retain a discretion (reviewable on *Wednesbury* principles) as to when to execute the warrant and it is within the lawful bounds of that discretion to delay the execution of the warrant until the investigation of the suspected criminal offence has been concluded: *Henderson v Chief Constable of Cleveland Police* [2001] EWCA Civ 225, [2001] 1 WLR 1103.
2. A justice may issue a duplicate warrant if he is satisfied that an application for the issue of a duplicate is justified, for example where the original has been destroyed or mislaid (*R v Leigh Justices, ex p Kara* (1980) 72 Cr App Rep 327).
3. For the execution of warrants of arrest in Scotland or Northern Ireland, see the Criminal Justice and Public Order Act 1994, Pt X—Cross-border enforcement—this PART, post; for the execution of warrants of arrest in the Isle of Man or Channel Islands, see s 126, post, and the Indictable Offences Act 1848, s 13, in PART VIII: title EXTRADITION, etc, post, and for the execution of a warrant of commitment in different parts of the United Kingdom for non-payment of a sum adjudged to be paid on conviction, see the Criminal Law Act 1977, ss 38A and 38B, this PART, ante.

1–2208A   125A. Civilian enforcement officers.   (1) A warrant to which this subsection applies may be executed anywhere in England and Wales by a civilian enforcement officer.

(2) In this section "civilian enforcement officer", in relation to a warrant, means a person who—

    (*a*) is employed by an authority of a prescribed[1] class which performs functions in relation to any area specified in the warrant; and

    (*b*) is authorised in the prescribed[1] manner to execute warrants.

(3) The warrants to which subsection (1) above applies are any warrant of arrest, commitment, detention or distress issued by a justice of the peace—

(*a*) under any provision specified[2] for the purposes of this subsection by an order made by the Lord Chancellor and the Secretary of State, acting jointly; or

(*b*) for the enforcement of a court order of any description so specified[2].

(3A) Subsection (1) also applies to any warrant of distress issued under Schedule 5 to the Courts Act 2003 by a court or fines officer.

(4) Where a warrant has been executed by a civilian enforcement officer, a written statement indicating—

(*a*) the name of the officer;

(*b*) the authority by which he is employed; and

(*c*) that he is authorised in the prescribed manner to execute warrants,

shall, on the demand of the person arrested, committed or detained or against whom distress is levied, be shown to him as soon as practicable.

(5) The power to make orders conferred by subsection (3) above shall be exercisable by statutory instrument which shall be subject to annulment in pursuance of a resolution of either House of Parliament.

[Magistrates' Courts Act 1980, s 125A, as inserted by the Access to Justice Act 1999, s 92 and amended by SI 2006/1737.]

---

1. Local authorities, police authorities and magistrates' courts committees are prescribed authorities and for the manner in which employees of such authorities may be authorised to execute such warrants, see the Magistrates' Courts (Civilian Enforcement Officers) Rules 1990, in this PART, post.

2. See the Magistrates' Courts Warrants (Specification of Provisions) Order 2000, in this PART, post.

1-2208B   125B. Execution by approved enforcement agency.   (1) A warrant to which section 125A(1) above applies may also be executed anywhere in England and Wales—

(*a*) by an individual who is an approved enforcement agency;

(*b*) by a director of a company which is an approved enforcement agency;

(*c*) by a partner in a partnership which is an approved enforcement agency; or

(*d*) by an employee of an approved enforcement agency who is authorised in writing by the agency to execute warrants.

(2) In this section "approved enforcement agency", in relation to a warrant, means a person or body approved under section 31A of the Justices of the Peace Act 1997 by the magistrates' courts committee for the petty sessions area of the justice (or any of the justices) who issued the warrant.

(3) Failure by a magistrates' courts committee to comply with any provision of, or made under, section 31A(2) to (5) of the Justices of the Peace Act 1997 does not of itself render unlawful the execution of a warrant.

(4) Where a warrant has been executed by a person mentioned in subsection (1) above, a written statement indicating the matters specified in subsection (5) below shall, on the demand of the person arrested, committed or detained or against whom distress is levied, be shown to him as soon as practicable.

(5) The matters referred to in subsection (4) above are—

(*a*) the name of the person by whom the warrant was executed;

(*b*) if he is a director of, or partner in, an approved enforcement agency, the fact that he is a director of, or partner in, that agency;

(*c*) if he is an employee of an approved enforcement agency, the fact that he is an employee authorised in writing by that agency to execute warrants; and

(*d*) the fact that his name, or (where paragraph (*b*) or (*c*) above applies) that of the agency indicated, is contained in the register maintained under section 31A(4) of the Justices of the Peace Act 1997 by the magistrates' courts committee concerned.

[Magistrates' Courts Act 1980, s 125B, as inserted by the Access to Justice Act 1999, s 93.]

1-2208BA   125BA. Powers of persons authorised under section 125A or 125B.   Schedule 4A to this Act, which confers powers on persons authorised under section 125A or 125B for the purpose of executing warrants for the enforcement of fines and other orders, shall have effect.

[Magistrates' Courts Act 1980, s 125BA, as inserted by the Domestic Violence, Crime and Victims Act 2004, s 27.]

1-2208C   125C. Disclosure of information for enforcing warrants.   (1) Basic personal information held by a relevant public authority may, on the application of a justices' chief executive, be supplied by the authority to him (or to a justices' clerk appointed by, or member of the staff of, his magistrates' courts committee who is specified in the application) for the purpose of facilitating the enforcement of a section 125A(1) warrant which is so specified.

(2) In this section—

"basic personal information" means a person's name, date of birth or national insurance number or the address (or any of the addresses) of a person;

"relevant public authority" means a Minister of the Crown, government department, local authority or chief officer of police specified in an order[1] made by the Lord Chancellor; and "a section 125A(1) warrant" means a warrant to which section 125A(1) above applies and which has been issued by a justice of the peace to whom the justices' chief executive making the application is chief executive.

(3) Information supplied to any person under subsection (1) above, or this subsection, for the purpose of facilitating the enforcement of a section 125A(1) warrant may be supplied by him for that purpose to—

(a) any person entitled to execute the warrant;

(b) any employee of a body or person who, for the purposes of section 125B above, is an approved enforcement agency in relation to the warrant; or

(c) any person who is the justices' chief executive, a justices' clerk or a member of the staff of the magistrates' courts committee whose justices' chief executive made the application for the information.

(4) A person who intentionally or recklessly—

(a) discloses information supplied to him under this section otherwise than as permitted by subsection (3) above; or

(b) uses information so supplied otherwise than for the purpose of facilitating the enforcement of the section 125A(1) warrant concerned,

commits an offence.

(5) But it is not an offence under subsection (4) above—

(a) to disclose any information in accordance with any enactment or order of a court or for the purposes of any proceedings before a court; or

(b) to disclose any information which has previously been lawfully disclosed to the public.

(6) A person guilty of an offence under subsection (4) above is liable—

(a) on summary conviction, to a fine not exceeding the statutory maximum; or

(b) on conviction on indictment, to a fine.

(7) The power to make orders conferred by subsection (2) above shall be exercisable by statutory instrument which shall be subject to annulment in pursuance of a resolution of either House of Parliament.

[Magistrates' Courts Act 1980, s 125C, as inserted by the Access to Justice Act 1999, s 94.]

---

1. The Secretary of State for Social Security has been specified by the Enforcement of Warrants (Disclosure of Information) Order 2000, SI 2000/3277.

1–2208CA 125CA. Power to make disclosure order.   (1) A magistrates' court may make a disclosure order if satisfied that it is necessary to do so for the purpose of executing a warrant to which this section applies.

(2) This section applies to a warrant of arrest, commitment, detention or distress issued by a justice of the peace in connection with the enforcement of a fine or other order imposed or made on conviction.

(3) A disclosure order is an order requiring the person to whom it is directed to supply the designated officer for the court with any of the following information about the person to whom the warrant relates—

(a) his name, date of birth or national insurance number;

(b) his address (or any of his addresses).

(4) A disclosure order may be made only on the application of a person entitled to execute the warrant.

(5) This section applies to the Crown as it applies to other persons.

[Magistrates' Courts Act 1980, s 125CA, as inserted by the Domestic Violence, Crime and Victims Act 2004, s 28.]

1–2208CB 125CB Use of information supplied under disclosure order.   (1) Information supplied to a person under a disclosure order, or under this subsection, may be supplied by him to—

(a) the applicant for the order or any other person entitled to execute the warrant concerned;

(b) any employee of a body or person who, for the purposes of section 125B above, is an approved enforcement agency in relation to the warrant;

(c) any justices' clerk or other person appointed under section 2(1) of the Courts Act 2003.

(2) A person who intentionally or recklessly—

(a) discloses information supplied under a disclosure order otherwise than as permitted by subsection (1) above, or

(b) uses information so supplied otherwise than for the purpose of facilitating the execution of the warrant concerned,

commits an offence.

(3) But it is not an offence under subsection (2) above—

(a) to disclose any information in accordance with any enactment or order of a court or for the purposes of any proceedings before a court; or (*b*)   to disclose any information which has previously been lawfully disclosed to the public.

(4)   A person guilty of an offence under subsection (2) above is liable—

(*a*)   on summary conviction, to a fine not exceeding the statutory maximum;

(*b*)   on conviction on indictment, to a fine.

(5)   In this section "disclosure order" has the meaning given by section 125CA(3) above.

[Magistrates' Courts Act 1980, s 125CB, as inserted by the Domestic Violence, Crime and Victims Act 2004, s 28.]

1-2208D   125D. Execution by person not in possession of warrant.   (1) A warrant to which section 125A(1) above applies may be executed by any person entitled to execute it even though it is not in his possession at the time.

(2)   A warrant to which this subsection applies (and which is not a warrant to which section 125A(1) above applies) may be executed by a constable even though it is not in his possession at the time.

(3)   Subsection (2) above applies to—

(*a*)   a warrant to arrest a person in connection with an offence;

(*b*)   a warrant under section 186(3) of the Army Act 1955, section 186(3) of the Air Force Act 1955, section 105(3) of the Naval Discipline Act 1957 or Schedule 2 to the Reserve Forces Act 1996 (desertion etc);

(*c*)   a warrant under section 102 or 104 of the General Rate Act 1967 (insufficiency of distress);

(*d*)   a warrant under section 47(8) of the Family Law Act 1996 (failure to comply with occupation order or non-molestation order);

(*e*)   a warrant under paragraph 4 of Schedule 3 to the Crime and Disorder Act 1998 (unwilling witnesses);

(*f*)   a warrant under paragraph 3(2) of Schedule 1 to the Powers of Criminal Courts (Sentencing) Act 2000 (offenders referred to court by youth offender panel); and

(*g*)   a warrant under section 55, 76, 93, 97 or 97A above.

(4)   Where by virtue of this section a warrant is executed by a person not in possession of it, it shall, on the demand of the person arrested, committed or detained or against whom distress is levied, be shown to him as soon as practicable.

[Magistrates' Courts Act 1980, s 125D, as inserted by the Access to Justice Act 1999, s 96.]

1-2209   126. Execution of certain warrants outside England and Wales.   Sections 12 to 14 of the Indictable Offences Act 1848[1] (which relate, among other things, to the execution in Scotland, Northern Ireland, the Isle of Man and the Channel Islands of warrants of arrest for the offences referred to in those sections) shall, so far as applicable, apply to—

(*a*)   warrants of arrest issued under section 1 above for offences other than those referred to in the said sections 12 to 14;

(*b*)   warrants of arrest issued under section 13 above;

(*c*)   warrants of arrest issued under section 97 above other than warrants issued in bastardy proceedings to arrest a witness;

(*cc*)   warrants of arrest issued under section 97A above;

(*d*)   warrants of commitment issued under this Act;

(*e*)   warrants of arrest issued under paragraph 4 of Schedule 3 to the Crime and Disorder Act 1998;

(*f*)   warrants of arrest issued under paragraph 3(2) of Schedule 1 to the Powers of Criminal Courts (Sentencing) Act 2000 (offender referred to court by youth offender panel).

[Magistrates' Courts Act 1980, s 126 as amended by the Crime and Disorder Act 1998, Sch 8, the Youth Justice and Criminal Evidence Act 1999, Sch 4, the Powers of Criminal Courts (Sentencing) Act 2000, Sch 11.]

---

1.   Section 12 (English warrants may be backed in Ireland and vice versa) and s 14 (English or Irish warrants may be backed in Scotland) are repealed by the Criminal Justice and Public Order Act 1994, Sch 11 and replaced by the provisions of Pt X—Cross-border enforcement—of that Act, this PART, post. Section 13 of the Indictable Offences Act 1848 which relates to the Isle of Man and the Channel Islands is printed, post, in PART VIII: title EXTRADITION, etc.

Limitation of time

1-2210   127. Limitation of time[1].   (1) Except as otherwise expressly provided by any enactment and subject to subsection (2) below, a magistrates' court shall not try an information or hear a complaint unless the information was laid, or the complaint made, within 6 months from the time when the offence was committed, or the matter of complaint arose[2].

(2)   Nothing in—

(*a*)   subsection (1) above; or

(*b*)   subject to subsection (4) below, any other enactment (however framed or worded) which, as regards any offence to which it applies, would but for this section impose a time-limit on the power of a magistrates' court to try an information summarily or impose a limitation on the time for taking summary proceedings,

shall apply in relation to any indictable offence[3].

(3)   Without prejudice to the generality of paragraph (*b*) of subsection (2) above, that paragraph

includes enactments which impose a time-limit that applies only in certain circumstances (for example, where the proceedings are not instituted by or with the consent of the Director of Public Prosecutions or some other specified authority).

(4) Where, as regards any indictable offence, there is imposed by any enactment (however framed or worded, and whether falling within subsection (2)(*b*) above or not) a limitation on the time for taking proceedings on indictment for that offence no summary proceedings for that offence shall be taken after the latest time for taking proceedings on indictment.

[Magistrates' Courts Act 1980, s 127.]

---

1. For detailed commentary on limitation of time see para 1–387, ante.
2. Where proceedings are taken by way of complaint for an order in civil contempt proceedings under s 63(3) of this Act, this section shall not apply to the complaint (Contempt of Court Act 1981, Sch 3).
3. "Indictable offence" means an offence which, if committed by an adult, is triable on indictment, whether it is exclusively so triable or triable either way (Interpretation Act 1978, Sch 1, in PART II: EVIDENCE, post). Accordingly, there is no time limit on the summary trial of an offence which is triable either way (*Kemp v Liebherr–GB Ltd* [1987] 1 All ER 885, [1987] 1 WLR 67). Section 127(2)–(4) does not apply to an offence under the Merchant Shipping Act 1995 (Merchant Shipping Act 1995, s 274, in PART VII: TRANSPORT: title MERCHANT SHIPPING, post).

Remand

1–2211 128. Remand in custody or on bail. (1) Where a magistrates' court has power to remand any person[1], then, subject to section 4 of the Bail Act 1976 and to any other enactment[2] modifying that power, the court may—

(*a*) remand him in custody[3], that is to say, commit him to custody[4] to be brought before the court[5], subject to subsection (3A) below, at the end of the period of remand or at such earlier time as the court may require; or

(*b*) where it is inquiring into or trying an offence alleged to have been committed by that person or has convicted him of an offence, remand him on bail in accordance with the Bail Act 1976, that is to say, by directing[6] him to appear as provided in subsection (4) below; or

(*c*) except in a case falling within paragraph (*b*) above, remand him on bail by taking from him a recognizance (with or without sureties[7]) conditioned as provided in that subsection;

and may, in a case falling within paragraph (*c*) above, instead of taking recognizances in accordance with that paragraph, fix the amount of the recognizances with a view to their being taken subsequently in accordance with section 119 above.

(1A) Where—

(*a*) on adjourning a case under section 5, 10(1), 17C or 18(4) above the court proposes to remand or further remand a person in custody; and

(*b*) he is before the court; and

(*c*) repealed;

(*d*) he is legally represented in that court,

it shall be the duty of the court—

(i) to explain the effect of subsections (3A) and (3B) below to him in ordinary language; and

(ii) to inform him in ordinary language that, notwithstanding the procedure for a remand without his being brought before a court, he would be brought before a court for the hearing and determination of at least every fourth application for his remand, and of every application for his remand heard at a time when it appeared to the court that he had no legal representative acting for him in the case.

(1B) For the purposes of subsection (1A) above a person is to be treated as legally represented in a court if, but only if, he has the assistance of a legal representative to represent him in the proceedings in that court.

(1C) After explaining to an accused as provided by subsection (1A) above the court shall ask him whether he consents to the hearing and determination of such applications in his absence.

(2) Where the court fixes the amount of a recognizance under subsection (1) above or section 8(3) of the Bail Act 1976 with a view to its being taken subsequently the court shall in the meantime commit the person so remanded to custody in accordance with paragraph (*a*) of the said subsection (1).

(3) Where a person is brought[8] before the court after remand, the court may further remand him.

(3A) Subject to subsection (3B) below, where a person has been remanded in custody and the remand was not a remand under section 128A below for a period exceeding 8 clear days, the court may further remand him (otherwise than in the exercise of the power conferred by that section) on an adjournment under section 5, 10(1), 17C or 18(4) above without his being brought before it if it is satisfied—

(*a*) that he gave his consent, either in response to a question under subsection (1C) above or otherwise, to the hearing and determination in his absence of any application for his remand on an adjournment of the case under any of those provisions; and

(*b*) that he has not by virtue of this subsection been remanded without being brought before the court on more than two such applications immediately preceding the application which the court is hearing; and

(*c*) Repealed;

(*d*) that he has not withdrawn his consent to their being so heard and determined.

(3B) The court may not exercise the power conferred by subsection (3A) above if it appears to the court, on an application for a further remand being made to it, that the person to whom the application relates has no legal representative acting for him in the case (whether present in court or not).

(3C) Where—

(a) a person has been remanded in custody on an adjournment of a case under section 5, 10(1), 17C or 18(4) above; and
(b) an application is subsequently made for his further remand on such an adjournment; and
(c) he is not brought before the court which hears and determines the application; and
(d) that court is not satisfied as mentioned in subsection (3A) above,

the court shall adjourn the case and remand him in custody for the period for which it stands adjourned.

(3D) An adjournment under subsection (3C) above shall be for the shortest period that appears to the court to make it possible for the accused to be brought before it.

(3E) Where—

(a) on an adjournment of a case under section 5, 10(1), 17C or 18(4) above a person has been remanded in custody without being brought before the court; and
(b) it subsequently appears—

(i) to the court which remanded him in custody; or
(ii) to an alternate magistrates' court to which he is remanded under section 130 below,

that he ought not to have been remanded in custody in his absence, the court shall require him to be brought before it at the earliest time that appears to the court to be possible.

(4) Where a person is remanded on bail under subsection (1) above the court may, where it remands him on bail in accordance with the Bail Act 1976 direct him to appear or, in any other case, direct that his recognizance be conditioned for his appearance—

(a) before that court[5] at the end of the period of remand; or
(b) at every time and place to which during the course of the proceedings the hearing may be from time to time adjourned;

and, where it remands him on bail conditionally on his providing a surety during an inquiry into an offence alleged to have been committed by him, may direct that the recognizance of the surety be conditioned to secure that the person so bailed appears—

(c) at every time and place to which during the course of the proceedings the hearing may be from time to time adjourned and also before the Crown Court in the event of the person so bailed being committed for trial there.

(5) Where a person is directed to appear or a recognizance is conditioned for a person's appearance in accordance with paragraph (b) or (c) of subsection (4) above, the fixing at any time of the time for him next to appear shall be deemed to be a remand; but nothing in this subsection or subsection (4) above shall deprive the court of power at any subsequent hearing to remand him afresh[9].

(6) Subject to the provisions of sections 128A and 129 below, a magistrates' court shall not remand a person for a period exceeding 8 clear days[10], except that—

(a) if the court remands him on bail, it may remand him for a longer period[11] if he and the other party consent;
(b) where the court adjourns a trial under section 10(3) above[12] or section 11 of the Powers of Criminal Courts (Sentencing) Act 2000, the court may remand him for the period of the adjournment;
(c) where a person is charged with an offence triable either way, then, if it falls to the court to try the case summarily but the court is not at the time so constituted, and sitting in such a place, as will enable it to proceed with the trial, the court may remand him until the next occasion on which it will be practicable for the court to be so constituted[13], and to sit in such a place, as aforesaid, notwithstanding that the remand is for a period exceeding 8 clear days.

(7) A magistrates' court having power to remand a person in custody may, if the remand is for a period not exceeding 3 clear days[14], commit him to detention at a police station.

(8) Where a person is committed to detention at a police station under subsection (7) above—

(a) he shall not be kept in such detention unless there is a need for him to be so detained for the purposes of inquiries into other offences[15];
(b) if kept in such detention, he shall be brought back before the magistrates' court which committed him as soon as that need ceases;
(c) he shall be treated as a person in police detention to whom the duties under section 39 of the Police and Criminal Evidence Act 1984 (responsibilities in relation to persons detained) relate;
(d) his detention shall be subject to periodic review at the times set out in section 40 of that Act (review of police detention).

[Magistrates' Courts Act 1980, s 128 as amended by the Criminal Justice Act 1982, Sch 9, the Police and Criminal Evidence Act 1980, s 48, the Criminal Justice Act 1988, Sch 15, the Courts and Legal Services Act 1990, Sch 18, the Criminal Procedure and Investigations Act 1996, ss 49, 52 and Sch 5 and the Powers of Criminal Courts (Sentencing) Act 2000, Sch 9.]

1. Powers to remand arise under the following sections of this Act: ss 5(1), 10(4), 15(2), 18(4), 30(1), 55(5) and s 21C(3) of the Football Spectators Act 1989..

2. See s 129, post.

3. The power to remand in custody may be exercised without the necessity for sworn evidence being given (*R v Guest, ex p Metropolitan Police Comr* [1961] 3 All ER 1118, 126 JP 21). This is subject to the requirements of art 5(3) of the European Convention on Human Rights. See para 1–1570 above.

4. "Commit to custody" is defined by s 150(1), post.

5. Justices may remand a defendant to appear before a magistrates' court sitting in a different petty sessional division of the same county (*R v Avon Magistrates' Courts Committee, ex p Bath Law Society* [1988] QB 409, [1988] 2 WLR 137, 151 JP 825).

6. Where the accused is detained in custody for other reasons, a "direction" under sub-paragraph (*b*) does not impose on the governor of the prison where the accused is detained a duty to produce him before the court on the date specified in the direction (*R v Governor of Brixton Prison, ex p Walsh* [1985] AC 154, [1984] 2 All ER 609, 149 JP 175, HL).

7. The Queen's Bench Divisional Court has expressed disapproval of a solicitor acting as a surety for his client (*R v Scott-Jervis* (1876) Times, 20 November).

8. See s 129, post, where the defendant cannot appear because of illness or accident.

9. The power to remand "afresh" empowers a court, notwithstanding a direction or a recognizance for "continuous bail", to reconsider remand in custody or on bail with sureties in a larger amount or different sureties.

10. "Eight clear days" means that eight days intervene between the day of remand and the day on which the person remanded is to appear before the court, eg from a Monday to the Wednesday of the following week. See also s 131(1), post, which enables a longer remand of a defendant already serving a custodial sentence.

11. But where the person remains in custody because sureties have not entered into recognizances, he must be brought before the court in accordance with a direction on the warrant of commitment at the end of eight clear days or earlier time (Magistrates' Courts Rules 1981, r 23, Criminal Procedure Rules 2005, Part 18, this PART: STATUTORY INSTRUMENTS AND PRACTICE DIRECTIONS ON PROCEDURE, post).

12. Section 10(3) relates to an adjournment for inquiries or to determine the most suitable method of dealing with the case; s 30 relates to remand for medical examination.

13. A single justice who forms the opinion that the case is a proper one for summary trial (see s 25, ante) would employ this provision.

14. But in the case of a child or young person the period must not exceed 24 hours (Children and Young Persons Act 1969, s 23(14), in PART V: YOUTH COURTS, post).

15. The words "other offences" are not to be given a restricted meaning but include offences relating to those with which the accused has already been charged. On an application to remand into police custody, s 128(8)(*a*) requires merely that the court is told whatever is directly pertinent to the question whether a need exists for the accused to be detained at a police station for the purpose of enquiries into other offences (*R v Bailey and Smith* (1993) 97 Cr App Rep 365).

1–2212   128A. Remands in custody for more than eight days. (1) The Secretary of State may by order[1] made by statutory instrument provide that this section shall have effect—

(*a*) in an area specified in the order; or
(*b*) in proceedings of a description so specified,

in relation to any accused person ("the accused").

(2) A magistrates' court may remand the accused in custody for a period exceeding 8 clear days if—

(*a*) it has previously remanded him in custody for the same offence; and
(*b*) he is before the court,

but only if, after affording the parties an opportunity to make representations, it has set a date on which it expects that it will be possible for the next stage in the proceedings, other than a hearing relating to a further remand in custody or on bail, to take place, and only—

(i) for a period ending not later than that date; or
(ii) for a period of 28 clear days,

whichever is the less.

(3) Nothing in this section affects the right of the accused to apply for bail during the period of the remand.

(4) A statutory instrument containing an order under this section shall not be made unless a draft of the instrument has been laid before Parliament and been approved by a resolution of each House.
[Magistrates' Courts Act 1980, s 128A, as inserted by the Criminal Justice Act 1988, s 155 and amended by the Criminal Procedure and Investigations Act 1996, s 52 and Sch 5.]

1. The Magistrates' Courts (Remands in Custody) Order, 1991, SI 1991/2667 amended by SI 1997/35 and SI 2005/617, provides that this section applies throughout England and Wales in relation to persons of any age.

1–2213   129. Further remand. (1) If a magistrates' court is satisfied[1] that any person who has been remanded is unable by reason of illness or accident to appear or be brought before the court at the expiration of the period for which he was remanded, the court may, in his absence, remand him for a further time; and section 128(6) above shall not apply.

(2) Notwithstanding anything in section 128(1) above, the power of a court under subsection (*l*) above to remand a person on bail for a further time—

(*a*) where he was granted bail in criminal proceedings, includes power to enlarge the recognizance of any surety for him to a later time;
(*b*) where he was granted bail otherwise than in criminal proceedings, may be exercised by enlarging his recognizance and those of any sureties[2] for him to a later time.

(3) Where a person remanded on bail[3] is bound to appear before a magistrates' court at any time and the court has no power to remand him under subsection (1) above, the court may in his absence—

   (a) where he was granted bail in criminal proceedings, appoint a later time as the time at which he is to appear and enlarge the recognizances of any sureties for him to that time;

   (b) where he was granted bail otherwise than in criminal proceedings, enlarge his recognizance and those of any sureties for him to a later time;

and the appointment of the time or the enlargement of his recognizance shall be deemed to be a further remand.

   (4) Where a magistrates' court commits a person for trial on bail and the recognizance of any surety for him has been conditioned in accordance with paragraph *(a)* of subsection (4) of section 128 above the court may, in the absence of the surety, enlarge his recognizance so that he is bound to secure that the person so committed for trial appears also before the Crown Court.

[Magistrates' Courts Act 1980, s 129.]

---

   1. The court must have been given solid grounds on which it can found a reliable opinion (*R v Liverpool City Justices, ex p Grogan* (1990) 155 JP 450).

   2. Notice of the enlargement of the recognizance must be given to principal and sureties (Magistrates' Courts Rules 1981, r 84, Criminal Procedure Rules 2005, Part 19, this PART: STATUTORY INSTRUMENTS AND PRACTICE DIRECTIONS ON PROCEDURE, post).

   3. Unlike sub-s (1) which applies to a person remanded either in custody or on bail.

1–2214   130. Transfer of remand hearings.   (1) A magistrates' court adjourning a case under section 5, 10(1), 17C or 18(4) above, and remanding the accused in custody, may, if he has attained the age of 17, order that he be brought up for any subsequent remands before an alternate magistrates' court nearer to the prison where he is to be confined while on remand.

   (2) The order shall require the accused to be brought before the alternate court at the end of the period of remand or at such earlier time as the alternate court may require.

   (3) While the order is in force, the alternate court shall, to the exclusion of the court which made the order, have all the powers in relation to further remand (whether in custody or on bail) and the grant of a right to representation funded by the Legal Services Commission as part of the Criminal Defence Service which that court would have had but for the order.

   (4) The alternate court may, on remanding the accused in custody, require him to be brought before the court which made the order at the end of the period of remand or at such earlier time as that court may require; and, if the alternate court does so, or the accused is released on bail, the order under subsection (1) above shall cease to be in force.

   (4A) Where a magistrates' court is satisfied as mentioned in section 128(3A) above—

   (a) subsection (1) above shall have effect as if for the words "he be brought up for any subsequent remands before" there were substituted the words "applications for any subsequent remands be made to";

   (b) subsection (2) above shall have effect as if for the words "the accused to be brought before" there were substituted the words "an application for a further remand to be made to"; and

   (c) subsection (4) above shall have effect as if for the words "him to be brought before" there were substituted the words "an application for a further remand to be made to".

   (5) Schedule 5 to this Act shall have effect to supplement this section.

[Magistrates' Courts Act 1980, s 130 as amended by the Criminal Justice Act 1982, Sch 9, the Criminal Procedure and Investigations Act 1996, s 49 and the Access to Justice Act 1999, Sch 4.]

1–2215   131. Remand of accused already in custody.   (1) When a magistrates' court remands an accused person in custody and he is already detained under a custodial sentence, the period for which he is remanded may be up to 28 clear days.

   (2) But the court shall inquire as to the expected date of his release from that detention; and if it appears that it will be before 28 clear days have expired, he shall not be remanded in custody for more than 8 clear days or (if longer) a period ending with that date.

   (2A) Where the accused person is serving a sentence of imprisonment to which an intermittent custody order under section 183 of the Criminal Justice Act 2003 relates, the reference in subsection (2) to the expected date of his release is to be read as a reference to the expected date of his next release on licence.

   (3) *Repealed.*

[Magistrates' Courts Act 1980, s 131 as amended by the Criminal Justice Act 1982, Schs 9 and 16 and the Criminal Justice Act 2003, Sch 32.]

Restrictions on imprisonment[1]

1–2216   132. Minimum term.   A magistrates' court shall not impose imprisonment[2] for less than 5 days.

[Magistrates' Courts Act 1980, s 132.]

---

   1. A sentence of imprisonment shall not be passed in a person's absence (s 11(3), ante).

   2. But note ss 135, 136, post (*detention* for short periods). There is no power to order a sentence of imprisonment to commence before the date of its pronouncement; (compare *R v Gilbert* [1975] 1 All ER 742, [1975] 1 WLR 1012, 139 JP 273—Crown Court).

1–2217   133. Consecutive terms of imprisonment[1].   (1) Subject to section 84 of the Powers of Criminal Courts (Sentencing) Act 2000, of the Crime and Disorder Act 1998[2] a magistrates' court imposing imprisonment[3] or a sentence of detention in a young offender institution on any person may order that the term of imprisonment or detention in a young offender institution shall commence on the expiration of any other term of imprisonment or detention in a young offender institution imposed by that or any other court; but where a magistrates' court imposes two or more terms of imprisonment or detention in a young offender institution to run consecutively the aggregate of such terms shall not, subject to the provisions of this section, exceed 6 months.

(2) If two or more of the terms imposed by the court are imposed in respect of an offence triable either way[4] which was tried summarily otherwise than in pursuance of section 22(2) above, the aggregate of the terms so imposed and any other terms imposed by the court may exceed 6 months but shall not, subject to the following provisions of this section, exceed 12 months[5].*

(2A) In relation to the imposition of terms of detention in a young offender institution subsection (2) above shall have effect as if the reference to an offence triable either way were a reference to such an offence or an offence triable only on indictment.**

(3) The limitations imposed by the preceding subsections shall not operate to reduce the aggregate of the terms that the court may impose in respect of any offences below the term which the court has power to impose[6] in respect of any one of those offences.

(4) Where a person has been sentenced by a magistrates' court to imprisonment and a fine for the same offence, a period of imprisonment imposed for non-payment of the fine, or for want of sufficient distress to satisfy the fine, shall not be subject to the limitations imposed by the preceding subsections.

(5) For the purposes of this section a term of imprisonment shall be deemed to be imposed in respect of an offence if it is imposed as a sentence or in default of payment of a sum adjudged to be paid by the conviction or for want of sufficient distress to satisfy such a sum.

[Magistrates' Courts Act 1980, s 133 as amended by the Criminal Justice Act 1982, Sch 14, the Criminal Justice Act 1988, Schs 8 and 15, the Crime and Disorder Act 1998, Schs 8 and 10 and the Powers of Criminal Courts (Sentencing) Act 2000, Sch 9.]

---

*Repealed by the Criminal Justice Act 2003, Sch 3 from a date to be appointed.
**Repealed by the Criminal Justice and Court Services Act 2000, Sch 7, Sch 8 from a date to be appointed.
1. For an analysis of the use of consecutive terms in practice, and complicated effect of this section and case law on fines enforcement, see post, PART III: SENTENCING, para 3–246 et seq. Section 133 of the Magistrates' Court Act 1980 does not apply directly to detention and training orders; therefore, the court may impose consecutive detention and training orders for summary offences to an aggregate that exceeds six months: *C v DPP* [2001] EWHC Admin 453, [2001] Crim LR 671, DC.
2. See this PART post.
3. "Impose imprisonment", is defined in s 150(1), post.
4. For meaning of "offence triable either way", see the Interpretation Act 1978, Sch 1, in PART II: EVIDENCE, post.
For the application of this subsection to consecutive terms of detention in a young offender institution see s 97(4) of the Powers of Criminal Courts (Sentencing) Act 2000 in PART III: SENTENCING, post.
5. The restrictions in s 133 apply only to terms imposed by the court and not to activating a suspended sentence (*R v Chamberlain* (1991) 156 JP 440, CA); thus in an appropriate case, implemented suspended sentences may be consecutive to terms imposed by the court so as to exceed 12 months. Similarly, justices who order the return to prison of an offender under section 40 of the Criminal Justice Act 1991 do not thereby pass a sentence of imprisonment on him and are entitled to pass the maximum sentence permitted by section 133 of the 1980 Act to run consecutively to a period of return ordered under s 40 of the 1991 Act (*R v Worthing Justices, ex p Varley* [1998] 1 WLR 819n, 161 JP 748, [1997] Crim LR 688).
6. Note the maximum terms set out in ss 31 and 78 of the Powers of Criminal Courts (Sentencing) Act 2000 in PART III: SENTENCING, post (general limit of six months for an offence) and s 33 of the 1980 Act (three months limit in "small value" procedure under s 22), ante.

Detention for short periods

1–2218   135. Detention of offender for one day in court-house or police station. (1) A magistrates' court that has power to commit to prison a person[1] convicted of an offence, or would have that power but for section 82 or 88 above, may order him to be detained[2] within the precincts of the court-house or at any police station until such hour, not later than 8 o'clock in the evening of the day on which the order is made, as the court may direct, and, if it does so, shall not, where it has power to commit him to prison, exercise that power.

(2) A court shall not make such an order under this section as will deprive the offender of a reasonable opportunity of returning to his abode on the day of the order.

(3) This section shall have effect in relation to a person aged 18 or over but less than 21 as if references in it to prison were references to detention under section 108 of the Powers of Criminal Courts (Sentencing) Act 2000.*

[Magistrates' Courts Act 1980, s 135 as amended by the Criminal Justice Act 1982, Sch 14, the Criminal Justice Act 1991, Sch 8 and the Powers of Criminal Courts (Sentencing) Act 2000, Sch 9.]

---

*Repealed by the Criminal Justice and Court Services Act 2000, Sch 7, Sch 8 from a date to be appointed.
1. A magistrates' court has no power to commit a person under 21 years of age to prison (Criminal Justice Act 1982, s 1 in PART III: SENTENCING, STATUTES ON SENTENCING, post), but as to persons aged 18 and under 21 see sub-s (3), post. Detention may be ordered on a fine defaulter without allowing time for payment, or holding a means inquiry, or first considering the report of a person who has exercised supervision.
2. This is not imprisonment. It should be described as "detention" in the court register.

1–2219   136. Committal to custody overnight at police station for non-payment of sum adjudged by conviction. (1) A magistrates' court that has power to commit to prison a person[1] in default of payment of a sum adjudged to be paid by a summary conviction, or would have that power but for section 82 or 88 above, may issue a warrant for his detention[2] in a police station, and, if it does so, shall not, where it has power to commit him to prison, exercise that power.

(2) A warrant under this section, unless the sum adjudged to be paid by the conviction is sooner paid—

(*a*) shall authorise the person executing it to arrest the defaulter and take him to a police station, and

(*b*) shall require the officer in charge of the station to detain him there until 8 o'clock in the morning of the day following that on which he is arrested, or, if he is arrested between midnight and 8 o'clock in the morning, until 8 o'clock in the morning of the day on which he is arrested.

(3) Notwithstanding subsection (2)(*b*) above, the officer may release the defaulter at any time within 4 hours before 8 o'clock in the morning if the officer thinks it expedient to do so in order to enable him to go to his work or for any other reason appearing to the officer to be sufficient.

(4) This section shall have effect in relation to a person aged 18 or over but less than 21 as if references in it to prison were references to detention under section 108 of the Powers of Criminal Courts (Sentencing) Act 2000 (detention of persons aged 18 to 20 for default).*

[Magistrates' Courts Act 1980, s 136 as amended by the Criminal Justice Act 1982, Sch 14, the Criminal Justice Act 1988, s 65, the Criminal Justice Act 1991, Sch 8, the Powers of Criminal Courts (Sentencing) Act 2000, Sch 9 and the Access to Justice Act, 1999, s 95(2).]

---

*Repealed by the Criminal Justice and Court Services Act 2000, Sch 7, Sch 8 from a date to be appointed.**

1. A magistrates' court has no power to commit a person under 21 years of age to prison (Powers of Criminal Courts (Sentencing) Act 2000, s 89 in PART III: SENTENCING, STATUTES ON SENTENCING, post), but as to persons aged 18 and under 21, see sub-s (4), post. Detention may be ordered on a fine defaulter without allowing time for payment, or holding a means inquiry, or first considering the report of a person who has exercised supervision.

2. This is not imprisonment. It should be described as "detention" in the court register.

3. Local authorities, police authorities and magistrates' courts committees are prescribed authorities and for the manner in which employees of such authorities may be authorised to execute such warrants, see the Magistrates' Courts (Civilian Fine Enforcement Officers) (No 2) Rules 1990, SI 1990/2260, in this PART, post.

Fees, fines, forfeitures, etc

1–2230 137. Fees. *Repealed.*

1–2231 138. Remission of fees. *Repealed.*

1–2232 139. Disposal of sums adjudged to be paid by conviction. A justices' chief executive shall apply moneys received by him on account of a sum adjudged to be paid by a summary conviction as follows—

(*a*) in the first place in payment of any compensation adjudged by the conviction to be paid to any person;

(*b*) in the second place in payment of any costs so adjudged to be paid to the prosecutor; and

(*c*) the balance to the fund to which, or the person to whom he is required to pay the sum by section 60 of the Justices of the Peace Act 1997 or any other enactment relating to the sum.

[Magistrates' Courts Act 1980, s 139 as amended by the Justices of the Peace Act 1997, Sch 5 and the Access to Justice Act 1999, Sch 13.]

1–2233 140. Disposal of non-pecuniary forfeitures. Subject to any enactment relating to customs or excise, anything other than money forfeited on a conviction by a magistrates' court or the forfeiture of which may be enforced by a magistrates' court shall be sold or otherwise disposed of in such manner as the court may direct; and the proceeds shall be applied as if they were a fine imposed under the enactment on which the proceedings for the forfeiture are founded.

[Magistrates' Courts Act 1980, s 140.]

Clerks to justices

1–2234 141. Clerks to justices. (1) Any reference in this Act to a clerk of any magistrates' court shall be construed as a reference to the clerk to the justices for the petty sessions area for which the court is acting, or was acting at the relevant time.

(2) Where there is more than one clerk to the justices for any petty sessions area, anything that this Act requires or authorises to be done by or to the clerk to the justices shall or may be done by or to any of the clerks or by or to such of the clerks as the magistrates' courts committee having power over the appointment of clerks to justices for that area generally or in any particular case or cases may direct.

(3) *Repealed.*

[Magistrates' Courts Act 1980, s 141 as amended by the Police and Magistrates' Courts Act 1994, Sch 9.]

Power to rectify mistakes, etc

1–2235 142. Power of magistrates' court to re-open cases to rectify mistakes etc[1]. (1) A magistrates' court may vary or rescind[2] a sentence or other order[3] imposed or made by it when dealing with an offender if it appears to the court to be in the interests of justice to do so; and it is hereby declared that this power extends to replacing a sentence or order which for any reason[4] appears to be invalid by another which the court has power to impose or make.

(1A) The power conferred on a magistrates' court by subsection (1) above shall not be exercisable in relation to any sentence or order imposed or made by it when dealing with an offender if—

(*a*) the Crown Court has determined an appeal against—

   (i)   that sentence or order;
   (ii) the conviction in respect of which that sentence or order was imposed or made; or
   (iii) any other sentence or order imposed or made by the magistrates' court when dealing with the offender in respect of that conviction (including a sentence or order replaced by that sentence or order); or

(*b*) the High Court has determined a case stated for the opinion of that court on any question arising in any proceeding leading to or resulting from the imposition or making of the sentence or order.

(2) Where a person is convicted[5] by a magistrates' court and it subsequently appears to the court that it would be in the interests of justice[6] that the case should be heard again by different justices, the court may so direct.

(2A) The power conferred on a magistrates' court by subsection (2) above shall not be exercisable in relation to a conviction if—

(*a*) the Crown Court has determined an appeal against—

   (i)   the conviction; or
   (ii) any sentence or order imposed or made by the magistrates' court when dealing with the offender in respect of the conviction; or

(*b*) the High Court has determined a case stated for the opinion of that court on any question arising in any proceeding leading to or resulting from the conviction.

(3) Where a court gives a direction under subsection (2) above—

(*a*) the conviction and any sentence or other order imposed or made in consequence thereof shall be of no effect; and

(*b*) section 10(4) above shall apply as if the trial of the person in question had been adjourned.

(4) *Repealed.*

(5) Where a sentence or order is varied under subsection (1) above, the sentence or other order, as so varied, shall take effect from the beginning of the day on which it was originally imposed or made, unless the court otherwise directs.

[Magistrates' Courts Act 1980, s 142 as amended by the Criminal Appeal Act 1995, s 26 and Sch 3.]

---

1. This section applies only to criminal proceedings, as to whether justices have jurisdiction to rectify an order made in civil proceedings, see para 1–754, ante.

2. This power extends only to cases where the defendant has been found guilty, and not where he has been acquitted (*R v Gravesend Justices, ex p Dexter* [1977] Crim LR 298). Likewise, the power does not extend to a case where the prosecution has withdrawn the charges (*Coles v East Penwith Justices* (1998) 162 JP 687). However, a court may rescind a hospital order made under s 37(3) of the Mental Health Act 1983 where although not convicted of the offence, the court is satisfied he "did the act" as for the purposes of s 142 he is to be treated as an "offender" (*R v Thames Magistrates' Court, ex p Ramadan* [1999] 1 Cr App Rep 386, 163 JP 428, [1999] Crim LR 498, DC). The wide powers conferred by s 142 include the power to review the issue of a warrant of overnight detention pursuant to s 136 of the 1980 Act for non-payment of a fine (*R v Sheffield City Justices, ex p Foster* (1999) Times, 2 November, DC). In the absence of any specific provision, an application for the variation or rescission of a sentence or order may be made by the offender or by the prosecution or the court may, of its own motion, reconsider a sentence. If the matter were raised otherwise than by the offender he should, in our opinion, be given notice of when the court proposed to consider reviewing the sentence.

3. Remittal to the adult court is legally defective in the case of an offence triable only on indictment, and such an order can be rescinded under s 142 of the Magistrates' Courts Act 1980: *R (on the application of Denny) v Acton Youth Court Justices (DPP, interested party)* [2004] EWHC 948 (Admin), [2004] 2 ALL ER 961, (2003) 168 JP 388, [2004] Crim LR 959.

4. This will not include increasing the sentence for the offence because of misconduct of the offender in the dock after sentence has been passed; any contempt should be dealt with separately; see *R v Powell* (1985) 7 Cr App Rep (S) 247. But where justices have erred in passing sentence, they may reconvene for the purpose of re-considering the sentence and thereafter increase that sentence (*Jane v Broome* (1987) Times, 2 November). However, it is important to bear in mind the principle of finality in sentencing. While it is possible that the failure of a magistrates' court to be aware of material factors at the time of sentencing is such that it is in the interests of justice for sentence to be reconsidered, it will only be in very rare circumstances that it will be appropriate to do so, particularly if the increase in sentence brings the possibility of custody (*Holmes v Liverpool City Justices* [2004] EWHC 3131 (Admin), 169 JP 306).

5. Nothing in this section operates to prevent a court acting under its common law powers to amend a plea from "guilty" to "not guilty" at any time before final adjudication: see *S (an infant) v Manchester City Recorder* [1971] AC 481, [1969] 3 All ER 1230, 134 JP 3; to hear and adjudicate upon a (summary) case wrongly committed for trial (*Bannister v Clarke* [1920] 3 KB 598, 85 JP 12); to commit for trial following an acquittal for an offence triable only on indictment (*R v West* [1964] 1 QB 15, [1962] 2 All ER 624, 126 JP 352); to re-try a case where some irregularity has vitiated the proceedings (*R v Marsham, ex p Pethick Lawrence* [1912] 2 KB 362, 76 JP 284); or, generally, to deal with a matter when the hearing or sentence was a nullity (*R v Norfolk Justices, ex p DPP* [1950] 2 KB 558, [1950] 2 All ER 42, 114 JP 312; *R v Warwick Quarter Sessions, ex p Patterson* (1971) 115 Sol Jo 484).

6. The purpose of s 142 is to rectify mistakes. It is generally to be regarded as a slip rule and the power under the section cannot be extended to cover situations beyond those akin to a mistake. Accordingly, it is wrong to employ s 142(2) as a method by which a defendant can obtain a rehearing in circumstances where he could not appeal to the Crown Court by reason of his unequivocal plea of guilty (*R v Croydon Youth Court, ex p DPP* [1997] 2 Cr App Rep 411). When exercising its discretion as to whether the interests of justice require a rehearing, the court must act on proper judicial grounds; accordingly, the late arrival at court of a defendant was held not to be a proper ground for refusing a rehearing (*R v Camberwell Green Magistrates' Court, ex p Ibrahim* (1984) 148 JP 400). While delay in making an application under s 142 is always likely to be harmful and is a factor to be taken into account, justices should not reject an application on that ground alone and must consider judicially all the relevant circumstances (*R v Ealing Magistrates' Court, ex p Sahota* (1997)

162 JP 73). However, in *R v Gwent Magistrates' Court, ex p Carey* (1996) 160 JP 613, it was held that justices were entrusted with a broad discretion and were entitled to take into account the fact that the defendant failed to appear through his own fault and that the witnesses would be inconvenienced by ordering a re-trial. The justices could also properly take into account the fact that the defendant was not being deprived of a fair trial by way of appeal in the Crown Court.

Power to alter sums specified in certain provisions

1–2236　143. Power to alter sums specified in certain provisions. (1) If it appears to the Secretary of State that there has been a change in the value of money since the relevant date, he may by order substitute for the sum or sums for the time being specified in any provision mentioned in subsection (2) below such other sum or sums as appear to him justified by the change.

(2) The said provisions are—

(*a*)　section 22(1) above;

(*aa*)　section 24(3) and (4) above;

(*b*)　the definition of "the prescribed sum" in section 32(9) above;

(*c*)　paragraph (*a*) of section 33(1) above;

(*ca*)　section 34(3)(*b*) above;

(*cb*)　section 131(1) of the Powers of Criminal Courts (Sentencing) Act 2000 (limit on compensation order of magistrates' court);

(*d*)　section 135 of that Act; (limit on fine imposed on young offender by magistrates' court);

(*da*)　section 1AB(3) of the Crime and Disorder Act 1998 (failure to comply with individual support order);

(*dd*)　section 59B(3) above;

(*e*)　the Table in paragraph 1 of Schedule 4 to this Act.

(*f*)　any provision mentioned in Schedule 6A to this Act;

(*g*)　paragraph 11(2) of Schedule 5A to the Army Act 1955 and to the Air Force Act 1955 (compensation orders);

(*h*)　paragraph 14(1) of that Schedule and paragraph 14(1) of Schedule 4A to the Naval Discipline Act 1957 (recognizance from parents and guardians);

(*i*)　*Repealed*;

(*j*)　the Table in section 139(4) of the Powers of Criminal Courts (Sentencing) Act 2000;

(*k*)　section 8(1)(*b*) of the Armed Forces Act 1976 (maximum fine awarded by Standing Civilian Courts);

(*l*)–(*n*)　*Repealed*;

(*o*)　section 37(2) of the Criminal Justice Act 1982;

(*p*)　section 150(2) and (3) of the Powers of Criminal Courts (Sentencing) Act 2000 (recognisance from parents or guardians);

(*q*)　column 5 or 6 of Schedule 4 to the Misuse of Drugs Act 1971 so far as the column in question relates to the offences under provisions of that Act specified in column 1 of that Schedule in respect of which the maximum fines were increased by Part II of Schedule 8 to the Criminal Justice and Public Order Act 1994.

(3) In subsection (1) above "the relevant date" means—

(*a*)　the date of the coming into force of section 17 of the Criminal Justice Act 1991 (increase of certain maxima); or

(*b*)　where the sums specified in a provision mentioned in subsection (2) above have been substituted by an order under subsection (1) above, the date of that order.

(4), (5)　*Repealed.*

(6) An order under subsection (1) above—

(*a*)　shall be made by statutory instrument subject to annulment in pursuance of a resolution of either House of Parliament and may be revoked by a subsequent order thereunder; and

(*b*)　shall not affect the punishment for an offence committed before that order comes into force.

[Magistrates' Courts Act 1980, s 143 as amended by the Criminal Justice Act 1982, s 48, the Cinemas Act 1985, Sch 2, the Criminal Justice Act 1988, Sch 16, the Children Act 1989, Sch 15, the Criminal Justice Act 1991, Sch 11, the Maintenance Enforcement Act 1991, Sch 2, the Criminal Justice and Public Order Act 1994, s 157, the Powers of Criminal Courts (Sentencing) Act 2000, Sch 9 and the Criminal Justice Act 2003, s 323.]

Rules

1–2237　144. Rule committee and rules of procedure[1]*. (A1) The Lord Chancellor may appoint a rule committee for magistrates' courts.

(1) The Lord Chief Justice may on the advice of or after consultation with the rule committee, and with the concurrence of the Lord Chancellor, make rules for regulating and prescribing, except in relation to—

(*a*)　any criminal cause or matter, or

(*b*)　family proceedings,

the procedure and practice to be followed in magistrates' courts and by justices' clerks and and designated officers for magistrates' courts

(1A) If the Lord Chancellor does not agree rules made by the Lord Chief Justice, the Lord Chancellor must give the Lord Chief Justice and the rules committee written reasons for doing so.

(2) The rule committee shall consist of the Lord Chief Justice, the President of the Family Division

of the High Court, the Senior District Judge (Chief Magistrate) and such number of other persons appointed by the Lord Chancellor as he may, after consulting the Lord Chief Justice, determine.

(3) Among the members of the committee appointed by the Lord Chancellor there shall be at least—*

(za) one District Judge (Magistrates' Courts);
(a) one justices' clerk;
(b) one person who has a Supreme Court** qualification (within the meaning of section 71 of the Courts and Legal Services Act 1990); and
(c) one person who has been granted by an authorised body, under Part II of that Act, the right to conduct litigation in relation to all proceedings in the Supreme Court**.

(4) The power to make rules conferred by this section shall be exercisable by statutory instrument which shall be subject to annulment by resolution of either House of Parliament.

(4A) The Lord Chief Justice may nominate a judicial office holder (as defined in section 109(4) of the Constitutional Reform Act 2005) to exercise his functions under this section.

(5) *Repealed.*

[Magistrates' Courts Act 1980, s 144 as amended by the Courts and Legal Services Act 1990, Sch 18, the Access to Justice Act 1999, Schs 11 and 13,the Courts Act 2003, Sch 8 and the Constitutional Reform Act 2005, Sch 4.]

*Words in sub-ss (2) repealed by the Courts Act 2003, Sch 8 from a date to be appointed.
**Amended by the Constitutional Reform Act 2005, Sch 4 from a date to be appointed.
1. This provision applies only to the power to make rules in respect of civil proceedings; provision for the Criminal Procedure Rules and Family Procedure Rules is made by the Courts Act 2003, ss 69 and 75, in this PART, post.

1–2237A   144A. Rules to be made if required by Lord Chancellor.   (1) This section applies if the Lord Chancellor gives the Lord Chief Justice written notice that he thinks it is expedient for rules made under section 144 to include provision that would achieve a purpose specified in the notice.

(2) The Lord Chief Justice must make such rules as he considers necessary to achieve the specified purpose.

(3) Those rules must be—

(a) made within a reasonable period after the Lord Chancellor gives notice to the Lord Chief Justice;
(b) made in accordance with section 144.

(4) The Lord Chief Justice may nominate a judicial office holder (as defined in section 109(4) of the Constitutional Reform Act 2005) to exercise his functions under this section.

[Magistrates' Courts Act 1980, s 144A as inserted by the Constitutional Reform Act 2005, Sch 4.]

1–2238   145. Rules: supplementary provisions.   (1) The power to make rules conferred by section 144 above shall, without prejudice to the generality of subsection (1) of that section, include power to make provision—

(a) as to the practice and procedure of justices in exercising functions preliminary or incidental to proceedings before a magistrates' court;
(aa) *Repealed;*
(b) as to the service and execution of process issued by or for the purposes of a magistrates' court, including the service and execution in England and Wales of process issued in other parts of the United Kingdom;
(c) as to the keeping of records of proceedings before magistrates' courts and the manner in which things done in the course of, or as preliminary or incidental to, any such proceedings, or any proceedings on appeal from a magistrates' court to the Crown Court, may be proved in any legal proceedings;
(d) *Repealed;*
(e) *Repealed;*
(f) *Repealed;*
(g) as to what magistrates' court shall have jurisdiction to hear any complaint;
(h) as to the matters additional to those specified in section 53 above on complaint for which a magistrates' court shall have power to make an order with the consent of the defendant without hearing evidence;
(i) *Repealed.*

(2) Where any Act expressly confers jurisdiction on any magistrates' court to hear a complaint, rules made under subsection (1)(g) above shall not take away that jurisdiction, but may extend it to any other magistrates' court.

(3) Any Act passed before 16th December 1949[1], in so far as that Act relates to matters about which rules may be made under section 144 above, shall have effect subject to any rules so made and may be amended or repealed by the rules accordingly; but nothing in the said section shall authorise the rules to reduce the number of justices required for any purpose by any Act.

(4) *Repealed.*

(5) Any rules, directions, forms or other instrument having effect immediately before this subsection comes into force as if contained in rules made under section 15 of the Justices of the Peace Act 1949 by virtue of section 15(8) of that Act (rules etc which previously had effect under the

enactments repealed by Part II of Schedule 7 to that Act) shall have effect as if contained in rules made under section 144 above.

[Magistrates' Courts Act 1980, s 145 as amended by the Courts and Legal Services Act 1990, Sch 18, the Police and Magistrates' Courts Act 1994, Schs 8 and 9, the Criminal Procedure and Investigations Act 1996, s 65 and Sch 5 and the Courts Act 2003, Sch 8.]

---

1. Certain Acts passed after this date contain provisions whereby they are deemed to have been passed before this date.

**1–2239	145A. Rules: costs order against legal representative.**	(1) In any civil proceedings, a magistrates' court may disallow or (as the case may be) order the legal or other representative concerned to meet the whole of any wasted costs or such part of them as may be determined in accordance with rules[1].

(2) In subsection (1), "wasted costs" means any costs incurred by a party—

(*a*)	as a result of any improper, unreasonable or negligent act or omission on the part of any legal or other representative or any employee of such a representative; or

(*b*)	which, in the light of any such act or omission occurring after they were incurred, the court considers it is unreasonable to expect that party to pay.

(3) In this section "legal or other representative", in relation to any proceedings, means any person who is exercising a right of audience, or a right to conduct litigation, on behalf of any party to the proceedings.

(4) Rules[1] made by virtue of this section may, in particular, make provision as to the destination of any payment required to be made under the rules (including provision for the reimbursement of sums paid by the Legal Services Commission).

(5) Rules[1] made by virtue of this section—

(*a*)	shall require a magistrates' court which proposes to act under the rules against a legal or other representative to allow him a reasonable opportunity to appear before it and show cause why it should not do so,

(*b*)	shall provide that action may be taken under the rules either on the application of any party to the proceedings or on the motion of the court;

(*c*)	shall provide that no such action shall be taken after the end of the period of six months beginning with the date on which the proceedings are disposed of by the court; and

(*d*)	shall provide that a legal or other representative against whom action is taken under the rules may appeal to the Crown Court.

[Magistrates' Courts Act 1980, s 145A, as inserted by the Courts and Legal Services Act 1990, s 112 and the Access to Justice Act 1999, Sch 4.]

---

1. See the Magistrates' Courts (Costs Against Legal Representatives in Civil Proceedings) Rules 1991, post.

Rules about youth courts

**1–2240	146. Rules relating to youth court panels and composition of youth courts.**	*Repealed.*

Occasional court-houses

**1–2241	147. Occasional court-house.**	*Repealed.*

Interpretation

**1–2242	148. "Magistrates' court".**	(1) In this Act the expression "magistrates' court"[1] means any justice or justices of the peace acting under any enactment or by virtue of his or their commission or under the common law.

(2) Except where the contrary is expressed, anything authorised or required by this Act to be done by, to or before the magistrates' court by, to or before which any other thing was done, or is to be done, may be done by, to or before any magistrates' court acting for the same petty sessions area as that court.

[Magistrates' Courts Act 1980, s 148.]

---

1. The expression includes justices sitting as licensing justices (*Jeffrey v Evans* [1964] 1 All ER 536, [1964] 1 WLR 505, 128 JP 252; approved *R v East Riding Quarter Sessions, ex p Newton* [1968] 1 QB 43, [1967] 3 All ER 118).

**1–2243	149. Isles of Scilly.**	*Repealed.*

**1–2244	150. Interpretation of other terms.**	(1) In this Act, unless the context otherwise requires, the following expressions have the meaning hereby assigned to them, that is to say—

"Act" includes local Act;

"bail in criminal proceedings" has the same meaning as in the Bail Act 1976;

"collection order" means an order made under Part 4 of Schedule 5 to the Courts Act 2003;

"commit to custody" means commit to prison or, where any enactment authorises or requires committal to some other place of detention instead of committal to prison, to that other place;

"committal proceedings" mean proceedings before a magistrates' court acting as examining justices;*

"family proceedings" has the meaning assigned to it by section 65 above;

"enactment" includes an enactment contained in a local Act or in any order, regulation or other instrument having effect by virtue of an Act;

"fine", except for the purposes of any enactment imposing a limit on the amount of any fine, includes any pecuniary penalty or pecuniary forfeiture or pecuniary compensation[1] payable under a conviction;

"the fines officer", in relation to a person subject to a collection order, means any fines officer working at the fines office specified in that order;

"impose imprisonment" means pass a sentence of imprisonment or fix a term of imprisonment for failure to pay any sum of money, or for want of sufficient distress to satisfy any sum of money, or for failure to do or abstain from doing anything required to be done or left undone;

"legal representative" means an authorised advocate or authorised litigator, as defined by section 119(1) of the Courts and Legal Services Act 1990;

"magistrates' court maintenance order" means a maintenance order enforceable by a magistrates' court;

"maintenance order" means any order specified in Schedule 8 to the Administration of Justice Act 1970 and includes such an order which has been discharged, if any arrears are recoverable thereunder;

"prescribed" means prescribed by rules of court[2];**

"sentence" does not include a committal in default of payment of any sum of money, or for want of sufficient distress to satisfy any sum of money, or for failure to do or abstain from doing anything required to be done or left undone;

"sum enforceable as a civil debt" means—

(a) any sum recoverable summarily as a civil debt which is adjudged to be paid by the order of a magistrates' court;

(b) any other sum expressed by this or any other Act to be so enforceable;

"transfer of fine order" has the meaning assigned to it by section 89 above.

(2) Except where the contrary is expressed or implied, anything required or authorised by this Act to be done by justices may, where two or more justices are present, be done by one of them on behalf of the others.

(3) Any reference in this Act to a sum adjudged to be paid by a conviction or order of a magistrates' court shall be construed as including a reference to any costs, damages or compensation adjudged to be paid by the conviction or order of which the amount is ascertained by the conviction or order; but this subsection does not prejudice the definition of "sum adjudged to be paid by a conviction" contained in subsection (8) of section 81 above for the purposes of that section.

(4) Where the age of any person at any time is material for the purposes of any provision of this Act regulating the powers of a magistrates' court, his age at the material time shall be deemed to be or to have been that which appears to the court after considering any available evidence to be or to have been his age at that time[3].

(5) Except where the context otherwise requires, any reference in this Act to an offence shall be construed as including a reference to an alleged offence; and any reference in this Act to an offence committed, completed or begun anywhere shall be construed as including a reference to an offence alleged to have been committed, completed or begun there.

(6) References in this Act to an offence punishable with imprisonment or punishable on summary conviction with imprisonment shall be construed without regard to any prohibition or restriction imposed by or under this or any other Act on imprisonment of young offenders.

(7) The provisions of this Act authorising a magistrates' court on conviction of an offender to pass a sentence or make an order instead of dealing with him in any other way shall not be construed as taking away any power to order him to pay costs, damages or compensation.

[Magistrates' Courts Act 1980, s 150 as amended by the Local Government Act 1985, s 12, the Family Law Reform Act 1987, Schs 2 and 4, the Children Act 1989, Sch 11, the Courts and Legal Services Act 1990, Sch 18, the Local Government (Wales) Act 1994, Sch 2, SI 1996/674 and 675, the Justices of the Peace Act 1997, Sch 5, the Access to Justice Act 1999, Schs 10, 11 and 15,the Courts Act 2003, Sch 8 and SI 2006/1737.]

---

*Repealed by the Criminal Justice Act 2003, Sch 3 from a day to be appointed.
**Definition "public prosecutor" inserted by the Criminal Justice Act 2003, Sch 36 from a date to be appointed.
1. Arrears expressed to be recoverable as a penalty are not a penalty for the purposes of this definition and thus may not be mitigated under s 34, ante (*Leach v Lichfield* [1960] 3 All ER 739, [1960] 1 WLR 1392, 125 JP 115). This definition does not apply for the purposes of remission under s 85, ante.
2. Rules were formerly made under s 15 of the Justice of the Peace Act 1949.
3. A person attains a particular age at the commencement of the relevant anniversary of the date of his birth; s 9 of the Family Law Reform Act 1969, post.

Miscellaneous

1–2245 151. Application of Act to distress for rates. (1) Justices may state a case under this Act when called upon to issue a warrant of distress for any rate other than a rate within the meaning of the General Rate Act 1967[1].

(2) Sections 79(2) and 100[2] above shall apply to proceedings for the non-payment of any rate to which subsection (1) above applies as they apply to proceedings for the non-payment of a sum adjudged to be paid by a magistrates' court.

(3) Except as provided in the preceding provisions of this section, the power of justices to issue a warrant of distress for a rate, the form and execution of such a warrant and the committal of persons for want of sufficient distress to satisfy a rate shall not be subject to the provisions of this Act.
[Magistrates' Courts Act 1980, s 151.]

---

1. The General Rate Act 1967 has been repealed with effect from 31 March 1990; community charges and non-domestic rates were thereafter governed by the Local Government Finance Act 1988 and then council tax by the Local Government Finance Act 1992, post, in PART VIII: title LOCAL GOVERNMENT.

2. These sections refer respectively to reduction of detention on part payment, and admissibility of a statement of wages.

1–2246   152. Saving for youth courts.   The provisions of this Act relating to the constitution, place of sitting and procedure of magistrates' courts shall, in their application to youth courts, have effect subject to any provision contained in rules of court or any enactment regulating the constitution, place of sitting or procedure of youth courts.
[Magistrates' Courts Act 1980, s 152 as amended by the Criminal Justice Act 1991, s 70 and the Courts Act 2003, Sch 8.]

1–2247   153. Magistrates' court may sit on Sundays and public holidays.   *Repealed.*

Repeals, short title etc

1–2248   154. Consequential amendments, transitional provisions, repeals, etc.   (4) Nothing in this Act shall be taken as prejudicing the operation of sections 16 and 17 of the Interpretation Act 1978 (which relate to the effect of repeals).

1–2249   155. Short title, extent and commencement.   (1) This Act may be cited as the Magistrates' Courts Act 1980.

(2) The following provisions of this Act extend to Scotland—

(a) sections 8 (except subsection (9)), 12(13), 83(3), 90 and 91 and this section; and
(b) section 154 and Schedules 7, 8 and 9 so far as they relate to any enactment extending to Scotland.

(3) The following provisions of this Act extend to Northern Ireland—

(a) sections 83(3), 90 and 91 and this section; and
(b) section 154 and Schedules 7, 8 and 9 so far as they relate to an enactment extending to Northern Ireland.

(4) The provisions of section 126 above have the same extent as the sections of the Indictable Offences Act 1848 to which they refer.

(5) *Repealed.*

(6) Except as stated in subsections (2) to (5) above, and except so far as relates to the interpretation or commencement of the provisions mentioned in those subsections, this Act extends to England and Wales only.

(7) This Act shall come into force on such date as the Secretary of State may appoint by order made by statutory instrument.
[Magistrates' Courts Act 1980, s 155 amended by the Statute Law (Repeals) Act 1993, Sch 1 and the Criminal Justice and Public Order Act 1994, Sch 5.]

Section 17   SCHEDULE 1
OFFENCES TRIABLE EITHER WAY BY VIRTUE OF SECTION 17

(*Amended by the Criminal Attempts Act 1981, Sch, the Housing (Consequential Provisions) Act 1985, Sch 1, the Wages Act 1986, Sch 5, the Criminal Justice Act 1988, Sch 16, the Electricity Act 1989, Sch 18 and the Statute Law (Repeals) Act 1989, Sch 1, the Criminal Justice Act 2003, s 320 and the Sexual Offences Act 2003, Sch 7*)

1–2250   1. Offences at common law of public nuisance.
     1A. An offence at common law of outraging public decency.
     2. Offences under section 8 of the Disorderly Houses Act 1751 (appearing to be keeper of bawdy house etc).
     3. Offences consisting in contravention of section 13 of the Statutory Declarations Act 1835 (administration by a person of an oath etc touching matters in which he has no jurisdiction).
     4. Offences under section 36 of the Malicious Damage Act 1861 (obstructing engines or carriages on railways).
     5. Offences under the following provisions of the Offences against the Person Act 1861—

(a) section 16 (threats to kill);
(b) section 20 (inflicting bodily injury, with or without a weapon);
(c) section 26 (not providing apprentices or servants with food etc);
(d) section 27 (abandoning or exposing child);
(e) section 34 (doing or omitting to do anything so as to endanger railway passengers);
(f) section 36 (assaulting a clergyman at a place of worship etc);
(g) section 38 (assault with intent to resist apprehension);
(h) section 47 (assault occasioning bodily harm);
(i) section 57 (bigamy);
(j) section 60 (concealing the birth of a child).

     6. Offences under section 20 of the Telegraph Act 1868 (disclosing or intercepting messages).
     7. Offences under section 13 of the Debtors Act 1869 (transactions intended to defraud creditors).

8. Offences under section 5 of the Public Stores Act 1875 (obliteration of marks with intent to conceal).

9. Offences under section 12 of the Corn Returns Act 1882 (false returns).

10. *Repealed*[1].

11. Offences under section 3 of the Submarine Telegraph Act 1885 (damaging submarine cables).

12. Offences under section 13 of the Stamp Duties Management Act 1891 (offences in relation to dies and stamps).

13. Offences under section 8(2) of the Cremation Act 1902 (making false representations etc with a view to procuring the burning of any human remains).

14. All offences under the Perjury Act 1911 except offences under—

(*a*)   section 1 (perjury in judicial proceedings);
(*b*)   section 3 (false statements etc with reference to marriage);
(*c*)   section 4 (false statements etc as to births or deaths).

15. *Repealed.*

16. Offences under section 17 of the Deeds of Arrangement Act 1914 (trustee making preferential payments).

17. *Repealed.*

18[2]**.** Offences under section 8(2) of the Census Act 1920 (disclosing census information).

19. Offences under section 36 of the Criminal Justice Act 1925 (forgery of passports etc).

20. Offences under section 11 of the Agricultural Credits Act 1928 (frauds by farmers).

21. *Repealed.*

22. *Repealed.*

23. *Repealed.*

24. *Repealed.*

25. *Repealed*[3].

26. The following offences under the Criminal Law Act 1967—

(*a*)   offences under section 4(1) (assisting offenders); and
(*b*)   offences under section 5(1) (concealing arrestable offences and giving false information),

where the offence to which they relate is triable either way.

27. *Repealed.*

28. All indictable offences[4] under the Theft Act 1968 except—

(*a*)   robbery, aggravated burglary, blackmail and assault with intent to rob;
(*b*)   burglary comprising the commission of, or an intention to commit, an offence which is triable only on indictment;
(*c*)   burglary in a dwelling if any person in the dwelling was subjected to violence or the threat of violence[5].

29. Offences under the following provisions of the Criminal Damage Act 1971—

section 1(1) (destroying or damaging property);
section 1(1) and (3) (arson);
section 2 (threats to destroy or damage property);
section 3 (possession anything with intent to destroy or damage property).

30. Offences in relation to stamps issued for the purpose of national insurance under the provisions of any enactments as applied to those stamps.

31. *Repealed.*

32. *Repealed.*

33. Aiding, abetting, counselling or procuring the commission of any offence listed in the preceding paragraphs of this Schedule except paragraph 26.

34. *Repealed.*

35. Any offence consisting in the incitement to commit an offence triable either way except an offence mentioned in paragraph 33.

---

1. Repealed by the Electricity Act 1989, Sch 18.

2. As a result of amendments made by the Census (Confidentiality) Act 1991, s 1, s 8(2) of the Census Act 1920 has been replaced by new provisions which create an offence which is triable either way, thereby rendering obsolete para 18 of this Schedule.

3. Repealed by the Housing (Consequential Provisions) Act 1985, Sch 1.

4. Including the offence of aggravated vehicle-taking under s 12A of the Theft Act 1968 (Aggravated Vehicle-Taking Act 1992, s 1(2)). Certain offences of domestic burglary within the meaning of s 111 of the Powers of Criminal Courts (Sentencing) Act 2000 will not be triable either way and triable only on indictment if the accused has on two previous occasions been convicted of a domestic burglary; see the Powers of Criminal Courts (Sentencing) Act 2000, s 111 in PART III: SENTENCING, post.

5. This includes where violence is offered in the course of the whole incident alleged to constitute the dwelling house burglary e.g. where the violence is offered in the course of the householder's attempts to prevent the defendant from leaving the premises. Matters of scale or degree of violence or discretion are irrelevant for the purpose of this provision (*R v McGrath* [2003] EWCA Crim 2062, [2004] 1 Cr App R 15, 167 JP 554, [2004] Crim LR 142).

1–2251   Section 22

SCHEDULE 2

OFFENCES FOR WHICH THE VALUE INVOLVED IS RELEVANT TO THE MODE OF TRIAL

Offence	Value involved	How measured

1. Offences under section 1 of the Criminal Damage Act 1971 (destroying or damaging property'), excluding any offence committed by destroying or damaging property by fire.	As regards property alleged to have been destroyed, its value.
	
	As regards property alleged to have been damaged, the value of the alleged damage.
		What the property would probably have cost to buy in the open market at the material time.
		
		(a) If immediately after the material time the damage was capable of repair—
		  (i) what would probably then have been the market price for the repair of the damage, or
		  (ii) what the property alleged to have been damaged would probably have cost to buy in the open market at the material time,
		
		  whichever is the less; or
		
		(b) if immediately after the material time the damage was beyond repair, what the said property would probably have cost to buy in the open market at the material time.

2. The following offences, namely— (a) aiding, abetting, counselling or procuring the commission of any offence mentioned in paragraph 1 above; (b) attempting to commit any offence so mentioned; and (c) inciting another to commit any offence so mentioned.	The value indicated in paragraph 1 above for the offence alleged to have been aided, abetted, counselled or procured, or attempted or incited.	As for the corresponding entry in paragraph 1 above.

3. Offences under section 12A of the Theft Act 1968 (aggravated vehicle-taking) where no allegation is made under subsection (1)(b) other than of damage, whether to the vehicle or other property or both.	The total value of the damage alleged to have been caused.	(1) In the case of damage to any property other than the vehicle involved in the offence, as for the corresponding entry in paragraph 1 above, substituting a reference to the time of the accident concerned for any reference to the material time.
		
		(2) In the case of damage to the vehicle involved in the offence—
		(a) if immediately after the vehicle was recovered the damage was capable of repair—
		  (i) what would probably then have been the market price for the repair of the damage, or
		  (ii) what the vehicle would probably have cost to buy in the open market immediately before it was unlawfully taken, whichever is the less; or
		(b) if immediately after the vehicle was recovered the damage was beyond repair, what the vehicle would probably have cost to buy in the open market immediately before it was unlawfully taken.

1   Although the Schedule makes no distinction between offences under s 1 of the Criminal Damage Act 1971, *simpliciter* and offences under sub-ss (2) and (3), the provision is to be treated as only applying to simple criminal damage charged under sub-s (1) (*R v Burt* (1996) 161 JP 77).

Section 46

SCHEDULE 3
CORPORATIONS

(As amended by the Criminal Justice Act 1991, s 25 and the Criminal Procedure and Investigations Act 1996, Sch 1.)

1–2260 **1.** (1) A magistrates' court may commit a corporation for trial by an order in writing[1] empowering the prosecutor to prefer a bill of indictment in respect of the offence named in the order.

(2) An order under this paragraph shall not prohibit the inclusion in the bill of indictment of counts that under section 2 of the Administration of Justice (Miscellaneous Provisions) Act 1933 may be included in the bill in substitution for, or in addition to, counts charging the offence named in the order.

2. A representative[2] may on behalf of a corporation—

(a) make before examining justices such representations as could be made by an accused who is not a corporation;

(b) consent to the corporation being tried summarily;

(c) enter a plea of guilty or not guilty on the trial by a magistrates' court of an information.

3. (1) Where a representative appears, any requirement of this Act that anything shall be done in the presence of the accused, or shall be read or said to the accused, shall be construed as a requirement that that thing shall be done in the presence of the representative or read or said to the representative.

(2) Where a representative does not appear, any such requirement, and any requirement that the consent of the accused shall be obtained for summary trial, shall not apply.

4. (1) Notification or intimation for the purposes of subsections (2) and (3) of section 12 above may be given on behalf of a corporation by a director or the secretary of the corporation; and those subsections shall apply in relation to a notification or intimation purporting to be so given as they apply to a notification or intimation purporting to be given by an individual accused.

(2) In this paragraph "director", in relation to a corporation which is established by or under any enactment for the purpose of carrying on under national ownership any industry or part of an industry or undertaking and whose affairs are managed by the members thereof, means a member of that corporation.

5. *Repealed.*

6. Subject to the preceding provisions of this Schedule, the provisions of this Act relating to the inquiry into, and trial of, indictable offences shall apply to a corporation as they apply to an adult.

7. Where a corporation and an individual who has attained the age of 17 are jointly charged before a magistrates' court with an offence triable either way, the court shall not try either of the accused summarily unless each of them consents to be so tried.

8. Subsection (6) of section 33 of the Criminal Justice Act 1925 shall apply to a representative for the purposes of this Schedule as it applies to a representative for the purposes of that section.

---

1. This provision requiring the certificate of committal of a corporation to be in Form 19 is directory not mandatory (*R v Nelson Group Services (Maintenance) Ltd* [1998] 4 All ER 331, [1999] 1 WLR 1526, CA). For form of order, see Form 19 in PART IX: PRECEDENTS AND FORMS, post.

2. A corporation appearing by solicitor may not be subject to these restrictions, but it is advisable for the solicitor to be appointed the corporation's representative (cf *R v Birmingham and Gloucester Rly Co, Re LCC and London Tramways Co, R v Manchester Corpn and R v Ascanio Puck & Co and Paice* (1912) 76 JP 487).

Section 76

SCHEDULE 4
MAXIMUM PERIODS OF IMPRISONMENT IN DEFAULT OF PAYMENT

(As amended by the Criminal Justice Act 1982, Sch 14, SI 1984/447, the Criminal Justice Act 1988, s 60 and the Criminal Justice Act 1991, s 23 and Sch 11.)

1–2261 **1.** Subject to the following provisions of this Schedule, the periods set out in the second column of the following Table shall be the maximum periods[1] applicable respectively to the amounts set out opposite thereto, being amounts due at the time the imprisonment or detention is imposed.

TABLE[2]

AN AMOUNT NOT EXCEEDING £200	7 DAYS
AN AMOUNT EXCEEDING £200 BUT NOT EXCEEDING £500	14 DAYS
AN AMOUNT EXCEEDING £500 BUT NOT EXCEEDING £1,000	28 DAYS
AN AMOUNT EXCEEDING £1,000 BUT NOT EXCEEDING £2,500	45 DAYS
AN AMOUNT EXCEEDING £2,500 BUT NOT EXCEEDING £5,000	3 MONTHS
AN AMOUNT EXCEEDING £5,000 BUT NOT EXCEEDING £10,000	6 MONTHS
AN AMOUNT EXCEEDING £10,000	12 MONTHS

2. (1) Where the amount due at the time imprisonment or detention is imposed is so much of a sum adjudged to be paid by a summary conviction as remains due after part payment, then, subject to sub-paragraph (2) below, the maximum period[3] applicable to the amount shall be the period applicable to the whole sum reduced by such number of days as bears to the total number of days therein the same proportion as the part paid bears to the whole sum.

(2) In calculating the reduction required under sub-paragraph (1) above any fraction of a day shall be left out of account and the maximum period shall not be reduced to less than seven days.

3. The maximum period applicable to a sum of any amount enforceable as a civil debt shall be 6 weeks.

---

1. If the aggregate of terms of imprisonment imposed consecutively for several sums due exceeds the statutory maximum for the total sum outstanding, a separate warrant in respect of each committal must be issued (*R v Midhurst Justices, ex p Seymour* (1983) 147 JP 266).

2. This table applies to sums enforceable by a magistrates' court by imprisonment, except the non-payment of a rate (see s 151(3), ante), subject to the rule that the maximum period applicable to a sum enforceable as a civil debt (see para 3, infra) or arrears under a magistrates' court maintenance order (see s 93, ante) is six weeks.

3. For example, where a person is ordered to pay £400 he may be ordered in default of payment to undergo

imprisonment for 14 days, but where he has paid instalments amounting to, say, £160 and makes default in payment of £240 only, the imprisonment to be imposed should not be 14 days, but a proportion corresponding to the unpaid balance, namely, 9 days; but the period shall not be reduced to less than 7 days. Note the difference between this calculation and that under s 79(2) and (3), ante (reduction of imprisonment ordered after part payment).

Section 125BA　　　　　　　　　　SCHEDULE 4A
POWERS OF AUTHORISED OFFICERS EXECUTING WARRANTS

(As inserted by the Domestic Violence, Crime and Victims Act 2004, Sch 4.)

Meaning of "authorised officer" etc

1–2261A　1. In this Schedule—

"authorised officer", in relation to a warrant, means a person who is entitled to execute the warrant by virtue of—

(*a*)　section 125A of this Act (civilian enforcement officers); or
(*b*)　section 125B of this Act (approved enforcement agencies);

"premises" includes any place and, in particular, includes—

(*a*)　any vehicle, vessel, aircraft or hovercraft;
(*b*)　any offshore installation within the meaning of the Mineral Workings (Offshore Installations) Act 1971; and
(*c*)　any tent or movable structure.

Entry to execute warrant of arrest etc

2. (1)　An authorised officer may enter and search any premises for the purpose of executing a warrant of arrest, commitment or detention issued in proceedings for or in connection with any criminal offence.

(2)　The power may be exercised—

(*a*)　only to the extent that it is reasonably required for that purpose; and
(*b*)　only if the officer has reasonable grounds for believing that the person whom he is seeking is on the premises.

(3)　In relation to premises consisting of two or more separate dwellings, the power is limited to entering and searching—

(*a*)　any parts of the premises which the occupiers of any dwelling comprised in the premises use in common with the occupiers of any other such dwelling; and
(*b*)　any such dwelling in which the officer has reasonable grounds for believing that the person whom he is seeking may be.

Entry to levy distress

3. (1)　An authorised officer may enter and search any premises for the purpose of executing a warrant of distress issued under section 76 of this Act for default in paying a sum adjudged to be paid by a conviction.

(2)　The power may be exercised only to the extent that it is reasonably required for that purpose.

Searching arrested persons

4. (1)　This paragraph applies where a person is arrested in pursuance of a warrant of arrest, commitment or detention issued in proceedings for or in connection with any criminal offence.

(2)　An authorised officer may search the arrested person, if he has reasonable grounds for believing that the arrested person may present a danger to himself or others.

(3)　An authorised officer may also search the arrested person for anything which he might use to assist him to escape from lawful custody.

(4)　The power conferred by sub-paragraph (3) above may be exercised—

(*a*)　only if the officer has reasonable grounds for believing that the arrested person may have concealed on him anything of a kind mentioned in that sub-paragraph; and
(*b*)　only to the extent that it is reasonably required for the purpose of discovering any such thing.

(5)　The powers conferred by this paragraph to search a person are not to be read as authorising the officer to require a person to remove any of his clothing in public other than an outer coat, a jacket or gloves; but they do authorise the search of a person's mouth.

(6)　An officer searching a person under sub-paragraph (2) above may seize and retain anything he finds, if the officer has reasonable grounds for believing that the person searched might use it to cause physical injury to himself or to any other person.

(7)　An officer searching a person under sub-paragraph (3) above may seize and retain anything he finds, if he has reasonable grounds for believing that the person might use it to assist him to escape from lawful custody.

Use of force

5. An authorised officer may use reasonable force, if necessary, in the exercise of a power conferred on him by this Schedule.

Section 130　　　　　　　　　　SCHEDULE 5
TRANSFER OF REMAND HEARINGS

(As amended by the Criminal Justice Act 1982, Sch 9.)

1–2262　1. A court which, on adjourning a case, makes an order under section 130(1) of this Act is not required at that time to fix the time and place at which the case is to be resumed but shall do so as soon as practicable after the order ceases to be in force.

2. Where an order under subsection (1) of section 130 of this Act is made in the course of proceedings which, for the purposes of section 8 of this Act, are committal proceedings, proceedings relating to the accused before the alternate court are also committal proceedings for those purposes.

3. A court making an order under subsection (1) of section 130 of this Act or remanding the accused under subsection (4) shall at once notify the terms of the order or remand to the court before which the accused is to be brought for the hearing on any application for a subsequent remand or, as the case may be, before which any such application is to be made without his being brought before it.

4. A person to whom an order under section 130(1) of this Act applies shall, if released on bail, be bailed to appear before the court which made the order.

5. Section 130 of this Act and this Schedule have effect notwithstanding anything in sections 5, 10 or 18(4) of this Act.

1–2266

SCHEDULE 6A[1]

FINES THAT MAY BE ALTERED UNDER SECTION 143

(As substituted by the Criminal Justice Act 1991, Sch 4 and as amended by the Powers of Criminal Courts (Sentencing) Act 2000, Sch 9 and Sch 12.)

Enactment	Maximum fine
ATTACHMENT OF EARNINGS ACT 1971(c.32)	
Section 23(3) (judge's fine)	£250
MAGISTRATES' COURTS ACT 1980 (c.43)	
Section 63(3)(*a*) (disobedience of orders other than payment of money)	£5,000
Section 97(4) (refusal to give evidence etc.)	£2,500
CONTEMPT OF COURT ACT 1981(c.49)	
Section 12(2) (contempt in face of magistrates' court)	£2,500
Section 14(2) (contempt in an inferior court)	£2,500
COUNTY COURTS ACT 1984 (c.28)	
Section 55(2) (neglect or refusal to give evidence)	£1,000
Section 118(1) (contempt in face of court)	£2,500
CORONERS ACT 1988 (c.13)	
Sections 10(1) and (2) and 21(5) (refusal to give evidence etc.)	£1,000
POWERS OF CRIMINAL COURTS (SENTENCING) ACT 2000 (c 6)	
Section 123(3) (failure to comply with suspended sentence supervision order)	£1,000*
In Schedule 3, paragraphs 4(1) and 5(1) (failure to comply with certain community orders)	£1,000**
In Schedule 5, paragraph 2(1) (failure to comply with attendance centre order or attendance centre rules)	£1,000
In Schedule 7, paragraph 2(2) (failure to comply with supervision order)	£1,000*

*Repealed by the Criminal Justice Act 2003, Sch 37, from a date to be appointed.
**Repealed by the Criminal Justice and Court Services Act 2000, Sch 7, Sch 8 from a date to be appointed.

Section 154　　　　　　　　　　SCHEDULE 8

TRANSITIONAL PROVISIONS AND SAVINGS

Interpretation

1–2267　1. In this Schedule references to the old enactments are to enactments repealed or amended by this Act and references to the appointed day are to the day on which this Act comes into force.

Proceedings commenced before appointed day

2. (1) Where proceedings were commenced before the appointed day, the old enactments relating to the proceedings continue to apply and nothing in this Act affects those enactments[1].

(2) Without prejudice to the generality of sub-paragraph (1) above, the old enactments relating to proceedings which continue in force by virtue of it include any provision of those enactments which creates an offence, which relates to civil or criminal procedure, which relates to the punishment for an offence, or which relates to enforcing, appealing against, questioning, varying or rescinding anything ordered or done in the proceedings.

Offences committed before appointed day

3. (1) This paragraph applies where proceedings are commenced under this Act in relation to an offence committed before the appointed day.

(2) Nothing in this Act renders a person liable to punishment by way of fine or imprisonment for the offence which differs from the punishment to which he would have been liable if this Act had not been passed and proceedings for the offence had been commenced under the old enactments.

(3) Nothing in this Act renders a person liable to pay compensation under a compensation order in respect of the offence which differs from the compensation he would have been liable to pay if this Act had not been passed and proceedings for the offence had been commenced under the old enactments.

(4) The provisions of this Act corresponding to the old enactments relating to punishment and compensation are to be construed accordingly.

Other matters: general

4. Paragraphs 5 and 6 below have effect subject to paragraphs 2 and 3 above.

5. Without prejudice to any express amendment made by this Act, a reference in an enactment or other document, whether express or implied, to an enactment repealed by this Act shall, unless the context otherwise requires, be construed as, or as including, a reference to this Act or to the corresponding provision of this Act.

6. Where a period of time specified in an enactment repealed by this Act is current at the commencement of this Act, this Act shall have effect as if the corresponding provision of it had been in force when that period began to run.

Saving for transitionals in orders

7. (1) This paragraph applies where any provision of an old enactment—

(a) was brought into force by order which made transitional provision in connection with the provision brought into force, or

(b) fell to be brought into force by order which could have made transitional provision in connection with the provision brought into force, if this Act had not been passed.

(2) In that case, an order under section 155(7) of this Act may make corresponding transitional provision in connection with any provision of this Act corresponding to that of the old enactment.

Savings of amendments

8. Notwithstanding the repeal by this Act of the Magistrates' Courts Act 1952, the amendments made in other enactments ("the amended enactments") by that Act shall, to the extent that they had effect immediately before the coming into force of this Act, continue to have effect subject to any amendment of any of the amended enactments by this Act.

Savings for Local Government Act 1972

9. The provisions of this Act shall have effect without prejudice to the exercise of any power conferred by section 67 of the Local Government Act 1972 (consequential and transitional arrangements relating to Part IV), section 252 of that Act (general power to adapt Acts and instruments) or section 254 of that Act (consequential and supplementary provision); and any such power which, if this Act had not been passed, would have been exercisable in relation to an enactment repealed by this Act shall be exercisable in the like manner and to the like extent in relation to the corresponding provision (if any) of this Act.

10. *Scotland.*

1. Notwithstanding this provision, a memorandum of conviction which in error referred to s 37 of this Act instead of s 28 of the Magistrates' Courts Act 1952 was held not to have invalidated the committal for sentence (*R v Folkestone and Hythe Juvenile Court Justices, ex p R (a juvenile)* [1981] 3 All ER 840, [1981] 1 WLR 1501, 74 Cr App Rep 58).

Imprisonment (Temporary Provisions) Act 1980
(1980 c 57)

PART II[1]
OTHER PROVISIONS

1–2370 6. Detention in the custody of a constable. (1) This section applies to any person in the custody of a constable whose duty it is to take him to a prison, remand centre★, secure training centre, Borstal institution or detention centre in which his detention is authorised by law, and shall be deemed always to have applied to persons in the custody of a constable in those circumstances.

(2) It is hereby declared that where it is for any reason not practicable to secure the admission of a person to whom this section applies to the prison, remand centre★, secure training centre, young offender institution in which his detention is so authorised, he may lawfully be detained in the custody of a constable until such time as he can be admitted there or is required to appear before a court.

(3) Any reference in this section to a constable includes a reference to a prisoner custody officer (within the meaning of Part IV of the Criminal Justice Act 1991) acting in pursuance of prisoner escort arrangements (within the meaning of that Part).

(4) Any reference in this section to a constable includes a reference to a custody officer (within the meaning of section 12 of the Criminal Justice and Public Order Act 1994) acting in pursuance of escort arrangements (within the meaning of Schedule 1 to that Act).

[Imprisonment (Temporary Provisions) Act 1980, s 6, as amended by the Criminal Justice Act 1988, s 123(6), Sch 8, Pt I and the Criminal Justice and Public Order Act 1994, s 94 and Sch 10.]

★Repealed by the Criminal Justice and Court Services Act 2000, Sch 7 from a date to be appointed.
1. Despite the citation of this Act, Pt II is of permanent duration.

1–2371 8. *Duration, expiry and revival of Part I, etc.*

Criminal Attempts Act 1981
(1981 c 47)

PART I[1]
ATTEMPTS ETC

Attempt

1–2410 1. Attempting to commit an offence. (1) If, with intent[2] to commit an offence to which this section applies, a person does an act which is more than merely preparatory[3] to the commission of the offence, he is guilty of attempting to commit the offence[4].

(1A) Subject to section 8 of the Computer Misuse Act 1990 (relevance of external law), if this subsection applies to an act, what the person doing it had in view shall be treated as an offence to which this section applies.

(1B) Subsection (1A) above applies to an act if—

(*a*) it is done in England and Wales; and

(*b*) it would fall within subsection (1) above as more than merely preparatory to the commission of an offence under section 3 of the Computer Misuse Act 1990 but for the fact that the offence, if completed, would not be an offence triable in England and Wales.

(2) A person may be guilty of attempting to commit an offence to which this section applies even though the facts are such that the commission of the offence is impossible[5].

(3) In any case where—

(*a*) apart from this subsection a person's intention would not be regarded as having amounted to an intent to commit an offence; but

(*b*) if the facts of the case had been as he believed them to be, his intention would be so regarded,

then, for the purposes of subsection (1) above, he shall be regarded as having had an intent to commit that offence.

(4) This section applies to any offence which, if it were completed, would be triable in England and Wales as an indictable offence[6], other than—

(*a*) conspiracy (at common law or under section 1 of the Criminal Law Act 1977 or any other enactment);

(*b*) aiding, abetting, counselling, procuring or suborning the commission of an offence[7];

(*c*) offences under section 4(1) (assisting offenders) or 5(1) (accepting or agreeing to accept consideration for not disclosing information about an arrestable offence) of the Criminal Law Act 1967.

[Criminal Attempts Act 1981, s 1 as amended by the Computer Misuse Act 1990, s 7.]

---

1. Part I contains ss 1–7.

2. Foresight of consequences might be something from which the court can infer intent but it is not to be equated with intent; see *R v Pearman* [1985] RTR 39, CA. On a charge of attempting to damage property, "recklessness" is not acceptable as an alternative to "intent" for the purposes of this section (*R v Millard and Vernon* [1987] Crim LR 393, CA).

3. It is a question of fact whether the defendant has gone beyond mere preparation and embarked on the commission of the offence (*R v Gullefer* [1990] 3 All ER 882, [1990] 1 WLR 1063n, CA). The line of demarcation between acts which are merely preparatory and acts which may amount to an attempt is not always clear or easy to recognize. There is no rule of thumb test. However, an accurate paraphrase of the statutory test is to ask whether the available evidence, if accepted, could show that a defendant has done an act which shows that he has actually tried to commit the offence in question, or whether he has only got ready or put himself in a position or equipped himself to do so; see *R v Geddes* (1996) 160 JP 697, [1996] Crim LR 894; *R v Nash* [1999] Crim LR 308, CA (letter not containing overtly sexual invitation merely preparatory to offence of attempting to procure act of gross indecency). On a charge of attempted rape, it is not necessary for the prosecution to prove that the defendant had with the requisite intent necessarily gone as far as to attempt physical penetration of the victim's vagina (*A-G's Reference (No 1 of 1992)* [1993] 2 All ER 190, [1993] 96 Cr App Rep 298). Providing a false name and address on a form used for credit-worthiness inquiries does not make a person guilty of attempting to obtain services by deception (*R v Widdowson* [1986] RTR 124, [1986] Crim LR 233, CA).

4. If on the facts as the defendant believed them to be, an offence would have been committed, but on the true facts the commission of such an offence was impossible, the defendant may nevertheless be convicted of an offence under s 1 of this Act. Accordingly, where a person says he is dealing in prohibited goods namely drugs, contained in a suitcase, and analysis shows that the suitcase contains harmless vegetable matter, he may rightly be convicted (*R v Shivpuri* [1987] AC 1, [1986] 2 All ER 334, 150 JP 353, HL).

5. As to the wording of the charge where the accused was seen putting a hand into someone's handbag, it would seem best to charge with attempting to steal from a handbag rather than to use phrases like "steal some or all of the contents of a handbag" thus avoiding evidential difficulties if the owner of the handbag is not available later to give evidence (*R v Smith and Smith* [1986] Crim LR 166, CA).

6. This includes a "scheduled offence" mentioned in Sch 2 to the Magistrates' Courts Act 1980, notwithstanding that under s 22(2) of that Act it must be proceeded with as if the offence were triable only summarily, because these provisions do not mean that such an offence is in law a summary offence (*R v Bristol Magistrates' Court, ex p E* [1998] 3 All ER 798, [1999] 1 WLR 390, [1999] 1 Cr App Rep 144, 163 JP 56, [1999] Crim LR 161).

7. The effect of this subsection is to exclude an attempt to aid, abet, counsel or procure an offence from criminal liability, but to retain liability under s 1(1) of the Act for acts of aiding and abetting an attempted crime (*R v Dunnington* [1984] QB 472, [1984] 1 All ER 676, 148 JP 316, CA).

1–2411   1A. Extended jurisdiction in relation to certain attempts[1]. (1) If this section applies to an act, what the person doing the act had in view shall be treated as an offence to which section 1(1) above applies.

(2) This section applies to an act if—

(*a*) it is done in England and Wales, and

(*b*) it would fall within section 1(1) above as more than merely preparatory to the commission of a Group A offence but for the fact that that offence, if completed, would not be an offence triable in England and Wales.

(3) In this section "Group A offence" has the same meaning as in Part 1 of the Criminal Justice Act 1993.

(4) Subsection (1) above is subject to the provisions of section 6 of the Act of 1993 (relevance of external law).

(5) Where a person does any act to which this section applies, the offence which he commits shall for all purposes be treated as the offence of attempting to commit the relevant Group A offence.

[Criminal Attempts Act 1981, s 1A, as inserted by the Criminal Justice Act 1993, s 5.]

1. At the date of going to press this section which is to be inserted in this Act by the Criminal Justice Act 1993, s 5, had not been brought into force.

1–2412   2. Application of procedural and other provisions to offences under s 1.   (1) Any provision to which this section applies shall have effect with respect to an offence under section 1 above of attempting to commit an offence as it has effect with respect to the offence attempted.

(2) This section applies to provisions of any of the following descriptions made by or under any enactment (whenever passed)—

(a)   provisions whereby proceedings may not be instituted or carried on otherwise than by, or on behalf or with the consent of, any person (including any provisions which also make other exceptions to the prohibition);

(b)   provisions conferring power to institute proceedings;

(c)   provisions as to the venue of proceedings;

(d)   provisions whereby proceedings may not be instituted after the expiration of a time limit;

(e)   provisions conferring a power of arrest or search;

(f)   provisions conferring a power of seizure and detention of property;

(g)   provisions whereby a person may not be convicted or committed for trial on the uncorroborated evidence of one witness (including any provision requiring the evidence of not less than two credible witnesses);

(h)   provisions conferring a power of forfeiture, including any power to deal with anything liable to be forfeited;

(i)   provisions whereby, if an offence committed by a body corporate is proved to have been committed with the consent or connivance of another person, that person also is guilty of the offence.

[Criminal Attempts Act 1981, s 2.]

Specific offences of attempt

1–2413   3. Offences of attempt under other enactments.   (1) Subsections (2) to (5) below shall have effect, subject to subsection (6) below and to any inconsistent provision in any other enactment, for the purpose of determining whether a person is guilty of an attempt under a special statutory provision.

(2) For the purposes of this Act an attempt under a special statutory provision is an offence which—

(a)   is created by an enactment other than section 1 above, including an enactment passed after this Act; and

(b)   is expressed as an offence of attempting to commit another offence (in this section referred to as "the relevant full offence").

(3) A person is guilty of an attempt under a special statutory provision if, with intent to commit the relevant full offence, he does an act which is more than merely preparatory to the commission of that offence.

(4) A person may be guilty of an attempt under a special statutory provision even though the facts are such that the commission of the relevant full offence is impossible.

(5) In any case where—

(a)   apart from this subsection a person's intention would not be regarded as having amounted to an intent to commit the relevant full offence; but

(b)   if the facts of the case had been as he believed them to be, his intention would be so regarded,

then, for the purposes of subsection (3) above, he shall be regarded as having had an intent to commit that offence.

(6) Subsections (2) to (5) above shall not have effect in relation to an act done before the commencement of this Act.

[Criminal Attempts Act 1981, s 3.]

Trial etc of offences of attempt

1–2414   4. Trial and penalties.   (1) A person guilty by virtue of section 1 above of attempting to commit an offence shall—

(a)   if the offence attempted is murder or any other offence the sentence for which is fixed by law, be liable on conviction on indictment to imprisonment for life; and

(b)   if the offence attempted is indictable but does not fall within paragraph (a) above, be liable on conviction on indictment to any penalty to which he would have been liable on conviction on indictment of that offence; and

(c)   if the offence attempted is triable either way, be liable on summary conviction to any penalty to which he would have been liable on summary conviction of that offence.

(2) In any case in which a court may proceed to summary trial of an information charging a person with an offence and an information charging him with an offence under section 1 above of attempting to commit it or an attempt under a special statutory provision, the court may, without his consent, try the informations together.

(3) Where, in proceedings against a person for an offence under section 1 above, there is evidence

sufficient in law to support a finding that he did an act falling within subsection (1) of that section, the question whether or not his act fell within that subsection is a question of fact.

(4) Where, in proceedings against a person for an attempt under a special statutory provision, there is evidence sufficient in law to support a finding that he did an act falling within subsection (3) of section 3 above, the question whether or not his act fell within that subsection is a question of fact.

(5) Subsection (1) above shall have effect—

(a) repealed
(b) notwithstanding anything—

   (i) in section 32(1) (no limit to fine on conviction on indictment) of the Criminal Law Act 1977; or
   (ii) in section 78(1) and (2) (maximum of six month's imprisonment on summary conviction unless express provision made to the contrary) of the Powers of Criminal Courts (Sentencing) Act 2000.*

[Criminal Attempts Act 1981, s 4, as amended by the Powers of Criminal Courts (Sentencing) Act 2000, Sch 9 and the Sexual Offences Act 2003, Sch 7.]

*Substituted by the Criminal Justice Act 2003, s 304, from a date to be appointed.

Supplementary

1–2415   6. Effect of Part I on common law.   (1) The offence of attempt at common law and any offence at common law of procuring materials for crime are hereby abolished for all purposes not relating to acts done before the commencement of this Act.

(2) Except as regards offences committed before the commencement of this Act, references in any enactment passed before this Act which fall to be construed as references to the offence of attempt at common law shall be construed as references to the offence under section 1 above.

[Criminal Attempts Act 1981, s 6.]

PART II[1]
SUSPECTED PERSONS, ETC

1–2416   8. *Abolition of offence of loitering etc with intent.*

1–2417   9. Interference with vehicles.   (1) A person is guilty of the offence of vehicle interference if he interferes with a motor vehicle or trailer or with anything carried in or on a motor vehicle or trailer with the intention that an offence specified in subsection (2) below shall be committed by himself or some other person.

(2) The offences mentioned in subsection (1) above are—

(a) theft of the motor vehicle or trailer or part of it;
(b) theft of anything carried in or on the motor vehicle or trailer; and
(c) an offence under section 12(1) of the Theft Act 1968 (taking and driving away without consent);

and, if it is shown that a person accused of an offence under this section intended that one of those offences should be committed, it is immaterial that it cannot be shown which it was.

(3) A person guilty of an offence under this section shall be liable on summary conviction to imprisonment for a term not exceeding **three months** or to a fine not exceeding **level 4** on the standard scale or to both.

(4) *(Repealed)*.

(5) In this section "motor vehicle" and "trailer" have the meanings assigned to them by section 185(1) of the Road Traffic Act 1988.

[Criminal Attempts Act 1981, s 9 as amended by the Criminal Justice Act 1982, s 46, the Police and Criminal Evidence Act 1984, Sch 7, and the Road Traffic (Consequential Provisions) Act 1988, Sch 3.]

1. Part II contains ss 8 and 9.

Contempt of Court Act 1981
(1981 c 49)

Strict liability

1–2430   1. The strict liability rule.   In this Act "the strict liability rule" means the rule of law whereby conduct may be treated as a contempt of court as tending to interfere with the course of justice in particular legal proceedings regardless of intent to do so.

[Contempt of Court Act 1981, s 1.]

1–2431   2. Limitation of scope of strict liability.   (1) The strict liability rule applies only in relation to publications, and for this purpose "publication" includes any speech, writing, programme included in a programme service or other communication in whatever form, which is addressed to the public at large or any section of the public.

(2) The strict liability rule applies only to a publication which creates a substantial risk[1] that the course of justice[2] in the proceedings in question will be seriously impeded or prejudiced.

(3) The strict liability rule applies to a publication only if the proceedings in question are active within the meaning of this section at the time of the publication.

(4) Schedule 1 applies for determining the times at which proceedings are to be treated as active within the meaning of this section.

(5) In this section "programme service" has the same meaning as in the Broadcasting Act 1990.
[Contempt of Court Act 1981, s 2 as amended by the Cable and Broadcasting Act 1984, Sch 5 and the Broadcasting Act 1990, Sch 20.]

---

1. The phrase "substantial risk" is intended to exclude a risk that is only remote (*A-G v English* [1983] 1 AC 116, [1982] 2 All ER 903). The risk must be a practical risk and not a theoretical one (*A-G v Guardian Newspapers Ltd* [1992] 3 All ER 38). Each case depends on its own facts, but the place of trial, the nature of the proposed publication and the proximity of the publication to the date of trial are factors of considerable importance in assessing whether the criteria set out in s 2 are met (*A-G v News Group Newspapers Ltd* [1987] QB 1, [1986] 2 All ER 833). For an extended exposition of the principles governing the application of the strict liability rule see the judgment of SCHIEMANN J in *A-G v MGN Ltd* [1997] 1 All ER 456, DC.

2. Contempt may be proved not only if the publication might prejudice the jury but also where the defendant's response to the prosecution might be influenced for example by impelling the accused to adopt a course in his own defence which he does not wish to adopt. However, on the facts, where an accused had clearly intimated an intention to plead guilty, the risk created by a newspaper article indicating that the accused had stated that she would not be denying the charges was not proved to be substantial (*A-G v Unger* [1998] 1 Cr App Rep 308).

1–2432   3. Defence of innocent publication or distribution.   (1) A person is not guilty of contempt of court under the strict liability rule as the publisher of any matter to which that rule applies if at the time of publication (having taken all reasonable care) he does not know and has no reason to suspect that relevant proceedings are active.

(2) A person is not guilty of contempt of court under the strict liability rule as the distributor of a publication containing any such matter if at the time of distribution (having taken all reasonable care) he does not know that it contains such matter and has no reason to suspect that it is likely to do so.

(3) The burden of proof of any fact tending to establish a defence afforded by this section to any person lies upon that person.

(4) *Repealed.*
[Contempt of Court Act 1981, s 3 as amended by the Statute Law (Repeals) Act 2004.]

1–2433   4. Contemporary reports of proceedings.   (1) Subject to this section a person is not guilty of contempt of court under the strict liability rule in respect of a fair and accurate report of legal proceedings held in public[1], published contemporaneously and in good faith.

(2) In any such proceedings[2] the court may, where it appears to be necessary[3] for avoiding a substantial risk[4] of prejudice to the administration of justice in those proceedings, or in any other proceedings pending or imminent, order[2] that the publication of any report of the proceedings, or any part of the proceedings, be postponed for such period as the court thinks necessary for that purpose.

(2A) Where in proceedings for any offence which is an administration of justice offence for the purposes of section 54 of the Criminal Procedure and Investigations Act 1996 (acquittal tainted by an administration of justice offence) it appears to the court that there is a possibility that (by virtue of that section) proceedings may be taken against a person for an offence of which he has been acquitted, subsection (2) of this section shall apply as if those proceedings were pending or imminent.

(3) For the purposes of subsection (1) of this section a report of proceedings shall be treated as published contemporaneously—

(*a*) in the case of a report of which publication is postponed pursuant to an order under subsection (2) of this section, if published as soon as practicable after that order expires;

(*b*) in the case of a report of committal proceedings of which publication is permitted by virtue only of subsection (3) of section 8 of the Magistrates' Courts Act 1980, if published as soon as practicable after publication is so permitted.*

(4) *Repealed.*
[Contempt of Court Act 1981, s 4 as amended by the Criminal Procedure and Investigations Act 1996, s 57, the Defamation Act 1996, Sch 2 and the Statute Law (Repeals) Act 2004.]

---

*New paras (*b*) and (*c*) substituted by the Criminal Justice Act 2003, Sch 3 from a date to be appointed.

1. A film of the arrest of a defendant is not within the scope of this phrase and should not therefore be the subject of an order under sub-s (2) below by magistrates; the proper remedy if proceedings seem likely to be prejudiced is to seek an injunction in the High Court (*R v Rhuddlan Justices, ex p HTV Ltd* [1986] Crim LR 329).

2. Section 4 (2) applies to committal proceedings before justices, notwithstanding the special provisions in s 8 of the Magistrates' Courts Act 1980; a court should not make a blanket order, but should satisfy itself that the order is no wider than necessary for the prevention of prejudice to the administration of justice (*R v Horsham Justices, ex p Farquharson* [1982] QB 762, [1982] 2 All ER 269, [1982] 2 WLR 430; applied in *Re Central Independent Television plc* [1991] 1 All ER 347, [1991] 1 WLR 4, 92 Cr App Rep 154, CA). As a matter of general policy, in committal proceedings justices should be slow to make an order under s 4(2) imposing reporting restrictions additional to those set out in s 8 of the Magistrates' Courts Act 1980; see *R v Beaconsfield Magistrates' Court, ex p Westminster Press Ltd* (1994) 158 JP 1055. Justices have a discretionary power to hear representations from the press when contemplating the making of or continuing of an order under s 4(2) (*R v Clerkenwell Magistrates' Court, ex p Telegraph plc* [1993] 2 All ER 183, (1992) 157 JP 554, (1993) 97 Cr App Rep 18). The prosecution has a duty to ensure, with the court itself, that the accused has a fair trial which is not liable to be set aside later for an irregularity so that in an application for an order under s 4(2) the prosecution in an objective

and nonpartisan spirit, should give the court such assistance as it can on the proper principles to be applied (*ex p News Group Newspapers Ltd* (1999) Times, 21 May, CA).

Any order must be committed to writing, stating its precise scope, the time at which it shall cease to have effect, if appropriate, and the specific purpose of making the order; the Press should normally be given notice in some form that an order has been made, but the onus rests with the Press to see that no breach of any order occurs, and to make enquiry in case of doubt (*Practice Direction (criminal: consolidated)* [2002] para V.54, in this PART, post.) In some cases it may be appropriate for the court to make plain whether and to what extent the making and the terms of the order can be published; see *A-G v Guardian Newspapers Ltd (No 3)* [1992] 1 WLR 874.

3. In forming a view whether it is necessary to make an order for avoiding such a risk, a court will have regard to the competing public considerations of ensuring a fair trial and of open justice (*Telegraph plc, ex p* [1994] Crim LR 114, CA). That a restriction is "necessary" in the terms of this sub-s ie to avoid prejudice must be distinguished from "necessary" in art 10(2) of the European Convention on Human Rights where sanctions under considerations of public policy may come into play. Applications under s 4(2) should be approached in three stages (1) would reporting give rise to a "not insubstantial" risk of prejudice; if so (2) would a s 4(2) order eliminate it, could the risk be overcome by less restrictive means; (3) would the degree of risk contemplated be tolerable as the "lesser of two evils" (*Ex p The Telegraph Group plc* [2001] EWCA Crim 1075, [2001] 1 WLR 1983).

4. In determining whether publication would cause a substantial risk of prejudice to a future trial a court should credit the jury with the will and ability to abide by the judge's direction to decide the case only on the evidence before them (*Telegraph plc, ex p* [1994] Crim LR 114, CA).

1–2434   5. Discussion of public affairs.   A publication made as or as part of a discussion in good faith of public affairs or other matters of general public interest is not to be treated as a contempt of court under the strict liability rule if the risk of impediment or prejudice to particular legal proceedings is merely incidental to the discussion[1].
[Contempt of Court Act 1981, s 5.]

---

1. For consideration of the effect of this section, see *A-G v English* [1983] 1 AC 116, [1982] 2 All ER 903.

1–2435   6. Savings.   Nothing in the foregoing provisions of this Act—

(*a*)   prejudices any defence available at common law to a charge of contempt of court under the strict liability rule;

(*b*)   implies that any publication is punishable as contempt of court under that rule which would not be so punishable apart from those provisions;

(*c*)   restricts liability for contempt of court in respect of conduct intended to impede or prejudice the administration of justice.
[Contempt of Court Act 1981, s 6.]

1–2436   7. Consent required for institution of proceedings.   Proceedings for a contempt of court under the strict liability rule (other than Scottish proceedings) shall not be instituted except by or with the consent of the Attorney General or on the motion of a court having jurisdiction to deal with it.
[Contempt of Court Act 1981, s 7.]

Other aspects of law and procedure

1–2437   8. Confidentiality of jury's deliberations.   (1) Subject to subsection (2) below, it is a contempt of court to obtain, disclose[1] or solicit any particulars of statements made, opinions expressed, arguments advanced or votes cast by members of a jury in the course of their deliberations in any legal proceedings.

(2) This section does not apply to any disclosure of any particulars—

(*a*)   in the proceedings in question for the purpose of enabling the jury to arrive at their verdict, or in connection with the delivery of that verdict, or

(*b*)   in evidence in any subsequent proceedings for an offence alleged to have been committed in relation to the jury in the first mentioned proceedings,

or to the publication of any particulars so disclosed.

(3) Proceedings for a contempt of court under this section (other than Scottish proceedings) shall not be instituted except by or with the consent of the Attorney General or on the motion of a court having jurisdiction to deal with it.
[Contempt of Court Act 1981, s 8.]

---

1. The prohibition in s 8(1) against the disclosure of deliberations made by members of a jury in the course of legal proceedings is not limited to the disclosure of information by a juror, but extends to a further revelation of that information by publication in a newspaper where the facts published were not already well known (*A-G v Associated Newspapers Ltd* (1994) 99 Cr App Rep 131, [1994] Crim LR 672, HL). A solicitor who wishes to take statements from jurors should seek the leave of the court (*R v Mickleburgh* [1995] 1 Cr App Rep 297, CA). Although s 8 does not fetter a court or an appeal court from making an investigation as to the conduct of a trial, the court is restricted in its inquiry into what happened in the jury's deliberations by the longstanding rule of the common law that what occurred in the jury room is secret (*R v Mirza* [2004] UKHL 2, [2004] AC 1118, [2004] 1 All ER 925, [2004] 2 Cr App R 8, [2004] Crim LR 1041).

It is not a contempt for a juror who has concerns about the jury's deliberations to disclose to the court or the court authorities what was said or done during the jury's deliberations with the intention of prompting an investigation. But it is a contempt if he discloses the deliberations to a third party who has no authority to receive the disclosure on behalf of the court (*A-G v Scotcher* [2005] UKHL 36, [2005] 3 All ER 1).

1–2438　9. Use of tape recorders[1].　(1) Subject to subsection (4) below, it is a contempt of court—

(a) to use in court, or bring into court for use, any tape recorder or other instrument for recording sound, except with the leave of the court;

(b) to publish a recording of legal proceedings made by means of any such instrument, or any recording derived directly or indirectly from it, by playing it in the hearing of the public or any section of the public, or to dispose of it or any recording so derived, with a view to such publication;

(c) to use any such recording in contravention of any conditions of leave granted under paragraph (a).

(2) Leave under paragraph (a) of subsection (1) may be granted or refused at the discretion of the court, and if granted may be granted subject to such conditions as the court thinks proper with respect to the use of any recording made pursuant to the leave; and where leave has been granted the court may at the like discretion withdraw or amend it either generally or in relation to any particular part of the proceedings.

(3) Without prejudice to any other power to deal with an act of contempt under paragraph (a) of subsection (1), the court may order the instrument, or any recording made with it, or both, to be forfeited; and any object so forfeited shall (unless the court otherwise determines on application by a person appearing to be the owner) be sold or otherwise disposed of in such manner as the court may direct.

(4) This section does not apply to the making or use of sound recordings for purposes of official transcripts of proceedings.
[Contempt of Court Act 1981, s 9.]

---

1. See *Practice Direction (criminal: consolidated)* [2002] para I.2, in this PART, post.

1–2439　10. Sources of information.　No court may require a person to disclose, nor is any person guilty of contempt of court for refusing to disclose, the source of information contained in a publication for which he is responsible, unless it be established to the satisfaction of the court that disclosure is necessary[1] in the interests of justice or national security or for the prevention of disorder or crime.
[Contempt of Court Act 1981, s 10.]

---

1. For the jurisdiction to order disclosure of the identity of a source and the relationship between s 10 of the 1981 Act and art 10 of the European Convention on Human Rights, see *Ashworth Hospital Authority v MGN Ltd* [2001] 1 All ER 991, [2001] 1 WLR 515, CA.

1–2440　11. Publication of matters exempted from disclosure in court.　In any case where a court (having power to do so) allows[1] a name or other matter to be withheld from the public in proceedings before the court, the court may give such directions[2] prohibiting the publication of that name or matter in connection with the proceedings as appear to the court to be necessary for the purpose for which it was so withheld.
[Contempt of Court Act 1981, s 11.]

---

1. The circumstances in which it is appropriate to allow a name or other matter to be withheld are rare; see *R v Malvern Justices, ex p Evans* [1988] QB 540, [1988] 1 All ER 371, 87 Cr App Rep 19, and para **1–113 Open court**, ante. It is a misuse of this section to prohibit publication of the address of the defendant if the court is motivated solely by its sympathy for the defendant's well being and not for reasons to do with the administration of justice; see *R v Malvern Justices, ex p Evans, supra*; and *R v Evesham Justices, ex p McDonagh* [1988] QB 553, [1988] 1 All ER 371, 87 Cr App Rep 28. Similarly, it is a misuse of the section to make an order prohibiting publication of the defendant's name and address and those of his business on account of the economic damage which might be done to the business (*R v Dover Justices, ex p Dover District Council and Wells* (1991) 156 JP 433, [1992] Crim LR 371).

As to the confidentiality of family proceedings and the appropriateness of the use of s 11 to prevent disclosure of any or all the information given in a private hearing, see *Clibbery v Allan* [2002] EWCA 45, [2002] Fam 261, [2002] 1 All ER 865, [2002] 2 WLR 1511, [2002] 1 FCR 385.

2. A court does not have power to make a direction prohibiting the publication of a name or other matter, unless the court has first allowed the name or other matter to be withheld from the public in the proceedings; accordingly, if the name or matter is mentioned in the proceedings the court has no jurisdiction to make a direction under s 11 (*R v Arundel Justices, ex p Westminster Press Ltd* [1985] 2 All ER 390, [1985] 1 WLR 708, 149 JP 299). When hearing an application for an order prohibiting publication of an address, it is generally necessary to hear the reasons in camera (*R v Tower Bridge Magistrates' Court, ex p Osborne* (1987) 152 JP 310, [1988] Crim LR 382). Any order must be committed to writing, stating its precise scope, the time at which it shall cease to have effect, if appropriate, and the specific purpose of making the order; the Press should normally be given notice in some form that an order has been made, but the onus rests with the Press to see that no breach of any order occurs, and to make enquiry in case of doubt (See *Practice Direction (criminal: consolidated)* [2002] para I.3, in this PART, post.).

1–2441　12. Offences of contempt of magistrates' courts[1].　(1) A magistrates' court has jurisdiction under this section to deal with any person who—

(a) wilfully[2] insults[3] the justice or justices, any witness before or officer of the court or any solicitor or counsel having business in the court, during his or their sitting or attendance in court or in going to or returning from the court; or

(b) wilfully interrupts the proceedings of the court[4] or otherwise misbehaves in court.

(2) In any such case the court may order[5] any officer of the court[6], or any constable, to take the offender into custody and detain him until the rising of the court; and the court may, if it thinks fit,

commit[7] the offender to custody[8] for a specified period not exceeding **one month** or impose on him a fine not exceeding £2,500 on the standard scale, or both[9].

(2A) A fine imposed under subsection (2) above shall be deemed, for the purposes of any enactment, to be a sum adjudged to be paid by a conviction.

(3) *Repealed.*

(4) A magistrates' court may at any time revoke an order of committal made under subsection (2) and, if the offender is in custody, order his discharge.

(5) Section 135 of the Powers of Criminal Courts (Sentencing) Act 2000 (limit on fines in respect of young persons) and the following provisions of the Magistrates' Courts Act 1980 apply in relation to an order under this section as they apply in relation to a sentence on conviction or finding of guilty of an offence, and those provisions of the Magistrates' Court Act 1980 are sections 75 to 91 (enforcement); section 108[10] (appeal to Crown Court); section 136 (overnight detention in default of payment); and section 142(1) (power to rectify mistakes).

[Contempt of Court Act 1981, s 12 as amended by the Criminal Justice Act 1982, s 37 and Sch 16, SI 1984/447, the Criminal Justice Act 1991, Sch 4, the Criminal Justice Act 1993, Sch 3 and the Powers of Criminal Courts (Sentencing) Act 2000, Sch 9.]

---

1. For a detailed consideration of the provisions of this section, which closely resembles s 157 of the County Courts Act 1959 (now s 118 of the County Courts Act 1984), and relevant authorities, see (1983) 147 JP Jo 531 et seq. And see para 1–116 Contempt of court, ante.

2. A person "wilfully" interrupts the proceedings of the court if he commits the acts causing the interruption deliberately with the intention that they should interrupt the proceedings of the court or if, knowing that there is a risk that his acts will interrupt the proceedings, he nevertheless goes on deliberately to do those acts (*Bodden v Metropolitan Police Comr* [1989] 3 All ER 833, [1990] 2 WLR 76, 154 JP 217, CA).

3. A threat made to a witness does not amount to an insult for the purposes of this paragraph (*R v Havant Justices, ex p Palmer* (1985) 149 JP 609). Whilst drawing on s 12 for guidance as to the use of the Crown Court's inherent powers the Divisional Court has held that a wolf whistle directed at a juror was potentially insulting, offensive and an interference with the court (*R v Powell* (1993) 98 Cr App Rep 224, CA).

4. The first part of paragraph (*b*) is aimed at interruptions of the proceedings by acts done inside or outside the court, and a distinction is drawn between such contempt and other misbehaviour in the latter part of the paragraph, which is punishable only if it occurs in the court; see *Bodden v Metropolitan Police Comr* [1989] 3 All ER 833, [1990] 2 WLR 76, 154 JP 217, CA.

5. This includes all incidental powers necessary to enable the court to exercise the jurisdiction in a judicial manner. Accordingly, a court whose proceedings were interrupted by the use of a loud-hailer in a demonstration outside the court was justified in causing a constable to bring the person responsible before it, if it had reasonable grounds for believing that the proceedings were being wilfully interrupted (*Bodden v Metropolitan Police Comr* [1990] 2 QB 397, [1989] 3 All ER 833, 154 JP 217, CA).

6. This reference has effect as if it referred to any court security officer assigned to the court-house in which the court is sitting (Criminal Justice Act 1991, Sch 11, para 29); the terms "court security officer" and "court-house" are defined by s 92(1) of that Act, in PART III: SENTENCING, post.

7. An order under this section does not amount to a summary conviction; accordingly s 83(1) Powers of Criminal Courts (Sentencing) Act 2000 (restrictions on imposing sentences of imprisonment on persons not legally represented) does not apply (*R v Newbury Justices, ex p Du Pont* (1983) 148 JP 248, 78 Cr App Rep 255) nor may courts make a probation order (*R v Palmer* [1992] 3 All ER 289 [1992] 1 WLR 568, 156 JP 667, CA Nevertheless contemnors should have the opportunity to be legally represented, see *Practice Note – Contempt of Court* at para 1–116 ante.

8. This power is subject to statutory restrictions prohibiting the committal of young offenders to custody (*R v Selby Justices, ex p Frame* [1991] 2 All ER 344, [1991] 2 WLR 965). The power to order detention for contempt under the Criminal Justice Act 1982, s 9 is now restricted to offenders over the age of 18. As a result, the powers of the court to deal with contempt where the offender is under the age of 18 are very limited (*R v Byas* (1995) 16 Cr App Rep (S) 869, [1995] Crim LR 439, CA).

9. In view of the fact that there will be no information before the court, that the court may subsequently have to consider whether the offender has purged his contempt, and that the justices will be the only respondents to an appeal to the Crown Court, we would suggest that when making an order under subsection (2), the justices state what their findings of fact are, and where appropriate the process of reasoning by which they arrived at those findings of fact; see *R v Goult* (1982) 76 Cr App Rep 140.

10. As the application of s 108 of the Magistrates' Courts Act 1980 is confined to an order under s 12, it would appear that the jurisdiction of the Crown Court does not extend to hearing an appeal against the finding of contempt itself; see *R v Havant Justices, ex p Palmer* (1985) 149 JP 609. See, however, the right of appeal to the High Court under s 13 of the Administration of Justice Act 1960, ante, to which Part 52 of the Civil Procedure Rules 1998, post applies.

Penalties for contempt and kindred offences

1-2442   14. Proceedings in England and Wales.   (1) In any case where a court has power to commit a person to prison for contempt[1] of court[2] and (apart from this provision) no limitation applies to the period of committal, the committal shall (without prejudice to the power of the court to order his earlier discharge) be for a fixed term, and that term shall not on any occasion exceed two years[3] in the case of committal by a superior court, or one month in the case of committal by an inferior court.

(2) In any case where an inferior court has power to fine a person for contempt of court and (apart from this provision) no limit applies to the amount of the fine, the fine shall not on any occasion exceed £2,500.

(2A) In the exercise of jurisdiction to commit for contempt of court or any kindred offence the court shall not deal with the offender by making an order under section 60 of the Powers of Criminal Courts (Sentencing) Act 2000 (an attendance centre order) if it appears to the court, after considering any available evidence, that he is under 17 years of age.

(2A)[4] A fine imposed under subsection (2) above shall be deemed, for the purposes of any enactment, to be a sum adjudged to be paid by a conviction.

(3) *Repealed.*

(4) Each of the superior courts shall have the like power to make a hospital order or guardianship order under section 37 of the Mental Health Act 1983 or an interim hospital order under section 38 of that Act in the case of a person suffering from mental illness or severe mental impairment who could otherwise be committed to prison for contempt of court as the Crown Court has under that section in the case of a person convicted of an offence.

(4A)[5] Each of the superior courts shall have the like power to make an order under section 35 of the said Act of 1983 (remand for report on accused's mental condition) where there is reason to suspect that a person who could be committed to prison for contempt of court is suffering from mental illness or severe mental impairment as the Crown Court has under that section in the case of an accused person within the meaning of that section.

(4A)[5] For the purposes of the preceding provisions of this section a county court shall be treated as a superior court and not as an inferior court.

(5) The enactments specified in Part III of Schedule 2 shall have effect subject to the amendments set out in that Part, being amendments relating to the penalties and procedure in respect of certain offences of contempt in coroners' courts, county courts and magistrates' courts.
[Contempt of Court Act 1981, s 14, as amended by the Criminal Justice Act 1982, Schs 14 and 16, the Mental Health (Amendment) Act 1982, Sch 3, the Mental Health Act 1983, Sch 4, the County Courts (Penalties for Contempt) Act 1983, s 1, SI 1984/447, the Criminal Justice Act 1991, Sch 4, the Criminal Justice Act 1993, Sch 3 and the Powers of Criminal Courts (Sentencing) Act 2000, Sch 9.]

---

1. This will include civil contempts (*Linnett v Coles* [1987] QB 555, [1986] 3 All ER 652, 84 Cr App Rep 227, CA).
2. The offence of absconding whilst on bail is not a contempt of court to be dealt with under this section; the Bail Act 1976, s 6(7) provides the penalty (*R v Reader* (1986) 84 Cr App Rep 294, CA).
3. This provision does not enable a superior court on any occasion to impose consecutive sentences which cumulatively exceed two years *(Re R (a minor) (contempt: sentence)* [1994] 2 All ER 144). Moreover, a court may not on the same occasion both activate a suspended sentence and impose a new sentence for contempt of court which together exceed the maximum of two years (*Villiers v Villiers* [1994] 2 All ER 149, [1994] 1 FLR 647).
4. This subsection added by the Criminal Justice Act 1991, Sch 4, and substituted by the Criminal Justice Act 1993, Sch 3, appears to have been inadvertently given a duplicate number (2A).
5. The first subsection (4A) printed here was inserted by the Mental Health (Amendment) Act 1982, Sch 3, and the second subsection (4A) was inserted by the County Courts (Penalties for Contempt) Act 1983, s 1.

1-2443 15. *Scotland.*

1-2444 16. Enforcement of fines imposed by certain superior courts.   (1) Payment of a fine for contempt of court imposed by a superior court, other than the Crown Court or one of the courts specified in subsection (4) below, may be enforced upon the order of the court—

(a) in like manner as a judgment of the High Court for the payment of money; or
(b) in like manner as a fine imposed by the Crown Court.

(2) Where payment of a fine imposed by any court falls to be enforced as mentioned in paragraph (a) of subsection (1)—

(a) the court shall, if the fine is not paid in full forthwith or within such time as the court may allow, certify to Her Majesty's Remembrancer the sum payable;
(b) Her Majesty's Remembrancer shall thereupon proceed to enforce payment of that sum as if it were due to him as a judgment debt.

(3) Where payment of a fine imposed by any court falls to be enforced as mentioned in paragraph (b) of subsection (1), the provisions of sections 139 and 140 of the Powers of Criminal Courts (Sentencing) Act 2000 shall apply as they apply to a fine imposed by the Crown Court.

(4) Subsection (1) of this section does not apply to fines imposed by the criminal division of the Court of Appeal or by the House of Lords★ on appeal from that division.

(5) The Fines Act 1833 shall not apply to a fine to which subsection (1) of this section applies.

(6) *Repealed.*
[Contempt of Court Act 1981, s 16 as amended by the Supreme Court Act 1981, Sch 7, the Industrial Tribunals Act 1996, Sch 3 and the Powers of Criminal Courts (Sentencing) Act 2000, Sch 9.]

★Words substituted by the Constitutional Reform Act 2005, Sch 11 from a date to be appointed.

1-2445 17. Disobedience to certain orders of magistrates' courts.   (1) The powers of a magistrates' court under subsection (3) of section 63 of the Magistrates' Courts Act 1980 (punishment by fine or committal for disobeying an order to do anything other than the payment of money or to abstain from doing anything) may be exercised either of the court's own motion or by order on complaint.

(2) In relation to the exercise of those powers the provisions of the Magistrates' Court Act 1980 shall apply subject to the modifications set out in Schedule 3 to this Act.
[Contempt of Court Act 1981, s 17.]

Supplemental

1-2446 18. *Northern Ireland.*

1–2447   19. Interpretation.   In this Act—

"court" includes any tribunal or body exercising the judicial power of the State, and "legal proceedings" shall be construed accordingly;

"publication" has the meaning assigned by subsection (1) of section 2, and "publish" (except in section 9) shall be construed accordingly;

"Scottish proceedings" means proceedings before any court, including the Courts-Martial Appeal Court★, the Restrictive Practices Court and the Employment Appeal Tribunal, sitting in Scotland, and includes proceedings before the House of Lords★★ in the exercise of any appellate jurisdiction over proceedings in such a court;

"the strict liability rule" has the meaning assigned by section 1;

"superior court" means the Court of Appeal, the High Court, the Crown Court, the Courts-Martial Appeal Court★, the Restrictive Practices Court, the Employment Appeal Tribunal and any other court exercising in relation to its proceedings powers equivalent to those of the High Court, and includes the House of Lords in the exercise of its appellate jurisdiction★★.

[Contempt of Court Act 1981, s 19 as amended by the Cable and Broadcasting Act 1984, Sch 5 and the Broadcasting Act 1990, Schs 20 and 21.]

★**Words substituted by the Armed Forces Act 2006, Sch 16 from a date to be appointed.**
★★**Words substituted by the Constitutional Reform Act 2005, Sch 11 from a date to be appointed.**

1–2448   20. *Tribunals of Inquiry.*

SCHEDULES

Section 2   SCHEDULE 1
TIMES WHEN PROCEEDINGS ARE ACTIVE FOR PURPOSES OF SECTION 2

(*As amended by the Mental Health Act 1983, Sch 4, the Mental Health (Scotland) Act 1984, Sch 3, the Prosecution of Offences Act, 1985 Sch 1, the Criminal Procedure and Investigations Act 1996, s 57,the Powers of Criminal Courts (Sentencing) Act 2000, Sch 9 and SSI 2005/465.*)

Preliminary

1–2449   1. In this Schedule "criminal proceedings" means proceedings against a person in respect of an offence, not being appellate proceedings or proceedings commenced by motion for committal or attachment in England and Wales or Northern Ireland; and "appellate proceedings" means proceedings on appeal from or for the review of the decision of a court in any proceedings.

2. Criminal, appellate and other proceedings are active within the meaning of section 2 at the times respectively prescribed by the following paragraphs of this Schedule; and in relation to proceedings in which more than one of the steps described in any of those paragraphs is taken, the reference in that paragraph is a reference to the first of those steps.

Criminal proceedings

3. Subject to the following provisions of this Schedule, criminal proceedings are active from the relevant initial step specified in paragraph 4 or 4A until concluded as described in paragraph 5.

4. The initial steps of criminal proceedings are—

(a)   arrest without warrant;
(b)   the issue, or in Scotland the grant, of a warrant for arrest;
(c)   the issue of summons to appear, or in Scotland the grant of a warrant to cite;
(d)   the service of an indictment or other document specifying the charge;
(e)   except in Scotland, oral charge.

4A. Where as a result of an order under section 54 of the Criminal Procedure and Investigations Act 1996 (acquittal tainted by an administration of justice offence) proceedings are brought against a person for an offence of which he has previously been acquitted, the initial step of the proceedings is a certification under subsection (2) of that section; and paragraph 4 has effect subject to this.

5. Criminal proceedings are concluded—

(a)   by acquittal or, as the case may be, by sentence;
(b)   by any other verdict, finding, order or decision which puts an end to the proceedings;
(c)   by discontinuance or by operation of law.

6. The references in paragraph 5(a) to sentence includes any order or decision consequent on conviction or finding of guilt which disposes of the case, either absolutely or subject to future events, and a deferment of sentence under section 1 of the Powers of Criminal Courts (Sentencing) Act 2000, section 219 or 432 of the Criminal Procedure (Scotland) Act 1975 or Article 14 of the Treatment of Offenders (Northern Ireland) Order 1976.

7. Proceedings are discontinued within the meaning of paragraph 5(c)—

(a)   in England and Wales or Northern Ireland, if the charge or summons is withdrawn or a *nolle prosequi* entered;
(aa) in England and Wales, if they are discontinued by virtue of the Prosecution of Offences Act 1985;
(b)   in Scotland, if the proceedings are expressly abandoned by the prosecutor or are deserted *simpliciter*;
(c)   in the case of proceedings in England and Wales or Northern Ireland commenced by arrest without warrant, if the person arrested is released, otherwise than on bail, without having been charged.

8. Criminal proceedings before a court-martial or standing civilian court are not concluded until the completion of any review of finding or sentence.

9. Criminal proceedings in England and Wales or Northern Ireland cease to be active if an order is made for the charge to lie on the file, but become active again if leave is later given for the proceedings to continue.

9A. Where proceedings in England and Wales have been discontinued by virtue of section 23 of the Prosecution of Offences Act 1985, but notice is given by the accused under subsection (7) of that section to the effect that he wants the proceedings to continue, they become active again with the giving of that notice.

10. Without prejudice to paragraph 5(*b*) above, criminal proceedings against a person cease to be active—

(a) if the accused is found to be under a disability such as to render him unfit to be tried or unfit to plead or, in Scotland, is found to be insane in bar of trial; or

(b) if a hospital order is made in his case under section 51(5) of the Mental Health Act 1983 or paragraph (*b*) of subsection (2) of section 62 of the Mental Health Act (Northern Ireland) 1961 or, in Scotland, where an assessment order or a treatment order ceases to have effect by virtue of sections 52H or 52R respectively of the Criminal Procedure (Scotland) Act 1995,

but become active again if they are later resumed.

11. Criminal proceedings against a person which become active on the issue or the grant of a warrant for his arrest cease to be active at the end of the period of twelve months beginning with the date of the warrant unless he has been arrested within that period, but become active again if he is subsequently arrested.

Other proceedings at first instance

12. Proceedings other than criminal proceedings and appellate proceedings are active from the time when arrangements for the hearing are made or, if no such arrangements are previously made, from the time the hearing begins, until the proceedings are disposed of or discontinued or withdrawn; and for the purposes of this paragraph any motion or application made in or for the purposes of any proceedings, and any pre-trial review in the county court, is to be treated as a distinct proceeding.

13. In England and Wales or Northern Ireland arrangements for the hearing of proceedings to which paragraph 12 applies are made within the meaning of that paragraph—

(a) in the case of proceedings in the High Court for which provision is made by rules of court for setting down for trial, when the case is set down;

(b) in the case of any proceedings, when a date for the trial or hearing is fixed.

14. *Scotland.*

Appellate proceedings

15. Appellate proceedings are active from the time when they are commenced—

(a) by application for leave to appeal or apply for review, or by notice of such an application;

(b) by notice of appeal or of application for review;

(c) by other originating process,

until disposed of or abandoned, discontinued or withdrawn.

16. Where, in appellate proceedings relating to criminal proceedings, the court—

(a) remits the case to the court below; or

(b) orders a new trial or a *venire de novo*, or in Scotland grants authority to bring a new prosecution,

any further or new proceedings which result shall be treated as active from the conclusion of the appellate proceedings.

Section 17   SCHEDULE 3
APPLICATION OF MAGISTRATES' COURTS ACT 1980 TO CIVIL CONTEMPT PROCEEDINGS UNDER SECTION
63(3)

(As amended by the Family Law Act 1996, Sch 8.)

1–2460 **1.** (1) Where the proceedings are taken of the court's own motion the provisions of the Act listed in this sub-paragraph shall apply as if a complaint had been made against the person against whom the proceedings are taken, and subject to the modifications specified in sub-paragraphs (2) and (3) below. The enactments so applied are—

section 51 (issue of summons)
section 53(1) and (2) (procedure on hearing)
section 54 (adjournment)
section 55 (non-appearance of defendant)
section 97(1) (summons to witness)
section 101 (onus of proving exceptions etc)
section 121(1) and (3)(*a*) (constitution and place of sitting of court)
section 123 (defect in process).

(2) In section 55, in subsection (1) for the words "the complainant appears but the defendant does not" there shall be substituted the words "the defendant does not appear", and in subsection (2) the words "if the complaint has been substantiated on oath, and" shall be omitted.

(3) In section 123, in subsections (1) and (2) the words "adduced on behalf of the prosecutor or complainant" shall be omitted.

2. Where the proceedings are taken by way of complaint for an order, section 127 of the Act (limitation of time) shall not apply to the complaint.

3. Whether the proceedings are taken of the court's own motion or by way of complaint for an order, subsection (3) of section 55 shall apply as if the following words were added at the end of the subsection—

"or, having been arrested under section 47 of the Family Law Act 1996 in connection with the matter of the complaint, is at large after being remanded under subsection (7)(*b*) or (10) of that section."

Supreme Court Act 1981
(1981 c 54)

PART I[1]
CONSTITUTION OF SUPREME COURT

1–2560

1–7 The Supreme Court of England and Wales consists of the Court of Appeal, the High Court of Justice and the Crown Court; the Lord Chancellor is president of the Supreme Court. Provision is made for the constitution of these courts; Court of Appeal divided into the criminal division under the Lord Chief Justice and the civil division under the Master of the Rolls. The three divisions of the High Court are the Chancery Division under the Lord Chancellor, the Queen's Bench Division under the Lord Chief Justice and the Family Division under the President of the Family Division[2]. Provision is made for the Patents, Admiralty and Commercial Courts, and power by Order in Council to alter Divisions or transfer certain courts to different Divisions.

[Supreme Court Act 1981, ss 1–7 amended by the Access to Justice Act 1999, s 69—summarised.]

---

1. Part I contains ss 1–14.
2. Schedule 1 of the Supreme Court Act 1981 sets out the distribution of business in the High Court.

The Crown Court

1–2561 8. The Crown Court. (1) The jurisdiction of the Crown Court shall be exercisable by—

(a) any judge of the High Court; or
(b) any Circuit judge , Recorder or District Judge (Magistrates' Courts);
(c) subject to and in accordance with the provision of sections 74 and 75(2), a judge of the High Court, Circuit judge or Recorder sitting with not more than four justices of the peace,

and any such persons when exercising the jurisdiction of the Crown Court shall be judges of the Crown Court[1].

(2) A justice of the peace is not disqualified from acting as a judge of the Crown Court merely because the proceedings are not at a place within the local justice area to which he is assigned or because the proceedings are not related to that area in any other way.3)When the Crown Court sits in the City of London it shall be known as the Central Criminal Court; and the Lord Mayor of the City and any Alderman of the City shall be entitled to sit as judges of the Central Criminal Court with any judge of the High Court or any Circuit judge or Recorder.

[Supreme Court Act 1981, s 8 as amended by the Courts Act 2003, s 65 and Sch 8.]

---

1. The Lord Chancellor may request a judge or former judge of the Court of Appeal to act in the Crown Court, or a Circuit judge to act in the High Court or in the criminal division of the Court of Appeal (s 9). A judge of the Supreme Court or Crown Court is not disqualified from acting as such by reason of being a ratepayer or taxpayer (s 14). The justices are to take part in the decision making and a majority decision, even if it excludes the professional judge, prevails except that in matters of law the justices must defer to the views of the presiding judge (*R v Orpin* [1975] QB 283, [1974] 2 All ER 1121).

PART II[1]
JURISDICTION

Other particular fields of jurisdiction

1–2562 28. Appeals from Crown Court and inferior courts. (1) Subject to subsection (2), any order, judgment or other decision of the Crown Court may be questioned by any party to the proceedings, on the ground that it is wrong in law or is in excess of jurisdiction[2], by applying to the Crown Court to have a case stated by that court for the opinion of the High Court.

(2) Subsection (1) shall not apply to—

(a) a judgment or other decision[3] of the Crown Court relating to trial on indictment; or
(b) any decision of that court under the Betting, Gaming and Lotteries Act 1963, the Gaming Act 1968, or the Local Government (Miscellaneous Provisions) Act 1982 which, by any provision of any of those Acts, is to be final[4].

(3) Subject to the provisions of this Act and to rules of court, the High Court shall, in accordance with section 19(2), have jurisdiction to hear and determine—

(a) any application, or any appeal (whether by way of case stated or otherwise), which it has power to hear and determine under or by virtue of this or any other Act; and
(b) all such other appeals as it had jurisdiction to hear and determine immediately before the commencement of this Act.

(4) In subsection (2)(a) the reference to a decision of the Crown Court relating to trial on indictment does not include a decision relating to an order under section 17 of the Access to Justice Act 1999.

[Supreme Court Act 1981, s 28 as amended by the Local Government (Miscellaneous Provisions) Act 1982, Sch 3 and the Access to Justice Act 1999, Sch 4 and the Licensing Act 2003, Sch 7.]

1. Part II contains ss 15–52.

2. A discretionary sentence may be wrong in law or in excess of jurisdiction if it is harsh and oppressive or so far outside the normal sentence imposed for the offence as to enable the Divisional Court to hold that the sentence involves an error of law (*R v Crown Court at St Albans, ex p Cinnamond* [1981] QB 480, [1981] 1 All ER 802; explained in *R v Crown Court at Acton, ex p Bewley* (1988) 152 JP 327, 10 Cr App Rep (S) 105). For power of the High Court to vary a sentence of a magistrates' court or the Crown Court on judicial review, see s 43, post, and notes thereto.

3. "Decision" means a final decision and accordingly the High Court has no jurisdiction to hear an appeal from the Crown Court by way of case stated on a ruling made in a criminal case until the proceedings in the Crown Court have been concluded (*Loade v DPP* [1990] 1 QB 1052, [1990] 1 All ER 36, 153 JP 674).

4. However, such decision may be the subject of an application to the High Court for judicial review; see s 29(3), post, and *Westminster City Council v Lunepalm Ltd* (1985) Times, 10 December.

1–2562A 28A. Proceedings on case stated by magistrates' court or Crown Court. (1) This section applies where a case is stated for the opinion of the High Court—

 (*a*) by a magistrates' court under section 111 of the Magistrates' Courts Act 1980; or
 (*b*) by the Crown Court under section 28(1) of this Act.

(2) The High Court may, if it thinks fit, cause the case to be sent back for amendment and, where it does so, the case shall be amended accordingly.

(3) The High Court shall hear and determine the question arising on the case (or the case as amended) and shall—

 (*a*) reverse[1], affirm or amend the determination in respect of which the case has been stated; or
 (*b*) remit the matter to the magistrates' court, or the Crown Court, with the opinion of the High Court,

and may make such other order in relation to the matter (including as to costs) as it thinks fit.

(4) Except as provided by the Administration of Justice Act 1960 (right of appeal to House of Lords in criminal cases), a decision of the High Court under this section is final.

[Supreme Court Act 1981, s 28A inserted by the Statute Law (Repeals) Act 1993, Sch 2, substituted by the Access to Justice Act 1999, s 108.]

---

1. On an appeal by way of case stated, the Divisional Court may grant leave for a defendant to amend a "due diligence" notice under s 21 of the Food Safety Act 1981 to include an employee by whose default an offence is alleged to have been committed and quash the conviction (*Kilhey Court Hotels Ltd v Wigan Metropolitan Borough Council* [2004] EWHC 2890 (Admin), 169 JP 1).

1–2563 29. Mandatory, prohibiting and quashing orders. (1) The orders of mandamus, prohibition and certiorari shall be known instead as mandatory, prohibiting and quashing orders respectively.

(1A) The High Court shall have jurisdiction to make mandatory, prohibiting and quashing orders[1] in those classes of case in which, immediately before 1st May 2004, it had jurisdiction to make orders of mandamus, prohibition and certiorari respectively.

(3) In relation to the jurisdiction of the Crown Court, other than its jurisdiction in matters relating to trial on indictment[2], the High Court shall have all such jurisdiction to make mandatory, prohibiting or quashing orders as the High Court possesses in relation to the jurisdiction of an inferior court.

(3A) The High Court shall have no jurisdiction to make mandatory, prohibiting or quashing orders in relation to the jurisdiction of a court-martial in matters relating to—

 (*a*) trial by court-martial for an offence, or
 (*b*) appeals from a Standing Civilian Court;

and in this subsection "court-martial" means a court-martial under the Army Act 1955, the Air Force Act 1955 or the Naval Discipline Act 1957.

(4) The power of the High Court under any enactment to require justices of the peace or a judge or officer of a county court to do any act relating to the duties of their respective offices, or to require a magistrates' court to state a case for the opinion of the High Court, in any case where the High Court formerly had by virtue of any enactment jurisdiction to make a rule absolute, or an order, for any of those purposes, shall be exercisable by order of mandatory order.

(5) In any statutory provision—

 (*a*) references to mandamus or to a writ or order of mandamus shall be read as references to a mandatory order;
 (*b*) references to prohibition or to a writ or order of prohibition shall be read as references to a prohibiting order;
 (*c*) references to certiorari or to a writ or order of certiorari shall be read as references to a quashing order; and
 (*d*) references to the issue or award of a writ of mandamus, prohibition or certiorari shall be read as references to the making of the corresponding mandatory, prohibiting or quashing order.

(6) In subsection (3) the reference to the Crown Court's jurisdiction in matters relating to trial on indictment does not include its jurisdiction relating to orders under section 17 of the Access to Justice Act 1999.

[Supreme Court Act 1981, s 29, as amended by the Access to Justice Act 1999, Sch 4 and the Armed Forces Act 2001, s 23(1) and SI 2004/1033.]

1. For the purposes of making a quashing order for error on the face of the record, the "record" is not restricted to the formal order but extends to the reasons given by the judge in his oral judgment and set out in the official transcript thereof (*R v Crown Court at Knightsbridge, ex p International Sporting Club (London) Ltd* [1982] QB 304, [1981] 3 All ER 417).

2. Judicial review may not review a costs order following trial on indictment (*Ex p Meredith* [1973] 2 All ER 234, [1973] 1 WLR 435, 137 JP 485), even where a circuit judge acted wrongly in directing solicitors to pay costs personally, without giving them an opportunity to be heard (*R v Martin Smith* [1975] QB 531, [1974] 1 All ER 651, 138 JP 257). Moreover, a decision by a Crown Court Judge not to make a defendant's costs order following his direction that a verdict of not guilty be entered on the prosecution offering no evidence against the defendant constituted "a matter relating to trial on indictment" and was not therefore subject to judicial review (*R v Harrow Crown Court, ex p Perkins* (1998) 162 JP 527). The High Court does not have jurisdiction to review a decision of the Crown Court to refuse legal aid for a trial on indictment (*R v Crown Court at Chichester, ex p Abodunrin and Sogbanmu* (1984) 149 JP 54, [1984] Crim LR 240), nor may it review a decision, to remit any sums due from, or to order repayment of any sums paid by, a defendant under a legal aid contribution order. However, the High Court may review a legal aid contribution order, made by a magistrates' court or the Crown Court, since such an order is not a matter "relating to trial on indictment" (*Sampson v Crown Court at Croydon* [1987] 1 All ER 609, [1987] 1 WLR 194, 84 Cr App Rep 376). Whether the High Court may review the making or refusal to make an order under s 39 of the Children and Young Persons Act 1933 would seem to depend on the stage of the proceedings and whether the order would have influence on the *trial* in contrast to the proceedings as a whole (*R v Crown Court at Manchester, ex p H* [2000] 2 All ER 166, [2000] 1 WLR 760, [2000] 1 Cr App Rep 262; contrast *R v Crown Court at Winchester, ex p B* [1999] 4 All ER 53, [1999] 1 WLR 788, DC.

The interpretation previously placed on s 29(3) is not incompatible with a Convention right; all that can be said is that in some cases breaches of a Convention right by a trial judge may not be capable of review, but that does not bring about a further independent breach of a Convention right and s 3 of the Human Rights Act 1998 does not, therefore, compel the court to interpret s 29(3) differently from previous decisions: *R v Crown Court at Canterbury, ex p Regentford Ltd* (2001) Times, 6 February.

The High Court does not have power to review an order of the Crown Court that counts of an indictment should lie on the file (*R v Central Criminal Court, ex p Raymond* [1986] 2 All ER 379, [1986] 1 WLR 710, 83 Cr App Rep 94), but the section does not exclude an order entreating a recognizance of a surety as that could not affect the conduct of any trial on indictment in any way and the Divisional Court could thus review the order; *Re Smalley* [1985] AC 622, [1985] 1 All ER 769, 149 JP 319, HL. In cases where the facts are complicated, appeals to the Divisional Court should be by way of case stated (*R v Felixstowe Justices, ex p Baldwin* [1981] 1 All ER 596, 72 Cr App Rep 131).

1–2564   31. Application for judicial review.   (1) An application to the High Court for one or more of the following forms of relief, namely—

(*a*)   a mandatory, prohibiting or quashing order;
(*b*)   a declaration or injunction under subsection (2); or
(*c*)   an injunction under section 30 restraining a person not entitled to do so from acting in an office to which that section applies,

shall be made in accordance with rules of court by a procedure to be known as an application for judicial review.

(2) A declaration may be made or an injunction granted under this subsection in any case where an application for judicial review, seeking that relief, has been made and the High Court considers that, having regard to—

(*a*)   the nature of the matters in respect of which relief may be granted by mandatory, prohibiting or quashing orders;
(*b*)   the nature of the persons and bodies against whom relief may be granted by such orders; and
(*c*)   all the circumstances of the case,

it would be just and convenient for the declaration to be made or the injunction to be granted, as the case may be.

(3) No application for judicial review shall be made unless the leave of the High Court has been obtained in accordance with rules of court; and the court shall not grant leave to make such an application unless it considers that the applicant has a sufficient interest in the matter to which the application relates.

(4) On an application for judicial review the High Court may award to the applicant damages, restitution or the recovery of a sum due if—

(*a*)   the application includes a claim for such an award arising from any matter to which the application relates; and
(*b*)   the court is satisfied that such an award would have been made if the claim had been made in an action begun by the applicant at the time of making the application.

(5) If, on an application for judicial review seeking a quashing order, the High Court quashes the decision to which the application relates, the High Court may remit the matter to the court, tribunal or authority concerned, with a direction to reconsider it and reach a decision in accordance with the findings of the High Court.

(6) Where the High Court considers that there has been undue delay in making an application for judicial review, the court may refuse to grant—

(*a*)   leave for the making of the application; or
(*b*)   any relief sought on the application,

if it considers that the granting of the relief sought would be likely to cause substantial hardship to, or substantially prejudice the rights of, any person or would be detrimental to good administration.

(7) Subsection (6) is without prejudice to any enactment or rule of court which has the effect of limiting the time within which an application for judicial review may be made.
[Supreme Court Act 1981, s 31 as amended by SI 2004/1033.]

Powers

1–2565   41. Wards of court.   (1) Subject to the provisions of this section, no minor shall be made a ward of court except by virtue of an order to that effect made by the High Court.

(2) Where an application is made for such an order in respect of a minor, the minor shall become a ward of court on the making of the application, but shall cease to be a ward of court at the end of such period as may be prescribed unless within that period an order has been made in accordance with the application.

(2A) Subsection (2) does not apply with respect to a child who is the subject of a care order (as defined by section 105 of the Children Act 1989).

(3) The High Court may, either upon an application in that behalf or without such an application, order that any minor who is for the time being a ward of court shall cease to be a ward of court.
[Supreme Court Act 1981, s 41 as amended by the Children Act 1989, Sch 13.]

1–2566   42. Restriction of vexatious[1] legal proceedings.   (1) If, on an application made by the Attorney General under this section, the High Court is satisfied that any person has habitually and persistently[2] and without any reasonable ground—

(a) instituted vexatious civil proceedings, whether in the High Court or any inferior court, and whether against the same person or against different persons; or

(b) made vexatious applications in any civil proceedings, whether in the High Court or any inferior court, and whether instituted by him or another, or

(c) instituted vexatious prosecutions (whether against the same person or different persons),

the court may, after hearing that person or giving him an opportunity of being heard, order—

(i) that no legal proceedings shall without the leave of the High Court be instituted by him in any court; and

(ii) that any legal proceedings instituted by him in any court before the making of the order shall not be continued by him without the leave of the High Court; and

(iii) that no application (other than an application for leave under this section) shall without the leave of the High Court be made by him in any legal proceedings instituted, whether by him or another, in any court.

(1A) In this section—

"civil proceedings order" means an order that—

(a) no civil proceedings shall without the leave[3] of the High Court be instituted in any court by the person against whom the order is made;

(b) any civil proceedings instituted by him in any court before the making of the order shall not be continued by him without the leave of the High Court; and

(c) no application (other than one for leave under this section) shall be made by him, in any civil proceedings instituted in any court by any person, without the leave of the High Court;

"criminal proceedings order" means an order that—

(a) no information shall be laid before a justice of the peace by the person against whom the order is made without the leave of the High Court; and

(b) no application for leave to prefer a bill of indictment shall be made by him without the leave of the High Court; and

"all proceedings order" means an order which has the combined effect of the two other orders.

(2) An order under subsection (1) may provide that it is to cease to have effect at the end of a specified period, but shall otherwise remain in force indefinitely.

(3) Leave for the institution or continuance of, or for the making of an application in, any civil proceedings by a person who is the subject of an order for the time being in force under subsection (1) shall not be given unless the High Court is satisfied that the proceedings or application are not an abuse of the process of the court in question and that there are reasonable grounds for the proceedings or application.

(3A) Leave for the laying of an information or for an application for leave to prefer a bill of indictment by a person who is the subject of an order for the time being in force under subsection (1) shall not be given unless the High Court is satisfied that the institution of the prosecution is not an abuse of the criminal process and that there are reasonable grounds for the institution of the prosecution by the applicant.

(4) No appeal shall lie from a decision of the High Court refusing leave required by virtue of this section.

(5) A copy of any order made under subsection (1) shall be published in the London Gazette.
[Supreme Court Act 1981, s 42 as amended by the Prosecution of Offences Act 1985, s 24.]

---

1. Principles for courts dealing with vexatious litigants' applications were set out in *Re C* (1989) Times, 14 November.

2. The words "habitually and persistently" connote an element of repetition which does not need to be over a long period (*A-G v Barker* [2000] 2 FCR 1).

3. Where an application for leave to apply for judicial review under CPR 1998, r 54.4 is made by a person who is subject to an order under this section, the matter should be placed before one of the judges who habitually deal with applications for leave under CPR 1998, Part 54, who should consider the matter on the footing that he is faced with both an application under s 42 for leave to institute civil proceedings and an application under Part 54 for leave to apply for judicial review (*R v Highbury Corner Magistrates' Court, ex p Ewing* [1991] 3 All ER 192, [1991] 1 WLR 388, CA).

1–2567 43. Power of High Court to vary sentence on application for quashing order.
(1) Where a person who has been sentenced for an offence—

(a) by a magistrates' court; or

(b) by the Crown Court after being convicted of the offence by a magistrates' court and committed to the Crown Court for sentence; or

(c) by the Crown Court on appeal against conviction or sentence,

applies to the High Court in accordance with section 31 for a quashing order to remove the proceedings of the magistrates' court or the Crown Court into the High Court, then, if the High Court determines that the magistrates' court or the Crown Court had no power to pass the sentence[1], the High Court may, instead of quashing the conviction, amend it by substituting for the sentence passed any sentence which the magistrates' court or, in a case within paragraph (b), the Crown Court had power to impose.

(2) Any sentence passed by the High Court by virtue of this section in substitution for the sentence passed in the proceedings of the magistrates' court or the Crown Court shall, unless the High Court otherwise directs, begin to run from the time when it would have begun to run if passed in those proceedings; but in computing the term of the sentence, any time during which the offender was released on bail in pursuance of section 37(1)(d) of the Criminal Justice Act 1948 shall be disregarded.

(3) Subsections (1) and (2) shall, with the necessary modifications, apply in relation to any order of a magistrates' court or the Crown Court which is made on, but does not form part of, the conviction[2] of an offender as they apply in relation to a conviction and sentence.
[Supreme Court Act 1981, s 43 as amended by SI 2004/1033.]

---

1. A sentence which, although in itself lawful, is so very much outside the range of sentences normally passed as to be in excess of the court's jurisdiction may be wrong in law; see *R v Crown Court at St Albans, ex p Cinnamond* [1981] QB 480, [1981] 1 All ER 802. But this will apply only to a very unusual and rare circumstance, and a person who seeks to have a sentence of justices or the Crown Court reviewed upon the basis that the sentence is too severe will need to show that the sentence was by any acceptable standard truly astonishing; see *R v Crown Court at Acton, ex p Bewley* (1988) 152 JP 327, 10 Cr App Rep (S) 105.
2. Section 43(3) is not apt to cover an order subsequent to conviction made for a new intervening cause such as wilful refusal or culpable neglect to pay a financial penalty made on a conviction. *R v St Helen's Justices, ex p Jones* [1999] 2 All ER 73, sub nom *R v Stoke on Trent Justices, ex p Wilby* [1998] 163 JP 369. For the power of the High Court to vary committal in default, see now s 43ZA, post.

1–2567A 43ZA. Power of High Court to vary committal in default. (1) Where the High Court quashes the committal of a person to prison or detention by a magistrates' court or the Crown Court for—

(a) a default in paying a sum adjudged to be paid by a conviction; or

(b) want of sufficient distress to satisfy such a sum,

the High Court may deal with the person for the default or want of sufficient distress in any way in which the magistrates' court or Crown Court would have power to deal with him if it were dealing with him at the time when the committal is quashed.

(2) If the High Court commits him to prison or detention, the period of imprisonment or detention shall, unless the High Court otherwise directs, be treated as having begun when the person was committed by the magistrates' court or the Crown Court (except that any time during which he was released on bail shall not be counted as part of the period).
[Supreme Court Act 1981, s 43ZA as inserted by the Access to Justice Act 1999, s 62.]

THE CROWN COURT

1–2568 45. General jurisdiction of Crown Court. (1) The Crown Court shall be a superior court of record.

(2) Subject to the provisions of this Act, there shall be exercisable by the Crown Court—

(a) all such appellate and other jurisdiction as is conferred on it by or under this or any other Act; and

(b) all such other jurisdiction as was exercisable by it immediately before the commencement of this Act.

(3) Without prejudice to subsection (2), the jurisdiction of the Crown Court shall include all such powers and duties as were exercisable or fell to be performed by it immediately before the commencement of this Act.

(4) Subject to section 8 of the Criminal Procedure (Attendance of Witnesses) Act 1965 (substitution in criminal cases of procedure in that Act for procedure by way of subpoena) and to any provision contained in or having effect under this Act, the Crown Court shall, in relation to the attendance and examination of witnesses, any contempt of court, the enforcement of its orders and all other matters incidental to its jurisdiction, have the like powers, rights, privileges and authority as the High Court.

(5) The specific mention elsewhere in this Act of any jurisdiction covered by subsections (2) and (3) shall not derogate from the generality of those subsections.
[Supreme Court Act 1981, s 45.]

1–2569 46. Exclusive jurisdiction of Crown Court in trial on indictment. (1) All proceedings on indictment shall be brought before the Crown Court.

(2) The jurisdiction of the Crown Court with respect to proceedings on indictment shall include jurisdiction in proceedings on indictment for offences wherever committed, and in particular proceedings on indictment for offences within the jurisdiction of the Admiralty of England.
[Supreme Court Act 1981, s 46.]

1–2569A   46A. Offences committed on ships and abroad.   Sections 280, 281 and 282 of the Merchant Shipping Act 1995 (offences on ships and abroad by British citizens and others) apply in relation to other offences under the law of England and Wales as they apply in relation to offences under that Act or instruments under that Act.
[Supreme Court Act 1981, s 46A, as inserted by the Merchant Shipping Act 1995, Sch 13.]

1–2570   47. Sentences and other orders of Crown Court when dealing with offenders.
Repealed.

1–2571   48. Appeals to Crown Court.   (1) The Crown Court may, in the course of hearing any appeal, correct any error or mistake in the order or judgment incorporating the decision which is the subject of the appeal[1].
(2) On the termination of the hearing of an appeal the Crown Court[2]—

(a) may confirm, reverse or vary any part[3] of the decision appealed against, including a determination not to impose a separate penalty in respect of an offence; or
(b) may remit[4] the matter with its opinion[5] thereon to the authority whose decision is appealed against; or
(c) may make such other order[6] in the matter as the court thinks just, and by such order exercise any power which the said authority might have exercised.

(3) Subsection (2) has effect subject to any enactment relating to any such appeal which expressly limits or restricts the powers of the court on the appeal.
(4) Subject to section 11(6) of the Criminal Appeal Act 1995, if the appeal is against a conviction or a sentence, the preceding provisions of this section shall be construed as including power to award any punishment, whether more or less severe than that awarded by the magistrates' court whose decision is appealed against, if that is a punishment which that magistrates' court might have awarded.
(5) This section applies whether or not the appeal is against the whole of the decision.
(6) In this section "sentence" includes any order made by a court when dealing with an offender, including—

(a) a hospital order under Part III of the Mental Health Act 1983, with or without a restriction order, and an interim hospital order under that Act; and
(b) a recommendation for deportation made when dealing with an offender.

(7) The fact that an appeal is pending against an interim hospital order under the said Act of 1983 shall not affect the power of the magistrates' court that made it to renew or terminate the order or to deal with the appellant on its termination; and where the Crown Court quashes such an order but does not pass any sentence or make any other order in its place the Court may direct the appellant to be kept in custody or released on bail pending his being dealt with by that magistrates' court.
(8) Where the Crown Court makes an interim hospital order by virtue of subsection (2)—

(a) the power of renewing or terminating the order and of dealing with the appellant on its termination shall be exercisable by the magistrates' court whose decision is appealed against and not by the Crown Court; and
(b) that magistrates' court shall be treated for the purposes of section 38(7) of the said Act of 1983 (absconding offenders) as the court that made the order.
[Supreme Court Act 1981, s 48 as amended by the Mental Health (Amendment) Act 1982, Sch 3, the Mental Health Act 1983, Sch 4, the Criminal Justice Act 1988, s 156 and the Criminal Appeal Act 1995, Sch 2.]

---

1. The words "the decision which is the subject of the appeal" mean the whole of the decision made by the justices on the occasion on which the conviction or sentence appealed against was made. Accordingly where the Crown Court allows an appeal in relation to a driving disqualification for one offence, it may vary sentences by adding penalty points for other offences not specifically appealed against but which were dealt with by the justices at the same time as the offence the subject matter of the appeal (*Dutta v Westcott* [1987] QB 291, [1986] 3 All ER 381).
2. Where an appeal against conviction by a magistrates' court has been abandoned before the hearing of the appeal has commenced, the Crown Court has no jurisdiction to increase the sentence imposed by the justices (*R v Gloucester Crown Court, ex p Betteridge* (1997) 161 JP 721, [1998] Crim LR 218).
3. Therefore, the Crown Court, when dismissing an appeal may vary any order made by the magistrates as to the payment by the defendant to the prosecutor in respect of proceedings before the magistrates (*Johnson v RSPCA* (2000) 164 JP 345, DC).
4. This will be appropriate, for instance, where a magistrates' court has wrongly entered an ambiguous plea as a plea of guilty (see *R v Durham Quarter Sessions, ex p Virgo* [1952] 2 QB 1, [1952] 1 All ER 466, 116 JP 157); but the Crown Court must make proper enquiry as to what took place in the magistrates' court and may only remit if it finds that an equivocal plea was entered (*R v Marylebone Justices, ex p Westminster City Council* [1971] 1 All ER 1025, [1971] 1 WLR 567, 135 JP 239).
5. In this context, the opinion of the Crown Court is an order which the lower court is bound to follow (*R v Tottenham Justices, ex p Rubens* [1970] 1 All ER 879, [1970] 1 WLR 800, 134 JP 285). Such an order has the effect of setting aside the justices' earlier decisions, so that they are no longer *functus officio* but rather are under a duty to proceed in accordance with the direction of the Crown Court (*R v Customs and Excise Comrs, ex p Wagstaff* (1997) 162 JP 186, [1998] Crim LR 287).
6. As to scope of these words, see *Fulham Metropolitan Borough Council v Santilli* [1933] 2 KB 357, 97 JP 174. Where a

suspended sentence of imprisonment is ordered, the operational period will run from the date the order is made by the Crown Court (*R v Burn* [1976] Crim LR 754).

GENERAL PROVISIONS
Law and equity

1–2672   49. Concurrent administration of law and equity.   (1) Subject to the provisions of this or any other Act, every court exercising jurisdiction in England or Wales in any civil cause or matter shall continue to administer law and equity on the basis that, wherever there is any conflict or variance between the rules of equity and the rules of the common law with reference to the same matter, the rules of equity shall prevail.

(2) Every such court shall give the same effect as hitherto—

(*a*)   to all equitable estates, titles, rights, reliefs, defences and counterclaims, and to all equitable duties and liabilities; and

(*b*)   subject thereto, to all legal claims and demands and all estates, titles, rights, duties, obligations and liabilities existing by the common law or by any custom or created by any statute,

and, subject to the provisions of this or any other Act, shall so exercise its jurisdiction in every cause or matter before it as to secure that, as far as possible, all matters in dispute between the parties are completely and finally determined, and all multiplicity of legal proceedings with respect to any of those matters is avoided.

(3) Nothing in this Act shall affect the power of the Court of Appeal or the High Court to stay any proceedings before it, where it thinks fit to do so, either of its own motion or on the application of any person, whether or not a party to the proceedings.
[Supreme Court Act 1981, s 49.]

Costs

1–2673   51. Costs in civil division of Court of Appeal, High Court and county courts.
(1) Subject to the provisions of this or any other enactment and to rules of court, the costs of and incidental to all proceedings in—

(*a*)   the civil division of the Court of Appeal;
(*b*)   the High Court; and
(*c*)   any county court,

shall be in the discretion of the court.

(2) Without prejudice to any general power to make rules of court, such rules may make provision for regulating matters relating to the costs of those proceedings including, in particular, prescribing scales of costs to be paid to legal or other representatives or for securing that the amount awarded to a party in respect of the costs to be paid by him to such representatives is not limited to what would have been payable by him to them if he had not been awarded costs.

(3) The court shall have full power to determine by whom and to what extent the costs are to be paid.

(4) In subsections (1) and (2) "proceedings" includes the administration of estates and trusts.

(5) Nothing in subsection (1) shall alter the practice in any criminal cause, or in bankruptcy.

(6) In any proceedings mentioned in subsection (1), the court may disallow, or (as the case may be) order the legal or other representative concerned to meet, the whole of any wasted costs or such part of them as may be determined in accordance with rules of court.

(7) In subsection (6), "wasted costs" means any costs incurred by a party[1]—

(*a*)   as a result of any improper, unreasonable or negligent act or omission on the part of any legal or other representative or any employee of such a representative; or

(*b*)   which, in the light of any such act or omission occurring after they were incurred, the court considers it is unreasonable to expect that party to pay.

(8) Where—

(*a*)   a person has commenced proceedings in the High Court; but
(*b*)   those proceedings should, in the opinion of the court, have been commenced in a county court in accordance with any provision made under section 1 of the Courts and Legal Services Act 1990 or by or under any other enactment,

the person responsible for determining the amount which is to be awarded to that person by way of costs shall have regard to those circumstances.

(9) Where, in complying with subsection (8), the responsible person reduces the amount which would otherwise be awarded to the person in question—

(*a*)   the amount of that reduction shall not exceed 25 per cent; and
(*b*)   on any taxation of the costs payable by that person to his legal representative, regard shall be had to the amount of the reduction.

(10) The Lord Chancellor may by order amend subsection (9)(*a*) by substituting, for the percentage for the time being mentioned there, a different percentage.

(11) Any such order shall be made by statutory instrument and may make such transitional or incidental provision as the Lord Chancellor considers expedient.

(12) No such statutory instrument shall be made unless a draft of the instrument has been approved by both Houses of Parliament.

(13) In this section "legal or other representative", in relation to a party to proceedings, means any person exercising a right of audience or right to conduct litigation on his behalf[2].

[Supreme Court Act 1981, s 51 as substituted by the Courts and Legal Services Act 1990, s 4 and the Access to Justice Act 1999, s 31.]

---

1. "Party", in relation to any proceedings, includes any person who pursuant to or by virtue of rules of court or any other statutory provision has been served with notice of, or has intervened in, those proceedings (Supreme Court Act 1981, s 151(1)). The term "party" is not an open-ended category and is limited to a person who has been served with notice of or has intervened in proceedings by virtue of rules of court or other statutory provision (*R v Camden London Borough Council, ex p Martin* [1997] 1 All ER 307, [1997] 1 WLR 359, [1997] 1 FLR 950).
2. This subsection is intended to make plain that no liability can attach to any practitioner not involved in the litigation giving rise to the claim and does not mean that a wasted costs order may not be made against the legal representative of the opposing party: *Medcalf v Mardell* [2002] UKHL 27, [2003] 1 AC 120, [2002] 3 All ER 721.

1–2681　52. Costs in Crown Court. (1) Rules of court may authorise the Crown Court to award costs and may regulate any matters relating to costs of proceedings in that court, and in particular may make provision as to—

(a) any discretion to award costs;
(b) the taxation of costs, or the fixing of a sum instead of directing a taxation, and as to the officer of the court or other person by whom costs are to be taxed;
(c) a right of appeal from any decision on the taxation of costs, whether to a Taxing Master of the Supreme Court or to any other officer or authority;
(d) a right of appeal to the High Court, subject to any conditions specified in the rules, from any decision on an appeal brought by virtue of paragraph (c);
(e) the enforcement of an order for costs; and
(f) the charges or expenses or other disbursements which are to be treated as costs for the purposes of the rules.

(2) The costs to be dealt with by rules made in pursuance of this section may, where an appeal is brought to the Crown Court from the decision of a magistrates' court, or from the decision of any other court or tribunal, include costs in the proceedings in that court or tribunal.

(2A) Subsection (6) of section 51 applies in relation to any civil proceedings in the Crown Court as it applies in relation to any proceedings mentioned in subsection (1) of that section.

(3) Nothing in this section authorises the making of rules about the payment of costs out of central funds, whether under Part II of the Prosecution of Offences Act 1985 or otherwise, but rules made in pursuance of this section may make any such provision as in relation to costs of proceedings in the Crown Court, is contained in section 18 of that Act or in regulations made under section 19 of that Act (awards of party and party costs in criminal proceedings).

(4) Rules made in pursuance of this section may amend or repeal all or any of the provisions of any enactment about costs between party and party in criminal or other proceedings in the Crown Court, being an enactment passed before, or contained in, Part II of the Prosecution of Offences Act 1985.

(5) Rules made in pursuance of this section shall have effect subject to the provisions of section 41 of, and Schedule 9 to, the Administration of Justice Act 1970 (method of enforcing orders for costs).

[Supreme Court Act 1981, s 52 as amended by the Prosecution of Offences Act 1985, Sch 1, the Courts and Legal Services Act 1990, s 4 and SI 2004/2035.]

PART III[1]
PRACTICE AND PROCEDURE

THE CROWN COURT
Composition of court

1–2682　73. General provisions. (1) Subject to the provisions of sections 8(1)(c), 74 and 75(2) as respects courts comprising justices of the peace, all proceedings in the Crown Court shall be heard and disposed of before a single judge of that court.

(2) Rules of court[2] may authorise or require a judge of the High Court, Circuit judge or Recorder, in such circumstances as are specified by the rules, at any stage to continue with any proceedings with a court from which any one or more of the justices initially constituting the court has withdrawn, or is absent for any reason.

(3) Where a judge of the High Court, Circuit judge or Recorder sits with justices of the peace he shall preside, and—

(a) the decision of the Crown Court may be a majority decision[3]; and
(b) if the members of the court are equally divided, the judge of the High Court, Circuit judge or Recorder shall have a second and casting vote.

[Supreme Court Act 1981, s 73 as amended by SI 2004/2035.]

---

1. Part III contains ss 53–87.
2. See r 4 of the Crown Court Rules 1982, this PART: STATUTORY INSTRUMENTS AND PRACTICE DIRECTIONS ON PROCEDURE, post.

3. The majority may exclude the professional judge but the justices must defer to the views of the presiding judge in matters of law (*R v Orpin* [1975] QB 283, [1974] 2 All ER 1121, 138 JP 651). Care must be taken by the presiding judge to ensure that consultation with the lay justices is a reality; see *R v Newby* [1984] Crim LR 509.

1–2683 74. Appeals and committals for sentence.   (1) On any hearing by the Crown Court—

(*a*) of any appeal;

(*b*) (*Repealed*),

the Crown Court shall consist of a judge of the High Court or a Circuit judge or a Recorder who, subject to the following provisions of this section, shall sit with not less than two nor more than four justices of the peace[1].

(2) Rules of court[2] may, with respect to hearings falling within subsection (1)—

(*a*) prescribe the number of justices of the peace constituting the court (within the limits mentioned in that subsection); and

(*b*) prescribe the qualifications to be possessed by any such justices of the peace;

and the rules may make different provision for different descriptions of cases, different places of sitting or other different circumstances.

(3) Rules of court[3] may authorise or require a judge of the High Court, Circuit judge or Recorder, in such circumstances as are specified by the rules, to enter on, or at any stage to continue with, any proceedings with a court not comprising the justices required by subsections (1) and (2).

(4) The Lord Chancellor may from time to time, having regard to the number of justices, or the number of justices with any prescribed qualifications, available for service in the Crown Court, give directions providing that, in such descriptions of proceedings as may be specified by the Lord Chancellor, the provisions of subsections (1) and (2) shall not apply.

(5) Directions under subsection (4) may frame descriptions of proceedings by reference to the place of trial, or by reference to the time of trial, or in any other way.

(6) No decision of the Crown Court shall be questioned on the ground that the court was not constituted as required by or under subsection (1) and (2) unless objection was taken by or on behalf of a party to the proceedings not later than the time when the proceedings were entered on, or when the alleged irregularity began.

(7) Rules of court may make provision as to the circumstances in which—

(*a*) a person concerned with a decision appealed against is to be disqualified from hearing the appeal;

(*b*) (*Repealed*); and

(*c*) proceedings on the hearing of an appeal are to be valid notwithstanding that any person taking part in them is disqualified.

[Supreme Court Act 1981, s 74 as amended by the Access to Justice Act 1999, s 79 and Sch 15 and SI 2004/2035.]

---

1. The justices are to take part in the decision making and a majority decision, even if it excludes the professional judge, prevails except that in matters of law the justices must defer to the views of the presiding judge (*R v Orpin* [1975] QB 283, [1974] 2 All ER 1121, 138 JP 651).

2. See r 3 of the Crown Court Rules 1982, Criminal Procedure Rules 2005, Part 63, this PART: STATUTORY INSTRUMENTS AND PRACTICE DIRECTIONS ON PROCEDURE, post.

3. See r 4 of the Crown Court Rules 1982, Criminal Procedure Rules 2005, Part 63, this PART: STATUTORY INSTRUMENTS AND PRACTICE DIRECTIONS ON PROCEDURE, post.

Distribution of business

1–2684 75. Allocation of cases according to composition of court, etc.   (1) The cases or classes of cases in the Crown Court suitable for allocation respectively to a judge of the High Court and to a Circuit judge or Recorder, and all other matters relating to the distribution of Crown Court business, shall be determined in accordance with directions given by or on behalf of the Lord Chief Justice with the concurrence of the Lord Chancellor.

(2) Subject to section 74(1), the cases or classes of cases in the Crown Court suitable for allocation to a court comprising justices of the peace (including those by way of trial on indictment which are suitable for allocation to such a court) shall be determined in accordance with directions[1] given by or on behalf of the Lord Chief Justice with the concurrence of the Lord Chancellor.

[Supreme Court Act 1981, s 75.]

---

1. Directions given in accordance with this provision are set out in *Practice Direction (criminal: consolidated)* [2002] para III.21, in this PART, post.

1–2685 76. Committal for trial: alteration of place of trial*.   (1) Without prejudice to the provisions of this Act about the distribution of Crown Court business, the Crown Court may give directions, or further directions, altering the place of any trial on indictment, whether by varying the decision of a magistrates' court under section 7 of the Magistrates' Courts Act 1980 or by substituting some other place for the place specified in a notice under section 4 of the Criminal Justice Act 1987 (notices of transfer from magistrates' court to Crown Court) or by varying a previous decision of the Crown Court.*

(2) Directions under subsection (1) may be given on behalf of the Crown Court by an officer of the court.

(2A) Where a preparatory hearing has been ordered under section 7 of the Criminal Justice Act

1987, directions altering the place of trial may be given under subsection (1) at any time before the time when the jury are sworn.

(2B) The reference in subsection (2A) to the time when the jury are sworn includes the time when the jury would be sworn but for the making of an order under Part 7 of the Criminal Justice Act 2003.

(3) The defendant or the prosecutor, if dissatisfied with the place of trial as fixed by the magistrates' court, as specified in a notice under section 4 of the Criminal Justice Act 1987 or as fixed by the Crown Court, may apply to the Crown Court for a direction, or further direction, varying the place of trial; and the court shall take the matter into consideration and may comply with or refuse the application, or give a direction not in compliance with the application, as the court thinks fit.*

(4) *Repealed.*

(5) In this section "relevant transfer provision" means—

(a)   section 4 of the Criminal Justice Act 1987, or
(b)   section 53 of the Criminal Justice Act 1991.*

[Supreme Court Act 1981, s 76 as amended by the Criminal Justice Act 1987, Sch 2, the Criminal Justice and Public Order Act 1994, Sch 9, the Courts Act 2003 and the Criminal Justice Act 2003, Sch 36.]

---

    *Heading and sub-ss (1) and (3) amended and sub-s (5) repealed by the Criminal Justice Act 2003, Sch 3, from a date to be appointed.

1–2686   77. Committal* for trial: date of trial.   (1) Criminal Procedure Rules shall prescribe the minimum and the maximum period* which may elapse between a person's committal for trial or the giving of a notice of transfer under a relevant transfer provision* and the beginning of the trial; and such rules may make different provision for different places of trial and for other different circumstances.

(2) The trial of a person committed by a magistrates' court or in respect of whom a notice of transfer under a relevant transfer provision has been given*—

(a)   shall not begin until the prescribed[1] minimum period has expired except with his consent and the consent of the prosecutor; and**
(b)   shall not begin later than the expiry of the prescribed[1] maximum period unless a judge of the Crown Court otherwise orders.[2]

(3) For the purposes of this section the prescribed minimum and maximum periods*** shall begin with the date of committal for trial or of a notice of transfer* and the trial shall be taken to begin when the defendant is arraigned.

[Supreme Court Act 1981, s 77 as amended by the Criminal Justice Act 1987, Sch 2.]

---

    *Words substituted by the Criminal Justice Act 2003 , Sch 3 from a date to be appointed.
    **Repealed by the Prosecution of Offences Act 1985, Sch 2, when in force.
    ***Amended by the Prosecution of Offences Act 1985, Sch 2, when in force.
    1. See the Criminal Procedure Rules 2005, Part 39, this PART: STATUTORY INSTRUMENTS AND PRACTICE DIRECTIONS ON PROCEDURE, post.
    2. This section is directory and not mandatory; failure to observe the section does not deprive the Crown Court of the power to extend the eight week period from the date of committal specified by the Criminal Procedure Rules 2005, Part 39, nor does such a failure render a trial, lawfully conducted, a nullity (*R v Spring Hill Prison Governor, ex p Sohi* [1988] 1 All ER 424, [1988] 1 WLR 596, 86 Cr App Rep 382).

Sittings

1–2687   78. Sittings.   (1) Any Crown Court business may be conducted at any place in England or Wales, and the sittings of the Crown Court at any place may be continuous or intermittent or occasional.

(2) Judges of the Crown Court may sit simultaneously to take any number of different cases in the same or different places, and may adjourn cases from place to place at any time.

(3) The places at which the Crown Court sits, and the days and times at which the Crown Court sits at any place, shall be determined in accordance with directions[1] given by the Lord Chancellor.

[Supreme Court Act 1981, s 78.]

---

    1. Directions given in accordance with this provision are set out in this PART: STATUTORY INSTRUMENTS AND PRACTICE DIRECTIONS ON PROCEDURE, post.

Other provisions

1–2688   79. Practice and procedure in connection with indictable offences and appeals.
(1) All enactments and rules of law relating to procedure in connection with indictable offences shall continue to have effect in relation to proceedings in the Crown Court.

(2) Without prejudice to the generality of subsection (1), that subsection applies in particular to—

(a)   the practice by which, on any one indictment, the taking of pleas, the trial by jury and the pronouncement of judgment may respectively be by or before different judges;
(b)   the release, after respite of judgment, of a convicted person on recognizance[1] to come up for judgment if called on, but meanwhile to be of good behaviour;
(c)   the manner of trying any question relating to the breach of a recognizance;

(*d*) the manner of execution of any sentence on conviction, or the manner in which any other judgment or order given in connection with trial on indictment may be enforced.

(3) The customary practice and procedure[2] with respect to appeals to the Crown Court, and in particular any practice as to the extent to which an appeal is by way of rehearing of the case, shall continue to be observed.
[Supreme Court Act 1981, s 79.]

---

1. There is a power for the Crown Court to add conditions, unlike a binding over in a magistrates' court where it seems the only conditions may be to keep the peace and to be of good behaviour. A condition restricting the right of residence will not contravene art 48 of the EEC treaty forbidding discrimination on the grounds of nationality (*R v Saunders* [1980] QB 72, [1979] 2 All ER 267).
2. It is an established practice that an appellant can appear by counsel if he wishes, and is under no strict legal obligation to be present in person if he does not wish to be so; *R v Crown Court at Croydon, ex p Clair* [1986] 2 All ER 716, [1986] 1 WLR 746. Where an appeal against sentence has not been abandoned by the appellant or by leave of the court, the Crown Court is entitled to hear the appeal in the absence of the appellant or any representative on his behalf (*R v Crown Court at Guildford, ex p Brewer* (1987) 152 JP 147).

1–2689 80. Process to compel appearance. (1) Any direction to appear and any condition of a recognizance to appear before the Crown Court, and any summons or order to appear before that court, may be so framed as to require appearance at such time and place as may be directed by the Crown Court, and if a time or place is specified in the direction, condition, summons or order, it may be varied by any subsequent direction of the Crown Court.

(2) Where an indictment has been signed although the person charged has not been committed for trial, the Crown Court may issue a summons requiring that person to appear before the Crown Court, or may issue a warrant for his arrest.

(3) Section 4 of the Summary Jurisdiction (Process) Act 1881 (execution of process of English courts in Scotland) shall apply to process issued under this section as it applies to process issued under the Magistrates' Courts Act 1980 by a magistrates' court.
[Supreme Court Act 1981, s 80.]

1–2690 81. Bail[1]. (1) The Crown Court may, subject to section 25 of the Criminal Justice and Public Order Act 1994, grant bail to any person—

(*a*) who has been committed in custody for appearance before the Crown Court or in relation to whose case a notice of transfer has been given under a relevant transfer provision* or who has been sent in custody to the Crown Court for trial under section 51 of the Crime and Disorder Act 1998; or**
(*b*) who is in custody[2] pursuant to a sentence imposed by a magistrates' court, and who has appealed to the Crown Court against his conviction or sentence; or
(*c*) who is in the custody of the Crown Court pending the disposal of his case by that court; or
(*d*) who, after the decision of his case by the Crown Court, has applied to that court for the statement of a case for the High Court on that decision; or
(*e*) who has applied to the High Court for a quashing order to remove proceedings in the Crown Court in his case into the High Court, or has applied to the High Court for leave to make such an application; or
(*f*) to whom the Crown Court has granted a certificate under section 1(2) or 11(1A) of the Criminal Appeal Act 1968[3] or under subsection (1B) below; or
(*g*) who has been remanded in custody by a magistrates' court[4] on adjourning a case under section 11 of the Powers of Criminal Courts (Sentencing) Act 2000 (remand for medical examination) or—

  (i) section 5 (adjournment of inquiry into offence);*
  (ii) section 10 (adjournment of trial);
  (iii) section 18 (initial procedure on information against adult for offence triable either way);*
  (iv) *repealed*

of the Magistrates' Courts Act 1980;
and the time during which a person is released on bail under any provision of this subsection shall not count as part of any term of imprisonment or detention under his sentence.*

(1A) The power conferred by subsection (1)(*f*) does not extend to a case to which section 12 or 15 of the Criminal Appeal Act 1968 (appeal against verdict of not guilty by reason of insanity or against findings that the accused is under a disability and that he did the act or made the omission charged against him) applies.

(1B) A certificate under this subsection is a certificate that a case is fit for appeal on a ground which involves a question of law alone.

(1C) The power conferred by subsection (1)(*f*) is to be exercised—

(*a*) where the appeal is under section 1 or 9 of the Criminal Appeal Act 1968, by the judge who tried the case; and
(*b*) where it is under section 10 of that Act, by the judge who passed the sentence.

(1D) The power may only be exercised within twenty-eight days from the date of the conviction appealed against, or in the case of appeal against sentence, from the date on which sentence was passed or, in the case of an order made or treated as made on conviction, from the date of the making of the order.

(1E) The power may not be exercised if the appellant has made an application to the Court of Appeal for bail in respect of the offence or offences to which the appeal relates.

(1F) It shall be a condition of bail granted in the exercise of the power that, unless a notice of appeal has previously been lodged in accordance with subsection (1) of section 18 of the Criminal Appeal Act 1968—

(a) such a notice shall be so lodged within the period specified in subsection (2) of that section; and

(b) not later than 14 days from the end of that period, the appellant shall lodge with the Crown Court a certificate from the registrar of criminal appeals that a notice of appeal was given within that period.

(1G) If the Crown Court grants bail to a person in the exercise of the power, it may direct him to appear—

(a) if a notice of appeal is lodged within the period specified in section 18(2) of the Criminal Appeal Act 1968 at such time and place as the Court of Appeal may require; and

(b) if no such notice is lodged within that period, at such time and place as the Crown Court may require.

(1H) Where the Crown Court grants a person bail under subsection (1)(g) it may direct him to appear at a time and place which the magistrates' court could have directed and the recognizance of any surety shall be conditioned accordingly.

(1J) The Crown Court may only grant bail to a person under subsection (1)(g) if the magistrates' court which remanded him in custody has certified under section 5(6A) of the Bail Act 1976 that it heard full argument on his application for bail before it refused the application.

(2) Provision may be made by rules of court as respects the powers of the Crown Court relating to bail, including any provision—

(a) except in the case of bail in criminal proceedings (within the meaning of the Bail Act 1976), allowing the court instead of requiring a person to enter into a recognizance, to consent to his giving other security;

(b) allowing the court to direct that a recognizance shall be entered into or other security given before a magistrates' court or a justice of the peace, or, if the rules so provide, a person of such other description as is specified in the rules;

(c) prescribing the manner in which a recognizance is to be entered into or other security given, and the persons by whom and the manner in which the recognizance or security may be enforced;

(d) authorising the recommittal, in such cases and by such courts or justices as may be prescribed by the rules, of persons released from custody in pursuance of the powers;

(e) making provision corresponding to sections 118 and 119 of the Magistrates' Courts Act 1980 (varying or dispensing with requirements as to sureties, and postponement of taking recognizances).

(3) Any reference in any enactment to a recognizance shall include, unless the context otherwise requires, a reference to any other description of security given instead of a recognizance, whether in pursuance of subsection (2)(a) or otherwise.

(4) The Crown Court, on issuing a warrant for the arrest of any person, may endorse the warrant for bail, and in any such case—

(a) the person arrested under the warrant shall, unless the Crown Court otherwise directs, be taken to a police station; and

(b) the officer in charge of the station shall release him from custody if he, and any sureties required by the endorsement and approved by the officer, enter into recognizances of such amount as may be fixed by the endorsement:

Provided that in the case of bail in criminal proceedings (within the meaning of the Bail Act 1976) the person arrested shall not be required to enter into a recognizance.

(5) A person in custody in pursuance of a warrant issued by the Crown Court with a view to his appearance before that court shall be brought forthwith before either the Crown Court or a magistrates' court.

(6) A magistrates' court shall have jurisdiction, and a justice of the peace may act, under or in pursuance of rules under subsection (2) whether or not the offence was committed, or the arrest was made, within the court's area, or the area for which he was appointed.

(7) In subsection (1) above "relevant transfer provision" means—

(a) section 4 of the Criminal Justice Act 1987, or

(b) section 53 of the Criminal Justice Act 1991.**

[Supreme Court Act 1981, s 81 as amended by the Criminal Justice Act 1982, ss 29 and 60, the Criminal Justice Act 1987, Sch 2, the Criminal Procedure (Insanity and Unfitness to Plead) Act 1991, Sch 3, the Criminal Justice and Public Order Act 1994, Schs 9 and 10, the Crime and Disorder Act 1998, Sch 8, the Powers of Criminal Courts (Sentencing) Act 2000, Sch 9 and Sch 12, SI 2004/1033 and 2004/2035.]

---

*Words substituted or inserted by the Cirminal Justice Act 2003, Sch 3 from a date to be appointed.
**Sub-sections (1)(a) and (g) amended and sub-s (7) repealed by the Criminal Justice Act 2003, Sch 3, and

sub-s(1)(g)(ii) amended by the Powers of Criminal Courts (Sentencing) Act 2000, Sch 9, from dates to be appointed.
   1. For the position under the European Convention on Human Rights relating to bail see para **1–1560** above.
   2. It would appear that a juvenile who was subject to a care order following a finding of guilt is "in custody" for the purposes of this section, and bail may be granted pending appeal; see *R v P* (1979) 144 JP 39.
   3. See also *Practice Direction (criminal: consolidated)* [2002] para IV.50, (not reproduced in this work).
   4. The Criminal Procedure Rules 2005, Part 19, this PART: STATUTORY INSTRUMENTS ON PROCEDURE, post apply. See *Practice Direction (criminal: consolidated)* [2002] para V.53, in this PART, post and note particularly the need to attach to the application to the Crown Court a copy of the certificate of the magistrates that they heard full argument on bail.

1–2691   82. Duties of officers of Crown Court.   (1) The officers of the Crown Court shall be responsible for the keeping of the records of the proceedings of the court, the signing of indictments, the notification to the parties or their legal advisers of the place and time appointed for any proceedings, and such other formal or administrative matters as may be specified by directions given by the Lord Chancellor.
   (2) Officers of the Crown Court shall in particular give effect to any orders or directions of the court for taking into custody, and detaining, any person committing contempt of court, and shall execute any order or warrant duly issued by the court for the committal of any person to prison for contempt of court.
[Supreme Court Act 1981, s 82.]

1–2692   83. Right of audience for solicitors in certain Crown Court centres.   *Repealed.*

RULES OF COURT

1–2693   84. *Power to make rules of court*[1].

   1. See in particular, the Civil Procedure Rules 1998 and the Criminal Procedure Rules 2005, this PART: STATUTORY INSTRUMENTS AND PRACTICE DIRECTIONS ON PROCEDURE, post.

PART VI[1]
MISCELLANEOUS AND SUPPLEMENTARY

Miscellaneous provisions

1–2694   140. Enforcement of fines and forfeited recognizances.   (1) Payment of a fine imposed, or sum due under a recognizance forfeited, by the High Court or the civil division of the Court of Appeal may be enforced upon the order of the court—
   (*a*)   in like manner as a judgment of the High Court for the payment of money; or
   (*b*)   in like manner as a fine imposed by the Crown Court.
   (3) Where payment of a fine or other sum falls to be enforced as mentioned in paragraph (*b*) of subsection (1) upon an order of the High Court or the civil division of the Court of Appeal under that subsection, the provisions of sections 139 and 140 of the Powers of Criminal Courts (Sentencing) Act 2000 shall apply to that fine or other sum as they apply to a fine imposed by the Crown Court.
   (5) In this section, and in sections 139 and 140 of the Powers of Criminal Courts (Sentencing) Act 2000 as extended by this section, "fine" includes a penalty imposed in civil proceedings.
[Supreme Court Act 1981, s 140(1), (3), (5), as amended by the Powers of Criminal Courts (Sentencing) Act 2000, Sch 9.]

   1. Part VI contains ss 129–153.

Police and Criminal Evidence Act 1984[1]

(1984 c 60)

PART I[2]
POWERS TO STOP AND SEARCH[3]

1–2695   1. Power of constable to stop and search persons, vehicles[4], etc.   (1) A constable may exercise any power conferred by this section—
   (*a*)   in any place to which at the time when he proposes to exercise the power the public or any section of the public has access, on payment or otherwise, as of right or by virtue of express or implied permission; or
   (*b*)   in any other place[5] to which people have ready access at the time when he proposes to exercise the power but which is not a dwelling.
   (2) Subject to subsection (3) to (5) below, a constable—
   (*a*)   may search—

   (i)   any person[6] or vehicle[7];
   (ii)   anything which is in or on a vehicle,

   for stolen or prohibited articles, any article to which subsection (8A) below applies or any firework to which subsection (8B) below applies; and

(b) may detain a person[6] or vehicle[7] for the purpose of such a search.

(3) This section does not give a constable power to search a person[8] or vehicle or anything in or on a vehicle unless he has reasonable grounds for suspecting[9] that he will find stolen or prohibited articles, any article to which subsection (8A) below applies or any firework to which subsection (8B) below applies.

(4) If a person is in a garden or yard occupied with and used for the purposes of a dwelling or on other land so occupied and used, a constable may not search him in the exercise of the power conferred by this section unless the constable has reasonable grounds for believing—

(a) that he does not reside in the dwelling; and
(b) that he is not in the place in question with the express or implied permission of a person who resides in the dwelling.

(5) If a vehicle is in a garden or yard occupied with and used for the purposes of a dwelling or on other land so occupied and used, a constable may not search the vehicle or anything in or on it in the exercise of the power conferred by this section unless he has reasonable grounds for believing—

(a) that the person in charge of the vehicle does not reside in the dwelling; and
(b) that the vehicle is not in the place in question with the express or implied permission of a person who resides in the dwelling.

(6) If in the course of such a search a constable discovers an article which he has reasonable grounds for suspecting to be a stolen or prohibited article, any article to which subsection (8A) below applies or any firework to which subsection (8B) below applies, he may seize it.

(7) An article is prohibited for the purposes of this Part of this Act if it is—

(a) an offensive weapon; or
(b) an article—

    (i) made or adapted for use in the course of or in connection with an offence to which this sub-paragraph applies; or
    (ii) intended by the person having it with him for such use by him or by some other person.

(8) The offences to which subsection (7)(b)(i) above applies are—

(a) burglary;
(b) theft;
(c) offences under section 12 of the Theft Act 1968 (taking motor vehicle or other conveyance without authority);
(d) offences under section 15 of that Act (obtaining property by deception); and*
(e) offences under section 1 of the Criminal Damage Act 1971 (destroying or damaging property).

(8A) This subsection applies to any article in relation to which a person has committed, or is committing or is going to commit an offence under section 139 of the Criminal Justice Act 1988.

(8B) This subsection applies to any firework which a person possesses in contravention of a prohibition imposed by fireworks regulations.

(8C) In this section—

(a) "firework" shall be construed in accordance with the definition of "fireworks" in section 1(1) of the Fireworks Act 2003; and
(b) "fireworks regulations" has the same meaning as in that Act.

(9) In this Part of this Act "offensive weapon" means[10] any article—

(a) made or adapted for use for causing injury to persons; or
(b) intended by the person having it with him for such use by him or by some other person.

[Police and Criminal Evidence Act 1984, s 1 as amended by the Criminal Justice Act 1988, s 140, the Criminal Justice Act 2003, s 1 and Sch 37 and the Serious Organised Crime and Police Act 2005, s 115.]

---

*Substituted by the Fraud Act 2006, Sch 1 from a date to be appointed.

1. Under the Human Rights Act 1998, police officers come within the definition of a public authority because they carry out functions of a public nature. It follows that it is unlawful for any police officer to act in any way which is incompatible with a right protected by the European Convention on Human Rights: see s 6(1) of the Act. Any person who claims that a public authority has acted (or proposes to act) in a way which is incompatible with a Convention right may bring proceedings against the authority or rely on the Convention rights or rights concerned in any legal proceedings: see s7(1) of the Act.

2. Part I contains ss 1–7.

3. See the Code of Practice for the Exercise by Police Officers of Statutory Powers of Stop and Search (Code of Practice A), in PART II: STATUTORY INSTRUMENTS ON EVIDENCE, post. The exercise of stop and search powers may raise issues of compliance with art 5 (the right to liberty), art 8 (the right to respect for private life) and art 14 (the prohibition on discrimination) of the European Convention on Human Rights.

4. Sections 1 to 3 and other search provisions are not necessary if a search is conducted with consent. For search of premises see ss 8 and 17 post, and note definition of "premises" for that purpose in s 23, which can include a vehicle. See also search of a person arrested and premises where he was, under s 32, post, and also power to search detained persons and to take samples etc, s 54 et seq, post. Code of Practice A applies to practically all such powers and not just those under this Act. The Code itself requires that a copy of it must be readily available at all police stations for consultation by police officers, detained persons and members of the public.

5. These are places to which there is no general public access but which are accessible from public areas.

6. The constable may use reasonable force (s 117, post).

7. Note also the power to stop a mechanically propelled vehicle, exerciseable by a constable in uniform (Road Traffic

Act 1988, s 163 in PART VII: TRANSPORT, ROAD TRAFFIC, post), and provisions for road checks, ss 4 and 6, post. This section applies to vessels, aircraft and hovercraft (s 2(10), post).

8. There is no general power to stop persons: see *Collins v Wilcock* [1984] 3 All ER 374, [1984] 1 WLR 1172.

9. "Reasonable grounds for suspicion" is explained in paras 2.3 and 2.4 the Code of Practice for the Exercise by Police Officers of Statutory Powers of Stop and Search (Code of Practice A); the Code envisages questioning before search as that may lead to a satisfactory explanation making the search unnecessary.

10. Compare the definition in the Prevention of Crime Act 1953, s 1 in PART VIII: OFFENSIVE WEAPONS, post.

1–2696   2. Provisions relating to search under section 1 and other powers.   (1) A constable who detains a person or vehicle in the exercise—

(a) of the power conferred by section 1 above; or
(b) of any other power—

   (i) to search a person without first arresting him; or
   (ii) to search a vehicle without making an arrest,

need not conduct a search if it appears to him subsequently—

   (i) that no search is required; or
   (ii) that a search is impracticable.

(2) If a constable contemplates a search, other than a search of an unattended vehicle, in the exercise—

(a) of the power conferred by section 1 above; or
(b) of any other power, except the power conferred by section 6 below and the power conferred by section 27(2) of the Aviation Security Act 1982[1]—

   (i) to search a person without first arresting him; or
   (ii) to search a vehicle without making an arrest,

it shall be his duty[2], subject to subsection (4) below, to take reasonable steps before he commences the search to bring to the attention of the appropriate person—

   (i) if the constable is not in uniform, documentary evidence that he is a constable; and
   (ii) whether he is in uniform or not, the matters specified in subsection (3) below;

and the constable shall not commence the search until he has performed that duty.

(3) The matters referred to in subsection (2)(ii) above are—

(a) the constable's name and the name of the police station to which he is attached;
(b) the object of the proposed search;
(c) the constable's grounds for proposing to make it; and
(d) the effect of section 3(7) or (8) below, as may be appropriate.

(4) A constable need not bring the effect of section 3(7) or (8) below to the attention of the appropriate person if it appears to the constable that it will not be practicable to make the record in section 3(1) below.

(5) In this section "the appropriate person" means—

(a) if the constable proposes to search a person, that person; and
(b) if he proposes to search a vehicle, or anything in or on a vehicle, the person in charge of the vehicle.

(6) On completing a search of an unattended vehicle or anything in or on such a vehicle in the exercise of any such power as is mentioned in subsection (2) above a constable shall leave a notice—

(a) stating that he has searched it;
(b) giving the name of the police station to which he is attached;
(c) stating that an application for compensation for any damage caused by the search may be made to that police station; and
(d) stating the effect of section 3(8) below.

(7) The constable shall leave the notice inside the vehicle unless it is not reasonably practicable to do so without damaging the vehicle.

(8) The time for which a person or vehicle may be detained for the purposes of such a search is such time as is reasonably required to permit a search to be carried out either at the place where the person or vehicle was first detained or nearby.

(9) Neither the power conferred by section 1 above nor any other power to detain and search a person without first arresting him or to detain and search a vehicle without making an arrest is to be construed—

(a) as authorising a constable to require a person to remove any of his clothing in public other than an outer coat, jacket or gloves[3]; or
(b) as authorising a constable not in uniform to stop a vehicle.

(10) This section and section 1 above apply to vessels[4], aircraft and hovercraft as they apply to vehicles.

[Police and Criminal Evidence Act 1984, s 2.]

---

1. See para **7–5472**.
2. The Code of Practice for the Exercise by Police Officers of Statutory Powers of Stop and Search (Code of Practice A), para 3.11 requires the officer to take reasonable steps to bring this information to the notice of the person who, or

whose vehicle, is to be searched, and who does not understand: this includes establishing whether a person with him can interpret. Failure to act in accordance with his duty may make the constable's behaviour actionable (cf *Christie v Leachinsky* [1947] AC 573, [1947] 1 All ER 567, 111 JP 224, HL and *Pedro v Diss* [1981] 2 All ER 59, 145 JP 445) or evidence may be excluded; see s 78, post.

3. This provision is amplified by the Code of Practice referred to above, para 3.5 and Notes for Guidance thereon. Intimate searches are dealt with in s 55, post.

4. Defined in s 118 (1), post.

1-2697 3. Duty to make records concerning searches. (1) Where a constable has carried out a search in the exercise of any such power as is mentioned in section 2(1) above, other than a search—

(*a*) under section 6 below; or

(*b*) under section 27(2) of the Aviation Security Act 1982,

he shall make a record of it in writing unless it is not practicable to do so.

(2) If—

(*a*) a constable is required by subsection (1) above to make a record of a search; but

(*b*) it is not practicable to make the record on the spot,

he shall make it as soon as practicable after the completion of the search.

(3) The record of a search of a person shall include a note of his name[1], if the constable knows it, but a constable may not detain a person to find out his name.

(4) If a constable does not know the name of a person whom he has searched, the record of the search shall include a note otherwise describing that person.

(5) The record of a search of a vehicle shall include a note describing the vehicle.

(6) The record of a search of a person or a vehicle—

(*a*) shall state—

(i) the object of the search;

(ii) the grounds[2] for making it;

(iii) the date and time when it was made;

(iv) the place where it was made;

(v) whether anything, and if so what, was found;

(vi) whether any, and if so what, injury to a person or damage to property appears to the constable to have resulted from the search; and

(*b*) shall identify the constable making it.

(7) If a constable who conducted a search of a person made a record of it, the person who was searched shall be entitled to a copy of the record if he asks for one before the end of the period specified in subsection (9) below.

(8) If—

(*a*) the owner of a vehicle which has been searched or the person who was in charge of the vehicle at the time when it was searched asks for a copy of the record of the search before the end of the period specified in subsection (9) below; and

(*b*) the constable who conducted the search made a record of it,

the person who made the request shall be entitled to a copy.

(9) The period mentioned in subsections (7) and (8) above is the period of 12 months beginning with the date on which the search was made.

(10) The requirements imposed by this section with regard to records of searches of vehicles shall apply also to records of searches of vessels, aircraft and hovercraft.

[Police and Criminal Evidence Act 1984, s 3.]

---

1. The Code of Practice for the Exercise by Police Officers of Statutory Powers of Stop and Search (Code of Practice A), para 4.5 also requires a note to be made of the self-defined ethnicity of every person stopped according to the categories used in the 2001 census and listed in Annex B.

2. This must explain the reason for suspecting the person concerned, briefly but informatively, whether by reference to his behaviour or other circumstances: (Code of Practice A), para 4.6.

1-2698 4. Road checks. (1) This section shall have effect in relation to the conduct of road checks by police officers for the purpose of ascertaining whether a vehicle is carrying—

(*a*) a person who has committed an offence other than a road traffic offence or a vehicle excise offence;

(*b*) a person who is a witness to such an offence;

(*c*) a person intending to commit such an offence; or

(*d*) a person who is unlawfully at large.

(2) For the purposes of this section a road check consists of the exercise in a locality of the power conferred by section 163 of the Road Traffic Act 1988[1] in such a way as to stop[2] during the period for which its exercise in that way in that locality continues all vehicles or vehicles selected by any criterion.

(3) Subject to subsection (5) below, there may only be such a road check if a police officer of the rank of superintendent or above authorises it in writing.

(4) An officer may only authorise a road check under subsection (3) above—

(*a*) for the purpose specified in subsection (1)(*a*) above, if he has reasonable grounds—

(i)   for believing that the offence is an indictable offence; and
(ii) for suspecting that the person is, or is about to be, in the locality in which vehicles would be stopped if the road check were authorised;

(b) for the purpose specified in subsection (1)(b) above, if he has reasonable grounds for believing that the offence is an indictable offence ;
(c) for the purpose specified in subsection (1)(c) above, if he has reasonable grounds—

(i)   for believing that the offence would be an indictable offence ; and
(ii) for suspecting that the person is, or is about to be, in the locality in which vehicles would be stopped if the road check were authorised;

(d) for the purpose specified in subsection (1)(d) above, if he has reasonable grounds for suspecting that the person is, or is about to be, in that locality.

(5) An officer below the rank of superintendent may authorise such a road check if it appears to him that it is required as a matter of urgency for one of the purposes specified in subsection (1) above.

(6) If an authorisation is given under subsection (5) above, it shall be the duty of the officer who gives it—

(a) to make a written record of the time at which he gives it; and
(b) to cause an officer of the rank of superintendent or above to be informed that it has been given.

(7) The duties imposed by subsection (6) above shall be performed as soon as it is practicable to do so.

(8) An officer to whom a report is made under subsection (6) above may, in writing, authorise the road check to continue.

(9) If such an officer considers that the road check should not continue, he shall record in writing—

(a) the fact that it took place; and
(b) the purpose for which it took place.

(10) An officer giving an authorisation under this section shall specify the locality in which vehicles are to be stopped.

(11) An officer giving an authorisation under this section, other than an authorisation under subsection (5) above—

(a) shall specify a period, not exceeding seven days, during which the road check may continue; and
(b) may direct that the road check—

(i)   shall be continuous; or
(ii) shall be conducted at specified times,

during that period.

(12) If it appears to an officer of the rank of superintendent or above that a road check ought to continue beyond the period for which it has been authorised he may, from time to time, in writing specify a further period, not exceeding seven days, during which it may continue.

(13) Every written authorisation shall specify—

(a) the name of the officer giving it;
(b) the purpose of the road check; and
(c) the locality in which vehicles are to be stopped.

(14) The duties to specify the purposes of a road check imposed by subsections (9) and (13) above include duties to specify any relevant indictable offence.

(15) Where a vehicle is stopped in a road check, the person in charge of the vehicle at the time when it is stopped shall be entitled to obtain a written statement of the purpose of the road check if he applies for such a statement not later than the end of the period of twelve months from the day on which the vehicle was stopped.

(16) Nothing in this section affects the exercise by police officers of any power to stop vehicles for purposes other than those specified in subsection (1) above.

[Police and Criminal Evidence Act 1984, s 4, as amended by the Road Traffic (Consequential Provisions) Act 1988, Sch 3, the Vehicle Excise and Registration Act 1994, Sch 3 and the Serious Organised Crime and Police Act 2005, Sch 7.]

---

1. See para **4–1590**. The police officer must be in uniform.
2. See also *Moss v McLachlan* (1984) 149 JP 167, [1985] IRLR 76. As to subsequent powers of arrest and search, see s 1, ante and ss 17, 32, post.

1–2699 **5.** *Reports of recorded searches and of road checks.—Information to be included in annual reports.*

1–2700 **6. Statutory undertakers etc.**   (1) A constable employed by statutory undertakers[1] may stop, detain and search any vehicle before it leaves a goods area included in the premises of the statutory undertakers.

(1A) Without prejudice to any powers under subsection (1) above, a constable employed by the Strategic Rail Authority may stop, detain and search any vehicle before it leaves a goods area which is included in the premises of any successor of the British Railways Board and is used wholly or mainly for the purposes of a relevant undertaking.

(2) In this section "goods area" means any area used wholly or mainly for the storage or handling of goods; and "successor of the British Railways Board" and "relevant undertaking" have the same meaning as in the Railways Act 1993 (Consequential Modifications) Order 1999.

(3)–(4) *Repealed.*

[Police and Criminal Evidence Act 1984, s 6 as amended by SI 1999/1998, SI 2001/57, the Transport Act 2000, s 217 and the Energy Act 2004, Sch 23.]

---

1. Defined in s 7(3), post. The Code of Practice for the Exercise by Police Officers of Statutory Powers of Stop and Search (Code of Practice A), para 3.11 does not apply to powers under s 6(1); see the general introduction to Code of Practice A. See also Code of Practice A paras 4.11 ff for the recording of encounters not governed by statutory powers.

1–2701   7. Part I—supplementary.   (1) The following enactments shall cease to have effect—

   (*a*)   section 8 of the Vagrancy Act 1824;
   (*b*)   section 66 of the Metropolitan Police Act 1839;
   (*c*)   section 11 of the Canals (Offences) Act 1840;
   (*d*)   section 19 of the Pedlars Act 1871;
   (*e*)   section 33 of the County of Merseyside Act 1980; and
   (*f*)   section 42 of the West Midlands County Council Act 1980.

(2) There shall also cease to have effect—

   (*a*)   so much of any enactment contained in an Act passed before 1974, other than—

      (i)   an enactment contained in a public general Act; or
      (ii) an enactment relating to statutory undertakers,

      as confers power on a constable to search for stolen or unlawfully obtained goods; and

   (*b*)   so much of any enactment relating to statutory undertakers as provides that such a power shall not be exercisable after the end of a specified period.

(3) In this Part of this Act "statutory undertakers" means persons authorised by any enactment to carry on any railway, light railway, road transport, water transport, canal, inland navigation, dock or harbour undertaking.

[Police and Criminal Evidence Act 1984, s 7.]

PART II[1]
POWERS OF ENTRY, SEARCH AND SEIZURE[2]

Search warrants[3]

1–2702   8. Power of justice of the peace to authorise entry and search of premises.   (1) If on an application made by a constable a justice of the peace is satisfied[4] that there are reasonable grounds for believing—

   (*a*)   that an indictable offence has been committed; and
   (*b*)   that there is material on premises mentioned in subsection (1A) below which is likely to be of substantial value (whether by itself or together with other material) to the investigation of the offence; and
   (*c*)   that the material is likely to be relevant evidence; and
   (*d*)   that it does not consist of or include items subject to legal privilege, excluded material or special procedure material[5]; and
   (*e*)   that any of the conditions specified in subsection (3) below applies in relation to each set of premises specified in the application,

he may issue a warrant[6] authorising a constable to enter and search the premises.

(1A) The premises referred to in subsection (1)(b) above are—

   (*a*)   one or more sets of premises specified in the application (in which case the application is for a "specific premises warrant"); or
   (*b*)   any premises occupied or controlled by a person specified in the application, including such sets of premises as are so specified (in which case the application is for an "all premises warrant").

(1B) If the application is for an all premises warrant, the justice of the peace must also be satisfied—

   (*a*)   that because of the particulars of the offence referred to in paragraph (a) of subsection (1) above, there are reasonable grounds for believing that it is necessary to search premises occupied or controlled by the person in question which are not specified in the application in order to find the material referred to in paragraph (b) of that subsection; and
   (*b*)   that it is not reasonably practicable to specify in the application all the premises which he occupies or controls and which might need to be searched.

(1C) The warrant may authorise entry to and search of premises on more than one occasion if, on the application, the justice of the peace is satisfied that it is necessary to authorise multiple entries in order to achieve the purpose for which he issues the warrant.

(1D) If it authorises multiple entries, the number of entries authorised may be unlimited, or limited to a maximum.

(2) A constable may seize[7] and retain anything for which a search has been authorised under subsection (1) above.

(3) The conditions mentioned in subsection (1)(*e*) above are—

(*a*) that it is not practicable to communicate with any person entitled to grant entry to the premises;

(*b*) that it is practicable to communicate with a person entitled to grant entry to the premises but it is not practicable to communicate with any person entitled to grant access to the evidence;

(*c*) that entry to the premises will not be granted unless a warrant is produced;

(*d*) that the purpose of a search may be frustrated or seriously prejudiced unless a constable arriving at the premises can secure immediate entry to them.

(4) In this Act "relevant evidence", in relation to an offence, means anything that would be admissible in evidence at a trial for the offence.

(5) The power to issue a warrant conferred by this section is in addition to any such power otherwise conferred.

(6) This section applies in relation to a relevant offence (as defined in section 28D(4) of the Immigration Act 1971) as it applies in relation to an indictable offence
[Police and Criminal Evidence Act 1984, s 8 as amended by the Immigration and Asylum Act 1999, Sch 14 and the Serious Organised Crime and Police Act 2005, ss 113 and 114 and Sch 7.]

---

1. Part II contains ss 8–23 and applies only to constables. The statutory powers of other persons remain unaffected by these provisions.
2. See the Code of Practice for Searches of Premises by Police Officers and the Seizure of Property Found by Police Officers on Persons or Premises (Code of Practice B), in PART II: STATUTORY INSTRUMENTS ON EVIDENCE, post. The exercise of powers of entry, search and seizure may raise issues of compliance with art 8 (the right to respect for private life) and art 14 (the prohibition on discrimination) of the European Convention on Human Rights. Any entry, search and seizure will breach art 8 (the right to respect for private and family life, home and correspondence) unless it is "in accordance with the law", pursues one or more of the legitimate aims referred to in art 8(2) and is "necessary in a democratic society" to achieve the aim or aims in question.
3. Entry and search without a search warrant is dealt with by s 17, et seq. Entry and search may, of course, be made with consent. Any consent should generally be in writing: see Code of Practice for the Searching of Premises by Police Officers and the Seizure of Property Found by Police Officers on Persons or Premises, Code B in PART II: STATUTORY INSTRUMENTS ON EVIDENCE, post, paras 5.1–5.4. If entry is obstructed, the constable may use reasonable force (s 117, post). This section deals with search for evidential material: other statutory provisions are unaffected. Note that the Code referred to above governs searches with the occupier's consent as well as searches under ss 15, 17, 18, 32 and Sch 1, post: note also the requirement that a full record of searches be kept (paras 8.1–9.1).
4. The criteria set out in s 8(1) are directed to the state of mind of the justice when he is being asked to issue the warrant. Accordingly, the justice to whom an application for a search warrant is made must consider whether the application raises the issue of legal professional privilege and, if the officer making the application does not volunteer information on the specific issue of privilege, the justice should ask whether the material sought consists of or includes items subject to such privilege. If there are reasonable grounds for believing that the material sought includes items subject to privilege, the targeted material will have to be redefined in such a way as to enable the justice to be satisfied that there are no longer reasonable grounds for such a belief, otherwise he cannot issue the warrant (*R v Chesterfield Justices, ex p Bramley* [2000] 1 All ER 411, [2000] 2 WLR 409, [2000] 1 Cr App Rep 486, [2000] Crim LR 385, DC).
5. For the meaning of "items subject to legal privilege", "excluded material" and "special procedure material" see ss 10, 11, 14 below, and for procedure for obtaining a search warrant involving such items, see s 9 below.
   A justice faced with a case where he cannot be satisfied that there are reasonable grounds for believing that the material sought does not include any items which are, prima facie, subject to legal privilege, or any material which is, prima facie, special procedure material, should refuse the application under s 8 and leave the applicant to proceed under s 9; see *R v Guildhall Magistrates' Court, ex p Primlaks Holdings Co (Panama) Inc* [1990] 1 QB 261, [1989] 2 WLR 841, DC. It is not a bar to the issue or execution of a warrant that the police may have to sift material and may encounter material which is subject to legal privilege or is special procedure material. Such material would be outside the scope of the search (*R v Leeds Magistrates' Court, ex p Dumbleton* [1993] Crim LR 866).
6. Section 8 must be read as being subject to s 15, post which provides safeguards in the form of stipulated procedural requirements. It is not a condition precedent to the granting of a search warrant under s 8 that other methods of obtaining the material have been tried without success (*R v Billericay Justices and Dobbyn, ex p Frank Harris (Coaches) Ltd* [1991] Crim LR 472).
7. Note s 19, which supplements the power of seizure. The effect of s 8(1) and (2) is to limit what may be seized under a warrant issued under s 8, and those executing such a warrant must not lose sight of the requirement that even though material may fall within the description in the warrant, its seizure still has to fall within what is permitted by s 8(1) and (2): see *R v Chief Constable of Warwickshire Constabulary, ex p Fitzpatrick* [1998] 1 All ER 65, [1999] 1 WLR 564, [1998] Crim LR 290. To decide how much of the available material falls within the scope of the warrant the constable must look at the documents to ascertain if any of them consists of special procedure material or is legally privileged.
   Part 2 of the Criminal Justice and Police Act 2001 (see this PART, post) was enacted to deal with the difficulties faced by the police and other law enforcement agencies where material was found on premises and it was reasonably believed to be or to contain material that could lawfully be seized, but it was not reasonably practicable to make that determination on the premises, or the material that they were entitled to seize was inextricably linked with other material that they could not seize. (It was held in *R v Chesterfield Justices, ex p Bramley* [2000] QB 576, [2000] 1 All ER 411, [2000] Cr App Rep 486 that the police were not entitled to seize material under PACE for the purpose of sifting it elsewhere). In these circumstances, the power of seizure is extended by Part 2 to include power to seize so much of the material as it is necessary to remove to make the required determination or separation. Like, additional powers of seizure are provided in respect of searches of the person. These powers are exercisable only where there is an existing power of seizure, which are listed in Sch 1 to the 2001 Act. In addition to those used by the police, they include powers available to the Serious Fraud Office and various other law enforcement agencies.

1–2703   9. Special provisions as to access.   (1) A constable may obtain access to excluded material or special procedure material for the purposes of a criminal investigation by making an application under Schedule 1 below and in accordance with that Schedule[1].

(2) Any Act[2] (including a local Act) passed before this Act under which a search of premises for the purposes of a criminal investigation could be authorised by the issue of a warrant to a constable shall cease to have effect so far as it relates to the authorisation of searches—

(a) for items subject to legal privilege; or
(b) for excluded material; or
(c) for special procedure material consisting of documents or records other than documents.

(2A) Section 4 of the Summary Jurisdiction (Process) Act 1881 (c 24) (which includes provision for the execution of process of English courts in Scotland) and section 29 of the Petty Sessions (Ireland) Act 1851 (c 93) (which makes equivalent provision for execution in Northern Ireland) shall each apply to any process issued by a circuit judge under Schedule 1 to this Act as it applies to process issued by a magistrates' court under the Magistrates' Courts Act 1980 (c 43).
[Police and Criminal Evidence Act 1984, s 9, as amended by the Criminal Justice and Police Act 2001, s 86(1).]

---

1. This involves making an application to a circuit judge for an order to produce material or to give access to it. Note however that once a constable is lawfully on premises, for example with consent or with a warrant under s 8, he may seize excluded material or special procedure material by virtue of s 19, post. The proper way of challenging such an order is by judicial review (*R v Crown Court at Liverpool, ex p Wimpey plc* [1991] Crim LR 635). It is not necessary for the police to rely on the procedure in s 9 where the person holding the records makes voluntary disclosure (*R v Singleton* [1995] 1 Cr App Rep 431, [1995] Crim LR 236, CA).
2. This does not preclude the endorsement under s 4 of the Summary Jurisdiction (Process) Act 1881 of a warrant issued in Scotland to search for protected material (*R v Manchester Stipendiary Magistrate, ex p Granada Television Ltd* [2000] 1 All ER 135, [2000] 2 WLR 1, CA).

1–2704   10. Meaning of "items subject to legal privilege".   (1) Subject to subsection (2) below, in this Act "items subject to legal privilege" means—

(a) communications[1] between a professional legal adviser and his client or any person representing his client made in connection with the giving of legal advice[2] to the client;
(b) communications[3] between a professional legal adviser and his client or any person representing his client or between such an adviser or his client or any such representative and any other person made in connection with or in contemplation of legal proceedings and for the purposes of such proceedings[3]; and
(c) items[4] enclosed with or referred to in such communications and made—
  (i) in connection with the giving of legal advice; or
  (ii) in connection with or in contemplation of legal proceedings and for the purposes of such proceedings,

when they are in the possession of a person who is entitled to possession of them.
(2) Items held with the intention of furthering a criminal purpose are not items subject to legal privilege[5].
[Police and Criminal Evidence Act 1984, s 10.]

---

1. The record of time on a solicitor's attendance note, on a time sheet or a fee record, is not a communication since it records nothing which passes between the solicitor and client, and has nothing to do with the giving of legal advice (*R v Crown Court at Manchester, ex p Rogers* [1999] 4 All ER 35, [1999] 1 WLR 832, DC).
2. The records of a conveyancing transaction itself are not privileged, but correspondence between the solicitor and his client regarding the conveyance would be privileged if it contained advice (*R v Crown Court at Inner London Sessions, ex p Baines & Baines* [1988] QB 579, [1987] 3 All ER 1025, 87 Cr App Rep 111).
3. This will include an application form for legal aid made in contemplation of legal proceedings (*R v Crown Court at Snaresbrook, ex p DPP* [1988] QB 532, [1988] 1 All ER 315, 86 Cr App Rep 227). Forged documents, or copies of such documents, are not made in connection with legal proceedings; to come within the paragraph documents must be lawfully made (*R v Leeds Magistrates' Court, ex p Dumbleton* [1993] Crim LR 866).
4. A sample of a defendant's blood provided by him to his doctor in criminal proceedings was held to be an item covered by s 10(1)(c) and subject to legal privilege; accordingly, the defendant was entitled to object to its production or to opinion based upon it being admitted in evidence (*R v R* [1994] 4 All ER 260, [1994] 1 WLR 758, [1995] 1 Cr App Rep 183, CA).
5. Since legal privilege is the privilege of the client and not that of his solicitor and since "a criminal purpose" in s 10(2) refers to any criminal purpose, the relevant intention referred to in s 10(2) includes that of the client or a third party. Accordingly, documents held by a solicitor which were intended by his client to be used to further a criminal purpose, such as the laundering of the proceeds of drug trafficking, were not subject to legal privilege (*R v Central Criminal Court, ex p Francis & Francis a firm*) [1989] AC 346, [1988] 1 All ER 677, 87 Cr App Rep 104, DC; affd [1989] AC 346, [1988] 3 All ER 775, 88 Cr App Rep 213, HL). See also *R (Hallinan Blackburn Gittings & Nott (a firm)) v Crown Court at Middlesex Guildhall* [2004] EWHC 2726 (Admin), [2005] 1 WLR 766 (witness statement taken by defending solicitors from person claiming to be present at defendant's arrest – evidence coming to light of conspiracy to pervert the course of justice involving the defendant, the statement maker and another, which was freestanding and independent in the sense it did not require a judgment to be made in relation to the issues in the trial – judge entitled to conclude that the statement (and other associated items) were not covered by legal professional privilege). If legal privilege is lost by virtue of s 10(2), it does not follow that no express or implied undertaking to hold in confidence can exist; therefore, such an item may still fall within the meaning of special procedure material, see *R v Guildhall Magistrates' Court, ex p Primlaks Holdings Co (Panama) Inc* [1990] 1 QB 261, [1989] 2 WLR 841, DC.

1–2705   11. Meaning of "excluded material".   (1) Subject to the following provisions of this section, in this Act "excluded material" means—

(a) personal records[1] which a person has acquired or created in the course of any trade, business, profession or other occupation or for the purposes of any paid or unpaid office and which he holds in confidence;

(b) human tissue or tissue fluid which has been taken for the purposes of diagnosis or medical treatment and which a person holds in confidence;

(c) journalistic[2] material which a person holds in confidence and which consists—

(i) of documents[3]; or
(ii) of records other than documents.

(2) A person holds material other than journalistic material[2] in confidence for the purposes of this section if he holds it subject—

(a) to an express or implied undertaking to hold it in confidence; or
(b) to a restriction on disclosure or an obligation of secrecy contained in any enactment, including an enactment contained in an Act passed after this Act.

(3) A person holds journalistic material[2] in confidence for the purposes of this section if—

(a) he holds it subject to such an undertaking, restriction or obligation; and
(b) it has been continuously held (by one or more persons) subject to such an undertaking, restriction or obligation since it was first acquired or created for the purposes of journalism.

[Police and Criminal Evidence Act 1984, s 11.]

1. "Personal records" is defined in s 12 below.
2. "Journalistic material" is defined in s 13 below.
3. "Document" is defined in s 118 below.

1–2706 12. Meaning of "personal records". In this Part of this Act "personal records" means documentary and other records concerning an individual (whether living or dead) who can be identified from them and relating—

(a) to his physical or mental health;
(b) to spiritual counselling or assistance given or to be given to him; or
(c) to counselling or assistance given or to be given to him, for the purposes of his personal welfare, by any voluntary organisation or by any individual who—

(i) by reason of his office or occupation has responsibilities for his personal welfare; or
(ii) by reason of an order of a court has responsibilities for his supervision.

[Police and Criminal Evidence Act 1984, s 12.]

1–2707 13. Meaning of "journalistic material". (1) Subject to subsection (2) below, in this Act "journalistic material" means material acquired or created for the purposes of journalism.

(2) Material is only journalistic material for the purposes of this Act if it is in the possession of a person who acquired or created it for the purposes of journalism.

(3) A person who receives material from someone who intends that the recipient shall use it for the purposes of journalism is to be taken to have acquired it for those purposes.

[Police and Criminal Evidence Act 1984, s 13.]

1–2708 14. Meaning of "special procedure material". (1) In this Act "special procedure material" means—

(a) material to which subsection (2) below applies; and
(b) journalistic material, other than excluded material.

(2) Subject to the following provisions of this section, this subsection applies to material[1], other than items subject to legal privilege and excluded material, in the possession of a person who—

(a) acquired or created it in the course of any trade, business, profession or other occupation or for the purpose of any paid or unpaid office; and
(b) holds it subject—

(i) to an express or implied undertaking to hold it in confidence; or
(ii) to a restriction or obligation such as is mentioned in section 11(2)(b) above.

(3) Where material is acquired—

(a) by an employee from his employer and in the course of his employment; or
(b) by a company from an associated company,

it is only special procedure material if it was special procedure material immediately before the acquisition.

(4) Where material is created by an employee in the course of his employment, it is only special procedure material if it would have been special procedure material had his employer created it.

(5) Where material is created by a company on behalf of an associated company, it is only special procedure material if it would have been special procedure material had the associated company created it.

(6) A company is to be treated as another's associated company for the purposes of this section if it would be so treated under section 416 of the Income and Corporation Taxes Act 1988.

[Police and Criminal Evidence Act 1984, s 14.]

1. Forged material cannot be created or acquired in the course of a solicitor's profession, neither can it be held in confidence (*R v Leeds Magistrates' Court, ex p Dumbleton* [1993] Crim LR 866).

1–2709   15. Search warrants—safeguards[1]. (1) This section and section 16 below have effect in relation to the issue to constables[2] under any enactment, including an enactment contained in an Act passed after this Act, of warrants to enter and search premises[3]; and an entry on or search of premises[3] under a warrant is unlawful unless it[4] complies with this section and section 16 below.

(2) Where a constable applies[5] for any such warrant, it shall be his duty—

(*a*) to state—

(i)   the ground on which he makes the application;

(ii) the enactment under which the warrant would be issued; and

(iii) if the application is for a warrant authorising entry and search on more than one occasion, the ground on which he applies for such a warrant, and whether he seeks a warrant authorising an unlimited number of entries, or (if not) the maximum number of entries desired;

(*b*) to specify the matters set out in subsection (2A) below; and

(*c*) to identify, so far as is practicable, the articles or persons to be sought.

(2A) The matters which must be specified pursuant to subsection (2)(*b*) above are—

(*a*) if the application relates to one or more sets of premises specified in the application, each set of premises which it is desired to enter and search;

(*b*) if the application relates to any premises occupied or controlled by a person specified in the application—

(i)   as many sets of premises which it is desired to enter and search as it is reasonably practicable to specify;

(ii) the person who is in occupation or control of those premises and any others which it is desired to enter and search;

(iii) why it is necessary to search more premises than those specified under sub-paragraph (i); and

(iv) why it is not reasonably practicable to specify all the premises which it is desired to enter and search.

(3) An application for such a warrant shall be made ex parte and supported by an information in writing[6].

(4) The constable shall answer on oath[7] any question that the justice of the peace or judge hearing the application asks him[8].

(5) A warrant shall authorise an entry on one occasion only unless it specifies that it authorises multiple entries.

(5A) If it specifies that it authorises multiple entries, it must also specify whether the number of entries authorised is unlimited, or limited to a specified maximum.

(6) A warrant—

(*a*) shall specify—

(i)   the name of the person who applies for it;

(ii) the date on which it is issued;

(iii) the enactment under which it is issued; and

(iv) each set of premises to be searched, or (in the case of an all premises warrant) the person who is in occupation or control of premises to be searched, together with any premises under his occupation or control which can be specified and which are to be searched; and

(*b*) shall identify, so far as is practicable, the articles or persons to be sought.

(7) Two copies shall be made of a warrant[9]warrant[9] (see section 8(1A)(*a*) above) which specifies only one set of premises and does not authorise multiple entries; and as many copies as are reasonably required may be made of any other kind of warrant.

((8) The copies shall be clearly certified as copies.

[Police and Criminal Evidence Act 1984, s 15 as amended by the Serious Organised Crime and Police Act 2005, ss 113 and 114 and SI 2005/3496.]

---

1. For further guidance on and forms of application and warrants, see Home Office Circular 56/2005, relevant parts of which are reproduced in PART IX FORMS AND PRECEDENTS, post.

2. The search warrant must be executed by the police and there is no power for the police to delegate the execution to a government agency, despite the fact that such agency may be primarily responsible for obtaining the search warrant; see *R v Reading Justices, Chief Constable of Avon and Somerset and Intervention Board for Agricultural Produce, ex p South West Meat Ltd* [1992] Crim LR 672.

3. "Premises" is defined in s 23 below. Notwithstanding the definition of "premises" in s 23, where a constable knows that premises include or consist of dwellings in separate occupation, in the context of s 15(2) Ord (6) he is required to specify the premises which it is desired to enter and search (*R v South Western Magistrates' Court, ex p Cofie* [1997] 1 WLR 885, 161 JP 69, DC.)

4. The word "it" probably refers to the warrant, so that an entry on premises or a search is unlawful unless the warrant complies with ss 15 and 16; see *R v Longman* [1988] 1 WLR 619, CA.

5. The Code of Practice for the Searching of Premises by Police Officers and the Seizure of Property Found by Police Officers on Persons or Premises (Code of Practice B), paras 3.1–3.5 in PART II: STATUTORY INSTRUMENTS ON EVIDENCE, post, imposes some important preliminary requirements on a police officer intending to apply for a search warrant. Where the search involves co-operation between the police and other agencies, the police must not delegate their powers in an unacceptable fashion; there may be the need to define the object of the search with precision and to limit the number of persons accompanying the police officer. Anyone accompanying the police should not exceed their authority (*R v Reading Justices, ex p South West Meat Ltd* [1992] Crim LR 672).

6. Code of Practice B para 3.6 requires the information to show (i) the enactment under which the application is made; (ii) as specifically as is reasonably practicable the premises to be searched and the object of the search; and (iii) the grounds on which the application is made (including, where the purpose of the proposed search is to find evidence of an alleged offence, an indication of how the evidence relates to the investigation). The justice must ensure that the material with which he is provided is sufficient so that he can properly say that the requirements set out in the relevant enactment are satisfied, but that does not mean that in every case the material that is put in the application has to be the sort of full material that one would see in a pleading or other such document: *R (on the application of R Cruickshank Ltd) v Chief Constable of Kent* [2001] EWHC Admin 123, [2001] Crim LR 990. The articles to be identified in the warrant by virtue of s 15(6)(*b*), post, must also be identified in the same terms in the information (*R v Central Criminal Court and British Railways Board, ex p A J D Holdings Ltd, Royle and Stanley Ltd* [1992] Crim LR 669).

7. Or affirmation: see Oaths Act 1978, s 5, para **2–1193**, post.

8. Provided the safeguards in the relevant legislation are complied, it is unreasonable to expect magistrates considering an application for a search warrant to make notes where they accept an information as containing all the material upon which they rely. If a particular matter is elicited in the course of questioning the deponent, it is desirable to make a note of that matter for the benefit a person who wishes to challenge the legality of the warrant and for the protection of the magistrates and the police (*R (Cronin) v Sheffield Magistrates' Court* [2002] EWHC 2568 (Admin), [2003] 1 WLR 752, 166 JP 777).

9. The making of copies and their certification should be carried out by the judge or magistrate who issues the search warrant (*R v Chief Constable of Lancashire, ex p Parker* [1993] 2 All ER 56, [1993] 2 WLR 428, 97 Cr App Rep 90).

1–2710   16. Execution of warrants[1].   (1) A warrant to enter and search premises[2] may be executed by any constable.

(2) Such a warrant may authorise persons to accompany any constable who is executing it.

(2A) A person so authorised has the same powers as the constable whom he accompanies in respect of—

(*a*)   the execution of the warrant, and
(*b*)   the seizure of anything to which the warrant relates.

(2B) But he may exercise those powers only in the company, and under the supervision, of a constable.

(3) Entry and search under a warrant must be within three months from the date of its issue.

(3A) If the warrant is an all premises warrant, no premises which are not specified in it may be entered or searched unless a police officer of at least the rank of inspector has in writing authorised them to be entered.

(3B) No premises may be entered or searched for the second or any subsequent time under a warrant which authorises multiple entries unless a police officer of at least the rank of inspector has in writing authorised that entry to those premises.

(4) Entry and search under a warrant must be at a reasonable hour unless it appears to the constable executing it that the purpose of a search may be frustrated on an entry at a reasonable hour.

(5) Where the occupier of premises[2] which are to be entered and searched is present at the time when a constable seeks to execute a warrant to enter and search them, the constable[3]—

(*a*)   shall identify himself to the occupier and, if not in uniform, shall produce[4] to him documentary evidence that he is a constable;
(*b*)   shall produce[4] the warrant to him; and
(*c*)   shall supply him with a copy of it.

(6) Where—

(*a*)   the occupier of such premises[2] is not present at the time when a constable seeks to execute such a warrant; but
(*b*)   some other person who appears to the constable to be in charge of the premises[2] is present,

subsection (5) above shall have effect as if any reference to the occupier were a reference to that other person.

(7) If there is no person present who appears to the constable to be in charge of the premises[2], he shall leave a copy of the warrant in a prominent place on the premises[2].

(8) A search under a warrant may only be a search to the extent required for the purpose for which the warrant was issued[5].

(9) A constable executing a warrant shall make an endorsement on it stating—

(*a*)   whether the articles or persons sought were found; and
(*b*)   whether any articles were seized, other than articles which were sought and,

unless the warrant is a warrant specifying one set of premises only, he shall do so separately in respect of each set of premises entered and searched, which he shall in each case state in the endorsement.

(10) A warrant shall be returned to the appropriate person mentioned in subsection (10A) below—

(*a*)   when it has been executed; or
(*b*)   in the case of a specific premises warrant which has not been executed, or an all premises warrant, or any warrant authorising multiple entries, upon the expiry of the period of three months referred to in subsection (3) above or sooner.

(10A) The appropriate person is—

(*a*)   if the warrant was issued by a justice of the peace, the designated officer for the local justice area in which the justice was acting when he issued the warrant;
(*b*)   if it was issued by a judge, the appropriate officer of the court from which he issued it.

(11) A warrant which is returned under subsection (10) above shall be retained for 12 months from its return—

    (a) by the designated officer for the local justice area, if it was returned under paragraph (i) of that subsection; and

    (b) by the appropriate officer, if it was returned under paragraph (ii).

(12) If during the period for which a warrant is to be retained the occupier of premises[2] to which it relates asks to inspect it, he shall be allowed to do so.

[Police and Criminal Evidence Act 1984, s 16 as amended by the Access to Justice Act 1999, s 90, the Criminal Justice Act 2003, s 2, the Courts Act 2003, Sch 8 and the Serious Organised Crime and Police Act 2005, ss 113 and 114 and SI 2005/3496.]

---

1. Save in exceptional circumstances, it is not in the public interest that legitimate investigative procedures by the police, such as the execution of search warrants should be accompanied by representatives of the media encouraged immediately to publish what they have seen *(R v Marylebone Magistrates' Court, ex p Amdrell Ltd* (1998) 162 JP 719, DC).

2. "Premises" is defined in s 23 below. The constable may use reasonable force; see s 117, post. He must leave the premises secure; see the Code of Practice B para 6.13.

3. Where there are reasonable grounds to believe that to alert the occupier would frustrate the object of the search, the constable is not required to fulfil the obligations listed in this subsection before entering the premises; but at the very earliest after entry and before search he should announce his identity, if not in uniform produce the warrant card and produce the search warrant *(R v Longman* [1988] 1 WLR 619, CA).

4. A warrant or warrant card is produced when the occupier is given an opportunity to inspect it *(R v Longman* [1988] 1 WLR 619, CA). The original warrant, as signed by the judge or magistrate, together with any schedule attached to the warrant, must be produced; see *R v Chief Constable of the Lancashire Constabulary, ex p Parker* [1993] 2 All ER 56, [1993] 2 WLR 428, 97 Cr App Rep 90.

5. Note however that an arrest may enable the scope of a search to be extended: see s 32, post. Section 16(8) is not restricted merely to the method of search but applies, subject to the *de minimis* principle, where articles are seized for which the warrant issued under s 8, ante, has provided no authority. By virtue of s 15(1), ante, the consequence of a breach of s 16(8) is to make the whole search unlawful so that there will have been a trespass to land as well as to goods; see *R v Chief Constable of Warwickshire Constabulary, ex p Fitzpatrick* [1998] 1 All ER 65, [1999] 1 WLR 564, [1998] Crim LR 290.

Entry and search without search warrant[1]

1–2711 17. Entry for purpose of arrest, etc. (1) Subject to the following provisions of this section, and without prejudice to any other enactment, a constable may enter and search any premises[2] for the purpose—

    (a) of executing—

        (i) a warrant of arrest[3] issued in connection with or arising out of criminal proceedings; or

        (ii) a warrant of commitment[3] issued under section 76 of the Magistrates' Courts Act 1980[4];

    (b) of arresting a person for an indictable offence;

    (c) of arresting a person for an offence under—

        (i) section 1 (prohibition of uniforms in connection with political objects) of the Public Order Act 1936;

        (ii) any enactment contained in sections 6 to 8 or 10 of the Criminal Law Act 1977 (offences relating to entering and remaining on property);

        (iii) section 4 of the Public Order Act 1986 (fear or provocation of violence);

        (iiia) section 4 (driving etc when under influence of drink or drugs) or 163 (failure to stop when required to do so by constable in uniform) of the Road Traffic Act 1988;

        (iiib) section 27 of the Transport and Works Act 1992 (which relates to offences involving drink or drugs);

        (iv) section 76 of the Criminal Justice and Public Order Act 1994 (failure to comply with interim possession order);*

    (ca) of arresting, in pursuance of section 32(1A) of the Children and Young Persons Act 1969, any child or young person who has been remanded or committed to local authority accommodation under section 23(1) of that Act;

    (caa) of arresting a person for an offence to which section 61 of the Animal Health Act 1981 applies;

    (cb) of recapturing any person who is, or is deemed for any purpose to be, unlawfully at large while liable to be detained—

        (i) in a prison, remand centre, young offender institution or secure training centre, or

        (ii) in pursuance of section 92 of the Powers of Criminal Courts (Sentencing) Act 2000 (dealing with children and young persons guilty of grave crimes), in any other place;

    (d) of recapturing any person whatever who is unlawfully at large and whom he is pursuing[5]; or

    (e) of saving life or limb or preventing serious damage to property.

(2) Except for the purpose specified in paragraph (e) of subsection (1) above, the powers of entry and search conferred by this section—

    (a) are only exercisable if the constable has reasonable grounds for believing that the person whom he is seeking is[6] on the premises[2]; and

    (b) are limited, in relation to premises[2] consisting of two or more separate dwellings, to powers to enter and search—

    (i) any parts of the premises[2] which the occupiers of any dwelling comprised in the premises use in common with the occupiers of any other such dwelling; and

    (ii) any such dwelling in which the constable has reasonable grounds for believing that the person whom he is seeking may be.

  (3) The powers of entry and search[7] conferred by this section are only exercisable for the purposes specified in subsection (1)(*c*)(ii) or (iv) above by a constable in uniform.

  (4) The power of search conferred by this section is only a power to search to the extent that is reasonably required for the purpose for which the power of entry is exercised.

  (5) Subject to subsection (6) below, all the rules of common law under which a constable has power to enter premises without a warrant are hereby abolished[8].

  (6) Nothing in subsection (5) above affects any power of entry to deal with or prevent a breach of the peace[9]peace[9].

[Police and Criminal Evidence Act 1984, s 17 as amended by the Public Order Act 1986, Schs 2 and 3, the Criminal Justice and Public Order Act 1994, Sch 10, the Prisoners (Return to Custody) Act 1995, s 2, the Powers of Criminal Courts (Sentencing) Act 2000, Sch 9,the Police Reform Act 2002, s 49 and the Serious Organised Crime and Police Act 2005, s 111.]

---

*New para (c)(v) inserted by the Animal Welfare Act 2006, s 24 from a date to be appointed.
  1. Search warrants are dealt with by s 8 et seq, ante. Entry may, of course, be made with consent, but any such consent should generally be in writing: see Code of Practice B paras 5.1–5.4 in PART II: STATUTORY INSTRUMENTS ON EVIDENCE, post. If entry is obstructed, the constable may use reasonable force (s 117, post). Statutory powers to enter for other purposes, for example to observe the conduct of licensed premises, are unaffected by this section. As to search of a person on arrest, and search of premises where he was see s 32, post.
  2. "Premises" is defined in s 23 below. Provisions of Code of Practice B apply: note particularly the requirement to keep full records (paras 8.1–9.1).
  3. The warrant need not be in the constable's possession when he executes it: Magistrates' Courts Act 1980, s 125(3) in this PART, ante.
  4. That is, where default is made in paying a sum adjudged to be paid by a conviction or order of a magistrates' court: see para **1–2126**, ante.
  5. "Pursuing" connotes an act of pursuit, a chase, however short in time and distance (*D'Souza v DPP* [1992] 4 All ER 545, [1992] 1 WLR 1073, 96 Cr App Rep 278, HL).
  6. It is unclear whether or not this would cover the case where the constable has reasonable grounds to believe only that the person he is seeking *may be* on the premises: see *Keegan v Chief Constable of Merseyside Police* [2003] EWCA Civ 936, [2003] 1 WLR 2187 at paras 23 and 40.
  7. Note also the power of seizure under s 19, post.
  8. Section 17(5) has nothing whatever to do with the power of police officers to search premises for evidence once a person has been arrested; it was intended to abolish only the common law powers relating to entry for the purpose of arrest (per Lord Rodger in *R (on the application of Rottman) v Metropolitan Police Comr* [2002] UKHL 20, [2002] AC 692, [2002] 2 All ER 865, [2002] 2 WLR 1315 at paras 108–9).
  9. See, for example, *Thomas v Sawkins* [1935] 2 KB 249, [1935] All ER Rep 655, 99 JP 295; *R v Howell* [1982] QB 416, [1981] 3 All ER 383. But see *McLeod v United Kingdom* (1998) 27 EHRR 493 for the position under the European Convention on Human Rights.

1–2712   **18. Entry and search after arrest.**   (1) Subject to the following provisions of this section, a constable may enter[1] and search any premises[2] occupied or controlled by a person who is under arrest for an indictable offence, if he has reasonable grounds for suspecting that there is on the premises evidence, other than items subject to legal privilege[3], that relates—

  (*a*) to that offence; or

  (*b*) to some other indictableindictable offence which is connected with or similar to that offence.

  (2) A constable may seize[4] and retain anything for which he may search under subsection (1) above.

  (3) The power to search conferred by subsection (1) above is only a power to search to the extent that is reasonably required for the purpose of discovering such evidence.

  (4) Subject to subsection (5) below, the powers conferred by this section may not be exercised unless an officer of the rank of inspector or above has authorised them in writing.

  (5) A constable may conduct a search under subsection (1)—

  (*a*) before the person is taken to a police station or released on bail under section 30A, and

  (*b*) without obtaining an authorisation under subsection (4),

if the condition in subsection (5A) is satisfied.

  (5A) The condition is that the presence of the person at a place (other than a police station) is necessary for the effective investigation of the offence.

  (6) If a constable conducts a search by virtue of subsection (5) above, he shall inform an officer of the rank of inspector or above that he has made the search as soon as practicable after he has made it.

  (7) An officer who—

  (*a*) authorises a search; or

  (*b*) is informed of a search under subsection (6) above, shall make a record in writing—

    (i) of the grounds for the search; and

    (ii) of the nature of the evidence that was sought.

  (8) If the person who was in occupation or control of the premises[2] at the time of the search is in police detention at the time the record is to be made, the officer shall make the record as part of his custody record.

[Police and Criminal Evidence Act 1984, s 18 as amended by the Police Reform Act 2002, Sch 7, the Criminal Justice Act 2003, Sch 1 and the Serious Organised Crime and Police Act 2005, Sch 7.]

1. A constable who proposes to enter premises by force and is in possession of an authorisation given under s18(4) must explain to the occupier, in so far as it is practicable to do so, the reason why he intends so to act (*Linehan v DPP* [2000] Crim LR 861, DC). See also *R (on the application of Odewale) v DPP* CO/1381/2000 (justices are not entitled to infer that a police officer was carrying out a lawful search pursuant to s 18 from the bare fact that he stated in evidence that he was carrying out such a search).

2. "Premises" is defined in s 23 below. Provisions of Code of Practice B in PART II: STATUTORY INSTRUMENTS ON EVIDENCE, post, apply.

3. "Items subject to legal privilege" is defined in s 10 above. Section 19(6) shall not apply to the powers of seizure conferred by the Criminal Justice and Police Act 2001, s 50(2) and s 51(2). At the time of going to press these provisions are not in force.

4. Note s 19 below which supplements this power of seizure.

Seizure, etc

1–2713   19. General power of seizure, etc[1].   (1) The powers conferred by subsections (2), (3) and (4) below are exercisable by a constable who is lawfully on any premises[2].

(2) The constable may seize anything which is on the premises[2] if he has reasonable grounds for believing—

(a) that it has been obtained in consequence of the commission of an offence; and
(b) that it is necessary to seize it in order to prevent it being concealed, lost, damaged, altered or destroyed.

(3) The constable may seize anything which is on the premises[2] if he has reasonable grounds for believing—

(a) that it is evidence in relation to an offence which he is investigating or any other offence[3]; and
(b) that it is necessary to seize it in order to prevent the evidence being concealed, lost, altered or destroyed.

(4) The constable may require any information which is stored in any electronic form and is accessible from the premises[2] to be produced in a form in which it can be taken away and in which it is visible and legible or from which it can readily be produced in a visible and legible form if he has reasonable grounds for believing—

(a) that—
    (i)   it is evidence in relation to an offence which he is investigating or any other offence; or
    (ii) it has been obtained in consequence of the commission of an offence; and
(b) that it is necessary to do so in order to prevent it being concealed, lost, tampered with or destroyed.

(5) The powers conferred by this section are in addition to any power otherwise conferred.

(6) No power of seizure conferred on a constable under any enactment (including an enactment contained in an Act passed after this Act) is to be taken to authorise the seizure of an item which the constable exercising the power has reasonable grounds for believing to be subject to legal privilege[4].

[Police and Criminal Evidence Act 1984, s 19, as amended by the Criminal Justice and Police Act 2001, Sch 2.]

1. The police are under a duty as bailees to take reasonable care, in all the circumstances, of any articles which are seized under this section (*Sutcliffe v Chief Constable of West Yorkshire* (1995) 159 JP 770, [1996] RTR 86, CA).

2. "Premises" is defined in s 23 below. The powers of seizure conferred by s 18(2), ante, and s 19(3) extend to the seizure of the whole premises where it is physically possible to seize and retain the premises in their totality, and practical considerations make such a seizure desirable. Accordingly, the police may remove premises such as tents, vehicles or caravans to a police station for the purpose of preserving evidence (*Cowan v Metropolitan Police Comr* [2000] 1 All ER 504, [2000] 1 WLR 254, CA). The effect of the Act is that entry may lawfully be made with consent, or warrant, or under a statutory power; it may otherwise lead to an application to exclude evidence (s 78, post) and may be actionable as a trespass. If consent is given, then withdrawn, rights of search and seizure cease unless and until there is an arrest (ss 18 and 32, post) or a search warrant is issued (s 8, ante) or there is supervening statutory authority for it (s 17, ante).

3. This relates to domestic offences and not to offences allegedly committed outside the United Kingdom (*R v Southwark Crown Court, ex p Sorsky Defries* [1996] Crim LR 195). However, a police officer who has arrested a person in or on his premises pursuant to a warrant of arrest issued under s 8 of the Extradition Act 1989 has a common law power to search those premises for, and to seize, any goods or documents which he reasonably believes to be material evidence in relation to the extradition crime for which the warrant was issued (though, because ss 18 and 19 of PACE apply only to domestic offences, this common law power has none of the disciplines created by s 18 attached to it) (*R (on the application of Rottman) v Metropolitan Police Comr* [2002] UKHL 20, [2002] AC 692, [2002] 2 All ER 865, [2002] 2 WLR 1315).

4. "Item subject to legal privilege" is defined in s 10 above. Section 19(6) does not apply to the power of search conferred by the Criminal Justice and Police Act 2001, s 50(2) and s 51(2).

1–2714   20. Extension of powers of seizure to computerised information.   (1) Every power of seizure which is conferred by an enactment to which this section applies on a constable who has entered premises[1] in the exercise of a power conferred by an enactment shall be construed as including a power to require any information stored in any electronic form and accessible from the premises to be produced in a form in which it can be taken away and in which it is visible and legible or from which it can readily be produced in a visible and legible form.

(2) This section applies—

(a) to any enactment contained in an Act passed before this Act;
(b) to sections 8 and 18 above;

(c)   to paragraph 13 of Schedule 1 to this Act; and
(d)   to any enactment contained in an Act passed after this Act.
[Police and Criminal Evidence Act 1984, s 20, as amended by the Criminal Justice and Police Act 2001, Sch 2.]

---

1. "Premises" is defined in s 23 below.

1–2725   21. Access and copying[1]. (1) A constable who seizes anything in the exercise of a power conferred by any enactment, including an enactment contained in an Act passed after this Act, shall, if so requested by a person showing himself—

(a)   to be the occupier of premises on which it was seized; or
(b)   to have had custody or control of it immediately before the seizure,

provide that person with a record of what he seized.

(2) The officer shall provide the record within a reasonable time from the making of the request for it.

(3) Subject to subsection (8) below, if a request for permission to be granted access to anything which—

(a)   has been seized by a constable; and
(b)   is retained by the police for the purpose of investigating an offence,

is made to the officer in charge of the investigation by a person who had custody or control of the thing immediately before it was so seized or by someone acting on behalf of such a person, the officer shall allow the person who made the request access to it under the supervision of a constable.

(4) Subject to subsection (8) below, if a request for a photograph or copy of any such thing is made to the officer in charge of the investigation by a person who had custody or control of the thing immediately before it was so seized, or by someone acting on behalf of such a person, the officer shall—

(a)   allow the person who made the request access to it under the supervision of a constable for the purpose of photographing or copying it; or
(b)   photograph or copy it, or cause it to be photographed or copied.

(5) A constable may also photograph or copy, or have photographed or copied, anything which he has power to seize, without a request being made under sub-section (4) above.

(6) Where anything is photographed or copied under subsection (4)(b) above, the photograph or copy shall be supplied to the person who made the request.

(7) The photograph or copy shall be so supplied within a reasonable time from the making of the request.

(8) There is no duty under this section to grant access to, or to supply a photograph or copy of, anything if the officer in charge of the investigation for the purposes of which it was seized has reasonable grounds for believing that to do so would prejudice—

(a)   that investigation;
(b)   the investigation of an offence other than the offence for the purposes of investigation which the thing was seized; or
(c)   any criminal proceedings which may be brought as a result of—

(i)   the investigation of which he is in charge; or
(ii)   any such investigation as is mentioned in paragraph (b) above.

(9) The references to a constable in subsections (1), (2), (3)(a) and (5) include a person authorised under section 16(2) to accompany a constable executing a warrant.
[Police and Criminal Evidence Act 1984, s 21 as amended by the Criminal Justice Act 2003, Sch 1.]

---

1. For the purposes of ss 21 and 22 of this Act, an investigation into whether any person has benefited from any criminal conduct or into the extent or whereabouts of the proceeds of any criminal conduct shall be treated (so far as that would not otherwise be the case) as if it were an investigation of, or in connection with, an offence (Proceeds of Crime Act 1995, s 15(2)).

1–2726   22. Retention[1]. (1) Subject to subsection (4) below, anything which has been seized by a constable or taken away by a constable following a requirement made by virtue of section 19 or 20 above may be retained[2] so long as is necessary in all the circumstances.

(2) Without prejudice to the generality of subsection (1) above—

(a)   anything seized for the purposes of a criminal investigation may be retained[3], except as provided by subsection (4) below—

(i)   for use as evidence at a trial for an offence; or
(ii)   for forensic examination or for investigation in connection with an offence; and

(b)   anything may be retained[4] in order to establish its lawful owner, where there are reasonable grounds for believing that it has been obtained in consequence of the commission of an offence.

(3) Nothing seized on the ground that it may be used—

(a)   to cause physical injury to any person;
(b)   to damage property;

(c)   to interfere with evidence; or

(d)   to assist in escape from police detention or lawful custody,

may be retained when the person from whom it was seized is no longer in police detention or the custody of a court or is in the custody of a court but has been released on bail.

(4)   Nothing may be retained for either of the purposes mentioned in subsection (2)(a) above if a photograph or copy would be sufficient for that purpose.

(5)   Nothing in this section affects any power of a court to make an order under section 1 of the Police (Property) Act 1897[5].

(6)   This section also applies to anything retained by the police under section 28H(5) of the Immigration Act 1971.

(7)   The reference in subsection (1) to anything seized by a constable includes anything seized by a person authorised under section 16(2) to accompany a constable executing a warrant.

[Police and Criminal Evidence Act 1984, s 22 as amended by the Immigration and Asylum Act 1999, Sch 14 and the Criminal Justice Act 2003, Sch 1.]

---

1. See note 1 to s 21, above. See the Criminal Justice and Police Act 2001, Part 2 this PART, post. These provisions (summarised at para **1-205**, ante) confer, by ss 50 and 51, additional powers of seizure of property in relation to searches carried out under existing powers. However, s 57 (retention of seized items) does not authorise the retention of any property which could not be retained under the provisions listed in s 57(1), which include s 22 of PACE, if the property was seized under the new powers (ie those conferred by ss 50 and 51) in reliance on one of those powers (ie those conferred by the provisions listed in s 57(1)). Section 57(4) further provides that nothing in any of the provisions listed in s 57(1) authorises the retention of anything after an obligation to return it has arisen under Part 2.

2. A customs officer retaining material under this section may make the material available to a foreign agency but may not part with it without further order (*R v Crown Court at Southwark, ex p Customs and Excise Comrs* [1990] 1 QB 650, [1989] 3 All ER 673, DC).

3. Subsection (2) must be read in conjunction with the rest of s 22, and it does not confer on the police power to retain unlawfully seized material (*R v Chief Constable of Lancashire, ex p Parker* [1993] 2 All ER 56, [1993] 2 WLR 428).

4. Where police officers seized a stolen vehicle then in the possession of C, who was its registered keeper, but C, though aware that the car was stolen, was not prosecuted, and the police were unable to trace anybody with a better title to the vehicle than C, C was entitled to the return of the vehicle once the purposes of s 22 had been exhausted: *Costello v Chief Constable of Derbyshire Constabulary* [2001] EWCA Civ 381, [2001] 3 All ER 150, [2001] 1 WLR 1437.

5. In PART VIII: POLICE, post: a claimant of the property may apply to a magistrates' court for an order for the delivery of the property to him.

Supplementary

1-2727   23. Meaning of "premises", etc.   In this Act—

"premises" includes any place and, in particular, includes—

     (a)   any vehicle, vessel, aircraft or hovercraft;

     (b)   any offshore installation; and

     (c)   any tent or movable structure; and

"offshore installation" has the meaning given to it by section 1 of the Mineral Workings (Offshore Installations) Act 1971.

[Police and Criminal Evidence Act 1984, s 23.]

PART III[1]

ARREST[2]

1-2728   24. Arrest without warrant: constables[3].   (1)   A constable may arrest[4] without a warrant—

     (a)   anyone who is about to commit an offence;

     (b)   anyone who is in the act of committing an offence;

     (c)   anyone whom he has reasonable grounds[5] for suspecting to be about to commit an offence;

     (d)   anyone whom he has reasonable grounds[5] for suspecting to be committing an offence.

(2)   If a constable has reasonable grounds[5] for suspecting that an offence has been committed, he may arrest without a warrant anyone whom he has reasonable grounds to suspect of being guilty of it.

(3)   If an offence has been committed, a constable may arrest without a warrant—

     (a)   anyone who is guilty of the offence;

     (b)   anyone whom he has reasonable grounds[5] for suspecting to be guilty of it.

(4)   But the power of summary arrest conferred by subsection (1), (2) or (3) is exercisable only if the constable has reasonable grounds for believing that for any of the reasons mentioned in subsection (5) it is necessary to arrest the person in question.

(5)   The reasons are—

     (a)   to enable the name of the person in question to be ascertained (in the case where the constable does not know, and cannot readily ascertain, the person's name, or has reasonable grounds for doubting whether a name given by the person as his name is his real name);

     (b)   correspondingly as regards the person's address;

     (c)   to prevent the person in question—

         (i)   causing physical injury to himself or any other person;

         (ii)   suffering physical injury;

         (iii)   causing loss of or damage to property;

(iv) committing an offence against public decency (subject to subsection (6)); or
(v) causing an unlawful obstruction of the highway;

(d) to protect a child or other vulnerable person from the person in question;
(e) to allow the prompt and effective investigation of the offence or of the conduct of the person in question;
(f) to prevent any prosecution for the offence from being hindered by the disappearance of the person in question.

(6) Subsection (5)(c)(iv) applies only where members of the public going about their normal business cannot reasonably be expected to avoid the person in question.
[Police and Criminal Evidence Act 1984, s 24 as substituted by the Serious Organised Crime and Police Act 2005, s 110.]

---

1. Part III contains ss 24–33 and is followed by Part IV dealing with detention.
This Part of the Act has been seen as following a trend towards arrest preceding full investigation, rather than coming at its end; this Act thus controls more precisely the power to detain. Following arrest, a person may be kept in detention initially for up to 24 hours (s 41, post) in order to secure or preserve evidence or to obtain it by questioning (see s 37(2) and note ss 42(1), 43(4)), and the police may enter and search his premises (s 18, ante). Note also the rights to have someone informed of the arrest (s 56, post) and to see a solicitor (s 58, post). For commentary on arrest, powers of arrest and police detention, see paras **1–220** to **1–223**, ante. The effect of ss 24–26 is to create a potential power of arrest for every offence.
2. See the Code of Practice for the Statutory Power of Arrest by Police Officers (Code of Practice G) andand the Code of Practice for the Detention, Treatment and Questioning of Persons by Police Officers (Code of Practice C), in PART II: STATUTORY INSTRUMENTS ON EVIDENCE, post. Powers of arrest are also governed by art 5 of the European Convention on Human Rights, which sets out three pre-conditions to a lawful arrest. They are—
  1. the arrest must be "lawful";
  2. the arrest must be "in accordance with a procedure prescribed by law"; and
  3. the grounds for arrest must fall within at least one of the paragraphs 5(1)(a) to (f) of art 5.
Paragraph 5(1)(c) provides for arrest on reasonable suspicion that an offence has been committed. The arrest must be for the purpose of bringing the person concerned before a "competent legal authority" which includes a magistrates' court. The words "reasonable suspicion" in art 5(1)(c) mean the existence of facts or information which would satisfy an objective observer that the person concerned may have committed the offence. Article 5(2) of the Convention requires that an arrested person be provided with the reasons for an arrest. The person concerned must be told "in simple, non-technical language that he can understand, the essential legal and factual grounds for his arrest so as to be able, if he sees fit, to apply to a court to challenge its lawfulness". See *Fox, Campbell and Hartley v United Kingdom* (1990) 13 EHRR 157.
3. This section has effect in relation to any offence whenever committed (Serious Organised Crime and Police Act 2005, s 111).
4. The arrested person must be told that he is under arrest, and usually told why: see s 28, post. Reasonable force may be used: see s 117, post, and indeed the use of force to resist lawful arrest may lead to a charge under the Police Act 1996, s 89 or indeed the Offences Against the Person Act 1861, s 38. The sanction of reasonable force under the Criminal Law Act 1967, s 3, ante, has not been repealed.
5. It is implicit in these provisions that the constable must not only have reasonable grounds for suspecting or believing that an offence has been committed, but must in fact do so. Moreover, the constable must reasonably suspect the existence of facts amounting to an offence of a kind which he has in mind, so as to be able to comply with s 28(3), post, by informing the suspect of the ground for the arrest; see *Chapman v DPP* (1988) 153 JP 27, 89 Cr App Rep 190. The critical question to be asked in all cases is what is in the mind of the arresting officer; he can never be a mere "conduit" for somebody else: *O'Hara v Chief Constable of the Royal Ulster Constabulary* [1997] AC 286, [1997] 1 All ER 129, [1997] 1 Cr App Rep 447, HL (where it was held that the mere fact that an arresting officer had been instructed by a superior officer to effect the arrest was not capable of amounting to reasonable grounds for the necessary suspicion required by s 12(1) of the Prevention of Terrorism (Temporary Provisions) Act 1984). Conversely, however, where the arresting officer's suspicion is formed on the basis of a police national computer entry, that entry is likely to provide the necessary objective justification: *Hough v Chief Constable of Staffordshire* [2001] EWCA Civ 39, 165 JPN 54.

1–2728A   **24A. Arrest without warrant: other persons**[1]. (1) A person other than a constable may arrest[2] without a warrant—

(a) anyone who is in the act of committing an indictable offence;
(b) anyone whom he has reasonable grounds for suspecting to be committing an indictable offence.

(2) Where an indictable offence has been committed[3], a person other than a constable may arrest without a warrant—

(a) anyone who is guilty[4] of the offence;
(b) anyone whom he has reasonable grounds for suspecting to be guilty[4] of it.

(3) But the power of summary arrest conferred by subsection (1) or (2) is exercisable only if—

(a) the person making the arrest has reasonable grounds for believing that for any of the reasons mentioned in subsection (4) it is necessary to arrest the person in question; and
(b) it appears to the person making the arrest that it is not reasonably practicable for a constable to make it instead.

(4) The reasons are to prevent the person in question—

(a) causing physical injury to himself or any other person;
(b) suffering physical injury;
(c) causing loss of or damage to property; or
(d) making off before a constable can assume responsibility for him.★
[Police and Criminal Evidence Act 1984, s 24A as inserted by the Serious Organised Crime and Police Act 2005, s 110.]

*New sub-s (5) inserted by the Racial and Religious Hatred Act 2006, s 2 from a date to be appointed.

1. This section has effect in relation to any offence whenever committed (Serious Organised Crime and Police Act 2005, s 111).

2. A private person effecting an arrest should take the arrested person to a constable as soon as possible (implied by s 30(1)(b), post), and see *John Lewis & Co Ltd v Tims* [1952] AC 676, [1952] 1 All ER 1203, HL (shoplifter can be taken to manager for decision to prosecute).

Reasonable force may be used: the sanction of reasonable force under the Criminal Law Act 1967, s 3, ante, has not been repealed.

3. If in fact no offence has been committed, a private person arresting will be liable in a civil action, however reasonable his grounds of suspicion may be: see *Walters v W H Smith & Son Ltd* [1914] 1 KB 595: compare this with the greater powers exercisable by a constable under s 24.

4. The offence must have been committed in order for the arrest to be valid; an acquittal invalidates the arrest (*R v Self* [1992] 3 All ER 476, [1992] 1 WLR 657, 156 JP 397, CA).

1-2730   26. Repeal of statutory powers of arrest without warrant or order. (1) Subject to subsection (2) below, so much of any Act (including a local Act) passed before this Act as enables a constable[1]—

    (a) to arrest a person for an offence without a warrant; or

    (b) to arrest a person otherwise than for an offence without a warrant or an order of a court,

shall cease to have effect.

(2) Nothing in subsection (1) above affects the enactments specified in Schedule 2 to this Act.
[Police and Criminal Evidence Act 1984, s 26.]

---

1. Other persons' powers are unaffected: see eg Customs and Excise Management Act 1979, s 138(1).

1-2731   27. Fingerprinting of certain offenders. (1) If a person—

    (a) has been convicted of a recordable offence;

    (b) has not at any time been in police detention for the offence; and

    (c) has not had his fingerprints taken—

        (i) in the course of the investigation of the offence by the police; or

        (ii) since the conviction,

any constable may at any time not later than one month[1] after the date of the conviction require him to attend a police station in order that his fingerprints may be taken[2].

(1A) Where a person convicted of a recordable offence has already had his fingerprints taken as mentioned in paragraph (c) of subsection (1) above, that fact (together with any time when he has been in police detention for the offence) shall be disregarded for the purposes of that subsection if—

    (a) the fingerprints taken on the previous occasion do not constitute a complete set of his fingerprints; or

    (b) some or all of the fingerprints taken on the previous occasion are not of sufficient quality to allow satisfactory analysis, comparison or matching.

(1B) Subsections (1) and (1A) above apply—

    (a) where a person has been given a caution in respect of a recordable offence which, at the time of the caution, he has admitted; or

    (b) where a person has been warned or reprimanded under section 65 of the Crime and Disorder Act 1998 (c 37) for a recordable offence,

as they apply where a person has been convicted of an offence, and references in this section to a conviction shall be construed accordingly.

(2) A requirement under subsection (1) above—

    (a) shall give the person a period of at least 7 days[1] within which he must so attend; and

    (b) may direct him to so attend at a specified time of day or between specified times of day[1].

(3) Any constable may arrest without warrant a person who has failed to comply with a requirement under subsection (1) above.

(4) The Secretary of State may by regulations[3] make provision for recording in national police records convictions for such offences as are specified in the regulations.

(4A) *Repealed.*

(5) Regulations under this section shall be made by statutory instrument and shall be subject to annulment in pursuance of a resolution of either House of Parliament.
[Police and Criminal Evidence Act 1984, s 27 as amended by the Crime and Disorder Act 1998, Sch 8 and the Criminal Justice and Police Act 2001, s 78 and Sch 7.]

---

1. If a person is convicted on the 1st of the month, the constable has until the end of the 2nd of the following month to make the requirement: if at, say, 6 pm on the 2nd he notifies the offender that he requires attendance at, say, noon within the next seven days, his power of arrest will not arise until after noon on the 9th. One month after 31st January is 28th February (or 29th in a leap year); one month after 30th April is 30th May. See post, para **2-744 Time** in PART II: EVIDENCE.

2. Section 61 below makes more general provision for fingerprinting.

3. The National Police Records (Recordable Offences) Regulations 2000, SI 2000/1139 amended by SI 2003/2823 and SI 2005/3106 provide that there may be recorded in national police records:

(*a*) convictions for; and
(*b*) cautions, reprimands and warnings given in respect of, any offence punishable with imprisonment and any offence specified in the Schedule to the Regulations. The reference to an offence punishable with imprisonment shall be construed without regard to any prohibition or restriction imposed by or under any enactment on the punishment of young offenders. Where a person is convicted of a recordable offence, there may also be recorded any conviction of his for any other offence of which he is convicted in the same proceedings (reg 3).

Regulation 3   SCHEDULE
SPECIFIED OFFENCES

The following offences are specified for the purposes of section 27(4) of the Police and Criminal Evidence Act 1984, that is to say, an offence under:

1   section 5 of the Children and Young Persons Act 1933 (offence of giving intoxicating liquor to children under five);
2   section 11 of the Children and Young Persons Act 1933 (offence of exposing children under twelve to risk of burning);
3. section 12 of the Children and Young Persons Act 1933 (offence of failing to provide for safety of children at entertainments);
4   section 91 of the Criminal Justice Act 1967 (offence of drunkenness in a public place);
5   section 167 of the Criminal Justice and Public Order Act 1994 (offence of touting for hire car services);
6   section 2 of the Crossbows Act 1987 (offence of purchasing or hiring a crossbow or part of a crossbow by person under the age of seventeen);
7   section 3 of the Crossbows Act 1987 (offence of possessing a crossbow or parts of a crossbow by unsupervised person under the age of seventeen);
8   section 5(6) of the Firearms Act 1968 (offence of failing to deliver up authority to possess prohibited weapon or ammunition);
9   section 22(3) of the Firearms Act 1968 (offence of possessing an assembled shotgun by unsupervised person under the age of fifteen);
10   section 22(4) of the Firearms Act 1968 (offence of possessing an air weapon or ammunition for an air weapon by unsupervised person under the age of fourteen);
11   section 22(5) of the Firearms Act 1968 (offence of possessing in a public place an air weapon by unsupervised person under the age of seventeen);
12   section 2 of the Football (Offences) Act 1991 (offence of throwing missiles);
13   section 3 of the Football (Offences) Act 1991 (offence of indecent or racialist chanting);
14   section 4 of the Football (Offences) Act 1991 (offence of unlawfully going on to the playing area);
15   section 30 of the Game Act 1831 (offences of trespassing in daytime on land in search of game, etc);
16   section 31 of the Game Act 1831 (offence of refusal of person trespassing in daytime on land in search of game to give his name and address);
17   section 32 of the Game Act 1831 (offence of five or more persons being found armed in daytime in search of game and using violence or refusal of such persons to give name and address);
18   section 12 of the Licensing Act 1872 (offence of being drunk in highway or public place);
19   section 59(5) of the Licensing Act 2003 (offence of obstructing an authorised person inspecting premises before the grant of a licence etc);
20   section 82(6) of the Licensing Act 2003 (offence of failing to notify change of name or alteration of rules of club);
21   section 96(5) of the Licensing Act 2003 (offence of obstructing an authorised person inspecting premises before the grant of a certificate etc);
22   section 108(3) of the Licensing Act 2003 (offence of obstructing an authorised person exercising a right of entry where a temporary event notice has been given);
23   section 123(2) of the Licensing Act 2003 (offence of failing to notify licensing authority of convictions during application period);
24   section 128(6) of the Licensing Act 2003 (offence of failing to notify court of personal licence);
24A section 138(1) of the Licensing Act 2003 (offence of keeping alcohol on premises for unauthorised sale etc);
24B section 140(1) of the Licensing Act 2003 (offence of allowing disorderly conduct on licensed premises etc);
24C section 141(1) of the Licensing Act 2003 (offence of selling alcohol to a person who is drunk);
24D section 142(1) of the Licensing Act 2003 (offence of obtaining alcohol for a person who is drunk);
24E section 143(1) of the Licensing Act 2003 (offence of failing to leave licensed premises etc);
24F section 144(1) of the Licensing Act 2003 (offence of keeping smuggled goods);
24G section 145(1) of the Licensing Act 2003 (offence of allowing unaccompanied children on certain premises);
24H section 146(1) and (3) of the Licensing Act 2003 (offence of selling alcohol to children);
24I section 147(1) of the Licensing Act 2003 (offence of allowing sale of alcohol to children);
24J section 149(1), (3) and (4) of the Licensing Act 2003 (offence of purchasing alcohol by or on behalf of children);
24K section 150(1) and (2) of the Licensing Act 2003 (offence of consumption of alcohol on relevant premises by children);
24L section 151(1), (2) and (4) of the Licensing Act 2003 (offence of delivering alcohol to children);
24M section 152 (1) of the Licensing Act 2003 (offence of send a child to obtain alcohol);
24N section 153(1) of the Licensing Act 2003 (offence of allowing unsupervised sales by children);
24O section 158(1) of the Licensing Act 2003 (offence of making false statements);
24P section 160(4) of the Licensing Act 2003 (offence of allowing premises to remain open following a closure order);
24Q section 179(4) of the Licensing Act 2003 (offence of obstructing authorised person exercising rights of entry to investigate licensable activities);
25   paragraph 21 of Schedule 3 to the Local Government (Miscellaneous Provisions) Act 1982 (offence of making false statement in connection with an application for a sex establishment licence);
26   *Revoked.*
27   article 44 of the Nursing and Midwifery Order 2001 (offence of falsely claiming a professional qualification etc.);
28   section 1 of the Night Poaching Act 1828 (offence of taking or destroying game or rabbits by night, or entering any land for that purpose);
29   section 90(2) of the Police Act 1996 (offence of wearing police uniform with intent to deceive);
30   section 90(3) of the Police Act 1996 (offence of unlawful possession of article of police uniform);
31   section 5 of the Public Order Act 1986 (offence of causing harassment, alarm or distress);
32   section 11 of the Public Order Act 1986 (offence of failing to give advance notice of public procession);
33   section 12(5) of the Public Order Act 1986 (offence of failing to comply with conditions imposed on a public procession);
34   section 13(8) of the Public Order Act 1986 (offence of taking part in a prohibited public procession);
35   section 14(5) of the Public Order Act 1986 (offence of failing to comply with conditions imposed on a public assembly);

36 section 14B(2) of the Public Order Act 1986 (offence of taking part in a prohibited assembly);
37 section 14C(3) of the Public Order Act 1986 (offence of failing to comply with directions);
38 section 6 of the Road Traffic Act 1988 (offence of failing to provide specimen of breath);
39 section 25 of the Road Traffic Act 1988 (penalisation of tampering with vehicles);
40 section 1 of the Sexual Offences Act 1985 (offence of kerb crawling);
41 section 2 of the Sexual Offences Act 1985 (offence of persistently soliciting women for the purpose of prostitution);
42 section 1(2) of the Sporting Events (Control of Alcohol Etc) Act 1985 (offence of allowing alcohol to be carried on public vehicles on journey to or from designated sporting event);
43 section 1(4) of the Sporting Events (Control of Alcohol Etc) Act 1985 (offence of being drunk on public vehicles on journey to or from designated sporting event);
44 section 1A(2) of the Sporting Events (Control of Alcohol Etc) Act 1985 (offence of allowing alcohol to be carried in vehicles on journey to or from designated sporting event);
45 section 2(2) of the Sporting Events (Control of Alcohol Etc) Act 1985 (offence of trying to enter designated sports ground while drunk);
46–49 *Revoked.*50section 1 of the Street Offences Act 1959 (offence of loitering or soliciting for purposes of prostitution);
51 *Revoked.*
52 section 12(5) of the Theft Act 1968 (offence of taking or riding a pedal cycle without owner's consent);
53 section 3 of the Vagrancy Act 1824 (offence of begging); and
54 section 4 of the Vagrancy Act 1824 (offence of persistent begging).

1–2732   28. Information to be given on arrest.   (1) Subject to subsection (5) below, where a person is arrested, otherwise than by being informed that he is under arrest, the arrest is not lawful unless the person arrested is informed that he is under arrest as soon as is practicable after his arrest[1].

(2) Where a person is arrested by a constable, subsection (1) above applies regardless of whether the fact of the arrest is obvious.

(3) Subject to subsection (5) below, no arrest is lawful unless the person arrested is informed of the ground for the arrest[2] at the time of, or as soon as is practicable after, the arrest.

(4) Where a person is arrested by a constable, subsection (3) above applies regardless of whether the ground for the arrest is obvious.

(5) Nothing in this section is to be taken to require a person to be informed—

(a) that he is under arrest; or
(b) of the ground for the arrest,

if it was not reasonably practicable for him to be so informed by reason of his having escaped from arrest before the information could be given.
[Police and Criminal Evidence Act 1984, s 28.]

1. Note also the requirement to caution in the Code of Practice for the Detention, Treatment and Questioning of Persons by Police Officers Code of Practice C, para 10.4 in PART II: STATUTORY INSTRUMENTS ON EVIDENCE, post.
An unauthorised taker of a motor vehicle, who was detained by an automatic device fitted to the vehicle which he had taken, was held to have been lawfully arrested because the police arrived on the scene quickly, and told the defendant he had been arrested and the reasons for his arrest (*Dawes v DPP* [1994] RTR 209, [1995] 1 Cr App Rep 65).
2. Where an arrest arose from the theft of a chequebook and a number of cheques from a jacket and the subsequent cashing of a cheque for almost all the funds in the account concerned, and the suspect had been at the premises at the time of the theft and had been identified by the victim as being at the victim's bank at the material time, but the arresting officer did not indicate any of these circumstances but simply arrested the suspect for "theft of cheques", there was a failure to comply with the requirements of s 28(3): *Wilson v Chief Constable of Lancashire Constabulary* [2000] All ER (D) 1949, CA. It is not enough for a constable to say that the arrest is due to the fact that the defendant has refused to give his name and address, he must indicate the offence alleged; the phrase "at the time of . . . the arrest" includes a reasonable time before the arrest (*Nicholas v Parsonage* [1987] RTR 199). When a police officer makes an arrest which he is lawfully entitled to make but is unable at the time to state the ground because it is impracticable to do so, it is his duty to maintain the arrest until it is practicable to inform the arrested person of that ground. If, when it does become practicable, he fails to do so, then the arrest is unlawful, but that does not mean that acts, which were previously done and were, when done, done in the execution of duty, become, retrospectively, acts which were not done in the execution of duty (*DPP v Hawkins* [1988] 3 All ER 673, [1988] 1 WLR 1166, 152 JP 518, DC).

1–2733   29. Voluntary attendance at police station, etc.   Where for the purpose of assisting with an investigation a person attends voluntarily[1] at a police station or at any other place where a constable is present or accompanies a constable to a police station or any such other place without having been arrested—

(a) he shall be entitled to leave at will unless he is placed under arrest[2];
(b) he shall be informed at once that he is under arrest if a decision is taken by a constable to prevent him from leaving at will.
[Police and Criminal Evidence Act 1984, s 29.]

1. The Code of Practice for the Detention, Treatment and Questioning of Persons by Police Officers (Code of Practice C) in PART II: STATUTORY INSTRUMENTS ON EVIDENCE, paras 3.21–3.22, 10.2 makes provision for the treatment of such persons, including when they attend and are cautioned.
2. Time then begins to run, limiting the period of detention without charge: see s 41(2)(c), post.

1–2734   30. Arrest elsewhere than at police station.   (1) Subsection (1A) applies where a person is, at any place other than a police station—

(a) arrested by a constable for an offence, or
(b) taken into custody by a constable after being arrested for an offence by a person other than a constable.

(1A) The person must be taken by a constable to a police station as soon as practicable[1] after the arrest.

(1B) Subsection (1A) has effect subject to section 30A (release on bail) and subsection (7) (release without bail).

(2) Subject to subsections (3) and (5) below, the police station to which an arrested person is taken under subsection (1A) above shall be a designated police station[2].

(3) A constable to whom this subsection applies may take an arrested person to any police station unless it appears to the constable that it may be necessary to keep the arrested person in police detention for more than six hours.

(4) Subsection (3) above applies—

(a) to a constable who is working in a locality covered by a police station which is not a designated police station[2]; and

(b) to a constable belonging to a body of constables maintained by an authority other than a police authority.

(5) Any constable may take an arrested person to any police station if—

(a) either of the following conditions is satisfied—

  (i) the constable has arrested him without the assistance of any other constable and no other constable is available to assist him;

  (ii) the constable has taken him into custody from a person other than a constable without the assistance of any other constable and no other constable is available to assist him; and

(b) it appears to the constable that he will be unable to take the arrested person to a designated police station[2] without the arrested person injuring himself, the constable or some other person.

(6) If the first police station to which an arrested person is taken after his arrest is not a designated police station[2], he shall be taken to a designated police station[2] not more than six hours after his arrival at the first police station unless he is released previously.

(7) A person arrested by a constable at any place other than a police station must be released without bail if the condition in subsection (7A) is satisfied.

(7A) The condition is that, at any time before the person arrested reaches a police station, a constable is satisfied that there are no grounds for keeping him under arrest or releasing him on bail under section 30A.

(8) A constable who releases a person under subsection (7) above shall record the fact that he has done so.

(9) The constable shall make the record as soon as is practicable after the release.

(10) Nothing in subsection (1A) or in section 30A prevents a constable delaying taking a person to a police station or releasing him on bail if the condition in subsection (10A) is satisfied.

(10A) The condition is that the presence of the person at a place (other than a police station) is necessary in order to carry out such investigations as it is reasonable to carry out immediately.

(11) Where there is any such delay the reasons for the delay must be recorded when the person first arrives at the police station or (as the case may be) is released on bail.

(12) Nothing in subsection (1A) or section 30A above shall be taken to affect—

(a) paragraphs 16(3) or 18(1) of Schedule 2 to the Immigration Act 1971[4];

(b) section 34(1) of the Criminal Justice Act 1972[5]; or

(c) any provision of the Terrorism Act 2000.

(13) Nothing in subsection (10) above shall be taken to affect paragraph 18(3) of Schedule 2 to the Immigration Act 1971[3].

[Police and Criminal Evidence Act 1984, s 30 as amended by the Prevention of Terrorism (Temporary Provisions) Act 1989, Sch 8, the Terrorism Act 2000, s 125 and the Criminal Justice Act 2003, s 4.]

---

1. Failure to do so may lead to exclusion of evidence under s 78: the court will take into account the overall fairness of the proceedings; see *R v Kerawalla* [1991] Crim LR 451, CA.

2. "Designated police station" is defined in s 35 below.

3. This does not mean that the constable has carte blanche to administer interrogation of the kind which ought properly to be reserved for the police station and for the rules applying under this Act and the Codes of Practice. Even where a constable is justified in delaying taking a suspect to the police station, he is not entitled to ask a lengthy series of questions on matters which ought properly to be asked where the relevant statutory provisions and codes apply. If justices believe the opportunity had been abused to circumvent the Code, they may exclude the evidence on the ground of unfairness under s 78 of the Act (*R v Khan* [1993] Crim LR 54).

4. See para **8–17692** (refusal of leave to enter).

5. See para **3–721** (detoxification centres).

1–2734A   30A. Bail elsewhere than at police station.   (1) A constable may release on bail a person who is arrested or taken into custody in the circumstances mentioned in section 30(1).

(2) A person may be released on bail under subsection (1) at any time before he arrives at a police station.

(3) A person released on bail under subsection (1) must be required to attend a police station.

(4) No other requirement may be imposed on the person as a condition of bail.

(5) The police station which the person is required to attend may be any police station.

[Police and Criminal Evidence Act 1984, s 30A as inserted by the Criminal Justice Act 2003, s 4.]

1–2734B   30B. Bail under section 30A: notices.   (1) Where a constable grants bail to a person under section 30A, he must give that person a notice in writing before he is released.

(2) The notice must state—

(*a*) the offence for which he was arrested, and

(*b*) the ground on which he was arrested.

(3) The notice must inform him that he is required to attend a police station.

(4) It may also specify the police station which he is required to attend and the time when he is required to attend.

(5) If the notice does not include the information mentioned in subsection (4), the person must subsequently be given a further notice in writing which contains that information.

(6) The person may be required to attend a different police station from that specified in the notice under subsection (1) or (5) or to attend at a different time.

(7) He must be given notice in writing of any such change as is mentioned in subsection (6) but more than one such notice may be given to him.

[Police and Criminal Evidence Act 1984, s 30B as inserted by the Criminal Justice Act 2003, s 4.]

1–2734C   30C. Bail under section 30A: supplemental.   (1) A person who has been required to attend a police station is not required to do so if he is given notice in writing that his attendance is no longer required.

(2) If a person is required to attend a police station which is not a designated police station he must be—

(*a*) released, or

(*b*) taken to a designated police station,

not more than six hours after his arrival.

(3) Nothing in the Bail Act 1976 applies in relation to bail under section 30A.

(4) Nothing in section 30A or 30B or in this section prevents the re-arrest without a warrant of a person released on bail under section 30A if new evidence justifying a further arrest has come to light since his release.

[Police and Criminal Evidence Act 1984, s 30C as inserted by the Criminal Justice Act 2003, s 4.]

1–2734CA   30CA. Bail under section 30A: variation of conditions by police.   (1) Where a person released on bail under section 30A(1) is on bail subject to conditions—

(*a*) a relevant officer at the police station at which the person is required to attend, or

(*b*) where no notice under section 30B specifying that police station has been given to the person, a relevant officer at the police station specified under section 30B(4A)(*c*),

may, at the request of the person but subject to subsection (2), vary the conditions.

(2) On any subsequent request made in respect of the same grant of bail, subsection (1) confers power to vary the conditions of the bail only if the request is based on information that, in the case of the previous request or each previous request, was not available to the relevant officer considering that previous request when he was considering it.

(3) Where conditions of bail granted to a person under section 30A(1) are varied under subsection (1)—

(*a*) paragraphs (*a*) to (*d*) of section 30A(3A) apply,

(*b*) requirements imposed by the conditions as so varied must be requirements that appear to the relevant officer varying the conditions to be necessary for any of the purposes mentioned in paragraphs (*a*) to (*d*) of section 30A(3B), and

(*c*) the relevant officer who varies the conditions must give the person notice in writing of the variation.

(4) Power under subsection (1) to vary conditions is, subject to subsection (3)(*a*) and (*b*), power—

(*a*) to vary or rescind any of the conditions, and

(*b*) to impose further conditions.

(5) In this section "relevant officer", in relation to a designated police station, means a custody officer but, in relation to any other police station—

(*a*) means a constable, or a person designated as a staff custody officer under section 38 of the Police Reform Act 2002, who is not involved in the investigation of the offence for which the person making the request under subsection (1) was under arrest when granted bail under section 30A(1), if such a constable or officer is readily available, and

(*b*) if no such constable or officer is readily available—

(i) means a constable other than the one who granted bail to the person, if such a constable is readily available, and

(ii) if no such constable is readily available, means the constable who granted bail.*

[Police and Criminal Evidence Act 1984, s 30CA as inserted by the Police and Justice Act 2006, Sch 6.]

---

*Inserted by the Police and Justice Act 2006, Sch 6, from a date to be appointed:

1–2734CA   30CB. Bail under section 30A: variation of conditions by court.   (1) Where a person released on bail under section 30A(1) is on bail subject to conditions, a magistrates' court may, on an application by or on behalf of the person, vary the conditions if—

(a)   the conditions have been varied under section 30CA(1) since being imposed under section 30A(3B),

(b)   a request for variation under section 30CA(1) of the conditions has been made and refused, or

(c)   a request for variation under section 30CA(1) of the conditions has been made and the period of 48 hours beginning with the day when the request was made has expired without the request having been withdrawn or the conditions having been varied in response to the request.

(2)   In proceedings on an application for a variation under subsection (1), a ground may not be relied upon unless—

(a)   in a case falling within subsection (1)(a), the ground was relied upon in the request in response to which the conditions were varied under section 30CA(1), or

(b)   in a case falling within paragraph (b) or (c) of subsection (1), the ground was relied upon in the request mentioned in that paragraph,

but this does not prevent the court, when deciding the application, from considering different grounds arising out of a change in circumstances that has occurred since the making of the application.

(3)   Where conditions of bail granted to a person under section 30A(1) are varied under subsection (1)—

(a)   paragraphs (a) to (d) of section 30A(3A) apply,

(b)   requirements imposed by the conditions as so varied must be requirements that appear to the court varying the conditions to be necessary for any of the purposes mentioned in paragraphs (a) to (d) of section 30A(3B), and

(c)   that bail shall not lapse but shall continue subject to the conditions as so varied.

(4)   Power under subsection (1) to vary conditions is, subject to subsection (3)(a) and (b), power—

(a)   to vary or rescind any of the conditions, and

(b)   to impose further conditions.*

[Police and Criminal Evidence Act 1984, s 30CB as inserted by the Police and Justice Act 2006, Sch 6.]

---

*Inserted by the Police and Justice Act 2006, Sch 6, from a date to be appointed:

1–2734D   30D.   Failure to answer to bail under section 30A.   (1)   A constable may arrest without a warrant a person who—

(a)   has been released on bail under section 30A subject to a requirement to attend a specified police station, but

(b)   fails to attend the police station at the specified time.

(2)   A person arrested under subsection (1) must be taken to a police station (which may be the specified police station or any other police station) as soon as practicable after the arrest.

(3)   In subsection (1), "specified" means specified in a notice under subsection (1) or (5) of section 30B or, if notice of change has been given under subsection (7) of that section, in that notice.

(4)   For the purposes of—

(a)   section 30 (subject to the obligation in subsection (2)), and

(b)   section 31,

an arrest under this section is to be treated as an arrest for an offence.

[Police and Criminal Evidence Act 1984, s 30D as inserted by the Criminal Justice Act 2003, s 4.]

1–2735   31.   Arrest for further offence[1].   Where—

(a)   a person—

(i)   has been arrested for an offence; and

(ii)   is at a police station in consequence of that arrest; and

(b)   it appears to a constable that, if he were released from that arrest, he would be liable to arrest for some other offence,

he shall be arrested for that other offence.

[Police and Criminal Evidence Act 1984, s 31.]

---

1.   This provision is designed to prevent artificial extension of detention periods by successive arrests: see also s 41(4), post.

1–2736   32.   Search upon arrest.   (1)   A constable may search an arrested person[1], in any case where the person to be searched has been arrested at a place other than a police station, if the constable has reasonable grounds for believing that the arrested person may present a danger to himself or others.

(2)   Subject to subsections (3) to (5) below, a constable shall also have power in any such case—

(a)   to search the arrested person for anything—

(i)   which he might use to assist him to escape from lawful custody; or (ii)　which might be evidence relating to an offence[2]; and

(b)　if the offence for which he has been arrested is an indictable offence, to enter and search any premises[3] in which he was when arrested or immediately before he was arrested for evidence relating to the offence.

(3)　The power to search conferred by subsection (2) above is only a power to search to the extent that is reasonably required for the purpose of discovering any such thing or any such evidence.

(4)　The powers conferred by this section to search a person are not to be construed as authorising a constable to require a person to remove any of his clothing in public other than an outer coat, jacket or gloves but they do authorise a search of a person's mouth.

(5)　A constable may not search a person in the exercise of the power conferred by subsection (2)(a) above unless he has reasonable grounds for believing that the person to be searched may have concealed on him anything for which a search is permitted under that paragraph.

(6)　A constable may not search premises in the exercise of the power conferred by subsection (2)(b) above unless he has reasonable grounds for believing that there is evidence for which a search is permitted under that paragraph on the premises[3].

(7)　In so far as the power of search conferred by subsection (2)(b) above relates to premises consisting of two or more separate dwellings, it is limited to a power to search—

(a)　any dwelling in which the arrest took place or in which the person arrested was immediately before his arrest; and

(b)　any parts of the premises which the occupier of any such dwelling uses in common with the occupiers of any other dwellings comprised in the premises.

(8)　A constable searching a person in the exercise of the power conferred by subsection (1) above may seize and retain anything he finds, if he has reasonable grounds for believing that the person searched might use it to cause physical injury to himself or to any other person.

(9)　A constable searching a person in the exercise of the power conferred by subsection (2)(a) above may seize[4] and retain anything he finds, other than an item subject to legal privilege, if he has reasonable grounds for believing—

(a)　that he might use it to assist him to escape from lawful custody; or

(b)　that it is evidence of an offence or has been obtained in consequence of the commission of an offence.

(10)　Nothing in this section shall be taken to affect the power conferred by section 43 of the Terrorism Act 2000.

[Police and Criminal Evidence Act 1984, s 32 as amended by the Prevention of Terrorism (Temporary Provisions) Act 1989, Sch 8, the Criminal Justice and Public Order Act 1994, s 59, the Terrorism Act 2000, s 125 and the Serious Organised Crime and Police Act 2005, Sch 7.]

1.　See also s 54 (search by custody officer in order to record everything which an arrested person has with him, and to seize articles), and s 55 (intimate searches). Reasonable force may be used: s 117, post.

2.　In *R v Churchill* [1989] Crim LR 226, where a person was arrested on suspicion of burglary, and the police requested the keys to his car but he refused to hand them over, it was held, on the facts of that case, that the police had acted beyond their powers of search under s 32(2) because the keys were not evidence relating to the suspected offence of burglary.

3.　It will be a question of fact in every case where the power under s 32 has been exercised whether that was the genuine reason why the police officers made their entry and search; if it is established the search was conducted unlawfully, the court will have to rule on the admissibility of evidence obtained as a result of the search having regard to ss 32 and 78 of this Act; see *R v Beckford* (1991) 94 Cr App Rep 43, CA. Note power to search premises under s 18, ante after arrest for an arrestable offence, which is somewhat wider in the allowable scope of the search. The Code of Practice for the Searching of Premises by Police Officers and the Seizure of Property Found by Police Officers on Persons or Premises (in PART II: STATUTORY INSTRUMENTS ON EVIDENCE, post), applies to searches under s 32.

For a discussion on the relationship between the powers under ss 18 and 32 of PACE, see the speech of Lord Rodger in *R (on the application of Rottman) v Metropolitan Police Comr* [2002] UKHL 20, [2002] 2 All ER 865, [2002] 2 WLR 1315 at paras 87–88, where his lordship expressed the opinion that s 18 dealt, at least primarily, with the position where the person is under arrest for an arrestable offence at a police station, and the powers to enter and search premises where someone was arrested, or where he had been immediately before his arrest, were to be found in s 32, even though the premises in question were the person's home.

4.　This is supplemented by the seizure power under s 19, ante.

PART IV[1]
DETENTION[2]

Detention—conditions and duration

1-2738　34. Limitations on police detention.　(1) A person arrested for an offence[3] shall not be kept in police detention[4] except in accordance with the provisions of this Part of this Act.

(2)　Subject to subsection (3) below, if at any time a custody officer[5]—

(a)　becomes aware, in relation to any person in police detention, that the grounds[6] for the detention of that person have ceased to apply; and

(b)　is not aware of any other grounds[6] on which the continued detention of that person could be justified under the provisions of this Part of this Act,

it shall be the duty of the custody officer[5], subject to subsection (4) below, to order his immediate release from custody[7].

(3)　No person in police detention shall be released except on the authority of a custody officer at the police station where his detention was authorised or, if it was authorised at more than one station, a custody officer at the station where it was last authorised.

(4) A person who appears to the custody officer[5] to have been unlawfully at large when he was arrested is not to be released under subsection (2) above.

(5) A person whose release is ordered under subsection (2) above shall be released without bail[6] unless it appears to the custody officer[4]—

(a) that there is need for further investigation of any matter in connection with which he was detained at any time during the period of his detention; or

(b) that, in respect of any such matter, proceedings may be taken against him or he may be reprimanded or warned under section 65 of the Crime and Disorder Act 1998,

and, if it so appears, he shall be released on bail[8],

(6) For the purposes of this Part of this Act a person arrested under section 6(D) of the Road Traffic Act 1988[9] or section 30(2) of the Transport and Works Act 1992 (c 42) is arrested for an offence.

(7) For the purposes of this Part a person who—

(a) attends a police station to answer to bail granted under section 30A,

(b) returns to a police station to answer to bail granted under this Part, or

(c) is arrested under section 30D or 46A,

is to be treated as arrested for an offence and that offence is the offence in connection with which he was granted bail.

[Police and Criminal Evidence Act 1984, s 34, as amended by the Road Traffic (Consequential Provisions) Act 1988, Sch 3, the Criminal Justice and Public Order Act 1994, s 29, the Criminal Justice and Court Services Act 2000, s 56 and the Police Reform Act 2002, s 53(1), the Railways and Transport Safety Act 2003, Sch 7 and the Criminal Justice Act 2003, Sch 1.]

---

*Repealed and "6D" substituted by the Railways and Transport Safety Act 2003, Sch 7, as from a date to be appointed.

1. Part IV contains ss 34–52.
2. See the Code of Practice for the Detention, Treatment and Questioning of Persons by Police Officers (Code of Practice C), in PART II: STATUTORY INSTRUMENTS ON EVIDENCE, post. Under the Human Rights Act 1998, these provisions relating to detention, so far as it is possible to do so, must be read and given effect in a way which is compatible with the Convention rights; in particular art 5 (the right to liberty) of the Convention. See also *Addison v Chief Constable of the West Midlands Police* (Note) [2004] 1 WLR 29.

1–2739 35. Designated police stations. (1) The chief officer of police for each police area shall designate the police stations in his area which, subject to sections 30(3) and (5), 30A(5) and 30D(2), are to be the stations in that area to be used for the purpose of detaining arrested persons.

(2) A chief officer's duty under subsection (1) above is to designate police stations appearing to him to provide enough accommodation for that purpose.

(2A) The Chief Constable of the British Transport Police Force may designate police stations which (in addition to those designated under subsection (1) above) may be used for the purpose of detaining arrested persons.

(3) Without prejudice to section 12 of the Interpretation Act 1978 (continuity of duties) a chief officer—

(a) may designate a station which was not previously designated; and

(b) may direct that a designation of a station previously made shall cease to operate.

(4) In this Act "designated police station" means a police station for the time being designated under this section.

[Police and Criminal Evidence Act 1984, s 35 amended by the Anti-terrorism, Crime and Security Act 2001, Sch 7 and the Criminal Justice Act 2003, Sch 1.]

1–2740 36. Custody officers at police stations. (1) One or more custody officers shall be appointed for each designated police station[1].

(2) A custody officer for a police station designated under section 35(1) above shall be appointed—

(a) by the chief officer of police for the area in which the designated police station is situated; or

(b) by such other police officer as the chief officer of police for that area may direct.

(2A) A custody officer for a police station designated under section 35(2A) above shall be appointed—

(a) by the Chief Constable of the British Transport Police Force; or

(b) by such other member of that Force as that Chief Constable may direct.

(3) No officer may be appointed a custody officer unless he is of at least the rank of sergeant.

(4) An officer of any rank may perform the functions of a custody officer at a designated police station if a custody officer is not readily available to perform them.

(5) Subject to the following provisions of this section and to section 39(2) below, none of the functions of a custody officer in relation to a person shall be performed by an officer who at the time when the function falls to be performed is involved in the investigation of an offence for which that person is in police detention at that time[2].

(6) Nothing in subsection (5) above is to be taken to prevent a custody officer—

    (*a*) performing any function assigned to custody officers—

        (i) by this Act; or

        (ii) by a code of practice[3] issued under this Act;

    (*b*) carrying out the duty imposed on custody officers by section 39 below;

    (*c*) doing anything in connection with the identification of a suspect; or

    (*d*) doing anything under sections 7 and 8 of the Road Traffic Act 1988[4].

    (7) Where an arrested person is taken to a police station which is not a designated police station[5], the functions in relation to him which at a designated police station would be the functions of a custody officer shall be performed—

    (*a*) by an officer who is not involved in the investigation of an offence for which he is in police detention, if such an officer is readily available; and

    (*b*) if no such officer is readily available, by the officer who took him to the station or any other officer.

    (7A) Subject to subsection (7B), subsection (7) applies where a person attends a police station which is not a designated station to answer to bail granted under section 30A as it applies where a person is taken to such a station.

    (7B) Where subsection (7) applies because of subsection (7A), the reference in subsection (7)(b) to the officer who took him to the station is to be read as a reference to the officer who granted him bail.

    (8) References to a custody officer in the following provisions of this Act include references to an officer other than a custody officer who is performing the functions of a custody officer by virtue of subsection (4) or (7) above.

    (9) Where by virtue of subsection (7) above an officer of a force maintained by a police authority who took an arrested person to a police station is to perform the functions of a custody officer in relation to him, the officer shall inform an officer who—

    (*a*) is attached to a designated police station; and

    (*b*) is of at least the rank of inspector,

that he is to do so.

    (10) The duty imposed by subsection (9) above shall be performed as soon as it is practicable to perform it.*

[Police and Criminal Evidence Act 1984, s 36, as amended by the Road Traffic (Consequential Provisions) Act 1988, Sch 3 and the Criminal Justice Act 2003, Sch 1.]

---

*Repealed by the Serious Organised Crime and Police Act 2005, Sch 7 from a date to be appointed.

    1. Section 36(1) means that a chief constable has a duty to appoint one custody officer for each designated police station and a discretion, which has to be exercised reasonably, to appoint more than one custody officer at a designated police station (*Vince v Chief Constable of Dorset Police* [1993] 2 All ER 321, CA).

    2. A strategem used by the police to obtain admissions whereby the custody officer co-operated with the investigating officers in placing the defendants in the same bugged cell, but not so as to be oppressive or to render the admissions unreliable, was held not to be in breach of s 36(5) of the Act or the Codes of Practice (*R v Bailey and Smith* (1993) 97 Cr App Rep 365 and see *R v Roberts (Stephen)* [1997] 1 Cr App Rep 217, [1997] Crim LR 222, CA).

    3. See the Code of Practice for the Detention, Treatment and Questioning of Persons by Police Officers (Code of Practice C) in PART II: STATUTORY INSTRUMENTS ON EVIDENCE, post.

    4. That is, requiring the provision of specimens for analysis or test.

    5. "Designated police station" is defined in s 35 above.

1-2741   37. Duties of custody officer before charge.   (1) Where—

    (*a*) a person is arrested for an offence—

        (i) without a warrant; or

        (ii) under a warrant not endorsed for bail,

    (*b*) *Repealed,*

the custody officer[1] at each police station where he is detained after his arrest[2] shall determine whether he has before him sufficient evidence to charge that person with the offence for which he was arrested and may detain him at the police station for such period as is necessary to enable him to do so[3].

    (2) If the custody officer determines that he does not have such evidence before him, the person arrested shall be released either on bail or without bail[4], unless the custody officer has reasonable grounds for believing that his detention without being charged is necessary to secure or preserve evidence relating to an offence for which he is under arrest or to obtain such evidence by questioning him[5].

    (3) If the custody officer has reasonable grounds for so believing, he may authorise the person arrested to be kept in police detention[6].

    (4) Where a custody officer authorises a person who has not been charged to be kept in police detention, he shall, as soon as is practicable, make a written record[7] of the grounds for the detention.

    (5) Subject to subsection (6) below, the written record shall be made in the presence of the person arrested who shall at that time be informed by the custody officer of the grounds for his detention.

    (6) Subsection (5) above shall not apply where the person arrested is, at the time when the written record is made—

    (*a*) incapable of understanding what is said to him;

(*b*)   violent or likely to become violent; or

(*c*)   in urgent need of medical attention.

(7)   Subject to section 41(7) below, if the custody officer determines that he has before him sufficient evidence to charge the person arrested with the offence for which he was arrested, the person arrested—

(*a*)   shall be released without charge and on bail[4] for the purpose of enabling the Director of Public Prosecutions to make a decision under section 37B below,

(*b*)   shall be released without charge and on bail but not for that purpose,

(*c*)   shall be released without charge and without bail, or

(*d*)   shall be charged[8].

(7A)   The decision as to how a person is to be dealt with under subsection (7) above shall be that of the custody officer.

(7B)   Where a person is released under subsection (7)(*a*) above, it shall be the duty of the custody officer to inform him that he is being released to enable the Director of Public Prosecutions to make a decision under section 37B below.

(8)   Where—

(*a*)   a person is released under subsection (7)(*b*) or (*c*) above; and

(*b*)   at the time of his release a decision whether he should be prosecuted for the offence for which he was arrested has not been taken,

it shall be the duty of the custody officer so to inform him.*

(8A)   Subsection (8B) applies if the offence for which the person is arrested is one in relation to which a sample could be taken under section 63B below and the custody officer—

(*a*)   is required in pursuance of subsection (2) above to release the person arrested and decides to release him on bail, or

(*b*)   decides in pursuance of subsection (7)(a) or (b) above to release the person without charge and on bail.

(8B)   The detention of the person may be continued to enable a sample to be taken under section 63B, but this subsection does not permit a person to be detained for a period of more than 24 hours after the relevant time.

(9)   If the person arrested is not in a fit state to be dealt with under subsection (7) above, he may be kept in police detention until he is.

(10)   The duty imposed on the custody officer under subsection (1) above shall be carried out by him as soon as practicable after the person arrested arrives at the police station or, in the case of a person arrested at the police station, as soon as practicable after the arrest.

(11)–(14)   *Repealed.*

(15)   In this Part of this Act—

"arrested juvenile" means a person arrested with or without a warrant who appears to be under the age of 17;

"endorsed for bail" means endorsed with a direction for bail in accordance with section 117(2) of the Magistrates' Courts Act 1980[9].

[Police and Criminal Evidence Act 1984, s 37 as amended by the Children Act 1989, Schs 13 and 15, the Criminal Justice Act 1991, s 72, the Criminal Justice and Public Order Act 1994, s 29 and Sch 11,the Criminal Justice Act 2003, Sch 2 and the Serious Organised Crime and Police Act 2005, Sch 7.]

---

1.   Section 36 above, provides for the appointment of custody officers. Where there are several offences, the custody officer may decide each one differently.

2.   It is not necessary for a custody officer to satisfy himself that the arrest was lawful before he can hold a person in lawful custody as he is entitled to assume that the arrest was lawful. Where it is subsequently ascertained that the initial arrest was unlawful what is done thereafter in the execution of his duty is not invalidated, see *DPP v L* [1999] Crim LR 752, DC.

3.   The person may be detained only up to 24 hours from the relevant time (s 41); thereafter the provisions of ss 42–44 limit detention to serious arrestable offences. The custody officer must inform the detained person of his rights to have someone informed of his arrest, to consult a solicitor and to consult the Codes of Practice, and give him a written notice of these rights as well as the right to a copy of the custody record, if need be using an interpreter: Code of Practice for the Detention, Treatment and Questioning of Persons by Police Officers (Code of Practice C in PART II: STATUTORY INSTRUMENTS ON EVIDENCE, post), paras 3.1, 3.2, 3.5. Note also the requirements of paras 3.12–3.20 in relation to special groups of detained persons such as those who are deaf, juveniles, mentally disordered, blind or unable to read.

4.   "Bail" is defined in s 47, post.

5.   The same grounds apply to authorisation of continued detention (s 42), and to warrants and extended warrants of further detention (ss 43, 44). Compare the wider grounds for keeping in police detention after charge, in s 38(1), post. Compare also the identical provisions in s 47(5) for police detention without charge, and thereunder (sub-s (6)) prior detention will count and so should arguably count here. Note the requirement in Code of Practice C referred to above as to cautioning (paras 10.1 to 10.13) and interviewing (paras 11.1A to 15.6), also Annex B relating to delay in notifying arrest or allowing access to legal advice, Annex C relating to the restriction on drawing adverse inferences from silence and terms of the caution when the restriction applies, Annex D relating to written statements under caution; and the summary of provisions relating to mentally ill and mentally handicapped persons in Annex E.

6.   The provisions of s 40, post, as to reviews, will apply.

7.   Code of Practice C, referred to above, makes provision for the keeping of custody records.

8.   As to arrangements after charge, see ss 38 and 46, post. In *R v Stafford Magistrates' Court, ex p Customs and Excise Comrs* [1991] 2 QB 339, [1991] 2 All ER 201, 154 JP 865 it was held (not following *R v Ealing Justices, ex p Dixon* [1989] 2 All ER 1050, 153 JP 505, DC) that a customs officer who investigated the commission of an offence, arrested a person and took him to a police station to be charged by a custody officer under this section did not thereby surrender conduct of

the prosecution since the proceedings were instituted by the Commissioners of Customs and Excise under specific statutory authority and they were entitled to prosecute independently of the Director of Public Prosecutions. *R v Stafford Magistrates' Court* was approved in *R (Hunt) v Criminal Cases Review Commission* [2001] QB 1108, [2001] 2 WLR 319, [2001] 2 Cr App Rep 76, [2001] Crim LR 324, DC (Inland Revenue could prosecute following charging by the police).

    9. See para **1–2200.**

1–2741A   37A. Guidance.   (1) The Director of Public Prosecutions may issue guidance—

    (*a*)   for the purpose of enabling custody officers to decide how persons should be dealt with under section 37(7) above or 37C(2) below, and

    (*b*)   as to the information to be sent to the Director of Public Prosecutions under section 37B(1) below.

    (2) The Director of Public Prosecutions may from time to time revise guidance issued under this section.

    (3) Custody officers are to have regard to guidance under this section in deciding how persons should be dealt with under section 37(7) above or 37C(2) below.

    (4) A report under section 9 of the Prosecution of Offences Act 1985 (report by DPP to Attorney General) must set out the provisions of any guidance issued, and any revisions to guidance made, in the year to which the report relates.

    (5) The Director of Public Prosecutions must publish in such manner as he thinks fit—

    (*a*)   any guidance issued under this section, and

    (*b*)   any revisions made to such guidance.

    (6) Guidance under this section may make different provision for different cases, circumstances or areas.

[Police and Criminal Evidence Act 1984, s 37A as inserted by the Criminal Justice Act 2003, Sch 2.]

1–2741B   37B. Consultation with the Director of Public Prosecutions.   (1) Where a person is released on bail under section 37(7)(*a*) above, an officer involved in the investigation of the offence shall, as soon as is practicable, send to the Director of Public Prosecutions such information as may be specified in guidance under section 37A above.

    (2) The Director of Public Prosecutions shall decide whether there is sufficient evidence to charge the person with an offence.

    (3) If he decides that there is sufficient evidence to charge the person with an offence, he shall decide—

    (*a*)   whether or not the person should be charged and, if so, the offence with which he should be charged, and

    (*b*)   whether or not the person should be given a caution and, if so, the offence in respect of which he should be given a caution.

    (4) The Director of Public Prosecutions shall give written notice of his decision to an officer involved in the investigation of the offence.

    (5) If his decision is—

    (*a*)   that there is not sufficient evidence to charge the person with an offence, or

    (*b*)   that there is sufficient evidence to charge the person with an offence but that the person should not be charged with an offence or given a caution in respect of an offence,

a custody officer shall give the person notice in writing that he is not to be prosecuted.

    (6) If the decision of the Director of Public Prosecutions is that the person should be charged with an offence, or given a caution in respect of an offence, the person shall be charged or cautioned accordingly.

    (7) But if his decision is that the person should be given a caution in respect of the offence and it proves not to be possible to give the person such a caution, he shall instead be charged with the offence.

    (8) For the purposes of this section, a person is to be charged with an offence either—

    (*a*)   when he is in police detention after returning to a police station to answer bail or is otherwise in police detention at a police station, or

    (*b*)   in accordance with section 29 of the Criminal Justice Act 2003.

    (9) In this section "caution" includes—

    (*a*)   a conditional caution within the meaning of Part 3 of the Criminal Justice Act 2003, and

    (*b*)   a warning or reprimand under section 65 of the Crime and Disorder Act 1998.

[Police and Criminal Evidence Act 1984, s 37B as inserted by the Criminal Justice Act 2003, Sch 2.]

1–2741C   37C. Breach of bail following release under section 37(7)(*a*).   (1) This section applies where—

    (*a*)   a person released on bail under section 37(7)(*a*) above or subsection (2)(*b*) below is arrested under section 46A below in respect of that bail, and

    (*b*)   at the time of his detention following that arrest at the police station mentioned in section 46A(2) below, notice under section 37B(4) above has not been given.

    (2) The person arrested—

    (*a*)   shall be charged, or

(b) shall be released without charge, either on bail or without bail.

(3) The decision as to how a person is to be dealt with under subsection (2) above shall be that of a custody officer.

(4) A person released on bail under subsection (2)(b) above shall be released on bail subject to the same conditions (if any) which applied immediately before his arrest.

[Police and Criminal Evidence Act 1984, s 37C as inserted by the Criminal Justice Act 2003, Sch 2.]

1–2741CA   37CA. Breach of bail following release under section 37(7)(b). (1) This section applies where a person released on bail under section 37(7)(b) above or subsection (2)(b) below—

(a) is arrested under section 46A below in respect of that bail, and
(b) is being detained following that arrest at the police station mentioned in section 46A(2) below.

(2) The person arrested—

(a) shall be charged, or
(b) shall be released without charge, either on bail or without bail.

(3) The decision as to how a person is to be dealt with under subsection (2) above shall be that of a custody officer.

(4) A person released on bail under subsection (2)(b) above shall be released on bail subject to the same conditions (if any) which applied immediately before his arrest.*

[Police and Criminal Evidence Act 1984, s 37CA as inserted by the Police and Justice Act 2006, Sch 6.]

---

*Inserted by the Police and Justice Act 2006, Sch 6, from a date to be appointed:

1–2741D   37D. Release under section 37(7)(a): further provision. (1) Where a person is released on bail under section 37(7)(a) or section 37C(2)(b) above, a custody officer may subsequently appoint a different time, or an additional time, at which the person is to attend at the police station to answer bail.

(2) The custody officer shall give the person notice in writing of the exercise of the power under subsection (1).

(3) The exercise of the power under subsection (1) shall not affect the conditions (if any) to which bail is subject.

(4) Where a person released on bail under section 37(7)(a) or 37C(2)(b) above returns to a police station to answer bail or is otherwise in police detention at a police station, he may be kept in police detention to enable him to be dealt with in accordance with section 37B or 37C above or to enable the power under subsection (1) above to be exercised.

(5) If the person is not in a fit state to enable him to be so dealt with or to enable that power to be exercised, he may be kept in police detention until he is.

(6) Where a person is kept in police detention by virtue of subsection (4) or (5) above, section 37(1) to (3) and (7) above (and section 40(8) below so far as it relates to section 37(1) to (3)) shall not apply to the offence in connection with which he was released on bail under section 37(7)(a) or 37C(2)(b) above.

[Police and Criminal Evidence Act 1984, s 37D as inserted by the Criminal Justice Act 2003, Sch 2.]

1–2742   38. Duties of custody officer after charge*. (1) Where a person arrested for an offence otherwise than under a warrant endorsed for bail is charged[1] with an offence, the custody officer[2] shall, subject to section 25 of the Criminal Justice and Public Order Act 1994, order his release[3] from police detention, either on bail or without bail[4], unless—

(a) if the person arrested is not an arrested juvenile—

  (i) his name or address cannot be ascertained or the custody officer has reasonable grounds for doubting whether a name or address furnished by him as his name or address is his real name or address;

  (ii) the custody officer has reasonable grounds for believing that the person arrested will fail to appear in court to answer to bail;

  (iii) in the case of a person arrested for an imprisonable offence, the custody officer has reasonable grounds for believing that the detention of the person arrested is necessary to prevent him from committing an offence;

  (iiia) in a case where a sample may be taken from the person under section 63B below, the custody officer has reasonable grounds for believing that the detention of the person is necessary to enable the sample to be taken from him;

  (iv) in the case of a person arrested for an offence which is not an imprisonable offence, the custody officer has reasonable grounds for believing that the detention of the person arrested is necessary to prevent him from causing physical injury to any other person or from causing loss of or damage to property;

  (v) the custody officer has reasonable grounds for believing that the detention of the person arrested is necessary to prevent him from interfering with the administration of justice or with the investigation of offences or of a particular offence; or

  (vi) the custody officer has reasonable grounds for believing that the detention of the person arrested is necessary for his own protection;

(b) if he is an arrested juvenile—

    (i) any of the requirements of paragraph (*a*) above is satisfied (but, in the case of paragraph (a)(iiia) above, only if the arrested juvenile has attained the minimum age)); or
    (ii) the custody officer has reasonable grounds for believing that he ought to be detained in his own interests.

(2) If the release of a person arrested is not required by subsection (1) above, the custody officer may authorise him to be kept in police detention[6] but may not authorise a person to be kept in police detention by virtue of subsection (1)(a)(iiia) after the end of the period of six hours beginning when he was charged with the offence.

(2A) The custody officer, in taking the decisions required by subsection (1)(*a*) and (*b*) above (except (*a*)(i) and (vi) and (*b*)(ii)), shall have regard to the same considerations as those which a court is required to have regard to in taking the corresponding decisions under paragraph 2(1) of Part I of Schedule 1 to the Bail Act 1976 (disregarding paragraph 2(2) of that Part).

(3) Where a custody officer authorises a person who has been charged to be kept in police detention, he shall, as soon as practicable, make a written record[7] of the grounds for the detention.

(4) Subject to subsection (5) below, the written record shall be made in the presence of the person charged who shall at that time be informed by the custody officer of the grounds for his detention.

(5) Subsection (4) above shall not apply where the person charged is, at the time when the written record is made—

    (*a*) incapable of understanding what is said to him;
    (*b*) violent or likely to become violent; or
    (*c*) in urgent need of medical attention.

(6) Where a custody officer authorises an arrested juvenile to be kept in police detention under subsection (1) above, the custody officer shall, unless he certifies—

    (*a*) that, by reason of such circumstances as are specified in the certificate, it is impracticable for him to do so; or
    (*b*) in the case of an arrested juvenile who has attained the age of 12 years[8], that no secure accommodation is available and that keeping him in other local authority accommodation would not be adequate to protect the public from serious harm from him,

secure that the arrested juvenile is moved to local authority accommodation.

(6A) In this section—

"local authority accommodation" means accommodation provided by or on behalf of a local authority (within the meaning of the Children Act 1989).*
"minimum age" means the age specified in section 63B(3)(*b*) below;
"secure accommodation" means accommodation provided for the purpose of restricting liberty;
"sexual offence" means an offence specified in Part 2 of Schedule 15 to the Criminal Justice Act 2003;
"violent offence" means murder or an offence specified in Part 1 of that Schedule;

and any reference, in relation to an arrested juvenile charged with a violent or sexual offence, to protecting the public from serious harm from him shall be construed as a reference to protecting members of the public from death or serious personal injury, whether physical or psychological, occasioned by further such offences committed by him.

(6B) Where an arrested juvenile is moved to local authority accommodation under subsection (6) above, it shall be lawful for any person acting on behalf of the authority to detain him.

(7) A certificate made under subsection (6) above in respect of an arrested juvenile shall be produced to the court before which he is first brought thereafter.

(7A) In this section "imprisonable offence" has the same meaning as in Schedule 1 to the Bail Act 1976.

(8) In this Part of this Act "local authority" has the same meaning as in the Children Act 1989[9].
[Police and Criminal Evidence Act 1984, s 38 as amended by the Children Act 1989, Sch 13, the Criminal Justice Act 1991, s 59, the Criminal Justice and Public Order Act 1994, s 28 and Sch 10, the Powers of Criminal Courts (Sentencing) Act 2000, Sch 9, the Criminal Justice and Court Services Act 2000, s 57 and the Criminal Justice Act 2003, s 5 and Sch 36.]

---

*Section 5 of the Criminal Justice Act 2003 amends s 38 to provide for the drug testing of under-18s). At the time of going to press these amendments had been brought into force in the police areas of: Cleveland; Greater Manchester; Humberside; Merseyside; Metropolitan Police District; Nottinghamshire; and West Yorkshire: (see the Criminal Justice Act 2003 (Commencement No 5) Order 2004, SI 2004/1867.
  1. As to the charging of detained persons, see the Code of Practice for the Detention, Treatment and Questioning of Persons by Police Officers (Code of Practice C in PART II: STATUTORY INSTRUMENTS ON EVIDENCE, post), paras 16.1 to 16.10.
  2. Section 36 above, provides for the appointment of custody officers.
  3. Note the separate power to detain an unfit driver under s 10 of the Road Traffic Act 1988 in PART VII: TRANSPORT title ROAD TRAFFIC, post.
  4. "Bail" is defined in s 47 below.
  5. As to the police areas in which the testing of persons in police detention is in force, see note to s 63B, post.
  6. The provisions of s 40 as to reviews will apply: see s 40(10), post.
  7. Code of Practice C referred to above, paras 2.1A to 2.7, makes provision for the keeping of custody records.
  8. The age of "12 years" is substituted for the age of "15 years" by the Criminal Justice and Public Order Act 1994, s 24, when in force.
  9. See s 105(1) of the Children Act 1989, in PART VI: FAMILY LAW, post.

1–2743 39. Responsibilities in relation to persons detained. (1) Subject to subsections (2) and (4) below, it shall be the duty of the custody officer[1] at a police station to ensure—

(a) that all persons in police detention at that station are treated in accordance with this Act and any code of practice[2] issued under it and relating to the treatment of persons in police detention; and

(b) that all matters relating to such persons which are required by this Act or by such codes of practice to be recorded are recorded in the custody records[3] relating to such persons.

(2) If the custody officer, in accordance with any code of practice issued under this Act, transfers or permits the transfer of a person in police detention—

(a) to the custody of a police officer investigating an offence for which that person is in police detention; or

(b) to the custody of an officer who has charge of that person outside the police station,

the custody officer shall cease in relation to that person to be subject to the duty imposed on him by subsection (1)(a) above; and it shall be the duty of the officer to whom the transfer is made to ensure that he is treated in accordance with the provisions of this Act and of any such codes of practice[2] as are mentioned in subsection (1) above.

(3) If the person detained is subsequently returned to the custody of the custody officer, it shall be the duty of the officer investigating the offence to report to the custody officer as to the manner in which this section and the codes of practice[2] have been complied with while that person was in his custody.

(4) If an arrested juvenile is moved to local authority accommodation under section 38(6) above, the custody officer shall cease in relation to the person to be subject to the duty imposed on him by subsection (1) above.

(5) *Repealed.*

(6) Where—

(a) an officer of higher rank than the custody officer gives directions relating to a person in police detention; and

(b) the directions are at variance—

(i) with any decision made or action taken by the custody officer in the performance of a duty imposed on him under this Part of this Act; or

(ii) with any decision or action which would but for the directions have been made or taken by him in the performance of such a duty,

the custody officer shall refer the matter at once to an officer of the rank of superintendent or above who is responsible for the police station for which the custody officer is acting as custody officer.*

[Police and Criminal Evidence Act 1984, s 39 as amended by the Children Act 1989, Schs 13 and 15.]

---

*Amended by the Serious Organised Crime and Police Act 2005, Sch 7 from a date to be appointed.
 1. Section 36 above, provides for the appointment of custody officers.
 2. See the Code of Practice for the Detention, Treatment and Questioning of Persons by Police Officers (Code of Practice C), and the Code of Practice for the Identification of Persons by Police Officers (Code of Practice D) in PART II: STATUTORY INSTRUMENTS ON EVIDENCE, post.
 3. See Code of Practice C, referred to above, paras 2.1A to 2.7.

1–2744 40. Review of police detention. (1) Reviews of the detention[1] of each person in police detention[2] in connection with the investigation of an offence shall be carried out periodically in accordance with the following provisions of this section—

(a) in the case of a person who has been arrested and charged, by the custody officer[3]; and

(b) in the case of a person who has been arrested but not charged, by an officer[4] of at least the rank of inspector who has not been directly involved in the investigation.

(2) The officer to whom it falls to carry out a review is referred to in this section as a "review officer".

(3) Subject to subsection (4) below—

(a) the first review shall be not later than six hours after the detention was first authorised[5];

(b) the second review shall be not later than nine hours after the first;

(c) subsequent reviews shall be at intervals of not more than nine hours.

(4) A review may be postponed—

(a) if, having regard to all the circumstances prevailing at the latest time for it specified in subsection (3) above, it is not practicable to carry out the review at that time;

(b) without prejudice to the generality of paragraph (a) above—

(i) if at that time the person in detention is being questioned by a police officer and the review officer is satisfied that an interruption of the questioning for the purpose of carrying out the review would prejudice the investigation in connection with which he is being questioned; or

(ii) if at that time no review officer is readily available.

(5) If a review is postponed under subsection (4) above it shall be carried out as soon as practicable after the latest time specified for it in subsection (3) above.

(6) If a review is carried out after postponement under subsection (4) above, the fact that it was so carried out shall not affect any requirement of this section as to the time at which any subsequent review is to be carried out.

(7) The review officer shall record the reasons for any postponement of a review in the custody record[6].

(8) Subject to subsection (9) below, where the person whose detention is under review has not been charged before the time of the review, section 37(1) to (6) above shall have effect in relation to him, but with [the modifications specified in subsection (8A).]

(8A) The modifications are—

(a) the substitution of references to the person whose detention is under review for references to the person arrested;

(b) the substitution of references to the review officer for references to the custody officer; and

(c) in subsection (6), the insertion of the following paragraph after paragraph (a)—
"(aa)asleep;".

(9) Where a person has been kept in police detention by virtue of section 37(9) or 37D(5) above, section 37(1) to (6) shall not have effect in relation to him but it shall be the duty of the review officer to determine whether he is yet in a fit state.

(10) Where the person whose detention is under review has been charged before the time of the review, section 38(1) to (6B) above shall have effect in relation to him, but with the modifications specified in subsection (10A).

(10A) The modifications are—

(a) the substitution of a reference to the person whose detention is under review for any reference to the person arrested or to the person charged; and

(b) in subsection (5), the insertion of the following paragraph after paragraph (a)—

"(aa)asleep;".

(11) Where—

(a) an officer of higher rank than the review officer gives directions relating to a person in police detention; and

(b) the directions are at variance—

(i)   with any decision made or action taken by the review officer in the performance of a duty imposed on him under this Part of this Act; or

(ii) with any decision or action which would but for the directions have been made or taken by him in the performance of such a duty,

the review officer shall refer the matter at once to an officer of the rank of superintendent or above who is responsible for the police station for which the review officer is acting as review officer in connection with the detention.

(12) Before determining whether to authorise a person's continued detention the review officer shall give—

(a) that person (unless he is asleep); or

(b) any solicitor representing him who is available at the time of the review,

an opportunity[7] to make representations to him about the detention.

(13) Subject to subsection (14) below, the person whose detention is under review or his solicitor may make representations under subsection (12) above either orally or in writing.

(14) The review officer may refuse to hear oral representations from the person whose detention is under review if he considers that he is unfit to make such representations by reason of his condition or behaviour.

[Police and Criminal Evidence Act 1984, s 40, as amended by the Police Reform Act 2002, s 52 and the Criminal Justice Act 2003, Sch 2.]

---

1. The duties of the review officer conducting a review before charge are as shown as the duties of the custody officer under s 37; those of the custody officer conducting a review after charge are as set out in s 38.

2. "Police detention" is defined in s 118(2) below.

3. Section 36 above, provides for the appointment of custody officers.

4. The review of police detention cannot be conducted by a video link, but must be conducted by an officer who is physically present at the police station where the person whose detention is under review is detained (*R v Chief Constable of Kent Constabulary, ex p Kent Police Federation Joint Branch Board* [2000] 2 Cr App Rep 196, [2000] Crim LR 857). See, however, ss 40A and 45A below. At the time of going to press these provisions are not yet in force

5. Detention is authorised under s 37(1)–(3) (before charge) and s 38(2) (after charge) ante; police detention as defined by s 118(2) may well have begun before such authorisation and time limits under ss 41–44 for holding someone run from "the relevant time" as defined in s 41, and not from the time of authorisation which is significant only in relation to the timing of reviews under s 40.

6. The Code of Practice for the Detention, Treatment and Questioning of Persons by Police Officers (Code of Practice C in PART II: STATUTORY INSTRUMENTS ON EVIDENCE, post) paras 2.1A to 2.7 makes detailed provision for custody records.

7. Code of Practice C referred to above, para 15.3 extends this to the appropriate adult or other persons having an interest in the person's welfare.

1-2754A 40A. Use of a telephone for review under s 40. (1) A review under section 40(1)(b) may be carried out by means of a discussion, conducted by telephone, with one or more persons at the police station where the arrested person is held.

(2) But subsection (1) does not apply if—

(a) the review is of a kind authorised by regulations under section 45A to be carried out using video-conferencing facilities; and

(b) it is reasonably practicable to carry it out in accordance with those regulations.

(3) Where any review is carried out under this section by an officer who is not present at the station where the arrested person is held—

(a) any obligation of that officer to make a record in connection with the carrying out of the review shall have effect as an obligation to cause another officer to make the record;

(b) any requirement for the record to be made in the presence of the arrested person shall apply to the making of that record by that other officer; and

(c) the requirements under section 40(12) and (13) above for—

(i) the arrested person, or

(ii) a solicitor representing him,

to be given any opportunity to make representations (whether in writing or orally) to that officer shall have effect as a requirement for that person, or such a solicitor, to be given an opportunity to make representations in a manner authorised by subsection (4) below.

(4) Representations are made in a manner authorised by this subsection—

(a) in a case where facilities exist for the immediate transmission of written representations to the officer carrying out the review, if they are made either—

(i) orally by telephone to that officer; or

(ii) in writing to that officer by means of those facilities;

and

(b) in any other case, if they are made orally by telephone to that officer.

(5) In this section 'video-conferencing facilities' has the same meaning as in section 45A below.

[Police and Criminal Evidence Act 1984, s 40A as inserted by the Criminal Justice and Police Act 2001, s 73 and the Criminal Justice Act 2003, s 6.]

1–2755   41. Limits on period of detention without charge.   (1) Subject to the following provisions of this section and to sections 42 and 43 below, a person shall not be kept in police detention[1] for more than 24 hours without being charged.

(2) The time from which the period of detention of a person is to be calculated (in this Act referred to as "the relevant time")—

(a) in the case of a person to whom this paragraph applies, shall be—

(i) the time at which that person arrives at the relevant police station; or

(ii) the time 24 hours after the time of that person's arrest,

whichever is the earlier;

(b) in the case of a person arrested outside England and Wales, shall be—

(i) the time at which that person arrives at the first police station to which he is taken in the police area in England or Wales in which the offence for which he was arrested is being investigated; or

(ii) the time 24 hours after the time of that person's entry into England and Wales,

whichever is the earlier;

(c) in the case of a person[2] who—

(i) attends voluntarily at a police station; or

(ii) accompanies a constable to a police station without having been arrested,

and is arrested at the police station, the time of his arrest;

(ca) in the case of a person who attends a police station to answer to bail granted under section 30A, the time when he arrives at the police station;

(d) in any other case, except where subsection (5) below applies, shall be the time at which the person arrested arrives at the first police station to which he is taken after his arrest.

(3) Subsection (2)(a) above applies to a person if—

(a) his arrest is sought in one police area in England and Wales;

(b) he is arrested in another police area; and

(c) he is not questioned[3] in the area in which he is arrested in order to obtain evidence in relation to an offence for which he is arrested;

and in sub-paragraph (I) of that paragraph "the relevant police station" means the first police station to which he is taken in the police area in which his arrest was sought.

(4) Subsection (2) above shall have effect in relation to a person arrested under section 31 above as if every reference in it to his arrest or his being arrested were a reference to his arrest or his being arrested for the offence for which he was originally arrested.

(5) If—

(a) a person is in police detention in a police area in England and Wales ("the first area"); and

(b)   his arrest for an offence is sought in some other police area in England and Wales ("the second area"); and

(c)   he is taken to the second area for the purposes of investigating that offence, without being questioned in the first area in order to obtain evidence in relation to it,

the relevant time shall be—

(i)   the time 24 hours after he leaves the place where he is detained in the first area; or

(ii)   the time at which he arrives at the first police station to which he is taken in the second area,

whichever is the earlier.

(6)   When a person who is in police detention is removed to hospital because he is in need of medical treatment, any time during which he is being questioned in hospital or on the way there or back by a police officer for the purpose of obtaining evidence relating to an offence shall be included in any period which falls to be calculated for the purposes of this Part of this Act, but any other time while he is in hospital or on his way there or back shall not be so included.

(7)   Subject to subsection (8) below, a person who at the expiry of 24 hours after the relevant time is in police detention and has not been charged shall be released at that time either on bail or without bail[4].

(8)   Subsection (7) above does not apply to a person whose detention for more than 24 hours after the relevant time has been authorised or is otherwise permitted in accordance with section 42 or 43 below.

(9)   A person released under subsection (7) above shall not be re-arrested without a warrant[5] for the offence for which he was previously arrested unless new evidence justifying a further arrest has come to light since his release; but this subsection does not prevent an arrest under section 46A below.

[Police and Criminal Evidence Act 1984, s 41 as amended by the Criminal Justice and Public Order Act 1994, s 29 and the Criminal Justice Act 2003, Sch 1.]

---

1.   "Police detention" is defined in s 118(2) below.
2.   Note the safeguards contained in s 29, ante.
3.   See the Code of Practice for the Detention, Treatment and Questioning of Persons by Police Officers (Code of Practice C in PART II: STATUTORY INSTRUMENTS ON EVIDENCE, post), para 14.1.
4.   "Bail" is defined in s 47, post.
5.   Note similar provisions in ss 42(11) and 43(19). If a warrant is requested in these circumstances we would advise justices to consider whether they, too, should require new evidence to be shown. Rearrest would appear to lead to a fresh period of police detention beginning with a new "relevant time" under s 41(2).

1–2756   42. Authorisation of continued detention.   (1) Where a police officer of the rank of superintendent or above who is responsible for the police station at which a person is detained has reasonable grounds for believing that—

(a)   the detention of that person without charge is necessary to secure or preserve evidence relating to an offence for which he is under arrest or to obtain such evidence by questioning him;

(b)   an offence for which he is under arrest is a serious indictable offence; and

(c)   the investigation is being conducted diligently and expeditiously,

he may authorise[1] the keeping of that person in police detention[2] for a period expiring at or before 36 hours after the relevant time[3]time[3].

(2)   Where an officer such as is mentioned in subsection (1) above has authorised the keeping of a person in police detention for a period expiring less than 36 hours after the relevant time[3], such an officer may authorise the keeping of that person in police detention for a further period expiring not more than 36 hours after that time if the conditions specified in subsection (1) above are still satisfied when he gives the authorisation.

(3)   If it is proposed to transfer a person in police detention to another police area, the officer determining whether or not to authorise keeping him in detention under subsection (1) above shall have regard to the distance and the time the journey would take.

(4)   No authorisation under subsection (1) above shall be given in respect of any person—

(a)   more than 24 hours after the relevant time[3]; or

(b)   before the second review of his detention under section 40 above has been carried out.

(5)   Where an officer authorises the keeping of a person in police detention under subsection (1) above, it shall be his duty—

(a)   to inform that person of the grounds for his continued detention; and

(b)   to record the grounds in that person's custody record[4].

(6)   Before determining whether to authorise the keeping of a person in detention under subsection (1) or (2) above, an officer shall give—

(a)   that person; or

(b)   any solicitor representing him who is available at the time when it falls to the officer to determine whether to give the authorisation,

an opportunity[5] to make representations to him about the detention.

(7)   Subject to subsection (8) below, the person in detention or his solicitor may make representations under subsection (6) above either orally or in writing.

(8)   The officer to whom it falls to determine whether to give the authorisation may refuse to hear

oral representations from the person in detention if he considers that he is unfit to make such representations by reason of his condition or behaviour.

(9) Where—

(a) an officer authorises the keeping of a person in detention under subsection (1) above; and
(b) at the time of the authorisation he has not yet exercised a right conferred on him by section 56 or 58 below,

the officer—

(i) shall inform him of that right;
(ii) shall decide whether he should be permitted to exercise it;
(iii) shall record the decision in his custody record; and
(iv) if the decision is to refuse to permit the exercise of the right, shall also record the grounds for the decision in that record.

(10) Where an officer has authorised the keeping of a person who has not been charged in detention under subsection (1) or (2) above, he shall be released from detention, either on bail or without bail, not later than 36 hours after the relevant time[3], unless—

(a) he has been charged with an offence; or
(b) his continued detention is authorised or otherwise permitted in accordance with section 43 below.

(11) A person released under subsection (10) above shall not be re-arrested without a warrant[6] for the offence for which he was previously arrested unless new evidence justifying a further arrest has come to light since his release; but this subsection does not prevent an arrest under section 46A below.

[Police and Criminal Evidence Act 1984, s 42 as amended by the Criminal Justice and Public Order Act 1994, s 29, the Criminal Justice Act 2003, s 7 and the Serious Organised Crime and Police Act 2005, Sch 7.]

1. Regardless of any such authorisation, a person may be kept for up to 24 hours (s 41(1), ante), but a refusal of authorisation will necessitate the custody officer considering release (s 34(2), ante) or charge (s 37(7), ante), unless the refusal was solely because the authorisation was not being conducted diligently and expeditiously. Where it is clear that long detention is going to be necessary, consideration should be given to applying to a magistrates' court for a warrant of further detention under s 43, in place of the application under s 42, but note that in this event the exercise of rights under ss 56 and 58, post, cannot be delayed.
2. "Police detention" is defined in s 118(2) below.
3. "Relevant time" is defined in s 41(2), ante.
4. Code of Practice for the Detention, Treatment and Questioning of Persons by Police Officers (Code of Practice C in PART II: STATUTORY INSTRUMENTS ON EVIDENCE, post), paras 2.1A–2.7 makes provision for custody records.
5. Code of Practice C referred to above, para 15.3A extends the categories of persons who may make representations. This appears to be a mandatory provision and failure to allow representations at the time should lead to the detention being held invalid; see [1988] Crim LR 296.
6. Note similar provisions in ss 41(9) and 43(19). If a warrant is requested in these circumstances, we would advise justices to consider whether they, too, should require new evidence to be shown. Rearrest would appear to lead to a fresh period of police detention beginning with a new "relevant time" under s 41(2).

1–2757 43. Warrants of further detention. (1) Where, on an application on oath[1] made by a constable and supported by an information, a magistrates' court[2] is satisfied that there are reasonable grounds for believing that the further detention of the person to whom the application relates is justified, it may issue a warrant of further detention authorising the keeping of that person in police detention.

(2) A court may not hear an application for a warrant of further detention unless the person to whom the application relates—

(a) has been furnished with a copy of the information; and
(b) has been brought before the court for the hearing.

(3) The person to whom the application relates shall be entitled to be legally represented at the hearing and, if he is not so represented but wishes to be so represented—

(a) the court shall adjourn the hearing to enable him to obtain representation; and
(b) he may be kept in police detention during the adjournment.

(4) A person's further detention is only justified for the purposes of this section or section 44 below if—

(a) his detention without charge is necessary to secure or preserve evidence relating to an offence for which he is under arrest or to obtain such evidence by questioning him;
(b) an offence for which he is under arrest is an indictable offence; and
(c) the investigation is being conducted diligently and expeditiously.

(5) Subject to subsection (7) below, an application for a warrant of further detention may be made—

(a) at any time before the expiry of 36 hours after the relevant time[3]; or
(b) in a case where—

(i) it is not practicable for the magistrates' court to which the application will be made to sit at the expiry of 36 hours[4] after the relevant time[3]; but
(ii) the court will sit during the 6 hours following the end of that period,

at any time before the expiry of the said 6 hours.

(6) In a case to which subsection (5)(*b*) above applies—

(*a*) the person to whom the application relates may be kept in police detention until the application is heard; and

(*b*) the custody officer shall make a note in that person's custody record[5]—

    (i) of the fact that he was kept in police detention for more than 36 hours after the relevant time[3]; and

    (ii) of the reason why he was so kept.

(7) If—

(*a*) an application for a warrant of further detention is made after the expiry of 36 hours after the relevant time[3]; and

(*b*) it appears to the magistrates' court that it would have been reasonable for the police to make it before the expiry of that period,

the court shall dismiss the application.

(8) Where on an application such as is mentioned in subsection (1) above a magistrates' court is not satisfied that there are reasonable grounds for believing that the further detention of the person to whom the application relates is justified, it shall be its duty—

(*a*) to refuse the application; or

(*b*) to adjourn the hearing of it until a time not later than 36 hours after the relevant time[3].

(9) The person to whom the application relates may be kept in police detention during the adjournment.

(10) A warrant of further detention shall—

(*a*) state the time at which it is issued;

(*b*) authorise the keeping in police detention of the person to whom it relates for the period stated in it.

(11) Subject to subsection (12) below, the period stated in a warrant of further detention shall be such period as the magistrates' court thinks fit, having regard to the evidence before it.

(12) The period shall not be longer than 36 hours.

(13) If it is proposed to transfer a person in police detention to a police area other than that in which he is detained when the application for a warrant of further detention is made, the court hearing the application shall have regard to the distance and the time the journey would take.

(14) Any information submitted in support of an application under this section shall state—

(*a*) the nature of the offence for which the person to whom the application relates has been arrested;

(*b*) the general nature of the evidence on which that person was arrested;

(*c*) what inquiries relating to the offence have been made by the police and what further inquiries are proposed by them;

(*d*) the reasons for believing the continued detention of that person to be necessary for the purposes of such further inquiries.

(15) Where an application under this section is refused, the person to whom the application relates shall forthwith be charged or, subject to subsection (16) below, released, either on bail or without bail[7].

(16) A person need not be released under subsection (15) above—

(*a*) before the expiry of 24 hours after the relevant time[3]; or

(*b*) before the expiry of any longer period for which his continued detention is or has been authorised under section 42 above.

(17) Where an application under this section is refused, no further application shall be made under this section in respect of the person to whom the refusal relates, unless supported by evidence which has come to light since the refusal.

(18) Where a warrant of further detention is issued, the person to whom it relates shall be released from police detention, either on bail[6] or without bail, upon or before the expiry of the warrant unless he is charged.

(19) A person released under subsection (18) above shall not be re-arrested without a warrant[7] for the offence for which he was previously arrested unless new evidence justifying a further arrest has come to light since his release; but this subsection does not prevent an arrest under section 46A below.

[Police and Criminal Evidence Act 1984, s 43 as amended by the Criminal Justice and Public Order Act 1994, s 29 and the Serious Organised Crime and Police Act 2005, Sch 7.]

---

1. Or on affirmation: see the Oaths Act 1978, s 5 (para **2–1193**, post). The Code of Practice for the Detention, Treatment and Questioning of Persons by Police Officers (Code of Practice C in PART II: STATUTORY INSTRUMENTS ON EVIDENCE, post) makes it clear that applications should be made between 10 am and 9 pm, if possible during normal court hours, and that it will not be practicable for a court to sit specially outside the hours of 10 am to 9 pm. Any likely requirements for a special sitting should be notified to the Clerk to the Justices while the court is sitting, if at all possible (see Notes for Guidance, Note 15D of the Code).

2. "Magistrates' Court" is defined in s 45 below. The application may be made at any time before the expiry of 36 hours after the relevant time (sub-s (5) below) and the warrant may authorise further detention for up to 36 hours (sub-ss

(11) and (12) below); thus it is not necessary to obtain an authorisation under s 42, ante, first; where, however, enquiries seem likely to end by the expiry of 36 hours from the relevant time, authorisation under s 42 will generally be more convenient than an application under s 43.

3. "Relevant time" is defined in s 41(2), ante.

4. This section is not limited to a situation where the court is not sitting at all; where justices are sitting, they have a discretion whether to hear such an application as soon as it is made, or to wait, provided they do not do so for longer than six hours after the 36 hour period expires (*R v Slough Justices, ex p Stirling* (1987) 151 JP 603, [1987] Crim LR 576).

5. Code of Practice C referred to above, paras 2.1A–2.7 makes provision for custody records.

6. "Bail" is defined in s 47, post.

7. Note similar provisions in ss 41(9) and 42(11). If a warrant is requested in these circumstances, we would advise justices to consider whether they, too, should require new evidence to be shown. Rearrest would appear to lead to a fresh period of police detention beginning with a new "relevant time" under s 41(2).

1–2758   44. Extension of warrants of further detention.   (1) On an application on oath made by a constable and supported by an information a magistrates' court may extend a warrant of further detention issued under section 43 above if it is satisfied that there are reasonable grounds for believing that the further detention of the person to whom the application relates is justified.

(2) Subject to subsection (3) below, the period for which a warrant of further detention may be extended shall be such period as the court thinks fit, having regard to the evidence before it.

(3) The period shall not—

(a) be longer than 36 hours; or

(b) end later than 96 hours after the relevant time[1].

(4) Where a warrant of further detention has been extended under subsection (1) above, or further extended under this subsection, for a period ending before 96 hours after the relevant time[1], on an application such as is mentioned in that subsection a magistrates' court may further extend the warrant if it is satisfied as there mentioned; and subsections (2) and (3) above apply to such further extensions as they apply to extensions under subsection (1) above.

(5) A warrant of further detention shall, if extended or further extended under this section, be endorsed with a note of the period of the extension.

(6) Subsections (2), (3) and (14) of section 43 above shall apply to an application made under this section as they apply to an application made under that section.

(7) Where an application under this section is refused, the person to whom the application relates shall forthwith be charged or, subject to subsection (8) below, released, either on bail or without bail[2].

(8) A person need not be released under subsection (7) above before the expiry of any period for which a warrant of further detention issued in relation to him has been extended or further extended on an earlier application made under this section.

[Police and Criminal Evidence Act 1984, s 44.]

———

1. "Relevant time" is defined in s 41(2), ante.
2. "Bail" is defined in s 47, post.

1–2759   45. Detention before charge—supplementary.   (1) In sections 43 and 44 of this Act "magistrates' court" means a court consisting of two or more justices of the peace[1] sitting otherwise than in open court.

(2) Any reference in this Part of this Act to a period of time or a time of day is to be treated as approximate only.

[Police and Criminal Evidence Act 1984, s 45.]

———

1. Or a District Judge (Magistrates' Courts), see the Justices of the Peace Act 1997, s 10D, post.

1–2759A   45A. Use of video-conferencing facilities for decisions about detention.   (1) Subject to the following provisions of this section, the Secretary of State may by regulations provide that, in the case of an arrested person who is held in a police station, some or all of the functions mentioned in subsection (2) may be performed (notwithstanding anything in the preceding provisions of this Part) by an officer who—

(a) is not present in that police station; but

(b) has access to the use of video-conferencing facilities that enable him to communicate with persons in that station.

(2) Those functions are—

(a) the functions in relation to an arrested person taken, or answering bail at, to a police station that is not a designated police station which, in the case of an arrested person taken to a station that is a designated police station, are functions of a custody officer under section 37, 38 or 40 above; and

(b) the function of carrying out a review under section 40(1)(b) above (review, by an officer of at least the rank of inspector, of the detention of person arrested but not charged).

(3) Regulations under this section shall specify the use to be made in the performance of the functions mentioned in subsection (2) above of the facilities mentioned in subsection (1) above.

(4) Regulations under this section shall not authorise the performance of any of the functions mentioned in subsection (2)(a) above by such an officer as is mentioned in subsection (1) above unless he is a custody officer for a designated police station.

(5) Where any functions mentioned in subsection (2) above are performed in a manner authorised by regulations under this section—

(a) any obligation of the officer performing those functions to make a record in connection with the performance of those functions shall have effect as an obligation to cause another officer to make the record; and

(b) any requirement for the record to be made in the presence of the arrested person shall apply to the making of that record by that other officer.

(6) Where the functions mentioned in subsection (2)(b) are performed in a manner authorised by regulations under this section, the requirements under section 40(12) and (13) above for—

(a) the arrested person, or

(b) a solicitor representing him,

to be given any opportunity to make representations (whether in writing or orally) to the person performing those functions shall have effect as a requirement for that person, or such a solicitor, to be given an opportunity to make representations in a manner authorised by subsection (7) below.

(7) Representations are made in a manner authorised by this subsection—

(a) in a case where facilities exist for the immediate transmission of written representations to the officer performing the functions, if they are made either—

(i) orally to that officer by means of the video-conferencing facilities used by him for performing those functions; or

(ii) in writing to that officer by means of the facilities available for the immediate transmission of the representations;

and

(b) in any other case if they are made orally to that officer by means of the video-conferencing facilities used by him for performing the functions.

(8) Regulations under this section may make different provision for different cases and may be made so as to have effect in relation only to the police stations specified or described in the regulations.

(9) Regulations under this section shall be made by statutory instrument and shall be subject to annulment in pursuance of a resolution of either House of Parliament.

(10) Any reference in this section to video-conferencing facilities, in relation to any functions, is a reference to any facilities (whether a live television link or other facilities) by means of which the functions may be performed with the officer performing them, the person in relation to whom they are performed and any legal representative of that person all able to both see and to hear each other.
[Police and Criminal Evidence Act 1984, s 45A as inserted by the Criminal Justice and Police Act 2001, s 73 and the Criminal Justice Act 2003, Sch 1.]

Detention—miscellaneous

1–2760   **46. Detention after charge.**   (1) Where a person—

(a) is charged[1] with an offence; and

(b) after being charged—

(i) is kept in police detention; or

(ii) is detained by a local authority in pursuance of arrangements made under section 38(6) above,

he shall be brought before a magistrates' court[2] in accordance with the provisions of this section.

(2) If he is to be brought before a magistrates' court in the local justice area in which the police station at which he was charged is situated, he shall be brought before such a court as soon as is practicable and in any event not later than the first sitting after he is charged with the offence.

(3) If no magistrates' court in that area is due to sit either on the day on which he is charged or on the next day, the custody officer for the police station at which he was charged shall inform the designated officer for the area that there is a person in the area to whom subsection (2) above applies.

(4) If the person charged is to be brought before a magistrates' court in the local justice area other than that in which the police station at which he was charged is situated, he shall be removed to that area as soon as is practicable and brought before such a court as soon as is practicable after his arrival in the area and in any event not later than the first sitting of a magistrates' court in that area after his arrival in the area.

(5) If no magistrates' court in that area is due to sit either on the day on which he arrives in the area or on the next day—

(a) he shall be taken to a police station in the area; and

(b) the custody officer at that station shall inform the designated officer for the area that there is a person in the area to whom subsection (4) applies.

(6) Subject to subsection (8) below, where the designated officer for a local justice area has been informed—

(a) under subsection (3) above that there is a person in the area to whom subsection (2) above applies; or

(b) under subsection (5) above that there is a person in the area to whom subsection (4) above applies, the justices' chief executive shall arrange[3] for a magistrates' court to sit not later than the day next following the relevant day.

(7) In this section "the relevant day"—

(*a*) in relation to a person who is to be brought before a magistrates' court in the local justice area in which the police station at which he was charged is situated, means the day on which he was charged; and

(*b*) in relation to a person who is to be brought before a magistrates' court for in any other local justice area, means the day on which he arrives in the area.

(8) Where the day next following the relevant day is Christmas Day, Good Friday or a Sunday, the duty of the designated officer under subsection (6) above is a duty to arrange for a magistrates' court to sit not later than the first day after the relevant day which is not one of those days[4].

(9) Nothing in this section requires a person who is in hospital to be brought before a court if he is not well enough.

[Police and Criminal Evidence Act 1984, s 46 amended by the Access to Justice Act 1999, s 90, SI 2001/618 and the Courts Act 2003, Sch 8.]

---

1. As to the charging of detained persons, see the Code of Practice for the Detention, Treatment and Questioning of Persons by Police Officers (Code of Practice C in PART II: STATUTORY INSTRUMENTS ON EVIDENCE, post) paras 16.1 to 16.10.

2. The overriding duty of the police under this section is to bring the person charged before a court as soon as practicable, and the justices' chief executive, in accordance with sub-s (6), shall arrange for a court to sit. It is not open to the magistrates' courts committee to make a decision binding on the justices of the area how such justices should exercise their discretion whether or not to hold court sittings on Saturdays or Bank Holidays (*R v Avon Magistrates' Courts Committee, ex p Broome* (1988) 152 JP 529, [1988] Crim LR 618).

3. The justices' chief executive is subject to a mandatory statutory duty and that duty cannot be overridden or attenuated by any direction of his justices. Nevertheless, in exercising that duty he should give effect to the wishes of his justices which may be expressed by general guidelines or on a case to case basis. Considerations which might properly influence their decision would be the legitimate interests of the defendant and, in particular, the need to bring him before a court as soon as practicable. Considerations of cost, convenience and good administration are also relevant as these may affect the police, the Crown Prosecution Service or the defendant's representatives; see *R v Avon Magistrates' Courts Committee, ex p Broome* (1988) 152 JP 529, [1988] Crim LR 618.

4. A court may nevertheless sit on any day of the year if it thinks fit: Magistrates' Courts Act 1980, s 153, ante.

1–2760ZA   46ZA. Persons granted live link bail.   (1) This section applies in relation to bail granted under this Part subject to the duty mentioned in section 47(3)(*b*) ("live link bail").

(2) An accused person who attends a police station to answer to live link bail is not to be treated as in police detention for the purposes of this Act.

(3) Subsection (2) does not apply in relation to an accused person if—

(*a*) at any time before the beginning of proceedings in relation to a live link direction under section 57C of the Crime and Disorder Act 1998 in relation to him, he informs a constable that he does not intend to give his consent to the direction;

(*b*) at any such time, a constable informs him that a live link will not be available for his use for the purposes of that section;

(*c*) proceedings in relation to a live link direction under that section have begun but he does not give his consent to the direction; or

(*d*) the court determines for any other reason not to give such a direction.

(4) If any of paragraphs (*a*) to (*d*) of subsection (3) apply in relation to a person, he is to be treated for the purposes of this Part—

(*a*) as if he had been arrested for and charged with the offence in connection with which he was granted bail, and

(*b*) as if he had been so charged at the time when that paragraph first applied in relation to him.

(5) An accused person who is arrested under section 46A for failing to attend at a police station to answer to live link bail, and who is brought to a police station in accordance with that section, is to be treated for the purposes of this Part—

(*a*) as if he had been arrested for and charged with the offence in connection with which he was granted bail, and

(*b*) as if he had been so charged at the time when he is brought to the station.

(6) Nothing in subsection (4) or (5) affects the operation of section 47(6).★

[Police and Criminal Evidence Act 1984, s 46ZA as inserted by the Police and Justice Act 2006, Sch 6.]

★Inserted by the Police and Justice Act 2006, Sch 6, from a date to be appointed:

1–2760A   46A. Power of arrest for failure to answer to police bail.   (1) A constable may arrest without a warrant any person who, having been released on bail under this Part of this Act subject to a duty to attend at a police station, fails to attend at that police station at the time appointed for him to do so.

(1A) A person who has been released on bail under section 37(7)(*a*) or 37C(2)(*b*) above may be arrested without warrant by a constable if the constable has reasonable grounds for suspecting that the person has broken any of the conditions of bail.

(2) A person who is arrested under this section shall be taken to the police station appointed as the place at which he is to surrender to custody as soon as practicable after the arrest.

(3) For the purposes of—

(a) section 30 above (subject to the obligation in subsection (2) above), and

(b) section 31 above,

an arrest under this section shall be treated as an arrest for an offence.

[Police and Criminal Evidence Act 1984, s 46A as inserted by the Criminal Justice and Public Order Act 1994, s 29 and the Criminal Justice Act 2003, Sch 2.]

1–2761 47. Bail after arrest. (1) Subject to the following provisions of this section, a release on bail of a person under this Part of this Act shall be a release on bail granted in accordance with sections 3, 3A, 5 and 5A of the Bail Act 1976[1] as they apply to bail granted by a constable.

(1A) The normal powers to impose conditions of bail shall be available to him where a custody officer releases a person on bail under section 37(7)(a) above or section 38(1) above (including that subsection as applied by section 40(10) above) but not in any other cases.

In this subsection, "the normal powers to impose conditions of bail" has the meaning given in section 3(6) of the Bail Act 1976.

(1B) No application may be made under section 5B of the Bail Act 1976 if a person is released on bail under section 37(7)(a) or 37C(2)(b) above.

(1C) Subsections (1D) to (1F) below apply where a person released on bail under section 37(7)(a) or 37C(2)(b) above is on bail subject to conditions.

(1D) The person shall not be entitled to make an application under section 43B of the Magistrates' Courts Act 1980.

(1E) A magistrates' court may, on an application by or on behalf of the person, vary the conditions of bail; and in this subsection "vary" has the same meaning as in the Bail Act 1976.

(1F) Where a magistrates' court varies the conditions of bail under subsection (1E) above, that bail shall not lapse but shall continue subject to the conditions as so varied.

(2) Nothing in the Bail Act 1976 shall prevent the re-arrest[2] without warrant of a person released on bail subject to a duty to attend at a police station if new evidence justifying a further arrest has come to light since his release.

(3) Subject to subsections (3A) and (4) below, in this Part of this Act references to "bail" are references to bail subject to a duty—

(a) to appear before a magistrates' court at such time and such place; or

(b) to attend at such police station at such time,

as the custody officer may appoint.

(3A) Where a custody officer grants bail to a person subject to a duty to appear before a magistrates' court, he shall appoint for the appearance—

(a) a date which is not later than the first sitting of the court after the person is charged with the offence; or

(b) where he is informed by the designated officer for the relevant local justice area that the appearance cannot be accommodated until a later date, that later date.

(4) Where a custody officer has granted bail to a person subject to a duty to appear at a police station, the custody officer may give notice in writing to that person that his attendance at the police station is not required.

(5) *(Repealed)*.

(6) Where a person who has been granted bail under this Part and either has attended at the police station in accordance with the grant of bail or has been arrested under section 46A above is detained at a police station, any time during which he was in police detention prior to being granted bail shall be included as part of any period which falls to be calculated under this Part of this Act.

(7) Where a person who was released on bail under this Part subject to a duty to attend at a police station is re-arrested[1], the provisions of this Part of this Act shall apply to him as they apply to a person arrested for the first time; but this subsection does not apply to a person who is arrested under section 46A above or has attended a police station in accordance with the grant of bail (and who accordingly is deemed by section 34(7) above to have been arrested for an offence).

(8) *Amendments to the Magistrates' Courts Act 1980, ss 43, 117.*

[Police and Criminal Evidence Act 1984, s 47 as amended by the Criminal Justice and Public Order Act 1994, ss 27 and 29, and Sch 11, the Crime and Disorder Act 1998, s 46, the Access to Justice Act 1999, s 90, the Criminal Justice Act 2003, Schs 1 and 2 and the Courts Act 2003, Sch 8.]

---

1. See this PART, *ante*. Note the power under s 3(4) of the Bail Act 1976 to require the provision of a surety or sureties before release, and the power under s 3A to impose conditions. See also the Magistrates' Courts Act 1980 s 43, this PART, *ante*, enabling a court to fix a later time for appearance before it and to enlarge recognizances, as well as provision therein for the enforcement of recognizances taken to ensure appearance at a police station.

2. Thus re-arrest will lead to a fresh period of police detention beginning with a new "relevant time" under s 41(2); otherwise the period of detention after surrender to bail will be added on to the period already established after arrest and up to release on bail.

1–2761A 47A. Early administrative hearings conducted by justices' clerks. Where a person has been charged with an offence at a police station, any requirement imposed under this Part for the person to appear or be brought before a magistrates' court shall be taken to be satisfied if the person

appears or is brought before a justices' clerk in order for the clerk to conduct a hearing under section 50 of the Crime and Disorder Act 1998 (early administrative hearings).
[Police and Criminal Evidence Act 1984, s 47A as inserted by the Crime and Disorder Act 1998, Sch 8 and amended by the Courts Act 2003, Sch 8.]

1–2762   50. *Records of detention.—Information to be kept and included in annual reports.*

1–2763   51. Savings.   Nothing in this Part of this Act shall affect—

(a) the powers conferred on immigration officers by section 4 of and Schedule 2 to the Immigration Act 1971 (administrative provisions as to control on entry etc);

(b) the powers conferred by virtue of section 41 of, or Schedule 7 to, the Terrorism Act 2000 (powers of arrest and detention);

(c) any duty of a police officer under—

(i) section 129, 190 or 202 of the Army Act 1955 (duties of governors of prisons and others to receive prisoners, deserters, absentees and persons under escort);

(ii) section 129, 190 or 202 of the Air Force Act 1955 (duties of governors of prisons and others to receive prisoners, deserters, absentees and persons under escort);

(iii) section 107 of the Naval Discipline Act 1957 (duties of governors of civil prisons etc); or

(iv) paragraph 5 of Schedule 5 to the Reserve Forces Act 1980 (duties of governors of civil prisons); or

(d) any right of a person in police detention to apply for a writ of habeas corpus or other prerogative remedy.
[Police and Criminal Evidence Act 1984, s 51 as amended by the Prevention of Terrorism (Temporary Provisions) Act 1989, Sch 8 and the Terrorism Act 2000, s 125.]

PART V[1]
QUESTIONING AND TREATMENT OF PERSONS BY POLICE[2]

1–2764   53. Abolition of certain powers of constables to search[3] persons.   (1) Subject to subsection (2) below, there shall cease to have effect any Act (including a local Act) passed before this Act in so far as it authorises—

(a) any search by a constable of a person in police detention at a police station; or

(b) an intimate search of a person by a constable;

and any rule of common law which authorises a search such as is mentioned in paragraph (a) or (b) above is abolished.

(2) (*Repealed*).
[Police and Criminal Evidence Act 1984, s 53 as amended by the Prevention of Terrorism (Temporary Provisions) Act 1989, Sch 9.]

---

1. Part V contains ss 53–65.
2. The Code of Practice for the Detention, Treatment and Questioning of Persons by Police Officers (Code of Practice C) is printed in PART II: STATUTORY INSTRUMENTS ON EVIDENCE, post. It must be readily available at all police stations (para 1.2).
3. Note the powers to stop and search in Part I of this Act, ante, and search upon arrest in s 32, ante.

1–2765   54. Searches of detained persons.   (1) The custody officer at a police station shall ascertain everything which a person has with him when he is—

(a) brought to the station after being arrested elsewhere or after being committed to custody by an order or sentence of a court; or

(b) arrested at the station or detained there, as a person falling within section 34(7), under section 37 above.

(2) The custody officer may record or cause to be recorded all or any of the things which he ascertains under subsection (1).

(2A) In the case of an arrested person, any such record may be made as part of his custody record[1].(3)Subject to subsection (4) below, a custody officer may seize[2] and retain any such thing or cause any such thing to be seized and retained[3].

(4) Clothes and personal effects may only be seized if the custody officer—

(a) believes that the person from whom they are seized may use them—

(i) to cause physical injury to himself or any other person;

(ii) to damage property;

(iii) to interfere with evidence; or

(iv) to assist him to escape; or

(b) has reasonable grounds for believing that they may be evidence relating to an offence.

(5) Where anything is seized, the person from whom it is seized shall be told the reason for the seizure unless he is—

(a) violent or likely to become violent; or

(b) incapable of understanding what is said to him.

(6) Subject to subsection (7) below, a person may be searched[4] if the custody officer considers it

necessary to enable him to carry out his duty under subsection (1) above and to the extent that the custody officer considers necessary for that purpose.

(6A) A person who is in custody at a police station or is in police detention otherwise than at a police station may at any time be searched in order to ascertain whether he has with him anything which he could use for any of the purposes specified in subsection (4)(*a*) above.

(6B) Subject to subsection (6C) below, a constable may seize and retain, or cause to be seized and retained, anything found on such a search.

(6C) A constable may only seize clothes and personal effects in the circumstances specified in subsection (4) above.

(7) An intimate search[5] may not be conducted under this section.

(8) A search under this section shall be carried out by a constable.

(9) The constable carrying out a search shall be of the same sex as the person searched.

[Police and Criminal Evidence Act 1984, s 54, as amended by the Criminal Justice Act 1988, s 147, the Criminal Justice and Public Order Act 1994, Sch 10 and the Criminal Justice Act 2003, s 8.]

---

1. The Code of Practice for the Detention, Treatment and Questioning of Persons by Police Officers (Code of Practice C in PART II: STATUTORY INSTRUMENTS ON EVIDENCE, post) paras 2.1A–2.7 makes provision for custody records.

2. Items subject to legal privilege may not be seized: s 19(6), ante.

3. It may be retained so long as is necessary in all the circumstances (s 22(1)), ante; note also the Magistrates' Courts Act 1980 s 48 (return of property at court's direction).

4. For power of search upon arrest see s 32, ante. Reasonable force may be used: s 117, post. As to intimate searches, see s 55 below, and also Annex A to Code of Practice C (referred to above) which deals with intimate and strip searches. See also the power to search persons under s 164 of the Customs and Excise Management Act 1979, exercisable by an officer as defined by that Act.

5. "Intimate search" is defined by s 118 below.

1–2765A 54A. Searches and examination to ascertain identity.

(1) If an officer of at least the rank of inspector authorises it, a person who is detained in a police station may be searched or examined, or both—

(*a*) for the purpose of ascertaining whether he has any mark that would tend to identify him as a person involved in the commission of an offence; or

(*b*) for the purpose of facilitating the ascertainment of his identity.

(2) An officer may only give an authorisation under subsection (1) for the purpose mentioned in paragraph (*a*) of that subsection if—

(*a*) the appropriate consent to a search or examination that would reveal whether the mark in question exists has been withheld; or

(*b*) it is not practicable to obtain such consent.

(3) An officer may only give an authorisation under subsection (1) in a case in which subsection (2) does not apply if—

(*a*) the person in question has refused to identify himself; or

(*b*) the officer has reasonable grounds for suspecting that that person is not who he claims to be.

(4) An officer may give an authorisation under subsection (1) orally or in writing but, if he gives it orally, he shall confirm it in writing as soon as is practicable.

(5) Any identifying mark found on a search or examination under this section may be photographed—

(*a*) with the appropriate consent; or

(*b*) if the appropriate consent is withheld or it is not practicable to obtain it, without it.

(6) Where a search or examination may be carried out under this section, or a photograph may be taken under this section, the only persons entitled to carry out the search or examination, or to take the photograph, are constables.

(7) A person may not under this section carry out a search or examination of a person of the opposite sex or take a photograph of any part of the body of a person of the opposite sex.

(8) An intimate search may not be carried out under this section.

(9) A photograph taken under this section—

(*a*) may be used by, or disclosed to, any person for any purpose related to the prevention or detection of crime, the investigation of an offence or the conduct of a prosecution; and

(*b*) after being so used or disclosed, may be retained but may not be used or disclosed except for a purpose so related.

(10) In subsection—

(*a*) the reference to crime includes a reference to any conduct which—

(i) constitutes one or more criminal offences (whether under the law of a part of the United Kingdom or of a country or territory outside the United Kingdom); or

(ii) is, or corresponds to, any conduct which, if it all took place in any one part of the United Kingdom, would constitute one or more criminal offences;

and

(*b*) the references to an investigation and to a prosecution include references, respectively, to any investigation outside the United Kingdom of any crime or suspected crime and to a prosecution brought in respect of any crime in a country or territory outside the United Kingdom.

(11) In this section—

(*a*) references to ascertaining a person's identity include references to showing that he is not a particular person; and

(*b*) references to taking a photograph include references to using any process by means of which a visual image may be produced, and references to photographing a person shall be construed accordingly.

(12) In this section "mark" includes features and injuries; and a mark is an identifying mark for the purposes of this section if its existence in any person's case facilitates the ascertainment of his identity or his identification as a person involved in the commission of an offence.

(13) Nothing in this section applies to a person arrested under an extradition arrest power.[1]

[Police and Criminal Evidence Act 1984, s 54A, as inserted by the Anti-terrorism, Crime and Security Act 2001, s 90(1) and amended by the Police Reform Act 2002, s 107(1) and the Extradition Act 2003, s 169.]

---

1. Subsection (13) does not apply in relation to extradition requests received or extraditions made on or before 31 December 2003.

1–2766   55. Intimate searches[1]. (1) Subject to the following provisions of this section, if an officer of at least the rank of inspector has reasonable grounds for believing—

(*a*) that a person who has been arrested and is in police detention may have concealed on him anything which—

(i)   he could use to cause physical injury to himself or others; and

(ii) he might so use while he is in police detention or in the custody of a court; or

(*b*) that such a person—

(i)   may have a Class A drug concealed on him; and

(ii) was in possession of it with the appropriate criminal intent before his arrest,

he may authorise an intimate search of that person.

(2) An officer may not authorise an intimate search[1] of a person for anything unless he has reasonable grounds for believing that it cannot be found without his being intimately searched.

(3) An officer may give an authorisation under subsection (1) above orally or in writing but, if he gives it orally, he shall confirm it in writing as soon as is practicable.

(3A) A drug offence search shall not be carried out unless the appropriate consent has been given in writing.

(3B) Where it is proposed that a drug offence search be carried out, an appropriate officer shall inform the person who is to be subject to it—

(*a*) of the giving of the authorisation for it; and

(*b*) of the grounds for giving the authorisation.

(4) An intimate search[1] which is only a drug offence search shall be by way of examination by a suitably qualified person.

(5) Except as provided by subsection (4) above, an intimate search[1] shall be by way of examination by a suitably qualified person unless an officer of at least the rank of inspector considers that this is not practicable.

(6) An intimate search[1] which is not carried out as mentioned in subsection (5) above shall be carried out by a constable.

(7) A constable may not carry out an intimate search[1] of a person of the opposite sex.

(8) No intimate search[1] may be carried out except—

(*a*) at a police station;

(*b*) at a hospital;

(*c*) at a registered medical practitioner's surgery; or

(*d*) at some other place used for medical purposes.

(9) An intimate search[1] which is only a drug offence search may not be carried out at a police station.

(10) If an intimate search[1] of a person is carried out, the custody record[2] relating to him shall state—

(*a*) which parts of his body were searched; and

(*b*) why they were searched.

(10A) If the intimate search is a drug offence search, the custody record relating to that person shall also state—

(*a*) the authorisation by virtue of which the search was carried out;

(*b*) the grounds for giving the authorisation; and

(*c*) the fact that the appropriate consent was given.

(11) The information required to be recorded by subsections (10) and (10A) above shall be recorded as soon as practicable after the completion of the search.

(12) The custody officer at a police station may seize and retain anything which is found on an intimate search[1] of a person, or cause any such thing to be seized and retained—

(a) if he believes that the person from whom it is seized may use it—

    (i)   to cause physical injury to himself or any other person;

    (ii) to damage property;

    (iii) to interfere with evidence; or

    (iv) to assist him to escape; or

(b) if he has reasonable grounds for believing that it may be evidence relating to an offence.

(13) Where anything is seized under this section, the person from whom it is seized shall be told the reason for the seizure unless he is—

(a) violent or likely to become violent; or

(b) incapable of understanding what is said to him.

(13A) Where the appropriate consent to a drug offence search of any person was refused without good cause, in any proceedings against that person for an offence—

(a) the court, in determining whether there is a case to answer;

(b) a judge, in deciding whether to grant an application made by the accused under paragraph 2 of Schedule 3 to the Crime and Disorder Act 1998 (applications for dismissal); and

(c) the court or jury, in determining whether that person is guilty of the offence charged,

may draw such inferences from the refusal as appear proper.

(14)–(16) *Information about searches to be included in annual reports.*

(17) In this section—

"the appropriate criminal intent" means an intent to commit an offence under—

(a) section 5(3) of the Misuse of Drugs Act 1971 (possession of controlled drug with intent to supply to another); or

(b) section 68(2) of the Customs and Excise Management Act 1979 (exportation etc with intent to evade a prohibition or restriction);

"appropriate officer" means—

(a) a constable,

(b) a person who is designated as a detention officer in pursuance of section 38 of the Police Reform Act 2002 if his designation applies paragraph 33D of Schedule 4 to that Act, or

(c) a person who is designated as a staff custody officer in pursuance of section 38 of that Act if his designation applies paragraph 35C of Schedule 4 to that Act;

"Class A drug" has the meaning assigned to it by section 2(1)(b) of the Misuse of Drugs Act 1971;

"drug offence search" means an intimate search for a Class A drug which an officer has authorised by virtue of subsection (1)(b) above; and

"suitably qualified person" means—

(a) a registered medical practitioner; or

(b) a registered nurse.★

[Police and Criminal Evidence Act 1984, s 55 as amended by the Criminal Justice Act 1988, Sch 15, the Police Act 1996, Sch 7, the Police Act 1997, Sch 9, the Criminal Justice and Police Act 2001, s 79 and the Drugs Act 2005, s 3.]

---

1. "Intimate search" is defined by s 118 below. See also Annex A to the Code of Practice for the Detention, Treatment and Questioning of Persons by Police Officers (Code of Practice C in PART II: STATUTORY INSTRUMENTS ON EVIDENCE, post) for detailed provisions for an intimate search or a strip search. Reasonable force may be used: see s 117, post.

2. Code of Practice C referred to above makes provision for custody records.

1-2766A   55A. X-rays and ultrasound scans. (1) If an officer of at least the rank of inspector has reasonable grounds for believing that a person who has been arrested for an offence and is in police detention—

(a) may have swallowed a Class A drug, and

(b) was in possession of it with the appropriate criminal intent before his arrest,

the officer may authorise that an x-ray is taken of the person or an ultrasound scan is carried out on the person (or both).

(2) An x-ray must not be taken of a person and an ultrasound scan must not be carried out on him unless the appropriate consent has been given in writing.

(3) If it is proposed that an x-ray is taken or an ultrasound scan is carried out, an appropriate officer must inform the person who is to be subject to it—

(a) of the giving of the authorisation for it, and

(b) of the grounds for giving the authorisation.

(4) An x-ray may be taken or an ultrasound scan carried out only by a suitably qualified person and only at—

(a) a hospital,

(b) a registered medical practitioner's surgery, or

(c) some other place used for medical purposes.

(5) The custody record of the person must also state—

(a)   the authorisation by virtue of which the x-ray was taken or the ultrasound scan was carried out,

(b)   the grounds for giving the authorisation, and

(c)   the fact that the appropriate consent was given.

(6) The information required to be recorded by subsection (5) must be recorded as soon as practicable after the x-ray has been taken or ultrasound scan carried out (as the case may be).

(7) Every annual report—

(a)   under section 22 of the Police Act 1996, or

(b)   made by the Commissioner of Police of the Metropolis,

must contain information about x-rays which have been taken and ultrasound scans which have been carried out under this section in the area to which the report relates during the period to which it relates.

(8) The information about such x-rays and ultrasound scans must be presented separately and must include—

(a)   the total number of x-rays;

(b)   the total number of ultrasound scans;

(c)   the results of the x-rays;

(d)   the results of the ultrasound scans.

(9) If the appropriate consent to an x-ray or ultrasound scan of any person is refused without good cause, in any proceedings against that person for an offence—

(a)   the court, in determining whether there is a case to answer,

(b)   a judge, in deciding whether to grant an application made by the accused under paragraph 2 of Schedule 3 to the Crime and Disorder Act 1998 (applications for dismissal), and

(c)   the court or jury, in determining whether that person is guilty of the offence charged,

may draw such inferences from the refusal as appear proper.

(10) In this section "the appropriate criminal intent", "appropriate officer", "Class A drug" and "suitably qualified person" have the same meanings as in section 55 above.

[Police and Criminal Evidence Act 1984, s 55A as inserted by the Drugs Act 2005, s 5.]

1–2767 56. Right to have someone informed when arrested.   (1) When a person has been arrested and is being held in custody in a police station or other premises, he shall be entitled, if he so requests, to have one friend or relative or other person who is known to him or who is likely to take an interest in his welfare told, as soon as is practicable except to the extent that delay is permitted by this section, that he has been arrested and is being detained there.

(2) Delay is only permitted—

(a)   in the case of a person who is in police detention for an indictable offence; and

(b)   if an officer of at least the rank of inspector authorises it.

(3) In any case the person in custody must be permitted to exercise the right conferred by subsection (1) above within 36 hours from the relevant time, as defined in section 41(2) above.

(4) An officer may give an authorisation under subsection (2) above orally or in writing but, if he gives it orally, he shall confirm it in writing as soon as is practicable.

(5) Subject to subsection (5A) below an officer may only authorise delay where he has reasonable grounds for believing that telling the named person of the arrest—

(a)   will lead to interference with or harm to evidence connected with an indictable offence or interference with or physical injury to other persons; or

(b)   will lead to the alerting of other persons suspected of having committed such an offence but not yet arrested for it; or

(c)   will hinder the recovery of any property obtained as a result of such an offence.

(5A) An officer may also authorise delay where he has reasonable grounds for believing that—

(a)   the person detained for the indictable offence has benefited from his criminal conduct, and

(b)   the recovery of the value of the property constituting the benefit will be hindered by telling the named person of the arrest.

(5B) For the purposes of subsection (5A) above the question whether a person has benefited from his criminal conduct is to be decided in accordance with Part 2 of the Proceeds of Crime Act 2002.

(6) If a delay is authorised—

(a)   the detained person shall be told the reason for it; and

(b)   the reason shall be noted on his custody record[1].

(7) The duties imposed by subsection (6) above shall be performed as soon as is practicable.

(8) The rights conferred by this section on a person detained at a police station or other premises are exercisable whenever he is transferred from one place to another; and this section applies to each subsequent occasion on which they are exercisable as it applies to the first such occasion.

(9) There may be no further delay in permitting the exercise of the right conferred by subsection (1) above once the reason for authorising delay ceases to subsist.

(10) Nothing in this section applies to a person arrested or detained under the terrorism provisions.

[Police and Criminal Evidence Act 1984, s 56 as amended by the Drug Trafficking Offences Act 1986, s 32, the

Criminal Justice Act 1988, s 99, the Terrorism Act 2000, s 125, the Criminal Justice and Police Act 2001, s 74, the Proceeds of Crime Act 2002, s 456 and the Serious Organised Crime and Police Act 2005, Sch 7.]

---

1. Code of Practice for the Detention, Treatment and Questioning of Persons by Police Officers, (Code of Practice C in PART II: STATUTORY INSTRUMENTS ON EVIDENCE) paras 2.1A to 2.7 makes provision for custody records: see also paras 5.1 to 5.8—right not to be held incommunicado—and Annex B—delay in notifying arrest or allowing access to legal advice.

1-2768 57. *Additional rights of children and young persons.*—*Amendments to Children and Young Persons Act* 1933, *s* 34(2).

1-2769 58. Access to legal advice[1]. (1) A person arrested and held in custody[2] in a police station or other premises[3] shall be entitled, if he so requests, to consult a solicitor privately at any time[4].

(2) Subject to subsection (3) below, a request under subsection (1) above and the time at which it was made shall be recorded in the custody record[5].

(3) Such a request need not be recorded in the custody record of a person who makes it at a time while he is at a court after being charged with an offence.

(4) If a person makes such a request, he must be permitted to consult a solicitor as soon as is practicable[6] except to the extent that delay is permitted by this section.

(5) In any case he must be permitted to consult a solicitor within 36 hours from the relevant time, as defined in section 41(2) above.

(6) Delay in compliance with a request is only permitted—

(*a*) in the case of a person who is in police detention for an indictable offence ; and

(*b*) if an officer of at least the rank[7] of superintendent authorises it.

(7) An officer may give an authorisation under subsection (6) above orally or in writing but, if he gives it orally, he shall confirm it in writing as soon as is practicable.

(8) Subject to subsection (8A) below an officer may only authorise delay where he has reasonable grounds for believing[8] that the exercise of the right conferred by subsection (1) above at the time when the person detained desires to exercise it—

(*a*) will lead to interference with or harm to evidence connected with an indictable offence or interference with or physical injury to other persons; or

(*b*) will lead to the alerting of other persons suspected of having committed such an offence but not yet arrested for it; or

(*c*) will hinder the recovery of any property obtained as a result of such an offence.

(8A) An officer may also authorise delay where he has reasonable grounds for believing that—

(*a*) the person detained for the indictable offence has benefited from his criminal conduct, and

(*b*) the recovery of the value of the property constituting the benefit will be hindered by the exercise of the right conferred by subsection (1) above.

(8B) For the purposes of subsection (8A) above the question whether a person has benefited from his criminal conduct is to be decided in accordance with Part 2 of the Proceeds of Crime Act 2002.

(9) If delay is authorised—

(*a*) the detained person shall be told the reason for it; and

(*b*) the reason shall be noted on his custody record[5].

(10) The duties imposed by subsection (9) above shall be performed as soon as is practicable.

(11) There may be no further delay in permitting the exercise of the right conferred by subsection (1) above once the reason for authorising delay ceases to subsist.

(12) Nothing in this section applies to a person arrested or detained under the terrorism provisions. [Police and Criminal Evidence Act 1984, s 58 as amended by the Drug Trafficking Offences Act 1986, s 32, the Criminal Justice Act 1988, s 99, the Terrorism Act 2000, s 125, the Proceeds of Crime Act 2002, s 456 and the Serious Organised Crime and Police Act 2005, Sch 7.]

---

1. There is a right of access to legal advice under art 6 of the European Convention on Human Rights which applies, with limited qualifications, at the stage of preliminary investigations by the police. See *Murray v United Kingdom* (1996) 22 EHRR 29. In addition, it is a requirement of art 6(3)(*c*) of the Convention that communications between a lawyer and his client are private and confidential: *S v Switzerland* (1991) 14 EHRR 670, though the Convention does not exist to be invoked where the deprivation is theoretical or illusory: *R (on the application of M) v Metropolitan Police Comr*, (*R (on the application of La Rose) v Metropolitan Police Comr*) [2002] Crim LR 215 (in M's case no consultation room at a police station; therefore, the interview took place in a cell where, allegedly, privacy was not assured due to the wicket in the door and, allegedly, communication and eye contact were difficult).
2. This does not apply to a person who is in custody after being remanded in custody by a magistrates' court except in special circumstances, eg where the defendant is the subject of continuing investigations for other offences. Nevertheless, a person held in custody in cells at a courthouse has a common law right, on request, to be permitted to consult a solicitor as soon as is practicable (*R v Chief Constable of South Wales, ex p Merrick* [1994] 2 All ER 560, [1994] 1 WLR 663).
3. The relevant provisions of the Police and Criminal Evidence Act 1984 and Code of Practice C are restricted to persons under arrest and at a police station or elsewhere in the charge of a constable. Neither is there any obligation under the jurisprudence on the European Convention on Human Rights to inform a suspect that he has a right to *free* legal advice. Accordingly, there was no impropriety where a trading standards officer gave a suspect the opportunity to seek legal advice but did not inform him of the availability of legal aid and advice: *R (Beale) v South East Wiltshire Magistrates* [2002] EWHC 2961 (Admin), 167 JP 41.
4. See the Code of Practice for the Detention, Treatment and Questioning of Persons by Police Officers, (Code of Practice C in PART II: STATUTORY INSTRUMENTS ON EVIDENCE, post), paras 6.1 to 6.17 and Annex B for the operation

of this right. Note also the provisions relating to a citizen of an independent Commonwealth country, or a foreign national (paras 7.1 to 7.5).

Where there has been a breach of s 58 it is nevertheless open to the court to balance all the circumstances and to decide whether or not there existed such an adverse effect on the fairness of the proceedings that justice required the evidence to be excluded in accordance with s 78 of this Act. Accordingly, where a suspect who was denied access to a solicitor showed by his conduct he was aware of his rights and there were grounds on which to conclude that the solicitor's advice would not have added anything to the suspect's knowledge of his rights, it was held the court was entitled to admit evidence of the suspect's admission notwithstanding the breach of s 58 (*R v Dunford* (1990) 91 Cr App Rep 150, [1990] NLJR 517, CA). See also *R v Dunn* (1990) 91 Cr App Rep 237, [1990] NLJR 599, CA (evidence of admissions made by the accused in circumstances where there were clear breaches of the Code of Practice admitted in view of fact that a clerk representing the accused's solicitor was present when the admissions were made).

5. Code of Practice C referred to above, paras 2.1A to 2.7 makes provision for custody records.

6. The right to consult a solicitor as soon as is practicable does not require the police to delay taking a specimen of breath, blood or urine under s 7(1) of the Road Traffic Act 1988 (*DPP v Billington* [1988] 1 All ER 435, [1988] 1 WLR 535, 152 JP 1).

7. In justifying his decision the officer will have to refer to specific circumstances including evidence as to the person detained or the actual solicitor sought to be consulted, and these circumstances will be rare; the grounds could not ever be successfully advanced in relation to solicitors generally (*R v Samuel* [1988] QB 615, [1988] 2 All ER 135, [1988] 2 WLR 920, 152 JP 253, CA). If the right is denied, that can lead to the exclusion of evidence obtained at unlawful interviews, either by exercising the power under s 78 (unfair evidence) or s 76 (confession obtained by oppression) in PART II: EVIDENCE, post.

8. The holder of an acting rank is to be treated, so far as authority and powers are concerned, as if he were the holder of the substantive rank; see *R v Alladice* [1988] Crim LR 608, CA.

1–2770   60. *Tape-recording of interviews.*—*Duty of Secretary of State to issue code of practice and make an Order*[1].

1. The Police and Criminal Evidence Act 1984 (Codes of Practice) Order 2005, SI 2005/3503 (draft codes laid before Parliament 8 November 2005) appointed 1 January 2006 as the date on which Codes A–G came into operation. The Police and Criminal Evidence act 1984 (Code of Practice C and Code of Practice H) Order 2006, SI 2006/1938 appointed 25 July 2006 as the date of which a revised Code C and new Code H (detention, treatment and questioning by police officers of persons arrested under section 41 of the Terrorism Act 2000) (draft codes laid before Parliament on 14 June 2006) came into operation. The Police and Criminal Evidence Act 1984 (Codes of Practice) (Revisions to Code A) Order 2006, SI 2006/2165 appointed 31 August 2006 as the date on which revisions to Code of Practice A laid in draft before Parliament on 10 August 2006 came into operation. Code of Practice E (tape recording of interviews with suspects) was made under this section and requires interviews in respect of indictable offences to be tape recorded. See also the Code of Practice on Tape Recording Interviews with Suspects (Code of Practice E), in PART II: EVIDENCE – STATUTORY INSTRUMENTS ON EVIDENCE, and notes to s 66, post and in relation to those detained under Sch 7 to, or s 41 of, the Terrorism Act 2000, see the Code of Practice on Audio Recording of Interviews) (No 2) Order 2001, SI 2001/189.

1–2770A   60A. Visual recording of interviews. *Power of Secretary of State to issue Code of Practice and make an Order*[1].

1. Section 60A was inserted by the Criminal Justice and Police Act 2001, s 76. Its purpose is to remove any doubt as to the legality of video recording of interviews where the interviewee objects to such recording. The Police and Criminal Evidence Act 1984 (Visual Recording of Interviews) (Certain Police Areas) Order 2002, SI 2002/1069 and the No 2 Order 2002, SI 2002/2527 required the visual recording of interviews held by police officers at the following police stations: (interviews commencing after midnight on 7 May 2002) Basingstoke, Portsmouth, Southampton, Chatham, Gravesend, Tonbridge, Bromley, Collingdale, Edmonton, Redditch, Telford and Worcester; (interviews commencing after midnight on 29 October 2002) Harlow, Colchester and Southend. These Orders were revoked with effect from 1 November 2003 by the Police and Criminal Evidence Act 1984 (Visual Recording of Interviews) (Certain Police Areas) (Revocation) Order 2003, SI 2003/2463 so that visual recording of interviews ceased to be mandatory.

The Police and Criminal Evidence Act 1984 (Codes of Practice) Order 2005, SI 2005/3503 (draft codes laid before Parliament 8 November 2005) appointed 1 January 2006 as the date on which Codes A–G came into operation. The Police and Criminal Evidence act 1984 (Code of Practice C and Code of Practice H) Order 2006, SI 2006/1938 appointed 25 July 2006 as the date of which a revised Code C and new Code H (detention, treatment and questioning by police officers of persons arrested under section 41 of the Terrorism Act 2000) (draft codes laid before Parliament on 14 June 2006) came into operation. The Police and Criminal Evidence Act 1984 (Codes of Practice) (Revisions to Code A) Order 2006, SI 2006/2165 appointed 31 August 2006 as the date on which revisions to Code of Practice A laid in draft before Parliament on 10 August 2006 came into operation. Code of Practice F (visual recording of interviews held by police officers at police stations) was made under this section.

See also the Code of Practice on Visual Recording with Sound of Interviews with Suspects (Code of Practice F), in PART II: EVIDENCE – STATUTORY INSTRUMENTS ON EVIDENCE,, and notes to s 66, post.

1–2771   61. Fingerprinting.   (1) Except as provided by this section no person's fingerprints[1] may be taken without the appropriate consent[1].

(2) Consent to the taking of a person's fingerprints must be in writing if it is given at a time when he is at a police station.

(3) The fingerprints of a person detained at a police station may be taken without the appropriate consent if—

(*a*) he is detained in consequence of his arrest for a recordable offence; and

(*b*) he has not had his fingerprints taken in the course of the investigation of the offence by the police.

(3A) Where a person mentioned in paragraph (a) of subsection (3) or (4) has already had his fingerprints taken in the course of the investigation of the offence by the police, that fact shall be disregarded for the purposes of that subsection if—

(*a*) the fingerprints taken on the previous occasion do not constitute a complete set of his fingerprints; or

(b) some or all of the fingerprints taken on the previous occasion are not of sufficient quality to allow satisfactory analysis, comparison or matching (whether in the case in question or generally).

(4) The fingerprints of a person detained at a police station may be taken without the appropriate consent if—

(a) he has been charged with a recordable offence or informed that he will be reported for such an offence; and

(b) he has not had his fingerprints taken in the course of the investigation of the offence by the police.

(4A) The fingerprints of a person who has answered to bail at a court or police station may be taken without the appropriate consent at the court or station if—

(a) the court, or

(b) an officer of at least the rank of inspector,

authorises them to be taken.

(4B) A court or officer may only give an authorisation under subsection (4A) if—

(a) the person who has answered to bail has answered to it for a person whose fingerprints were taken on a previous occasion and there are reasonable grounds for believing that he is not the same person; or

(b) the person who has answered to bail claims to be a different person from a person whose fingerprints were taken on a previous occasion.

(5) An officer may give an authorisation under subsection (4A) above orally or in writing but, if he gives it orally, he shall confirm it in writing as soon as is practicable.

(6) Any person's fingerprints may be taken without the appropriate consent if—

(a) he has been convicted of a recordable offence;

(b) he has been given a caution in respect of a recordable offence which, at the time of the caution, he has admitted; or

(c) he has been warned or reprimanded under section 65 of the Crime and Disorder Act 1998 (c 37) for a recordable offence.

(7) In a case where by virtue of subsection (3), (4) or (6) above a person's fingerprints are taken without the appropriate consent—

(a) he shall be told the reason before his fingerprints are taken; and

(b) the reason shall be recorded as soon as is practicable after the fingerprints are taken.

(7A) If a person's fingerprints are taken at a police station, whether with or without the appropriate consent—

(a) before the fingerprints are taken, an officer shall inform him that they may be the subject of a speculative search; and

(b) the fact that the person has been informed of this possibility shall be recorded as soon as is practicable after the fingerprints have been taken.

(8) If he is detained at a police station when the fingerprints are taken, the reason for taking them and, in the case falling within subsection (7A) above, the fact referred to in paragraph (b) of that subsection shall be recorded on his custody record[2].

(8A) Where a person's fingerprints are taken electronically, they must be taken only in such manner, and using such devices, as the Secretary of State has approved for the purposes of electronic fingerprinting.[*]

(8B) The power to take the fingerprints of a person detained at a police station without the appropriate consent shall be exercisable by any constable.

(9) Nothing in this section—

(a) affects any power conferred by paragraph 18(2) of Schedule 2 to the Immigration Act 1971, section 141 of the Immigration and Asylum Act 1999 or regulations mad under section 144 of that Act; or

(b) applies to a person arrested or detained under the terrorism provisions[1].

(10) Nothing in this section applies to a person arrested under an extradition arrest power.[3][**]

[Police and Criminal Evidence Act 1984, s 61 as amended by the Prevention of Terrorism (Temporary Provisions) Act 1989, Sch 8, the Criminal Justice and Public Order Act 1994, Sch 10, the Police Reform Act 2002, Sch 7 and the Criminal Justice and Police Act 2001, s 78 and the Extradition Act 2003, s 169.]

---

*Reproduced as prospectively inserted by the Criminal Justice and Police Act 2001, s 78.
**Amended by the Serious Organised Crime and Police Act 2005, Sch 7 from a date to be appointed.

1. "Fingerprints", "appropriate consent", "terrorism provisions" are defined in s 65 below. The Code of Practice for the Identification of Persons by Police Officers, (Code of Practice D in PART II: STATUTORY INSTRUMENTS ON EVIDENCE, post) paras 4.1 to 4.15 makes detailed provision for the taking of fingerprints.

2. The Code of Practice for the Detention, Treatment and Questioning of Persons by Police Officers (Code of Practice C in PART II: STATUTORY INSTRUMENTS ON EVIDENCE, post), paras 2.1A to 2.7, makes provision for custody records.

3. Subsection (10) does not apply in relation to extradition requests received or extraditions made on or before 31 December 2003.

1–2771A   61A. Impressions of footwear.   (1) Except as provided by this section, no impression of a person's footwear may be taken without the appropriate consent.

(2) Consent to the taking of an impression of a person's footwear must be in writing if it is given at a time when he is at a police station.

(3) Where a person is detained at a police station, an impression of his footwear may be taken without the appropriate consent if—

(*a*) he is detained in consequence of his arrest for a recordable offence, or has been charged with a recordable offence, or informed that he will be reported for a recordable offence; and

(*b*) he has not had an impression taken of his footwear in the course of the investigation of the offence by the police.

(4) Where a person mentioned in paragraph (*a*) of subsection (3) above has already had an impression taken of his footwear in the course of the investigation of the offence by the police, that fact shall be disregarded for the purposes of that subsection if the impression of his footwear taken previously is—

(*a*) incomplete; or

(*b*) is not of sufficient quality to allow satisfactory analysis, comparison or matching (whether in the case in question or generally).

(5) If an impression of a person's footwear is taken at a police station, whether with or without the appropriate consent—

(*a*) before it is taken, an officer shall inform him that it may be the subject of a speculative search; and

(*b*) the fact that the person has been informed of this possibility shall be recorded as soon as is practicable after the impression has been taken, and if he is detained at a police station, the record shall be made on his custody record.

(6) In a case where, by virtue of subsection (3) above, an impression of a person's footwear is taken without the appropriate consent—

(*a*) he shall be told the reason before it is taken; and

(*b*) the reason shall be recorded on his custody record as soon as is practicable after the impression is taken.

(7) The power to take an impression of the footwear of a person detained at a police station without the appropriate consent shall be exercisable by any constable.

(8) Nothing in this section applies to any person—

(*a*) arrested or detained under the terrorism provisions;

(*b*) arrested under an extradition arrest power.

[Police and Criminal Evidence Act 1984, s 61A as inserted by the Serious Organised Crime and Police Act 2005, s 118.]

1–2772   62. Intimate samples.   (1) Subject to section 63B below, an intimate sample[1] may be taken from a person in police detention only—

(*a*) if a police officer of at least the rank of inspector authorises it to be taken; and

(*b*) if the appropriate consent[1] is given.

(1A) An intimate sample may be taken from a person who is not in police detention but from whom, in the course of the investigation of an offence two or more non-intimate samples suitable for the same means of analysis have been taken which have proved insufficient—

(*a*) if a police officer of at least the rank of inspector authorises it to be taken; and

(*b*) if the appropriate consent is given.

(2) An officer may only give an authorisation under subsection (1) or (1A) above if he has reasonable grounds—

(*a*) for suspecting the involvement of the person from whom the sample is to be taken in a recordable offence; and

(*b*) for believing that the sample will tend to confirm or disprove his involvement.

(3) An officer may give an authorisation under subsection (1) or (1A) above orally or in writing but, if he gives it orally, he shall confirm it in writing as soon as is practicable.

(4) The appropriate consent must be given in writing.

(5) Where—

(*a*) an authorisation has been given; and

(*b*) it is proposed that an intimate sample shall be taken in pursuance of the authorisation,

an officer shall inform the person from whom the sample is to be taken—

(i) of the giving of the authorisation; and

(ii) of the grounds for giving it.

(6) The duty imposed by subsection (5)(ii) above includes a duty to state the nature of the offence in which it is suspected that the person from whom the sample is to be taken has been involved.

(7) If an intimate sample is taken from a person—

(*a*) the authorisation by virtue of which it was taken;

(b) the grounds for giving the authorisation; and
(c) the fact that the appropriate consent was given,

shall be recorded as soon as is practicable after the sample is taken.

(7A) If an intimate sample is taken from a person at a police station—

(a) before the sample is taken, an officer shall inform him that it may be the subject of a speculative search; and
(b) the fact that the person has been informed of this possibility shall be recorded as soon as practicable after the sample has been taken.

(8) If an intimate sample is taken from a person detained at a police station, the matters required to be recorded by subsection (7) or (7A) above shall be recorded in his custody record[2].

(9) In the case of an intimate sample which is a dental impression, the sample may be taken from a person only by a registered dentist.

(9A) In the case of any other form of intimate sample, except in the case of a sample of urine, the sample may be taken from a person only by—

(a) a registered medical practitioner; or
(b) a registered health care professional.

(10) Where the appropriate consent to the taking of an intimate sample from a person was refused without good cause, in any proceedings against that person for an offence—

(a) the court, in determining—

(i) whether to commit that person for trial; or
(ii) whether there is a case to answer; and

(aa) a judge, in deciding whether to grant an application made by the accused under—

(i) section 6 of the Criminal Justice Act 1987 (application for dismissal of charge of serious fraud in respect of which notice of transfer has been given under section 4 of that Act); or
(ii) paragraph 5 of Schedule 6 to the Criminal Justice Act 1991 (application for dismissal of charge of violent or sexual offence involving child in respect of which notice of transfer has been given under section 53 of that Act); and

(b) the court or jury, in determining whether that person is guilty of the offence charged,

may draw such inferences from the refusal as appear proper.

(11) Nothing in this section applies to the taking of a specimen for the purposes of any of the provisions of sections 4 to 11 of the Road Traffic Act 1988[3] or of sections 26 to 38 of the Transport and Works Act 1992.

(12) Nothing in this section applies to a person arrested or detained under the terrorism provisions; and subsection (1A) shall not apply where the non-intimate samples mentioned in that subsection were taken under paragraph 10 of Schedule 8 to the Terrorism Act 2000.[4]

[Police and Criminal Evidence Act 1984, s 62, as amended by the Road Traffic (Consequential Provisions) Act 1988, Sch 3, the Criminal Justice and Public Order Act 1994, s 54, and Schs 9, 10 and 11, the Criminal Justice and Court Services Act 2000, Sch 7, the Terrorism Act 2000, Sch 15, the Criminal Justice and Police Act 2001, s 80 and the Police Reform Act 2002, ss 53 and 54.]

---

1. "Intimate sample" and "appropriate consent" are defined by s 65 post. The Code of Practice for the Identification of Persons by Police Officers (Code of Practice D in PART II: STATUTORY INSTRUMENTS ON EVIDENCE, post), paras 6.1 to 6.12 makes detailed provision for the taking of samples.

Where an intimate sample is lawfully obtained under s 62 in the course of one investigation, the results of the analysis of the sample are admissible in proceedings resulting from a separate investigation into a different offence (*R v Kelt* [1994] 2 All ER 780, [1994] 1 WLR 765).

2. Code of Practice for the Detention, Treatment and Questioning of Persons by Police Officers (Code of Practice C in PART II: STATUTORY INSTRUMENTS ON EVIDENCE, post), paras 2.1A to 2.7 makes provision for custody records.

3. These are the driving with excess alcohol provisions.

4. Sub-section in force as from 19 February 2001 except in relation to a person detained prior to that date.

1–2773 63. Other samples. (1) Except as provided by this section, a non-intimate sample[1] may not be taken from a person without the appropriate consent[1].

(2) Consent to the taking of a non-intimate sample must be given in writing.

(2A) A non-intimate sample may be taken from a person without the appropriate consent if two conditions are satisfied.

(2B) The first is that the person is in police detention in consequence of his arrest for a recordable offence.

(2C) The second is that—

(a) he has not had a non-intimate sample of the same type and from the same part of the body taken in the course of the investigation of the offence by the police, or
(b) he has had such a sample taken but it proved insufficient.

(3) A non-intimate sample may be taken from a person without the appropriate consent if—

(a) he is being held in custody by the police on the authority of a court; and
(b) an officer of at least the rank of inspector authorises it to be taken without the appropriate consent.

(3A) A non-intimate sample may be taken from a person (whether or not he is in police detention or held in custody by the police on the authority of a court) without the appropriate consent if—

(*a*) he has been charged with a recordable offence or informed that he will be reported for such an offence; and

(*b*) either he has not had a non-intimate sample taken from him in the course of the investigation of the offence by the police or he has had a non-intimate sample taken from him but either it was not suitable for the same means of analysis or, though so suitable, the sample proved insufficient.

(3B) A non-intimate sample may be taken from a person without the appropriate consent if he has been convicted of a recordable offence.

(3C) A non-intimate sample may also be taken from a person without the appropriate consent if he is a person to whom section 2 of the Criminal Evidence (Amendment) Act 1997 applies (persons detained following acquittal on grounds of insanity or finding of unfitness to plead).

(4) An officer may only give an authorisation under subsection (3) above if he has reasonable grounds—

(*a*) for suspecting the involvement of the person from whom the sample is to be taken in a recordable offence; and

(*b*) for believing that the sample will tend to confirm or disprove his involvement.

(5) An officer may give an authorisation under subsection (3) above orally or in writing but, if he gives it orally, he shall confirm it in writing as soon as is practicable.

(5A) An officer shall not give an authorisation under subsection (3) above for the taking from any person of a non-intimate sample consisting of a skin impression if—

(*a*) a skin impression of the same part of the body has already been taken from that person in the course of the investigation of the offence; and

(*b*) the impression previously taken is not one that has proved insufficient.

(6) Where—

(*a*) an authorisation has been given; and

(*b*) it is proposed that a non-intimate sample shall be taken in pursuance of the authorisation,

an officer shall inform the person from whom the sample is to be taken—

(i) of the giving of the authorisation; and

(ii) of the grounds for giving it.

(7) The duty imposed by subsection (6)(ii) above includes a duty to state the nature of the offence in which it is suspected that the person from whom the sample is to be taken has been involved.

(8) If a non-intimate sample is taken from a person by virtue of subsection (3) above—

(*a*) the authorisation by virtue of which it was taken; and

(*b*) the grounds for giving the authorisation,

shall be recorded as soon as is practicable after the sample is taken.

(8A) In a case where by virtue of subsection (2A), (3A), (3B) or (3C) above a sample is taken from a person without the appropriate consent—

(*a*) he shall be told the reason before the sample is taken; and

(*b*) the reason shall be recorded as soon as practicable after the sample is taken.

(8B) If a non-intimate sample is taken from a person at a police station, whether with or without the appropriate consent—

(*a*) before the sample is taken, an officer shall inform him that it may be the subject of a speculative search; and

(*b*) the fact that the person has been informed of this possibility shall be recorded as soon as practicable after the sample has been taken.

(9) If a non-intimate sample is taken from a person detained at a police station, the matters required to be recorded by subsection (8) or (8A) or (8B) above shall be recorded in his custody record[2].

(9ZA) The power to take a non-intimate sample from a person without the appropriate consent shall be exercisable by any constable.

(9A) Where a non-intimate sample consisting of a skin impression is taken electronically from a person, it must be taken only in such manner, and using such devices, as the Secretary of State has approved for the purpose of the electronic taking of such an impression.*

(10) Nothing in this section applies to a person arrested or detained under the terrorism provisions.[4]

(11) Nothing in this section applies to a person arrested under an extradition arrest power.[5]

[Police and Criminal Evidence Act 1984, s 63 as amended by the Criminal Justice and Public Order Act 1994, s 55 and Sch 10, the Criminal Evidence (Amendment) Act 1997, ss 1 and 2, the Criminal Justice and Police Act 2001, s 80, the Police Reform Act 2002, Sch 7 and the Criminal Justice and Police Act 2001, s 80(1), the Terrorism Act 2000, Sch 15 and the Extradition Act 2003, s 169.]

---

*Sub-section reproduced as prospectively inserted by the Criminal Justice and Police Act 2001, s 80(4).

1. "Non-intimate sample" and "appropriate consent" are defined in s 65 below. The Code of Practice for the

Identification of Persons by Police Officers (Code of Practice D in PART II: STATUTORY INSTRUMENTS ON EVIDENCE, post) paras 6.1 to 6.12 makes detailed provision for the taking of samples.

2. The Code of Practice for the Detention, Treatment and Questioning of Persons by Police Officers (Code of Practice C in PART II: STATUTORY INSTRUMENTS ON EVIDENCE, post) paras 2.1A to 2.7 makes provision for custody records.

3. See this PART, post.

4. Sub-section in force as from 19 February 2001 except in relation to a person detained prior to that date.

5. Subsection (11) does not apply in relation to extradition requests received or extraditions made on or before 31 December 2003.

1–2774   63A. Fingerprints and samples: supplementary provisions. (1) Where a person has been arrested on suspicion of being involved in a recordable offence or has been charged with such an offence or has been informed that he will be reported for such an offence, fingerprints, impressions of footwear or samples or the information derived from samples taken under any power conferred by this Part of this Act from the person may be checked against—

(*a*) other fingerprints, impressions of footwear or samples to which the person seeking to check has access and which are held by or on behalf of any one or more relevant law-enforcement authorities or which are held in connection with or as a result of an investigation of an offence;

(*b*) information derived from other samples if the information is contained in records to which the person seeking to check has access and which are held as mentioned in paragraph (*a*) above.*

(1A) In subsection (1)* above "relevant law-enforcement authority" means—

(*a*) a police force;

(*b*) the Serious Organised Crime Agency;

(*c*) repealedrepealed;

(*d*) a public authority (not falling within paragraphs (*a*) to (*c*)) with functions in any part of the British Islands which consist of or include the investigation of crimes or the charging of offenders;

(*e*) any person with functions in any country or territory outside the United Kingdom which—

(i) correspond to those of a police force; or

(ii) otherwise consist of or include the investigation of conduct contrary to the law of that country or territory, or the apprehension of persons guilty of such conduct;

(*f*) any person with functions under any international agreement which consist of or include the investigation of conduct which is—

(i) unlawful under the law of one or more places,

(ii) prohibited by such an agreement, or

(iii) contrary to international law,

or the apprehension of persons guilty of such conduct.

(1B) The reference in subsection (1A) above to a police force is a reference to any of the following—

(*a*) any police force maintained under section 2 of the Police Act 1996 (c 16) (police forces in England and Wales outside London);

(*b*) the metropolitan police force;

(*c*) the City of London police force;

(*d*) any police force maintained under or by virtue of section 1 of the Police (Scotland) Act 1967 (c 77);

(*e*) the Police Service of Northern Ireland;

(*f*) the Police Service of Northern Ireland Reserve;

(*g*) the Ministry of Defence Police;

(*h*) the Royal Navy Regulating Branch;

(*i*) the Royal Military Police;

(*j*) the Royal Air Force Police;

(*k*) the Royal Marines Police;

(*l*) the British Transport Police;

(*m*) the States of Jersey Police Force;

(*n*) the salaried police force of the Island of Guernsey;

(*o*) the Isle of Man Constabulary.

(1C) Where—

(*a*) fingerprints, impressions of footwear or samples have been taken from any person in connection with the investigation of an offence but otherwise than in circumstances to which subsection (1) above applies, and

(*b*) that person has given his consent in writing to the use in a speculative search of the fingerprints, of the impressions of footwear or of the samples and of information derived from them,

the fingerprints or impressions of footwear or, as the case may be, those samples and that information may be checked against any of the fingerprints, impressions of footwear, samples or information mentioned in paragraph (*a*) or (*b*) of that subsection.

(1D) A consent given for the purposes of subsection (1C) above shall not be capable of being withdrawn.

(2) Where a sample of hair other than pubic hair is to be taken the sample may be taken either by

cutting hairs or by plucking hairs with their roots so long as no more are plucked than the person taking the sample reasonably considers to be necessary for a sufficient sample.

(3) Where any power to take a sample is exercisable in relation to a person the sample may be taken in a prison or other institution to which the Prison Act 1952 applies.

(3A) Where—

(a) the power to take a non-intimate sample under section 63(3B) above is exercisable in relation to any person who is detained under Part III of the Mental Health Act 1983 in pursuance of—

(i) a hospital order or interim hospital order made following his conviction for the recordable offence in question, or

(ii) a transfer direction given at a time when he was detained in pursuance of any sentence or order imposed following that conviction, or

(b) the power to take a non-intimate sample under section 63(3C) above is exercisable in relation to any person,

the sample may be taken in the hospital in which he is detained under that Part of that Act.

Expressions used in this subsection and in the Mental Health Act 1983 have the same meaning as in that Act.

(3B) Where the power to take a non-intimate sample under section 63(3B) above is exercisable in relation to a person detained in pursuance of directions of the Secretary of State under section 92 of the Powers of Criminal Courts (Sentencing) Act 2000 the sample may be taken at the place where he is so detained.

(4) Any constable may, within the allowed period, require a person who is neither in police detention nor held in custody by the police on the authority of a court to attend a police station in order to have a sample taken where—

(a) the person has been charged with a recordable offence or informed that he will be reported for such an offence and either he has not had a sample taken from him in the course of the investigation of the offence by the police or he has had a sample so taken from him but either it was not suitable for the same means of analysis or, though so suitable, the sample proved insufficient; or

(b) the person has been convicted of a recordable offence and either he has not had a sample taken from him since the conviction or he has had a sample taken from him (before or after his conviction) but either it was not suitable for the same means of analysis or, though so suitable, the sample proved insufficient.

(5) The period allowed for requiring a person to attend a police station for the purpose specified in subsection (4) above is—

(a) in the case of a person falling within paragraph[1], one month beginning with the date of the charge or of his being informed as mentioned in that paragraph or one month beginning with the date on which the appropriate officer is informed of the fact that the sample is not suitable for the same means of analysis or has proved insufficient, as the case may be;

(b) in the case of a person falling within paragraph[2], one month beginning with the date of the conviction or one month beginning with the date on which the appropriate officer is informed of the fact that the sample is not suitable for the same means of analysis or has proved insufficient, as the case may be.

(6) A requirement under subsection (4) above—

(a) shall give the person at least 7 days within which he must so attend; and

(b) may direct him to attend at a specified time of day or between specified times of day.

(7) Any constable may arrest without a warrant a person who has failed to comply with a requirement under subsection (4) above.

(8) In this section "the appropriate officer" is—

(a) in the case of a person falling within subsection (4)(a), the officer investigating the offence with which that person has been charged or as to which he was informed that he would be reported;

(b) in the case of a person falling within subsection (4)(b), the officer in charge of the police station from which the investigation of the offence of which he was convicted was conducted.*

[Police and Criminal Evidence Act 1984, s 63A, as inserted by the Criminal Justice and Public Order Act 1994, s 56 and amended by the Criminal Procedure and Investigations Act 1996, s 64, the Criminal Evidence (Amendment) Act 1997, ss 3 and 4, the Powers of Criminal Courts (Sentencing) Act 2000, Sch 9 and the Criminal Justice and Police Act 2001, s 81 and the Serious Organised Crime and Police Act 2005, s 118.]

---

*Sub-s (1ZA) inserted and sub-s (1A) amended by the **Serious Organised Crime and Police Act 2005, s 117** from a date to be appointed.

1–2774A 63B. Testing for presence of Class A drugs. (1) A sample of urine or a non-intimate sample may be taken from a person in police detention for the purpose of ascertaining whether he has any specified Class A drug in his body if—

(a) either the arrest condition or the charge condition is met;

(b) both the age condition and the request condition are met; and

(c)   the notification condition is met in relation to the arrest condition, the charge condition or the age condition (as the case may be).

(1A) The arrest condition is that the person concerned has been arrested for an offence but has not been charged with that offence and either—

(a)   the offence is a trigger offence; or
(b)   a police officer of at least the rank of inspector has reasonable grounds for suspecting that the misuse by that person of a specified Class A drug caused or contributed to the offence and has authorised the sample to be taken.

(2)   The charge condition is either—

(a)   that the person concerned has been charged with a trigger offence; or
(b)   that the person concerned has been charged with an offence and a police officer of at least the rank of inspector, who has reasonable grounds for suspecting that the misuse by that person of any specified Class A drug caused or contributed to the offence, has authorised the sample to be taken.

(3)   The age condition is—

(a)   if the arrest condition is met, that the person concerned has attained the age of 18;

(b)   if the charge condition is met, that he has attained the age of 14.4)The request condition is that a police officer has requested the person concerned to give the sample.

(4A) The notification condition is that—

(a)   the relevant chief officer has been notified by the Secretary of State that appropriate arrangements have been made for the police area as a whole, or for the particular police station, in which the person is in police detention, and
(b)   the notice has not been withdrawn.

(4B) For the purposes of subsection (4A) above, appropriate arrangements are arrangements for the taking of samples under this section from whichever of the following is specified in the notification—

(a)   persons in respect of whom the arrest condition is met;
(b)   persons in respect of whom the charge condition is met;
(c)   persons who have not attained the age of 18.

(5)   Before requesting the person concerned to give a sample, an officer must—

(a)   warn him that if, when so requested, he fails without good cause to do so he may be liable to prosecution, and
(b)   in a case within subsection (1A)(b) or (2)(b) above, inform him of the giving of the authorisation and of the grounds in question.

(5A) In the case of a person who has not attained the age of 17—

(a)   the making of the request under subsection (4) above;
(b)   the giving of the warning and (where applicable) the information under subsection (5) above; and
(c)   the taking of the sample,

may not take place except in the presence of an appropriate adult.

(5B) If a sample is taken under this section from a person in respect of whom the arrest condition is met no other sample may be taken from him under this section during the same continuous period of detention but—

(a)   if the charge condition is also met in respect of him at any time during that period, the sample must be treated as a sample taken by virtue of the fact that the charge condition is met;
(b)   the fact that the sample is to be so treated must be recorded in the person's custody record.

(5C) Despite subsection (1)(a) above, a sample may be taken from a person under this section if—

(a)   he was arrested for an offence (the first offence),
(b)   the arrest condition is met but the charge condition is not met,
(c)   before a sample is taken by virtue of subsection (1) above he would (but for his arrest as mentioned in paragraph (d) below) be required to be released from police detention,
(d)   he continues to be in police detention by virtue of his having been arrested for an offence not falling within subsection (1A) above, and
(e)   the sample is taken before the end of the period of 24 hours starting with the time when his detention by virtue of his arrest for the first offence began.

(5D) A sample must not be taken from a person under this section if he is detained in a police station unless he has been brought before the custody officer.

(6)   A sample may be taken under this section only by a person prescribed by regulations[1] made by the Secretary of State by statutory instrument.

No regulations shall be made under this subsection unless a draft has been laid before, and approved by resolution of, each House of Parliament.

(6A) The Secretary of State may by order made by statutory instrument amend—

(a) paragraph (a) of subsection (3) above, by substituting for the age for the time being specified a different age specified in the order, or different ages so specified for different police areas so specified;

(b) paragraph (b) of that subsection, by substituting for the age for the time being specified a different age specified in the order.

(6B) A statutory instrument containing an order under subsection (6A) above shall not be made unless a draft of the instrument has been laid before, and approved by a resolution of, each House of Parliament.

(7) Information obtained from a sample taken under this section may be disclosed—

(a) for the purpose of informing any decision about granting bail in criminal proceedings (within the meaning of the Bail Act 1976) to the person concerned;

(aa) for the purpose of informing any decision about the giving of a conditional caution under Part 3 of the Criminal Justice Act 2003 to the person concerned;

(b) where the person concerned is in police detention or is remanded in or committed to custody by an order of a court or has been granted such bail, for the purpose of informing any decision about his supervision;

(c) where the person concerned is convicted of an offence, for the purpose of informing any decision about the appropriate sentence to be passed by a court and any decision about his supervision or release;

(ca) for the purpose of an assessment which the person concerned is required to attend by virtue of section 9(2) or 10(2) of the Drugs Act 2005;

(cb) for the purpose of proceedings against the person concerned for an offence under section 12(3) or 14(3) of that Act;

(d) for the purpose of ensuring that appropriate advice and treatment is made available to the person concerned.

(8) A person who fails without good cause to give any sample which may be taken from him under this section shall be guilty of an offence.

(9) *Repealed.*

(10) In this section—

"appropriate adult", in relation to a person who has not attained the age of 17, means—

(a) his parent or guardian or, if he is in the care of a local authority or voluntary organisation, a person representing that authority or organisation; or

(b) a social worker of a local authority; or

(c) if no person falling within paragraph (a) or (b) is available, any responsible person aged 18 or over who is not a police officer or a person employed by the police;

"relevant chief officer" means—

(a) in relation to a police area, the chief officer of police of the police force for that police area; or

(b) in relation to a police station, the chief officer of police of the police force for the police area in which the police station is situated.

[Police and Criminal Evidence Act 1984, s 63B as inserted by the Criminal Justice and Courts Services Act 2000, s 57, the Criminal Justice Act 2003, s 5, the Children Act 2004, Sch 5 and the Drugs Act 2005, s 7 and Schs 1 and 2.]

---

1. The Police and Criminal Evidence Act 1984 (Drug Testing of Persons in Police Detention) (Prescribed Persons) Regulations 2001, SI 2001/2645 have been made.

1–2774B   63C. Testing for presence of Class A drugs: supplementary. (1) A person guilty of an offence under section 63B above shall be liable on summary conviction to imprisonment for a term not exceeding three months*, or to a fine not exceeding level 4 on the standard scale, or to both.

(2) A police officer may give an authorisation under section 63B above orally or in writing but, if he gives it orally, he shall confirm it in writing as soon as is practicable.

(3) If a sample is taken under section 63B above by virtue of an authorisation, the authorisation and the grounds for the suspicion shall be recorded as soon as is practicable after the sample is taken.

(4) If the sample is taken from a person detained at a police station, the matters required to be recorded by subsection (3) above shall be recorded in his custody record.

(5) Subsections (11) and (12) of section 62 above apply for the purposes of section 63B above as they do for the purposes of that section; and section 63B above does not prejudice the generality of sections 62 and 63 above.

(6) In section 63B above—

"Class A drug" and "misuse" have the same meanings as in the Misuse of Drugs Act 1971;

"specified" (in relation to a Class A drug) and "trigger offence" have the same meanings as in Part III of the Criminal Justice and Court Services Act 2000.**

[Police and Criminal Evidence Act 1984, s 63C as inserted by the Criminal Justice and Court Services Act 2000, s 57.]

---

*"51 weeks" substituted by the **Criminal Justice Act 2003, Sch 26, from a date to be appointed.**
In force in relation to the police districts of: **Nottinghamshire, Staffordshire and the Metropolitan police

district (SI 2001/2232); Bedfordshire, Devon and Cornwall, Lancashire, Merseyside, South Yorkshire and North Wales (SI 2002/1149); Avon and Somerset, Greater Manchester, Thames Valley and West Yorkshire (SI 2002/1862); Cleveland and Humber (SI 2003/709); Cambridgeshire, Leicestershire, Northumbria and West Midlands (SI 2004/780); and Gwent, Northamptonshire and South Wales (SI 2005/596).

1–2775   64. Destruction of fingerprints[1] and samples[2]. (1A) Where—

  (a) fingerprints, impressions of footwear or samples are taken from a person in connection with the investigation of an offence, and

  (b) subsection (3) below does not require them to be destroyed,

the fingerprints, impressions of footwear or samples may be retained after they have fulfilled the purposes for which they were taken but shall not be used by any person except for purposes related to the prevention or detection of crime, the investigation of an offence, the conduct of a prosecution or the identification of a deceased person or of the person from whom a body part came.

  (1B) In subsection (1A) above—

  (a) the reference to using a fingerprint or an impression of footwear includes a reference to allowing any check to be made against it under section 63A(1) or (1C) above and to disclosing it to any person;

  (b) the reference to using a sample includes a reference to allowing any check to be made under section 63A(1) or (1C) above against it or against information derived from it and to disclosing it or any such information to any person;

  (c) the reference to crime includes a reference to any conduct which—

    (i) constitutes one or more criminal offences (whether under the law of a part of the United Kingdom or of a country or territory outside the United Kingdom); or

    (ii) is, or corresponds to, any conduct which, if it all took place in any one part of the United Kingdom, would constitute one or more criminal offences;

  and

  (d) the references to an investigation and to a prosecution include references, respectively, to any investigation outside the United Kingdom of any crime or suspected crime and to a prosecution brought in respect of any crime in a country or territory outside the United Kingdom.★

  (2) *Repealed.*

  (3) If—

  (a) fingerprints, impressions of footwear or samples are taken from a person in connection with the investigation of an offence; and

  (b) that person is not suspected of having committed the offence,

they must, except as provided in the following provisions of this section, be destroyed as soon as they have fulfilled the purpose for which they were taken[3].

  (3AA) Samples, fingerprints and impressions of footwear are not required to be destroyed under subsection (3) above if—

  (a) they were taken for the purposes of the investigation of an offence of which a person has been convicted; and

  (b) a sample, fingerprint, (or as the case may be) an impression of footwear was also taken from the convicted person for the purposes of that investigation.

  (3AB) Subject to subsection (3AC) below, where a person is entitled under subsection (3) above to the destruction of any fingerprint, impression of footwear or sample taken from him (or would be but for subsection (3AA) above), neither the fingerprint, nor the impression of footwear, nor the sample, nor any information derived from the sample, shall be used—

  (a) in evidence against the person who is or would be entitled to the destruction of that fingerprint, impression of footwear or sample; or

  (b) for the purposes of the investigation of any offence;

and subsection (1B) above applies for the purposes of this subsection as it applies for the purposes of subsection (1A) above.

  (3AC) Where a person from whom a fingerprint, impression of footwear or sample has been taken consents in writing to its retention—

  (a) that sample need not be destroyed under subsection (3) above;

  (b) subsection (3AB) above shall not restrict the use that may be made of the fingerprint or sample or, in the case of a sample, of any information derived from it; and

  (c) that consent shall be treated as comprising a consent for the purposes of section 63A(1C) above;

and a consent given for the purpose of this subsection shall not be capable of being withdrawn.★

  (3AD) For the purposes of subsection (3AC) above it shall be immaterial whether the consent is given at, before or after the time when the entitlement to the destruction of the fingerprint, impression of footwear or sample arises.

  (4) *Repealed.*

  (5) If fingerprints or impressions of footwear are destroyed—

  (a) any copies of the fingerprints or impressions of footwear shall also be destroyed; and (*b*) any chief officer of police controlling access to computer data relating to the fingerprints or impressions of footwear shall make access to the data impossible, as soon as it is practicable to do so.

(6) A person who asks to be allowed to witness the destruction of his fingerprints or impressions of footwear or copies of them shall have a right to witness it.

(6A) If—

(*a*) subsection (5)(*b*) above falls to be complied with; and

(*b*) the person to whose fingerprints or impressions of footwear the data relate asks for a certificate that it has been complied with,

such a certificate shall be issued to him, not later than the end of the period of three months beginning with the day on which he asks for it, by the responsible chief officer of police or a person authorised by him or on his behalf for the purposes of this section.

(6B) In this section—

"the responsible chief officer of police" means the chief officer of police in whose police area the computer data were put on to the computer.

(7) Nothing in this section—

(*a*) affects any power conferred by paragraph 18(2) of Schedule 2 to the Immigration Act 1971 or section 20 of the Immigration and Asylum Act 1999 (c 33) (disclosure of police information to the Secretary of State for use for immigration purposes); or

(*b*) applies to a person arrested or detained under the terrorism provisions.

[Police and Criminal Evidence Act 1984, s 64 as amended by the Criminal Justice Act 1988, s 148, the Criminal Justice and Public Order Act 1994, s 57, the Police Act 1996, Sch 7 and the Criminal Justice and Police Act 2001, ss 82, 137 and the Serious Organised Crime and Police Act 2005, s 118.]

---

*. Amended by the Serious Organised Crime and Police Act 2005, Sch 7 from a date to be appointed.

1. Section 64 was substantially amended by the Criminal Justice and Police Act 2001, s 82. The purpose was to remove the requirement of destruction and to provide that fingerprints and samples lawfully taken on suspicion of involvement in an offence or under the Terrorism Act could be used in the investigation of other offences. As to the use of fingerprints and samples that should have been destroyed before the commencement of s 82, see fn 3 infra and the Criminal Justice and Police Act 2001, s 82(6), this PART, post.

If the retention of fingerprints and DNA samples under s 64(1A) of the 1984 Act constitutes an interference with respect for private life under art 8(1) of the ECHR, the interference is modest and is objectively justified under art 8(2) as being necessary for the prevention of crime and the protection of the rights of others; nor does an issue of discrimination contrary to art 14 arise as between those who have not been required to provide fingerprints and samples and those who have: *Regina (S) v Chief Constable of the South Yorkshire Police, Regina (Marper) v Chief Constable of the South Yorkshire Police* [2004] UKHL 39, [2004] 4 ALL ER 193, [2004] 1 WLR 2196.

2. See also the Code of Practice for the Identification of Persons by Police Officers (Code of Practice D in PART II: STATUTORY INSTRUMENTS ON EVIDENCE, post) as regards fingerprints.

3. There was a requirement under the former s 64(1), for which subsections (1A) and (1B) were substituted by the Criminal Justice and Police Act 2001, s 82(2), to destroy any fingerprints or samples taken from a person in connection with the investigation of an offence if he was subsequently cleared of that offence, and the former s 64(3B), for which provision together with the former (3A) s 82(2) substituted subsections (3AA)–(3AD), prohibited the use of information derived from any such fingerprint or sample in evidence against that person or for the purposes of any investigation of an offence. However, it was held in *A-G's Reference (No 3 of 1999)* [2001] AC 91, [2001] 2 WLR 56 that this prohibition did not make evidence obtained as a result of failure to comply with it inadmissible, but left it to the discretion of the court whether or not to exclude the evidence under s 78 of PACE.

As to the retention of fingerprints and samples that should have been destroyed prior to the coming into effect on 11 May 2001 of the changes made to s 64 by the Criminal Justice and Police Act 2001, and as to the use information derived from such samples, see the Criminal Justice and Police Act, s 82(6), this PART, post.

1–2775A   64A. Photographing of suspects etc.   (1) A person who is detained at a police station may be photographed—

(*a*) with the appropriate consent; or

(*b*) if the appropriate consent is withheld or it is not practicable to obtain it, without it.

(1A) A person falling within subsection (1B) below may, on the occasion of the relevant event referred to in subsection (1B), be photographed elsewhere than at a police station—

(*a*) with the appropriate consent; or

(*b*) if the appropriate consent is withheld or it is not practicable to obtain it, without it.

(1B) A person falls within this subsection if he has been—

(*a*) arrested by a constable for an offence;

(*b*) taken into custody by a constable after being arrested for an offence by a person other than a constable;

(*c*) made subject to a requirement to wait with a community support officer under paragraph 2(3) or (3B) of Schedule 4 to the Police Reform Act 2002 ("the 2002 Act");

(*d*) given a penalty notice by a constable in uniform under Chapter 1 of Part 1 of the Criminal Justice and Police Act 2001, a penalty notice by a constable under section 444A of the Education Act 1996, or a fixed penalty notice by a constable in uniform under section 54 of the Road Traffic Offenders Act 1988;

(*e*) given a notice in relation to a relevant fixed penalty offence (within the meaning of paragraph 1 of Schedule 4 to the 2002 Act) by a community support officer by virtue of a designation applying that paragraph to him; or

(f)   given a notice in relation to a relevant fixed penalty offence (within the meaning of paragraph 1 of Schedule 5 to the 2002 Act) by an accredited person by virtue of accreditation specifying that that paragraph applies to him.

(2) A person proposing to take a photograph of any person under this section—

(a)   may, for the purpose of doing so, require the removal of any item or substance worn on or over the whole or any part of the head or face of the person to be photographed; and

(b)   if the requirement is not complied with, may remove the item or substance himself.

(3) Where a photograph may be taken under this section, the only persons entitled to take the photograph are constables.

(4) A photograph taken under this section—

(a)   may be used by, or disclosed to, any person for any purpose related to the prevention or detection of crime, the investigation of an offence or the conduct of a prosecution or to the enforcement of a sentence; and

(b)   after being so used or disclosed, may be retained but may not be used or disclosed except for a purpose so related.

(5) In subsection (4)—

(a)   the reference to crime includes a reference to any conduct which—

     (i)   constitutes one or more criminal offences (whether under the law of a part of the United Kingdom or of a country or territory outside the United Kingdom); or

     (ii)   is, or corresponds to, any conduct which, if it all took place in any one part of the United Kingdom, would constitute one or more criminal offences;

     and

(b)   the references to an investigation and to a prosecution include references, respectively, to any investigation outside the United Kingdom of any crime or suspected crime and to a prosecution brought in respect of any crime in a country or territory outside the United Kingdom; and

(c)   "sentence" includes any order made by a court in England and Wales when dealing with an offender in respect of his offence.

(6) References in this section to taking a photograph include references to using any process by means of which a visual image may be produced; and references to photographing a person shall be construed accordingly.

(6A) In this section, a "photograph" includes a moving image, and corresponding expressions shall be construed accordingly.

(7) Nothing in this section applies to a person arrested under an extradition arrest power.[1]

[Police and Criminal Evidence Act 1984, s 64A, as inserted by the Anti-terrorism, Crime and Security Act 2001, s 92 and amended by the Police Reform Act 2002, Sch 7 and the Extradition Act 2003, s 169 and the Serious Organised Crime and Police Act 2005, s 116.]

---

1. Subsection (7) does not apply in relation to extradition requests received or extraditions made on or before 31 December 2003.

1–2776   65. Part V—supplementary.   (1) In this Part of this Act—

"analysis", in relation to a skin impression, includes comparison and matching;

"appropriate consent" means—

(a)   in relation to a person who has attained the age of 17 years, the consent of that person;

(b)   in relation to a person who has not attained that age but has attained the age of 14 years, the consent of that person and his parent or guardian; and

(c)   in relation to a person who has not attained the age of 14 years, the consent of his parent or guardian[1];

"extradition arrest power" means any of the following—

(a)   a Part 1 warrant (within the meaning given by the Extradition Act 2003) in respect of which a certificate under section 2 of that Act has been issued;

(b)   section 5 of that Act;

(c)   a warrant issued under section 71 of that Act;

(d)   a provisional warrant (within the meaning given by that Act);

"fingerprints", in relation to any person, means a record (in any form and produced by any method) of the skin pattern and other physical characteristics or features of—

(a)   any of that person's fingers; or

(b)   either of his palms;

"intimate sample" means

(a)   a sample of blood, semen or any other tissue fluid, urine or pubic hair;

(b)   a dental impression;

(c)   a swab taken from any part of a person's genitals (including pubic hair) or from a person's body orifice other than the mouth;

"intimate search" means a search which consists of the physical examination of a person's body orifices[2] other than the mouth;

"non-intimate sample" means—

(a) a sample of hair other than pubic hair;
(b) a sample taken from a nail or from under a nail;
(c) a swab taken from any part of a person's body other than a part from which a swab taken would be an intimate sample;
(d) saliva;
(e) a skin impression;

"registered dentist" has the same meaning as in the Dentists Act 1984;

"registered health care professional" means a person (other than a medical practitioner) who is—

(a) a registered nurse; or
(b) a registered member of a health care profession which is designated for the purposes of this paragraph by an order[3] made by the Secretary of State;

"skin impression", in relation to any person, means any record (other than a fingerprint) which is a record (in any form and produced by any method) of the skin pattern and other physical characteristics or features of the whole or any part of his foot or of any other part of his body;

"speculative search", in relation to a person's fingerprints or samples, means such a check against other fingerprints or samples or against information derived from other samples as is referred to in section 63A(1) above;

"sufficient" and "insufficient", in relation to a sample, means (subject to subsection (2) below) sufficient or insufficient (in point of quantity or quality) for the purpose of enabling information to be produced by the means of analysis used or to be used in relation to the sample;

"the terrorism provisions" means section 41 of the Terrorism Act 2000, and any provision of Schedule 7 to that Act conferring a power of arrest or detention; and

"terrorism" has the meaning assigned to it by section 1 of that Act;

Repealed.

(1A) A health care profession is any profession mentioned in section 60(2) of the Health Act 1999 (c 8) other than the profession of practising medicine and the profession of nursing.

(1B) An order under subsection (1) shall be made by statutory instrument and shall be subject to annulment in pursuance of a resolution of either House of Parliament.

(2) References in this Part of this Act to a sample's proving insufficient include references to where, as a consequence of—

(a) the loss, destruction or contamination of the whole or any part of the sample,
(b) any damage to the whole or a part of the sample, or
(c) the use of the whole or a part of a sample for an analysis which produced no results or which produced results some or all of which must be regarded, in the circumstances, as unreliable,

the sample has become unavailable or insufficient for the purpose of enabling information, or information of a particular description, to be obtained by means of analysis of the sample.

[Police and Criminal Evidence Act 1984, s 65 as amended by the Drug Trafficking Offences Act 1986, s 32, the Criminal Justice Act 1988, Schs 15 and 16, the Prevention of Terrorism (Temporary Provisions) Act 1989, Sch 8, the Criminal Justice and Public Order Act 1994, ss 58 and 59, the Drug Trafficking Act 1994, Sch 1, the Terrorism Act 2000, s 125, the Criminal Justice and Police Act 2001, ss 78 and 80, the Police Reform Act 2002, s 54, the Proceeds of Crime Act 2002, Sch 12, the Extradition Act 2003, s 169 and the Serious Organised Crime and Police Act 2005, s 119.]

---

1. If he is in care, this means obtaining the consent of the local authority or voluntary organisation caring for him: s 118(1), post.
2. This definition requires that there should be some physical intrusion into a body orifice, some physical examination rather than mere visual examination or any attempt to cause the person to extrude what was contained in the body through one of its orifices; see *R v Hughes* [1994] 1 WLR 876, 99 Cr App Rep 160, CA, a decision in relation to a similar definition previously contained in s 118(1) of this Act before it was amended by the Criminal Justice and Public Order Act 1994, Sch 11.
3. The Registered Health Care Profession (Designation) Order 2003, SI 2003/2461 has been made which designates the profession of paramedics.

PART VI[1]
CODES OF PRACTICE—GENERAL

1–2787 **66. Codes of practice.** (1) The Secretary of State shall issue codes of practice[2] in connection with—

(a) the exercise by police officers of statutory powers—

(i) to search a person without first arresting him;
(ii) to search a vehicle without making an arrest; or
(iii) to arrest a person;

(b) the detention, treatment, questioning and identification of persons by police officers;
(c) searches of premises by police officers; and
(d) the seizure of property found by police officers on persons or premises.

(2) Codes shall (in particular) include provision in connection with the exercise by police officers of powers under section 63B above[3].

[Police and Criminal Evidence Act 1984, s 66, as amended by the Criminal Justice and Court Services Act 2000, s 57 and the Serious Organised Crime and Police Act 2005, s 110.]

---

1. Part VI contains ss 66 and 67.

2. Codes of Practice in relation to these matters have been issued and are printed post, in PART II: EVIDENCE – STATUTORY INSTRUMENTS ON EVIDENCE.

The Police and Criminal Evidence Act 1984 (Codes of Practice) Order 2005, SI 2005/3503 (draft codes laid before Parliament 8 November 2005) appointed 1 January 2006 as the date on which Codes A–G came into operation. Code E (tape recording of interviews with suspects) was made under s 60, ante. Code F (visual recording of interviews held by police officers at police stations) was made under s 60A, ante. The Police and Criminal Evidence act 1984 (Code of Practice C and Code of Practice H) Order 2006, SI 2006/1938 appointed 25 July 2006 as the date of which a revised Code C and new Code H (detention, treatment and questioning by police officers of persons arrested under section 41 of the Terrorism Act 2000) (draft codes laid before Parliament on 14 June 2006) came into operation. The Police and Criminal Evidence Act 1984 (Codes of Practice) (Revisions to Code A) Order 2006, SI 2006/2165 appointed 31 August 2006 as the date on which revisions to Code of Practice A laid in draft before Parliament on 10 August 2006 came into operation.

3. As to the police areas in which the testing of persons in police detention is in force, see note to s 63B, ante.

1-2788 **67. Codes of practice—supplementary.** (1)–(7C) *Provisions for the issue of codes of practice.*

(8) *Repealed.*

(9) Persons[1] other than police officers who are charged with the duty of investigating offences or charging offenders shall in the discharge of that duty have regard to any relevant provision of a code.

(9A) Persons on whom powers are conferred by—

(*a*) any designation under section 38 or 39 of the Police Reform Act 2002 (c 30) (police powers for police authority employees), or

(*b*) any accreditation under section 41 of that Act (accreditation under community safety accreditation schemes),

shall have regard to any relevant provision of a code in the exercise or performance of the powers and duties conferred or imposed on them by that designation or accreditation.

(10) A failure on the part—

(*a*) of a police officer to comply with any provision of a code;

(*b*) of any person other than a police officer who is charged with the duty of investigating offences or charging offenders to have regard to any relevant provision of a code in the discharge of that duty, or

(*c*) of a person designated under section 38 or 39 or accredited under section 41 of the Police Reform Act 2002 (c 30) to have regard to any relevant provision of a code in the exercise or performance of the powers and duties conferred or imposed on him by that designation or accreditation,

shall not of itself render him liable to any criminal or civil proceedings.

(11) In all criminal and civil proceedings any code shall be admissible in evidence; and if any provision of a code appears to the court or tribunal conducting the proceedings to be relevant to any question arising in the proceedings it shall be taken into account in determining that question.

(12) *Inclusion of courts-martial, etc.*

[Police and Criminal Evidence Act 1984, s 67 as amended by the Police and Magistrates' Courts Act 1994, s 37(1)(a), Police Act 1996, Sch 9, the Armed Forces Act 1996, Sch 1, the Criminal Justice and Police Act 2001, s 7, the Armed Forces Act 2001, Sch 7, the Police Reform Act 2002, Schs 7 and 8 and the Criminal Justice Act 2003, s 11 and Sch 37.]

---

1. It is a question of fact for the court to decide whether a person is charged with the duty of investigating offences (*Joy v Federation against Copyright Theft Ltd* [1993] Crim LR 588). A store detective may fall into this category of person (*R v Bayliss* (1993) 157 JP 1062, 98 Cr App Rep 235), but a head teacher does not *(DPP v G (duty to investigate)* (1997) Times, 24 November).

PART VII[1]

DOCUMENTARY EVIDENCE IN CRIMINAL PROCEEDINGS

1-2789

---

1. Part VII contains ss 68–72. For this Part see PART II: EVIDENCE, post.

PART VIII[1]

EVIDENCE IN CRIMINAL PROCEEDINGS—GENERAL

---

1. Part VIII contains ss 73–82 For this Part, see PART II: EVIDENCE, post.

PART XI[1]
MISCELLANEOUS AND SUPPLEMENTARY

1–2790   **113–114.** *Application of Act to Armed Forces[2] and to Customs and Excise[2].*

---

1. Part XI contains ss 113–122.
2. The Act is applied to the Armed Forces by SI 2006/2015; the following Codes of Practice (laid in draft before Parliament on 5 September 2003) under Pt VI were brought into force for the Armed Forces by the Police and Criminal Evidence Act 1984 (Codes of Practice) (Armed Forces) Order 2003, SI 2003/2315 with effect from 30 September 2003:
    (*a*)   Code of Practice A – the exercise by the Service Police of statutory powers of stop and search;
    (*b*)   Code of Practice B – the exercise by the Service Police of statutory powers for the entry and search of premises and the seizure of property found on persons and premises by the Service Police; and
    (*c*)   the Commanding Officer's Code of Practice.
The Police and Criminal Evidence Act 1984 (Application to Customs and Excise) Order 1985, SI 1985/1800, amended by SI 1987/439 and SI 1995/3217 as amended, is printed in this PART: STATUTORY INSTRUMENTS AND PRACTICE DIRECTIONS ON PROCEDURE, post.

1–2790A   **114A.** *Power to apply Act to officers of the Secretary of State etc*[1]

---

1. This section, which was inserted by the Criminal Justice and Police Act 2001, s 85, empowers the Secretary of State to direct by order that the provisions of this Act and of Sch 1 in so far as they relate to special procedure material shall apply, with such modifications as may be specified, to certain DTI investigations. See the Police and Criminal Evidence Act 1984 (Department of Trade and Industry Investigations) Order 2002, SI 2002/2326 amended by SI 2005/3389.

1–2791   **116. Meaning of "serious arrestable offence".**   *Repealed by the Serious Organised Crime and Police Act 2005, Sch 17.*

1–2792   **117. Power of constable to use reasonable force.**   Where any provision of this Act—

    (*a*)   confers a power on a constable; and
    (*b*)   does not provide that the power may only be exercised with the consent of some person, other than a police officer,

the officer may use reasonable force[1], if necessary, in the exercise of the power.
[Police and Criminal Evidence Act 1984, s 117.]

---

1. This section and s 17, ante, together allow a constable to use reasonable force, if necessary, to enter and search any premises for the purpose of arresting a person for an indictable offence. However, when exercising such power a constable is obliged to inform the occupier of the premises of the proper reason why entry is required, unless circumstances make it impossible, impracticable or undesirable to give the resaon: see *O'Loughlin v Chief Constable of Essex* [1998] 1 WLR 374.

1–2793   **118. General interpretation.**   (1) In this Act—

"British Transport Police Force" means the constables appointed under section 53 of the British Transport Commission Act 1949 (c xxix);
"designated police station" has the meaning assigned to it by section 35 above;
"document" means anything in which information of any description is recorded;
"item subject to legal privilege" has the meaning assigned to it by section 10 above;
"parent or guardian" means—

    (*a*)   in the case of a child or young person in the care of a local authority, that authority;
    (*b*)   *Repealed*;

"premises" has the meaning assigned to it by section 23 above;
"recordable offence" means any offence to which regulations under section 27 above apply;
"vessel" includes any ship, boat, raft or other apparatus constructed or adapted for floating on water.

   (2)   Subject to subsection (2A) a person is in police detention for the purposes of this Act if—

    (*a*)   he has been taken to a police station after being arrested for an offence or after being arrested under section 41 of the Terrorism Act 2000, or
    (*b*)   he is arrested at a police station after attending voluntarily at the station or accompanying a constable to it,

and is detained there or is detained elsewhere in the charge of a constable[1], except that a person who is at a court after being charged is not in police detention for those purposes.

   (2A)   Where a person is in another's lawful custody by virtue of paragraph 22, 34(1) or 35(3) of Schedule 4 to the Police Reform Act 2002, he shall be treated as in police detention.
[Police and Criminal Evidence Act 1984, s 118 as amended by the Prevention of Terrorism (Temporary Provisions) Act 1989, Sch 8, the Children Act 1989, Sch 15, the Criminal Justice and Public Order Act 1994, Sch 11, the Civil Evidence Act 1995, Sch 1, the Terrorism Act 2000, s 125, the Police Reform Act 2002, s 107, the Anti-terrorism, Crime and Security Act 2001, Sch 7 and the Serious Organised Crime and Police Act, Sch 7.]

---

1. Thus a person who has been arrested and is on his way to the police station, or is helping with investigations under s 30(10), ante, is not in police detention for the purposes of this Act, nor is a person who has not been arrested and is voluntarily at a police station, nor is a person who has been taken directly to a hospital after arrest; but if he was taken to a hospital from a police station, the circumstances may then amount to police detention: note s 41(6), ante.

SCHEDULES

Section 9

SCHEDULE 1
SPECIAL PROCEDURE

(As amended by the Criminal Justice and Police Act 2001, Sch 2 and the Serious Organised Crime and Police Act, Sch 7.)

Making of orders by circuit judge

1-2794   1. If on an application[1] made by a constable a circuit judge is satisfied that one or other of the sets of access conditions is fulfilled, he may[2] make an order under paragraph 4 below.*

2. The first set of access conditions is fulfilled if—

(a)   there are reasonable grounds for believing[3]—

    (i)   that an indictable offence has been committed;

    (ii)   that there is material which consists of special procedure material or includes special procedure material and does not also include excluded material on premises specified in the application, or on premises occupied or controlled by a person specified in the application (including all such premises on which there are reasonable grounds for believing that there is such material as it is reasonably practicable so to specify);

    (iii) that the material is likely to be of substantial value (whether by itself or together with other material) to the investigation in connection with which the application is made; and

    (iv)   that the material is likely to be relevant evidence;

(b)   other methods[4] of obtaining the material—

    (i)   have been tried without success; or

    (ii)   have not been tried because it appeared that they were bound to fail; and

(c)   it is in the public interest[5], having regard—

    (i)   to the benefit likely to accrue to the investigation if the material is obtained; and

    (ii)   to the circumstances under which the person in possession of the material holds it,

that the material should be produced or that access to it should be given.

3. The second set of access conditions is fulfilled if—

(a)   there are reasonable grounds for believing that there is material which consists of or includes excluded material or special procedure material on premises specified in the application, or on premises occupied or controlled by a person specified in the application (including all such premises on which there are reasonable grounds for believing that there is such material as it is reasonably practicable so to specify);

(b)   but for section 9(2) above a search of such premises for that material could have been authorised by the issue of a warrant to a constable under an enactment other than this Schedule; and

(c)   the issue of such a warrant would have been appropriate.

4. An order under this paragraph is an order that the person who appears to the circuit judge to be in possession of the material to which the application relates shall—*

(a)   produce it to a constable for him to take away; or

(b)   give a constable access to it,

not later than the end of the period of seven days from the date of the order or the end of such longer period as the order may specify.

5. Where the material consists of information stored in any electronic form—

(a)   an order under paragraph 4(a) above shall have effect as an order to produce the material in a form in which it can be taken away and in which it is visible and legible or from which it can readily be produced in a visible and legible form; and

(b)   an order under paragraph 4(b) above shall have effect as an order to give a constable access to the material in a form in which it is visible and legible.

6. For the purposes of sections 21 and 22 above material produced in pursuance of an order under paragraph 4(a) above shall be treated as if it were material seized by a constable.

Notices of applications for orders

7. An application for an order under paragraph 4 above shall be made inter partes[6].

8. Notice[7] of an application for such an order may be served on a person either by delivering it to him or by leaving it at his proper address or by sending it by post to him in a registered letter or by the recorded delivery service.

9. Such a notice may be served[8]—

(a)   on a body corporate, by serving it on the body's secretary or clerk or other similar officer; and

(b)   on a partnership, by serving it on one of the partners.

10. For the purposes of this Schedule, and of section 7 of the Interpretation Act 1978 in its application to this Schedule, the proper address of a person, in the case of secretary or clerk or other similar officer of a body corporate, shall be that of the registered or principal office of that body, in the case of a partner of a firm shall be that of the principal office of the firm, and in any other case shall be the last known address of the person to be served.

11. Where notice of an application for an order under paragraph 4 above has been served on a person, he shall not conceal, destroy, alter or dispose[9] of the material to which the application relates except—

(a)   with the leave of a judge; or

(b)   with the written permission of a constable,

until—

(i) the application is dismissed or abandoned; or
(ii) he has complied with an order under paragraph 4 above made on the application.

Issue of warrants by circuit judge

12. If on an application made by a constable[10] a circuit judge—*

(a) is satisfied—

(i) that either set of access conditions is fulfilled; and
(ii) that any of the further conditions set out in paragraph 14 below is also fulfilled in relation to each set of premises specified in the application; or

(b) is satisfied—

(i) that the second set of access conditions is fulfilled; and
(ii) that an order under paragraph 4 above relating to the material has not been complied with,

he may issue a warrant authorising a constable to enter and search the premises or (as the case may be) all premises occupied or controlled by the person referred to in paragraph 2(a)(ii) or 3(a), including such sets of premises as are specified in the application (an "all premises warrant").

12A. The judge may not issue an all premises warrant unless he is satisfied—

(a) that there are reasonable grounds for believing that it is necessary to search premises occupied or controlled by the person in question which are not specified in the application, as well as those which are, in order to find the material in question; and
(b) that it is not reasonably practicable to specify all the premises which he occupies or controls which might need to be searched.

13. A constable may seize and retain anything for which a search has been authorised under paragraph 12 above.

14. The further conditions mentioned in paragraph 12(a)(ii) above are—

(a) that it is not practicable to communicate with any person entitled to grant entry to the premises;
(b) that it is practicable to communicate with a person entitled to grant entry to the premises but it is not practicable to communicate with any person entitled to grant access to the material;
(c) that the material contains information which—

(i) is subject to a restriction or obligation such as is mentioned in section 11(2)(b) above; and
(ii) is likely to be disclosed in breach of it if a warrant is not issued;

(d) that service of notice of an application for an order under paragraph 4 above may seriously prejudice the investigation.

15. (1) If a person fails to comply with an order under paragraph 4 above, a circuit judge may deal with him as if he had committed a contempt of the Crown Court.*
(2) Any enactment relating to contempt of the Crown Court shall have effect in relation to such a failure as if it were such a contempt.

Costs

16. The costs of any application under this Schedule and of anything done or to be done in pursuance of an order made under it shall be in the discretion of the judge.**

---

*Amended by the Courts Act 2003, Sch 4 from a date to be appointed.
**New para 17 inserted by the Serious Organised Crime and Police Act, Sch 7 from a date to be appointed.
1. The police are not required to provide the evidence in support of the application in advance of the hearing (*R v Crown Court at Inner London Sessions, ex p Baines & Baines* [1988] QB 579, [1987] 3 All ER 1025, 87 Cr App Rep 111).
2. Although the risk of self-incrimination is to be taken into account in the exercise of the judge's discretion, an order can be made even though it will or may oblige the person against whom it is directed to incriminate himself: *R v Central Criminal Court, ex p Bright; R v Central Criminal Court, ex p Alton; R v Central Criminal Court, ex p Rusbridger* [2001] 2 All ER 244, [2001] 1 WLR 1134, [2001] EMLR 79, DC.
3. A judge cannot, generally speaking, proceed on the basis of a bare assertion by a police officer; the judge must be satisfied personally that the statutory requirements have been established and thus he cannot simply ask himself whether the decision of the applicant police officer is reasonable: *R v Central Criminal Court, ex p Bright; R v Central Criminal Court, ex p Alton; R v Central Criminal Court, ex p Rusbridger* [2001] 2 All ER 244, [2001] 1 WLR 1134, [2001] EMLR 79, DC.
4. The judge should not make an order under the Schedule unless he is satisfied that the application is substantially the last resort and that other practical methods of obtaining disclosure have been exhausted without success (*R v Crown Court at Lewes, ex p Hill* (1990) 93 Cr App Rep 60).
5. For consideration of this condition, see *R v Crown Court at Bristol, ex p Bristol Press and Picture Agency Ltd* (1986) 85 Cr App Rep 190. See also *R v Central Criminal Court, ex p Bright; R v Central Criminal Court, ex p Alton; R v Central Criminal Court, ex p Rusbridger* [2001] 2 All ER 244, [2001] 1 WLR 1134, [2001] EMLR 79, DC, where it was held that para 2(c) is not open-ended and is restricted to the matters to which it refers.
6. There is no requirement that the accused person should be given notice (*R v Crown Court at Leicester, ex p DPP* [1987] 3 All ER 654, [1987] 1 WLR 1371).
7. The notice, or a document accompanying it, should specify details of the material which is sought to be produced or to which access is to be given (*R v Central Criminal Court, ex p Adegbesan* [1986] 3 All ER 113, [1986] 1 WLR 1292), but the notice will not be invalid if it omits that information, provided the information is conveyed orally to the person concerned either at the time when the notice is served or beforehand (*R v Crown Court at Manchester, ex p Taylor* [1988] 2 All ER 769, [1988] 1 WLR 705).
8. Where the police are proceeding to obtain information from an unincorporated body, it would seem that they should name an officer of that body as the person against whom they are moving by way of application; see *R v Central Criminal Court, ex p Adegbesan* [1986] 3 All ER 113, [1986] 1 WLR 1292.
9. Where a company is served with notice of an application pursuant to s 9 of and Sch 1 to the Police and Criminal Evidence Act 1984 for an order to produce special procedure material in the form of e-mails addressed to a particular customer and the notice warns that the company cannot destroy or dispose of that material except with the leave of the court and, due to its auto deletion system (for reasons of storage) the company can only comply by transferring copies of

the e-mails to another e-mail address, which amounts to an offence under s 1 of the Regulation of Investigatory Powers Act 2000, the company has implicit power to preserve the e-mails and this provides it with lawful authority for the purposes of s 1(5)(c) of that Act (*R (NTL Group Ltd) v Crown Court at Ipswich* [2002] EWHC 1585 (Admin), [2003] QB 131, [2002] 3 WLR 1173, [2003] 1 Cr App Rep 225).

10. See also the requirements of para 2.7 of the Code of Practice for the Searching of Premises by Police Officers and the Seizure of Property Found by Police Officers on Persons or Premises (Code of Practice (*b*) in PART II: STATUTORY INSTRUMENTS ON EVIDENCE, post).

SCHEDULE 1A
SPECIFIC OFFENCES WHICH ARE ARRESTABLE OFFENCES

1–2794A   *Repealed by the Serious Organised Crime and Police Act 2005, Sch 17.*

Section 26   SCHEDULE 2
PRESERVED POWERS OF ARREST

(*As amended by the Representation of the People Act 1985, s 25(1), the Road Traffic (Consequential Provisions) Act 1988, Sch 1, the Prevention of Terrorism (Temporary Provisions) Act 1989, Sch 9, the Children Act 1989, Schs 13 and 15, the Civil Contigencies Act 2004, Sch 3 and the Serious Organised Crime and Police Act 2005, Sch 7.*)

1–2795

1952 c 52	Section 49 of the Prison Act 1952.
1952 c 67	Section 13 of the Visiting Forces Act 1952.
1955 c 18	Sections 186 and 190B of the Army Act 1955.
1955 c 19	Sections 186 and 190B of the Air Force Act 1955.
1957 c 53	Sections 104 and 105 of the Naval Discipline Act 1957.
1969 c 54	Section 32 of the Children and Young Persons Act 1969.
1971 c 77	Section 24(2) of the Immigration Act 1971 and paragraphs 17, 24 and 33 of Schedule 2 and paragraph 7 of Schedule 3 to that Act.
1976 c 63	Section 7 of the Bail Act 1976.
1983 c 2	Rule 36 in Schedule 1 to the Representation of the People Act 1983.
1983 c 20	Sections 18, 35(10), 36(8), 38(7), 136(1) and 138 of the Mental Health Act 1983.
1984 c 47	Section 5(5) of the Repatriation of Prisoners Act 1984.

Section 70   SCHEDULE 3[1]
PROVISIONS SUPPLEMENTARY TO SECTIONS 68 AND 69

1–2796

---

1. For Schedule 3, see PART II: EVIDENCE, post.

Section 116   SCHEDULE 5
SERIOUS ARRESTABLE OFFENCES

1–2797 *Repealed by the Serious Organised Crime and Police Act 2005, Sch 17.*

Prosecution of Offences Act 1985[1]
(1985 c 23)

PART I[2]
THE CROWN PROSECUTION SERVICE

1–2900 **1, 2.** The Director of Public Prosecutions, who is appointed by the Attorney General, is head of the Crown Prosecution Service[3]. England and Wales is divided into areas each with a Chief Crown Prosecutor. Crown Prosecutors employed in the Service may give consents or take steps required by any enactment from the Director.
[Prosecution of Offences Act 1985, ss 1, 2 as amended by the Courts and Legal Services Act 1990, Sch 10 and by the Access to Justice Act 1999, Sch 15, summarised.]

---

1. At the date of going to press, only Sch 1, para 11, and Sch 2 so far as those provisions relate to the Supreme Court Act 1981, s 77, had not been brought into force. As to commencement orders made, see s 31, post.
2. Part I contains ss 1–15.
3. By virtue of s 2(5) of the Crown Proceedings Act 1947, the Crown Prosecution Service is immune from any action in negligence in respect of acts or omissions in discharging its responsibilities of a judicial nature. Nevertheless, that immunity does not extend to any failure of the Crown Prosecution Service to carry out its general administrative responsibility or practice as prosecutor to keep the court informed as to the state of an adjourned criminal case, or its particular responsibility to the accused to whom it owes a duty of care (*Welsh v Chief Constable of the Merseyside Police* [1993] 1 All ER 692).

By the Crown Prosecution Service Inspectorate Act 2000, the Attorney General is required to appoint a person as Her Majesty's Chief Inspector of the Crown Prosecution Service and the Chief Inspector shall inspect or arrange for the inspection of the operation of the Crown Prosecution Service.

1–2901 **3. Functions of the Director.** (1) The Director shall discharge his functions under this or any other enactment under the superintendence of the Attorney General.

(2) It shall be the duty of the Director[1], subject to any provisions contained in the Criminal Justice Act 1987—

(a) to take over the conduct of all criminal proceedings instituted[2] by an immigration officer (as defined for the purposes of the Immigration Act 1971) acting in his capacity as such an officer;

(aa) to take over the conduct of any criminal proceedings instituted by an immigration officer (as defined for the purposes of the Immigration Act 1971) acting in his capacity as such an officer;

(b) to institute and have the conduct of criminal proceedings in any case where it appears to him that—

   (i) the importance or difficulty of the case makes it appropriate that proceedings should be instituted by him; or

   (ii) it is otherwise appropriate for proceedings to be instituted by him;

(ba) to institute and have the conduct of any criminal proceedings in any case where the proceedings relate to the subject-matter of a report a copy of which has been sent to him under paragraph 23 or 24 of Schedule 3 to the Police Reform Act 2002 (c 30) (reports on investigations into conduct of persons serving with the police);

(c) to take over the conduct of all binding over proceedings instituted on behalf of a police force (whether by a member of that force or by any other person);

(d) to take over the conduct of all proceedings begun by summons issued under section 3 of the Obscene Publications Act 1959 (forfeiture of obscene articles);

(e) to give, to such extent as he considers appropriate advice to police forces on all matters relating to criminal offences;

(ea) to have the conduct of any extradition proceedings;

(eb) to give, to such extent as he considers appropriate, and to such persons as he considers appropriate, advice on any matters relating to extradition proceedings or proposed extradition proceedings;

(ec) to give, to such an extent as he considers appropriate, advice to immigration officers on matters relating to criminal offences;

(f) to appear for the prosecution, when directed by the court to do so, on any appeal under—

   (i) section 1 of the Administration of Justice Act 1960 (appeal from the High Court in criminal cases);

   (ii) Part I or Part II of the Criminal Appeal Act 1968 (appeals from the Crown Court to the criminal division of the Court of Appeal and thence to the House of Lords*); or

   (iii) section 108 of the Magistrates' Courts Act 1980 (right of appeal to Crown Court) as it applies, by virtue of subsection (5) of section 12 of the Contempt of Court Act 1981, to orders made under section 12 (contempt of magistrates' courts);

(fa) To have the conduct of applications for orders under section 1C of the Crime and Disorder Act 1998 (orders made on conviction of certain offences) and section 14A of the Football Spectators Act 1989 (banning orders made on conviction of certain offences);

(fb) where it appears to him appropriate to do so, to have the conduct of applications under section 1CA(3) of the Crime and Disorder Act 1998 for the variation or discharge of orders made under section 1C of that Act;

(fc) where it appears to him appropriate to do so, to appear on any application under section 1CA of that Act made by a person subject to an order under section 1C of that Act for the variation or discharge of the order;

(g) to discharge such other functions[3] as may from time to time be assigned to him by the Attorney General in pursuance of this paragraph.

(2A) Subsection (2)(ea) above does not require the Director to have the conduct of any extradition proceedings in respect of a person if he has received a request not to do so and—

(a) in a case where the proceedings are under Part 1 of the Extradition Act 2003, the request is made by the authority which issued the Part 1 warrant in respect of the person;

(b) in a case where the proceedings are under Part 2 of that Act, the request is made on behalf of the territory to which the person's extradition has been requested.

(3) In this section—

"the court" means—

   (a) in the case of an appeal to or from the criminal division of the Court of Appeal, that division;

   (b) in the case of an appeal from a Divisional Court of the Queen's Bench Division, the Divisional Court; and

   (c) in the case of an appeal against an order of a magistrates' court, the Crown Court;

"Police force" means any police force maintained by a police authority under the Police Act 1996, and any other body of constables for the time being specified by order[4] made by the Secretary of State for the purposes of this section; and

"specified proceedings" means proceedings which fall within any category for the time being specified by order[5] made by the Attorney General for the purposes of this section.

(4) The power to make orders under subsection (3) above shall be exercisable by statutory instrument subject to annulment in pursuance of a resolution of either House of Parliament.

[Prosecution of Offences Act 1985, s 3 as amended by the Criminal Justice Act 1987, Sch 2, the Police Act 1996,

Sch 7, the Police Act 1997, Sch 9, the Immigration and Asylum Act 1999, s 164, the Anti-Social Behaviour Act 2003, Sch 3, the Extradition Act 2003, s 190, Police Reform Act 2002, Sch 7, the Immigration and Asylum Act 1999, s 164, the Asylum and Immigration (Treatments of Claimants, etc) Act 2004, s 7 and the Serious Organised Crime and Police Act 2005, s 140 and Sch 4.]

---

*Words substituted by the Constitutional Reform Act 2005, Sch 9 from a date to be appointed.
1. A decision by the Director to consent to a prosecution is not amenable to judicial review in the absence of dishonesty, mala fides or an exceptional circumstance (*R v DPP, ex p Kebilene* [2002] 2 AC 326, [1999] 4 All ER 801).

The Director has no power to give an undertaking that he will not consent to the prosecution of a crime yet to be committed (*R (on the application of Pretty) v DPP* [2001] UKHL 61, [2002] 1 AC 800, [2002] 1 All ER 1, [2002] 1 FCR 1).
The Director cannot lawfully delegate to any person not being a Crown Prosecutor the decision whether in any criminal proceedings the evidence is sufficient to proceed and/or the prosecution is in the public interest (*R v DPP, ex p First Division Association* [1988] NLJR 158).
2. As to when proceedings in relation to an offence are instituted, see s 15(2), post. It has been held that once a person has been arrested without warrant and charged by the police, it is not open to a private prosecutor to take over the conduct of the prosecution (*R v Ealing Magistrates' Court, ex p Dixon* [1989] 2 All ER 1050, 153 JP 505, DC). However, this decision was not followed in *R v Stafford Magistrates' Court, ex p Customs and Excise Comrs* (1990) 154 JP 865, where the Divisional Court expressed the view that proceedings could only be said to have been instituted on behalf of a police force when it was the police who had investigated, arrested and brought the arrested person to the custody officer. The decision in the *Stafford* case was followed in *R v Croydon Justices, ex p Holmberg* (1992) 157 JP 277, [1992] Crim LR 892, where it was held that the seeking of police assistance of itself does not necessarily turn what are in truth proceedings brought by a local authority into police proceedings. In *R (Hunt) v Criminal Cases Review Commission* [2001] QB 1108, [2001] 2 WLR 319, [2001] 2 Cr App R 76, [DC, the court approved the decisions in *R v Stafford Magistrates' Court* and *R v Croydon Justices* and disapproved *R v Ealing Justices*.
Section 28 of the Criminal Justice Act 2003 (see this Part, post) introduces Sch 2 to that Act, which makes significant changes to the charging of offenders by means of amendments to the Police and Criminal Evidence Act 1984. The effect is that where the custody officer is of the opinion that a suspect should be charged or cautioned, and the suspect is a suitable candidate for bail, the suspect will generally be granted bail pending a decision by the Crown Prosecution Service on whether he should be charged or cautioned or not further proceeded against. Only in minor cases will the police make the charging decision. If the offender is not suitable for bail a Duty Inspector may authorise a charge in an emergency but a prosecutor must be informed as soon as possible for authority to proceed with the prosecution. Since, in custody cases, there may not be sufficient time to obtain all the relevant evidence before the charging decision must be taken, a lower threshold test of 'reasonable suspicion' of the commission of the offence will be applied.
These changes are prospective. However, it is anticipated that the new charging regime will be operating in 14 priority areas by 31 October 2004, and will be implemented nationwide by April 2007.
3. By an assignment dated 10 December 1996, the Attorney General has assigned to the Director of Public Prosecutions the following three functions:

(i) the conduct in England and Wales of applications made by foreign states, Commonwealth countries or colonies for extradition of persons from the United Kingdom;
(ii) the conduct of proceedings relating to appeals by way of case stated and to applications for writs of Habeas Corpus ad Subjiciendum whether by representing a party or by intervention where it appears to the Director that the issues involved relate to the conduct of proceedings falling within the statutory functions of the Director of Public Prosecutions under the Prosecution of Offences Act 1985 or any other enactment;
(iii) the conduct of proceedings under s 2 of the Dogs Act 1871 instituted on behalf of a police force (whether by a member of that force or by any other person).
4. The following bodies of constables have been specified by SI 1985/1956: British Transport Police Force, City of London Police, Dover Harbour Board Police, Falmouth Docks Police, Felixstowe Dock and Railway Company Police, Manchester Dock Police Force, Mersey Tunnel law enforcement officers, Metropolitan Police Force, Milford Docks Police, Ministry of Defence Police, Port of Bristol Police, Port of Liverpool Police, Port of London Authority Police, Royal Parks Constabulary (England), Tees and Hartlepool Port Authority Harbour Police, United Kingdom Atomic Energy Authority Constabulary.
5. The Prosecution of Offences Act 1985 (Specified Proceedings) Order 1999, SI 1999/904, has been made. It specifies the following offences:—
1. Fixed penalty offences within the meaning of section 51(1) of the Road Traffic Offenders Act 1988.
2. The offence under s 29(1) of the Vehicle Excise and Registration Act 1994.
3. The offences under sections 17(2), 18(3), 24(3), 26(1) and (2), 29, 31(1), 42(*b*), 47(1), 87(2), 143, 164(6) and (9), 165(3) and (6), 168 and 172(3) of the Road Traffic Offenders Act 1988.
4. All offences under the Road Traffic Regulation Act 1984 other than those under sections 35A(2), 43(5) and (12), 47(3), 52(1), 108(3), 115(1) and (2), 116(1) and 129(3) or those mentioned in paragraph 1 above.
5. The offences arising by contravention of Regulations 3(9)(*a*) (involving a pedal cycle) and 3(9)(*b*) and 4(27), (28) and (30) of the Royal and Other Open Spaces Regulations 1977, SI 1997/1639.
It provides that where a summons has been issued for one of these offences, proceedings cease to be specified when the summons is served unless the documents described in s 12(3)(*b*) of the Magistrates' Courts Act 1980 are served with the summons; also that proceedings cease to be specified if at any time a magistrates' court begins to receive evidence in those proceedings (for the purpose of this paragraph nothing read out before the court under s 12(7) of the 1980 Act shall be regarded as evidence).

1–2903   5. Conduct of prosecutions on behalf of the Service. (1) The Director may at any time appoint a person who has a general qualification (within the meaning of section 71 of the Courts and Legal Services Act 1990) to institute or take over the conduct of such criminal proceedings or extradition proceedings[1] as the Director may assign to him.

(2) Any person conducting proceedings assigned to him under this section shall have all the powers of a Crown Prosecutor but shall exercise those powers subject to any instructions given to him by a Crown Prosecutor.
[Prosecution of Offences Act 1985, s 5 as amended by the Courts and Legal Services Act 1990, Sch 10 and the Extradition Act 2003, s 190.]

---

1. Words "or extradition proceedings" do not apply in relation to extradition requests received or extraditions made on or before 31 December 2003.

1–2904   6. Prosecutions instituted and conducted otherwise than by the Service.   (1) Subject to subsection (2) below, nothing in this Part shall preclude any person from instituting any criminal proceedings or conducting any criminal proceedings to which the Director's duty to take over the conduct of proceedings does not apply[1].

(2) Where criminal proceedings are instituted in circumstances in which the Director is not under a duty to take over their conduct, he may nevertheless do so at any stage.

[*Prosecution of Offences Act 1985, s 6.*]

---

1. Section 6(1) does not confer a right to have documents produced by the Crown Prosecution Service in aid of a private prosecution (*R v DPP, ex p Hallas* (1987) 87 Cr App Rep 340).

The effect of s 6(1) is to preclude a person from bringing a private prosecution in cases covered by s 3(2)(*a*), (*c*) and (*d*), but not in the residuary category of s 3(2)(*b*). So far as s 3(2)(*b*) cases are concerned, there is nothing to preclude a private prosecution (*R v Bow Street Stipendiary Magistrate, ex p South Coast Shipping Co Ltd* [1993] 1 All ER 219, [1993] 2 WLR 621, 96 Cr App Rep 405).

1–2905   7. Delivery of recognizances etc to Director.   (1) Where the Director or any Crown Prosecutor gives notice to any justice of the peace that he has instituted, or is conducting, any criminal proceedings, the justice shall—

(*a*)   at the prescribed time and in the prescribed manner; or

(*b*)   in a particular case, at the time and in the manner directed by the Attorney General;

send him every recognizance, information, certificate, deposition, document and thing connected with those proceedings which the justice is required by law to deliver to the appropriate officer of the Crown Court.

(2) The Attorney General may make regulations for the purpose of supplementing this section; and in subsection (1) above "prescribed" means prescribed by the regulations.

(3) The Director or, as the case may be, Crown Prosecutor shall—

(*a*)   subject to the regulations, cause anything which is sent to him under subsection (1) above to be delivered to the appropriate officer of the Crown Court; and

(*b*)   be under the same obligation (on the same payment) to deliver to an applicant copies of anything so sent as that officer.

(4) It shall be the duty of every justices' chief executive to send to the Director, in accordance with the regulations, a copy of the information and of any depositions and other documents relating to any case in which—

(*a*)   a prosecution for an offence before a magistrates' court for which he is the justices' chief executive is withdrawn or is not proceeded with within a reasonable time;

(*b*)   the Director does not have the conduct of the proceedings; and

(*c*)   there is some ground for suspecting that there is no satisfactory reason for the withdrawal or failure to proceed.

[*Prosecution of Offences Act 1985, s 7 as amended by the Access to Justice Act 1999, s 90.*]

1–2906   7A. Powers of non-legal staff.   (1) The Director may designate, for the purposes of this section, members of the staff of the Crown Prosecution Service who are not Crown Prosecutors.

(2) Subject to such exceptions (if any) as may be specified in the designation, a person so designated shall have such of the following as may be so specified, namely—

(*a*)   the powers and rights of audience of a Crown Prosecutor in relation to—

(i)   applications for, or relating to, bail in criminal proceedings;

(ii)   the conduct of criminal proceedings in magistrates' courts other than trials;

(*b*)   the powers of such a Prosecutor in relation to the conduct of criminal proceedings not falling within paragraph (*a*)(ii) above.

(3) A person so designated shall exercise any such powers subject to instructions given to him by the Director.

(4) Any such instructions may be given so as to apply generally.

(5) For the purposes of this section—

(*a*)   "bail in criminal proceedings" has the same meaning as it would have in the Bail Act 1976 by virtue of the definition in section 1 of that Act if in that section "offence" did not include an offence to which subsection (6) below applies;

(*b*)   "criminal proceedings" does not include proceedings for an offence to which subsection (6) below applies; and

(*c*)   a trial begins with the opening of the prosecution case after the entry of a plea of not guilty and ends with the conviction or acquittal of the accused.

(6) This subsection applies to an offence if it is triable only on indictment, or is an offence—

(*a*)   for which the accused has elected to be tried on indictment;

(*b*)   which a magistrates' court has decided is more suitable to be so tried; or

(*c*)   in respect of which a notice of transfer has been given under section 4 of the Criminal Justice Act 1987 or section 53 of the Criminal Justice Act 1991.★

(7) Details of the following for any year, namely—

(a) the criteria applied by the Director in determining whether to designate persons under this section;
(b) the training undergone by persons so designated; and
(c) any general instructions given by the Director under subsection (4) above,

shall be set out in the Director's report under section 9 of this Act for that year.
[Prosecution of Offences Act 1985, s 7A, as inserted by the Courts and Legal Services Act 1990, s 114 and substituted by the Crime and Disorder Act 1998, s 53.]

---

*Sub-s (6): substituted by the Criminal Justice Act 2003, Sch 3:

"**(6) This section applies to an offence if it is triable only on indictment or is an offence for which the accused has been sent for trial.**"
In force (in relation to cases sent for trial under the Crime and Disorder Act 1998, ss 51 or 51A(3)(*d*)): 9 May 2005; (for remaining purposes): to be appointed: see the Criminal Justice Act 2003, s 336(3).

1–2907 10. Guidelines for Crown Prosecutors. (1) The Director shall[1] issue a Code[2] for Crown Prosecutors giving guidance on general principles to be applied by them—

(a) in determining, in any case—

  (i) whether proceedings for an offence should be instituted or, where proceedings have been instituted, whether they should be discontinued; or
  (ii) what charges should be preferred; and

(b) in considering, in any case, representations to be made by them to any magistrates' court about the mode of trial suitable for that case.

(2) The Director may from time to time make alterations in the Code.
(3) The provisions of the Code shall be set out in the Director's report under section 9 of this Act for the year in which the Code is issued; and any alteration in the Code shall be set out in his report under that section for the year in which the alteration is made.
[Prosecution of Offences Act 1985, s 10.]

---

1. It has been stated, obiter, that the fact that there is a duty under s 10 to issue a code does not necessarily mean that the Director may not ever give guidance as to how prosecutorial discretion will be exercised in regard to particular offences (*R (on the application of Pretty) v DPP* [2001] UKHL 61, [2002] 1 AC 800, [2002] 1 All ER 1, [2002] 1 FCR 1).
2. See this PART, STATUTORY INSTRUMENTS AND PRACTICE DIRECTIONS ON PROCEDURE, post.

1–2908 14. Control of certain fees and expenses etc paid by the Service. (1) The Attorney General may, with the approval of the Treasury, by regulations[1] make such provision as he considers appropriate in relation to—

(a) the fees of any legal representative briefed to appear on behalf of the Service in any criminal proceedings or extradition proceedings[2]; and
(b) the costs and expenses of witnesses attending to give evidence at the instance of the Service and, subject to subsection (1A) below, of any other person who in the opinion of the Service necessarily attends for the purpose of the case otherwise than to give evidence.

(1A) The power conferred on the Attorney General by subsection (1)(*b*) above only relates to the costs and expenses of an interpreter if the interpreter is required because of the lack of English of a person attending to give evidence at the instance of the Service.
(1B) In subsection (1)(*b*) above "attending" means attending at the court or elsewhere.
(2) The regulations may, in particular—

(a) prescribe scales or rates of fees, costs or expenses; and
(b) specify conditions for the payment of fees, costs or expenses.

(3) Regulations made under subsection (1)(*b*) above may provide that scales or rates of costs and expenses shall be determined by the Attorney General with the consent of the Treasury.
[Prosecution of Offences Act 1985, s 14, as amended by the Criminal Justice Act 1988, s 166, the Courts and Legal Services Act 1990, Sch 18 and the Extradition Act 2003, s 190.]

---

1. The Crown Prosecution Service (Witnesses' Allowances) Regulations 1988, SI 1988/1862.
2. Words "or extradition proceedings" do not apply in relation to extradition requests received or extraditions made on or before 31 December 2003.

1–2909 15. Interpretation of Part I. (1) In this Part—

"binding over proceedings" means any proceedings instituted (whether by way of complaint under section 115 of the Magistrates' Courts Act 1980 or otherwise) with a view to obtaining from a magistrate's court an order requiring a person to enter into a recognizance to keep the peace or to be of good behaviour;
"Director" means the Director of Public Prosecutions;
"extradition proceedings" means proceedings under the Extradition Act 2003[1];
"legal representative" means an authorised advocate or authorised litigator, as defined by section 119(1) of the Courts and Legal Services Act 1990;
"police force" has the same meaning as in section 3 of this Act;

"prosecution functions" means functions which by virtue of this Part become functions of the
Director;

"public authority" has the same meaning as in section 17 of this Act;★

"Service" means the Crown Prosecution Service; and

"solicitor" means a solicitor of the Supreme Court.

(2) For the purposes of this Part, proceedings in relation to an offence are instituted—

(a) where a justice of the peace issues a summons under section 1 of the Magistrates' Courts Act
1980, when the information for the offence is laid before him;

(b) where a justice of the peace issues a warrant for the arrest of any person under that section,
when the information for the offence is laid before him;

(c) where a person is charged with the offence after being taken into custody without a warrant,
when he is informed of the particulars of the charge;

(d) where a bill of indictment is preferred under section 2 of the Administration of Justice
(Miscellaneous Provisions) Act 1933 in a case falling within paragraph (b) of subsection 2 of
that section, when the bill of indictment is preferred before the court;

and where the application of this subsection would result in there being more than one time for the
institution of the proceedings, they shall be taken to have been instituted at the earliest of those times.

(3) For the purposes of this Part, references to the conduct of any proceedings include references
to the proceedings being discontinued and to the taking of any steps (including the bringing of
appeals and making of representations in respect of applications for bail) which may be taken in
relation to them.

(4) For the purposes of sections 3(2)(b), 5, 6 and 7(1) of this Act, binding over proceedings shall
be taken to be criminal proceedings.

(5) For the purposes of section 5 of this Act, proceedings begun by summons issued under section
3 of the Obscene Publications Act 1959 (forfeiture of obscene articles) shall be taken to be criminal
proceedings.

(6), (7) *Transferred functions.*

[Prosecution of Offences Act 1985, s 15 as amended by the Courts and Legal Services Act 1990, Schs 18 and 20,
the Employment Rights Act 1996, Sch 1 and the Extradition Act 2003, s 190.]

**★New definitions "public prosecutor, "requisition" and "written charge" and sub-ss(2)(ba) inserted by
the Criminal Justice Act 2003, Sch 36, from a date to be appointed.**

1. Definition "extradition proceedings" does not apply in relation to extradition requests received or extraditions made
on or before 31 December 2003.

PART II[1]
COSTS IN CRIMINAL CASES[2]

Award of costs out of central funds

1–2910   16. Defence costs. (1) Where—

(a) an information laid[3] before a justice of the peace for any area, charging any person with an
offence, is not proceeded with;

(b) a magistrates' court inquiring into an indictable offence as examining justices determines not
to commit the accused[4] for trial;

(c) a magistrates' court dealing summarily with an offence dismisses the information;

that court[5] or, in a case falling within paragraph (a) above, a magistrates' court for that area, may[6]
make an order in favour of the accused[4] for a payment to be made out of central funds in respect of
his costs (a "defendant's costs order").

(2) Where—

(a) any person is not tried for an offence for which he has been indicted or committed for trial; or

(aa) a notice of transfer is given under a relevant transfer provision but a person in relation to
whose case it is given is not tried on a charge to which it relates; or

(b) any person is tried on indictment and acquitted on any count in the indictment;

the Crown Court may make a defendant's costs order in favour of the accused.

(3) Where a person convicted of an offence by a magistrates' court appeals to the Crown Court
under section 108 of the Magistrates' Courts Act 1980 (right of appeal against conviction or sentence)
and, in consequence of the decision on appeal—

(a) his conviction is set aside; or

(b) a less severe punishment is awarded;

the Crown Court may make a defendant's costs order in favour of the accused.[7]

(4), (4A), (5) *Defendant's costs order in Court of Appeal, Queen's Bench Divisional Court, House of
Lords.*

(6) A defendant's costs order shall, subject to the following provisions of this section, be for the
payment out of central funds, to the person in whose favour the order is made, of such amount as the
court considers reasonably sufficient[8] to compensate him for any expenses[9] properly incurred[10] by
him in the proceedings.

(7) Where a court makes a defendant's costs order but is of the opinion that there are circumstances

which make it inappropriate that the person in whose favour the order is made should recover the full amount mentioned in subsection (6) above, the court shall—

(*a*)   assess what amount would, in its opinion, be just and reasonable; and
(*b*)   specify that amount in the order.

(8) *Repealed.*

(9) Subject to subsection (7) above, the amount to be paid out of central funds in pursuance of a defendant's costs order shall—

(*a*)   be specified in the order, in any case where the court considers it appropriate for the amount to be so specified and the person in whose favour the order is made agrees the amount; and
(*b*)   in any other case, be determined in accordance with regulations made by the Lord Chancellor for the purposes of this section.

(10) Subsection (6) above shall have effect, in relation to any case falling within subsection (1)(*a*) or 2(*a*) above, as if for the words "in the proceedings" there were substituted the words "in or about the defence".

(11) Where a person ordered to be retried is acquitted at his retrial, the costs which may be ordered to be paid out of central funds under this section shall include—

(*a*)   any costs which, at the original trial, could have been ordered to be so paid under this section if he had been acquitted; and
(*b*)   if no order was made under this section in respect of his expenses on appeal, any sums for the payment of which such an order could have been made.

(12) In subsection (2)(*aa*) "relevant transfer provision" means—

(*a*)   section 4 of the Criminal Justice Act 1987, or
(*b*)   section 53 of the Criminal Justice Act 1991.

[Prosecution of Offences Act 1985, s 16 as amended by the Criminal Justice Act 1987, Sch 2, the Legal Aid Act 1988, Sch 6, the Criminal Procedure (Insanity and Unfitness to Plead) Act 1991, Sch 3 and the Criminal Justice and Public Order Act 1994, Sch 9.]

1. Part II contains ss 16–21.

2. No "right" to costs or expenses can be read into the European Convention on Human Rights, but decisions about costs where an information is not proceeded with or a defendant is acquitted can raise issues relating to the presumption of innocence under art 6(2). In *Minelli v Switzerland* (1983) 5 EHRR 554 a breach of art 6(2) was found where a court ordered a defendant to pay part of the prosecutor's costs on the basis that if the case had progressed to trial, he would "very probably" have been found guilty. See further *Sekanina v Austria* (1993) 17 EHRR 221 and *Byrne v United Kingdom* (1998) EHRLR 626.

3. The power to award costs is not excluded merely because the information has been laid outside the limitation period prescribed by s 127 of the Magistrates' Courts Act 1980 (*Patel and Patel v Blakey* (1987) 151 JP 532, [1987] Crim LR 683).

4. The term "accused" may include the "parent" or "guardian" of a child or young person in s 55 of the Children and Young Persons Act 1933 thereby enabling a local authority to apply for a defendant's costs order (*R v Preston Crown Court, ex p Lancashire County Council* [1998] 3 All ER 765,[1999] 1 WLR 142, DC).

5. The power to make a defendant's costs order is not limited to the court as originally constituted so that where for example the court which has dismissed an information adjourns a further information for sentence the court as subsequently constituted may make a costs order in respect of the proceedings which have been dismissed (*R v Liverpool Magistrates' Court, ex p Abiaka* (1999) 163 JP 497, DC).

6. See detailed commentary on costs orders in para **1–800** et seq in PART I: MAGISTRATES' COURTS, PROCEDURE, ante, and para **3–522 Costs** in PART III: SENTENCING, post.

7. The court should also give reasons for its decision on the costs of the appeal (unless the reasons are obvious, such as costs following the event), and where an appeal against conviction or sentence succeeds the Crown Court should normally award costs in the appellant's favour unless there are positive reasons for not doing so: *Cunningham v Crown Court at Exeter* [2003] EWHC 184 (Admin), (2003) 167 JP 93, [2003] Crim LR 340 sub nom *R (on the application of Cunningham) v Exeter Crown Court* [2003] EWHC 184 (Admin), [2003] 2 Cr App R (S) 64).

8. This refers to the level of compensation due rather than whether a solicitor of less experience would be sufficient (*R (Hale) v Southport Justices* (2002) Times 29 January, DC).

9. It is reasonable to instruct a solicitor of four years' standing to defend a charge of common assault (*R (Hale) v Southport Justices* (2002) Times, 29 January, DC). While costs in respect of the hours expended by a defendant personally in defeating a prosecution against him are not "expenses properly incurred", there may be included in the defendant's costs order other expenses and disbursements incurred by the defendant as a litigant. Moreover, the fact that the defendant's solicitor has submitted his claim for costs and disbursements does not rule out a further claim for expenses and disbursements incurred by the defendant himself (*R v Bedlington Magistrates' Court, ex p Wilkinson* (1999) 164 JP 156). Where a defendant is legally aided, there is no power to make a defendant's costs order under this section authorising the payment of fees of defence counsel who was not included in the legal aid order (*R v Liverpool Crown Court, ex p the Lord Chancellor* (1993) 158 JP 821). Where a solicitor defended himself, it was held under previous legislation that "expenses" could include his own fees and disbursements (*R v Stafford Stone and Eccleshall Magistrates' Court ex p Robinson* [1988] 1 All ER 430, [1988] 1 WLR 369, 152 JP 153). Similarly, an acquitted barrister may have the costs of preparing his defence but not the costs of his appearance at the hearing (*Khan v Lord Chancellor* [2003] EWHC 12 (QB), [2003] 2 All ER 367, [2003] 1 WLR 2385). There is no power to award interest on a costs order of any kind in criminal proceedings (*Westminster City Council v Wingrove* [1991] 1 QB 652, [1991] 2 WLR 708, 155 JP 303).

10. The taxing authority has first to resolve whether work has been actually and reasonably done under reg 7(1)(*a*) and then consider what sum is reasonably sufficient to compensate the applicant for the expenses properly incurred (*R v Leeds Magistrates' Court, ex p Castle* [1991] Crim LR 770). For the purpose of determining whether leading counsel's fee should be allowed under a defendant's costs order, the test to be applied is whether the defendant acted reasonably in employing leading counsel and not whether the case could have been conducted adequately by a senior solicitor or junior counsel (*R v Dudley Magistrates' Court, ex p Power City Stores Ltd* (1990) 154 JP 654, [1990] NLJR 361, DC and see also *Wraith v Sheffield Forgemasters* [1998] 1 All ER 82, [1998] 1 WLR 132, [1998] 1 FLR 265, CA (where "out of area" solicitors instructed the test is whether the client acted reasonably in instructing that firm) and *Jones v Secretary of State for Wales* [1997] 2 All ER 507, DC (expense rate for specialist firm of provincial solicitors).

A defendant has 'properly incurred' costs where he is under a contractual liability to pay his solicitor even though there might be little prospect of any payment being recovered (*R (on the application of McCormick) v Liverpool City Magistrates' Court* [2001] 2 All ER 705, 165 JP 362, DC).

1–2911   17. Prosecution costs.   (1) Subject to subsection (2) below, the court may—

(*a*)   in any proceedings in respect of an indictable offence; and
(*b*)   in any proceedings before a Divisional Court of the Queen's Bench Division or the House of Lords in respect of a summary offence;

order the payment out of central funds of such amount as the court considers reasonably sufficient to compensate the prosecutor for any expenses properly incurred by him in the proceedings.

(2) No order under this section may be made in favour of—

(*a*)   a public authority; or
(*b*)   a person acting—

(i)   on behalf of a public authority; or
(ii) in his capacity as an official appointed by such an authority.

(3) Where a court makes an order under this section but is of the opinion that there are circumstances which make it inappropriate that the prosecution should recover the full amount mentioned in subsection (1) above, the court shall—

(*a*)   assess what amount would, in its opinion, be just and reasonable; and
(*b*)   specify that amount in the order.

(4) Subject to subsection (3) above, the amount to be paid out of central funds in pursuance of an order under this section shall—

(*a*)   be specified in the order, in any case where the court considers it appropriate for the amount to be so specified and the prosecutor agrees the amount; and
(*b*)   in any other case, be determined in accordance with regulations made by the Lord Chancellor for the purposes of this section.

(5) Where the conduct of proceedings to which subsection (1) above applies is taken over by the Crown Prosecution Service, that subsection shall have effect as if it referred to the prosecutor who had the conduct of the proceedings before the intervention of the Service and to expenses incurred by him up to the time of intervention.

(6) In this section "public authority" means—

(*a*)   a police force within the meaning of section 3 of this Act;
(*b*)   the Crown Prosecution Service or any other government department;
(*c*)   a local authority or other authority or body constituted for purposes of—

(i)   the public service or of local government; or
(ii) carrying on under national ownership any industry or undertaking or part of an industry or undertaking; or

(*d*)   any other authority or body whose members are appointed by Her Majesty or by any Minister of the Crown or government department or whose revenues consist wholly or mainly of money provided by Parliament.

[Prosecution of Offences Act 1985, s 17.]

Award of costs against accused

1–2912   18. Award of costs against accused.   (1) Where—

(*a*)   any person is convicted of an offence before a magistrates' court;
(*b*)   the Crown Court dismisses an appeal against such a conviction or against the sentence imposed on that conviction; or
(*c*)   any person is convicted of an offence before the Crown Court;

the court may make such order as to costs to be paid by the accused to the prosecutor as it considers just and reasonable[1].

(2) and (6) *Court of Appeal.*

(3) The amount to be paid by the accused in pursuance of an order under this section shall be specified in the order.

(4) Where any person is convicted of an offence before a magistrates' court and—

(*a*)   under the conviction the court orders payment of any sum as a fine, penalty, forfeiture or compensation; and
(*b*)   the sum so ordered to be paid does not exceed £5;

the court shall not order the accused to pay any costs under this section unless in the particular circumstances of the case it considers it right to do so.

(5) Where any person under the age of eighteen is convicted of an offence before a magistrates' court, the amount of any costs ordered to be paid by the accused under this section shall not exceed the amount of any fine imposed on him.

[Prosecution of Offences Act 1985, s 18, as amended by the Criminal Justice Act 1987, Sch 2 and the Criminal Justice and Public Order Act 1994, Sch 9.]

1. Where a case is resolved on a guilty plea to a charge and the defendant would have paid a fixed penalty for the offence concerned if one had been offered, justices should either not award costs or give reasons why they were awarding costs having regard to that fact: *R (on the application of Ritson) v County Durham Magistrates' Court* (2001) 165 JPN 514. In the absence of any provision for taxation of the prosecution costs, the prosecution should serve details of its costs on the defence in order to give the defence the opportunity to make representations. In exceptional cases, a full hearing to resolve any objections may be necessary. Costs ordered to be paid by the defendant may include costs incurred in the course of the investigation of the offence (*R v Associated Octel Ltd* [1996] 1 Cr App Rep (S) 435, [1997] Crim LR 144). When the Crown Court dismisses an appeal against sentence the power to make an order for costs to be paid by the accused to the prosecutor includes a power to vary an order made by the magistrates' court requiring the accused to pay the costs of the prosecutor in relation to the proceedings in the magistrates' court (*Hamilton-Johnson v RSPCA* [2000] 2 Cr App Rep (S) 390, 164 JP 345, DC).

Where multiple defendants have been prosecuted, a sentencing court is entitled to order any defendant to pay a contribution to prosecution costs that exceeds those costs that relate to him alone where he was more responsible for the criminal conduct that led to the convictions than his co-defendants (*R v Fresha Bakeries* [2002] EWCA Crim 1451, [2002] All ER (D) 408 (May), [2002] JPN 479.

Other awards

1–2913   19. Provision for orders as to costs in other circumstances. (1) The Lord Chancellor may by regulations[1] make provision empowering magistrates' courts, the Crown Court and the Court of Appeal, in any case where the court is satisfied that one party to criminal proceedings has incurred costs as a result of an unnecessary or improper act or omission by, or on behalf of, another party to the proceedings, to make an order as to the payment of those costs.

(2) and (5) *Content of regulations.*

(3) The Lord Chancellor may by regulations[1] make provision for the payment out of central funds, in such circumstances and in relation to such criminal proceedings as may be specified, of such sums as appear to the court to be reasonably necessary—

- (*a*) to compensate any witness in the proceedings, and any other person who in the opinion of the court necessarily attends for the purpose of the proceedings otherwise than to give evidence, for the expense, trouble or loss of time properly incurred in or incidental to his attendance;
- (*b*) to cover the proper expenses of an interpreter who is required because of the accused's lack of English;
- (*c*) to compensate a duly qualified medical practitioner who—
  - (i) makes a report otherwise than in writing for the purpose of section 11 of the Powers of Criminal Courts (Sentencing) Act 2000 (remand for medical examination); or
  - (ii) makes a written report to a court in pursuance of a request to which section 32(2) of the Criminal Justice Act 1967 (report by medical practitioner on medical condition of offender) applies;

  for the expenses properly incurred in or incidental to his reporting to the court;
- (*d*) to cover the proper fee or costs of a person appointed by the Crown Court under section 4A of the Criminal Procedure (Insanity) Act 1964 to put the case for the defence.
- (*e*) to cover the proper fee or costs of a legal representative appointed under section 38(4) of the Youth Justice and Criminal Evidence Act 1999 (defence representation for purposes of cross-examination) and any expenses properly incurred in providing such a person with evidence or other material in connection with his appointment.

(3A) In subsection (3)(*a*) above "attendance" means attendance at the court or elsewhere.

(4) *Court of Appeal.*

[Prosecution of Offences Act 1985, s 19 as amended by the Criminal Justice Act 1988, s 166, the Legal Aid Act 1988, Schs 5 and 6, the Criminal Procedure (Insanity and Unfitness to Plead) Act 1991, Sch 3, the Youth Justice and Criminal Evidence Act 1999, Sch 7 and the Powers of Criminal Courts (Sentencing) Act 2000, Sch 9.]

---

1. See the Costs in Criminal Cases (General) Regulations 1986, reg 3, this PART: STATUTORY INSTRUMENTS ON PROCEDURE, post.

1–2914   19A. Costs against legal representatives, etc. (1) In any criminal proceedings[1]—

- (*a*) the Court of Appeal;
- (*b*) the Crown Court; or
- (*c*) a magistrates' court,

may disallow, or (as the case may be) order the legal or other representative concerned to meet, the whole of any wasted costs or such part of them as may be determined in accordance with regulations[2].

(2) Regulations[2] shall provide that a legal or other representative against whom action is taken by a magistrates' court under subsection (1) may appeal to the Crown Court and that a legal or other representative against whom action is taken by the Crown Court under subsection (1) may appeal to the Court of Appeal.

(3) In this section—

"legal or other representative", in relation to any proceedings, means a person who is exercising a right of audience, or a right to conduct litigation, on behalf of any party to the proceedings;

"regulations" means regulations made by the Lord Chancellor; and

"wasted costs" means any costs incurred by a party—

(*a*) as a result of any improper, unreasonable or negligent act or omission on the part of any representative or any employee of a representative; or

(*b*) which, in the light of any such act or omission occurring after they were incurred, the court considers it is unreasonable to expect that party to pay.

[Prosecution of Offences Act 1985, s 19A, as inserted by the Courts and Legal Services Act 1990, s 111.]

---

1. It has been held that the words "in any criminal proceedings" are wide enough to cover proceedings initiated by summons for the attendance of a witness before the Crown Court to produce a document. A party served with a witness summons and who served a notice of application asking the court to declare the summons to be of no effect was thus a party to criminal proceedings whose costs could be the subject of a wasted costs order (*Re a Solicitor (Wasted Costs Order)* [1996] 3 FCR 365, [1996] 1 FLR 40).

2. See post the Costs in Criminal Cases (General) Regulations 1986, Pt IIA which deals with wasted costs orders; see also para **1–643 Costs**, ante and para **3–522 Costs**, post.

1–2914A 19B. Provision for award of costs against third parties. (1) The Lord Chancellor may by regulations make provision empowering magistrates' courts, the Crown Court and the Court of Appeal to make a third party costs order if the condition in subsection (3) is satisfied.

(2) A "third party costs order" is an order as to the payment of costs incurred by a party to criminal proceedings by a person who is not a party to those proceedings ("the third party").

(3) The condition is that—

(*a*) there has been serious misconduct (whether or not constituting a contempt of court) by the third party, and

(*b*) the court considers it appropriate, having regard to that misconduct, to make a third party costs order against him.

(4) Regulations made under this section may, in particular—

(*a*) specify types of misconduct in respect of which a third party costs order may not be made;

(*b*) allow the making of a third party costs order at any time;

(*c*) make provision for any other order as to costs which has been made in respect of the proceedings to be varied on, or taken account of in, the making of a third party costs order;

(*d*) make provision for account to be taken of any third party costs order in the making of any other order as to costs in respect of the proceedings.

(5) Regulations made under this section in relation to magistrates' courts must provide that the third party may appeal to the Crown Court against a third party costs order made by a magistrates' court.

(6) Regulations made under this section in relation to the Crown Court must provide that the third party may appeal to the Court of Appeal against a third party costs order made by the Crown Court.

[Prosecution of Offences Act 1985, s 19B inserted by the Courts Act 2003, s 93.]

1–2915 20 *Regulations.—Lord Chancellor may make regulations for carrying Part II of the Act into effect.*[Prosecution of Offences Act 1985, s 20 amended by the Legal Aid 1988, Sch 5, the Courts and Legal Services Act 1990, Sch 18, SI 1992/709 and the Justices of the Peace Act 1997, Sch 5, summarised.]

1–2916 21. Interpretation, etc. (1) In this Part—

"accused" and "appellant", in a case where section 44A of the Criminal Appeal Act 1968 (death of convicted person) applies, include the person approved under that section;

"defendant's costs order" has the meaning given in section 16 of this Act;

"legally assisted person", in relation to any proceedings, means a person to whom a right to representation funded by the Legal Services Commission as part of the Criminal Defence Service has been granted for the purposes of the proceedings;

"proceedings" includes—

(*a*) proceedings in any court below; and

(*b*) in relation to the determination of an appeal by any court, any application made to that court for leave to bring the appeal; and

"witness" means any person properly attending to give evidence, whether or not he gives evidence or is called at the instance of one of the parties or of the court, but does not include a person attending as a witness to character only unless the court has certified that the interests of justice required his attendance.

(2), (3) *Court of Appeal.*

(4) For the purposes of sections 16 and 17 of this Act, the costs of any party to proceedings shall be taken to include the expense of compensating any witness for the expenses, trouble or loss of time properly incurred in or incidental to his attendance.

(4A) Where one party to any proceedings is a legally assisted person then—

(*a*) for the purposes of sections 16 and 17 of this Act, his costs shall be taken not to [the cost of representation funded for him by the Legal Services Commission as part of the Criminal Defence Service; and

(b) for the purposes of sections 18 to 19B of this Act, his costs shall be taken to include the cost of representation funded for him by the Legal Services Commission as part of the Criminal Defence Service.

(5) Where, in any proceedings in a criminal cause or matter or in either of the cases mentioned in subsection (6) below, an interpreter is required because of the accused's lack of English, the expenses properly incurred on his employment shall not be treated as costs of any part to the proceedings.

(6) The cases are—

(a) where an information charging the accused with an offence is laid before a justice of the peace but not proceeded with and the expenses are incurred on the employment of the interpreter for the proceedings on the information; and

(b) where the accused is committed for trial but* not tried and the expenses are incurred on the employment of the interpreter for the proceedings in the Crown Court.

[Prosecution of Offences Act 1985, s 21, as amended by the Legal Aid Act 1988, Schs 5 and 6, the Criminal Appeal Act 1995, Sch 2, the Access to Justice Act 1999, Sch 15, the Criminal Justice and Public Order Act 1994, Sch 4 and the Courts Act 2003, Sch 8.]

---

*Amended by the Criminal Justice and Public Order Act 1994, Sch 4, from a date to be appointed.

PART III[1]

MISCELLANEOUS

1–2917   22. Power of Secretary of State to set time limits in relation to preliminary stages of criminal proceedings. (1) The Secretary of State may by regulations[2] make provision, with respect to any specified preliminary stage[3] of proceedings for an offence, as to the maximum period—

(a) to be allowed to the prosecution to complete that stage;

(b) during which the accused may, while awaiting completion of that stage, be—

   (i) in the custody of a magistrates' court; or

   (ii) in the custody of the Crown Court;

   in relation to that offence.

(2) The Regulations may, in particular—

(a) be made so as to apply only in relation to proceedings instituted in specified areas, or proceedings of, or against persons of, specified classes or descriptions;

(b) make different provision with respect to proceedings instituted in different areas, or different provision with respect to proceedings of, or against persons of, different classes or descriptions;

(c) make such provision with respect to the procedure to be followed in criminal proceedings as the secretary of State considers appropriate in consequence of any other provision of the regulations;

(d) provide for the Magistrates' Courts Act 1980 and the Bail Act 1976 to apply in relation to cases to which custody or overall time limits apply subject to such modifications as may be specified (being modifications which the Secretary of State considers necessary in consequence of any provision made by the regulations); and

(e) make such transitional provision in relation to proceedings instituted before the commencement of any provision of the regulations as the Secretary of State considers appropriate.

(3) The appropriate[4] court may, at any time before the expiry[5] of a time limit imposed by the regulations, extend[6], or further extend, that limit; but the court shall not do so unless it is satisfied[7]—

(a) that the need for the extension is due to—

   (i) the illness or absence of the accused, a necessary witness, a judge or a magistrate;

   (ii) a postponement which is occasioned by the ordering by the court of separate trials in the case of two or more accused or two or more offences; or

   (iii) some other good and sufficient cause[8]; and

(b) that the prosecution[9] has acted with all due diligence[10] and expedition.

(4) Where, in relation to any proceedings for an offence, an overall time limit has expired before the completion of the stage of the proceedings to which the limit applies, the appropriate court shall stay the proceedings.

(5) Where—

(a) a person escapes from the custody of a magistrates' court or the Crown Court before the expiry of a custody time limit which applies in his case; or

(b) a person who has been released on bail in consequence of the expiry of a custody time limit—

   (i) fails to surrender himself into the custody of the court at the appointed time; or

   (ii) is arrested by a constable on a ground mentioned in section 7(3)(b) of the Bail Act 1976 (breach, or likely breach, of conditions of bail);

the regulations shall, so far as they provide for any custody time limit in relation to the preliminary stage in question, be disregarded.

(6) Subsection (6A) below applies where

(a) a person escapes from the custody of a magistrates' court or the Crown Court; or (*b*)   a person who has been released on bail fails to surrender himself into the custody of the court at the appointed time;

and is accordingly unlawfully at large for any period.

(6A)   The following, namely—

(*a*)   the period for which the person is unlawfully at large; and

(*b*)   such additional period (if any) as the appropriate court may direct, having regard to the disruption of the prosecution occasioned by—

(i)   the person's escape or failure to surrender; and

(ii)   the length of the period mentioned in paragraph (*a*) above,

shall be disregarded, so far as the offence in question is concerned, for the purposes of the overall time limit which applies in his case in relation to the stage which the proceedings have reached at the time of the escape or, as the case may be, at the appointed time.

(7)   Where a magistrates' court decides to extend, or further extend, a custody or overall time limit, or to give a direction under subsection (6A) above, the accused may appeal against the decision to the Crown Court.

(8)   Where a magistrates' court refuses to extend, or further extend, a custody or overall time limit, or to give a direction under subsection (6A) above, the prosecution may appeal against the refusal to the Crown Court.

(9)   An appeal under subsection (8) above may not be commenced after the expiry of the limit in question; but where such an appeal is commenced before the expiry of the limit the limit shall be deemed not to have expired before the determination or abandonment of the appeal.

(10)   Where a person is convicted of an offence in any proceedings, the exercise, in relation to any preliminary stage of those proceedings, of the power conferred by subsection (3) above shall not be called into question in any appeal against that conviction.

(11)   In this section—

"appropriate court" means—

(*a*)   where the accused has been committed for trial, sent for trial under section 51 of the Crime and Disorder Act 1998 or indicted for the offence, the Crown Court; and

(*b*)   in any other case, the magistrates' court specified in the summons or warrant in question or, where the accused has already appeared or been brought before a magistrates' court, a magistrates' court for the same area;

"custody" includes local authority accommodation to which a person is remanded or committed by virtue of section 23 of the Children and Young Persons Act 1969, and references to a person being committed to custody shall be construed accordingly;

"custody of the Crown Court" includes custody to which a person is committed in pursuance of—

(*a*)   section 6 of the Magistrates' Courts Act 1980 (magistrates' court committing accused for trial); or

(*b*)   section 43A of that Act (magistrates' court dealing with a person brought before it following his arrest in pursuance of a warrant issued by the Crown Court); or;

(*c*)   section 5(3)(*a*) of the Criminal Justice Act 1987 (custody after transfer order in fraud case); or;

(*d*)   paragraph 2(1)(*a*) of Schedule 6 to the Criminal Justice Act 1991 (custody after transfer order in certain cases involving children);*

"custody of a magistrates' court"[11] means custody to which a person is committed in pursuance of section 128 of the Magistrates' Courts Act 1980 (remand);

"custody time limit" means a time limit imposed by regulations made under subsection (1)(*b*) above or, where any such limit has been extended by a court under subsection (3) above, the limit as so extended;

"preliminary stage", in relation to any proceedings, does not include any stage after the start of the trial (within the meaning given by subsections (11A) and (11B) below);

"overall time limit" means a time limit imposed by regulations made under subsection (1)(*a*) above or, where any such limit has been extended by a court under subsection (3) above, the limit as so extended; and

"specified" means specified in the regulations.

(11ZA)   For the purposes of this section, proceedings for an offence shall be taken to begin when the accused is charged with the offence or, as the case may be, an information is laid charging him with the offence.

(11A)   For the purposes of this section, the start of a trial on indictment shall be taken to occur at the time when a jury is sworn to consider the issue of guilt or fitness to plead or, if the court accepts a plea of guilty before the time when a jury is sworn, when that plea is accepted; but this is subject to section 8 of the Criminal Justice Act 1987 and section 30 of the Criminal Procedure and Investigations Act 1996 (preparatory hearings).

(11AA)   The references in subsection (11A) above to the time when a jury is sworn include the time when that jury would be sworn but for the making of an order under Part 7 of the Criminal Justice Act 2003.

(11B)   For the purposes of this section, the start of a summary trial shall be taken to occur—

(*a*) when the court begins to hear evidence for the prosecution at the trial or to consider whether to exercise its power under section 37(3) of the Mental Health Act 1983 (power to make hospital order without convicting the accused), or

(*b*) if the court accepts a plea of guilty without proceeding as mentioned above, when that plea is accepted.

(12) For the purposes of the application of any custody time limit in relation to a person who is in the custody of a magistrates' court or the Crown Court—

(*a*) all periods during which he is in the custody of a magistrates' court in respect of the same offence shall be aggregated and treated as a single continuous period; and

(*b*) all periods during which he is in the custody of the Crown Court in respect of the same offence shall be aggregated and treated similarly.

(13) For the purposes of section 29(3) of the Supreme Court Act 1981** (High Court to have power to make prerogative orders in relation to jurisdiction of Crown Court in matters which do not relate to trial on indictment) the jurisdiction conferred on the Crown Court by this section shall be taken to be part of its jurisdiction in matters other than those relating to trial on indictment.
[Prosecution of Offences Act 1985, s 22 as amended by the Criminal Justice Act 1988, Sch 15, the Criminal Justice Act 1991, Sch 11, the Criminal Justice and Public Order Act 1994, Sch 9, the Criminal Procedure and Investigations Act 1996, s 71, the Crime and Disorder Act 1998, s 43, the Access to Justice Act 1999, s 67 and the Criminal Justice Act 2003, Sch 36.]

---

*Definition substituted by the Criminal Justice Act 2003, Sch 3. In force (in relation to cases sent for trial under the Crime and Disorder Act 1998, ss 51 or 51A(3)(d)) as from 9 May 2005; in force for remaining purposes from a date to be appointed.
**Words substituted by the Constitutional Reform Act, Sch 11 from a date to be appointed.
1. Part III contains ss 22–28.
2. The Prosecution of Offences (Custody Time Limits) Regulations 1987, this PART: STATUTORY INSTRUMENTS ON PROCEDURE, post, have been made.
3. For the meaning of "preliminary stage", see s 22(11), post. Applying that definition, on the expiry of a custody time limit in the Crown Court the right of the defendant to be granted bail continues only until arraignment and not until the commencement of the trial (*R v Croydon Crown Court, ex p Lewis* (1994) 158 JP 886). As the preliminary stage of proceedings in the Crown Court ends when the jury is sworn in to consider the issue of guilt, the custody time limit does not continue contingently through the trial against the event of it aborting. Nor does it extend to the period between trial and retrial, where the retrial has not been directed by the Court of Appeal (*R v Crown Court at Leeds, ex p Whitehead* (1999) 164 JP 102, DC).
4. "Appropriate court" is defined in subsection (11). Where the accused has been committed for trial or indicted for the offence, and an application for an extension of the custody time-limit has been refused by a judge of the Crown Court acting under a fundamental and critical misapprehension of the facts, it is not an abuse of process of the court for the prosecution, before expiry of the existing time-limit, to make a fresh application, if possible, to the same judge or, if that is not possible, to the senior judge available to hear it (*R v Crown Court at Bradford, ex p Crossling* (1999) 163 JP 821, [2000] 1 Cr App Rep 463, [2000] Crim LR 171).
5. For this purpose, the custody period begins at the close of the day during which the accused person is first remanded and expires at the relevant midnight thereafter (*R v Governor of Canterbury Prison, ex p Craig* [1991] 2 QB 195, [1990] 2 All ER 654, 154 JP 137). Once a custody time limit has expired without an application to extend having been made, magistrates have no power to grant an extension of time but must grant bail: a defendant may, however, subsequently be committed for trial in custody when the time limit in reg 5(3) of the Prosecution of Offences (Custody Time Limits) Regulations 1987 (post) will apply (*R v Sheffield Justices, ex p Turner* [1991] 2 QB 472, [1991] 1 All ER 858, 155 JP 173).
Once the custody time limit has expired, the accused is unlawfully detained and an order for his release may be obtained from the court. However, it does not follow that in the absence of any such order the prison governor will be guilty of falsely imprisoning the accused because the governor is neither entitled nor bound to release the accused without an order of the court; see *Olutu v Home Office* [1997] 1 All ER 385. Before justices decide which of a number of trials that are ready to start should begin first, they should be given information as to the statutory time limits that apply for each case (*Re C* (2000) 164 JP 693, DC).
6. Proper compliance requires that (*a*) the prosecutor makes his application for an extension clearly and unmistakably; (*b*) the defence have an opportunity to raise objections and make representations; (*c*) the chairman of the bench announces in the clearest possible terms the order made by the court and gives details of it; and (*d*) the clerk of the court ensures that a proper record is made of the order (*Re Ward, Ward and Bond* (1990) 155 JP 181, [1991] Crim LR 558).
7. The court should be satisfied on the balance of probabilities (*R v Governor of Canterbury Prison, ex p Craig* [1991] 2 QB 195, [1990] 2 All ER 654, 154 JP 137). The procedure for applying for an extension of the custody time limits may be more informal than a normal trial process and, that being so, it is unnecessary to comply with the formal rules of evidence; but the prosecution must satisfy the justices that it is a proper application and, insofar as it is necessary for the defendant to test any aspect of the application, then the means must be provided for him to do that, though this will not normally require formal disclosure of the sort that is appropriate prior to the trial: *Wildman v DPP* [2001] EWCA Admin 14, [2001] Crim LR 565, (2001) The Times, February 8.
8. Bail Act considerations are not properly to be considered when the court addresses the question of whether there is a good and sufficient cause to extend the custody time limit; the two regimes are separate and different: *R (on the application of Eliot) v Crown Court at Reading* [2001] EWHC Admin 464, [2002] 1 Cr App Rep 3, [2001] 4 All ER 625. A proper and reasonable requirement of the defence for time to consider the case may be a good and sufficient cause for an extension of the time limit, provided the prosecution has acted with all due expedition; see *McKay White v DPP* [1989] Crim LR 375. The desirability of trying co-defendants together is capable of being a good and sufficient cause for extension of the custody time limit (*R v Central Criminal Court, ex p Abu-Wardeh* [1997] 1 All ER 159, 161 JP 142). The protection of a member of the public from violence is capable of being a good and sufficient cause (*R v Crown Court at Neaves* (1992) 157 JP 80), but the correctness of this decision was doubted in *R v Central Criminal Court, ex p Abu-Wardeh* [1997] 1 All ER 159, 161 JP 142. However, neither the seriousness of the charge nor the shortness of the extension sought constitute "good and sufficient cause" (*R v Governor of Winchester Prison, ex p Roddie* [1991] 2 All ER 931, [1991] 1 WLR 303). The words "good and sufficient cause" are neither constrained nor defined in the Act and the phrase is not suitable for judicial definition; lack of a court or a judge could come within it (*R v Crown Court at Norwich, ex p Cox* (1993) 97 Cr App Rep 145, 157 JP 593, CA, followed in *R v Central Criminal Court, ex p Abu-Wardeh* [1997] 1 All ER 159, 161 JP 142, *R v Manchester Crown Court, ex p McDonald* [1999] 1 WLR 841, and *Regina (Gibson) v Crown Court at Winchester (Crown Prosecution Service)* [2004] EWHC 361 (Admin), [2004] 3 ALL ER 475, [2004] 1 WLR 1623, [2004] 2 Cr App R 14),

but an adjournment to investigate an expedited trial date has been held not to be (*R v Crown Court at Maidstone, ex p Schulz and Steinkellner* (1992) 157 JP 601).

9. The words "before the expiry of a time limit imposed by the regulations" mean "before the expiry of a time limit imposed by the regulations as extended, if appropriate, by the court": *R (on the application of Haque) v Central Criminal Court* [2003] EWHC Admin. 2457, [2004] Crim LR 298. "Prosecution" for this purpose includes those collectively responsible, namely the police and the Crown Prosecution Service, for the distinct stages in the conduct of the prosecution; see *R v Crown Court at Birmingham, ex p Ricketts* [1991] RTR 105, [1990] Crim LR 745. A forensic science laboratory is not part of the prosecution for the purposes of s 22. However, that fact does not entitle the prosecution, in the form of the police or the Crown Prosecution Service, or any other prosecuting authority, to refrain from taking any action and to disclaim responsibility for delay by a forensic science laboratory in producing evidence. A prosecuting authority is obliged to do all in its power to ensure, so far as it reasonably can, that the necessary evidence is available within the relevant custody time limits (*R v Central Criminal Court, ex p Johnson* [1999] 2 Cr App Rep 51).

10. The matters to be considered by a court in determining whether to extend custody time limits were summarised in *R v Crown Court at Manchester, ex p MacDonald* [1999] 1 All ER 805, [1999] 1 WLR 841, [1999] 1 Cr App Rep 409, DC, and include the following—

(*a*) the court must give full weight to the overriding purpose of this subjection namely

  (i) to ensure that the periods for which unconvicted defendants are held in custody are as short as reasonable and practically possible;
  (ii) to ensure the prosecution prepare cases for trial with all the due diligence and expedition;
  (iii) to invest the court with a power and duty to control any extension of the prescribed maximum period;

(*b*) the prosecution must satisfy the court on the balance of probabilities that the conditions in s 22(2) are met;
(*c*) the court cannot grant an extension on the nod, even if the parties agree, it must address its mind to s 22(3);
(*d*) whether it is necessary to call evidence will depend on the circumstances of the case;
(*e*) the maximum time limits are a maximum not a target;
(*f*) the prosecution need not show that every stage of preparation of the case has been accomplished as quickly and efficiently as humanly possible, nor should it be assumed that all involved on the prosecution side have been able to give the case in question their undivided attention. What is required is such diligence and expedition as would be shown by a competent prosecutor conscious of his duty to bring the case to trial as quickly as reasonably and fairly possible;
(*g*) the court will not pay attention to pretexts such as chronic staff shortages, overwork, sickness, absenteeism or matters of that kind;
(*h*) seriousness of the charge or the need to protect the public cannot of itself be a good and sufficient cause nor is it a good cause that the extension is only for a short period (as to this see also *R v Sheffield Crown Court, ex p Headley* [2000] 2 Cr App R1, [2000] Crim LR 374, CA).

When a contested application is made for the extension of a custody time limit and the issue turns wholly or in part on whether the prosecution have acted with all due diligence and expedition, a detailed chronology, preferably agreed, should be provided to the court which is to rule on that issue (*R v Crown Court at Chelmsford, ex p Mills* (1999) 164 JP 1).

The requirements of "good and sufficient cause" and the prosecution acting with "all due diligence and expedition" are linked, but that does not mean that the court is obliged to refuse the extension of a custody time limit because the prosecution is shown to have been guilty of avoidable delay where that delay has had no effect whatever on the ability of the prosecution and the defence to be ready for trial on a predetermined trial date; ie lack of due diligence and expedition on some matters will not prevent an extension of custody time limits if that is not the cause of the need for the extension (see *Ex p Bagoutie* (1999) The Times 31 May; and *Regina (Gibson) v Crown Court at Winchester (Crown Prosecution Service)* [2004] EWHC 361 (Admin), [2004] 1 WLR 1623, [2004] 2 Cr App R 14).

When ruling on an application, the court should not only state its decision but also its reasons for reaching it and, if an extension is granted, for holding the conditions in s 23(3) to be satisfied. These provisions create a rigorous regime and impose important burdens on the prosecution. Accordingly, once the prosecution judge a piece of evidence as likely to be of importance, they should ensure that it is made available to the defence swiftly (*R v Central Criminal Court, ex p Behbehani* [1994] Crim LR 352). Where the court has imposed an obligation to produce certain information within a specified period it is open to the defendant, while that obligation is in place, to explore whether the prosecution is pursuing its inquiries with due diligence; but in a complex investigation it is unrealistic to expect a prosecutor who is seeking an extension of the custody time limit to be armed with detailed information as to every aspect of the inquiry and, if the defence require such detail, reasonable notice has to be given, and if it is not, the court may decide that at least for the time being general information will suffice (*R (on the application of Smith) v Woolwich Crown Court* [2002] EWHC 995 (Admin), [2002] Crim LR 915). Due diligence was lacking where the court laid down a timetable for service of forensic evidence, but the officer in charge of the case and the person in charge of forensic investigations set their own timetable and the evidence was not actually served until 12 weeks after the deadline set by the court (*R (on the application of Holland) v Crown Court at Leeds* [2002] EWHC 1862 (Admin), [2003] Crim LR 272).

The test of due expedition must be judged objectively, and it is not sufficient that the prosecution have done their best in difficult circumstances (see *R v Governor of Winchester Prison, ex p Roddie* [1991] 2 All ER 931, [1991] 1 WLR 303). In deciding whether there is good and sufficient cause to grant the extension, reference must be made to the presence or absence of all due expedition at the stage to which the custody time limit relates (*R v Birmingham Crown Court, ex p Bell* (1997) 161 JP 345, [1997] 2 Cr App Rep 363). Delay does not necessarily mean lack of due expedition; there may be delays for a number of perfectly legitimate reasons and delays readily explained. Lack of due expedition, whilst it must import some delay, also has to involve a different concept, in other words, some lack of responsibility on the part of those having the conduct of the prosecution; per Farquharson LJ in *R v Crown Court at Birmingham, ex p Ricketts* [1991] RTR 105, [1990] Crim LR 745. The court is not called upon to hear evidence concerning the manner in which preparation for the committal or trial has been conducted since the question of "due expedition" is one solely for the justices (*R v Crown Court at Norwich, ex p Parker* (1992) 156 JP 818, 96 Cr App Rep 68, [1992] Crim LR 500). The duty of the prosecution to act with due expedition requires the defence to have time to consider and achieve a s 6(1) or s 6(2) committal within the custody time limits and is not restricted to the possibility of achieving an uncontested committal within those time limits (*R v Leeds Crown Court, ex p Briggs (No 2)* [1998] 2 Cr App Rep 424, [1998] Crim LR 746, sub nom *R v Leeds Crown Court, ex p Briggs* (1998) 162 JP 623, DC.

Section 25 of the Criminal Justice and Public Order Act 1994 continues to have effect after the expiration of a defendant's custody time limit, and the fact that the prosecution has failed to satisfy the court that it has acted with all due diligence for the purpose of obtaining an extension of the custody time limit does not mean that the prosecution has failed to display "special diligence in the conduct of the proceedings" such as to breach article 5(3) of the Convention; the time span covered by art 5(3) is different from that which is laid down for custody time limits (*R (O) v Crown Court at Harrow* [2003] EWHC 868 (Admin), [2003] 1 WLR 2756).

11. The custody time limits apply equally to a person who remains in custody because of inability to meet a condition to be complied with before release on bail (*Re Ofili* [1995] Crim LR 880).

1–2917A   22A. Additional time limits for persons under 18.   (1) The Secretary of State may by regulations[1] make provision—

(a)   with respect to a person under the age of 18 at the time of his arrest in connection with an offence, as to the maximum period to be allowed for the completion of the stage beginning with his arrest and ending with the date fixed for his first appearance in court in connection with the offence ("the initial stage");

(b)   with respect to a person convicted of an offence who was under that age at the time of his arrest for the offence or (where he was not arrested for it) the laying of the information charging him with it, as to the period within which the stage between his conviction and his being sentenced for the offence should be completed.

(2)   Subsection (2) of section 22 above applies for the purposes of regulations under subsection (1) above as if—

(a)   the reference in paragraph (d) to custody or overall time limits were a reference to time limits imposed by the regulations; and

(b)   the reference in paragraph (e) to proceedings instituted before the commencement of any provisions of the regulations were a reference to a stage begun before that commencement.

(3)   A magistrates' court may, at any time before the expiry of the time limit imposed by the regulations under subsection (1)(a) above ("the initial stage time limit"), extend, or further extend, that limit; but the court shall not do so unless it is satisfied—

(a)   that the need for the extension is due to some good and sufficient cause; and

(b)   that the investigation has been conducted, and (where applicable) the prosecution has acted, with all due diligence and expedition.

(4)   Where the initial stage time limit (whether as originally imposed or as extended or further extended under subsection (3) above) expires before the person arrested is charged with the offence, he shall not be charged with it unless further evidence relating to it is obtained, and—

(a)   if he is then under arrest, he shall be released;

(b)   if he is then on bail under Part IV of the Police and Criminal Evidence Act 1984, his bail (and any duty or conditions to which it is subject) shall be discharged.

(5)   Where the initial stage time limit (whether as originally imposed or as extended or further extended under subsection (3) above) expires after the person arrested is charged with the offence but before the date fixed for his first appearance in court in connection with it, the court shall stay the proceedings.

(6)   Where—

(a)   a person escapes from arrest; or

(b)   a person who has been released on bail under Part IV of the Police and Criminal Evidence Act 1984 fails to surrender himself at the appointed time,

and is accordingly unlawfully at large for any period, that period shall be disregarded, so far as the offence in question is concerned, for the purposes of the initial stage time limit.

(7)   Subsections (7) to (9) of section 22 above apply for the purposes of this section, at any time after the person arrested has been charged with the offence in question, as if any reference (however expressed) to a custody or overall time limit were a reference to the initial stage time limit.

(8)   Where a person is convicted of an offence in any proceedings, the exercise of the power conferred by subsection (3) above shall not be called into question in any appeal against that conviction.

(9)   Any reference in this section (however expressed) to a person being charged with an offence includes a reference to the laying of an information charging him with it.

[Prosecution of Offences Act 1985, s 22A as inserted by the Crime and Disorder Act 1998, s 44.]

---

1.   The Prosecution of Offences (Youth Courts Time Limits) Regulations 1999, SI 1999/ 917 were made and applied to certain court areas but were revoked by the Prosecution of Offences (Youth Courts Time Limits) (Revocation and Transitional Provision) Regulations 2003, SI 2003/917 with effect from 22 April 2003.

1–2917B   22B. Re-institution of proceedings stayed under section 22(4) or 22A(5).   (1) This section applies where proceedings for an offence ("the original proceedings") are stayed by a court under section 22(4) or 22A(5) of this Act.

(2)   If—

(a)   in the case of proceedings conducted by the Director, the Director or a Chief Crown Prosecutor so directs;

(b)   in the case of proceedings conducted by the Director of the Serious Fraud Office, the Commissioners of Inland Revenue or the Commissioners of Customs and Excise, that Director or those Commissioners so direct; or

(c)   in the case of proceedings not conducted as mentioned in paragraph (a) or (b) above, a person designated for the purpose by the Secretary of State so directs,

fresh proceedings for the offence may be instituted within a period of three months (or such longer period as the court may allow) after the date on which the original proceedings were stayed by the court.

(3)   Fresh proceedings shall be instituted as follows—

    (*a*) where the original proceedings were stayed by the Crown Court[1], by preferring a bill of indictment;

    (*b*) where the original proceedings were stayed by a magistrates' court, by laying an information.

    (4) Fresh proceedings may be instituted in accordance with subsections (2) and (3)(*b*) above notwithstanding anything in section 127(1) of the Magistrates' Courts Act 1980 (limitation of time).

    (5) Where fresh proceedings are instituted, anything done in relation to the original proceedings shall be treated as done in relation to the fresh proceedings if the court so directs or it was done—

    (*a*) by the prosecutor in compliance or purported compliance with section 3, 4, 7 or 9 of the Criminal Procedure and Investigations Act 1996; or

    (*b*) by the accused in compliance or purported compliance with section 5 or 6 of that Act.

    (6) Where a person is convicted of an offence in fresh proceedings under this section, the institution of those proceedings shall not be called into question in any appeal against that conviction.
[Prosecution of Offences Act 1985, s 22B as inserted by the Crime and Disorder Act 1998, s 45.]

---

    1. Where proceedings are stayed by the Crown Court as the result of an appeal they are not, for the purposes of this provision, stayed by the Crown Court and the proceedings can be re-instituted by laying a fresh information (*R (on the application of the Director of Public Prosecutions) v Croydon Youth Court* [2003] EWHC 2240 (Admin), CO/1930/2003, (2003) 167 JPN 482).

1–2918   23. Discontinuance of proceedings in magistrates' courts.   (1) Where the Director of Public Prosecutions has the conduct of proceedings for an offence, this section applies in relation to the preliminary stages of those proceedings.

    (2) In this section "preliminary stage" in relation to proceedings for an offence does not include—

    (*a*) in the case of a summary offence, any stage of the proceedings after the court has begun to hear evidence for the prosecution at the trial;*

    (*b*) in the case of an indictable offence, any stage of the proceedings after—

        (i) the accused has been committed for trial; or

        (ii) the court has begun to hear evidence for the prosecution at a summary trial of the offence;*

    (*c*) in the case of any offence, any stage of the proceedings after the accused has been sent for trial under section 51 of the Crime and Disorder Act 1998 (no committal proceedings for indictable-only and related offences).*

    (3) Where, at any time during the preliminary stages of the proceedings, the Director gives notice under this section to the justices' chief executive for** the court that he does not want the proceedings to continue, they shall be discontinued[1] with effect from the giving of that notice but may be revived by notice given by the accused under subsection (7) below.

    (4) Where, in the case of a person charged with an offence after being taken into custody without a warrant, the Director gives him notice, at a time when no magistrates' court has been informed of the charge, that the proceedings against him are discontinued, they shall be discontinued with effect from the giving of that notice.

    (5) The Director shall, in any notice given under subsection (3) above, give reasons for not wanting the proceedings to continue.

    (6) On giving any notice under subsection (3) above the Director shall inform the accused of the notice and of the accused's right to require the proceedings to be continued; but the Director shall not be obliged to give the accused any indication of his reasons for not wanting the proceedings to continue.

    (7) Where the Director has given notice under subsection (3) above, the accused shall, if he wants the proceedings to continue, give notice to that effect to the justices' chief executive for** the court within the prescribed period; and where notice is so given the proceedings shall continue as if no notice had been given by the Director under subsection (3) above.

    (8) Where the justices' chief executive for** the court has been so notified by the accused he shall inform the Director.

    (9) The discontinuance of any proceedings by virtue of this section shall not prevent the institution of fresh proceedings in respect of the same offence.

    (10) In this section "prescribed" means prescribed by Criminal Procedure Rules[2].
[Prosecution of Offences Act 1985, s 23 as amended by the Crime and Disorder Act 1998, Sch 8, the Access to Justice Act 1999, Sch 13 and the Courts Act 2003, Sch 8.]

    ***In sub-s (2) paras (*a*)–(*c*) substituted by the Criminal Justice Act 2003, Sch 3 from a date to be appointed.**
    ****In sub-ss (3), (7) and (8) words "designated officer to" substituted by the Courts Act 2003, Sch 8 from a date to be appointed.**
    1. The power of discontinuance is additional to the other powers of the prosecutor to offer no evidence or to withdraw a charge, without or if required with the consent of the court (*Cooke v DPP and Brent Justices* (1991) 156 JP 497).
    2. See the Criminal Procedure Rules 2005, Part 8, in this PART, post.

1–2918A   23A. Discontinuance of proceedings after accused has been sent for trial.   (1) This section applies where—

    (*a*) the Director of Public Prosecutions, or a public authority (within the meaning of section 17 of this Act), has the conduct of proceedings for an offence; and (*b*) the accused has been sent for trial under section 51 of the Crime and Disorder Act 1998 for the offence.

(2) Where, at any time before the indictment is preferred, the Director or authority gives notice under this section to the Crown Court sitting at the place specified in the notice under section 51(7) of the Crime and Disorder Act 1998 that he or it does not want the proceedings to continue, they shall be discontinued with effect from the giving of that notice.

(3) The Director or authority shall, in any notice given under subsection (2) above, give reasons for not wanting the proceedings to continue.

(4) On giving any notice under subsection (2) above the Director or authority shall inform the accused of the notice; but the Director or authority shall not be obliged to give the accused any indication of his reasons for not wanting the proceedings to continue.

(5) The discontinuance of any proceedings by virtue of this section shall not prevent the institution of fresh proceedings in respect of the same offence.

[Prosecution of Offences Act 1985, s 23A as inserted by the Crime and Disorder Act 1998, Sch 8.]

1–2919 25. Consents to prosecutions etc. (1) This section applies to any enactment[1] which prohibits the institution or carrying on of proceedings for any offence except—

(*a*) with the consent (however expressed) of a Law Officer of the Crown or the Director; or
(*b*) where the proceedings are instituted or carried on by or on behalf of a Law Officer of the Crown or the Director;

and so applies whether or not there are other exceptions to the prohibition (and in particular whether or not the consent is an alternative to the consent of any other authority or person).

(2) An enactment to which this section applies—

(*a*) shall not prevent the arrest without warrant, or the issue or execution of a warrant for the arrest, of a person for any offence, or the remand in custody or on bail of a person charged with any offence; and
(*b*) shall be subject to any enactment concerning the apprehension or detention of children or young persons.

(3) In this section "enactment" includes any provision having effect under or by virtue of any Act; and this section applies to enactments whenever passed or made.

[Prosecution of Offences Act 1985, s 25.]

1. In *R v Whale and Lockton* [1991] Crim LR 692, CA, proceedings under s 4 of the Explosive Substances Act 1883 were "instituted" for the purposes of s 7 of that Act (as substituted) when the case proceeded beyond the formalities of charging and ensuing remands to the committal proceedings.

1–2920 26. Consents to be admissible in evidence. Any document purporting to be the consent of a Law Officer of the Crown, the Director or a Crown Prosecutor for, or to—

(*a*) the institution of any criminal proceedings; or
(*b*) the institution of criminal proceedings in any particular form;

and to be signed by a Law Officer of the Crown, the Director or, as the case may be, a Crown Prosecutor shall be admissible as prima facie evidence without further proof.

[Prosecution of Offences Act 1985, s 26.]

PART IV[1]

SUPPLEMENTAL

1–2931 29. Regulations. (1) Any power to make regulations under this Act shall be exercisable by statutory instrument subject to annulment in pursuance of a resolution of either House of Parliament.

(2) Any such regulations may make different provisions with respect to different cases or classes of case.

[Prosecution of Offences Act 1985, s 29.]

1. Part IV contains ss 29–31.

1–2932 30. *Expenses*.

1–2933 31. Short title commencement and extent etc. (1) This Act may be cited as the Prosecution of Offences Act 1985.

(2) The following provisions of this Act come into force on its passing—

(*a*) this Part (other than subsections (5) and (6) below);
(*b*) sections 11 to 13; and
(*c*) section 15, so far as it applies in relation to sections 11 to 13;

and the remaining provisions of this Act shall come into force on such day as the Lord Chancellor or Secretary of State may by order[1] made by statutory instrument appoint.

(3) An order under subsection (2) above may—

(*a*) appoint different days for different purposes and relation to proceedings instituted in different areas; and (*b*) contain such transitional and supplementary provisions as appear to the Lord Chancellor or, as the case may be, Secretary of State to be necessary or expedient.

(4) Paragraphs (*a*) and (*c*) of section 3(2) of this Act shall not apply in relation to proceedings instituted before their commencement and paragraph (*d*) of section 3(2) shall not apply in relation to proceedings begun by a summons issued before its commencement.

(5) Schedule 1 to this Act shall have effect for the purpose of making minor and consequential amendments in other enactments.

(6) The enactments specified in Schedule 2 to this Act (which include certain provisions which are already spent) are hereby repealed to the extent set out in the third column of that Schedule.

(7) This Act does not extend to Scotland or Northern Ireland.

[Prosecution of Offences Act 1985, s 31.]

---

1. See the Prosecution of Offences Act 1985 (Commencement No 1) Order 1985, SI 1985/1849; (Commencement No 2) Order 1986, SI 1986/1029 and (Commencement No 3) Order 1986, SI 1986/1334.

Criminal Justice Act 1987

(1987 c 38)

Part I[1]
Fraud

Serious Fraud Office

1–3040 1. The Serious Fraud Office.   (1) A Serious Fraud Office shall be constituted for England and Wales and Northern Ireland.

(2) The Attorney General shall appoint a person to be the Director of the Serious Fraud Office (referred to in this Part of this Act as "the Director"), and he shall discharge his functions under the superintendence of the Attorney General.

(3) The Director may investigate any suspected offence which appears to him on reasonable grounds to involve serious or complex fraud[2].

(4) The Director may, if he thinks fit, conduct any such investigation in conjunction either with the police or with any other person who is, in the opinion of the Director, a proper person to be concerned in it.

(5) The Director may—

(*a*) institute and have the conduct of any criminal proceedings which appear to him to relate to such fraud; and

(*b*) take over the conduct of any such proceedings at any stage.

(6) The Director shall discharge such other functions in relation to fraud as may from time to time be assigned to him by the Attorney General.

(7) The Director may designate for the purposes of subsection (5) above any member of the Serious Fraud Office who is—

(*a*) a barrister in England and Wales or Northern Ireland;

(*b*) a solicitor of the Supreme Court; or

(*c*) a solicitor of the Supreme Court of Judicature of Northern Ireland.

(8) Any member so designated shall, without prejudice to any functions which may have been assigned to him in his capacity as a member of that Office, have all the powers of the Director as to the institution and conduct of proceedings but shall exercise those powers under the direction of the Director.

(9)–(11) *Repealed.*

(12)–(14) *Northern Ireland.*

(15) Schedule 1 to this Act shall have effect.

(16) For the purposes of this section (including that Schedule) references to the conduct of any proceedings include references to the proceedings being discontinued and to the taking of any steps (including the bringing of appeals and making of representations in respect of applications for bail) which may be taken in relation to them.

(17) *Northern Ireland.*

[Criminal Justice Act 1987, s 1 as amended by the Access to Justice Act 1999, Sch 15.]

---

1. Part I contains ss 1–12.

2. Section 1(3) only confers a power to investigate; it does not impose a positive duty on the director to investigate so that, by proceeding to prosecute, he may pre-empt the eventual trial venue in favour of the UK where it appears that the Convention rights of a suspect may be violated by trial elsewhere: *R (on the application of Bermingham) v Director of the Serious Fraud Office* [2006] EWHC 200, [2006] 3 All ER 239.

1–3041 2. Director's investigation powers.   (1) The powers of the Director under this section shall be exercisable, but only for the purposes of an investigation under section 1 above or, on a request made by an authority entitled to make such a request, in any case in which it appears to him that there is good reason to do so for the purpose of investigating the affairs, or any aspect of the affairs, of any person.

(1A) The authorities entitled to request the Director to exercise his powers under this section are—

(*a*) the Attorney-General of the Isle of Man, Jersey or Guernsey, acting under legislation corresponding to section 1 of this Act and having effect in the Island whose Attorney-General makes the request; and

(*b*) the Secretary of State acting under section 15(2) of the Crime (International Co-operation) Act 2003, in response to a request received by him from a person mentioned in section 13(2) of that Act (an "overseas authority").

(1B) The Director shall not exercise his powers on a request from the Secretary of State acting in response to a request received from an overseas authority within subsection (1A)(*b*) above unless it appears to the Director on reasonable grounds that the offence in respect of which he has been requested to obtain evidence involves serious or complex fraud.

(2) The Director may by notice in writing require the person whose affairs are to be investigated ("the person under investigation"[1]) or any other person whom he has reason to believe has relevant information to answer questions or otherwise furnish information with respect to any matter relevant to the investigation at a specified place and either at a specified time or forthwith[2].

(3) The Director may by notice in writing require the person under investigation[1] or any other person[3] to produce at such place as may be specified in the notice and either forthwith or at such time as may be so specified, any specified documents which appear to the Director to relate to any matter relevant to the investigation or any documents of a specified description which appear to him so to relate; and—

(*a*) if any such documents are produced, the Director may—

(i)   take copies or extracts from them;
(ii) require the person producing them to provide an explanation of any of them;

(*b*) if any such documents are not produced, the Director may require the person who was required to produce them to state, to the best of his knowledge and belief, where they are.

(4) Where, on information on oath laid by a member of the Serious Fraud Office[4], a justice of the peace is satisfied, in relation to any documents, that there are reasonable grounds for believing—

(*a*) that—

(i)   a person has failed to comply with an obligation under this section to produce them;
(ii)   it is not practicable to serve a notice under subsection (3) above in relation to them; or
(iii) the service of such a notice in relation to them might seriously prejudice the investigation; and

(*b*) that they are on premises specified in the information,

he may issue such a warrant as is mentioned in subsection (5) below.

(5) The warrant referred to above is a warrant authorising any constable—

(*a*) to enter (using such force as is reasonably necessary for the purpose) and search the premises, and

(*b*) to take possession of any documents appearing to be documents of the description specified in the information or to take in relation to any documents so appearing any other steps which may appear to be necessary for preserving them and preventing interference with them.

(6) Unless it is not practicable in the circumstances, a constable executing a warrant issued under subsection (4) above shall be accompanied by an appropriate person.

(6A) Where an appropriate person accompanies a constable, he may exercise the powers conferred by subsection (5) but only in the company, and under the supervision, of the constable.

(7) In this section "appropriate person" means—

(*a*) a member of the Serious Fraud Office; or
(*b*) some person who is not a member of that Office but whom the Director has authorised to accompany the constable.

(8) A statement by a person in response to a requirement imposed by virtue of this section may only be used in evidence against him—

(*a*) on a prosecution for an offence under subsection (14) below; or
(*b*) on a prosecution for some other offence where in giving evidence he makes a statement inconsistent with it.

(8AA) However, the statement may not be used against that person by virtue of paragraph (*b*) of subsection (8) unless evidence relating to it is adduced, or a question relating to it is asked, by or on behalf of that person in the proceedings arising out of the prosecution.

(8A) Any evidence obtained by the Director for use by an overseas authority shall be given to the overseas authority which requested it or given to the Secretary of State for forwarding to that overseas authority).

(8B) *Repealed.*

(8C) Where any evidence obtained by the Director for use by an overseas authority consists of a document the original or a copy shall be forwarded and where it consists of any other article the article itself or a description, photograph or other representation of it shall be forwarded as may be necessary in order to comply with the request of the overseas authority.

(8D) The references in subsections (8A) to (8C) above to evidence obtained by the Director include references to evidence obtained by him by virtue of the exercise by a constable, in the course of a search authorised by a warrant issued under subsection (4) above, of powers conferred by section 50 of the Criminal Justice and Police Act 2001.

(9) A person shall not under this section be required to disclose any information or produce any document which he would be entitled to refuse to disclose or produce on grounds of legal professional privilege in proceedings in the High Court, except that a lawyer may be required to furnish the name and address of his client.

(10) A person shall not under this section be required to disclose information or produce a document in respect of which he owes an obligation of confidence by virtue of carrying on any banking business unless—

(a) the person to whom the obligation of confidence is owed consents to the disclosure or production; or

(b) the Director has authorised the making of the requirement or, if it is impracticable for him to act personally, a member of the Serious Fraud Office designated by him for the purposes of this subsection has done so.

(11) Without prejudice to the power of the Director to assign functions to members of the Serious Fraud Office, the Director may authorise any competent investigator (other than a constable) who is not a member of that Office to exercise on his behalf all or any of the powers conferred by this section, but no such authority shall be granted except for the purpose of investigating the affairs, or any aspect of the affairs, of a person specified in the authority.

(12) No person shall be bound to comply with any requirement imposed by a person exercising powers by virtue of any authority granted under subsection (11) above unless he has, if required to do so, produced evidence of his authority.

(13) Any person who without reasonable excuse fails to comply with a requirement imposed on him under this section shall be guilty of an offence and liable on summary conviction to imprisonment for a term not exceeding **six months** or to a fine not exceeding **level 5** on the standard scale or to both.

(14) A person who, in purported compliance with a requirement under this section—

(a) makes a statement which he knows to be false or misleading in a material particular; or

(b) recklessly makes a statement which is false or misleading in a material particular,

shall be guilty of an offence.

(15) A person guilty of an offence under subsection (14) above shall[5]—

(a) on conviction on indictment, be liable to imprisonment for a term not exceeding **two years** or to a **fine** or to both; and

(b) on summary conviction, be liable to imprisonment for a term not exceeding **six months** or to a fine not exceeding **the statutory maximum**, or to both.

(16) Where any person—

(a) knows or suspects that an investigation by the police or the Serious Fraud Office into serious or complex fraud is being or is likely to be carried out; and

(b) falsifies, conceals, destroys or otherwise disposes of, or causes or permits the falsification, concealment, destruction or disposal of documents which he knows or suspects are or would be relevant to such an investigation,

he shall be guilty of an offence unless he proves that he had no intention of concealing the facts disclosed by the documents from persons carrying out such an investigation.

(17) A person guilty of an offence under subsection (16) above shall[4]—

(a) on conviction on indictment, be liable to imprisonment for a term not exceeding **7 years** or to a **fine** or to both; and

(b) on summary conviction, be liable to imprisonment for a term not exceeding **6 months** or to a fine not exceeding **the statutory maximum** or to both.

(18) In this section, "documents" includes information recorded in any form and, in relation to information recorded otherwise than in legible form, references to its production include references to producing a copy of the information in legible form; and "evidence" (in relation to subsections (1A)(b), (8A), and (8C) above) includes documents and other articles.

(19) *Scotland; Northern Ireland.*

[Criminal Justice Act 1987, s 2 as amended by the Criminal Justice Act 1988, s 143 and Sch 15, the Criminal Justice and Public Order Act 1994, s 164 and the Youth Justice and Criminal Evidence Act 1999, Sch 3 and the Criminal Justice and Police Act 2001, Sch 2.]

---

1. The powers of the Director under this section do not come to an end when the person under investigation has been charged; accordingly, the Director is entitled to compel such person to answer questions and no caution is appropriate (*Smith v Director of Serious Fraud Office* [1992] 3 All ER 456, [1992] 3 WLR 66, HL).

2. Where the Secretary of State receives a request under s 4 of the Criminal Justice (International Co-operation) Act 1990 for assistance in obtaining evidence in the UK for use overseas, and he refers that request to the Director pursuant to s 4(2A), the Director has the full range of powers under s 2(2): *R (Evans) v Director of the Serious Fraud Office* [2002] EWHC 2304 (Admin), [2003] 1 WLR 299. The starting position is that the letter of request is confidential and is not a disclosable; justice must be done to the recipients of notices issued under s 2(2), but those needs can normally be met by giving information as to the nature of the criminal investigation concerned: *R (Evans)*, supra.

3. The Director is authorised by s 2(3) to require office-holders, namely liquidators or receivers, to produce transcripts

of examinations and affirmations in evidence in examinations which they have conducted; see *Re Arrows Ltd (No 4)* [1993] 3 All ER 861.

4. The following principles were stated in *R (Energy Financing Team Ltd) v Bow Street Magistrates' Court (Practice Note)* [2005] EWHC 1626 (Admin), [2006] 1 WLR 1316: (*a*) before seeking or granting a warrant under s 2(4) it is necessary to consider whether some lesser measure, such as a notice under s 2(3) of the Act, will suffice. If such a notice will not suffice, consideration should be given to the possibility of obtaining the documents from an alternative untainted source, such as a bank, but where that would involve many inquiries of many institutions which might or might not be willing and able to produce the information required, the need to assist the investigating authority to make progress with its overall investigation may well render resort to alternative sources impracticable; (*b*) where the Director of the SFO is seeking a warrant pursuant to a request from abroad for mutual legal assistance the warrant need not reflect precisely the wording of the letter or letters of request. The Director has a duty to decide for himself how best to give effect to the request in furtherance of the overall investigation, and if that means going further than the letter of request he is entitled to do so; (*c*) a warrant should be drafted with sufficient precision to enable both those who execute it and those whose property is affected by it to know whether any individual document or class of documents falls within it. If that is done the specificity required will be no less than would be required for a notice under s 2(3) of the Act were it practicable to serve such a notice; and (*d*) a warrant drawn in wide terms will not simply be fishing if it is directed to support an investigation which has apparent merit.

It was further held that the applicant for a warrant must give full assistance to the district judge, including drawing to his or her attention anything that militates against the issue of a warrant. It is desirable to give the district judge time to pre-read the material relied upon, namely the sworn information, usually supported by the letter or letters of request and the draft warrant. It is important for the purposes of any subsequent review for the Director or his representative to be able to say whether that was done. If the applicant supplements the material already provided, that should be noted, as should the decision of the district judge, which should be briefly reasoned. A tape-recording of the proceedings is the best form of record, but if that is impracticable the applicant must prepare a note which can be submitted to the judge for approval if any issue arises as to the way in which the warrant was obtained. Once a warrant has been executed it cannot be reconsidered by the district judge; the only remedy is judicial review. As to what should be disclosed about the proceedings before the district judge and of the material that was laid, to assist a person affected by the warrant to consider whether or not to seek relief, see paras 24 and 30.

5. For procedure in respect of this offence which is triable either way, see the Magistrates' Courts Act 1980, ss 17A–21, this PART, ante.

1–3042   3. Disclosure of information.   (1) Where any information subject to an obligation of secrecy under the Taxes Management Act 1970 has been disclosed by the Commissioners of Inland Revenue or an officer of those Commissioners to any member of the Serious Fraud Office for the purposes of any prosecution of an offence relating to inland revenue, that information may be disclosed by any member of the Serious Fraud Office—

(*a*)   for the purposes of any prosecution of which that Office has the conduct;

(*b*)   to any member of the Crown Prosecution Service for the purposes of any prosecution of an offence relating to inland revenue; and

(*c*)   to the Director of Public Prosecutions for Northern Ireland for the purposes of any prosecution of an offence relating to inland revenue,

but not otherwise.

(2) Where the Serious Fraud Office has the conduct of any prosecution of an offence which does not relate to inland revenue, the court may not prevent the prosecution from relying on any evidence under section 78 of the Police and Criminal Evidence Act 1984 (discretion to exclude unfair evidence) by reason only of the fact that the information concerned was disclosed by the Commissioners of Inland Revenue or an officer of those Commissioners for the purposes of any prosecution of an offence relating to inland revenue.

(3) Where any information is subject to an obligation of secrecy imposed by or under any enactment other than an enactment contained in the Taxes Management Act 1970, the obligation shall not have effect to prohibit the disclosure of that information to any person in his capacity as a member of the Serious Fraud Office but any information disclosed by virtue of this subsection may only be disclosed by a member of the Serious Fraud Office for the purposes of any prosecution in England and Wales, Northern Ireland or elsewhere and may only be disclosed by such a member if he is designated by the Director for the purposes of this subsection.

(4) Without prejudice to his power to enter into agreements apart from this subsection, the Director may enter into a written agreement for the supply of information to or by him subject, in either case, to an obligation not to disclose the information concerned otherwise than for a specified purpose.

(5) Subject to subsections (1) and (3) above and to any provision of an agreement for the supply of information which restricts the disclosure of the information supplied, information obtained by any person in his capacity as a member of the Serious Fraud Office may be disclosed by any member of that Office designated by the Director for the purposes of this subsection—

(*a*)   to any government department or Northern Ireland department or other authority or body discharging its functions on behalf of the Crown (including the Crown in right of Her Majesty's Government in Northern Ireland);

(*b*)   to any competent authority;

(*c*)   for the purposes of any criminal investigation or criminal proceedings, whether in the United Kingdom or elsewhere; and

(*d*)   for the purposes of assisting any public or other authority for the time being designated for the purposes of this paragraph by an order made by the Secretary of State to discharge any functions which are specified in the order.

(6) The following are competent authorities for the purposes of subsection (5) above—

(a) an inspector appointed under Part XIV of the Companies Act 1985 or Part XV of the Companies (Northern Ireland) Order 1986;
(b) an Official Receiver;
(c) the Accountant in Bankruptcy;
(d) the Official Receiver for Northern Ireland;
(e) a person appointed under—

    (i) section 167 of the Financial Services and Markets Act 2000 (general investigations),
    (ii) section 168 of that Act (investigations in particular cases),
    (iii) section 169(1)(b) of that Act (investigation in support of overseas regulator),
    (iv) section 284 of that Act (investigations into affairs of certain collective investment schemes), or
    (v) regulations made as a result of section 262(2)(k) of that Act (investigations into open-ended investment companies),

to conduct an investigation;

(f) a body corporate established in accordance with section 212(1) of the Financial Services and Markets Act 2000 (compensation scheme manager);
(l) any body having supervisory, regulatory or disciplinary functions in relation to any profession or any area of commercial activity;
(m) any person or body having, under the law of any country or territory outside the United Kingdom, functions corresponding to any of the functions of any person or body mentioned in any of the foregoing paragraphs;
(n) any person or body having, under the Treaty on European Union or any other treaty to which the United Kingdom is a party, the function of receiving information of the kind in question;
(o) any person or body having, under the law of any country or territory outside the United Kingdom, the function of receiving information relating to the proceeds of crime.

(7) An order under subsection (5)(d) above may impose conditions subject to which, and otherwise restrict the circumstances in which, information may be disclosed under that paragraph.
[Criminal Justice Act 1987, s 3, as amended by the Criminal Justice Act 1988, Sch 15, the Criminal Justice Act 1993, Sch 6, SI 2001/3649 and the Crime (International Co-operation) Act 2003, s 80.]

Transfer of cases to Crown Court

1–3043 4. Notices of transfer and designated authorities. (1) If—

(a) a person has been charged with an indictable offence; and
(b) in the opinion of an authority designated by subsection (2) below or of one of such an authority's officers acting on the authority's behalf the evidence of the offence charged—

    (i) would be sufficient for the person charged to be committed for trial; and
    (ii) reveals a case of fraud of such seriousness or complexity that it is appropriate that the management of the case should without delay be taken over by the Crown Court; and

(c) before the magistrates' court in whose jurisdiction the offence has been charged begins to inquire into the case as examining justices, the authority or one of the authority's officers acting on the authority's behalf gives the court a notice (in this Act referred to as a "notice of transfer") certifying that opinion,

the functions of the magistrates' court shall cease in relation to the case, except as provided by section 5(3), (7A) and (8) below and by paragraph 2 of Schedule 3 to the Access to Justice Act 1999.
(2) The authorities mentioned in subsection (1) above (in this Act referred to as "designated authorities") are—

(a) the Director of Public Prosecutions;
(b) the Director of the Serious Fraud Office;
(c) the Commissioners of Inland Revenue;
(d) the Commissioners of Customs and Excise; and
(e) the Secretary of State.

(3) A designated authority's decision to give notice of transfer shall not be subject to appeal or liable to be questioned in any court.
(4) This section and sections 5 and 6 below shall not apply in any case in which section 51 of the Crime and Disorder Act 1998 (no committal proceedings for indictable-only offences) applies.
[Criminal Justice Act 1987, s 4 as amended by the Criminal Justice Act 1988, s 144, the Legal Aid Act 1988, Sch 5, the Criminal Justice and Public Order Act 1994, Sch 9 and the Crime and Disorder Act 1998, Sch 8.]

1–3044 5. Notices of transfer—procedure[1]. (1) A notice of transfer shall specify the proposed place of trial[2] and in selecting that place the designated authority shall have regard to the considerations to which section 7 of the Magistrates' Courts Act 1980 requires a magistrates' court committing a person for trial to have regard when selecting the place at which he is to be tried.
(2) A notice of transfer shall specify the charge or charges to which it relates and include or be accompanied by such additional matter as regulations under subsection (9) below may require.
(3) If a magistrates' court has remanded a person to whom a notice of transfer relates in custody, it shall have power, subject to section 4 of the Bail Act 1976 and regulations under section 22 of the Prosecution of Offences Act 1985—

(a)   to order that he shall be safely kept in custody until delivered in due course of law; or

(b)   to release him on bail in accordance with the Bail Act 1976, that is to say, by directing him to appear before the Crown Court for trial;

and where his release on bail is conditional on his providing one or more surety or sureties and, in accordance with section 8(3) of the Bail Act 1976, the court fixes the amount in which the surety is to be bound with a view to his entering into his recognizance subsequently in accordance with subsections (4) and (5) or (6) of that section, the court shall in the meantime make an order such as is mentioned in paragraph (a) of this subsection.

(4) If the conditions specified in subsection (5) below are satisfied, a court may exercise the powers conferred by subsection (3) above in relation to a person charged without his being brought before it in any case in which by virtue of section 128(3A) of the Magistrates' Courts Act 1980 it would have power further to remand him on an adjournment such as is mentioned in that subsection.

(5) The conditions mentioned in subsection (4) above are—

(a)   that the person in question has given his written consent to the powers conferred by subsection (3) above being exercised without his being brought before the court; and

(b)   that the court is satisfied that, when he gave his consent, he knew that the notice of transfer had been issued.

(6) Where notice of transfer is given after a person to whom it relates has been remanded on bail to appear before a magistrates' court on an appointed day, the requirement that he shall so appear shall cease on the giving of the notice, unless the notice states that it is to continue.

(7) Where the requirement that a person to whom the notice of transfer relates shall appear before a magistrates' court ceases by virtue of subsection (6) above, it shall be his duty to appear before the Crown Court at the place specified by the notice of transfer as the proposed place of trial or at any place substituted for it by a direction under section 76 of the Supreme Court Act 1981.

(7A) If the notice states that the requirement is to continue, when a person to whom the notice relates appears before the magistrates' court, the court shall have—

(a)   the powers and duty conferred on a magistrates' court by subsection (3) above, but subject as there provided; and

(b)   power to enlarge, in the surety's absence, a recognizance conditioned in accordance with section 128(4)(a) of the Magistrates' Courts Act 1980 so that the surety is bound to secure that the person charged appears also before the Crown Court.

(8) For the purposes of the Criminal Procedure (Attendance of Witnesses) Act 1965—

(a)   any magistrates' court for the petty sessions area for which the court from which a case was transferred sits shall be treated as examining magistrates; and

(b)   a person indicated in the notice of transfer as a proposed witness shall be treated as a person who has been examined by the court.

(9) The Attorney General—

(a)   shall by regulations[3] make provision requiring the giving of a copy of a notice of transfer, together with copies of the documents containing the evidence (including oral evidence) on which any charge to which it relates is based—

    (i)   to any person to whom the notice of transfer relates; and

    (ii)   to the Crown Court sitting at the place specified by the notice of transfer as the proposed place of trial; and*

(b)   may by regulations[3] make such further provision in relation to notices of transfer, including provision as to the duties of a designated authority in relation to such notices, as appears to him to be appropriate.

(9A) Regulations under subsection (9)(a) above may provide that there shall be no requirement for copies of documents to accompany the copy of the notice of transfer if they are referred to, in documents sent with the notice of transfer, as having already been supplied.*

(10) The power to make regulations conferred by subsection (9) above shall be exercisable by statutory instrument subject to annulment in pursuance of a resolution of either House of Parliament.

(11) Any such regulations may make different provision with respect to different cases or classes of case.**

[Criminal Justice Act 1987, s 5 as amended by the Criminal Justice Act 1988, s 144 and the Criminal Procedure and Investigations Act 1996, s 45.]

---

   *Section 5(9)(a) is printed as prospectively amended by, and s 5(9A) as inserted by, the Criminal Procedure and Investigations Act 1996, s 45. Until the amendment of s 5(9)(a) takes effect for the words "copies of the documents containing the evidence (including oral evidence)" there shall be substituted the words "a statement of the evidence".

   **Repealed by the Criminal Justice Act 2003, Sch 3, from a date to be appointed.

   1. See the Magistrates' Courts (Notices of Transfer) Rules 1988, this Part: Statutory Instruments on Procedure.

   2. The place of trial specified in a notice of transfer shall be one of the Crown Court centres specified in the *Practice Direction (criminal: consolidated)* [2002] para III.21, in this Part, post.

   3. The Criminal Justice Act 1987 (Notice of Transfer) Regulations 1988/1691 amended by SI 1997/737 and SI 2001/444 have been made: a notice of transfer, with a statement of its effect, must be given to the defendant, the Crown Court and (if the defendant is in custody) the prison governor.

1–3045 **6. Applications for dismissal.** (1) Where notice of transfer has been given, any person to whom the notice relates, at any time before he is arraigned (and whether or not an indictment has been preferred against him), may apply orally or in writing to the Crown Court sitting at the place specified by the notice of transfer as the proposed place of trial for the charge, or any of the charges, in the case to be dismissed; and the judge shall dismiss a charge (and accordingly quash a count relating to it in any indictment preferred against the applicant) if it appears to him that the evidence against the applicant would not be sufficient for a jury properly to convict him[1].

(2) No oral application may be made under subsection (1) above unless the applicant has given the Crown Court sitting at the place specified by the notice of transfer as the proposed place of trial written notice of his intention to make the application.

(3) Oral evidence may be given on such an application only with the leave of the judge or by his order, and the judge shall give leave or make an order only if it appears to him, having regard to any matters stated in the application for leave, that the interests of justice require him to do so.

(4) If the judge gives leave permitting, or makes an order requiring, a person to give oral evidence, but he does not do so, the judge may disregard any document indicating the evidence that he might have given.

(5) Dismissal of the charge, or all the charges, against the applicant shall have the same effect as a refusal by examining magistrates to commit for trial, except that no further proceedings may be brought on a dismissed charge except by means of the preferment of a voluntary bill of indictment.

(6) Crown Court Rules[2] may make provision for the purposes of this section and, without prejudice to the generality of this subsection—

(a)   as to the time or stage in the proceedings at which anything required to be done is to be done (unless the court grants leave to do it at some other time or stage);
(b)   as to the contents and form of notices or other documents;
(c)   as to the manner in which evidence is to be submitted; and
(d)   as to persons to be served with notices or other material.

[Criminal Justice Act 1987, s 6, as substituted by the Criminal Justice Act 1988, s 144.]

---

1. The exercise required of the judge is to assess the weight of the evidence. He must not substitute himself for the jury, and the question is not whether the defendant should be convicted, but the sufficiency of the evidence. Where the evidence is largely documentary and the case depends on the conclusions or inferences to be drawn from it, the judge has to assess the conclusions or inferences that the prosecution is proposing to ask the jury to draw and to decide whether it seems to him that the jury could properly come to those conclusions and draw those inferences: *R (on the application of the IRC) v Crown Court at Kingston* [2001] EWHC Admin 581, [2001 4 All ER 721.
2. See the Criminal Procedure Rules 2005, Part 13, in this PART, post..

Preparatory hearings

1–3046 **7. Power to order preparatory hearing[1].** (1) Where it appears to a judge of the Crown Court that the evidence on an indictment reveals a case of fraud of such seriousness or complexity that substantial benefits are likely to accrue from a hearing (in this Act referred to as a "preparatory hearing") before the the time when the jury are sworn, , for the purpose of—

(a)   identifying issues which are likely to be material to the verdict of the jury;
(b)   assisting their comprehension of any such issues;
(c)   expediting the proceedings before the jury; or

(d)   assisting the judge's management of the trial,*he may order that such a hearing shall be held.

[Criminal Justice Act 1987, s 7(1) as amended by the Criminal Justice and Public Order Act 1994, Sch 9, the Criminal Procedure and Investigations Act 1996, Sch 3 and the Criminal Justice Act 2003, Sch 36.]

---

*Paras (a)–(c) substituted by the Criminal Justice Act 2003, s 45 from a date to be appointed.
1. See the Criminal Procedure Rules 2005, Part 15, in this PART, post.

1–3047 **8–10.** *Supplementary provisions as to preparatory hearings.*

Reporting restrictions

1–3048 **11. Restrictions on reporting.** (1) Except as provided by this section—

(a)   no written report of proceedings falling within subsection (2) below shall be published in Great Britain;
(b)   no report of proceedings falling within subsection (2) below shall be included in a relevant programme for reception in Great Britain.

(2) The following proceedings fall within this subsection—

(a)   an application under section 6(1) above;
(b)   a preparatory hearing;
(c)   an application for leave to appeal in relation to such a hearing;
(d)   an appeal in relation to such a hearing.

(3) The judge dealing with an application under section 6(1) above may order that subsection (1) above shall not apply, or shall not apply to a specified extent, to a report of the application.

(4) The judge dealing with a preparatory hearing may order that subsection (1) above shall not apply, or shall not apply to a specified extent, to a report of—

(a) the preparatory hearing, or
(b) an application to the judge for leave to appeal to the Court of Appeal under section 9(11) above in relation to the preparatory hearing.

(5) The Court of Appeal may order that subsection (1) above shall not apply, or shall not apply to a specified extent, to a report of—

(a) an appeal to the Court of Appeal under section 9(11) above in relation to a preparatory hearing,
(b) an application to that Court for leave to appeal to it under section 9(11) above in relation to a preparatory hearing, or
(c) an application to that Court for leave to appeal to the House of Lords under Part II of the Criminal Appeal Act 1968 in relation to a preparatory hearing.

(6) The House of Lords may order that subsection (1) above shall not apply, or shall not apply to a specified extent, to a report of—

(a) an appeal to that House under Part II of the Criminal Appeal Act 1968 in relation to a preparatory hearing, or
(b) an application to that House for leave to appeal to it under Part II of the Criminal Appeal Act 1968 in relation to a preparatory hearing.

(7) Where there is only one accused and he objects to the making of an order under subsection (3), (4), (5) or (6) above the judge or the Court of Appeal or the House of Lords shall make the order if (and only if) satisfied after hearing the representations of the accused that it is in the interests of justice to do so; and if the order is made it shall not apply to the extent that a report deals with any such objection or representations.

(8) Where there are two or more accused and one or more of them objects to the making of an order under subsection (3), (4), (5) or (6) above the judge or the Court of Appeal or the House of Lords shall make the order if (and only if) satisfied after hearing the representations of each of the accused that it is in the interests of justice to do so; and if the order is made it shall not apply to the extent that a report deals with any such objection or representations.

(9) Subsection (1) above does not apply to—

(a) the publication of a report of an application under section 6(1) above, or
(b) the inclusion in a relevant programme of a report of an application under section 6(1) above,

where the application is successful.

(10) Where—

(a) two or more persons are jointly charged, and
(b) applications under section 6(1) above are made by more than one of them,

subsection (9) above shall have effect as if for the words "the application is" there were substituted "all the applications are".

(11) Subsection (1) above does not apply to—

(a) the publication of a report of an unsuccessful application made under section 6(1) above,
(b) the publication of a report of a preparatory hearing,
(c) the publication of a report of an appeal in relation to a preparatory hearing or of an application for leave to appeal in relation to such a hearing,
(d) the inclusion in a relevant programme of a report of an unsuccessful application made under section 6(1) above,
(e) the inclusion in a relevant programme of a report of a preparatory hearing, or
(f) the inclusion in a relevant programme of a report of an appeal in relation to a preparatory hearing or of an application for leave to appeal in relation to such a hearing,

at the conclusion of the trial of the accused or of the last of the accused to be tried.

(12) Subsection (1) above does not apply to a report which contains only one or more of the following matters—

(a) the identity of the court and the name of the judge;
(b) the names, ages, home addresses and occupations of the accused and witnesses;
(c) any relevant business information;
(d) the offence or offences, or a summary of them, with which the accused is or are charged;
(e) the names of counsel and solicitors in the proceedings;
(f) where the proceedings are adjourned, the date and place to which they are adjourned;
(g) any arrangements as to bail;
(h) whether a right to representation funded by the Legal Services Commission as part of the Criminal Defence Service was granted to the accused or any of the accused.

(13) The addresses that may be published or included in a relevant programme under subsection (12) above are addresses—

(a) at any relevant time, and

(b)   at the time of their publication or inclusion in a relevant programme,

and "relevant time" here means a time when events giving rise to the charges to which the proceedings relate occurred.

(14)   The following is relevant business information for the purposes of subsection (12) above—

(a)   any address used by the accused for carrying on a business on his own account;
(b)   the name of any business which he was carrying on on his own account at any relevant time;
(c)   the name of any firm in which he was a partner at any relevant time or by which he was engaged at any such time;
(d)   the address of any such firm;
(e)   the name of any company of which he was a director at any relevant time or by which he was otherwise engaged at any such time;
(f)   the address of the registered or principal office of any such company;
(g)   any working address of the accused in his capacity as a person engaged by any such company,

and here "engaged" means engaged under a contract of service or a contract for services, and "relevant time" has the same meaning as in subsection (13) above.

(15)   Nothing in this section affects any prohibition or restriction imposed by virtue of any other enactment on a publication or on matter included in a programme.

(16)   In this section—

(a)   "publish", in relation to a report, means publish the report, either by itself or as part of a newspaper or periodical, for distribution to the public;
(b)   expressions cognate with "publish" shall be construed accordingly;
(c)   "relevant programme" means a programme included in a programme service, within the meaning of the Broadcasting Act 1990.

[Criminal Justice Act 1987, s 11, as substituted by the Criminal Procedure and Investigations Act 1996, Sch 3 and the Access to Justice Act 1999, Sch 4.]

1–3048A   11A. Offences in connection with reporting.   (1) If a report is published or included in a relevant programme in contravention of section 11 above each of the following persons is guilty of an offence—

(a)   in the case of a publication of a written report as part of a newspaper or periodical, any proprietor, editor or publisher of the newspaper or periodical;
(b)   in the case of a publication of a written report otherwise than as part of a newspaper or periodical, the person who publishes it;
(c)   in the case of the inclusion of a report in a relevant programme, any body corporate which is engaged in providing the service in which the programme is included and any person having functions in relation to the programme corresponding to those of an editor of a newspaper.

(2)   A person guilty of an offence under this section is liable on summary conviction to a fine of an amount not exceeding **level 5** on the standard scale.

(3)   Proceedings for an offence under this section shall not be instituted in England and Wales otherwise than by or with the consent of the Attorney General.

(4)   Subsection (16) of section 11 above applies for the purposes of this section as it applies for the purposes of that.

[Criminal Justice Act 1987, s 11A, as inserted by the Criminal Procedure and Investigations Act 1996, Sch 3.]

Conspiracy to defraud

1–3049   12. Charges of and penalty for conspiracy to defraud.   (1) If—

(a)   a person agrees with any other person or persons that a course of conduct shall be pursued; and
(b)   that course of conduct will necessarily amount to or involve the commission of any offence or offences by one or more of the parties to the agreement if the agreement is carried out in accordance with their intentions,

the fact that it will do so shall not preclude a charge of conspiracy to defraud being brought against any of them in respect of the agreement.

(2)   *Repealed.*

(3)   A person guilty of conspiracy to defraud is liable on conviction on indictment to imprisonment for a term not exceeding **10 years** or a **fine** or both.

[Criminal Justice Act 1987, s 12.]

PART II[1]
GENERAL AND SUPPLEMENTARY

_____

1. Part II contains ss 13–18.

1–3050   17–18. *Extent; citation.*

SCHEDULES

Section 1   SCHEDULE 1
THE SERIOUS FRAUD OFFICE

(As amended by the Criminal Justice Act 1988, s 166 and Sch 15 and the Justice (Northern Ireland) Act 2002, Sch 13.)

General

1–3051 **1.** There shall be paid to the Director of the Serious Fraud Office such remuneration as the Attorney General may, with the approval of the Treasury, determine.

2. The Director shall appoint such staff for the Serious Fraud Office as, with the approval of the Treasury as to numbers, remuneration and other terms and conditions of service, he considers necessary for the discharge of his functions.

3. (1) As soon as practicable after 4th April in any year the Director shall make to the Attorney General a report on the discharge of his functions during the year ending with that date.

(2) The Attorney General shall lay before Parliament a copy of every report received by him under sub-paragraph (1) above and shall cause every such report to be published.

Procedure

4. (1) Where any enactment (whenever passed) prohibits the taking of any step—

(a) except by the Director of Public Prosecutions or except by him or another; or
(b) without the consent of the Director of Public Prosecutions or without his consent or the consent of another,

it shall not prohibit the taking of any such step by the Director of the Serious Fraud Office.

(2) In this paragraph references to the Director of Public Prosecutions include references to the Director of Public Prosecutions for Northern Ireland.

5. (1) Where the Director has the conduct of any criminal proceedings in England and Wales, the Director of Public Prosecutions shall not in relation to those proceedings be subject to any duty by virtue of section 3(2) of the Prosecution of Offences Act 1985.

(2) *Repealed.*

6. (1) Where the Director or any member of the Serious Fraud Office designated for the purposes of section 1(5) above ("designated official") gives notice to any justice of the peace that he has instituted, or is conducting, any criminal proceedings in England and Wales, the justice shall—

(a) at the prescribed time and in the prescribed manner; or
(b) in a particular case, at the time and in the manner directed by the Attorney General;

send him every recognizance, information, certificate, deposition, document and thing connected with those proceedings which the justice is required by law to deliver to the appropriate officer of the Crown Court.

(2) *Northern Ireland.*

(3) The Attorney General may make regulations for the purpose of supplementing this paragraph; and in this paragraph "prescribed" means prescribed by the regulations.

(4) The Director or, as the case may be, designated official shall—

(a) subject to the regulations, cause anything which is sent to him under this paragraph to be delivered to the appropriate officer of the Crown Court; and
(b) be under the same obligation (on the same payment) to deliver to an applicant copies of anything so sent as that officer.

7. (1) The Attorney General may make regulations requiring the chief officer of any police force to which the regulations are expressed to apply to give to the Director information with respect to every offence of a kind prescribed by the regulations which is alleged to have been committed in his area and in respect of which it appears to him that there is a prima facie case for proceedings.

(2) The regulations may also require every such chief officer to give to the Director such information as the Director may require with respect to such cases or classes of case as he may from time to time specify.

8. (1) The Attorney General may, with the approval of the Treasury, by regulations[1] make such provision as he considers appropriate in relation to—

(a) the fees of counsel briefed to appear on behalf of the Serious Fraud Office in any criminal proceedings; and
(b) the costs and expenses of witnesses attending to give evidence at the instance of the Serious Fraud Office and, subject to sub-paragraph (2) below, of any other person who in the opinion of that Office necessarily attends for the purpose of the case otherwise than to give evidence.

(2) The power conferred on the Attorney General by sub-paragraph (1)(b) above only relates to the costs and expenses of an interpreter if he is required because of the lack of English of a person attending to give evidence at the instance of the Serious Fraud Office.

(3) The regulations may, in particular—

(a) prescribe scales or rates of fees, costs or expenses; and
(b) specify conditions for the payment of fees, costs or expenses.

(4) Regulations made under sub-paragraph (1)(b) above may provide that scales or rates of costs and expenses shall be determined by the Attorney General with the consent of the Treasury.

(5) In sub-paragraph (1)(b) above "attends" means attends at the court or elsewhere.

9. (1) Any power to make regulations under this Schedule shall be exercisable by statutory instrument subject to annulment in pursuance of a resolution of either House of Parliament.

(2) Any such regulations may make different provisions with respect to different cases or classes of case.

---

1. The Serious Fraud Office (Witnesses' Etc Allowances) Regulations 1988, SI 1988/1863, have been made.

Criminal Justice Act 1988[1]

(1988 c 33)

PART V[2]

JURISDICTION, IMPRISONMENT, FINES, ETC

Jurisdiction

1–3160   40. Power to join in indictment count for common assault etc.   (1) A count charging a person with a summary offence to which this section applies may be included in an indictment if the charge—

(*a*) is founded on the same facts or evidence as a count charging an indictable offence[3]; or

(*b*) is part of a series of offences of the same or similar character as an indictable offence[4] which is also charged,

but only if (in either case) the facts or evidence relating to the offence were disclosed to a magistrates' court inquiring into the offence as examining justices[5] or are disclosed by material which, in pursuance of regulations made under paragraph 1 of Schedule 3 to the Crime and Disorder Act 1998 (procedure where person sent for trial under section 51), has been served on the person charged.

(2) Where a count charging an offence to which this section applies is included in an indictment, the offence shall be tried in the same manner as if it were an indictable offence; but the Crown Court may only deal with the offender in respect of it in a manner in which a magistrates' court could have dealt[6] with him.

(3) The offences to which this section applies are—

(*a*) common assault[7];

(*aa*) an offence under section 90(1) of the Criminal Justice Act 1991 (assaulting a prisoner custody officer);

(*ab*) an offence under section 13(1) of the Criminal Justice and Public Order Act 1994 (assaulting a secure training centre custody officer);

(*b*) an offence under section 12(1) of the Theft Act 1968[8] (taking motor vehicle or other conveyance without authority etc);

(*c*) an offence under section 103(1)(*b*) of the Road Traffic Act 1988[9] (driving a motor vehicle while disqualified);

(*d*) an offence mentioned in the first column of Schedule 2 to the Magistrates' Courts Act 1980[10] (criminal damage etc) which would otherwise be triable only summarily by virtue of section 22(2) of that Act; and

(*e*) any summary offence specified under subsection (4) below.

(4) The Secretary of State may by order made by statutory instrument specify for the purposes of this section any summary offence which is punishable with imprisonment or involves obligatory or discretionary disqualification from driving.

(5) A statutory instrument containing an order under this section shall be subject to annulment in pursuance of a resolution of either House of Parliament.

[Criminal Justice Act 1988, s 40, as amended by the Road Traffic (Consequential Provisions) Act 1988, Sch 3, the Criminal Justice and Public Order Act 1994, Sch 9, the Criminal Procedure and Investigations Act 1996, Sch 1 and the Crime and Disorder Act 1998, Sch 8.]

---

1. The Criminal Justice Act 1988 is printed partly in PART I and partly in PARTS II AND IV of this Manual. Parts II and III of the Act—Documentary and other provisions about evidence in criminal proceedings are contained in PART II: EVIDENCE; PART XI, ss 134 to 138—Torture— are contained in PART VIII: title PERSONS, OFFENCES, AGAINST; ss 139 to 142—Articles with blades or points and offensive weapons—are contained in PART VIII: title OFFENSIVE WEAPONS, and s 160—Possession of indecent photograph of child—is contained in PART VIII: title SEXUAL OFFENCES, post.

2. PART V contains ss 37–70.

3. An offence of driving while disqualified and an offence of having an offensive weapon which were committed at the same time as the defendant drove along were held to be founded on the same facts or evidence (*R v Bird* [1996] RTR 22, CA).

4. It is necessary for the summary offence to be linked to an indictable offence, and not another summary offence; see *R v Callaghan* (1991) 155 JP 965, [1992] Crim LR 191, CA.

5. The provisions of this section do not apply to proceedings transferred for trial under s 53 of the Criminal Justice Act 1991 (*R v T and K* [2001] 1 Cr App Rep 446, 165 JP 306, [2001] Crim LR 398, CA).

6. The 3-month custodial limit that applies to offences of criminal damage that fall to be tried only summarily by virtue of s 22 of the Magistrates' Courts Act 1980 (**1–2051**, *ante*) does not apply where a determination under that provision has not been made and the offence has been added to the indictment under s 40; though, the Crown Court, when determining the appropriate sentence, will regard the value of the damage caused as a significant factor (*R v Alden* [2002] EWCA Crim 421, [2003] Crim LR 417).

However, where criminal damage charges that form a series and involve an aggregate value of which is less than the relevant sum are transferred with other offences under s 51 of the Crime and Disorder Act 1998, the summary maxima of 3 months per offence and 6 months in the aggregate apply (*R v Gwynn* [2002] EWCA Crim 2951, [2003] Crim LR 421). An offender convicted by the Crown Court under s 40 may be made the subject of a hospital order by the Crown Court, but the power of the Crown Court to "deal with the offender ... in a manner in which the magistrates' could have dealt with him" should, in the circumstances, be read as extending to and including the power of the magistrates' court to commit to the Crown Court under s 43 of the Powers of Criminal Courts Act 1973. Accordingly, when dealing with an offender who has been convictcd under s 40, the Crown Court may make a hospital order with a restriction order (*R v Avbunudje* [1999] Crim LR 336, [1999] 2 Cr App Rep (S) 189).

7. This includes an offence under s 39 of the Criminal Justice Act 1988 alleging battery (*R v Lynsey* [1995] 3 All ER 654, [1995] 2 Cr App Rep 667, 159 JP 437, CA).

8. See PART VIII: title THEFT, post.

9. See Part VII: Transport, title Road Traffic, post.

10. See this Part, ante. Although s 22 of the Magistrates' Courts Act 1980 provides that an offence of criminal damage is triable summarily where the amount of damage is small, it does not thereby affect the classification of the offence as triable either way, as provided by s 17 and paragraph 29 of Sch 1 to that Act, and by the definition of an "offence triable either way" in Sch 1 to the Interpretation Act 1978 (*R v Fennell* (2000) 164 JP 386, [2000] 1 WLR 2011, [2000] Crim LR 677, CA, followed in *R v Alden* [2002] EWCA Crim 421, [2002] 2 Cr App Rep (S) 326, 166 JP 234, [2002] Crim LR 417).

1-3161   41. Power of Crown Court to deal with summary offence where person committed for either way offence.

(1) Where a magistrates' court commits a person to the Crown Court for trial on indictment for an offence triable either way[1] or a number of such offences, it may also commit him for trial for any summary offence with which he is charged and which—

(*a*)   is punishable with imprisonment or involves obligatory or discretionary disqualification from driving; and

(*b*)   arises out of circumstances which appear to the court to be the same as or connected with those giving rise to the offence, or one of the offences, triable either way,

whether or not evidence relating to that summary offence appears on the depositions or written statements in the case; and the trial of the information charging the summary offence shall then be treated as if the magistrates' court had adjourned it under section 10 of the Magistrates' Court Act 1980 and had not fixed the time and place for its resumption.

(2) Where a magistrates' court commits a person to the Crown Court for trial on indictment for a number of offences triable either way and exercises the power conferred by subsection (1) above in respect of a summary offence, the magistrates' court shall give the Crown Court and the person who is committed for trial a notice stating which of the offences triable either way appears to the court to arise out of circumstances which are the same as or connected with those giving rise to the summary offence.

(3) A magistrates' court's decision to exercise the power conferred by subsection (1) above shall not be subject to appeal or liable to be questioned in any court.

(4) The committal of a person under this section in respect of an offence to which section 40 above applies shall not preclude the exercise in relation to the offence of the power conferred by that section; but where he is tried on indictment for such an offence, the functions of the Crown Court under this section in relation to the offence shall cease.

(5) If he is convicted[2] on the indictment, the Crown Court shall consider whether the conditions specified in subsection (1) above were satisfied.

(6) If it considers that they were satisfied, it shall state to him the substance of the summary offence and ask him whether he pleads guilty or not guilty.

(7) If he pleads guilty, the Crown Court shall convict him, but may deal with him in respect of that offence only in a manner in which a magistrates' court could have dealt with him.

(8) If he does not plead guilty, the powers of the Crown Court shall cease[3] in respect of the offence except as provided by subsection (9) below.

(9) If the prosecution inform the Court that they would not desire to submit evidence on the charge relating to the summary offence, the Court shall dismiss it.

(10) The Crown Court shall inform the justices' chief executive for the magistrates' court of the outcome of any proceedings under this section.

(11) Where the Court of Appeal allows an appeal against conviction of an offence triable either way which arose out of circumstances which were the same as or connected with those giving rise to a summary offence of which the appellant was convicted under this section—

(*a*)   it shall set aside his conviction of the summary offence and give the justices' chief executive for the magistrates' court notice that it has done so; and

(*b*)   it may direct that no further proceedings in relation to the offence are to be undertaken;

and the proceedings before the Crown Court in relation to the offence shall thereafter be disregarded for all purposes.

(12) A notice under subsection (11) above shall include particulars of any direction given under paragraph (*b*) of that subsection in relation to the offence.

[Criminal Justice Act 1988, s 41 as amended by the Access to Justice Act 1999, Schs 13 and 15.]

1. This power is not available to a magistrates' court committing an offence triable only on indictment for trial: see *R v Miall* [1992] 3 All ER 153, [1992] 2 WLR 883, 155 JP 875, CA. Nevertheless, where a count charging an offence has been properly joined in the indictment, pursuant to s 40, ante, a conviction on that count is to be treated as a conviction on the indictment for the purposes of s 41(5) (*R v Bird* [1996] RTR 22, CA).

2. The power of the Crown Court to deal with a summary offence under this section arises only if the defendant is convicted of an indictable offence. If the defendant is acquitted of the indictable offence, or pleads not guilty to the summary offence, the Crown Court's powers cease, and the case is then sent back to the justices, unless the Crown Court dismisses it under s 41(9); see *R v Foote* (1991) 156 JP 99, [1991] Crim LR 909, CA. Nevertheless, where a count charging an offence has been properly joined in the indictment, pursuant to s 40, ante, a conviction on that count is to be treated as a conviction on the indictment for the purposes of s 41(5) (*R v Bird* [1996] RTR 22, CA).

3. However, Crown Court judges have the powers of District Judges (Magistrates' Courts); therefore, even though the Crown Court lacks jurisdiction the judge may deal with the offence without remitting it to a magistrates' court: see Courts Act 2003, s 66, this Part, ante.

1-3162   50. Suspended and partly suspended sentences on certain civilians in courts-martial and Standing Civilian Courts.

(1) The Secretary of State may by order made by statutory instrument make such provision as appears to him to be appropriate—

(a) to give courts-martial and Standing Civilian Courts power to pass suspended and partly suspended sentences of imprisonment on civilians to whom this section applies; and

(b) to give courts power to deal with offenders in respect of suspended and partly suspended sentences passed by courts-martial and Standing Civilian Courts.

(2) This section applies to the following civilians—

(a) persons to whom Part II of the Army Act 1955 applies by virtue of section 209 of that Act;

(b) persons to whom Part II of the Air Force Act 1955 applies by virtue of section 209 of that Act; and

(c) persons to whom Parts I and II of the Naval Discipline Act 1957 apply by virtue of section 118 of that Act.

(3) An order under this section—

(a) may amend—

    (i) the Army Act 1955;
    (ii) the Air Force Act 1955;
    (iii) the Naval Discipline Act 1957; and
    (iv) the Armed Forces Act 1976;

(b) may apply, with or without modifications, any enactment contained in—

    (i) the Criminal Justice Act 2003;
    (ii) the Criminal Law Act 1977; or
    (iii) any other Act not mentioned in paragraph (a) above; and

(c) may make such incidental or consequential provision as the Secretary of State considers necessary or expedient.

(4) Without prejudice to the generality of this section, an order under this section may make—

(a) provision prohibiting a court which passes a suspended sentence on a person from making an order under paragraph 4 of Schedule 5A to the Army Act 1955 or the Air Force Act 1955 or paragraph 4 of Schedule 4A to the Naval Discipline Act 1957 (community supervision orders) in respect of another offence; and

(b) provision restricting the powers conferred by sections 110 and 113 of the Army Act 1955 and the Air Force Act 1955 (confirmation and review) and sections 70 and 71 of the Naval Discipline Act 1957 (review).

(5) A statutory instrument containing an order under this section shall be subject to annulment in pursuance of a resolution of either House of Parliament.

[Criminal Justice Act 1988, s 50, as amended by the Powers of Criminal Courts (Sentencing) Act 2000, Sch 9.]

Maximum fines under subordinate legislation

1–3163   51. Statutory maximum as penalty on summary conviction for offences triable either way in subordinate legislation.   (1) For any offence triable either way under a subordinate instrument made before the commencement of this section, the maximum fine which may be imposed on summary conviction shall by virtue of this subsection be the statutory maximum unless the offence is one for which by virtue of the instrument a larger maximum fine may be imposed on summary conviction.

(2) Where apart from this section the maximum fine would be one amount in the case of a first conviction and a different amount in the case of a second or subsequent conviction, subsection (1) above shall apply irrespective of whether the conviction is a first, second or subsequent one.

(3) Subsection (1) above shall not affect so much of any instrument as (in whatever words) makes a person liable on summary conviction to a fine not exceeding a specified amount for each period of a specified length during which a continuing offence is continued after conviction or the occurrence of any other specified event.

(4) Where there is under any enactment (however framed or worded) contained in an Act passed before the commencement of this section a power by subordinate instrument to impose penal provisions, being a power which allows the creation of offences triable either way, the maximum fine which may in the exercise of that power be authorised on summary conviction in respect of an offence triable either way shall by virtue of this subsection be the statutory maximum unless some larger maximum fine can be authorised on summary conviction of such an offence by virtue of an enactment contained in an Act passed before the commencement of this section.

(5) Where there is under any enactment (however framed or worded) contained in an Act passed before the commencement of this section a power by subordinate instrument to create offences triable either way, the maximum fine for an offence triable either way so created may be expressed as a fine not exceeding the statutory maximum.

(6) Subsection (5) above has effect in relation to exercises of powers before as well as after the commencement of this section.

(7) Nothing in this section shall affect the punishment for an offence committed before the commencement of this section.

(8) In this section and sections 52, 53, 55, 57 and 59 below "fine" includes a pecuniary penalty but does not include a pecuniary forfeiture or pecuniary compensation.

[Criminal Justice Act 1988, s 51.]

1–3164 52. Penalties on conviction for summary offences under subordinate legislation —conversion of references to amounts to references to levels on scale. (1) Where under a relevant subordinate instrument the maximum fine on conviction of a summary offence specified in the instrument is an amount shown in the second column of the standard scale, the reference in the instrument to the amount of the maximum fine shall be construed as a reference to the level in the first column of the standard scale corresponding to that amount.

(2) In subsection (1) above "relevant subordinate instrument" means any instrument made by virtue of an enactment or instrument after 30th April 1984 and before the commencement of this section.

(3) Subsection (1) above shall not affect so much of any instrument as (in whatever words) makes a person liable on summary conviction to a fine not exceeding a specified amount for each period of a specified length during which a continuing offence is continued after conviction or the occurrence of any other specified event.

(4) Where there is—

(a) under any enactment (however framed or worded) contained in an Act passed before the commencement of this section;

(b) under any instrument (however framed or worded) made by virtue of such an enactment,

a power to provide by subordinate instrument that a person, as regards any summary offence (whether or not created by the instrument) shall be liable on conviction to a fine, a person may be so made liable to a fine not exceeding a specified level on the standard scale.

(5) Subsection (4) above has effect in relation to exercises of powers before as well as after the commencement of this section.
[Criminal Justice Act 1988, s 52.]

1–3165 53. Powers to specify maximum fines for summary offences under subordinate instruments—conversion of references to amounts to references to levels on scale —England and Wales. (1) Where an instrument which was made under an enactment on or after 11th April 1983 but before this section came into force confers on any authority other than a harbour authority a power by subordinate instrument to make a person liable to a fine on conviction of a summary offence of an amount shown in the second column of the standard scale, as that scale had effect when the instrument was made, a reference to the level in the first column of the standard scale which then corresponded to that amount shall be substituted for the reference in the instrument conferring the power to the amount of the fine.

(2) If an order under section 143 of the Magistrates' Courts Act 1980 alters the sums specified in section 37(2) of the Criminal Justice Act 1982, the second reference to the standard scale in subsection (1) above is to be construed as a reference to that scale as it has effect by virtue of the order.

(3) This section shall not affect so much of any instrument as (in whatever words) makes a person liable on summary conviction to a maximum fine not exceeding a specified amount for each period of a specified length during which a continuing offence is continued.
[Criminal Justice Act 1988, s 53.]

1–3166 55. Fines under secondary subordinate instruments—England and Wales. (1) This section applies to any instrument (however framed or worded) which—

(a) was made before 11th April 1983 (the date of the commencement of sections 35 to 50 of the Criminal Justice Act 1982); and

(b) confers on any authority other than a harbour authority a power by subordinate instrument to make a person, as regards any summary offence (whether or not created by the latter instrument), liable on conviction to a maximum fine of a specified amount not exceeding £1,000,

but does not affect so much of any such instrument as (in whatever words) confers a power by subordinate instrument to make a person liable on conviction to a fine for each period of a specified length during which a continuing offence is continued.

(2) The maximum fine to which a subordinate instrument made by virtue of an instrument to which this section applies may provide that a person shall be liable on conviction of a summary offence is—

(a) if the specified amount is less than £25, level 1 on the standard scale;
(b) if it is £25 or more but less than £50, level 2;
(c) if it is £50 or more but less than £200, level 3;
(d) if it is £200 or more but less than £400, level 4; and
(e) if it is £400 or more, level 5.

(3) Subject to subsection (5) below, where an instrument to which this section applies confers a power by subordinate instrument to make a person, as regards a summary offence, liable on conviction to a fine in respect of a specified quantity or a specified number of things, that fine shall be treated for the purposes of this section as being the maximum fine to which a person may be made liable by virtue of the instrument.

(4) Where an instrument to which this section applies confers a power to provide for different

maximum fines in relation to different circumstances or persons of different descriptions, the amounts specified as those maximum fines are to be treated separately for the purposes of this section.

(5) Where an instrument to which this section applies confers a power by subordinate instrument to make a person, as regards a summary offence, liable on conviction to a fine in respect of a specified quantity or a specified number of things but also confers a power by subordinate instrument to make a person, as regards such an offence, liable on conviction to an alternative fine, this section shall have effect in relation—

(*a*)   to the alternative fine; and

(*b*)   to any amount that the instrument specifies as the maximum fine for which a subordinate instrument made in the exercise of the power conferred by it may provide,

as well as in relation to the fine mentioned in subsection (3) above.

(6)   Section 36 of the Criminal Justice Act 1982 (abolition of enhanced penalties under subordinate instruments) shall have effect as if the references in it to an Act included references to an instrument and the reference in subsection (2) to the coming into force of the section were a reference, in relation to an instrument conferring a power such as is mentioned in subsection (1), to the coming into force of this section.

[Criminal Justice Act 1988, s 55.]

1–3167   57. Powers of harbour authorities to provide for maximum fines up to level 4 on standard scale.   (1) Where a harbour authority is empowered to provide—

(*a*)   in an instrument made by virtue of an enactment; or

(*b*)   in an instrument made by virtue of an instrument made under an enactment,

that a person, as regards any summary offence (whether or not created by the instrument), shall be liable on conviction to a fine not exceeding an amount less than **level 4** on the standard scale, the power shall extend by virtue of this section to making him liable to a fine not exceeding **level 4**.

(2)   Where any enactment or instrument ("the enabling legislation") (however expressed) provides that a person who contravenes any provision of an instrument ("a regulatory instrument") made by a harbour authority—

(*a*)   by virtue of the enabling legislation; or

(*b*)   by virtue of an instrument made under the enabling legislation,

shall be guilty of a summary offence and liable on conviction to a fine not exceeding an amount less than **level 4** on the standard scale, the power conferred by the enabling legislation shall by virtue of this section enable the harbour authority to provide in a regulatory instrument that a person, as regards any summary offence created by the regulatory instrument, shall be liable on summary conviction to a fine not exceeding **level 4**.

[Criminal Justice Act 1988, s 57.]

Exceptionally high maximum fines

1–3168   59. Power to alter exceptionally high maximum fines.   (1) The Secretary of State may by order amend an enactment or subordinate instrument specifying a sum to which this subsection applies so as to substitute for that sum such other sum as appears to him—

(*a*)   to be justified by a change in the value of money appearing to him to have taken place since the last occasion on which the sum in question was fixed; or

(*b*)   to be appropriate to take account of an order altering the standard scale which has been made or is proposed to be made.

(2)   Subsection (1) above applies to any sum which—

(*a*)   is specified as the maximum fine which may be imposed on conviction of a summary offence; and

(*b*)   is higher than **level 5** on the standard scale.

(3)   The Secretary of State may by order amend an enactment or subordinate instrument specifying a sum to which this subsection applies so as to substitute for that sum such other sum as appears to him—

(*a*)   to be justified by a change in the value of money appearing to him to have taken place since the last occasion on which the sum in question was fixed; or

(*b*)   to be appropriate to take account of an order made or proposed to be made altering the statutory maximum.

(4)   Subsection (3) above applies to any sum which—

(*a*)   is specified as the maximum fine which may be imposed on summary conviction of an offence triable either way; and

(*b*)   is higher than the statutory maximum.

(5)   An order under this section—

(*a*)   shall be made by statutory instrument subject to annulment in pursuance of a resolution of either House of Parliament; and

(*b*)   shall not affect the punishment for an offence committed before it comes into force.

(6)   In this section—

"enactment" includes an enactment contained in an Act passed after this Act; and
"subordinate instrument" includes an instrument made after the passing of this Act.
[Criminal Justice Act 1988, s 59.]

1–3169 67. Fines imposed and recognizances forfeited by coroners. (1) A fine imposed by a coroner, including a fine so imposed before this section comes into force, shall be treated for the purpose of its collection, enforcement and remission as having been imposed by the magistrates' court for the area in which the coroner's court was held, and the coroner shall as soon as practicable after imposing the fine give particulars of the fine to the justices' chief executive for that court.

(2) A coroner shall proceed in the like manner under subsection (1) above in relation to a recognizance forfeited at an inquest held before him, including a recognizance so forfeited before this section comes into force, as if he had imposed a fine upon the person forfeiting that recognizance, and subsection (1) above shall apply accordingly.
[Criminal Justice Act 1988, s 67, as amended by the Access to Justice Act 1999, Sch 13.]

PART VI
CONFISCATION OF THE PROCEEDS OF AN OFFENCE

1–3170 *Repealed.*

PART VII[1]
COMPENSATION BY COURT AND CRIMINAL INJURIES COMPENSATION BOARD

1–3217

1. Part VII contains ss 104–117. Sections 104–107 amend the law relating to compensation orders and make provision for the application of the proceeds of forfeited property for the benefit of victims; such amendments have been incorporated in the relevant statutes elsewhere in this work. Sections 108–117, which are not printed in this work, make fresh provision for the payment of compensation by the Criminal Injuries Compensation Board.

PART VIII[1]
AMENDMENTS OF LAW RELATING TO JURIES

1–3218

1. Part VIII contains ss 118–122 which are not reproduced in this work.

PART IX[1]
YOUNG OFFENDERS

1–3219

1. Part IX contains ss 123–130. Part IX amends the law relating to young offenders and the amendments arising from this Part have been incorporated in the relevant statutes elsewhere in this work.

PART X[1]
PROBATION AND THE PROBATION SERVICE, ETC

1–3220

1. Part X contains s 131 which amends the Bail Act 1976 with respect to bail—hostel conditions.

PART XI[1]
MISCELLANEOUS

Miscarriages of justice

1–3221 133. Compensation for miscarriages of justice[2]. (1) Subject to subsection (2) below, when a person has been convicted of a criminal offence and when subsequently his conviction has been reversed or he has been pardoned on the ground that a new or newly discovered fact shows beyond reasonable doubt that there has been a miscarriage of justice[3], the Secretary of State shall pay compensation for the miscarriage of justice to the person who has suffered punishment as a result of such conviction or, if he is dead, to his personal representatives, unless the non-disclosure of the unknown fact was wholly or partly attributable to the person convicted.

(2) No payment of compensation under this section shall be made unless an application for such compensation has been made to the Secretary of State.

(3) The question whether there is a right to compensation under this section shall be determined by the Secretary of State.

(4) If the Secretary of State determines that there is a right to such compensation, the amount of the compensation shall be assessed by an assessor appointed by the Secretary of State.

(4A) In assessing so much of any compensation payable under this section to or in respect of a person as is attributable to suffering, harm to reputation or similar damage, the assessor shall have regard in particular to—

(a) the seriousness of the offence of which the person was convicted and the severity of the punishment resulting from the conviction;

(b) the conduct of the investigation and prosecution of the offence; and

(c) any other convictions of the person and any punishment resulting from them.

(5) In this section "reversed" shall be construed as referring to a conviction having been quashed—

(a) on an appeal out of time; or

(b) on a reference—

    (i) under the Criminal Appeal Act 1995; or

    (ii) *Scotland*;

    (iii) *Repealed*; or

(c) on an appeal under section 7 of the Terrorism Act 2000; or

(d) on an appeal under section 12 of the Prevention of Terrorism Act 2005.

(6) For the purposes of this section a person suffers punishment as a result of a conviction when sentence is passed on him for the offence of which he was convicted.

(7) Schedule 12[4] shall have effect.

[Criminal Justice Act 1988, s 133 as amended by the Criminal Appeal Act 1995, s 28 and Schs 2 and 3, the Terrorism Act 2000, s 7 and the Prevention of Terrorism Act 2005, s 12.]

---

1. Part XI contains ss 133 to 167. Sections 134 to 138—Torture— are printed in PART VIII: title PERSONS, OFFENCES AGAINST; ss 139 to 142—Articles with blades or points and offensive weapons—are printed in PART VIII: title OFFENSIVE WEAPONS, post, and s 160—Possession of indecent photograph of child—is printed in PART VIII: title SEXUAL OFFENCES, post. Of the remaining provisions in Part XI, only those relevant to magistrates' courts are printed here.

2. Compensation under this section is not payable where there has been an abuse of executive power prior to commencement of the trial process but where there had been no failure in the trial process: *R (Mullen) v Secretary of State for the Home Department* [2004] UKHL 18, [2005] 1 AC 1, [2004] 3 All ER 65, [2004] Crim LR 837, [2004] 2 WLR 1140. The Secretary of State operates an ex gratia scheme of compensation for persons who do not fall within s 133.

3. This section is concerned with facts that emerge after the normal appellate process has been exhausted and is not engaged where facts are disclosed between conviction and appeal. Further, the new or newly discovered fact has to be the principal, if not the only reason for quashing the conviction (*R (Murphy) v Secretary of State for the Home Department* [2005] EWHC 140 (Admin), [2005] 2 All ER 763, [2005] 1 WLR 3516).

4. Schedule 12 is not reproduced in this manual.

Provisions relating to Customs and Excise

1–3222 **150.** *Bail for persons in customs detention*[1]*.—Amendment of the Police and Criminal Evidence Act 1984, s 114.*

---

1. At the date of going to press, s 150 had not been brought into force.

1–3223 **151. Customs and Excise power of arrest**[1]**.** (1) If—

(a) a person—

    (i) has been released on bail in criminal proceedings for an offence falling within subsection (4) below; and

    (ii) is under a duty to surrender into customs detention; and

(b) an officer of Customs and Excise has reasonable grounds for believing that that person is not likely to surrender to custody,

he may be arrested without warrant by an officer of Customs and Excise.

(2) A person arrested in pursuance of subsection (1) above shall be brought as soon as practicable and in any event within 24 hours after his arrest before a justice of the peace.

(3) In reckoning for the purposes of subsection (2) above any period of 24 hours, no account shall be taken of Christmas Day, Good Friday or any Sunday.

(4) The offences that fall within this subsection are—

(a) an offence against section 5(2) of the Misuse of Drugs Act 1971[2] (possession of controlled drugs);

(b) a drug trafficking offence;

(c) a money laundering offence.

(5) In this section and section 152 below "drug trafficking offence" means any offence which is specified in—

(a) paragraph 1 of Schedule 2 to the Proceeds of Crime Act 2002 (drug trafficking offences), or

(b) so far as it relates to that paragraph, paragraph 10 of that Schedule.

(6) In this section "money laundering offence" means any offence which by virtue of section 415 of the Proceeds of Crime Act 2002 is a money laundering offence for the purposes of Part 8 of that Act.

[Criminal Justice Act 1988, s 151 as amended by the Drug Trafficking Act 1994, Sch 1, the Proceeds of Crime Act 2002, Sch 11 and SI 2005/886.]

---

1. At the date of going to press, s 151, apart from sub-s (5), had not been brought into force.

2. See PART VIII: title MEDICINE AND PHARMACY, post.

1–3224   152. Remands of suspected drug offenders to detention. (1) Subject—

(*a*) to subsection (2) below; and
(*b*) to section 4 of the Bail Act 1976[1],

where—

(i)   a person is brought before a magistrates' court on a charge of an offence against section 5(2) of the Misuse of Drugs Act 1971 or a drug trafficking offence; and
(ii) the court has power to remand him,

it shall have power, if it considers it appropriate to do so, to remand him to customs detention, that is to say, commit him to the custody of a customs officer for a period not exceeding 192 hours.

(1A) In subsection (1) the power of a magistrates' court to remand a person to customs detention for a period not exceeding 192 hours includes power to commit the person to the custody of a constable to be detained for such a period.

(2) This section does not apply where a charge is brought against a person under the age of 17.

(3)–(4) *Northern Ireland.*

[Criminal Justice Act 1988, s 152 as amended by the Proceeds of Crime Act 2002, Sch 11 and the Drugs Act 2005, s 8.]

---

1. See this PART, ante.

PART XII[1]
GENERAL AND SUPPLEMENTARY

1–3225   170. *Minor and consequential amendments and repeals.*

---

1. Part XII contains ss 168–173.

1–3226   171–173. *Commencement, Extent, Citation.*

SCHEDULE 4

1–3227 *Repealed.*

Criminal Justice (International Co-operation) Act 1990[1]
(1990 c 5)

PART I[2]
CRIMINAL PROCEEDINGS AND INVESTIGATIONS
Mutual service of process

1–3430   1. Service of overseas process in United Kingdom. *Repealed.*

---

1. This Act shall come into force on such day or days as may be appointed by the Secretary of State (s 32). Part I of and Sch 1 to the Act which are printed here were brought into force on 10 June 1991 by the Criminal Justice (International Co-operation) Act 1990 (Commencement No 1) Order 1991, SI 1991/1072.

Part I of the Act relates to criminal proceedings and investigations and is contained in this PART; Parts II to IV of the Act appear in PART VIII: title MEDICINE AND PHARMACY, post.

2. Part I contains ss 1–11.

1–3431   2. Service of United Kingdom process overseas. *Repealed.*

Mutual provision of evidence

1–3432   3. Overseas evidence for use in United Kingdom. *Repealed.*

1–3433   4. United Kingdom evidence for use overseas. *Repealed.*

1–3434   5. Transfer of United Kingdom prisoner to give evidence or assist investigation overseas. (1) The Secretary of State may, if he thinks fit, issue a warrant providing for any person ("a prisoner") serving a sentence in a prison or other institution to which the Prison Act 1952 or the Prisons (Scotland) Act 1989 applies to be transferred to a country or territory outside the United Kingdom for the purpose—

(*a*) of giving evidence in criminal proceedings there; or
(*b*) of being identified in, or otherwise by his presence assisting, such proceedings or the investigation of an offence.

(2) No warrant shall be issued under this section in respect of any prisoner unless he has consented to being transferred as mentioned in subsection (1) above and that consent may be given either—

(*a*) by the prisoner himself; or

(b) in circumstances in which it appears to the Secretary of State inappropriate, by reason of the prisoner's physical or mental condition or his youth, for him to act for himself, by a person appearing to the Secretary of State to be an appropriate person to act on his behalf;

but a consent once given shall not be capable of being withdrawn after the issue of the warrant.

(3) The effect of a warrant under this section shall be to authorise—

(a) the taking of the prisoner to a place in the United Kingdom and his delivery at a place of departure from the United Kingdom into the custody of a person representing the appropriate authority of the country or territory to which the prisoner is to be transferred; and

(b) the bringing of the prisoner back to the United Kingdom and his transfer in custody to the place where he is liable to be detained under the sentence to which he is subject.

(3A) A warrant under this section has effect in spite of section 127(1) of the Army Act 1955, section 127(1) of the Air Force Act 1955 or section 82A(1) of the Naval Discipline Act 1957 (restriction on removing persons out of the United Kingdom who are serving military sentences).

(4) Where a warrant has been issued in respect of a prisoner under this section he shall be deemed to be in legal custody at any time when, being in the United Kingdom or on board a British ship, British aircraft or British hovercraft, he is being taken under the warrant to or from any place or being kept in custody under the warrant.

(5) A person authorised by or for the purposes of the warrant to take the prisoner to or from any place or to keep him in custody shall have all the powers, authority, protection and privileges—

(a) of a constable in the part of the United Kingdom in which that person is for the time being; or

(b) if he is outside the United Kingdom, of a constable in the part of the United Kingdom to or from which the prisoner is to be taken under the warrant.

(6) If the prisoner escapes or is unlawfully at large, he may be arrested without warrant by a constable and taken to any place to which he may be taken under the warrant issued under this section.

(7) In subsection (4) above—

"British aircraft" means a British-controlled aircraft within the meaning of section 92 of the Civil Aviation Act 1982 (application of criminal law to aircraft) or one of Her Majesty's aircraft;

"British hovercraft" means a British-controlled hovercraft within the meaning of that section as applied in relation to hovercraft by virtue of provisions made under the Hovercraft Act 1968 or one of Her Majesty's hovercraft;

"British ship" means a British ship for the purposes of the Merchant Shipping Act 1995 or one of Her Majesty's ships;

and in this subsection references to Her Majesty's aircraft, hovercraft or ships are references to aircraft, hovercraft or, as the case may be, ships belonging to or exclusively employed in the service of Her Majesty in right of the Government of the United Kingdom.

(8) In subsection (6) above "constable", in relation to any part of the United Kingdom, means any person who is a constable in that or any other part of the United Kingdom or any person who, at the place in question has, under any enactment including subsection (5) above, the powers of a constable in that or any other part of the United Kingdom.

(9) This section applies to a person in custody awaiting trial or sentence and a person committed to prison for default in paying a fine as it applies to a prisoner and the reference in subsection (3)(b) above to a sentence shall be construed accordingly.

(10) *Northern Ireland.*

[Criminal Justice (International Co-operation) Act 1990, s 5 as amended by the Merchant Shipping Act 1995, Sch 13 and the Crime (International Co-operation) Act 2003, Sch 5.]

1–3435   6. Transfer of overseas prisoner to give evidence or assist investigation in the United Kingdom.   (1) This section has effect where—

(a) a witness order has been made or a witness summons or citation issued in criminal proceedings in the United Kingdom in respect of a person ("a prisoner") who is detained in custody in a country or territory outside the United Kingdom by virtue of a sentence or order of a court or tribunal exercising criminal jurisdiction in that country or territory; or

(b) it appears to the Secretary of State that it is desirable for a prisoner to be identified in, or otherwise by his presence to assist, such proceedings or the investigation in the United Kingdom of an offence.

(2) If the Secretary of State is satisfied that the appropriate authority in the country or territory where the prisoner is detained will make arrangements for him to come to the United Kingdom to give evidence pursuant to the witness order, witness summons or citation or, as the case may be, for the purpose mentioned in subsection (1)(b) above, he may issue a warrant under this section.

(3) No warrant shall be issued under this section in respect of any prisoner unless he has consented to being brought to the United Kingdom to give evidence as aforesaid or, as the case may be, for the purpose mentioned in subsection (1)(b) above but a consent once given shall not be capable of being withdrawn after the issue of the warrant.

(4) The effect of the warrant shall be to authorise—

(a) the bringing of the prisoner to the United Kingdom;

(b) the taking of the prisoner to, and his detention in custody at, such place or places in the United Kingdom as are specified in the warrant; and

(c) the returning of the prisoner to the country or territory from which he has come.

(5) Subsections (4) to (8) of section 5 above shall have effect in relation to a warrant issued under this section as they have effect in relation to a warrant issued under that section.

(6) A person shall not be subject to the Immigration Act 1971 in respect of his entry into or presence in the United Kingdom in pursuance of a warrant under this section but if the warrant ceases to have effect while he is still in the United Kingdom—

(a) he shall be treated for the purposes of that Act as if he has then illegally entered the United Kingdom; and

(b) the provisions of Schedule 2 to that Act shall have effect accordingly except that paragraph 20(1) (liability of carrier for expenses of custody etc. of illegal entrant) shall not have effect in relation to directions for his removal given by virtue of this subsection.

(7) This section applies to a person detained in custody in a country or territory outside the United Kingdom in consequence of having been transferred there—

(a) from the United Kingdom under the Repatriation of Prisoners Act 1984; or

(b) under any similar provision or arrangement from any other country or territory,

as it applies to a person detained as mentioned in subsection (1) above.
[Criminal Justice (International Co-operation) Act 1990, s 6.]

Additional co-operation powers

1–3436   7. Search etc for material relevant to overseas investigation. *Repealed.*

1–3437   8. Search etc for material relevant to overseas investigation: Scotland. . *Repealed.*

1–3438   9. Enforcement of overseas forfeiture orders.   (1) Her Majesty may by Order[1] in Council provide for the enforcement in the United Kingdom of any order which—

(a) is made by a court in a country or territory outside the United Kingdom designated for the purposes of this section by the Order in Council; and

(b) is for the forfeiture and destruction, or the forfeiture and other disposal, of anything in respect of which an offence to which this section applies has been committed or which was used or intended for use in connection with the commission of such an offence.

(1A) Without prejudice to the generality of subsection (1) above the provision that may be made by virtue of that subsection includes provision which, for the purpose of facilitating the enforcement of any order that may be made, has effect at times before there is an order to be enforced[2].

(2) Without prejudice to the generality of subsection (1) above an Order in Council under this section may provide for the registration by a court in the United Kingdom of any order as a condition of its enforcement and prescribe requirements to be satisfied before an order can be registered.

(3) An Order in Council under this section may include such supplementary and incidental provisions as appear to Her Majesty to be necessary or expedient and may apply for the purposes of the Order (with such modifications as appear to Her Majesty to be appropriate) any provisions relating to confiscation or forfeiture orders under any other enactment.

(4) An Order in Council under this section may make different provision for different cases.

(5) An Order in Council under this section shall be subject to annulment in pursuance of a resolution of either House of Parliament.

(6) This section applies to any offence which corresponds to or is similar to—

(a) an offence under the law of England and Wales;

(b) an offence under the law of Scotland; or

(c) an offence under the law of Northern Ireland.
[Criminal Justice (International Co-operation) Act 1990, s 9 as amended by the Criminal Justice Act 1993, s 21, the Drug Trafficking Act 1994, Sch 1, the Proceeds of Crime Act 1995, s 14, the Criminal Justice (Scotland) Act 1995, Sch 6, the Criminal Procedure (Consequential Provisions) (Scotland) Act 1995, Sch 4 and the Serious Organised Crime and Police Act 2005, s 95.]

---

1. See the Criminal Justice (International Co-operation) Act 1990 (Enforcement of Overseas Forfeiture Orders) Order 2005, SI 2005/3180.
2. Section 9 is deemed always to have had effect with the insertion of sub-s (1A) by the Proceeds of Crime Act 1995 (Proceeds of Crime Act 1995, s 14).

Supplementary

1–3439   10. Rules of court.   (1) Provision may be made by rules[1] of court for any purpose for which it appears to the authority having power to make the rules that it is necessary or expedient that provision should be made in connection with any of the provisions of this Part of this Act.

(2) Rules made for the purposes of Schedule 1 to this Act may, in particular, make provision with respect to the persons entitled to appear or take part in the proceedings to which that Schedule applies and for excluding the public from any such proceedings.

(3) An Order in Council under section 9 above may authorise the making of rules of court for any purpose specified in the Order.

(4) Rules of court made under this section by the High Court in Scotland shall be made by Act of Adjournal.

(5) This section is without prejudice to the generality of any existing power to make rules.
[Criminal Justice (International Co-operation) Act 1990, s 10.]

1. The Magistrates' Courts (Criminal Justice (International Co-operation) Rules 1991, this PART: STATUTORY INSTRUMENTS AND PRACTICE DIRECTIONS ON PROCEDURE, post, have been made.

1–3440   11. Application to courts-martial etc.. *Repealed.*

SCHEDULES

Section 4(6)   SCHEDULE 1
UNITED KINGDOM EVIDENCE FOR USE OVERSEAS: PROCEEDINGS OF NOMINATED COURT
Repealed.

Bail (Amendment) Act 1993
(1993 c 26)

1–3447   1. Prosecution right of appeal.   (1) Where a magistrates' court grants bail to a person who is charged with, or convicted of, an offence punishable by imprisonment, the prosecution may appeal to a judge of the Crown Court against the granting of bail.

(1A) Where a magistrates' court grants bail to a person in connection with extradition proceedings, the prosecution may appeal to a judge of the Crown Court against the granting of bail.

(2) Subsection (1) above applies only where the prosecution is conducted—

(*a*) by or on behalf of the Director of Public Prosecutions; or
(*b*) by a person who falls within such class or description of person as may be prescribed[1] for the purposes of this section by order made by the Secretary of State.

(3) An appeal under subsection (1) or (1A) may be made only if—

(*a*) the prosecution made representations that bail should not be granted; and
(*b*) the representations were made before it was granted.

(4) In the event of the prosecution wishing to exercise the right of appeal set out in subsection (1) or (1A) above, oral notice[2] of appeal shall be given to the court which has granted bail at the conclusion of the proceedings in which such bail has been granted and before the release from custody of the person concerned.

(5) Written notice of appeal shall thereafter be served on the court which has granted bail and the person concerned within two hours of the conclusion of such proceedings.

(6) Upon receipt from the prosecution of oral notice of appeal from its decision to grant bail the court which has granted bail shall remand in custody the person concerned, until the appeal is determined or otherwise disposed of.

(7) Where the prosecution fails, within the period of two hours[3] mentioned in subsection (5) above, to serve one or both of the notices required by that subsection, the appeal shall be deemed to have been disposed of.

(8) The hearing of an appeal under subsection (1) or (1A) above against a decision of the court to grant bail shall be commenced within forty-eight hours[4], excluding weekends and any public holiday (that is to say, Christmas Day, Good Friday or a bank holiday), from the date on which oral notice of appeal is given.

(9) At the hearing of any appeal by the prosecution under this section, such appeal shall be by way of re-hearing, and the judge hearing any such appeal may remand[5] the person concerned in custody or may grant bail subject to such conditions (if any) as he thinks fit.

(10) In relation to a child or young person (within the meaning of the Children and Young Persons Act 1969)—

(*a*) the reference in subsection (1) above to an offence punishable by imprisonment is to be read as a reference to an offence which would be so punishable in the case of an adult; and
(*b*) the references in subsections (6) and (9) above to remand in custody are to be read subject to the provisions of section 23 of the Act of 1969[6] (remands to local authority accommodation).

(11) The power to make an order under subsection (2) above shall be exercisable by statutory instrument and any instrument shall be subject to annulment in pursuance of a resolution of either House of Parliament.

(12) In this section—

"extradition proceedings" means proceedings under the Extradition Act 2003;
"magistrates' court" and "court" in relation to extradition proceedings means a District Judge (Magistrates' Courts) designated in accordance with section 67 or section 139 of the Extradition Act 2003;
"prosecution" in relation to extradition proceedings means the person acting on behalf of the territory to which extradition is sought.

[Bail (Amendment) Act 1993, s 1 as amended by the Extradition Act 2003, s 200 and the Criminal Justice Act 2003, ss 18 and 200.]

---

1. The following prosecuting authorities have been prescribed by the Bail (Amendment) Act 1993 (Prescription of Prosecuting Authorities) Order 1994, SI 1994/1438: the Director of the Serious Fraud Office and any person designated under s 1(7) of the Criminal Justice Act 1987; Secretary of State for Trade and Industry; Secretary of State for Social Security; the Post Office; the Director of Revenue and Customs Prosecutions and any person designated under s 37(1) of the Commissioners for Revenue and Customs Act 2005.

2. In order to exercise the right of appeal, it is not necessary for the prosecution to give oral notice the moment that the last word is said in the proceedings; it has been held that giving oral notice to the clerk of the court 5 minutes after the conclusion of the proceedings and after the justices have left the court building is sufficient (*R v Isleworth Crown Court, ex p Clarke* [1998] 1 Cr App Rep 257).

3. If the prosecutor has given himself ample time to serve the notice on the defendant, has used all due diligence to do so, but has been defeated by circumstances out of his control, and the delay has not caused any prejudice to the defendant, s 1(7) will not defeat the making of an appeal (*R (on the application of Jeffrey) v Crown Court at Warwick* [2002] EWHC 2469 (Admin), [2002] All ER (D) 340 (Nov), [2002] JPN 942).

4. The provisions of s 1(8) are mandatory. However, the requirements of this subsection are that the appeal must be commenced within two working days of the date of the decision of the magistrates' court rather than literally within 48 hours of the moment upon which oral notice had been given by the prosecutor (*R v Crown Court at Middlesex Guildhall, ex p Okoli* [2001] 1 Cr App Rep 1, 165 JP 144, [2000] Crim LR 921, DC).

5. Where the judge decides to remand the person concerned in custody, he should be invited by the prosecution to stipulate a period of remand in custody which complies with the provisions of ss 128, 128A and 129 of the Magistrates' Courts Act 1980 (this PART, ante); see *Re Bone* (1994) 159 JP 111 and *Re Szakal* [2000] 1 Cr App Rep 248, CA.

6. See PART V: YOUTH COURTS, post.

1–3448   2. *Citation, commencement and extent.*

Criminal Justice Act 1993[1]

(1993 c 36)

PART I[2]

JURISDICTION

1–3449   1. Offences to which this Part applies. (1) This Part applies to two groups of offences—

(a) any offence mentioned in subsection (2) (a "Group A offence"); and
(b) any offence mentioned in subsection (3) (a "Group B offence").

(2) The Group A offences are—

(a) an offence under any of the following provisions of the Theft Act 1968—

section 1 (theft);
section 15 (obtaining property by deception);*
section 15A (obtaining a money transfer by deception);*
section 16 (obtaining pecuniary advantage by deception);*
section 17 (false accounting);
section 19 (false statements by company directors, etc);
section 20(2) (procuring execution of valuable security by deception);*
section 21 (blackmail);
section 22 (handling stolen goods);
section 24A (retaining credits from dishonest sources, etc.);

(b) an offence under either of the following provisions of the Theft Act 1978—

section 1 (obtaining services by deception);
section 2 (avoiding liability by deception);*

(c) an offence under any of the following provisions of the Forgery and Counterfeiting Act 1981—

section 1 (forgery);
section 2 (copying a false instrument);
section 3 (using a false instrument);
section 4 (using a copy of a false instrument);
section 5 (offences which relate to money orders, share certificates, passports, etc);
section 14 (offences of counterfeiting notes and coins);
section 15 (offences of passing etc counterfeit notes and coins);
section 16 (offences involving the custody or control of counterfeit notes and coins);
section 17 (offences involving the making or custody or control of counterfeiting materials and implements);
section 20 (prohibition of importation of counterfeit notes and coins);
section 21 (prohibition of exportation of counterfeit notes and coins)

(ca) an offence under section 25 of the Identity Cards Act 2006;
(d) the common law offence of cheating in relation to the public revenue.

(3) The Group B offences are—

(a) conspiracy to commit a Group A offence;
(b) conspiracy to defraud;

    (*c*)   attempting to commit a Group A offence;
    (*d*)   incitement to commit a Group A offence.

    (4) The Secretary of State may by order amend subsection (2) or (3) by adding or removing any offence.

    (5) The power to make such an order shall be exercisable by statutory instrument.

    (6) No order shall be made under subsection (4) unless a draft of it has been laid before and approved by a resolution of each House of Parliament.

[Criminal Justice Act 1993, s 1 as amended by the Theft (Amendment) Act 1996, s 3,SI 2000/1878 and the Identity Cards Act 2006, s 30]

---

    *Repealed and para (2)(*bb*) inserted by the Fraud Act 2006, Sch 1 from a date to be appointed.
    1. The Criminal Justice Act 1993 is printed partly in PART I and partly in PART VII of this manual. Part I of the Act, ss 1 to 6—Jurisdiction—and certain provisions of Parts VI—Miscellaneous—and VII—Supplementary—are printed below in this PART: MAGISTRATES' COURTS, PROCEDURE. Part V of the Act, ss 52 to 64—Insider Dealing—is printed in PART VIII: title COMPANIES, post. For commencement provisions, see s 78 and notes thereto, post.
    2. Part I contains ss 1–6.

1–3450 **2. Jurisdiction in respect of Group A offences.** (1) For the purposes of this Part, "relevant event", in relation to any Group A offence, means any act or omission or other event (including any result of one or more acts or omissions) proof of which is required for conviction of the offence.*

    (2) For the purpose of determining whether or not a particular event is a relevant event in relation to a Group A offence, any question as to where it occurred is to be disregarded.

    (3) A person may be guilty of a Group A offence if any of the events which are relevant events in relation to the offence occurred in England and Wales.

[Criminal Justice Act 1993, s 2.]

---

    *Subsection (1) amended and subs (1A) inserted by the Fraud Act 2006, Sch 1 from a date to be appointed.

1–3451 **3. Questions immaterial to jurisdiction in the case of certain offences.** (1) A person may be guilty of a Group A or Group B offence whether or not—

    (*a*)   he was a British citizen at any material time;
    (*b*)   he was in England and Wales at any such time.

    (2) On a charge of conspiracy to commit a Group A offence, or on a charge of conspiracy to defraud in England and Wales, the defendant may be guilty of the offence whether or not—

    (*a*)   he became a party to the conspiracy in England and Wales;
    (*b*)   any act or omission or other event in relation to the conspiracy occurred in England and Wales.

    (3) On a charge of attempting to commit a Group A offence, the defendant may be guilty of the offence whether or not—

    (*a*)   the attempt was made in England and Wales;
    (*b*)   it had an effect in England and Wales.

    (4) Subsection (1)(*a*) does not apply where jurisdiction is given to try the offence in question by an enactment which makes provision by reference to the nationality of the person charged.

    (5) Subsection (2) does not apply in relation to any charge under the Criminal Law Act 1977 brought by virtue of section 1A of that Act.

    (6) Subsection (3) does not apply in relation to any charge under the Criminal Attempts Act 1981 brought by virtue of section 1A of that Act.

[Criminal Justice Act 1993, s 3.]

1–3452 **4. Rules for determining certain jurisdictional questions relating to the location of events.** In relation to a Group A or Group B offence—

    (*a*)   there is an obtaining of property in England and Wales if the property is either despatched from or received at a place in England and Wales; and
    (*b*)   there is a communication in England and Wales of any information, instruction, request, demand or other matter if it is sent by any means—

        (i)   from a place in England and Wales to a place elsewhere; or
        (ii) from a place elsewhere to a place in England and Wales.

[Criminal Justice Act 1993, s 4.]

1–3453 **5. Conspiracy, attempt and incitement.** (1) *Repealed.*

    (2) *Amendments.*

    (3) A person may be guilty of conspiracy to defraud if—

    (*a*)   a party to the agreement constituting the conspiracy, or a party's agent, did anything in England and Wales in relation to the agreement before its formation, or
    (*b*)   a party to it became a party in England and Wales (by joining it either in person or through an agent), or

(c) a party to it, or a party's agent, did or omitted anything in England and Wales in pursuance of it,

and the conspiracy would be triable in England and Wales but for the fraud which the parties to it had in view not being intended to take place in England and Wales.

    (4) A person may be guilty of incitement to commit a Group A offence if the incitement—

    (a) takes place in England and Wales; and

    (b) would be triable in England and Wales but for what the person charged had in view not being an offence triable in England and Wales.

    (5) Subsections (3) and (4) are subject to section 6.

[Criminal Justice Act 1993, s 5, as amended by the Criminal Justice (Terrorism and Conspiracy) Act 1998, Schs 1 and 2.]

1–3454   6. Relevance of external law. (1) A person is guilty of an offence triable by virtue of section 5(3), only if the pursuit of the agreed course of conduct would at some stage involve—

    (a) an act or omission by one or more of the parties, or

    (b) the happening of some other event,

constituting an offence under the law in force where the act, omission or other event was intended to take place.

    (2) A person is guilty of an offence triable by virtue of section 1A of the Criminal Attempts Act 1981, or by virtue of section 5(4), only if what he had in view would involve the commission of an offence under the law in force where the whole or any part of it was intended to take place.

    (3) Conduct punishable under the law in force in any place is an offence under that law for the purposes of this section, however it is described in that law.

    (4) Subject to subsection (6), a condition specified in subsection (1) or (2) shall be taken to be satisfied unless, not later than rules of court may provide, the defence serve on the prosecution a notice—

    (a) stating that, on the facts as alleged with respect to the relevant conduct, the condition is not in their opinion satisfied;

    (b) showing their grounds for that opinion; and

    (c) requiring the prosecution to show that it is satisfied.

    (5) In subsection (4) "the relevant conduct" means—

    (a) where the condition in subsection (1) is in question, the agreed course of conduct; and

    (b) where the condition in subsection (2) is in question, what the defendant had in view.

    (6) The court, if it thinks fit, may permit the defence to require the prosecution to show that the condition is satisfied without the prior service of a notice under subsection (4).

    (7) In the Crown Court, the question whether the condition is satisfied shall be decided by the judge alone.

    (8) The following paragraph shall be inserted in section 9(3) of the Criminal Justice Act 1987 (preparatory hearing in a case of serious fraud), before paragraph (b)—

    "(aa) a question arising under section 6 of the Criminal Justice Act 1993 (relevance of external law to certain charges of conspiracy, attempt and incitement);".

[Criminal Justice Act 1993, s 6 as amended by the Criminal Justice (Terrorism and Conspiracy) Act 1998, Schs 1 and 2.]

PART II[1]

DRUG TRAFFICKING OFFENCES

1–3455

_____

1. Part II contains ss 7–26. Section 21(3) repealed by the Proceeds of Crime Act 2002, Sch 12.

PART III

PROCEEDS OF CRIMINAL CONDUCT

1–3456

    Repealed.

PART IV[1]

FINANCING ETC OF TERRORISM

1–3457

_____

1. Part IV contains ss 36–51. Amendments made by Pt IV have been incorporated in the Prevention of Terrorism (Temporary Provisions) Act 1989 in PART VIII: title PERSONS, OFFENCES AGAINST, post.

PART V[1]
INSIDER DEALING

1–3458

---

1. Part V contains ss 52–64. Part V is printed in PART VIII: title COMPANIES, *post*.

PART VI[1]
MISCELLANEOUS

1–3459 71. Offences in connection with taxation etc in the EC. (1) A person who, in the United Kingdom, assists in or induces any conduct outside the United Kingdom which involves the commission of a serious offence against the law of another member State is guilty of an offence under this section if—

(a) the offence involved is one consisting in or including the contravention of provisions of the law of that member State which relate to any of the matters specified in subsection (2);

(b) the offence involved is one consisting in or including the contravention of other provisions of that law so far as they have effect in relation to any of those matters; or

(c) the conduct is such as to be calculated to have an effect in that member State in relation to any of those matters.

(2) The matters mentioned in subsection (1) are—

(a) the determination, discharge or enforcement of any liability for a Community duty or tax;

(b) the operation of arrangements under which reliefs or exemptions from any such duty or tax are provided or sums in respect of any such duty or tax are repaid or refunded;

(c) the making of payments in pursuance of Community arrangements made in connection with the regulation of the market for agricultural products and the enforcement of the conditions of any such payments;

(d) the movement into or out of any member State of anything in relation to the movement of which any Community instrument imposes, or requires the imposition of, any prohibition or restriction; and

(e) such other matters in relation to which provision is made by any Community instrument as the Secretary of State may by order specify.

(3) For the purposes of this section—

(a) an offence against the law of a member State is a serious offence if provision is in force in that member State authorising the sentencing, in some or all cases, of a person convicted of that offence to imprisonment for a maximum term of twelve months or more; and

(b) the question whether any conduct involves the commission of such an offence shall be determined according to the law in force in the member State in question at the time of the assistance or inducement.

(4) In any proceedings against any person for an offence under this section it shall be a defence for that person to show—

(a) that the conduct in question would not have involved the commission of an offence against the law of the member State in question but for circumstances of which he had no knowledge; and

(b) that he did not suspect or anticipate the existence of those circumstances and did not have reasonable grounds for doing so.

(5) For the purposes of any proceedings for an offence under this section, a certificate purporting to be issued by or on behalf of the government of another member State which contains a statement, in relation to such times as may be specified in the certificate—

(a) that a specified offence existed against the law of that member State,

(b) that an offence against the law of that member State was a serious offence within the meaning of this section,

(c) that such an offence consists in or includes the contravention of particular provisions of the law of that member State,

(d) that specified provisions of the law of that member State relate to, or are capable of having an effect in relation to, particular matters,

(e) that specified conduct involved the commission of a particular offence against the law of that member State, or

(f) that a particular effect in that member State in relation to any matter would result from specified conduct,

shall, in the case of a statement falling within paragraphs (a) to (d), be conclusive of the matters stated and, in the other cases, be evidence, and in Scotland sufficient evidence, of the matters stated.

(6) A person guilty of an offence under this section shall be liable[2]—

(a) on summary conviction, to a penalty of **the statutory maximum** or to imprisonment for a term not exceeding **six months** or to **both**; or

(b) on conviction on indictment, to a **penalty** of any amount or to imprisonment for a term not exceeding **seven years** or to **both**.

(7) Sections 145 to 152 and 154 of the Customs and Excise Management Act 1979[3] (general provisions as to legal proceedings) shall apply as if this section were contained in that Act; and an offence under this section shall be treated for all purposes as an offence for which a person is liable to be arrested under the customs and excise Acts.

(8) The power of the Secretary of State to make an order under subsection (2)(e) shall be exercisable by statutory instrument; and no such order shall be made unless a draft of the order has been laid before, and approved by a resolution of, each House of Parliament.

(9) In this section—

"another member State" means a member State other than the United Kingdom;
"Community duty or tax" means any of the following, that is to say—

   (a) any Community customs duty;
   (b) an agricultural levy of the Economic Community;
   (c) value added tax under the law of another member State;
   (d) any duty or tax on tobacco products, alcoholic liquors or hydrocarbon oils which, in another member State, corresponds to any excise duty;
   (e) any duty, tax or other charge not falling within paragraphs (a) to (d) of this definition which is imposed by or in pursuance of any Community instrument on the movement of goods into or out of any member State;

"conduct" includes acts, omissions and statements;
"contravention" includes a failure to comply; and
"the customs and excise Acts" has the same meaning as in the Customs and Excise Management Act 1979[3].

(10) References in this section, in relation to a Community instrument, to the movement of anything into or out of a member State include references to the movement of anything between member States and to the doing of anything which falls to be treated for the purposes of that instrument as involving the entry into, or departure from, the territory of the Community of any goods (within the meaning of that Act of 1979).
[Criminal Justice Act 1993, s 71.]

---

1. Part VI contains ss 65–77.
2. For procedure in respect of this offence which is triable either way, see s 147 of the Customs and Excise Management Act 1979, in PART VIII: title CUSTOMS AND EXCISE, post, and the Magistrates' Courts Act 1980, ss 17A–21, in this PART, ante.
3. See PART VIII: title CUSTOMS AND EXCISE, post.

PART VII[1]
SUPPLEMENTARY

1–3460 78. Commencement etc. (1) Sections 70 and 71 shall come into force at the end of the period of two months beginning with the day on which this Act is passed.

(2) Sections 68, 69, 75, 76 and 79(1) to (12), paragraph 2 of Schedule 5 and, in so far as relating to the Criminal Procedure (Scotland) Act 1975 and the Prisoners and Criminal Proceedings (Scotland) Act 1993, Schedule 6, shall come into force on the passing of this Act.

(3) The other provisions of this Act shall come into force on such day as may be appointed by the Secretary of State by an order[2] made by statutory instrument.

(4) Different days may be appointed under subsection (3) for different provisions and different purposes.

(5) Nothing in any provision in Part I applies to any act, omission or other event occurring before the coming into force of that provision.

(6) Where a person is charged with a relevant offence which was committed before the coming into force of a provision of Part II, Part III, or (as the case may be) Part IV, that provision shall not affect the question whether or not that person is guilty of the offence and, where it confers a power on the court, shall not apply in proceedings instituted before the coming into force of that provision.

(7) *Repealed.*
(8) *Repealed.*
(9) In subsection (6) "relevant offence" means an offence in relation to which provision is made by Part II, Part III or Part IV, other than an offence created by that Part.
(10) An order under subsection (3) may contain such transitional provisions and savings as the Secretary of State considers appropriate.
(11) *Repealed.*
(12) *Repealed.*
[Criminal Justice Act 1993, s 78, as amended by the Criminal Justice and Public Order Act 1994, Sch 9, the Drug Trafficking Act 1994, Sch 3, the Northern Ireland (Emergency Provisions) Act 1996, Sch 7 and the Terrorism Act 2000, Sch 16.]

---

1. Part VII contains ss 78 and 79.
2. At the date of going to press, the following commencement orders had been made:

Criminal Justice Act 1993 (Commencement No 1) Order 1993, SI 1993/1968;
Criminal Justice Act 1993 (Commencement No 2) (Transitional Provisions and Savings) (Scotland) Order 1993, SI 1993/2035 (relating only to Scotland);

Criminal Justice Act 1993 (Commencement No 3) Order 1993, SI 1993/2734;
Criminal Justice Act 1993 (Commencement No 4) Order 1994, SI 1994/71;
Criminal Justice Act 1993 (Commencement No 5) Order 1994, SI 1994/242;
Criminal Justice Act 1993 (Commencement No 6) Order 1994, SI 1994/700;
Criminal Justice Act 1993 (Commencement No 7) Order 1994, SI 1994/1951;
Criminal Justice Act 1993 (Commencement No 8) Order 1995, SI 1995/43;
Criminal Justice Act 1993 (Commencement No 9) Order 1995, SI 1995/1958;
Criminal Justice Act 1993 (Commencement No 10) Order 1999, SI 1999/1189;
Criminal Justice Act 1993 (Commencement No 11) Order 1999, SI 1999/1499.

1–3461　79. Short title, extent etc.　(1) This Act may be cited as the Criminal Justice Act 1993.

(2) The following provisions of this Act extend to the United Kingdom—

Part V;
sections 21(1) and (3)(*h*), 23, 45 to 51, 70 to 72, 77, 78 and this section;
Schedules 1 and 2; and
paragraphs 4 and 6 of Schedule 4.

(3) The following provisions of this Act extend only to Great Britain—

sections 21(3)(*e*), 29 to 32, 34(1), 35, 67(1) and 73; and
paragraph 3 of Schedule 4.

(4) The following provisions of this Act extend only to Scotland—

sections 17, 19, 20(2), 21(3)(*c*) and (*d*), 22(2), 24(12) to (15), 26(2), 33, 68, 69, 75 and 76; and
paragraph 2 of Schedule 4.

(5) Sections 21(3)(*f*) and 34(2) and paragraph 5 of Schedule 4 extend to Scotland and Northern Ireland only.

(6) *Repealed.*

(7) *Repealed.*[1]

(8) The provisions of Schedules 5 and 6 have the same extent as the provisions on which they operate.

(9) Otherwise, this Act extends to England and Wales only.

(10) Her Majesty may by Order in Council direct that such provisions of this Act as may be specified in the Order shall extend, with such exceptions and modifications as appear to Her Majesty to be appropriate, to any colony.

(11) *Repealed.*

(12) An Order in Council under paragraph 1(1)(*b*) of Schedule 1 to the Northern Ireland Act 1974 (legislation for Northern Ireland in the interim period) which contains a statement that it is made only for purposes corresponding to purposes of any of sections 16, 18 and 29 to 32—

(*a*)　shall not be subject to paragraph 1(4) and (5) of that Schedule (affirmative resolution of both Houses of Parliament); but

(*b*)　shall be subject to annulment in pursuance of a resolution of either House of Parliament.

(13) Schedule 5 (consequential amendments) shall have effect.

(14) The repeals and revocations set out in Schedule 6 (which include the repeal of two enactments which are spent) shall have effect.

[Criminal Justice Act 1993, s 79 as amended by the Drug Trafficking Act 1994, Schs 1 and 3 and the Northern Ireland (Emergency Provisions) Act 1996, Sch 7 and the Extradition Act 2003, Sch 4.]

---

1. The repeal of sub-s (7) does not apply in relation to extradition requests received or extraditions made on or before 31 December 2003.

Criminal Justice and Public Order Act 1994[1]

(1994 c 33)

PART II[2]

BAIL

1–3530　25. No bail for defendants charged with or convicted of homicide or rape after previous conviction of such offences[3].　(1) A person who in any proceedings has been charged with or convicted of an offence to which this section applies in circumstances to which it applies shall be granted bail in those proceedings only if the court or, as the case may be, the constable considering the grant of bail is satisfied that there are exceptional circumstances which justify it[4].

(2) This section applies, subject to subsection (3) below, to the following offences, that is to say—

(*a*)　murder;
(*b*)　attempted murder;
(*c*)　manslaughter;
(*d*)　rape under the law of Scotland or Northern Ireland;
(*e*)　an offence under section 1 of the Sexual Offences Act 1956 (rape);
(*f*)　an offence under section 1 of the Sexual Offences Act 2003 (rape);
(*g*)　an offence under section 2 of that Act (assault by penetration);

(*h*) an offence under section 4 of that Act (causing a person to engage in sexual activity without consent), where the activity caused involved penetration within subsection (4)(a) to (d) of that section;

(*i*) an offence under section 5 of that Act (rape of a child under 13);

(*j*) an offence under section 6 of that Act (assault of a child under 13 by penetration);

(*k*) an offence under section 8 of that Act (causing or inciting a child under 13 to engage in sexual activity), where an activity involving penetration within subsection (3)(a) to (d) of that section was caused;

(*l*) an offence under section 30 of that Act (sexual activity with a person with a mental disorder impeding choice), where the touching involved penetration within subsection (3)(a) to (d) of that section;

(*m*) an offence under section 31 of that Act (causing or inciting a person, with a mental disorder impeding choice, to engage in sexual activity), where an activity involving penetration within subsection (3)(a) to (d) of that section was caused;

(*n*) an attempt to commit an offence within any of paragraphs (*d*) to (*m*).

(3) This section applies to a person charged with or convicted of any such offence only if he has been previously convicted by or before a court in any part of the United Kingdom of any such offence or of culpable homicide and, in the case of a previous conviction of manslaughter or of culpable homicide, if he was then sentenced to imprisonment or, if he was then a child or young person, to long-term detention under any of the relevant enactments.

(4) This section applies whether or not an appeal is pending against conviction or sentence.

(5) In this section—

"conviction" includes—

(*a*) a finding that a person is not guilty by reason of insanity;

(*b*) a finding under section 4A(3) of the Criminal Procedure (Insanity) Act 1964 (cases of unfitness to plead) that a person did the act or made the omission charged against him; and

(*c*) a conviction of an offence for which an order is made discharging the offender absolutely or conditionally;

and "convicted" shall be construed accordingly; and

"the relevant enactments" means—

(*a*) as respects England and Wales, section 91 of the Powers of Criminal Courts (Sentencing) Act 2000;

(*b*) as respects Scotland, sections 205(1) to (3) and 208 of the Criminal Procedure (Scotland) Act 1995;

(*c*) as respects Northern Ireland, section 73(2) of the Children and Young Persons Act (Northern Ireland) 1968.

(6) This section does not apply in relation to proceedings instituted before its commencement.

[Criminal Justice and Public Order Act 1994, s 25 as amended by the Criminal Procedure (Consequential Provisions) (Scotland) Act 1995, Sch 4, the Crime and Disorder Act 1998, s 56, the Powers of Criminal Courts (Sentencing) Act 2000, Sch 9, the Sexual Offences Act 2003, Sch 6 and the Criminal Justice Act 2003, Sch 32.]

---

1. The Criminal Justice and Public Order Act 1994 is printed partly in PART I and partly in PARTS II, V AND VIII of this Manual. For provisions of the Act which are not printed in this PART, reference should be made to the following table:

Provision of Act	*Subject matter*	*PART and title within this Manual*
Part I, ss 1–24	*Young offenders—secure training orders etc*	PART V: YOUTH COURTS
Part III, ss 31–39	Evidence	PART II: EVIDENCE
Part V, ss 61–80	Public order: collective trespass or nuisance on land	PART VIII: title PROPERTY, OFFENCES AGAINST

Other provisions of the Act which amend earlier legislation have been incorporated in the text of those statutes as appropriate. For the commencement provisions of the Act, see s 172, post, and notes thereto. Of the provisions of the Act printed below in this PART, only s 168 had not been brought fully into force at the date of going to press on 1 January 2000.

2. Part II contains ss 25–30.

3. This section may be applied in a way which is compatible with the ECHR Article 5 if the court nevertheless takes all the relevant circumstances into account, see Law Commission Consultation Paper No 157, *Bail and the Human Rights Act 1998.*

Section 25 continues to have effect after the expiration of a defendant's custody time limit, and the fact that the prosecution has failed to satisfy the court that it has acted with all due diligence for the purpose of obtaining an extension of the custody time limit does not mean that the prosecution has failed to display "special diligence in the conduct of the proceedings" such as to breach article 5(3) of the Convention; the time span covered by art 5(3) is different from that which is laid down for custody time limits: *R (O) v Crown Court at Harrow* [2003] EWHC 868 (Admin), [2003] 1 WLR 2756.

4. As to the application of this section upon the expiry of, and refusal to extend, a custody time limit, it was held as follows in *R (O) v Crown Court at Harrow* [2006] UKHL 42, [2006] 3 WLR 195: s 25 was to be read as placing an evidential burden upon a defendant to whom the section applied to adduce material supporting the existence of exceptional circumstances justifying the grant of bail; that when the defendant's custody time limit had expired and the court had refused to extend it because of the prosecution's failure to act with all due diligence and expedition within the meaning of s 22(3)(*b*) of the 1985 Act, the defendant's continued detention in custody did not automatically amount to a violation of art 5(3), and a finding of lack of due diligence on the part of the prosecution did not automatically equate to a breach of the right to trial within a reasonable time; s 25 should be construed essentially as a guide to the proper operation of the Bail Act 1976, and it operated to disapply the ordinary requirement under the 1987 Regulations that bail should be granted automatically to any defendant whose custody time limit had expired, and so applied was compatible with art 5(3).

PART III[1]
COURSE OF JUSTICE: EVIDENCE, PROCEDURE, ETC
Procedure, jurisdiction and powers of magistrates' courts

1–3532   45. Extension of procedures enabling magistrates' courts to deal with cases in which accused pleads guilty.   The amendments to the Magistrates' Courts Act 1980 specified in Schedule 5 (being amendments designed principally to extend the procedures applicable in magistrates' courts when the accused pleads guilty) shall have effect.
[Criminal Justice and Public Order Act 1994, s 45.]

1. Part III contains ss 31–53.

1–3533   46. Criminal damage, etc as summary offence—relevant sum.   (1) In subsection (1) of section 22 of the Magistrates' Courts Act 1980 (under which, where an offence of or related to criminal damage or, in certain circumstances, an offence of aggravated vehicle-taking, is charged and it appears clear to the magistrates' court that the value involved does not exceed the relevant sum, the court is to proceed as if the offence were triable only summarily) in the second paragraph (which states the relevant sum), for "£2,000" there shall be substituted "£5,000".
   (2) Subsection (1) above does not apply to an offence charged in respect of an act done before this section comes into force.
[Criminal Justice and Public Order Act 1994, s 46.]

Sentencing: guilty pleas
1–3534   48. Reduction in sentences for guilty pleas.   *Repealed.*

Intimidation, etc, of witnesses, jurors and others
1–3535   51. Intimidation, etc, of witnesses, jurors and others[1].   (1) A person commits an offence[2] if—

   (a) he does an act which intimidates[3], and is intended to intimidate, another person ("the victim");
   (b) he does the act knowing or believing that the victim is assisting in the investigation of an offence or is a witness or potential witness or a juror or potential juror in proceedings for an offence; and
   (c) he does it intending thereby to cause the investigation[4] or the course of justice to be obstructed, perverted or interfered with.

   (2) A person commits an offence if—

   (a) he does an act which harms[5] or would harm, and is intended to harm, another person or, intending to cause another person to fear harm, he threatens to do an act which would harm that other person,
   (b) he does or threatens to do the act knowing or believing that the person harmed or threatened to be harmed ("the victim"), or some other person, has assisted in an investigation into an offence or has given evidence or particular evidence in proceedings for an offence, or has acted as a juror or concurred in a particular verdict in proceedings for an offence; and
   (c) does or threatens to do it because of that knowledge or belief.

   (3) For the purposes of subsections (1) and (2) it is immaterial that the act is or would be done, or that the threat is made—

   (a) otherwise than in the presence of the victim, or
   (b) to a person other than the victim.

   (4) The harm that may be done or threatened may be financial as well as physical (whether to the person or a person's property) and similarly as respects an intimidatory act which consists of threats.
   (5) The intention required by subsection (1)(c) and the motive required by subsection (2)(c) above need not be the only or the predominating intention or motive with which the act is done or, in the case of subsection (2), threatened.
   (6) A person guilty of an offence under this section shall be liable[6]—

   (a) on conviction on indictment, to imprisonment for a term not exceeding **five years** or a **fine** or both;
   (b) on summary conviction, to imprisonment for a term not exceeding **six months** or a fine not exceeding **the statutory maximum** or both.

   (7) If, in proceedings against a person for an offence under subsection (1) above, it is proved that he did an act falling within paragraph (a) with the knowledge or belief required by paragraph (b), he shall be presumed, unless the contrary is proved, to have done the act with the intention required by paragraph (c) of that subsection.
   (8) If, in proceedings against a person for an offence under subsection (2) above, it is proved that within the relevant period—

   (a) he did an act which harmed, and was intended to harm, another person, or
   (b) intending to cause another person fear of harm, he threatened to do an act which would harm that other person,

and that he did the act, or (as the case may be) threatened to do the act, with the knowledge or belief required by paragraph (*b*), he shall be presumed, unless the contrary is proved, to have done the act or (as the case may be) threatened to do the act with the motive required by paragraph (*c*) of that subsection.

(9) In this section—

"investigation into an offence" means such an investigation by the police or other person charged with the duty of investigating offences or charging offenders;

"offence" includes an alleged or suspected offence;

"potential", in relation to a juror, means a person who has been summoned for jury service at the court at which proceedings for the offence are pending; and*

"the relevant period"—

    (*a*) in relation to a witness or juror in any proceedings for an offence, means the period beginning with the institution of the proceedings and ending with the first anniversary of the conclusion of the trial or, if there is an appeal or a reference under section 9 or 11 of the Criminal Appeal Act 1995, of the conclusion of the appeal;

    (*b*) in relation to a person who has or is believed by the accused to have, assisted in an investigation into an offence, but was not also a witness in proceedings for an offence, means the period of one year beginning with any act of his, or any act believed by the accused to be an act of his, assisting in the investigation; and

    (*c*) in relation to a person who both has or is believed by the accused to have, assisted in the investigation into an offence and was a witness in proceedings for the offence, means the period beginning with any act of his, or any act believed by the accused to be an act of his, assisting in the investigation and ending with the anniversary mentioned in paragraph (*a*) above.

(10) For the purposes of the definition of the relevant period in subsection (9) above—

(*a*) proceedings for an offence are instituted at the earliest of the following times—

    (i) when a justice of the peace issues a summons or warrant under section 1 of the Magistrates' Courts Act 1980 in respect of the offence;*

    (ii) when a person is charged with the offence after being taken into custody without a warrant;

    (iii) when a bill of indictment is preferred by virtue of section 2(2)(*b*) of the Administration of Justice (Miscellaneous Provisions) Act 1933;

(*b*) proceedings at a trial of an offence are concluded with the occurrence of any of the following, the discontinuance of the prosecution, the discharge of the jury without a finding otherwise than in circumstances where the proceedings are continued without a jury, the acquittal of the accused or the sentencing of or other dealing with the accused for the offence of which he was convicted; and

(*c*) proceedings on an appeal are concluded on the determination of the appeal or the abandonment of the appeal.

(11) This section is in addition to, and not in derogation of, any offence subsisting at common law.

[Criminal Justice and Public Order Act 1994, s 51 as amended by the Criminal Appeal Act 1995, Sch 2 and the Youth Justice and Criminal Evidence Act 1999, Sch 4.]

---

*New definitions in sub-s (9) and para (*a*)(*ia*) inserted in sub-s (10) inserted by the **Criminal Justice Act 2003, Sch 36 from a date to be appointed.**

1. See also the Criminal Justice and Police Act 2001, ss 39–41, which create two new offences intended to increase protection for witnesses in all proceedings other than proceedings for a criminal offence.

2. The prosecution must prove that there was an investigation under way, not merely that the defendant believed there to be one (*R v Singh* [2000] 1 Cr App Rep 31, [1999] Crim LR 681, CA).

3. Although "to intimidate" normally means to put someone in fear, another meaning is "to force to or deter from some action by threats or violence" and this embraces a shade of meaning whereby the intimidator does not in fact succeed in putting the victim in fear although some element of threat or violence is necessary so that mere pressure by itself is insufficient. An act may amount to intimidation and thus intimidate, even though the victim is sufficiently steadfast not to be intimidated (*R v Patrascu* [2004] EWCA Crim 2417, [2004] 4 All ER 1066, [2005] 1 WLR 3344, [2005] 1 Cr App R 35).

4. The ambit of s 51(1) is not limited by sub-s (3), and the common law principle that a principal may commit an offence through an innocent agent applies; accordingly, a person who makes a threat against a witness to a third party, intending that the third party should convey the threat to the witness, is guilty of an offence contrary to s 51(1), provided that all the other statutory ingredients of the offence are satisfied (*A-G's Reference (No 1 of 1999)* [1999] 3 WLR 769, 163 JP 769).

5. "Harm" other than financial harm or damage to property (for which see sub-s (4)) means physical harm, and spitting at a witness in the absence of evidence of physical or psychiatric injury is not capable of being "harm" for the purposes of this provision (*R v Normanton* [1998] Crim LR 220, CA).

6. For procedure in respect of an offence which is triable either way, see the Magistrates' Courts Act 1980, ss 17A–21, this PART, ante.

PART IV[1]

POLICE POWERS

Powers of police to stop and search

1-3536   60. Powers to stop and search in anticipation of violence[2]. (1) If a police officer of or above the rank of inspector reasonably believes—

(*a*) that incidents involving serious violence may take place in any locality in his police area, and that it is expedient to give an authorisation under this section to prevent their occurrence, or

(*b*) that persons are carrying dangerous instruments or offensive weapons in any locality in his police area without good reason,

he may give an authorisation that the powers[3] conferred by this section are to be exercisable at any place within that locality for a specified period not exceeding 24 hours.

(2) *Repealed.*

(3) If it appears to an officer of or above the rank of superintendent that it is expedient to do so, having regard to offences which have, or are reasonably suspected to have, been committed in connection with any activity falling within the authorisation, he may direct that the authorisation shall continue in being for a further 24 hours.

(3A) If an inspector gives an authorisation under subsection (1) he must, as soon as it is practicable to do so, cause an officer of or above the rank of superintendent to be informed.

(4) This section confers on any constable in uniform power—

(*a*) to stop any pedestrian and search him or anything carried by him for offensive weapons or dangerous instruments;

(*b*) to stop any vehicle and search the vehicle, its driver and any passenger for offensive weapons or dangerous instruments.

(4A) *Repealed.**

(5) A constable may, in the exercise of the powers conferred by subsection (4) above, stop any person or vehicle and make any search he thinks fit whether or not he has any grounds for suspecting that the person or vehicle is carrying weapons or articles of that kind.

(6) If in the course of a search under this section a constable discovers a dangerous instrument or an article which he has reasonable grounds for suspecting to be an offensive weapon, he may seize it.

(7) This section applies (with the necessary modifications) to ships, aircraft and hovercraft as it applies to vehicles.

(8) A person who fails

(*a*) to stop, or to stop a vehicle; or

(*b*) to remove an item worn by him,*

when required to do so by a constable in the exercise of his powers under this section shall be liable on summary conviction to imprisonment for a term not exceeding **one month*** or to a fine not exceeding **level 3** on the standard scale or both.

(9) Any authorisation under this section shall be in writing signed by the officer giving it and shall specify the grounds on which it is given and the locality in which and the period during which the powers conferred by this section are exercisable and a direction under subsection (3) above shall also be given in writing or, where that is not practicable, recorded in writing as soon as it is practicable to do so.

(9A) The preceding provisions of this section, so far as they relate to an authorisation by a member of the British Transport Police Force (including sone who for the time being has the same powers and privileges as a member of a police force for a police area), shall have effect as if the references to a locality in his police area were references to a place specified in section 31(1)(*a*) to (*f*) of the Railways and Transport Safety Act 2003.

(10) Where a vehicle is stopped by a constable under this section, the driver shall be entitled to obtain a written statement that the vehicle was stopped under the powers conferred by this section if he applies for such a statement not later than the end of the period of twelve months from the day on which the vehicle was stopped.

(10A) A person who is searched by a constable under this section shall be entitled to obtain a written statement that he was searched under the powers conferred by this section if he applies for such a statement not later than the end of the period of twelve months from the day on which he was searched.

(11) In this section—

"British Transport Police Force" means the constables appointed under section 53 of the British Transport Commission Act 1949;

"dangerous instruments" means instruments which have a blade or are sharply pointed;

"offensive weapon" has the meaning given by section 1(9) of the Police and Criminal Evidence Act 1984 or, in relation to Scotland, section 47(4) of the Criminal Law (Consolidation) (Scotland) Act 1995; and

"vehicle" includes a caravan as defined in section 29(1) of the Caravan Sites and Control of Development Act 1960.

(11A) For the purposes of this section, a person carries a dangerous instrument or an offensive weapon if he has it in his possession.

(12) The powers conferred by this section are in addition to and not in derogation of, any power otherwise conferred.

[Criminal Justice and Public Order Act 1994, s 60 as amended by the Knives Act 1997, s 8, the Crime and Disorder Act 1998, s 25, the Anti-terrorism, Crime and Security Act 2001, Sch 7 and SI 2004/1573.]

***Repealed in relation to England by the Anti-terrorism, Crime and Security Act 2001, Sch 8. With regards Scotland, repealed from a date to be appointed.**

**Words "51 weeks" substituted by Criminal Justice Act 2003, Sch 26 from a date to be appointed.

1. Part IV contains ss 54–60.

2. The exercise of stop and search powers may raise issues of compliance with art 5 (the right to liberty), art 8 (the right to respect for private life) and art 14 (the prohibition on discrimination) of the European Convention on Human Rights.

3. The powers of search conferred by s 60 (the exercise of the power conferred by s 60(4A) does not give rise to a search: see infra) are governed by the requirements of s 2 of the Police and Criminal Evidence Act 1984, this Part, ante, which provides, *inter alia*, that a police constable shall not commence a search until he has taken reasonable steps to bring to the attention of the person to be searched his name and the name of the police station to which he is attached; the object of the proposed search; his grounds for proposing to make it; and an indication that he is going to make a record, of which the individual can in due course, if necessary, obtain a copy (*Osman v DPP* (1999) 163 JP 725).

1–3536A 60AA. Powers to require removal of disguises. (1) Where—

(a) an authorisation under section 60 is for the time being in force in relation to any locality for any period, or

(b) an authorisation under subsection (3) that the powers conferred by subsection (2) shall be exercisable at any place in a locality is in force for any period,

those powers shall be exercisable at any place in that locality at any time in that period.

(2) This subsection confers power[1] on any constable in uniform—

(a) to require any person to remove any item which the constable reasonably believes that person is wearing wholly or mainly for the purpose of concealing his identity;

(b) to seize[2] any item which the constable reasonably believes any person intends to wear wholly or mainly for that purpose.

(3) If a police officer of or above the rank of inspector reasonably believes—

(a) that activities may take place in any locality in his police area that are likely (if they take place) to involve the commission of offences, and

(b) that it is expedient, in order to prevent or control the activities, to give an authorisation under this subsection,

he may give an authorisation that the powers conferred by this section shall be exercisable at any place within that locality for a specified period not exceeding twenty-four hours.

(4) If it appears to an officer of or above the rank of superintendent that it is expedient to do so, having regard to offences which—

(a) have been committed in connection with the activities in respect of which the authorisation was given, or

(b) are reasonably suspected to have been so committed,

he may direct that the authorisation shall continue in force for a further twenty-four hours.

(5) If an inspector gives an authorisation under subsection, he must, as soon as it is practicable to do so, cause an officer of or above the rank of superintendent to be informed.

(6) Any authorisation under this section—

(a) shall be in writing and signed by the officer giving it; and

(b) shall specify—

(i) the grounds on which it is given;

(ii) the locality in which the powers conferred by this section are exercisable;

(iii) the period during which those powers are exercisable;

and a direction under subsection (4) shall also be given in writing or, where that is not practicable, recorded in writing as soon as it is practicable to do so.

(7) A person who fails to remove an item worn by him when required to do so by a constable in the exercise of his power under this section shall be liable, on summary conviction, to imprisonment for a term not exceeding one month or to a fine not exceeding level 3 on the standard scale or both[2].

(8) The preceding provisions of this section, so far as they relate to an authorisation by a member of the British Transport Police Force (including one who for the time being has the same powers and privileges as a member of a police force for a police area), shall have effect as if references to a locality or to a locality in his police area were references to any locality in or in the vicinity of any policed premises, or to the whole or any part of any such premises.

(9) In this section "British Transport Police Force" and "policed premises" each has the same meaning as in section 60.

(10) The powers conferred by this section are in addition to, and not in derogation of, any power otherwise conferred.

(11) This section does not extend to Scotland.

[Criminal Justice and Public Order Act 1994, s 60AA as inserted by the Anti-terrorism, Crime and Security Act 2001, s 94(1).]

---

1. It was held in relation to the former power to require removal of disguises (ie s 60(4A) of this Act, which was repealed by Sch 8 to the Anti-terrorism, Crime and Security Act 2001) that its exercise did not give rise to a power of search; therefore, the power did not have to be exercised pursuant to s 2(2)(b) and (3) of PACE (*DPP v Amery* [2002] Crim LR 142).

2. For retention of items seized, see note to s 60A, post.

1–3536B 60A. Retention and disposal of things seized under section 60. (1) Any things seized by a constable under section 60 or 60AA may be retained in accordance with regulations made by the Secretary of State under this section.

(2) The Secretary of State may make regulations[1] regulating the retention and safe keeping, and the disposal and destruction in prescribed circumstances, of such things.

(3) Regulations under this section may make different provisions for different classes of things or for different circumstances.

(4) The power to make regulations under this section shall be exercisable by statutory instrument which shall be subject to annulment in pursuance of a resolution of either House of Parliament.

[Criminal Justice and Public Order Act 1994, s 60A as inserted by the Crime and Disorder Act 1998, s 26 and amended by the Anti-terrorism, Crime and Security Act 2001, s 94(2).]

---

1. The Police (Retention and Disposal of Items Seized) Regulations 2002, SI 2002/1372 have been made which apply to any item which has been seized by a constable under s 60 or 60AA of the 1994 Act, unless it is an item of property to which the Police (Property) Regulations 1997 apply.

1–3536C   60B. *Scotland*

PART X[1]
CROSS-BORDER ENFORCEMENT

1–3537   136. Execution of warrants. (1) A warrant issued in England, Wales or Northern Ireland for the arrest of a person charged with an offence may (without any endorsement) be executed in Scotland by any constable of any police force of the country of issue or of the country of execution, or by a constable appointed under section 53 of the British Transport Commission Act 1949, as well as by any other persons within the directions in the warrant.

(2) A warrant issued in—

(*a*) Scotland; or
(*b*) Northern Ireland,

for the arrest of a person charged with an offence may (without any endorsement) be executed in England or Wales by any constable of any police force of the country of issue or of the country of execution as well as by any other persons within the directions in the warrant.

(3) A warrant issued in—

(*a*) England or Wales; or
(*b*) Scotland,

for the arrest of a person charged with an offence may (without any endorsement) be executed in Northern Ireland by any constable of any police force of the country of issue or of the country of execution, or by a constable appointed udner section 53 of the British Transport Commission Act 1949, as well as by any other persons within the directions in the warrant.

(4) A person arrested in pursuance of a warrant shall be taken, as soon as reasonably practicable, to any place to which he is committed by, or may be conveyed under, the warrant.

(5) A constable executing a warrant—

(*a*) under subsection (1), (2)(*b*) or (3)(*a*) of this section may use reasonable force and shall have the powers of search conferred by section 139;
(*b*) under subsection (2)(*a*) or (3)(*b*) of this section shall have the same powers and duties, and the person arrested the same rights, as they would have had if execution had been in Scotland by a constable of a police force in Scotland.

(6) Any other person within the directions in a warrant executing that warrant under this section shall have the same powers and duties, and the person arrested the same rights, as they would have had if execution had been in the country of issue by the person within those directions.

(7) This section applies as respects—

(*a*) a warrant of commitment and a warrant to arrest a witness issued by a judicial authority in England, Wales or Northern Ireland as it applies to a warrant for arrest; and
(*b*) a warrant for committal, a warrant to imprison (or to apprehend and imprison) and a warrant to arrest a witness issued by a judicial authority in Scotland as it applies to a warrant for arrest.

(7A) This section applies as respects a warrant issued under paragraph 3(2) of Schedule 1 to the Powers of Criminal Courts (Sentencing) Act 2000 (warrant for arrest of offender referred back to court by youth offender panel) as it applies to a warrant issued in England or Wales for the arrest of a person charged with an offence.

(8) In this section "judicial authority" means any justice of the peace or the judge of any court exercising jurisdiction in criminal proceedings; and any reference to a part of the United Kingdom in which a warrant may be executed includes a reference to the adjacent sea and other waters within the seaward limits of the territorial sea.

[Criminal Justice and Public Order Act 1994, s 136, as amended by the Youth Justice and Criminal Evidence Act 1999, Sch 4 , the Powers of Criminal Courts (Sentencing) Act 2000, Sch 9 and the Anti-terrorism, Crime and Security Act 2001, Sch 7.]

---

1. Part X contains ss 135–140.

1–3538   137. Cross-border powers of arrest etc[1]. (1) If the condition applicable to this subsection is satisfied, any constable of a police force in England and Wales who has reasonable grounds for suspecting that an offence has been committed or attempted in England or Wales and that the suspected person is in Scotland or in Northern Ireland may arrest without a warrant the suspected person wherever he is in Scotland or in Northern Ireland.

(2) If the condition applicable to this subsection is satisfied, any constable of a police force in Scotland who has reasonable grounds for suspecting that an offence has been committed or attempted in Scotland and that the suspected person is in England or Wales or in Northern Ireland may, as respects the suspected person, wherever he is in England or Wales or in Northern Ireland, exercise the same powers of arrest or detention as it would be competent for him to exercise were the person in Scotland.

(2A) The powers conferred by subsections (1) and (2) may be exercised in England and Wales and Scotland by a constable appointed under section 53 of the British Transport Commission Act 1949.

(3) If the conditions applicable to this subsection are satisfied, any constable of a police force in Northern Ireland who has reasonable grounds for suspecting that an offence has been committed or attempted in Northern Ireland and that the suspected person is in England or Wales or in Scotland may arrest without a warrant the suspected person wherever he is in England or Wales or in Scotland.

(4) The condition applicable to subsection (1) above is that it appears to the constable that it would have been lawful for him to have exercised the powers had the suspected person been in England and Wales.

(5) The condition applicable to subsection (2) above is that it appears to the constable that it would have been lawful for him to have exercised the powers had the suspected person been in Scotland.

(6) The conditions applicable to subsection (3) above are—

(a)   that the suspected offence is an arrestable offence; or

(b)   that, in the case of any other offence, it appears to the constable that service of a summons is impracticable or inappropriate for any of the reasons specified in subsection (3) of section 138.

(7) It shall be the duty of a constable who has arrested or, as the case may be, detained, a person under this section—

(a)   if he arrested him in Scotland, to take the person arrested either to the nearest convenient designated police station in England or in Northern Ireland or to a designated police station in a police area in England and Wales or in Northern Ireland in which the offence is being investigated;

(b)   if he arrested him in England or Wales, to take the person arrested to the nearest convenient police station in Scotland or to a police station within a sheriffdom in which the offence is being investigated or to the nearest convenient designated police station in Northern Ireland or to a designated police station in Northern Ireland in which the offence is being investigated;

(c)   if he detained him in England or Wales, to take the person detained to either such police station in Scotland as is mentioned in paragraph (b) above, or to the nearest convenient designated police station in England or Wales;

(d)   if he arrested him in Northern Ireland, to take the person arrested either to the nearest convenient designated police station in England or Wales or to a designated police station in a police area in England and Wales in which the offence is being investigated or to the nearest convenient police station in Scotland or to a police station within a sheriffdom in which the offence is being investigated;

(e)   if he detained him in Northern Ireland, to take the person detained to either such police station in Scotland as is mentioned in paragraph (b) above, or to the nearest convenient designated police station in Northern Ireland;

and to do so as soon as reasonably practicable.

(8) A constable—

(a)   arresting a person under subsection (1) or (3) above, may use reasonable force and shall have the powers of search conferred by section 139;

(b)   arresting a person under subsection (2) above shall have the same powers and duties, and the person arrested the same rights, as they would have had if the arrest had been in Scotland; and

(c)   detaining a person under subsection (2) above shall act in accordance with the provisions applied by subsection (2) (as modified by subsection (6)) of section 138.

(9) In this section—

"arrestable offence" has the same meaning as in the Police and Criminal Evidence (Northern Ireland) Order 1989 ("the 1989 Order");

"designated police station" has the same meaning as in the Police and Criminal Evidence Act 1984 or, in relation to Northern Ireland, as in the 1989 Order; and

"constable of a police force", in relation to Northern Ireland, means a member of the the Police Service of Northern Ireland or the Police Service of Northern Ireland Reserve.

(10) This section shall not prejudice any power of arrest conferred apart from this section.

[Criminal Justice and Public Order Act 1994, s 137, as amended by the Anti-terrorism, Crime and Security Act 2001, s 127(2)(f) and the Police (Northern Ireland) Act 2000, s 78(2)(d) and the Serious Organised Crime and Police Act 2005, Sch 7.]

1. The exercise of cross-border powers of arrest may raise issues of compliance with art 5 of the European Convention on Human Rights. See para **1–2728** above.

1–3539   138. Powers of arrest etc: supplementary provisions.   (1) The following provisions have effect to supplement section 137 ("the principal section").

(2) Where a person is detained under subsection (2) of the principal section, subsections (2) to (8) of section 14 (detention and questioning at police station), subsections (1), (2) and (4) to (6) of section 15 (rights of person arrested or detained) and section 18 (prints, samples etc. in criminal investigations) of the Criminal Procedure (Scotland) Act 1995 shall apply to detention under that subsection of the principal section as they apply to detention under subsection (1) of the said section 2, but with the modifications mentioned in subsection (6) below.

(3) The reasons referred to in subsection (6)(*b*) of the principal section are that—

(*a*) the name of the suspected person is unknown to, and cannot readily be ascertained by, the constable;

(*b*) the constable has reasonable grounds for doubting whether a name furnished by the suspected person as his name is his real name;

(*c*) either—

(i) the suspected person has failed to furnish a satisfactory address for service; or

(ii) the constable has reasonable grounds for doubting whether an address furnished by the suspected person is a satisfactory address for service;

(*d*) the constable has reasonable grounds for believing that arrest is necessary to prevent the suspected person—

(i) causing physical injury to himself or any other person;

(ii) suffering physical injury;

(iii) causing loss of or damage to property;

(iv) committing an offence against public decency; or

(v) causing an unlawful obstruction of a highway or road; or

(*e*) the constable has reasonable grounds for believing that arrest is necessary to protect a child or other vulnerable person from the suspected person.

(4) For the purposes of subsection (3) above an address is a satisfactory address for service if it appears to the constable—

(*a*) that the suspected person will be at it for a sufficiently long period for it to be possible to serve him with process; or

(*b*) that some other person specified by the suspected person will accept service of process for the suspected person at it.

(5) Nothing in subsection (3)(*d*) above authorises the arrest of a person under sub-paragraph (iv) of that paragraph except where members of the public going about their normal business cannot reasonably be expected to avoid the person to be arrested.

(6) The following are the modifications of sections 14 and 15 of the said Act of 1995 which are referred to in subsection (2) above—

(*a*) in section 14—

(i) in subsection (2), the reference to detention being terminated not more than six hours after it begins shall be construed as a reference to its being terminated not more than four hours after the person's arrival at the police station to which he is taken under subsection (7)(*c*) of the principal section; and

(ii) in subsections (6) and (9), references to "other premises" shall be disregarded; and

(*b*) in subsections (1) and (2) of section 15, references to "other premises" shall be disregarded.

[Criminal Justice and Public Order Act 1994, s 138 as amended by the Criminal Procedure (Consequential Provisions) (Scotland) Act 1995, Sch 4 and the Serious Organised Crime and Police Act 2005, Sch 7.]

1–3540   139. Search powers available on arrests under sections 136 and 137.   (1) The following powers are available to a constable in relation to a person arrested under section 136(1), (2)(*b*) or (3)(*a*) or 137(1) or (3).

(2) A constable to whom this section applies may search the person if the constable has reasonable grounds for believing that the person may present a danger to himself or others.

(3) Subject to subsections (4) to (6) below, a constable to whom this section applies may—

(*a*) search the person for anything—

(i) which he might use to assist him to escape from lawful custody; or

(ii) which might be evidence relating to an offence; and

(*b*) enter and search any premises in which the person was when, or was immediately before, he was arrested for evidence relating to the offence for which he was arrested.

(4) The power to search conferred by subsection (3) above is only a power to search to the extent that is reasonably required for the purpose of discovering any such thing or any such evidence.

(5) The powers conferred by this section to search a person are not to be construed as authorising

a constable to require a person to remove any of his clothing in public other than an outer coat, jacket, headgear, gloves or footwear but they do authorise a search of a person's mouth.

(6) A constable may not search a person in the exercise of the power conferred by subsection (3)(*a*) above unless he has reasonable grounds for believing that the person to be searched may have concealed on him anything for which a search is permitted under that paragraph.

(7) A constable may not search premises in the exercise of the power conferred by subsection (3)(*b*) above unless he has reasonable grounds for believing that there is evidence for which a search is permitted under that paragraph.

(8) In so far as the power of search conferred by subsection (3)(*b*) above relates to premises consisting of two or more separate dwellings, it is limited to a power to search—

(*a*) any dwelling in which the arrest took place or in which the person arrested was immediately before his arrest; and

(*b*) any parts of the premises which the occupier of any such dwelling uses in common with the occupiers of any other dwellings comprised in the premises.

(9) A constable searching a person in the exercise of the power conferred by subsection (2) above may seize and retain anything he finds, if he has reasonable grounds for believing that the person searched might use it to cause physical injury to himself or to any other person.

(10) A constable searching a person in the exercise of the power conferred by subsection (3)(*a*) above may seize and retain anything he finds, other than an item subject to legal privilege, if he has reasonable grounds for believing—

(*a*) that he might use it to assist him to escape from lawful custody; or

(*b*) that it is evidence of an offence, or has been obtained in consequence of the commission of an offence.

(11) Nothing in this section shall be taken to affect the power conferred by section 43 of the Terrorism Act 2000.

(12) In this section—

"item subject to legal privilege" has the meaning given to it—

(*a*) as respects anything in the possession of a person searched in England and Wales, by section 10 of the Police and Criminal Evidence Act 1984;

(*b*) as respects anything in the possession of a person searched in Scotland, by section 412 of the Proceeds of Crime Act 2002;

(*c*) as respects anything in the possession of a person searched in Northern Ireland, by Article 12 of the Police and Criminal Evidence (Northern Ireland) Order 1989;

"premises" includes any place and, in particular, includes—

(*a*) any vehicle, vessel, aircraft or hovercraft;

(*b*) any offshore installation; and

(*c*) any tent or movable structure; and

"offshore installation" has the meaning given to it by section 1 of the Mineral Workings (Offshore Installation) Act 1971.

[Criminal Justice and Public Order Act 1994, s 139, as amended by the Terrorism Act 2000, Sch 15 and the Proceeds of Crime Act 2002, Sch 11.]

1–3541 140. Reciprocal powers of arrests. (1) Where a constable of a police force in England and Wales would, in relation to an offence, have power to arrest a person in England or Wales under section 24 of the Police and Criminal Evidence Act 1984 (arrestable offences and non-arrestable offences in certain circumstances) a constable of a police force in Scotland or in Northern Ireland shall have the like power of arrest in England and Wales.

(2) Where a constable of a police force in Scotland or in Northern Ireland arrests a person in England or Wales by virtue of subsection (1) above—

(*a*) the constable shall be subject to requirements to inform the arrested person that he is under arrest and of the grounds for it corresponding to the requirements imposed by section 28 of that Act;

(*b*) the constable shall be subject to a requirement to take the arrested person to a police station corresponding to the requirement imposed by section 30 of that Act and so also as respects the other related requirements of that section; and

(*c*) the constable shall have powers to search the arrested person corresponding to the powers conferred by section 32 of that Act.

(3) Where a constable of a police force in Scotland would, in relation to an offence, have power to arrest a person in Scotland, a constable of a police force in England and Wales or in Northern Ireland shall have the like power of arrest in Scotland.

(4) Where a constable of a police force in England and Wales or in Northern Ireland arrests a person in Scotland by virtue of subsection (3) above, the arrested person shall have the same rights and the constable the same powers and duties as they would have were the constable a constable of a police force in Scotland.

(5) Where a constable of a police force in Northern Ireland would, in relation to an offence, have power to arrest a person in Northern Ireland under Article 26(6) or (7) or 27 of the Police and Criminal Evidence (Northern Ireland) Order 1989 (arrestable offences and non-arrestable offences

in certain circumstances) a constable of a police force in England and Wales or Scotland shall have the like power of arrest in Northern Ireland.

(6) Where a constable of a police force in England and Wales or in Scotland arrests a person in Northern Ireland by virtue of subsection (5) above—

(a) the constable shall be subject to requirements to inform the arrested person that he is under arrest and of the grounds for it corresponding to the requirements imposed by Article 30 of that Order;

(b) the constable shall be subject to a requirement to take the arrested person to a police station corresponding to the requirement imposed by Article 32 of that Order and so as respects the other related requirements of that Article; and

(c) the constable shall have powers to search the arrested person corresponding to the powers conferred by Article 34 of that Order.

(6A) The references in subsections (1) and (2) to a constable of a police force in Scotland, and the references in subsections (3) and (4) to a constable of a police force in England and Wales, include a constable appointed under section 53 of the British Transport Commission Act 1949 (c xxix).

(7) In this section "constable of a police force", in relation to Northern Ireland, means a member of the Police Service of Northern Ireland or the Police Service of Northern Ireland Reserve.

[Criminal Justice and Public Order Act 1994, s 140, as amended by the Anti-terrorism, Crime and Security Act 2001, Sch 7, the Police (Northern Ireland) Act 2000, s 78 and the Serious Organised Crime and Police Act 2005, Sch 7.]

1–3542 141. Aid of one police force by another. (1) The chief officer of police of a police force in England and Wales may, on the application of the chief officer of a police force in Scotland or the chief constable of the Royal Ulster Constabulary in Northern Ireland, provide constables or other assistance for the purpose of enabling the Scottish force or the Royal Ulster Constabulary to meet any special demand on its resources.

(2) The chief officer of a police force in Scotland may, on the application of the chief officer of police of a police force in England and Wales or the chief constable of the Royal Ulster Constabulary in Northern Ireland, provide constables or other assistance for the purpose of enabling the English or Welsh force or the Royal Ulster Constabulary to meet any special demand on its resources.

(3) The chief constable of the Royal Ulster Constabulary in Northern Ireland may, on the application of the chief officer of police of a police force in England and Wales or the chief officer of a police force in Scotland, provide constables or other assistance for the purpose of enabling the English or Welsh force or the Scottish force to meet any special demand on its resources.

(4) If it appears to the Secretary of State to be expedient in the interests of public safety or order that any police force should be reinforced or should receive other assistance for the purpose of enabling it to meet any special demand on its resources, and that satisfactory arrangements under subsection (1), (2) or (3) above cannot be made, or cannot be made in time, he may direct the chief officer of police of any police force in England and Wales, the chief officer of any police force in Scotland or the chief constable of the Royal Ulster Constabulary, as the case may be, to provide such constables or other assistance for that purpose as may be specified in the direction.

(5) While a constable is provided under this section for the assistance of another police force he shall, notwithstanding any enactment,—

(a) be under the direction and control of the chief officer of police of that other force (or, where that other force is a police force in Scotland or the Royal Ulster Constabulary in Northern Ireland, of its chief officer or the chief constable of the Royal Ulster Constabulary respectively); and

(b) have in any place the like powers and privileges as a member of that other force therein as a constable.

(6) The police authority maintaining a police force for which assistance is provided under this section shall pay to the police authority maintaining the force from which that assistance is provided such contribution as may be agreed upon between those authorities or, in default of any such agreement, as may be provided by any agreement subsisting at the time between all police authorities generally, or, in default of such general agreement, as may be determined by the Secretary of State.

(7) Any expression used in the Police Act 1964, the Police (Scotland) Act 1967 or the Police Act (Northern Ireland) 1970 and this section in its application to England and Wales, Scotland and Northern Ireland respectively has the same meaning in this section as in that Act.

(8) In this section "constable of a police force", in relation to Northern Ireland, means a member of the Royal Ulster Constabulary or the Royal Ulster Constabulary Reserve.

[Criminal Justice and Public Order Act 1994, s 141.]

PART XII[1]

MISCELLANEOUS AND GENERAL

Increase in certain penalties

1–3544 157. *Increase in penalties for certain offences.*

---

1. Part XII contains ss 149–172.

Ticket touts

1–3545   166. Sale of tickets by unauthorised persons. (1) It is an offence for an unauthorised person to sell, or offer or expose for sale, a ticket for a designated football match in any public place or place to which the public has access or, in the course of a trade or business, in any other place.

(2) For this purpose—

(a) a person is "unauthorised" unless he is authorised in writing to sell tickets for the match by the home club or by the organisers of the match;

(b) a "ticket" means anything which purports to be a ticket; and

(c) a "designated football match" means a football match of a description, or a particular football match, for the time being designated for the purposes of Part I of the Football Spectators Act 1989 or which is a regulated football match for the purposes of Part II of that Act.

(3) A person guilty of an offence under this section is liable on summary conviction to a fine not exceeding **level 5** on the standard scale.

(4) *Repealed.*

(5) Section 32 of the Police and Criminal Evidence Act 1984 (search of persons and premises (including vehicles) upon arrest) shall have effect, in its application in relation to an offence under this section, as if the power conferred on a constable to enter and search any vehicle extended to any vehicle which the constable has reasonable grounds for believing was being used for any purpose connected with the offence.

(6) The Secretary of State may by order made by statutory instrument apply this section, with such modifications as he thinks fit, to such sporting event or category of sporting event for which 6,000 or more tickets are issued for sale as he thinks fit.

(7) An order under subsection (6) above may provide that —

(a) a certificate (a "ticket sale certificate") signed by a duly authorised officer certifying that 6,000 or more tickets were issued for sale for a sporting event is conclusive evidence of that fact;

(b) an officer is duly authorised if he is authorised in writing to sign a ticket sale certificate by the home club or the organisers of the sporting event; and

(c) a document purporting to be a ticket sale certificate shall be received in evidence and deemed to be such a certificate unless the contrary is proved.

(8) Where an order has been made under subsection (6) above, this section also applies, with any modifications made by the order, to any part of the sporting event specified or described in the order, provided that 6,000 or more tickets are issued for sale for the day on which that part of the event takes place.★

[Criminal Justice and Public Order Act 1994, s 166 as amended by the Football (Offences and Disorder) Act 1999, s 10, the Football (Disorder) Act 2000, Schs 2 and 3 and the Serious Organised Crime and Police Act 2005, Sch 7.]

★Amended by the Violent Crime Reduction Act 2006, s 53 from a date to be appointed.

1–3545A   166A. Supplementary provision relating to sale and disposal of tickets on internet.
(1) Nothing in section 166 makes it an offence for a service provider established outside of the United Kingdom to do anything in the course of providing information society services.

(2) If—

(a) a service provider established in the United Kingdom does anything in an EEA State other than the United Kingdom in the course of providing information society services, and

(b) the action, if done in England and Wales, would constitute an offence falling within section 166(1),

the service provider shall be guilty in England and Wales of an offence under that section.

(3) A service provider is not capable of being guilty of an offence under section 166 in respect of anything done in the course of providing so much of an information society service as consists in—

(a) the transmission in a communication network of information falling within subsection (4), or

(b) the storage of information provided by a recipient of the service,

except where subsection (5) applies.

(4) Information falls within this subsection if—

(a) it is provided by a recipient of the service; and

(b) it is the subject of automatic, intermediate and temporary storage which is solely for the purpose of making the onward transmission of the information to other recipients of the service at their request more efficient.

(5) This subsection applies at any time in relation to information if—

(a) the service provider knew when that information was provided that it contained material contravening section 166; or

(b) that information is stored at that time (whether as mentioned in subsection (3)(b) or (4)) in consequence of the service provider's failure expeditiously to remove the information, or to disable access to it, upon obtaining actual knowledge that the information contained material contravening section 166.

(6) In this section—

"the Directive" means Directive 2000/31/EC of the European Parliament and of the Council of 8 June 2000 on certain legal aspects of information society services, in particular electronic commerce, in the Internal Market (Directive on electronic commerce);

"information society services"—

(a) has the meaning set out in Article 2(a) of the Directive (which refers to Article 1(2) of Directive 98/34/EC of the European Parliament and of the Council of 22 June 1998 laying down a procedure for the provision of information in the field of technical standards and regulations, as amended by Directive 98/48/EC of 20 July 1998); and

(b) is summarised in recital 17 of the Directive as covering "any service normally provided for remuneration, at a distance, by means of electronic equipment for the processing (including digital compression) and storage of data, and at the individual request of a recipient of a service";

"EEA State" means a state which is for the time being a member State, Norway, Iceland or Liechtenstein;

"recipient of the service" means any person who, for professional ends or otherwise, uses an information society service, in particular for the purposes of seeking information or making it accessible;

"service provider" means any person providing an information society service.*

[Criminal Justice and Public Order Act 1994, s 166A as inserted by the Violent Crime Reduction Act 2006, s 53.]

---

*Inserted by the Violent Crime Reduction Act 2006, s 53 from a date to be appointed.

Taxi touts

1–3546   167. Touting for hire car services.   (1) Subject to the following provisions, it is an offence, in a public place, to solicit persons to hire vehicles to carry them as passengers.

(2) Subsection (1) above does not imply that the soliciting must refer to any particular vehicle nor is the mere display of a sign on a vehicle that the vehicle is for hire soliciting within that subsection.

(3) No offence is committed under this section where soliciting persons to hire licensed taxis is permitted by a scheme under section 10 of the Transport Act 1985 (schemes for shared taxis) whether or not supplemented by provision made under section 13 of that Act (modifications of the taxi code).

(4) It is a defence for the accused to show that he was soliciting for passengers to be carried at separate fares by public service vehicles for public service vehicles on behalf of the holder of a PSV operator's licence for those vehicles whose authority he had at the time of the alleged offence.

(5) A person guilty of an offence under this section shall be liable on summary conviction to a fine not exceeding **level 4** on the standard scale.

(6) In this section—

"public place" includes any highway and any other premises or place to which at the material time the public have or are permitted to have access (whether on payment or otherwise); and

"public service vehicle" and "PSV operator's licence" have the same meaning as in Part II of the Public Passenger Vehicles Act 1981.

(7) *Repealed.*

[Criminal Justice and Public Order Act 1994, s 167 amended by the Transport Act 2000, s 265(3) and the Serious Organised Crime and Police Act 2005, Sch 7.]

General

1–3547   168. Minor and consequential amendments and repeals.   (1) The enactments mentioned in Schedule 9 to this Act shall have effect with the amendments there specified (being minor amendments).

(2) The enactments mentioned in Schedule 10 to this Act shall have effect with the amendments there specified (amendments consequential on the foregoing provisions of this Act).

(3) The enactments mentioned in Schedule 11 to this Act (which include enactments which are spent) are repealed or revoked to the extent specified in the third column of that Schedule.

[Criminal Justice and Public Order Act 1994, s 168.]

1–3548   172. Short title, commencement and extent.   (1) This Act may be cited as the Criminal Justice and Public Order Act 1994.

(2) With the exception of section 82 and, subject to subsection (4) below, this Act shall come into force on such day as the Secretary of State or, in the case of sections 52 and 53, the Lord Chancellor may appoint by order[1] made by statutory instrument, and different days may be appointed for different provisions or different purposes.

(3) Any order under subsection (2) above may make such transitional provisions and savings as appear to the authority making the order necessary or expedient in connection with any provision brought into force by the order.

(4) The following provisions and their related amendments, repeals and revocations shall come into force on the passing of this Act, namely sections 5 to 15 (and Schedules 1 and 2), 61, 63, 65, 68 to 71, 77 to 80, 81, 83, 90, Chapters I and IV of Part VIII, sections 142 to 148, 150, 158(1), (3) and (4), 166, 167, 171, paragraph 46 of Schedule 9 and this section.

(5) No order shall be made under subsection (6) of section 166 above unless a draft of the order has been laid before, and approved by a resolution of, each House of Parliament.

(6) For the purposes of subsection (4) above—

(a) the following are the amendments related to the provisions specified in that subsection, namely, in Schedule 10, paragraphs 26, 35, 36, 59 60 and 63(1), (3), (4) and (5);

(b) the repeals and revocations related to the provisions specified in that subsection are those specified in the Note at the end of Schedule 11.

(7) Except as regards any provisions applied under section 39 and subject to the following provisions, this Act extends to England and Wales only.

(8) Sections 47(3), 49, 60 to 67, 70, 71, 81, 82, 146(4), 157(1), 163, 169 and 170 also extend to Scotland.

(9) Section 83(1) extends to England and Wales and Northern Ireland.

(10) This section, sections 68, 69, 83(3) to (5), 88 to 92, 136 to 141, 156, 157(2), (3), (4), (5) and (9), 158, 159, 161, 162, 164, 165, 168, 171 and Chapter IV of Part VIII extend to the United Kingdom and sections 158 and 159 also extend to the Channel Islands and the Isle of Man.

(11) Sections 93, 95 and 101(8), so far as relating to the delivery of prisoners to or from premises situated in a part of the British Islands outside England and Wales, extend to that part of those Islands.

(12) Sections 102(1) to (3), 104, 105 and 117, so far as relating to the transfer of prisoners to or from premises situated in a part of the British Islands outside Scotland, extend to that part of those Islands, but otherwise Chapter II of Part VIII extends to Scotland only.

(13) Sections 47(4), 83(2), 84(5) to (7), 87, Part IX, sections 145(2), 146(2), 148, 151(2), 152(2), 153, 157(7) and 160(2) extend to Scotland only.

(14) Sections 118, 120, 121 and 125, so far as relating to the delivery of prisoners to or from premises situated in a part of the British Islands outside Northern Ireland, extend to that part of those islands, but otherwise Chapter III of Part VIII extends to Northern Ireland only.

(15) Sections 53, 84(8) to (11), 85(4) to (6), 86(2), 145(3), 147 and 157(8) extend to Northern Ireland only.

(16) Where any enactment is amended, repealed or revoked by Schedule 9, 10 or 11 to this Act the amendment, repeal or revocation has the same extent as that enactment; except that Schedules 9 and 11 do not extend to Scotland in so far as they relate to section 17(1) of the Video Recordings Act 1984.

[Criminal Justice and Public Order Act 1994, s 172.]

---

1. At the date of going to press, the following commencement orders had been made: Criminal Justice and Public Order Act 1994 (Commencement No 1) Order 1994, SI 1994/2935, (Commencement No 2) Order 1994, SI 1994/ 3192, and (Commencement No 3) Order 1994, SI 1994/3258, (Commencement No 5 and Transitional Provisions) Order 1995, SI 1995/127, (Commencement No 6) Order 1995, SI 1995/721, (Commencement No 7) Order 1995, SI 1995/1378, (Commencement No 8 and Transitional Provision) Order 1995, SI 1995/1957 (Commencement No 9) Order 1996, SI 1996/625, (Commencement No 10) Order 1996, SI 1996/1608, (Commencement No 11 and Transitional Provision) Order 1997, SI 1997/882 and (Commencement No 12 and Transitional Provision) Order 1998, SI 1998/277. The Criminal Justice and Public Order Act 1994 (Commencement No 4) Order 1995, SI 1995/24, extends only to Northern Ireland.

Criminal Appeal Act 1995[1]
(1995 c 35)

1–3549

PART I[2]
THE COURT OF APPEAL

---

1. This Act amends provisions relating to appeals and references to the Court of Appeal in criminal cases and establishes a Criminal Cases Review Commission.

Under the Human Rights Act 1998, this Act, so far as it is possible to do so, must be read and given effect in a way which is compatible with the Convention rights. The European Convention on Human Rights does not guarantee a right of appeal as such. This is provided for by art 2 of Protocol 7 (which has not yet entered force). However, where a right of appeal is provided in domestic law, whether on grounds of fact or law, art 6 (fair trial) applies. The manner of application will depend on the nature of the hearing and some art 6 guarantees, such as the right to an oral hearing and the right to be present, are less strictly applied in appeal proceedings, particularly where the only issues raised are points of law. In general, where an appeal involves an assessment of disputed questions of fact, the requirements of fairness are more akin to those of a criminal trial. See *Monnell and Morris v United Kingdom* (1987) 10 EHRR 205, *Ekbatani v Sweden* (1988) 13 EHRR 504, *Andersson v Sweden* (1991) 15 EHRR 218 and *Helmers v Sweden* (1991) 15 EHRR 285.

2. Part I contains ss 1–7.

PART II[1]
THE CRIMINAL CASES REVIEW COMMISSION
The Commission

1–3550 **8. The Commission.** (1) There shall be a body corporate to be known as the Criminal Cases Review Commission.

(2) The Commission shall not be regarded as the servant or agent of the Crown or as enjoying any status, immunity or privilege of the Crown; and the Commission's property shall not be regarded as property of, or held on behalf of, the Crown.

(3) The Commission shall consist of not fewer than eleven members.

(4) The members of the Commission shall be appointed by Her Majesty on the recommendation of the Prime Minister.

(5) At least one third of the members of the Commission shall be persons who are legally qualified; and for this purpose a person is legally qualified if—

(*a*) he has a ten year general qualification, within the meaning of section 71 of the Courts and Legal Services Act 1990, or

(*b*) he is a member of the Bar of Northern Ireland, or solicitor of the Supreme Court of Northern Ireland, of at least ten years' standing.*

(6) At least two thirds of the members of the Commission shall be persons who appear to the Prime Minister to have knowledge or experience of any aspect of the criminal justice system and of them at least one shall be a person who appears to him to have knowledge or experience of any aspect of the criminal justice system in Northern Ireland; and for the purposes of this subsection the criminal justice system includes, in particular, the investigation of offences and the treatment of offenders.

(7) Schedule 1 (further provisions with respect to the Commission) shall have effect.
[Criminal Appeal Act 1995, s 8.]

***Amended by the Constitutional Reform Act 2005, Sch 11 from a date to be appointed.**
1. Part II contains ss 8–25.

References to Court

1–3550A 9. Cases dealt with on indictment in England and Wales. (1) Where a person has been convicted of an offence on indictment in England and Wales, the Commission—

(*a*) may at any time refer the conviction to the Court of Appeal, and

(*b*) (whether or not they refer the conviction) may at any time refer to the Court of Appeal any sentence (not being a sentence fixed by law) imposed on, or in subsequent proceedings relating to, the conviction.

(2) A reference under subsection (1) of a person's conviction shall be treated for all purposes as an appeal by the person under section 1 of the 1968 Act against the conviction.

(3) A reference under subsection (1) of a sentence imposed on, or in subsequent proceedings relating to, a person's conviction on an indictment shall be treated for all purposes as an appeal by the person under section 9 of the 1968 Act against—

(*a*) the sentence, and

(*b*) any other sentence (not being a sentence fixed by law) imposed on, or in subsequent proceedings relating to, the conviction or any other conviction on the indictment.

(4) On a reference under subsection (1) of a person's conviction on an indictment the Commission may give notice to the Court of Appeal that any other conviction on the indictment which is specified in the notice is to be treated as referred to the Court of Appeal under subsection (1).

(5) Where a verdict of not guilty by reason of insanity has been returned in England and Wales in the case of a person, the Commission may at any time refer the verdict to the Court of Appeal; and a reference under this subsection shall be treated for all purposes as an appeal by the person under section 12 of the 1968 Act against the verdict.

(6) Where in England and Wales there have been findings that a person is under a disability and that he did the act or made the omission charged against him, the Commission may at any time refer either or both of those findings to the Court of Appeal; and a reference under this subsection shall be treated for all purposes as an appeal by the person under section 15 of the 1968 Act against the finding or findings referred.
[Criminal Appeal Act 1995, s 9 as amended by the Domestic Violence, Crime and Victims Act 2004, Sch 10.]

1–3551 10. *Cases dealt with on indictment in Northern Ireland.*

1–3551A 11. Cases dealt with summarily in England and Wales. (1) Where a person has been convicted of an offence by a magistrates' court in England and Wales, the Commission—

(*a*) may at any time refer the conviction to the Crown Court, and

(*b*) (whether or not they refer the conviction) may at any time refer to the Crown Court any sentence imposed on, or in subsequent proceedings relating to, the conviction.

(2) A reference under subsection (1) of a person's conviction shall be treated for all purposes as an appeal by the person under section 108(1) of the Magistrates' Courts Act 1980 against the conviction (whether or not he pleaded guilty).

(3) A reference under subsection (1) of a sentence imposed on, or in subsequent proceedings relating to, a person's conviction shall be treated for all purposes as an appeal by the person under section 108(1) of the Magistrates' Courts Act 1980 against—

(*a*) the sentence, and

(b) any other sentence imposed on, or in subsequent proceedings relating to, the conviction or any related conviction.

(4) On a reference under subsection (1) of a person's conviction the Commission may give notice to the Crown Court that any related conviction which is specified in the notice is to be treated as referred to the Crown Court under subsection (1).

(5) For the purposes of this section convictions are related if they are convictions of the same person by the same court on the same day.

(6) On a reference under this section the Crown Court may not award any punishment more severe than that awarded by the court whose decision is referred.

(7) The Crown Court may grant bail to a person whose conviction or sentence has been referred under this section; and any time during which he is released on bail shall not count as part of any term of imprisonment or detention under his sentence.

[Criminal Appeal Act 1995, s 11.]

1–3552   12. *Cases dealt with summarily in Northern Ireland.**

*New ss 12A and 12B inserted by the Armed Forces Act 2006, Sch 11 from a date to be appointed.

1–3552A   13. Conditions for making of references.   (1) A reference of a conviction, verdict, finding or sentencing shall not be made under any of sections 9 to 12 unless—*

(a) the Commission consider that there is a real possibility that the conviction, verdict, finding or sentence would not be upheld were the reference to be made,

(b) the Commission so consider—

(i) in the case of a conviction, verdict or finding, because of an argument, or evidence, not raised in the proceedings which led to it or on any appeal or application for leave to appeal against it, or

(ii) in the case of a sentence, because of an argument on a point of law, or information, not so raised, and

(c) an appeal against the conviction, verdict, finding or sentence has been determined or leave to appeal against it has been refused.

(2) Nothing in subsection (1)(b)(i) or (c) shall prevent the making of a reference if it appears to the Commission that there are exceptional circumstances which justify making it.

[Criminal Appeal Act 1995, s 13.]

*Amended by the Armed Forces Act 2006, Sch 11 from a date to be appointed.

1–3553   14. Further provisions about references.   (1) A reference of a conviction, verdict, finding or sentence may be made under any of sections 9 to 12 either after an application has been made by or on behalf of the person to whom it relates or without an application having been so made.

(2) In considering whether to make a reference of a conviction, verdict, finding or sentence under any of sections 9 to 12 the Commission shall have regard to—

(a) any application or representations made to the Commission by or on behalf of the person to whom it relates,

(b) any other representations made to the Commission in relation to it, and

(c) any other matters which appear to the Commission to be relevant.

(3) In considering whether to make a reference under section 9 or 10 the Commission may at any time refer any point on which they desire the assistance of the Court of Appeal to that Court for the Court's opinion on it; and on a reference under this subsection the Court of Appeal shall consider the point referred and furnish the Commission with the Court's opinion on the point.

(4) Where the Commission make a reference under any of sections 9 to 12 the Commission shall—

(a) give to the court to which the reference is made a statement of the Commission's reasons for making the reference, and

(b) send a copy of the statement to every person who appears to the Commission to be likely to be a party to any proceedings on the appeal arising from the reference.

(5) Where a reference under any of sections 9 to 12 is treated as an appeal against any conviction, verdict, finding or sentence, the appeal may be on any ground relating to the conviction, verdict, finding or sentence (whether or not the ground is related to any reason given by the Commission for making the reference).[1]

(6) In every case in which—

(a) an application has been made to the Commission by or on behalf of any person for the reference under any of sections 9 to 12 of any conviction, verdict, finding or sentence, but

(b) the Commission decide not to make a reference of the conviction, verdict, finding or sentence,

the Commission shall give a statement of the reasons for their decision to the person who made the application.*

[Criminal Appeal Act 1995, s 14.]

*Section amended by the Armed Forces Act 2006, Sch 11 from a date to be appointed.

1. Once a party has the benefit of a reference, he may add whatever grounds of appeal he considers appropriate, even matters rejected by the CCRC or which were not considered by them: *R v Smith (Wallace Duncan) (No 3)* [2002] EWCA Crim 2907, [2003] 1 Cr App Rep 648, [2003] Crim LR 398.

Investigations and assistance

1–3553A   15. Investigations for Court of Appeal.   Where a direction is given by the Court of Appeal under section 23A(1) of the 1968 Act or section 25A(1) of the 1980 Act the Commission shall investigate the matter specified in the direction in such manner as the Commission think fit.

(2) Where, in investigating a matter specified in such a direction, it appears to the Commission that—

(*a*) another matter (a "related matter") which is relevant to the determination of the appeal or application for leave to appeal by the Court of Appeal ought, if possible, to be resolved before the appeal or application for leave to appeal is determined by that Court, and

(*b*) an investigation of the related matter is likely to result in the Court's being able to resolve it,

the Commission may also investigate the related matter.

(3) The Commission shall—

(*a*) keep the Court of Appeal informed as to the progress of the investigation of any matter specified in a direction under section 23A(1) of the 1968 Act or section 25A(1) of the 1980 Act, and

(*b*) if they decide to investigate any related matter, notify the Court of Appeal of their decision and keep the Court informed as to the progress of the investigation.

(4) The Commission shall report to the Court of Appeal on the investigation of any matter specified in a direction under section 23A(1) of the 1968 Act or section 25A(1) of the 1980 Act when—

(*a*) they complete the investigation of that matter and of any related matter investigated by them, or

(*b*) they are directed to do so by the Court of Appeal,

whichever happens first.

(5) A report under subsection (4) shall include details of any inquiries made by or for the Commission in the investigation of the matter specified in the direction or any related matter investigated by them.

(6) Such a report shall be accompanied—

(*a*) by any statements and opinions received by the Commission in the investigation of the matter specified in the direction or any related matter investigated by them, and

(*b*) subject to subsection (7), by any reports so received.

(7) Such a report need not be accompanied by any reports submitted to the Commission under section 20(6) by an investigating officer.*

[Criminal Appeal Act 1995, s 15 as amended by the Criminal Justice Act 2003, Sch 36.]

*Section amended by the Armed Forces Act 2006, Sch 11 from a date to be appointed.

1–3554   16. Assistance in connection with prerogative of mercy.   (1) Where the Secretary of State refers to the Commission any matter which arises in the consideration of whether to recommend the exercise of Her Majesty's prerogative of mercy in relation to a conviction and on which he desires their assistance, the Commission shall—

(*a*) consider the matter referred, and

(*b*) give to the Secretary of State a statement of their conclusions on it;

and the Secretary of State shall, in considering whether so to recommend, treat the Commission's statement as conclusive of the matter referred.

(2) Where in any case the Commission are of the opinion that the Secretary of State should consider whether to recommend the exercise of Her Majesty's prerogative of mercy in relation to the case they shall give him the reasons for their opinion.*

[Criminal Appeal Act 1995, s 16.]

*New sub-s (3) inserted by the Armed Forces Act 2006, Sch 11 from a date to be appointed.

Supplementary powers

1–3554A   17. Power to obtain documents etc.   (1) This section applies where the Commission believe that a person serving in a public body has possession or control of a document or other material which may assist the Commission in the exercise of any of their functions.

(2) Where it is reasonable to do so, the Commission may require the person who is the appropriate person in relation to the public body—

(*a*) to produce the document or other material to the Commission or to give the Commission access to it, and

(b) to allow the Commission to take away the document or other material or to make and take away a copy of it in such form as they think appropriate,

and may direct that person that the document or other material must not be destroyed, damaged or altered before the direction is withdrawn by the Commission.

(3) The documents and other material covered by this section include, in particular, any document or other material obtained or created during any investigation or proceedings relating to—

(a) the case in relation to which the Commission's function is being or may be exercised, or

(b) any other case which may be in any way connected with that case (whether or not any function of the Commission could be exercised in relation to that other case).

(4) The duty to comply with a requirement under this section is not affected by any obligation of secrecy or other limitation on disclosure (including any such obligation or limitation imposed by or by virtue of an enactment) which would otherwise prevent the production of the document or other material to the Commission or the giving of access to it to the Commission.

[Criminal Appeal Act 1995, s 17.]

1–3555 18. Government documents etc. relating to current or old cases. (1) Section 17 does not apply to any document or other material in the possession or control of a person serving in a government department if the document or other material—

(a) is relevant to a case to which this subsection applies, and

(b) is in the possession or control of the person in consequence of the Secretary of State's consideration of the case.

(2) Subsection (1) applies to a case if the Secretary of State—

(a) is, immediately before the day on which the repeal by this Act of section 17 of the 1968 Act or of section 14 of the 1980 Act comes into force, considering the case with a view to deciding whether to make a reference under that section or whether to recommend the exercise of Her Majesty's prerogative of mercy in relation to a conviction by a magistrates' court, or

(b) has at any earlier time considered the case with a view to deciding whether to make such a reference or whether so to recommend.★

(3) The Secretary of State shall give to the Commission any document or other material which—

(a) contains representations made to him in relation to any case to which this subsection applies, or

(b) was received by him in connection with any such case otherwise than from a person serving in a government department,

and may give to the Commission any document or other material which is relevant to any such case but does not fall within paragraph (a) or (b).

(4) Subsection (3) applies to a case if—

(a) the Secretary of State is, immediately before the day on which the repeal by this Act of section 17 of the 1968 Act or of section 14 of the 1980 Act comes into force, considering the case with a view to deciding whether to make a reference under that section or whether to recommend the exercise of Her Majesty's prerogative of mercy in relation to a conviction by a magistrates' court, or

(b) the Secretary of State has at any earlier time considered the case with a view to deciding whether to make such a reference, or whether so to recommend, and the Commission at any time notify him that they wish subsection (3) to apply to the case.★

[Criminal Appeal Act 1995, s 18.]

★**New para (2)(c) and sub-ss (5), (6) inserted by the Armed Forces Act 2006, Sch 11 from a date to be appointed.**

1–3555A 19. Power to require appointment of investigating officers. (1) Where the Commission believe that inquiries should be made for assisting them in the exercise of any of their functions in relation to any case they may require the appointment of an investigating officer to carry out the inquiries.

(2) Where any offence to which the case relates was investigated by persons serving in a public body, a requirement under this section may be imposed—

(a) on the person who is the appropriate person in relation to the public body, or

(b) where the public body has ceased to exist, on any chief officer of police or on the person who is the appropriate person in relation to any public body which appears to the Commission to have functions which consist of or include functions similar to any of those of the public body which has ceased to exist.

(3) Where no offence to which the case relates was investigated by persons serving in a public body, a requirement under this section may be imposed on any chief officer of police.

(4) A requirement under this section imposed on a chief officer of police may be—

(a) a requirement to appoint a person serving in the police force in relation to which he is the chief officer of police, or

(b) a requirement to appoint a person serving in another police force selected by the chief officer.

(5) A requirement under this section imposed on a person who is the appropriate person in relation to a public body other than a police force may be—

(a) a requirement to appoint a person serving in the public body, or

(b) a requirement to appoint a person serving in a police force, or in a public body (other than a police force) having functions which consist of or include the investigation of offences, selected by the appropriate person.

(6) The Commission may direct—

(a) that a person shall not be appointed, or

(b) that a police force or other public body shall not be selected,

under subsection (4) or (5) without the approval of the Commission.

(7) Where an appointment is made under this section by the person who is the appropriate person in relation to any public body, that person shall inform the Commission of the appointment; and if the Commission are not satisfied with the person appointed they may direct that—

(a) the person who is the appropriate person in relation to the public body shall, as soon as is reasonably practicable, select another person in his place and notify the Commission of the proposal to appoint the other person, and

(b) the other person shall not be appointed without the approval of the Commission.

[Criminal Appeal Act 1995, s 19.]

---

*Section amended by the Armed Forces Act 2006, Sch 11 from a date to be appointed.

1–3556 20. Inquiries by investigating officers. (1) A person appointed as the investigating officer in relation to a case shall undertake such inquiries as the Commission may from time to time reasonably direct him to undertake in relation to the case.

(2) A person appointed as an investigating officer shall be permitted to act as such by the person who is the appropriate person in relation to the public body in which he is serving.

(3) Where the chief officer of an England and Wales police force appoints a member of the Police Service of Northern Ireland as an investigating officer, the member appointed shall have in England and Wales the same powers and privileges as a member of the police force has there as a constable; and where the Chief Constable of the Police Service of Northern Ireland appoints a member of an England and Wales police force as an investigating officer, the member appointed shall have in Northern Ireland the same powers and privileges as a member of the Police Service of Northern Ireland has there as a constable.

(4) The Commission may take any steps which they consider appropriate for supervising the undertaking of inquiries by an investigating officer.

(5) The Commission may at any time direct that a person appointed as the investigating officer in relation to a case shall cease to act as such; but the making of such a direction shall not prevent the Commission from imposing a requirement under section 19 to appoint another investigating officer in relation to the case.

(6) When a person appointed as the investigating officer in relation to a case has completed the inquiries which he has been directed by the Commission to undertake in relation to the case, he shall—

(a) prepare a report of his findings,

(b) submit it to the Commission, and

(c) send a copy of it to the person by whom he was appointed.

(7) When a person appointed as the investigating officer in relation to a case submits to the Commission a report of his findings he shall also submit to them any statements, opinions and reports received by him in connection with the inquiries which he was directed to undertake in relation to the case.

[Criminal Appeal Act 1995, s 20 as amended by the Police (Northern Ireland) Act 2000, s 78.]

1–3556A 21. Other powers. Sections 17 to 20 are without prejudice to the taking by the Commission of any steps which they consider appropriate for assisting them in the exercise of any of their functions including, in particular—

(a) undertaking, or arranging for others to undertake, inquiries, and

(b) obtaining, or arranging for others to obtain, statements, opinions and reports.

[Criminal Appeal Act 1995, s 21.]

1–3557 22. Meaning of "public body" etc. (1) In sections 17, 19 and 20 and this section "public body" means—

(a) any police force,

(b) any government department, local authority or other body constituted for purposes of the public service, local government or the administration of justice, or

(c) any other body whose members are appointed by Her Majesty, any Minister or any government department or whose revenues consist wholly or mainly of money provided by Parliament or appropriated by Measure of the Northern Ireland Assembly.

(2) In sections 19 and 20 and this section—

(a) "police force" includes the Police Service of Northern Ireland and the Police Service of Northern Ireland Reserve and any body of constables maintained otherwise than by a police authority,

(b) references to the chief officer of police

(i) in relation to the Police Service of Northern Ireland and the Police Service of Northern Ireland Reserve, are to the Chief Constable of the Service, and

(ii) *repealed*

(iii) in relation to any other police force maintained otherwise than by a police authority, are to the Chief Constable, and

(c) references to an England and Wales police force are to a police force maintained under section 2 of the Police Act 1996, the metropolitan police force or the City of London police force,

(d) *repealed* and

(e) *repealed.*

(3) In section 18 and this section—

(a) references to a government department include a Northern Ireland department and the Public Prosecution Service for Northern Ireland, and

(b) "Minister" means a Minister of the Crown as defined by section 8 of the Ministers of the Crown Act 1975 but also includes the head of a Northern Ireland department.

(4) In sections 17, 19 and 20 "the appropriate person" means—

(a) in relation to a police force, the chief officer of police,

(aa) in relation to the Serious Organised Crime Agency, the Director General of that Agency,

(b) in relation to the Crown Prosecution Service, the Director of Public Prosecutions,

(c) in relation to Public Prosecution Service for Northern Ireland, the Director of Public Prosecution Service for Northern Ireland,

(d) in relation to the Serious Fraud Office, the Director of the Serious Fraud Office,

(e) in relation to Her Majesty's Revenue and Customs, the Commissioners for Her Majesty's Revenue and Customs,

(f) in relation to the Revenue and Customs Prosecutions Office, the Director of Revenue and Customs Prosecutions,

(g) in relation to any government department not within any of the preceding paragraphs, the Minister in charge of the department, and

(h) in relation to any public body not within any of the preceding paragraphs, the public body itself (if it is a body corporate) or the person in charge of the public body (if it is not).

(5) *Repealed.**

[Criminal Appeal Act 1995, s 22 as amended by the Police Act 1996, Sch 7, the Police Act 1997, Sch 9, the Police (Northern Ireland) Act 2000, s 78, the Justice (Northern Ireland) Act 2002, Sch 12, the Commissioners for Revenue and Customs Act 2005, Sch 4, and the Serious Organised Crime and Police Act 2005, Sch 4.]

*Section amended by the Armed Forces Act 2006, Sch 11 from a date to be appointed.

Disclosure of information

1–3557A 23. Offence of disclosure. (1) A person who is or has been a member or employee of the Commission shall not disclose any information obtained by the Commission in the exercise of any of their functions unless the disclosure of the information is excepted from this section by section 24.

(2) A person who is or has been an investigating officer shall not disclose any information obtained by him in his inquiries unless the disclosure of the information is excepted from this section by section 24.

(3) A member of the Commission shall not authorise—

(a) the disclosure by an employee of the Commission of any information obtained by the Commission in the exercise of any of their functions, or

(b) the disclosure by an investigating officer of any information obtained by him in his inquiries,

unless the authorisation of the disclosure of the information is excepted from this section by section 24.

(4) A person who contravenes this section is guilty of an offence and liable on summary conviction to a fine of an amount not exceeding **level 5** on the standard scale.

[Criminal Appeal Act 1995, s 23.]

1–3558 24. Exceptions from obligations of non-disclosure. (1) The disclosure of information, or the authorisation of the disclosure of information, is excepted from section 23 by this section if the information is disclosed, or is authorised to be disclosed—

(a) for the purposes of any criminal, disciplinary or civil proceedings,

(b) in order to assist in dealing with an application made to the Secretary of State for compensation for a miscarriage of justice,

(c) by a person who is a member or an employee of the Commission either to another person who is a member or an employee of the Commission or to an investigating officer,

(d) by an investigating officer to a member or an employee of the Commission,

(e) in any statement or report required by this Act,
(f) in or in connection with the exercise of any function under this Act, or
(g) in any circumstances in which the disclosure of information is permitted by an order made by the Secretary of State.

(2) The disclosure of information is also excepted from section 23 by this section if the information is disclosed by an employee of the Commission, or an investigating officer, who is authorised to disclose the information by a member of the Commission.

(3) The disclosure of information, or the authorisation of the disclosure of information, is also excepted from section 23 by this section if the information is disclosed, or is authorised to be disclosed, for the purposes of—

(a) the investigation of an offence, or
(b) deciding whether to prosecute a person for an offence,

unless the disclosure is or would be prevented by an obligation of secrecy or other limitation on disclosure (including any such obligation or limitation imposed by or by virtue of an enactment) arising otherwise than under that section.

(4) Where the disclosure of information is excepted from section 23 by subsection (1) or (2), the disclosure of the information is not prevented by any obligation of secrecy or other limitation on disclosure (including any such obligation or limitation imposed by or by virtue of an enactment) arising otherwise than under that section.

(5) The power to make an order under subsection (1)(g) is exercisable by statutory instrument which shall be subject to annulment in pursuance of a resolution of either House of Parliament.
[Criminal Appeal Act 1995, s 24.]

1–3558A   25. Consent to disclosure.   (1) Where a person on whom a requirement is imposed under section 17 notifies the Commission that any information contained in any document or other material to which the requirement relates is not to be disclosed by the Commission without his prior consent, the Commission shall not disclose the information without such consent.

(2) Such consent may not be withheld unless—

(a) (apart from section 17) the person would have been prevented by any obligation of secrecy or other limitation on disclosure from disclosing the information to the Commission, and
(b) it is reasonable for the person to withhold his consent to disclosure of the information by the Commission.

(3) An obligation of secrecy or other limitation on disclosure which applies to a person only where disclosure is not authorised by another person shall not be taken for the purposes of subsection (2)(a) to prevent the disclosure by the person of information to the Commission unless—

(a) reasonable steps have been taken to obtain the authorisation of the other person, or
(b) such authorisation could not reasonably be expected to be obtained.
[Criminal Appeal Act 1995, s 25.]

1–3558B

PART III[1]
OTHER PROVISIONS
Powers of magistrates' courts to rectify mistakes

----

1. Part III contains ss 26–28.

PART IV[1]
SUPPLEMENTARY

1–3559   29. Minor and consequential amendments and repeals.   (1) Schedule 2 (minor and consequential amendments) shall have effect.

(2) The enactments specified in Schedule 3 (which include spent provisions) are repealed to the extent specified in the third column of that Schedule.
[Criminal Appeal Act 1995, s 29.]

----

1. Part IV contains ss 29–34.

1–3560   30. Interpretation.   (1) In this Act—

"the 1968 Act" means the Criminal Appeal Act 1968,
"the 1980 Act" means the Criminal Appeal (Northern Ireland) Act 1980,
"the Commission" means the Criminal Cases Review Commission,
"enactment" includes an enactment comprised in Northern Ireland legislation, and
"investigating officer" means a person appointed under section 19 to carry out inquiries.

(2) In this Act "sentence"—

(a) in section 9 has the same meaning as in the 1968 Act,
(b) in section 10 has the same meaning as in Part I of the 1980 Act,

    (c)　in section 11 has the same meaning as in section 108 of the Magistrates' Courts Act 1980, and

    (d)　in section 12 has the same meaning as in Article 140(1) of the Magistrates' Courts (Northern Ireland) Order 1981.*

[Criminal Appeal Act 1995, s 30.]

*****Section amended by the Armed Forces Act 2006, Sch 11 from a date to be appointed.**

1–3561　32. Commencement

1–3562　33. Extent.　(1) The provisions of Parts I and III and of Schedules 2 and 3 have the same extent as the enactments which they amend or repeal.

    (2) Section 8 and Schedule 1 and sections 13 to 25 extend only to England and Wales and Northern Ireland.

    (3) Sections 9 and 11 extend only to England and Wales.

    (4) Sections 10 and 12 extend only to Northern Ireland.*

[Criminal Appeal Act 1995, s 33.]

*****Section amended by the Armed Forces Act 2006, Sch 11 from a date to be appointed.**

1–3562A　34. Short title.　This Act may be cited as the Criminal Appeal Act 1995.

[Criminal Appeal Act 1995, s 34.]

SCHEDULES

Section 8

SCHEDULE 1
THE COMMISSION: FURTHER PROVISIONS

1–3563　1–6. *Membership; members and employees and procedure.*

Evidence

    7. A document purporting to be—

    (a)　duly executed under the seal of the Commission, or

    (b)　signed on behalf of the Commission,

shall be received in evidence and, unless the contrary is proved, taken to be so executed or signed.

    8–9. *Annual reports and accounts; expenses.*

Criminal Procedure and Investigations Act 1996[1]

(1996 c 25)

PART I[2]
DISCLOSURE

Introduction

1–3581　1. Application of this Part.　(1) This Part applies where—

    (a)　a person is charged with a summary offence in respect of which a court proceeds to summary trial and in respect of which he pleads not guilty,

    (b)　a person who has attained the age of 18 is charged with an offence which is triable either way, in respect of which a court proceeds to summary trial and in respect of which he pleads not guilty, or

    (c)　a person under the age of 18 is charged with an indictable offence in respect of which a court proceeds to summary trial and in respect of which he pleads not guilty.

    (2) This Part also applies where—

    (a)　a person is charged with an indictable offence and he is committed for trial for the offence concerned,

    (b)　a person is charged with an indictable offence and proceedings for the trial of the person on the charge concerned are transferred to the Crown Court by virtue of a notice of transfer given under section 4 of the Criminal Justice Act 1987 (serious or complex fraud),

    (c)　a person is charged with an indictable offence and proceedings for the trial of the person on the charge concerned are transferred to the Crown Court by virtue of a notice of transfer served on a magistrates' court under section 53 of the Criminal Justice Act 1991 (certain cases involving children),

    (cc)　a person is charged with an offence for which he is sent for trial under section 51 (no committal proceedings for indictable-only offences) of the Crime and Disorder Act 1998,

    (d)　a count charging a person with a summary offence is included in an indictment under the authority of section 40 of the Criminal Justice Act 1988 (common assault etc), or

    (e)　a bill of indictment charging a person with an indictable offence is preferred under the authority of section 2(2)(b) of the Administration of Justice (Miscellaneous Provisions) Act

1933 (bill preferred by direction of Court of Appeal, or by direction or with consent of a judge) or

(f) a bill of indictment charging a person with an indictable offence is preferred under section 22B(3)(a) of the Prosecution of Offences Act 1985.

(3) This Part applies in relation to alleged offences into which no criminal investigation[3] has begun before the appointed day.

(4) For the purposes of this section a criminal investigation is an investigation which police officers or other persons have a duty to conduct with a view to it being ascertained—

(a) whether a person should be charged with an offence, or
(b) whether a person charged with an offence is guilty of it.

(5) The reference in subsection (3) to the appointed day is to such day as is appointed for the purposes of this Part by the Secretary of State by order[4].
[Criminal Procedure and Investigations Act 1996, s 1 as amended by Crime and Disorder Act 1998, Sch 8.]

---

*A new sub-s (6) is inserted by the Sexual Offences (Protected Material) Act 1997, s 9, in PART VIII: SEXUAL OFFENCES, post, when in force.

1. Under the Human Rights Act 1998, this Act, so far as it is possible to do so, must be read and given effect in a way which is compatible with the Convention rights. There is a general requirement under art 6 of the European Convention on Human Rights that "all material evidence for or against the accused" be disclosed before trial: see *Edwards v United Kingdom* (1992) 15 EHRR 417 at para 36. In *Jespers v Belgium* (1981) 27 DR 61 the European Commission of Human Rights held that the "equality of arms" principle imposed on prosecuting and investigating authorities an obligation to disclose any material in their possession, or to which they could gain access, which may assist the accused in exonerating himself or in obtaining a reduction in sentence. Where disclosure is not made, the court must assess the impact of non-disclosure on the fairness of the trial as a whole: see *R v Stratford Justices, ex p Imbert* [1999] 2 Cr App Rep 276. But, it is submitted, there is nothing to prevent a magistrates' court ordering disclosure where fairness dictates that such a step be taken.

2. Part I contains ss 1–21.

3. A "criminal investigation" may begin before a crime has actually been committed so that for example where the police, acting on information, mount a surveillance operation before 1 April 1997, but the offence is not actually committed until after that date, the provisions of Parts I and II of the Act will not apply to the subsequent criminal proceedings. (*R v Uxbridge Magistrates' Court, ex p Patel* (1999) 164 JP 209, [2000] Crim LR 383, DC not following *R v Norfolk Stipendiary Magistrate, ex p Keable* [1998] Crim LR 510, DC).

4. The day appointed for the purposes of Pt I of the Act was 1 April 1997 (Criminal Procedure and Investigations Act 1996 (Appointed Day No 3) Order 1997, SI 1997/682).

1–3582 2. General interpretation. (1) References to the accused are to the person mentioned in section 1(1) or (2).

(2) Where there is more than one accused in any proceedings this Part applies separately in relation to each of the accused.

(3) References to the prosecutor are to any person acting as prosecutor, whether an individual or a body.

(4) References to material are to material of all kinds, and in particular include references to—

(a) information, and
(b) objects of all descriptions.

(5) References to recording information are to putting it in a durable or retrievable form (such as writing or tape).

(6) This section applies for the purpose of this Part.
[Criminal Procedure and Investigations Act 1996, s 2.]

The main provisions

1–3583 3. Initial duty of prosecutor to disclose. (1) The prosecutor must—

(a) disclose to the accused any prosecution material which has not previously been disclosed to the accused and which might reasonably be considered capable of undermining the case for the prosecution against the accused or of assisting the case for the accused, or
(b) give to the accused a written statement that there is no material of a description mentioned in paragraph (a).

(2) For the purposes of this section prosecution material is material—

(a) which is in the prosecutor's possession, and came into his possession in connection with the case for the prosecution against the accused[1], or
(b) which, in pursuance of a code operative under Part II, he has inspected in connection with the case for the prosecution against the accused.

(3) Where material consists of information which has been recorded in any form the prosecutor discloses it for the purposes of this section—

(a) by securing that a copy is made of it and that the copy is given to the accused[2], or
(b) if in the prosecutor's opinion that is not practicable or not desirable, by allowing the accused to inspect it at a reasonable time and a reasonable place or by taking steps to secure that he is allowed to do so;

and a copy may be in such form as the prosecutor thinks fit and need not be in the same form as that in which the information has already been recorded.

(4) Where material consists of information which has not been recorded the prosecutor discloses it for the purposes of this section by securing that it is recorded in such form as he thinks fit and—

    (a)   by securing that a copy is made of it and that the copy is given to the accused, or

    (b)   if in the prosecutor's opinion that is not practicable or not desirable, by allowing the accused to inspect it at a reasonable time and a reasonable place or by taking steps to secure that he is allowed to do so.

(5) Where material does not consist of information the prosecutor discloses it for the purposes of this section by allowing the accusedto inspect it at a reasonable time and a reasonable place or by taking steps to secure that he is allowed to do so.

(6) Material must not be disclosed under this section to the extent that the court, on an application by the prosecutor, concludes it is not in the public interest to disclose it and orders accordingly[3].

(7) Material must not be disclosed under this section to the extent that it is material the disclosure of which is prohibited by section 17 of the Regulation of Investigatory Powers Act 2000.

(8) The prosecutor must act under this section during the period which, by virtue of section 12, is the relevant period for this section.

[Criminal Procedure and Investigations Act 1996, s 3 as amended by the Regulation of Investigatory Powers Act 2000, Sch 4 and the Criminal Justice Act 2003, s 32 and Sch 36.]

---

1. Thus, there is no obligation under s 3 (or s 7) to disclose material that formed part of other criminal proceedings, but that is not an end of the matter; the Crown has a duty to act fairly: *R v C* [2001] EWCA Crim 1529. The words 'in connection with the case for the prosecution against the accused' are to be widely construed in relation to the prosecutor's duty of primary disclosure and the route by which material comes into the possession of the prosecutor is irrelevant. Such material is not required to be part of the prosecution case nor is the material limited to that arising during preparation of the prosecution case (*R v Reid* [2002] EWCA Crim 1806, [2002] 1 Cr App Rep 21, [2002] Crim LR 211).

2. By virtue of s 1(6), sub-ss (3) and (5) do not apply in relation to any disclosure required by ss 3, 7 or 9 of this Act where the material is "protected material" (ie material relating to the victim of a sexual offence); disclosure is regulated by the Sexual Offences (Protected Material) Act 1997, in PART VIII: SEXUAL OFFENCES, post.

3. For a case involving a conflict between the principles governing disclosure by the prosecution and the narrower principles governing 3rd party disclosure, see *R v Brushett* [2001] Crim LR 471, CA (which concerned disclosure of social services files on prosecution witnesses).

1–3584   4. Initial duty to disclose: further provisions.   (1) This section applies where—

    (a)   the prosecutor acts under section 3, and

    (b)   before so doing he was given a document in pursuance of provision included, by virtue of section 24(3), in a code operative under Part II.

(2) In such a case the prosecutor must give the document to the accused at the same time as the prosecutor acts under section 3.

[Criminal Procedure and Investigations Act 1996, s 4 as amended by the Criminal Justice Act 2003, Sch 36.]

1–3585   5. Compulsory disclosure by accused.   (1) Subject to subsections (2) to (4), this section applies where—*

    (a)   this Part applies by virtue of section 1(2), and

    (b)   the prosecutor complies with section 3 or purports[1] to comply with it.

(2) Where this Part applies by virtue of section 1(2)(b), this section does not apply unless—

    (a)   a copy of the notice of transfer, and

    (b)   copies of the documents containing the evidence,

have been given to the accused under regulations made under section 5(9) of the Criminal Justice Act 1987.*

(3) Where this Part applies by virtue of section 1(2)(c), this section does not apply unless—

    (a)   a copy of the notice of transfer, and

    (b)   copies of the documents containing the evidence,

have been given to the accused under regulations made under paragraph 4 of Schedule 6 to the Criminal Justice Act 1991.*

(3A) Where this Part applies by virtue of section 1(2)(cc), this section does not apply unless—

    (a)   copies of the documents containing the evidence have been served on the accused under regulations made under paragraph 1 of Schedule 3 to the Crime and Disorder Act 1998; and

    (b)   a copy of the notice under subsection (7) of section 51* of that Act has been served on him under that subsection.

(4) Where this Part applies by virtue of section 1(2)(e), this section does not apply unless the prosecutor has served on the accused a copy of the indictment and a copy of the set of documents containing the evidence which is the basis of the charge.

(5) Where this section applies, the accused must give a defence statement[2] to the court and the prosecutor.*

(5A) Where there are other accused in the proceedings and the court so orders, the accused must also give a defence statement to each other accused specified by the court.

(5B) The court may make an order under subsection (5A) either of its own motion or on the application of any party.

(5C) A defence statement that has to be given to the court and the prosecutor (under subsection (5)) must be given during the period which, by virtue of section 12, is the relevant period for this section.**

(5D) A defence statement that has to be given to a co-accused (under subsection (5A)) must be given within such period as the court may specify.

(6)–(9) *Repealed.*

[Criminal Procedure and Investigations Act 1996, s 5 as amended by the Crime and Disorder Act 1998, Sch 8 and the Criminal Justice Act 2003, Schs 3 and 36.]

---

*Subsections (2) and (3) repealed, subs (3A) amended and subss (5A)–(5D) inserted by the Criminal Justice Act 2003, Sch 3 from a date to be appointed.

**Subsection (5C) in force for certain purposes 24 July 2006, for remaining purposes from a date to be appointed.

1. Where there is no material to disclose, the relevant date is when the prosecutor sends a letter to that effect (*DPP v Wood* [2006] EWHC 32 (Admin), 170 JP 177).

2. Where the accused's solicitor purports to give a defence statement under s 5 or 6 or 6B, or a statement of the kind mentioned in s 6B(4), the statement shall, unless the contrary be proved, be deemed to be given with the authority of the accused: see s 6E(1) below, which was inserted by s 36 of the Criminal Justice Act 2005 to overcome the difficulties of unsigned defence statements identified in *R v Wheeler* [2001] 1 Cr App Rep 150, 164 JP 565, [2001] Crim LR 744, CA. Although there are defence statements which are so deficient in their fulfilment of the statutory requirements that they cannot properly be termed defence statements at all, there are real dangers of injustice in treating deficient written defence statements as so wholly ineffective as to be non-existent in reality and this to remove the court's jurisdiction to make an order under s 8 (*DPP v Wood* [2006] EWHC 32 (Admin), 170 JP 177).

1–3586   6. Voluntary disclosure by accused.   (1) This section applies where—

(*a*) this Part applies by virtue of section 1(1), and
(*b*) the prosecutor complies with section 3 or purports[1] to comply with it.

(2) The accused—

(*a*) may give a defence statement[2] to the prosecutor, and
(*b*) if he does so, must also give such a statement to the court.

(3) *Repealed.*

(4) If the accused gives a defence statement under this section he must give it during the period which, by virtue of section 12, is the relevant period for this section.

[Criminal Procedure and Investigations Act 1996, s 6 as amended by the Criminal Justice Act 2003, Sch 36.]

---

1. Where there is no material to disclose, the relevant date is when the prosecutor sends a letter to that effect (*DPP v Wood* [2006] EWHC 32 (Admin)).

2. See note 2 to s 5, ante.

1–3586A   6A. Contents of defence statement.   (1) For the purposes of this Part a defence statement is a written statement—

(*a*) setting out the nature of the accused's defence, including any particular defences on which he intends to rely,
(*b*) indicating the matters of fact on which he takes issue with the prosecution,
(*c*) setting out, in the case of each such matter, why he takes issue with the prosecution, and
(*d*) indicating any point of law (including any point as to the admissibility of evidence or an abuse of process) which he wishes to take, and any authority on which he intends to rely for that purpose.

(2) A defence statement that discloses an alibi must give particulars of it, including—

(*a*) the name, address and date of birth of any witness the accused believes is able to give evidence in support of the alibi, or as many of those details as are known to the accused when the statement is given;
(*b*) any information in the accused's possession which might be of material assistance in identifying or finding any such witness in whose case any of the details mentioned in paragraph (*a*) are not known to the accused when the statement is given.

(3) For the purposes of this section evidence in support of an alibi is evidence tending to show that by reason of the presence of the accused at a particular place or in a particular area at a particular time he was not, or was unlikely to have been, at the place where the offence is alleged to have been committed at the time of its alleged commission.

(4) The Secretary of State may by regulations make provision as to the details of the matters that, by virtue of subsection (1), are to be included in defence statements.*

[Criminal Procedure and Investigations Act 1996, s 6A as inserted by the Criminal Justice Act 2003, s 33.]

---

*New ss 6B–6D inserted by the Criminal Justice Act 2003, ss 33–35 from a date to be appointed.

1–3586E   6E. Disclosure by accused: further provisions.   (1) Where an accused's solicitor purports to give on behalf of the accused—

(*a*) a defence statement under section 5, 6 or 6B, or
(*b*) a statement of the kind mentioned in section 6B(4),

the statement shall, unless the contrary is proved, be deemed to be given with the authority of the accused.

(2) If it appears to the judge at a pre-trial hearing that an accused has failed to comply fully with section 5, 6B or 6C, so that there is a possibility of comment being made or inferences drawn under section 11(5), he shall warn the accused accordingly.

(3) In subsection (2) "pre-trial hearing" has the same meaning as in Part 4 (see section 39).

(4) The judge in a trial before a judge and jury—

(*a*) may direct that the jury be given a copy of any defence statement, and

(*b*) if he does so, may direct that it be edited so as not to include references to matters evidence of which would be inadmissible.

(5) A direction under subsection (4)—

(*a*) may be made either of the judge's own motion or on the application of any party;

(*b*) may be made only if the judge is of the opinion that seeing a copy of the defence statement would help the jury to understand the case or to resolve any issue in the case.

(6) The reference in subsection (4) to a defence statement is a reference—

(*a*) where the accused has given only an initial defence statement (that is, a defence statement given under section 5 or 6), to that statement;

(*b*) where he has given both an initial defence statement and an updated defence statement (that is, a defence statement given under section 6B), to the updated defence statement;

(*c*) where he has given both an initial defence statement and a statement of the kind mentioned in section 6B(4), to the initial defence statement. the Criminal Justice Act 2003, ss 331, 332, Sch 3

[Criminal Procedure and Investigations Act 1996, s 6E as inserted by the Criminal Justice Act 2003, s 36.]

1–3587   7. Secondary disclosure by prosecutor.   *Repealed.*

1–3587A   7A. Continuing duty of prosecutor to disclose.   (1) This section applies at all times—

(*a*) after the prosecutor has complied with section 3 or purported to comply with it, and

(*b*) before the accused is acquitted or convicted or the prosecutor decides not to proceed with the case concerned.

(2) The prosecutor must keep under review the question whether at any given time (and, in particular, following the giving of a defence statement) there is prosecution material which—

(*a*) might reasonably be considered capable of undermining the case for the prosecution against the accused or of assisting the case for the accused, and

(*b*) has not been disclosed to the accused.

(3) If at any time there is any such material as is mentioned in subsection (2) the prosecutor must disclose it to the accused as soon as is reasonably practicable (or within the period mentioned in subsection (5)(a), where that applies).

(4) In applying subsection (2) by reference to any given time the state of affairs at that time (including the case for the prosecution as it stands at that time) must be taken into account.

(5) Where the accused gives a defence statement under section 5, 6 or 6B—

(*a*) if as a result of that statement the prosecutor is required by this section to make any disclosure, or further disclosure, he must do so during the period which, by virtue of section 12, is the relevant period for this section;

(*b*) if the prosecutor considers that he is not so required, he must during that period give to the accused a written statement to that effect.

(6) For the purposes of this section prosecution material is material—

(*a*) which is in the prosecutor's possession and came into his possession in connection with the case for the prosecution against the accused, or

(*b*) which, in pursuance of a code operative under Part 2, he has inspected in connection with the case for the prosecution against the accused.

(7) Subsections (3) to (5) of section 3 (method by which prosecutor discloses) apply for the purposes of this section as they apply for the purposes of that.

(8) Material must not be disclosed under this section to the extent that the court, on an application by the prosecutor, concludes it is not in the public interest to disclose it and orders accordingly.

(9) Material must not be disclosed under this section to the extent that it is material the disclosure of which is prohibited by section 17 of the Regulation of Investigatory Powers Act 2000 (c 23).

[Criminal Procedure and Investigations Act 1996, s 7A as inserted by the Criminal Justice Act 2003, s 37.]

1–3588   8. Application by accused for disclosure.   (1) This section applies where the accused has given a defence statement[1] under section 5, 6 or 6B and the prosecutor has complied with section 7A(5) or has purported to comply with it or has failed to comply with it.

(2) If the accused has at any time reasonable cause to believe that there is prosecution material which is required by section 7A to be disclosed to him and has not been, he may apply to the court for an order requiring the prosecutor to disclose it to him.

(3) For the purposes of this section prosecution material[2] is material—

(a) which is in the prosecutor's possession and came into his possession in connection with the case for the prosecution against the accused,

(b) which, in pursuance of a code operative under Part II, he has inspected in connection with the case for the prosecution against the accused, or

(c) which falls within subsection (4).

(4) Material falls within this subsection if in pursuance of a code operative under Part II the prosecutor must, if he asks for the material, be given a copy of it or be allowed to inspect it in connection with the case for the prosecution against the accused.

(5) Material must not be disclosed under this section to the extent that the court, on an application by the prosecutor, concludes it is not in the public interest to disclose it and orders accordingly.

(6) Material must not be disclosed under this section to the extent that it is material the disclosure of which is prohibited by section 17 of the Regulation of Investigatory Powers Act 2000.

[Criminal Procedure and Investigations Act 1996, s 8 as amended by the Regulation of Investigatory Powers Act 2000, Sch 4 and the Criminal Justice Act 2003, s 38.]

---

1. Where there is no material to disclose, the relevant date is when the prosecutor sends a letter to that effect (*DPP v Wood* [2006] EWHC 32 (Admin), 170 JP 177).

2. Intoximeters UK did not become part of the CPS because it had supplied the intoximeter device to the police force and had certain continuing obligations to the police under contract. Nor has the CPS the right to inspect Intoximeters records (*DPP v Wood* [2006] EWHC 32 (Admin), 170 JP 177).

1–3589   9. Continuing duty of prosecutor to disclose.   *Repealed.*

1–3590   10. Prosecutor's failure to observe time limits.   (1) This section applies if the prosecutor—

(a) purports to act under section 3 after the end of the period which, by virtue of section 12, is the relevant period for section 3, or

(b) purports to act under section 7A(5) after the end of the period which, by virtue of section 12, is the relevant period for section 7A.

(2) Subject to subsection (3), the failure to act during the period concerned does not on its own constitute grounds for staying the proceedings for abuse of process.

(3) Subsection (2) does not prevent the failure constituting such grounds if it involves such delay by the prosecutor that the accused is denied a fair trial.

[Criminal Procedure and Investigations Act 1996, s 10 as amended by the Criminal Justice Act 2003, s 331, Sch 36.]

1–3591   11. Faults in disclosure by accused.   (1) This section applies in the three cases set out in subsections (2), (3) and (4).

(2) The first case is where section 5 applies and the accused—

(a) fails to give an initial defence statement,

(b) gives an initial defence statement but does so after the end of the period which, by virtue of section 12, is the relevant period for section 5,

(c) is required by section 6B to give either an updated defence statement or a statement of the kind mentioned in subsection (4) of that section but fails to do so,

(d) gives an updated defence statement or a statement of the kind mentioned in section 6B(4) but does so after the end of the period which, by virtue of section 12, is the relevant period for section 6B,

(e) sets out inconsistent defences in his defence statement, or

(f) at his trial—

   (i) puts forward a defence which was not mentioned in his defence statement or is different from any defence set out in that statement,

   (ii) relies on a matter which, in breach of the requirements imposed by or under section 6A, was not mentioned in his defence statement,

   (iii) adduces evidence in support of an alibi without having given particulars of the alibi in his defence statement, or

   (iv) calls a witness to give evidence in support of an alibi without having complied with section 6A(2)(a) or (b) as regards the witness in his defence statement.

(3) The second case is where section 6 applies, the accused gives an initial defence statement, and the accused—

(a) gives the initial defence statement after the end of the period which, by virtue of section 12, is the relevant period for section 6, or

(b) does any of the things mentioned in paragraphs (c) to (f) of subsection (2).

(4) The third case is where the accused—

(a) gives a witness notice but does so after the end of the period which, by virtue of section 12, is the relevant period for section 6C, or

(b) at his trial calls a witness (other than himself) not included, or not adequately identified, in a witness notice.

(5) Where this section applies—

    (*a*)   the court or any other party may make such comment as appears appropriate;

    (*b*)   the court or jury may draw such inferences as appear proper in deciding whether the accused is guilty of the offence concerned.

    (6)   Where—

    (*a*)   this section applies by virtue of subsection (2)(*f*)(ii) (including that provision as it applies by virtue of subsection (3)(*b*)), and

    (*b*)   the matter which was not mentioned is a point of law (including any point as to the admissibility of evidence or an abuse of process) or an authority,

comment by another party under subsection (5)(*a*) may be made only with the leave of the court.

    (7)   Where this section applies by virtue of subsection (4), comment by another party under subsection (5)(*a*) may be made only with the leave of the court.

    (8)   Where the accused puts forward a defence which is different from any defence set out in his defence statement, in doing anything under subsection (5) or in deciding whether to do anything under it the court shall have regard—

    (*a*)   to the extent of the differences in the defences, and

    (*b*)   to whether there is any justification for it.

    (9)   Where the accused calls a witness whom he has failed to include, or to identify adequately, in a witness notice, in doing anything under subsection (5) or in deciding whether to do anything under it the court shall have regard to whether there is any justification for the failure.

    (10)   A person shall not be convicted of an offence solely on an inference drawn under subsection (5).

    (11)   Where the accused has given a statement of the kind mentioned in section 6B(4), then, for the purposes of subsections (2)(*f*)(ii) and (iv), the question as to whether there has been a breach of the requirements imposed by or under section 6A or a failure to comply with section 6A(2)(*a*) or (*b*) shall be determined—

    (*a*)   by reference to the state of affairs at the time when that statement was given, and

    (*b*)   as if the defence statement was given at the same time as that statement.

    (12)   In this section—

    (*a*)   "initial defence statement" means a defence statement given under section 5 or 6;

    (*b*)   "updated defence statement" means a defence statement given under section 6B;

    (*c*)   a reference simply to an accused's "defence statement" is a reference—

       (i)   where he has given only an initial defence statement, to that statement;

       (ii)   where he has given both an initial and an updated defence statement, to the updated defence statement;

       (iii)   where he has given both an initial defence statement and a statement of the kind mentioned in section 6B(4), to the initial defence statement;

    (*d*)   a reference to evidence in support of an alibi shall be construed in accordance with section 6A(3);

    (*e*)   "witness notice" means a notice given under section 6C.*

[Criminal Procedure and Investigations Act 1996, s 11 as substituted by the Criminal Justice Act 2003, s 39.]

---

*In force except in so far as relating to sub-ss (4), (7), (11): 4 April 2005.

    1. 'Defence statement' is a general term which includes the nature of the defence, matters on which issue is being taken and the reasons for so doing; it is not confined to 'defence' in a narrow legal definition. Therefore cross examination may take place on differences in the defence at the trial and the defence statement even though the defendant may still be relying on the same legal defence (*R v Tibbs* [2000] 2 Cr App Rep 309, [2001] Crim LR 759, CA).

    2. 'Comment' does not include cross examination for which no leave is required (*R v Tibbs* [2000] 2 Cr App Rep 309, [2001] Crim LR 759, CA).

Time limits

1-3592   12. Time limits.   (1) This section has effect for the purpose of determining the relevant period for sections 3, 5, 6, 6B, 6C and 7A(5).

    (2)   Subject to subsection (3), the relevant period is a period beginning and ending with such days as the Secretary of State prescribes by regulations[1] for the purposes of the section concerned.

    (3)   The regulations may do one or more of the following—

    (*a*)   provide that the relevant period for any section shall if the court so orders be extended (or further extended) by so many days as the court specifies;

    (*b*)   provide that the court may only make such an order if an application is made by a prescribed person and if any other prescribed conditions are fulfilled;

    (*c*)   provide that an application may only be made if prescribed conditions are fulfilled;

    (*d*)   provide that the number of days by which a period may be extended shall be entirely at the court's discretion;

    (*e*)   provide that the number of days by which a period may be extended shall not exceed a prescribed number;

    (*f*)   provide that there shall be no limit on the number of applications that may be made to extend a period;

(g) provide that no more than a prescribed number of applications may be made to extend a period;

and references to the relevant period for a section shall be construed accordingly.

(4) Conditions mentioned in subsection (3) may be framed by reference to such factors as the Secretary of State thinks fit.

(5) Without prejudice to the generality of subsection (4), so far as the relevant period for section 3 or 7A(5) is concerned—

(a) conditions may be framed by reference to the nature or volume of the material concerned;
(b) the nature of material may be defined by reference to the prosecutor's belief that the question of non-disclosure on grounds of public interest may arise.

(6) In subsection (3) "prescribed" means prescribed by regulations under this section.
[Criminal Procedure and Investigations Act 1996, s 12 as amended by the Criminal Justice Act 2003, Sch 36.]

---

1. See the Criminal Procedure and Investigations Act 1996 (Defence Disclosure Time Limits) Regulations 1997, in this PART: STATUTORY INSTRUMENTS ON PROCEDURE, post.

1–3593 13. Time limits: transitional.   (1) As regards a case in relation to which no regulations under section 12 have come into force for the purposes of section 3, section 3(8) shall have effect as if it read—

"(8) The prosecutor must act under this section as soon as is reasonably practicable after—

(a) the accused pleads not guilty (where this Part applies by virtue of section 1(1)),
(b) the accused is committed for trial (where this Part applies by virtue of section 1(2)(a)),
(c) the proceedings are transferred (where this Part applies by virtue of section 1(2)(b) or (c),*
(ca) copies of the documents containing the evidence on which the charge or charges are based are served on the accused (where this Part applies by virtue of section 1(2)(cc)),
(cc) *Repealed.*
(d) the count is included in the indictment (where this Part applies by virtue of section 1(2)(d)), or
(e) the bill of indictment is preferred (where this Part applies by virtue of section 1(2)(e) or (f))."

(2) As regards a case in relation to which no regulations under section 12 have come into force for the purposes of section 7A, section 7A(5) shall have effect as if—

(a) in paragraph (a) for the words from "during the period" to the end, and
(b) in paragraph (b) for "during that period",

there were substituted "as soon as is reasonably practicable after the accused gives the statement in question".
[Criminal Procedure and Investigations Act 1996, s 13 as amended by the Crime and Disorder Act 1998, Sch 8, the Access to Justice Act 1999, s 67 and Sch 15 and the Criminal Justice Act 2003, Sch 36.]

---

*Repealed by the Criminal Justice Act 2003, Sch 3 from a date to be appointed.

Public interest

1–3594 14. Public interest: review for summary trials.   (1) This section applies where this Part applies by virtue of section 1(1).

(2) At any time—

(a) after a court makes an order under section 3(6), 7A(8) or 8(5), and
(b) before the accused is acquitted or convicted or the prosecutor decides not to proceed with the case concerned,

the accused may apply to the court for a review of the question whether it is still not in the public interest to disclose material affected by its order.

(3) In such a case the court must review that question, and if it concludes that it is in the public interest to disclose material to any extent—

(a) it shall so order, and
(b) it shall take such steps as are reasonable to inform the prosecutor of its order.

(4) Where the prosecutor is informed of an order made under subsection (3) he must act accordingly having regard to the provisions of this Part (unless he decides not to proceed with the case concerned).
[Criminal Procedure and Investigations Act 1996, s 14 as amended by the Criminal Justice Act 2003, Sch 36.]

1–3595 15. Public interest: review in other cases.   (1) This section applies where this Part applies by virtue of section 1(2).

(2) This section applies at all times—

(a) after a court makes an order under section 3(6), 7A(8) or 8(5), and
(b) before the accused is acquitted or convicted or the prosecutor decides not to proceed with the case concerned.

(3) The court must keep under review the question whether at any given time it is still not in the public interest to disclose material affected by its order.

(4) The court must keep the question mentioned in subsection (3) under review without the need for an application; but the accused may apply to the court for a review of that question.

(5) If the court at any time concludes that it is in the public interest to disclose material to any extent—

(a) it shall so order, and

(b) it shall take such steps as are reasonable to inform the prosecutor of its order.

(6) Where the prosecutor is informed of an order made under subsection (5) he must act accordingly having regard to the provisions of this Part (unless he decides not to proceed with the case concerned).

[Criminal Procedure and Investigations Act 1996, s 15 as amended by the Criminal Justice Act 2003, Sch 36.]

1–3596   16. Applications: opportunity to be heard.   (1) Where—

(a) an application is made under section 3(6), 7A(8) or 8(5), 14(2) or 15(4),

(b) a person claiming to have an interest in the material applies to be heard by the court, and

(c) he shows that he was involved (whether alone or with others and whether directly or indirectly) in the prosecutor's attention being brought to the material,

the court must not make an order under section 3(6), 7A(8) or 8(5), 14(3) or 15(5) (as the case may be) unless the person applying under paragraph (b) has been given an opportunity to be heard.

[Criminal Procedure and Investigations Act 1996, s 15 as amended by the Criminal Justice Act 2003, Sch 36.]

Confidentiality

1–3597   17. Confidentiality of disclosed information[1].   (1) If the accused is given or allowed to inspect a document or other object under—

(a) section 3, 4, 7A, 14 or 15, or

(b) an order under section 8,

then, subject to subsections (2) to (4), he must not use or disclose it or any information recorded in it.

(2) The accused may use or disclose the object or information—

(a) in connection with the proceedings for whose purposes he was given the object or allowed to inspect it,

(b) with a view to the taking of further criminal proceedings (for instance, by way of appeal) with regard to the matter giving rise to the proceedings mentioned in paragraph (a), or

(c) in connection with the proceedings first mentioned in paragraph (b).

(3) The accused may use or disclose—

(a) the object to the extent that it has been displayed to the public in open court, or

(b) the information to the extent that it has been communicated to the public in open court;

but the preceding provisions of this subsection do not apply if the object is displayed or the information is communicated in proceedings to deal with a contempt of court under section 18.

(4) If—

(a) the accused applies to the court for an order granting permission to use or disclose the object or information, and

(b) the court makes such an order,

the accused may use or disclose the object or information for the purpose and to the extent specified by the court.

(5) An application under subsection (4) may be made and dealt with at any time, and in particular after the accused has been acquitted or convicted or the prosecutor has decided not to proceed with the case concerned; but this is subject to rules made by virtue of section 19(2).

(6) Where—

(a) an application is made under subsection (4), and

(b) the prosecutor or a person claiming to have an interest in the object or information applies to be heard by the court,

the court must not make an order granting permission unless the person applying under paragraph (b) has been given an opportunity to be heard.

(7) References in this section to the court are to—

(a) a magistrates' court, where this Part applies by virtue of section 1(1);

(b) the Crown Court, where this Part applies by virtue of section 1(2).

(8) Nothing in this section affects any other restriction or prohibition on the use or disclosure of an object or information, whether the restriction or prohibition arises under an enactment (whenever passed) or otherwise.

[Criminal Procedure and Investigations Act 1996, s 17 as amended by the Criminal Justice Act 2003, Sch 36.]

---

1. By virtue of s 1(6) of this Act, this section does not apply to disclosures regulated by the Sexual Offences (Protected Material) Act 1997, in PART VIII: title SEXUAL OFFENCES, post.

1–3598   18. Confidentiality: contravention[1]. (1) It is a contempt of court for a person knowingly to use or disclose an object or information recorded in it if the use or disclosure is in contravention of section 17.

(2) The following courts have jurisdiction to deal with a person who is guilty of a contempt under this section—

  (a) a magistrates' court, where this Part applies by virtue of section 1(1);
  (b) the Crown Court, where this Part applies by virtue of section 1(2).

(3) A person who is guilty of a contempt under this section may be dealt with as follows—

  (a) a magistrates' court may commit him to custody for a specified period not exceeding six months or impose on him a fine not exceeding £5,000 or both;
  (b) the Crown Court may commit him to custody for a specified period not exceeding two years or impose a fine on him or both.

(4) If—

  (a) a person is guilty of a contempt under this section, and
  (b) the object concerned is in his possession,

the court finding him guilty may order that the object shall be forfeited and dealt with in such manner as the court may order.

(5) The power of the court under subsection (4) includes power to order the object to be destroyed or to be given to the prosecutor or to be placed in his custody for such period as the court may specify.

(6) If—

  (a) the court proposes to make an order under subsection (4), and
  (b) the person found guilty, or any other person claiming to have an interest in the object, applies to be heard by the court,

the court must not make the order unless the applicant has been given an opportunity to be heard.

(7) If—

  (a) a person is guilty of a contempt under this section, and
  (b) a copy of the object concerned is in his possession,

the court finding him guilty may order that the copy shall be forfeited and dealt with in such manner as the court may order.

(8) Subsections (5) and (6) apply for the purposes of subsection (7) as they apply for the purposes of subsection (4), but as if references to the object were references to the copy.

(9) An object or information shall be inadmissible as evidence in civil proceedings if to adduce it would in the opinion of the court be likely to constitute a contempt under this section; and "the court" here means the court before which the civil proceedings are being taken.

(10) The powers of a magistrates' court under this section may be exercised either of the court's own motion or by order on complaint.
[Criminal Procedure and Investigations Act 1996, s 18.]

---

1. By virtue of s 1(6) of this Act, this section does not apply to disclosures regulated by the Sexual Offences (Protected Material) Act 1997, in PART VIII: title SEXUAL OFFENCES, post.

Other provisions

1–3599   19. Rules of court[1]. (1) The power to make Criminal Procedure Rules includes power to make provision mentioned in subsection (2).

(2) The provision is provision as to the practice and procedure to be followed in relation to—

  (a) proceedings to deal with a contempt of court under section 18;
  (b) an application under section 3(6), 5(5B), 6B(6), 6E(5), 7A(8), 8(2) or (5), 14(2), 15(4), 16(b), 17(4) or (6)(b) or 18(6);
  (c) an application under regulations made under section 12;
  (d) an order under section 3(6), 5(5B), 6B(6), 6E(5), 7A(8), 8(2) or (5), 14(3), 17(4) or 18(4) or (7);
  (e) an order under section 15(5) (whether or not an application is made under section 15(4));
  (f) an order under regulations made under section 12.

(3) Criminal Procedure Rules made by virtue of subsection (2)(a) above may contain or include provision equivalent to Schedule 3 to the Contempt of Court Act 1981 (proceedings for disobeying magistrates' court order) or such provision for modifications

(4) Rules made by virtue of subsection (2)(b) in relation to an application under section 17(4) may include provision—

  (a) that an application to a magistrates' court must be made to a particular magistrates' court;
  (b) that an application to the Crown Court must be made to the Crown Court sitting at a particular place;
  (c) requiring persons to be notified of an application.

(5) Rules made by virtue of this section may make different provision for different cases or classes of case.

[Criminal Procedure and Investigations Act 1996, s 19 as amended by the Courts Act 2003, Sch 8, the Criminal Justice Act 2003, Sch 36 and the Constitutional Reform Act 2005, Sch 4.]

---

1. See the Criminal Procedure Rules 2005, Parts 25 and 26 in this Part, post.

1–3600　20. Other statutory rules as to disclosure.　(1) A duty under any of the disclosure provisions shall not affect or be affected by any duty arising under any other enactment with regard to material to be provided to or by the accused or a person representing him; but this is subject to subsection (2).

(2) *Repealed.*

(3) The power to make Criminal Procedure Rules includes power to make, with regard to any proceedings before a magistrates' court which relate to an alleged offence, provision for—

(a) requiring any party to the proceedings to disclose to the other party or parties any expert evidence which he proposes to adduce in the proceedings;

(b) prohibiting a party who fails to comply in respect of any evidence with any requirement imposed by virtue of paragraph (a) from adducing that evidence without the leave of the court.

(4) Rules made by virtue of subsection (3)—

(a) may specify the kinds of expert evidence to which they apply;

(b) may exempt facts or matters of any description specified in the rules.

(5) For the purposes of this section—

(a) the disclosure provisions are sections 3 to 8;

(b) "enactment" includes an enactment comprised in subordinate legislation (which here has the same meaning as in the Interpretation Act 1978).

[Criminal Procedure and Investigations Act 1996, s 20 as amended by the Courts Act 2003, Sch 8 and the Criminal Justice Act 2003, Sch 36.]

1–3602　21. Common law rules as to disclosure.　(1) Where this Part applies as regards things falling to be done after the relevant time in relation to an alleged offence, the rules of common law which—

(a) were effective immediately before the appointed day, and

(b) relate to the disclosure of material by the prosecutor,

do not apply as regards things falling to be done after that time in relation to the alleged offence.

(2) Subsection (1) does not affect the rules of common law as to whether disclosure is in the public interest.

(3) References in subsection (1) to the relevant time are to the time when—

(a) the accused pleads not guilty (where this Part applies by virtue of section 1(1)),

(b) the accused is committed for trial (where this Part applies by virtue of section 1(2)(a)),

(c) the proceedings are transferred (where this Part applies by virtue of section 1(2)(b) or (c)),

(d) the count is included in the indictment (where this Part applies by virtue of section 1(2)(d)), or

(e) the bill of indictment is preferred (where this Part applies by virtue of section 1(2)(e)).

(4) The reference in subsection (1) to the appointed day is to the day appointed under section 1(5).

[Criminal Procedure and Investigations Act 1996, s 21.]

1–3602A　21A. Code of practice for police interviews of witnesses notified by accused.
(1) The Secretary of State shall prepare a code of practice which gives guidance to police officers, and other persons charged with the duty of investigating offences, in relation to the arranging and conducting of interviews of persons—

(a) particulars of whom are given in a defence statement in accordance with section 6A(2), or

(b) who are included as proposed witnesses in a notice given under section 6C

(2) The code must include (in particular) guidance in relation to—

(a) information that should be provided to the interviewee and the accused in relation to such an interview;

(b) the notification of the accused's solicitor of such an interview;

(c) the attendance of the interviewee's solicitor at such an interview;

(d) the attendance of the accused's solicitor at such an interview;

(e) the attendance of any other appropriate person at such an interview taking into account the interviewee's age or any disability of the interviewee.

(3) Any police officer or other person charged with the duty of investigating offences who arranges or conducts such an interview shall have regard to the code.

(4) In preparing the code, the Secretary of State shall consult—

(a) to the extent the code applies to England and Wales—

(i) any person who he considers to represent the interests of chief officers of police;

(ii) the General Council of the Bar;

      (iii) the Law Society of England and Wales;
      (iv) the Institute of Legal Executives;

  (*b*) to the extent the code applies to Northern Ireland—

      (i)   the Chief Constable of the Police Service of Northern Ireland;
      (ii) the General Council of the Bar of Northern Ireland;
      (iii) the Law Society of Northern Ireland;

  (*c*) such other persons as he thinks fit.

  (5) The code shall not come into operation until the Secretary of State by order so provides.

  (6) The Secretary of State may from time to time revise the code and subsections (4) and (5) shall apply to a revised code as they apply to the code as first prepared.

  (7) An order bringing the code into operation may not be made unless a draft of the order has been laid before each House of Parliament and approved by a resolution of each House.

  (8) An order bringing a revised code into operation shall be laid before each House of Parliament if the order has been made without a draft having been so laid and approved by a resolution of each House.

  (9) When an order or a draft of an order is laid in accordance with subsection (7) or (8), the code to which it relates shall also be laid.

  (10) No order or draft of an order may be laid until the consultation required by subsection (4) has taken place.

  (11) A failure by a person mentioned in subsection (3) to have regard to any provision of a code for the time being in operation by virtue of an order under this section shall not in itself render him liable to any criminal or civil proceedings.

  (12) In all criminal and civil proceedings a code in operation at any time by virtue of an order under this section shall be admissible in evidence.

  (13) If it appears to a court or tribunal conducting criminal or civil proceedings that—

  (*a*) any provision of a code in operation at any time by virtue of an order under this section, or
  (*b*) any failure mentioned in subsection (11),

is relevant to any question arising in the proceedings, the provision or failure shall be taken into account in deciding the question.

[Criminal Procedure and Investigations Act 1996, s 21A as inserted by the Criminal Justice Act 2003, s 40.]

PART II[1]
CRIMINAL INVESTIGATIONS

1–3603 **22. Introduction.** (1) For the purposes of this Part a criminal investigation is an investigation conducted by police officers with a view to it being ascertained—

  (*a*) whether a person should be charged with an offence, or
  (*b*) whether a person charged with an offence is guilty of it.

  (2) In this Part references to material are to material of all kinds, and in particular include references to—

  (*a*) information, and
  (*b*) objects of all descriptions.

  (3) In this Part references to recording information are to putting it in a durable or retrievable form (such as writing or tape).

[Criminal Procedure and Investigations Act 1996, s 22.]

---

  1. PART II contains ss 22–27.

1–3604 **23. Code of practice.** (1) The Secretary of State shall prepare a code of practice[1] containing provisions designed to secure—

  (*a*) that where a criminal investigation is conducted all reasonable steps are taken for the purposes of the investigation and, in particular, all reasonable lines of inquiry are pursued;
  (*b*) that information which is obtained in the course of a criminal investigation and may be relevant to the investigation is recorded;
  (*c*) that any record of such information is retained;
  (*d*) that any other material which is obtained in the course of a criminal investigation and may be relevant to the investigation is retained;
  (*e*) that information falling within paragraph (*b*) and material falling within paragraph (*d*) is revealed to a person who is involved in the prosecution of criminal proceedings arising out of or relating to the investigation and who is identified in accordance with prescribed provisions;
  (*f*) that where such a person inspects information or other material in pursuance of a requirement that it be revealed to him, and he requests that it be disclosed to the accused, the accused is allowed to inspect it or is given a copy of it;
  (*g*) that where such a person is given a document indicating the nature of information or other material in pursuance of a requirement that it be revealed to him, and he requests that it be disclosed to the accused, the accused is allowed to inspect it or is given a copy of it;

(h)   that the person who is to allow the accused to inspect information or other material or to give him a copy of it shall decide which of those (inspecting or giving a copy) is appropriate;

(i)   that where the accused is allowed to inspect material as mentioned in paragraph (f) or (g) and he requests a copy, he is given one unless the person allowing the inspection is of opinion that it is not practicable or not desirable to give him one;

(j)   that a person mentioned in paragraph (e) is given a written statement that prescribed activities which the code requires have been carried out.

(2)   the code may include provision—

(a)   that a police officer identified in accordance with prescribed provisions must carry out a prescribed activity which the code requires;

(b)   that a police officer so identified must take steps to secure the carrying out by a person (whether or not a police officer) of a prescribed activity which the code requires;

(c)   that a duty must be discharged by different people in succession in prescribed circumstances (as where a person dies or retires).

(3)   The code may include provision about the form in which information is to be recorded.

(4)   The code may include provision about the manner in which and the period for which—

(a)   a record of information is to be retained, and

(b)   any other material is to be retained;

and if a person is charged with an offence the period may extend beyond a conviction or an acquittal.

(5)   The code may include provision about the time when, the form in which, the way in which, and the extent to which, information or any other material is to be revealed to the person mentioned in subsection (1)(e).

(6)   The code must be so framed that it does not apply to material intercepted in obedience to a warrant issued under section 2 of the Interception of Communications Act 1985 or under the authority of an interception warrant under section 5 of the Regulation of Investigatory Powers Act 2000.

(7)   The code may—

(a)   make different provision in relation to different cases or descriptions of case;

(b)   contain exceptions as regards prescribed cases or descriptions of case.

(8)   In this section "prescribed" means prescribed by the code.

[Criminal Procedure and Investigations Act 1996, s 23 as amended by the Regulation of Investigatory Powers Act 2000, Sch 4.]

---

1. The Code of Practice under Pt II of the Act, which is printed in this PART: STATUTORY INSTRUMENTS AND PRACTICE DIRECTIONS ON PROCEDURE, post, was brought into force on 4 April 2005 (Criminal Procedure and Investigations Act 1996 (Code of Practice) Order 2005, SI 2005/985.

1–3605 24. Examples of disclosure provisions.   (1) This section gives examples of the kinds of provision that may be included in the code by virtue of section 23(5).

(2)   The code may provide that if the person required to reveal material has possession of material which he believes is sensitive he must give a document which—

(a)   indicates the nature of that material, and

(b)   states that he so believes.

(3)   The code may provide that if the person required to reveal material has possession of material which is of a description prescribed under this subsection and which he does not believe is sensitive he must give a document which—

(a)   indicates the nature of that material, and

(b)   states that he does not so believe.

(4)   The code may provide that if—

(a)   a document is given in pursuance of provision contained in the code by virtue of subsection (2), and

(b)   a person identified in accordance with prescribed provisions asks for any of the material,

the person giving the document must give a copy of the material asked for to the person asking for it or (depending on the circumstances) must allow him to inspect it.

(5)   The code may provide that if—

(a)   a document is given in pursuance of provision contained in the code by virtue of subsection (3),

(b)   all or any of the material is of a description prescribed under this subsection, and

(c)   a person is identified in accordance with prescribed provisions as entitled to material of that description,

the person giving the document must give a copy of the material of that description to the person so identified or (depending on the circumstances) must allow him to inspect it.

(6)   The code may provide that if—

(a)   a document is given in pursuance of provision contained in the code by virtue of subsection (3),

(*b*) all or any of the material is not of a description prescribed under subsection (5), and
(*c*) a person identified in accordance with prescribed provisions asks for any of the material not of that description,

the person giving the document must give a copy of the material asked for to the person asking for it or (depending on the circumstances) must allow him to inspect it.

(7) The code may provide that if the person required to reveal material has possession of material which he believes is sensitive and of such a nature that provision contained in the code by virtue of subsection (2) should not apply with regard to it—

(*a*) that provision shall not apply with regard to the material,
(*b*) he must notify a person identified in accordance with prescribed provisions of the existence of the material, and
(*c*) he must allow the person so notified to inspect the material.

(8) For the purposes of this section material is sensitive to the extent that its disclosure under Part I would be contrary to the public interest.

(9) In this section "prescribed" means prescribed by the code.
[Criminal Procedure and Investigations Act 1996, s 24.]

1–3606   25. Operation and revision of code.   (1) When the Secretary of State has prepared a code under section 23—

(*a*) he shall publish it in the form of a draft,
(*b*) he shall consider any representations made to him about the draft, and
(*c*) he may modify the draft accordingly.

(2) When the Secretary of State has acted under subsection (1) he shall lay the code before each House of Parliament, and when he has done so he may bring it into operation on such day as he may appoint by order[1].

(3) A code brought into operation under this section shall apply in relation to suspected or alleged offences into which no criminal investigation has begun before the day so appointed.

(4) The Secretary of State may from time to time revise a code previously brought into operation under this section; and the preceding provisions of this section shall apply to a revised code as they apply to the code as first prepared.
[Criminal Procedure and Investigations Act 1996, s 25.]

---

1. For the current Code, see note to s 23, ante. The day appointed for the purposes of s 25(2) is the day which was appointed for the purposes of Pt I of the Act, namely 1 April 1997 (Criminal Procedure and Investigations Act 1996 (Code of Practice) (No 2) Order 1997, SI 1997/1033).

1–3607   26. Effect of code.   (1) A person other than a police officer who is charged with the duty of conducting an investigation with a view to it being ascertained—

(*a*) whether a person should be charged with an offence, or
(*b*) whether a person charged with an offence is guilty of it,

shall in discharging that duty have regard to any relevant provision of a code which would apply if the investigation were conducted by police officers.

(2) A failure—

(*a*) by a police officer to comply with any provision of a code for the time being in operation by virtue of an order under section 25, or
(*b*) by a person to comply with subsection (1),

shall not in itself render him liable to any criminal or civil proceedings.

(3) In all criminal and civil proceedings a code in operation at any time by virtue of an order under section 25 shall be admissible in evidence.

(4) If it appears to a court or tribunal conducting criminal or civil proceedings that—

(*a*) any provision of a code in operation at any time by virtue of an order under section 25, or
(*b*) any failure mentioned in subsection (2)(*a*) or (*b*),

is relevant to any question arising in the proceedings, the provision or failure shall be taken into account in deciding the question.
[Criminal Procedure and Investigations Act 1996, s 26.]

1–3608   27. Common law rules as to criminal investigations.   (1) Where a code prepared under section 23 and brought into operation under section 25 applies in relation to a suspected or alleged offence, the rules of common law which—

(*a*) were effective immediately before the appointed day, and
(*b*) relate to the matter mentioned in subsection (2),

shall not apply in relation to the suspected or alleged offence.

(2) The matter is the revealing of material—

(*a*) by a police officer or other person charged with the duty of conducting an investigation with a view to it being ascertained whether a person should be charged with an offence or whether a person charged with an offence is guilty of it;

   (*b*)   to a person involved in the prosecution of criminal proceedings.

   (3) In subsection (1) "the appointed day" means the day appointed under section 25 with regard to the code as first prepared.

[Criminal Procedure and Investigations Act 1996, s 27.]

PART III[1]

PREPARATORY HEARINGS

Introduction

1–3609   **28. Introduction.**   (1) This Part applies in relation to an offence if—

   (*a*)   on or after the appointed day the accused is committed for trial, or sent for trial under section 51 of the Crime and Disorder Act 1998, for the offence concerned,

   (*b*)   proceedings for the trial on the charge concerned are transferred to the Crown Court on or after the appointed day, or

   (*c*)   a bill of indictment relating to the offence is preferred on or after the appointed day under the authority of section 2(2)(*b*) of the Administration of Justice (Miscellaneous Provisions) Act 1933 (bill preferred by direction of Court of Appeal, or by direction or with consent of a judge).

   (2) References in subsection (1) to the appointed day are to such day as is appointed for the purposes of this section by the Secretary of State by order[2].

   (3) If an order under this section so provides, this Part applies only in relation to the Crown Court sitting at a place or places specified in the order.

   (4) References in this Part to the prosecutor are to any person acting as prosecutor, whether an individual or a body.

[Criminal Procedure and Investigations Act 1996, s 28 as amended by the Crime and Disorder Act 1998, Sch 8.]

---

   1. Part III contains ss 28–38.

   2. The appointed day for the purposes of s 28 was 15 April 1997 (Criminal Procedure and Investigations Act 1996 (Appointed Day No 4) Order 1997, SI 1997/1019).

1–3610   **29. Power to order preparatory hearing[1].**   (1) Where it appears to a judge of the Crown Court that an indictment reveals a case of such complexity, a case of such seriousness or a case whose trial is likely to be of such length, that substantial benefits are likely to accrue from a hearing—

   (*a*)   before the time when the jury are sworn, and

   (*b*)   for any of the purposes mentioned in subsection (2),

he may order that such a hearing (in this Part referred to as a preparatory hearing[2]) shall be held.

   (1A) A judge of the Crown Court may also order that a preparatory hearing shall be held if an application to which section 45 of the Criminal Justice Act 2003 applies (application for trial without jury) is made.

   (1B) An order that a preparatory hearing shall be held must be made by a judge of the Crown Court in every case which (whether or not it falls within subsection (1) or (1A)) is a case in which at least one of the offences charged by the indictment against at least one of the persons charged is a terrorism offence.

   (1C) An order that a preparatory hearing shall be held must also be made by a judge of the Crown court in every case which (whether or not it falls within subsection (1) or (1A)) is a case in which—

   (*a*)   at least one of the offences charged by the indictment against at least one of the persons charged is an offence carrying a maximum of at least 10 years' imprisonment; and

   (*b*)   it appears to the judge that evidence on the indictment reveals that conduct in respect of which that offence is charged had a terrorist connection.

   (2) The purposes are those of—

   (*a*)   identifying issues which are likely to be material to the determinations and findings which are likely to be required during the trial,

   (*b*)   if there is to be a jury, assisting their comprehension of those issues and expediting the proceedings before them[3],

   (*c*)   determining an application to which section 45 of the Criminal Justice Act 2003 applies,

   (*d*)   assisting the judge's management of the trial,

   (*e*)   considering questions as to the severance or joinder of charges.★

   (3) In a case in which it appears to a judge of the Crown Court that evidence on an indictment reveals a case of fraud of such seriousness or complexity as is mentioned in section 7 of the Criminal Justice Act 1987 (preparatory hearings in cases of serious or complex fraud)—

   (*a*)   the judge may make an order for a preparatory hearing under this section only if he is required to do so by subsection (1B) or (1C);

   (*b*)   before making an order in pursuance of either of those subsections, he must determine whether to make an order for a preparatory hearing under that section; and

   (*c*)   he is not required by either of those subsections to make an order for a preparatory hearing under this section if he determines that an order should be made for a preparatory hearing under that section;

and, in a case in which an order is made for a preparatory hearing under that section, requirements imposed by those subsections apply only if that order ceases to have effect.

(4) An order that a preparatory hearing shall be held may be made—

    (*a*)   on the application of the prosecutor,

    (*b*)   on the application of the accused or, if there is more than one, any of them, or

    (*c*)   of the judge's own motion.

(5) The reference in subsection (1)(*a*) to the time when the jury are sworn includes the time when the jury would be sworn but for the making of an order under Part 7 of the Criminal Justice Act 2003.

(6) In this section "terrorism offence" means—

    (*a*)   an offence under section 11 or 12 of the Terrorism Act 2000 (c 11) (offences relating to proscribed organisations);

    (*b*)   an offence under any of sections 15 to 18 of that Act (offences relating to terrorist property);

    (*c*)   an offence under section 38B of that Act (failure to disclose information about acts of terrorism);

    (*d*)   an offence under section 54 of that Act (weapons training);

    (*e*)   an offence under any of sections 56 to 59 of that Act (directing terrorism, possessing things and collecting information for the purposes of terrorism and inciting terrorism outside the United Kingdom);

    (*f*)   an offence in respect of which there is jurisdiction by virtue of section 62 of that Act (extra-territorial jurisdiction in respect of certain offences committed outside the United Kingdom for the purposes of terrorism etc);

    (*g*)   an offence under Part 1 of the Terrorism Act 2006 (miscellaneous terrorist related offences);

    (*h*)   conspiring or attempting to commit a terrorism offence;

    (*i*)   incitement to commit a terrorism offence.

(7) For the purposes of this section an offence carries a maximum of at least 10 years' imprisonment if—

    (*a*)   it is punishable, on conviction on indictment, with imprisonment; and

    (*b*)   the maximum term of imprisonment that may be imposed on conviction on indictment of that offence is 10 years or more or is imprisonment for life.

(8) For the purposes of this section conduct has a terrorist connection if it is or takes place in the course of an act of terrorism or is for the purposes of terrorism.

(9) In subsection (8) "terrorism" has the same meaning as in the Terrorism Act 2000 (see section 1 of that Act).

[Criminal Procedure and Investigations Act 1996, s 29 as amended by the Criminal Justice Act 2003, s 309 and the Terrorism Act 2006, s 16.]

---

*Subsection (5)(*a*)–(*e*) as substituted by the Criminal Justice Act 2003, s 45 in force for certain purposes 24 July 2006, for remaining purposes from a date to be appointed.

1. For there to be a preparatory hearing under these provisions the case must meet the requirements of complexity or length of trial. Where these criteria are not satisfied, the provisions for interlocutory appeal will not apply: *R v W, P and S* [2003] EWCA Crim 814, [2003] Crim LR 546. It was held in *A- G's Reference (No 1 of 2004), R v Edwards* [2004] EWCA Crim 1025, [2004] 1 WLR 2111 that the decision to hold a preparatory, rather than a pre-trial, hearing required an informed judgment and close attention to the statutory provisions which created the jurisdiction to order such a hearing. Before ordering a preparatory hearing, the judge must identify factors relevant to the criteria, whether complexity, or likely length, or both, bearing in mind the specific, but limited, purposes identified in s 29(2) of the Criminal Procedure and Investigations Act 1996. The decision cannot not be made solely on the basis of a study of the terms or length of the specific indictment but should include a consideration of the evidence which is likely to be called at trial. If the judge has addressed those issues and has decided to proceed with a preparatory hearing on the basis that the potential advantages outweighed the disadvantages, the Court of Appeal will be reluctant to set aside that decision. If, however, there is no relevant material on which the judge can properly have concluded that the case falls within s 29(1), there is no jurisdiction to order a preparatory hearing and the Court of Appeal has no jurisdiction to hear an interlocutory appeal against that decision, although, in such circumstances, the Court of Appeal is not precluded from inviting argument and making observations about the substantive issue for the assistance of the Crown Court, if it sees fit.

2. Although it is appropriate in most cases where there are several defendants charged on the same indictment for there to be one preparatory hearing, there is nothing to prevent the court ordering a separate preparatory hearing in respect of one defendant jointly charged in the same indictment (*Re Kanaris* [2003] UKHL 2, [2003] 1 All ER 593, [2003] 1 WLR 443, [2003] 2 Cr App Rep 1).

3. A ruling on a submission of abuse of process does not fall within any of the purposes of sub-section (2), but a ruling excluding evidence under s 78 of PACE is to be treated as for the purpose of expediting the proceedings before the jury: *R v Claydon* [2001] EWCA Crim 1359, [2004] 1 WLR 1575, [2004] Crim LR 476.

1–3611   30. Start of trial and arraignment.   (1) If a judge orders a preparatory hearing—

    (*a*)   the trial shall start with that hearing, and

    (*b*)   arraignment shall take place at the start of that hearing, unless it has taken place before then.

[Criminal Procedure and Investigations Act 1996, s 30.]

1–3612   31. The preparatory hearing.   (1) At the preparatory hearing the judge may exercise any of the powers specified in this section.

(2) The judge may adjourn a preparatory hearing from time to time.

(3) He may make a ruling as to—

    (*a*)   any question as to the admissibility of evidence;

   (b)   any other question of law relating to the case;

   (c)   any question as to the severance or joinder of charges.

(4) He may order the prosecutor—

   (a)   to give the court and the accused or, if there is more than one, each of them a written statement (a case statement) of the matters falling within subsection (5);

   (b)   to prepare the prosecution evidence and any explanatory material in such a form as appears to the judge to be likely to aid comprehension by a jury and to give it in that form to the court and to the accused or, if there is more than one, to each of them;

   (c)   to give the court and the accused or, if there is more than one, each of them written notice of documents the truth of the contents of which ought in the prosecutor's view to be admitted and of any other matters which in his view ought to be agreed;

   (d)   to make any amendments of any case statement given in pursuance of an order under paragraph (a) that appear to the judge to be appropriate, having regard to objections made by the accused or, if there is more than one, by any of them.

(5) The matters referred to in subsection (4)(a) are—

   (a)   the principal facts of the case for the prosecution;

   (b)   the witnesses who will speak to those facts;

   (c)   any exhibits relevant to those facts;

   (d)   any proposition of law on which the prosecutor proposes to rely;

   (e)   the consequences in relation to any of the counts in the indictment that appear to the prosecutor to flow from the matters falling within paragraphs (a) to (d).

(6) Where a judge has ordered the prosecutor to give a case statement and the prosecutor has complied with the order, the judge may order the accused or, if there is more than one, each of them—

   (a)   *repealed*;

   (b)   to give the court and the prosecutor written notice of any objections that he has to the case statement;

   (c)   *repealed*.

(7) Where a judge has ordered the prosecutor to give notice under subsection (4)(c) and the prosecutor has complied with the order, the judge may order the accused or, if there is more than one, each of them to give the court and the prosecutor a written notice stating—

   (a)   the extent to which he agrees with the prosecutor as to documents and other matters to which the notice under subsection (4)(c) relates, and

   (b)   the reason for any disagreement.

(8) A judge making an order under subsection (6) or (7) shall warn the accused or, if there is more than one, each of them of the possible consequence under section 34 of not complying with it.

(9) If it appears to a judge that reasons given in pursuance of subsection (7) are inadequate, he shall so inform the person giving them and may require him to give further or better reasons.

(10) An order under this section may specify the time within which any specified requirement contained in it is to be complied with.

(11) An order or ruling made under this section shall have effect throughout the trial, unless it appears to the judge on application made to him that the interests of justice require him to vary or discharge it.

[Criminal Procedure and Investigations Act 1996, s 31 as amended by the Criminal Justice Act 2003, s 310 and Sch 36.]

1–3613   **32. Orders before preparatory hearing.**   (1) This section applies where—

   (a)   a judge orders a preparatory hearing, and

   (b)   he decides that any order which could be made under section 31(4) to (7) at the hearing should be made before the hearing.

(2) In such a case—

   (a)   he may make any such order before the hearing (or at the hearing), and

   (b)   section 31(4) to (11) shall apply accordingly.

[Criminal Procedure and Investigations Act 1996, s 32.]

1–3614   **33. Criminal Procedure Rules[1].**   (1) Criminal Procedure Rules may provide that except to the extent that disclosure is required—

   (a)   by rules under section 81 of the Police and Criminal Evidence Act 1984 (expert evidence), or

   (b)   by section 5(7) of this Act,

anything required to be given by an accused in pursuance of a requirement imposed under section 31 need not disclose who will give evidence.

(2) Criminal Procedure Rules may make provision as to the minimum or maximum time that may be specified under section 31(10).

[Criminal Procedure and Investigations Act 1996, s 33 as amended by the Courts Act 2003, Sch 8.]

---

1. See the Criminal Procedure Rules 2005, Parts 15 and 65 in this PART, *post*.

1–3615   34. Later stages of trial.   (1) Any party may depart from the case he disclosed in pursuance of a requirement imposed under section 31.

(2) Where—

(*a*)   a party departs from the case he disclosed in pursuance of a requirement imposed under section 31, or

(*b*)   a party fails to comply with such a requirement,

the judge or, with the leave of the judge, any other party may make such comment as appears to the judge or the other party (as the case may be) to be appropriate and the jury or, in the case of a trial without a jury, the judge may draw such inference as appears proper.

(3) In doing anything under subsection (2) or in deciding whether to do anything under it the judge shall have regard—

(*a*)   to the extent of the departure or failure, and

(*b*)   to whether there is any justification for it.

(4) Except as provided by this section, in the case of a trial with a jury no part—

(*a*)   of a statement given under section 31(6)(*a*), or

(*b*)   of any other information relating to the case for the accused or, if there is more than one, the case for any of them, which was given in pursuance of a requirement imposed under section 31,

may be disclosed at a stage in the trial after the jury have been sworn without the consent of the accused concerned.

[Criminal Procedure and Investigations Act 1996, s 34 as amended by the Criminal Justice Act 2003, Sch 36.]

Appeals

1–3616   35. *Appeals to Court of Appeal.*

1–3617   36. *Appeals to House of Lords.*

Reporting restrictions

1–3618   37. Restrictions on reporting.   (1) Except as provided by this section—

(*a*)   no written report of proceedings falling within subsection (2) shall be published in Great Britain;

(*b*)   no report of proceedings falling within subsection (2) shall be included in a relevant programme for reception in Great Britain.

(2) The following proceedings fall within this subsection—

(*a*)   a preparatory hearing;

(*b*)   an application for leave to appeal in relation to such a hearing;

(*c*)   an appeal in relation to such a hearing.

(3) The judge dealing with a preparatory hearing may order that subsection (1) shall not apply, or shall not apply to a specified extent, to a report of—

(*a*)   the preparatory hearing, or

(*b*)   an application to the judge for leave to appeal to the Court of Appeal under section 35(1) in relation to the preparatory hearing.

(4) The Court of Appeal may order that subsection (1) shall not apply, or shall not apply to a specified extent, to a report of—

(*a*)   an appeal to the Court of Appeal under section 35(1) in relation to a preparatory hearing,

(*b*)   an application to that Court for leave to appeal to it under section 35(1) in relation to a preparatory hearing, or

(*c*)   an application to that Court for leave to appeal to the House of Lords under Part II of the Criminal Appeal Act 1968 in relation to a preparatory hearing.

(5) The House of Lords may order that subsection (1) shall not apply, or shall not apply to a specified extent, to a report of—

(*a*)   an appeal to that House under Part II of the Criminal Appeal Act 1968 in relation to a preparatory hearing, or

(*b*)   an application to that House for leave to appeal to it under Part II of the Criminal Appeal Act 1968 in relation to a preparatory hearing.

(6) Where there is only one accused and he objects to the making of an order under subsection (3), (4) or (5) the judge or the Court of Appeal or the House of Lords shall make the order if (and only if) satisfied after hearing the representations of the accused that it is in the interests of justice to do so; and if the order is made it shall not apply to the extent that a report deals with any such objection or representations.

(7) Where there are two or more accused and one or more of them objects to the making of an order under subsection (3), (4) or (5) the judge or the Court of Appeal or the House of Lords shall make the order if (and only if) satisfied after hearing the representations of each of the accused that it

is in the interests of justice to do so; and if the order is made it shall not apply to the extent that a report deals with any such objection or representations.

(8) Subsection (1) does not apply to—

(a) the publication of a report of a preparatory hearing,

(b) the publication of a report of an appeal in relation to a preparatory hearing or of an application for leave to appeal in relation to such a hearing,

(c) the inclusion in a relevant programme of a report of a preparatory hearing, or

(d) the inclusion in a relevant programme of a report of an appeal in relation to a preparatory hearing or of an application for leave to appeal in relation to such a hearing,

at the conclusion of the trial of the accused or of the last of the accused to be tried.

(9) Subsection (1) does not apply to a report which contains only one or more of the following matters—

(a) the identity of the court and the name of the judge;

(b) the names, ages, home addresses and occupations of the accused and witnesses;

(c) the offence or offences, or a summary of them, with which the accused is or are charged;

(d) the names of counsel and solicitors in the proceedings;

(e) where the proceedings are adjourned, the date and place to which they are adjourned;

(f) any arrangements as to bail;

(g) whether a right to representation funded by the Legal Services Commission as part of the Criminal Defence Service was granted to the accused or any of the accused.

(10) The addresses that may be published or included in a relevant programme under subsection (9) are addresses—

(a) at any relevant time, and

(b) at the time of their publication or inclusion in a relevant programme;

and "relevant time" here means a time when events giving rise to the charges to which the proceedings relate occurred.

(11) Nothing in this section affects any prohibition or restriction imposed by virtue of any other enactment on a publication or on matter included in a programme.

(12) In this section—

(a) "publish", in relation to a report, means publish the report, either by itself or as part of a newspaper or periodical, for distribution to the public;

(b) expressions cognate with "publish" shall be construed accordingly;

(c) "relevant programme" means a programme included in a programme service, within the meaning of the Broadcasting Act 1990.

[Criminal Procedure and Investigations Act 1996, s 37, as amended by the Access to Justice Act 1999, Sch 4.]

1–3619 38. Offences in connection with reporting.   (1) If a report is published or included in a relevant programme in contravention of section 37 each of the following persons is guilty of an offence—

(a) in the case of a publication of a written report as part of a newspaper or periodical, any proprietor, editor or publisher of the newspaper or periodical;

(b) in the case of a publication of a written report otherwise than as part of a newspaper or periodical, the person who publishes it;

(c) in the case of the inclusion of a report in a relevant programme, any body corporate which is engaged in providing the service in which the programme is included and any person having functions in relation to the programme corresponding to those of an editor of a newspaper.

(2) A person guilty of an offence under this section is liable on summary conviction to a fine of an amount not exceeding **level 5** on the standard scale.

(3) Proceedings for an offence under this section shall not be instituted in England and Wales otherwise than by or with the consent of the Attorney General.

(4) Subsection (12) of section 37 applies for the purposes of this section as it applies for the purposes of that.

[Criminal Procedure and Investigations Act 1996, s 38.]

PART IV[1]
RULINGS

1–3620 39. Meaning of pre-trial hearing.   (1) For the purposes of this Part a hearing is a pre-trial hearing if it relates to a trial on indictment and it takes place—

(a) after the accused has been committed for trial for the offence concerned, after the accused has been sent for trial for the offence under section 51 of the Crime and Disorder Act 1998, or after the proceedings for the trial have been transferred to the Crown Court, and

(b) before the start of the trial.

(2) For the purposes of this Part a hearing is also a pre-trial hearing if—

(a) it relates to a trial on indictment to be held in pursuance of a bill of indictment preferred under the authority of section 2(2)(b) of the Administration of Justice (Miscellaneous Provisions)

Act 1933 (bill preferred by direction of Court of Appeal, or by direction or with consent of a judge), and
(*b*) it takes place after the bill of indictment has been preferred and before the start of the trial.

(3) For the purposes of this section the start of a trial on indictment occurs at the time when a jury is sworn to consider the issue of guilt or fitness to plead or, if the court accepts a plea of guilty before the time when a jury is sworn, when that plea is accepted, but this is subject to section 8 of the Criminal Justice Act 1987 and section 30 of this Act (preparatory hearings).
(4) The references in subsection (3) to the time when a jury is sworn include the time when that jury would be sworn but for the making of an order under Part 7 of the Criminal Justice Act 2003.
[Criminal Procedure and Investigations Act 1996, s 39 as amended by the Crime and Disorder Act 1998, Sch 8 and the Criminal Justice Act 2003, Sch 36.]

1. Part IV contains ss 39–43. Part IV applies to pre-trial hearings beginning on or after the 1 October 1996; see s 43, post.

1–3621   40. Power to make rulings.   (1) A judge may make at a pre-trial hearing a ruling as to—
(*a*) any question as to the admissibility of evidence;
(*b*) any other question of law relating to the case concerned.

(2) A ruling may be made under this section—
(*a*) on an application by a party to the case, or
(*b*) of the judge's own motion.

(3) Subject to subsection (4), a ruling made under this section has binding effect from the time it is made until the case against the accused or, if there is more than one, against each of them is disposed of; and the case against an accused is disposed of if—
(*a*) he is acquitted or convicted, or
(*b*) the prosecutor decides not to proceed with the case against him.

(4) A judge may discharge or vary (or further vary) a ruling made under this section if it appears to him that it is in the interests of justice to do so; and a judge may act under this subsection—
(*a*) on an application by a party to the case, or
(*b*) of the judge's own motion.

(5) No application may be made under subsection (4)(*a*) unless there has been a material change of circumstances since the ruling was made or, if a previous application has been made, since the application (or last application) was made.
(6) The judge referred to in subsection (4) need not be the judge who made the ruling or, if it has been varied, the judge (or any of the judges) who varied it.
(7) For the purposes of this section the prosecutor is any person acting as prosecutor, whether an individual or a body.
[Criminal Procedure and Investigations Act 1996, s 40.]

1–3622   41. Restrictions on reporting.   (1) Except as provided by this section—
(*a*) no written report of matters falling within subsection (2) shall be published in Great Britain;
(*b*) no report of matters falling within subsection (2) shall be included in a relevant programme for reception in Great Britain.

(2) The following matters fall within this subsection—
(*a*) a ruling made under section 40;
(*b*) proceedings on an application for a ruling to be made under section 40;
(*c*) an order that a ruling made under section 40 be discharged or varied or further varied;
(*d*) proceedings on an application for a ruling made under section 40 to be discharged or varied or further varied.

(3) The judge dealing with any matter falling within subsection (2) may order that subsection (1) shall not apply, or shall not apply to a specified extent, to a report of the matter.
(4) Where there is only one accused and he objects to the making of an order under subsection (3) the judge shall make the order if (and only if) satisfied after hearing the representations of the accused that it is in the interests of justice to do so; and if the order is made it shall not apply to the extent that a report deals with any such objection or representations.
(5) Where there are two or more accused and one or more of them objects to the making of an order under subsection (3) the judge shall make the order if (and only if) satisfied after hearing the representations of each of the accused that it is in the interests of justice to do so; and if the order is made it shall not apply to the extent that a report deals with any such objection or representations.
(6) Subsection (1) does not apply to—
(*a*) the publication of a report of matters, or
(*b*) the inclusion in a relevant programme of a report of matters,
at the conclusion of the trial of the accused or of the last of the accused to be tried.
(7) Nothing in this section affects any prohibition or restriction imposed by virtue of any other enactment on a publication or on matter included in a programme.
(8) In this section—

(a) "publish", in relation to a report, means publish the report, either by itself or as part of a newspaper or periodical, for distribution to the public;

(b) expressions cognate with "publish" shall be construed accordingly;

(c) "relevant programme" means a programme included in a programme service, within the meaning of the Broadcasting Act 1990.

[Criminal Procedure and Investigations Act 1996, s 41.]

1-3623   **42. Offences in connection with reporting.**   (1) If a report is published or included in a relevant programme in contravention of section 41 each of the following persons is guilty of an offence—

(a) in the case of a publication of a written report as part of a newspaper or periodical, any proprietor, editor or publisher of the newspaper or periodical;

(b) in the case of a publication of a written report otherwise than as part of a newspaper or periodical, the person who publishes it;

(c) in the case of the inclusion of a report in a relevant programme, any body corporate which is engaged in providing the service in which the programme is included and any person having functions in relation to the programme corresponding to those of an editor of a newspaper.

(2) A person guilty of an offence under this section is liable on summary conviction to a fine of an amount not exceeding **level 5** on the standard scale.

(3) Proceedings for an offence under this section shall not be instituted in England and Wales otherwise than by or with the consent of the Attorney General.

(4) Subsection (8) of section 41 applies for the purposes of this section as it applies for the purposes of that.

[Criminal Procedure and Investigations Act 1996, s 42.]

1-3624   **43. Application of this Part.**   (1) This Part applies in relation to pre-trial hearings beginning on or after the appointed day.

(2) The reference in subsection (1) to the appointed day is to such day as is appointed for the purposes of this section by the Secretary of State by order[1].

[Criminal Procedure and Investigations Act 1996, s 43.]

---

1. 1 October 1996 was appointed for this purpose (Criminal Procedure and Investigation Act 1996 (Appointed Day No 1) Order 1996, SI 1996/2343).

1-3625

PART V[1]

COMMITTAL, TRANSFER, ETC.

---

1. Part V contains ss 44–47.

1-3626

PART VI[1]

MAGISTRATES' COURTS

---

1. Part VI contains ss 48–53.

PART VII[1]

MISCELLANEOUS AND GENERAL

Tainted acquittals[2]

1-3635   **54. Acquittals tainted by intimidation etc.**   (1) This section applies where—

(a) a person has been acquitted of an offence, and

(b) a person has been convicted of an administration of justice offence involving interference with or intimidation of a juror or a witness (or potential witness) in any proceedings which led to the acquittal.

(2) Where it appears to the court before which the person was convicted that—

(a) there is a real possibility that, but for the interference or intimidation, the acquitted person would not have been acquitted, and

(b) subsection (5) does not apply,

the court shall certify that it so appears.

(3) Where a court certifies under subsection (2) an application may be made to the High Court for an order quashing the acquittal, and the Court shall make the order if (but shall not do so unless) the four conditions in section 55 are satisfied.

(4) Where an order is made under subsection (3) proceedings may be taken against the acquitted person for the offence of which he was acquitted.

(5) This subsection applies if, because of lapse of time or for any other reason, it would be contrary to the interests of justice to take proceedings against the acquitted person for the offence of which he was acquitted.

(6) For the purposes of this section the following offences are administration of justice offences—

(a) the offence of perverting the course of justice;

(b) the offence under section 51(1) of the Criminal Justice and Public Order Act 1994 (intimidation etc. of witnesses, jurors and others);

(c) an offence of aiding, abetting, counselling, procuring, suborning or inciting another person to commit an offence under section 1 of the Perjury Act 1911.

(7) This section applies in relation to acquittals in respect of offences alleged to be committed on or after the appointed day.

(8) The reference in subsection (7) to the appointed day is to such day as is appointed for the purposes of this section by the Secretary of State by order[3].

[Criminal Procedure and Investigations Act 1996, s 54.]

---

1. Part VII contains ss 54–81.
2. See the Criminal Procedure Rules 2005, Part 40 in this PART, post.
3. The appointed day for the purposes of s 54 was 15 April 1997 (Criminal Procedure and Investigations Act 1996 (Appointed Day No 4) Order 1997, SI 1997/1019).

1–3636   55. Conditions for making order.   (1) The first condition is that it appears to the High Court likely that, but for the interference or intimidation, the acquitted person would not have been acquitted.

(2) The second condition is that it does not appear to the Court that, because of lapse of time or for any other reason, it would be contrary to the interests of justice to take proceedings against the acquitted person for the offence of which he was acquitted.

(3) The third condition is that it appears to the Court that the acquitted person has been given a reasonable opportunity to make written representations to the Court.

(4) The fourth condition is that it appears to the Court that the conviction for the administration of justice offence will stand.

(5) In applying subsection (4) the Court shall—

(a) take into account all the information before it, but

(b) ignore the possibility of new factors coming to light.

(6) Accordingly, the fourth condition has the effect that the Court shall not make an order under section 54(3) if (for instance) it appears to the Court that any time allowed for giving notice of appeal has not expired or that an appeal is pending.

[Criminal Procedure and Investigations Act 1996, s 55.]

1–3637   56. Time limits for proceedings.   (1) Where—

(a) an order is made under section 54(3) quashing an acquittal,

(b) by virtue of section 54(4) it is proposed to take proceedings against the acquitted person for the offence of which he was acquitted, and

(c) apart from this subsection, the effect of an enactment would be that the proceedings must be commenced before a specified period calculated by reference to the commission of the offence,

in relation to the proceedings the enactment shall have effect as if the period were instead one calculated by reference to the time the order is made under section 54(3).

(2) Subsection (1)(c) applies however the enactment is expressed so that (for instance) it applies in the case of—

(a) *repealed*

(b) section 127(1) of the Magistrates' Courts Act 1980 (magistrates' court not to try information unless it is laid within 6 months from time when offence committed);

(c) an enactment that imposes a time limit only in certain circumstances (as where proceedings are not instituted by or with the consent of the Director of Public Prosecutions).

[Criminal Procedure and Investigations Act 1996, s 56 as amended by the Sexual Offences Act 2003, Sch 7.]

1–3638   57. Tainted acquittals: supplementary.   (1) Section 45 of the Offences Against the Person Act 1861 (which releases a person from criminal proceedings in certain circumstances) shall have effect subject to section 54(4) of this Act.

(2)–(4) *Amendment of the Contempt of Court Act 1981.*

[Criminal Procedure and Investigations Act 1996, s 57.]

Derogatory assertions

1–3639   58. Orders in respect of certain assertions.   (1) This section applies where a person has been convicted of an offence and a speech in mitigation is made by him or on his behalf before—

(a) a court determining what sentence should be passed on him in respect of the offence, or

(b) a magistrates' court determining whether he should be committed to the Crown Court for sentence.

(2) This section also applies where a sentence has been passed on a person in respect of an offence and a submission relating to the sentence is made by him or on his behalf before—

(a) a court hearing an appeal against or reviewing the sentence, or

(b) a court determining whether to grant leave to appeal against the sentence.

(3) Where it appears to the court that there is a real possibility that an order under subsection (8) will be made in relation to the assertion, the court may make an order under subsection (7) in relation to the assertion.

(4) Where there are substantial grounds for believing—

(a) that an assertion forming part of the speech or submission is derogatory to a person's character (for instance, because it suggests that his conduct is or has been criminal, immoral or improper), and

(b) that the assertion is false or that the facts asserted are irrelevant to the sentence,

the court may make an order under subsection (8) in relation to the assertion.

(5) An order under subsection (7) or (8) must not be made in relation to an assertion if it appears to the court that the assertion was previously made—

(a) at the trial at which the person was convicted of the offence, or

(b) during any other proceedings relating to the offence.

(6) Section 59 has effect where a court makes an order under subsection (7) or (8).

(7) An order under this subsection—

(a) may be made at any time before the court has made a determination with regard to sentencing;

(b) may be revoked at any time by the court;

(c) subject to paragraph (b), shall cease to have effect when the court makes a determination with regard to sentencing.

(8) An order under this subsection—

(a) may be made after the court has made a determination with regard to sentencing, but only if it is made as soon as is reasonably practicable after the making of the determination;

(b) may be revoked at any time by the court;

(c) subject to paragraph (b), shall cease to have effect at the end of the period of 12 months beginning with the day on which it is made;

(d) may be made whether or not an order has been made under subsection (7) with regard to the case concerned.

(9) For the purposes of subsection (7) and (8) the court makes a determination with regard to sentencing—

(a) when it determines what sentence should be passed (where this section applies by virtue of subsection (1)(a));

(b) when it determines whether the person should be committed to the Crown Court for sentence (where this section applies by virtue of subsection (1)(b));

(c) when it determines what the sentence should be (where this section applies by virtue of subsection (2)(a));

(d) when it determines whether to grant leave to appeal (where this section applies by virtue of subsection (2)(b)).

[Criminal Procedure and Investigations Act 1996, s 58.]

1–3640 59. Restriction on reporting of assertions. (1) Where a court makes an order under section 58(7) or (8) in relation to any assertion, at any time when the order has effect the assertion must not—

(a) be published in Great Britain in a written publication available to the public, or

(b) be included in a relevant programme for reception in Great Britain.

(2) In this section—

"relevant programme" means a programme included in a programme service, within the meaning of the Broadcasting Act 1990;

"written publication" includes a film, a soundtrack and any other record in permanent form but does not include an indictment or other document prepared for use in particular legal proceedings.

(3) For the purposes of this section an assertion is published or included in a programme if the material published or included—

(a) names the person about whom the assertion is made or, without naming him, contains enough to make it likely that members of the public will identify him as the person about whom it is made, and

(b) reproduces the actual wording of the matter asserted or contains its substance.

[Criminal Procedure and Investigations Act 1996, s 59.]

1–3641 60. Reporting of assertions: offences. (1) If an assertion is published or included in a relevant programme in contravention of section 59, each of the following persons is guilty of an offence—

(a) in the case of publication in a newspaper or periodical, any proprietor, any editor and any publisher of the newspaper or periodical;

(b)   in the case of publication in any other form, the person publishing the assertion;

(c)   in the case of an assertion included in a relevant programme, any body corporate engaged in providing the service in which the programme is included and any person having functions in relation to the programme corresponding to those of an editor of a newspaper.

(2) A person guilty of an offence under this section is liable on summary conviction to a fine of an amount not exceeding **level 5** on the standard scale.

(3) Where a person is charged with an offence under this section it is a defence to prove that at the time of the alleged offence—

(a)   he was not aware, and neither suspected nor had reason to suspect, that an order under section 58(7) or (8) had effect at that time, or

(b)   he was not aware, and neither suspected nor had reason to suspect, that the publication or programme in question was of, or (as the case may be) included, the assertion in question.

(4) Where an offence under this section committed by a body corporate is proved to have been committed with the consent or connivance of, or to be attributable to any neglect on the part of—

(a)   a director, manager, secretary or other similar officer of the body corporate, or

(b)   a person purporting to act in any such capacity,

he as well as the body corporate is guilty of the offence and liable to be proceeded against and punished accordingly.

(5) In relation to a body corporate whose affairs are managed by its members "director" in subsection (4) means a member of the body corporate.

(6) Subsection (2) and (3) of section 59 apply for the purposes of this section as they apply for the purposes of that.

[Criminal Procedure and Investigations Act 1996, s 60.]

1–3642   61. Reporting of assertions: commencement and supplementary.   (1) Section 58 applies where the offence mentioned in subsection (1) or (2) of that section is committed on or after the appointed day.

(2) The reference in subsection (1) to the appointed day is to such day as is appointed for the purposes of this section by the Secretary of State by order[1].

(3) Nothing in section 58 or 59 affects any prohibition or restriction imposed by virtue of any other enactment on a publication or on matter included in a programme.

(4) Nothing in section 58 or 59 affects section 3 of the Law of Libel Amendment Act 1888 (privilege of newspaper reports of court proceedings).

(5) Section 8 of the Law of Libel Amendment Act 1888 (order of judge required for prosecution for libel published in a newspaper) does not apply to a prosecution for an offence under section 60.

(6) *Amendment of s 159 of the Criminal Justice Act 1988 (appeal to Court of Appeal against orders restricting reports etc).*

[Criminal Procedure and Investigations Act 1996, s 61.]

---

1. The day appointed for the purposes of s 61 was 1 April 1997 (Criminal Procedure and Investigations Act 1996 (Appointed Day No 3) Order 1997, SI 1997/682).

Evidence: special provisions

1–3643   62. Television links and video recordings.   (1) In section 32 of the Criminal Justice Act 1988 (evidence through television links) the following subsections shall be inserted after subsection (3B)—

"(3C) Where—

(a)   the court gives leave for a person to give evidence through a live television link, and

(b)   the leave is given by virtue of subsection (1)(b) above,

then, subject to subsection (3D) below, the person concerned may not give evidence otherwise than through a live television link.

(3D) In a case falling within subsection (3C) above the court may give permission for the person to give evidence otherwise than through a live television link if it appears to the court to be in the interests of justice to give such permission.

(3E) Permission may be given under subsection (3D) above—

(a)   on an application by a party to the case, or

(b)   of the court's own motion;

but no application may be made under paragraph (a) above unless there has been a material change of circumstances since the leave was given by virtue of subsection (1)(b) above."

(2) In section 32A of the Criminal Justice Act 1988 (video recordings of testimony from child witnesses) the following subsections shall be inserted after subsection (6)—

"(6A) Where the court gives leave under subsection (2) above the child witness shall not give relevant evidence (within the meaning given by subsection (6D) below) otherwise than by means of the video recording; but this is subject to subsection (6B) below.

(6B) In a case falling within subsection (6A) above the court may give permission for the child witness to give relevant evidence (within the meaning given by subsection (6D) below) otherwise than by means of the video recording if it appears to the court to be in the interests of justice to give such permission.

(6C) Permission may be given under subsection (6B) above—

(a) on an application by a party to the case, or
(b) of the court's own motion;

but no application may be made under paragraph (a) above unless there has been a material change of circumstances since the leave was given under subsection (2) above.

(6D) For the purposes of subsections (6A) and (6B) above evidence is relevant evidence if—

(a) it is evidence in chief on behalf of the party who tendered the video recording, and
(b) it relates to matter which, in the opinion of the court, is dealt with in the recording and which the court has not directed to be excluded under subsection (3) above."

(3) This section applies where the leave concerned is given on or after the appointed day.
(4) The reference in subsection (3) to the appointed day is to such day as is appointed for the purposes of this section by the Secretary of State by order[1].*
[Criminal Procedure and Investigations Act 1996, s 62.]

---

*Repealed in relation to England and Wales, by the Youth Justice and Criminal Evidence Act 1999, s 68 and Sch 6, with effect from 24 July 2002, with regards Northern Ireland, repealed with effect from a date to be appointed: see the Criminal Evidence (Northern Ireland) Order 1999 (SI 1999/2789).
1. At the date of going to press no order appointing a day for the purpose of s 62(4) had been made.

1–3647   66. Summons to witness to attend Crown Court. *Amendment of s 2 and other provisions of the Criminal Procedure (Attendance of Witnesses) Act 1965.*

1–3648   67. Witness summons: securing attendance of witness. *Amendment of s 4(1) of the Criminal Procedure (Attendance of Witnesses) Act 1965.*

Other miscellaneous provisions

1–3649   68. Use of written statements and depositions at trial. Schedule 2 to this Act (which relates to the use at the trial of written statements and depositions admitted in evidence in committal proceedings) shall have effect.
[Criminal Procedure and Investigations Act 1996, s 68.]

General

1–3656   75. Time when alleged offence committed. (1) Subsection (2) applies for the purposes of sections 52(3) and 54(7).
(2) Where an offence is alleged to be committed over a period of more than one day, or at some time during a period of more than one day, it must be taken to be alleged to be committed on the last of the days in the period.
(3) Subsection (2) applies for the purposes of section 61(1) as if "alleged to be" (in each place) were omitted.
[Criminal Procedure and Investigations Act 1996, s 75.]

1–3657   76. Power of magistrates' courts. In section 148(2) of the Magistrates' Courts Act 1980 (power of court to act where another may act) the reference to that Act includes a reference to this Act.
[Criminal Procedure and Investigations Act 1996, s 76.]

1–3658   77. Orders and regulations. (1) This section concerns the powers of the Secretary of State to make orders or regulations under this Act.
(2) Any power to make an order or regulations may be exercised differently in relation to different areas or in relation to other different cases or descriptions of case.
(3) Any order or regulations may include such supplementary, incidental, consequential or transitional provisions as appear to the Secretary of State to be necessary or expedient.
(4) Any power to make an order or regulations shall be exercisable by statutory instrument.
(5) No regulations or order under section 6A or 25 shall have effect unless approved by a resolution of each House of Parliament.
(6) A statutory instrument containing—

(a) an order under section 78, or
(b) regulations (other than regulations under section 6A),

shall be subject to annulment in pursuance of a resolution of either House of Parliament.[1]
[Criminal Procedure and Investigations Act 1996, s 77 as amended by the Criminal Justice Act 2003, Sch 36.]

---

1. Subordinate legislation made under this section: SI 1999/716 and SI 1999/718.

1–3659   78. *Application to armed forces*

1–3660   79. Extent. (1) This Act does not extend to Scotland, with the exception of—

(a) sections 37, 38, 41, 42, 59, 60, 61(3), 63, 72, 73, 74(2) and (3) and 78, this section and section 81;

(b) paragraphs 6 and 7 of Schedule 3, and paragraph 8 of that Schedule so far as it relates to paragraphs 6 and 7;

(c) paragraph 5 of Schedule 5;

(d) paragraph 12 of Schedule 5 so far as it relates to provisions amending section 11 of the Criminal Justice Act 1987.

(2) Section 73 extends only to Scotland.

(3) Parts III and VI and sections 44, 47, 65, 67, 68 and 71 do not extend to Northern Ireland.

(4) In its application to Northern Ireland, this Act has effect subject to the modifications set out in Schedule 4.

(5) Section 74(2) and (3) extend to any place where proceedings before courts martial may be held.

(6) Section 78 extends as follows—

(a) so far as it relates to proceedings, it extends to any place where such proceedings may be held;

(b) so far as it relates to investigations, it extends to any place where such investigations may be conducted.

[Criminal Procedure and Investigations Act 1996, s 79.]

1–3661 80. Repeals. The provisions mentioned in Schedule 5 are repealed (or revoked) to the extent specified in column 3, but subject to any provision of that Schedule.

[Criminal Procedure and Investigations Act 1996, s 80.]

1–3662 81. Citation. This Act may be cited as the Criminal Procedure and Investigations Act 1996.

[Criminal Procedure and Investigations Act 1996, s 81.]

SCHEDULES

1–3663

Section 47

SCHEDULE 1
COMMITTAL PROCEEDINGS

Section 68

SCHEDULE 2*
STATEMENTS AND DEPOSITIONS

(*Amended by the Courts Act 2003, Sch 8.*)

Statements

1–3688 1. (1) Sub-paragraph (2) applies if—

(a) a written statement has been admitted in evidence in proceedings before a magistrates' court inquiring into an offence as examining justices,

(b) in those proceedings a person has been committed for trial,

(c) for the purposes of section 5A of the Magistrates' Courts Act 1980 the statement complied with section 5B of that Act prior to the committal for trial,

(d) the statement purports to be signed by a justice of the peace, and

(e) sub-paragraph (3) does not prevent sub-paragraph (2) applying.

(2) Where this sub-paragraph applies the statement may without further proof be read as evidence on the trial of the accused, whether for the offence for which he was committed for trial or for any other offence arising out of the same transaction or set of circumstances.

(3) Sub-paragraph (2) does not apply if—

(a) it is proved that the statement was not signed by the justice by whom it purports to have been signed,

(b) the court of trial at its discretion orders that sub-paragraph (2) shall not apply, or

(c) a party to the proceedings objects to sub-paragraph (2) applying.

(4) If a party to the proceedings objects to sub-paragraph (2) applying the court of trial may order that the objection shall have no effect if the court considers it to be in the interests of justice so to order.

Depositions

1–3689 2. (1) Sub-paragraph (2) applies if—

(a) in pursuance of section 97A of the Magistrates' Courts Act 1980 (summons or warrant to have evidence taken as a deposition etc.) a person has had his evidence taken as a deposition for the purposes of proceedings before a magistrates' court inquiring into an offence as examining justices,

(b) the deposition has been admitted in evidence in those proceedings,

(c) in those proceedings a person has been committed for trial,

(d) for the purposes of section 5A of the Magistrates' Courts Act 1980 the deposition complied with section 5C of that Act prior to the committal for trial,

(e) the deposition purports to be signed by the justice before whom it purports to have been taken, and

(f) sub-paragraph (3) does not prevent sub-paragraph (2) applying.

(2) Where this sub-paragraph applies the deposition may without further proof be read as evidence on the trial

of the accused, whether for the offence for which he was committed for trial or for any other offence arising out of the same transaction or set of circumstances.

(3) Sub-paragraph (2) does not apply if—

(*a*)　it is proved that the deposition was not signed by the justice by whom it purports to have been signed,

(*b*)　the court of trial at its discretion orders that sub-paragraph (2) shall not apply, or

(*c*)　a party to the proceedings objects to sub-paragraph (2) applying.

(4) If a party to the proceedings objects to sub-paragraph (2) applying the court of trial may order that the objection shall have no effect if the court considers it to be in the interests of justice so to order.

Signatures

1–3690　**3.** (1) A justice who signs a certificate authenticating one or more relevant statements or depositions shall be treated for the purposes of paragraphs 1 and 2 as signing the statement or deposition or (as the case may be) each of them.

(2) For this purpose—

(*a*)　a relevant statement is a written statement made by a person for the purposes of proceedings before a magistrates' court inquiring into an offence as examining justices;

(*b*)　a relevant deposition is a deposition made in pursuance of section 97A of the Magistrates' Courts Act 1980 for the purposes of such proceedings.

Time limit for objection

1–3691　**4.** Criminal Procedure Rules make provision—

(*a*)　requiring an objection under paragraph 1(3)(*c*) or 2(3)(*c*) to be made within a period prescribed in the rules;

(*b*)　allowing the court of trial at its discretion to permit such an objection to be made outside any such period.

Retrial

1–3692　**5.** In Schedule 2 to the Criminal Appeal Act 1968 (procedural and other provisions applicable on order for retrial) in paragraph 1 for the words from "section 13(3)" to "before the original trial" there shall be substituted "paragraphs 1 and 2 of Schedule 2 to the Criminal Procedure and Investigations Act 1996 (use of written statements and depositions) shall not apply to any written statement or deposition read as evidence at the original trial".

Repeals

1–3693　**6.** (1) Section 13(3) of the Criminal Justice Act 1925 (which relates to depositions taken before examining justices and is superseded by paragraph 2 above) shall be omitted.

(2) Section 7 of the Criminal Justice Act 1967 (which is superseded by paragraph 3 above) shall be omitted.

Commencement

1–3694　**7.** This Schedule shall have effect in accordance with provision made by the Secretary of State by order.

---

*　**Repealed by the Criminal Justice Act 2003, Sch 3 from a date to be appointed.**

1–3695　　　　　　　　　　　SCHEDULE 3
　　　　　　　　　　　　　　FRAUD

Criminal Evidence (Amendment) Act 1997[1]

(1997 c 17)

Extension of power to take non-intimate body samples without consent

1–3701　**1. Persons imprisoned or detained by virtue of pre-existing conviction for sexual offence etc.**　(1) This section has effect for removing, in relation to persons to whom this section applies, the restriction on the operation of section 63(3B) of the Police and Criminal Evidence Act 1984 (power to take non-intimate samples without the appropriate consent from persons convicted of recordable offences)—

(*a*)　which is imposed by the subsection (10) inserted in section 63 by section 55(6) of the Criminal Justice and Public Order Act 1994, and

(*b*)　by virtue of which section 63(3B) does not apply to persons convicted before 10 April 1995.

(2) *Amendment of s 63 of the 1984 Act.*

(3) This section applies to a person who was convicted of a recordable offence before 10 April 1995 if—

(*a*)　that offence was one of the offences listed in Schedule 1 to this Act (which lists certain sexual, violent and other offences), and

(*b*)　at the relevant time he is serving a sentence of imprisonment in respect of that offence.

(4) This section also applies to a person who was convicted of a recordable offence before 10 April 1995 if—

- (*a*) that offence was one of the offences listed in Schedule 1 to this Act, and
- (*b*) at the relevant time he is detained under Part III of the Mental Health Act 1983 in pursuance of—
  - (i) a hospital order or interim hospital order made following that conviction, or
  - (ii) a transfer direction given at a time when he was serving a sentence of imprisonment in respect of that offence.

Expressions used in this subsection and in the Mental Health Act 1983 have the same meaning as in that Act.

(5) Where a person convicted of a recordable offence before 10 April 1995 was, following his conviction for that and any other offence or offences, sentenced to two or more terms of imprisonment (whether taking effect consecutively or concurrently), he shall be treated for the purposes of this section as serving a sentence of imprisonment in respect of that offence at any time when serving any of those terms.

(6) For the purposes of this section, references to a person serving a sentence of imprisonment include references—

- (*a*) to his being detained in any institution to which the Prison Act 1952 applies in pursuance of any other sentence or order for detention imposed by a court in criminal proceedings, or
- (*b*) to his being detained (otherwise than in any such institution) in pursuance of directions of the Secretary of State under section 92 of the Powers of Criminal Courts (Sentencing) Act 2000;

and any reference to a term of imprisonment shall be construed accordingly.
[Criminal Evidence (Amendment) Act 1997, s 1 as amended by the Powers of Criminal Courts (Sentencing) Act 2000, Sch 9.]

---

1. This Act makes provision extending the categories of persons from whom non-intimate body samples may be taken without consent under Pt V of the Police and Criminal Evidence Act 1984.

1–3702   2. Persons detained following acquittal on grounds of insanity or finding of unfitness to plead.   (1) This section has effect for enabling non-intimate samples to be taken from persons under section 63 of the 1984 Act without the appropriate consent where they are persons to whom this section applies.

(2) *Amendment of s 63 of the 1984 Act.*

(3) This section applies to a person if—

- (*a*) at the relevant time he is detained under Part III of the Mental Health Act 1983 in pursuance of an order made under—
  - (i) section 5(2)(*a*) of the Criminal Procedure (Insanity) Act 1964 or section 6 or 14 of the Criminal Appeal Act 1968 (findings of insanity or unfitness to plead), or
  - (ii) section 37(3) of the Mental Health Act 1983 (power of magistrates' court to make hospital order without convicting accused), and
- (*b*) that order was made on or after the date of the passing of this Act in respect of a recordable offence.

(4) This section also applies to a person if—

- (*a*) at the relevant time he is detained under Part III of the Mental Health Act 1983 in pursuance of an order made under—
  - (i) any of the provisions mentioned in subsection (3)(*a*), or
  - (ii) section 5(1) of the Criminal Procedure (Insanity) Act 1964 as originally enacted, and
- (*b*) that order was made before the date of the passing of this Act in respect of any offence listed in Schedule 1 to this Act.

(5) Subsection (4)(*a*)(i) does not apply to any order made under section 14(2) of the Criminal Appeal Act 1968 as originally enacted.

(6) For the purposes of this section an order falling within subsection (3) or (4) shall be treated as having been made in respect of an offence of a particular description—

- (*a*) if, where the order was made following—
  - (i)   a finding of not guilty by reason of insanity, or
  - (ii) a finding that the person in question was under a disability and did the act or made the omission charged against him, or
  - (iii) a finding for the purposes of section 37(3) of the Mental Health Act 1983 that the person in question did the act or made the omission charged against him, or
  - (iv) (in the case of an order made under section 5(1) of the Criminal Procedure (Insanity) Act 1964 as originally enacted) a finding that he was under a disability,

  that finding was recorded in respect of an offence of that description; or

- (*b*) if, where the order was made following the Court of Appeal forming such opinion as is mentioned in section 6(1) or 14(1) of the Criminal Appeal Act 1968, that opinion was formed on an appeal brought in respect of an offence of that description.

(7) In this section any reference to an Act "as originally enacted" is a reference to that Act as it

had effect without any of the amendments made by the Criminal Procedure (Insanity and Unfitness to Plead) Act 1991.

[Criminal Evidence (Amendment) Act 1997, s 2.]

Supplementary

1–3703   5. Interpretation.   In this Act—

"the 1984 Act" means the Police and Criminal Evidence Act 1984;

"appropriate consent" has the meaning given by section 65 of the 1984 Act;

"non-intimate sample" has the meaning given by section 65 of the 1984 Act;

"recordable offence" means any offence to which regulations under section 27 of the 1984 Act (fingerprinting) apply;

"the relevant time" means, in relation to the exercise of any power to take a non-intimate sample from a person, the time when it is sought to take the sample.

[Criminal Evidence (Amendment) Act 1997, s 5.]

1–3704   6. Short title, repeal and extent.   (1) This Act may be cited as the Criminal Evidence (Amendment) Act 1997.

(2) For ease of reference sections 63 and 63A of the 1984 Act, as amended by sections 1 to 4 above, are set out in Schedule 2 to this Act.

(3) Section 55(6) of the Criminal Justice and Public Order Act 1994 is repealed.

(4) This Act extends to England and Wales only.

[Criminal Evidence (Amendment) Act 1997, s 6.]

SCHEDULES

Section 1   SCHEDULE 1
                                    LIST OF OFFENCES

Sexual offences and offences of indecency

1–3705   1. Any offence under the Sexual Offences Act 1956, other than an offence under section 30, 31 or 33 to 36 of that Act.

2. Any offence under section 128 of the Mental Health Act 1959 (intercourse with mentally handicapped person by hospital staff etc).

3. Any offence under section 1 of the Indecency with Children Act 1960 (indecent conduct towards young child).

4. Any offence under section 54 of the Criminal Law Act 1977 (incitement by man of his grand-daughter, daughter or sister under the age of 16 to commit incest with him).

5. Any offence under section 1 of the Protection of Children Act 1978.

Violent and other offences

1–3706   6. Any of the following offences—

(a)   murder;
(b)   manslaughter;
(c)   false imprisonment; and
(d)   kidnapping.

7. Any offence under any of following provisions of the Offences Against the Person Act 1861—

(a)   section 4 (conspiring or soliciting to commit murder);
(b)   section 16 (threats to kill);
(c)   section 18 (wounding with intent to cause grievous bodily harm);
(d)   section 20 (causing grievous bodily harm);
(e)   section 21 (attempting to choke etc in order to commit or assist in the committing of any indictable offence);
(f)   section 22 (using chloroform etc to commit or assist in the committing of any indictable offence);
(g)   section 23 (maliciously administering poison etc so as to endanger life or inflict grievous bodily harm);
(h)   section 24 (maliciously administering poison etc with intent to injure etc); and
(i)   section 47 (assault occasioning actual bodily harm).

8. Any offence under either of the following provisions of the Explosive Substances Act 1883—

(a)   section 2 (causing explosion likely to endanger life or property); and
(b)   section 3 (attempt to cause explosion, or making or keeping explosive with intent to endanger life or property).

9. Any offence under section 1 of the Children and Young Persons Act 1933 (cruelty to persons under 16).

10. Any offence under section 4(1) of the Criminal Law Act 1967 (assisting offender) committed in relation to the offence of murder.

11. Any offence under any of the following provisions of the Firearms Act 1968—

(a)   section 16 (possession of firearm with intent to injure);
(b)   section 17 (use of firearm to resist arrest); and
(c)   section 18 (carrying firearm with criminal intent).

12. Any offence under either of the following provisions of the Theft Act 1968—

(a)   section 9 (burglary); and
(b)   section 10 (aggravated burglary);

and any offence under section 12A of that Act (aggravated vehicle-taking) involving an accident which caused the death of any person.

13. Any offence under section 1 of the Criminal Damage Act 1971 (destroying or damaging property) required to be charged as arson.

14. Any offence under section 2 of the Child Abduction Act 1984 (abduction of child by person other than parent).

Conspiracy, incitement and attempts

1–3707 **15.** Any offence under section 1 of the Criminal Law Act 1977 of conspiracy to commit any of the offences mentioned in paragraphs 1 to 14.

16. Any offence under section 1 of the Criminal Attempts Act 1981 of attempting to commit any of those offences.

17. Any offence of inciting another to commit any of those offences.

1–3708

Section 6   SCHEDULE 2

SECTIONS 63 AND 63A OF THE POLICE AND CRIMINAL EVIDENCE ACT 1984, AS AMENDED

Justices of the Peace Act 1997[1]

(1997 c 25)

1–3709

_____

1. This Act has been repealed by the Courts Act 2003 (see this PART, post).

Crime and Disorder Act 1998[1]

(1998 c 37)

PART I[2]

PREVENTION OF CRIME AND DISORDER

CHAPTER 1[3]

ENGLAND AND WALES

Crime and disorder: general

1–3804 **1. Anti-social behaviour orders.** (1) An application[4] for an order under this section may be made by a relevant authority if it appears to the authority that the following conditions are fulfilled with respect to any person[5] aged 10 or over, namely—

(a) that the person has acted, since the commencement date, in an anti-social manner, that is to say, in a manner that caused or was likely to cause[6] harassment, alarm or distress to one or more persons not of the same household as himself[7]; and

(b) that such an order is necessary to protect relevant persons from further anti-social acts by him.

(1A) In this section and sections 1B, 1CA,1E and 1F "relevant authority" means—

(a) the council for a local government area;

(aa) in relation to England, a county council;

(b) the chief officer of police of any police force maintained for a police area;

(c) the chief constable of the British Transport Police Force;

(d) any person registered under section 1 of the Housing Act 1996 (c 52) as a social landlord who provides or manages any houses or hostel in a local government area; or

(e) a housing action trust established by order in pursuance of section 62 of the Housing Act 1988.

(1B) In this section "relevant persons" means—

(a) in relation to a relevant authority falling within paragraph (a) of subsection (1A), persons within the local government area of that council;

(aa) in relation to a relevant authority falling within paragraph (aa) of subsection (1A), persons within the county of the county council.

(b) in relation to a relevant authority falling within paragraph (b) of that subsection, persons within the police area;

(c) in relation to a relevant authority falling within paragraph (c) of that subsection—

(i) persons who are within or likely to be within a place specified in section 31(1)(a) to (f) of the railways and Transport Safety Act 2003 in a local government area; or

(ii) persons who are within or likely to be within such a place;

(d) in relation to a relevant authority falling within paragraph (d) or (e) of that subsection—

(i) persons who are residing in or who are otherwise on or likely to be on premises provided or managed by that authority; or

(ii) persons who are in the vicinity of or likely to be in the vicinity of such premises.*

(2) *Repealed.*

(3) Such an application shall be made by complaint to a magistrates' court[8].

(4) If, on such an application, it is proved that the conditions mentioned in subsection (1) above are fulfilled, the magistrates' court may make an order under this section (an "anti-social behaviour order") which prohibits the defendant from doing anything described in the order[9].

(5) For the purpose of determining whether the condition mentioned in subsection (1)(a) above is fulfilled, the court shall disregard any act of the defendant which he shows was reasonable in the circumstances.

(6) The prohibitions[10] that may be imposed by an anti-social behaviour order are those necessary for the purpose of protecting persons (whether relevant persons or persons elsewhere in England and Wales) from further anti-social acts by the defendant.

(7) An anti-social behaviour order shall have effect for a period (not less than two years) specified in the order or until further order.

(8) Subject to subsection (9) below, the applicant or the defendant may apply[11] by complaint to the court which made an anti-social behaviour order for it to be varied or discharged by a further order.

(9) Except with the consent of both parties, no anti-social behaviour order shall be discharged before the end of the period of two years beginning with the date of service[11] of the order.

(10) If without reasonable excuse[13] a person does anything which he is prohibited from doing by an anti-social behaviour order, he is guilty of an offence and liable[14]—

(a) on summary conviction, to imprisonment for a term not exceeding **six months** or to a fine not exceeding the **statutory maximum**, or to both; or

(b) on conviction on indictment, to imprisonment for a term not exceeding **five years** or to a **fine**, or to both.

(10A) The following may bring proceedings for an offence under subsection (10)—

(a) a council which is a relevant authority;

(b) the council for the local government area in which a person in respect of whom an anti-social behaviour order has been made resides or appears to reside.

(10B) If proceedings for an offence under subsection (10) are brought in a youth court section 47(2) of the Children and Young Persons Act 1933 (c 12) has effect as if the persons entitled to be present at a sitting for the purposes of those proceedings include one person authorised to be present by a relevant authority.

(10C) In proceedings for an offence under subsection (10), a copy of the original anti-social behaviour order, certified as such by the proper officer of the court which made it, is admissible as evidence of its having been made and of its contents to the same extent that oral evidence of those things is admissible in those proceedings.

(10D) In relation to proceedings brought against a child or a young person for an offence under subsection (10)—

(a) section 49 of the Children and Young Persons Act 1933 (restrictions on reports of proceedings in which children and young persons are concerned) does not apply in respect of the child or young person against whom the proceedings are brought;

(b) section 45 of the Youth Justice and Criminal Evidence Act 1999 (power to restrict reporting of criminal proceedings involving persons under 18) does so apply.

(10E) If, in relation to any such proceedings, the court does exercise its power to give a direction under section 45 of the Youth Justice and Criminal Evidence Act 1999, it shall give its reasons for doing so.

(11) Where a person is convicted of an offence under subsection (10) above, it shall not be open to the court by or before which he is so convicted to make an order under subsection (1)(b) (conditional discharge) of section 12 of the Powers of Criminal Courts (Sentencing) Act 2000 in respect of the offence.

(12) In this section—

"British Transport Police Force" means the force of constables appointed under section 53 of the British Transport Commission Act 1949 (c xxix);

"child" and "young person" shall have the same meaning as in the Children and Young Persons Act 1933;

"the commencement date" means the date of the commencement of this section[15];

"local government area" means—

(a) in relation to England, a district or London borough, the City of London, the Isle of Wight and the Isles of Scilly;

(b) in relation to Wales, a county or county borough.

[Crime and Disorder Act 1998, s 1 as amended by the Powers of Criminal Courts (Sentencing) Act 2000, Sch 9, the Police Reform Act 2002, s 61, the Anti-social Behaviour Act 2003, s 85, SI 2004/1573 and the Serious Organised Crime and Police Act 2005, ss 140 and 142.]

---

1. The Crime and Disorder Act 1998 is reproduced partly in PART I and partly in PART III and PART V of this manual. For commencement provisions: see s 121 post.

2. PART I contains ss 1 to 27.

3. Chapter 1 contains ss 1 to 18.

4. While in some or perhaps in many cases it might worthwhile to involve the proposed defendant before a decision is made apply for an order, the authority is not required to do so; it is for it to consider whether it makes practical sense to do so (*Wareham v Purbeck District Council* [2005] EWHC 358 (Admin), 169 JP 217).

5. Where the child is in the care of a local authority which is making the application there will be a conflict of interest which will arise from its duties under s 22 of the Children Act 1989. The local authority must comply with its duty under s 22(4) of the Children Act 1989 to ascertain the child's wishes and feelings and those of a person with parental responsibility and any other relevant person. A report should be prepared for the authority by those officers discharging the authority's care duties in respect of the child but not as a report for the anti-social behaviour panel but as a report for the authority on behalf of the child. This report should be considered before an application for an ASBO is made and any decision to apply for an order should be communicated to all concerned. The social worker should not participate in the decision by the authority. Social workers for the authority should be available as witnesses if requested by the child. Save in exceptional circumstances no court should make an order without someone from social services who can speak to the issue. The solicitor with responsibility for the authority's application should not attend meeting with the child's solicitor and social services representatives and once a decision has been made to make an application there should be no contact on the issue between the team seeking the application and the social services section without the solicitor for the child being informed and consenting. Orders should contain prohibitions directed to the anti-social behaviour but care should be taken not to include negative prohibitions which amount to mandatory orders to do something: *R (M) v Sheffield Magistrates' Court* [2004] EWHC 1830 (Admin), 169 JP 557, [2005] 1 FLR 81.

6. To show that the behaviour "caused harassment (etc)" it is probably necessary to show to hear evidence from one of the harassed (etc) victims, whereas the "was likely" alternative enables police witnesses to demonstrate that there were potential victims present who it was likely were caused harassment (etc); even then it is a matter for the court to decide whether an ASBO is necessary to protect relevant persons from further anti-social acts as required by s 1(1)(b): *R (on the application of Gosport Borough Council) v Fareham Magistrates' Court* [2006] EWHC 3047 (Admin), (2006) 171 1 JP 102.

7. Sub-s (1)(a) does not require proof of intent to cause harassment etc or, where the conduct of a number of persons was involved, that a sole defendant was acting in concert with them. Where harassment, alarm or distress were caused by a number of people, including the defendant, it does not require proof that the defendant's conduct of its own should have been of a sufficiently aggravated nature to cause harassment, alarm or distress or, if not, that she should have in some way shared responsibility with the others for their aggravated conduct. Therefore, on the facts, an anti-social behaviour order could apply to the activities of a street prostitute (*Chief Constable of Lancashire v Potter* [2003] 42 LS Gaz R 31, QBD).

The court is able to receive evidence of acts committed before the beginning of the limitation period of 6 months specified in s 127 of the Magistrates' Courts Act 1980 in relation to both limbs: *R (on the application of Chief Constable of West Mercia Constabulary) v Boorman* [2005] EWHC Admin 2559, (2005) 169 JP 669. However, "if, for instance, the pre-period behaviour was so outrageous, so dramatic that it put into the shadow some less serious behaviour committed within-time, then it might well be that it would be quite wrong to consider it; there would be the danger of an effective circumvention of the limitation period" (*R (on the application of Chief Constable of West Mercia Constabularly) v Boorman*, supra, at para 13).

8. The hearing of a complaint in relation to an anti-social behaviour order is before the adult court but (except in the case of interim orders) all practicable steps should be taken to constitute such a court with justices qualified to sit in the youth court, see the *Practice Direction (Magistrates' Courts: Anti-Social Behaviour Orders: Composition of Benches)*, in this PART: STATUTORY INSTRUMENTS AND PRACTICE DIRECTIONS ON PROCEDURE, post.

9. The date of the order is the date on which it is pronounced in court and not the date on which the document comes into existence as a result of the pronouncement (*R (on the application of Walking) v DPP* [2003] EWHC Admin 3139, (2004) 168 JP 65).

Proceedings under s 1(1) are civil, not criminal, both as a matter of domestic law and for the purposes of art 6, their true purpose being preventative, accordingly, hearsay evidence is admissible; magistrates must, however, apply, in relation to s 1(1)(a), the criminal standard of proof, though the inquiry under s 1(1)(b) does not involve a standard of proof but is an exercise of judgment or evaluation (*R (on the application of McCann) v Crown Court at Manchester, Clingham v Kensington and Chelsea Royal London Borough Council* [2002] UKHL 39, [2003] 1 AC 787, [2002] 4 All ER 593, [2002] 3 WLR 1313). Evidence of a police officer of complaints made to him about the behaviour of the defendant is hearsay but is admissible in accordance with the provisions of the Civil Evidence Act 1995. The fact that some of the evidence is hearsay, without the possibility of cross-examination does not have the automatic result that the trial is not a fair trial as art 6(1) of the European Convention on Human Rights requires. The court will have to consider what weight to give to the evidence in the light of the criticisms which can be made of hearsay evidence *(R v Marylebone Magistrates' Court, ex p C* [2001] EWHC Admin 1, 165 JP 322).

A term preventing a person from leaving or travelling between specified premises during specified periods satisfies the requirement that an anti-social behaviour order should be substantially prohibitory in nature: *R (Lonergan) v Crown Court at Lewes (Secretary of State for the Home Department intervening)* [2005] EWHC 457 (Admin), [2005] 2 All ER 362, [2005] 1 WLR 2570.

As to the circumstances in which an order should be made under s 39 of the Children and Young Persons Act 1933 preventing the identification of a child or young person involved in proceedings for an anti-social behaviour order, see para **5–23** post and *R (on the application of T) v Crown Court at St Albans* [2002] EWHC 1129 (Admin), [2002] All ER (D) 308 (May), [2002] JPN 478 (evidence as to the effect of publicity on an offender's family is not, prima facie, a relevant matter).

Post ASBO publicity It is implicit in the terms of the 1998 Act that there is power for the police and the local authority to publicize the making of an ASBO, its terms and the person to whom it applies. Publicity may be aimed at achieving the following objects: to inform, to reassure, to assist in enforcing the existing orders by policing and to inhibit the behaviour of those against whom the orders have been made, or to deter others. However, such publicity may infringe the rights of the person concerned under article 8.1 of the Human Rights Convention especially if photographs are used. The authorities should therefore consider the Convention rights of those against whom orders are made, and of the wider public (including past and potential victims of anti-social behaviour) and if this is recorded, it should then be clear that the publicity is confined to what is reasonable and proportionate, and the possibility of judicial review should be eliminated (*R (on the application of Stanley, Marshall and Kelly) v Metropolitan Police Comr* [2004] EWHC 2229 (Admin), 168 JP 623).

10. Although the statute requires the ASBO to be substantially and not just formally prohibitory, a restraint upon leaving or travelling between specified premises between particular times meets that test, and there is nothing legally objectionable in the making of a curfew provision in an ASBO if it is necessary for protection: *R (on the application of Lonergan) v Lewes Crown Court* [2005] EWHC 457 (Admin), [2005] All ER (D) 382 (Mar).

A prohibition from "committing any criminal offence" is too wide and is consequently invalid: *R (on the application of W) v DPP* [2005] EDWCA Civ 1333, (2005) 169 JP 435. Similarly, a provision "not to act in an anti-social manner" is too wide; however, a court order is valid until it is set aside on appeal, and an alleged breach must be considered even though the prohibition said to have been breached would be liable to be struck out on appeal: *CPS v T* [2006] EWHC 728 (Admin), (2006) 170 JP 470.

However, a prohibition from carrying any knife or bladed article in a public place, which was intended to cover behaviour which was not caught by the criminal law (ie carrying penknives that might be less than 3 inches long) was lawful; similarly, a prohibition from associating with another where there was no reciprocal prohibition in relation to that other was lawful where the person subject to the order behaved in an anti-social manner when in that other's company: *Hills v Chief Constable of Essex* [2006] EWHC 2633 (Admin), [2007] 171 JP 14.

11. The Magistrates' Courts (Anti-social Behaviour Orders) Rules 2002, this PART, post, provide forms in relation to

anti-social behaviour orders under s 1 and interim orders under s 1D of this Act and make provision for applications to vary or discharge such orders. For orders made on conviction in criminal proceedings, see s 1C, post.

12. The order is, however, the order pronounced in court, and the order is not invalid if the document subsequently served is at variance with the former and states a period of less than two years: *Walking v DPP* [2003] EWHC 3139 (Admin), (2004) 168 JP 65.

13. A defence of ignorance or misunderstanding of the terms of an ASBO is not an impermissible reliance on an error of law but a question of fact and a value judgement as to its reasonableness. Accordingly, in the Crown Court, except where the case is so clear, it will usually be for the jury to decide whether the defence is made out and a defendant should not be deprived of the opportunity to present his defence at the trial: *R v Nicholson* [2006] EWCA Crim 1518, [2006] 1 WLR 2857, [2006] 2 Cr App R 30, 170 JP 573.

14. For procedure in respect of this offence which is triable either way, see the Magistrates' Court Act 1980, ss 17A–21, this PART ante.

Where an ABSO contains a term that is "plainly invalid", but the defendant does not appeal or seek a variation of the order and he is returned to court for breaching the term, it had been held in *R (on the application of W) v DPP*, supra, that, applying the propositions propounded by the House of Lords in relation to the vires of byelaws (*Boddington v British Transport Police* [1999] 2 AC 143), the court could consider submissions on validity and should have done so in the present case. However, in the subsequent decision in *DPP v T* [2006] EWHC 728 (Admin), [2006] 3 All ER 471, [2007] 1 WLR 209, [2006] 3 FCR 183, which concerned a provision "not to act in an anti-social manner", it was held, first, that the normal rule in relation to an order of the court was that it had to be treated as valid and be obeyed unless and until it was set aside. Even if the order should not have been made in the first place, a person might be liable for any breach of it committed before it was set aside. Secondly, the person against whom an ASBO was made had a full opportunity to challenge that order on appeal or to apply to vary it. During the intervening period it could not be treated as a nullity and of no legal effect. The policy consideration that the magistrates' court had jurisdiction to determine issues of the validity of a byelaw or an administrative decision was wholly absent when the issue was the validity of the order of the court. Thus, it had not been open to the district judge, as a matter of jurisdiction, to rule that the original order was invalid. He had been entitled, however, to consider whether the provision lacked sufficient clarity to warrant a finding that the respondent's conduct amounted to a breach of the order; whether the lack of clarity provided a reasonable excuse for non-compliance with the order; and whether, if a breach was established, it was appropriate in the circumstances to impose any penalty for the breach.

An order is to be treated as a valid order unless and until it is varied; but where the breach relates to a prohibition that is plainly invalid because it is too wide the court can consider submissions to that effect just in the same way that the court can consider submissions concerning the vires of a byelaw without the need for prior or concurrent proceedings in the High Court for the purpose of identifying and declaring the order's invalidity: *R (on the application of W) v DPP*, supra.

15. Ie 1 April 1999 (SI 1998/3263).

1–3804A 1A. Power of Secretary of State to add to relevant authorities. (1) The Secretary of State may by order provide that the chief officer of a body of constables maintained otherwise than by a police authority is, in such cases and circumstances as may be prescribed by the order, to be a relevant authority for the purposes of section 1 above.

(2) The Secretary of State may by order[1]—

(a) provide that a person or body of any other description specified in the order is, in such cases and circumstances as may be prescribed by the order, to be a relevant authority for the purposes of such of sections 1 above and 1B, 1CA and 1E below as are specified in the order; and

(b) prescribe the description of persons who are to be "relevant persons" in relation to that person or body.

[Crime and Disorder Act 1998, s 1A as inserted by the Police Reform Act 2002, s 62(1) and amended by the Serious Organised Crime and Police Act 2005, s 139.]

1. The Crime and Disorder Act 1998 (Relevant Authorities and Relevant Persons) Order 2006, SI 2006/2137 has been made which provides for the Environment Agency and Transport for London to be relevant authorities.

1–3804AA 1AA. Individual support orders. (1) Where a court makes an anti-social behaviour order in respect of a defendant who is a child or young person when that order is made, it must consider whether the individual support conditions are fulfilled.

(2) If it is satisfied that those conditions are fulfilled, the court must make an order under this section ("an individual support order") which—

(a) requires the defendant to comply, for a period not exceeding six months, with such requirements as are specified in the order; and

(b) requires the defendant to comply with any directions given by the responsible officer with a view to the implementation of the requirements under paragraph (a) above.

(3) The individual support conditions are—

(a) that an individual support order would be desirable in the interests of preventing any repetition of the kind of behaviour which led to the making of the anti-social behaviour order;

(b) that the defendant is not already subject to an individual support order; and

(c) that the court has been notified[1] by the Secretary of State that arrangements for implementing individual support orders are available in the area in which it appears to it that the defendant resides or will reside and the notice has not been withdrawn.

(4) If the court is not satisfied that the individual support conditions are fulfilled, it shall state in open court that it is not so satisfied and why it is not.

(5) The requirements that may be specified under subsection (2)(a) above are those that the court considers desirable in the interests of preventing any repetition of the kind of behaviour which led to the making of the anti-social behaviour order.

(6) Requirements included in an individual support order, or directions given under such an order by a responsible officer, may require the defendant to do all or any of the following things—

(*a*) to participate in activities specified in the requirements or directions at a time or times so specified;

(*b*) to present himself to a person or persons so specified at a place or places and at a time or times so specified;

(*c*) to comply with any arrangements for his education so specified.

(7) But requirements included in, or directions given under, such an order may not require the defendant to attend (whether at the same place or at different places) on more than two days in any week; and "week" here means a period of seven days beginning with a Sunday.

(8) Requirements included in, and directions given under, an individual support order shall, as far as practicable, be such as to avoid—

(*a*) any conflict with the defendant's religious beliefs; and

(*b*) any interference with the times, if any, at which he normally works or attends school or any other educational establishment.

(9) Before making an individual support order, the court shall obtain from a social worker of a local authorityor a member of a youth offending team any information which it considers necessary in order—

(*a*) to determine whether the individual support conditions are fulfilled, or

(*b*) to determine what requirements should be imposed by an individual support order if made,

and shall consider that information.

(10) In this section and section 1AB below "responsible officer", in relation to an individual support order, means one of the following who is specified in the order, namely—

(*a*) a social worker of a local authority;

(*b*) a person nominated by a person appointed as chief education officer under section 532 of the Education Act 1996 (c 56);

(*c*) a member of a youth offending team.

[Crime and Disorder Act 1998, s 1AA as inserted by the Criminal Justice Act 2003, s 322 and amended by the Children Act 2004, Sch 5.]

---

1. Notification by the Secretary of State that arrangements for implementing individual support orders were available to all magistrates' courts as from 1 May 2004 has been given by HOC 25/2004.

1–3804AB   1AB. Individual support orders: explanation, breach, amendment etc. (1) Before making an individual support order, the court shall explain to the defendant in ordinary language—

(*a*) the effect of the order and of the requirements proposed to be included in it;

(*b*) the consequences which may follow (under subsection (3) below) if he fails to comply with any of those requirements; and

(*c*) that the court has power (under subsection (6) below) to review the order on the application either of the defendant or of the responsible officer.

(2) The power of the Secretary of State under section 174(4) of the Criminal Justice Act 2003 includes power by order to—

(*a*) prescribe cases in which subsection (1) above does not apply; and

(*b*) prescribe cases in which the explanation referred to in that subsection may be made in the absence of the defendant, or may be provided in written form.

(3) If the person in respect of whom an individual support order is made fails without reasonable excuse to comply with any requirement included in the order, he is guilty of an offence and liable on summary conviction to a fine not exceeding—

(*a*) if he is aged 14 or over at the date of his conviction, £1,000;

(*b*) if he is aged under 14 then, £250.

(4) No referral order under section 16(2) or (3) of the Powers of Criminal Courts (Sentencing) Act 2000 (referral of young offenders to youth offender panels) may be made in respect of an offence under subsection (3) above.

(5) If the anti-social behaviour order as a result of which an individual support order was made ceases to have effect, the individual support order (if it has not previously ceased to have effect) ceases to have effect when the anti-social behaviour order does.

(6) On an application made by complaint by—

(*a*) the person subject to an individual support order, or

(*b*) the responsible officer,

the court which made the individual support order may vary or discharge it by a further order.

(7) If the anti-social behaviour order as a result of which an individual support order was made is varied, the court varying the anti-social behaviour order may by a further order vary or discharge the individual support order.]

[Crime and Disorder Act 1998, s 1AB as inserted by the Criminal Justice Act 2003, s 322.]

1–3804B   1B. Orders in county court proceedings. (1) This section applies to any proceedings in a county court ("the principal proceedings").

(2) If a relevant authority—

(a) is a party to the principal proceedings, and

(b) considers that a party to those proceedings is a person in relation to whom it would be reasonable for it to make an application under section 1,

it may make an application in those proceedings for an order under subsection (4).

(3) If a relevant authority—

(a) is not a party to the principal proceedings, and

(b) considers that a party to those proceedings is a person in relation to whom it would be reasonable for it to make an application under section 1,

it may make an application to be joined to those proceedings to enable it to apply for an order under subsection (4) and, if it is so joined, may apply for such an order.*

(3A) Subsection (3B) applies if a relevant authority is a party to the principal proceedings and considers—

(a) that a person who is not a party to the proceedings has acted in an anti-social manner, and

(b) that the person's anti-social acts are material in relation to the principal proceedings.*

(3B) The relevant authority may—

(a) make an application for the person mentioned in subsection (3A)(a) to be joined to the principal proceedings to enable an order under subsection (4) to be made in relation to that person;

(b) if that person is so joined, apply for an order under subsection (4).*

(3C) But a person must not be joined to proceedings in pursuance of subsection (3B) unless his anti-social acts are material in relation to the principal proceedings.*

(4) If, on an application for an order under this subsection, it is proved that the conditions mentioned in section 1(1) are fulfilled as respects that other party, the court may make an order which prohibits him from doing anything described in the order.

(5) Subject to subsection (6), the person against whom an order under this section has been made and the relevant authority on whose application that order was made may apply to the county court which made an order under this section for it to be varied or discharged by a further order.

(6) Except with the consent of the relevant authority and the person subject to the order, no order under this section shall be discharged before the end of the period of two years beginning with the date of service of the order.

(7) Subsections (5) to (7) and (10) to (12) of section 1 apply for the purposes of the making and effect of orders made under this section as they apply for the purposes of the making and effect of anti-social behaviour orders.

[Crime and Disorder Act 1998, s 1B as inserted by the Police Reform Act 2002, s 63 and amended by the Anti-social Behaviour Act 2003, s 85.]

---

*New sub-ss (3A)–(3C) in force in so far as relating to persons aged 18 or over and in relation to applications for orders made at certain specified county courts, for remaining purposes from a date to be appointed.

1–3804C   **1C. Orders on conviction in criminal proceedings[1].** (1) This section applies where a person (the "offender") is convicted of a relevant offence.

(2) If the court considers—

(a) that the offender has acted, at any time since the commencement date, in an anti-social manner, that is to say in a manner that caused or was likely to cause harassment, alarm or distress to one or more persons not of the same household as himself, and

(b) that an order[2] under this section is necessary[3] to protect persons in any place in England and Wales from further anti-social acts by him,

it may make an order which prohibits the offender from doing anything described in the order.

(3) The court may make an order under this section—

(a) if the prosecutor asks it to do so, or

(b) if the court thinks it is appropriate to do so.

(3A) For the purpose of deciding whether to make an order under this section the court may consider evidence led by the prosecution and the defence.

(3B) It is immaterial whether evidence led in pursuance of subsection (3A) would have been admissible in the proceedings in which the offender was convicted.

(4) An order under this section shall not be made except—

(a) in addition to a sentence imposed in respect of the relevant offence; or

(b) in addition to an order discharging him conditionally.

(4A) The court may adjourn any proceedings in relation to an order under this section even after sentencing the offender.

(4B) If the offender does not appear for any adjourned proceedings, the court may further adjourn the proceedings or may issue a warrant for his arrest.

(4C) But the court may not issue a warrant for the offender's arrest unless it is satisfied that he has had adequate notice of the time and place of the adjourned proceedings.

(5) An order under this section takes effect on the day on which it is made, but the court may

provide in any such order that such requirements of the order as it may specify shall, during any period when the offender is detained in legal custody, be suspended until his release from that custody.

(6)–(8) *Repealed.*

(9) Subsections (7), (10, (10C), (10D), (10E) and (11) of section 1 apply for the purposes of the making and effect of orders made by virtue of this section as they apply for the purposes of the making and effect of anti-social behaviour orders.

(9A) The council for the local government area in which a person in respect of whom an anti-social behaviour order has been made resides or appears to reside may bring proceedings under section 1(10) (as applied by subsection (9) above) for breach of an order under subsection (2) above.

(9B) Subsection (9C) applies in relation to proceedings in which an order under subsection (2) is made against a child or young person who is convicted of an offence.

(9C) In so far as the proceedings relate to the making of the order—

(a) section 49 of the Children and Young Persons Act 1933 (c 12) (restrictions on reports of proceedings in which children and young persons are concerned) does not apply in respect of the child or young person against whom the order is made;

(b) section 39 of that Act (power to prohibit publication of certain matter) does so apply.

(10) In this section—

"child" and "young person" have the same meaning as in the Children and Young Persons Act 1933 (c 12)

"the commencement date" has the same meaning as in section 1 above;

"the court" in relation to an offender means—

(a) the court by or before which he is convicted of the relevant offence; or

(b) if he is committed to the Crown Court to be dealt with for that offence, the Crown Court; and

"relevant offence" means an offence committed after the coming into force of section 64 of the Police Reform Act 2002 (c 30).

[Crime and Disorder Act 1998, s 1C as inserted by the Police Reform Act 2002, s 64, and amended by the Anti-social Behaviour Act 2003, s 86 and the Serious Organised Crime and Police Act 2005, ss 139–141.]

---

1. See paras **3–210 Order made under s 1C of the Crime and Disorder Act 1998** and **5–44A Order made under s 1C of the Crime and Disorder Act 1998**.

2. There is no harm, so far as minor offences are concerned, in the court reminding offenders that certain matters constitute criminal conduct by the order containing terms which prohibit conduct which would amount to specific offences under the criminal law, but the Court of Appeal would only encourage the inclusion of comparatively minor criminal offences in the terms of such orders: *R v Parkin* [2004] EWCA Crim 287, [2004] 2 Cr App Rep (S) 343, [2004] Crim LR 490.

3. Where a custodial sentence is passed in excess of a few months and the offender is liable to be released on licence, the circumstances will be limited in which it will be demonstrated that an order under this section is required although there may be circumstances in which geographical restrictions imposed by an order may usefully supplement licence conditions: *R v Parkin* [2004] EWCA Crim 287, [2004] 2 Cr App Rep (S) 343, [2004] Crim LR 490. Making an order for the object of increasing the penalty for future offences is not permissible. Such an order should not be a normal part of sentencing particularly where the offences are not themselves specifically involving harassment, alarm or distress: *R v Kirby* [2005] EWCA Crim 1228, [2005] Crim LR 732.

1–3804CA   1CA. Variation and discharge of orders under section 1C.   (1) An offender subject to an order under section 1C may apply to the court which made it for it to be varied or discharged.

(2) If he does so, he must also send written notice of his application to the Director of Public Prosecutions.

(3) The Director of Public Prosecutions may apply to the court which made an order under section 1C for it to be varied or discharged.

(4) A relevant authority may also apply to the court which made an order under section 1C for it to be varied or discharged if it appears to it that—

(a) in the case of variation, the protection of relevant persons from anti-social acts by the person subject to the order would be more appropriately effected by a variation of the order;

(b) in the case of discharge, that it is no longer necessary to protect relevant persons from anti-social acts by him by means of such an order.

(5) If the Director of Public Prosecutions or a relevant authority applies for the variation or discharge of an order under section 1C, he or it must also send written notice of the application to the person subject to the order.

(6) In the case of an order under section 1C made by a magistrates' court, the references in subsections (1), (3) and (4) to the court by which the order was made include a reference to any magistrates' court acting in the same local justice area as that court.

(7) No order under section 1C shall be discharged on an application under this section before the end of the period of two years beginning with the day on which the order takes effect, unless—

(a) in the case of an application under subsection (1), the Director of Public Prosecutions consents, or

(b) in the case of an application under subsection (3) or (4), the offender consents.

[Crime and Disorder Act 1998, s 1CA as inserted by the Serious Organised Crime and Police Act 2005, s 140.]

1–3804D   1D. Interim orders¹. (1) This section applies where—

(a)   an application is made for an anti-social behaviour order;

(b)   an application is made for an order under section 1B;

(c)   a request is made by the prosecution for an order under section 1C; or

(d)   the court is minded to make an order under section 1C of its own motion.

(2) If, before determining the application or request, or before deciding whether to make an order under section 1C of its own motion, the court considers that it is just to make an order under this section pending the determination of that application or request or before making that decision, it may make such an order.

(3) An order under this section is an order which prohibits the defendant from doing anything described in the order.

(4) An order under this section—

(a)   shall be for a fixed period;

(b)   may be varied, renewed or discharged;

(c)   shall, if it has not previously ceased to have effect, cease to have effect on the determination of the application or request mentioned in subsection (1), or on the court's making a decision as to whether or not to make an order under section 1C of its own motion.

(5) In relation to cases to which this section applies by virtue of paragraph (a) or (b) of subsection (1), subsections (6), (8) and (10) to (12) of section 1 apply for the purposes of the making and effect of orders under this section as they apply for the purposes of the making and effect of anti-social behaviour orders.

(6) In relation to cases to which this section applies by virtue of paragraph (c) or (d) of subsection (1)—

(a)   subsections (6) and (10) to (12) of section 1 apply for the purposes of the making and effect of orders under this section as they apply for the purposes of the making and effect of anti-social behaviour orders; and

(b)   section 1CA applies for the purposes of the variation or discharge of an order under this section as it applies for the purposes of the variation or discharge of an order under section 1C.

[Crime and Disorder Act 1998, s 1D as inserted by the Police Reform Act 2002, s 66 and amended by the Serious Organised Crime and Police Act 2005, s 139.]

1. The Magistrates' Courts (Anti-social Behaviour Orders) Rules 2002, this PART, post make provision for procedure and forms in relation to interim anti-social behaviour orders under s 1D of this Act.

2. The procedure for making a without notice interim ASBO in accordance with r 5 of the Magistrates' Courts (Anti-Social Behaviour Orders) Rules 2002, SI 2002/2784 is lawful and does not engage art 6(1) of the European Convention on Human Rights. The criterion for the decision whether to make an interim order is whether it is just to do so which involves consideration of all relevant circumstances, including the fact that the application has been made without notice: *R (on the application of M) v Secretary of State for Constitutional Affairs and Lord Chancellor* [2004] EWCA Civ 312, [2004] 2 All ER 531, [2004] 1 WLR 2298, 168 JP 529 (affirming the decision at first instance which additionally held that in the balancing exercise protection of the public should be weighed against impact on the individual. Considerations which weigh in favour of an order must be sufficiently serious and in the case of an individual under 18 the young person's best interests are a primary consideration when considering whether it is just to make an order: *R (on the application of Kenny) v Leeds Magistrates' Court* [2003] EWHC 2963 (Admin), [2004] 1 All ER 1333, 168 JP 125).

1–3804E   1E. Consultation requirements. (1) This section applies to—

(a)   applications for an anti-social behaviour order; and

(b)   applications for an order under section 1B.

(2) Before making an application to which this section applies, the council for a local government area shall consult the chief officer of police of the police force maintained for the police area within which that local government area lies.

(3) Before making an application to which this section applies, a chief officer of police shall consult the council for the local government area in which the person in relation to whom the application is to be made resides or appears to reside.

(4) Before making an application to which this section applies, a relevant authority other than a council for a local government area or a chief officer of police shall consult—

(a)   the council for the local government area in which the person in relation to whom the application is to be made resides or appears to reside; and

(b)   the chief officer of police of the police force maintained for the police area within which that local government area lies.

(5) Subsection (4)(a) does not apply if the relevant authority is a county council for a county in which there are no districts.

[Crime and Disorder Act 1998, s 1E as inserted by the Police Reform Act 2002, s 66, and amended by the Anti-social Behaviour Act 2003, s 85.]

1–3804F   1F. Contracting out of local authority functions. *Power of Secretary of State to authorise by order a relevant authority to contract out functions.*

1–3804G   1G. Intervention orders.   (1) This section applies if, in relation to a person who has attained the age of 18, a relevant authority—

(*a*)   makes an application for an anti-social behaviour order or an order under section 1B above (the behaviour order),

(*b*)   has obtained from an appropriately qualified person a report relating to the effect on the person's behaviour of the misuse of controlled drugs or of such other factors as the Secretary of State by order prescribes, and

(*c*)   has engaged in consultation with such persons as the Secretary of State by order[1] prescribes for the purpose of ascertaining that, if the report recommends that an order under this section is made, appropriate activities will be available.

(2) The relevant authority may make an application to the court which is considering the application for the behaviour order for an order under this section (an intervention order).

(3) If the court—

(*a*)   makes the behaviour order, and

(*b*)   is satisfied that the relevant conditions are met,

it may also make an intervention order.

(4) The relevant conditions are—

(*a*)   that an intervention order is desirable in the interests of preventing a repetition of the behaviour which led to the behaviour order being made (trigger behaviour);

(*b*)   that appropriate activities relating to the trigger behaviour or its cause are available for the defendant;

(*c*)   that the defendant is not (at the time the intervention order is made) subject to another intervention order or to any other treatment relating to the trigger behaviour or its cause (whether on a voluntary basis or by virtue of a requirement imposed in pursuance of any enactment);

(*d*)   that the court has been notified by the Secretary of State that arrangements for implementing intervention orders are available in the area in which it appears that the defendant resides or will reside and the notice has not been withdrawn.

(5) An intervention order is an order which—

(*a*)   requires the defendant to comply, for a period not exceeding six months, with such requirements as are specified in the order, and

(*b*)   requires the defendant to comply with any directions given by a person authorised to do so under the order with a view to the implementation of the requirements under paragraph (a) above.

(6) An intervention order or directions given under the order may require the defendant—

(*a*)   to participate in the activities specified in the requirement or directions at a time or times so specified;

(*b*)   to present himself to a person or persons so specified at a time or times so specified.

(7) Requirements included in, or directions given under, an intervention order must, as far as practicable, be such as to avoid—

(*a*)   any conflict with the defendant's religious beliefs, and

(*b*)   any interference with the times (if any) at which he normally works or attends an educational establishment.

(8) If the defendant fails to comply with a requirement included in or a direction given under an intervention order, the person responsible for the provision or supervision of appropriate activities under the order must inform the relevant authority of that fact.

(9) The person responsible for the provision or supervision of appropriate activities is a person of such description as is prescribed by order[1] made by the Secretary of State.

(10) In this section—

"appropriate activities" means such activities, or activities of such a description, as are prescribed by order[1] made by the Secretary of State for the purposes of this section;

"appropriately qualified person" means a person who has such qualifications or experience as the Secretary of State by order[1] prescribes;

"controlled drug" has the same meaning as in the Misuse of Drugs Act 1971;

"relevant authority" means a relevant authority for the purposes of section 1 above.

(11) An order under this section made by the Secretary of State may make different provision for different purposes.

(12) This section and section 1H below apply to a person in respect of whom a behaviour order has been made subject to the following modifications—

(*a*)   in subsection (1) above paragraph (a) must be ignored;

(*b*)   in subsection (2) above, for "is considering the application for" substitute "made";

(*c*)   in subsection (3) above paragraph (a), the word "and" following it and the word "also" must be ignored.]

[Crime and Disorder Act 1998, s 1G as inserted by the Drugs Act 2005, s 20.]

---

1. The Crime and Disorder Act 1998 (Intervention Orders) Order 2006, SI 2006/2138 has been made.

1–3804H   1H. Intervention orders: explanation, breach, amendment etc.   (1) Before making an intervention order the court must explain to the defendant in ordinary language—

    (a) the effect of the order and of the requirements proposed to be included in it,

    (b) the consequences which may follow (under subsection (3) below) if he fails to comply with any of those requirements, and

    (c) that the court has power (under subsection (5) below) to review the order on the application either of the defendant or of the relevant authority.

(2) The power of the Secretary of State under section 174(4) of the Criminal Justice Act 2003 includes power by order to—

    (a) prescribe cases in which subsection (1) does not apply, and

    (b) prescribe cases in which the explanation referred to in that subsection may be made in the absence of the defendant, or may be provided in written form.

(3) If a person in respect of whom an intervention order is made fails without reasonable excuse to comply with any requirement included in the order he is guilty of an offence and liable on summary conviction to a fine not exceeding level 4 on the standard scale.

(4) If the behaviour order as a result of which an intervention order is made ceases to have effect, the intervention order (if it has not previously ceased to have effect) ceases to have effect when the behaviour order does.

(5) On an application made by—

    (a) a person subject to an intervention order, or

    (b) the relevant authority,

the court which made the intervention order may vary or discharge it by a further order.

(6) An application under subsection (5) made to a magistrates' court must be made by complaint.

(7) If the behaviour order as a result of which an intervention order was made is varied, the court varying the behaviour order may by a further order vary or discharge the intervention order.

(8) Expressions used in this section and in section 1G have the same meaning in this section as in that section.

[Crime and Disorder Act 1998, s 1H as inserted by the Drugs Act 2005, s 20.]

1–3804I   1I. Special measures for witnesses.   (1) This section applies to the following proceedings—

    (a) any proceedings in a magistrates' court on an application for an anti-social behaviour order,

    (b) any proceedings in a magistrates' court or the Crown Court so far as relating to the issue whether to make an order under section 1C, and

    (c) any proceedings in a magistrates' court so far as relating to the issue whether to make an order under section 1D.

(2) Chapter 1 of Part 2 of the Youth Justice and Criminal Evidence Act 1999 (special measures directions in the case of vulnerable and intimidated witnesses) shall apply in relation to any such proceedings as it applies in relation to criminal proceedings, but with—

    (a) the omission of the provisions of that Act mentioned in subsection (3) (which make provision appropriate only in the context of criminal proceedings), and

    (b) any other necessary modifications.

(3) The provisions are—

    (a) section 17(4),

    (b) section 21(1)(b) and (5) to (7),

    (c) section 22(1)(b) and (2)(b) and (c),

    (d) section 27(10), and

    (e) section 32.

(4) Any rules of court made under or for the purposes of Chapter 1 of Part 2 of that Act shall apply in relation to proceedings to which this section applies—

    (a) to such extent as may be provided by rules of court, and

    (b) subject to such modifications as may be so provided.

(5) Section 47 of that Act (restrictions on reporting special measures directions etc) applies, with any necessary modifications, in relation to—

    (a) a direction under section 19 of the Act as applied by this section, or

    (b) a direction discharging or varying such a direction,

and sections 49 and 51 of that Act (offences) apply accordingly.

[Crime and Disorder Act 1998, s 1I as inserted by the Serious Organised Crime and Police Act 2005, s 143.]

1–3805   2. Sex offender orders.   *Repealed.*

1–3805A   2A. Interim orders: sex offenders.   *Repealed.*

1–3805B   2B. Sex offender orders made in Scotland or Northern Ireland.   *Repealed.*

1–3806   3. Sex offender orders: supplemental.   *Repealed.*

1–3807   4. Appeals against orders.   (1) An appeal shall lie to the Crown Court against the making by a magistrates' court of an anti-social behaviour order, an individual support order, an order under section 1D above.

(2) On such an appeal the Crown Court—

(a) may make such orders as may be necessary to give effect to its determination of the appeal; and

(b) may also make such incidental or consequential orders as appear to it to be just.

(3) Any order of the Crown Court made on an appeal under this section (other than one directing that an application be re-heard by a magistrates' court) shall, for the purposes of section 1(8), 1AB(6) be treated as if it were an order of the magistrates' court from which the appeal was brought and not an order of the Crown Court.

[Crime and Disorder Act 1998, s 4 as amended by the Police Reform Act 2002, ss 65 and 68 and the Sexual Offences Act 2003, Schs 6 and 7.]

1–3808   5. Authorities responsible for strategies.   (1) Subject to the provisions of this section, the functions conferred by section 6 below shall be exercisable in relation to each local government area[1] by the responsible authorities, that is to say—

(a) the council for the area and, where the area is a district and the council is not a unitary authority, the council for the county which includes the district;

(b) every chief officer of police any part of whose police area lies within the area;

(c) every police authority any part of whose police area so lies;

(d) every fire and rescue authority any part of whose area so lies;

(e) if the local government area is in England, every Primary Care Trust the whole or any part of whose area so lies; and

(f) if the local government area is in Wales, every health authority the whole or any part of whose area so lies.

(1A) The Secretary of State may by order[2] provide in relation to any two or more local government areas in England—

(a) that the functions conferred by sections 6 to 7 below are to be carried out in relation to those areas taken together as if they constituted only one area; and

(b) that the persons who for the purposes of this Chapter are to be taken to be responsible authorities in relation to the combined area are the persons who comprise every person who (apart from the order) would be a responsible authority in relation to any one or more of the areas included in the combined area.

(1B) The Secretary of State shall not make an order under subsection (1A) above unless—

(a) an application for the order has been made jointly by all the persons who would be the responsible authorities in relation to the combined area or the Secretary of State has first consulted those persons; and

(b) he considers it would be in the interests of reducing crime and disorder, or of combatting the misuse of drugs, to make the order.

(2) In exercising those functions, the responsible authorities shall act in co-operation with the following persons and bodies, namely—

(a) *revoked*;

(b) every local probation board any part of whose area lies within the area;

(c) every person or body of a description which is for the time being prescribed by order[1] of the Secretary of State under this subsection; and

(d) where they are acting in relation to an area in Wales, every person or body which is of a description which is for the time being prescribed by an order under this subsection of the National Assembly for Wales;

and it shall be the duty of those persons and bodies to co-operate in the exercise by the responsible authorities of those functions.

(3) The responsible authorities shall also invite the participation in their exercise of those functions of at least one person or body of each description which is for the time being prescribed by order[3] of the Secretary of State under this subsection and, in the case of the responsible authorities for an area in Wales, of any person or body of a description for the time being prescribed by an order under this subsection of the National Assembly for Wales.

(4) In this section and sections 6 and 7 below "local government area" means—

(a) in relation to England, each district or London borough, the City of London, the Isle of Wight and the Isles of Scilly;

(b) in relation to Wales, each county or county borough.

(5) In this section—

"fire and rescue authority" means—

(a) a fire and rescue authority constituted by a scheme under section 2 of the Fire and Rescue Services Act 2004 or a scheme to which section 4 of that Act applies;

(b) a metropolitan county fire and rescue authority; or

(c) the London Fire and Emergency Planning Authority; and

"police authority" means—

(a) any police authority established under section 3 of the Police Act 1996 (c 16); or

(b) the Metropolitan Police Authority.

[Crime and Disorder Act 1998, s 5 as amended by SI 2000/90, the Criminal Justice and Court Services Act 2000, Sch 7, the Police Reform Act 2002, ss 63, 97 and s 107, the Fire and Rescue Services Act 2004, Sch 1 and the Civil Contingencies Act 2004, Sch 2.]

1. "Section 5(1) shall have effect in relation to a local government area in England at any time when that area or a part of it comprises or contains an area that is not included in the area of a Primary Care Trust, as if the reference to a Primary Care Trust the whole or part of whose area lies within the local government area included a reference to any health authority or strategic health authority whose area comprises or includes the area for which there is no Primary Care Trust." (Police Reform Act 2002, s 97(15)).

2. The Crime and Disorder Act 1998 (Responsible Authorities) Order 2005, SI 2005/1789 and the Crime and Disorder Act 1998 (Responsible Authorities) (No 2) Order 2005, SI 2005/3343 have been made.

3. The Crime and Disorder Strategies (Prescribed Descriptions) Order 1998, SI 1998/2452 amended by SI 1998/2513, SI 1999/483, SI 2000/300 and SI 2005/2929 (revoked to the extent that it applies to England) and the Crime and Disorder Strategies (Prescribed Descriptions) (England) Order 2004, SI 2004/118 have been made.

1–3809　6. Formulation and implementation of strategies.　(1) The responsible authorities for a local government area shall, in accordance with the provisions of section 5 above and this section, formulate and implement, for each relevant period,

(a) in the case of an area in England—

(i) a strategy for the reduction of crime and disorder in the area; and

(ii) a strategy for combatting the misuse of drugs in the area;

and

(b) in the case of an area in Wales—

(i) a strategy for the reduction of crime and disorder in the area; and

(ii) a strategy for combatting substance misuse in the area.

(1A) In determining what matters to include or not to include in their strategy for combatting substance misuse, the responsible authorities for an area in Wales shall have regard to any guidance issued for the purposes of this section by the National Assembly for Wales.

(2) Before formulating a strategy, the responsible authorities shall—

(a) carry out, taking due account of the knowledge and experience of persons in the area, a review—

(i) in the case of an area in England, of the levels and patterns of crime and disorder in the area and of the level and patterns of the misuse of drugs in the area; and

(ii) in the case of an area in Wales, of the levels and patterns of crime and disorder in the area and of the level and patterns of substance misuse in the area;*

(b) prepare an analysis of the results of that review;

(c) publish in the area a report of that analysis; and

(d) obtain the views on that report of persons or bodies in the area (including those of a description prescribed by order under section 5(3) above), whether by holding public meetings or otherwise.

(3) In formulating a strategy, the responsible authorities shall have regard to the analysis prepared under subsection (2)(b) above and the views obtained under subsection (2)(d) above.

(4) A strategy shall include—

(a) objectives to be pursued by the responsible authorities, by co-operating persons or bodies or, under agreements with the responsible authorities, by other persons or bodies; and

(b) long-term and short-term performance targets for measuring the extent to which such objectives are achieved.

(5) After formulating a strategy, the responsible authorities shall publish in the area a document which includes details of—

(a) co-operating persons and bodies;

(b) the review carried out under subsection (2)(a) above;

(c) the report published under subsection (2)(c) above; and

(d) the strategy, including in particular—

(i) the objectives mentioned in subsection (4)(a) above and, in each case, the authorities, persons or bodies by whom they are to be pursued; and

(ii) the performance targets mentioned in subsection (4)(b) above.

(6) While implementing a strategy, the responsible authorities shall keep it under review with a view to monitoring its effectiveness and making any changes to it that appear necessary or expedient.

(6A) Within one month of the end of each reporting period, the responsible authorities shall submit a report on the implementation of their strategies during that period—

(*a*) in the case of a report relating to the strategies for an area in England, to the Secretary of State; and

(*b*) in the case of a report relating to the strategies for an area in Wales, to the Secretary of State and to the National Assembly for Wales.

(7) In this section—

"co-operating persons or bodies" means persons or bodies co-operating in the exercise of the responsible authorities' functions under this section;

"relevant period" means—

(*a*) the period of three years beginning with such day as the Secretary of State may by order appoint; and

(*b*) each subsequent period of three years.

"reporting period" means every period of one year which falls within a relevant period and which begins—

(*a*) in the case of the first reporting period in the relevant period, with the day on which the relevant period begins; and

(*b*) in any other case, with the day after the day on which the previous reporting period ends;

"substance misuse" includes the misuse of drugs or alcohol.**

[Crime and Disorder Act 1998, s 6 as amended by the Police Reform Act 2002, s 97.]

---

*Amended by the Clean Neighbourhoods and Environment Act 2005, s 1 from a date to be appointed.
**Substituted by the Police and Justice Act 2006, Sch 9 from a date to be appointed.

1–3809A   6A. Powers of the Secretary of State and National Assembly for Wales.   (1) The Secretary of State may, by order, require—

(*a*) the responsible authorities for local government areas to formulate any section 6 strategy of theirs for the reduction of crime and disorder so as to include, in particular, provision for the reduction of—

(i)   crime of a description specified in the order; or

(ii) disorder of a description so specified.

(*b*) the responsible authorities for local government areas in England to prepare any section 6 strategy of theirs for combatting the misuse of drugs so as to include in it a strategy for combatting, in the area in question, such other forms of substance misuse as may be specified or described in the order.

(2) After formulating any section 6 strategy (whether in a case in which there has been an order under subsection or in any other case), the responsible authorities for a local government area shall send both—

(*a*) a copy of the strategy, and

(*b*) a copy of the document which they propose to publish under section 6(5),

to the Secretary of State.

(3) It shall be the duty of the responsible authorities, when preparing any document to be published under section 6(5), to have regard to any guidance issued by the Secretary of State as to the form and content of the documents to be so published.

(4) If the responsible authorities for a local government area propose to make any changes to a section 6 strategy of theirs, they shall send copies of the proposed changes to the Secretary of State.

(5) In subsections (2) to (4)—

(*a*) references to the Secretary of State, in relation to responsible authorities for local government areas in Wales shall have effect as references to the Secretary of State and the National Assembly for Wales; and

(*b*) accordingly, guidance issued for the purposes of subsection (3) in relation to local government areas in Wales must be issued by the Secretary of State and that Assembly acting jointly.

(6) In this section—

"responsible authorities" and "local government area" have same meanings as in sections 5 and 6;

"section 6 strategy" means a strategy required to be formulated under section 6(1); and

"substance misuse" has the same meaning as in section 6.

[Crime and Disorder Act 1998, s 6A as inserted by the Police Reform Act 2002, s 98.]

1–3810   7. Supplemental.   (1) The responsible authorities for a local government area shall, whenever so required by the Secretary of State, submit to the Secretary of State a report on such matters connected with the exercise of their functions under section 6 above as may be specified in the requirement.

(2) A requirement under subsection (1) above may specify the form in which a report is to be given.

(3) The Secretary of State may arrange, or require the responsible authorities to arrange, for a

report under subsection (1) above to be published in such manner as appears to him to be appropriate.
[*Crime and Disorder Act 1998, s 7.*]

Youth crime and disorder

1–3811   8. Parenting orders[1]**.** (1) This section applies where, in any court proceedings—

(*a*)   a child safety order is made in respect of a child or the court determines on an application under section 12(6) below that a child has failed to comply with any requirement included in such an order;

(*aa*)   a parental compensation order is made in relation to a child's behaviour;★

(*b*)   an anti-social behaviour order or sex offender order is made in respect of a child or young person;

(*c*)   a child or young person is convicted of an offence; or

(*d*)   a person is convicted of an offence under section 443 (failure to comply with school attendance order) or section 444 (failure to secure regular attendance at school of registered pupil) of the Education Act 1996.

(2) Subject to subsection (3) and section 9(1) below, if in the proceedings the court is satisfied that the relevant condition is fulfilled, it may make a parenting order in respect of a person who is a parent or guardian of the child or young person or, as the case may be, the person convicted of the offence under section 443 or 444 ("the parent").

(3) A court shall not make a parenting order unless it has been notified[2] by the Secretary of State that arrangements for implementing such orders are available in the area in which it appears to the court that the parent resides or will reside and the notice has not been withdrawn.

(4) A parenting order[3] is an order which requires the parent—

(*a*)   to comply, for a period not exceeding twelve months, with such requirements as are specified in the order, and

(*b*)   subject to subsection (5) below, to attend, for a concurrent period not exceeding three months, such counselling or guidance programme as may be specified in directions given by the responsible officer.

(5) A parenting order may, but need not, include such a requirement as is mentioned in subsection (4)(*b*) above in any case where a parenting order under this section or any other enactment has been made in respect of the parent on a previous occasion.

(6) The relevant condition is that the parenting order would be desirable in the interests of preventing—

(*a*)   in a case falling within paragraph (*a*), (*aa*)★ or (*b*) of subsection (1) above, any repetition of the kind of behaviour which led to the child safety order, parental compensation order,★ anti-social behaviour order or sex offender order being made;

(*b*)   in a case falling within paragraph (*c*) of that subsection, the commission of any further offence by the child or young person;

(*c*)   in a case falling within paragraph (*d*) of that subsection, the commission of any further offence under section 443 or 444 of the Education Act 1996.

(7) The requirements that may be specified under subsection (4)(*a*) above are those which the court considers desirable in the interests of preventing any such repetition or, as the case may be, the commission of any such further offence.

(7A) A counselling or guidance programme which a parent is required to attend by virtue of subsection (4)(*b*) above may be or include a residential course but only if the court is satisfied—

(*a*)   that the attendance of the parent at a residential course is likely to be more effective than his attendance at a non-residential course in preventing any such repetition or, as the case may be, the commission of any such further offence, and

(*b*)   that any interference with family life which is likely to result from the attendance of the parent at a residential course is proportionate in all the circumstances.

(8) In this section and section 9 below "responsible officer", in relation to a parenting order, means one of the following who is specified in the order, namely—

(*a*)   an officer of a local probation board;

(*b*)   a social worker of a local authority; and

(*bb*)   a person nominated by a person appointed as director of children's services under section 18 of the Children Act 2004 or by a person appointed as chief education officer under section 532 of the Education Act 1996;★★

[*Crime and Disorder Act 1998, s 8 as amended by the Powers of Criminal Courts (Sentencing) Act 2000, Sch 9, the Courts and Legal Services Act 2000, s 73, the Anti-social Behaviour Act 2003, s 18 and the Children Act 2004, s 60 and Schs 2 and 5 and the Serious Organised Crime Act 2005, Sch 10.*]

★**New para (1)(*aa*) and references to it in subs (6) inserted by the Serious Organised Crime Act 2005, Sch 10 certain specified areas: 20 July 2006: see SI 2006/1871, art 2. In force for remaining purposes.**
★★**Sub-section (8) reproduced as amended by the Children Act 2004, Sch 2 from a date to be appointed.**
  1. See the narrative on parenting orders at para **5–47A** (in the case of parenting orders combined with referral orders, para **5–47AA**), in Part V: Youth Courts, post.

2. All courts in England and Wales were notified by Home Office letter dated 27 April 2000 that arrangements for implementing the parenting order were available in their area with effect from 1 June 2000.

3. For form of order, see the Magistrates' Courts (Parenting Orders) Rules 2004, also the Criminal Procedure Rules 2005, Part 50, in this PART, post.

1–3812   9. Parenting orders: supplemental.   (1) Where a person under the age of 16 is convicted of an offence, the court by or before which he is so convicted—

(a) if it is satisfied that the relevant condition is fulfilled, shall make a parenting order; and

(b) if it is not so satisfied, shall state in open court that it is not and why it is not.

(1A) The requirements of subsection (1) do not apply where the court makes a referral order in respect of the offence.

(1B) If an anti-social behaviour order is made in respect of a person under the age of 16 the court which makes the order—

(a) must make a parenting order if it is satisfied that the relevant condition is fulfilled;

(b) if it is not so satisfied, must state in open court that it is not and why it is not.

(2) Before making a parenting order—

(a) in a case falling within paragraph (a) of subsection (1) of section 8 above;

(b) in a case falling within paragraph (b) or (c) of that subsection, where the person concerned is under the age of 16; or

(c) in a case falling within paragraph (d) of that subsection, where the person to whom the offence related is under that age,

a court shall obtain and consider information about the person's family circumstances and the likely effect of the order on those circumstances.

(2A) In a case where a court proposes to make both a referral order in respect of a child or young person convicted of an offence and a parenting order, before making the parenting order the court shall obtain and consider a report by an appropriate officer—

(a) indicating the requirements proposed by that officer to be included in the parenting order;

(b) indicating the reasons why he considers those requirements would be desirable in the interests of preventing the commission of any further offence by the child or young person; and

(c) if the child or young person is aged under 16, containing the information required by subsection (2) above.

(2B) In subsection (2A) above "an appropriate officer" means—

(a) an officer of a local probation board;

(b) a social worker of a local authority; or

(c) a member of a youth offending team.

(3) Before making a parenting order, a court shall explain to the parent in ordinary language—

(a) the effect of the order and of the requirements proposed to be included in it;

(b) the consequences which may follow (under subsection (7) below) if he fails to comply with any of those requirements; and

(c) that the court has power (under subsection (5) below) to review the order on the application either of the parent or of the responsible officer.

(4) Requirements specified in, and directions given under, a parenting order shall, as far as practicable, be such as to avoid—

(a) any conflict with the parent's religious beliefs; and

(b) any interference with the times, if any, at which he normally works or attends an educational establishment.

(5) If while a parenting order is in force it appears to the court which made it, on the application of the responsible officer or the parent, that it is appropriate to make an order under this subsection, the court may make an order discharging the parenting order or varying it—

(a) by cancelling any provision included in it; or

(b) by inserting in it (either in addition to or in substitution for any of its provisions) any provision that could have been included in the order if the court had then had power to make it and were exercising the power.

(6) Where an application under subsection (5) above for the discharge of a parenting order is dismissed, no further application for its discharge shall be made under that subsection by any person except with the consent of the court which made the order.

(7) If while a parenting order is in force the parent without reasonable excuse fails to comply with any requirement included in the order, or specified in directions given by the responsible officer, he shall be liable on summary conviction to a fine not exceeding level 3 on the standard scale.

(7A) In this section "referral order" means an order under section 16(2) or (3) of the Powers of Criminal Courts (Sentencing) Act 2000 (referral of offender to youth offender panel).

[Crime and Disorder Act 1998, s 9 as amended by the Powers of Criminal Courts (Sentencing) Act 2000, Sch 9, the Anti-social Behaviour Act 2003, s 85, the Criminal Justice Act 2003, Sch 34 and the Children Act 2004, Sch 5.]

1–3813 **10. Appeals against parenting orders.** (1) An appeal shall lie—

(a) to the High Court against the making of a parenting order by virtue of paragraph (a) of subsection (1) of section 8 above; and

(b) to the Crown Court against the making of a parenting order by virtue of paragraph (b) of that subsection.

(2) On an appeal under subsection (1) above the High Court or the Crown Court—

(a) may make such orders as may be necessary to give effect to its determination of the appeal; and

(b) may also make such incidental or consequential orders as appear to it to be just.

(3) Any order of the High Court or the Crown Court made on an appeal under subsection (1) above (other than one directing that an application be re-heard by a magistrates' court) shall, for the purposes of subsections (5) to (7) of section 9 above, be treated as if it were an order of the court from which the appeal was brought and not an order of the High Court or the Crown Court.

(4) A person in respect of whom a parenting order is made by virtue of section 8(1)(c) above shall have the same right of appeal against the making of the order as if—

(a) the offence that led to the making of the order were an offence committed by him; and

(b) the order were a sentence passed on him for the offence.

(5) A person in respect of whom a parenting order is made by virtue of section 8(1)(d) above shall have the same right of appeal against the making of the order as if the order were a sentence passed on him for the offence that led to the making of the order.

(6) The Lord Chancellor may, with the concurrence of the Lord Chief Justice, by order make provision as to the circumstances in which appeals under subsection (1)(a) above may be made against decisions taken by courts on questions arising in connection with the transfer, or proposed transfer, of proceedings by virtue of any order under paragraph 2 of Schedule 11 (jurisdiction) to the Children Act 1989 ("the 1989 Act").

(7) Except to the extent provided for in any order made under subsection (6) above, no appeal may be made against any decision of a kind mentioned in that subsection.

(8) The Lord Chief Justice may nominate a judicial office holder (as defined in section 109(4) of the Constitutional Reform Act 2005) to exercise his functions under this section.

[Crime and Disorder Act 1998, s 10 as amended by the Constitutional Reform Act 2005, Sch 4.]

1–3814 **11. Child safety orders[1].** (1) Subject to subsection (2) below, if a magistrates' court, on the application of a local authority, is satisfied that one or more of the conditions specified in subsection (3) below are fulfilled with respect to a child under the age of 10, it may make an order (a "child safety order") which—

(a) places the child, for a period (not exceeding the permitted maximum) specified in the order, under the supervision of the responsible officer; and

(b) requires the child to comply with such requirements as are so specified.

(2) A court shall not make a child safety order unless it has been notified[2] by the Secretary of State that arrangements for implementing such orders are available in the area in which it appears that the child resides or will reside and the notice has not been withdrawn.

(3) The conditions are—

(a) that the child has committed an act which, if he had been aged 10 or over, would have constituted an offence;

(b) that a child safety order is necessary for the purpose of preventing the commission by the child of such an act as is mentioned in paragraph (a) above;

(c) that the child has contravened a ban imposed by a curfew notice; and

(d) that the child has acted in a manner that caused or was likely to cause harassment, alarm or distress to one or more persons not of the same household as himself.

(4) The maximum period permitted for the purposes of subsection (1)(a) above is twelve months.

(5) The requirements that may be specified under subsection (1)(b) above are those which the court considers desirable in the interests of—

(a) securing that the child receives appropriate care, protection and support and is subject to proper control; or

(b) preventing any repetition of the kind of behaviour which led to the child safety order being made.

(6) Proceedings under this section or section 12 below shall be family proceedings for the purposes of the 1989 Act or section 65 of the Magistrates' Courts Act 1980 ("the 1980 Act"); and the standard of proof applicable to such proceedings shall be that applicable to civil proceedings.

(7) In this section "local authority" has the same meaning as in the 1989 Act.

(8) In this section and section 12 below, "responsible officer", in relation to a child safety order, means one of the following who is specified in the order, namely—

(a) a social worker of a local authority; and

(b) a member of a youth offending team.

[Crime and Disorder Act 1998, s 11 as amended by the Children Act 2004, Sch 5.]

1. For commentary on child safety orders, see para **6–175B** in PART VI: FAMILY LAW, post.
2. All courts in England and Wales were notified by Home Office Letter dated 27 April 2000 that parenting orders were available in their area from 1 June 2000.

1–3815   12. Child safety orders: supplemental.   (1) Before making a child safety order, a magistrates' court shall obtain and consider information about the child's family circumstances and the likely effect of the order on those circumstances.

(2) Before making a child safety order, a magistrates' court shall explain to the parent or guardian of the child in ordinary language—

(*a*) the effect of the order and of the requirements proposed to be included in it;
(*b*) the consequences which may follow (under subsection (6) below) if the child fails to comply with any of those requirements; and
(*c*) that the court has power (under subsection (4) below) to review the order on the application either of the parent or guardian or of the responsible officer.

(3) Requirements included in a child safety order shall, as far as practicable, be such as to avoid—

(*a*) any conflict with the parent's religious beliefs; and
(*b*) any interference with the times, if any, at which the child normally attends school.

(4) If while a child safety order is in force in respect of a child it appears to the court which made it, on the application of the responsible officer or a parent or guardian of the child, that it is appropriate to make an order under this subsection, the court may make an order discharging the child safety order or varying it—

(*a*) by cancelling any provision included in it; or
(*b*) by inserting in it (either in addition to or in substitution for any of its provisions) any provision that could have been included in the order if the court had then had power to make it and were exercising the power.

(5) Where an application under subsection (4) above for the discharge of a child safety order is dismissed, no further application for its discharge shall be made under that subsection by any person except with the consent of the court which made the order.

(6) Where a child safety order is in force and it is proved to the satisfaction of the court which made it or another magistrates' court acting in the same local justice area, on the application of the responsible officer, that the child has failed to comply with any requirement included in the order, the court—

(*a*) *repealed*
(*b*) may make an order varying the order—

    (i) by cancelling any provision included in it; or
    (ii) by inserting in it (either in addition to or in substitution for any of its provisions) any provision that could have been included in the order if the court had then had power to make it and were exercising the power.

(7) *Repealed.*
[Crime and Disorder Act 1998, s 12 as amended by SI 2005/886 and the Children Act 2004, Sch 5.]

1–3816   13. Appeals against child safety orders.   (1) An appeal shall lie to the High Court against the making by a magistrates' court of a child safety order; and on such an appeal the High Court—

(*a*) may make such orders as may be necessary to give effect to its determination of the appeal; and
(*b*) may also make such incidental or consequential orders as appear to it to be just.

(2) Any order of the High Court made on an appeal under this section (other than one directing that an application be re-heard by a magistrates' court) shall, for the purposes of subsections (4) to (6) of section 12 above, be treated as if it were an order of the magistrates' court from which the appeal was brought and not an order of the High Court.

(3) Subsections (6) and (7) of section 10 above shall apply for the purposes of subsection (1) above as they apply for the purposes of subsection (1)(*a*) of that section.
[Crime and Disorder Act 1998, s 13.]

1–3816A   13A. Parental compensation orders.   (1) A magistrates' court may make an order under this section (a "parental compensation order") if on the application of a local authority it is satisfied, on the civil standard of proof—

(*a*) that the condition mentioned in subsection (2) below is fulfilled with respect to a child under the age of 10; and
(*b*) that it would be desirable to make the order in the interests of preventing a repetition of the behaviour in question.

(2) The condition is that the child has taken, or caused loss of or damage to, property in the course of—

(*a*) committing an act which, if he had been aged 10 or over, would have constituted an offence; or

(b) acting in a manner that caused or was likely to cause harassment, alarm or distress to one or more persons not of the same household as himself.

(3) A parental compensation order is an order which requires any person specified in the order who is a parent or guardian of the child (other than a local authority) to pay compensation of an amount specified in the order to any person or persons specified in the order who is, or are, affected by the taking of the property or its loss or damage.

(4) The amount of compensation specified may not exceed £5,000 in all.

(5) The Secretary of State may by order amend subsection (4) above so as to substitute a different amount.

(6) For the purposes of collection and enforcement, a parental compensation order is to be treated as if it were a sum adjudged to be paid on the conviction by the magistrates' court which made the order of the person or persons specified in the order as liable to pay the compensation.

(7) In this section and sections 13B and 13C below, "local authority" has the same meaning as in the 1989 Act.*

[Crime and Disorder Act 1998, s 13A as inserted by the Serious Organised Crime Act 2005, Sch 10.]

*Sections 13A–E in force in relation to certain specified areas: 20 July 2006: see SI 2006/1871, art 2. In force for remaining purposes from a date to be appointed.

1–3816B   13B. Parental compensation orders: the compensation.   (1) When specifying the amount of compensation for the purposes of section 13A(3) above, the magistrates' court shall take into account—

(a) the value of the property taken or damaged, or whose loss was caused, by the child;

(b) any further loss which flowed from the taking of or damage to the property, or from its loss;

(c) whether the child, or any parent or guardian of his, has already paid any compensation for the property (and if so, how much);

(d) whether the child, or any parent or guardian of his, has already made any reparation (and if so, what it consisted of);

(e) the means of those to be specified in the order as liable to pay the compensation, so far as the court can ascertain them;

(f) whether there was any lack of care on the part of the person affected by the taking of the property or its loss or damage which made it easier for the child to take or damage the property or to cause its loss.

(2) If property taken is recovered before compensation is ordered to be paid in respect of it—

(a) the court shall not order any such compensation to be payable in respect of it if it is not damaged;

(b) if it is damaged, the damage shall be treated for the purposes of making a parental compensation order as having been caused by the child, regardless of how it was caused and who caused it.

(3) The court shall specify in the order how and by when the compensation is to be paid (for example, it may specify that the compensation is to be paid by instalments, and specify the date by which each instalment must be paid).

(4) For the purpose of ascertaining the means of the parent or guardian, the court may, before specifying the amount of compensation, order him to provide the court, within such period as it may specify in the order, such a statement of his financial circumstances as the court may require.

(5) A person who without reasonable excuse fails to comply with an order under subsection (4) above is guilty of an offence and is liable on summary conviction to a fine not exceeding level 3 on the standard scale.

(6) If, in providing a statement of his financial circumstances pursuant to an order under subsection (4) above, a person—

(a) makes a statement which he knows to be false in a material particular;

(b) recklessly provides a statement which is false in a material particular; or

(c) knowingly fails to disclose any material fact,

he is liable on summary conviction to a fine not exceeding level 4 on the standard scale.

(7) Proceedings in respect of an offence under subsection (6) above may, despite anything in section 127(1) of the 1980 Act (limitation of time), be commenced at any time within two years from the date of the commission of the offence or within six months of its first discovery by the local authority, whichever period expires earlier.*

[Crime and Disorder Act 1998, s 13B as inserted by the Serious Organised Crime Act 2005, Sch 10.]

*Sections 13A–E in force in relation to certain specified areas: 20 July 2006: see SI 2006/1871, art 2. In force for remaining purposes from a date to be appointed.

1–3816C   13C. Parental compensation orders: supplemental.   (1) Before deciding whether or not to make a parental compensation order in favour of any person, the magistrates' court shall take into account the views of that person about whether a parental compensation order should be made in his favour.

(2) Before making a parental compensation order, the magistrates' court shall obtain and consider

information about the child's family circumstances and the likely effect of the order on those circumstances.

(3) Before making a parental compensation order, a magistrates' court shall explain to the parent or guardian of the child in ordinary language—

(*a*) the effect of the order and of the requirements proposed to be included in it;

(*b*) the consequences which may follow (under subsection (4)(b) below) as a result of failure to comply with any of those requirements;

(*c*) that the court has power (under subsection (4)(a) below) to review the order on the application either of the parent or guardian or of the local authority.

(4) A magistrates' court which has made a parental compensation order may make an order under subsection (5) below if while the order is in force—

(*a*) it appears to the court, on the application of the local authority, or the parent or guardian subject to the order, that it is appropriate to make an order under subsection (5); or

(*b*) it is proved to the satisfaction of the court, on the application of the local authority, that the parent or guardian subject to it has failed to comply with any requirement included in the order.

(5) An order under this subsection is an order discharging the parental compensation order or varying it—

(*a*) by cancelling any provision included in it; or

(*b*) by inserting in it (either in addition to or in substitution for any of its provisions) any provision that could have been included in the order if the court had then had power to make it and were exercising the power.

(6) Where an application under subsection (4) above for the discharge of a parental compensation order is dismissed, no further application for its discharge shall be made under that subsection by any person except with the consent of the court which made the order.

(7) References in this section to the magistrates' court which made a parental compensation order include any magistrates' court acting in the same local justice area as that court.*

[Crime and Disorder Act 1998, s 13C as inserted by the Serious Organised Crime Act 2005, Sch 10.]

---

*Sections 13A–E in force in relation to certain specified areas: 20 July 2006: see SI 2006/1871, art 2. In force for remaining purposes from a date to be appointed.

1–3816D   13D. Parental compensation orders: appeal.   (1) If a magistrates' court makes a parental compensation order, the parent or guardian may appeal against the making of the order, or against the amount of compensation specified in the order.

(2) The appeal lies to the Crown Court.

(3) On the appeal the Crown Court—

(*a*) may make such orders as may be necessary to give effect to its determination of the appeal;

(*b*) may also make such incidental or consequential orders as appear to it to be just.

(4) Any order of the Crown Court made on an appeal under this section (other than one directing that an application be re-heard by a magistrates' court) shall, for the purposes of section 13C above, be treated as if it were an order of the magistrates' court from which the appeal was brought and not an order of the Crown Court.

(5) A person in whose favour a parental compensation order is made shall not be entitled to receive any compensation under it until (disregarding any power of a court to grant leave to appeal out of time) there is no further possibility of an appeal on which the order could be varied or set aside.*

[Crime and Disorder Act 1998, s 13D as inserted by the Serious Organised Crime Act 2005, Sch 10.]

---

*Sections 13A–E in force in relation to certain specified areas: 20 July 2006: see SI 2006/1871, art 2. In force for remaining purposes from a date to be appointed.

1–3816E   13E. Effect of parental compensation order on subsequent award of damages in civil proceedings.   (1) This section has effect where—

(*a*) a parental compensation order has been made in favour of any person in respect of any taking or loss of property or damage to it; and

(*b*) a claim by him in civil proceedings for damages in respect of the taking, loss or damage is then to be determined.

(2) The damages in the civil proceedings shall be assessed without regard to the parental compensation order, but the claimant may recover only an amount equal to the aggregate of the following—

(*a*) any amount by which they exceed the compensation; and

(*b*) a sum equal to any portion of the compensation which he fails to recover.

(3) The claimant may not enforce the judgment, so far as it relates to such a sum as is mentioned in subsection (2)(b) above, without the permission of the court.*

[Crime and Disorder Act 1998, s 13E as inserted by the Serious Organised Crime Act 2005, Sch 10.]

Sections 13A–E in force in relation to certain specified areas: 20 July 2006: see SI 2006/1871, art 2. In force for remaining purposes from a date to be appointed.

1–3817   14. Local child curfew schemes[1].   (1) A local authority or a chief officer of police may make a scheme (a "local child curfew scheme") for enabling the authority or (as the case may be) the officer—

    (*a*) subject to and in accordance with the provisions of the scheme; and

    (*b*) if, after such consultation as is required by the scheme, the authority or (as the case may be) the officer considers it necessary to do so for the purpose of maintaining order,

to give a notice imposing, for a specified period (not exceeding 90 days), a ban to which subsection (2) below applies.

    (2) This subsection applies to a ban on children of specified ages (under 16) being in a public place within a specified area—

    (*a*) during specified hours (between 9 pm and 6 am); and

    (*b*) otherwise than under the effective control of a parent or a responsible person aged 18 or over.

    (3) Before making a local child curfew scheme, a local authority shall consult—

    (*a*) every chief officer of police any part of whose police area lies within its area; and

    (*b*) such other persons or bodies as it considers appropriate.

    (3A) Before making a local child curfew scheme, a chief officer of police shall consult—

    (*a*) every local authority any part of whose area lies within the area to be specified; and

    (*b*) such other persons or bodies as he considers appropriate.

    (4) A local child curfew scheme shall, if made by a local authority, be made under the common seal of the authority.

    (4A) A local child curfew scheme shall not have effect until it is confirmed by the Secretary of State.

    (5) The Secretary of State—

    (*a*) may confirm, or refuse to confirm, a local child curfew scheme submitted under this section for confirmation; and

    (*b*) may fix the date on which such a scheme is to come into operation;

and if no date is so fixed, the scheme shall come into operation at the end of the period of one month beginning with the date of its confirmation.

    (6) A notice given under a local child curfew scheme (a "curfew notice") may specify different hours in relation to children of different ages.

    (7) A curfew notice shall be given—

    (*a*) by posting the notice in some conspicuous place or places within the specified area; and

    (*b*) in such other manner, if any, as appears to the local authority or (as the case may be) the chief officer of police to be desirable for giving publicity to the notice.

    (8) In this section—

"local authority" means—

    (*a*) in relation to England, the council of a district or London borough, the Common Council of the City of London, the Council of the Isle of Wight and the Council of the Isles of Scilly;

    (*b*) in relation to Wales, the council of a county or county borough;

"public place" has the same meaning as in Part II of the Public Order Act 1986.
[Crime and Disorder Act 1998, s 14 amended by the Criminal Justice and Police Act 2001, s 49.]

---

    1. Amended by the Criminal Justice and Police Act 2001, s 48 and s 49, respectively, to increase the maximum age of children that may be subject to local child curfew schemes from 9 to 15, and to empower the police to initiate a local child curfew scheme.

1–3818   15. Contravention of curfew notices.   (1) Subsections (2) and (3) below apply where a constable has reasonable cause to believe that a child is in contravention of a ban imposed by a curfew notice.

    (2) The constable shall, as soon as practicable, inform the local authority for the area that the child has contravened the ban.

    (3) The constable may remove the child to the child's place of residence unless he has reasonable cause to believe that the child would, if removed to that place, be likely to suffer significant harm.

    (4) *Amendment of the Children Act 1989.*
[Crime and Disorder Act 1998, s 15.]

1–3819   16. Removal of truants to designated premises etc.   (1) This section applies where a local authority—

    (*a*) designates premises in a police area ("designated premises") as premises to which children and young persons of compulsory school age may be removed under this section; and

    (*b*) notifies the chief officer of police for that area of the designation.

(2) A police officer of or above the rank of superintendent may direct that the powers conferred on a constable by subsection (3) below—

(*a*) shall be exercisable as respects any area falling within the police area and specified in the direction; and

(*b*) shall be so exercisable during a period so specified;

and references in that subsection to a specified area and a specified period shall be construed accordingly.

(3) If a constable has reasonable cause to believe that a child or young person found by him in a public place in a specified area during a specified period—

(*a*) is of compulsory school age; and

(*b*) is absent from a school without lawful authority,

the constable may remove the child or young person to designated premises, or to the school from which he is so absent.

(3A) Subsection (2) shall have effect in relation to The British Transport Police Force; and for that purpose the reference to any area falling within the police area shall be treated as a reference to any area in a place specified in section 31(1)(a) to (f) of the Railways and Transport Safety Act 2003.

(4) A child's or young person's absence from a school shall be taken to be without lawful authority unless it falls within subsection (3) (leave, sickness, unavoidable cause or day set apart for religious observance) of section 444 of the Education Act 1996.

(5) In this section—

"British Transport Police" means the force of constables appointed under section 53 of the British Transport Commission Act 1949 (c xxix);

"local authority" means—

(*a*) in relation to England, a county council, a district council whose district does not form part of an area that has a county council, a London borough council or the Common Council of the City of London;

(*b*) in relation to Wales, a county council or a county borough council;

"public place" has the same meaning as in section 14 above;

"school" has the same meaning as in the Education Act 1996.

[Crime and Disorder Act 1998, s 16 as amended by the Police Reform Act 2002, s 75 and SI 2004/1573.]

---

1. Amended by the Criminal Justice and Police Act 2001, s 48 and s 49, respectively, to increase the maximum age of children that may be subject to local child curfew schemes from 9 to 15, and to empower the police to initiate a local child curfew scheme.

Miscellaneous and supplemental

1–3820   17. Duty to consider crime and disorder implications.   (1) Without prejudice to any other obligation imposed on it, it shall be the duty of each authority to which this section applies to exercise its various functions with due regard to the likely effect of the exercise of those functions on, and the need to do all that it reasonably can to prevent, crime and disorder in its area.

(2) This section applies to a local authority, a joint authority, the London Fire and Emergency Planning Authority, a fire and rescue authority constituted by a scheme under section 2 of the Fire and Rescue Services Act 2004 or a scheme to which section 4 of that Act applies, a police authority, a National Park authority and the Broads Authority.

(3) In this section—

"local authority" means a local authority within the meaning given by section 270(1) of the Local Government Act 1972 or the Common Council of the City of London;

"joint authority" has the same meaning as in the Local Government Act 1985;

"National Park authority" means an authority established under section 63 of the Environment Act 1995.

[Crime and Disorder Act 1998, s 17 as amended by the Greater London Authority Act 1999, Sch 29, the Police Reform Act 2002, s 97 and the Fire and Rescue Services Act 2004, Sch 1.]

1–3820A   17A. Sharing of information.   (1) A relevant authority is under a duty to disclose to all other relevant authorities any information held by the authority which is of a prescribed description, at such intervals and in such form as may be prescribed.

(2) In subsection (1) "prescribed" means prescribed in regulations made by the Secretary of State.

(3) The Secretary of State may only prescribe descriptions of information which appears to him to be of potential relevance in relation to the reduction of crime and disorder in any area of England and Wales (including anti-social or other behaviour adversely affecting the local environment in that area).

(4) Nothing in this section requires a relevant authority to disclose any personal data (within the meaning of the Data Protection Act 1998).

(5) In this section "relevant authority" means an authority in England and Wales which is for the time being a relevant authority for the purposes of section 115.

[Crime and Disorder Act 1998, s 17A as inserted by the Police and Justice Act 2006, Sch 9.]

*Inserted by the Police and Justice Act 2006, Sch 9 from a date to be appointed.

1–3821 **18. Interpretation etc of Chapter I.** (1) In this Chapter—

"anti-social behaviour order" has the meaning given by section 1(4) above;

"chief officer of police" has the meaning given by section 101(1) of the Police Act 1996;

"child safety order" has the meaning given by section 11(1) above;

"curfew notice" has the meaning given by section 14(6) above;

"individual support order" has the meaning given by section 1AA(2) above;

"local child curfew scheme" has the meaning given by section 14(1) above;

"parental compensation order" has the meaning given by section 13A(1) above;*

"parenting order" has the meaning given by section 8(4) above;

"police area" has the meaning given by section 1(2) of the Police Act 1996;

"police authority" has the meaning given by section 101(1) of that Act;

"responsible officer"—

   (*za*) in relation to an individual support order, has the meaning given by section 1AA(10)) above;

   (*a*) in relation to a parenting order, has the meaning given by section 8(8) above;

   (*b*) in relation to a child safety order, has the meaning given by section 11(8) above;*

"serious harm" shall be contrued in accordance with section 224 of the Criminal Justice Act 2003;

"sex offender order" has the meaning given by section 2(3) above.

(2) *Repealed.*

(3) Where directions under a parenting order are to be given by a probation officer, the probation officer shall be an officer appointed for or assigned to the local justice area within which it appears to the court that the child or, as the case may be, the parent resides or will reside.

(4) Where the supervision under a child safety order is to be provided, or directions under an individual support order or a parenting order are to be given, by—

   (*a*) a social worker of a local authority; or

   (*b*) a member of a youth offending team,

the social worker or member shall be a social worker of, or a member of a youth offending team established by, the local authority within whose area it appears to the court that the child, defendant or parent, as the case may be, resides or will reside.

(5) For the purposes of this Chapter the Inner Temple and the Middle Temple form part of the City of London.

[Crime and Disorder Act 1998, s 18 as amended by the Powers of Criminal Courts (Sentencing) Act 2000, Sch 9, the Criminal Justice Act 2003, s 323 and Sch 32, SI 2005/886, the Children Act 2004, Sch 5 and the Serious Organised Crime and Police Act 2005, Sch 10.]

---

*Definition "parental compensation order" inserted by the Serious Organised Crime and Police Act 2005, Sch 10 in force in relation to certain specified areas: 20 July 2006: see SI 2006/1871, art 2. In force for remaining purposes

PART II[1]

CRIMINAL LAW

Racially-aggravated offences[2]: England and Wales

1–3822 **28. Meaning of "racially or religiously aggravated".** (1) An offence is racially[3] or religiously aggravated for the purposes of sections 29 to 32 below if—

   (*a*) at the time of committing the offence, or immediately before or after doing so, the offender demonstrates towards the victim of the offence hostility based on the victim's membership[4] (or presumed membership) of a racial or religious group; or

   (*b*) the offence is motivated (wholly or partly) by hostility towards members of a racial or religious group based on their membership[3] of that group.

(2) In subsection (1)(*a*) above—

"membership", in relation to a racial or religious group, includes association with members of that group;

"presumed" means presumed by the offender.

(3) It is immaterial for the purposes of paragraph (*a*) or (*b*) of subsection (1) above whether or not the offender's hostility is also based, to any extent, on any other factor not mentioned in that paragraph.

(4) In this section "racial group" means a group of persons defined by reference to race, colour, nationality (including citizenship) or ethnic or national origins.

(5) In this section "religious group" means a group of persons defined by reference to religious belief or lack of religious belief.

[Crime and Disorder Act 1998, s 28, as amended by the Anti-terrorism, Crime and Security Act 2001, s 39(1)–(4).]

---

1. Part II contains ss 28–36.
2. The mischiefs attacked by the aggravated versions of these offences are racism and xenophobia. Their essence is the

denial of equal respect and dignity to people who were seen as "other" which is more deeply hurtful, damaging and disrespectful to the victims than the simple versions of the offences. It is also damaging to the community as a whole by denying acceptance to members of certain groups for reasons they can do nothing about (*R v Rogers* (2007) Times, 1 March, HL).

3. For the offence to be aggravated in accordance with this section, the defendant must first form a view that the victim is a member of a racial group within the definition in sub-s (4). Then he must say something which demonstrates hostility towards the victim based on membership of that group.

The statute intends a broad, non-technical approach rather than a construction which invites nice distinctions. So that it does not matter, for example, whether the use of the word "Paki" demonstrated hostility to all who came from the Indian Sub-continent or simply those who came from Pakistan. It is also the same whether the group is defined exclusively by reference to what its members are not, eg some description implying they are not British such as "bloody foreigners" or inclusively by reference to what they are eg "bloody Spaniards". However, to demonstrate hostility no particular words need be used. The necessary hostility can be demonstrated in ways such as the wearing of a swastika or the singing of certain songs, although it will normally be proved by some well known terms of abuse.

Accordingly, those who were not of a British origin do constitute a "racial group" as do "foreigners". Whether the evidence proves that the offender's conduct demonstrated hostility to such a group, or was motivated by such hostility is a question of fact for the court (*R v Rogers* (2007) Times, 1 March, HL). In an earlier authority, the word "immigrant doctor" itself was held to be specific enough to denote membership of a "racial group" within the meaning in sub-s (4) of the 1998 Act where the court was satisfied that in the factual context the defendant's hostility was based his perception of the victim's non-Britishness derived from his race and/or his colour and/or his nationality and/or his ethnic or national origins (*A-G's Reference (No 4 of 2004)* [2005] EWCA Crim 889, [2005] 1 WLR 2810).4. Cases may arise where it is legitimate to require the prosecution to make clear whether it is proceeding under subpara (*a*), or (*b*), or both: *G v DPP and T v DPP* [2004] EWHC 183 (Admin), (2004) 168 JP 313.

The hostility must be towards the victim as a member of a racial group. Where the hostility is towards the victim's conduct such as associating with members of another racial group, then, depending on the facts, the conduct may not amount to being "racially aggravated", see *DPP v Pal* [2000] Crim LR 756, DC. Whilst it may be unusual, and may be more difficult to establish that the hostility is of racial, ethnic or national origin, a person may show hostility to his own kind, whether racial, ethnic or national (*R v White* [2001] EWCA Crim 216, [2001] 1 WLR 1352, [2001] Crim LR 576).

1-3823   29. Racially or religiously aggravated assaults.   (1) A person is guilty of an offence under this section if he commits—

   (*a*) an offence under section 20 of the Offences Against the Person Act 1861 (malicious wounding or grievous bodily harm);

   (*b*) an offence under section 47 of that Act (actual bodily harm); or

   (*c*) common assault,

which is racially or religiously aggravated for the purposes of this section.

(2) A person guilty of an offence falling within subsection (1)(*a*) or (*b*) above shall be liable[1]—

   (*a*) on summary conviction, to imprisonment for a term not exceeding **six months** or to a fine not exceeding the **statutory maximum**, or to both;

   (*b*) on conviction on indictment, to imprisonment for a term not exceeding **seven years** or to a **fine**, or to both.

(3) A person guilty of an offence falling within subsection (1)(*c*) above shall be liable[1]—

   (*a*) on summary conviction, to imprisonment for a term not exceeding **six months** or to a fine not exceeding the **statutory maximum**, or to both;

   (*b*) on conviction on indictment, to imprisonment for a term not exceeding **two years** or to a **fine**, or to both.

[Crime and Disorder Act 1998, s 29, as amended by the Anti-terrorism, Crime and Security Act 2001, s 39(5).]

---

1. For procedure in respect of this offence which is triable either way, see the Magistrates' Courts Act 1980, ss 17A to 21 this PART ante.

1-3824   30. Racially or religiously aggravated criminal damage.   (1) A person is guilty of an offence under this section if he commits an offence under section 1(1) of the Criminal Damage Act 1971 (destroying or damaging property belonging to another) which is racially or religiously aggravated for the purposes of this section.

(2) A person guilty of an offence under this section shall be liable[1]—

   (*a*) on summary conviction, to imprisonment for a term not exceeding **six months** or to a fine not exceeding the **statutory maximum**, or to both;

   (*b*) on conviction on indictment, to imprisonment for a term not exceeding **fourteen years** or to a **fine**, or to both.

(3) For the purposes of this section, section 28(1)(*a*) above shall have effect as if the person to whom the property belongs or is treated as belonging for the purposes of that Act were the victim of the offence.

[Crime and Disorder Act 1998, s 30, as amended by the Anti-terrorism, Crime and Security Act 2001, s 39(5).]

---

1. For procedure in respect of this offence which is triable either way, see the Magistrates' Courts Act 1980, ss 17A to 21 this PART ante.

1-3825   31. Racially or religiously aggravated public order offences.   (1) A person is guilty of an offence under this section if he commits—

   (*a*) an offence under section 4 of the Public Order Act 1986 (fear or provocation of violence);

   (*b*) an offence under section 4A of that Act (intentional harassment, alarm or distress); or

   (*c*) an offence under section 5 of that Act (harassment, alarm or distress), which is racially or religiously aggravated for the purposes of this section.

(2) *Repealed.*

(3) *Repealed.*

(4) A person guilty of an offence falling within subsection (1)(*a*) or (*b*) above shall be liable[2]—

(*a*) on summary conviction, to imprisonment for a term not exceeding **six months** or to a fine not exceeding the **statutory maximum**, or to both;

(*b*) on conviction on indictment, to imprisonment for a term not exceeding **two years** or to a **fine**, or to both.

(5) A person guilty of an offence falling within subsection (1)(*c*) above shall be liable on summary conviction to a fine not exceeding **level 4** on the standard scale.

(6) If, on the trial on indictment of a person charged with an offence falling within subsection (1)(*a*) or (*b*) above, the jury find him not guilty of the offence charged, they may find him guilty of the basic offence mentioned in that provision.

(7) For the purposes of subsection (1)(*c*) above, section 28(1)(*a*) above shall have effect as if the person likely to be caused harassment, alarm or distress were the victim of the offence.

[Crime and Disorder Act 1998, s 31, as amended by the Anti-terrorism, Crime and Security Act 2001, s 39(5) and the Serious Organised Crime and Police Act 2005, Sch 7.]

---

1. The warning is not an ingredient of the offence, but merely a prerequisite to the exercise of the power of arrest: *DPP v Chippendale* [2004] EWHC 464 (Admin), [2004] Crim LR 755.

2. For procedure in respect of this offence which is triable either way, see the Magistrates' Courts Act 1980, ss 17A to 21 this PART ante.

1–3826 **32. Racially or religiously aggravated harassment etc.** (1) A person is guilty of an offence under this section if he commits—

(*a*) an offence under section 2 of the Protection from Harassment Act 1997 (offence of harassment); or

(*b*) an offence under section 4 of that Act (putting people in fear of violence),

which is racially or religiously aggravated for the purposes of this section.

(2) *Repealed.*

(3) A person guilty of an offence falling within subsection (1)(*a*) above shall be liable[1]—

(*a*) on summary conviction, to imprisonment for a term not exceeding **six months** or to a fine not exceeding the **statutory maximum**, or to both;

(*b*) on conviction on indictment, to imprisonment for a term not exceeding **two years** or to a **fine**, or to both.

(4) A person guilty of an offence falling within subsection (1)(*b*) above shall be liable—

(*a*) on summary conviction, to imprisonment for a term not exceeding **six months** or to a fine not exceeding the **statutory maximum**, or to both;

(*b*) on conviction on indictment, to imprisonment for a term not exceeding **seven years** or to a **fine**, or to both.

(5) If, on the trial on indictment of a person charged with an offence falling within subsection (1)(*a*) above, the jury find him not guilty of the offence charged, they may find him guilty of the basic offence mentioned in that provision.

(6) If, on the trial on indictment of a person charged with an offence falling within subsection (1)(*b*) above, the jury find him not guilty of the offence charged, they may find him guilty of an offence falling within subsection (1)(*a*) above.

(7) Section 5 of the Protection from Harassment Act 1997 (restraining orders) shall have effect in relation to a person convicted of an offence under this section as if the reference in subsection (1) of that section to an offence under section 2 or 4 included a reference to an offence under this section.

[Crime and Disorder Act 1998, s 32, as amended by the Anti-terrorism, Crime and Security Act 2001, s 39(5) and the Police Reform Act 2002, s 108.]

---

1. For procedure in respect of this offence which is triable either way, see the Magistrates' Courts Act 1980, ss 17A–21 this PART ante.

PART III[1]
CRIMINAL JUSTICE SYSTEM
Time limits etc

1–3827 **43. Time limits.** (1) In subsection (2) of section 22 (time limits in relation to criminal proceedings) of the Prosecution of Offences Act 1985 ("the 1985 Act"), for paragraphs (*a*) and (*b*) there shall be substituted the following paragraphs—

"(*a*) be made so as to apply only in relation to proceedings instituted in specified areas, or proceedings of, or against persons of, specified classes or descriptions;

(*b*) make different provision with respect to proceedings instituted in different areas, or different provision with respect to proceedings of, or against persons of, different classes or descriptions;".

(2) For subsection (3) of that section there shall be substituted the following subsection—

"(3) The appropriate court may, at any time before the expiry of a time limit imposed by the regulations, extend, or further extend, that limit; but the court shall not do so unless it is satisfied—

    (*a*) that the need for the extension is due to—

        (i) the illness or absence of the accused, a necessary witness, a judge or a magistrate;

        (ii) a postponement which is occasioned by the ordering by the court of separate trials in the case of two or more accused or two or more offences; or

        (iii) some other good and sufficient cause; and

    (*b*) that the prosecution has acted with all due diligence and expedition."

(3) In subsection (4) of that section, for the words from "the accused" to the end there shall be substituted the words "the appropriate court shall stay the proceedings".

(4) In subsection (6) of that section—

    (*a*) for the word "Where" there shall be substituted the words "Subsection (6A) below applies where"; and

    (*b*) for the words from "the overall time limit" to the end there shall be substituted the words "and is accordingly unlawfully at large for any period."

(5) After that subsection there shall be inserted the following subsection—

"(6A) The following, namely—

    (*a*) the period for which the person is unlawfully at large; and

    (*b*) such additional period (if any) as the appropriate court may direct, having regard to the disruption of the prosecution occasioned by—

        (i) the person's escape or failure to surrender; and

        (ii) the length of the period mentioned in paragraph (*a*) above,

shall be disregarded, so far as the offence in question is concerned, for the purposes of the overall time limit which applies in his case in relation to the stage which the proceedings have reached at the time of the escape or, as the case may be, at the appointed time."

(6) In subsection (7) of that section, after the words "time limit," there shall be inserted the words "or to give a direction under subsection (6A) above,".

(7) In subsection (8) of that section, after the words "time limit" there shall be inserted the words ", or to give a direction under subsection (6A) above,".

(8) After subsection (11) of that section there shall be inserted the following subsection—

"(11ZA) For the purposes of this section, proceedings for an offence shall be taken to begin when the accused is charged with the offence or, as the case may be, an information is laid charging him with the offence."

[Crime and Disorder Act 1998, s 43.]

---

1. Part III consists of ss 37–57.

1–3828   44. Additional time limits for persons under 18.   After section 22 of the 1985 Act there shall be inserted the following section—

"22A. Additional time limits for persons under 18.   (1) The Secretary of State may by regulations make provision—

    (*a*) with respect to a person under the age of 18 at the time of his arrest in connection with an offence, as to the maximum period to be allowed for the completion of the stage beginning with his arrest and ending with the date fixed for his first appearance in court in connection with the offence ("the initial stage");

    (*b*) with respect to a person convicted of an offence who was under that age at the time of his arrest for the offence or (where he was not arrested for it) the laying of the information charging him with it, as to the period within which the stage between his conviction and his being sentenced for the offence should be completed.

(2) Subsection (2) of section 22 above applies for the purposes of regulations under subsection (1) above as if—

    (*a*) the reference in paragraph (*d*) to custody or overall time limits were a reference to time limits imposed by the regulations; and

    (*b*) the reference in paragraph (*e*) to proceedings instituted before the commencement of any provisions of the regulations were a reference to a stage begun before that commencement.

(3) A magistrates' court may, at any time before the expiry of the time limit imposed by the regulations under subsection (1)(*a*) above ("the initial stage time limit"), extend, or further extend, that limit; but the court shall not do so unless it is satisfied—

    (*a*) that the need for the extension is due to some good and sufficient cause; and

    (*b*) that the investigation has been conducted, and (where applicable) the prosecution has acted, with all due diligence and expedition.

(4) Where the initial stage time limit (whether as originally imposed or as extended or further

extended under subsection (3) above) expires before the person arrested is charged with the offence, he shall not be charged with it unless further evidence relating to it is obtained, and—

(a) if he is then under arrest, he shall be released;
(b) if he is then on bail under Part IV of the Police and Criminal Evidence Act 1984, his bail (and any duty or conditions to which it is subject) shall be discharged.

(5) Where the initial stage time limit (whether as originally imposed or as extended or further extended under subsection (3) above) expires after the person arrested is charged with the offence but before the date fixed for his first appearance in court in connection with it, the court shall stay the proceedings.

(6) Where—

(a) a person escapes from arrest; or
(b) a person who has been released on bail under Part IV of the Police and Criminal Evidence Act 1984 fails to surrender himself at the appointed time,

and is accordingly unlawfully at large for any period, that period shall be disregarded, so far as the offence in question is concerned, for the purposes of the initial stage time limit.

(7) Subsections (7) to (9) of section 22 above apply for the purposes of this section, at any time after the person arrested has been charged with the offence in question, as if any reference (however expressed) to a custody or overall time limit were a reference to the initial stage time limit.

(8) Where a person is convicted of an offence in any proceedings, the exercise of the power conferred by subsection (3) above shall not be called into question in any appeal against that conviction.

(9) Any reference in this section (however expressed) to a person being charged with an offence includes a reference to the laying of an information charging him with it."

[Crime and Disorder Act 1998, s 44.]

1–3829 45. Re-institution of stayed proceedings.   After section 22A of the 1985 Act there shall be inserted the following section—

"22B. Re-institution of proceedings stayed under section 22(4) or 22A(5).   (1) This section applies where proceedings for an offence ("the original proceedings") are stayed by a court under section 22(4) or 22A(5) of this Act.

(2) If—

(a) in the case of proceedings conducted by the Director, the Director or a Chief Crown Prosecutor so directs;
(b) in the case of proceedings conducted by the Director of the Serious Fraud Office, the Commissioners of Inland Revenue or the Commissioners of Customs and Excise, that Director or those Commissioners so direct; or
(c) in the case of proceedings not conducted as mentioned in paragraph (a) or (b) above, a person designated for the purpose by the Secretary of State so directs,

fresh proceedings for the offence may be instituted within a period of three months (or such longer period as the court may allow) after the date on which the original proceedings were stayed by the court.

(3) Fresh proceedings shall be instituted as follows—

(a) where the original proceedings were stayed by the Crown Court, by preferring a bill of indictment;
(b) where the original proceedings were stayed by a magistrates' court, by laying an information.

(4) Fresh proceedings may be instituted in accordance with subsections (2) and (3)(b) above notwithstanding anything in section 127(1) of the Magistrates' Courts Act 1980 (limitation of time).

(5) Where fresh proceedings are instituted, anything done in relation to the original proceedings shall be treated as done in relation to the fresh proceedings if the court so directs or it was done—

(a) by the prosecutor in compliance or purported compliance with section 3, 4, 7 or 9 of the Criminal Procedure and Investigations Act 1996; or
(b) by the accused in compliance or purported compliance with section 5 or 6 of that Act.

(6) Where a person is convicted of an offence in fresh proceedings under this section, the institution of those proceedings shall not be called into question in any appeal against that conviction."

[Crime and Disorder Act 1998, s 45.]

1–3830 46. Date of first court appearance in bail cases.   (1) In subsection (3) of section 47 of the 1984 Act (bail after arrest), for the words "subsection (4)" there shall be substituted the words "subsections (3A) and (4)".

(2) After that subsection there shall be inserted the following subsection—

"(3A) Where a custody officer grants bail to a person subject to a duty to appear before a magistrates' court, he shall appoint for the appearance—

(*a*) a date which is not later than the first sitting of the court after the person is charged with the offence; or

(*b*) where he is informed by the clerk to the justices for the relevant petty sessions area that the appearance cannot be accommodated until a later date, that later date."

[Crime and Disorder Act 1998, s 46.]

1–3831   49. Powers of magistrates' courts exercisable by single justice etc.   (1) The following powers of a magistrates' court for any area may be exercised by a single justice of the peace for that area, namely—

(*a*) to extend bail or to impose or vary conditions of bail;

(*b*) to mark an information as withdrawn;

(*c*) to dismiss an information, or to discharge an accused in respect of an information, where no evidence is offered by the prosecution;

(*d*) to make an order for the payment of defence costs out of central funds;

(*e*) to request a pre-sentence report following a plea of guilty and, for that purpose, to give an indication of the seriousness of the offence;

(*f*) to request a medical report and, for that purpose, to remand the accused in custody or on bail;

(*g*) to remit an offender to another court for sentence;

(*h*) where a person has been granted police bail to appear at a magistrates' court, to appoint an earlier time for his appearance;

(*i*) to extend, with the consent of the accused, a custody time limit or an overall time limit;

(*j*) *repealed*;

(*k*) where an accused has been convicted of an offence, to order him to produce his driving licence;

(*l*) to give a direction prohibiting the publication of matters disclosed or exempted from disclosure in court;

(*m*) to give, vary or revoke directions for the conduct of a trial, including directions as to the following matters, namely—

  (i)   the timetable for the proceedings;

  (ii) the attendance of the parties;

  (iii) the service of documents (including summaries of any legal arguments relied on by the parties);

  (iv) the manner in which evidence is to be given; and

(*n*) to give, vary or revoke orders for separate or joint trials in the case of two or more accused or two or more informations.

(2) Criminal Procedure Rules may, subject to subsection (3) below, provide that any of the things which, by virtue of subsection (1) above, are authorised to be done by a single justice of the peace for any area may, subject to any specified restrictions or conditions, be done by a justices' clerk for that area.

(3) Criminal Procedure Rules which make such provision as is mentioned in subsection (2) above shall not authorise a justices' clerk—

(*a*) without the consent of the prosecutor and the accused, to extend bail on conditions other than those (if any) previously imposed, or to impose or vary conditions of bail;

(*b*) to give an indication of the seriousness of an offence for the purposes of a pre-sentence report;

(*c*) to remand the accused in custody for the purposes of a medical report or, without the consent of the prosecutor and the accused, to remand the accused on bail for those purposes on conditions other than those (if any) previously imposed;

(*d*) to give a direction prohibiting the publication of matters disclosed or exempted from disclosure in court; or

(*e*) without the consent of the parties, to give, vary or revoke orders for separate or joint trials in the case of two or more accused or two or more informations.

(4) Before making any Criminal Procedure Rules which make such provision as is mentioned in subsection (2) above in relation to any area, the Criminal Procedure Rule Committee shall consult justices of the peace and justices' clerks for that area.

(5) In this section and section 50 below "justices' clerk" has the same meaning as in section 144 of the 1980 Act.

[Crime and Disorder Act 1998, s 49, as amended by the Access to Justice Act 1999, Sch 15 and SI 2004/2035.]

1–3832   50. Early administrative hearings.   (1) Where a person ("the accused") has been charged with an offence at a police station, the magistrates' court before whom he appears or is brought for the first time in relation to the charge may, unless the accused falls to be dealt with under section 51 below,★ consist of a single justice.

(2) At a hearing conducted by a single justice under this section the accused shall be asked whether he wishes to be granted a right to representation funded by the Legal Services Commission as part of the Criminal Defence Service.★

(2A) Where the accused wishes to be granted such a right, the Legal Services Commission shall decide whether or not to grant him that right.**

(3) At such a hearing the single justice—

(a) may exercise, subject to subsection (2) above, such of his powers as a single justice as he thinks fit; and

(b) on adjourning the hearing, may remand the accused in custody or on bail.

(4) This section applies in relation to a justices' clerk as it applies in relation to a single justice; but nothing in subsection (3)(b) above authorises such a clerk to remand the accused in custody or, without the consent of the prosecutor and the accused, to remand the accused on bail on conditions other than those (if any) previously imposed.

(4A) A hearing conducted by a single justice under this section may be—

(a) adjourned to enable the decision mentioned in subsection (2A) above to be taken, and

(b) subsequently resumed by a single justice.**

(5) *Repealed.****

[Crime and Disorder Act 1998, s 50, as amended by the Access to Justice Act 1999, Schs 4 and 15 and SI 2006/2493.]

---

*Sub-s (1): words underlined repealed by the Criminal Justice Act 2003, Sch 37 from a date to be appointed.
**Subsection (2), as substituted, and (2A) and (4A) in force 2 October 2006, except in relation to applications for representation orders received before that date: see SI 2006/2493, regs 1, 6.
***New s 50A inserted by the Criminal Justice Act 2003, Sch 3 from a date to be appointed.

1–3833 51. Sending cases to the Crown Court: adults. (1) Where an adult appears or is brought before a magistrates' court ("the court") charged[1] with an offence and any of the conditions mentioned in subsection (2) below is satisfied, the court shall send him forthwith to the Crown Court for trial for the offence[2].

(2) Those conditions are—

(a) that the offence is an offence triable only on indictment other than one in respect of which notice has been given under section 51B or 51C below;

(b) that the offence is an either-way offence and the court is required under section 20(9)(b), 21, 23(4)(b) or (5) or 25(2D) of the Magistrates' Courts Act 1980 to proceed in relation to the offence in accordance with subsection (1) above;

(c) that notice is given to the court under section 51B or 51C below in respect of the offence.

(3) Where the court sends an adult for trial under subsection (1) above, it shall at the same time send him to the Crown Court for trial for any either-way or summary offence with which he is charged and which—

(a) (if it is an either-way offence) appears to the court to be related to the offence mentioned in subsection (1) above; or

(b) (if it is a summary offence) appears to the court to be related to the offence mentioned in subsection (1) above or to the either-way offence, and which fulfils the requisite condition (as defined in subsection (11) below).

(4) Where an adult who has been sent for trial under subsection (1) above subsequently appears or is brought before a magistrates' court charged with an either-way or summary offence which—

(a) appears to the court to be related to the offence mentioned in subsection (1) above; and

(b) (in the case of a summary offence) fulfils the requisite condition,

the court may send him forthwith to the Crown Court for trial for the either-way or summary offence.

(5) Where—

(a) the court sends an adult ("A") for trial under subsection (1) or (3) above;

(b) another adult appears or is brought before the court on the same or a subsequent occasion charged jointly with A with an either-way offence; and

(c) that offence appears to the court to be related to an offence for which A was sent for trial under subsection (1) or (3) above,

the court shall where it is the same occasion, and may where it is a subsequent occasion, send the other adult forthwith to the Crown Court for trial for the either-way offence.

(6) Where the court sends an adult for trial under subsection (5) above, it shall at the same time send him to the Crown Court for trial for any either-way or summary offence with which he is charged and which—

(a) (if it is an either-way offence) appears to the court to be related to the offence for which he is sent for trial; and

(b) (if it is a summary offence) appears to the court to be related to the offence for which he is sent for trial or to the either-way offence, and which fulfils the requisite condition.

(7) Where—

(a) the court sends an adult ("A") for trial under subsection (1), (3) or (5) above; and

(b) a child or young person appears or is brought before the court on the same or a subsequent occasion charged jointly with A with an indictable offence for which A is sent for trial under subsection (1), (3) or (5) above, or an indictable offence which appears to the court to be related to that offence,

the court shall, if it considers it necessary in the interests of justice to do so, send the child or young person forthwith to the Crown Court for trial for the indictable offence.

(8) Where the court sends a child or young person for trial under subsection (7) above, it may at the same time send him to the Crown Court for trial for any indictable or summary offence with which he is charged and which—

(a) (if it is an indictable offence) appears to the court to be related to the offence for which he is sent for trial; and

(b) (if it is a summary offence) appears to the court to be related to the offence for which he is sent for trial or to the indictable offence, and which fulfils the requisite condition.

(9) Subsections (7) and (8) above are subject to sections 24A and 24B of the Magistrates' Courts Act 1980 (which provide for certain cases involving children and young persons to be tried summarily).

(10) The trial of the information charging any summary offence for which a person is sent for trial under this section shall be treated as if the court had adjourned it under section 10 of the 1980 Act and had not fixed the time and place for its resumption.

(11) A summary offence fulfils the requisite condition if it is punishable with imprisonment or involves obligatory or discretionary disqualification from driving.

(12) In the case of an adult charged with an offence—

(a) if the offence satisfies paragraph (c) of subsection (2) above, the offence shall be dealt with under subsection (1) above and not under any other provision of this section or section 51A below;

(b) subject to paragraph (a) above, if the offence is one in respect of which the court is required to, or would decide to, send the adult to the Crown Court under—

(i) subsection (5) above; or
(ii) subsection (6) of section 51A below,

the offence shall be dealt with under that subsection and not under any other provision of this section or section 51A below.

(13) The functions of a magistrates' court under this section, and its related functions under section 51D below, may be discharged by a single justice.*

[Crime and Disorder Act 1998, s 51 as substituted by the Criminal Justice Act 2003, Sch 3.]

---

*Reproduced as substituted by the Criminal Justice Act 2003, Sch 3, in force for certain purposes 4 April 2005 and for remaining purposes to be appointed.

1. The word 'charged' does not refer only to charges preferred at a police station or by the laying of an information, but includes charges preferred by addition or substitution at or after the accused's first court appearance (*R (Salubi) v Bow Street Magistrates' Court* [2002] EWHC 919 (Admin), [2002] 1 WLR 3073).

2. The court's duty under s 51 of the Crime and Disorder Act 1998 to send indictable only cases to the Crown Court forthwith does not preclude it from staying the proceedings as an abuse of process, but it will be appropriate to do so only in rare cases where the defence establishes bad faith or serious misconduct (possible instances of which could include the addition of an unmeritorious indictable-only charge in the late stages of committal proceedings for either way offences, solely to overcome custody time limits or evidential difficulties that would otherwise delay or defeat a committal); relatively novel or complex points should normally be left for resolution in the Crown Court or High Court (*R (Salubi) v Bow Street Magistrates' Court*, supra).

The existence of the duty in sub-s (1) is not dependent of the fulfilment of the sub-s (7) duty although it might be that such a failure might give rise to due process arguments if prejudice or unfairness were occasioned (*R v McGrath* [2003] EWCA Crim 2062, [2004] 1 Cr App R 15, 167 JP 554, [2004] Crim LR 142).

Notwithstanding that the magistrates' court has selected the place of trial when sending a person to the Crown Court for trial under this section, the Crown Court has the power to alter the place of trial under s 76 of the Supreme Court Act 1981 (*R v Crown Court at Croydon, ex p Britton* (2000) 164 JP 729, DC).

As to the effect of mistaken belief that an offence of burglary was triable only on indictment because of previous convictions, see *R v Ashton,R v Draz, R v O'Reilly* [2006] EWCA Crim 794, [2006] Cr App R 15 (the subsequent use in the Crown Court of para 7 of Sch 3 to this Act was valid, notwithstanding that no indictment had been preferred) (Cf *R v Haye* [2002] EWCA Crim 2476, [2003] Crim LR 287.)

1–3833A   51A. Sending cases to the Crown Court: children and young persons.   (1) This section is subject to sections 24A and 24B of the Magistrates' Courts Act 1980 (which provide for certain offences involving children or young persons to be tried summarily).

(2) Where a child or young person appears or is brought before a magistrates' court ("the court") charged with an offence and any of the conditions mentioned in subsection (3) below is satisfied, the court shall send him forthwith to the Crown Court for trial for the offence.

(3) Those conditions are—

(a) that the offence falls within subsection (12) below;

(b) that the offence is such as is mentioned in subsection (1) of section 91 of the Powers of Criminal Courts (Sentencing) Act 2000 (other than one mentioned in paragraph (d) below in relation to which it appears to the court as mentioned there) and the court considers that if he is found guilty of the offence it ought to be possible to sentence him in pursuance of subsection (3) of that section;

(c) that notice is given to the court under section 51B or 51C below in respect of the offence;

(*d*) that the offence is a specified offence (within the meaning of section 224 of the Criminal Justice Act 2003) and it appears to the court that if he is found guilty of the offence the criteria for the imposition of a sentence under section 226(3) or 228(2) of that Act would be met.

(4) Where the court sends a child or young person for trial under subsection (2) above, it may at the same time send him to the Crown Court for trial for any indictable or summary offence with which he is charged and which—

(*a*) (if it is an indictable offence) appears to the court to be related to the offence mentioned in subsection (2) above; or
(*b*) (if it is a summary offence) appears to the court to be related to the offence mentioned in subsection (2) above or to the indictable offence, and which fulfils the requisite condition (as defined in subsection (9) below).

(5) Where a child or young person who has been sent for trial under subsection (2) above subsequently appears or is brought before a magistrates' court charged with an indictable or summary offence which—

(*a*) appears to the court to be related to the offence mentioned in subsection (2) above; and
(*b*) (in the case of a summary offence) fulfils the requisite condition,

the court may send him forthwith to the Crown Court for trial for the indictable or summary offence.

(6) Where—

(*a*) the court sends a child or young person ("C") for trial under subsection (2) or (4) above; and
(*b*) an adult appears or is brought before the court on the same or a subsequent occasion charged jointly with C with an either-way offence for which C is sent for trial under subsection (2) or (4) above, or an either-way offence which appears to the court to be related to that offence,

the court shall where it is the same occasion, and may where it is a subsequent occasion, send the adult forthwith to the Crown Court for trial for the either-way offence.

(7) Where the court sends an adult for trial under subsection (6) above, it shall at the same time send him to the Crown Court for trial for any either-way or summary offence with which he is charged and which—

(*a*) (if it is an either-way offence) appears to the court to be related to the offence for which he was sent for trial; and
(*b*) (if it is a summary offence) appears to the court to be related to the offence for which he was sent for trial or to the either-way offence, and which fulfils the requisite condition.

(8) The trial of the information charging any summary offence for which a person is sent for trial under this section shall be treated as if the court had adjourned it under section 10 of the 1980 Act and had not fixed the time and place for its resumption.

(9) A summary offence fulfils the requisite condition if it is punishable with imprisonment or involves obligatory or discretionary disqualification from driving.

(10) In the case of a child or young person charged with an offence—

(*a*) if the offence satisfies any of the conditions in subsection (3) above, the offence shall be dealt with under subsection (2) above and not under any other provision of this section or section 51 above;
(*b*) subject to paragraph (*a*) above, if the offence is one in respect of which the requirements of subsection (7) of section 51 above for sending the child or young person to the Crown Court are satisfied, the offence shall be dealt with under that subsection and not under any other provision of this section or section 51 above.

(11) The functions of a magistrates' court under this section, and its related functions under section 51D below, may be discharged by a single justice.

(12) An offence falls within this subsection if—

(*a*) it is an offence of homicide; or
(*b*) each of the requirements of section 51A(1) of the Firearms Act 1968 would be satisfied with respect to—

(i) the offence; and
(ii) the person charged with it,

if he were convicted of the offence.

[Crime and Disorder Act 1998, s 51A as inserted by the Criminal Justice Act 2003, Sch 3.]

---

*Reproduced as substituted by the Criminal Justice Act 2003, Sch 3, in force for except as relating to sub-s(3)(a)–(c) 4 April 2005 and for remaining purposes to be appointed. Section 51B and 51C inserted from a date to be appointed.

1–3833D   **51D. Notice of offence and place of trial.**   (1) The court shall[1] specify in a notice—

(*a*) the offence or offences for which a person is sent for trial under section 51 or 51A above; and
(*b*) the place at which he is to be tried (which, if a notice has been given under section 51B above, must be the place specified in that notice).

(2) A copy of the notice shall be served on the accused and given to the Crown Court sitting at that place.

(3) In a case where a person is sent for trial under section 51 or 51A above for more than one offence, the court shall specify in that notice, for each offence—

(*a*) the subsection under which the person is so sent; and

(*b*) if applicable, the offence to which that offence appears to the court to be related.

(4) Where the court selects the place of trial for the purposes of subsection (1) above, it shall have regard to—

(*a*) the convenience of the defence, the prosecution and the witnesses;

(*b*) the desirability of expediting the trial; and

(*c*) any direction given by or on behalf of the Lord Chief Justice with the concurrence of the Lord Chancellor under section 75(1) of the Supreme Court Act 1981.

[Crime and Disorder Act 1998, s 51D as inserted by the Criminal Justice Act 2003, Sch 3.]

---

*Reproduced as substituted by the Criminal Justice Act 2003, Sch 3, in force in relation to cases sent under sub-s 51A(3)(*d*) 4 April 2005 and for remaining purposes to be appointed.

1. In relation to the provision that this supersedes (the former s 51(7) of the CDA 1998) it has been held that a technical defect in the notice does not invalidate the sending: *Bentham v Governor of HM Prison Wandsworth* [2006] EWHC 121 (Admin), [2006] Crim LR 855.

1–3833E 51E. Interpretation of sections 50A to 51D. For the purposes of sections 50A to 51D above—

(*a*) "adult" means a person aged 18 or over, and references to an adult include a corporation;

(*b*) "either-way offence" means an offence triable either way;

(*c*) an either-way offence is related to an indictable offence if the charge for the either-way offence could be joined in the same indictment as the charge for the indictable offence;

(*d*) a summary offence is related to an indictable offence if it arises out of circumstances which are the same as or connected with those giving rise to the indictable offence."

[Crime and Disorder Act 1998, s 51E as inserted by the Criminal Justice Act 2003, Sch 3.]

---

*Reproduced as substituted by the Criminal Justice Act 2003, Sch 3, in force in relation to cases sent under sub-s 51A(3)(*d*) 4 April 2005 and for remaining purposes to be appointed.

1–3834 52. Provisions supplementing section 51. (1) Subject to section 4 of the Bail Act 1976, section 41 of the 1980 Act, regulations under section 22 of the 1985 Act and section 25 of the 1994 Act, the court may send a person for trial under section 51 above—

(*a*) in custody, that is to say, by committing him to custody there to be safely kept until delivered in due course of law; or

(*b*) on bail in accordance with the Bail Act 1976, that is to say, by directing him to appear before the Crown Court for trial.

(2) Where—

(*a*) the person's release on bail under subsection (1)(*b*) above is conditional on his providing one or more sureties; and

(*b*) in accordance with subsection (3) of section 8 of the Bail Act 1976, the court fixes the amount in which a surety is to be bound with a view to his entering into his recognisance subsequently in accordance with subsections (4) and (5) or (6) of that section,

the court shall in the meantime make an order such as is mentioned in subsection (1)(*a*) above.

(3) The court shall treat as an indictable offence for the purposes of section 51 above an offence which is mentioned in the first column of Schedule 2 to the 1980 Act (offences for which the value involved is relevant to the mode of trial) unless it is clear to the court, having regard to any representations made by the prosecutor or the accused, that the value involved does not exceed the relevant sum.

(4) In subsection (3) above "the value involved" and "the relevant sum" have the same meanings as in section 22 of the 1980 Act (certain offences triable either way to be tried summarily if value involved is small).

(5) A magistrates' court may adjourn any proceedings under section 51 above, and if it does so shall remand the accused.

(6) Schedule 3 to this Act (which makes further provision in relation to persons sent to the Crown Court for trial under section 51 above) shall have effect.

[Crime and Disorder Act 1998, s 52.]

Miscellaneous

PART 3A

LIVE LINKS FOR ACCUSED'S ATTENDANCE AT CERTAIN PRELIMINARY AND SENTENCING HEARINGS

1–3835 57A. Introductory. (1) This Part—

(*a*) applies to preliminary hearings and sentencing hearings in the course of proceedings for an offence; and

(b) enables the court in the circumstances provided for in sections 57B, 57C and 57E to direct the use of a live link for securing the accused's attendance at a hearing to which this Part applies.

(2) The accused is to be treated as present in court when, by virtue of a live link direction under this Part, he attends a hearing through a live link.

(3) In this Part—

"custody"—

    (a) includes local authority accommodation to which a person is remanded or committed by virtue of section 23 of the Children and Young Persons Act 1969; but

    (b) does not include police detention;

"live link" means an arrangement by which a person (when not in the place where the hearing is being held) is able to see and hear, and to be seen and heard by, the court during a hearing (and for this purpose any impairment of eyesight or hearing is to be disregarded);

"police detention" has the meaning given by section 118(2) of the Police and Criminal Evidence Act 1984;

"preliminary hearing" means a hearing in the proceedings held before the start of the trial (within the meaning of subsection (11A) or (11B) of section 22 of the 1985 Act) including, in the case of proceedings in the Crown Court, a preparatory hearing held under—

    (a) section 7 of the Criminal Justice Act 1987 (cases of serious or complex fraud); or

    (b) section 29 of the Criminal Procedure and Investigations Act 1996 (other serious, complex or lengthy cases);

"sentencing hearing" means any hearing following conviction which is held for the purpose of—

    (a) proceedings relating to the giving or rescinding of a direction under section 57E;

    (b) proceedings (in a magistrates' court) relating to committal to the Crown Court for sentencing; or

    (c) sentencing the offender or determining how the court should deal with him in respect of the offence.

[Crime and Disorder Act 1998, s 57A as inserted by the Police and Justice Act 2006, s 45.]

1–3835A **57B. Use of live link at preliminary hearings where accused is in custody.** (1) This section applies in relation to a preliminary hearing in a magistrates' court or the Crown Court.

(2) Where it appears to the court before which the preliminary hearing is to take place that the accused is likely to be held in custody during the hearing, the court may give a live link direction under this section in relation to the attendance of the accused at the hearing.

(3) A live link direction under this section is a direction requiring the accused, if he is being held in custody during the hearing, to attend it through a live link from the place at which he is being held.

(4) If a hearing takes place in relation to the giving or rescinding of such a direction, the court may require or permit a person attending the hearing to do so through a live link.

(5) The court shall not give or rescind such a direction (whether at a hearing or otherwise) unless the parties to the proceedings have been given the opportunity to make representations.

(6) If in a case where it has power to do so a magistrates' court decides not to give a live link direction under this section, it must—

    (a) state in open court its reasons for not doing so; and

    (b) cause those reasons to be entered in the register of its proceedings.

[Crime and Disorder Act 1998, s 57B as inserted by the Police and Justice Act 2006, s 45.]

1–3835B **57C. Use of live link at preliminary hearings where accused is at police station.** (1) This section applies in relation to a preliminary hearing in a magistrates' court.

(2) Where subsection (3) or (4) applies to the accused, the court may give a live link direction in relation to his attendance at the preliminary hearing.

(3) This subsection applies to the accused if—

    (a) he is in police detention at a police station in connection with the offence; and

    (b) it appears to the court that he is likely to remain at that station in police detention until the beginning of the preliminary hearing.

(4) This subsection applies to the accused if he is at a police station in answer to live link bail in connection with the offence.

(5) A live link direction under this section is a direction requiring the accused to attend the preliminary hearing through a live link from the police station.

(6) But a direction given in relation to an accused to whom subsection (3) applies has no effect if he does not remain in police detention at the police station until the beginning of the preliminary hearing.

(7) A live link direction under this section may not be given unless the accused has given his consent to the court.

(8) A magistrates' court may rescind a live link direction under this section at any time before or during a hearing to which it relates.

(9) A magistrates' court may require or permit—

    (a) the accused to give or withhold consent under subsection (7) through a live link; and

(b) any party to the proceedings who wishes to make representations in relation to the giving or rescission of a live link direction under this section to do so through a live link.

(10) Where a live link direction under this section is given in relation to an accused person who is answering to live link bail he is to be treated as having surrendered to the custody of the court (as from the time when the direction is given).

(11) In this section, "live link bail" means bail granted under Part 4 of the Police and Criminal Evidence Act 1984 subject to the duty mentioned in section 47(3)(b) of that Act."

[Crime and Disorder Act 1998, s 57C as inserted by the Police and Justice Act 2006, s 45.]

1–3835C 57D. Continued use of live link for sentencing hearing following a preliminary hearing. (1) Subsection (2) applies where—

(a) a live link direction under section 57B or 57C is in force;
(b) the accused is attending a preliminary hearing through a live link by virtue of the direction;
(c) the court convicts him of the offence in the course of that hearing (whether by virtue of a guilty plea or an indication of an intention to plead guilty); and
(d) the court proposes to continue the hearing as a sentencing hearing in relation to the offence.

(2) The accused may continue to attend through the live link by virtue of the direction if—

(a) the hearing is continued as a sentencing hearing in relation to the offence;
(b) the accused consents to his continuing to attend through the live link; and
(c) the court is satisfied that it is not contrary to the interests of justice for him to do so.

(3) But the accused may not give oral evidence through the live link during a continued hearing under subsection (2) unless—

(a) he consents to give evidence in that way; and
(b) the court is satisfied that it is not contrary to the interests of justice for him to give it in that way.

[Crime and Disorder Act 1998, s 57D as inserted by the Police and Justice Act 2006, s 45.]

1–3835D 57E. Use of live link in sentencing hearings. (1) This section applies where the accused is convicted of the offence.

(2) If it appears to the court by or before which the accused is convicted that it is likely that he will be held in custody during any sentencing hearing for the offence, the court may give a live link direction under this section in relation to that hearing.

(3) A live link direction under this section is a direction requiring the accused, if he is being held in custody during the hearing, to attend it through a live link from the place at which he is being held.

(4) Such a direction—

(a) may be given by the court of its own motion or on an application by a party; and
(b) may be given in relation to all subsequent sentencing hearings before the court or to such hearing or hearings as may be specified or described in the direction.

(5) The court may not give such a direction unless—

(a) the offender has given his consent to the direction; and
(b) the court is satisfied that it is not contrary to the interests of justice to give the direction.

(6) The court may rescind such a direction at any time before or during a hearing to which it relates if it appears to the court to be in the interests of justice to do so (but this does not affect the court's power to give a further live link direction in relation to the offender).
The court may exercise this power of its own motion or on an application by a party.

(7) The offender may not give oral evidence while attending a hearing through a live link by virtue of this section unless—

(a) he consents to give evidence in that way; and
(b) the court is satisfied that it is not contrary to the interests of justice for him to give it in that way.

(8) The court must—

(a) state in open court its reasons for refusing an application for, or for the rescission of, a live link direction under this section; and
(b) if it is a magistrates' court, cause those reasons to be entered in the register of its proceedings.

[Crime and Disorder Act 1998, s 57E as inserted by the Police and Justice Act 2006, s 45.]

PART V[1]
MISCELLANEOUS AND SUPPLEMENTAL

Supplemental

1–3836 114. Orders and regulations. (1) Any power of a Minister of the Crown or of the National Assembly for Wales to make an order or regulations under this Act—

(a) is exercisable by statutory instrument; and
(b) includes power to make such transitional provision as appears to him necessary or expedient in connection with any provision made by the order or regulations.

(2) A statutory instrument containing an order under section 1A, 1G, 5(1A), (2) or (3), 6A(1) or

10(6) above (other than one made by the National Assembly for Wales), or containing regulations under paragraph 1 of Schedule 3 to this Act, shall be subject to annulment in pursuance of a resolution of either House of Parliament.

(3) No order under section 1F, 135A(5),* 38(5) or 41(6) above shall be made unless a draft of the order has been laid before and approved by a resolution of each House of Parliament.**

[Crime and Disorder Act 1998, s 114 as amended by the Powers of Criminal Courts (Sentencing) Act 2000, Sch 9,the Police Reform Act 2002, s 97 and the Serious Organised Crime and Police Act 2005, s 142 **the Drugs Act 2005, s 20**.]

---

*"135A(5)" inserted by the Serious Organised Crime and Police Act 2005, Sch 10 in force in relation to certain specified areas: 20 July 2006: see SI 2006/1871, art 2. In force for remaining purposes from a date to be appointed.

1. Part V contains ss 97–121.

1–3837   115. Disclosure of information.   (1) Any person who, apart from this subsection, would not have power to disclose information—

(a)   to a relevant authority; or
(b)   to a person acting on behalf of such an authority,

shall have power to do so in any case where the disclosure is necessary or expedient for the purposes of any provision of this Act.

(2) In subsection (1) above "relevant authority" means—

(a)   the chief officer of police for a police area in England and Wales;
(b)   the chief constable of a police force maintained under the Police (Scotland) Act 1967;
(c)   a police authority within the meaning given by section 101(1) of the Police Act 1996;
(d)   a local authority, that is to say—

  (i)   in relation to England, a county council, a district council, a London borough council, a parish council or the Common Council of the City of London;
  (ii)   in relation to Wales, a county council or a county borough council, a county borough council or a community council;
  (iii)   in relation to Scotland, a council constituted under section 2 of the Local Government etc (Scotland) Act 1994;

(da)   a person registered under section 1 of the Housing Act 1996 as a social landlord;
(e)   a probation committee in England and Wales;
(ee)   a Strategic Health Authority;
(f)   a health authority;
(g)   a Primary Care Trust.

[Crime and Disorder Act 1998, s 115 as amended by SI 2000/90, SI 2002/2306 and SI 2002/2469, the Police Reform Act 2002, s 97 and the Housing Act 2004, s 219.]

1–3838   116. Transitory provisions.   (1) The Secretary of State may by order provide that, in relation to any time before the commencement of section 73 above, a court shall not make an order under—

(a)   section 1 of the 1994 Act (secure training orders); or
(b)   subsection (3)(a) of section 4 of that Act (breaches of supervision requirements),

unless it has been notified by the Secretary of State that accommodation at a secure training centre, or accommodation provided by a local authority for the purpose of restricting the liberty of children and young persons, is immediately available for the offender, and the notice has not been withdrawn.

(2) An order under this section may provide that sections 2 and 4 of the 1994 Act shall have effect, in relation to any such time, as if—

(a)   for subsections (2) and (3) of section 2 there were substituted the following subsection—

"(2) Where accommodation for the offender at a secure training centre is not immediately available—

  (a)   the court shall commit the offender to accommodation provided by a local authority for the purpose of restricting the liberty of children and young persons until such time as accommodation for him at such a centre is available; and
  (b)   the period of detention in the centre under the order shall be reduced by the period spent by the offender in the accommodation so provided.";

(b)   in subsection (5) of that section, for the words "subsections (2)(a)(ii) and (4)(b) apply" there were substituted the words "subsection (4)(b) applies";
(c)   for subsection (8) of that section there were substituted the following subsection—

"(8) In this section "local authority" has the same meaning as in the Children Act 1989."; and

(d)   in subsection (4) of section 4, for the words "paragraphs (a), (b) and (c) of subsection (2) and subsections (5), (7) and (8) of section 2" there were substituted the words "paragraphs (a) and (b) of subsection (2) and subsections (7) and (8) of section 2".

(3) In relation to any time before the commencement of section 73 above, section 4 of the 1994 Act shall have effect as if after subsection (4) there were inserted the following subsection—

"(4A) A fine imposed under subsection (3)(*b*) above shall be deemed, for the purposes of any enactment, to be a sum adjudged to be paid by a conviction."

(4) In relation to any time before the commencement of section 73 above, section 1B of the 1982 Act (special provision for offenders under 18) shall have effect as if—

(*a*) in subsection (4), immediately before the words "a total term" there were inserted the words "a term or (in the case of an offender to whom subsection (6) below applies)";

(*b*) in subsection (5)—

    (i) immediately before the words "total term" there were inserted the words "term or (as the case may be)"; and

    (ii) for the words "the term" there were substituted the word "it"; and

(*c*) for subsection (6) there were substituted the following subsection—

"(6) This subsection applies to an offender sentenced to two or more terms of detention in a young offender institution which are consecutive or wholly or partly concurrent if—

(*a*) the sentences were passed on the same occasion; or

(*b*) where they were passed on different occasions, the offender has not been released under Part II of the Criminal Justice Act 1991 at any time during the period beginning with the first and ending with the last of those occasions;

and in subsections (4) and (5) above "the total term", in relation to such an offender, means the aggregate of those terms."

(5) In this section "local authority" has the same meaning as in the 1989 Act.

[Crime and Disorder Act 1998, s 116.]

1–3839   117. General interpretation.   (1) In this Act—

"the 1933 Act" means the Children and Young Persons Act 1933;
"the 1969 Act" means the Children and Young Persons Act 1969;
"the 1973 Act" means the Powers of Criminal Courts Act 1973;
"the 1980 Act" means the Magistrates' Courts Act 1980;
"the 1982 Act" means the Criminal Justice Act 1982;
"the 1984 Act" means the Police and Criminal Evidence Act 1984;
"the 1985 Act" means the Prosecution of Offences Act 1985;
"the 1989 Act" means the Children Act 1989;
"the 1991 Act" means the Criminal Justice Act 1991;
"the 1994 Act" means the Criminal Justice and Public Order Act 1994;
"the 1997 Act" means the Crime (Sentences) Act 1997;
"caution" has the same meaning as in Part V of the Police Act 1997;
"child" means a person under the age of 14,
"custodial sentence" has the same meaning as in the Powers of Criminal Courts (Sentencing) Act 2000;
"guardian" has the same meaning as in the 1933 Act;
"local probation board" means a local probation board established under section 4 of the Criminal Justice and Court Services Act 2000;
"prescribed" means prescribed by an order made by the Secretary of State;
"young person" means a person who has attained the age of 14 and is under the age of 18;
"youth offending team" means a team established under section 39 above.

(2) In this Act—

"the 1993 Act" means the Prisoners and Criminal Proceedings (Scotland) Act 1993; and
"the 1995 Act" means the Criminal Procedure (Scotland) Act 1995.

(3) For the purposes of this Act, the age of a person shall be deemed to be that which it appears to the court to be after considering any available evidence.

[Crime and Disorder Act 1998, s 117 as amended by the Powers of Criminal Courts (Sentencing) Act 2000, Sch 9, the Criminal Justice and Court Services Act 2000, Sch 7 and SI 2005/886.]

1–3840   119. Minor and consequential amendments.   The enactments mentioned in Schedule 8[1] to this Act shall have effect subject to the amendments there specified, being minor amendments and amendments consequential on the provisions of this Act.

[Crime and Disorder Act 1998, s 119.]

---

1. Schedule 8 is not reproduced in this work.

1–3841   120. Transitional provisions, savings and repeals.   (1) The transitional provisions and savings contained in Schedule 9[1] to this Act shall have effect; but nothing in this subsection shall be taken as prejudicing the operation of sections 16 and 17 of the Interpretation Act 1978 (which relate to the effect of repeals).

(2) The enactments specified in Schedule 10[1] to this Act, which include some that are spent, are hereby repealed to the extent specified in the third column of that Schedule.

[Crime and Disorder Act 1998, s 120.]

1. Schedule 9, see post.
2. Schedule 10 is not reproduced in this work.

1–3842   121. Short title, commencement and extent.   (1) This Act may be cited as the Crime and Disorder Act 1998.

(2) This Act, except this section, sections 109 and 111(8) above and paragraphs 55, 99 and 117 of Schedule 8 to this Act, shall come into force on such day as the Secretary of State may by order[1] appoint; and different days may be appointed for different purposes or different areas.

(3) Without prejudice to the provisions of Schedule 9 to this Act, an order under subsection (2) above may make such transitional provisions and savings as appear to the Secretary of State necessary or expedient in connection with any provision brought into force by the order.

(4) Subject to subsections (5) to (12) below, this Act extends to England and Wales only.

(5) The following provisions extend to Scotland only, namely—

(a) Chapter II of Part I;
(b) section 33;
(c) Chapter II of Part IV;
(d) sections 108 to 112 and 117(2); and
(e) paragraphs 55, 70, 71, 98 to 108, 115 to 124 and 140 to 143 of Schedule 8 and section 119 above so far as relating to those paragraphs.

(6) The following provisions also extend to Scotland, namely—

(a) Chapter III of Part I;
(b) section 36(3) to (5);
(c) section 65(9);
(d) section 115;
(e) paragraph 3 of Schedule 3 to this Act and section 52(6) above so far as relating to that paragraph;
(f) *repealed*;
(g) paragraphs 1, 7(1) and (3), 14(1) and (2), 35, 36, 45, 135, 136 and 138 of Schedule 8 to this Act and section 119 above so far as relating to those paragraphs; and
(h) this section.

(7) Sections 36(1), (2)(a), (b) and (d) and (6)(b) and section 118 above extend to Northern Ireland only.

(8) Section 36(3)(b), (4) and (5) above, paragraphs 7(1) and (3), 45, 135 and 138 of Schedule 8 to this Act, section 119 above so far as relating to those paragraphs and this section also extend to Northern Ireland.

(9) Section 36(5) above, paragraphs 7(1) and (3), 45 and 134 of Schedule 8 to this Act, section 119 above so far as relating to those paragraphs and this section also extend to the Isle of Man.

(10) Section 36(5) above, paragraphs 7(1) and (3), 45 and 135 of Schedule 8 to this Act, section 119 above so far as relating to those paragraphs and this section also extend to the Channel Islands.

(11) The repeals in Schedule 10 to this Act, and section 120(2) above so far as relating to those repeals, have the same extent as the enactments on which the repeals operate.

(12) And in Schedule 1 to the 1997 Act—

(a) paragraph 14 (restricted transfers between the United Kingdom and the Channel Islands) as applied in relation to the Isle of Man; and
(b) paragraph 19 (application of Schedule in relation to the Isle of Man),

apply to the amendments of that Schedule made by paragraph 135 of Schedule 8 to this Act.
[Crime and Disorder Act 1998, s 121 as amended by the Powers of Criminal Courts (Sentencing) Act 2000, Sch 12 and the Criminal Justice Act 2003, Sch 32.]

---

1. At the date of going to press, the following commencement orders which are reproduced in this PART post, had been made: Crime and Disorder Act 1998 (Commencement No 1) Order 1998, SI 1998/1883, the Crime and Disorder Act 1998 (Commencement No 2 and Transitional Provisions) Order 1998, SI 1998/2327, amended by 1998/2412, the Crime and Disorder Act 1998 (Commencement No 3 and Appointed Day) Order 1998, SI 1998/3263, the Crime and Disorder Act 1998 (Commencement No 4) Order 1999, SI 1999/1279, the Crime and Disorder Act 1998 (Commencement No 5) Order 1999, SI 1999/2976, the Crime and Disorder Act 1998 (Commencement No 6) Order 1999, SI 1999/3426, the Crime and Disorder Act 1998 (Commencement No 7) Order 2000, SI 2000/924, the Crime and Disorder Act 1998 (Commencement No 8) Order 2000, SI 2000/3283.

SCHEDULE 3
PROCEDURE WHERE PERSONS ARE SENT FOR TRIAL UNDER SECTION 51

(As amended by the Access to Justice Act 1999, s 67 and Schs 4, 13 and 15, the Powers of Criminal Courts (Sentencing) Act 2000, Sch 9, the Criminal Justice Act 2003, Schs 36 and 37, SI 2005/886 and the Serious Organised Crime and Police Act 2005, s 169.)

Regulations

1–3843   1. (1) The Attorney General shall by regulations[1] provide that, where a person is sent for trial under section 51* of this Act on any charge or charges, copies of the documents containing the evidence on which the charge or charges are based shall—

(*a*) be served on that person; and
(*b*) be given to the Crown Court sitting at the place specified in the notice under subsection (7) of that section★

before the expiry of the period prescribed by the regulations; but the judge may at his discretion extend or further extend that period.

(2) The regulations[1] may make provision as to the procedure to be followed on an application for the extension or further extension of a period under sub-paragraph (1) above.

★Words inserted or substituted by the Criminal Justice Act 2003, Sch 3 from a date to be appointed.
1. The Crime and Disorder Act 1998 (Service of Prosecution Evidence) Regulations 2005, SI 2005/902 have been made which provide that copies of the documents containing the evidence on which the charge or charges are based shall be served on the person sent for trial and given to the Crown Court within 70 days from the date of the sending of the person for trial or, in the case of a person committed to custody, 50 days.
Oral or written application may be made by the prosecutor to the Crown Court to extend or further this period. In relation to a former version of these regulations it was held that failure to comply with the 42-day time limit which was then applicable does not render the prosecution a nullity, and the Crown Court can grant an extension of time on an application by the prosecution made outside the 42-day time limit (*Fehily v Governor of HM Prison Wandsworth* [2002] EWHC 1295 Admin, [2003] Cr App R 10).

Applications for dismissal

1–3844 **2.** (1) A person who is sent for trial under section 51★ of this Act on any charge or charges may, at any time—

(*a*) after he is served with copies of the documents containing the evidence on which the charge or charges are based; and
(*b*) before he is arraigned (and whether or not an indictment has been preferred against him),

apply orally or in writing to the Crown Court sitting at the place specified in the notice under subsection (7) of that section★ for the charge, or any of the charges, in the case to be dismissed.

(2) The judge shall dismiss a charge (and accordingly quash any count relating to it in any indictment preferred against the applicant) which is the subject of any such application if it appears to him that the evidence against the applicant would not be sufficient for him to be properly convicted [1].

(3) No oral application may be made under sub-paragraph (1) above unless the applicant has given to the Crown Court sitting at the place in question written notice of his intention to make the application.

(4) Oral evidence may be given on such an application only with the leave of the judge or by his order; and the judge shall give leave or make an order only if it appears to him, having regard to any matters stated in the application for leave, that the interests of justice require him to do so.★

(5) If the judge gives leave permitting, or makes an order requiring, a person to give oral evidence, but that person does not do so, the judge may disregard any document indicating the evidence that he might have given.★

(6) If the charge, or any of the charges, against the applicant is dismissed—

(*a*) no further proceedings may be brought on the dismissed charge or charges except by means of the preferment of a voluntary bill of indictment; and
(*b*) unless the applicant is in custody otherwise than on the dismissed charge or charges, he shall be discharged.

(7) Criminal Procedure Rules may make provision for the purposes of this paragraph and, without prejudice to the generality of this sub-paragraph, may make provision—

(*a*) as to the time or stage in the proceedings at which anything required to be done is to be done (unless the court grants leave to do it at some other time or stage);
(*b*) as to the contents and form of notices or other documents;
(*c*) as to the manner in which evidence is to be submitted; and
(*d*) as to persons to be served with notices or other material.

★Words inserted or substituted in sub-paras (1)–(3), sub-paras (4) and (5) repealed by the Criminal Justice Act 2003, Sch 3 from a date to be appointed.
1. A decision to dismiss is not amenable to judicial review: *R (Snelgrove) v Crown Court at Woolwich* [2004] EWHC 2172 (Admin), [2005] 1 WLR 3223, [2005] 1 Cr App R 18.

Reporting restrictions

1–3845 **3.** (1) Except as provided by this paragraph, it shall not be lawful—

(*a*) to publish in Great Britain★ a written report of an application under paragraph 2(1) above; or
(*b*) to include in a relevant programme for reception in Great Britain★ a report of such an application,

if (in either case) the report contains any matter other than that permitted by this paragraph.

(2) An order that sub-paragraph (1) above shall not apply to reports of an application under paragraph 2(1) above may be made by the judge dealing with the application.

(3) Where in the case of two or more accused one of them objects to the making of an order under sub-paragraph (2) above, the judge shall make the order if, and only if, he is satisfied, after hearing the representations of the accused, that it is in the interests of justice to do so.

(4) An order under sub-paragraph (2) above shall not apply to reports of proceedings under sub-paragraph (3) above, but any decision of the court to make or not to make such an order may be contained in reports published or included in a relevant programme before the time authorised by sub-paragraph (5) below.

(5) It shall not be unlawful under this paragraph to publish or include in a relevant programme a report of an application under paragraph 2(1) above containing any matter other than that permitted by sub-paragraph (8) below where the application is successful.

(6) Where—

(a) two or more persons were jointly charged; and
(b) applications under paragraph 2(1) above are made by more than one of them,

sub-paragraph (5) above shall have effect as if for the words "the application is" there were substituted the words "all the applications are".

(7) It shall not be unlawful under this paragraph to publish or include in a relevant programme a report of an unsuccessful application at the conclusion of the trial of the person charged, or of the last of the persons charged to be tried.

(8) The following matters may be contained in a report published or included in a relevant programme without an order under sub-paragraph (2) above before the time authorised by sub-paragraphs (5) and (6) above, that is to say—

(a) the identity of the court and the name of the judge;
(b) the names, ages, home addresses and occupations of the accused and witnesses;*
(c) the offence or offences, or a summary of them, with which the accused is or are charged;
(d) the names of counsel and solicitors engaged in the proceedings;
(e) where the proceedings are adjourned, the date and place to which they are adjourned;
(f) the arrangements as to bail;
(g) whether a right to representation funded by the Legal Services Commission as part of the Criminal Defence Service was granted to the accused or any of the accused.

(9) The addresses that may be published or included in a relevant programme under sub-paragraph (8) above are addresses—

(a) at any relevant time; and
(b) at the time of their publication or inclusion in a relevant programme.*

(10) If a report is published or included in a relevant programme in contravention of this paragraph, the following persons, that is to say—

(a) in the case of a publication of a written report as part of a newspaper or periodical, any proprietor, editor or publisher of the newspaper or periodical;
(b) in the case of a publication of a written report otherwise than as part of a newspaper or periodical, the person who publishes it;
(c) in the case of the inclusion of a report in a relevant programme, any body corporate which is engaged in providing the service in which the programme is included and any person having functions in relation to the programme corresponding to those of the editor of a newspaper;

shall be liable on summary conviction to a fine not exceeding level 5 on the standard scale.

(11) Proceedings for an offence under this paragraph shall not, in England and Wales, be instituted otherwise than by or with the consent of the Attorney General.*

(12) Sub-paragraph (1) above shall be in addition to, and not in derogation from, the provisions of any other enactment with respect to the publication of reports of court proceedings.

(13) In this paragraph—

"publish", in relation to a report, means publish the report, either by itself or as part of a newspaper or periodical, for distribution to the public;
"relevant programme" means a programme included in a programme service (within the meaning of the Broadcasting Act 1990);
"relevant time" means a time when events giving rise to the charges to which the proceedings relate occurred.

---

*Words substituted and new sub-paras (8)(bb), (9) and (11A) inserted by the Criminal Justice Act 2003, Sch 3 from a date to be appointed.

Power of justice to take depositions etc[1]

1–3846 **4.** (1) Sub-paragraph (2) below applies where a justice of the peace for any commission area is satisfied that—

(a) any person in England and Wales ("the witness") is likely to be able to make on behalf of the prosecutor a written statement containing material evidence, or produce on behalf of the prosecutor a document or other exhibit likely to be material evidence, for the purposes of proceedings for an offence for which a person has been sent for trial under section 51* of this Act by a magistrates' court for that area; and
(b) it is in the interests of justice to issue a summons under this paragraph to secure the attendance of the witness to have his evidence taken as a deposition or to produce the document or other exhibit.

(2) In such a case the justice shall issue a summons directed to the witness requiring him to attend before a justice at the time and place appointed in the summons, and to have his evidence taken as a deposition or to produce the document or other exhibit.

(3) If a justice of the peace is satisfied by evidence on oath of the matters mentioned in sub-paragraph (1) above, and also that it is probable that a summons under sub-paragraph (2) above would not procure the result required by it, the justice may instead of issuing a summons issue a warrant to arrest the witness and to bring him before a justice at the time and place specified in the warrant.

(4) A summons may also be issued under sub-paragraph (2) above if the justice is satisfied that the witness is outside the British Islands, but no warrant may be issued under sub-paragraph (3) above unless the justice is satisfied by evidence on oath that the witness is in England and Wales.

(5) If—

(a) the witness fails to attend before a justice in answer to a summons under this paragraph;
(b) the justice is satisfied by evidence on oath that the witness is likely to be able to make a statement or produce a document or other exhibit as mentioned in sub-paragraph (1)(a) above;
(c) it is proved on oath, or in such other manner as may be prescribed, that he has been duly served with the summons and that a reasonable sum has been paid or tendered to him for costs and expenses; and
(d) it appears to the justice that there is no just excuse for the failure,

the justice may issue a warrant to arrest the witness and to bring him before a justice at the time and place specified in the warrant.

(6) Where—

(*a*) a summons is issued under sub-paragraph (2) above or a warrant is issued under sub-paragraph (3) or (5) above; and

(*b*) the summons or warrant is issued with a view to securing that the witness has his evidence taken as a deposition,

the time appointed in the summons or specified in the warrant shall be such as to enable the evidence to be taken as a deposition before the relevant date.

(7) If any person attending or brought before a justice in pursuance of this paragraph refuses without just excuse to have his evidence taken as a deposition, or to produce the document or other exhibit, the justice may do one or both of the following—

(*a*) commit him to custody until the expiration of such period not exceeding one month as may be specified in the summons or warrant or until he sooner has his evidence taken as a deposition or produces the document or other exhibit;

(*b*) impose on him a fine not exceeding £2,500.

(8) A fine imposed under sub-paragraph (7) above shall be deemed, for the purposes of any enactment, to be a sum adjudged to be paid by a conviction.

(9) If in pursuance of this paragraph a person has his evidence taken as a deposition, the designated officer for the justice concerned shall as soon as is reasonably practicable send a copy of the deposition to the prosecutor and the Crown Court.

(10) If in pursuance of this paragraph a person produces an exhibit which is a document, the designated officer for the justice concerned shall as soon as is reasonably practicable send a copy of the document to the prosecutor and the Crown Court.

(11) If in pursuance of this paragraph a person produces an exhibit which is not a document, the designated officer for the justice concerned shall as soon as is reasonably practicable inform the prosecutor and the Crown Court of that fact and of the nature of the exhibit.

(12) In this paragraph—

"prescribed" means prescribed by Criminal Procedure Rules;
"the relevant date" has the meaning given by paragraph 1(2) above.*

---

*Words "or 51A" inserted in sub-para (1) and in sub-para (12) definition "the relevant date" substituted by the Criminal Justice Act 2003, Sch 3 from a date to be appointed.

1. The procedure of taking a deposition from a witness, pursuant to para 4 of Sch 3 to the 1998 Act, is a proceeding in open court, though justices may exceptionally exclude persons from the taking of the deposition or otherwise modify the procedure that will assist in the reception of the evidence or it is in the interests of justice to do so: *R (on the application of the Crown Prosecution Service) v Bolton Magistrates' Court* [2003] EWHC 2697 (Admin), [2004] 1 WLR 835. [2004] Cr App R 33.

The lawyer representing the defendant in the proceedings for which the deposition is sought is entitled to attend the hearing to take the deposition unless there is some special reason justifying his exclusion; cross-examination, however, should generally be left until the Crown Court trial, though there may be cases where the reluctant witness is likely to be unavailable at the Crown Court, or can perhaps be spared attendance there if one or two questions are asked and in such a situation it would be open to the justice to permit cross-examination: *R (on the application of the Crown Prosecution Service) v Bolton Magistrates' Court*, supra.

Where a witness who has been summonsed to give a deposition under para 4 refuses to answer questions on the ground of self-incrimination that claim must be the subject of a proper investigation by the justices in respect of every question for which it is claimed and before acceding to such a claim the court should satisfy itself, from the circumstances of the case and the nature of the evidence which the witness is called to give, that there is a real and appreciable danger to the witness with reference to the ordinary operation of the law in the ordinary course of things, and not a danger of an imaginary or insubstantial character; reliance by a witness on legal advice is not capable without more of amounting to just excuse for a claim to privilege: *Regina (Crown Prosecution Service) v Bolton Magistrates' Court*, supra.

Use of depositions as evidence

1-3847 **5.** (1) Subject to sub-paragraph (3) below, sub-paragraph (2) below applies where in pursuance of paragraph 4 above a person has his evidence taken as a deposition.

(2) Where this sub-paragraph applies the deposition may without further proof be read as evidence on the trial of the accused, whether for an offence for which he was sent for trial under section 51* of this Act or for any other offence arising out of the same transaction or set of circumstances.

(3) Sub-paragraph (2) above does not apply if—

(*a*) it is proved that the deposition was not signed by the justice by whom it purports to have been signed;
(*b*) the court of trial at its discretion orders that sub-paragraph (2) above shall not apply; or
(*c*) a party to the proceedings objects to sub-paragraph (2) above applying.

(4) *Repealed.*

---

*Words "or 51A" inserted in sub-para (1) by the Criminal Justice Act 2003, Sch 3 from a date to be appointed.

Power of Crown Court to deal with summary offence

1-3848 **6.** (1) This paragraph applies where a magistrates' court has sent a person for trial under section 51* of this Act for offences which include a summary offence.

(2) If the person is convicted on the indictment, the Crown Court shall consider whether the summary offence is related to the offence that is triable only on indictment or, as the case may be, any of the offences that are so triable[1]*.

(3) If it considers that the summary offence is so related, the court shall state to the person the substance of the offence and ask him whether he pleads guilty or not guilty.

(4) If the person pleads guilty, the Crown Court shall convict him, but may deal with him in respect of the summary offence only in a manner in which a magistrates' court could have dealt with him.

(5) If he does not plead guilty, the powers of the Crown Court shall cease in respect of the summary offence except as provided by sub-paragraph (6) below.

(6) If the prosecution inform the court that they would not desire to submit evidence on the charge relating to the summary offence, the court shall dismiss it.

(7) The Crown Court shall inform the designated officer for the magistrates' court of the outcome of any proceedings under this paragraph.

(8) If the summary offence is one to which section 40 of the Criminal Justice Act 1988 applies, the Crown Court may exercise in relation to the offence the power conferred by that section; but where the person is tried on indictment for such an offence, the functions of the Crown Court under this paragraph in relation to the offence shall cease.

(9) Where the Court of Appeal allows an appeal against conviction of an indictable-only* offence which is related to a summary offence of which the appellant was convicted under this paragraph—

(a) it shall set aside his conviction of the summary offence and give the clerk of the magistrates' court notice that it has done so; and

(b) it may direct that no further proceedings in relation to the offence are to be undertaken;

and the proceedings before the Crown Court in relation to the offence shall thereafter be disregarded for all purposes.

(10) A notice under sub-paragraph (9) above shall include particulars of any direction given under paragraph (b) of that sub-paragraph in relation to the offence.

(11) *Repealed.*

(12) An offence is related to another offence for the purposes of this paragraph if it arises out of circumstances which are the same as or connected with those giving rise to the other offence.

---

*Words "or 51A" inserted in sub-para (1) and in sub-paras (2) and (9) words substituted by the Criminal Justice Act 2003, Sch 3 from a date to be appointed.

1. The words "so triable" relate to "triable on indictment" not "triable only on indictment" so that where an indictment for an offence triable either way is substituted for an offence triable only on indictment, the Crown Court has jurisdiction under this provision to deal with a related summary offence (*R v Nembard* [2002] EWCA Crim 134, 166 JP 363).

Procedure where no indictable-only offence remains

1–3849   7. (1) Subject to paragraph 13 below, this paragraph applies where—

(a) a person has been sent for trial under section 51* of this Act but has not been arraigned; and

(b) the person is charged on an indictment which (following amendment of the indictment, or as a result of an application under paragraph 2 above, or for any other reason) includes no offence that is triable only on indictment*[1].

(2) Everything that the Crown Court is required to do under the following provisions of this paragraph must be done with the accused present in court.

(3) The court shall cause to be read to the accused each count of the indictment that charges an offence triable either way.*

(4) The court shall then explain to the accused in ordinary language that, in relation to each of those offences, he may indicate whether (if it were to proceed to trial) he would plead guilty or not guilty, and that if he indicates that he would plead guilty the court must proceed as mentioned in sub-paragraph (6) below.

(5) The court shall then ask the accused whether (if the offence in question were to proceed to trial) he would plead guilty or not guilty.

(6) If the accused indicates that he would plead guilty the court shall proceed as if he had been arraigned on the count in question and had pleaded guilty.

(7) If the accused indicates that he would plead not guilty, or fails to indicate how he would plead, the court shall consider* whether the offence is more suitable for summary trial or for trial on indictment.

(8) Subject to sub-paragraph (6) above, the following shall not for any purpose be taken to constitute the taking of a plea—

(a) asking the accused under this paragraph whether (if the offence were to proceed to trial) he would plead guilty or not guilty;

(b) an indication by the accused under this paragraph of how he would plead.*

---

*Words inserted substituted in sub-paras (1) and (7), word inserted in sub-para (3) and new sub-para (9) inserted by the Criminal Justice Act 2003, Sch 3 from a date to be appointed.

1. Where a case was sent to the Crown Court under s 51 of this Act in the mistaken belief that previous convictions made a charge of burglary triable only on indictment, the subsequent use of para 7 to determine mode of trial was not invalid because an indictment had not been preferred: *R v Ashton, R v Draz, R v O'Reilly* [2006] EWCA Crim 794, [2006] Crim.App.R. 15.

1–3850   8. (1) Subject to paragraph 13 below, this paragraph applies in a case where—

(a) a person has been sent for trial under section 51* of this Act but has not been arraigned;

(b) he is charged on an indictment which (following amendment of the indictment, or as a result of an application under paragraph 2 above, or for any other reason) includes no offence that is triable only on indictment*;

(c) he is represented by a legal representative;

(d) the Crown Court considers that by reason of his disorderly conduct before the court it is not practicable for proceedings under paragraph 7 above to be conducted in his presence; and

(e) the court considers that it should proceed in his absence.

(2) In such a case—

(a) the court shall cause to be read to the representative each count of the indictment that charges an offence triable either way;*

(b) the court shall ask the representative whether (if the offence in question were to proceed to trial) the accused would plead guilty or not guilty;

(c) if the representative indicates that the accused would plead guilty the court shall proceed as if the accused had been arraigned on the count in question and had pleaded guilty;

(d) if the representative indicates that the accused would plead not guilty, or fails to indicate how the accused would plead, the court shall consider* whether the offence is more suitable for summary trial or for trial on indictment.

(3) Subject to sub-paragraph (2)(c) above, the following shall not for any purpose be taken to constitute the taking of a plea—

(a) asking the representative under this section whether (if the offence were to proceed to trial) the accused would plead guilty or not guilty;

(b) an indication by the representative under this paragraph of how the accused would plead.

---

*Words inserted in sub-paras (1) and (2)(a) and words substituted in sub-paras (1) and (2)(d) by the Criminal Justice Act 2003, Sch 3 from a date to be appointed.

1–3851 9. (1) This paragraph applies where the Crown Court is required by paragraph 7(7) or 8(2)(d) above to consider* the question whether an offence is more suitable for summary trial or for trial on indictment.

(2) Before considering the question, the court shall afford first the prosecutor and then the accused an opportunity to make representations as to which mode of trial would be more suitable.*

(3) In considering the question, the court shall have regard to—

(a) any representations made by the prosecutor or the accused;

(b) the nature of the case;

(c) whether the circumstances make the offence one of a serious character;

(d) whether the punishment which a magistrates' court would have power to impose for it would be adequate; and

(e) any other circumstances which appear to the court to make it more suitable for the offence to be dealt tried in one way rather than the other.*

---

*Word substituted in sub-para (1), sub-paras (2) and (3) substituted and new sub-paras (4) and (5) inserted by the Criminal Justice Act 2003, Sch 3 from a date to be appointed.

1–3852 10. (1) This paragraph applies (unless excluded by paragraph 15 below) where the Crown Court considers that an offence is more suitable for summary trial.

(2) The court shall explain to the accused in ordinary language—

(a) that it appears to the court more suitable for him to be tried summarily for the offence, and that he can either consent to be so tried or, of if he wishes, be tried by a jury; and

(b) that if he is tried summarily and is convicted by the magistrates' court, he may be committed for sentence to the Crown Court under section 3 of the Powers of Criminal Courts (Sentencing) Act 2000 if the convicting court is of such opinion as is mentioned in subsection (2) of that section.*

(3) After explaining to the accused as provided by sub-paragraph (2) above the court shall ask him whether he wishes to be tried summarily or by a jury*, and—

(a) if he indicates that he wishes to be tried summarily, shall remit him for trial to a magistrates' court acting for the place where he was sent to the Crown Court for trial;

(b) if he does not give such an indication, shall retain its functions in relation to the offence and proceed accordingly.

---

*Sub-paragraph (2) and words in sub-para (3) substituted by the Criminal Justice Act 2003, Sch 3 from a date to be appointed.

1–3853 11. If the Crown Court considers that an offence is more suitable for trial on indictment*, the court—

(a) shall tell the accused that it has decided that it is more suitable for him to be tried for the offence by a jury; and

(b) shall retain its functions in relation to the offence and proceed accordingly.

---

*Words substituted by the Criminal Justice Act 2003, Sch 3 from a date to be appointed.

1–3854 12. (1) Where the prosecution is being carried on by the Attorney General, the Solicitor General or the Director of Public Prosecutions and he applies for an offence which may be tried on indictment to be so tried—

(a) sub-paragraphs (4) to (8) of paragraph 7, sub-paragraphs (2)(b) to (d) and (3) of paragraph 8 and paragraphs 9 to 11 above shall not apply; and

(b) the Crown Court shall retain its functions in relation to the offence and proceed accordingly.

(2) The power of the Director of Public Prosecutions under this paragraph to apply for an offence to be tried on indictment shall not be exercised except with the consent of the Attorney General.*

---

*Repealed by the Criminal Justice Act 2003, Sch 3 from a date to be appointed.

1–3855 13. (1) This paragraph applies, in place of paragraphs 7 to 12 above, in the case of a child or young person who—

(a) has been sent for trial under section 51* of this Act but has not been arraigned; and
(b) is charged on an indictment which (following amendment of the indictment, or as a result of an application under paragraph 2 above, or for any other reason) includes no offence that is triable only on indictment*.

(2) The Crown Court shall remit the child or young person for trial to a magistrates' court acting for the place where he was sent to the Crown Court for trial unless—

(a) he is charged with such an offence as is mentioned in subsection (1) or (2) of section 91 of the Powers of Criminal Courts (Sentencing) Act 2000 (punishment of certain grave crimes) and the Crown Court considers that if he is found guilty of the offence it ought to be possible to sentence him in pursuance of subsection (3) of that section; or
(b) he is charged jointly with an adult with an offence triable either way and the Crown Court considers it necessary in the interests of justice that they both be tried for the offence in the Crown Court.*

(3) In sub-paragraph (2) above "adult" has the same meaning as in section 51 of this Act.*

---

*Words in sub-para (1) substituted, words in sub-para (2) repealed and sub-para (3) substituted by the Criminal Justice Act 2003, Sch 3 from a date to be appointed.

Procedure for determining whether offences of criminal damage etc are summary offences

1–3856 **14.** (1) This paragraph applies where the Crown Court has to determine, for the purposes of this Schedule, whether an offence which is listed in the first column of Schedule 2 to the 1980 Act (offences for which the value involved is relevant to the mode of trial) is a summary offence.
(2) The court shall have regard to any representations made by the prosecutor or the accused.
(3) If it appears clear to the court that the value involved does not exceed the relevant sum, it shall treat the offence as a summary offence.
(4) If it appears clear to the court that the value involved exceeds the relevant sum, it shall treat the offence as an indictable offence.
(5) If it appears to the court for any reason not clear whether the value involved does or does not exceed the relevant sum, the court shall ask the accused whether he wishes the offence to be treated as a summary offence.
(6) Where sub-paragraph (5) above applies—

(a) if the accused indicates that he wishes the offence to be treated as a summary offence, the court shall so treat it;
(b) if the accused does not give such an indication, the court shall treat the offence as an indictable offence.

(7) In this paragraph "the value involved" and "the relevant sum" have the same meanings as in section 22 of the 1980 Act (certain offences triable either way to be tried summarily if value involved is small).

Power of Crown Court, with consent of legally-represented accused, to proceed in his absence

1–3857 **15.** (1) The Crown Court may proceed in the absence of the accused in accordance with such of the provisions of paragraphs 9 to 14 above as are applicable in the circumstances if—

(a) the accused is represented by a legal representative who signifies to the court the accused's consent to the proceedings in question being conducted in his absence; and
(b) the court is satisfied that there is good reason for proceeding in the absence of the accused.

(2) Sub-paragraph (1) above is subject to the following provisions of this paragraph which apply where the court exercises the power conferred by that sub-paragraph.
(3) If, where the court has considered* as required by paragraph 7(7) or 8(2)(d) above, it appears to the court that an offence is more suitable for summary trial, paragraph 10 above shall not apply and—

(a) if the legal representative indicates that the accused wishes to be tried summarily, the court shall remit the accused for trial to a magistrates' court acting for the place where he was sent to the Crown Court for trial;
(b) if the legal representative does not give such an indication, the court shall retain its functions and proceed accordingly.

(4) If, where the court has considered* as required by paragraph 7(7) or 8(2)(d) above, it appears to the court that an offence is more suitable for trial on indictment, paragraph 11 above shall apply with the omission of paragraph (a).
(5) Where paragraph 14 above applies and it appears to the court for any reason not clear whether the value involved does or does not exceed the relevant sum, sub-paragraphs (5) and (6) of that paragraph shall not apply and—

(a) the court shall ask the legal representative whether the accused wishes the offence to be treated as a summary offence;
(b) if the legal representative indicates that the accused wishes the offence to be treated as a summary offence, the court shall so treat it;
(c) if the legal representative does not give such an indication, the court shall treat the offence as an indictable offence.

---

*In Sub-paras (3) and (4) "decided" substituted by the Criminal Justice Act 2003, Sch 3 from a date to be appointed.

Section 120(1)   SCHEDULE 9
TRANSITIONAL PROVISIONS AND SAVINGS

(As amended by the Powers of Criminal Courts (Sentencing) Act 2000, Schs 9 and 12.)

Presumption of incapacity

1–3858 **1.** Nothing in section 34 of this Act shall apply in relation to anything done before the commencement of that section.

Effect of child's silence at trial

  2. Nothing in section 35 of this Act shall apply where the offence was committed before the commencement of that section.

  3. *Repealed.*

  4. *Repealed.*

Young offenders: cautions

  5. (1) Any caution given to a child or young person before the commencement of section 65 of this Act shall be treated for the purposes of subsections (2) and (4) of that section as a reprimand.

  (2) Any second or subsequent caution so given shall be treated for the purposes of paragraphs (*a*) and (*b*) of subsection (3) of that section as a warning.

Abolition of secure training orders

  6. In relation to any time before the commencement of subsection (7) of section 73 of this Act, section 9A of the 1997 Act shall have effect as if after subsection (1) there were inserted the following subsection—

  "(1A) Section 9 above applies to periods of detention which offenders are liable to serve under secure training orders as it applies to sentences of imprisonment."

Sentencing guidelines

  7. (1) Section 80 of this Act does not apply by virtue of subsection (1)(*a*) of that section in any case where the Court is seised of the appeal before the commencement of that section.

  (2) In this paragraph "the Court" and "seised" have the same meanings as in that section.

Confiscation orders on committal for sentence

  8. Section 83 of this Act does not apply where the offence was committed before the commencement of that section.*

Football spectators: failure to comply with reporting duty

  9. Section 84 of this Act does not apply where the offence was committed before the commencement of that section.

Power to release short-term prisoners on licence

  10. (1) Section 99 of this Act does not apply in relation to a prisoner who, immediately before the commencement of that section, has served one or more days more than the requisite period for the term of his sentence.

  (2) In this paragraph "the requisite period" has the same meaning as in section 34A of the 1991 Act (which is inserted by section 99 of this Act).

Early release: two or more sentences

  11. (1) Where the terms of two or more sentences passed before the commencement of section 101 of this Act have been treated, by virtue of section 51(2) of the 1991 Act, as a single term for the purposes of Part II of that Act, they shall continue to be so treated after that commencement.

  (2) Subject to sub-paragraph (1) above, section 101 of this Act applies where one or more of the sentences concerned were passed after that commencement.

Recall to prison of short-term prisoners

  12. (1) Sub-paragraphs (2) to (7) below have effect in relation to any prisoner whose sentence, or any part of whose sentence, was imposed for an offence committed before the commencement of section 103 of this Act.

  (2) The following provisions of this Act do not apply, namely—

  (*a*) section 103;

  (*b*) paragraphs 83(1)(*b*) and 88(3)(*a*) of Schedule 8 to this Act and section 119 so far as relating to those paragraphs; and

  (*c*) section 120(2) and Schedule 10 so far as relating to the repeal of section 38 of the 1991 Act and the repeals in sections 37(1) and 45(4) of that Act.

  (3) Section 33 of the 1991 Act has effect as if, in subsection (3)(*b*) (as amended by paragraph 80(1) of Schedule 8 to this Act), for the words "section 39(1) or (2)" there were substituted the words "section 38(2) or 39(1) or (2)".

  (4) Section 33A of the 1991 Act (as inserted by paragraph 81 of Schedule 8 to this Act) has effect as if—

  (*a*) in subsection (1), for the words "section 38A(1) or 39(1) or (2)" there were substituted the words "section 38(2) or 38A(1)"; and

  (*b*) in subsection (3), for the words "section 39(1) or (2)", in both places where they occur, there were substituted the words "section 38(2)".

(5) Section 34A of the 1991 Act (as inserted by section 99 of this Act) has effect as if, in subsection (2)(*g*), for the words "section 39(1) or (2)" there were substituted the words "section 38(2)".

(6) Section 40A of the 1991 Act (as inserted by section 105 of this Act) has effect as if, in subsection (1), for the word "39" there were substituted the word "38".

(7) Section 44 of the 1991 Act (as substituted by section 59 of this Act) has effect as if—

(*a*) in subsections (3) and (4), after the words "subject to" there were inserted the words "any suspension under section 38(2) above or, as the case may be,"; and

(*b*) in subsection (7), for the words "sections 37(5) and 39(1) and (2)" there were substituted the words "section 37(5), 38(2) and 39(1) and (2)".

(8) Section 45 of the 1991 Act has effect as if, in subsection (3) (as amended by paragraph 88(2) of Schedule 8 to this Act), for the words "section 39(1) or (2)" there were substituted the words "section 38(2) or 39(1) or (2)".

(9) For the purposes of this paragraph and paragraph 13 below, consecutive sentences, or sentences that are wholly or partly concurrent, shall be treated as parts of a single sentence.

Release on licence following recall to prison

13. Section 104 of this Act does not apply in relation to a prisoner whose sentence, or any part of whose sentence, was imposed for an offence committed before the commencement of that section.

Release on licence following return to prison

14. (1) Section 105 of this Act does not apply where the new offence was committed before the commencement of that section.

(2) In this paragraph "the new offence" has the same meaning as in section 116 of the Powers of Criminal Courts (Sentencing) Act 2000.

Remand time: two or more sentences

15. (1) Where the terms of two or more sentences passed before the commencement of paragraph 11 of Schedule 8 to this Act have been treated, by virtue of section 104(2) of the Criminal Justice Act 1967, as a single term for the purposes of section 67 of that Act, they shall continue to be so treated after that commencement.

(2) Subject to sub-paragraph (1) above, paragraph 11 of Schedule 8 to this Act applies where one or more of the sentences concerned were passed after that commencement.

*Repealed by the Proceeds of Crime Act 2002, Sch 12 from a date to be appointed.

Government of Wales Act 1998
(1998 c 38)

Introduction

1–3859   21. Introductory. The Assembly shall have the functions which are—

(*a*) transferred to, or made exercisable by, the Assembly by virtue of this Act, or
(*b*) conferred or imposed on the Assembly by or under this Act or any other Act.*

[Government of Wales Act 1998, s 21.]

*Repealed by the Government of Wales Act 2006, Sch 12 as from immediately after the ordinary election held in 2007.
1. Part II contains ss 21–45.

Transfer of Ministerial functions to Assembly

1–3860   22. Transfer of Ministerial functions. (1) Her Majesty may by Order in Council—

(*a*) provide for the transfer to the Assembly of any function so far as exercisable by a Minister of the Crown in relation to Wales,
(*b*) direct that any function so far as so exercisable shall be exercisable by the Assembly concurrently with the Minister of the Crown, or
(*c*) direct that any function so far as exercisable by a Minister of the Crown in relation to Wales shall be exercisable by the Minister only with the agreement of, or after consultation with, the Assembly.

(2)–(5) Further provisions concerning Orders in Council.*

[Government of Wales Act 1998, s 22.]

*Repealed by the Government of Wales Act 2006, Sch 12 as from immediately after the ordinary election held in 2007.

Ancillary powers etc

1–3861   38. Legal proceedings. Where the Assembly considers it appropriate for the promotion or protection of the public interest it may institute in its own name, defend or appear in any legal proceedings relating to matters with respect to which any functions of the Assembly are exercisable.
[Government of Wales Act 1998, s 38.]

Supplementary

1–3862   43. Construction of references to Ministers and departments. (1) So far as may be necessary for the purpose or in consequence of the exercise by the Assembly of any of its functions, any reference in any enactment or other document to—

(a)   a Minister of the Crown, or
(b)   a government department,

(whether by name or in general terms) shall be construed as being or including a reference to the Assembly.

(2) References in any enactment to property vested in or held for the purposes of a government department shall be construed as including references to property vested in or held for the purposes of the Assembly (and in relation to property so vested or held the Assembly shall be deemed to be a government department for the purposes of any enactment).

(3) In this section "enactment" includes an enactment—

(a)   contained in an Act passed after this Act, or
(b)   made after the passing of this Act.★

[Government of Wales Act 1998, s 43.]

1–3863   44. Parliamentary procedures for subordinate legislation. (1) This section applies where a function to make subordinate legislation (including a function conferred or imposed by, or after the passing of, this Act) has been transferred to, or made exercisable by, the Assembly by an Order in Council under section 22.

(2) Subject to subsections (4) and (5), any relevant Parliamentary procedural provision relating to the function shall not have effect in relation to the exercise of the function by the Assembly.

(3) For the purposes of this Act "relevant Parliamentary procedural provision" means provision—

(a)   requiring any instrument made in the exercise of the function, or a draft of any such instrument, to be laid before Parliament or either House of Parliament,
(b)   for the annulment or approval of any such instrument or draft by or in pursuance of a resolution of either House of Parliament or of both Houses,
(c)   prohibiting the making of any such instrument without that approval,
(d)   for any such instrument to be a provisional order (that is, an order which requires to be confirmed by Act of Parliament), or
(e)   requiring any order (within the meaning of the Statutory Orders (Special Procedure) Act 1945) to be subject to special parliamentary procedure.

(4) Subsection (2) does not apply in the case of any instrument made in the exercise of the function, or a draft of any such instrument, if it—

(a)   contains subordinate legislation made or to be made by a Minister of the Crown or government department (whether or not jointly with the Assembly),
(b)   contains (or confirms or approves) subordinate legislation relating to an English border area, or
(c)   contains (or confirms or approves) subordinate legislation relating to a cross-border body (and not relating only to the exercise of functions, or the carrying on of activities, by the body in or with respect to Wales or a part of Wales).

(5) Where a function transferred to, or made exercisable by, the Assembly by an Order in Council under section 22 is subject to a provision of the description specified in subsection (3)(e), the Order in Council may provide that—

(a)   any order made by the Assembly in the exercise of the function, or
(b)   any order so made in circumstances specified in the Order in Council,

is to be subject to special parliamentary procedure.

(6) In this section "make" includes confirm or approve and related expressions (except "made exercisable") shall be construed accordingly; but an instrument (or draft) does not fall within subsection (4)(a) just because it contains subordinate legislation made (or to be made) by the Assembly with the agreement of a Minister of the Crown or government department.★

[Government of Wales Act 1998, s 44.]

PART V[1]
OTHER PROVISIONS ABOUT THE ASSEMBLY
Community law, human rights and international obligations

1–3864   106. Community law. (1) A Community obligation of the United Kingdom is also an obligation of the Assembly if and to the extent that, the obligation could be implemented (or enabled to be implemented) or complied with by the exercise by the Assembly of any of its functions.

(2) Subsection (1) does not apply in the case of a Community obligation of the United Kingdom if—

(a) it is an obligation to achieve a result defined by reference to a quantity (whether expressed as an amount, proportion or ratio or otherwise), and

(b) the quantity relates to the United Kingdom (or to an area including the United Kingdom or to an area consisting of a part of the United Kingdom which includes the whole or part of Wales).

(3) But if such a Community obligation could (to any extent) be implemented (or enabled to be implemented) or complied with by the exercise by the Assembly of any of its functions, a Minister of the Crown may by order provide for the achievement by the Assembly (in the exercise of its functions) of so much of the result to be achieved under the Community obligation as is specified in the order.

(4) The order may specify the time by which any part of the result to be achieved by the Assembly is to be achieved.

(5) No order shall be made by a Minister of the Crown under subsection (3) unless he has consulted the Assembly.

(6) Where an order under subsection (3) is in force in relation to a Community obligation, to the extent that the Community obligation involves achieving what is specified in the order it is also an obligation of the Assembly (enforceable as if it were an obligation of the Assembly under subsection (1)).

(7) The Assembly has no power—

(a) to make, confirm or approve any subordinate legislation, or

(b) to do any other act,

so far as the subordinate legislation or act is incompatible with Community law or an obligation under subsection (6).*

[Government of Wales Act 1998, s 106.]

---

*Repealed by the Government of Wales Act 2006, Sch 12 as from immediately after the ordinary election held in 2007.
1. Part V contains ss 106–125.

1–3865   107. Human rights.   (1) The Assembly has no power—

(a) to make, confirm or approve any subordinate legislation, or

(b) to do any other act,

so far as the subordinate legislation or act is incompatible with any of the Convention rights.

(2) Subsection (1) does not enable a person—

(a) to bring any proceedings in a court or tribunal, or

(b) to rely on any of the Convention rights in any such proceedings,

in respect of an act unless he would be a victim for the purposes of Article 34 of the Convention if proceedings were brought in the European Court of Human Rights in respect of that act.

(3) Subsection (2) does not apply to the Attorney General, the Assembly, the Advocate General for Scotland or the Attorney General for Northern Ireland.*

(4) Subsection (1)—

(a) does not apply to an act which, by virtue of subsection (2) of section 6 of the Human Rights Act 1998, is not unlawful under subsection (1) of that section, and

(b) does not enable a court or tribunal to award in respect of an act any damages which it could not award on finding the act unlawful under that subsection.

(5) In this Act "the Convention rights" has the same meaning as in the Human Rights Act 1998 and in subsection (2) "the Convention" has the same meaning as in that Act.**

[Government of Wales Act 1998, s 107.]

---

*Sub-section (3) amended by the Justice (Northern Ireland) Act 2002, Sch 7, when in force.
**Repealed by the Government of Wales Act 2006, Sch 12 as from immediately after the ordinary election held in 2007.

1–3866   108. International obligations.   (1) If a Minister of the Crown considers that any action proposed to be taken by the Assembly would be incompatible with any international obligation, he may by order direct that the proposed action shall not be taken.

(2) If a Minister of the Crown considers that any action capable of being taken by the Assembly is required for the purpose of giving effect to any international obligation, he may by order direct the Assembly to take the action.

(3) If a Minister of the Crown considers that any subordinate legislation made, or which could be revoked, by the Assembly is incompatible with any international obligation, he may by order revoke the legislation.

(4) An order under subsection (3) may include provision for the order to have effect from a date earlier than that on which it is made; but—

(*a*) such a provision shall not affect any rights or liabilities acquired or incurred before the date on which the order is made, and

(*b*) no person shall be guilty of an offence merely because of such a provision.

(5) An order under subsection (1), (2) or (3) may contain any appropriate consequential, incidental, supplementary or transitional provisions or savings.

(6) In this section "international obligation" means an international obligation of the United Kingdom other than—

(*a*) an obligation under Community law, or

(*b*) an obligation not to act (or fail to act) in a way which is incompatible with any of the Convention rights.

(7) A Minister of the Crown may make an order containing provision such as is specified in subsection (8) where—

(*a*) an international obligation is an obligation to achieve a result defined by reference to a quantity (whether expressed as an amount, proportion or ratio or otherwise), and

(*b*) the quantity relates to the United Kingdom (or to an area including the United Kingdom or to an area consisting of a part of the United Kingdom which includes the whole or part of Wales).

(8) The provision referred to in subsection (7) is provision for the achievement by the Assembly (in the exercise of its functions) of so much of the result to be achieved under the international obligation as is specified in the order.

(9) The order may specify the time by which any part of the result to be achieved by the Assembly is to be achieved.

(10) Where an order under subsection (7) is in force in relation to an international obligation, references to the international obligation in subsections (1) to (3) are to an obligation to achieve so much of the result to be achieved under the international obligation as is specified in the order by the time or times so specified.

(11) No order shall be made by a Minister of the Crown under subsection (2), (3) or (7) unless he has consulted the Assembly.

(12) In this section "action" includes making, confirming or approving subordinate legislation.*
[Government of Wales Act 1998, s 108.]

---

*Repealed by the Government of Wales Act 2006, Sch 12 as from immediately after the ordinary election held in 2007.

Decisions about Assembly functions

1–3867   109. Resolution of devolution issues.   Schedule 8 (which makes provision about devolution issues) has effect.*
[Government of Wales Act 1998, s 109.]

---

*Repealed by the Government of Wales Act 2006, Sch 12 as from immediately after the ordinary election held in 2007.

1–3868   110. Power to vary retrospective decisions.   (1) This section applies where any court or tribunal decides that the Assembly did not have the power to make a provision of subordinate legislation which it has purported to make.

(2) The court or tribunal may make an order—

(*a*) removing or limiting any retrospective effect of the decision, or

(*b*) suspending the effect of the decision for any period and on any conditions to allow the defect to be corrected.

(3) In determining whether to make an order under this section, the court or tribunal shall (among other things) have regard to the extent to which persons who are not parties to the proceedings would otherwise be adversely affected by the decision.

(4) Where a court or tribunal is considering whether to make an order under this section, it shall order notice (or intimation) of that fact to be given to the relevant law officer and the Assembly (unless he or it is a party to the proceedings).

(5) Where the relevant law officer or the Assembly is given notice (or intimation) under subsection (4), he or it may take part as a party in the proceedings so far as they relate to the making of the order.

(6) In deciding any question as to costs or expenses, the court or tribunal may—

(*a*) take account of any additional expense which it considers that any party to the proceedings has incurred as a result of the participation of any person in pursuance of subsection (5), and

(*b*) award the whole or part of the additional expense as costs or expenses to the party who incurred it (whether or not it makes an order under this section and whatever the terms of any such order it does. make).

(7) Any power to make provision for regulating the procedure before any court or tribunal shall include power to make provision for the purposes of this section including, in particular, provision

for determining the manner in which and the time within which any notice (or intimation) is to be given.

(8) In this section "the relevant law officer" means—

(a) in relation to proceedings in England and Wales, the Attorney General,
(b) in relation to proceedings in Scotland, the Advocate General for Scotland, and
(c) in relation to proceedings in Northern Ireland, the Attorney General for Northern Ireland;

and in subsection (1) "make" includes confirm or approve.* **

[Government of Wales Act 1998, s 110.]

---

*Sub-section (8) para (c) amended by the Justice (Northern Ireland) Act 2002, Sch 7, when in force.
**Repealed by the Government of Wales Act 2006, Sch 12 as from immediately after the ordinary election held in 2007.

Miscellaneous

1–3869 122. English and Welsh texts of Assembly instruments. (1) The English and Welsh texts of any subordinate legislation made by the Assembly which is in both English and Welsh when made shall be treated for all purposes as being of equal standing.

(2) The Assembly may by order provide in respect of any Welsh word or phrase that, where it appears in the Welsh text of any subordinate legislation made by the Assembly, it is to be taken as having the same meaning as the English word or phrase specified in relation to it in the order.

(3) An order under subsection (2) may, in respect of any Welsh word or phrase, make different provision for different purposes.

(4) Subordinate legislation made by the Assembly shall, subject to any provision to the contrary contained in it, be construed in accordance with any order under subsection (2).*

[Government of Wales Act 1998, s 122.]

---

*Repealed by the Government of Wales Act 2006, Sch 12 as from immediately after the ordinary election held in 2007.

1–3869A 150. Abolition of Residuary Body for Wales. (1) Paragraph 18 of Schedule 13 to the Local Government (Wales) Act 1994 (provisions for winding up of Residuary Body for Wales) is amended as follows.

(2) In sub-paragraph (2) (meaning of "the transitional period" within which the Residuary Body must try to complete its work and at the end of which it is to be wound up), for "period of five years beginning with the establishment of the Residuary Body" substitute "period beginning with the establishment of the Residuary Body and ending with 31st March 1999."

(3) Omit—

(a) in sub-paragraph (3), "Subject to sub-paragraph (4),", and
(b) sub-paragraph (4),

(under which the Secretary of State may specify a period longer than the transitional period as the period at the end of which the Residuary Body is to be wound up).

(4) For sub-paragraphs (5) to (7) (duty of Residuary Body to submit scheme for its winding up and to make arrangements for transfers etc and power of Secretary of State to make orders) substitute—

"(5) The Residuary Body shall, before the end of the period of three months beginning with the day on which the Government of Wales Act 1998 is passed, submit to the Secretary of State a scheme for the winding up of the Residuary Body.

(6) The scheme shall include in relation to the Residuary Body's remaining functions, property, rights and liabilities—

(a) a statement of arrangements made by the Residuary Body for their transfer by the Residuary Body to another body or bodies,
(b) proposals for their transfer by the Secretary of State to another body or bodies, or
(c) such a statement in relation to some of them and such proposals in relation to the rest.

(7) The Secretary of State may by order make provision for giving effect to the scheme (with or without modifications) and for the transfer of functions, property, rights and liabilities of the Residuary Body to another body or bodies (whether or not as proposed in the scheme)."

[Government of Wales Act 1998, s 150.]

PART VII[1]
SUPPLEMENTARY

1–3870 151. Power to amend enactments. (1) The Secretary of State may by order make in any enactment—

(a) contained in an Act passed before or in the same session as this Act, or
(b) made before the passing of this Act or in the session in which this Act is passed,

such amendments or repeals as appear to him to be appropriate in consequence of this Act.

(2) An Order in Council under section 22 may include any provision that may be included in an order under subsection (1).★

[Government of Wales Act 1998, s 151.]

★Amended by the Government of Wales Act 2006, Sch 12 as from immediately after the ordinary election held in 2007.

1. Part VII contains ss 151–159.

1–3871   152. *Repeals*

1–3872   153. *Transitional provisions etc*

1–3872   154. *Orders and directions*★

★Repealed by the Government of Wales Act 2006, Sch 12 as from immediately after the ordinary election held in 2007.

1–3873   155. Interpretation.   (1) In this Act—

"Community law" means—

(a) all the rights, powers, liabilities, obligations and restrictions from time to time created or arising by or under the Community Treaties, and

(b) all the remedies and procedures from time to time provided for by or under the Community Treaties,

"delegate" includes further delegate,
"enactment" includes subordinate legislation,
"functions" includes powers and duties,
"Minister of the Crown" includes the Treasury,
"subordinate legislation" has the same meaning as in the Interpretation Act 1978, and
"Wales" includes the sea adjacent to Wales out as far as the seaward boundary of the territorial sea;

and related expressions shall be construed accordingly.

(2) The Secretary of State may by order determine, or make provision for determining, for the purposes of the definition of "Wales" any boundary between—

(a) the parts of the sea which are to be treated as adjacent to Wales, and

(b) those which are not,

and may make different determinations or provision for different purposes; and an Order in Council under section 22 may include any provision that may be included in an order under this subsection.

(3) In this Act "financial year" means the twelve months ending with 31st March; and the first financial year of the Assembly is the financial year ending with the 31st March following the day of the first ordinary election.

(4) Section 13 of the National Audit Act 1983 (interpretation of references to the Committee of Public Accounts) applies for the purposes of this Act as for those of that Act.★

[Government of Wales Act 1998, s 155.]

★Section amended by the Government of Wales Act 2006, Sch 12 as from immediately after the ordinary election held in 2007.

1–3874   156. *Defined expressions*★

★Repealed by the Government of Wales Act 2006, Sch 12 as from immediately after the ordinary election held in 2007.

1–3875   157. *Financial provisions*

1–3876   158. Commencement.   (1) Parts I and II, the provisions of Part III other than sections 50 and 51, Parts IV to VI and section 152 (and Schedule 18) shall not come into force until such day as the Secretary of State may by order appoint[1].

(2) Different days may be appointed under this section for different purposes.

[Government of Wales Act 1998, s 158.]

---

1. The following commencement orders have been made: (No 1) SI 1999/2244; (No 2) 1998/2789; (No 3) SI 1999/782 and (No 5) SI 1999/1290.

1–3877   159. *Short title*

Section 109

SCHEDULE 8
DEVOLUTION ISSUES★

PART I
PRELIMINARY

1–3878   **1.** (1) In this Schedule "devolution issue" means—

(a) a question whether a function is exercisable by the Assembly,

(b) a question whether a purported or proposed exercise of a function by the Assembly is, or would be, within the powers of the Assembly (including a question whether a purported or proposed exercise of a function by the Assembly is, or would be, outside its powers by virtue of section 106(7) or 107(1)),

(c) a question whether the Assembly has failed to comply with a duty imposed on it (including a question whether the Assembly has failed to comply with any obligation which is an obligation of the Assembly by virtue of section 106(1) or (6)), or

(d) a question whether a failure to act by the Assembly is incompatible with any of the Convention rights.

(2) In this Schedule—

(a) "the Judicial Committee" means the Judicial Committee of the Privy Council, and

(b) "civil proceedings" means any proceedings other than criminal proceedings.

★Schedule repealed by the Government of Wales Act 2006, Sch 12 as from immediately after the ordinary election held in 2007.

1–3879   **2.** A devolution issue shall not be taken to arise in any proceedings merely because of any contention of a party to the proceedings which appears to the court or tribunal before which the proceedings take place to be frivolous or vexatious.

PART II
PROCEEDINGS IN ENGLAND AND WALES

Application of Part II

1–3880   **3.** This Part of this Schedule applies in relation to devolution issues in proceedings in England and Wales.

Institution of proceedings

1–3881   **4.** (1) Proceedings for the determination of a devolution issue may be instituted by the Attorney General.

(2) Sub-paragraph (1) does not limit any power to institute proceedings exercisable apart from that sub-paragraph by any person.

Notice of devolution issue

1–3882   **5.** (1) A court or tribunal shall order notice of any devolution issue which arises in any proceedings before it to be given to the Attorney General and the Assembly (unless a party to the proceedings).

(2) A person to whom notice is given in pursuance of sub-paragraph (1) may take part as a party in the proceedings, so far as they relate to a devolution issue.

Reference of devolution issue to High Court or Court of Appeal

1–3883   **6.** A magistrates' court may refer any devolution issue which arises in civil proceedings before it to the High Court.

1–3884   **7.** (1) A court may refer any devolution issue which arises in civil proceedings before it to the Court of Appeal.

(2) Sub-paragraph (1) does not apply—

(a) to a magistrates' court, the Court of Appeal or the House of Lords, or

(b) to the High Court if the devolution issue arises in proceedings on a reference under paragraph 6.

1–3885   **8.** A tribunal from which there is no appeal shall refer any devolution issue which arises in proceedings before it to the Court of Appeal; and any other tribunal may make such a reference.

1–3886   **9.** A court, other than the Court of Appeal or the House of Lords, may refer any devolution issue which arises in criminal proceedings before it to—

(a) the High Court if the proceedings are summary proceedings, or

(b) the Court of Appeal if the proceedings are proceedings on indictment.

References from Court of Appeal to Judicial Committee

1–3887   **10.** The Court of Appeal may refer any devolution issue which arises in proceedings before it (otherwise than on a reference under paragraph 7, 8 or 9) to the Judicial Committee.

Appeals from superior courts to Judicial Committee

1–3888   **11.** An appeal against a determination of a devolution issue by the High Court or the Court of Appeal on a reference under paragraph 6, 7, 8 or 9 shall lie to the Judicial Committee, but only—

(a)   with leave of the court concerned, or
(b)   failing such leave, with special leave of the Judicial Committee.

PART III
PROCEEDINGS IN SCOTLAND

1–3889
PART IV
PROCEEDINGS IN NORTHERN IRELAND

1–3890
PART V
GENERAL

Proceedings in the House of Lords

1–3891   29. Any devolution issue which arises in judicial proceedings in the House of Lords shall be referred to the Judicial Committee unless the House considers it more appropriate, having regard to all the circumstances, that they should determine the issue.

Direct references to Judicial Committee

1–3892   30. (1) The relevant law officer or the Assembly may require any court or tribunal to refer to the Judicial Committee any devolution issue which has arisen in any proceedings before it to which he or it is a party.
(2) In sub-paragraph (1) "the relevant law officer" means—

(a)   in relation to proceedings in England and Wales, the Attorney General,
(b)   in relation to proceedings in Scotland, the Advocate General for Scotland, and
(c)   in relation to proceedings in Northern Ireland, the Attorney General for Northern Ireland.*

*Repealed and new words inserted by the Justice (Northern Ireland) Act 2002, Sch 7 with effect from a date to be appointed.

1–3893   31. (1) The Attorney General or the Assembly may refer to the Judicial Committee any devolution issue which is not the subject of proceedings.
(2) Where a reference is made under sub-paragraph (1) by the Attorney General in relation to a devolution issue which relates to the proposed exercise of a function by the Assembly—

(a)   the Attorney General shall notify the Assembly of that fact, and
(b)   the Assembly shall not exercise the function in the manner proposed during the period beginning with the receipt of the notification and ending with the reference being decided or otherwise disposed of.

The Judicial Committee

1–3894   32. Any decision of the Judicial Committee in proceedings under this Schedule—

(a)   shall be stated in open court, and
(b)   shall be binding in all legal proceedings (other than proceedings before the Judicial Committee).

1–3895   33. No member of the Judicial Committee shall sit and act as a member of the Judicial Committee in proceedings under this Schedule unless he holds or has held—

(a)   the office of a Lord of Appeal in Ordinary, or
(b)   high judicial office as defined in section 25 of the Appellate Jurisdiction Act 1876 (ignoring for this purpose section 5 of the Appellate Jurisdiction Act 1887).

1–3896   34. (1) Her Majesty may by Order in Council—

(a)   confer on the Judicial Committee in relation to proceedings under this Schedule such powers as appear to be appropriate,
(b)   apply the Judicial Committee Act 1833 in relation to proceedings under this Schedule with exceptions and modifications, and
(c)   make rules for regulating the procedure with respect to proceedings under this Schedule before the Judicial Committee[1].

(2) An Order in Council under this paragraph may contain any appropriate consequential, incidental, supplementary or transitional provisions or savings (including provisions in the form of amendments or repeals of enactments).
(3) No recommendation shall be made to Her Majesty in Council to make an Order in Council under this paragraph which contains provisions in the form of amendments or repeals of enactments contained in an Act unless a draft of the statutory instrument containing the Order in Council has been laid before, and approved by a resolution of, each House of Parliament.
(4) A statutory instrument containing an Order in Council which makes provision falling within sub-paragraph (1)(a) or (b) shall (unless a draft of it has been approved by a resolution of each House of Parliament) be subject to annulment in pursuance of a resolution of either House of Parliament.

1. The Judicial Committee (Devolution Issues) Rules 1999 have been made, in this PART, post.

Costs

1–3897 35. (1) A court or tribunal before which any proceedings take place may take account of any additional expense of the kind mentioned in sub-paragraph (3) in deciding any question as to costs or expenses.

(2) In deciding any such question, the court or tribunal may award the whole or part of the additional expense as costs or expenses to the party who incurred it (whatever the decision on the devolution issue).

(3) The additional expense is any additional expense which the court or tribunal considers that any party to the proceedings has incurred as a result of the participation of any person in pursuance of paragraph 5, 14 or 24.

Procedure of courts and tribunals

1–3898 36. Any power to make provision for regulating the procedure before any court or tribunal shall include power to make provision for the purposes of this Schedule including, in particular, provision—

(a) for prescribing the stage in the proceedings at which a devolution issue is to be raised or referred,

(b) for the staying or sisting of proceedings for the purpose of any proceedings under this Schedule, and

(c) for determining the manner in which and the time within which any notice or intimation is to be given.

References to be for decision

1–3899 37. Any function conferred by this Schedule to refer a devolution issue to a court shall be construed as a function of referring the issue to the court for decision.

Scotland Act 1998

(1998 c 46)

PART II[1]

THE SCOTTISH ADMINISTRATION

Ministerial functions

1–3900 52. Exercise of functions.   (1) Statutory functions may be conferred on the Scottish Ministers by that name.

(2) Statutory functions of the Scottish Ministers, the First Minister or the Lord Advocate shall be exercisable on behalf of Her Majesty.

(3) Statutory functions of the Scottish Ministers shall be exercisable by any member of the Scottish Executive.

(4) Any act or omission of, or in relation to, any member of the Scottish Executive shall be treated as an act or omission of, or in relation to, each of them; and any property acquired, or liability incurred, by any member of the Scottish Executive shall be treated accordingly.

(5) Subsection (4) does not apply in relation to the exercise of—

(a) functions conferred on the First Minister alone, or

(b) retained functions of the Lord Advocate.

(6) In this Act, "retained functions" in relation to the Lord Advocate means—

(a) any functions exercisable by him immediately before he ceases to be a Minister of the Crown, and

(b) other statutory functions conferred on him alone after he ceases to be a Minister of the Crown.

(7) In this section, "statutory functions" means functions conferred by virtue of any enactment.
[Scotland Act 1998, s 52.]

---

1. Part II contains ss 44–63.

1–3901 53. General transfer of functions.   (1) The functions mentioned in subsection (2) shall, so far as they are exercisable within devolved competence, be exercisable by the Scottish Ministers instead of by a Minister of the Crown.

(2) Those functions are—

(a) those of Her Majesty's prerogative and other executive functions which are exercisable on behalf of Her Majesty by a Minister of the Crown,

(b) other functions conferred on a Minister of the Crown by a prerogative instrument, and

(c) functions conferred on a Minister of the Crown by any pre-commencement enactment,

but do not include any retained functions of the Lord Advocate.

(3) In this Act, "pre-commencement enactment" means—

(a) an Act passed before or in the same session as this Act and any other enactment made before the passing of this Act,

(b) an enactment made, before the commencement of this section, under such an Act or such other enactment,

(c) subordinate legislation under section 106, to the extent that the legislation states that it is to be treated as a pre-commencement enactment.

(4) This section and section 54 are modified by Part III of Schedule 4.
[Scotland Act 1998, s 53.]

1–3902   54. Devolved competence.   (1) References in this Act to the exercise of a function being within or outside devolved competence are to be read in accordance with this section.

(2) It is outside devolved competence—

(*a*) to make any provision by subordinate legislation which would be outside the legislative competence of the Parliament if it were included in an Act of the Scottish Parliament, or

(*b*) to confirm or approve any subordinate legislation containing such provision.

(3) In the case of any function other than a function of making, confirming or approving subordinate legislation, it is outside devolved competence to exercise the function (or exercise it in any way) so far as a provision of an Act of the Scottish Parliament conferring the function (or, as the case may be, conferring it so as to be exercisable in that way) would be outside the legislative competence of the Parliament.

[Scotland Act 1998, s 54.]

1–3903   55. Functions exercisable with agreement.   (1) A statutory provision, or any provision not contained in an enactment, which provides for a Minister of the Crown to exercise a function with the agreement of, or after consultation with, any other Minister of the Crown shall cease to have effect in relation to the exercise of the function by a member of the Scottish Executive by virtue of section 53.

(2) In subsection (1) "statutory provision" means any provision in a pre-commencement enactment other than paragraph 5 or 15 of Schedule 32 to the Local Government, Planning and Land Act 1980 (designation of enterprise zones).

[Scotland Act 1998, s 55.]

1–3904   56. Shared powers

1–3905   57. Community law and Convention rights.   (1) Despite the transfer to the Scottish Ministers by virtue of section 53 of functions in relation to observing and implementing obligations under Community law, any function of a Minister of the Crown in relation to any matter shall continue to be exercisable by him as regards Scotland for the purposes specified in section 2(2) of the European Communities Act 1972.

(2) A member of the Scottish Executive has no power to make any subordinate legislation, or to do any other act, so far as the legislation or act is incompatible with any of the Convention rights or with Community law.

(3) Subsection (2) does not apply to an act of the Lord Advocate—

(*a*) in prosecuting any offence, or

(*b*) in his capacity as head of the systems of criminal prosecution and investigation of deaths in Scotland,

which, because of subsection (2) of section 6 of the Human Rights Act 1998, is not unlawful under subsection (1) of that section.

[Scotland Act 1998, s 57.]

PART V[1]
MISCELLANEOUS AND GENERAL

Juridical

1–3906   98. Devolution issues.   Schedule 6 (which makes provision in relation to devolution issues) shall have effect.

[Scotland Act 1998, s 98.]

---

1. Part V contains ss 81–111.

1–3907   103. The Judicial Committee[1].   (1) Any decision of the Judicial Committee in proceedings under this Act shall be stated in open court and shall be binding in all legal proceedings (other than proceedings before the Committee).

(2) No member of the Judicial Committee shall sit and act as a member of the Committee in proceedings under this Act unless he holds or has held—

(*a*) the office of a Lord of Appeal in Ordinary, or

(*b*) high judicial office as defined in section 25 of the Appellate Jurisdiction Act 1876 (ignoring for this purpose section 5 of the Appellate Jurisdiction Act 1887).

(3) Her Majesty may by Order in Council—

(*a*) confer on the Judicial Committee in relation to proceedings under this Act such powers as Her Majesty considers necessary or expedient,

(*b*) apply the Judicial Committee Act 1833 in relation to proceedings under this Act with exceptions or modifications, (*c*) make rules for regulating the procedure in relation to proceedings under this Act before the Judicial Committee.

(4) In this section "proceedings under this Act" means proceedings on a question referred to the Judicial Committee under section 33 or proceedings under Schedule 6.
[Scotland Act 1998, s 103.]

---

1. The Judicial Committee (Devolution Issues) Rules 1999 have been made which regulate procedure before the Judicial Committee, in this PART, post.

Supplementary powers

1–3908   111. Regulation of Tweed and Esk fisheries.   (1) Her Majesty may by Order in Council make provision for or in connection with the conservation, management and exploitation of salmon, trout, eels and freshwater fish in the Border rivers[1].

(2) An Order under subsection (1) may—

(*a*) exclude the application of section 53 in relation to any Border rivers function,
(*b*) confer power to make subordinate legislation.

(3) In particular, provision may be made by such an Order—

(*a*) conferring any function on a Minister of the Crown, the Scottish Ministers or a public body in relation to the Border rivers,
(*b*) for any Border rivers function exercisable by any person to be exercisable instead by a person (or another person) mentioned in paragraph (*a*),
(*c*) for any Border rivers function exercisable by any person to be exercisable concurrently or jointly with, or with the agreement of or after consultation with, a person (or another person) mentioned in paragraph (*a*).

(4) In this section—

"the Border rivers" means the Rivers Tweed and Esk,
"Border rivers function" means a function conferred by any enactment, so far as exercisable in relation to the Border rivers,
"conservation", in relation to salmon, trout, eels and freshwater fish, includes the protection of their environment,
"eels", "freshwater fish", "salmon" and "trout" have the same meanings as in the Salmon and Freshwater Fisheries Act 1975,
"the River Tweed" has the same meaning as in section 39 of the Salmon and Freshwater Fisheries Act 1975,
"the River Esk" means the river of that name which, for part of its length, constitutes the border between England and Scotland including—

(*a*) its tributary streams (which for this purpose include the River Sark and its tributary streams), and
(*b*) such waters on the landward side of its estuary limits as are determined by an Order under subsection (1), together with its banks;

and references to the Border rivers include any part of the Border rivers.
(5) An Order under subsection (1) may modify the definitions in subsection (4) of the River Tweed and the River Esk.
[Scotland Act 1998, s 111.]

---

1. The Scotland Act 1998 (Border Rivers) Order 1999, SI 1999/1746 and the Scotland Act 1998 (River Tweed) Order 2006, SI 2006/2913 have been made.

PART VI[1]
SUPPLEMENTARY

Final provisions

1–3909   130. Commencement.   (1) Sections 19 to 43, Parts II to V, sections 117 to 124 and section 125 (except so far as relating to paragraphs 10, 11, 19 and 23(1) and (6) of Schedule 8) shall come into force on such day as the Secretary of State may by order appoint[2].

(2) Different days may be appointed under this section for different purposes.
[Scotland Act 1998, s 130.]

---

1. Part VI contains ss 112–132.
2. Various dates have been appointed by the Scotland Act 1998 (Commencement) Order 1998, SI 1998/3178.

1–3910   131. *Extent*

1–3911   132. *Short title*

SCHEDULE 6
DEVOLUTION ISSUES

PART I
PRELIMINARY

1–3912　**1.** In this Schedule "devolution issue" means—

(a) a question whether an Act of the Scottish Parliament or any provision of an Act of the Scottish Parliament is within the legislative competence of the Parliament,

(b) a question whether any function (being a function which any person has purported, or is proposing, to exercise) is a function of the Scottish Ministers, the First Minister or the Lord Advocate,

(c) a question whether the purported or proposed exercise of a function by a member of the Scottish Executive is, or would be, within devolved competence,

(d) a question whether a purported or proposed exercise of a function by a member of the Scottish Executive is, or would be, incompatible with any of the Convention rights or with Community law,

(e) a question whether a failure to act by a member of the Scottish Executive is incompatible with any of the Convention rights or with Community law,

(f) any other question about whether a function is exercisable within devolved competence or in or as regards Scotland and any other question arising by virtue of this Act about reserved matters.

1–3913　**2.** A devolution issue shall not be taken to arise in any proceedings merely because of any contention of a party to the proceedings which appears to the court or tribunal before which the proceedings take place to be frivolous or vexatious.

PART II
PROCEEDINGS IN SCOTLAND

PART III
PROCEEDINGS IN ENGLAND AND WALES

Application of Part III

1–3914　**14.** This Part of this Schedule applies in relation to devolution issues in proceedings in England and Wales.

Institution of proceedings

1–3915　**15.** (1) Proceedings for the determination of a devolution issue may be instituted by the Attorney General.
(2) The Lord Advocate may defend any such proceedings.
(3) This paragraph is without prejudice to any power to institute or defend proceedings exercisable apart from this paragraph by any person.

Notice of devolution issue

1–3916　**16.** A court or tribunal shall order notice of any devolution issue which arises in any proceedings before it to be given to the Attorney General and the Lord Advocate (unless the person to whom the notice would be given is a party to the proceedings).

1–3917　**17.** A person to whom notice is given in pursuance of paragraph 16 may take part as a party in the proceedings, so far as they relate to a devolution issue.

Reference of devolution issue to High Court or Court of Appeal

1–3918　**18.** A magistrates' court may refer any devolution issue which arises in proceedings (other than criminal proceedings) before it to the High Court.

1–3919　**19.** (1) A court may refer any devolution issue which arises in proceedings (other than criminal proceedings) before it to the Court of Appeal.
(2) Sub-paragraph (1) does not apply to—

(a) a magistrates' court, the Court of Appeal or the House of Lords, or

(b) the High Court if the devolution issue arises in proceedings on a reference under paragraph 18.

1–3920　**20.** A tribunal from which there is no appeal shall refer any devolution issue which arises in proceedings before it to the Court of Appeal; and any other tribunal may make such a reference.

1–3921　**21.** A court, other than the House of Lords or the Court of Appeal, may refer any devolution issue which arises in criminal proceedings before it to—

(a) the High Court (if the proceedings are summary proceedings), or

(b) the Court of Appeal (if the proceedings are proceedings on indictment).

References from Court of Appeal to Judicial Committee

1–3922　**22.** The Court of Appeal may refer any devolution issue which arises in proceedings before it (otherwise than on a reference under paragraph 19, 20 or 21) to the Judicial Committee.

Appeals from superior courts to Judicial Committee

1–3923　**23.** An appeal against a determination of a devolution issue by the High Court or the Court of Appeal on a reference under paragraph 18, 19, 20 or 21 shall lie to the Judicial Committee, but only with leave of the High Court or (as the case may be) the Court of Appeal or, failing such leave, with special leave of the Judicial Committee.

Part IV
Proceedings in Northern Ireland

Part V
General

Proceedings in the House of Lords

1-3924　32. Any devolution issue which arises in judicial proceedings in the House of Lords shall be referred to the Judicial Committee unless the House considers it more appropriate, having regard to all the circumstances, that it should determine the issue.

Direct references to Judicial Committee

1-3925　33. The Lord Advocate, the Advocate General, the Attorney General or the Attorney General for Northern Ireland may require any court or tribunal to refer to the Judicial Committee any devolution issue which has arisen in proceedings before it to which he is a party.

1-3926　34. The Lord Advocate, the Attorney General, the Advocate General or the Attorney General for Northern Ireland may refer to the Judicial Committee any devolution issue which is not the subject of proceedings.

1-3927　35. (1) This paragraph applies where a reference is made under paragraph 34 in relation to a devolution issue which relates to the proposed exercise of a function by a member of the Scottish Executive.
　　(2) The person making the reference shall notify a member of the Scottish Executive of that fact.
　　(3) No member of the Scottish Executive shall exercise the function in the manner proposed during the period beginning with the receipt of the notification under sub-paragraph (2) and ending with the reference being decided or otherwise disposed of.
　　(4) Proceedings relating to any possible failure by a member of the Scottish Executive to comply with sub-paragraph (3) may be instituted by the Advocate General.
　　(5) Sub-paragraph (4) is without prejudice to any power to institute proceedings exercisable apart from that sub-paragraph by any person.

Expenses

1-3928　36. (1) A court or tribunal before which any proceedings take place may take account of any additional expense of the kind mentioned in sub-paragraph (3) in deciding any question as to costs or expenses.
　　(2) In deciding any such question, the court or tribunal may award the whole or part of the additional expense as costs or (as the case may be) expenses to the party who incurred it (whatever the decision on the devolution issue).
　　(3) The additional expense is any additional expense which the court or tribunal considers that any party to the proceedings has incurred as a result of the participation of any person in pursuance of paragraph 6, 17 or 27.

Procedure of courts and tribunals

1-3929　37. Any power to make provision for regulating the procedure before any court or tribunal shall include power to make provision for the purposes of this Schedule including, in particular, provision—

　　(*a*) for prescribing the stage in the proceedings at which a devolution issue is to be raised or referred,
　　(*b*) for the sisting or staying of proceedings for the purpose of any proceedings under this Schedule, and
　　(*c*) for determining the manner in which and the time within which any intimation or notice is to be given.

Interpretation

1-3930　38. Any duty or power conferred by this Schedule to refer a devolution issue to a court shall be construed as a duty or (as the case may be) power to refer the issue to the court for decision.

Access to Justice Act 1999[1]
(1999 c 22)

Part I[2]
Legal Services Commission

Commission

1-3931　1. Legal Services Commission. (1) There shall be a body known as the Legal Services Commission (in this Part referred to as "the Commission").
　　(2) The Commission shall have the functions relating to—

　　(*a*) the Community Legal Service, and
　　(*b*) the Criminal Defence Service,

which are conferred or imposed on it by the provisions of this Act or any other enactment.
　　(3)–(5) *Members of the Commission: constitution and appointment*
　　(6) Schedule 1[3] (which makes further provision about the Commission) has effect.
[Access to Justice Act 1999, s 1 as amended by SI 2005/3429.]

---

1. Parts II and III of the Access to Justice Act 1999 (Funding and Provision of Legal Services) are set out in Part VIII: title Solicitors, below. For commencement of this Act, see s 108, below, and notes thereto.
2. Part I comprises ss 1–26.
3. Schedule 1 is not reproduced in this work.

Community Legal Service

1–3934   4. Community Legal Service.   (1) The Commission shall establish, maintain and develop a service known as the Community Legal Service for the purpose of promoting the availability to individuals of services of the descriptions specified in subsection (2) and, in particular, for securing (within the resources made available, and priorities set, in accordance with this Part) that individuals have access to services that effectively meet their needs.

(2) The descriptions of services referred to in subsection (1) are—

(*a*) the provision of general information about the law and legal system and the availability of legal services,

(*b*) the provision of help by the giving of advice as to how the law applies in particular circumstances,

(*c*) the provision of help in preventing, or settling or otherwise resolving, disputes about legal rights and duties,

(*d*) the provision of help in enforcing decisions by which such disputes are resolved, and

(*e*) the provision of help in relation to legal proceedings not relating to disputes.

(3) Services which the Commission is required to fund as part of the Criminal Defence Service do not fall within subsection (2).

(4) Every person who exercises any function relating to the Community Legal Service shall have regard to the desirability of exercising it, so far as is reasonably practicable, so as to—

(*a*) promote improvements in the range and quality of services provided as part of the Community Legal Service and in the ways in which they are made accessible to those who need them,

(*b*) secure that the services provided in relation to any matter are appropriate having regard to its nature and importance, and

(*c*) achieve the swift and fair resolution of disputes without unnecessary or unduly protracted proceedings in court.

(5) The Commission shall fund services of the descriptions specified in subsection (2) as part of the Community Legal Service in accordance with the following sections.

(6) The Commission shall also inform itself about the need for, and the provision of, services of the descriptions specified in subsection (2) and about the quality of the services provided and, in co-operation with such authorities and other bodies and persons as it considers appropriate—

(*a*) plan what can be done towards meeting that need by the performance by the Commission of its functions, and

(*b*) facilitate the planning by other authorities, bodies and persons of what can be done by them to meet that need by the use of any resources available to them;

and the Commission shall notify the Lord Chancellor of what it has done under this subsection.

(7) The Commission may set and monitor standards in relation to services of the descriptions specified in subsection (2).

(8) In particular, the Commission may accredit, or authorise others to accredit, persons or bodies providing services of the descriptions specified in subsection (2); and any system of accreditation shall include provision for the monitoring of the services provided by accredited persons and bodies and for the withdrawal of accreditation from any providing services of unsatisfactory quality.

(9) The Commission may charge—

(*a*) for accreditation,

(*b*) for monitoring the services provided by accredited persons and bodies, and

(*c*) for authorising accreditation by others;

and persons or bodies authorised to accredit may charge for accreditation, and for such monitoring, in accordance with the terms of their authorisation.

(10) The Lord Chancellor may by order require the Commission to discharge the functions in subsections (6) to (9) in accordance with the order.

[Access to Justice Act 1999, s 4, as amended by SI 2005/3429.]

1–3935   5. Funding of services.   (1) The Commission shall establish and maintain a fund known as the Community Legal Service Fund from which it shall fund services as part of the Community Legal Service.

(2) The Lord Chancellor —

(*a*) shall pay to the Commission the sums which he determines are appropriate for the funding of services by the Commission as part of the Community Legal Service, and

(*b*) may determine the manner in which and times at which the sums are to be paid to the Commission and may impose conditions on the payment of the sums.

(3) In making any determination under subsection (2) the Lord Chancellor shall take into account (in addition to such other factors as he considers relevant) the need for services of the descriptions specified in subsection (2) of section 4 as notified to him by the Commission under subsection (6) of that section.

(4) The Lord Chancellor shall lay before each House of Parliament a copy of every determination under subsection (2)(*a*).

(5) The Commission shall pay into the Community Legal Service Fund—

(*a*) sums received from the Lord Chancellor under subsection (2), and
(*b*) sums received by the Commission by virtue of regulations under section 10 or 11.

(6) The Lord Chancellor may by direction impose requirements on the Commission as to the descriptions of services to be funded from any specified amount paid into the Community Legal Service Fund.

(7) In funding services as part of the Community Legal Service the Commission shall aim to obtain the best possible value for money.
[Access to Justice Act 1999, s 5, as amended by SI 2005/3429.]

1–3936   6. Services which may be funded.   (1) The Commission shall set priorities in its funding of services as part of the Community Legal Service and the priorities shall be set—

(*a*) in accordance with any directions given by the Lord Chancellor, and
(*b*) after taking into account the need for services of the descriptions specified in section 4(2).

(2) Subject to that (and to subsection (6)), the services which the Commission may fund as part of the Community Legal Service are those which the Commission considers appropriate.

(3) The Commission may fund services as part of the Community Legal Service by—

(*a*) entering into contracts with persons or bodies for the provision of services by them,
(*b*) making payments to persons or bodies in respect of the provision of services by them,
(*c*) making grants or loans to persons or bodies to enable them to provide, or facilitate the provision of, services,
(*d*) establishing and maintaining bodies to provide, or facilitate the provision of, services,
(*e*) making grants or loans to individuals to enable them to obtain services,
(*f*) itself providing services, or
(*g*) doing anything else which it considers appropriate for funding services.

(4) The Lord Chancellor may by order[1] require the Commission to discharge the function in subsection (3) in accordance with the order[1].

(5) The Commission may fund as part of the Community Legal Service different descriptions of services or services provided by different means—

(*a*) in relation to different areas or communities in England and Wales, and
(*b*) in relation to descriptions of cases.

(6) The Commission may not fund as part of the Community Legal Service any of the services specified in Schedule 2.

(7) Regulations[2] may amend that Schedule by adding new services or omitting or varying any services.

(8) The Lord Chancellor —

(*a*) may by direction require the Commission to fund the provision of any of the services specified in Schedule 2 in circumstances specified in the direction, and
(*b*) may authorise the Commission to fund the provision of any of those services in specified circumstances or, if the Commission request him to do so, in an individual case.

(9) The Lord Chancellor shall either—

(*a*) publish, or
(*b*) require the Commission to publish,

any authorisation under subsection (8)(*b*) unless it relates to an individual case (in which case he or the Commission may publish it if appropriate).
[Access to Justice Act 1999, s 6, as amended by SI 2005/3429.]

1. See the Community Legal Service (Funding) Order 2000 and the Community Legal Service (Funding) (Counsel in Family Proceedings) Order 2001, in this PART, post.
2. The Community Legal Service (Scope) Regulations 2000, SI 2000/822 which amend Sch 2 to this Act.

1–3937   7. Individuals for whom services may be funded.   (1) The Commission may only fund services for an individual as part of the Community Legal Service if his financial resources are such that, under regulations[1], he is an individual for whom they may be so funded.

(2) Regulations[1] may provide that, in prescribed circumstances and subject to any prescribed conditions, services of a prescribed description may be so funded for individuals without reference to their financial resources.

(3) Regulations[1] under this section may include provision requiring the furnishing of information.
[Access to Justice Act 1999, s 7.]

1. The Community Legal Service (Financial) Regulations 2000 in this PART, post have been made and make provision for the assessment of the financial resources of the client in order to determine eligibility to receive funded services and to assess any contribution to be made.

1–3938 **8. Code about provision of funded services.** (1) The Commission shall prepare a code setting out the criteria according to which it is to decide whether to fund (or continue to fund) services as part of the Community Legal Service for an individual for whom they may be so funded and, if so, what services are to be funded for him.

(2) In settling the criteria to be set out in the code the Commission shall consider the extent to which they ought to reflect the following factors—

(a) the likely cost of funding the services and the benefit which may be obtained by their being provided,

(b) the availability of sums in the Community Legal Service Fund for funding the services and (having regard to present and likely future demands on that Fund) the appropriateness of applying them to fund the services,

(c) the importance of the matters in relation to which the services would be provided for the individual,

(d) the availability to the individual of services not funded by the Commission and the likelihood of his being able to avail himself of them,

(e) if the services are sought by the individual in relation to a dispute, the prospects of his success in the dispute,

(f) the conduct of the individual in connection with services funded as part of the Community Legal Service (or an application for funding) or in, or in connection with, any proceedings,

(g) the public interest, and

(h) such other factors as the Lord Chancellor may by order require the Commission to consider.

(3) The criteria set out in the code shall reflect the principle that in many family disputes mediation will be more appropriate than court proceedings.

(4) The code shall seek to secure that, where more than one description of service is available, the service funded is that which (in all the circumstances) is the most appropriate having regard to the criteria set out in the code.

(5) The code shall also specify procedures for the making of decisions about the funding of services by the Commission as part of the Community Legal Service, including—

(a) provision about the form and content of applications for funding,

(b) provision imposing conditions which must be satisfied by an individual applying for funding,

(c) provision requiring applicants to be informed of the reasons for any decision to refuse an application,

(d) provision for the giving of information to individuals whose applications are refused about alternative ways of obtaining or funding services, and

(e) provision establishing procedures for appeals against decisions about funding and for the giving of information about those procedures.

(6) The code may make different provision for different purposes.

(7) The Commission may from time to time prepare a revised version of the code.

(8) Before preparing the code the Commission shall undertake such consultation as appears to it to be appropriate; and before revising the code the Commission shall undertake such consultation as appears to it to be appropriate unless it considers that it is desirable for the revised version to come into force without delay.

(9) The Lord Chancellor may by order require the Commission to discharge its functions relating to the code in accordance with the order.

[Access to Justice Act 1999, s 8, as amended by SI 2005/3429.]

1–3939 **9. Procedure relating to funding code.** (1) After preparing the code or a revised version of the code the Commission shall send a copy to the Lord Chancellor.

(2) If he approves it he shall lay it before each House of Parliament.

(3) The Commission shall publish—

(a) the code as first approved by the Lord Chancellor, and

(b) where he approves a revised version, either the revisions or the revised code as appropriate.

(4) The code as first approved by the Lord Chancellor shall not come into force until it has been approved by a resolution of each House of Parliament.

(5) A revised version of the code which does not contain changes in the criteria set out in the code shall not come into force until it has been laid before each House of Parliament.

(6) Subject as follows, a revised version of the code which does contain such changes shall not come into force until it has been approved by a resolution of each House of Parliament.

(7) Where the Lord Chancellor considers that it is desirable for a revised version of the code containing such changes to come into force without delay, he may (when laying the revised version before Parliament) also lay before each House a statement of his reasons for so considering.

(8) In that event the revised version of the code—

(a) shall not come into force until it has been laid before each House of Parliament, and

(b) shall cease to have effect at the end of the period of 120 days beginning with the day on which it comes into force unless a resolution approving it has been made by each House (but without that affecting anything previously done in accordance with it).

[Access to Justice Act 1999, s 9, as amended by SI 2005/3429.]

1–3940 10. Terms of provision of funded services. (1) An individual for whom services are funded by the Commission as part of the Community Legal Service shall not be required to make any payment in respect of the services except where regulations[1] otherwise provide.

(2) Regulations[2] may provide that, in prescribed circumstances, an individual for whom services are so funded shall—

(a) pay a fee of such amount as is fixed by or determined under the regulations,

(b) if his financial resources are, or relevant conduct is, such as to make him liable to do so under the regulations, pay the cost of the services or make a contribution in respect of the cost of the services of such amount as is so fixed or determined, or

(c) if the services relate to a dispute and he has agreed to make a payment (which may exceed the cost of the services) only in specified circumstances, make in those circumstances a payment of the amount agreed, or determined in the manner agreed, by him;

and in paragraph (b) "relevant conduct" means conduct in connection with the services (or any application for their funding) or in, or in connection with, any proceedings in relation to which they are provided.

(3) The regulations[1] may include provision for any amount payable in accordance with the regulations to be payable by periodical payments or one or more capital sums, or both.

(4) The regulations[1] may also include provision for the payment by an individual of interest (on such terms as may be prescribed) in respect of—

(a) any loan made to him by the Commission as part of the Community Legal Service,

(b) any payment in respect of the cost of services required by the regulations to be made by him later than the time when the services are provided, or

(c) so much of any payment required by the regulations to be made by him which remains unpaid after the time when it is required to be paid.

(5) The regulations[1] shall include provision for the repayment to an individual of any payment made by him in excess of his liability under the regulations.

(6) The regulations[1] may—

(a) include provision requiring the furnishing of information, and

(b) make provision for the determination of the cost of services for the purposes of the regulations.

(7) Except so far as regulations[1] otherwise provide, where services have been funded by the Commission for an individual as part of the Community Legal Service—

(a) sums expended by the Commission in funding the services (except to the extent that they are recovered under section 11), and

(b) other sums payable by the individual by virtue of regulations under this section,

shall constitute a first charge on any property recovered or preserved by him (whether for himself or any other person) in any proceedings or in any compromise or settlement of any dispute in connection with which the services were provided.

(8) Regulations[1] may make provision about the charge, including—

(a) provision as to whether it is in favour of the Commission or the body or person by whom the services were provided, and

(b) provision about its enforcement.

[Access to Justice Act 1999, s 10.]

---

1. The Community Legal Service (Costs) Regulations 2000, SI 2000/441 have been made.
2. The Community Legal Service (Financial) Regulations 2000, SI 2000/516, and the Community Legal Service (Costs) Regulations 2000, SI 2000/441, have been made.

1–3941 11. Costs in funded cases. (1) Except in prescribed[1] circumstances, costs ordered against an individual in relation to any proceedings or part of proceedings funded for him shall not exceed the amount (if any) which is a reasonable one for him to pay having regard to all the circumstances including—

(a) the financial resources of all the parties to the proceedings, and

(b) their conduct in connection with the dispute to which the proceedings relate;

and for this purpose proceedings, or a part of proceedings, are funded for an individual if services relating to the proceedings or part are funded for him by the Commission as part of the Community Legal Service.

(2) In assessing for the purposes of subsection (1) the financial resources of an individual for whom services are funded by the Commission as part of the Community Legal Service, his clothes and household furniture and the tools and implements of his trade shall not be taken into account, except so far as may be prescribed[2].

(3) Subject to subsections (1) and (2), regulations[3] may make provision about costs in relation to proceedings in which services are funded by the Commission for any of the parties as part of the Community Legal Service.

(4) The regulations[3] may, in particular, make provision—

(a) specifying the principles to be applied in determining the amount of any costs which may be awarded against a party for whom services are funded by the Commission as part of the Community Legal Service,

(b) limiting the circumstances in which, or extent to which, an order for costs may be enforced against such a party,

(c) as to the cases in which, and extent to which, such a party may be required to give security for costs and the manner in which it is to be given,

(d) requiring the payment by the Commission of the whole or part of any costs incurred by a party for whom services are not funded by the Commission as part of the Community Legal Service,

(e) specifying the principles to be applied in determining the amount of any costs which may be awarded to a party for whom services are so funded,

(f) requiring the payment to the Commission, or the person or body by which the services were provided, of the whole or part of any sum awarded by way of costs to such a party, and

(g) as to the court, tribunal or other person or body by whom the amount of any costs is to be determined and the extent to which any determination of that amount is to be final.

[Access to Justice Act 1999, s 11.]

---

1. See the Community Legal Service (Cost Protection) Regulations 2000 in this PART, post.
2. The Community Legal Service (Costs) Regulations 2000 in this PART, post have been made.
3. The Community Legal Service (Costs) Regulations 2000 and the Community Legal Service (Cost Protection) Regulations 2000 have been made in this PART, post.

1–3942

Criminal Defence Service

12. Criminal Defence Service. (1) The Commission shall establish, maintain and develop a service known as the Criminal Defence Service for the purpose of securing that individuals involved in criminal investigations or criminal proceedings have access to such advice, assistance and representation as the interests of justice require.

(2) In this Part "criminal proceedings" means—

(a) proceedings before any court for dealing with an individual accused of an offence[1],

(b) proceedings before any court for dealing with an individual convicted of an offence[1] (including proceedings in respect of a sentence or order),

(c) proceedings for dealing with an individual under the Extradition Act 2003,

(d) proceedings for binding an individual over to keep the peace or to be of good behaviour under section 115 of the Magistrates' Courts Act 1980 and for dealing with an individual who fails to comply with an order under that section,

(e) proceedings on an appeal brought by an individual under section 44A of the Criminal Appeal Act 1968,

(f) proceedings for contempt committed, or alleged to have been committed, by an individual in the face of a court, and

(g) such other proceedings concerning an individual, before any such court or other body, as may be prescribed[2].

(3) The Commission shall fund services as part of the Criminal Defence Service in accordance with sections 13 to 15.

(4) The Commission may accredit, or authorise others to accredit, persons or bodies providing services which may be funded by the Commission as part of the Criminal Defence Service; and any system of accreditation shall include provision for the monitoring of the services provided by accredited persons and bodies and for the withdrawal of accreditation from any providing services of unsatisfactory quality.

(5) The Commission may charge—

(a) for accreditation,

(b) for monitoring the services provided by accredited persons and bodies, and

(c) for authorising accreditation by others;

and persons or bodies authorised to accredit may charge for accreditation, and for such monitoring, in accordance with the terms of their authorisation.

(6) The Lord Chancellor may by order require the Commission to discharge the functions in subsections (4) and (5) in accordance with the order.

[Access to Justice Act 1999, s 12, as amended by the Extradition Act, s 182 and SI 2005/3429.]

---

1. Condemnation proceedings under the Customs and Excise Management Act 1979, Sch 3 are not proceedings in respect of an offence (*R (Mudie) v Kent Magistrates' Court* [2003] EWCA Civ 237, [2003] 2 All ER 631).
2. See the Criminal Defence Service (General) (No 2) Regulations 2001, in this PART, post.

1–3943 13. Advice and assistance. (1) The Commission shall fund such advice and assistance as it considers appropriate—

(a) for individuals who are arrested and held in custody at a police station or other premises, and

(b) in prescribed[1] circumstances, for individuals who—

(i) are not within paragraph (a) but are involved in investigations which may lead to criminal proceedings,

(ii) are before a court or other body in such proceedings, or

(iii) have been the subject of such proceedings;

and the assistance which the Commission may consider appropriate includes assistance in the form of advocacy.

(2) The Commission may comply with the duty imposed by subsection (1) by—

(*a*) entering into contracts with persons or bodies for the provision of advice or assistance by them,

(*b*) making payments to persons or bodies in respect of the provision of advice or assistance by them,

(*c*) making grants or loans to persons or bodies to enable them to provide, or facilitate the provision of, advice or assistance,

(*d*) establishing and maintaining bodies to provide, or facilitate the provision of, advice or assistance,

(*e*) making grants to individuals to enable them to obtain advice or assistance,

(*f*) employing persons to provide advice or assistance, or

(*g*) doing anything else which it considers appropriate for funding advice and assistance.

(3) The Lord Chancellor may by order[2] require the Commission to discharge the function in subsection (2) in accordance with the order[2].

(4) The Commission may fund advice and assistance by different means—

(*a*) in different areas in England and Wales, and

(*b*) in relation to different descriptions of cases.

[Access to Justice Act 1999, s 13, as amended by the Criminal Defence Service (Advice and Assistance) Act 2001 and SI 2005/3429.]

---

1. See the Criminal Defence Service (General) (No 2) Regulations 2001, in this PART, post.
2. The Criminal Defence Service (Funding) Order 2001 has been made, in this PART, post. See the Criminal Defence Service (Funding) Order 2001 and the Criminal Defence Service (Representation Order Appeals) Regulations 2001, in this PART, post.

1–3944   14. Representation.   (1) Schedule 3 (which makes provision about the grant of a right to representation in criminal proceedings) has effect; and the Commission shall fund representation to which an individual has been granted a right in accordance with that Schedule.

(2) Subject to the following provisions, the Commission may comply with the duty imposed by subsection (1) by—

(*a*) entering into contracts with persons or bodies for the provision of representation by them,

(*b*) making payments to persons or bodies in respect of the provision of representation by them,

(*c*) making grants or loans to persons or bodies to enable them to provide, or facilitate the provision of, representation,

(*d*) establishing and maintaining bodies to provide, or facilitate the provision of, representation,

(*e*) making grants to individuals to enable them to obtain representation,

(*f*) employing persons to provide representation, or

(*g*) doing anything else which it considers appropriate for funding representation.

(3) The Lord Chancellor—

(*a*) shall by order make provision about the payments which may be made by the Commission in respect of any representation provided by non-contracted private practitioners, and

(*b*) may by order make any other provision requiring the Commission to discharge the function in subsection (2) in accordance with the order.

(4) For the purposes of subsection (3)(*a*) representation is provided by a non-contracted private practitioner if it is provided, otherwise than pursuant to a contract entered into by the Commission, by a person or body which is neither—

(*a*) a person or body in receipt of grants or loans made by the Commission as part of the Criminal Defence Service, nor

(*b*) the Commission itself or a body established or maintained by the Commission.

(5) The provision which the Lord Chancellor is required to make by order under subsection (3)(*a*) includes provision for reviews of, or appeals against, determinations required for the purposes of the order.

(6) The Commission may fund representation by different means—

(*a*) in different areas in England and Wales, and

(*b*) in relation to different descriptions of cases.

[Access to Justice Act 1999, s 14, as amended by SI 2005/3429.]

1–3945   15. Selection of representative.   (1) An individual who has been granted a right to representation in accordance with Schedule 3 may select any representative or representatives willing to act for him; and, where he does so, the Commission is to comply with the duty imposed by section 14(1) by funding representation by the selected representative or representatives.

(2) Regulations[1] may provide that in prescribed circumstances—

(*a*) the right conferred by subsection (1) is not to apply in cases of prescribed descriptions,

(b)   an individual who has been provided with advice or assistance funded by the Commission under section 13 by a person whom he chose to provide it for him is to be taken to have selected that person as his representative pursuant to that right,

(c)   that right is not to include a right to select a representative of a prescribed description,

(d)   that right is to select only a representative of a prescribed description,

(e)   that right is to select not more than a prescribed number of representatives to act at any one time, and

(f)   that right is not to include a right to select a representative in place of a representative previously selected.

(3) Regulations under subsection (2)(b) may prescribe circumstances in which an individual is to be taken to have chosen a person to provide advice or assistance for him.

(4) Regulations under subsection (2) may not provide that only a person employed by the Commission, or by a body established and maintained by the Commission, may be selected.

(5) Regulations[2] may provide that in prescribed circumstances the Commission is not required to fund, or to continue to fund, representation for an individual by a particular representative (but such provision shall not prejudice any right of the individual to select another representative).

(6) The circumstances which may be prescribed by regulations under subsection (2) or (5) include that a determination has been made by a prescribed body or person.
[Access to Justice Act 1999, s 15.]

---

1. See the Criminal Defence Service (General) (No 2) Regulations 2001, in this PART, post.
2. See the Criminal Defence Service (Choice in Very High Cost Cases) Regulations 2001, in this PART, post.

1–3946   16. Code of conduct.   (1) The Commission shall prepare a code of conduct to be observed by employees of the Commission, and employees of any body established and maintained by the Commission, in the provision of services as part of the Criminal Defence Service.

(2) The code shall include—

(a)   duties to avoid discrimination,

(b)   duties to protect the interests of the individuals for whom services are provided,

(c)   duties to the court,

(d)   duties to avoid conflicts of interest, and

(e)   duties of confidentiality,

and duties on employees who are members of a professional body to comply with the rules of the body.

(3) The Commission may from time to time prepare a revised version of the code.

(4) Before preparing or revising the code the Commission shall consult the Law Society and the General Council of the Bar and such other bodies or persons as it considers appropriate.

(5) After preparing the code or a revised version of the code the Commission shall send a copy to the Lord Chancellor.

(6) If he approves it he shall lay it before each House of Parliament.

(7) The Commission shall publish—

(a)   the code as first approved by the Lord Chancellor, and

(b)   where he approves a revised version, either the revisions or the revised code as appropriate.

(8) The code, and any revised version of the code, shall not come into force until it has been approved by a resolution of each House of Parliament.
[Access to Justice Act 1999, s 16, as amended by and SI 2005/3429.]

1–3947   17. Terms of provision of funded services.   (1) An individual for whom services are funded by the Commission as part of the Criminal Defence Service shall not be required to make any payment in respect of the services except where subsection (2) applies or regulations under section 17A otherwise provide.

(2) Where representation for an individual in respect of criminal proceedings in any court other than a magistrates' court is funded by the Commission as part of the Criminal Defence Service, the court may, subject to regulations under subsection (3), make an order requiring him to pay some or all of the cost of any representation so funded for him (in proceedings in that or any other court), except insofar as he has already been ordered under regulations under section 17A to pay that cost.

(3) Regulations[1] may make provision about—

(a)   the descriptions of individuals against whom an order under subsection (2) may be made,

(b)   the circumstances in which such an order may be made and the principles to be applied in deciding whether to make such an order and the amount to be paid,

(c)   the determination of the cost of representation for the purposes of the making of such an order,

(d)   the furnishing of information and evidence to the court or the Commission for the purpose of enabling the court to decide whether to make such an order and (if so) the amount to be paid,

(e)   prohibiting individuals who are required to furnish information or evidence from dealing with property until they have furnished the information or evidence or until a decision whether to make an order, or the amount to be paid, has been made,

   (f)   the person or body to which, and manner in which, payments required by such an order must be made and what that person or body is to do with them, and

   (g)   the enforcement of such an order (including provision for the imposition of charges in respect of unpaid amounts).

[Access to Justice Act 1999, s 17 as amended by the Criminal Defence Service Act 2006, s 3.]

---

   1. See the Criminal Defence Service (Recovery of Defence Costs Orders) Regulations 2001, in this PART, post.

1–3947A   17A. Contribution orders.   (1) Regulations may provide that, in prescribed circumstances, where—

   (a)   an individual has been granted a right to representation, and

   (b)   his financial resources are such as to make him liable under the regulations to do so,

the relevant authority shall order him to pay the cost of his representation or to make a contribution in respect of that cost of such amount as is fixed by or determined under the regulations.

   (2) Regulations under subsection (1) may include—

   (a)   provision requiring the furnishing of information;

   (b)   provision for the determination of the cost of representation for the purposes of liability under a contribution order;

   (c)   provision enabling the relevant authority to require that an amount payable under a contribution order be paid by periodical payments or one or more capital sums, or both;

   (d)   provision for the payment by an individual of interest (on such terms as may be prescribed) in respect of—

      (i)   any payment in respect of the cost of representation required by a contribution order to be made by him later than the time when the representation is provided;

      (ii)   so much of any payment which he is required by a contribution order to make which remains unpaid after the time when it is required to be made;

   (e)   provision about the enforcement of any liability under a contribution order, including provision for the withdrawal of the individual's right to representation in certain circumstances;

   (f)   provision for the variation or revocation of contribution orders;

   (g)   provision for an appeal to lie to such court or other person or body as may be prescribed against a contribution order;

   (h)   such transitional provision as the Lord Chancellor may consider appropriate.

   (3) Regulations under subsection (1) shall include provision for the repayment to an individual of any payment made by him in excess of his liability under a contribution order.

   (4) Regulations under subsection (1) shall provide that an order made under the regulations may not order the payment of costs to the extent that they are already the subject of an order under section 17(2).

   (5) Regulations under subsection (1) may—

   (a)   be made so as to have effect only for a specified period not exceeding 12 months;

   (b)   provide that their provisions are to apply only in relation to one or more prescribed areas.

   (6) In this section, "contribution order" means an order under regulations under subsection (1).

[Access to Justice Act 1999, s 17A as inserted by the Criminal Defence Service Act 2006, s 3.]

1–3948   18. Funding.   (1) The Lord Chancellor shall pay to the Commission such sums as are required to meet the costs of any advice, assistance and representation funded by the Commission as part of the Criminal Defence Service.

   (2) The Lord Chancellor may—

   (a)   determine the manner in which and times at which the sums referred to in subsection (1) shall be paid to the Commission, and

   (b)   impose conditions on the payment of the sums.

   (3) In funding services as part of the Criminal Defence Service the Commission shall aim to obtain the best possible value for money.

[Access to Justice Act 1999, s 18, as amended by SI 2005/3429.]

Supplementary

1–3949   19. Foreign law.   (1) The Commission may not fund as part of the Community Legal Service or Criminal Defence Service services relating to any law other than that of England and Wales, unless any such law is relevant for determining any issue relating to the law of England and Wales.

   (2) But the Lord Chancellor may, if it appears to him necessary to do so for the purpose of fulfilling any obligation imposed on the United Kingdom by any international agreement, by order[1] specify that there may be funded as part of the Community Legal Service or Criminal Defence Service (or both) services relating to the application of such other law as may be specified in the order.

[Access to Justice Act 1999, s 19, as amended by SI 2005/3429.]

---

   1. The Community Legal Service (Funding) Order 2000 in this PART, post has been made.

1–3950   20. Restriction of disclosure of information.   (1) Subject to the following provisions of this section, information which is furnished—

   (*a*)   to the Commission or any court, tribunal or other person or body on whom functions are imposed or conferred by or under this Part, and

   (*b*)   in connection with the case of an individual seeking or receiving services funded by the Commission as part of the Community Legal Service or Criminal Defence Service,

shall not be disclosed except as permitted by subsection (2).

   (2)   Such information may be disclosed—

   (*a*)   for the purpose of enabling or assisting the Commission to discharge any functions imposed or conferred on it by or under this Part,

   (*b*)   for the purpose of enabling or assisting the Lord Chancellor to discharge any functions imposed or conferred on him by or under this Part,

   (*c*)   for the purpose of enabling or assisting any court, tribunal or other person or body to discharge any functions imposed or conferred on it by or under this Part,

   (*d*)   except where regulations otherwise provide, for the purpose of the investigation or prosecution of any offence (or suspected offence) under the law of England and Wales or any other jurisdiction,

   (*e*)   in connection with any proceedings relating to the Community Legal Service or Criminal Defence Service, or

   (*f*)   for the purpose of facilitating the proper performance by any tribunal of disciplinary functions.

   (3)   Subsection (1) does not limit the disclosure of—

   (*a*)   information in the form of a summary or collection of information so framed as not to enable information relating to any individual to be ascertained from it, or

   (*b*)   information about the amount of any grant, loan or other payment made to any person or body by the Commission.

   (4)   Subsection (1) does not prevent the disclosure of information for any purpose with the consent of the individual in connection with whose case it was furnished and, where he did not furnish it himself, with that of the person or body who did.

   (4A)   Subsection (1) does not prevent the disclosure of information after the end of the restricted period, if—

   (*a*)   the disclosure is by a person who is, or is acting on behalf of a person who is, a public authority for the purposes of the Freedom of Information Act 2000, and

   (*b*)   the information is not held by the authority on behalf of another person.

   (4B)   The restricted period is the period of one hundred years starting at the end of the calendar year in which a record containing the information was first created.

   (5)   A person who discloses any information in contravention of this section shall be guilty of an offence and liable on summary conviction to a fine not exceeding **level 4** on the standard scale.

   (6)   Proceedings for an offence under this section shall not be brought without the consent of the Director of Public Prosecutions.

   (7)   Nothing in this section applies to information furnished to a person providing services funded as part of the Community Legal Service or the Criminal Defence Service by or on behalf of an individual seeking or receiving such services.

[Access to Justice Act 1999, s 20, as amended by SI 2005/3429 and SI 2004/3363.]

1–3951   21. Misrepresentation etc.   (1) Any person who—

   (*a*)   intentionally fails to comply with any requirement imposed by virtue of this Part as to the information to be furnished by him, or

   (*b*)   in furnishing any information required by virtue of this Part makes any statement or representation which he knows or believes to be false,

shall be guilty of an offence.

   (2)   A person guilty of an offence under subsection (1) is liable on summary conviction to—

   (*a*)   a fine not exceeding **level 4** on the standard scale, or

   (*b*)   imprisonment for a term not exceeding **three months**,

or to both.

   (3)   Proceedings in respect of an offence under subsection (1) may (despite anything in the Magistrates' Courts Act 1980) be brought at any time within the period of six months beginning with the date on which evidence sufficient in the opinion of the prosecutor to justify a prosecution comes to his knowledge.

   (4)   But subsection (3) does not authorise the commencement of proceedings for an offence at a time more than two years after the date on which the offence was committed.

   (5)   A county court shall have jurisdiction to hear and determine any action brought by the Commission to recover loss sustained by reason of—

   (*a*)   the failure of any person to comply with any requirement imposed by virtue of this Part as to the information to be furnished by him, or (*b*)   a false statement or false representation made by any person in furnishing any information required by virtue of this Part.

[Access to Justice Act 1999, s 21.]

1–3952   22. Position of service providers and other parties etc.   (1) Except as expressly provided by regulations[1], the fact that services provided for an individual are or could be funded by the Commission as part of the Community Legal Service or Criminal Defence Service shall not affect—

(*a*)   the relationship between that individual and the person by whom they are provided or any privilege arising out of that relationship, or

(*b*)   any right which that individual may have to be indemnified in respect of expenses incurred by him by any other person.

(2) A person who provides services funded by the Commission as part of the Community Legal Service or Criminal Defence Service shall not take any payment in respect of the services apart from—

(*a*)   that made by way of that funding, and

(*b*)   any authorised by the Commission to be taken.

(3) The withdrawal of a right to representation previously granted to an individual shall not affect the right of any person who has provided to him services funded by the Commission as part of the Criminal Defence Service to remuneration for work done before the date of the withdrawal.

(4) Except as expressly provided by regulations, any rights conferred by or by virtue of this Part on an individual for whom services are funded by the Commission as part of the Community Legal Service or Criminal Defence Service in relation to any proceedings shall not affect—

(*a*)   the rights or liabilities of other parties to the proceedings, or

(*b*)   the principles on which the discretion of any court or tribunal is normally exercised.

(5) Regulations[2] may make provision about the procedure of any court or tribunal in relation to services funded by the Commission as part of the Community Legal Service or Criminal Defence Service.

(6) Regulations[2] made under subsection (5) may in particular authorise the exercise of the functions of any court or tribunal by any member or officer of that or any other court or tribunal.

[Access to Justice Act 1999, s 22.]

---

1. See the Legal Services Commission (Disclosure of Information) Regulations 2000, SI 2000/442 amended by SI 2001/857 which waive the rules of privilege and confidentiality regarding disclosure of information relating to the cases of clients or former clients funded by the Commission. See also the Community Legal Service (Costs) Regulations 2000 in this PART, post.

2. See the Community Legal Service (Costs) Regulations 2000 in this PART, post.

1–3953   23. Guidance.   (1) The Lord Chancellor may give guidance to the Commission as to the manner in which he considers it should discharge its functions.

(2) The Commission shall take into account any such guidance when considering the manner in which it is to discharge its functions.

(3) Guidance may not be given under this section in relation to individual cases.

(4) The Lord Chancellor shall either—

(*a*)   publish, or

(*b*)   require the Commission to publish,

any guidance given under this section.

[Access to Justice Act 1999, s 23, as amended by SI 2005/3429.]

1–3954   24. Consequential amendments.   Schedule 4 (which makes amendments consequential on this Part) has effect.

[Access to Justice Act 1999, s 24.]

1–3955   25. Orders, regulations and directions.   (1) Any power of the Lord Chancellor under this Part to make an order or regulations is exercisable by statutory instrument.

(2) Before making any remuneration order relating to the payment of remuneration to barristers or solicitors the Lord Chancellor shall consult the General Council of the Bar and the Law Society.

(3) When making any remuneration order the Lord Chancellor shall have regard to—

(*a*)   the need to secure the provision of services of the description to which the order relates by a sufficient number of competent persons and bodies,

(*b*)   the cost to public funds, and

(*c*)   the need to secure value for money.

(4) In subsections (2) and (3) "remuneration order" means an order under section 6(4), 13(3) or 14(3) which relates to the payment by the Commission of remuneration—

(*a*)   for the provision of services by persons or bodies in individual cases, or

(*b*)   by reference to the provision of services by persons or bodies in specified numbers of cases.

(5) No directions may be given by the Lord Chancellor to the Commission under this Part in relation to individual cases.

(6) Any directions given by the Lord Chancellor to the Commission under this Part may be varied or revoked.

(7) The Lord Chancellor shall either—

(a) publish, or

(b) require the Commission to publish,

any directions given by him under this Part.

(8) Orders, regulations and directions of the Lord Chancellor under this Part may make different provision for different purposes (including different areas).

(9) No order shall be made under section 2 or 8 or paragraph 5(3) of Schedule 3, and no regulations shall be made under section 6(7), 11(1) or (4)(b) or (d) or 15(2)(a) or (5) or or paragraph 2A or 4 of Schedule 3, unless a draft of the order or regulations has been laid before, and approved by a resolution of, each House of Parliament.

(9A) The first regulations under section 17A or paragraph 3B of Schedule 3 shall not be made unless a draft of the regulations has been laid before, and approved by a resolution of, each House of Parliament.

(10) A statutory instrument containing any other order or regulations under this Part shall be subject to annulment in pursuance of a resolution of either House of Parliament.

[Access to Justice Act 1999, s 25, as amended by SI 2005/3429 and the Criminal Defence Service Act 2006, ss 1–3.]

1–3956   26. Interpretation.   In this Part—

"the Commission" means the Legal Services Commission,

"the Community Legal Service Fund" has the meaning given by section 5(1),

"criminal proceedings" has the meaning given in section 12(2),

"prescribed" means prescribed by regulations and "prescribe" shall be construed accordingly,

"regulations" means regulations made by the Lord Chancellor, and

"relevant authority" means such person or body as may be prescribed, and

"representation" means representation for the purposes of proceedings and includes the assistance which is usually given by a representative in the steps preliminary or incidental to any proceedings and, subject to any time limits which may be prescribed, advice and assistance as to any appeal.

[Access to Justice Act 1999, s 26, as amended by SI 2005/3429 and the Criminal Defence Service Act 2006, s 2.]

1–3957

PART IV[1]

APPEALS, COURTS, JUDGES AND COURT PROCEEDINGS

----

1. Part IV comprises ss 54–73.

1–3958

PART V[1]

MAGISTRATES AND MAGISTRATES' COURTS

----

1. Part V comprises ss 74–97.

Justices' chief executives, justices' clerks and staff

1–3964   90. Transfer of clerks' functions to chief executives.   (1) Schedule 13[1] (which makes amendments transferring administrative functions of justices' clerks to justices' chief executives) has effect.

(2) The Lord Chancellor may by order made by statutory instrument make provision for the transfer of other administrative functions of justices' clerks to justices' chief executives.

(3) An order under subsection (2) may contain amendments of enactments.

(4) A statutory instrument containing an order under subsection (2) shall be subject to annulment in pursuance of a resolution of either House of Parliament.

(5) For the purposes of this section the administrative functions of justices' clerks are all of their functions apart from those which are legal functions within the meaning given by section 48(2) of the Justices of the Peace Act 1997.

[Access to Justice Act 1999, s 90.]

1–3965   91. Accounting etc functions of chief executives[1].   *Amendment of the Justices of the Peace Act 1997.*

----

1. The amendments made by s 91 have been incorporated in the provisions of the Justices of the Peace Act 1997, this PART, ante.

1–3966

PART VI[1]

IMMUNITY AND INDEMNITY

Justices and their clerks

----

1. Part VI comprises ss 98–104.

PART VII[1]
SUPPLEMENTARY

1–3975   105. Transitional provisions and savings.   Schedule 14[2] (transitional provisions and savings) has effect.
[Access to Justice Act 1999, s 105.]

---

1. Part VII comprises ss 105–110.
2. See, post.

1–3976   106. Repeals and revocations.   Schedule 15 (repeals and revocations) has effect.
[Access to Justice Act 1999, s 106.]

1–3977   107. Crown application.   This Act binds the Crown.
[Access to Justice Act 1999, s 107.]

1–3978   108. Commencement.   (1) Subject to subsections (2) and (3), the preceding provisions of this Act shall come into force on such day as the Lord Chancellor or Secretary of State may by order[1] made by statutory instrument appoint; and different days may be appointed for different purposes and, in the case of section 67(2), for different areas.

(2) Section 45 shall come into force on the day on which this Act is passed.

(3) The following provisions shall come into force at the end of the period of two months beginning with the day on which this Act is passed—

(a) in Part II, sections 32 to 34,
(b) Part IV, apart from section 66 and Schedule 9 and sections 67(2) and 71,
(c) in Part V, sections 74 to 76, 81, 82, 84, 86 and 87 and Schedule 10,
(d) in Part VI, section 104,
(e) Schedule 14,
(f) in Schedule 15, Part III and Part V(1) and (5), apart from the provisions specified in subsection (4), and
(g) section 107.

(4) The provisions excepted from subsection (3)(f) are the repeal of section 67(8) of the Magistrates' Courts Act 1980 (and that in Schedule 11 to the Children Act 1989) contained in Part V(1) of Schedule 15.
[Access to Justice Act 1999, s 108, as amended by SI 2003/1887.]

---

1. The following commencement orders have been made: Access to Justice Act 1999 (Commencement No 1) Order 1999, SI 1999/2657; Access to Justice Act 1999 (Commencement No 2 and Transitional Provisions) Order 1999, SI 1999/3344; Access to Justice Act 1999 (Commencement No 3, Transitional Provisions and Savings) Order 2000, SI 2000/7741; Access to Justice Act 1999 (Commencement No 4 and Transitional Provisions) Order 2000, SI 2000/19202; Access to Justice Act 1999 (Commencement No 5 and Transitional Provisions) Order 2000, SI 2000/32803; Access to Justice Act 1999 (Commencement No 6 and Transitional Provisions) Order 2001, SI 2001/1684; Access to Justice Act 1999 (Commencement No 7, Transitional Provisions and Savings) Order 2001, SI 2001/9165; Access to Justice Act 1999 (Commencement No 8) Order 2001, SI 2001/1655; Access to Justice Act 1999 (Commencement No 9 and Transitional Provisions) (Scotland) Order 2003, SSI 2003/207; Access to Justice Act 1999 (Commencement No 10) Order 2003, SI 2003/1241; and Access to Justice Act 1999 (Commencement No 11) Order 2003, SI 2003/2571. Functions under this Part of this Act, so far as exercisable by the Secretary of State, were transferred to the Lord Chancellor by the Transfer of Functions (Lord Chancellor and Secretary of State) Order 2005, SI 2005/3429, arts 3(1)(c), 4, 5.

1–3979   109. Extent.   (1) Sections 32 to 34 and 73(2) extend to Scotland.

(2) Sections 98(2) and (3) and 104(2) extend to Northern Ireland.

(3) Sections 68, 101, 102 and 103 extend to England and Wales, Scotland and Northern Ireland.

(4) The other provisions of this Act which make amendments or repeals or revocations in other enactments also have the same extent as the enactments which they amend or repeal or revoke.

(5) Subject to subsection (4), the provisions of this Part (including paragraph 1, but not the rest, of Schedule 14) extend to England and Wales, Scotland and Northern Ireland.

(6) Subject to the preceding provisions, this Act extends to England and Wales.

(7) For the purposes of the Scotland Act 1998 this Act, so far as it extends to Scotland, shall be taken to be a pre-commencement enactment within the meaning of that Act.
[Access to Justice Act 1999, s 109.]

1–3980   110. Short title.   This Act may be cited as the Access to Justice Act 1999.
[Access to Justice Act 1999, s 110.]

1–3981

Section 1

SCHEDULE 1
LEGAL SERVICES COMMISSION

1–3982

SCHEDULE 2
COMMUNITY LEGAL SERVICE: EXCLUDED SERVICES

(*As amended by the Child Support, Pensions and Social Security Act 2000, Sch 8, SI 2000/822, the Anti-terrorism, Crime and Security Act 2001, s 2(1), the Proceeds of Crime Act 2002, ss 456, 457, the Nationality, Immigration and Asylum Act 2002, s 116, SI 2003/1887, 2004/1055, SI 2005/2008 and the Adoption and Children Act 2002, Sch 3.*)
The services which may not be funded as part of the Community Legal Service are as follows.

1. Services consisting of the provision of help (beyond the provision of general information about the law and the legal system and the availability of legal services) in relation to—

(*a*) allegations of negligently caused injury or death, other than allegations relating to clinical negligence,
(*aa*) allegations of negligently caused damage to property,
(*b*) conveyancing,
(*c*) boundary disputes,
(*d*) the making of wills,
(*e*) matters of trust law,*
(*f*) defamation or malicious falsehood,
(*g*) matters of company or partnership law,
(*h*) other matters arising out of the carrying on of a business, or
(*i*) attending an interview on behalf of the Secretary of State with a view to his reaching a decision on a claim for asylum (as defined by section 167(1) of the Immigration and Asylum Act 1999).

2. Advocacy in any proceedings except—
(1) proceedings in—

(*a*) the House of Lords in its judicial capacity,**
(*b*) the Judicial Committee of the Privy Council in the exercise of its jurisdiction under the Government of Wales Act 1998, the Scotland Act 1998 or the Northern Ireland Act 1998,**
(*c*) the Court of Appeal,
(*d*) the High Court,
(*e*) any county court,
(*f*) the Employment Appeal Tribunal,
(*g*) any Mental Health Review Tribunal,
(*h*) the Asylum and Immigration Tribunal,
(*ha*) the Special Immigration Appeals Commission, or
(*i*) the Proscribed Organisations Appeal Commission.

(2) proceedings in the Crown Court—

(*a*) for the variation or discharge of an order under section 5 of the Protection from Harassment Act 1997,
(*b*) which relate to an order under section 10 of the Crime and Disorder Act 1998,
(*c*) *repealed*,
(*d*) which relate to an order under paragraph 6 or Schedule 1 to the Anti-terrorism, Crime and Security Act 2001, or
(*e*) under the Proceeds of Crime Act 2002 to the extent specified in paragraph 3.

(3) proceedings in a magistrates' court—

(*a*) under section 43 or 47 of the National Assistance Act 1948, section 22 of the Maintenance Orders Act 1950, section 4 of the Maintenance Orders Act 1958 or section 106 of the Social Security Administration Act 1992,
(*b*) under Part I of the Maintenance Orders (Reciprocal Enforcement) Act 1972 relating to a maintenance order made by a court of a country outside the United Kingdom,
(*c*) in relation to an application for leave of the court to remove a child from a person's custody under section 36 of the Adoption and Children Act 2002 or in which the making of a placement order or adoption order (within the meaning of the Adoption and Children Act 2002) or an order under section 41 or 84 of that Act is opposed by any party to the proceedings,*
(*d*) for or in relation to an order under Part I of the Domestic Proceedings and Magistrates' Courts Act 1978 or Schedule 6 to the Civil Partnership Act 2004,
(*da*) under section 55A of the Family Law Act 1986 (declarations of parentage),
(*e*) under the Children Act 1989,
(*f*) under section 30 of the Human Fertilisation and Embryology Act 1990,
(*g*) under section 20 of the Child Support Act 1991,
(*h*) under Part IV of the Family Law Act 1996,
(*i*) for the variation or discharge of an order under section 5 of the Protection from Harassment Act 1997,
(*j*) under section 8 or 11 of the Crime and Disorder Act 1998,
(*k*) for an order or direction under paragraph 3, 5, 6, 9 or 10 of Schedule 1 to the Anti-terrorism, Crime and Security Act 2001,
(*l*) for an order or direction under section 295, 297, 298, 301 or 302 of the Proceeds of Crime Act 2002, and

(4) proceedings before any person to whom a case is referred (in whole or in part) in any proceedings within paragraphs (1) to (3).

3. (1) These are the proceedings under the Proceeds of Crime Act 2002—

(*za*) an application under section 42 for a restraint order;
(*a*) an application under section 42(3) to vary or discharge a restraint order or an order under section 41(7);
(*b*) proceedings which relate to a direction under section 54(3) or 56(3) as to the distribution of funds in the hands of a receiver;
(*c*) an application under section 62 relating to action taken or proposed to be taken by a receiver;
(*d*) an application under section 63 to vary or discharge an order under any of sections 48 to 53 for the appointment of or conferring powers on a receiver;
(*e*) an application under section 72 or 73 for the payment of compensation;
(*f*) proceedings which relate to an order under section 298 for the forfeiture of cash;
(*g*) an application under section 351(3), 362(3), 369(3) or 375(2) to vary or discharge certain orders made under Part 8.

(2) But sub-paragraph (1) does not authorise the funding of the provision of services to a defendant (within the meaning of Part 1 of that Act) in relation to—

(a) proceedings mentioned in paragraph (b);
(b) an application under section 73 for the payment of compensation if the confiscation order was varied under section 29.

---

*New sub-paras (ea) and (eb) inserted by the Mental Capacity Act 2005, Sch 6, from a date to be appointed.
**Sub-para (1)(a) substituted and sub-para (1)(b) repealed by the Constitutional Reform Act 2005, Schs 9 and 18, from a date to be appointed.

1–3983

Section 14

SCHEDULE 3

CRIMINAL DEFENCE SERVICE: RIGHT TO REPRESENTATION

(*As amended by SI 2004/2035, SI 2005/3429 and the Criminal Defence Service Act 2006, ss 1, 2*).

Individuals to whom right may be granted

1. (1) A right to representation for the purposes of any kind of criminal proceedings before a court may be granted to an individual such as is mentioned in relation to that kind of proceedings in section 12(2).
(2) A right to representation for the purposes of criminal proceedings may also be granted to an individual to enable him to resist an appeal to the Crown Court otherwise than in an official capacity.
(3) In this Schedule "court" includes any body before which criminal proceedings take place.

Grant of right by court[2]

2. (1) A court before which any criminal proceedings take place, or are to take place, has power to grant a right to representation in respect of those proceedings.
(2) Where a right to representation is granted for the purposes of criminal proceedings it includes the right to representation for the purposes of any related bail proceedings and any preliminary or incidental proceedings; and regulations may make provision specifying whether any proceedings are or are not to be regarded as preliminary or incidental.
(3) A court also has power to grant a right to representation for the purposes of criminal proceedings before another court in such circumstances as may be prescribed.
(4) The form of the application for a grant of a right to representation under this paragraph, and the form of the grant of such a right, shall be such as may be prescribed.
(5) Subject to sub-paragraph (5A), a right to representation in respect of proceedings may be withdrawn by any court before which the proceedings take place; and a court must consider whether to withdraw a right to representation in such circumstances as may be prescribed.*
(5A) Sub-paragraph (5) does not apply where the Commission has power to withdraw the right to representation in respect of the proceedings.
(6) The powers of a magistrates' court for any area under this paragraph may be exercised by a single justice of the peace for the area.
(7) Repealed.*

Grant of right by commission

2A. (1) Regulations may—

(a) provide that the Commission shall have power to grant rights to representation in respect of criminal proceedings of a prescribed description;
(b) provide that the Commission shall, except in such circumstances as may be prescribed, have power to withdraw any rights to representation granted in respect of proceedings of a description prescribed under paragraph (a).

(2) In sub-paragraph (1)(a), the reference to criminal proceedings does not include proceedings prescribed under section 12(2)(g).
(3) Regulations under sub-paragraph (1) may make such consequential amendment or repeal of any enactment, including an enactment contained in subordinate legislation (within the meaning of the Interpretation Act 1978), as the Lord Chancellor may consider appropriate.
3. (1) Regulations[1] may provide that the Commission shall have power to grant rights to representation in respect of any one or more of the descriptions of proceedings prescribed under section 12(2)(g), and to withdraw any rights to representation granted by it.
3A. (1) The form of the grant of a right to representation under paragraph 2A or 3 shall be such as may be prescribed.
(2) Regulations under paragraph 2A or 3 may make such transitional provision as the Lord Chancellor may consider appropriate.

Financial eligibility

3B. (1) Power under this Schedule to grant a right to representation may only be exercised in relation to an individual whose financial resources appear to the relevant authority to be such that, under regulations, he is eligible to be granted such a right.
(2) Power under this Schedule to withdraw a right to representation shall be exercised in relation to an individual if it appears to the relevant authority—

(a) that his financial resources are not such that, under regulations, he is eligible to be granted such a right, or
(b) that he has failed, in relation to the right, to comply with regulations under this paragraph about the furnishing of information.

(3) Regulations may make provision for exceptions from sub-paragraph (1) or (2).
(4) Regulations under this paragraph may include—

(*a*) provision requiring the furnishing of information;
(*b*) provision for the notification of decisions about the application of—

    (i) sub-paragraph (1) or (2), or
    (ii) regulations under sub-paragraph (3);

(*c*) provision for the review of such decisions;
(*d*) such transitional provision as the Lord Chancellor may consider appropriate.

(5) The provision which may be made under sub-paragraph (4)(*c*) includes provision prescribing circumstances in which the person or body reviewing a decision may refer a question to the High Court for its decision.

(6) Section 16 of the Supreme Court Act 1981 (appeals from the High Court) shall not apply to decisions of the High Court on a reference under regulations under this paragraph.

Appeals

4. Except where regulations[2] otherwise provide, an appeal shall lie to such court or other person or body as may be prescribed against a decision to refuse to grant a right to representation or to withdraw a right to representation.

Criteria for grant of right

5. (1) Any question as to whether power to grant a right to representation should be exercised shall be determined according to the interests of justice.

(2) In deciding what the interests of justice consist of in relation to any individual, the following factors must be taken into account—

(*a*) whether the individual would, if any matter arising in the proceedings is decided against him, be likely to lose his liberty or livelihood or suffer serious damage to his reputation,
(*b*) whether the determination of any matter arising in the proceedings may involve consideration of a substantial question of law,
(*c*) whether the individual may be unable to understand the proceedings or to state his own case,
(*d*) whether the proceedings may involve the tracing, interviewing or expert cross-examination of witnesses on behalf of the individual, and
(*e*) whether it is in the interests of another person that the individual be represented.

(3) The Lord Chancellor may by order amend sub-paragraph (2) by adding new factors or varying any factor.

(4) Regulations may prescribe circumstances in which the grant of a right to representation shall be taken to be in the interests of justice.

---

1. See generally the Criminal Defence Service (General) (No 2) Regulations 2001, in this PART, post.
2. See generally the Criminal Defence Service (Representation Order Appeals) Regulations 2001, in this PART, post.

1–3984

Section 24

SCHEDULE 4
AMENDMENTS CONSEQUENTIAL ON PART I[1]

---

1. The amendments relating to enactments that appear in this work have been incorporated as appropriate.

1–3988

Section 83

SCHEDULE 12
GREATER LONDON MAGISTRATES' COURTS AUTHORITY[1]

---

1. The amendments relating to enactments that appear in this work have been incorporated.

1–3989

Section 90

SCHEDULE 13
FUNCTIONS TRANSFERRED TO JUSTICES' CHIEF EXECUTIVES

1–3990

Section 105

SCHEDULE 14
TRANSITIONAL PROVISIONS AND SAVINGS

(As amended by SI 2003/1887and 2867).

PART I
GENERAL

1. (1) The Lord Chancellor or Secretary of State may by order made by statutory instrument make such transitional provisions and savings he considers appropriate in connection with the coming into force of any provision of this Act.

(2) Nothing in the following provisions of this Schedule limits sub-paragraph (1).

(3) Nothing in this Schedule limits the operation of sections 16 and 17 of the Interpretation Act 1978 (effect of repeals).

PART II
LEGAL SERVICES COMMISSION

PART III
LEGAL SERVICES

Regulations and rules for barristers and solicitors

14. (1) For the purposes of section 27 of the Courts and Legal Services Act 1990—

(a) the qualification regulations and rules of conduct of the General Council of the Bar at the time when section 36 of this Act comes into force shall (so far as relating to rights of audience) be deemed to have been approved in relation to the right specified in section 31(1) of that Act (as substituted by that section), and

(b) the qualification regulations and rules of conduct of the Law Society at that time shall (so far as relating to rights of audience) be deemed to have been approved in relation to the right specified in section 31(2)(a) of that Act (as so substituted).

(2) For the purposes of section 28 of that Act, the qualification regulations and rules of conduct of the Law Society at that time shall (so far as relating to rights to conduct litigation) be deemed to have been approved in relation to the right specified in section 31(2)(b) of that Act (as substituted by section 36 of this Act).

15. Where a person was called to the Bar or admitted as a solicitor before the coming into force of section 36 of this Act, he shall be taken for the purposes of determining for how many years he has had one of the qualifications listed in section 71(3) of the Courts and Legal Services Act 1990 as having been granted a right of audience before every court in relation to all proceedings on his call or admission.

Existing rights of solicitors in certain Crown Court centres

16. (1) If section 36 of this Act comes into force before the repeal by this Act of section 83 of the Supreme Court Act 1981, section 83 shall have effect until that repeal comes into force subject to the modifications specified in sub-paragraphs (2) and (3).

(2) Subsection (1) shall have effect as if for "may have rights of audience in the Crown Court" there were substituted "shall be entitled to exercise their right of audience in the Crown Court even though they do not satisfy the regulations of the Law Society relating to the education and training which solicitors must receive in order to exercise their right of audience in the Crown Court".

(3) Subsection (3) shall have effect as if for "with" there were substituted "who may exercise".

Authorised bodies

17. (1) An Order in Council made pursuant to a recommendation under section 29 of the Courts and Legal Services Act 1990 and in force immediately before the time when Schedule 5 to this Act comes into force shall have effect after that time (unless revoked) as if made pursuant to a recommendation under Part I of Schedule 4 to that Act as substituted by Schedule 5 to this Act.

(2) Any approval under Part II of Schedule 4 to the Courts and Legal Services Act 1990 in force immediately before the time when Schedule 5 to this Act comes into force shall have effect after that time as an approval under that Part of that Schedule as substituted by Schedule 5 to this Act.

District Judges (Magistrates' Courts): appointment

22. Any person who is a stipendiary magistrate or a metropolitan stipendiary magistrate immediately before the time when section 78 of this Act comes into force shall be treated as having been appointed to be a District Judge (Magistrates' Courts) at that time (unless he would have been required by reason of age to vacate his office at that time).

23. Any person who, immediately before the time when section 78 of this Act comes into force, is authorised under section 13(1)(a) or 19 of the Justices of the Peace Act 1997 to act as a stipendiary magistrate or metropolitan stipendiary magistrate shall be treated as having been appointed to be a Deputy District Judge (Magistrates' Courts) at that time for the remainder of the period for which he is so authorised.

District Judges (Magistrates' Courts): pensions

24. (1) For the purposes specified in sub-paragraph (2), a person who—

(a) is a stipendiary magistrate or metropolitan stipendiary magistrate immediately before the time when section 78 of this Act comes into force, and

(b) is at that time a member of a judicial pension scheme constituted by the Judicial Pensions Act 1981,

shall not be regarded as having been appointed (by virtue of paragraph 22) to be a District Judge (Magistrates' Courts) but shall instead be regarded as if he continued to be a stipendiary magistrate or metropolitan stipendiary magistrate.

(2) The purposes referred to in sub-paragraph (1) are those of—

(a) the Judicial Pensions Act 1981,

(b) any scheme constituted by that Act, and

(c) any enactment made by or under an Act which applies to such a scheme or to rights arising under such a scheme.

District Judges (Magistrates' Courts): retirement

25. For the purposes of section 26 of and Schedule 7 to the Judicial Pensions and Retirement Act 1993 (date of retirement for holders of a relevant office immediately before the time when section 26 came into force) a person who held the office of stipendiary magistrate or metropolitan stipendiary magistrate at any time during the period beginning when section 26 came into force and ending when Schedule 11 to this Act comes into force shall be treated as having held a relevant office at that time in spite of the amendment made to Schedule 5 to the Judicial Pensions and Retirement Act 1993 by Schedule 11 to this Act.

Pensions of inner London court staff

36. (1) The Lord Chancellor may by order made by statutory instrument[3] make provision about the provision of pensions for or in respect of persons who are or have been members of the inner London court staff.

(2) An order under this paragraph may include provision for, or in connection with—

(a) enabling persons to participate, or continue to participate, in any pension scheme and requiring their employers to make contributions under that scheme, and

(b) the administration or management of pension schemes or pension funds.

(3) Provision of the kind specified in sub-paragraph (2)(a) may—

(*a*) with the consent of the Minister for the Civil Service, include provision for section 1 of the Superannuation Act 1972 (pensions of civil servants etc) to apply to persons who are or have been members of the inner London court staff, or

(*b*) include provision for persons who have been members of the inner London court staff but who are employees of the Greater London Magistrates' Courts Authority by virtue of a scheme under paragraph 33 to be regarded as continuing to be members of the metropolitan civil staffs for the purposes of section 15 of the Superannuation (Miscellaneous Provisions) Act 1967 (pensions of metropolitan civil staffs).

(4) An order under this paragraph containing provision of the kind specified in sub-paragraph (3)(*a*) may also contain provision for such body or person as may be specified in the order to pay to the Minister for the Civil Service, at such times as he may direct, such sums as he may determine in respect of the increase attributable to such provision (so far as referable to that body or person) in the sums payable under the Superannuation Act 1972 out of money provided by Parliament.

(5) Where an order is made under this paragraph containing provision of the kind specified in sub-paragraph (3)(*a*), the Minister for the Civil Service may, to such extent and subject to such conditions as he thinks fit—

(*a*) delegate to any person the function of administering a scheme made under section 1 of the Superannuation Act 1972, so far as relating to persons who are or have been members of the inner London court staff, or

(*b*) authorise the exercise of that function (so far as so relating) by, or by employees of, any person.

(6) A person to whom the function of administering a scheme made under section 1 of the Superannuation Act 1972 is delegated under sub-paragraph (5)(*a*) may, to such extent and subject to such conditions as he may determine, authorise the exercise of that function by, or by employees of, any person.

(7) Where a person is authorised under sub-paragraph (5)(*b*) or (6) to exercise the function of administering a scheme made under section 1 of the Superannuation Act 1972, anything done or omitted to be done by or in relation to him (or an employee of his) in, or in connection with, the exercise or purported exercise of the function shall be treated for all purposes as done or omitted to be done by the person who authorised him.

(8) Sub-paragraph (7) does not apply for the purposes of—

(*a*) any criminal proceedings against the authorised person (or any employee of his), or

(*b*) any contract between him and the person who authorised him, so far as relating to the function.

(9) An order under this paragraph may provide that any enactment repealed by this Act shall continue to have effect for any purpose specified in the order with such modifications as may be so specified.

(10) A statutory instrument containing an order under this paragraph shall be subject to annulment in pursuance of a resolution of either House of Parliament.

(11) In this paragraph the "inner London court staff" means—

(*a*) the justices' chief executive employed by the magistrates' courts committee for the area consisting of the inner London boroughs,

(*b*) any justices' clerk for that area, and

(*c*) staff of the magistrates' courts committee for that area.

---

1. Immediately before abolition of ACLEC on 1 January 2000 by s 35 of the Access to Justice Act 1999, the ACLEC's property, rights and liabilities were transferred to the Lord Chancellor by the Lord Chancellor's Advisory Committee on Legal Education and Conduct (Provisions on Abolition) Order 1999, SI 1999/3296.

3. The Inner London Court Staff Pensions Order 2001, SI 2001/733 amended by SI 2001/1425 has been made. (See also the Greater London Magistrates' Courts Authority (Pensions) Order 2002, SI 2002/2143.)

1–3991

Section 106   SCHEDULE 15

REPEALS AND REVOCATIONS[1]

---

1. The repeals and revocations relating to enactments that appear in this work have been incorporated as appropriate.

Criminal Justice and Court Services Act 2000[1]

(2000 c 43)

PART I[2]

THE NEW SERVICES

CHAPTER I

NATIONAL PROBATION SERVICE FOR ENGLAND AND WALES

Introduction

1–3992   **1. Purposes of the Chapter.** (1) This Chapter has effect for the purposes of providing for—

(*a*) courts to be given assistance in determining the appropriate sentences to pass, and making other decisions, in respect of persons charged with or convicted of offences, and

(*b*) the supervision and rehabilitation of such persons.

(1A) This Chapter also has effect for the purposes of providing for—

(*a*) authorised persons to be given assistance in determining whether conditional cautions should be given and which conditions to attach to conditional cautions, and

(*b*) the supervision and rehabilitation of persons to whom conditional cautions are given.

(2) Subsection (1)(*b*) extends (in particular) to—

(a) giving effect to community orders,

(b) supervising persons released from prison on licence,

(c) providing accommodation in approved premises.

(3) Regulations[3] may extend the purposes mentioned in subsection (1) to include other prescribed purposes relating to persons charged with or convicted of offences.

(4) In this section "authorised person" and "conditional caution" have the same meaning as in Part 3 of the Criminal Justice Act 2003.

[*Criminal Justice and Court Services Act 2000*, s 1 as amended by the *Criminal Justice Act 2003*, s 26.]

---

1. This Act establishes a National Probation Service for England and Wales and a Children and Family Court Advisory and Support Service; makes further provision for the protection of children; makes further provision about dealing with persons suspected of, charged with or convicted of offences; amends the law relating to access to information held under Part III of the Road Traffic Act 1988.

2. Part I comprises ss 1 to 5.

3. The Local Probation Boards (Miscellaneous Provisions) Regulations 2001, in this PART, post, have been made.

1–3993   2. Aims of the Service.   (1) This section applies to—

(a) the functions of the Secretary of State under this Chapter,

(b) the functions of local probation boards, and officers of local probation boards, under this Act or any other enactment,

so far as they may be exercised for the purposes mentioned in section 1.

(2) In exercising those functions the person concerned must have regard to the following aims—

(a) the protection of the public,

(b) the reduction of re-offending,

(c) the proper punishment of offenders,

(d) ensuring offenders' awareness of the effects of crime on the victims of crime and the public,

(e) the rehabilitation of offenders.

[*Criminal Justice and Court Services Act 2000*, s 2.]

Functions

1–3994   3. Functions of the Secretary of State.   (1) The Secretary of State has the function of ensuring that provision is made throughout England and Wales for the purposes mentioned in section 1.

(2) The Secretary of State may make any payment he considers appropriate towards expenditure incurred by any person for any of those purposes.

(3) If he considers it appropriate, he may make any payment on conditions.

(4) The conditions may (among other things)—

(a) regulate the purposes for which the payment or any part of it may be used,

(b) require repayment to the Secretary of State in specified circumstances.

[*Criminal Justice and Court Services Act 2000*, s 3.]

1–3995   4. Local probation boards.   (1) For the purpose of implementing this Chapter, England and Wales shall be divided into areas.

(2) For each area there shall be a board (referred to in this Act as a local probation board) which is to exercise the functions conferred on it by virtue of this Act and any other enactment.

(3) Schedule 1[1] (which makes provision about the constitution of local probation boards, their powers and other matters relating to them) is to have effect.

(4) References in this Act or any other enactment to an officer of a local probation board are references to—

(a) any member of the staff of a local probation board appointed to exercise the functions of an officer of the board, and

(b) any other individual exercising functions of an officer of a local probation board by virtue of section 5(2).

(5) The initial areas for the purpose of implementing this Chapter are—

(a) the police areas listed in Schedule 1 to the Police Act 1996 (areas into which England and Wales, apart from London, is divided), and

(b) the area comprising the Metropolitan Police District and the City of London Police Area.

(6) The division of England and Wales into areas for that purpose may be altered from time to time by order made by the Secretary of State.

[*Criminal Justice and Court Services Act 2000*, s 4.]

---

1. See para **1–4073**.

1–3996   5. Functions of local probation boards.   (1) It is a function of a local probation board—

(a) to make arrangements for ensuring that sufficient provision is made in respect of its area for the purposes mentioned in section 1 and for ensuring the performance of any other functions conferred by virtue of this Act or any other enactment on the board,

(b) to make arrangements for ensuring the performance of any functions conferred by virtue of this Act or any other enactment on officers of the board,

and to implement, or ensure the implementation of, any arrangements it makes under this section.

(2) In addition to making arrangements for provision to be made by its staff, a local probation board may (for example)—

(a) make arrangements with organisations for provision to be made on the board's behalf by the organisations,

(b) make arrangements with individuals who are not members of the board's staff under which they may perform functions of officers of the board,

and arrangements under paragraph (a) may provide for the organisations to designate individuals who may perform functions of officers of the board.

(3) The provision that may be made in pursuance of such arrangements includes providing services to any person and, in particular—

(a) giving assistance to persons remanded on bail or for whom officers of the board have responsibilities,

(b) providing accommodation in approved premises for persons who have at any time been charged with or convicted of an offence.

(4) A local probation board may provide for its staff to co-operate with persons in its area who are concerned with the prevention or reduction of crime or with giving assistance to the victims of crime.

(5) Regulations[1] may confer further functions on local probation boards or officers of local probation boards.

(6) A local probation board may give grants or other financial assistance to any person only in pursuance of regulations[1].

(7) A local probation board—

(a) may make an arrangement with another local probation board under which it provides on behalf of the other board, in respect of the other board's area, any services which it could provide under this section in respect of its own area, and

(b) may charge the other local probation board for any services it provides in pursuance of the arrangement.

(8) It is for the Secretary of State to determine whether or not any provision made by a local probation board under this section is sufficient.

[Criminal Justice and Court Services Act 2000, s 5.]

---

1. The Local Probation Boards (Miscellaneous Provisions) Regulations 2001, in this PART, post, have been made.

1-3997   6. The inspectorate.   (1) The inspectorate, and the office of chief inspector, established under section 23 of the Probation Service Act 1993 (inspectorate of probation) shall continue in being, but—

(a) the members of the inspectorate are to be known as "Her Majesty's Inspectorate of the National Probation Service for England and Wales", and

(b) the chief inspector is to be known as "Her Majesty's Chief Inspector of the National Probation Service for England and Wales".

(2) The power to appoint a person to be chief inspector or one of the other members of the inspectorate is exercisable by the Secretary of State.

(3) The Secretary of State may determine—

(a) the number of members of the inspectorate,

(b) the remuneration, allowances or other amounts to be paid by him to or in respect of the members of the inspectorate.

(4) Below in this Chapter—

(a) references to the chief inspector are to Her Majesty's Chief Inspector of the National Probation Service for England and Wales,

(b) references to the members of the inspectorate are to the chief inspector and the other members of Her Majesty's Inspectorate of the National Probation Service for England and Wales.

[Criminal Justice and Court Services Act 2000, s 6.]

1-3998   7. Functions of inspectorate.   (1) The chief inspector must secure that the provision made in pursuance of arrangements made by each local probation board under section 5 is inspected by a member of the inspectorate.

(2) The Secretary of State may direct the members of the inspectorate to assess the provision made by reference to criteria specified in directions.

(3) A report of an inspection under subsection (1) must be sent to the Secretary of State.

(4) The Secretary of State may give directions as to—

(a) the information to be given in the report and the form in which it is to be given,

(b) the time by which the report is to be given.

(5) The Secretary of State must lay a copy of the report before each House of Parliament.

(6) The Secretary of State may give directions, in connection with the purposes mentioned in

section 1 or any related purposes, conferring further functions on the chief inspector and the other members of the inspectorate.
[Criminal Justice and Court Services Act 2000, s 7.]

Miscellaneous

1–3999 8. Support services.   (1) The Secretary of State may by order provide for any services to which, in his opinion, subsection (3) applies to be provided not by the staff of local probation boards but by others under arrangements made with the boards.

(2) The order may provide that only the Secretary of State, or an organisation or individual of a description specified in the order, may provide the services.

(3) This subsection applies to services—

(a) which are required by local probation boards in connection with the exercise of their functions, but

(b) which, with a view to obtaining better value for money or to improving the standard of the services or the efficiency of their provision, are better provided by persons other than the staff of local probation boards.

[Criminal Justice and Court Services Act 2000, s 8.]

1–4000 9. Approved premises.   (1) The Secretary of State may approve premises in which accommodation is provided—

(a) for persons granted bail in criminal proceedings (within the meaning of the Bail Act 1976), or

(b) for, or in connection with, the supervision or rehabilitation of persons convicted of offences.

(2) References in any enactment to an approved bail hostel or approved probation hostel are to be read as references to premises approved under this section.

(3) Regulations[1] may provide for the regulation, management and inspection of premises approved under this section.

(4) The Secretary of State may at any time make payments of any amount he considers appropriate towards the expenditure of any person in carrying on, or enlarging or improving, any premises if the premises are approved under this section or the payment is made with a view to their approval.
[Criminal Justice and Court Services Act 2000, s 9.]

---

1. The Criminal Justice and Court Services Act 2000 (Approved Premises) Regulations 2001, SI 2001/850 have been made.

1–4001 10. Default powers.   (1) The power conferred by this section is exercisable by the Secretary of State in respect of a local probation board if it appears to him that the board is failing to perform the functions conferred on it or that its arrangements for performing those functions do not represent good value for money.

(2) The Secretary of State may make an order (a "management order") in respect of the board.

(3) A management order may modify the application of Schedule 1 in relation to the board by—

(a) providing for the board to comprise persons determined in accordance with an arrangement made between the Secretary of State and an organisation (a "management arrangement"), and

(b) making any other modifications which appear to the Secretary of State to be necessary or expedient in consequence of that provision or of the management arrangement.

(4) A management order may provide for the persons determined in accordance with the management arrangement to replace all or any of the chairman, the chief officer and the other existing members of the board; and vacancies occurring among the replacements are to be filled in accordance with the management arrangement.

(5) The power to revoke a management order is exercisable at any time when the Secretary of State considers it necessary or expedient to revoke it.

(6) On the revocation of a management order, any person who is a member of the board by virtue of the order and the arrangement ceases to be a member; and, accordingly, any vacancy occurring by virtue of the revocation is to be filled in accordance with Schedule 1 (unless the Secretary of State makes a new management order).
[Criminal Justice and Court Services Act 2000, s 10.]

CHAPTER II
CHILDREN AND FAMILY COURT ADVISORY AND SUPPORT SERVICE

1–4002 11. Establishment of the Service.   (1) There shall be a body corporate to be known as the Children and Family Court Advisory and Support Service (referred to in this Part as the Service) which is to exercise the functions conferred on it by virtue of this Act and any other enactment.

(2) Schedule 2[1] (which makes provision about the constitution of the Service, its powers and other matters relating to it) is to have effect.

(3) References in this Act or any other enactment to an officer of the Service are references to—

(a) any member of the staff of the Service appointed under paragraph 5(1)(a) of that Schedule, and

(b) any other individual exercising functions of an officer of the Service by virtue of section 13(2) or (4).
[Criminal Justice and Court Services Act 2000, s 11.]

1. See para **1–4074**.

1–4003   12. Principal functions of the Service.   (1) In respect of family proceedings in which the welfare of children is or may be in question, it is a function of the Service to—

(a) safeguard and promote the welfare of the children,
(b) give advice to any court about any application made to it in such proceedings,
(c) make provision for the children to be represented in such proceedings,
(d) provide information, advice and other support for the children and their families.

(2) The Service must also make provision for the performance of any functions conferred on officers of the Service by virtue of this Act or any other enactment (whether or not they are exercisable for the purposes of the functions conferred on the Service by subsection (1))[1].

(3) Regulations[2] may provide for grants to be paid by the Service to any person for the purpose of furthering the performance of any of the Service's functions.

(4) The regulations may provide for the grants to be paid on conditions, including conditions—

(a) regulating the purposes for which the grant or any part of it may be used,
(b) requiring repayment to the Service in specified circumstances.

(5) In this section, "family proceedings" has the same meaning as in the Matrimonial and Family Proceedings Act 1984 and also includes any other proceedings which are family proceedings for the purposes of the Children Act 1989, but—

(a) references to family proceedings include (where the context allows) family proceedings which are proposed or have been concluded.
[Criminal Justice and Court Services Act 2000, s 12, as amended by the Adoption and Children Act 2002, Schs 3 and 5.]

1. Section 12(2) does not by its express language impose a duty upon CAFCASS to make provision to enable it, immediately on request by the court, to make available an officer of the service for appointment as a guardian; the relevant statutory provisions imply that, while CAFCASS should respond as soon as practicable after a request is made, there can be a gap between the request made by the court and CAFCASS making an officer available for appointment (*R v Children and Family Court Advisory and Support Service* [2003] EWHC 235 (Admin), [2003] 1 FLR 953).
2. The Children and Family Court Advisory and Support Service (Provision of Grants) Regulations 2001, SI 2001/697 have been made.

1–4004   13. Other powers of the Service.   (1) The Service may make arrangements with organisations under which the organisations perform functions of the Service on its behalf.

(2) Arrangements under subsection (1) may provide for the organisations to designate individuals who may perform functions of officers of the Service.

(3) But the Service may only make an arrangement under subsection (1) if it is of the opinion—

(a) that the functions in question will be performed efficiently and to the required standard, and
(b) that the arrangement represents good value for money.

(4) The Service may make arrangements with individuals under which they may perform functions of officers of the Service.

(5) The Service may commission, or assist the conduct of, research by any person into matters concerned with the exercise of its functions.
[Criminal Justice and Court Services Act 2000, s 13.]

1–4005   14. Provision of staff or services to other organisations.   (1) The Service may make arrangements with an organisation or individual under which staff of the Service may work for the organisation or individual.

(2) The Service may make arrangements with an organisation or individual under which any services provided to the Service by its staff are also made available to the organisation or individual.

(3) The Service may charge for anything done under arrangements under this section.
[Criminal Justice and Court Services Act 2000, s 14.]

1–4006   15. Right to conduct litigation and right of audience.   (1) The Service may authorise an officer of the Service of a prescribed[1] description—

(a) to conduct litigation in relation to any proceedings in any court,
(b) to exercise a right of audience in any proceedings before any court,

in the exercise of his functions.

(2) An officer of the Service exercising a right to conduct litigation by virtue of subsection (1)(a) who would otherwise have such a right by virtue of section 28(2)(a) of the Courts and Legal Services Act 1990 is to be treated as having acquired that right solely by virtue of this section.

(3) An officer of the Service exercising a right of audience by virtue of subsection (1)(b) who would otherwise have such a right by virtue of section 27(2)(a) of the Courts and Legal Services Act 1990 is to be treated as having acquired that right solely by virtue of this section.

(4) In this section and section 16, "right to conduct litigation" and "right of audience" have the same meanings as in section 119 of the Courts and Legal Services Act 1990.
[*Criminal Justice and Court Services Act 2000, s 15.*]

1. The Children and Family Court Advisory and Support Service (Conduct of Litigation and Exercise of Rights of Audience) Regulations 2001, SI 2001/698 prescribe an officer of the Service who is —

    (*a*) a barrister or a solicitor of the Supreme Court, or
    (*b*) employed (whether wholly or in part), or is otherwise engaged, to conduct litigation and is doing so in conjunction with an officer of the Service described in (*a*).

1–4007　16. Cross-examination of officers of the Service.　(1) An officer of the Service may, subject to rules of court, be cross-examined in any proceedings to the same extent as any witness.

(2) But an officer of the Service may not be cross-examined merely because he is exercising a right to conduct litigation or a right of audience granted in accordance with section 15.
[*Criminal Justice and Court Services Act 2000, s 16.*]

1–4008　17. Inspection[1]

1. Section 17 inserts new subsections in ss 62 and 63 of the Justices of the Peace Act 1997.

Chapter III
General

Property and staff

1–4009　18–23.　*These provisions are concerned with the transfer of staff and property.*

Provision for the protection of children

1–4015　24. Provision for the protection of children.　(1) The Protection of Children Act 1999 ("the 1999 Act") shall have effect as if the Service were a child care organisation within the meaning of that Act.

(2) Arrangements which the Service makes with an organisation under section 13(1) must provide that, before selecting an individual to be employed under the arrangements in a child care position, the organisation—

    (*a*) must ascertain whether the individual is included in any of the lists mentioned in section 7(1) of the 1999 Act, and
    (*b*) if he is included in any of those lists, must not select him for that employment.

(3) Such arrangements must provide that, if at any time the organisation has power to refer a relevant individual to the Secretary of State under section 2 of the 1999 Act (inclusion in list on reference following disciplinary action etc), the organisation must so refer him.
In this subsection, "relevant individual" means an individual who is or has been employed in a child care position under the arrangements.

(4) In this section, "child care position" and "employment" have the same meanings as in the 1999 Act.
[*Criminal Justice and Court Services Act 2000, s 24.*]

Interpretation

1–4016　25. Interpretation of Part I.　In this Part—

"approved premises" means premises approved under section 9,
"by virtue of" includes by or under,
"organisation" includes a public body and a private or voluntary organisation,
"prescribed" means prescribed by regulations,
"regulations"[1] means—

    (*a*) in the case of regulations under section 15, regulations made by the Lord Chancelleor, and
    (*b*) in any other case, regulations made by the Secretary of State.
[*Criminal Justice and Court Services Act 2000, s 25, as amended by SI 2003/3191.*]

1. The Children and Family Court Advisory and Support Service (Conduct of Litigation and Exercise of Rights of Audience) Regulations 2001, SI 2001/698 have been made.

Part II[1]
Protection of Children

Disqualification orders

1–4016A　26. Meaning of "offence against a child".　(1) For the purposes of this Part, an individual commits an offence against a child if—

    (*a*) he commits any offence mentioned in paragraph 1 of Schedule 4[2],
    (*b*) he commits against a child any offence mentioned in paragraph 2 of that Schedule, or

(c) he falls within paragraph 3 of that Schedule,

and references to being convicted of, or charged with, an offence against a child are to be read accordingly.

(2) The Secretary of State may by order amend Schedule 4 so as to add, modify or omit any entry.

[Criminal Justice and Court Services Act 2000, s 26.]

---

1. Part II comprises ss 26 to 42.
2. See below.

1–4017 27. Equivalent armed forces offences. (1) For the purposes of this Part, an individual is treated as being convicted of or (as the case may be) charged with an offence against a child if he is convicted of or charged with an equivalent armed forces offence.

(2) In subsection (1), "equivalent armed forces offence" means an armed forces offence constituted by an act or omission which—

(a) is an offence against a child, or

(b) would, if committed in England or Wales, be an offence against a child.

(3) In that subsection, "equivalent armed forces offence" also includes a civil offence of attempting to commit—

(a) an offence against a child, or

(b) an act that would, if committed in England or Wales, be an offence against a child.

(4) For the purpose of determining whether an offence is an equivalent armed forces offence, Schedule 4 shall have effect as if the words "or attempting" were omitted from paragraph 3(t).

(5) In this section, "civil offence" has the same meaning as in the Army Act 1955.

[Criminal Justice and Court Services Act 2000, s 27.]

1–4018 28. Disqualification from working with children: adults[1]. (1) This section applies where either of the conditions set out below is satisfied in the case of an individual.

(2) The first condition is that—

(a) the individual is convicted of an offence against a child committed when he was aged 18 or over, and

(b) a qualifying sentence is imposed by a senior court in respect of the conviction.

(3) The second condition is that—

(a) the individual is charged with an offence against a child committed when he was aged 18 or over, and

(b) a relevant order is made by a senior court in respect of the act or omission charged against him as the offence.

(4) Subject to subsection (5), the court must order the individual to be disqualified from working with children.

(5) An order shall not be made under this section if the court is satisfied[2], having regard to all the circumstances, that it is unlikely that the individual will commit any further offence against a child.

(6) If the court does not make an order under this section, it must state its reasons for not doing so and cause those reasons to be included in the record of the proceedings.

[Criminal Justice and Court Services Act 2000, s 28.]

---

1. A disqualification order pursuant to s 28 is not a "penalty" for the purposes of art 7 of the Convention; therefore, a disqualification order can be made in respect of offences committed before s 28 came into force (*R v Field* [2002] EWCA Crim 2913, [2003] 3 All ER 769, [2003] 1 WLR 882, [2003] 2 Cr App Rep 38.
2. The criminal standard "satisfied so as to be sure" does not apply to this provision which is intended primarily to apply to those who present a serious on-going risk of danger to children rather than, for example, a man who has been convicted of two isolated incidents many years ago without any sign of continuing offences (*R v MG* [2001] EWCA Crim 2308, [2002] 2 Cr App Rep (S) 1, [2002] 1 FLR 694). Though the standard of proof is the civil – balance of probabilities – standard, the court is entitled to go beyond the facts of the offence and to take into account, for example, a previous offence of violence and indifference to the well being of the victim (*R v Clayton* [2003] EWCA Crim 2161, [2004] 1 Cr App R (S) 201).

1–4019 29. Disqualification from working with children: juveniles. (1) This section applies where either of the conditions set out below is satisfied in the case of an individual.

(2) The first condition is that—

(a) the individual is convicted of an offence against a child committed at a time when the individual was under the age of 18, and

(b) a qualifying sentence is imposed by a senior court in respect of the conviction.

(3) The second condition is that—

(a) the individual is charged with an offence against a child committed at a time when the individual was under the age of 18, and

(b) a relevant order is made by a senior court in respect of the act or omission charged against him as the offence.

(4) If the court is satisfied, having regard to all the circumstances, that it is likely that the individual

will commit a further offence against a child, it must order the individual to be disqualified from working with children.

(5) If the court makes an order under this section, it must state its reasons for doing so and cause those reasons to be included in the record of the proceedings.
[Criminal Justice and Court Services Act 2000, s 29.]

1–4019A   29A. Disqualification at discretion of court: adults and juveniles.   (1) This section applies where—

(*a*) an individual is convicted of an offence against a child (whether or not committed when he was aged 18 or over),

(*b*) the individual is sentenced by a senior court, and

(*c*) no qualifying sentence is imposed in respect of the conviction.

(2) If the court is satisfied, having regard to all the circumstances, that it is likely that the individual will commit a further offence against a child, it may order the individual to be disqualified from working with children.

(3) If the court makes an order under this section, it must state its reasons for doing so and cause those reasons to be included in the record of the proceedings.
[Criminal Justice and Court Services Act 2000, s 29A as inserted by the Criminal Justice Act 2003, Sch 30.]

1–4019B   29B. Subsequent application for order under section 28 or 29.   (1) Where—

(*a*) section 28 applies but the court has neither made an order under that section nor complied with subsection (6) of that section, or

(*b*) section 29 applies but the court has not made an order under that section, and it appears to the prosecutor that the court has not considered the making of an order under that section,

the prosecutor may at any time apply to that court for an order under section 28 or 29.

(2) Subject to subsection (3), on an application under subsection (1)—

(*a*) in a case falling within subsection (1)(*a*), the court—

(i) must make an order under section 28 unless it is satisfied as mentioned in subsection (5) of that section, and

(ii) if it does not make an order under that section, must comply with subsection (6) of that section,

(*b*) in a case falling within subsection (1)(*b*), the court—

(i) must make an order under section 29 if it is satisfied as mentioned in subsection (4) of that section, and

(ii) if it does so, must comply with subsection (5) of that section.

(3) Subsection (2) does not enable or require an order under section 28 or 29 to be made where the court is satisfied that it had considered the making of an order under that section at the time when it imposed the qualifying sentence or made the relevant order.
[Criminal Justice and Court Services Act 2000, s 29B as inserted by the Criminal Justice Act 2003, Sch 30.]

1–4020   30. Sections 28 to 29B: supplemental.   (1) In sections 28 to 29B and this section—

"guardianship order" means a guardianship order within the meaning of the Army Act 1955, the Air Force Act 1955, the Naval Discipline Act 1957 or the Mental Health Act 1983,

"qualifying sentence" means—

(*a*) a sentence of imprisonment for a term of 12 months or more,

(*b*) *repealed*

(*c*) a sentence of detention during Her Majesty's pleasure,

(*d*) a sentence of detention for a period of 12 months or more under section 91 of the Powers of Criminal Courts (Sentencing) Act 2000 (offenders under 18 convicted of certain serious offences),

(*dd*) a sentence of detention under section 226 or 228 of the Criminal Justice Act 2003,

(*e*) a detention and training order for a term of 12 months or more,

(*f*) a sentence of detention for a term of 12 months or more imposed by a court-martial or the Courts-Martial Appeal Court,

(*g*) a hospital order within the meaning of the Mental Health Act 1983, or

(*h*) a guardianship order,

"relevant order" means—

(*a*) an order made by the Crown Court, the Court of Appeal, a court-martial or the Courts-Martial Appeal Court that the individual in question be admitted to hospital, or

(*b*) a guardianship order,

"senior court" means the Crown Court, the Court of Appeal, a court-martial or the Courts-Martial Appeal Court.

(2) The reference to detention in paragraph (*f*) of the above definition of "qualifying sentence" includes a reference to detention by virtue of a custodial order under—

(*a*) section 71AA of, or paragraph 10 of Schedule 5A to, the Army Act 1955,

(b) section 71AA of, or paragraph 10 of Schedule 5A to, the Air Force Act 1955,
(c) section 43AA of, or paragraph 10 of Schedule 4A to, the Naval Discipline Act 1957.

(3) In this Part, references to a sentence of imprisonment, or to a sentence of detention imposed by a court-martial or the Courts-Martial Appeal Court, include references to a suspended sentence.

(4) If, for the purpose of making an order under section 28 or 29, the court determines, after considering any available evidence, that an individual was, or was not, under the age of 18 at the time when the offence in question was committed, his age at that time shall be taken, for the purposes of that sections (and in particular for the purpose of determining any question as to the validity of the order), to be that which the court determined it to be.

(5) Below in this Part—

(a) references to a disqualification order are to an order under section 28, 29 or 29A,
(b) in relation to an individual on whom a sentence has been passed, or in relation to whom an order has been made, as mentioned in subsection (2) or (3) of section 28 or 29, references to his sentence are to that sentence or order
(c) in relation to an individual to whom section 29A applies and on whom a sentence has been passed, references to his sentence are to that sentence.

[Criminal Justice and Court Services Act 2000, s 30 as amended by Sch 8 of that Act and the Criminal Justice Act 2003, Sch 30.]

1–4021 31. Appeals. (1) An individual may appeal against a disqualification order—

(a) where the first condition mentioned in section 28 or 29 is satisfied in his case, as if the order were a sentence passed on him for the offence of which he has been convicted,
(b) where the second condition mentioned in section 28 or 29 is satisfied in his case, as if he had been convicted of an offence on indictment and the order were a sentence passed on him for the offence
(c) where an order is made under section 29A, as if the order were a sentence passed on him for the offence of which he has been convicted.

(2) In relation to a disqualification order made by a court-martial, subsection (1)(b) has effect as if the reference to conviction on indictment were a reference to conviction by a court-martial.

[Criminal Justice and Court Services Act 2000, s 31 as amended by the Criminal Justice Act 2003, Sch 30.]

1–4022 32. Review of disqualification. (1) Subject to section 33, an individual who is subject to a disqualification order may make an application to the Tribunal under this section.

(2) On an application under this section the Tribunal must determine whether or not the individual is to continue to be subject to the order.

(3) If the Tribunal is satisfied that the individual is suitable to work with children, it must direct that the order is to cease to have effect; otherwise it must dismiss the application.

[Criminal Justice and Court Services Act 2000, s 32.]

1–4023 33. Conditions for application under section 32. (1) An individual may only make an application under section 32 with the leave of the Tribunal.

(2) An application for leave under this section may not be made unless the appropriate conditions are satisfied in the individual's case.

(3) In the case of an individual who was under the age of 18 when he committed the offence against a child, the appropriate conditions are satisfied if—

(a) at least five years have elapsed since the relevant date, and
(b) in the period of five years ending with the time when he makes the application under this section, he has made no other such application.

(4) In the case of any other individual, the appropriate conditions are satisfied if—

(a) at least ten years have elapsed since the relevant date, and
(b) in the period of ten years ending with the time when he makes the application under this section, he has made no other such application.

(5) The Tribunal may not grant an application under this section unless it considers—

(a) that the individual's circumstances have changed since the order was made or, as the case may be, since he last made an application under this section, and
(b) that the change is such that leave should be granted.

(6) In this section, "the relevant date" means—

(a) in relation to an individual whose sentence is an actual term of custody, the day on which he is released or, if later, the day on which the disqualification order is made,
(b) in relation to an individual whose sentence is suspended and does not take effect, the day on which the disqualification order is made,
(c) in relation to an individual whose sentence is an order for admission to hospital—

(i) if he is detained in a hospital pursuant to the order, the day on which he ceases to be liable to be detained there, or
(ii) if he is not so detained, the day on which the disqualification order is made,

(d)   in relation to an individual whose sentence is a guardianship order, the day on which the disqualification order is made,

(e)   in relation to an individual not falling within any of paragraphs (a) to (d), the day on which the disqualification order is made.

(7)   In this section—

"actual term of custody" means a term of imprisonment or detention which is not suspended, or is suspended but takes effect,

"guardianship order" has the same meaning as in section 30,

"order for admission to hospital" means—

(a)   an order made by the Crown Court, the Court of Appeal, a court-martial or the Courts-Martial Appeal Court that the individual be admitted to hospital, or

(b)   a hospital order within the meaning of the Mental Health Act 1983.

(8)   In subsection (7) "detention" means detention (or detention and training)—

(a)   under any sentence or order falling within paragraphs (b) to (f) of the definition of "qualifying sentence" in section 30(1), or

(b)   under any sentence or order which would fall within those paragraphs if it were for a term or period of 12 months or more.

[Criminal Justice and Court Services Act 2000, s 33 as amended by the Criminal Justice Act 2003, Sch 30.]

1–4024   34. Restoration of disqualification order.   (1) If it appears to a chief officer of police or a director of social services of a local authority that the conditions set out in subsection (2) are satisfied in the case of an individual, the chief officer or (as the case may be) the director may apply to the High Court for an order under this section to be made in respect of the individual.

(2)   The conditions are that—

(a)   a disqualification order made in respect of the individual is no longer in force, and

(b)   the individual has acted in such a way (whether before or after the order ceased to be in force) as to give reasonable cause to believe that an order under this section is necessary to protect children in general, or any children in particular, from serious harm from him.

(3)   An application under this section may be made at any time after the disqualification order ceased to be in force.

(4)   If the High Court is satisfied that the conditions set out in subsection (2) are satisfied, it must order that the disqualification order is to be restored; otherwise it must dismiss the application.

(5)   Where an order is made under this section, section 33 has effect with the following modifications—

(a)   in subsection (3), the reference to the individual being under the age of 18 when he committed the offence against a child is to be read as a reference to his being under that age when the order under this section was made,

(b)   in subsections (3)(a) and (4)(a), references to the relevant date are to be read as references to the date on which the order under this section was made,

(c)   in subsection (5)(a), the reference to the individual's circumstances changing since the disqualification order was made is to be read as a reference to his circumstances changing since the order under this section was made.

(6)   For the purposes of this section a disqualification order is no longer in force if a direction under section 32(3) has been given in respect of it and it is not restored by virtue of an order under this section.

[Criminal Justice and Court Services Act 2000, s 34.]

Effect of disqualification from working with children

1–4025   35. Persons disqualified from working with children: offences.   (1) An individual who is disqualified from working with children is guilty of an offence if he knowingly applies for, offers to do, accepts or does any work in a regulated position.

(2)   An individual is guilty of an offence if he knowingly—

(a)   offers work in a regulated position to, or procures work in a regulated position for, an individual who is disqualified from working with children, or

(b)   fails to remove such an individual from such work.

(3)   It is a defence for an individual charged with an offence under subsection (1) to prove that he did not know, and could not reasonably be expected to know, that he was disqualified from working with children.

(4)   An individual is disqualified from working with children for the purposes of this Part if—

(a)   he is included (otherwise than provisionally) in the list kept under section 1 of the Protection of Children Act 1999 (individuals considered unsuitable to work with children),

(b)   he is subject to a direction under 142 of the Education Act 2002 (prohibition from teaching, &c), given on the grounds that he is unsuitable to work with children,

(c)   he is included, on the grounds that he is unsuitable to work with children, in any list kept by the Secretary of State or the National Assembly for Wales of persons disqualified under section 470 or 471 of the Education Act 1996, or

(d) he is subject to a disqualification order.

(5) *Repealed.*

(6) An individual who is guilty of an offence under this section is liable[1]—

(a) on summary conviction, to imprisonment for a term not exceeding **six months,** or to a fine not exceeding **the statutory maximum,** or to both,

(b) on conviction on indictment, to imprisonment for a term not exceeding **five years,** or to a **fine,** or to both.

[Criminal Justice and Court Services Act 2000, s 35, as amended by the Education Act 2002, Sch 21.]

---

1. For procedure in respect of this offence which is triable either way, see the Magistrates' Courts Act 1980, ss 17A–21, this Part, ante.

1–4026   36. Meaning of "regulated position".   (1) The regulated positions for the purposes of this Part are—

(a) a position whose normal duties include work in an establishment mentioned in subsection (2),

(b) a position whose normal duties include work on day care premises,

(c) a position whose normal duties include caring for, training, supervising or being in sole charge of children,

(d) a position whose normal duties involve unsupervised contact with children under arrangements made by a responsible person,

(e) a position whose normal duties include caring for children under the age of 16 in the course of the children's employment,

(f) a position a substantial part of whose normal duties includes supervising or training children under the age of 16 in the course of the children's employment,

(g) a position mentioned in subsection (6),

(h) a position whose normal duties include supervising or managing an individual in his work in a regulated position.

(2) The establishments referred to in subsection (1)(a) are—

(a) an institution which is exclusively or mainly for the detention of children,

(b) a hospital which is exclusively or mainly for the reception and treatment of children,

(c) a care home, residential care home, nursing home or private hospital which is exclusively or mainly for children,

(d) an educational institution,

(e) a children's home or voluntary home,

(f) a home provided under section 82(5) of the Children Act 1989.

(3) For the purposes of this section, work done on any premises is treated as not being done on day care premises to the extent that—

(a) it is done in a part of the premises in which children are not looked after, or

(b) it is done at times when children are not looked after there.

(4) The duties referred to in subsection (1)(c) and (d) do not include (respectively)—

(a) caring for, training, supervising or being in sole charge of children in the course of the children's employment, or

(b) duties involving contact with children in the course of the children's employment.

(5) The reference in subsection (1)(d) to unsupervised contact is to contact in the absence of any responsible person or carer; and in this subsection, "carer" means a person who holds a position such as is mentioned in subsection (1)(c).

(6) The positions mentioned in subsection (1)(g) are—

(a) member of the governing body of an educational institution,

(b) member of a relevant local government body,★

(c) director of social services of a local authority,★

(d) chief education officer of a local education authority,★

(e) charity trustee of a children's charity,

(f) member of the Youth Justice Board for England and Wales,

(fa) Children's Commissioner and deputy Children's Commissioner appointed under Part 1 of the Children Act 2004,

(g) Children's Commissioner for Wales or deputy Children's Commissioner for Wales,

(h) member, or chief executive, of the Children and Family Court Advisory and Support Service.

(7) For the purposes of subsection (6), a person is a member of a relevant local government body if—

(a) he is a member of, or of an executive of, a local authority and discharges any education functions, or social services functions, of a local authority,

(b) he is a member of an executive of a local authority which discharges any such functions,

(c) he is a member of—

(i) a committee of an executive of a local authority, or

(ii) an area committee, or any other committee, of a local authority, which discharges any such functions.

(8) In its application to Northern Ireland, subsection (6) is to be read as mentioning also the following positions—

(a) member, or director of social services, of a Health and Social Services Board established under Article 16 of the Health and Personal Social Services (Northern Ireland) Order 1972,

(b) member, or executive director of social work, of a Health and Social Services trust established under Article 10 of the Health and Personal Social Services (Northern Ireland) Order 1991,

(c) member, or chief education officer, of an education and library board established under Article 3 of the Education and Libraries (Northern Ireland) Order 1986,

(d) Commissioner for Children and Young People for Northern Ireland appointed under the Commissioner for Children and Young People (Northern Ireland) Order 2003.

(9) Any reference in subsection (7) to a committee includes a reference to any sub-committee which discharges any functions of that committee.

(10) For the purposes of subsection (1)(h), the holder of a position—

(a) only supervises an individual if he supervises the day-to-day performance of the individual's duties, and

(b) only manages an individual if the individual is directly responsible to him for the performance of his duties or he has authority to dismiss the individual.

(11) For the purposes of this section, a charity is a children's charity if the individuals who are workers for the charity normally include individuals working in regulated positions.

(12) For the purposes of this section, an individual is a worker for a charity if he does work under arrangements made by the charity; but the arrangements referred to in this subsection do not include any arrangements made for purposes which are merely incidental to the purposes for which the charity is established.

(13) For the purposes of this section, the following are responsible persons in relation to a child—

(a) the child's parent or guardian and any adult with whom the child lives,

(b) the person in charge of any establishment mentioned in subsection (2) in which the child is accommodated, is a patient or receives education, and any person acting on behalf of such a person,

(c) a person registered under Part XA of the Children Act 1989 for providing day care on premises on which the child is cared for, and**

(d) any person holding a position mentioned in subsection (6).

(14) In this section—

"area committee" has the same meaning as in section 18 of the Local Government Act 2000,

"detention" means detention by virtue of an order of a court or under an enactment,

"education functions", in relation to a local authority, means any functions with respect to education which are conferred on the authority in its capacity as a local education authority,

"executive", in relation to a local authority, has the same meaning as in Part II of the Local Government Act 2000,

"social services functions", in relation to a local authority, has the same meaning as in the Local Authority Social Services Act 1970.

(15) For the purpose of amending the definition of "regulated position", the Secretary of State may by order make any amendment of this section (apart from this subsection) which he thinks appropriate.

[Criminal Justice and Court Services Act 2000, s 36, as amended by SI 2003/439 and the Children Act 2004, Sch 1.]

---

*Paragraph (6)(ba) and words in paras (c) and (d) inserted by the Childcare Act 2006, Sch 2 from a date to be appointed.
**Paragraph (13)(c) substituted, by paras (c), (ca), by the Childcare Act 2006, Sch 2 from a date to be appointed.

1-4027 37. Disqualification in Scotland or Northern Ireland

1-4028 38. Rehabilitation of offenders. (1) Where a disqualification order is made in respect of an individual's conviction of an offence, the rehabilitation period which, in accordance with section 6 of the Rehabilitation of Offenders Act 1974, is applicable to the conviction is to be determined as if that order had not been made; and a disqualification order is not a sentence for the purposes of that Act.

(2) In this section, "conviction" has the same meaning as in that Act.

[Criminal Justice and Court Services Act 2000, s 38.]

Indecent conduct towards children

1-4029 39. Extension of offence: conduct towards 14 and 15 year olds. *Repealed.*

1-4030 40. *Extension of corresponding Northern Ireland offence: conduct towards 14 to 16 year olds*

1–4031   41. Indecent photographs of children: increase of maximum penalties[1]

1. These amendments took effect on 11 January 2001: see SI 2000/3302.

General

1–4032   42. Interpretation of Part II.   (1) In this Part—

"armed forces offence" means an offence under section 70 of the Army Act 1955, section 70 of the Air Force Act 1955 or section 42 of the Naval Discipline Act 1957,

"care home" has the same meaning as in the Care Standards Act 2000,

"charity" and "charity trustee" have the same meanings as in the Charities Act 1993,

"child" means a person under the age of 18,

"children's home" has—

(a) in relation to England and Wales, the same meaning as in the Care Standards Act 2000,

(b) in relation to Northern Ireland, the meaning which would be given by Article 90(1) of the Children (Northern Ireland) Order 1995 if, in Article 91(2) of that Order, sub-paragraphs (a), (f) and (g) and the words after sub-paragraph (h) were omitted,

"Class A drug" has the same meaning as in the Misuse of Drugs Act 1971,

"day care premises" means premises in respect of which a person is registered under Part XA of the Children Act 1989 for providing day care,★

"disqualification order" has the meaning given by section 30,

"educational institution" means an institution which is exclusively or mainly for the provision of full-time education to children,

"employment" means paid employment, whether under a contract of service or apprenticeship or under a contract for services,

"hospital" has—

(a) in relation to England and Wales, the meaning given by section 128(1) of the National Health Service Act 1977,

(b) in relation to Northern Ireland, the meaning given by Article 2(2) of the Health and Personal Social Services (Northern Ireland) Order 1972,

"local authority" has the same meaning as in the Education Act 1996,

"nursing home" has the meaning given by Article 16 of the Registered Homes (Northern Ireland) Order 1992,

"private hospital" has the meaning given by Article 90(2) of the Mental Health (Northern Ireland) Order 1986,

"residential care home" has the meaning given by Article 3 of the Registered Homes (Northern Ireland) Order 1992,

"the Tribunal" means the tribunal established by section 9 of the Protection of Children Act 1999,

"voluntary home" has the meaning given by Article 74(1) of the Children (Northern Ireland) Order 1995,

"work" includes—

(a) work of any kind, whether paid or unpaid and whether under a contract of service or apprenticeship, under a contract for services, or otherwise than under a contract, and

(b) an office established by or by virtue of an enactment,

and "working" is to be read accordingly.

(2) In this Part references, in relation to a suspended sentence, to taking effect are to taking effect by virtue of—

(a) an order or direction under section 91 of the Naval Discipline Act 1957 or section 119 of the Powers of Criminal Courts (Sentencing) Act 2000, or

(b) the determination of the suspension under section 120 of the Army Act 1955 or section 120 of the Air Force Act 1955.

[Criminal Justice and Court Services Act 2000, s 42.]

★**Definition "day care premises" substituted by the Childcare Act 2006, Sch 2 from a date to be appointed.**

PART III[1]
DEALING WITH OFFENDERS
CHAPTER I
COMMUNITY SENTENCES
Renaming certain community orders

1–4033   43–54.   *These provisions are concerned with community orders and insert or amend provisions in other legislation.*

1–4045   55. Regulation of community orders.   (1) Regulations made by the Secretary of State may provide for—

    (*a*)   the supervision of persons subject to community rehabilitation orders or community punishment and rehabilitation orders,

    (*b*)   the arrangements to be made by local probation boards for persons subject to community punishment orders, or community punishment and rehabilitation orders, to perform work and the performance of such work.

    (2)   In particular, they may regulate the functions of—

    (*a*)   officers of local probation boards and members of youth offending teams who are responsible for the supervision of offenders subject to community rehabilitation orders, and

    (*b*)   officers of local probation boards or other persons who are, in relation to persons subject to community punishment orders, responsible officers (within the meaning of section 46(13) of the Powers of Criminal Courts (Sentencing) Act 2000).

    (3)   Regulations made by virtue of subsection (1)(*b*) may, in particular, make provision—

    (*a*)   limiting the number of hours of work to be done by a person on any one day,

    (*b*)   as to the reckoning of hours worked and the keeping of work records, and

    (*c*)   for the payment of travelling and other expenses in connection with the performance of work.

[Criminal Justice and Court Services Act 2000, s 55.]

CHAPTER II

MISCELLANEOUS

Young offenders: reprimands and warnings

1–4046   56. *Reprimands and warnings*[1]

    1. Section 56 amends s 65 of the Crime and Disorder Act 1998 and s 34 of the Police and Criminal Evidence Act 1984.

Police powers: drugs

1–4047   57. *Testing persons in police detention*[1]

    1. Section 57 inserted new ss 63B and 63C in the Police and Criminal Evidence Act 1984 and made consequential amendments to ss 38 and 66 of that Act (see this PART, ante). At the time of going to press these provisions had not been brought into force in relation to the following police areas: Cheshire; City of London; Cumbria; Derbyshire; Dorset; Durham; Essex; Gloucestershire; Hampshire; Hertfordshire; Kent; Lincolnshire; Norfolk; Northamptonshire; North Yorkshire; Suffolk; Surrey; Sussex; Warwickshire; West Mercia; Wiltshire; Dyfed Powys; Gwent; and South Wales.

Bail

1–4048   58. *Right to bail: relevance of drug misuse*[1]

    1. Section 58 amends s 4 of the Bail Act 1976.

Detention

1–4049   59. Remand centres[1]**.**   In section 43(1) of the Prison Act 1952 (places of detention provided by Secretary of State), paragraph (*a*) (remand centres) is to cease to have effect.

[Criminal Justice and Court Services Act 2000, s 59.]

    1. At the time of going to press s 59 had not been brought into force.

1–4050   60. *Life sentences: tariffs*[1]

    1. Section 60 inserts a new s 82A in the Powers of Criminal Courts (Sentencing) Act 2000.

1–4051   61. Abolition of sentences of detention in a young offender institution, custody for life, etc.   (1) No court is to pass a sentence of detention in a young offender institution or a sentence of custody for life, and no court is to make a custodial order except in relation to a person who is aged at least 17 but under 18.

    (2)   No court is to commit a person to be detained under section 108 of the Powers of Criminal Courts (Sentencing) Act 2000 (detention of persons aged at least 18 but under 21 for default or contempt) or make an order fixing a term of detention under that section.

    (3)   A person who—

    (*a*)   has been sentenced (before the coming into force of this section) to a term of detention in a young offender institution, to custody for life or to a custodial order, and

    (*b*)   is aged at least 18 but under 21,

may be detained in a young offender institution, or in a prison, determined by the Secretary of State.

(4) A person—

(a) who has been committed (before the coming into force of this section) to be detained under section 108 of the Powers of Criminal Courts (Sentencing) Act 2000 or in respect of whom an order fixing a term of detention under that section has been made (before the coming into force of this section), and

(b) who is aged under 21,

may be detained in a young offender institution, or in a prison, determined by the Secretary of State.

(5) A person who has been sentenced to imprisonment and is aged under 21 may be detained—

(a) in a prison, or

(b) in a young offender institution in which one or more persons mentioned in subsection (3) or (4) are detained,

determined by the Secretary of State.

(6) A determination of the Secretary of State under this section may be made in respect of an individual or any description of individuals.

(7) The repeal by this Act of section 106(1) of the Powers of Criminal Courts (Sentencing) Act 2000 (interaction of sentences of detention in a young offender institution) does not affect the validity of any order made, or having effect as if made, under paragraph (b) of that subsection.

(8) In this section—

"court" includes a court-martial and a Standing Civilian Court,
"custodial order" means an order under—

(a) section 71AA of, or paragraph 10 of Schedule 5A to, the Army Act 1955,

(b) section 71AA of, or paragraph 10 of Schedule 5A to, the Air Force Act 1955,

(c) section 43AA of, or paragraph 10 of Schedule 4A to, the Naval Discipline Act 1957.

(9) On the coming into force of this section—

(a) paragraph (b) of the definition of "qualifying sentence" in section 30(1), and

(b) paragraph (b) of the definition of "relevant sentence" in section 69(7),

are omitted.
[Criminal Justice and Court Services Act 2000, s 61.]

Release of prisoners on licence etc

1–4052 62. Release on licence etc: conditions as to monitoring. (1) This section applies where a sentence of imprisonment has been imposed on a person and, by virtue of any enactment—

(a) the Secretary of State is required to, or may, release the person from prison, and

(b) the release is required to be, or may be, subject to conditions (whether conditions of a licence or any other conditions, however expressed).

(2) The conditions may include—

(a) conditions for securing the electronic monitoring of his compliance with any other conditions of his release,

(b) conditions for securing the electronic monitoring of his whereabouts (otherwise than for the purpose of securing his compliance with other conditions of his release).

(3) In relation to a prisoner released under section 34A(3) of the Criminal Justice Act 1991 (power to release short-term prisoners on licence) the monitoring referred to in subsection (2)(a) does not include the monitoring of his compliance with conditions imposed under section 37A of that Act (curfew conditions).

(4) The Secretary of State may make rules about the conditions that may be imposed by virtue of this section.

(5) In this section, "sentence of imprisonment" includes—

(a) a detention and training order,

(b) a sentence of detention in a young offender institution,

(c) a sentence of detention under section 90 of the Powers of Criminal Courts (Sentencing) Act 2000 (detention at Her Majesty's pleasure),

(d) a sentence of detention under section 91 of that Act (detention of offenders under 18 convicted of certain serious offences),

(e) a sentence of custody for life under section 93 or 94 of that Act,

and "prison" shall be construed accordingly.
[Criminal Justice and Court Services Act 2000, s 62.]

1–4053 63. *Supervision of young offenders after release*[1]

---

1. Section 63 inserts new subsections (5A)–(5D) and (9) in s 65 of the Criminal Justice Act 1991.

1–4054 64. Release on licence etc: drug testing requirements. (1) This section applies where—

(a) the Secretary of State releases from prison a person aged 18 or over on whom a sentence of imprisonment has been imposed for a trigger offence, and

(b) the release is subject to conditions (whether conditions of a licence or any other conditions, however expressed).

(2) For the purpose of determining whether the person is complying with any of the conditions, they may include the following requirement.

(3) The requirement is that the person must provide, when instructed to do so by an officer of a local probation board or a person authorised by the Secretary of State, any sample mentioned in the instruction for the purpose of ascertaining whether he has any specified Class A drug in his body.

(4) The function of giving such an instruction is to be exercised in accordance with guidance given from time to time by the Secretary of State; and regulations made by the Secretary of State may regulate the provision of samples in pursuance of such an instruction.

(5) In this section, "sentence of imprisonment" includes—

(a) a detention and training order,

(b) a sentence of detention in a young offender institution,

(c) a sentence of detention under section 90 of the Powers of Criminal Courts (Sentencing) Act 2000 (detention at Her Majesty's pleasure),

(d) a sentence of detention under section 91 of that Act (detention of offenders under 18 convicted of certain serious offences),

(e) a sentence of custody for life under section 93 or 94 of that Act,

and "prison" shall be construed accordingly.★
[Criminal Justice and Court Services Act 2000, s 64.]

★Section amended by the Criminal Justice Act 2003, s 266 and Sch 37 from a date to be appointed.

1–4055   65. *Short-term prisoners: release subject to curfew conditions*[1]

1. Section 65 inserts a new sub-para (*da*) in s 34A(2) of the Criminal Justice Act 1991.

Sexual or violent offenders

1–4056   66. Amendments of the Sex Offenders Act 1997 *Repealed.*

1–4057   67. Arrangements for assessing etc risks posed by certain offenders. *Repealed.*

1–4058   68. Section 67: interpretation. *Repealed.*

1–4059   69. Duties of local probation boards in connection with victims of certain offences. *Repealed.*

CHAPTER III
SUPPLEMENTARY

1–4060   70. Interpretation, etc.   (1) In this Part—

"Class A drug" has the same meaning as in the Misuse of Drugs Act 1971,

"specified", in relation to a Class A drug, means specified by an order made by the Secretary of State,

"trigger offence" has the meaning given by Schedule 6[1].

(2) The Secretary of State may by order amend Schedule 6 so as to add, modify or omit any description of offence.

(3) In this Part (except in section 69), references to release include temporary release.

(4) In section 163 of the Powers of Criminal Courts (Sentencing) Act 2000 (general definitions), at the appropriate places there are inserted—

""specified Class A drug" has the same meaning as in Part III of the Criminal Justice and Court Services Act 2000",

""trigger offence" has the same meaning as in Part III of the Criminal Justice and Court Services Act 2000".

(5) Section 53 does not apply in relation to any community order made before that section comes into force.
[Criminal Justice and Court Services Act 2000, s 70.]

---

1. See below.

PART IV
GENERAL AND SUPPLEMENTARY

CHAPTER I
GENERAL

1–4061   71. Access to driver licensing records.   (1) The Secretary of State may make any information held by him for the purposes of Part III of the Road Traffic Act 1988 available to the

Police Information Technology Organisation for use by constables and members of the staff of the Serious Organised Crime Agency.

(2) In respect of any information made available to the Organisation under subsection (1), the Secretary of State may by regulations[1]—

(a) determine the purposes for which constables and members of the staff of the Serious Organised Crime Agency may be given access to the information,

(b) determine the circumstances in which any of the information to which they have been given access may be further disclosed by them.

(3) Before making any regulations applying in respect of constables in police forces in Scotland, the Secretary of State must, to the extent to which the regulations will so apply, consult the Scottish Ministers.

(4) In this section, —

"constables" includes—

(a) persons employed by a police authority under section 15(1) of the Police Act 1996 who are under the direction and control of the chief officer of police of the police force maintained by that authority,

(b) persons employed by a police authority under section 9(1) of the Police (Scotland) Act 1967 who are under the direction and control of the chief constable of the police force maintained for the authority's area,

(c) police support staff (within the meaning of the Police (Northern Ireland) Act 2000), and

(d) persons employed by the British Transport Police Authority under section 27(1) of the Railways and Transport Safety Act 2003 who are under the direction and control of the Chief Constable of the British Transport Police Force

"information" means information held in any form.

(5) Section 105(2)(b) of that Act (power by regulations to make particulars with respect to persons who are disqualified etc available for use by the police) is to cease to have effect[2].

[Criminal Justice and Court Services Act 2000, s 71 as amended by the Serious Organised Crime and Police Act 2005, s 123 and Sch 4.]

---

1. See the Motor Vehicles (Access to Driver Licensing Records) Regulations 2001, SI 2001/3343 which specify the following purposes (reg 2):

(a) the prevention, investigation or prosecution of a contravention of any provision of the following enactments—

(i) the Road Traffic Act 1988;
(ii) the Road Traffic Offenders Act 1988;
(iii) the Road Traffic (Northern Ireland) Order 1981;
(iv) the Road Traffic (Northern Ireland) Order 1995; and
(v) the Road Traffic Offenders (Northern Ireland) Order 1996;

(b) ascertaining whether a person has had an order made in relation to him under—

(i) section 40B(1) or (5) (disqualification from driving: further provision) of the Child Support Act 1991;
(ii) section 248A(1) (general power to disqualify offenders) or 248B(2) (power to disqualify fine defaulters) of the Criminal Procedure (Scotland) Act 1995; or
(iii) section 39(1) (offenders) or 40(2) (fine defaulters) of the Crime (Sentences) Act 1997.

And the following circumstances (reg 3) namely that the information is passed to an employee of a police authority for any purpose ancillary to, or connected with, the use of the information by constables.

2. At the time of going to press s 71(5) had not been brought into force.

1–4062 **72.** *Failure to secure regular attendance at school*[1]

---

1. Section 72 inserts new subsections (1A), (8A) and (8B) in s 44 of the Education Act 1996.

1–4063 **73.** *Parenting orders: responsible officer*[1]

---

1. Section 73 inserts a new sub-para 8(8)(bb) in the Crime and Disorder Act 1998.

1–4064 **74. Amendments.** Schedule 7[1] (which makes minor and consequential amendments) is to have effect.

[Criminal Justice and Court Services Act 2000, s 74.]

---

1. See below.

1–4065 **75. Repeals.** The enactments specified in Schedule 8 are repealed to the extent specified.

[Criminal Justice and Court Services Act 2000, s 75.]

CHAPTER II
SUPPLEMENTARY

1–4066 **76. Subordinate legislation.** (1) This section applies to any power conferred by this Act onSecretary of State to make regulations, rules or an order.

(2) The power, unless it is a power to make an order under section 19, 20 or 23, shall be exercisable by statutory instrument.

(3) The power may be exercised so as to make different provision for different purposes or different areas.

(4) The power includes power to make—

    (a)   any supplementary, incidental or consequential provision, and

    (b)   any transitory, transitional or saving provision,

which the Minister exercising the power considers necessary or expedient.

(5) An order—

    (a)   making any provision by virtue of section 10, 26(2), 36(15), 57(5) or 70(2), or

    (b)   making any provision by virtue of section 77(2) which adds to, replaces or omits any part of the text of an Act,

may only be made if a draft of the statutory instrument containing the order has been laid before and approved by resolution of each House of Parliament.

(6) Any other statutory instrument made in exercise of a power to which this section applies shall be subject to annulment in pursuance of a resolution of either House of Parliament.

(7) Subsection (6) does not apply to a statutory instrument containing an order—

    (a)   revoking an order made by virtue of section 10, or

    (b)   made by virtue only of section 80.

[Criminal Justice and Court Services Act 2000, s 76 as amended by the Constitutional Reform Act 2005, Sch 18.]

1–4067   77. Supplementary and consequential provision, etc.   (1) The Secretary of State may by order[1] make—

    (a)   any supplementary, incidental or consequential provision,

    (b)   any transitory, transitional or saving provision,

which he considers necessary or expedient for the purposes of, in consequence of or for giving full effect to any provision of this Act.

(2) The provision which may be made under subsection (1) includes provision amending or repealing any enactment, instrument or document.

[Criminal Justice and Court Services Act 2000, s 77 as amended by the Constitutional Reform Act 2005, Sch 18.]

---

   1. The Children and Family Court Advisory and Support Service (Miscellaneous Amendments) Order 2002, SI 2002/3220 has been made.

1–4068   78. General interpretation.   (1) In this Act—

    "community order" has the meaning given by section 33 of the Powers of Criminal Courts (Sentencing) Act 2000,

    "enactment" includes an enactment contained in subordinate legislation,

    "functions" includes powers and duties,

    "local probation board" has the meaning given by section 4,

    "subordinate legislation" has the same meaning as in the Interpretation Act 1978.

(2) In this Act, "enactment" means an enactment whenever passed or made; but in this Part it means—

    (a)   an Act passed before, or in the same Session as, this Act, and

    (b)   subordinate legislation made before the passing of this Act.

[Criminal Justice and Court Services Act 2000, s 78.]

1–4069   79. *Expenses*

1–4070   80. Commencement.   (1) This Act shall come into force on such day as the Lord Chancellor or the Secretary of State may by order[1] appoint.

(2) Different days may be appointed under this section for different purposes and different areas.

(3) Subsection (1) does not apply to—

    (a)   sections 19 to 22,

    (b)   section 60,

    (c)   this Chapter,

    (d)   in Schedule 7, paragraphs 15(1)(e) and (2), 18(3)(c)(i) and (4), 22(1)(e) and (2), 25(3)(c)(i) and (4), 29(1)(e) and (2), 32(3)(c)(i) and (4), 135 to 138, 142, 144 to 148 and 203(3) and (4),

    (e)   the repeals mentioned in the note to Schedule 8.

[Criminal Justice and Court Services Act 2000, s 80.]

---

   1. The following commencement orders have been made: Criminal Justice and Court Services Act 2000 (Commencement No 1) Order 2000, SI 2000/3302; Criminal Justice and Court Services Act 2000 (Commencement No 2) Order 2001, SI 2001/340; Criminal Justice and Court Services Act 2000 (Commencement No 3) Order 2001, SI 2001/562; Criminal Justice and Court Services Act 2000 (Commencement No 4) Order 2001, SI 2001/919; Criminal Justice and Court Services Act 2000 (Commencement No 5) (Scotland) Order 2001, SSI 2001/166; Criminal Justice and Court Services Act 2000 (Commencement No 6) Order 2001, SI 2001/1651; Criminal Justice and Court Services Act

2000 (Commencement No 7) Order 2001, SI 2001/2232; Criminal Justice and Court Services Act 2000 (Commencement No 8) Order 2001, SI 2001/3385; Criminal Justice and Court Services Act 2000 (Commencement No 9) Order 2002, SI 2002/1149; Criminal Justice and Court Services Act 2000 (Commencement No 10) Order 2002, SI 2002/1862; Criminal Justice and Court Services Act 2000 (Commencement No 11) Order 2003, SI 2003/709; Criminal Justice and Court Services Act 2000 (Commencement No 12) Order 2004, SI 2004/780; Criminal Justice and Court Services Act 2000 (Commencement No 13) Order 2004, SI 2004/2171; Criminal Justice and Court Services Act 2000 (Commencement No 14) Order 2005, SI 2005/596; and Criminal Justice and Court Services Act 2000 (Commencement No 15) Order 2005, SI 2005/3054.

1–4071 81. Extent. (1) Subject to the following provisions, this Act extends to England and Wales only.

(2) Subsection (1) does not apply to—

(a) sections 26 to 33, so far as they relate to the making of orders by, or orders made by, courts-martial or the Courts-Martial Appeal Court,

(b) section 60, and paragraphs 135 to 138, 142 and 144 to 148 of Schedule 7, so far as they relate to sentences passed by a court-martial,

(c) section 61 so far as it relates to sentences passed by a court-martial or a Standing Civilian Court,

(d) section 66 and Schedule 5,

(e) section 71,

(f) this Chapter,

(g) paragraphs 17 and 19 of Schedule 2,

(h) any amendment by Schedule 7 of the Army Act 1955, the Air Force Act 1955 or the Naval Discipline Act 1957,

(i) paragraph 159 of Schedule 7.

(3) Sections 35, 36 and 41 extend to England and Wales and Northern Ireland.

(4) Section 40 extends to Northern Ireland only.

(5) The amendment or repeal by Schedule 7 or 8 of an enactment extending to Scotland or Northern Ireland extends also to Scotland or, as the case may be, Northern Ireland.

(6) For the purposes of the Scotland Act 1998, any provision of section 66 and Schedule 5 and, so far as relating to those provisions and extending to Scotland, any provision of this Chapter is to be taken to be a pre-commencement enactment within the meaning of that Act.

[Criminal Justice and Court Services Act 2000, s 81.]

1–4072 82. Short title. This Act may be cited as the Criminal Justice and Court Services Act 2000.

[Criminal Justice and Court Services Act 2000, s 82.]

SCHEDULE 1
LOCAL PROBATION BOARDS

(As amended by the Constitutional Reform Act 2005, Sch 4 and the Courts Act 2003, Sch 8.)

Section 4

Constitution

1–4073 1. A local probation board shall be a body corporate.

2. (1) A local probation board is to consist of a chairman, a chief officer and not less than five other members.

(2) One of the other members is to be appointed by Lord Chief Justice, after consulting the Lord Chancellor from among the judges of the Crown Court (being a judge of the High Court, a Circuit judge, a Recorder or a District Judge (Magistrates' Courts)).

(3) The chairman, the chief officer and the other members are to be appointed by the Secretary of State.

(4) Regulations[1] may make provision as to their appointment (including the number, or limits on the number, of members who may be appointed and any conditions to be fulfilled for appointment as a member).

(5) Regulations[2] made by virtue of sub-paragraph (4) and coming into force on or after the coming into force of section 4 must make provision—

(a) for the selection procedure for the chairman, the chief officer and the other members of the board who are to be appointed by the Secretary of State to include selection panels,

(b) in the case of the chief officer, for the board to be represented on any selection panel making a final recommendation to the Secretary of State.

(6) Regulations[2] must provide, so far as it is practicable to do so, for the persons appointed to be representative of the local community in the board's area and to live or work (or to have lived or worked) in that area.

(7) Below in this Schedule, "member" includes the chairman and chief officer (where the context allows).

(8) The Lord Chief Justice may nominate a judicial office holder (as defined in section 109(4) of the Constitutional Reform Act 2005) to exercise his functions under sub-paragraph (2).

Tenure of members

3. (1) A person is to hold and vacate office as a member in accordance with the terms of the instrument appointing him.

(2) A person may at any time resign office as a member by giving written notice to the Secretary of State or, as the case may be, the Lord Chancellor.

(3) The Secretary of State or, as the case may be, the Lord Chancellor may remove a member from office by giving written notice to him.

(3A) The power conferred by sub-paragraph (3) may be exercised by the Lord Chancellor to remove a person appointed by him by virtue of paragraph 2(2) only with the concurrence of the Lord Chief Justice.

(4) Regulations¹ may make provision as to the tenure of office of the members (including the circumstances in which they cease to hold office or may be removed or suspended from office).

(5) The chief officer is to be treated for the purposes of the Employment Rights Act 1996 as if he were in Crown employment (within the meaning of that Act).

(6) Sub-paragraphs (1) to (3) have effect subject to sub-paragraph (5) and any regulations made by virtue of sub-paragraph (4).

Chairman's report

4. Regulations may require the chairman to make a report to the Secretary of State about the performance of the other members, or any of them, and may confer other functions on the chairman.

Remuneration etc

5. (1) It is for the Secretary of State to pay, or make provision for paying, to or in respect of any person who is or has been a member—

(a) any remuneration, fees or expenses,
(b) any pension, allowance or gratuity,

determined by him.

(2) If the Secretary of State determines that there are special circumstances that make it right for a person ceasing to hold office as a member otherwise than on the expiration of his term of office to receive compensation, the Secretary of State may pay an amount of compensation determined by him to that person.

Procedure

6. Regulations² may provide for—

(a) the establishment and functions of committees and sub-committees (including committees and sub-committees which consist of or include persons who are not members),
(b) the procedure of the boards and of any committees or sub-committees of the boards (including quorum and the validation of proceedings in the event of vacancies or defects in appointment).

Secretary and Treasurer

7. Regulations² shall provide—

(a) for each local probation board to appoint a secretary or treasurer (including the conditions to be fulfilled for appointment),
(b) for the tenure of office of a secretary or treasurer so appointed (including the circumstances in which he ceases to hold office or may be removed or suspended from office).

Staff

8. (1) A local probation board may appoint staff on terms and conditions determined by the local probation board as to—

(a) any remuneration, fees or expenses,
(b) any pension, allowance or gratuity.

(2) But—

(a) a determination under this paragraph requires the approval of the Secretary of State,
(b) the Secretary of State may give directions as to the appointment of staff of a description specified in the directions,
(c) the Secretary of State may give directions as to the qualifications, experience or training of staff.

Delegation of functions

9. A local probation board may arrange for a committee, sub-committee or member to discharge functions of the board.

10. Regulations² may provide for prescribed functions or other powers of a local probation board to be exercised by the chief officer on behalf of the board.

Payments to boards

11. (1) The Secretary of State may pay to a local probation board any amount he considers appropriate.

(2) If he considers it appropriate, he may make any payment on conditions.

(3) The conditions may (among other things)—

(a) regulate the purposes for which the payment or any part of it may be used,
(b) require repayment to the Secretary of State in specified circumstances.

Supervision

12. (1) Functions and other powers of local probation boards must be performed in accordance with any directions given to them by the Secretary of State.

(2) A local probation board must provide the Secretary of State with any information relating to the performance of its functions or other powers which he may from time to time require.

Ancillary powers

13. (1) Subject to any directions given by the Secretary of State, a local probation board may do anything which appears to it to be necessary or expedient for the purpose of, or in connection with, the exercise of its functions.

(2) That includes, in particular—

(a) holding property,
(b) entering into contracts,
(c) investing sums not immediately required for the purpose of performing its functions,
(d) accepting gifts.

(3) But a local probation board—

(a) may not hold land (though it may manage it),
(b) may not borrow money, whether by way of overdraft or otherwise, without the approval of the Secretary of State.

(4) Approval under this paragraph may be either general or special.

Directions

14. (1) Different directions may be given under this Chapter for different purposes.
(2) Directions under this Chapter may be either general or special.
(3) Directions under this Chapter may apply in relation to local probation boards generally or in relation to one or more local probation boards identified in the directions.

Annual plan

15. (1) A local probation board must, before the beginning of each financial year—

(a) prepare a plan setting out how it intends to exercise its functions in that year, having regard to the circumstances prevailing in its area, and dealing with any other matter which the Secretary of State by directions requires it to deal with in respect of that year,
(b) send a copy of the plan to the Secretary of State.

(2) If the plan does not appear to the Secretary of State to be satisfactory, he may direct the local probation board to modify it.

Reports

16. (1) A local probation board must—

(a) make a report to the Secretary of State on the performance of its functions during each financial year, and
(b) arrange for the report to be published.

(2) The Secretary of State may give directions as to—

(a) the information to be given in the report and the form in which it is to be given,
(b) the time by which the report is to be made,
(c) the form and manner in which the report is to be published.

Accounts

17. (1) A local probation board must—

(a) keep proper accounts and proper records in relation to the accounts,
(b) prepare in respect of each financial year of the board a statement of accounts.

(2) The Comptroller and Auditor General may examine any accounts of a local probation board, any records relating to the accounts and any auditor's report on them.
(3) In the Audit Commission Act 1998—

(a) in section 11(2) (consideration of reports and recommendations), for paragraph (f) there is substituted—

"(f) local probation boards established under section 4 of the Criminal Justice and Court Services Act 2000",
(b) in Schedule 2 (accounts subject to audit), for paragraph 1(p) there is substituted—

"(p) a local probation board established under section 4 of the Criminal Justice and Court Services Act 2000".

(4) The Secretary of State must prepare in respect of each financial year consolidated accounts of the local probation boards and send them, not later than the time specified in directions given by the Treasury, to the Comptroller and Auditor General.
(5) The Comptroller and Auditor General must examine and certify the consolidated accounts and lay copies of them, together with his report on them, before the House of Commons.

Complaints

18. Regulations[2] may require each local probation board to make and publicise arrangements for dealing with complaints made by or on behalf of prescribed persons in relation to things done under the arrangements made by the board under section 5.

Status

19. A local probation board is not to be regarded as the servant or agent of the Crown, or as enjoying any status, privilege or immunity of the Crown; and its property is not to be regarded as property of, or property held on behalf of, the Crown.

Interpretation

20. "Financial year", in this Schedule, means—

(a) the period beginning with the date on which the local probation board is established and ending with the next following 31st March, and

(b) each successive period of twelve months.

---

1. The Local Probation Boards (Appointments and Miscellaneous Provisions) Regulations 2000 and the Local Probation Boards (Appointments and Miscellaneous Provisions) Regulations 2001, have been made, in this PART, post.
2. The Local Probation Boards (Miscellaneous Provisions) Regulations 2001 and the Local Probation Boards (Appointments and Miscellaneous Provisions) Regulations 2001, in this PART, post, have been made.

SCHEDULE 2
CHILDREN AND FAMILY COURT ADVISORY AND SUPPORT SERVICE

(As amended by SI 2003/3191.)

Section 11

Constitution

1–4074   **1.** The Service is to consist of a chairman, and not less than ten other members, appointed by the Secretary of State.

2. (1) Regulations[1] may provide—

(a) for the appointment of the chairman and other members and for the co-option by the Service for particular purposes of additional members (including the number, or limits on the number, of persons who may be appointed or co-opted and any conditions to be fulfilled for appointment or co-option),

(b) for the tenure of office of the chairman and other members and any co-opted members (including the circumstances in which they cease to hold office or may be removed or suspended from office).

(2) References below in this Schedule to members of the Service do not include co-opted members.

Remuneration etc of members

3. (1) The Service may pay, or make provision for paying, to or in respect of any person who is or has been the chairman or another member—

(a) any remuneration, fees or expenses,

(b) any pension, allowance or gratuity,

determined by the Secretary of State.

(2) The Service may, to any extent determined by the Secretary of State, reimburse any co-opted members for any expenses or loss of earnings.

(3) Where a person ceases to be chairman or another member of the Service otherwise than on the expiry of his term of office and it appears to the Secretary of State that there are circumstances which make it right for that person to receive compensation, the Service may pay that person an amount determined by the Secretary of State.

Procedure

4. Regulations[1] may provide for—

(a) the establishment and functions of committees (including committees which include persons who are not the chairman or another member of the Service),

(b) the procedure of the Service and of any of its committees (including quorum and the validation of proceedings in the event of vacancies or defects in appointment).

Staff and other officers

5. (1) The Service may appoint—

(a) staff to perform the functions of officers of the Service, and

(b) other staff.

(2) Regulations may make provision as to the qualifications, experience or training to be required of officers of the Service (whether or not appointed under sub-paragraph (1)(a)).

(3) One of the staff appointed under sub-paragraph (1)(b) is to be the chief executive.

(4) The Service must not appoint a person—

(a) as chief executive, or

(b) as a member of the staff of a description specified in a direction given by the Secretary of State,

without the approval of the Secretary of State.

6. (1) Staff of the Service are to be appointed on terms and conditions determined by the Service as to—

(a) any remuneration, fees or expenses,

(b) any pension, allowance or gratuity.

(2) It is for the Service to determine the terms and conditions of any arrangements under section 13(4) under which individuals perform the functions of officers of the Service.

(3) But a determination under this paragraph requires the approval of the Secretary of State.

Delegation

7. The Service may arrange for the chairman or any other member to discharge functions of the Service on its behalf.

Payments to the Service

8. (1) The Secretary of State may, at any time, pay to the Service any amount he considers appropriate.

(2) If he considers it appropriate, he may make any payment on conditions.

Supervision

9. (1) Functions and other powers of the Service, and functions of any officer of the Service, must be performed in accordance with any directions given by the Secretary of State.

(2) In particular, the directions may make provision for the purpose of ensuring that the services provided are of appropriate quality and meet appropriate standards.

(3) The Service must provide the Secretary of State with any information relating to the performance of its functions which he may from time to time require.

Ancillary powers

10. (1) Subject to any directions given by the Secretary of State, the Service may do anything which appears to it to be necessary or expedient for the purpose of, or in connection with, the exercise of its functions.

(2) That includes, in particular—

(*a*) holding land and other property,
(*b*) entering into contracts,
(*c*) investing sums not immediately required for the purpose of performing its functions,
(*d*) accepting gifts.

(3) But the Service may not borrow money, whether by way of overdraft or otherwise, without the approval of the Secretary of State.

Directions

11. (1) Different directions may be given under this Schedule for different purposes.

(2) Directions under this Schedule may be either general or special.

Reports and accounts

12. (1) The Service must make a report to the Secretary of State in respect of each financial year on the performance of its functions.

(2) The Secretary of State may give directions as to—

(*a*) the information to be given in the report and the form in which it is to be given, and
(*b*) the time by which the report is to be given.

(3) The Secretary of State must—

(*a*) lay a copy of the report before each House of Parliament,
(*b*) arrange for the report to be published in a manner he considers appropriate.

13. (1) The Service must—

(*a*) keep proper accounts and proper records in relation to the accounts,
(*b*) prepare in respect of each financial year of the Service a statement of accounts, and
(*c*) send copies of the statement to the Secretary of State and to the Comptroller and Auditor General before the end of the month of August next following the financial year to which the statement relates.

(2) The statement of accounts must comply with any directions given by the Secretary of State as to—

(*a*) the information to be contained in it,
(*b*) the manner in which the information contained in it is to be presented,
(*c*) the methods and principles according to which the statement is to be prepared,

and must contain any additional information the Secretary of State may require to be provided for the information of Parliament.

(3) The Service must, in accordance with directions given by the Secretary of State—

(*a*) appoint an auditor who is not a member of the Service's staff, and
(*b*) ensure that the auditor makes a report to the Secretary of Stateabout the preparation of the accounts and about the statement of accounts.

(4) The Comptroller and Auditor General must examine, certify and report on the statement of accounts and must lay copies of the statement and of his report before each House of Parliament.

14. "Financial year", in this Schedule, means—

(*a*) the period beginning with the date on which the Service is established and ending with the next following 31st March, and
(*b*) each successive period of twelve months.

Complaints

15. The Service must make and publicise a scheme for dealing with complaints made by or on behalf of prescribed persons in relation to the performance by the Service and its officers of their functions.

Status

16. The Service is not to be regarded as the servant or agent of the Crown, or as enjoying any status, privilege or immunity of the Crown; and its property is not to be regarded as property of, or property held on behalf of, the Crown.

General

17. In Schedule 2 to the Parliamentary Commissioner Act 1967 (departments etc subject to investigation), at the appropriate place there is inserted—

"Children and Family Court Advisory and Support Service".

18. (1) Employment with the Service shall be included in the kinds of employment to which a scheme under section 1 of the Superannuation Act 1972 can apply.

(2) The Service must pay to the Minister for the Civil Service, at such times as he may direct, such sums as he

may determine in respect of any increase attributable to sub-paragraph (1) in the sums payable out of money provided by Parliament under the Superannuation Act 1972.

19. In Part II of Schedule 1 to the House of Commons Disqualification Act 1975 (bodies of which all members are disqualified), at the appropriate place there is inserted—

"The Children and Family Court Advisory and Support Service".

1. The Children and Family Court Advisory and Support Service (Membership, Committee and Procedure) Regulations 2005, SI 2005/433have been made.

1-4075   SCHEDULE 3
                              TRANSFER OF PROPERTY

                              SCHEDULE 4
                 MEANING OF "OFFENCE AGAINST A CHILD"

(As amended by the Nationality, Immigration and Asylum Act 2002, s 146, the Sexual Offences Act 2003, Schs 6 and 7 and the Asylum and Immigration (Treatment of Claimants, etc) Act).

Section 26
1-4076   1. The offences mentioned in paragraph (*a*) of subsection (1) of section 26 are—

   (*a*) an offence under section 1 of the Children and Young Persons Act 1933 (cruelty to children),
   (*b*) an offence under section 1 of the Infanticide Act 1938 (infanticide),
   (*c*) *repealed*
   (*d*) *repealed*
   (*e*) *repealed*
   (*f*) *repealed*
   (*g*) *repealed*
   (*h*) *repealed*
   (*i*) *repealed*
   (*j*) an offence under section 1 of the Protection of Children Act 1978 (indecent photographs of children),
   (*k*) an offence under section 1 of the Child Abduction Act 1984 (abduction of child by parent),
   (*l*) an offence under section 160 of the Criminal Justice Act 1988 (possession of indecent photograph of child),
   (*m*) an offence under any of sections 5 to 26 and 47 to 50 of the Sexual Offences Act 2003 (offences against children).

2. The offences mentioned in paragraph (*b*) of that subsection are—

   (*a*) murder,
   (*b*) manslaughter,
   (*c*) kidnapping,
   (*d*) false imprisonment,
   (*e*) an offence under section 18 or 20 of the Offences against the Person Act 1861 (wounding and causing grievous bodily harm),
   (*f*) an offence under section 47 of that Act (assault occasioning actual bodily harm),
   (*g*) *repealed*
   (*h*) *repealed*
   (*i*) *repealed*
   (*j*) *repealed*
   (*k*) *repealed*
   (*l*) *repealed*
   (*m*) *repealed*
   (*n*) an offence under any of sections 1 to 4, 30 to 41, 52, 53, 57 to 61, 66 and 67 of the Sexual Offences Act 2003 (offences against children);
   (*o*) an offence under section 4 of the Asylum and Immigration (Treatment of Claimants, etc) Act 2004 (Trafficking peope for exploitation).

3. A person falls within this paragraph if—

   (*a*) he commits an offence under section 16 of the Offences against the Person Act 1861 (threats to kill) by making a threat to kill a child,
   (*b*) *repealed*
   (*c*) *repealed*
   (*d*) *repealed*
   (*e*) *repealed*
   (*f*) *repealed*
   (*g*) *repealed*
   (*h*) *repealed*
   (*i*) *repealed*
   (*j*) *repealed*
   (*k*) *repealed*
   (*l*) *repealed*
   (*m*) *repealed*
   (*n*) *repealed*
   (*o*) *repealed*
   (*p*) *repealed*
   (*q*) *repealed*
   (*r*) *repealed*
   (*s*) he commits an offence under section 4(3) of the Misuse of Drugs Act 1971 by—

      (i) supplying or offering to supply a Class A drug to a child,
      (ii) being concerned in the supplying of such a drug to a child, or
      (iii) being concerned in the making to a child of an offer to supply such a drug,

   (*sa*) he commits an offence under section 62 or 63 of the Sexual Offences Act 2003 (committing an offence or trespasssing with intent to commit a sexual offence) in a case where the intended offence was an offence against a child,

(t) he commits an offence of—

    (i) aiding, abetting, counselling, procuring or inciting the commission of an offence against a child, or

    (ii) conspiring or attempting to commit such an offence.

SCHEDULE 5
AMENDMENTS OF THE SEX OFFENDERS ACT 1997[1]

1. The amendments made to the Sex Offenders Act 1997 have all been brought into force and are noted in that Act.

SCHEDULE 6
TRIGGER OFFENCES

(As amended by SI 2004/1892)

Section 70

1–4077   **1.** Offences under the following provisions of the Theft Act 1968 are trigger offences:

section 1 (theft)
section 8 (robbery)
section 9 (burglary)
section 10 (aggravated burglary)
section 12 (taking motor vehicle or other conveyance without authority)
section 12A (aggravated vehicle-taking)
section 15 (obtaining property by deception)*
section 22 (handling stolen goods)
section 25 (going equipped for stealing, etc)

2. Offences under the following provisions of the Misuse of Drugs Act 1971 are trigger offences, if committed in respect of a specified Class A drug:

section 4 (restriction on production and supply of controlled drugs)
section 5(2) (possession of controlled drug)
section 5(3) (possession of controlled drug with intent to supply)

3. An offence under section 1(1) of the Criminal Attempts Act 1981 is a trigger offence, if committed in respect of an offence under any of the following provisions of the Theft Act 1968;

section 1 (theft)
section 8 (robbery)
section 9 (burglary)
section 15 (obtaining property by deception)
section 22 (handling stolen goods)

4. Offences under the following provisions of the Vagrancy Act 1824 are trigger offences;

section 3 (begging)section 4 (persistent begging)

*Words underlined repealed by the Fraud Act 2006, Sch 1 from a date to be appointed.

SCHEDULE 7
MINOR AND CONSEQUENTIAL AMENDMENTS

1–4080

SCHEDULE 8
REPEALS

Criminal Justice and Police Act 2001[1]
(2001 c 16)

PART 1[2]
PROVISIONS FOR COMBATTING CRIME AND DISORDER

CHAPTER 1[3]
ON THE SPOT PENALTIES FOR DISORDERLY BEHAVIOUR

Offences to which this Chapter applies

1–4100   **1. Offences leading to penalties on the spot.**   (1) For the purposes of this Chapter "penalty offence" means an offence committed under any of the provisions mentioned in the first column of the following Table and described, in general terms, in the second column:

Offence creating provision	Description of offence
Section 12 of the Licensing Act 1872 (c 94)	Being drunk in a highway, other public place or licensed premises
Section 80 of the Explosives Act 1875 (c 17)	Throwing fireworks in a thoroughfare*
Section 55 of the British Transport Commission Act 1949 (c xxix)	Trespassing on a railway
Section 56 of the British Transport Commission Act 1949 (c xxix)	Throwing stones etc at trains or other things on railways

Offence creating provision	Description of offence
Section 91 of the Criminal Justice Act 1967 (c 80)	Disorderly behaviour while drunk in a public place
Section 5(2) of the Criminal Law Act 1967 (c 58)	Wasting police time or giving false report
Section 1 of the Theft Act 1968 (c 60)	Theft
Section 1(1) of the Criminal Damage Act 1971 (c 48)	Destroying or damaging property
Section 5 of the Public Order Act 1986 (c 64)	Behaviour likely to cause harassment, alarm or distress
Section 87 of the Environmental Protection Act 1990 (c 43)	Depositing and leaving litter
Section 12 of this Act	Consumption of alcohol in designated public place
Section 127(2) of the Communications Act 2003	Using public electronic communications network in order to cause annoyance, inconvenience or needless anxiety
Section 11 of the Fireworks Act 2003 (c 22)	Contravention of a prohibition or failure to comply with a requirement imposed by or under fireworks regulations or making false statements
Section 141 of the Licensing Act 2003 (c 17)	Sale of alcohol to a person who is drunk
Section 146(1) and (3) of the Licensing Act 2003 (c 17)	Sale of alcohol to children
Section 149 of the Licensing Act 2003 (c 17)	Purchase of alcohol by or on behalf of children
Section 149(4) of the Licensing Act 2003	Buying or attempting to buy alcohol for consumption on licensed premises, etc by child
Section 150 of the Licensing Act 2003 (c 17)	Consumption of alcohol by children or allowing such consumption
Section 151 of the Licensing Act 2003 (c 17)	Delivering alcohol to children or allowing such delivery
Section 49 of the Fire and Rescue Services Act 2004 (c 21)	Knowingly giving a false alarm of fire

(2)–(5) *Power of the Secretary of State to amend, add or remove entries in s 1(1).*
[Criminal Justice and Police Act 2001, s 1 as amended by SI 2002/1934, the Fire and Rescue Services Act 2004, Sch 1, the Communications Act 2003, Sch 17, SI 2004/2540 and SI 2005/3048.]

*Repealed by the Fireworks Act 2003, Schedule from a date to be appointed.
1. Part 1 of this Act makes provision for: a range of low-level, anti-social offences associated with disorderly conduct to be dealt with by way of fixed penalty; combating alcohol consumption in designated public places; closure of certain licensed premises due to disorder or disturbance; and also amends the law in relation to sales of alcohol to persons under 18 and drunkenness or disorder on licensed premises. Part I also empowers courts to make travel restrictions in relation to certain offenders convicted of drug trafficking offences; creates new offences of intimidating or harming witnesses; amends the law on harassment and malicious communications; creates new offences relating to the placing of advertisements for prostitution; and extends local child curfew schemes. Part 2 is concerned with the seizure of property from persons or premises and the return or retention of seized property. Part 3 makes various amendments to the Police and Criminal Act 1984 and the Terrorism Act 2000. Part 4 is concerned with police training. Part 5 is concerned with police organisation. Part 6 amends the law relating to remands, committals and miscellaneous matters. These parts are reproduced or noted in the relevant sections of this work. For commencement provisions see s 138, post. At the time of going to press the following commencement orders had been made: Commencement provisions: s 138(2)–(4); Criminal Justice and Police Act 2001 (Commencement No 1) Order 2001, SI 2001/2223; Criminal Justice and Police Act 2001 (Commencement No 2) Order 2001, SI 2001/3150; Criminal Justice and Police Act 2001 (Commencement No 3) Order 2001, SI 2001/3736; Criminal Justice and Police Act 2001 (Commencement No 4 and Transitional Provisions) Order 2002, SI 2002/3441; Criminal Justice and Police Act 2001 (Commencement No 5) Order 2002, SI 2002/533; Criminal Justice and Police Act 2001 (Commencement No 6) Order 2002, SI 2002/1097; Criminal Justice and Police Act 2001 (Commencement No 7) Order 2002, SI 2002/2050; Criminal Justice and Police Act 2001 (Commencement No 8) Order 2002, SI 2002/3032; Criminal Justice and Police Act 2001 (Commencement No 9) Order 2003, SI 2003/708; and Criminal Justice and Police Act 2001 (Commencement No 10) Order 2004, SI 2004/1376.
2. Part 1 contains ss 1–49.
3. Chapter 1 contains ss 1–11.

Penalty notices and penalties

1–4101   2. Penalty notices. (1) A constable who has reason to believe that a person aged 10[1] or over has committed a penalty offence may give him a penalty notice in respect of the offence.
(2) Unless the notice is given in a police station, the constable giving it must be in uniform.
(3) At a police station, a penalty notice may be given only by an authorised constable.
(4) In this Chapter "penalty notice" means a notice offering the opportunity, by paying a penalty in accordance with this Chapter, to discharge any liability to be convicted of the offence to which the notice relates.
(5) "Authorised constable" means a constable authorised, on behalf of the chief officer of police for the area in which the police station is situated, to give penalty notices.
(6) The Secretary of State may by order—

(*a*) amend subsection (1) by substituting for the age for the time being specified in that subsection a different age which is not lower than 10, and

(*b*) if that different age is lower than 16, make provision as follows—

    (i) where a person whose age is lower than 16 is given a penalty notice, for a parent or guardian of that person to be notified of the giving of the notice, and

    (ii) for that parent or guardian to be liable to pay the penalty under the notice.

(7) The provision which may be made by virtue of subsection (6)(*b*) includes provision amending, or applying (with or without modifications), this Chapter or any other enactment (whenever passed or made).

(8) The power conferred by subsection (6) is exercisable by statutory instrument[2].

(9) No order shall be made under subsection (6) unless a draft of the order has been laid before and approved by a resolution of each House of Parliament.

[Criminal Justice and Police Act 2001, s 2, as amended by the Anti-social Behaviour Act 2003, s 87 and SI 2004/3166.]

---

1. The age of "10" was substituted for "16" by the Penalties for Disorderly Behaviour (Amendment of Minimum Age) Order 2004, in this PART, post, as from 26 December 2004.

2. For procedure in respect of a person under the age of 16 who is given a penalty notice, see the Penalties for Disorderly Behaviour (Amendment of Minimum Age) Order 2004, in this PART, post.

1–4102   **3. Amount of penalty and form of penalty notice.**   (1) The penalty payable in respect of a penalty offence is such amount as the Secretary of State may specify by order[1].

(1A) The Secretary of State may specify different amounts for persons of different ages.

(2) But the Secretary of State may not specify an amount which is more than a quarter of the amount of the maximum fine for which a person is liable on summary conviction of the offence.★

(3) A penalty notice must—

(*a*) be in the prescribed form;

(*b*) state the alleged offence;

(*c*) give such particulars of the circumstances alleged to constitute the offence as are necessary to provide reasonable information about it;

(*d*) specify the suspended enforcement period (as to which see section 5) and explain its effect;

(*e*) state the amount of the penalty;

(*f*) state the designated officer for a local justice area to whom, and the address at which, the penalty may be paid; and

(*g*) inform the person to whom it is given of his right to ask to be tried for the alleged offence and explain how that right may be exercised.

(4) "Prescribed" means prescribed[2] by regulations made by the Secretary of State.

(5) The power to make regulations or an order conferred by this section is exercisable by statutory instrument.

(6) Such an instrument shall be subject to annulment in pursuance of a resolution of either House of Parliament.

[Criminal Justice and Police Act 2001, s 3 as amended by the Anti-social Behaviour Act 2003, s 87, the Courts Act 2003, Sch 8 and SI 2004/2540.]

★Amended and new sub-s (2A) inserted by the Domestic Violence, Crime and Victims Act 2004, s 15 from a date to be appointed.

1. The following orders have been made: Penalties for Disorderly Behaviour (Amount of Penalty) Order 2002, SI 2002/1837; Penalties for Disorderly Behaviour (Amount of Penalty) (Amendment) Order 2004, SI 2004/316; Penalties for Disorderly Behaviour (Amount of Penalty) (Amendment No 2) Order 2004, SI 2004/2468; Penalties for Disorderly Behaviour (Amount of Penalty) (Amendment No 3) Order 2004, SI 2004/3167; and Penalties for Disorderly Behaviour (Amount of Penalty) (Amendment) Order 2005, SI 2005/581. The amounts of the fixed penalties are set out below.

2. The Penalties for Disorderly Behaviour (Form of Penalty Notice) Regulations 2002, SI 2002/1838The Penalties for Disorderly Behaviour (Form of Penalty Notice) (Amendment) Regulations 2005, SI 2005/630 have been made.

SCHEDULE

(*As amended by SI 2004/316, 2468 and 3371 and SI 2005/581.*)

Article 2

PART I

OFFENCES ATTRACTING PENALTY OF £80 FOR PERSONS 16 AND OVER, OR £40 FOR PERSONS UNDER 16

Offence creating provision	Description of offence
Section 80 of the Explosives Act 1875 (c 17)	Throwing fireworks in a thoroughfare
Section 31 of the Fire Services Act 1947 (c 41)	Knowingly giving a false alarm to a fire brigade
Section 169A of the Licensing Act 1964 (c 26)	Sale of alcohol to a person under 18
Section 169C(2) and (3) of the Licensing Act 1964 (c 26)	Buying or attempting to buy alcohol for a person under 18
Section 169F of the Licensing Act 1964 (c 26)	Delivery of alcohol to a person under 18 or allowing such delivery
Section 172(3) of the Licensing Act 1964 (c 26)	Selling alcohol to a drunken person
Section 5(2) of the Criminal Law Act 1967 (c 58)	Wasting police time or giving false report

Offence creating provision	Description of offence
Section 91 of the Criminal Justice Act 1967 (c 80)	Disorderly behaviour while drunk in a public place
Section 1 of the Theft Act 1968 (c 60)	Theft
Section 1(1) of the Criminal Damage Act 1971 (c 48)	Destroying or damaging property
Section 5 of the Public Order Act 1986 (c 64)	Behaviour likely to cause harassment, alarm or distress
Section 127(2) of the Communications Act 2003 (c 21)	Using a public electronic communications network in order to cause annoyance, inconvenience or needless anxiety
Section 11 of the Fireworks Act 2003 (c 22)	Contravention of a prohibition or failure to comply with a requirement imposed by or under fireworks regulations or making false statements
Section 49 of the Fire and Rescue Services Act 2004 (c 21)	Knowingly giving a false alarm to a person acting on behalf of a fire and rescue authority

PART II

OFFENCES ATTRACTING PENALTY OF £50 FOR PERSONS 16 AND OVER, OR £30 FOR PERSONS UNDER 16

Offence creating provision	Description of offence
Section 12 of the Licensing Act 1872 (c 94)	Being drunk in a highway, other public place or licensed premises
Section 55 of the British Transport Commission Act 1949 (c xxix)	Trespassing on a railway
Section 56 of the British Transport Commission Act 1949 (c xxix)	Throwing stones etc at trains or other things on railways
Section 169C(1) of the Licensing Act 1964 (c 26)	Buying or attempting to buy alcohol by a person under 18
Section 168E of the Licensing Act 1964 (c 26)	Consumption of alcohol by a person under 18 or allowing such consumption
Section 87 of the Environmental Protection Act 1990 (c 43)	Depositing and leaving litter
Section 12 of the Criminal Justice and Police Act 2001 (c 16)	Consumption of alcohol in designated public place

---

[1]   See the Penalties for Disorderly Behaviour (Form of Penalty Notice) Regulations 2002, SI 2002/1838 amended by SI 2004/3193 and SI 2005/630.

1–4103   4. Effect of penalty notice.   (*1*) This section applies if a penalty notice is given to a person ("A") under section 2.

(2) If A asks to be tried for the alleged offence, proceedings may be brought against him.

(3) Such a request must be made by a notice given by A—

(*a*) in the manner specified in the penalty notice; and

(*b*) before the end of the period of suspended enforcement (as to which see section 5).

(4) A request which is made in accordance with subsection (3) is referred to in this Chapter as a "request to be tried".

(5) If, by the end of the suspended enforcement period—

(*a*) the penalty has not been paid in accordance with this Chapter, and

(*b*) A has not made a request to be tried,

a sum equal to one and a half times the amount of the penalty may be registered under section 8 for enforcement against A as a fine[1].
[Criminal Justice and Police Act 2001, s 4.]

---

1. Subs (5) has been modified in relation to a young penalty recipient, by the Penalties for Disorderly Behaviour (Amendment of Minimum Age) Order 2004, SI 2004/3166, art 6(1), (2).

1–4104   5. General restriction on proceedings.   (1) Proceedings for the offence to which a penalty notice relates may not be brought until the end of the period of 21 days beginning with the date on which the notice was given ("the suspended enforcement period")[1].

(2) If the penalty is paid before the end of the suspended enforcement period, no proceedings may be brought for the offence.

(3) Subsection (1) does not apply if the person to whom the penalty notice was given has made a request to be tried.
[Criminal Justice and Police Act 2001, s 5.]

---

1. Subs (1) has been modified in relation to a young penalty recipient, by the Penalties for Disorderly Behaviour (Amendment of Minimum Age) Order 2004, SI 2004/3166, art 6(1), (3).

1–4105   6. *Power of the Secretary of State to issue guidance.*

Procedure

1–4106   7. Payment of penalty.   (1) If a person to whom a penalty notice is given decides to pay the penalty, he must pay it to the justices' chief executive specified in the notice[1].

587   *Criminal Justice and Police Act 2001*   **1–4110**

(2) Payment of the penalty may be made by properly addressing, pre-paying and posting a letter containing the amount of the penalty (in cash or otherwise).

(3) Subsection (4) applies if a person—

(*a*) claims to have made payment by that method, and

(*b*) shows that his letter was posted.

(4) Unless the contrary is proved, payment is to be regarded as made at the time at which the letter would be delivered in the ordinary course of post.

(5) Subsection (2) is not to be read as preventing the payment of a penalty by other means.

(6) A letter is properly addressed for the purposes of subsection (2) if it is addressed in accordance with the requirements specified in the penalty notice.

[Criminal Justice and Police Act 2001, s 7.]

---

1. Subs (1) has been modified, in relation to a young penalty recipient, by the Penalties for Disorderly Behaviour (Amendment of Minimum Age) Order 2004, SI 2004/3166, art 6(1), (4).

1–4107   8. Registration certificates. (1) The chief officer of police[1] may, in respect of any registrable sum, issue a certificate (a "registration certificate") stating that the sum is registrable for enforcement against the defaulter as a fine.

(2) If that officer issues a registration certificate, he must cause it to be sent to the justices' chief executive for the petty sessions area in which the defaulter appears to that officer to reside.

(3) A registration certificate must—

(*a*) give particulars of the offence to which the penalty notice relates, and

(*b*) state the name and last known address of the defaulter and the amount of the registrable sum.

(4) "Registrable sum" means a sum that may be registered under this section as a result of section 4(5).

(5) "Defaulter" means the person against whom that sum may be registered.

[Criminal Justice and Police Act 2001, s 8.]

---

1. Defined to include the Chief Constable of the British Transport Police. See s 11, post.

1–4109   9. Registration of sums payable in default. (1) If the justices' chief executive for a petty sessions area receives a registration certificate, he must register the registrable sum for enforcement as a fine in that area by entering it in the register of a magistrates' court acting for that area.

(2) But if it appears to him that the defaulter does not reside in that area—

(*a*) subsection (1) does not apply to him; but

(*b*) he must cause the certificate to be sent to the person appearing to him to be the appropriate justices' chief executive.

(3) A justices' chief executive registering a sum under this section for enforcement as a fine, must give the defaulter notice of the registration.

(4) The notice must—

(*a*) specify the amount of the sum registered, and

(*b*) give the information with respect to the offence, and the authority for registration, which was included in the registration certificate under section 8.

(5) If a sum is registered in a magistrates' court as a result of this section, any enactment referring (in whatever terms) to a fine imposed, or other sum adjudged to be paid, on conviction by such a court applies as if the registered sum were a fine imposed by that court on the conviction of the defaulter on the date on which the sum was registered.

[Criminal Justice and Police Act 2001, s 9.]

1–4110   10. Enforcement of fines. (1) In this section—

"fine" means a sum which is enforceable as a fine as a result of section 9; and "proceedings" means proceedings for enforcing a fine.

(2) Subsection (3) applies if, in any proceedings, the defaulter claims that he was not the person to whom the penalty notice concerned was issued[1].

(3) The court may adjourn the proceedings for a period of not more than 28 days for the purpose of allowing that claim to be investigated.

(4) On the resumption of proceedings that have been adjourned under subsection (3), the court must accept the defaulter's claim unless it is shown, on a balance of probabilities, that he was the recipient of the penalty notice[1].

(5) The court may set aside a fine in the interests of justice.

(6) If the court does set a fine aside it must—

(*a*) give such directions for further consideration of the case as it considers appropriate; or

(*b*) direct that no further action is to be taken in respect of the allegation that gave rise to the penalty notice concerned.

[Criminal Justice and Police Act 2001, s 10.]

1. Subss (2) and (4) have been modified in relation to a young penalty recipient, by the Penalties for Disorderly Behaviour (Amendment of Minimum Age) Order 2004, SI 2004/3166, art 6(1), (5), (6).

Interpretation

1–4111   11. Interpretation of Chapter 1.   In this Chapter—

"chief officer of police" includes the Chief Constable of the British Transport Police;

"defaulter" has the meaning given in section 8(5);

"penalty notice" has the meaning given in section 2(4);

"penalty offence" has the meaning given in section 1(1);

"registrable sum" has the meaning given in section 8(4).

[Criminal Justice and Police Act 2001, s 11.]

CHAPTER 2[1]

PROVISIONS FOR COMBATTING ALCOHOL-RELATED DISORDER

Alcohol consumption in designated public places

1–4112   12. Alcohol consumption in designated public places.   (1) Subsection (2) applies if a constable reasonably believes that a person is, or has been, consuming alcohol in a designated public place[2] or intends to consume alcohol in such a place.

(2) The constable may require the person concerned—

(*a*) not to consume in that place anything which is, or which the constable reasonably believes to be, alcohol;

(*b*) to surrender anything in his possession which is, or which the constable reasonably believes to be, alcohol or a container for alcohol.

(3) A constable may dispose of anything surrendered to him under subsection (2) in such manner as he considers appropriate.

(4) A person who fails without reasonable excuse to comply with a requirement imposed on him under subsection (2) commits an offence and is liable on summary conviction to a fine not exceeding level 2 on the standard scale.

(5) A constable who imposes a requirement on a person under subsection (2) shall inform the person concerned that failing without reasonable excuse to comply with the requirement is an offence.

(6) *Repealed.*

[Criminal Justice and Police Act 2001, s 12 as amended by the Police Reform Act 2002, Sch 8 and the Licensing Act 2003, Schs 6 and 7.]

1. Chapter 2 contains ss 12–32.
2. As to places which are not designated public places, see s 14, post.

1–4113   13. Designated public places.   (1) A place is, subject to section 14, a designated public place if it is—

(*a*) a public place in the area of a local authority[1]; and

(*b*) identified in an order made by that authority under subsection (2).

(2) A local authority may for the purposes of subsection (1) by order identify any public place[2] in their area if they are satisfied that—

(*a*) nuisance or annoyance to members of the public or a section of the public; or

(*b*) disorder;

has been associated with the consumption of alcohol in that place.

(3) The power conferred by subsection (2) includes power—

(*a*) to identify a place either specifically or by description;

(*b*) to revoke or amend orders previously made.

(4) The Secretary of State shall by regulations[3] prescribe the procedure to be followed in connection with the making of orders under subsection (2).

(5) Regulations under subsection (4) shall, in particular, include provision requiring local authorities to publicise the making and effect of orders under subsection (2).

(6) Regulations under subsection (4) shall be made by statutory instrument which shall be subject to annulment in pursuance of a resolution of either House of Parliament.

[Criminal Justice and Police Act 2001, s 13 as amended by the Licensing Act 2003, Sch 6.]

1. Defined in s 16(2), post.
2. Defined in s 16(1), post.
3. The Local Authorities (Alcohol Consumption in Designated Public Places) Regulations 2001, SI 2001/2831 have been made.

1–4114   14. Places which are not designated public places.   (1) A place is not a designated public place or a part of such a place if it is—

(*a*) premises in respect of which a premises licence or club premises certificate, within the meaning of the Licensing Act 2003, has effect;

(b) a place within the curtilage of premises within paragraph (a);

(c) premises which by virtue of Part 5 of the Licensing Act 2003 may for the time being be used for the supply of alcohol or which, by virtue of that Part, could have been so used within the last 20 minutes;

(e) a place where facilities or activities relating to the sale or consumption of alcohol are for the time being permitted by virtue of a permission granted under section 115E of the Highways Act 1980 (c 66) (highway related uses).

(2) *Repealed.*

[Criminal Justice and Police Act 2001, s 14 as amended by the Licensing Act 2003, Sch 6.]

1–4115 15. Effect of sections 12 to 14 on byelaws. (1) Subsections (2) and (3) apply to any byelaw which—

(a) prohibits, by the creation of an offence, the consumption in a particular public place of alcohol (including any liquor of a similar nature which falls within the byelaw); or

(b) makes any incidental, supplementary or consequential provision (whether relating to the seizure or control of containers or otherwise).

(2) In so far as any byelaw to which this subsection applies would, apart from this subsection, have effect in relation to any designated public place, the byelaw—

(a) shall cease to have effect in relation to that place; or

(b) where it is made after the order under section 13(2), shall not have effect in relation to that place.

(3) In so far as any byelaw made by a local authority and to which this subsection applies still has effect at the end of the period of 5 years beginning with the day on which this subsection comes into force, it shall cease to have effect at the end of that period in relation to any public place.

[Criminal Justice and Police Act 2001, s 15 as amended by the Licensing Act 2003, Sch 6.]

1–4116 16. Interpretation of sections 12 to 15. (1) In sections 12 to 15, unless the context otherwise requires—

"designated public place" has the meaning given by section 13(1);

"alcohol" has the same meaning as in the Licensing Act 2003;

"public place" means any place to which the public or any section of the public has access, on payment or otherwise, as of right or by virtue of express or implied permission; and

"supply of alcohol" has the meaning given by section 14 of the Licensing Act 2003.

(2) In sections 12 to 15 "local authority" means—

(a) in relation to England—

(i) a unitary authority;

(ii) a district council so far as they are not a unitary authority;

(b) in relation to Wales, a county council or a county borough council.

(3) In subsection (2) "unitary authority" means—

(a) the council of a county so far as they are the council for an area for which there are no district councils;

(b) the council of any district comprised in an area for which there is no county council;

(c) a London borough council;

(d) the Common Council of the City of London in its capacity as a local authority;

(e) the Council of the Isles of Scilly.

[Criminal Justice and Police Act 2001, s 16 as amended by the Licensing Act 2003, Sch 6.]

*Substituted by "alcohol" by the Licensing Act 2003, Sch 6, from a date to be appointed.

1–4117 17, 18. *Repealed.*

Closure of unlicensed premises[1]

1–4119 19. Closure notices. (1) Where a constable is satisfied that any premises are being, or within the last 24 hours have been, used for the unauthorised sale of alcohol for consumption on, or in the vicinity of, the premises, he may serve under subsection (3) a notice in respect of the premises.

(2) Where a local authority is satisfied that any premises in the area of the authority are being, or within the last 24 hours have been, used for the unauthorised sale of alcohol for consumption on, or in the vicinity of, the premises, the authority may serve under subsection (3) a notice in respect of the premises.

(3) A notice under subsection (1) or (2) ("a closure notice") shall be served by the constable or local authority concerned on a person having control of, or responsibility for, the activities carried on at the premises.

(4) A closure notice shall also be served by the constable or local authority concerned on any person occupying another part of any building or other structure of which the premises form part if the constable or (as the case may be) the local authority concerned reasonably believes, at the time of serving notice under subsection (3), that the person's access to the other part of the building or other

structure would be impeded if an order under section 21 providing for the closure of the premises were made.

(5) A closure notice may also be served by a constable or the local authority concerned on—

(a) any other person having control of, or responsibility for, the activities carried on at the premises;

(b) any person who has an interest in the premises.

(6) A closure notice shall—

(a) specify the alleged use of the premises and the grounds on which the constable or (as the case may be) the local authority concerned is satisfied as mentioned in subsection (1) or (as the case may be) subsection (2);

(b) state the effect of section 20; and

(c) specify the steps which may be taken to ensure that the alleged use of the premises ceases or (as the case may be) does not recur.

(7) A closure notice served by a constable or local authority may be cancelled by a notice of cancellation served by a constable or (as the case may be) the local authority concerned.

(8) Any such notice of cancellation shall have effect as soon as it is served by a constable or (as the case may be) the authority concerned on at least one person on whom the closure notice was served.

(9) The constable or (as the case may be) the local authority concerned shall also serve the notice of cancellation on any other person on whom the closure notice was served.

(10) For the purposes of subsections (3) and (5) a person having control of, or responsibility for, the activities carried on at the premises includes a person who—

(a) derives or seeks to derive profit from the carrying on of the activities;

(b) manages the activities;

(c) employs any person to manage the activities; or

(d) is involved in the conduct of the activities.

[Criminal Justice and Police Act 2001, s 19 as amended by the Licensing Act 2003, Sch 6.]

---

1. Sections 19–28 of the Criminal Justice and Police Act 2001 provide the police and local authorities with power to serve closure notices, and subsequently to seek closure orders, in respect of unlicensed premises that are used for the sale of alcohol. The provisions are modelled on the scheme contained in the City of Westminster Act 1996 (not reproduced in this work), which allows the police and local authorities to close down unlicensed sex establishments.

1–4120   20. Applications for closure orders.   (1) Where a closure notice has been served under section 19(3), a constable or (as the case may be) the local authority concerned may make a complaint to a justice of the peace for an order under section 21 (a "closure order").

(2) A complaint under subsection (1) shall be made not less than seven days, and not more than six months, after the service of the closure notice under section 19(3).

(3) No complaint shall be made under subsection (1) if the constable or (as the case may be) the local authority is satisfied that—

(a) the use of the premises for the unauthorised sale of alcohol for consumption on, or in the vicinity of, the premises has ceased; and

(b) there is no reasonable likelihood that the premises will be so used in the future.

(4) Where a complaint has been made to a justice of the peace under subsection (1), the justice may issue a summons to answer to the complaint.

(5) The summons shall be directed to—

(a) the person on whom the closure notice was served under section 19(3); and

(b) any other person on whom the closure notice was served under section 19(5)(a).

(6) Where a summons is served in accordance with subsections (4) and (5), a notice stating the date, time and place at which the complaint will be heard shall be served on all persons on whom the closure notice was served under section 19(4) and (5)(b).

(7) The procedure on a complaint for a closure order shall (except as otherwise provided) be in accordance with the Magistrates' Courts Act 1980 (c 43).

[Criminal Justice and Police Act 2001, s 20 as amended by the Licensing Act 2003, Sch 6 and SI 2005/886.]

1–4121   21. Closure orders.   (1) On hearing a complaint made under section 20(1), the court may make such order as it considers appropriate if it is satisfied that—

(a) the closure notice was served under section 19(3); and

(b) the premises continue to be used for the unauthorised sale of alcohol for consumption on, or in the vicinity of, the premises or there is a reasonable likelihood that the premises will be so used in the future.

(2) An order under this section may, in particular, require—

(a) the premises in respect of which the closure notice was served to be closed immediately to the public and to remain closed until a constable or (as the case may be) the local authority concerned makes a certificate under section 22(1);

(b) the use of the premises for the unauthorised sale of alcohol for consumption on, or in the vicinity of, the premises to be discontinued immediately;

(c) any defendant to pay into court such sum as the court determines and that the sum will not be released by the court to that person until the other requirements of the order are met.

(3) An order of the kind mentioned in subsection (2)(a) may, in particular, include such conditions as the court considers appropriate relating to—

(a) the admission of persons onto the premises;

(b) the access by persons to another part of any building or other structure of which the premises form part.

(4) The complainant shall, as soon as practicable after the making of an order under this section, give notice of the order by fixing a copy of it in a conspicuous position on the premises in respect of which it was made.

(5) A sum which has been ordered to be paid into court under this section shall be paid to the designated officer for the court.

[Criminal Justice and Police Act 2001, s 21 as amended by the Courts Act 2003, Sch 8 and the Licensing Act 2003, Sch 6.]

1–4122   22. Termination of closure orders by constable or local authority.   (1) Where a closure order has been made, a constable or (as the case may be) the local authority concerned may make a certificate to the effect that the constable or (as the case may be) the authority is satisfied that the need for the order has ceased.

(2) Where such a certificate has been made, the closure order shall cease to have effect.

(3) Where a closure order containing provision of the kind mentioned in section 21(2)(c) ceases to have effect by virtue of the making of a certificate under subsection (1), any sum paid into court by a defendant under the closure order shall be released by the court.

(4) Subject to this, a closure order may include such provision as the court considers appropriate for dealing with any consequences which would arise if the order were to cease to have effect by virtue of the making of a certificate under subsection (1).

(5) The constable or (as the case may be) the local authority concerned shall, as soon as practicable after the making of a certificate under subsection (1)—

(a) serve a copy of it on the person against whom the closure order has been made and the justices' chief executive for the court which made the order; and

(b) fix a copy of it in a conspicuous position on the premises in respect of which the order was made.

(6) The constable or (as the case may be) the local authority concerned shall also serve a copy of the certificate on any person who requests such a copy.

[Criminal Justice and Police Act 2001, s 22.]

1–4123   23. Discharge of closure orders by the court.   (1) Where a closure order has been made—

(a) any person on whom the closure notice concerned was served under section 19; or

(b) any person who has an interest in the premises in respect of which the closure order was made but on whom no closure notice was served,

may make a complaint to a justice of the peace acting for the petty sessions area in which the premises are situated for an order that the closure order be discharged.

(2) The court may not make an order under subsection (1) unless it is satisfied that the need for the closure order has ceased.

(3) Where a complaint has been made to a justice of the peace under subsection (1), the justice may issue a summons directed to such constable as he considers appropriate or (as the case may be) the local authority concerned requiring that person to appear before the magistrates' court to answer to the complaint.

(4) Where a summons is served in accordance with subsection (3), a notice stating the date, time and place at which the complaint will be heard shall be served on all persons on whom the closure notice concerned was served under section 19 (other than the complainant).

(5) The procedure on a complaint for an order under this section shall (except as otherwise provided) be in accordance with the Magistrates' Courts Act 1980 (c 43).

[Criminal Justice and Police Act 2001, s 23.]

1–4124   24. Appeals.   (1) An appeal against a closure order, an order under section 23(1) or a decision not to make an order under section 23(1) may be brought to the Crown Court at any time before the end of the period of 21 days beginning with the day on which the order or (as the case may be) the decision was made.

(2) An appeal under this section against a closure order may be brought by—

(a) any person on whom the closure notice concerned was served under section 19; or

(b) any person who has an interest in the premises in respect of which the closure order was made but on whom no closure notice was so served.

(3) On an appeal under this section the Crown Court may make such order as it considers appropriate.

[Criminal Justice and Police Act 2001, s 24.]

1–4125   25. Enforcement of closure orders.   (1) Where a closure order has been made, a constable or an authorised person may (if necessary using reasonable force)—

(a)   at any reasonable time enter the premises concerned; and

(b)   having so entered the premises, do anything reasonably necessary for the purpose of securing compliance with the order.

(2)   A constable or an authorised person seeking to enter any premises in exercise of his powers under subsection (1) shall, if required by or on behalf of the owner or occupier or person in charge of the premises, produce evidence of his identity, and of his authority, before entering the premises.

(3)   Any person who intentionally obstructs a constable or an authorised person in the exercise of his powers under this section shall be guilty of an offence and shall be liable on summary conviction—

(a)   where the offence was committed in respect of a constable, to imprisonment for a term not exceeding <u>one month</u>★ or to a fine not exceeding level 5 on the standard scale or to both;

(b)   where the offence was committed in respect of an authorised person, to a fine not exceeding level 5 on the standard scale.

(4)   A person who, without reasonable excuse, permits premises to be open in contravention of a closure order shall be guilty of an offence and shall be liable on summary conviction to imprisonment for a term not exceeding <u>three months</u>★ or to a fine not exceeding £20,000 or to both.

(5)   A person who, without reasonable excuse, otherwise fails to comply with, or does an act in contravention of, a closure order shall be guilty of an offence and shall be liable on summary conviction to imprisonment for a term not exceeding three months or to a fine not exceeding level 5 on the standard scale or to both.

(6)   In this section "an authorised person" means a person authorised for the purposes of this section by a local authority in respect of premises situated in the area of the authority.
[Criminal Justice and Police Act 2001, s 25.]

★Prospectively increased to 51 weeks by the Criminal Justice Act 2003, ss 280 and 336, respectively.

1–4126   26. Offences by body corporate.   (1) Where an offence under section 25 committed by a body corporate is proved to have been committed with the consent or connivance of, or to be attributable to any neglect on the part of, a director, manager, secretary or other similar officer of the body corporate, he as well as the body corporate commits the offence and shall be liable to be proceeded against and punished accordingly.

(2)   Where the affairs of a body corporate are managed by its members, subsection (1) applies in relation to the acts and defaults of a member in connection with his functions of management as if he were a director of the body corporate.
[Criminal Justice and Police Act 2001, s 26.]

1–4127   27. Service of notices.   (1) Any document required or authorised by virtue of sections 19 to 26 to be served on any person may be served—

(a)   by delivering it to him or by leaving it at his proper address or by sending it by post to him at that address;

(b)   if the person is a body corporate other than a limited liability partnership, by serving it in accordance with paragraph (a) on the secretary of the body;

(c)   if the person is a limited liability partnership, by serving it in accordance with paragraph (a) on a member of the partnership; or

(d)   if the person is a partnership, by serving it in accordance with paragraph (a) on a partner or a person having the control or management of the partnership business.

(2)   For the purposes of this section and section 7 of the Interpretation Act 1978 (c 30) (service of documents by post) in its application to this section, the proper address of any person on whom a document is to be served shall be his last known address, except that—

(a)   in the case of service on a body corporate (other than a limited liability partnership) or its secretary, it shall be the address of the registered or principal office of the body;

(b)   in the case of service on a limited liability partnership or a member of the partnership, it shall be the address of the registered or principal office of the partnership;

(c)   in the case of service on a partnership or a partner or a person having the control or management of a partnership business, it shall be the address of the principal office of the partnership.

(3)   For the purposes of subsection (2) the principal office of a company constituted under the law of a country or territory outside the United Kingdom or of a partnership carrying on business outside the United Kingdom is its principal office within the United Kingdom.

(4)   Subsection (5) applies if a person to be served under sections 19 to 26 with any document by another has specified to that other an address within the United Kingdom other than his proper address (as determined under subsection (2)) as the one at which he or someone on his behalf will accept documents of the same description as that document.

(5)   In relation to that document, that address shall be treated as his proper address for the purposes of this section and section 7 of the Interpretation Act 1978 (c 30) in its application to this section, instead of that determined under subsection (2).

(6)   Where the address of the person on whom a document is to be served under sections 19 to 26

cannot be ascertained after reasonable inquiry, the document shall be taken to be duly served if a copy of it is fixed in a conspicuous position on the premises which are alleged to have been used for the unauthorised sale of alcohol.

(7) Where the name of the person on whom a document is to be served under sections 19 to 26 cannot be ascertained after reasonable inquiry, the document shall be taken to be duly served if it is served in accordance with this section using an appropriate description for the person concerned.

(8) This section does not apply to any document if rules of court make provision about its service.

[Criminal Justice and Police Act 2001, s 27 as amended by the Licensing Act 2003, Sch 6.]

1–4128   28. Sections 19 to 27: interpretation.   (1) In sections 19 to 27 and this section—*

"alcohol" has the same meaning as in the Licensing Act 2003;

"closure notice" means a notice under section 19(1) or (2);

"closure order" means an order under section 21;

"notice" means notice in writing;

"premises" includes any land or other place (whether enclosed or otherwise);

"sale" includes exposure for sale; and

"unauthorised sale", in relation to any alcohol, means any supply of the alcohol (within the meaning of section 14 of the Licensing Act 2003) which—

(a) is a licensable activity within the meaning of that Act, but

(b) is made otherwise than under and in accordance with an authorisation (within the meaning of section 136 of that Act).

(2) In sections 19 to 27 "local authority" means—

(a) in relation to England—

(i)   a county council;

(ii) a district council;

(iii) a London borough council;

(iv) the Common Council of the City of London in its capacity as a local authority;

(v)   the Council of the Isles of Scilly;

(b) in relation to Wales, a county council or a county borough council.

(3) References in sections 19 to 27 to a person who has an interest in the premises are references to any person who is the owner, leaseholder or occupier of the premises.

[Criminal Justice and Police Act 2001, s 28 as amended by the Licensing Act 2003, Sch 6.]

CHAPTER 3[1]
OTHER PROVISIONS FOR COMBATTING CRIME AND DISORDER
Travel restrictions on drug trafficking offenders

1–4129   33. Power to make travel restriction orders[2].   (1) This section applies where—

(a) a person ("the offender") has been convicted by any court of a post-commencement drug trafficking offence;

(b) the court has determined that it would be appropriate to impose a sentence of imprisonment for that offence; and

(c) the term of imprisonment which the court considers appropriate is a term of four years or more.

(2) It shall be the duty of the court, on sentencing the offender—

(a) to consider whether it would be appropriate for the sentence for the offence to include the making of a travel restriction order in relation to the offender;

(b) if the court determines that it is so appropriate, to make such travel restriction order in relation to the offender as the court thinks suitable in all the circumstances (including any other convictions of the offender for post-commencement drug trafficking offences in respect of which the court is also passing sentence); and

(c) if the court determines that it is not so appropriate, to state its reasons for not making a travel restriction order.

(3) A travel restriction order is an order that prohibits the offender from leaving the United Kingdom at any time in the period which—

(a) begins with the offender's release from custody; and

(b) continues after that time for such period of not less than two years as may be specified in the order.

(4) A travel restriction order may contain a direction to the offender to deliver up, or cause to be delivered up, to the court any UK passport held by him; and where such a direction is given, the court shall send any passport delivered up in pursuance of the direction to the Secretary of State at such address as the Secretary of State may determine.*

(5) Where the offender's passport is held by the Secretary of State by reason of the making of any direction contained in a travel restriction order, the Secretary of State (without prejudice to any other power or duty of his to retain the passport)—

(a) may retain it for so long as the prohibition imposed by the order applies to the offender, and is not for the time being suspended; and

(b) shall not return the passport after the prohibition has ceased to apply, or when it is suspended, except where the passport has not expired and an application for its return is made to him by the offender.*

(6) In this section "post-commencement"—

(a) except in relation to an offence that is a drug trafficking offence by virtue of an order under section 34(1)(c), means committed after the coming into force of this section; and

(b) in relation to an offence that is a drug trafficking offence by virtue of such an order, means committed after the coming into force of that order.

(7) References in this section to the offender's release from custody are references to his first release from custody after the imposition of the travel restriction order which is neither—

(a) a release on bail; nor

(b) a temporary release for a fixed period.

(8) In this section "UK passport" means a United Kingdom passport within the meaning of the Immigration Act 1971 (c 77).*

[Criminal Justice and Police Act 2001, s 33.]

---

*Amended by the Identity Cards Act 2006, s 39 from a date to be appointed.

1. Chapter 3 contains ss 33–49.

2. This section imposes a duty on the court, where a person has been convicted of a drug trafficking offence and a term of imprisonment of at least four years is appropriate, to consider whether it would also be appropriate to make a travel restriction order in relation to the offender. Such an order prohibits the offender from leaving the UK at any time while it is in force. The order begins on the offender's release from custody and continues for such period of not less than two years as may be specified. The order may contain a direction requiring the offender to deliver up his passport. In *R v Mee* [2004] EWCA Crim 629, [2004] 2 Cr App R (S) 434 the Court of Appeal gave general guidance on the making of travel restriction orders. Such an order is not intended to be a substitute for the appropriate term of imprisonment for the offence. Its purpose is to prevent or reduce the risk of offending following release. It is not confined to importation cases, though such cases are the most apt for its use. The fact that an offender has imported drugs once may not give rise to a risk that he will do so again following his release. Large, sophisticated importations from a country well known to be a source of supply obviously gives rise to different considerations. If the need for an order arises, proportionality and fairness requires a balanced approach to the length of the order. The weight to be given to personal factors, such as future employment and personal life, is affected by s 35. The length of an order should be measured to the defendant by reference to his age., previous convictions, the risk of re-offending, family contacts and employment considerations. The length should be such as that which is required to protect the public in the light of the risk presented by the facts. The section does not contemplate an order that applies only to certain parts of the world.

1–4130 **34. Meaning of 'drug trafficking offence'.** (1) In section 33 "drug trafficking offence" means any of the following offences (including one committed by aiding, abetting, counselling or procuring)—

(a) an offence under section 4(2) or (3) of the Misuse of Drugs Act 1971 (c 38) (production and supply of controlled drugs);

(b) an offence under section 20 of that Act (assisting in or inducing commission outside United Kingdom of an offence punishable under a corresponding law);

(c) any such other offence under that Act as may be designated by order made by the Secretary of State;

(d) an offence under—

(i) section 50(2) or (3) of the Customs and Excise Management Act 1979 (c 2) (improper importation),

(ii) section 68(2) of that Act (exportation), or

(iii) section 170 of that Act (fraudulent evasion),

in connection with a prohibition or restriction on importation or exportation having effect by virtue of section 3 of the Misuse of Drugs Act 1971 (c 38);

(e) an offence under section 1 of the Criminal Law Act 1977 (c 45) or Article 9 of the Criminal Attempts and Conspiracy (Northern Ireland) Order 1983 (SI 1983/1120 (NI 13)), or in Scotland at common law, of conspiracy to commit any of the offences in paragraphs (a) to (d) above;

(f) an offence under section 1 of the Criminal Attempts Act 1981 (c 47) or Article 3 of the Criminal Attempts and Conspiracy (Northern Ireland) Order 1983, or in Scotland at common law, of attempting to commit any of those offences; and

(g) an offence under section 19 of the Misuse of Drugs Act 1971 (c 38) or at common law of inciting another person to commit any of those offences.

(2) The power to make an order under subsection (1)(c) shall be exercisable by statutory instrument; and no such order shall be made unless a draft of it has been laid before Parliament and approved by a resolution of each House.

(3) An order under subsection (1)(c) may provide, in relation to any offence designated by such an order, that it is to be treated as so designated only—

(a) for such purposes, and

(b) in cases where it was committed in such manner or in such circumstances,

as may be described in the order.
[Criminal Justice and Police Act 2001, s 34.]

1–4131   35. Revocation and suspension of a travel restriction order. (1) Subject to the following provisions of this section, the court by which a travel restriction order has been made in relation to any person under section 33 may—

(a) on an application made by that person at any time which is—

    (i) after the end of the minimum period, and

    (ii) is not within three months after the making of any previous application for the revocation of the prohibition,

revoke the prohibition imposed by the order with effect from such date as the court may determine; or

(b) on an application made by that person at any time after the making of the order, suspend the prohibition imposed by the order for such period as the court may determine.

(2) A court to which an application for the revocation of the prohibition imposed on any person by a travel restriction order is made shall not revoke that prohibition unless it considers that it is appropriate to do so in all the circumstances of the case and having regard, in particular, to—

(a) that person's character;

(b) his conduct since the making of the order; and

(c) the offences of which he was convicted on the occasion on which the order was made.

(3) A court shall not suspend the prohibition imposed on any person by a travel restriction order for any period unless it is satisfied that there are exceptional circumstances, in that person's case, that justify the suspension on compassionate grounds of that prohibition for that period.

(4) In making any determination on an application for the suspension of the prohibition imposed on any person by a travel restriction order, a court (in addition to considering the matters mentioned in subsection (3)) shall have regard to—

(a) that person's character;

(b) his conduct since the making of the order;

(c) the offences of which he was convicted on the occasion on which the order was made; and

(d) any other circumstances of the case that the court considers relevant.

(5) Where the prohibition imposed on any person by a travel restriction order is suspended, it shall be the duty of that person—

(a) to be in the United Kingdom when the period of the suspension ends; and

(b) if the order contains a direction under section 33(4), to surrender, before the end of that period, any passport returned or issued to that person, in respect of the suspension, by the Secretary of State;

and a passport that is required to be surrendered under paragraph (b) shall be surrendered to the Secretary of State in such manner or by being sent to such address as the Secretary of State may direct at the time when he returns or issues it.*

(6) Where the prohibition imposed on any person by a travel restriction order is suspended for any period under this section, the end of the period of the prohibition imposed by the order shall be treated (except for the purposes of subsection (7)) as postponed (or, if there has been one or more previous suspensions, further postponed) by the length of the period of suspension.

(7) In this section "the minimum period"—

(a) in the case of a travel restriction order imposing a prohibition for a period of four years or less, means the period of two years beginning at the time when the period of the prohibition began;

(b) in the case of a travel restriction order imposing a prohibition of more than four years but less than ten years, means the period of four years beginning at that time; and

(c) in any other case, means the period of five years beginning at that time.

[Criminal Justice and Police Act 2001, s 35.]

---

*Amended by the Identity Cards Act 2006, s 39 from a date to be appointed.

1–4132   36. Offences of contravening orders. (1) A person who leaves the United Kingdom at a time when he is prohibited from leaving it by a travel restriction order is guilty of an offence and liable[1]—

(a) on summary conviction to imprisonment for a term not exceeding six months or to a fine not exceeding the statutory maximum, or to both;

(b) on conviction on indictment, to imprisonment for a term not exceeding five years or to a fine, or to both.

(2) A person who is not in the United Kingdom at the end of a period during which a prohibition imposed on him by a travel restriction order has been suspended shall be guilty of an offence and liable—

(a) on summary conviction, to imprisonment for a term not exceeding six months or to a fine not exceeding the statutory maximum, or to both;

(b)   on conviction on indictment, to imprisonment for a term not exceeding five years or to a fine, or to both.

(3)   A person who fails to comply with—

(a)   a direction contained in a travel restriction order to deliver up a passport to a court, or to cause such a passport to be delivered up, or

(b)   any duty imposed on him by section 35(5)(b) to surrender a passport to the Secretary of State,

shall be guilty of an offence and liable, on summary conviction, to imprisonment for a term not exceeding six months or to a fine not exceeding level 5 on the standard scale, or to both.★

(4)   This section has effect subject to section 37(3).

[Criminal Justice and Police Act 2001, s 36.]

★Amended by the Identity Cards Act 2006, s 39 from a date to be appointed.

1.   For procedure in respect of this offence, which is triable either way, see the Magistrates' Courts Act 1980, ss 17A–21, in PART 1: MAGISTRATES' COURTS, PROCEDURE, ante.

1–4133   **37.   Savings for powers to remove a person from the United Kingdom.**   (1)   A travel restriction order made in relation to any person shall not prevent the exercise in relation to that person of any prescribed removal power.

(2)   A travel restriction order made in relation to any person shall remain in force, notwithstanding the exercise of any prescribed removal power in relation to that person, except in so far as either—

(a)   the Secretary of State by order otherwise provides; or

(b)   the travel restriction order is suspended or revoked under section 35.

(3)   No person shall be guilty of an offence under section 36 in respect of any act or omission required of him by an obligation imposed in the exercise of a prescribed removal power.

(4)   In this section "a prescribed removal power" means any such power conferred by or under any enactment as—

(a)   consists in a power to order or direct the removal of a person from the United Kingdom; and

(b)   is designated for the purposes of this section by an order[1] made by the Secretary of State.

(5)   An order under subsection (2)(a) or (4) shall be made by statutory instrument subject to annulment in pursuance of a resolution of either House of Parliament.

(6)   An order under subsection (2)(a)—

(a)   may make different provision for different cases; and

(b)   may contain such incidental, supplemental, consequential and transitional provision as the Secretary of State thinks fit.

(7)   References in this section to a person's removal from the United Kingdom include references to his deportation, extradition, repatriation, delivery up or other transfer to a place outside the United Kingdom.

[Criminal Justice and Police Act 2001, s 37.]

---

1.   The Sch to the Travel Restriction Order (Prescribed Removal Powers) Order 2002, SI 2002/313 prescribes the following removal powers:

     Colonial Prisoners Removal Act 1884 (c 31) – Section 3(1).
     United Nations Act 1946 (c 45) – Powers to order or direct the removal of a person from the United Kingdom conferred by Orders in Council made in exercise of the power contained in section 1(1).
     Backing of Warrants (Republic of Ireland) Act 1965 (c 45) – Section 2(1).
     Immigration Act 1971 (c 77) – Section 5(1); Schedule 2, paragraphs 8, 9, 10, 12, 13 and 14; Schedule 3, paragraph 1.
     Mental Health Act 1983 (c 20) – Section 86(2)(a) and (b).
     Repatriation of Prisoners Act 1984 (c 47) – Sections 1(1), 2 and 4(1).
     Extradition Act 1989 (c 33) – Section 12(1) and Schedule 1, paragraph 8(2).
     Criminal Justice (International Co-operation) Act 1990 (c 5) – Section 5.
     Immigration and Asylum Act 1999 (c 33) – Section 10.
     Immigration (European Economic Area) Regulations 2000 (2000/2326) – Regulation 21(3).
     International Criminal Court Act 2001 (c 17) – Sections 5, 7, 15, 21, 32 and 43.

Use of controlled drugs

1–4134   **38.**   *Permitting use of controlled drugs on premises.*   **Repealed.**

Intimidating, harming and threatening witnesses etc

1–4135   **39.   Intimidation of witnesses[1].**   (1)   A person commits an offence if—

(a)   he does an act which intimidates, and is intended to intimidate, another person ("the victim");

(b)   he does the act—

    (i)   knowing or believing that the victim is or may be a witness in any relevant proceedings[2]; and

    (ii)   intending, by his act, to cause the course of justice to be obstructed, perverted or interfered with;

and

(c)   the act is done after the commencement of those proceedings.

(2) For the purposes of subsection (1) it is immaterial—

(a)   whether or not the act that is done is done in the presence of the victim;
(b)   whether that act is done to the victim himself or to another person; and
(c)   whether or not the intention to cause the course of justice to be obstructed, perverted or interfered with is the predominating intention of the person doing the act in question.

(3) If, in proceedings against a person for an offence under this section, it is proved—

(a)   that he did any act that intimidated, and was intended to intimidate, another person, and
(b)   that he did that act knowing or believing that that other person was or might be a witness in any relevant proceedings that had already commenced,

he shall be presumed, unless the contrary is shown, to have done the act with the intention of causing the course of justice to be obstructed, perverted or interfered with.

(4) A person guilty of an offence under this section shall be liable[3]—

(a)   on conviction on indictment, to imprisonment for a term not exceeding five years or to a fine, or to both;
(b)   on summary conviction, to imprisonment for a term not exceeding six months or to a fine not exceeding the statutory maximum, or to both.

(5) References in this section to a witness, in relation to any proceedings, include references to a person who provides, or is able to provide, any information or any document or other thing which might be used as evidence in those proceedings or which (whether or not admissible as evidence in those proceedings)—

(a)   might tend to confirm evidence which will be or might be admitted in those proceedings;
(b)   might be referred to in evidence given in those proceedings by another witness; or
(c)   might be used as the basis for any cross examination in the course of those proceedings.

(6) References in this section to doing an act include references to issuing any threat (whether against a person or his finances or property or otherwise), or making any other statement.

(7) This section is in addition to, and not in derogation of, any offence subsisting at common law.
[Criminal Justice and Police Act 2001, s 39.]

---

1. Sections 39–41 create 2 new offences intended to increase protection for witnesses in all proceedings other than proceedings for a criminal offence, which are covered by the Criminal Justice and Public Order Act 1994, s 51 (see this PART, ante).
2. Defined in s 41, post.
3. For procedure in respect of this offence, which is triable either way, see the Magistrates' Courts Act 1980, ss 17A–21, in PART 1: MAGISTRATES' COURTS, PROCEDURE, ante.

1–4136   40. Harming witnesses etc.   (1) A person commits an offence if, in circumstances falling within subsection (2)—

(a)   he does an act which harms, and is intended to harm, another person; or
(b)   intending to cause another person to fear harm, he threatens to do an act which would harm that other person.

(2) The circumstances fall within this subsection if—

(a)   the person doing or threatening to do the act does so knowing or believing that some person (whether or not the person harmed or threatened or the person against whom harm is threatened) has been a witness in relevant proceedings; and
(b)   he does or threatens to do that act because of that knowledge or belief.

(3) If, in proceedings against a person for an offence under this section, it is proved that, within the relevant period—

(a)   he did an act which harmed, and was intended to harm, another person, or
(b)   intending to cause another person to fear harm, he threatened to do an act which would harm that other person,

and that he did the act, or (as the case may be) threatened to do the act, with the knowledge or belief required by paragraph (a) of subsection (2), he shall be presumed, unless the contrary is shown, to have done the act, or (as the case may be) threatened to do the act, because of that knowledge or belief.

(4) For the purposes of this section it is immaterial—

(a)   whether or not the act that is done or threatened, or the threat that is made, is or would be done or is made in the presence of the person who is or would be harmed or of the person who is threatened;
(b)   whether or not the motive mentioned in subsection (2)(b) is the predominating motive for the act or threat; and
(c)   whether the harm that is done or threatened is physical or financial or is harm to a person or to his property.

(5) A person guilty of an offence under this section shall be liable[1]—

(a) on conviction on indictment, to imprisonment for a term not exceeding five years or to a fine, or to both;

(b) on summary conviction, to imprisonment for a term not exceeding six months or to a fine not exceeding the statutory maximum, or to both.

(6) In this section "the relevant period", in relation to an act done, or threat made, with the knowledge or belief that a person has been a witness in any relevant proceedings, means the period that begins with the commencement of those proceedings and ends one year after they are finally concluded.

(7) References in this section to a witness, in relation to any proceedings, include references to a person who has provided any information or any document or other thing which was or might have been used as evidence in those proceedings or which (whether or not it was admissible as evidence in those proceedings)—

(a) tended to confirm or might have tended to confirm any evidence which was or could have been given in those proceedings;

(b) was or might have been referred to in evidence given in those proceedings by another witness; or

(c) was or might have been used as the basis for any cross examination in the course of those proceedings.

(8) This section is in addition to, and not in derogation of, any offence subsisting at common law.
[Criminal Justice and Police Act 2001, s 40.]

---

1. For procedure in respect of this offence, which is triable either way, see the Magistrates' Courts Act 1980, ss 17A–21, in Part I: Magistrates' Courts, Procedure, ante.

1–4137 **41. Relevant proceedings.** (1) A reference in section 39 or 40 to relevant proceedings is a reference to any proceedings in or before the Court of Appeal, the High Court, the Crown Court or any county court or magistrates' court which—

(a) are not proceedings for an offence; and

(b) were commenced after the coming into force of that section.

(2) For the purposes of any reference in section 39 or 40 or this section to the commencement of any proceedings relevant proceedings are commenced (subject to subsection (5)) at the earliest time at which one of the following occurs—

(a) an information is laid or application, claim form, complaint, petition, summons or other process made or issued for the purpose of commencing the proceedings;

(b) any other step is taken by means of which the subject matter of the proceedings is brought for the first time (whether as part of the proceedings or in anticipation of them) before the court.

(3) For the purposes of any reference in section 39 or 40 to the time when any proceedings are finally concluded, relevant proceedings are finally concluded (subject to subsection (4))—

(a) if proceedings for an appeal against, or an application for a review of, those proceedings or of any decision taken in those proceedings are brought or is made, at the time when proceedings on that appeal or application are finally concluded;

(b) if the proceedings are withdrawn or discontinued, at the time when they are withdrawn or discontinued; and

(c) in any other case, when the court in or before which the proceedings are brought finally disposes of all the matters arising in those proceedings.

(4) Relevant proceedings shall not be taken to be finally concluded by virtue of subsection (3)(a) where—

(a) the matters to which the appeal or application relate are such that the proceedings in respect of which it is brought or made continue or resume after the making of any determination on that appeal or application; or

(b) a determination made on that appeal or application requires those proceedings to continue or to be resumed.

(5) Where, after having appeared to be finally concluded, any relevant proceedings continue by reason of—

(a) the giving of permission to bring an appeal after a fixed time for appealing has expired,

(b) the lifting of any stay in the proceedings,

(c) the setting aside, without an appeal, of any judgment or order, or

(d) the revival of any discontinued proceedings,

sections 39 and 40 and this section shall have effect as if the proceedings had concluded when they appeared to, but as if the giving of permission, the lifting of the stay, the setting aside of the judgment or order or, as the case may be, the revival of the discontinued proceedings were the commencement of new relevant proceedings
[Criminal Justice and Police Act 2001, s 41.]

Further provisions about intimidation etc

1–4138 **42. Police direction stopping the harassment etc of a person in his home.** (1) Subject to the following provisions of this section, a constable who is at the scene may give a direction under this section to any person if—

(a) that person is present outside or in the vicinity of any premises that are used by any individual ("the resident") as his dwelling[1];

(b) that constable believes, on reasonable grounds, that that person is present there for the purpose (by his presence or otherwise) of representing to the resident or another individual (whether or not one who uses the premises as his dwelling), or of persuading the resident or such another individual—

(i) that he should not do something that he is entitled or required to do; or
(ii) that he should do something that he is not under any obligation to do;

and

(c) that constable also believes, on reasonable grounds, that the presence of that person (either alone or together with that of any other persons who are also present)—

(i) amounts to, or is likely to result in, the harassment of the resident; or
(ii) is likely to cause alarm or distress to the resident.

(2) A direction under this section is a direction requiring the person to whom it is given to do all such things as the constable giving it may specify as the things he considers necessary to prevent one or both of the following—

(a) the harassment of the resident; or
(b) the causing of any alarm or distress to the resident.

(3) A direction under this section may be given orally; and where a constable is entitled to give a direction under this section to each of several persons outside, or in the vicinity of, any premises, he may give that direction to those persons by notifying them of his requirements either individually or all together.

(4) The requirements that may be imposed by a direction under this section include—

(a) a requirement to leave the vicinity of the premises in question, and
(b) a requirement to leave that vicinity and not to return to it within such period as the constable may specify, not being longer than 3 months;

and (in either case) the requirement to leave the vicinity may be to do so immediately or after a specified period of time.

(5) A direction under this section may make exceptions to any requirement imposed by the direction, and may make any such exception subject to such conditions as the constable giving the direction thinks fit; and those conditions may include—

(a) conditions as to the distance from the premises in question at which, or otherwise as to the location where, persons who do not leave their vicinity must remain; and
(b) conditions as to the number or identity of the persons who are authorised by the exception to remain in the vicinity of those premises.

(6) The power of a constable to give a direction under this section shall not include—

(a) any power to give a direction at any time when there is a more senior-ranking police officer at the scene; or
(b) any power to direct a person to refrain from conduct that is lawful under section 220 of the Trade Union and Labour Relations (Consolidation) Act 1992 (c 52) (right peacefully to picket a work place);

but it shall include power to vary or withdraw a direction previously given under this section.

(7) Any person who knowingly fails to comply with a requirement in a direction given to him under this section (other than a requirement under subsection (4)(b)) shall be guilty of an offence and liable, on summary conviction, to imprisonment for a term not exceeding three months or to a fine not exceeding level 4 on the standard scale, or to both.

(7A) Any person to whom a constable has given a direction including a requirement under subsection (4)(b) commits an offence if he—

(a) returns to the vicinity of the premises in question within the period specified in the direction beginning with the date on which the direction is given; and
(b) does so for the purpose described in subsection (1)(b).

(7B) A person guilty of an offence under subsection (7A) shall be liable, on summary conviction, to imprisonment for a term not exceeding 51 weeks or to a fine not exceeding level 4 on the standard scale, or to both.

(7C) In relation to an offence committed before the commencement of section 281(5) of the Criminal Justice Act 2003 (alteration of penalties for summary offences), the reference in subsection (7B) to 51 weeks is to be read as a reference to 6 months.

(8) *Repealed.*

(9) In this section "dwelling" has the same meaning as in Part 1 of the Public Order Act 1986 (c 64).

[Criminal Justice and Police Act 2001, s 42 as amended by the Serious Organised Crime and Police Act 2005, s 127.]

---

1. Defined in s 42(9).

1–4138A   **42A. Offence of harassment etc of a person in his home.**   (1) A person commits an offence if—

   (a)   that person is present outside or in the vicinity of any premises that are used by any individual ("the resident") as his dwelling;

   (b)   that person is present there for the purpose (by his presence or otherwise) of representing to the resident or another individual (whether or not one who uses the premises as his dwelling), or of persuading the resident or such another individual—

     (i)   that he should not do something that he is entitled or required to do; or

     (ii)   that he should do something that he is not under any obligation to do;

   (c)   that person—

     (i)   intends his presence to amount to the harassment of, or to cause alarm or distress to, the resident; or

     (ii)   knows or ought to know that his presence is likely to result in the harassment of, or to cause alarm or distress to, the resident; and

   (d)   the presence of that person—

     (i)   amounts to the harassment of, or causes alarm or distress to, any person falling within subsection (2); or

     (ii)   is likely to result in the harassment of, or to cause alarm or distress to, any such person.

   (2) A person falls within this subsection if he is—

   (a)   the resident,

   (b)   a person in the resident's dwelling, or

   (c)   a person in another dwelling in the vicinity of the resident's dwelling.

   (3) The references in subsection (1)(c) and (d) to a person's presence are references to his presence either alone or together with that of any other persons who are also present.

   (4) For the purposes of this section a person (A) ought to know that his presence is likely to result in the harassment of, or to cause alarm or distress to, a resident if a reasonable person in possession of the same information would think that A's presence was likely to have that effect.

   (5) A person guilty of an offence under this section shall be liable, on summary conviction, to imprisonment for a term not exceeding 51 weeks or to a fine not exceeding level 4 on the standard scale, or to both.

   (6) In relation to an offence committed before the commencement of section 281(5) of the Criminal Justice Act 2003 (alteration of penalties for summary offences), the reference in subsection (5) to 51 weeks is to be read as a reference to 6 months.

   (7) In this section "dwelling" has the same meaning as in Part 1 of the Public Order Act 1986.

[Criminal Justice and Police Act 2001, s 42A as inserted by the Serious Organised Crime and Police Act 2005, s 126.]

1–4139   **43.** *Malicious communications*[1]

---

     1. Amends s 1 of the Malicious Communications Act 1988.

1–4140   **44.** *Collective harassment*[1]

---

     1. Amends s 7 of the Protection from Harassment Act 1997.

1–4141   **45.** *Addresses of directors and secretaries of companies*[1]

---

     1. Amends the Companies Act 1985 as to the addresses of directors and secretaries of companies.

Advertisements relating to prostitution

1–4142   **46. Placing of advertisement relating to prostitution.**   (1) A person commits an offence if—

   (a)   he places on, or in the immediate vicinity of, a public telephone an advertisement relating to prostitution, and

   (b)   he does so with the intention that the advertisement should come to the attention of any other person or persons.

   (2) For the purposes of this section, an advertisement is an advertisement relating to prostitution if it—

   (a)   is for the services of a prostitute, whether male or female; or

   (b)   indicates that premises are premises at which such services are offered.

   (3) In any proceedings for an offence under this section, any advertisement which a reasonable person would consider to be an advertisement relating to prostitution shall be presumed to be such an advertisement unless it is shown not to be.

(4) A person guilty of an offence under this section is liable on summary conviction to imprisonment for a term not exceeding six months or to a fine not exceeding level 5 on the standard scale, or both.

(5) In this section—

"public telephone" means—

    (*a*) any telephone which is located in a public place and made available for use by the public, or a section of the public, and

    (*b*) where such a telephone is located in or on, or attached to, a kiosk, booth, acoustic hood, shelter or other structure, that structure; and

"public place" means any place to which the public have or are permitted to have access, whether on payment or otherwise, other than—

    (*a*) any place to which children under the age of 16 years are not permitted to have access, whether by law or otherwise, and

    (*b*) any premises which are wholly or mainly used for residential purposes.

(6) *Repealed.*

[Criminal Justice and Police Act 2001, s 46 as amended by the Police Reform Act 2002, Sch 8.]

1–4143 47. Application of section 46 by order to public structures. (1) The Secretary of State may, by order, provide for section 46 to apply in relation to any public structure of a description specified in the order as it applies in relation to a public telephone.

(2) In this section—

"public structure" means any structure that—

    (*a*) is provided as an amenity for the use of the public or a section of the public, and

    (*b*) is located in a public place; and

"public place" and "public telephone" have the same meaning as in section 46.

(3) *Repealed.*

(4) The power to make an order under this section is exercisable by statutory instrument.

(5) No order may be made under this section unless a draft of the order has been laid before, and approved by a resolution of, each House of Parliament.

[Criminal Justice and Police Act 2001, s 47as amended by the Serious Organised Crime and Police Act 2005, s 111.]

1–4144 48–49

These provisions extend local child curfew schemes to older children and make various other amendments to such schemes.

PART 2[1]
POWERS OF SEIZURE
Additional powers of seizure[2]

1–4145 50. Additional powers of seizure from premises. (1) Where—

    (*a*) a person who is lawfully on any premises finds anything on those premises that he has reasonable grounds for believing may be or may contain something for which he is authorised to search on those premises,

    (*b*) a power of seizure to which this section applies or the power conferred by subsection (2) would entitle him, if he found it, to seize[3] whatever it is that he has grounds for believing that thing to be or to contain, and

    (*c*) in all the circumstances, it is not reasonably practicable for it to be determined, on those premises—

        (i) whether what he has found is something that he is entitled to seize, or

        (ii) the extent to which what he has found contains something that he is entitled to seize,

that person's powers of seizure shall include power under this section to seize so much of what he has found as it is necessary to remove from the premises to enable that to be determined.

(2) Where—

    (*a*) a person who is lawfully on any premises finds anything on those premises ("the seizable property") which he would be entitled to seize but for its being comprised in something else that he has (apart from this subsection) no power to seize,

    (*b*) the power under which that person would have power to seize the seizable property is a power to which this section applies, and

    (*c*) in all the circumstances it is not reasonably practicable for the seizable property to be separated, on those premises, from that in which it is comprised,

that person's powers of seizure shall include power under this section to seize both the seizable property and that from which it is not reasonably practicable to separate it.

(3) The factors to be taken into account in considering, for the purposes of this section, whether

or not it is reasonably practicable on particular premises for something to be determined, or for something to be separated from something else, shall be confined to the following—

   (a) how long it would take to carry out the determination or separation on those premises;

   (b) the number of persons that would be required to carry out that determination or separation on those premises within a reasonable period;

   (c) whether the determination or separation would (or would if carried out on those premises) involve damage to property;

   (d) the apparatus or equipment that it would be necessary or appropriate to use for the carrying out of the determination or separation; and

   (e) in the case of separation, whether the separation—

      (i) would be likely, or

      (ii) if carried out by the only means that are reasonably practicable on those premises, would be likely,

to prejudice the use of some or all of the separated seizable property for a purpose for which something seized under the power in question is capable of being used.

(4) Section 19(6) of the 1984 Act and Article 21(6) of the Police and Criminal Evidence (Northern Ireland) Order 1989 (SI 1989/1341 (NI 12)) (powers of seizure not to include power to seize anything that a person has reasonable grounds for believing is legally privileged) shall not apply to the power of seizure conferred by subsection (2).

(5) This section applies to each of the powers of seizure specified in Part 1 of Schedule 1.

(6) Without prejudice to any power conferred by this section to take a copy of any document, nothing in this section, so far as it has effect by reference to the power to take copies of documents under section 28(2)(b) of the Competition Act 1998 (c 41), shall be taken to confer any power to seize any document.

[Criminal Justice and Police Act 2001, s 50.]

---

1. Part 2 contains ss 50–70. At the date of going to press, these provisions are not yet in force.
2. See this PART, para **1–205**, ante, for a summary of these powers.
3. In Part 2 "seize" includes "take a copy of": see s 63(1), post.

1–4146   **51. Additional powers of seizure from the person.**   (1) Where—

   (a) a person carrying out a lawful search of any person finds something that he has reasonable grounds for believing may be or may contain something for which he is authorised to search,

   (b) a power of seizure to which this section applies or the power conferred by subsection (2) would entitle him, if he found it, to seize whatever it is that he has grounds for believing that thing to be or to contain,

   (c) in all the circumstances it is not reasonably practicable for it to be determined, at the time and place of the search—

      (i) whether what he has found is something that he is entitled to seize, or

      (ii) the extent to which what he has found contains something that he is entitled to seize,

that person's powers of seizure shall include power under this section to seize so much of what he has found as it is necessary to remove from that place to enable that to be determined.

(2) Where—

   (a) a person carrying out a lawful search of any person finds something ("the seizable property") which he would be entitled to seize but for its being comprised in something else that he has (apart from this subsection) no power to seize,

   (b) the power under which that person would have power to seize the seizable property is a power to which this section applies, and

   (c) in all the circumstances it is not reasonably practicable for the seizable property to be separated, at the time and place of the search, from that in which it is comprised,

that person's powers of seizure shall include power under this section to seize both the seizable property and that from which it is not reasonably practicable to separate it.

(3) The factors to be taken into account in considering, for the purposes of this section, whether or not it is reasonably practicable, at the time and place of a search, for something to be determined, or for something to be separated from something else, shall be confined to the following—

   (a) how long it would take to carry out the determination or separation at that time and place;

   (b) the number of persons that would be required to carry out that determination or separation at that time and place within a reasonable period;

   (c) whether the determination or separation would (or would if carried out at that time and place) involve damage to property;

   (d) the apparatus or equipment that it would be necessary or appropriate to use for the carrying out of the determination or separation; and

   (e) in the case of separation, whether the separation—

      (i) would be likely, or

      (ii) if carried out by the only means that are reasonably practicable at that time and place, would be likely, to prejudice the use of some or all of the separated seizable property for a purpose for which something seized under the power in question is capable of being used.

(4) Section 19(6) of the 1984 Act and Article 21(6) of the Police and Criminal Evidence (Northern Ireland) Order 1989 (SI 1989/1341 (NI 12)) (powers of seizure not to include power to seize anything a person has reasonable grounds for believing is legally privileged) shall not apply to the power of seizure conferred by subsection (2).

(5) This section applies to each of the powers of seizure specified in Part 2 of Schedule 1.
[Criminal Justice and Police Act 2001, s 51.]

1–4147 52. Notice of exercise of power under s 50 or 51. (1) Where a person exercises a power of seizure conferred by section 50, it shall (subject to subsections (2) and (3)) be his duty, on doing so, to give to the occupier of the premises a written notice—

(a) specifying what has been seized in reliance on the powers conferred by that section;
(b) specifying the grounds on which those powers have been exercised;
(c) setting out the effect of sections 59 to 61;
(d) specifying the name and address of the person to whom notice of an application under section 59(2) to the appropriate judicial authority in respect of any of the seized property must be given; and
(e) specifying the name and address of the person to whom an application may be made to be allowed to attend the initial examination required by any arrangements made for the purposes of section 53(2).

(2) Where it appears to the person exercising on any premises a power of seizure conferred by section 50—

(a) that the occupier of the premises is not present on the premises at the time of the exercise of the power, but
(b) that there is some other person present on the premises who is in charge of the premises,

subsection (1) of this section shall have effect as if it required the notice under that subsection to be given to that other person.

(3) Where it appears to the person exercising a power of seizure conferred by section 50 that there is no one present on the premises to whom he may give a notice for the purposes of complying with subsection (1) of this section, he shall, before leaving the premises, instead of complying with that subsection, attach a notice such as is mentioned in that subsection in a prominent place to the premises.

(4) Where a person exercises a power of seizure conferred by section 51 it shall be his duty, on doing so, to give a written notice to the person from whom the seizure is made—

(a) specifying what has been seized in reliance on the powers conferred by that section;
(b) specifying the grounds on which those powers have been exercised;
(c) setting out the effect of sections 59 to 61;
(d) specifying the name and address of the person to whom notice of any application under section 59(2) to the appropriate judicial authority in respect of any of the seized property must be given; and
(e) specifying the name and address of the person to whom an application may be made to be allowed to attend the initial examination required by any arrangements made for the purposes of section 53(2).

(5) The Secretary of State may by regulations made by statutory instrument, after consultation with the Scottish Ministers, provide that a person who exercises a power of seizure conferred by section 50 shall be required to give a notice such as is mentioned in subsection (1) of this section to any person, or send it to any place, described in the regulations.

(6) Regulations under subsection (5) may make different provision for different cases.

(7) A statutory instrument containing regulations under subsection (5) shall be subject to annulment in pursuance of a resolution of either House of Parliament.
[Criminal Justice and Police Act 2001, s 52.]

Return or retention of seized property

1–4148 53. Examination and return of property seized under s 50 or 51. (1) This section applies where anything has been seized under a power conferred by section 50 or 51.

(2) It shall be the duty of the person for the time being in possession of the seized property in consequence of the exercise of that power to secure that there are arrangements in force which (subject to section 61) ensure—

(a) that an initial examination of the property is carried out as soon as reasonably practicable after the seizure;
(b) that that examination is confined to whatever is necessary for determining how much of the property falls within subsection (3);
(c) that anything which is found, on that examination, not to fall within subsection (3) is separated from the rest of the seized property and is returned as soon as reasonably practicable after the examination of all the seized property has been completed; and

(*d*) that, until the initial examination of all the seized property has been completed and anything which does not fall within subsection (3) has been returned, the seized property is kept separate from anything seized under any other power.

(3) The seized property falls within this subsection to the extent only—

(*a*) that it is property for which the person seizing it had power to search when he made the seizure but is not property the return of which is required by section 54;

(*b*) that it is property the retention of which is authorised by section 56; or

(*c*) that it is something which, in all the circumstances, it will not be reasonably practicable, following the examination, to separate from property falling within paragraph (*a*) or (*b*).

(4) In determining for the purposes of this section the earliest practicable time for the carrying out of an initial examination of the seized property, due regard shall be had to the desirability of allowing the person from whom it was seized, or a person with an interest in that property, an opportunity of being present or (if he chooses) of being represented at the examination.

(5) In this section, references to whether or not it is reasonably practicable to separate part of the seized property from the rest of it are references to whether or not it is reasonably practicable to do so without prejudicing the use of the rest of that property, or a part of it, for purposes for which (disregarding the part to be separated) the use of the whole or of a part of the rest of the property, if retained, would be lawful.

[Criminal Justice and Police Act 2001, s 53.]

1–4149　54. Obligation to return items subject to legal privilege.　(1) If, at any time after a seizure of anything has been made in exercise of a power of seizure to which this section applies—

(*a*) it appears to the person for the time being having possession of the seized property in consequence of the seizure that the property—

    (i)　is an item subject to legal privilege, or

    (ii)　has such an item comprised in it,

    and

(*b*) in a case where the item is comprised in something else which has been lawfully seized, it is not comprised in property falling within subsection (2),

it shall be the duty of that person to secure that the item is returned as soon as reasonably practicable after the seizure.

(2) Property in which an item subject to legal privilege is comprised falls within this subsection if—

(*a*) the whole or a part of the rest of the property is property falling within subsection (3) or property the retention of which is authorised by section 56; and

(*b*) in all the circumstances, it is not reasonably practicable for that item to be separated from the rest of that property (or, as the case may be, from that part of it) without prejudicing the use of the rest of that property, or that part of it, for purposes for which (disregarding that item) its use, if retained, would be lawful.

(3) Property falls within this subsection to the extent that it is property for which the person seizing it had power to search when he made the seizure, but is not property which is required to be returned under this section or section 55.

(4) This section applies—

(*a*) to the powers of seizure conferred by sections 50 and 51;

(*b*) to each of the powers of seizure specified in Parts 1 and 2 of Schedule 1; and

(*c*) to any power of seizure (not falling within paragraph (*a*) or (*b*)) conferred on a constable by or under any enactment, including an enactment passed after this Act.

[Criminal Justice and Police Act 2001, s 54.]

1–4150　55. Obligation to return excluded and special procedure material.　(1) If, at any time after a seizure of anything has been made in exercise of a power to which this section applies—

(*a*) it appears to the person for the time being having possession of the seized property in consequence of the seizure that the property—

    (i)　is excluded material or special procedure material, or

    (ii)　has any excluded material or any special procedure material comprised in it,

(*b*) its retention is not authorised by section 56, and

(*c*) in a case where the material is comprised in something else which has been lawfully seized, it is not comprised in property falling within subsection (2) or (3),

it shall be the duty of that person to secure that the item is returned as soon as reasonably practicable after the seizure.

(2) Property in which any excluded material or special procedure material is comprised falls within this subsection if—

(*a*) the whole or a part of the rest of the property is property for which the person seizing it had power to search when he made the seizure but is not property the return of which is required by this section or section 54; and (*b*) in all the circumstances, it is not reasonably practicable for that material to be separated from the rest of that property (or, as the case may be, from that part of it) without prejudicing the use of the rest of that property, or that part of it, for purposes for which (disregarding that material) its use, if retained, would be lawful.

(3) Property in which any excluded material or special procedure material is comprised falls within this subsection if—

(*a*) the whole or a part of the rest of the property is property the retention of which is authorised by section 56; and

(*b*) in all the circumstances, it is not reasonably practicable for that material to be separated from the rest of that property (or, as the case may be, from that part of it) without prejudicing the use of the rest of that property, or that part of it, for purposes for which (disregarding that material) its use, if retained, would be lawful.

(4) This section applies (subject to subsection (5)) to each of the powers of seizure specified in Part 3 of Schedule 1.

(5) In its application to the powers of seizure conferred by—

(*a*) *Repealed.*
(*b*) section 56(5) of the Drug Trafficking Act 1994 (c 37),
(*c*) Article 51(5) of the Proceeds of Crime (Northern Ireland) Order 1996 (SI 1996/1299 (NI 6)), and
(*d*) section 352(4) of the Proceeds of Crime Act 2002,

this section shall have effect with the omission of every reference to special procedure material.

(6) In this section, except in its application to—

(*a*) the power of seizure conferred by section 8(2) of the 1984 Act,
(*b*) the power of seizure conferred by Article 10(2) of the Police and Criminal Evidence (Northern Ireland) Order 1989 (SI 1989/1341 (NI 12)),
(*c*) each of the powers of seizure conferred by the provisions of paragraphs 1 and 3 of Schedule 5 to the Terrorism Act 2000 (c 11), and
(*d*) the power of seizure conferred by paragraphs 15 and 19 of Schedule 5 to that Act of 2000, so far only as the power in question is conferred by reference to paragraph 1 of that Schedule,

"special procedure material" means special procedure material consisting of documents or records other than documents.

[Criminal Justice and Police Act 2001, s 55, as amended by the Proceeds of Crime Act 2002, Schs 11 and 12.]

1–4151   56. Property seized by constables etc.   (1) The retention of—

(*a*) property seized on any premises by a constable who was lawfully on the premises,
(*b*) property seized on any premises by a relevant person who was on the premises accompanied by a constable, and
(*c*) property seized by a constable carrying out a lawful search of any person,

is authorised by this section if the property falls within subsection (2) or (3).

(2) Property falls within this subsection to the extent that there are reasonable grounds for believing—

(*a*) that it is property obtained in consequence of the commission of an offence; and
(*b*) that it is necessary for it to be retained in order to prevent its being concealed, lost, damaged, altered or destroyed.

(3) Property falls within this subsection to the extent that there are reasonable grounds for believing—

(*a*) that it is evidence in relation to any offence; and
(*b*) that it is necessary for it to be retained in order to prevent its being concealed, lost, altered or destroyed.

(4) Nothing in this section authorises the retention (except in pursuance of section 54(2)) of anything at any time when its return is required by section 54.*

(4A) Subsection (1)(*a*) includes property seized on any premises—

(*a*) by a person authorised under section 16(2) of the 1984 Act to accompany a constable executing a warrant, or
(*b*) by a person accompanying a constable under section 2(6) of the Criminal Justice Act 1987 in the execution of a warrant under section 2(4) of that Act.

(5) In subsection (1)(*b*) the reference to a relevant person's being on any premises accompanied by a constable is a reference only to a person who was so on the premises under the authority of—

(*a*) a warrant under section 448 of the Companies Act 1985 (c 6) authorising him to exercise together with a constable the powers conferred by subsection (3) of that section;
(*b*) a warrant under Article 441 of the Companies (Northern Ireland) Order 1986 (SI 1986/1032 (NI 6)) authorising him to exercise together with a constable the powers conferred by paragraph (3) of that Article;
(*c*)–(*e*) *repealed.*

[Criminal Justice and Police Act 2001, s 56, as amended by SI 2001/3649 and the Criminal Justice Act 2003, Sch 1.]

1–4152   57. Retention of seized items.   (1) This section has effect in relation to the following provisions (which are about the retention of items which have been seized and are referred to in this section as "the relevant provisions")—

(a)   section 22 of the 1984 Act;
(b)   Article 24 of the Police and Criminal Evidence (Northern Ireland) Order 1989 (SI 1989/1341 (NI 12));
(c)   section 20CC(3) of the Taxes Management Act 1970 (c 9);
(d)   paragraph 4 of Schedule 9 to the Weights and Measures (Northern Ireland) Order 1981 (SI 1981/231 (NI 10));
(e)   repealed;
(f)   section 448(6) of the Companies Act 1985 (c 6);
(g)   paragraph 4 of Schedule 7 to the Weights and Measures (Packaged Goods) Regulations 2006;
(h)   repealed;
(i)   Article 441(6) of the Companies (Northern Ireland) Order 1986;
(j)   section 43(4) of the Banking Act 1987;
(k)   section 40(4) of the Human Fertilisation and Embryology Act 1990 (c 37);
(l)   repealed;
(m)   paragraph 7(2) of Schedule 9 to the Data Protection Act 1998 (c 29);
(n)   section 28(7) of the Competition Act 1998 (c 41);
(o)   section 176(8) of the Financial Services and Markets Act 2000 (c 8);
(p)   paragraph 7(2) of Schedule 3 to the Freedom of Information Act 2000 (c 36);
(q)   paragraph 5(4) of Schedule 5 to the Human Tissue Act 2004.★

(2) The relevant provisions shall apply in relation to any property seized in exercise of a power conferred by section 50 or 51 as if the property had been seized under the power of seizure by reference to which the power under that section was exercised in relation to that property.

(3) Nothing in any of sections 53 to 56 authorises the retention of any property at any time when its retention would not (apart from the provisions of this Part) be authorised by the relevant provisions.

(4) Nothing in any of the relevant provisions authorises the retention of anything after an obligation to return it has arisen under this Part.

[Criminal Justice and Police Act 2001, s 57, as amended by SI 2001/3649 and the Human Tissue Act 2004, Sch 6.]

★New para (r) inserted by the Animal Wlefare ACr 2006, Sch 3 from a date to be appointed.

1–4153   58. Person to whom seized property is to be returned.   (1) Where—

(a)   anything has been seized in exercise of any power of seizure, and
(b)   there is an obligation under this Part for the whole or any part of the seized property to be returned,

the obligation to return it shall (subject to the following provisions of this section) be an obligation to return it to the person from whom it was seized.

(2) Where—

(a)   any person is obliged under this Part to return anything that has been seized to the person from whom it was seized, and
(b)   the person under that obligation is satisfied that some other person has a better right to that thing than the person from whom it was seized,

his duty to return it shall, instead, be a duty to return it to that other person or, as the case may be, to the person appearing to him to have the best right to the thing in question.

(3) Where different persons claim to be entitled to the return of anything that is required to be returned under this Part, that thing may be retained for as long as is reasonably necessary for the determination in accordance with subsection (2) of the person to whom it must be returned.

(4) References in this Part to the person from whom something has been seized, in relation to a case in which the power of seizure was exercisable by reason of that thing's having been found on any premises, are references to the occupier of the premises at the time of the seizure.

(5) References in this section to the occupier of any premises at the time of a seizure, in relation to a case in which—

(a)   a notice in connection with the entry or search of the premises in question, or with the seizure, was given to a person appearing in the occupier's absence to be in charge of the premises, and
(b)   it is practicable, for the purpose of returning something that has been seized, to identify that person but not to identify the occupier of the premises,

are references to that person.

[Criminal Justice and Police Act 2001, s 58.]

Remedies and safeguards

1–4154   **59.** *Application to the appropriate judicial authority*[1]

1. This section gives anyone with a relevant interest in the seized property the right to apply to the appropriate judicial authority (defined in s 64 below) for its return.

1–4155   **60.** *Cases where duty to secure arises*[1]

1. Where property has been seized under s 50 or s 51 a duty to secure arises where an application is made under s 59 and one of the conditions set out in s 60(2) or (3) is satisfied.

1–4156   **61.** *The duty to secure*[1]

1. This defines the duty to secure. In particular, the duty ensures that the person in possession of the seized property does not examine or copy it without the consent of the applicant or in accordance with the directions of the Court.

1–4157   **62.** *Use of inextricably linked property*[1]

1. This section provides that inextricably linked property shall not, except to the extent that its use is necessary to facilitate the use in any investigation or proceedings of property of which the inextricably linked property forms part, be examined or copied or put to any other use without the consent of the person from whom it was seized.

Construction of Part 2

1–4158   **63. Copies.** (1) Subject to subsection (3)—

(a) in this Part, "seize" includes "take a copy of", and cognate expressions shall be construed accordingly;

(b) this Part shall apply as if any copy taken under any power to which any provision of this Part applies were the original of that of which it is a copy; and

(c) for the purposes of this Part, except sections 50 and 51, the powers mentioned in subsection (2) (which are powers to obtain hard copies etc of information which is stored in electronic form) shall be treated as powers of seizure, and references to seizure and to seized property shall be construed accordingly.

(2) The powers mentioned in subsection (1)(c) are any powers which are conferred by—

(a) section 19(4) or 20 of the 1984 Act;

(b) Article 21(4) or 22 of the Police and Criminal Evidence (Northern Ireland) Order 1989 (SI 1989/1341 (NI 12));

(c) section 46(3) of the Firearms Act 1968 (c 27);

(d) section 43(5)(aa) of the Gaming Act 1968 (c 65);

(e) section 20C(3A) of the Taxes Management Act 1970 (c 9);

(f) section 32(6)(b) of the Food Safety Act 1990 (c 16);

(g) Article 34(6)(b) of the Food Safety (Northern Ireland) Order 1991 (SI 1991/762 (NI 7));

(h) section 28(2)(f) of the Competition Act 1998 (c 41); or

(i) section 8(2)(c) of the Nuclear Safeguards Act 2000 (c 5).

(3) Subsection (1) does not apply to section 50(6) or 57.

[Criminal Justice and Police Act 2001, s 63.]

1–4159   **64. Meaning of "appropriate judicial authority".** (1) Subject to subsection (2), in this Part "appropriate judicial authority" means—

(a) in relation to England and Wales and Northern Ireland, a judge of the Crown Court;

(b) in relation to Scotland, a sheriff.

(2) In this Part "appropriate judicial authority", in relation to the seizure of items under any power mentioned in subsection (3) and in relation to items seized under any such power, means—

(a) in relation to England and Wales and Northern Ireland, the High Court;

(b) in relation to Scotland, the Court of Session.

(3) Those powers are—

(a) the powers of seizure conferred by—

(i) section 448(3) of the Companies Act 1985 (c 6);

(ii) Article 441(3) of the Companies (Northern Ireland) Order 1986 (SI 1986/1032 (NI 6)); and

(iii) section 28(2) of the Competition Act 1998;

(aa) the power of seizure conferred by section 352(4) of the Proceeds of Crime Act 2002, if the power is exercisable for the purposes of a civil recovery investigation (within the meaning of Part 8 of that Act);

(b) any power of seizure conferred by section 50, so far as that power is exercisable by reference to any power mentioned in paragraph (a).

[Criminal Justice and Police Act 2001, s 64, as amended by the Proceeds of Crime Act 2002, Sch 11.]

1-4160 65. Meaning of "legal privilege"[1]. (1) Subject to the following provisions of this section, references in this Part to an item subject to legal privilege shall be construed—

(a) for the purposes of the application of this Part to England and Wales, in accordance with section 10 of the 1984 Act (meaning of "legal privilege");

(b) *Application to Scotland.**

(c) *Application to Northern Ireland.*

(2) In relation to property which has been seized in exercise, or purported exercise, of—

(a) the power of seizure conferred by section 28(2) of the Competition Act 1998, or

(b) so much of any power of seizure conferred by section 50 as is exercisable by reference to that power,

references in this Part to an item subject to legal privilege shall be read as references to a privileged communication within the meaning of section 30 of that Act.

(3) In relation to property which has been seized in exercise, or purported exercise, of—

(a) the power of seizure conferred by section 20C of the Taxes Management Act 1970 (c 9), or

(b) so much of any power of seizure conferred by section 50 as is exercisable by reference to that power,

references in this Part to an item subject to legal privilege shall be construed in accordance with section 20C(4A) of that Act.

(3A) In relation to property which has been seized in exercise, or purported exercise, of—

(a) the power of seizure conferred by section 352(4) of the Proceeds of Crime Act 2002, or

(b) so much of any power of seizure by section 50 as is exercisable by reference to that power,

references in this Part to an item subject to legal privilege shall be read as references to privileged material within the meaning of section 345(2) of that Act.

(4) An item which is, or is comprised in, property which has been seized in exercise, or purported exercise, of the power of seizure conferred by section 448(3) of the Companies Act 1985 (c 6) shall be taken for the purposes of this Part to be an item subject to legal privilege if, and only if, the seizure of that item was in contravention of section 452(2) of that Act (privileged information).

(5) *Northern Ireland.*

(6) An item which is, or is comprised in, property which has been seized in exercise, or purported exercise, of the power of seizure conferred by sub-paragraph (2) of paragraph 3 of Schedule 2 to the Timeshare Act 1992 (c 35) shall be taken for the purposes of this Part to be an item subject to legal privilege if, and only if, the seizure of that item was in contravention of sub-paragraph (4) of that paragraph (privileged documents).

(7) An item which is, or is comprised in, property which has been seized in exercise, or purported exercise, of the power of seizure conferred by paragraph 1 of Schedule 9 to the Data Protection Act 1998 (c 29) shall be taken for the purposes of this Part to be an item subject to legal privilege if, and only if, the seizure of that item was in contravention of paragraph 9 of that Schedule (privileged communications).

(8) An item which is, or is comprised in, property which has been seized in exercise, or purported exercise, of the power of seizure conferred by paragraph 1 of Schedule 3 to the Freedom of Information Act 2000 (c 36) shall be taken for the purposes of this Part to be an item subject to legal privilege if, and only if, the seizure of that item was in contravention of paragraph 9 of that Schedule (privileged communications).

(9) An item which is, or is comprised in, property which has been seized in exercise, or purported exercise, of so much of any power of seizure conferred by section 50 as is exercisable by reference to a power of seizure conferred by—

(a) section 448(3) of the Companies Act 1985,

(b) Article 441(3) of the Companies (Northern Ireland) Order 1986,

(c) paragraph 3(2) of Schedule 2 to the Timeshare Act 1992,

(d) paragraph 1 of Schedule 9 to the Data Protection Act 1998, or

(e) paragraph 1 of Schedule 3 to the Freedom of Information Act 2000,

shall be taken for the purposes of this Part to be an item subject to legal privilege if, and only if, the item would have been taken for the purposes of this Part to be an item subject to legal privilege had it been seized under the power of seizure by reference to which the power conferred by section 50 was exercised.

[Criminal Justice and Police Act 2001, s 65, as amended by the Proceeds of Crime Act 2002, Sch 11.]

---

1. This section provides a definition of 'legal privilege' that is based in part on the meaning of that term in the relevant power listed in Sch 1. Thus, the meaning of that term varies according to which of those powers is in point.

1-4161 66. General interpretation of Part 2. (1) In this Part—

"appropriate judicial authority" has the meaning given by section 64;

"documents" includes information recorded in any form;

"item subject to legal privilege" shall be construed in accordance with section 65;

"premises" includes any vehicle, stall or moveable structure (including an offshore installation) and any other place whatever, whether or not occupied as land;

"offshore installation" has the same meaning as in the Mineral Workings (Offshore Installations) Act 1971 (c 61);

"return", in relation to seized property, shall be construed in accordance with section 58, and cognate expressions shall be construed accordingly;

"seize", and cognate expressions, shall be construed in accordance with section 63(1) and subsection (5) below;

"seized property", in relation to any exercise of a power of seizure, means (subject to subsection (5)) anything seized in exercise of that power; and

"vehicle" includes any vessel, aircraft or hovercraft.

(2) In this Part references, in relation to a time when seized property is in any person's possession in consequence of a seizure ("the relevant time"), to something for which the person making the seizure had power to search shall be construed—

(a) where the seizure was made on the occasion of a search carried out on the authority of a warrant, as including anything of the description of things the presence or suspected presence of which provided grounds for the issue of the warrant;

(b) where the property was seized in the course of a search on the occasion of which it would have been lawful for the person carrying out the search to seize anything which on that occasion was believed by him to be, or appeared to him to be, of a particular description, as including—

(i) anything which at the relevant time is believed by the person in possession of the seized property, or (as the case may be) appears to him, to be of that description; and

(ii) anything which is in fact of that description;

(c) where the property was seized in the course of a search on the occasion of which it would have been lawful for the person carrying out the search to seize anything which there were on that occasion reasonable grounds for believing was of a particular description, as including—

(i) anything which there are at the relevant time reasonable grounds for believing is of that description; and

(ii) anything which is in fact of that description;

(d) where the property was seized in the course of a search to which neither paragraph (b) nor paragraph (c) applies, as including anything which is of a description of things which, on the occasion of the search, it would have been lawful for the person carrying it out to seize otherwise than under section 50 and 51; and

(e) where the property was seized on the occasion of a search authorised under section 82 of the Terrorism Act 2000 (c 11) (seizure of items suspected to have been, or to be intended to be, used in commission of certain offences), as including anything—

(i) which is or has been, or is or was intended to be, used in the commission of an offence such as is mentioned in subsection (3)(a) or (b) of that section; or

(ii) which at the relevant time the person who is in possession of the seized property reasonably suspects is something falling within sub-paragraph (i).

(3) For the purpose of determining in accordance with subsection (2), in relation to any time, whether or to what extent property seized on the occasion of a search authorised under section 9 of the Official Secrets Act 1911 (c 28) (seizure of evidence of offences under that Act having been or being about to be committed) is something for which the person making the seizure had power to search, subsection (1) of that section shall be construed—

(a) as if the reference in that subsection to evidence of an offence under that Act being about to be committed were a reference to evidence of such an offence having been, at the time of the seizure, about to be committed; and

(b) as if the reference in that subsection to reasonable ground for suspecting that such an offence is about to be committed were a reference to reasonable ground for suspecting that at the time of the seizure such an offence was about to be committed.

(4) References in subsection (2) to a search include references to any activities authorised by virtue of any of the following—

(a) section 28(1) of the Trade Descriptions Act 1968 (c 29) (power to enter premises and to inspect and seize goods and documents);

(b) section 29(1) of the Fair Trading Act 1973 (c 41) (power to enter premises and to inspect and seize goods and documents);

(c) paragraph 9 of the Schedule to the Prices Act 1974 (c 24) (powers of entry and inspection);

(d) section 162(1) of the Consumer Credit Act 1974 (c 39) (powers of entry and inspection);

(e) section 11(1) of the Estate Agents Act 1979 (c 38) (powers of entry and inspection);

(f) Schedule 9 to the Weights and Measures (Northern Ireland) Order 1981 (SI 1981/231 (NI 10));

(g) section 79 of the Weights and Measures Act 1985 (c 72) or Schedule 7 to the Weights and Measures (Packaged Goods) Regulations 2006 (powers of entry and inspection etc);

(h) section 29 of the Consumer Protection Act 1987 (c 43) (powers of search etc);

(*i*) Article 22 of the Consumer Protection (Northern Ireland) Order 1987 (SI 1987/2049 (NI 20));

(*j*) section 32(5) of the Food Safety Act 1990 (c 16) (power to inspect records relating to a food business);

(*k*) paragraph 3 of the Schedule to the Property Misdescriptions Act 1991 (c 29) (powers of seizure etc);

(*l*) Article 33(6) of the Food Safety (Northern Ireland) Order 1991 (SI 1991/762 (NI 7));

(*m*) paragraph 3 of Schedule 2 to the Timeshare Act 1992 (c 35) (powers of officers of enforcement authority).

(*n*) paragraph 2 of Schedule 5 to the Human Tissue Act 2004 (entry and inspection of licensed premises);

(*o*) regulation 22 of the General Product Safety Regulations 2005 (powers of entry and search etc).*

(5) References in this Part to a power of seizure include references to each of the powers to take possession of items under—

(*a*) *repealed*;

(*b*) section 448(3) of the Companies Act 1985 (c 6);

(*c*) *repealed*;

(*d*) Article 441(3) of the Companies (Northern Ireland) Order 1986 (SI 1986/1032 (NI 6));

(*e*) *repealed*;

(*f*) section 2(5) of the Criminal Justice Act 1987 (c 38);

(*g*) section 40(2) of the Human Fertilisation and Embryology Act 1990 (c 37);

(*h*) section 28(2)(*c*) of the Competition Act 1998 (c 41); and

(*i*) section 176(5) of the Financial Services and Markets Act 2000 (c 8);

and references in this Part to seizure and to seized property shall be construed accordingly.

(6) In this Part, so far as it applies to England and Wales—

(*a*) references to excluded material shall be construed in accordance with section 11 of the 1984 Act (meaning of "excluded material"); and

(*b*) references to special procedure material shall be construed in accordance with section 14 of that Act (meaning of "special procedure material").

(7) In this Part, so far as it applies to Northern Ireland—

(*a*) references to excluded material shall be construed in accordance with Article 13 of the Police and Criminal Evidence (Northern Ireland) Order 1989 (SI 1989/1341 (NI 12)) (meaning of "excluded material"); and

(*b*) references to special procedure material shall be construed in accordance with Article 16 of that Order (meaning of "special procedure material").

(8) References in this Part to any item or material being comprised in other property include references to its being mixed with that other property.

(9) In this Part "enactment" includes an enactment contained in Northern Ireland legislation.

[Criminal Justice and Police Act 2001, s 66, as amended by SI 2001/3649, SI 2005/1803 and the Human Tissue Act 2004, Sch 6.]

---

*New para (*p*) inserted by the Animal Welfare Act 2006, Sch 3 from a date to be appointed.**

Supplemental provisions of Part 2

1–4162 67. Application to customs officers. The powers conferred by section 114(2) of the 1984 Act and Article 85(1) of the Police and Criminal Evidence (Northern Ireland) Order 1989 (application of provisions relating to police officers to customs officers) shall have effect in relation to the provisions of this Part as they have effect in relation to the provisions of that Act or, as the case may be, that Order.

[Criminal Justice and Police Act 2001, s 67.]

1–4163 68. *Application to Scotland*

1–4164 69. Application to powers designated by order. (1) The Secretary of State may by order[1]—

(*a*) provide for any power designated by the order to be added to those specified in Schedule 1 or section 63(2);

(*b*) make any modification of the provisions of this Part which the Secretary of State considers appropriate in consequence of any provision made by virtue of paragraph (*a*);

(*c*) make any modification of any enactment making provision in relation to seizures, or things seized, under a power designated by an order under this subsection which the Secretary of State considers appropriate in consequence of any provision made by virtue of that paragraph.

(2) Where the power designated by the order made under subsection (1) is a power conferred in relation to Scotland, the Secretary of State shall consult the Scottish Ministers before making the order.

(3) The power to make an order under subsection (1) shall be exercisable by statutory instrument;

and no such order shall be made unless a draft of it has been laid before Parliament and approved by a resolution of each House.

(4) In this section "modification" includes any exclusion, extension or application.
[Criminal Justice and Police Act 2001, s 69.]

---

1. The Criminal Justice and Police Act 2001 (Powers of Seizure) Order 2003, SI 2003/934 have been made.

1–4165 70. Consequential applications and amendments of enactments. Schedule 2 (which applies enactments in relation to provision made by this Part and contains minor and consequential amendments) shall have effect.
[Criminal Justice and Police Act 2001, s 70.]

PART 3[1]

POLICE AND CRIMINAL EVIDENCE AND THE TERRORISM ACT[2]

1–4166 82. Restriction on use and destruction of fingerprints and samples. (6) The fingerprints, samples and information the retention and use of which, in accordance with the amended provisions of section 64 of the 1984 Act, is authorised by this section include—

(a) fingerprints and samples the destruction of which should have taken place before the commencement of this section, but did not; and

(b) information deriving from any such samples or from samples the destruction of which did take place, in accordance with that section, before the commencement of this section.
[Criminal Justice and Police Act 2001, s 82.]

---

1. Part 3 contains ss 71–86.

2. These provisions make various amendments to the Police and Criminal Evidence Act 1984 (see this PART, ante) and the Terrorism Act 2000 (see PART 8, post).

PART 6[1]

MISCELLANEOUS AND SUPPLEMENTAL

Supplemental

1–4171 135. *Ministerial expenditure etc*

1–4172 136. General interpretation. In this Act—

"the 1984 Act" means the Police and Criminal Evidence Act 1984 (c 60);
"the 1996 Act" means the Police Act 1996 (c 16); and
"the 1997 Act" means the Police Act 1997 (c 50).
[Criminal Justice and Police Act 2001, s 136.]

1–4173 137. Repeals. The enactments and instruments mentioned in Schedule 7 (which include spent provisions) are hereby repealed or (as the case may be) revoked to the extent specified in the second column of that Schedule.*
[Criminal Justice and Police Act 2001, s 137.]

---

*In force in so far as it relates to the entries in Sch 7 referred to in paragraph (m) below.

1–4174 138. Short title, commencement and extent. (1) This Act may be cited as the Criminal Justice and Police Act 2001.

(2) The provisions of this Act, other than this section and sections 42 and 43, 81 to 85, 109, 116(7) and 119(7), shall come into force on such day as the Secretary of State may by order made by statutory instrument appoint; and different days may be appointed under this subsection for different purposes[1].

(3) An order under subsection (2) may contain such savings as the Secretary of State thinks fit.

(4) Section 85 comes into force at the end of the period of two months beginning with the day on which this Act is passed.

(5) Subject to subsections (6) to (12), this Act extends to England and Wales only.

(6) The following provisions of this Act extend to the United Kingdom—

(a) sections 33 to 38;
(b) Part 2;
(c) section 86(1) and (2);
(d) repealed;
(e) section 127; and
(f) section 136 and this section.

(7) Except in so far as it contains provision relating to the matters mentioned in section 745(1) of the Companies Act 1985 (c 6) (companies registered or incorporated in Northern Ireland or outside Great Britain), section 45 extends to Great Britain only.

(8) Section 126 extends to Great Britain only.

(9) Sections 29, 39 to 41, 72, 75, 84 and 134 extend to England and Wales and Northern Ireland only.

(10) Section 83 extends to Northern Ireland only.

(11) Section 86(3) has the same extent as section 27 of the Petty Sessions (Ireland) Act 1851 (c 93).

(12) An amendment, repeal or revocation contained in Schedule 4, 6 or 7 has the same extent as the enactment or instrument to which it relates.

[Criminal Justice and Police Act 2001, s 138 as amended by the Serious Organised Crime and Police Act 2005, Sch 4.]

---

1. Commencement provisions: s 138(2)–(4); Criminal Justice and Police Act 2001 (Commencement No 1) Order 2001, SI 2001/2223; Criminal Justice and Police Act 2001 (Commencement No 2) Order 2001, SI 2001/3150; Criminal Justice and Police Act 2001 (Commencement No 3) Order 2001, SI 2001/3736; Criminal Justice and Police Act 2001 (Commencement No 4 and Transitional Provisions) Order 2002, SI 2002/3441; Criminal Justice and Police Act 2001 (Commencement No 5) Order 2002, SI 2002/533; Criminal Justice and Police Act 2001 (Commencement No 6) Order 2002, SI 2002/1097; Criminal Justice and Police Act 2001 (Commencement No 7) Order 2002, SI 2002/2050; Criminal Justice and Police Act 2001 (Commencement No 8) Order 2002, SI 2002/3032; Criminal Justice and Police Act 2001 (Commencement No 9) Order 2003, SI 2003/708; and Criminal Justice and Police Act 2001 (Commencement No 10) Order 2004, SI 2004/1376.

1–4175

Sections 50, 51 & 55   SCHEDULE 1
                                    POWERS OF SEIZURE

(As amended by SI 2001/3649, the Proceeds of Crime Act 2002, Schs 11 and 12, SI 2003/934, the Enterprise Act 2003, s 194, the Extradition Act 2003, s 165, the Licensing Act 2003, Schs 6 and 7, the Crime (International Co-operation) Act 2003, Sch 6, the Human Tissue Act 2004, Sch 6, SI 2005/1803, the Licensing Act 203, Sch 7, the Serious Organised Crime and Police Act 2005, s 68, the Terrorism Act 2006, s 28 and SI 2006/659.)

PART 1
POWERS TO WHICH SECTION 50 APPLIES

Police and Criminal Evidence Act 1984 (c 60)

1. Each of the powers of seizure conferred by the provisions of Part 2 or 3 of the 1984 Act (police powers of entry, search and seizure).

Police and Criminal Evidence (Northern Ireland) Order 1989 (SI 1989/1341 (NI 12))

2. Each of the powers of seizure conferred by the provisions of Parts 3 and 4 of the Police and Criminal Evidence (Northern Ireland) Order 1989 (police powers of entry, search and seizure).

Official Secrets Act 1911 (c 28)

3. The power of seizure conferred by section 9(1) of the Official Secrets Act 1911 (seizure of evidence that an offence under that Act has been or is about to be committed).

Children and Young Persons (Harmful Publications) Act 1955 (c 28)

4. The power of seizure conferred by section 3(1) of the Children and Young Persons (Harmful Publications) Act 1955 (seizure of copies of work to which that Act applies etc).

Obscene Publications Act 1959 (c 66)

5. Each of the powers of seizure conferred by section 3(1) and (2) of the Obscene Publications Act 1959 (power to search for and seize obscene materials and documents relating to a connected business).

Betting, Gaming and Lotteries Act 1963 (c 2)

6. The power of seizure conferred by section 51(1) of the Betting, Gaming and Lotteries Act 1963 (seizure of evidence of offences under that Act).*

7. Repealed.

Firearms Act 1968 (c 27)

8. The power of seizure conferred by section 46 of the Firearms Act 1968 (seizure of firearms etc).

Trade Descriptions Act 1968 (c 29)

9. Each of the powers of seizure conferred by section 28(1)(*c*) and (*d*) of the Trade Descriptions Act 1968 (seizure of evidence of offences under that Act etc).

Theft Act 1968 (c 60)

10. The power of seizure conferred by section 26(3) of the Theft Act 1968 (seizure of goods suspected of being stolen).

Gaming Act 1968 (c 65)

11. The power of seizure conferred by section 43(5) of the Gaming Act 1968 (seizure of evidence of offences under that Act).*

Theft Act (Northern Ireland) 1969 (c 16 NI))

12. The power of seizure conferred by section 25(3) of the Theft Act (Northern Ireland) 1969 (seizure of goods suspected of being stolen).

Taxes Management Act 1970 (c 9)

13. The power of seizure conferred by section 20C of the Taxes Management Act 1970 (seizure of evidence of offences involving serious fraud).

Misuse of Drugs Act 1971 (c 38)

14. Each of the powers of seizure conferred by the provisions of section 23(2) and (3) of the Misuse of Drugs Act 1971 (power to search for and seize controlled drugs and related documents).

Immigration Act 1971 (c 77)

15. Each of the powers of seizure conferred by the provisions of sections 28D(3), 28E(5) and 28F(6) of the Immigration Act 1971 (seizure of evidence of offences under that Act).

Fair Trading Act 1973 (c 41)

16. Each of the powers of seizure conferred by the provisions of section 29(1)(c) and (d) of the Fair Trading Act 1973 (seizure of evidence of offences under section 23 of that Act etc).

Biological Weapons Act 1974 (c 6)

17. Each of the powers of seizure conferred by the provisions of section 4(1)(b), (c) and (d) of the Biological Weapons Act 1974 (seizures under a warrant).

Prices Act 1974 (c 24)

18. Each of the powers of seizure conferred by the provisions of paragraph 9(2) to the Schedule to the Prices Act 1974 (seizure of evidence of offences in connection with price regulation, price marking and price range notices).**

Consumer Credit Act 1974 (c 39)

19. Each of the powers of seizure conferred by the provisions of section 162(1)(c) and (d) of the Consumer Credit Act 1974 (seizure of evidence of offences under that Act etc).

Lotteries and Amusements Act 1976 (c 32)

20. The power of seizure conferred by section 19 of the Lotteries and Amusements Act 1976 (seizure of evidence of offences under that Act).*

Protection of Children Act 1978 (c 37)

21. The power of seizure conferred by section 4(2) of the Protection of Children Act 1978 (seizure of indecent photographs or pseudo-photographs of children).

Protection of Children (Northern Ireland) Order 1978 (SI 1978/1047 (NI 17))

22. The power of seizure conferred by Article 4(1) of the Protection of Children (Northern Ireland) Order 1978 (seizure of indecent photographs or pseudo-photographs of children).

Customs and Excise Management Act 1979 (c 2)

23. The power of seizure conferred by section 118C(4) of the Customs and Excise Management Act 1979 (seizure of evidence of fraud offences).

Estate Agents Act 1979 (c 38)

24. The power of seizure conferred by section 11(1)(c) of the Estate Agents Act 1979 (seizure of evidence of offences under that Act).

Indecent Displays (Control) Act 1981 (c 42)

25. The power of seizure conferred by section 2(3) of the Indecent Displays (Control) Act 1981 (seizure of indecent matter believed to have been used in the commission of an offence under that Act).

Forgery and Counterfeiting Act 1981 (c 45)

26. Each of the powers of seizure conferred by the provisions of sections 7(1) and 24(1) of the Forgery and Counterfeiting Act 1981 (seizure of forgeries and counterfeits and of things used for making them etc).

Betting and Gaming Duties Act 1981 (c 63)

27. The power of seizure conferred by paragraph 16(2) of Schedule 1 to the Betting and Gaming Duties Act 1981 (seizure of evidence of offences in connection with general gaming duty).
28. The power of seizure conferred by paragraph 17(2) of Schedule 3 to that Act (seizure of evidence of offences in connection with bingo duty etc).
29. The power of seizure conferred by paragraph 17(2) of Schedule 4 to that Act (seizure of evidence of offences in connection with the provision of amusement machines).

Firearms (Northern Ireland) Order 1981 (SI 1981/155 (NI 2))

30. The power of seizure conferred by Article 45 of the Firearms (Northern Ireland) Order 1981 (seizure of firearms etc).***

Weights and Measures (Northern Ireland) Order 1981 (SI 1981/231 (NI 10))

31. The power of seizure conferred by paragraph 4 of Schedule 9 to the Weights and Measures (Northern Ireland) Order 1981.

32. *Repealed.*

Dogs (Northern Ireland) Order 1983 (SI 1983/764 (NI 8))

33. The power of seizure conferred by Article 25C(2) of the Dogs (Northern Ireland) Order 1983 (seizure of evidence of offences).

Video Recordings Act 1984 (c 39)

34. The power of seizure conferred by section 17(2) of the Video Recordings Act 1984 (seizure of evidence of offences under that Act).

Companies Act 1985 (c 6)

35. The power of seizure conferred by section 448(3) of the Companies Act 1985 (seizure of documents which have not been produced in compliance with a requirement etc).

Weights and Measures Act 1985 (c 72)

36. The power of seizure conferred by section 79(2)(*b*) of the Weights and Measures Act 1985 (seizure of evidence of offences under that Act, except Part 5).

37. *Repealed.*

Betting, Gaming, Lotteries and Amusements (Northern Ireland) Order 1985 (SI 1985/1204 (NI 11))

38. The power of seizure conferred by Article 180(4) of the Betting, Gaming, Lotteries and Amusements (Northern Ireland) Order 1985 (seizure of evidence of offences under that Order).

Protection of Military Remains Act 1986 (c 35)

39. The power of seizure conferred by section 6(3) of the Protection of Military Remains Act 1986 (seizure of evidence of offences under that Act etc).

40. *Repealed.*

Greater London Council (General Powers) Act 1986 (c iv)

41. Any power of seizure conferred by virtue of section 12 of the Greater London Council (General Powers) Act 1986 (seizure of items which may be subject to forfeiture).

Companies (Northern Ireland) Order 1986 (SI 1986/1032 (NI 6))

42. The power of seizure conferred by Article 441(3) of the Companies (Northern Ireland) Order 1986 (seizure of evidence of offences etc).

43. *Repealed.*

Criminal Justice Act 1987 (c 38)

44. The power of seizure conferred by section 2(5) of the Criminal Justice Act 1987 (seizure of documents for the purposes of an investigation under section 1 of that Act).

Consumer Protection Act 1987 (c 43)

45. Each of the powers of seizure conferred by the provisions of section 29(4), (5) and (6) of the Consumer Protection Act 1987 (seizure for the purposes of ascertaining whether safety provisions have been contravened etc).

Consumer Protection (Northern Ireland) Order 1987 (SI 1987/2049 (NI 20))

46. Each of the powers of seizure conferred by the provisions of Article 22(3) and (4) of the Consumer Protection (Northern Ireland) Order 1987 (seizure for purposes of ascertaining whether safety provisions have been contravened).

47. *Repealed.*

Copyright, Designs and Patents Act 1988 (c 48)

48. The powers of seizure conferred by sections 109(4), 200(3A) and 297B(4) of the Copyright, Designs and Patents Act 1988 (seizure of evidence relating to offences concerning infringing copies, illicit recordings and unauthorised decoders).

49. *Repealed.*

Food Safety Act 1990 (c 16)

50. The power of seizure conferred by section 32(6) of the Food Safety Act 1990 (seizure of evidence for the purposes of proceedings under that Act).

Computer Misuse Act 1990 (c 18)

51. The power of seizure conferred by section 14(4) of the Computer Misuse Act 1990 (seizure of evidence of offences under that Act).

Human Fertilisation and Embryology Act 1990 (c 37)

52. The power of seizure conferred by section 40(2) of the Human Fertilisation and Embryology Act 1990 (seizure of evidence of offences under that Act).

Property Misdescriptions Act 1991 (c 29)

53. The power of seizure conferred by paragraph 3(3) of the Schedule to the Property Misdescriptions Act 1991 (seizure of evidence of offences under section 1 of that Act).

Dangerous Dogs Act 1991 (c 65)

54. The power of seizure conferred by section 5(2) of the Dangerous Dogs Act 1991 (seizure of evidence of offences under that Act).

Food Safety (Northern Ireland) Order 1991 (SI 1991/762 (NI 7))

55. The power of seizure conferred by Article 33(7) of the Food Safety (Northern Ireland) Order 1991 (seizure of evidence of offences under that Order).

Timeshare Act 1992 (c 35)

56. The power of seizure conferred by paragraph 3(2) of Schedule 2 to the Timeshare Act 1992 (seizure of evidence of offences).

Finance Act 1994 (c 9)

57. The power of seizure conferred by paragraph 4(3) of Schedule 7 to the Finance Act 1994 (seizure of evidence of offences relating to insurance premium tax).

Value Added Tax Act 1994 (c 23)

58. The power of seizure conferred by paragraph 10(3) of Schedule 11 to the Value Added Tax Act 1994 (seizure of evidence of fraudulent evasion of VAT etc).

Trade Marks Act 1994 (c 26)

58A. The power of seizure conferred by section 92A(4) of the Trade Marks Act 1994 (seizure of evidence relating to offences concerning unauthorised use of a trade mark, etc in relation to goods).

Drug Trafficking Act 1994 (c 37)

59. The power of seizure conferred by section 56(5) of the Drug Trafficking Act 1994 (seizure of material likely to be of substantial value to an investigation into drug trafficking).

Chemical Weapons Act 1996 (c 6)

60. Each of the powers of seizure conferred by the provisions of section 29(2)(c), (d) and (e) of the Chemical Weapons Act 1996 (seizure of evidence of offences under that Act).

Finance Act 1996 (c 8)

61. The power of seizure conferred by paragraph 5(2) of Schedule 5 to the Finance Act 1996 (seizure of evidence of offences relating to landfill tax).

Proceeds of Crime (Northern Ireland) Order 1996 (SI 1996/1299 (NI 9))

62. The power of seizure conferred by Article 51(5) of the Proceeds of Crime (Northern Ireland) Order 1996 (seizure of material relevant to investigation).

Knives Act 1997 (c 21)

63. The power of seizure conferred by section 5(2) of the Knives Act 1997 (seizure of publications consisting of or containing prohibited material).

Nuclear Explosions (Prohibitions and Inspections) Act 1998 (c 7)

64. Each of the powers of seizure conferred by the provisions of section 10(2)(c), (d) and (e) of the Nuclear Explosions (Prohibitions and Inspections) Act 1998 (seizure of evidence of offences under that Act).

Data Protection Act 1998 (c 29)

65. The power of seizure conferred by paragraph 1 of Schedule 9 to the Data Protection Act 1998 (seizure of evidence of contravention of data protection principles etc).

Landmines Act 1998 (c 33)

66. Each of the powers of seizure conferred by the provisions of section 18(3)(c), (d) and (e) of the Landmines Act 1998 (seizure of evidence of offences under that Act).

Competition Act 1998 (c 41)

67. Each of the powers of seizure conferred by section 28(2) of the Competition Act 1998 (seizure of documents or information).

Nuclear Safeguards Act 2000 (c 5)

68. The power of seizure conferred by section 8(2) of the Nuclear Safeguards Act 2000 (seizure of evidence of offences under that Act etc).

Financial Services and Markets Act 2000 (c 8)

69. The power of seizure conferred by section 176(5) of the Financial Services and Markets Act 2000 (seizure of documents or information not supplied in compliance with a requirement etc).

Terrorism Act 2000 (c 11)

70. The power of seizure conferred by section 82(3) of the Terrorism Act 2000 (power of constable in Northern Ireland to seize items used or intended for use in the commission of certain offences).
71. Each of the powers of seizure conferred by the provisions of paragraphs 1, 3, 11, 15 and 19 of Schedule 5 to that Act (powers for use in terrorism investigations).

Finance Act 2000 (c 17)

72. The power of seizure conferred by paragraph 130(2) of Schedule 6 to the Finance Act 2000 (seizure of evidence of offences relating to climate change levy).

Freedom of Information Act 2000 (c 36)

73. The power of seizure conferred by paragraph 1 of Schedule 3 to the Freedom of Information Act 2000.

International Criminal Court Act 2001 (c 17)

73A¹. The power of seizure conferred by paragraph 9 of Schedule 5 to the International Criminal Court Act 2001 (seizure of evidence in connection with offences under that Act).

Proceeds of Crime Act 2002 (c 29)

73A¹. The power of seizure conferred by section 352(4) of the Proceeds of Crime Act 2002 (seizure of material likely to be of substantial value to certain investigations).

Enterprise Act 2002

73B. The power of seizure conferred by section 194(2) of the Enterprise Act 2002 (seizure of documents for the purposes of an investigation under section 192(1) of that Act).

Crime (International Co-operation) Act 2003

73C. The power of seizure conferred by sections 17 and 22 of the Crime (International Co-operation) Act 2003 (seizure of evidence relevant to overseas investigation or offence).

Extradition Act 2003 (c 41)

73D. The powers of seizure conferred by sections 156(5), 160(5), 161(4), 162(6) and (7) and 164(6) and (7) of the Extradition Act 2003 (seizure in connection with extradition).

Human Tissue Act 2004 (c 30)

73E. Each of the powers of seizure conferred by the provisions of paragraph 5(1) (seizure of material relevant to licensing functions) and (2) (seizure of evidence of offences) of Schedule 5 to the Human Tissue Act 2004.****

Serious Organised Crime and Police Act 2005

73F. The power of seizure conferred by section 66 of the Serious Organised Crime and Police Act 2005 (seizure of documents for purposes of investigation by DPP or other Investigating Authority).**** *****

General Product Safety Regulations 2005

73G. Each of the powers of seizure conferred by the provisions of regulation 22(4) to (6) of the General Product Safety Regulations 2005 (seizure for the purposes of ascertaining whether safety provisions have been contravened etc).
73H. The power of seizure conferred by section 28 of the Terrorism Act 2006.

Licensing Act 2003

74**.** The power of seizure conferred by section 90 of the Licensing Act 2003 (seizure of documents relating to club).

---

*Paras 6, 11 and 20: repealed by the Gambling Act 2005, Sch 16 from a date to be appointed.
**Para 18A: inserted by the Consumer Credit Act 2006, s 51 from a date to be appointed.
***Para 30: substituted by the Firearms (Northern Ireland) Order 2004, SI 2004/702, from a date to be appointed.
****Para 74 inserted by the Licensing Act 2003, s 198(1), Sch 6 to be renumbered as second para 73E by the Gambling Act 2005, s 356(1), Sch 16 from a date to be appointed. Para 73I inserted by the Animal Welfare Act 2006, Sch 3 from a date to be appointed.
*****Second para 73F inserted by the Gambling Act 2005, Sch 16, from a date to be appointed.
1. First para 73A inserted by SI 2003/934, second by the Proceeds of Crime Act 2002, Sch 12.

PART 2
POWERS TO WHICH SECTION 51 APPLIES
Police and Criminal Evidence Act 1984 (c 60)

74. Each of the powers of seizure conferred by the provisions of Part 3 of the 1984 Act (police powers of search and seizure on arrest).

Police and Criminal Evidence (Northern Ireland) Order 1989 (SI 1989/1341 (NI 12))

75. Each of the powers of seizure conferred by the provisions of Part 4 of the Police and Criminal Evidence (Northern Ireland) Order 1989 (police powers of seizure on arrest).

Firearms Act 1968 (c 27)

76. The power of seizure conferred by section 46 of the Firearms Act 1968 (seizure of firearms etc).

Misuse of Drugs Act 1971 (c 38)

77. Each of the powers of seizure conferred by the provisions of section 23(2) and (3) of the Misuse of Drugs Act 1971 (power to search for and seize controlled drugs and related documents).

Immigration Act 1971 (c 77)

78. The power of seizure conferred by section 28G(7) of the Immigration Act 1971 (seizure of evidence of offences under that Act etc).

Biological Weapons Act 1974 (c 6)

79. Each of the powers of seizure conferred by the provisions of section 4(1)(*b*), (*c*) and (*d*) of the Biological Weapons Act 1974 (seizures under a warrant).

Firearms (Northern Ireland) Order 1981 (SI 1981/155 (NI 2))

80. The power of seizure conferred by Article 45 of the Firearms (Northern Ireland) Order 1981 (seizure of firearms etc).*

Criminal Justice and Public Order Act 1994 (c 33)

81. The power of seizure conferred by section 139(10) of the Criminal Justice and Public Order Act 1994 (seizure of items found in searching persons arrested under certain cross-border powers).

Terrorism Act 2000 (c 11)

82. The power of seizure conferred by section 43(4) of the Terrorism Act 2000 (seizure on the occasion of a search of a suspected terrorist).
83. Each of the powers of seizure conferred by the provisions of paragraphs 1, 3, 11, 15 and 19 of Schedule 5 to the Terrorism Act 2000 (powers for use in terrorism investigations).

Extradition Act 2003 (c 41)

83A. The powers of seizure conferred by section 163(6) and (7) of the Extradition Act 2003 (seizure in connection with extradition).

*****Paragraph 80 substituted by the Firearms (Northern Ireland) Order 2004, SI 2004/702, Sch 7 from a date to be appointed.**

1–4176

PART 3
POWERS TO WHICH SECTION 55 APPLIES
Police and Criminal Evidence Act 1984 (c 60)

84. The power of seizure conferred by section 8(2) of the 1984 Act (police power, on exercise of search warrant, to seize property searched for).

Police and Criminal Evidence (Northern Ireland) Order 1989 (SI 1989/1341 (NI 12))

85. The power of seizure conferred by Article 10(2) of the Police and Criminal Evidence (Northern Ireland) Order 1989 (police power, on exercise of search warrant, to seize property searched for).

Official Secrets Act 1911 (c 28)

86. The power of seizure conferred by section 9(1) of the Official Secrets Act 1911 (seizure of evidence that an offence under that Act has been or is about to be committed).

Children and Young Persons (Harmful Publications) Act 1955 (c 28)

87. The power of seizure conferred by section 3(1) of the Children and Young Persons (Harmful Publications) Act 1955 (seizure of copies of work to which that Act applies etc).

Obscene Publications Act 1959 (c 66)

88. Each of the powers of seizure conferred by section 3(1) and (2) of the Obscene Publications Act 1959 (power to search for and seize obscene materials and documents relating to a connected business).

Betting, Gaming and Lotteries Act 1963 (c 2)

89. The power seizure conferred by section 51 of the Betting, Gaming and Lotteries Act 1963 (seizure of evidence of offences under that Act).
90. *Repealed.*

Firearms Act 1968 (c 27)

91. The power of seizure conferred by section 46 of the Firearms Act 1968 (seizure of firearms etc).

Theft Act 1968 (c 60)

92. The power of seizure conferred by section 26(3) of the Theft Act 1968, (power to search for and seize goods suspected of being stolen).

Gaming Act 1968 (c 65)

93. The power of seizure conferred by section 43(5) of the Gaming Act 1968 (seizure of evidence of offences under that Act).

Theft Act (Northern Ireland) 1969 (c 16 (NI))

94. The power of seizure conferred by section 25(3) of the Theft Act (Northern Ireland) 1969 (seizure of goods suspected of being stolen).

Immigration Act 1971 (c 77)

95. The power of seizure conferred by section 28D(3) of the Immigration Act 1971 (seizure of evidence of offences under that Act).

Biological Weapons Act 1974 (c 6)

96. Each of the powers of seizure conferred by the provisions of section 4(1)(*b*), (*c*) and (*d*) of the Biological Weapons Act 1974 (seizures under a warrant).

Lotteries and Amusements Act 1976 (c 32)

97. The power of seizure conferred by section 19 of the Lotteries and Amusements Act 1976 (seizure of evidence of offences under that Act).

Protection of Children Act 1978 (c 37)

98. The power of seizure conferred by section 4(2) of the Protection of Children Act 1978 (seizure of indecent photographs or pseudo-photographs of children).

Protection of Children (Northern Ireland) Order 1978 (SI 1978/1047 (NI 17))

99. The power of seizure conferred by Article 4(1) of the Protection of Children (Northern Ireland) Order 1978 (seizure of indecent photographs or pseudo-photographs of children).

Indecent Displays (Control) Act 1981 (c 42)

100. The power of seizure conferred by section 2(3) of the Indecent Displays (Control) Act 1981 (seizure of indecent matter believed to have been used in the commission of an offence under that Act).

Forgery and Counterfeiting Act 1981 (c 45)

101. Each of the powers of seizure conferred by the provisions of sections 7(1) and 24(1) of the Forgery and Counterfeiting Act 1981 (seizure of forgeries and counterfeits and of things used for making them etc).

Firearms (Northern Ireland) Order 1981 (SI 1981/155 (NI 2))

102. The power of seizure conferred by Article 45 of the Firearms (Northern Ireland) Order 1981 (seizure of firearms etc).*

Video Recordings Act 1984 (c 39)

103. The power of seizure conferred by section 17(2) of the Video Recordings Act 1984 (seizure of evidence of offences under that Act).

Betting, Gaming, Lotteries and Amusements (Northern Ireland) Order 1985 (SI 1985/1204 (NI 11))

104. The power of seizure conferred by Article 180(4) of the Betting, Gaming, Lotteries and Amusements (Northern Ireland) Order 1985 (seizure of evidence of offences under that Order).
105. *Repealed.*

Copyright, Designs and Patents Act 1988 (c 48)

106. The powers of seizure conferred by sections 109(4), 200(3A) and 297B(4) of the Copyright, Designs and Patents Act 1988 (seizure of evidence relating to offences concerning infringing copies, illicit reocrodings and unauthorised decoders).

Computer Misuse Act 1990 (c 18)

107. The power of seizure conferred by section 14(4) of the Computer Misuse Act 1990 (seizure of evidence of offences under that Act).

Trade Marks Act 1994 (c 26)

107A. The power of seizure conferred by section 92A(4) of the Trade Marks Act 1994 (seizure of evidence relating to offences concerning unauthorised use of a trade mark, etc in relation to goods).

Drug Trafficking Act 1994 (c 37)

108. The power of seizure conferred by section 56(5) of the Drug Trafficking Act 1994 (seizure of material likely to be of substantial value to an investigation into drug trafficking).

Terrorism Act 2000 (c 11)

109. (1) Each of the powers of seizure conferred by the provisions of paragraphs 1 and 3 of Schedule 5 to the Terrorism Act 2000 (powers for use in terrorism investigations).

(2) Each of the powers of seizure conferred by paragraphs 15 and 19 of Schedule 5 to that Act, so far only as the power in question is conferred by reference to paragraph 1 of that Schedule.

Proceeds of Crime Act 2002 (c 29)

110. The power of seizure conferred by section 352(4) of the Proceeds of Crime Act 2002 (seizure of material likely to be of substantial value to certain investigations).**

*Paragraph 102 substituted by the Firearms (Northern Ireland) Order 2004, SI 2004/702, Sch 7 from a date to be appointed.
**Second para 110 inserted by the Licensing Act 2003, Sch 7, when in force.

1–4177

Section 70

SCHEDULE 2
APPLICATIONS AND MINOR AND CONSEQUENTIAL AMENDMENTS
(Amended by SI 2001/3649)

PART 1
APPLICATION OF ENACTMENTS[1]

1. Paragraphs 1–10 ensure that the various provisions relating to testing, access, compensation and forfeiture in relation to items seized under the legislation specified in those paragraphs will also apply where material is seized under s 50 and the search giving rise to the use of the s 50 power was under the specified legislation. Paragraph 11 ensures that any provision restricting the disclosure of information obtained through the exercise of a power of seizure specified in Part 1 or Part 2 of Sch 1, or any provision that confers power to restrict such disclosure, shall also apply to information obtained under s 50 or s 51 in reliance on the power in question.

Notice of tests

1. Section 30 of the Trade Descriptions Act 1968 (c 29) (notice of test) shall apply in relation to items seized under section 50 of this Act in reliance on the power of seizure conferred by section 28(1) of that Act as it applies in relation to items seized in pursuance of that Act.

2. Section 31 of the Fair Trading Act 1973 (c 41) (notice of test) shall apply in relation to items seized under section 50 of this Act in reliance on the power of seizure conferred by section 29(1) of that Act as it applies in relation to items seized in pursuance of Part 2 of that Act.

3. Section 30(6) and (7) of the Consumer Protection Act 1987 (c 43) (provision about the testing of seized goods) shall apply in relation to items seized under section 50 of this Act in reliance on the power of seizure conferred by section 29 of that Act as it applies in relation to items seized under section 29 of that Act.

4. Article 23(6) and (7) of the Consumer Protection (Northern Ireland) Order 1987 (SI 1987/2049 (NI 20)) (provision about the testing of seized goods) shall apply in relation to items seized under section 50 of this Act in reliance on the power of seizure conferred by Article 22 of that Order as it applies in relation to items seized under that Article.

Access to seized items

5. Subject to section 61 of this Act, section 11(3) of the Estate Agents Act 1979 (c 38) (access to items seized under that section) shall apply in relation to items seized under section 50 of this Act in reliance on the power of seizure conferred by section 11 of that Act as it applies in relation to items seized under section 11 of that Act.

Compensation for seizure and detention

6. Section 32 of the Fair Trading Act 1973 (c 41) (compensation for seizure and detention) shall apply in relation to the seizure of items under section 50 of this Act in reliance on the power of seizure conferred by section 29(1) of that Act, and the retention of those items, as it applies in relation to the seizure and detention of goods under section 29 of that Act.

7. Section 163 of the Consumer Credit Act 1974 (c 39) (compensation for seizure and detention) shall apply in relation to the seizure of items under section 50 of this Act in reliance on the power of seizure conferred by section 162(1) of that Act, and the retention of those items, as it applies in relation to the seizure and detention of goods under section 162 of that Act.

8. Section 34 of the Consumer Protection Act 1987 (compensation for seizure and detention) shall apply in relation to the seizure of items under section 50 of this Act in reliance on the power of seizure conferred by section 29 of that Act, and the retention of those items, as it applies in relation to the seizure and detention of goods under section 29 of that Act.

9. Article 26 of the Consumer Protection (Northern Ireland) Order 1987 (compensation for seizure and detention) shall apply in relation to the seizure of items under section 50 of this Act in reliance on the power of seizure conferred by Article 22 of that Order, and the retention of those items, as it applies in relation to the seizure and detention of goods under that Article.

Forfeiture of seized items

10. (1) The provisions mentioned in sub-paragraph (2) (which are about the forfeiture etc of items which have been seized) shall apply in relation to an item seized under section 50 as if the item had been seized under the power of seizure in reliance on which it was seized.

(2) Those provisions are—

(a)   section 3(3) of the Obscene Publications Act 1959 (c 66);
(b)   sections 4(3) and 5 of the Protection of Children Act 1978 (c 37);
(c)   Article 5 of the Protection of Children (Northern Ireland) Order 1978 (SI 1978/1047 (NI 17));
(d)   sections 7(2) and 24(2) of the Forgery and Counterfeiting Act 1981 (c 45).

Disclosure of information

11. Any provision which—

(a)   restricts the disclosure, or permits the disclosure only for limited purposes or in limited circumstances, of information obtained through the exercise of a power of seizure specified in Part 1 or 2 of Schedule 1, or
(b)   confers power to make provision which does either or both of those things,

shall apply in relation to information obtained under section 50 or 51 in reliance on the power in question as it applies in relation to information obtained through the exercise of that power.

Interpretation

12. For the purposes of this Part of this Schedule, an item is seized, or information is obtained, under section 50 or 51 in reliance on a power of seizure if the item is seized, or the information obtained, in exercise of so much of any power conferred by that section as is exercisable by reference to that power of seizure.

1–4178

PART 2
MINOR AND CONSEQUENTIAL AMENDMENTS

13. (1) In each of the provisions mentioned in sub-paragraph (2) (which confer powers to require the production of information contained in a computer in a visible and legible form)—

(a)   for "contained in a computer" there shall be substituted "stored in any electronic form"; and
(b)   after "in which it is visible and legible" there shall be inserted "or from which it can readily be produced in a visible and legible form".

(2) Those provisions are—

(a)   sections 19(4) and 20(1) of the 1984 Act;
(b)   Articles 21(4) and 22(1) of the Police and Criminal Evidence (Northern Ireland) Order 1989 (SI 1989/1341 (NI 12));
(c)   section 43(5)(aa) of the Gaming Act 1968 (c 65);
(d)   section 20C(3A) of the Taxes Management Act 1970 (c 9);
(e)   section 118D(4) of the Customs and Excise Management Act 1979 (c 2);
(f)   paragraph 11(4) of Schedule 11 to the Value Added Tax Act 1994 (c 23);
(g)   paragraph 4A(4) of Schedule 7 to the Finance Act 1994 (c 9);
(h)   paragraph 7(4) of Schedule 5 to the Finance Act 1996 (c 8);
(i)   paragraph 131(4) of Schedule 6 to the Finance Act 2000 (c 17).

14. In paragraph 5 of Schedule 1 to each of the 1984 Act and the Police and Criminal Evidence (Northern Ireland) Order 1989 (SI 1989/1341 (NI 12)) (power to require the production of information contained in a computer in a visible and legible form)—

(a)   for "contained in a computer" there shall be substituted "stored in any electronic form"; and
(b)   in paragraph (a), after "in which it is visible and legible" there shall be inserted "or from which it can readily be produced in a visible and legible form".

15. In section 46(3) of the Firearms Act 1968 (c 27) (power to require the production of information kept by means of a computer in a visible and legible form)—

(a)   for "kept by means of a computer" there shall be substituted "stored in any electronic form"; and
(b)   after "in which it is visible and legible" there shall be inserted "or from which it can readily be produced in a visible and legible form".

16. (1) In each of the provisions mentioned in sub-paragraph (2) (which confer power to require the production in legible form of information recorded otherwise than in legible form), after "information in legible form" there shall be inserted ", or in a form from which it can readily be produced in visible and legible form".

(2) Those provisions are—

(a)–(d)   repealed.

17. In sections 434(6) and 447(9) of the Companies Act 1985 (c 6) and Articles 427(6) and 440(9) of the Companies (Northern Ireland) Order 1986 (SI 1986/1032 (NI 6)) (power to require the production in legible form of information recorded otherwise than in legible form), at the end there shall be inserted ", or in a form from which it can readily be produced in visible and legible form".

18. In section 32 of the Food Safety Act 1990 (c 16) (powers of entry), in subsections (5) and (6)(b), for "kept by means of a computer" there shall be substituted "stored in any electronic form".

19. In Article 33 of the Food Safety (Northern Ireland) Order 1991 (SI 1991/762 (NI 7)) (powers of entry), in paragraphs (6) and (7)(b), for "kept by means of a computer" there shall be substituted "stored in any electronic form".

20. In paragraph 3(1)(b) of the Schedule to the Property Misdescriptions Act 1991 (c 29) and paragraph 3(1)(b) of Schedule 2 to the Timeshare Act 1992 (c 35) (powers to require the production of information contained in a computer in a visible and legible documentary form)—

(*a*) after "form" there shall be inserted "or from which it can readily be produced in a visible and legible form"; and
(*b*) for "contained in a computer" there shall be substituted "stored in any electronic form".

21. In sections 27(5)(*e*) and 28(2)(*f*) of the Competition Act 1998 (c 41) (power to require the production of information held in a computer in a visible and legible form)—

(*a*) for "held in a computer" there shall be substituted "stored in any electronic form"; and
(*b*) after "in which it is visible and legible" there shall be inserted "or from which it can readily be produced in a visible and legible form".

22. In section 8(2)(*c*) of the Nuclear Safeguards Act 2000 (c 5) (power to require the production of information which is held in electronic form in a form in which it can be read and copied), after "copy it" there shall be inserted ", or from which it can readily be produced in a form in which he can read and copy it".

23. In section 2 of the Criminal Justice Act 1987 (c 38) (investigation powers of the Director of the Serious Fraud Office), after subsection (8C) there shall be inserted—

"(8D) The references in subsections (8A) to (8C) above to evidence obtained by the Director include references to evidence obtained by him by virtue of the exercise by a constable, in the course of a search authorised by a warrant issued under subsection (4) above, of powers conferred by section 50 of the Criminal Justice and Police Act 2001."

24. In section 7 of the Criminal Justice (International Co-operation) Act 1990 (c 5) (search etc for material relevant to overseas investigation), after subsection (8) there shall be inserted—

"(8A) Subject to subsection (8B) below, the reference in subsection (4) above to evidence seized by a constable by virtue of this section shall be taken to include a reference to evidence seized by a constable by virtue of the exercise, in the course of a search authorised by a warrant issued by virtue of this section, of powers conferred by section 50 of the Criminal Justice and Police Act 2001.

(8B) Nothing in subsection (8A) above requires any evidence to be furnished to the Secretary of State—

(*a*) before it has been found, on the completion of any examination required to be made by arrangements under subsection (2) of section 53 of the Criminal Justice and Police Act 2001, to be property which falls within subsection (3) of that section (property which may be retained after examination); or
(*b*) at a time when it constitutes property in respect of which a person is required to ensure that arrangements such as are mentioned in section 61(1) of that Act (duty to secure) are in force."

25. In section 8 of the Criminal Justice (International Co-operation) Act 1990 (which makes similar provision for Scotland) after subsection (6) there shall be added—

"(7) Subject to subsection (8) below, the reference in subsection (2) above to evidence seized by a constable by virtue of this section shall be taken to include a reference to evidence seized by a constable by virtue of the exercise, in the course of a search authorised by a warrant issued by virtue of this section, of powers conferred by section 50 of the Criminal Justice and Police Act 2001.

(8) Nothing in subsection (7) above requires any evidence to be furnished to the Lord Advocate—

(*a*) before it has been found, on the completion of any examination required to be made by arrangements under subsection (2) of section 53 of the Criminal Justice and Police Act 2001, to be property which falls within subsection (3) of that section (property which may be retained after examination); or
(*b*) at a time when it constitutes property in respect of which a person is required to ensure that arrangements such as are mentioned in section 61(1) of that Act (duty to secure) are in force."

26. Section 426 of the Financial Services and Markets Act 2000 (c 8) (consequential and supplementary provision) shall have effect as if the provisions referred to in subsection (2)(*b*) of that section included the provisions of this Part of this Act.

27. In paragraph 29(1)(*a*) of Schedule 5 to the Terrorism Act 2000 (c 11) (conditions for grant of warrant), for "28" there shall be substituted "22".

Crime (International Co-operation) Act 2003[1]

(2003 c 32)

PART 1[2]
MUTUAL ASSISTANCE IN CRIMINAL MATTERS

CHAPTER 1[3]
Mutual Service of Process[4] etc

Service of overseas process in the UK

1–4179   1. Service of overseas process.   (1) The power conferred by subsection (3) is exercisable where the Secretary of State receives any process or other document to which this section applies from the government of, or other authority in, a country outside the United Kingdom, together with a request for the process or document to be served on a person in the United Kingdom.

(2) This section applies—

(*a*) to any process issued or made in that country for the purposes of criminal proceedings,
(*b*) to any document issued or made by an administrative authority in that country in administrative proceedings,
(*c*) to any process issued or made for the purposes of any proceedings on an appeal before a court in that country against a decision in administrative proceedings,
(*d*) to any document issued or made by an authority in that country for the purposes of clemency proceedings.

(3) The Secretary of State may cause the process or document to be served by post or, if the

request is for personal service, direct the chief officer of police for the area in which that person appears to be to cause it to be personally served on him.

(4) In relation to any process or document to be served in Scotland, references in this section to the Secretary of State are to be read as references to the Lord Advocate.

[Crime (International Co-operation) Act 2003, s 1.]

---

1. This Act implements various UK commitments in relation to policing and judicial co-operation. It includes the legislative provisions necessary to enable the UK's partial participation in the Schlengen Convention, which was designed to facilitate free movement of persons within the EU by the removal of internal border controls. To compensate for the lifting of controls, a serious of measures to enhance police and judicial co-operation was agreed. The formal integration of the Schlengen Convention into the EU treaty structure occurred with the Treaty of Amsterdam 1997. The Act also implements several Framework Decisions of the EU in the field of Justice and Home Affairs policy. The purpose of Framework Decisions is to approximate the laws and regulations of the Member States (though the choice of forms and methods is left to national authorities).

Part 1 of the Act deals with mutual legal assistance and the evidence aspects of the 2003 Framework Decision. It implements the unrepealed mutual legal assistance provisions of the Schlengen Convention and those of the Convention on Mutual Assistance in Criminal Matters 2000. Part 1 re-enacts and updates the provisions of Part 1 of the Criminal Justice (International Co-operation) Act 1990 to widen the range of cases in which the UK is able to request or to offer assistance. Part 1 also implements the 2001 Protocol, which enables the provision of a wider range of banking information than before. Part 1 additionally introduces the mutual recognition of freezing orders on evidence. The mutual legal assistance provisions of Part 1 apply to all other countries, except for certain new provisions that are limited to 'participating countries', defined to include all EU countries (provided they are participating in the relevant instruments).

Part 2 of the Act concerns terrorist acts and threats and it gives effect to art 9 of the 2002 Framework Decision (much of the substance of which has previously been brought into effect in UK legislation).

Part 3 concerns road traffic. The Convention provides for EU wide recognition of disqualifications imposed in any Member State. The Convention will come into effect when it has been ratified by all the Member States, but there is also provision for implementation on a bilateral basis between Member States. Part 3 also introduces new measures to prevent drivers banned in Northern Ireland from obtaining a British driving licence, and vice versa.

Part 4 contains miscellaneous provisions. These include the disclosure of information by the Serious Fraud Office, four different areas of the Schlengen Convention and false monetary instruments.

With the exception of the provisions of Chapter 2 of Part 5, the Act will be brought into force in accordance with commencement orders made under s 94. At the time of going to press the following commencement orders had been made: Crime (International Co-operation) Act 2003 (Commencement No 1) Order 2004, SI 2004/786; Crime (International Co-operation) Act 2003 (Commencement No 2) Order, SI 2004/2624; and Crime (International Co-operation) Act 2003 (Commencement No 3) Order 2006, SI 2006/2811. The first brought into force the majority of the Act's provisions. The second brought into force the provisions concerned with mutual recognition of driver licensing and disqualification between Great Britain and Northern Ireland and giving effect in Great Britain to driving disqualifications imposed in the Isle of Man, the Channel Islands and Gibraltar. The third brought into force ss 32–26 and 42–46. The provisions that have not yet been brought into force are: ss 10–12, 20–25, 37–41, 54–75, 86–87, 89, Schs 3 and 4 and parts of Schs 5 and 6.

2. Part 1 contains ss 1–51.

3. Chapter 1 contains ss 1–6.

4. "Process" is defined in s 51(3), post.

1–4180   2. Service of overseas process: supplementary. (1) Subsections (2) and (3) apply to any process served in a part of the United Kingdom by virtue of section 1 requiring a person to appear as a party or attend as a witness.

(2) No obligation under the law of that part to comply with the process is imposed by virtue of its service.

(3) The process must be accompanied by a notice—

(a) stating the effect of subsection (2),

(b) indicating that the person on whom it is served may wish to seek advice as to the possible consequences of his failing to comply with the process under the law of the country where it was issued or made, and

(c) indicating that under that law he may not be accorded the same rights and privileges as a party or as a witness as would be accorded to him in proceedings in the part of the United Kingdom in which the process is served.

(4) Where a chief officer of police causes any process or document to be served under section 1, he must at once—

(a) tell the Secretary of State (or, as the case may be, the Lord Advocate) when and how it was served, and

(b) (if possible) provide him with a receipt signed by the person on whom it was served.

(5) Where the chief officer of police is unable to cause any process or document to be served as directed, he must at once inform the Secretary of State (or, as the case may be, the Lord Advocate) of that fact and of the reason.

[Crime (International Co-operation) Act 2003, s 2.]

1–4181

Service of UK process abroad

3. General requirements for service of process. (1) This section applies to any process issued or made for the purposes of criminal proceedings by a court in England and Wales or Northern Ireland.

(2) The process may be issued or made in spite of the fact that the person on whom it is to be served is outside the United Kingdom.

(3) Where the process is to be served outside the United Kingdom and the person at whose

request it is issued or made believes that the person on whom it is to be served does not understand English, he must—

    (*a*) inform the court of that fact, and

    (*b*) provide the court with a copy of the process, or of so much of it as is material, translated into an appropriate language.

    (4) Process served outside the United Kingdom requiring a person to appear as a party or attend as a witness—

    (*a*) must not include notice of a penalty,

    (*b*) must be accompanied by a notice giving any information required to be given by rules of court[1].

    (5) If process requiring a person to appear as a party or attend as a witness is served outside the United Kingdom, no obligation to comply with the process under the law of the part of the United Kingdom in which the process is issued or made is imposed by virtue of the service.

    (6) Accordingly, failure to comply with the process does not constitute contempt of court and is not a ground for issuing a warrant to secure the attendance of the person in question.

    (7) But the process may subsequently be served on the person in question in the United Kingdom (with the usual consequences for non-compliance).

[Crime (International Co-operation) Act 2003, s 3.]

---

    1. See the Magistrates' Courts (Crime (International Co-operation) Rules 2004, in this PART, post.

1–4182 **4. Service of process otherwise than by post.** (1) Process to which section 3 applies may, instead of being served by post, be served[1] on a person outside the United Kingdom in accordance with arrangements made by the Secretary of State.

    (2) But where the person is in a participating country, the process may be served in accordance with those arrangements only if one of the following conditions is met.

    (3) The conditions are—

    (*a*) that the correct address of the person is unknown,

    (*b*) that it has not been possible to serve the process by post,

    (*c*) that there are good reasons for thinking that service by post will not be effective or is inappropriate.

[Crime (International Co-operation) Act 2003, s 4.]

---

    1. For proof of service under this section, see the Magistrates' Courts (Crime (International Co-operation)) Rules 2004, in this PART, post.

1–4183 **5.** *General requirements for effecting Scottish citation etc*

1–4184 **6.** *Effecting Scottish citation etc otherwise than by post*

CHAPTER 2[1]
MUTUAL PROVISION OF EVIDENCE

Assistance in obtaining evidence abroad

1–4185 **7. Requests for assistance in obtaining evidence abroad.** (1) If it appears to a judicial authority in the United Kingdom on an application made by a person mentioned in subsection (3)—

    (*a*) that an offence has been committed or that there are reasonable grounds for suspecting that an offence has been committed, and

    (*b*) that proceedings in respect of the offence have been instituted or that the offence is being investigated,

the judicial authority may request assistance under this section.

    (2) The assistance that may be requested under this section is assistance in obtaining outside the United Kingdom any evidence specified in the request for use in the proceedings or investigation.

    (3) The application may be made—

    (*a*) in relation to England and Wales and Northern Ireland, by a prosecuting authority,

    (*b*) in relation to Scotland, by the Lord Advocate or a procurator fiscal,

    (*c*) where proceedings have been instituted, by the person charged in those proceedings.

    (4) The judicial authorities are—

    (*a*) in relation to England and Wales, any judge or justice of the peace,

    (*b*) in relation to Scotland, any judge of the High Court or sheriff,

    (*c*) in relation to Northern Ireland, any judge or resident magistrate.

    (5) In relation to England and Wales or Northern Ireland, a designated prosecuting authority may itself request assistance under this section if—

    (*a*) it appears to the authority that an offence has been committed or that there are reasonable grounds for suspecting that an offence has been committed, and (*b*)   the authority has instituted proceedings in respect of the offence in question or it is being investigated.

"Designated" means designated by an order[2] made by the Secretary of State.

(6) In relation to Scotland, the Lord Advocate or a procurator fiscal may himself request assistance under this section if it appears to him—

(*a*)   that an offence has been committed or that there are reasonable grounds for suspecting that an offence has been committed, and

(*b*)   that proceedings in respect of the offence have been instituted or that the offence is being investigated.

(7) If a request for assistance under this section is made in reliance on Article 2 of the 2001 Protocol (requests for information on banking transactions) in connection with the investigation of an offence, the request must state the grounds on which the person making the request considers the evidence specified in it to be relevant for the purposes of the investigation.
[Crime (International Co-operation) Act 2003, s 7.]

---

1. Chapter 2 contains ss 7–28.
2. The Crime (International Co-operation) Act 2003 (Designation of Prosecuting Authorities) Order 2004, SI 2004/1034 amended by SI 2004/1747 and SI 2005/1130, has been made.

1–4186   8. Sending requests for assistance.   (1) A request for assistance under section 7 may be sent[1]—

(*a*)   to a court exercising jurisdiction in the place where the evidence is situated, or

(*b*)   to any authority recognised by the government of the country in question as the appropriate authority for receiving requests of that kind.

(2) Alternatively, if it is a request by a judicial authority or a designated prosecuting authority it may be sent to the Secretary of State (in Scotland, the Lord Advocate) for forwarding to a court or authority mentioned in subsection (1).

(3) In cases of urgency, a request for assistance may be sent to—

(*a*)   the International Criminal Police Organisation, or

(*b*)   any body or person competent to receive it under any provisions adopted under the Treaty on European Union,

for forwarding to any court or authority mentioned in subsection (1).
[Crime (International Co-operation) Act 2003, s 8.]

---

1. Where a request for assistance under s 7 of the Act is made by a justice of the peace the justices' clerk must send a copy of the letter of request to the Secretary of State as soon as practicable after the request has been made, see the Magistrates' Courts (Crime (International Co-operation) Rules 2004, in this PART, post.

1–4187   9. Use of evidence obtained.   (1) This section applies to evidence obtained pursuant to a request for assistance under section 7.

(2) The evidence may not without the consent of the appropriate overseas authority be used for any purpose other than that specified in the request.

(3) When the evidence is no longer required for that purpose (or for any other purpose for which such consent has been obtained), it must be returned to the appropriate overseas authority, unless that authority indicates that it need not be returned.

(4) In exercising the discretion conferred by section 25 of the Criminal Justice Act 1988 (c 33) or Article 5 of the Criminal Justice (Evidence, Etc.) (Northern Ireland) Order 1988 (SI 1988/1847 (NI 17)) (exclusion of evidence otherwise admissible) in relation to a statement contained in the evidence, the court must have regard—

(*a*)   to whether it was possible to challenge the statement by questioning the person who made it, and

(*b*)   if proceedings have been instituted, to whether the local law allowed the parties to the proceedings to be legally represented when the evidence was being obtained.

(5) In Scotland, the evidence may be received in evidence without being sworn to by witnesses, so far as that may be done without unfairness to either party.

(6) In this section, the appropriate overseas authority means the authority recognised by the government of the country in question as the appropriate authority for receiving requests of the kind in question.
[Crime (International Co-operation) Act 2003, s 9.]

1–4188   10. Domestic freezing orders.   (1) If it appears to a judicial authority in the United Kingdom, on an application made by a person mentioned in subsection (4)—

(*a*)   that proceedings in respect of a listed offence have been instituted or such an offence is being investigated,

(*b*)   that there are reasonable grounds to believe that there is evidence in a participating country which satisfies the requirements of subsection (3), and

(*c*)   that a request has been made, or will be made, under section 7 for the evidence to be sent to the authority making the request, the judicial authority may make a domestic freezing order in respect of the evidence.

(2) A domestic freezing order is an order for protecting evidence which is in the participating country pending its transfer to the United Kingdom.

(3) The requirements are that the evidence—

(a) is on premises specified in the application in the participating country,
(b) is likely to be of substantial value (whether by itself or together with other evidence) to the proceedings or investigation,
(c) is likely to be admissible in evidence at a trial for the offence, and
(d) does not consist of or include items subject to legal privilege.

(4) The application may be made—

(a) in relation to England and Wales and Northern Ireland, by a constable,
(b) in relation to Scotland, by the Lord Advocate or a procurator fiscal.

(5) The judicial authorities are—

(a) in relation to England and Wales, any judge or justice of the peace,
(b) in relation to Scotland, any judge of the High Court or sheriff,
(c) in relation to Northern Ireland, any judge or resident magistrate.

(6) This section does not prejudice the generality of the power to make a request for assistance under section 7.

[Crime (International Co-operation) Act 2003, s 10.]

1–4189 11. Sending freezing orders. (1) A domestic freezing order made in England and Wales or Northern Ireland is to be sent to the Secretary of State for forwarding to—

(a) a court exercising jurisdiction in the place where the evidence is situated, or
(b) any authority recognised by the government of the country in question as the appropriate authority for receiving orders of that kind.

(2) A domestic freezing order made in Scotland is to be sent to the Lord Advocate for forwarding to such a court or authority.

(3) The judicial authority is to send the order to the Secretary of State or the Lord Advocate before the end of the period of 14 days beginning with its being made.

(4) The order must be accompanied by a certificate giving the specified information and, unless the certificate indicates when the judicial authority expects such a request to be made, by a request under section 7 for the evidence to be sent to the authority making the request.

(5) The certificate must include a translation of it into an appropriate language of the participating country (if that language is not English).

(6) The certificate must be signed by or on behalf of the judicial authority who made the order and must include a statement as to the accuracy of the information given in it.

The signature may be an electronic signature.

[Crime (International Co-operation) Act 2003, s 11.]

1–4190 12. Variation or revocation of freezing orders. (1) The judicial authority that made a domestic freezing order may vary or revoke it on an application by a person mentioned below.

(2) The persons are—

(a) the person who applied for the order,
(b) in relation to England and Wales and Northern Ireland, a prosecuting authority,
(c) in relation to Scotland, the Lord Advocate,
(d) any other person affected by the order.

[Crime (International Co-operation) Act 2003, s 12.]

Assisting overseas authorities to obtain evidence in the UK

1–4191 13. Requests for assistance from overseas authorities. (1) Where a request for assistance in obtaining evidence in a part of the United Kingdom is received by the territorial authority for that part, the authority may[1]—

(a) if the conditions in section 14 are met, arrange for the evidence to be obtained under section 15, or
(b) direct that a search warrant be applied for under or by virtue of section 16 or 17 or, in relation to evidence in Scotland, 18.

(2) The request for assistance may be made only by—

(a) a court exercising criminal jurisdiction, or a prosecuting authority, in a country outside the United Kingdom,
(b) any other authority in such a country which appears to the territorial authority to have the function of making such requests for assistance,
(c) any international authority mentioned in subsection (3).

(3) The international authorities are—

(a) the International Criminal Police Organisation,

(b)   any other body or person competent to make a request of the kind to which this section applies under any provisions adopted under the Treaty on European Union.
[Crime (International Co-operation) Act 2003, s 13.]

---

1. The exercise of the Secretary of State's discretion under this section and ss 14(1) and 15(1) is susceptible to judicial review. However his duties are procedural and ministerial and any decision is no more than a decision to subject the request to a judicial process (*R (Hafner) v Secretary of State for the Home Department* [2006] EWHC 1259 (Admin), [2006] 3 All ER 382).

1–4192   14. Powers to arrange for evidence to be obtained. (1) The territorial authority may arrange for evidence to be obtained under section 15 if the request for assistance in obtaining the evidence is made in connection with—

(a)   criminal proceedings or a criminal investigation, being carried on outside the United Kingdom,
(b)   administrative proceedings[1], or an investigation into an act punishable in such proceedings, being carried on there,
(c)   clemency proceedings[1], or proceedings on an appeal before a court against a decision in administrative proceedings, being carried on, or intended to be carried on, there.

(2)   In a case within subsection (1)(a) or (b), the authority may arrange for the evidence to be so obtained only if the authority is satisfied—

(a)   that an offence under the law of the country in question has been committed or that there are reasonable grounds for suspecting that such an offence has been committed, and
(b)   that proceedings in respect of the offence have been instituted in that country or that an investigation into the offence is being carried on there.

An offence includes an act punishable in administrative proceedings.

(3)   The territorial authority is to regard as conclusive a certificate as to the matters mentioned in subsection (2)(a) and (b) issued by any authority in the country in question which appears to him to be the appropriate authority to do so.

(4)   If it appears to the territorial authority that the request for assistance relates to a fiscal offence in respect of which proceedings have not yet been instituted, the authority may not arrange for the evidence to be so obtained unless—

(a)   the request is from a country which is a member of the Commonwealth or is made pursuant to a treaty to which the United Kingdom is a party, or
(b)   the authority is satisfied that if the conduct constituting the offence were to occur in a part of the United Kingdom, it would constitute an offence in that part.
[Crime (International Co-operation) Act 2003, s 14.]

---

1. Defined in s 51(1), post.

1–4193   15. Nominating a court etc to receive evidence. (1) Where the evidence is in England and Wales or Northern Ireland, the Secretary of State may by a notice nominate a court to receive any evidence to which the request relates which appears to the court to be appropriate for the purpose of giving effect to the request.

(2)   But if it appears to the Secretary of State that the request relates to an offence involving serious or complex fraud, he may refer the request (or any part of it) to the Director of the Serious Fraud Office for the Director to obtain any evidence to which the request or part relates which appears to him to be appropriate for the purpose of giving effect to the request or part.

(3)   Where the evidence is in Scotland, the Lord Advocate may by a notice nominate a court to receive any evidence to which the request relates which appears to the court to be appropriate for the purpose of giving effect to the request.

(4)   But if it appears to the Lord Advocate that the request relates to an offence involving serious or complex fraud, he may give a direction under section 27 of the Criminal Law (Consolidation) (Scotland) Act 1995 (c 39) (directions applying investigatory provisions).

(5)   Schedule 1 is to have effect in relation to proceedings before a court nominated under this section.
[Crime (International Co-operation) Act 2003, s 15.]

1–4194   16. Extension of statutory search powers in England and Wales and Northern Ireland. (1) Part 2 of the Police and Criminal Evidence Act 1984 (c 60) (powers of entry, search and seizure) is to have effect as if references to indictable offences in section 8 of, and Schedule 1 to, that Act included any conduct which—

(a)   constitutes an offence under the law of a country outside the United Kingdom, and
(b)   would, if it occurred in England and Wales, constitute an indictable offence.

(2)   But an application for a warrant or order by virtue of subsection (1) may be made only—

(a)   in pursuance of a direction given under section 13, or
(b)   if it is an application for a warrant or order under section 8 of, or Schedule 1 to, that Act by a constable for the purposes of an investigation by an international joint investigation team of which he is a member.

(3)   Part 3 of the Police and Criminal Evidence (Northern Ireland) Order 1989 (SI 1989/ 1341

(NI12)) (powers of entry, search and seizure) is to have effect as if references to serious arrestable offences in Article 10 of, and Schedule 1 to, that Order included any conduct which—

(a) constitutes an offence under the law of a country outside the United Kingdom, and
(b) would, if it occurred in Northern Ireland, constitute a serious arrestable offence.

(4) But an application for a warrant or order by virtue of subsection (3) may be made only—

(a) in pursuance of a direction given under section 13, or
(b) if it is an application for a warrant or order under Article 10 of, or Schedule 1 to, that Order, by a constable for the purposes of an investigation by an international joint investigation team of which he is a member.

(5) In this section, "international joint investigation team" has the meaning given by section 88(7) of the Police Act 1996 (c 16).

[Crime (International Co-operation) Act 2003, s 16 as amended by the Serious Organised Crime and Police Act 2005, Sch 3.]

1–4195   17. Warrants in England and Wales or Northern Ireland.   (1) A justice of the peace may issue a warrant under this section if he is satisfied, on an application made by a constable, that the following conditions are met.

(2) But an application for a warrant under subsection (1) may be made only in pursuance of a direction given under section 13.

(3) The conditions are that—

(a) criminal proceedings have been instituted against a person in a country outside the United Kingdom or a person has been arrested in the course of a criminal investigation carried on there,
(b) the conduct constituting the offence which is the subject of the proceedings or investigation would (if it occurred in England and Wales) constitute an indictable offence, or (if it occurred in Northern Ireland) constitute an arrestable offence, and
(c) there are reasonable grounds for suspecting that there is on premises in England and Wales or (as the case may be) Northern Ireland occupied or controlled by that person evidence relating to the offence.

"Arrestable offence" has the same meaning as in (Northern Ireland) Order 1989 (SI 1989/1341 (NI 12)).

(4) A warrant under this section may authorise a constable—

(a) to enter the premises in question and search the premises to the extent reasonably required for the purpose of discovering any evidence relating to the offence,
(b) to seize and retain any evidence for which he is authorised to search.

[Crime (International Co-operation) Act 2003, s 17 as amended by the Serious Organised Crime and Police Act 2005, Sch 7.]

1–4196   18. *Warrants in Scotland*

1–4197   19. Seized evidence.   (1) Any evidence seized by a constable under or by virtue of section 16, 17 or 18 is to be sent to the court or authority which made the request for assistance or to the territorial authority for forwarding to that court or authority.

(2) So far as may be necessary in order to comply with the request for assistance—

(a) where the evidence consists of a document, the original or a copy is to be sent, and
(b) where the evidence consists of any other article, the article itself or a description, photograph or other representation of it is to be sent.

(3) This section does not apply to evidence seized under or by virtue of section 16(2)(b) or (4)(b) or 18(2)(b).

[Crime (International Co-operation) Act 2003, s 19.]

Overseas freezing orders

1–4198   20. Overseas freezing orders.   (1) Section 21 applies where an overseas freezing order made by a court or authority in a participating country[1] is received from the court or authority which made or confirmed the order by the territorial authority for the part of the United Kingdom in which the evidence to which the order relates is situated.

(2) An overseas freezing order is an order—

(a) for protecting, pending its transfer to the participating country, evidence which is in the United Kingdom and may be used in any proceedings or investigation in the participating country, and
(b) in respect of which the following requirements of this section are met.

(3) The order must have been made by—

(a) a court exercising criminal jurisdiction in the country,
(b) a prosecuting authority in the country,
(c) any other authority in the country which appears to the territorial authority to have the function of making such orders.

(4) The order must relate to—

(*a*) criminal proceedings instituted in the participating country in respect of a listed offence, or
(*b*) a criminal investigation being carried on there into such an offence.

(5) The order must be accompanied by a certificate which gives the specified information; but a certificate may be treated as giving any specified information which is not given in it if the territorial authority has the information in question.

(6) The certificate must—

(*a*) be signed by or on behalf of the court or authority which made or confirmed the order,
(*b*) include a statement as to the accuracy of the information given in it,
(*c*) if it is not in English, include a translation of it into English (or, if appropriate, Welsh).

The signature may be an electronic signature.

(7) The order must be accompanied by a request for the evidence to be sent to a court or authority mentioned in section 13(2), unless the certificate indicates when such a request is expected to be made.

(8) References below in this Chapter to an overseas freezing order include its accompanying certificate.

[Crime (International Co-operation) Act 2003, s 20.]

---

1. Defined in s 51(1), post.

1–4199   21. Considering the order.   (1) In relation to England and Wales and Northern Ireland, where this section applies the Secretary of State must—

(*a*) by a notice nominate a court in England and Wales or (as the case may be) Northern Ireland to give effect to the overseas freezing order,
(*b*) send a copy of the overseas freezing order to the nominated court and to the chief officer of police for the area in which the evidence is situated,
(*c*) tell the chief officer which court has been nominated.

(2) In relation to Scotland, where this section applies the Lord Advocate must—

(*a*) by a notice nominate a sheriff to give effect to the overseas freezing order,
(*b*) send a copy of the overseas freezing order to the sheriff and to the procurator fiscal.

In relation to Scotland, references below in this section and in sections 22 to 25 to the nominated court are to be read as references to the nominated sheriff.

(3) The nominated court is to consider the overseas freezing order on its own initiative within a period prescribed by rules of court.

(4) Before giving effect to the overseas freezing order, the nominated court must give the chief officer of police or (as the case may be) the procurator fiscal an opportunity to be heard.

(5) The court may decide not to give effect to the overseas freezing order only if, in its opinion, one of the following conditions is met.

(6) The first condition is that, if the person whose conduct is in question were charged in the participating country with the offence to which the overseas freezing order relates or in the United Kingdom with a corresponding offence, he would be entitled to be discharged under any rule of law relating to previous acquittal or conviction.

(7) The second condition is that giving effect to the overseas freezing order would be incompatible with any of the Convention rights (within the meaning of the Human Rights Act 1998 (c 42)).

[Crime (International Co-operation) Act 2003, s 21.]

1–4200   22. Giving effect to the order.   (1) The nominated court is to give effect to the overseas freezing order by issuing a warrant authorising a constable—

(*a*) to enter the premises to which the overseas freezing order relates and search the premises to the extent reasonably required for the purpose of discovering any evidence to which the order relates, and
(*b*) to seize and retain any evidence for which he is authorised to search.

(2) But, in relation to England and Wales and Northern Ireland, so far as the overseas freezing order relates to excluded material or special procedure material the court is to give effect to the order by making a production order.

(3) A production order is an order for the person who appears to the court to be in possession of the material to produce it to a constable before the end of the period of seven days beginning with the date of the production order or such longer period as the production order may specify.

(4) The constable may take away any material produced to him under a production order; and the material is to be treated for the purposes of section 21 of the Police and Criminal Evidence Act 1984 (c 60) or (as the case may be) Article 23 of the Police and Criminal Evidence (Northern Ireland) Order 1989 (SI 1989/1341 (NI 12)) (access and copying) as if it had been seized by the constable.

(5) If a person fails to comply with a production order, the court may (whether or not it deals with the matter as a contempt of court) issue a warrant under subsection (1) in respect of the material to which the production order relates.

(6) Section 409 of the Proceeds of Crime Act 2002 (c 29) (jurisdiction of sheriff) has effect for the purposes of subsection (1) as if that subsection were included in Chapter 3 of Part 8 of that Act.
[Crime (International Co-operation) Act 2003, s 22.]

1–4201 23. Postponed effect.   The nominated court may postpone giving effect to an overseas freezing order in respect of any evidence—

(a) in order to avoid prejudicing a criminal investigation which is taking place in the United Kingdom, or

(b) if, under an order made by a court in criminal proceedings in the United Kingdom, the evidence may not be removed from the United Kingdom.
[Crime (International Co-operation) Act 2003, s 23.]

1–4202 24. Evidence seized under the order.   (1) Any evidence seized by or produced to the constable under section 22 is to be retained by him until he is given a notice under subsection (2) or authorised to release it under section 25.

(2) If—

(a) the overseas freezing order was accompanied by a request for the evidence to be sent to a court or authority mentioned in section 13(2), or

(b) the territorial authority subsequently receives such a request,

the territorial authority may by notice require the constable to send the evidence to the court or authority that made the request.
[Crime (International Co-operation) Act 2003, s 24.]

1–4203 25. Release of evidence held under the order.   (1) On an application made by a person mentioned below, the nominated court may authorise the release of any evidence retained by a constable under section 24 if, in its opinion—

(a) the condition in section 21(6) or (7) is met, or

(b) the overseas freezing order has ceased to have effect in the participating country.

(2) In relation to England and Wales and Northern Ireland, the persons are—

(a) the chief officer of police to whom a copy of the order was sent,

(b) the constable,

(c) any other person affected by the order.

(3) In relation to Scotland, the persons are—

(a) the procurator fiscal to whom a copy of the order was sent,

(b) any other person affected by the order.

(4) If the territorial authority decides not to give a notice under section 24(2) in respect of any evidence retained by a constable under that section, the authority must give the constable a notice authorising him to release the evidence.
[Crime (International Co-operation) Act 2003, s 25.]

General

1–4204 26. Powers under warrants.   (1) A court in England and Wales or Northern Ireland, or a justice of the peace, may not issue a warrant under section 17 or 22 in respect of any evidence unless the court or justice has reasonable grounds for believing that it does not consist of or include items subject to legal privilege, excluded material or special procedure material.

(2) Subsection (1) does not prevent a warrant being issued by virtue of section 22(5) in respect of excluded material or special procedure material.

(3) *Amends Sch 1 to the Criminal Justice and Police Act 2001.*

(4) References in this Chapter to evidence seized by a person by virtue of or under any provision of this Chapter include evidence seized by a person by virtue of section 50 of the Criminal Justice and Police Act 2001 (additional powers of seizure), if it is seized in the course of a search authorised by a warrant issued by virtue of or under the provision in question.

(5) Subsection (4) does not require any evidence to be sent to the territorial authority or to any court or authority—

(a) before it has been found, on the completion of any examination required to be made by arrangements under section 53(2) of the Criminal Justice and Police Act 2001, to be property within subsection (3) of that section (property which may be retained after examination), or

(b) at a time when it constitutes property in respect of which a person is required to ensure that arrangements such as are mentioned in section 61(1) of that Act (duty to secure) are in force.
[Crime (International Co-operation) Act 2003, s 26.]

1–4205 27. Exercise of powers by others.   (1) The Treasury may by order[1] provide, in relation to England and Wales or Northern Ireland—

(a) for any function conferred on the Secretary of State (whether or not in terms) under sections 10, 11 and 13 to 26 to be exercisable instead in prescribed circumstances by the Commissioners of Customs and Excise, (*b*) for any function conferred on a constable under those sections to be exercisable instead in prescribed circumstances by a customs officer or a person acting under the direction of such an officer.

"Prescribed" means prescribed by the order.

(2) The Secretary of State may by order provide, in relation to England and Wales or Northern Ireland—

(*a*) for any function conferred on him under sections 13 to 26 to be exercisable instead in prescribed circumstances by a prescribed person,

(*b*) for any function conferred on a constable under those sections to be exercisable instead in prescribed circumstances by a prescribed person.

"Prescribed" means prescribed by the order.

(3) Subsection (2)(*b*) does not apply to any powers exercisable by virtue of section 16(2)(*b*) or (4)(*b*).

[Crime (International Co-operation) Act 2003, s 27.]

---

1. The Crime (International Co-operation) Act 2003 (Exercise of Functions) Order 2005, SI 2005/425 has been made which provides that certain functions under the Act may be performed by Commissioners of Customs and Excise and customs officers.

1-4206   28. Interpretation of Chapter 2.   (1) In this Chapter—

"domestic freezing order" has the meaning given by section 10(2),

"notice" means a notice in writing,

"overseas freezing order" has the meaning given by section 20,

"premises" has the same meaning as in the Police and Criminal Evidence Act 1984 (c 60), Chapter 3 of Part 8 of the Proceeds of Crime Act 2002 (c 29) or the Police and Criminal Evidence (Northern Ireland) Order 1989 (SI 1989/1341 (NI 12)) (as the case may be),

"the relevant Framework Decision" means the Framework Decision on the execution in the European Union of orders freezing property or evidence adopted by the Council of the European Union on 22nd July 2003.

(2) The following provisions have effect for the purposes of this Chapter.

(3) In relation to England and Wales and Northern Ireland, "items subject to legal privilege", "excluded material" and "special procedure material" have the same meaning as in the Police and Criminal Evidence Act 1984 or (as the case may be) the Police and Criminal Evidence (Northern Ireland) Order 1989.

(4) In relation to Scotland, "items subject to legal privilege" has the same meaning as in Chapter 3 of Part 8 of the Proceeds of Crime Act 2002.

(5) A listed offence means—

(*a*) an offence described in Article 3(2) of the relevant Framework Decision, or

(*b*) an offence prescribed or of a description prescribed by an order made by the Secretary of State.

(6) An order prescribing an offence or a description of offences under subsection (5)(*b*) may require, in the case of an overseas freezing order, that the conduct which constitutes the offence or offences would, if it occurred in a part of the United Kingdom, constitute an offence in that part.

(7) Specified information, in relation to a certificate required by section 11(4) or 20(5), means—

(*a*) any information required to be given by the form of certificate annexed to the relevant Framework Decision, or

(*b*) any information prescribed by an order made by the Secretary of State.

(8) In relation to Scotland, references to the Secretary of State are to be read as references to the Scottish Ministers.

(9) The territorial authority—

(*a*) in relation to evidence in England and Wales or Northern Ireland, is the Secretary of State,

(*b*) in relation to evidence in Scotland, is the Lord Advocate.

[Crime (International Co-operation) Act 2003, s 28.]

CHAPTER 3[1]
HEARING EVIDENCE THROUGH TELEVISION LINKS OR BY TELEPHONE

1-4207   29. Hearing witnesses abroad through television links.   (1) The Secretary of State may by order provide for section 32(1A) of the Criminal Justice Act 1988 (c 33) or Article 80A(4) of the Police and Criminal Evidence (Northern Ireland) Order 1989 (SI 1989/1341 (NI 12)) (proceedings in which evidence may be given through television link) to apply to any further description of criminal proceedings, or to all criminal proceedings.

(2) The Scottish Ministers may by order provide for section 273(1) of the Criminal Procedure (Scotland) Act 1995 (c 46) (proceedings in which evidence may be given through television link) to apply to any further description of criminal proceedings, or to all criminal proceedings.

[Crime (International Co-operation) Act 2003, s 29 as amended by SI 2005/1965.]

---

1. Chapter 3 contains ss 29–31.

1–4208   30. Hearing witnesses in the UK through television links. (1) This section applies where the Secretary of State receives a request, from an authority mentioned in subsection (2) ("the external authority"), for a person in the United Kingdom to give evidence through a live television link in criminal proceedings before a court in a country outside the United Kingdom.

Criminal proceedings include any proceedings on an appeal before a court against a decision in administrative proceedings.

(2) The authority referred to in subsection (1) is the authority in that country which appears to the Secretary of State to have the function of making requests of the kind to which this section applies.

(3) Unless he considers it inappropriate to do so, the Secretary of State must by notice in writing nominate a court in the United Kingdom where the witness may be heard in the proceedings in question through a live television link.

(4) Anything done by the witness in the presence of the nominated court which, if it were done in proceedings before the court, would constitute contempt of court is to be treated for that purpose as done in proceedings before the court.

(5) Any statement made on oath by a witness giving evidence in pursuance of this section is to be treated for the purposes of—

   (a)   section 1 of the Perjury Act 1911 (c 6),
   (b)   Article 3 of the Perjury (Northern Ireland) Order 1979 (SI 1979/1714 (NI 19)),
   (c)   sections 44 to 46 of the Criminal Law (Consolidation) (Scotland) Act 1995 (c 39) or, in relation to Scotland, any matter pertaining to the common law crime of perjury,

as made in proceedings before the nominated court.

(6) Part 1 of Schedule 2 (evidence given by television link) is to have effect.

(7) Subject to subsections (4) and (5) and the provisions of that Schedule, evidence given pursuant to this section is not to be treated for any purpose as evidence given in proceedings in the United Kingdom.

(8) In relation to Scotland, references in this section and Part 1 of Schedule 2 to the Secretary of State are to be read as references to the Lord Advocate.
[Crime (International Co-operation) Act 2003, s 30.]

1–4209   31. Hearing witnesses in the UK by telephone. (1) This section applies where the Secretary of State receives a request, from an authority mentioned in subsection (2) ("the external authority") in a participating country, for a person in the United Kingdom to give evidence by telephone in criminal proceedings before a court in that country.

Criminal proceedings include any proceedings on an appeal before a court against a decision in administrative proceedings.

(2) The authority referred to in subsection (1) is the authority in that country which appears to the Secretary of State to have the function of making requests of the kind to which this section applies.

(3) A request under subsection (1) must—

   (a)   specify the court in the participating country,
   (b)   give the name and address of the witness,
   (c)   state that the witness is willing to give evidence by telephone in the proceedings before that court.

(4) Unless he considers it inappropriate to do so, the Secretary of State must by notice in writing nominate a court in the United Kingdom where the witness may be heard in the proceedings in question by telephone.

(5) Anything done by the witness in the presence of the nominated court which, if it were done in proceedings before the court, would constitute contempt of court is to be treated for that purpose as done in proceedings before the court.

(6) Any statement made on oath by a witness giving evidence in pursuance of this section is to be treated for the purposes of—

   (a)   section 1 of the Perjury Act 1911 (c 6),
   (b)   Article 3 of the Perjury (Northern Ireland) Order 1979 (SI 1979/1714 (NI 19)),
   (c)   sections 44 to 46 of the Criminal Law (Consolidation) (Scotland) Act 1995 (c 39) or, in relation to Scotland, any matter pertaining to the common law crime of perjury,

as made in proceedings before the nominated court.

(7) Part 2 of Schedule 2 (evidence given by telephone link) is to have effect.

(8) Subject to subsections (5) and (6) and the provisions of that Schedule, evidence given in pursuance of this section is not to be treated for any purpose as evidence given in proceedings in the United Kingdom.

(9) In relation to Scotland, references in this section to the Secretary of State are to be read as references to the Lord Advocate.
[Crime (International Co-operation) Act 2003, s 31.]

CHAPTER 4[1]
INFORMATION ABOUT BANKING TRANSACTIONS

Requests for information about banking transactions in England and Wales and Northern Ireland for use abroad

1–4210 32. Customer information. (1) This section applies where the Secretary of State receives a request from an authority mentioned in subsection (2) for customer information to be obtained in relation to a person who appears to him to be subject to an investigation in a participating country into serious criminal conduct.

(2) The authority referred to in subsection (1) is the authority in that country which appears to the Secretary of State to have the function of making requests of the kind to which this section applies.

(3) The Secretary of State may—

(a) direct a senior police officer[2] to apply, or arrange for a constable to apply, for a customer information order,

(b) direct a senior customs officer to apply, or arrange for a customs officer to apply, for such an order.

(4) A customer information order is an order made by a judge[2] that a financial institution[2] specified in the application for the order must, on being required to do so by notice in writing given by the applicant for the order, provide any such customer information as it has relating to the person specified in the application.

(5) A financial institution which is required to provide information under a customer information order must provide the information to the applicant for the order in such manner, and at or by such time, as the applicant requires.

(6) Section 364 of the Proceeds of Crime Act 2002 (c 29) (meaning of customer information), except subsections (2)(f) and (3)(i), has effect for the purposes of this section as if this section were included in Chapter 2 of Part 8 of that Act.

(7) A customer information order has effect in spite of any restriction on the disclosure of information (however imposed).

(8) Customer information obtained in pursuance of a customer information order is to be given to the Secretary of State and sent by him to the authority which made the request.

[Crime (International Co-operation) Act 2003, s 32.]

1. Chapter 4 contains ss 32–46.
2. Defined in s 46, post.

1–4211 33. Making, varying or discharging customer information orders. (1) A judge may make a customer information order, on an application made to him pursuant to a direction under section 32(3), if he is satisfied that—

(a) the person specified in the application is subject to an investigation in the country in question,
(b) the investigation concerns conduct which is serious criminal conduct[1],
(c) the conduct constitutes an offence in England and Wales or (as the case may be) Northern Ireland, or would do were it to occur there, and
(d) the order is sought for the purposes of the investigation.

(2) The application may be made ex parte to a judge in chambers.

(3) The application may specify—

(a) all financial institutions,
(b) a particular description, or particular descriptions, of financial institutions, or
(c) a particular financial institution or particular financial institutions.

(4) The court[1] may discharge or vary a customer information order on an application made by—

(a) the person who applied for the order,
(b) a senior police officer,
(c) a constable authorised by a senior police officer to make the application,
(d) a senior customs officer,
(e) a customs officer authorised by a senior customs officer to make the application.

[Crime (International Co-operation) Act 2003, s 33.]

1. Defined in s 46, post.

1–4212 34. Offences. (1) A financial institution is guilty of an offence if without reasonable excuse it fails to comply with a requirement imposed on it under a customer information order.

(2) A financial institution guilty of an offence under subsection (1) is liable on summary conviction to a fine not exceeding level 5 on the standard scale.

(3) A financial institution is guilty of an offence if, in purported compliance with a customer information order, it—

(a) makes a statement which it knows to be false or misleading in a material particular, or
(b) recklessly makes a statement which is false or misleading in a material particular.

(4) A financial institution guilty of an offence under subsection (3) is liable—

(a) on summary conviction, to a fine not exceeding the statutory maximum, or
(b) on conviction on indictment, to a fine[1].
[Crime (International Co-operation) Act 2003, s 34.]

---

1. For procedure in respect of offences triable either way, see s 17A–21 of the MAGISTRATES' COURTS ACT 1980 in PART 1: MAGISTRATES' COURTS. PROCEDURE, ante.

1–4213   35. Account information.   (1) This section applies where the Secretary of State receives a request from an authority mentioned in subsection (2) for account information to be obtained in relation to an investigation in a participating country into criminal conduct.

(2) The authority referred to in subsection (1) is the authority in that country which appears to the Secretary of State to have the function of making requests of the kind to which this section applies.

(3) The Secretary of State may—

(a) direct a senior police officer to apply, or arrange for a constable to apply, for an account monitoring order,

(b) direct a senior customs officer to apply, or arrange for a customs officer to apply, for such an order.

(4) An account monitoring order is an order made by a judge that a financial institution specified in the application for the order must, for the period stated in the order, provide account information of the description specified in the order to the applicant in the manner, and at or by the time or times, stated in the order.

(5) Account information is information relating to an account or accounts held at the financial institution specified in the application by the person so specified (whether solely or jointly with another).

(6) An account monitoring order has effect in spite of any restriction on the disclosure of information (however imposed).

(7) Account information obtained in pursuance of an account monitoring order is to be given to the Secretary of State and sent by him to the authority which made the request.
[Crime (International Co-operation) Act 2003, s 35.]

1–4214   36. Making, varying or discharging account monitoring orders.   (1) A judge may make an account monitoring order, on an application made to him in pursuance of a direction under section 35(3), if he is satisfied that—

(a) there is an investigation in the country in question into criminal conduct, and
(b) the order is sought for the purposes of the investigation.

(2) The application may be made ex parte to a judge in chambers.
(3) The application may specify information relating to—

(a) all accounts held by the person specified in the application for the order at the financial institution so specified,
(b) a particular description, or particular descriptions, of accounts so held, or
(c) a particular account, or particular accounts, so held.

(4) The court may discharge or vary an account monitoring order on an application made by—

(a) the person who applied for the order,
(b) a senior police officer,
(c) a constable authorised by a senior police officer to make the application,
(d) a senior customs officer,
(e) a customs officer authorised by a senior customs officer to make the application.

(5) Account monitoring orders have effect as if they were orders of the court.
[Crime (International Co-operation) Act 2003, s 36.]

1–4215   (*Sections 37–41 make corresponding provisions in relation to Scotland for customer information and account monitoring orders.*)

Disclosure of information

1–4216   42. Offence of disclosure.   (1) This section applies where—

(a) a financial institution is specified in a customer information order or account monitoring order made in any part of the United Kingdom, or
(b) the Secretary of State or the Lord Advocate receives a request under section 13 for evidence to be obtained from a financial institution in connection with the investigation of an offence in reliance on Article 2 (requests for information on banking transactions) of the 2001 Protocol.

(2) If the institution, or an employee of the institution, discloses any of the following information, the institution or (as the case may be) the employee is guilty of an offence.
(3) That information is—

(a) that the request to obtain customer information or account information, or the request mentioned in subsection (1)(b), has been received,

(b)   that the investigation to which the request relates is being carried out, or
(c)   that, in pursuance of the request, information has been given to the authority which made the request.

(4)   An institution guilty of an offence under this section is liable—

(a)   on summary conviction, to a fine not exceeding the statutory maximum,
(b)   on conviction on indictment, to a fine[1].

(5)   Any other person guilty of an offence under this section is liable—

(a)   on summary conviction, to imprisonment for a term not exceeding six months or to a fine not exceeding the statutory maximum, or to both,
(b)   on conviction on indictment, to imprisonment for a term not exceeding five years or to a fine, or to both.

[Crime (International Co-operation) Act 2003, s 42.]

---

1. For procedure in respect of offences triable either way, see s 17A–21 of the MAGISTRATES' COURTS ACT 1980 in PART 1: MAGISTRATES' COURTS. PROCEDURE, ante.

Requests for information about banking transactions for use in UK

1–4217   43. Information about a person's bank account.   (1) If it appears to a judicial authority in the United Kingdom, on an application made by a prosecuting authority, that—

(a)   a person is subject to an investigation in the United Kingdom into serious criminal conduct,
(b)   the person holds, or may hold, an account at a bank which is situated in a participating country, and
(c)   the information which the applicant seeks to obtain is likely to be of substantial value for the purposes of the investigation,

the judicial authority may request assistance under this section.
(2)   The judicial authorities are—

(a)   in relation to England and Wales, any judge or justice of the peace,
(b)   in relation to Scotland, any sheriff,
(c)   in relation to Northern Ireland, any judge or resident magistrate.

(3)   If it appears to a prosecuting authority mentioned in subsection (4) that paragraphs (a) to (c) of subsection (1) are met, the authority may itself request assistance under this section.
(4)   The prosecuting authorities are—

(a)   in relation to England and Wales and Northern Ireland, a prosecuting authority designated by an order made by the Secretary of State,
(b)   in relation to Scotland, the Lord Advocate or a procurator fiscal.

(5)   The assistance that may be requested under this section is any assistance in obtaining from a participating country one or more of the following—

(a)   information as to whether the person in question holds any accounts at any banks situated in the participating country,
(b)   details of any such accounts,
(c)   details of transactions carried out in any period specified in the request in respect of any such accounts.

(6)   A request for assistance under this section must—

(a)   state the grounds on which the authority making the request thinks that the person in question may hold any account at a bank which is situated in a participating country and (if possible) specify the bank or banks in question,
(b)   state the grounds on which the authority making the request considers that the information sought to be obtained is likely to be of substantial value for the purposes of the investigation, and
(c)   include any information which may facilitate compliance with the request.

(7)   For the purposes of this section, a person holds an account if—

(a)   the account is in his name or is held for his benefit, or
(b)   he has a power of attorney in respect of the account.

In relation to Scotland, a power of attorney includes a factory and commission.
[Crime (International Co-operation) Act 2003, s 43.]

1–4218   44. Monitoring banking transactions.   (1) If it appears to a judicial authority in the United Kingdom, on an application made by a prosecuting authority, that the information which the applicant seeks to obtain is relevant to an investigation in the United Kingdom into criminal conduct, the judicial authority may request assistance under this section.
(2)   The judicial authorities are—

(a)   in relation to England and Wales, any judge or justice of the peace,
(b)   in relation to Scotland, any sheriff,
(c)   in relation to Northern Ireland, any judge or resident magistrate.

(3) If it appears to a prosecuting authority mentioned in subsection (4) that the information which it seeks to obtain is relevant to an investigation into criminal conduct, the authority may itself request assistance under this section.

(4) The prosecuting authorities are—

(a) in relation to England and Wales and Northern Ireland, a prosecuting authority designated by an order made by the Secretary of State,

(b) in relation to Scotland, the Lord Advocate or a procurator fiscal.

(5) The assistance that may be requested under this section is any assistance in obtaining from a participating country details of transactions to be carried out in any period specified in the request in respect of any accounts at banks situated in that country.

[Crime (International Co-operation) Act 2003, s 44.]

1–4219   45. Sending requests for assistance.   (1) A request for assistance under section 43 or 44, other than one to which subsection (3) or (4) applies, is to be sent to the Secretary of State for forwarding—

(a) to a court specified in the request and exercising jurisdiction in the place where the information is to be obtained, or

(b) to any authority recognised by the participating country in question as the appropriate authority for receiving requests for assistance of the kind to which this section applies.

(2) But in cases of urgency the request may be sent to a court referred to in subsection (1)(a).

(3) Such a request for assistance by the Lord Advocate is to be sent to a court or authority mentioned in subsection (1)(a) or (b).

(4) Such a request for assistance by a sheriff or a procurator fiscal is to be sent to such a court or authority, or to the Lord Advocate for forwarding to such a court or authority.

[Crime (International Co-operation) Act 2003, s 45.]

General

1–4220   46. Interpretation of Chapter 4.   (1) In this Chapter—

"the court" means the Crown Court or, in Scotland, the sheriff,

"senior police officer" means a police officer who is not below the rank of superintendent and

"senior customs officer" means a customs officer who is not below the grade designated by the Commissioners of Customs and Excise as equivalent to that rank.

(2) The following provisions apply for the purposes of this Chapter.

(3) Serious criminal conduct means conduct which constitutes—

(a) an offence to which paragraph 3 of Article 1 (request for information on bank accounts) of the 2001 Protocol applies, or

(b) an offence specified in an order made by the Secretary of State or, in relation to Scotland, the Scottish Ministers for the purpose of giving effect to any decision of the Council of the European Union under paragraph 6 of that Article.

(4) A financial institution—

(a) means a person who is carrying on business in the regulated sector, and

(b) in relation to a customer information order or an account monitoring order, includes a person who was carrying on business in the regulated sector at a time which is the time to which any requirement for him to provide information under the order is to relate.

"Business in the regulated sector" is to be interpreted in accordance with Schedule 9 to the Proceeds of Crime Act 2002 (c 29).

(5) A judge means—

(a) in relation to England and Wales, a judge entitled to exercise the jurisdiction of the Crown Court,

(b) in relation to Northern Ireland, a Crown Court judge.

[Crime (International Co-operation) Act 2003, s 46.]

CHAPTER 5[1]
TRANSFER OF PRISONERS

1–4221   (*Sections 47 and 48 provide for the transfer of UK prisoners to assist investigations in participating countries and vice versa.*)

---

1. Chapter 5 contains ss 47–48.

CHAPTER 6[1]
SUPPLEMENTARY

1–4222   49. Rules of court.   (1) Provision may be made by rules of court[1] as to the practice and procedure to be followed in connection with proceedings under this Part.

(2) Rules of court made under this section by the High Court in Scotland are to be made by Act of Adjournal.

(3) The power to make rules of court under this section does not prejudice any existing power to make rules.

[Crime (International Co-operation) Act 2003, s 49.]

---

1. Chapter 6 contains ss 49–51.
2. The Magistrates' Courts (Crime (International Co-operation)) Rules 2004 have been made, in this Part, post.

1–4223 50. Subordinate legislation. (1) Any power to make an order conferred by this Part on the Secretary of State, the Treasury or the Scottish Ministers is exercisable by statutory instrument.

(2) Such an order may make different provision for different purposes.

(3) A statutory instrument (other than an instrument to which subsection (5) applies) containing an order made by the Secretary of State or the Treasury is to be subject to annulment in pursuance of a resolution of either House of Parliament.

(4) A statutory instrument (other than an instrument to which subsection (5) applies) containing an order made by the Scottish Ministers is to be subject to annulment in pursuance of a resolution of the Scottish Parliament.

(5) A statutory instrument containing an order under section 51(2)(*b*) designating a country other than a member State is not to be made unless—

(*a*) in the case of an order to be made by the Secretary of State, a draft of the instrument has been laid before, and approved by resolution of, each House of Parliament,

(*b*) in the case of an order to be made by the Scottish Ministers, a draft of the instrument has been laid before, and approved by resolution of, the Scottish Parliament.

[Crime (International Co-operation) Act 2003, s 50.]

1–4224 51. General interpretation. (1) In this Part—

"the 1990 Act" means the Criminal Justice (International Co-operation) Act 1990 (c 5),

"the 2001 Protocol" means the Protocol to the Mutual Legal Assistance Convention, established by Council Act of 16th October 2001 (2001/C326/01),

"administrative proceedings" means proceedings outside the United Kingdom to which Article 3(1) of the Mutual Legal Assistance Convention applies (proceedings brought by administrative authorities in respect of administrative offences where a decision in the proceedings may be the subject of an appeal before a court),

"chief officer of police"—

(*a*) in relation to any area in Scotland, means the chief constable for the police force maintained for that area,

(*b*) in relation to any area in Northern Ireland, means the Chief Constable of the Police Service of Northern Ireland,

"clemency proceedings" means proceedings in a country outside the United Kingdom, not being proceedings before a court exercising criminal jurisdiction, for the removal or reduction of a penalty imposed on conviction of an offence,

"country" includes territory,

"court" includes a tribunal,

"criminal proceedings" include criminal proceedings outside the United Kingdom in which a civil order may be made,

"customs officer" means an officer commissioned by the Commissioners of Customs and Excise under section 6(3) of the Customs and Excise Management Act 1979 (c 2),

"evidence" includes information in any form and articles, and giving evidence includes answering a question or producing any information or article,

"the Mutual Legal Assistance Convention" means the Convention on Mutual Assistance in Criminal Matters established by Council Act of 29th May 2000 (2000/C197/01),

"the Schengen Convention" means the Convention implementing the Schengen Agreement of 14th June 1985.

(2) A participating country, in relation to any provision of this Part, means—

(*a*) a country other than the United Kingdom which is a member State on a day appointed for the commencement of that provision, and

(*b*) any other country designated by an order made by the Secretary of State or, in relation to Scotland, the Scottish Ministers.

(3) In this Part, "process", in relation to England and Wales and Northern Ireland, means any summons or order issued or made by a court and includes—

(*a*) any other document issued or made by a court for service on parties or witnesses,

(*b*) any document issued by a prosecuting authority outside the United Kingdom for the purposes of criminal proceedings.

(4) In this Part, "process", in relation to service in Scotland, means a citation by a court or by a prosecuting authority, or an order made by a court, and includes any other document issued or made as mentioned in subsection (3)(*a*) or (*b*).

[Crime (International Co-operation) Act 2003, s 51.]

PART 2[1]
TERRORIST ACTS AND THREATS: JURISDICTION

1–4225   (*Part 2 inserts new provisions in the Terrorism Act 2000 and the Anti-terrorism, Crime and Security Act 2001.*)

1. Part 2 contains ss 52–53.

PART 3[1]
ROAD TRAFFIC

CHAPTER 1[2]
CONVENTION[3] ON DRIVING DISQUALIFICATIONS

Road traffic offences in UK

1–4226   54. Application of section 55.   (1) Section 55 applies where—

(*a*)   an individual ("the offender") who is normally resident in a member State other than the United Kingdom is convicted of an offence mentioned in Schedule 3,

(*b*)   no appeal is outstanding in relation to the offence, and

(*c*)   the driving disqualification condition is met in relation to the offence.

(2)   The driving disqualification condition is met—

(*a*)   in relation to an offence mentioned in Part 1 of Schedule 3, if an order of disqualification is made in respect of the offence,

(*b*)   in relation to an offence mentioned in Part 2 of that Schedule, if an order of disqualification for a period not less than the minimum period is made in respect of the offence.

(3)   The minimum period is—

(*a*)   a period of six months, or

(*b*)   where the State in which the offender normally resides is a prescribed State, a shorter period equal to the period prescribed in relation to the State.

(4)   Section 55 does not apply in prescribed circumstances.

(5)   For the purposes of this section no appeal is outstanding in relation to an offence if—

(*a*)   no appeal is brought against an offender's conviction of the offence, or any order made on his conviction, within the time allowed for making such appeals, or

(*b*)   such an appeal is brought and the proceedings on appeal are finally concluded.

[Crime (International Co-operation) Act 2003, s 54.]

1. Part 2 contains ss 54–79. At the time of going to press on the provisions of Chapter 2 (ss 76–79) were in force.
2. Part 2 contains ss 45–75.
3. "Convention" refers to the Convention drawn up on the basis of Article K.3 of the Treaty on European Union on Driving Disqualifications signed on 17 June, 1998: see 74(1), post.

1–4227   55. Duty to give notice to foreign authorities of driving disqualification of a non-UK resident.   (1) Where this section applies, the appropriate Minister must give the central authority of the State in which the offender is normally resident a notice under this section.

(2)   A notice under this section must—

(*a*)   give the name, address and date of birth of the offender,

(*b*)   give particulars of the offence,

(*c*)   state that no appeal is outstanding in relation to it,

(*d*)   give particulars of the disqualification,

(*e*)   state whether or not the offender took part in the proceedings in which the disqualification was imposed,

(*f*)   state that the offender has been informed that any decision made for the purposes of the convention on driving disqualifications will have no effect on the disqualification.

(3)   A notice under this section may contain such other information as the appropriate Minister considers appropriate.

(4)   A notice under this section must be accompanied by the original or a certified copy of the order of disqualification.

(5)   Where the offender did not take part in the proceedings mentioned in subsection (2)(*e*), a notice under this section must also be accompanied by evidence that the offender was duly notified of those proceedings.

(6)   Where the offender is the holder of a Community licence, a notice under this section must also be accompanied by the licence unless it has been returned to the driver—

(*a*)   under section 91A(7)(*b*)(ii) of the Road Traffic Offenders Act 1988 (c 53), or

(*b*)   under Article 92A(7)(*b*)(ii) of the Road Traffic Offenders (Northern Ireland) Order 1996 (SI 1996/1320 (NI 10)).

(7)   Where the period of disqualification is reduced by virtue of section 34A of that Act or Article 36 of that Order, the appropriate Minister must give the central authority particulars of the reduction.

(8) Where the disqualification is removed by an order under section 42 of that Act or Article 47 of that Order, the appropriate Minister must give the central authority particulars of the removal.

(9) The appropriate Minister must provide—

(a) the central authority, or

(b) the competent authority of the State mentioned in subsection (1),

with any further information which it requires for the purposes of the convention on driving disqualifications.

[Crime (International Co-operation) Act 2003, s 55.]

Disqualification in respect of road traffic offences outside UK

1–4228   56. Application of section 57.   (1) Section 57 applies where—

(a) an individual ("the offender") who is normally resident in the United Kingdom is convicted in another member State of an offence falling within subsection (5),

(b) no appeal is outstanding in relation to the offence,

(c) the driving disqualification condition is met in relation to the offence, and

(d) the offender was duly notified of the proceedings ("the relevant proceedings") in which the disqualification was imposed and was entitled to take part in them.

(2) The driving disqualification condition is met—

(a) in relation to an offence falling within subsection (5)(a), if, as a result of the offence, the offender is disqualified in the State in which the conviction is made,

(b) in relation to an offence falling within subsection (5)(b), if, as a result of the offence, the offender is disqualified in that State for a period not less than the minimum period.

(3) For the purposes of this section an offender is disqualified in a State if he is disqualified in that State for holding or obtaining a licence to drive a motor vehicle granted under the law of that State (however the disqualification is described under that law).

(4) The minimum period is—

(a) a period of six months, or

(b) where the State in which the conviction is made is a prescribed State, a shorter period equal to the period prescribed in relation to that State.

(5) An offence falls within this subsection if it is constituted by—

(a) conduct falling within any of paragraphs 1 to 5 of the Annex to the convention on driving disqualifications, or

(b) other conduct which constitutes a road traffic offence for the purposes of that convention.

(6) Section 57 does not apply if the relevant proceedings were brought later than the time at which summary proceedings for any corresponding offence under the law of the part of the United Kingdom in which the offender is normally resident could have been brought.

(7) An offence is a corresponding offence if—

(a) the conduct constituting the offence outside the United Kingdom took place in any part of the United Kingdom, and

(b) that conduct is, or corresponds to, conduct which would constitute an offence under the law of that part.

(8) The appropriate Minister may make regulations treating offences under the law of a part of the United Kingdom as corresponding to offences under the law of a member State other than the United Kingdom.

(9) For the purposes of this section no appeal is outstanding in relation to an offence if—

(a) no appeal is brought against an offender's conviction of the offence, or any decision made as a result of his conviction, within the time allowed for making such appeals, or

(b) such an appeal is brought and the proceedings on appeal are finally concluded.

[Crime (International Co-operation) Act 2003, s 56.]

1–4229   57. Recognition in United Kingdom of foreign driving disqualification.   (1) Where this section applies, the appropriate Minister—

(a) must give the offender a notice under this section if the unexpired period of the foreign disqualification is not less than one month, and

(b) may give him a notice under this section if that period is less than one month.

(2) The unexpired period of the foreign disqualification is—

(a) the period of the foreign disqualification, less

(b) any period of that disqualification which is treated by regulations made by the appropriate Minister as having been served in the State in which the offender was convicted.

(3) The provision which may be made by regulations under subsection (2)(b) includes provision for treating any period during which a central authority or competent authority of a State has seized a licence without returning it as a period which has been served in that State.

(4) If the appropriate Minister gives the offender a notice under this section, the offender is disqualified in each part of the United Kingdom—

(a) for the relevant period, and

(b) if the foreign disqualification is also effective until a condition is satisfied, until the condition or a corresponding prescribed condition is satisfied.

(5) The relevant period is the period which—

(a) begins at the end of the period of 21 days beginning with the day on which the notice is given, and

(b) is equal to the unexpired period of the foreign disqualification.

(6) But if the foreign disqualification is at any time removed otherwise than in prescribed circumstances, the offender ceases to be disqualified in each part of the United Kingdom from that time.

(7) The appropriate Minister may make regulations substituting a longer period for the period for the time being mentioned in subsection (5)(a).

(8) Where the foreign disqualification is for life—

(a) the condition in subsection (1)(a) is to be treated as satisfied, and

(b) the other references in this section and section 58 to the unexpired period of the foreign disqualification are to be read as references to a disqualification for life.

[Crime (International Co-operation) Act 2003, s 57.]

1–4230   **58. Notice under section 57.**   (1) A notice under section 57 must—

(a) give particulars of the offence in respect of which the foreign disqualification was imposed and the period of that disqualification,

(b) state that the offender is disqualified in each part of the United Kingdom for a period equal to the unexpired period of the foreign disqualification,

(c) state the date from which, and period for which, he is disqualified,

(d) give particulars of any relevant condition mentioned in section 57(4)(b),

(e) give details of his right to appeal under section 59.

(2) A notice under section 57 must be in writing.

(3) A notice under section 57 may contain such other information as the appropriate Minister considers appropriate.

[Crime (International Co-operation) Act 2003, s 58.]

Appeals

1–4231   **59. Appeal against disqualification.**   (1) A person who is disqualified by virtue of section 57 may, after giving notice to the appropriate Minister of his intention to do so, appeal to the appropriate court against the disqualification.

(2) The appropriate court is—

(a) in relation to England and Wales, a magistrates' court acting for the petty sessions area in which the applicant resides,

(b) in relation to Scotland, the sheriff within whose jurisdiction the applicant resides,

(c) in relation to Northern Ireland, a court of summary jurisdiction acting for the petty sessions district in which the applicant resides.

(3) The appeal must be made before the end of the period of 21 days beginning with the day on which the notice under section 57 is given to the applicant.

(4) But the appropriate Minister may make regulations substituting a longer period for the period for the time being mentioned in subsection (3).

(5) If the appropriate court is satisfied that section 57 does not apply to the applicant's case, it must allow the appeal.

(6) Otherwise it must dismiss the appeal.

(7) Where on an appeal against the disqualification the appeal is allowed, the court by which the appeal is allowed must send notice of that fact to the appropriate Minister.

(8) The notice must—

(a) be sent in such manner and to such address, and

(b) contain such particulars,

as the appropriate Minister may determine.

[Crime (International Co-operation) Act 2003, s 59.]

1–4232   **60. Power of appellate courts in England and Wales to suspend disqualification.**

(1) This section applies where a person is disqualified by virtue of section 57.

(2) Where the person appeals to a magistrates' court against the disqualification, the court may, if it thinks fit, suspend the disqualification.

(3) Where the person makes an application in respect of the decision of the court under section 111 of the Magistrates' Courts Act 1980 (c 43) (statement of case), the High Court may, if it thinks fit, suspend the disqualification.

(4) Where the person has appealed, or applied for leave to appeal, to the House of Lords under section 1 of the Administration of Justice Act 1960 (c 65) from any decision of the High Court which is material to the disqualification, the High Court may, if it thinks fit, suspend the disqualification.

(5) Any power of a court under this section to suspend the disqualification is a power to do so on such terms as the court thinks fit.

(6) Where, by virtue of this section, a court suspends the disqualification, it must send notice of the suspension to the Secretary of State.

(7) The notice must—

(a) be sent in such manner and to such address, and

(b) contain such particulars,

as the Secretary of State may determine.

[Crime (International Co-operation) Act 2003, s 60.]

1–4233   **61.** *Power of appellate courts in Scotland to suspend disqualification*

1–4234   **62.** *Power of appellate courts in Northern Ireland to suspend disqualification*

Production of licence

1–4235   **63. Production of licence: Great Britain.**   (1) A person who—

(a) is given a notice under section 57 by the Secretary of State, and

(b) is the holder of a licence,

must deliver his licence and its counterpart to the Secretary of State before the end of the period of 21 days beginning with the day on which the notice is given.

(2) The Secretary of State may make regulations substituting a longer period for the period for the time being mentioned in subsection (1).

(3) If—

(a) a person delivers a current receipt for his licence and its counterpart to the Secretary of State within the period for the time being mentioned in subsection (1), and

(b) on the return of his licence and its counterpart immediately delivers them to the Secretary of State,

the duty under subsection (1) is to be taken as satisfied.

"Receipt" means a receipt issued under section 56 of the Road Traffic Offenders Act 1988 (c 53).

(4) Subsection (1) does not apply if the competent authority of the relevant State—

(a) has the licence and its counterpart, or

(b) has delivered them to the Secretary of State.

(5) The relevant State is the State in which the offence in relation to which the notice was given was committed.

(6) If the holder of a licence does not deliver his licence and its counterpart to the Secretary of State as required by subsection (1), he is guilty of an offence.

(7) A person is not guilty of an offence under subsection (6) if he satisfies the court that he has applied for a new licence and has not received it.

In relation to the holder of a Northern Ireland licence or Community licence, a new licence includes the counterpart of such a licence.

(8) A person guilty of an offence under subsection (6) is liable on summary conviction to a fine not exceeding level 3 on the standard scale.

(9) "Licence" means a Great Britain licence, a Northern Ireland licence or a Community licence.

[Crime (International Co-operation) Act 2003, s 63.]

1–4236   **64.** *Production of licence: Northern Ireland*

1–4237   **65. Production of licence: Community licence holders.**   (1) This section applies where—

(a) the holder of a Community licence is disqualified by virtue of section 57, and

(b) the licence is sent to the Secretary of State or the Department under section 63 or 64.

(2) The Secretary of State or (as the case may be) the Department must send—

(a) the holder's name and address, and

(b) particulars of the disqualification,

to the licensing authority in the EEA State in respect of which the licence was issued.

(3) But subsection (2) does not apply if the EEA State is the same as the State in which the offence in relation to which the holder is disqualified was committed.

(4) The Secretary of State or (as the case may be) the Department must return the licence to the holder—

(a) on the expiry of the relevant period of the disqualification (within the meaning of section 57), or

(b) if earlier, on being satisfied that the holder has left Great Britain or (as the case may be) Northern Ireland and is no longer normally resident there.

(5) But subsection (4) does not apply at any time where—

(*a*) the Secretary of State or the Department would otherwise be under a duty under paragraph (*a*) of that subsection to return the licence, and

(*b*) the holder would not at that time be authorised by virtue of section 99A(1) of the Road Traffic Act 1988 (c 52) or Article 15A(1) of the Road Traffic (Northern Ireland) Order 1981 (SI 1981/154 (NI 1)) to drive in Great Britain or Northern Ireland a motor vehicle of any class.

(6) In that case the Secretary of State or (as the case may be) the Department must—

(*a*) send the licence to the licensing authority in the EEA State in respect of which it was issued, and

(*b*) explain to that authority the reasons for so doing.

(7) "EEA State" has the same meaning as in Part 3 of the Road Traffic Act 1988.
[Crime (International Co-operation) Act 2003, s 65.]

Disqualification

1–4238 66. Effect of disqualification by virtue of section 57. Where the holder of a Great Britain licence or Northern Ireland licence is disqualified by virtue of section 57, the licence is to be treated as revoked with effect from the beginning of the period of disqualification.
[Crime (International Co-operation) Act 2003, s 66.]

1–4239 67. Rule for determining end of period of disqualification. In determining the expiration of the period for which a person is disqualified by virtue of section 57, any time during which—

(*a*) the disqualification is suspended, or

(*b*) he is not disqualified,

is to be disregarded.
[Crime (International Co-operation) Act 2003, s 67.]

Endorsement

1–4240 68. Endorsement of licence: Great Britain. (1) This section applies where a person who is normally resident in Great Britain is disqualified by virtue of section 57.

(2) The Secretary of State must secure that particulars of the disqualification are endorsed on the counterpart of any Great Britain licence or of any Northern Ireland licence or Community licence which the person—

(*a*) may then hold, or

(*b*) may subsequently obtain,

until he becomes entitled under subsection (4) or (5) to have a Great Britain licence and its counterpart, or a counterpart of his Northern Ireland licence or Community licence, issued to him free from those particulars.

(3) On the issue to the person of—

(*a*) a new Great Britain licence, or

(*b*) a new counterpart of a Northern Ireland licence or Community licence,

those particulars must be entered on the counterpart of the new licence or the new counterpart unless he has become so entitled.

(4) The person is entitled to have issued to him with effect from the end of the period for which the endorsement remains effective a new Great Britain licence with a counterpart free from the endorsement if he—

(*a*) applies for a new licence under section 97(1) of the Road Traffic Act 1988 (c 52),

(*b*) surrenders any subsisting licence and its counterpart,

(*c*) pays the fee prescribed by regulations under Part 3 of that Act, and

(*d*) satisfies the other requirements of section 97(1).

(5) The person is entitled to have issued to him with effect from the end of that period a new counterpart of any Northern Ireland licence or Community licence then held by him free from the endorsement if he makes an application to the Secretary of State for that purpose in such manner as the Secretary of State may determine.

(6) The endorsement remains effective until four years have elapsed since he was convicted of the offence in relation to which he is disqualified by virtue of section 57.

(7) Where the person ceases to be disqualified by virtue of section 57(6), the Secretary of State must secure that the relevant particulars are endorsed on the counterpart of the Great Britain licence or of any Northern Ireland licence or Community licence previously held by him.
[Crime (International Co-operation) Act 2003, s 68.]

1–4241 69. *Endorsement of licence: Northern Ireland*

General

1–4242 70. Duty of appropriate Minister to inform competent authority. (1) This section applies where a competent authority of any State gives the appropriate Minister a notice under the convention on driving disqualifications in respect of any person.

(2) If the appropriate Minister gives a notice under section 57 to that person, he must give the competent authority particulars of the disqualification which arises by virtue of that section.

(3) If the appropriate Minister does not give such a notice, he must give his reasons to the competent authority.

[Crime (International Co-operation) Act 2003, s 70.]

1–4243   71. Notices.   (1) A notice authorised or required under this Chapter to be given by the appropriate Minister to an individual, or a Community licence required to be returned to its holder by section 65, may be given or returned to him by—

    (a)   delivering it to him,
    (b)   leaving it at his proper address, or
    (c)   sending it to him by post.

    (2) For the purposes of—

    (a)   subsection (1), and
    (b)   section 7 of the Interpretation Act 1978 (c 30) in its application to that subsection,

the proper address of any individual is his latest address as known to the appropriate Minister.

[Crime (International Co-operation) Act 2003, s 71.]

1–4244   72. Regulations: Great Britain.   (1) Any power to make regulations conferred by this Chapter on the Secretary of State is exercisable by statutory instrument.

    (2) A statutory instrument containing any such regulations is subject to annulment in pursuance of a resolution of either House of Parliament.

    (3) The regulations may make different provision for different purposes.

[Crime (International Co-operation) Act 2003, s 72.]

1–4245   73. *Regulations: Northern Ireland*

1–4246   74. Interpretation.   (1) In this Chapter—

"appropriate Minister" means—

    (a)   in relation to Great Britain, the Secretary of State,
    (b)   in relation to Northern Ireland, the Department,

"central authority", in relation to a State, means an authority designated by the State as a central authority for the purposes of the convention on driving disqualifications,
"Community licence"—

    (a)   in relation to Great Britain, has the same meaning as in Part 3 of the Road Traffic Act 1988 (c 52),
    (b)   in relation to Northern Ireland, has the same meaning as in Part 2 of the Road Traffic (Northern Ireland) Order 1981 (SI 1981/154 (NI 1)),

"competent authority", in relation to a State, means an authority which is a competent authority in relation to the State for the purposes of the convention on driving disqualifications,
"the convention on driving disqualifications" means the Convention drawn up on the basis of Article K.3 of the Treaty on European Union on Driving Disqualifications signed on 17th June 1998,
"counterpart"—

    (a)   in relation to Great Britain, has the same meaning as in Part 3 of the Road Traffic Act 1988 (c 52),
    (b)   in relation to Northern Ireland, has the same meaning as in Part 2 of the Road Traffic (Northern Ireland) Order 1981 (SI 1981/154 (NI1)),

"the Department" means the Department of the Environment,
"disqualified", except in section 56, means—

    (a)   in relation to Great Britain, disqualified for holding or obtaining a Great Britain licence,
    (b)   in relation to Northern Ireland, disqualified for holding or obtaining a Northern Ireland licence,

and "disqualification" is to be interpreted accordingly,
"foreign disqualification" means the disqualification mentioned in section 56,
"Great Britain licence" means a licence to drive a motor vehicle granted under Part 3 of the Road Traffic Act 1988,
"motor vehicle"—

    (a)   in relation to Great Britain, has the same meaning as in the Road Traffic Act 1988,
    (b)   in relation to Northern Ireland, has the same meaning as in the Road Traffic (Northern Ireland) Order 1995 (SI 1995/2994 (NI18)),

"Northern Ireland licence" means a licence to drive a motor vehicle granted under Part 2 of the Road Traffic (Northern Ireland) Order 1981,
"prescribed" means prescribed by regulations made by the appropriate Minister.

(2) In this Chapter a disqualification, or foreign disqualification, for life is to be treated as being for a period of not less than six months.
[Crime (International Co-operation) Act 2003, s 74.]

1–4247 75. Application to Crown. This Chapter applies to vehicles and persons in the public service of the Crown.
[Crime (International Co-operation) Act 2003, s 75.]

CHAPTER 2[1]
MUTUAL RECOGNITION WITHIN THE UNITED KINGDOM ETC
1–4248

----

1. Chapter 2 contains ss 76–79. These sections insert new provisions in, or make amendments to, the Road Traffic Act 1988 and the Road Traffic Offenders Act 1988, and are concerned with mutual recognition of driver licensing and disqualification between Great Britain and Northern Ireland and giving effect in Great Britain to driving disqualifications imposed in the Isle of Man, the Channel Islands and Gibraltar. The provisions of Chapter 2 came into force on 11 October 2004: see Crime (international Co-operation) Act 2003 (Commencement No 2) Order, SI 2004/2624.

PART 4[1]
MISCELLANEOUS
Information

1–4249 80. Disclosure of information by SFO. (*This section makes amendments to s 3 of the Criminal Justice Act 1987.*)

1–4250 81. Inspection of overseas information systems. (*This section inserts a new s 54A in the Data Protection Act 1998.*)

----

1. Part 4 contains ss 80–90.

Cross-border surveillance

1–4251 83. Foreign surveillance operations. (*This section inserts a new 76A in the Regulation of Investigatory Powers Act 2000.*)

1–4252 84. Assaults on foreign officers. (1) For the purposes of section 89 of the Police Act 1996 (c 16) (assaults on constables) any person who is carrying out surveillance in England and Wales under section 76A of the Regulation of Investigatory Powers Act 2000 (c 23) is to be treated as if he were acting as a constable in the execution of his duty.
(2) For the purposes of section 41 of the Police (Scotland) Act 1967 (c 77) (assaults on constables) any person who is carrying out surveillance in Scotland under section 76A of that Act of 2000 is to be so treated.
(3) For the purposes of section 66 of the Police (Northern Ireland) Act 1998 (c 32) (assaults on constables) any person who is carrying out surveillance in Northern Ireland under section 76A of that Act of 2000 is to be so treated.
[Crime (International Co-operation) Act 2003, s 84.]

1–4253 85. Liability in respect of foreign officers. *Repealed by the Serious Organised Crime and Police Act 2005, Sch 4.*

Extradition

1–4254 86. Schengen-building provisions of the 1996 Extradition Convention. *Repealed by the Extradition Act 2003 (Repeals) Order 2004, SI 2004/1897.*

1–4255 87. States in relation to which 1995 and 1996 Extradition Conventions not in force. *Repealed by the Extradition Act 2003 (Repeals) Order 2004, SI 2004/1897.*

False monetary instruments

1–4256 88. False monetary instruments: England and Wales and Northern Ireland. (*This section amends s 5 of the Forgery and Counterfeiting Act 1981.*)

1–4257 89. False monetary instruments: Scotland

Freezing of terrorist property

1–4258 90. Freezing of terrorist property. Schedule 4 is to have effect.
[Crime (International Co-operation) Act 2003, s 90.]

PART 5[1]

FINAL PROVISIONS

CHAPTER 1[2]

AMENDMENTS AND REPEALS

1–4259   91. Amendments and repeals.   (1) Schedule 5 (minor and consequential amendments) is to have effect.

(2) The enactments set out in Schedule 6 are repealed to the extent specified.

[Crime (International Co-operation) Act 2003, s 1.]

---

1. Part 5 contains ss 91-96.
2. Chapter 2 contains s 91 only.

CHAPTER 2[1]

MISCELLANEOUS

1–4260   92. Northern Ireland

1–4261   93. Supplementary and consequential provision.   (1) The appropriate Minister may by order[2] made by statutory instrument make—

(a)   any supplementary, incidental or consequential provision,

(b)   any transitory, transitional or saving provision,

which he considers necessary or expedient for the purposes of, in consequence of or for giving full effect to any provision of this Act.

(2) The appropriate Minister means—

(a)   in relation to any provision that would, if included in an Act of the Scottish Parliament, be within the legislative competence of that Parliament, the Scottish Ministers,

(b)   in relation to any other provision, the Secretary of State.

(3) The provision which may be made under subsection (1) includes provision amending or repealing any enactment or instrument.

(4) An order under this section may make different provision for different purposes.

(5) A statutory instrument (other than an instrument to which subsection (6) applies) containing an order under this section made by the Secretary of State is subject to annulment in pursuance of a resolution of either House of Parliament.

(6) A statutory instrument containing such an order which adds to, replaces or omits any part of the text of an Act is not to be made unless a draft of the instrument has been laid before, and approved by a resolution of, each House of Parliament.

(7) A statutory instrument (other than an instrument to which subsection (8) applies) containing an order under this section made by the Scottish Ministers is subject to annulment in pursuance of a resolution of the Scottish Parliament.

(8) A statutory instrument containing such an order which adds to, replaces or omits any part of the text of an Act or of an Act of the Scottish Parliament is not to be made unless a draft of the instrument has been laid before, and approved by a resolution of, the Scottish Parliament.

[Crime (International Co-operation) Act 2003, s 93.]

---

1. Chapter 2 contains ss 92–96.
2. The Crime (International Co-operation) Act 2003 (Savings) Order 2004, SI 2004/787 has been made.

1–4262   94. Commencement.   (1) This Act (except this Chapter and the provisions mentioned in subsection (3)) is to come into force on such day as the Secretary of State may by order made by statutory instrument appoint[1].

(2) Any day appointed for the purposes of Part 1 (other than sections 32 to 41), and the related amendments and repeals, is to be one decided by the Secretary of State and the Scottish Ministers.

(3) The following are to come into force on such day as the Scottish Ministers may by order made by statutory instrument appoint—

(a)   sections 37 to 41,

(b)   section 89.

(4) An order under this section may make different provision for different purposes.

[Crime (International Co-operation) Act 2003, s 94.]

---

1. For details of commencement orders made, and the provisions they brought into force, see the note to the title of the Act.

1–4263   95. Extent.   (1) Sections 32 to 36 extend only to England and Wales and Northern Ireland.

(2) Sections 37 to 41 extend only to Scotland.

[Crime (International Co-operation) Act 2003, s 95.]

1–4264   96. Short title.   This Act may be cited as the Crime (International Co-operation) Act 2003.

[Crime (International Co-operation) Act 2003, s 96.]

Section 15   SCHEDULE 1
                    PROCEEDINGS OF A NOMINATED COURT UNDER SECTION 15
1–4265

Securing attendance of witnesses

1. The court has the like powers for securing the attendance of a witness as it has for the purposes of other proceedings before the court.
2. (*Scotland*).

Power to administer oaths

3. The court may take evidence on oath.

Proceedings

4. Rules of court[1] under section 49 may, in particular, make provision in respect of the persons entitled to appear or take part in the proceedings and for excluding the public from the proceedings.

Privilege of witnesses

5. (1) A person cannot be compelled to give any evidence which he could not be compelled to give—

(*a*) in criminal proceedings in the part of the United Kingdom in which the nominated court exercises jurisdiction, or
(*b*) subject to sub-paragraph (2), in criminal proceedings in the country from which the request for the evidence has come.

(2) Sub-paragraph (1)(*b*) does not apply unless the claim of the person questioned to be exempt from giving the evidence is conceded by the court or authority which made the request.
(3) Where the person's claim is not conceded, he may be required to give the evidence to which the claim relates (subject to the other provisions of this paragraph); but the evidence may not be forwarded to the court or authority which requested it if a court in the country in question, on the matter being referred to it, upholds the claim.
(4) A person cannot be compelled to give any evidence if his doing so would be prejudicial to the security of the United Kingdom.
(5) A certificate signed by or on behalf of the Secretary of State or, where the court is in Scotland, the Lord Advocate to the effect that it would be so prejudicial for that person to do so is conclusive evidence of that fact.
(6) A person cannot be compelled to give any evidence in his capacity as an officer or servant of the Crown.
(7) Sub-paragraphs (4) and (6) are without prejudice to the generality of sub-paragraph (1).

Forwarding evidence

6. (1) The evidence received by the court is to be given to the court or authority that made the request or to the territorial authority for forwarding to the court or authority that made the request.
(2) So far as may be necessary in order to comply with the request—

(*a*) where the evidence consists of a document, the original or a copy is to be provided,
(*b*) where it consists of any other article, the article itself, or a description, photograph or other representation of it, is to be provided.

Supplementary

7. The Bankers' Books Evidence Act 1879 (c 11) applies to the proceedings as it applies to other proceedings before the court.
8. No order for costs may be made.

---

1. See the Magistrates' Courts (Crime (International Co-operation) Rules 2004, in this PART, post.

Sections 30 and 31   SCHEDULE 2
                    EVIDENCE GIVEN BY TELEVISION LINK OR TELEPHONE
                                PART 1
                    EVIDENCE GIVEN BY TELEVISION LINK
1–4266

Securing attendance of witnesses

1. The nominated court has the like powers for securing the attendance of the witness to give evidence through the link as it has for the purpose of proceedings before the court.
2. (*Scotland*).

Conduct of hearing

3. The witness is to give evidence in the presence of the nominated court.
4. The nominated court is to establish the identity of the witness.
5. The nominated court is to intervene where it considers it necessary to do so to safeguard the rights of the witness.
6. The evidence is to be given under the supervision of the court of the country concerned.
7. The evidence is to be given in accordance with the laws of that country and with any measures for the protection of the witness agreed between the Secretary of State and the authority in that country which appears to him to have the function of entering into agreements of that kind.
8. Rules of court[1] under section 49 must make provision for the use of interpreters.

Privilege of witness

9. (1) The witness cannot be compelled to give any evidence which he could not be compelled to give in criminal proceedings in the part of the United Kingdom in which the nominated court exercises jurisdiction.

(2) The witness cannot be compelled to give any evidence if his doing so would be prejudicial to the security of the United Kingdom.

(3) A certificate signed by or on behalf of the Secretary of State or, where the court is in Scotland, the Lord Advocate to the effect that it would be so prejudicial for that person to do so is to be conclusive evidence of that fact.

(4) The witness cannot be compelled to give any evidence in his capacity as an officer or servant of the Crown.

(5) Sub-paragraphs (2) and (4) are without prejudice to the generality of sub-paragraph (1).

Record of hearing

10. Rules of court[1] under section 49 must make provision—

(a) for the drawing up of a record of the hearing,
(b) for sending the record to the external authority.

---

1. See the Magistrates' Courts (Crime (International Co-operation) Rules 2004, in this PART, post.

PART 2
EVIDENCE GIVEN BY TELEPHONE

Notification of witness

11. The nominated court must notify the witness of the time when and the place at which he is to give evidence by telephone.

Conduct of hearing

12. The nominated court must be satisfied that the witness is willingly giving evidence by telephone.
13. The witness is to give evidence in the presence of the nominated court.
14. The nominated court is to establish the identity of the witness.
15. The evidence is to be given under the supervision of the court of the participating country.
16. The evidence is to be given in accordance with the laws of that country.
17. Rules of court under section 49 must make provision for the use of interpreters.

Section 54   SCHEDULE 3
OFFENCES FOR THE PURPOSES OF SECTION 54

PART 1
OFFENCES WHERE ORDER OF DISQUALIFICATION FOR A MINIMUM PERIOD UNNECESSARY

1–4267 **1.** (1) Manslaughter or culpable homicide by the driver of a motor vehicle.
(2) "Driver"—

(a) in relation to Great Britain, has the same meaning as in the Road Traffic Act 1988 (c 52),
(b) in relation to Northern Ireland, has the same meaning as in Article 2(2) of the Road Traffic (Northern Ireland) Order 1995 (SI 1995/2994 (NI 18)).

2. An offence under section 89(1) of the Road Traffic Regulation Act 1984 (c 27) or Article 43(1) of the Road Traffic Regulation (Northern Ireland) Order 1997 (SI 1997/276 (NI 2)) (exceeding speed limit).

3. An offence under any of the following sections of the Road Traffic Act 1988 or Articles of the Road Traffic (Northern Ireland) Order 1995—

(a) section 1 or Article 9 (causing death by dangerous driving),
(b) section 2 or Article 10 (dangerous driving),
(c) section 3 or Article 12 (careless, and inconsiderate, driving),
(d) section 3A or Article 14 (causing death by careless driving when under influence of drink or drugs),
(e) section 4 or Article 15 (driving, or being in charge, when under influence of drink or drugs),
(f) section 5 or Article 16 (driving, or being in charge, of a motor vehicle with alcohol concentration above prescribed limit),
(g) section 6 or Article 17 (failing to provide a specimen of breath for a breath test),
(h) section 7 or Article 18 (failing to provide specimen for analysis or laboratory test).

4. An offence under section 12 of the Road Traffic Act 1988 (motor racing and speed trials on public ways).
5. An offence under section 103(1)(b) of the Road Traffic Act 1988 or Article 167(1) of the Road Traffic (Northern Ireland) Order 1981 (SI 1981/154 (NI 1)) (driving while disqualified).
6. An offence under section 170(4) of the Road Traffic Act 1988 or Article 175(2) of the Road Traffic (Northern Ireland) Order 1981 (failing to stop after accident and give particulars or report of accident).

PART 2
OFFENCES WHERE ORDER OF DISQUALIFICATION FOR MINIMUM PERIOD NECESSARY

7. An offence which—

(a) is mentioned in Part 1 of Schedule 2 to the Road Traffic Offenders Act 1988 (c 53) or Part 1 of Schedule 1 to the Road Traffic Offenders (Northern Ireland) Order 1996 (SI 1996/1320 (NI 10)), but
(b) is not an offence mentioned in Part 1 of this Schedule.

1–4268   SCHEDULE 4
TERRORIST PROPERTY: FREEZING ORDERS

(*The Provisions of this Schedule amend or insert provisions in the Terrorism Act 2000.*)

1–4269   SCHEDULE 5
MINOR AND CONSEQUENTIAL AMENDMENTS

1–4270   SCHEDULE 6
REPEALS

Courts Act 2003[1]
(2003 c 39)

PART 1[2]
MAINTAINING THE COURT SYSTEM
The general duty

1–4271   **1. The general duty.**   (1) The Lord Chancellor is under a duty to ensure that there is an efficient and effective system to support the carrying on of the business of—

(a) the Supreme Court,
(b) county courts, and
(c) magistrates' courts,

and that appropriate services are provided for those courts.

(2) In this Part—

(a) "the Supreme Court" includes the district probate registries, and
(b) "magistrates' court" includes a committee of justices.

(3) In this Part references to the Lord Chancellor's general duty in relation to the courts are to his duty under this section.

(4) The Lord Chancellor must, within 18 months of the coming into force of this section, and afterwards annually, prepare and lay before both Houses of Parliament a report as to the way in which he has discharged his general duty in relation to the courts.
[Courts Act 2003, s 1.]

1. The Courts Act 2003 unified the court structure by abolishing magistrates' courts committees and bringing magistrates' courts within the Courts Service under the leadership of the Lord Chancellor. There continue, however, to be 'local justice areas' with their own chairmen and deputy chairmen, and justices' clerks and assistant clerks assigned to one or more such areas. The Act also provided for the appointment of fines officers, and accounting and banking in relation to fines, and made various changes to criminal and civil jurisdiction and procedure.

The Act further provided for the appointment of court security officers, who have powers of search, exclusion, etc.

CAFCASS and all courts of original jurisdiction now come under the same inspection regime. The Act made changes to judicial offices and styles, and enabled greater flexibility in the deployment of judicial resources.

The remainder of the Act was principally concerned with: the making of rules and practice directions; appeals; the collection of fines, including, inter alia, discounts for immediate payment or payment without default on the order and increases where default occurs (though subsequent compliance can avoid liability to pay the increase), and obligatory attachment of earnings and benefits for, respectively, employed and unemployed defaulters unless such an order would be impracticable or inappropriate, with other sanctions, including vehicle clamping and sale where default persists, or the discharge of fines by unpaid work; transitional arrangements; and repeals.

The majority of the Act's provisions were left to be brought into force in accordance with commencement orders made under s 110. At the date of going to press the following commencement orders had been made: Commencement provisions: s 110; Courts Act 2003 (Commencement No 1) Order 2003, SI 2003/3345; Courts Act 2003 (Commencement No 2) Order 2004, SI 2004/174; Courts Act 2003 (Commencement No 3 and Transitional Provisions) Order 2004, SI 2004/401; Courts Act 2003 (Commencement No 4) Order 2004, SI 2004/798; Courts Act 2003 (Commencement No 5) Order 2004, SI 2004/1104; Courts Act 2003 (Commencement No 6 and Savings) Order 2004, SI 2004/2066; Courts Act 2003 (Commencement No 7) Order 2004, SI 2004/2195; Courts Act 2003 (Commencement No 8, Savings and Consequential Provisions) Order 2004, SI 2004/3123; Courts Act 2003 (Commencement No 9, Savings, Consequential and Transitional Provisions) Order 2005, SI 2005/547, revoked by SI 2005/910; Courts Act 2003 (Commencement No 10) Order 2005, SI 2005/910; Courts Act 2003 (Commencement No 11 and Transitional Provision) Order 2005, SI 2005/2744; and Courts Act 2003 (Commencement No 12 and Transitional Provision) Order 2005, SI 2005/3518.

2. Part 1 contains ss 1–6.

Court staff and accommodation

1–4272   **2. Court officers, staff and services.**   (1) The Lord Chancellor may appoint such officers and other staff as appear to him appropriate for the purpose of discharging his general duty in relation to the courts.

(2) The civil service pension arrangements for the time being in force apply (with any necessary adaptations) to persons appointed under subsection (1) as they apply to other persons employed in the civil service of the State.

(3) "The civil service pension arrangements" means—

(a) the principal civil service pension scheme (within the meaning of section 2 of the Superannuation Act 1972 (c 11)), and
(b) any other superannuation benefits for which provision is made under or by virtue of section 1 of the 1972 Act for or in respect of persons in employment in the civil service of the State.

(4) Subject to subsections (5) and (6), the Lord Chancellor may enter into such contracts with other persons for the provision, by them or their sub-contractors, of officers, staff or services as appear to him appropriate for the purpose of discharging his general duty in relation to the courts.

(5) The Lord Chancellor may not enter into contracts for the provision of officers and staff to discharge functions which involve making judicial decisions or exercising any judicial discretion.

(6) The Lord Chancellor may not enter into contracts for the provision of officers and staff to carry out the administrative work of the courts unless an order made by the Lord Chancellor authorises him to do so.

(7) Before making an order under subsection (6) the Lord Chancellor must consult—

    (a)   the Lord Chief Justice,

    (b)   the Master of the Rolls,

    (c)   The President of the Queen's Bench Division,

    (d)   the President of the Family Division, and

    (d)   the Chancellor of the High Court,

as to what effect (if any) the order might have on the proper and efficient administration of justice.

(8) An order under subsection (6) may authorise the Lord Chancellor to enter into contracts for the provision of officers or staff to discharge functions—

    (a)   wholly or to the extent specified in the order,

    (b)   generally or in cases or areas specified in the order, and

    (c)   unconditionally or subject to the fulfilment of conditions specified in the order.

[Courts Act 2003, s 2 as amended by the Constitutional Reform Act 2005, Sch 4.]

1–4273   3. Provision of accommodation.   (1) The Lord Chancellor may provide, equip, maintain and manage such court-houses, offices and other accommodation as appear to him appropriate for the purpose of discharging his general duty in relation to the courts.

(2) The Lord Chancellor may enter into such arrangements for the provision, equipment, maintenance or management of court-houses, offices or other accommodation as appear to him appropriate for the purpose of discharging his general duty in relation to the courts.

(3) The powers under—

    (a)   section 2 of the Commissioners of Works Act 1852 (c 28) (acquisition by agreement), and

    (b)   section 228(1) of the Town and Country Planning Act 1990 (c 8) (compulsory acquisition),

to acquire land necessary for the public service are to be treated as including power to acquire land for the purpose of its provision under arrangements entered into under subsection (2).

(4) "Court-house" means any place where a court sits, including the precincts of any building in which it sits.

[Courts Act 2003, s 3.]

Courts boards

1–4274   4. Establishment of courts boards.   (1) England and Wales is to be divided into areas for each of which there is to be a courts board.

(2) The areas are to be those specified by an order[1] made by the Lord Chancellor.

(3) Each area established by an order under subsection (2) is to be known by such name as is specified in the order (but subject to subsection (4)).

(4) The Lord Chancellor may make orders altering the areas.

(5) "Altering", in relation to an area, includes (as well as changing its boundaries)—

    (a)   combining it with one or more other areas,

    (b)   dividing it between two or more other areas, and

    (c)   changing its name.

(5A) Before making any order under subsection (2) or (4), the Lord Chancellor must consult the Lord Chief Justice.

(6) Before making an order under subsection (4), the Lord Chancellor must consult any courts board affected by the proposed order.

(7) When making an order under subsection (2) the Lord Chancellor must have regard to the desirability of specifying areas which are the same as—

    (a)   the police areas listed in Schedule 1 to the Police Act 1996 (c 16) (division of England and Wales, except London, into police areas), and

    (b)   the area consisting of the Metropolitan Police District and the City of London police area.

(7A) The Lord Chief Justice may nominate a judicial office holder (as defined in section 109(4) of the Constitutional Reform Act 2005) to exercise his functions under this section.

(8) Schedule 1 contains provisions about the constitution and procedure of courts boards.

[Courts Act 2003, s 4 as amended by the Constitutional Reform Act 2005, Sch 4.]

---

1. The Courts Boards Areas Order 2004 has been made, in this PART, STATUTORY INSTRUMENTS ON PROCEDURE, post.

1–4275   5. Functions of courts boards.   (1) Each courts board is under a duty, in accordance with guidance under this section—

(a) to scrutinise, review and make recommendations about the way in which the Lord Chancellor is discharging his general duty in relation to the courts with which the board is concerned, and

(b) for the purposes mentioned in paragraph (a), to consider draft and final business plans relating to those courts.

(2) In discharging his general duty in relation to the courts, the Lord Chancellor must give due consideration to recommendations made by the boards under subsection (1).

(3) If the Lord Chancellor rejects a recommendation made by a courts board under subsection (1) as a result of the board's consideration of a final business plan, he must give the board his written reasons for so doing.

(4) The courts with which a courts board is concerned are—

(a) the Crown Court,

(b) county courts, and

(c) magistrates' courts,

in the board's area.

(5) The Lord Chancellor must, after consulting the Lord Chief Justice, prepare and issue the boards with guidance about how they should carry out their functions under subsection (1).

(6) The guidance may, after consulting the Lord Chief Justice, in particular contain provisions about the procedures to be followed in connection with draft and final business plans.

(7) The Lord Chancellor may from time to time issue the boards with revised guidance and revoke previous guidance.

(8) Guidance issued under this section must be laid before both Houses of Parliament.

(9) The Lord Chief Justice may nominate a judicial office holder (as defined in section 109(4) of the Constitutional Reform Act 2005) to exercise his functions under this section.

[Courts Act 2003, s 5 as amended by the Constitutional Reform Act 2005, Sch 4.]

1–4276

Abolition of magistrates' courts committees

6. Abolition of magistrates' courts committees, etc. (1) The Greater London Magistrates' Courts Authority (the magistrates' courts committee for Greater London) and all the magistrates' courts committees for areas of England and Wales outside Greater London are abolished.

(2) In consequence of that—

(a) England and Wales outside Greater London is no longer divided into magistrates' courts committee areas, and

(b) the office of justices' chief executive is abolished.

(3) Schedule 2 (abolition of magistrates' courts committees: transfers) has effect.

(4) The Justices of the Peace Act 1997 (c 25) ceases to have effect.

[Courts Act 2003, s 6.]

PART 2[1]

JUSTICES OF THE PEACE

The commission of the peace and local justice areas

1–4277   7. The commission of the peace for England and Wales. There shall be a commission of the peace for England and Wales—

(a) issued under the Great Seal, and

(b) addressed generally, and not by name, to all such persons as may from time to time hold office as justices of the peace for England and Wales.

[Courts Act 2003, s 7.]

---

1. Part 2 tcontains ss 7–42.

1–4278   8. Local justice areas. (1) England and Wales is to be divided into areas to be known as local justice areas.

(2) The areas are to be those specified by an order[1] made by the Lord Chancellor.

(3) Each local justice area established by order under subsection (2) is to be known by such name as is specified in the order (but subject to subsection (4)).

(4) The Lord Chancellor may make orders[2] altering local justice areas.

(5) "Altering", in relation to a local justice area, includes (as well as changing its boundaries)—

(a) combining it with one or more other local justice areas,

(b) dividing it between two or more other local justice areas, and

(c) changing its name.

(5A) Before making any order under subsection (2) or (4), the Lord Chancellor must consult the Lord Chief Justice.

(6) Before making an order under subsection (4) in relation to a local justice area the Lord Chancellor must consult—

(a) the justices of the peace assigned to the local justice area, (*b*) any courts board whose area includes the local justice area or a part of the local justice area, and

(*c*) unless the alteration consists only of a change of name, any local authorities whose area includes the local justice area or a part of the local justice area.

(7) "Local authority" means—

(*a*) any council of a county, a county borough, a London borough or a council of a district,

(*b*) the Common Council of the City of London, or

(*c*) a police authority established under section 3 of the Police Act 1996 (c 16) or the Metropolitan Police Authority.

(8) The Lord Chief Justice may nominate a judicial office holder (as defined in section 109(4) of the Constitutional Reform Act 2005) to exercise his functions under this section.
[Courts Act 2003, s 8 as amended by the Constitutional Reform Act 2005, Sch 4.]

---

1. The Local Justice Areas Order 2005 has been made, in this PART: STATUTORY INSTRUMENTS AND PRACTICE DIRECTIONS ON PROCEDURE, post.
2. The following Local Justice Areas Order has been made which also amends the Schedule to the Local Justice Areas Order 2005, in this PART, post: (No 1) Order 2006, SI 2006/1839.

Lay justices

1–4279   9. Meaning of "lay justice".   In this Act "lay justice" means a justice of the peace who is not a District Judge (Magistrates' Courts).
[Courts Act 2003, s 9.]

1–4280   10. Appointment of lay justices etc.   (1) Lay justices are to be appointed for England and Wales by the Lord Chancellor by instrument on behalf and in the name of Her Majesty.

(2) The Lord Chief Justice—

(*a*) must assign each lay justice to one or more local justice areas, and

(*b*) may change an assignment so as to assign the lay justice to a different local justice area or to different local justice areas.

(2A) The Lord Chancellor must ensure that arrangements for the exercise, so far as affecting any local justice area, of functions under subsections (1) and (2) include arrangements for consulting persons appearing to him to have special knowledge of matters relevant to the exercise of those functions in relation to that area.

(3) Every lay justice is, by virtue of his office, capable of acting as such in any local justice area (whether or not he is assigned to it); but he may do so only in accordance with arrangements made by or on behalf of the Lord Chief Justice.

(4) Rules[1] may make provision about the training courses to be completed before a person may exercise functions as a lay justice in any proceedings or class of proceedings specified in the rules.

(5) Subsection (3) is subject to section 12 (the supplemental list).

(6) The functions conferred on the Lord Chief Justice by subsections (2) and (3) may be exercised only after consulting the Lord Chancellor.

(7) The Lord Chief Justice may nominate a judicial office holder (as defined in section 109(4) of the Constitutional Reform Act 2005) to exercise his functions under subsection (2) or (3).
[Courts Act 2003, s 10 as amended by the Constitutional Reform Act 2005, Sch 4.]

---

1. The Justices of the Peace (Training and Appraisal) Rules 2005 have been made, in this PART: STATUTORY INSTRUMENTS AND PRACTICE DIRECTIONS ON PROCEDURE, post.

1–4281   11. Resignation and removal of lay justices.   (1) A lay justice may resign his office at any time.

(2) The Lord Chancellor may, with the concurrence of the Lord Chief Justice, remove a lay justice from his office by an instrument on behalf and in the name of Her Majesty—

(*a*) on the ground of incapacity or misbehaviour,

(*b*) on the ground of a persistent failure to meet such standards of competence as are prescribed by a direction given by the Lord Chancellor, with the concurrence of the Lord Chief Justice, or

(*c*) if he is satisfied that the lay justice is declining or neglecting to take a proper part in the exercise of his functions as a justice of the peace.
[Courts Act 2003, s 11.]

1–4282   12. The supplemental list.   (1) A list, to be known as "the supplemental list", must be kept in the office of the Clerk of the Crown in Chancery.

(2) A lay justice whose name is entered in the supplemental list is not qualified as a justice of the peace to do any act or to be a member of a committee or other body.

(3) No act or appointment is invalidated by reason of the disqualification of a lay justice under subsection (2).
[Courts Act 2003, s 12.]

1–4283   13. Entry of names in the supplemental list.   (1) Subject to subsections (2) and (3), the name of a lay justice who has reached 70 must be entered in the supplemental list.

(2) The name of a lay justice who, when he reaches 70, is chairman of the lay justices assigned to a local justice area need not be entered in the supplemental list until the term for which he is serving as chairman has ended.

(3) Where—

(a) proceedings are, or are expected to be, in progress on the day on which the lay justice reaches 70, and

(b) the lay justice is exercising functions in those proceedings as a justice of the peace,

the Lord Chief Justice may, with the concurrence of the Lord Chancellor, direct that the name of the lay justice need not be entered in the supplemental list until the proceedings have ended.

(4) The name of a lay justice must be entered in the supplemental list if—

(a) he applies for it to be entered, and

(b) the application is approved by the Lord Chancellor.

(5) The Lord Chancellor may, with the concurrence of the Lord Chief Justice, direct that the name of a lay justice is to be entered in the supplemental list on the ground of incapacity.

(6) The Lord Chief Justice may nominate a judicial office holder (as defined in section 109(4) of the Constitutional Reform Act 2005) to exercise his functions under subsection (3).

[Courts Act 2003, s 13 as amended by the Constitutional Reform Act 2005, Sch 4.]

1–4284   14. Removal of names from the supplemental list.   (1) A person's name must be removed from the supplemental list if he ceases to be a justice of the peace.

(2) A person's name must be removed from the supplemental list if—

(a) his name is in the list as a result of section 13(4) or (5), and

(b) the Lord Chancellor, with the concurrence of the Lord Chief Justice, directs its removal.

[Courts Act 2003, s 14 as amended by the Constitutional Reform Act 2005, Sch 4.]

1–4285   15. Lay justices' allowances.   (1) A lay justice is entitled to payments by way of—

(a) travelling allowance,

(b) subsistence allowance, and

(c) financial loss allowance.

(2) Allowances under this section are to be paid by the Lord Chancellor at rates determined by him.

(3) A lay justice's travelling allowance is an allowance in respect of expenditure—

(a) which is incurred by him on travelling, and

(b) which is necessarily incurred for the purpose of enabling him to perform his duties.

(4) A lay justice's subsistence allowance is an allowance in respect of expenditure—

(a) which is incurred by him on subsistence, and

(b) which is necessarily incurred for the purpose of enabling him to perform his duties.

(5) A lay justice's financial loss allowance is an allowance in respect of—

(a) any other expenditure incurred by reason of the performance of his duties, and

(b) any loss of earnings or social security benefits suffered by reason of the performance of his duties.

(6) A lay justice is not entitled to a payment under this section in respect of the performance of his duties if—

(a) a payment of a similar kind in respect of those duties may be made to him apart from this section, or

(b) entitlement to the payment is excluded by regulations made by the Lord Chancellor.

(7) For the purposes of this section the performance of a lay justice's duties includes taking a training course provided by or on behalf of the Lord Chief Justice.

(8) The Lord Chancellor may by regulations[1] make provision about the way in which this section is to be administered and may in particular make provision—

(a) prescribing sums (including tax credits) that are to be treated as social security benefits for the purposes of financial loss allowances,

(b) prescribing the particulars to be provided for claiming payment of allowances, and

(c) for avoiding duplication between payments under this section and under other arrangements where expenditure is incurred for more than one purpose.

(9) The Lord Chief Justice may nominate a judicial office holder (as defined in section 109(4) of the Constitutional Reform Act 2005) to exercise his functions under subsection (3).

[Courts Act 2003, s 15.]

---

1. See the Justices' Allowances Regulations 1976, in this PART: STATUTORY INSTRUMENTS AND PRACTICE DIRECTIONS ON PROCEDURE, post.

1–4286   **16. Records of lay justices.** (1) The Lord Chancellor—

(a) must appoint a person to be keeper of the rolls for each local justice area, and
(b) may appoint the same person to be keeper of the rolls for more than one local justice area.

(2) The keeper of the rolls for a local justice area must be notified, in such manner as the Lord Chancellor may direct, of—

(a) any assignment of a lay justice to the area,
(b) any change in an assignment of a lay justice as a result of which he ceases to be assigned to the area, and
(c) the fact that a lay justice assigned to the area has ceased to be a justice of the peace or that his name has been entered in or removed from the supplemental list.

(3) The keeper of the rolls for a local justice area must ensure that an accurate record is maintained of all lay justices for the time being assigned to the area.
(4) The Lord Chancellor must consult the Lord Chief Justice before—

(a) appointing a person under subsection (1), or
(b) giving a direction under subsection (2).

(5) The Lord Chief Justice may nominate a judicial office holder (as defined in section 109(4) of the Constitutional Reform Act 2005) to exercise his functions under this section.
[Courts Act 2003, s 16 as amended by the Constitutional Reform Act 2005, Sch 4.]

1–4287

Chairman and deputy chairmen and the bench

   17. Chairman and deputy chairmen: selection. (1) For each local justice area there is to be—

(a) a chairman of the lay justices assigned to the area, and
(b) one or more deputy chairmen of those lay justices,

chosen by them from among their number.
   (2) Rules[1] may make provision—

(a) subject to subsection (3), as to the term of office of the chairman and deputy chairmen, and
(b) as to the number of deputy chairmen to be elected for any area.

   (3) The Lord Chief Justice may, with the concurrence of the Lord Chancellor, authorise a lay justice to continue to hold office as chairman or deputy chairman for the purposes of specified proceedings which are, or are expected to be, in progress on the day on which the lay justice's office would otherwise end.
   (4) Any contested election for choosing the chairman or a deputy chairman is to be held by secret ballot.
   (5) Rules[1] may make provision for the purposes of this section and may in particular make provision—

(a) about the procedure for nominating candidates for election as a chairman or a deputy chairman;
(b) about the procedure at such an election.

   (6) The Lord Chief Justice may nominate a judicial office holder (as defined in section 109(4) of the Constitutional Reform Act 2005) to exercise his functions under subsection (3).
[Courts Act 2003, s as1as amended by the Constitutional Reform Act 2005, Sch 4.]

---

   1. The Justices of the Peace (Size and Chairmanship of Bench) Rules 2005 have been made, in this PART: STATUTORY INSTRUMENTS AND PRACTICE DIRECTIONS ON PROCEDURE, post.

1–4288   **18. Rights to preside and size of bench.** (1) If the chairman for a local justice area is present at a sitting or other meeting of lay justices assigned to or acting in the area, he must preside.
   (2) If, in the absence of the chairman, one or more of the deputy chairmen for a local justice area is present at a sitting or other meeting of lay justices assigned to or acting in that area he (or the most senior of them) must preside.
   (3) Neither subsection (1) nor subsection (2) applies if, in accordance with rules, the chairman or (as the case may be) the deputy chairman asks another of the lay justices to preside.
   (4) Subsections (1) and (2) do not confer on the chairman or a deputy chairman a right to preside in court if, under rules, he is ineligible to do so.
   (5) Subsections (1) and (2) do not confer on the chairman or a deputy chairman a right to preside—

(a) in a youth court or family proceedings court,
(b) at meetings of a committee or other body of justices of the peace which has its own chairman, or
(c) at sittings when a District Judge (Magistrates' Courts) is engaged as such in administering justice.

   (6) Rules[1] may make provision for the purposes of subsections (3) and (4) and may in particular make provision—

(a)   as to training courses to be completed by lay justices before they may preside in court,
(b)   as to—

   (i)   the approval of lay justices, in accordance with the rules, before they may preside in court,
   (ii)   the lay justices who may be so approved, and
   (iii)   the courts to which the approval relates, and

(c)   as to circumstances in which a lay justice may preside in court even though requirements imposed under paragraph (a) or (b) are not met in relation to him.

(7)   Rules[1] may also make provision—

(a)   specifying the maximum number of lay justices who may sit to deal with a case as a magistrates' court, and
(b)   as to the arrangements to be made for securing the presence on the bench of enough, but not more than enough, lay justices.
[Courts Act 2003, s 18.]

---

1. The Justices of the Peace (Training and Appraisal) Rules 2005 have been made, in this PART: STATUTORY INSTRUMENTS AND PRACTICE DIRECTIONS ON PROCEDURE, post.

Supplementary provisions about the bench

1–4289   19. Training, development and appraisal of lay justices.   (1) Rules[1] may (in addition to making provision under sections 10(4) and 18(6)) make provision for, or in connection with, the training, development and appraisal of lay justices.

(2)   Such rules may make provision for committees, constituted in accordance with the rules, to have such functions as may be specified in the rules, including, in particular—

(a)   providing advice and support to lay justices in connection with their functions as lay justices;
(b)   identifying the training needs of lay justices;
(c)   appraising lay justices and reporting on the results of appraisals;
(d)   giving or withholding approval for the purposes of section 18;
(e)   advising the Lord Chief Justice in relation to authorisations of lay justices as members of family proceedings courts or youth courts;
(f)   granting or revoking such authorisations on behalf of the Lord Chief Justice.

(3)   The Lord Chief Justice must ensure that training and training materials that appear to him, after consulting the Lord Chancellor, to be appropriate are provided for lay justices with a view to enabling them to comply with requirements as to training imposed by rules under section 10 or 18 or this section.

(4)   The Lord Chief Justice may nominate a judicial office holder (as defined in section 109(4) of the Constitutional Reform Act 2005) to exercise his functions under this section.
[Courts Act 2003, s 19 as amended by the Constitutional Reform Act 2005, Sch 4.]

---

1. The Justices of the Peace (Training and Appraisal) Rules 2005 have been made, in this PART: STATUTORY INSTRUMENTS AND PRACTICE DIRECTIONS ON PROCEDURE, post.

1–4290   20. Rules.   (1) In sections 10, 17, 18 and 19 "rules" means rules made by the Lord Chief Justice.

(2)   Before making any rules for the purposes of section 10, 17, 18 or 19 the Lord Chief Justice must consult—

(za)   Lord Chief Justice,
(a)   the Criminal Procedure Rule Committee,
(b)   the Family Procedure Rule Committee, and
(c)   the Magistrates' Courts Rule Committee.

(3)   The Lord Chief Justice may nominate a judicial office holder (as defined in section 109(4) of the Constitutional Reform Act 2005) to exercise his functions under this section.
[Courts Act 2003, s 20 as amended by the Constitutional Reform Act 2005, Sch 4.]

1–4291   21. Duty to consult lay justices on matters affecting them etc.   (1) The Lord Chief Justice must take all reasonable and practicable steps—

(a)   for ensuring that lay justices acting in a local justice area are kept informed of matters affecting them in the performance of their duties, and
(b)   for ascertaining their views on such matters.

(2)   The Lord Chief Justice may nominate a judicial office holder (as defined in section 109(4) of the Constitutional Reform Act 2005) to exercise his functions under this section.
[Courts Act 2003, s 21 as amended by the Constitutional Reform Act 2005, Sch 4.]

District Judges (Magistrates' Courts)

1–4292   22. Appointment etc.   (1) Her Majesty may, on the recommendation of the Lord Chancellor, appoint a person who has a 7 year general qualification to be a District Judge (Magistrates' Courts).

(2)   A District Judge (Magistrates' Courts) must, before acting as such, take the oath of allegiance

and judicial oath in accordance with the Promissory Oaths Act 1868 (c 72) and the Promissory Oaths Act 1871 (c 48).

(3) The Lord Chancellor may pay to a District Judge (Magistrates' Courts) such allowances as he may determine.

(4) Any such allowances are in addition to the salary charged on and paid out of the Consolidated Fund under section 9 of the Administration of Justice Act 1973 (c 15).

(5) The Lord Chancellor may, with the concurrence of the Lord Chief Justice, remove a District Judge (Magistrates' Courts) from office on the ground of incapacity or misbehaviour.
[Courts Act 2003, s 22 as amended by the Constitutional Reform Act 2005, Sch 4.]

1–4293   23. Senior District Judge (Chief Magistrate).   Her Majesty—

(a) may designate one of the District Judges (Magistrates' Courts) to be Senior District Judge (Chief Magistrate), and

(b) if she does so, may designate another of them to be the deputy of the Senior District Judge (Chief Magistrate).
[Courts Act 2003, s 23 as amended by the Constitutional Reform Act 2005, Sch 3.]

1–4294   24. Deputy District Judges (Magistrates' Courts).   (1) The Lord Chancellor may appoint a person who has a 7 year general qualification to be a Deputy District Judge (Magistrates' Courts) for such period as the Lord Chancellor considers appropriate (but subject to subsection (4)).

(2) A Deputy District Judge (Magistrates' Courts) must, before acting as such, take the oath of allegiance and judicial oath in accordance with the Promissory Oaths Act 1868 and the Promissory Oaths Act 1871.

(3) The Lord Chancellor may pay to a Deputy District Judge (Magistrates' Courts) such remuneration and allowances as he may determine.

(4) The Lord Chancellor may, with the concurrence of the Lord Chief Justice, remove a Deputy District Judge (Magistrates' Courts) from office on the ground of incapacity or misbehaviour.

(5) During the period of his appointment, a Deputy District Judge (Magistrates' Courts)—

(a) is to act as a District Judge (Magistrates' Courts), and

(b) is to be treated for all purposes (apart from appointment, tenure, remuneration, allowances and pensions) as if he were a District Judge (Magistrates' Courts).
[Courts Act 2003, s 24 as amended by the Constitutional Reform Act 2005, Sch 4.]

1–4295   25. District Judges (Magistrates' Courts) as justices of the peace.   (1) A District Judge (Magistrates' Courts) is by virtue of his office a justice of the peace for England and Wales.

(2) It is the duty of a District Judge (Magistrates' Courts) to act as a justice of the peace in any local justice area in accordance with arrangements made by the Lord Chief Justice, after consulting the Lord Chancellor.

(3) The Lord Chief Justice may nominate a judicial office holder (as defined in section 109(4) of the Constitutional Reform Act 2005) to exercise his functions under subsection (2).
[Courts Act 2003, s 25 as amended by the Constitutional Reform Act 2005, Sch 4.]

1–4296   26. District Judges (Magistrates' Courts) able to act alone.   (1) Nothing in the 1980 Act—

(a) requiring a magistrates' court to be composed of two or more justices, or

(b) limiting the powers of a magistrates' court when composed of a single justice,

applies to a District Judge (Magistrates' Courts).

(2) A District Judge (Magistrates' Courts) may—

(a) do any act, and

(b) exercise alone any jurisdiction,

which can be done or exercised by two justices, apart from granting or transferring a licence.

(3) Any enactment making provision ancillary to the jurisdiction exercisable by two justices of the peace also applies to the jurisdiction of a District Judge (Magistrates' Courts), unless the provision relates to granting or transferring a licence.

(4) This section does not apply to the hearing or determination of family proceedings (as defined by section 65 of the 1980 Act).

(5) "The 1980 Act" means the Magistrates' Courts Act 1980 (c 43).
[Courts Act 2003, s 26.]

Justices' clerks and assistant clerks

1–4297   27. Justices' clerks and assistant clerks.   (1) A justices' clerk is a person who is—

(a) appointed by the Lord Chancellor under section 2(1), and

(b) designated by the Lord Chancellor, after consulting with the Lord Chief Justice, as a justices' clerk.

(2) A person may be designated as a justices' clerk only if he—

(a) has a 5 year magistrates' court qualification,

(*b*) is a barrister or solicitor who has served for not less than 5 years as an assistant to a justices' clerk, or

(*c*) has previously been a justices' clerk.

(3) The Lord Chancellor—

(*a*) must, after consulting with the Lord Chief Justice, assign each justices' clerk to one or more local justice areas, and

(*b*) subject to subsections (4A) to (4C), may change an assignment so as to assign the justices' clerk to a different local justice area or to different local justice areas.

(4A) The Lord Chancellor may change an assignment of a justices' clerk so that he is no longer assigned to a local justice area ("the relevant area") only if the conditions in subsections (4B) and (4C) are met.

(4B) Before changing the assignment, the Lord Chancellor must consult—

(*a*) the chairman of the lay justices assigned to the relevant area, or

(*b*) if that is not possible or not practicable, the deputy chairman or such of the lay justices assigned to or acting in the relevant area as it appears to the Lord Chancellor appropriate to consult.

(4C) The Lord Chief Justice must agree to the change.

(5) An assistant to a justices' clerk is a person who is—

(*a*) appointed by the Lord Chancellor under section 2(1) or provided under a contract made by virtue of section 2(4), and

(*b*) designated by the Lord Chancellor as an assistant to a justices' clerk.

(6) The Lord Chancellor may by regulations provide that, subject to such exceptions as may be prescribed by the regulations[1], a person may be designated as an assistant to a justices' clerk only if he—

(*a*) has a 5 year magistrates' court qualification, or

(*b*) has such qualifications as may be prescribed by, or approved by the Lord Chancellor in accordance with, the regulations.

(6A) The Lord Chief Justice may nominate a judicial office holder (as defined in section 109(4) of the Constitutional Reform Act 2005) to exercise his functions under this section.

(7) In this Part "assistant clerk" is short for "assistant to a justices' clerk".

[Courts Act 2003, s 27 as amended by the Constitutional Reform Act 2005, Sch 4.]

---

1. The Assistants to Justices' Clerks Regulations 2006 have been made, in this PART: STATUTORY INSTRUMENTS AND PRACTICE DIRECTIONS ON PROCEDURE, post.

1–4298 28. Functions. (1) Rules[1] may make provision enabling things authorised to be done by, to or before a single justice of the peace to be done instead by, to or before a justices' clerk.

(2) Rules[1] may also make provision enabling things authorised to be done by, to or before a justices' clerk (whether by virtue of subsection (1) or otherwise) to be done instead by, to or before an assistant clerk.

(3) An enactment or rule of law which—

(*a*) regulates the exercise of any jurisdiction or powers of justices of the peace, or

(*b*) relates to things done in the exercise or purported exercise of any such jurisdiction or powers,

applies in relation to the exercise or purported exercise of any such jurisdiction or powers by a justices' clerk by virtue of subsection (1) as if he were a justice of the peace.

(4) The functions of a justices' clerk include giving advice to any or all of the justices of the peace to whom he is clerk about matters of law (including procedure and practice) on questions arising in connection with the discharge of their functions, including questions arising when the clerk is not personally attending on them.

(5) The powers of a justices' clerk include, at any time when he thinks he should do so, bringing to the attention of any or all of the justices of the peace to whom he is clerk any point of law (including procedure and practice) that is or may be involved in any question so arising.

(6) For the purposes of subsections (4) and (5) the functions of justices of the peace do not include functions as a judge of the Crown Court.

(7) Subsections (4) and (5) do not limit—

(*a*) the powers and duties of a justices' clerk, or

(*b*) the matters on which justices of the peace may obtain assistance from their clerk.

(8) In this section "rules" means rules[1] made by the Lord Chancellor with the concurrence of the Lord Chief Justice.

(9) Before making any rules for the purposes of this section the Lord Chancellor must consult—

(*a*) the Criminal Procedure Rule Committee,

(*b*) the Family Procedure Rule Committee, and

(*c*) the Magistrates' Courts Rule Committee.

(10) The Lord Chief Justice may nominate a judicial office holder (as defined in section 109(4) of the Constitutional Reform Act 2005) to exercise his functions under this section.

[Courts Act 2003, s 28 as amended by the Constitutional Reform Act 2005, Sch 4.]

1. The Justices' Clerk's Rules 2005 have been made, in this PART: STATUTORY INSTRUMENTS AND PRACTICE DIRECTIONS ON PROCEDURE, post.

1–4299   29. Independence.   (1) A justices' clerk exercising—

(a) a function exercisable by one or more justices of the peace,

(b) a function specified in section 28(4) or (5) (advice on matters of law, including procedure and practice), or

(c) a function as a member of the Criminal Procedure Rule Committee or the Family Procedure Rule Committee,

is not subject to the direction of the Lord Chancellor or any other person.

(2) An assistant clerk who is exercising any such function is not subject to the direction of any person other than a justices' clerk.
[Courts Act 2003, s 29.]

Places, dates and times of sittings

1–4300   30. Places, dates and times of sittings.   (1) The Lord Chancellor may, after consulting with the Lord Chief Justice, give directions as to the places in England and Wales at which magistrates' courts may sit.

(2) In exercising his powers under subsection (1), the Lord Chancellor shall have regard to the need to ensure that court-houses are accessible to persons resident in each local justice area.

(3) The Lord Chancellor may, with the concurrence of the Lord Chief Justice, give directions as to the distribution and transfer of the general business of magistrates' courts between the places specified in directions under subsection (1).

(4) Directions under subsection (3) may, in particular, contain provision that, where a person is charged with an offence and is being required to appear before a magistrates' court, the place where he is required to appear is one of the places described in subsection (5).

(5) The places are—

(a) a place in the local justice area in which the offence is alleged to have been committed;

(b) a place in the local justice area in which the person charged with the offence resides;

(c) a place in the local justice area in which the witnesses, or the majority of the witnesses, reside;

(d) a place where other cases raising similar issues are being dealt with.

(6) "The general business of magistrates' courts" does not include family proceedings (as defined in section 65 of the 1980 Act).

(7) The Lord Chancellor may, after consulting with the Lord Chief Justice, give directions as to the days on which and times at which magistrates' courts may sit.

(8) Subject to any directions under subsection (7), the business of magistrates' courts may be conducted on any day and at any time.

(9) The Lord Chief Justice may nominate a judicial office holder (as defined in section 109(4) of the Constitutional Reform Act 2005) to exercise his functions under this section.
[Courts Act 2003, s 30 as amended by the Constitutional Reform Act 2005, Sch 4.]

Protection and indemnification of justices and justices' clerks

1–4301   31. Immunity for acts within jurisdiction.   (1) No action lies against a justice of the peace in respect of what he does or omits to do—

(a) in the execution of his duty as a justice of the peace, and

(b) in relation to a matter within his jurisdiction.

(2) No action lies against a justices' clerk or an assistant clerk in respect of what he does or omits to do—

(a) in the execution of his duty as a justices' clerk or assistant clerk exercising, by virtue of an enactment, a function of a single justice of the peace, and

(b) in relation to a matter within his jurisdiction.
[Courts Act 2003, s 31.]

1–4302   32. Immunity for certain acts beyond jurisdiction.   (1) An action lies against a justice of the peace in respect of what he does or omits to do—

(a) in the purported execution of his duty as a justice of the peace, but

(b) in relation to a matter not within his jurisdiction,

if, but only if, it is proved that he acted in bad faith.

(2) An action lies against a justices' clerk or an assistant clerk in respect of what he does or omits to do—

(a) in the purported execution of his duty as a justices' clerk or assistant clerk exercising, by virtue of an enactment, a function of a single justice of the peace, but

(b) in relation to a matter not within his jurisdiction,

if, but only if, it is proved that he acted in bad faith.
[Courts Act 2003, s 32.]

1–4303 33. Striking out proceedings where action prohibited. (1) If an action is brought in circumstances in which section 31 or 32 provides that no action lies, a judge of the court in which the action is brought may, on the application of the defendant, strike out the proceedings in the action.

(2) If a judge strikes out proceedings under subsection (1), he may if he thinks fit order the person bringing the action to pay costs.
[Courts Act 2003, s 33.]

1–4304 34. Costs in legal proceedings. (1) A court may not order a justice of the peace to pay costs in any proceedings in respect of what he does or omits to do in the execution (or purported execution) of his duty as a justice of the peace.

(2) A court may not order—

(*a*) a justices' clerk, or
(*b*) an assistant clerk,

to pay costs in any proceedings in respect of what he does or omits to do in the execution (or purported execution) of his duty as a justices' clerk or assistant clerk exercising, by virtue of an enactment, a function of a single justice of the peace.

(3) But subsections (1) and (2) do not apply in relation to any proceedings in which a justice of the peace, justices' clerk or assistant clerk—

(*a*) is being tried for an offence or is appealing against a conviction, or
(*b*) is proved to have acted in bad faith in respect of the matters giving rise to the proceedings.

(4) A court which is prevented by subsection (1) or (2) from ordering a justice of the peace, justices' clerk or assistant clerk to pay costs in any proceedings may instead order the Lord Chancellor to make a payment in respect of the costs of a person in the proceedings.

(5) The Lord Chancellor may, after consulting with the Lord Chief Justice, make regulations[1] specifying—

(*a*) circumstances in which a court must or must not exercise the power conferred on it by subsection (4), and
(*b*) how the amount of any payment ordered under subsection (4) is to be determined.

(6) The Lord Chief Justice may nominate a judicial office holder (as defined in section 109(4) of the Constitutional Reform Act 2005) to exercise his functions under this section.
[Courts Act 2003, s 34 as amended by the Constitutional Reform Act 2005, Sch 4.]

---

1. The Justices and Justices' Clerks (Costs) Regulations 2001, in this PART: STATUTORY INSTRUMENTS AND PRACTICE DIRECTIONS ON PROCEDURE, post, continue to have effect as if made under this section by virtue of the Courts Act 2003 (Transitional Provisions, Savings and Consequential Provisions) Order 2005, SI 2005/911.

1–4305 35. Indemnity. (1) "Indemnifiable amounts", in relation to a justice of the peace, justices' clerk or assistant clerk, means—

(*a*) costs which he reasonably incurs in or in connection with proceedings in respect of anything done or omitted to be done in the exercise (or purported exercise) of his duty as a justice of the peace, justices' clerk or assistant clerk,
(*b*) costs which he reasonably incurs in taking steps to dispute a claim which might be made in such proceedings,
(*c*) damages awarded against him or costs ordered to be paid by him in such proceedings, or
(*d*) sums payable by him in connection with a reasonable settlement of such proceedings or such a claim.

(2) Indemnifiable amounts relate to criminal matters if the duty mentioned in subsection (1)(*a*) relates to criminal matters.

(3) The Lord Chancellor must indemnify a justice of the peace, justices' clerk or assistant clerk in respect of—

(*a*) indemnifiable amounts which relate to criminal matters, unless it is proved, in respect of the matters giving rise to the proceedings or claim, that he acted in bad faith, and
(*b*) other indemnifiable amounts if, in respect of the matters giving rise to the proceedings or claim, he acted reasonably and in good faith.

(4) The Lord Chancellor may indemnify a justice of the peace, justices' clerk or assistant clerk in respect of other indemnifiable amounts unless it is proved, in respect of the matters giving rise to the proceedings or claim, that he acted in bad faith.

(5) Any question whether, or to what extent, a person is to be indemnified under this section is to be determined by the Lord Chancellor.

(6) The Lord Chancellor may, if the person claiming to be indemnified so requests, make a determination for the purposes of this section with respect to—

(*a*) costs such as are mentioned in subsection (1)(*a*) or (*b*), or
(*b*) sums such as are mentioned in subsection (1)(*d*),

before the costs are incurred or the settlement in connection with which the sums are payable is made.

(7) But a determination under subsection (6) before costs are incurred—

(a)   is subject to such limitations (if any) as the Lord Chancellor thinks proper and to the subsequent determination of the costs reasonably incurred, and

(b)   does not affect any other determination which may fall to be made in connection with the proceedings or claim in question.

[Courts Act 2003, s 35.]

Fines officers and designated officers

1–4306   **36. Fines officers.**   Any reference in an enactment to a fines officer is to a person who is—

(a)   appointed by the Lord Chancellor under section 2(1) or provided under a contract made by virtue of section 2(4), and

(b)   designated as a fines officer by the Lord Chancellor.

[Courts Act 2003, s 36.]

1–4307   **37. Designated officers and magistrates' courts.**   (1) Any reference in an enactment to the designated officer, in relation to a magistrates' court, justice of the peace or local justice area, is to a person who is—

(a)   appointed by the Lord Chancellor under section 2(1) or provided under a contract made by virtue of section 2(4), and

(b)   designated by the Lord Chancellor in relation to that court, justice of the peace or area.

(2) In this section "magistrates' court" includes—

(a)   a committee of justices, and

(b)   when exercising a function exercisable by one or more justices of the peace—

(i)   a justices' clerk, and

(ii)   an assistant clerk.

[Courts Act 2003, s 37.]

Application of receipts of magistrates' courts etc

1–4308   **38. Application of receipts of designated officers.**   (1) The following are to be paid to the Lord Chancellor—

(a)   fines imposed by a magistrates' court,

(b)   sums which—

(i)   become payable by virtue of an order of a magistrates' court, and

(ii)   are by an enactment made applicable as fines (or any description of fines) imposed by a magistrates' court, and

(c)   all other sums received by—

(i)   a designated officer for a magistrates' court, or

(ii)   a designated officer for a local justice area,

in his capacity as such.

(2) "Fine" includes—

(a)   any pecuniary penalty, pecuniary forfeiture or pecuniary compensation payable under a conviction, and

(b)   any pecuniary forfeiture on conviction by, or under any order of, a magistrates' court so far as the forfeiture is converted into or consists of money.

(3) For the purposes of this section anything done by the Crown Court on appeal from a magistrates' court is to be treated as done by the magistrates' court.

(4) Any sums received by the Lord Chancellor under this section are to be paid by him into the Consolidated Fund.

[Courts Act 2003, s 38.]

1–4309   **39. Limits to requirements about application of receipts.**   (1) Section 38(1) is subject to section 139 of the 1980 Act (sums paid on summary conviction applied for payment of compensation and costs).

(2) Paragraphs (a) and (b) of section 38(1) do not apply to sums which, by or under any enactment, are directed to be paid to—

(a)   the Commissioners of Customs and Excise, or

(b)   officers of, or persons appointed by, the Commissioners.

(3) Those paragraphs also do not apply to sums which, by or under any enactment, are directed—

(a)   to be paid to or for the benefit of—

(i)   the party aggrieved or injured or a person described in similar terms, or

(ii)   the family or relatives of a person described in any such terms or of a person dying in consequence of an act or event which constituted or was the occasion of an offence,

(b)   to be applied in making good any default or repairing any damage or reimbursing any expenses (other than those of the prosecution), or

(c) to be paid to any person, if the enactment refers in terms to awarding or reimbursing a loss or to damages, compensation or satisfaction for loss, damage, injury or wrong.

(4) Paragraph (c) of section 38(1) does not apply to—

(a) sums to which a person other than the Lord Chancellor is by law entitled and which are paid to that person, or

(b) sums received by a designated officer on account of his salary or expenses as such.

(5) Any sum paid to the Lord Chancellor by virtue of paragraph (c) of section 38(1) is to be paid to him subject to being repaid to any person establishing his title to it.
[Courts Act 2003, s 39.]

1–4310   40. Regulations about payments, accounting and banking by designated officers. (1) The Lord Chancellor may, with the concurrence of the Treasury, make regulations—

(a) as to the times at which, and the manner in which, a designated officer is to pay sums payable by him in his capacity as such to the Lord Chancellor or any other person,

(b) requiring the keeping of accounts by designated officers in respect of sums received by them,

(c) as to the production, inspection and audit of accounts required to be kept, and

(d) requiring designated officers to use—

(i) specified banking arrangements or facilities, or

(ii) banking arrangements or facilities of a specified description,

in relation to sums received by them.

(2) Regulations under this section may make different provision in relation to different descriptions of designated officer.
[Courts Act 2003, s 40.]

Miscellaneous

1–4311   41. Disqualification of lay justices who are members of local authorities. (1) A lay justice who is a member of a local authority may not act as a member of the Crown Court or a magistrates' court in proceedings brought by or against, or by way of an appeal from a decision of—

(a) that local authority,

(b) a committee or officer of that local authority, or

(c) if that local authority is operating executive arrangements (within the meaning of Part 2 of the Local Government Act 2000 (c 22))—

(i) the executive of that local authority (within the meaning of that Part), or

(ii) any person acting on behalf of that executive.

(2) A lay justice who is a member of the Common Council of the City of London may not act as a member of the Crown Court or a magistrates' court in proceedings brought by or against, or by way of an appeal from a decision of—

(a) the Corporation of the City,

(b) the Common Council, or

(c) a committee or officer of the Corporation or the Common Council.

(3) A joint committee, joint board, joint authority or other combined body—

(a) of which a local authority, the Corporation or the Common Council is a member, or

(b) on which the local authority, the Corporation or the Council is represented,

is to be regarded for the purposes of this section as a committee of the local authority, Corporation or Common Council.

(4) Any reference in this section to an officer of—

(a) a local authority,

(b) the Corporation, or

(c) the Common Council,

is to a person employed or appointed by, or by a committee of, the local authority, Corporation or Common Council in the capacity in which he is employed or appointed to act.

(5) No act is invalidated merely because of the disqualification under this section of the person by whom it is done.

(6) "Local authority" means—

(a) a local authority within the meaning of the Local Government Act 1972 (c 70),

(b) a local authority constituted under section 2 of the Local Government etc (Scotland) Act 1994 (c 39),

(c) a police authority established under section 3 of the Police Act 1996 (c 16), the Metropolitan Police Authority or the Serious Organised Crime Agency

(d) the London Fire and Emergency Planning Authority,

(e) a joint authority established under Part 4 of the Local Government Act 1985 (c 51),

(f) a National Park Authority,

(g) the Broads Authority, or

(h) a housing action trust established under Part 3 of the Housing Act 1988 (c 50).

[Courts Act 2003, s 41 as amended by the Serious Organised Crime and Police Act 2005, Sch 4.]

1–4312   42. Effect of Act of Settlement on existing justices of the peace.   Nothing in section 3 of the Act of Settlement (1700 c 2) (certain persons born outside the United Kingdom) invalidates—

> (*a*)   any appointment, whether made before or after the passing of this Act, of a justice of the peace, or
>
> (*b*)   any act done by virtue of such an appointment.

[Courts Act 2003, s 42.]

PART 3[1]
MAGISTRATES' COURTS
Criminal jurisdiction and procedure

1–4313   43. Summons or warrant for suspected offender.   *Amends s 1 of the Magistrates' Courts Act 1980.*

---

    1. Part 3 contains ss 43–50.

1–4314   44. Trial of summary offences.   *Substitutes s 2 of the Magistrates' Courts Act 1980.*

1–4315   45. Power to make rulings at pre-trial hearings.   (1) Schedule 3 contains amendments of the 1980 Act relating to rulings at pre-trial hearings in magistrates' courts.

    (2) The amendments made by the Schedule apply in relation to pre-trial hearings beginning on or after the day on which it comes into force.

[Courts Act 2003, s 45.]

1–4316   46. Power to transfer criminal cases.   *Inserts new s 27A into and repeals s 3B of the Magistrates' Courts Act 1980.*

Civil jurisdiction and procedure

1–4317   47. Jurisdiction to issue summons and deal with complaints.   *Substitutes ss 51 and 52 of the Magistrates' Courts Act 1980.*

1–4318   48. Power to transfer civil proceedings (other than family proceedings).   *Substitutes s 57 of the Magistrates' Courts Act 1980.*

Family proceedings courts and youth courts

1–4319   49. Family proceedings courts.   *Substitutes s 67 and repeals s 68 of the Magistrates' Courts Act 1980.*

1–4320   50. Youth courts.   (1) *Substitutes new s 45 of the Children and Young Persons Act 1933* (constitution of youth courts).

    (2) Omit Schedule 2 to the 1933 Act (constitution of youth courts).

    (3) Omit section 146 of the 1980 Act (rules relating to youth court panels and the composition of youth courts).

    (4) "The 1933 Act" means the Children and Young Persons Act 1933 (c 12).

[Courts Act 2003, s 50.]

PART 4[1]
COURT SECURITY

1–4321   51. Court security officers.   (1) A court security officer is a person who is—

> (*a*)   appointed by the Lord Chancellor under section 2(1) or provided under a contract made by virtue of section 2(4), and
>
> (*b*)   designated by the Lord Chancellor as a court security officer.

    (2) The Lord Chancellor may by regulations[2] make provision as to—

> (*a*)   training courses to be completed by court security officers;
>
> (*b*)   conditions to be met before a person may be designated as a court security officer.

    (3) For the purposes of this Part a court security officer who is not readily identifiable as such (whether by means of his uniform or badge or otherwise), is not to be regarded as acting in the execution of his duty.

[Courts Act 2003, s 51.]

---

    1. Part 4 contains ss 51–57.

    2. The Court Security Officers (Designation) Regulations 2005 in this PART: STATUTORY INSTRUMENTS AND PRACTICE DIRECTIONS ON PROCEDURE*post*, have been made.

1–4322   52. Powers of search.   (1) A court security officer acting in the execution of his duty may search—

> (*a*)   any person who is in, or seeking to enter, a court building, and

(*b*) any article in the possession of such a person.

(2) Subsection (1) does not authorise the officer to require a person to remove any of his clothing other than a coat, jacket, headgear, gloves or footwear.

(3) In this Part "court building" means any building—

(*a*) where the business of any of the courts referred to in section 1 is carried on, and

(*b*) to which the public has access.

[Courts Act 2003, s 52.]

1–4323 53. Powers to exclude, remove or restrain persons. (1) A court security officer acting in the execution of his duty may exclude or remove from a court building, or a part of a court building, any person who refuses—

(*a*) to permit a search under section 52(1), or

(*b*) to surrender an article in his possession when asked to do so under section 54(1).

(2) A court security officer acting in the execution of his duty may—

(*a*) restrain any person who is in a court building, or

(*b*) exclude or remove any person from a court building, or a part of a court building,

if it is reasonably necessary to do so for one of the purposes given in subsection (3).

(3) The purposes are—

(*a*) enabling court business to be carried on without interference or delay;

(*b*) maintaining order;

(*c*) securing the safety of any person in the court building.

(4) A court security officer acting in the execution of his duty may remove any person from a courtroom at the request of a judge or a justice of the peace.

(5) The powers conferred by subsections (1), (2) and (4) include power to use reasonable force, where necessary.

[Courts Act 2003, s 53.]

1–4324 54. Surrender and seizure of articles. (1) If a court security officer acting in the execution of his duty reasonably believes that an article in the possession of a person who is in, or seeking to enter, a court building ought to be surrendered on any of the grounds given in subsection (3), he must ask the person to surrender the article.

(2) If the person refuses to surrender the article, the officer may seize it.

(3) The grounds are that the article—

(*a*) may jeopardise the maintenance of order in the court building (or a part of it),

(*b*) may put the safety of any person in the court building at risk, or

(*c*) may be evidence of, or in relation to, an offence.

[Courts Act 2003, s 54.]

1–4325 55. Powers to retain articles surrendered or seized. (1) Subject to subsection (2), a court security officer may retain an article which was—

(*a*) surrendered in response to a request under section 54(1), or

(*b*) seized under section 54(2),

until the time when the person who surrendered it, or from whom it was seized, is leaving the court building.

(2) If a court security officer reasonably believes that the article may be evidence of, or in relation to, an offence, he may retain it until—

(*a*) the time when the person who surrendered it, or from whom it was seized, is leaving the court building, or

(*b*) the end of the permitted period,

whichever is later.

(3) "The permitted period" means such period, not exceeding 24 hours from the time the article was surrendered or seized, as will enable the court security officer to draw the article to the attention of a constable.

[Courts Act 2003, s 55.]

1–4326 56. Regulations about retention of articles. (1) The Lord Chancellor may by regulations make provision as to—

(*a*) the provision to persons—

(i) by whom articles have been surrendered in response to a request under section 54(1), or

(ii) from whom articles have been seized under section 54(2),

of written information about the powers of retention of court security officers,

(*b*) the keeping of records about articles which have been so surrendered or seized,

(*c*) the period for which unclaimed articles have to be kept, and

(*d*) the disposal of unclaimed articles at the end of that period.

(2) "Unclaimed article" means an article—

(a) which has been retained under section 55,
(b) which a person is entitled to have returned to him,
(c) which has not been returned, and
(d) whose return has not been requested by a person entitled to it.
[Courts Act 2003, s 56.]

1–4327   57. Assaulting and obstructing court security officers.   (1) Any person who assaults a court security officer acting in the execution of his duty commits an offence.
(2) A person guilty of an offence under subsection (1) is liable on summary conviction to—

(a) a fine not exceeding level 5 on the standard scale, or
(b) imprisonment for a term not exceeding 6 months,

or to both.
(3) A person who resists or wilfully obstructs a court security officer acting in the execution of his duty commits an offence.
(4) A person guilty of an offence under subsection (3) is liable on summary conviction to a fine not exceeding level 3 on the standard scale.
[Courts Act 2003, s 57.]

PART 5[1]
INSPECTORS OF COURT ADMINISTRATION

1–4328   58. Inspectors of court administration etc.   (1) The Lord Chancellor may appoint such number of inspectors of court administration as he considers appropriate.
(2) They are to be known collectively as "Her Majesty's Inspectorate of Court Administration".
(3) The Lord Chancellor must appoint one of the persons so appointed to be Her Majesty's Chief Inspector of Court Administration.
(4) In this Part that person is referred to as "the Chief Inspector".
(5) The Lord Chancellor may make to or in respect of inspectors of court administration such payments by way of remuneration, allowances or otherwise as he may determine.
(6) In this Act—

(a) "CAFCASS" means the Children and Family Court Advisory and Support Service, and
(b) "CAFCASS functions" means the functions of CAFCASS and its officers.
[Courts Act 2003, s 58.]

---

1. Part 5 contains ss 58–61.

1–4329   59. Functions of inspectors.   (1) It is the duty of inspectors of court administration to—

(a) inspect and report to the Lord Chancellor[1] on the system that supports the carrying on of the business of the courts listed in subsection (2) and the services provided for those courts;
(b) inspect and report to the Lord Chancellor on the performance of CAFCASS functions;
(c) discharge any other particular functions which may be specified in connection with—

(i)   the courts listed in subsection (2), or
(ii) CAFCASS functions or related functions of any other person.

(2) The courts are—

(a) the Crown Court,
(b) county courts, and
(c) magistrates' courts.

(3) The Lord Chancellor may by order—

(a) add to the list in subsection (2) any court having jurisdiction in the United Kingdom, other than one having jurisdiction only in relation to Scotland or Northern Ireland, and
(b) remove any court from the list.

(4) "Specified" means specified in a direction given by the Lord Chancellor; but before giving any such direction the Lord Chancellor must consult the Chief Inspector.
(5) Nothing in this section is to be read as enabling inspectors to inspect persons—

(a) making judicial decisions, or
(b) exercising any judicial discretion.
[Courts Act 2003, s 59.]

---

1. The Lord Chancellor's functions in respect of CAFCASS were transferred to the Secretary of State by the Transfer of Functions (Children, Young People and Families) Order 2005, SI 2005/252 which made consequential amendments to this section.

1–4330   60. Functions of Chief Inspector.   (1) The Chief Inspector must make an annual report to the Lord Chancellor[1] as to the discharge of the functions of Her Majesty's Inspectorate of Court Administration.
(2) The Lord Chancellor may give directions as to—

(a) the information to be included in the report,

(*b*)   the form of the report, and

(*c*)   the time by which the report is to be made.

(3)   The Lord Chancellor must, within one month of receiving the annual report, lay a copy of it before both Houses of Parliament.

(4)   The Chief Inspector must report to the Lord Chancellor on any matter which the Lord Chancellor refers to him and which is connected with—

(*a*)   the courts listed in section 59(2), or

(*b*)   CAFCASS functions or related functions of any other person.

(5)   The Chief Inspector may designate an inspector of court administration to discharge his functions during any period when he is absent or unable to act.
[Courts Act 2003, s 60.]

---

1.   The Lord Chancellor's functions in respect of CAFCASS were transferred to the Secretary of State by the Transfer of Functions (Children, Young People and Families) Order 2005, SI 2005/252 which made consequential amendments to this section.

1–4331   61. Rights of entry and inspection.   (1) An inspector exercising functions under section 59 may enter—

(*a*)   any place of work occupied by persons provided under a contract made by the Lord Chancellor by virtue of section 2(4);

(*b*)   any premises occupied by CAFCASS.

(2)   An inspector exercising functions under section 59 may inspect and take copies of—

(*a*)   any records kept by persons provided under a contract made by the Lord Chancellor by virtue of section 2(4), or

(*b*)   any records kept by CAFCASS or other documents containing information relating to the performance of CAFCASS functions,

which he considers relevant to the discharge of his functions.

(3)   Subsection (1) does not entitle an inspector—

(*a*)   to be present when a court listed in section 59(2) is hearing proceedings in private, or

(*b*)   to attend any private deliberations of persons having jurisdiction to hear or determine any proceedings.

(4)   The records referred to in subsection (2) include records kept by means of a computer.

(5)   An inspector exercising the power under subsection (2) to inspect records—

(*a*)   is entitled to have access to, and inspect and check the operation of, any computer and associated apparatus or material which is or has been in use in connection with the records in question, and

(*b*)   may require—

    (i)   the person by whom or on whose behalf the computer is or has been used, or

   (ii)   any person having charge of, or otherwise concerned with the operation of, the computer, apparatus or material,

to afford him such reasonable assistance as he may require.

(6)   The powers conferred by subsections (1), (2) and (5) may be exercised at reasonable times only.
[Courts Act 2003, s 61.]

1–4331A   61A. Further provision about the inspectorate.   Schedule 3A (further provision about the inspectorate) has effect.*
[Courts Act 2003, s 61A as inserted by the Police and Justice Act 2006, s 32.]

---

*Inserted by the Police and Justice Act 2006, s 32 from a date to be appointed.

PART 6[1]
JUDGES
Offices, titles, styles etc

1–4332   62. Head and Deputy Head of Civil Justice.   (1) There is to be a Head of Civil Justice.

(2)   The Head of Civil Justice is—

(*a*)   the Master of the Rolls, or

(*b*)   if the Lord Chief Justice appoints another person, that person.

(3)   The Lord Chief Justice may appoint a person to be Deputy Head of Civil Justice.

(4)   The Lord Chief Justice must not appoint a person under subsection (2)(*b*) or (3) unless these conditions are met—

(*a*)   the Lord Chief Justice has consulted the Lord Chancellor;

(*b*)   the person to be appointed is one of the following—

    (i)   the Chancellor of the High Court;

(ii) an ordinary judge of the Court of Appeal.

(5) A person appointed under subsection (2)(*b*) or (3) holds the office to which he is appointed in accordance with the terms of his appointment.

(6) The Lord Chief Justice may nominate a judicial office holder (as defined in section 109(4) of the Constitutional Reform Act 2005) to exercise his functions under this section.

[Courts Act 2003, s 62 as substituted by the Constitutional Reform Act 2005, Sch 4.]

---

1. Part 6 contains ss 62–66.

1–4333　63. Ordinary judges of the Court of Appeal.　(1) In section 2 of the 1981 Act (the Court of Appeal), for subsection (3) substitute—

"(3) An ordinary judge of the Court of Appeal (including the vice-president, if any, of either division) shall be styled "Lord Justice of Appeal" or "Lady Justice of Appeal"."

(2) "The 1981 Act" means the Supreme Court Act 1981 (c 54).

[Courts Act 2003, s 63.]

1–4334　64. Power to alter judicial titles.　(1) The Lord Chancellor may by order—

(*a*) alter the name of an office listed in subsection (2);
(*b*) provide for or alter the way in which the holders of any of those offices are to be styled.

(2) The offices are—

Admiralty Registrar
Assistant Recorder
Chancellor of the High Court
Circuit judge
Deputy Circuit judge
Deputy district judge appointed under section 102 of the 1981 Act
Deputy district judge for a county court district
Deputy Head of Civil Justice*
Deputy Head of Family Justice
Deputy judge of the High Court
District judge for a county court district
District judge of the High Court
District judge of the principal registry of the Family Division
District probate registrar
Head of Civil Justice*
Head of Family Justice
Lord Chief Justice
Master of the Chancery Division
Master of the Court of Protection**
Master of the Queen's Bench Division
Master of the Rolls
Ordinary judge of the Court of Appeal*
President of the Courts of England and Wales
President of the Family Division
President of the Queen's Bench Division
Presiding Judge for a Circuit
Puisne judge of the High Court
Queen's Coroner and Attorney and Master of the Crown Office and Registrar of Criminal Appeals
Recorder
Registrar in Bankruptcy of the High Court*
Senior Presiding Judge for England and Wales
Taxing Master of the Supreme Court** ***
Vice-president of the Court of Appeal**
Vice-president of the Queen's Bench Division.

(3) The Lord Chancellor may also by order provide for or alter the way in which deputies or temporary additional officers appointed under section 91(1)(*a*) of the 1981 Act are to be styled.

(3A) The Lord Chancellor may make an order under this section only with the concurrence of the Lord Chief Justice.

(4) Before making an order under this section the Lord Chancellor must consult—

(*a*) *repealed*
(*b*) the Master of the Rolls,
(*ba*) the President of the Queen's Bench Division,
(*c*) the President of the Family Division, and
(*d*) the Chancellor of the High Court.

(5) An order under this section may make such provision as the Lord Chancellor considers necessary in consequence of any provision made under subsection (1) or (3).

(6) The provision that may be made under subsection (5) includes provision amending, repealing or revoking any enactment.

(7) The Lord Chief Justice may nominate a judicial office holder (as defined in section 109(4) of the Constitutional Reform Act 2005) to exercise his functions under this section.
[Courts Act 2003, s 64 as amended by the Constitutional Reform Act 2005, Sch 4.]

*Entries "Deputy Head of Criminal Justice" and "Head of Criminal Justice" inserted by the Constitutional Reform Act 2005, Sch 4, from a date to be appointed.
**Entry "Master of the Court of Protection" repealed and entries "President of the Court of Protection", "Senior Judge of the Court of Protection" and "Vice-president of the Court of Protection" inserted by the Mental Capacity Act 2005, Sch 6, from a date to be appointed.
***In entry "Taxing Master of the Supreme Court" words underlined repealed and "Senior Courts" substituted by the Constitutional Reform Act 2005, Sch 11 from a date to be appointed.

Flexibility in deployment of judicial resources

1-4335   65. District Judges (Magistrates' Courts) as Crown Court judges etc. (1) In section 8(1) of the 1981 Act (persons who are judges of the Crown Court), in paragraph (*b*) for "or Recorder" substitute ", Recorder or District Judge (Magistrates' Courts)".
(2) Schedule 4 contains amendments conferring functions on District Judges (Magistrates' Courts).
(3) References in any enactment, instrument or other document to a district judge or deputy district judge do not include—

(*a*) a District Judge (Magistrates' Courts), or
(*b*) a Deputy District Judge (Magistrates' Courts).
[Courts Act 2003, s 65.]

1-4336   66. Judges having powers of District Judges (Magistrates' Courts). (1) Every holder of a judicial office specified in subsection (2) has the powers of a justice of the peace[1] who is a District Judge (Magistrates' Courts) in relation to—

(*a*) criminal causes and matters, and
(*b*) family proceedings as defined by section 65 of the 1980 Act.

(2) The offices are—

(*a*) judge of the High Court;
(*b*) deputy judge of the High Court;
(*c*) Circuit judge;
(*d*) deputy Circuit judge;
(*e*) recorder.

(3) For the purposes of section 45 of the 1933 Act, every holder of a judicial office specified in subsection (2) is qualified to sit as a member of a youth court.
(4) For the purposes of section 67 of the 1980 Act—

(*a*) a judge of the High Court or a deputy judge of the High Court is qualified to sit as a member of a family proceedings court to hear family proceedings of any description, and
(*b*) a Circuit judge, deputy Circuit judge or recorder is qualified to sit as a member of a family proceedings court to hear family proceedings of any description if he has been nominated to do so by the President of the Family Division.
[Courts Act 2003, s 66.]

1. Where a case was erroneously committed to the Crown Court for sentence (the prior consent of the DPP, which was a prerequisite to the prosecution, had not been obtained by that stage, though it was given subsequently), it was unnecessary for the judge to use s 66 to exercise the powers of a district judge and re-commit the offender; the judge should instead have considered whether it was Parliament's intention that such a failure rendered the proceedings a nullity (however, the judge had been entitled to use his powers under s 66 and had been entitled, thereafter, to pass sentence): *R v Ashton, R v Draz, R v O'Reilly* [2006] EWCA Crim 794, [2006] Crim.App.R. 15.

1-4337   67. Removal of restriction on Circuit judges sitting on certain appeals

PART 7[1]
PROCEDURE RULES AND PRACTICE DIRECTIONS
Criminal Procedure Rules and practice directions

1-4338   68. Meaning of "criminal court". In this Part "criminal court" means—

(*a*) the criminal division of the Court of Appeal;
(*b*) when dealing with any criminal cause or matter—

(i) the Crown Court;
(ii) a magistrates' court.
[Courts Act 2003, s 68.]

1. Part 7 contains ss 68–85. Sections 69, 70–73, 78–80, 92, 102, and 107–109 have been amended by Sch 4 to the Constitutional Reform Act 2005, which also inserted new ss 72A and 79A.

1–4339   69. Criminal Procedure Rules.   (1) There are to be rules of court (to be called "Criminal Procedure Rules") governing the practice and procedure to be followed in the criminal courts.

(2) Criminal Procedure Rules are to be made by a committee known as the Criminal Procedure Rule Committee.

(3) The power to make Criminal Procedure Rules includes power to make different provision for different cases or different areas, including different provision—

(a) for a specified court or description of courts, or
(b) for specified descriptions of proceedings or a specified jurisdiction.

(4) Any power to make or alter Criminal Procedure Rules is to be exercised with a view to securing that—

(a) the criminal justice system is accessible, fair and efficient, and
(b) the rules are both simple and simply expressed.
[Courts Act 2003, s 69.]

1–4340   70. Criminal Procedure Rule Committee.   (1) The Criminal Procedure Rule Committee is to consist of—

(a) the Lord Chief Justice, and
(b) the persons currently appointed by the Lord Chancellor under subsection (2).★

(2) The Lord Chancellor must appoint★—

(a) a person nominated by the Secretary of State,
(b) three persons each of whom is either a judge of the High Court or a judge of the Court of Appeal,
(c) two Circuit judges with particular experience of sitting in criminal courts,
(d) one District Judge (Magistrates' Courts),
(e) one lay justice,
(f) one justices' clerk,
(g) the Director of Public Prosecutions or a person nominated by the Director,
(h) two persons who have a Supreme Court★ qualification and who have particular experience of practice in criminal courts,
(i) two persons who—

   (i) have been granted by an authorised body, under Part 2 of the 1990 Act, the right to conduct litigation in relation to all proceedings in the Supreme Court★, and
   (ii) have particular experience of practice in criminal courts,

(j) one person who appears to represent the Association of Chief Police Officers, and
(k) two persons who appear to represent voluntary organisations with a direct interest in the work of criminal courts.

(3) Before appointing a person under subsection (2)(b) to (f), the Lord Chancellor must consult the Lord Chief Justice.★

(4) The Criminal Procedure Rule Committee is to be chaired by the Lord Chief Justice; and one of the judges appointed under subsection (2)(b) is to be his deputy.

(5) The Lord Chancellor may reimburse—

(a) the travelling and out-of-pocket expenses of the members of the Criminal Procedure Rule Committee, and
(b) authorised travelling and out-of-pocket expenses of persons invited to participate in the work of the Committee.★

(6) "The 1990 Act" means the Courts and Legal Services Act 1990 (c 41).★
[Courts Act 2003, s 70 as amended by SI 2005/2625.]

★**Amended by the Constitutional Reform Act 2005, Sch 4 from a date to be appointed.**

1–4341   71. Power to change certain requirements relating to Committee.   (1) The Lord Chancellor may by order[1]—

(a) amend section 70(2) (persons to be appointed to Committee by Lord Chancellor), and
(b) make consequential amendments in any other provision of section 70.

(2) Before making an order under this section the Lord Chancellor must consult the Lord Chief Justice.
[Courts Act 2003, s 71.]

1. Section 70 of this Act has been amended by the Criminal Procedure Rule Committee (Amendment of Constitution) Order 2005, SI 2005/2625.

1–4342   72. Process for making Criminal Procedure Rules.   (1) The Criminal Procedure Rule Committee must, before making Criminal Procedure Rules—

(a) consult such persons as they consider appropriate, and
(b) meet (unless it is inexpedient to do so).

(2) Rules made by the Criminal Procedure Rule Committee must be—

(a) signed by a majority of the members of the Committee, and
(b) submitted to the Lord Chancellor.

(3) The Lord Chancellor may, with the concurrence of the Secretary of State, allow, disallow or alter rules so made.

(4) Before altering rules so made the Lord Chancellor must consult the Committee.

(5) Rules so made, as allowed or altered by the Lord Chancellor—

(a) come into force on such day as the Lord Chancellor directs, and
(b) are to be contained in a statutory instrument to which the Statutory Instruments Act 1946 (c 36) applies as if the instrument contained rules made by a Minister of the Crown.

(6) Subject to subsection (7), a statutory instrument containing Criminal Procedure Rules is subject to annulment in pursuance of a resolution of either House of Parliament.

(7) A statutory instrument containing rules altered by the Lord Chancellor is of no effect unless approved by a resolution of each House of Parliament before the day referred to in subsection (5)(a).
[Courts Act 2003, s 72.]

1–4343   73. Power to amend legislation in connection with the rules.   The Lord Chancellor may, with the concurrence of the Secretary of State, by order amend, repeal or revoke any enactment to the extent that he considers necessary or desirable—

(a) in order to facilitate the making of Criminal Procedure Rules, or
(b) in consequence of section 69 or 72 or Criminal Procedure Rules.
[Courts Act 2003, s 73.]

1–4344   74. Practice directions as to practice and procedure of the criminal courts.   (1) The Lord Chief Justice may, with the concurrence of the Lord Chancellor, give directions as to the practice and procedure of the criminal courts.

(2) Directions as to the practice and procedure of the criminal courts may not be given by anyone other than the Lord Chief Justice without the approval of the Lord Chief Justice and the Lord Chancellor.

(3) The power to give directions under subsection (1) includes power—

(a) to vary or revoke directions as to the practice and procedure of the criminal courts (or any of them), whether given by the Lord Chief Justice or any other person,
(b) to give directions containing different provision for different cases (including different areas), and
(c) to give directions containing provision for a specific court, for specific proceedings or for a specific jurisdiction.

(4) Nothing in this section prevents the Lord Chief Justice, without the concurrence of the Lord Chancellor, giving directions which contain guidance as to law or making judicial decisions.
[Courts Act 2003, s 74.]

Family Procedure Rules and practice directions

1–4345   75. Family Procedure Rules.   (1) There are to be rules of court (to be called "Family Procedure Rules") governing the practice and procedure to be followed in family proceedings in—

(a) the High Court,
(b) county courts, and
(c) magistrates' courts.

(2) Family Procedure Rules are to be made by a committee known as the Family Procedure Rule Committee.

(3) "Family proceedings", in relation to a court, means proceedings in that court which are family proceedings as defined by either—

(a) section 65 of the 1980 Act, or
(b) section 32 of the Matrimonial and Family Proceedings Act 1984 (c 42).

(4) The power to make Family Procedure Rules includes power to make different provision for different areas, including different provision—

(a) for a specified court or description of courts, or
(b) for specified descriptions of proceedings or a specified jurisdiction.

(5) Any power to make or alter Family Procedure Rules is to be exercised with a view to securing that—

(a) the family justice system is accessible, fair and efficient, and
(b) the rules are both simple and simply expressed.
[Courts Act 2003, s 75.]

1–4346   76. Further provision about scope of Family Procedure Rules.   (1) Family Procedure Rules may not be made in respect of matters which may be dealt with in probate rules made by the President of the Family Division, with the concurrence of the Lord Chancellor, under section 127 of the 1981 Act.

(2) Family Procedure Rules may—

(a) modify or exclude the application of any provision of the County Courts Act 1984 (c 28), and

(b) provide for the enforcement in the High Court of orders made in a divorce county court.

(3) Family Procedure Rules may modify the rules of evidence as they apply to family proceedings in any court within the scope of the rules.

(4) Family Procedure Rules may apply any rules of court (including in particular Civil Procedure Rules) which relate to—

(a) courts which are outside the scope of Family Procedure Rules, or

(b) proceedings other than family proceedings.

(5) Any rules of court, not made by the Family Procedure Rule Committee, which apply to proceedings of a particular kind in a court within the scope of Family Procedure Rules may be applied by Family Procedure Rules to family proceedings in such a court.

(6) In subsections (4) and (5) "rules of court" includes any provision governing the practice and procedure of a court which is made by or under an enactment.

(7) Where Family Procedure Rules may be made by applying other rules, the other rules may be applied—

(a) to any extent,

(b) with or without modification, and

(c) as amended from time to time.

(8) Family Procedure Rules may, instead of providing for any matter, refer to provision made or to be made about that matter by directions.
[Courts Act 2003, s 76.]

1–4347 77. Family Procedure Rule Committee. (1) The Family Procedure Rule Committee is to consist of—

(a) the President of the Family Division, and

(b) the persons currently appointed by the Lord Chancellor under subsection (2).

(2) The Lord Chancellor must appoint—

(a) two judges of the Supreme Court, at least one of whom must be a puisne judge attached to the Family Division,

(b) one Circuit judge,

(c) one district judge of the principal registry of the Family Division,

(d) one district judge appointed under section 6 of the County Courts Act 1984 (c 28),

(e) one District Judge (Magistrates' Courts),

(f) one lay justice,

(g) one justices' clerk,

(h) one person who has—

(i) a Supreme Court qualification, and

(ii) particular experience of family practice in the High Court,

(i) one person who has—

(i) a Supreme Court qualification, and

(ii) particular experience of family practice in county courts,

(j) one person who has—

(i) a Supreme Court qualification, and

(ii) particular experience of family practice in magistrates' courts,

(k) one person who—

(i) has been granted by an authorised body, under Part 2 of the 1990 Act, the right to conduct litigation in relation to all proceedings in the Supreme Court, and

(ii) has particular experience of family practice in the High Court,

(l) one person who—

(i) has been so granted that right, and

(ii) has particular experience of family practice in county courts,

(m) one person who—

(i) has been so granted that right, and

(ii) has particular experience of family practice in magistrates' courts,

(n) one person nominated by CAFCASS, and

(o) one person with experience in and knowledge of the lay advice sector or the system of justice in relation to family proceedings.

(3) Before appointing a person under subsection (2), the Lord Chancellor must consult the President of the Family Division.

(4) Before appointing a person under subsection (2)(a), the Lord Chancellor must consult the Lord Chief Justice.

(5) Before appointing a person under subsection (2)(*h*) to (m), the Lord Chancellor must consult any body which—

  (*a*) has members eligible for appointment under the provision in question, and
  (*b*) is an authorised body for the purposes of section 27 or 28 of the 1990 Act.

(6) The Lord Chancellor may reimburse the members of the Family Procedure Rule Committee their travelling and out-of-pocket expenses.
[Courts Act 2003, s 77.]

1–4348   78. Power to change certain requirements relating to Committee.   (1) The Lord Chancellor may by order—

  (*a*) amend section 77(2) (persons to be appointed to Committee by Lord Chancellor), and
  (*b*) make consequential amendments in any other provision of section 77.

(2) Before making an order under this section the Lord Chancellor must consult the President of the Family Division.
[Courts Act 2003, s 78.]

1–4349   79. Process for making Family Procedure Rules.   (1) The Family Procedure Rule Committee must, before making Family Procedure Rules—

  (*a*) consult such persons as they consider appropriate, and
  (*b*) meet (unless it is inexpedient to do so).

(2) Rules made by the Family Procedure Rule Committee must be—

  (*a*) signed by a majority of the members of the Committee, and
  (*b*) submitted to the Lord Chancellor.

(3) The Lord Chancellor may allow, disallow or alter rules so made.
(4) Before altering rules so made the Lord Chancellor must consult the Committee.
(5) Rules so made, as allowed or altered by the Lord Chancellor—

  (*a*) come into force on such day as the Lord Chancellor directs, and
  (*b*) are to be contained in a statutory instrument to which the Statutory Instruments Act 1946 (c 36) applies as if the instrument contained rules made by a Minister of the Crown.

(6) Subject to subsection (7), a statutory instrument containing Family Procedure Rules is subject to annulment in pursuance of a resolution of either House of Parliament.
(7) A statutory instrument containing rules altered by the Lord Chancellor is of no effect unless approved by a resolution of each House of Parliament before the day referred to in subsection (5)(*a*).
[Courts Act 2003, s 79.]

1–4350   80. Power to amend legislation in connection with the rules.   The Lord Chancellor may by order amend, repeal or revoke any enactment to the extent that he considers necessary or desirable—

  (*a*) in order to facilitate the making of Family Procedure Rules, or
  (*b*) in consequence of section 75, 76 or 79 or Family Procedure Rules.
[Courts Act 2003, s 80.]

1–4351   81. Practice directions relating to family proceedings.   (1) The President of the Family Division may, with the concurrence of the Lord Chancellor, give directions as to the practice and procedure of—

  (*a*) county courts, and
  (*b*) magistrates' courts,

in family proceedings.

(2) Directions as to the practice and procedure of those courts in family proceedings may not be given by anyone other than the President of the Family Division without the approval of the President of the Family Division and the Lord Chancellor.
(3) The power to give directions under subsection (1) includes power—

  (*a*) to vary or revoke directions as to the practice and procedure of magistrates' courts and county courts (or any of them) in family proceedings, whether given by the President of the Family Division or any other person,
  (*b*) to give directions containing different provision for different cases (including different areas), and
  (*c*) to give directions containing provision for a specific court, for specific proceedings or for a specific jurisdiction.
[Courts Act 2003, s 81.]

Civil Procedure Rules

1–4352   82. Civil Procedure Rules[1]

---

1. Substitutes a new s 1(3) of the Civil Procedure Act 1997 (not reproduced in this work).

1–4353   83. Civil Procedure Rule Committee[1]

1. Substitutes new s 2(1)(*a*) and (*b*), s 2(2)(*a*), (*g*) and (*h*) of the Civil Procedure Act 1997 (not reproduced in this work).

1–4354   84. Power to change certain requirements relating to Committee[1]

1. Amends the Civil Procedure Act 1997, s 2 (not reproduced in this work).

1–4355   85. Process for making Civil Procedure Rules[1]

1. Inserts a new s 2A in the Civil Procedure Act 1997 (not reproduced in this work).

PART 8[1]

MISCELLANEOUS

Provisions relating to criminal procedure and appeals

1–4356   86–91. (*These provisions deal with procedural and appellate matters that are not relevant to magistrates' courts.*)

Fees and costs

1–4357   92. Fees.   (1) The Lord Chancellor may with the consent of the Treasury by order[2] prescribe fees[3] payable in respect of anything dealt with by—

    (*a*) the <u>Supreme Court</u>,*
    (*b*) county courts, and
    (*c*) magistrates' courts.

    (2) An order under this section may, in particular, contain provision as to—

    (*a*) scales or rates of fees;
    (*b*) exemptions from or reductions in fees;
    (*c*) remission of fees in whole or in part.

    (3) When including any provision in an order under this section, the Lord Chancellor must have regard to the principle that access to the courts must not be denied.

    (4) The Lord Chancellor may not under this section prescribe fees which he or another authority has power to prescribe apart from this section.

    (5) Before making an order under this section, the Lord Chancellor must consult—

    (*a*)   the Lord Chief Justice;
    (*b*)   the Master of the Rolls;
    (ba) the President of the Queen's Bench Division;
    (*c*)   the President of the Family Division;
    (*d*)   the Chancellor of the High Court;
    (*e*)   the Head of Civil Justice;
    (*f*)   the Deputy Head of Civil Justice (if there is one).

    (6) Before making an order under this section in relation to civil proceedings, the Lord Chancellor must consult the Civil Justice Council.

    (7) The Lord Chancellor must take such steps as are reasonably practicable to bring information about fees to the attention of persons likely to have to pay them.

    (8) Fees payable under this section are recoverable summarily as a civil debt.

    (9) Subsection (10) applies in relation to an authority which has power to prescribe fees payable in any of the courts referred to in subsection (1).

    (10) Nothing in this section prevents the authority from applying to any extent provisions contained in an order made under this section; and an instrument made in exercise of the power is to be read (unless the contrary intention appears) as applying those provisions as amended from time to time.

[Courts Act 2003, s 92 as amended by the Constitutional Reform Act 2005, Sch 4.]

---

*Amended by the Constitutional Reform Act 2005, Sch 4 from a date to be appointed.

1. Part 8 contains ss 86–106.
2. As regards proceedings in magistrates' courts, the Magistrates' Courts Fees Order 2005, SI 2005/3444 has been made, in this PART, STATUTORY INSTRUMENTS AND PRACTICE DIRECTIONS ON PROCEDURE, post.
3. There is no summary way of recovering before justices the fees which are chargeable. The person who made the application or initiated the proceedings, or at whose request the business was done, is liable for the fees according to the table in force, and an action may be maintained in the county court of the district in which such person resides, or where the cause of action arose for recovery of such fees, although the person complained against was convicted in a penalty and costs, and committed to prison for non-payment (*Drew v Harris* (1849) 14 JP 26). A justices' clerk is not bound, it seems, to issue a summons, or warrant, or other document, or to take a recognizance until the fee be paid (34 JP 316). See *Wray v Chapman* (1850) 14 QB 742, 14 JP 95, and *Ex p Reddish* (1856) 20 JP 101. It is a well known principle of law that where a public officer is required to perform a certain duty, he is not entitled to make any charge for doing that duty unless some

charge is distinctly provided for him by enactment of law, and that in the absence of such enactment he must do the duty for nothing (*per* Cave J, *Re Howe* (1887) 18 QBD 573). The Secretary of State advised the Birmingham City justices, 29 July 1899, that it would not be a proper course for a magistrate to pursue to receive and retain fees in respect of work done as a justice at his own house, and further that it would not be becoming to take clerk's fees for the purpose of handling them to such clerk unless there should be some exceptional ground for such action on his part, and on August 11, 1899, in reply to a second letter, he expressed an opinion that a justice could not impose or collect fees for administering oaths when the justice's clerk was not present (43 Sol Jo 815, 63 JP 665).

1–4358   93. Award of costs against third parties.   *Inserts new s 19B in the Prosecution of Offences Act 1985.*

1–4359   94. Award of costs in appeals under Proceeds of Crime Act 2002.   *Amends the Proceeds of Crime Act 2002.*

Fines

1–4360   95. Fixing of fines: failure to furnish statement of financial circumstances.   *Amends s 20A of the Criminal Justice Act 1991 and s 128(5) of the Powers of Criminal Courts (Sentencing) Act 2000.*

1–4361   96. Recovery of fines etc by deductions from income support: failure to provide information.   *Amends s 24 of the Criminal Justice Act 1991.*

1–4362   97. Collection of fines and discharge of fines by unpaid work.   (1) Schedule 5 contains provisions about the collection of fines.

   (2) Schedule 6 contains provisions about the discharge of fines by means of unpaid work.

   (3) Subsections (4) to (9) apply in relation to each of those Schedules.

   (4) The Schedule is to have effect only in accordance with—

   (*a*) subsections (5) and (6) (pilot schemes), or

   (*b*) subsections (7) to (9) (power to make pilot schemes, or modified versions of pilot schemes, permanent after completion of pilots).

   (5) The Lord Chancellor may by order[1] provide that the Schedule is to have effect in relation to the local justice area or areas specified in the order for the period specified in the order[2].

   (6) An order under subsection (5) may make provision modifying the Schedule, or any enactment in connection with the operation of the Schedule, in relation to the specified local justice area or areas and the specified period.

   (7) The Lord Chancellor may, at the end of the relevant period, by order provide that the Schedule is to have effect—

   (*a*) in all local justice areas, and

   (*b*) indefinitely.

   (8) "The relevant period" means—

   (*a*) if one order has been made under subsection (5) in relation to the Schedule, the period specified in the order;

   (*b*) if more than one order has been made under subsection (5) in relation to the Schedule, the period which, out of the periods so specified, ends at the latest date.

   (9) An order under subsection (7) may make such amendments of—

   (*a*) the Schedule, and

   (*b*) any other enactments,

as appear to the Lord Chancellor appropriate in the light of the operation of the Schedule in accordance with the order made under subsection (5) (pilot schemes).
[Courts Act 2003, s 97.]

---

   1. The Collection of Fines (Pilot Scheme) and Discharge of Fines by Unpaid Work (Pilot Schemes) (Amendment) Order 2006, in this PART, post, has been made which makes provision for the piloting of various provisions of Sch 5 on a national basis for periods ending on 2 July 2006. Supplementary provisions for implementing the pilots schemes is made by the Fines Collection Regulations 2006, in this PART, post.
   2. The Discharge of Fines by Unpaid Work (Pilot Schemes) Order 2004, in this PART: STATUTORY INSTRUMENTS AND PRACTICE DIRECTIONS ON PROCEDURE, post provides that Schedule 6 to the Courts Act 2003 (Discharge of Fines by Unpaid Work) is to have effect in relation to the following petty sessions areas specified in the Schedule to the Order for the period beginning on 21st September 2004 and ending on 31 March 2007: *Cambridgeshire*: Peterborough, Huntingdon, Wisbech; *South Yorkshire*: Sheffield, Barnsley; *Cheshire*: Halton, Warrington; *Cumbria*: Kendal (South Lakeland), Barrow (Furness and District); *Devon and Cornwall*: South Devon; Central Devon; East Cornwall; West Cornwall; *Gloucestershire*: Gloucester; Stroud; Forest of Dean.

Register of judgments etc and execution of writs

1–4363   98. Register of judgments and orders etc.   (1) A register is to be kept, in accordance with regulations[1], of—

   (*a*) judgments entered in the High Court;

   (*b*) judgments entered in county courts;

(*c*) administration orders made under section 112 of the County Courts Act 1984 (c 28) (power of county courts to make administration orders);

(*d*) orders restricting enforcement made under section 112A of that Act (power of county courts to restrict enforcement of debts in lieu of administration order);

(*e*) sums which are, for the purposes of the 1980 Act, sums adjudged to be paid by a conviction or order of a magistrates' court.

(2) "Regulations" means regulations made by the Lord Chancellor for the purposes of this section.

(3) The regulations may—

(*a*) provide for prescribed classes of judgments, orders or adjudged sums to be exempt from registration;

(*b*) prescribe circumstances in which judgments, orders or adjudged sums (or classes of them) are to be exempt from registration;

(*c*) prescribe circumstances in which an entry in the register is to be cancelled;

(*d*) in the case of sums adjudged to be paid by conviction of a magistrates' court, provide for sums to be registered only in prescribed circumstances or subject to prescribed conditions.

(4) The Lord Chancellor may fix charges to be made for—

(*a*) making information in an entry in the register available for inspection;

(*b*) carrying out an official search of the register;

(*c*) supplying a certified copy of information in an entry in the register.

(5) The proceeds of those charges are to be applied in paying the expenses incurred in maintaining the register; and any surplus is to be paid into the Consolidated Fund.

(6) If there is in force an agreement between the Lord Chancellor and a body corporate relating to the keeping by that body corporate of the register the register is to be kept by that body corporate.

(7) If, under subsection (6), the register is kept by a body corporate—

(*a*) the Lord Chancellor may recover from the body corporate any expenses incurred by the Lord Chancellor in connection with the supply of information to that body for the purposes of the register,

(*b*) subsection (4) applies as if it enabled the Lord Chancellor to fix the maximum charges to be made (instead of the charges to be made), and

(*c*) subsection (5) does not apply.

(8) If subsection (6) ceases to apply to a body corporate as a result of the termination (for any reason) of the agreement, the Lord Chancellor may require the information contained in the entries in the register to be transferred to such person as he may direct.
[Courts Act 2003, s 98.]

---

1. The Register of Fines Regulations 2003 and the Register of Fines, Judgments, Orders and Fines Regulations 2005 have been made in this PART: STATUTORY INSTRUMENTS AND PRACTICE DIRECTIONS ON PROCEDURE, post.

1–4364   99–101. *These provisions deal with matters that are not relevant to magistrates' courts.*

1–4365   102–106. *Northern Ireland.*

PART 9[1]
FINAL PROVISIONS

1–4366   107. Interpretation. (1) In this Act—

"the 1933 Act" means the Children and Young Persons Act 1933 (c 12);
"the 1968 Act" means the Criminal Appeal Act 1968 (c 19);
"the 1978 Act" means the Judicature (Northern Ireland) Act 1978 (c 23);
"the 1980 Act" means the Magistrates' Courts Act 1980 (c 43);
"the 1981 Act" means the Supreme Court Act 1981 (c 54);
"the 1990 Act" means the Courts and Legal Services Act 1990 (c 41);
"the 1997 Act" means the Civil Procedure Act 1997 (c 12).

(2) In this Act the following have the meaning given by section 71 of the 1990 Act—

"5 year magistrates' court qualification";
"7 year general qualification";
"Supreme Court qualification".

(3) In this Act "criminal court" has the meaning given by section 68.

(4) In this Act "judge", except where the context otherwise requires, means a person holding an office listed in subsection (2) of section 64 (power to alter judicial titles).

(5) In this Act "lay justice" has the meaning given by section 9.

(6) In this Act "Magistrates' Courts Rule Committee" means the committee appointed by the Lord Chancellor under section 144 of the 1980 Act.

(7) In this Act "Minister of the Crown" has the same meaning as in the Ministers of the Crown Act 1975 (c 26).

(8) In this Act "enactment" includes subordinate legislation and, except where otherwise provided,

any reference to an enactment is to an enactment whenever passed or made; and "subordinate legislation" here has the same meaning as in the Interpretation Act 1978 (c 30).

(9) In sections 102(6) and 109(5)(*b*) "enactment" also includes Northern Ireland legislation (whenever passed or made); and "Northern Ireland legislation" here has the same meaning as in the Interpretation Act 1978.
[Courts Act 2003, s 107.]

---

1. Part 9 contains ss 107–112.

1–4367 108. Rules, regulations and orders. (1) Any power of the Lord Chancellor to make rules, regulations or orders under this Act is exercisable by statutory instrument.

(2) None of the orders and regulations mentioned in subsection (3) may be made unless a draft of the statutory instrument containing the order or regulations has been laid before, and approved by a resolution of, each House of Parliament.

(3) The orders and regulations are—

(*a*) the first order to be made under section 4 (areas of courts boards);
(*b*) regulations under section 34(5) (costs in legal proceedings);
(*c*) an order under—

    (i) section 73 or 80 (powers to amend enactments in connection with Criminal Procedure Rules and Family Procedure Rules), or
    (ii) section 109 (power to make consequential provision etc),

which contains any provision (whether alone or with other provisions) amending or repealing any Act or provision of an Act;

(*d*) an order under section 97(7) to (9) (power to make permanent provision about collection of fines and discharge of fines by unpaid work);
(*e*) regulations under Schedule 1;
(*f*) regulations under Schedule 6 relating to the prescribed hourly sum.

(4) A statutory instrument containing—

(*a*) the first order to be made under section 8 (local justice areas), or
(*b*) regulations under section 40 (payments, accounting and banking by designated officers),

is to be laid before Parliament after being made.

(5) Any other statutory instrument, apart from one containing an order under section 110 (commencement), is subject to annulment in pursuance of a resolution of either House of Parliament.

(6) Any power of the Lord Chancellor to make rules, regulations[1] or orders under this Act includes power to make—

(*a*) any supplementary, incidental or consequential provision, and
(*b*) any transitory, transitional or saving provision,

which he considers necessary or expedient.

(7) Nothing in this section applies to—

(*a*) rules made under Part 7 (Criminal Procedure and Family Procedure Rules), or
(*b*) an order made under section 102 (power to alter judicial titles: Northern Ireland).
[Courts Act 2003, s 108.]

---

1. The Register of Fines Regulations 2003 have been made in this PART: STATUTORY INSTRUMENTS AND PRACTICE DIRECTIONS ON PROCEDURE, post.

The Courts Act 2003 (Continuing Provision of Court-houses) Regulations 2005, SI 2005/562 have been made which make arrangements between the Lord Chancellor and the relevant councils in respect of the Justice Rooms in the City of London and the Guildhall, Kingston on Thames. Also the Courts Act 2003 (Transitional Provisions, Savings and Consequential Provisions) Order 2005, SI 2005/911 amended by SI 2006/680 has been made. The Courts Act 2003 (Revocations, Savings and Transitional Provisions) Order 2005, SI 2005/2804 has been made, see note to s 108, ante.

1–4368 109. Minor and consequential amendments, repeals, etc. (1) Schedule 8 contains minor and consequential amendments.

(2) Schedule 9 contains transitional provisions and savings.
(3) Schedule 10 contains repeals.
(4) The Lord Chancellor may by order[1] make—

(*a*) any supplementary, incidental or consequential provision, and
(*b*) any transitory, transitional or saving provision,

which he considers necessary or expedient for the purposes of, in consequence of, or for giving full effect to any provision of this Act.

(5) An order[1] under subsection (4) may, in particular—

(*a*) provide for any provision of this Act which comes into force before another such provision has come into force to have effect, until that other provision has come into force, with such modifications as are specified in the order, and
(*b*) amend, repeal or revoke any enactment other than one contained in an Act passed in a Session after that in which this Act is passed.

(6) The amendments that may be made under subsection (5)(*b*) are in addition to those made by or under any other provision of this Act.
[Courts Act 2003, s 109.]

1. The Courts Act 2003 (Consequential Amendments) Order 2004, SI 2004/2035 made a number of amendments to primary legislation consequential to the introduction of Criminal Procedure Rules and Family Procedure Rules under ss 68–70 and ss 75–77 respectively. In general, powers to make procedural rules in any criminal cause or matter and in family proceedings in pre-existing legislative provisions were repealed by the 2003 Act, Schs 8 and 10. The 2004 Order substituted in primary legislation references to the new rules and repealed redundant provisions. Although the 2004 Order came into force on 1 September 2004, it did not affect the general operation of the enactments amended or repealed by the 2004 Order until the first Criminal Procedure Rules or Family Procedure Rules came into force, as appropriate.
  The Courts Act 2003 (Consequential Provisions) (No 2) Order 2005, SI 2005/617 amended by SI 2006/1970 has been made which inter alia substituted for "justices' chief executive" the words "designated officer for a local justice area" and "local justice area" for "petty sessions area" and similar expressions in subordinate legislation. It also revoked the Magistrates' Courts (Remands in Custody) Order 1989, SI 1989/970. The Courts Act 2003 (Consequential Provisions) Order 2005, SI 2005/886 made analogous consequential amendments to primary legislation. The Courts Act 2003 (Transitional Provisions, Savings and Consequential Provisions) Order 2005, SI 2005/911 amended by SI 2006/680 made provision for continuity following the abolition of justices' chief executives and petty sessional areas and for the continued effect of certain rules and regulations made under repealed enactments. The Courts Act 2003 (Consequential and Transitional Provisions) Order 2005, SI 2005/1012 made consequential and transitional amendments in relation to civilian enforcement officers. The Courts Act 2003 (Revocations, Savings and Transitional Provisions) Order 2005, SI 2005/2804 revoked inter alia the Magistrates' Courts (Adoption) Rules 1984, SI 1984/611 with savings and transitional povisions in consequence of the implementation of the Adoption and Children Act 2002 and because the replacement rules were made under the Courts Act 2003 so that the 1984 did not automatically become spent.

1–4369 110. Commencement. (1) Subject to subsection (2), this Act comes into force in accordance with provision made by order by the Lord Chancellor.
  (2) Subsection (1) does not apply to section 42, 94, 107, 108, 109(4) to (6), this section or section 111 or 112.
  (3) An order under this section may appoint different days for different provisions and different purposes.[1]
[Courts Act 2003, s 110.]

1. At the date of going to press the following commencement orders had been made: Commencement provisions: s 110; Courts Act 2003 (Commencement No 1) Order 2003, SI 2003/3345; Courts Act 2003 (Commencement No 2) Order 2004, SI 2004/174; Courts Act 2003 (Commencement No 3 and Transitional Provisions) Order 2004, SI 2004/401; Courts Act 2003 (Commencement No 4) Order 2004, SI 2004/798; Courts Act 2003 (Commencement No 5) Order 2004, SI 2004/1104; Courts Act 2003 (Commencement No 6 and Savings) Order 2004, SI 2004/2066; Courts Act 2003 (Commencement No 7) Order 2004, SI 2004/2195; Courts Act 2003 (Commencement No 8, Savings and Consequential Provisions) Order 2004, SI 2004/3123; Courts Act 2003 (Commencement No 9, Savings, Consequential and Transitional Provisions) Order 2005, SI 2005/547, revoked by SI 2005/910; Courts Act 2003 (Commencement No 10) Order 2005, SI 2005/910; Courts Act 2003 (Commencement No 11 and Transitional Provision) Order 2005, SI 2005/2744; and Courts Act 2003 (Commencement No 12 and Transitional Provision) Order 2005, SI 2005/3518.

1–4370 111. Extent. (1) Subject to subsections (2) and (3), this Act extends only to England and Wales.
  (2) Subsection (1) does not apply to section 59(3), 90, 91, 100, 101, 102, 103, 104, 105, 106 or 109.
  (3) Subject to any provision made in Schedule 8, the amendments and repeals made by Schedules 4, 8 and 10 have the same extent as the enactments to which they relate.
[Courts Act 2003, s 111.]

1–4371 112. Short title. This Act may be cited as the Courts Act 2003.
[Courts Act 2003, s 112.]

1–4372
Section 4 **SCHEDULE 1**[1]
CONSTITUTION AND PROCEDURE OF COURTS BOARDS
Constitution

1. The members of each courts board are to be appointed by the Lord Chancellor.
2. Each board must have—
(*a*) at least one member who is a judge,
(*b*) at least two members who are lay justices, each of whom is assigned to a local justice area the whole or a part of which is included in the board's area,
(*c*) at least two other members who are persons appearing to the Lord Chancellor to have appropriate knowledge or experience of the work of the courts in the area for which the board acts, and
(*d*) at least two more members who are persons appearing to the Lord Chancellor to be representative of people living in that area,
and may have such other members of a description mentioned in sub-paragraphs (*a*) to (*d*) as the Lord Chancellor considers appropriate.
3. Regulations[2] may make provision in relation to the appointment of members of courts boards, including in particular provision about the procedures to be followed in connection with appointments.

Chairman

4. Regulations[2] may make provision as to the selection of one of the members of each courts board to be its chairman.

Tenure of office

5. (1) Regulations[2] may make provision as to—

(*a*) the term of office of chairmen and members of courts boards;
(*b*) their resignation, suspension or removal.

(2) Subject to the regulations, a person is to hold and vacate office as a member of a courts board in accordance with the terms of the instrument appointing him.

Payments in respect of expenses, etc

6. The Lord Chancellor may make such payments to or in respect of members of courts boards by way of reimbursement of expenses, allowances and remuneration as he may determine.

Procedure

7. Regulations[2] may make provision about—

(*a*) the procedure of courts boards (including quorum);
(*b*) the validation of proceedings in the event of a vacancy among the members of a courts board or a defect in the appointment of a member.

Interpretation

8. In this Schedule "regulations" means regulations made by the Lord Chancellor.

---

1. Section 4 of and Sch 1 to the Courts Act 2004 were brought into force on 1 June 2004 by the Courts Act (Commencement No 4) Order, SI 2004/798.
2. The Courts Boards (Appointment and Procedure) Regulations 2004 have been made in this PART, STATUTORY INSTRUMENTS ON PROCEDURE, post.

1–4373

Section 6

SCHEDULE 2
ABOLITION OF MAGISTRATES' COURTS COMMITTEES: TRANSFERS

PART 1
PROPERTY TRANSFER SCHEMES

Property transfer schemes: general

1. (1) The Lord Chancellor may make a scheme[1] or schemes for the transfer to him or another Minister of the Crown of any property, rights or liabilities—

(*a*) to which magistrates' courts committees are entitled or subject immediately before the appointed day, or
(*b*) to which any of the persons specified in sub-paragraph (2) is entitled or subject immediately before the appointed day and which then subsist for the purposes of, or in connection with, or are otherwise attributable to, magistrates' courts.

(2) The persons are—

(*a*) an authority which is a responsible authority for the purposes of the Justices of the Peace Act 1997;
(*b*) the Receiver for the Metropolitan Police District;
(*c*) the council of an outer London borough;
(*d*) the Common Council of the City of London;
(*e*) a police authority established under section 3 of the Police Act 1996;
(*f*) a local probation board;
(*g*) any other body which acts under any enactment or instrument for public purposes and not for its own profit.

(3) Without prejudice to the generality of paragraph (*b*) of sub-paragraph (1), any property, rights or liabilities are to be treated as falling within that paragraph if the Lord Chancellor issues a certificate to that effect.
(4) In this Schedule "property transfer scheme" means a scheme under sub-paragraph (1).
(5) In this Part of this Schedule "the appointed day" means—

(*a*) in the case of the transfer of property, rights or liabilities to which magistrates' courts committees are entitled or subject, the day immediately before the abolition day;
(*b*) in any other case, the day specified in the scheme.

(6) On the day which is the appointed day in relation to property, rights or liabilities to which provisions of a property transfer scheme apply, the property, rights and liabilities are transferred and vest in accordance with those provisions.
(7) In this Schedule "the abolition day" means the day appointed under section 110(1) for the coming into force of section 6(1) (abolition of magistrates' courts committees).

---

1. As to the limits of this power and the position where a magistrates' court formed only part of the building concerned, see *R (Lord Chancellor) v Chief Land Registrar* [2005] EWHC 1706 (Admin), [2006] 1 QB 795, [2006] 2 WLR 1118.

Property transfer schemes and terminated contracts of employment

2. A property transfer scheme may not transfer rights or liabilities under a contract of employment, except where the rights or liabilities—

   (*a*) are those to which a magistrates' courts committee is entitled or subject, and

   (*b*) relate to a person whose contract of employment was terminated before the appointed day.

Property transfer schemes: supplementary

3. (1) A property transfer scheme may provide for the creation of rights, or the imposition of liabilities, in relation to property transferred by the scheme.

(2) A property transfer scheme may provide for the apportionment or division of any property, rights or liabilities.

(3) A property transfer scheme may—

   (*a*) specify property, rights or liabilities to be transferred under or in accordance with the scheme, or

   (*b*) provide for property, rights or liabilities to be transferred to be determined in accordance with the scheme.

4. (1) A property transfer scheme has effect in relation to the property, rights and liabilities to which it applies despite any provision (of whatever nature) which would otherwise prevent, penalise or restrict the transfer of any of the property, rights and liabilities.

(2) A right of pre-emption, right of reverter or other similar right is not to operate or become exercisable as a result of a transfer under a property transfer scheme.

(3) In the case of such a transfer, any such right has effect as if the transferee were the same person in law as the transferor and as if the transfer had not taken place.

5. (1) Such compensation as is just is to be paid to a third party in respect of any right which would, apart from paragraph 4, have operated in favour of, or become exercisable by, him but which, in consequence of the operation of that paragraph, cannot subsequently operate in his favour or become exercisable by him.

(2) Any compensation payable by virtue of sub-paragraph (1) is to be paid by the transferor, by the transferee or by both.

(3) A property transfer scheme may provide for the determination of any disputes as to—

   (*a*) whether, and (if so) how much, compensation is payable by virtue of sub-paragraph (1), and

   (*b*) the person to whom or by whom it is to be paid.

(4) "Third party" means a person other than the transferor or the transferee.

6. Paragraphs 4 and 5 apply in relation to the creation of rights in relation to property as they apply in relation to a transfer of property; and references to the transferor and the transferee are to be read accordingly.

7. A certificate issued by the Lord Chancellor that any property, rights or liabilities have, or have not, been transferred under or in accordance with a property transfer scheme is conclusive evidence of the transfer, or of the fact that there has not been a transfer.

Stamp duty

8. (1) Stamp duty is not chargeable in respect of a transfer or grant effected under or in accordance with a property transfer scheme.

(2) No instrument made or executed for the purposes of such a transfer or grant is to be treated as duly stamped unless—

   (*a*) it has, in accordance with section 12 of the Stamp Act 1891, been stamped with a particular stamp denoting that it is not chargeable with that duty or that it is duly stamped, or

   (*b*) it is stamped with the duty to which it would be liable, apart from this paragraph.

Supplementary provisions in property transfer scheme

9. A property transfer scheme may make such supplemental, consequential or transitional provision for the purposes of, or in connection with, a transfer made by the scheme as the Lord Chancellor considers appropriate.

PART 2
STAFF TRANSFERS

Interpretation

10. In this Part of this Schedule—

   (*a*) "TUPE" means the Transfer of Undertakings (Protection of Employment) Regulations 1981 (SI 1981/1794),

   (*b*) "the appointed day" means the day immediately before the abolition day,

   (*c*) references to a responsible authority are to an authority which is a responsible authority under the Justices of the Peace Act 1997,

   (*d*) references to a responsible authority's relevant functions are to its functions under that Act, and

   (*e*) references to a transferred employee are to an employee transferred to the Lord Chancellor's employment by virtue of paragraph 11 or 12.

Application of TUPE

11. For the purposes of TUPE—

   (*a*) the functions of each magistrates' courts committee are to be treated as transferred on the appointed day from the committee to the Lord Chancellor, and

   (*b*) each such transfer is to be treated as the transfer of an undertaking.

12. (1) For the purposes of TUPE—

   (*a*) the relevant functions of each responsible authority are to be treated as transferred on the appointed day from the authority to the Lord Chancellor,

   (*b*) each such transfer is to be treated as the transfer of an undertaking, and

   (*c*) each person falling within sub-paragraph (2) (but no other person) is to be treated as employed in the undertaking immediately before the appointed day.

(2) A person falls within this sub-paragraph if—

(a) immediately before the appointed day he is employed by the responsible authority under a contract of employment,
(b) he spends a substantial part of his time on duties connected with the relevant functions of the authority, and
(c) the Lord Chancellor certifies that in his opinion it is expedient that the person be transferred to the Lord Chancellor's employment.

(3) Where TUPE applies by virtue of this paragraph, it applies as if regulation 5(4B) were omitted.

13. A reference in any enactment to a person appointed under section 2(1) includes a transferred employee.

Restrictions on employment of aliens not to apply to transferred employees

14. Nothing in—

(a) section 3 of the Act of Settlement,
(b) section 6 of the Aliens Restriction (Amendment) Act 1919, or
(c) any rules prescribing requirements as to nationality which must be satisfied in the case of persons employed in a civil capacity under the Crown,

applies to the employment of a transferred employee by the Lord Chancellor following his transfer by virtue of paragraph 11 or 12.

Compensation for responsible authorities

15. The Lord Chancellor may, to the extent he thinks fit, compensate a responsible authority in respect of costs incurred by the authority as a result of this Act in respect of a person who—

(a) immediately before the appointed day is employed by the authority under a contract of employment, and
(b) spends part of his time on duties connected with the relevant functions of the authority,

but who is not transferred to the Lord Chancellor's employment by virtue of paragraph 12.

PART 3
MISCELLANEOUS AND SUPPLEMENTARY
Continuing provision of court-houses, accommodation etc

16. (1) The Lord Chancellor may by regulations provide that any petty sessional court-house or other accommodation specified in the regulations which immediately before the abolition day was being provided by—

(a) the council of an outer London borough, or
(b) the Common Council of the City of London,

pursuant to regulations made under paragraph 35 of Schedule 14 to the Access to Justice Act 1999 shall on and after that day be provided by that council to the Lord Chancellor for the performance of his functions under section 3.

(2) Regulations under sub-paragraph (1) may—

(a) prescribe terms and conditions, including conditions as to payment, on which any court-house or other accommodation is to be provided, and
(b) prohibit a council providing a court-house or other accommodation under sub-paragraph (1) from altering or extending it without the consent of the Lord Chancellor.

Assistance

17. It is the duty of each magistrates' courts committee, and each person falling within paragraph 1(2) to provide the Lord Chancellor with such information or assistance as he may reasonably require for the purposes of, or in connection with—

(a) the exercise of any powers exercisable by him in relation to a property transfer scheme, or
(b) Part 2 of this Schedule.

1–4374

SCHEDULE 3
PRE-TRIAL HEARINGS IN MAGISTRATES' COURTS
Inserted new ss 8A–8D into the Magistrates' Courts Act 1980.

1–4374A

Section 61A

SCHEDULE 3A*
FURTHER PROVISION ABOUT THE INSPECTORS OF COURT ADMINISTRATION
Delegation of functions

1. (1) An inspector of court administration may delegate any of his functions (to such extent as he may determine) to another public authority.

(2) If an inspector of court administration delegates the carrying out of an inspection under sub-paragraph (1) it is nevertheless to be regarded for the purposes of this Part as carried out by the inspector.

(3) In this Schedule "public authority" includes any person certain of whose functions are functions of a public nature.

*Inserted by the Police and Justice Act 2006, s 32 from a date to be appointed.

Inspection programmes and inspection frameworks

2. (1) The Chief Inspector shall from time to time, or at such times as the Lord Chancellor may specify by order, prepare—

    (a) a document setting out what inspections he proposes to carry out (an "inspection programme");

    (b) a document setting out the manner in which he proposes to carry out his functions of inspecting and reporting (an "inspection framework").

  (2) Before preparing an inspection programme or an inspection framework the Chief Inspector shall consult the Lord Chancellor, the Lord Chief Justice of England and Wales and (subject to sub-paragraph (3))—

    (a) Her Majesty's Chief Inspector of Prisons,

    (b) Her Majesty's Chief Inspector of Constabulary,

    (c) Her Majesty's Chief Inspector of the Crown Prosecution Service,

    (d) Her Majesty's Chief Inspector of the National Probation Service for England and Wales,

    (e) Her Majesty's Chief Inspector of Education, Children's Services and Skills,

    (f) the Commission for Healthcare Audit and Inspection,

    (g) the Commission for Social Care Inspection,

    (h) the Audit Commission for Local Government and the National Health Service in England and Wales,

    (i) the Auditor General for Wales, and

    (j) any other person or body specified by an order made by the Lord Chancellor,

and he shall send to each of those persons or bodies a copy of each programme or framework once it is prepared.

  (3) The requirement in sub-paragraph (2) to consult, and to send copies to, a person or body listed in paragraphs (a) to (j) of that sub-paragraph is subject to any agreement made between the Chief Inspector and that person or body to waive the requirement in such cases or circumstances as may be specified in the agreement.

  (4) The Lord Chancellor may by order specify the form that inspection programmes or inspection frameworks are to take.

  (5) Nothing in any inspection programme or inspection framework is to be read as preventing the inspectors of court administration from making visits without notice.

Inspections by other inspectors of organisations within inspectors' remit

3. (1) If—

    (a) a person or body within sub-paragraph (2) is proposing to carry out an inspection that would involve inspecting a specified organisation, and

    (b) the Chief Inspector considers that the proposed inspection would impose an unreasonable burden on that organisation, or would do so if carried out in a particular manner,

the Chief Inspector shall, subject to sub-paragraph (6), give a notice to that person or body not to carry out the proposed inspection, or not to carry it out in that manner.

  (2) The persons or bodies within this sub-paragraph are—

    (a) the Audit Commission for Local Government and the National Health Service in England and Wales;

    (b) any other person or body specified by an order made by the Lord Chancellor.

  (3) In sub-paragraph (1)(a) "specified organisation" means a person or body specified by an order made by the Lord Chancellor.

  (4) A person or body may be specified under sub-paragraph (3) only if it exercises functions in relation to any matter falling with the scope of the duties of the inspectors of court administration under section 59 of this Act.

  (5) A person or body may be specified under sub-paragraph (3) in relation to particular functions that it has.

In the case of a person or body so specified, sub-paragraph (1)(a) is to be read as referring to an inspection that would involve inspecting the discharge of any of its functions in relation to which it is specified.

  (6) The Lord Chancellor may by order specify cases or circumstances in which a notice need not, or may not, be given under this paragraph.

  (7) Where a notice is given under this paragraph, the proposed inspection is not to be carried out, or (as the case may be) is not to be carried out in the manner mentioned in the notice.

This is subject to sub-paragraph (8).

  (8) The Lord Chancellor, if satisfied that the proposed inspection—

    (a) would not impose an unreasonable burden on the organisation in question, or

    (b) would not do so if carried out in a particular manner,

may give consent to the inspection being carried out, or being carried out in that manner.

  (9) The Lord Chancellor may by order make provision supplementing that made by this paragraph, including in particular—

    (a) provision about the form of notices;

    (b) provision prescribing the period within which notices are to be given;

    (c) provision prescribing circumstances in which notices are, or are not, to be made public;

    (d) provision for revising or withdrawing notices;

    (e) provision for setting aside notices not validly given.

Co-operation

4. The inspectors of court administration shall co-operate with—

    (a) Her Majesty's Chief Inspector of Prisons,

    (b) Her Majesty's Inspectors of Constabulary,

    (c) Her Majesty's Chief Inspector of the Crown Prosecution Service,

    (d) Her Majesty's Inspectorate of the National Probation Service for England and Wales,

    (e) Her Majesty's Chief Inspector of Education, Children's Services and Skills,

    (f) the Commission for Healthcare Audit and Inspection,

    (g) the Commission for Social Care Inspection,

    (h) the Audit Commission for Local Government and the National Health Service in England and Wales,

    (i) the Auditor General for Wales, and

    (j) any other public authority specified by an order made by the Lord Chancellor,

where it is appropriate to do so for the efficient and effective discharge of the inspectors' functions.

Joint action

5. (1) The inspectors of court administration may act jointly with another public authority where it is appropriate to do so for the efficient and effective discharge of the inspectors' functions.

(2) The Chief Inspector, acting jointly with the chief inspectors within sub-paragraph (3), shall prepare a document (a "joint inspection programme") setting out—

(a) what inspections the inspectors of court administration propose to carry out in the exercise of the power conferred by sub-paragraph (1), and

(b) what inspections the chief inspectors within sub-paragraph (3) (or their inspectorates) propose to carry out in the exercise of any corresponding powers conferred on them.

(3) The chief inspectors within this sub-paragraph are—

(a) Her Majesty's Chief Inspector of Prisons;
(b) Her Majesty's Chief Inspector of Constabulary;
(c) Her Majesty's Chief Inspector of the Crown Prosecution Service;
(d) Her Majesty's Chief Inspector of the National Probation Service for England and Wales.

(4) A joint inspection programme must be prepared from time to time or at such times as the Secretary of State, the Lord Chancellor and the Attorney General may jointly direct.

(5) Sub-paragraphs (2), (3) and (5) of paragraph 2 apply to a joint inspection programme as they apply to a document prepared under that paragraph.

(6) The Secretary of State, the Lord Chancellor and the Attorney General may by a joint direction specify the form that a joint inspection programme is to take.

Assistance for other public authorities

6. (1) The inspectors of court administration may if they think it appropriate to do so provide assistance to any other public authority for the purpose of the exercise by that authority of its functions.

(2) Assistance under this paragraph may be provided on such terms (including terms as to payment) as the Chief Inspector thinks fit.

1–4375

Section 65   SCHEDULE 4
            FURTHER FUNCTIONS CONFERRED ON DISTRICT JUDGES (MAGISTRATES' COURTS)

Criminal Justice Act 1967 (c 80)

1. In section 9(5) (requirement for author of written statement to give evidence in person), for "by a puisne judge of the High Court, a Circuit judge or Recorder sitting alone" substitute

"by any of the following sitting alone—

(a) a puisne judge of the High Court;
(b) a Circuit judge;
(c) a District Judge (Magistrates' Courts);
(d) a Recorder."

Taxes Management Act 1970 (c 9)

2. In—

(a) section 20D(1)(a) (meaning of "the appropriate judicial authority" in relation to England and Wales), and
(b) paragraph 9(2)(a) of Schedule 1AA (sanction for failure to comply with order under section 20BA),

after "Circuit judge" insert "or a District Judge (Magistrates' Courts)".

Juries Act 1974 (c 23)

3. In section 9B, for subsection (3) (meaning of "the judge" for purposes of discharge of person incapable of acting effectively as juror) substitute—

"(3) In this section and section 10 "the judge" means—

(a) a judge of the High Court,
(b) a Circuit judge,
(c) a District Judge (Magistrates' Courts), or
(d) a Recorder."

4. In section 10 (discharge of summons in case of doubt as to capacity to act effectively as juror) omit "and for this purpose "the judge" means any judge of the High Court or any Circuit judge or Recorder".

Police and Criminal Evidence Act 1984 (c 60)

5. In section 9(2A) (application of enactments relating to execution of process in Scotland or Northern Ireland to processes issued by a Circuit judge under Schedule 1 to 1984 Act), for "circuit judge" substitute "judge".

6. (1) In Schedule 1 (applications for access to excluded or special procedure material) for "circuit judge", in each place, substitute "judge".

(2) After paragraph 16 insert—

"17. Interpretation. In this Schedule "judge" means a Circuit judge or a District Judge (Magistrates' Courts)."

Computer Misuse Act 1990 (c 18)

7. In section 14(1) (search warrants for offences under section 1) after "a Circuit judge" insert "or a District Judge (Magistrates' Courts)".

Data Protection Act 1998 (c 29)

8. In Schedule 9 (powers of entry and inspection) in paragraph 1(1) after "circuit judge" insert "or a District Judge (Magistrates' Courts)".

Terrorism Act 2000 (c 11)

9. In Schedule 5 (terrorist investigations: information)—

(*a*) in paragraphs 5(1) and (5), 6(1), 10(1), 11(1), 12(1) and (2) and 13(1), after "Circuit judge" insert "or a District Judge (Magistrates' Courts)", and

(*b*) in paragraphs 5(4)(*a*) and 7(1)(*b*), after "Circuit judge" insert "or the District Judge (Magistrates' Courts)".

10. In Schedule 6 (financial information), in paragraph 3(*a*), after "Circuit judge" insert "or a District Judge (Magistrates' Courts)".

11. In Schedule 6A (account monitoring orders), in paragraph 1(2)(*a*), for "a Circuit judge," substitute "a Circuit judge or a District Judge (Magistrates' Courts),".

Regulation of Investigatory Powers Act 2000 (c 23)

12. In Schedule 2 (persons who have the appropriate permission), in paragraph 1(1)(*a*), after "Circuit judge" insert "or a District Judge (Magistrates' Courts)".

Freedom of Information Act 2000 (c 36)

13. In Schedule 3 (powers of entry and inspection), in paragraph 1(1), after "Circuit judge" insert "or a District Judge (Magistrates' Courts)".

International Criminal Court Act 2001 (c 17)

14. In Schedule 5 (investigation of proceeds of ICC crime) in paragraphs 1(1) and 8 for "a Circuit judge or, in Northern Ireland, a county court judge" substitute

"—

(*a*) a Circuit judge or a District Judge (Magistrates' Courts), or

(*b*) in Northern Ireland, a county court judge,".

Armed Forces Act 2001 (c 19)

15. In section 6(2)(*a*) (applications for access to excluded or special procedure material), for "circuit judges" substitute "judges".

1–4376

Section 97(1)

SCHEDULE 5
COLLECTION OF FINES AND OTHER SUMS IMPOSED ON CONVICTION

(As amended by the Disability Discrimination Act 2005, Sch 1 and SI 2006/1737.)

PART 1
INTRODUCTORY

Application of Schedule

1. This Schedule applies if a person aged 18 or over ("P") is liable to pay a sum which is or is treated for the purposes of Part 3 of the 1980 Act as a sum adjudged to be paid by a conviction of a magistrates' court.

Meaning of "the sum due"

2. (1) In this Schedule "the sum due" means the sum adjudged to be paid as mentioned in paragraph 1.

(2) For the purposes of this Schedule—

a "fine" does not include any pecuniary forfeiture or pecuniary compensation payable on conviction; and

"a sum required to be paid by a compensation order" means any sum required to be paid by an order made under section 130(1) of the Powers of Criminal Courts (Sentencing) Act 2000.

Meaning of "existing defaulter" etc

3. (1) For the purposes of this Schedule, P is an existing defaulter if it is shown that—

(*a*) repealed,

(*b*) the sum due or any other sum is registered for enforcement against him as a fine under—

(i) section 71 of the Road Traffic Offenders Act 1988,

(ii) section 9 of the Criminal Justice and Police Act 2001, or

(iii) any other enactment specified in fines collection regulations,

(*c*) he is in default on a collection order in respect of another sum falling within paragraph 1, or

(*d*) he is in default in payment of another sum falling within paragraph 1 but in respect of which no collection order has been made.

(2) For the purposes of this Schedule, P's existing default can be disregarded only if he shows that there was an adequate reason for it.

(3) Sub-paragraph (2) is subject to sub-paragraph (4).

(4) Where a sum is registered for enforcement against P as mentioned in sub-paragraph (1)(*b*), P's existing default is not one which can be disregarded for the purposes of the following provisions of this Schedule.

(5) Repealed..

(6) *Repealed.*

(7) "Collection order" means an order made under Part 4 of this Schedule.

PART 2

IMMEDIATE PAYMENT OF FINES: DISCOUNTS

Repealed.

PART 3

ATTACHMENT OF EARNINGS ORDERS AND APPLICATIONS FOR BENEFIT DEDUCTIONS

Application of Part

7. (1) This Part does not apply where the court is hearing P's case following an appeal under paragraph 23, 32 or 37(9).

(2) In the following provisions of this Part, "the relevant court" means—

(a) the court which is imposing the liability to pay the sum due, or
(b) the magistrates' court responsible for enforcing payment of the sum due.

(3) For the purposes of this Schedule—

(a) an attachment of earnings order, or
(b) an application for benefit deductions,

is an order or application to secure the payment of the whole of the sum due.

Attachment of earnings order or application for benefit deductions where P is liable to pay compensation

7A. (1) This paragraph applies if the sum due consists of or includes a sum required to be paid by a compensation order.

(2) The relevant court must make an attachment of earnings order if it appears to the court—

(a) that P is in employment, and
(b) that it is not impracticable or inappropriate to make the order.

(3) The relevant court must make an application for benefit deductions if it appears to the court—

(a) that P is entitled to a relevant benefit, and
(b) that it is not impracticable or inappropriate to make the application.

(4) If it appears to the court that (apart from this sub-paragraph) both sub-paragraph (2) and sub-paragraph (3) would apply, the court must make either an attachment of earnings order or an application for benefit deductions.

Attachment of earnings order or application for benefit deductions without P's consent

8. (1) This paragraph applies if—

(a) paragraph 7A does not apply, and
(b) the relevant court concludes that P is an existing defaulter and that his existing default (or defaults) cannot be disregarded.

(2) The court must make an attachment of earnings order if it appears to the court—

(a) that P is in employment, and
(b) that it is not impracticable or inappropriate to make the order.

(3) The court must make an application for benefit deductions if it appears to the court—

(a) that P is entitled to a relevant benefit, and
(b) that it is not impracticable or inappropriate to make the application.

(4) If it appears to the court that (apart from this sub-paragraph) both sub-paragraph (2) and sub-paragraph (3) would apply, the court must make either an attachment of earnings order or an application for benefit deductions.

Attachment of earnings order or application for benefit deductions with P's consent

9. (1) This paragraph applies if—

(a) paragraph 7A does not apply, and
(b) the relevant court concludes that P is not an existing defaulter or, if he is, that his existing default (or defaults) can be disregarded.

(2) The court may make—

(a) an attachment of earnings order, or
(b) an application for benefit deductions,

if P consents.

Meaning of "relevant benefit" and "application for benefit deductions"

10. In this Schedule—

(a) "relevant benefit" means a benefit from which the Secretary of State may make deductions by virtue of section 24 of the Criminal Justice Act 1991 (recovery of fines etc by deductions from income support etc), and
(b) "application for benefit deductions", in relation to a relevant benefit, means an application to the Secretary of State asking him to deduct sums from any amounts payable to P by way of the benefit.

PART 4
MAKING OF COLLECTION ORDERS

Application of Part

11. (1) This Part applies whether or not the relevant court has made an attachment of earnings order or an application for benefit deductions under Part 3 of this Schedule.

(2) In this Part "the relevant court" has the same meaning as in Part 3 of this Schedule.

Court's power to make a collection order

12. (1) The relevant court must make an order ("a collection order") relating to the payment of the sum due, unless it appears to the court that it is impracticable or inappropriate to make the order.

(2) If P is subject to a collection order, the powers of any court to deal with P's liability to pay the sum due are subject to the provisions of this Schedule and to fines collection regulations.

Contents of collection orders: general

13. (1) The collection order must—

(a) state the amount of the sum due,

(aa) where that sum consists of or includes a fine or a sum required to be paid by a compensation order, state—

     (i) the amount of the fine, or the amount required to be paid by the compensation order (or, if applicable, the amount of the fine and the amount required to be paid by the compensation order), and

     (ii) the amount of any other part of the sum due,

(b) state the court's conclusions as to whether P is an existing defaulter and if so whether the existing default (or defaults) can be disregarded,

(c) if the court has made an attachment of earnings order or an application for benefit deductions, state that fact,

(d) specify the fines office to which the order is allocated, and

(e) contain information about the effect of the order.

(2) In this Schedule "the fines officer", in relation to P, means any fines officer working at the fines office specified in the collection order.

Contents of collection orders: no attachment of earnings order etc made

14. (1) If the relevant court has not under Part 3 made an attachment of earnings order or an application for benefit deductions, the collection order must state the payment terms.

(2) "The payment terms" means—

(a) a term requiring P to pay the sum due within a specified period, or

(b) terms requiring P to pay the sum due by instalments of specified amounts on or before specified dates.

Contents of collection orders: attachment of earnings order etc made

15. (1) If the court has under Part 3 of this Schedule made an attachment of earnings order or an application for benefit deductions, the collection order must state the reserve terms.

(2) "The reserve terms" means terms of a description mentioned in paragraph 14(2) but which (subject to paragraphs 31, 32 and 39) are to have effect if the attachment of earnings order or application for benefit deductions fails.

When an attachment of earnings order fails

16. For the purposes of this Schedule, an attachment of earnings order fails if—

(a) P's employer fails to comply with the order, or

(b) the order is discharged at a time when P remains liable to pay any part of the sum due.

When an application for benefit deductions fails

17. For the purposes of this Schedule, an application for benefit deductions fails if—

(a) the application is withdrawn,

(b) the Secretary of State decides not to make deductions,

(c) an appeal against a decision of the Secretary of State to make deductions succeeds, or

(c) the Secretary of State ceases to make deductions at a time when P remains liable to pay any part of the sum due.

PART 5
DISCOUNT WHERE COLLECTION ORDER MADE

Repealed.

PART 6
VARIATION OF COLLECTION ORDERS CONTAINING PAYMENT TERMS

Application of Part

21. This Part applies if the court has made a collection order and the order contains payment terms.

Application to fines officer for variation of order or attachment of earnings order etc

22. (1) P may, at any time—

(*a*) after the collection order is made and before Part 7 applies, and
(*b*) when he is not in default on the order,

apply to the fines officer under this paragraph.

(2) P may apply for—

(*a*) the payment terms to be varied, or
(*b*) an attachment of earnings order or application for benefit deductions to be made.

(3) No application may be made under sub-paragraph (2)(*a*) unless—

(*a*) there has been a material change in P's circumstances since the collection order was made (or the payment terms were last varied under this paragraph), or
(*b*) P is making further information about his circumstances available.

(4) On an application under sub-paragraph (2)(*a*), the fines officer may decide—

(*a*) to vary the payment terms in P's favour, or
(*b*) not to vary them.

(5) On an application under sub-paragraph (2)(*b*), the fines officer may decide—

(*a*) to make an attachment of earnings order or application for benefit deductions, or
(*b*) not to do so.

(6) If he decides to make an order or application he must vary the collection order so that it states reserve terms.
(7) The reserve terms must not be less favourable to P than the payment terms.
(8) A decision of the fines officer under this paragraph must be in writing, dated and delivered to P.
(9) Subject to paragraph 23, the effect of—

(*a*) a decision under sub-paragraph (4)(*a*), and
(*b*) a variation under sub-paragraph (6),

is that the collection order has effect as varied by the fines officer.

Appeal against decision of fines officer

23.—(1) P may, within 10 working days from the date of a decision under paragraph 22, appeal to the magistrates' court against the decision.
(2) On an appeal under this paragraph the magistrates' court may—

(*a*) confirm or vary the payment terms (or the reserve terms),
(*b*) if the appeal is against a decision on an application under paragraph 22(2)(*b*) or if P consents, make an attachment of earnings order or an application for benefit deductions, or
(*c*) discharge the collection order and exercise any of its standard powers in respect of persons liable to pay fines.

(3) If the court makes an attachment of earnings order or an application for benefit deductions, it must vary the collection order so that it states reserve terms.

Nature of power to vary terms of collection order

24.—(1) A power to vary the payment terms of a collection order includes power to—

(*a*) substitute terms requiring P to pay by specified instalments on or before specified dates for a term requiring P to pay within a specified period, or
(*b*) substitute a term requiring P to pay within a specified period for terms requiring P to pay the sum due by specified instalments on or before specified dates.

(2) Subject to sub-paragraph (1), a power to vary the payment terms of a collection order under which the sum due is required to be paid within a specified period is a power to vary the date on or before which the sum due is to be paid.
(3) Subject to sub-paragraph (1), a power to vary the payment terms of a collection order under which the sum due is required to be paid by specified instalments on or before specified dates is a power to vary—

(*a*) the number of instalments payable;
(*b*) the amount of any instalment;
(*c*) the date on or before which any instalment is required to be paid.

(4) This paragraph applies in relation to the variation of the reserve terms as it applies in relation to the payment terms.

Meaning of "in default on a collection order"

24A. For the purposes of this Schedule, P is in default on a collection order if he fails to pay any amount due under the payment terms (or, if they have effect, the reserve terms) on or before the date on which it is required to be paid.

PART 7
EFFECT OF FIRST DEFAULT ON COLLECTION ORDER CONTAINING PAYMENT TERMS

Application of Part

25. This Part applies on the first occasion on which P is in default on a collection order containing payment terms and none of the following is pending—

(*a*) an application under paragraph 22 (application to fines officer for variation of order or for attachment of earnings order etc);

(b) an appeal under paragraph 23 (appeal against decision of fines officer);

(c) a reference under paragraph 42 (power of fines officer to refer case to magistrates' court).

Attachment of earnings order or application for benefit deductions to be made

26. (1) The fines officer must make an attachment of earnings order if it appears to him—

(a) that P is in employment, and

(b) that it is not impracticable or inappropriate to make the order.

(2) The fines officer must make an application for benefit deductions if it appears to him—

(a) that P is entitled to a relevant benefit, and

(b) that it is not impracticable or inappropriate to make the application.

(3) If it appears to the fines officer that (apart from this sub-paragraph) both sub-paragraph (1) and sub-paragraph (2) would apply, he must make either an attachment of earnings order or an application for benefit deductions.

27, 28. *REPEALED.*

PART 8
OPERATION OF COLLECTION ORDERS CONTAINING RESERVE TERMS

Application of Part

29. This Part applies if—

(a) a collection order contains reserve terms, and

(b) the attachment of earnings order or application for benefit deductions made under Part 3 or 6 fails.

Requirement to notify P on failure of an attachment of earnings order etc

30. The fines officer must deliver to P a notice ("a payment notice") informing P—

(a) that the order or application has failed and the reserve terms have effect,

(b) what P has to do to comply with the reserve terms, and

(c) of his right to make applications under paragraph 31.

Application to fines officer for variation of reserve terms

31. (1) P may, at any time—

(a) after the date of a payment notice under paragraph 30 and before a further steps notice is delivered to him under paragraph 37, and

(b) when he is not in default on the collection order,

apply to the fines officer for the reserve terms to be varied.

(2) No application may be made under sub-paragraph (1) unless—

(a) there has been a material change in P's circumstances since the reserve terms were set (or last varied under this paragraph), or

(b) P is making further information about his circumstances available.

(3) On such an application being made, the fines officer may decide—

(a) to vary the reserve terms in P's favour, or

(b) not to vary them.

(4) A decision of the fines officer under this paragraph must be in writing, dated and delivered to P.

(5) Subject to paragraph 32, the effect of a decision under sub-paragraph (3)(a) is that the collection order has effect with the reserve terms varied in the way decided by the fines officer.

Appeal against decision of fines officer

32. (1) P may, within 10 working days from the date of a decision under paragraph 31(3), appeal to the magistrates' court against the decision.

(2) On an appeal under this paragraph the magistrates' court may—

(a) confirm or vary the reserve terms, or

(b) discharge the order and exercise any of its standard powers in respect of persons liable to pay fines or other sums.

33, 34. *Repealed.*

PART 9
FURTHER STEPS

35, 36. *Repealed.*

Functions of fines officer in relation to defaulters: referral or further steps notice

37. (1) This paragraph applies if—

(a) P is in default on a collection order,

(b) paragraph 26 does not apply, and

(c) none of the following is pending—

(i) an application under paragraph 31(1) (application to fines officer for variation and reserve terms),

(ii) an appeal under paragraph 32(1) (appeal against decision of fines officer),

(iii) a reference under paragraph 42 (power of fines officer to refer case to magistrates' court).

(2)–(5) *Repealed.*(6)The fines officer must—

(*a*) refer P's case to the magistrates' court, or
(*b*) deliver to P a notice (a "further steps notice") that he intends to take one or more of the steps listed in paragraph 38.

(7) Any steps that the fines officer intends to take must be specified in the notice.
(8) A further steps notice must be in writing and dated.
(9) P may, within 10 working days from the date of the further steps notice, appeal to the magistrates' court against it.

The range of further steps available against defaulters

38. (1) The steps referred to in paragraphs 37(6)(*b*) and 39(3) and (4) (powers to take further steps) are—

(*a*) issuing a warrant of distress for the purpose of levying the sum due;
(*b*) registering the sum in the register of judgments and orders required to be kept by section 98;
(*c*) making an attachment of earnings order or an application for benefit deductions;
(*d*) subject to sub-paragraph (3), making a clamping order;
(*e*) taking proceedings by virtue of section 87(1) of the 1980 Act (enforcement of payment of fines by High Court and county court).

(2) A clamping order is an order—

(*a*) that a motor vehicle be fitted with an immobilisation device ("clamped"), and
(*b*) which complies with any requirements that are imposed by fines collection regulations under paragraph 46 with respect to the making of clamping orders.

(3) A clamping order must not be made except in relation to a vehicle which is registered under the Vehicle Excise and Registration Act 1994 in P's name.

Powers of court

39. (1) This paragraph applies if the magistrates' court is hearing P's case following—

(*a*) repealed,
(*b*) a referral under paragraph 37(6)(*a*) (functions of fines officer in relation to defaulters), or
(*c*) an appeal under paragraph 37(9) (appeal against a further steps notice).

(2) *Repealed.*
(3) On a referral falling within sub-paragraph (1)*b*), the court may—

(*a*) vary the payment terms (or the reserve terms);
(*b*) take any of the steps listed in paragraph 38;
(*c*) discharge the order and exercise any of its standard powers in respect of persons liable to pay fines or other sums.

(4) On an appeal against a further steps notice, the court may—

(*a*) confirm or quash the notice;
(*b*) vary the notice so as to specify any step listed in paragraph 38;
(*c*) vary the payment terms (or the reserve terms);
(*d*) discharge the order and exercise any of its standard powers in respect of persons liable to pay fines or other sums.

Implementation of further steps notice

40. If—

(*a*) P does not appeal within 10 working days against a further steps notice, or
(*b*) he does so but the further steps notice is confirmed or varied,

any step specified in the notice (or the notice as varied) may be taken.

Power to order sale of clamped vehicle

41. (1) This paragraph applies if—

(*a*) a motor vehicle has been clamped under a clamping order, and
(*b*) at the end of the period specified in fines collection regulations under paragraph 46 any part of the sum due is unpaid.

(2) The magistrates' court may order that—

(*a*) the vehicle is to be sold or otherwise disposed of in accordance with those regulations, and
(*b*) any proceeds are to be applied in accordance with those regulations in discharging P's liability in respect of the sum due.

Power of fines officer to refer case to magistrates' court

42. (1) The fines officer may refer a case to the magistrates' court at any time during the period which—

(*a*) begins the day after the collection order is made, and
(*b*) ends with the date on which—

(i) the sum due (including any increase to which he remains liable) is paid, or
(ii) the order is discharged.

(2) On a referral under this paragraph, the court may—

(a)   confirm or vary the payment terms (or the reserve terms),
(b)   exercise any of its standard powers in respect of persons liable to pay fines or other sums, or
(c)   exercise a power it could exercise under any other paragraph.

(2A)   Where the court exercises any of its standard powers under sub-paragraph (2)(b) it may also discharge the order.

(3)   Fines collection regulations may provide for the fines officer to have the power to issue a summons for the purpose of ensuring that P attends a magistrates' court to whom P's case has been referred under this paragraph or paragraph 37.

Increase in fine by court

42A.   (1)   This paragraph applies where—

(a)   P is in default on a collection order,
(b)   the sum due consists of or includes a fine, and
(c)   the fines officer has referred P's case to the court—

     (i)   under paragraph 37(6)(a), or
     (ii)   after taking any of the steps listed in paragraph 38.

(2)   Where the court is satisfied that the default is due to P's wilful refusal or culpable neglect, the court may increase the fine which is the subject of the order.

(3)   But the court may not increase any other sum which is the subject of the order.

(4)   The amount of the increase is to be determined in accordance with fines collection regulations but must not be greater than 50% of the fine.

(5)   The increase is given effect by treating it as part of the fine imposed on P by his conviction.

PART 10
SUPPLEMENTARY PROVISIONS
Fines collection regulations

43.   In this Schedule "fines collection regulations" means regulations[1] made by the Lord Chancellor for the purpose of giving effect to this Schedule.

44.   (1)   Fines collection regulations may, for the purpose of giving effect to this Schedule and section 97 so far as it relates to this Schedule, make provision modifying (or applying with modifications) any enactment which relates to fines or the enforcement of payment of sums falling within paragraph 1.

(2)   The enactments which may be so modified (or applied with modifications) include enactments containing offences.

(3)   Fines collection regulations may make different provision for different cases.

45.   Fines collection regulations may, for the purpose of giving effect to the powers to make attachment of earnings orders, make provision as to the method for calculating the amounts which are to be deducted from P's earnings.

46.   (1)   Fines collection regulations may, for the purpose of giving effect to the powers to make clamping orders and to order the sale of clamped motor vehicles, make provision in connection with—

(a)   the fitting of immobilisation devices;
(b)   the fitting of immobilisation notices to motor vehicles to which immobilisation devices have been fitted;
(c)   the removal and storage of motor vehicles;
(d)   the release of motor vehicles from immobilisation devices or from storage (including the conditions to be met before the vehicle is released);
(e)   the sale or other disposal of motor vehicles not released.

(2)   Fines collection regulations must provide that an immobilisation device may not be fitted to a vehicle—

(a)   which displays a current disabled person's badge or a current recognised badge, or
(b)   in relation to which there are reasonable grounds for believing that it is used for the carriage of a disabled person.

(3)   In this Schedule—

"disabled person's badge" means a badge issued, or having effect as if issued, under regulations made under section 21 of the Chronically Sick and Disabled Persons Act 1970 (badges for display on motor vehicles used by disabled persons);

"immobilisation device" has the same meaning as in section 104(9) of the Road Traffic Regulation Act 1984 (immobilisation of vehicles illegally parked);

"motor vehicle" means a mechanically propelled vehicle intended or adapted for use on roads, except that section 189 of the Road Traffic Act 1988 (exceptions for certain vehicles) applies for the purposes of this Schedule as it applies for the purposes of the Road Traffic Acts;

"recognised badge" has the meaning given by section 21A of the Chronically Sick and Disabled Persons Act 1970 (recognition of badges issued outside Great Britain).

47.   *Repealed.*

Offences of providing false information, failing to disclose information etc

48.   (1)   P commits an offence if, in providing a statement of his financial circumstances to a fines officer in response to a relevant request, he—

(a)   makes a statement which he knows to be false in a material particular,
(b)   recklessly provides a statement which is false in a material particular, or
(c)   knowingly fails to disclose any material fact.

(2)   A person guilty of an offence under sub-paragraph (1) is liable on summary conviction to a fine not exceeding level 4 on the standard scale.

(3)   P commits an offence if he fails to provide a statement of his financial circumstances to a fines officer in response to a relevant request.

(4) A person guilty of an offence under sub-paragraph (3) is liable on summary conviction to a fine not exceeding level 2 on the standard scale.

(5) A relevant request is a request for information about P's financial circumstances which—

(a) is made by a fines officer, and

(b) is expressed to be made for the purpose of determining whether or how the fines officer should vary the payment terms (or the reserve terms) of a collection order in P's favour.

(6) Proceedings in respect of an offence under this paragraph may be commenced at any time within—

(a) 2 years from the date of the commission of the offence, or

(b) 6 months from its first discovery by the prosecutor,

whichever ends first.

Offence of meddling with vehicle clamp

49. (1) A person commits an offence if he removes or attempts to remove—

(a) an immobilisation device, or

(b) an immobilisation notice,

fitted or fixed to a motor vehicle in accordance with a clamping order made under a further steps notice or under paragraph 39(3)(b) (powers of court).

(2) A person guilty of an offence under this paragraph is liable on summary conviction to a fine not exceeding level 3 on the standard scale.

Meaning of "standard powers in respect of persons liable to pay fines or other sums"

50. In this Schedule "standard powers in respect of persons liable to pay fines or other sums" means any power that a magistrates' court would have had if P had not been subject to a collection order but had been liable to pay the sum due.

Meaning of references to pending appeals

51. For the purposes of this Schedule the period during which an appeal under this Schedule is pending is to be treated as including the period within which the appeal may be brought (regardless of whether it is in fact brought).

Meaning of "10 working days"

52. In this Schedule "10 working days" means any period of 10 days not including—

(a) Saturday or Sunday,

(b) Christmas Day or Good Friday, or

(c) any day which is a bank holiday in England and Wales under the Banking and Financial Dealings Act 1971.

Meaning of "the magistrates' court"

53. In this Schedule "the magistrates' court", in relation to a collection order, means any magistrates' court acting in the local justice area in which the court which made the order was sitting.

---

1. The Fines Collection Regulations 2006 have been made, in this PART, post.

1–4377

Section 97(2)

SCHEDULE 6
DISCHARGE OF FINES BY UNPAID WORK

Introductory

1. (1) This Schedule applies if a person aged 18 or over ("P") is liable to pay a sum which is or is treated for the purposes of Part 3 of the 1980 Act as a sum adjudged to be paid by conviction of a magistrates' court.

(2) In this Schedule—

"the prescribed[1] hourly sum" means such sum as may be prescribed by regulations;

"regulations" means regulations made under this Schedule by the Lord Chancellor;

"the relevant court" means—

(a) the court imposing the liability to pay the relevant sum, or

(b) if that liability has previously been imposed, the magistrates' court responsible for enforcing payment of the relevant sum;

"the relevant sum" means the sum for which P is liable as mentioned in sub-paragraph (1), but excluding any pecuniary compensation, any pecuniary forfeiture or any sum due in respect of prosecution costs.

Cases where work order may be made

2. (1) The relevant court may, on the application of a fines officer or of its own motion, make an order under this Schedule (a "work order") where—

(a) it appears to the court that in view of P's financial circumstances all the following methods of enforcing payment of the relevant sum are likely to be impracticable or inappropriate—

(i) a warrant of distress under section 76 of the 1980 Act,

(ii) an application to the High Court or county court for enforcement under section 87 of the 1980 Act,

(iii) an order under section 88 of the 1980 Act,

(iv) an attachment of earnings order,

(v) an application for deductions to be made by virtue of section 24 of the Criminal Justice Act 1991 (recovery of fines etc by deductions from income support etc), and

(vi) a collection order under Schedule 5,

(*b*) it appears to the court that P is a suitable person to perform unpaid work under this Schedule, and
(*c*) P consents to the making of the order.

(2) A court which is considering the making of a work order may issue a summons requiring P to appear before the court.

(3) A magistrates' court which is considering the making of a work order may order P to give to the court, within a specified period, such a statement of his means as the court may require.

(4) Subsections (2) to (4) of section 84 of the 1980 Act (offences in respect of statement of means) apply to an order made under sub-paragraph (3) as they apply to an order made under subsection (1) of that section.

Provisions of order

3. (1) A work order is an order requiring P to perform unpaid work for a specified number of hours, in accordance with instructions to be given by the fines officer, in order to discharge by virtue of this Schedule his liability for the relevant sum.

(2) The order must also—

(*a*) state the amount of the relevant sum,
(*b*) specify a fines office to which the order is allocated, and
(*c*) specify a person ("the supervisor") who is to act as supervisor in relation to P.

(3) The specified number of hours is to be determined by dividing the relevant sum by the prescribed hourly sum and, where the result is not a whole number, adjusting the result upwards to the next whole number.

(4) A work order must specify a date ("the specified date") not later than which the required hours of unpaid work must be performed.

(5) In the following provisions of this Schedule "the fines officer", in relation to P, means any fines officer working at the fines office specified in the work order.

Effect of order on enforcement of payment

4. (1) Where a work order has been made in respect of the relevant sum, payment of that sum may not be enforced against P unless the order is revoked.

(2) On making a work order, the court must revoke any order relating to the enforcement of the payment of the relevant sum.

Appointment of, and duties of, supervisor

5. (1) A person may not be appointed as the supervisor without his consent.

(2) It is the duty of the supervisor—

(*a*) to monitor P's compliance with the requirements of the work order, and
(*b*) to provide the court with such information as the court may require relating to P's compliance with those requirements.

Obligations of person subject to work order, and effect of compliance

6. (1) Where a work order is in force, P must perform for the number of hours specified in the order such work, at such places and at such times as he may be instructed by the fines officer.

(2) The fines officer must ensure, as far as practicable, that any instructions given to P in pursuance of the work order are such as to avoid—

(*a*) any conflict with P's religious beliefs, and
(*b*) any interference with the times, if any, at which he normally works or attends school or any other educational establishment.

(3) If not later than the specified date P performs work in accordance with the instructions of the fines officer for the specified number of hours, his liability to pay the relevant sum is discharged.

Effect of payment

7. (1) Where a work order has been made in respect of any sum—

(*a*) on payment of the whole of the sum to any person authorised to receive it, the work order ceases to have effect, and
(*b*) on payment of part of the sum to any such person, the number of hours specified in the order is to be taken to be reduced by a proportion corresponding to that which the part paid bears to the whole of the relevant sum.

(2) In calculating any reduction required by sub-paragraph (1)(*b*), any fraction of an hour is to be disregarded.

Revocation or variation of order

8. (1) If, on the application of the fines officer, it appears to the relevant court that P is failing or has failed to comply with a work order without reasonable excuse, the court must revoke the order.

(2) If, on the application of the fines officer, it appears to the relevant court—

(*a*) that P has failed to comply with a work order but has a reasonable excuse for the failure, or
(*b*) that, because of a change in circumstances since the order was made, P is unlikely to be able to comply with a work order,

the court may revoke the order or postpone the specified date.

(3) The relevant court may of its own motion revoke a work order if it appears to the court that, because of a change in circumstances since the order was made, P is unlikely to be able to comply with the order.

(4) A work order may be revoked under any of sub-paragraphs (1) to (3), or varied under sub-paragraph (2), before the specified date (as well as on or after that date).

(5) Regulations[2] may provide for the fines officer to have the power to issue a summons for the purpose of ensuring that P attends the court to which an application has been made under sub-paragraph (1) or (2).

Allowing for work done

9. (1) If it appears to the court revoking a work order under paragraph 8(1), (2) or (3) that P has performed at least one hour of unpaid work in accordance with the instructions of the fines officer, the court must by order specify the number of hours of work that have been performed; and for this purpose any fraction of an hour is to be disregarded.

(2) Where the court has specified a number of hours under this paragraph, P's liability to pay the relevant sum is discharged to the extent of the prescribed hourly sum in respect of each hour.

Effect of revocation

10. (1) Where a work order is revoked under paragraph 8(1), (2) or (3), immediate payment of the relevant sum (subject to any reduction under paragraph 9(2)) may be enforced against P.

(2) Sub-paragraph (1) does not limit the court's power, on or after the revocation of the work order, to allow time for payment or to direct payment by instalments.

Order not directly enforceable

11. The obligations of P under a work order are not enforceable against him except by virtue of paragraph 10(1).

Evidence of supervisor

12. (1) This paragraph applies where—

(*a*) it falls to a court to determine whether P has performed unpaid work in accordance with a work order, and
(*b*) the court is satisfied—

  (i) that the supervisor is likely to be able to give evidence that may assist the court in determining that matter, and
  (ii) that the supervisor will not voluntarily attend as a witness.

(2) The court may issue a summons directed to that person requiring him to attend before the court at the time and place appointed in the summons to give evidence.

Provision of information

13. Regulations may—

(*a*) require a work order to contain prescribed information,
(*b*) require the court making a work order to give a copy of the order to such persons as may be prescribed, and
(*c*) require the court revoking or varying a work order to give notice of the revocation or variation to such persons as may be prescribed.

---

1. The sum of £6 has been prescribed by the Discharge of Fines by Unpaid Work (Prescribed Hourly Sum) Regulations 2004, SI 2004/2196.
2. The Discharge of Fines By Unpaid Work (Issue of Summons) Regulations 2004, SI 2004/2197 provide that a fines officer may issue a summons for this purpose.

1–4378   SCHEDULE 7
                              HIGH COURT WRITS OF EXECUTION

1–4379   SCHEDULE 8
                           MINOR AND CONSEQUENTIAL AMENDMENTS

This schedule makes numerous, minor and consequential amendments. Those which effect statutory provisions reproduced in this work will be shown in the statutes concerned when they take effect.

1–4380

Section 109(2)   SCHEDULE 9
                           TRANSITIONAL PROVISIONS AND SAVINGS

Interpretation

1. In this Schedule "the JPA 1997" means the Justices of the Peace Act 1997.

Orders contracting out the provision of officers and staff

2. Any order which, immediately before section 2 comes into force, was in force under section 27(3) of the Courts Act 1971, including, in particular, any order made under section 27(3) by virtue of—

(*a*) section 4(7) of the Taxes Management Act 1970, or
(*b*) section 82(3) of the Value Added Tax Act 1994,

shall have effect as if made under section 2 for the purpose of discharging the Lord Chancellor's general duty in relation to the courts (and may be amended or revoked accordingly).

Local justice areas

3. The first order under section 8 must specify as a local justice area each area which was a petty sessions area immediately before the time when that section comes into force.

Appointment and assignment of lay justices

4. A person who, immediately before section 10 comes into force, was a justice of the peace for a commission area under section 5 of the JPA 1997 shall be treated as having been—

(*a*) appointed under section 10(1) as a lay justice for England and Wales, and

(*b*) assigned under section 10(2)(*a*) to the local justice area which—

     (i) is specified as such in the first order under section 8, and

     (ii) immediately before section 10 comes into force, was the petty sessions area in and for which he ordinarily acted.

The supplemental list

5. (1) The existing supplemental list shall have effect as the supplemental list required to be kept by section 12; and any name which, immediately before that section comes into force, was included in that list under a provision listed in column 1 of the table shall be treated as having been entered in the list under the provision listed in column 2—

Provision of the JPA 1997	Provision of this Act
Section 7(2)	Section 13(1)
Section 7(4)	Section 13(5)
Section 7(6)	Section 13(4)

(2) "The existing supplemental list" means the supplemental list having effect under the JPA 1997 immediately before section 12 comes into force.

Keepers of the rolls

6. A person who, immediately before section 16 comes into force, was under section 25 of the JPA 1997 keeper of the rolls for a commission area shall be treated as having been appointed under section 16 as keeper of the rolls for each local justice area which—

(*a*) is specified as such in the first order under section 8, and

(*b*) immediately before section 16 comes into force, formed part of, or consisted of, that commission area.

Chairman and deputy chairmen of the bench

7. A person who, immediately before section 17 comes into force, was under section 22 of the JPA 1997 the chairman (or a deputy chairman) of the justices for a petty sessions area shall be treated as having been chosen under section 17 as the chairman (or a deputy chairman) of the lay justices assigned to the corresponding local justice area specified in the first order under section 8.

Senior District Judge (Chief Magistrate)

8. (1) The person who, immediately before section 23 comes into force, was under section 10A of the JPA 1997 the Senior District Judge (Chief Magistrate) shall be treated as having been designated as such under section 23(*a*).

(2) A person who, immediately before section 23 comes into force, was under section 10A of the JPA 1997 the deputy of the Senior District Judge (Chief Magistrate) shall be treated as having been designated as such under section 23(*b*).

Justices' clerks and assistant clerks

9. A person who—

(*a*) immediately before section 27 comes into force, was a justices' clerk for a petty sessions area (or areas), and

(*b*) is transferred to the Lord Chancellor's employment by virtue of paragraph 11 of Schedule 2,

shall be treated as having been designated as a justices' clerk under section 27(1)(*b*) and assigned under section 27(3)(*a*) to the corresponding local justice area (or areas) specified in the first order under section 8.

10. A person who—

(*a*) immediately before section 27 comes into force, was employed to assist a justices' clerk by acting as a clerk in court in proceedings before a justice or justices, and

(*b*) is transferred to the Lord Chancellor's employment by virtue of paragraph 11 of Schedule 2,

shall be treated as having been designated as an assistant to a justices' clerk under section 27(5)(*b*).

11. (1) Any regulations made under—

(*a*) section 42 of the Justices of the Peace Act 1949 (compensation in connection with Parts 2 and 3 of the 1949 Act), or

(*b*) paragraph 16 of Schedule 3 to the Justices of the Peace Act 1968 (compensation in connection with section 1 of the 1968 Act),

and in force immediately before paragraph 20 of Schedule 4 to the JPA 1997 is repealed by this Act shall continue to have effect and may be revoked or amended despite the repeal by the Justices of the Peace Act 1979 of the provisions under which they were made.

(2) The power to make amendments by virtue of sub-paragraph (1) of regulations falling within paragraph (*a*) of that sub-paragraph shall extend to making provision—

(*a*) for compensation to or in respect of persons falling within sub-paragraph (3) to be payable if such persons suffer loss of employment, or loss or diminution of emoluments, attributable to anything done under Part 2;

(*b*) for the determination by persons other than magistrates' courts committees of claims for compensation to be made;

(c) for the payment by the Lord Chancellor of compensation payable under the regulations.

(3) A person falls within this sub-paragraph if—

(a) on 2nd February 1995 he held the office of justices' clerk or was employed to assist a justices' clerk, and
(b) is transferred to the Lord Chancellor's employment by virtue of paragraph 11 of Schedule 2.

(4) A person who under regulations made by virtue of sub-paragraph (2)(a) is entitled to compensation in respect of anything done under Part 2 is not entitled to compensation in respect of that thing under a scheme made under section 1 of the Superannuation Act 1972 by virtue of section 2(2)(a) of that Act.

Family proceedings courts

12. Any justice of the peace who, immediately before section 49 comes into force, was qualified to sit as a member of a family proceedings court shall be treated as having been authorised to do so by the Lord Chancellor under section 67 of the 1980 Act (as substituted by section 49).

Youth courts

13. Any justice of the peace who, immediately before section 50 comes into force, was qualified to sit as a member of a youth court shall be treated as having been authorised to do so by the Lord Chancellor under section 45 of the 1933 Act (as substituted by section 50).

Inspectors of court administration

14. Any person who, immediately before section 58 comes into force, was an inspector of the magistrates' courts service under section 62 of the JPA 1997 shall be treated as having been appointed as an inspector of court administration under section 58(1).

Collection of fines and discharge of fines by unpaid work

15[1]. (1) This paragraph applies if section 97 and Schedule 5 are brought into force before section 8.
(2) Section 97 and Schedule 5 have effect in relation to the period ending with the date on which section 8 comes into force as if any reference to a local justice area were a reference to a petty sessions area.

1. In force on (or in some areas before) 5 April 2004: see Courts Act 2003 (Commencement No 2) Order SI 2004/174.

Register of judgments and orders

16. The register having effect under section 73 of the County Courts Act 1984 immediately before section 98 comes into force shall be treated as part of the register required to be kept under section 98.

SCHEDULE 10
REPEALS

1–4381   (The repeals contained in this schedule which effect statutory provisions reproduced in this work will be shown in the statutes concerned when they take effect.)

Criminal Justice Act 2003[1]
(2003 c 44)

PART 1[2]
AMENDMENTS OF POLICE AND CRIMINAL EVIDENCE ACT 1984

1–4382   1. Extension of powers to stop and search.   (1) In this Part, "the 1984 Act" means the Police and Criminal Evidence Act 1984 (c 60).
(2) *Adds offences under s 1 of the Criminal Damage Act 1971 to s 1(8) of PACE: see this PART, ante.*
[Criminal Justice Act 2003, s 1.

---

1. The Criminal Justice Act 2003 fundamentally reformed the law on criminal procedure, evidence and sentencing. The Act is in 14 Parts and also contains 38 Schedules. In summary:

PART 1 makes amendments to the Police and Criminal Evidence Act 1984.
PART 2 makes amendments to the Bail Act 1976.
PART 3 introduces "conditional cautions".
PART 4 amends the law on charging and introduces a new method of instituting criminal proceedings.
PART 5 amends the law on disclosure.
PART 6 is concerned with the allocation and sending of offences.
PART 7 introduces trials on indictment without a jury.
PART 8 is concerned with live links.
PART 9 introduces prosecution appeals.
PART 10 provides for retrial for certain serious offences.
PART 11 reforms the law on evidence, in particular as to bad character and hearsay. This is reproduced in PART II: EVIDENCE, post.
PART 12 substantially revises the law on sentencing. This is reproduced in Part III, Sentencing, post.
PART 13 contains miscellaneous provisions.
PART 14 deals with general matters.
The vast majority of the Act's provisions were left to be brought into force in accordance with Commencement Orders made under s 336. At the time of going to press the following Commencement Orders had been made: Criminal Justice Act 2003 (Commencement No 1) Order 2003, SI 2003/3282; Criminal Justice Act 2003 (Commencement No 2 and Saving Provisions) Order 2004, SI 2004/81; Criminal Justice Act 2003 (Commencement No 3 and Transitional Provisions) Order 2004, SI 2004/829; Criminal Justice Act 2003 (Commencement No 4 and Saving Provisions) Order 2004,

SI 2004/1629; Criminal Justice Act 2003 (Commencement No 5) Order 2004, SI 2004/1867; the Criminal Justice Act 2003 (Commencement No 6 and Transitional Provisions) Order 2004, SI 2004/3033; the Criminal Justice Act 2003 (Commencement No 7) Order, SI 2005/373; the Criminal Justice Act 2003 (Commencement No 8 and Transitional and Saving Provisions) Order 2005, SI 2005/950; the Criminal Justice Act 2003 (Commencement No 9) Order 2005, SI 2005/1267; and Criminal Justice Act 2003 (Commencement No 10 and Saving Provisions) Order 2005, SI 2005/1817; Criminal Justice Act 2003 (Commencement No 11) Order 2005, SI 2005/3055; Criminal Justice Act 2003 (Commencement No 12) Order 2006, SI 2006/751; Criminal Justice Act 2003 (Commencement No 13 and Transitional Provisions) Order 2006. SI 2006/1835; Criminal Justice Act 2003 (Commencement No 14 and Transitional Provision) Order 2006, SI 2006/3217; and Criminal Justice Act 2003 (Commencement No 15) Order 2006, SI 2006/3422. See also: the Criminal Justice Act 2003 (Commencement No 8 and Transitional and Saving Provisions) Order 2005 (Supplementary Provisions) Order 2005, SI 2005/2122.

The first order brought into force some of the provisions of Part 12 dealing with custodial sentences so as to enable intermittent custody orders to be made and administered. The second order brought into force most of the provisions of Part 1 (amendments to PACE), some of the provisions of Part 4 (Charging, etc), various code and rule-making provisions, and assorted other provisions. The third order brought into force further provisions of Part 1, most of the provisions of Part 2 relating to bail, and assorted other provisions. The fourth order brought into force most of the provisions of Part 3 relating to conditional cautions, and assorted other provisions. The fifth order brought into force the provisions of s 5 (drug-testing for under-18s) in the police areas of: Cleveland; Greater Manchester; Humberside; Merseyside; Metropolitan Police District; Nottinghamshire; and West Yorkshire (see, now, the eleventh order). The sixth order brought into force the 'bad character' provisions of Part 11. The seventh order brought into force miscellaneous, primarily sentencing provisions. The eighth order brought into force some of the disclosure provisions of Part 5; the hearsay provisions of Part 11; the dangerous offender sentencing provisions of Part 12, together with some of the related allocation and committal provisions; the suspended sentence, deferment of sentence, community order (prospectively, in the case of young offenders); release on licence, crediting for time on remand, and some general sentencing provisions of Part 12; and sundry other provisions. The ninth order brought into force provisions relating to the sending of persons to the Crown Court for trial and the committal of dangerous young offenders to the Crown Court for sentence. (The tenth order is concerned with Northern Ireland only.) The eleventh order brought into force drug-testing for under-eighteens to the extent it was not already in force. The twelfth order ss 328 and 332 so far as they relate to certain amendments and repeals concerning criminal record certificates. The thirteenth order brought into force s 33(1), so far as it inserts a new subs (5C) of s 5 of the Criminal Procedure and Investigations Act 1996, but with respect only to criminal investigations began on or after 4 April 2005 (and provisions in relation to jury tampering that are not reproduced in this work). The fourteenth order brought into force ss 14 and 16, which make amendments (with transitional provisions) to Part 1 of Sch 1 to the Bail Act 1976. The fifteenth order is concerned with Northern Ireland.

Many of the provisions that have been brought into force, especially those concerned with sentencing, are subject to transitional arrangements; and while most of the Act is now in force some key provisions – eg those dealing with "custody plus" – still await implementation.

2. Part 1 contains ss 1–12.

1-4383   2. Warrants to enter and search. *Inserts new s 16(2A) and 2(B) in PACE: see this* PART, *ante.*

1-4384   3. Arrestable offences. *Repealed.*

1-4385   4. Bail elsewhere than at police station. *Makes various amendments to s 30 of PACE and inserts new ss 30A–30D: see this* PART, *ante.*

1-4386   5. Drug testing for under-eighteens. (1) The 1984 Act is amended as follows.
(2) In section 38 (duties of custody officer after charge)—

(*a*) in subsection (1)—

  (i) for sub-paragraph (iiia) of paragraph (*a*) there is substituted—

    "(iiia)except in a case where (by virtue of subsection (9) of section 63B below) that section does not apply, the custody officer has reasonable grounds for believing that the detention of the person is necessary to enable a sample to be taken from him under that section;",

  (ii) in sub-paragraph (i) of paragraph (*b*), after "satisfied" there is inserted " (but, in the case of paragraph (*a*)(iiia) above, only if the arrested juvenile has attained the minimum age)",

(*b*) in subsection (6A), after the definition of "local authority accommodation" there is inserted—
""minimum age" means the age specified in section 63B(3) below;".

(3) In section 63B (testing for presence of Class A drugs)—

(*a*) repealed
(*b*) after subsection (5) there is inserted—

  "(5A) In the case of a person who has not attained the age of 17—

    (*a*) the making of the request under subsection (4) above;
    (*b*) the giving of the warning and (where applicable) the information under subsection (5) above; and
    (*c*) the taking of the sample,

may not take place except in the presence of an appropriate adult.",

(*c*) after subsection (6) there is inserted—

  "(6A) The Secretary of State may by order made by statutory instrument amend subsection (3) above by substituting for the age for the time being specified a different age specified in the order.

  (6B) A statutory instrument containing an order under subsection (6A) above shall not be made unless a draft of the instrument has been laid before, and approved by a resolution of, each House of Parliament.'',

(*d*) after subsection (8) there is inserted—

"(9) In relation to a person who has not attained the age of 18, this section applies only where—

(*a*) the relevant chief officer has been notified by the Secretary of State that arrangements for the taking of samples under this section from persons who have not attained the age of 18 have been made for the police area as a whole, or for the particular police station, in which the person is in police detention; and

(*b*) the notice has not been withdrawn.

(10) In this section—

"appropriate adult", in relation to a person who has not attained the age of 17, means—

(*a*) his parent or guardian or, if he is in the care of a local authority or voluntary organisation, a person representing that authority or organisation; or

(*b*) a social worker of a local authority social services department; or

(*c*) if no person falling within paragraph (*a*) or (*b*) is available, any responsible person aged 18 or over who is not a police officer or a person employed by the police;

"relevant chief officer" means—

(*a*) in relation to a police area, the chief officer of police of the police force for that police area; or

(*b*) in relation to a police station, the chief officer of police of the police force for the police area in which the police station is situated.''

[Criminal Justice Act 2003, s 5 as amended by the Drugs Act 2005, Sch 1.]

1–4387   6. Use of telephones for review of police detention.   *Substitutes new s 40A(1) and (2) of PACE: see this PART, ante.*

1–4388   7. Limits on period of detention without charge.   *Substitutes new s 42(1)(b) of PACE: see this PART, ante.*

1–4389   8. Property of detained persons.   *Amends s 54 of PACE: see this PART, ante.*

1–4390   9. Taking fingerprints without consent.   *Amends s 61 of PACE: see this PART, ante.*

1–4391   10. Taking non-intimate samples without consent.   (1) Section 63 of the 1984 Act (other samples) is amended as follows.

(2) After subsection (2) (consent to be given in writing) there is inserted—

"(2A) A non-intimate sample may be taken from a person without the appropriate consent if two conditions are satisfied.

(2B) The first is that the person is in police detention in consequence of his arrest for a recordable offence.

(2C) The second is that—

(*a*) he has not had a non-intimate sample of the same type and from the same part of the body taken in the course of the investigation of the offence by the police, or

(*b*) he has had such a sample taken but it proved insufficient.''

(3) In subsection (3)(*a*) (taking of samples without appropriate consent) the words "is in police detention or" are omitted.

(4) In subsection (3A) (taking of samples without appropriate consent after charge) for '' (whether or not he falls within subsection (3)(*a*) above)'' there is substituted '' (whether or not he is in police detention or held in custody by the police on the authority of a court)''.

(5) In subsection (8A) (reasons for taking of samples without consent) for "subsection (3A)'' there is substituted "subsection (2A), (3A)''.

[Criminal Justice Act 2003, s 10.]

1–4392   11. Codes of practice.   *Substitutes new s 67 and amends s 113 of PACE: see this PART, ante.*

1–4393   12. Amendments related to Part 1.   Schedule 1 (which makes amendments related to the provisions of this Part) has effect.

[Criminal Justice Act 2003, s 12.]

PART 2[1]
BAIL

1–4394   13. Grant and conditions of bail.   *Amends ss 3(6), 3 A(5), and paras 8(3) of Part 1 and 5(4) of Part 2 of Sch 1 to the Bail Act 1976: see this PART, ante.*

---

1. Part 2 contains ss 13–21.

1–4395   14. Offences committed on bail[1]. *This section substituted a new para 2A of, and inserted a new para 9AA in, Part 1 of Sch 1 to the Bail Act 1976.*

1–4396   15. Absconding by persons released on bail[1]. *This section substituted a new para 6 of, and inserted a new para 9AB in, Part 1 of Sch 1 to the Bail Act 1976.*

1–4397   16. Appeal to Crown Court. (1) This section applies where a magistrates' court grants bail to a person ("the person concerned") on adjourning a case under—

- (a)   section 10 of the Magistrates' Courts Act 1980 (c 43) (adjournment of trial),
- (b)   section 17C of that Act (intention as to plea: adjournment),
- (c)   section 18 of that Act (initial procedure on information against adult for offence triable either way),
- (d)   section 24C of that Act (intention as to plea by child or young person: adjournment),
- (e)   section 52(5) of the Crime and Disorder Act 1998 (c 37) (adjournment of proceedings under section 51 etc), or
- (f)   section 11 of the Powers of Criminal Courts (Sentencing) Act 2000 (c 6) (remand for medical examination).

(2) Subject to the following provisions of this section, the person concerned may appeal to the Crown Court against any condition of bail falling within subsection (3).

(3) A condition of bail falls within this subsection if it is a requirement—

- (a)   that the person concerned resides away from a particular place or area,
- (b)   that the person concerned resides at a particular place other than a bail hostel,
- (c)   for the provision of a surety or sureties or the giving of a security,
- (d)   that the person concerned remains indoors between certain hours,
- (e)   imposed under section 3(6ZAA) of the 1976 Act (requirements with respect to electronic monitoring), or
- (f)   that the person concerned makes no contact with another person.

(4) An appeal under this section may not be brought unless subsection (5) or (6) applies.

(5) This subsection applies if an application to the magistrates' court under section 3(8)(a) of the 1976 Act (application by or on behalf of person granted bail) was made and determined before the appeal was brought.

(6) This subsection applies if an application to the magistrates' court—

- (a)   under section 3(8)(b) of the 1976 Act (application by constable or prosecutor), or
- (b)   under section 5B(1) of that Act (application by prosecutor),

was made and determined before the appeal was brought.

(7) On an appeal under this section the Crown Court may vary the conditions of bail.

(8) Where the Crown Court determines an appeal under this section, the person concerned may not bring any further appeal under this section in respect of the conditions of bail unless an application or a further application to the magistrates' court under section 3(8)(a) of the 1976 Act is made and determined after the appeal.

[Criminal Justice Act 2003, s 16.]

1–4398   17. Appeals to High Court. (1) In section 22(1) of the Criminal Justice Act 1967 (c 80) (extension of power of High Court to grant, or vary conditions of, bail)—

- (a)   after "Where" there is inserted " (a)", and
- (b)   after "proceedings,", in the second place where it occurs, there is inserted

"and

- (b)   it does so where an application to the court to state a case for the opinion of the High Court is made,".

(2) The inherent power of the High Court to entertain an application in relation to bail where a magistrates' court—

- (a)   has granted or withheld bail, or
- (b)   has varied the conditions of bail,

is abolished.

(3) The inherent power of the High Court to entertain an application in relation to bail where the Crown Court has determined—

- (a)   an application under section 3(8) of the 1976 Act, or
- (b)   an application under section 81(1)(a), (b), (c) or (g) of the Supreme Court Act 1981 (c 54),

is abolished.

(4) The High Court is to have no power to entertain an application in relation to bail where the Crown Court has determined an appeal under section 16 of this Act.

(5) The High Court is to have no power to entertain an application in relation to bail where the Crown Court has granted or withheld bail under section 88 or 89 of this Act.

(6) Nothing in this section affects—

- (a)   any other power of the High Court to grant or withhold bail or to vary the conditions of bail, or (*b*) any right of a person to apply for a writ of habeas corpus or any other prerogative remedy.

(7) Any reference in this section to an application in relation to bail is to be read as including—

(*a*) an application for bail to be granted,
(*b*) an application for bail to be withheld,
(*c*) an application for the conditions of bail to be varied.

(8) Any reference in this section to the withholding of bail is to be read as including a reference to the revocation of bail.

[Criminal Justice Act 2003, s 17.]

1–4399 18. Appeal by prosecution.   (1) Section 1 of the Bail (Amendment) Act 1993 (c 26) (prosecution right of appeal) is amended as follows.

(2) For subsection (1) (prosecution may appeal to Crown Court judge against bail in case of offence punishable by imprisonment for five years or more etc) there is substituted—

"(1) Where a magistrates' court grants bail to a person who is charged with, or convicted of, an offence punishable by imprisonment, the prosecution may appeal to a judge of the Crown Court against the granting of bail."

(3) In subsection (10)(*a*) for "punishable by a term of imprisonment" there is substituted "punishable by imprisonment".

[Criminal Justice Act 2003, s 18.]

1–4400 19. Drug users: restriction on bail.   *Inserts new ss (6C)–(6F) in s 3 of, and makes further amendments to Part 1 of Sch 1 to, the Bail Act 1976: see this PART, ante.*

1–4401 20. Supplementary amendments to the Bail Act 1976.   *Makes supplementary amendments to Part 1 of Sch 1 to the Bail Act 1976: see this PART, ante.*

1–4402 21. Interpretation of Part 2.   In this Part—

"bail" means bail in criminal proceedings (within the meaning of the 1976 Act),
"bail hostel" has the meaning given by section 2(2) of the 1976 Act,
"the 1976 Act" means the Bail Act 1976 (c 63),
"vary" has the same meaning as in the 1976 Act.

[Criminal Justice Act 2003, s 21.]

PART 3[1]
CONDITIONAL CAUTIONS

1–4403 22. Conditional cautions.   (1) An authorised person may give a conditional caution to a person aged 18 or over ("the offender") if each of the five requirements in section 23 is satisfied.

(2) In this Part "conditional caution" means a caution which is given in respect of an offence committed by the offender and which has conditions attached to it with which the offender must comply.

(3) The conditions which may be attached to such a caution are those which have either or both of the following objects—

(*a*) facilitating the rehabilitation of the offender,
(*b*) ensuring that he makes reparation for the offence.

(4) In this Part "authorised person" means—

(*a*) a constable,
(*b*) an investigating officer, or
(*c*) a person authorised by a relevant prosecutor for the purposes of this section.

[Criminal Justice Act 2003, s 22.]

––––––––––––––––––––––
1. Part 3 contains ss 22–27.

1–4404 23. The five requirements.   (1) The first requirement is that the authorised person has evidence that the offender has committed an offence.

(2) The second requirement is that a relevant prosecutor decides—

(*a*) that there is sufficient evidence to charge the offender with the offence, and
(*b*) that a conditional caution should be given to the offender in respect of the offence.

(3) The third requirement is that the offender admits to the authorised person that he committed the offence.

(4) The fourth requirement is that the authorised person explains the effect of the conditional caution to the offender and warns him that failure to comply with any of the conditions attached to the caution may result in his being prosecuted for the offence.

(5) The fifth requirement is that the offender signs a document which contains—

(*a*) details of the offence,
(*b*) an admission by him that he committed the offence,
(*c*) his consent to being given the conditional caution, and

    (*d*)   the conditions attached to the caution.
[Criminal Justice Act 2003, s 23.]

1-4404A   23A.   Financial penalties.   (1) A condition that the offender pay a financial penalty (a "financial penalty condition") may not be attached to a conditional caution given in respect of an offence unless the offence is one that is prescribed, or of a description prescribed, in an order made by the Secretary of State.

    (2) An order under subsection (1) must prescribe, in respect of each offence or description of offence in the order, the maximum amount of the penalty that may be specified under subsection (5)(*a*).

    (3) The amount that may be prescribed in respect of any offence must not exceed—

    (*a*)   one quarter of the amount of the maximum fine for which a person is liable on summary conviction of the offence, or

    (*b*)   £250,

whichever is the lower.

    (4) The Secretary of State may by order amend subsection (3) by—

    (*a*)   substituting a different fraction in paragraph (*a*);
    (*b*)   substituting a different figure in paragraph (*b*).

    (5) Where a financial penalty condition is attached to a conditional caution, a relevant prosecutor must also specify—

    (*a*)   the amount of the penalty,
    (*b*)   the designated officer for a local justice area to whom the penalty is to be paid, and
    (*c*)   the address of that officer.

    (6) To comply with the condition, the offender must pay the penalty to the specified officer.

    (7) The offender may pay a sum in respect of the penalty by pre-paying and posting a letter containing that sum (in cash or otherwise) to the address specified under subsection (5)(*c*).

    (8) If a person—

    (*a*)   claims to have made payment by the method described in subsection (7), and
    (*b*)   shows that his letter was posted,

then, unless the contrary is proved, payment is to be regarded as made at the time at which the letter would be delivered in the ordinary course of post.

    (9) Subsection (7) is not to be read as preventing payment by other means.*
[Criminal Justice Act 2003, s 23A as inserted by the Police and Justice Act 2006, s 17.]

---

    *Inserted by the Police and Justice Act 2006, s 17 from a date to be appointed.

1-4405   24.   Failure to comply with conditions.   (1) If the offender fails, without reasonable excuse, to comply with any of the conditions attached to the conditional caution, criminal proceedings may be instituted against the person for the offence in question.

    (2) The document mentioned in section 23(5) is to be admissible in such proceedings.

    (3) Where such proceedings are instituted, the conditional caution is to cease to have effect.
[Criminal Justice Act 2003, s 24.]

1-4405A   24A.   Arrest for failure to comply.   (1) If a constable has reasonable grounds for believing that the offender has failed, without reasonable excuse, to comply with any of the conditions attached to the conditional caution, he may arrest him without warrant.

    (2) A person arrested under this section must be—

    (*a*)   charged with the offence in question,
    (*b*)   released without charge and on bail to enable a decision to be made as to whether he should be charged with the offence, or
    (*c*)   released without charge and without bail (with or without any variation in the conditions attached to the caution).

    (3) Subsection (2) also applies in the case of—

    (*a*)   a person who, having been released on bail under subsection (2)(*b*), returns to a police station to answer bail or is otherwise in police detention at a police station;
    (*b*)   a person who, having been released on bail under section 30A of the 1984 Act (bail elsewhere than at police station) as applied by section 24B below, attends at a police station to answer bail or is otherwise in police detention at a police station;
    (*c*)   a person who is arrested under section 30D or 46A of the 1984 Act (power of arrest for failure to answer to police bail) as applied by section 24B below.

    (4) Where a person is released under subsection (2)(*b*), the custody officer must inform him that he is being released to enable a decision to be made as to whether he should be charged with the offence in question.

    (5) A person arrested under this section, or any other person in whose case subsection (2) applies, may be kept in police detention—

    (*a*)   to enable him to be dealt with in accordance with that subsection, or (*b*) where applicable, to enable the power under section 37D(1) of the 1984 Act (power of custody officer to appoint a different or additional time for answering to police bail), as applied by section 24B below, to be exercised.

If the person is not in a fit state to enable him to be so dealt with, or to enable that power to be exercised, he may be kept in police detention until he is.

(6) The power under subsection (5)(a) includes power to keep the person in police detention if it is necessary to do so for the purpose of investigating whether he has failed, without reasonable excuse, to comply with any of the conditions attached to the conditional caution.

(7) Subsection (2) must be complied with as soon as practicable after the person arrested arrives at the police station or, in the case of a person arrested at the police station, as soon as practicable after the arrest.

(8) Subsection (2) does not require a person who—

(*a*) falls within subsection (3)(*a*) or (*b*), and
(*b*) is in police detention in relation to a matter other than the conditional caution,

to be released if he is liable to be kept in detention in relation to that other matter.

(9) In this Part—

"the 1984 Act" means the Police and Criminal Evidence Act 1984;
"police detention" has the same meaning as in the 1984 Act (see section 118(2) of that Act).★
[Criminal Justice Act 2003, s 24A as inserted by the Police and Justice Act 2006, s 18.]

★Inserted by the Police and Justice Act 2006, s 18 from a date to be appointed.

1–4405B   24B. Application of PACE provisions.   (1) In the case of a person arrested under section 24A, the provisions of the 1984 Act specified in subsection (2) apply, with the modifications specified in subsection (3) and with such further modifications as are necessary, as they apply in the case of a person arrested for an offence.

(2) The provisions are—

(*a*) section 30 (arrest elsewhere than at police station);
(*b*) sections 30A to 30D (bail elsewhere than at police station);
(*c*) section 31 (arrest for further offence);
(*d*) section 34(1) to (5) (limitations on police detention);
(*e*) section 36 (custody officers at police stations);
(*f*) section 37(4) to (6) (record of grounds for detention);
(*g*) section 38 (duties of custody officer after charge);
(*h*) section 39 (responsibilities in relation to persons detained);
(*i*) section 55A (x-rays and ultrasound scans).

(3) The modifications are—

(*a*) in section 30CA(5)(*a*), for the reference to being involved in the investigation of the offence mentioned in that provision substitute a reference to being involved—

(i) in the investigation of the offence in respect of which the person was given the conditional caution, or
(ii) in investigating whether the person has failed, without reasonable excuse, to comply with any of the conditions attached to the conditional caution;

(*b*) in section 36(5) and (7), for the references to being involved in the investigation of an offence for which the person is in police detention substitute references to being involved—

(i) in the investigation of the offence in respect of which the person was given the conditional caution, or
(ii) in investigating whether the person has failed, without reasonable excuse, to comply with any of the conditions attached to the conditional caution;

(*c*) in section 38(1)(*a*)(iii) and (iv), for "arrested for" substitute "charged with";
(*d*) in section 39(2) and (3), for the references to an offence substitute references to a failure to comply with conditions attached to the conditional caution.

(4) Section 40 of the 1984 Act (review of police detention) applies to a person in police detention by virtue of section 24A above as it applies to a person in police detention in connection with the investigation of an offence, but with the following modifications—

(*a*) omit subsections (8) and (8A);
(*b*) in subsection (9), for the reference to section 37(9) or 37D(5) substitute a reference to the second sentence of section 24A(5) above.

(5) The following provisions of the 1984 Act apply to a person released on bail under section 24A(2)(b) above as they apply to a person released on bail under section 37 of that Act—

(*a*) section 37D(1) to (3) (power of custody officer to appoint a different or additional time for answering to police bail);
(*b*) section 46A (power of arrest for failure to answer to police bail);
(*c*) section 47 (bail after arrest).

(6) Section 54 of the 1984 Act (searches of detained persons) applies in the case of a person who

falls within subsection (3) of section 24A above and is detained in a police station under that section as it applies in the case of a person who falls within section 34(7) of that Act and is detained at a police station under section 37.

(7) Section 54A of the 1984 Act (searches and examination to ascertain identity) applies with the following modifications in the case of a person who is detained in a police station under section 24A above—

    (*a*)   in subsections (1)(*a*) and (12), after "as a person involved in the commission of an offence" insert "or as having failed to comply with any of the conditions attached to his conditional caution";

    (*b*)   in subsection (9)(*a*), after "the investigation of an offence" insert ", the investigation of whether the person in question has failed to comply with any of the conditions attached to his conditional caution".★

[Criminal Justice Act 2003, s 24B as inserted by the Police and Justice Act 2006, s 18.]

★Inserted by the Police and Justice Act 2006, s 18 from a date to be appointed.

1–4406   25. Code of practice. *The Secretary of State to prepare a Code of Practice in relation to conditional cautions*[1].

---

1. The Criminal Justice Act 2003 (Conditional Cautions: Code of Practice) Order 2004, SI 2004/1683 has been made which came into force on 3 July 2004 and which brought into force on the same day the code of practice entitled "Conditional Cautions" laid before Parliament on 19 April 2004.

1–4407   26. Assistance of National Probation Service. (1) Section 1 of the Criminal Justice and Court Services Act 2000 (c 43) (purposes of Chapter 1) is amended as follows.

(2) After subsection (1) there is inserted—

"(1A) This Chapter also has effect for the purposes of providing for—

    (*a*)   authorised persons to be given assistance in determining whether conditional cautions should be given and which conditions to attach to conditional cautions, and

    (*b*)   the supervision and rehabilitation of persons to whom conditional cautions are given."

(3) After subsection (3) there is inserted—

"(4) In this section "authorised person" and "conditional caution" have the same meaning as in Part 3 of the Criminal Justice Act 2003."

[Criminal Justice Act 2003, s 26.]

1–4408   27. Interpretation of Part 3. In this Part—

"authorised person" has the meaning given by section 22(4),

"conditional caution" has the meaning given by section 22(2),

"investigating officer" means a person designated as an investigating officer under section 38 of the Police Reform Act 2002 (c 30),

"the offender" has the meaning given by section 22(1),

"relevant prosecutor"[1] means—

    (*a*)   the Attorney General,

    (*b*)   the Director of the Serious Fraud Office,

    (*c*)   the Director of Public Prosecutions,

    (*d*)   a Secretary of State,

    (*e*)   the Commissioners of Inland Revenue,

    (*f*)   the Commissioners of Customs and Excise, or

    (*g*)   a person who is specified in an order made by the Secretary of State as being a relevant prosecutor for the purposes of this Part.

[Criminal Justice Act 2003, s 27.]

---

1. At the date of going to press only (*a*) and (*c*) below had been appointed (see the Criminal Justice Act 2003 (Commencement No 4 and Saving Provisions) Order 2004, SI 2004/1629); and some amendments and repeals have been made by the Commissioners for Revenue and Customs Act 2005.

PART 4[1]
CHARGING ETC

1–4409   28. Charging or release of persons in police detention. Schedule 2 (which makes provision in relation to the charging or release of persons in police detention) shall have effect.

[Criminal Justice Act 2003, s 28.]

---

1. Part 3 contains ss 28–31.

1–4410   29. New method of instituting proceedings[1]. (1) A public prosecutor may institute criminal proceedings against a person by issuing a document (a "written charge") which charges the person with an offence.

(2) Where a public prosecutor issues a written charge, it must at the same time issue a document

(a "requisition") which requires the person to appear before a magistrates' court to answer the written charge.

(3) The written charge and requisition must be served on the person concerned, and a copy of both must be served on the court named in the requisition.

(4) In consequence of subsections (1) to (3), a public prosecutor is not to have the power to lay an information for the purpose of obtaining the issue of a summons under section 1 of the Magistrates' Courts Act 1980 (c 43).

(5) In this section "public prosecutor" means—

(a)　a police force or a person authorised by a police force to institute criminal proceedings,

(b)　the Director of the Serious Fraud Office or a person authorised by him to institute criminal proceedings,

(c)　the Director of Public Prosecutions or a person authorised by him to institute criminal proceedings,

(ca)　the Director of Revenue and Customs Prosecutions or a person authorised by him to institute criminal proceedings,

(cb)　the Director General of the Serious Organised Crime Agency or a person authorised by him to institute criminal proceedings,

(d)　the Attorney General or a person authorised by him to institute criminal proceedings,

(e)　a Secretary of State or a person authorised by a Secretary of State to institute criminal proceedings,

(f)　the Commissioners of Inland Revenue or a person authorised by them to institute criminal proceedings,

(g)　the Commissioners of Customs and Excise or a person authorised by them to institute criminal proceedings, or

(h)　a person specified in an order made by the Secretary of State for the purposes of this section or a person authorised by such a person to institute criminal proceedings.

(6) In subsection (5) "police force" has the meaning given by section 3(3) of the Prosecution of Offences Act 1985 (c 23).

[Criminal Justice Act 2003, s 29 as amended by the Commissioners for Revenue and Customs Act 2005, Sch 4 and the Serious Organised Crime and Police Act 2005, Sch 4.]

---

1. At the date of going to press s 29 was not in force.

1–4411　30. Further provision about new method[1]. (1) Criminal Procedure Rules may make—

(a)　provision as to the form, content, recording, authentication and service of written charges or requisitions, and

(b)　such other provision in relation to written charges or requisitions as appears to the Criminal Procedure Rule Committee to be necessary or expedient.

(2) Without limiting subsection (1), the provision which may be made by virtue of that subsection includes provision—

(a)　which applies (with or without modifications), or which disapplies, the provision of any enactment relating to the service of documents,

(b)　for or in connection with the issue of further requisitions.

(3) *Repealed.*

(4) Nothing in section 29 affects—

(a)　the power of a public prosecutor to lay an information for the purpose of obtaining the issue of a warrant under section 1 of the Magistrates' Courts Act 1980 (c 43),

(b)　the power of a person who is not a public prosecutor to lay an information for the purpose of obtaining the issue of a summons or warrant under section 1 of that Act, or

(c)　any power to charge a person with an offence whilst he is in custody.

(5) Except where the context otherwise requires, in any enactment contained in an Act passed before this Act—

(a)　any reference (however expressed) which is or includes a reference to an information within the meaning of section 1 of the Magistrates' Courts Act 1980 (c 43) (or to the laying of such an information) is to be read as including a reference to a written charge (or to the issue of a written charge),

(b)　any reference (however expressed) which is or includes a reference to a summons under section 1 of the Magistrates' Courts Act 1980 (or to a justice of the peace issuing such a summons) is to be read as including a reference to a requisition (or to a public prosecutor issuing a requisition).

(6) Subsection (5) does not apply to section 1 of the Magistrates' Courts Act 1980.

(7) The reference in subsection (5) to an enactment contained in an Act passed before this Act includes a reference to an enactment contained in that Act as a result of an amendment to that Act made by this Act or by any other Act passed in the same Session as this Act.

(8) In this section "public prosecutor", "requisition" and "written charge" have the same meaning as in section 29.

[Criminal Justice Act 2003, s 30 as amended by SI 2004/2035.]

1. At the date of going to press s 30 was not in force.

1–4412 31. Removal of requirement to substantiate information on oath. *Amends ss 1 and 13 of the Magistrates' Courts Act 1980 by removing the requirement to substantiate an information on oath before the issue of, respectively, a warrant in the first instance and a warrant for failing to appear.*

PART 5[1]
DISCLOSURE

1–4413 32. Initial duty of disclosure by prosecutor. In the Criminal Procedure and Investigations Act 1996 (c 25) (in this Part referred to as "the 1996 Act"), in subsection (1)(*a*) of section 3 (primary disclosure by prosecutor)—

   (*a*) for "in the prosecutor's opinion might undermine" there is substituted "might reasonably be considered capable of undermining";
   (*b*) after "against the accused" there is inserted "or of assisting the case for the accused".
[Criminal Justice Act 2003, s 32.]

1. Part 5 contains ss 32–40. The provisions of this Part are in force save as to the insertion of new s 11(4), (7) and (11) of the Criminal Procedure and Investigations Act 1996, but are of no effect in relation to alleged offences into which a criminal investigation within the meaning of s 1(4) of the 1996 Act had begun before 4 April, 2005: see the Criminal Justice Act 2003 (Commencement No 8 and Transitional and Saving Provisions) Order 2005, SI 2005/950.

1–4414 33. Defence disclosure. (1) In section 5 of the 1996 Act (compulsory disclosure by accused), after subsection (5) there is inserted—

"(5A) Where there are other accused in the proceedings and the court so orders, the accused must also give a defence statement to each other accused specified by the court.
   (5B) The court may make an order under subsection (5A) either of its own motion or on the application of any party.
   (5C) A defence statement that has to be given to the court and the prosecutor (under subsection (5)) must be given during the period which, by virtue of section 12, is the relevant period for this section.
   (5D) A defence statement that has to be given to a co-accused (under subsection (5A)) must be given within such period as the court may specify."
   (2) After section 6 of that Act there is inserted—

"6A. Contents of defence statement. (1) For the purposes of this Part a defence statement is a written statement—

   (*a*) setting out the nature of the accused's defence, including any particular defences on which he intends to rely,
   (*b*) indicating the matters of fact on which he takes issue with the prosecution,
   (*c*) setting out, in the case of each such matter, why he takes issue with the prosecution, and
   (*d*) indicating any point of law (including any point as to the admissibility of evidence or an abuse of process) which he wishes to take, and any authority on which he intends to rely for that purpose.

   (2) A defence statement that discloses an alibi must give particulars of it, including—

   (*a*) the name, address and date of birth of any witness the accused believes is able to give evidence in support of the alibi, or as many of those details as are known to the accused when the statement is given;
   (*b*) any information in the accused's possession which might be of material assistance in identifying or finding any such witness in whose case any of the details mentioned in paragraph (*a*) are not known to the accused when the statement is given.

   (3) For the purposes of this section evidence in support of an alibi is evidence tending to show that by reason of the presence of the accused at a particular place or in a particular area at a particular time he was not, or was unlikely to have been, at the place where the offence is alleged to have been committed at the time of its alleged commission.
   (4) The Secretary of State may by regulations make provision as to the details of the matters that, by virtue of subsection (1), are to be included in defence statements."
   (3) After section 6A of that Act (inserted by subsection (2) above) there is inserted—

"6B. Updated disclosure by accused. (1) Where the accused has, before the beginning of the relevant period for this section, given a defence statement under section 5 or 6, he must during that period give to the court and the prosecutor either—

   (*a*) a defence statement under this section (an "updated defence statement"), or
   (*b*) a statement of the kind mentioned in subsection (4).

   (2) The relevant period for this section is determined under section 12.
   (3) An updated defence statement must comply with the requirements imposed by or under section 6A by reference to the state of affairs at the time when the statement is given.
   (4) Instead of an updated defence statement, the accused may give a written statement stating that he has no changes to make to the defence statement which was given under section 5 or 6.

(5) Where there are other accused in the proceedings and the court so orders, the accused must also give either an updated defence statement or a statement of the kind mentioned in subsection (4), within such period as may be specified by the court, to each other accused so specified.

(6) The court may make an order under subsection (5) either of its own motion or on the application of any party."

[Criminal Justice Act 2003, s 33.]

1–4415   34. Notification of intention to call defence witnesses.   After section 6B of the 1996 Act (inserted by section 33 above) there is inserted—

"6C. Notification of intention to call defence witnesses.   (1) The accused must give to the court and the prosecutor a notice indicating whether he intends to call any persons (other than himself) as witnesses at his trial and, if so—

(a)   giving the name, address and date of birth of each such proposed witness, or as many of those details as are known to the accused when the notice is given;

(b)   providing any information in the accused's possession which might be of material assistance in identifying or finding any such proposed witness in whose case any of the details mentioned in paragraph (a) are not known to the accused when the notice is given.

(2) Details do not have to be given under this section to the extent that they have already been given under section 6A(2).

(3) The accused must give a notice under this section during the period which, by virtue of section 12, is the relevant period for this section.

(4) If, following the giving of a notice under this section, the accused—

(a)   decides to call a person (other than himself) who is not included in the notice as a proposed witness, or decides not to call a person who is so included, or

(b)   discovers any information which, under subsection (1), he would have had to include in the notice if he had been aware of it when giving the notice,

he must give an appropriately amended notice to the court and the prosecutor."

[Criminal Justice Act 2003, s 34.]

1–4416   35. Notification of names of experts instructed by defendant.   After section 6C of the 1996 Act (inserted by section 34 above) there is inserted—

"6D. Notification of names of experts instructed by accused.   (1) If the accused instructs a person with a view to his providing any expert opinion for possible use as evidence at the trial of the accused, he must give to the court and the prosecutor a notice specifying the person's name and address.

(2) A notice does not have to be given under this section specifying the name and address of a person whose name and address have already been given under section 6C

(3) A notice under this section must be given during the period which, by virtue of section 12, is the relevant period for this section."

[Criminal Justice Act 2003, s 35.]

1–4417   36. Further provisions about defence disclosure.   After section 6D of the 1996 Act (inserted by section 35 above) there is inserted—

"6E. Disclosure by accused: further provisions.   (1) Where an accused's solicitor purports to give on behalf of the accused—

(a)   a defence statement under section 5, 6 or 6B, or

(b)   a statement of the kind mentioned in section 6B(4),

the statement shall, unless the contrary is proved, be deemed to be given with the authority of the accused.

(2) If it appears to the judge at a pre-trial hearing that an accused has failed to comply fully with section 5, 6B or 6C, so that there is a possibility of comment being made or inferences drawn under section 11(5), he shall warn the accused accordingly.

(3) In subsection (2) "pre-trial hearing" has the same meaning as in Part 4 (see section 39).

(4) The judge in a trial before a judge and jury—

(a)   may direct that the jury be given a copy of any defence statement, and

(b)   if he does so, may direct that it be edited so as not to include references to matters evidence of which would be inadmissible.

(5) A direction under subsection (4)—

(a)   may be made either of the judge's own motion or on the application of any party;

(b)   may be made only if the judge is of the opinion that seeing a copy of the defence statement would help the jury to understand the case or to resolve any issue in the case.

(6) The reference in subsection (4) to a defence statement is a reference—

(a)   where the accused has given only an initial defence statement (that is, a defence statement given under section 5 or 6), to that statement;

(b)   where he has given both an initial defence statement and an updated defence statement (that is, a defence statement given under section 6B), to the updated defence statement;

(c)   where he has given both an initial defence statement and a statement of the kind mentioned in section 6B(4), to the initial defence statement."

[Criminal Justice Act 2003, s 36.]

1-4418   37. Continuing duty of disclosure by prosecutor.   Before section 8 of the 1996 Act there is inserted—

"7A.   Continuing duty of prosecutor to disclose.   (1) This section applies at all times—

(a)   after the prosecutor has complied with section 3 or purported to comply with it, and

(b)   before the accused is acquitted or convicted or the prosecutor decides not to proceed with the case concerned.

(2)   The prosecutor must keep under review the question whether at any given time (and, in particular, following the giving of a defence statement) there is prosecution material which—

(a)   might reasonably be considered capable of undermining the case for the prosecution against the accused or of assisting the case for the accused, and

(b)   has not been disclosed to the accused.

(3)   If at any time there is any such material as is mentioned in subsection (2) the prosecutor must disclose it to the accused as soon as is reasonably practicable (or within the period mentioned in subsection (5)(a), where that applies).

(4)   In applying subsection (2) by reference to any given time the state of affairs at that time (including the case for the prosecution as it stands at that time) must be taken into account.

(5)   Where the accused gives a defence statement under section 5, 6 or 6B—

(a)   if as a result of that statement the prosecutor is required by this section to make any disclosure, or further disclosure, he must do so during the period which, by virtue of section 12, is the relevant period for this section;

(b)   if the prosecutor considers that he is not so required, he must during that period give to the accused a written statement to that effect.

(6)   For the purposes of this section prosecution material is material—

(a)   which is in the prosecutor's possession and came into his possession in connection with the case for the prosecution against the accused, or

(b)   which, in pursuance of a code operative under Part 2, he has inspected in connection with the case for the prosecution against the accused.

(7)   Subsections (3) to (5) of section 3 (method by which prosecutor discloses) apply for the purposes of this section as they apply for the purposes of that.

(8)   Material must not be disclosed under this section to the extent that the court, on an application by the prosecutor, concludes it is not in the public interest to disclose it and orders accordingly.

(9)   Material must not be disclosed under this section to the extent that it is material the disclosure of which is prohibited by section 17 of the Regulation of Investigatory Powers Act 2000 (c 23)."

[Criminal Justice Act 2003, s 37.]

1-4419   38. Application by defence for disclosure.   In section 8 of the 1996 Act (application by accused for disclosure), for subsections (1) and (2) there is substituted—

"(1)   This section applies where the accused has given a defence statement under section 5, 6 or 6B and the prosecutor has complied with section 7A(5) or has purported to comply with it or has failed to comply with it.

(2)   If the accused has at any time reasonable cause to believe that there is prosecution material which is required by section 7A to be disclosed to him and has not been, he may apply to the court for an order requiring the prosecutor to disclose it to him."

[Criminal Justice Act 2003, s 38.]

1-4420   39. Faults in defence disclosure.   For section 11 of the 1996 Act there is substituted—

"11.   Faults in disclosure by accused.   (1) This section applies in the three cases set out in subsections (2), (3) and (4).

(2)   The first case is where section 5 applies and the accused—

(a)   fails to give an initial defence statement,

(b)   gives an initial defence statement but does so after the end of the period which, by virtue of section 12, is the relevant period for section 5,

(c)   is required by section 6B to give either an updated defence statement or a statement of the kind mentioned in subsection (4) of that section but fails to do so,

(d)   gives an updated defence statement or a statement of the kind mentioned in section 6B(4) but does so after the end of the period which, by virtue of section 12, is the relevant period for section 6B,

(e)   sets out inconsistent defences in his defence statement, or (*f*)　at his trial—

(i)　puts forward a defence which was not mentioned in his defence statement or is different from any defence set out in that statement,

(ii)　relies on a matter which, in breach of the requirements imposed by or under section 6A, was not mentioned in his defence statement,

(iii)　adduces evidence in support of an alibi without having given particulars of the alibi in his defence statement, or

(iv)　calls a witness to give evidence in support of an alibi without having complied with section 6A(2)(*a*) or (*b*) as regards the witness in his defence statement.

(3)　The second case is where section 6 applies, the accused gives an initial defence statement, and the accused—

(*a*)　gives the initial defence statement after the end of the period which, by virtue of section 12, is the relevant period for section 6, or

(*b*)　does any of the things mentioned in paragraphs (*c*) to (*f*) of subsection (2).

(4)　The third case is where the accused—

(*a*)　gives a witness notice but does so after the end of the period which, by virtue of section 12, is the relevant period for section 6C, or

(*b*)　at his trial calls a witness (other than himself) not included, or not adequately identified, in a witness notice.

(5)　Where this section applies—

(*a*)　the court or any other party may make such comment as appears appropriate;

(*b*)　the court or jury may draw such inferences as appear proper in deciding whether the accused is guilty of the offence concerned.

(6)　Where—

(*a*)　this section applies by virtue of subsection (2)(*f*)(ii) (including that provision as it applies by virtue of subsection (3)(*b*)), and

(*b*)　the matter which was not mentioned is a point of law (including any point as to the admissibility of evidence or an abuse of process) or an authority,

comment by another party under subsection (5)(*a*) may be made only with the leave of the court.

(7)　Where this section applies by virtue of subsection (4), comment by another party under subsection (5)(*a*) may be made only with the leave of the court.

(8)　Where the accused puts forward a defence which is different from any defence set out in his defence statement, in doing anything under subsection (5) or in deciding whether to do anything under it the court shall have regard—

(*a*)　to the extent of the differences in the defences, and

(*b*)　to whether there is any justification for it.

(9)　Where the accused calls a witness whom he has failed to include, or to identify adequately, in a witness notice, in doing anything under subsection (5) or in deciding whether to do anything under it the court shall have regard to whether there is any justification for the failure.

(10)　A person shall not be convicted of an offence solely on an inference drawn under subsection (5).

(11)　Where the accused has given a statement of the kind mentioned in section 6B(4), then, for the purposes of subsections (2)(*f*)(ii) and (iv), the question as to whether there has been a breach of the requirements imposed by or under section 6A or a failure to comply with section 6A(2)(*a*) or (*b*) shall be determined—

(*a*)　by reference to the state of affairs at the time when that statement was given, and

(*b*)　as if the defence statement was given at the same time as that statement.

(12)　In this section—

(*a*)　"initial defence statement" means a defence statement given under section 5 or 6;

(*b*)　"updated defence statement" means a defence statement given under section 6B;

(*c*)　a reference simply to an accused's "defence statement" is a reference—

(i)　where he has given only an initial defence statement, to that statement;

(ii)　where he has given both an initial and an updated defence statement, to the updated defence statement;

(iii)　where he has given both an initial defence statement and a statement of the kind mentioned in section 6B(4), to the initial defence statement;

(*d*)　a reference to evidence in support of an alibi shall be construed in accordance with section 6A(3);

(*e*)　"witness notice" means a notice given under section 6C"

[Criminal Justice Act 2003, s 39.]

1–4421　40. Code of practice for police interviews of witnesses notified by accused. *Inserts new s 21A in the Police Act 1996.*

PART 6[1]
ALLOCATION AND SENDING OF OFFENCES

1–4422   41. Allocation of offences triable either way, and sending cases to Crown Court.
Schedule 3 (which makes provision in relation to the allocation and other treatment of offences triable either way, and the sending of cases to the Crown Court) shall have effect.

> 1   Part 6 contains ss 41–42. Section 42 came into force on 22 January 2004: see the Criminal Justice Act 2003 (Commencement No 2 and Saving Provisions) Order 2004, SI 2004/81.
> [Criminal Justice Act 2003, s 41.]

1–4423   42. Mode of trial for certain firearms offences: transitory arrangements.   *Section 42 amends ss 24 and 25 of the Magistrates' Courts Act 1980: see this* PART, *ante.*

PART 7[1]
TRIALS ON INDICTMENT WITHOUT A JURY

1–4424

> 1. Part 7 contains ss 43–50. Part 7 provides for the possibility of trial on indictment without jury in cases of serious or complex fraud and cases where there is a danger of jury tampering. The provisions of Part 7 are not reproduced in this work.

PART 8[1]
LIVE LINKS

1–4425   51. Live links in criminal proceedings[2].   (1) A witness (other than the defendant) may, if the court so directs, give evidence through a live link in the following criminal proceedings.

(2) They are—

(a) a summary trial,
(b) an appeal to the Crown Court arising out of such a trial,
(c) a trial on indictment,
(d) an appeal to the criminal division of the Court of Appeal,
(e) the hearing of a reference under section 9 or 11 of the Criminal Appeal Act 1995 (c 35),
(f) a hearing before a magistrates' court or the Crown Court which is held after the defendant has entered a plea of guilty, and
(g) a hearing before the Court of Appeal under section 80 of this Act.

(3) A direction may be given under this section—

(a) on an application by a party to the proceedings, or
(b) of the court's own motion.

(4) But a direction may not be given under this section unless—

(a) the court is satisfied that it is in the interests of the efficient or effective administration of justice for the person concerned to give evidence in the proceedings through a live link,
(b) it has been notified by the Secretary of State that suitable facilities for receiving evidence through a live link are available in the area in which it appears to the court that the proceedings will take place, and
(c) that notification has not been withdrawn.

(5) The withdrawal of such a notification is not to affect a direction given under this section before that withdrawal.

(6) In deciding whether to give a direction under this section the court must consider all the circumstances of the case.

(7) Those circumstances include in particular—

(a) the availability of the witness,
(b) the need for the witness to attend in person,
(c) the importance of the witness's evidence to the proceedings,
(d) the views of the witness,
(e) the suitability of the facilities at the place where the witness would give evidence through a live link,
(f) whether a direction might tend to inhibit any party to the proceedings from effectively testing the witness's evidence.

(8) The court must state in open court its reasons for refusing an application for a direction under this section and, if it is a magistrates' court, must cause them to be entered in the register of its proceedings.
[Criminal Justice Act 2003, s 51.]

> 1. Part 8 contains ss 51–56.
> 2. At the time of going to press s 51 was not in force.

1–4426   52. Effect of, and rescission of, direction[1].   (1) Subsection (2) applies where the court gives a direction under section 51 for a person to give evidence through a live link in particular proceedings.

(2) The person concerned may not give evidence in those proceedings after the direction is given otherwise than through a live link (but this is subject to the following provisions of this section).

(3) The court may rescind a direction under section 51 if it appears to the court to be in the interests of justice to do so.

(4) Where it does so, the person concerned shall cease to be able to give evidence in the proceedings through a live link, but this does not prevent the court from giving a further direction under section 51 in relation to him.

(5) A direction under section 51 may be rescinded under subsection (3)—

(a) on an application by a party to the proceedings, or

(b) of the court's own motion.

(6) But an application may not be made under subsection (5)(a) unless there has been a material change of circumstances since the direction was given.

(7) The court must state in open court its reasons—

(a) for rescinding a direction under section 51, or

(b) for refusing an application to rescind such a direction,

and, if it is a magistrates' court, must cause them to be entered in the register of its proceedings.
[Criminal Justice Act 2003, s 52.]

---

1. At the time of going to press s 52 was not in force.

1–4427 53. Magistrates' courts permitted to sit at other locations. (1) This section applies where—

(a) a magistrates' court is minded to give a direction under section 51 for evidence to be given through a live link in proceedings before the court, and

(b) suitable facilities for receiving such evidence are not available at any petty-sessional court-house in which the court can (apart from subsection (2)) lawfully sit.

(2) The court may sit for the purposes of the whole or any part of the proceedings at any place at which such facilities are available and which has been appointed for the purposes of this section by the justices acting for the petty sessions area for which the court acts.

(3) A place appointed under subsection (2) may be outside the petty sessions area for which it is appointed; but (if so) it shall be deemed to be in that area for the purpose of the jurisdiction of the justices acting for that area.
[Criminal Justice Act 2003, s 53.]

1–4428 54. Warning to jury

1–4429 55. Rules of court. (1) Criminal Procedure Rules may make such provision as appears to the Criminal Procedure Rule Committeethem to be necessary or expedient for the purposes of this Part.

(2) Criminal Procedure Rules may in particular make provision—

(a) as to the procedure to be followed in connection with applications under section 51 or 52, and

(b) as to the arrangements or safeguards to be put in place in connection with the operation of live links.

(3) The provision which may be made by virtue of subsection (2)(a) includes provision—

(a) for uncontested applications to be determined by the court without a hearing,

(b) for preventing the renewal of an unsuccessful application under section 51 unless there has been a material change of circumstances,

(c) for the manner in which confidential or sensitive information is to be treated in connection with an application under section 51 or 52 and in particular as to its being disclosed to, or withheld from, a party to the proceedings.

(4) Nothing in this section is to be taken as affecting the generality of any enactment conferring power to make Criminal Procedure Rules.
[Criminal Justice Act 2003, s 55 as amended by SI 2004/2035.]

1–4430 56. Interpretation of Part 8. (1) In this Part—

"legal representative" means an authorised advocate or authorised litigator (as defined by section 119(1) of the Courts and Legal Services Act 1990 (c 41)),

"petty-sessional court-house" has the same meaning as in the Magistrates' Courts Act 1980 (c 43),

"petty sessions area" has the same meaning as in the Justices of the Peace Act 1997 (c 25),

"witness", in relation to any criminal proceedings, means a person called, or proposed to be called, to give evidence in the proceedings.

(2) In this Part "live link" means a live television link or other arrangement by which a witness, while at a place in the United Kingdom which is outside the building where the proceedings are being held, is able to see and hear a person at the place where the proceedings are being held and to be seen and heard by the following persons.

(3) They are—

(a) the defendant or defendants,
(b) the judge or justices (or both) and the jury (if there is one),
(c) legal representatives acting in the proceedings, and
(d) any interpreter or other person appointed by the court to assist the witness.

(4) The extent (if any) to which a person is unable to see or hear by reason of any impairment of eyesight or hearing is to be disregarded for the purposes of subsection (2).

(5) Nothing in this Part is to be regarded as affecting any power of a court—

(a) to make an order, give directions or give leave of any description in relation to any witness (including the defendant or defendants), or
(b) to exclude evidence at its discretion (whether by preventing questions being put or otherwise).

[Criminal Justice Act 2003, s 56 as amended by SI 2004/2035.]

PART 9[1]
PROSECUTION APPEALS

1–4431   71. Restrictions on reporting.   (1) Except as provided by this section no publication shall include a report of—

(a) anything done under section 58, 59, 62, 63 or 64,
(b) an appeal under this Part,
(c) an appeal under Part 2 of the 1968 Act in relation to an appeal under this Part, or
(d) an application for leave to appeal in relation to an appeal mentioned in paragraph (b) or (c).

(2) The judge may order that subsection (1) is not to apply, or is not to apply to a specified extent, to a report of—

(a) anything done under section 58, 59, 62, 63 or 64, or
(b) an application to the judge for leave to appeal to the Court of Appeal under this Part.

(3) The Court of Appeal may order that subsection (1) is not to apply, or is not to apply to a specified extent, to a report of—

(a) an appeal to the Court of Appeal under this Part,
(b) an application to that Court for leave to appeal to it under this Part, or
(c) an application to that Court for leave to appeal to the House of Lords under Part 2 of the 1968 Act.

(4) The House of Lords may order that subsection (1) is not to apply, or is not to apply to a specified extent, to a report of—

(a) an appeal to that House under Part 2 of the 1968 Act, or
(b) an application to that House for leave to appeal to it under Part 2 of that Act.

(5) Where there is only one defendant and he objects to the making of an order under subsection (2), (3) or (4)—

(a) the judge, the Court of Appeal or the House of Lords are to make the order if (and only if) satisfied, after hearing the representations of the defendant, that it is in the interests of justice to do so, and
(b) the order (if made) is not to apply to the extent that a report deals with any such objection or representations.

(6) Where there are two or more defendants and one or more of them object to the making of an order under subsection (2), (3) or (4)—

(a) the judge, the Court of Appeal or the House of Lords are to make the order if (and only if) satisfied, after hearing the representations of each of the defendants, that it is in the interests of justice to do so, and
(b) the order (if made) is not to apply to the extent that a report deals with any such objection or representations.

(7) Subsection (1) does not apply to the inclusion in a publication of a report of—

(a) anything done under section 58, 59, 62, 63 or 64,
(b) an appeal under this Part,
(c) an appeal under Part 2 of the 1968 Act in relation to an appeal under this Part, or
(d) an application for leave to appeal in relation to an appeal mentioned in paragraph (b) or (c),

at the conclusion of the trial of the defendant or the last of the defendants to be tried.

(8) Subsection (1) does not apply to a report which contains only one or more of the following matters—

(a) the identity of the court and the name of the judge,
(b) the names, ages, home addresses and occupations of the defendant or defendants and witnesses,
(c) the offence or offences, or a summary of them, with which the defendant or defendants are charged,
(d) the names of counsel and solicitors in the proceedings,
(e) where the proceedings are adjourned, the date and place to which they are adjourned,

(f) any arrangements as to bail,

(g) whether a right to representation funded by the Legal Services Commission as part of the Criminal Defence Service was granted to the defendant or any of the defendants.

(9) The addresses that may be included in a report by virtue of subsection (8) are addresses—

(a) at any relevant time, and

(b) at the time of their inclusion in the publication.

(10) Nothing in this section affects any prohibition or restriction by virtue of any other enactment on the inclusion of any matter in a publication.

(11) In this section—

"programme service" has the same meaning as in the Broadcasting Act 1990 (c 42),

"publication" includes any speech, writing, relevant programme or other communication in whatever form, which is addressed to the public at large or any section of the public (and for this purpose every relevant programme is to be taken to be so addressed), but does not include an indictment or other document prepared for use in particular legal proceedings,

"relevant time" means a time when events giving rise to the charges to which the proceedings relate are alleged to have occurred,

"relevant programme" means a programme included in a programme service.

[Criminal Justice Act 2003, s 71.]

---

1. Part 9 contains ss 57–74. Part 9 provides for prosecution appeals to the Court of Appeal in respect of certain judicial rulings in relation to trials on indictment. The provisions confer two types of rights of appeal: general and evidentiary. In relation to the former, the prosecution may appeal only if it accepts effectively that an unsuccessful appeal will result in the acquittal of the accused in relation to the offence or offences in question. In relation to the latter, the evidentiary ruling must be made before the close of the prosecution's case and leave to appeal will not be granted unless the ruling significantly weakens the prosecution's case in relation to the offence of offences in question. The provisions of Part 9 are not reproduced in this work, save for those dealing with restrictions on reporting.

1–4432 72. Offences in connection with reporting. (1) This section applies if a publication includes a report in contravention of section 71.

(2) Where the publication is a newspaper or periodical, any proprietor, editor or publisher of the newspaper or periodical is guilty of an offence.

(3) Where the publication is a relevant programme—

(a) any body corporate or Scottish partnership engaged in providing the programme service in which the programme is included, and

(b) any person having functions in relation to the programme corresponding to those of an editor of a newspaper,

is guilty of an offence.

(4) In the case of any other publication, any person publishing it is guilty of an offence.

(5) If an offence under this section committed by a body corporate is proved—

(a) to have been committed with the consent or connivance of, or

(b) to be attributable to any neglect on the part of,

an officer, the officer as well as the body corporate is guilty of the offence and liable to be proceeded against and punished accordingly.

(6) In subsection (5), "officer" means a director, manager, secretary or other similar officer of the body, or a person purporting to act in any such capacity.

(7) If the affairs of a body corporate are managed by its members, "director" in subsection (6) means a member of that body.

(8) Where an offence under this section is committed by a Scottish partnership and is proved to have been committed with the consent or connivance of a partner, he as well as the partnership shall be guilty of the offence and shall be liable to be proceeded against and punished accordingly.

(9) A person guilty of an offence under this section is liable on summary conviction to a fine not exceeding level 5 on the standard scale.

(10) Proceedings for an offence under this section may not be instituted—

(a) in England and Wales otherwise than by or with the consent of the Attorney General, or

(b) in Northern Ireland otherwise than by or with the consent of—

(i) before the relevant date, the Attorney General for Northern Ireland, or

(ii) on or after the relevant date, the Director of Public Prosecutions for Northern Ireland.

(11) In subsection (10) "the relevant date" means the date on which section 22(1) of the Justice (Northern Ireland) Act 2002 (c 26) comes into force.

[Criminal Justice Act 2003, s 72.]

PART 10[1]
RETRIAL FOR SERIOUS OFFENCES

1–4433 82. Restrictions on publication in the interests of justice. (1) Where it appears to the Court of Appeal that the inclusion of any matter in a publication would give rise to a substantial risk of prejudice to the administration of justice in a retrial, the court may order that the matter is not to be included in any publication while the order has effect.

(2) In subsection (1) "retrial" means the trial of an acquitted person for a qualifying offence pursuant to any order made or that may be made under section 77.

(3) The court may make an order under this section only if it appears to it necessary in the interests of justice to do so.

(4) An order under this section may apply to a matter which has been included in a publication published before the order takes effect, but such an order—

(a)   applies only to the later inclusion of the matter in a publication (whether directly or by inclusion of the earlier publication), and

(b)   does not otherwise affect the earlier publication.

(5) After notice of an application has been given under section 80(1) relating to the acquitted person and the qualifying offence, the court may make an order under this section only—

(a)   of its own motion, or

(b)   on the application of the Director of Public Prosecutions.

(6) Before such notice has been given, an order under this section—

(a)   may be made only on the application of the Director of Public Prosecutions, and

(b)   may not be made unless, since the acquittal concerned, an investigation of the commission by the acquitted person of the qualifying offence has been commenced by officers.

(7) The court may at any time, of its own motion or on an application made by the Director of Public Prosecutions or the acquitted person, vary or revoke an order under this section.

(8) Any order made under this section before notice of an application has been given under section 80(1) relating to the acquitted person and the qualifying offence must specify the time when it ceases to have effect.

(9) An order under this section which is made or has effect after such notice has been given ceases to have effect, unless it specifies an earlier time—

(a)   when there is no longer any step that could be taken which would lead to the acquitted person being tried pursuant to an order made on the application, or

(b)   if he is tried pursuant to such an order, at the conclusion of the trial.

(10) Nothing in this section affects any prohibition or restriction by virtue of any other enactment on the inclusion of any matter in a publication or any power, under an enactment or otherwise, to impose such a prohibition or restriction.

(11) In this section—

"programme service" has the same meaning as in the Broadcasting Act 1990 (c 42),

"publication" includes any speech, writing, relevant programme or other communication in whatever form, which is addressed to the public at large or any section of the public (and for this purpose every relevant programme is to be taken to be so addressed), but does not include an indictment or other document prepared for use in particular legal proceedings,

"relevant programme" means a programme included in a programme service.

[Criminal Justice Act 2003, s 82.]

---

1. Part 10 contains ss 75–97. The provisions of Part 10 provide for the possibility of retrial following acquittal of a "qualifying offence" (ie an offence listed in Pt 1 of Sch 5). The acquittal need not have been in the UK, and the acquittal may have taken place before or after the commencement of Pt 10. The Court of Appeal must order a retrial if the relevant conditions, namely as to new and compelling evidence and the interests of justice, are met. The provisions of Pt 10 are not reproduced in this work, save for those dealing with restrictions on reporting, the authorisation of investigations, arrest, charge, bail and interpretation.

1–4434   83. Offences in connection with publication restrictions.   (1) This section applies if—

(a)   an order under section 82 is made, whether in England and Wales or Northern Ireland, and

(b)   while the order has effect, any matter is included in a publication, in any part of the United Kingdom, in contravention of the order.

(2) Where the publication is a newspaper or periodical, any proprietor, editor or publisher of the newspaper or periodical is guilty of an offence.

(3) Where the publication is a relevant programme—

(a)   any body corporate or Scottish partnership engaged in providing the programme service in which the programme is included, and

(b)   any person having functions in relation to the programme corresponding to those of an editor of a newspaper,

is guilty of an offence.

(4) In the case of any other publication, any person publishing it is guilty of an offence.

(5) If an offence under this section committed by a body corporate is proved—

(a)   to have been committed with the consent or connivance of, or

(b)   to be attributable to any neglect on the part of,

an officer, the officer as well as the body corporate is guilty of the offence and liable to be proceeded against and punished accordingly.

(6) In subsection (5), "officer" means a director, manager, secretary or other similar officer of the body, or a person purporting to act in any such capacity.

(7) If the affairs of a body corporate are managed by its members, "director" in subsection (6) means a member of that body.

(8) Where an offence under this section is committed by a Scottish partnership and is proved to have been committed with the consent or connivance of a partner, he as well as the partnership shall be guilty of the offence and shall be liable to be proceeded against and punished accordingly.

(9) A person guilty of an offence under this section is liable on summary conviction to a fine not exceeding level 5 on the standard scale.

(10) Proceedings for an offence under this section may not be instituted—

(a) in England and Wales otherwise than by or with the consent of the Attorney General, or
(b) in Northern Ireland otherwise than by or with the consent of—

(i) before the relevant date, the Attorney General for Northern Ireland, or
(ii) on or after the relevant date, the Director of Public Prosecutions for Northern Ireland.

(11) In subsection (10) "the relevant date" means the date on which section 22(1) of the Justice (Northern Ireland) Act 2002 (c 26) comes into force.
[Criminal Justice Act 2003, s 83.]

Retrial

1–4435   84. Retrial.   (1) Where a person—

(a) is tried pursuant to an order under section 77(1), or
(b) is tried on indictment pursuant to an order under section 77(3),

the trial must be on an indictment preferred by direction of the Court of Appeal.

(2) After the end of 2 months after the date of the order, the person may not be arraigned on an indictment preferred in pursuance of such a direction unless the Court of Appeal gives leave.

(3) The Court of Appeal must not give leave unless satisfied that—

(a) the prosecutor has acted with due expedition, and
(b) there is a good and sufficient cause for trial despite the lapse of time since the order under section 77.

(4) Where the person may not be arraigned without leave, he may apply to the Court of Appeal to set aside the order and—

(a) for any direction required for restoring an earlier judgment and verdict of acquittal of the qualifying offence, or
(b) in the case of a person acquitted elsewhere than in the United Kingdom, for a declaration to the effect that the acquittal is a bar to his being tried for the qualifying offence.

(5) An indictment under subsection (1) may relate to more than one offence, or more than one person, and may relate to an offence which, or a person who, is not the subject of an order or declaration under section 77.

(6) Evidence given at a trial pursuant to an order under section 77(1) or (3) must be given orally if it was given orally at the original trial, unless—

(a) all the parties to the trial agree otherwise,
(b) section 116 applies, or
(c) the witness is unavailable to give evidence, otherwise than as mentioned in subsection (2) of that section, and section 114(1)(d) applies.

(7) At a trial pursuant to an order under section 77(1), paragraph 5 of Schedule 3 to the Crime and Disorder Act 1998 (c 37) (use of depositions) does not apply to a deposition read as evidence at the original trial.
[Criminal Justice Act 2003, s 84.]

Investigations

1–4436   85. Authorisation of investigations.   (1) This section applies to the investigation of the commission of a qualifying offence by a person—

(a) acquitted in proceedings within section 75(1) of the qualifying offence, or
(b) acquitted elsewhere than in the United Kingdom of an offence the commission of which as alleged would have amounted to or included the commission (in the United Kingdom or elsewhere) of the qualifying offence.

(2) Subject to section 86, an officer may not do anything within subsection (3) for the purposes of such an investigation unless the Director of Public Prosecutions—

(a) has certified that in his opinion the acquittal would not be a bar to the trial of the acquitted person in England and Wales for the qualifying offence, or
(b) has given his written consent to the investigation (whether before or after the start of the investigation).

(3) The officer may not, either with or without the consent of the acquitted person—

(a) arrest or question him,
(b) search him or premises owned or occupied by him,
(c) search a vehicle owned by him or anything in or on such a vehicle,

(d)   seize anything in his possession, or

(e)   take his fingerprints or take a sample from him.

(4)   The Director of Public Prosecutions may only give his consent on a written application, and such an application may be made only by an officer who—

(a)   if he is an officer of the metropolitan police force or the City of London police force, is of the rank of commander or above, or

(b)   in any other case, is of the rank of assistant chief constable or above.

(5)   An officer may make an application under subsection (4) only if—

(a)   he is satisfied that new evidence has been obtained which would be relevant to an application under section 76(1) or (2) in respect of the qualifying offence to which the investigation relates, or

(b)   he has reasonable grounds for believing that such new evidence is likely to be obtained as a result of the investigation.

(6)   The Director of Public Prosecutions may not give his consent unless satisfied that—

(a)   there is, or there is likely as a result of the investigation to be, sufficient new evidence to warrant the conduct of the investigation, and

(b)   it is in the public interest for the investigation to proceed.

(7)   In giving his consent, the Director of Public Prosecutions may recommend that the investigation be conducted otherwise than by officers of a specified police force or specified team of customs and excise officers.

[Criminal Justice Act 2003, s 85.]

1–4437   86. Urgent investigative steps.   (1) Section 85 does not prevent an officer from taking any action for the purposes of an investigation if—

(a)   the action is necessary as a matter of urgency to prevent the investigation being substantially and irrevocably prejudiced,

(b)   the requirements of subsection (2) are met, and

(c)   either—

(i)   the action is authorised under subsection (3), or

(ii)   the requirements of subsection (5) are met.

(2)   The requirements of this subsection are met if—

(a)   there has been no undue delay in applying for consent under section 85(2),

(b)   that consent has not been refused, and

(c)   taking into account the urgency of the situation, it is not reasonably practicable to obtain that consent before taking the action.

(3)   An officer of the rank of superintendent or above may authorise the action if—

(a)   he is satisfied that new evidence has been obtained which would be relevant to an application under section 76(1) or (2) in respect of the qualifying offence to which the investigation relates, or

(b)   he has reasonable grounds for believing that such new evidence is likely to be obtained as a result of the investigation.

(4)   An authorisation under subsection (3) must—

(a)   if reasonably practicable, be given in writing;

(b)   otherwise, be recorded in writing by the officer giving it as soon as is reasonably practicable.

(5)   The requirements of this subsection are met if—

(a)   there has been no undue delay in applying for authorisation under subsection (3),

(b)   that authorisation has not been refused, and

(c)   taking into account the urgency of the situation, it is not reasonably practicable to obtain that authorisation before taking the action.

(6)   Where the requirements of subsection (5) are met, the action is nevertheless to be treated as having been unlawful unless, as soon as reasonably practicable after the action is taken, an officer of the rank of superintendent or above certifies in writing that he is satisfied that, when the action was taken—

(a)   new evidence had been obtained which would be relevant to an application under section 76(1) or (2) in respect of the qualifying offence to which the investigation relates, or

(b)   the officer who took the action had reasonable grounds for believing that such new evidence was likely to be obtained as a result of the investigation.

[Criminal Justice Act 2003, s 86.]

Arrest, custody and bail

1–4438   87. Arrest and charge.   (1) Where section 85 applies to the investigation of the commission of an offence by any person and no certification has been given under subsection (2) of that section—

(a)	a justice of the peace may issue a warrant to arrest that person for that offence only if satisfied by written information that new evidence has been obtained which would be relevant to an application under section 76(1) or (2) in respect of the commission by that person of that offence, and

(b)	that person may not be arrested for that offence except under a warrant so issued.

(2)	Subsection (1) does not affect section 89(3)(b) or 91(3), or any other power to arrest a person, or to issue a warrant for the arrest of a person, otherwise than for an offence.

(3)	Part 4 of the 1984 Act (detention) applies as follows where a person—

(a)	is arrested for an offence under a warrant issued in accordance with subsection (1)(a), or

(b)	having been so arrested, is subsequently treated under section 34(7) of that Act as arrested for that offence.

(4)	For the purposes of that Part there is sufficient evidence to charge the person with the offence for which he has been arrested if, and only if, an officer of the rank of superintendent or above (who has not been directly involved in the investigation) is of the opinion that the evidence available or known to him is sufficient for the case to be referred to a prosecutor to consider whether consent should be sought for an application in respect of that person under section 76.

(5)	For the purposes of that Part it is the duty of the custody officer at each police station where the person is detained to make available or known to an officer at that police station of the rank of superintendent or above any evidence which it appears to him may be relevant to an application under section 76(1) or (2) in respect of the offence for which the person has been arrested, and to do so as soon as practicable—

(a)	after the evidence becomes available or known to him, or

(b)	if later, after he forms that view.

(6)	Section 37 of that Act (including any provision of that section as applied by section 40(8) of that Act) has effect subject to the following modifications—

(a)	in subsection (1)—

(i)	for "determine whether he has before him" there is substituted "request an officer of the rank of superintendent or above (who has not been directly involved in the investigation) to determine, in accordance with section 87(4) of the Criminal Justice Act 2003, whether there is";

(ii)	for "him to do so" there is substituted "that determination to be made";

(b)	in subsection (2)—

(i)	for the words from "custody officer determines" to "before him" there is substituted "officer determines that there is not such sufficient evidence";

(ii)	the word "custody" is omitted from the second place where it occurs;

(c)	in subsection (3)—

(i)	the word "custody" is omitted;

(ii)	after "may" there is inserted "direct the custody officer to";

(d)	in subsection (7) for the words from "the custody officer" to the end of that subsection there is substituted "an officer of the rank of superintendent or above (who has not been directly involved in the investigation) determines, in accordance with section 87(4) of the Criminal Justice Act 2003, that there is sufficient evidence to charge the person arrested with the offence for which he was arrested, the person arrested shall be charged.";

(e)	subsections (7A), (7B) and (8) do not apply;

(f)	after subsection (10) there is inserted—

"(10A) The officer who is requested by the custody officer to make a determination under subsection (1) above shall make that determination as soon as practicable after the request is made.".

(7)	Section 40 of that Act has effect as if in subsections (8) and (9) of that section after " (6)" there were inserted "and (10A)".

(8)	Section 42 of that Act has effect as if in subsection (1) of that section for the words from "who" to "detained" there were substituted " (who has not been directly involved in the investigation)".

[Criminal Justice Act 2003, s 87.]

**1–4439	88. Bail and custody before application.**	(1) In relation to a person charged in accordance with section 87(4)—

(a)	section 38 of the 1984 Act (including any provision of that section as applied by section 40(10) of that Act) has effect as if, in subsection (1), for "either on bail or without bail" there were substituted "on bail",

(b)	section 47(3) of that Act does not apply and references in section 38 of that Act to bail are references to bail subject to a duty to appear before the Crown Court at such place as the custody officer may appoint and at such time, not later than 24 hours after the person is released, as that officer may appoint, and

(c)	section 43B of the Magistrates' Courts Act 1980 (c 43) does not apply.

(2) Where such a person is, after being charged—

(a) kept in police detention, or
(b) detained by a local authority in pursuance of arrangements made under section 38(6) of the 1984 Act,

he must be brought before the Crown Court as soon as practicable and, in any event, not more than 24 hours after he is charged, and section 46 of the 1984 Act does not apply.

(3) For the purpose of calculating the period referred to in subsection (1) or (2), the following are to be disregarded—

(a) Sunday,
(b) Christmas Day,
(c) Good Friday, and
(d) any day which is a bank holiday under the Banking and Financial Dealings Act 1971 (c 80) in the part of the United Kingdom where the person is to appear before the Crown Court as mentioned in subsection (1) or, where subsection (2) applies, is for the time being detained.

(4) Where a person appears or is brought before the Crown Court in accordance with subsection (1) or (2), the Crown Court may either—

(a) grant bail for the person to appear, if notice of an application is served on him under section 80(2), before the Court of Appeal at the hearing of that application, or
(b) remand the person in custody to be brought before the Crown Court under section 89(2).

(5) If the Crown Court grants bail under subsection (4), it may revoke bail and remand the person in custody as referred to in subsection (4)(b).

(6) In subsection (7) the "relevant period", in relation to a person granted bail or remanded in custody under subsection (4), means—

(a) the period of 42 days beginning with the day on which he is granted bail or remanded in custody under that subsection, or
(b) that period as extended or further extended under subsection (8).

(7) If at the end of the relevant period no notice of an application under section 76(1) or (2) in relation to the person has been given under section 80(1), the person—

(a) if on bail subject to a duty to appear as mentioned in subsection (4)(a), ceases to be subject to that duty and to any conditions of that bail, and
(b) if in custody on remand under subsection (4)(b) or (5), must be released immediately without bail.

(8) The Crown Court may, on the application of a prosecutor, extend or further extend the period mentioned in subsection (6)(a) until a specified date, but only if satisfied that—

(a) the need for the extension is due to some good and sufficient cause, and
(b) the prosecutor has acted with all due diligence and expedition.
[Criminal Justice Act 2003, s 88.]

1–4440   89. Bail and custody before hearing.   (1) This section applies where notice of an application is given under section 80(1).

(2) If the person to whom the application relates is in custody under section 88(4)(b) or (5), he must be brought before the Crown Court as soon as practicable and, in any event, within 48 hours after the notice is given.

(3) If that person is not in custody under section 88(4)(b) or (5), the Crown Court may, on application by the prosecutor—

(a) issue a summons requiring the person to appear before the Court of Appeal at the hearing of the application, or
(b) issue a warrant for the person's arrest,

and a warrant under paragraph (b) may be issued at any time even though a summons has previously been issued.

(4) Where a summons is issued under subsection (3)(a), the time and place at which the person must appear may be specified either—

(a) in the summons, or
(b) in a subsequent direction of the Crown Court.

(5) The time or place specified may be varied from time to time by a direction of the Crown Court.

(6) A person arrested under a warrant under subsection (3)(b) must be brought before the Crown Court as soon as practicable and in any event within 48 hours after his arrest, and section 81(5) of the Supreme Court Act 1981 (c 54) does not apply.

(7) If a person is brought before the Crown Court under subsection (2) or (6) the court must either—

(a) remand him in custody to be brought before the Court of Appeal at the hearing of the application, or
(b) grant bail for him to appear before the Court of Appeal at the hearing.

(8) If bail is granted under subsection (7)(*b*), the Crown Court may revoke the bail and remand the person in custody as referred to in subsection (7)(*a*).

(9) For the purpose of calculating the period referred to in subsection (2) or (6), the following are to be disregarded—

(*a*) Sunday,
(*b*) Christmas Day,
(*c*) Good Friday, and
(*d*) any day which is a bank holiday under the Banking and Financial Dealings Act 1971 (c 80) in the part of the United Kingdom where the person is for the time being detained.

[Criminal Justice Act 2003, s 89.]

1–4441 90. Bail and custody during and after hearing.   (1) The Court of Appeal may, at any adjournment of the hearing of an application under section 76(1) or (2)—

(*a*) remand the person to whom the application relates on bail, or
(*b*) remand him in custody.

(2) At a hearing at which the Court of Appeal—

(*a*) makes an order under section 77,
(*b*) makes a declaration under subsection (4) of that section, or
(*c*) dismisses the application or makes a declaration under subsection (3) of that section, if it also gives the prosecutor leave to appeal against its decision or the prosecutor gives notice that he intends to apply for such leave,

the court may make such order as it sees fit for the custody or bail of the acquitted person pending trial pursuant to the order or declaration, or pending determination of the appeal.

(3) For the purpose of subsection (2), the determination of an appeal is pending—

(*a*) until any application for leave to appeal is disposed of, or the time within which it must be made expires;
(*b*) if leave to appeal is granted, until the appeal is disposed of.

(4) Section 4 of the Bail Act 1976 (c 63) applies in relation to the grant of bail under this section as if in subsection (2) the reference to the Crown Court included a reference to the Court of Appeal.

(5) The court may at any time, as it sees fit—

(*a*) revoke bail granted under this section and remand the person in custody, or
(*b*) vary an order under subsection (2).

[Criminal Justice Act 2003, s 90.]

1–4442 91. Revocation of bail.   (1) Where—

(*a*) a court revokes a person's bail under this Part, and
(*b*) that person is not before the court when his bail is revoked,

the court must order him to surrender himself forthwith to the custody of the court.

(2) Where a person surrenders himself into the custody of the court in compliance with an order under subsection (1), the court must remand him in custody.

(3) A person who has been ordered to surrender to custody under subsection (1) may be arrested without a warrant by an officer if he fails without reasonable cause to surrender to custody in accordance with the order.

(4) A person arrested under subsection (3) must be brought as soon as practicable, and, in any event, not more than 24 hours after he is arrested, before the court and the court must remand him in custody.

(5) For the purpose of calculating the period referred to in subsection (4), the following are to be disregarded—

(*a*) Sunday,
(*b*) Christmas Day,
(*c*) Good Friday,
(*d*) any day which is a bank holiday under the Banking and Financial Dealings Act 1971 (c 80) in the part of the United Kingdom where the person is for the time being detained.

[Criminal Justice Act 2003, s 91.]

Part 10: supplementary

1–4443 92. Functions of the DPP.   (1) Section 1(7) of the Prosecution of Offences Act 1985 (c 23) (DPP's functions exercisable by Crown Prosecutor) does not apply to the provisions of this Part other than section 85(2)(*a*).

(2) In the absence of the Director of Public Prosecutions, his functions under those provisions may be exercised by a person authorised by him.

(3) An authorisation under subsection (2)—

(*a*) may relate to a specified person or to persons of a specified description, and
(*b*) may be general or relate to a specified function or specified circumstances.

[Criminal Justice Act 2003, s 92.]

1-4444 93. Rules of court. (1) Rules of court may make such provision as appears to the authority making them to be necessary or expedient for the purposes of this Part.

(2) Without limiting subsection (1), rules of court may in particular make provision as to procedures to be applied in connection with sections 76 to 82, 84 and 88 to 90.

(3) Nothing in this section is to be taken as affecting the generality of any enactment conferring power to make rules of court.

[Criminal Justice Act 2003, s 93.]

1-4445 94. Armed Forces: Part 10

1-4446 95. Interpretation of Part 10. (1) In this Part—

"the 1984 Act" means the Police and Criminal Evidence Act 1984 (c 60),

"acquittal" and related expressions are to be read in accordance with section 75(7),

"customs and excise officer" means an officer as defined by section 1(1) of the Customs and Excise Management Act 1979 (c 2), or a person to whom section 8(2) of that Act applies,

"new evidence" is to be read in accordance with section 78(2),

"officer", except in section 83, means an officer of a police force or a customs and excise officer,

"police force" has the meaning given by section 3(3) of the Prosecution of Offences Act 1985 (c 23),

"prosecutor" means an individual or body charged with duties to conduct criminal prosecutions,

"qualifying offence" has the meaning given by section 75(8).

(2) Subject to rules of court made under section 53(1) of the Supreme Court Act 1981 (c 54) (power by rules to distribute business of Court of Appeal between its civil and criminal divisions)—

(a) the jurisdiction of the Court of Appeal under this Part is to be exercised by the criminal division of that court, and

(b) references in this Part to the Court of Appeal are to be construed as references to that division.

(3) References in this Part to an officer of a specified rank or above are, in the case of a customs and excise officer, references to an officer of such description as—

(a) appears to the Commissioners of Customs and Excise to comprise officers of equivalent rank or above, and

(b) is specified by the Commissioners for the purposes of the provision concerned.

[Criminal Justice Act 2003, s 95.]

1-4447 96. Application of Part 10 to Northern Ireland

1-4448 97. Application of Criminal Appeal Acts to proceedings under Part 10

PART 13[1]
MISCELLANEOUS

Detention of suspected terrorists

1-4449 306. Limit on period of detention without charge of suspected terrorists. *Amends Sch 8 to the Terrorism Act 2000. Section 306 came into force on 20 January 2004: see the Criminal Justice Act 2003 (Commencement No 2 and Saving Provisions) Order 2004, SI 2004/81.*

¹ Part 13 contains ss 306–329.

Enforcement of legislation on endangered species

1-4450 307. Enforcement of regulations implementing Community legislation on endangered species. (1) In this section—

"the 1972 Act" means the European Communities Act 1972 (c 68);

"relevant Community instrument" means—

(a) Council Regulation 338/97/EC on the protection of species of wild fauna and flora by regulating the trade therein, and

(b) Commission Regulation 1808/01/EC on the implementation of the Council Regulation mentioned in paragraph (a).

(2) Regulations made under section 2(2) of the 1972 Act for the purpose of implementing any relevant Community instrument may, notwithstanding paragraph 1(1)(d) of Schedule 2 to the 1972 Act, create offences punishable on conviction on indictment with imprisonment for a term not exceeding five years.

(3) In relation to Scotland and Northern Ireland, regulations made under section 2(2) of the 1972 Act for the purpose of implementing any relevant Community instrument may, notwithstanding paragraph 1(1)(d) of Schedule 2 to the 1972 Act, create offences punishable on summary conviction with imprisonment for a term not exceeding six months.

(4) In Scotland, a constable may arrest without a warrant a person—

(a) who has committed or attempted to commit an offence under regulations made under section 2(2) of the 1972 Act for the purpose of implementing any relevant Community instrument, or (*b*)   whom he has reasonable grounds for suspecting to have committed or to have attempted to commit such an offence.

(5)   Until the coming into force of paragraph 3 of Schedule 27 (which amends paragraph 1 of Schedule 2 to the 1972 Act), subsection (3) has effect—

(*a*)   with the omission of the words "in relation to Scotland and Northern Ireland", and

(*b*)   as if, in relation to England and Wales, the definition of "relevant Community instrument" also included Council Directive 92/43/EEC on the conservation of natural habitats and wild fauna and flora as amended by the Act of Accession to the European Union of Austria, Finland and Sweden and by Council Directive 97/62/EC

(6)   Any reference in this section to a Community instrument is to be read—

(*a*)   as a reference to that instrument as amended from time to time, and

(*b*)   where any provision of that instrument has been repealed, as including a reference to any instrument that re-enacts the repealed provision (with or without amendment).
[Criminal Justice Act 2003, s 307.]

Miscellaneous provisions about criminal proceedings

1–4451   **308. Non-appearance of defendant: plea of guilty.**   In section 12 of the Magistrates' Courts Act 1980 (c 43) (non-appearance of accused: plea of guilty) subsection (1)(*a*)(i) (which excludes offences punishable with imprisonment for term exceeding 3 months) is omitted.
[Criminal Justice Act 2003, s 308.]

1–4452   **309. Preparatory hearings for serious offences not involving fraud**

1–4453   **310. Preparatory hearings to deal with severance and joinder of charges**

1–4454   **311. Reporting restrictions for preparatory hearings**

1–4455   **312. Awards of costs**

1–4456   **313. Extension of investigations by Criminal Cases Review Commission in England and Wales**

1–4457   **314. Extension of investigations by Criminal Cases Review Commission in Northern Ireland**

1–4458   **315. Appeals following reference by Criminal Cases Review Commission**

1–4459   **316. Power to substitute conviction of alternative offence on appeal in England and Wales**

1–4460   **317. Power to substitute conviction of alternative offence on appeal in Northern Ireland**

1–4461   **318. Substitution of conviction on different charge on appeal from court-martial**

1–4462   **319. Appeals against sentences in England and Wales.**   (1) The Criminal Appeal Act 1968 (c 19) is amended as follows.

(2) In section 10 (appeal against sentence in certain cases) for subsection (3) there is substituted—

"(3) An offender dealt with for an offence before the Crown Court in a proceeding to which subsection (2) of this section applies may appeal to the Court of Appeal against any sentence passed on him for the offence by the Crown Court."

(3) In section 11 (supplementary provisions as to appeal against sentence) after subsection (6) there is inserted—

"(7) For the purposes of this section, any two or more sentences are to be treated as passed in the same proceeding if—

(*a*)   they are passed on the same day; or

(*b*)   they are passed on different days but the court in passing any one of them states that it is treating that one together with the other or others as substantially one sentence."
[Criminal Justice Act 2003, s 319.]

Outraging public decency

1–4463   **320. Offence of outraging public decency triable either way.**   (*Makes the offence of outraging public decency triable either way. Section 320 came into force on 20 January 2004, but without application to offences committed before that date: see the Criminal Justice Act 2003 (Commencement No 2 and Saving Provisions) Order 2004, SI 2004/81.*)

Jury service

1–4464　321. Jury service

Individual support orders

1–4465　322. Individual support orders.　*Inserts ss 1AA and 1AB in the Crime and Disorder Act 1998.*

1–4466　323. Individual support orders: consequential amendments.　*Makes various consequential amendments to the Crime and Disorder Act 1998.*

Parenting orders and referral orders

1–4467　324. Parenting orders and referral orders.　*Introduces Sch 34, which makes provision in relation to the interaction between parenting orders made under ss 8–10 of the Crime and Disorder Act 1998 and referral orders made under Pt 3 of the Powers of Criminal Courts Act 2000.*

Assessing etc risks posed by sexual or violent offenders

1–4468　325. Arrangements for assessing etc risks posed by certain offenders.　(1) In this section—

"relevant sexual or violent offender" has the meaning given by section 327;
"responsible authority", in relation to any area, means the chief officer of police, the local probation board for that area and the Minister of the Crown exercising functions in relation to prisons, acting jointly.

(2) The responsible authority for each area must establish arrangements for the purpose of assessing and managing the risks posed in that area by—

(*a*)　relevant sexual and violent offenders, and
(*b*)　other persons who, by reason of offences committed by them (wherever committed), are considered by the responsible authority to be persons who may cause serious harm to the public.

(3) In establishing those arrangements, the responsible authority must act in co-operation with the persons specified in subsection (6); and it is the duty of those persons to co-operate in the establishment by the responsible authority of those arrangements, to the extent that such co-operation is compatible with the exercise by those persons of their functions under any other enactment.

(4) Co-operation under subsection (3) may include the exchange of information.

(5) The responsible authority for each area ("the relevant area") and the persons specified in subsection (6) must together draw up a memorandum setting out the ways in which they are to co-operate.

(6) The persons referred to in subsections (3) and (5) are—

(*a*)　every youth offending team established for an area any part of which falls within the relevant area,
(*b*)　the Ministers of the Crown exercising functions in relation to social security, child support, war pensions, employment and training,
(*c*)　every local education authority any part of whose area falls within the relevant area,
(*d*)　every local housing authority or social services authority any part of whose area falls within the relevant area,
(*e*)　every registered social landlord which provides or manages residential accommodation in the relevant area in which persons falling within subsection (2)(*a*) or (*b*) reside or may reside,
(*f*)　every Health Authority or Strategic Health Authority any part of whose area falls within the relevant area,
(*g*)　every Primary Care Trust or Local Health Board any part of whose area falls within the relevant area,
(*h*)　every NHS trust any part of whose area falls within the relevant area, and
(*i*)　every person who is designated by the Secretary of State by order for the purposes of this paragraph as a provider of electronic monitoring services.

(7) The Secretary of State may by order amend subsection (6) by adding or removing any person or description of person.

(8) The Secretary of State may issue guidance to responsible authorities on the discharge of the functions conferred by this section and section 326.

(9) In this section—

"local education authority" has the same meaning as in the Education Act 1996 (c 56);
"local housing authority" has the same meaning as in the Housing Act 1985 (c 68);
"Minister of the Crown" has the same meaning as in the Ministers of the Crown Act 1975 (c 26);
"NHS trust" has the same meaning as in the National Health Service Act 1977 (c 49);
"prison" has the same meaning as in the Prison Act 1952 (c 52);
"registered social landlord" has the same meaning as in Part 1 of the Housing Act 1996 (c 52);

"social services authority" means a local authority for the purposes of the Local Authority Social
   Services Act 1970 (c 42).
[Criminal Justice Act 2003, s 325.]

1–4469   326. Review of arrangements.   (1) The responsible authority for each area must keep the
arrangements established by it under section 325 under review with a view to monitoring their
effectiveness and making any changes to them that appear necessary or expedient.

   (2) The responsible authority for any area must exercise their functions under subsection (1) in
consultation with persons appointed by the Secretary of State as lay advisers in relation to that
authority.

   (3) The Secretary of State must appoint two lay advisers under subsection (2) in relation to each
responsible authority.

   (4) The responsible authority must pay to or in respect of the persons so appointed such
allowances as the Secretary of State may determine.

   (5) As soon as practicable after the end of each period of 12 months beginning with 1st April, the
responsible authority for each area must—

   (a) prepare a report on the discharge by it during that period of the functions conferred by section
        325 and this section, and
   (b) publish the report in that area.

   (6) The report must include—

   (a) details of the arrangements established by the responsible authority, and
   (b) information of such descriptions as the Secretary of State has notified to the responsible
        authority that he wishes to be included in the report.
[Criminal Justice Act 2003, s 326.]

1–4470   327. Section 325: interpretation.   (1) For the purposes of section 325, a person is a
relevant sexual or violent offender if he falls within one or more of subsections (2) to (5).

   (2) A person falls within this subsection if he is subject to the notification requirements of Part 2
of the Sexual Offences Act 2003 (c 42).

   (3) A person falls within this subsection if—

   (a) he is convicted by a court in England or Wales of murder or an offence specified in Schedule
        15, and
   (b) one of the following sentences is imposed on him in respect of the conviction—

        (i)   a sentence of imprisonment for a term of 12 months or more,
        (ii)   a sentence of detention in a young offender institution for a term of 12 months or more,
        (iii) a sentence of detention during Her Majesty's pleasure,
        (iv)   a sentence of detention for public protection under section 226,
        (v)   a sentence of detention for a period of 12 months or more under section 91 of the
               Sentencing Act (offenders under 18 convicted of certain serious offences),
        (vi)   a sentence of detention under section 228,
        (vii) a detention and training order for a term of 12 months or more, or
        (viii) a hospital or guardianship order within the meaning of the Mental Health Act 1983 (c
               20).

   (4) A person falls within this subsection if—

   (a) he is found not guilty by a court in England and Wales of murder or an offence specified in
        Schedule 15 by reason of insanity or to be under a disability and to have done the act charged
        against him in respect of such an offence, and
   (b) one of the following orders is made in respect of the act charged against him as the offence—

        (i)   an order that he be admitted to hospital, or
        (ii) a guardianship order within the meaning of the Mental Health Act 1983.

   (5) A person falls within this subsection if—

   (a) the first condition set out in section 28(2) or 29(2) of the Criminal Justice and Court Services
        Act 2000 (c 43) or the second condition set out in section 28(3) or 29(3) of that Act is
        satisfied in his case, or
   (b) an order under section 29A of that Act has been made in respect of him.

   (6) In this section "court" does not include a service court, as defined by section 305(1).
[Criminal Justice Act 2003, s 327.]

Criminal record certificates

1–4471   328. Criminal record certificates: amendments of Part 5 of Police Act 1997

Civil proceedings brought by offenders

1–4472   329. Civil proceedings for trespass to the person brought by offender

PART 14[1]
GENERAL

1-4473   330.   Orders and rules.   (1)   This section applies to—

(a)   any power conferred by this Act on the Secretary of State to make an order or rules;
(b)   the power conferred by section 168 on the Lord Chief Justice to make an order.

(2)   The power is exercisable by statutory instrument.

(2A)   Where a statutory instrument is made by the Lord Chief Justice in the exercise of the power referred to in subsection (1)(b), the Statutory Instruments Act 1946 applies to the instrument as if it contained an order made by a Minister of the Crown.

(3)   The power—

(a)   may be exercised so as to make different provision for different purposes or different areas, and
(b)   may be exercised either for all the purposes to which the power extends, or for those purposes subject to specified exceptions, or only for specified purposes.

(4)   The power includes power to make—

(a)   any supplementary, incidental or consequential provision, and
(b)   any transitory, transitional or saving provision,

which the Minister making the instrument considers necessary or expedient.

(5)   A statutory instrument containing—

(a)   an order under any of the following provisions—

section 25(5),
section 103,
section 161(7),
section 178,
section 197(3),
section 223,
section 246(5),
section 260,
section 267,
section 269(6),
section 281(2),
section 283(1),
section 291,
section 301(5),
section 325(7), and
paragraph 5 of Schedule 31,

(b)   an order under section 336(3) bringing section 43 into force,
(c)   an order making any provision by virtue of section 333(2)(b) which adds to, replaces or omits any part of the text of an Act, or
(d)   rules under section 240(4)(a),

may only be made if a draft of the statutory instrument has been laid before, and approved by a resolution of, each House of Parliament.

(6)   Any other statutory instrument made in the exercise of a power to which this section applies is subject to annulment in pursuance of a resolution of either House of Parliament.

(7)   Subsection (6) does not apply to a statutory instrument containing only an order made under one or more of the following provisions—

section 202(3)(b),
section 215(3),
section 253(5),
section 325(6)(i), and
section 336.

[Criminal Justice Act 2003, s 330 as amended by the Constitutional Reform Act 2005, s 146, Schs 4 and 18.]

1.   Part 14 contains ss 330–339.

1-4474   331.   Further minor and consequential amendments.   Schedule 36 (further minor and consequential amendments) shall have effect.
[Criminal Justice Act 2003, s 331.]

1-4475   332.   Repeals.   Schedule 37 (repeals) shall have effect.
[Criminal Justice Act 2003, s 332.]

1-4476   333.   Supplementary and consequential provision, etc.   (1)   The Secretary of State may by order[1] make—

(a)   any supplementary, incidental or consequential provision, and
(b)   any transitory, transitional or saving provision,

which he considers necessary or expedient for the purposes of, in consequence of, or for giving full effect to any provision of this Act.

(2) An order under subsection (1) may, in particular—

(a) provide for any provision of this Act which comes into force before another such provision has come into force to have effect, until that other provision has come into force, with such modifications as are specified in the order, and

(b) amend or repeal—

    (i) any Act passed before, or in the same Session as, this Act, and
    (ii) subordinate legislation made before the passing of this Act.

(3) Nothing in this section limits the power by virtue of section 330(4)(b) to include transitional or saving provision in an order under section 336.

(4) The amendments that may be made under subsection (2)(b) are in addition to those made by or under any other provision of this Act.

(5) In this section "subordinate legislation" has the same meaning as in the Interpretation Act 1978 (c 30).

(6) Schedule 38 (which contains transitory and transitional provisions and savings) shall have effect.

[Criminal Justice Act 2003, s 333.]

---

1. The Criminal Justice Act 2003 (Sentencing) (Transitory Provisions) Order 2005, SI 2005/643 has been made.

1–4477   334. Provision for Northern Ireland

1–4478   335. Expenses

1–4479   336. Commencement.   (1) The following provisions of this Act come into force on the passing of this Act—

section 168(1) and (2),
section 183(8),
section 307(1) to (3), (5) and (6),
section 330,
section 333(1) to (5),
sections 334 and 335,
this section and sections 337, 338 and 339, and
the repeal in Part 9 of Schedule 37 of section 81(2) and (3) of the Countryside and Rights of Way Act 2000 (c 37) (and section 332 so far as relating to that repeal), and
paragraphs 1 and 6 of Schedule 38 (and section 333(6) so far as relating to those paragraphs).

(2) The following provisions of this Act come into force at the end of the period of four weeks beginning with the day on which this Act is passed—

Chapter 7 of Part 12 (and Schedules 21 and 22);
section 303(b)(i) and (ii);
paragraphs 42, 43(3), 66, 83(1) to (3), 84 and 109(2), (3)(b), (4) and (5) of Schedule 32 (and section 304 so far as relating to those provisions);
Part 8 of Schedule 37 (and section 332 so far as relating to that Part of that Schedule).

(3) The remaining provisions of this Act come into force in accordance with provision made by the Secretary of State by order[1].

(4) Different provision may be made for different purposes and different areas.

[Criminal Justice Act 2003, s 336.]

---

1. At the time of going to press the following Commencement Orders had been made: Criminal Justice Act 2003 (Commencement No 1) Order 2003, SI 2003/3282; Criminal Justice Act 2003 (Commencement No 2 and Saving Provisions) Order 2004, SI 2004/81; Criminal Justice Act 2003 (Commencement No 3 and Transitional Provisions) Order 2004, SI 2004/829; Criminal Justice Act 2003 (Commencement No 4 and Saving Provisions) Order 2004, SI 2004/1629; Criminal Justice Act 2003 (Commencement No 5) Order 2004, SI 2004/1867; the Criminal Justice Act 2003 (Commencement No 6 and Transitional Provisions) Order 2004, SI 2004/3033; the Criminal Justice Act 2003 (Commencement No 7) Order, SI 2005/373; the Criminal Justice Act 2003 (Commencement No 8 and Transitional and Saving Provisions) Order 2005, SI 2005/950; the Criminal Justice Act 2003 (Commencement No 9) Order 2005, SI 2005/1267; and Criminal Justice Act 2003 (Commencement No 10 and Saving Provisions) Order 2005, SI 2005/1817; Criminal Justice Act 2003 (Commencement No 11) Order 2005, SI 2005/3055; Criminal Justice Act 2003 (Commencement No 12) Order 2006, SI 2006/751; Criminal Justice Act 2003 (Commencement No 11) Order 2005, SI 2005/3055; Criminal Justice Act 2003 (Commencement No 12) Order 2006, SI 2006/751; Criminal Justice Act 2003 (Commencement No 13 and Transitional Provisions) Order 2006, SI 2006/1835; and Criminal Justice Act 2003 (Commencement No 14 and Transitional Provision) Order 2006, SI 2006/3217. See also: the Criminal Justice Act 2003 (Commencement No 8 and Transitional and Saving Provisions) Order 2005 (Supplementary Provisions) Order 2005, SI 2005/2122.

1–4480   337. Extent.   (1) Subject to the following provisions of this section and to section 338, this Act extends to England and Wales only.

(2)–(9) *Provisions extending to Scotland and Northern Ireland.*

(10)–(13) *Provisions relating to service courts.*

[Criminal Justice Act 2003, s 337.]

1–4481   338. Channel Islands and Isle of Man

1–4482   339. Short title.   This Act may be cited as the Criminal Justice Act 2003.

1–4483   SCHEDULE 1
                          AMENDMENTS RELATED TO PART 1

1–4484   SCHEDULE 2
                  CHARGING OR RELEASE OF PERSONS IN POLICE DETENTION

1–4485
   Section 41   SCHEDULE 3[1]
      ALLOCATION OF CASES TRIABLE EITHER WAY, AND SENDING CASES TO THE CROWN COURT ETC

                                           PART 1
                                  PRINCIPAL AMENDMENTS

                            Magistrates' Courts Act 1980 (c 43)

   1. The Magistrates' Courts Act 1980 is amended as follows.

   ---

   1. Paragraphs 18, 23, 27 and 28 are in force for certain purposes: see the Criminal Justice Act 2003 (Commencement No 8 and Transitional and Saving Provisions) Order 2005, SI 2005/950.
   2. (1) Section 17A (initial indication as to plea) is amended as follows.
   (2) For paragraph (*b*) of subsection (4) there is substituted—

   "(*b*) he may (unless section 17D(2) below were to apply) be committed to the Crown Court under section 3 or (if applicable) 3A of the Powers of Criminal Courts (Sentencing) Act 2000 if the court is of such opinion as is mentioned in subsection (2) of the applicable section."

   (3) After subsection (9) there is inserted—

   "(10) If in respect of the offence the court receives a notice under section 51B or 51C of the Crime and Disorder Act 1998 (which relate to serious or complex fraud cases and to certain cases involving children respectively), the preceding provisions of this section and the provisions of section 17B below shall not apply, and the court shall proceed in relation to the offence in accordance with section 51 or, as the case may be, section 51A of that Act."
   3. After section 17C there is inserted—

   "17D. Maximum penalty under section 17A(6) or 17B(2)(c) for certain offences.   (1) If—

   (*a*) the offence is a scheduled offence (as defined in section 22(1) below);
   (*b*) the court proceeds in relation to the offence in accordance with section 17A(6) or 17B(2)(*c*) above; and
   (*c*) the court convicts the accused of the offence,

   the court shall consider whether, having regard to any representations made by him or by the prosecutor, the value involved (as defined in section 22(10) below) appears to the court to exceed the relevant sum (as specified for the purposes of section 22 below).
   (2) If it appears to the court clear that the value involved does not exceed the relevant sum, or it appears to the court for any reason not clear whether the value involved does or does not exceed the relevant sum—

   (*a*) subject to subsection (4) below, the court shall not have power to impose on the accused in respect of the offence a sentence in excess of the limits mentioned in section 33(1)(*a*) below; and
   (*b*) sections 3 and 4 of the Powers of Criminal Courts (Sentencing) Act 2000 shall not apply as regards that offence.

   (3) Subsections (9) to (12) of section 22 below shall apply for the purposes of this section as they apply for the purposes of that section (reading the reference to subsection (1) in section 22(9) as a reference to subsection (1) of this section).
   (4) Subsection (2)(*a*) above does not apply to an offence under section 12A of the Theft Act 1968 (aggravated vehicle-taking).

   17E. Functions under sections 17A to 17D capable of exercise by single justice.   (1) The functions of a magistrates' court under sections 17A to 17D above may be discharged by a single justice.
   (2) Subsection (1) above shall not be taken as authorising—

   (*a*) the summary trial of an information (otherwise than in accordance with section 17A(6) or 17B(2)(*c*) above); or
   (*b*) the imposition of a sentence,

   by a magistrates' court composed of fewer than two justices."
   4. In section 18 (initial procedure on information against adult for offence triable either way), for subsection (5) there is substituted—

   "(5) The functions of a magistrates' court under sections 19 to 23 below may be discharged by a single justice, but this subsection shall not be taken as authorising—

   (*a*) the summary trial of an information (otherwise than in accordance with section 20(7) below); or
   (*b*) the imposition of a sentence,

   by a magistrates' court composed of fewer than two justices."
   5. For section 19 (court to begin by considering which mode of trial appears more suitable) there is substituted—

   "19. Decision as to allocation.   (1) The court shall decide whether the offence appears to it more suitable for summary trial or for trial on indictment.
   (2) Before making a decision under this section, the court—

(a) shall give the prosecution an opportunity to inform the court of the accused's previous convictions (if any); and

(b) shall give the prosecution and the accused an opportunity to make representations as to whether summary trial or trial on indictment would be more suitable.

(3) In making a decision under this section, the court shall consider—

(a) whether the sentence which a magistrates' court would have power to impose for the offence would be adequate; and

(b) any representations made by the prosecution or the accused under subsection (2)(b) above,

and shall have regard to any allocation guidelines (or revised allocation guidelines) issued as definitive guidelines under section 170 of the Criminal Justice Act 2003.

(4) Where—

(a) the accused is charged with two or more offences; and

(b) it appears to the court that the charges for the offences could be joined in the same indictment or that the offences arise out of the same or connected circumstances,

subsection (3)(a) above shall have effect as if references to the sentence which a magistrates' court would have power to impose for the offence were a reference to the maximum aggregate sentence which a magistrates' court would have power to impose for all of the offences taken together.

(5) In this section any reference to a previous conviction is a reference to—

(a) a previous conviction by a court in the United Kingdom; or

(b) a previous finding of guilt in—

    (i) any proceedings under the Army Act 1955, the Air Force Act 1955 or the Naval Discipline Act 1957 (whether before a court-martial or any other court or person authorised under any of those Acts to award a punishment in respect of any offence); or

    (ii) any proceedings before a Standing Civilian Court.

(6) If, in respect of the offence, the court receives a notice under section 51B or 51C of the Crime and Disorder Act 1998 (which relate to serious or complex fraud cases and to certain cases involving children respectively), the preceding provisions of this section and sections 20, 20A and 21 below shall not apply, and the court shall proceed in relation to the offence in accordance with section 51(1) of that Act."

6. For section 20 (procedure where summary trial appears more suitable) there is substituted—

"20. Procedure where summary trial appears more suitable. (1) If the court decides under section 19 above that the offence appears to it more suitable for summary trial, the following provisions of this section shall apply (unless they are excluded by section 23 below).

(2) The court shall explain to the accused in ordinary language—

(a) that it appears to the court more suitable for him to be tried summarily for the offence;

(b) that he can either consent to be so tried or, if he wishes, be tried on indictment; and

(c) in the case of a specified offence (within the meaning of section 224 of the Criminal Justice Act 2003), that if he is tried summarily and is convicted by the court, he may be committed for sentence to the Crown Court under section 3A of the Powers of Criminal Courts (Sentencing) Act 2000 if the committing court is of such opinion as is mentioned in subsection (2) of that section.

(3) The accused may then request an indication ("an indication of sentence") of whether a custodial sentence or non-custodial sentence would be more likely to be imposed if he were to be tried summarily for the offence and to plead guilty.

(4) If the accused requests an indication of sentence, the court may, but need not, give such an indication.

(5) If the accused requests and the court gives an indication of sentence, the court shall ask the accused whether he wishes, on the basis of the indication, to reconsider the indication of plea which was given, or is taken to have been given, under section 17A or 17B above.

(6) If the accused indicates that he wishes to reconsider the indication under section 17A or 17B above, the court shall ask the accused whether (if the offence were to proceed to trial) he would plead guilty or not guilty.

(7) If the accused indicates that he would plead guilty the court shall proceed as if—

(a) the proceedings constituted from that time the summary trial of the information; and

(b) section 9(1) above were complied with and he pleaded guilty under it.

(8) Subsection (9) below applies where—

(a) the court does not give an indication of sentence (whether because the accused does not request one or because the court does not agree to give one);

(b) the accused either—

    (i) does not indicate, in accordance with subsection (5) above, that he wishes; or

    (ii) indicates, in accordance with subsection (5) above, that he does not wish,

to reconsider the indication of plea under section 17A or 17B above; or

(c) the accused does not indicate, in accordance with subsection (6) above, that he would plead guilty.

(9) The court shall ask the accused whether he consents to be tried summarily or wishes to be tried on indictment and—

(a) if he consents to be tried summarily, shall proceed to the summary trial of the information; and

(b) if he does not so consent, shall proceed in relation to the offence in accordance with section 51(1) of the Crime and Disorder Act 1998.

20A. Procedure where summary trial appears more suitable: supplementary. (1) Where the case is dealt with in accordance with section 20(7) above, no court (whether a magistrates' court or not) may impose a custodial sentence for the offence unless such a sentence was indicated in the indication of sentence referred to in section 20 above.

(2) Subsection (1) above is subject to sections 3A(4), 4(8) and 5(3) of the Powers of Criminal Courts (Sentencing) Act 2000.

(3) Except as provided in subsection (1) above—

(a) an indication of sentence shall not be binding on any court (whether a magistrates' court or not); and
(b) no sentence may be challenged or be the subject of appeal in any court on the ground that it is not consistent with an indication of sentence.

(4) Subject to section 20(7) above, the following shall not for any purpose be taken to constitute the taking of a plea—

(a) asking the accused under section 20 above whether (if the offence were to proceed to trial) he would plead guilty or not guilty; or
(b) an indication by the accused under that section of how he would plead.

(5) Where the court gives an indication of sentence under section 20 above, it shall cause each such indication to be entered in the register.

(6) In this section and in section 20 above, references to a custodial sentence are to a custodial sentence within the meaning of section 76 of the Powers of Criminal Courts (Sentencing) Act 2000, and references to a non-custodial sentence shall be construed accordingly.''

7. For section 21 (procedure where trial on indictment appears more suitable) there is substituted—

''**21. Procedure where trial on indictment appears more suitable.** If the court decides under section 19 above that the offence appears to it more suitable for trial on indictment, the court shall tell the accused that the court has decided that it is more suitable for him to be tried on indictment, and shall proceed in relation to the offence in accordance with section 51(1) of the Crime and Disorder Act 1998.''

8. (1) Section 23 (power of court, with consent of legally represented accused, to proceed in his absence) is amended as follows.

(2) In subsection (4)—

(a) for the words preceding paragraph (a) there is substituted "If the court decides under section 19 above that the offence appears to it more suitable for trial on indictment then—", and
(b) in paragraph (b), for the words from "to inquire" to the end there is substituted "in relation to the offence in accordance with section 51(1) of the Crime and Disorder Act 1998.''.

(3) For subsection (5) there is substituted—

''(5) If the court decides under section 19 above that the offence appears to it more suitable for trial on indictment, section 21 above shall not apply and the court shall proceed in relation to the offence in accordance with section 51(1) of the Crime and Disorder Act 1998.''

9. (1) Section 24 (summary trial of information against child or young persons for indictable offence), as amended by section 42 of this Act, is amended as follows.

(2) For subsection (1) there is substituted—

''(1) Where a person under the age of 18 years appears or is brought before a magistrates' court on an information charging him with an indictable offence he shall, subject to sections 51 and 51A of the Crime and Disorder Act 1998 and to sections 24A and 24B below, be tried summarily.''

(3) Subsections (1A) and (2) are omitted.

10. After section 24 there is inserted—

''**24A. Child or young person to indicate intention as to plea in certain cases.** (1) This section applies where—

(a) a person under the age of 18 years appears or is brought before a magistrates' court on an information charging him with an offence other than one falling within section 51A(12) of the Crime and Disorder Act 1998 ("the 1998 Act"); and
(b) but for the application of the following provisions of this section, the court would be required at that stage, by virtue of section 51(7) or (8) or 51A(3)(b), (4) or (5) of the 1998 Act to determine, in relation to the offence, whether to send the person to the Crown Court for trial (or to determine any matter, the effect of which would be to determine whether he is sent to the Crown Court for trial).

(2) Where this section applies, the court shall, before proceeding to make any such determination as is referred to in subsection (1)(b) above (the "relevant determination"), follow the procedure set out in this section.

(3) Everything that the court is required to do under the following provisions of this section must be done with the accused person in court.

(4) The court shall cause the charge to be written down, if this has not already been done, and to be read to the accused.

(5) The court shall then explain to the accused in ordinary language that he may indicate whether (if the offence were to proceed to trial) he would plead guilty or not guilty, and that if he indicates that he would plead guilty—

(a) the court must proceed as mentioned in subsection (7) below; and
(b) (in cases where the offence is one mentioned in section 91(1) of the Powers of Criminal Courts (Sentencing) Act 2000) he may be sent to the Crown Court for sentencing under section 3B or (if applicable) 3C of that Act if the court is of such opinion as is mentioned in subsection (2) of the applicable section.

(6) The court shall then ask the accused whether (if the offence were to proceed to trial) he would plead guilty or not guilty.

(7) If the accused indicates that he would plead guilty, the court shall proceed as if—

(a) the proceedings constituted from the beginning the summary trial of the information; and
(b) section 9(1) above was complied with and he pleaded guilty under it,

and, accordingly, the court shall not (and shall not be required to) proceed to make the relevant determination or to proceed further under section 51 or (as the case may be) section 51A of the 1998 Act in relation to the offence.

(8) If the accused indicates that he would plead not guilty, the court shall proceed to make the relevant determination and this section shall cease to apply.

(9) If the accused in fact fails to indicate how he would plead, for the purposes of this section he shall be taken to indicate that he would plead not guilty.

(10) Subject to subsection (7) above, the following shall not for any purpose be taken to constitute the taking of a plea—

(*a*) asking the accused under this section whether (if the offence were to proceed to trial) he would plead guilty or not guilty;

(*b*) an indication by the accused under this section of how he would plead.

24B. Intention as to plea by child or young person: absence of accused. (1) This section shall have effect where—

(*a*) a person under the age of 18 years appears or is brought before a magistrates' court on an information charging him with an offence other than one falling within section 51A(12) of the Crime and Disorder Act 1998;

(*b*) but for the application of the following provisions of this section, the court would be required at that stage to make one of the determinations referred to in paragraph (*b*) of section 24A(1) above ("the relevant determination");

(*c*) the accused is represented by a legal representative;

(*d*) the court considers that by reason of the accused's disorderly conduct before the court it is not practicable for proceedings under section 24A above to be conducted in his presence; and

(*e*) the court considers that it should proceed in the absence of the accused.

(2) In such a case—

(*a*) the court shall cause the charge to be written down, if this has not already been done, and to be read to the representative;

(*b*) the court shall ask the representative whether (if the offence were to proceed to trial) the accused would plead guilty or not guilty;

(*c*) if the representative indicates that the accused would plead guilty the court shall proceed as if the proceedings constituted from the beginning the summary trial of the information, and as if section 9(1) above was complied with and the accused pleaded guilty under it;

(*d*) if the representative indicates that the accused would plead not guilty the court shall proceed to make the relevant determination and this section shall cease to apply.

(3) If the representative in fact fails to indicate how the accused would plead, for the purposes of this section he shall be taken to indicate that the accused would plead not guilty.

(4) Subject to subsection (2)(*c*) above, the following shall not for any purpose be taken to constitute the taking of a plea—

(*a*) asking the representative under this section whether (if the offence were to proceed to trial) the accused would plead guilty or not guilty;

(*b*) an indication by the representative under this section of how the accused would plead.

24C. Intention as to plea by child or young person: adjournment. (1) A magistrates' court proceeding under section 24A or 24B above may adjourn the proceedings at any time, and on doing so on any occasion when the accused is present may remand the accused.

(2) Where the court remands the accused, the time fixed for the resumption of proceedings shall be that at which he is required to appear or be brought before the court in pursuance of the remand or would be required to be brought before the court but for section 128(3A) below.

24D. Functions under sections 24A to 24C capable of exercise by single justice. (1) The functions of a magistrates' court under sections 24A to 24C above may be discharged by a single justice.

(2) Subsection (1) above shall not be taken as authorising—

(*a*) the summary trial of an information (other than a summary trial by virtue of section 24A(7) or 24B(2)(*c*) above); or

(*b*) the imposition of a sentence,

by a magistrates' court composed of fewer than two justices."

11. (1) Section 25 (power to change from summary trial to committal proceedings and vice versa), as amended by section 42 of this Act, is amended as follows.

(2) In subsection (1), for " (2) to (4)" there is substituted " (2) to (2D)".

(3) For subsection (2) there is substituted—

"(2) Where the court is required under section 20(9) above to proceed to the summary trial of the information, the prosecution may apply to the court for the offence to be tried on indictment instead.

(2A) An application under subsection (2) above—

(*a*) must be made before the summary trial begins; and

(*b*) must be dealt with by the court before any other application or issue in relation to the summary trial is dealt with.

(2B) The court may grant an application under subsection (2) above but only if it is satisfied that the sentence which a magistrates' court would have power to impose for the offence would be inadequate.

(2C) Where—

(*a*) the accused is charged on the same occasion with two or more offences; and

(*b*) it appears to the court that they constitute or form part of a series of two or more offences of the same or a similar character,

subsection (2B) above shall have effect as if references to the sentence which a magistrates' court would have power to impose for the offence were a reference to the maximum aggregate sentence which a magistrates' court would have power to impose for all of the offences taken together.

(2D) Where the court grants an application under subsection (2) above, it shall proceed in relation to the offence in accordance with section 51(1) of the Crime and Disorder Act 1998."

(4) Subsections (3) to (8) are omitted.

12. For subsections (1) and (2) of section 26 (power to issue summons to accused in certain circumstances) there is substituted—

"(1) Where, in the circumstances mentioned in section 23(1)(a) above, the court is not satisfied that there is good reason for proceeding in the absence of the accused, the justice or any of the justices of which the court is composed may issue a summons directed to the accused requiring his presence before the court.

(2) In a case within subsection (1) above, if the accused is not present at the time and place appointed for the proceedings under section 19 or section 22(1) above, the court may issue a warrant for his arrest."

13. In section 33 (maximum penalties on summary conviction in pursuance of section 22), in subsection (1), paragraph (b) and the word "and" immediately preceding it are omitted.

14. Section 42 (restriction on justices sitting after dealing with bail) shall cease to have effect.

Crime and Disorder Act 1998 (c 37)

15. The Crime and Disorder Act 1998 is amended as follows.

16. In section 50 (early administrative hearings), in subsection (1) (court may consist of single justice unless accused falls to be dealt with under section 51), the words "unless the accused falls to be dealt with under section 51 below" are omitted.

17. After section 50 there is inserted—

"50A. Order of consideration for either-way offences. (1) Where an adult appears or is brought before a magistrates' court charged with an either-way offence (the "relevant offence"), the court shall proceed in the manner described in this section.

(2) If notice is given in respect of the relevant offence under section 51B or 51C below, the court shall deal with the offence as provided in section 51 below.

(3) Otherwise—

(a) if the adult (or another adult with whom the adult is charged jointly with the relevant offence) is or has been sent to the Crown Court for trial for an offence under section 51(2)(a) or 51(2)(c) below—

(i) the court shall first consider the relevant offence under subsection (3), (4), (5) or, as the case may be, (6) of section 51 below and, where applicable, deal with it under that subsection;

(ii) if the adult is not sent to the Crown Court for trial for the relevant offence by virtue of sub-paragraph (i) above, the court shall then proceed to deal with the relevant offence in accordance with sections 17A to 23 of the 1980 Act;

(b) in all other cases—

(i) the court shall first consider the relevant offence under sections 17A to 20 (excluding subsections (8) and (9) of section 20) of the 1980 Act;

(ii) if, by virtue of sub-paragraph (i) above, the court would be required to proceed in relation to the offence as mentioned in section 17A(6), 17B(2)(c) or 20(7) of that Act (indication of guilty plea), it shall proceed as so required (and, accordingly, shall not consider the offence under section 51 or 51A below);

(iii) if sub-paragraph (ii) above does not apply—

(a) the court shall consider the relevant offence under sections 51 and 51A below and, where applicable, deal with it under the relevant section;

(b) if the adult is not sent to the Crown Court for trial for the relevant offence by virtue of paragraph (a) of this sub-paragraph, the court shall then proceed to deal with the relevant offence as contemplated by section 20(9) or, as the case may be, section 21 of the 1980 Act.

(4) Subsection (3) above is subject to any requirement to proceed as mentioned in subsections (2) or (6)(a) of section 22 of the 1980 Act (certain offences where value involved is small).

(5) Nothing in this section shall prevent the court from committing the adult to the Crown Court for sentence pursuant to any enactment, if he is convicted of the relevant offence."

18. *Substitutes s 51 and inserts news ss 51A–51E into the Crime and Disorder Act 1998 (ss 51B and 51C not yet in force).*

51B. Notices in serious or complex fraud cases. (1) A notice may be given by a designated authority under this section in respect of an indictable offence if the authority is of the opinion that the evidence of the offence charged—

(a) is sufficient for the person charged to be put on trial for the offence; and

(b) reveals a case of fraud of such seriousness or complexity that it is appropriate that the management of the case should without delay be taken over by the Crown Court.

(2) That opinion must be certified by the designated authority in the notice.

(3) The notice must also specify the proposed place of trial, and in selecting that place the designated authority must have regard to the same matters as are specified in paragraphs (a) to (c) of section 51D(4) below.

(4) A notice under this section must be given to the magistrates' court at which the person charged appears or before which he is brought.

(5) Such a notice must be given to the magistrates' court before any summary trial begins.

(6) The effect of such a notice is that the functions of the magistrates' court cease in relation to the case, except—

(a) for the purposes of section 51D below;

(b) as provided by paragraph 2 of Schedule 3 to the Access to Justice Act 1999; and

(c) as provided by section 52 below.

(7) The functions of a designated authority under this section may be exercised by an officer of the authority acting on behalf of the authority.

(8) A decision to give a notice under this section shall not be subject to appeal or liable to be questioned in any court (whether a magistrates' court or not).

(9) In this section "designated authority" means—

(a) the Director of Public Prosecutions;
(b) the Director of the Serious Fraud Office;
(c) the Commissioners of the Inland Revenue;
(d) the Commissioners of Customs and Excise; or
(e) the Secretary of State.

51C. Notices in certain cases involving children. (1) A notice may be given by the Director of Public Prosecutions under this section in respect of an offence falling within subsection (3) below if he is of the opinion—

(a) that the evidence of the offence would be sufficient for the person charged to be put on trial for the offence;
(b) that a child would be called as a witness at the trial; and
(c) that, for the purpose of avoiding any prejudice to the welfare of the child, the case should be taken over and proceeded with without delay by the Crown Court.

(2) That opinion must be certified by the Director of Public Prosecutions in the notice.
(3) This subsection applies to an offence—

(a) which involves an assault on, or injury or a threat of injury to, a person;
(b) under section 1 of the Children and Young Persons Act 1933 (cruelty to persons under 16);
(c) under the Sexual Offences Act 1956, the Protection of Children Act 1978 or the Sexual Offences Act 2003;
(d) of kidnapping or false imprisonment, or an offence under section 1 or 2 of the Child Abduction Act 1984;
(e) which consists of attempting or conspiring to commit, or of aiding, abetting, counselling, procuring or inciting the commission of, an offence falling within paragraph (a), (b), (c) or (d) above.

(4) Subsections (4), (5) and (6) of section 51B above apply for the purposes of this section as they apply for the purposes of that.
(5) The functions of the Director of Public Prosecutions under this section may be exercised by an officer acting on behalf of the Director.
(6) A decision to give a notice under this section shall not be subject to appeal or liable to be questioned in any court (whether a magistrates' court or not).
(7) In this section "child" means—

(a) a person who is under the age of 17; or
(b) any person of whom a video recording (as defined in section 63(1) of the Youth Justice and Criminal Evidence Act 1999) was made when he was under the age of 17 with a view to its admission as his evidence in chief in the trial referred to in subsection (1) above.

19. (1) After section 52 there is inserted—

"52A. Restrictions on reporting. (1) Except as provided by this section, it shall not be lawful—

(a) to publish in the United Kingdom a written report of any allocation or sending proceedings in England and Wales; or
(b) to include in a relevant programme for reception in the United Kingdom a report of any such proceedings,

if (in either case) the report contains any matter other than that permitted by this section.

(2) Subject to subsections (3) and (4) below, a magistrates' court may, with reference to any allocation or sending proceedings, order that subsection (1) above shall not apply to reports of those proceedings.
(3) Where there is only one accused and he objects to the making of an order under subsection (2) above, the court shall make the order if, and only if, it is satisfied, after hearing the representations of the accused, that it is in the interests of justice to do so.
(4) Where in the case of two or more accused one of them objects to the making of an order under subsection (2) above, the court shall make the order if, and only if, it is satisfied, after hearing the representations of the accused, that it is in the interests of justice to do so.
(5) An order under subsection (2) above shall not apply to reports of proceedings under subsection (3) or (4) above, but any decision of the court to make or not to make such an order may be contained in reports published or included in a relevant programme before the time authorised by subsection (6) below.
(6) It shall not be unlawful under this section to publish or include in a relevant programme a report of allocation or sending proceedings containing any matter other than that permitted by subsection (7) below—

(a) where, in relation to the accused (or all of them, if there are more than one), the magistrates' court is required to proceed as mentioned in section 20(7) of the 1980 Act, after the court is so required;
(b) where, in relation to the accused (or any of them, if there are more than one), the court proceeds other than as mentioned there, after conclusion of his trial or, as the case may be, the trial of the last to be tried.

(7) The following matters may be contained in a report of allocation or sending proceedings published or included in a relevant programme without an order under subsection (2) above before the time authorised by subsection (6) above—

(a) the identity of the court and the name of the justice or justices;
(b) the name, age, home address and occupation of the accused;
(c) in the case of an accused charged with an offence in respect of which notice has been given to the court under section 51B above, any relevant business information;
(d) the offence or offences, or a summary of them, with which the accused is or are charged;
(e) the names of counsel and solicitors engaged in the proceedings;
(f) where the proceedings are adjourned, the date and place to which they are adjourned;
(g) the arrangements as to bail;
(h) whether a right to representation funded by the Legal Services Commission as part of the Criminal Defence Service was granted to the accused or any of the accused.

(8) The addresses that may be published or included in a relevant programme under subsection (7) above are addresses—

(a)   at any relevant time; and

(b)   at the time of their publication or inclusion in a relevant programme.

(9)   The following is relevant business information for the purposes of subsection (7) above—

(a)   any address used by the accused for carrying on a business on his own account;

(b)   the name of any business which he was carrying on on his own account at any relevant time;

(c)   the name of any firm in which he was a partner at any relevant time or by which he was engaged at any such time;

(d)   the address of any such firm;

(e)   the name of any company of which he was a director at any relevant time or by which he was otherwise engaged at any such time;

(f)   the address of the registered or principal office of any such company;

(g)   any working address of the accused in his capacity as a person engaged by any such company;

and here "engaged" means engaged under a contract of service or a contract for services.

(10)   Subsection (1) above shall be in addition to, and not in derogation from, the provisions of any other enactment with respect to the publication of reports of court proceedings.

(11)   In this section—

"allocation or sending proceedings" means, in relation to an information charging an indictable offence—

(a)   any proceedings in the magistrates' court at which matters are considered under any of the following provisions—

(i)   sections 19 to 23 of the 1980 Act;

(ii)   section 51, 51A or 52 above;

(b)   any proceedings in the magistrates' court before the court proceeds to consider any matter mentioned in paragraph (a) above; and

(c)   any proceedings in the magistrates' court at which an application under section 25(2) of the 1980 Act is considered;

"publish", in relation to a report, means publish the report, either by itself or as part of a newspaper or periodical, for distribution to the public;

"relevant programme" means a programme included in a programme service (within the meaning of the Broadcasting Act 1990);

"relevant time" means a time when events giving rise to the charges to which the proceedings relate occurred.

52B. Offences in connection with reporting.   (1) If a report is published or included in a relevant programme in contravention of section 52A above, each of the following persons is guilty of an offence—

(a)   in the case of a publication of a written report as part of a newspaper or periodical, any proprietor, editor or publisher of the newspaper or periodical;

(b)   in the case of a publication of a written report otherwise than as part of a newspaper or periodical, the person who publishes it;

(c)   in the case of the inclusion of a report in a relevant programme, any body corporate which is engaged in providing the service in which the programme is included and any person having functions in relation to the programme corresponding to those of the editor of a newspaper.

(2)   A person guilty of an offence under this section is liable on summary conviction to a fine not exceeding level 5 on the standard scale.

(3)   Proceedings for an offence under this section shall not, in England and Wales, be instituted otherwise than by or with the consent of the Attorney General.

(4)   Proceedings for an offence under this section shall not, in Northern Ireland, be instituted otherwise than by or with the consent of the Attorney General for Northern Ireland.

(5)   Subsection (11) of section 52A above applies for the purposes of this section as it applies for the purposes of that section.".

(2)   In section 121 (short title, commencement and extent)—

(a)   in subsection (6), after paragraph (b) there is inserted—

"(bb)sections 52A and 52B;", and

(b)   in subsection (8), after " (5) above," there is inserted "sections 52A and 52B above,".

20.   (1) Schedule 3 (procedure where persons are sent for trial under section 51 of the Crime and Disorder Act 1998) is amended as follows.

(2)   In paragraph 1(1)—

(a)   after "51" there is inserted "or 51A", and

(b)   in paragraph (b), for "subsection (7) of that section" there is substituted "section 51D(1) of this Act".

(3)   In paragraph 2—

(a)   in sub-paragraph (1)—

(i)   after "51" there is inserted "or 51A", and

(ii)   for "subsection (7) of that section" there is substituted "section 51D(1) of this Act", and

(b)   sub-paragraphs (4) and (5) are omitted.

(4)   In paragraph 4, in sub-paragraph (1)(a), after "51" there is inserted "or 51A".

(5)   In paragraph 5, in sub-paragraph (2), after "51" there is inserted "or 51A".

(6)   Paragraph 6 is amended as follows—

(a)   in sub-paragraph (1), after "51" there is inserted "or 51A",

(b)   in sub-paragraph (2), for the words from the second "offence" to the end there is substituted "indictable offence for which he was sent for trial or, as the case may be, any of the indictable offences for which he was so sent", and

(c)   in sub-paragraph (9), for "indictable-only" there is substituted "indictable".

(7)   In paragraph 7—

(a) in sub-paragraph (1)(*a*), after "51" there is inserted "or 51A",
(b) in sub-paragraph (1)(*b*), for "offence that is triable only on indictment" there is substituted "main offence",
(c) in sub-paragraph (3), after "each" there is inserted "remaining",
(d) in sub-paragraph (7), for "consider" there is substituted "decide", and
(e) after sub-paragraph (8) there is inserted—

"(9) In this paragraph, a "main offence" is—

    (a) an offence for which the person has been sent to the Crown Court for trial under section 51(1) of this Act; or
    (b) an offence—

        (i) for which the person has been sent to the Crown Court for trial under subsection (5) of section 51 or subsection (6) of section 51A of this Act ("the applicable subsection"); and
        (ii) in respect of which the conditions for sending him to the Crown Court for trial under the applicable subsection (as set out in paragraphs (*a*) to (*c*) of section 51(5) or paragraphs (*a*) and (*b*) of section 51A(6)) continue to be satisfied."

(8) In paragraph 8—

(a) in sub-paragraph (1)(*a*), after "51" there is inserted "or 51A",
(b) in sub-paragraph (1)(*b*), for "offence that is triable only on indictment" there is substituted "main offence (within the meaning of paragraph 7 above)",
(c) in sub-paragraph (2)(*a*), after "each" there is inserted "remaining", and
(d) in sub-paragraph (2)(*d*), for "consider" there is substituted "decide".

(9) In paragraph 9—

(a) in sub-paragraph (1), for "consider" there is substituted "decide", and
(b) for sub-paragraphs (2) and (3), there is substituted—

"(2) Before deciding the question, the court—

    (a) shall give the prosecution an opportunity to inform the court of the accused's previous convictions (if any); and
    (b) shall give the prosecution and the accused an opportunity to make representations as to whether summary trial or trial on indictment would be more suitable.

(3) In deciding the question, the court shall consider—

    (a) whether the sentence which a magistrates' court would have power to impose for the offence would be adequate; and
    (b) any representations made by the prosecution or the accused under sub-paragraph (2)(*b*) above,

and shall have regard to any allocation guidelines (or revised allocation guidelines) issued as definitive guidelines under section 170 of the Criminal Justice Act 2003.

(4) Where—

    (a) the accused is charged on the same occasion with two or more offences; and
    (b) it appears to the court that they constitute or form part of a series of two or more offences of the same or a similar character;

sub-paragraph (3)(*a*) above shall have effect as if references to the sentence which a magistrates' court would have power to impose for the offence were a reference to the maximum aggregate sentence which a magistrates' court would have power to impose for all of the offences taken together.

(5) In this paragraph any reference to a previous conviction is a reference to—

    (a) a previous conviction by a court in the United Kingdom, or
    (b) a previous finding of guilt in—

        (i) any proceedings under the Army Act 1955, the Air Force Act 1955 or the Naval Discipline Act 1957 (whether before a court-martial or any other court or person authorised under any of those Acts to award a punishment in respect of any offence), or
        (ii) any proceedings before a Standing Civilian Court."

(10) In paragraph 10—

(a) for sub-paragraph (2), there is substituted—

"(2) The court shall explain to the accused in ordinary language—

    (a) that it appears to the court more suitable for him to be tried summarily for the offence;
    (b) that he can either consent to be so tried or, if he wishes, be tried on indictment; and
    (c) in the case of a specified offence (within the meaning of section 224 of the Criminal Justice Act 2003), that if he is tried summarily and is convicted by the court, he may be committed for sentence to the Crown Court under section 3A of the Powers of Criminal Courts (Sentencing) Act 2000 if the committing court is of such opinion as is mentioned in subsection (2) of that section.", and
(b) in sub-paragraph (3), for "by a jury" there is substituted "on indictment".

(11) In paragraph 11, in sub-paragraph (*a*), for "by a jury" there is substituted "on indictment".
(12) Paragraph 12 shall cease to have effect.
(13) In paragraph 13—

(a) in sub-paragraph (1)(*a*), after "51" there is inserted "or 51A",
(b) in sub-paragraph (1)(*b*), for "offence that is triable only on indictment" there is substituted "main offence",
(c) in sub-paragraph (2), the words from "unless" to the end are omitted, and
(d) for sub-paragraph (3) there is substituted—

"(3) In this paragraph, a "main offence" is—

    (a) an offence for which the child or young person has been sent to the Crown Court for trial under section 51A(2) of this Act; or

(b) an offence—

    (i) for which the child or young person has been sent to the Crown Court for trial under subsection (7) of section 51 of this Act; and

    (ii) in respect of which the conditions for sending him to the Crown Court for trial under that subsection (as set out in paragraphs (a) and (b) of that subsection) continue to be satisfied."

(14) In paragraph 15, in each of sub-paragraphs (3) and (4), for "considered" there is substituted "decided".

Powers of Criminal Courts (Sentencing) Act 2000 (c 6)

21. The Powers of Criminal Courts (Sentencing) Act 2000 is amended as follows.

22. For section 3 (committal for sentence on summary trial of offence triable either way) there is substituted—

"3. Committal for sentence on indication of guilty plea to serious offence triable either way.

(1) Subject to subsection (4) below, this section applies where—

(a) a person aged 18 or over appears or is brought before a magistrates' court ("the court") on an information charging him with an offence triable either way ("the offence");

(b) he or his representative indicates under section 17A or (as the case may be) 17B of the Magistrates' Courts Act 1980 (initial procedure: accused to indicate intention as to plea), but not section 20(7) of that Act, that he would plead guilty if the offence were to proceed to trial; and

(c) proceeding as if section 9(1) of that Act were complied with and he pleaded guilty under it, the court convicts him of the offence.

(2) If the court is of the opinion that—

(a) the offence; or

(b) the combination of the offence and one or more offences associated with it,

was so serious that the Crown Court should, in the court's opinion, have the power to deal with the offender in any way it could deal with him if he had been convicted on indictment, the court may commit him in custody or on bail to the Crown Court for sentence in accordance with section 5(1) below.

(3) Where the court commits a person under subsection (2) above, section 6 below (which enables a magistrates' court, where it commits a person under this section in respect of an offence, also to commit him to the Crown Court to be dealt with in respect of certain other offences) shall apply accordingly.

(4) This section does not apply in relation to an offence as regards which this section is excluded by section 17D of the Magistrates' Courts Act 1980 (certain offences where value involved is small).

(5) The preceding provisions of this section shall apply in relation to a corporation as if—

(a) the corporation were an individual aged 18 or over; and

(b) in subsection (2) above, the words "in custody or on bail" were omitted."

23. After section 3 there is inserted—

"3A. Committal for sentence of dangerous adult offenders. (1) This section applies where on the summary trial of a specified offence triable either way a person aged 18 or over is convicted of the offence.

(2) If, in relation to the offence, it appears to the court that the criteria for the imposition of a sentence under section 225(3) or 227(2) of the Criminal Justice Act 2003 would be met, the court must commit the offender in custody or on bail to the Crown Court for sentence in accordance with section 5(1) below.

(3) Where the court commits a person under subsection (2) above, section 6 below (which enables a magistrates' court, where it commits a person under this section in respect of an offence, also to commit him to the Crown Court to be dealt with in respect of certain other offences) shall apply accordingly.

(4) In reaching any decision under or taking any step contemplated by this section—

(a) the court shall not be bound by any indication of sentence given in respect of the offence under section 20 of the Magistrates' Courts Act 1980 (procedure where summary trial appears more suitable); and

(b) nothing the court does under this section may be challenged or be the subject of any appeal in any court on the ground that it is not consistent with an indication of sentence.

(5) Nothing in this section shall prevent the court from committing a specified offence to the Crown Court for sentence under section 3 above if the provisions of that section are satisfied.

(6) In this section, references to a specified offence are to a specified offence within the meaning of section 224 of the Criminal Justice Act 2003.

3B. Committal for sentence on indication of guilty plea by child or young person. (1) This section applies where—

(a) a person aged under 18 appears or is brought before a magistrates' court ("the court") on an information charging him with an offence mentioned in subsection (1) of section 91 below ("the offence");

(b) he or his representative indicates under section 24A or (as the case may be) 24B of the Magistrates' Courts Act 1980 (child or young person to indicate intention as to plea in certain cases) that he would plead guilty if the offence were to proceed to trial; and

(c) proceeding as if section 9(1) of that Act were complied with and he pleaded guilty under it, the court convicts him of the offence.

(2) If the court is of the opinion that—

(a) the offence; or

(b) the combination of the offence and one or more offences associated with it,

was such that the Crown Court should, in the court's opinion, have power to deal with the offender as if the provisions of section 91(3) below applied, the court may commit him in custody or on bail to the Crown Court for sentence in accordance with section 5A(1) below.

(3) Where the court commits a person under subsection (2) above, section 6 below (which enables a magistrates' court, where it commits a person under this section in respect of an offence, also to commit him to the Crown Court to be dealt with in respect of certain other offences) shall apply accordingly.

3C. Committal for sentence of dangerous young offenders.   (1) This section applies where on the summary trial of a specified offence a person aged under 18 is convicted of the offence.

(2) If, in relation to the offence, it appears to the court that the criteria for the imposition of a sentence under section 226(3) or 228(2) of the Criminal Justice Act 2003 would be met, the court must commit the offender in custody or on bail to the Crown Court for sentence in accordance with section 5A(1) below.

(3) Where the court commits a person under subsection (2) above, section 6 below (which enables a magistrates' court, where it commits a person under this section in respect of an offence, also to commit him to the Crown Court to be dealt with in respect of certain other offences) shall apply accordingly.

(4) Nothing in this section shall prevent the court from committing a specified offence to the Crown Court for sentence under section 3B above if the provisions of that section are satisfied.

(5) In this section, references to a specified offence are to a specified offence within the meaning of section 224 of the Criminal Justice Act 2003."

24. (1) Section 4 (committal for sentence on indication of guilty plea to offence triable either way) is amended as follows.

(2) For subsection (1)(b), there is substituted—

"(b) he or (where applicable) his representative indicates under section 17A, 17B or 20(7) of the Magistrates' Courts Act 1980 that he would plead guilty if the offence were to proceed to trial; and".

(3) In subsection (1)(c), for "the Magistrates' Courts Act 1980" there is substituted "that Act".

(4) After subsection (1) there is inserted—

"(1A) But this section does not apply to an offence as regards which this section is excluded by section 17D of that Act (certain offences where value involved is small)."

(5) For subsection (3), there is substituted—

"(3) If the power conferred by subsection (2) above is not exercisable but the court is still to determine to, or to determine whether to, send the offender to the Crown Court for trial under section 51 or 51A of the Crime and Disorder Act 1998 for one or more related offences—

(a) it shall adjourn the proceedings relating to the offence until after it has made those determinations; and
(b) if it sends the offender to the Crown Court for trial for one or more related offences, it may then exercise that power."

(6) In subsection (4)(b), after "section 3(2)" there is inserted "or, as the case may be, section 3A(2)".

(7) After subsection (7) there is inserted—

"(8) In reaching any decision under or taking any step contemplated by this section—

(a) the court shall not be bound by any indication of sentence given in respect of the offence under section 20 of the Magistrates' Courts Act 1980 (procedure where summary trial appears more suitable); and
(b) nothing the court does under this section may be challenged or be the subject of any appeal in any court on the ground that it is not consistent with an indication of sentence."

25. After section 4 there is inserted—

"4A. Committal for sentence on indication of guilty plea by child or young person with related offences.   (1) This section applies where—

(a) a person aged under 18 appears or brought before a magistrates' court ("the court") on an information charging him with an offence mentioned in subsection (1) of section 91 below ("the offence");
(b) he or his representative indicates under section 24A or (as the case may be) 24B of the Magistrates' Courts Act 1980 (child or young person to indicate intention as to plea in certain cases) that he would plead guilty if the offence were to proceed to trial; and
(c) proceeding as if section 9(1) of that Act were complied with and he pleaded guilty under it, the court convicts him of the offence.

(2) If the court has sent the offender to the Crown Court for trial for one or more related offences, that is to say one or more offences which, in its opinion, are related to the offence, it may commit him in custody or on bail to the Crown Court to be dealt with in respect of the offence in accordance with section 5A(1) below.

(3) If the power conferred by subsection (2) above is not exercisable but the court is still to determine to, or to determine whether to, send the offender to the Crown Court for trial under section 51 or 51A of the Crime and Disorder Act 1998 for one or more related offences—

(a) it shall adjourn the proceedings relating to the offence until after it has made those determinations; and
(b) if it sends the offender to the Crown Court for trial for one or more related offences, it may then exercise that power.

(4) Where the court—

(a) under subsection (2) above commits the offender to the Crown Court to be dealt with in respect of the offence; and
(b) does not state that, in its opinion, it also has power so to commit him under section 3B(2) or, as the case may be, section 3C(2) above,

section 5A(1) below shall not apply unless he is convicted before the Crown Court of one or more of the related offences.

(5) Where section 5A(1) below does not apply, the Crown Court may deal with the offender in respect of the offence in any way in which the magistrates' court could deal with him if it had just convicted him of the offence.

(6) Where the court commits a person under subsection (2) above, section 6 below (which enables a magistrates' court, where it commits a person under this section in respect of an offence, also to commit him to the Crown Court to be dealt with in respect of certain other offences) shall apply accordingly.

(7) Section 4(7) above applies for the purposes of this section as it applies for the purposes of that section."

26. For section 5 (power of Crown Court on committal for sentence under sections 3 and 4) there is substituted—

"5. Power of Crown Court on committal for sentence under sections 3, 3A and 4.   (1) Where an offender is committed by a magistrates' court for sentence under section 3, 3A or 4 above, the Crown Court shall inquire into the circumstances of the case and may deal with the offender in any way in which it could deal with him if he had just been convicted of the offence on indictment before the court.

(2) In relation to committals under section 4 above, subsection (1) above has effect subject to section 4(4) and (5) above.

(3) Section 20A(1) of the Magistrates' Courts Act 1980 (which relates to the effect of an indication of sentence under section 20 of that Act) shall not apply in respect of any specified offence (within the meaning of section 224 of the Criminal Justice Act 2003)—

(*a*)   in respect of which the offender is committed under section 3A(2) above; or

(*b*)   in respect of which—

   (i)   the offender is committed under section 4(2) above; and

   (ii)   the court states under section 4(4) above that, in its opinion, it also has power to commit the offender under section 3A(2) above."

27. After section 5 there is inserted—

"5A. Power of Crown Court on committal for sentence under sections 3B, 3C and 4A.   (1) Where an offender is committed by a magistrates' court for sentence under section 3B, 3C or 4A above, the Crown Court shall inquire into the circumstances of the case and may deal with the offender in any way in which it could deal with him if he had just been convicted of the offence on indictment before the court.

(2) In relation to committals under section 4A above, subsection (1) above has effect subject to section 4A(4) and (5) above."

28. In section 6 (committal for sentence in certain cases where offender committed in respect of another offence), in subsection (4)(*b*), for "3 and 4" there is substituted "3 to 4A".

PART 2
MINOR AND CONSEQUENTIAL AMENDMENTS

This Part of Sch 3 makes numerous, minor and consequential amendments. Those which effect statutory provisions reproduced in this work will be shown in the statutes concerned when they take effect.

Anti-social Behaviour Act 2003[1]
(2003 c 38)

PART 1[2]
PREMISES WHERE DRUGS USED UNLAWFULLY

1–4507   1. Closure notice[3].   (1) This section applies to premises if a police officer not below the rank of superintendent (the authorising officer) has reasonable grounds for believing[4]—

(*a*)   that at any time during the relevant period the premises[3] have been used in connection with the unlawful use, production or supply of a Class A controlled drug, and

(*b*)   that the use of the premises is associated with the occurrence of disorder or serious nuisance to members of the public.

(2) The authorising officer may authorise the issue of a closure notice in respect of premises to which this section applies if he is satisfied—

(*a*)   that the local authority[3] for the area in which the premises are situated has been consulted;

(*b*)   that reasonable steps have been taken to establish the identity of any person who lives on the premises or who has control of or responsibility for or an interest in the premises.

(3) An authorisation under subsection (2) may be given orally or in writing, but if it is given orally the authorising officer must confirm it in writing as soon as it is practicable.

(4) A closure notice must—

(*a*)   give notice that an application will be made under section 2 for the closure of the premises;

(*b*)   state that access to the premises by any person other than a person who habitually resides in the premises or the owner of the premises is prohibited;

(*c*)   specify the date and time when and the place at which the application will be heard;

(*d*)   explain the effects of an order made in pursuance of section 2;

(*e*)   state that failure to comply with the notice amounts to an offence;

(*f*)   give information about relevant advice providers.

(5) The closure notice must be served by a constable.

(6) Service is effected by—

(*a*)   fixing a copy of the notice to at least one prominent place on the premises,

(*b*)   fixing a copy of the notice to each normal means of access to the premises,

(*c*)   fixing a copy of the notice to any outbuildings which appear to the constable to be used with or as part of the premises,

(*d*)   giving a copy of the notice to at least one person who appears to the constable to have control of or responsibility for the premises, and

(*e*)   giving a copy of the notice to the persons identified in pursuance of subsection (2)(*b*) and to any other person appearing to the constable to be a person of a description mentioned in that subsection.

(7) The closure notice must also be served on any person who occupies any other part of the building or other structure in which the premises are situated if the constable reasonably believes at the time of serving the notice under subsection (6) that the person's access to the other part of the building or structure will be impeded if a closure order[3] is made under section 2.

(7A) For the purpose of subsection (6)(*a*) a constable may enter any premises to which this section applies, using reasonable force if necessary.

(8) It is immaterial whether any person has been convicted of an offence relating to the use, production or supply of a controlled drug.

(9) The Secretary of State may by regulations specify premises or descriptions of premises to which this section does not apply.

(10) The relevant period is the period of three months ending with the day on which the authorising officer considers whether to authorise the issue of a closure notice in respect of the premises.

(11) Information about relevant advice providers is information about the names of and means of contacting persons and organisations in the area that provide advice about housing and legal matters.

[Anti-social Behaviour Act 2003, s 1 as amended by the Drugs Act 2005, Sch 1.]

1. This Act implements further measures against anti-social behaviour by providing, inter alia, for: the closure of premises in which Class A drugs have been unlawfully used; applications by social landlords for injunctions, possession and eviction orders and the demotion of certain tenancies; firmer action against the parents of truanting children or children evicted from school for anti-social behaviour by making available fixed penalties and parenting orders; the dispersal of groups and removal of persons under 16 to their homes; changes to firearms legislation; the closure of noisy premises; penalty notices for graffiti and fly-positing; changes to the law relating to public assemblies, raves and trespass; a complaints procedure, etc, regarding high hedges; additional categories of organisations becoming able to apply for anti-social behaviour orders and other amendments as to the circumstances in which such orders may be made; and the issue of penalty notices for certain anti-social offences against 16 and 17 year-olds.

The Act will be brought into force in accordance with Commencement Orders made under s 93. At the time of going to press the following orders had been made: Anti-social Behaviour Act 2003 (Commencement No 1 and Transitional Provisions) Order 2003, SI 2003/3300; Anti-social Behaviour Act 2003 (Commencement No 2) Order 2004, SI 2004/690; Anti-social Behaviour Act 2003 (Commencement No 1) (Wales) Order 2004, SI 2004/999; Anti-social Behaviour Act 2003 (Commencement No 3 and Savings) Order 2004, SI 2004/1502; Anti-social Behaviour Act 2003 (Commencement No 4) Order 2004, SI 2004/2168 amended by SI 2006/835; Anti-social Behaviour Act 2003 (Commencement No 2 and Savings) (Wales) Order 2004, SI 2004/2557; Anti-social Behaviour Act 2003 (Commencement No 3) (Wales) Order 2004, SI 2004/3238; Anti-social Behaviour Act 2003 (Commencement No 5) (England) Order 2005, SI 2005/710; Anti-social Behaviour Act 2003 (Commencement No 4) (Wales) Order 2005, SI 2005/1225; Anti-social Behaviour Act 2003 (Commencement No 6) (England) Order 2006, SI 2006/393; Anti-Social Behaviour Act 2003 (Commencement No 4) (Amendment) Order 2006, SI 2006/835; and Anti-social Behaviour Act 2003 (Commencement No 5) (Wales) Order 2006, SI 2006/1278. Most of the provisions of the Act are now in force.

2. Part 1 contains ss 1–11. The provisions of Pt 1 came into force on 20 January 2004.

3. Defined in s 11, post.

4. A closure notice is an administrative act and the officer may rely on hearsay and on any material which is relevant whatever its source: *R (Errington) v Metropolitan Police Authority* [2006] EWHC 1155 (Admin), 171 JP 89.

1–4508   2. Closure order[1]. (1) If a closure notice has been issued under section 1 a constable must apply under this section to a magistrates' court for the making of a closure order.

(2) The application must be heard by the magistrates' court not later than 48 hours after the notice was served in pursuance of section 1(6)(*a*).

(3) The magistrates' court may make a closure order if and only if it is satisfied that each of the following paragraphs applies—

(*a*) the premises in respect of which the closure notice was issued have been used in connection with the unlawful use, production or supply of a Class A controlled drug;

(*b*) the use of the premises is associated with the occurrence of disorder or serious nuisance to members of the public;

(*c*) the making of the order is necessary to prevent the occurrence of such disorder or serious nuisance for the period specified in the order.

(4) A closure order is an order that the premises in respect of which the order is made are closed to all persons for such period (not exceeding three months) as the court decides.

(5) But the order may include such provision as the court thinks appropriate relating to access to any part of the building or structure of which the premises form part.

(6) The magistrates' court may adjourn the hearing on the application for a period of not more than 14 days[2] to enable—

(*a*) the occupier of the premises,

(*b*) the person who has control of or responsibility for the premises, or

(*c*) any other person with an interest in the premises,

to show why a closure order should not be made.

(7) If the magistrates' court adjourns the hearing under subsection (6) it may order that the closure notice continues in effect until the end of the period of the adjournment.

(8) A closure order may be made in respect of all or any part of the premises in respect of which the closure notice was issued.

(9) It is immaterial whether any person has been convicted of an offence relating to the use, production or supply of a controlled drug.

[Anti-social Behaviour Act 2003, s 2.]

1. Proceedings for a closure order are civil in nature: *Metropolitan Police Comr v Hooper* [2005] EWHC 199 (Admin), [2005] 4 All ER 1095, [2005] 1 WLR 1995, (2005) 169 JP 409. The standard of proof to be applied to the matters specified in s 2(3)(a) and (b) is the civil standard, ie proof on the balance of probabilities: *Chief Constable of Merseyside Police v Harrison (Secretary of State for the Home Department intervening)* [2006] EWHC 1106 (Admin), [2007] 1 QB 79, [2006] 3 WLR 171, (2006) 170 JP 523. However, the procedure for bringing civil proceedings by way of complaint does not seem to be appropriate as the closure notice is not against a person but in respect of premises. Section 2 has its own procedural provisions. There is no particular form for the making of an application to the magistrates' court. The closure notice has informed persons with an interest in the premises when and where the application to the court will be heard. There is therefore no need for a summons. At the hearing, the court should satisfy itself that copies of the notice have been served so that anyone who would be adversely affected by it and entitled to make representations had been, so far as was reasonably practicable, identified and served. If the notice does not contain the necessary information about the hearing, the magistrates are likely to indicate that they are not prepared to continue with any hearing until the notice is put in proper form. Provided those affected have been notified of the hearing, shortcomings in the notice (such as the reliance by the officer on "reasonable suspicion" rather than "reasonable grounds for believing") do not affect the jurisdiction of the magistrates to hear an application but may preclude criminal proceedings under s 4(1) or (2) in so far as they are dependant on the validity of the notice. As regards proceedings under s 2, it is for the court to satisfy itself whether an order is needed having heard the evidence: *R (Errington) v Metropolitan Police Authority* [2006] EWHC 1155 (Admin), 171 JP 89.

The following guidance on service of evidence, the use of hearsay, hearsay notices and disclosure was given in *R (on the application of Cleary) v Highbury Corner Magistrates' Court* [2006] EWHC 1869 (Admin), [2007] 1 All ER 270:

(1) Fairness requires that the police must normally serve written versions of the evidence they propose to adduce in sufficient time before the hearing to enable the defendant fairly to deal with it. The statutory intention is that the first hearing within 48 hours of the service of a closure notice should be an effective hearing if possible. If the evidence which the police propose to adduce is not served by the time of the first 48-hour hearing, or if it is not fully served, fairness requires that it should be served well in advance of the adjourned hearing.

(2) Credible direct evidence of a defendant in an application for a closure order may well carry greater weight than uncross-examined hearsay from an anonymous witness or several anonymous witnesses. Magistrates are more likely to be satisfied as to the statutory conditions for the making of an order if the application is supported by direct evidence of *witnesses* available for cross-examination, and if there is hearsay evidence, if what is served and adduced is first hand and complete. If what is relied on is oral statements to a police officer, the officer should give direct evidence of what was said and the circumstances in which it was said.

(3) Rule 3b of the Magistrates' Courts (Hearsay Evidence in Civil Proceedings) Rules 1999 provides that a party who desires to give hearsay evidence at a hearing must serve a hearsay notice not less than 21 days before the date fixed for the hearing. This fits ill with the timetable for closure applications. Therefore, if the police intend to rely on hearsay evidence they will have to make an application for a direction under r 3(2) to reduce the 21-day period. They will want to make the application at the first hearing and may need to serve an application to do so with the closure notice. If the court accedes to the application the period for serving the hearsay notice will need to be sufficiently in advance of the adjourned hearing to enable the defendant fairly to deal with it, including making an application under r 4c of the 1999 rules to call and cross-examine the maker of a statement whom it is not proposed to call.

(4) Standard disclosure under the CPR which requires a party to disclose only the documents on which he relies and documents which adversely affect his own case or support another party's case is a good guide to what is necessary and proportionate in relation to disclosure. The police should disclose documents which clearly and materially affect their case adversely or support the defendant's case.

2. While the engagement of Convention rights means that s 2 should not be read as excluding s 54 of the Magistrates' Courts Act 1980, s 54 should be resorted to only where no other way exists of avoiding a breach of a person's Convention rights and justices should otherwise not adjourn proceedings once or in total for more than the 14 days permitted by s 2: *Metropolitan Police Comr v Hooper*, supra. The ability to adjourn beyond 14 days was confirmed in *R (Turner) v Highbury Corner Magistrates' Court* [2005] EWHC 2568 (Admin), [2006] 1 WLR 220, (2006) 170 JP 93 in which it was held that, the court could exercise its general powers under s 54 of the 1980 Act to grant an adjournment if it were satisfied that the need for such an adjournment, in the interests of justice, overrode Parliament's intention that the proceedings should be concluded speedily. See further *R (on the application of Cleary v Highbury Corner Magistrates' Court*, supra.

1-4509   3. Closure order: enforcement.   (1) This section applies if a magistrates' court makes an order under section 2.

(2) A constable or an authorised person may—

(a)   enter the premises in respect of which the order is made;
(b)   do anything reasonably necessary to secure the premises against entry by any person.

(3) A person acting under subsection (2) may use reasonable force.

(4) But a constable or authorised person seeking to enter the premises for the purposes of subsection (2) must, if required to do so by or on behalf of the owner, occupier or other person in charge of the premises, produce evidence of his identity and authority before entering the premises.

(5) A constable or authorised person may also enter the premises at any time while the order has effect for the purpose of carrying out essential maintenance of or repairs to the premises.

(6) In this section and in section 4 an authorised person is a person authorised by the chief officer of police for the area in which the premises are situated.
[Anti-social Behaviour Act 2003, s 3.]

1-4510   4. Closure of premises: offences.   (1) A person commits an offence[1] if he remains on or enters premises in contravention of a closure notice.

(2) A person commits an offence[1] if—

(a)   he obstructs a constable or an authorised person acting under section 1(6) or 3(2),
(b)   he remains on premises in respect of which a closure order has been made, or
(c)   he enters the premises.

(3) A person guilty of an offence under this section is liable on summary conviction—

(a)   to imprisonment for a period not exceeding six months, or
(b)   to a fine not exceeding level 5 on the standard scale,

or to both such imprisonment and fine.

(4) But a person does not commit an offence under subsection (1) or subsection (2)(*b*) or (*c*) if he has a reasonable excuse for entering or being on the premises (as the case may be).

(5) *Repealed.*

[Anti-social Behaviour Act 2003, s 4 as amended by the Serious Organised Crime and Police Act 2005, Sch 7.]

---

1. It is a defence in so far as it relates to s 1(6) that the closure notice was invalid: *R (Errington) v Metropolitan Police Authority* [2006] EWHC 1155 (Admin), 171 JP 89.

1–4511 5. Extension and discharge of closure order. (1) At any time before the end of the period for which a closure order is made or extended a constable may make a complaint to an appropriate justice of the peace for an extension or further extension of the period for which it has effect.

(2) But a complaint must not be made unless it is authorised by a police officer not below the rank of superintendent—

(*a*) who has reasonable grounds for believing that it is necessary to extend the period for which the closure order has effect for the purpose of preventing the occurrence of disorder or serious nuisance to members of the public, and

(*b*) who is satisfied that the local authority has been consulted about the intention to make the complaint.

(3) If a complaint is made to a justice of the peace under subsection (1) the justice may issue a summons directed to—

(*a*) the persons on whom the closure notice relating to the closed premises was served under subsection (6)(*d*) or (*e*) or (7) of section 1;

(*b*) any other person who appears to the justice to have an interest in the closed premises but on whom the closure notice was not served,

requiring such person to appear before the magistrates' court to answer to the complaint.

(4) If the court is satisfied that the order is necessary to prevent the occurrence of disorder or serious nuisance for a further period it may extend the period for which the order has effect by a period not exceeding three months.

(5) But a closure order must not have effect for more than six months.

(6) Any of the following persons may make a complaint to an appropriate justice of the peace for an order that a closure order is discharged—

(*a*) a constable;

(*b*) the local authority;

(*c*) a person on whom the closure notice relating to the closed premises was served under subsection (6)(*d*) or (*e*) or (7) of section 1;

(*d*) a person who has an interest in the closed premises but on whom the closure notice was not served.

(7) If a complaint is made under subsection (6) by a person other than a constable the justice may issue a summons directed to such constable as he thinks appropriate requiring the constable to appear before the magistrates' court to answer to the complaint.

(8) The court must not make an order discharging a closure order unless it is satisfied that the closure order is no longer necessary to prevent the occurrence of disorder or serious nuisance to members of the public.

(9) If a summons is issued in accordance with subsection (3) or (7), a notice stating the date, time and place at which the complaint will be heard must be served on—

(*a*) the persons to whom the summons is directed if it is issued under subsection (3);

(*b*) the persons mentioned in subsection (6)(*c*) and (*d*) (except the complainant) if the summons is issued under subsection (7);

(*c*) such constable as the justice thinks appropriate (unless he is the complainant);

(*d*) the local authority (unless they are the complainant).

(10) An appropriate justice of the peace is a justice of the peace acting for the petty sessions area in which the premises in respect of which a closure order is made are situated.

[Anti-social Behaviour Act 2003, s 5.]

1–4512 6. Appeals[1]. (1) This section applies to—

(*a*) an order under section 2 or 5;

(*b*) a decision by a court not to make an order under either of those sections.

(2) An appeal against an order or decision to which this section applies must be brought to the Crown Court before the end of the period of 21 days beginning with the day on which the order or decision is made.

(3) An appeal against an order under section 2 or 5(4) may be brought by—

(*a*) a person on whom the closure notice relating to the closed premises was served under section 1(6)(*d*) or (*e*);

(*b*) a person who has an interest in the closed premises but on whom the closure notice was not served.

(4) An appeal against the decision of a court not to make such an order may be brought by—

(a) a constable;

(b) the local authority.

(5) On an appeal under this section the Crown Court may make such order as it thinks appropriate.
[Anti-social Behaviour Act 2003, s 6.]

---

1. It is important that appeals against closure orders are heard as soon as possible, ideally within a very few days of the lodging of the notice. Courts should take steps to ensure such appeals are given the necessary priority: *R (Errington) v Metropolitan Police Authority* [2006] EWHC 1155 (Admin), 171 JP 89.

1-4513   7. Access to other premises.   (1) This section applies to any person who occupies or owns any part of a building or structure—

(a) in which closed premises are situated, and

(b) in respect of which the closure order does not have effect.

(2) A person to whom this section applies may at any time while a closure order has effect apply to—

(a) the magistrates' court in respect of an order made under section 2 or 5;

(b) the Crown Court in respect of an order made under section 6.

(3) If an application is made under this section notice of the date, time and place of the hearing to consider the application must be given to every person mentioned in section 5(6).

(4) On an application under this section the court may make such order as it thinks appropriate in relation to access to any part of a building or structure in which closed premises are situated.

(5) It is immaterial whether any provision has been made as mentioned in section 2(5).
[Anti-social Behaviour Act 2003, s 7.]

1-4514   8. Reimbursement of costs.   (1) A police authority or a local authority which incurs expenditure for the purpose of clearing, securing or maintaining the premises in respect of which a closure order has effect may apply to the court which made the order for an order under this section.

(2) On an application under this section the court may make such order as it thinks appropriate in the circumstances for the reimbursement (in full or in part) by the owner of the premises of the expenditure mentioned in subsection (1).

(3) But an application for an order under this section must not be entertained unless it is made not later than the end of the period of three months starting with the day the closure order ceases to have effect.

(4) An application under this section must be served on—

(a) the police authority for the area in which the premises are situated if the application is made by the local authority;

(b) the local authority if the application is made by a police authority;

(c) the owner of the premises.
[Anti-social Behaviour Act 2003, s 8.]

1-4515   9. Exemption from liability for certain damages.   (1) A constable is not liable for relevant damages in respect of anything done or omitted to be done by him in the performance or purported performance of his functions under this Part.

(2) A chief officer of police is not liable for relevant damages in respect of anything done or omitted to be done by a constable under his direction or control in the performance or purported performance of the constable's functions under this Part.

(3) Subsections (1) and (2) do not apply—

(a) if the act or omission is shown to have been in bad faith;

(b) so as to prevent an award of damages made in respect of an act or omission on the ground that the act or omission was unlawful by virtue of section 6(1) of the Human Rights Act 1998 (c 42).

(4) This section does not affect any other exemption from liability for damages (whether at common law or otherwise).

(5) Relevant damages are damages in proceedings for judicial review or for the tort of negligence or misfeasance in public duty.
[Anti-social Behaviour Act 2003, s 9.]

1-4516   10. Compensation.   (1) This section applies to any person who incurs financial loss in consequence of—

(a) the issue of a closure notice, or

(b) a closure order having effect.

(2) A person to whom this section applies may apply to—

(a) the magistrates' court which considered the application for a closure order;

(*b*)   the Crown Court if the closure order was made or extended by an order made by that Court on an appeal under section 6.

(3)   An application under this section must not be entertained unless it is made not later than the end of the period of three months starting with whichever is the later of—

(*a*)   the day the court decides not to make a closure order;
(*b*)   the day the Crown Court dismisses an appeal against a decision not to make a closure order;
(*c*)   the day a closure order ceases to have effect.

(4)   On an application under this section the court may order the payment of compensation out of central funds if it is satisfied—

(*a*)   that the person had no connection with the use of the premises as mentioned in section 1(1),
(*b*)   if the person is the owner or occupier of the premises, that he took reasonable steps to prevent the use,
(*c*)   that the person has incurred financial loss as mentioned in subsection (1), and
(*d*)   having regard to all the circumstances it is appropriate to order payment of compensation in respect of that loss.

(5)   Central funds has the same meaning as in enactments providing for the payment of costs.
[Anti-social Behaviour Act 2003, s 10.]

1–4517   11. Interpretation.   (1)   References to a controlled drug and (however expressed) to the production or supply of a controlled drug must be construed in accordance with the Misuse of Drugs Act 1971 (c 38).

(2)   A Class A controlled drug is a controlled drug which is a Class A drug within the meaning of section 2 of that Act.

(3)   Premises includes—

(*a*)   any land or other place (whether enclosed or not);
(*b*)   any outbuildings which are or are used as part of the premises.

(4)   A closure notice is a notice issued under section 1.
(5)   A closure order is—

(*a*)   an order made under section 2;
(*b*)   an order extended under section 5;
(*c*)   an order made or extended under section 6 which has the like effect as an order made or extended under section 2 or 5 (as the case may be).

(6)   Each of the following is a local authority in relation to England—

(*a*)   a district council;
(*b*)   a London borough council;
(*c*)   a county council for an area for which there is no district council;
(*d*)   the Common Council of the City of London in its capacity as a local authority;
(*e*)   the Council of the Isles of Scilly.

(7)   Each of the following is a local authority in relation to Wales—

(*a*)   a county council;
(*b*)   a county borough council.

(8)   References to a local authority are to the local authority for the area in which premises—

(*a*)   to which a closure notice applies are situated;
(*b*)   in respect of which a closure order has effect are situated.

(9)   Closed premises are premises in respect of which a closure order has effect.
(10)   A person is the owner of premises if either of the following paragraphs applies to him—

(*a*)   he is a person (other than a mortgagee not in possession) who is for the time being entitled to dispose of the fee simple in the premises, whether in possession or in reversion;
(*b*)   he is a person who holds or is entitled to the rents and profits of the premises under a lease which (when granted) was for a term of not less than three years.

(11)   This section applies for the purposes of this Part.
[Anti-social Behaviour Act 2003, s 11.]

1–4518

PART 2[1]
HOUSING[2]

---

1.   Part 2 contains ss 12–17.
2.   This part inserts provisions in the Housing Acts 1985 and 1986. The later Act is amended for, inter alia, social landlords to obtain anti-social behaviour and other forms of injunction or exclusion orders. The earlier Act is amended to enable social landlords to seek the demotion of secure tenancies where tenants or their visitors have engaged or threatened to engage in anti-social behaviour or use of premises for unlawful purposes; the 1985 is further amended as to proceedings for possession in cases of alleged anti-social behaviour.

PART 3[1]

PARENTAL RESPONSIBILITIES

Parenting orders under the 1998 Act

1–4519   18.   Parenting orders under the 1998 Act[2]

---

    1. Part 3 contains ss 18–29. At the time of going to press, ss 18, 23, 25–29 were in force in relation to England and Wales, and ss 19–22 and 24 were in force in relation to England only: see the Anti-social Behaviour Act 2003 (Commencement No 1 and Transitional Provisions) Order 2003/3300.
    2. Section 18 amended s 8 of the Crime and Disorder Act 1998. See this PART, ante.

Truancy and exclusion from school

1–4520   19.   Parenting contracts in cases of exclusion from school or truancy.   (1) This section applies where a pupil has been excluded on disciplinary grounds from a relevant school for a fixed period or permanently.
    (2) This section also applies where a child of compulsory school age has failed to attend regularly at

    (*a*)   a relevant school at which he is a registered pupil;
    (*b*)   any place at which education is provided for him in the circumstances mentioned in subsection (1) of section 444ZA of the Education Act 1996, and
    (*c*)   any place at which he is required to attend in the circumstances mentioned in subsection (2) of that section.

    (3) A local education authority or the governing body of a relevant school may enter into a parenting contract with a parent of the pupil or child.
    (4) A parenting contract is a document which contains—

    (*a*)   a statement by the parent that he agrees to comply with such requirements as may be specified in the document for such period as may be so specified, and
    (*b*)   a statement by the local education authority or governing body that it agrees to provide support to the parent for the purpose of complying with those requirements.

    (5) The requirements mentioned in subsection (4) may include (in particular) a requirement to attend a counselling or guidance programme.
    (6) The purpose of the requirements mentioned in subsection (4)—

    (*a*)   in a case falling within subsection (1), is to improve the behaviour of the pupil,
    (*b*)   in a case falling within subsection (2), is to ensure that the child attends regularly at the relevant school at which he is a registered pupil.

    (7) A parenting contract must be signed by the parent and signed on behalf of the local education authority or governing body.
    (8) A parenting contract does not create any obligations in respect of whose breach any liability arises in contract or in tort.
    (9) Local education authorities and governing bodies of relevant schools must, in carrying out their functions in relation to parenting contracts, have regard to any guidance which is issued by the appropriate person from time to time for that purpose.
[Anti-social Behaviour Act 2003, s 19 as amended by the Education Act 2005, Sch 18.]

1–4521   20.   Parenting orders in cases of exclusion from school.   (1) This section applies where—

    (*a*)   a pupil has been excluded on disciplinary grounds from a relevant school for a fixed period or permanently, and
    (*b*)   such conditions as may be prescribed[1] in regulations made by the appropriate person are satisfied.

    (2) A local education authority may apply[2] to a magistrates' court for a parenting order in respect of a parent of the pupil.
    (3) If such an application is made, the court may make a parenting order in respect of a parent of the pupil if it is satisfied that making the order would be desirable in the interests of improving the behaviour of the pupil.
    (4) A parenting order is an order which requires the parent—

    (*a*)   to comply, for a period not exceeding twelve months, with such requirements as are specified in the order, and
    (*b*)   subject to subsection (5), to attend, for a concurrent period not exceeding three months, such counselling or guidance programme as may be specified in directions given by the responsible officer.

    (5) A parenting order under this section may, but need not, include a requirement mentioned in subsection (4)(*b*) in any case where a parenting order under this section or any other enactment has been made in respect of the parent on a previous occasion.
    (6) A counselling or guidance programme which a parent is required to attend by virtue of

subsection (4)(*b*) may be or include a residential course but only if the court is satisfied that the following two conditions are fulfilled.

(7) The first condition is that the attendance of the parent at a residential course is likely to be more effective than his attendance at a non-residential course in improving the behaviour of the pupil.

(8) The second condition is that any interference with family life which is likely to result from the attendance of the parent at a residential course is proportionate in all the circumstances.
[Anti-social Behaviour Act 2003, s 20.]

---

1. The Education (Parenting Orders) (England) Regulations 2004, SI 2004/182 and the Education (Parenting Orders) (Wales) Regulations 2006, SI 2006/1277 have been made.
2. Application is by way of complaint and for form of application and order, see the Magistrates' Courts (Parenting Orders) Rules 2004, in this Part, post.

1–4522   21. Parenting orders: supplemental.   (1) In deciding whether to make a parenting order under section 20, a court must take into account (amongst other things)—

(*a*) any refusal by the parent to enter into a parenting contract under section 19 in respect of the pupil in a case falling within subsection (1) of that section, or
(*b*) if the parent has entered into such a parenting contract, any failure by the parent to comply with the requirements specified in the contract.

(2) Before making a parenting order under section 20 in the case of a pupil under the age of 16, a court must obtain and consider information about the pupil's family circumstances and the likely effect of the order on those circumstances.

(3) Subsections (3) to (7) of section 9 of the Crime and Disorder Act 1998 (c 37) (supplemental provisions about parenting orders) are to apply in relation to a parenting order under section 20 as they apply in relation to a parenting order under section 8 of that Act.

(4) The appropriate person may by regulations[1] make provision as to how the costs associated with the requirements of parenting orders under section 20 (including the costs of providing counselling or guidance programmes) are to be borne.

(5) Local education authorities, head teachers and responsible officers must, in carrying out their functions in relation to parenting orders, have regard to any guidance which is issued by the appropriate person from time to time for that purpose.
[Anti-social Behaviour Act 2003, s 21.]

---

1. The Education (Parenting Orders) (England) Regulations 2004, SI 2004/182 and the Education (Parenting Orders) (Wales) Regulations 2006, SI 2006/1277, have been made.

1–4523   22. Parenting orders: appeals.   (1) An appeal lies to the Crown Court against the making of a parenting order under section 20.

(2) Subsections (2) and (3) of section 10 of the Crime and Disorder Act 1998 (appeals against parenting orders) are to apply in relation to an appeal under this section as they apply in relation to an appeal under subsection (1)(*b*) of that section.
[Anti-social Behaviour Act 2003, s 22.]

1–4524   23. Penalty notices for parents in cases of truancy[1]

---

1. Section 23 inserted new provisions in the Education Act 1996 to provide the option of a fixed penalty scheme for the offence of failing to secure the regular school attendance of a registered pupil. These provisions are reproduced in the 1996 Act (in Part VIII, Miscellaneous offences, Matters of complaint, etc post).

1–4525   24. Interpretation.   In this section and sections 19 to 21—

"the appropriate person" means—

(*a*) in relation to England, the Secretary of State, and
(*b*) in relation to Wales, the National Assembly for Wales,

"child of compulsory school age" has the same meaning as in the 1996 Act, and "child" is to be construed accordingly,
"head teacher" includes acting head teacher, teacher in charge and acting teacher in charge,
"local education authority" has the same meaning as in the 1996 Act,
"parent", in relation to a pupil or child, is to be construed in accordance with section 576 of the 1996 Act, but does not include a person who is not an individual,
"pupil" is to be construed in accordance with section 3(1) and (1A) of the 1996 Act,
"registered pupil" has the meaning given by section 434(5) of the 1996 Act,
"relevant school" means—

(*a*) a qualifying school as defined in section 1(3) of the Education Act 2002 (c 32), or
(*b*) a pupil referral unit as defined in section 19(2) of the 1996 Act,

"responsible officer", in relation to a parenting order, means one of the following who is specified in the order, namely—

(*a*) an officer of a local education authority, and

(*b*) a head teacher or a person nominated by a head teacher,

but a person falling within paragraph (*b*) may not be specified in the order without his consent,
"the 1996 Act" means the Education Act 1996 (c 56).
[Anti-social Behaviour Act 2003, s 24.]

Criminal conduct and anti-social behaviour

1–4526   25. Parenting contracts in respect of criminal conduct and anti-social behaviour.
(1) This section applies where a child or young person has been referred to a youth offending team.
(2) The youth offending team may enter into a parenting contract with a parent of the child or young person if a member of that team has reason to believe that the child or young person has engaged, or is likely to engage, in criminal conduct[1] or anti-social behaviour[1].
(3) A parenting contract is a document which contains—

(*a*) a statement by the parent that he agrees to comply with such requirements as may be specified in the document for such period as may be so specified, and
(*b*) a statement by the youth offending team that it agrees to provide support to the parent for the purpose of complying with those requirements.

(4) The requirements mentioned in subsection (3)(*a*) may include (in particular) a requirement to attend a counselling or guidance programme.
(5) The purpose of the requirements mentioned in subsection (3)(*a*) is to prevent the child or young person from engaging in criminal conduct or anti-social behaviour or further criminal conduct or further anti-social behaviour.
(6) A parenting contract must be signed by the parent and signed on behalf of the youth offending team.
(7) A parenting contract does not create any obligations in respect of whose breach any liability arises in contract or in tort.
(8) Youth offending teams must, in carrying out their functions in relation to parenting contracts, have regard to any guidance which is issued by the Secretary of State from time to time for that purpose.
[Anti-social Behaviour Act 2003, s 25.]

———————

1. Defined in s 29, post.

1–4526A   25A. Parenting contracts in respect of anti-social behaviour: local authorities.
(1) A local authority may enter into a parenting contract with a parent of a child or young person if—

(*a*) the local authority has reason to believe that the child or young person has engaged, or is likely to engage, in anti-social behaviour, and
(*b*) the child or young person resides, or appears to reside, in the local authority's area.

(2) A parenting contract is a document which contains—

(*a*) a statement by the parent that he agrees to comply with such requirements as may be specified in the document for such period as may be so specified, and
(*b*) a statement by the local authority that it agrees to provide support to the parent for the purpose of complying with those requirements.

(3) The requirements mentioned in subsection (2)(a) may include (in particular) a requirement to attend a counselling or guidance programme.
(4) The purpose of the requirements mentioned in subsection (2)(*a*) is to prevent the child or young person from engaging in anti-social behaviour or further anti-social behaviour.
(5) A parenting contract must be signed by the parent and signed on behalf of the local authority.
(6) A parenting contract does not create any obligations in respect of whose breach any liability arises in contract or in tort.
(7) In carrying out their functions in relation to parenting contracts—

(*a*) local authorities in England shall have regard to any guidance which is issued by the Secretary of State from time to time for that purpose;
(*b*) local authorities in Wales shall have regard to any guidance which is issued by the National Assembly for Wales from time to time for that purpose.*
[Criminal Justice Act 2003, s 25A as inserted by the Police and Justice Act 2006, s 23.]

———————

*Inserted by the Police and Justice Act 2006, s 23 from a date to be appointed.

1–4526B   25B. Parenting contracts in respect of anti-social behaviour: registered social landlords.   (1) A registered social landlord may enter into a parenting contract with a parent of a child or young person if—

(*a*) the registered social landlord has reason to believe that the child or young person—

(i)   has engaged in anti-social behaviour, or
(ii) is likely to engage in such behaviour,

and

  (b) that behaviour directly or indirectly relates to or affects the housing management functions of the registered social landlord (or, where paragraph (a)(ii) applies, would do so if the behaviour were engaged in).

 (2) A parenting contract is a document which contains—

  (a) a statement by the parent that he agrees to comply with such requirements as may be specified in the document for such period as may be so specified, and

  (b) a statement by the registered social landlord that it agrees to make arrangements for the provision of support to the parent for the purpose of complying with those requirements.

 (3) The requirements mentioned in subsection (2)(a) may include (in particular) a requirement to attend a counselling or guidance programme.

 (4) The purpose of the requirements mentioned in subsection (2)(a) is to prevent the child or young person from engaging in anti-social behaviour or further anti-social behaviour.

 (5) A parenting contract must be signed by the parent and signed on behalf of the registered social landlord.

 (6) A parenting contract does not create any obligations in respect of whose breach any liability arises in contract or in tort.

 (7) In carrying out their functions in relation to parenting contracts—

  (a) registered social landlords on the register maintained by the Housing Corporation shall have regard to any guidance which is issued by the Secretary of State from time to time for that purpose;

  (b) registered social landlords on the register maintained by the National Assembly for Wales shall have regard to any guidance which is issued by the Assembly from time to time for that purpose.*

[Criminal Justice Act 2003, s 25B as inserted by the Police and Justice Act 2006, s 23.]

*Inserted by the Police and Justice Act 2006, s 23 from a date to be appointed.

1–4527 26. Parenting orders in respect of criminal conduct and anti-social behaviour.
 (1) This section applies where a child or young person has been referred to a youth offending team.

 (2) A member of the youth offending team may apply[1] to a magistrates' court for a parenting order in respect of a parent of the child or young person.

 (3) If such an application is made, the court may make a parenting order in respect of a parent of the child or young person if it is satisfied—

  (a) that the child or young person has engaged in criminal conduct or anti-social behaviour, and

  (b) that making the order would be desirable in the interests of preventing the child or young person from engaging in further criminal conduct or further anti-social behaviour.

 (4) A parenting order is an order which requires the parent—

  (a) to comply, for a period not exceeding twelve months, with such requirements as are specified in the order, and

  (b) subject to subsection (5), to attend, for a concurrent period not exceeding three months, such counselling or guidance programme as may be specified in directions given by the responsible officer.

 (5) A parenting order under this section may, but need not, include a requirement mentioned in subsection (4)(b) in any case where a parenting order under this section or any other enactment has been made in respect of the parent on a previous occasion.

 (6) A counselling or guidance programme which a parent is required to attend by virtue of subsection (4)(b) may be or include a residential course but only if the court is satisfied that the following two conditions are fulfilled.

 (7) The first condition is that the attendance of the parent at a residential course is likely to be more effective than his attendance at a non-residential course in preventing the child or young person from engaging in further criminal conduct or further anti-social behaviour.

 (8) The second condition is that any interference with family life which is likely to result from the attendance of the parent at a residential course is proportionate in all the circumstances.

[Anti-social Behaviour Act 2003, s 26.]

---

 1. Application is by way of complaint and for form of application and order, see the Magistrates' Courts (Parenting Orders) Rules 2004, in this PART, post.

1–4527A 26A. Parenting orders in respect of anti-social behaviour: local authorities. (1) A local authority may apply for a parenting order in respect of a parent of a child or young person if—

  (a) the local authority has reason to believe that the child or young person has engaged in anti-social behaviour, and

  (b) the child or young person resides, or appears to reside, in the local authority's area.

An application for such an order may be made to a magistrates' court or, where section 26C so allows, to a county court.

 (2) If such an application is made, the court may make a parenting order in respect of a parent of the child or young person if it is satisfied—

(a) that the child or young person has engaged in anti-social behaviour, and
(b) that making the order would be desirable in the interests of preventing the child or young person from engaging in further anti-social behaviour.

(3) A parenting order is an order which requires the parent—

(a) to comply, for a period not exceeding twelve months, with such requirements as are specified in the order, and
(b) subject to subsection (4), to attend, for a concurrent period not exceeding three months, such counselling or guidance programme as may be specified in directions given by the responsible officer.

(4) A parenting order under this section may, but need not, include a requirement mentioned in subsection (3)(b) in any case where a parenting order under this section or any other enactment has been made in respect of the parent on a previous occasion.

(5) A counselling or guidance programme which a parent is required to attend by virtue of subsection (3)(b) may be or include a residential course but only if the court is satisfied that the following two conditions are fulfilled.

(6) The first condition is that the attendance of the parent at a residential course is likely to be more effective than his attendance at a non-residential course in preventing the child or young person from engaging in further anti-social behaviour.

(7) The second condition is that any interference with family life which is likely to result from the attendance of the parent at a residential course is proportionate in all the circumstances.

(8) A person is eligible to be the responsible officer in relation to a parenting order under this section only if he is—

(a) an officer of the local authority which applied for the order, or
(b) a person nominated by that authority or by a person or body requested by the authority to make a nomination.

A person may not be nominated under paragraph (b) without his consent.*
[Anti-social Behaviour Act 2003, s 26A as inserted by the Police and Justice Act 2006, s 24.]

*Inserted by the Police and Justice Act 2006, s 24 from a date to be appointed.

1–4527B   26B. Parenting orders in respect of anti-social behaviour: registered social landlords. (1) A registered social landlord may apply for a parenting order in respect of a parent of a child or young person if—

(a) the registered social landlord has reason to believe that the child or young person has engaged in anti-social behaviour, and
(b) the behaviour in question directly or indirectly relates to or affects the housing management functions of the registered social landlord.

An application for such an order may be made to a magistrates' court or, where section 26C so allows, to a county court.

(2) If such an application is made, the court may make a parenting order in respect of a parent of the child or young person if it is satisfied—

(a) that the child or young person has engaged in anti-social behaviour, and
(b) that making the order would be desirable in the interests of preventing the child or young person from engaging in further anti-social behaviour.

(3) A parenting order is an order which requires the parent—

(a) to comply, for a period not exceeding twelve months, with such requirements as are specified in the order, and
(b) subject to subsection (4), to attend, for a concurrent period not exceeding three months, such counselling or guidance programme as may be specified in directions given by the responsible officer.

(4) A parenting order under this section may, but need not, include a requirement mentioned in subsection (3)(b) in any case where a parenting order under this section or any other enactment has been made in respect of the parent on a previous occasion.

(5) A counselling or guidance programme which a parent is required to attend by virtue of subsection (3)(b) may be or include a residential course but only if the court is satisfied that the following two conditions are fulfilled.

(6) The first condition is that the attendance of the parent at a residential course is likely to be more effective than his attendance at a non-residential course in preventing the child or young person from engaging in further anti-social behaviour.

(7) The second condition is that any interference with family life which is likely to result from the attendance of the parent at a residential course is proportionate in all the circumstances.

(8) A registered social landlord must not make an application under this section without first consulting the local authority in whose area the child or young person in question resides or appears to reside.

(9) A person is eligible to be the responsible officer in relation to a parenting order under this section only if he is—

    (*a*)   an officer of the registered social landlord which applied for the order, or
    (*b*)   a person nominated by that registered social landlord.

A person may not be nominated under paragraph (*b*) without his consent.

(10) In deciding whom to nominate under subsection (9)(*b*) a registered social landlord must take into account the views of—

    (*a*)   the local authority mentioned in subsection (8), and
    (*b*)   such other persons or bodies as the registered social landlord thinks appropriate.*

[Anti-social Behaviour Act 2003, s 26B as inserted by the Police and Justice Act 2006, s 24.]

---

*Inserted by the Police and Justice Act 2006, s 23 from a date to be appointed.

26C. Applications under section 26A or 26B in county court proceedings

1–4528   27. Parenting orders: supplemental.   (1) In deciding whether to make a parenting order under section 26, a court must take into account (amongst other things)—

    (*a*)   any refusal by the parent to enter into a parenting contract under section 25 in respect of the child or young person, or
    (*b*)   if the parent has entered into such a parenting contract, any failure by the parent to comply with the requirements specified in the contract.

(2) Before making a parenting order under section 26 in the case of a child or a young person under the age of 16, a court must obtain and consider information about the child or young person's family circumstances and the likely effect of the order on those circumstances.

(3) Subsections (3) to (7) of section 9 of the 1998 Act (supplemental provisions about parenting orders) are to apply in relation to a parenting order under section 26 as they apply in relation to a parenting order under section 8 of that Act.

(4) Members of youth offending teams and responsible officers must, in carrying out their functions in relation to parenting orders, have regard to any guidance which is issued by the Secretary of State from time to time for that purpose.

[Anti-social Behaviour Act 2003, s 27.]

1–4529   28. Parenting orders: appeals.   (1) An appeal lies to the Crown Court against the making of a parenting order under section 26.

(2) Subsections (2) and (3) of section 10 of the 1998 Act (appeals against parenting orders) are to apply in relation to an appeal under this section as they apply in relation to an appeal under subsection (1)(*b*) of that section.

[Anti-social Behaviour Act 2003, s 28.]

28A. Contracting out of local authority functions.   *Secretary of State or National Assembly for Wales may by order provide for local authority to make arrangements with persons specified in the order for the exercise of its functions under ss 25A or 26A.*

1–4530   29. Interpretation and consequential amendment.   (1) In this section and sections 25 to 28—

"anti-social behaviour" means behaviour by a person which causes or is likely to cause harassment, alarm or distress to one or more other persons not of the same household as the person,

"child" has the same meaning as in the 1998 Act,

"criminal conduct" means conduct which—

    (*a*)   constitutes a criminal offence, or
    (*b*)   in the case of conduct by a person under the age of 10, would constitute a criminal offence if that person were not under that age,

"guardian" has the same meaning as in the Children and Young Persons Act 1933 (c 12),

"parent" includes guardian,

"responsible officer", in relation to a parenting order, means a member of a youth offending team who is specified in the order,

"the 1998 Act" means the Crime and Disorder Act 1998 (c 37),

"young person" has the same meaning as in the 1998 Act,

"youth offending team" means a team established under section 39 of the 1998 Act.

(2) In section 38(4) of the 1998 Act (meaning of "youth justice services") after paragraph (*e*) insert—

     "(ee) the performance by youth offending teams and members of youth offending teams of functions under sections 25 to 27 of the Anti-social Behaviour Act 2003;".

[Anti-social Behaviour Act 2003, s 29.]

PART 4[1]
DISPERSAL OF GROUPS ETC

1–4531   30. Dispersal of groups and removal of persons under 16 to their place of residence.
(1) This section applies where a relevant officer has reasonable grounds for believing—

(a) that any members of the public have been intimidated, harassed, alarmed or distressed as a result of the presence or behaviour of groups of two or more persons in public places in any locality in his police area (the "relevant locality"), and

(b) that anti-social behaviour[2] is a significant and persistent problem in the relevant locality.

(2) The relevant officer may give an authorisation that the powers conferred on a constable in uniform by subsections (3) to (6) are to be exercisable for a period specified in the authorisation which does not exceed 6 months.

(3) Subsection (4) applies if a constable in uniform has reasonable grounds for believing[3] that the presence or behaviour of a group of two or more persons in any public place in the relevant locality has resulted, or is likely to result, in any members of the public being intimidated, harassed, alarmed or distressed[4].

(4) The constable may give one or more of the following directions, namely—

(a) a direction requiring the persons in the group to disperse (either immediately or by such time as he may specify and in such way as he may specify),

(b) a direction requiring any of those persons whose place of residence is not within the relevant locality to leave the relevant locality or any part of the relevant locality (either immediately or by such time as he may specify and in such way as he may specify), and

(c) a direction prohibiting any of those persons whose place of residence is not within the relevant locality from returning to the relevant locality or any part of the relevant locality for such period (not exceeding 24 hours) from the giving of the direction as he may specify;

but this subsection is subject to subsection (5).

(5) A direction under subsection (4) may not be given in respect of a group of persons—

(a) who are engaged in conduct which is lawful under section 220 of the Trade Union and Labour Relations (Consolidation) Act 1992 (c 52), or

(b) who are taking part in a public procession of the kind mentioned in section 11(1) of the Public Order Act 1986 (c 64) in respect of which—

(i)   written notice has been given in accordance with section 11 of that Act, or

(ii) such notice is not required to be given as provided by subsections (1) and (2) of that section.

(6) If, between the hours of 9pm and 6am, a constable in uniform finds a person in any public place in the relevant locality who he has reasonable grounds for believing—

(a) is under the age of 16, and

(b) is not under the effective control of a parent or a responsible person aged 18 or over,

he may remove[5] the person to the person's place of residence unless he has reasonable grounds for believing that the person would, if removed to that place, be likely to suffer significant harm.

(7) In this section any reference to the presence or behaviour of a group of persons is to be read as including a reference to the presence or behaviour of any one or more of the persons in the group.
[Anti-social Behaviour Act 2003, s 30.]

---

1. Part 4 contains ss 30–36. The provisions of Part 4 came into force on 20 January 2004.
2. Defined in s 36, post.
3. Unless there are exceptional circumstances, a reasonable belief for the purposes of subs (3) must depend, at least in part, on some behaviour of the group indicating in some way or another harassment, intimidation, the cause of alarm or the cause of distress; otherwise, there would be an illegitimate intrusion of the rights of people to go where they pleased in public: *MB v Director of Public Prosecutions* [2006] EWHC 1888 (Admin), [2007] 171 JP 10.
4. Once an authorisation has been given, the powers under subs(3)–(6) may be exercised regardless of whether the purpose is the same as that for which the authorisation was given; public protests are not excluded from those provisions, but the use of the power to disperse protesters is subject to ECHR considerations: *R (on the application of Singh) v Chief Constable of the West Midlands Police* [2006] EWCA Civ 1118, (2006) 170 JP 765.
5. The word "remove" means "take away using reasonable force if necessary". The purpose for which the power is conferred is to protect children under the age of 16 within a designated dispersal area at night from the physical and social risks of anti-social behaviour by others. Another purpose is to prevent children from themselves participating in anti-social behaviour within a designated dispersal area at night. The section does not confer an arbitrary power to remove children who are not involved in , nor at risk from exposure to, actual or imminently anticipated anti-social behaviour. Children are free to go to the area without fear of being removed provided that they do not themselves participate in anti-social behaviour and provided they avoid others who are behaving anti-socially. The power must be exercised reasonably and constables must have regard to circumstances such as how young the child is; how late at night it is; whether the child is vulnerable or in distress; the child's explanation for his or her conduct and presence in the area; and the nature of the actual or imminently anticipated anti-social behaviour (*R (W) v Metropolitan Police Commissioner* [2006] EWCA Civ 458, [2006] 3 All ER 458, [2006] 3 WLR 1098).

1–4532   31. Authorisations: supplemental. (1) An authorisation—

(a) must be in writing,

(b) must be signed by the relevant officer giving it, and

(c) must specify—

  (i)   the relevant locality,
  (ii) the grounds[1] on which the authorisation is given, and
  (iii) the period during which the powers conferred by section 30(3) to (6) are exercisable.

(2) An authorisation may not be given without the consent of the local authority or each local authority whose area includes the whole or part of the relevant locality.

(3) Publicity must be given to an authorisation by either or both of the following methods—

(a) publishing an authorisation notice in a newspaper circulating in the relevant locality,
(b) posting an authorisation notice in some conspicuous place or places within the relevant locality.

(4) An "authorisation notice" is a notice which—

(a) states the authorisation has been given,
(b) specifies the relevant locality, and
(c) specifies the period during which the powers conferred by section 30(3) to (6) are exercisable.

(5) Subsection (3) must be complied with before the beginning of the period mentioned in subsection (4)(c).

(6) An authorisation may be withdrawn by—

(a) the relevant officer who gave it, or
(b) any other relevant officer whose police area includes the relevant locality and whose rank is the same as or higher than that of the relevant officer mentioned in paragraph (a).

(7) Before the withdrawal of an authorisation, consultation must take place with any local authority whose area includes the whole or part of the relevant locality.

(8) The withdrawal of an authorisation does not affect the exercise of any power pursuant to that authorisation which occurred prior to its withdrawal.

(9) The giving or withdrawal of an authorisation does not prevent the giving of a further authorisation in respect of a locality which includes the whole or any part of the relevant locality to which the earlier authorisation relates.

(10) In this section "authorisation" means an authorisation under section 30.
[Anti-social Behaviour Act 2003, s 31.]

---

1. This requires the written authorisation to state, "not merely that the relevant officer has reasonable grounds for believing that members of the public have been intimidated, harassed alarmed or distressed, and that there is a significant and persistent problem in the locality of anti-social behaviour, but to specify what those reasonable grounds are, if only in general terms": *Sierny v DPP* [2006] EWHC 716 (Admin), (2006) 170 JP 697, per Hallet J at 704B.

1–4533 32. Powers under section 30: supplemental. (1) A direction under section 30(4)—

(a) may be given orally,
(b) may be given to any person individually or to two or more persons together, and
(c) may be withdrawn or varied by the person who gave it.

(2) A person who knowingly contravenes a direction given to him under section 30(4) commits an offence and is liable on summary conviction to—

(a) a fine not exceeding level 4 on the standard scale, or
(b) imprisonment for a term not exceeding 3 months,

or to both.

(3) *Repealed.*

(4) Where the power under section 30(6) is exercised, any local authority whose area includes the whole or part of the relevant locality must be notified of that fact.
[Anti-social Behaviour Act 2003, s 32 as amended by the Serious Organised Crime and Police Act 2005, Sch 7.]

1–4534 33. Powers of community support officers[1]

---

1. Section 33 inserts new provisions in Pt 1 of Sch 4 to the Police Reform Act 2002.

1–4535 34. Code of practice. (1) The Secretary of State may issue a code of practice about—

(a) the giving or withdrawal of authorisations under section 30, and
(b) the exercise of the powers conferred by section 30(3) to (6).

(2) The Secretary of State may from time to time revise the whole or any part of a code of practice issued under this section.

(3) The Secretary of State must lay any code of practice issued by him under this section, and any revisions of such a code, before Parliament.

(4) In giving or withdrawing an authorisation under section 30, a relevant officer must have regard to any code of practice for the time being in force under this section.

(5) In exercising the powers conferred by section 30(3) to (6), a constable in uniform or community support officer must have regard to any code of practice for the time being in force under this section.

(6) A code of practice under this section may make different provision for different cases.

[Anti-social Behaviour Act 2003, s 34.]

1-4536   35. Authorisations by British Transport Police.   (1) For the purposes of the giving of an authorisation under section 30 by a relevant officer who is an officer of the British Transport Police Force, section 30(1) is to have effect as if for "in his police area" there were substituted "which forms part of property in relation to which he has all the powers and privileges of a constable by virtue of section 31(1)(*a*) to (*f*) of the Railways and Transport Safety Act 2003".

(2) Where such an authorisation is given by such an officer, section 31(6)(*b*) is to have effect as if for "whose police area includes the relevant locality" there were substituted "who is an officer of the British Transport Police Force".

[Anti-social Behaviour Act 2003, s 35.]

1-4537   36. Interpretation.   In this Part—

"anti-social behaviour" means behaviour by a person which causes or is likely to cause harassment, alarm or distress to one or more other persons not of the same household as the person,

"local authority" means—

     (*a*)   in relation to England, a district council, a county council that is the council for a county in which there are no district councils, a London borough council, the Common Council of the City of London or the Council of the Isles of Scilly,

     (*b*)   in relation to Wales, a county council or a county borough council,

"public place" means—

     (*a*)   any highway, and

     (*b*)   any place to which at the material time the public or any section of the public has access, on payment or otherwise, as of right or by virtue of express or implied permission,

"relevant locality" has the same meaning as in section 30,

"relevant officer" means a police officer of or above the rank of superintendent.

[Anti-social Behaviour Act 2003, s 36.]

PART 5[1]

FIREARMS

1-4538   37–38[2]

---

1. Part 5 contains ss 37–39. Sections 37 and 38 came into force on 20 January 2004. Section 39(1), (2), (3) in so far it relates to the purchase, acquisition, manufacture, sale or transfer of the prohibited weapon also came into force on that date. Section 39(3), subject to the following, to the extent that it was not already in force came into force on 30 April 2004. The qualification is that s 1(1)(*a*) of the Firearms Act 1968 shall not apply to a person who has in his possession any air rifle, air gun or air pistol which uses, or is designed or adapted for use with, a self-contained gas cartridge system where he has applied before 30 April 2004, for a certificate under Pt 2 of that Act and either that application is still being processed or any appeal in respect of it has not been determined (see the Anti-social Behaviour Act 2003 (Commencement No 1 and Transitional Provisions) Order 2003, arts 2 and 5).

2. These provisions amend the Firearms Act 1968 as to possession of an air weapon or imitation firearm in a public place, and as to the minimum age for the acquisition and possession of air weapons.

1-4539   39. Prohibition of certain air weapons.   (1)–(3) *Amend the Firearms Act 1968.*

(4) If at the time when subsection (3)[1] comes into force a person has in his possession an air rifle, air gun or air pistol of the kind described in section 5(1)(af) of the Firearms Act 1968 (inserted by subsection (3) above)—

     (*a*)   section 5(1) of that Act shall not prevent the person's continued possession of the air rifle, air gun or air pistol,

     (*b*)   section 1 of that Act shall apply, and

     (*c*)   a chief officer of police may not refuse to grant or renew, and may not revoke or partially revoke, a firearm certificate under Part II of that Act on the ground that the person does not have a good reason for having the air rifle, air gun or air pistol in his possession.

(5) But subsection (4)(*a*) to (*c*) shall not apply to possession in the circumstances described in section 8 of that Act (authorised dealing).

(6) *Amends s 1 of the Firearms (Amendment) Act 1988.*

[Anti-social Behaviour Act 2003, s 39.]

---

1. Subsection (3) inserts a new s 5(1)(*af*) in the Firearms Act 1968.

PART 6[1]
THE ENVIRONMENT

Noise

1–4540   40. Closure of noisy premises.   (1) The chief executive officer of the relevant local authority may make a closure order in relation to premises to which this section applies if he reasonably believes that—

(*a*)   a public nuisance is being caused by noise coming from the premises, and
(*b*)   the closure of the premises is necessary to prevent that nuisance.

(2)   This section applies to premises if—

(*a*)   a premises licence has effect in respect of them, or
(*b*)   a temporary event notice has effect in respect of them.

(3)   In this section "closure order" means an order which requires specified premises to be kept closed during a specified period which—

(*a*)   does not exceed 24 hours, and
(*b*)   begins when a manager of the premises receives written notice of the order.

(4)   A person commits an offence if without reasonable excuse he permits premises to be open in contravention of a closure order.

(5)   A person guilty of an offence under this section shall be liable on summary conviction to—

(*a*)   imprisonment for a term not exceeding three months,
(*b*)   a fine not exceeding £20,000, or
(*c*)   both.

[Anti-social Behaviour Act 2003, s 40.]

---

1. Part 6 contains ss 40–56. At the time of going to press, ss 48–52 were in force in England in relation to certain specified local authorities only: see the Anti-social Behaviour Act 2003 (Commencement No 2) Order, SI 2004/690.

1–4541   41. Closure of noisy premises: supplemental.   (1) Where a closure order is made in relation to premises, the chief executive officer of the relevant local authority—

(*a*)   may cancel the closure order by notice in writing to a manager of the premises,
(*b*)   shall cancel the order as soon as is reasonably practicable if he believes that it is no longer necessary in order to prevent a public nuisance being caused by noise coming from the premises, and
(*c*)   shall give notice of the order as soon as is reasonably practicable to the licensing authority for the area in which the premises are situated.

(2)   The chief executive officer of a local authority may authorise an environmental health officer of the authority to exercise a power or duty of the chief executive officer under section 40(1) or under subsection (1) above; and—

(*a*)   authority under this subsection may be general or specific, and
(*b*)   a reference in section 40(1) or subsection (1) above to a belief of the chief executive officer includes a reference to a belief of a person authorised under this subsection.

(3)   In section 40 and this section—

"chief executive officer" of an authority means the head of the paid service of the authority designated under section 4 of the Local Government and Housing Act 1989 (c 42),
"environmental health officer" of an authority means an officer authorised by the authority for the purpose of exercising a statutory function in relation to pollution of the environment or harm to human health,
"licensing authority" has the same meaning as in the Licensing Act 2003 (c 17),
"manager" in relation to premises means—

(*a*)   a person who holds a premises licence in respect of the premises,
(*b*)   a designated premises supervisor under a premises licence in respect of the premises,
(*c*)   the premises user in relation to a temporary event notice which has effect in respect of the premises, and
(*d*)   any other person who works at the premises in a capacity (paid or unpaid) which enables him to close them,

"premises licence" has the same meaning as in the Licensing Act 2003,
"relevant local authority" in relation to premises means an authority which has statutory functions, for the area in which the premises are situated, in relation to minimising or preventing the risk of pollution of the environment or of harm to human health, and
"temporary event notice" has the same meaning as in the Licensing Act 2003 (and is to be treated as having effect in accordance with section 170(6) of that Act).

[Anti-social Behaviour Act 2003, s 41.]

1–4542   42. Dealing with noise at night.   *Amends the Noise Act 1996.*

Penalty notices for graffiti and fly-posting

1–4543   43. Penalty notices for graffiti and fly-posting. (1) Where an authorised officer of a local authority has reason to believe that a person has committed a relevant offence in the area of that authority, he may give that person a notice offering him the opportunity of discharging any liability to conviction for that offence by payment of a penalty in accordance with the notice.

(2) But an authorised officer may not give a notice under subsection (1) if he considers that the commission of the offence—

(a)   in the case of a relevant offence falling within section 44(1)(c), also involves the commission of an offence under section 30 of the Crime and Disorder Act 1998 (c 37), or

(b)   in the case of any other relevant offence, was motivated (wholly or partly) by hostility—

(i)   towards a person based upon his membership (or presumed membership) of a racial or religious group, or

(ii)   towards members of a racial or religious group based on their membership of that group.

(3) In the case of a relevant offence falling within section 44(1)(f), an authorised officer may not give a notice to a person under subsection (1) in relation to the display of an advertisement unless he has reason to believe that that person personally affixed or placed the advertisement to, against or upon the land or object on which the advertisement is or was displayed.

(4) Where a person is given a notice under subsection (1) in respect of an offence—

(a)   no proceedings may be instituted for that offence (or any other relevant offence arising out of the same circumstances) before the expiration of the period of fourteen days following the date of the notice, and

(b)   he may not be convicted of that offence (or any other relevant offence arising out of the same circumstances) if before the expiration of that period he pays the penalty in accordance with the notice.

(5) A notice under subsection (1) must give such particulars of the circumstances alleged to constitute the offence as are necessary for giving reasonable information of the offence.

(6) A notice under subsection (1) must also state—

(a)   the period during which, by virtue of subsection (4), proceedings will not be instituted for the offence,

(b)   the amount of the penalty, and

(c)   the person to whom and the address at which the penalty may be paid.

(7) Without prejudice to payment by any other method, payment of a penalty in pursuance of a notice under subsection (1) may be made by pre-paying and posting a letter containing the amount of the penalty (in cash or otherwise) to the person mentioned in subsection (6)(c) at the address so mentioned.

(8) Where a letter is sent in accordance with subsection (7) payment is to be regarded as having been made at the time at which that letter would be delivered in the ordinary course of post.

(9) A notice under subsection (1) must be in such form as the appropriate person may by order prescribe.

(10) Subject to subsection (11), the penalty payable in pursuance of a notice under subsection (1) is £50.*

(11) The appropriate person may by order substitute a different amount for the amount for the time being specified in subsection (10).*

[Anti-social Behaviour Act 2003, s 43.]

---

*. **Repealed by the Clean Neighbourhoods and Environment Act 2005, Sch 5. In force in England; in force for certain purposes in relation to Wales, in force for remaining purposes from a date to be appointed.**

1–4543A   43A. Amount of penalty[1]. (1) The amount of a penalty payable in pursuance of a notice under section 43(1)—

(a)   is the amount specified by a relevant local authority in relation to its area (whether or not the penalty is payable to that or another authority), or

(b)   if no amount is so specified, is £75.

(2) In subsection (1)(a), "relevant local authority" means—

(a)   a district council in England;

(b)   a county council in England for an area for which there is no district council;

(c)   a London borough council;

(d)   the Common Council of the City of London;

(e)   the Council of the Isles of Scilly;

(f)   a county or county borough council in Wales.

(3) The local authority to which a penalty is payable in pursuance of a notice under section 43(1) may make provision for treating it as having been paid if a lesser amount is paid before the end of a period specified by the authority.

(4) The appropriate person may by regulations make provision in connection with the powers conferred under subsections (1)(a) and (3).

(5) Regulations under subsection (4) may (in particular)—

(a) require an amount specified under subsection (1)(a) to fall within a range prescribed in the regulations;

(b) restrict the extent to which, and the circumstances in which, a local authority can make provision under subsection (3).

(6) The appropriate person may by order substitute a different amount for the amount for the time being specified in subsection (1)(b).*

[Anti-social Behaviour Act 2003, s 43A as inserted by the Clean Neighbourhoods and Environment Act 2005, s 28.]

***In force in relation to England. In relation to Wales, in force for certain purposes only. SI 2006/2797, art 4(m) provides that this section shall come into force in relation to Wales for remaining purposes on the date on which the Environmental Offences (Fixed Penalties) (Miscellaneous Provisions) (Wales) Regulations 2007 come into force.**

1–4543B 43B. Penalty notices: power to require name and address*. (1) If an authorised officer of a local authority proposes to give a person a notice under section 43(1), the officer may require the person to give him his name and address.

(2) A person commits an offence if—

(a) he fails to give his name and address when required to do so under subsection (1), or

(b) he gives a false or inaccurate name or address in response to a requirement under that subsection.

(3) A person guilty of an offence under subsection (2) is liable on summary conviction to a fine not exceeding level 3 on the standard scale.

[Anti-social Behaviour Act 2003, s 43B as inserted by the Clean Neighbourhoods and Environment Act 2005, s 28.]

***In force in relation to England. In relation to Wales, SI 2006/2797, art 4(n) provides that this section shall come into force in relation to Wales on the date on which the Environmental Offences (Fixed Penalties) (Miscellaneous Provisions) (Wales) Regulations 2007 come into force.**

1–4544 44. Meaning of relevant offence. (1) "Relevant offence" means—

(a) an offence under paragraph 10 of section 54 of the Metropolitan Police Act 1839 (c 47) (affixing posters etc),

(b) an offence under section 20(1) of the London County Council (General Powers) Act 1954 (defacement of streets with slogans etc),

(c) an offence under section 1(1) of the Criminal Damage Act 1971 (c 48) (damaging property etc) which involves only the painting or writing on, or the soiling, marking or other defacing of, any property by whatever means,

(d) an offence under section 131(2) of the Highways Act 1980 (c 66) (including that provision as applied by section 27(6) of the Countryside Act 1968 (c 41)) which involves only an act of obliteration,

(e) an offence under section 132(1) of the Highways Act 1980 (painting or affixing things on structures on the highway etc),

(f) an offence under section 224(3) of the Town and Country Planning Act 1990 (c 8) (displaying advertisement in contravention of regulations).

(2) This section has effect for the purposes of the interpretation of section 43.

[Anti-social Behaviour Act 2003, s 44.]

1–4545 45. Penalty receipts. (1) Penalties which are payable in pursuance of notices under section 43(1) are payable to local authorities.

(2) In any proceedings a certificate which—

(a) purports to be signed by or on behalf of the person responsible for the financial affairs of a local authority, and

(b) states that payment of a penalty payable in pursuance of a notice under section 43(1) was or was not received by a date specified in the certificate,

is evidence of the facts stated.

(3) A local authority may use any sums it receives in respect of penalties payable to it in pursuance of notices under section 43(1) (its "penalty receipts") only for the purposes of functions of its that are qualifying functions.

(4) The following are qualifying functions for the purposes of this section—

(a) functions under section 43, and

(b) functions of a description specified in regulations made by the appropriate person.

(5) Regulations under subsection (4)(b) may (in particular) have the effect that a local authority may use its penalty receipts for the purposes of any of its functions.

(6) A local authority must supply the appropriate person with such information relating to its use of its penalty receipts as the appropriate person may require.

(7) The appropriate person may by regulations—

(a) make provision for what a local authority is to do with its penalty receipts—

(i) pending their being used for the purposes of qualifying functions of the authority;

(ii) if they are not so used before such time after their receipt as may be specified by the regulations;

(b) make provision for accounting arrangements in respect of a local authority's penalty receipts.

(8) The provision that may be made under subsection (7)(a)(ii) includes (in particular) provision for the payment of sums to a person (including the appropriate person) other than the local authority.

(9) Before making regulations under this section, the appropriate person must consult—

(a) the local authorities to which the regulations are to apply, and

(b) such other persons as the appropriate person considers appropriate.

[Anti-social Behaviour Act 2003, s 45.]

1–4546 46. Powers of police civilians. (1) In paragraph 1 of Schedule 4 to the Police Reform Act 2002 (c 30) (powers of community support officers to issue fixed penalty notices)—

(a) at the end of sub-paragraph (2)(c) omit "and", and

(b) after sub-paragraph (2)(c) insert—

"(ca) the power of an authorised officer of a local authority to give a notice under section 43(1) of the Anti-social Behaviour Act 2003 (penalty notices in respect of graffiti or fly-posting); and".

(2) In paragraph 1 of Schedule 5 to that Act (powers of accredited persons to issue fixed penalty notices)—

(a) at the end of sub-paragraph (2)(b) omit "and", and

(b) after sub-paragraph (2)(b) insert—

"(ba) the power of an authorised officer of a local authority to give a notice under section 43(1) of the Anti-social Behaviour Act 2003 (penalty notices in respect of graffiti or fly-posting); and".

[Anti-social Behaviour Act 2003, s 46.]

1–4547 47. Interpretation etc. (1) In this section and sections 43 and 45—

"advertisement" and "land" have the meanings given by section 336(1) of the Town and Country Planning Act 1990 (c 8),

"appropriate person" means—

(a) in relation to England, the Secretary of State, and

(b) in relation to Wales, the National Assembly for Wales,

"authorised officer", in relation to a local authority, means—

(a) an employee of the authority who is authorised in writing by the authority for the purpose of giving notices under section 43(1);

(b) any person who, in pursuance of arrangements made with the authority, has the function of giving such notices and is authorised in writing by the authority to perform that function; and

(c) any employee of such a person who is authorised in writing by the authority for the purpose of giving such notices,★

"local authority" means an authority in England and Wales which is a litter authority for the purposes of section 88 of the Environmental Protection Act 1990 (c 43),

"racial group" and "religious group" have the meanings given by section 28(4) and (5) of the Crime and Disorder Act 1998 (c 37).

(2) Section 28(2) of the Crime and Disorder Act 1998 is to apply for the purposes of section 43(2)(b)(i) as it applies for the purposes of section 28(1)(a) of that Act.

(3) The appropriate person may issue guidance—

(a) about the exercise of the discretion to give notices under section 43(1), and

(b) about the giving of such notices.

(4) The appropriate person may by regulations prescribe conditions to be satisfied by a person before a parish or community council may authorise him in writing for the purpose of giving notices under section 43(1).★

[Anti-social Behaviour Act 2003, s 47 as amended by the Clean Neighbourhoods and Environment Act 2005, s 30.]

★Definition of "authorised person" in subs(1) amended, and subs(4) added, by s 30 of the Clean Neighbourhoods and Environment Act 2005. These amendments are in force in relation to England. In relation to Wales, SI 2006/2797, art 4(o) provides that these amendments shall come into force (to the extent

(c) so as to prevent an award of damages made in respect of an act or omission on the ground that the act or omission was unlawful by virtue of section 6(1) of the Human Rights Act 1998 (c 42).

(4) This section does not affect any other exemption from liability (whether at common law or otherwise).

(5) Section 48(11) is to apply for the purposes of this section as it applies for the purposes of that section.
[Anti-social Behaviour Act 2003, s 52.]

Advertisements

1–4553 53. Display of advertisements in contravention of regulations. In section 224(3) of the Town and Country Planning Act 1990 (c 8) (offence of displaying advertisement in contravention of regulations) for "level 3", in both places where it occurs, substitute "level 4".
[Anti-social Behaviour Act 2003, s 53.]

Aerosol paints

1–4554 54. Sale of aerosol paint to children. (1) A person commits an offence if he sells an aerosol paint container to a person under the age of sixteen.

(2) In subsection (1) "aerosol paint container" means a device which—

(a) contains paint stored under pressure, and

(b) is designed to permit the release of the paint as a spray.

(3) A person guilty of an offence under this section shall be liable on summary conviction to a fine not exceeding level 4 on the standard scale.

(4) It is a defence for a person charged with an offence under this section in respect of a sale to prove that—

(a) he took all reasonable steps to determine the purchaser's age, and

(b) he reasonably believed that the purchaser was not under the age of sixteen.

(5) It is a defence for a person charged with an offence under this section in respect of a sale effected by another person to prove that he (the defendant) took all reasonable steps to avoid the commission of an offence under this section.
[Anti-social Behaviour Act 2003, s 54.]

1–4554A 54A. Enforcement of section 54. (1) It is the duty of every local weights and measures authority—

(a) to consider, at least once in every period of twelve months, the extent to which it is appropriate for the authority to carry out in their area a programme of enforcement action in relation to section 54; and

(b) to the extent that they consider it appropriate to do so, carry out such a programme.

(2) For the purposes of subsection (1), a programme of enforcement action in relation to section 54 is a programme involving all or any of the following—

(a) the bringing of prosecutions in respect of offences under that section;

(b) the investigation of complaints in respect of alleged offences under that section;

(c) the taking of other measures intended to reduce the incidence of offences under that section.
[Anti-social Behaviour Act 2003, s 54A as inserted by the Clean Neighbourhoods and Environment Act 2005, s 32.]

Waste and litter

1–4555 55. Unlawfully deposited waste etc. (1)–(3) *Amendments the Control of Pollution (Amendment) Act 1989.*

(4) *Inserts a new s 59A in the Environmental Protection Act 1990.*

(5) *Inserts a new s 71(4) in the Environmental Protection Act 1990.*

(6)–(8) *Amendments to s 108(15) of the Environment Act 1995.*
[Anti-social Behaviour Act 2003, s 55.]

1–4556 56. Extension of litter authority powers to take remedial action. (1) *Substitutes new sub-ss (10)–(12) for s 92(10) of the Environmental Protection Act 1990.*

PART 7[1]
PUBLIC ORDER AND TRESPASS

1–4557 57. Public assemblies. (*Amends the definition of "public assembly" in s 19 of the Public Order Act 1986.*)

---

1. Part 7 contains ss 57–64. Sections 57, 58 and 59 came into force on 20 January 2004. Sections 60–64 came into force on 27 February 2004.

1–4558 57. *Amends the definition of "public assembly" in s 19 of the Public Order Act 1986.*

1–4559   58.   *Amends s 63 of the Criminal Justice and Public Order Act 1994 (powers in relations to raves.)*

1–4560   59.   *Amendments to ss 68 and 69 of the Criminal Justice and Public Order Act 1994 (aggravated trespasser).*

1–4561   60–64.   *Inserts new ss 62A–62E in the Criminal Justice and Public Order Act 1994.*

PART 8[1]
HIGH HEDGES

Introductory

1–4562   65–68.   *(These provisions enable owners of adjacent property to complain to their local authority about the height of hedges on neighbouring land where (in summary) those hedges consist of two or more evergreens exceeding two metres in height and their height is such that they adversely affect reasonable enjoyment of the property.)*

1–4563   69. Remedial notices.   (1) For the purposes of this Part a remedial notice is a notice—

(a)   issued by the relevant authority in respect of a complaint to which this Part applies; and
(b)   stating the matters mentioned in subsection (2).

(2)   Those matters are—

(a)   that a complaint has been made to the authority under this Part about a high hedge specified in the notice which is situated on land so specified;
(b)   that the authority have decided that the height of that hedge is adversely affecting the complainant's reasonable enjoyment of the domestic property specified in the notice;
(c)   the initial action that must be taken in relation to that hedge before the end of the compliance period;
(d)   any preventative action that they consider must be taken in relation to that hedge at times following the end of that period while the hedge remains on the land; and
(e)   the consequences under sections 75 and 77 of a failure to comply with the notice.

(3)   The action specified in a remedial notice is not to require or involve—

(a)   a reduction in the height of the hedge to less than two metres above ground level; or
(b)   the removal of the hedge.

(4)   A remedial notice shall take effect on its operative date.
(5)   "The operative date" of a remedial notice is such date (falling at least 28 days after that on which the notice is issued) as is specified in the notice as the date on which it is to take effect.
(6)   "The compliance period" in the case of a remedial notice is such reasonable period as is specified in the notice for the purposes of subsection (2)(c) as the period within which the action so specified is to be taken; and that period shall begin with the operative date of the notice.
(7)   Subsections (4) to (6) have effect in relation to a remedial notice subject to—

(a)   the exercise of any power of the relevant authority under section 70; and
(b)   the operation of sections 71 to 73 in relation to the notice.

(8)   While a remedial notice has effect, the notice—

(a)   shall be a local land charge; and
(b)   shall be binding on every person who is for the time being an owner or occupier of the land specified in the notice as the land where the hedge in question is situated.

(9)   In this Part—

"initial action" means remedial action or preventative action, or both;
"remedial action" means action to remedy the adverse effect of the height of the hedge on the complainant's reasonable enjoyment of the domestic property in respect of which the complaint was made; and
"preventative action" means action to prevent the recurrence of the adverse effect.
[Anti-social Behaviour Act 2003, s 69.]

---

1. Part 8 contains ss 65–84.

1–4564   70. Withdrawal or relaxation of requirements of remedial notices

Appeals

1–4565   71. Appeals against remedial notices and other decisions of relevant authorities

1–4566   72. Appeals procedure[1]

---

1. See the High Hedges (Appeals) (Wales) Regulations 2004, SI 2004/3240; and High Hedges (Appeals) (England) Regulations 2005, SI 2005/711.

1–4567   **73. Determination or withdrawal of appeals**

Powers of entry

1–4568   **74. Powers of entry for the purposes of complaints and appeals.**   (1) Where, under this Part, a complaint has been made or a remedial notice has been issued, a person authorised by the relevant authority may enter the neighbouring land in order to obtain information required by the relevant authority for the purpose of determining—

    (*a*)   whether this Part applies to the complaint;
    (*b*)   whether to issue or withdraw a remedial notice;
    (*c*)   whether to waive or relax a requirement of a remedial notice;
    (*d*)   whether a requirement of a remedial notice has been complied with.

  (2)   Where an appeal has been made under section 71, a person authorised—

    (*a*)   by the appeal authority, or
    (*b*)   by a person appointed to determine appeals on its behalf,

may enter the neighbouring land in order to obtain information required by the appeal authority, or by the person so appointed, for the purpose of determining an appeal under this Part.

  (3)   A person shall not enter land in the exercise of a power conferred by this section unless at least 24 hours' notice of the intended entry has been given to every occupier of the land.

  (4)   A person authorised under this section to enter land—

    (*a*)   shall, if so required, produce evidence of his authority before entering; and
    (*b*)   shall produce such evidence if required to do so at any time while he remains on the land.

  (5)   A person who enters land in the exercise of a power conferred by this section may—

    (*a*)   take with him such other persons as may be necessary;
    (*b*)   take with him equipment and materials needed in order to obtain the information required;
    (*c*)   take samples of any trees or shrubs that appear to him to form part of a high hedge.

  (6)   If, in the exercise of a power conferred by this section, a person enters land which is unoccupied or from which all of the persons occupying the land are temporarily absent, he must on his departure leave it as effectively secured against unauthorised entry as he found it.

  (7)   A person who intentionally obstructs a person acting in the exercise of the powers under this section is guilty of an offence and shall be liable, on summary conviction, to a fine not exceeding level 3 on the standard scale.
[Anti-social Behaviour Act 2003, s 74.]

Enforcement powers etc

1–4569   **75. Offences.**   (1) Where—

    (*a*)   a remedial notice requires the taking of any action, and
    (*b*)   that action is not taken in accordance with that notice within the compliance period or (as the case may be) by the subsequent time by which it is required to be taken,

every person who, at a relevant time, is an owner or occupier of the neighbouring land is guilty of an offence and shall be liable, on summary conviction, to a fine not exceeding level 3 on the standard scale.

  (2)   In subsection (1) "relevant time"—

    (*a*)   in relation to action required to be taken before the end of the compliance period, means a time after the end of that period and before the action is taken; and
    (*b*)   in relation to any preventative action which is required to be taken after the end of that period, means a time after that at which the action is required to be taken but before it is taken.

  (3)   In proceedings against a person for an offence under subsection (1) it shall be a defence for him to show that he did everything he could be expected to do to secure compliance with the notice.

  (4)   In any such proceedings against a person, it shall also be a defence for him to show, in a case in which he—

    (*a*)   is not a person to whom a copy of the remedial notice was sent in accordance with a provision of this Part, and
    (*b*)   is not assumed under subsection (5) to have had knowledge of the notice at the time of the alleged offence,

that he was not aware of the existence of the notice at that time.

  (5)   A person shall be assumed to have had knowledge of a remedial notice at any time if at that time—

    (*a*)   he was an owner of the neighbouring land; and
    (*b*)   the notice was at that time registered as a local land charge.

  (6)   Section 198 of the Law of Property Act 1925 (c 20) (constructive notice) shall be disregarded for the purposes of this section.

  (7)   Where a person is convicted of an offence under subsection (1) and it appears to the court—

    (*a*)   that a failure to comply with the remedial notice is continuing, and
    (*b*)   that it is within that person's power to secure compliance with the notice,

the court may, in addition to or instead of imposing a punishment, order him to take the steps specified in the order for securing compliance with the notice.

(8) An order under subsection (7) must require those steps to be taken within such reasonable period as may be fixed by the order.

(9) Where a person fails without reasonable excuse to comply with an order under subsection (7) he is guilty of an offence and shall be liable, on summary conviction, to a fine not exceeding level 3 on the standard scale.

(10) Where a person continues after conviction of an offence under subsection (9) (or of an offence under this subsection) to fail, without reasonable excuse, to take steps which he has been ordered to take under subsection (7), he is guilty of a further offence and shall be liable, on summary conviction, to a fine not exceeding one-twentieth of that level for each day on which the failure has so continued.

[Anti-social Behaviour Act 2003, s 75.]

1–4570   76. Power to require occupier to permit action to be taken by owner.   Section 289 of the Public Health Act 1936 (c 49) (power of court to require occupier to permit work to be done by owner) shall apply with any necessary modifications for the purpose of giving an owner of land to which a remedial notice relates the right, as against all other persons interested in the land, to comply with the notice.

[Anti-social Behaviour Act 2003, s 76.]

1–4571   77. Action by relevant authority.   (1) This section applies where—

(a)   a remedial notice requires the taking of any action; and

(b)   that action is not taken in accordance with that notice within the compliance period or (as the case may be) after the end of that period when it is required to be taken by the notice.

(2) Where this section applies—

(a)   a person authorised by the relevant authority may enter the neighbouring land and take the required action; and

(b)   the relevant authority may recover any expenses reasonably incurred by that person in doing so from any person who is an owner or occupier of the land.

(3) Expenses recoverable under this section shall be a local land charge and binding on successive owners of the land and on successive occupiers of it.

(4) Where expenses are recoverable under this section from two or more persons, those persons shall be jointly and severally liable for the expenses.

(5) A person shall not enter land in the exercise of a power conferred by this section unless at least 7 days' notice of the intended entry has been given to every occupier of the land.

(6) A person authorised under this section to enter land—

(a)   shall, if so required, produce evidence of his authority before entering; and

(b)   shall produce such evidence if required to do so at any time while he remains on the land.

(7) A person who enters land in the exercise of a power conferred by this section may—

(a)   use a vehicle to enter the land;

(b)   take with him such other persons as may be necessary;

(c)   take with him equipment and materials needed for the purpose of taking the required action.

(8) If, in the exercise of a power conferred by this section, a person enters land which is unoccupied or from which all of the persons occupying the land are temporarily absent, he must on his departure leave it as effectively secured against unauthorised entry as he found it.

(9) A person who wilfully obstructs a person acting in the exercise of powers under this section to enter land and take action on that land is guilty of an offence and shall be liable, on summary conviction, to a fine not exceeding level 3 on the standard scale.

[Anti-social Behaviour Act 2003, s 77.]

1–4572   78. Offences committed by bodies corporate.   (1) Where an offence under this Part committed by a body corporate is proved to have been committed with the consent or connivance of, or to be attributable to any neglect on the part of—

(a)   a director, manager, secretary or other similar officer of the body corporate, or

(b)   any person who was purporting to act in any such capacity,

he, as well as the body corporate, shall be guilty of that offence and be liable to be proceeded against and punished accordingly.

(2) Where the affairs of a body corporate are managed by its members, subsection (1) applies in relation to the acts and defaults of a member in connection with his functions of management as if he were a director of the body corporate.

[Anti-social Behaviour Act 2003, s 78.]

Supplementary

1–4573   79. Service of documents.   (1) A notification or other document required to be given or sent to a person by virtue of this Part shall be taken to be duly given or sent to him if served in accordance with the following provisions of this section.

(2) Such a document may be served—

(a) by delivering it to the person in question;

(b) by leaving it at his proper address; or

(c) by sending it by post to him at that address.

(3) Such a document may—

(a) in the case of a body corporate, be served on the secretary or clerk of that body;

(b) in the case of a partnership, be served on a partner or a person having the control or management of the partnership business.

(4) For the purposes of this section and of section 7 of the Interpretation Act 1978 (c 30) (service of documents by post) in its application to this section, a person's proper address shall be his last known address, except that—

(a) in the case of a body corporate or their secretary or clerk, it shall be the address of the registered or principal office of that body; and

(b) in the case of a partnership or person having the control or the management of the partnership business, it shall be the principal office of the partnership.

(5) For the purposes of subsection (4) the principal office of—

(a) a company registered outside the United Kingdom, or

(b) a partnership carrying on business outside the United Kingdom,

shall be their principal office within the United Kingdom.

(6) If a person has specified an address in the United Kingdom other than his proper address within the meaning of subsection (4) as the one at which he or someone on his behalf will accept documents of a particular description, that address shall also be treated for the purposes of this section and section 7 of the Interpretation Act 1978 as his proper address in connection with the service on him of a document of that description.

(7) Where—

(a) by virtue of this Part a document is required to be given or sent to a person who is an owner or occupier of any land, and

(b) the name or address of that person cannot be ascertained after reasonable inquiry,

the document may be served either by leaving it in the hands of a person who is or appears to be resident or employed on the land or by leaving it conspicuously affixed to some building or object on the land.

[Anti-social Behaviour Act 2003, s 79.]

1–4574 80. Documents in electronic form. (1) A requirement of this Part—

(a) to send a copy of a remedial notice to a person, or

(b) to notify a person under section 68(4) of the reasons for the issue of a remedial notice,

is not capable of being satisfied by transmitting the copy or notification electronically or by making it available on a web-site.

(2) The delivery of any other document to a person (the "recipient") may be effected for the purposes of section 79(2)(a)—

(a) by transmitting it electronically, or

(b) by making it available on a web-site,

but only if it is transmitted or made available in accordance with subsection (3) or (5).

(3) A document is transmitted electronically in accordance with this subsection if—

(a) the recipient has agreed that documents may be delivered to him by being transmitted to an electronic address and in an electronic form specified by him for that purpose; and

(b) the document is a document to which that agreement applies and is transmitted to that address in that form.

(4) A document which is transmitted in accordance with subsection (3) by means of an electronic communications network shall, unless the contrary is proved, be treated as having been delivered at 9 a.m. on the working day immediately following the day on which it is transmitted.

(5) A document is made available on a web-site in accordance with this subsection if—

(a) the recipient has agreed that documents may be delivered to him by being made available on a web-site;

(b) the document is a document to which that agreement applies and is made available on a web-site;

(c) the recipient is notified, in a manner agreed by him, of—

(i) the presence of the document on the web-site;

(ii) the address of the web-site; and

(iii) the place on the web-site where the document may be accessed.

(6) A document made available on a web-site in accordance with subsection (5) shall, unless the contrary is proved, be treated as having been delivered at 9a.m. on the working day immediately following the day on which the recipient is notified in accordance with subsection (5)(c).

(7) In this section—

"electronic address" includes any number or address used for the purposes of receiving electronic communications;

"electronic communication" means an electronic communication within the meaning of the Electronic Communications Act 2000 (c 7) the processing of which on receipt is intended to produce writing;

"electronic communications network" means an electronic communications network within the meaning of the Communications Act 2003 (c 21);

"electronically" means in the form of an electronic communication;

"working day" means a day which is not a Saturday or a Sunday, Christmas Day, Good Friday or a bank holiday in England and Wales under the Banking and Financial Dealings Act 1971 (c 80).

[Anti-social Behaviour Act 2003, s 80.]

1–4575   81.   *Enables the making of regulations to amend certain provisions of s 80 as to documents in electronic form.*

1–4576   83.   *Enables the making of regulations to amend the scope of complaints relating to high hedges and how the latter are defined.*

1–4577   84. Crown application.   (1) This Part and any provision made under it bind the Crown.

(2) This section does not impose criminal liability on the Crown.

(3) Subsection (2) does not affect the criminal liability of persons in the service of the Crown.

[Anti-social Behaviour Act 2003, s 84.]

PART 9[1]
MISCELLANEOUS POWERS

1–4578

1. Part 9 contains ss 85–91. At the time of going to press, nearly all of these provisions were in force.

1–4579   85.   (1)–(8) *Various amendments to the Crime and Disorder Act 1998, ss 1, 1B, 1E and 9.*

(9) An order under section 93 below made in relation to subsection (5) above may make provision for that subsection to come into force—

(a)   for such period as is specified in the order;

(b)   on different days in respect of persons of different ages[1].

(10) Subsection (9) does not affect section 94(2) below.

(11) The making of an order as mentioned in subsection (9)(a) does not prevent the making of a further order under section 93 below—

(a)   whether for the same or a different purpose, or

(b)   in relation to the same area.

[Anti-social Behaviour Act 2003, s 85.]

1. Pursuant to this power, subs (5) was brought into force on 31 March 2004 in relation to persons aged 18 and over (SI 2004/690), otherwise on 1 Oct 2004 for a period of eighteen months in relation to applications for anti-social behaviour orders in specified county courts) (SI 2004/2168).

1–4580   86. Certain orders made on conviction of offences.   *Makes amendments to s 1C of the Crime and Disorder Act 1998, inserts new s 14A(3A)–(3B) in the Football Spectators Act 1989, and inserts new s 3(2)(fa) in the Prosecution of Offences Act 1985.*

1–4581   87. Penalty notices for disorderly behaviour by young persons.   *Makes amendments to the Criminal Justice and Police Act 2001.*

1–4582   88. Curfew orders and supervision orders.   Schedule 2 (which relates to curfew orders and supervision orders under the Powers of Criminal Courts (Sentencing) Act 2000 (c 6)) shall have effect[1].

[Anti-social Behaviour Act 2003, s 88.]

1. Section 88, in so far as it relates to para 2(2) of Sch 2, and para 2(2) of Sch 2, came into force on 30 September 2004 in relation to specified local authorities only: see the Anti-social Behaviour Act 2003 (Commencement No 4) Order 2004, SI 2004/2168.

1–4583   89. Extension of powers of community support officers etc.   *Makes various amendments to s 105 of, and Sch 4 to, the Police Reform Act 2002.*

1–4584   90. Report by local authority in certain cases where person remanded on bail.   *Inserts new s 23B in the Children and Young Persons Act 1969.*

1–4585   91. Proceedings under section 222 of the Local Government Act 1972: power of arrest attached to injunction

PART 10[1]
GENERAL

1–4586   92. Repeals.   Schedule 3 contains repeals.
[Anti-social Behaviour Act 2003, s 92.]

---

1. Part 10 contains ss 92–97. At the time of going to press s 92 was in force in so far as it relates to some only of the repeals specified in Schedule 3.

1–4587   93. Commencement.   (1) Except as provided in subsections (2) and (3), the preceding provisions of this Act (other than subsections (9) to (11) of section 85) come into force in accordance with provision made by the Secretary of State by order[1].

(2) Part 2 and sections 19 to 22, 24, 40 to 45, 47 to 52, 55, 56 and 91—

(a) so far as relating to England, come into force in accordance with provision made by the Secretary of State by order;

(b) so far as relating to Wales, come into force in accordance with provision made by the National Assembly for Wales by order.

(3) Part 8 comes into force—

(a) in relation to complaints about hedges situated in England, in accordance with provision made by the Secretary of State by order;

(b) in relation to complaints about hedges situated in Wales, in accordance with provision made by the National Assembly for Wales by order.

[Anti-social Behaviour Act 2003, s 93.]

---

1. At the time of going to press the following Commencement Orders had been made: Anti-social Behaviour Act 2003 (Commencement No 1 and Transitional Provisions) Order 2003, SI 2003/3300; Anti-social Behaviour Act 2003 (Commencement No 2) Order 2004, SI 2004/690; Anti-social Behaviour Act 2003 (Commencement No 1) (Wales) Order 2004, SI 2004/999; Anti-social Behaviour Act 2003 (Commencement No 3 and Savings) Order 2004, SI 2004/1502; Anti-social Behaviour Act 2003 (Commencement No 4) Order 2004, SI 2004/2168; Anti-social Behaviour Act 2003 (Commencement No 2 and Savings) (Wales) Order 2004, SI 2004/2557; Anti-social Behaviour Act 2003 (Commencement No 5) (England) Order 2005, SI 2005/710; Anti-social Behaviour Act 2003 (Commencement No 4) (Wales) Order 2005, SI 2005/1225; Anti-social Behaviour Act 2003 (Commencement No 6) (England) Order 2006, SI 2006/393; Anti-Social Behaviour Act 2003 (Commencement No 4) (Amendment) Order 2006, SI 2006/835; and Anti-social Behaviour Act 2003 (Commencement No 5) (Wales) Order 2006, SI 2006/1278..

1–4588   94. Orders and regulations.   (1) References in this section to subordinate legislation are to—

(a) an order of the Secretary of State or the National Assembly for Wales under this Act;
(b) regulations under this Act.

(2) Subordinate legislation—

(a) may make different provision for different purposes, different cases and different areas;
(b) may include incidental, supplemental, consequential, saving or transitional provisions (including provisions applying, with or without modification, provision contained in an enactment).

(3) A power to make subordinate legislation is exercisable by statutory instrument.

(4) A statutory instrument is subject to annulment in pursuance of a resolution of either House of Parliament if it contains subordinate legislation made by the Secretary of State other than—

(a) regulations under section 81 or 83; or
(b) an order under section 93.

(5) No regulations shall be made by the Secretary of State under section 81 or 83 (whether alone or with other provisions) unless a draft of the statutory instrument containing the regulations has been laid before, and approved by a resolution of, each House of Parliament.

[Anti-social Behaviour Act 2003, s 94.]

1–4589   95. Money

1–4590   96. Extent.   (1) Parts 1 to 4 and 6 to 9 extend to England and Wales only.

(2) Part 5 and this Part do not extend to Northern Ireland.

[Anti-social Behaviour Act 2003, s 96.]

1–4591   97. Short title.   This Act may be cited as the Anti-social Behaviour Act 2003.

[Anti-social Behaviour Act 2003, s 97.]

1–4592   SCHEDULE 1

This Schedule inserts a new Chapter 1A 'Demoted Tenancies' in the Housing Act 1996 and makes various amendments to the Housing Act 1985.

1-4593   SCHEDULE 2

This Schedule makes various amendments to the Powers of Criminal Courts (Sentencing) Act 2000, and makes consequential amendments to s 21 of the Children Act 1989 and Sch 7 to the 2000 Act. These will be noted in the enactments concerned when they take effect.

1-4594   SCHEDULE 3

Where these relate to enactments reproduced in this work they will be shown in the enactments concerned when they take effect.

Constitutional Reform Act 2005[1]
(2005 c 4)

PART 1[2]
THE RULE OF LAW

1-4595   **1. The rule of law.** This Act does not adversely affect—

   (*a*) the existing constitutional principle of the rule of law, or
   (*b*) the Lord Chancellor's existing constitutional role in relation to that principle.
[Constitutional Reform Act 2005, s 1.]

1. The Constitutional Reform Act received the Royal Assent on 24 March 23005. It modifies the office of Lord Chancellor and changes the ways in which some of the functions vested in that office are to be exercised. The Act abolishes the appellate jurisdiction of the House of Lords and establishes a new Supreme Court. It creates the Judicial Appointments Commission, and provides for judicial discipline in England and Wales. The Act also modifies the jurisdiction of the Judicial Committee of the Privy Council.

The Act contains 7 Parts and 18 Schedules.

Part 1 provides that the Act does not adversely affect the Rule of Law or the Lord Chancellor's role in relation to that principle.
Part 2 modifies the office of Lord Chancellor so that the office holder is no longer a judge nor exercises any judicial functions. It provides for the division of functions relating to the judiciary between the reformed ministerial office of Lord Chancellor and the Lord Chief Justice (and/or other senior judicial office holders, as appropriate). It also guarantees continued judicial independence.
Part 3 makes provision for the new Supreme Court.
Part 4 creates the Judicial Appointments Commission which will be responsible for selecting judges for the courts of England and Wales and members of certain tribunals.
Part 5 is concerned with judicial appointments and removals in relation to Northern Ireland.
Part 6 contains other provisions in relation to the judiciary.
Part 7 deals with general matters.

Most of the Act's provisions will be brought into force in accordance with commencement orders made under s 148. At the time of going to press, the following commencement orders had been made: Constitutional Reform Act 2005 (Commencement No 1) Order 2005, SI 2005/1431; Constitutional Reform Act 2005 (Commencement No 2) Order 2005, SI 2005/2284; Constitutional Reform Act 2005 (Commencement No 3) Order 2005, SI 2005/2505; Constitutional Reform Act 2005 (Commencement No 4) Order 2005, SI 2006/228; Constitutional Reform Act 2005 (Commencement No 5) Order 2006, SI 2006/1014; and Constitutional Reform Act 2005 (Commencement No 6) Order 2006, SI 2006/1537. With the exception of most of the provisions of part 3 (Supreme Court), nearly all of the provisions of the Act relating to England and Wales are in force.

2. Part 1 contains s 1.

PART 2[1]
ARRANGEMENTS TO MODIFY THE OFFICE OF LORD CHANCELLOR
Qualifications for office of Lord Chancellor

1-4596   **2. Lord Chancellor to be qualified by experience.** (1) A person may not be recommended for appointment as Lord Chancellor unless he appears to the Prime Minister to be qualified by experience.

(2) The Prime Minister may take into account any of these—

   (*a*) experience as a Minister of the Crown;
   (*b*) experience as a member of either House of Parliament;
   (*c*) experience as a qualifying practitioner;
   (*d*) experience as a teacher of law in a university;
   (*e*) other experience that the Prime Minister considers relevant.

(3) In this section "qualifying practitioner" means any of these—

   (*a*) a person who has a Senior Courts qualification, within the meaning of section 71 of the Courts and Legal Services Act 1990 (c 41);
   (*b*) an advocate in Scotland or a solicitor entitled to appear in the Court of Session and the High Court of Justiciary;
   (*c*) a member of the Bar of Northern Ireland or a solicitor of the Court of Judicature of Northern Ireland.
[Constitutional Reform Act 2005, s 2.]

1. Part 2 contains ss 2–22. Sections 4 and 18–22 came into force on commencement (see s 148, post).

Continued judicial independence

1–4597   3. Guarantee of continued judicial independence.   (1) The Lord Chancellor, other Ministers of the Crown and all with responsibility for matters relating to the judiciary or otherwise to the administration of justice must uphold the continued independence of the judiciary.

(2) Subsection (1) does not impose any duty which it would be within the legislative competence of the Scottish Parliament to impose.

(3) A person is not subject to the duty imposed by subsection (1) if he is subject to the duty imposed by section 1(1) of the Justice (Northern Ireland) Act 2002 (c 26).

(4) The following particular duties are imposed for the purpose of upholding that independence.

(5) The Lord Chancellor and other Ministers of the Crown must not seek to influence particular judicial decisions through any special access to the judiciary.

(6) The Lord Chancellor must have regard to—

(a) the need to defend that independence;

(b) the need for the judiciary to have the support necessary to enable them to exercise their functions;

(c) the need for the public interest in regard to matters relating to the judiciary or otherwise to the administration of justice to be properly represented in decisions affecting those matters.

(7) In this section "the judiciary" includes the judiciary of any of the following—

(a) the Supreme Court;

(b) any other court established under the law of any part of the United Kingdom;

(c) any international court.

(8) *Defines "International Court".*
[Constitutional Reform Act 2005, s 3.]

4. Guarantee of continued judicial independence: Northern Ireland

Representations by senior judges

1–4598   5. Representations to Parliament.   (1) The chief justice of any part of the United Kingdom may lay before Parliament written representations on matters that appear to him to be matters of importance relating to the judiciary, or otherwise to the administration of justice, in that part of the United Kingdom.

(2)–(4) *Concern Scotland and Northern Ireland.*
[Constitutional Reform Act 2005, s 5.]

1–4599   6. Representations to the Northern Ireland Assembly

Judiciary and courts in England and Wales

1–4600   7. President of the Courts of England and Wales.   (1) The Lord Chief Justice holds the office of President of the Courts of England and Wales and is Head of the Judiciary of England and Wales.

(2) As President of the Courts of England and Wales he is responsible—

(a) for representing the views of the judiciary of England and Wales to Parliament, to the Lord Chancellor and to Ministers of the Crown generally;

(b) for the maintenance of appropriate arrangements for the welfare, training and guidance of the judiciary of England and Wales within the resources made available by the Lord Chancellor;

(c) for the maintenance of appropriate arrangements for the deployment of the judiciary of England and Wales and the allocation of work within courts.

(3) The President of the Courts of England and Wales is president of the courts listed in subsection (4) and is entitled to sit in any of those courts.

(4) The courts are—

the Court of Appeal
the High Court
the Crown Court
the county courts
the magistrates' courts.

(5) In section 1 of the Supreme Court Act 1981 (c 54), subsection (2) (Lord Chancellor to be president of the Supreme Court of England and Wales) ceases to have effect.
[Constitutional Reform Act 2005, s 7.]

1–4600A   8. Head and Deputy Head of Criminal Justice.   (1) There is to be a Head of Criminal Justice.

(2) The Head of Criminal Justice is—

(a) the Lord Chief Justice, or

(b) if the Lord Chief Justice appoints another person, that person.

(3) The Lord Chief Justice may appoint a person to be Deputy Head of Criminal Justice.

(4) The Lord Chief Justice must not appoint a person under subsection (2)(*b*) or (3) unless these conditions are met—

(*a*) the Lord Chief Justice has consulted the Lord Chancellor;
(*b*) the person to be appointed is an ordinary judge of the Court of Appeal.

(5) A person appointed under subsection (2)(*b*) or (3) holds the office to which he is appointed in accordance with the terms of his appointment.
[Constitutional Reform Act 2005, s 8.]

1–4600B 9. Head and Deputy Head of Family Justice. (1) The President of the Family Division is Head of Family Justice.

(2) The Lord Chief Justice may appoint a person to be Deputy Head of Family Justice.

(3) The Lord Chief Justice must not appoint a person under subsection (2) unless these conditions are met—

(*a*) the Lord Chief Justice has consulted the Lord Chancellor;
(*b*) the person to be appointed is an ordinary judge of the Court of Appeal.

(4) A person appointed as Deputy Head of Family Justice holds that office in accordance with the terms of his appointment.
[Constitutional Reform Act 2005, s 9.]

Judiciary and courts in Northern Ireland

1–4600C 10, 11. *Concern Northern Ireland.*

Other provisions about the judiciary and courts

1–4600D 12. Powers to make rules. (1) Part 1 of Schedule 1 sets out a process for the exercise of rule-making powers.

(2) Part 2 of the Schedule contains amendments of Acts that contain rule-making powers.

(3) Those amendments—

(*a*) provide for those powers to be exercised in accordance with the process set out in Part 1 of the Schedule, and
(*b*) make consequential provision.
[Constitutional Reform Act 2005, s 12.]

1–4600E 13. Powers to give directions. (1) Part 1 of Schedule 2 sets out a process for the exercise of powers to give directions.

(2) Part 2 of the Schedule contains amendments of Acts that contain powers to give directions.

(3) Those amendments—

(*a*) provide for those powers to be exercised in accordance with the process set out in Part 1 of the Schedule, and
(*b*) make consequential provision.
[Constitutional Reform Act 2005, s 13.]

1–4600F 14. Transfer of appointment functions to Her Majesty. Schedule 3 provides for—

(*a*) Her Majesty instead of the Lord Chancellor to make appointments to certain offices, and
(*b*) the modification of enactments relating to those offices.
[Constitutional Reform Act 2005, s 14.]

1–4600G 15. Other functions of the Lord Chancellor and organisation of the courts. (1) Schedule 4 provides for—

(*a*) the transfer of functions to or from the Lord Chancellor,
(*b*) the modification of other functions of the Lord Chancellor,
(*c*) the modification of enactments relating to those functions, and
(*d*) the modification of enactments relating to the organisation of the courts.

(2) Schedule 5 makes similar provision about functions under legislation relating to Northern Ireland.
[Constitutional Reform Act 2005, s 15.]

1–4600H 16. Functions of the Lord Chief Justice during vacancy or incapacity. (1) This section applies during any period when—

(*a*) the office of Lord Chief Justice is vacant, or
(*b*) the Lord Chief Justice is incapacitated.

(2) During such a period—

(*a*) any function of the Lord Chief Justice may be exercised by the senior Head of Division;
(*b*) anything which falls to be done in relation to the Lord Chief Justice may be done in relation to the senior Head of Division.

(3) The senior Head of Division is—

(a) the Master of the Rolls, or
(b) the President of the Queen's Bench Division, if the office in paragraph (a) is vacant, or
(c) the President of the Family Division, if the offices in paragraphs (a) and (b) are vacant, or
(d) the Chancellor of the High Court, if the offices in paragraphs (a), (b) and (c) are vacant.

(4) For the purposes of this section—

(a) the Lord Chief Justice is to be regarded as incapacitated only if at least three of the Heads of Division declare in writing that they are satisfied that he is incapacitated;
(b) in such a case, the Lord Chief Justice is to be regarded as incapacitated until at least three of the Heads of Division declare in writing that they are satisfied that he is no longer incapacitated.

(5) In this section—

(a) "Lord Chief Justice" means the Lord Chief Justice of England and Wales;
(b) "incapacitated", in relation to the Lord Chief Justice, means unable to exercise the functions of that office;
(c) "Head of Division" means each of the office holders referred to in subsection (3).
[Constitutional Reform Act 2005, s 16.]

Lord Chancellor's oath

1–4600I 17. Lord Chancellor's oath

Speakership of the House of Lords

18. Speakership of the House of Lords

Functions subject to transfer, modification or abolition

1–4600J 19. Transfer, modification or abolition of functions by order. (1) The Lord Chancellor may by order make provision for any of these purposes—

(a) to transfer an existing function of the Lord Chancellor to another person;
(b) to direct that an existing function of the Lord Chancellor is to be exercisable concurrently with another person;
(c) to direct that an existing function of the Lord Chancellor exercisable concurrently with another person is to cease to be exercisable by the Lord Chancellor;
(d) to modify an existing function of the Lord Chancellor;
(e) to abolish an existing function of the Lord Chancellor.

(2) An order under subsection (1) may in particular—

(a) amend or repeal any of the following—

(i) an enactment other than one contained in an Act passed, or Northern Ireland legislation passed or made, after the Session in which this Act is passed;
(ii) subordinate legislation other than subordinate legislation made under an Act passed, or Northern Ireland legislation passed or made, after the Session in which this Act is passed;
(iii) any other instrument or document, including a prerogative instrument;

(b) include—

(i) any supplementary, incidental or consequential provision, and
(ii) any transitory, transitional or saving provision,

which the Lord Chancellor considers necessary or expedient for the purposes of, in consequence of, or for giving full effect to, provision made under subsection (1).

(3) The amendments that may be made by virtue of subsection (2)(a) are in addition to those made by or under any other provision of this Act.

(4) An order under subsection (1) may not include provision that may be made under section 1(1) of the Ministers of the Crown Act 1975 (c 26) (power to transfer functions to other Ministers etc).

(5) An order under subsection (1) may not be made in relation to any function of the Lord Chancellor that is within Schedule 7.

(6) An order under subsection (1) may amend Schedule 7 so as to include any function which, by virtue of provision in the order—

(a) becomes exercisable by the Lord Chancellor concurrently with another person, or
(b) is modified.

(7) An order under subsection (1) may not, to the extent that it amends Schedule 7, be revoked by another order under subsection (1).

(8) In this section—

"existing function" means any function other than one that is conferred by—

(a) an Act passed, or Northern Ireland legislation passed or made, after the Session in which this Act is passed, or
(b) subordinate legislation made under an Act passed, or Northern Ireland legislation passed or made, after the Session in which this Act is passed;

"prerogative instrument" means an Order in Council, warrant, charter or other instrument made
under the prerogative.
[Constitutional Reform Act 2005, s 19.]

1–4600K   20. Protected functions not transferable under Ministers of the Crown Act 1975.
(1) The Ministers of the Crown Act 1975 (c 26) is amended as follows.
(2) In section 1 (power by Order in Council to transfer functions of Ministers), after subsection
(5) insert—

"(6) This section does not apply to the functions of the Lord Chancellor that are within
Schedule 7 to the Constitutional Reform Act 2005.
(7) An Order in Council under this section may amend Schedule 7 to the Constitutional
Reform Act 2005 so as to include any function which, by virtue of provision in the Order in
Council—
(*a*) is transferred to the Lord Chancellor,
(*b*) becomes exercisable by the Lord Chancellor concurrently with another person, or
(*c*) remains exercisable by the Lord Chancellor but ceases to be exercisable concurrently with
another person.
(8) An Order in Council under this section may not, to the extent that it amends Schedule 7 to
the Constitutional Reform Act 2005, be revoked by another Order in Council under this section."
(3) After section 5(3) (Orders under Act to be revocable) insert—

"(3A) Subsection (3) is subject to section 1(8)."
[Constitutional Reform Act 2005, s 20.]

1–4600L   21. Amendment of Schedule 7.   (1) The Lord Chancellor may by order amend
Schedule 7 so as to include within that Schedule any function of the Lord Chancellor under an
enactment, other than an enactment contained in an Act passed, or Northern Ireland legislation
passed or made, after the Session in which this Act is passed.
(2) For the purposes of subsection (1) it does not matter whether a function of the Lord
Chancellor is exercisable by him alone or concurrently with another person.
(3) An order made under this section may not be revoked by an order made under this section.
[Constitutional Reform Act 2005, s 21.]

Supplementary

1–4600M   22. Transfers: supplementary.   (1) This section applies where a function of the Lord
Chancellor is transferred to another person ("the transferee") by any provision of this Act or of an
order under section 19 ("the amending provision").
(2) Where the transferee is Her Majesty, references to the transferee in the following provisions of
this section are to be read as references to the Lord Chancellor.
(3) The transfer does not affect the validity of anything done (or having effect as if done) by or in
relation to the Lord Chancellor before the commencement of the amending provision.
(4) So far as is necessary in consequence of the transfer, an enactment or instrument passed or
made before the commencement of the provision has effect, subject to any amendment made by the
amending provision or any other provision of this Act, as if—
(*a*) a reference to the Lord Chancellor were a reference to the transferee;
(*b*) a reference to the Lord Chancellor's Department were a reference to the department of the
transferee;
(*c*) a reference to an officer of the Lord Chancellor were a reference to an officer of the transferee.
(5) Anything done by or in relation to the Lord Chancellor in connection with the function has
effect, so far as is necessary for continuing its effect after the commencement of the amending
provision, as if done by or in relation to the transferee.
(6) Anything which relates to the function and which is in the process of being done by or in
relation to the Lord Chancellor at the commencement of the amending provision may be continued
by or in relation to the transferee.
(7) Legal proceedings to which the Lord Chancellor is party in relation to the function at the
commencement of the amending provision may be continued by or against the transferee.
(8) Documents or forms printed for use in connection with the function may be used in connection
with it even though they contain (or are to be read as containing) references to the Lord Chancellor,
his Department or an officer of his.
(9) For the purposes of the use of any such documents after the commencement of the amending
provision, those references are to be read as references to the transferee, his department or an officer
of his.
[Constitutional Reform Act 2005, s 22.]

PART 3[1]
THE SUPREME COURT
The Supreme Court

1–4600N   23. The Supreme Court.   (1) There is to be a Supreme Court of the United Kingdom.
(2) The Court consists of 12 judges appointed by Her Majesty by letters patent.

(3) Her Majesty may from time to time by Order in Council amend subsection (2) so as to increase or further increase the number of judges of the Court.

(4) No recommendation may be made to Her Majesty in Council to make an Order under subsection (3) unless a draft of the Order has been laid before and approved by resolution of each House of Parliament.

(5) Her Majesty may by letters patent appoint one of the judges to be President and one to be Deputy President of the Court.

(6) The judges other than the President and Deputy President are to be styled "Justices of the Supreme Court".

(7) The Court is to be taken to be duly constituted despite any vacancy among the judges of the Court or in the office of President or Deputy President.

[Constitutional Reform Act 2005, s 23.]

---

1. Part 3 contains ss 23–60.

1–4600O   24. First members of the Court.   On the commencement of section 23—

     (a)   the persons who immediately before that commencement are Lords of Appeal in Ordinary become judges of the Supreme Court,

     (b)   the person who immediately before that commencement is the senior Lord of Appeal in Ordinary becomes the President of the Court, and

     (c)   the person who immediately before that commencement is the second senior Lord of Appeal in Ordinary becomes the Deputy President of the Court.

[Constitutional Reform Act 2005, s 24.]

Appointment of judges

1–4600P   25. Qualification for appointment.   (1) A person is not qualified to be appointed a judge of the Supreme Court unless he has (at any time)—

     (a)   held high judicial office for a period of at least 2 years, or

     (b)   been a qualifying practitioner for a period of at least 15 years.

(2) A person is a qualifying practitioner for the purposes of this section at any time when—

     (a)   he has a Senior Courts qualification, within the meaning of section 71 of the Courts and Legal Services Act 1990 (c 41),

     (b)   he is an advocate in Scotland or a solicitor entitled to appear in the Court of Session and the High Court of Justiciary, or

     (c)   he is a member of the Bar of Northern Ireland or a solicitor of the Court of Judicature of Northern Ireland.

[Constitutional Reform Act 2005, s 25.]

1–4600Q   26–60.   *These provisions are concerned with the selection of members of the Supreme Court; their terms of appointment, etc; staff, accommodation and other resources.*

PART 4[1]

JUDICIAL APPOINTMENTS AND DISCIPLINE

CHAPTER 1[2]

Commission and Ombudsman

1–4600R   61. The Judicial Appointments Commission.   (1) There is to be a body corporate called the Judicial Appointments Commission.

(2) Schedule 12 is about the Commission.

[Constitutional Reform Act 2005, s 61.]

---

1. Part 4 contains ss 61–122. Sections 65(1) – (3), 66 and 85(3), and for the purpose of making rules or regulations ss 115–118 and para 26 of Sch 12 and certain paras of Sch 4, are in force: see Constitutional Reform Act 2005 (Commencement No 3) Order 2005. SI 2005/2505).

2. Chapter 1 contains ss 61 and 62.

1–4600S   62. Judicial Appointments and Conduct Ombudsman.   (1) There is to be a Judicial Appointments and Conduct Ombudsman.

(2) Schedule 13 is about the Ombudsman.

[Constitutional Reform Act 2005, s 62.]

CHAPTER 2[1]

Appointments

General provisions

1–4600T   63. Merit and good character.   (1) Subsections (2) and (3) apply to any selection under this Part by the Commission or a selection panel ("the selecting body").

(2) Selection must be solely on merit.

(3) A person must not be selected unless the selecting body is satisfied that he is of good character.

[Constitutional Reform Act 2005, s 63.]

1. Chapter 2 contains ss 63–107.

1–4600U   64. Encouragement of diversity. (1) The Commission, in performing its functions under this Part, must have regard to the need to encourage diversity in the range of persons available for selection for appointments.

(2) This section is subject to section 63.

[Constitutional Reform Act 2005, s 64.]

1–4600V   65. Guidance about procedures. (1) The Lord Chancellor may issue guidance about procedures for the performance by the Commission or a selection panel of its functions of—

(a) identifying persons willing to be considered for selection under this Part, and

(b) assessing such persons for the purposes of selection.

(2) The guidance may, among other things, relate to consultation or other steps in determining such procedures.

(3) The purposes for which guidance may be issued under this section include the encouragement of diversity in the range of persons available for selection.

(4) The Commission and any selection panel must have regard to the guidance in matters to which it relates.

[Constitutional Reform Act 2005, s 65.]

1–4600W   66. Guidance: supplementary. (1) Before issuing any guidance the Lord Chancellor must—

(a) consult the Lord Chief Justice;

(b) after doing so, lay a draft of the proposed guidance before each House of Parliament.

(2) If the draft is approved by a resolution of each House of Parliament within the 40-day period the Lord Chancellor must issue the guidance in the form of the draft.

(3) In any other case the Lord Chancellor must take no further steps in relation to the proposed guidance.

(4) Subsection (3) does not prevent a new draft of the proposed guidance from being laid before each House of Parliament after consultation with the Lord Chief Justice.

(5) Guidance comes into force on such date as the Lord Chancellor may appoint by order.

(6) The Lord Chancellor may—

(a) from time to time revise the whole or part of any guidance and re-issue it;

(b) after consulting the Lord Chief Justice, by order revoke any guidance.

(7) In this section—

"40-day period" in relation to the draft of any proposed guidance means—

(a) if the draft is laid before one House on a day later than the day on which it is laid before the other House, the period of 40 days beginning with the later day, and

(b) in any other case, the period of 40 days beginning with the day on which the draft is laid before each House,

no account being taken of any period during which Parliament is dissolved or prorogued or during which both Houses are adjourned for more than 4 days;

"guidance" means guidance issued by the Lord Chancellor under section 65 and includes guidance which has been revised and re-issued.

[Constitutional Reform Act 2005, s 66.]

Lord Chief Justice and Heads of Division

1–4600X   67–105. *These provisions are concerned with the selection of: the Lord Chief and Heads of Divisions; Lords Justices of Appeal; and puisne judges and other office holders. They also deal with complaints to the Commission or to the Lord Chancellor, and complaints to the Judicial Appointments and Conduct Ombudsman.*

Miscellaneous

1–4600Y   106. Consultation on appointment of lay justices. In section 10 of the Courts Act 2003 (c 39) (appointment of lay justices etc) after subsection (2) insert—

"(2A) The Lord Chancellor must ensure that arrangements for the exercise, so far as affecting any local justice area, of functions under subsections (1) and (2) include arrangements for consulting persons appearing to him to have special knowledge of matters relevant to the exercise of those functions in relation to that area."

[Constitutional Reform Act 2005, s 106.]

1–4600Z   107. Disclosure of information to the Commission. (1) Information which is held by or on behalf of a permitted person (whether obtained before or after this section comes into force) may be disclosed to the Commission or a committee of the Commission for the purposes of selection under this Part.

(2) A disclosure under this section is not to be taken to breach any restriction on the disclosure of information (however imposed).

(3) But nothing in this section authorises the making of a disclosure—

(a) which contravenes the Data Protection Act 1998 (c 29), or

(b) which is prohibited by Part 1 of the Regulation of Investigatory Powers Act 2000 (c 23).

(4) This section does not affect a power to disclose which exists apart from this section.

(5) The following are permitted persons—

(a) a chief officer of police of a police force in England and Wales;

(b) a chief constable of a police force in Scotland;

(c) the Chief Constable of the Police Service of Northern Ireland;

(d) the Director General of the National Criminal Intelligence Service;

(e) the Director General of the National Crime Squad;

(f) the Commissioners of Inland Revenue;

(g) the Commissioners of Customs and Excise.

(6) The Lord Chancellor may by order[1] designate as permitted persons other persons who exercise functions which he considers are of a public nature (including a body or person discharging regulatory functions in relation to any description of activities).

(7) Information must not be disclosed under this section on behalf of the Commissioners of Inland Revenue or on behalf of the Commissioners of Customs and Excise unless the Commissioners concerned authorise the disclosure.

(8) The power to authorise a disclosure under subsection (7) may be delegated (either generally or for a specific purpose)—

(a) in the case of the Commissioners of Inland Revenue, to an officer of the Board of Inland Revenue,

(b) in the case of the Commissioners of Customs and Excise, to a customs officer.

(9) For the purposes of this section a customs officer is a person commissioned by the Commissioners of Customs and Excise under section 6(3) of the Customs and Excise Management Act 1979 (c 2).

[Constitutional Reform Act 2005, s 107.]

---

1. The Permitted Persons (Designation) Order 2006, SI 2006/679 has been made.

CHAPTER 3[1]
Discipline

Disciplinary powers

1–4601 108. Disciplinary powers. (1) Any power of the Lord Chancellor to remove a person from an office listed in Schedule 14 is exercisable only after the Lord Chancellor has complied with prescribed procedures (as well as any other requirements to which the power is subject).

(2) The Lord Chief Justice may exercise any of the following powers but only with the agreement of the Lord Chancellor and only after complying with prescribed procedures.

(3) The Lord Chief Justice may give a judicial office holder formal advice, or a formal warning or reprimand, for disciplinary purposes (but this section does not restrict what he may do informally or for other purposes or where any advice or warning is not addressed to a particular office holder).

(4) He may suspend a person from a judicial office for any period during which any of the following applies—

(a) the person is subject to criminal proceedings;

(b) the person is serving a sentence imposed in criminal proceedings;

(c) the person has been convicted of an offence and is subject to prescribed procedures in relation to the conduct constituting the offence.

(5) He may suspend a person from a judicial office for any period if—

(a) the person has been convicted of a criminal offence,

(b) it has been determined under prescribed procedures that the person should not be removed from office, and

(c) it appears to the Lord Chief Justice with the agreement of the Lord Chancellor that the suspension is necessary for maintaining confidence in the judiciary.

(6) He may suspend a person from office as a senior judge for any period during which the person is subject to proceedings for an Address.

(7) He may suspend the holder of an office listed in Schedule 14 for any period during which the person—

(a) is under investigation for an offence, or

(b) is subject to prescribed procedures.

(8) While a person is suspended under this section from any office he may not perform any of the functions of the office (but his other rights as holder of the office are not affected).

[Constitutional Reform Act 2005, s 108.]

1. Part 2 contains ss 108–121.

1–4601A   109. Disciplinary powers: interpretation.   (1) This section has effect for the purposes of section 108.

(2) A person is subject to criminal proceedings if in any part of the United Kingdom proceedings against him for an offence have been begun and have not come to an end, and the times when proceedings are begun and come to an end for the purposes of this subsection are such as may be prescribed.

(3) A person is subject to proceedings for an Address from the time when notice of a motion is given in each House of Parliament for an Address for the removal of the person from office, until the earliest of the following events—

(a) either notice is withdrawn;

(b) either motion is amended so that it is no longer a motion for an address for removal of the person from office;

(c) either motion is withdrawn, lapses or is disagreed to;

(d) where an Address is presented by each House, a message is brought to each House from Her Majesty in answer to the Address.

(4) "Judicial office" means—

(a) office as a senior judge, or

(b) an office listed in Schedule 14;

and "judicial office holder" means the holder of a judicial office.

(5) "Senior judge" means any of these—

(a) Master of the Rolls;

(b) President of the Queen's Bench Division;

(c) President of the Family Division;

(d) Chancellor of the High Court;

(e) Lord Justice of Appeal;

(f) puisne judge of the High Court.

(6) "Sentence" includes any sentence other than a fine (and "serving" is to be read accordingly).

(7) The times when a person becomes and ceases to be subject to prescribed procedures for the purposes of section 108(4) or (7) are such as may be prescribed.

(8) "Under investigation for an offence" has such meaning as may be prescribed.

[Constitutional Reform Act 2005, s 109.]

Applications for review and references

1–4601B   110. Applications to the Ombudsman.   (1) This section applies if an interested party makes an application to the Ombudsman for the review of the exercise by any person of a regulated disciplinary function, on the grounds that there has been—

(a) a failure to comply with prescribed procedures, or

(b) some other maladministration.

(2) The Ombudsman must carry out a review if the following three conditions are met.

(3) The first condition is that the Ombudsman considers that a review is necessary.

(4) The second condition is that—

(a) the application is made within the permitted period,

(b) the application is made within such longer period as the Ombudsman considers appropriate in the circumstances, or

(c) the application is made on grounds alleging undue delay and the Ombudsman considers that the application has been made within a reasonable time.

(5) The third condition is that the application is made in a form approved by the Ombudsman.

(6) But the Ombudsman may not review the merits of a decision made by any person.

(7) If any of the conditions in subsections (3) to (5) is not met, or if the grounds of the application relate only to the merits of a decision, the Ombudsman—

(a) may not carry out a review, and

(b) must inform the applicant accordingly.

(8) In this section and sections 111 to 113, "regulated disciplinary function" means any of the following—

(a) any function of the Lord Chancellor that falls within section 108(1);

(b) any function conferred on the Lord Chief Justice by section 108(3) to (7);

(c) any function exercised under prescribed procedures in connection with a function falling within paragraph (a) or (b).

(9) In this section, in relation to an application under this section for a review of the exercise of a regulated disciplinary function—

"interested party" means—

(a) the judicial office holder in relation to whose conduct the function is exercised, or

(b) any person who has made a complaint about that conduct in accordance with prescribed procedures;

"permitted period" means the period of 28 days beginning with the latest of—

(a) the failure or other maladministration alleged by the applicant;

(b) where that failure or maladministration occurred in the course of an investigation, the applicant being notified of the conclusion or other termination of that investigation;

(c) where that failure or maladministration occurred in the course of making a determination, the applicant being notified of that determination.

(10) References in this section and section 111 to the exercise of a function include references to a decision whether or not to exercise the function.

[Constitutional Reform Act 2005, s 110.]

1–4601C   111.   Review by the Ombudsman.

(1) Where the Ombudsman is under a duty to carry out a review on an application under section 110, he must—

(a) on the basis of any findings he makes about the grounds for the application, decide to what extent the grounds are established;

(b) decide what if any action to take under subsections (2) to (7).

(2) If he decides that the grounds are established to any extent, he may make recommendations to the Lord Chancellor and Lord Chief Justice.

(3) A recommendation under subsection (2) may be for the payment of compensation.

(4) Such a recommendation must relate to loss which appears to the Ombudsman to have been suffered by the applicant as a result of any failure or maladministration to which the application relates.

(5) If the Ombudsman decides that a determination made in the exercise of a function under review is unreliable because of any failure or maladministration to which the application relates, he may set aside the determination.

(6) If a determination is set aside under subsection (5)—

(a) the prescribed procedures apply, subject to any prescribed modifications, as if the determination had not been made, and

(b) for the purposes of those procedures, any investigation or review leading to the determination is to be disregarded.

(7) Subsection (6) is subject to any direction given by the Ombudsman under this subsection—

(a) for a previous investigation or review to be taken into account to any extent, or

(b) for any investigation or review which may form part of the prescribed procedures to be undertaken, or undertaken again.

(8) This section is subject to section 112.

[Constitutional Reform Act 2005, s 111.]

1–4601D   112.   Reports on reviews.

(1) In this section references to the Ombudsman's response to an application are references to the findings and decisions referred to in section 111(1).

(2) Before determining his response to an application the Ombudsman must prepare a draft of a report of the review carried out on the application.

(3) The draft report must state the Ombudsman's proposed response.

(4) The Ombudsman must submit the draft report to the Lord Chancellor and the Lord Chief Justice.

(5) If the Lord Chancellor or the Lord Chief Justice makes a proposal that the Ombudsman's response to the application should be changed, the Ombudsman must consider whether or not to change it to give effect to that proposal.

(6) The Ombudsman must produce a final report that sets out—

(a) the Ombudsman's response to the application, including any changes made to it to give effect to a proposal under subsection (5);

(b) a statement of any proposal under subsection (5) that is not given effect to.

(7) The Ombudsman must send a copy of the final report to each of the Lord Chancellor and the Lord Chief Justice.

(8) The Ombudsman must also send a copy of the final report to the applicant, but that copy must not include information—

(a) which relates to an identified or identifiable individual other than the applicant, and

(b) whose disclosure by the Ombudsman to the applicant would (apart from this subsection) be contrary to section 139.

(9) Each copy must be signed by the Ombudsman.

(10) No part of the Ombudsman's response to an application has effect until he has complied with subsections (2) to (9).

[Constitutional Reform Act 2005, s 112.]

1–4601E   113.   References to the Ombudsman relating to conduct.

(1) The Ombudsman must investigate any matter referred to him by the Lord Chancellor or the Lord Chief Justice that relates to the exercise of one or more regulated disciplinary functions.

(2) A matter referred to the Ombudsman under subsection (1) may relate to the particular exercise of a regulated disciplinary function or to specified descriptions of the exercise of such functions.
[Constitutional Reform Act 2005, s 113.]

1–4601F   114. Reports on references.   (1) Where the Ombudsman carries out an investigation under section 113 he must prepare a draft of a report of the investigation.

(2) If the investigation relates to a matter which is the subject of a review on an application under section 110, subsection (1) applies only when the Ombudsman has sent a copy of the final report on that review to the Lord Chancellor, the Lord Chief Justice and the applicant.

(3) The draft report must state the Ombudsman's proposals as to—

(a) the findings he will make;

(b) any recommendations he will make for action to be taken by any person in relation to the matter subject to investigation.

(4) Those findings and recommendations are referred to in this section as the Ombudsman's response on the investigation.

(5) The Ombudsman must submit the draft report to the Lord Chancellor and the Lord Chief Justice.

(6) If the Lord Chancellor or the Lord Chief Justice makes a proposal that the Ombudsman's response on the investigation should be changed, the Ombudsman must consider whether or not to change it to give effect to that proposal.

(7) The Ombudsman must produce a final report that sets out—

(a) the Ombudsman's response on the investigation, including any changes made to it to give effect to a proposal under subsection (6);

(b) a statement of any proposal under subsection (6) that is not given effect to.

(8) The Ombudsman must send a copy of the final report to each of the Lord Chancellor and the Lord Chief Justice.

(9) Each copy must be signed by the Ombudsman.
[Constitutional Reform Act 2005, s 114.]

General

1–4601G   115. Regulations about procedures.   The Lord Chief Justice may, with the agreement of the Lord Chancellor, make regulations[1] providing for the procedures that are to be followed in—

(a) the investigation and determination of allegations by any person of misconduct by judicial office holders;

(b) reviews and investigations (including the making of applications or references) under sections 110 to 112.
[Constitutional Reform Act 2005, s 115.]

---

1. The Judicial Discipline (Prescribed Procedures) Regulations 2006, SI 2006/676 have been made.

1–4601H   116. Contents of regulations.   (1) Regulations under section 115(a) may include provision as to any of the following—

(a) circumstances in which an investigation must or may be undertaken (on the making of a complaint or otherwise);

(b) steps to be taken by a complainant before a complaint is to be investigated;

(c) the conduct of an investigation, including steps to be taken by the office holder under investigation or by a complainant or other person;

(d) time limits for taking any step and procedures for extending time limits;

(e) persons by whom an investigation or part of an investigation is to be conducted;

(f) matters to be determined by the Lord Chief Justice, the Lord Chancellor, the office holder under investigation or any other person;

(g) requirements as to records of investigations;

(h) requirements as to confidentiality of communications or proceedings;

(i) requirements as to the publication of information or its provision to any person.

(2) The regulations—

(a) may require a decision as to the exercise of functions under section 108, or functions mentioned in subsection (1) of that section, to be taken in accordance with findings made pursuant to prescribed procedures;

(b) may require that prescribed steps be taken by the Lord Chief Justice or the Lord Chancellor in exercising those functions or before exercising them.

(3) Where regulations under section 115(a) impose any requirement on the office holder under investigation or on a complainant, a person contravening the requirement does not incur liability other than liability to such procedural penalty if any (which may include the suspension or dismissal of a complaint)—

(a) as may be prescribed by the regulations, or

(b) as may be determined by the Lord Chief Justice and the Lord Chancellor or either of them in accordance with provisions so prescribed.

(4) Regulations under section 115 may—

(a) provide for any prescribed requirement not to apply if the Lord Chief Justice and the Lord Chancellor so agree;

(b) make different provision for different purposes.

(5) Nothing in this section limits the generality of section 115.
[Constitutional Reform Act 2005, s 116.]

1–4601I   117. Procedural rules.   (1) Regulations under section 115 may provide for provision of a prescribed description that may be included in the regulations to be made instead by rules made by the Lord Chief Justice with the agreement of the Lord Chancellor.

(2) But the provision that may be made by rules does not include—

(a) provision within section 116(2);

(b) provision made for the purposes of section 108(7) or (8) or 116(3).

(3) The rules are to be published in such manner as the Lord Chief Justice may determine with the agreement of the Lord Chancellor.
[Constitutional Reform Act 2005, s 117.]

1–4601J   118. Extension of discipline provisions to other offices.   (1) This Chapter applies in relation to an office designated by the Lord Chancellor under this section as it would apply if the office were listed in Schedule 14.

(2) The Lord Chancellor may by order[1] designate any office, not listed in Schedule 14, the holder of which he has power to remove from office.

(3) An order under this section may be made only with the agreement of the Lord Chief Justice.
[Constitutional Reform Act 2005, s 118.]

---

1 The Discipline of Coroners (Designation) Order 2006, SI 2006/677 has been made.

1–4601K   119. Delegation of functions.   (1) The Lord Chief Justice may nominate a judicial office holder (as defined in section 109(4)) to exercise any of his functions under the relevant sections.

(2) The relevant sections are—

(a) section 108(3) to (7);

(b) section 111(2);

(c) section 112;

(d) section 116(3)(b).

[Constitutional Reform Act 2005, s 119.]

120, 121   *Scotland and Northern Ireland*

These provisions concern Scotland and Northern Ireland.

CHAPTER 4
INTERPRETATION OF PART 4

1–4601L   122. Interpretation of Part 4.   In this Part—

"appoint" includes nominate or designate (and "appointment" is to be read accordingly);
the "Commission" means the Judicial Appointments Commission;
"Head of Division" means any of these—

(a) the Master of the Rolls;

(b) the President of the Queen's Bench Division;

(c) the President of the Family Division;

(d) the Chancellor of the High Court;

"High Court" means the High Court in England and Wales;
"high judicial office" has the meaning given by section 60;
"lay member" of the Commission has the meaning given by paragraph 4 of Schedule 12;
"Lord Chief Justice", unless otherwise stated, means the Lord Chief Justice of England and Wales;
"Lord Justice of Appeal" means a Lord Justice of Appeal in England and Wales;
"office" includes a position of any description;
the "Ombudsman" means the Judicial Appointments and Conduct Ombudsman;
"prescribed" means prescribed by regulations under section 115 or, subject to section 117(2), by rules under section 117;
"vacancy" in relation to an office to which one of sections 68, 77 and 86 applies, means a vacancy arising on a holder of the office vacating it at any time after the commencement of that section.
[Constitutional Reform Act 2005, s 122.]

PART 5[1]
JUDICIAL APPOINTMENTS AND REMOVALS: NORTHERN IRELAND

PART 5[1]
JUDICIAL APPOINTMENTS AND REMOVALS: NORTHERN IRELAND

PART 6[2]
OTHER PROVISIONS RELATING TO THE JUDICIARY

PART 7[3]
GENERAL

1–4601M   139. Confidentiality.   (1) A person who obtains confidential information, or to whom confidential information is provided, under or for the purposes of a relevant provision must not disclose it except with lawful authority.

(2) These are the relevant provisions—

(a) sections 26 to 31;
(b) Part 4;
(c) regulations and rules under Part 4.

(3) Information is confidential if it relates to an identified or identifiable individual (a "subject").

(4) Confidential information is disclosed with lawful authority only if and to the extent that any of the following applies—

(a) the disclosure is with the consent of each person who is a subject of the information (but this is subject to subsection (5));
(b) the disclosure is for (and is necessary for) the exercise by any person of functions under a relevant provision;
(c) the disclosure is for (and is necessary for) the exercise of functions under section 11(3A) of the Supreme Court Act 1981 (c 54) or a decision whether to exercise them;
(d) the disclosure is for (and is necessary for) the exercise of powers to which section 108 applies, or a decision whether to exercise them;
(e) the disclosure is required, under rules of court or a court order, for the purposes of legal proceedings of any description.

(5) An opinion or other information given by one identified or identifiable individual (a) about another (b)—

(a) is information that relates to both;
(b) must not be disclosed to B without A's consent.

(6) This section does not prevent the disclosure with the agreement of the Lord Chancellor and the Lord Chief Justice of information as to disciplinary action taken in accordance with a relevant provision.

(7) This section does not prevent the disclosure of information which is already, or has previously been, available to the public from other sources.

(8) A contravention of this section in respect of any information is actionable, subject to the defences and other incidents applying to actions for breach of statutory duty.

(9) But it is actionable only at the suit of a person who is a subject of the information.
[Constitutional Reform Act 2005, s 139.]

---

1. Part 5 contains ss 123–136 and is concerned with Northern Ireland.
2. Part 6 contains ss 137 and 138, which are concerned with Parliamentary disqualification and the Judicial Committee of the Privy Council.
3. Part 7 contains ss 139–149.

1–4601N   140. "Enactment".   (1) In this Act "enactment" includes—

(a) an enactment contained in this Act;
(b) an enactment contained in a local, personal or private Act;
(c) except in sections 19 and 143, an enactment contained in subordinate legislation;

and any reference to an enactment includes a reference to an enactment whenever passed or made.

(2) In section 22 "enactment" also includes an enactment contained in, or in an instrument made under, Northern Ireland legislation.

(3) In Part 3 "enactment" also includes—

(a) an enactment comprised in, or in an instrument made under, an Act of the Scottish Parliament;
(b) an enactment contained in, or in an instrument made under, Northern Ireland legislation.

(4) In sections 19, 21 and 143 and in paragraph 3 of Schedule 7 "enactment" also includes—

(a) an enactment contained in Northern Ireland legislation;
(b) an enactment contained in a Measure of the Church Assembly or of the General Synod of the Church of England.
[Constitutional Reform Act 2005, s 140.]

1–4601O   141. "Subordinate legislation".   (1) In this Act "subordinate legislation" has the same meaning as in the Interpretation Act 1978 (c 30).

(2) In sections 19 and 143 "subordinate legislation" also includes an enactment contained in an instrument made under Northern Ireland legislation.
[Constitutional Reform Act 2005, s 141.]

1–4601P　142. General interpretation. In this Act—

"functions" includes powers and duties;

"Minister of the Crown" has the same meaning as in the Ministers of the Crown Act 1975 (c 26).
[Constitutional Reform Act 2005, s 142.]

1–4601Q　143. Supplementary provision etc. (1) The Lord Chancellor may by order make—

(a)　any supplementary, incidental or consequential provision, and

(b)　any transitory, transitional or saving provision,

which he considers necessary or expedient for the purposes of, in consequence of, or for giving full effect to, any provision of this Act.

(2) An order under this section may in particular—

(a)　provide for any provision of this Act which comes into force before another such provision has come into force to have effect, until that other provision has come into force, with such modifications as are specified in the order;

(b)　amend or repeal any of the following—

(i)　an enactment other than one contained in an Act passed, or Northern Ireland legislation passed or made, after the Session in which this Act is passed;

(ii)　subordinate legislation other than subordinate legislation made under an Act passed, or Northern Ireland legislation passed or made, after the Session in which this Act is passed;

(iii)　any other instrument or document, including a prerogative instrument;

(c)　amend or repeal an enactment or subordinate legislation, whenever passed or made, in consequence of section 59.

(3) The amendments that may be made by virtue of subsection (2)(b) are in addition to those made by or under any other provision of this Act.

(4) In this section "prerogative instrument" means an Order in Council, warrant, charter or other instrument made under the prerogative.
[Constitutional Reform Act 2005, s 143.]

1–4601R　144. Orders and regulations. (1) Any power of a Minister of the Crown to make an order or regulations under this Act is exercisable by statutory instrument, except where subsection (2) applies.

(2) Any power of the Lord Chancellor to make an order under section 19(1) or 143 amending an enactment contained in, or in an instrument made under, Northern Ireland legislation is exercisable by statutory rule for the purposes of the Statutory Rules (Northern Ireland) Order 1979 (SI 1979/1573 (NI 12)).

(3) Regulations under section 115, 120(5) or 121(5) are to be made in the form of a statutory instrument to which the Statutory Instruments Act 1946 (c 36) applies as if the regulations were made by a Minister of the Crown.

(4) A statutory instrument to which this subsection applies may not be made unless a draft of the instrument has been laid before and approved by a resolution of each House of Parliament.

(5) Subsection (4) applies to a statutory instrument which contains any of the following—

(a)　an order under section 85(3)(a) or (b) which amends Part 1 of Schedule 14;

(b)　an order under section 19(1) which amends a public general Act, except where the only such amendment is the inclusion in Schedule 7 of a function of the Lord Chancellor;

(c)　an order under section 19(1) which amends subordinate legislation of which a draft was required to be laid before and approved by a resolution of each House of Parliament, except where the only such amendment consists of provision that falls within subsection (2)(b) of section 19;

(d)　an order under section 143 which amends a public general Act;

(e)　an order under paragraph 5 of Schedule 12.

(6) In any other case a statutory instrument containing an order or regulations under this Act, unless it contains only an order under section 66(5) or 148, is subject to annulment in pursuance of a resolution of either House of Parliament.

(7) A statutory rule made under a power to which subsection (2) applies is subject to annulment in pursuance of a resolution of either House of Parliament.
[Constitutional Reform Act 2005, s 144.]

1–4601S　145. Minor and consequential amendments. Schedule 17 (minor and consequential amendments) has effect.
[Constitutional Reform Act 2005, s 145.]

1–4601T　146. Repeals and revocations. The provisions listed in Schedule 18 are repealed or revoked to the extent specified.
[Constitutional Reform Act 2005, s 146.]

1–4601U   147. Extent.   (1) Sections 7, 8 and 9 extend to England and Wales only.

(2) Section 6 and Part 5 extend to Northern Ireland only.

(3) Any amendment, repeal or revocation made by this Act has the same extent as the provision to which it relates.

(4) Subject to subsections (1) to (3), this Act extends to Northern Ireland.

[Constitutional Reform Act 2005, s 147.]

1–4601V   148. Commencement.   (1) This Act, except the following provisions, comes into force in accordance with provision to be made by the Lord Chancellor by order[1].

(2) The provisions excepted from subsection (1) are—

(a)   section 4;
(b)   sections 18 to 22;
(c)   sections 140 to 144;
(d)   section 147;
(e)   this section;
(f)   section 149;
(g)   Schedules 6 and 7.

(3) Section 4 comes into force in accordance with provision to be made by the Secretary of State by order.

(4) An order by which section 23(1) comes into force at any time may not be made unless the Lord Chancellor is satisfied that the Supreme Court will at that time be provided with accommodation in accordance with written plans that he has approved.

(5) The Lord Chancellor may approve plans only if, having consulted the Lords of Appeal in Ordinary holding office at the time of the approval, he is satisfied that accommodation in accordance with the plans will be appropriate for the purposes of the Court.

(6) An order under this section may make different provision for different purposes.

[Constitutional Reform Act 2005, s 148.]

---

1. The following commencement orders have been made: Constitutional Reform Act 2005 (Commencement No 1) Order 2005, SI 2005/1431; Constitutional Reform Act 2005 (Commencement No 2) Order 2005, SI 2005/2284; Constitutional Reform Act 2005 (Commencement No 3) Order 2005, SI 2005/2505; Constitutional Reform Act 2005 (Commencement No 4) Order 2005, SI 2006/228; Constitutional Reform Act 2005 (Commencement No 5) Order 2005, SI 2006/1014 and Constitutional Reform Act 2005 (Commencement No 6) Order 2006, SI 2006/1537 (Northern Ireland only).

1–4601W   149. Short title.   This Act may be cited as the Constitutional Reform Act 2005.

[Constitutional Reform Act 2005, s 14.]

1–4601X   SCHEDULE 1
                                      POWERS TO MAKE RULES

                                           SCHEDULE 2
                                   POWERS TO GIVE DIRECTIONS

                                           SCHEDULE 3
                        TRANSFER OF APPOINTMENT FUNCTIONS TO HER MAJESTY

1–4601Y

Section 15   SCHEDULE 4
        OTHER FUNCTIONS OF THE LORD CHANCELLOR AND ORGANISATION OF THE COURTS

                          Children and Young Persons Act 1933 (c 12)

20. (1) Section 45 of the Children and Young Persons Act 1933 (youth courts) (as amended by section 50 of the Courts Act 2003 (c 39)) is amended as follows.

(2) In subsection (3) for "Lord Chancellor or a person acting on his behalf" substitute "Lord Chief Justice, with the concurrence of the Lord Chancellor,".

(3) In subsection (4) for "Lord Chancellor may" substitute "Lord Chief Justice may, with the concurrence of the Lord Chancellor,".

(4) In subsection (5) after "Lord Chancellor" insert "or Lord Chief Justice".

(5) After subsection (8) insert—

"(9) The Lord Chief Justice may nominate a judicial office holder (as defined in section 109(4) of the Constitutional Reform Act 2005) to exercise his functions under subsection (3) or (4) or his powers under rules under subsection (4)."

                              Magistrates' Courts Act 1980 (c 43)

99. The Magistrates' Courts Act 1980 is amended as follows.

100. (1) Section 3B (transfer of trials of summary offences) is amended as follows.

(2) In subsection (3) for "Lord Chancellor may" substitute "Lord Chief Justice may, with the concurrence of the Lord Chancellor,".

(3) After subsection (4) insert—

"(5) The Lord Chief Justice may nominate a judicial office holder (as defined in section 109(4) of the Constitutional Reform Act 2005) to exercise his functions under subsection (3)."

101. (1) Section 67 (Family Proceedings Courts) (as substituted by section 49(1) of the Courts Act 2003 (c 39)) is amended as follows.

(2) In subsection (3) for "Lord Chancellor or a person acting on his behalf" substitute "Lord Chief Justice".

(3) In subsection (4) for "Lord Chancellor may by rules" substitute "Lord Chief Justice may, after consulting the Lord Chancellor, by rules".

(4) In subsection (5) for "Lord Chancellor" substitute "Lord Chief Justice".

(5) After subsection (8) insert—

"(9) The Lord Chief Justice may nominate a judicial office holder (as defined in section 109(4) of the Constitutional Reform Act 2005) to exercise his functions under subsection (3) or (4) or the powers conferred on him by rules under subsection (4)."

102. (1) Section 144 (rule committee and rules of procedure) is amended as follows.

(2) Before subsection (1) insert—

"(A1) The Lord Chancellor may appoint a rule committee for magistrates' courts."

(3) In subsection (1)—

(*a*) for the words from the beginning to "and may on" substitute "The Lord Chief Justice may on";
(*b*) after "consultation with the rule committee" insert ", and with the concurrence of the Lord Chancellor,".

(4) After subsection (1) insert—

"(1A) If the Lord Chancellor does not agree rules made by the Lord Chief Justice, the Lord Chancellor must give the Lord Chief Justice and the rules committee written reasons for doing so."

(5) In subsection (2) for "he may determine" substitute "he may, after consulting the Lord Chief Justice, determine".

(6) After subsection (4) insert—

"(4A) The Lord Chief Justice may nominate a judicial office holder (as defined in section 109(4) of the Constitutional Reform Act 2005) to exercise his functions under this section."

103. After section 144 insert—

"**144A. Rules to be made if required by Lord Chancellor.** (1) This section applies if the Lord Chancellor gives the Lord Chief Justice written notice that he thinks it is expedient for rules made under section 144 to include provision that would achieve a purpose specified in the notice.

(2) The Lord Chief Justice must make such rules as he considers necessary to achieve the specified purpose.

(3) Those rules must be—

(*a*) made within a reasonable period after the Lord Chancellor gives notice to the Lord Chief Justice;
(*b*) made in accordance with section 144.

(4) The Lord Chief Justice may nominate a judicial office holder (as defined in section 109(4) of the Constitutional Reform Act 2005) to exercise his functions under this section."

Courts Act 2003 (c 39)

308. The Courts Act 2003 is amended as follows.

309. (1) In section 2 (Court officers, staff and services), in subsection (7) for paragraphs (*c*) and (*d*) substitute—

"(*c*) the President of the Queen's Bench Division,
(*d*) the President of the Family Division, and
(*e*) the Chancellor of the High Court."

310. (1) Section 4 (establishment of courts boards) is amended as follows.

(2) After subsection (5) insert—

"(5A) Before making any order under subsection (2) or (4), the Lord Chancellor must consult the Lord Chief Justice."

(3) After subsection (7) insert—

"(7A) The Lord Chief Justice may nominate a judicial office holder (as defined in section 109(4) of the Constitutional Reform Act 2005) to exercise his functions under this section."

311. (1) Section 5 (functions of courts boards) is amended as follows.

(2) In subsection (5) after "Lord Chancellor must" insert ", after consulting the Lord Chief Justice,".

(3) In subsection (7) after "Lord Chancellor may" insert ", after consulting the Lord Chief Justice,".

(4) After subsection (8) insert—

"(9) The Lord Chief Justice may nominate a judicial office holder (as defined in section 109(4) of the Constitutional Reform Act 2005) to exercise his functions under this section."

312. (1) Section 8 (local justice areas) is amended as follows.

(2) After subsection (5) insert—

"(5A) Before making any order under subsection (2) or (4), the Lord Chancellor must consult the Lord Chief Justice."

(3) After subsection (7) insert—

"(8) The Lord Chief Justice may nominate a judicial office holder (as defined in section 109(4) of the Constitutional Reform Act 2005) to exercise his functions under this section."

313. (1) Section 10 (appointment of lay justices etc) is amended as follows.

(2) In subsection (2) for "Lord Chancellor" substitute "Lord Chief Justice".

(3) In subsection (3) for "or on behalf of the Lord Chancellor" substitute "Lord Chief Justice".

(4) After subsection (5) insert—

"(6) The functions conferred on the Lord Chief Justice by subsections (2) and (3) may be exercised only after consulting the Lord Chancellor.

(7) The Lord Chief Justice may nominate a judicial office holder (as defined in section 109(4) of the Constitutional Reform Act 2005) to exercise his functions under subsection (2) or (3)."

314. In section 11 (resignation and removal of lay justices), in subsection (2)—

(a) after "Lord Chancellor may" insert ", with the concurrence of the Lord Chief Justice,";
(b) in paragraph (b) after "Lord Chancellor" insert "with the concurrence of the Lord Chief Justice".

315. (1) Section 13 (entry of names in the supplemental list) is amended as follows.
(2) In subsection (3) for "Lord Chancellor may" substitute "Lord Chief Justice may, with the concurrence of the Lord Chancellor,".
(3) In subsection (5) after "Lord Chancellor may" insert ", with the concurrence of the Lord Chief Justice,".
(4) After subsection (5) insert—

"(6) The Lord Chief Justice may nominate a judicial office holder (as defined in section 109(4) of the Constitutional Reform Act 2005) to exercise his functions under subsection (3)."
316. In section 14 (removal of names from the supplemental list), in subsection (2)(b) after "Lord Chancellor" insert ", with the concurrence of the Lord Chief Justice,".
317. (1) Section 15 (lay justices' allowances) is amended as follows.
(2) In subsection (7) for "Lord Chancellor" substitute "Lord Chief Justice".
(3) After subsection (8) insert—

"(9) The Lord Chief Justice may nominate a judicial office holder (as defined in section 109(4) of the Constitutional Reform Act 2005) to exercise his functions under subsection (7)."
318. In section 16 (records of lay justices), after subsection (3) insert—

"(4) The Lord Chancellor must consult the Lord Chief Justice before—

(a) appointing a person under subsection (1), or
(b) giving a direction under subsection (2).

(5) The Lord Chief Justice may nominate a judicial office holder (as defined in section 109(4) of the Constitutional Reform Act 2005) to exercise his functions under this section."
319. (1) Section 17 (chairman and deputy chairmen) is amended as follows.
(2) In subsection (3) for "Lord Chancellor, or a person acting on his behalf, may" substitute "Lord Chief Justice may, with the concurrence of the Lord Chancellor,".
(3) After subsection (5) insert—

"(6) The Lord Chief Justice may nominate a judicial office holder (as defined in section 109(4) of the Constitutional Reform Act 2005) to exercise his functions under this section."
320. (1) Section 19 (training, development and appraisal of lay justices) is amended as follows.
(2) In subsection (2) for "Lord Chancellor" in each place substitute "Lord Chief Justice".
(3) In subsection (3)—

(a) for "Lord Chancellor" substitute "Lord Chief Justice";
(b) for "appropriate training and training materials" substitute "training and training materials that appear to him, after consulting the Lord Chancellor, to be appropriate".

(4) After subsection (3) insert—

"(4) The Lord Chief Justice may nominate a judicial office holder (as defined in section 109(4) of the Constitutional Reform Act 2005) to exercise his functions under this section."
321. (1) Section 20 (rules) is amended as follows.
(2) In subsection (1) for "Lord Chancellor" substitute "Lord Chief Justice".
(3) In subsection (2)—

(a) for "Lord Chancellor" substitute "Lord Chief Justice";
(b) before paragraph (a) insert—

"(za)the Lord Chancellor,".

(4) After subsection (2) insert—

"(3) The Lord Chief Justice may nominate a judicial office holder (as defined in section 109(4) of the Constitutional Reform Act 2005) to exercise his functions of making the rules referred to in this section."
322. (1) Section 21 (duty to consult lay justices on matters affecting them etc) is amended as follows.
(2) That section becomes subsection (1) of section 21.
(3) In that subsection after "Lord Chancellor" insert "and the Lord Chief Justice".
(4) After that subsection insert—

"(2) The Lord Chief Justice may nominate a judicial office holder (as defined in section 109(4) of the Constitutional Reform Act 2005) to exercise his functions under this section."
323. In section 22 (appointment of District Judges (Magistrates' Courts)), in subsection (5) after "Lord Chancellor may" insert ", with the concurrence of the Lord Chief Justice,".
324. In section 24 (Deputy District Judges (Magistrates' Courts)), in subsection (4) after "Lord Chancellor may" insert ", with the concurrence of the Lord Chief Justice,".
325. (1) Section 25 (District Judges (Magistrates' Courts) as justices of the peace) is amended as follows.
(2) In subsection (2), leave out "or on behalf of the Lord Chancellor" and insert "the Lord Chief Justice, after consulting the Lord Chancellor".
(3) After subsection (2) insert—

"(3) The Lord Chief Justice may nominate a judicial office holder (as defined in section 109(4) of the Constitutional Reform Act 2005) to exercise his functions under subsection (2)."
326. (1) Section 27 (justices' clerks and assistant clerks) is amended as follows.
(2) In subsection (1)(b) after "Lord Chancellor" insert ", after consulting the Lord Chief Justice,".
(3) In subsection (3)—

(a) in paragraph (a) after "must" insert ", after consulting the Lord Chief Justice,";
(b) in paragraph (b) for "subsection (4)" substitute "subsections (4A) to (4C)".

(4) For subsection (4) substitute—

"(4A) The Lord Chancellor may change an assignment of a justices' clerk so that he is no longer assigned to a local justice area ("the relevant area") only if the conditions in subsections (4B) and (4C) are met.
(4B) Before changing the assignment, the Lord Chancellor must consult—

(a) the chairman of the lay justices assigned to the relevant area, or
(b) if that is not possible or not practicable, the deputy chairman or such of the lay justices assigned to or acting in the relevant area as it appears to the Lord Chancellor appropriate to consult.

(4C) The Lord Chief Justice must agree to the change."
(5) After subsection (6) insert—

"(6A) The Lord Chief Justice may nominate a judicial office holder (as defined in section 109(4) of the Constitutional Reform Act 2005) to exercise his functions under this section."
327. (1) Section 28 (functions) is amended as follows.
(2) In subsection (8) after "Lord Chancellor" insert "with the concurrence of the Lord Chief Justice".
(3) After subsection (9) insert—

"(10) The Lord Chief Justice may nominate a judicial office holder (as defined in section 109(4) of the Constitutional Reform Act 2005) to exercise his functions under this section."
328. (1) Section 30 (places, dates and times of sittings) is amended as follows.
(2) In subsection (1) after "Lord Chancellor may" insert ", after consulting the Lord Chief Justice,".
(3) In subsection (7) after "Lord Chancellor may" insert ", after consulting the Lord Chief Justice,".
(4) After subsection (8) insert—

"(9) The Lord Chief Justice may nominate a judicial office holder (as defined in section 109(4) of the Constitutional Reform Act 2005) to exercise his functions under subsection (1) or (7)."
329. (1) Section 34 (costs in legal proceedings) is amended as follows.
(2) In subsection (5) after "Lord Chancellor may" insert ", after consulting the Lord Chief Justice,".
(3) After subsection (5) insert—

"(6) The Lord Chief Justice may nominate a judicial office holder (as defined in section 109(4) of the Constitutional Reform Act 2005) to exercise his functions under this section."
330. For section 62 substitute—

"62. Head and Deputy Head of Civil Justice.   (1) There is to be a Head of Civil Justice.
(2) The Head of Civil Justice is—

(a) the Master of the Rolls, or
(b) if the Lord Chief Justice appoints another person, that person.

(3) The Lord Chief Justice may appoint a person to be Deputy Head of Civil Justice.
(4) The Lord Chief Justice must not appoint a person under subsection (2)(b) or (3) unless these conditions are met—

(a) the Lord Chief Justice has consulted the Lord Chancellor;
(b) the person to be appointed is one of the following—

(i) the Chancellor of the High Court;
(ii) an ordinary judge of the Court of Appeal.

(5) A person appointed under subsection (2)(b) or (3) holds the office to which he is appointed in accordance with the terms of his appointment.
(6) The Lord Chief Justice may nominate a judicial office holder (as defined in section 109(4) of the Constitutional Reform Act 2005) to exercise his functions under this section."
331. (1) Section 64 (power to alter judicial titles) is amended as follows.
(2) In subsection (2)—

(a) omit "Vice-Chancellor";
(b) insert at the appropriate place—

(i) "Chancellor of the High Court";
(ii) "Deputy Head of Civil Justice";
(iii) "Deputy Head of Criminal Justice";
(iv) "Deputy Head of Family Justice";
(v) "Head of Civil Justice";
(vi) "Head of Criminal Justice";
(vii) "Head of Family Justice";
(viii)"President of the Courts of England and Wales";
(ix) "President of the Queen's Bench Division".

(3) After subsection (3) insert—

"(3A) The Lord Chancellor may make an order under this section only with the concurrence of the Lord Chief Justice."
(4) In subsection (4)—

(a) omit paragraph (a);
(b) for paragraphs (c) and (d) substitute—

"(ba)the President of the Queen's Bench Division,
(c) the President of the Family Division, and
(d) the Chancellor of the High Court."

(5) After subsection (6) insert—

"(7) The Lord Chief Justice may nominate a judicial office holder (as defined in section 109(4) of the Constitutional Reform Act 2005) to exercise his functions under this section."
332. In section 69 (Criminal Procedure Rules), in subsection (4) omit "or alter".
333. (1) Section 70 (Criminal Procedure Rule Committee) is amended as follows.
(2) In subsection (1) for paragraph (b) substitute—

"(b) the persons currently appointed in accordance with subsections (1A) and (1B)."

(3) After subsection (1) insert—

"(1A) The Lord Chief Justice must appoint the persons falling within paragraphs (*a*) to (*e*) of subsection (2).

(1B) The Lord Chancellor must appoint the persons falling within paragraphs (*f*) to (*k*) of subsection (2)."

(4) In subsection (2) for "The Lord Chancellor must appoint" substitute "The persons to be appointed in accordance with subsections (1A) and (1B) are".

(5) For subsection (3) substitute—

"(3) Before appointing a person in accordance with subsection (1A), the Lord Chief Justice must consult the Lord Chancellor.

(3A) Before appointing a person in accordance with subsection (1B), the Lord Chancellor must consult the Lord Chief Justice."

(6) After subsection (5) insert—

"(5A) The Lord Chief Justice may nominate a judicial office holder (as defined in section 109(4) of the Constitutional Reform Act 2005) to exercise his functions under this section."

334. (1) Section 71 (power to change certain requirements relating to Committee) is amended as follows.

(2) In subsection (1) for paragraph (*a*) substitute—

"(*a*) amend section 70(2) or (3A), and".

(3) For subsection (2) substitute—

"(2) The Lord Chancellor may make an order under this section only with the concurrence of the Lord Chief Justice.

(3) The Lord Chief Justice may nominate a judicial office holder (as defined in section 109(4) of the Constitutional Reform Act 2005) to exercise his functions under this section."

335. (1) Section 72 (process for making Criminal Procedure Rules) is amended as follows.

(2) For subsections (3) and (4) substitute—

"(3) The Lord Chancellor may, with the concurrence of the Secretary of State, allow or disallow rules so made.

(4) If the Lord Chancellor disallows rules, he must give the Committee written reasons for doing so."

(3) In subsection (5) for ", as allowed or altered" substitute "and allowed".

336. After section 72 insert—

"**72A. Rules to be made if required by Lord Chancellor.** (1) This section applies if the Lord Chancellor gives the Criminal Procedure Rules Committee written notice that he thinks it is expedient for Criminal Procedure Rules to include provision that would achieve a purpose specified in the notice.

(2) The Committee must make such rules as it considers necessary to achieve the specified purpose.

(3) Those rules must be—

(*a*) made within a reasonable period after the Lord Chancellor gives notice to the Committee;

(*b*) made in accordance with section 72.

(4) The Lord Chancellor may not give notice under subsection (1) unless the Secretary of State agrees."

337. (1) Section 73 (power to amend legislation in connection with Criminal Procedure Rules) is amended as follows.

(2) That section becomes subsection (1) of section 73.

(3) In that subsection after "Secretary of State" insert "and after consulting the Lord Chief Justice".

(4) After that subsection insert—

"(2) The Lord Chief Justice may nominate a judicial office holder (as defined in section 109(4) of the Constitutional Reform Act 2005) to exercise his functions under this section."

338. In section 75 (Family Procedure Rules), in subsection (5) omit "or alter".

339. (1) Section 77 (Family Procedure Rule Committee) is amended as follows.

(2) In subsection (1) for paragraph (*b*) substitute—

"(*b*) the persons currently appointed in accordance with subsections (1A) and (1B)."

(3) After subsection (1) insert—

"(1A) The Lord Chief Justice must appoint the persons falling within paragraphs (*a*) to (*f*) of subsection (2).

(1B) The Lord Chancellor must appoint the persons falling within paragraphs (*g*) to (*o*) of subsection (2)."

(4) In subsection (2) for "The Lord Chancellor must appoint" substitute "The persons to be appointed in accordance with subsections (1A) and (1B) are".

(5) In subsection (3) for "under subsection (2), Lord Chancellor must consult" substitute "in accordance with subsection (1A), the Lord Chief Justice must consult the Lord Chancellor and".

(6) Omit subsection (4).

(7) In subsection (5) for "under subsection (2)(*h*) to (*m*), the Lord Chancellor must consult" substitute "in accordance with subsection (1B), the Lord Chancellor must consult the Lord Chief Justice and, if the person falls within any of paragraphs (*h*) to (*m*) of subsection (2), must also consult".

(8) After section (6) insert—

"(7) The Lord Chief Justice may nominate a judicial office holder (as defined in section 109(4) of the Constitutional Reform Act 2005) to exercise his functions under this section."

340. (1) Section 78 (power to change certain requirements relating to Committee) is amended as follows.

(2) In subsection (1)(*a*) after "Lord Chancellor" insert "or Lord Chief Justice".

(3) After subsection (1) insert—

"(1A) The Lord Chancellor may make an order under this section only with the concurrence of the Lord Chief Justice."

(4) After subsection (2) insert—

"(3) The Lord Chief Justice may nominate a judicial office holder (as defined in section 109(4) of the Constitutional Reform Act 2005) to exercise his functions under this section."

341. (1) Section 79 (process for making Family Procedure Rules) is amended as follows.

(2) For subsections (3) and (4) substitute—

"(3) The Lord Chancellor may allow or disallow rules so made.

(4) If the Lord Chancellor disallows rules, he must give the Committee written reasons for doing so."

(3) In subsection (5) for ", as allowed or altered" substitute "and allowed".
342. After section 79 insert—

"79A. Rules to be made if required by Lord Chancellor. (1) This section applies if the Lord Chancellor gives the Family Procedure Rules Committee written notice that he thinks it is expedient for Family Procedure Rules to include provision that would achieve a purpose specified in the notice.
(2) The Committee must make such rules as it considers necessary to achieve the specified purpose.
(3) Those rules must be—
   (a) made within a reasonable period after the Lord Chancellor gives notice to the Committee;
   (b) made in accordance with section 79."

343. (1) Section 80 (power to amend legislation in connection with the rules) is amended as follows.
(2) That section becomes subsection (1) of section 80.
(3) In that subsection after "Lord Chancellor may" insert ", after consulting the Lord Chief Justice,".
(4) After that subsection insert—
"(2) The Lord Chief Justice may nominate a judicial office holder (as defined in section 109(4) of the Constitutional Reform Act 2005) to exercise his functions under this section."
344. (1) Section 81 (practice directions relating to family proceedings) is amended as follows.
(2) In subsection (1), before paragraph (a) insert—
"(za)the civil division of the Court of Appeal,
(zb) the High Court,".
(3) After subsection (2) insert—
"(2A) Directions as to the practice and procedure of any relevant court in family proceedings (whether given under subsection (1) or otherwise) may provide for any matter which, by virtue of paragraph 3 of Schedule 1 to the Civil Procedure Act 1997, may be provided for by Civil Procedure Rules."
(4) In subsection (3) for "magistrates' courts and county courts (or any of them)" substitute "any relevant court".
(5) After subsection (4) (inserted by paragraph 9(5) of Schedule 2 to this Act) insert—
"(5) In this section—
"Civil Procedure Rules" has the same meaning as in the Civil Procedure Act 1997;
"relevant court" means a court listed in subsection (1)."
345. In section 92 (fees), in subsection (5) for paragraphs (c) and (d) substitute—
"(ba)the President of the Queen's Bench Division;
(c) the President of the Family Division;
(d) the Chancellor of the High Court;".
346. (1) Section 102 (power to alter judicial titles: Northern Ireland) is amended as follows.
(2) Omit subsection (4).
(3) After subsection (6) insert—
"(6A) The Lord Chancellor may make an order under this section only with the concurrence of the Lord Chief Justice.
(6B) The Lord Chief Justice may nominate any of the following to exercise his functions under subsection (6A)—
   (a) the holder of one of the offices listed in Schedule 1 to the Justice (Northern Ireland) Act 2002;
   (b) a Lord Justice of Appeal (as defined in section 88 of that Act)."
347. In section 107 (interpretation), in subsection (6) omit "by the Lord Chancellor".
348. In section 108 (rules, regulations and orders), in subsections (1) and (6) after "Lord Chancellor" insert "or Lord Chief Justice".
349. (1) Section 109 (minor and consequential amendments etc) is amended as follows.
(2) After subsection (4) insert—
"(4A) The following paragraphs apply to the making of provision that relates to England and Wales in an order under subsection (4)—
   (a) before deciding what provision it is necessary or expedient to make, the Lord Chancellor must consult the Lord Chief Justice of England and Wales;
   (b) before making the order, the Lord Chancellor must consult the Lord Chief Justice of England and Wales.
(4B) The following paragraphs apply to the making of provision that relates to Northern Ireland in an order under subsection (4)—
   (a) before deciding what provision it is necessary or expedient to make, the Lord Chancellor must consult the Lord Chief Justice of Northern Ireland;
   (b) before making the order, the Lord Chancellor must consult the Lord Chief Justice of Northern Ireland."
(3) After subsection (6) insert—
"(7) The Lord Chief Justice may nominate a judicial office holder (as defined in section 109(4) of the Constitutional Reform Act 2005) to exercise his functions under this section.
(8) The Lord Chief Justice of Northern Ireland may nominate any of the following to exercise his functions under this section—
   (a) the holder of one of the offices listed in Schedule 1 to the Justice (Northern Ireland) Act 2002;
   (b) a Lord Justice of Appeal (as defined in section 88 of that Act)."
350. (1) Schedule 1 (constitution and procedure of courts boards) is amended as follows.
(2) For paragraph 1 substitute—
"1. (1) The members of each courts board are to be appointed by the Lord Chancellor.

(2) The Lord Chancellor may appoint a member of a description mentioned in paragraph 2(*a*) only with the concurrence of the Lord Chief Justice."

(3) In paragraph 8 (meaning of regulations) after "Lord Chancellor" insert "after consulting the Lord Chief Justice".

(4) After paragraph 8 insert—

"9. The Lord Chief Justice may nominate a judicial office holder (as defined in section 109(4) of the Constitutional Reform Act 2005) to exercise his functions under this Schedule."

Criminal Justice Act 2003 (c 44)

356. The Criminal Justice Act 2003 is amended as follows.

357. (1) Section 167 (Sentencing Guidelines Council) is amended as follows.

(2) In subsection (1)(*b*)—

(*a*) for "Lord Chancellor" substitute "Lord Chief Justice";

(*b*) for "Lord Chief Justice" substitute "Lord Chancellor".

(3) After subsection (9) insert—

"(10) The Lord Chief Justice may nominate a judicial office holder (as defined in section 109(4) of the Constitutional Reform Act 2005) to exercise his functions under this section."

358. (1) Section 168 (Sentencing Guidelines Council: supplementary) is amended as follows.

(2) In subsection (1) for paragraphs (*b*) and (*c*) substitute—

"(*b*) enabling the Lord Chancellor to remove a judicial member from office, with the concurrence of the Lord Chief Justice, on the grounds of incapacity or misbehaviour, and

(*c*) enabling the Secretary of State to remove a non-judicial member from office on the grounds of incapacity or misbehaviour."

(3) For subsection (2) substitute—

"(1A) The following provisions apply to an order under subsection (1)—

(*a*) if the order includes provision falling within subsection (1)(*a*), the Lord Chancellor must consult the Lord Chief Justice about that provision before making the order;

(*b*) if the order includes provision falling within subsection (1)(*b*), the order may not be made unless the Lord Chief Justice agrees to the inclusion of that provision.

(1B) The Lord Chief Justice may, with the concurrence of the Lord Chancellor, by order make provision as to the proceedings of the Council."

(4) After subsection (5) insert—

"(6) The Lord Chief Justice may nominate a judicial office holder (as defined in section 109(4) of the Constitutional Reform Act 2005) to exercise his functions under subsection (1B)."

359. (1) Section 330 (orders and rules) is amended as follows.

(2) In subsection (1)(*b*) after "Lord Chancellor" insert "or the Lord Chief Justice".

(3) After subsection (2) insert—

"(2A) Where a statutory instrument is made by the Lord Chief Justice in the exercise of the power referred to in subsection (1)(*b*), the Statutory Instruments Act 1946 applies to the instrument as if it contained an order made by a Minister of the Crown."

1-4601Z

SCHEDULE 5
FUNCTIONS UNDER LEGISLATION RELATING TO NORTHERN IRELAND

SCHEDULE 6
SPEAKERSHIP OF THE HOUSE OF LORDS

SCHEDULE 7
PROTECTED FUNCTIONS OF THE LORD CHANCELLOR

SCHEDULE 8
SUPREME COURT SELECTION COMMISSIONS

SCHEDULE 9
AMENDMENTS RELATING TO JURISDICTION OF THE SUPREME COURT

SCHEDULE 10
PROCEEDINGS UNDER JURISDICTION TRANSFERRED TO SUPREME COURT

SCHEDULE 11
RENAMING OF THE SUPREME COURTS OF ENGLAND AND WALES AND NORTHERN IRELAND

SCHEDULE 12
THE JUDICIAL APPOINTMENTS COMMISSION

SCHEDULE 13
THE JUDICIAL APPOINTMENTS AND CONDUCT OMBUDSMAN

SCHEDULE 14
THE JUDICIAL APPOINTMENTS COMMISSION: RELEVANT OFFICES AND ENACTMENTS

SCHEDULE 15
NORTHERN IRELAND JUDICIAL APPOINTMENTS OMBUDSMAN

SCHEDULE 16
JUDICIAL COMMITTEE OF THE PRIVY COUNCIL

SCHEDULE 17[1]
MINOR AND CONSEQUENTIAL AMENDMENTS

1. Where these affect provisions reproduced in this work they will be shown in those provisions when they take effect.

SCHEDULE 18
REPEALS AND REVOCATIONS

Serious Organised Crime and Police Act 2005
(2005 c 15)

PART 1[1]
THE SERIOUS ORGANISED CRIME AGENCY

Establishment of SOCA, functions, general powers, administration and supervision, annual plans and strategy, liability for conduct of staff, disclosure of information, duty of police to assist SOCA, special powers of designated staff of constable etc.

1. Part 1 comprises ss 1–59 and Schs 1–4. For commencement of this Act, see s 178, post and orders made thereunder.

Annual plans and reports

1–4602　**6, 7.** *SOCA annual plan and publication of annual report.*

Central supervision and direction

8–16. *Duty of Secretary of State including determining strategic priorities, Codes of practice, reports to Secretary of State, action plans and inspections.*

Use and disclosure of information

32–37. *Disclosure of information, duty of police to pass information to, and assist, SOCA.*

Prosecutions

1–4602A　**38. Prosecution of offences investigated by SOCA.**　(1) The Director of Revenue and Customs Prosecutions—

(a) may institute and conduct criminal proceedings in England and Wales that arise out of a criminal investigation by SOCA relating to a designated offence, and

(b) must take over the conduct of criminal proceedings instituted by SOCA in England and Wales in respect of a designated offence.

(2) The Director of Revenue and Customs Prosecutions must provide such advice as he thinks appropriate, to such persons as he thinks appropriate, in relation to—

(a) a criminal investigation by SOCA relating to a designated offence, or

(b) criminal proceedings instituted in England and Wales that arise out of such an investigation.

(3) The Director of Public Prosecutions—

(a) may institute and conduct criminal proceedings in England and Wales that arise out of a criminal investigation by SOCA relating to a non-designated offence, and

(b) must take over the conduct of criminal proceedings instituted by SOCA in England and Wales in respect of such an offence.

But paragraph (b) does not apply where the Director of the Serious Fraud Office has the conduct of the proceedings.

(4) The Director of Public Prosecutions must provide such advice as he thinks appropriate, to such persons as he thinks appropriate, in relation to—

(a) a criminal investigation by SOCA relating to a non-designated offence, or

(b) criminal proceedings instituted in England and Wales that arise out of such an investigation.

(5) Sections 23 and 23A of the Prosecution of Offences Act 1985 (c 23) (power to discontinue proceedings) apply (with any necessary modifications) to proceedings conducted by the Director of Revenue and Customs Prosecutions in accordance with this section as they apply to proceedings conducted by the Director of Public Prosecutions.

(6) In the Commissioners for Revenue and Customs Act 2005 (c 11)—

(a) section 37(1) (prosecutors), and

(b) section 38(1) (conduct of prosecutions by appointed persons),

have effect as if the reference to section 35 of that Act included a reference to this section.

(7) For the purposes of this section and section 39—

(a) "criminal investigation" means any process—

(i) for considering whether an offence has been committed,

(ii) for discovering by whom an offence has been committed, or

(iii) as a result of which an offence is alleged to have been committed;

(b) an offence is a "designated offence" if criminal proceedings instituted by SOCA in respect of the offence fall (or, as the case may be, would fall) to be referred to the Director of Revenue and Customs Prosecutions by virtue of directions under section 39(1);

(c) "non-designated offence" means an offence which is not a designated offence;

(d) a reference to the institution of criminal proceedings is to be construed in accordance with section 15(2) of the Prosecution of Offences Act 1985 (c 23); and

(e) a reference to the institution of proceedings by SOCA includes a reference to their institution by the Director General of SOCA or a person authorised by him.

[Serious Organised Crime and Police Act 2005, s 38.]

39. Directions as to reference of cases and proceedings to appropriate prosecutor

1–4602B 40. Functions of Director of Revenue and Customs Prosecutions as to persons arrested for designated offence. (1) Sections 37 to 37B of the Police and Criminal Evidence Act 1984 (c 60) (duties of custody officers; guidance etc) have effect, in relation to a person arrested following a criminal investigation by SOCA relating to a designated offence, as if references to the Director of Public Prosecutions were references to the Director of Revenue and Customs Prosecutions.

(2) In subsection (1) the reference to a designated offence is to be read in accordance with section 38(7)(b) of this Act.

[Serious Organised Crime and Police Act 2005, s 40.]

CHAPTER 2

SOCA: SPECIAL POWERS OF DESIGNATED STAFF

Designations

1–4602C 43. Designation of SOCA staff as persons having powers of constable etc. (1) The Director General of SOCA may designate a member of the staff of SOCA as one or more of the following—

(a) a person having the powers of a constable;

(b) a person having the customs powers of an officer of Revenue and Customs;

(c) a person having the powers of an immigration officer.

(2) A designation under this section—

(a) may be made subject to any limitations specified in the designation (whether as to the powers exercisable by virtue of it, the purposes for which they are exercisable or otherwise); and

(b) has effect either for a period so specified or without limit of time.

(3) Subsection (2) applies subject to any modification or withdrawal of the designation under section 45.

(4) A member of SOCA's staff may be designated as a person having the powers mentioned in any of paragraphs (a) to (c) of subsection (1) whether or not—

(a) he already has (for any reason) any powers falling within any of those paragraphs, or

(b) he had any such powers before becoming a member of SOCA's staff.

(5) But a person may not be designated as a person having the powers mentioned in any of paragraphs (a) to (c) of subsection (1) unless the Director General is satisfied that that person—

(a) is capable of effectively exercising the powers that would be exercisable by virtue of the designation,

(b) has received adequate training in respect of the exercise of those powers, and

(c) is otherwise a suitable person to exercise those powers.

(6) Where an employee of SOCA—

(a) before becoming such an employee, held an office by virtue of which he had any powers falling within subsection (1)(a), (b) or (c), and

(b) has not resigned that office,

that office is to be treated as suspended so long as he remains in SOCA's employment, and revives if (and only if) on ceasing to be so employed he returns to service as the holder of that office.

(7) References in this section to the powers of a constable, the customs powers of an officer of Revenue and Customs or the powers of an immigration officer are to be read in accordance with sections 46 to 49.

[Serious Organised Crime and Police Act 2005, s 43.]

Powers exercisable

1–4602D 46. Person having powers of a constable. (1) This section applies to a member of SOCA's staff who is for the time being designated under section 43 as a person having the powers of a constable.

(2) The designated person has all the powers and privileges of a constable.

(3) Those powers and privileges are exercisable by the designated person—

(*a*) throughout England and Wales and the adjacent United Kingdom waters, and

(*b*) in accordance with section 47, in Scotland or Northern Ireland and the adjacent United Kingdom waters.

(4) If any of those powers and privileges, when exercisable by a constable, are subject to any territorial restrictions on their exercise, they are similarly subject to those restrictions when exercised by the designated person.

(5) If any of those powers and privileges, when exercisable by a constable, are exercisable elsewhere than in the United Kingdom or the adjacent United Kingdom waters, they are similarly exercisable by the designated person.

(6) The designated person also has any powers exercisable by virtue of subsection (7).

(7) Any enactment under which a constable may be authorised by warrant to exercise any power in relation to any matter has effect, for the purpose of enabling the designated person to be authorised to exercise the power in relation to any such matter, as if he were a constable.

(8) Subsections (2) to (7) have effect subject to any limitation specified in the designation under section 43(2).

(9) In this section references to the powers and privileges of a constable are references to the powers and privileges of a constable whether under any enactment or otherwise.

[Serious Organised Crime and Police Act 2005, s 46.]

1–4602E 48. Person having customs powers. (1) This section applies to a member of SOCA's staff who is for the time being designated under section 43 as a person having the customs powers of an officer of Revenue and Customs.

(2) The designated person has, in relation to any customs matter, the same powers as an officer of Revenue and Customs would have.

(3) The designated person also has any powers exercisable by virtue of subsection (4).

(4) Any enactment under which an officer of Revenue and Customs may be authorised by warrant to exercise any power in relation to any customs matter has effect, for the purpose of enabling the designated person to be authorised to exercise the power in relation to any such matter, as if he were an officer of Revenue and Customs.

(5) Where any power is exercisable by an officer of Revenue and Customs both—

(*a*) in relation to a customs matter, and

(*b*) in relation to any other matter,

it is exercisable by the designated person only in relation to the customs matter.

(6) Subsections (2) to (5) have effect subject to any limitation specified in the designation under section 43(2).

(7) In this section "customs matter" means any matter other than—

(*a*) a matter to which section 7 of the Commissioners for Revenue and Customs Act 2005 (c 11) applies (former Inland Revenue matters), or

(*b*) any tax or duty not mentioned in Schedule 1 to that Act (which lists such matters).

[Serious Organised Crime and Police Act 2005, s 48.]

1–4602F 49. Person having powers of an immigration officer. (1) This section applies to a member of SOCA's staff who is for the time being designated under section 43 as a person having the powers of an immigration officer.

(2) The designated person has, in relation to any matter in relation to which powers are exercisable by an immigration officer, the same powers as such an officer would have.

(3) The designated person also has any powers exercisable by virtue of subsection (4).

(4) Any enactment under which an immigration officer may be authorised by warrant to exercise any power in relation to any matter has effect, for the purpose of enabling the designated person to be authorised to exercise the power in relation to any such matter, as if he were an immigration officer.

(5) Subsections (2) to (4) have effect subject to any limitation specified in the designation under section 43(2).

(6) In this section "immigration officer" means a person who is an immigration officer within the meaning of the Immigration Act 1971 (c 77).

[Serious Organised Crime and Police Act 2005, s 49.]

Exercise of powers

1–4602G 50. Designations: supplementary. (1) If a designated person—

(*a*) exercises any power in relation to another person in reliance on his designation under section 43, or

(*b*) purports to do so,

he must produce evidence of his designation to the other person if requested to do so.

(2) A failure to comply with subsection (1) does not make the exercise of the power invalid.

(3) For the purpose of determining liability for the unlawful conduct of members of SOCA's staff, any conduct by a designated person in reliance, or purported reliance, on his designation is to be taken to be—

(*a*) if he is employed by SOCA, conduct in the course of his employment, or

(b) if he is a person to whom section 28 applies by virtue of subsection (3)(a) of that section, conduct falling within subsection (1) of that section.

(4) In the case of any unlawful conduct within subsection (3) which is a tort, SOCA is accordingly to be treated as a joint tortfeasor.

This subsection does not apply to Scotland.

[Serious Organised Crime and Police Act 2005, s 50.]

1–4602H   51. Assaults, obstruction or deception in connection with designations.   (1) A person commits an offence if he assaults—

(a) a designated person acting in the exercise of a relevant power, or

(b) a person who is assisting a designated person in the exercise of such a power.

(2) A person commits an offence if he resists or wilfully obstructs—

(a) a designated person acting in the exercise of a relevant power, or

(b) a person who is assisting a designated person in the exercise of such a power.

(3) A person commits an offence if, with intent to deceive—

(a) he impersonates a designated person,

(b) he makes any statement or does any act calculated falsely to suggest that he is a designated person, or

(c) he makes any statement or does any act calculated falsely to suggest that he has powers as a designated person that exceed the powers he actually has.

(4) A person guilty of an offence under subsection (1) or (3) is liable on summary conviction—

(a) to imprisonment for a term not exceeding 51 weeks[1], or

(b) to a fine not exceeding level 5 on the standard scale,

or to both.

(5) A person guilty of an offence under subsection (2) is liable on summary conviction—

(a) to imprisonment for a term not exceeding 51 weeks[2], or

(b) to a fine not exceeding level 3 on the standard scale,

or to both.

(6) In this section "relevant power", in relation to a designated person, means a power or privilege exercisable by that person by virtue of the designation under section 43.

(7) In the application of this section to Scotland the references to 51 weeks in subsections (4)(a) and (5)(a) are to be read as references to 12 months in each case.

(8) In the application of this section to Northern Ireland the references to 51 weeks are to be read as follows—

(a) in subsection (4)(a) the reference is to be read as a reference to 6 months, and

(b) in subsection (5)(a) the reference is to be read as a reference to 1 month.

[Serious Organised Crime and Police Act 2005, s 51.]

---

1. In relation to an offence committed before the commencement of s 281(5) of the Criminal Justice Act 2003 this is to be read as a reference to "6 months", s 175(3), post.

2. In relation to an offence committed before the commencement of s 281(5) of the Criminal Justice Act 2003 this is to be read as a reference to "1 month", s 175(3), post.

1–4602I   57. Assaults or obstruction in connection with joint investigation teams.   (1) This section applies where an international joint investigation team has been formed under the leadership of a member of SOCA's staff.

(2) A person commits an offence if he assaults a member of the team who is carrying out his functions as a member of the team.

(3) A person commits an offence if he resists or wilfully obstructs a member of the team who is carrying out his functions as a member of that team.

(4) A person guilty of an offence under subsection (2) is liable on summary conviction—

(a) to imprisonment for a term not exceeding 51 weeks[1], or

(b) to a fine not exceeding level 5 on the standard scale,

or to both.

(5) A person guilty of an offence under subsection (3) is liable on summary conviction—

(a) to imprisonment for a term not exceeding 51 weeks[2], or

(b) to a fine not exceeding level 3 on the standard scale,

or to both.

(6) In this section "international joint investigation team" means any investigation team formed in accordance with—

(a) any framework decision on joint investigation teams adopted under Article 34 of the Treaty on European Union,

(b) the Convention on Mutual Assistance in Criminal Matters between the Member States of the European Union and the Protocol to that Convention established in accordance with that Article of the Treaty, or (c)　any international agreement to which the United Kingdom is a party and which is specified in an order made by the Secretary of State.

(7)　In the application of this section to Scotland the references to 51 weeks in subsections (4)(a) and (5)(a) are to be read as references to 12 months in each case.

(8)　In the application of this section to Northern Ireland the references to 51 weeks are to be read as follows—

(a)　in subsection (4)(a) the reference is to be read as a reference to 6 months, and
(b)　in subsection (5)(a) the reference is to be read as a reference to 1 month.

[Serious Organised Crime and Police Act 2005, s 57.]

1.　In relation to an offence committed before the commencement of s 281(5) of the Criminal Justice Act 2003 this is to be read as a reference to "6 months", s 175(3), post.

2.　In relation to an offence committed before the commencement of s 281(5) of the Criminal Justice Act 2003 this is to be read as a reference to "1 month", s 175(3), post.

PART 2[1]

INVESTIGATIONS, PROSECUTIONS, PROCEEDINGS AND PROCEEDS OF CRIME

CHAPTER 1

INVESTIGATORY POWERS OF DPP, ETC

Introductory

1–4602J　60.　Investigatory powers of DPP etc.　(1)　This Chapter confers powers on—

(a)　the Director of Public Prosecutions,
(b)　the Director of Revenue and Customs Prosecutions,
(c)　the Lord Advocate, and
(d)　the Director of Public Prosecutions for Northern Ireland,

in relation to the giving of disclosure notices in connection with the investigation of offences to which this Chapter applies or in connection with a terrorist investigation.

(2)　The Director of Public Prosecutions may, to such extent as he may determine, delegate the exercise of his powers under this Chapter to a Crown prosecutor.

(3)　The Director of Revenue and Customs Prosecutions may, to such extent as he may determine, delegate the exercise of his powers under this Chapter to a Revenue and Customs Prosecutor.

(4)　The Lord Advocate may, to such extent as he may determine, delegate the exercise of his powers under this Chapter to a procurator fiscal.

(4A)　The Director of Public Prosecutions for Northern Ireland may, to such extent as he may determine, delegate the exercise of his powers under this Chapter to a Public Prosecutor.

(5)　In this Chapter "the Investigating Authority" means—

(a)　the Director of Public Prosecutions,
(b)　the Director of Revenue and Customs Prosecutions,
(c)　the Lord Advocate, or
(d)　the Director of Public Prosecutions for Northern Ireland,

(6)　But, in circumstances where the powers of any of those persons are exercisable by any other person by virtue of subsection (2), (3), (4) or (4A), references to "the Investigating Authority" accordingly include any such other person.

(7)　In this Chapter 'terrorist investigation' means an investigation of—

(a)　the commission, preparation or instigation of acts of terrorism,
(b)　any act or omission which appears to have been for the purposes of terrorism and which consists in or involves the commission, preparation or instigation of an offence, or
(c)　the commission, preparation or instigation of an offence under the Terrorism Act 2000 (c 11) or under Part 1 of the Terrorism Act 2006 other than an offence under section 1 or 2 of that Act.

[Serious Organised Crime and Police Act 2005, s 60 as amended by the Terrorism Act 2006, s 33 and the Northern Ireland (Miscellaneous Provisions) Act 2006, Sch 3.]

1.　Part 2 comprises ss 60–109 and Schs 5 and 6.

1–4602K　61.　Offences to which this Chapter applies.　(1)　This Chapter applies to the following offences—

(a)　any offence listed in Schedule 2 to the Proceeds of Crime Act 2002 (c 29) (lifestyle offences: England and Wales);
(b)　any offence listed in Schedule 4 to that Act (lifestyle offences: Scotland);
(ba)　any offence listed in Schedule 5 to that Act (lifestyle offences: Northern Ireland);
(c)　any offence under sections 15 to 18 of the Terrorism Act 2000 (c 11) (offences relating to fund-raising, money laundering etc);
(d)　any offence under section 170 of the Customs and Excise Management Act 1979 (c 2) (fraudulent evasion of duty) or section 72 of the Value Added Tax Act 1994 (c 23) (offences relating to VAT) which is a qualifying offence;

(e) any offence under section 17 of the Theft Act 1968 (c 60) or section 17 of the Theft Act (Northern Ireland) 1969 (false accounting), or any offence at common law of cheating in relation to the public revenue, which is a qualifying offence;

(f) any offence under section 1 of the Criminal Attempts Act 1981 (c 47) or Article 3 of the Criminal Attempts and Conspiracy (Northern Ireland) Order 1983, or in Scotland at common law, of attempting to commit any offence in paragraph (c) or any offence in paragraph (d) or (e) which is a qualifying offence;

(g) any offence under section 1 of the Criminal Law Act 1977 (c 45) or Article 9 of the Criminal Attempts and Conspiracy (Northern Ireland) Order 1983, or in Scotland at common law, of conspiracy to commit any offence in paragraph (c) or any offence in paragraph (d) or (e) which is a qualifying offence.

(h) in England and Wales—

    (i) any common law offence of bribery;

    (ii) any offence under section 1 of the Public Bodies Corrupt Practices Act 1889 (c 69) (corruption in office);

    (iii) the first two offences under section 1 of the Prevention of Corruption Act 1906 (c 34) (bribes obtained by or given to agents).

(2) For the purposes of subsection (1) an offence in paragraph (d) or (e) of that subsection is a qualifying offence if the Investigating Authority certifies that in his opinion—

(a) in the case of an offence in paragraph (d) or an offence of cheating the public revenue, the offence involved or would have involved a loss, or potential loss, to the public revenue of an amount not less than £5,000;

(b) in the case of an offence under section 17 of the Theft Act 1968 (c 60) or section 17 of the Theft Act (Northern Ireland) 1969, the offence involved or would have involved a loss or gain, or potential loss or gain, of an amount not less than £5,000.

(3) A document purporting to be a certificate under subsection (2) is to be received in evidence and treated as such a certificate unless the contrary is proved.

(4) The Secretary of State may by order—

(a) amend subsection (1), in its application to England and Wales or Northern Ireland, so as to remove an offence from it or add an offence to it;

(b) amend subsection (2), in its application to England and Wales or Northern Ireland, so as to—

    (i) take account of any amendment made by virtue of paragraph (a) above, or

    (ii) vary the sums for the time being specified in subsection (2)(a) and (b).

(5) The Scottish Ministers may by order—

(a) amend subsection (1), in its application to Scotland, so as to remove an offence from it or add an offence to it;

(b) amend subsection (2), in its application to Scotland, so as to—

    (i) take account of any amendment made by virtue of paragraph (a) above, or

    (ii) vary the sums for the time being specified in subsection (2)(a) and (b).

[Serious Organised Crime and Police Act 2005, s 61 as amended by SI 2006/1629 and the Northern Ireland (Miscellaneous Provisions) Act 2006, Sch 3.]

Disclosure notices

1–4602L 62. Disclosure notices. (1) If it appears to the Investigating Authority—

(a) that there are reasonable grounds for suspecting that an offence to which this Chapter applies has been committed,

(b) that any person has information (whether or not contained in a document) which relates to a matter relevant to the investigation of that offence, and

(c) that there are reasonable grounds for believing that information which may be provided by that person in compliance with a disclosure notice is likely to be of substantial value (whether or not by itself) to that investigation,

he may give, or authorise an appropriate person to give, a disclosure notice to that person.

(1A) If it appears to the Investigating Authority—

(a) that any person has information (whether or not contained in a document) which relates to a matter relevant to a terrorist investigation, and

(b) that there are reasonable grounds for believing that information which may be provided by that person in compliance with a disclosure notice is likely to be of substantial value (whether or not by itself) to that investigation,

he may give, or authorise an appropriate person to give, a disclosure notice to that person.

(2) In this Chapter "appropriate person" means—

(a) a constable,

(b) a member of the staff of SOCA who is for the time being designated under section 43, or

(c) an officer of Revenue and Customs.

But in the application of this Chapter to Northern Ireland, this subsection has effect as if paragraph (b) were omitted.

(3) In this Chapter "disclosure notice" means a notice in writing requiring the person to whom it is given to do all or any of the following things in accordance with the specified requirements, namely—

(a) answer questions with respect to any matter relevant to the investigation;
(b) provide information with respect to any such matter as is specified in the notice;
(c) produce such documents, or documents of such descriptions, relevant to the investigation as are specified in the notice.

(4) In subsection (3) "the specified requirements" means such requirements specified in the disclosure notice as relate to—

(a) the time at or by which,
(b) the place at which, or
(c) the manner in which,

the person to whom the notice is given is to do any of the things mentioned in paragraphs (a) to (c) of that subsection; and those requirements may include a requirement to do any of those things at once.

(5) A disclosure notice must be signed or counter-signed by the Investigating Authority.

(6) This section has effect subject to section 64 (restrictions on requiring information etc).

[Serious Organised Crime and Police Act 2005, s 62 as amended by the Terrorism Act 2006, s 33 and the Northern Ireland (Miscellaneous Provisions) Act 2006, Sch 3.]

1–4602M 63. Production of documents. (1) This section applies where a disclosure notice has been given under section 62.

(2) An authorised person may—

(a) take copies of or extracts from any documents produced in compliance with the notice, and
(b) require the person producing them to provide an explanation of any of them.

(3) Documents so produced may be retained for so long as the Investigating Authority considers that it is necessary to retain them (rather than copies of them) in connection with the investigation for the purposes of which the disclosure notice was given.

(4) If the Investigating Authority has reasonable grounds for believing—

(a) that any such documents may have to be produced for the purposes of any legal proceedings, and
(b) that they might otherwise be unavailable for those purposes,

they may be retained until the proceedings are concluded.

(5) If a person who is required by a disclosure notice to produce any documents does not produce the documents in compliance with the notice, an authorised person may require that person to state, to the best of his knowledge and belief, where they are.

(6) In this section "authorised person" means any appropriate person who either—

(a) is the person by whom the notice was given, or
(b) is authorised by the Investigating Authority for the purposes of this section.

(7) This section has effect subject to section 64 (restrictions on requiring information etc).

[Serious Organised Crime and Police Act 2005, s 63.]

1–4602N 64. Restrictions on requiring information etc. (1) A person may not be required under section 62 or 63—

(a) to answer any privileged question,
(b) to provide any privileged information, or
(c) to produce any privileged document,

except that a lawyer may be required to provide the name and address of a client of his.

(2) A "privileged question" is a question which the person would be entitled to refuse to answer on grounds of legal professional privilege in proceedings in the High Court.

(3) "Privileged information" is information which the person would be entitled to refuse to provide on grounds of legal professional privilege in such proceedings.

(4) A "privileged document" is a document which the person would be entitled to refuse to produce on grounds of legal professional privilege in such proceedings.

(5) A person may not be required under section 62 to produce any excluded material (as defined by section 11 of the Police and Criminal Evidence Act 1984 (c 60) or, in relation to Northern Ireland, Article 13 of the Police and Criminal Evidence (Northern Ireland) Order 1989).

(6) In the application of this section to Scotland—

(a) subsections (1) to (5) do not have effect, but
(b) a person may not be required under section 62 or 63 to answer any question, provide any information or produce any document which he would be entitled, on grounds of legal privilege, to refuse to answer or (as the case may be) provide or produce.

(7) In subsection (6)(b), "legal privilege" has the meaning given by section 412 of the Proceeds of Crime Act 2002 (c 29).

(8) A person may not be required under section 62 or 63 to disclose any information or produce

any document in respect of which he owes an obligation of confidence by virtue of carrying on any banking business, unless—

 (*a*) the person to whom the obligation of confidence is owed consents to the disclosure or production, or

 (*b*) the requirement is made by, or in accordance with a specific authorisation given by, the Investigating Authority.

 (9) Subject to the preceding provisions, any requirement under section 62 or 63 has effect despite any restriction on disclosure (however imposed).

[Serious Organised Crime and Police Act 2005, s 64 and the Northern Ireland (Miscellaneous Provisions) Act 2006, Sch 3.]

1–4602O 65. Restrictions on use of statements. (1) A statement made by a person in response to a requirement imposed under section 62 or 63 ("the relevant statement") may not be used in evidence against him in any criminal proceedings unless subsection (2) or (3) applies.

 (2) This subsection applies where the person is being prosecuted—

 (*a*) for an offence under section 67 of this Act, or

 (*b*) for an offence under section 5 of the Perjury Act 1911 (c 6) (false statements made on oath otherwise than in judicial proceedings or made otherwise than on oath), or

 (*c*) for an offence under section 2 of the False Oaths (Scotland) Act 1933 (c 20) (false statutory declarations and other false statements without oath) or at common law for an offence of attempting to pervert the course, or defeat the ends, of justice, or

 (*d*) for an offence under Article 10 of the Perjury (Northern Ireland) Order 1979 (false statements made otherwise than on oath).

 (3) This subsection applies where the person is being prosecuted for some other offence and—

 (*a*) the person, when giving evidence in the proceedings, makes a statement inconsistent with the relevant statement, and

 (*b*) in the proceedings evidence relating to the relevant statement is adduced, or a question about it is asked, by or on behalf of the person.

[Serious Organised Crime and Police Act 2005, s 65 and the Northern Ireland (Miscellaneous Provisions) Act 2006, Sch 3.]

Enforcement

1–4602P 66. Power to enter and seize documents. (1) A justice of the peace may issue a warrant under this section if, on an information on oath laid by the Investigating Authority, he is satisfied—

 (*a*) that any of the conditions mentioned in subsection (2) is met in relation to any documents of a description specified in the information, and

 (*b*) that the documents are on premises so specified.

 (2) The conditions are—

 (*a*) that a person has been required by a disclosure notice to produce the documents but has not done so;

 (*b*) that it is not practicable to give a disclosure notice requiring their production;

 (*c*) that giving such a notice might seriously prejudice the investigation of an offence to which this Chapter applies.

 (3) A warrant under this section is a warrant authorising an appropriate person named in it—

 (*a*) to enter and search the premises, using such force as is reasonably necessary;

 (*b*) to take possession of any documents appearing to be documents of a description specified in the information, or to take any other steps which appear to be necessary for preserving, or preventing interference with, any such documents;

 (*c*) in the case of any such documents consisting of information recorded otherwise than in legible form, to take possession of any computer disk or other electronic storage device which appears to contain the information in question, or to take any other steps which appear to be necessary for preserving, or preventing interference with, that information;

 (*d*) to take copies of or extracts from any documents or information falling within paragraph (*b*) or (*c*);

 (*e*) to require any person on the premises to provide an explanation of any such documents or information or to state where any such documents or information may be found;

 (*f*) to require any such person to give the appropriate person such assistance as he may reasonably require for the taking of copies or extracts as mentioned in paragraph (*d*).

 (4) A person executing a warrant under this section may take other persons with him, if it appears to him to be necessary to do so.

 (5) A warrant under this section must, if so required, be produced for inspection by the owner or occupier of the premises or anyone acting on his behalf.

 (6) If the premises are unoccupied or the occupier is temporarily absent, a person entering the premises under the authority of a warrant under this section must leave the premises as effectively secured against trespassers as he found them.

 (7) Where possession of any document or device is taken under this section—

   (*a*) the document may be retained for so long as the Investigating Authority considers that it is necessary to retain it (rather than a copy of it) in connection with the investigation for the purposes of which the warrant was sought, or

   (*b*) the device may be retained for so long as he considers that it is necessary to retain it in connection with that investigation,

as the case may be.

   (8) If the Investigating Authority has reasonable grounds for believing—

   (*a*) that any such document or device may have to be produced for the purposes of any legal proceedings, and

   (*b*) that it might otherwise be unavailable for those purposes,

it may be retained until the proceedings are concluded.

   (9) Nothing in this section authorises a person to take possession of, or make copies of or take extracts from, any document or information which, by virtue of section 64, could not be required to be produced or disclosed under section 62 or 63.

   (10) In the application of this section to Scotland—

   (*a*) subsection (1) has effect as if, for the words from the beginning to "satisfied—", there were substituted "A sheriff may issue a warrant under this section, on the application of a procurator fiscal, if he is satisfied—";

   (*b*) subsections (1)(*a*) and (3)(*b*) have effect as if, for "in the information", there were substituted "in the application"; and

   (*c*) subsections (4) to (6) do not have effect.

   (11) In the application of this section to Northern Ireland—

   (*a*) subsection (1) has effect as if, for the words from the beginning to "laid", there were substituted "A lay magistrate may issue a warrant under this section if, on complaint on oath made"; and

   (*b*) subsections (1)(*a*) and (3)(*b*) have effect as if, for "in the information", there were substituted "in the complaint".

[Serious Organised Crime and Police Act 2005, s 66 and the Northern Ireland (Miscellaneous Provisions) Act 2006, Sch 3.]

1–4602Q 67. Offences in connection with disclosure notices or search warrants. (1) A person commits an offence if, without reasonable excuse, he fails to comply with any requirement imposed on him under section 62 or 63.

   (2) A person commits an offence if, in purported compliance with any requirement imposed on him under section 62 or 63—

   (*a*) he makes a statement which is false or misleading, and

   (*b*) he either knows that it is false or misleading or is reckless as to whether it is false or misleading.

   "False or misleading" means false or misleading in a material particular.

   (3) A person commits an offence if he wilfully obstructs any person in the exercise of any rights conferred by a warrant under section 66.

   (4) A person guilty of an offence under subsection (1) or (3) is liable on summary conviction—

   (*a*) to imprisonment for a term not exceeding 51 weeks[1], or

   (*b*) to a fine not exceeding level 5 on the standard scale,

or to both.

   (5) A person guilty of an offence under subsection (2) is liable[2]—

   (*a*) on conviction on indictment, to imprisonment for a term not exceeding two years or to a fine, or to both;

   (*b*) on summary conviction, to imprisonment for a term not exceeding 12 months[3] or to a fine not exceeding the statutory maximum, or to both.

   (6) In the application of this section to Scotland, the reference to 51 weeks in subsection (4)(*a*) is to be read as a reference to 12 months.

   (7) In the application of this section to Northern Ireland—

   (a) the reference to 51 weeks in subsection (4)(a) is to be read as a reference to 6 months; and

   (b) the reference to 12 months in subsection (5)(b) is to be read as a reference to 6 months.

[Serious Organised Crime and Police Act 2005, s 67 and the Northern Ireland (Miscellaneous Provisions) Act 2006, Sch 3.]

---

   1. In relation to an offence committed before the commencement of s 281(5) of the Criminal Justice Act 2003 this is to be read as a reference to "6 months", s 175(3), post.

   2. For procedure in respect of an offence triable either way, see the Magistrates' Courts Act 1980, ss 17A-21, in PART I: MAGISTRATES' COURTS, PROCEDURE, ante.

   3. In relation to an offence committed before the commencement of s 154(1) of the Criminal Justice Act 2003 this is to be read as a reference to "6 months", s 175(2), post.

Supplementary

1–4602R 69. Manner in which disclosure notice may be given. (1) This section provides for the manner in which a disclosure notice may be given under section 62.

(2) The notice may be given to a person by—

(a) delivering it to him,

(b) leaving it at his proper address,

(c) sending it by post to him at that address.

(3) The notice may be given—

(a) in the case of a body corporate, to the secretary or clerk of that body;

(b) in the case of a partnership, to a partner or a person having the control or management of the partnership business;

(c) in the case of an unincorporated association (other than a partnership), to an officer of the association.

(4) For the purposes of this section and section 7 of the Interpretation Act 1978 (c 30) (service of documents by post) in its application to this section, the proper address of a person is his usual or last-known address (whether residential or otherwise), except that—

(a) in the case of a body corporate or its secretary or clerk, it is the address of the registered office of that body or its principal office in the United Kingdom,

(b) in the case of a partnership, a partner or a person having the control or management of the partnership business, it is that of the principal office of the partnership in the United Kingdom, and

(c) in the case of an unincorporated association (other than a partnership) or an officer of the association, it is that of the principal office of the association in the United Kingdom.

(5) This section does not apply to Scotland.

[Serious Organised Crime and Police Act 2005, s 69.]

1–4602S   70. Interpretation of Chapter 1.   (1) In this Chapter—

"act of terrorism" includes anything constituting an action taken for the purposes of terrorism, within the meaning of the Terrorism Act 2000 (see section 1(5) of that Act);

"appropriate person" has the meaning given by section 62(2);

"the Investigating Authority" is to be construed in accordance with section 60(5) and (6);

"disclosure notice" has the meaning given by section 62(3);

"document" includes information recorded otherwise than in legible form;

"terrorism" has the same meaning as in the Terrorism Act 2000 (see section 1(1) to (4) of that Act);

"terrorist investigation" has the meaning given by section 60(7).

(2) In relation to information recorded otherwise than in legible form, any reference in this Chapter to the production of documents is a reference to the production of a copy of the information in legible form.

[Serious Organised Crime and Police Act 2005, s 70 as amended by the Terrorism Act 2006, s 33.]

CHAPTER 2
OFFENDERS ASSISTING INVESTIGATIONS AND PROSECUTIONS

1–4602T   71–75.   *Assistance by offender: immunity from prosecution, undertakings as to use of evidence, (in Crown Court proceedings) reduction in sentence, review of sentence, exclusion of public.*

CHAPTER 3
FINANCIAL REPORTING ORDERS

1–4602U   76. Financial reporting orders: making.   (1) A court sentencing or otherwise dealing with a person convicted of an offence mentioned in subsection (3) may also make a financial reporting order in respect of him.

(2) But it may do so only if it is satisfied that the risk of the person's committing another offence mentioned in subsection (3) is sufficiently high to justify the making of a financial reporting order.

(3) The offences are—

(a) an offence under any of the following provisions of the Theft Act 1968 (c 60)—

section 15 (obtaining property by deception),
section 15A (obtaining a money transfer by deception),
section 16 (obtaining a pecuniary advantage by deception),
section 20(2) (procuring execution of valuable security, etc),★

(b) an offence under either of the following provisions of the Theft Act 1978 (c 31)—

section 1 (obtaining services by deception),
section 2 (evasion of liability by deception),★

(c) any offence specified in Schedule 2 to the Proceeds of Crime Act 2002 (c 29) ("lifestyle offences").

(4) The Secretary of State may by order amend subsection (3) so as to remove an offence from it or add an offence to it.

(5) A financial reporting order—

(a) comes into force when it is made, and

(*b*) has effect for the period specified in the order, beginning with the date on which it is made.

(6) If the order is made by a magistrates' court, the period referred to in subsection (5)(*b*) must not exceed 5 years.

(7) Otherwise, that period must not exceed—

(*a*) if the person is sentenced to imprisonment for life, 20 years,
(*b*) otherwise, 15 years.

[Serious Organised Crime and Police Act 2005, s 76.]

---

*Substituted, by para (*aa*), by the Fraud Act 2006, Sch 1 as from a date to be appointed.

77. Financial reporting orders: making in Scotland

78. Financial reporting orders: making in Northern Ireland

1–4602V   79. Financial reporting orders: effect.   (1) A person in relation to whom a financial reporting order has effect must do the following.

(2) He must make a report, in respect of—

(*a*) the period of a specified length beginning with the date on which the order comes into force, and
(*b*) subsequent periods of specified lengths, each period beginning immediately after the end of the previous one.

(3) He must set out in each report, in the specified manner, such particulars of his financial affairs relating to the period in question as may be specified.

(4) He must include any specified documents with each report.

(5) He must make each report within the specified number of days after the end of the period in question.

(6) He must make each report to the specified person.

(7) Rules of court may provide for the maximum length of the periods which may be specified under subsection (2).

(8) In this section, "specified" means specified by the court in the order.

(9) In Scotland the specified person must be selected by the court from a list set out in an order made for the purposes of this section by the Scottish Ministers.

(10) A person who without reasonable excuse includes false or misleading information in a report, or otherwise fails to comply with any requirement of this section, is guilty of an offence and is liable on summary conviction to—

(*a*) imprisonment for a term not exceeding—

    (i) in England and Wales, 51 weeks[1],
    (ii) in Scotland, 12 months,
    (iii) in Northern Ireland, 6 months, or

(*b*) a fine not exceeding level 5 on the standard scale,

or to both.

[Serious Organised Crime and Police Act 2005, s 79.]

---

1. In relation to an offence committed before the commencement of s 281(5) of the Criminal Justice Act 2003 this is to be read as a reference to "6 months", s 175(3), post.

1–4602W   80. Financial reporting orders: variation and revocation.   (1) An application for variation or revocation of a financial reporting order may be made by—

(*a*) the person in respect of whom it has been made,
(*b*) the person to whom reports are to be made under it (see section 79(6)).

(2) The application must be made to the court which made the order.

(3) But if the order was made on appeal, the application must be made to the court which originally sentenced the person in respect of whom the order was made.

(4) If (in either case) that court was a magistrates' court, the application may be made to any magistrates' court acting in the same local justice area (or in Northern Ireland for the same county court division) as that court.

(5) Subsections (3) and (4) do not apply to Scotland.

[Serious Organised Crime and Police Act 2005, s 80.]

1–4602X   81. Financial reporting orders: verification and disclosure.   (1) In this section, "the specified person" means the person to whom reports under a financial reporting order are to be made.

(2) The specified person may, for the purpose of doing either of the things mentioned in subsection (4), disclose a report to any person who he reasonably believes may be able to contribute to doing either of those things.

(3) Any other person may disclose information to—

(*a*) the specified person, or

(*b*)   a person to whom the specified person has disclosed a report,

for the purpose of contributing to doing either of the things mentioned in subsection (4).

(4)   The things mentioned in subsections (2) and (3) are—

(*a*)   checking the accuracy of the report or of any other report made pursuant to the same order,
(*b*)   discovering the true position.

(5)   The specified person may also disclose a report for the purposes of—

(*a*)   the prevention, detection, investigation or prosecution of criminal offences, whether in the United Kingdom or elsewhere,
(*b*)   the prevention, detection or investigation of conduct for which penalties other than criminal penalties are provided under the law of any part of the United Kingdom or of any country or territory outside the United Kingdom.

(6)   A disclosure under this section does not breach—

(*a*)   any obligation of confidence owed by the person making the disclosure, or
(*b*)   any other restriction on the disclosure of information (however imposed).

(7)   But nothing in this section authorises a disclosure, in contravention of any provisions of the Data Protection Act 1998 (c 29), of personal data which are not exempt from those provisions.

(8)   In this section, references to a report include any of its contents, any document included with the report, or any of the contents of such a document.

[Serious Organised Crime and Police Act 2005, s 81.]

CHAPTER 4
PROTECTION OF WITNESSES AND OTHER PERSONS

1–4602Y   82. Protection of persons involved in investigations or proceedings.   (1) A protection provider may make such arrangements as he considers appropriate for the purpose of protecting a person of a description specified in Schedule 5 if—

(*a*)   the protection provider considers that the person's safety is at risk by virtue of his being a person of a description so specified, and
(*b*)   the person is ordinarily resident in the United Kingdom.

(2)   A protection provider may vary or cancel any arrangements made by him under subsection (1) if he considers it appropriate to do so.

(3)   If a protection provider makes arrangements under subsection (1) or cancels arrangements made under that subsection, he must record that he has done so.

(4)   In determining whether to make arrangements under subsection (1), or to vary or cancel arrangements made under that subsection, a protection provider must, in particular, have regard to—

(*a*)   the nature and extent of the risk to the person's safety,
(*b*)   the cost of the arrangements,
(*c*)   the likelihood that the person, and any person associated with him, will be able to adjust to any change in their circumstances which may arise from the making of the arrangements or from their variation or cancellation (as the case may be), and
(*d*)   if the person is or might be a witness in legal proceedings (whether or not in the United Kingdom), the nature of the proceedings and the importance of his being a witness in those proceedings.

(5)   A protection provider is—

(*a*)   a chief officer of a police force in England and Wales;
(*b*)   a chief constable of a police force in Scotland;
(*c*)   the Chief Constable of the Police Service of Northern Ireland;
(*d*)   the Director General of SOCA;
(*e*)   any of the Commissioners for Her Majesty's Revenue and Customs;
(*f*)   the Director of the Scottish Drug Enforcement Agency;*
(*g*)   a person designated by a person mentioned in any of the preceding paragraphs to exercise his functions under this section.

(6)   The Secretary of State may, after consulting the Scottish Ministers, by order amend Schedule 5 so as to add, modify or omit any entry.

(7)   Nothing in this section affects any power which a person has (otherwise than by virtue of this section) to make arrangements for the protection of another person.

[Serious Organised Crime and Police Act 2005, s 82.]

*****Substituted by the Police, Public Order and Criminal Justice (Scotland) Act 2006, s 101, Sch 6 as from a date to be appointed.**

83. Joint arrangements

84. Transfer of responsibility to other protection provider

85. Duty to assist protection providers

1–4602Z   86. Offence of disclosing information about protection arrangements.   (1) A person commits an offence if—

   (a)   he discloses information which relates to the making of arrangements under section 82(1) or to the implementation, variation or cancellation of such arrangements, and

   (b)   he knows or suspects that the information relates to the making of such arrangements or to their implementation, variation or cancellation.

  (2) A person who commits an offence under this section is liable[1]—

   (a)   on conviction on indictment, to imprisonment for a term not exceeding two years, to a fine or to both;

   (b)   on summary conviction, to imprisonment for a term not exceeding 12 months[2], to a fine not exceeding the statutory maximum or to both.

  (3) In the application of this section to Scotland or Northern Ireland, the reference in subsection (2)(b) to 12 months is to be read as a reference to 6 months.

[Serious Organised Crime and Police Act 2005, s 86.]

---

1. For procedure in respect of an offence triable either way, see the Magistrates' Courts Act 1980, ss 17A–21, in PART I: MAGISTRATES' COURTS, PROCEDURE, ante.

2. In relation to an offence committed before the commencement of s 154(1) of the Criminal Justice Act 2003 this is to be read as a reference to "6 months", s 175(2), post.

1–4603   87. Defences to liability under section 86.   (1) A person (P) is not guilty of an offence under section 86 if—

   (a)   at the time when P disclosed the information, he was or had been a protected person,

   (b)   the information related only to arrangements made for the protection of P or for the protection of P and a person associated with him, and

   (c)   at the time when P disclosed the information, it was not likely that its disclosure would endanger the safety of any person.

  (2) A person (d) is not guilty of an offence under section 86 if—

   (a)   D disclosed the information with the agreement of a person (P) who, at the time the information was disclosed, was or had been a protected person,

   (b)   the information related only to arrangements made for the protection of P or for the protection of P and a person associated with him, and

   (c)   at the time when D disclosed the information, it was not likely that its disclosure would endanger the safety of any person.

  (3) A person is not guilty of an offence under section 86 if he disclosed the information for the purposes of safeguarding national security or for the purposes of the prevention, detection or investigation of crime.

  (4) A person is not guilty of an offence under section 86 if—

   (a)   at the time when he disclosed the information, he was a protection provider or involved in the making of arrangements under section 82(1) or in the implementation, variation or cancellation of such arrangements, and

   (b)   he disclosed the information for the purposes of the making, implementation, variation or cancellation of such arrangements.

  (5) The Secretary of State may by order make provision prescribing circumstances in which a person who discloses information as mentioned in section 86(1) is not guilty in England and Wales or in Northern Ireland of an offence under that section.

  (6) The Scottish Ministers may by order make provision prescribing circumstances in which a person who discloses information as mentioned in section 86(1) is not guilty in Scotland of an offence under that section.

  (7) If sufficient evidence is adduced to raise an issue with respect to a defence under or by virtue of this section, the court or jury must assume that the defence is satisfied unless the prosecution proves beyond reasonable doubt that it is not.

[Serious Organised Crime and Police Act 2005, s 87.]

1–4603A   88. Offences of disclosing information relating to persons assuming new identity. (1) A person (P) commits an offence if—

   (a)   P is or has been a protected person,

   (b)   P assumed a new identity in pursuance of arrangements made under section 82(1),

   (c)   P discloses information which indicates that he assumed, or might have assumed, a new identity, and

   (d)   P knows or suspects that the information disclosed by him indicates that he assumed, or might have assumed, a new identity.

  (2) A person (d) commits an offence if—

   (a)   D discloses information which relates to a person (P) who is or has been a protected person,

   (b)   P assumed a new identity in pursuance of arrangements made under section 82(1),

   (c)   the information disclosed by D indicates that P assumed, or might have assumed, a new identity, and

(d)   D knows or suspects—

     (i)   that P is or has been a protected person, and
     (ii)   that the information disclosed by D indicates that P assumed, or might have assumed, a new identity.

(3)   A person who commits an offence under this section is liable[1]—

(a)   on conviction on indictment, to imprisonment for a term not exceeding two years, to a fine or to both;
(b)   on summary conviction, to imprisonment for a term not exceeding 12 months, to a fine not exceeding the statutory maximum or to both.

(4)   In the application of this section to Scotland or Northern Ireland, the reference in subsection (3)(b) to 12 months is to be read as a reference to 6 months.
[Serious Organised Crime and Police Act 2005, s 88.]

---

     1.   For procedure in respect of an offence triable either way, see the Magistrates' Courts Act 1980, ss 17A–21, in PART I: MAGISTRATES' COURTS, PROCEDURE, ante.
     2.   In relation to an offence committed before the commencement of s 154(1) of the Criminal Justice Act 2003 this is to be read as a reference to "6 months", s 175(2), post.

1–4603B   89. Defences to liability under section 88.   (1) P is not guilty of an offence under section 88(1) if, at the time when he disclosed the information, it was not likely that its disclosure would endanger the safety of any person.
     (2) D is not guilty of an offence under section 88(2) if—

(a)   D disclosed the information with the agreement of P, and
(b)   at the time when D disclosed the information, it was not likely that its disclosure would endanger the safety of any person.

(3)   D is not guilty of an offence under section 88(2) if he disclosed the information for the purposes of safeguarding national security or for the purposes of the prevention, detection or investigation of crime.
     (4) D is not guilty of an offence under section 88(2) if—

(a)   at the time when he disclosed the information, he was a protection provider or involved in the making of arrangements under section 82(1) or in the implementation, variation or cancellation of such arrangements, and
(b)   he disclosed the information for the purposes of the making, implementation, variation or cancellation of such arrangements.

(5)   The Secretary of State may by order make provision prescribing circumstances in which a person who discloses information as mentioned in subsection (1) or (2) of section 88 is not guilty in England and Wales or in Northern Ireland of an offence under that subsection.
     (6) The Scottish Ministers may by order make provision prescribing circumstances in which a person who discloses information as mentioned in subsection (1) or (2) of section 88 is not guilty in Scotland of an offence under that subsection.
     (7) If sufficient evidence is adduced to raise an issue with respect to a defence under or by virtue of this section, the court or jury must assume that the defence is satisfied unless the prosecution proves beyond reasonable doubt that it is not.
[Serious Organised Crime and Police Act 2005, s 89.]

1–4603C   90. Protection from liability.   (1) This section applies if—

(a)   arrangements are made for the protection of a person under section 82(1), and
(b)   the protected person assumes a new identity in pursuance of the arrangements.

(2)   No proceedings (whether civil or criminal) may be brought against a person to whom this section applies in respect of the making by him of a false or misleading representation if the representation—

(a)   relates to the protected person, and
(b)   is made solely for the purpose of ensuring that the arrangements made for him to assume a new identity are, or continue to be, effective.

(3)   The persons to whom this section applies are—

(a)   the protected person;
(b)   a person who is associated with the protected person;
(c)   a protection provider;
(d)   a person involved in the making of arrangements under section 82(1) or in the implementation, variation or cancellation of such arrangements.

[Serious Organised Crime and Police Act 2005, s 90.]

91. Transitional provision

92. Transitional provision: supplemental

1–4603D   93. Provision of information.   (1) This section applies if—

(a) a protection provider makes arrangements under section 82(1), or

(b) a protection provider determines under section 91(5) that it is appropriate to treat arrangements to which that section applies as having been made under section 82(1).

(2) The protection provider must inform the person to whom the arrangements relate of the provisions of this Chapter as they apply in relation to the arrangements.

(3) If the protection provider considers that the person would be unable to understand the information, by reason of his age or of any incapacity, the information must instead be given to a person who appears to the protection provider—

(a) to be interested in the welfare of the person to whom the arrangements relate, and

(b) to be the appropriate person to whom to give the information.

(4) If arrangements are made jointly under section 82(1) (by virtue of section 83), the protection providers involved in the arrangements must nominate one of those protection providers to perform the duties imposed by this section.
[Serious Organised Crime and Police Act 2005, s 93.]

1–4603E   94. Interpretation of Chapter 4.   (1) This section applies for the purposes of this Chapter.

(2) "Protection provider" is to be construed in accordance with section 82.

(3) A person is a protected person if—

(a) arrangements have been made for his protection under subsection (1) of section 82, and

(b) the arrangements have not been cancelled under subsection (2) of that section.

(4) A person is associated with another person if any of the following apply—

(a) they are members of the same family;

(b) they live in the same household;

(c) they have lived in the same household.

(5) A person assumes a new identity if either or both of the following apply—

(a) he becomes known by a different name;

(b) he makes representations about his personal history or circumstances which are false or misleading.

(6) A reference to a person who is a witness in legal proceedings includes a reference to a person who provides any information or any document or other thing which might be used in evidence in those proceedings or which (whether or not admissible as evidence in those proceedings)—

(a) might tend to confirm evidence which will or might be admitted in those proceedings,

(b) might be referred to in evidence given in those proceedings by another witness, or

(c) might be used as the basis for any cross examination in the course of those proceedings,

and a reference to a person who might be, or to a person who has been, a witness in legal proceedings is to be construed accordingly.

(7) A reference to a person who is a witness in legal proceedings does not include a reference to a person who is an accused person in criminal proceedings unless he is a witness for the prosecution and a reference to a person who might be, or to a person who has been, a witness in legal proceedings is to be construed accordingly.

(8) A reference to a person who is or has been a member of staff of an organisation includes a reference to a person who is or has been seconded to the organisation to serve as a member of its staff.

(9) "The Scottish Drug Enforcement Agency" and "the Director" of that Agency have the meanings given by section 42(2).*
[Serious Organised Crime and Police Act 2005, s 94.]

*Substituted by the Police, Public Order and Criminal Justice (Scotland) Act 2006, s 101, Sch 6 as from a date to be appointed.

CHAPTER 5
INTERNATIONAL OBLIGATIONS

1–4603EA   96. Mutual assistance in freezing property or evidence.   *Secretary of State may make regulations for purpose of implementing international obligations.*

CHAPTER 6
PROCEEDS OF CRIME

1–4603F   97. Confiscation orders by magistrates' courts.   (1) The Secretary of State may by order make such provision as he considers appropriate for or in connection with enabling confiscation orders under—

(a) Part 2 of the Proceeds of Crime Act 2002 (c 29) (confiscation: England and Wales), or

(b) Part 4 of that Act (confiscation: Northern Ireland),

to be made by magistrates' courts in England and Wales or Northern Ireland (as the case may be).

(2) But an order under subsection (1) may not enable such a confiscation order to be made by any magistrates' court in respect of an amount exceeding £10,000.

(3) An order under subsection (1) may amend, repeal, revoke or otherwise modify any provision of Part 2 or 4 of the 2002 Act or any other enactment relating to, or to things done under or for the purposes of, either (or any provision) of those Parts.

[Serious Organised Crime and Police Act 2005, s 97.]

98. Civil recovery: freezing orders

99. Civil recovery: interim receivers' expenses etc

1–4603G   100–109.   *Amendments to money laundering provisions of the Proceeds of Crime Act 2002.*

PART 3[1]
POLICE POWERS ETC
Powers of arrest

1–4603H   110, 111.   *Amend the Police and Criminal Evidence Act 1984, ss 24 and 25 (powers of arrest) and makes consequential amendments.*

---

1. Part 3 comprises ss 110–124 and Schs 7–9.

Exclusion zones

1–4603I   112. Power to direct a person to leave a place.   (1) A constable may direct a person to leave a place if he believes, on reasonable grounds, that the person is in the place at a time when he would be prohibited from entering it by virtue of—

(a) an order to which subsection (2) applies, or

(b) a condition to which subsection (3) applies.

(2) This subsection applies to an order which—

(a) was made, by virtue of any enactment, following the person's conviction of an offence, and

(b) prohibits the person from entering the place or from doing so during a period specified in the order.

(3) This subsection applies to a condition which—

(a) was imposed, by virtue of any enactment, as a condition of the person's release from a prison in which he was serving a sentence of imprisonment following his conviction of an offence, and

(b) prohibits the person from entering the place or from doing so during a period specified in the condition.

(4) A direction under this section may be given orally.

(5) Any person who knowingly contravenes a direction given to him under this section is guilty of an offence and liable on summary conviction to imprisonment for a term not exceeding 51 weeks[1] or to a fine not exceeding level 4 on the standard scale, or to both.

(6) *Repealed.*

(7) *Repealed.*

(8) In subsection (3)(a)—

(a) "sentence of imprisonment" and "prison" are to be construed in accordance with section 62(5) of the Criminal Justice and Court Services Act 2000 (c 43);

(b) the reference to a release from prison includes a reference to a temporary release.

(9) In this section, "place" includes an area.

(10) This subsection applies whether or not the order or condition mentioned in subsection (1) was made or imposed before or after the commencement of this section.

[Serious Organised Crime and Police Act 2005, s 112 as amended by s 174 of the same Act.]

---

1. In relation to an offence committed before the commencement of s 281(5) of the Criminal Justice Act 2003 this is to be read as a reference to "4 months", s 175(3), post.

Search warrants

1–4603J   113, 114.   *Amends the Police and Criminal Evidence Act 1984.*

Fireworks

115. Power to stop and search for prohibited fireworks.   *Amends the Police and Criminal Evidence Act 1984, s 1.*

Photographing of suspects etc

116. Photographing of suspects etc.   *Amends the Police and Criminal Evidence Act 1984, s 64A.*

Fingerprints and footwear impressions

1–4603K **117. Fingerprints.** (1) Section 61 of PACE (fingerprinting) is amended as provided in subsections (2) to (4).

(2) After subsection (6) insert—

"(6A) A constable may take a person's fingerprints without the appropriate consent if—

(*a*) the constable reasonably suspects that the person is committing or attempting to commit an offence, or has committed or attempted to commit an offence; and

(*b*) either of the two conditions mentioned in subsection (6B) is met.

(6B) The conditions are that—

(*a*) the name of the person is unknown to, and cannot be readily ascertained by, the constable;

(*b*) the constable has reasonable grounds for doubting whether a name furnished by the person as his name is his real name.

(6C) The taking of fingerprints by virtue of subsection (6A) does not count for any of the purposes of this Act as taking them in the course of the investigation of an offence by the police."

(3) In subsection (7), for "or (6)" substitute ", (6) or (6A)".

(4) In subsection (7A)—

(*a*) after "police station," insert "or by virtue of subsection (6A) at a place other than a police station,",

(*b*) in paragraph (*a*), after "an officer" insert "(or, in a subsection (6A) case, the constable)".

(5) In section 63A of PACE (fingerprints and samples: supplementary provisions)—

(*a*) after subsection (1) insert—

"(1ZA) Fingerprints taken by virtue of section 61(6A) above may be checked against other fingerprints to which the person seeking to check has access and which are held by or on behalf of any one or more relevant law-enforcement authorities or which are held in connection with or as a result of an investigation of an offence.",

(*b*) in subsection (1A), after "subsection (1)" insert "and (1ZA)".

(6) Section 64 of PACE (destruction of fingerprints and samples) is amended as follows.

(7) In subsection (1A), for "or the conduct of a prosecution" substitute ", the conduct of a prosecution or the identification of a deceased person or of the person from whom a body part came".

(8) After subsection (1B) insert—

"(1BA) Fingerprints taken from a person by virtue of section 61(6A) above must be destroyed as soon as they have fulfilled the purpose for which they were taken."

(9) In subsection (3AB), for "subsection (3)" substitute "subsection (1BA) or (3)".

(10) in subsection (3AC)—

(*a*) in paragraph (*a*), after "that" insert "fingerprint or",

(*b*) at the end add the following new sentence—

"This subsection does not apply to fingerprints taken from a person by virtue of section 61(6A) above."

[Serious Organised Crime and Police Act 2005, s 117.]

118. Impressions of footwear. *Inserts s 61A into the Police and Criminal Evidence Act 1984.*

Intimate samples

119. Intimate samples. *Amends the Police and Criminal Evidence Act 1984, s 65.*

Custody officers

1–4603L **120. Staff custody officers: designation.** (1) Section 38 of the Police Reform Act 2002 (c 30) (police powers for police authority employees) is amended as provided in subsections (2) to (4).

(2) In subsection (2), after paragraph (*d*) add—

"(*e*) staff custody officer."

(3) In subsection (6), after paragraph (*d*) add—

"(*e*) in the case of a person designated as a staff custody officer, Part 4A."

(4) After subsection (9) add—

"(10) References in this section, section 42 or section 46(4) to powers and duties conferred or imposed on a designated person, or to a designated person's being authorised or required to do anything by virtue of a designation under this section, or to a power or duty exercisable by a designated person in reliance on or by virtue of a designation under this section are, in the case of a staff custody officer at a police station designated under section 35(1) of the 1984 Act, references to those things in relation to him after his appointment as a custody officer for that police station under section 36(2) of that Act."

(5) After Part 4 of Schedule 4 to the Police Reform Act 2002 (powers exercisable by police civilians) insert—

"Part 4A
Staff Custody Officers
Exercise of functions of custody officers

35A. (1) Where a designation applies this paragraph to any person, he may (subject to sub-paragraph (2)) perform all the functions of a custody officer under the 1984 Act (except those under section 45A(4) of that Act) and under any other enactment which confers functions on such a custody officer.

(2) But in relation to a police station designated under section 35(1) of the 1984 Act, the person must first also be appointed a custody officer for that police station under section 36(2) of that Act.

(3) A person performing the functions of a custody officer by virtue of a designation under this paragraph (together with, if appropriate, an appointment as such) shall have all the powers and duties of a custody officer.

(4) Except in sections 36 and 45A(4) of the 1984 Act, references in any enactment to a custody officer within the meaning of that Act include references to a person performing the functions of a custody officer by virtue of a designation under this paragraph."

[Serious Organised Crime and Police Act 2005, s 120.]

1–4603M   121. Custody officers: amendments to PACE. (1) Section 36 of PACE (custody officers at police stations) is amended as provided in subsections (2) to (6).

(2) For subsection (3) substitute—

"(3) No person may be appointed a custody officer unless—

(*a*) he is a police officer of at least the rank of sergeant; or
(*b*) he is a staff custody officer."

(3) In subsection (5), for "an officer" substitute "an individual".

(4) In subsection (7)—

(*a*) in paragraph (*a*)—

(i) after "by an officer" insert "or a staff custody officer",
(ii) for "such an officer" substitute "such a person",

(*b*) in paragraph (*b*), for "such officer" substitute "such person".

(5) In subsection (8)—

(*a*) after "in" insert "section 34 above or in",
(*b*) for "an officer" substitute "a person".

(6) After subsection (10) add—

"(11) In this section, "staff custody officer" means a person who has been designated as such under section 38 of the Police Reform Act 2002."

(7) In section 39 of PACE (responsibilities in relation to persons detained)—

(*a*) in subsection (6)(*a*), after "custody officer" insert "(or, if the custody officer is a staff custody officer, any police officer or any police employee)",
(*b*) after subsection (6) add—

"(7) In subsection (6) above—

"police employee" means a person employed under section 15 of the Police Act 1996;
"staff custody officer" has the same meaning as in the Police Reform Act 2002."

[Serious Organised Crime and Police Act 2005, s 121.]

Designated and accredited persons

122. Powers of designated and accredited persons. *Amends the Police Reform Act 2002.*

Provision of information for use by police staff

123. Provision of information for use by police staff. *Amends the Criminal Justice and Court Services Act 2000 and the Vehicles (Crime) Act 2001.*

Interpretation of Part 3

1–4603N   124. Interpretation of Part 3. In this Part, "PACE" means the Police and Criminal Evidence Act 1984 (c 60).

[Serious Organised Crime and Police Act 2005, s 124.]

Part 4[1]
Public Order and Conduct in Public Places etc

---

1. Part 4 comprises ss 125–144 and Sch 10 and is reproduced in Part VIII: title Public Meeting and Public Order, post.

PART 5[1]

MISCELLANEOUS

Vehicle registration and insurance and road traffic offences

1–4603O   150–156.   *Amendments to road traffic legislation concerning offences of using an incorrectly registered vehicle, power of constables etc. to require production of registration documents, power to seize etc. vehicles driven without licence or insurance, making information about insurance status of vehicles available to constables[2], extension of power to take specimens of breath at the roadside, payments by the Secretary of State to police authorities in relation to the prevention, detection and enforcement of certain traffic offences.*

---

1. Part 5 comprises ss 145–171 and Schs 11–15. Sections 145–149 are reproduced in PART VIII: title PUBLIC MEETING AND PUBLIC ORDER, post.
2. The Disclosure of Vehicle Insurance Information Regulations 2005, SI 2005/2833 have been made under the powers in s 152.

Local policing information

1–4603P   157. Publication of local policing information.   *Amends the Police Act 1996, s 1.*

Other miscellaneous police matters

158. Responsibilities in relation to the health and safety etc of police.   *Amends the Health and Safety at Work Act 1974, s 51A.*

159. Investigations: accelerated procedure in special cases

160. Investigations: deaths and serious injuries during or after contact with the police

Royal Parks etc

161. Abolition of Royal Parks Constabulary

162. Regulation of specified parks

Criminal record checks

1–4603Q   163. Criminal record certificates.   (1) Sections 113 and 115 of the Police Act 1997 (c 50) (criminal record certificates) are omitted.
    (2) Before section 114 of that Act insert—

"113A. Criminal record certificates.   (1) The Secretary of State must issue a criminal record certificate to any individual who—

(*a*) makes an application in the prescribed manner and form, and
(*b*) pays in the prescribed manner any prescribed fee.

(2) The application must—

(*a*) be countersigned by a registered person, and
(*b*) be accompanied by a statement by the registered person that the certificate is required for the purposes of an exempted question.

(3) A criminal record certificate is a certificate which—

(*a*) gives the prescribed details of every relevant matter relating to the applicant which is recorded in central records, or
(*b*) states that there is no such matter.

(4) The Secretary of State must send a copy of a criminal record certificate to the registered person who countersigned the application.

(5) The Secretary of State may treat an application under this section as an application under section 113B if—

(*a*) in his opinion the certificate is required for a purpose prescribed under subsection (2) of that section,
(*b*) the registered person provides him with the statement required by that subsection, and
(*c*) the applicant consents and pays to the Secretary of State the amount (if any) by which the fee payable in relation to an application under that section exceeds the fee paid in relation to the application under this section.

(6) In this section—

"central records" means such records of convictions and cautions held for the use of police forces generally as may be prescribed;
"exempted question" means a question in relation to which section 4(2)(*a*) or (*b*) of the Rehabilitation of Offenders Act 1974 (effect of rehabilitation) has been excluded by an order of the Secretary of State under section 4(4) of that Act;
"relevant matter" means—

(*a*)   a conviction within the meaning of the Rehabilitation of Offenders Act 1974, including a spent conviction, and

(*b*)   a caution.

"113B. Enhanced criminal record certificates.   (1) The Secretary of State must issue an enhanced criminal record certificate to any individual who—

(*a*)   makes an application in the prescribed manner and form, and

(*b*)   pays in the prescribed manner any prescribed fee.

(2)   The application must—

(*a*)   be countersigned by a registered person, and

(*b*)   be accompanied by a statement by the registered person that the certificate is required for a prescribed purpose.

(3)   An enhanced criminal record certificate is a certificate which—

(*a*)   gives the prescribed details of every relevant matter relating to the applicant which is recorded in central records and any information provided in accordance with subsection (4), or

(*b*)   states that there is no such matter or information.

(4)   Before issuing an enhanced criminal record certificate the Secretary of State must request the chief officer of every relevant police force to provide any information which, in the chief officer's opinion—

(*a*)   might be relevant for the purpose described in the statement under subsection (2), and

(*b*)   ought to be included in the certificate.

(5)   The Secretary of State must also request the chief officer of every relevant police force to provide any information which, in the chief officer's opinion—

(*a*)   might be relevant for the purpose described in the statement under subsection (2),

(*b*)   ought not to be included in the certificate, in the interests of the prevention or detection of crime, and

(*c*)   can, without harming those interests, be disclosed to the registered person.

(6)   The Secretary of State must send to the registered person who countersigned the application—

(*a*)   a copy of the enhanced criminal record certificate, and

(*b*)   any information provided in accordance with subsection (5).

(7)   The Secretary of State may treat an application under this section as an application under section 113A if in his opinion the certificate is not required for a purpose prescribed under subsection (2).

(8)   If by virtue of subsection (7) the Secretary of State treats an application under this section as an application under section 113A, he must refund to the applicant the amount (if any) by which the fee paid in relation to the application under this section exceeds the fee payable in relation to an application under section 113A.

(9)   In this section—

"central records", "exempted question", and "relevant matter" have the same meaning as in section 113A;

"relevant police force", in relation to an application under this section, means a police force which is a relevant police force in relation to that application under regulations made by the Secretary of State.

(10)   For the purposes of this section references to a police force include any of the following—

(*a*)   the Royal Navy Regulating Branch;

(*b*)   the Royal Marines Police;

(*c*)   the Royal Military Police;

(*d*)   the Royal Air Force Police;

(*e*)   the Ministry of Defence Police;

(*f*)   the National Criminal Intelligence Service;

(*g*)   the National Crime Squad;

(*h*)   the British Transport Police;

(*i*)   the Civil Nuclear Constabulary;

(*j*)   the States of Jersey Police Force;

(*k*)   the salaried police force of the Island of Guernsey;

(*l*)   the Isle of Man Constabulary;

(*m*)   a body with functions in any country or territory outside the British Islands which correspond to those of a police force in any part of the United Kingdom,

and any reference to the chief officer of a police force includes the person responsible for the direction of a body mentioned in this subsection.

(11)   For the purposes of this section each of the following must be treated as if it were a police force—

(*a*) the Commissioners for Her Majesty's Revenue and Customs (and for this purpose a reference to the chief officer of a police force must be taken to be a reference to any one of the Commissioners);

(*b*) the Serious Organised Crime Agency (and for this purpose a reference to the chief officer of a police force must be taken to be a reference to the Director General of the Agency);

(*c*) such other department or body as is prescribed (and regulations may prescribe in relation to the department or body the person to whom a reference to the chief officer is to be taken to be).

113C. Criminal record certificates: suitability relating to children. (1) If an application under section 113A or 113B is accompanied by a children's suitability statement the criminal record certificate or enhanced criminal record certificate (as the case may be) must also state—

(*a*) whether the applicant is included in a specified children's list;

(*b*) if he is included in such a list, such details of his inclusion as may be prescribed;

(*c*) whether he is subject to a specified children's direction;

(*d*) if he is subject to such a direction, the grounds on which it was given and such details as may be prescribed of the circumstances in which it was given.

(2) A children's suitability statement is a statement by the registered person that the certificate is required for the purpose of considering—

(*a*) the applicant's suitability to be employed, supplied to work, found work or given work in a position (whether paid or unpaid) within subsection (5),

(*b*) the applicant's suitability to be a foster parent or to adopt a child,

(*c*) the applicant's suitability to be a child's special guardian for the purposes of sections 14A and 14C of the Children Act 1989,

(*d*) the applicant's suitability to have a child placed with him by virtue of section 70 of the Children (Scotland) Act 1995 or by virtue of section 5(2), (3) and (4) of the Social Work (Scotland) Act 1968, or

(*e*) the suitability of a person living in the same household as the applicant to be a person mentioned in paragraph (*b*) or (*c*) or to have a child placed with him as mentioned in paragraph (*d*).

(3) Each of the following is a specified children's list—

(*a*) the list kept under section 1 of the Protection of Children Act 1999;

(*b*) the list kept under section 1(1) of the Protection of Children (Scotland) Act 2003;

(*c*) the list kept under Article 3 of the Protection of Children and Vulnerable Adults (Northern Ireland) Order 2003;

(*d*) any list kept for the purposes of regulations under Article 70(2)(*e*) or 88A(2)(*b*) of the Education and Libraries (Northern Ireland) Order 1986;

(*e*) any such other list as the Secretary of State specifies by order if he thinks that the list corresponds to a list specified in paragraphs (*a*) to (*c*) and is kept in pursuance of a country or territory outside the United Kingdom.

(4) Each of the following is a specified children's direction—

(*a*) a direction under section 142 of the Education Act 2002;

(*b*) anything which the Secretary of State specifies by order which he thinks corresponds to such a direction and which is done for the purposes of the law of Scotland or of Northern Ireland or of a country or territory outside the United Kingdom.

(5) A position falls within this subsection if it is any of the following—

(*a*) a child care position within the meaning of the Protection of Children Act 1999;

(*b*) a child care position within the meaning of the Protection of Children (Scotland) Act 2003;

(*c*) a child care position within the meaning of Chapter 1 of Part 2 of the Protection of Children and Vulnerable Adults (Northern Ireland) Order 2003;

(*d*) a position, employment or further employment in which may be prohibited or restricted by regulations under Article 70(2)(*e*) or 88A(2)(*b*) of the Education and Libraries (Northern Ireland) Order 1986;

(*e*) a position which involves work to which section 142 of the Education Act 2002 applies;

(*f*) a position of such other description as may be prescribed.

(6) An order under subsection (4)(*b*) may make such modifications of subsection (1)(*d*) as the Secretary of State thinks necessary or expedient in consequence of the order.

113D. Criminal record certificates: suitability relating to adults. (1) If an application under section 113A or 113B is accompanied by an adults' suitability statement the criminal record certificate or enhanced criminal record certificate (as the case may be) must also state—

(*a*) whether the applicant is included in a specified adults' list;

(*b*) if he is included in such a list, such details of his inclusion as may be prescribed.

(2) An adults' suitability statement is a statement by the registered person that the certificate is required for the purpose of considering the applicant's suitability to be employed, supplied to

work, found work or given work in a position (whether paid or unpaid) falling within subsection (4).

(3) Each of the following is a specified adults' list—

(a) the list kept under section 81 of the Care Standards Act 2000;
(b) the list kept under Article 35 of the Protection of Children and Vulnerable Adults (Northern Ireland) Order 2003;
(c) any such other list as the Secretary of State specifies by order if he thinks that the list corresponds to a list specified in paragraph (a) or (b) and is kept in pursuance of the law of Scotland or of a country or territory outside the United Kingdom.

(4) A position falls within this subsection if it is any of the following—

(a) a care position within the meaning of Part 7 of the Care Standards Act 2000;
(b) a care position within the meaning of Part 3 of the Protection of Children and Vulnerable Adults (Northern Ireland) Order 2003;
(c) a position concerned with providing a care service (as defined by section 2(1) of the Regulation of Care (Scotland) Act 2001);
(d) a position of such other description as may be prescribed.

113E. Criminal record certificates: specified children's and adults' lists: urgent cases.
(1) Subsection (2) applies to an application under section 113A or 113B if—

(a) it is accompanied by a children's suitability statement,
(b) the registered person requests an urgent preliminary response, and
(c) the applicant pays in the prescribed manner such additional fee as is prescribed in respect of the application.

(2) The Secretary of State must notify the registered person—

(a) if the applicant is not included in a specified children's list, of that fact;
(b) if the applicant is included in such a list, of the details prescribed for the purposes of section 113C(1)(b) above;
(c) if the applicant is not subject to a specified children's direction, of that fact;
(d) if the applicant is subject to such a direction, of the grounds on which the direction was given and the details prescribed for the purposes of section 113C(1)(d) above.

(3) Subsection (4) applies to an application under section 113A or 113B if—

(a) it is accompanied by an adults' suitability statement,
(b) the registered person requests an urgent preliminary response, and
(c) the applicant pays in the prescribed manner such additional fee as is prescribed in respect of the application.

(4) The Secretary of State must notify the registered person either—

(a) that the applicant is not included in a specified adults' list, or
(b) that a criminal record certificate or enhanced criminal record certificate will be issued in due course.

(5) In this section—

"criminal record certificate" has the same meaning as in section 113A;
"enhanced criminal record certificate" has the same meaning as in section 113B;
"children's suitability statement", "specified children's direction" and "specified children's list" have the same meaning as in section 113C;
"adults' suitability statement" and "specified adults' list" have the same meaning as in section 113D.

113F. Criminal record certificates: supplementary. (1) References in sections 113C(2) and 113D(2) to considering the applicant's suitability to be employed, supplied to work, found work or given work in a position falling within section 113C(5) or 113D(4) include references to considering—

(a) for the purposes of Part 10A of the Children Act 1989 (child minding and day care in England and Wales), the applicant's suitability to look after or be in regular contact with children under the age of eight;
(b) for the purposes of that Part of that Act, in the case of an applicant for or holder of a certificate under section 79W of that Act, or a person prescribed under subsection (4) of that section, his suitability to look after children within the meaning of that section;
(c) the applicant's suitability to be registered for child minding or providing day care under section 71 of the Children Act 1989 or Article 118 of the Children (Northern Ireland) Order 1995 (child minding and day care);
(d) for the purposes of section 3 of the Teaching and Higher Education Act 1998 (registration of teachers with the General Teaching Council for England or the General Teaching Council for Wales) or of section 6 of the Teaching Council (Scotland) Act 1965 (registration of teachers with the General Teaching Council for Scotland), the applicant's suitability to be a teacher;

(e) the applicant's suitability to be registered under Part 2 of the Care Standards Act 2000 (establishments and agencies);

(f) the applicant's suitability to be registered under Part 4 of that Act (social care workers);

(g) the applicant's suitability to be registered under Part 1 of the Regulation of Care (Scotland) Act 2001 (applications by persons seeking to provide a care service);

(h) the applicant's suitability to be registered under Part 3 of that Act (social workers and other social service workers);

(i) the applicant's application to have a care service, consisting of the provision of child minding or the day care of children, registered under Part 1 of that Act (care services);

(j) the applicant's suitability to be registered under Part 1 of the Health and Personal Social Services Act (Northern Ireland) 2001 (social care workers);

(k) the applicant's suitability to be registered under Part 3 of the Health and Personal Social Services (Quality, Improvement and Regulation) (Northern Ireland) Order 2003 (regulation of establishments and agencies).

(2) The power to make an order under section 113C or 113D is exercisable by statutory instrument, but no such order may be made unless a draft of the order has been laid before and approved by a resolution of each House of Parliament.

(3) If the power mentioned in subsection (2) is exercised by the Scottish Ministers, the reference in that subsection to each House of Parliament must be construed as a reference to the Scottish Parliament."

(3) Schedule 14 (which makes consequential amendments to Part 5 of the Police Act 1997 (c 50)) has effect.

(4) If section 115(1) of the Adoption and Children Act 2002 (c 38) comes into force before the preceding provisions of this section, the Secretary of State may by order apply Part 5 of the Police Act 1997 subject to such modifications as he thinks necessary or expedient for the purpose of enabling a certificate or statement to be issued under section 113 or 115 of that Act of 1997 in connection with consideration by a court of whether to make a special guardianship order under section 14A of the Children Act 1989 (c 41).

[Serious Organised Crime and Police Act 2005, s 163.]

1–4603R   164. Criminal records checks: verification of identity.   (1) Section 118 of the Police Act 1997 (evidence of identity) is amended as follows.

(2) In subsection (1) after "117" insert "or 120".

(3) After subsection (2) insert—

"(2A) For the purpose of verifying evidence of identity supplied in pursuance of subsection (1) the Secretary of State may obtain such information as he thinks is appropriate from data held—

(a) by the United Kingdom Passport Agency;

(b) by the Driver and Vehicle Licensing Agency;

(c) by Driver and Vehicle Licensing Northern Ireland;

(d) by the Secretary of State in connection with keeping records of national insurance numbers;

(e) by such other persons or for such purposes as is prescribed."

[Serious Organised Crime and Police Act 2005, s 164.]

1–4603S   165. Certain references to police forces.   (1) In section 119 of the Police Act 1997 (c 50) (sources of information),

(a) in subsection (3) for "the prescribed fee" substitute "such fee as he thinks appropriate";

(b) after subsection (5) insert—

"(6) For the purposes of this section references to a police force include any body mentioned in subsections (10)(a) to (i) and (11) of section 113B and references to a chief officer must be construed accordingly.

(7) In the case of such a body the reference in subsection (3) to the appropriate police authority must be construed as a reference to such body as is prescribed."

(2) In each version of section 120A of that Act (as inserted respectively by section 134(1) of the Criminal Justice and Police Act 2001 (c 16) and section 70 of the Criminal Justice (Scotland) Act 2003 (asp 7)), after subsection (5) insert—

"(6) For the purposes of this section references to a police force include any body mentioned in subsections (10)(a) to (i) and (11) of section 113B and references to a chief officer must be construed accordingly."

(3) In section 124A of that Act (offences relating to disclosure of information) (inserted by section 328 of and paragraphs 1 and 11 of Schedule 35 to the Criminal Justice Act 2003 (c 44)), after subsection (5) insert—

"(6) For the purposes of this section the reference to a police force includes any body mentioned in subsections (10)(a) to (i) and (11) of section 113B and the reference to a chief officer must be construed accordingly."

[Serious Organised Crime and Police Act 2005, s 165.]

1–4603T   166–168.   *Scotland, Northern Ireland, Channel Islands and Isle of Man.*

Witness summonses

169. Powers of Crown Court and Magistrates' Court to issue witness summons. *Amends s 2 of the Criminal Procedure (Attendance of Witnesses) Act 1965 and s 97 of the Magistrates' Courts Act 1980.*

170. Powers of courts-martial etc to issue warrants of arrest in respect of witnesses

Private Security Industry Act 2001: Scotland

171. Private Security Industry Act 2001: Scottish extent

PART 6[1]
FINAL PROVISIONS

1–4603U   **172. Orders and regulations**

173. Supplementary, incidental, consequential etc provision

174. Minor and consequential amendments, repeals and revocations

1–4603V   **175. Penalties for offences: transitional modification for England and Wales.**
(1) This section contains transitional modifications in respect of penalties for certain offences committed in England or Wales.

(2) In relation to an offence committed before the commencement of section 154(1) of the Criminal Justice Act 2003 (c 44) (general limit on magistrates' court's power to impose imprisonment), the references in the following provisions to periods of imprisonment of 12 months are to be read as references to periods of imprisonment of 6 months—

> section 67(5)(*b*);
> section 86(2)(*b*);
> section 88(3)(*b*);
> section 147(1)(*a*).

(3) In relation to an offence committed before the commencement of section 281(5) of the Criminal Justice Act 2003 (alteration of penalties for summary offences), the references in the following provisions of this Act to periods of imprisonment of 51 weeks are to be read as references to the periods of imprisonment specified in respect of those provisions as follows—

Section	*Modified period of imprisonment*
section 51(4)(*a*)	6 months
section 51(5)(*a*)	1 month
section 57(4)(*a*)	6 months
section 57(5)(*a*)	1 month
section 67(4)(*a*)	6 months
section 79(10)(*a*)(i)	6 months
section 112(5)	4 months
section 128(5)(*a*)	6 months
section 136(1)	3 months
section 136(3)(*a*)	3 months
section 136(4)	3 months

[Serious Organised Crime and Police Act 2005, s 175.]

---

1. Part 1 comprises ss 172–179 and Schs 16–17.

176. Expenses

1–4603W   **177. Interpretation.** (1) In this Act "SOCA" means the Serious Organised Crime Agency.

(2) In this Act "enactment" includes—

> (*a*) an enactment contained in or made under an Act of the Scottish Parliament or Northern Ireland legislation, and
> (*b*) an enactment comprised in subordinate legislation (within the meaning of the Interpretation Act 1978 (c 30)).

(3) In this Act references to enactments include enactments passed or made after the passing of this Act.

(4) Subsections (2) and (3) apply except where the context otherwise requires.
[Serious Organised Crime and Police Act 2005, s 177.]

1–4603X   **178. Commencement.** (1) The following provisions come into force on the day on which this Act is passed—

(*a*)   sections 117(7) (and section 117(6) so far as relates to it), 158, 167, 172, 173, 176, 177, this section and section 179, and

(*b*)   Part 1 of Schedule 17 and (so far as it relates to that Part of that Schedule) section 174(2).

(2)   Section 163(4) comes into force at the end of the period of three months beginning with the day on which this Act is passed.

(3)   Sections 77 and 156 come into force on such day as the Scottish Ministers may by order appoint.

(4)   So far as they extend to Scotland—

(*a*)   Chapter 1 of Part 2,

(*b*)   sections 79 to 81,

(*c*)   Chapter 4 of Part 2 (including Schedule 5),

(*d*)   sections 163 to 166, and

(*e*)   Schedule 14,

come into force on such day as the Scottish Ministers may by order appoint.

(5)   So far as they relate—

(*a*)   to sections 113 and 115 of the Police Act 1997 (c 50) as those sections apply to Scotland;

(*b*)   to section 125 of that Act, to the Regulation of Care (Scotland) Act 2001 (asp 8), to the Protection of Children (Scotland) Act 2003 (asp 5) and to the Criminal Justice (Scotland) Act 2003 (asp 7),

section 174(2) and Schedule 17 come into force on such day as the Scottish Ministers may by order appoint.

(6)   The following provisions come into force on such day as the Scottish Ministers may by order appoint after consulting the Secretary of State—

(*a*)   section 96 so far as it has effect for the purpose of conferring functions on the Scottish Ministers, and

(*b*)   section 171 and Schedule 15.

(7)   The following provisions come into force on such day as the Secretary of State may by order appoint after consulting the Scottish Ministers—

(*a*)   sections 95, 98(2), 99(2) and (3), 100, 101 and 107, and

(*b*)   paragraphs 1 and 6 of Schedule 6, and section 109 so far as relating to those paragraphs.

(8)   Otherwise, this Act comes into force on such day as the Secretary of State may by order[1] appoint.

(9)   Different days may be appointed for different purposes or different areas.

(10)   The Secretary of State may by order make such provision as he considers appropriate for transitory, transitional or saving purposes in connection with the coming into force of any provision of this Act.

(11)   The power conferred by subsection (10) is exercisable by the Scottish Ministers (rather than the Secretary of State) in connection with any provision of this Act which comes into force by order made by the Scottish Ministers.

[Serious Organised Crime and Police Act 2005, s 178.]

---

1. The following commencement orders have been made: (No 1) SI 2005/1521; (No 2) SI 2005/2026; (No 3) SI 2005/3136; (No 4 and Transitory Provision) SI 2005/3495; (No 5 and Transitional and Transitory Provisions and Savings) SI 2006/378; (No 6 and Appointed Day), SI 2006/1085; (No 7) SSI 2006/381; (No 8), SI 2006/1871 amended by SI 2006/2182; (No 9) SI 2006/2182. At the date of going to press the following provisions were in force:

—   ss 117(6) and (7), 158,167, 172, 173, 176-179, Sch 17 (part) (7 April 2005);

—   ss 95–97, 99–101, 103-108, 112, 115,119, 122(7), 123-131, 132(7), 133, 134(1)(6), (9), (10), 138–143, 145-155, 157–159, 161, 162(1), (2), (4), 164, 165(1)(*a*), 166(2), 168, 169, 174 (part), 175, Schs 8 (part), 9 (part), 11, 12, 13 17 (part) (1 July 2005);

—   ss 163(4), 164 (7 July 2005);

—   ss 116(1) and (3)–(5), 161, 122(1)–(6), 132(1)–(6), 134(7), (8), Sch 6 (part) (1 August 2005);

—   ss 1(3), 8–10, 17, 18, 27, 39, 42, 44(2), 52, 54, 58, 59, 98, 110, 111, 113, 114, 116(2), 118, 122(7), Schs 3, 4 (part), 6 (part), 7, 9 (part), 16, 17 (part) (1 January 2006);

—   ss 1(1), (2) (part), 6, 43, 44(1), 55(1), (2), Sch 1 (part), Sch 2 (part), (1 March 2006); 1(1) and (2), Sch 1 (so far as not already in force, 2 to 5 and 7, 11 to 16, 19 to 26, 28 to 38, 40, 41 and 45 to 51, 53, 55, Sch 2 (so far as not already in force, 56 and 57, 59, Sch 4 (except paras 42, 170, 171 and 172, 76 and 78, 174(2) , Sch 17 (repeals) (1 April 2006);

—   ss 163(1), (2) (save to the extent it relates to—(i) s 113B(10)(*a*) to (*i*) and (*m*) of the Police Act 1997; (ii) s 113C(3)(*b*) to (*d*) of the Police Act 1997; (iii) s 113D(3)(*b*) of the Police Act 1997; and (iv) s 113E(1) and (2) of the Police Act 1997), (3), 165 (fully), 174(2) (part), Sch 14 (part), Sch 17 (part)

—   s 161 (1), (2) and, to the extent not already in force, subs (5); s 174(2) in so far as it relates to the following entries in Sch 17: para 27D and the cross-heading before it of Sch 1 to the Regulation of Investigatory Powers Act 2000; s 82(1)(*f*) and (5) of the Police Reform Act 2002; paras 9, 10 and 12 in Part 2 of Sch 13 (8 May 2006);

—   s 102 (15 May 2006);

—   s 144 and Sch 10 (20 July 2006 in the following areas: Hampshire, Hertfordshire, Nottinghamshire and Worcestershire; Leicester and York; Gateshead and South Tyneside; Southwark and Wandsworth;

—   s 161 insofar as it relates to s 113B (10)(*h*) of the Police Act 1997 (25 September 2005).

179. Short title and extent

1–4603Y

Section 163   SCHEDULE 14
AMENDMENTS OF PART 5 OF POLICE ACT 1997

1. Part 5 of the Police Act 1997 (c 50) (certificates of criminal records etc) is amended as follows.
2. In section 114(3) for "Section 113(3) to (5)" substitute "Sections 113A(3) to (6) and 113C to 113F".
3. In section 116—

(a) in the application to Scotland of subsection (2)(b) for "to which subsection (3) or (4) of section 115 applies" substitute "of such description as may be prescribed";
(b) in subsection (3) for "Section 115(6) to (10)" substitute "Sections 113B(3) to (11) and 113C to 113F".

4. In section 119—

(a) in subsection (1A) for "section 113(3A) or (3C) or (3EA) or (3EC)" substitute "section 113C(3) or 113D(3)";
(b) in subsection (2) for "115" substitute "113B".

5. In section 119A(2) for the words from "under" to "adults)" substitute "in a list mentioned in section 113C(3) or 113D(3)".
6. In section 120—

(a) in subsection (3)(b) for "113 or 115" substitute "113A or 113B";
(b) in subsection (5)(b) for "113 or 115" substitute "113A or 113B";
(c) in subsection (7) for "113" substitute "113A".

7. In section 120ZA(4)(b) for "113 or 115" substitute "113A or 113B".
8. In section 120A (as inserted by section 134(1) of the Criminal Justice and Police Act 2001 (c 16))—

(a) in subsection (3)(b) for "section 113(3A) or (3C) or (3EA) or (3EC)" substitute "section 113C(3) or 113D(3)";
(b) in subsection (5) for "113" substitute "113A".

9. In section 120A (as inserted by section 70 of the Criminal Justice (Scotland) Act 2003 (asp 7))—

(a) in subsection (3)(a) for "113" substitute "113A";
(b) in subsection (3)(b) for "113(3C)" substitute "113C(3) or 113D(3)";
(c) after subsection (6) (as inserted by section 165(2) of this Act) insert—

"(7) In the case of such a body the reference in subsection (5) to a police authority must be construed as a reference to such body as is prescribed."
10. In section 121 for "under section 114(2), 115(4) or (10), 116(2), 122(1) or (2) or 125" substitute "in relation to the making of regulations or orders".
11. In section 122(3) and (4)(b) for "113 or 115" substitute "113A or 113B".
12. In section 124—

(a) in subsections (1), (2), (3), (4) and (6) for "113 or 115" substitute "113A or 113B";
(b) in subsection (5) for "115(8)" substitute "113B(5)";
(c) in subsection (6)(e) for "113" substitute "113A".

13. In section 124B—

(a) in subsection (1) for "113" substitute "113A";
(b) in subsection (3) for "113(5)" substitute "113A(6)".

14. In section 125, at the end add—

"(6) If the power mentioned in subsection (1) is exercised by the Scottish Ministers, the reference in subsection (3) to each House of Parliament must be construed as a reference to the Scottish Parliament."

SCHEDULE 15
PRIVATE SECURITY INDUSTRY ACT 2001: SCOTTISH EXTENT

1–4603Z

Section 174   SCHEDULE 16
REMAINING MINOR AND CONSEQUENTIAL AMENDMENTS (SEARCH WARRANTS)

Incitement to Disaffection Act 1934 (c 56)

1. In section 2 of the Incitement to Disaffection Act 1934 (which makes provision about search warrants), in subsection (2), for "one month" substitute "three months".

Public Order Act 1936 (1 Edw 8 & 1 Geo 6 c 6)

2. In section 2 of the Public Order Act 1936 (prohibition of quasi-military organisations), in subsection (5), for "one month" substitute "three months".

Wireless Telegraphy Act 1949 (c 54)

3. In section 15 of the Wireless Telegraphy Act 1949 (entry and search of premises), in subsection (1), for "one month" substitute "three months".

Licensing Act 1964 (c 26)

4. Until their repeal by the Licensing Act 2003 (c 17), the following provisions of the Licensing Act 1964 have effect as if for "one month" there were substituted "three months"—

section 54 (search warrants relating to clubs),
section 85(1) (search warrants relating to parties organised for gain),
section 187(1) (search warrants relating to sale of alcohol).

Biological Weapons Act 1974 (c 6)

5. *Amends section 4 of the Biological Weapons Act 1974.*

Copyright, Designs and Patents Act 1988 (c 48)

6. (1) The Copyright, Designs and Patents Act 1988 is amended as follows.
(2) In section 109 (search warrants), in subsection (3)(*b*), for "28 days" substitute "three months".
(3) In section 200 (search warrants), in subsection (3)(*b*), for "28 days" substitute "three months".
(4) In section 297B (search warrants), in subsection (3)(*b*), for "28 days" substitute "three months".

Computer Misuse Act 1990 (c 18)

7. In section 14 of the Computer Misuse Act 1990 (search warrants), in subsection (3)(*b*), for "twenty-eight days" substitute "three months".

Trade Marks Act 1994 (c 26)

8. In section 92A of the Trade Marks Act 1994 (search warrants), in subsection (3)(*b*), for "28 days" substitute "three months".

1–4603ZA

Section 174

SCHEDULE 17
REPEALS AND REVOCATIONS

PART 1
REPEALS COMING INTO FORCE ON ROYAL ASSENT

Short title and chapter	Extent of repeal
Police Reform Act 2002 (c 30)	Section 95. In Schedule 8, the reference to section 5 of the Police (Health and Safety) Act 1997 (c 42).

PART 2
OTHER REPEALS AND REVOCATIONS

Short title and chapter or title and number	Extent of repeal or revocation
Unlawful Drilling Act 1819 (60 Geo 3 & 1 Geo 4 c 1)	In section 2, the words ", or for any other person acting in their aid or assistance,".
Vagrancy Act 1824 (c 83)	Section 6.
Railway Regulation Act 1842 (c 55)	Section 17.
Companies Clauses Consolidation Act 1845 (c 16)	In section 156, the words ", and all persons called by him to his assistance,".
Railways Clauses Consolidation Act 1845 (c 20)	Sections 104 and 154.
Licensing Act 1872 (c 94)	In section 12, the words "may be apprehended, and".
Public Stores Act 1875 (c 25)	Section 12(1).
London County Council (General Powers) Act 1894 (c ccxii)	In section 7, the words "and any person called to the assistance of such constable or person authorised".
London County Council (General Powers) Act 1900 (c cclxviii)	In section 27, the words "and any person called to the assistance of such constable or officer".
Licensing Act 1902 (c 28)	In section 1, the words "apprehended and". In section 2(1), the words "may be apprehended, and".
Protection of Animals Act 1911 (c 27)	Section 12(1).
Official Secrets Act 1911 (c 28)	Section 6.
Public Order Act 1936 (1 Edw 8 & 1 Geo 6 c 6)	Section 7(3).
Army Act 1955 (3 & 4 Eliz 2 c 18)	Section 83BC(2)(*k*).
Air Force Act 1955 (3 & 4 Eliz 2 c 19)	Section 83BC(2)(*k*).
Naval Discipline Act 1957 (c 53)	Section 52IJ(2)(*k*).
Public Records Act 1958 (c 51)	In Schedule 1, in Part 2 of the Table at the end of paragraph 3, the entries relating to the Service Authorities for the National Crime Squad and the National Criminal Intelligence Service.
Street Offences Act 1959 (c 57)	Section 1(3).
Trustee Investments Act 1961 (c 62)	In section 11(4), in paragraph (*a*), the words ", the Service Authority for the National Crime Squad", and paragraph (*e*). In Part 2 of Schedule 1, paragraph 9(da).
Parliamentary Commissioner Act 1967 (c 13)	In Schedule 2, the entries relating to the Service Authorities for the National Crime Squad and the National Criminal Intelligence Service.
Police (Scotland) Act 1967 (c 77)	In section 33, in subsections (3) and (4), the words "and the National Criminal Intelligence Service". Section 38A(1)(ba).

Short title and chapter or title and number	Extent of repeal or revocation
	In section 41(4)(*a*), the words "or by a member of the National Criminal Intelligence Service or of the National Crime Squad".
Criminal Justice Act 1967 (c 80)	In section 91(1), the words "may be arrested without warrant by any person and".
Leasehold Reform Act 1967 (c 88)	Section 28(5)(bc).
Ministry of Housing and Local Government Provisional Order Confirmation (Greater London Parks and Open Spaces) Act 1967 (c xxix)	In Article 19 of the Order set out in the Schedule, the words "and any person called to the assistance of such constable or officer".
Theft Act 1968 (c 60)	Section 25(4).
Port of London Act 1968 (c xxxii)	In section 2, the definition of "arrestable offence". Section 170.
Employment Agencies Act 1973 (c 35)	In section 13(7)(*f*), the words ", the Service Authority for the National Criminal Intelligence Service, the Service Authority for the National Crime Squad".
House of Commons Disqualification Act 1975 (c 24)	Section 1(1)(da). In Schedule 1, in Part 2, the entries relating to the Service Authorities for the National Crime Squad and the National Criminal Intelligence Service.
Northern Ireland Assembly Disqualification Act 1975 (c 25)	Section 1(1)(da). In Schedule 1, in Part 2, the entries relating to the Service Authorities for the National Crime Squad and the National Criminal Intelligence Service.
Sex Discrimination Act 1975 (c 65)	In section 17(7), in the definition of "chief officer of police", paragraph (aa), in the definition of "police authority", paragraph (aa) and, in the definition of "police fund" the words from ", in relation to" (in the second place where they occur) to "the Police Act 1997".
Police Pensions Act 1976 (c 35)	In section 11(5), in paragraph (*a*) of the definition of "central service", "(ca), (cb),".
Race Relations Act 1976 (c 74)	In section 76B, subsection (1) and, in subsection (2), the word "also". In Schedule 1A, in Part 1, paragraphs 59 and 60 and, in Part 3, the entry relating to the Director General of the National Crime Squad.
Criminal Law Act 1977 (c 45)	Section 6(6). Section 7(6). Section 8(4). Section 9(7). In section 10(5), the words "A constable in uniform,".
Theft Act 1978 (c 31)	Section 3(4).
Health and Safety at Work (Northern Ireland) Order 1978 (SI 1978/1039 (NI 9))	In Article 47A(2), sub-paragraph (*b*).
Animal Health Act 1981 (c 22)	Section 61(1). Section 62(1).
Local Government (Miscellaneous Provisions) Act 1982 (c 30)	In Schedule 3, paragraph 24.
Aviation Security Act 1982 (c 36)	Section 28(3).
Stock Transfer Act 1982 (c 41)	In Schedule 1, in paragraph 7(1), paragraph (bb) and the word "or" before it.
Police and Criminal Evidence Act 1984 (c 60)	Section 5(1A). In section 15(2)(*a*)(i), the word "and" at the end. Section 25. Section 55(14A). In section 66(1)(*a*)(i), the word "or" at the end. Section 116. In section 118(1), the definition of "arrestable offence". In Schedule 1, in paragraph 14(*a*), the words "to which the application relates". Schedule 1A. In Schedule 2, the entries relating to the Military Lands Act 1892 (c 43), the Protection of Animals Act 1911 (c 27), the Public Order Act 1936 (1 Edw 8 & 1 Geo 6 c. 6), the Street Offences Act 1959 (c 57), the Criminal Law Act 1977 (c 45) and the Animal Health Act 1981 (c 22). Schedule 5. In Schedule 6, paragraph 17.
Prosecution of Offences Act 1985 (c 23)	In section 3(3), in the definition of "police force", the words ", the National Crime Squad".
Sporting Events (Control of Alcohol etc) Act 1985 (c 57)	In section 7(2), the words ", and may arrest such a person".
Public Order Act 1986 (c 64)	Section 3(6). Section 4(3). Section 4A(4).

Short title and chapter or title and number	Extent of repeal or revocation
	Section 5(4) and (5).
	Section 12(7).
	Section 13(10).
	Section 14(7).
	Section 14B(4).
	Section 14C(4).
	Section 18(3).
Ministry of Defence Police Act 1987 (c 4)	In section 2B(3), in the definitions of "chief officer" and "relevant force", paragraphs (c) and (d).
Criminal Justice Act 1988 (c 33)	Section 140(1)(a) and (b).
	In Schedule 15, paragraphs 98 and 102.
Road Traffic Act 1988 (c 52)	Section 4(6) to (8).
	In section 124(2), the definitions of "chief officer of police", "police authority" and "police force".
	Section 144(2)(ba).
	Section 163(4).
Road Traffic (Consequential Provisions) Act 1988 (c 54)	In Schedule 3, paragraph 27(5).
Football Spectators Act 1989 (c 37)	Section 2(4).
Aviation and Maritime Security Act 1990 (c 31)	In section 22(4)(b), sub-paragraph (iii) and the word "or" before it.
	In Schedule 3, paragraph 8.
Football (Offences) Act 1991 (c 19)	Section 5(1).
Road Traffic Act 1991 (c 40)	In Schedule 4, paragraph 39.
Local Government Finance Act 1992 (c 14)	In section 43(7)(b), ", (5A)".
Transport and Works Act 1992 (c 42)	Section 30(1) and (3).
	Section 40.
Trade Union and Labour Relations (Consolidation) Act 1992 (c 52)	Section 241(3).
Tribunals and Inquiries Act 1992 (c 53)	In section 7(2), after "36A", "(a) or (b)".
	In Schedule 1, in paragraph 36A, "(a)" and sub-paragraph (b).
Criminal Justice and Public Order Act 1994 (c 33)	Section 61(5).
	Section 62B(4).
	Section 63(8).
	Section 65(5).
	Section 68(4).
	Section 69(5).
	Section 76(7).
	Section 85(1), (2) and (3).
	Section 155.
	Section 166(4).
	Section 167(7).
	In Schedule 10, paragraph 59.
Drug Trafficking Act 1994 (c 37)	In Schedule 1, paragraph 9 and, in paragraph 25, the words "section 9(6) of" and the words after "1990".
Criminal Appeal Act 1995 (c 35)	In section 22(2), in paragraph (a), the words ", the National Crime Squad", paragraph (b)(ii) and paragraphs (d) and (e).
Criminal Procedure (Consequential Provisions) (Scotland) Act 1995 (c 40)	In Schedule 4, paragraph 76(2).
Disability Discrimination Act 1995 (c 50)	In the section 64A inserted by the Disability Discrimination Act 1995 (Amendment) Regulations 2003 (SI 2003/1673), in subsection (7), in the definitions of "chief officer of police", "police authority" and "police fund", paragraph (b).
Reserve Forces Act 1996 (c 14)	In Schedule 2, paragraph 2(1).
Police Act 1996 (c 16)	Section 23(8).
	Section 24(5).
	In section 54(2), the words "the National Criminal Intelligence Service and the National Crime Squad".
	Section 55(7).
	Section 59(8).
	Section 60(2A).
	Section 61(1)(aa) and (ba).
	In section 62, subsection (1)(aa) and (ab), the subsection (1A) inserted by paragraph 82(2) of Schedule 9 to the Police Act 1997, and subsections (1B) and (1C).
	In section 63, subsections (1A) and (1B).
	In section 64, subsections (4A) and (4B).
	In section 88(5)(b), the words "or section 23 of the Police Act 1997".
	In section 89(4)(a), the words "or by a member of the National Crimina Intelligence Service or of the National Crime Squad".
	Section 97(1)(ca) and (cb).

Short title and chapter or title and number	*Extent of repeal or revocation*
	In section 98, in subsections (2) and (3), the words "or the Director General of the National Crime Squad" and "or the National Crime Squad", subsection (3A), in subsection (4) the words "or the National Crime Squad" and "or the Director General of the National Crime Squad", in subsection (5) the words "or the National Crime Squad" (in both places) and "or the Director General of the National Crime Squad" and subsection (6A).
Employment Rights Act 1996 (c 18)	Section 50(2)(ca).
Offensive Weapons Act 1996 (c 26)	Section 1(1).
Public Order (Amendment) Act 1996 (c 59)	The whole Act.
Juries (Northern Ireland) Order 1996 (SI 1996/1141 (NI 6))	In Schedule 2, the entry relating to members of the National Criminal Intelligence Service, members of the Service Authority for the National Criminal Intelligence Service and persons employed by the Authority.
Employment Rights (Northern Ireland) Order 1996 (SI 1996/1919 (NI 16))	Article 67KA(3)(b).
	Article 72A(2)(b).
	Article 169A(2)(b).
Confiscation of Alcohol (Young Persons) Act 1997 (c 33)	Section 1(5).
Police (Health and Safety) Act 1997 (c 42)	In section 5(3), in the definition of "relevant authority" paragraphs (c) and (d), in the definition of "relevant fund" paragraphs (b) and (c) and, in the definition of "responsible officer", paragraph (b).
Police Act 1997 (c 50)	Sections 1 to 87.
	Sections 89 and 90.
	In section 93(6), paragraphs (d) and (e).
	In section 94, in subsection (1) paragraph (c) and the word "or" before it and subsections (3) and (4)(c).
	In section 111, in subsection (1), paragraphs (c) and (d), in subsection (2), paragraphs (d) and (e) and, in subsection (3), paragraphs (c) and (d).
	Section 113.
	Section 115.
	In section 125 as it applies to Scotland, subsection (3) and, in subsection (4), the words "to which subsection (3) does not apply".
	In section 137(2), paragraphs (b) and (c).
	Schedules 1 to 2A.
	In Schedule 9, paragraphs 1, 4 to 6, 11, 14(b), 15, 16, 20, 26, 29(2), 30(2), 31, 44, 46 to 48, 54, 58 to 62, 69, 70, 71(2)(a), (c), (d) and (3), 73, 74, 76, 77, 79 to 84, 86(3) and (4), 87, 88 and 92.
Police (Health and Safety) (Northern Ireland) Order 1997 (SI 1997/1774 (NI 6))	In Article 7(3), in the definition of "the relevant authority", sub-paragraph (b), in the definition of "the relevant fund", sub-paragraph (a) and, in the definition of "the responsible officer", sub-paragraph (b).
Police (Northern Ireland) Act 1998 (c 32)	Section 27(1)(b).
	In section 42, in subsection (1) ", (3)", and subsection (7).
	In Schedule 4, paragraph 22.
Crime and Disorder Act 1998 (c 37)	In section 1C, subsections (6) to (8).
	Section 27(1).
	Section 31(2) and (3).
	Section 113.
Protection of Children Act 1999 (c 14)	Section 8.
Terrorism Act 2000 (c 11)	In Schedule 15, paragraph 5(11).
Care Standards Act 2000 (c 14)	Section 90.
	Section 102.
	Section 104.
	In Schedule 4, paragraph 25.
Regulation of Investigatory Powers Act 2000 (c 23)	In section 33, in subsection (1) the words ", the National Criminal Intelligence Service or the National Crime Squad" and ", Service or Squad", in subsection (3) the words ", the National Criminal Intelligence Service or the National Crime Squad" and (in both places) ", Service or Squad" and, in subsection (6), in paragraph (e) the words "and also of the National Criminal Intelligence Service" and paragraph (f).
	In section 34, subsections (5) and (6)(c).
	In section 45(6), paragraphs (d) and (e).
	In section 56(1), in the definition of "chief officer of police", paragraphs (j) and (k)
	Section 75(6)(b).
	In section 76A(11)(c) the words "the National Crime Squad or".
	In Schedule 1, paragraph 27D and the cross-heading before it.
	In Schedule 4, paragraph 8(4)(c) and (5).

Short title and chapter or title and number	Extent of repeal or revocation
	Football (Disorder) Act 2000 (c 25)
	Section 2.
	In Schedule 2, paragraph 2.
Police (Northern Ireland) Act 2000 (c 32)	In Schedule 6, in paragraph 20, sub-paragraphs (4) to (7).
Freedom of Information Act 2000 (c 36)	In section 23(3), the word "and" at the end of paragraph (*k*).
	In Schedule 1, in Part 6, the entries relating to the National Crime Squad and the Service Authority for the National Crime Squad.
Criminal Justice and Court Services Act 2000 (c 43)	In Schedule 7, paragraph 77.
Health and Social Care Act 2001 (c 15)	Section 19.
Criminal Justice and Police Act 2001 (c 16)	Section 42(8).
	Section 47(3).
	In section 104, subsection (3), in subsection (4) paragraph (*c*) and the word "and" before it, and subsection (8).
	In section 107, subsections (1)(*c*) and (4).
	Sections 108 to 121.
	Section 138(6)(*d*).
	In Schedule 4, paragraph 7(3)(*b*).
	Schedule 5.
	In Schedule 6, paragraphs 1 to 21, 55, 56, 60, 61 and 77.
Anti-terrorism, Crime and Security Act 2001 (c 24)	Section 39(8).
Regulation of Care (Scotland) Act 2001 (asp 8)	In Schedule 3, paragraph 21.
International Development Act 2002 (c 1)	In Schedule 3, paragraphs 3(3), 11(3) and 12(3).
National Health Service Reform and Health Care Professions Act 2002 (c 17)	In Schedule 2, paragraph 64.
Proceeds of Crime Act 2002 (c 29)	In section 313(1), paragraphs (*c*) and (*d*).
	In section 330, subsection (5)(*b*), and, in subsection (9)(*b*), the words after "employment".
	Section 331(5)(*b*).
	In section 332(1) and (3), "337 or".
	Section 332(5)(*b*).
	In section 337(5)(*b*), the words after "employment".
	In section 338, subsection (1)(*b*) (except the word "and" at the end) and, in subsection (5)(*b*), the words after "employment".
	Section 339(5) and (6).
	In section 447(3)(*a*), the word "or" at the end.
	In Schedule 11, paragraphs 3(3), 14(4), 30(3) and (4) and 34(3) and (4).
Police Reform Act 2002 (c 30)	Section 8.
	In section 9(3)(*e*) the words "is or".
	In section 10, in subsection (1), at the end of paragraph (*e*) the word "and", in paragraph (*f*) the words "the National Criminal Intelligence Service, the National Crime Squad and", in subsection (3), paragraph (*a*) and, in paragraph (*d*), the words "the National Criminal Intelligence Service, the National Crime Squad or" and, in subsection (7), the word "or" at the end of paragraph (*a*).
	In section 15(6), the words from "or, as the case may be" to the end of the subsection.
	Section 25.
	In section 38, subsection (3), in subsection (4) the words "or a Director General" and, in subsection (7), the words "or of a Service Authority".
	Section 42(4) and (8).
	In section 45, in subsection (1) the words "and by Directors General", in subsection (3) paragraphs (*a*), (*b*), (*d*) and (*e*) and, in subsection (5), the words "or a Director General".
	In section 47(1), the definitions of "Director General" and "Service Authority".
	Section 48.
	Section 49(1).
	In section 82, subsection (1)(*c*) and (*f*), in subsection (2), paragraph (*c*) and the word "or" before it, subsection (3)(*d*) and subsection (5).
	Sections 85 to 91.
	Section 93.
	In section 102, in subsection (2), paragraphs (*c*) and (*d*) and, in subsection (5), paragraphs (*b*) and (*c*).
	In section 103, subsections (2) and (3) and, in subsection (6), the words ", the NCIS service fund or the NCS service fund,".
	Section 108(7)(*e*).
	Schedule 1.

Short title and chapter or title and number	Extent of repeal or revocation
	In Schedule 4, paragraph 2(5)(*a*) and (7), and in paragraph 36(1), paragraph (*b*) and the word "and" before it.
	In Schedule 5, in paragraph 1(2)(aa), the words "except in respect of an offence under section 12 of the Licensing Act 1872 or section 91 of the Criminal Justice Act 1967".
	Schedule 6.
	In Schedule 7, paragraphs 16, 17, 19(2) and (3), 21 and 22(2).
Education Act 2002 (c 32)	Part 2 of Schedule 12.
	In Schedule 13, paragraphs 7 and 8.
	In Schedule 21, paragraphs 72 and 73.
Adoption and Children Act 2002 (c 38)	Section 135.
	In Schedule 3, paragraph 93.
Licensing Act 2003 (c 17)	In Schedule 6, paragraphs 93 and 116.
Aviation (Offences) Act 2003 (c 19)	Section 1(1).
	Communications Act 2003 (c 21)
	Section 181(1).
Crime (International Co-operation) Act 2003 (c 32)	In section 17(3), the words "the Police and Criminal Evidence Act 1984 (c 60) or (as the case may be)".
	Section 85.
Anti-social Behaviour Act 2003 (c 38)	Section 4(5).
	Section 23(5).
	Section 32(3).
	Section 37(3).
	Courts Act 2003 (c 39)
	In Schedule 8, paragraphs 12 and 281(2).
Sexual Offences Act 2003 (c 42)	In Schedule 6, paragraph 28(3) and (4).
Criminal Justice Act 2003 (c 44)	Section 3.
	In Schedule 35, paragraphs 3 and 4.
Protection of Children (Scotland) Act 2003 (asp 5)	Section 12.
Criminal Justice (Scotland) Act 2003 (asp 7)	Section 70(3).
Protection of Children and Vulnerable Adults (Northern Ireland) Order 2003 (SI 2003/417 (NI 4))	Article 17(4) to (6).
	Article 47(3) to (5).
Energy Act 2004 (c 20)	In section 59(3), in the definition of "chief officer", paragraphs (*c*) and (*d*) and, in the definition of "relevant force", paragraphs (*c*) and (*d*).
	In Schedule 14, paragraph 11(*b*).
Domestic Violence, Crime and Victims Act 2004 (c 28)	Section 10(1).
	In Schedule 10, paragraph 24.
Hunting Act 2004 (c 37)	Section 7.
Prevention of Terrorism Act 2005 (c 2)	Section 9(9).
Serious Organised Crime and Police Act 2005 (c 15)	Section 112(6) and (7).
	Section 126(2) and (3).
	Section 130(1).
	Section 136(5).

Violent Crime Reduction Act 2006[1]

(2006 c 38)

PART 1[2]
ALCOHOL-RELATED VIOLENCE AND DISORDER

CHAPTER 1[3]
Drinking Banning Orders

Introductory

1–4604   **1. Drinking banning orders.**   (1) A drinking banning order is an order that prohibits the individual against whom it is made ("the subject") from doing the things described in the order.

(2) Such an order may impose any prohibition on the subject which is necessary for the purpose of protecting other persons from criminal or disorderly conduct[4] by the subject while he is under the influence of alcohol.

(3) The prohibitions imposed by such an order must include such prohibition as the court making it considers necessary, for that purpose, on the subject's entering—

    (*a*) premises in respect of which there is a premises licence[5] authorising the use of the premises for the sale of alcohol by retail; and

    (*b*) premises in respect of which there is a club premises certificate[5] authorising the use of the premises for the supply of alcohol to members or guests.

(4) A drinking banning order may not impose a prohibition on the subject that prevents him—

(*a*) from having access to a place where he resides;

(*b*) from attending at any place which he is required to attend for the purposes of any employment of his or of any contract of services to which he is a party;

(*c*) from attending at any place which he is expected to attend during the period for which the order has effect for the purposes of education or training or for the purpose of receiving medical treatment; or

(*d*) from attending at any place which he is required to attend by any obligation imposed on him by or under an enactment or by the order of a court or tribunal.

(5) Expressions used in subsection (3) and in the Licensing Act 2003 (c 17) or in a Part of that Act have the same meanings in that subsection as in that Act or Part.

[Violent Crime Reduction Act 2006, s 1.]

---

1. The Violent Crime Reduction Act 2006 is reproduced partly in PART I and partly in PART VIII of this Manual. For the provisions of the Act which are not printed in this PART, reference should be made to the following: ss 28–41, 49–51 and Sch 1, in the title FIREARMS, post; ss 42–48 in the title OFFENSIVE WEAPONS, post; ss 52–53; Sch 3 in the title PUBLIC MEETING AND PUBLIC ORDER and ss 54–58 and Sch 4 in the title SEXUAL OFFENCES, in PART VIII, post.

This Act is brought into effect in accordance with s 66, post, and orders made thereunder, see post.

2. Part 1 comprises ss 1–27.

3. Chapter 1 comprises ss 1–14.

4. This includes protecting their property from unlawful loss or damage, see s 14(2), post.

5. For "premises licence" and "club premises certificate", see the Licensing Act 2003, in PART VIII: title LOCAL GOVERNMENT, post.

1–4604A   2. Duration of drinking banning orders.   (1) A drinking banning order has effect for a period specified in the order ("the specified period"), which must be not less than two months and not more than two years.

(2) A drinking banning order may provide that different prohibitions contained in the order have effect for different periods; but, in each case, the period ("the prohibition period") must be not less than two months and not more than two years.

(3) A drinking banning order may include provision for—

(*a*) the order, or

(*b*) a prohibition contained in it,

to cease to have effect before the end of the specified period or the prohibition period if the subject satisfactorily completes the approved course specified in the order.

(4) Provision under subsection (3) must fix the time at which the order or the prohibition will cease to have effect if the subject satisfactorily completes the specified approved course as whichever is the later of—

(*a*) the time specified in the order in accordance with subsection (5); and

(*b*) the time when he does satisfactorily complete that course.

(5) The time specified for the purposes of subsection (4)(*a*) must be a time after the expiry of at least half the specified period or (as the case may be) the prohibition period.

(6) Provision under subsection (3) may be included in a drinking banning order only if—

(*a*) the court making the order is satisfied that a place on the specified approved course will be available for the subject; and

(*b*) the subject has agreed to the inclusion of the provision in question in the order.

(7) Before making provision under subsection (3), the court must inform the subject in ordinary language (whether in writing or otherwise) about—

(*a*) the effect of including the provision in the order;

(*b*) what, in general terms, attendance on the course will involve if he undertakes it;

(*c*) any fees he will be required to pay for the course if he undertakes it; and

(*d*) when he will have to pay any such fees.

(8) Where a court makes a drinking banning order which does not include provision under subsection (3), it must give its reasons for not including such provision in open court.

(9) The Secretary of State may by regulations amend subsection (5) so as to modify the earliest time (after the completion of the specified approved course) when by virtue of that subsection—

(*a*) a drinking banning order, or

(*b*) a prohibition contained in such an order,

may cease to have effect.

[Violent Crime Reduction Act 2006, s 2.]

Orders made on application

1–4604B   3. Orders on an application to magistrates' court.   (1) An application to a magistrates' court for the making of a drinking banning order against an individual may be made by a relevant authority if—

(*a*) it appears to the authority that the conditions in subsection (2) are satisfied with respect to the individual; and (*b*)   the individual is aged 16 or over.

(2)   The conditions are—

(*a*)   that the individual has, after the commencement of this section, engaged in criminal or disorderly conduct while under the influence of alcohol; and

(*b*)   that such an order is necessary to protect other persons from further conduct by him of that kind while he is under the influence of alcohol.

(3)   An application under this section to a magistrates' court has to be made by complaint.

(4)   Before making an application under this section, a relevant authority must consult the appropriate persons.

(5)   If, on an application under this section with respect to an individual, it is proved that the conditions in subsection (2) are satisfied in his case, the magistrates' court may make a drinking banning order against him.

(6)   Nothing in this section affects the operation of section 127 of the Magistrates' Courts Act 1980 (c 43) (limitation of time in respect of informations laid or complaints made in magistrates' court).

[Violent Crime Reduction Act 2006, s 3.]

4. Orders in county court proceedings

Chapter 2[1]
Alcohol Disorder Zones

1–4604C   15. Power to impose charges on licence holders etc in zones.   *Secretary may, by regulations, make provision for the imposition by a local authority of charges to be paid to the authority by those who hold premises licences and club premises certificates for the sale or supply of alcohol.*

---

1. Chapter 2 comprises ss 15–20.

1–4604D   16. Designation of alcohol disorder zones.   (1) A local authority may by order designate a locality in their area as an alcohol disorder zone if they are satisfied—

(*a*)   that there has been nuisance or annoyance to members of the public, or a section of the public, or disorder, in or near that locality;

(*b*)   that the nuisance, annoyance or disorder is associated with the consumption of alcohol in that locality or with the consumption of alcohol supplied at premises in that locality;

(*c*)   that there is likely to be a repetition of nuisance, annoyance or disorder that is so associated; and

(*d*)   that subsection (8) allows the making of the order.

(2)   Before designating a locality as an alcohol disorder zone, a local authority must publish a notice—

(*a*)   setting out their proposal to designate the locality; and

(*b*)   inviting persons interested to make representations about the proposal, and about what might be included in the action plan under subsection (4).

(3)   That notice must require the representations to be made before the end of the period of 28 days beginning with the day after publication of the notice.

(4)   As soon as reasonably practicable after the end of the period for making representations about a proposal by a local authority to designate a locality, the local authority and the local chief officer of police must—

(*a*)   prepare a document ("the action plan") setting out the steps the taking of which would, in their opinion, make the designation of the locality unnecessary;

(*b*)   publish the action plan in such manner as they consider appropriate for bringing it to the attention of persons likely to be interested in it; and

(*c*)   send a copy of the plan to every person who holds—

(i)   a premises licence authorising the use of premises in the locality for the sale of alcohol by retail; or

(ii)   a club premises certificate by virtue of which authorisation is given to the use of premises in the locality for the supply of alcohol to members or guests.

(5)   The steps set out in the action plan may include the establishment and maintenance of a scheme for the making of payments to the local authority.

(6)   The action plan must also contain proposals by—

(*a*)   the local authority in whose area the locality to which the proposed designation relates is situated, and

(*b*)   the local chief officer of police,

about what action they will take in relation to that locality if the plan is implemented.

(7)   The power of the Secretary of State to make regulations under subsection (2) of section 15 shall be exercisable in relation to sums received by a local authority in accordance with a scheme established under an action plan as it is exercisable in relation to sums received by a local authority in respect of charges imposed by virtue of regulations under that section.

(c)   after subsection (4) insert—

"(4A) This subsection applies to an order under section 147A(9) if it appears to the Secretary of State that the power to make the order is being exercised for purposes that are not confined to the increase of the maximum fine to take account of changes in the value of money."

(4) A sale of alcohol is not to count for the purposes of the offence under section 147A of the Licensing Act 2003 (c 17) if it took place before the commencement of this section.

[Violent Crime Reduction Act 2006, s 23.]

1–4604L 24. Closure notices for persistently selling alcohol to children.   (1) *Inserts ss 169A and 169B into the Licensing Act 2003.*

(2) In subsection (1) of section 170 of that Act (exemptions from liability)—

(a)   for "A constable is not" substitute "Neither a constable nor a trading standards officer is"; and

(b)   at the end insert "or of his functions in relation to a closure notice".

(3) For subsection (2) of that section substitute—

"(2) Neither a chief officer of police nor a local weights and measures authority is liable for relevant damages in respect of any act or omission of a person in the performance or purported performance, while under the direction or control of such a chief officer or local weights and measures authority—

(a)   of a function of that person in relation to a closure order, or any extension of it; or

(b)   of a function in relation to a closure notice."

(4) After subsection (4) of that section insert—

"(4A) In this section references to a constable include references to a person exercising the powers of a constable by virtue of a designation under section 38 of the Police Reform Act 2002 (community support officers etc); and, in relation to such a person, the first reference in subsection (2) to a chief officer of police has effect as a reference to a police authority."

(5) In section 171(5) of that Act (expressions defined for the purposes of Part 8),

(a)   after the definition of "appropriate person" insert—

""closure notice" has the meaning given in section 169A;"

(b)   after the definition of "extension" insert—

""local weights and measures authority' has the meaning given by section 69 of the Weights and Measures Act 1985;"

(c)   after the definition of "senior police officer" insert—

""trading standards officer", in relation to any premises to which a premises licence relates, means a person authorised by a local weights and measures authority to act in the area where those premises are situated in relation to proposed prohibitions contained in closure notices;".

(6) In Part 1 of Schedule 4 to the Police Reform Act 2002 (c 30) (powers of community support officers), after paragraph 5 insert—

"Power to serve closure notice for licensed premises persistently selling to children

5A.   Where a designation applies this paragraph to any person, that person shall have—

(a)   within the relevant police area, and

(b)   if it appears to him as mentioned in subsection (7) of section 169A of the Licensing Act 2003 (closure notices served on licensed premises persistently serving children),

the capacity of a constable under that subsection to be the person by whose delivery of a closure notice that notice is served."

[Violent Crime Reduction Act 2006, s 24.]

Door supervision at licensed premises

1–4604M 25. Mandatory premises licence condition: door supervision.   (1) Section 21 of the Licensing Act 2003 (c 17) (mandatory condition: door supervision) is amended as follows.

(2) In subsection (1) for "be licensed by the Security Industry Authority" substitute

"—

(a)   be authorised to carry out that activity by a licence granted under the Private Security Industry Act 2001; or

(b)   be entitled to carry out that activity by virtue of section 4 of that Act."

(3) In subsection (3) in paragraph (a), at the end insert "and which is licensable conduct for the purposes of that Act (see section 3(2) of that Act)".

[Violent Crime Reduction Act 2006, s 25.]

Alcohol related disorder in public places

1–4604N 26. Designated public places.   (1) Section 14 of the Criminal Justice and Police Act 2001 (c 16) (places which are not designated public places) is amended as follows.

(2) In subsection (1)—

(a) for paragraph (a) substitute—

"(a) premises in respect of which a premises licence has effect which authorises the premises to be used for the sale or supply of alcohol;

(aa) premises in respect of which a club premises certificate has effect which certifies that the premises may be used by the club for the sale or supply of alcohol;"

(b) in paragraph (b), after "(a)" insert "or (aa)";

(c) in paragraph (c), for "20" substitute "30".

(3) After subsection (1) insert—

"(1A) Subsection (1B) applies to premises falling within subsection (1)(a) if—

(a) the premises licence is held by a local authority in whose area the premises or part of the premises is situated; or

(b) the premises licence is held by another person but the premises are occupied by such an authority or are managed by or on behalf of such an authority.

(1B) Subsection (1) prevents premises to which this subsection applies from being, or being part of, a designated public place only—

(a) at times when it is being used for the sale or supply of alcohol; and

(b) at times falling within 30 minutes after the end of a period during which it has been so used.

(1C) In this section "premises licence and "club premises certificate" have the same meaning as in the Licensing Act 2003."

[Violent Crime Reduction Act 2006, s 26.]

1–4604O   27. Directions to individuals who represent a risk of disorder. (1) If the test in subsection (2) is satisfied in the case of an individual aged 16 or over who is in a public place, a constable in uniform may give a direction to that individual—

(a) requiring him to leave the locality of that place; and

(b) prohibiting the individual from returning to that locality for such period (not exceeding 48 hours) from the giving of the direction as the constable may specify.

(2) That test is—

(a) that the presence of the individual in that locality is likely, in all the circumstances, to cause or to contribute to the occurrence of alcohol-related crime or disorder in that locality, or to cause or to contribute to a repetition or continuance there of such crime or disorder; and

(b) that the giving of a direction under this section to that individual is necessary for the purpose of removing or reducing the likelihood of there being such crime or disorder in that locality during the period for which the direction has effect or of there being a repetition or continuance in that locality during that period of such crime or disorder.

(3) A direction under this section—

(a) must be given in writing;

(b) may require the individual to whom it is given to leave the locality in question either immediately or by such time as the constable giving the direction may specify;

(c) must clearly identify the locality to which it relates;

(d) must specify the period for which the individual is prohibited from returning to that locality;

(e) may impose requirements as to the manner in which that individual leaves the locality, including his route; and

(f) may be withdrawn or varied (but not extended so as to apply for a period of more than 48 hours) by a constable.

(4) A constable may not give a direction under this section that prevents the individual to whom it is given—

(a) from having access to a place where he resides;

(b) from attending at any place which he is required to attend for the purposes of any employment of his or of any contract of services to which he is a party;

(c) from attending at any place which he is expected to attend during the period to which the direction applies for the purposes of education or training or for the purpose of receiving medical treatment; or

(d) from attending at any place which he is required to attend by any obligation imposed on him by or under an enactment or by the order of a court or tribunal.

(5) A constable who gives a direction under this section must make a record of—

(a) the terms of the direction and the locality to which it relates;

(b) the individual to whom it is given;

(c) the time at which it is given;

(d) the period during which that individual is required not to return to the locality.

(6) A person who fails to comply with a direction under this section is guilty of an offence and shall be liable, on summary conviction, to a fine not exceeding level 4 on the standard scale.

(7) In section 64A of the Police and Criminal Evidence Act 1984 (c 60) (power to photograph suspects), in subsection (1B), after paragraph (*c*) insert—

"(ca) given a direction by a constable under section 27 of the Violent Crime Reduction Act 2006;".

(8) In this section "public place" means—

(*a*) a highway; or

(*b*) any place to which at the material time the public or any section of the public has access, on payment or otherwise, as of right or by virtue of express or implied permission;

and for this purpose "place" includes a place on a means of transport.

[Violent Crime Reduction Act 2006, s 27.]

PART 3[1]

MISCELLANEOUS

Other

1–4604P 59. Limitation period for anti-social behaviour orders.   (1) In section 1 of the Crime and Disorder Act 1998 (c 37) (anti-social behaviour orders), after subsection (5) insert—

"(5A) Nothing in this section affects the operation of section 127 of the Magistrates' Courts Act 1980 (limitation of time in respect of informations laid or complaints made in magistrates' court)."

(2) In Article 3 of the Anti-Social Behaviour (Northern Ireland) Order 2004 (SI 2004/1988 (NI 12)) (anti-social behaviour orders), after paragraph (4) insert—

"(4A) Nothing in this Article affects the operation of Article 78 of the Magistrates' Courts (Northern Ireland) Order 1981 (limitation of time in respect of complaints made in courts of summary jurisdiction)."

[Violent Crime Reduction Act 2006, s 59.]

---

1. Part 3 comprises ss 52–63 and Schs 3 and 4.

1–4604Q 60. Parenting orders.   (1) The Crime and Disorder Act 1998 is amended as follows.

(2) In section 8 (parenting orders)—

(*a*) in subsections (1)(*b*) and (6)(*a*) for "sex offender order" substitute "sexual offences prevention order"; and

(*b*) after subsection (8) insert—

"(9) In this section "sexual offences prevention order" means an order under section 104 of the Sexual Offences Act 2003 (sexual offences prevention orders)."

(3) In section 18(1) (interpretation etc of Chapter 1 of Part 1), omit the definition of "sex offender order".

(4) The amendments made by subsection (2) have effect in relation to court proceedings in which an order under section 104 of the Sexual Offences Act 2003 (c 42) is made before the passing of this Act, as well as those in which such an order is made after that.

[Violent Crime Reduction Act 2006, s 60.]

1–4604R 61. Committal of young persons of unruly character.   In section 23(1) of the Children and Young Persons Act 1969 (c 54) (remand to local authority accommodation etc of young persons of unruly character)—

(*a*) in paragraph (*a*), for "commits him for trial or" substitute "sends him for trial or commits him for";

(*b*) for "the remand or committal", substitute "the remand, sending or committal";

(*c*) for "a reference to a committal", substitute "a reference to such a sending or a committal".

[Violent Crime Reduction Act 2006, s 61.]

1–4604S 62. Offering or agreeing to re-programme a mobile telephone.   In section 1(1) of the Mobile Telephones (Re-programming) Act 2002 (c 31) (offence of re-programming mobile telephone etc), omit "or" at the end of paragraph (*a*) and after paragraph (*b*) insert—

"(*c*) he offers or agrees to change, or interfere with the operation of, a unique device identifier, or

(*d*) he offers or agrees to arrange for another person to change, or interfere with the operation of, a unique device identifier."

[Violent Crime Reduction Act 2006, s 62.]

1–4604T 63. Removal of sports grounds etc from private security industry regulation.   In section 4 of the Private Security Industry Act 2001 (c 12) (exemptions from licensing requirement) after subsection (5) insert—

"(6) A relevant employee who engages in licensable conduct shall not be guilty of an offence under section 3 in respect of that conduct if it is carried out in connection with the use of a certified sports ground or certified sports stand for purposes for which its safety certificate has effect.

(7) An employee for a visiting team who engages in licensable conduct shall not be guilty of an offence under section 3 in respect of that conduct if—

(a) it is carried out in connection with the use of a certified sports ground or certified sports stand for purposes for which its safety certificate has effect; and

(b) that visiting team is involved in the activities for which the ground is being used, or which the stand is being used to view.

(8) In subsection (7) a reference to a person being an employee for a visiting team is a reference to his being a relevant employee in relation to the visitors' ground, or in relation to a certified sports stand contained in the visitors' premises.

(9) In this section "a relevant employee", in relation to a certified sports ground or certified sports stand, means a person employed by—

(a) the holder of its safety certificate;

(b) a person who manages the ground or stand or occupies the premises where it is or owns an interest in those premises;

(c) a company which is in the same group as a company falling within paragraph (b).

(10) In this section a reference to the use of a certified sports ground for purposes for which the safety certificate has effect is a reference to—

(a) the use of the ground for activities specified in a general safety certificate in force in respect of the use of that ground; or

(b) the use of the ground, on an occasion specified in a special safety certificate which is so in force, for activities specified in that certificate.

(11) In this section a reference to the use of a certified sports stand for purposes for which the safety certificate has effect is a reference to—

(a) the use of the stand for viewing activities specified in a general safety certificate in force in respect of the use of that stand; or

(b) the use of the stand, on an occasion specified in a special safety certificate which is so in force, for viewing activities specified in that certificate.

(12) In this section—

"certified sports ground" means a sports ground in respect of which a safety certificate is in force;

"certified sports stand" means a sports stand in respect of which a safety certificate is in force;

"company", "holding company" and "subsidiary" have the same meanings as in section 736 of the Companies Act 1985 (c 6);

"group", in relation to a company, means a holding company and all of its subsidiaries;

"safety certificate", "general safety certificate" and "special safety certificate"—

(a) in relation to a sports ground, have the same meanings as in the Safety of Sports Grounds Act 1975 (see sections 1(4) and 17(1) of that Act); and

(b) in relation to a sports stand, have the same meanings as in Part 3 of the Fire Safety and Safety of Places of Sport Act 1987 (see section 26(2) and (11) of that Act);

"sports ground" has the same meaning as in that Act of 1975 (see section 17(1) of that Act);

"sports stand" means a stand within the meaning of Part 3 of that Act of 1987 (see section 26(11) of that Act);

"visiting team", in relation to a certified sports ground ("the home ground") or a certified sports stand contained in any premises ("the home premises") means a team which uses as its base, or as one of its bases, any premises which are either—

(a) a certified sports ground which is not the home ground ("the visitors' ground"); or

(b) premises which are not the home premises and which contain a certified sports stand ("the visitors' premises");

"visitors' ground" and "visitors' premises", in relation to a visiting team, have the meanings given by the previous definition."

[Violent Crime Reduction Act 2006, s 63.]

PART 4[1]
GENERAL

64. Expenses

65. Repeals

1–4604U   **66. Short title, commencement and extent.**   (1) This Act may be cited as the Violent Crime Reduction Act 2006.

(2) This Act, other than—

(a) this section;

(b) section 25;

(c) section 56;

(*d*)   section 60 and the repeal in section 18(1) of the Crime and Disorder Act 1998 (c 37); and
(*e*)   section 63,

shall come into force on such day as the relevant national authority may by order[2] made by statutory instrument appoint; and different days may be appointed for different purposes, including different areas.

(3)–(8) *Commencement orders may be made by the Secretary of State, National Assembly for Wale; extent.*
[Violent Crime Reduction Act 2006, s 66.]

---

1. Part 4 comprises ss 64–66 and Sch 5.
2. The following commencement order has been made: (No 1) SI 2007/74 which brought into force ss 42, 54, 55, 57 and Sch 4 on 12 February 2007.

1–4604V

Section 65

SCHEDULE 5
REPEALS

Short title and chapter	Extent of repeal
Firearms Act 1968 (c 27)	In section 3(1)(*a*), the word "or" at the end. Section 23(4). In section 40(2), the words from "to firearms" to "therein". In section 51A(1)(*a*)(i), the word "or" at the end. In Part 1 of Schedule 6, the entry for section 23(4). In paragraph 7 of Part 2 of Schedule 6, the words "or (4)". In paragraph 8 of Part 2 of Schedule 6, the words "or (4)" in the second place they appear.
Licensed Premises (Exclusion of Certain Persons) Act 1980 (c 32)	The whole Act.
Magistrates' Courts Act 1980 (c 43)	In section 24(1B), the "or" at the end of paragraph (*a*).
Mental Health Act 1983 (c 20)	In section 37(1A), the "or" at the end of paragraph (*b*).
Criminal Justice Act 1988 (c 33)	In section 36(2)(*b*), the "or" at the end of sub-paragraph (ii). Section 141(3).
Football Spectators Act 1989 (c 37)	In section 1— (*a*) subsection (3); (*b*) in subsection (4), paragraph (*b*) and the word "and" immediately preceding it; (*c*) subsections (5) and (8A). Sections 2 to 7. In section 10— (*a*) in subsection (8), paragraph (*c*) and the word "or" immediately preceding it; (*b*) in subsection (12), paragraph (*b*). In section 14A(4C), the word "But". In section 14E— (*a*) in subsection (3), the words ", unless it appears to the court that there are exceptional circumstances,"; (*b*) subsection (4).In section 19(2B)(*b*), the words "and the order imposes a requirement as to the surrender by him of his passport". In section 22A(1), the definition of "declaration of relevance". In Schedule 1, in paragraph 1(*a*), "2(1), 5(7)".In section 27— (*a*) in subsection (4), the words "section 3 or"; (*b*) subsection (5).
Criminal Justice Act 1991 (c 53)	In Schedule 11, paragraph 23.
Criminal Justice and Public Order Act 1994 (c 33)	In section 166— (*a*) in subsection (2)(*a*), the words "by the home club or"; (*b*) in subsection (7)(*b*), the words "the home club or". In the table in Part 3 of Schedule 8, the entry relating to offences under section 19 of the Firearms Act 1968 (c 27).
Criminal Procedure (Consequential Provisions) (Scotland) Act 1995 (c 40)	In Schedule 4, paragraph 29.
Data Protection Act 1998 (c 29)	In Schedule 15, paragraph 9.
Crime and Disorder Act 1998 (c 37)	In section 18(1), the definition of "sex offender order". In section 51A(12), the "or" at the end of paragraph (*b*).
Football (Offences and Disorder) Act 1999 (c 21)	Section 2(3).
Access to Justice Act 1999 (c 22)	In Schedule 13— (*a*) paragraph 94; (*b*) in paragraph 158, the words "7(7)(*b*) and".
Powers of Criminal Courts (Sentencing) Act 2000 (c 6)	In section 164(3), the "or" at the end of paragraph (*b*). In Schedule 9, paragraph 60.
Football (Disorder) Act 2000 (c 25)	Section 5(2). In Schedule 2, paragraphs 12, 13 and 20.
Football (Disorder) (Amendment) Act 2002 (c 12)	The whole Act.
Mobile Telephones (Re-programming) Act 2002 (c 31)	In section 1(1)(*a*), the word "or" at the end.

Short title and chapter	Extent of repeal
Licensing Act 2003 (c 17)	In Schedule 6, paragraph 74.
Anti-social Behaviour Act 2003 (c 38)	Section 37(3).
	In section 38, subsections (2), (4), (5)(*a*) to (*c*) and (5)(*e*).
Courts Act 2003 (c 39)	In Schedule 8, the unnumbered paragraph after paragraph 200 and paragraph 331.
Criminal Justice Act 2003 (c 44)	In section 150, the "or" at the end of paragraph (*c*).
	In Schedule 26, paragraphs 27 and 41.

Police and Justice Act 2006
(2006 c 48)

PART 1[1]
POLICE REFORM

National Policing Improvement Agency

1–4605   1. National Policing Improvement Agency

---

1. Part 1 comprises ss 1–9 and Schs 1–5. For commencement of this Act, see s 53 and notes thereto.

Police forces and police authorities

1–4605A   2. Amendments to the Police Act 1996.   Schedule 2 (which makes amendments to the Police Act 1996 (c 16)) has effect.
[Police and Justice Act 2006, s 2.]

Community support officers etc

1–4605B   7. Standard powers and duties of community support officers.   (1) In section 38 of the Police Reform Act 2002 (c 30) (police powers for police authority employees), after subsection (5) there is inserted—

"(5A) A person designated under this section as a community support officer shall also have the standard powers and duties of a community support officer (see section 38A(2))."

(2) *Inserts s 38A into the Police Reform Act 2002.*

1–4605C   8. Community support officers: power to deal with truants.   In Schedule 4 to the Police Reform Act 2002 (exercise of police powers etc by civilians), after paragraph 4B there is inserted—

"Power to remove truants to designated premises etc

4C. Where a designation applies this paragraph to any person, that person shall—

  (*a*)   as respects any area falling within the relevant police area and specified in a direction under section 16(2) of the Crime and Disorder Act 1998, but

  (*b*)   only during the period specified in the direction,

have the powers conferred on a constable by section 16(3) of that Act (power to remove truant found in specified area to designated premises or to the school from which truant is absent)."
[Police and Justice Act 2006, s 8.]

1–4605D   9. Exercise of police powers by civilians.   Schedule 5, which—

makes amendments consequential on section 7 (standard powers and duties of community support officers), and

makes other minor amendments in connection with the exercise of police powers by civilians,

has effect.
[Police and Justice Act 2006, s 9.]

PART 2[1]
POWERS OF POLICE ETC

Police powers

1–4605E   10. Police bail.   Schedule 6, which amends provisions in the Police and Criminal Evidence Act 1984 (c 60) that relate to bail—

  (*a*)   granted by a constable elsewhere than at a police station, or

  (*b*)   granted at a police station,

has effect.
[Police and Justice Act 2006, s 10.]

1. Part 2 comprises ss 10–18 and Schs 6–7.

11. Power to detain pending DPP's decision about charging.   *Amends s 37 of the Police and Criminal Evidence Act 1984.*

12. Power to stop and search at aerodromes.   *Inserts new s 24B into the Aviation Security Act 1982.*

Information from registers of death

1–4605F   **13. Supply of information to police etc by Registrar General.**   *Registrar General may supply information to police, Ministry of Defence Police, British Transport Police, Civil Nuclear Constabulary and the Scottish Crime and Drug Enforcement Agency, Serious Organised Crime Agency or person specified by order.*

Travel and freight information

1–4605G   **14. Information-gathering powers: extension to domestic flights and voyages.**
(1) The Immigration, Asylum and Nationality Act 2006 (c 13) is amended as follows.

(2) In section 32 (police powers to gather information relating to flights and voyages to or from the United Kingdom), in subsection (1) (ships and aircraft to which section applies), for paragraphs (*a*) and (*b*) there is substituted—

> "(*a*) arriving, or expected to arrive, at any place in the United Kingdom (whether from a place in the United Kingdom or from outside the United Kingdom), or
> (*b*) leaving, or expected to leave, from any place in the United Kingdom (whether for a place in the United Kingdom or for outside the United Kingdom)."

(3) In each of section 32(5) (interpretation of section) and section 33(5) (police powers to gather information about freight entering or leaving the United Kingdom: interpretation of section), after paragraph (*c*) there is inserted

> ", and
> (*d*) "ship" includes—
>   (i) every description of vessel used in navigation, and
>   (ii) hovercraft."

(4) In section 36 (duty to share travel and freight information), in subsection (9) (interpretation of section), after the definition of "Revenue and Customs purposes" there is inserted

> ", and
> "ship" includes—
>   (*a*) every description of vessel used in navigation, and
>   (*b*) hovercraft."

(5) In section 38 (disclosure of travel and freight information for security purposes), after subsection (5) there is inserted—

> "(5A) In subsection (4) "ship" includes—
>   (*a*) every description of vessel used in navigation, and
>   (*b*) hovercraft."

[Police and Justice Act 2006, s 14.]

Fixed penalty notices

1–4605H   **15. Accreditation of weights and measures inspectors.**   *Inserts s 41A and Sch 5A into the Police Reform Act 2002.*

16. Power to apply accreditation schemes

Inserts s 41B into the Police Reform Act 2002.

Conditional cautions

1–4605I   **17. Conditional cautions: types of condition.**   (1) Part 3 of the Criminal Justice Act 2003 (c 44) (conditional cautions) is amended as set out in subsections (2) to (4).

(2) In section 22, for subsection (3) (types of conditions that may be attached to cautions) there is substituted—

> "(3) The conditions which may be attached to such a caution are those which have one or more of the following objects—
>   (*a*) facilitating the rehabilitation of the offender;
>   (*b*) ensuring that the offender makes reparation for the offence;
>   (*c*) punishing the offender."

(3) After that subsection there is inserted—

"(3A) The conditions which may be attached to a conditional caution include—

(a) (subject to section 23A) a condition that the offender pay a financial penalty;

(b) a condition that the offender attend at a specified place at specified times.

"Specified" means specified by a relevant prosecutor.

(3B) Conditions attached by virtue of subsection (3A)(b) may not require the offender to attend for more than 20 hours in total, not including any attendance required by conditions attached for the purpose of facilitating the offender's rehabilitation.

(3C) The Secretary of State may by order amend subsection (3B) by substituting a different figure."

(4) *Inserts s 23A into the Criminal Justice Act 2003.*

(5) In section 330 of that Act (orders subject to affirmative resolution procedure), in subsection (5)—

(a) in paragraph (a), before "section 25(5)" there is inserted—

"section 22(3C),";

(b) after that paragraph there is inserted—

"(aa) an order under section 23A(4) which makes provision—

(i)   increasing the fraction in section 23A(3)(a), or

(ii) increasing the figure in section 23A(3)(b) by more than is necessary to reflect changes in the value of money,".

[Police and Justice Act 2006, s 17.]

1–4605J   18. Arrest for failing to comply with conditional caution. (1) *Inserts ss 24A and 24B into the Criminal Justice Act 2003.*

(2) The reference in subsection (1) of section 24A of the Criminal Justice Act 2003 (c 44) (inserted by subsection (1) above) to a failure to comply with conditions attached to a conditional caution is to any such failure occurring on or after the day on which this section comes into force. [Police and Justice Act 2006, s 18.]

PART 3[1]

CRIME AND ANTI-SOCIAL BEHAVIOUR

Crime and disorder

1–4605K   19. Local authority scrutiny of crime and disorder matters. (1) Every local authority shall ensure that it has a committee (the "crime and disorder committee") with power—

(a) to review or scrutinise decisions made, or other action taken, in connection with the discharge by the responsible authorities of their crime and disorder functions;

(b) to make reports or recommendations to the local authority with respect to the discharge of those functions.

"The responsible authorities" means the bodies and persons who are responsible authorities within the meaning given by section 5 of the Crime and Disorder Act 1998 (c 37) (authorities responsible for crime and disorder strategies) in relation to the local authority's area.

(2) Where by virtue of subsection (1)(b) the crime and disorder committee makes a report or recommendations it shall provide a copy—

(a) to each of the responsible authorities, and

(b) to each of the persons with whom, and bodies with which, the responsible authorities have a duty to co-operate under section 5(2) of the Crime and Disorder Act 1998 ("the co-operating persons and bodies").

(3) Where a member of a local authority ("the councillor") is asked to consider a local crime and disorder matter by a person who lives or works in the area that the councillor represents—

(a) the councillor shall consider the matter and respond to the person who asked him to consider it, indicating what (if any) action he proposes to take;

(b) the councillor may refer the matter to the crime and disorder committee.

In this subsection and subsections (4) to (6) "local authority" does not include the county council for an area for which there are district councils.

(4) Where a member of a local authority operating executive arrangements declines to refer a matter to the crime and disorder committee under subsection (3)(b), the person who asked him to consider it may refer the matter to the executive of that authority.

(5) Where a matter is referred under subsection (4) to the executive of a local authority—

(a) the executive shall consider the matter and respond to the person who referred the matter to it, indicating what (if any) action it proposes to take;

(b) the executive may refer the matter to the crime and disorder committee.

(6) The crime and disorder committee shall consider any local crime and disorder matter—

(a) referred to it by a member of the local authority in question (whether under subsection (3)(b) or not), or

(b) referred to it under subsection (5),

and may make a report or recommendations to the local authority with respect to it.

(7) Where the crime and disorder committee makes a report or recommendations under subsection (6) it shall provide a copy to such of the responsible authorities and to such of the co-operating persons and bodies as it thinks appropriate.

(8) An authority, person or body to which a copy of a report or recommendations is provided under subsection (2) or (7) shall—

(a) consider the report or recommendations;

(b) respond to the crime and disorder committee indicating what (if any) action it proposes to take;

(c) have regard to the report or recommendations in exercising its functions.

(9) In the case of a local authority operating executive arrangements—

(a) the crime and disorder committee is to be an overview and scrutiny committee of the authority (within the meaning of Part 2 of the Local Government Act 2000 (c 22));

(b) a reference in subsection (1)(b) or (6) to making a report or recommendations to the local authority is to be read as a reference to making a report or recommendations to the local authority or the executive.

(10) Schedule 8 (which makes further provision about the crime and disorder committees of local authorities not operating executive arrangements, made up of provision corresponding to that made by section 21 of the Local Government Act 2000 and particular provision for the City of London) has effect.

(11) In this section—

"crime and disorder functions" means functions conferred by or under section 6 of the Crime and Disorder Act 1998 (c 37) (formulation and implementation of crime and disorder strategies);

"executive arrangements" means executive arrangements under Part 2 of the Local Government Act 2000;

"local authority" means—

(a) in relation to England, a county council, a district council, a London borough council, the Common Council of the City of London or the Council of the Isles of Scilly;

(b) in relation to Wales, a county council or a county borough council;

"local crime and disorder matter", in relation to a member of a local authority, means a matter concerning—

(a) crime and disorder (including in particular forms of crime and disorder that involve anti-social behaviour or other behaviour adversely affecting the local environment) in the area represented by the member, or

(b) the misuse of drugs, alcohol and other substances in that area.

[Police and Justice Act 2006, s 19.]

---

1. Part 3 comprises ss 19–27 and Schs 8–10.

1–4605L　20. Guidance and regulations regarding crime and disorder matters. *Secretary of State and National Assembly for Wales may issue guidance.*

1–4605M　21. Joint crime and disorder committees. In section 5 of the Crime and Disorder Act 1998 (c 37) (authorities responsible for crime and disorder strategies), after subsection (1B) there is inserted—

"(1C) An order under subsection (1A) above—

(a) may require the councils for the local government areas in question to appoint a joint committee of those councils (the "joint crime and disorder committee") and to arrange for crime and disorder scrutiny functions in relation to any (or all) of those councils to be exercisable by that committee;

(b) may make provision applying any of the relevant provisions, with or without modifications, in relation to a joint crime and disorder committee.

(1D) In subsection (1C)—

"crime and disorder scrutiny functions", in relation to a council, means functions that are, or, but for an order under subsection (1A) above, would be, exercisable by the crime and disorder committee of the council under section 19 of the Police and Justice Act 2006 (local authority scrutiny of crime and disorder matters);

"the relevant provisions" means—

(a) section 19 of the Police and Justice Act 2006;

(b) section 20 of that Act and any regulations made under that section;

(c) Schedule 8 to that Act;

(d) section 21 of the Local Government Act 2000."

[Police and Justice Act 2006, s 21.]

1–4605N   22. Amendments to the Crime and Disorder Act 1998. Schedule 9 (which contains amendments to the Crime and Disorder Act 1998 (c 37) in relation to crime and disorder strategies and other matters relating to the reduction of crime and disorder) has effect.
[Police and Justice Act 2006, s 22.]

Parenting contracts and parenting orders

1–4605O   23. Parenting contracts: local authorities and registered social landlords. (1) *Inserts ss 25A and 25B into the Anti-social Behaviour Act 2003.*

(2) In section 29(1) of that Act (interpretation of sections 25 to 29) the following definitions are inserted at the appropriate places—

""housing accommodation" has the meaning given by section 153E(9) of the Housing Act 1996;";

""housing management functions", in relation to a registered social landlord, include—

(*a*) functions conferred by or under any enactment;
(*b*) the powers and duties of the landlord as the holder of an estate or interest in housing accommodation;";

""local authority" means—

(*a*) a county council in England;
(*b*) a metropolitan district council;
(*c*) a non-metropolitan district council for an area for which there is no county council;
(*d*) a London borough council;
(*e*) the Common Council of the City of London;
(*f*) the Council of the Isles of Scilly;
(*g*) a county council or county borough council in Wales;";

""registered social landlord" means a body registered as such under Chapter 1 of Part 1 of the Housing Act 1996;".
[Police and Justice Act 2006, s 23.]

1–4605P   24. Parenting orders: local authorities and registered social landlords. *Inserts s 26A–26C into the Anti-social Behaviour Act 2003.*

25. Contracting out of local authority functions with regard to parenting contracts and parenting orders. *Inserts s 28A into the Anti-social Behaviour Act 2003.*

Injunctions

26, 27. *Anti-social behaviour injunctions in county court proceedings*

PART 4[1]
INSPECTORATES

1–4605Q   32. Her Majesty's Inspectorate of Court Administration. *Inserts new s 61A and Sch 3A in the Courts Act 2003.*

---

1. Part 4 comprises ss 28–33.

PART 5[1]
MISCELLANEOUS

Bail offences

1–4605R   34. Sentences of imprisonment for bail offences. (1) Part 12 of the Criminal Justice Act 2003 (c 44) (sentencing) is amended as follows.

(2) In section 195 (interpretation of terms used in Chapter 3), for the definition of "sentence of imprisonment" there is substituted—

""sentence of imprisonment" does not include a sentence of imprisonment passed in respect of a summary conviction for an offence under section 6(1) or (2) of the Bail Act 1976."

(3) In section 237 (meaning of "fixed-term prisoner" for purposes of Chapter 6), after subsection (1) there is inserted—

"(1A) In subsection (1)(*a*) "sentence of imprisonment" does not include a sentence of imprisonment passed in respect of a summary conviction for an offence under section 6(1) or (2) of the Bail Act 1976."

(4) In section 257 (additional days for disciplinary offences), after subsection (2) there is inserted—

"(3) For the purposes of this section "fixed-term prisoner" includes a person serving a sentence of imprisonment passed in respect of an offence under section 6(1) or (2) of the Bail Act 1976."

(5) In section 258 (early release for fine defaulters and contemnors), after subsection (1) there is inserted—

"(1A) This section also applies to a person serving a sentence of imprisonment passed in respect of a summary conviction for an offence under section 6(1) or (2) of the Bail Act 1976."

(6) In section 305(1) (interpretation of Part 12), in paragraph (c) of the definition of "sentence of imprisonment", at the end there is inserted "(including contempt of court or any kindred offence)".

[Police and Justice Act 2006, s 34.]

---

1. Part 5 comprises ss 34–48 and Schs 11–13.

Computer misuse

1–4605S 35. Unauthorised access to computer material.   (1) In the Computer Misuse Act 1990 (c 18) ("the 1990 Act"), section 1 (offence of unauthorised access to computer material) is amended as follows.

(2) In subsection (1)—

(a) in paragraph (a), after "any computer" there is inserted ", or to enable any such access to be secured";

(b) in paragraph (b), after "secure" there is inserted ", or to enable to be secured,".

(3) For subsection (3) there is substituted—

"(3) A person guilty of an offence under this section shall be liable—

(a) on summary conviction in England and Wales, to imprisonment for a term not exceeding 12 months or to a fine not exceeding the statutory maximum or to both;

(b) on summary conviction in Scotland, to imprisonment for a term not exceeding six months or to a fine not exceeding the statutory maximum or to both;

(c) on conviction on indictment, to imprisonment for a term not exceeding two years or to a fine or to both."

[Police and Justice Act 2006, s 35.]

1–4605T 36. Unauthorised acts with intent to impair operation of computer, etc.   For section 3 of the 1990 Act (unauthorised modification of computer material) there is substituted—

"3. Unauthorised acts with intent to impair, or with recklessness as to impairing, operation of computer, etc.   (1) A person is guilty of an offence if—

(a) he does any unauthorised act in relation to a computer;

(b) at the time when he does the act he knows that it is unauthorised; and

(c) either subsection (2) or subsection (3) below applies.

(2) This subsection applies if the person intends by doing the act—

(a) to impair the operation of any computer;

(b) to prevent or hinder access to any program or data held in any computer;

(c) to impair the operation of any such program or the reliability of any such data; or

(d) to enable any of the things mentioned in paragraphs (a) to (c) above to be done.

(3) This subsection applies if the person is reckless as to whether the act will do any of the things mentioned in paragraphs (a) to (d) of subsection (2) above.

(4) The intention referred to in subsection (2) above, or the recklessness referred to in subsection (3) above, need not relate to—

(a) any particular computer;

(b) any particular program or data; or

(c) a program or data of any particular kind.

(5) In this section—

(a) a reference to doing an act includes a reference to causing an act to be done;

(b) "act" includes a series of acts;

(c) a reference to impairing, preventing or hindering something includes a reference to doing so temporarily.

(6) A person guilty of an offence under this section shall be liable—

(a) on summary conviction in England and Wales, to imprisonment for a term not exceeding 12 months or to a fine not exceeding the statutory maximum or to both;

(b) on summary conviction in Scotland, to imprisonment for a term not exceeding six months or to a fine not exceeding the statutory maximum or to both;

(c) on conviction on indictment, to imprisonment for a term not exceeding ten years or to a fine or to both."

[Police and Justice Act 2006, s 36.]

---

37. Making, supplying or obtaining articles for use in computer misuse offences.   *Inserts s 3A into the Computer Misuse Act 1990.*

1–4605U   38. Transitional and saving provision.   (1) The amendments made by—

(*a*) subsection (2) of section 35, and
(*b*) paragraphs 19(2), 25(2) and 29(2) of Schedule 14,

apply only where every act or other event proof of which is required for conviction of an offence under section 1 of the 1990 Act takes place after that subsection comes into force.

(2) The amendments made by—

(*a*) subsection (3) of section 35, and
(*b*) paragraphs 23, 24, 25(4) and (5), 26, 27(2) and (7) and 28 of Schedule 14,

do not apply in relation to an offence committed before that subsection comes into force.

(3) An offence is not committed under the new section 3 unless every act or other event proof of which is required for conviction of the offence takes place after section 36 above comes into force.

(4) In relation to a case where, by reason of subsection (3), an offence is not committed under the new section 3—

(*a*) section 3 of the 1990 Act has effect in the form in which it was enacted;
(*b*) paragraphs 19(3), 25(3) to (5), 27(4) and (5) and 29(3) and (4) of Schedule 14 do not apply.

(5) An offence is not committed under the new section 3A unless every act or other event proof of which is required for conviction of the offence takes place after section 37 above comes into force.

(6) In the case of an offence committed before section 154(1) of the Criminal Justice Act 2003 (c 44) comes into force, the following provisions have effect as if for "12 months" there were substituted "six months"—

(*a*) paragraph (*a*) of the new section 1(3);
(*b*) paragraph (*a*) of the new section 2(5);
(*c*) subsection (6)(*a*) of the new section 3;
(*d*) subsection (5)(*a*) of the new section 3A.

(7) In this section—

(*a*) "the new section 1(3)" means the subsection (3) substituted in section 1 of the 1990 Act by section 35 above;
(*b*) "the new section 2(5)" means the subsection (5) substituted in section 2 of the 1990 Act by paragraph 17 of Schedule 14 to this Act;
(*c*) "the new section 3" means the section 3 substituted in the 1990 Act by section 36 above;
(*d*) "the new section 3A" means the section 3A inserted in the 1990 Act by section 37 above.

[Police and Justice Act 2006, s 38.]

Forfeiture of indecent photographs of children

1–4605V   39. Forfeiture of indecent photographs of children: England and Wales.   (1) The Protection of Children Act 1978 (c 37) is amended as follows.

(2) In section 4 (entry, search and seizure)—

(*a*) subsection (3) is omitted;
(*b*) for subsection (4) there is substituted—

"(4) In this section "premises" has the same meaning as in the Police and Criminal Evidence Act 1984 (see section 23 of that Act)."

(3) For section 5 (forfeiture) there is substituted—

"5. Forfeiture.   The Schedule to this Act makes provision about the forfeiture of indecent photographs and pseudo-photographs."

(4) At the end of the Act there is inserted the Schedule set out in Schedule 11 to this Act.

(5) The amendment made by paragraph (*b*) of subsection (2) has effect only in relation to warrants issued under section 4 of the Protection of Children Act 1978 after the commencement of that paragraph.

(6) The amendments made by subsections (2)(*a*), (3) and (4) and Schedule 11 have effect whether the property in question was lawfully seized before or after the coming into force of those provisions.

This is subject to subsection (7).

(7) Those amendments do not have effect in a case where the property has been brought before a justice of the peace under section 4(3) of the Protection of Children Act 1978 before the coming into force of those provisions.

[Police and Justice Act 2006, s 39.]

40. Forfeiture of indecent photographs of children: Northern Ireland

Independent Police Complaints Commission

41. Immigration and asylum enforcement functions: complaints and misconduct

Extradition

42. Amendments to the Extradition Act 2003 etc

1–4605X 43. Designation of United States of America. (1) In article 3(2) of the Extradition Act 2003 (Designation of Part 2 Territories) Order 2003 (SI 2003/3334) (territories designated for the purposes of sections 71, 73, 84 and 86 of the Extradition Act 2003) the entry for the United States of America is omitted.

(2) An order bringing subsection (1) into force is not to be made—

(a) within the period of 12 months beginning with the day on which this Act is passed, or

(b) if instruments of ratification of the 2003 treaty have been exchanged.

In this subsection "the 2003 treaty" means the Extradition Treaty between the United Kingdom of Great Britain and Northern Ireland and the United States of America signed at Washington on 31st March 2003.

(3) Subject to subsection (2), if after the end of the period mentioned in subsection (2)(a) a resolution is made by each House of Parliament that subsection (1) should come into force, the Secretary of State shall make an order under section 53 bringing it into force.

(4) An order made by virtue of subsection (3) must bring subsection (1) into force no later than one month after the day on which the resolutions referred to in subsection (3) are made or, if they are made on different days, the day on which the later resolution is made.

(5) If subsection (1) is brought into force, it does not affect the power of the Secretary of State to make a further order under section 71(4), 73(5), 84(7) or 86(7) of the Extradition Act 2003 amending article 3 of the Extradition Act 2003 (Designation of Part 2 Territories) Order 2003 so as to add a reference to the United States of America.

(6) An order such as is mentioned in subsection (5) may include provision repealing this section.
[Police and Justice Act 2006, s 43.]

Repatriation of prisoners

44. Transfer of prisoner under international arrangements not requiring his consent

Live links

45. Attendance by accused at certain preliminary or sentencing hearings. *Inserts Part 3A into the Crime and Disorder Act 1998.*

1–4605Y 46. Live link bail. (1) The Police and Criminal Evidence Act 1984 (c 60) is amended as follows.

(2) After section 34(7) (persons who are to be treated as arrested) there is inserted—

"(8) Subsection (7) does not apply in relation to a person who is granted bail subject to the duty mentioned in section 47(3)(b) and who either—

(a) attends a police station to answer to such bail, or

(b) is arrested under section 46A for failing to do so,

(provision as to the treatment of such persons for the purposes of this Part being made by section 46ZA)."

(3) *Inserts s 46ZA into the Police and Criminal Evidence Act 1984.*

(4) In section 46A (power of arrest for failure to answer to police bail) after subsection (1) there is inserted—

"(1ZA) The reference in subsection (1) to a person who fails to attend at a police station at the time appointed for him to do so includes a reference to a person who—

(a) attends at a police station to answer to bail granted subject to the duty mentioned in section 47(3)(b), but

(b) leaves the police station at any time before the beginning of proceedings in relation to a live link direction under section 57C of the Crime and Disorder Act 1998 in relation to him, without informing a constable that he does not intend to give his consent to the direction."

(5) In section 47 (bail after arrest)—

(a) in subsection (3), for paragraphs (a) and (b) and the words following them there is substituted—

"(a) to appear before a magistrates' court at such time and such place as the custody officer may appoint;

(b) to attend at such police station as the custody officer may appoint at such time as he may appoint for the purposes of—

(i) proceedings in relation to a live link direction under section 57C of the Crime and Disorder Act 1998 (use of live link direction at preliminary hearings where accused is at police station); and

(ii) any preliminary hearing in relation to which such a direction is given; or

(c) to attend at such police station as the custody officer may appoint at such time as he may appoint for purposes other than those mentioned in paragraph (b).";

(b) in subsection (7), at the end there is inserted "or to a person to whom section 46ZA(4) or (5) applies".

(6) In section 54 (searches of detained persons), in subsection (1)(*b*), after "37 above" there is inserted "or as a person to whom section 46ZA(4) or (5) applies".
[Police and Justice Act 2006, s 46.]

47. Evidence of vulnerable accused.   *Inserts Chapter 1A into the Youth Justice and Criminal Evidence Act 1999.*

48. Appeals under Part 1 of the Criminal Appeal Act 1968

PART 6[1]
SUPPLEMENTAL

1–4605Z   49. Orders and regulations

---

1. Part 6 comprises ss 49–55 and Schs 14–15.

---

50. Money

51. Power to make consequential and transitional provision etc

1–4606   52. Amendments and repeals.   Schedules 14 (minor and consequential amendments) and 15 (repeals and revocations) have effect.
[Police and Justice Act 2006, s 52.]

1–4606A   53. Commencement.   (1) Subject to subsections (2) to (9)—

(*a*) Parts 1 to 5, and
(*b*) section 52 (and Schedules 14 and 15),

come into force in accordance with provision made by order[1] by the Secretary of State.
(2) Subsection (1) does not apply to—

(*a*) section 43(2) to (6);
(*b*) paragraph 6 of Schedule 13;
(*c*) paragraphs 7(3)(*a*), 14, 15 and 24 to 26 of Schedule 2 (and section 2 so far as relating to those paragraphs);
(*d*) paragraphs 34, 39, 47, 49 and 59 of Schedule 14;
(*e*) the repeals in Part 1(*b*) of Schedule 15 that relate to the paragraphs mentioned in paragraphs (*c*) and (*d*);
(*f*) section 52 so far as relating to any of those paragraphs and repeals.
[Police and Justice Act 2006, s 53(1), (2).]

---

1. The following commencement order has been made under this provision: (No 1, Transitional and Saving Provisions) Order 2006, SI 2006/3364 amended by SI 2007/29 which brought into force the following provisions on 15 January 2007: ss 2 (part), 11, 42 (part), 44, 44 (other than inserting s 57C in the Crime and Disorder Act 1998), 47, 48, 52 (part), Schs 2 (part), 13 (except paras 4, 5 and 6), 14 (part) and 15 (part).

---

(3)–(10) *Further provision for commencement by orders made by the Scottish Ministers and the National Assembly for Wales.*

54. Extent

55. Short title

1–4606B
Section 2   SCHEDULE 2
                   AMENDMENTS TO THE POLICE ACT 1996

Supplementary

7. (1) Regulations under this Schedule may make transitional, consequential, incidental and supplemental provision or savings.
(2) A statutory instrument containing regulations under this Schedule shall be subject to annulment in pursuance of a resolution of either House of Parliament.

Police authorities: objectives, plans and reports

9. After section 6ZA (inserted by paragraph 8) there is inserted—

"**6ZB. Plans by police authorities.**   (1) Before the beginning of each financial year every police authority shall issue a plan (a "policing plan") setting out—

(*a*) the authority's objectives ("policing objectives") for the policing of its area during that year; and
(*b*) the proposed arrangements for the policing of that area for the period of three years beginning with that year.

(2) Policing objectives shall be so framed as to be consistent with any strategic priorities determined under section 37A.

(3) Before determining policing objectives, a police authority shall—

(a) consult the relevant chief officer of police, and
(b) consider any views obtained by the authority in accordance with arrangements made under section 96.

(4) A draft of a policing plan required to be issued by a police authority under this section shall be prepared by the relevant chief officer of police and submitted by him to the authority for it to consider.

The authority shall consult the relevant chief officer of police before issuing a policing plan which differs from the draft submitted by him under this subsection.

(5) The Secretary of State may by regulations make provision supplementing that made by this section.

(6) The regulations may make provision (further to that made by subsection (3)) as to persons who are to be consulted, and matters that are to be considered, before determining policing objectives.

(7) The regulations may contain provision as to—

(a) matters to be dealt with in policing plans (in addition to those mentioned in subsection (1));
(b) persons who are to be consulted, and matters that are to be considered, in preparing policing plans;
(c) modification of policing plans;
(d) persons to whom copies of policing plans are to be sent.

(8) Before making regulations under this section the Secretary of State must consult—

(a) the Association of Police Authorities,
(b) the Association of Chief Police Officers, and
(c) such other persons as he thinks fit.

(9) Regulations under this section may make different provision for different police authorities.

(10) A statutory instrument containing regulations under this section shall be subject to annulment in pursuance of a resolution of either House of Parliament.

(11) In this section "the relevant chief officer of police", in relation to a police authority, means the chief officer of police of the police force maintained by that authority.

6ZC. Reports by police authorities. (1) The Secretary of State may by order require police authorities to issue reports concerning the policing of their areas.

(2) An order under this section may contain provision as to—

(a) the periods to be covered by reports, and, as regards each period, the date by which reports are to be issued;
(b) the matters to be dealt with in reports;
(c) persons to whom copies of reports are to be sent.

(3) Before making an order under this section the Secretary of State must consult—

(a) the Association of Police Authorities,
(b) the Association of Chief Police Officers, and
(c) such other persons as he thinks fit.

(4) An order under this section may make different provision for different police authorities.

(5) A statutory instrument containing an order under this section shall be subject to annulment in pursuance of a resolution of either House of Parliament."

10. The following sections are repealed—

section 6A (three-year strategy plans);
section 7 (local policing objectives);
section 8 (local policing plans);
section 9 (annual reports by police authorities).

11. In section 9A (general functions of Commissioner of Police of the Metropolis), in subsection (2), for the words after "shall have regard" there is substituted

"to—

(a) any arrangements involving the metropolitan police force that are made by virtue of section 6ZA(2)(b);
(b) the policing plan issued by the Metropolitan Police Authority under section 6ZB."

12. In section 10 (general functions of chief constables), in subsection (2), for the words after "shall have regard" there is substituted

"to—

(a) any arrangements involving his force that are made by virtue of section 6ZA(2)(b);
(b) the policing plan issued by the police authority for his area under section 6ZB."

13. (1) Section 96B (national and international functions: application of requirements relating to reports etc) is amended as follows.

(2) In subsection (2), for "section 7(1) shall have effect as if the reference" there is substituted "section 6ZB(1) shall have effect as if a reference".

(3) Subsection (3) is repealed.

(4) In subsection (4), for "section 9(1)" there is substituted "section 6ZC(1)".

Appointment of deputy chief constables etc

20. (1) A reference in subordinate legislation (within the meaning of the Interpretation Act 1978 (c 30)) to the clerk to a police authority has effect as a reference to the chief executive of the authority.

(2) A person holding office as clerk to a police authority on the commencement of paragraph 18 continues in that office as chief executive of the authority.

(3) In this paragraph "police authority" means—

(a) a police authority established under section 3 of the Police Act 1996 (c 16);
(b) the Metropolitan Police Authority.

Jurisdiction of special constables

21. (1) Section 30 (jurisdiction of constables) is amended as follows.
(2) For subsection (2) (jurisdiction of special constables) there is substituted—

"(2) A special constable shall have all the powers and privileges of a constable throughout England and Wales
and the adjacent United Kingdom waters."
(3) Subsections (3) and (4) are omitted.

Secretary of State's strategic functions in relation to police authorities

24. Sections 36A (National Policing Plan) and 37 (setting of objectives for police authorities) are repealed.
25. Before section 38 there is inserted—

"37A. Setting of strategic priorities for police authorities.   (1) The Secretary of State may determine
strategic priorities for the policing of the areas of all police authorities to which this section applies.
(2) Before determining any such priorities the Secretary of State shall consult—

(a) the Association of Police Authorities, and
(b) the Association of Chief Police Officers.

(3) The Secretary of State shall arrange for any priorities determined under this section to be published in
such manner as he considers appropriate.
(4) The police authorities to which this section applies are those established under section 3 and the
Metropolitan Police Authority."

1–4606C

Section 9

SCHEDULE 5
EXERCISE OF POLICE POWERS BY CIVILIANS

1. The Police Reform Act 2002 (c 30) is amended as follows.
2. (1) Section 38 (police powers for police authority employees) is amended as follows.
(2) In subsection (4)(c) (person not to be designated unless adequately trained), after "conferred" there is
inserted "or imposed".
(3) Before subsection (6) there is inserted—

"(5B) The reference in subsection (4)(c) to the powers and duties to be conferred or imposed on a person by
virtue of his designation, so far as it is a reference to the standard powers and duties of a community support
officer, is a reference to the powers and duties that at the time of the person's designation are the standard
powers and duties of a community support officer."
(4) After subsection (6) there is inserted—

"(6A) Subsection (6) has effect subject to subsections (5A) and (8)."
3. (1) Section 42 (supplementary provisions relating to designations etc) is amended as follows.
(2) Before subsection (1) there is inserted—

"(A1) A person who exercises or performs any power or duty in relation to any person in reliance on his
designation under section 38 as a community support officer, or who purports to do so, shall produce to that
person evidence of his designation, if requested to do so.
(B1) A person who exercises or performs any non-standard power or duty in relation to any
person in reliance on his designation under section 38 as a community support officer, or who purports to do
so, shall produce to that person evidence that the power or duty has been conferred or imposed on him, if
requested to do so.
(C1) For the purposes of subsection (B1), a power or duty is "non-standard" if it is not one of the standard
powers and duties of a community support officer."
(3) After subsection (1) there is inserted—

"(1A) Subsection (1) does not apply to a person who exercises or performs any power or duty in reliance on
his designation under section 38 as a community support officer, or who purports to do so."
4. In section 105 (orders and regulations), in subsection (3)(b), after "section 19(3)" there is inserted ",
38A(4)".
5. (1) Schedule 4 (powers exercisable by police civilians) is amended as follows.
(2) In paragraph 1(3) (community support officers: power to issue fixed penalty notices: definition of "relevant
fixed penalty offence")—

(a) in paragraph (a), for "1(2)(a) to (d)" there is substituted "(2)(a) to (e)";
(b) in paragraph (b), for "that person's designation as an offence he" there is substituted "a designation by
which this paragraph is applied to the designated person as an offence which the designated person".

(3) In paragraph 1A(2) (community support officers: power to require name and address: confining the power),
for "Such a designation may specify that, in relation to that person, the application of sub-paragraph (3)" there is
substituted "A designation by which this paragraph is applied to a person may specify that the application of sub-
paragraph (3) by that designation to that person".
(4) In paragraph 2(3A)(b) (community support officers: powers under byelaws to remove persons from places),
for "under paragraph 1A" there is substituted "applying paragraph 1A to the CSO,".
(5) In paragraph 2(4) (person required to wait with community support officer may be given choice to go to
police station), for "this Part of this Schedule applies" there is substituted "this paragraph is applied".
(6) In paragraph 2(6) (meaning of "relevant offence"), in the words after paragraph (b), after "may provide
that" there is inserted ", for the purposes of this paragraph as applied to that person by that designation,".
(7) In paragraph 2(8) (application of paragraph 2 by other provisions effective only where paragraph 2 is itself
applied to community support officer)—

(a)　for "or 7A(8)" there is substituted ", 7A(8) or 7C(2)";
(b)　"under this paragraph" is omitted.

(8)　In paragraph 4 (power to use reasonable force to detain or control person required to wait with community support officer)—

(a)　in sub-paragraph (1), for "This paragraph applies" there is substituted "Sub-paragraph (3) applies";
(b)　in sub-paragraph (1)(b), for "sets out the matters" there is substituted "sets out matters";
(c)　in sub-paragraph (2), for "as the matters" there is substituted "as matters".

(9)　In paragraph 7B(2)(a) (community support officer's power to seize controlled drugs found in person's possession), for the words from "(whether" to the end there is substituted "(whether or not the CSO finds it in the course of searching the person by virtue of any paragraph of this Part of this Schedule being applied to the CSO by a designation); and".

(10)　In paragraphs 34(2) and 35(4) (escort officer's powers to carry out non-intimate searches of persons), for "designation under" there is substituted "application of".

(11)　In paragraph 35A (staff custody officer to have powers of a custody officer), in each of sub-paragraphs (3) and (4), for "under" there is substituted "applying".

(12)　In paragraph 36(1)(a) (meaning of "the relevant police area"), for "designation" there is substituted "person designated".

(13)　In paragraph 36, for sub-paragraphs (2) and (3) there is substituted—

"(2)　In Part 1 of this Schedule "a designation" means—

(a)　a designation under section 38, or
(b)　an order under section 38A(1) (and, accordingly, the power to make such an order—

(i)　is extended by paragraphs 1(3)(b), 1A(2) and (7), 2(6) and 4(1)(b), but
(ii)　is subject to paragraphs 2(2), 4(2) and 11B(5)).

(2A)　In Parts 2 and 4A of this Schedule "a designation" means a designation under section 38.
(3)　In Parts 3 and 4 of this Schedule "a designation" means a designation under section 38 or 39."

6. (1)　Paragraph 1 of Schedule 5 (power of accredited persons to issue fixed penalty notices) is amended as follows.

(2)　In sub-paragraph (2) (powers conferred on a person when paragraph 1 is applied to him), in the words before paragraph (a) (which refer to a relevant offence), after "relevant" there is inserted "fixed penalty".

(3)　In sub-paragraph (3)(a) (meaning of "relevant fixed penalty offence" in paragraph 1), for "(c)" there is substituted "(d)".

1–4606D

Section 10　　　　　　　　　　SCHEDULE 6
　　　　　　　　　　　　　　POLICE BAIL

PART 1
INTRODUCTORY

1. The Police and Criminal Evidence Act 1984 (c 60) is amended as follows.

PART 2
POLICE BAIL GRANTED ELSEWHERE THAN AT POLICE STATION

Power to impose conditions on granting bail

2. In section 30A (bail elsewhere than at police station), for subsection (4) (no condition of bail may be imposed other than requirement to attend police station) there is substituted—

"(3A)　Where a constable releases a person on bail under subsection (1)—

(a)　no recognizance for the person's surrender to custody shall be taken from the person,
(b)　no security for the person's surrender to custody shall be taken from the person or from anyone else on the person's behalf,
(c)　the person shall not be required to provide a surety or sureties for his surrender to custody, and
(d)　no requirement to reside in a bail hostel may be imposed as a condition of bail.

(3B)　Subject to subsection (3A), where a constable releases a person on bail under subsection (1) the constable may impose, as conditions of the bail, such requirements as appear to the constable to be necessary—

(a)　to secure that the person surrenders to custody,
(b)　to secure that the person does not commit an offence while on bail,
(c)　to secure that the person does not interfere with witnesses or otherwise obstruct the course of justice, whether in relation to himself or any other person, or
(d)　for the person's own protection or, if the person is under the age of 17, for the person's own welfare or in the person's own interests.

(4)　Where a person is released on bail under subsection (1), a requirement may be imposed on the person as a condition of bail only under the preceding provisions of this section."

Contents of notice given to person released on bail

3. In section 30B (bail under section 30A: notices), after subsection (4) there is inserted—

"(4A)　If the person is granted bail subject to conditions under section 30A(3B), the notice also—

(a)　must specify the requirements imposed by those conditions,
(b)　must explain the opportunities under sections 30CA(1) and 30CB(1) for variation of those conditions, and
(c)　if it does not specify the police station at which the person is required to attend, must specify a police station at which the person may make a request under section 30CA(1)(b)."

Variation of bail conditions

4. *Inserts s 30CA, 30CB into the Police and Criminal Evidence Act 1984.*

Power of arrest for breach of bail conditions

5. (1) Section 30D (failure to answer to bail under section 30A) is amended as follows.

(2) After subsection (2) there is inserted—

"(2A) A person who has been released on bail under section 30A may be arrested without a warrant by a constable if the constable has reasonable grounds for suspecting that the person has broken any of the conditions of bail.

(2B) A person arrested under subsection (2A) must be taken to a police station (which may be the specified police station mentioned in subsection (1) or any other police station) as soon as practicable after the arrest."

(3) In subsection (4)(*a*) (arrest under section 30D treated for purposes of section 30 as arrest for offence, subject to obligation in subsection (2)), for "obligation in subsection (2)" there is substituted "obligations in subsections (2) and (2B)".

PART 3

POLICE BAIL GRANTED AT POLICE STATION BEFORE CHARGE

Power to impose conditions on bail granted under section 37(2) or (7)(b)

6. In section 47(1A) (where person released on bail under Part 4, normal powers to impose conditions of bail are available only where release is under section 37(7)(*a*) or 38(1)), for "37(7)(*a*)" there is substituted "37".

Power of arrest for breach of conditions of bail granted under section 37(2) or (7)(b)

7. In section 46A(1A) (person released on bail under section 37(7)(*a*) or 37C(2)(*b*) may be arrested without warrant if suspected of breaking conditions of bail), for "37(7)(*a*) or 37C(2)(*b*)" there is substituted "37, 37C(2)(*b*) or 37CA(2)(*b*)".

Dealing with person arrested for breach of conditions of bail granted under section 37(7)(b)

8. *Inserts s 37CA into the Police and Criminal Evidence Act 1984.*

Time for person to answer bail granted under section 37(2) or (7)(b) or 37CA(2)(b)

9. (1) In section 37D(1) (release on bail under section 37(7)(*a*) or 37C(2)(*b*): appointment of different or additional time to answer bail), for "37(7)(*a*) or section 37C(2)(*b*)" there is substituted "37, 37C(2)(*b*) or 37CA(2)(*b*)".

(2) In the heading to section 37D, for "**under section 37(7)(*a*)**" there is substituted "**on bail under section 37**".

Dealing with person released on bail under section 37(7)(b) or 37CA(2)(b)

10. (1) Section 37D (release under section 37(7)(*a*): further provision) is amended as follows.

(2) For subsection (5) (person not fit to be dealt with as mentioned in subsection (4) to be detained until fit) there is substituted—

"(4A) Where a person released on bail under section 37(7)(*b*) or 37CA(2)(*b*) above returns to a police station to answer bail or is otherwise in police detention at a police station, he may be kept in police detention to enable him to be dealt with in accordance with section 37CA above or to enable the power under subsection (1) above to be exercised.

(5) If the person mentioned in subsection (4) or (4A) above is not in a fit state to enable him to be dealt with as mentioned in that subsection or to enable the power under subsection (1) above to be exercised, he may be kept in police detention until he is."

(3) In subsection (6) (application of section 37 where person detained under section 37D)—

(*a*) after "subsection (4)" there is inserted ", (4A)";

(*b*) for "37(7)(*a*) or 37C(2)(*b*)" there is substituted "37(7), 37C(2)(*b*) or 37CA(2)(*b*)".

Applications to court where person released on bail under section 37(2) or (7)(b) or 37CA(2)(b)

11. In section 47(1B) and (1C) (applications to court where person on bail under section 37(7)(*a*) or 37C(2)(*b*)), for "37(7)(*a*) or 37C(2)(*b*)" there is substituted "37, 37C(2)(*b*) or 37CA(2)(*b*)".

SCHEDULE 7

Inserts Sch 5A into the Police Reform Act 2002.

1–4606E

Section 19 SCHEDULE 8

FURTHER PROVISION ABOUT CRIME AND DISORDER COMMITTEES OF CERTAIN LOCAL AUTHORITIES

Introductory

1. (1) This Schedule applies in relation to a local authority that is not operating executive arrangements under Part 2 of the Local Government Act 2000 (c 22).

(2) In this Schedule "local authority" and "crime and disorder committee" have the same meaning as in section 19.

Functions of crime and disorder committees

2. (1) The crime and disorder committee of a local authority may not discharge any functions other than its functions under section 19 or this Schedule.

(2) In the case of a committee of a local authority that acts as its crime and disorder committee and also acts in one or more other capacities, the reference in sub-paragraph (1) to the crime and disorder committee is a reference to that committee in its capacity as crime and disorder committee.

Appointment of sub-committees

3. (1) The crime and disorder committee of a local authority—

(a) may appoint one or more sub-committees, and
(b) may arrange for the discharge of any of its functions by any such sub-committee.

(2) A sub-committee of the crime and disorder committee may not discharge any functions other than those conferred on it under sub-paragraph (1)(b).

Meetings etc

4. A local authority shall make arrangements—

(a) for enabling a member of the crime and disorder committee of the authority to ensure that a matter that is relevant to the functions of the committee is included in the agenda for, and is discussed at, a meeting of the committee, and
(b) for enabling a member of a sub-committee of such a committee to ensure that a matter that is relevant to the functions of the sub-committee is included in the agenda for, and is discussed at, a meeting of the sub-committee.

5. The crime and disorder committee of a local authority, or a sub-committee of such a committee, may include persons who are not members of the authority, but (subject to section 20(6)) such persons are not entitled to vote, at a meeting of such a committee or sub-committee, on any question that falls to be decided at that meeting.

Power to compel attendance etc

6. (1) The crime and disorder committee of a local authority or a sub-committee of such a committee—

(a) may require members or officers of the authority to attend before it to answer questions;
(b) may invite other persons to attend meetings of the committee.

(2) A member or officer of a local authority shall comply with any requirement made under sub-paragraph (1)(a).

(3) A person is not obliged by sub-paragraph (2) to answer any question that he would be entitled to refuse to answer in or for the purposes of proceedings in a court in England and Wales.

Miscellaneous and supplemental

7. The crime and disorder committee of a local authority, or a sub-committee of such a committee, is to be treated as a committee or sub-committee of a principal council for the purposes of Part 5A of the Local Government Act 1972 (c 70) (access to meetings and documents of certain authorities, committees and sub-committees).

8. The crime and disorder committee of a local authority, or a sub-committee of such a committee, is to be treated as a body to which section 15 of the Local Government and Housing Act 1989 (c 42) (duty to allocate seats to political groups) applies.

9. Subsections (2) and (5) of section 102 of the Local Government Act 1972 (appointment of committees) apply to the crime and disorder committee of a local authority, or a sub-committee of such a committee, as they apply to a committee appointed under that section.

Application to the City of London

10. Paragraph 8 does not apply to the crime and disorder committee of the Common Council or to a sub-committee of that committee.

11. (1) The Common Council may discharge its duty under section 19(1) by itself acting as the crime and disorder committee of the Council, and sub-paragraphs (2) to (4) apply if it does so.

(2) In section 19 or 20 or this Schedule, or in section 5 of the Crime and Disorder Act 1998 (c 37) (authorities responsible for crime and disorder strategies), a reference to the crime and disorder committee of a local authority includes a reference to the Common Council in its capacity as crime and disorder committee.

(3) Paragraph 2, in its application to the Common Council, has effect with the omission of sub-paragraph (2).

(4) Paragraph 9, in its application to the Common Council, applies only so far as it relates to sub-committees.

12. In paragraphs 10 and 11 "the Common Council" means the Common Council of the City of London.

1–4606F

Section 22   SCHEDULE 9
                     AMENDMENTS TO THE CRIME AND DISORDER ACT 1998

1. The Crime and Disorder Act 1998 (c 37) is amended as follows.
2. (1) Section 5 (authorities responsible for strategies) is amended as follows.
(2) In subsection (1), after "functions conferred by" there is inserted "or under".
(3) In subsection (1A)(a), for "by sections 6 to 7" there is substituted "by or under section 6 or by section 7".
(4) In subsection (1B)(b), after "drugs" there is inserted ", alcohol and other substances".
(5) After subsection (5) there is inserted—

"(6) The appropriate national authority may by order amend this section by—

(a) adding an entry for any person or body to the list of authorities in subsection (1),
(b) altering or repealing an entry for the time being included in the list, or
(c) adding, altering or repealing provisions for the interpretation of entries in the list.

(7) In this section the "appropriate national authority", in relation to a person or body, means—

(a) the National Assembly for Wales, if all the functions of the person or body are devolved Welsh functions;

(b) the Secretary of State and the Assembly acting jointly, if the functions of the person or body include devolved Welsh functions and other functions; and

(c) the Secretary of State, if none of the functions of the person or body are devolved Welsh functions.

(8) In subsection (7), "devolved Welsh functions" means functions which are dischargeable only in relation to Wales and relate to matters in relation to which the Assembly has functions."

3. For sections 6 and 6A there is substituted—

"6. Formulation and implementation of strategies. (1) The responsible authorities for a local government area shall, in accordance with section 5 and with regulations made under subsection (2), formulate and implement—

(a) a strategy for the reduction of crime and disorder in the area (including anti-social and other behaviour adversely affecting the local environment); and

(b) a strategy for combatting the misuse of drugs, alcohol and other substances in the area.

(2) The appropriate national authority may by regulations make further provision as to the formulation and implementation of a strategy under this section.

(3) Regulations under subsection (2) may in particular make provision for or in connection with—

(a) the time by which a strategy must be prepared and the period to which it is to relate;

(b) the procedure to be followed by the responsible authorities in preparing and implementing a strategy (including requirements as to the holding of public meetings and other consultation);

(c) the conferring of functions on any one or more of the responsible authorities in relation to the formulation and implementation of a strategy;

(d) matters to which regard must be had in formulating and implementing a strategy;

(e) objectives to be addressed in a strategy and performance targets in respect of those objectives;

(f) the sharing of information between responsible authorities;

(g) the publication and dissemination of a strategy;

(h) the preparation of reports on the implementation of a strategy.

(4) The provision which may be made under subsection (2) includes provision for or in connection with the conferring of functions on a committee of, or a particular member or officer of, any of the responsible authorities.

(5) The matters referred to in subsection (3)(d) may in particular include guidance given by the appropriate national authority in connection with the formulation or implementation of a strategy.

(6) Provision under subsection (3)(e) may require a strategy to be formulated so as to address (in particular)—

(a) the reduction of crime or disorder of a particular description; or

(b) the combatting of a particular description of misuse of drugs, alcohol or other substances.

(7) Regulations under this section may make—

(a) different provision for different local government areas;

(b) supplementary or incidental provision.

(8) For the purposes of this section any reference to the implementation of a strategy includes—

(a) keeping it under review for the purposes of monitoring its effectiveness; and

(b) making any changes to it that appear necessary or expedient.

(9) In this section the "appropriate national authority" is—

(a) the Secretary of State, in relation to strategies for areas in England;

(b) the National Assembly for Wales, in relation to strategies for combatting the misuse of drugs, alcohol or other substances in areas in Wales;

(c) the Secretary of State and the Assembly acting jointly, in relation to strategies for combatting crime and disorder in areas in Wales."

4. (1) Section 17 (duty to consider crime and disorder implications) is amended as follows.

(2) In subsection (1), for "crime and disorder in its area" there is substituted—

"(a) crime and disorder in its area (including anti-social and other behaviour adversely affecting the local environment); and

(b) the misuse of drugs, alcohol and other substances in its area."

(3) For subsection (2) there is substituted—

"(2) This section applies to each of the following—

a local authority;

a joint authority;

the London Fire and Emergency Planning Authority;

a fire and rescue authority constituted by a scheme under section 2 of the Fire and Rescue Services Act 2004 or a scheme to which section 4 of that Act applies;

a metropolitan county fire authority;

a police authority;

a National Park authority;

the Broads Authority."

(4) After subsection (3) there is inserted—

"(4) The appropriate national authority may by order amend this section by—

(a) adding an entry for any person or body to the list of authorities in subsection (2),

(b) altering or repealing any entry for the time being included in the list, or

(c) adding, altering or repealing provisions for the interpretation of entries in the list.

(5) In subsection (4) "the appropriate national authority" has the same meaning as in section 5."

5. *Inserts s 17A into the Crime and Disorder Act 1998.*

6. (1) Section 114 (orders and regulations) is amended as follows.

(2) In subsection (2)—

(*a*) ", 6A(1)" is omitted;

(*b*) after "regulations under" there is inserted "section 6 or 17A or".

(3) In subsection (3)—

(*a*) after "1F," there is inserted "5(6),";

(*b*) for "38(5) or 41(6)" there is substituted "17(4), 38(5), 41(6) or 115(3)".

(4) After that subsection there is inserted—

"(4) The Secretary of State must consult the National Assembly for Wales before making an order under section 5(6), 17(4) or 115(3) that relates to a person or body any of whose functions are dischargeable in relation to Wales (not being functions of the kind referred to in section 5(8))."

7. (1) Section 115 (disclosure of information) is amended as follows.

(2) In subsection (2), for "subsection (1) above" there is substituted "this section", and at the end there is inserted—

"(*h*) the London Fire and Emergency Planning Authority;

(*i*) a fire and rescue authority constituted by a scheme under section 2 of the Fire and Rescue Services Act 2004 or a scheme to which section 4 of that Act applies;

(*j*) a metropolitan county fire and rescue authority."

(3) After that subsection there is inserted—

"(3) The appropriate national authority may by order amend this section so far as it extends to England and Wales by—

(*a*) adding an entry for any person or body to the list of authorities in subsection (2),

(*b*) altering or repealing any entry for the time being included in the list, or

(*c*) adding, altering or repealing provisions for the interpretation of entries in the list.

(4) In subsection (3) "the appropriate national authority" has the same meaning as in section 5."

SCHEDULE 11

Inserts Schedule into the Protection of Children Act 1978.

1–4606G

Section 42   SCHEDULE 13

EXTRADITION

Restriction on extradition in cases where trial in United Kingdom more appropriate

4. (1) In section 11 (bars to extradition)—

(*a*) at the end of subsection (1) there is inserted—

"(*j*) forum.";

(*b*) in subsection (2), for the words from "12" to "apply" there is substituted "12 to 19B apply".

(2) *Inserts s 19B into the Extradition Act 2003.*

5. (1) In section 79 (bars to extradition)—

(*a*) at the end of subsection (1) there is inserted—

"(*e*) forum.";

(*b*) in subsection (2), for "Sections 80 to 83" there is substituted "Sections 80 to 83A".

(2) *Inserts s 83A into the Extradition Act 2003.*

6. (1) An order bringing paragraph 4 or 5 into force is not to be made within the period of 12 months beginning with the day on which this Act is passed.

(2) If after the end of that period a resolution is made by each House of Parliament that paragraphs 4 and 5 (or either of them) should come into force, the Secretary of State shall make an order under section 53 bringing the paragraphs (or paragraph) into force.

(3) An order made by virtue of sub-paragraph (2) must bring the provisions in question into force no later than one month after the day on which the resolutions referred to in that sub-paragraph are made or, if they are made on different days, the day on which the later resolution is made.

1–4606H

Section 52   SCHEDULE 14[1]

MINOR AND CONSEQUENTIAL AMENDMENTS

Criminal Damage Act 1971 (c 48)

2. In section 10 of the Criminal Damage Act 1971 (interpretation), after subsection (4) there is inserted—

"(5) For the purposes of this Act a modification of the contents of a computer shall not be regarded as damaging any computer or computer storage medium unless its effect on that computer or computer storage medium impairs its physical condition."

---

1. Reproduced are those unimplemented amendments relating to provisions contained in this manual.

Bail Act 1976 (c 63)

5. In subsection (1) of—

   (*a*)   section 3A of the Bail Act 1976 (conditions of bail in case of police bail), and
   (*b*)   section 5A of that Act (supplementary provisions in cases of police bail),

after "Part IV of the Police and Criminal Evidence Act 1984" there is inserted "or Part 3 of the Criminal Justice Act 2003".

Local Government (Miscellaneous Provisions) Act 1982 (c 30)

7. In Schedule 3 to the Local Government (Miscellaneous Provisions) Act 1982 (control of sex establishments), in paragraph 1(*b*)(ii), for "section 5 of" there is substituted "the Schedule to".

Aviation Security Act 1982 (c 36)

8. (1) Part 3 of the Aviation Security Act 1982 (policing of airports) is amended as follows.
   (2) In the heading to that Part, for "AIRPORTS" there is substituted "AERODROMES".
   (3) Between section 24B (inserted by section 12 above) and section 25 of that Act there is inserted—

"Policing of designated airports".

   (4) Subsections (1), (4) and (5) of section 27 of that Act (prevention of theft at designated airports) are omitted.

Police and Criminal Evidence Act 1984 (c 60)

9. In section 37 of the Police and Criminal Evidence Act 1984 (duties of custody officer before charge), in subsection (7B)—

   (*a*)   for "released under subsection (7)(*a*)" there is substituted "dealt with under subsection (7)(*a*)";
   (*b*)   after "he is being released" there is inserted ", or (as the case may be) detained,".

10. (1) Section 37B of that Act (consultation with the Director of Public Prosecutions) is amended as follows.
   (2) In subsection (1), for "released on bail under section 37(7)(*a*)" there is substituted "dealt with under section 37(7)(*a*)".
   (3) In subsection (4), for "shall give written notice" there is substituted "shall give notice".
   (4) After that subsection there is inserted—

"(4A) Notice under subsection (4) above shall be in writing, but in the case of a person kept in police detention under section 37(7)(*a*) above it may be given orally in the first instance and confirmed in writing subsequently."
   (5) In subsection (8), for paragraph (*a*) there is substituted—

   "(*a*)   when he is in police detention at a police station (whether because he has returned to answer bail, because he is detained under section 37(7)(*a*) above or for some other reason), or".

11. In section 64A of that Act (photographing of suspects etc), in subsection (1B), after paragraph (*f*) there is inserted

   "; or
   (*g*)   given a notice in relation to a relevant fixed penalty offence (within the meaning of Schedule 5A to the 2002 Act) by an accredited inspector by virtue of accreditation specifying that paragraph 1 of Schedule 5A to the 2002 Act applies to him."

Criminal Justice Act 1988 (c 33)

14. In section 142 of the Criminal Justice Act 1988 (power of justice of the peace to authorise entry and search of premises for offensive weapons), in subsection (3), for "subsection (1)(*b*)" there is substituted "subsection (1)(*c*)".

Computer Misuse Act 1990 (c 18)

17. In section 2 of the Computer Misuse Act 1990 (unauthorised access with intent to commit or facilitate commission of further offences), for subsection (5) there is substituted—

"(5) A person guilty of an offence under this section shall be liable—

   (*a*)   on summary conviction in England and Wales, to imprisonment for a term not exceeding 12 months or to a fine not exceeding the statutory maximum or to both;
   (*b*)   on summary conviction in Scotland, to imprisonment for a term not exceeding six months or to a fine not exceeding the statutory maximum or to both;
   (*c*)   on conviction on indictment, to imprisonment for a term not exceeding five years or to a fine or to both."

18. In the heading to section 4 of that Act (territorial scope of offences under that Act), for **"offences under this Act"** there is substituted **"offences under sections 1 to 3"**.
19. (1) Section 5 of that Act (significant links with domestic jurisdiction) is amended as follows.
   (2) In subsection (2), for paragraph (*b*) there is substituted—

   "(*b*)   that any computer containing any program or data to which the accused by doing that act secured or intended to secure unauthorised access, or enabled or intended to enable unauthorised access to be secured, was in the home country concerned at that time."

   (3) In subsection (3)—

   (*a*)   in paragraph (*a*), for "he did the act which caused the unauthorised modification" there is substituted "he did the unauthorised act (or caused it to be done)";

(*b*) for paragraph (*b*) there is substituted—

"(*b*) that the unauthorised act was done in relation to a computer in the home country concerned."

20. In section 6 of that Act (territorial scope of inchoate offences)—

(*a*) in the heading, for **"offences under this Act"** there is substituted **"offences under sections 1 to 3"**;
(*b*) in subsections (1) and (3), for "offence under this Act" there is substituted "offence under section 1, 2 or 3 above".

21. In section 7 of that Act (territorial scope of inchoate offences related to offences under external law)—

(*a*) in the heading, for **"offences under this Act"** there is substituted **"offences under sections 1 to 3"**;
(*b*) in subsection (4), for "offence under this Act" there is substituted, in each place, "offence under section 1, 2 or 3 above".

22. In section 9 of that Act (British citizenship immaterial), in paragraphs (*a*) and (*d*) of subsection (2), for "offence under this Act" there is substituted "offence under section 1, 2 or 3 above".

23. Section 11 of that Act (proceedings for offences under section 1) is repealed.

24. Section 12 of that Act (conviction of an offence under section 1 in proceedings for an offence under section 2 or 3) is repealed.

26. Section 14 of that Act (search warrants for offences under section 1) is repealed.

29. (1) Section 17 of that Act (interpretation) is amended as follows.

(2) In subsection (2), after "such access" there is inserted "or to enable such access to be secured".

(3) Subsection (7) is omitted.

(4) For subsection (8) there is substituted—

"(8) An act done in relation to a computer is unauthorised if the person doing the act (or causing it to be done)—

(*a*) is not himself a person who has responsibility for the computer and is entitled to determine whether the act may be done; and
(*b*) does not have consent to the act from any such person.

In this subsection "act" includes a series of acts."

Police Act 1996 (c 16)

30. In section 91 of the Police Act 1996 (offence of causing disaffection amongst members of police forces etc), after subsection (2) there is inserted—

"(3) Liability under subsection (1) for any behaviour is in addition to any civil liability for that behaviour."

Employment Rights Act 1996 (c 18)

31. In section 50 of the Employment Rights Act 1996 (right to time off for public duties), for paragraph (*c*) of subsection (2) there is substituted—

"(*c*) a police authority established under section 3 of the Police Act 1996 or the Metropolitan Police Authority,".

Crime and Disorder Act 1998 (c 37)

36. In section 38(4) of the Crime and Disorder Act 1998 (meaning of "youth justice services"), in paragraph (ee), for "sections 25 to 27" there is substituted "sections 25, 26 and 27".

Youth Justice and Criminal Evidence Act 1999 (c 23)

37. (1) The Youth Justice and Criminal Evidence Act 1999 is amended as follows.

(2) In the cross-heading before section 47 (restrictions on reporting directions under Chapter 1 or 2 of Part 2) and in the heading to that section, for "Chapter I or II" there is substituted "Chapter 1, 1A or 2".

(3) In section 47, in subsection (2)(*a*), after "section 19", in the first place it occurs, there is inserted ", 33A".

Police Reform Act 2002 (c 30)

41. In section 40 of that Act (community safety accreditation schemes), subsection (7) is omitted.

42. In section 41 of that Act (accreditation under community safety accreditation schemes), after subsection (4) there is inserted—

"(4A) A chief officer of police may not grant accreditation under this section to a weights and measures inspector."

43. (1) Section 42 of that Act (supplementary provisions relating to designations and accreditations) is amended as follows.

(2) In subsection (1), after "section 41" there is inserted "or 41A".

(3) In subsection (3)—

(*a*) after "or 41" there is inserted "or an accreditation to any weights and measures inspector under section 41A";
(*b*) after "accredited person" there is inserted "or the accredited inspector".

(4) After subsection (6) there is inserted—

"(6A) Where the accreditation of a weights and measures inspector under section 41A is modified or withdrawn, the chief officer giving notice of the modification or withdrawal shall send a copy of the notice to the local weights and measures authority by which the inspector was appointed."

(5) After subsection (10) there is inserted—

"(11) For the purposes of determining liability for the unlawful conduct of weights and measures inspectors, conduct by such an inspector in reliance or purported reliance on an accreditation under section 41A shall be taken to be conduct in the course of his duties as a weights and measures inspector; and, in the case of a tort, the local weights and measures authority by which he was appointed shall fall to be treated as a joint tortfeasor accordingly."

44. (1) Section 46 of that Act (offences against designated and accredited persons etc) is amended as follows.

(2) In subsections (1) and (2)—

(*a*) before the "or" following paragraph (*b*) there is inserted—

"(ba)an accredited inspector in the execution of his duty,";

(*b*) in paragraph (*c*), after "accredited person" there is inserted "or an accredited inspector".

(3) In subsection (3)—

(*a*) in paragraph (*a*), for "or an accredited person" there is substituted ", an accredited person or an accredited inspector";

(*b*) in paragraph (*b*), for "or that he is an accredited person" there is substituted ", that he is an accredited person or that he is an accredited inspector";

(*c*) in paragraph (*c*), after "accredited person" there is inserted "or as an accredited inspector".

(4) In subsection (4), for "or accredited person" there is substituted ", accredited person or accredited inspector".

45. In section 47 of that Act (interpretation of Chapter 1), in subsection (1) the following definitions are inserted at the appropriate places—

""accredited inspector" means a weights and measures inspector in relation to whom an accreditation under section 41A is for the time being in force;";

""weights and measures inspector" means an inspector of weights and measures appointed under section 72(1) of the Weights and Measures Act 1985."

Anti-social Behaviour Act 2003 (c 38)

53. In the heading to section 25 of the Anti-social Behaviour Act 2003 (parenting contracts in respect of criminal conduct and anti-social behaviour), at the end there is inserted "**: youth offending teams**".

54. (1) Section 26 of that Act (parenting orders in respect of criminal conduct and anti-social behaviour) is amended as follows.

(2) In the heading, at the end there is inserted "**: youth offending teams**".

(3) After subsection (8) there is inserted—

"(9) A person is eligible to be the responsible officer in relation to a parenting order under this section only if he is a member of a youth offending team."

55. (1) Section 27 of that Act (parenting orders: supplemental) is amended as follows.

(2) In subsections (1) and (2), for "section 26" there is substituted "section 26, 26A or 26B".

(3) In subsection (1)(*a*), for "section 25" there is substituted "section 25, 25A or 25B".

(4) In subsection (3), for "in relation to a parenting order under section 26 as they apply" there is substituted—

"in relation to—

(*a*) a parenting order under section 26,

(*b*) a parenting order under section 26A, or

(*c*) a parenting order under section 26B,

as they apply".

(5) After subsection (3) there is inserted—

"(3A) Proceedings for an offence under section 9(7) of the 1998 Act (parenting orders: breach of requirement etc) as applied by subsection (3)(*b*) above may be brought by—

(*a*) the local authority for the area where the child or young person resides or appears to reside, or

(*b*) (if different) the local authority for the area where the person alleged to be in breach resides or appears to reside."

(6) For subsection (4) there is substituted—

"(4) In carrying out their functions in relation to parenting orders—

(*a*) members of youth offending teams,

(*b*) local authorities in England,

(*c*) registered social landlords on the register maintained by the Housing Corporation, and

(*d*) responsible officers in relation to parenting orders made on the application of local authorities in England or of registered social landlords on that register,

must have regard to any guidance which is issued by the Secretary of State from time to time for that purpose.

(4A) In carrying out their functions in relation to parenting orders—

(*a*) local authorities in Wales,

(*b*) registered social landlords on the register maintained by the National Assembly for Wales, and

(*c*) responsible officers in relation to parenting orders made on the application of local authorities in Wales or of registered social landlords on that register,

must have regard to any guidance which is issued by the National Assembly for Wales from time to time for that purpose."

56. (1) Section 28 of that Act (parenting orders: appeals) is amended as follows.

(2) In subsection (1), for "under section 26" there is substituted "by a magistrates' court under section 26, 26A or 26B".

(3) After that subsection there is inserted—

"(1A) An appeal lies to the High Court against the making of a parenting order by a county court under section 26A or 26B."

(4) In subsection (2), for "subsection (1)(*b*)" there is substituted "subsection (1)".

57. In section 29(1) of that Act (interpretation of sections 25 to 29), in the definition of "responsible officer", for the words after "means" there is substituted "the person who is specified as such in the order,".

1–4606I

Section 52

SCHEDULE 15
REPEALS AND REVOCATIONS

PART 1
POLICE REFORM

PART 2
POWERS OF POLICE ETC

Short title and chapter	Extent of repeal
Aviation Security Act 1982 (c 36)	Section 27(1), (4) and (5).
Police and Criminal Evidence Act 1984 (c 60)	In section 64A(1B), the word "or" preceding paragraph (*f*).
Criminal Justice Act 2003 (c 44)	In section 25(2), the word "and" preceding paragraph (*h*).
Immigration, Asylum and Nationality Act 2006 (c 13)	In sections 32(5) and 33(5), the word "and" preceding paragraph (*c*).
	In section 36(9), the word "and" preceding the definition of "Revenue and Customs purposes".

PART 3
CRIME AND ANTI-SOCIAL BEHAVIOUR

Short title and chapter	Extent of repeal
Crime and Disorder Act 1998 (c 37)	In section 114(2), ", 6A(1)".
Powers of Criminal Courts (Sentencing) Act 2000 (c 6)	In Schedule 9, paragraph 199.
Police Reform Act 2002 (c 30)	Section 97(7) to (12).
	Section 98.
Anti-social Behaviour Act 2003 (c 38)	Section 13(4)(*b*).
	Section 91.
Clean Neighbourhoods and Environment Act 2005 (c 16)	Section 1.

Statutory Instruments and Practice Directions on Procedure

The Justices, the Justices' Clerk and Committees

Justices' Allowances Regulations 1976[1]
(SI 1976/117 amended by SI 1976/2118 and SI 1985/1383)

1–4620   **2.** (1) In these Regulations unless the context otherwise requires—

"authority" means any authority responsible by virtue of paragraph 8(4) of Schedule 1 to the Act, for the payment of allowances under that paragraph;

"the Act" means the Administration of Justice Act 1973.

(2) The Interpretation Act [1978] shall apply to the interpretation of these Regulations as it applies to the interpretation of an Act of Parliament, and as if these Regulations and the Regulations revoked by these Regulations were Acts of Parliament.

---

1. Made under Pt III of Sch 1 to the Administration of Justice Act 1973, and varied by Lord Chancellor's Department Circulars.

1–4621   **3.** *Repeals.*

1–4622   **4.** The rate of travelling and subsistence allowance payable under paragraph 8 of Schedule 1 to the Act to a justice of the peace for any area in England or Wales in respect of expenditure on travelling, or, as the case may be, on subsistence, necessarily incurred by him for the purpose of enabling him to perform any of his duties as a justice shall be the rates set out in Schedules 1 and 2 to these Regulations respectively.

1–4623   **5.** (1) The rate of financial loss allowance payable under paragraph 8 of Schedule 1 to the Act[1] to a justice of the peace for any area in England or Wales where for the purpose of enabling him to perform any of his duties as a justice there is incurred by him any expenditure (other than expense on account of travelling or subsistence) to which he would not otherwise be subject or there is suffered by him any loss of earnings or of benefit under the enactments relating to social security which he would otherwise have made or received shall be the amount of that expenditure or loss:

(a) **£34.69 (£45.65** for the self employed) for any period not exceeding 4 hours;

(b) **£69.38 (£91.30** for the self employed) for any period exceeding 4 hours but not exceeding 24 hours;

(c) for a period exceeding 24 hours, **£69.38 (£91.30** for the self employed) for each period of 24 hours plus the amount specified above which is appropriate to the remainder of the period[2].

(2) For the purposes of paragraph (1) above, a justice shall not be treated as having incurred any expenditure or suffered any loss for the purpose of enabling him to perform any of his duties as a justice in so far as the expenditure was also incurred or the loss also suffered for the purpose of enabling the justice to perform an approved duty within the meaning of the Local Government Act 1972.

---

1. See now the Justices of the Peace Act 1979, s 12(1) this PART, ante.
2. These sums were substituted by Court Service Circular 166/2002 and with effect from 1 October 2002. As indicated, in recognition of the fact that financial loss allowance for self-employed is taxable, the allowances have been grossed up at the standard rate of tax.

1–4624   **6.** A justice who desires to claim financial loss, travelling or subsistence allowance shall complete and submit to the authority an application in the appropriate form set out in Schedule 3 to these Regulations or in a form substantially to the like effect.

1–4625   **7.** An authority shall, so far as practicable, arrange for the issue to a justice of a ticket, or a document which can be exchanged for a ticket, to cover a journey in respect of which a travelling allowance would otherwise fall to be paid.

1–4626   **8.** (1) An authority shall keep a record of every payment made under paragraph 8 of Schedule 1 to the Act showing the amount and nature of the payment and the name of the justice to whom it is paid; and payments made in respect of duties as chairman, deputy chairman or member of the Crown Court shall be kept separate from other payments in the said record.

(2) For the purposes of this Regulation, expenditure incurred in the issue to a justice of a ticket or other document under Regulation 7 of these Regulations shall be deemed to be an amount paid to that justice.

1–4627   **9.** Where any expenditure or loss entitles a person to receive an allowance under paragraph 8 of Schedule 1 to the Act in respect of duties as a justice and an allowance of the same nature, by whatever name called, under any other enactment in respect of duties in respect of some other capacity, the aggregate amount which that person shall be entitled to receive under the said paragraph 8 on account of the said expenditure or loss shall be reduced by the aggregate amount received by him on that account under the other enactment, and any claim made under the said paragraph 8 shall contain particulars of any amount so received or claimed, or which it is intended to claim, under the other enactment.

Regulation 4   SCHEDULE 1[1]
                        RATES OF TRAVELLING ALLOWANCE

1–4628   **1.** (1) The rate for travel by public service shall be the amount of the fare of the class in which the justice chooses to travel, but, subject to any supplementary allowances payable under sub-paragraph (2) of this paragraph, shall not exceed the lowest available first class fare.

(2) The rate payable under the foregoing sub-paragraph shall, if the justice so claims, be increased by supplementary allowances not exceeding the expenditure incurred on deposit or porterage of luggage, on reservation of seats, or on Pullman Car or similar supplements (other than expenditure on refreshment or sleeping accommodation).

2. The rate for travel by hired motor vehicle shall be—

(a) in cases of urgency or where no public service is reasonably available, the amount of the fare and any reasonable gratuity paid; and

(b) in any other case, the amount of the fare for travel by the appropriate public service.

3. (1) *Obsolete.*

(2) The rate for travel by a justices' own motor car and motor cycle shall be—

(a) for the use of a motor vehicle of cylinder capacity up to and including 1,100 cubic centimetres, **30.98p** a mile;

(b) for the use of a motor vehicle of cylinder capacity of 1,101 cubic centimetres to 1,549 cubic centimetres, **39.90p** a mile;

(c) for the use of a motor vehicle of cylinder capacity exceeding 1,550 cubic centimetres **50.65p** a mile;

(d) *Revoked.*

Provided that a 5,000 mile per annum threshold shall be applied after which a standard rate of **26.13p** a mile shall have effect.

(3) The appropriate rate specified in the foregoing provisions of this paragraph shall, if the justice so claims, be increased—

(a) in respect of the carriage of each passenger, not exceeding four, to whom a travelling allowance would otherwise be payable under any enactment:

(i) by not more than **1·0p** a mile;

(ii) *Obsolete;*

(b) in the case of an absence overnight from the usual place of residence, by the amount of any expenditure incurred on garaging a motor vehicle, not exceeding **29·0p** a night in the case of a motor car or tri-car or **17·5p** a night in the case of a vehicle of any other type;

(c) in any case, by the amount of any expenditure incurred on tolls, ferries or parking fees.

(4) For the purposes of this paragraph—

"motor cycle combination" means a motor cycle with a side car;
"motor cycle" means a motor cycle without a side car.

4. The rate for travel by air shall not exceed the fare paid but, subject thereto, shall be the rate applicable to travel by the appropriate public service together with an allowance equivalent to the amount of any saving in subsistence allowance consequent upon travel by air.

5. In this Schedule "public service" means any service provided for travel by the public by railway, ship, vessel, omnibus, trolley vehicle or tramway.

---

1. This Schedule is printed as varied by Home Office Circular No 26/1981, dated 13 March 1981, No 77/1981 dated 18 August 1981, No 9/1983, dated 11 January 1983, No 27/1984, dated 24 April 1984, No 4/1985, dated 5 February 1985, No 2/1986, dated 10 January 1986, No 4/1987, dated 27 March 1987, No 4/1988, dated 19 January 1988, No 19/1989, dated 15 February 1989, No 52/1990, dated 11 June 1990 and No 68/1991 dated 28 August 1991, Lord Chancellor's Department Circular No MCD (93) 9 dated 12 November 1993, No MCD (94) 6 dated 22 August 1994, No 13/96, dated 15 December 1995, No 3/96, dated 21 August 1996, No 1/97, dated 22 August 1997, F3/42/10, dated 3 September 1998, F3/42/10, dated 11 August 1999 and F3/42/10, dated 21 August 2000 *Court Business* effective 1 October 2002.

With effect from 1 September 1997 a new allowance has been introduced for justices who travel to and from court by bicycle. The bicycle allowance payable is **6·9p** per mile (LCD Circular 1/97, dated 22 August 1997, F3/42/10, dated 3 September 1998, F3/42/10, dated 11 August 1999 and F3/42/10, dated 21 August 2000).

Regulation 4   SCHEDULE 2[1]
                  RATES OF SUBSISTENCE ALLOWANCE

1–4629   **1.** (1) The rate of subsistence allowance shall be—

(a) in the case of an absence, not involving an absence overnight, from the usual place of residence—

     (i) of more than four but not more than eight hours, **£6·77**;
     (ii) of more than eight but not more than twelve hours, **£9.44**;
     (iii) of more than twelve hours, **£17.82**;
     (iv) *obsolete*;

(b) in the case of an absence overnight from the usual place of residence, **£79.82**;
     or for such an absence overnight in Greater London area **£91.04**.

(2) Any rate determined under the preceding sub-paragraph shall be deemed to cover a continuous period of absence of twenty-four hours.

2. (1) The rates specified in the preceding paragraph shall be reduced by an appropriate amount in respect of any meal provided free of charge by any local authority during the period to which the allowance relates.

(2) In the preceding sub-paragraph "local authority" means the corporation of the City of London, a county council, a district council, a London borough council or a parish or community council.

3. (1) When main meals (i.e. a full breakfast, lunch or dinner) are taken on trains during a period for which there is entitlement to day subsistence, the reasonable cost of the meals (including VAT), may be reimbursed in full, within the limits specified below. Where the cost of meals taken on trains is reimbursed, the rate of day subsistence allowance for that period of duty shall not exceed the maximum payable if the period of absence from the usual place of residence were reduced by 4 hours in respect of each meal taken.

(2) The limitations of reimbursement are:

(a) absence of more than 4 but not more than 8 hours, the cost of 1 main meal;
(b) absence of more than 8 hours but not more than 12 hours, the cost of 2 main meals;
(c) absence of more than 12 hours, the cost of 3 main meals.

---

1. See note 1 to Sch 1, ante.

Local Probation Boards (Appointment) Regulations 2000[1]

(SI 2000/3342 as amended by SI 2001/786, SI 2005/617 and SI 2006/2664)

1–4800   **1.** These Regulations may be cited as the Local Probation Boards (Appointment) Regulations 2000 and shall come into force on 22nd January 2001.

---

1. Made by the Lord Chancellor under paras 2(4) and (6) and 3(4) of Schedule 1 to the Criminal Justice and Court Services Act 2000.

1–4801   **2.** A local probation board shall have a maximum of 15 members.

1–4802   **3.** A member of a local probation board shall be at least eighteen years of age on appointment.

1–4803   **4.** The following shall not be appointed as a member of a local probation board:

(a) a person employed under a contract of employment with a local probation board; or
(b) a person who is subject to the notification requirements of Part 1 of the Sex Offenders Act 1997.

1–4804   **5.** (1) Persons appointed to a local probation board shall, so far as practicable, be representative of the local community in the board's area.

(2) *Revoked.*

(3) Persons appointed to a local probation board shall, so far as practicable, live or work (or have lived or worked) in the board's area.

1–4805   **6.** A member of a local probation board other than the chief officer shall be appointed for a term not exceeding three years and shall be eligible for re-appointment.

1–4806   **7.** Save for a chief officer, no person shall serve more than two terms as a member of a local probation board.

1–4807   **8.** (1) The Secretary of State may suspend, or remove, from office a member of a local probation board, by giving notice in writing on one of the following grounds:

(*a*)   subject to paragraph (2) below, that he has failed to attend board meetings for a continuous period of six months without the consent of the board;

(*b*)   that he has been convicted of a criminal offence;

(*c*)   that he has become subject to the notification requirements of Part I of the Sex Offenders Act 1997;

(*d*)   that a bankruptcy order has been made against him, or his estate has been sequestrated or he has made a composition or arrangement with, or granted a trust deed for, his creditors; or

(*e*)   that it is considered that he is unable or unfit to discharge his functions as a member.

(2) A member of a local probation board shall not be removed from office under paragraph (1)(*a*) above if in the opinion of the Secretary of State he has good reason for the non-attendance.

Local Probation Boards (Miscellaneous Provisions) Regulations 2001

(SI 2001/786 as amended by SI 2001/1035, SI 2005/2114 and SI 2006/2664)

1–4808   **1. Citation, commencement and interpretation.**   (1) These Regulations may be cited as the Local Probation Boards (Miscellaneous Provisions) Regulations 2001 and shall come into force on 1st April 2001.

(2) In these Regulations, "the 2000 Act" means the Criminal Justice and Court Services Act 2000.

1–4809   **2. Purposes of the National Probation Service for England and Wales.**   The purposes of the National Probation Service for England and Wales mentioned in section 1(1) of the 2000 Act are hereby extended under section 1(3) of that Act to include the giving of information relating to the judicial and custodial process to:

(*a*)   the victim of a person convicted of an offence; and

(*b*)   a person claiming to be the victim of a person charged with an offence.

1–4809A   **3. Fares incurred in reporting.**   A local probation board may, in a case of hardship, pay the cost of fares necessarily incurred by a person under the supervision of an officer of the board in reporting to the officer or presenting himself elsewhere in accordance with instructions given by the officer.

1–4809B   **4. Financial assistance.**   Where a person is subject to the supervision of a local probation board, the board may grant that person any financial assistance which it considers necessary and which is not available from any other source.

1–4809C   **5. Delegation to chief officers.**   (1) Subject to paragraph (2), the power of a local probation board to appoint and dismiss staff below the level of assistant chief officer and to conduct disciplinary and grievance hearings in relation to such staff is hereby prescribed under paragraph 10 of Schedule 1 to the 2000 Act for the purpose of being exercised by the chief officer on behalf of the board.

(2) Paragraph (1) shall not prevent the board from arranging for the carrying out of the said power by a person other than the chief officer where the chief officer is for any reason unavailable to do so.

(3) Nothing in this regulation shall prevent a local probation board from hearing an appeal from a person employed or formerly employed by the board in relation to any disciplinary or grievance matter concerning that person.

1–4809D   **6. Complaints.**   (1) A local probation board shall make and publicise arrangements for dealing with complaints.

(2) The following persons are prescribed under paragraph 18 of Schedule 1 to the 2000 Act for the purpose of complaints being made by or on behalf of such persons in relation to things done under arrangements made by the board under section 5 of that Act:

(*a*)   persons in respect of whom the local probation board has had responsibility for writing a pre-sentence report;

(*b*)   persons convicted of offences who are, or have been, under the supervision of a local probation board or who are or have been provided with accommodation in premises approved by the Secretary of State in accordance with section 9 of the 2000 Act;

(*c*)   victims of persons convicted of offences;

(*d*)   persons who have suffered physical injury or distress or theft of or damage to their property as a result of the conduct of a person subject to a community order or released from prison on licence whilst undertaking activities under the supervision of an officer of a local probation board; and

(e) the immediate family of a person falling within sub-paragraph (*a*), (*b*), (*c*) or (*d*) above where that person has died; and for this purpose, "immediate family" means the parents, spouse, civil partner, cohabitee, siblings or children of a person falling within (*a*), (*b*), (*c*) or (*d*) above.

1–4809E 7. Audit committees. (1) Each local probation board shall establish an audit committee.

(2) The audit committee shall be responsible for reviewing the financial management and probity of the local probation board.

(3) An audit committee shall have a maximum of 6 members, of whom at least 4 shall also be members of the local probation board.

(4) The quorum of an audit committee shall be not less than 3.

(5) Where the number of members attending a meeting of an audit committee who are not also members of the local probation board exceeds the number of committee members attending the meeting who are also members of the board, any decision made by the committee must be ratified by the board in order to take effect.

(6) The chairman of an audit committee must be appointed by the local probation board.

(7) Neither the chairman of a local probation board nor the chief officer of the board may be appointed as the chairman of the audit committee.

1–4809F 8. Meetings of local probation boards. (1) Subject to the provision of these Regulations, a local probation board may establish its own procedures and the procedures of its committees and sub-committees.

(2) The quorum of a local probation board shall not be less than 5.

(3) A local probation board shall meet at least four times a year and, so far as practicable, shall meet at least ten times a year.

(4) A local probation board shall meet in public, except where the board resolves to meet in private in accordance with a scheme that has been approved by the Secretary of State.

1–4809G 9. Secretary or treasurer. (1) Each local probation board shall appoint a secretary and a treasurer who shall, subject to paragraph (3) below, each hold office in accordance with the terms of his appointment.

(2) A member of a local probation board shall not be appointed as the secretary or treasurer to the board.

(3) A secretary or treasurer to a local probation board may be suspended or removed from office by resolution of the board.

(4) A person appointed as treasurer on or after 1st April 2001 shall be a member of one or more of the bodies mentioned in section 113(3) of the Local Government Finance Act 1988.

Local Probation Boards (Appointments and Miscellaneous Provisions) Regulations 2001[1]
(SI 2001/1035 amended by SI 2006/680)

1–4810 1. Citation and commencement. These Regulations may be cited as the Local Probation Boards (Appointments and Miscellaneous Provisions) Regulations 2001 and shall come into force on 10th April 2001.

---

1. Made by the Secretary of State, in exercise of the powers conferred upon him by ss 4(3) and 25 of and paras 2(4), (5) and (6) and 6 of Sch 1 to the Criminal Justice and Court Services Act 2000.

1–4811 2. Applications for appointment to local probation boards. (1) The procedure for the appointment of the chairman, chief officer and other members of local probation boards, except the member to be appointed by the Lord Chief Justice, shall be in accordance with the following provisions of these Regulations.

(2) A person seeking appointment to a local probation board shall apply on a form provided for the purpose by the Secretary of State.

(3) The completed application form shall be submitted to the Secretary of State within the time set for such applications.

(4) In the case of an application for the post of chief officer, candidates who on the basis of the completed application form appear to the Secretary of State to be best qualified for the post shall be referred for assessment of their suitability to an assessment centre established for the purpose by the Secretary of State.

(5) Paragraph (4) above shall not apply in relation to a temporary appointment to fill a vacancy in the post of chief officer where it appears to the Secretary of State that the period for which the person appointed will hold the post is not likely to exceed 12 months.

(6) The Secretary of State shall not make an appointment except on the recommendation of a selection panel appointed under regulation 3 below.

(7) In paragraphs (1) to (4) above references to the Secretary of State, except for the second reference in paragraph (4), include a reference to a person providing services to him.

1–4812 3. Selection panels. (1) Selection panels shall be established by the Secretary of State in accordance with this regulation.

(2) Subject to paragraph (3) below, a selection panel shall consist of a chairman and two or more other members appointed by the Secretary of State.

(3) Where the panel is considering the appointment of a chief officer, one of the members shall be appointed from the members of the local probation board on which the person appointed as chief officer will serve.

(4) The Secretary of State shall—

(a) provide the selection panel with such accommodation and assistance as they may reasonably require; and

(b) meet any expenses of the panel in the exercise of their functions.

1–4813   4. Functions of selection panel.   (1) A selection panel shall interview any person who has applied to the Secretary of State for appointment to a local probation board and who either—

(a) in the case of a candidate to whom regulation 2(4) applies (applications for post of chief officer), has been selected as a suitable candidate at an assessment centre in accordance with that regulation; or

(b) in the case of any other candidate, has been referred to the panel by the Secretary of State or a person providing services to him.

(2) All candidates selected for interview in accordance with paragraph (1) above shall be notified in writing by a person acting on behalf of the selection panel of the date, time and place of the interview.

(3) The notification shall be sent to the candidate at least 5 days before the date set for the interview.

(4) A person who has been notified in accordance with the provisions of this regulation but who fails to attend for interview at the date, time and place notified to him must be given the opportunity to explain his absence and be given an alternative date for the interview where it appears to the selection panel appropriate to do so.

(5) When the selection panel has completed interviews of the candidates, other than for the post of chief officer, it shall draw up a short list of the candidates, if any, considered suitable for appointment.

(6) The short list shall be submitted to the Secretary of State.

(7) Where a selection panel has completed interviews of candidates for the post of chief officer, it shall determine which, if any, of the candidates interviewed it considers suitable for the post, and if more than one candidate is selected, it shall prepare a list naming the suitable candidates in order of merit.

(8) A selection panel shall inform the Secretary of State of its decision under paragraph (7) above and supply him with a copy of any list prepared in accordance with that paragraph.

1–4814   5. Appointments.   (1) Appointments other than for the post of chief officer made by the Secretary of State to a local probation board must be made from the short list of candidates submitted to him by the selection panel for that board under regulation 4(6) above and must, so far as practicable, be made from candidates who live or work in the area of the board to which the appointments are to be made and who are representative of the local community in that board's area.

(2) Any person appointed chief officer by the Secretary of State must be a person who was selected by the selection panel as being the only or the most suitable candidate for the post.

(3) Where a person on a list prepared by a selection panel rejects or fails to take up an offer of appointment as chief officer, the next person on the list (if any) shall be regarded as the most suitable.

1–4815   6. Re-advertising unfilled posts.   Where the Secretary of State makes no appointment to a post for which candidates were interviewed by a selection panel, the post shall be re-advertised.

1–4816   7. Audit committees.   (1) Regulation 7 of the Local Probation Boards (Miscellaneous Provisions) Regulations 2001 is amended in accordance with the following paragraphs of this regulation.

(2) For paragraph (4) there is substituted—

"(4) The quorum of an audit committee shall be not less than 3.".

(3) For paragraph (6) there is substituted—

"(6) The chairman of an audit committee must be appointed by the local probation board.".

Courts Boards Areas Order 2004[1]
(SI 2004/1192 amended by SI 2004/1303)

1–4820   1   Citation and commencement.   This Order may be cited as the Court Boards Areas Order 2004 and shall come into force on 1st June 2004.

---

1. Made by the Lord Chancellor, in exercise of the powers conferred upon him by s 4(2) of the Courts Act 2003, having regard to the desirability of specifying areas which are the same as the police areas listed in Sch 1 to the Police Act 1996 and the area consisting of the Metropolitan Police District and the City of London police area, a draft of which has, in accordance with s 108(2) and (3) of the Courts Act 2003, been laid before and approved by resolution of each House of Parliament.

1–4821 **2.** Each of the areas respectively named in column 1, and specified in column 2 of Table 1 of the Schedule to this Order, is a courts board area in England.

1–4822 **3.** Each of the areas respectively named in column 1, and specified in column 2 of Table 2 of the Schedule to this Order, is a courts board area in Wales.

1–4823   SCHEDULE

TABLE 1
ENGLAND

Avon and Somerset	The county of Somerset and the non-metropolitan districts of Bath and North East Somerset, Bristol, North Somerset and South Gloucestershire
Bedfordshire	The county of Bedfordshire and the non-metropolitan district of Luton
Cambridgeshire	The county of Cambridgeshire and the non-metropolitan district of Peterborough
Cheshire	The county of Cheshire and the non-metropolitan districts of Halton and Warrington
Cleveland	The non-metropolitan districts of Hartlepool, Middlesbrough, Redcar and Cleveland and Stockton-on-Tees
Cumbria	The county of Cumbria
Derbyshire	The county of Derbyshire and the non-metropolitan district of Derby
Devon and Cornwall	The counties of Devon and Cornwall, the non-metropolitan districts of Plymouth and Torbay and the Isles of Scilly
Dorset	The county of Dorset and the non-metropolitan districts of Bournemouth and Poole
Durham	The county of Durham and the non-metropolitan district of Darlington
Essex	The county of Essex and the non-metropolitan districts of Southend-on-Sea and Thurrock
Gloucestershire	The county of Gloucestershire
Greater Manchester	The metropolitan districts of Bolton, Bury, Manchester, Oldham, Rochdale, Salford, Stockport, Tameside, Trafford and Wigan
Hampshire	The counties of Hampshire and Isle of Wight and the non-metropolitan districts of Portsmouth and Southampton
Hertfordshire	The county of Hertfordshire
Humberside	The non-metropolitan districts of the East Riding of Yorkshire, Kingston upon Hull, North East Lincolnshire and North Lincolnshire
Kent	The county of Kent and the non-metropolitan district of Medway
Lancashire	The county of Lancashire and the non-metropolitan districts of Blackburn with Darwen and Blackpool
Leicestershire	The county of Leicestershire and the non-metropolitan districts of Leicester and Rutland
Lincolnshire	The county of Lincolnshire
London	Greater London
Merseyside	The metropolitan districts of Knowsley, Liverpool, St. Helens, Sefton and Wirral
Norfolk	The county of Norfolk
Northamptonshire	The county of Northamptonshire
Northumbria	The county of Northumberland and the metropolitan districts of Gateshead, Newcastle upon Tyne, North Tyneside, South Tyneside and Sunderland
North Yorkshire	The county of North Yorkshire and the non-metropolitan district of York
Nottinghamshire	The county of Nottinghamshire and the non-metropolitan district of Nottingham
South Yorkshire	The metropolitan districts of Barnsley, Doncaster, Rotherham and Sheffield
Staffordshire	The county of Staffordshire and the non-metropolitan district of Stoke-on-Trent
Suffolk	The county of Suffolk
Surrey	The county of Surrey
Sussex	The counties of East Sussex and West Sussex and the non-metropolitan district of Brighton and Hove
Thames Valley	The counties of Buckinghamshire and Oxfordshire and the non-metropolitan districts of Bracknell Forest, Milton Keynes Reading, Slough, West Berkshire, Windsor and Maidenhead and Wokingham
Warwickshire	The county of Warwickshire
West Mercia	The counties of Shropshire and Worcestershire and the non-metropolitan districts of Herefordshire and Telford and The Wrekin
West Midlands	The metropolitan districts of Birmingham, Coventry, Dudley, Sandwell, Solihull, Walsall and Wolverhampton
West Yorkshire	The metropolitan districts of Bradford, Calderdale, Kirklees, Leeds and Wakefield
Wiltshire	The county of Wiltshire and the non-metropolitan district of Swindon

TABLE 2
WALES

Dyfed Powys	The counties of Ceredigion, Carmarthenshire, Pembrokeshire and Powys
Gwent	The county of Monmouthshire and the county boroughs of Blaenau Gwent, Caerphilly, Newport and Torfaen
North Wales	The counties of the Isle of Anglesey, Gwynedd, Denbighshire and Flintshire and the county boroughs of Conwy and Wrexham
South Wales	The counties of Cardiff and Swansea and the county boroughs of Bridgend, Merthyr Tydfil, Neath Port Talbot, Rhondda Cynon Taff and the Vale of Glamorgan

Courts Boards (Appointments and Procedure) Regulations 2004[1]
(SI 2004/1193 as amended by SI 2006/1016)

1–4830 **1. Citation and commencement.** These Regulations may be cited as the Courts Boards (Appointments and Procedure) Regulations 2004 and shall come into force on 1st June 2004.

---

1. Made by the Lord Chancellor, in exercise of the powers conferred upon him by paras 3, 4, 5 and 7 of Sch 1 to the Courts Act 2003, a draft of which has been laid before and approved by resolution of each House of Parliament.

1–4831 **2.** In these Regulations—

"courts board area" means the area to which a courts board relates, as specified and named in an order made under section 4 of the Act;
"the Act" means the Courts Act 2003.

1–4832 **3. Appointment of members of courts boards.** No courts board may comprise more than twelve members.

1–4833 **4. Appointment of courts board appointments advisory panels.** (1) In any case in which these Regulations indicate that functions are to be discharged in respect of a courts board by or in relation to a courts board appointments advisory panel, the Lord Chancellor shall appoint such a panel in accordance with the provisions of this regulation.

(2) A courts board appointments advisory panel shall comprise—

(a) except as provided by paragraph (3), a person in the civil service of the state who appears to the Lord Chancellor to be appropriate for this purpose;

(b) a person who has been trained in a manner approved by the Commissioner for Public Appointments to act as an independent appointments assessor; and

(c) except as provided by paragraph (4), a member of the courts board in respect of which the functions mentioned in paragraph (1) are to be discharged.

(3) In any case where an appointment to a courts board appointments advisory panel is to be made prior to the commencement of section 2(1) and of paragraph 13 of Schedule 2 to the Act, a person appointed under paragraph (2)(a) shall be a person either in the civil service of the state or in the employment of a magistrates' courts committee who appears to the Lord Chancellor to be appropriate for this purpose.

(4) In any case in which either there are no members of a courts board for the relevant area or it appears to the Lord Chancellor that no member of the relevant courts board may reasonably be appointed to a courts board appointments advisory panel, he shall instead appoint some other person who appears to him to have appropriate knowledge or experience of the working of the courts in the relevant courts board area.

1–4834 **5. Appointment of members of courts boards who are not judges.** (1) This regulation has effect in relation to the appointment of members of courts boards except for those to which regulation 6 applies, and except as provided by regulation 8.

(2) The Lord Chancellor must not make such appointments otherwise than in accordance with this regulation.

(3) Where he is considering making an appointment, the Lord Chancellor must—

(a) identify, and publish in such manner as he considers appropriate—

(i) the qualities and abilities which in his view are likely to be the most relevant, and
(ii) any experience and qualifications which in his view are likely to be relevant,

in considering the suitability of candidates to be appointed; and

(b) identify the candidates from among whom the appointment may be made.

(4) Before taking the steps set out in paragraph (3), the Lord Chancellor must consult a person who has been trained in a manner approved by the Commissioner for Public Appointments to act as an independent appointments assessor.

(5) Before making an appointment, the Lord Chancellor must notify a courts board appointments advisory panel of—

(a) the matters and candidates which he has identified under paragraph (3) above, and
(b) which of the descriptions mentioned in sub-paragraphs (b) to (d) of paragraph 2 of Schedule 1 to the Act he considers requires to be satisfied in the case of the person to be appointed (the "relevant description").

(6) On being notified under paragraph (5), a courts board appointments advisory panel must consider the extent to which each candidate—

(a) satisfies the relevant description, and
(b) taking into account the matters which the Lord Chancellor has identified under sub-paragraph (3)(a), appears to it to be a suitable person to be appointed,

and must accordingly make such recommendations about appointment to the Lord Chancellor as it considers appropriate.

(7) The Lord Chancellor must supply a courts board appointments advisory panel with such further information as it reasonably requires for the purpose of discharging its functions under paragraph (6).

(8) Before making an appointment, the Lord Chancellor must take into account the recommendations made under paragraph (6).

1–4835   6. Appointment of members of courts boards who are judges.   (1) This regulation applies in the case of any appointment of a member of a courts board who is a judge.

(2) The Lord Chancellor must not make an appointment to which this regulation applies unless the person to be appointed has been recommended to him by the Lord Chief Justice as suitable for that appointment.

1–4836   7. Selection of chairmen of courts boards.   (1) The Lord Chancellor is to select one of the members of each courts board to be its chairman.

(2) Where he is considering selecting a chairman, the Lord Chancellor must identify, and publish in such manner as he considers appropriate—

(a)   the qualities and abilities which in his view are likely to be the most relevant, and

(b)   any experience and qualifications which in his view are likely to be relevant,

in considering the suitability of candidates to be appointed.

(3) Before taking the steps set out in paragraph (2), the Lord Chancellor must consult a person who has been trained in a manner approved by the Commissioner for Public Appointments to act as an independent appointments assessor.

(4) Except as provided by regulation 10, before selecting a member of a courts board to be its chairman, the Lord Chancellor must consult a courts board appointments advisory panel.

1–4837   8. Term of office of members of courts boards.   (1) A courts board member shall be appointed for a fixed term not exceeding three years.

(2) On expiry of a member's term of office, the Lord Chancellor may, subject to paragraphs (2A) and (3), re-appoint that member to serve a further term.

(2A) The Lord Chancellor must not re-appoint a judge under paragraph (2) unless the Lord Chief Justice concurs.

(3) No member of a courts board may be re-appointed more than twice.

(4) Regulation 5 does not apply to a re-appointment under paragraph (2).

1–4838   9. Resignation, suspension or removal of members of courts boards.   (1) A member of a courts board may resign his office at any time by giving notice in writing to the Lord Chancellor.

(2) The Lord Chancellor may by giving notice in writing suspend or remove from office a member of a courts board on one of the following grounds—

(a)   that he has been charged with or convicted of a criminal offence either—

(i)   in respect of conduct which is alleged to have taken place since his appointment, or

(ii)   which was not disclosed, or is in respect of conduct which was not disclosed, in response to any relevant request made by the Lord Chancellor before his appointment;

(b)   that he has failed to attend courts board meetings for a continuous period of six months without the prior approval of the board;

(c)   that he is unable or unfit to carry out his functions as a member of a courts board;

(d)   that he has otherwise failed to carry out his functions as a member of a courts board or acted in a manner incompatible with his membership.

(2A) The Lord Chancellor must not suspend or remove a judge under paragraph (2) unless the Lord Chief Justice concurs.

(3) Where the Lord Chancellor gives notice in writing suspending or removing a member from office, that member's term of office shall be suspended or cease, as the case may be, from the date on which the notice is given by the Lord Chancellor.

1–4839   10. Tenure of office of chairmen of courts boards.   (1) A member selected to be a chairman of a courts board shall be appointed by the Lord Chancellor to hold that office for a fixed term.

(2) On expiry of a member's term of office as chairman, the Lord Chancellor may select and re-appoint that member to serve a further term as chairman.

(3) Regulation 7 does not apply to selection and re-appointment under paragraph (2).

(4) A chairman of a courts board may resign from that office at any time by giving notice in writing to the Lord Chancellor.

(5) Where the Lord Chancellor gives notice in writing under regulation 9 suspending or removing a chairman's membership of a courts board, his term of office as chairman shall also be suspended or cease, as the case may be, from the date on which the notice is given by the Lord Chancellor.

1–4840   11. Procedure of courts boards.   (1) Each courts board must decide the number of its members, not being fewer than four, which will constitute its quorum.

(2) Where a decision of a courts board is to be made by voting—

(a)   each member present at the meeting has one vote; and

(b)   where there is an equality of votes, the member presiding at the meeting has an additional, casting vote.

(3) Meetings of a courts board shall be presided over by—

(a)   the chairman; or

(*b*) where no chairman is present, a member elected to preside by those members present at the meeting.

1-4841   12. Proceedings of a courts board shall not be invalidated by reason of a vacancy among its members or of a defect in the appointment of a member or in the selection of its chairman.

1-4842   13. Delegation by Lord Chief Justice. The Lord Chief Justice may nominate a judicial office holder (as defined in section 109(4) of the Constitutional Reform Act 2005) to exercise his functions under these Regulations.

Justices of the Peace (Size and Chairmanship of Bench) Rules 2005[1]
(SI 2005/553)

1-4860   1. Citation and commencement. These Rules may be cited as the Justices of the Peace (Size and Chairmanship of Bench) Rules 2005 and shall come into force on 1 April 2005.

---

1. Made by the Lord Chancellor, in exercise of the powers conferred upon him by s 17 of the Courts Act 2003 and after consultation with the Criminal Procedure Rule Committee, the Family Procedure Rule Committee, and the Magistrates' Courts Rule Committee, in accordance with s 20(2) of the Courts Act 2003.

1-4861   2. Interpretation. In these Rules—

"election meeting" means a meeting held in accordance with rule 11;
"justice" means, in relation to a local justice area, a justice who is assigned to that area;
"justices' clerk" in relation to a local justice area, means a justices' clerk assigned to that area and includes any person acting as such;
"reserve vote" means a vote cast in accordance with rule 7(6);
"the schedule" means the Schedule to these Rules;
references to a ballot are references to a ballot conducted under these Rules;
references to a postal ballot are references to a postal ballot conducted under rule 7.

1-4862   3. Size of bench. (1) Subject to paragraph (2), the number of justices sitting to deal with a case as a magistrates' court shall not be greater than three.
(2) Paragraph (1) shall not apply to a magistrates' court sitting as a youth court, a family proceedings court or a licensing or betting licensing committee.

1-4863   4. Presiding justices. (1) A justice may preside before he has been included on a list of approved court chairmen only if—
(*a*) he is under the supervision of a justice who is on the list of approved court chairmen; and
(*b*) he has completed the chairman training courses prescribed by the BTDC
(2) In this rule, "list of approved court chairmen" means a list kept by a Bench Training and Development Committee in accordance with rule 13 of the Justices of the Peace (Training and Appraisal) Rules 2005.

1-4864   5. Elections. (1) The justices for each local justice area shall each year elect from among themselves a chairman and one or more deputy chairmen.
(2) Subject to paragraph (3), a secret ballot shall be held in accordance with these Rules for the election of a chairman and for the election of deputy chairmen.
(3) Paragraph (2) shall not apply where, as the case may be, the chairman or all the deputy chairmen required to fill the number of offices available have been elected under rule 6(8).
(4) A justice is eligible to vote in an election if—
(*a*) in the case of an election by postal ballot, the justice is assigned to that local justice area at the date the notices seeking nominations are posted; and
(*b*) in the case of an election held at an election meeting, the justice is assigned to that local justice area at the date of the meeting.

1-4865   6. Nomination procedure. (1) The justices' clerk shall give written notice, in accordance with paragraph (2), to each justice eligible to vote in a postal ballot.
(2) The notice shall—
(*a*) notify the recipient that he may submit to the justices' clerk nominations in writing for the offices of chairman and deputy chairman, the number of which will have been determined under rule 11(2)(*b*);
(*b*) specify a closing date for receipt of nominations;
(*c*) specify the date, time and place of the election meeting;
(*d*) be posted by first class post at least 28 days before the closing date for receipt of nominations (including the date of posting but excluding the closing date for receipt of nominations); and
(*e*) not be posted earlier than 12 weeks, nor later than 9 weeks, before the date of the election meeting (including the date of posting but excluding the date of the election meeting).
(3) A justice may not be nominated without his consent.
(4) Each nomination must be proposed and seconded by justices eligible to vote in a postal

ballot and shall contain the full names and signatures of the proposer, seconder and justice nominated.

(5) The justices' clerk shall satisfy himself that each nomination received fulfils the requirements of paragraph (4) but shall not disclose the names of proposers and seconders.

(6) If a justice nominated for election as chairman wishes, should he not be elected chairman, to be nominated for election as deputy chairman, his nomination shall contain a statement to that effect signed by the proposer, seconder and justice nominated.

(7) If the statement referred to in paragraph (6) is included in a nomination for chairman, that nomination shall be treated as a nomination for the office of chairman and for the office of deputy chairman (but a justice may not hold both offices at the same time).

(8) Where—

(a) only one justice is nominated for election as chairman, that justice shall be elected chairman (and his nomination, if any, to the office of deputy chairman shall be treated as having been withdrawn);

(b) the number of justices nominated to the office of deputy chairman equals or is less than the number of offices available, those justices shall be elected to the office of deputy chairman.

(9) Nominations withdrawn before the date of posting the ballot papers shall be disregarded when determining the number of nominations for the purposes of paragraph (8).

(10) If a justice is elected to the office of deputy chairman under paragraph (8)(b) and is subsequently elected chairman, he shall not take up the office of deputy chairman and his nomination for that office shall be treated as having been withdrawn before the closing date for receipt of completed ballot papers.

(11) If a chairman or deputy chairman is elected under paragraph (8), the justices' clerk shall give written notice, in accordance with paragraph (12), to each justice eligible to vote in a postal ballot of the name of the justice or justices elected.

(12) The notice under paragraph (11) shall be sent by first class post at least 28 days before the date of the election meeting (including the date of posting but excluding the date of the election meeting).

(13) Where a justice who has been nominated for election to the office of chairman or deputy chairman ceases to be a justice at any time after nomination up to (and including) the closing date for receipt of completed ballot papers, his nomination shall be treated as having been withdrawn when he ceased to be a justice.

(14) A nomination cannot be withdrawn after the closing date for receipt of completed ballot papers.

1–4866   7. Conduct of postal ballot.   (1) Where nominations are received under rule 6 and have not been withdrawn before the date of posting the ballot papers, the secret ballot held under rule 5(2) shall be a postal ballot held in accordance with this rule.

(2) The justices' clerk shall—

(a) where there is to be an election of a chairman, prepare ballot papers which contain a list in alphabetical order of the justices nominated as chairman;

(b) where there is to be an election of a deputy chairman or deputy chairmen, prepare ballot papers which contain a list in alphabetical order of the justices nominated as deputy chairman; and

(c) send by first class post to each justice eligible to vote in a postal ballot one ballot paper for each election.

(3) There must be—

(a) at least 21 days between the date of posting the ballot papers and the closing date for receipt of completed ballot papers (including the date of posting but excluding the closing date for receipt of completed ballot papers); and

(b) at least 7 days between the closing date for receipt of completed ballot papers and the date of the election meeting (including the closing date for receipt of completed ballot papers but excluding the date of the election meeting).

(4) Each justice who votes shall write "X" on the appropriate ballot paper—

(a) against the name of the justice who is his choice to be chairman,

(b) where a single deputy chairman is to be elected, against the name of the justice who is his choice to be deputy chairman, and

(c) where more than one deputy chairman is to be elected, against the names of as many justices as are his choice to be deputy chairmen, provided that the number of votes so cast does not exceed the number of deputy chairmen to be elected.

(5) Paragraph (6) applies in the case of a justice who votes, where—

(a) the nomination of a candidate has, by virtue of rule 6(7), been treated as a nomination for the office of chairman and for the office of deputy chairman,

(b) the justice has voted for that person as a candidate for the office of deputy chairman,

(c) the justice has cast the maximum number of votes for the office of deputy chairman permitted under paragraph (4) above, and

(d) there remain candidates for the office of deputy chairman for whom the justice has not voted.

(6) In a case to which this paragraph applies, a justice may, in addition to the votes he has already cast, cast a reserve vote by writing "R" on the appropriate ballot paper against the name

of the justice who is his choice to be deputy chairman in the event that any other justice for whom he has voted as his choice to be deputy chairman is elected to be chairman.

(7) A justice who votes shall return his ballot paper to the justices' clerk by post or by hand.

(8) A ballot shall not be invalidated by reason of—

(a) a ballot paper not being received by a justice eligible to vote in a postal ballot; or

(b) a completed ballot paper not being received by the justices' clerk.

(9) As soon as practicable after the closing date for receipt of the completed ballot papers, the justices' clerk shall—

(a) determine the result of the postal ballot for election as chairman; and

(b) then, subject to paragraph (10), determine the result of the postal ballot for election to the office of deputy chairman.

(10) Where a chairman is not elected before the election meeting, the result of the postal ballot for the election to the office of deputy chairman shall not be determined until after a chairman has been elected at the election meeting.

(11) When the result of the postal ballot has been determined, the justices' clerk shall—

(a) immediately notify the candidates of the result, and

(b) either give the justices written notice of the result before the election meeting or announce it at the meeting.

1–4867 8. Determining result of postal ballot for election of chairman. (1) This rule applies for determining the result of the postal ballot for the election of chairman.

(2) Subject to paragraph (3), the justice who has received the highest number of the votes cast shall be elected chairman.

(3) If two or more justices have received equally the highest number of votes, the justices' clerk shall, at the election meeting, decide between them by lot and paragraph (4) applies.

(4) Where this paragraph applies—

(a) the justice on whom the lot falls shall be elected chairman; and

(b) the justices' clerk shall, at the election meeting, announce the name of the justice so elected.

1–4868 9. Determining result of postal ballot for election of deputy chairmen. (1) This rule applies for determining the result of the postal ballot for the election of one or more deputy chairmen.

(2) In this rule, "requisite number" means the number of deputy chairmen to be elected.

(3) Except as provided by paragraph (8), reserve votes are not to be counted for the purposes of this rule.

(4) The requisite number of justices who have received the highest numbers of votes cast shall be elected deputy chairmen.

(5) If—

(a) two or more justices have received an equal number of votes (the "tied candidates"); and

(b) taking into account the election of any justice who has received a higher number of votes than the tied candidates -

(i) the election of one or more of the tied candidates is necessary to make up the requisite number, but

(ii) the election of all of the tied candidates would exceed the requisite number,

the justices' clerk shall, at the election meeting, decide by lot which of the tied candidates is to be elected, and paragraph (6) applies.

(6) A justice on whom the lot falls shall be elected deputy chairman and the justices' clerk shall, at the election meeting, announce the name of any justice so elected.

(7) If a justice has been elected chairman and his name was included on a ballot paper for the election of deputy chairman, all the votes for him as deputy chairman shall be disregarded and shall no longer be counted as votes.

(8) Where a justice has—

(a) cast a vote for a candidate which has been disregarded under paragraph (7) or under rule 12(1), and

(b) cast a reserve vote for any other candidate,

the reserve vote shall be counted as a vote for the purposes of this rule.

(9) If any deputy chairmen remain to be elected, the justices shall elect them at the election meeting in accordance with the provisions of the schedule.

(10) The election referred to in paragraph (9) shall be by secret ballot unless paragraph 3 of the schedule applies.

1–4869 10. Election where no or insufficient nominations. Where—

(a) no nomination for the office of chairman is received under rule 6 or where all nominations for that office are withdrawn at any time up to (and including) the closing date for receipt of completed ballot papers; or

(b) fewer nominations for the office of deputy chairman are received under rule 6 than the number of deputy chairmen to be elected; or

(c) one or more nominations for the office of deputy chairman are withdrawn at any time up to (and including) the closing date for receipt of completed ballot papers with the result that the remaining number of nominations for that office falls below the number of deputy chairmen to be elected,

the justices shall by secret ballot elect the chairman or the number of deputy chairmen that have still to be elected at the election meeting in accordance with the provisions of the schedule.

1–4870   11. Election meeting.   (1) The justices for each local justice area shall hold an election meeting in October every year.
(2) At the election meeting—

(*a*)   where rule 7(10) applies, the justices' clerk shall determine the result of the postal ballot for the election to the office of deputy chairman and shall announce the name of the justice or justices who has or have been elected to that office; and
(*b*)   the justices shall decide the number of deputy chairmen to be elected to take office in the year commencing on 1st January after the next election meeting.

(3) Where a chairman and one or more deputy chairmen are to be elected at the election meeting, the result of the election to the office of chairman shall be announced before the election to the office of deputy chairman.

1–4871   12. Miscellaneous provisions about ballots.   (1) If a justice withdraws his nomination on the date of posting the ballot papers or at any time after that date up to (and including) the closing date for receipt of completed ballot papers, all the votes for that justice shall be disregarded and shall no longer be counted as votes.
(2) Where a ballot paper—

(*a*)   is returned unmarked; or
(*b*)   in a postal ballot is marked—

(i)   by writing otherwise than as indicated by rule 7(4) or 7(6), or
(ii)   in such a manner that there is doubt as to the intention of the voter; or

(*c*)   in a ballot held at a meeting, is marked in such a manner that there is doubt as to the identity of the justice or justices for whom the vote is cast,

the ballot paper or the vote (as the case may be) shall be rejected when the votes are counted.
(3)   There shall be no disclosure as to how any justice voted in any ballot.
(4)   The justices' clerk shall—

(*a*)   keep a note of the date that a ballot paper was received by him; and
(*b*)   keep the ballot papers received for a period of 12 months commencing with the date of the election meeting.

1–4872   13. Period of office and eligibility for re-election.   (1) A chairman or (as the case may be) deputy chairman elected under these Rules shall, subject to rule 14(3) and (9), hold office for one year beginning on 1st January after his election and shall, subject to paragraphs (3), (4) and (5), be eligible for re-election.
(2) In paragraphs (3) and (4) "previous chairman" means a justice who has held office as chairman of the justices.
(3) A previous chairman shall not be eligible for re-election as chairman if, on 1st January after the election, he will have held such office for periods totalling more than two years unless at least six years have elapsed since he last held office.
(4) In any event, a previous chairman shall not be eligible for re-election as chairman if, on 1st January after the election, he will have held such office for periods totalling more than five years.
(5) A justice who has held office as deputy chairman shall not be eligible for re-election as deputy chairman if on 1st January after the election he will have held such office for periods totalling more than five years.
(6) Any period served as chairman or deputy chairman, as the case may be, before 1 April 2005 shall not count towards the maximum periods of service permitted by paragraphs (3), (4) and (5).

1–4873   14. Vacancy in office.   (1) If the office of chairman or deputy chairman becomes or is about to become vacant for any reason, the justices' clerk shall give written notice sent by first class post as soon as practicable to each justice eligible to vote in a postal ballot that he may submit nominations in writing to the justices' clerk for another chairman or deputy chairman (as the case may be).
(2) Rule 6(3), (4) and (5) shall apply to a nomination made under this rule as it applies to a nomination made under rule 5.
(3) If only one nomination is received, the justice nominated shall hold office for the remainder of the term of the appointment of the justice whom he replaces.
(4) If more than one nomination is received, the justices shall by secret ballot elect another chairman or deputy chairman (as the case may be).
(5) The ballot shall be a postal ballot except that—

(*a*)   the ballot papers shall be posted by first class post as soon as practicable;
(*b*)   there shall be at least 7 days between the date of posting the ballot papers and the closing date for receipt of completed ballot papers (including the date of posting but excluding the closing date for receipt of completed ballot papers);
(*c*)   rule 7(1), (3), (9) and (10) shall not apply;

(*d*) as soon as practicable after the closing date for receipt of completed ballot papers, the justices' clerk shall determine the result of the ballot;

(*e*) rules 8(3), 9(5) and 9(6) shall be read as if the decision by lot shall take place before at least 3 justices (instead of at the election meeting) and the names of the justice or justices elected shall be notified to the justices by post as soon as practicable (instead of being announced at the election meeting).

(6) Where no nomination for a vacancy is received, the justices' clerk shall as soon as practicable, convene a meeting of the justices for the local justice area.

(7) At that meeting, the justices shall by secret ballot elect another chairman or deputy chairman (as the case may be).

(8) The provisions of the schedule shall apply to the election with the following modifications—

(*a*) the list of justices shall comprise the names of all the justices for the local justice area on the date of the meeting (excluding, in the case of an election to the office of deputy chairman, the name of any justice who holds office as chairman or deputy chairman);

(*b*) references to the election meeting in the schedule shall be read as references to the meeting held under this rule.

(9) Any justice elected under this rule shall hold office for the remainder of the term of the appointment of the justice whom he replaces.

(10) Any period served as chairman or deputy chairman by virtue of this rule shall not count towards the maximum period of service permitted by rule 13(3), (4) and (5).

1–4874   15. Absence of justice entitled to preside.   The justices present may appoint one of their number to preside in court to deal with any case in the absence of a justice entitled to preside under rule 4, if—

(*a*) before making such an appointment, the justices present are satisfied as to the suitability for this purpose of the justice proposed; and

(*b*) the justice proposed has completed or is undergoing a chairman training course in accordance with rules made under section 18 of the Courts Act 2003, unless by reason of illness, circumstances unforeseen when the justices to sit were chosen, or other emergency no such justice is present.

1–4875   16. Transitional provisions.   Appointments made under the Justices of the Peace (Size and Chairmanship of Bench) Rules 2002 shall continue for the term specified in those Rules, as if they were still in force.

1–4876

Rule 9(9)

SCHEDULE 1
PROCEDURE FOR ELECTIONS

List of justices
1. The justices' clerk shall compile a list of justices as specified in paragraphs 2, 4 and 5.
2. Where rule 9(7) applies, the list shall comprise the names of the justices who were nominated for the office of deputy chairman excluding the name of any justices who have been elected chairman or deputy chairman.
3. If the number of justices whose names are on the list described in paragraph 2 equals or is less than the number of offices available, the justices whose names are on the list shall be elected to the office of deputy chairman without a ballot.
4. Where rule 10(*a*) applies, the list shall comprise the names of all the justices for the local justice area on the date of the election meeting.
5. Where rule 10(*b*) or (*c*) applies, the list shall comprise the names of all the justices for the local justice area on the date of the election meeting excluding the name of any justice or justices who have been elected chairman or deputy chairman.
Conduct of ballot
6. The justices' clerk shall—

(*a*) prepare ballot papers containing the list of justices in alphabetical order; and
(*b*) hand to each justice present at the election meeting and eligible to vote in a postal ballot—

(i) where there is to be an election of a chairman, one ballot paper for the election of chairman;
(ii) where there is to be an election of a deputy chairman or deputy chairman, one ballot paper for that election.

7. Each justice who votes shall write X on the appropriate ballot paper against the name of the justice he wishes to be chairman and the name of the justice or justices he wishes to be deputy chairman or deputy chairmen (as the case may be).
8. Immediately after the ballot has been closed, the justices' clerk shall collect the ballot papers and count the votes.
Election of chairman
9. Except as mentioned below, the justice who has received a majority of the votes cast shall be elected chairman.
10. Where no justice receives a majority after the first ballot, up to two further ballots shall be held.
11. If, following two further ballots, no justice has obtained a majority, the justice who has received the most votes in aggregate in the three ballots shall be elected chairman.
12. If, after three ballots, two or more justices have received the same number of votes in aggregate, so that the addition of a vote to those cast would entitle one of them to be elected, the justices' clerk shall immediately decide between them by lot and shall proceed as if the justice on whom the lot falls had received an additional vote.
13. Where a ballot (other than the third ballot) has been inconclusive the justices' clerk shall announce the fact and state the names of the justices for whom votes have been cast and the number of votes each justice received.

14. Where a ballot has been conclusive the justices' clerk shall announce the result.

Election of deputy chairman

15. The result of the ballot for the election to the office of deputy chairman shall be ascertained by counting the votes given to each justice. The justice or justices (if there is to be more than one deputy chairman) who has or have received the most votes shall be elected to the office of deputy chairman.

16. If—

(a) two or more justices obtain an equal number of votes; and

(b) the addition of a vote to those cast for any one or more of those justices would entitle him or them to be elected,

the justices' clerk shall immediately decide between those justices by lot and proceed as if any justice on whom the lot falls had received an additional vote.

Justices of the Peace (Training and Appraisal) Rules 2005

(SI 2005/564 amended by SI 2006/680)

1–4880 1. Citation and commencement. These Rules may be cited as the Justices of the Peace (Training and Appraisal) Rules 2005 and shall come into force on 1 April 2005.

---

1. Made by the Lord Chancellor, in exercise of the powers conferred upon him by sections 10,18 and 19 of the Courts Act 2003], and after consultation with the Criminal Procedure Rule Committee, the Family Procedure Rule Committee and the Magistrates' Courts Rule Committee in accordance with section 20(2) of the Courts Act 2003.

1–4881 2. Interpretation. In these Rules —

"a BTDC" means a Bench Training and Development Committee established in accordance with these Rules; and references to justices, in relation to a BTDC, mean justices assigned to the local justice area or areas for which the BTDC is established;

"approved court chairman" means a justice approved by the BTDC to preside in magistrates' courts other than family proceedings courts, youth courts, or licensing or betting licensing committees in accordance with rule 13;

"courts board area" means an area of England and Wales for which there is a courts board under section 4 of the Courts Act 2003;

"election meeting" means a meeting held in accordance with rule 11 of the Justices of the Peace (Size and Chairmanship of Bench) Rules 2005;

"justice" means a lay justice and, in relation to a local justice area, means a justice who is assigned to that area;

"justices' clerk", in relation to a local justice area, means a justices' clerk assigned to that area and includes any person acting as such;

"an MATC" means a Magistrates' Area Training Committee, established in accordance with these Rules.

1–4882 3. Formation of a BTDC. There shall be a BTDC for each local justice area.

1–4883 4. Membership of a BTDC. (1) The membership of the BTDC shall consist of three, six or nine justices for the local justice area, appointed in accordance with this rule.

(2) The membership of the BTDC shall rotate by one third in each calendar year.

(3) Except as mentioned in rules 5(2), 9(3) and 9(4), a member of the BTDC shall be appointed to hold office for a term of three years beginning on 1st January following his appointment.

(4) At each election meeting the justices shall—

(a) elect the members of the BTDC or choose a panel of justices who shall select the members of the BTDC; and

(b) decide the method of filling casual vacancies.

(5) The BTDC shall hold a meeting as soon as practicable after 1st January of each year.

(6) At that meeting the members shall, where rule 5 or rule 8(2) applies, decide the length of their terms of office and if they are unable to agree, the length of their terms shall be determined by lot conducted by the justices' clerk.

(7) At that meeting, the members of the BTDC shall appoint a chairman, whose term of office shall expire on 31 December of each year.

(8) Subject to rule 6, the BTDC may re-appoint a chairman.

(9) The justices' clerk may attend the meetings of the BTDC but, except where he is required to act under paragraph (6), may act in an advisory capacity only.

(10) A chairman of the justices elected under the Justices of the Peace (Size and Chairmanship of Bench) Rules 2005 shall not be a member of the BTDC for the local justice area for which he was appointed.

(11) Appointments to BTDCs made under the Justices of the Peace (Size and Chairmanship of Bench) Rules 2002 shall continue for the term specified in those Rules, as if they were still in force.

1–4884 5. Change of number of members of BTDC. (1) At an election meeting the justices may decide, subject to rule 4(1), to increase or reduce the number of members of the BTDC.

(2) If the justices decide to increase or reduce the number of members of the BTDC in accordance with paragraph (1)—

  (*a*) all the existing members of the BTDC shall retire at the end of the calendar year in which the decision is made;

  (*b*) members of the BTDC appointed in that year shall hold office from 1st January in the following year for the following periods—

    (i) one year, in the case of one third of the members;

    (ii) two years, in the case of one third of the members; and

    (iii) three years, in the case of the remaining one third of the members.

1–4885   6. Limit on length of service as member of BTDC.   (1) A justice may not serve as a member of a BTDC for more than a total of nine years.

  (2) A member of the BTDC shall be eligible for reappointment if, at the end of his most recent term of office, he will have served as a member of the BTDC for a period or periods totalling less than nine years.

  (3) If, on a date before the end of the period specified in rule 4(3) or (as the case may be) rules 5(2)(*b*) or 8(2)(*b*), a member will have served as a member of the BTDC for nine years, that member's term of office shall end on that date.

1–4886   7. Quorum of a BTDC meeting.   A BTDC meeting shall be quorate if:

  (*a*) where the BTDC has six or nine members, there are three members at the meeting; or

  (*b*) where the BTDC has three members, there are two members at the meeting.

1–4887   8. Establishment of combined BTDC.   (1) The justices for two or more local justice areas may establish a combined BTDC, and—

  (*a*) the provisions of these Rules shall apply to such a BTDC as they apply to a BTDC for a single local justice area, subject to such modifications to rule 4(4) and rule 9(1) as are agreed by the justices for the local justice areas concerned; and

  (*b*) the justices for the local justice areas concerned shall, subject to rule 4(1), decide the number of members of such a BTDC.

  (2) If the justices for two or more local justice areas establish a combined BTDC in accordance with paragraph (1)—

  (*a*) all the existing members of the BTDCs which are combined to make the combined BTDC shall retire at the end of the calendar year in which the decision is made;

  (*b*) members of the combined BTDC appointed in that year shall hold office from 1st January in the following year for the following periods—

    (i) one year, in the case of one third of the members;

    (ii) two years, in the case of one third of the members; and

    (iii) three years, in the case of the remaining one third of the members.

1–4888   9. Casual vacancy.   (1) If a casual vacancy arises, it shall be filled as soon as practicable in accordance with the method of filling casual vacancies decided in accordance with rule 4(4)(*b*).

  (2) If, but for rule 6(3), a member would have served for a longer term, a casual vacancy arises when that member's term of office ends.

  (3) A member appointed to fill a casual vacancy described in paragraph (2) shall serve for the remaining part of the period for which the member he is replacing would, but for rule 6(3), have served.

  (4) A member appointed to fill a casual vacancy, other than described in paragraph (2), shall serve for the remaining part of the period for which the member he is replacing was appointed.

  (5) Any period served by virtue of paragraphs (3) and (4) shall not count towards the period of nine years' service referred to in rule 6.

1–4889   10. Functions of a BTDC.   (1) Each BTDC shall—

  (*a*) establish a scheme for appraising justices;

  (*b*) identify the training needs of justices and, no later than 30th of September in each year, give the relevant MATC a report of those training needs; and

  (*c*) maintain a list of approved court chairmen.

  (2) In paragraph (1), the relevant MATC means the MATC for the Courts Board area in which the local justice area covered by the BTDC is located.

1–4890   11. Appraisal of justices.   (1) Every BTDC shall establish a scheme to appraise the performance on the bench of the justices, such as will enable it to—

  (*a*) determine their training and development needs;

  (*b*) report to the MATC on their training needs; and

  (*c*) maintain a list of approved court chairmen in accordance with rules 13 and 14.

  (2) The BTDC shall select justices to conduct appraisals ("the appraising justices") and it may also arrange for a justice assigned to a different area to conduct appraisals.

  (3) The BTDC shall determine the intervals at which justices are to be appraised, having regard to the requirements of rule 14.

  (4) The BTDC shall establish a procedure for conducting appraisals, which shall include the following elements—

(a) the notification that will be given to the justice to be appraised ("the appraised justice");
(b) a procedure for the appraising justice to record his assessment and for notifying the appraised justice and the BTDC of that assessment;
(c) a procedure for enabling the appraised justice to discuss the assessment with the appraising justice and a procedure enabling the appraised justice to challenge the assessment to a person other than the appraising justice;
(d) the time limits for these procedures.
(5) The BTDC shall publish its scheme to the justices.

1–4891 12. Required training courses. A justice shall not perform any of the following functions unless he has completed a training course approved by the Lord Chief Justice in respect of that function—

(a) sitting as a justice in the adult court;
(b) sitting as a chairman in the adult court;
(c) sitting as a justice in the family proceedings court;
(d) sitting as a chairman in the family proceedings court;
(e) sitting as a justice in the youth court; and
(f) sitting as a chairman in the youth court.

1–4892 13. List of approved court chairmen. (1) A BTDC shall maintain a list of approved court chairmen.
(2) The BTDC shall consider the number of approved court chairmen necessary to—

(a) enable each court to sit under the chairmanship of an approved court chairman; and
(b) ensure that each approved court chairman has the opportunity to sit as chairman sufficiently often to maintain an appropriate level of competence.

(3) The BTDC—

(a) shall regularly review the list of approved court chairmen; and
(b) may at any time remove a justice's name from, or add a justice's name to, the list.

1–4893 14. Inclusion in list of approved court chairmen. A justice may only be included in the list of approved court chairmen if:

(a) he has been appraised as competent to sit in the adult court—
  (i) in two appraisals, and
  (ii) the most recent of those appraisals took place within the three years preceding the date when the BTDC considers the suitability of the justice for inclusion in the list of approved court chairmen;
(b) he has completed a chairmanship training course in accordance with rule 12(b);
(c) he has been appraised on a minimum of three and a maximum of six separate occasions, by a different appraising justice on at least one such occasion, while presiding in court in accordance with rule 4 of the Justices of the Peace (Size and Chairmanship of Bench) Rules 2005; and
(d) the BTDC has decided to add the justice concerned to the list of approved court chairmen.

1–4894 15. Inclusion of justices assigned to other local justice areas on the list of approved court chairmen. A BTDC may include a justice in the list of approved court chairmen for its local justice area without complying with rule 14, if—

(a) the justice is or was assigned to another local justice area and is now assigned to its local justice area, and
(b) immediately before he was assigned to its local justice area he was included in the list of approved court chairmen for the other area.

1–4895 16. Formation of a Magistrates' Area Training Committee. (1) From 1st January 2006, but subject to paragraphs (3) and (4), there shall be a Magistrates' Area Training Committee for each courts board area.
(2) The schedule to these Rules makes transitional provision for the establishment of MATCs.
(3) On or after 1 January 2006—

(a) an MATC may apply to the Lord Chancellor to establish more than one MATC in its courts board area; and
(b) if, after consulting the Lord Chief Justice, the Lord Chancellor agrees to the application, he shall determine the membership of the MATCs and the terms of office of its members, having regard as far as practicable to the requirements of rules 17 and 19.

(4) The MATCs for two or more courts board areas may establish a combined MATC and the composition of a combined MATC shall be in accordance with rule 18.

1–4896 17. Membership of an MATC. (1) The membership of an MATC established under rule 16(1) shall consist of justices assigned within the courts board area (referred to in this rule and rules 18 and 19 as "justice members") and other members, as follows—

(a) enough justices for them to be a majority of the membership;
(b) a justices' clerk assigned to a local justice area within the courts board area;

(*c*)   a District Judge (Magistrates' Courts) who sits regularly in the courts board area, if such a judge is available;

(*d*)   a designated family judge, if such a judge is available;

(*e*)   a Crown Court liaison judge, if such a judge is available.

(2) There shall be no maximum number of justice members.

(3) The MATC may appoint additional justice members and shall do so where it is necessary for the MATC to comply with paragraph (1)(*a*).

(4) If the number of justice members has fallen so that paragraph 1(*a*) is not complied with, the MATC may nevertheless act for the purpose of appointing additional justice members.

(5) The justice members shall include —

(*a*)   every BTDC chairman whose bench is in the courts board area, and

(*b*)   a justice nominated by the Magistrates' Association.

(6) If there is more than one justices' clerk assigned within the courts board area, the Area Director for the courts board area shall appoint one of them to the MATC.

(7) At its first meeting of the calendar year, the MATC shall appoint a chairman from amongst its justice members.

(8) The Area Director may attend the meetings of the MATC in an advisory capacity only.

1–4897   18. Composition of a combined MATC.   (1) The membership of a combined MATC shall consist of justices within the courts board areas for which the combined MATC is established ("the MATC area") and other members, as follows—

(*a*)   enough justices for them to be a majority of the membership;

(*b*)   a justices' clerk assigned within each of the courts board areas for which the MATC is established;

(*c*)   a District Judge (Magistrates' Courts) who sits regularly in the MATC area, if such a judge is available;

(*d*)   a designated family judge, if such a judge is available;

(*e*)   a Crown Court liaison judge, if such a judge is available.

(2) There shall be no maximum number of justice members.

(3) The MATC may appoint additional justice members and shall do so where it is necessary for the MATC to comply with paragraph 1(*a*).

(4) If the number of justice members has fallen so that paragraph 1(*a*) is not complied with, the MATC may nevertheless act for the purpose of appointing additional justice members.

(5) The justice members shall include—

(*a*)   every BTDC chairman whose bench is within the MATC area, and

(*b*)   a justice nominated by the Magistrates' Association.

(6) The Area Directors for the MATC area may attend the meetings of the MATC in an advisory capacity only.

1–4898   19. Term of office of members of MATC.   (1) The term of office for a BTDC chairman as a member of an MATC shall be the same as his term of office as BTDC chairman.

(2) The justice nominated by the Magistrates' Association shall have a renewable term of office of three years, but may not serve for more than a total of six years.

(3) Any justice member who is not a BTDC chairman shall have a renewable term of office of three years, but may not serve for more than a total of six years.

(4) The chairman of the MATC shall have a renewable term of office, which shall expire on 31 December of each year.

(5) This rule—

(*a*)   applies to members of an MATC which is combined under rule 16(4); and

(*b*)   where a member of a combined MATC has previously served in an MATC, the length of that previous service shall count for the purposes of paragraphs (2) and (3).

1–4899   20. Quorum of an MATC meeting.   An MATC meeting shall be quorate if:

(*a*)   the number of members present at the meeting is a number which, if multiplied by four, exceeds the total number of members of the MATC, and

(*b*)   a majority of members present are justices.

1–4900   21. Functions of an MATC.   (1) An MATC shall—

(*a*)   consider the training needs identified by BTDCs in accordance with rule 10(*b*), and

(*b*)   produce, no later than the end of February each year, a training plan for the period of the following April to March.

(2) The content of the training plan shall include —

(*a*)   the proposed types of training;

(*b*)   the number of justices who are to receive training;

(*c*)   the place or places where the training is likely to be provided;

(*d*)   the proposed dates of the training.

(3) Each MATC shall also provide, no later than 30 September each year, an annual report to the Lord Chief Justice on training which was undertaken in the preceding April to March, which shall include:

(a) information on the types of training that have taken place in that period;
(b) an evaluation of the training that has taken place;
(c) the cost of the training;
(d) information on the number of magistrates who attended the training; and
(e) any substantial respects in which the training that has taken place has differed from the training that was proposed in the training plan for that period.

(4) An MATC, when producing a training plan under paragraph (1)(b) or providing an annual report under paragraph (3), shall have regard to any guidance issued by the Lord Chief Justice as to the form or content of the training plan or report.

22. Delegation of functions by the Lord Chief Justice.   The Lord Chief Justice may nominate a judicial office holder (as defined in section 109(4) of the Constitutional Reform Act 2005) to exercise his functions under these Rules.

1–4901

Rule 16   SCHEDULE 1

Transitional Provisions About Magistrates Area Training Committees
1. The following persons may meet, during the period starting on 1st April 2005 and ending on 31st December 2005, for the purposes mentioned in paragraph 2:

(a) each BTDC chairman whose bench is within the courts board area for which the MATC is established;
(b) a justice nominated by the Magistrates' Association; and
(c) a justice's clerk assigned within the courts board area for which the MATC is established.

2. The persons mentioned in paragraph 1 shall:

(a) appoint one of the justices to act as chairman for the period ending on 31 December 2005;
(b) appoint as many additional justices to be members as they judge will be needed for the MATC to comply with rule 17(1)(a); and
(c) prepare a draft training plan in respect of the period from 1 April 2006 to 31 March 2007.

Local Justice Areas Order 2005[1]
(SI 2005/554 amended by SI 2006/1839 and 2315)

1–4910   1. Citation and commencement.   This Order may be cited as the Local Justice Areas Order 2005 and shall come into force on 1st April 2005.

---

1. Made by the Lord Chancellor, in exercise of the powers conferred upon him by s 8 of the Courts Act 2003.

1–4911   2. Local Justice Areas.   The local justice areas into which England and Wales is divided are specified in the Schedule to this Order.

1–4912

Article 2   SCHEDULE

Local Justice Areas in England & Wales

Alnwick	Neath Port Talbot
Ashby-de-la-Zouch	New Forest
Barking and Dagenham	Newark and Southwell
Barnet	Newcastle-upon-Tyne District
Barnsley District	Newcastle and Ogmore
Bath and Wansdyke	Newham
Batley and Dewsbury	North East Essex
Bedford and Mid Bedfordshire	North West Essex
Berwick-upon-Tweed	North Avon
Beverley and the Wolds	North Devon
Bexley	North Durham
Birmingham	North East Derbyshire and Dales
Blackburn, Darwen and Ribble Valley	North East Hampshire
Bolton	North East Suffolk
Boston	North Hertfordshire
Bourne and Stamford	North Kent
Bradford	North Lincolnshire
Brent	North Norfolk
Bridlington	North Sefton District
Bristol	North Somerset
Bromley	North Staffordshire
Bromsgrove and Redditch	North Surrey
Burnley, Pendle and Rossendale	North Tyneside District
Bury	North West Hampshire
Calderdale	North West Surrey
Cambridge	North West Wiltshire
Camden and Islington	Northallerton and Richmond
Cardiff	Northampton
Carlisle and District	Northern Oxfordshire
Carmarthen	Norwich
Central and South West Staffordshire	Nottingham
Central Buckinghamshire	Oldham
Central Devon	Ormskirk

Local Justice Areas in England & Wales

Central Hertfordshire
Central Kent
Central Norfolk
Ceredigion
Chester, Ellesmere Port and Neston
Chorley
City of London
City of Salford
City of Westminster
Conwy
Corby
Coventry District
Croydon
Cynon Valley
Daventry
De Brychieniog
Denbighshire
Dinefwr
Doncaster
Dudley
Ealing
East Berkshire
East Cambridgeshire
East Cornwall
East Dorset
East Hertfordshire
East Kent
Eden
Elloes
Enfield
Fenland
Flintshire
Furness and District
Fylde Coast
Gainsborough
Gateshead District
Gloucestershire
Goole and Howdenshire
Grantham
Great Yarmouth
Greenwich and Lewisham
Grimsby and Cleethorpes
Gwent
Gwynedd
Hackney and Tower Hamlets
Halton
Hammersmith and Fulham and Kensington and Chelsea
Chelsea
Haringey
Harrogate
Harrow Gore
Hartlepool
Havering
Herefordshire
High Peak
Hillingdon
Houghton-le-Spring
Hounslow
Huddersfield
Hull and Holderness
Huntingdonshire
Hyndburn
Isle of Wight
Keighley
Kettering
Kidderminster
Kingston-upon-Thames
Knowsley
Lambeth and Southwark
Lancaster
Langbaurgh East
Leeds District
Leicester
Lincoln District
Liverpool
Llanelli
Loughborough
Luton and South Bedfordshire
Macclesfield
Manchester City
Mansfield
Market Bosworth

Oxford
Pembrokeshire
Peterborough
Plymouth District
Pontefract
Preston
Radnorshire and North Brecknock
Reading
Redbridge
Richmond-upon-Thames
Rochdale, Middleton and Heywood
Rotherham
Scarborough
Sedgemoor
Selby
Wakefield
Walsall and Aldridge
Waltham Forest
Wandsworth
Warley
Warrington
Warwickshire
Wellingborough
West Allerdale and Keswick
West Berkshire
West Bromwich
West Cornwall
West Dorset
Sheffield
Shrewsbury and North Shropshire
Skegness
Skipton
Sleaford
Solihull
South East Essex
South West Essex
South Cheshire
South Devon
South Durham
South East Hampshire
South East Northumberland
South East Staffordshire
South East Suffolk
South East Surrey
South East Wiltshire
South Hampshire
South Lakeland
South Norfolk
South Pembrokeshire
South Ribble
South Sefton District
South Somerset
South Tyneside District
South West Surrey
South Worcestershire
Southampton
Southern Derbyshire
Southern Oxfordshire
St Helens
Stockport
Stourbridge and Halesowen
Sunderland
Sussex (Central)
Sussex (Eastern)
Sussex (Northern)
Sussex (Western)
Sutton
Sutton Coldfield
Swansea County
Swindon
Tameside
Taunton Deane and West Somerset
Teesside
Telford and South Shropshire
Towcester
Trafford
Tynesdale
Vale of Glamorgan
Vale Royal
West Hertfordshire
West Norfolk
West Suffolk

Local Justice Areas in England & Wales

Market Harborough and Lutterworth
Melton, Belvoir and Rutland
Mendip
Merthyr Tydfil
Merton
Mid-North Essex
Mid-South Essex
Milton Keynes
Miskin
Montgomeryshire

Whitehaven
Wigan and Leigh
Wirral
Wolds
Wolverhampton
Worksop and Retford
Wrexham Maelor
Wycombe and Beaconsfield
Ynys Môn/Anglesey
York

Court Security Officers (Designation) Regulations 2005[1]
(SI 2005/588)

1–4920   1. Citation and commencement.   These Regulations may be cited as the Court Security Officers (Designation) Regulations 2005 and shall come into force on 1st April 2005.

---

1. Made by the Lord Chancellor, in exercise of the powers conferred upon him by s 51 of the Courts Act 2003.

1–4921   2. Training requirements for court security officers.   (1) Before a person may be designated as a court security officer, he must provide the Lord Chancellor with documentary evidence that he has completed one or more training courses which include instruction in the following —

(a) the duties and powers of a court security officer;
(b) risk assessment;
(c) safe working practices;
(d) managing stress when dealing with threatening situations;
(e) techniques for restraining a person and removing them from a building.

(2) Where the Lord Chancellor has designated a person as a court security officer, he may subsequently require that person to undergo —

(a) further training in any of the matters mentioned in paragraph (1);
(b) training in any other matter which the Lord Chancellor determines,

and the Lord Chancellor may make different determinations in respect of different officers, courts, court buildings and areas.

1–4922   3. Proof of identity and other requirements.   Before a person may be designated as a court security officer, the Lord Chancellor must take the following steps:

(a) obtain proof of the person's identity;
(b) obtain a declaration from that person as to whether he has any unspent criminal offences within the meaning of the Rehabilitation of Offenders Act 1974; and
(c) make criminal records check.

Assistants to Justices' Clerks Regulations 2006[1]
(SI 2006/3405)

1–4923   1. Citation and Commencement.   These Regulations may be cited as the Assistants to Justices' Clerks Regulations 2006 and shall come into force on 9 January 2007.

---

1. Made by the Lord Chancellor, in exercise of the powers conferred upon him by s 27(6) of the Courts Act 2003.

2. Revocation

1–4924   3. Qualifications needed by assistant clerks.   An assistant clerk may be employed as a clerk in court only if he is a barrister or solicitor of the Supreme Court or has passed the necessary examinations for either of those professions, or has been granted an exemption in relation to any examination by the appropriate examining body.

1–4925   4.   Notwithstanding the provisions of regulation 3 above, the Lord Chancellor may designate any person be employed as a clerk in court for such period not exceeding six months as he may specify if he is satisfied—

(a) that the person so specified is, in the circumstances, a suitable person to be employed as a clerk in court, and
(b) that no other arrangements can reasonably be made for the hearing of proceedings before the court.

1–4926   5. Unqualified assistant clerks.   (1) The Lord Chancellor may designate a person who is not qualified under regulation 3 above to perform the functions mentioned in paragraph (2) below.

(2) A person designated under paragraph (1) above may carry out the functions contained in paragraphs 7, 8, 9(*a*), 10 to 11 (with the exception of enlarging sureties), 15, 24, 25, 26B and 27 to 36 in the Schedule to the Justices' Clerks Rules 2005, to the extent that they are performed out of court, provided that that person has been specifically authorised by the justices' clerk for that purpose.

Legal Services

Community Legal Service (Costs) Regulations 2000[1]

(SI 2000/441 as amended by SI 2001/822 and 3649, SI 2003/649 and SI 2005/2114 and 3504)

PART I
GENERAL

1–5648   1. Citation and commencement.   These Regulations may be cited as the Community Legal Service (Costs) Regulations 2000 and shall come into force on 1st April 2000.

---

1. Made by the Lord Chancellor in exercise of powers conferred on him by ss 10, 11(2), (3) 4(*a*), (*c*), (*e*)–(*g*), 22(1), (5), (6) of the Access to Justice Act 1999.

2. Interpretation.   In these Regulations:

"the Act" means the Access to Justice Act 1999;

"certificate" means a certificate issued under the Funding Code certifying a decision to fund services for the client;

"child" means a person under 18;

"client" means an individual who receives funded services;

"Commission" means the Legal Services Commission established under section 1 of the Act;

"costs judge" has the same meaning as in the CPR;

"costs order" means an order that a party pay all or part of the costs of proceedings;

"costs order against the Commission" means an order, made under regulation 5 of the Community Legal Service (Cost Protection) Regulations 2000 (but not one under regulation 6 of those Regulations), that the Commission pay all or part of the costs of a party to proceedings who has not received funded services in relation to those proceedings under a certificate, other than a certificate which has been revoked;

"cost protection" means the limit on costs awarded against a client set out in section 11(1) of the Act;

"court" includes any tribunal having the power to award costs in favour of, or against, a party;

"CPR" means the Civil Procedure Rules 1998, and a reference to a Part or rule, prefixed by "CPR", means the Part or rule so numbered in the CPR;

"Financial Regulations" means the Community Legal Service (Financial) Regulations 2000;

"Funding Code" means the code approved under section 9 of the Act;

"full costs" means, where a section 11(1) costs order is made against a client, the amount of costs which that client would, but for section 11(1) of the Act, have been ordered to pay;

"funded services" means services which are provided directly for a client and funded for that client by the Commission as part of the Community Legal Service under sections 4 to 11 of the Act;

"litigation friend" has the meaning given by CPR 21;

"partner", in relation to a party to proceedings, means a person with whom that party lives as a couple, and includes a person with whom the party is not currently living but from whom he is not living separate and apart;

"patient" means a person who by reason of mental disorder within the meaning of the Mental Health Act 1983 is incapable of managing and administering his own affairs;

"proceedings" include proceedings in any tribunal which is a court, as defined, in this paragraph;

"receiving party" means a party in favour of whom a costs order is made;

"Regional Director" means any Regional Director appointed by the Commission in accordance with the Funding Code and any other person authorised to act on his behalf, except a supplier;

"rules of court", in relation to a tribunal, means rules or regulations made by the authority having power to make rules or regulations regulating the practice and procedure of that tribunal and, in relation to any court, includes practice directions;

"section 11(1) costs order" means a costs order against a client where cost protection applies;

"solicitor" means solicitor or other person who is an authorised litigator within the meaning of section 119(1) of the Courts and Legal Services Act 1990;

"statement of resources" means:

(*a*) a statement, verified by a statement of truth, made by a party to proceedings setting out:

(i) his income and capital and financial commitments during the previous year and, if applicable, those of his partner;

(ii) his estimated future financial resources and expectations and, if applicable, those of his partner; and

(iii) a declaration stating whether he, and if applicable his partner, has deliberately foregone or deprived himself of any resources or expectations, together (If applicable and as far as is practical) with details of those resources or expectations and the manner in which they have been foregone or dprived;

(iv) particulars of any application for funding made by him in connection with the proceedings; and

(v) any other facts relevant to the determination of his resources; or

(b) a statement, verified by a statement of truth, made by a client receiving funded services, setting out the information provided by the client under regulation 6 of the Financial Regulations, and stating that there has been no significant change in the client's financial circumstances since the date on which the information was provided or, as the case may be, details of any such change;

"statement of truth" has the same meaning as in CPR Part 22;

"supplier" means any person or body providing funded services to the client, including any authorised advocate (within the meaning of section 119(1) of the Courts and Legal Services Act 1990) engaged by the client's solicitor to act in proceedings.

3. Effect of these Regulations. Nothing in these Regulations shall be construed, in relation to proceedings where one or more parties are receiving, or have received, funded services, as:

(a) requiring a court to make a costs order where it would not otherwise have made a costs order; or

(b) affecting the court's power to make a wasted costs order against a legal representative.

4. Termination of retainer where funding is withdrawn. (1) The following paragraphs of this regulation apply where funding is withdrawn by revoking or discharging the client's certificate.

(2) Subject to paragraphs (3) and (4), on the revocation or discharge of the client's certificate, the retainer of any supplier acting under that certificate shall terminate immediately.

(3) Termination of retainers under paragraph (2) shall not take effect unless and until any procedures under the Funding Code for review of the decision to withdraw the client's funding are concluded, and confirm the decision to withdraw funding.

(4) The solicitor's retainer shall not terminate until he has complied with any procedures under the Funding Code that require him to send or serve notices.

PART II
COSTS ORDERS AGAINST CLIENT AND AGAINST COMMISSION

1–5649 5. Application of regulations 6 to 13. Regulations 6 to 13 apply only where cost protection applies.

6. Security for costs. Where in any proceedings a client is required to give security for costs, the amount of that security shall not exceed the amount (if any) which is a reasonable one having regard to all the circumstances, including the client's financial resources and his conduct in relation to the dispute to which the proceedings relate.

7. Assessment of resources. (1) The first £100,000 of the value of the client's interest in the main or only dwelling in which he resides shall not be taken into account in having regard to the client's resources for the purposes of section 11(1) of the Act.

(2) Where, but only to the extent that, the court considers that the circumstances are exceptional, having regard in particular to the quantity or value of the items concerned, the court may take into account the value of the client's clothes and household furniture, or the tools and implements of his trade, in having regard to the client's resources for the purposes of section 11(1) of the Act.

(3) Subject to paragraph (4), in having regard to the resources of a party for the purposes of section 11(1) of the Act, the resources of his partner shall be treated as his resources.

(4) The resources of a party's partner shall not be treated as that party's resources if the partner has a contrary interest in the dispute in respect of which the funded services are provided.

(5) Where a party is acting in a representative, fiduciary or official capacity, the court shall not take the personal resources of the party into account for the purposes of section 11(1) of the Act, but shall have regard to the value of any property or estate, or the amount of any fund out of which he is entitled to be indemnified, and may also have regard to the resources of the persons, if any, including that party where appropriate, who are beneficially interested in that property, estate or fund.

(6) For the purposes of section 11(1) of the Act, where a party is acting as a litigation friend to a client who is a child or patient, the court shall not take the personal resources of the litigation friend into account in assessing the resources of the client.

8. Statements of resources. (1) Any person who is a party to proceedings in which another party is a client may make a statement of resources, and file it with the court.

(2) A person making and filing a statement of resources under paragraph (1) shall serve a copy of it on the client.

(3) Where a copy of a statement of resources has been served under paragraph (2) not less

than seven days before the date fixed for a hearing at which the amount to be paid under a section 11(1) costs order falls, or may fall, to be decided, the client shall also make a statement of resources, and shall produce it at that hearing.

9. Procedures for ordering costs against client and Commission. (1) Where the court is considering to make a section 11(1) costs order, it shall consider whether, but for cost protection, it would have made a costs order against the client and, if so, whether it would, on making the costs order, have specified the amount to be paid under that order.

(2) If the court considers that it would have made a costs order against the client, but that it would not have specified the amount to be paid under it, the court shall, when making the section 11(1) costs order:

(a) specify the amount (if any) that the client is to pay under that order if, but only if:

(i)   it considers that it has sufficient information before it to decide what amount is, in that case, a reasonable amount for the client to pay, in accordance with section 11(1) of the Act; and

(ii) it is satisfied that, if it were to determine the full costs at that time, they would exceed the amount referred to in sub-paragraph (i);

(b) otherwise, it shall not specify the amount the client is to pay under the section 11(1) costs order.

(3) If the court considers that it would have made a costs order against the client, and that it would have specified the amount to be paid under it, the court shall, when making the section 11(1) costs order:

(a) specify the amount (if any) that the client is to pay under that order if, but only if, it considers that it has sufficient information before it to decide what amount is, in that case, a reasonable amount for the client to pay, in accordance with section 11(1) of the Act;

(b) otherwise, it shall not specify the amount the client is to pay under the section 11(1) costs order.

(4) Any order made under paragraph (3) shall state the amount of the full costs.

(5) The amount (if any) to be paid by the client under an order made under paragraph (2)(b) or paragraph (3)(b), and any application for a costs order against the Commission, shall be determined in accordance with regulation 10, and at any such determination following an order made under paragraph (2)(b), the amount of the full costs shall also be assessed.

(6) Where the court makes a section 11(1) costs order that does not specify the amount which the client is to pay under it, it may also make findings of fact, as to the parties' conduct in the proceedings or otherwise, relevant to the determination of that amount, and those findings shall be taken into consideration in that determination.

10. (1) The following paragraphs of this regulation apply where the amount to be paid under a section 11(1) costs order, or an application for a costs order against the Commission, is to be determined under this regulation, by virtue of regulation 9(5).

(2) The receiving party may, within three months after a section 11(1) costs order is made, request a hearing to determine the costs payable to him.

(3) A request under paragraph (2) shall be accompanied by:

(a) if the section 11(1) costs order does not state the full costs, the receiving party's bill of costs, which shall comply with any requirements of relevant rules of court relating to the form and content of a bill of costs where the court is assessing a party's costs;

(b) unless the conditions set out in paragraph (3A) are satisfied, a statement of resources; and

(c) if the receiving party is seeking, or, subject to the determination of the amount to be paid under the section 11(1) costs order, may seek, a costs order against the Commission, written notice to that effect.

(3A) The conditions referred to in paragraph (3)(b) above are that—

(a) the court is determining an application for a costs order against the Commission;

(b) the costs were not incurred in a court of first instance.

(4) The receiving party shall file the documents referred to in paragraph (3) with the court and at the same time serve copies of them:

(a) on the client, if a determination of costs payable under section 11(1) of the Act is sought; and

(b) on the Regional Director, if notice has been given under paragraph (3)(c).

(5) Where documents are served on the client under paragraph (4)(a), the client shall make a statement of resources.

(6) The client shall file the statement of resources made under paragraph (5) with the court, and serve copies of it on the receiving party and, if notice has been given under paragraph (3)(c), on the Regional Director, not more than 21 days after the client receives a copy of the receiving party's statement of resources.

(7) The client may, at the same time as filing and serving a statement of resources under paragraph (6), file, and serve on the same persons, a statement setting out any points of dispute in relation to the bill of costs referred to in paragraph (3)(a).

(8) If the client, without good reason, fails to file a statement of resources in accordance with paragraph (6), the court shall determine the amount which the client shall be required to pay under the section 11(1) costs order (and, if relevant, the full costs), having regard to the statement made by the receiving party, and the court need not hold an oral hearing for such determination.

(9) If the client files a statement of resources in accordance with paragraph (6), or the period for filing such notice expires, or if the costs payable by the client have already been determined, the court shall set a date for the hearing and, at least 14 days before that date, serve notice of it on:

(*a*) the receiving party;

(*b*) the client (unless the costs payable by the client have already been determined); and

(*c*) if a costs order against the Commission is or may be sought, the Regional Director.

(10) The court's functions under this regulation may be exercised:

(*a*) in relation to proceedings in the House of Lords, by the Clerk to the Parliaments;

(*b*) in relation to proceedings in the Court of Appeal, High Court or a county court, a costs judge or a district judge;

(*c*) in relation to proceedings in a magistrates' court, by a single justice or by the justices' clerk;

(*d*) in relation to proceedings in the Employment Appeal Tribunal, by the Registrar of that Tribunal.

(11) The amount of costs to be determined under this regulation may include the costs incurred in relation to a request made under this regulation.

10A. (1) Subject to paragraph (2), where the court makes a section 11(1) costs order but does not specify the amount which the client is to pay under it, the court may order the client to pay an amount on account of the costs which are the subject of the order.

(2) The court may order a client to make a payment on account of costs under this regulation only if it has sufficient information before it to decide the minimum amount which the client is likely to be ordered to pay on a determination under regulation 10.

(3) The amount of the payment on account of costs shall not exceed the minimum amount which the court decides that the client is likely to be ordered to pay on such a determination.

(4) Where the court orders a client to make a payment on account of costs—

(*a*) it shall order the client to make the payment into court; and

(*b*) the payment shall remain in court unless and until the court—

    (i) makes a determination under regulation 10 of the amount which the client should pay to the receiving party under the section 11(1) costs order, and orders the payment on account or part of it to be paid to the receiving party in satisfaction or part satisfaction of the client's liability under that order; or

    (ii) makes an order under paragraph (5)(*b*) or (5)(*c*) of this regulation that the payment on account or part of it be repaid to the client.

(5) Where a client has made a payment on account of costs pursuant to an order under paragraph (1) of this regulation—

(*a*) the receiving party shall request a hearing under regulation 10 to determine the amount of costs payable to him;

(*b*) if the receiving party fails to request such a hearing within the time permitted by regulation 10(2), the payment on account shall be repaid to the client;

(*c*) if upon the hearing under regulation 10 the amount of costs which it is determined that the client should pay is less than the amount of the payment on account, the difference shall be repaid to the client.

11. Appeals, etc. (1) Subject to the following paragraphs of this regulation, and to regulation 12, any determination made under regulation 9 or regulation 10 shall be final.

(2) Any party with a financial interest in an assessment of the full costs may appeal against that assessment, if and to the extent that that party would, but for these Regulations, be entitled to appeal against an assessment of costs by the court in which the relevant proceedings are taking place.

(3) Where, under regulation 9(2)(*a*), the court has specified the amount which a client is required to pay under a section 11(1) costs order, the client may apply to the court for a determination of the full costs and if, on that determination, the amount of the full costs is less than the amount which the court previously specified under regulation 9(2)(*a*), the client shall instead be required to pay the amount of the full costs.

(4) The receiving party or the Commission may appeal, on a point of law, against the making of a costs order against the Commission (including the amount of costs which the Commission is required to pay under the order), or against the court's refusal to make such an order.

12. Variation and late determination of amount of costs. (1) The following paragraphs of this regulation apply where the court makes a section 11(1) costs order.

(2) Where the amount (if any) which the client is required to pay under the section 11(1) costs order, together with the amount which the Commission is required to pay under any costs order against the Commission, is less than the full costs, the receiving party may, on the ground set out in paragraph (4)(*a*), apply to the court for an order varying the amount which the client is required to pay under the section 11(1) costs order.

(3) Where the court has not specified the amount to be paid under the section 11(1) costs order, and the receiving party has not, within the time limit in regulation 10(2), applied to have that amount determined in accordance with regulation 10, the receiving party may, on any of the grounds set out in paragraph (4), apply for a determination of the amount that the client is required to pay.

(4) The grounds referred to in paragraphs (2) and (3) are the grounds that:

(a) there has been a significant change in the client's circumstances since the date of the order;

(b) material additional information as to the client's financial resources is available, and that information could not with reasonable diligence have been obtained by the receiving party in time to make an application in accordance with regulation 10; or

(c) there were other good reasons justifying the receiving party's failure to make an application within the time limit in regulation 10(2).

(5) Any application under paragraph (2) or (3) shall be made by the receiving party within six years from the date on which the section 11(1) costs order is first made.

(6) On any application under paragraph (2), the order may be varied as the court thinks fit, but the amount of costs ordered (excluding any costs ordered to be paid under paragraph (9)) shall not exceed the amount of the full costs as stated in any previous order of the court.

(7) When the amount which the client is required to pay under the section 11(1) costs order has been determined under regulation 9(2)(a), and the receiving party applies under paragraph (2) for an order varying that amount:

(a) the receiving party shall file with the application under paragraph (2) his bill of costs, which shall comply with any requirements of relevant rules of court relating to the form and content of a bill of costs where the court is assessing a party's costs; and

(b) the court shall, when determining the application, assess the full costs.

(8) Where the receiving party has received funded services in relation to the proceedings, the Commission may make an application under paragraph (2) or paragraph (3), and:

(a) when making the application the Commission shall file with the court a statement of the receiving party's costs or, if those costs have not been assessed, the receiving party's bill of costs; and

(b) paragraphs (4) to (6) shall apply to that application as if "the Commission" were substituted for "the receiving party" in those paragraphs.

(9) The amount of costs to be determined under this regulation may include the costs incurred in relation to an application made under this regulation.

13. Rights to appear. (1) The Regional Director may appear at:

(a) any hearing in relation to which notice has been given under regulation 10(3)(c);

(b) the hearing of any appeal under regulation 11(4); or

(c) the hearing of any application under regulation 12(8).

(2) The Regional Director may, instead of appearing under paragraph (1), give evidence in the form of a written statement to the court, verified by a statement of truth.

(3) The Regional Director shall file with the court any statement under paragraph (2), and serve a copy on the receiving party, not less than seven days before the hearing to which it relates.

Part III
PROPERTY AND COSTS RECOVERED FOR A FUNDED CLIENT

1–5650 14. Application of this Part. (1) In this Part:

"the awarded sum" means the amount of costs to be paid in accordance with a client's costs order or a client's costs agreement;

"client's costs order" and "client's costs agreement" mean, respectively, an order and an agreement that another party to proceedings or prospective proceedings pay all or part of the costs of a client;

"Fund" means the Community Legal Service Fund established under section 5 of the Act;

"the funded sum" means the amount of remuneration payable by the Commission to a supplier for the relevant work under a contract or any other arrangements that determine that supplier's remuneration, including those that apply by virtue of article 4 of the Community Legal Service (Funding) Order 2000; and, where funding is provided by the Commission under a contract which does not differentiate between the remuneration for the client's case and remuneration for other cases, means such part of the remuneration payable under the contract as may be specified in writing by the Commission as being the funded sum;

"relevant work" means the funded services provided in relation to the dispute or proceedings to which the client's costs order or client's costs agreement relates;

"remuneration" includes fees and disbursements and value added tax on fees and disbursements;

"statutory charge" means the charge created by section 10(7) of the Act.

15. Amount of costs under client's costs order or client's costs agreement. (1) Subject to the following paragraphs of this regulation, the amount of the costs to be paid under a client's costs order or client's costs agreement shall, subject to regulation 16, be determined on the same basis as it would be if the costs were to be paid to a person who had not received funded services.

(2) Subject to paragraph (3), the amount of the awarded sum shall not be limited to the amount of the funded sum by any rule of law which limits the costs recoverable by a party to proceedings to the amount he is liable to pay to his legal representatives.

(3) Paragraph (2) applies only to the extent that the Commission has authorised the supplier

under section 22(2)(*b*) of the Act to take payment for the relevant work other than that funded by the Commission.

16. Costs of serving notices and other documents. The amount of costs to be paid under a client's costs order or client's costs agreement may include costs incurred in filing with the court, or serving on any other party to proceedings, notices or any other documents in accordance with these Regulations, the Financial Regulations or the Funding Code.

17. Application of regulations 18 to 24. (1) Regulations 18 to 24 apply only where funded services have been provided under a certificate.

(2) If the client is no longer being represented by a solicitor, all money to which regulation 18(1) applies shall be paid (or repaid) to the Commission, and all references in regulations 18(1) and 19 to the client's solicitor shall be construed as references to the Commission.

18. Money recovered to be paid to solicitor. (1) Subject to the following paragraphs of this regulation, and to regulation 17(2), all money payable to or recovered by a client in connection with a dispute by way of damages, costs or otherwise, whether or not proceedings were begun, and whether under an order of the court or an agreement or otherwise, shall be paid to the client's solicitor, and only the client's solicitor shall be capable of giving a good discharge for that money.

(2) Paragraph (1) shall not apply to:

(*a*) any periodical payment of maintenance; or

(*b*) any money recovered or preserved by a client in any proceedings which:

    (i) has been paid into, or remains in, court, and is invested for the client's benefit; and

    (ii) under regulation 50 of the Financial Regulations, is not subject to the statutory charge.

(3) Where the client's solicitor has reason to believe that an attempt may be made to circumvent the provisions of paragraph (1), he shall inform the Commission immediately.

19. Notice to third parties. (1) Where money is payable under regulation 18, and that money is payable by a trustee in bankruptcy, a trustee or assignee of a deed of arrangement, a liquidator of a company in liquidation, a trustee of a pension fund or any other third party ("the third party") the client's solicitor shall send to the third party notice that funded services have been funded for the client by the Commission.

(2) Notice under paragraph (1) shall operate as a request by the client that money payable under regulation 18 be paid to his solicitor, and shall be a sufficient authority for that purpose.

20. Solicitor to pay money recovered to Commission. (1) The client's solicitor shall forthwith:

(*a*) inform the Regional Director of any money or other property recovered or preserved, and send him a copy of the order or agreement by virtue of which the property was recovered or preserved;

(*b*) subject to the following paragraphs of this regulation, pay to the Commission all money or other property received by him under regulation 18.

(2) Paragraph (1)(*b*) shall not apply to any money or other property to which the statutory charge does not apply, by virtue of the Financial Regulations.

(3) Where he considers it essential to protect the client's interests or welfare, the Regional Director shall pay, or direct the client's solicitor to pay, to the client any money received by way of any interim payment made in accordance with an order made under CPR rule 25.6, or in accordance with an agreement having the same effect as such an order.

(4) The Regional Director may direct the client's solicitor to:

(*a*) pay to the Commission under paragraph (1)(*b*) only such sums as, in the Regional Director's opinion, should be retained by the Commission in order to safeguard its interests; and

(*b*) pay any other money to the client.

(5) Where the solicitor pays money to the Commission in accordance with this regulation, he shall identify what sums relate respectively to:

(*a*) costs;

(*b*) damages;

(*c*) interest on costs; and

(*d*) interest on damages.

21. Postponement of statutory charge. (1) In this regulation:

"conveyancer" means a solicitor or any other person who lawfully provides conveyancing services;

"family proceedings" means proceedings which arise out of family relationships, including proceedings in which the welfare of children is determined. Family proceedings also include all proceedings under any one or more of the following:

    (*a*) the Matrimonial Causes Act 1973;

    (*b*) the Inheritance (Provision for Family and Dependants) Act 1975;

    (*c*) the Adoption Act 1976;

    (*d*) the Domestic Proceedings and Magistrates' Courts Act 1978;

    (*e*) Part III of the Matrimonial and Family Proceedings Act 1984;

(f) Parts I, II and IV of the Children Act 1989;
(g) Part IV of the Family Law Act 1996;
(ga) the Adoption and Children Act 2002;
(h) the inherent jurisdiction of the High Court in relation to children; and
(i) the Civil Partnership Act 2004;

"purchase money" means money recovered or preserved by the client in family proceedings which, by virtue of an order of the court or an agreement, is to be used to purchase a home to be used by the client or the client's dependants, and "the purchased property" means the property purchased or to be purchased with that money.

(2) The following paragraphs of this regulation apply, and (subject to paragraph (6)) regulation 20(1)(b) does not apply, where the Commission decides to postpone enforcement of the statutory charge under regulation 52 of the Financial Regulations.

(3) The solicitor may release the purchase money to the seller or the seller's representative on completion of the purchase of the purchased property; and shall as soon as practicable provide the Commission with sufficient information to enable it to protect its interest in accordance with regulation 52(1)(c) of the Financial Regulations.

(4) The client's solicitor may release the purchase money to a conveyancer acting for the client in the purchase of the purchased property, if he is satisfied that adequate steps have been, or will be, taken to protect the interests of the Commission.

(5) The steps referred to in paragraph (4) shall include, but are not limited to, the securing of an undertaking from the conveyancer referred to in that paragraph to:

(a) provide the information referred to in paragraph (3); and
(b) repay the purchase money under paragraph (6).

(6) Where the purchase of the purchased property has not been completed within 12 months after the date of the Commission's decision referred to in paragraph (2), or such longer period as the Commission considers reasonable, regulation 20(1)(b) shall apply and the purchase money shall accordingly be repaid to the Commission.

22. Retention and payment out of money by the Commission. (1) The Commission shall deal with the money paid to it under this Part in accordance with this regulation.

(2) The Commission shall retain:

(a) an amount equal to the costs incurred in taking steps under regulation 23;
(b) an amount equal to that part of the funded sum already paid to the supplier in respect of the relevant work; and
(c) where costs are paid to the Commission together with interest, an amount equal to that interest, less the amount of any interest payable to the supplier under paragraph (3)(b)(ii).

(3) The Commission shall pay to the supplier:

(a) any outstanding amount of the funded sum payable to him in respect of the relevant work;
(b) where costs are ordered or agreed to be paid to the client, and those costs are received by the Commission, and those costs (less any amount retained under paragraph (2)(a) or payable under paragraph (5)) exceed the funded sum:

(i) an amount equal to the amount of the excess; and
(ii) where those costs are paid to the Commission together with interest, an amount equal to the interest attributable to the excess referred to in sub-paragraph (i).

(4) Paragraph (5) applies where a solicitor has acted on behalf of the client in proceedings before that client receives funded services in respect of the same proceedings, or has a lien on any documents necessary to proceedings to which a client is a party, and has handed them over subject to the lien, but applies only so far as is consistent with the express terms of any contract between the Commission and the solicitor.

(5) Where the solicitor referred to in paragraph (4) gives the Commission written notice that this paragraph applies, the Commission shall pay to that solicitor the costs to which that solicitor would have been entitled if those costs had been assessed on an indemnity basis.

(6) Where the amount of costs payable under paragraph (5) have not been assessed by the court, they may instead be assessed by the Commission.

(7) Where the amount received by the Commission, less any amount retained under paragraph (2)(a), is insufficient to meet the funded sum and any sum payable under paragraph (5), the Commission shall apportion the amount received proportionately between the two.

(8) The Commission shall pay all the money paid to it under this Part, which is not paid or retained under paragraphs (2) to (5), to the client.

23. Enforcement of orders etc in favour of client. (1) Where, in relation to any dispute to which a client is a party, whether or not proceedings are begun:

(a) an order or agreement is made providing for the recovery or preservation of property by the client (whether for himself or any other person); or
(b) there is a client's costs order or client's costs agreement

the Commission may take any steps, including proceedings in its own name, as may be necessary to enforce or give effect to that order or agreement.

(2) A client may, with the consent of the Regional Director, take proceedings to give effect to an order or agreement under which he is entitled to recover or preserve money or other property.

(3) Subject to paragraph (4), the client's solicitor may take proceedings for the recovery of costs where a client's costs order or a client's costs agreement has been made.

(4) Where the client's costs order or client's costs agreement relates wholly or partly to costs incurred in carrying out work which is remunerated, or to be remunerated, in the funded sum, but those costs have not been reimbursed by payment from any other party in favour of the client, the solicitor shall require the consent of the Regional Director before taking proceedings to which paragraph (3) refers.

(5) Where the Commission takes proceedings, it may authorise any person to make a statement, file a proof or take any other step in the proceedings in its name.

(6) The costs incurred by the Commission in taking any step to enforce an order or agreement where paragraph (1) applies shall be a first charge on any property or sum so recovered.

24. Interest on damages. (1) Where the Commission receives damages paid in favour of a client it shall, subject to the following paragraphs, pay to the client a sum representing gross interest earned while the damages are being held by the Commission.

(2) Without prejudice to its other powers to invest money, the Commission shall maintain and may deposit damages to which this regulation refers in one general account at a deposit-taker.

(3) The rate of interest payable to the client under this regulation shall be 0.5% per annum less than the rate payable on damages deposited in the general account.

(4) The Commission shall not be required to pay interest where the damages received do not exceed £500 or where the period during which they are held by the Commission is less than 28 days.

(5) Interest shall be payable for the period beginning on the third business day after the date on which damages are received by the Commission to and including the date on which the Commission determines the amount to be paid under regulation 22(8).

(6) In this regulation:

"business day" means a day other than a Saturday, a Sunday, Christmas Day, Good Friday or a bank holiday under the Banking and Financial Dealings Act 1971;

"deposit taker" means the Bank of England, or the branch, situated in England or Wales, of either—

(a) a person with permission under Part 4 of the Financial Services and Markets Act 2000 to accept deposits, or

(b) an EEA firm of the kind mentioned in paragraph 5(b) of Schedule 3 to that Act, which has permission under paragraph 15 of that Schedule (as a result of qualifying for authorisation under paragraph 12(1) of that Schedule) to accept deposits;

"general account" means an interest bearing account opened in the name of the Commission, the title of which does not identify any client.

(7) The definition of "deposit taker" in paragraph (6) must be read with—

(a) section 22 of the Financial Services and Markets Act 2000;

(b) any relevant order under that section; and

(c) Schedule 22 to that Act.

Community Legal Service (Financial) Regulations 2000[1]

(SI 2000/516 as amended by SI 2001/950, 2996, 2997, 3663 and 3929, SI 2002/709 and 1766, SI 2003/650 and 2838, SI 2004/1748 and 2899, SI 2005/589, 1097, 1793 and 3504 and SI 2006/713 and 2363)

PART I
GENERAL

1–5651   1. Citation and commencement. These Regulations may be cited as the Community Legal Service (Financial) Regulations 2000 and shall come into force on 1st April 2000.

---

1. Made by the Lord Chancellor in Exercise of powers conferred on him by ss 7 and 10 of the Access to Justice Act 1999.

2. Interpretation. (1) In these Regulations, unless the context requires otherwise:

"the Act" means the Access to Justice Act 1999;

"application" means an application to receive funded services, made by or on behalf of a client in accordance with the Funding Code;

"assessing authority" means:

(a) the Commission, where the client's eligibility under regulation 5(6) is being assessed;

(b) otherwise, the supplier;

"asylum claim" means a claim that it would be contrary to the United Kingdom's obligations under the Convention relating to the Status of Refugees done at Geneva on 28th July 1951 and the protocol to the Convention or to Article 3 of the Convention for the Protection of Human Rights and Fundamental Freedoms, agreed by the Council of Europe at Rome on 4th November 1950, for the claimant to be removed from or required to leave the United Kingdom;

"certificate" means a certificate issued under the Funding Code certifying a decision to fund services for the client;

"client" means an individual who applies for or receives funded services and, in the case of actual or contemplated proceedings, is a party or prospective party to the proceedings;

"clinical negligence proceedings" means proceedings which include:

(a) a claim for damages in respect of breach of a duty of care or trespass to the person committed in the course of the provision of clinical or medical services (including dental or nursing services); or

(b) a claim for damages in respect of alleged professional negligence in the conduct of such a claim;

"Commission" means the Legal Services Commission established under section 1 of the Act;

"CPR" means the Civil Procedure Rules 1998, and a reference to a Part or a rule, prefixed by "CPR", means the Part or rule so numbered in the CPR;

"disposable income" and "disposable capital" mean, respectively, the income and capital of the person concerned, calculated in accordance with regulations 16 to 37;

"family proceedings" means proceedings which arise out of family relationships, including proceedings in which the welfare of children is determined. Family proceedings also include all proceedings under any one or more of the following:

(a) the Matrimonial Causes Act 1973;

(b) the Inheritance (Provision for Family and Dependents) Act 1975;

(c) the Adoption Act 1976;

(d) the Domestic Proceedings and Magistrates' Courts Act 1978;

(e) Part III of the Matrimonial and Family Proceedings Act 1984;

(f) Parts I, II and IV of the Children Act 1989;

(g) Part IV of the Family Law Act 1996;

(ga) the Adoption and Children Act 2002;

(gb) the Civil Partnership Act 2004; and

(h) the inherent jurisdiction of the High Court in relation to children;

"Funding Code" means the code approved under section 9 of the Act;

"funded services" means services which are provided directly for a client and funded for that client by the Commission as part of the Community Legal Service under sections 4 to 11 of the Act;

"immigration matter" means any relevant matter as defined in section 82 of the Immigration and Asylum Act 1999;

"the Independent Living Funds" means the Independent Living Fund, the Independent Living (Extension) Fund and the Independent Living (1993) Fund;

"the Independent Living Fund" means the charitable trust established out of funds provided by the Secretary of State for the purpose of providing financial assistance to those persons incapacitated by or otherwise suffering from very severe disablement who are in need of such assistance to enable them to live independently;

"the Independent Living (Extension) Fund" means the Trust of that name established by a deed dated 25th February 1993 and made between the Secretary of State for Social Security of the one part and Robin Glover Wendt and John Fletcher Shepherd of the other part;

"the Independent Living (1993) Fund" means the Trust of that name established by a deed dated 25th February 1993 and made between the Secretary of State for Social Security of the one part and Robin Glover Wendt and John Fletcher Shepherd of the other part;"

"the Lord Chancellor's Authorisation" means the Lord Chancellor's Authorisation on funding for representation at inquests issued in November 2001 under section 6(8)(b) of the Act, as amended from time to time;

"Multi-Party Action" means any action or actions, in which a number of clients have causes of action, which involve common issues of fact or law arising out of the same cause or event;

"partner" except in the expression "partner in a business" means a person with whom the person concerned lives as a couple, and includes a person with whom the person concerned is not currently living but from whom he is not living separate and apart;

"personal injury proceedings" means proceedings for damages in respect of death or any disease or impairment of the client's physical or mental condition, excluding proceedings for clinical negligence;

"person concerned" means the person:

(a) whose eligibility is to be assessed; or

(b) whose resources are to be treated as the resources of the client under these Regulations;

"solicitor" means solicitor or other person who is an authorised litigator within the meaning of section 119(1) of the Courts and Legal Services Act 1990;

"supplier" means the solicitor, mediator or agency being requested to provide or providing funded services to the client;

"wider public interest" means the potential of proceedings to produce real benefits for individuals other than the client (other than any general benefits which normally flow from proceedings of the type in question).

(2) References to the levels of service listed in paragraph (3) shall be construed as references to the application for, or receipt or provision of, those levels of service in accordance with the Funding Code.

(3) The levels of service referred to in paragraph (2) are:

(a) Legal Help;

   (b) Help at Court;
   (c) Legal Representation;
   (d) Family Mediation;
   (e) Help with Mediation;
   (f) General Family Help;
   (g) *revoked*;
   (h) *revoked*.

PART II
ELIGIBILITY, ASSESSMENT AND CONTRIBUTIONS

1–5652 **3. Financial eligibility.** (1) The following services shall be available without reference to the client's financial resources:

   (a) services consisting exclusively of the provision of general information about the law and legal system and the availability of legal services;

   (b) legal advice consisting of such amount of Legal Help, and Help at Court as is authorised under a contract to be provided without reference to the client's financial resources;

   (c) Legal Representation in proceedings under the Children Act 1989 applied for by or on behalf of:

      (i) a child in respect of whom an application is made for an order under:

         (a) section 31 (care or supervision order);
         (b) section 43 (child assessment order);
         (c) section 44 (emergency protection order); or
         (d) section 45 (extension or discharge of emergency protection order);

      (ii) a parent of such a child, or a person with parental responsibility for such a child within the meaning of the Children Act 1989; or

      (iii) a child who is brought before a court under section 25 (use of accommodation for restricting liberty) who is not, but wishes to be, legally represented before the court;

   (d) Legal Representation, applied for by or on behalf of any of the parties referred to in subparagraph (c) in proceedings related to any proceedings in sub-paragraph (c) which are being heard together with those proceedings or in which an order is being sought as an alternative to an order in those proceedings;

   (e) Legal Representation in proceedings before a Mental Health Review Tribunal under the Mental Health Act 1983, where the client's case or application to the Tribunal is, or is to be, the subject of the proceedings;

   (f) Legal Representation by a solicitor in England and Wales of a person whose application under the Hague Convention or the European Convention has been submitted to the Central Authority in England and Wales under section 3(2) or 14(2) of the Child Abduction and Custody Act 1985; and

   (g) Legal Representation of a person who:

      (i) appeals to a magistrates' court against the registration of, or the refusal to register, a maintenance order made in a Hague Convention country under the Maintenance Orders (Reciprocal Enforcement) Act 1972; or

      (ii) applies for the registration of a judgment under section 4 of the Civil Jurisdiction and Judgments Act 1982; or

      (iii) applies for the registration of a judgment under Council Regulation (EC) No 44/2001 of 22nd December 2000 on jurisdiction and the recognition and enforcement of judgments in civil and commercial matters or

      (iv) applies for either the registration of or the registration and enforcement of a judgment under Council Regulation (EC) No 2201/2003 of 27 November 2003 on jurisdiction and the recognition and enforcement of judgments in matrimonial matters and the matters of parental responsibility

     and who benefited from complete or partial assistance with, or exemption from, costs or expenses in the country in which the maintenance order was made or the judgment was given;

   (h) such services as are funded through grants under section 6(3)(c) of the Act except where the terms of the grant provide otherwise;

   (i) Legal Help or Legal Representation for a person who is subject to a control order, consisting of advice in connection with that order, help with an application to the Secretary of State under section 7(1) of the Prevention of Terrorism Act 2005, or representation in control order proceedings.

  (2) In this regulation:

"Central Authority" has the same meaning as in sections 3 and 14 of the Child Abduction and Custody Act 1985;

"control order" and "control order proceedings" have the same meanings as in the Prevention of Terrorism Act 2005;

"European Convention" means the convention defined in section 12(1) of the Child Abduction and Custody Act 1985;

"Hague Convention" means the convention defined in section 1(1) of the Child Abduction and Custody Act 1985;

"Hague Convention country" has the same meaning as in the Reciprocal Enforcement of Maintenance Orders (Hague Convention Countries) Order 1993; and

"the Maintenance Orders (Reciprocal Enforcement) Act 1972" means that Act as applied with such exceptions, adaptations and modifications as are specified in the Reciprocal Enforcement of Maintenance Orders (Hague Convention Countries) Order 1993.

4. (1) Subject to regulation 3, the assessing authority to which an application is made shall determine the financial eligibility of the client in accordance with these Regulations.

(2) Where the assessing authority is satisfied that the client is in receipt, directly or indirectly, of—

(a) income support,

(b) income-based jobseeker's allowance, or

(c) guarantee state pension credit (under section 1(3)(a) of the State Pension Credit Act 2002),

he shall be eligible for all the levels of service listed in regulation 2(3) without making (where applicable) any contributions.

(3) Where the assessing authority is satisfied that the client is in receipt, directly or indirectly, of support provided under section 4 or 95 of the Immigration and Asylum Act 1999, he shall be eligible for—

(a) Legal Help in relation to an asylum claim or immigration matter;

(b) the High Court in respect of an application under section 103A of the Nationality, Immigration and Asylum Act 2002.

5. (1) This regulation has effect subject to regulations 3, 4 and 5A.

(2) A client is eligible for Legal Representation before—

(a) the Asylum and Immigration Tribunal; and

(b) the High Court in respect of an application under section 103A of the Nationality, Immigration and Asylum Act 2002,

if his monthly disposable income does not exceed £649 and his disposable capital does not exceed £3,000, except in cases to which paragraph (2A) applies.

(2A) A client is eligible for Legal Representation in respect of an asylum claim before—

(a) the Asylum and Immigration Tribunal; and

(b) the High Court in respect of an application under section 103A of the Nationality, Immigration and Asylum Act 2002,

if his monthly disposable income does not exceed £649 and his disposable capital does not exceed £8,000.

(3) A client is eligible for Legal Help, Help at Court and Family Mediation if his monthly disposable income does not exceed £649 and his disposable capital does not exceed £8,000.

(4) A client who is eligible for Family Mediation under paragraph (3) shall also be eligible for Help with Mediation in relation to family mediation.

(5) A client is eligible for Legal Representation in respect of family proceedings before a magistrates' court, other than proceedings under the Children Act 1989 or Part IV of the Family Law Act 1996, if his disposable income does not exceed £649 per month, but a person may be refused such services where:

(a) his disposable capital exceeds £8,000; and

(b) it appears to the assessing authority that the probable cost of the funded services to which the application relates would not exceed the contribution payable by him under regulation 38.

(6) A client is eligible for Legal Representation (other than as provided for in paragraphs (2) and (5)), General Family Help, and for such other services as are required or authorised by the Lord Chancellor to be funded under section 6(8) of the Act, if his disposable income does not exceed £649 per month, but a person may be refused such services where:

(a) his disposable capital exceeds £8,000; and

(b) it appears to the assessing authority that the probable cost of the funded services to which the application relates would not exceed the contribution payable to him under regulation 38.

5A. (1) For the purposes of this regulation, "gross income" means total income from all sources, before any deductions are made other than those payments which are to be disregarded under regulation 19, and any housing benefit paid under the Social Security Contributions and Benefits Act 1992.

(2) This regulation does not apply to any applications to which regulation 4(2) applies.

(3) In relation to the calculation of gross income:

(a) regulations 6, 10, 11, 12 and 15 shall apply as if "gross income" were substituted for "disposable income" each time it appears; and

(b) regulations 21 and 23 shall not apply.

(4) Subject to paragraph (5) and regulation 3, where the gross monthly income of the person concerned exceeds £2,350, the assessing authority shall refuse any application for funded services.

(5) Where the person concerned has more than four dependant children in respect of whom he receives child benefit, the sum referred to in paragraph (4) shall be increased by £145 in respect of the fifth and each subsequent child.

5B. Waiver of eligibility limit in Multi-Party Actions of wider public interest. (1) *Revoked.*

(2) Paragraph (3) applies where:

   (*a*) the Commission funds Legal Representation in a Multi-Party Action which it considers has a significant wider public interest; and

   (*b*) the Commission considers it cost-effective to fund those services only in relation to specific issues within the Multi-Party Action.

(3) Where this paragraph applies, the Commission may, if it considers it equitable to do so, disapply the eligibility limits in regulations 5(6) and 5A.

5C. Waiver of eligibility limit in certain inquests. (1) This regulation applies to an application for the funding of services in relation to an inquest into the death of a member of the immediate family of the client.

(2) Where this regulation applies—

   (*a*) the Commission may, if it considers it equitable to do so, request the Lord Chancellor to disapply the eligibility limits in regulations 5(3), 5(6) and 5A in respect of an application for funding which falls outside the scope of the Lord Chancellor's Authorisation;

   (*b*) the Commission may, if it considers it equitable to do so, disapply the eligibility limits in regulations 5(3), 5(6) and 5A in respect of an application for funding which falls within the scope of the Lord Chancellor's Authorisation.

(3) In considering whether to make such a request or waiver, the Commission shall have regard in particular to any applicable Convention rights under Article 2 of Schedule 1 to the Human Rights Act 1998.

(4) On receipt of a request under paragraph (2)(*a*) the Lord Chancellor may, if he thinks it equitable, disapply the eligibility limits.

5D. Waiver of eligibility limit and contributions in cross-border disputes. (1) This regulation applies to an application to the Commission by a client domiciled or habitually resident in another Member State for the funding of services in relation to a cross-border dispute.

(2) Where this regulation applies, the Commission must—

   (*a*) disapply the relevant eligibility limits in regulations 5 and 5A if the client proves that he is unable to pay the cost of proceedings in England and Wales in relation to the dispute as a result of differences in the cost of living between the client's Member State of domicile or habitual residence and England and Wales; and

   (*b*) waive part or all of any contributions payable under regulation 38, if and to such extent as the client proves that he is unable to pay them as a result of such differences in the cost of living.

(3) In this regulation—

"cross-border dispute" means a dispute where a client is domiciled or habitually resident in a Member State other than the Member State where the court is sitting or where the decision is to be enforced;

"Member State" means a member state of the European Union except Denmark.

For the purposes of this regulation the Member State in which a client is domiciled shall be determined in accordance with Article 59 of Council Regulation (EC) No 44/2001 of 22 December 2000 on jurisdiction and the recognition and enforcement of judgments in civil and commercial matters.

5E. Waiver of eligibility limit in proceedings for protection from harm to the person. (1) This regulation applies to an application by a client for the funding of Legal Representation in proceedings where the client seeks—

   (*a*) an injunction or other order for protection from harm to the person; or

   (*b*) committal for breach of any such order.

(2) Where this regulation applies the Commission may, if it considers it equitable to do so, disapply the disposable income limit in regulation 5(5) or 5(6).

6. Where an application is made, the client shall provide the assessing authority with the information necessary to enable it to:

   (*a*) determine whether he satisfies the conditions set out in regulation 4; and

   (*b*) calculate, where relevant, his disposable income and disposable capital and those of any other person concerned.

7. (1) The assessing authority shall, subject to regulation 4(2):

   (*a*) calculate the disposable income and disposable capital of the person concerned in accordance with regulations 16 to 37;

   (*b*) calculate the gross income of the person concerned in accordance with regulation 5A; and

   (*c*) calculate any contribution payable in accordance with regulations 38 and 39.

(2) When calculating:

   (*a*) disposable income for the purposes of regulation 5(2), (3), (5) or (6); or

   (*b*) gross income for the purposes of regulation 5A

the period of calculation shall be one month.

(3) For the purposes of this regulation and regulation 15, one month means the period of one

calendar month which ends on the date on which the application is made, or such other equivalent period as the Commission considers appropriate.

(4) Where the assessing authority calculates that a client has disposable income or disposable capital of an amount which makes him ineligible to receive funded services, it shall refuse the application.

8. The supplier shall not provide any funded services to the client prior to the assessment of resources in accordance with regulation 7 other than:

(*a*) in accordance with Funding Code procedures; or

(*b*) where authorisation to do so is given by the Commission in a contract.

9. Where the assessing authority is the supplier, any question arising under regulations 10 to 41 shall be decided by the supplier and the supplier, in deciding any such question, shall have regard to any guidance which may from time to time be given by the Commission as to the application of these Regulations.

10. Application in representative, fiduciary or official capacity. Where the client is acting only in a representative, fiduciary or official capacity, the assessing authority shall, in calculating his disposable income and disposable capital, and the amount of any contribution to be made:

(*a*) assess the value of any property or estate or the amount of any fund out of which he is entitled to be indemnified; and

(*b*) unless it considers that he might benefit from the proceedings, disregard his personal resources.

11. Resources of other persons. (1) Subject to paragraph (2), in calculating the disposable income and disposable capital of the client, the resources of his partner shall be treated as his resources.

(2) The resources of the client's partner shall not be treated as his resources if he has a contrary interest in the dispute in respect of which the application is made.

(3) Except where eligibility is being assessed under regulation 5(6), where the client is a child the resources of a parent, guardian or any other person who is responsible for maintaining him, or who usually contributes substantially to his maintenance, shall be treated as his resources, unless, having regard to all the circumstances, including the age and resources of the child and any conflict of interest, it appears inequitable to do so.

(4) Where it appears to the assessing authority that:

(*a*) another person is or has been or is likely to be, substantially maintaining the person concerned, or

(*b*) any of the resources of another person have been or are likely to be made available to the person concerned, and may assess or estimate the value of those resources as well as it is able.

the assessing authority may treat all or any part of the resources of that other person as the resources of the person concerned, and may assess or estimate the value of those resources as well as it is able.

(5) In this regulation and regulation 12, "person" includes a company, partnership, body of trustees and any body of persons, whether corporate or not corporate.

12. Deprivation or conversion of resources. If it appears to the assessing authority that the person concerned has, with intent to reduce the amount of his disposable income or disposable capital, whether for the purpose of making himself eligible to receive funded services, reducing his liability to pay a contribution, or otherwise:

(*a*) directly or indirectly deprived himself of any resources,

(*b*) transferred any resources to another person, or

(*c*) converted any part of his resources into resources which under these Regulations are to be wholly or partly disregarded,

the resources which he has so deprived himself of, transferred or converted shall be treated as part of his resources or as not so converted as the case may be.

13. Duty to report change in financial circumstances. The client shall forthwith inform the assessing authority of any change in his financial circumstances (or those of any other person concerned) of which he is, or should reasonably be, aware, which has occurred since any assessment of his resources, and which might affect the terms on which the client was assessed as eligible to receive funded services.

14. Amendment of assessment due to error or receipt of new information. Where:

(*a*) it appears to the assessing authority that there has been an error in the assessment of a person's resources or contribution, or in any calculation or estimate upon which such assessment was based, or

(*b*) new information which is relevant to the assessment has come to light,

the assessing authority may make an amended assessment, and may take such steps as appear equitable to give effect to it in relation to any period during which funded services have already been provided.

15. Further assessments. (1) Where the eligibility of the person concerned was assessed under regulation 5(6) and it appears that his circumstances may have altered so that:

    (a) his normal disposable income may have increased by an amount greater than £60 or decreased by an amount greater than £25, or

    (b) his disposable capital may have increased by an amount greater than £750,

the assessing authority shall, subject to paragraph (6), make a further assessment of the person's resources and contribution (if any) in accordance with these Regulations.

(2) For the purposes of the further assessment, the period of calculation shall be the period of one month following the date of the change of circumstances or such other period of one month as the assessing authority considers to be appropriate.

(3) Where a further assessment is made, the amount or value of every resource of a capital nature acquired since the date of the original application shall be ascertained as at the date of receipt of that resource.

(4) Any capital contribution which becomes payable as a result of a further assessment shall be payable in respect of the cost of the funded services, including costs already incurred.

(5) Where a certificate is discharged as a result of a further assessment of capital, the assessing authority may require a contribution to be paid in respect of costs already incurred.

(6) The assessing authority may decide not to make a further assessment under paragraph (1) if it considers such a further assessment inappropriate, having regard in particular to the period during which funded services are likely to continue to be provided to the client.

16. Calculation of income. The income of the person concerned from any source shall be taken to be the income which that person may reasonably expect to receive (in cash or in kind) during the period of calculation, but where the eligibility of the person concerned is being assessed under regulation 5(6), in calculating such income the Commission may have regard to his average income during such other period as it considers appropriate.

17. (1) The income from a trade, business or gainful occupation other than an occupation at a wage or salary shall be deemed to be whichever of the following the assessing authority considers more appropriate and practicable:

    (a) the profits which have accrued or will accrue to the person concerned in respect of the period of calculation; or

    (b) the drawings of the person concerned.

(2) In calculating the profits under paragraph (1)(a):

    (a) the assessing authority may have regard to the profits of the last accounting period of such trade, business or gainful occupation for which accounts have been prepared; and

    (b) there shall be deducted all sums necessarily expended to earn those profits, but no deduction shall be made in respect of the living expenses of the person concerned or any member of his family or household, except in so far as that person is wholly or mainly employed in that trade or business and such living expenses form part of his remuneration.

18. (1) For the purposes of this regulation, "national insurance contributions" means contributions under Part 1 of the Social Security Contributions and Benefits Act 1992.

(2) In calculating the disposable income of the person concerned, any income tax and national insurance contributions paid or, in the case of an assessment under regulation 5(6), payable on that income in respect of the period of calculation shall be deducted.

19. In calculating the disposable income or the gross income of the person concerned, the following payments shall be disregarded:

    (a) under the Social Security Contributions and Benefits Act 1992:

        (i) disability living allowance;

        (ii) attendance allowance paid under section 64 or Schedule 8 paragraphs 4 or 7(2);

        (iii) constant attendance allowance paid under section 104 as an increase to a disablement pension;

        (iv) any payment made out of the social fund;

        (v) carer's allowance;

        (vi) council tax benefit;

    (b) any payment made under the Community Care (Direct Payments) Act 1996 or under regulations made under section 57 of the Health and Social Care Act 2001 (direct payments)[1]; and

    (c) so much of any back to work bonus received under section 26 of the Jobseekers Act 1995 as is by virtue of that section to be treated as payable by way of jobseeker's allowance.

    (d) severe disablement allowance paid under the Social Security (Severe Disablement Allowance) Regulations 1984;

    (e) exceptionally severe disablement allowance paid under the Personal Injuries (Civilians) Scheme 1983;

    (f) all pensions paid under the Naval, Military and Air Forces etc (Disability and Death) Service Pensions Order 1983; and

    (g) to the extent that it exceeds the relevant figure referred to in regulation 20(2)(b), any financial support paid under an agreement for the care of a foster child entered into in accordance with regulation 5(6) of the Foster Placement (Children) Regulations 1991;

    (h) any payment made out of the Independent Living Funds.

20. (1) For the purposes of this regulation, "the Schedule" means Schedule 2 to the Income Support (General) Regulations 1987.

(2) Subject to paragraph (3), in calculating the disposable income of the person concerned there shall be a deduction at or equivalent to the following rates (as they applied at the beginning of the period of calculation):

(*a*) in respect of the maintenance of his partner, the difference between the income support allowance for a couple both aged not less than 18 (which is specified in column 2 of paragraph 1(3)(c) of the Schedule), and the allowance for a single person aged not less than 25 (which is specified in column 2 of paragraph 1(1)(*e*) of the Schedule); and

(*b*) in respect of the maintenance of any dependent child or dependent relative of his, where such persons are members of his household:

(i) in the case of a dependent child or a dependent relative aged 15 or under at the beginning of the period of calculation, the amount specified at (*a*) in column 2 in paragraph 2(1) of the Schedule; and

(ii) in the case of a dependent child or a dependent relative aged 16 or over at the beginning of the period of calculation, the amount specified at (*b*) in column 2 in paragraph 2(1) of the Schedule.

(3) The assessing authority may reduce any rate provided by virtue of paragraph (1) by taking into account the income and other resources of the dependent child or dependent relative to such extent as appears to the assessing authority to be equitable.

(4) In ascertaining whether a child is a dependent child or whether a person is a dependent relative for the purposes of this regulation, regard shall be had to their income and other resources.

21. Where the person concerned is making and, throughout such period as the assessing authority considers adequate, has regularly made payments for the maintenance of:

(*a*) a former partner;

(*b*) a child; or

(*c*) a relative

who is not a member of his household, a reasonable amount shall be deducted in respect of such payments.

22. *Revoked.*

23. (1) Where the income of the person concerned consists, wholly or partly, of a wage or salary from employment, there shall be deducted—

(*a*) the sum of £45 per month; and

(*b*) where it would be reasonable to do so, an amount to provide for the care of any dependant child living with the person concerned during the time that person is absent from home by reason of his employment.

(2) Where the income of the person consists, wholly or partly, of income from a trade, business or gainful occupation other than an occupation at a wage or salary, there shall be deducted, where it would be reasonable to do so, an amount to provide for the care of any dependant child living with the person concerned during the time that person is absent from home whilst he is engaged in that trade, business or gainful occupation.

24. (1) *Revoked.*

(2) Paragraphs (3) to (5) apply only if the person concerned is a householder.

(3) In calculating the disposable income of the person concerned, the net rent payable by him in respect of his main or only dwelling, or such part of it as is reasonable in the circumstances, shall be deducted; and the assessing authority shall decide which is the main dwelling where the person concerned resides in more than one dwelling.

(4) For the purpose of this regulation, "net rent" includes:

(*a*) any monthly rent payable;

(*b*) any monthly instalment (whether of interest or capital) in respect of a debt secured by a mortgage or charge on the property.

(5) In calculating the amount of net rent payable, there shall be deducted:

(*a*) any housing benefit paid under the Social Security Contributions and Benefits Act 1992;

(*b*) any proceeds of sub-letting any part of the premises; and

(*c*) an amount reasonably attributable to any person other than the person concerned, his partner or any dependent, who is accommodated in the premises otherwise than as a sub-tenant.

(6) If the person concerned is not a householder, a reasonable amount in respect of the cost of his living accommodation shall be deducted.

(7) If no deduction has been made under regulation 20(2), the maximum amount to be deducted under paragraph (3) or, as the case may be, (6) shall be £545.

25. *Revoked.*

26. Subject to the provisions of these Regulations, in calculating the disposable capital of the person concerned, the amount or value of every resource of a capital nature belonging to him on the date on which the application is made shall be included.

27. In so far as any resource of a capital nature does not consist of money, its value shall be taken to be:

(*a*) the amount which that resource would realise if sold; or

(*b*) the value assessed in such other manner as appears to the assessing authority to be equitable.

28. Where money is due to the person concerned, whether it is payable immediately or otherwise and whether payment is secured or not, its value shall be taken to be its present value.

29. The value to the person concerned of any life insurance or endowment policy shall be taken to be the amount which he could readily borrow on the security of that policy.

30. Other than in circumstances which are exceptional having regard in particular to the quantity or value of the items concerned, nothing shall be included in the disposable capital of the person concerned in respect of:

(a) the household furniture and effects of the main or only dwelling house occupied by him;

(b) articles of personal clothing; and

(c) the tools and equipment of his trade, unless they form part of the plant or equipment of a business to which the provisions of regulation 31 apply.

30A. Subject to regulation 31, in calculating the value of the interest of the person concerned in any resource of a capital nature which he owns jointly or in common with any other person, the assessing authority may treat that resource as being owned—

(a) in equal shares; or

(b) in such other proportions as appear to the assessing authority to be equitable.

31. (1) Where eligibility is being assessed under regulation 5(6), paragraphs (2) to (4) apply.

(2) Where the person concerned is the sole owner of or partner in a business, the value of the business to him shall be taken to be the greater of:

(a) such sum, or his share of such sum, as could be withdrawn from the assets of his business without substantially impairing its profits or normal development; and

(b) such sum as that person could borrow on the security of his interest in the business without substantially injuring its commercial credit.

(3) Where the person concerned stands in relation to a company in a position analogous to that of a sole owner or partner in a business, the assessing authority may, instead of ascertaining the value of his stocks, shares, bonds or debentures in that company, treat that person as if he were a sole owner or partner in a business and calculate the amount of his capital in respect of that resource in accordance with paragraph (2).

(4) Where the person concerned owns solely, jointly or in common with other persons, any interest on the termination of a prior estate, whether

(a) legal or equitable;

(b) vested or contingent;

(c) in reversion or remainder; and

(d) whether in real or personal property or in a trust or other fund

the value of such interest shall be calculated in such manner as is both equitable and practicable.

(5) Where eligibility is being assessed other than under regulation 5(6), the sums mentioned in this regulation shall be disregarded.

32. (1) In calculating the disposable capital of the client, the value of any interest in land shall be taken to be the amount for which that interest could be sold less, subject to paragraphs (2) and (3), the amount of any debt secured by a mortgage or charge on the property.

(2) The total amount to be deducted under this regulation on an assessment of the client's disposable capital shall not exceed £100,000 in respect of all secured debts.

(3) Where—

(a) the interests in land which are taken into account in an assessment of the client's disposable capital include interests in both—

(i) the main or only dwelling in which the client resides; and

(ii) one or more other properties, and

(b) debts totalling more than £100,000 are secured on the main or only dwelling and one or more of the other properties,

the deduction to be made under this regulation shall be made in respect of the debts secured on the other properties first.

(4) Where the client resides in more than one dwelling, the assessing authority shall decide which is the main dwelling for the purposes of this regulation and regulations 32A and 32B.

32A. (1) In calculating the disposable capital of the client, the amount or value of the subject matter of the dispute to which the application relates shall, subject to paragraphs (2) and (3), be disregarded.

(2) Where eligibility is being assessed under regulation 5(5) or 5(6), the total amount to be disregarded under this regulation shall not exceed £100,000.

(3) Where eligibility is being assessed under regulation 5(5) or 5(6), if—

(a) the subject matter of the dispute includes interests of the client in—

(i) the main or only dwelling in which the client resides; and

(ii) other resources of a capital nature, and

(b) the total value of those interests (after the application of regulation 32) exceeds £100,000,

the assessing authority shall disregard the value of the client's interest in his main or only dwelling first.

32B. (1) In calculating the disposable capital of the client, the value (after the application of regulations 32 and 32A) of his interest (if any) in the main or only dwelling in which he resides shall, subject to paragraph (2), be disregarded.

(2) The amount to be disregarded under this regulation shall not exceed £100,000.

33. In calculating the disposable capital of the person concerned, there shall be disregarded:

(a) so much of any back to work bonus received under section 26 of the Jobseekers Act 1995 as is by virtue of that section to be treated as payable by way of jobseeker's allowance; and

(b) the whole of any payment made out of the social fund under the Social Security Contributions and Benefits Act 1992 or any arrears of payments made under the Community Care (Direct Payments) Act 1996 or under regulations made under section 57 of the Health and Social Care Act 2001 (direct payments);

(c) the whole of any payment made out of the Independent Living Funds.

34. *Revoked.*

35. (1) Where—

(a) eligibility is being assessed under regulation 5(2), 5(3), 5(5) or 5(6);

(b) the client or any other person concerned is aged 60 or over; and

(c) the total monthly disposable income (excluding any net income derived from capital) of the client and any other person concerned is less than the first figure prescribed in regulation 38(2)(a), that is, £279,

the amount of capital shown in the following table shall be disregarded:

monthly disposable income (excluding net income derived from capital	amount of capital disregard
up to £25	£100,000
£26–50	£90,000
£51–75	£80,000
£76–100	£70,000
£101–125	£60,000
£126–150	£50,000
£151–175	£40,000
£176–200	£30,000
£201–225	£20,000
£226–279	£10,000

(2) *Revoked.*

36. Where eligibility is being assessed under regulation 5(5) or 5(6), in calculating the disposable capital of the person concerned, any interim payment made to him in any court proceedings may be disregarded.

37. Where eligibility is being assessed under regulation 5(5) or 5(6), in calculating the disposable capital of the person concerned, any capital resource may be disregarded where:

(a) he is restrained from dealing with that resource by order of the court;

(b) he has requested the court which made the order to release part or all of that resource for use in connection with the proceedings to which the application for funding relates; and

(c) that request has been refused.

38. Contributions. (1) Subject to regulation 15, all contributions shall be:

(a) assessed at the beginning of the case; and

(b) payable to the assessing authority.

(2) Subject to regulation 4(2), a person whose eligibility is assessed under regulation 5(5) or 5(6) shall make the following contributions:

(a) where his monthly disposable income exceeds £279—

(i) one quarter of any such income between £275 and £411 inclusive;

(ii) one third of any such income between £412 and £545 inclusive; and

(iii) one half of his remaining disposable income; and

(b) where his disposable capital exceeds £3,000, a contribution of the lesser of the excess and the sum which the assessing authority considers to be the likely maximum cost of the funded services.

(3) All contributions under paragraph (2)(a) shall be payable monthly throughout the period the certificate is in force.

(4) All contributions under paragraph (2)(b) shall be payable upon assessment.

(5) Paragraph (6) applies where:

(a) eligibility is being assessed under regulation 5(5) or 5(6); and

(b) the Commission considers that:

(i) there are other persons or bodies, including those who have the same or a similar interest to the client or who might benefit from any proceedings, who can reasonably be expected to contribute to the cost of the funded services; or

(ii) some other source of funding exists which could be used to contribute to that cost.

(6) Where this paragraph applies, the Commission may add a reasonable additional amount to the contribution (if any) due from the client.

(7) The Commission may subsequently vary the amount of any additional contribution payable under paragraph (6).

(8) Paragraph (9) applies where the Commission funds Legal Representation in proceedings which it considers to have a significant wider public interest and either:

(a) the Commission considers it cost-effective to fund those services for a specified claimant or claimants, but not for other claimants or potential claimants who might benefit from the litigation; or

(b) the Commission is funding those services in a Multi-Party Action and it considers it cost-effective to fund those services only in relation to specific issues within that action.

(8A) Paragraph (9) also applies where the Commission funds services in relation to an inquest into the death of a member of the immediate family of the client.

(9) Where this paragraph applies, the Commission may, if it considers it equitable to do so, waive part or all of the contributions payable under this regulation, except where paragraph (10) applies.

(10) Where under section 6(8)(b) of the Act the Lord Chancellor authorises the Commission to fund services in relation to an inquest into the death of a member of the immediate family of the client, the Lord Chancellor may, if he considers it equitable to do so, waive part or all of the contributions payable under this regulation.

39. Where more than one certificate is in force in respect of the client at any one time, contributions from income under only one certificate shall be payable, and the Commission may decide under which certificate contributions shall be paid.

40. (1) Where a certificate has been discharged or revoked and the contribution made by the client exceeds the net cost of the funded services, the excess shall be refunded to the client.

(2) The net cost of the funded services means the cost paid by the Commission less any costs recovered by the Commission from another party.

(3) Where funding is provided by the Commission under a contract which does not differentiate between the remuneration for the client's case and remuneration for other cases, or require the cost of individual cases to be assessed, the reference in paragraph (2) to the cost paid by the Commission shall be construed as a reference to such part of the remuneration payable under the contract as may be specified in writing by the Commission.

(4) For the purposes of this regulation and regulation 43, where a certificate is discharged the cost of any assessment proceedings under CPR Part 47 or of taxation in the House of Lords shall not be included as part of the cost of the funded services, and the cost of drawing up a bill is not part of the cost of assessment proceedings.

41. Where the Commission has revoked a certificate in accordance with Part 15 of the Funding Code:

(a) the client shall pay to the Commission all costs paid or payable by it under the certificate, less any amount already paid by way of contribution; and

(b) the solicitor shall have the right to recover from the client the difference between the amount paid or payable to him by the Commission and the full amount of his costs assessed on the indemnity basis under CPR rule 44.4.

PART III
THE STATUTORY CHARGE

1–5653   42. Calculation of the statutory charge.   In regulations 43 to 53:

"relevant dispute" means the dispute in connection with which funded services are provided;

"relevant proceedings" means proceedings in connection with which funded services are provided;

"recovered", in relation to property or money, means property or money recovered or preserved by a client, whether for himself or for any other person;

"statutory charge" means the charge created by section 10(7) of the Act in respect of the amount defined in regulation 43; and

"success fee" is defined in accordance with section 58 of the Courts and Legal Services Act 1990.

43. (1) Subject to paragraphs (3), (4) and (5) , where any money or property is recovered for a client in a relevant dispute or proceedings, the amount of the statutory charge shall be the aggregate of the sums referred to in section 10(7)(a) and (b) of the Act.

(2) For the purposes of this regulation:

(a) the sum referred to in section 10(7)(a) shall be defined in accordance with regulation 40(2) to (4), less any contribution paid by the client;

(b) the sum referred to in section 10(7)(b) shall include:

(i) any interest payable under regulation 52; and

(ii) any sum which the client has agreed to pay only in specific circumstances under section 10(2)(c) of the Act.

(3) Subject to paragraph (4), the amount of the charge created by section 10(7) of the Act shall not include sums expended by the Commission in funding any of the following services:

(a) Legal Help;
(b) Help at Court;
(c) Family Mediation; or
(d) Help with Mediation.

(4) Paragraph (3)(a) and (b) does not apply where the funded services are given in relation to

family, clinical negligence or personal injury proceedings or a dispute which may give rise to such proceedings.

(5) Where Legal Help is provided as part of the family advice and information networks pilot, the amount of the statutory charge shall not exceed the sum which would have been expended by the Commission, had the Legal Help been provided otherwise than as a part of that pilot.

44. Exemptions from the statutory charge. (1) The charge created by section 10(7) of the Act shall not apply to any of the following:

(a) any periodical payment of maintenance;

(b) other than in circumstances which are exceptional having regard in particular to the quantity or value of the items concerned, the client's clothes or household furniture or the tools or implements of his trade;

(c) any sum or sums ordered to be paid under section 5 of the Inheritance (Provision for Family and Dependents) Act 1975 or Part IV of the Family Law Act 1996;

(d) revoked;

(e) one-half of any redundancy payment within the meaning of Part XI of the Employment Rights Act 1996 recovered by the client;

(f) any payment of money made in accordance with an order made by the Employment Appeal Tribunal (excluding an order for costs);

(g) where the statutory charge is in favour of the supplier, the client's main or only dwelling; or

(h) any sum, payment or benefit which, by virtue of any provision of or made under an Act of Parliament, cannot be assigned or charged.

(2) Revoked.

(4) In paragraph (1)(a), "maintenance" means money or money's worth paid towards the support of a former partner, child or any other person for whose support the payer has previously been responsible or has made payments.

45. (1) Subject to paragraph (2), the statutory charge shall be in favour of the Commission.

(2) Subject to paragraph (3), where it relates to the cost of Legal Help or Help at Court, the statutory charge shall be in favour of the supplier.

(3) Where Legal Help or Help at Court has been provided, the statutory charge shall be in favour of the Commission if it attaches to money or property recovered after a certificate has been granted in relation to the same matter.

46. Supplier's authority to waive statutory charge. (1) This regulation applies only where the statutory charge is in favour of the supplier.

(2) The Commission may grant a supplier authority, either in respect of individual cases or generally, to waive either all or part of the amount of the statutory charge where its enforcement would cause grave hardship or distress to the client or would be unreasonably difficult because of the nature of the property.

47. Waiver of charge in case of wider public interest. (1) Revoked.

(2) Paragraph (3) applies where:

(a) the Commission funds Legal Representation in proceedings which it considers have a significant wider public interest; and

(b) the Commission considers it cost-effective to fund those services for a specified claimant or claimants, but not for other claimants or potential claimants who might benefit from the litigation.

(3) Where this paragraph applies, the Commission may, if it considers it equitable to do so, waive some or all of the amount of the statutory charge.

48. Application of regulations 49 to 53. Regulations 49 to 53 apply only in relation to a statutory charge in favour of the Commission.

49. Operation of statutory charge where certificate revoked or discharged. (1) Where a certificate has been revoked or discharged, section 10(7) of the Act shall apply to any money or property recovered as a result of the client continuing to pursue the relevant dispute or take, defend or be a party to the relevant proceedings.

(2) In paragraph (1), "client" means the person whose certificate has been revoked or discharged, or, as the case may be, his personal representatives, trustee in bankruptcy or the Official Receiver.

50. Operation of statutory charge on money in court. (1) Paragraph (2) applies where any money recovered by a client in any proceedings is ordered to be paid into or remain in court and invested for the benefit of the client.

(2) Where this paragraph applies, the statutory charge shall attach only to such part of the money as, in the opinion of the Commission, will be sufficient to safeguard the interests of the Commission, and the Commission shall notify the court in writing of the amount so attached.

51. Enforcement of statutory charge. Subject to regulation 52, the Commission may enforce the statutory charge in any manner which would be available to a chargee in respect of a charge given between parties.

52. (1) Where the condition in regulation 52A is satisfied the Commission may postpone the enforcement of the statutory charge where:

(a) by order of the court or agreement it relates to property to be used as a home by the client or his dependents, or, where the relevant proceedings were family proceedings, to money to pay for such a home;

(b) the Commission is satisfied that the property in question will provide such security for the statutory charge as it considers appropriate; and

(c) as soon as it is possible to do so, the Commission registers a charge under the Land Registration Act 2002 to secure the amount in regulation 43 or, as appropriate, takes equivalent steps (whether in England and Wales or in any other jurisdiction) to protect its interest in the property.

(2) Where the client wishes to purchase a property in substitution for the property over which a charge is registered under paragraph (1)(c), the Commission may release the charge if the conditions in paragraph (1)(b) and (c) are satisfied.

(3) Where the enforcement of the statutory charge is postponed, interest shall accrue for the benefit of the Commission in accordance with regulation 53.

(4) Without prejudice to the provisions of the Land Registration Act 2002 and the Land Charges Act 1972, all conveyances and acts done to defeat, or operating to defeat, any charge shall, except in the case of a bona fide purchaser for value without notice, be void as against the Commission.

52A. The Commission may only postpone enforcement of the statutory charge if it appears to the Commission that it would be unreasonable for the client to repay the amount of the charge.

52B. (1) The Commission may review any decision to postpone enforcement of the charge at any time and, unless it appears to the Commission that it would be unreasonable for the client to repay the amount of the charge which has been postponed, it shall either—

(i) proceed to enforce the charge; or

(ii) where the conditions in regulation 52(1) (a) to (c) are satisfied continue to postpone enforcement of the charge, in which case the provisions of regulation 52(3) shall also continue to apply.

(2) If the Commission continues to postpone enforcement under paragraph (1) (ii) it may do so on such terms or conditions as to repayment of the amount of the charge by way of interim payments of either capital or interest or both, or otherwise, as appear to the Commission to be appropriate.

53. Payment and recovery of interest. (1) Where interest is payable by the client under regulation 52, that interest shall continue to accrue until the amount of the statutory charge is paid.

(2) The client may make interim payments of interest or capital in respect of the outstanding amount of the statutory charge, but no interim payment shall be used to reduce the capital outstanding while any interest remains outstanding.

(3) Where interest is payable by the client under regulation 52:

(a) it shall run from the date when the charge is first registered;

(b) the applicable rate shall be—

(i) 8% per annum until 31st March 2002;
(ii) 5% per annum from 1st April 2002 until 30th September 2005;
(iii) 8% per annum from 1st October 2005;

(c) *revoked*;
(d) *revoked*; and
(e) the capital on which it is calculated shall be the lesser of:

(i) the amount of the statutory charge outstanding from time to time, less any interest accrued by virtue of regulation 52(3), or
(ii) the value of the property recovered at the time of such recovery.

Community Legal Service (Funding) Order 2000[1]

(SI 2000/627 as amended by SI 2000/1541, 2001/831 and 2996 and SI 2003/651 and 851, SI 2004/597 and 2900, SI 2005/571, 2114 and 3504 and SI 2006/2366)

1–5654 **1. Citation and commencement.** This Order may be cited as the Community Legal Service (Funding) Order 2000 and shall come into force on 1st April 2000.

1. Made by the Lord Chancellor in exercise of powers conferred on him by ss 6(4), 19, 105 of and, Sch 14 Pt I para 1 to the Access to Justice Act 1999.

2. Interpretation. (1) In this Order:

"the Act" means the Access to Justice Act 1999;

"assessing authority" means, where remuneration is payable by the Commission under a contract, the authority to which it falls at any time to assess that remuneration (including assessing by way of appeal), and shall include a Director of the Commission, or the Commission's Costs Committee or Cost Appeals Committee, or the court;

"certificate" means a certificate issued under the Funding Code certifying a decision to fund services for the client;

"client" means an individual who receives funded services;

"clinical negligence proceedings" means proceedings which include:

- (a) a claim for damages in respect of breach of a duty of care or trespass to the person committed in the course of the provision of clinical or medical services (including dental or nursing services); or
- (b) a claim for damages in respect of alleged professional negligence in the conduct of such a claim;

"Commission" means the Legal Services Commission established under section 1 of the Act;

"family proceedings" means proceedings, other than proceedings for judicial review, which arise out of family relationships, including proceedings in which the welfare of children is determined, and including all proceedings under one or more of the following:

- (a) the Matrimonial Causes Act 1973;
- (b) the Inheritance (Provision for Family and Dependants) Act 1975;
- (c) the Adoption Act 1976;
- (d) the Domestic Proceedings and Magistrates' Courts Act 1978;
- (e) Part III of the Matrimonial and Family Proceedings Act 1984;
- (f) Parts I, II and IV of the Children Act 1989;
- (g) Part IV of the Family Law Act 1996;
- (ga) the Adoption and Children Act 2002;
- (h) the inherent jurisdiction of the High Court in relation to children; and
- (i) the Civil Partnership Act 2004;

"fund" means the Community Legal Service Fund established under section 5 of the Act;

"funded services" means services which are provided directly for a client and funded for that client by the Commission as part of the Community Legal Service under sections 4 to 11 of the Act;

"Funding Code" means the code approved under section 9 of the Act;

"group litigation" means litigation of a number of claims which give rise to common or related issues of fact or law;

"immigration proceedings" means any proceedings relating to immigration, nationality or asylum in:

- (a) the House of Lords;
- (b) the Court of Appeal;
- (c) the High Court; or before
- (d) the Asylum and Immigration Tribunal;

"personal injury proceedings" means proceedings in which there is a claim for damages in respect of death or any disease or impairment of a person's physical or mental condition, excluding proceedings for clinical negligence or proceedings arising from the disrepair of, eviction from or obligation to allow quiet enjoyment of residential premises.

(2) References to the levels of service listed in paragraph (3) shall be construed as references to the receipt or provision of those levels of service granted in accordance with the Funding Code.

(3) The levels of service referred to in paragraph (2) are:

- (a) Legal Help;
- (b) Help at Court;
- (c) Legal Representation;
- (d) Help with Mediation; and
- (e) General Family Help.

(4) In this Order, any reference to the provisions of the Civil Legal Aid (General) Regulations 1989 shall be construed as though they were amended as follows:

- (a) any reference to "assisted person" shall be replaced by a reference to "client";
- (b) any reference to "authorised summary proceedings" shall be replaced by a reference to "proceedings in a magistrates' court";
- (c) in regulation 59, the words "legal aid" shall be replaced by "Legal Services Commission";
- (d) in regulations 84 and 107, any reference to "regulation 83" shall be replaced by a reference to "regulation 4 of the Community Legal Service (Costs) Regulations 2000";
- (e) in regulation 102, the words "or the Funding Code" shall be inserted after "these Regulations";
- (f) in regulation 104, the words "or the Crown Court" shall be inserted after "magistrates' court";
- (g) in regulation 106A, the words "legal aid only costs" shall be replaced by "costs payable from the Community Legal Service Fund only"; and
- (h) in regulation 113(3), the words "section 16(6) of the Act" shall be replaced by "section 10(7) of the Access to Justice Act 1999".

3. Funding of services—Direct payments. (1) The Commission may only fund services as part of the Community Legal Service under section 6(3)(b) of the Act as follows:

(a) where a certificate was granted before 1st April 2001, to make payments in respect of the provision of Legal Representation in actual or contemplated proceedings other than the following:

    (i)   personal injury;

    (ii)   clinical negligence;

    (iii)   family;

    (iv)   immigration; or

    (v)   before a Mental Health Review Tribunal;

(b) where authorisation has been given in an individual case under section 6(8)(b) of the Act.

(2) The Commission may only fund services as part of the Community Legal Service under section 6(3)(e) of the Act where authorisation for such funding has been given in an individual case under section 6(8)(b) of the Act.

    4. Where the Commission funds services under article 3(1)(a), the provisions of regulations 48, 59 to 63, 84, 100 to 102, 104 to 107A, 108 to 110, 112, 113(1), (2) and (4), 119(1), 122 and 149(7) of the Civil Legal Aid (General) Regulations 1989 shall apply.

5. Remuneration under contracts.   (1) Paragraph (2) applies to contracts which have not been awarded:

(a)   after competitive tendering as to price has taken place; or

(b)   in relation to a particular case (including group litigation or potential group litigation); or

(ba) as part of any pilot which provides for remuneration by way of one or more standard fees;

(c)   as part of the housing possession court duty scheme; or

(d)   as part of the alternative methods of delivery pilot;

(e)   as part of the family advice and information networks pilot;

(f)   as part of the fast track asylum decision and appeals process pilot; or

(g)   as part of the Community Legal Advice Centres and Community Legal Advice Networks.

(2) Subject to paragraphs (1) and (2A), any contract for the provision of funded services under section 6(3)(a) of the Act which provides for the levels of service in this article ("a relevant contract") shall provide for payment by the Commission to be at rates no higher than the rates in the following paragraphs.

(2A) Where any relevant contract provides for payment for a unit of work to be based on an average value of units of work previously carried out, paragraph (2) shall not apply but the rates applied in calculating that average value shall be no higher than rates 2.5% greater than the rates in the following paragraphs.

(3) Subject to paragraphs (3A) to (3C), in relation to:

(a)   Legal Help; and

(b)   Help at Court

payment shall be at rates no higher than those provided in Schedule 6, paragraphs 1 and 2 of the Legal Advice and Assistance Regulations 1989.

(3A) In relation to Legal Help and Help at Court within any category of work mentioned in paragraph (3B)(a) which is authorised as a specific category in the schedule to the contract with the Commission under which it is provided, payment shall, subject to paragraph (7B), be at rates no higher than those set out in Part I to the Schedule.

(3AA) In relation to Legal Help and Help at Court within any category of work mentioned in paragraph (3B)(b) which is authorised as a specific category in the schedule to the contract with the Commission under which it is provided, payment shall, subject to paragraph (4A), be at rates no higher than those set out in Part II of the Schedule.

(3B) The categories of work mentioned—

(a)   in paragraph (3A) are: immigration, mental health, education, public law, actions against the police etc and community care; and

(b)   in paragraph (3AA) are: family, housing and employment.

(3C) In relation to any Legal Help and Help at Court provided in accordance with a contract with the Commission to which neither paragraph (3A) nor (3AA) applies, payment shall be at rates no higher than those set out in Part III of the Schedule.

(4) In relation to Help with Mediation payment shall be at rates no higher than those set out in Part IV of the Schedule.

(4A) In relation to—

(a)   Legal Representation before a Mental Health Review Tribunal or, subject to paragraph (4B), before the Asylum and Immigration Tribunal; or

(b)   Legal Help or Help at Court provided within the housing category of work to an applicant on a review by a local authority under section 202 of the Housing Act 1996 (but not advice as to whether the applicant should pursue the review) or to a defendant to a possession claim in a county court.

payment shall be at rates no higher than those set out in Part V of the Schedule provided that where advocacy is carried out as part of any service referred to in sub-paragraph (b) payment shall be no higher than the rate set out there for preparation.

(4B) Paragraph (4A) shall not apply in relation to Legal Representation before the Asylum and Immigration Tribunal—

(a)   where the assessing authority considers that a case either—

    (i)   raises an exceptionally novel or complex point of law; or

   (ii) has significant potential to produce real benefits for individuals other than the client (other than benefits to the public at large which normally flow from proceedings of the type in question);

   (b) on an application under section 103A of the Nationality, Immigration and Asylum Act 2002 which is considered by a member of the Tribunal pursuant to paragraph 30 of Schedule 2 to the Asylum and Immigration (Treatment of Claimants, etc) Act 2004; or

   (c) in proceedings for the reconsideration of an appeal pursuant to an order under section 103A.

(5) In relation to General Family Help, payment shall be at rates no higher than the relevant rates provided in the Legal Aid in Family Proceedings (Remuneration) Regulations 1991.

(6) In relation to Legal Representation (other than as provided for in paragraph (4A), or where paragraph (4A) does not apply by virtue of paragraph (4B), or the Legal Representation referred to in paragraphs (7) or (7A), payment shall be at rates no higher than whichever of those provided by the Legal Aid in Civil Proceedings (Remuneration) Regulations 1994 or the Legal Aid in Family Proceedings (Remuneration) Regulations 1991 would have been applicable if the representation had been provided under Part IV of the Legal Aid Act 1988.

(7) Paragraph (6) shall not apply to Legal Representation before—

   (a) Special Commissioners of Income Tax or General Commissioners of Income Tax;

   (b) a VAT and duties tribunal constituted by Schedule 12 to the Value Added Tax Act 1994;

   (c) the tribunal constituted by section 9 of the Protection of Children Act 1999; or

   (d) the High Court on an application under section 103A of the Nationality, Immigration and Asylum Act 2002.

(7A) In relation to Legal Representation for any proceedings under the Proceeds of Crime Act 2002 in the Crown Court or a magistrates' court, payment shall be at rates no higher than those set out for magistrates' court proceedings in Schedule 2A to the Legal Aid in Family Proceedings (Remuneration) Regulations 1991.

(7B) The maximum rate applicable in relation to any specialist immigration work shall be 5% greater than the maximum rate which would be applicable to that work but for this paragraph.

(7C) In paragraph (7B)—

"maximum rate" means a rate specified by this article as the rate that may not be exceeded in relation to payment by the Commission under a contract for the provision of funded services;

"specialist immigration work" means work carried out by a member of the Legal Services Commission's Immigration and Asylum Accreditation Scheme who is accredited to level 3 of that Scheme where—

   (a) immigration is authorised as a specific category of work in the schedule to the contract with the Commission under which it is provided; and

   (b) that work is within the category of immigration.

(8) Where any item in the Schedule is applicable to a fee-earner, the figure to be applied shall be—

   (a) the figure in the column headed "London Region" if that fee-earner's office is situated in the Commission's London Region;

   (b) otherwise, the figure in the column headed "Outside Region".

6. Where a contract entered into by the Commission in accordance with section 6(3)(a) of the Act provides that the procedures for assessing the remuneration payable by the Commission shall be the same as those set out in the Civil Legal Aid (General) Regulations 1989, the Legal Aid in Civil Proceedings (Remuneration) Regulations 1994, or the Legal Aid in Family Proceedings (Remuneration) Regulations 1991, the court shall assess the remuneration accordingly.

7. Foreign Law. The Commission may fund as part of the Community Legal Service Legal Help relating to the preparation of applications for transmission under the provisions of the European Agreement on the Transmission of Applications for Legal Aid and under Council Directive 2002/8/EC of 27th January 2003.

1–5654A   SCHEDULE

PART I

LEGAL HELP AND HELP AT COURT—IMMIGRATION, MENTAL HEALTH, ACTIONS AGAINST THE POLICE ETC, PUBLIC LAW, EDUCATION AND COMMUNITY CARE

	London Region	Outside London
Preparation	£57.35 per hour	£52.55 per hour
Travel and waiting	£30.30 per hour	£29.45 per hour
Letters written and telephone calls	£4.40 per item	£4.10 per item

PART II

LEGAL HELP AND HELP AT COURT—FAMILY, HOUSING AND EMPLOYMENT

	London Region	Outside London
Preparation	£53.10 per hour	£50.05 per hour
Travel and waiting	£28.05 per hour	£28.05 per hour
Letters written and telephone calls	£4.10 per item	£3.95 per item

PART III
LEGAL HELP AND HELP AT COURT—OTHER WORK CARRIED OUT UNDER CONTRACT

	London Region	Outside London
Preparation	£50.70 per hour	£47.80 per hour
Travel and waiting	£26.80 per hour	£26.80 per hour
Letters written and telephone calls	£3.90 per item	£3.75 per item

PART IV
HELP WITH MEDIATION

	London Region	Outside London
Preparation	£64.10 per hour	£59.95 per hour
Travel and waiting	£28.05 per hour	£28.05 per hour
Letters written and telephone calls	£4.30 per item	£4.30 per item

PART V
LEGAL REPRESENTATION—IMMIGRATION AND MENTAL HEALTH

LEGAL HELP AND HELP AT COURT—HOMELESSNESS REVIEWS AND POSSESSION PROCEEDINGS

	London Region	Outside London
Preparation	£61.20 per hour	£57.25 per hour
Travel and waiting	£30.30 per hour	£29.45 per hour
Letters written and telephone calls	£4.40 per item	£4.10 per item
Advocacy	£69.60 per hour	£69.60 per hour
Attending tribunal with counsel (Mental Health Review Tribunal only)	£32.55 per hour	£32.55 per hour

Community Legal Service (Cost Protection) Regulations 2000[1]

(SI 2000/824 as amended by SI 2001/823 and 3812 and SI 2005/2006)

1–5655 **1. Citation and commencement.** These Regulations may be cited as the Community Legal Service (Cost Protection) Regulations 2000 and shall come into force on 1st April 2000.

1. Made by the Lord Chancellor in exercise of powers conferred on him by s 11(1), (3), (4)(b), (d) of the Access to Justice Act 1999.

2. Interpretation. (1) In these Regulations:

"the Act" means the Access to Justice Act 1999;

"certificate" means a certificate issued under the Funding Code certifying a decision to fund services for the client and "emergency certificate" means a certificate certifying a decision to fund Legal Representation for the client in a case of emergency;

"client" means an individual who receives funded services;

"Commission" means the Legal Services Commission established under section 1 of the Act;

"costs judge" has the same meaning as in the Civil Procedure Rules 1998;

"costs order" means an order that a party pay all or part of the costs of proceedings;

"cost protection" means the limit on costs awarded against a client set out in section 11(1) of the Act;

"court" includes any tribunal having the power to award costs in favour of, or against, a party;

"family proceedings" means—

　(a) all proceedings under any one or more of the following—

　　(i) the Matrimonial Causes Act 1973;
　　(ii) the Domestic Proceedings and Magistrates' Courts Act 1978;
　　(iii) Part III of the Matrimonial and Family Proceedings Act 1984;
　　(iv) the Child Abduction and Custody Act 1985;
　　(v) Parts I and II of and Schedule 1 to the Children Act 1989;
　　(vi) section 53 of and Schedule 7 to the Family Law Act 1996; and

　(b) proceedings which arise out of family relationships under either or both of the following—

　　(i) the Inheritance (Provision for Family and Dependants) Act 1975;
　　(ii) the Trusts of Land and Appointment of Trustees Act 1996;

"family relationships" has the same meaning as in the Funding Code which came into force on 1st April 2000 and the Funding Code Guidance published on 1st April 2000 by the Commission for the purpose of making decisions under the Funding Code;

"full costs" means, where a section 11(1) costs order is made against a client, the amount of costs which that client would, but for section 11(1) of the Act, have been ordered to pay;

"funded proceedings" means proceedings (including prospective proceedings) in relation to which the client receives funded services or, as the case may be, that part of proceedings during which the client receives funded services;

"funded services" means services which are provided directly for a client and funded for that client by the Commission as part of the Community Legal Service under sections 4 to 11 of the Act;

"Funding Code" means the code approved under section 9 of the Act;

"non-funded party" means a party to proceedings who has not received funded services in relation to those proceedings under a certificate, other than a certificate which has been revoked;

"partner" means a person with whom the person concerned lives as a couple, and includes a person with whom the person concerned is not currently living but from whom he is not living separate and apart;

"proceedings" include proceedings in any tribunal which is a court, as defined in this paragraph;

"receiving party" means a party in favour of whom a costs order is made;

"section 11(1) costs order" means a costs order against a client where cost protection applies;

"solicitor" means a solicitor or another person who is an authorised litigator within the meaning of section 119(1) of the Courts and Legal Services Act 1990.

(2) References to the levels of service listed in paragraph (3) shall be construed as references to the receipt or provision of those levels of service granted in accordance with the Funding Code.

(3) The levels of service referred to in paragraph (2) are:

(a) Legal Help;
(b) Help at Court;
(c) Legal Representation;
(d) General Family Help and Help with Mediation;
(e) revoked;
(f) revoked.

3. Cost protection. (1) Cost protection shall not apply in relation to such parts of proceedings, or prospective proceedings, as are funded for the client by way of:

(a) Help at Court;
(b) revoked;
(c) subject to paragraph (2), Legal Help;
(d) General Family Help and Help with Mediation in family proceedings;
(e) Legal Representation in amily proceedings.

(2) Subject to paragraph (4), where the client receives Legal Help, but later receives Legal Representation or General Family Help or Help with Mediation in respect of the same dispute, other than Legal Representation in family proceedings or General Family Help or Help with Mediation in family proceedings, cost protection shall apply, both in respect of:

(a) the costs incurred by the receiving party before the commencement of proceedings which, as regards the client, are funded proceedings by virtue of the client's receipt of Legal Help, and

(b) the costs incurred by the receiving party in the course of proceedings which, as regards the client, are funded proceedings by virtue of the client's receipt of Legal Representation, General Family Help or Help with Mediation.

(3) Subject to paragraph (4), cost protection shall apply only to costs incurred by the receiving party in relation to proceedings which, as regards the client, are funded proceedings, and:

(a) where work is done before the issue of a certificate, cost protection shall (subject to paragraphs (2) and (5)) apply only to costs incurred after the issue of the certificate;

(b) where funding is withdrawn by discharging the client's certificate, cost protection shall apply only to costs incurred before the date when funded services under the certificate ceased to be provided.

(4) Where funding is withdrawn by revoking the client's certificate, cost protection shall not apply, either in respect of work done before or after the revocation.

(5) Cost protection shall apply to work done immediately before the grant of an emergency certificate, other than an emergency certificate granted in relation to family proceedings, if:

(a) no application for such a certificate could be made because the Commission's office was closed; and

(b) the client's solicitor applies for an emergency certificate at the first available opportunity, and the certificate is granted.

4. Enforcement of costs order against client. Where, in a case where costs protection applies, for the purpose of enforcing a costs order against a client (alone or together with any other judgment or order), a charging order under section 1 of the Charging Orders Act 1979 is made in respect of the client's interest in the main or only dwelling in which he resides:

(a) that charging order shall operate to secure the amount payable under the costs order (including, without limitation, any interest) only to the extent of the amount (if any) by which the proceeds of sale of the client's interest in the dwelling (having deducted any mortgage debts) exceed £100,000; and

(b) an order for the sale of the dwelling shall not be made in favour of the person in whose favour the charging order is made.

5. Costs order against Commission. (1) The following paragraphs of this regulation apply where:

(a) funded services are provided to a client in relation to proceedings;
(b) those proceedings are finally decided in favour of a non-funded party; and
(c) cost protection applies.

(2) The court may, subject to the following paragraphs of this regulation, make an order for the payment by the Commission to the non-funded party of the whole or any part of the costs incurred by him in the proceedings (other than any costs that the client is required to pay under a section 11(1) costs order).

(3) An order under paragraph (2) may only be made if all the conditions set out in sub-paragraphs (a), (b), (c) and (d) are satisfied:

(a) a section 11(1) costs order is made against the client in the proceedings, and the amount (if any) which the client is required to pay under that costs order is less than the amount of the full costs;
(b) unless there is a good reason for the delay,the non-funded party makes a request under regulation 10(2) of the Community Legal Service (Costs) Regulations 2000 within three months of the making of the section 11(1) costs order;
(c) as regards costs incurred in a court of first instance, the proceedings were instituted by the client, the non-funded party is an individual, and the court is satisfied that the non-funded party will suffer financial hardship unless the order is made; and
(d) in any case, the court is satisfied that it is just and equitable[1] in the circumstances that provision for the costs should be made out of public funds.

(3A) An order under paragraph (2) may be made—

(a) in relation to proceedings in the House of Lords, by the Clerk to the Parliaments;
(b) in relation to proceedings in the Court of Appeal, High Court or a county court, by a costs judge or a district judge;
(c) in relation to proceedings in a magistrates' court, by a single justice or by the justices' clerk;
(d) in relation to proceedings in the Employment Appeal Tribunal, by the Registrar of that tribunal.

(4) Where the client receives funded services in connection with part only of the proceedings, the reference in paragraph (2) to the costs incurred by the non-funded party in the relevant proceedings shall be construed as a reference to so much of those costs as is attributable to the part of the proceedings which are funded proceedings.

(5) Where a court decides any proceedings in favour of the non-funded party and an appeal lies (with or without permission) against that decision, any order made under this regulation shall not take effect:

(a) where permission to appeal is required, unless the time limit for applications for permission to appeal expires without permission being granted;
(b) where permission to appeal is granted or is not required, unless the time limit for appeal expires without an appeal being brought.

(6) Subject to paragraph (7), in determining whether the conditions in paragraph (3)(c) and (d) are satisfied, the court shall have regard to the resources of the non-funded party and of his partner.

(7) The court shall not have regard to the resources of the partner of the non-funded party if the partner has a contrary interest in the funded proceedings.

(8) Where the non-funded party is acting in a representative, fiduciary or official capacity and is entitled to be indemnified in respect of his costs from any property, estate or fund, the court shall, for the purposes of paragraph (3), have regard to the value of the property, estate or fund and the resources of the persons, if any, including that party where appropriate, who are beneficially interested in that property, estate or fund.

6. Orders for costs against Commission—Litigation Support. *Revoked.*

7. Effect of these Regulations. (1) No order to pay costs in favour of a non-funded party shall be made against the Commission in respect of funded proceedings except in accordance with these Regulations, and any costs to be paid under such an order shall be paid out of the Community Legal Service Fund.

(2) Nothing in these Regulations shall be construed, in relation to proceedings where one or more parties are receiving, or have received, funded services, as:

(a) requiring a court to make a costs order where it would not otherwise have made a costs order; or
(b) affecting the court's power to make a wasted costs order against a legal representative.

---

1. The justice or justices' clerk should proceed on the basis that it is "just and equitable" that the commission should stand behind its "client" unless he or she is aware of facts which render that result unjust or inequitable(*R v Secretary of State for the Home Department, ex p Gunn* [2001] EWCA Civ 891, [2001] 3 All ER 481, [2001] 1 WLR 1634).

Criminal Defence Service (Funding) Order 2001[1]

(SI 2001/855 amended by SI 2001/1143, 1256 and 3341, SI 2002/714, SI 2003/642, SI 2004/2045, 2005/2621 and SI 2006/389)

1-5656   1. Citation and commencement.   This Order may be cited as the Criminal Defence Service (Funding) Order 2001 and shall come into force on 2nd April 2001.

---

1. Made by the Lord Chancellor in exercise of the powers conferred on him by ss 13(3), 14(3), 105 and Sch 14 para 9 of the Access to Justice Act 1999.

2. Interpretation.   In this Order:

"the Act" means the Access to Justice Act 1999;

"advocate" means a barrister, or a solicitor who has obtained a higher courts advocacy qualification in accordance with regulations and rules of conduct of the Law Society;

"appropriate category", in relation to a Very High Cost Case, means the category to which the case is assigned in accordance with article 14;

"appropriate officer" means:

in the case of proceedings in the civil division of the Court of Appeal, the head of the civil appeals office;

in the case of proceedings in the criminal division of the Court of Appeal, the registrar of criminal appeals ("the registrar");

in the case of proceedings in the High Court, a Costs Judge;

in the case of proceedings in the Crown Court, an officer appointed by the Lord Chancellor;

in respect of advice or assistance as to an appeal from the Crown Court to the Court of Appeal, (except in the case of an appeal under section 9(11) of the Criminal Justice Act 1987) where, on the advice of any representative assigned, notice of appeal is given, or application for leave to appeal is made, whether or not such appeal is later abandoned, the registrar;

in respect of advice or assistance as to an appeal to the Courts-Martial Appeal Court, the registrar;

in respect of advice or assistance as to an appeal from the Court of Appeal to the House of Lords, where the appeal is not lodged with the House of Lords, the registrar; and

in any other case, the Commission

and, in any case, includes an officer designated by the appropriate officer to act on his behalf in that regard;

"CDS Regulations" means regulations made under Part I of the Act relating to the Criminal Defence Service;

"the Commission" means the Legal Services Commission established under section 1 of the Act;

"the Contract" means the General Criminal Contract, published by the Commission in February 2001, as amended on 12th March 2001;

"Costs Committee" means a committee appointed under arrangements made by the Commission to deal with, inter alia, applications for appeal against, or review of, assessments of costs;

"funded services" means services which are provided directly for a client and funded for that client as part of the Criminal Defence Service under sections 12 to 18 of the Act;

"a representation order" means a document granting a right to representation;

"a representative" means a solicitor or a barrister;

"VAT" means Value Added Tax; and

"a Very High Cost Case" is a case where if the case proceeds to trial, that trial would be likely to last for 41 days or longer, and any question as to whether the case fulfils this criterion shall be determined by the Commission.

3. Funding of services—Lord Chancellor.   (1) Except as provided in paragraph (2), the duty of the Commission under section 14(1) of the Act shall, until 1st April 2003, have effect as a duty of the Lord Chancellor in relation to representation in:

   (a)   criminal proceedings in the House of Lords;
   (b)   proceedings in the Court of Appeal; and
   (c)   proceedings in the Crown Court.

(2) Paragraph (1) does not apply to:

   (a)   any proceedings in the Crown Court which are prescribed under section 12(2)(*g*) of the Act;
   (b)   any Very High Cost Case which is the subject of an individual contract for the provision of funded services; or
   (c)   any proceedings in which representation is provided by a person employed by the Commission for that purpose.

4. Other than where the case is remitted back to the magistrates' court, where a case is sent for trial to the Crown Court under section 51 of the Crime and Disorder Act 1998, any fees in relation to work carried out in the magistrates' court shall be assessed and paid together with the Crown Court fees for that case.

4A. The fees referred to in article 4 for work carried out in the magistrates' court shall be assessed and paid at the rate set out in the Contract as appropriate to that category of work.

5. Remuneration in respect of the proceedings mentioned in article 3(1) shall be in accordance with the provisions of Schedules 1 to 4.

6. *Revoked.*

7. Funding of services—Legal Services Commission. The Commission may only fund services as part of the Criminal Defence Service under section 13(2)(*b*) or 14(2)(*b*) of the Act where representation is provided in proceedings referred to in section 12(2)(*f*) of the Act (proceedings for contempt in the face of a court).

8. Except as provided in article 9, where the Commission funds services as part of the Criminal Defence Service under section 13(2)(*a*) or 14(2)(*a*) of the Act, remuneration shall be at rates no higher than those set out in Part E of the Specification to the Contract.

9. Subject to article 9A, where services are provided in a Very High Cost Case which is the subject of an individual contract for the provision of funded services, remuneration for that case shall be at rates no higher than those set out for the appropriate category and the appropriate level of fee earner in Schedule 5.

9A. (1) This article applies to Very High Cost Cases in respect of which a representation order has been made on or before 1st July 2004.

(2) Where this article applies, the Commission may elect to apply the provisions for remuneration in:

(*a*) Schedule 4, to the whole or any part of an advocate's claim for costs,

(*b*) Schedule 2, to the whole or any part of a solicitor's claim for costs so far as they are not met by (*a*),

which would otherwise be subject to remuneration in accordance with article 9.

10. Proceedings for contempt. (1) Subject to article 11, remuneration in proceedings referred to in section 12(2)(*f*) of the Act shall be at the rate of £72.75 per day.

(2) Where representation in such proceedings is provided by two legal representatives, remuneration shall be at the rate of £46.50 per day for the representative appearing as an advocate, and £26.25 per day for the other representative.

11. (1) A representative may, when he claims remuneration for work done in respect of proceedings referred to in section 12(2)(*f*) of the Act, claim that there are exceptional circumstances which justify remuneration greater than the standard fee specified in article 10.

(2) If the appropriate officer decides that there are such exceptional circumstances, he may allow the representative such fee as appears to him to be reasonable (having regard to the standard fee) for such work as appears to him to have been reasonably done.

(3) If the appropriate officer decides that there are no such exceptional circumstances, the standard fee shall apply.

(4) The fee allowed to a representative (other than an advocate) under this article shall not exceed the rates set out in Schedule 2 as appropriate to the type of work, the court in which the proceedings took place, the grade and the situation of the office of the fee-earner who did the work.

(5) In the application of paragraph (4), the rates appropriate to the Crown Court shall apply to proceedings in all courts other than the magistrates' courts

(6) Where a court grants representation to a person for the purposes of proceedings for contempt, it may assign to him, for the purposes of those proceedings, any representative who is within the precincts of the court.

(7) Where the fee-earner who did the work was not assigned by the court under sub-paragraph (6), the fee allowed for his work shall not exceed the rate set out in Schedule 2 as appropriate to the lowest grade of fee-earner which the appropriate officer considers would have been competent to do the work.

(8) The total of the fees allowed to an advocate under this article in respect of proceedings covered by any one representation order shall not exceed the amounts set out in Schedule 3 as appropriate to a single junior counsel instructed in an appeal to the Crown Court against conviction.

12. The provisions of Schedule 1 shall apply with the necessary modifications to the remuneration payable to any representative under articles 10 and 11.

13. Where a representation order has been made in respect of any proceedings, the representative shall not receive or be a party to the making of any payment for work done in connection with those proceedings except such payments as may be made:

(*a*) by the Lord Chancellor or the Commission; or

(*b*) in respect of any expenses or fees incurred in:

(i) preparing, obtaining or considering any report, opinion or further evidence, whether provided by an expert witness or otherwise; or

(ii) obtaining any transcripts or recordings

where an application under CDS Regulations for an authority to incur such fees or expenses has been refused by the Costs Committee.

14. Very High Cost Cases—assignment of cases to categories and solicitors to levels. (1) The Commission shall assign each case which is a Very High Cost Case to one of the four categories referred to in Schedule 5, according to its complexity, importance and subject matter.

(2) The Commission shall assign each solicitor or other fee earner (other than a barrister acting as an advocate) providing funded services in relation to a case which is a Very High Cost Case to one of the three levels referred to in Schedule 5.

1–5657　　　　　　　　　　SCHEDULE 1

1. General. (1) Costs in respect of work done under a representation order to which this Schedule applies shall be determined by the appropriate officer in accordance with this Schedule.

(2) In determining costs, the appropriate officer shall, subject to the provisions of this Schedule:

(a) take into account all the relevant circumstances of the case including the nature, importance, complexity or difficulty of the work and the time involved; and

(b) allow a reasonable amount in respect of all work actually and reasonably done.

2. Interim payment of disbursements. (1) A solicitor may submit a claim to the appropriate officer for payment of a disbursement for which he has incurred liability in criminal proceedings in the Crown Court in accordance with the provisions of this paragraph.

(2) A claim for payment may be made where:

(a) a solicitor has obtained prior authority to incur expenditure of £100 or more under CDS Regulations; and

(b) he has incurred such a liability.

(3) Without prejudice to paragraph 13(4), a claim under sub-paragraph (1) shall not exceed the maximum fee authorised under the prior authority.

(4) A claim for payment under sub-paragraph (1) may be made at any time before the solicitor submits a claim for costs under paragraph 11(2).

(5) A claim under sub-paragraph (1) shall be submitted to the appropriate officer in such form and manner as he may direct and shall be accompanied by the authority to incur expenditure and any invoices or other documents in support of the claim.

(6) The appropriate officer shall allow the disbursement subject to the limit in sub-paragraph (3) above if it appears to have been reasonably incurred in accordance with the prior authority.

(7) Where the appropriate officer allows the disbursement, he shall notify the solicitor and, where the disbursement includes the fees or charges of any person, that person, of the amount payable, and shall authorise payment to the solicitor accordingly.

(8) Paragraphs 20 to 22 (redetermination etc) shall not apply to a payment under this paragraph.

3. Interim disbursements and final determination of costs. (1) On a final determination of costs, paragraphs 11(2) and (3)(e) and 13 shall apply notwithstanding that a payment has been made under paragraph 2.

(2) Where the amount found to be due under paragraph 13 in respect of a disbursement is less than the amount paid under paragraph 2 ("the interim disbursement"), the appropriate officer shall deduct the difference from the sum otherwise payable to the solicitor on the determination of costs, and where the amount due under paragraph 13 exceeds the interim disbursement, the appropriate officer shall add the difference to the amount otherwise payable to the solicitor.

4. Interim payments in cases awaiting determination. (1) The appropriate officer shall make an interim payment in respect of a claim for costs in criminal proceedings in the Crown Court in accordance with the following provisions of this paragraph.

(2) Entitlement to a payment arises in respect of a claim for costs:

(a) in the case of a solicitor, where the total claim for costs is £4,000 or more (exclusive of VAT);

(b) in the case of an advocate, where the basic fee claimed is £4,000 or more (exclusive of VAT); and

(c) where the claim for costs is for less than the amounts mentioned in (a) or (b) but is related to any claim falling under (a) or (b).

(3) Entitlement to a payment under sub-paragraph (1) shall not arise until three months have elapsed from the earlier of:

(a) the date on which the bill is ready to tax; or

(b) three months after the conclusion of the last of any related proceedings

(4) A bill shall be regarded as being ready to tax on the date on which it is received by the appropriate officer for determination except that where there are related claims for costs all the bills relating thereto shall be regarded as ready to tax on the date the last bill is received.

(5) A representative may submit a claim for an interim payment under this paragraph if no payment has been made under sub-paragraph (1) and six months have elapsed from the conclusion of the proceedings against the defendant whom he represented under the representation order.

(6) For the purposes of this paragraph, proceedings are related to each other in the circumstances set out in sub-paragraph (7) and claims for costs are related to each other in the circumstances set out in sub-paragraph (8).

(7) Proceedings are related to each other:

(a) where different proceedings involving the same defendant are prepared, heard or dealt with together; or

(b) where proceedings involving more than one defendant arose out of the same incident, so that the defendants are charged, tried or disposed of together.

(8) The following claims for costs are related to each other:

(a) the claims of representatives acting in the same proceedings for a defendant;

(b) the claims of any representative acting in any proceedings mentioned in sub-paragraph (7)(a); and

(c) the claims of all the representatives acting for the defendants in the circumstances mentioned in sub-paragraph (7)(b).

(9) No payment shall be made under this paragraph unless (subject to paragraph 23) the representative has submitted a claim in accordance with the provisions of paragraphs 11(1) and 14(1).

5. Amount of interim payments in cases awaiting determination. (1) Where entitlement to a payment arises under paragraph 4, the amount payable shall be 40 per cent of the total claim for costs, less any sum already paid.

(2) Paragraphs 20 to 22 (redetermination etc) shall not apply to a payment under this paragraph.

6. Staged payments in long Crown Court cases. (1) A representative may submit a claim to the appropriate officer for a staged payment of his fees in relation to criminal proceedings in the Crown Court.

(2) Where a claim is submitted in accordance with the provisions of this paragraph, a staged payment shall be allowed where the appropriate officer is satisfied:

(a) that the claim relates to fees for a period of preparation of 100 hours or more, for which the representative will, subject to final determination of the costs payable, be entitled to be paid in accordance with this Schedule; and

(b) that the period from committal or transfer for trial (or from the date of the representation order, if later) to the conclusion of the Crown Court proceedings will be likely to exceed 12 months, having regard, amongst other matters, to the number of defendants, the anticipated pleas and the weight and complexity of the case.

(3) In this paragraph "preparation" means:

(a) all work falling within the definition of "preparation" in paragraph 1(1) of Schedule 4;

(b) attendance at pre-trial reviews and other hearings (other than a pleas and directions hearing) prior to the main hearing;

(c) preparation of applications, statements or notices for the purposes of section 6 or 9(5) of the Criminal Justice Act 1987; and

(d) all preparation within the meaning of paragraph 12(1)(a) not falling within the preceding sub-paragraphs,

and is limited to preparation done before the trial, except in proceedings in which a preparatory hearing has been ordered under section 8 of the Criminal Justice Act 1987, in which case it is limited to preparation done before the date on which the jury is sworn (or on which it became certain, by reason of pleas of guilty or otherwise, that the matter would not proceed to trial).

(4) The amount to be allowed for preparation falling within sub-paragraph (3)(a), (b) or (c) shall be computed by reference to the number of hours of preparation which it appears to the appropriate officer, without prejudice to the final determination of the costs payable, has been reasonably done, multiplied by the relevant hourly rate, namely:

(a) in the case of an advocate who is a Queen's Counsel, the hourly rate for subsidiary fees for Queen's Counsel in the Crown Court prescribed in Table 2 in Schedule 3;

(b) in the case of an advocate instructed as leading junior counsel pursuant to an order made under CDS Regulations, 75 per cent of the hourly rate for subsidiary fees for Queen's Counsel in the Crown Court prescribed in Table 2 in Schedule 3;

(c) in the case of any other advocate, the hourly rate for subsidiary fees for junior counsel in the Crown Court prescribed in Table 1 in Schedule 3.

(5) The amount to be allowed for preparation falling within sub-paragraph (3)(d) shall be computed by reference to the number of hours of preparation which it appears to the appropriate officer, without prejudice to the final determination of the costs payable, has been reasonably done, multiplied by the relevant hourly rate prescribed in Schedule 2 Part 1, applicable to the class of work and the grade and office location of the fee-earner.

(6) A claim shall be submitted in such form and manner as the appropriate officer may direct, including such case plan as he may require for the purposes of sub-paragraph (2)(a).

(7) A representative may claim further staged payments in accordance with this paragraph in respect of further periods of preparation exceeding 100 hours which were not included in an earlier claim.

(8) Paragraphs 20 to 22 (redetermination etc) shall not apply to a payment under this paragraph.

7. Interim payments for attendance at trial and refreshers. (1) Subject to sub-paragraph (1A), a representative may submit a claim to the appropriate officer for an interim payment in respect of attendance at court or refreshers where a Crown Court trial lasts for a qualifying period.

(1A) No claim may be submitted for an interim payment in respect of work for which a graduated fee calculated in accordance with Schedule 4 Part 2 is payable and, if a claim is so submitted, no interim payment shall be allowed in respect of that work.

(2) Where a claim is submitted in accordance with the provisions of this paragraph, an interim payment shall, without prejudice to the final determination of the costs payable, be allowed:

(a) to a solicitor where he or a fee-earner representing him has attended at court on each day of the relevant qualifying period;

(b) to an advocate where he has done work falling within paragraph 6(2)(b) or (c) of Schedule 4 on each day of the relevant qualifying period.

(3) The qualifying period for the purposes of this paragraph shall be:

(a) 20 days for an interim payment allowed under sub-paragraph (2)(a); and

(b) 26 days for an interim payment allowed under sub-paragraph (2)(b) where a case does not qualify for a graduated fee under paragraph 2(2) of Schedule 4,

and a day shall qualify as part of the relevant qualifying period, whether or not the days within the qualifying period are continuous, if the hearing begins at any time on that day.

(4) The amount payable in respect of each day which qualifies as part of the qualifying period shall be:

(a) in the case of a solicitor:

(i) where the hearing begins before and ends after the luncheon adjournment, five times the hourly rate for a trainee or fee-earner of equivalent experience attending court where more than one representative is assigned as prescribed in Schedule 2 Part 1;

(ii) where the hearing begins and ends before the luncheon adjournment, or begins after the luncheon adjournment, two and a half times the hourly rate referred to in (i) above;

(b) in the case of an advocate who is a Queen's Counsel, the maximum amount of the full day refresher fee for Queen's Counsel in the Crown Court prescribed in Table 2 in Schedule 3;

(c) in the case of an advocate instructed as leading junior counsel pursuant to an order made under CDS Regulations, 75 per cent of the maximum amount of the full day refresher fee for Queen's Counsel in the Crown Court prescribed in Table 2 in Schedule 3;

(d) in the case of an advocate retained solely for the purpose of making a note of any hearing, one-half of the maximum amount of the full day refresher fee for junior counsel in the Crown Court prescribed in Table 1 in Schedule 3;

(e) in the case of any other advocate, the maximum amount of the full day refresher fee for junior counsel in the Crown Court prescribed in Table 1 in Schedule 3.

(5) A claim for an interim payment may be made in respect of a qualifying period and shall be submitted in such form and manner as the appropriate officer may direct.

(6) Further interim payments under this paragraph may be claimed if the trial lasts for further qualifying periods

(7) A representative who has obtained prior approval under CDS Regulations for the incurring of travelling or accommodation expenses may, at the same time as he submits a claim for an interim payment under this paragraph, submit a claim for an interim payment of all such expenses incurred to date (less any expenses previously recovered by him by way of interim payment under this paragraph).

(8) A claim under sub-paragraph 7 shall be submitted in such form and manner as the appropriate officer may direct, and shall be supported by such evidence of the expense claimed as he may require.

(9) Paragraphs 20 to 22 (redetermination etc) shall not apply to a payment under this paragraph.

8. Advance payments for early preparation in Crown Court cases. (1) An advance payment under this paragraph shall be payable in respect of every case in the Crown Court in which:

    (a) a pleas and directions hearing or plea and case management hearing is held;

    (b) on or before the date of the pleas and directions hearing or plea and case management hearing, a representation order has been made providing for an advocate to represent the assisted person at the trial and a person ("the trial advocate") has been instructed for that purpose; and

    (c) the trial advocate satisfies the appropriate officer that, in his capacity as the trial advocate, and at least 5 days before the date of the pleas and directions hearing or plea and case management hearing, he has done work of all the types listed in paragraphs (a) to (d) of the definition of "preparation" in paragraph 1(1) of Schedule 4 (whether or not he also does work of those types afterwards), unless at the pleas and directions hearing or plea and case management hearing the assisted person pleads guilty to all counts or the prosecution declares an intention not to proceed to trial.

(2) Subject to sub-paragraph (3), the amount of the advance payment under this sub-paragraph in respect of any such case shall be:

    (a) £250 where the trial advocate is a Queen's Counsel;

    (b) £170 where the trial advocate is not a Queen's Counsel but appears as a leader to another trial advocate;

    (c) £100 for any other trial advocate.

(3) Where the same trial advocate is instructed in two or more cases which are to be heard concurrently the advance payment shall be the amount specified in sub-paragraph (2) in respect of the first case and twenty per cent of that amount in respect of each of the other cases

(4) In this paragraph, a "case" means proceedings against any one assisted person on one or more counts of a single indictment.

9. Hardship payments. (1) The appropriate officer may allow a hardship payment to a representative in the circumstances set out in sub-paragraph (2), subject to the other provisions of this paragraph.

(2) Those circumstances are that the representative:

    (a) represents the assisted person in proceedings in the Crown Court;

    (b) applies for such payment, in such form and manner as the appropriate officer may direct, not less than six months after he was first instructed in those proceedings (or in any related proceedings, if he was instructed in those proceedings earlier than in the proceedings to which the application relates);

    (c) is not, at the date of the application, entitled to any payment under paragraph 4 (interim payments in cases awaiting determination), 6 (staged payments) or 7 (interim payments);

    (d) is unlikely to receive final payment in respect of the proceedings, as determined under paragraph 12 or 15, within the three months following the application for the hardship payment; and

    (e) satisfies the appropriate officer that, by reason of the circumstance in paragraph (d), he is likely to suffer financial hardship.

(3) Every application for a hardship payment shall be accompanied by such information and documents as the appropriate officer may require as evidence of:

    (a) the work done by the representative in relation to the proceedings up to the date of the application; and

    (b) the likelihood of financial hardship.

(4) The amount of any hardship payment shall be in the discretion of the appropriate officer, but shall not exceed such sum as would be reasonable remuneration for the work done by the representative in the proceedings up to the date of the application.

(5) No hardship payment shall be made if it appears to the appropriate officer that the sum which would be reasonable remuneration for the representative, or the sum required to relieve his financial hardship, is less than £5,000 (excluding any VAT).

(6) Any hardship payment shall be set off against the remuneration finally payable to the representative under paragraph 12 or 15.

(7) The question of whether proceedings are related to each other for the purposes of this paragraph shall be determined in accordance with paragraph 4(7).

10. Computation of final claim. (1) At the conclusion of a case in which one or more payments have been made to a representative under paragraph 6, 7, 8 or 9, he shall submit a claim under paragraph 11 or 14 for the determination of his overall remuneration, whether or not such a claim will result in any payment additional to those already made.

(2) In the determination of the amount payable to a representative under paragraph 12 or 15, the appropriate officer shall deduct the amount of any advance payment made under paragraph 6, 7, 8 or 9 in respect of the same case from the amount that would otherwise be payable; and, if the amount of the advance payment is greater than the amount that would otherwise be payable, the appropriate officer shall be entitled to recover the amount of the difference, either by way of repayment by the representative or by way of deduction from any other amount that may be due to him.

11. Claims for costs by solicitors. (1) Subject to paragraph 23, no claim by a solicitor for costs in respect of work done under a representation order shall be entertained unless he submits it within three months of the conclusion of the proceedings to which it relates

(2) Subject to sub-paragraph (3), a claim for costs shall be submitted to the appropriate officer in such form and manner as he may direct and shall be accompanied by the representation order and any receipts or other documents in support of any disbursement claimed.

(3) A claim shall:

(a) summarise the items of work done by a fee-earner in respect of which fees are claimed according to the classes specified in paragraph 12(1);

(b) state, where appropriate, the dates on which the items of work were done, the time taken, the sums claimed and whether the work was done for more than one assisted person;

(c) specify, where appropriate, the fee-earner who undertook each of the items of work claimed;

(d) give particulars of any work done in relation to more than one indictment or a retrial; and

(e) specify any disbursements claimed, the circumstances in which they were incurred and the amounts claimed in respect of them.

(4) Where the solicitor claims that paragraph 4 of Schedule 2 Part 1 should be applied in relation to an item of work, he shall give full particulars in support of his claim.

(5) The solicitor shall specify any special circumstances which should be drawn to the attention of the appropriate officer.

(6) The solicitor shall supply such further particulars, information and documents as the appropriate officer may require.

(7) Where a representation order has been made in respect of any proceedings where a defendant has been acquitted and granted a defendant's costs order under section 16 of the Prosecution of Offences Act 1985, the solicitor shall certify that no claim for costs incurred before the representation order was made has been or will be made from central funds in relation to that work.

12. Determination of solicitors' fees. (1) The appropriate officer may allow work done by fee-earners in the following classes:

(a) preparation, including taking instructions, interviewing, witnesses, ascertaining the prosecution case, advising on plea and mode of trial, preparing and perusing documents, dealing with letters and telephone calls which are not routine, preparing for advocacy, instructing an advocate and expert witnesses, conferences, consultations, views and work done in connection with advice on appeal or case stated;

(b) advocacy, including applications for bail and other applications to the court;

(c) attending at court where an advocate is assigned, including conferences with the advocate at court;

(d) travelling and waiting; and

(e) dealing with routine letters written and routine telephone calls

(2) The appropriate officer shall consider the claim, any further particulars, information or documents submitted by the solicitor under paragraph 11 and any other relevant information and shall allow:

(a) such work as appears to him to have been reasonably done under the representation order (including any representation or advice which is deemed to be work done under that order) by a fee-earner, classifying such work according to the classes specified in sub-paragraph (1) as he considers appropriate; and

(b) such time in each class of work allowed by him (other than routine letters written and routine telephone calls) as he considers reasonable.

(3) Subject to sub-paragraph 4, in any proceedings which are specified in paragraph 1(2) of Schedule 2 Part 2, the appropriate officer shall proceed in accordance with the provisions of paragraph 3 of that Part of that Schedule.

(4) In any proceedings in the Crown Court:

(a) in respect of the classes of work specified in paragraph 6(2) of Schedule 4 (whether or not the proceedings are ones to which that Schedule applies), the appropriate officer shall proceed in accordance with the provisions of paragraph 15 as if the fee-earner who did the work had been a barrister;

(b) in respect of all other classes of work, the provisions of this paragraph shall apply.

(5) Subject to sub-paragraph (2), (3), (4) and (6), the appropriate officer shall allow fees for work allowed by it under this paragraph in accordance with Schedule 2 Part 1.

(6) In the case of criminal proceedings in the Crown Court and the Court of Appeal, the fees allowed in accordance with Part 1 of Schedule 2 shall be those appropriate to such of the following grades of fee-earner as the appropriate officer considers reasonable:

(a) senior solicitor;

(b) solicitor, legal executive or fee earner of equivalent experience;

(c) trainee or fee-earner of equivalent experience.

(7) In relation to hearings specified in sub-paragraph (8), work of the class specified in sub-paragraph (1)(c) shall only be allowed in the following circumstances:

(a) if the assisted person is charged with an offence included in Class 1 or Class 2 as determined pursuant to section 75(2) of the Supreme Court Act 1981*;

(b) if the proceedings have been instituted or taken over by the Serious Fraud Office, or are before the Crown Court by reason of a notice of transfer given under section 4 of the Criminal Justice Act 1987;

(c) if the assisted person was a child or a young person within the meaning of section 107 of the Children and Young Persons Act 1933 at the time when the Crown Court acquired jurisdiction in the case (by committal, notice of transfer or otherwise);

(d) if the assisted person was unable to understand the proceedings or give adequate instructions to his advocate because of his inadequate knowledge of English, mental illness or other mental or physical disability;

(e) if the assisted person was likely if convicted to receive a custodial sentence; or

(f) if the case has been certified as requiring attendance for the whole or any part of the hearing in accordance with sub-paragraphs (10A) and (10B)

(8) The following hearings in the Crown Court are specified for the purpose of sub-paragraph (7): trials, hearings of cases listed for pleas of guilty following a pleas and direction hearing, sentence hearings following committals for sentence and the hearing of appeals against conviction or sentence.

(9) The circumstances referred to in sub-paragraph (7)(e) shall only justify the allowing of attendance on:

(a) a day of a trial on which it was reasonably expected that the assisted person would be sentenced if convicted; and

(b) if different, the day on which the assisted person was in fact sentenced

and where a doubt arises whether attendance should be allowed by reason of that circumstance, the doubt shall be resolved in the assisted person's favour.

(10) The circumstances referred to in sub-paragraph (7)(*f*) shall only justify the allowing of attendance to the extent specified in the representation order.

(10A) A judge of the Crown Court shall have power to certify that attendance on the advocate instructed in the proceedings is required for the whole or any part of a hearing and, in deciding whether a case should be so certified, the judge shall have regard to the following factors, in addition to any other factors which he considers to be relevant:

(*a*) on which days (if any) the attendance of a significant number of defence witnesses is likely to be required;
(*b*) where the hearing is a trial, the amount of documentary evidence likely to be adduced on behalf of the defence;
(*c*) the likelihood of the legally assisted person disrupting the proceedings if the advocate were to appear alone;
(*d*) whether the advocate represents more than one legally assisted person;
(*e*) on which days (if any) the advocate is likely to require notes of the proceedings to be taken for the proper conduct of the defence.

(10B) An application for a certificate under sub-paragraph (10A) may be made at or at any time after the pleas and directions hearing or plea and case management hearing or, if there is to be no pleas and directions hearing or plea and case management hearing, at or at any time after the listing of the first hearing of the case; and in either case the application may be made orally or in writing.

(11) This paragraph applies to work in respect of which standard fees are payable under Part 2 of Schedule 2, or a graduated or fixed fee is payable under Schedule 4 only to the extent that that Part or that Schedule specifically so provide.

(12) *Revoked.*
(13) *Revoked.*

13. Determination of solicitors' disbursements. (1) Subject to the provisions of this paragraph, the appropriate officer shall allow such disbursements claimed under paragraph 11 as appears to him to have been reasonably incurred, provided that:

(*a*) if they are abnormally large by reason of the distance of the court or the assisted person's residence or both from the solicitors' place of business, reimbursement of the expenses may be limited to what otherwise would, having regard to all the circumstances, be a reasonable amount; and
(*b*) in the case of an appeal to the Court of Appeal, the cost of a transcript, or any part thereof, of the proceedings in the court from which the appeal lies obtained otherwise than through the registrar shall not be allowed except where the appropriate officer considers that it is reasonable in all the circumstances for such disbursement to be allowed.

(2) No question as to the propriety of any step or act in relation to which prior authority has been obtained under CDS Regulations shall be raised on any determination of costs, unless the solicitor knew or ought reasonably to have known that the purpose for which the authority was given had failed or had become irrelevant or unnecessary before the costs were incurred.

(3) Where costs are reasonably incurred in accordance with and subject to the limit imposed by a prior authority given under CDS Regulations, no question shall be raised on any determination of costs as to the amount of the payment to be allowed for the step or act in relation to which the authority was given.

(4) Where costs are incurred in taking any steps or doing any act for which authority may be given under CDS Regulations, without such authority having been given or in excess of any fee so authorised, payment in respect of those costs may nevertheless be allowed on a determination of costs

14. Claims for fees by an advocate. (1) Subject to sub-paragraph (1A) and paragraph 23, no claim by an advocate for fees for work done under a representation order shall be entertained unless he submits it within three months of the conclusion of the proceedings to which the representation order relates

(1A) Where a confiscation hearing under section 2 of the Drug Trafficking Act 1994 or section 71 of the Criminal Justice Act 1988 is to be held more than 28 days after:

(*a*) the conclusion of the trial to which the representation order relates; or
(*b*) the entering of a guilty plea

a claim by an advocate for a graduated fee calculated in accordance with Schedule 4 shall be entertained as soon as the trial has concluded or the guilty plea has been entered.

(2) A claim for fees shall be submitted to the appropriate officer in such form and manner as he may direct.
(3) A claim shall:

(*a*) summarise the items of work in respect of which fees are claimed according to the classes of fee specified in paragraph 15(5);
(*b*) state the dates on which the items of work were done, the time taken where appropriate, the sums claimed and whether the work was done for more than one assisted person;
(*c*) give particulars of any work done in relation to more than one indictment or a retrial.

(4) Where an advocate claims that:

(*a*) it would be inappropriate to allow a standard fee under paragraph 15(2); or
(*b*) paragraph 15(6) should be applied in relation to an item of work

he shall give full particulars in support of his claim.

(5) Where there are any special circumstances which should be drawn to the attention of the appropriate officer, the advocate shall specify them.

(6) The advocate shall supply such further particulars, information and documents as the appropriate officer may require.

15. Determination of advocate's fees. (1) The appropriate officer shall consider the claim, any further particulars and information submitted by an advocate under paragraph 14 and any other relevant information and shall allow such work as appears to him to have been reasonably done.

(2) In any proceedings specified in paragraph 2 or 3 of Schedule 4, the appropriate officer shall allow a graduated or fixed fee calculated in accordance with that Schedule in respect of all such work allowed by it as falls into the classes specified in paragraph 6(2) of that Schedule.

(3) Where in any proceedings specified in paragraph 2 of Schedule 4, the trial judge makes adverse observations concerning the advocate's conduct of the case, the appropriate officer may reduce any fee which would otherwise be payable in accordance with that Schedule by such proportion as he shall see fit, having

first given the advocate the opportunity to make representations about the extent to which the fee should be reduced.

(4) Where it appears to the appropriate officer that the fixed fee allowed by Schedule 4 in respect of any proceedings specified in paragraph 3 of that Schedule would be inappropriate taking into account all of the relevant circumstances of the case, he may instead allow fees in accordance with sub-paragraphs (5) and (6) below.

(5) The appropriate officer may, except in relation to work for which a graduated or fixed fee is allowed under subparagraph (2), allow any of the following classes of fee to an advocate in respect of work allowed by him under this paragraph:

(a) a basic fee for preparation including preparation for a pre-trial review and, where appropriate, the first day's hearing including, where they took place on that day, short conferences, consultations, applications and appearances (including bail applications), views and any other preparation;

(b) a refresher fee for any day or part of a day during which a hearing continued, including, where they took place on that day, short conferences, consultations, applications and appearances (including bail applications), views and any other preparation;

(c) subsidiary fees for:

(i) attendance at conferences, consultations and views not covered by (a) or (b);

(ii) written advice on evidence, plea, appeal, case stated or other written work; and

(iii) attendance at pre-trial reviews, applications and appearances (including bail applications and adjournments for sentence) not covered by (a) or (b).

(6) In the case of proceedings in the Crown Court, the appropriate officer shall, except in relation to work for which a graduated or fixed fee is allowed under sub-paragraph (2), allow such fees in respect of such work as he considers reasonable in such amounts as he may determine in accordance with Schedule 3, provided that where it appears to the appropriate officer, taking into account all the relevant circumstances of the case, that owing to the exceptional circumstances of the case the amount payable by way of fees in accordance with Part 2 of Schedule 3 would not provide reasonable remuneration for some or all of the work he has allowed, he may allow such amounts as appear to him to be reasonable remuneration for the relevant work.

(7) In the case of proceedings in the Court of Appeal, the appropriate officer shall allow such fees in respect of such work as he considers reasonable in such amount as appears to him to be reasonable remuneration for such work.

(8) Where prior authority has been obtained to instruct a Queen's Counsel alone no question as to the propriety of that act shall be raised on any determination of the advocate's fees, unless the solicitor knew or ought reasonably to have known that the purpose for which the authority was given had failed or become irrelevant or unnecessary before the fees were incurred.

(9) Where:

(a) a representation order provides for representation by a sole advocate other than a Queen's Counsel, and a Queen's Counsel agrees to appear as the sole advocate; or

(b) a representation order provides for representation by two advocates other than Queen's Counsel, and a Queen's Counsel agrees to appear as a leading junior that Queen's Counsel shall be treated for all the purposes of this Schedule as having been instructed under that order, and his remuneration shall be determined as if he were not a Queen's Counsel.

16. (1) Subject to sub-paragraph (2), where the court has disallowed the whole or any part of any wasted costs under section 19A of the Prosecution of Offences Act 1985 the appropriate officer, in determining costs in respect of work done by the representatives against whom the wasted costs order was made, shall deduct the amount of the order from the amount otherwise payable in accordance with this Schedule.

(2) Where the appropriate officer, in accordance with this Schedule, is minded to disallow any amount of a claim for work done to which the wasted costs order relates, he shall disallow that amount or the amount of the wasted costs order, whichever is the greater.

17. Payment of costs. (1) Having determined the costs payable to a representative in accordance with this Schedule, the appropriate officer shall notify the representative of the costs payable and authorise payment accordingly.

(2) Where the costs payable under sub-paragraph (1) are varied as a result of any review, redetermination or appeal made or brought pursuant to this Schedule:

(a) where the costs are increased, the appropriate officer shall authorise payment of the increase;

(b) where the costs are decreased, the representative shall repay the amount of such decrease; and

(c) where the payment of any costs of the representative is ordered under paragraph 21(14) or 22(8) or Schedule 2 Part 2 paragraph 8(4), the appropriate officer shall authorise payment.

18. Recovery of overpayments. (1) This paragraph applies where a representative is entitled to be paid a certain sum ("the amount due") by virtue of the provisions of this Schedule and, for whatever reason, he is paid an amount greater than that sum.

(2) Where the circumstances in sub-paragraph (1) arise, the appropriate officer may:

(a) require immediate repayment of the amount in excess of the amount due ("the excess amount") and the representative shall on demand repay the excess amount to the appropriate officer; or

(b) deduct the excess amount from any other sum which is or becomes payable to the representative by virtue of the provisions of this Schedule.

(3) The appropriate officer may proceed under sub-paragraph (2)(b) without first proceeding under sub-paragraph (2)(a).

(4) Sub-paragraph (2) shall apply notwithstanding that the representative to whom the excess amount was paid is exercising, or may exercise, a right under paragraphs 20 to 22.

19. Notification of costs. For the purposes of an order which may be made under section 17 of the Act, other than where the proceedings are in the magistrates' court only, having determined the costs payable to a representative in accordance with this Schedule, the appropriate officer shall notify the court before which the proceedings are heard of the amount determined in each case.

20. Redetermination of costs by appropriate officer. (1) Where:

(a) a representative is dissatisfied with the costs (other than the standard fees allowed under Schedule 2 Part 2 or graduated or fixed fees allowed under Schedule 4) determined in accordance with the provisions of this Schedule by the appropriate officer;

(b) an advocate in proceedings in the Crown Court is dissatisfied with the decision that Schedule 4 does or does not apply to those proceedings or with the calculation of the remuneration payable under that Schedule; or

(c) an advocate in proceedings in the Crown Court is dissatisfied with the decision not to allow one of the following fees, or with the number of hours allowed in the calculation of such a fee, namely:

    (i) a special preparation fee under paragraph 17 of Schedule 4;
    (ii) a wasted preparation fee under paragraph 18 of Schedule 4; or
    (iii) an hourly fee under sub-paragraph (a) or (b) of paragraph 19(1) of Schedule 4, paragraph 29 of Schedule 4 or paragraph 30 of Schedule 4; or

(d) an advocate in proceedings in the Crown Court is dissatisfied with the classification, under paragraph 5 of Schedule 4, of an offence not specifically listed in the Table of Offences at the end of Schedule 4 Part 5 but deemed to fall within Class H]

he may apply to the appropriate officer to reclassify the offence, to redetermine those costs or to review that decision as the case may be.

(2) Subject to paragraph 23, the application shall be made within 21 days of the receipt of notification of the costs payable under paragraph 17, by giving notice in writing to the appropriate officer specifying the matters in respect of which the application is made and the grounds of objection and shall be made in such form and manner as the appropriate officer may direct.

(3) The notice of application shall be accompanied by the particulars, information and documents supplied under paragraph 11 or 14, as appropriate.

(4) The notice of application shall state whether the applicant wishes to appear or to be represented and, if the applicant so wishes, the appropriate officer shall notify the applicant of the time at which he is prepared to hear him or his representative.

(5) The applicant shall supply such further particulars, information and documents as the appropriate officer may require.

(6) The appropriate officer shall:

(a) redetermine the costs, whether by way of confirmation, or increase or decrease in the amount previously determined; or

(b) review the decision to allow standard fees under paragraph 15(2), and confirm it, or allow fees in accordance with paragraph 15(5) and (6),

in the light of the objections made by the applicant or on his behalf and shall notify the applicant of his decision.

(7) The applicant may request the appropriate officer to give reasons in writing for his decision and the appropriate officer shall comply with any such request.

(8) Subject to paragraph 23, any request under sub-paragraph (7) shall be made within 21 days of receiving notification of the decision.

21. Appeals to a Costs Judge. (1) Where the appropriate officer has given his reasons for his decisions under paragraph 20, a representative who is dissatisfied with that decision may appeal to a Costs Judge.

(2) Subject to paragraph 23, an appeal shall be instituted within 21 days of the receipt of the appropriate officer's reasons, by giving notice in writing to the Senior Costs Judge.

(3) The appellant shall send a copy of any notice given under sub-paragraph (2) to the appropriate officer.

(4) The notice of appeal shall be accompanied by:

(a) a copy of the written representations given under paragraph 20(2);
(b) the appropriate officer's reasons for his decision given under paragraph 20(7); and
(c) the particulars, information and documents supplied to the appropriate officer under paragraph 20.

(5) The notice of appeal shall:

(a) be in such form as the Senior Costs Judge may direct;
(b) specify separately each item appealed against, showing (where appropriate) the amount claimed for the item, the amount determined and the grounds of the objection to the determination; and
(c) state whether the appellant wishes to appear or to be represented or whether he will accept a decision given in his absence.

(6) The Senior Costs Judge may, and if so directed by the Lord Chancellor either generally or in a particular case shall, send to the Lord Chancellor a copy of the notice of appeal together with copies of such other documents as the Lord Chancellor may require.

(7) With a view to ensuring that the public interest is taken into account, the Lord Chancellor may arrange for written or oral representations to be made on his behalf and, if he intends to do so, he shall inform the Senior Costs Judge and the appellant.

(8) Any written representations made on behalf of the Lord Chancellor under sub-paragraph (7) shall be sent to the Senior Costs Judge and the appellant and, in the case of oral representations, the Senior Costs Judge and the appellant shall be informed of the grounds on which such representations will be made.

(9) The appellant shall be permitted a reasonable opportunity to make representations in reply.

(10) The Costs Judge shall inform the appellant (or his representative) and the Lord Chancellor, where representations have been or are to be made on his behalf, of the date of any hearing and, subject to the provisions of this paragraph, may give directions as to the conduct of the appeal.

(11) The Costs Judge may consult the trial judge or the appropriate officer and may require the appellant to provide any further information which he requires for the purpose of the appeal and, unless the Costs Judge otherwise directs, no further evidence shall be received on the hearing of the appeal and no ground of objection shall be valid which was not raised under paragraph 20.

(12) The Costs Judge shall have the same powers as the appropriate officer under this Schedule and, in the exercise of such powers, may:

(a) alter the redetermination of the appropriate officer in respect of any sum allowed, whether by increase or decrease as he thinks fit;
(b) confirm the decision to allow standard fees under paragraph 15(2) or allow fees in accordance with paragraph 15(5) and (6).

(13) The Costs Judge shall communicate his decision and the reasons for it in writing to the appellant, the Lord Chancellor and the appropriate officer.

(14) Except where he confirms or decreases the sums redetermined under paragraph 20 or confirms a

decision to allow standard fees, the Costs Judge may allow the appellant a sum in respect of part or all of any reasonable costs (including any fee payable in respect of an appeal) incurred by him in connection with the appeal.

22. Appeals to the High Court. (1) A representative who is dissatisfied with the decision of a Costs Judge on an appeal under paragraph 21 may apply to a Costs Judge to certify a point of principle of general importance.

(2) Subject to paragraph 23, an application under sub-paragraph (1) shall be made within 21 days of notification of a Costs Judge's decision under sub-paragraph 21(13).

(3) Where a Costs Judge certifies a point of principle of general importance, the representative may appeal to the High Court against the decision of a Costs Judge on an appeal under paragraph 21, and the Lord Chancellor shall be a respondent to such an appeal.

(4) Subject to paragraph 23, an appeal under sub-paragraph (3) shall be instituted within 21 days of receiving a Costs Judge's certificate under sub-paragraph (1).

(5) Where the Lord Chancellor is dissatisfied with the decision of a Costs Judge on an appeal under paragraph 21, he may, if no appeal has been made by the representative under sub-paragraph (3), appeal to the High Court against that decision, and the representative shall be a respondent to the appeal.

(6) Subject to paragraph 23, an appeal under sub-paragraph (5) shall be instituted within 21 days of receiving notification of the Costs Judge's decision under paragraph 21(13).

(7) An appeal under sub-paragraph (3) or (5) shall be brought in the Queen's Bench Division, follow the procedure set out in Part 52 of the Civil Procedure Rules 1998, and shall be heard and determined by a single judge whose decision shall be final.

(8) The judge shall have the same powers as the appropriate officer and a Costs Judge under this Schedule and may reverse, affirm or amend the decision appealed against or make such other order as he thinks fit.

23. Time limits. (1) Subject to sub-paragraph (2), the time limit within which any act is required or authorised to be done may, for good reason, be extended:

(a) in the case of acts required or authorised to be done under paragraph 21 or 22, by a Costs Judge or the High Court as the case may be; and

(b) in the case of acts required or authorised to be done by a representative under any other paragraph, by the appropriate officer.

(2) Where a representative without good reason has failed (or, if an extension were not granted, would fail) to comply with a time limit, the appropriate officer, a Costs Judge or the High Court, as the case may be, may, in exceptional circumstances, extend the time limit and shall consider whether it is reasonable in the circumstances to reduce the costs; provided that the costs shall not be reduced unless the representative has been allowed a reasonable opportunity to show cause orally or in writing why the costs should not be reduced.

(3) A representative may appeal to a Costs Judge against a decision made under this paragraph by an appropriate officer and such an appeal shall be instituted within 21 days of the decision being given by giving notice in writing to the Senior Costs Judge specifying the grounds of appeal.

24. House of Lords. (1) In the case of proceedings in the House of Lords, the costs payable to a representative under sections 13 or 14 of the Act shall be determined by such officer as may be prescribed by order of the House of Lords

(2) Subject to paragraph (1), this Schedule shall not apply to proceedings in the House of Lords

---

*Amended by the Constitutional Reform Act 2005, Sch 11 from a date to be appointed.

1–5658   SCHEDULE 2
SOLICITORS' FEES

PART 1
FEES DETERMINED UNDER PARAGRAPH 12 OF SCHEDULE 1

1. Subject to paragraphs 2 and 3, for proceedings in the Crown Court and Court of Appeal the appropriate officer shall allow fees for work allowed by it under paragraph 12 of Schedule 1 at the following prescribed rates:

Class of work	Grade of fee-earner	Rate	
Preparation	Senior solicitor	£53.00 per hour—	(£55.75 per hour for a fee-earner whose office is situated within the London region of the Commission)
	Solicitor, legal executive or fee-earner of equivalent experience	£45.00 per hour—	(£47.25 per hour for a fee-earner whose office is situated within the London region of the Commission)
	Trainee or fee-earner of equivalent experience	£29.75 per hour—	(£34.00 per hour for a fee-earner whose office is situated within the London region of the Commission)
Advocacy (other than in the Crown Court)	Senior solicitor	£64.00 per hour	
	Solicitor	£56.00 per hour	
Attendance at court where more than one representative assigned	Senior solicitor	£42.25 per hour	
	Solicitor, legal executive or fee-earner of equivalent experience	£34.00 per hour	
	Trainee or fee-earner of equivalent experience	£20.50 per hour	

Class of work	Grade of fee-earner	Rate	
Travelling and waiting	Senior solicitor	£24.75 per hour	
	Solicitor, legal executive or fee-earner of equivalent experience	£24. 75 per hour	
	Trainee or fee-earner of equivalent experience	£12.50 per hour	
Routine letters written and routine telephone calls		£3.45 per item—	(£3.60 per item for a fee-earner whose office is situated within the London region of the Commission)

2. In relation to any hearing specified in paragraph 12(8) of Schedule 1, the fee specified in paragraph 1 for attendance at court where an advocate is assigned shall only be payable in the circumstances and to the extent provided by paragraphs 12(7) to (10) of that Schedule.

3. In respect of any item of work, the appropriate officer may allow fees at less than the relevant prescribed rate specified in paragraph 1 where it appears to him reasonable to do so having regard to the competence and despatch with which the work was done.

4. (1) Upon a determination the appropriate officer may, subject to the provisions of this paragraph, allow fees at more than the relevant prescribed rate specified in paragraph 1 for preparation, advocacy (other than in the Crown Court), attendance at court where more than one representative is assigned, routine letters written and routine telephone calls, in respect of offences in Class A, B, C, D, G or I in the Table of Offences at the end of Part 5 of Schedule 4.

(1A) The appropriate officer may allow fees at more than the prescribed rate where it appears to him, taking into account all the relevant circumstances of the case, that—

(a) the work was done with exceptional competence, skill or expertise;
(b) the work was done with exceptional despatch; or
(c) the case involved exceptional circumstances or complexity.

(1B) Paragraph 5 of Schedule 4 applies to solicitors in respect of proceedings in the Crown Court and Court of Appeal as it applies to advocates.

(2) Where the appropriate officer considers that any item or class of work should be allowed at more than the prescribed rate, he shall apply to that item or class of work a percentage enhancement in accordance with the following provisions of this paragraph.

(3) In determining the percentage by which fees should be enhanced above the prescribed rate the appropriate officer should have regard to:

(a) the degree of responsibility accepted by the solicitor and his staff;
(b) the care, speed and economy with which the case was prepared; and
(c) the novelty, weight and complexity of the case.

(4) The percentage above the relevant prescribed rate by which fees for work may be enhanced shall not exceed 100 per cent.

(5) *Revoked.*

(6) The appropriate officer may have regard to the generality of proceedings to which this Order applies in determining what is exceptional within the meaning of this paragraph.

PART 2
STANDARD FEES IN THE CROWN COURT

1. Application. (1) Subject to sub-paragraphs (3) and (4), this Part of this Schedule applies to the fees for work done by a fee-earner regardless of his grade in relation to the proceedings in the Crown Court specified in sub-paragraph (2).

(2) The following proceedings are specified for the purpose of sub-paragraph (1):

(a) committals for trial in which the indictment consisted of counts in respect of an offence which is classified as a Class 3 or 4 offence in accordance with directions given by the Lord Chief Justice under section 75 of the Supreme Court Act 1981 and*

(i) where the trial (including any case prepared for trial in which no jury was sworn) lasted two days or less and at the time of listing was reasonably expected to last two days or less; or
(ii) where the case was listed and disposed of as a plea of guilty;

(b) appeals against conviction;
(c) appeals against sentence; and
(d) committals for sentence (including proceedings which arose out of a breach of an order of the Crown Court, proceedings in which a sentence was deferred and other similar matters).

(3) Where in any proceedings specified in sub-paragraph (2), the trial judge:

(a) is dissatisfied with the solicitor's conduct of the case; or
(b) considers that, for exceptional reasons, the fees should be determined under paragraph 12 of Schedule 1

he may direct that the fees should be determined under paragraph 12 and in that event this Part of this Schedule shall not apply.

(4) If a solicitor so elects, he may claim standard fees under this Part of this Schedule in respect of work done by him notwithstanding that the proceedings in relation to which the work was done are not specified in sub-paragraph (2), and the provisions of this Part of this Schedule shall apply to such a claim with the necessary modifications, save that, where a solicitor elects to claim the principal standard fee for preparation in respect of a trial which lasted more than two days, he shall be paid that fee (together with the appropriate standard fee for the other classes of work specified in paragraph (4)(2)) and paragraph 2 shall not apply.

(5) In relation to any hearing specified in paragraph 12(8) of Schedule 1, the fee specified in the Table for attendance at court where an advocate was assigned shall only be payable in the circumstances and to the extent provided by paragraph 12(7) to 12(10) of Schedule 1.

(6) For the purposes of this Part of this Schedule, the standard fees which are payable and the classes of work for which such fees may be paid are specified in paragraph 4 and the "lower fee limit" and the "higher fee limit" have the meanings given by paragraph 4(3).

2. Allowance of standard fees. (1) The appropriate officer shall allow the standard fee for preparation which has been claimed by a solicitor (together with the appropriate standard fees for the other classes of work specified in paragraph 4(2)) unless, where the principal standard fee for preparation has been claimed, such a fee is considered to be excessive, in which case the lower standard fee shall be allowed.

(2) A solicitor who has been allowed the lower standard fee instead of the principal fee claimed may:

(a) accept that lower fee;

(b) request the appropriate officer in writing to review his decision; or

(c) provide the appropriate officer with a detailed claim in the form directed by him requesting that the fees for preparation be determined under paragraph 12 of Schedule 1.

(3) Where the appropriate officer is requested to review his decision under sub-paragraph (2)(b), the officer shall either:

(a) allow the principal fee; or

(b) request the solicitor to provide a detailed claim in the form directed by him.

(4) Where a solicitor fails to make a request under sub-paragraph (2)(b) or to supply a detailed claim for the purposes of sub-paragraph (2)(c) or (3)(b) within six weeks of the decision to allow the lower fee or the request to supply a detailed claim, whichever is the later, the decision to allow the lower standard fee shall be deemed to be confirmed.

3. (1) Where a solicitor:

(a) submits a claim for determination under paragraph 12 of Schedule 1 in a case to which paragraph 1(2) applies; or

(b) disputes the allowance of the lower standard fee and provides a detailed claim under paragraph 2(2)(c) or (3)(b)

the appropriate officer shall first determine fees for preparation work within the meaning of paragraph 4(2)(a) of this Part of this Schedule.

(2) If the fees so determined are:

(a) less than the lower fee limit, the appropriate officer shall allow and pay the lower standard fee together with the standard fees for all other classes of work specified in paragraph 4(2);

(b) not less than the lower fee limit and not more than the upper fee limit, the appropriate officer shall allow and pay the principal standard fee together with the standard fees for all other classes of works specified in paragraph 4(2);

(c) more than the upper fee limit, no standard fees shall be payable and all fees shall be determined in accordance with paragraph 12 of Schedule 1.

4. Standard fees. (1) The classes of work for which standard fees shall be payable are those specified in sub-paragraph (2) and the fees for classes of work which are not so specified shall be determined in accordance with paragraph 12 of Schedule 1.

(2) The classes of work specified for the purposes of sub-paragraph (1) are:

(a) preparation within the meaning of paragraph 12(1)(a) of Schedule 1 but including routine letters written and telephone calls, within the meaning of paragraph 12(1)(e) of that Schedule;

(b) attendance at court (including waiting) where more than one representative is assigned;

(c) travelling, other than to undertake work for which standard fees are not payable. For the purpose of this paragraph, "travelling" shall be deemed to include waiting in connection with preparation work, within the meaning of sub-paragraph (2)(a) above.

(3) The standard fees payable under this Part of this Schedule are the fees specified in the Table below and in this Part of this Schedule the "lower fee limit" and the "upper fee limit" mean the lower and upper fee limits specified in the Table.

TABLE

PREPARATION

Type of proceedings		Lower standard fee	Lower fee limit	Principal standard fee	Upper fee limit
Jury trials (including any case prepared for trial in which no jury was sworn)	London rate	£129.50	£179	£249.50	£312
		£139.00	£186	£261.50	£326
Guilty pleas	London rate	£81.50	£110	£175.00	£226
		£87.50	£114	£185.50	£235
Appeals against conviction	London rate	£51.00	£68	£153.00	£233
		£54.50	£70	£159.00	£244
Appeals against sentence	London rate	£36.25	£52	£93.00	£131
		£39.25	£54	£98.00	£135
Committals for sentence	London rate	£42.50	£51	£97.75	£141
		£45.00	£53	£103.00	£145
Attendance at court (including waiting) where more than one representative assigned		£21.40	per hour		
Travelling		£18.50	per hour		

(4) A solicitor shall be entitled to the "London rate" of the standard fees specified in the Table where his office is situated within the London region of the Commission.

(5) The hourly rate specified in the Table for attendance at court shall, subject to sub-paragraph (6), be paid in respect of the period of time beginning 30 minutes before the case was listed, and ending:

(a) where the client was present at court, 15 minutes after the hearing ended on that day; or

(b) where the client was not present at court, when the hearing ended on that day

and save in exceptional circumstances, shall not be payable during the luncheon adjournment.

(6) Where a fee-earner attends a court centre for the purpose of more than one case, the solicitor may claim

the attendance fee in respect of the second or subsequent case only for the time actually spent in attendance in addition to the time for which payment is made under sub-paragraph (5).

(7) The hourly rate specified in the Table shall be paid for time spent travelling (within the meaning of sub-paragraph (2)(c)).

(8) Where a solicitor acts for more than one defendant, the appropriate officer shall allow whichever of the appropriate standard preparation fees is the greater and increase that fee by 20 per cent for each additional defendant, but no percentage increase shall be made to the standard fees for attendance at court and travelling.

(9) Where a solicitor acts for a defendant in respect of more than one:

(a) indictment;
(b) appeal against conviction;
(c) appeal against sentence; or
(d) committal for sentence

or in respect of any combination of (a) to (d) above, the appropriate officer shall allow whichever of the appropriate standard preparation fees is the greater and increase that fee by 20 per cent for each additional indictment, appeal or committal for sentence as the case may be.

(10) Where a solicitor prepares a case with a view to an advocate appearing at the substantive hearing without the solicitor or his representative attending court, the standard preparation fee payable after any increase required by paragraphs (8) or (9) shall be further increased by:

(a) £60.00 in a case which is prepared for trial, whether or not a trial takes place (£64.00 for a solicitor whose office is situated within the London region of the Commission); and
(b) £30.00 in every other case (£32.00 for a solicitor whose office is situated within the London region of the Commission).

(11) Where a fee-earner listens to a recording of an interview conducted under a code issued by the Secretary of State under section 60 of the Police and Criminal Evidence Act 1984, the standard preparation fee payable after application of any increase required by paragraph 8 or 9 shall be further increased by £10.90 for every 10 minutes of the total running time of all recordings or parts thereof listened to and by the same amount for any remaining period.

(12) Where the standard fee payable is increased by virtue of sub-paragraph (8), (9), (10) or (11), then for the purposes of paragraphs 3, 6 and 8:

(a) the upper fee limit shall be increased by the same amount by which the principal standard fee has been increased; and
(b) the lower fee limit shall be increased by the same amount by which the standard fee has been increased.

5. Disbursements. Nothing in this Part of this Schedule applies to disbursements, which shall be determined in accordance with paragraph 13 of Schedule 1.

6. Re-determinations and appeals. (1) A solicitor who is dissatisfied with a decision on a determination under paragraph 3 may apply for the costs to be re-determined and, subject to sub-paragraph (2), the provisions of paragraph 20(2) to (8) of Schedule 1 shall apply with the necessary modifications to an application under this paragraph as they apply to an application under paragraph 20 of Schedule 1.

(2) On a re-determination under this paragraph, the appropriate officer shall determine the fees for preparation work within the meaning of paragraph 4(2)(a) and if the fees as so determined are:

(a) less than the lower fee limit, the lower standard fee shall be allowed together with the standard fees for all other classes of work specified in paragraph 4(2);
(b) not less than the lower fee limit and not more than the upper fee limit, the principal standard fee shall be allowed together with the standard fees for all other classes of work specified in paragraph 4(2);
(c) more than the upper fee limit, the fees for all classes of work shall be determined in accordance with paragraph 12 of Schedule 1.

7. Irrespective of any dispute under paragraph 2 as to whether the principal standard fee should have been allowed instead of the lower standard fee, where a solicitor is satisfied with a decision to allow a standard fee but contends that:

(a) a standard fee which is not apt for the type of work done has been allowed; or
(b) the provisions of paragraph 4(4) to (12) have been incorrectly applied

he may, within six weeks of receipt of notification of the decision, make a written request setting out his reasons why the decision should be reviewed and, if the appropriate officer confirms his decision, written reasons shall be given.

8. (1) A solicitor may appeal to a Costs Judge where he is dissatisfied with:

(a) a decision on a re-determination under paragraph 6; or
(b) a decision on a review under paragraph 7.

(2) Where a solicitor appeals to a Costs Judge in respect of a decision under paragraph 6, the Costs Judge shall determine the fees for preparation within the meaning of paragraph 4(2)(a) and if the fees so determined are:

(a) less than the lower fee limit, the lower standard fee shall be allowed by the Costs Judge together with the standard fees for all other classes of work specified in paragraph 4(2);
(b) not less than the lower fee limit and not more than the upper fee limit, the principal standard fee shall be allowed by the Costs Judge together with the standard fees for all other classes of work specified in paragraph 4(2);
(c) more than the upper fee limit, the fees for all classes of work shall be determined by the Costs Judge in accordance with paragraph 12 of Schedule 1.

(3) Where a solicitor appeals to a Costs Judge in respect of a decision made on a review under paragraph 7, the Costs Judge shall allow whichever standard fee he considers to be apt for the type of work done or, as the case may be, re-apply the provisions of paragraph 4(4) to (12).

(4) Where a Costs Judge allows an appeal in whole or in part, he may allow the solicitor a sum in respect of part or all of any reasonable costs (including any fee payable in respect of the appeal) incurred by him in connection with the appeal.

(5) This paragraph only applies to appeals in proceedings for which standard fees are payable and the provisions of paragraph 21 of Schedule 1 shall apply to appeals in proceedings for which standard fees are not payable.

(6) Subject to the foregoing provisions of this paragraph, the provisions of paragraphs 21 to 23 of Schedule

1 relating to appeals by solicitors shall apply with the necessary modifications to appeals in proceedings for which standard fees are payable under this Part of this Schedule as they apply to appeals in proceedings for which standard fees are not payable.

---

*Amended by the Constitutional Reform Act 2005, Sch 11 from a date to be appointed.

1–5659

SCHEDULE 3
COUNSEL'S FEES

1. The appropriate officer shall allow such fee in respect of an item of work allowed under paragraph 15(6) of Schedule 1, not exceeding the maximum amount specified in respect of that item of work, as appears to it to provide reasonable remuneration.

2. Where an hourly rate is specified in a Table in this part of this Schedule in respect of an item of work allowed under paragraph 15(6) of Schedule 1, the appropriate officer shall determine any fee for such work in accordance with that hourly rate; provided that the fee determined shall not be less than the minimum amount specified.

3. Where a refresher fee is claimed in respect of less than a full day, the appropriate officer shall allow such fee as appears to him reasonable having regard to the fee which would be allowable for a full day.

4. The fees allowed to junior counsel for proceedings in the Crown Court arising out of a breach of an order of the Crown Court or other similar matter shall not exceed the maximum amounts specified for "committals for sentence".

5. Paragraph 25 of Schedule 4 shall apply where an advocate's fees are determined in accordance with this Part of this Schedule as it applies where a graduated or fixed fee is allowed in accordance with Schedule 4.

TABLE 1: JUNIOR COUNSEL

Type of proceedings	Basic fee	Full day refresher fee	Subsidiary fees		
			Attendance at consultations, conferences & views	Written work	Attendance at pre-trial reviews, applications and other appearances
Jury trials	Maximum amount: £545.50				
Cases prepared for trial in which no jury is sworn	Maximum amount: £317.75				
Guilty pleas	Maximum amount: £192.25	Maximum amount: £178.75	£33.50 per hour Minimum amount: £16.75	Maximum amount: £58.25	Maximum amount: £110.00
Appeals against conviction	Maximum amount: £210.00				
Appeals against sentence	Maximum amount: £107.50				
Committals for sentence	Maximum amount: £107.50				

TABLE 2: QUEEN'S COUNSEL

Type of proceedings	Basic fee	Full day refresher fee	Subsidiary fees		
			Attendance at consultations, conferences and views	Written work	Attendance at pre-trial reviews, applications and other appearances
All cases	Maximum amount: £5,400.00	Maximum amount: £330.50	£62.50 per hour Minimum amount: £32.00	Maximum amount: £119.50	Maximum amount: £257.50

1–5659A

SCHEDULE 4
FEES FOR ADVOCACY IN THE CROWN COURT

PART 1
DEFINITION AND SCOPE

1. (1) In this Schedule:

"trial advocate" means a person instructed in accordance with a representation order to represent the assisted person at the main hearing in any case including a Queen's Counsel or a leading junior counsel so instructed after the hearing at which pleas are taken;

"case" means proceedings in the Crown Court against any one assisted person:

(a) on one or more counts of a single indictment;

(b) arising out of a single notice of appeal against conviction or sentence, or a single committal for sentence, whether on one or more charges; or

(c) arising out of a single alleged breach of an order of the Crown Court

and a case falling within paragraph (c) shall be treated as a separate case from the proceedings in which the order was made;

"cracked trial" and "guilty plea" have the meaning given in paragraph 9(3), (4) and (5) of this Schedule;

"main hearing" means:

(a) in relation to a case which goes to trial, the trial;

(b) in relation to a guilty plea, the hearing at which pleas are taken or, where there is more than one such hearing, the last such hearing;

(bb) in relation to a cracked trial, the hearing at which—

(i) the case becomes a cracked trial by meeting the conditions in paragraph 9(3) or (4), whether or not any pleas were taken at that hearing; or

(ii) a formal verdict of not guilty was entered as a result of the prosecution offering no evidence under the administrative procedure, whether or not the parties were required by the court to attend the hearing;

(c) in relation to an appeal against conviction or sentence, the hearing of the appeal;

(d) in relation to proceedings arising out of a committal for sentence, the sentencing hearing; and

(e) in relation to proceedings arising out of an alleged breach of an order of the Crown Court, the final hearing;

"Newton Hearing" means a hearing at which evidence is heard for the purpose of determining the sentence of a convicted person in accordance with the principles of *R v Newton* (1982) 77 Cr App Rep 13;

"preparation" means work of any of the following types when done by a trial advocate:

(a) reading the papers in the case;

(b) (revoked)

(c) contact with prosecution representatives;

(d) written or oral advice on plea;

(e) researching the law, preparation for examination of witnesses and preparation of oral submissions for the main hearing;

(f) viewing exhibits or undisclosed material at police stations;

(g) (revoked)

(h) written advice on evidence;

(i) written and oral advice on appeal (where covered under the same representation order as the main hearing);

(j) preparation of written submissions, notices or other documents for use at the main hearing; and

(k) views.

(2) For the purpose of this Schedule, the number of pages of prosecution evidence shall include all witness statements, documentary and pictorial exhibits and records of interview with the assisted person and with other defendants forming part of the committal or served prosecution documents or included in any notice of additional evidence.

(3) In the case of proceedings on indictment in the Crown Court initiated otherwise than by committal for trial, the appropriate officer shall determine the number of pages of prosecution evidence as nearly in accordance with the preceding sub-paragraph as the nature of the case permits

(4) A reference to the Table of Offences in this Schedule refers to the Table of Offences at the end of Part 5 and a reference to a Class of Offence in this Schedule refers to the Class in which that offence is listed in the Table of Offences.

2. (1) Subject to the following sub-paragraphs of this paragraph and to paragraph 4, this Schedule applies to every case on indictment.

(2) This Schedule does not apply to a case which goes to trial where the trial exceeds 40 days, unless:

(a) it was accepted by the court at the pleas and directions hearing or plea and case management hearing that the trial would not exceed 40 days but it did; or

(b) the Commission was notified and accepted that the trial would not exceed 40 days but it did; or

(c) the Commission has made an election under article 9A to apply this Schedule to the whole or any part of a Very High Cost Case.

(3) *Revoked.*

(4) *Revoked.*

(5) Where following a trial an order was made for a new trial and the same trial advocate appeared for an assisted person at both trials then, in respect of the new trial, the trial advocate shall receive a graduated fee calculated in accordance with paragraph 7 except that each of the elements of the formula set out in paragraph 7 shall be reduced by:

(a) forty per cent, where the new trial started within one calendar month of the conclusion of the first trial; and

(b) twenty five per cent, where the new trial did not start within one calendar month of the conclusion of the first trial;

except for the refresher element which shall not be so reduced.

(5A) Where following a trial an order was made for a new trial and a different trial advocate appeared for the assisted person at each trial then, in respect of each trial, the trial advocate shall receive a graduated fee calculated in accordance with paragraph 7.

(6) Where following a case on indictment a Newton hearing takes place:

(a) the case shall for all the purposes of this Schedule be treated as having gone to trial;
(b) the length of trial shall be taken to be the combined length of the main hearing and of the Newton hearing;
(c) the provisions of this Schedule relating to cracked trials and guilty pleas shall not apply; and
(d) no fee shall be payable under paragraph 15 in respect of that hearing.

(7) A case on indictment which is discontinued at the pleas and directions hearing or plea and case management hearing other than by reason of pleas of guilty being entered shall for all purposes of this Schedule be treated as a guilty plea.

3. This Schedule also applies to the following proceedings in the Crown Court, subject to paragraph 4:

(a) an appeal against conviction or sentence;
(b) a sentence hearing following a committal for sentence to the Crown Court; and
(c) proceedings arising out of an alleged breach of an order of the Crown Court (whether or not this Schedule applies to the proceedings in which the order was made).

4. This Schedule does not apply to any case where:

(a) the representation order provides for the services of more than two trial advocates; or
(b) the length of the main hearing, or the combined length of the main hearing and of any hearing to which paragraph 2(6), 13 or 14 applies exceeds 40 days, unless:

    (i) it was accepted by the court at the pleas and directions hearing or plea and case management hearing that the trial would not exceed 40 days but it did; or
    (ii) the Commission was notified and accepted that the trial would not exceed 40 days but it did; or
    (iii) the Commission has made an election under article 9A to apply this Schedule to the whole or any part of a Very High Cost Case.

5. (1) *Revoked*.

(2) For the purposes of this Schedule:

(a) every indictable offence falls within the Class under which it is listed in the Table of Offences and, subject to sub-paragraph (3) below, indictable offences not specifically so listed shall be deemed to fall within Class H;
(b) conspiracy to commit an indictable offence contrary to section 1 of the Criminal Law Act 1977, incitement to commit an indictable offence and attempts to commit an indictable offence contrary to section 1 of the Criminal Attempts Act 1981, fall within the same Class as the substantive offence to which they relate;
(c) where the Table specifies that the Class within which an offence falls depends on whether that value involved exceeds a stated limit, the value shall be presumed not to exceed that limit unless the person claiming remuneration proves otherwise to the satisfaction of the appropriate officer;
(d) where more than one count of the indictment is for an offence in relation to which the Class depends on the value involved, that value shall be taken to be the total value involved in all those offences, so however that where two or more counts relate to the same property the value of that property shall be taken into account once only; and
(e) where an entry in the Table of Offences specifies an offence as being contrary to a statutory provision, then subject to any express limitation in the entry that entry shall include every offence contrary to that statutory provision whether or not the words of description in the entry are apt to cover all such offences;
(f) where in a case on indictment there is a hearing to determine the question of whether an assisted person is unfit to plead or unfit to stand trial, that hearing falls within the same Class as the indictable offence to which it relates or within Class D, whichever the trial advocate shall elect; and
(g) where in a case on indictment a restriction order is made under section 41 of the Mental Health Act 1983, the offence falls within Class A, regardless of the Class under which the offence would be listed in the Table of Offences but for this paragraph.

(3) If an advocate in proceedings in the Crown Court is dissatisfied with the classification within Class H of an indictable offence not listed in the Table of Offences, he may apply to the appropriate officer to reclassify the offence.

6. (1) The classes of work for which a graduated or fixed fee calculated in accordance with the following paragraphs of this Schedule shall be allowed in accordance with paragraph 15(2) are those specified in sub-paragraph (2), and the fees for classes of work which are not so specified shall be determined in accordance with paragraph 15.

(2) The classes of work specified for the purposes of sub-paragraph (1) are:

(a) all preparation not falling within sub-paragraph (c) below;
(b) advocacy on the first day of the main hearing;
(c) preparation and advocacy on the second and subsequent days of the main hearing;
(d) appearing at the pleas and directions hearing or plea and case management hearing, if any;
(e) appearing at any other hearings and applications;
(f) listening to or viewing evidence recorded on disc, tape or video cassette;
(g) attending conferences with expert witnesses.

PART 2

GRADUATED FEES FOR TRIAL

7. (1) The amount of the graduated fee for a single trial advocate representing one assisted person being tried on one indictment in the Crown Court shall be calculated according to the following formulae:

(a) for trials not exceeding 10 days and trials lasting 26 to 40 days—

$$G = B + (d \times D) + (e \times E) + (w \times W) + (d \times R); \text{ and}$$

(b) for trials lasting 11 to 25 days—

$$G = B + (d \times D) + (e \times E) + (w \times W) + (d \times R) + d \times (D \times (d-9) \times g).$$

(2) In the formulae in sub-paragraph (1):G is the amount of the graduated fee;

B is the basic fee specified in paragraph 8 as appropriate to the offence for which the assisted person is tried and the category of trial advocate instructed;

d is the number of days or parts of a day by which the trial exceeds one day;

e is the number of pages of prosecution evidence excluding the first 50 up to a maximum of 10,000;

w is the number of prosecution witnesses excluding the first 10;

D is the length of trial uplifts specified in paragraph 8 as appropriate to the offence for which the assisted person is tried and the category of trial advocate instructed;

E is the evidence uplift specified in paragraph 8 as appropriate to the offence for which the assisted person is tried and the category of trial advocate instructed;

W is the witness uplift specified in paragraph 8 as appropriate to the offence for which the assisted person is tried and the category of trial advocate instructed;

R is the refresher specified in paragraph 8 as appropriate to the offence for which the assisted person is tried and the category of trial advocate instructed;

g is the length of trial gradient specified in paragraph 8 as appropriate to the offence for which the assisted person is tried and the category of trial advocate instructed.

8. For the purposes of paragraph 7 the basic fee, refresher, length of trial gradient, length of trial uplift, evidence uplift and witness uplift appropriate to any offence shall be those specified in the Table below as appropriate to the Class within which that offence falls according to paragraph 5, the length of trial and the category of trial advocate instructed.

TABLE OF FEES AND UPLIFTS

(A) TRIALS (1–10 DAYS)—QUEEN'S COUNCIL

Offence falling within	Basic fee	Refresher	Length of trial uplift: per day	Evidence uplift: per page	Witnesses uplift: per witness
Class A	£1,618.75	£453.25	£685.13	£1.45	£6.16
Class B	£853.13	£319.38	£481.25	£2.17	£14.37
Class C	£853.13	£319.38	£481.25	£2.17	£14.37
Class D	£853.13	£319.38	£481.25	£2.17	£14.37
Class E	£853.13	£319.38	£481.25	£2.17	£14.37
Class F	£853.13	£319.38	£481.25	£2.17	£14.37
Class G	£853.13	£319.38	£481.25	£2.17	£14.37
Class H	£853.13	£319.38	£481.25	£2.17	£14.37
Class I	£853.13	£319.38	£481.25	£2.17	£14.37

(B) TRIALS (1–10 DAYS)—OTHER TRIAL ADVOCATES

Offence falling within	Basic fee	Refresher	Length of trial uplift: per day	Evidence uplift: per page	Witnesses uplift: per witness
Class A	£740	£207	£313	£0.66	£2.82
Class B	£250	£136	£143	£1.48	£12.22
Class C	£250	£136	£143	£1.48	£12.22
Class D	£390	£146	£220	£0.99	£6.57
Class E	£210	£124	£109	£1.21	£5.10
Class F	£210.	£124	£109	£1.21	£5.10
Class G	£370	£146	£210	£2.02	£16.64
Class H	£250.	£136	£143	£1.48	£12.22
Class I	£250	£136	£143	£1.48	£12.22

(c) TRIALS (11–25 DAYS)—QUEEN'S COUNSEL

Offence falling within	Basic fee	Refresher	Length of trial uplift: per day	Evidence uplift: per page	Witnesses uplift: per witness	Length of trial gradient
Class A	£1,618.75	£453.25	£856.63	£1.82	£7.70	0%
Class B	£853.13	£319.38	£602	£2.71	£17.96	0%
Class C	£853.13	£319.38	£602	£2.71	£17.96	0%
Class D	£853.13	£319.38	£602	£2.71	£17.96	0%
Class E	£853.13	£319.38	£602	£2.71	£17.96	0%
Class F	£853.13	£319.38	£602	£2.71	£17.96	0%
Class G	£853.13	£319.38	£602	£2.71	£17.96	0%
Class H	£853.13	£319.38	£602	£2.71	£17.96	0%
Class I	£853.13	£319.38	£602	£2.71	£17.96	0%

(D) Trials (11–25 days) — other trial advocates

Offence falling within	Basic fee	Refresher	Length of trial uplift: per day	Evidence uplift: per page	Witnesses uplift: per witness	Length of trial gradient
Class A	£740	£311	£376	£0.79	£3.38	0%
Class B	£250	£204	£172	£1.78	£14.66	0%
Class C	£250	£204	£172	£1.78	£14.66	0%
Class D	£390	£219	£264	£1.19	£7.88	0%
Class E	£210	£186	£131	£1.45	£6.12	0%
Class F	£210	£186	£131	£1.45	£6.12	0%
Class G	£370	£219	£252	£2.42	£19.97	0%
Class H	£250	£204	£172	£1.78	£14.66	0%
Class I	£250	£204	£172	£1.78	£14.66	0%

(E) Trials (26–40 days) — Queen's Counsel

Offence falling within	Basic fee	Refresher	Length of trial uplift: per day	Evidence uplift: per page	Witnesses uplift: per witness
Class A	£1,618.75	£453.25	£856.63	£1.82	£7.70
Class B	£853.13	£319.38	£602	£2.71	£17.56
Class C	£853.13	£319.38	£602	£2.71	£17.56
Class D	£853.13	£319.38	£602	£2.71	£17.56
Class E	£853.13	£319.38	£602	£2.71	£17.56
Class F	£853.13	£319.38	£602	£2.71	£17.56
Class G	£853.13	£319.38	£602	£2.71	£17.56
Class H	£853.13	£319.38	£602	£2.71	£17.56
Class I	£853.13	£319.38	£602	£2.71	£17.56

(F) Trials (26–40 days) — other trial advocates

Offence falling within	Basic fee	Refresher	Length of trial uplift: per day	Evidence uplift: per page	Witnesses uplift: per witness
Class A	£740	£311	£376	£0.79	£3.38
Class B	£250	£204	£172	£1.78	£14.66
Class C	£250	£204	£172	£1.78	£14.66
Class D	£390	£219	£264	£1.19	£7.88
Class E	£210	£186	£131	£1.45	£6.12
Class F	£210	£186	£131	£1.45	£6.12
Class G	£370	£219	£252	£2.42	£19.97
Class H	£250	£204	£172	£1.78	£14.66
Class I	£250	£204	£172	£1.78	£14.66

Part 3
Graduated Fees for Guilty Pleas and Cracked Trials

9. (1) The amount of the graduated fee for a single trial advocate representing one assisted person in a guilty plea or cracked trial shall be the basic fee specified in paragraph 10 as appropriate to the offence with which the assisted person is charged, the category of trial advocate instructed and whether the case is a guilty plea or a cracked trial, increased by the evidence and witness uplifts.

(2) The evidence and witness uplifts shall be calculated in accordance with the Table in paragraph 10.

(3) A case on indictment in which a pleas and directions hearing or plea and case management hearing takes place is a cracked trial if it fulfils the following conditions:

(a) the matter did not proceed to trial (whether by reason of pleas of guilty or for other reasons) or the prosecution offered no evidence, and

(b)

(i) in respect of one or more counts to which the assisted person pleaded guilty, he did not so plead at the pleas and directions hearing or plea and case management hearing; or

(ii) in respect of one or more counts which were not proceeded with, the prosecution did not, before or at the pleas and directions hearing or plea and case management hearing, declare an intention of not proceeding with them.

(4) A case on indictment in which no pleas and directions hearing or plea and case management hearing takes place is a cracked trial if it was listed for trial but the case was disposed of without a trial (whether by reason of pleas of guilty or for other reasons) or the prosecution offered no evidence.

(5) A case on indictment is a guilty plea if it was disposed of without a trial because the assisted person pleaded guilty to one or more counts and is not a cracked trial.

10. (1) Subject to sub-paragraphs (2) and (3) of this paragraph ,for the purposes of paragraph 9 the basic fee and evidence and witness uplifts appropriate to any offence shall be those specified in the Table below as appropriate to the class within which that offence falls according to paragraph 5 and the category of trial advocate instructed.

TABLE OF FEES AND UPLIFTS

(A) GUILTY PLEA AND TRIALS THAT CRACK IN THE FIRST THIRD — QUEEN'S COUNSEL

Offence falling within	Basic fee	Evidence uplift Per page (pages 1 to 1,000)	Evidence uplift Per page (pages 1,001 to 10,000)
Class A	£1,214.50	£2.18	£1.09
Class B	£639.63	£1.93	£0.96
Class C	£639.63	£1.37	£0.68
Class D	£639.63	£3.06	£1.53
Class E	£639.63	£0.98	£0.49
Class F	£639.63	£1.29	£0.65
Class G	£639.63	£1.71	£0.85
Class H	£639.63	£1.77	£0.88
Class I	£639.63	£1.72	£0.86

(B) TRIALS THAT CRACK BEYOND THE FIRST THIRD — QUEEN'S COUNSEL

Offence falling within	Basic fee	Evidence uplift per page (pages 1 to 1,000)	Witness uplift per witness (witnesses 11 to 80)	A case that cracks in the second third — Evidence uplift per page (pages 1,001 to 10,000)	A case that cracks in the last third — Evidence uplift per page (pages 1,001 to 10,000)	A case that cracks in the second third — Witness uplift (witnesses in excess of 80)	A case that cracks in the last third — Witness uplift (witnesses in excess of 80)
Class A	£1,618.75	£4.36	£19.57	£1.44	£4.36	£4.89	£19.57
Class B	£853.13	£3.86	£26.14	£1.28	£3.86	£6.54	£26.14
Class C	£853.13	£2.74	£21.40	£0.90	£2.74	£5.36	£21.40
Class D	£853.13	£6.12	£43.41	£2.02	£6.12	£10.85	£43.41
Class E	£853.13	£1.96	£15.01	£0.65	£1.96	£3.75	£15.01
Class F	£853.13	£2.57	£19.44	£0.85	£2.57	£4.87	£19.44
Class G	£853.13	£3.41	£23.02	£1.13	£3.41	£5.76	£23.02
Class H	£853.13	£3.53	£23.35	£1.16	£3.53	£5.84	£23.35
Class I	£853.13	£3.45	£23.92	£1.14	£3.45	£5.99	£23.92]

(C) GUILTY PLEAS AND TRIALS THAT CRACK IN THE FIRST THIRD — OTHER TRIAL ADVOCATES

Offence falling within	Basic fee	Evidence uplift per page (pages 1 to 1,000)	Evidence uplift per page (pages 1,001 to 10,000)
Class A	£555	£1.14	£0.57
Class B	£188	£0.99	£0.50
Class C	£188	£0.74	£0.37
Class D	£293	£1.45	£0.72
Class E	£158	£0.43	£0.22
Class F	£158	£0.66	£0.33
Class G	£278	£1.25	£0.63
Class H	£188	£0.67	£0.33
Class I	£188	£0.52	£0.26

(D) TRIALS THAT CRACK BEYOND THE FIRST THIRD — OTHER TRIAL ADVOCATES

Offence falling within	Basic fee	Evidence uplift per page (pages 1 to 250)	Evidence uplift per page (pages 251 to 1,000)	Witness uplift per witness (witnesses 11 to 80)	A case that cracks in the second third — Evidence uplift per page (pages 1,001 to 10,000)	A case that cracks in the last third — Evidence uplift per page (pages 1,001 to 10,000)	A case that cracks in the second third — Witness uplift (witnesses in excess of 80)	A case that cracks in the last third — Witness uplift (witnesses in excess of 80)
Class A	£740.00	£4.91	£2.28	£11.53	£0.75	£2.28	£2.88	£11.53
Class B	£250.00	£4.27	£1.99	£23.29	£0.66	£1.99	£5.82	£23.29
Class C	£250.00	£3.17	£1.47	£34.69	£0.49	£1.47	£8.67	£34.69
Class D	£390.00	£6.22	£2.89	£28.79	£0.95	£2.89	£7.20	£28.79
Class E	£210.00	£1.86	£0.87	£11.91	£0.29	£0.87	£2.98	£11.91
Class F	£210.00	£2.86	£1.33	£9.39	£0.44	£1.33	£2.35	£9.39
Class G	£370.00	£5.39	£2.51	£22.55	£0.83	£2.51	£5.64	£22.55
Class H	£250.00	£2.87	£1.34	£31.30	£0.44	£1.34	£7.83	£31.30
Class I	£250.00	£2.24	£1.04	£18.85	£0.34	£1.04	£4.71	£18.85]

(2) Where the trial of a case does not commence on the date first fixed or, if it is entered in a warned list, the case is not taken and disposed of from the first warned list in which it is entered, the basic fee and evidence and witness uplifts for the offence shall be those specified for the last third in the Table in sub-paragraph (1) above.

(3) In this paragraph references to the first, second and last third are references to the first, second and last third—

(i) where a case is first listed for trial on a fixed date, of the period of time beginning after the date the case is so listed and ending before the date so fixed,

(ii) where the case is first placed in a warned list, of the period of time beginning after the date on which the case is so placed and ending before the date of the start of that warned list, and

where the number of days in this period of time cannot be divided by three equally, any days remaining after such division shall be added to the last third.

PART 4
FIXED AND HOURLY FEES

11. (1) The basic fee payable for any person for appearing at a hearing that was listed as a pleas and directions hearing or plea and case management hearing or a pre-trial review shall be that set out in the Table following paragraph 22 as appropriate to the category of trial advocate or other advocate but where a fee is also payable under sub-paragraph (2), an amount equal to that fee shall be deducted from the fee payable under this sub-paragraph.

(2) The basic fee payable to any person for entering a paper plea and directions shall be that set out in the Table following paragraph 22.

(3) This paragraph does not apply to a pleas and directions hearing or plea and case management hearing which is or forms part of the main hearing in a case.

12. (1) The fixed fee set out in the Table following paragraph 22 as appropriate to the category of trial advocate shall be payable where:

(a) the assisted person fails to attend any hearing at which the trial advocate appears;
(b) at that hearing a bench warrant is issued for the arrest of the assisted person; and
(c) that warrant is not executed within the three months beginning on the date on which it was issued.

(2) The fixed fee set out in the Table following paragraph 22 as appropriate to the category of trial advocate shall be payable in respect of each occasion on which the case was listed for trial but did not proceed on the day for which it was listed (other than by reason of an application for postponement by the prosecution or the defence).

13. (1) This paragraph applies to:

(a) the hearing of an application to stay the indictment or any count on the ground that the proceedings constitute an abuse of the process of the court;
(b) any hearing relating to the question of whether any material should be disclosed by the prosecution to the defence or the defence to the prosecution (whether or not any claim to public interest immunity is made); and
(c) the hearing of an application under section 2(1) of the Criminal Procedure (Attendance of Witnesses) Act 1965 for disclosure of material held by third parties;
(d) any hearing relating to the question of the admissibility as evidence of any material.

(2) Where a hearing to which this paragraph applies is held on any day of the main hearing of a case on indictment, no separate fee shall be payable in respect of attendance at the hearing, but the hearing shall be included in the length of the main hearing for the purpose of calculating remuneration.

(3) Where a hearing to which this paragraph applies is held prior to the first or only day of the main hearing, it shall not be included in the length of the main hearing for the purpose of calculating remuneration and the trial advocate or other advocate shall be remunerated for attendance at such a hearing:

(a) in respect of any day where the hearing begins before and ends after the luncheon adjournment, at the daily rate set out in the Table following paragraph 22 as appropriate to the category of trial advocate or other advocate and length of the trial;
(b) in respect of any day where the hearing begins and ends before the luncheon adjournment, or begins after the luncheon adjournment, at the half-daily rate set out in the Table following paragraph 22 as appropriate to the category of trial advocate or other advocate and length of the trial.

14. (1) This paragraph applies to:

(a) a hearing to which the court proceeds under section 2 of the Drug Trafficking Act 1994;
(b) a hearing to which the court proceeds under section 71 of the Criminal Justice Act 1988; and
(c) a hearing to which the court proceeds under Part 2 of the Proceeds of Crime Act 2002.

(2) A hearing to which this paragraph applies shall not be included in the length of the main hearing or of any sentencing hearing for the purpose of calculating remuneration, and the trial advocate or other advocate shall be remunerated for attendance at such a hearing:

(a) in respect of any day where the hearing begins before and ends after the luncheon adjournment, at the daily rate set out in the Table following paragraph 22 as appropriate to the category of trial advocate or other advocate and length of the trial; and
(b) in respect of any day where the hearing begins and ends before the luncheon adjournment, or begins after the luncheon adjournment, at the half-daily rate set out in the Table following paragraph 22 as appropriate to the category of trial advocate or other advocate and length of the trial.

15. (1) The fee payable to any person for appearing at a hearing to which this paragraph applies shall be that set out in the Table following paragraph 22 as appropriate to the category of person appearing and the circumstances of the hearing.

(2) This paragraph applies to the following hearings:

(a) a sentencing hearing following a case on indictment to which this Schedule applies, where sentence has been deferred under section 1 of the Powers of Criminal Courts (Sentencing) Act 2000;
(b) a sentencing hearing following a case on indictment to which this Schedule applies, other than a hearing within paragraph (a) or a sentencing hearing forming part of the main hearing.

16. A fee under this paragraph, of the amount set out in the Table following paragraph 22 as appropriate to the category of the person appearing, shall be payable to any person (whether the trial advocate or not) for appearing in the following hearings in a case on indictment or in any proceedings specified in paragraph 3 of this Schedule, when not forming part of the main hearing or a hearing for which a fee is provided elsewhere in this Schedule:

(a) the hearing of a case listed for plea which is adjourned for trial;

(b) any hearing (other than a trial, a pleas and directions hearing, a plea and case management hearing or a pre-trial review) which is listed but cannot proceed because of the failure of the assisted person or a witness to attend, the unavailability of a pre-sentence report or other good reason;

(c) bail, custody time limit applications and other applications; and

(d) the hearing of the case listed for mention only, including applications relating to the date of the trial.

16A. The fixed fee set out in the Table following paragraph 22 as appropriate to the category of trial advocate shall be payable in respect of each occasion on which the case was listed for trial but did not proceed on the day for which it was listed by reason of an application for postponement by the prosecution or the defence.

17. (1) Where this paragraph applies, a special preparation fee may be claimed in addition to the graduated fee payable under this Schedule.

(2) This paragraph applies where, in any case on indictment in the Crown Court in respect of which a graduated fee is payable under this Schedule, it has been necessary for the trial advocate to do work by way of preparation substantially in excess of the amount normally done for cases of the same type because the case involves a very unusual or novel point of law or factual issue.

(3) The amount of the special preparation fee shall be calculated from the number of hours' preparation in excess of the amount normally done for cases of the same type, using the rates of hourly fees set out in the table following paragraph 22 as appropriate to the category of trial advocate and length of the trial.

(4) A trial advocate claiming a special preparation fee shall supply such information and documents as may be required by the appropriate officer as proof of the unusual nature or novelty of the point of law or factual issue and of the number of hours of preparation.

17A. (1) Where this paragraph applies, a special preparation fee may be claimed in addition to the graduated fee payable under this Schedule.

(2) This paragraph applies where, in any case on indictment in the Crown Court in respect of which a graduated fee is payable under this Schedule, the pages of prosecution evidence as defined in paragraph 1(2) in Part 1 of this Schedule exceeds 10,000 and the appropriate officer considers it reasonable to make a payment in excess of the graduated fee payable under this Schedule.

(3) The amount of the special preparation fee shall be calculated from the number of hours' preparation in excess of the amount normally done for cases of the same type, using the rates of hourly fees set out in the table following paragraph 22 as appropriate to the category of trial advocate and length of the trial.

(4) A trial advocate claiming a special preparation fee shall supply such information and documents as may be required by the appropriate officer in support of his claim.

18. (1) A wasted preparation fee may be claimed where a trial advocate instructed in any case to which this paragraph applies is prevented from representing the assisted person in the main hearing by any of the following circumstances:

(a) the trial advocate is instructed to appear in other proceedings at the same time as the main hearing in the case and has been unable to secure a change of date for either the main hearing or the other proceedings;

(b) the date fixed for the main hearing is changed by the court despite the trial advocate's objection;

(c) the trial advocate has withdrawn from the case with the leave of the court because of his professional code of conduct or to avoid embarrassment in the exercise of his profession;

(d) the trial advocate has been dismissed by his client;

(e) the trial advocate is obliged to attend at any place by reason of a judicial office held by him or other public duty.

(2) This paragraph applies to every case on indictment to which this Schedule applies provided that:

(a) the case goes to trial, and the trial lasts for five days or more; or

(b) the case is a cracked trial, and the number of pages of prosecution evidence exceeds 150.

(3) The amount of the wasted preparation fee shall be calculated from the number of hours of preparation reasonably carried out by the trial advocate, using the rates for hourly fees set out in the Table following paragraph 22 as appropriate to the category of trial advocate and length of the trial; but no such fee shall be payable unless the number of hours of preparation is eight or more.

(4) A trial advocate claiming a wasted preparation fee shall supply such information and documents as may be required by the appropriate officer as proof of the circumstances in which he was prevented from representing the assisted person and of the number of hours of preparation.

19. (1) The hourly fee set out in the Table following paragraph 22 as appropriate to the category of trial advocate and length of the trial shall be payable in respect of work of the following types, provided that the trial advocate satisfies the appropriate officer that the work was reasonably necessary, namely:

(a) attendance by the trial advocate at conferences with prospective or actual expert witnesses; or

(aa) attendance by the trial advocate at one view per case for up to one hour (exclusive of travelling time); or

(b) travel for the purpose of attending a view, or a conference with the assisted person, where the appropriate officer is satisfied that the assisted person was unable or could not reasonably have been expected to attend a conference at the trial advocate's office or chambers; or

(c) attendance by the trial advocate at pre-trial conferences with the assisted person not held at court, provided that such conferences do not exceed the number and length set out in sub-paragraph (1A);

and where that fee is allowed the trial advocate shall also be paid the reasonable expenses of travelling to and from the conference.

(1A) The number and length of conferences for which the hourly fee set out in sub-paragraph (1) above shall be payable is as follows:

(a) for trials that do not exceed 10 days, cracked trials where it was accepted by the court at the pleas and directions hearing or plea and case management hearing that the trial would not exceed 10 days and any guilty pleas, one conference not exceeding 2 hours;

(b) for trials lasting not less than 11 and not more than 15 days and cracked trials where it was accepted by the court at the pleas and directions hearing or the plea and case management hearing that the trial would last not less than 11 days and not more than 15 days, two conferences each not exceeding 2 hours;

(c) for trials lasting not less than 16 and not more than 20 days and cracked trials where it was accepted by the court at the pleas and directions hearing or the plea and case management hearing that the trial would last not less than 16 days and not more than 20 days, 3 conferences each not exceeding 2 hours;

(d) for trials lasting not less than 21 and not more than 25 days and cracked trials where it was accepted by the court at the pleas and directions hearing or the plea and case management hearing that the trial would last not less than 21 days and not more than 25 days, 4 conferences each not exceeding 2 hours;

(e) for trials lasting not less than 26 days and not more than 35 days and cracked trials where it was accepted by the court at the pleas and directions hearing or the plea and case management hearing that the trial would last not less than 26 days and not more than 35 days, 5 conferences each not exceeding 2 hours;

(f) for trials lasting not less than 36 days and not more than 40 days and cracked trials where it was accepted by the court at the pleas and directions hearing or the plea and case management hearing that the trial would last not less than 36 days and not more than 40 days, 6 conferences each not exceeding 2 hours;

(g) for trials lasting not less than 26 days and not more than 35 days, where the Commission has made an election under article 9A to apply this Schedule, 5 conferences each not exceeding 2 hours; and

(h) for trials lasting not less than 36 days, where the Commission has made an election under article 9A to apply this Schedule, 6 conferences each not exceeding 2 hours.

(2) In any case on indictment, a trial advocate shall be entitled to a fee in accordance with the Table following paragraph 22 for the number of periods or parts of a period of 10 minutes of running time of any disc, tape or video cassette or part thereof which he listens to or views as part of the evidence in the case.

20. The additional fee set out in the Table following paragraph 22 shall be payable in respect of each day of the main hearing in any case mentioned in paragraph 2 on which the trial advocate appears unattended by the representative.

21. (1) Subject to paragraph 15(4) of Schedule 1, and to paragraph 23(2), the remuneration payable to a trial advocate instructed in any case mentioned in paragraph 3 shall be the fixed fee set out in the Table following paragraph 22.

(2) Where the trial advocate appears in any case mentioned in paragraph 3 unattended by a representative, he shall be entitled to the additional fee set out in that Table.

22. The remuneration payable to a representative retained solely for the purpose of making a note of any hearing shall be the daily fee set out in the Table following this paragraph.

TABLE

Type of work	Paragraph providing for fee	Fee for Queen's Counsel £	Fee for leading advocate (other than Queen's Counsel) £	Fee for junior or soe advocate (other than Queen's Counsel) £
Paper Pleas and directions basic fee		30.00	30.00	30.00
Pleas and directions hearing or plea and case management hearing or pre-trial review—basic fee	11(1)	188.00	127.00	100.00
Attendance where bench warrant issued	12(1)	250.00	170.00	100.00
Appearing at listed trial that did not proceed—basic fee	12(2)	275.00	187.00	110.00
Work for which daily or half daily fee is payable	13 and 14	Guilty pleas, cracked trials and trials lasting 1–10 days: 330.00 per day 185.00 per half day Trials lasting 11–25 days and trials lasting 26–40 days: 495.00 per day 277.50 per half day	Guilty pleas, cracked trials and trials lasting 1–10 days: 250.00 per day 140.00 per half day Trials lasting 11–25 days and trials lasting 26–40 days: 375.00 per day 210.00 per half day	Guilty pleas, cracked trials and trials lasting 1–10 days: 178.25 per day 99.50 per half day Trials lasting 11–25 days and trials lasting 26–40 days: 267.45 per day 149.25 per half day
Appearing at deferred sentencing hearing	15(2)(a)	300.00	204.00	120.00
Appearing at other sentencing hearing	15(2)(b)	150.00	102.00	60.00
Other appearances	16	116.00	79.00	46.50
Appearing at listed trial that did not proceed because of adjournment application	16A	116.00	79.00	55.00
Work for which hourly fee is payable	17, 18, 19(1) and (2), 29 and 30	Guilty pleas, cracked trials and trials lasting 1–10 days: 62.50 per hour Trials lasting 11–25 days and trials lasting 26–40 days: 75.00 per hour	Guilty pleas, cracked trials and trials lasting 1–10 days: 47.00 per hour Trials lasting 11–25 days and trials lasting 26–40 days: 56.40 per hour	Guilty pleas, cracked trials and trials lasting 1–10 days: 33.50 per hour Trials lasting 11–25 days and trials lasting 26–40 days: 40.20 per hour
Listening to or viewing tapes etc	19(3)	27.15 per 10 minutes	18.50 per 10 minutes	10.90 per 10 minutes
Additional fee for unattended advocate, case within paragraph 2	20	38.50 per day	38.50 per day	38.50 per day
Appearing in appeal against conviction	21(1)	292.25	199.00	117.00

Type of work	Paragraph providing for fee	Fee for Queen's Counsel	Fee for leading advocate (other than Queen's Counsel)	Fee for junior or sole advocate (other than Queen's Counsel)
		£	£	£
Appearing at a committal for sentence hearing	21(1)	184.50	125.00	85.00
Appearing within other cases within paragraph 3	21(1)	184.50	125.00	73.50
Additional fee for unattended advocate	21(2)	19.25	19.25	19.25
Noting brief	22	–	–	100.00 per day

PART 5

MISCELLANEOUS

23. (1) Where an assisted person is charged with more than one offence on one indictment, the graduated fee payable to the trial advocate shall be based on whichever of those offences he shall select for the purposes
(2) Where two or more cases to which this Schedule applies involving the same trial advocate are heard concurrently (whether involving the same or different assisted persons):

(a) the trial advocate shall select one case ("the principal case"), which shall be treated for the purposes of remuneration in accordance with the previous paragraphs of this Schedule;
(b) in respect of the main hearing in each of the other cases the trial advocate shall be paid a fixed fee of twenty per cent of:

(i) the basic fee for the principal case, where that is a case falling within paragraph 2, or
(ii) the fixed fee for the principal case, where that is a case falling within paragraph 3.

(3) Where a person appears at a hearing specified in paragraph 11, 12(2), 13, 14, 15, 16(a) or (b) or 16A, forming part of two or more cases involving different assisted persons, he shall be paid:

(a) in respect of the first such case, the fixed fee for that hearing specified in the Table following paragraph 22; and
(b) in respect of each of the other cases, twenty per cent of that fee.

(4) Subject to sub-paragraphs (1) to (3), where a person appears at a hearing forming part of two or more cases, he shall be paid the fixed fee for that hearing specified in the Table following paragraph 22 in respect of one such case, without any increase in respect of the other cases
24. (1) Where in any case on indictment two trial advocates are instructed to represent the same assisted person:

(a) if the leading advocate is a Queen's Counsel, he shall receive the same graduated fee as if he were appearing alone;
(b) if the leading advocate is not a Queen's Counsel, he shall receive the proportion of the graduated fee payable to Queen's Counsel appearing alone calculated by dividing that fee by 875 and multiplying the product by 750;
(c) in either case, the junior advocate shall receive the proportion of the graduated fee payable to a Queen's Counsel appearing alone calculated by dividing that fee by 875 and multiplying the product by 500.

(2) Where the assisted person is represented by a single trial advocate and another person charged on the same indictment with an offence falling within the same class is represented by two trial advocates, the single trial advocate shall receive the same graduated fee as if he were appearing as junior to another trial advocate.
(3) Sub-paragraph (2) shall not apply where the charge which the single trial advocate is instructed to defend (or where there is more than one such charge, the charge forming the basis of remuneration in accordance with paragraph 23(1)) is for an offence falling within Class A.
25. Where a person is instructed to appear in court which is not within 40 kilometres of his office or chambers, the appropriate officer may allow an amount for travelling and other expenses incidental to that appearance; provided that the amount shall not be greater than the amount, if any, which would be payable to a trial advocate from the nearest local Bar or the nearest advocate's office (whichever is the nearer) unless the person instructed to appear has obtained prior approval under CDS Regulations for the incurring of such expenses or can justify his attendance having regard to all the relevant circumstances of the case.
26. Where a trial exceeds 40 days, the trial advocate shall receive:

(a) a graduated fee calculated in accordance with the formula in paragraph 7(1)(a) as if the trial had lasted 40 days; and
(b) the refresher specified in paragraph 8 as appropriate to the offence increased by:

(i) forty per cent for each of the days by which the trial exceeds 40 days but does not exceed 50 days; and
(ii) fifty per cent for each of the days by which the trial exceeds 50 days.

27. Where in any case a hearing is held to determine the question of whether the assisted person is unfit to plead or to stand trial or where there is a subsequent trial of the issue once the assisted person has been found unfit (a "fitness hearing"):

(a) if a trial on indictment is held at any time thereafter, the length of the fitness hearing shall be included in determining the length of the trial for the calculation of the graduated fee in accordance with Part 2 of this Schedule;
(b) if a trial on indictment is not held thereafter by reason of the assisted person being found unfit to plead or to stand trial, the trial advocate shall receive either a graduated fee calculated in accordance with Part 2 of this Schedule as appropriate to the length of the fitness hearing or a graduated fee calculated in accordance with Part 3 of this Schedule as appropriate for representing an assisted person in a cracked trial, whichever the trial advocate shall elect; and

(c) if at any time the assisted person pleads guilty to the indictable offence, the trial advocate shall be paid either a graduated fee calculated in accordance with Part 2 of this Schedule as appropriate to the length of the fitness hearing or a graduated fee calculated in accordance with Part 3 of this Schedule as appropriate for representing an assisted person in a guilty plea, whichever the trial advocate shall elect.

28. (1) Where in any case on indictment an advocate is retained solely for the purpose of cross-examining a vulnerable witness under sections 34 and 35 of the Youth Justice and Criminal Evidence Act 1999, he shall receive a graduated fee calculated in accordance with Part 2 of this Schedule.

(2) For the purposes of this paragraph the length of trial uplift and refresher shall be as set out in the Table following paragraph 8 as appropriate to the number of days of attendance at court by the advocate.

29. (1) Where in any case on indictment a person is assigned under a representation order solely for the purpose of providing written or oral advice, he shall be paid in respect of that advice a fee calculated from the reasonable number of hours of preparation for that advice using the rates of hourly fees set out in the table following paragraph 22 as appropriate to the category of trial advocate and length of trial.

(2) A person claiming a fee for advice under this paragraph may apply to the appropriate officer to redetermine the fee under paragraph 20(1)(c) of Schedule 1 and he shall supply such information and documents as may be required by the appropriate officer as proof of the number of hours of preparation.

30. (1) Where in any case on indictment a person is assigned under a representation order to appear at a sentencing hearing solely for the purpose of applying to the court to mitigate the assisted person's sentence, he shall be paid in respect of that appearance the fee payable under paragraph 15 as appropriate to the nature of the sentencing hearing together with a fee calculated from the reasonable number of hours of preparation for that appearance using the rates of hourly fees set out in the table following paragraph 22 as appropriate to the category of trial advocate and length of trial.

(2) A person claiming an hourly preparation fee under this paragraph may apply to the appropriate officer to redetermine such hourly fee under paragraph 20(1)(c) of Schedule 1 and he shall supply such information and documents as may be required by the appropriate officer as proof of the number of hours of preparation.

TABLE OF OFFENCES

Offence	Contrary to	Year and chapter
Class A: Homicide and related grave offences		
Murder	Common law	
Manslaughter	Common law	
Soliciting to murder	Offences against the Person Act 1861 s 4	1861 c 100
Child destruction	Infant Life (Preservation) Act 1929 s 1(1)	1929 c 34
Infanticide	Infanticide Act 1938 s 1(1)	1938 c 36
Causing explosion likely to endanger life or property	Explosive Substances Act 1883 s 2	1883 c 3
Attempt to cause explosion, making or keeping explosive etc	Explosive Substances Act 1883 s 3	as above
Class B: Offences involving serious violence or damage, and serious drugs offences		
Kidnapping	Common law	
False imprisonment	Common law	
Aggravated criminal damage	Criminal Damage Act 1971 s 1(2)	1971 c 48
Aggravated arson	Criminal Damage Act 1971 s 1(2), (3)	as above
Arson (where value exceeds £30,000)	Criminal Damage Act 1971 s 1(3)	as above
Possession of firearm with intent to endanger life	Firearms Act 1968 s 16	1968 c 27
Use of firearm to resist arrest	Firearms Act 1968 s 17	as above
Possession of firearm with criminal intent	Firearms Act 1968 s 18	as above
Possession or acquisition of certain prohibited weapons etc	Firearms Act 1968 s 5	1968 c 27
Aggravated burglary	Theft Act 1968 s 10	1968 c 60
Armed robbery	Theft Act 1968 s 8(1)	as above
Assault with weapon with intent to rob	Theft Act 1968 s 8(2)	as above
Blackmail	Theft Act 1968 s 21	as above
Riot	Public Order Act 1986 s 1	1986 c 64
Violent disorder	Public Order Act 1986 s 2	as above
Contamination of goods with intent	Public Order Act 1986 s 38	as above
Causing death by dangerous driving	Road Traffic Act 1988 s 1	1988 c 52
Causing death by careless driving while under the influence of drink or drugs	Road Traffic Act 1988 s 3A	as above
Aggravated vehicle taking resulting in death	Theft Act 1968 s 12A	1968 c 60
Causing danger to road users	Road Traffic Act 1988 s 22A	1988 c 52
Attempting to choke, suffocate, strangle etc	Offences against the Person Act 1861 s 21	1861 c 100
Causing miscarriage by poison, instrument	Offences against the Person Act 1861 s 58	as above
Making threats to kill	Offences against the Person Act 1861 s 16	as above
Wounding or grievous bodily harm with intent to cause grievous bodily harm etc	Offences against the Person Act 1861 s 18	as above
Endangering the safety of railway passengers	Offences against the Person Act 1861 ss 32, 33, 34	as above
Impeding persons endeavouring to escape wrecks	Offences against the Person Act 1861 s 17	as above
Administering chloroform, laudanum etc	Offences against the Person Act 1861 s 22	as above
Administering poison etc so as to endanger life	Offences against the Person Act 1861 s 23	as above
Cruelty to persons under 16	Children and Young Persons Act 1933 s 1	1933 c 12
Aiding and abetting suicide	Suicide Act 1961 s 2	1961 c 60
Placing wood etc on railway	Malicious Damage Act 1861 s 35	1861 c 97
Exhibiting false signals etc	Malicious Damage Act 1861 s 47	as above
Prison mutiny	Prison Security Act 1992 s 1	1992 c 25
Assaulting prison officer whilst possessing firearm etc	Criminal Justice Act 1991 s 90	1991 c 53

Offence	Contrary to	Year and chapter
Acquiring, possessing etc the proceeds of criminal conduct	Criminal Justice Act 1988 s 93	1988 c 33
Producing or supplying a Class A or B drug	Misuse of Drugs Act 1971 s 4	1971 c 38
Possession of a Class A or B drug with intent to supply	Misuse of Drugs Act 1971 s 5(3)	as above
Manufacture and supply of scheduled substances	Criminal Justice (International Co-operation) Act 1990 s 12	1990 c 5
Fraudulent evasion of controls on Class A and B drugs	Customs and Excise Management Act 1979 ss 1, 70(2)(b), (c)	1979 c 2
Illegal importation of Class A and B drugs	Customs and Excise Management Act 1979 s 50	as above
Offences in relation to proceeds of drug trafficking	Drug Trafficking Act 1994 ss 49, 50 and 51	1994 c 37
Offences in relation to money laundering investigations	Drug Trafficking Act 1994 ss 52 and 53	as above
Practitioner contravening drug supply regulations	Misuse of Drugs Act 1971 ss 12 and 13	1971 c 38
Cultivation of cannabis plant	Misuse of Drugs Act 1971 s 6	as above
Occupier knowingly permitting drugs offences etc	Misuse of Drugs Act 1971 s 8	as above
Activities relating to opium	Misuse of Drugs Act 1971 s 9	as above
Drug trafficking offences at sea	Criminal Justice (International Co-operation) Act 1990 s 18	1990 c 5
Firing on Revenue vessel	Customs and Excise Management Act 1979 s 85	1979 c 2
Making or possession of explosive in suspicious circumstances	Explosive Substances Act 1883 s 4(1)	1883 c 3
Causing bodily injury by explosives	Offences against the Person Act 1861 s 28	1861 c 100
Using explosive or corrosives with intent to cause grievous bodily harm	Offences against the Person Act 1861 s 29	as above
Hostage taking	Taking of Hostages Act 1982 s 1	1982 c 28
Assisting another to retain proceeds of terrorist activities	Northern Ireland (Emergency Provisions) Act 1991 s 53	1991 c 24
Concealing or transferring proceeds of terrorist activities	Northern Ireland (Emergency Provisions) Act 1991 s 54	as above
Offences against international protection of nuclear material	Nuclear Material (Offences) Act 1983 s 2	1983 c 18
Placing explosives with intent to cause bodily injury	Offences against the Person Act 1861 s 30	1861 c 100
Membership of prescribed organisations	Terrorism Act 2000 s 11	2000 c 11
Support or meeting of prescribed organisations	Terrorism Act 2000 s 12	as above
Uniform of prescribed organisations	Terrorism Act 2000 s 13	as above
Fund-raising for terrorism	Terrorism Act 2000 s 15	as above
Other offences involving money or property to be used for terrorism	Terrorism Act 2000 ss 16-18	as above
Disclosure prejudicing, or interference of material relevant to, investigation of terrorism	Terrorism Act 2000 s 39	as above
Weapons training	Terrorism Act 2000 s 54	as above
Directing terrorist organisation	Terrorism Act 2000 s 56	as above
Possession of articles for terrorist purposes	Terrorism Act 2000 s 57	as above
Unlawful collection of information for terrorist purposes	Terrorism Act 2000 s 58	as above
Incitement of terrorism overseas	Terrorism Act 2000 s 59	as above
Endangering the safety of an aircraft	Aviation Security Act 1982 s 2(1)(b)	1982 c 36
Racially-aggravated arson (not endangering life)	Crime and Disorder Act 1998 s 30(1)	1998 c 37

Class C: Lesser offences involving violence or damage, and less serious drugs offences

Offence	Contrary to	Year and chapter
Robbery (other than armed robbery)	Theft Act 1968 s 8(1)	1968 c 60
Unlawful wounding	Offences against the Person Act 1861 s 20	1861 c 100
Assault occasioning actual bodily harm	Offences against the Person Act 1861 s 47	as above
Concealment of birth	Offences against the Person Act 1861 s 60	as above
Abandonment of children under two	Offences against the Person Act 1861 s 27	as above
Arson (other than aggravated arson) where value does not exceed £30,000	Criminal Damage Act 1971 s 1(3)	1971 c 48
Criminal damage (other than aggravated criminal damage)	Criminal Damage Act 1971 s 1(1)	as above
Possession of firearm without certificate	Firearms Act 1968 s 1	1968 c 27
Carrying loaded firearm in public place	Firearms Act 1968 s 19	as above
Trespassing with a firearm	Firearms Act 1968 s 20	as above
Shortening of shotgun or possession of shortened shotgun	Firearms Act 1968 s 4	as above
Shortening of smooth bore gun	Firearms Amendment Act 1988 s 6(1)	1988 c 45
Possession or acquisition of shotgun without certificate	Firearms Act 1968 s 2	1968 c 27
Possession of firearms by person convicted of crime	Firearms Act 1968 s 21(4)	as above
Acquisition by or supply of firearms to person denied them	Firearms Act 1968 s 21(5)	as above

Offence	Contrary to	Year and chapter
Dealing in firearms	Firearms Act 1968 s 3	as above
Failure to comply with certificate when transferring firearm	Firearms Act 1968 s 42	as above
Permitting an escape	Common law	
Rescue	Common law	
Escaping from lawful custody without force	Common law	
Breach of prison	Common law	
Harbouring escaped prisoners	Criminal Justice Act 1961 s 22	1961 c 39
Assisting prisoners to escape	Prison Act 1952 s 39	1952 c 52
Fraudulent evasion of agricultural levy	Customs and Excise Management Act 1979 s 68A(1) and (2)	1979 c 2
Offender armed or disguised	Customs and Excise Management Act 1979 s 86	as above
Making threats to destroy or damage property	Criminal Damage Act 1971 s 2	1971 c 48
Possessing anything with intent to destroy or damage property	Criminal Damage Act 1971 s 3	as above
Child abduction by connected person	Child Abduction Act 1984 s 1	1984 c 37
Child abduction by other person	Child Abduction Act 1984 s 2	as above
Bomb hoax	Criminal Law Act 1977 s 51	1977 c 45
Cutting away buoys etc	Malicious Damage Act 1861 s 48	1861 c 97
Producing or supplying Class C drug	Misuse of Drugs Act 1971 s 4	1971 c 38
Possession of a Class C drug with intent to supply	Misuse of Drugs Act 1971 s 5(3)	as above
Fraudulent evasion of controls on Class C drugs	Customs and Excise Management Act 1979 s 170(2)(b), (c)	1979 c 2
Illegal importation of Class C drugs	Customs and Excise Management Act 1979 s 50	as above
Possession of Class A drug	Misuse of Drugs Act 1971 s 5(2)	1971 c 38
Failure to disclose knowledge or suspicion of money laundering	Drug Trafficking Offences Act 1986 s 26B	1986 c 32
Tipping-off in relation to money laundering investigations	Drug Trafficking Offences Act 1986 s 26C	as above
Assaults on officers saving wrecks	Offences against the Person Act 1861 s 37	1861 c 100
Attempting to injure or alarm the Sovereign	Treason Act 1842 s 2	1842 c 51
Assisting illegal entry or harbouring persons	Immigration Act 1971 s 25	1971 c 77
Administering poison with intent to injure etc	Offences against the Person Act 1861 s 24	1861 c 100
Neglecting to provide food for or assaulting servants etc	Offences against the Person Act 1861 s 26	as above
Setting spring guns with intent to inflict grievous bodily harm	Offences against the Person Act 1861 s 31	as above
Supplying instrument etc to cause miscarriage	Offences against the Person Act 1861 s 59	as above
Failure to disclose information about terrorism	Terrorism Act 2000 s 19	2000 c 11
Circumcision of females	Prohibition of Female Circumcision Act 1985 s 1	1985 c 38
Breaking or injuring submarine telegraph cables	Submarine Telegraph Act 1885 s 3	1885 c 49
Failing to keep dogs under proper control resulting in injury	Dangerous Dogs Act 1991 s 3	1991 c 65
Making gunpowder etc to commit offences	Offences against the Person Act 1861 s 64	1861 c 100
Stirring up racial hatred	Public Order Act 1986 ss 18-23	1986 c 64
[Racially-aggravated assault	Crime and Disorder Act 1998 s 29(1)	1998 c 37]
[Racially-aggravated criminal damage	Crime and Disorder Act 1998 s 30(1)	1998 c 37]

Class D: Serious sexual offences, offences against children

Rape	Sexual Offences Act 1956 s 1(1)	1956 c 69
Administering drugs to obtain intercourse	Sexual Offences Act 1956 s 4	as above
Sexual intercourse with girl under 13	Sexual Offences Act 1956 s 5	as above
Sexual intercourse with girl under 16	Sexual Offences Act 1956 s 6	as above
Sexual intercourse with defective	Sexual Offences Act 1956 s 7	as above
Procurement of a defective	Sexual Offences Act 1956 s 9	as above
Incest	Sexual Offences Act 1956 ss 10 and 11	as above
Buggery of person under 16 or animal	Sexual Offences Act 1956 s 12	as above
Gross indecency between male of 21 or over and male under 16	Sexual Offences Act 1956 s 13	as above
Indecent assault on a woman	Sexual Offences Act 1956 s 14	as above
Indecent assault on a man	Sexual Offences Act 1956 s 15	as above
Abuse of position of trust	Sexual Offences (Amendment) Act 2000 s 3	2000 c 44
Indecency with children under 14	Indecency with Children Act 1960 s 1(1)	1960 c 33
Taking, having etc indecent photographs of children	Protection of Children Act 1978 s 1	1978 c 37
Assault with intent to commit buggery	Sexual Offences Act 1956 s 16	1956 c 69
Abduction of woman by force	Sexual Offences Act 1956 s 17	as above
Permitting girl under 13 to use premises for sexual intercourse	Sexual Offences Act 1956 s 25	as above
Man living on earnings of prostitution	Sexual Offences Act 1956 s 30	as above
Woman exercising control over prostitute	Sexual Offences Act 1956 s 31	as above
Living on earnings of male prostitution	Sexual Offences Act 1967 s 5	1967 c 60
Incitement to commit incest	Criminal Law Act 1977 s 54	1977 c 45

Offence	Contrary to	Year and chapter
Allowing or procuring child under 16 to go abroad to perform	Children and Young Persons Act 1933 ss 25, 26	1933 c 12
Sexual intercourse with patients	Mental Health Act 1959 s 128	1959 c 72
Ill-treatment of persons of unsound mind	Mental Health Act 1983 s 127	1983 c 20
Abduction of unmarried girl under 18 from parent	Sexual Offences Act 1956 s 19	1956 c 69
Abduction of unmarried girl under 16 from parent	Sexual Offences Act 1956 s 20	as above
Abduction of defective from parent	Sexual Offences Act 1956 s 21	as above
Procuration of girl under 21	Sexual Offences Act 1956 s 23	as above
Permitting girl under 16 to use premises for intercourse	Sexual Offences Act 1956 s 26	as above
Permitting defective to use premises for intercourse	Sexual Offences Act 1956 s 27	as above
Causing or encouraging prostitution of girl under 16	Sexual Offences Act 1956 s 28	as above
Causing or encouraging prostitution of defective	Sexual Offences Act 1956 s 29	as above

Class E: Burglary etc

Burglary (domestic)	Theft Act 1968 s 9(3)(a)	1968 c 60
Going equipped to steal	Theft Act 1968 s 25	as above
Burglary (non-domestic)	Theft Act 1968 s 9(3)(b)	as above

Classes F and G: Other offences of dishonesty
The following offences are always in Class F

Destruction of registers of births etc	Forgery Act 1861 s 36	1861 c 98
Making false entries in copies of registers sent to register	Forgery Act 1861 s 37	as above

The following offences are always in Class G

Undischarged bankrupt being concerned in a company	Insolvency Act 1986 s 360	1986 c 45
Counterfeiting notes and coins	Forgery and Counterfeiting Act 1981 s 14	1981 c 45
Passing counterfeit notes and coins	Forgery and Counterfeiting Act 1981 s 15	as above
Offences involving custody or control of counterfeit notes and coins	Forgery and Counterfeiting Act 1981 s 16	as above
Making, custody or control of counterfeiting materials etc	Forgery and Counterfeiting Act 1981 s 175	as above
Illegal importation: counterfeit notes or coins	Customs and Excise Management Act 1979 s 50	1979 c 2
Fraudulent evasion: counterfeit notes or coins	Customs and Excise Management Act 1979 s 170(2)(b), (c)	as above

The following offences are in Class G if the value involved exceeds £30,000 and in Class F otherwise

VAT offences	Value Added Tax Act 1994 s 72(1)–(8)	1994 c 23
Fraudulent evasion of duty	Customs and Excise Management Act 1979 s 170(1)(b)	1979 c 2
Theft	Theft Act 1968 s 1	1968 c 60
Removal of articles from places open to the public	Theft Act 1968 s 11	as above
Abstraction of electricity	Theft Act 1968 s 13	as above
Obtaining property by deception	Theft Act 1968 s 15	as above
Obtaining pecuniary advantage by deception	Theft Act 1968 s 16	as above
False accounting	Theft Act 1968 s 17	as above
Handling stolen goods	Theft Act 1968 s 22	as above
Obtaining services by deception	Theft Act 1978 s 1	1978 c 31
Evasion of liability by deception	Theft Act 1978 s 2	as above
Illegal importation: not elsewhere specified	Customs and Excise Management Act 1979 s 50	1979 c 2
Counterfeiting Customs documents	Customs and Excise Management Act 1979 s 168	as above
Fraudulent evasion: not elsewhere specified	Customs and Excise Management Act 1979 s 170(2)(b), (c)	as above
Forgery	Forgery and Counterfeiting Act 1981 s 1	1981 c 45
Copying false instrument with intent	Forgery and Counterfeiting Act 1981 s 2	as above
Using a false instrument	Forgery and Counterfeiting Act 1981 s 3	as above
Using a copy of a false instrument	Forgery and Counterfeiting Act 1981 s 4	as above
Custody or control of false instruments etc	Forgery and Counterfeiting Act 1981 s 5	as above
Offences in relation to dies or stamps	Stamp Duties Management Act 1891 s 13	1891 c 38
Counterfeiting of dies or marks	Hallmarking Act 1973 s 6	1973 c 43
Fraudulent application of trade mark	Trade Marks Act 1938 s 58A	1938 c 22

Class H: Miscellaneous lesser offences

[Breach of anti-social behaviour order	Crime and Disorder Act 1998 s 1(10)	1998 c 37
Breach of sex offender order	Crime and Disorder Act 1998 s 2(8)	1998 c 37
Racially-aggravated public order offence	Crime and Disorder Act 1998 s 31(1)	1998 c 37
Racially-aggravated harassment/putting another in fear of violence	Crime and Disorder Act 1998 s 32(1)	1998 c 37
Having an article with a blade or point in a public place	Criminal Justice Act 1988 s 139	1988 c 33

Offence	Contrary to	Year and chapter
Breach of harassment injunction	Protection from Harassment Act 1997 s 3(6)	1997 c 40
Putting people in fear of violence	Protection from Harassment Act 1997 s 4(1)	1997 c 40
Breach of restraining order	Protection from Harassment Act 1997 s 5(5)	1997 c 40
Being drunk on an aircraft	Civil Aviation Act 1982 s 60 and 61	1982 c 16
Possession of offensive weapon	Prevention of Crime Act 1953 s 1	1953 c 14
Affray	Public Order Act 1986 s 3	1986 c 64
Assault with intent to resist arrest	Offences against the Person Act 1861 s 38	1861 c 100
Unlawful eviction and harassment of occupier	Protection from Eviction Act 1977 s 1	1977 c 43
Obscene articles intended for publication for gain	Obscene Publications Act 1964 s 1	1964 c 74
Gross indecency between males (other than where one is 21 or over and the other is under 16)	Sexual Offences Act 1956 s 13	1956 c 69
Solicitation for immoral purposes	Sexual Offences Act 1956 s 32	As above
Buggery of males of 16 or over otherwise than in private	Sexual Offences Act 1956 s 12	As above
Acts outraging public decency	Common law	
Offences of publication of obscene matter	Obscene Publications Act 1959 s 2	1959 c 66
Keeping a disorderly house	Common law; Disorderly Houses Act 1751 s 8	25 Geo 2 c 36
Indecent display	Indecent Displays (Control) Act 1981 s 1	1981 c 42
Presentation of obscene performance	Theatres Act 1968 s 2	1968 c 54
Procurement of intercourse by threats etc	Sexual Offences Act 1956 s 2	1956 c 69
Causing prostitution of women	Sexual Offences Act 1956 s 22	As above
Detention of woman in brothel or other premises	Sexual Offences Act 1956 s 24	As above
Procurement of a woman by false pretences	Sexual Offences Act 1956 s 3	As above
Procuring others to commit homosexual acts	Sexual Offences Act 1967 s 4	1967 c 60
Trade description offences (9 offences)	Trade Descriptions Act 1968 ss 1, 8, 9, 12, 13, 14, 18	1968 c 29
Absconding by person released on bail	Bail Act 1976 s 6(1), (2)	1976 c 63
Misconduct endangering ship or persons on board ship	Merchant Shipping Act 1970 s 27	1970 c 36
Obstructing engine or carriage on railway	Malicious Damage Act 1861 s 36	1861 c 97
Offences relating to the safe custody of controlled drugs	Misuse of Drugs Act 1971 s 11	1971 c 38
Possession of Class B or C drug	Misuse of Drugs Act 1971 s 5(2)	As above
Wanton or furious driving	Offences against the Person Act 1861 s 35	1861 c 100
Dangerous driving	Road Traffic Act 1988 s 2	1988 c 52
Forgery and misuse of driving documents	Public Passenger Vehicles Act 1981 s 65	1981 c 14
Forgery of driving documents	Road Traffic Act 1960 s 233	1960 c 59
Forgery etc of licences and other documents	Road Traffic Act 1988 s 173	1988 c 52
Mishandling or falsifying parking documents etc	Road Traffic Regulation Act 1984 s 115	1984 c 27
Aggravated vehicle taking	Theft Act 1968 s 12A	1968 c 60
Forgery, alteration, fraud of licences etc	Vehicle (Excise) Act 1971 s 26	1971 c 10
Making off without payment	Theft Act 1978 s 3	1978 c 31
Agreeing to indemnify sureties	Bail Act 1976 s 9(1)	1976 c 63
Sending prohibited articles by post	Post Office Act 1953 s 11	1953 c 36
Impersonating Customs officer	Customs and Excise Management Act 1979 s 3	1979 c 2
Obstructing Customs officer	Customs and Excise Management Act 1979 s 16	As above

Class I: Offences against public justice and similar offences

Conspiring to commit offences outside the United Kingdom	Criminal Justice (Terrorism and Conspiracy) Act 1998 s 5	1998
Perverting the course of public justice	Common law	
Perjuries (7 offences)	Perjury Act 1911 ss 1–7(2)	1911 c 6
Corrupt transactions with agents	Prevention of Corruption Act 1906 s 1	1906 c 34
Corruption in public office	Public Bodies Corrupt Practices Act 1889 s 1	1889 c 69
Embracery	Common law	
Fabrication of evidence with intent to mislead a tribunal	Common law	
Personation of jurors	Common law	
Concealing an arrestable offence	Criminal Law Act 1967 s 5	1967 c 45
Assisting offenders	Criminal Law Act 1967 s 4(1)	as above
False evidence before European Court	European Communities Act 1972 s 11	1972 c 68
Personating for purposes of bail etc	Forgery Act 1861 s 34	1861 c 60
Intimidating a witness, juror etc	Criminal Justice and Public Order Act 1994 s 51(1)	1994 c 33
Harming, threatening to harm a witness, juror etc	Criminal Justice and Public Order Act 1994 s 51(2)	as above
Prejudicing a drug trafficking investigation	Drug Trafficking Act 1994 s 58(1)	1994 c 37
Giving false statements to procure cremation	Cremation Act 1902 s 8(2)	1902 c 8
False statement tendered under section 9 of the Criminal Justice Act 1967	Criminal Justice Act 1967 s 89	1967 c 80
Making a false statement to obtain interim possession order	Criminal Justice and Public Order Act 1994 s 75(1)	1994 c 33

Offence	Contrary to	Year and chapter
Making false statement to resist making of interim possession order	Criminal Justice and Public Order Act 1994 s 75(2)	as above
False statement tendered under section 102 of the Magistrates' Courts Act 1980	Magistrates' Courts Act 1980 s 106	1980 c 43
Making false statement to authorised officer	Trade Descriptions Act 1968 s 29(2)	1968 c 29

1–5659B

SCHEDULE 5

VERY HIGH COST CASES

Table 1 Hourly rates for preparation

Column 1	Column 2	Column 3	Column 4	Column 5	Column 6
Solicitor, employed barrister, legal executive or other fee earner	**Category 1 cases (fraud and terrorism only)**	**Category 2 cases**	**Category 3 cases**	**Category 4 cases (non-fraud only)**	**Standard rates**
£ per hour	**£ per hour**	**£ per hour**	**£ per hour**	**£ per hour**	
Level A	180	140	110	110	55.75
Level B	140	110	90	90	47.25
Level C	100	80	70	70	34.00
Pupil/junior	50	40	35	35	
Counsel					
Queen's Counsel	180	140	110	110	
Leading junior advocate	140	110	90	90	
Led junior advocate	100	80	70	70	
Junior advocate alone	110	90	80	80	
Second led junior advocate	70	55	50	-	
Solicitor Advocate					
Leading level A	180	140	110	110	
Led level A	140	110	90	90	
Leading level B	140	110	90	90	
Led level B	115	95	75	75	
Level A alone	145	120	100	100	
Level B alone	125	105	85	85	
Second advocate	70	55	50	50	

1.1. In circumstances where the Commission considers the work undertaken not to be of the exceptional nature appropriate to a Very High Cost Case, the standard rates of pay set out in column 6 of Table 1 in this Schedule will apply.

Table 2 Hourly rates for non-preparatory work

Type of work	Level	Rate (£ per hour)
Attendance at court	A	42.25
	B	34.00
	C	20.50
Travel and waiting	A	25.00
	B	25.00
	C	25.00

2.1. The Commission may enhance by up to 100%:

    (*a*) in exceptional circumstances, the applicable rate for attendance at court in Table 2 in this Schedule; and
    (*b*) in very exceptional circumstances, the applicable rate for travel and waiting in Table 2 in this Schedule.

Table 3 Daily rates for advocacy

Column 1	Column 2	Column 3	Column 4	Column 5
	Category 1 cases (fraud and terrorism only)	**Category 2 cases**	**Category 3 cases**	**Category 4 cases (non-fraud only)**
	£ per day	**£ per day**	**£ per day**	**£ per day**
Queen's Counsel	600	600	600	600
Leading junior	450	450	450	450
Led junior	300	300	300	300
Junior alone	330	330	330	330
Second led junior	150	150	150	-
Noter	125	125	125	125

3.1. Solicitor advocates will be paid the appropriate rate for a leading junior, a led junior, or a junior alone, as set out in Table 3 of this Schedule.

3.2. The full daily rate in Table 3 of this Schedule will be allowed if the advocate is in court for more than $3\frac{1}{2}$ hours; half that rate will be allowed if he is in court for $3\frac{1}{2}$ hours or less

Table 4 Preliminary hearings

	Amount payable for hearing £
Queen's Counsel	140
Leading junior	100
Led junior	70
Junior alone	80
Second led junior	40
Noter	35

4.1. The rates in Table 4 of this Schedule will only apply where the hearing lasts two hours or less; otherwise the daily or half daily rate payable under Table 3 of this Schedule and paragraphs 3.1 and 3.2.

Criminal Defence Service (Recovery of Defence Costs Orders) Regulations 2001[1]

(SI 2001/856 amended by SI 2002/713, SI 2003/643, SI 2004/1195 and SI 2005/2783)

1–5660   **1. Citation and commencement.** These Regulations may be cited as the Criminal Defence Service (Recovery of Defence Costs Orders) Regulations 2001 and shall come into force on 2nd April 2001.

1. Made by the Lord Chancellor in exercise of the powers conferred on him by s 17 of the Access to Justice Act 1999.

1–5661   **2. Interpretation.** In these Regulations:

"the Act" means the Access to Justice Act 1999;
"appropriate officer" means:

in the case of the Crown Court, the court manager; and
in the case of the Court of Appeal or the House of Lords, the registrar of criminal appeals

and, in either case, includes an officer designated by him to act on his behalf in that regard;

"the Commission" means the Legal Services Commission established under section 1 of the Act;
"the Criminal Defence Service" means the Criminal Defence Service established under section 12 of the Act;
"funded defendant" means an individual who has received representation in respect of criminal proceedings before any court which is funded by the Commission or the Lord Chancellor as part of the Criminal Defence Service; and
"representation order" means a document granting a right to representation, and includes any other representation order under which representation has been provided for the funded defendant in the same proceedings.

1–5662   **3.** (1) Where an individual receives representation in respect of criminal proceedings which is funded by the Commission or the Lord Chancellor as part of the Criminal Defence Service, the court before which the proceedings are heard, other than a magistrates' court, shall make an order requiring him to pay some or all of the cost of any representation so funded for him in the circumstances set out in these Regulations.

(2) An order of the type mentioned in paragraph (1) shall be known as a Recovery of Defence Costs Order (an "RDCO").

1–5663   **4.** (1) The judge hearing the case shall make an RDCO against a funded defendant except as provided in paragraph (2).

(2) An RDCO shall not be made against a funded defendant who:

(a) has appeared in the magistrates' court only;
(b) is committed for sentence to the Crown Court;
(c) is appealing against sentence to the Crown Court; or
(d) has been acquitted, other than in exceptional circumstances.

1–5664   **5.** (1) An RDCO may be made up to a maximum amount of the full cost of the representation incurred in any court under the representation order.

(2) An RDCO may provide for payment to be made forthwith, or in specified instalments.

1–5665   **6.** Except in the circumstances mentioned in regulation 4(2)(a), (b) or (c), such information and evidence as is required by the court or the Commission with regard to the financial resources of a funded defendant shall be provided.

1–5666   7. (1) Where a representation order has been made or is being considered, the court or the appropriate officer may refer the financial resources of the funded defendant to the Commission for a report, and the Commission shall produce such a report.

(2) In compiling a report under this regulation, the Commission may investigate the financial resources of the funded defendant and may subsequently require him to provide further information or evidence, and details of any change in his financial circumstances.

1–5667   8. (1) Without prejudice to regulation 9(1)(*a*), where it appears to the judge, the appropriate officer or the Commission that:

(*a*)   the funded defendant has directly or indirectly transferred any resources to another person;
(*b*)   another person is or has been maintaining him in any proceedings; or
(*c*)   any of the resources of another person are or have been made available to him

the judge, the appropriate officer or the Commission (as the case may be) may assess or estimate the value of the resources of that other person and may treat all or any of such resources as those of the funded defendant.

(2) In this regulation, "person" includes a company, partnership, body of trustees and any body of persons whether corporate or not corporate.

1–5668   9. (1) Except as provided in paragraph (2), for the purpose of calculating the financial resources of the funded defendant:

(*a*)   the amount or value of every source of income and every resource of a capital nature available to him may be taken into account; and
(*b*)   the financial resources of the funded defendant's partner shall be treated as the financial resources of the funded defendant.

(2) Other than in exceptional circumstances, the following assets of the funded defendant shall not be taken into account:

(*a*)   the first £3,000 of capital available to him;
(*b*)   the first £100,000 of equity in his principal residence; and
(*c*)   his income, where the court or the Commission are satisfied that his gross annual income does not exceed £25,250.

(3) In this regulation, "funded defendant's partner" means a person with whom the funded defendant lives as a couple, and includes a person with whom the funded defendant is not currently living but from whom he is not living separate and apart.

1–5669   10. Where he is requested to do so by the judge, the solicitor for the funded defendant shall provide an estimate of the total costs which are likely to be incurred under the representation order.

1–5670   11. At the conclusion of the relevant proceedings, the judge shall :

(*a*)   subject to regulation 4(2), make an RDCO;
(*b*)   where an RDCO may be made under regulation 4(2)(*d*), consider whether it is reasonable in all the circumstances of the case to make such an order

1–5671   12. Where the judge considers that it is, or may be, reasonable to make an RDCO, he may:

(*a*)   make the order; or
(*b*)   if further information is required in order to decide whether to make the order:

(i)   adjourn the making of the order; and
(ii)   order that any further information which is required should be provided.

1–5672   13. Where information is required under regulation 6, 7(2) or 12(*b*)(ii) and such information fails to be provided, an RDCO shall be made for the full cost of the representation incurred under the representation order.

1–5673   14. (1) The solicitor for the funded defendant shall inform the Commission if it subsequently transpires that the costs incurred under the representation order were lower than the amount ordered to be paid under an RDCO.

(2) In the circumstances mentioned in paragraph (1), where the funded defendant has paid the amount ordered to be paid under the RDCO, the balance shall be repaid to him.

1–5674   15. The judge may make an order prohibiting an individual who is required to furnish information or evidence from dealing with property where:

(*a*)   information has failed to be provided in accordance with these Regulations;
(*b*)   he considers that there is a real risk that relevant property will be disposed of; or
(*c*)   at the conclusion of the case, the assessment of the costs incurred under the representation order or of the financial resources of the funded defendant has not yet been completed.

1–5675   16. Any payment required to be made under an RDCO shall be made to the Commission in accordance with the order.

1–5676 17. The Commission may enforce an RDCO in any manner which would be applicable to a civil debt between parties, and may add any costs incurred in connection with the enforcement to the amount to be paid under the RDCO.

Community Legal Service (Funding) (Counsel in Family Proceedings) Order 2001[1]

(SI 2001/1077 amended by SI 2003/2590, SI 2005/184, 2114 and 3504 and SI 2006/2364)

PART I
GENERAL

1–5677 1. Citation and commencement. This Order may be cited as the Community Legal Service (Funding) (Counsel in Family Proceedings) Order 2001 and shall come into force on 1st May 2001.

2. Interpretation. In this Order:

"the Act" means the Access to Justice Act 1999;

"Advocates Meeting" means an Advocates Meeting held in accordance with paragraph 4.5 or 5.2 of the Children Act Protocol and the expression "Advocates Meeting" does not include communications between the advocates under paragraph 5.2 other than a meeting;

"assessment of costs" means the determination of all costs and disbursements due under the relevant certificate in relation to proceedings in which counsel has submitted a claim for payment under this Order;

"business accounts" includes accounts relating to trusts and investments whether or not those accounts are maintained for the purposes of, or in connection with, a business;

"care proceedings" means proceedings under Part IV of the Children Act 1989;

"Case Management Conference" means a Case Management Conference held in accordance with step 4 of the Children Act Protocol;

"certificate" means a certificate issued under the Funding Code certifying a decision to fund services for the client;

"Children Act Protocol" means the Protocol annexed to the Practice Direction *(Care Cases: Judicial Continuity and Judicial Case Management)* made by the President of the Family Division;

"client" means an individual who receives funded services from the Commission as part of the Community Legal Service under sections 4 to 11 of the Act;

"the Commission" means the Legal Services Commission established under section 1 of the Act;

"committal hearing" means any hearing to determine whether a person should be committed to prison;

"Cost Appeals Committee" means a committee appointed by the Commission for the purpose of considering appeals from the Costs Committee;

"Costs Committee" means a committee appointed by the Commission for the purpose of considering appeals in relation to costs, whether under this Order or generally;

"counsel" means a barrister in independent practice;

"Director" means any Director appointed by the Commission under the Funding Code and includes any person authorised to act on his behalf, other than a solicitor authorised by contract to determine applications on behalf of the Commission;

"family proceedings" means proceedings, other than proceedings for judicial review, which arise out of family relationships, including proceedings in which the welfare of children is determined, and including all proceedings under one or more of the following:

(a) the Matrimonial Causes Act 1973;
(b) revoked
(c) the Adoption Act 1976;
(d) the Domestic Proceedings and Magistrates' Courts Act 1978;
(e) Part III of the Matrimonial and Family Proceedings Act 1984;
(f) Parts I to V of the Children Act 1989;
(g) Part IV of the Family Law Act 1996;
(ga) the Adoption and Children Act 2002;
(h) the inherent jurisdiction of the High Court in relation to children; and
(i) the Civil Partnership Act 2004;

but excluding proceedings under either the Inheritance (Provision for Family and Dependants) Act 1975 or the Trusts of Land and Appointment of Trustees Act 1996;

"function F1" has the meaning set out in article 2A;

"function F2" has the meaning set out in article 2B;
"function F3" has the meaning set out in article 2C;
"function F4" has the meaning set out in article 2D;
"function F5" has the meaning set out in article 2E;

"Funding Code" means the code approved under section 9 of the Act;

"harm" has the same meaning as in section 31(9) of the Children Act 1989 and the question of whether harm is significant shall be determined in accordance with section 31(10) of that Act;

"Independent Funding Adjudicator" means an adjudicator appointed by the Commission to carry out functions under the Funding Code;

"the main hearing" means the hearing at which the substantive issues are listed to be determined and are considered by the court;

"mental disorder" has the same meaning as in section 1(2) of the Mental Health Act 1983;

"Pre-Hearing Review" means a Pre-Hearing Review held in accordance with step 5 of the Children Act Protocol;

"the primary hearing unit" means the first day of the main hearing;

"the secondary hearing unit" means any day of the main hearing other than the first.

3. Transitional provisions.   This Order applies to all fees mentioned in article 4(2) payable to counsel under a certificate granted on or after 1st May 2001, and such fees payable under a certificate granted before that date shall be treated as if this Order had not been made.

4. Scope.   (1) In respect of proceedings to which this Order applies, the Commission shall fund services as part of the Community Legal Service in accordance with the provisions of the following articles.

(2) Subject to article 3 and paragraphs (3) to (6), and to any limitations on the relevant certificate, this Order applies to counsel's fees in respect of all family proceedings in the High Court, county courts and magistrates' courts.

(3) This Order does not apply to proceedings where the length of the main hearing exceeds 10 days.

(4) This Order does not apply to appeals to:

(*a*) the Divisional Court of the High Court;

(*b*) the Court of Appeal; or

(*c*) the House of Lords.

(5) Where the Commission issues a High Cost Case Contract under the Funding Code, this Order applies except to the extent that the terms of such contract provide otherwise.

(6) Nothing in this Order shall affect any determination of the amount of costs payable under an order or agreement which provides that another party to proceedings or prospective proceedings shall pay all or part of the costs of a client.

5. Graduated fees.   (1) The amount of the graduated fee for counsel shall be the base fee or the hearing unit fee, as appropriate, in respect of the function for which the fee is claimed, which is specified in the Schedules to this Order as applicable to the category of proceedings and the counsel instructed, increased by any:

(*a*) settlement supplement ("SS") or additional payment;

(*b*) special issue payment ("SIP"); and

(*c*) court bundle payment;

so specified.

(2) The total graduated fee, as set out in paragraph (1), shall be increased by 33% in respect of all work carried out while the proceedings are in the High Court.

6. Mixed and multiple claims.   (1) Only one base fee may be claimed in respect of each of functions F1 and F4 in relation to any single set of proceedings.

(2) Where counsel carries out work relating to more than one category of proceedings within the same function in a single set of proceedings, he may claim the fee for one category only.

(3) Counsel shall specify the category of proceedings upon which the fee payable under this Order is to be based when he submits his claim for payment.

(4) For the purposes of this Order, applications to the court constitute a single set of proceedings irrespective of whether they are made separately or together, where they are:

(*a*) heard together or consecutively; and

(*b*) treated by the court as a single set of proceedings.

7. Representation of more than one party.   Subject to article 9(1)(*c*), where counsel represents more than one party in the same set of proceedings, payment shall be made as if counsel represented a single party.

---

1. Made by the Lord Chancellor in exercise of powers conferred on him by s 6(4) of the Access to Justice Act 1999.

PART II

RULES REGARDING FEES

1–5678 8. Hearing units.   (1) Where:

(*a*) preparatory work for a hearing is carried out but that hearing does not take place; or

(*aa*) in care proceedings, the advocates concerned are able to discuss all relevant matters without the need for an Advocates Meeting under paragraph 5.2 of the Children Act Protocol; or

(*b*) preparatory work for the main hearing is carried out but counsel is prevented from representing his client because:

(i)   he has withdrawn from the proceedings with the permission of the court because of his professional code of conduct or to avoid embarrassment in the exercise of his profession; or
(ii) he has been dismissed by his client

one half of the relevant hearing unit fee, without special issue payments or court bundle payments, shall be paid and for the purposes of this paragraph "hearing" shall, in care proceedings, include a Case Management Conference or a Pre-Hearing Review.

(2) For the purpose of functions F2 and F3:

(a) one hearing unit fee shall be paid for each period of two and a half hours or less for which the hearing continues;
(b) the hearing shall:

(i)   subject to paragraph (2A), commence at the time at which it is listed to begin or at the time at which counsel is specifically directed by the court to attend for that particular hearing, whichever is earlier;
(ii) end when it concludes or at 5pm, whichever is earlier; and
(iii) take no account of any luncheon adjournment; and

(c) where a hearing continues after 5pm and concludes on that same day, an additional one half of the hearing unit fee shall be paid in respect of the time on that day after 5pm.

(2A) For the purpose of function F3, where, in care proceedings, an Advocates Meeting is held on the same day as a Case Management Conference or Pre-Hearing Review, a hearing unit fee shall be paid as if the Advocates Meeting and the Case Management Conference or (as the case may be) Pre-Hearing Review together formed a single hearing, beginning at the time when the Advocates Meeting began and ending when the Case Management Conference or (as the case may be) Pre-Hearing Review ended.

(3) For the purpose of function F5:

(a) where the hearing takes place on one day, the primary hearing unit fee shall be paid for the period from the time at which the hearing begins until 5pm on that day;
(b) where the hearing takes place over more than one day, whether by reason of being adjourned, split or otherwise:

(i)   the hearing on the first day shall be paid at the primary hearing unit rate; and
(ii) the hearing on any subsequent date shall be paid at the secondary hearing unit rate; and

(c) where a hearing continues after 5pm and ends on that same day, an additional one half of the appropriate hearing unit fee (whether primary or secondary) shall be paid in respect of the time on that day after 5pm.
(d) where, in care proceedings, the same counsel attends both the Pre-Hearing Review and the main hearing on behalf of a client, a function F5 primary hearing unit fee shall be paid in respect of the Pre-Hearing Review and the main hearing shall be paid at the secondary hearing unit rate;
(e) where, in care proceedings, counsel makes written submissions as to orders consequential to the main hearing an additional secondary hearing unit fee shall be paid.

9. Special issue payments.   (1) A special issue may arise where the proceedings involve, or, with regard to sub-paragraphs (e) to (g), are alleged to involve:

(a) a litigant in person;
(b) more than two parties;
(c) representation of more than one child by counsel submitting a claim for payment under this Order;
(ca) representation of a person who has difficulty:

(i)   giving instruction, or
(ii) understanding advice,

attributable to a mental disorder or to a significant impairment of intelligence or social functioning;

(cb) representation of:

(i)   a parent or parents of a child who is the subject of proceedings, or
(ii) another person (including a child) against whom allegations are made that he has caused or is likely to cause significant harm to a child;

(cc) analysis of the business accounts of an individual, partnership or company;
(cd) in respect of proceedings which fall within paragraph 4 of Schedule 2, one or more experts;
(d) in respect of proceedings which fall within paragraphs 1, 2 or 3 of Schedule 2, more than one expert;
(e) a relevant foreign element;
(f) relevant assets which are not or may not be under the exclusive control of any of the parties; or
(g) a party who has or may have been involved in the following:

(i)   conduct by virtue of which a child who is the subject of the proceedings has, may have or might suffer very significant harm; or
(ii) intentional conduct which has, could have or might significantly reduce the assets available for distribution by the court.

(2) The judge hearing the case shall, at the conclusion of the relevant hearing, certify on a form provided for that purpose any special issues mentioned in paragraph (1)(*a*) to (*cb*)(i), and any mentioned in paragraph (1)(*cb*)(i) to (*g*) which were of substance and relevant to any of the issues before the court at that hearing.

(3) The decision of the judge under paragraph (2) shall be final save on a point of law.

(4) In relation to functions F2, F3 and F5:

(*a*) a special issue payment shall be made for each special issue certified;

(*b*) such payment shall equate to the percentage applicable to each special issue multiplied by the total hearing unit fees applicable to the function in which the issue arises, as specified in Schedule 1.

(5) In relation to functions F1 and F4

(*a*) counsel may, when he submits his claim for payment, claim a special issue payment in respect of any special issue which arises;

(*b*) such payment shall equate to the percentage of the single base fee applicable to the function in which the issue arises which is specified in Schedule 1 for that special issue.

(6) The Director shall, in considering any claim made under paragraph (5), consider whether the work in question was reasonably carried out and, in respect of any special issues mentioned in paragraph (1)(*d*) to (*g*), whether the issue was of substance and relevant to any of the issues before the court.

(7) *Revoked.*

(8) *Revoked.*

10. Financial Dispute Resolution hearing payments. In respect of a set of proceedings which include proceedings for ancillary relief, an additional payment shall be paid at a rate of £150 in respect of Queen's Counsel, and £60 in respect of counsel other than Queen's Counsel, in respect of the Financial Dispute Resolution hearing in function F3.

10A. In respect of care proceedings, an additional payment shall be paid at a rate of £206.25 in respect of Queen's Counsel, and £82.50 in respect of counsel other than Queen's Counsel, in respect of the Case Management Conference in function F3.

11. Court bundle payments. (1) A court bundle payment shall be made:

(*a*) where the court bundle comprises between 176 and 350 pages;

(*b*) where the court bundle comprises comprises more than 350 pages; and

(*c*) in addition to the payment under sub-paragraph (*b*) as a special preparation fee in accordance with article 16 where the court bundle comprises more than 700 pages.

(2) Where there is no court bundle, equivalent provisions to those in paragraph (1) shall apply to counsel's brief.

12. Early settlement payments. (1) Subject to paragraphs (2) and (3), one settlement supplement shall be paid, as a percentage of the base fee or the hearing unit fee, as appropriate, applicable to the function in which the settlement takes place, where a settlement takes place which leads to the resolution of the set of proceedings.

(2) Subject to paragraph (3), no settlement supplement shall be paid in respect of a settlement which takes place in:

(*a*) function F1;

(*b*) function F4;

(*c*) the primary hearing unit of function F5 where the proceedings have been listed for less than 2 days; or

(*d*) the secondary hearing unit of function F5.

(3) In respect of a set of proceedings which include proceedings for ancillary relief, an additional payment shall be paid at a rate of £171.88 in respect of Queen's Counsel, and £68.75 in respect of counsel other than Queen's Counsel, where a settlement takes place in function F1 which leads to the resolution of the set of proceedings.

13. Incidental items. An incidental item payment may be claimed, where it was reasonably and necessarily incurred, in respect of the following:

(*a*) listening to or viewing evidence recorded on tape, disc or video cassette, once in respect of each item, at a rate of £10.90 per 10 minutes running time; and

(*b*)

(i) time spent travelling, at an hourly rate of £13.60;

(ii) incurring travel expenses at a mileage rate of 45p per mile or at the rate of the cheapest second class fare reasonably available, as appropriate; and

(iii) incurring hotel expenses at an overnight subsistence rate of £85.25 in respect of hotels situated within the London Region of the Commission and £55.25 elsewhere.

14. Replacement counsel. Where one counsel replaces another during the course of a function, payment shall be made to the replacement counsel and shall be divided by agreement between them.

15. Applications after the main hearing. (1) Claims for payment in respect of work carried out after the main hearing shall be paid at the appropriate function rate.

(2) For the purposes of this Order, an appeal from a District Judge to a Circuit Judge or a High Court Judge, and all work relating thereto including but not limited to an advice on appeal, shall be treated as the commencement of a new set of proceedings.

16. Special preparation fee. (1) Where this article applies, counsel may claim a special preparation fee in addition to the graduated fee payable under this Order.

(2) This article applies where:

(a) the proceedings to which the relevant certificate relates involve exceptionally complex issues of law or fact, or was otherwise an exceptional case of its nature; or

(b) in public law children proceedings, in relation to work carried out within the secondary hearing unit of function F5, where the main hearing is split so that a period of at least four months elapses between its commencement and the time at which it resumes

such that it has been necessary for counsel to carry out work by way of preparation substantially in excess of the amount normally carried out for proceedings of the same type; or

(c) the court bundle comprises more than 700 pages.

(3) The amount of the special preparation fee shall be calculated by multiplying the number of hours of preparation in excess of the amount normally carried out for proceedings of the same type, by an hourly rate of £100.50 in respect of Queen's Counsel, and £40.20 in respect of counsel other than Queen's Counsel.

(4) Where counsel claims a special preparation fee for work carried out within functions F1 and F4, or within functions F2, F3 and F5 where no hearing takes place, he shall, when submitting his claim for payment, supply such information and documents as may be required by the Director as proof of the complexity of the relevant issues of law or fact and of the number of hours of preparation, and the Director shall decide what special preparation fee, if any, shall be paid.

(5) Where counsel claims a special preparation fee for work carried out within functions F2, F3 and F5 he shall apply accordingly to the judge hearing the case at the relevant hearing, who shall decide what additional fee, if any, shall be paid, and whose decision shall be final save on a point of law.

17. Claims for payment. (1) Claims for payment in respect of work to which this Order applies shall be submitted to the Director and shall contain full details of the claim and copies of all relevant documents.

(2) Counsel may submit a claim for payment:

(a) when the proceedings to which the certificate relates are concluded;

(b) when the certificate under which the work has been carried out is discharged or revoked and any review by the Commission or the Independent Funding Adjudicator has been completed;

(c) when he has completed all work in respect of which he has been instructed up to and including function F2 or F3, as appropriate;

(d) when he has completed all work in respect of which he has been instructed in function F5; and

(e) where he has received no instructions from the instructing solicitor for a period of 3 months.

(3) Only one claim for payment may be submitted under paragraph (2)(c) in respect of any one set of proceedings.

(4) Only one claim for payment may be submitted in respect of function F4 in respect of any one set of proceedings.

(5) Any claim for payment may include a claim in respect of all work carried out in the proceedings for which counsel has not previously submitted a claim.

(6) Counsel shall submit his claim for payment within 3 months of the discharge or revocation of the certificate to which it relates and, if he fails to do so, the Director may reduce the amount payable under this Order; provided that the amount payable shall not be reduced unless counsel has been allowed a reasonable opportunity to show cause in writing why the amount should not be reduced.

(7) Any claim for payment shall include a claim in respect of all special issue payments, court bundle payments, settlement supplements and additional payments in respect of any functions for which the base fee or hearing unit fee, as appropriate, has been claimed and no later claim may be made in this respect.

(8) The Director shall consider claims for payment under this Order and all relevant information and shall pay counsel such sums as are properly and reasonably due under this Order for work carried out within the scope of any relevant certificate or contract.

(9) No claims for payment on account of sums payable under this Order may be made.

18. Appeals. (1) If counsel is dissatisfied with any decision of the Director with regard to the assessment of his fees under this Order, he may, within 21 days of the date of the assessment, (or such longer period as the Director may allow) make written representations to the Costs Committee by way of an appeal.

(2) In any appeal under paragraph (1) the Costs Committee shall review the assessment and shall confirm, increase or decrease the amount assessed.

(3) If counsel is dissatisfied with the decision of the Costs Committee he may, within 21 days of the date of the reviewed assessment, apply to that Committee to certify a point of principle of general importance.

(4) Where the Costs Committee certifies a point of principle of general importance, counsel

may, within 21 days of the date of the certification, appeal in writing to the Cost Appeals Committee against the reviewed assessment.

(5) If the Director is dissatisfied with any reviewed assessment under paragraph (2), he may, within 21 days of the date of such reviewed assessment, certify a point of principle of general importance and appeal in writing to the Cost Appeals Committee.

(6) In any appeal under paragraph (5) the Director shall serve notice of the appeal on counsel who may, within 21 days of the date of such notice, make written representations to the Cost Appeals Committee.

(7) In any appeal under paragraph (4) or (5) the Cost Appeals Committee shall review the decision of the Costs Committee and shall confirm, increase or decrease the reviewed assessment.

19. Review of payments.   (1) Subject to the provisions of this article and article 4, payments under this Order shall be final payments.

(2) Nothing in this Order shall affect any right of a client with a financial interest in an assessment of costs to make representations after the conclusion of the set of proceedings with regard to such payments.

(3) Representations under paragraph (2) above may include representations as to the use of counsel in proceedings and as to the sums payable to counsel under this Order.

(4) Where a contract entered into by the Commission in accordance with section 6(3)(*a*) of the Act includes rules for the assessment of costs in proceedings in which fees have been paid or are payable to counsel under this Order, and such costs are to be assessed by the court, the court shall carry out such assessment in accordance with those rules.

(5) Where in any assessment of costs it appears that payments made to counsel are in excess of the amount properly and reasonably due to counsel under this Order or any relevant certificate, counsel's fees shall be reduced accordingly.

(6) Where in any assessment of costs payment to counsel under this Order alone would exceed any limit set by the Commission on the total costs payable under the relevant certificate or contract, counsel's fees shall be reduced accordingly.

(7) Counsel shall be informed of any reduction in his fees under this article and shall have the same rights to make representations with regard to any such reduction as would a solicitor, in accordance with the relevant rules of court, contract and regulations, as applicable.

(8) Where payment has been made under this Order which is in excess of the amount properly and reasonably due to counsel, the Commission may recover the excess payment either by way of repayment by counsel or by way of deduction from any other sum which may be due to him.

SCHEDULE 1
TABLES OF FEES

1–5679   **1.** In respect of the proceedings mentioned in paragraph 1 of Schedule 2, the amount of the graduated fee shall be as follows:

(*a*) in respect of Queen's Counsel:

	Base fee	Hearing unit fee	SS	CBP$_1$	CBP$_2$
F1	£150	—	—	£40	£79
F2	—	£287.50	100%	£47	£94
F4	£125	—	—	£33	£67
F5 primary	—	£800	10%	£221	£442
F5 secondary	—	£550	—	£135	£271
Special Issue Payments					
Litigant in person		5%			
More than two parties		5%			
More than one child		5%			
More than one expert		10%			
Foreign		0%			
Assets		0%			
Conduct		0%			

1 where the court bundle comprises between 176 and 350 pages
   2 where the court bundle comprises more than 350 pages

(*b*) in respect of counsel other than Queen's Counsel:

	Base fee	Hearing unit fee	SS	CBP$_1$	CBP$_2$
F1	£60	—	—	£16	£32
F2	—	£115	100%	£19	£37.50
F4	£50	—	—	£13	£27
F5 primary	—	£320	10%	£88	£177
F5 secondary	—	£220	—	£54	£108
Special Issue Payments					
Litigant in person		5%			
More than two parties		5%			
More than one child		5%			
More than one expert		10%			
Foreign		0%			
Assets		0%			
Conduct		0%			

  1 where the court bundle comprises between 176 and 350 pages
  2 where the court bundle comprises more than 350 pages

2. In respect of proceedings mentioned in paragraph 2 of Schedule 2, the amount of the graduated fee shall be as follows:

(*a*) in respect of Queen's Counsel:

	Base fee	Hearing unit fee	SS	CBP₁	CBP₂
F1	£175	—	—	£40	£79
F2	—	£212.50	100%	£47	£94
F3	—	£412.50	100%	£82	£165
F4	£150	—	—	£33	£67
F5 primary	—	£1,075	20%	£221	£442
F5 secondary	—	£575	—	£135	£271
Special Issue Payments					
Litigant in person		40%			
More than two parties		40%			
More than one child		5%			
More than one expert		20%			
Foreign		30%			
Assets		0%			
Conduct		50%			

  1 where the court bundle comprises between 176 and 350 pages
  2 where the court bundle comprises more than 350 pages

(*b*) in respect of counsel other than Queen's Counsel:

	Base fee	Hearing unit fee	SS	CBP₁	CBP₂
F1	£70	—	—	£16	£32
F2	—	£85	100%	£19	£37.50
F3	—	£165	100%	£33	£66
F4	£60	—	—	£13	£27
F5 primary	—	£430	20%	£88	£177
F5 secondary	—	£230	—	£54	£108
Special Issue Payments					
Litigant in person		40%			
More than two parties		40%			
More than one child		5%			
More than one expert		20%			
Foreign		30%			
Assets		0%			
Conduct		50%			

  1 where the court bundle comprises between 176 and 350 pages
  2 where the court bundle comprises more than 350 pages

3. In respect of proceedings mentioned in paragraph 3 of Schedule 2, the amount of the graduated fee shall be as follows:

(*a*) in respect of Queen's Counsel:

	Base fee	Hearing unit fee	SS	CBP₁	CBP₂
F1	£150	—	—	£40	£79
F2	—	£187.50	100%	£47	£94
F3	—	£300	100%	£82	£165
F4	£125	—	—	£33	£67
F5 primary	—	£812.50	10%	£221	£442
F5 secondary	—	£550	—	£135	£271
Special Issue Payments					
Litigant in person		30%			
More than two parties		30%			
More than one child		5%			
More than one expert		50%			
Foreign		30%			
Assets		0%			
Conduct		50%			

  1 where the court bundle comprises between 176 and 350 pages
  2 where the court bundle comprises more than 350 pages

(*b*) in respect of counsel other than Queen's Counsel:

	Base fee	Hearing unit fee	SS	CBP₁	CBP₂
F1	£60	—	—	£16	£32
F2	—	£75	100%	£19	£37.50
F3	—	£120	100%	£33	£66
F4	£50	—	—	£13	£27
F5 primary	—	£325	10%	£88	£177

	Base fee	Hearing unit fee	SS	CBP$_1$	CBP$_2$
F5 secondary	—	£220	—	£54	£108
Special Issue Payments					
Litigant in person		30%			
More than two parties		30%			
More than one child		5%			
More than one expert		50%			
Foreign		30%			
Assets		0%			
Conduct		50%			

1   where the court bundle comprises between 176 and 350 pages
2   where the court bundle comprises more than 350 pages

4. In respect of proceedings mentioned in paragraph 4 of Schedule 2, the amount of the graduated fee shall be as follows:

(a) in respect of Queen's Counsel:

	Base fee	Hearing unit fee	SS	CBP$_1$	CBP$_2$
F1	£150	—	—*	£40	£79
F2	—	£162.50	50%	£47	£94
F3	—	£300	50%	£82	£165
F4	£125	—	—	£33	£67
F5 primary	—	£812.50	10%	£221	£442
F5 secondary	—	£550	—	£135	£271
Special Issue Payments					
Litigant in person		10%			
More than two parties		10%			
More than one child		5%			
More than one expert		10%			
Foreign		25%			
Assets		50%			
Conduct		50%			

*   see article 12(3)
1   where the court bundle comprises between 176 and 350 pages
2   where the court bundle comprises more than 350 pages

(b) in respect of counsel other than Queen's Counsel:

	Base fee	Hearing unit fee	SS	CBP$_1$	CBP$_2$
F1	£60	—	—*	£16	£32
F2	—	£65	50%	£19	£37.50
F3	—	£120	50%	£33	£66
F4	£50	—	—	£13	£27
F5 primary	—	£325	10%	£88	£177
F5 secondary	—	£220	—	£54	£108
Special Issue Payments					
Litigant in person		10%			
More than two parties		10%			
More than one child		5%			
More than one expert		10%			
Foreign		25%			
Assets		50%			
Conduct		50%			

*   see article 12(3)
1   where the court bundle comprises between 176 and 350 pages
2   where the court bundle comprises more than 350 pages

SCHEDULE 2
CATEGORIES OF PROCEEDINGS

1–5680   **1.** Category of proceedings: family injunctions.

Family proceedings (other than those for ancillary relief) for an injunction, committal order, or other order for the protection of a person (other than proceedings for the protection of children within paragraph 2).

2. Category of proceedings: public law children.

Family proceedings under Parts III, IV or V of the Children Act 1989, adoption proceedings (including applications to free for adoption), proceedings under the Child Abduction and Custody Act 1985, and other family proceedings within the inherent jurisdiction of the High Court concerning the welfare of children (other than proceedings for ancillary relief).

3. Category of proceedings: private law children.

Family proceedings between individuals concerning the welfare of children (other than those for ancillary relief or within paragraph 2).

4. Category of proceedings: ancillary relief and all other family proceedings.

All other family proceedings not within paragraphs 1 to 3.

Criminal Defence Service (Choice in Very High Cost Cases) Regulations 2001[1]

(SI 2001/1169 amended by SI 2004/598 and 3345)

1-5688   **1. Citation and commencement.** These Regulations may be cited as the Criminal Defence Service (Choice in Very High Cost Cases) Regulations 2001 and shall come into force on 2nd April 2001.

_____

1. Made by the Lord Chancellor in exercise of powers conferred on him by s 15(5) of the Access to Justice Act 1999.

1-5689   **2. Interpretation.** In these Regulations:

"the Commission" means the Legal Services Commission established under section 1 of the Access to Justice Act 1999;

"current representatives" means the representatives named on the representation order and any advocate currently instructed in the case;

"funded services" means services which are provided directly for a client and funded for that client as part of the Criminal Defence Service under sections 12 to 18 of the Access to Justice Act 1999;

"representation order" means a document granting a right to representation; and

"a Very High Cost Case" is a case where if the case proceeds to trial, that trial would be likely to last for 41 days or longer, and any question as to whether the case fulfils this criterion shall be determined by the Commission; and

1-5690   **3. Choice of representative in Very High Cost Cases.** (1) Paragraph (2) applies where:

(a) a representation order has been granted in relation to a Very High Cost Case; and

(b) the Commission proposes to enter into an individual contract for the provision of funded services in relation to that case; and either

(c) the Commission serves notice that it does not propose to enter into such a contract with any, or all, of the current representatives; or

(d) any or all of the current representatives serves notice that they do not propose to enter into such a contract.

(2) Where this paragraph applies:

(a) the Commission is no longer required to fund representation by the relevant current representative referred to in paragraph (1)(c) or (d);

(b) the person in whose favour the representation order was granted may select a different representative chosen in accordance with The Criminal Defence Service (General) Regulations; and

(c) the Commission may amend the representation order accordingly.

Criminal Defence Service (General) (No 2) Regulations 2001[1]

(SI 2001/1437 amended by SI 2002/712 and 2785, SI 2003/644 and 2378, SI 2004/1196, 1748 and 2046, SI 2005/2784 and SI 2006/2490)

Part I
General

1-5691   **1. Citation and commencement.** These Regulations may be cited as the Criminal Defence Service (General) (No 2) Regulations 2001 and shall come into force on the day after the day on which they are made, but regulations 4 and 5 shall have effect from and including 2nd April 2001 as if these Regulations had come into force on that date.

_____

1. Made by the Lord Chancellor in exercise of powers conferred on him by the Access to Justice Act 1999, ss 12, 13, 15, 20 and Sch 3.

2. Interpretation. In these Regulations:

"the Act" means the Access to Justice Act 1999;

"advocacy assistance" means assistance in the form of advocacy;

"advocate" means:

    a barrister; or

    a solicitor who has obtained a higher courts advocacy qualification in accordance with regulations and rules of conduct of the Law Society;

"assisted person" means a person in receipt of funded services;

"appropriate officer" means:

    in the case of the Crown Court, the court manager;

    in the case of a magistrates' court, the justices' clerk or designated officer; and

    in the case of the Court of Appeal, the Courts-Martial Appeal Court or the House of Lords, the registrar of criminal appeals or the head of the Civil Appeals Office and, in any case, includes an officer designated by him to act on his behalf in that regard;

"the Commission" means the Legal Services Commission established under section 1 of the Act;

"the Costs Committee" means a committee appointed under arrangements made by the Commission to deal with, inter alia, applications for appeal against, or review of, assessments of costs;

"the Financial Services and Markets Tribunal" means the Tribunal established under section 132 of the Financial Services and Markets Act;

"funded services" means services which are provided directly for an individual and funded for that individual as part of the Criminal Defence Service established under sections 12 to 18 of the Act;

"judge of the court" means, in relation to a magistrates' court, a single justice;

"representation order" means a document granting a right to representation under section 14 of the Act;

"tax credit" means a tax credit under the Tax Credits Act 2002 and "working tax credit" and "child tax credit" shall be construed in accordance with section 1(1) and (2) of that Act;

"a very high cost case" is a case where if the case proceeds to trial, that trial would be likely to last for 41 days or longer, and any question as to whether the case fulfils this criterion shall be determined by the Commission; and

"volunteer" means a person who, for the purpose of assisting with an investigation, attends voluntarily at a police station or a customs office, or at any other place where a constable or customs officer is present, or accompanies a constable or customs officer to a police station or a customs office or any other such place, without having been arrested.

PART II
SCOPE

1–5692 3. Criminal proceedings.   (1) For the purposes of this regulation, "the 1998 Act" means the Crime and Disorder Act 1998 .

(2) The following proceedings are criminal proceedings for the purposes of section 12(2)(*g*) of the Act:

(*a*) civil proceedings in a magistrates' court arising from failure to pay a sum due or to obey an order of that court where such failure carries the risk of imprisonment;

(*b*) proceedings under sections 1, 1D and 4 of the 1998 Act relating to anti-social behaviour orders;*

(*ba*) proceedings under sections 1G and 1H of the 1998 Act relating to intervention orders, in which an application for an anti-social behaviour order has been made;

(*c*) proceedings under section 8(1)(*b*) of the 1998 Act relating to parenting orders made where an anti-social behaviour order or a sex offender order is made in respect of a child;

(*d*) proceedings under section 8(1)(*c*) of the 1998 Act relating to parenting orders made on the conviction of a child;

(*e*) proceedings under section 9(5) of the 1998 Act to discharge or vary a parenting order made as mentioned in sub-paragraph (*c*) or (*d*);

(*f*) proceedings under section 10 of the 1998 Act to appeal against a parenting order made as mentioned in sub-paragraph (*c*) or (*d*);

(*g*) proceedings under sections 14B, 14D, 14G, 14H, 21B and 21D of the Football Spectators Act 1989 (banning orders and references to a court);

(*h*) proceedings under section 137 of the Financial Services and Markets Act 2000 to appeal against a decision of the Financial Services and Markets Tribunal;

(*i*) proceedings under sections 2, 5 and 6 of the Anti-social Behaviour Act 2003 relating to tclosure orders;

(*j*) proceedings under sections 20, 22, 26 and 28 of the Anti-Social Behaviour Act 2003 relating to parenting orders in cases of exclusion from school and parenting orders in respect of criminal conduct and anti-social behaviour;

(*k*) proceedings under sections 97, 100 and 101 of the Sexual Offences Act 2003 relating to notification orders and interim notification orders;

(*l*) proceedings under sections 104, 108, 109 and 110 of the Sexual Offences Act 2003 relating to sexual offences prevention orders and interim sexual offences prevention orders;

(*m*) proceedings under sections 114, 118 and 119 of the Sexual Offences Act 2003 relating to foreign travel orders;

(*n*) proceedings under sections 123, 125, 126 and 127 of the Sexual Offences Act 2003 relating to risk of sexual harm orders and interim risk of sexual harm orders;

(*o*) proceedings under Part 1A of Schedule 1 to the Powers of Criminal Courts (Sentencing) Act 2000 relating to parenting orders for failure to comply with orders under section 20 of that Act; and.*

(3) Proceedings:

(*a*) in the Crown Court, following committal for sentence by a magistrates' court;

(*b*) to quash an acquittal under the Criminal Procedure and Investigations Act 1996; and

(*c*) for confiscation and forfeiture in connection with criminal proceedings under RSC Order 115 in Schedule 1 to the Civil Procedure Rules 1998

are to be regarded as incidental to the criminal proceedings from which they arise.

(4) Applications for judicial review or habeas corpus relating to any criminal investigations or proceedings are not to be regarded as incidental to such criminal investigations or proceedings.

4. Advice and assistance—scope. The Commission shall fund such advice and assistance, including advocacy assistance, as it considers appropriate in relation to any individual who:

(a) is the subject of an investigation which may lead to criminal proceedings;

(b) is the subject of criminal proceedings;

(c) requires advice and assistance regarding his appeal or potential appeal against the outcome of any criminal proceedings or an application to vary a sentence;

(d) requires advice and assistance regarding his sentence;

(e) requires advice and assistance regarding his application or potential application to the Criminal Cases Review Commission;

(f) requires advice and assistance regarding his treatment or discipline in prison (other than in respect of actual or contemplated proceedings regarding personal injury, death or damage to property);

(g) is the subject of proceedings before the Parole Board;

(h) requires advice and assistance regarding representations to the Home Office in relation to a mandatory life sentence or other parole review;

(i) is a witness in criminal proceedings and requires advice regarding self-incrimination; or

(j) is a volunteer" or

(k) is detained under Schedule 7 to the Terrorism Act 2000.

4A. Advice given prior to the grant of a representation order in the Crown Court shall be deemed to have been given under that order where:

(a) the interests of justice required that the advice was provided as a matter of urgency;

(b) there was no undue delay in making the application for a representation order; and

(c) the advice was given by the representative who was subsequently assigned under the representation order.

5. Advice and assistance—financial eligibility. (1) The following advice and assistance may be granted without reference to the financial resources of the individual:

(a) all advice and assistance provided to an individual who is arrested and held in custody at a police station or other premises;

(b) all advocacy assistance before a magistrates' court or the Crown Court;

(c) all advice and assistance provided by a court duty solicitor in accordance with his contract with the Commission;

(d) all advice and assistance provided to a volunteer during his period of voluntary attendance;

(e) all advice and assistance provided to an individual being interviewed in connection with a serious service offence; and

(f) all advice and assistance provided in respect of an individual who is the subject of an identification procedure carried out by means of video recordings in connection with that procedure, notwithstanding the individual's non-attendance at a police station at the time the procedure is carried out.

(2) For the purposes of paragraph (1), a serious service offence is an offence under the Army Act 1955, the Air Force Act 1955 or the Naval Discipline Act 1957 which cannot be dealt with summarily.

(3) Advocacy assistance may be granted to an individual regarding his treatment or discipline in prison (other than in respect of actual or contemplated proceedings regarding personal injury, death or damage to property), or where he is the subject of proceedings before the Parole Board, if his weekly disposable income does not exceed £194 and his disposable capital does not exceed £3,000.

(4) Except where paragraph (1) applies, the Commission, or a person acting on behalf of the Commission where such function has been delegated in accordance with section 3(4) of the Act, shall determine the financial eligibility of the individual in accordance with the following paragraphs.

(5) Except where paragraph (1) or (3) applies, an individual is eligible for advice and assistance if his weekly disposable income does not exceed £92 and his disposable capital does not exceed £1,000.

(6) The Commission shall assess the disposable income and disposable capital of the individual and, where appropriate, of any person whose financial resources may be treated as those of the individual, in accordance with Schedule 1 to these Regulations.

(7) Where the Commission is satisfied that any person whose disposable income is to be assessed under paragraph (6) is directly or indirectly in receipt of any qualifying benefit, it shall take that person's disposable income as not exceeding the sum for the time being specified in paragraph (3) or (5), as appropriate.

(8) The following are qualifying benefits for the purposes of paragraph (7):

(a) income support;

(b) income-based jobseeker's allowance;

(c) working tax credit claimed together with child tax credit where the gross annual income is not more than £14,213;

(d) working tax credit with a disability element or severe disability element (or both) where the gross annual income is not more than £14,213; and

(e) guarantee credit under section 1(3)(a) of the State Pension Credit Act 2002.

(9) Where the Commission is satisfied that any person whose disposable capital is to be assessed in accordance with paragraph (3) is directly or indirectly in receipt of income support or income-based jobseeker's allowance or guarantee state pension credit, it shall take that person's disposable capital as not exceeding the capital sum for the time being specified in paragraph (3).

PART III

APPLICATIONS FOR REPRESENTATION ORDERS

1–5693   **6. Representation order.**   (1) The date of any representation order is the date on which the application for the grant of such an order is received in accordance with these Regulations.

(2) Any application for the grant of a representation order in respect of proceedings in the Crown Court or the Court of Appeal which are mentioned in section 12(2)(a) to (f) of the Act and in regulation 3(2)(h), shall be made in accordance with regulations 9 and 10.

(3) Any application for the grant of a representation order in respect of the proceedings mentioned in regulation 3(2) (criminal proceedings for the purposes of section 12(2)(g) of the Act), except those mentioned in regulation 3(2)(h):

    (a) shall be made to the Commission; and

    (b) may be granted only by the Commission or a person acting on behalf of the Commission where such function has been delegated in accordance with section 3(4) of the Act.

(4) Where an application under paragraph (3) is refused, the Commission shall provide to the applicant:

    (a) written reasons for the refusal; and

    (b) details of the appeal process.

(5) Where the person who requires representation is aged less than 18, the application for the grant of a representation order may be made by his parent or guardian on his behalf.

(6) The appropriate officer of each court shall keep a record of every application to that court for a representation order, and of its outcome.

(7) The appropriate officer shall send to the Lord Chancellor such information from the record mentioned in paragraph (6) as the Lord Chancellor may request.

7. General power to grant representation.   The court, a judge of the court, the head of the Civil Appeals Office, or the registrar of criminal appeals may grant a representation order at any stage of criminal proceedings (other than criminal proceedings in a magistrates' court) in the circumstances set out in these Regulations whether or not an application has been made for such an order.

8. Proceedings in a magistrates' court.   *Revoked.*

9. Proceedings in the Crown Court.   (1) Other than where regulation 6(3) applies, an application for a representation order in respect of proceedings in the Crown Court may be made, where an application for such an order in respect of the proceedings in a magistrates' court has not been made or has been refused:

    (a) orally or in writing to the Crown Court;

    (b) in writing to the appropriate officer of that court;

    (c) in writing to a magistrates' court at the conclusion of any proceedings in that magistrates' court;

    (d) in writing to a magistrates' court inquiring into the offence as examining justices or sending for trial under section 51 of the Crime and Disorder Act 1998;

    (e) where a magistrates' court has been given a notice of transfer under section 4 of the Criminal Justice Act 1987 (serious fraud cases), in writing to the appropriate officer of that magistrates' court;

    (f) in the case of an appeal to the Crown Court from a magistrates' court, in writing to the appropriate officer of that magistrates' court;

    (g) where the applicant was committed for trial in the Crown Court under section 6(2) of the Magistrates' Courts Act 1980, in writing to the appropriate officer of the magistrates' court ordering the committal; and

    (h) in the case of a retrial ordered under section 7 of the Criminal Appeal Act 1968, orally or in writing to the court ordering the retrial.

(2) An application for a representation order in respect of representations to the High Court against a voluntary bill of indictment may be made:

    (a) in writing to the appropriate officer of the Crown Court; or

    (b) orally to the judge considering the voluntary bill

and where any such order is granted it shall also apply to any proceedings to which the applicant is indicted.

(3) Where an application is made to the court, it may refer it to the appropriate officer for determination.

(4) Where an application is refused, the appropriate officer shall provide to the applicant:

    (a) written reasons for the refusal; and

    (b) details of the appeal process.

10. Proceedings in the Court of Appeal and the House of Lords. (1) An application for a representation order in respect of proceedings in the Court of Appeal or the House of Lords may be made:

(a) orally to the Court of Appeal, or a judge of the court; or

(b) in writing to the Court of Appeal, a judge of the court, or the appropriate officer of the court.

(2) Where an application is made to the court, it may refer it to a judge or the appropriate officer for determination.

(3) Where an application is made to a judge, he may refer it to the registrar for determination.

(4) The appropriate officer may:

(a) grant the application; or

(b) refer it to the court or a judge of the court.

(5) A representation order shall not be granted until notice of leave to appeal has been given in respect of the proceedings which are the subject of the application.

(6) Where a representation order is granted in respect of proceedings in the Court of Appeal, a judge or the appropriate officer may specify the stage of the proceedings at which the representation order shall take effect.

(7) The House of Lords may not grant a representation order in respect of any proceedings.

PART IV

SELECTION OF REPRESENTATIVE

1-5694 **11. Representation in magistrates' courts and some Crown Court proceedings.** (1) The right conferred by section 15(1) of the Act, as regards representation in respect of any proceedings to which this regulation applies, shall be exercisable only in relation to those representatives who are:

(a) employed by the Commission to provide such representation; or

(b) authorised to provide such representation under a crime franchise contract with the Commission which commences on or after 2nd April 2001 and specifies the rate of remuneration for such representation.

(2) This regulation applies to:

(a) any criminal proceedings in a magistrates' court;

(b) any proceedings in the Crown Court mentioned in regulation 3(2);

(c) any appeal by way of case stated from a magistrates' court; and

(d) any proceedings which are preliminary or incidental to proceedings mentioned in sub-paragraphs (a) to (c).

(3) This regulation does not apply to proceedings referred to in section 12(2)(f) of the Act (proceedings for contempt in the face of a court).

12. Advocates in magistrates' courts. (1) A representation order for the purposes of proceedings before a magistrates' court may only include representation by an advocate in the case of:

(a) any indictable offence, including an offence which is triable either way; or

(b) proceedings under section 9 of, or paragraph 6 of Schedule 1 to, the Extradition Act 1989

where the court is of the opinion that, because of circumstances which make the proceedings unusually grave or difficult, representation by both a solicitor and an advocate would be desirable.

(2) A representation order for the purposes of proceedings before a magistrates' court may not include representation by an advocate other than as provided in paragraph (1).

13. Representation in the Crown Court, Court of Appeal and House of Lords. (1) Subject to paragraph (2) and regulation 11, the right conferred by section 15(1) of the Act, as regards representation in respect of any proceedings in the Crown Court (other than proceedings mentioned in regulation 3(2)), Court of Appeal or House of Lords, shall be exercisable only in relation to those representatives who are:

(a) employed by the Commission to provide such representation; or

(b) authorised to provide such representation under a crime franchise contract with the Commission" or

(c) in respect of an appeal from the Financial Services and Markets Tribunal, the representatives of the assisted person before the Court of Appeal.

(2) Where the Commission has determined that representation in a very high cost serious fraud case shall be provided by members of the Serious Fraud Panel, such right shall be limited to representatives who are for the time being members of that Panel.

(3) For the purposes of this regulation:

(a) a very high cost serious fraud case is a very high cost case with regard to which the offence with which the defendant is charged is primarily or substantially founded on allegations of fraud or other serious financial impropriety, or involves complex financial transactions; and

(b) the Serious Fraud Panel is a panel of solicitors appointed under arrangements made by the Commission to deal with such cases.

(4) This regulation does not apply to any proceedings referred to in section 12(2)(f) of the Act.

14. Advocates in the Crown Court, Court of Appeal and House of Lords. (1) A representation order may provide for the services of a Queen's Counsel or of more than one advocate in respect of the whole or any specified part of any proceedings only in the cases specified and in the manner provided for by the following paragraphs of this regulation; and in this regulation "junior counsel" means any advocate other than a Queen's Counsel.

(2) Subject to paragraphs (3) to (9), a representation order may provide for the services of a Queen's Counsel or of more than one advocate in any of the following terms:

  (a) a Queen's Counsel alone;

  (b) where two advocates are required:

    (i) a Queen's Counsel with a junior counsel;

    (ii) a Queen's Counsel with a noting junior counsel;

    (iii) two junior counsel; or

    (iv) a junior counsel with a noting junior counsel;

  (c) where three advocates are required:

    (i) in any of the terms provided for in sub-paragraph (b) plus an extra junior counsel; or

    (ii) in any of the terms provided for in sub-paragraph (b) plus an extra noting junior counsel.

(3) A representation order relating to proceedings in the Crown Court may be made in the terms of paragraph (2)(a) if and only if:

  (a) in the opinion of the court the case for the assisted person involves substantial novel or complex issues of law or fact which could not be adequately presented except by a Queen's Counsel; and

  (b) either:

    (i) a Queen's Counsel or senior Treasury counsel has been instructed on behalf of the prosecution; or

    (ii) the case for the assisted person is exceptional compared with the generality of cases involving similar offences.

(4) A representation order relating to proceedings in the Crown Court may be made in the terms of paragraph (2)(b)(iii) or (iv) if and only if:

  (a) in the opinion of the court the case for the assisted person involves substantial novel or complex issues of law or fact which could not be adequately presented by a single advocate; and

  (b) either:

    (i) two or more advocates have been instructed on behalf of the prosecution;

    (ii) the case for the assisted person is exceptional compared with the generality of cases involving similar offences;

    (iii) the number of prosecution witnesses exceeds 80; or

    (iv) the number of pages of prosecution evidence exceeds 1,000

and for this purpose the number of pages of prosecution evidence shall include all witness statements, documentary and pictorial exhibits and records of interview with the assisted person and with other defendants forming part of the committal documents or included in any notice of additional evidence.

(5) A representation order relating to proceedings in the Crown Court may be made in the terms of paragraph (2)(b)(i) or (ii) if and only if:

  (a) in the opinion of the court the case for the assisted person involves substantial novel or complex issues of law or fact which could not be adequately presented except by a Queen's Counsel assisted by junior counsel; and

  (b) either:

    (i) the case for the assisted person is exceptional compared with the generality of cases involving similar offences; or

    (ii) a Queen's Counsel or senior Treasury counsel has been instructed on behalf of the prosecution and one of the conditions in paragraph (4)(b)(i), (iii) or (iv) is satisfied.

(6) A representation order may be made in the terms of paragraph (2)(c) if and only if:

  (a) the proceedings arise from a prosecution brought by the Serious Fraud Office;

  (b) the court making the order considers that three advocates are required; and

  (c) in the case of proceedings in the Crown Court, the conditions in paragraph (4) or (5) are satisfied.

(7) The fact that a Queen's Counsel has been or is proposed to be assigned under this regulation shall not by itself be a reason for making an order in any of the terms provided for by paragraph (2)(b) or (c).

(8) Where a Queen's Counsel has been or is proposed to be assigned under this regulation, no order in any of the terms provided for by paragraph (2)(b) or (c) shall be made where the case relates to an appeal to the Court of Appeal or to the House of Lords and it appears to the court at the time of making the order that representation can properly be undertaken by a Queen's Counsel alone.

(9) No order shall be made or amended so as to provide for representation:

(a) in the terms of paragraph (2)(b) unless the court making the order is of the opinion that the assisted person could not be adequately represented under an order in the terms of paragraph (2)(a);

(b) in the terms of paragraph (2)(b)(i) unless the court making the order is of the opinion that the assisted person could not be adequately represented under an order in the terms of paragraph (2)(b)(ii), (iii) or (iv);

(c) in the terms of paragraph (2)(b)(ii) unless the court making the order is of the opinion that the assisted person could not be adequately represented under an order in the terms of paragraph (2)(b)(iii) or (iv);

(d) in the terms of paragraph (2)(b)(iii) unless the court making the order is of the opinion that the assisted person could not be adequately represented under an order in the terms of paragraph (2)(b)(iv);

(e) in any of the terms provided for by paragraph (2)(c)(i) unless the court making the order is of the opinion that the assisted person could not be adequately represented under the corresponding order under paragraph (2)(c)(ii).

(10) Every application for a representation order in any of the terms provided for by paragraph (2), or for an amendment under paragraph (15), shall be in writing specifying:

(a) the terms of the order sought and the grounds of the application; and

(b) which of the conditions in paragraphs (3), (4), (5), (6) and (9) is relied upon in support of the order sought, and on what grounds it is contended that each such condition is fulfilled.

(11) A court may, before making a representation order in the terms provided for by paragraph (2) or amending the order under paragraph (15), require written advice from any advocate already assigned to the applicant on the question of what representation is needed in the proceedings.

(12) A court making a decision whether to make an order under paragraph (2) or to amend an order under paragraph (15) shall make annotations to the written application under paragraph (10), stating whether each of the conditions relied upon in support of the order made or sought is fulfilled.

(13) Subject to paragraph (14), a decision to make or amend a representation order so as to provide for the services of a Queen's Counsel or of more than one advocate may only be made:

(a) in the course of a trial or of a preliminary hearing, pre-trial review or pleas and directions hearing, by the judge presiding at that trial or hearing;

(b) where the proceedings are in the Crown Court, by a High Court judge, the resident judge of the Crown Court or (in the absence of the resident judge) a judge nominated for that purpose by the presiding judge of the circuit; or

(c) where the proceedings are in the Court of Appeal, by the registrar, a High Court judge or a judge of the Court of Appeal.

(14) A magistrates' court which may grant a representation order as respects any proceedings in the Crown Court by virtue of these Regulations may make:

(a) a representation order providing for the services of a Queen's Counsel without a junior counsel where the proceedings are a trial for murder and the order is made upon committal, transfer or sending for trial; or

(b) a representation order providing for the services of a Queen's Counsel with one junior counsel where the prosecution is brought by the Serious Fraud Office and the order is made upon receiving a notice of transfer under section 4 of the Criminal Justice Act 1987

but shall have no other power to make an order under this regulation.

(15) In proceedings to which paragraph (3), (4), (5) or (6) applies, a representation order may be amended:

(a) in any terms provided for by paragraph (2) in accordance with the provisions of this regulation; or

(b) to provide for representation by one junior counsel only.

(16) In every case in which a representation order is made under this regulation for the provision of funded services in terms provided for by paragraph (2)(b) or (c), it shall be the duty of:

(a) each representative:

(i) to keep under review the need for more than one advocate to be present in court or otherwise providing services; and

(ii) to consider whether the representation order should be amended as provided for in paragraph (15);

(b) Queen's Counsel, where the services of a Queen's Counsel are provided, to keep under review the question whether he could act alone.

(17) It shall be the duty of each representative, if of the opinion that the representation order should be amended as provided for in paragraph (15), to notify that opinion in writing:

(a) to the other representatives for the assisted person; and

(b) to the court

and the court shall, after considering the opinion and any representations made by any other representatives for the assisted person, determine whether and in what manner the representation order should be amended.

15. The court may grant a representation order for representation by an advocate alone:

(a) in any proceedings referred to in section 12(2)(f) of the Act;

(b) in respect of an appeal to the Court of Appeal or the Courts-Martial Appeal Court; or
(c) in cases of urgency where it appears to the court that there is no time to instruct a solicitor:
  (i) in respect of an appeal to the Crown Court; or
  (ii) in proceedings in which a person is committed to or appears before the Crown Court for trial or sentence, or appears or is brought before that court to be dealt with.

16. Change of representative.   (1) Where a representation order has been granted an application may be made to the court before which the proceedings are heard to select a representative in place of a representative previously selected, and any such application shall state the grounds on which it is made.

(2) The court may:
(a) grant the application where:
  (i) the representative considers himself to be under a duty to withdraw from the case in accordance with his professional rules of conduct and, in such a case, the representative shall provide details of the nature of such duty;
  (ii) there is a breakdown in the relationship between the assisted person and the representative such that effective representation can no longer be provided and, in such a case, the representative shall provide details of the nature of such breakdown;
  (iii) through circumstances beyond his control, the representative is no longer able to represent the assisted person; or
  (iv) some other substantial compelling reason exists; or
(b) refuse the application.

16A.   Where an individual who is granted a right to representation is one of two or more co-defendants whose cases are to be heard together, that individual must select the same representative as a co-defendant unless there is, or is likely to be, a conflict of interest.

PART V
WITHDRAWAL OF REPRESENTATION

1–5695 **17.** (1) Where any charge or proceedings against the assisted person are varied, the court before which the proceedings are heard or, in respect of any proceedings mentioned in regulation 3(2)(a) to (g), the Commission, must—
(a) consider whether the interests of justice continue to require that he be represented in respect of the varied charge or proceedings; and
(b) withdraw the representation order if the interests of justice do not so require.

(1A) The court before which the proceedings are heard or, in respect of any proceedings mentioned in regulation 3(2)(a) to (g), the Commission, must consider whether to withdraw the representation order in any of the following circumstances—
(a) where the assisted person declines to accept the order in the terms which are offered;
(b) otherwise at the request of the assisted person; or
(c) where the representative named in the representation order declines to continue to represent the assisted person.

(2) Where representation is withdrawn, the appropriate officer or the Commission, as appropriate, shall provide written notification to the assisted person and to the solicitor (or, where there was no solicitor assigned, to the advocate), who shall inform any assigned advocate (or, where notification is given to the advocate, any other assigned advocate).

(3) On any subsequent application by the assisted person for a representation order in respect of the same proceedings,
(a) he must declare the withdrawal of the previous representation order and the reason for it; and
(b) where the representation order was withdrawn in the circumstances set out in paragraph (1) or paragraph (1A)(a) or (b) and a representation order is subsequently granted, the court or the Commission, as appropriate, must select the same representative, unless it considers that there are good reasons why it should select a different representative.

PART VI
MISCELLANEOUS

1–5696 **18. Transfer of documents.**   Where an individual is committed or sent for trial by a lower court to a higher court, or appeals or applies for leave to appeal from a lower court to a higher court, the appropriate officer of the lower court shall send to the appropriate officer of the higher court the following documents:
(a) a copy of any representation order previously made in respect of the same proceedings; and
(b) a copy of any application for a representation order which has been refused.

19. Authorisation of expenditure.   (1) Where it appears to the solicitor necessary for the proper conduct of proceedings in the Crown Court for costs to be incurred under the representation order by taking any of the following steps:
(a) obtaining a written report or opinion of one or more experts;
(b) employing a person to provide a written report or opinion (otherwise than as an expert);
(c) obtaining any transcripts or recordings; or

(*d*) performing an act which is either unusual in its nature or involves unusually large expenditure

he may apply to the Costs Committee for prior authority to do so.

(2) The Commission may authorise a person acting on behalf of the Costs Committee to grant prior authority in respect of any application made under paragraph (1).

(3) Where the Costs Committee or a person acting on its behalf authorises the taking of any step specified in paragraph (1), it shall also authorise the maximum to be paid in respect of that step.

20. A representative assigned to an assisted person in any proceedings in the Crown Court may apply to the court for prior authority for the incurring of travelling and accommodation expenses in order to attend at the trial or other main hearing in those proceedings.

21. (1) No question as to the propriety of any step, or as to the amount of the payment within the maximum authorised, with regard to which prior authority has been given under regulation 19 or 20 or under any contract, shall be raised on any determination of costs unless the representative knew or should reasonably have known that the purpose for which it was given had become unnecessary.

(2) Payment may be allowed on a determination of costs in respect of any step with regard to which prior authority may be given, notwithstanding that no such authority was given or that the maximum authorised was exceeded.

22. Restriction on payment.   Where a representation order has been made, the assisted person's solicitor or advocate, whether acting under a representation order or otherwise, shall not receive or be a party to the making of any payment for work done in connection with the proceedings in respect of which the representation order was made except such payments as may be made:

(*a*) by the Lord Chancellor or the Commission; or
(*b*) in respect of any expenses or fees incurred in:

    (i) preparing, obtaining or considering any report, opinion or further evidence, whether provided by an expert witness or otherwise; or
    (ii) obtaining any transcripts or recordings

where an application for an authority to incur such fees or expenses has been refused by the Costs Committee.

23. Notification of very high cost cases.   (1) This regulation applies to very high cost cases where funded services are provided.

(2) Any solicitor who has conduct of a case which is a very high cost case shall notify the Commission in writing accordingly as soon as is practicable.

(3) Where a solicitor fails to comply with the provisions of this regulation without good reason, and as a result there is a loss to public funds, the court or Costs Committee, as appropriate, may refuse payment of his costs up to the extent of such loss.

(4) No payment under paragraph (3) shall be refused unless the solicitor has been given a reasonable opportunity to show why it should not be refused.

24. Duty to report abuse.   Notwithstanding the relationship between or rights of a representative and client or any privilege arising out of such relationship, where the representative for an applicant or assisted person knows or suspects that that person:

(*a*) has intentionally failed to comply with any provision of regulations made under the Act concerning the information to be furnished by him; or
(*b*) in furnishing such information has knowingly made a false statement or false representation

the representative shall immediately report the circumstances to the Commission.

25. Revocation.   The Criminal Defence Service (General) Regulations 2001 are revoked.

SCHEDULE 1
ASSESSMENT OF RESOURCES

1-5697   1. In this Schedule, unless the context otherwise requires:

"capital" means the amount or value of every resource of a capital nature;
"income" means the total income from all sources which the person concerned has received or may reasonably expect to receive in respect of the seven days up to and including the date of his application;
"partner" means a person with whom the person concerned lives as a couple, and includes a person with whom the person concerned is not currently living but from whom he is not living separate and apart;
"the person concerned" means the person whose disposable capital and disposable income are to be assessed;
"supplier" means the solicitor or firm of solicitors being requested to provide or providing funded services to the individual.

2. Any question arising under this Schedule shall be decided by the supplier to whom the individual has applied and that supplier, in deciding any such question, shall have regard to any guidance which may from time to time be given by the Commission as to the application of this Schedule.

3. The disposable capital and disposable income of the person concerned shall be the capital and income as assessed by the supplier after deducting any sums which are to be left out of account or for which allowance is to be made under the provisions of this Schedule.

4. Where the person concerned is a child, the resources of a parent, guardian or any other person who is responsible for maintaining him, or who usually contributes substantially to his maintenance, shall be treated

as his resources, unless, having regard to all the circumstances including the age and resources of the child and any conflict of interest, it appears inequitable to do so.

5. If it appears to the supplier that the person concerned has, with intent to reduce the amount of his disposable capital or disposable income, whether for the purpose of making himself eligible for advice and assistance or otherwise:

(a) directly or indirectly deprived himself of any resources; or
(b) converted any part of his resources into resources which are to be left out of account wholly or partly

the resources of which he has so deprived himself or which he has so converted shall be treated as part of his resources or as not so converted as the case may be.

6. (1) In calculating the capital and income of the person concerned, the resources of his partner shall be treated as his resources unless:

(a) the partner has a contrary interest in the matter in respect of which he is seeking advice and assistance; or
(b) in all the circumstances of the case it would be inequitable or impractical to do so.

(2) In calculating the capital and income of the person concerned, there shall be left out of account so much of any back to work bonus received under section 26 of the Jobseekers Act 1995 as is by virtue of that section to be treated as payable by way of a jobseeker's allowance.

7. In calculating the capital of the person concerned:

(a) there shall be left out of account the value of his household furniture and effects, of his clothes and of tools and implements of his trade;
(b) the value of any interest in land shall be taken to be the amount for which that interest could be sold less the amount of any mortgage debt or hereditable security, subject to the following:

(i) in calculating the value of his interests, the total amount to be deducted in respect of all mortgage debts or hereditable securities shall not exceed £100,000;
(ii) in making the deductions in sub-paragraph (i), any mortgage debt or hereditable security in respect of the main or only dwelling shall be deducted last; and
(iii) the first £100,000 of the value of his interest (if any) in the main or only dwelling in which he resides, after the application of sub-paragraphs (i) and (ii), shall be disregarded;

(c) where the person concerned resides in more than one dwelling, the supplier shall decide which is the main dwelling; and
(d) where the person concerned has living with him one or more of the following persons, namely, a partner whose resources are required to be aggregated with his, a dependent child or a dependent relative wholly or substantially maintained by him, a deduction shall be made of £335 in respect of the first person, £200 in respect of the second and £100 in respect of each further person.

8. (1) In calculating the disposable income of the person concerned, there shall be left out of account:

(a) any income tax paid or payable on income treated under the provisions of this Schedule as his income;
(b) any contributions estimated to have been paid under Part I of the Social Security Contributions and Benefits Act 1992 during or in respect of the seven days up to and including the date of the application for advice and assistance;
(c) the following payments made under the Social Security Contributions and Benefits Act 1992:

(i) disability living allowance;
(ii) attendance allowance paid under section 64;
(iii) constant attendance allowance paid under section 104 or paragraph 4 or 7(2) of Schedule 8 as an increase to a disablement pension; and
(iv) any payment made out of the social fund; and

(d) any payment made under the Community Care (Direct Payments) Act 1996 or under regulations made under section 57 of the Health and Social Care Act 2001 (direct payments).

(2) Subject to sub-paragraph (3), in calculating the disposable income of the person concerned there shall be a deduction at or equivalent to the following rates (as they applied at the beginning of the period of calculation):

(a) in respect of the maintenance of his partner, the difference between the income support allowance for a couple both aged not less than 18 (which is specified in column 2 of paragraph 1(3)(c) of Schedule 2 to the Income Support (General) Regulations 1987, and the allowance for a single person aged not less than 25 (which is specified in column 2 of paragraph 1(1)(e) of that Schedule); and
(b) in respect of the maintenance of any dependant child or dependant relative of his, where such persons are members of his household:

(i) in the case of a dependant child or a dependant relative aged 15 or under at the beginning of the period of calculation, the amount specified at (a) in column 2 in paragraph 2(1) of the Schedule referred to in sub-paragraph (a); and
(ii) in the case of a dependant child or a dependant relative aged 16 or over at the beginning of the period of calculation, the amount specified at (b) in column 2 in paragraph 2(1) of that Schedule.

(3) The supplier may reduce any rate provided by virtue of paragraph (2) by taking into account the income and other resources of the dependant child or dependant relative to such extent as appears to him to be equitable.

(4) In ascertaining whether a child is a dependant child or whether a person is a dependant relative for the purposes of this paragraph, regard shall be had to their income and other resources.

9. If the person concerned is making bona fide payments for the maintenance of a former partner, a child or a relative who is not (in any such case) a member of his household, there shall be a deduction of such payment as was or will be made in respect of the seven days up to and including the date of the application for advice and assistance.

10. Where it appears to the supplier that there has been some error or mistake in the assessment of the disposable income or disposable capital of the person concerned, he may reassess the disposable income or disposable capital or, as the case may be, amend the assessment and in the latter case the amended assessment shall for all purposes be substituted for the original assessment.

Criminal Defence Service (Financial Eligibility) Regulations 2006[1]
(SI 2006/2492)

1-5699　1. Citation and commencement. These Regulations may be cited as the Criminal Defence Service (Financial Eligibility) Regulations 2006 and come into force on 2nd October 2006.

---

1. Made by the Lord Chancellor in exercise of the powers conferred by s 26 of, and para 3B of Schedule 3 to, the Access to Justice Act 1999.

1-5700　2. Interpretation. (1) In these Regulations—

"the Act" means the Access to Justice Act 1999;

"child care costs" means the costs of care which is provided by one or more of the following care providers—

　(a) a school on school premises, out of school hours;
　(b) a local authority, out of school hours—

　　(i) for children who are not disabled, in respect of the period beginning on their eighth birthday and ending on the day preceding the first Monday in September following their 15th birthday;
　　(ii) for children who are disabled, in respect of the period beginning on their eighth birthday and ending on the day preceding the first Monday in September following their 16th birthday;

　(c) a child care provider approved in accordance with the Tax Credit (New Category of Care Provider) Regulations 1999;
　(d) persons registered under Part XA of the Children Act 1989;
　(e) persons referred to in paragraph 1 or 2 of Schedule 9A to the Children Act 1989, in schools or establishments referred to in those paragraphs;
　(f) persons prescribed in regulations made pursuant to section 12(4) of the Tax Credits Act 2002;

　other than costs paid in respect of the child's compulsory education or by the individual to his partner (or vice versa) in respect of any child for whom either or any of them is responsible in accordance with regulation 10 of the Council Tax Benefit Regulations 2006, or in respect of care provided by a relative of the child wholly or mainly in the child's home;

"the Commission" means the Legal Services Commission established under section 1 of the Act;

"gross annual income" means total annual income, as at the date of the application for a representation order, from all sources, other than the receipt of any of the following—

　(a) any of the following payments made under the Social Security Contributions and Benefits Act 1992—

　　(i) attendance allowance paid under section 64;
　　(ii) severe disablement allowance;
　　(iii) carer's allowance;
　　(iv) disability living allowance;
　　(v) constant attendance allowance paid under section 104 or paragraph 4 or 7(2) of Schedule 8 as an increase to a disablement pension;
　　(vi) council tax benefit;
　　(vii) any payment made out of the social fund;

　(b) any direct payments made under the Community Care, Services for Carers and Children's Services (Direct Payments) (England) Regulations 2003 or the Community Care, Services for Carers and Children's Services (Direct Payments) (Wales) Regulations 2004;
　(c) any exceptionally severe disablement allowance paid under the Personal Injuries (Civilians) Scheme 1983;
　(d) any pensions paid under the Naval, Military and Air Forces etc (Disablement and Death) Service Pensions Order 2006;
　(e) any Independent Living Funds payments;
　(f) any financial support paid under an agreement for the care of a foster child;

"the Independent Living Funds" means the Independent Living Fund, the Independent Living (Extension) Fund and the Independent Living (1983) Fund;

"the Independent Living Fund" means the charitable trust established out of funds provided by the Secretary of State for the purpose of providing financial assistance to those persons incapacitated by or otherwise suffering from very severe disablement who are in need of such assistance to enable them to live independently;

"the Independent Living (Extension) Fund" means the Trust of that name established by a deed dated 25th February 1993 and made between the Secretary of State for Social Security of the one part and Robin Glover Wendt and John Fletcher Shepherd of the other part;

"the Independent Living (1993) Fund" means the Trust of that name established by a deed dated 25th February 1993 and made between the Secretary of State for Social Security of the one part and Robin Glover Wendt and John Fletcher Shepherd of the other part;

"partner" means a person with whom the individual lives as a couple, and includes a person with whom the individual is not currently living but from whom he is not living separate and apart;

"period of calculation" means the period of one year ending on the date on which an application for a representation order is made;

"representation authority" means the Commission or a court officer or other person to whom the Commission, in accordance with section 3(4) of the Act, has delegated its functions under paragraph 2A of Schedule 3 to the Act;

"representation order" means a document granting a right to representation under section 14 of the Act.

(2) Subject to the proviso in regulation 7(1), in these Regulations a reference to the financial resources, income or financial circumstances of the individual includes a reference to the financial resources, income or financial circumstances of his partner.

1–5701 3. Scope.   These Regulations apply to those criminal proceedings which—

(a) are referred to in section 12(2)(a) to (f) of the Act and in regulation 3(2) (other than sub-paragraph (h)) of the Criminal Defence Service (General) (No 2) Regulations 2001; and

(b) are in a magistrates' court.

1–5702 4. Relevant authority.   The representation authority is the relevant authority for the purposes of section 26 of, and paragraph 3B of Schedule 3 to, the Act.

1–5703 5. Assessment by representation authority.   (1) The representation authority must assess whether the financial resources of the individual are such that he is eligible to be granted a representation order in accordance with this regulation and regulations 7 to 10.

(2) The representation authority must treat an individual who at the date of the application is under the age of 16 or who is under the age of 18 and in full-time education as financially eligible for a representation order, and paragraphs (3) to (5) of this regulation and regulations 7 to 14 do not apply in such a case.

(3) Where the representation authority is satisfied that the individual is directly or indirectly in receipt of a qualifying benefit, it must take his gross annual income as not exceeding the sum specified for the time being in regulation 9(2).

(4) The following are qualifying benefits for the purposes of paragraph (3)—

(a) income support;

(b) income-based jobseeker's allowance;

(c) guarantee credit under section 1(3)(a) of the State Pension Credit Act 2002.

(5) Except where paragraph (2) or (3) applies, the representation authority must calculate the gross annual income and, if applicable, the annual disposable income of the individual in accordance with regulations 7 to 10.

1–5704 6. Furnishing evidence.   The representation authority may at any time require the individual to provide documentary evidence in support of his application.

1–5705 7. Resources of other persons.   (1) In calculating the income of the individual, the representation authority must treat the resources of his partner as his resources, unless the partner has a contrary interest in the proceedings in respect of which he is seeking a representation order.

(2) Where it appears to the representation authority that—

(a) another person is or has been or is likely to be substantially maintaining the individual or his partner; or

(b) any of the resources of another person have been or are likely to be made available to the individual or his partner,

the representation authority may assess or estimate the value of the resources of that other person and may treat all or any part of them as the resources of the individual.

1–5706 8. Deprivation etc of resources.   If it appears to the representation authority that the individual or his partner has, with intent to reduce the amount of his resources, whether for the purpose of making the individual eligible for a representation order or otherwise—

(a) directly or indirectly deprived himself of any resources; or

(b) transferred any resources to another person,

the resources of which he has so deprived himself, or which he has transferred, are to be treated as part of the individual's resources.

1–5707 9. Financial eligibility.   (1) Where an individual applies for a representation order, the representation authority must calculate the gross annual income of the individual and, where he has a partner or has children living in his household, must divide the total according to the scale set out in the Schedule to these Regulations.

(2) An individual is eligible for a representation order if his gross annual income, as adjusted under paragraph (1) where appropriate, is £11,590 or less.

(3) An individual is not eligible for a representation order if his gross annual income, as adjusted under paragraph (1) where appropriate, is £20,740 or more.

1–5708 10. (1) Where an individual's gross annual income, as adjusted under regulation 9(1) where appropriate, is more than £11,590 and less than £20,740, the representation authority must calculate the individual's annual disposable income in accordance with paragraph (2).

(2) There are to be deducted from the individual's gross annual income—

(a) any income tax paid or payable in respect of the period of calculation;

(b) any contributions estimated to have been paid under Part 1 of the Social Security Contributions and Benefits Act 1992, in respect of the period of calculation;

(c) any council tax paid or payable in respect of the period of calculation;

(d) either—

(i) any annual rent or annual payment (whether of interest or capital) in respect of a mortgage debt or hereditable security, payable by him in respect of his only or main dwelling, less any housing benefit paid under the Social Security Contributions and Benefits Act 1992; or

(ii) the annual cost of his living accommodation;

(e) any child care costs paid or payable in respect of the period of calculation;

(f) if the individual is making bona fide payments for the maintenance of a former partner or of a child or a relative who is not (in such case) a member of his household, the amount of such payments paid or payable in respect of the period of calculation;

(g) an amount representing cost of living expenses in respect of the period of calculation, being either—

(i) £5,304; or

(ii) if the individual has a partner or has children living in his household, an amount calculated in accordance with the scale set out in the Schedule to these Regulations.

(3) An individual is eligible for a representation order if his annual disposable income, as calculated under this regulation, does not exceed £3,156.

1–5709 11. Duty to report change in financial circumstances. (1) An individual who has been granted a representation order must—

(a) forthwith inform the representation authority of any change in his financial circumstances of which he is aware, which has occurred since any calculation of his resources and which might affect his eligibility for a representation order; and

(b) inform the representation authority of any change in his financial circumstances of which he should reasonably be aware, which has occurred since any calculation of his resources and which might affect his eligibility for a representation order.

(2) Where, as a result of any such change, the individual is no longer financially eligible for a representation order, the representation authority must withdraw the grant of representation.

1–5710 12. Re-calculation of income following error etc. Where—

(a) it appears to the representation authority that there has been some error in the calculation of the individual's income; or

(b) new information which is relevant to the application has come to light (whether under regulation 11 or otherwise),

the representation authority must re-calculate the income and, if the individual is no longer financially eligible for a representation order, must withdraw the order.

1–5711 13. Renewal of application. An individual who has been refused a representation order on the grounds that his financial resources are not such that he is eligible for such an order may renew his application if, but only if, there is a change in his financial circumstances which might affect his eligibility for a representation order.

1–5712 14. Review of decision. (1) An individual who has been refused a representation order on the grounds that his financial resources are not such that he is eligible for such an order may apply for a review of the decision—

(a) to the representation authority, on the ground that there has been a miscalculation of his income or an administrative error; or

(b) to the Commission, on the ground that he does not have sufficient means to pay for the cost of legal assistance, notwithstanding that his financial resources are such that he is not eligible for a representation order under these Regulations.

(2) An application for a review must be made on such form as the Commission may specify.

(3) Where the grounds of the application are those mentioned in paragraph (1)(b), the individual must provide full particulars of his income and expenditure and a certificate by a solicitor as to the individual's likely costs of the proceedings.

(4) Where—

(a) the grounds of the application are those mentioned in paragraph (1)(a); and

(b) the representation authority is not the Commission,

the representation authority may refer the application to the Commission for its decision.

(5) On a review the representation authority or the Commission (as the case may be) must uphold the decision or grant the individual a representation order.

(6) The Commission may, if it thinks that the application raises a question of such importance that it should be decided by the High Court, refer that question to the High Court for its decision.

1–5713   15. Withdrawal of representation order. Where the individual fails to comply with a requirement under regulation 6 and a representation order has been granted, the representation authority must withdraw the order unless it is satisfied that there are good reasons why it should not do so.

1–5714   16. Transitional provisions. An application for a representation order which is received before 2nd October 2006 is to be dealt with as if these Regulations had not been made.

1–5715   SCHEDULE
                        SCALE FOR THE PURPOSES OF REGULATIONS 9(1) AND 10(2)(G)(II)

For the purposes of regulation 9(1), add the relevant figure below to 1.00 and divide the individual's gross annual income by the total.

For the purpose of regulation 10(2)(g)(ii), add the relevant figure below to 1.00 and multiply £5,304 by the total.

A partner	0.64
Each child of the individual in his household, aged 0–1	0.15
Each child, as above, aged 2–4	0.30
Each child, as above, aged 5–7	0.34
Each child, as above, aged 8–10	0.38
Each child, as above, aged 11–12	0.41
Each child, as above, aged 13–15	0.44
Each child, as above, aged 16–18	0.59

Criminal Defence Service (Representation Orders and Consequential Amendments) Regulations 2006[1]
(SI 2006/2493)

1–5716   1. Citation and commencement. These Regulations may be cited as the Criminal Defence Service (Representation Orders and Consequential Amendments) Regulations 2006 and come into force on 2nd October 2006.

1. Made by the Lord Chancellor in exercise of the powers conferred by s 26 of, and paras 2A and 3A(2) of Schedule 3 to, the Access to Justice Act 1999.

1–5717   2. Interpretation. In these Regulations—

"the Act" means the Access to Justice Act 1999;

"the Commission" means the Legal Services Commission established under section 1 of the Act;

"relevant proceedings" means criminal proceedings which—

(a)   are mentioned in section 12(2)(a) to (f) of the Act; and

(b)   are in a magistrates' court;

"representation authority" means the Commission or a court officer or other person to whom the Commission, in accordance with section 3(4) of the Act, has delegated its functions under paragraph 2A of Schedule 3 to the Act;

"representation order" means a document granting a right to representation under section 14 of the Act.

1–5718   3. Proceedings in which representation order may be granted. The Commission may, at any stage of the proceedings, grant to an individual a representation order in respect of relevant proceedings.

1–5719   4. Extension of representation order. A representation order granted to an individual extends to—

(a)   the Crown Court, if the proceedings continue there; and

(b)   any proceedings incidental to the proceedings,

but does not extend to an appeal.

1–5720   5. Withdrawal of representation order. (1) Where any charge or proceedings against the individual are varied, the representation authority must—

(a)   consider whether the interests of justice require that he be represented in respect of the varied charge or proceedings; and

(b)   withdraw the representation order if the interests of justice do not so require.

(2) The representation authority must consider whether to withdraw the representation order in any of the following circumstances—

(a)   where the individual declines to accept the order in the terms on which it is granted;

(b)   otherwise at the request of the individual; or

(c)   where the representative named in the representation order declines to continue to represent the individual.

1–5721   6. Transitional provisions

7–10. Consequential amendments

Criminal Defence Service (Representation Orders: Appeals etc) Regulations 2006[1]

(SI 2006/2494)

1–5722   1. Citation and commencement. These Regulations may be cited as the Criminal Defence Service (Representation Orders: Appeals etc) Regulations 2006 and come into force on 2nd October 2006.

_____

1. Made by the Lord Chancellor in exercise of the powers conferred by s 26 of, and para 4 of Schedule 3 to, the Access to Justice Act 1999.

1–5723   2. Interpretation. In these Regulations—

"the Act" means the Access to Justice Act 1999;
"appropriate officer" means—

in a magistrates' court, the justices' clerk or the designated officer;
in the Crown Court, a court manager or a court officer designated by him to act on his behalf for the purposes of these Regulations;
in the Court of Appeal—

the Registrar of Criminal Appeals or the Head of the Civil Appeals Office, as appropriate; or
in either case, a court officer designated by him to act on his behalf for the purposes of these Regulations;

"the Commission" means the Legal Services Commission established under section 1 of the Act;
"representation authority" has the same meaning as in the Criminal Defence Service (Representation Orders and Consequential Amendments) Regulations 2006;
"representation order" means a document granting a right to representation under section 14 of the Act.

1–5724   3. General provisions. (1) An appeal or a renewed application under these Regulations must be made on such form as is from time to time specified—

(a) in the case of appeals, and renewed applications under regulation 8, by the Commission; and
(b) in the case of renewed applications under regulations 6 and 7, by the Lord Chancellor.

(2) The individual must provide such further particulars and documents as the person or body determining the appeal or renewed application may require in relation to his appeal or application.
(3) An appeal or a renewed application will be determined without a hearing unless the person or body determining the appeal or application directs otherwise.
(4) Where an application is referred under regulation 6(2)(b), 7(2)(b) or 9(3)(b), it is to be treated thereafter as if it were an appeal.
(5) Written reasons must be given for any decision on an appeal or a renewed application.
(6) The date of any representation order granted on an appeal or a renewed application under these Regulations—

(a) in proceedings in the Court of Appeal, is the date on which the original application for the order was received, subject to regulation 10(6) of the Criminal Defence Service (General) (No 2) Regulations 2001; and
(b) in other proceedings, is the date on which the original application was received.

1–5725   4. Appeals: magistrates' courts. (1) In this regulation "court" means the magistrates' court in which the proceedings in respect of which the individual is seeking a representation order are being or are to be heard and includes a single justice.
(2) An individual may appeal to the court against a decision to refuse to grant a representation order made on the grounds that the interests of justice do not require such an order to be granted.
(3) The court must either—

(a) uphold the decision; or
(b) decide that it would be in the interests of justice for a representation order to be granted.

(4) Where the court makes a decision under paragraph (3)(b), the individual may apply to the representation authority for a representation order; and—

(a) if the individual states in writing, verified by a statement of truth, that his financial resources have not changed since the date of his original application so as to make him financially ineligible for a representation order, the representation authority must grant the order; or
(b) if his financial resources may have so changed, the representation authority—

(i) must determine whether the individual is financially eligible to be granted a representation order in accordance with the Criminal Defence Service (Financial Eligibility) Regulations 2006; and
(ii) if he is so eligible, must grant the order.

1–5726 5. An appeal does not lie against a decision to refuse to grant a representation order in respect of proceedings in a magistrates' court made on the grounds that the individual is not financially eligible to be granted such an order.

1–5737 **6. Renewals of application where representation order refused: Crown Court.** (1) An individual whose application for the grant of a representation order in respect of proceedings in the Crown Court has been refused on the grounds that the interests of justice do not require such an order to be granted may make a renewed application to the appropriate officer who, or court which, refused the application.

(2) Where a renewed application is made to the appropriate officer, he may—

(a) grant the order; or

(b) refer the application—

(i) in the Crown Court, to a judge of the Crown Court; or

(ii) in a magistrates' court, to the court or a District Judge (Magistrates' Court),

who may grant the order or refuse the application.

7. Renewals of application where representation order refused: Court of Appeal

1–5728 **8. Renewals of application where representation order refused: Commission.** An individual whose application for the grant of a representation order in respect of proceedings, other than proceedings in a magistrates' court, has been refused by the Commission on the grounds that the interests of justice do not require such an order to be granted may make a renewed application to the Commission, which may grant the order or refuse the application.

1–5729 **9. Withdrawals of representation order.** (1) An individual whose representation order has been withdrawn may apply on one occasion to the person who, or body which, withdrew the order to set aside the withdrawal.

(2) Any application must be made on such form as is from time to time specified—

(a) by the Commission, in the case of withdrawal by the Commission or by the representation authority in proceedings in a magistrates' court; and

(b) by the Lord Chancellor, in the case of withdrawal by the appropriate officer or the court in proceedings in the Crown Court or the Court of Appeal.

(3) Where an application is made to the appropriate officer, he may—

(a) set aside the withdrawal; or

(b) refer the application—

(i) in a magistrates' court, to the court or a District Judge (Magistrates' Court);

(ii) in the Crown Court, to a judge of the Crown Court; or

(iii) in the Court of Appeal, to a judge of the Court of Appeal,

who may set aside the withdrawal or refuse the application.

10. Transitional provisions

11. Revocation

Practice and Procedure

Magistrates' Courts (Attachment of Earnings) Rules 1971[1]
(SI 1971/809 amended by SI 2001/615 and SI 2003/1236)

1–5794 1. *Citation and operation.*

---

1. Made under s 15 of the Justices of the Peace Act 1949, as extended by s 122 of the Magistrates' Courts Act 1952, s 5 of the Justices of the Peace Act 1968, and ss 6(3), 9(3), 12(1), 17(3), 19(2), 20(4) and 26(2) of the Attachment of Earnings Act 1971. See now Magistrates' Courts Act 1980, ss 144, 145 and 154.

1–5795 **2. Interpretation.** (1) Sections 2 and 25(1) of the Act shall apply to the interpretation of these Rules as they apply to the interpretation of the Act.

(2) The Interpretation Act 1978 shall apply to the interpretation of these Rules as it applies to the interpretation of an Act of Parliament.

(3) Any reference in these Rules to "the Act" is a reference to the Attachment of Earnings Act 1971.

(4) Any reference in these Rules to any enactment or rule is a reference to that enactment or rule as amended by any enactment or rule.

(5) *Revoked.*

(6) Any reference in these Rules to an attachment of earnings order shall be construed subject to the provisions of Rule 23.

1–5796 3. *Revocation.*

1–5797   4. Jurisdiction as respects complaints for an attachment of earnings order. A magistrates' court shall have jurisdiction to hear a complaint for an attachment of earnings order if it would have jurisdiction to enforce payment of any arrears under the related maintenance order.

1–5798   5.   *Revoked.*

1–5799   6. Service of orders and notices. (1) Where a magistrates' court makes an attachment of earnings order or an order varying or discharging such an order, the justices' chief executive for the court shall cause a copy of the order to be served on the employer and shall send a copy of the order to the debtor.

(2) Where an attachment of earnings order made by a magistrates' court ceases to have effect as provided in section 8 or 11 of the Act, notice of cessation shall be given to the employer.

(3) The notice required by the preceding paragraph shall be given by the justices' chief executive for the magistrates' court—

(a)   which made or confirmed the maintenance order (in a case to which section 11(1)(*c*) of the Act applies):

(b)   in which the maintenance order is registered under any enactment (in a case to which section 11(1)(*a*), (*b*) or (*d*) of the Act applies);

(c)   which issued the warrant of commitment or exercised the power conferred by section 65(2) of the Magistrates' Courts Act 1952[1] (in a case to which section 8 of the Act applies).

---

1.   See now the Magistrates' Courts Act 1980, s 77(2).

1–5800   7. Particulars of debtor. The particulars of the debtor for the purpose of enabling him to be identified which, so far as they are known, are to be included in an attachment of earnings order under section 6(3) of the Act shall be—

(a)   full name and address;

(b)   place of work;

(c)   nature of work and works number, if any.

1–5801   8. Notice of application for appropriate variation order. The justices' chief executive for a magistrates' court, by which an application under section 10 of the Act for the appropriate variation of an attachment of earnings order is to be heard, shall give notice in writing of the time and place appointed for the hearing of the application to the person entitled to receive payment under the related maintenance order (whether directly or through the officer of any court).

1–5802   9. Jurisdiction as respects complaints for the discharge and variation of attachment of earnings order. (1) This Rule shall apply to a complaint for the discharge or variation of an attachment of earnings order except where the related maintenance order—

(a)   is an affiliation order to which section 88(2)(*a*) of the Children and Young Persons Act 1933[1] applies;

(b)   is an order made under section 87[2] of that Act;

(c)   is an order made under section 43 of the National Assistance Act 1948;

(d)   is an order made under section 30 of the Children and Young Persons Act 1963[3].

(2) Where a complaint is made to a justice of the peace[4] acting for the same petty sessions area as the court which made the attachment of earnings order and it appears to him that—

(a)   the person in whose favour the attachment of earnings order was made, or

(b)   the debtor,

is for the time being in some petty sessions area other than that for which the justice is acting, or that the complainant is the justices' chief executive for a magistrates' court acting for such other area, then, if it appears to the justice that the complaint may be more conveniently dealt with by a magistrates' court acting for that other area, he may cause the justices' chief executive for the court to send the complaint by post to the justices' chief executive for the other court and for that purpose shall write down the complaint, if this has not already been done.

(3) On receipt by the clerk of a magistrates' court of a complaint under the preceding paragraph, he shall bring the complaint before the Court and the court shall issue a summons requiring the person appropriate under section 19(4) of the Act to appear before it, and shall hear and determine the complaint.

---

1.   Replaced by s 49(4) of the Child Care Act 1980 (now repealed).
2.   Replaced by s 47 of the Child Care Act 1980 (now repealed).
3.   Replaced by s 51 of the Child Care Act 1980 (now repealed).
4.   The complaint may also be made to a justices' clerk (Justices' Clerks Rules 1999, this Part, post) who may determine that the complaint be dealt with by another magistrates' court (r 22(2)(*b*), post).

1–5803   10. Complaints for variation or discharge of attachment of earnings orders against persons outside United Kingdom. (1) Where a complaint for the variation or discharge of an attachment of earnings order is made against a person who resides outside the United Kingdom and that person does not appear at the time and place appointed for the hearing of the complaint, then, subject to paragraph (2) of this Rule, the court may, if it thinks it reasonable in all the circumstances to do so, proceed to hear and determine the complaint in accordance with section 20(3) of the Act if it is proved to the satisfaction of the court that the complainant has taken any of the following steps to give the person against whom the complaint is made notice of the complaint and of the time and place appointed for the hearing thereof, that is to say—

(a)   has caused written notice of the matters aforesaid to be delivered to the said person;

(b)   has caused written notice of the matters aforesaid to be sent by post addressed to the said person at his last known or usual place of abode or at his place of business or at some other address at which there is ground for believing that it will reach him; or

(c)   has caused notice of the matters aforesaid to be inserted in one or more newspapers on one or more occasions.

(2) Where it is proposed to take any such steps as are mentioned in subparagraph (b) or (c) of the preceding paragraph, the complainant shall apply for directions to a justice of the peace[1] acting for the same petty sessions area as the court by which the complaint is to be heard, and the taking of such steps shall be effective for the purposes of this Rule only if they were taken in accordance with the directions given by the said justice.

(3) Paragraph (1) of Rule 55 of the Magistrates' Courts Rules 1968[2] shall apply for the purposes of proving the delivery of a written notice in pursuance of sub-paragraph (a) of paragraph (1) of this Rule as it applies for the purpose of proving the service of a summons.

In relation to a solemn declaration made outside the United Kingdom, paragraph (1) of the said Rule 55[2], as applied by this paragraph, shall have effect as if for the reference to the authorities mentioned in the said paragraph (1) there were substituted a reference to a consular officer of Her Majesty's Government in the United Kingdom or any person for the time being authorised by law, in the place where the declarant is, to administer an oath for any judicial or other legal purpose.

(4) Paragraph (2) of the said Rule 55[2] shall apply for the purpose of proving the sending of a written notice in pursuance of sub-paragraph (b) of paragraph (1) of this Rule, or the insertion of a notice in a newspaper in pursuance of sub-paragraph (c) thereof, as it applies for the purpose of proving the service of any process, provided, as respects the insertion of a notice in a newspaper, that a copy of the newspaper containing the notice is annexed to the certificate.

---

1. Or justices' clerk: r 22(2), post.
2. See now r 67 of the Magistrates' Courts Rules 1981.

1–5804   **11. Complaints by debtors for variation or discharge of attachment of earnings orders against persons who cannot be found.**   (1) Where a complaint by the debtor for the variation or discharge of an attachment of earnings order is made against a person and that person does not appear at the time and place appointed for the hearing of the complaint, then, subject to paragraph (2) of this Rule, the court may, if it thinks it reasonable in all the circumstances to do so, proceed to hear and determine the complaint, notwithstanding the absence of proof that that person had knowledge of the summons as required by Rule 82(2) of the Magistrates' Courts Rules 1968[1], if it is proved to the satisfaction of the court that the summons in respect of the complaint was served in accordance with the provisions of Rule 82(1) (b) or (c) of those Rules[1] and the complainant has caused notice of the complaint and of the time and place appointed for the hearing thereof to be inserted in one or more newspapers on one or more occasions.

(2) Where it is proposed to rely upon the provisions of the preceding paragraph of this Rule, the complainant shall apply for directions to a justice of the peace[2] acting for the same petty sessions area as the court by which the complaint is to be heard, and the giving of notice in a newspaper shall be effective for the purposes of this Rule only if the notice was given in accordance with the directions given by the said justice.

(3) Paragraph (2) of Rule 55 of the Magistrates' Courts Rules 1968[3] shall apply for the purpose of proving the insertion of a notice in a newspaper in pursuance of paragraph (1) of this rule as it applies for the purpose of proving the service of any process, provided that a copy of the newspaper containing the notice is annexed to the certificate.

---

1. See now r 99 of the Magistrates' Courts Rules 1981.
2. Or justices' clerk: r 22(2)(c), post.
3. See now r 67(2) of the 1981 Rules.

1–5805   **12. Variation of attachment of earnings order on change of employment.**   Where an attachment of earnings order has lapsed under section 9(4) of the Act on the debtor's ceasing to be in the employment of the person to whom the order was directed and it appears to a magistrates' court[1], acting for the same petty sessions area as the court which made the order, that the debtor has subsequently entered the employment of a person (whether the same as before or another), the court may, of its own motion, vary the order by directing it to that person and may make any consequential amendment to the order made necessary by this variation.

---

1. Or justices' clerk: r 22(2)(c), post.

1–5806   **13. Discharge of attachment of earnings order by court of its own motion.**   (1) Where it appears to a magistrates' court[1] acting for the same petty sessions areas as the magistrates' court which made the attachment of earnings order that the debtor is not in the employment of the person to whom the order is directed and that the likelihood of the debtor's entering the employment of any person is not such as to justify preserving the order, the court may, of its own motion, discharge the order.

(2) Where a magistrates' court has made an attachment of earnings order and, by virtue of

section 7, 21 or 30 of the Matrimonial Proceedings and Property Act 1970[2], the related maintenance order ceases to have effect because of the remarriage of the person entitled to receive payments under it, a magistrates' court acting for the same petty sessions area as that court may, of its own motion, discharge the attachment of earnings order, if there are no arrears to be recovered.

---

    1. Or justices' clerk: r 22(2)(c), post.
    2. Section 30 of the 1970 Act amended s 7 of the Matrimonial Proceedings (Magistrates' Courts) Act 1960, by adding sub-ss (4) to (6) thereto.

1–5807   14. Temporary variation of protected earnings rate.   (1) A justice of the peace[1] acting for the same petty sessions area as the magistrates' court which made the attachment of earnings order may, on a written application made by the debtor on the ground of a material change in the debtor's resources and needs since the order was made or last varied, by order (hereinafter referred to as a temporary variation order) vary the attachment of earnings order for a period of not more than four weeks by an increase of the protected earnings rate.

    (2) *Revoked.*

    (3) The justices' chief executive for the magistrates' court which made the attachment of earnings order shall cause a copy of any temporary order to be served on the employer and shall give him notice if the temporary variation order is discharged and the justices' chief executive shall also send a copy to the person entitled to receive payments under the related maintenance order (whether directly or through an officer of any court).

    (4) Where an application for the variation or discharge of an attachment of earnings order is made to a magistrates' court and there is in existence a temporary variation order in respect of the attachment of earnings order, the court may, of its own motion, discharge the temporary variation order.

---

    1. Or justices' clerk: r 22(2)(e), post.

1–5808   15. Consolidated attachment orders.   (1) In this Rule references to an attachment of earnings order are references to such an order made by a magistrates' court and do not include such an order made to secure payments under a magistrates' court maintenance order.

    (2) Where a magistrates' court has power to make more than one attachment of earnings order in respect of the liabilities of a debtor, it may make a consolidated attachment order to discharge those liabilities.

    (3) Where a magistrates' court has power to make an attachment of earnings order in respect of a debtor who is already subject to such an order (whether or not it is itself a consolidated attachment order) made by any magistrates' court, the court may, subject to the provisions of this Rule, discharge the existing order and make a consolidated attachment order in respect of that debtor.

    (4) Where two or more attachment of earnings orders (whether or not they are themselves consolidated attachment orders) made by magistrates' courts are in existence in respect of one debtor, a magistrates' court acting for the same petty sessions area as one of those courts may, subject to the provisions of this Rule, discharge the existing orders and make a consolidated attachment order in respect of that debtor.

    (5) A magistrates' court may exercise the powers conferred under paragraphs (2) to (4) of this Rule either of its own motion or on the application of the debtor.

    (6) A debtor may apply to a magistrates' court for a consolidated attachment order—

    (i) in a case to which paragraph (2) or (3) of this Rule applies, during the hearing of the proceedings for the enforcement of the fine or other liability;

    (ii) in a case to which paragraph (4) of this Rule applies, by complaint.

    (7) Where an employer applies in writing to the clerk of a magistrates' court which has power to make a consolidated attachment order requesting the court to make such an order, the clerk shall bring the application before the court, and, if it appears to the court that the application is justified, the court shall proceed as if it had determined of its own motion to make such an order.

    (8) Before a magistrates' court exercises of its own motion the powers conferred under paragraph (4) of this Rule, it shall cause written notice to be given to the debtor of his right to make representations to the court.

    (9) Where a magistrates' court has power to make a consolidated attachment order under paragraph (3) or (4) of this Rule and a relevant attachment of earnings order has been made by a magistrates' court acting for another petty sessions area, the first mentioned court shall cause notice to be given to the clerk of the second mentioned court and shall not discharge that attachment of earnings order unless the enforcement of the sum to which the order relates is transferred to the first mentioned court under section 72 of the Magistrates' Courts Act 1952[1] (transfer of fines), paragraph 7 of Schedule 3 to the Legal Aid Act 1974 (transfer of enforcement of legal aid contribution orders) or Rule 16 of these Rules as the case may be.

    (10) Where a magistrates' court makes a consolidated attachment order, it shall specify in the order such normal deduction rate as the court thinks reasonable and this rate may be less than the sum of the normal deduction rates specified in any attachment of earnings orders discharged by the court.

---

    1. See now Magistrates' Courts Act 1980, ss 89 and 90, ante.

1–5809   16. Transfer of fines etc with view to making consolidated attachment order.   (1) Where a magistrates' court has made or has power to make an attachment of earnings order to secure—

    (*a*) the payment of any sum adjudged to be paid by a conviction or treated (by any enactment relating to the collection and enforcement of fines, costs, compensation or forfeited recognisances) as so adjudged to be paid, or

    (*b*) the payment of any sum required to be paid by a legal aid contribution order,

and a magistrates' court acting for some other petty sessions area has made an attachment of earnings order in respect of the debtor, then, if the debtor does not reside in either petty sessions area, the first mentioned court[1] may make an order making payment of that sum enforceable in the petty sessions area for which the second mentioned court acted.

(2) As from the date on which an order is made under paragraph (1) of this Rule with respect to any sum, all functions under any enactment relating to that sum which, if no such order had been made, would have been exercisable by the court which made the order, shall be exercisable by a court acting for the petty sessions area specified in the order, or the justices' chief executive for that court, as the case may be, and not otherwise.

(3) The making of an order under paragraph (1) of this Rule with respect to any sum shall not prejudice the power to make a subsequent order with respect to that sum under that paragraph or under section 72 or 72A of the Magistrates' Courts Act 1952[2] or paragraph 7 of Schedule 3 to the Legal Aid Act 1974.

---

    1. Or the justices' clerk of that court: r 22(2)(*f*), post.
    2. See now Magistrates' Courts Act 1980, ss 89 and 90, ante.

1–5810   **17. Disposal of sums paid under consolidated attachment orders.**   (1) A justices' chief executive for a magistrates' court receiving a payment under a consolidated attachment order shall, subject to paragraph (2) below, apply the money in payment of the sums secured by the order, paying first any sums previously secured by an attachment of earnings order which was discharged in consequence of the making of the consolidated attachment order.

(2) Where two or more attachment of earnings orders were discharged in consequence of the making of the consolidated attachment order the sums due under the orders shall be paid in the chronological order of the orders.

1–5811   **18. Method of making payment under attachment of earnings order.**   (1) A justices' chief executive for a magistrates' court to whom any payment under an attachment of earnings order is to be made shall notify the employer and the person entitled to receive payments under the related maintenance order of the hours during which, and the place at which, payments are, subject to the provisions of this Rule, to be made and received.

(2) If an employer sends by post any payments under an attachment of earnings order to a justices' chief executive for a magistrates' court, he shall do so at his own risk and expense.

(3) A justices' chief executive for a magistrates' court may send by post any payment under an attachment of earnings order to the person entitled to receive payments under the related maintenance order at the request and at the risk of that person.

1–5812   **19. Payments under attachment of earnings order after imprisonment imposed.** (1) Where imprisonment or other detention has been imposed for the purpose of enforcing a maintenance order, the justices' chief executive for a magistrates' court to whom any payment under a related attachment of earnings order is to be made—

    (*a*) in relation to such a payment shall be a person authorised to receive the said payment for the purposes of section 67(2) of the Magistrates' Courts Act 1952[1] (which relates to release from custody and reduction of detention on payment);

    (*b*) on receiving such a payment shall notify the person authorised for the said purposes by Rule 45(1) of the Magistrates' Courts Rules 1968[2] of the sum received.

(2) Where a person receives notice of the receipt of a sum under the preceding paragraph of this Rule, he shall note the receipt of that sum on the warrant of commitment, if any, held by him.

---

    1. See now the Magistrates' Courts Act 1980, s 79(2).
    2. See now r 55 of the Magistrates' Courts Rules 1981.

1–5813   **20. Service of orders and notices.**   Where under section 14 of the Act (which relates to statements of earnings, etc) an order is directed to the debtor or to a person appearing to be an employer of the debtor or where under these Rules a copy of an order is to be served or a notice is to be given to any person—

    (*a*) service may be effected on, or notice may be given to a person, other than a corporation, by delivering it to the person to whom it is directed or by sending it by post in a letter addressed to him at his last known or usual place of abode, or, in the case of an employer or a person appearing to be an employer of the debtor, at his place of business;

    (*b*) service may be effected on, or notice given to, a corporation by delivering the document at, or sending it to—

        (i) such office or place as the corporation may, for the purpose of this Rule, have specified in writing to the court in relation to the debtor or to a class or description of person to which he belongs, or

        (ii) the registered office of the corporation if that office is in England and Wales or, if there is no registered office in England and Wales, any place therein where the corporation trades or conducts its business.

1-5814 21. County Court records. (1) Where a justices' chief executive for a magistrates' court causes a copy of an order or notice to be given to any person under Rule 6 of these Rules, he shall cause a copy of the order or notice to be given also to the County Court Registrar for the district in which the debtor resides.

(2) Where the justices' chief executive for a magistrates' court which has made an attachment of earnings order is informed of a debtor's change of address, he shall notify the new address to the County Court Registrar for the district in which the debtor resided before the change of address.

1-5815 22. Justices' clerks. (1) The things specified in paragraph (2) of this Rule, being things authorised to be done by, to or before a single justice of the peace for a petty sessions area, may be done by, to or before the justices' clerk for that area.

(2) The things referred to in paragraph (1) above are—

(a) the power to make an order under section 14(1) or (2) of the Act (power of court to obtain statements of earnings, etc) before the hearing of an application to a magistrates' court for an attachment of earnings order, or for the variation or discharge of such an order;

(b) the determination that a complaint for the discharge or variation of an attachment of earnings order be dealt with by a magistrates' court acting for another petty sessions area in accordance with Rule 9 of these Rules;

(c) the giving of directions under Rule 10 or 11 of these Rules;

(d) the discharge or variation by the court of its own motion of an attachment of earnings order in accordance with Rule 12 or 13 of these Rules;

(e) the temporary variation of an attachment of earnings order by an increase of the protected earnings rate in accordance with Rule 14 of these Rules;

(f) the making of an order under Rule 16 of these Rules (transfer of fines etc with view to making consolidated attachment order).

1-5816 23. Application of these Rules to attachment of earnings orders in respect of fines etc. (1) In the application of these Rules to attachment of earnings orders to secure—

(a) the payment of any sum adjudged to be paid by a conviction or treated (by any enactment relating to the collection and enforcement of fines, costs, compensation or forfeited recognisances) as so adjudged to be paid, or

(b) the payment of any sum required to be paid by a legal aid contribution order,

the exceptions and modifications specified in the following provisions of this Rule shall apply.

(2) Rules 4, 8, 9, 10, 11 and 19 shall not apply.

(3) *Revoked.*

(4) Rule 14 (temporary variation of protected earnings rate) shall have effect as if in paragraph (3) the words "and the justices' chief executive shall also send a copy to the person entitled to receive payments under the related maintenance order (whether directly or through an officer of any court)" were omitted.

(5) Rule 18 (method of making payment under attachment of earnings order) shall have effect as if in paragraph (1) the words "and the person entitled to receive payments under the related maintenance order" and paragraph (3) were omitted.

1-5817 24. *Revoked.*

1-5818 *Schedule revoked.*

Magistrates' Courts Rules 1981[1]

(SI 1981/552 amended by SI 1982/245, 1983/523, 1984/1552, 1985/1695 and 1944, 1986/1332, SI 1988/2132, SI 1989/300 and 384, SI 1990/336, 1190, 2260, SI 1991/1991, SI 1992/457, 709, 729 and 2072, SI 1993/1183, SI 1994/1481 and 3154, SI 1995/585 and 2619, SI 1997/706, SI 1998/2167 and 3046, SI 1999/2765, SI 2001/167 and 610, SI 2003/423 and 1236, Courts Act 2003, Sch 8 and SI 2004/2993, 2005/617 and 2930)

GENERAL

1-5930 1. *Citation, operation and revocation.*

---

1. Made by the Lord Chancellor in exercise of the power conferred on him by s 144 of the Magistrates' Courts Act 1980, as extended by s 145 of that Act.

Note: these rules are revoked in relation to criminal proceedings, see now the Criminal Procedure Rules 2005, in this PART, POST.

Interpretation

1-5931 2. (1) In these Rules—

"the Act of 1978" means the Domestic Proceedings and Magistrates' Courts Act 1978;

"the Act of 1980" means the Magistrates' Courts Act 1980;

"the Act of 1989" means the Children Act 1989;

"the Act of 2000" means the Powers of Criminal Courts (Sentencing) Act 2000;

"*the Act of 1998*" means the Crime and Disorder Act 1998[1];

"child" means a person who has not attained the age of 18;

"court computer system" means a computer or computer system which is used to assist to discharge and record the business of the court;

"electronic signature" is as much of anything in electronic form as

(a) is incorporated into or otherwise logically associated with any electronic communication or electronic data; and

(b) purports to be so incorporated or associated for the purpose of being used in establishing the authenticity of the communication or data, the integrity of the communication or data, or both;

"judgment summons" has the meaning assigned to it by rule 58.

(2) In these Rules "representation order" has the meaning assigned to it by section 14 of the Access to Justice Act 1999.

(3) In these Rules a reference to the person with whom a child has his home shall be construed in accordance with the Act of 1989, except that, in the case of any child in the care of a local authority, the local authority shall be treated for the purposes of these Rules as the person with whom the child has his home.

(4) In these Rules a reference to "the authorised persons for the area in which they are employed" is a reference to the persons employed by an authority which performs its functions within that area who are authorised to execute warrants within that area in pursuance of rule 3 of the Magistrates' Courts (Civilian Fine Enforcement Officers) (No 2) Rules 1990.

(5) Any requirement in these Rules that a document shall be in the prescribed form shall be construed as a requirement that the document shall be in the form prescribed in that behalf by rules[2] made under section 144 of the Act of 1980, or a form to like effect.

(6) In these Rules any reference to a rule shall be construed as a reference to a rule contained in these Rules; and any reference in a rule to a paragraph shall be construed as a reference to a paragraph of that rule.

(7) Subject to rules 15 and 99, where these Rules require a document to be given or sent, or a notice to be communicated in writing, it may, with the consent of the addressee, be sent by electronic communication.

(8) Electronic communication means a communication transmitted (whether from one person to another, from one device to another or from a person to a device or vice versa)—

(a) by means of a telecommunication system (within the meaning of the Telecommunications Act 1984); or

(b) by other means but while in an electronic form.

---

1. Words in italics inserted by the Magistrates' Courts (Modification) Rules 1998, SI 1998/3046 in respect of those areas from which a person is sent for trial under s 51 of the Crime and Disorder Act 1998.

2. See the Magistrates' Courts (Forms) Rules 1981, set out in full in PART IX: PRECEDENTS AND FORMS, post.

Saving for the Family Proceedings Courts (Children Act 1989) Rules 1991 and the Family Proceedings Courts (Matrimonial Proceedings etc) Rules 1991

1–5932 3. The provisions of these Rules shall have effect subject to the provisions of the Family Proceedings Courts (Children Act 1989) Rules 1991 and the Family Proceedings Courts (Matrimonial Proceedings etc) Rules 1991.

INFORMATION AND COMPLAINT

Information and complaint

1–5933 4. (1) An information[1] may be laid or complaint made by the prosecutor or complainant in person or by his counsel or solicitor or other person authorised in that behalf.

(2) Subject to any provision of the Act of 1980 and any other enactment an information or complaint need not be in writing or on oath.

(3) It shall not be necessary in an information or complaint to specify or negative an exception, exemption, proviso, excuse or qualification, whether or not it accompanies the description of the offence or matter of complaint contained in the enactment creating the offence or on which the complaint is founded.

DEPOSITION ETC. OF RELUCTANT WITNESS

1–5933A 4A–13A. *Revoked.*

SUMMARY TRIAL OF INFORMATION AND HEARING OF COMPLAINT

Order of evidence and speeches: complaint

1–5943 14. (1) On the hearing of a complaint, except where the court determines under section 53(3) of the Act of 1980 to make the order with the consent of the defendant without hearing evidence, the complainant shall call his evidence, and before doing so may address the court.

(2) At the conclusion of the evidence for the complainant the defendant may address the court, whether or not he afterwards calls evidence[1].

(3) At the conclusion of the evidence, if any, for the defence, the complainant may call evidence to rebut[2] that evidence.

(4) At the conclusion of the evidence for the defence and the evidence, if any, in rebuttal, the defendant may address the court if he has not already done so.

(5) Either party may, with the leave of the court, address the court a second time, but where the court grants leave to one party it shall not refuse leave to the other[3].

(6) Where the defendant obtains leave to address the court for a second time his second address shall be made before the second address, if any, of the complainant.

---

1. This right is retained even if the defendant has previously submitted that in law there is no case to answer (*Disher v Disher* [1965] P 31, [1963] 3 All ER 933). The court may dismiss the case at the conclusion of the complainant's case either of its own motion or upon a submission to that effect and, in either event the complainant's solicitor must be given an opportunity to address the court before such dismissal (*Mayes v Mayes* [1971] 2 All ER 397, 135 JP 487).

In civil proceedings unsworn statements cannot be received in evidence in the absence of agreement or statutory provision; the defendant has no right to make a statement not on oath in lieu of giving evidence (*Aggas v Aggas* [1971] 2 All ER 1497, 135 JP 484).

2. In civil cases, the right to call "rebutting evidence" corresponds with a similar right in criminal trials (see note to r 13, ante). For evidence in rebuttal, see 17 *Halsbury's Laws of England* (4th edn), para 18.

3. The terms of para (5) are such that the complainant may be allowed to address the court a second time even if the defendant does not wish to do so.

Adjournment of trial of information

1-5944   15. *Revoked.*

Record of Adjudication

1-5945   16. (1) A record of summary conviction or order made on complaint required for an appeal or other legal purpose may be in the form of certified extract from the court register.

(2) *Revoked.*

---

1. See Forms 38 and 101 in PART IX: PRECEDENTS AND FORMS, post, cd-rom only.

1-5946   17–22. *Revoked.*

REMAND

Remand on bail for more than 8 days where sureties have not entered into recognizances

1-5952   23. Where the court, with a view to a person's being remanded on bail under paragraph (*a*) of section 128(6) of the Act of 1980 for a period exceeding 8 days, has fixed the amount of the recognizances to be taken for that purpose but commits that person to custody because the recognizances of the sureties have not yet been taken, the warrant of commitment shall direct the governor or keeper of the prison or place to which he is committed to bring him before the court at the end of 8 clear days or at such earlier time as may be specified in the warrant, unless in the meantime the sureties have entered into their recognizances.

Revoked.

1-5953   24–33. *Revoked.*

APPEAL TO MAGISTRATES' COURT

Appeal to be by complaint

1-5963   34. Where under any enactment[1] an appeal lies to a magistrates' court against the decision or order of a local authority or other authority, or other body or person, the appeal shall be by way of complaint for an order[2].

---

1. Many enactments which give a right of appeal to a magistrates' court against a decision of a local authority or other authority, prescribe the procedure in the same terms as this rule, eg Public Health Act 1936, s 300; Food Safety Act 1990, s 37(3). Other enactments do not prescribe any procedure, eg Caravan Sites and Control of Development Act 1960, s 7. The effect of this rule is to secure that procedure shall be uniform in every case of appeal to a magistrates' court.

2. Section 53 of the Magistrates' Courts Act 1980 this PART, ante, will apply. Any appeal is by way of re-hearing, and evidence will thus be heard on the same basis as was presented to the body from which the appeal is brought, thus the court may be required to hear evidence which would not be admissible in normal judicial proceedings. See *Westminster City Council v Zestfair Ltd* (1989) 153 JP 613, 88 LGR 288. However, as the appeal is by way of rehearing the court is entitled to consider all the relevant evidence including that arising between the original decision appealed against and the appeal (*Rushmoor Borough Council v Richards* (1996) 160 LG Rev 460, DC).

AFFILIATION ORDERS

1-5964   35. *Revoked.*

1-5965   35A. *Revoked.*

DOMESTIC PROCEEDINGS

1-5966   36–37. *Revoked.*

Certification of records

1–5967 **38.** For the purposes of section 84(2) of the Act of 1978 (which provides that a copy of any record made by virtue of section 84 of the reasons for a decision of a magistrates' court shall, if certified by such officer of the court as may be prescribed, be admissible as evidence of those reasons) the certifying officer shall be the justices' chief executive for the magistrates' court concerned.

ORDERS FOR PERIODICAL PAYMENTS

Method of making periodical payments

1–5968 **39.** (1) Where a magistrates' court makes a means of payment order, the clerk of the court shall record on the order for periodical payments[1] to which the means of payment order relates, the means of payment which the court has ordered and the justices' chief executive shall notify in writing, as soon as practicable, the person liable to make payments under the order of how payments are to be made.

(2) Where the court orders that payments by the debtor to the creditor are to be made to the justices' chief executive for the court or to the justices' chief executive for any other magistrates' court under section 59(3)(*b*) of the Act of 1980, the justices' chief executive to whom the payments are ordered to be made shall notify the person liable to make the payments of the hours during which, and the place at which, payments are to be made.

(3) The justices' chief executive for the court to whom any periodical payments are made shall send them by post[2] to—

(*a*) the person entitled to them; or
(*b*) if the person entitled to them is a child, to the child or to the person with whom the child has his home:

Provided that the justices' chief executive may—

(*a*) at the request of the person entitled to the payments; or
(*b*) if the person entitled to them is a child, at the request of the child or the person with whom the child has his home,

make other arrangements for making the payments.

(4) If a person makes any periodical payments to a justices' chief executive for a magistrates' court otherwise than in person at the office of the justices' chief executive, he shall do so at his own risk and expense.

(5) Where the court orders that payments by the debtor to the creditor be made by a method of payment falling within section 59(6) of the Act of 1980 (standing order, etc), the justices' chief executive for the court shall notify the person liable to make payments under the order of the number and location of the account into which the payments should be made.

(6) Where the designated officer for the magistrates' court receives an application from an interested party under section 20ZA(2) of the Act of 1978, paragraph 36(1) of Schedule 6 to the Civil Partnership Act 2004, section 60(4) of the Act of 1980 or paragraph 6A(2) of Schedule 1 to the Children Act 1989 for the method of payment to be varied, the justices' chief executive shall notify in writing, as soon as practicable, that party and, where practicable, any other interested party, of the result of the application, including any decision to refer the matter to the court; where the clerk of the court grants the application, he shall record the variation on the order for periodical payments to which the variation relates.

(7) In this rule "means of payment order" means an order of a magistrates' court under paragraphs (*a*) to (*d*) of section 59(3) of the Act of 1980.

---

1. For restrictions on the amount that can offered in coin ("legal tender"), see the Coinage Act 1971, s 2, in PART VIII, title CURRENCY, post.
2. The Secretary of State in HO Circular 214/1971 took the view that the cost of payment by post by cheque may reasonably be borne by the court.

1–5969 **40.** *Revoked.*

Revocation, variation, etc, of orders for periodical payments

1–5970 **41.** (1) This rule shall apply to a complaint for the revocation, discharge, revival, alteration or variation of a magistrates' court maintenance order or order enforceable as a magistrates' court maintenance order[1], but shall not apply—

(*a*) where jurisdiction is confined by paragraph (*a*) of subsection (2) of section 88 of the Children and Young Persons Act 1933[2] to courts appointed for the commission area where the person liable is residing;
(*b*) where an order has been made under the proviso to subsection (4) of that section[2];
(*c*) to a contribution order[3];
(*d*) to a complaint for an order under section 26(4) of the Children Act 1948[4];
(*e*) to a complaint for an order under section 22(1)[5] of the Maintenance Orders Act 1950.

(2) A complaint to which this rule applies may be made to a justice of the peace acting for the same petty sessions area as the responsible court[6] or to a justice of the peace[7] acting for the petty sessions area where the complainant is for the time being.

(3) A justice of the peace[7] shall not take action on a complaint to which this rule applies unless either the complainant has furnished him with written particulars—

(a) of the nature of the evidence that the complainant proposes to adduce at the hearing of the complaint and the names and addresses and, if known to him, the occupations of his witnesses; and

(b) of the occupations of the complainant and defendant and the address of the complainant and last address of the defendant known to the complainant,

or the justice[7] is acting for the same petty sessions area as the responsible court and it appears to him that the last address of the defendant known to the complainant is within that area.

(4) Where a complaint to which this rule applies is made to a justice of the peace[7] acting for the same petty sessions area as the responsible court, and it appears to him that either of the places stated in the said particulars as being the addresses of the complainant and defendant is within another petty sessions area, then, if the justice[7] determines that the complaint could more conveniently[8] be dealt with by a magistrates' court acting for that other petty sessions area, he shall cause the justices' chief executive for the responsible court to send by post to the justices' chief executive for that other court the complaint[9], the said particulars and a copy of any relevant record of reasons for a decision kept in pursuance of rule 36.

(5) Where the places stated in the said particulars as being the addresses of the complainant and the defendant appear to the justice to be outside the petty sessions area for which the justice is acting and in other and different petty sessions areas, the reference in the last preceding paragraph to another petty sessions area shall be construed as a reference to such one of those other areas aforesaid as appears to the justice convenient.

(6) On receipt by the justices' chief executive for a magistrates' court of a complaint, the particulars and a copy of any relevant record of reasons under paragraph (4), he shall bring the complaint before the court, and the court shall issue a summons requiring the defendant to appear before it, and shall hear and determine the complaint.

(7) Where a complaint to which this rule applies is made to a justice of the peace acting for a petty sessions area other than that for which the responsible court acts, the justice shall cause the justices' chief executive for the magistrates' court acting for that other petty sessions area to send the complaint, the said particulars and the said copy of any relevant record of reasons by post to the justices' chief executive for the responsible court; and the justices' chief executive for the responsible court shall bring the complaint before the court; and thereupon paragraphs (4) to (6) shall have effect as if the complaint had been made and the particulars and the copy of any relevant record of reasons furnished to a justice of the peace acting for the same petty sessions area as the responsible court.

(8) Notwithstanding the foregoing provisions of this rule, a justice to whom a complaint is made may refer the complaint to the responsible court which may, in such case or when the complaint is brought before the court in accordance with paragraph (6), cause the complaint, the particulars and the copy of any relevant record of reasons to be sent by post to the justices' chief executive for the court which made the original order and that clerk and that court shall proceed in accordance with the provisions of paragraph (6).

(9) Where a magistrates' court makes an order on a complaint to which this rule applies affecting an order made by another magistrates' court or affecting an order under which payments are made to the justices' chief executive for another magistrates' court, the justices' chief executive for the first-mentioned court shall cause a copy of the order to be sent to the justices' chief executive for that other court.

(10) In this rule "responsible court" means—

(a) where payments under the order are made to the justices' chief executive for a magistrates' court, that court;

(b) where payments are not so made, the court which made the order.

---

1. The rule applies to an affiliation order, a maintenance order made under the Matrimonial Proceedings (Magistrates' Courts) Act 1960, a High Court or county court maintenance order registered in a magistrates' court under the Maintenance Orders Act 1958 (see Magistrates' Courts (Maintenance Orders Act 1958) Rules 1959, r 9, post), an order for the recovery by a local authority of the cost of assistance (National Assistance Act 1948, s 43), an order for the recovery of expenditure on benefit from person liable for maintenance (Social Security Administration Act 1992, s 106).

2. The Children and Young Persons Act 1933, s 88(2)(a) was repealed and replaced by the Child Care Act 1980, s 49(4), and similarly s 88(4) of the 1933 Act by s 49(5)–(7) of the 1980 Act, now repealed by the Children Act 1989, Sch 15.

3. A contribution order is made under the Children Act 1989, Sch 2, Pt III, in PART IV: FAMILY LAW, post.

4. The Children Act 1948, s 26(4) was repealed and replaced by the Child Care Act 1980, ss 50(5) and 87(1) now repealed by the Children Act 1989, Sch 15.

5. This section relates to the discharge and variation of maintenance order, between England, Scotland and Northern Ireland.

6. The term "responsible court", which is defined in para (9), infra, has been substituted for the reference to the court which made the order (the "original court"), with the effect that it is now the court through which payments are made which decides venue (whether or not this is the "original court"). Paragraph (8) enables a complaint made at a court other than the "original court", to be sent to the "original court" for hearing in appropriate cases.

7. A complaint not on oath may, instead, be made to a justices' clerk who may also make the determination as to venue under the Justices' Clerks Rules 1999, Schedule, para (37), post.

8. The rule does not require parties to be given the opportunity of making representations, but the court should allow them to do so when the interests of fairness so require (*R v Wareham Magistrates' Court, ex p Seldon* [1988] 1 All ER 746, [1988] 1 WLR 825).

9. It is pointed out in Home Office Circular (278/1947) that it is desirable in order that the other court may be in a position to deal with the matter that any necessary further information should be transmitted at the same time as the complaint is sent. It may, for instance, be relevant to the consideration of an application for enforcement of arrears for the other court to know whether the defendant has made default in payment on

previous occasions and how he has been dealt with. Again, on an application for variation of the amount of the order it would be helpful to the court which has to deal with the application to know what were the circumstances of the defendant at the time when the order was made or was previously varied; and where the application is for variation of some other provision of the order the court would also be helped by knowing the circumstances in which this provision was included in the order. It will be for the justices' chief executive for the transmitting court to decide what information should be sent with the complaint in any individual case, but the Secretary of State would suggest that the guiding principle should be that such information should be sent as it would in his opinion be desirable that the original court should have if it were dealing with the complaint. This practice was commended in *John v John* [1959] 1 All ER 389, 123 JP 143.

1–5971 42. *Revoked.*

Service of copy of order

1–5972 43. Where a magistrates' court makes, revokes, discharges, suspends, revives, alters or varies a magistrates' court maintenance order or order enforceable as a magistrates' court maintenance order or allows time or further time for payment of a lump sum under any such order or orders payment of a lump sum under any such order to be paid by instalments or varies any such order for payment by instalments the court shall cause a copy of its order to be served on the defendant by delivering it to him or by sending it by post[1] in a letter addressed to him at his last known or usual place of abode.

---

1. See presumption of due delivery in s 7 of the Interpretation Act 1978, in Part II: Evidence, post.

Remission of sums due under order

1–5973 44. (1) Before remitting the whole or any part of a sum due under a magistrates' court maintenance order or an order enforceable as a magistrates' court maintenance order under section 95 of the Act of 1980, the court shall, except save where it appears to it to be unnecessary or impracticable to do so, cause the person in whose favour the order is made or, if that person is a child, the child or the person with whom the child has his home to be notified[1] of its intention and shall afford to such person a reasonable opportunity to make representations to the court, either orally at an adjourned hearing of the complaint for enforcement or in writing and such representations shall be considered by the court.

(2) Any written representations may be considered by the court if they purport to be signed by or on behalf of the person in whose favour the order is made or, if that person is a child, by or on behalf of the child or the person with whom the child has his home.

---

1. If there is a failure to give notice, as required, the High Court may entertain an application for judicial review to quash the order remitting arrears; see *R v Dover Magistrates' Court, ex p Kidner* [1983] 1 All ER 475, 147 JP 254. However, a party to whom such notice has not been given should normally pursue their remedy by way of case stated (*R v Bristol Magistrates, ex p Hodge* [1996] 4 All ER 924, [1997] 2 WLR 756, [1997] 1 FCR 412, [1997] 1 FLR 88).

The requirement for the court to notify the person concerned of its intention applies as much to a party who is present before the court as it does to an absent party; see *A v A (Remission of Arrears: Procedure)* [1996] 1 FCR 629. The court must also notify that person of its intention notwithstanding that the party, at an earlier date, has signed a statement acknowledging the court's power to remit arrears when requesting the clerk to the justices to take enforcement action (*R v Bristol Magistrates' Court, ex p Hodge* [1996] 4 All ER 924, [1997] 2 WLR 756, [1997] 1 FCR 412, [1997] 1 FLR 88).

Duty of designated officer to notify subsequent marriage or formation of civil partnership] of person entitled to payments under a maintenance order

1–5974 45. (1) Where the designated officer for a magistrates' court to whom any payments under an order to which this rule applies are required to be made is notified in writing by or on behalf of the person entitled to payments under such an order, the person liable to make payments under such an order or the personal representatives of either of those persons that the person so entitled has subsequently married or formed a civil partnership, the designated officer shall forthwith in writing so notify the designated officer for or other appropriate officer of each of the courts mentioned in paragraph (2) for which he is not the designated officer.

(2) The courts referred to in paragraph (1) are—

(a) any court which has made a relevant order or, in the case of a provisional order made under section 3 of the Maintenance Orders (Facilities for Enforcement) Act 1920 or section 3 of the Maintenance Orders (Reciprocal Enforcement) Act 1972, the court which confirmed the order;

(b) if a relevant order has been transmitted abroad for registration under section 2 of the said Act of 1920 or section 2 of the said Act of 1972 the court in which the order is registered, and

(c) if a complaint for the enforcement of a relevant order has been sent to a court under rule 59(2), that court.

(3) This rule applies to an order of a kind mentioned in paragraph (4) and an attachment of earnings order made to secure payments under an order of that kind, and in paragraph (2) "relevant order" means any such order to which the payments referred to in paragraph (1) relate.

(4) The kinds of order referred to in paragraph (3) are orders to which the following provisions apply—

(a) section 38 of the Matrimonial Causes Act 1973;

(b) section 4(2) of the Act of 1978;

(*c*)   paragraph 65 of Schedule 5 to the Civil Partnership Act 2004; and
(*d*)   paragraph 26(2) of Schedule 6 to the Civil Partnership Act 2004.

SATISFACTION, ENFORCEMENT AND APPLICATION OF PAYMENTS

1-5975   **46.** *Revoked.*

Registration and notification of financial penalty enforcement order

1-5976   **47.** (1) The justices' chief executive for a magistrates' court receiving a financial penalty enforcement order made by the Defence Council or an officer authorised by them shall cause the said order to be registered in his courts by means of a memorandum entered in the register kept pursuant to rule 66 and signed by him and shall send notice in writing to the Defence Council or the authorised officer, as appropriate, stating that the order has been so registered.

(2) Where a financial penalty enforcement order has been registered in accordance with the provisions of paragraph (1), the clerk shall forthwith serve on the person against whom the order was made a notice of registration in the prescribed form.

(3) A notice required by paragraph (2) shall be served on the person by delivering it to him or by sending it by post addressed to him at the address shown on the financial penalty enforcement order.

(4) In this rule "financial penalty enforcement order" means an order made under section 133A(1) of the Army Act 1955, section 133A(1) of the Air Force Act 1955 or section 128F(1) of the Naval Discipline Act 1957.

To whom payments are to be made

1-5977   **48.** (1) A person adjudged by the conviction of a magistrates' court to pay any sum shall, unless the court otherwise directs, pay that sum, or any instalment of that sum, to the justices' chief executive for the court.

(2) Where payment of any sum or instalment of any sum adjudged to be paid by the conviction or order of a magistrates' court is made to any person[1] other than the justices' chief executive for the court, that person, unless he is the person to whom the court has directed payment to be made or, in the case of a child, is the person with whom the child has his home, shall, as soon as may be, account for and, if the clerk so requires, pay over the sum or instalment to the justices' chief executive for the court.

(3) Where payment of any sum adjudged to be paid by the conviction or order of a magistrates' court, or any instalment of such a sum, is directed to be made to the justices' chief executive for some other magistrates' court, the justices' chief executive for the court that adjudged the sum to be paid shall pay over any sums received by him on account of the said sum or instalment to the justices' chief executive for that other court.

---

1. For instance, the person exercising supervision under the Magistrates' Courts Act 1980, s 88, ante.

Duty of clerk to give receipt

1-5978   **49.** The justices' chief executive for a magistrates' court shall give or send a receipt to any person who makes a payment to him in pursuance of a conviction or order of a magistrates' court and who asks for a receipt.

Application for further time

1-5979   **51.** An application under section 75(2) of the Act of 1980, or section 22 of the Act of 1978 or paragraph 41 of Schedule 6 to the Civil Partnership Act 2004 may, unless the court requires the applicant to attend, be made in writing.

1-5980   **52-52A.** *Revoked.*

Notice to defendant before enforcing order

1-5982   **53.** (1) A warrant of distress shall not be issued for failure to pay a sum enforceable as a civil debt[1] unless the defendant has been previously served with a copy of the minute of the order, or the order was made in his presence and the warrant is issued on that occasion.

(2) A warrant of commitment shall not be issued for disobedience to an order of a magistrates' court unless the defendant has been previously served with a copy of the minute of the order, or the order was made in his presence and the warrant is issued on that occasion:
Provided that this paragraph shall not apply to—

(*a*)   an order to pay money[2], or
(*b*)   an expedited order under section 16(2) and (6) of the Act of 1978.

(3) A copy of the minute of the order shall be served under this rule by delivering it to the defendant or by sending it to him by post[3] in a letter addressed to him at his last known or usual place of abode.

(4) In relation to an order under section 16 of the Act of 1978 (other than an expedited order under subsections (2) and (6) of that section) paragraphs (2) and (3) shall have effect as if for the references to a copy of the minute of the order there were substituted references to a copy of the order.

1. Note that this paragraph relates only to procedure in civil debt (see Magistrates' Court Act, 1980, s 58 this PART, ante). Nowhere is it specifically required that an order enforceable as an affiliation order shall be served on the defendant before proceedings are taken to enforce the order, but in the fifteen days that must elapse before enforcement proceedings are taken (see Magistrates' Court Act, 1980, s 93, ante) it is usual to serve a copy of the order. Further, by r 43, supra, it is provided that a copy of the order shall be served on a defendant who is neither present nor legally represented at the hearing.

2. For orders other than for the payment of money, see Magistrates' Courts Act 1980, s 63, this PART, ante.

3. See presumption of due delivery in s 7 of the Interpretation Act 1978, in PART II, post.

Execution of distress warrant[1]

1–5983 54.—(1) A warrant of distress issued for the purpose of levying a sum[2] adjudged to be paid by a summary conviction or order—

    (a) shall name or otherwise describe the person against whom the distress is to be levied;

    (b) shall be directed to the constables of the police area in which the warrant is issued or to the civilian enforcement officers for the area in which they are employed, or to a person named in the warrant and shall, subject to, and in accordance with, the provisions of this rule, require them to levy the said sum by distress and sale of the goods[3] belonging to the said person;

    (c) may where it is directed to the constables of a police area, instead of being executed by any of those constables, be executed by any person under the direction of a constable.

(2) The warrant shall authorise the person charged with the execution of it to take as well any money as any goods of the person against whom the distress is levied; and any money so taken shall be treated as if it were the proceeds of the sale of goods taken under the warrant.

(3) The warrant shall require the person charged with the execution to pay the sum to be levied to the justices' chief executive for the court that issued the warrant.

(3A) A warrant to which this rule applies may be executed by the persons to whom it was directed or by any of the following persons, whether or not the warrant was directed to them—

    (a) a constable for any police area in England and Wales, acting in his own police area;

    (b) where the warrant is one to which section 125A of the Act of 1980 applies, a civilian enforcement officer within the meaning of section 125A of the Act of 1980;

    (c) where the warrant is one to which section 125A of the Act of 1980 applies, any of the individuals described in section 125B(1) of the Act of 1980;

and in this rule any reference to the person charged with the execution of a warrant includes any of the above persons who is for the time being authorised to execute the warrant, whether or not they have the warrant in their possession at the time.

(3B) A person executing a warrant of distress shall—

    (a) either—

        (i) if he has the warrant with him, show it to the person against whom the distress is levied, or

        (ii) otherwise, state where the warrant is and what arrangements may be made to allow the person against whom distress is levied to inspect it;

    (b) explain, in ordinary language, the sum for which distress is levied and the reason for the distress;

    (c) where the person executing the warrant is one of the persons referred to in paragraph (3A)(b) or (c) above, show the person against whom distress is levied a written statement under section 125A(4) of 125B(4) as appropriate; and

    (d) in any case, show documentary proof of his identity.

(4) There shall not be taken under the warrant the clothing or bedding of any person or his family or the tools, books, vehicles or other equipment which he personally needs to use in his employment, business or vocation, provided that in this paragraph the word "person" shall not include a corporation."

(5) The distress levied under any such warrant as aforesaid shall be sold within such period beginning not earlier than the 6th day after the making of the distress as may be specified in the warrant, or if no period is specified in the warrant, within a period beginning on the 6th day and ending on the 14th day after the making of the distress:

Provided that with the consent in writing of the person against whom the distress is levied the distress may be sold before the beginning of the said period.

(5A) The clerk of the court which issued the warrant may, on the application of the person charged with the execution of it, extend the period within which the distress must be sold by any number of days not exceeding 60; but following the grant of such an application there shall be no further variation or extension of that period.

(6) The said distress shall be sold by public auction or in such other manner as the person against whom the distress is levied may in writing allow.

(7) Notwithstanding anything in the preceding provisions of this rule, the said distress shall not be sold if the sum for which the warrant was issued and the charges of taking and keeping the distress have been paid.

(8) Subject to any direction to the contrary in the warrant, where the distress is levied on household goods, the goods shall not, without the consent in writing of the person against whom the distress is levied, be removed from the house until the day of sale; and so much of the goods shall be impounded as is in the opinion of the person executing the warrant sufficient to satisfy the distress, by affixing to the articles impounded a conspicuous mark[4].

(9) The constable or other person charged with the execution of any such warrant as aforesaid shall cause the distress to be sold, and may deduct out of the amount realised by the sale all costs and charges incurred in effecting the sale; and he shall return to the owner the balance, if any, after retaining the amount of the sum for which the warrant was issued and the proper costs and charges of the execution of the warrant.

(10) The constable or other person charged with the execution of any such warrant as aforesaid shall as soon as practicable send to the justices' chief executive for the court that issued it a written account[5] of the costs and charges[6] incurred in executing it; and the justices' shall allow the person against whom the distress was levied to inspect the account within one month after the levy of the distress at any reasonable time to be appointed by the court.

(11) If any person pays or tenders to the constable or other person charged with the execution of any such warrant as aforesaid the sum mentioned in the warrant, or produces a receipt for that sum given by the justices' chief executive for the court that issued the warrant, and also pays the amount of the costs and charges of the distress up to the time of the payment or tender or the production of the receipt, the constable or other person as aforesaid shall not execute the warrant, or shall cease to execute it, as the case may be.

---

1. Revoked in relation to criminal proceedings, see now the Criminal Procedure Rules 2005, in this PART, post.

2. Where the fine and costs are not to exceed a fixed sum, the further costs of enforcing payment by distress warrant may be added (*Cook v Plaskett* (1882) 47 JP 265).

3. Goods seized by a constable under a distress warrant are in *custodia legis*, and a landlord has no right to distrain or make a claim upon them. The Landlord and Tenant Act 1709, s 1, which requires the sheriff to pay the landlord his arrears of rent before the removal of goods under an execution, has no application to goods seized by a constable in the execution of a justice's warrant of distress (*Potts v Hickman* [1941] AC 2112, [1940] 4 All ER 491, 105 JP 26). Water fittings let for hire are not the subject of distress (Water Act 1945, s 35(2)); nor are gas fittings let for hire and marked with a sufficient mark indicating ownership of a public gas supplier (Gas Act 1986, Sch 5, para 19, in PART VIII: title ENERGY, post). Similar protection is given to electrical plant etc belonging to a public electricity supplier (Electricity Act 1989, Sch 6, para 9, in PART VIII: title ENERGY, post).

4. For offence of removing goods so marked, or defacing or removing the mark, see Magistrates' Courts Act 1980, s 78(4), ante.

5. For form of account, see Form 50 in PART IX: PRECEDENTS AND FORMS, post, cd-rom only.

6. For offence of exacting excessive costs and charges, see Magistrates' Courts Act 1980, s 78(5), ante.

Payment after imprisonment imposed

1–5984 **55.** (1) The persons authorised for the purposes of section 79(2) of the Act of 1980 to receive a part payment are—

(a) unless there has been issued a warrant of distress or commitment, the justices' chief executive for the court enforcing payment of the sum, or any person appointed under section 88 of that Act to supervise the offender;

(b) where the issue of a warrant of commitment has been suspended on conditions which provide for payment to be made to the justices' chief executive for some other magistrates' court, that chief executive;

(c) any constable holding a warrant of distress or commitment or, where the warrant is directed to some other person, that person;

(d) the governor or keeper of the prison or place in which the defaulter is detained, or other person having lawful custody of the defaulter:

Provided that—

(i) the said governor or keeper shall not be required to accept any sum tendered in part payment under the said subsection (2) except on a week-day between 9 o'clock in the morning and 5 o'clock in the afternoon; and

(ii) no person shall be required to receive in part payment under the said subsection (2) an amount which, or so much of an amount as, will not procure a reduction of the period for which the defaulter is committed or ordered to be detained.

(2) Where a person having custody of a defaulter receives payment of any sum he shall note receipt of the sum on the warrant of commitment.

(3) Where the justices' chief executive for a court other than the court enforcing payment of the sums receives payment of any sum he shall inform the justices' chief executive for the other court.

(4) Where a person appointed under section 88 of the Act of 1980 to supervise an offender receives payment of any sum, he shall send it forthwith to the justices' chief executive for the court which appointed him.

(5) *Obsolete*[1].

---

1. Section 134 of the Magistrates' Courts Act 1980 has been repealed by the Criminal Justice Act 1988, s 49, and, therefore, r 55(5) has ceased to have effect.

Order for supervision

1–5985 **56–57A.** *Revoked.*

Civil debt: judgment summons

1–5987 **58.** (1) A summons[1] issued on a complaint made for the purposes of section 96 of the Act of 1980 (in these rules referred to as a "judgment summons") shall be served on the judgment debtor personally:

Provided that if a justice of the peace is satisfied by evidence on oath that prompt personal service of the summons is impracticable, he may allow[2] the summons to be served in such a way as he may think just[3].

(2) Unless the judgment debtor appears and consents to an immediate hearing, the court shall not hear the complaint unless the summons was served at least 3 clear days before the hearing[4].

(3) Service of a judgment summons outside the commission area for which the justice issuing the summons acted may, without prejudice to any other[5] provision of these rules enabling service of a summons to be proved, be proved by affidavit.

1. See Form 108 in PART IX: PRECEDENTS AND FORMS, post, cd-rom only.
2. The usual practice is for the justice to endorse this permission on the back of the summons reciting that he is satisfied on the points set out in the Rule.
3. This is usually spoken of a "substituted service" and may be by ordinary post, service on the defendant's wife or business partner or other person who is known to have contact with him, or service by advertisement. What will be "just" in the circumstances, is entirely within the justices' discretion. The usual procedure for service of a summons does not apply to a judgment summons (see r 99(9), post).
4. This is the minimum period: where substituted service is allowed the justices may think it just to allow a longer period.
5. Service may be proved in manner provided by r 67, post.

Enforcement of affiliation orders, etc

1–5988 **59.** (1) Subject to the following provisions of this rule, a complaint[1] for the enforcement of a magistrates' court maintenance order, or an order enforceable as a magistrates' court maintenance order[2], shall be heard by the court that made the order:
Provided that—

(a) where—
  (i) the complainant is the person in whose favour the order was made or, if that person is a child, is the child or the person with whom the child had his home; and
  (ii) the complainant resides in a petty sessions area other than that for which the court acts; and
  (iii) payment is directed to be made either to the complainant or the justices' chief executive for a magistrates' court for that petty sessions area,
    the complaint may be heard by the last-mentioned court;

(b) where the complainant is the justices' chief executive for a magistrates' court, the complaint may be heard by that court.

(2) Where a complaint is made to a justice of the peace[3] for the enforcement of such an order as aforesaid and it appears to him that the defendant is for the time being in some petty sessions area other than that for which the justice[3] is acting and that the order may be more conveniently enforced by a magistrates' court acting for that area, the justice shall cause the justices' chief executive for the court to send the complaint[3] by post to the justices' chief executive for a magistrates' court acting for that other petty sessions area, and for that purpose shall write down the complaint if this has not already been done.

(3) On receipt by the justices' chief executive for a magistrates' court of a complaint sent under the last preceding paragraph, he shall bring it before the court; and the court shall issue a summons or warrant[4] for procuring the appearance of the defendant before it, and shall hear and determine the complaint.

(4) If, after a complaint has been sent to the justices' chief executive for a magistrates' court under this rule, the justices' chief executive for the court to which the complaint was made receives any payment under the order, he shall forthwith send[5] by post to the justices' chief executive to whom the complaint was sent a certificate of the amount of the payment and of the date when it was made.

(5) If, after a complaint has been sent as aforesaid, payment under the order is made, not to the justices' chief executive for the court to which the complaint was originally made, but to the person specified in the order or, in the case of a child, to the person with whom the child has his home, that person shall forthwith inform the justices' chief executive of the amount and date as aforesaid and the justices' chief executive shall forthwith send a certificate of the amount and date as required by the last preceding paragraph.

(6) A certificate under this rule purporting to be signed by the justices' chief executive for the court to which the complaint was originally made shall be admissible as evidence on the hearing of the complaint that the amount specified in the certificate was paid on the date so specified.

(7) This rule shall not apply—

(a) where jurisdiction is confined by section 88(2)(a) of the Children and Young Persons Act 1933[6], to courts having jurisdiction in the place where the person liable is residing;
(b) to a contribution order[7].

1. Note the provisions of the Magistrates' Courts Act 1980, s 99, ante; enabling proof of non-payment by means of certificate or statutory declaration.
2. A list of orders enforceable as magistrates' court maintenance orders is noted to the Magistrates' Courts Act 1980, s 93(1), this PART, ante.
3. A complaint not on oath may be made to a justices' clerk who may also make the determination as to venue: Justices' Clerks Rules 1999, Schedule, para 37, post.
4. Ordinarily, the complaint need not be in writing (r 4, ante), but this rule requires that it shall be set down in writing if it is to be transmitted to another court. The other court is empowered to issue a summons or warrant (see para (3), infra), but cannot issue a warrant unless the complaint is substantiated on oath

(Magistrates' Courts Act 1980, s 93(5), ante). It is recommended therefore that a complaint sent to another court shall always be on oath, and the court receiving a complaint should be sure it has been substantiated on oath before issuing a warrant.

5. In Home Office Circular (278/1947) the Secretary of State draws attention to the importance of the observance of the provisions of this sub-paragraph, relating to the transmission to the other court of information as to any payments made after the complaint for recovery of payments under the order has been transmitted to that court. If that court does not receive this information, and the defendant when he appears before it claims to have made such payments, the court may have difficulty in deciding the matter and delay may result by reason of the adjournment of the hearing in order that inquiries may be made.

6. Superseded by s 51 of the Child Care Act 1980, now repealed by the Children Act 1989, Sch 15.

7. A contribution order is made under the Children Act 1989, Sch 2, Pt III, in PART IV: FAMILY LAW, post.

Enforcement where periodical payments made under more than one order

1–5989 60. (1) Where periodical payments are required to be made to any person by another person under more than one periodical payments order, proceedings for the recovery of the payments may be brought by way of one complaint. Any such complaint shall indicate the payments due under each order referred to in the complaint.

(2) Any sum paid to the justices' chief executive for a magistrates' court on any date by a person liable to make payments under 2 or more periodical payments orders which is less than the total sum required to be paid on that date to that chief executive by that person in respect of those orders (being orders one of which requires payments to be made for the benefit of a child to the person with whom the child has his home and one or more of which requires payments to be made to that person either for his own benefit or for the benefit of another child who has his home with him) shall be apportioned between the orders in proportion to the amounts respectively due under each order over a period of one year and if, as a result of the apportionment, the payments under any such order are no longer in arrears the residue shall be applied to the amount due under the other order or (if there is more than one other order) shall be apportioned as aforesaid between the other orders.

(3) For the purposes of calculating the apportionment of any sum under paragraph (2)—

(a) a month shall be treated as consisting of 4 weeks; and

(b) a year shall be treated as consisting of 52 weeks.

Notice of adjudication on complaint for enforcement of affiliation order, etc

1–5990 61. A magistrates' court shall give notice in writing to the complainant of its adjudication on a complaint for the enforcement of a magistrates' court maintenance order, or order enforceable as a magistrates' court maintenance order, unless the complainant is present or is the justices' chief executive for the court.

Particulars relating to payment of lump sum under affiliation order, etc to be entered in register

1–5991 62. Where a magistrates' court allows time for payment of a lump sum required to be paid under a magistrates' court maintenance order, or order enforceable as a magistrates' court maintenance order, or orders that any such lump sum shall be paid by instalments or varies the number of instalments payable, the amount of any instalment payable or the date on which any instalment becomes payable, particulars thereof shall be entered in the register or in any separate record kept for the purpose of recording particulars of lump sum payments.

Notice of date of reception in custody and discharge

1–5992 63. (1) Where in proceedings to enforce a magistrates' court maintenance order, or an order enforceable as a magistrates' court maintenance order[1], the defendant is committed to custody, then on his discharge the governor or keeper of the prison or place of detention shall send to the justices' chief executive for the court that committed the defendant a certificate showing the dates of the defendant's reception and discharge; and that chief executive shall, if the payments under the order are required to be made to the justices' chief executive for any other court, send the certificate to the last-mentioned justices' chief executive.

(2) Where a magistrates' court issues a warrant of commitment for a default in paying a sum adjudged to be paid by a summary conviction then on the discharge of the defaulter the governor or keeper of the prison or place of detention shall send to the justices' chief executive for the court a certificate showing the dates of the defaulter's reception and discharge.

1. This rule applies to an affiliation order, a maintenance order made under the Matrimonial Proceedings (Magistrates' Courts) Act 1960, an order for the maintenance of a child under the Guardianship of Minors Acts 1971 and 1973, an order made under s 47 (contribution order) or s 49 (empowering local authority to collect money under affiliation order) of the Child Care Act 1980, an order for the recovery by a local authority of the cost of assistance (National Assistance Act 1948, s 43), an order for the recovery of cost of benefit (Supplementary Benefits Act 1976, s 18) and an order under the Domestic Proceedings and Magistrates' Courts Act 1978. A similar procedure is recommended in Home Office Circular No 73/1957, dated 16 April 1957, in relation to fines, etc, lost by committal. Justices' clerks are asked not to make entries "lost by committal" in their accounts until notification has been received from the prison that the prisoner has been discharged without payment.

1–5993 64–65. *Revoked.*

REGISTER

Register of convictions, etc

1–5995 66. (1) The justices' chief executive for every magistrates' court shall keep a register[1] in which there shall be entered—

(a) a minute or memorandum[2] of every adjudication[3] of the court;
(b) a minute or memorandum[2] of every other proceeding or thing required by these rules or any other enactment[4] to be so entered.

(2) The register may be stored in electronic form on the court computer system and entries in the register shall include, where relevant, the following particulars—

(a) the name of the informant, complainant or applicant;
(b) the name and date of birth (if known) of the defendant or respondent;
(c) the nature of offence, matter of complaint or details of the application;
(d) the date of offence or matter of complaint;
(e) the plea or consent to order; and
(f) the minute of adjudication.

(3) Particulars of any entry relating to a decision about bail or the reasons for any such decisions or the particulars of any certificate granted under section 5(6A) of the Bail Act 1976 may be made in a book separate from that in which the entry recording the decision itself is made, but any such separate book shall be regarded as forming part of the register.

(3A) Where, by virtue of subsection (3A) of section 128 of the Act of 1980, an accused gives his consent to the hearing and determination in his absence of any application for his remand on an adjournment of the case under sections 5, 10(1) or 18(4) of that Act, the court shall cause the consent of the accused, and the date on which it was notified to the court, to be entered in the register.

(3B) Where any consent mentioned in paragraph (3A) is withdrawn, the court shall cause the withdrawal of the consent and the date on which it was notified to the court to be entered in the register.

(4) On the summary trial of an information the accused's plea shall be entered in the register.

(5) Where a court tries any person summarily in any case in which he may be tried summarily only with his consent, the court shall cause his consent to be entered in the register and, if the consent is signified by a person representing him in his absence, the court shall cause that fact also to be entered in the register.

(6) Where a person is charged before a magistrates' court with an offence triable either way the court shall cause the entry in the register to show whether he was present when the proceedings for determining the mode of trial were conducted and, if they were conducted in his absence, whether they were so conducted by virtue of section 18(3) of the Act of 1980 (disorderly conduct on his part) or by virtue of section 23(1) of that Act (consent signified by person representing him).

(7) In any case to which section 22 of the Act of 1980 (certain offences triable either way to be tried summarily if value involved is small) applies, the court shall cause its decision as to the value involved or, as the case may be, the fact that it is unable to reach such a decision to be entered in the register.

(8) Where a court has power under section 53(3) of the Act of 1980 to make an order with the consent of the defendant without hearing evidence, the court shall cause any consent of the defendant to the making of the order to be entered in the register.

(9) In the case of conviction or dismissal, the register shall clearly show the nature of the offence of which the accused is convicted or, as the case may be, the nature of the offence charged in the information that is dismissed.

(10) An entry of a conviction in the register shall state the date of the offence.

(10A) Where a court is required under section 130(3) of the Act of 2000 to give reasons for not making a compensation order the court shall cause the reasons given to be entered in the register.

(10B) Where a court passes a custodial sentence, the court shall cause a statement of whether it obtained and considered a pre-sentence report before passing sentence to be entered in the register.

(11) *Revoked.*

(11A) *Revoked.*

(12) Every register shall be open to inspection during reasonable hours by any justice of the peace, or any person authorised in that behalf by a justice of the peace or the Lord Chancellor[8].

---

1. For rules relating to the register in adoption proceedings, see the Magistrates' Courts (Adoption) Rules 1984, r 32, post, and as to the youth court register, see the Magistrates' Courts (Children and Young Persons) Rules 1992, rr 25 and 29 and Form 54 in PART IX: FORMS (Youth Courts), cd-rom only.
2. For admissibility in evidence of a certified extract from the register, see r 68, post.
3. This includes the dismissal of a complaint: see *Baker v Baker* [1961] 2 All ER 746. It is not the entry in the register which makes or contributes to the making of the conviction or order. That has already been done (*R v Manchester Justices, ex p Lever* [1937] 2 KB 96, [1937] 3 All ER 4, 101 JP 407). The clerk's duty relating to entries in the register was considered in *R v Huntingdon Justices, ex p Simpkin and Coombes* (1959) 123 JP 166; a verbal inaccuracy in an entry in the register may be corrected by the clerk within the scope of his duty. If the court convicts of part only of the offence charged, e.g. theft of one only of a number of articles charged, the adjudication should show what the defendant has been convicted of (*Machent v Quinn* [1970] 2 All ER 255, 134 JP 501).
4. See ante, rr 20, 28, 29.
5. See Form 148 in PART IX: PRECEDENTS AND FORMS, post, cd-rom only.
6. This means the clerk who was actually acting as justices' chief executive for the court during proceedings to which the entry relates even if he were not the clerk to the justices.
7. By a justice sitting "out of court", as an examining justice (see Magistrates' Courts Act 1980, s 4(2), statutory exception or where ends of justice not served by sitting in open court) or sitting in an occasional court house (Magistrates' Court Act, 1980, s 147).
8. The Home Secretary by circular letter, 9 February, 1893 (57 JP Jo 105), requested clerks to justices to offer

facilities to police officers to enable them to prepare the annual returns of crime and to assist them with advice if the occasion should require it, and suggested that for this purpose the officers preparing the returns should have access to the register to enable them to correct their notes or returns.

1–5996 66A. *Revoked.*

Registration of certificate issued under section 70 of the Road Traffic Offenders Act 1988

1–5997 66B. The justices' chief executive for every magistrates' court shall register receipt of a registration certificate issued under section [70 of the Road Traffic Offenders Act 1988] in a book separate from the register kept under rule 66 but any such book shall be regarded as forming part of the register.

EVIDENCE—GENERAL

Proof of service, handwriting, etc

1–6010 67. (1) The service on any person of a summons, process, notice or document required or authorised to be served in any proceedings before a magistrates' court, and the handwriting or seal of a justice of the peace or other person on any warrant, summons, notice, process or documents issued or made in any such proceedings, may be proved in any legal proceedings by a document purporting to be a solemn declaration in the prescribed form[1] made before a justice of the peace, commissioner for oaths, justices' chief executive for a magistrates' court or registrar of a county court or a sheriff or sheriff clerk (in Scotland) or a justices' chief executive for petty sessions (in Northern Ireland).

(2) The service of any process or other document required or authorised to be served may be proved[2] in any proceedings before a magistrates' court by a document purporting to be a certificate[1] signed by the person by whom the service was effected.

(3) References in paragraph (2) to the service of any process shall, in their application to a witness summons, be construed as including references to the payment or tender to the witness of his costs and expenses.

(4) Any process or other document produced by the court computer system on a given day shall be sufficient evidence that the process or other document was sent to the person to whom it is addressed within 2 days of it being produced, unless the contrary is proved.

---

1. See Forms 142–145 in PART IX: PRECEDENTS AND FORMS, post; and see Magistrates' Courts Act 1980, s 107, for offence of making a false statement in a declaration or certificate.
2. A certificate of service is not conclusive proof that a summons has been properly served, and the Crown Court may have jurisdiction to hear an appeal on the basis that an appellant was never served with the summons although the court was in possession of a certificate of service: see *Maher v Gower (formerly Kubilius)* (1981) 12 Fam Law 32, 126 Sol Jo 65.

Proof of proceedings

1–6011 68. The register[1] of a magistrates' court, or an extract[2] from the register certified by the justices' chief executive as a true extract, shall be admissible[3] in any legal proceedings as evidence of the proceedings of the court entered in the register.

---

1. This will include a note of the matters referred to in rr 20, 28, 29, ante.
2. For form of extract, see Form 154 in PART IX: PRECEDENTS AND FORMS, post.
3. The identity with the proof of conviction of the person charged may be proved by finger-print evidence (Criminal Justice Act 1948, s 39, post).

Proof that magistrates' court maintenance orders, etc, have not been revoked, etc

1–6012 69. A certificate purporting to be signed by the designated officer for a magistrates' court, and stating that no minute or memorandum of an order revoking, discharging, suspending, reviving, altering or varying a magistrates' court maintenance order, or order enforceable as a magistrates' court maintenance order or an order made under Part I of the Act of 1978 or under Schedule 6 to the Civil Partnership Act 2004, enforceable otherwise than as a magistrates' court maintenance order made by the court is entered in the register of the court shall, in any proceedings relating to the enforcement of the order or the revocation, discharge, suspension, revival, alteration or variation of the order, be evidence that the order has not been revoked, discharged, suspended, revived, altered or varied.

EVIDENCE—CRIMINAL PROCEEDINGS

1–6013 70–73. *Revoked.*

APPEAL TO CROWN COURT

Documents to be sent to Crown Court

1–6017 74. (1) A justices' chief executive for a magistrates' court shall as soon as practicable send[1] to the appropriate officer of the Crown Court[2] any notice of appeal[3] to the Crown Court given to the justices' chief executive for the court.

(2) The justices' chief executive for a magistrates' court shall send to the appropriate officer of the Crown Court, with the notice of appeal[4], a copy of the extract of the magistrates' court register relating to that decision[5] and of the last known or usual place of abode of the parties to the appeal.

(3) Where any person, having given notice of appeal to the Crown Court, has been granted bail[6] for the purposes of the appeal the justices' chief executive for the court from whose decision the appeal is brought shall before the day fixed for the hearing of the appeal send to the appropriate officer of the Crown Court—

    (a) in the case of bail in criminal proceedings, a copy of the record made in pursuance of section 5 of the Bail Act 1976 relating to such bail;

    (b) in the case of bail otherwise than in criminal proceedings, the recognizance entered into by the appellant relating to such bail.

(4) Where, in any such case as is referred to in paragraph 3(b), the recognizance in question has been entered into otherwise than before the magistrates' court from whose decision the appeal is brought, or the justices' chief executive for that court, the person who took the recognizance shall send it forthwith to that chief executive.

(5) Where a notice of appeal is given in respect of a hospital order or guardianship order made under section 37 of the Mental Health Act 1983, the justices' chief executive for the magistrates' court from which the appeal is brought shall send with the notice to the appropriate officer of the Crown Court any written evidence considered by the court under subsection (1)(a) of the said section 37.

(6) Where a notice of appeal is given in respect of an appeal against conviction by a magistrates' court the justices' chief executive for the court shall send with the notice to the appropriate officer of the Crown Court any admission of facts made for the purposes of the summary trial under section 10 of the Criminal Justice Act 1967.

(7) Where a notice of appeal is given in respect of an appeal against sentence by a magistrates' court, and where that sentence was a custodial sentence, the justices' chief executive for the court shall send with the notice to the appropriate officer of the Crown Court a statement of whether the magistrates' court obtained and considered a pre-sentence report before passing such sentence.

---

1. The requirements of this rule should be complied with even where the notice of appeal is given after twenty-one days have expired; it will be for the Crown Court to decide whether or not to extend the time for appealing (see Crown Court Rules 1982, r 7, post).
2. The appropriate officer of the Crown Court shall enter the appeal and give notice to the appellant, to the other party to the appeal, and to the clerk to the magistrates' court as to the date, time and place fixed for the hearing of the appeal (Crown Court Rules 1982, r 8 post).
3. In a case where the provisions of the Road Traffic (New Drivers) Act 1995 apply, notice of the appeal must be given by the magistrates' court to the Secretary of State for Transport in accordance with the New Drivers (Appeals Procedure) Regulations 1997, in PART VII, TRANSPORT, title ROAD TRAFFIC, post.
4. Generally, for procedure on appeal to the Crown Court, see the Crown Court Rules 1982, post.
5. See the Magistrates' Courts Act 1980, s 113, this PART, ante.

Abandonment of appeal

1–6018 75. Where notice to abandon an appeal has been given by the appellant, any recognizance conditioned for the appearance of the appellant at the hearing of the appeal shall have effect as if conditioned for the appearance of the appellant before the court from whose decision the appeal was brought at a time and place to be notified to the appellant by the justices' chief executive for that court.

CASE STATED[1]
Application to state case

1–6019 76. (1) An application under section 111(1) of the Act of 1980 shall be made in writing and signed by or on behalf of the applicant and shall identify the question or questions of law or jurisdiction on which the opinion of the High Court is sought.

(2) Where one of the questions on which the opinion of the High Court is sought is whether there was evidence on which the magistrates' court could come to its decision, the particular finding of fact made by the magistrates' court which it is claimed cannot be supported by the evidence before the magistrates' court shall be specified in such application.

(3) Any such application shall be sent to the justices' chief executive for the magistrates' court whose decision is questioned.

---

1. For detailed commentary on case stated, see this PART, ante, para **1–765** and see also Rules of the Supreme Court Ord 56, post.

Consideration of draft case

1–6020 77. (1) Within 21 days after receipt of an application made in accordance with rule 76, the justices' chief executive for the magistrates' court whose decision is questioned shall, unless the justices refuse to state a case under section 111(5) of the Act of 1980, send[1] a draft case in which are stated the matters required under rule 81 to the applicant or his solicitor and shall send a copy thereof to the respondent or his solicitor.

(2) Within 21 days after receipt of the draft case under paragraph (1), each party may make representations thereon. Any such representations shall be in writing and signed by or on behalf of the party making them and shall be sent[1] to the clerk.

(3) Where the justices refuse to state a case under section 111(5) of the Act and they are

required by the High Court by order of mandamus under section 111(6) to do so, this rule shall apply as if in paragraph (1)—

    (*a*) for the words "receipt of an application made in accordance with rule 76" there were substituted the words "the date on which an order of mandamus under section 111(6) of the Act of 1980 is made"; and

    (*b*) the words "unless the justices refuse to state a case under section 111(5) of the Act of 1980" were omitted.

---

1. Note r 80 as to service.

Preparation and submission of final case

1–6021 78. (1) Within 21 days after the latest day on which representations may be made under rule 77, the justices whose decision is questioned shall make such adjustments, if any, to the draft case prepared for the purposes of that rule as they think fit, after considering any such representations, and shall state[1] and sign the case.

(2) A case may be stated on behalf of the justices whose decision is questioned by any 2 or more of them and may, if the justices so direct, be signed on their behalf by their clerk.

(3) Forthwith after the case has been stated and signed the justices' chief executive for the court shall send it to the applicant or his solicitor, together with any statement required by rule 79.

---

1. The case must comply with r 81, post, and should be in Form 155 in PART IX: PRECEDENTS AND FORMS, post (*Practice Direction* [1972] 1 All ER 286).

Extension of time limits

1–6022 79. (1) If the justices' chief executive for a magistrates' court is unable to send to the applicant a draft case under paragraph (1) of rule 77 within the time required by that paragraph, he shall do so as soon as practicable thereafter and the provisions of that rule shall apply accordingly; but in that event the justices' chief executive shall attach to the draft case, and to the final case when it is sent to the applicant or his solicitor under rule 78(3), a statement of the delay and the reasons therefor.

(2) If the justices' chief executive for a magistrates' court receives an application in writing from or on behalf of the applicant or the respondent for an extension of the time within which representations on the draft case may be made under paragraph (2) of rule 77, together with reasons in writing therefor, the clerk of the magistrates' court may by notice in writing sent to the applicant or respondent as the case may be by the justices' chief executive extend the time and the provisions of that paragraph and of rule 78 shall apply accordingly; but in that event the justices' chief executive shall attach to the final case, when it is sent to the applicant or his solicitor under rule 78(3), a statement of the extension and the reasons therefor.

(3) If the justices are unable to state a case within the time required by paragraph (1) of rule 78, they shall do so as soon as practicable thereafter and the provisions of that rule shall apply accordingly; but in that event the clerk shall attach to the final case, when it is sent to the applicant or his solicitor under rule 78(3), a statement of the delay and the reasons therefor.

Service of documents

1–6023 80. Any document required by rules 76 to 79 to be sent to any person shall either be delivered to him or be sent by post in a registered letter or by recorded delivery service and, if sent by post to an applicant or respondent, shall be addressed to him at his last known or usual place of abode.

Content of case

1–6024 81. (1) A case stated by the magistrates' court shall state the facts found by the court and the question or questions of law or jurisdiction on which the opinion of the High Court is sought.

(2) Where one of the questions on which the opinion of the High Court is sought is whether there was evidence on which the magistrates' court could come to its decision, the particular finding of fact which it is claimed cannot be supported by the evidence before the magistrates' court shall be specified in the case.

(3) Unless one of the questions on which the opinion of the High Court is sought is whether there was evidence on which the magistrates' court could come to its decision, the case shall not contain a statement of evidence[1].

---

1. Save where the condition set out in r 81(3) is satisfied, a statement of the evidence should not be included. Moreover, the High Court is not competent to receive with the case stated notes of evidence; see *Cotgreave and Cotgreave v Cheshire County Council* (1992) 157 JP 85.

RECOGNIZANCES AND BAIL

Recognizance to keep the peace, etc, taken by one court and discharged by another

1–6025 82. Where a magistrates' court acting for any petty sessions area makes an order under section 116 of the Act of 1980 discharging a recognizance entered into before a magistrates' court acting for any other petty sessions area, the justices' chief executive for the court that orders the recognizance to be discharged shall send a copy of the order of discharge to the justices' chief executive for the court acting for that other petty sessions area.

Application to vary order for sureties or dispense with them

1–6026   **83.** Where a person has been committed to custody in default of finding sureties and the order to find sureties was made at the instance of another person, an application under section 118 of the Act of 1980 shall be made by complaint[1] against that other person.

---

1. That is to say, by complaint on which is issued a summons calling upon the other person to show cause why the amount of the recognizance should not be varied or the sureties dispensed with.

Notice of enlargement of recognizances

1–6027   **84.** (1) If a magistrates' court before which any person is bound by a recognizance to appear enlarges the recognizance to a later time under section 129 of the Act in his absence, it shall give him and his sureties, if any, notice thereof[1].

(2) If a magistrates' court, under section 129(4) of the Act of 1980, enlarges the recognizance of a surety for a person committed for trial on bail, it shall give the surety notice thereof[2].

---

1. See Form 131, in PART IX: PRECEDENTS AND FORMS, post.
2. See Form 132 in PART IX: PRECEDENTS AND FORMS, post.

1–6027A   **84A–85.** *Revoked.*

Requirements to be complied with before release

1–6029   **86.** (1) Where a magistrates' court has fixed the amount[1] in which a person (including any surety) is to be bound by a recognizance, the recognizance may be entered into—

    (a)   in the case of a surety in connection with bail in criminal proceedings where the accused is in a prison or other place of detention, before the governor or keeper of the prison or place as well as before the persons mentioned in section 8(4)(a) of the Bail Act 1976;

    (b)   in any other case, before a justice of the peace[2], a justices' clerk[2], a justices' chief executive, a police officer[2] who either is of the rank of inspector or above or is in charge of a police station or, if the person to be bound is in a prison or other place of detention, before the governor or keeper of the prison or place; or

    (c)   where a person other than a police officer is authorised under section 125A or 125B of the Act of 1980 to execute a warrant of arrest providing for a recognizance to be entered into by the person arrested (but not by any other person), before the person executing the warrant.

(2) The justices' chief executive for a magistrates' court which has fixed the amount in which a person (including any surety) is to be bound by a recognizance or, under section 3(5), (6) or (6A) of the Bail Act 1976, imposed any requirement to be complied with before a person's release on bail or any condition of bail shall issue a certificate showing the amount and conditions, if any, of the recognizance or, as the case may be, containing a statement of the requirement or condition of bail; and a person authorised to take the recognizance or do anything in relation to the compliance with such requirement or condition of bail shall not be required to take or do it without production of the certificate as aforesaid.

(3) If any person proposed as a surety for a person committed to custody by a magistrates' court produces to the governor or keeper of the prison or other place of detention in which the person so committed is detained a certificate to the effect that he is acceptable as a surety, signed by any of the justices composing the court or the justices' chief executive for the court and signed in the margin by the person proposed as surety, the governor or keeper shall take the recognizance of the person so proposed.

(4) Where the recognizance of any person committed to custody by a magistrates' court or of any surety of such a person is taken by any person other than the court which committed the first-mentioned person to custody, the person taking the recognizance shall send it to the justices' chief executive for that court:

Provided that, in the case of a surety, if the person committed has been committed to the Crown Court for trial or under any of the enactments mentioned in rule 17(1), the person taking the recognizance shall send it to the appropriate officer of the Crown Court.

---

1. The power to fix the amount where recognizances are to be entered into later is contained in the Magistrates' Courts Act 1980, s 119, ante.
2. Not necessarily in the same county or place.

Notice to governor of prison, etc where release from custody is ordered

1–6030   **87.** Where a magistrates' court has, with a view to the release on bail of a person in custody, fixed the amount in which he or any surety of such a person shall be bound or, under section 3(5), (6) or (6A) of the Bail Act 1976, imposed any requirement to be complied with before his release or any condition of bail—

    (a)   the justices' chief executive for the court shall give notice thereof to the governor or keeper of the prison or place where that person is detained by sending him such a certificate[1] as is mentioned in rule 86(2);

(*b*) any person authorised to take the recognizance of a surety or do anything in relation to the compliance with such requirement shall, on taking or doing it, send notice thereof by post to the said governor or keeper and, in the case of a recognizance of a surety, shall give a copy of the notice to the surety.

---

1. See Forms 126 and 127 in PART IX: PRECEDENTS AND FORMS, post.

Release when recognizances have been taken or requirements complied with

1–6031 88. Where a magistrates' court has, with a view to the release on bail of a person in custody, fixed the amount in which he or any surety of such a person shall be bound or, under section 3(5) or (6) of the Bail Act 1976, imposed any requirement to be complied with before his release and given notice thereof in accordance with these Rules to the governor or keeper of the prison or place where that person is detained, the governor or keeper shall, when satisfied that the recognizances of all sureties required have been taken and that all such requirements have been complied with—

    (*a*) in the case of bail in criminal proceedings, unless he is in custody for some other cause, release him;

    (*b*) in the case of bail otherwise than in criminal proceedings, take the recognizances of that person if this has not already been done and, unless he is in custody for some other cause, release him.

1–6032 89–93. *Revoked.*

Procedure where prosecution appeals against a decision to grant bail

1–6036A 93A–93B. *Revoked.*

WARRANT
Committal to custody to be by warrant

1–6037 94. A justice of the peace shall not commit any person to a prison, young offender institution or a remand centre, or to a police station under section 128(7) of the Act of 1980, or to customs detention under section 152 of the Criminal Justice Act 1988 except by a warrant[1] of commitment.

---

1. It is unnecessary for it to be under seal. The operation of para (2) is reflected in the prescribed forms. See forms in PART IX: PRECEDENTS AND FORMS, post.

Warrant to be signed

1–6038 95. Except where signature by the justices' chief executive for a magistrates' court is permitted by rule 109 or by the Magistrates' Courts (Forms) Rules 1981 every warrant under the Act of 1980 shall be signed by the justice issuing it.

1–6038A 95A. *Revoked.*

Warrant of arrest

1–6039 96. (1) A warrant[1] issued by a justice of the peace for the arrest of any person shall require the persons to whom it is directed, that is to say, the constables of the police area in which the warrant is issued, or the civilian enforcement officers[2] for the area in which they are employed, or any persons named in that behalf in the warrant, to arrest the person against whom the warrant is issued.

(2) The warrant shall name or otherwise describe the person for whose arrest it is issued, and shall contain a statement[3] of the offence charged in the information or, as the case may be, the ground on which the warrant is issued.

(3) A warrant to which this rule applies may be executed by the persons to whom it was directed or by any of the following persons, whether or not the warrant was directed to them—

    (*a*) a constable for any police area in England and Wales, acting in his own police area;

    (*b*) where the warrant is one to which section 125A of the Act of 1980 applies, a civilian enforcement officer within the meaning of section 125A of the Act of 1980;

    (*c*) where the warrant is one to which section 125A of the Act of 1980 applies, any of the individuals described in section 125B(1) of the Act of 1980;

and in this rule any reference to the person charged with the execution of a warrant includes any of the above persons who is for the time being authorised to execute the warrant, whether or not they have the warrant in their possession at the time.

(4) A person executing a warrant of arrest shall, upon arresting the person against whom the warrant is issued—

    (*a*) either

        (i) if he has the warrant with him, show it to the person against whom the warrant is issued, or

        (ii) otherwise, state where the warrant is and what arrangements may be made to allow the person arrested to inspect it;

(b) explain, in ordinary language, the offence or default with which the person is charged and the reason for the arrest;

(c) where the person executing the warrant is one of the persons referred to in paragraph (3)(b) or (c) above, show the person arrested a written statement under section 125A(4) or 125B(4) as appropriate; and

(d) in any case, show documentary proof of his identity.

(5) A warrant of arrest issued under any of the provisions in paragraph (6) shall cease to have effect when—

(a) the sum in respect of which the warrant is issued is paid to the person charged with the execution of the warrant;

(b) that sum is tendered to and refused by the person charged with the execution of the warrant; or

(c) a receipt for that sum given by—

   (i) the justices' chief executive for the court which issued the warrant; or

   (ii) the charging or billing authority,

is produced to the person charged with the execution of the warrant.

(6) Those provisions are—

(a) sections 83(1), 83(2), 86(4) and 93(5) of the Act of 1980;

(b) Revoked.

(c) regulation 17(5)(b) of the Non-Domestic Rating (Collection and Enforcement) (Local Lists) Regulations 1989; and

(d) regulation 48(5)(b) of the Council Tax (Administration and Enforcement) Regulations 1992.

---

1. See forms in PART IX: PRECEDENTS AND FORMS, post. For backing of an English warrant for execution in the Isles of Man, Guernsey, Jersey, Alderney or Sark and *vice versa*, see Indictable Offences Act 1848, s 13 in PART VIII: title EXTRADITION etc, post. For the execution of a warrant of arrest in Scotland or Northern Ireland, see the Criminal Justice and Public Order Act 1994, Pt X, this PART, post.
2. Defined by r 2(4), ante.
3. The form in which the offence is to be stated is dealt with in r 100, post.

Warrant of commitment

1–6040 **97.** (1) A warrant of commitment[1] or detention, other than a warrant committing a person to customs detention under section 152 of the Criminal Justice Act 1988, issued by a justice of the peace—

(a) shall name or otherwise describe the person committed or detained;

(b) shall contain a statement of the offence[2] with which the person committed or detained is charged, or of which he has been convicted, or of any other ground on which he is committed;

(c) shall be directed to a person named in the warrant or to the constables of the police area in which the warrant is issued or to the civilian enforcement officers[3] for the area in which they are employed and to the governor or keeper of the prison or place of detention specified in the warrant, and shall require—

   (i) the named person or the constables or civilian enforcement officers[3] to arrest the person committed or detained, if he is at large, and convey him to that prison or place and deliver him with the warrant to the governor or keeper;

   (ii) the governor or keeper to keep in his custody the person committed or detained until that person be delivered in due course of law, or until the happening of an event specified in the warrant, or for the period specified in the warrant, as the case may be.

(1A) A warrant issued by a justice of the peace committing a person to customs detention under section 152 of the Criminal Justice Act 1988—

(a) shall name or otherwise describe the person committed;

(b) shall contain a statement of the offence with which the person committed is charged;

(c) shall be directed to the officers of Her Majesty's Customs and Excise and shall require those officers to keep the person committed in their custody, unless in the meantime he be otherwise delivered in due course of law, for a period (not exceeding 192 hours) specified in the warrant.

(1B) A warrant of commitment or detention other than a warrant committing a person to customs detention under section 152 of the Criminal Justice Act 1988 may be executed by the persons to whom it was directed or by any of the following persons, whether or not the warrant was directed to them—

(a) a constable for any police area in England and Wales, acting in his own police area;

(b) where the warrant is one to which section 125A of the Act of 1980 applies, a civilian enforcement officer within the meaning of section 125A of the Act of 1980;

(c) where the warrant is one to which section 125A of the Act of 1980 applies, any of the individuals described in section 125B(1) of the Act of 1980;

and in this rule any reference to the person charged with the execution of a warrant includes any of the above persons who is for the time being authorised to execute the warrant, whether or not they have the warrant in their possession at the time.

(1C) A person executing a warrant of commitment or detention shall, upon arresting the person against whom the warrant is issued—

(a) either

    (i) if he has the warrant with him, show it to the person against whom the warrant is issued, or

    (ii) otherwise, state where the warrant is and what arrangements may be made to allow the person against whom the warrant was issued to inspect it;

(b) explain, in ordinary language, the offence or default with which the person is charged and the reason for the commitment or detention;

(c) where the person executing the warrant is one of the persons referred to in paragraph (1B)(b) or (c) above, show the person against whom the warrant was issued a written statement under section 125A(4) or 125B(4) as appropriate; and

(d) in any case, show documentary proof of his identity.

(2) A warrant of commitment or detention other than a warrant committing a person to customs detention under section 152 of the Criminal Justice Act 1988, may be executed by conveying the person committed or detained to any prison or place of detention in which he may lawfully be detained and delivering him there together with the warrant; and, so long as any person is detained in any such prison or place other than that specified in the warrant, the warrant shall have effect as if that other prison or place were the prison or place specified in it.

(3) Notwithstanding the preceding provisions of this rule, a warrant of commitment or detention issued in pursuance of a valid conviction, or of a valid order requiring the person committed or detained to do or abstain from doing anything, shall not, if it alleges that the person committed or detained has been convicted, or ordered to do or abstain from doing that thing, be held void[4] by reason of any defect in the warrant.

(4) The governor or keeper of the prison or place of detention at which any person is delivered in pursuance of a warrant of commitment or detention shall give to the constable or other person making the delivery a receipt for that person.

(5) Notwithstanding the preceding provisions of this rule, a warrant of a justice of the peace to commit to custody any person who to the justice's knowledge is already detained in a prison or other place of detention shall be delivered to the governor or keeper of the prison or place of detention in which that person is detained.

(6) A warrant of commitment or detention issued under any of the provisions in paragraph (7) shall cease to have effect if, at any time before the person for whose commitment or detention the warrant was issued is placed in custody—

(a) the sum in respect of which the warrant is issued, together with the costs and charges, if any, of the commitment, is paid to the person charged with the execution of the warrant;

(b) that sum is tendered to and refused by the person charged with the execution of the warrant; or

(c) a receipt for that sum given by—

    (i) the justices' chief executive for the court which issued the warrant; or

    (ii) the charging or billing authority,

    is produced to the person charged with the execution of the warrant.

(7) Those provisions are:

(a) sections 76 and 136 of the Act of 1980;

(b) section 40 of the Child Support Act 1991;

(c) *Revoked.*

(d) regulation 16(3)(a) of the Non-Domestic Rating (Collection and Enforcement) (Local Lists) Regulations 1989; and

(e) regulation 47(3)(a) of the Council Tax (Administration and Enforcement) Regulations 1992.

(8) A warrant of commitment issued for the enforcement of a maintenance order to which Part I of the Maintenance Orders Act 1958 applies shall cease to have effect if, at any time when the defendant is not already detained in pursuance of the warrant, the person charged with the execution of the warrant is informed—

(a) that an application for registration of the order has been granted under section 2 of the Maintenance Orders Act 1958; or

(b) that notice seeking the cancellation of such registration has been given under section 5 of that Act.

---

1. See Forms in PART IX: PRECEDENTS AND FORMS, post, and in Magistrates' Courts (Maintenance Orders Act 1958) Rules 1959, PART IV: FAMILY LAW, post.

2. Where the warrant is issued on committal for trial, it may set out a number of offences and will be treated as several and distinct warrants for all the offences (*R v Phillips, R v Quayle* [1939] 1 KB 63, [1938] 3 All ER 674).

3. See note 3 to r 96, supra.

4. The issue of a warrant of commitment is a judicial act, and if the power to issue it is dependent on a sum of money not having been paid, *certiorari* will lie to quash a warrant issued in error after payment of the money (*R v Doherty, ex p Isaacs* (1910) 74 JP 304).

SUMMONS

Form of summons

1–6041 **98.** (1) A summons shall be signed[1] by the justice[2] issuing it or state his name and be authenticated by the signature of the justices' chief executive for a magistrates' court.

(2) A summons requiring a person to appear before a magistrates' court to answer to an

information or complaint shall state shortly the matter of the information or complaint and shall state the time and place at which the defendant is required by the summons to appear.

(3) A single summons may be issued against a person in respect of several informations or complaints; but the summons shall state the matter of each information or complaint separately and shall have effect as several summonses, each issued in respect of one information or complaint.

(4) In this rule where a signature is required, an electronic signature incorporated into the document shall satisfy this requirement.

---

1. It is unnecessary that it shall also be sealed. The signature may be affixed by means of a rubber stamped facsimile not only by the justice himself but also by a justices' clerk's assistant with the authority, general or specific, of the justice (*R v Brentford Justices, ex p Catlin* [1975] QB 455, [1975] 2 All ER 201, 139 JP 516).

2. Or justices' clerk acting under the Justices' Clerks Rules 2005, post. For the justices' clerk's power to delegate his functions under the Justices' Clerks Rules 2005 to a person appointed by a magistrates' courts committee to assist him, see the 1999 Rules, r 3, this PART, post. Although a summons must be authorised individually by a justice or by the justices' clerk (or a person appointed to assist him) and must bear the signature of the person who issued it the task can be lightened by batches of complaints having similar characteristics being assembled and placed before a single individual, and the task of signing can be performed vicariously by the use of a facsimile signature on a rubber stamp.

Service of summons, etc

1–6042 **99.** (1) Service[1] of a summons[2] issued by a justice of the peace on a person other than a corporation may be effected[3]—

(a) by delivering[4] it to the person to whom it is directed; or
(b) by leaving it for him with some person at his last known or usual place of abode[5]; or
(c) by sending it by post[6] in a letter addressed to him at his last known or usual place of abode.

(2) *Revoked.*

(3) Service for the purposes of the Act of 1980 of a summons[7] issued by a justice of the peace on a corporation may be effected by delivering[4] it at, or sending it by post[8] to, the registered office of the corporation, if that office is in the United Kingdom, or, if there is no registered office in the United Kingdom, any place in the United Kingdom where the corporation trades or conducts its business.

(4) Paragraph (3) shall have effect in relation to a document (other than a summons) issued by a justice of the peace as it has effect in relation to a summons so issued, but with the substitution of references to England and Wales for the references to the United Kingdom.

(5) Any summons or other document served[9] in manner authorised by the preceding provisions of this rule shall, for the purposes of any enactment other than the Act of 1980 or these Rules requiring a summons or other document to be served in any particular manner, be deemed to have been as effectively served as if it had been served in that manner; and nothing in this rule shall render invalid the service of a summons or other document in that manner.

(6) Sub-paragraph (c) of paragraph (1) shall not authorise the service by post of—

(a) a summons[10] requiring the attendance of any person to give evidence or produce a document or thing; or
(b) a summons issued under any enactment relating to the liability of members of the naval, military or air forces[11] of the Crown for the maintenance of their husbands, wives or civil partners, as the case may be, and children, whether legitimate or illegitimate.

(7) In the case of a summons issued on an application for an order under section 16 or 17(1) of the Act of 1978 (powers of court to make orders for the protection of a party to a marriage or a child of the family) service of the summons shall not be effected in manner authorised by sub-paragraph (b) or (c) of paragraph (1) unless a justice of the peace is satisfied by evidence on oath that prompt personal service of the summons is impracticable and allows service to be effected in such manner.

(8) Where this rule or any other of these Rules provides that a summons or other document may be sent by post to a person's last known or usual place of abode that rule shall have effect as if it provided also for the summons or other document to be sent in the manner specified in the rule to an address given by that person for that purpose.

(9) This rule shall not apply to a judgment[12] summons.

---

1. For manner of proving service, see r 67, ante. A summons may be served on a Sunday since the repeal of the Sunday Observance Act 1677; see Home Office Circular No 274/1969.

2. Other than a judgment summons (see para (9), infra).

3. Note that the rule does not require that the summons shall be served by a constable. A summons requiring a person charged with an offence to appear before a court in England or Wales may be served on him without endorsement in Scotland or Northern Ireland (Criminal Law Act 1977, s 39, ante). Subject to s 15 of the Maintenance Orders Act 1950, a summons in respect of civil proceedings issued by a justice in England or Wales may be served in Scotland after endorsement by a court of summary jurisdiction in Scotland (Summary Jurisdiction (Process) Act 1881, s 4 ante). There is no corresponding provision to s 4 of the 1881 Act for the service of a summons in civil proceedings on a defendant in Northern Ireland. However, process in proceedings for a maintenance order may be served in both Scotland and Northern Ireland in accordance with s 15 of the Maintenance Orders Act 1950, in PART IV, title FAMILY LAW, post.

4. The Rules make no provision for service by fax, but in considering a similar gap in the Rules of the Supreme Court, it was decided that if it was proved that a legible document came into the hands of the party to be served, and the Rules were otherwise complied with, that was good service: see *Ralux NV/SA v Spencer Mason* (1989) Times, 18 May, CA.

5. "Place of abode" does not include a shop nor a lock-up office where the party sought to be served does

not reside (*R v Lilley, ex p Taylor* (1910) 75 JP 95; *R v Rhodes, ex p McVittie* (1915) 79 JP 527), but note the provision in para (8) enabling service at an address given for the purpose.

6. Certain summonses may not be served by post (see para (6), infra).

7. Notwithstanding the apparently wide application of r 99(3), it would seem that a summons relating to civil proceedings should be endorsed in accordance with the Summary Jurisdiction (Process) Act 1881, ante, before being served at the registered office of a corporation, if that office is in Scotland, since s 39 of the Criminal Law Act 1977, which gave rise to the amendment of this rule providing for service on a corporation throughout the UK, only applies where an offence is alleged. Alternatively, the summons may be served on a company registered in Scotland by leaving it at or sending it by post to the principal place of business of the company in England, in accordance with s 725 of the Companies Act 1985, in PART VIII, title COMPANIES, post.

8. See s 7 of the Interpretation Act 1978, in PART II, post.

9. Note that this does not apply to a judgment summons (see para (9), infra).

10. The reason for this exception is that in the event of the witness' failure to attend, a warrant may be issued on proof on oath that the summons was served and conduct money tendered (see Magistrates' Courts Act, 1980, s 97, ante).

11. See PART VIII, title ARMED FORCES, post; provisions in the Naval Discipline Act 1957, s 101(1), the Army Act 1955, s 153(1), and the Air Force Act 1955, s 153(1), empower service by registered post, without prejudice to any other method of service. Although r 99(6)(*b*) disapplies service by post on a member of the armed forces, it does not restrict service under either r 99(1)(*a*) or (*b*); see *Smith v Chuter* [1989] FCR 171, [1989] 1 FLR 93.

12. For service of a judgment summons, see r 58, ante.

FORM IN WHICH OFFENCE MAY BE STATED IN DOCUMENTS

1–6043   **100.** *Revoked.*

MISCELLANEOUS

1–6044   **101–101A.** *Revoked.*

1–6045   **102.** *Revoked.*

1–6046   **103.** *Revoked.*

1–6047   **104–104C.** *Revoked.*

Application for alteration of maintenance agreement under s 35 of Matrimonial Causes Act 1973 or under paragraph 69 of Schedule 5 to the Civil Partnership Act 2004

1–6049   **105.** An application to a magistrates' court under section 35 of the Matrimonial Causes Act 1973, under paragraph 69 of Schedule 5 to the Civil Partnership Act 2004 for the alteration of a maintenance agreement shall be by complaint.

Proceedings against person outside the United Kingdom on application for variation, etc of certain maintenance orders

1–6050   **106.** (1) The period referred to in section 41(2A) of the Maintenance Orders (Reciprocal Enforcement) Act 1972 (which provides that, subject to certain conditions, a magistrates' court may, if it is satisfied that the respondent has been outside the United Kingdom during such period as may be prescribed by rules, proceed on an application made under sections 11B or 11C of the Guardianship of Minors Act 1971 notwithstanding that the respondent has not been served with the summons) shall be the whole of the period beginning one month before the making of the application and ending with the date of the hearing.

(2) Before proceeding in any such case as is referred to in the said section 41(2A), the court shall be satisfied that, in addition to the matter referred to in those subsections, the applicant has taken steps to notify the respondent of the making of the application and of the time and place appointed for the hearing by—

(*a*) causing a notice in writing to that effect to be delivered to the respondent; or

(*b*) causing a notice in writing to that effect to be sent by post addressed to the respondent at his last known or usual place of abode or at his place of business or at such other address at which there is ground for believing that it will reach the respondent, in accordance with directions given for the purpose by a justice of the peace acting for the same petty sessions area as that of the court; or

(*c*) causing a notice to that effect to be inserted in one or more newspapers, in accordance with directions given as aforesaid;

and that it is reasonable in all the circumstances to proceed in the absence of the respondent.

(3) In any such case as is referred to in the said section 41(2A), the court shall not make the order for which the application is made unless it is satisfied that during the period of 6 months immediately preceding the making of the application the respondent was continuously outside the United Kingdom or was not in the United Kingdom on more than 30 days and that, having regard to any communication to the court in writing purporting to be from the respondent, it is reasonable in all the circumstances so to do.

(4) Paragraph (1) of rule 67 of these Rules shall apply for the purpose of proving the delivery of a written notice in pursuance of paragraph (2)(*a*) as it applies for the purpose of proving the service of a summons.

In relation to a solemn declaration made outside the United Kingdom, paragraph (1) of the said rule 67 as applied by this paragraph, shall have effect as if for the reference to the authorities mentioned in the said paragraph (1) there were substituted a reference to a consular officer of

Her Majesty's Government in the United Kingdom or any person for the time being authorised by law, in the place where the declarant is, to administer an oath for any judicial or other legal purpose.

(5) Paragraph (2) of the said rule 67 shall apply for the purpose of proving the sending of a written notice in pursuance of paragraph (2)(*b*) or the insertion of a notice in a newspaper in pursuance of paragraph (2)(*c*) as it applies for the purpose of proving the service of any process, provided, as respects the insertion of a notice in a newspaper, that a copy of the newspaper containing the notice is annexed to the certificate.

Application for summons to witness or warrant for his arrest

1–6051 **107.** (1) An application for the issue of a summons or warrant under section 97 or 97A of the Act of 1980 *or paragraph 4 of Schedule 3 to the Act of 1998*[1] may be made by the applicant in person or by his counsel or solicitor.

(2) An application for the issue of such a summons may be made by delivering or sending the application in writing to the clerk to the magistrates' court.

1. Words in italics inserted by the Magistrates' Courts (Modification) Rules 1998, SI 1998/3046 in respect of those areas from which a person is sent for trial under s 51 of the Crime and Disorder Act 1998.

1–6052 **108.** *Revoked.*

Signature of forms prescribed by rules made under the Act of 1980

1–6053 **109.** (1) Subject to paragraph (2), where any form prescribed by Rules made or having effect as if made under section 144 of the Act of 1980 contains provision for signature by a justice of the peace only, the form shall have effect as if it contained provision in the alternative for signature by the justices' chief executive for a magistrates' court.

(2) This rule shall not apply to any form of warrant, other than a warrant of commitment or of distress, or to any form prescribed in the Magistrates' Courts (Forms) Rules 1981.

(3) In this rule where a signature is required on a form or warrant other than an arrest, remand or commitment warrant, an electronic signature incorporated into the document will satisfy this requirement.

1–6054 **110–114.** *Revoked.*

Crown Court Rules 1982[1]

(SI 1982/1109 amended by SI 1984/699, SI 1986/2151, SI 1988/952, 1322, 1635, 2131 and 2160, SI 1989/299 and 1103, SI 1990/2157, 1991/1288, SI 1992/1847, SI 1994/1480 and 3153, SI 1995/2618, SI 1997/701, SI 1998/2168 and SI 1999/598, 2838 and 3040, SI 2000/2093, 2987 and 3362, SI 2001/193, 614 and 4012, SI 2002/1688, 2783 and 2997, SI 2003/422, 639 and 1664, SI 2004/1047, 1292 and 2991, Courts Act 2003, Sch 8)

PART I
INTRODUCTION

1–6070 **1.** *Citation, commencement, revocations and transitionals.*

1. Made in exercise of powers conferred by s 9(3) of the Juries Act 1974, ss 5(1) and 8(4) of the Bail Act 1976 and ss 52, 73(2), 74(2), (3) and (7) 77, 81(2), 84(1) and (2), 86 and 87(5) of the Supreme Court Act 1981.

Interpretation

1–6071 **2.** (1) In these Rules, unless the context otherwise requires, any reference to a judge is a reference to a judge of the High Court or a Circuit judge or a Recorder; "justice" means a justice of the peace; and "Taxing Master" means a Master of the Supreme Court (Taxing Office).

(2) In these Rules any reference to a Rule or Schedule shall be construed as a reference to a Rule contained in these Rules or, as the case may be, to a Schedule thereto; and any reference in a Rule to a paragraph shall be construed as a reference to a paragraph of that Rule.

PART II
JUSTICES AS JUDGES OF CROWN COURT[1]
Number and qualification of justices

1–6072 **3.** (1) Subject to the provisions of Rule 4 and to any directions under section 74(4) of the Supreme Court Act 1981, on any proceedings to which a subsequent paragraph of this Rule applies, the number of justices sitting to hear the proceedings and the qualification of those justices shall be as specified in that paragraph.

(2) On the hearing of an appeal against a decision of licensing justices under the Licensing Act 1964, the Crown Court shall consist of a judge sitting with four justices, each of whom is a member of a licensing committee appointed under Schedule 1 to that Act and two (but not more than two) of whom are justices for the petty sessions area in which the premises to which the appeal relates are situated[2].

(3) On the hearing of an appeal against a decision of any authority under the Betting, Gaming and Lotteries Act 1963 or the Gaming Act 1968, the Crown Court shall consist of a judge sitting with four justices, two (but not more than two) of whom are justices for the petty sessions area in which the premises to which the appeal relates are situated.

(4) On the hearing of an appeal from a youth court, the Crown Court shall consist of a judge sitting with two justices each of whom is a member of a youth court panel and who are chosen so that the Court shall include a man and a woman.

(5) On the hearing of an appeal from a magistrates' court under section 8 of the Affiliation Proceedings Act 1957, the Crown Court shall consist of a judge sitting with two justices each of whom is a member of a domestic court panel and who are chosen so that the Court shall include a man and a woman.

---

1. Revoked in relation to criminal proceedings, see now the Criminal Procedure Rules 2005, in this PART, post.
2. It has been held that r 3(2), in so far as it requires the tribunal to include 2 licensing justices from the petty sessions area in which the premises concerned are situated, does not comply with the art 6(1) requirement of an independent and impartial tribunal and that the procedure cannot be saved by the availability of judicial review: *R (on the application of Smith) v Crown Court at Lincoln, R (on the application of the Chief Constable of Lancashire) v Crown Court at Preston* [2001] EWHC Admin 928, [2002] 1 WLR 1332.

Dispensations for special circumstances

1–6073   4. (1) The Crown Court may enter on any appeal notwithstanding that the Court is not constituted as required by section 74(1) of the Supreme Court Act 1981 or Rule 3 if it appears to the judge that the Court could not be so constituted without unreasonable delay and the Court includes—

(a) in a case to which paragraph (2) of that Rule applies, at least two justices each of whom is a member of a committee specified in that paragraph, provided that the Court includes a justice for the petty sessions area so specified and a justice for some other area;

(b) in a case to which paragraph (3) of that Rule applies, at least two justices including a justice for the petty sessions area so specified and a justice for some other area;

(c) in a case to which paragraph (4) of that Rule applies, one justice who is a member of a youth court panel;

(d) in a case to which paragraph (5) of that Rule applies, one justice who is a member of a domestic court panel;

(e) in any other case, one justice:

Provided that the judge may sit without one or both of the justices required by sub-paragraphs (a) and (b) above if the parties appearing at the hearing of the appeal agree.

(2) *Revoked.*

(3) The Crown Court may at any stage continue with any proceedings with a Court from which any one or more of the justices initially comprising the Court has withdrawn, or is absent for any reason.

Disqualifications

1–6074   5. A justice of the peace shall not sit in the Crown Court on the hearing of an appeal in a matter[1] on which he adjudicated.

---

1. This rule will preclude a licensing justice from sitting in the Crown Court on an appeal from a decision of the licensing committee of which he was a member. The prohibition contained in this rule is not exhaustive in the context of a licensing justice's disqualification from sitting, and it does not imply that there are no other circumstances where a justice is also disqualified on the basis of a previous connection with the case; see *R v Crown Court at Bristol, ex p Cooper* [1990] 2 All ER 193, [1990] 1 WLR 1031, CA.

PART III
APPEALS TO THE CROWN COURT[1]

Application of Part III

1–6075   6. (1) Subject to the following provisions of this Rule, this Part of these Rules shall apply to every appeal which by or under any enactment lies to the Crown Court from any court, tribunal or person except any appeal against a decision of a magistrates' court under section 22(7) or (8) of the Prosecution of Offences Act 1985 or under section 1 of the Bail (Amendment) Act 1993.

(2) Without prejudice to Rule 7(5), this Part of these Rules shall have effect subject to the provisions of the enactments specified in Part I of Schedule 3 (being enactments which make special procedural provisions in respect of certain appeals)[2], and those enactments shall have effect subject to the amendments set out in Part II of that Schedule (being amendments reproducing amendments made by Rule 6(2) of, and Part II of Schedule 1 to, the Crown Court Rules 1971).

---

1. Revoked in relation to criminal proceedings, see now the Criminal Procedure Rules 2005, in this PART, post.
2. The effect of this provision is any special procedure in the enactments listed in Pt I of Sch 3 will prevail over the provisions of these Rules but certain of those enactments have been amended by Pt II of the Schedule, eg by extending the time for notice of appeal to 21 days.

Notice of appeal

1–6076   7. (1) An appeal shall be commenced by the appellant's giving notice of appeal in accordance with the following provisions of this Rule.

(2) The notice required by the preceding paragraph shall be in writing and shall be given[1]—

(a) in a case where the appeal is against a decision of a magistrates' court, to the justices' chief executive for the magistrates' court;

(b) in the case of an appeal under section 67B or 81B of the Licensing Act 1964 against a decision of licensing justices, to the chief executive to the justices;

(c) in any other case, to the appropriate officer of the Crown Court;

(d) in the case of an appeal against a decision of a juvenile court in proceedings to which Part III of the Magistrates' Courts (Children and Young Persons) Rules 1988 applies (care proceedings and proceedings relating to care or supervision orders), to any person (other than the appellant) to whom notice of the proceedings in the juvenile court was given in pursuance of Rule 14(3) of the said Rules and to any other person who made representations to the juvenile court in those proceedings in pursuance of Rule 19(1) of those rules; and

(e) in any case, to any other party to the appeal[2].

(3) Notice of appeal shall be given[1] not later than 21 days after the day on which the decision appealed against is given and, for this purpose, where the court has adjourned the trial of an information after conviction, that day shall be the day on which the court sentences or otherwise deals with the offender:

Provided that, where a court exercises its power to defer sentence under section 1(1) of the Powers of Criminal Courts Act 1973, that day shall, for the purposes of an appeal against conviction, be the day on which the court exercises that power.

(4) A notice of appeal shall state—

(a) in the case of an appeal arising out of a conviction by a magistrates' court, whether the appeal is against conviction or sentence or both; and

(b) in the case of an appeal under an enactment listed in Part III of Schedule 3, the grounds of appeal.

(5) The time for giving notice of appeal (whether prescribed under paragraph (3), or under an enactment listed in Part I of Schedule 3) may be extended[3], either before or after it expires, by the Crown Court, on an application made in accordance with paragraph (6).

(6) An application for an extension of time shall be made in writing, specifying the grounds of the application and sent to the appropriate officer of the Crown Court.

(7) Where the Crown Court extends the time for giving notice of appeal, the appropriate officer of the Crown Court shall give notice[4] of the extension to—

(a) the appellant;

(b) in the case of an appeal from a decision of a magistrates' court, to the justices' chief executive for that court;

(c) in the case of an appeal under section 67B or 81B of the Licensing Act 1964 from a decision of licensing justices, to the chief executive to the justices,

and the appellant shall give notice of the extension to any other party to the appeal and, in the case of an appeal against a decision of a juvenile court in proceedings to which Part III of the Magistrates' Courts (Children and Young Persons) Rules 1988 applies, to any other person required to be given notice of the appeal in pursuance of paragraph 2(d) above.

---

1. See r 28 post, as to service.

2. It would appear that the removal of "third party proceedings" under s 100 of the Food Act 1984 and their replacement by ss 20 and 21 of the Food Safety Act 1990 removes the need to involve the former "third party" who is now liable to have proceedings taken direct against him.

3. It would appear that the Crown Court may extend the time either in relation to a notice previously given (though out of time) or in relation to a notice not yet given. The clerk of a magistrates' court should accept any notice of appeal notwithstanding that it is out of time. It will be good practice for him to notify the appellant of his right to apply for an extension of time to the Crown Court. Where the Crown Court refuses an extension of time, it should give a brief statement why (*Re Worth (application for judicial review)* (1979) 1 FLR 159).

4. It is submitted that a notice of appeal given out of time requires an extension of time by the Crown Court to perfect its validity; therefore, until notice of the extension has been received by the clerk of the magistrates' court, there does not arise the courts' power to release the appellant from custody under the Magistrates' Courts Act 1980, s 113, ante.

Entry of appeal and notice of hearing

1–6077 **8.** On receiving notice of appeal, the appropriate officer of the Crown Court shall enter the appeal and give notice of the time and place of the hearing to—

(a) the appellant;

(b) any other party to the appeal;

(c) in the case of an appeal from a decision of a magistrates' court, to the justices' chief executive for that court;

(d) in the case of an appeal under section 67B or 81B of the Licensing Act 1964 from a decision of licensing justices, to the chief executive to the justices;

(e) in the case of an appeal under paragraph 7 of Schedule 1 to the Anti-terrorism Crime and Security Act 2001,

(i) to any person to whom notice of the order for continued detention of cash was given in accordance with paragraph 3(4) of Schedule 1 to that Act and who has not been joined as a party to the case, and,

(ii) to any person who has made an application under paragraph 9(1) of Schedule 1 to that Act and who has not been joined as a party to the case,

(f) in the case of an appeal under section 299 of the Proceeds of Crime Act 2002,

> (i) to any person to whom notice of the order for continued detention of the cash was given in accordance with section 295(8) of that Act and who has not been joined as a party to the case, and
>
> (ii) to any person who has made an application under section 301 of that Act and who has not been joined as a party to the case,

and, in the case of an appeal against a decision of a juvenile court in proceedings to which Part III of the Magistrates' Courts (Children and Young Persons) Rules 1988 applies, the appellant shall give notice of the time and place of the hearing to any other person to whom notice of the appeal has been given in pursuance of Rule 7(2)(d).

1-6078   9–10B. *Spent.*

Abandonment of appeal[1]

1-6082   11. (1) Without prejudice to the power of the Crown Court to give leave for an appeal to be abandoned[2], an appellant may abandon[3] an appeal by giving notice[4] in writing, in accordance with the following provisions of this Rule, not later than the third day before the day fixed for hearing the appeal.

(2) The notice required by the preceding paragraph shall be given—

> (a) in a case where the appeal is against a decision of a magistrates' court, to the justices' chief executive for the magistrates' court;
>
> (b) in the case of an appeal under section 21 of the Licensing Act 1964, or in the case of an appeal under 67B or 81B of that Act against a decision of licensing justices, to the chief executive to the licensing justices;
>
> (c) in any other case, to the appropriate officer of the Crown Court; and
>
> (d) in any case, to any other party to the appeal and to any other person to whom notice of appeal was required to be given by Rule 7(2)(d);

and, in the case of an appeal mentioned in sub-paragraph (a) or (b), the appellant shall send a copy of the notice to the appropriate officer of the Crown Court.

(3) For the purposes of determining whether notice of abandonment was given in time there shall be disregarded any Saturday, Sunday and any day which is specified to be a bank holiday in England and Wales under section 1(1) of the Banking and Financial Dealings Act 1971.

---

1. Revoked in relation to criminal proceedings, see now the Criminal Procedure Rules 2005, in this PART, post. Where an appellant persistently fails to appear for the appeal hearing and provides no evidence for the cause of the failure, the Crown Court has a discretion to proceed in his absence where he is represented by counsel and he (the defendant) is under no strict legal obligation to be present in person; the Crown Court may not, however, treat a course of action that is intended to frustrate the course of the proceedings as amounting, in fact, to an abandonment of the appeal: *R (on the application of Hayes) v Crown Court at Chelmsford* [2003] EWHC 73 (Admin), (2003) 167 JP 65, [2003] Crim LR 400.

2. Leave to withdraw an abandonment can only be given where the abandonment was given in circumstances which make it a nullity (*R v Crown Court at Knightsbridge, ex p Customs and Excise Comrs* [1986] Crim LR 324).

3. An appellant, who has been granted bail by a magistrates' court pending an appeal, but who then persistently fails to appear for the appeal hearing without providing any evidence for the cause of that failure, thereby frustrating the appeal process, is not to be regarded as de facto abandoning his appeal; the appropriate remedy where an appellant has deliberately absented himself is to hear the appeal in his absence (*R (on the application of Haynes) v Crown Court at Chelmsford* [2003] EWHC 73 (Admin), (2003) 167 JP 65).

4. Where an appellant fails to comply with the requirements of this Rule, the judge has a discretion to allow the abandonment of the appeal (*R v Crown Court at Manchester, ex p Welby* (1981) 73 Cr App Rep 248).

PART IIIA
APPEALS UNDER THE BAIL (AMENDMENT) ACT 1993

1-6082A   11A. *Revoked.*

PART IV
COSTS BETWEEN PARTIES IN CROWN COURT[1]

Jurisdiction to award costs

1-6083   12. (1) Subject to the provisions of section 109(1) of the Magistrates' Courts Act 1980 (power of magistrates' courts to award costs on abandonment of appeals from magistrates' courts) and sections 22(4) and 81B(4) of the Licensing Act 1964 (application of section 109(1) of the Act of 1980 to appeals under sections 21 and 81B of the Act of 1964), no party shall be entitled to recover any costs of any proceedings in the Crown Court from any other party to the proceedings except under an order of the Court.

(2) Subject to section 4 of the Costs in Criminal Cases Act 1973[2] and to the following provisions of this Rule, the Crown Court may make such order for the costs as it thinks just[3].

(3) In the case of an appeal under section 21 or 67B of the Licensing Act 1964—

> (a) no order for costs shall be made on the abandonment of an appeal by giving notice under Rule 11[4];
>
> (b) no order for costs shall be made against a person who appeared before the licensing justices and opposed the grant of the justices' licence unless he appeared at the hearing of the appeal and opposed the appeal;

(c) if the appeal, not being an appeal against the grant of a justices' licence, is dismissed, the Court shall order the appellant to pay to the justices against whose decision he has appealed, or such person as those justices may appoint, such sum by way of costs as is, in the opinion of the Court, sufficient to indemnify the justices from all costs and charges to which they have been put in consequence of his having given notice of appeal.

(4) In the case of an appeal under section 81B of the Licensing Act 1964 against a decision of licensing justices, no order for costs shall be made on the abandonment of an appeal by giving notice under Rule 11.

(5) No order for costs shall be made on the abandonment of an appeal from a magistrates' court by giving notice under Rule 11[5].

(6) Without prejudice to the generality of paragraph (2), the Crown Court may make an order for costs on dismissing an appeal where the appellant has failed to proceed with the appeal or on the abandonment of an appeal not being an appeal to which paragraph (3), (4) or (5) applies.

---

1. Revoked in relation to criminal proceedings, see now the Criminal Procedure Rules 2005, in this PART, post.
2. Repealed and replaced by Pt II of the Prosecution of Offences Act 1985.
3. There is no rule of practice that costs do, or do not, follow the event in a betting licensing appeal. The appropriate order of costs will depend on what the Crown Court considers to be just on the facts of the particular case (*R v Crown Court at Stafford, ex p Wilf Gilbert* [1999] 2 All ER 955).
4. The power to order costs lies with the justices under the Magistrates' Courts Act 1980, s 109(2), ante, as applied by s 22(4) of the Licensing Act 1964.
5. The power to order costs lies with the magistrates' court under the Magistrates' Courts Act 1980, s 109(2), this PART, ante.

Costs in proceedings from which appeal is brought

1–6084   **13.** Where an appeal is brought to the Crown Court from the decision of a magistrates' court or a tribunal and the appeal is successful, the Crown Court may make any order as to the costs of the proceedings in the magistrates' court or tribunal which that court or tribunal had power to make.

Taxation

1–6085   **14.** (1) Where under these Rules the Crown Court has made an order for the costs of any proceedings to be paid by a party and the Court has not fixed a sum, the amount of the costs to be paid shall be ascertained as soon as practicable by the appropriate officer of the Crown Court (hereinafter referred to as the taxing authority).

(2) On a taxation under the preceding paragraph or under section 4(2) of the Costs in Criminal Cases Act 1973[1], there shall be allowed the costs reasonably incurred in or about the prosecution and conviction or the defence, as the case may be.

---

1. Now repealed, see Pt II of the Prosecution of Offences Act 1985.

Review by taxing authority

1–6086   **15.** (1) Any party dissatisfied with the taxation of any costs by the taxing authority under section 4(2)[1] of the Costs in Criminal Cases Act 1973 or Rule 14 may apply to the taxing authority to review his decision.

(2) The application shall be made by giving notice to the taxing authority and to any other party to the taxation within 14 days of the taxation, specifying the items in respect of which the application is made and the grounds of objection.

(3) Any party to whom notice is given under the preceding paragraph may within 14 days of the service of the notice deliver to the taxing authority answers in writing to the objections specified in that notice to the taxing authority and, if he does, shall send copies to the applicant for the review and to any other party to the taxation.

(4) The taxing authority shall reconsider his taxation in the light of the objections and answers, if any, of the parties and any oral representations made by or on their behalf and shall notify them of the result of his review.

---

1. Now repealed, see Pt II of the Prosecution of Offences Act 1985.

Further review by Taxing Master

1–6087   **16.** (1) Any party dissatisfied with the result of a review of taxation under Rule 15 may, within 14 days of receiving notification thereof, request the taxing authority to supply him with reasons in writing for his decision and may within 14 days of the receipt of such reasons apply to the Chief Taxing Master for a further review and shall, in that case, give notice of the application to the taxing authority and to any other party to the taxation, to whom he shall also give a copy of the reasons given by the taxing authority.

(2) Such application shall state whether the applicant wishes to appear or be represented, or whether he will accept a decision given in his absence and shall be accompanied by a copy of the notice given under Rule 15, of any answer which may have been given under paragraph (3) thereof and of the reasons given by the taxing authority for his decision, together with the bill of costs and full supporting documents.

(3) A party to the taxation who receives notice of an application under this Rule shall inform

the Chief Taxing Master whether he wishes to appear or be represented at a further review, or whether he will accept a decision given in his absence.

(4) The further review shall be conducted by a Taxing Master and if the applicant or any other party to the taxation has given notice of his intention to appear or be represented, the Taxing Master shall inform the parties (or their agents) of the date on which the further review will take place.

(5) Before reaching his decision the Taxing Master may consult the judge who made the order for costs and the taxing authority, and, unless the Taxing Master otherwise directs, no further evidence shall be received on the hearing of the further review; and no ground of objection shall be valid which was not raised on the review under Rule 15.

(6) In making his review, the Taxing Master may alter the assessment of the taxing authority in respect of any sum allowed, whether by increase or decrease.

(7) The Taxing Master shall communicate the result of the further review to the parties and to the taxing authority.

Appeal to High Court judge

1–6088   **17.** (1) Any party dissatisfied with the result of a further review under Rule 16 may, within 14 days of receiving notification thereof, appeal by originating summons to a judge of the Queen's Bench Division of the High Court if, and only if, the Taxing Master certifies that the question to be decided involves a point of principle of general importance.

(2) On the hearing of the appeal the judge may reverse, affirm or amend the decision appealed against or make such other order as he thinks appropriate.

Supplementary provisions

1–6089   **18.** (1) On a further review or an appeal to a judge of the High Court the Taxing Master or judge may make such order as he thinks just in respect of the costs of the hearing of the further review or the appeal, as the case may be.

(2) The time prescribed by Rule 15, 16 or 17 may be extended by the taxing authority, Taxing Master or judge of the High Court on such terms as he thinks just.

PART V
MISCELLANEOUS[1]

1–6090   **19–25**

---

1. Revoked in relation to criminal proceedings, see now the Criminal Procedure Rules 2005, in this PART, post.

Application to Crown Court to state case

1–6104   **26.** (1) An application under section 28 of the Supreme Court Act 1981 to the Crown Court to state a case for the opinion of the High Court shall be made in writing to the appropriate officer of the Crown Court within 21 days after the date of the decision in respect of which the application is made.

(2) The application shall state the ground on which the decision of the Crown Court is questioned.

(3) After making the application, the applicant shall forthwith send a copy of it to the parties to the proceedings in the Crown Court.

(4) On receipt of the application, the appropriate officer of the Crown Court shall forthwith send it to the judge who presided at the proceedings in which the decision was made.

(5) On receipt of the application, the judge shall inform the appropriate officer of the Crown Court as to whether or not he has decided to state a case and that officer shall give notice in writing to the applicant of the judge's decision.

(6) If the judge considers that the application is frivolous, he may refuse to state a case and shall in that case, if the applicant so requires, cause a certificate stating the reasons for the refusal to be given to him.

(7) If the judge decides to state a case, the procedure to be followed shall, unless the judge in a particular case otherwise directs, be the procedure set out in paragraphs (8) to (12).

(8) The applicant shall, within 21 days of receiving the notice referred to in paragraph (5), draft a case and send a copy of it to the appropriate officer of the Crown Court and to the parties to the proceedings in the Crown Court.

(9) Each party to the proceedings in the Crown Court shall, within 21 days of receiving a copy of the draft case under paragraph (8), either—

(a) give notice in writing to the applicant and the appropriate officer of the Crown Court that he does not intend to take part in the proceedings before the High Court; or

(b) indicate in writing on the copy of the draft case that he agrees with it and send the copy to the appropriate officer of the Crown Court; or

(c) draft an alternative case and send it, together with the copy of the applicant's case, to the appropriate officer of the Crown Court.

(10) The judge shall consider the applicant's draft case and any alternative draft case sent to the appropriate officer of the Crown Court under paragraph (9)(c).

(11) If the Crown Court so orders, the applicant shall, before the case is stated and delivered to him, enter before an officer of the Crown Court into a recognizance, with or without sureties and

in such sum as the Crown Court considers proper, having regard to the means of the applicant, conditioned to prosecute the appeal without delay.

(12) The judge shall state and sign a case within 14 days after either—

(a) the receipt of all the documents required to be sent to the appropriate officer of the Crown Court under paragraph (9); or

(b) the expiration of the period of 21 days referred to in that paragraph,

whichever is the sooner.

(13) A case stated by the Crown Court shall state the facts found by the Crown Court, the submissions of the parties (including any authorities relied on by the parties during the course of those submissions), the decision of the Crown Court in respect of which the application is made and the question on which the opinion of the High Court is sought.

(14) Any time limit referred to in this Rule may be extended[1] either before or after it expires by the Crown Court.

(15) If the judge decides not to state a case but the stating of a case is subsequently required by the High Court by order of *mandamus*, paragraphs (7) to (14) shall apply to the stating of the case save that—

(a) in paragraph (7) the words "If the judge decides to state a case" shall be omitted; and

(b) in paragraph (8) for the words "receiving the notice referred to in paragraph (5)" there shall be substituted the words "the day on which the order of *mandamus* was made".

---

1. The use of the expression "Crown Court" rather than "judge" reflects the possibility, not that the justices have to be involved, but that a judge other than the one who had heard the appeal may consider the relevant application. Where following an acquittal in the Crown Court on appeal from a magistrates' court, the prosecution seek an extension of the 21 day time limit in r 26(1) in which they may apply to the Court for a case to be stated, the Crown Court should not grant the extension without giving the defendant the opportunity to make representations on the subject (*DPP v Coleman* [1998] 1 All ER 912, [1998] 2 Cr App Rep 7).

Business in chambers

1–6105 27. (1) The jurisdiction of the Crown Court specified in the following paragraph may be exercised by a judge of the Crown Court sitting in chambers.

(2) The said jurisdiction is—

(a) hearing applications for bail[1];

(b) issuing a summons or warrant;

(c) hearing any application relating to procedural matters preliminary or incidental to proceedings in the Crown Court, including applications relating to legal aid;

(d) jurisdiction under rule 7(7), 9, 23, 25, 26 or 39;

(e) hearing applications under subsection (3) of section 22 of the Prosecution of Offences Act 1985 for the extension or further extension of a time limit imposed by regulations made under subsection (1) of that section;

(f) hearing an appeal brought by an accused under subsection (7) of the said section 22 against a decision of a magistrates' court to extend, or further extend, such a time limit or brought by the prosecution under subsection (8) thereof against a decision of a magistrates' court to refuse to extend, or further extend, such a time limit.

(g) hearing appeals under section 1 of the Bail (Amendment) Act 1993.

(h) *jurisdiction under Rule 24ZA*[2].

---

1. This may be incompatible with art 5(3) of the European Convention on Human Rights. The case law of the European Court of Human Rights is inconsistent on the issue: see *Neumeister v Austria* (1968) 1 EHRR 91 cf *De Wilde, Ooms and Versyp v Belgium* (1971) 1 EHRR 373.

2. Words in italics inserted by the Crown Court (Modification) Rules 1998, SI 1998/3047 in respect of those areas from which a person is sent for trial under s 51 of the Crime and Disorder Act 1998.

1–6106 27A. *Revoked.*

Service of documents

1–6107 28. Any notice or other document which is required by these Rules to be given to any person may be served personally on that person or sent to him by post[1] at his usual or last known residence or place of business in England or Wales or, in the case of a company, at the company's registered office in England or Wales.

---

1. See presumption of due delivery in s 7 of the Interpretation Act 1978, in Part II: Evidence, post.

1–6108 33–37A. *Revoked.*

References to the European Court

1–6109 57. (1) In this Rule "order" means an order referring a question to the European Court for a preliminary ruling under Article 177 of the Treaty establishing the Economic Community, Article 150 of the Treaty establishing Euratom or Article 41 of the Treaty establishing the Coal and Steel Community.

(2) An order may be made by the Crown Court of its own motion or on application by a party to proceedings in the Crown Court.

(3) An order shall set out in a schedule the request for the preliminary ruling of the European

Court, and the Crown Court may give directions as to the manner and form in which the schedule is to be prepared.

(4) When an order has been made, a copy shall be sent to the senior master of the Supreme Court (Queen's Bench Division) for transmission to the Registrar of the European Court.

(5) The proceedings in which an order is made shall, unless the Crown Court otherwise determines, be adjourned until the European Court has given a preliminary ruling on the question referred to it.

(6) Nothing in paragraph (5) shall be taken as preventing the Crown Court from deciding any preliminary or incidental question which may arise in the proceedings after an order is made and before a preliminary ruling is given by the European Court.

1–6110　　　　　　　　　　SCHEDULE 1

(Amended by SI 1994/2218, SI 1995/952, SI 1996/644, SI 1998/2401 and SI 2001/1180 and 3425)

Revocations

1–6111　　　　　　　　　　SCHEDULE 2

Transitional Provisions

1–6112

Rules 6 and 7　　　　　　　　SCHEDULE 3

Enactments relating to Appeals to Crown Court

(Amended by SI 2001/4012, SI 2002/2997 and SI 2004/1047.)

Part I

Enactments making Special Provisions about Procedure on Appeals to Crown Court

Chapter	Act	Section or Schedule
1957 c 56	The Housing Act 1957 (a)	Section 14(5) (a).
1963 c 2	The Betting, Gaming and Lotteries Act 1963	Schedule 1, paragraphs 21, 28
		Schedule 2, paragraph 6.
		Schedule 3, paragraph 13.
1963 c 33	The London Government Act 1963	Schedule 12, paragraph 19(4).
1964 c 26	The Licensing Act 1964	Sections 22, 50, 67B, 81B, 146, 154.
1967 c 9	The General Rate Act 1967	Section 7(1).
1968 c 27	The Firearms Act 1968	Section 44.
		Schedule 5 Part II.
1968 c 54	The Theatres Act 1968	Section 14(4).
1968 c 65	The Gaming Act 1968	Schedule 2, paragraphs 29, 31, 45, 46, 50, 61.
		Schedule 3, paragraphs 12, 13, 15, 16.
		Schedule 7, paragraphs 11, 20.
		Schedule 9, paragraph 11.
1969 c 54	The Children and Young Persons Act 1969	Section 21(5).
1976 c 32	The Lotteries and Amusements Act 1976	Schedule 1, paragraph 5.
		Schedule 3, paragraph 8.
1976 c 70	The Land Drainage Act 1976	Section 77.

Part II

Amendments to Enactments specified in Part 1

Part III

Appeals in which the Notice of Appeal is to State the Grounds of Appeal

Chapter	Act	Section or Schedule
1957 c 56	The Housing Act 1957[1]	Section 14(5).
1963 c 2	The Betting, Gaming and Lotteries Act 1963	Schedule 1, paragraphs 21, 28.
		Schedule 2, paragraph 6.
		Schedule 3, paragraph 13.
1963 c 33	The London Government Act 1963	Schedule 12, paragraph 19(2).
1964 c 26	The Licensing Act 1964	Sections 22, 50, 67B, 81B, 146, 154.
1967 c 9	The General Rate Act 1967[2]	Section 7(1).
1968 c 54	The Theatres Act 1968	Section 14(4).
1968 c 65	The Gaming Act 1968	Schedule 2, paragraphs 29, 31, 45, 46, 50, 61.
		Schedule 3, paragraphs 12, 13, 15, 16.
		Schedule 7, paragraphs 11, 20.
		Schedule 9, paragraph 11.
1976 c 32	The Lotteries and Amusements Act 1976	Schedule 1, paragraph 5.
		Schedule 3, paragraph 8.
1982 c 30	The Local Government (Miscellaneous Provisions) Act 1982	Section 5.
		Schedule 1, paragraph 17.
		Schedule 3, paragraph 27.
		Schedule 4, paragraph 6.
1982 c 33	The Cinematograph (Amendment) Act 1982	Section 4.
2001 c 24	The Anti-terrorism, Crime and Security Act 2001[3]	Schedule 1, paragraph 7.
2002 c 29	The Proceeds of Crime Act 2002[3]	Section 299
2003 c 44	The Criminal Justice Act 2003[3]	Section 16

1. See the Housing Act 1985, s 229 which has, in turn, been repealed by Sch 12 of the LGHA 1989.
2. Following the repeal of the General Rate Act 1967 with effect from 31 March 1990 an aggrieved person may appeal under s 23 of the Local Government Finance Act 1988 to a valuation and community charge tribunal.
3. See now the Criminal Procedure Rules 2005, in this PART, post.

1–6113   *Schedules 4–14*
Revoked.

Police and Criminal Evidence Act 1984 (Application to Customs and Excise) Order 1985[1]

(SI 1985/1800 amended by SI 1987/439, SI 1995/3217, SI 1996/1860 and SI 2005/3389)

1–6140   **1.** *Citation, commencement.*

1. Made under s 114(2) of the Police and Criminal Evidence Act 1984.

1–6141   **2.** (1) In this Order, unless the context otherwise requires—

"the Act" means the Police and Criminal Evidence Act 1984;
"assigned matter" has the meaning given to it by section 1 of the Customs and Excise Management Act 1979;
"the customs and excise Acts" has the meaning given to it by section 1 of the Customs and Excise Management Act 1979;
"customs office" means a place for the time being occupied by Her Majesty's Customs and Excise;
"officer" means a person commissioned by the Commissioners of Customs and Excise under section 6(3) of the Customs and Excise Management Act 1979.

(2) A person is in customs detention for the purpose of this Order if—

(a) he has been taken to a customs office after being arrested for an offence; or
(b) he is arrested at a customs office after attending voluntarily at the office or accompanying an officer to it,

and is detained there or is detained elsewhere in the charge of an officer, and nothing shall prevent a detained person from bring transferred between customs detention and police detention.

1–6142   **3.** (1) Subject to the modifications in paragraphs (2) and (3) of this article, in articles 4 to 12 below and in Schedule 2 to this Order, the provisions of the Act contained in Schedule 1 to this Order which relate to investigations of offences conducted by police officers or to persons detained by the police shall apply to investigations conducted by officers of Customs and Excise of offences which relate to assigned matters, and to persons detained by such officers.
(2) The Act shall have effect as if the words and phrases in Column 1 of Part 1 of Schedule 2 to this Order were replaced by the substitute words and phrases in Column 2 of that Part.
(3) Where in the Act any act or thing is to be done by a constable of a specified rank, that act or thing shall be done by an officer of at least the grade specified in Column 2 of Part 2 of Schedule 2 to this Order, and the Act shall be interpreted as if the substituted grade were specified in the Act.

1–6143   **4.** Nothing in the application of the Act to Customs and Excise shall be construed as conferring upon an officer any power—

(a) to charge a person with any offence;
(b) to release a person on bail;
(c) to detain a person for an offence after he has been charged with that offence.

1–6144   **5.** (1) Where in the Act a constable is given power to seize and retain any thing found upon a lawful search of person or premises, an officer shall have the same power notwithstanding that the thing found is not evidence of an offence in relation to an assigned matter.
(2) Nothing in the application of the Act to Customs and Excise shall be construed to prevent any thing lawfully seized by a person under any enactment from being accepted and retained by an officer.
(3) Section 21 of the Act (access and copying) shall not apply to any thing seized as liable to forfeiture under the customs and excise Acts.

1–6145   **6.** In its application by virtue of article 3 above the Act shall have effect as if the following section were inserted after section 14—

"**14A.** Material in the possession of a person who acquired or created it in the course of any trade, business, profession or other occupation or for the purpose of any paid or unpaid office and which relates to an assigned matter, as defined in section 1 of the Customs and Excise Management Act 1979, is neither excluded material nor special procedure material for the purposes of any enactment such as is mentioned in section 9(2) above.".

1–6146   7. Section 18(1) of the Act shall be modified as follows—

"**18.** (1) Subject to the following provisions of this section, an officer of Customs and Excise may enter and search any premises occupied or controlled by a person who is under arrest for any indictable offence which relates to an assigned matter, as defined in section 1 of the Customs and Excise Management Act 1979, if he has reasonable grounds for suspecting that there is on the premises evidence, other than items subject to legal privilege, that relates—

     (*a*)   to that offence; or

     (*b*)   to some other indictable offence which is connected with or similar to that offence.".

1–6147   8. *Annual report.*

1–6148   9. (1) Section 55 of the Act shall have effect as if it related only to things such as are mentioned in subsection (1)(*a*) of that section.

     (2) *Annual report.*

1–6149   10. Section 77(3) of the Act shall be modified to the extent that the definition of "independent person" shall, in addition to the persons mentioned therein, also include an officer or any other person acting under the authority of the Commissioners of Customs and Excise.

1–6150   11. Where any provision of the Act as applied to Customs and Excise—

     (*a*)   confers a power on an officer, and

     (*b*)   does not provide that the power may only be exercised with the consent of some person other than an officer,

the officer may use reasonable force, if necessary, in the exercise of the power.

1–6151   12. Section 24(2) of the Act shall apply without prejudice to section 138(1) of the Customs and Excise Management Act 1979, section 72(9) of the Value Added Tax Act 1994, section 20 of and paragraph 4 of Schedule 3 to the Criminal Justice (International Co-operation) Act 1990, or any other enactment, including any enactment contained in subordinate legislation, for the time being in force which confers upon officers of Customs and Excise the power to arrest or detain persons.

1–6152

(Article 3)   SCHEDULE 1

          Provisions of the Act applied to Customs and Excise

Section 8.
Section 9 and Schedule 1.
Section 15.
Section 16.
Section 17(1)(*b*), (2), (4).
Section 18 subject to the modification in article 7 hereof.
Section 19.
Section 20.
Section 21 subject to the modifications in article 5 hereof.
Section 22(1) to (4).
Section 24(2), subject to the modification in article 12 hereof.
Section 28.
Section 29.
Section 30(1) to (4)(*a*) and (5) to (11).
Section 31.
Section 32(1) to (9) subject to the modifications in article 5 hereof.
Section 34(1) to (5).
Section 35.
Section 36.
Section 37.
Section 39.
Section 40.
Section 41.
Section 42.
Section 43.
Section 44.
Section 50 subject to the modification in article 8 hereof.
Section 51(*d*).
Section 52.
Section 54.
Section 55 subject to the modifications in articles 5 and 9 hereof.
Section 56(1) to (9)[1].
Section 57(1) to (9).
Section 58(1) to (11)[1].
Section 62.
Section 63.
Section 64(1) to (6).
Section 107.

---

1. Without prejudice to s 20(2) of the Interpretation Act 1978, this Order applies to ss 56 and 58 of the Police and Criminal Evidence Act 1984, this Part, ante, as those sections have effect by virtue of s 32 of the Drug

Trafficking Offences Act 1986 (Drug Trafficking Offences Act 1986, s 32(4) and the Criminal Justice Act 1988, s 99).

1–6153

(Article 3)   SCHEDULE 2

PART 1

Substitution of equivalent words and phrases in the Act./S-P1

Where in the Act a word or phrase specified in Column 1 below is used, in the application of the Act to Customs and Excise, there shall be substituted the equivalent word or phrase in Column 2 below—

Column 1	Column 2
WORDS AND PHRASES USED IN THE ACT	SUBSTITUTED WORDS AND PHRASES
area	collection
chief officer	collector
constable	officer
designated police station	designated customs office
officer of a force maintained by a police authority	officer
police area	collection
police detention (except in section 118 and in section 39(1)(*a*) the second time the words occur)	customs detention
police force	HM Commissioners of Customs and Excise
police officer	officer
police station	customs office
rank	title
station	customs office
the police	HM Customs and Excise

PART 2

Equivalent titles of officers.

Where in the Act an act or thing is to be done by a constable of the rank specified in Column 1 below, that same act or thing shall, in the application of the Act to Customs and Excise, be done by an officer of at least an equivalent title specified in Column 2 below—

Column 1	Column 2
Rank of constable	*Title of officer*
sergeant	Anti-Smuggling Officer (2); Cargo Team Leader (1); Cargo Team Member (3); Drug Dog Unit Team Leader; EFIT Team Member; EVO (2); LVOIT Officer (1); PSD Team Member (1); Road Fuel Testing Officer; Specialist Investigator (1); or any other officer within job bands 5 or 6
inspector	Anti-Smuggling Team Leader; Cargo Team Leader (2); EFIT Team Leader; EVU Team Leader; LVOIT Officer (2); PSD Team Manager; Road Fuel Control Officer; Specialist Investigator (2); Specialist Investigator (3); or any other officer within job bands 7 or 8
superintendent	Anti-Smuggling Manager; Cargo Operational Manager; Investigation Team Leader; PSD Operations Manager; or any other officer within job band 9
[Chief Inspector	Anti-Smuggling Team Leader; Cargo Team Leader (2); EFIT Team Leader; EVU Team Leader; LVOIT Officer (2); PSD Team Manager; Road Fuel Control Officer; Specialist Investigator (2); Specialist Investigator (3); or any other officer within job bands 7 or 8]

The abbreviations used in Column 2 above shall have the following meaning—

     "PSD" shall mean "Passenger Services Division"
     "EFIT" shall mean "Excise Fraud Investigation Team"
     "EVO" shall mean "Excise Verification Officer"
     "EVU" shall mean "Excise Verification Unit"
     "LVOIT" shall mean "Local Value Added Tax Office Investigation Team".

The job bands referred to in Column 2 above are set from time to time by the Commissioners of Customs and Excise.

Costs in Criminal Cases (General) Regulations 1986[1]

(SI 1986/1335 as amended by SI 1991/789, SI 1992/323, SI 1992/2956, SI 1999/2096, SI 2000/2094, SI 2001/611, SI 2004/2408 and SI 2005/617 and 2622)

PART I
PRELIMINARY

1–6170   **1.** *Citation and commencement.*

     1. Made by the Lord Chancellor under ss 19 and 20 of the Prosecution of Offences Act 1985.

1–6171   **2.** *Revocation.*

PART II
COSTS UNNECESSARILY OR IMPROPERLY INCURRED

Unnecessary or improper acts and omissions

1–6172   **3.** (1) Subject to the provisions of this regulation, where at any time during criminal proceedings[1]—

     (*a*) a magistrates' court,
     (*b*) the Crown Court, or
     (*c*) the Court of Appeal

is satisfied that costs have been incurred in respect of the proceedings[2] by one of the parties as a result of an unnecessary or improper[3] act or omission by, or on behalf of, another party to the proceedings, the court may, after hearing the parties, order[4] that all or part of the costs so incurred by that party shall be paid to him by the other party.

     (2) Before making an order under paragraph (1), the court shall take into account any other order as to costs (including any legal aid order) which has been made in respect of the proceedings.

     (3) An order made under paragraph (1) shall specify[5] the amount of costs to be paid in pursuance of the order.

     (4) Where an order under paragraph (1) has been made, the court may take that order into account when making any other order as to costs in respect of the proceedings.

     (5) No order under paragraph (1) shall be made by a magistrates' court which requires a person under the age of seventeen who has been convicted of an offence to pay an amount by way of costs which exceeds the amount of any fine imposed on him.

---

     1. This will not prevent the court from entertaining an application for costs after notice of discontinuance has been sent by the prosecutor (*DPP v Denning* [1991] 2 QB 532, [1991] 3 All ER 439, 155 JP 1003, DC).

     2. The phrase "in respect of the proceedings" includes the whole proceedings. Where a notice of discontinuance has been served, justices still have power, after hearing the parties, to make an order for costs under reg 3(1) (*DPP v Denning* [1991] 2 QB 532, [1991] 3 All ER 439, 155 JP 1003, DC).

     3. The word "improper" does not denote some grave impropriety, but is intended to cover an act or omission which would not have occurred if the party concerned had conducted his case properly (*DPP v Denning* [1991] 2 QB 532, [1991] 3 All ER 439, 155 JP 1003, DC).

     4. Any order for costs to be paid by the accused under this provision shall be treated for the purposes of collection and enforcement as if it had been adjudged to be paid on conviction, whereas an order for costs to be paid by the prosecutor shall be enforceable as if it were for the payment of money recoverable summarily as a civil debt (Administration of Justice Act 1970, s 41 and Sch 9, this PART, ante). As to enforcement of such orders, see generally the Magistrates' Courts Act 1980, Pt III, and, in particular, as respects enforcement of a civil debt, see the Magistrates' Courts Act 1980, ss 92 and 96, and the Administration of Justice Act 1970, s 12, this PART, ante.

     5. Before specifying the amount of costs the court should show any bill of costs which is submitted to the other party and invite representations; see *Hutber v Gabriele* (1997) Times, 19 August.

PART IIA
WASTED COSTS ORDERS

Application and definitions

1–6173   **3A.** This Part of these Regulations applies to action taken by a court under section 19A of the Act and in this Part of these regulations—

     "wasted costs order" means any action taken by a court under section 19A of the Act; and
     "interested party" means the party benefiting from the wasted costs order and, where he was receiving services funded for him as part of the Criminal Defence Service, or an order for

the payment of costs out of central funds was made in his favour, shall include the authority responsible for determining costs payable in respect of work done under the representation order or out of central funds as the case may be.

General[1]

1–6174   3B. (1) A wasted costs order may provide for the whole or any part of the wasted costs to be disallowed or ordered to be paid and the court shall specify the amount of such costs.

(2) Before making a wasted costs order the court shall allow the legal or other representative and any party to the proceedings to make representations[1].

(3) When making a wasted costs order the court may take into account any other order as to costs in respect of the proceedings and may take the wasted costs order into account when making any other such order.

(4) Where a wasted costs order has been made the court shall notify any interested party of the order and the amount disallowed or ordered to be paid.

---

1. Before making a wasted costs order, reference should be made to the *Practice Direction (Costs: Criminal proceedings)* [2004] this PART, post. The Court of Appeal, in *Re a Barrister (wasted costs order) (No 1 of 1991)* [1992] 3 All ER 429, gave further guidance in the following terms:

(1) There is a clear need for any court intending to exercise the wasted costs jurisdiction to formulate carefully and concisely the complaint and grounds upon which such an order may be sought. These measures are draconian, and, as in contempt proceedings, the grounds must be clear and particular.
(2) Where necessary a transcript of the relevant part of the proceedings under discussion should be available. A transcript of any wasted costs hearing must be made.
(3) A defendant involved in a case where such proceedings are contemplated should be present if, after discussion with counsel, it is thought that his interests may be affected. And he should certainly be present and represented if the matter might affect the course of his trial. Regulation 3(b)(2) furthermore requires that before a wasted costs order is made "the court shall allow the legal or other representative and any party to the proceedings to make representations". There may be cases where it may be appropriate for counsel for the Crown to be present.
(4) A three-stage test or approach is recommended when a wasted costs order is contemplated. (i) Has there been an improper, unreasonable or negligent act or omission? (ii) As a result have any costs been incurred by a party? (iii) If the answers to (i) and (ii) are Yes, should the court exercise its discretion to disallow or order the representative to meet the whole or any part of the relevant costs, and if so what specific sum is involved?
(5) It is inappropriate to propose any deal or settlement that the representative might forgo fees. The court must formally state its complaint and invite the representative to make his own comments. After any other party has been heard the court should give its formal ruling.
(6) As is indicated above, the court must specify the sum to be disallowed or ordered.

At a trial the prosecution should be in a position to deal with any defences that arise; where, therefore, on the day set for the trial of the offence (speeding) the prosecutor sought an adjournment to obtain the transcript of an authority (which was concerned with identification) on which the defence intended to rely, the fact that the justices granted the adjournment did not mean that an adjournment was necessary for justice to be done and it was open to the justices to make a wasted costs order (though to award £1750 was unreasonable and the court substituted the sum of £400) (*DPP v Cheshire Justices* [2002] EWHC 466 (Admin), (2002) JPN 198).

Appeals

1–6175   3C. (1) A legal or other representative against whom the wasted costs order is made may appeal—

(a) in the case of an order made by a magistrates' court, to the Crown Court, and
(b) in the case of an order made at first instance by the Crown Court, to the Court of Appeal.

(2) Subject to paragraph (4), an appeal shall be instituted within 21 days of the wasted costs order being made by the appellant's giving notice in writing to the court which made the order, stating the grounds of appeal.

(3) The appellant shall serve a copy of the notice of appeal and grounds, including any application for an extension of time in which to appeal, on any interested party.

(4) The time limit within which an appeal may be instituted may, for good reason, be extended before or after it expires—

(a) in the case of an appeal to the Crown Court, by a judge of that court;
(b) in the case of an appeal to the Court of Appeal, a judge of the High Court or Court of Appeal, or by the Registrar of Criminal Appeals,

and in each case the court to which the appeal is made shall give notice of the extension to the appellant, the court which made the wasted costs order and any interested party.

(5) The court shall give notice of the hearing date to the appellant, the court which made the wasted costs order and any interested party and shall allow the interested party to make representations which may be made orally or in writing.

(6) The court may affirm, vary or revoke the order as it thinks fit and shall notify its decision to the appellant, any interested party and the court which made the order.

Recovery of sums due under a wasted costs order

1–6176   3D. Where the person required to make a payment in respect of sums due under a wasted costs order fails to do so, the payment may be recovered summarily as a sum adjudged to be paid as a civil debt by order of a magistrates' court by the party benefiting from the order, save that where he was receiving services funded for him as part of the Criminal Defence Service or an order for the payment of costs out of central funds was made in his favour, the power to recover shall be exercisable by the Lord Chancellor.

PART IIB
THIRD PARTY COSTS ORDERS

1–6176A 3E. Application and definitions. (1) This Part of these Regulations applies where there are, or have been criminal proceedings in a magistrates' court, the Crown Court or the Court of Appeal.

(2) In this Part of these Regulations—

"court" means the court in which the criminal proceedings are taking, or took, place;

"interested party" means the party benefiting from the third party costs order and, where he was receiving services funded for him as part of the Criminal Defence Service, shall include the authority responsible for determining costs payable in respect of work done under the representation order or out of central funds as the case may be;

"party" means a party to the criminal proceedings;

"third party" means a person who is not a party;

"third party costs order" means an order as to the payment, by a third party, of costs incurred by a party in accordance with regulation 3F.

1–6176B 3F. General. (1) If—

(*a*) there has been serious misconduct (whether or not constituting a contempt of court) by a third party; and

(*b*) the court considers it appropriate, having regard to that misconduct, to make a third party costs order against him

the court may order the third party to pay all or part of the costs incurred or wasted by any party as a result of the misconduct.

(2) The court may make a third party costs order—

(*a*) subject to paragraph (3), at any time during or after the criminal proceedings; and

(*b*) on the application of any party or of its own initiative (but not otherwise).

(3) The court shall make a third party costs order during the proceedings only if it decides that there are good reasons to do so, rather than making the order after the proceedings, and it shall notify the parties and the third party of those reasons and allow any of them to make representations.

(4) Before making a third party costs order the court shall allow the third party and any party to make representations and may hear evidence.

(5) When making a third party costs order the court may vary or take into account any other order as to costs in respect of the criminal proceedings and may take the third party costs order into account when making any other order as to costs in respect of the criminal proceedings.

(6) A third party costs order shall specify the amount of costs to be paid in pursuance of the order.

(7) When a third party costs order has been made the court shall notify the third party and any interested party of the order and the amount ordered to be paid.

1–6176C 3G. Procedure for third party costs orders. (1) This regulation applies where a party ("the applicant") applies to the court for a third party costs order or the court decides that it might make a third party costs order of its own initiative.

(2) In this regulation—

"appropriate officer" means—

(*a*) in relation to a magistrates' court, a designated officer (as defined in section 37(1) of the Courts Act 2003);

(*b*) in relation to the Crown Court, an officer appointed by the Lord Chancellor; and

(*c*) in relation to the Court of Appeal, the Registrar of Criminal Appeals;

"serve" means serve in accordance with rules of court.

(3) An application for a third party costs order shall be in writing and shall contain—

(*a*) the name and address of the applicant;

(*b*) the names and addresses of the other parties;

(*c*) the name and address of the third party against whom the order is sought;

(*d*) the date of the end of the criminal proceedings;

(*e*) a summary of the facts upon which the applicant intends to rely in making the application, including details of the alleged misconduct of the third party.

(4) The application shall be sent to the appropriate officer and, upon receiving it, the appropriate officer shall serve copies of it on the third party and to the other parties.

(5) Where the court decides that it might make a third party costs order of its own initiative the appropriate officer shall serve notice in writing accordingly on the third party and the parties.

(6) At the same time as serving notice under paragraph (5) the appropriate officer shall serve a summary of the reasons why the court might make a third party costs order, including details of the alleged misconduct of the third party.

(7) When the appropriate officer serves copies of an application under paragraph (4) or serves notice under paragraph (5) he shall at the same time serve notice on the parties and the third party of the time and place fixed for the hearing.

(8) At the time notified the court may proceed in the absence of the third party and of any party if it is satisfied that they have been duly served with the notice given under paragraph (7) and the copy of the application or (as the case may be) the notices given under paragraphs (5) and (6), but the court may set aside any third party costs order if it is later shown that the third party did not receive them.

1–6176D 3H. Appeals. (1) A third party against whom a third party costs order is made may appeal—

(a) in the case of an order made by a magistrates' court, to the Crown Court; and
(b) in the case of an order made at first instance by the Crown Court, to the Court of Appeal.

(2) Subject to paragraph (4), an appeal shall be instituted within 21 days of the third party costs order being made by the appellant giving notice in writing to the court which made the order, stating the grounds of appeal.

(3) The appellant shall serve a copy of the notice of appeal and grounds, including any application for extension of time in which to appeal, on any interested party.

(4) The time limit within which an appeal may be instituted may, for good reason, be extended before or after it expires—

(a) in the case of an appeal to the Crown Court, by a judge of that court;
(b) in the case of an appeal to the Court of Appeal, by a judge of the High Court or Court of Appeal, or by the Registrar of Criminal Appeals,

and in each case the court to which the appeal is made ("the appeal court") shall give notice of the extension to the appellant, the court which made the third party costs order and any interested party.

(5) The appeal court shall give notice of the hearing date to the appellant, the court which made the third party costs order and any interested party and shall allow the interested party to make representations which may be made orally or in writing.

(6) The appeal court may affirm, vary or revoke the order as it thinks fit and shall notify its decision to the appellant, any interested party and the court which made the order.

1–6176E 3I. Recovery of sums due under a third party costs order. Where the person required to make a payment in respect of sums due under a third party costs order fails to do so, the payment may be recovered summarily as a sum adjudged to be paid as a civil debt by order of a magistrates' court by the party benefiting from the order, save that where he was receiving services funded for him as part of the Criminal Defence Service or an order for the payment of costs out of central funds was made in his favour, the power to recover shall be exercisable by the Lord Chancellor.

PART III
COSTS OUT OF CENTRAL FUNDS
Application and definitions

1–6177 4. This Part of these Regulations applies to costs payable out of central funds in pursuance of an order made under or by virtue of Part II of the Act and in this Part of these Regulations—

"applicant" means the person in whose favour a costs order has been made;
"appropriate authority" has the meaning assigned to it by regulation 5;
"costs judge" means a taxing master of the Supreme Court;
"costs order" means an order made under or by virtue of Part II of the Act for the payment of costs out of central funds;
"disbursements" do not include any payment made out of central funds to a witness, interpreter or medical practitioner in accordance with Part V of these Regulations;
"presiding judge" means the judge who presided at the hearing in respect of which the costs are payable; and

The appropriate authority

1–6178 5. (1) Costs shall be determined by the appropriate authority in accordance with these Regulations.

(2) Subject to paragraph (3), the appropriate authority shall be—

(a) the registrar of criminal appeals in the case of proceedings in the Court of Appeal,
(b) the master of the Crown Office in the case of proceedings in a Divisional Court of the Queen's Bench Division,
(c) an officer appointed by the Lord Chancellor in the case of proceedings in the Crown Court,
(d) the justices' clerk in the case of proceedings in a magistrates' court.

(3) The appropriate authority may appoint or authorise the appointment of determining officers to act on its behalf under these Regulations in accordance with directions given by it or on its behalf.

Claims for costs

1–6179 6. (1) Subject to regulation 12, no claim for costs shall be entertained unless it is submitted within three months of the date on which the costs order was made.

(2) Subject to paragraph (3), a claim for costs shall be submitted to the designated officer for the court, in the case of proceedings in a magistrates' court, or to the appropriate authority, in

the case of proceedings in any other court specified in regulation 5(2), in such form and manner as he or it may direct and shall be accompanied by receipts or other evidence of the applicant's payment[1] of the costs claimed, and any receipts or other documents in support of any disbursements claimed.

(3) A claim shall—

(a) summarise the items of work done by a solicitor;

(b) state, where appropriate, the dates on which items of work were done, the time taken and the sums claimed,

(c) specify any disbursements claimed, including counsel's fees, the circumstances in which they were incurred and the amounts claimed in respect of them and

(d) contain either full particulars, including the date and outcome, of any claim that regulation 44(7) of the Legal Aid in Criminal and Care Proceedings (General) Regulations 1989 should be applied in respect of any work comprised in the claim under these Regulations, or a certificate by the solicitor that he has not made, and will not make, any such claim.

(4) Where there are any special circumstances which should be drawn to the attention of the appropriate authority, the applicant shall specify them.

(5) The applicant shall supply such further particulars, information and documents as the appropriate authority may require.

---

1. This means where the defendant has made a payment, he should send in receipts or other evidence; it does not mean that he can obtain reimbursement only if he has made a payment (*R (on the application of McCormick) v Liverpool City Magistrates' Court* [2001] 2 All ER 705, 165 JP 362, DC).

Determination of costs

1–6180 7. (1) The appropriate authority shall consider the claim, any further particulars, information or documents submitted by the applicant under regulation 6 and shall allow such costs in respect of—

(a) such work as appears to it to have been actually and reasonably done; and

(b) such disbursements as appear to it to have been actually and reasonably incurred,

as it considers reasonably sufficient to compensate the applicant for any expenses properly incurred[1] by him in the proceedings.

(2) In determining costs under paragraph (1) the appropriate authority shall take into account all the relevant circumstances of the case including the nature, importance, complexity or difficulty of the work and the time involved.

(3) When determining costs for the purpose of this regulation, there shall be allowed a reasonable amount in respect of all costs reasonably incurred and any doubts which the appropriate authority may have as to whether the costs were reasonably incurred or were reasonable in amount shall be resolved against the applicant.

---

1. A defendant has "properly incurred" costs where he is under a contractual liability to pay his solicitor even though there might be little prospect of any payment being recovered *R (on the application of McCormick) v Liverpool City Magistrates' Court* [2001] 2 All ER 705, 165 JP 362, DC).

Payment of costs

1–6181 8. (1) When the appropriate authority has determined the costs payable to an applicant in accordance with these Regulations, the designated officer for the court, in the case of proceedings in a magistrates' court, or the appropriate authority, in the case of proceedings in any other court specified in regulation 5(2), shall notify the applicant of the costs payable and authorise payment accordingly.

(2) *Higher Courts.*

1–6182 9–11. *Determinations, appeals etc in Crown Court.*

Time limits

1–6183 12. (1) Subject to paragraph (2), the time limit within which there must be made or instituted—

(a) a claim for costs by an applicant under regulation 6, an application for a redetermination under regulation 9, or a request for an appropriate authority to give reasons for its decision on a redetermination under regulation 9;

(b) an appeal to a costs judge under regulation 10 or an application for a certificate under regulation 11; or

(c) an appeal to the High Court under regulation 11;

may, for good reason, be extended[1] by the appropriate authority, the Senior Costs Judge or the High Court, as the case may be.

(2) Where an applicant without good reason has failed (or, if an extension were not granted, would fail) to comply with a time limit, the appropriate authority, the Senior Costs Judge or the High Court, as the case may be, may, in exceptional circumstances, extend the time limit[2] and shall consider whether it is reasonable in the circumstances to reduce the costs; provided that the costs shall not be reduced unless the representative has been allowed a reasonable opportunity to show cause orally or in writing why the costs should not be reduced.

(3) An applicant may appeal to the Senior Costs Judge against a decision made under this

regulation by an appropriate authority in respect of proceedings other than proceedings before a magistrates' court and such an appeal shall be instituted within 21 days of the decision being given by giving notice in writing to the Senior Costs Judge specifying the grounds of appeal.

---

1. Regulation 12(1) applies to applications for extension of the time limit made both within and outside the time limit prescribed by reg 6, ante. Accordingly, where the application is made after the expiration of the time limit, that limit can be extended where there is good reason for the delay (*R v Clerk to the North Kent Justices, ex p McGoldrick & Co* (1995) 160 JP 30).

2. Regulation 12(2) is dealing with cases where there is no good reason for failure to comply with the time limit, in other words procedurally unmeritorious cases. The "exceptional circumstances" must relate to something other than explanations for failing to submit the application in time (*R v Clerk to the North Kent Justices, ex p McGoldrick & Co* (1995) 160 JP 30).

1–6184   **13.** *House of Lords.*

PART IIIA
FEES OF COURT APPOINTEES

1–6184A   **13A.** Subject to the following provisions of this Part, Part III of these Regulations shall apply, with any necessary modifications, to the determination of the proper fee or costs of a court appointee.

1–6184B   **13B.** For the purposes of this Part of the Regulations:—

(a) the reference to "solicitor in regulation 6(3)(a) and any reference to "applicant" in Part III shall be construed as including a reference to a court appointee;
(b) any reference to "costs" in Part III shall be construed as including a reference to the proper fee or costs of a court appointee; and
(c) the words after paragraph (b) in regulation 7(1) shall be omitted.

1–6184C   **13C.** In this Part of the Regulations "court appointee" means:—

(a) a person appointed by the Crown Court under section 4A of the Criminal Procedure (Insanity) Act 1964 to put the case for the defence;
(b) a legal representative appointed by the court under section 38(4) of the Youth Justice and Criminal Evidence Act 1999 to cross-examine a witness in the interests of the accused.

PART IV
MISCELLANEOUS APPLICATIONS OF THE ACT

1–6185   **14.** (1) Sections 17 and 18 of the Act shall apply to proceedings in the Crown Court in respect of a person committed by a magistrates' court to that Court—

(a) with a view to his being sentenced for an indictable offence in accordance with section 42 of the Powers of Criminal Courts Act 1973; or
(b) with a view to his being sentenced by the Crown Court under section 6(6) or 9(3) of the Bail Act 1976; or
(c) with a view to the making of a hospital order with an order restricting his discharge under Part III of the Mental Health Act 1983,

as they apply where a person is convicted in proceedings before the Crown Court.
(2) Section 18 of the Act shall apply to proceedings in the Crown Court—

(a) in respect of a person committed by a magistrates' court as an incorrigible rogue under section 5 of the Vagrancy Act 1824 as if he were committed for trial before the Crown Court and as if the committing court were examining justices; and
(b) in respect of an appeal under section 14 of the Vagrancy Act 1824 as if the hearing of the appeal were a trial on indictment and as if the magistrates' court from which the appeal was brought were examining justices.

(3) Section 18 of the Act shall apply to proceedings in a magistrates' court or the Crown Court—

(a) for dealing with an offender under Schedule 1, Part I, paragraph 1B and Schedule 2, Part II, paragraphs 3 and 4 of the Criminal Justice Act 1991 (orders for conditional discharge, community service orders, probation orders etc);
(b) under section 23(1) or 27 of the Powers of Criminal Courts Act 1973 for dealing with an offender in respect of a suspended sentence or for breach of a suspended sentence supervision order; or
(c) under section 19 of the Criminal Justice Act 1982 for dealing with an offender in respect of a breach of an attendance centre order,

as if the offender had been tried in those proceedings for the offence for which the order was made or the sentence passed.
(4) Section 16 of the Act shall apply to proceedings in a magistrates' court or the Crown Court in which it is alleged that an offender required to enter into a recognisance to keep the peace or be of good behaviour has failed to comply with a condition of that recognisance, as if that failure were an indictable offence.

PART V
ALLOWANCES TO WITNESSES

Definitions

1-6186   **15.** In this Part of these Regulations—

"expenses" include compensation to a witness for his trouble or loss of time and out of pocket expenses;

"proceedings in a criminal cause or matter" includes any case in which—

(a) an information charging the accused with an offence is laid before a justice of the peace for any area but not proceeded with; or

(b) the accused is committed for trial but not tried;

"professional witness" means a witness practising as a member of the legal or medical profession or as a dentist, veterinary surgeon or accountant who attends to give professional evidence as to matters of fact;

"private prosecutor" means any person in whose favour an order for the payment of costs out of central funds could be made under section 17 of the Act;

"the relevant amount" has the meaning assigned to it by regulation 17;

"witness" means any person properly attending to give evidence, whether or not he gives evidence or is called at the instance of one of the parties or of the court, but does not include—

(a) a person attending as a witness to character only unless the court has certified that the interests of justice required his attendance;

(b) a member of a police force attending court in his capacity as such;

(c) a full-time officer of an institution to which the Prison Act 1952 applies attending court in his capacity as such; or

(d) a prisoner in respect of any occasion on which he is conveyed to court in custody.

General

1-6187   **16.** (1) Where, in any proceedings in a criminal cause or matter in a magistrates' court, the Crown Court, a Divisional Court of the Queen's Bench Division, the Court of Appeal or the House of Lords—

(a) a witness attends at the instance of the accused, a private prosecutor or the court; or

(b) an interpreter is required because of the accused's lack of English; or

(c) a medical practitioner makes a report otherwise than in writing,

the expenses properly incurred by that witness, interpreter or medical practitioner shall be allowed out of central funds in accordance with this Part of these Regulations, unless the court directs that the expenses are not to be allowed out of central funds.

(2) Subject to paragraph (3), any entitlement to an allowance under this Part of these Regulations shall be the same whether the witness, interpreter or medical practitioner attends on the same day in one case or more than one case.

(3) Paragraph (2) shall not apply to allowances under regulation 25.

Determination of rates or scales of allowances payable out of central funds

1-6188   **17.** The Lord Chancellor shall, with the consent of the Treasury, determine the rates or scales of allowance payable out of central funds to witnesses, interpreters or medical practitioners and a reference in this Part of these Regulations to an allowance not exceeding the relevant amount means an amount calculated in accordance with the rates or scales so determined.

Witnesses other than professional or expert witnesses

1-6189   **18.** (1) A witness (other than a witness to whom regulation 19 or 20 applies) may be allowed—

(a) a loss allowance not exceeding the relevant amount in respect of

(i) any expenditure incurred (other than on travelling. lodging or subsistence) to which the witness would not otherwise be subject; or

(ii) any loss of earnings or benefit under the enactments relating to National Insurance; and

(b) a subsistence allowance not exceeding the relevant amount.

(2) Any other person who in the opinion of the court necessarily attends for the purpose of any proceedings otherwise than to give evidence may be allowed the same allowances under paragraph (1) as if he attended as a witness other than a professional or expert witness.

(3) Paragraph (2) shall not apply to—

(a) a member of a police force attending court in his capacity as such;

(b) a full-time officer of an institution to which the Prison Act 1952 applies attending court in his capacity as such, or

(c) a prisoner in respect of any occasion on which he is conveyed to court in custody.

Professional witnesses

1-6190   **19.** A professional witness may be allowed a professional witness allowance not exceeding the relevant amount.

Expert witnesses etc

1–6191 **20.**—(1) The court may make an allowance in respect of an expert witness for attending to give expert evidence and for work in connection with its preparation of such an amount as it may consider reasonable having regard to the nature and difficulty of the case and the work necessarily involved.

(2) Paragraph (1) shall apply, with the necessary modifications, to—

(*a*) an interpreter, or

(*b*) a medical practitioner who makes a report otherwise than in writing for the purpose of section 30 of the Magistrates' Courts Act 1980

as it applies to an expert witness.

Night allowances

1–6192 **21.**—(1) A professional or expert witness who is necessarily absent from his place of residence overnight may be allowed a night allowance not exceeding the relevant amount.

(2) An interpreter or medical practitioner who receives an allowance under regulation 20 may be allowed the same night allowance as if he attended as a professional or expert witness.

Seamen

1–6193 **22.**—(1) A seaman who is detained on shore as a witness may be allowed—

(*a*) an allowance not exceeding the relevant amount in respect of any loss of earnings, unless for special reasons the court allows a greater sum; and

(*b*) an allowance not exceeding the sum actually and reasonably incurred for his maintenance, for the time during which he is necessarily detained on shore.

(2) No allowance shall be paid under regulation 18 to a seaman who is paid an allowance under paragraph (1).

Prosecutors and defendants

1–6194 **23.** A person in whose favour an order is made under section 16, 17 or 19(4) of the Act may be allowed the same subsistence allowance and travelling expenses as if he attended as a witness other than a professional or expert witness.

Travelling expenses

1–6195 **24.**—(1) Subject to paragraphs (2) and (3), a witness who travels to or from court by public transport (including by air) may be allowed the fare actually paid.

(2) Unless the court otherwise directs, only the second class fare shall be allowed under paragraph (1) for travel by railway.

(3) A witness who travels to or from court by air may be allowed the fare actually paid only if—

(*a*) there was no reasonable alternative to travel by air and the class of fare paid was reasonable in all the circumstances; or

(*b*) travel by air was more economical in the circumstances taking into account any savings of time resulting from the adoption of such mode of travel and its consequent effect in reducing the amount of allowances payable under the other provisions of this Part of these Regulations,

and, where the air fare is not allowed, there may be allowed such amount as the court considers reasonable.

(4) A witness who travels to or from court by hired vehicle may be allowed—

(*a*) the fare actually paid and any reasonable gratuity so paid in a case of urgency or where public transport is not reasonably available; or

(*b*) in any other case, the amount of fare for travel by public transport.

(5) A witness who travels to or from court by private vehicle may be allowed an appropriate private vehicle allowance not exceeding the relevant amount.

(6) Where—

(*a*) a witness is in the opinion of the court suffering from a serious illness; or

(*b*) heavy exhibits have to be taken to court,

the court may allow reasonable additional sums in excess of those allowed under paragraphs (1) to (5).

(7) An interpreter or a medical practitioner who incurs travelling expenses in providing the court with a report otherwise than in writing may be allowed a travelling allowance not exceeding the relevant amount.

Written medical reports

1–6196 **25.**—(1) A medical practitioner who makes a written report to a court in pursuance of a request to which section 32(2) of the Criminal Justice Act 1967 applies may be allowed a medical report allowance not exceeding the relevant amount.

(2) A medical practitioner who makes a report to which paragraph (1) applies and incurs travelling expenses in connection with the preparation of that report may be allowed a travelling allowance not exceeding the relevant amount.

(3) Nothing in this regulation shall apply to a report by the medical officer of an institution to which the Prison Act 1952 applies.

PART VI
RECOVERY OF SUMS PAID OUT OF THE LEGAL AID FUND OR CENTRAL FUNDS
Directions by the Lord Chancellor

1-6197 26. (1) The Lord Chancellor shall recover in accordance with directions given by him any sums paid out as part of the Criminal Defence Service or central funds where a costs order has been made against a person in favour of—

(a) a person receiving services funded for him as part of the Criminal Defence Service, or
(b) a person in whose favour an order for the payment of costs out of central funds has been made.

(2) Directions given by the Lord Chancellor under this regulation may be given generally or in respect of a particular case and may require the payment of sums due under a costs order and stipulate the mode of payment and the person to whom payment is to be made.

(3) In this regulation and regulation 27 "costs order" shall include a wasted costs order as defined by regulation 3A, or a third party costs order as defined by regulation 3E, of these Regulations.

Recovery of sums due under a costs order

1-6198 27. Where the person required to make a payment in respect of sums due under a costs order fails to do so, the payment may be recovered summarily by the Lord Chancellor as a sum adjudged to be paid as a civil debt by order of a magistrates' court.

Costs in Criminal Cases (General) Regulations 1986—Rates of Allowances[1]

1-6199 In exercise of the powers conferred on the Lord Chancellor by section 20 of the Prosecution of Offences Act 1985, and with the consent of the Treasury, the relevant amounts payable under the Costs in Criminal Cases (General) Regulations 1986 shall be as set out below.

---

1. Includes all circulars up to and including the Guide to Allowances under Part V of the Costs in Criminal Cases (General) Regulations 1986 issued by Public Legal Services Division, Department for Constitutional Affairs in June 2005.

1-6200
Regulation 18—Ordinary Witness and other persons Financial Loss Allowance

Period of Absence	Maximum Amount with effect from 1.6.2005
Not exceeding 4 hours	£33.50
Exceeding 4 hours	£67.00

1-6201
Regulation 18—Ordinary Witness and other persons Subsistence Allowance

Period of Absence	Maximum Amount with effect from 1.8.2001
Not exceeding 5 hours	£2.25
Exceeding 5 hours but not exceeding 10 hours	£4.50
Over 10 hours	£9.75
Hotel (London, Birmingham, Manchester, Leeds, Liverpool or Newcastle Upon Tyne city centres)	£95.00 * Plus £21.00 Night Subsistence Allowance and £5.00 Personal Incidental Allowance with effect from 1.6.2005
Overnight (elsewhere)	£65.00 * Plus £21.00 Night Subsistence Allowance and £5.00 Personal Incidental Allowance with effect from 1.6.2005
	£25.00 only if with family or friends with effect from 1.6.2005

1–6202

Regulation 19—Professional Witness Allowances

(a) If the witness attends on any day to give evidence in one or more cases and does not claim the expenses of a person to take care of a practice during the absence, the professional witness allowance payable is—

Period of Absence	Maximum Amount with effect from 1.8.2001
Not exceeding 2 hours	£83.50
Exceeding 2 hours but not exceeding 4 hours	£117.00
Exceeding 4 hours but not exceeding 6 hours	£174.00
Exceeding 6 hours	234.00

(b) If the witness necessarily incurs and claims the expense of a person to take care of a practice during the absence, the allowance payable is—

Period of Absence	Maximum amount with effect from 6.5.2003
Not exceeding 2 hours	£89.00
Exceeding 2 hours but not exceeding 4 hours	£125.00
Exceeding 4 hours	£250.00

(In those cases where a locum is necessarily employed and it is not possible or practicable to employ the locum for only half a day, the full reimbursement of the costs of the locum should be made, subject to the maximum of £156·50 per day. Such payment is instead of, not in addition to the fee otherwise payable; proof of the expense incurred in connection with such a claim should be provided.)

1–6203

Regulation 20—Expert Witness and Interpreters Allowance[1]

A. EXPERT WITNESS	Maximum amount with effect from 6.5.2003
1. *Consultant medical practitioner, psychiatrist pathologist*	
Preparation (examination and report):	£70–£100 per hour
Attendance at court (full day)	£346–£500
2. *Fire expert (assessor), Explosives*	
Preparation	£50–£75 per hour
Attendance at court	£255–£365
3. *Forensic scientist (including questioned document examiner), surveyor, accountant, engineer, medical practitioner, architect, veterinary surgeon, meteorologist*	
Preparation	£47–£100 per hour
Attendance at court	£226–£490
4. *Fingerprint*	
Preparation	£32–£52 per hour
Attendance at court	£153–£256
B. OTHERS	
5. *Interpreter*	£25–£28[2] per hour (with a minimum of 3 hours for those employed regularly in this capacity)

1. The rates of these allowances are discretionary and the following amounts are those given in the *Guide to Allowances Under Part V of the Costs in Criminal Cases (General) Regulations 1986* (LCD–Criminal Defence Services (Remuneration) Legal Aid Division (4)) as amended by LCD Circular 78 of 2003.
2. With effect from 1 January 2002 as notified in LCD letter 2001/180 as amended by LCD Circular 78 of 2003.

1–6204

Regulation 21—Expert and Professional Witness and Interpreters Overnight Allowance

	Maximum Amount with effect from 1.8.2001
Hotel - London, Birmingham, Manchester, Leeds, Liverpool or Newcastle Upon Tyne city centres	£85.25
	* Plus £21.00 Night Subsistence Allowance and £5.00 Personal Incidental Allowance with effect from 1.6.2005
Overnight elsewhere	£55.25
	* Plus £21.00 Night Subsistence Allowance and £5.00 Personal Incidental Allowance if at a Hotel with effect from 1.6.2005
	£25.00 only if with family or friends with effect from 1.6.2005

1-6205

Regulation 22—*Seaman Missing Ship*
                                            Maximum Amount with effect from 23.5.1988
        Loss allowance   £29.70
Maintenance allowance—at the discretion of the court, but not exceeding the sum actually and
reasonably incurred.

1-6206

Regulation 24—*Travelling Allowances*
  (a) *Public Transport Rate*   Rate per mile with effect from 1.8.2001
       Motor-cycles   25p
       Motor cars   25p
  (b) *Standard Rate*   Rate per mile with effect from 1.8.2001
       Motor-cycles   45p
       Motor cars   45p
  (c) *Passenger Supplement*
       First passenger   2p
       Each additional passenger   1p
  (d) *Parking Fees and Congestion Charges*
       Fees and charges actually and reason-
       ably incurred
  (e) Pedal-cycle   6p with effect from 1.6.2005

1-6207

Regulation 25—*Written Medical Reports*

  (a) Report in pursuance of a request to which Section 32(2) of the Criminal Justice Act 1967
       applies—

                                            Maximum Amount with effect
                                            from 6.5.2003
       Consultant   £74.80
       Other registered medical practitioner £52.80
  (b) *Higher Fees*[1] (where more than 2 hours work necessarily undertaken)—

                                            Daily Maximum
       Consultant   £298.25
       Other registered medical practitioner £211.00
  (c) Examination and report to determine fitness for detention centre training—

       All registered medical practitioners £35.20

---

1. The fees provide generally for up to two hours' work, including any travelling time. In difficult cases where
more then two hours' work has necessarily been undertaken, higher fees (but not exceeding the daily maximum)
may be paid at the discretion of the appropriate officer of the court, but the appropriate officer should be satisfied
that payment of a higher fee is justified. In exceptional cases, a senior medical officer of the DHSS regional office
may be consulted for advice.

1-6208

Regulation 25(2)—*Mileage Allowance for Medical Practitioner*

                                            Maximum Amount with effect
       Motor-cycles   from 1.8.2001
                                            45p per mile
       Motor cars   45p per mile

Prosecution of Offences (Custody Time Limits) Regulations 1987[1]

(SI 1987/299 amended by SI 1988/164, SI 1989/767, SI 1989/1107, SI 1991/1515,
SI 1995/555, the Criminal Procedure and Investigations Act 1996, s 71, SI 1998/3037,
SI 1999/2744 and SI 2000/3284)

1-6220 **1.** *Citation and commencement.*

---

1. Made by the Secretary of State in exercise of the powers conferred on him by ss 22(1) and (2) and 29(2) of
the Prosecution of Offences Act 1985.

Interpretation

1-6221 **2.** (1) In these Regulations—

"the 1980 Act" means the Magistrates' Courts Act 1980;
"the 1985 Act" means the Prosecution of Offences Act 1985.

(2) In these Regulations, a reference to a person's first appearance in relation to proceedings in a magistrates' court for an offence is—

   (a) in a case where that person has made an application under section 43B of the 1980 Act, a reference to the time when he appears before the court on the hearing of that application;

   (b) in a case where that person appears or is brought before the court in pursuance of section 5B of the Bail Act 1976 and the decision which is to be, or has been, reconsidered under that section is the decision of a constable, a reference to the time when he so appears or is brought; and

   (c) in any other case, a reference to the time when first he appears or is brought before the court on an information charging him with that offence.

(3) In these Regulations any reference to the start of the trial shall be construed in accordance with section 22(11A) and (11B) of the 1985 Act.

(4) Any maximum period set by these Regulations during which a person may be in the custody of a court does not include the day on which the custody commenced.

(5) A custody time limit which would, apart from this paragraph, expire on any of the days to which this paragraph applies shall be treated as expiring on the next preceding day which is not one of those days.

The days to which this paragraph applies are Saturday, Sunday, Christmas Day, Good Friday and any day which under the Banking and Financial Dealings Act 1971 is a bank holiday in England and Wales.

Application

1–6222 **3.** *Revoked.*

Custody time limits in magistrates' courts

1–6223 **4.** (1) The maximum period during which a person accused of an indictable offence[1] other than treason may be in the custody of a magistrates' court in relation to that offence while awaiting completion of any preliminary stage of the proceedings specified in the following provisions of this Regulation shall be as stated in those provisions.

(2) Except as provided in paragraph (3) below, in the case of an offence triable either way[2] the maximum period of custody between the accused's first appearance and the start of summary trial or, as the case may be, the time when the court decides whether or not to commit the accused to the Crown Court for trial shall be 70 days.

(3) In the case of an offence triable either way[2] if, before the expiry of 56 days following the day of the accused's first appearance, the court decides to proceed to summary trial in pursuance of sections 19 to 24 of the 1980 Act the maximum period of custody between the accused's first appearance and the start of the summary trial shall be 56 days.

(4) In the case of an offence triable on indictment exclusively the maximum period of custody between the accused's first appearance and the time when the court decides whether or not to commit the accused to the Crown Court for trial, shall be 70 days.

(4A) In the case of a summary offence, the maximum period of custody beginning with the date of the accused's first appearance and ending with the date of the start of the summary trial shall be 56 days.

(5) The foregoing provisions of this regulation shall have effect as if any reference therein to the time when the court decides whether or not to commit the accused to the Crown Court for trial were a reference—

   (a) where a court proceeds to inquire into an information as examining justices in pursuance of section 6(1) of the 1980 Act, to the time when it begins to hear evidence for the prosecution at the inquiry;

   (b) where a notice has been given under section 4(1)(c) of the Criminal Justice Act 1987 (in these Regulations referred to as a "notice of transfer"), to the date on which notice of transfer was given.

---

1. Each offence undoubtedly attracts its own custody time limit (*R v Wirral District Magistrates' Court, ex p Meikle* (1990) 154 JP 1035, [1990] Crim LR 801). In the absence of bad faith the fact that a new offence is based upon the same facts as an earlier offence does not alter the principle that each offence has its own time limit (*R v Waltham Forest Magistrates' Court, ex p Lee and Lee* (1993) 97 Cr App Rep 287, [1993] Crim LR 522). See also *R v Crown Court at Leeds, ex p Wardle* [2001] UKHL 12, [2002] 1 AC 754, [2001] 2 All ER 1, [2001] 2 WLR 865, where the prosecution offered no evidence on a charge of murder on the day the custody time limit was due to expire but laid a charge of manslaughter; it was held that as this was a different offence in law it attracted its own custody time limit under reg 4(4) (though the position would be different if the new charge was simply a restatement of the other offence with different particulars, and the bringing of a new charge would be an abuse of process if the prosecution could not demonstrate on the facts that it was justified and the justices were satisfied it had been brought solely for the arbitrary and improper purpose of substituting a new custody time limit). It is desirable that the prosecutor should review all the evidence at the earliest possible moment to decide whether further charges should be brought and to comply with the original custody time limit if that is at all possible (*R v Wolverhampton Justices and Stafford Crown Court, ex p Uppal* (1994) 159 JP 86, [1995] Crim LR 223, DC). It is not permissible for the Crown Court to create an arraignment situation merely to evade custody time limits (*R v Maidstone Crown Court, ex p Hollstein* (1994) 159 JP 73).

2. "Offence triable either way" includes an offence which, although triable only on indictment in the case of an adult, is in the case of a child or young person triable summarily or on indictment under s 24 of the Magistrates' Courts Act 1980 whether or not it is so triable in respect of the particular accused (*R v Stratford Youth Court, ex p S* [1998] 1 WLR 1758 162 JP 552, [1999] Crim LR 146, DC).

Custody time limits in the Crown Court

1-6224 5. (1) *Revoked.*

(2) Where—

(a) a person accused of an indictable offence other than treason is committed to the Crown Court for trial; or

(b) a bill of indictment is preferred against a person under section 2(2)(b) of the Administration of Justice (Miscellaneous Provisions) Act 1933,

the maximum period during which he may be in the custody of the Crown Court in relation to that offence, or any other offence included in the indictment preferred against him, while awaiting the preliminary stage of the proceedings specified in the following provisions of this Regulation shall be as stated in those provisions.

(3) The maximum period of custody—

(a) between the time when the accused is committed for trial and the start of the trial; or

(b) where a bill of indictment is preferred against him under the said section 2(2)(b), between the preferment of the bill and the start of the trial,

shall, subject to the following provisions of this Regulation, be 112 days[1].

(4) Where, following a committal for trial, the bill of indictment preferred against the accused (not being a bill preferred under the said section 2(2)(b)) contains a count charging an offence for which he was committed for trial at that committal together with a count charging an offence for which he was committed for trial on a different occasion, paragraph (3) above applies in relation to each offence separately.

(5) Where, following a committal for trial, a bill of indictment is preferred under the said section 2(2)(b) and the bill does not contain a count charging an offence for which he was not committed for trial, the maximum period of custody between the preferment of the bill and the start of the trial shall be 112 days less any period, or the aggregate of any periods, during which the accused has, since the committal, been in the custody of the Crown Court in relation to an offence for which he was committed for trial.

(6) Where, following a committal for trial, the bill of indictment preferred against the accused (not being a bill preferred under the said section 2(2)(b)) contains a count charging an offence for which he was not committed for trial, the maximum period of custody—

(a) between the preferment of the bill and the start of the trial, or

(b) if the count was added to the bill after its preferment, between that addition and the start of the trial,

shall be 112 days less any period, or the aggregate of any periods, during which he has, since the committal, been in the custody of the Crown Court in relation to an offence for which he was committed for trial.

(6A) The foregoing provisions of this regulation shall have effect, where notice of transfer is given in respect of a case, as if references to committal for trial and to offences for which a person was or was not committed for trial included references to the giving of notice of transfer and to charges contained or not contained in the notice of transfer.

(6B) Where an accused is sent for trial under section 51 of the Crime and Disorder Act 1998 ("the 1998 Act"), the maximum period of custody between the accused being sent to the Crown Court by a magistrates' court for an offence and the start of the trial in relation to it, shall be 182 days less any period, or the aggregate of any periods, during which the accused has, since that first appearance for the offence, been in the custody of the magistrates' court.

(6C) Where, following a sending for trial under section 51 of the 1998 Act, a bill of indictment is preferred under the said section 2(2)(b) and the bill does not contain a count charging an offence for which he was not sent for trial, the maximum period of custody between the preferment of the bill and the start of the trial shall be the maximum period of custody as provided for in paragraph (6B) above (after making any deductions required by that paragraph) less any period, or the aggregate of any periods, during which the accused has, since he was sent for trial, been in the custody of the Crown Court in relation to an offence for which he was not sent for trial.

(6D) Where, following a sending for trial under section 51 of the 1998 Act, the bill of indictment preferred against the accused (not being a bill preferred under the said section 2(2)(b)) contains a count charging an offence for which he was not sent for trial, the maximum period of custody—

(a) between the preferment of the bill and the start of the trial, or

(b) if the count was added to the bill after its preferment, between that addition and the start of the trial,

shall be the maximum period of custody as provided for in paragraph (6B) above (after making any deductions required by that paragraph) less any period, or the aggregate of any periods, during which he has, since being sent for trial, been in the custody of the Crown Court in relation to the offence for which he was previously sent for trial.

(7) *Revoked.*

---

1. Even when an earlier time limit has expired and the defendant has been released on bail, he may still be committed in custody for trial with the new time limits applying (*R v Sheffield Justices, ex p Turner* [1991] 2 QB 472, [1991] 1 All ER 858, 155 JP 173).

Bail of expiry of Crown Court custody time limit

1-6225 6. (1) Subject to the following provisions of this Regulation where an accused who is in custody pending trial in the Crown Court has the benefit of a custody time limit under Regulation 5 above the prosecution shall—

(a) not less than 5 days before the expiry of the time limit give notice in writing to the appropriate officer of the Crown Court and to the accused or his representative stating whether or not it intends to ask the Crown Court to impose conditions on the grant of bail in respect of the accused and, if it intends to do so, the nature of the conditions to be sought; and

(b) make arrangement for the accused to be brought before the Crown Court within the period of 2 days preceding the expiry of the time limit.

(2) If the Crown Court is satisfied that it is not practicable in all the circumstances for the prosecution to comply with sub-paragraph (a) in paragraph (1) above, the Crown Court may direct that the prosecution need not comply with that sub-paragraph or that the minimum period of notice required by that sub-paragraph shall be such lesser minimum period as the Crown Court may specify.

(3) The prosecution need not comply with paragraph (1)(a) above if it has given notice under Regulation 7(2) below of its intention to make an application under section 22(3) of the 1985 Act.

(4) On receiving notice under paragraph (1)(a) above stating that the prosecution intends to ask the Crown Court to impose conditions on the grant of bail, the accused or his representative shall—

(a) give notice in writing to the appropriate officer of the Crown Court and to the prosecution that the accused wishes to be represented at the hearing of the application; or

(b) give notice in writing to the appropriate officer and to the prosecution stating that the accused does not oppose the application; or

(c) give to the appropriate officer, for the consideration of the Crown Court, a written statement of the accused's reasons for opposing the application, at the same time sending a copy of the statement to the prosecution.

(5) The Crown Court may direct that the prosecution need not comply with paragraph (1)(b) above.

(6) The Crown Court, on being notified that an accused who is in custody pending trial there has the benefit of a custody time limit under Regulation 5 above and that the time limit is about to expire, shall, subject to section 25 of the Criminal Justice and Public Order Act 1994 (exclusion of bail in cases of homicide and rape), grant him bail in accordance with the Bail Act 1976, as from the expiry of the time limit, subject to a duty to appear before the Crown Court for trial.

Application for extension of custody time limit

1–6226 **7.** (1) An application to a court for the extension or further extension of a custody time limit under section 22(3) of the 1985 Act may be made orally or in writing.

(2) Subject to paragraphs (3) and (4) below the prosecution shall[1]—

(a) not less than 5 days before making such an application in the Crown Court; and

(b) not less than 2 days before making such an application in a magistrates' court,

give notice in writing to the accused or his representative and to the proper officer of the court stating that it intends to make such an application.

(2A) In paragraph (2) above, "the proper officer of the court" means in relation to an application in the Crown Court the appropriate officer of the court and in relation to an application in a magistrates' court the clerk of the court.

(3) It shall not be necessary for the prosecution to comply with paragraph (2) above if the accused or his representative has informed the prosecution that he does not require such notice.

(4) If the court is satisfied[2] that it is not practicable in all the circumstances for the prosecution to comply with paragraph (2) above, the court may direct that the prosecution need not comply with that paragraph or that the minimum period of notice required by that paragraph to be given shall be such lesser minimum period as the court may specify.

---

1. This requirement to give notice is directory and not mandatory, and does not limit the power under s 22(3) of the Prosecution of Offences Act 1985 to extend the time limit at any time before its expiry (*R v Governor of Canterbury Prison, ex p Craig* [1991] 2 QB 195, [1990] 2 All ER 654, 154 JP 137, DC). A prison governor is not liable in tort for false imprisonment where a prisoner remains in prison after the custody time limit has expired through the failure of the prosecution to apply for an extension and in the absence of the prisoner's application for bail (*Oluto v Secretary of State for the Home Department* (1996) Times, 8 May).
2. The court should be satisfied on the balance of probabilities. The question of practicability should be viewed not as at the time when the matter is raised before the court, but against the whole background of the case (*R v Governor of Canterbury Prison, ex p Craig* [1991] 2 QB 195, [1990] 2 All ER 654, 154 JP 137, DC).

Application of Bail Act 1976

1–6227 **8.** (1) The Bail Act 1976 shall apply in relation to cases which a custody time limit applies subject to the modifications specified in paragraph (2) below, being modifications necessary in consequence of the foregoing provisions of these Regulations.

(2) That Act shall apply as if—

(a) in section 3 (general provisions) at the end there were inserted the following subsection—

"(10A) Where a custody time limit has expired this section shall have effect as if—

(a) subsections (4) and (5) (sureties and security for his surrender to custody) were omitted;
(b) in subsection (6) (conditions of bail) for the words "before release on bail or later" there were substituted the words "after release on bail"";

(*b*) in section 4 (general right to bail of accused persons and others) at the end there were inserted the following subsection—

"(8A) Where a custody time limit has expired this section shall have effect as if, in subsection (1), the words "except as provided in Schedule 1 to this Act" were omitted.";

(*c*) in section 7 (liability to arrest for absconding or breaking conditions of bail) at the end there were inserted the following subsection—

"(7) Where a custody time limit has expired this section shall have effect as if, in subsection (3), paragraphs (*a*) and (*c*) were omitted.".

Magistrates' Courts (Civilian Enforcement Officers) Rules 1990[1]
(SI 1990/2260 as amended by SI 2001/164 and SI 2005/1012)

1-6260   1. (1) *Citation.*
(2) In rule 4 below, the reference to "the principal Rules" is a reference to the Magistrates' Courts Rules 1981.

---

1. Made by the Lord Chancellor in exercise of the power conferred on him by s 144 of the Magistrates' Courts Act 1980.

1-6261   2. *Revoked.*

1-6262   3. (1) For the purposes of subsection (2) of section 125A of the Magistrates' Courts Act 1980 (warrants)—

(*a*) local authorities, police authorities and the Lord Chancellor are authorities of a prescribed class; and
(*b*) a person employed by any such authority is authorised in the prescribed manner to execute warrants to which those sections apply throughout England and Wales if he has been issued by or on behalf of the authority by which he is employed with an authorisation in writing in that behalf in a form suitable for identifying him to persons with whom he deals as a person so authorised.

(2) In paragraph (1) above, "local authorities" means—

(*a*) a district council,
(*b*) a London borough council, and
(*c*) a county council.

1-6263   4. *Revoked.*

Magistrates' Courts (Criminal Justice (International Co-operation)) Rules 1991[1]
(SI 1991/1074 amended by SI 1991/1074 and SI 2001/615)

1-6270   1. *Citation and commencement.*

---

1. Made by the Lord Chancellor, in exercise of the powers conferred on him by s 144 of the Magistrates' Courts Act 1980, as extended by s 145 of that Act and s 10 of the Criminal Justice (International Co-operation) Act 1990.

Interpretation

1-6271   2. In these Rules "the Act" means the Criminal Justice (International Co-operation) Act 1990.

Service of summons or order outside the United Kingdom

1-6272   3. Where a summons is issued or order is made by a magistrates' court in accordance with section 2(1) of the Act for service outside the United Kingdom it shall be sent by the justices' chief executive to the Secretary of State with a view to its being served there in accordance with arrangements made by the Secretary of State.

Proof of service of summons outside the United Kingdom

1-6273   4. (1) The service on any person of a summons issued under section 2(1) of the Act may be proved in any legal proceedings by a certificate given by or on behalf of the Secretary of State.
(2) A statement in any such certificate as is mentioned in paragraph (1) above:

(*a*) that a summons has been served;
(*b*) of the manner in which service was effected;
(*c*) of the date upon which a summons was served.

shall be admissible as evidence of any facts so stated.

Notice of application for letters of request

1–6274   5. Notice of an application under section 3(1) (overseas evidence for use in the United Kingdom) of the Act shall be given to the justices' chief executive for a magistrates' court and shall—

(a) be made in writing, save that the court may in exceptional circumstances dispense with the need for notice;

(b) state the particulars of the offence which it is alleged has been committed or the grounds upon which it is suspected that an offence has been committed;

(c) state whether proceedings in respect of the offence have been instituted or the offence is being investigated; and

(d) include particulars of the assistance requested in the form of a draft letter of request.

Hearing of application for letters of request

1–6275   6. (1) An application under section 3(1) of the Act—

(a) shall be heard in a petty-sessional court-house;

(b) may be heard *ex parte.*

(2) When hearing an application under section 3(1) of the Act the court may, if it thinks it necessary in the interests of justice, direct that the public be excluded from the court.

(3) The powers conferred on a magistrates' court by the preceding paragraph shall be in addition and without prejudice to any other powers of the court to hear proceedings in camera.

Letters of request in urgent cases

1–6276   7. Where in a case of urgency a magistrates' court sends a letter of request direct to any court or tribunal in accordance with section 3(5) of the Act, the justices' chief executive shall forthwith notify the Secretary of State of this and send with the notification a copy of the letter of request.

Proceedings before a nominated court

1–6277   8. (1) In proceedings before a nominated court pursuant to a notice under section 4(2) of the Act the court may, if it thinks it necessary in the interests of justice, direct that the public be excluded from the court.

(2) The powers conferred on a magistrates' court by the preceding paragraph shall be in addition and without prejudice to any other powers of the court to hear proceedings in camera.

Court register of proceedings before a nominated court

1–6278   9. (1) Where a magistrates' court receives evidence in proceedings pursuant to a notice under section 4(2) of the Act, the justices' chief executive shall note in the register—

(a) particulars of the proceedings;

(b) without prejudice to the generality of (a) above—

(i) which persons with an interest in the proceedings were present;

(ii) which of the said persons were represented and by whom;

(iii) whether any of the said persons were denied the opportunity of cross-examining a witness as to any part of his testimony.

(2) Such part of the register as relates to proceedings mentioned in paragraph (1) above shall be kept in a separate book.

(3) Save as authorised by the Secretary of State, or with the leave of the court, such part of the register as relates to proceedings mentioned in paragraph (1) above shall not be open to inspection by any person.

(4) When so requested by the Secretary of State, the justices' chief executive shall send to him a copy of an extract of the register as it relates to any proceedings mentioned in paragraph (1) above.

Magistrates' Courts (Costs Against Legal Representatives in Civil Proceedings) Rules 1991[1]

(SI 1991/2096 amended by SI 2001/615)

Citation, commencement and interpretation

1–6300   1. (1) *Citation.*

(2) In these Rules—

"interested party" means the party benefiting from the wasted costs order and, where he is a legally assisted person, within the meaning of section 2(11) of the 1988 Act, the Legal Aid Board;

"the 1988 Act" means the Legal Aid Act 1988;

"wasted costs order" means any action taken by a court under section 145A of the Magistrates' Courts Act 1980.

1. Made by the Lord Chancellor, in exercise of the powers conferred upon him by s 144 of the Magistrates' Courts Act 1980.

General

1–6301   **2.** (1) A wasted costs order may provide that the whole or any part of the wasted costs incurred by a party shall be disallowed or (as the case may be) met by the legal or other representative concerned and the court shall specify the amount of such costs.

(2) Subject to paragraph (7) below, a court may make a wasted costs order either on the application of a party to the proceedings or on its own motion and when doing so the justices' clerk shall make a record of the order in writing, and the reasons for the decision of the court.

(3) Before making a wasted costs order, the court shall allow the legal or other representative a reasonable opportunity to appear before it and show cause why the order should not be made.

(4) Subject to paragraphs (5) and (6) below, any payments which are required to be made by a legal or other representative under a wasted costs order shall be made to the party who has incurred the wasted costs.

(5) Where the party who has incurred wasted costs is receiving assistance by way of representation under Part III of the 1988 Act and which has been approved under regulation 22 of the Legal Advice and Assistance Regulations 1989, any payments which are required to be made by a legal or other representative under a wasted costs order shall be paid to the justices' chief executive in accordance with regulation 31 of those Regulations.

(6) Where the party who has incurred wasted costs is being granted representation under Part IV of the 1988 Act, any payments which are required to be made by a legal or other representative under a wasted costs order shall be paid to the justices' chief executive in accordance with regulation 89(*a*) of the Civil Legal Aid (General) Regulations 1989.

(7) A court shall not make a wasted costs order after the end of the period of six months beginning with the date on which the proceedings are disposed of by the court.

(8) Where a wasted costs order has been made, the justices' chief executive shall, as soon as practicable, serve a copy of the order on any interested party and on the legal or other representative concerned.

Appeals

1–6302   **3.** (1) A legal or other representative against whom a wasted costs order is made may appeal to the Crown Court.

(2) Subject to paragraph (4) below, an appeal shall be instituted within 21 days of the wasted costs order being made by the appellant giving notice in writing to the justices' chief executive for the court which made the order, stating the grounds of appeal.

(3) The appellant shall, as soon as practicable after instituting the appeal, serve a copy of the notice and grounds of appeal, including any application for an extension of the time in which to appeal granted under paragraph (4) below, on any interested party.

(4) The time limit within which an appeal may be instituted may, for good reason, be extended before or after it expires by a judge of the Crown Court and, where it is so extended, the court to which the appeal is made shall give notice of the extension to the appellant, the justices' chief executive for the court which made the wasted costs order and any interested party.

(5) The court to which the appeal is made shall give notice of the hearing date to the appellant, the justices' chief executive for the court which made the wasted costs order and any interested party and shall allow the interested party to make representations either orally or in writing.

(6) The court hearing the appeal may affirm, vary or revoke the order as it thinks fit and shall notify its decision to the appellant, any interested party and the justices' chief executive for the court which made the order.

Criminal Justice Act 1991 (Notice of Transfer) Regulations 1992[1]

(SI 1992/1670 amended by SI 1997/738, SI 1998/461 and SI 2001/444)

1–6340   **1.** (1) *Citation, commencement.*

(2) In these Regulations—

"the Director" means the Director of Public Prosecutions;

"notice of transfer" means a notice served under section 53(1) of the Criminal Justice Act 1991.

1. Made by the Attorney General, in exercise of the powers conferred on him by s 53(5) of and para 4 of Sch 6 to the Criminal Justice Act 1991.

Notice of transfer

1–6341   **2.** A notice of transfer served by or on behalf of the Director shall be in Form 1 in the Schedule to these Regulations, or in a form to the like effect.

Notice to defendant

1–6342   **3.** Where a notice of transfer is served by or on behalf of the Director, a copy of the notice shall be given by or on behalf of the Director to any person to whom the notice of transfer relates (or, if he is acting by a solicitor, to his solicitor) together with—

(a) a notice in Form 2 in the Schedule to these Regulations, or in a form to the like effect; and

(b) subject to regulation 3A below, copies of the documents containing the evidence (including oral evidence) on which any charge to which the notice of transfer relates is based.

1–6342A 3A. There shall be no requirement for copies of any documents referred to in the documents sent with the notice of transfer as having already been supplied to accompany the copy of the notice of transfer given in accordance with regulation 3 above.

Notice to Crown Court

1–6343 4. Where a notice of transfer is served by or on behalf of the Director, a copy of the notice shall be given by or on behalf of the Director to the appropriate officer of the Crown Court sitting at the place specified by the notice of transfer as the proposed place of trial together with—

(a) a copy of the notice referred to in paragraph (a) of regulation 3 above and copies of the material enclosed with that notice; and

(b) copies of the documents referred to in paragraph (b) of that regulation, including both those which accompanied the copy of the notice of transfer given to the person to whom the notice relates and those which had already been supplied.

Notice to prison governor etc

1–6344 5. Where a notice of transfer is served by or on behalf of the director, a copy of the notice shall be given by or on behalf of the Director to any person who has custody of any person to whom the notice of transfer relates together with a copy of the notice referred to in paragraph (a) of regulation 3 above.

1–6345

SCHEDULE

(Forms)

Criminal Procedure and Investigations Act 1996 (Defence Disclosure Time Limits) Regulations 1997[1]

(SI 1997/684)

1–6510 1. (1) *Citation and commencement.*

(2) These Regulations extend to England and Wales only.

(3) In these Regulations, the expression "the Act" means the Criminal Procedure and Investigations Act 1996.

---

1. Made by the Secretary of State, in pursuance of ss 12 and 77(2) and (4) of the Criminal Procedure and Investigations Act 1996.

1–6511 2. Subject to regulations 3, 4 and 5, the relevant period for sections 5 and 6 of the Act (disclosure by the accused) is a period beginning with the day on which the prosecutor complies, or purports to comply, with section 3 of that Act and ending with the expiration of 14 days from that day.

1–6512 3. (1) The period referred to in regulation 2 shall, if the court so orders, be extended by so many days as the court specifies.

(2) The court may only make such an order if an application which complies with paragraph (3) below is made by the accused before the expiration of the period referred to in regulation 2.

(3) An application under paragraph (2) above shall—

(a) state that the accused believes, on reasonable grounds, that it is not possible for him to give a defence statement under section 5 or, as the case may be, 6 of the Act during the period referred to in regulation 2;

(b) specify the grounds for so believing; and

(c) specify the number of days by which the accused wishes that period to be extended.

(4) The court shall not make an order under paragraph (1) above unless it is satisfied that the accused cannot reasonably give or, as the case may be, could not reasonably have given a defence statement under section 5 or, as the case may be, 6 of the Act during the period referred to in regulation 2.

(5) The number of days by which the period referred to in regulation 2 may be extended shall be entirely at the court's discretion.

1–6513 4. (1) Where the court has made an order under regulation 3(1), the period referred to in regulation 2 as extended in accordance with that order shall, if the court so orders, be further extended by so many days as the court specifies.

(2) Paragraphs (2) and (5) of regulation 3 shall, subject to paragraph (4) below, apply for the purposes of an order under paragraph (1) above as they apply for the purposes of an order under regulation 3(1).

(3) There shall be no limit on the number of applications that may be made under regulation 3(2) as applied by paragraph (2) above; and on a second or subsequent such application the court shall have the like powers under paragraph (1) above as on the first such application.

(4) In the application of regulation 3(2) to (5) in accordance with paragraph (2) above, any reference to the period referred to in regulation 2 shall be construed as a reference to that period as extended or, as the case may be, further extended by an order of the court under regulation 3(1) or paragraph (1) or (3) above.

1–6514   5. (1) Where the period referred to in regulation 2 or that period as extended or, as the case may be, further extended by an order of the court under regulation 3(1) or 4(1) or (3) would, apart from this regulation, expire on any of the days specified in paragraph (2) below, that period shall be treated as expiring on the next following day which is not one of those days.

(2) The days referred to in paragraph (1) above are Saturday, Sunday, Christmas Day, Good Friday and any day which under the Banking and Financial Dealings Act 1971 is a bank holiday in England and Wales.

Civil Procedure Rules 1998

(SI 1998/3132 amended by SI 2000/221 and 2092, SI 2001/256, SI 2003/364, 1329, 2113 and 3361, SI 2004/1306, SI 2005/352, 2292 and 3515 and SI 2006/1689[1])

CONTENTS

The following Rules are reproduced in part in this work

1. Reference is made only to those instruments which amend provisions reproduced in this work.

I GENERAL RULES ABOUT SERVICE

1–6563A   **6.1. Part 6 rules about service apply generally.**   The rules in this Part apply to the service of documents, except where—

(a) any other enactment, a rule in another Part, or a practice direction makes a different provision; or
(b) the court orders otherwise.

(For service in possession claims, see Part 55).

1–6563B   **6.2. Methods of service—general.**   (1) A document may be served by any of the following methods—

(a) personal service, in accordance with rule 6.4;
(b) first class post (or an alternative service which provides for delivery on the next working day);
(c) leaving the document at a place specified in rule 6.5;
(d) through a document exchange in accordance with the relevant practice direction; or
(e) by fax or other means of electronic communication in accordance with the relevant practice direction.

(Rule 6.8 provides for the court to permit service by an alternative method)
(2) A company may be served by any method permitted under this Part as an alternative to the methods of service set out in-

(a) section 725 of the Companies Act 1985 (service by leaving a document at or posting it to an authorised place);
(b) section 695 of that Act (service on overseas companies); and
(c) section 694A of that Act (service of documents on companies incorporated outside the UK and Gibraltar and having a branch inGreat Britain).

1–6563C   **6.3. Who is to serve.**   (1) The court will serve a document which it has issued or prepared except where—

(a) a rule provides that a party must serve the document in question;
(b) the party on whose behalf the document is to be served notifies the court that he wishes to serve it himself;
(c) a practice direction provides otherwise;
(d) the court orders otherwise; or
(e) the court has failed to serve and has sent a notice of non-service to the party on whose behalf the document is to be served in accordance with rule 6.11.

(2) Where the court is to serve a document, it is for the court to decide which of the methods of service specified in rule 6.2 is to be used.
(3) Where a party prepares a document which is to be served by the court, that party must file a copy for the court, and for each party to be served.

1–6563D   **6.4. Personal service.**   (1) A document to be served may be served personally, except as provided in paragraphs (2) and (2A).
(2) Where a solicitor—

(*a*) is authorised to accept service on behalf of a party; and
(*b*) has notified the party serving the document in writing that he is so authorised,

a document must be served on the solicitor, unless personal service is required by an enactment, rule, practice direction or court order.

(2A) In civil proceedings by or against the Crown, as defined in rule 66.1(2), documents required to be served on the Crown may not be served personally.

(3) A document is served personally on an individual by leaving it with that individual.

(4) A document is served personally on a company or other corporation by leaving it with a person holding a senior position within the company or corporation.

(The service practice direction sets out the meaning of "senior position")

(5) A document is served personally on a partnership where partners are being sued in the name of their firm by leaving it with—

(*a*) a partner; or
(*b*) a person who, at the time of service, has the control or management of the partnership business at its principal place of business.

1–6563E   6.5. Address for service.   (1) Except as provided by Section III of this Part (service out of the jurisdiction) a document must be served within the jurisdiction.

("Jurisdiction" is defined in rule 2.3)

(2) A party must give an address for service within the jurisdiction. Such address must include a full postcode, unless the court orders otherwise.

(Paragraph 2.4 of the Practice Direction to Part 16 contains provision about the content of an address for service).

(3) Where a party—

(*a*) does not give the business address of his solicitor as his address for service; and
(*b*) resides or carries on business within the jurisdiction,

he must give his residence or place of business as his address for service.

(4) Any document to be served—

(*a*) by first class post (or an alternative service which provides for delivery on the next working day);
(*b*) by leaving it at the place of service;
(*c*) through a document exchange;
(*d*) by fax or by other means of electronic communication,

must be sent or transmitted to, or left at, the address for service given by the party to be served.

(5) Where—

(*a*) a solicitor is acting for the party to be served; and
(*b*) the document to be served is not the claim form;

the party's address for service is the business address of his solicitor.

(Rule 6.13 specifies when the business address of a defendant's solicitor may be the defendant's address for service in relation to the claim form)

(6) Where—

(*a*) no solicitor is acting for the party to be served; and,
(*b*) the party has not given an address for service,

the document must be sent or transmitted to, or left at, the place shown in the following table.

(Rule 6.2 (2) sets out the statutory methods of service on a company)

Nature of party to be served	Place of service
Individual	Usual or last known residence.
Proprietor of a business	Usual or last known residence; or place of business or last known place of business
Individual who is suing or being sued in the name of a firm	Usual or last known residence; or principal or last known place of business of the firm
Corporation incorporated in England and Wales other than a company	Principal office of the corporation; or any place within the jurisdiction where the corporation carries on its activities and which has a real connection with the claim
Company registered in England and Wales	Principal office of the company; or any place of business of the company within the jurisdiction which has a real connection with the claim
Any other company or corporation	Any place within the jurisdiction where the corporation carries on its activities; or any place of business of the company within the jurisdiction

(7) This rule does not apply where an order made by the court under rule 6.8 (service by an alternative method) specifies where the document in question may be served.

(Rule 42.1 provides that if the business address of his solicitor is given that solicitor will be treated as acting for that party).

(8) In civil proceedings by or against the Crown, as defined in rule 66.1(2)—

(*a*) service on the Attorney General must be effected on the Treasury Solicitor;

(b) service on a government department must be effected on the solicitor acting for that department as required by section 18 of the Crown Proceedings Act 1947.

(The practice direction to Part 66 gives the list published under section 17 of that Act of the solicitors acting for the different government departments on whom service is to be effected, and of their addresses).

1–6563F   6.6. Service of documents on children and patients. (1) The following table shows the person on whom a document must be served if it is a document which would otherwise be served on a child or a patient—

Type of document	Nature of party	Person to be served
Claim form	Child who is not also a patient	One of the child's parents or guardians; or if there is no parent or guardian, the person with whom the child resides or in whose care the child is
Claim form	Patient	The person authorised under Part VII of the Mental Health Act 1983 to conduct the proceedings in the name of the patient or on his behalf; or if there is no person so authorised, the person with whom the patient resides or in whose care the patient is.
Application for an order appointing a litigation friend, where a child or patient has no litigation friend	Child or patient	See rule 21.8
Any other document	Child or patient	The litigation friend who is conducting proceedings on behalf of the child or patient

(2) The court may make an order permitting a document to be served on the child or patient, or on some person other than the person specified in the table in this rule.

(3) An application for an order under paragraph (2) may be made without notice.

(4) The court may order that, although a document has been served on someone other than the person specified in the table, the document is to be treated as if it had been properly served.

(5) This rule does not apply where the court has made an order under rule 21.2 (3) allowing a child to conduct proceedings without a litigation friend.

(Part 21 contains rules about the appointment of a litigation friend)

1–6563G   6.7. Deemed service. (1) A document which is served in accordance with these rules or any relevant practice direction shall be deemed[1] to be served on the day shown in the following table—

Method of service	Deemed day of service
First class post (or an alternative service which provides for delivery on the next working day)	The second day after it was posted
Document exchange	The second day after it was left at the document exchange
Delivering the document to or leaving it at a permitted address	The day after it was delivered to or left at the permitted address
Fax	If it is transmitted on a business day before 4 pm, on that day; or in any other case, on the business day after the day on which it is transmitted
Other electronic method	The second day after the day on which it is transmitted

(2) If a document is served personally—

(a) after 5 p.m., on a business day; or

(b) at any time on a Saturday, Sunday or a Bank Holiday,

it will be treated as being served on the next business day.

(3) In this rule—

"business day" means any day except Saturday, Sunday or a bank holiday; and
"bank holiday" includes Christmas Day and Good Friday.

1. The deemed day of service is not rebuttable by evidence that service had actually been effected on a different day (*Godwin v Swindon Borough Council* [2001] EWCA Civ 1478, [2001] 4 All ER 641, [2002] 1 WLR 997, followed in *Anderton v Clwyd County Council* [2002] EWCA Civ 933, [2002] 3 All ER 813). Saturday and Sunday are not excluded from the calculation of the deemed day of service by first class post; though there is a parenthetical reference to Rule 2.8 in Rule 6.7, the language of the former is not applicable to the latter (*Anderton v Clwyd County Council*, supra, disapproving dicta to the contrary effect in *Godwin v Swindon Borough Council*, supra, and *Sealy v Consignia plc* [2002] EWCA Civ 878, [2002] 3 All ER 801).)

1–6563H   6.8. Service by an alternative method. (1) Where it appears to the court that there is a good reason to authorise service by a method not permitted by these Rules, the court may make an order permitting service by an alternative method.

(2) An application for an order permitting service by an alternative method—

(a) must be supported by evidence; and

(b) may be made without notice.

(3) An order permitting service by an alternative method must specify—

(a) the method of service; and

(b) the date when the document will be deemed to be served.

1–6563I   6.9. Power of court to dispense with service. (1) The court may dispense[1] with service of a document.

(2) An application for an order to dispense with service may be made without notice.

1. It was held in *Anderton v Clwyd County Council* (which was applied in *Cranfield v Bridgegrove Ltd* [2003] EWCA Civ 656, [2003] 3 All ER 129) appeals [2002] EWCA Civ 933, [2002] 3 All ER 813 that the power to dispense with service of a claim form could be exercised retrospectively as well as prospectively, but it would be exercised retrospectively only in exceptional circumstances", and in that regard there was a sensible and relevant distinction between cases where (i) the claimant had not even attempted to serve a claim form by one of the permitted methods, and (ii) cases where the claimant had made an ineffective attempt to serve a claim form by one of the permitted methods, but the defendant did not dispute that he or his legal representatives had in fact received, and had their attention drawn to, the claim form by a permitted method of service within the period of 4 months (or any extension thereof that had been granted). To grant dispensation in the first case would constitute an impermissible attempt to circumvent the limitations in r 7.6(3) on the grant of extensions of time for service of the claim form. In the second case the defendant would not usually suffer prejudice as a result of the court dispensing with the formality of service of a document that had already come into his hands before the end of the period for service.

In *Wilkey v BBC* [2002] EWCA Civ 1561, [2002] 4 All ER 1177 it was held that in the second (category 2) case referred to in *Anderton*, discretion should ordinary be exercised in the claimant's favour *only* if the deemed late service occurred *before* the judgment in *Anderton*; in other cases a "strict approach" should generally be adopted.

1–6563J   6.10. Certificate of service. Where a rule, practice direction or court order requires a certificate of service, the certificate must state—

(a) that the document has not been returned undelivered; and

(b) the details set out in the following table—

Method of service	Details to be certified
Post	Date of posting
Personal	Date of personal service
Document exchange	Date of delivery to the document exchange
Delivery of document to or leaving it at a permitted place	Date when the document was delivered or left at the permitted place
Fax	Date and time of transmission
Other electronic means	Date of transmission and the means used
Alternative method permitted by the court	As required by the court

1–6563K   6.11. Notification of outcome of postal service by the court. Where—

(a) a document to be served by the court is served by post; and

(b) such document is returned to the court,

the court must send notification to the party who requested service stating that the document has been returned.

1–6563KA   6.11A. Notice of non-service by bailiff. Where—

(a) the court bailiff is to serve a document; and

(b) the bailiff is unable to serve it,

the court must send notification to the party who requested service.

II   SPECIAL PROVISIONS ABOUT SERVICE OF THE CLAIM FORM
6.12–6.16

III   SPECIAL PROVISIONS ABOUT SERVICE OUT OF THE JURISDICTION
6.17–6.31

PART 52

I GENERAL RULES ABOUT APPEALS

1–6563L   52.1. Scope and interpretation.   (1) The rules in this Part apply to appeals to—

   (*a*)   the civil division of the Court of Appeal;
   (*b*)   the High Court; and
   (*c*)   a county court.

   (2) This Part does not apply to an appeal in detailed assessment proceedings against a decision of an authorised court officer.
   (Rules 47.20 to 47.23 deal with appeals against a decision of an authorised court officer in detailed assessment proceedings)
   (3) In this Part—

   (*a*)   "appeal" includes an appeal by way of case stated;
   (*b*)   "appeal court" means the court to which an appeal is made;
   (*c*)   "lower court" means the court, tribunal or other person or body from whose decision an appeal is brought;
   (*d*)   "appellant" means a person who brings or seeks to bring an appeal;
   (*e*)   "respondent" means—

     (i)   a person other than the appellant who was a party to the proceedings in the lower court and who is affected by the appeal; and
     (ii)   a person who is permitted by the appeal court to be a party to the appeal; and

   (*f*)   "appeal notice" means an appellant's or respondent's notice.

   (4) This Part is subject to any rule, enactment or practice direction which sets out special provisions with regard to any particular category of appeal.

1–6563M   52.2 Parties to comply with the practice direction.   All parties to an appeal must comply with the relevant practice direction[1].

---
   1. See this PART, post.

1–6563N   52.3 to 52.5.   (*Appeals from county court or High Court*).

1–6563O   52.6. Variation of time.   (1) An application to vary the time limit for filing an appeal notice must be made to the appeal court.
   (2) The parties may not agree to extend any date or time limit set by—

   (*a*)   these Rules;
   (*b*)   the relevant practice direction; or
   (*c*)   an order of the appeal court or the lower court.

   (Rule 3.1(2)(*a*) provides that the court may extend or shorten the time for compliance with any rule, practice direction or court order (even if an application for extension is made after the time for compliance has expired))
   (Rule 3.1(2)(*b*) provides that the court may adjourn or bring forward a hearing)

1–6563P   52.7. Stay.   Unless—

   (*a*)   the appeal court or the lower court orders otherwise; or
   (*b*)   the appeal is from the Asylum and Immigration Tribunal,

an appeal shall not operate as a stay of any order or decision of the lower court.

1–6563Q   52.8. Amendment of appeal notice.   An appeal notice may not be amended without the permission of the appeal court.

1–6563R   52.9. Striking out appeal notices and setting aside or imposing conditions on permission to appeal.   (1) The appeal court may—

   (*a*)   strike out the whole or part of an appeal notice;
   (*b*)   set aside permission to appeal in whole or in part;
   (*c*)   impose or vary conditions upon which an appeal may be brought.

   (2) The court will only exercise its powers under paragraph (1) where there is a compelling reason for doing so.
   (3) Where a party was present at the hearing at which permission was given he may not subsequently apply for an order that the court exercise its powers under sub-paragraphs (1)(*b*) or (1)(*c*).

1–6563S   52.10 Appeal court's powers.   (1) In relation to an appeal the appeal court has all the powers of the lower court.
   (Rule 52.1(4) provides that this Part is subject to any enactment that sets out special provisions with regard to any particular category of appeal—where such an enactment gives a statutory power to a tribunal, person or other body it may be the case that the appeal court may not exercise that power on an appeal)
   (2) The appeal court has power to—

(a) affirm, set aside or vary any order or judgment made or given by the lower court;
(b) refer any claim or issue for determination by the lower court;
(c) order a new trial or hearing;
(d) make orders for the payment of interest;
(e) make a costs order.

(3) In an appeal from a claim tried with a jury the Court of Appeal may, instead of ordering a new trial—

(a) make an order for damages; or
(b) vary an award of damages made by the jury.

(4) The appeal court may exercise its powers in relation to the whole or part of an order of the lower court.
(Part 3 contains general rules about the court's case management powers)

1–6563T   **52.11. Hearing of appeals.**   (1) Every appeal will be limited to a review of the decision of the lower court unless—

(a) a practice direction makes different provision for a particular category of appeal; or
(b) the court considers that in the circumstances of an individual appeal it would be in the interests of justice to hold a re-hearing.

(2) Unless it orders otherwise, the appeal court will not receive—

(a) oral evidence; or
(b) evidence which was not before the lower court.

(3) The appeal court will allow an appeal where the decision of the lower court was—

(a) wrong; or
(b) unjust because of a serious procedural or other irregularity in the proceedings in the lower court.

(4) The appeal court may draw any inference of fact which it considers justified on the evidence.
(5) At the hearing of the appeal a party may not rely on a matter not contained in his appeal notice unless the appeal court gives permission.

II SPECIAL PROVISIONS APPLYING TO THE COURT OF APPEAL

1–6563U   **52.15. Judicial review appeals.**   (1) Where permission to apply for judicial review has been refused at a hearing in the High Court, the person seeking that permission may apply to the Court of Appeal for permission to appeal.
(2) An application in accordance with paragraph (1) must be made within 7 days of the decision of the High Court to refuse to give permission to apply for judicial review.
(3) On an application under paragraph (1), the Court of Appeal may, instead of giving permission to appeal, give permission to apply for judicial review.
(4) Where the Court of Appeal gives permission to apply for judicial review in accordance with paragraph (3), the case will proceed in the High Court unless the Court of Appeal orders otherwise.

1–6563V   **52.16. Who may exercise the powers of the Court of Appeal**

SECTION III – PROVISIONS ABOUT REOPENING APPEALS

1–6563W   **52.17. Reopening of final appeals**

PRACTICE DIRECTION – APPEALS[1]
This Practice Direction supplements Part 52.
CONTENTS OF THIS PRACTICE DIRECTION

1.1 This practice direction is divided into three sections:

Section I – General provisions about appeals
Section II – General provisions about statutory appeals and appeals by way of case stated
Section III –Provisions about specific appeals

---

1. For additional guidance on provisions where application for permission to appeal is dismissed on paper see *Hyams v Plender* [2001] 2 All ER 179, [2001] 1 WLR 32, CA.

SECTION I – GENERAL PROVISIONS ABOUT APPEALS

2.1 This practice direction applies to all appeals to which Part 52 applies except where specific provision is made for appeals to the Court of Appeal.
2.2 For the purpose only of appeals to the Court of Appeal from cases in family proceedings this Practice Direction will apply with such modifications as may be required.

GROUNDS FOR APPEAL
3.1 Rule 52.11(3) (a) and (b) sets out the circumstances in which the appeal court will allow an appeal.
3.2 The grounds of appeal should set out clearly the reasons why rule 52.11(3)(a) or (b) is said to apply.

PERMISSION TO APPEAL

APPELLANT'S NOTICE

5.1 An appellant's notice (N161) must be filed and served in all cases. Where an application for permission to appeal is made to the appeal court it must be applied for in the appellant's notice.

Extension of time for filing appellant's notice

5.2 If an appellant requires an extension of time for filing his notice the application must be made in the appellant's notice. The notice should state the reason for the delay and the steps taken prior to the application being made.

5.3 Where the appellant's notice includes an application for an extension of time and permission to appeal has been given or is not required the respondent has the right to be heard on that application. He must be served with a copy of the appellant's bundle. However, a respondent who unreasonably opposes an extension of time runs the risk of being ordered to pay the appellant's costs of that application.

5.4 If an extension of time is given following such an application the procedure at paragraphs 6.1 to 6.6 applies.

Applications

5.5 Notice of an application to be made to the appeal court for a remedy incidental to the appeal (eg an interim remedy under rule 25.1 or an order for security for costs) may be included in the appeal notice or in a Part 23 application notice.

(Rule 25.15 deals with security for costs of an appeal)

(Paragraph 10 *[11]* of this practice direction contains other provisions relating to applications)

Documents

5.6 The appellant must lodge the following documents with his appellant's notice in every case except where the appellant's notice relates to a refusal of permission to apply for judicial review (see paragraph 15.3 below):

(1) one additional copy of the appellant's notice for the appeal court; and
(2) one copy of the appellant's notice for each of the respondents ;
(3) one copy of any skeleton argument (see paragraph 5.9)
(4) a sealed copy of the order being appealed;
(5) any order giving or refusing permission to appeal, together with a copy of the reasons for that decision;
(6) any witness statements or affidavits in support of any application included in the appellant's notice; and
(7) a bundle of documents in support of the appeal– this should include copies of the documents referred to in paragraphs (1) to (6) and any other documents which the appellant reasonably considers necessary to enable the appeal court to reach its decision on the hearing of the application or appeal. Documents which are extraneous to the issues to be considered should be excluded. The other documents will, subject to paragraph 5.7, include:

(*a*) any affidavit or witness statement filed in support of the application for permission to appeal or the appeal,
(*b*) a suitable record of the reasons for judgment of the lower court (see paragraph 5.12);
(*c*) where permission to appeal has been given or permission is not required; any relevant transcript or note of evidence (see paragraph 5.15 below)
(*d*) statements of case,
(*e*) any application notice (or case management documentation) relevant to the subject of the appeal,
(*f*) in cases where the decision appealed was itself made on appeal, the first order, the reasons given and the appellant's notice of appeal from that order,
(*g*) in cases where the appeal is from a Tribunal, a copy of the Tribunal's reasons for the decision, a copy of the decision reviewed by the Tribunal and the reasons for the original decision
(*h*) in the case of judicial review or a statutory appeal, the original decision which was the subject of the application to the lower court
(*i*) relevant affidavits, witness statements, summaries, experts' reports and exhibits;
(*j*) any skeleton arguments relied on in the lower court; and
(*k*) such other documents as the court may direct.

5.7 Where it is not possible to file all the above documents, the appellant must indicate which documents have not yet been filed and the reasons why they are not currently available.

5.8 Where bundles comprise more than 150 pages excluding transcripts of judgment and other transcripts of the proceedings in the lower court only those documents which the court may reasonably be expected to pre-read should be included. A full set of documents should then be brought to the hearing for reference.

Skeleton arguments

5.9 (1) The appellant's notice must, subject to (2) and (3) below, be accompanied by a skeleton argument. Alternatively the skeleton argument may be included in the appellant's notice. Where the skeleton argument is so included it will not form part of the notice for the purposes of rule 52.8.

(2) Where it is impracticable for the appellant's skeleton argument to accompany the appellant's notice it must be lodged and served on all respondents within 14 days of filing the notice.

(3) An appellant who is not represented need not lodge a skeleton argument but is encouraged to do so since this will be helpful to the court.

Content of skeleton arguments

5.10 Skeleton arguments for the appeal court should contain a numbered list of points stated in no more than a few sentences which should both define and confine the areas of controversy. Each point should be followed by references to any documentation on which the appellant proposes to rely.

5.11 The appellant should consider what other information the appeal court will need. This may include a list of persons who feature in the case or glossaries of technical terms. A chronology of relevant events will be necessary in most appeals. In the case of points of law, authorities relied on should be cited with reference to the particular pages where the principle concerned is set out.

Suitable record of the judgment

5.12 Where the judgment to be appealed has been officially recorded by the court, an approved transcript of that record should accompany the appellant's notice. Photocopies will not be accepted for this purpose. However, where there is no officially recorded judgment, the following documents will be acceptable:

Written judgments

(1) Where the judgment was made in writing a copy of that judgment endorsed with the judge's signature.

Note of judgment

(2) When judgment was not officially recorded or made in writing a note of the judgment (agreed between the appellant's and respondent's advocates) should be submitted for approval to the judge whose decision is being appealed. If the parties cannot agree on a single note of the judgment, both versions should be provided to that judge with an explanatory letter. For the purpose of an application for permission to appeal the note need not be approved by the respondent or the lower court judge.

Advocates' notes of judgments where the appellant is unrepresented

(3) When the appellant was unrepresented in the lower court it is the duty of any advocate for the respondent to make his/her note of judgment promptly available, free of charge to the appellant where there is no officially recorded judgment or if the court so directs. Where the appellant was represented in the lower court it is the duty of his/her own former advocate to make his/her note available in these circumstances. The appellant should submit the note of judgment to the appeal court.

Reasons for Judgment in Tribunal cases

(4) A sealed copy of the Tribunal's reasons for the decision.

5.13 An appellant may not be able to obtain an official transcript or other suitable record of the lower court's decision within the time within which the appellant's notice must be filed. In such cases the appellant's notice must still be completed to the best of the appellant's ability on the basis of the documentation available. However it may be amended subsequently with the permission of the appeal court.

Advocate's notes of judgments

5.14 Advocates' brief (or, where appropriate, refresher) fee includes:
(1) remuneration for taking a note of the judgment of the court;
(2) having the note transcribed accurately;
(3) attempting to agree the note with the other side if represented;
(4) submitting the note to the judge for approval where appropriate;
(5) revising it if so requested by the judge, and
(6) providing any copies required for the appeal court, instructing solicitors and lay client; and
(7) providing a copy of his note to an unrepresented appellant.

Transcripts or Notes of Evidence

5.15 When the evidence is relevant to the appeal an official transcript of the relevant evidence must be obtained. Transcripts or notes of evidence are generally not needed for the purpose of determining an application for permission to appeal.

Notes of evidence

5.16 If evidence relevant to the appeal was not officially recorded, a typed version of the judge's notes of evidence must be obtained.

Transcripts at public expense

5.17 Where the lower court or the appeal court is satisfied that an unrepresented appellant is in such poor financial circumstances that the cost of a transcript would be an excessive burden the court may certify that the cost of obtaining one official transcript should be borne at public expense.

5.18 In the case of a request for an official transcript of evidence or proceedings to be paid for at public expense, the court must also be satisfied that there are reasonable grounds for appeal. Whenever possible a request for a transcript at public expense should be made to the lower court when asking for permission to appeal.

Filing and service of appellant's notice

5.19 Rule 52.4 sets out the procedure and time limits for filing and serving an appellant's notice. The appellant must file the appellant's notice at the appeal court within such period as may be directed by the lower court which should not normally exceed 28 days or, where the lower court directs no such period, within 14 days of the date of the decision that the appellant wishes to appeal.

Skeleton arguments must be filed with the appellant's notice whether they are included within the notice or accompany it except as provided by paragraph 5.9(2),

The fee must be paid at the time the notice is presented for filing

5.20 Where the lower court judge announces his decision and reserves the reasons for his judgment or order until a later date, he should, in the exercise of powers under rule 52.4(2)(*a*), fix a period for filing the appellant's notice at the appeal court that takes this into account.

5.21 Except where the appeal court orders otherwise, the appellant must serve a sealed copy of the appellant's notice, including any skeleton arguments on all respondents to the appeal in accordance with the timetable prescribed by rule 52.4(3) except where this requirement is modified by paragraph 5.9(2) in which case where the skeleton argument should be served as soon as it is lodged.

5.22 Unless the court otherwise directs a respondent need not take any action when served with an appellant's notice until such time as notification is given to him that permission to appeal has been given.

5.23 The court may dispense with the requirement for service of the notice on a respondent. Any application notice seeking an order under rule 6.9 to dispense with service should set out the reasons relied on and be verified by a statement of truth.

5.24 Where the appellant is applying for permission to appeal in his appellant's notice, there is no requirement at this stage for copies of the documents referred to at paragraph 5.6 to be served on the respondents. However, if permission has been given by the lower court or permission is not required, copies of all the documents must be served on the respondents with the appellant's notice.

(Paragraph 5.6 provides for certain documents to be filed with an appellant's notice.)

Amendment of Appeal Notice

5.25 An appeal notice may be amended with permission. Such an application to amend and any application in opposition will normally be dealt with at the hearing unless that course would cause unnecessary expense or delay in which case a request should be made for the application to amend to be heard in advance.

PROCEDURE AFTER PERMISSION IS OBTAINED

6.1 This paragraph sets out the procedure where:

(1) permission to appeal is given by the appeal court; or

(2) the appellant's notice is filed in the appeal court and-

    (*a*) permission was given by the lower court; or

    (*b*) permission is not required.

6.2 If the appeal court gives permission to appeal, copies of all the documents referred to at paragraph 5.6 must be served on the respondents within 7 days of receiving the order giving permission to appeal.

(Part 6 (service of documents) provides rules on service.)

6.3 The appeal court will send the parties-

(1) notification of-

    (*a*) the date of the hearing or the period of time (the "listing window") during which the appeal is likely to be heard; and

    (*b*) in the Court of Appeal, the date by which the appeal will be heard (the "hear by date");

(2) where permission is granted by the appeal court a copy of the order giving permission to appeal; and

(3) any other directions given by the court.

Appeal Questionnaire in the Court of Appeal

6.4 The Court of Appeal will send an Appeal Questionnaire to the appellant when it notifies him of the matters referred to in paragraph 6.3.

6.5 The appellant must complete and lodge the Appeal Questionnaire within 14 days of the date of the letter of notification of the matters in paragraph 6.3. The Listing Questionnaire must contain:

(1) if the appellant is legally represented, the advocate's time estimate for the hearing of the appeal;

(2) where a transcript of evidence is relevant to the appeal, confirmation that a transcript of evidence has been ordered where this is not already in the bundle of documents;

(3) confirmation that copies of the appeal bundle are being prepared and will be held ready for the use of the Court of Appeal and an undertaking that they will be supplied to the court on request. For the purpose of these bundles photocopies of the transcripts will be accepted

(4) confirmation that copies of the Appeal Questionnaire and the appeal bundle have been served on the respondents and the date of that service;

Time estimates

6.6 The time estimate included in an Appeal Questionnaire must be that of the advocate who will argue the appeal. It should exclude the time required by the court to give judgment. If the respondent disagrees with the time estimate, the respondent must inform the court within 7 days of receipt of the Appeal Questionnaire . In the absence of such notification the respondent will be deemed to have accepted the estimate proposed on behalf of the appellant.

RESPONDENT

7.1 A respondent who wishes to ask the appeal court to vary the order of the lower court in any way must appeal and permission will be required on the same basis as for an appellant.

7.2 A respondent who wishes only to request that the appeal court upholds the judgment or order of the lower court whether for the reasons given in the lower court or otherwise does not make an appeal and does not therefore require permission to appeal in accordance with rule 52.3(1).

7.3 A respondent who wishes to appeal or who wishes to ask the appeal court to uphold the order of the lower court for reasons different from or additional to those given by the lower court must file a respondent's notice.

Time limits

7.4 The time limits for filing a respondent's notice are set out in rule 52.5 (4) and (5).

7.5 Where an extension of time is required the extension must be requested in the respondent's notice and the reasons why the respondent failed to act within the specified time must be included.

Respondent's skeleton argument

7.6 The respondent must provide a skeleton argument for the court in all cases where he proposes to address arguments to the court. The respondent's skeleton argument may be included within a respondent's notice. Where a skeleton argument is included within a respondent's notice it will not form part of the notice for the purposes of rule 52.8.

7.7 Where the skeleton argument is not included within a respondent's notice it should be lodged and served no later than 21 days after the respondent receives the appellant's skeleton argument.

(Rule 52.5(4) sets out the period for filing and serving a respondent's notice)

Content of skeleton arguments

7.8 A respondent's skeleton argument must conform to the directions at paragraphs 5.10 and 5.11 above with any necessary modifications. It should, where appropriate, answer the arguments set out in the appellant's skeleton argument.

Applications within respondent's notices

7.9 A respondent may include an application within a respondent's notice in accordance with paragraph 5.5 above.

Filing respondent's notices and skeleton arguments

7.10 The respondent must lodge the following documents with his respondent's notice in every case:

(1) two additional copies of the respondent's notice for the appeal court

(2) one copy each for the appellant and any other respondents; and

(3) two copies of any skeleton arguments.

7.11 If the respondent does not file a respondent's notice, he will not be entitled, except with the permission of the court, to rely on any ground not relied on in the lower court.

7.12 If the respondent wishes to rely on any documents in addition to those filed by the appellant he must prepare a supplemental bundle and lodge it at the appeal court with his respondent's notice. He must serve a copy of the supplemental bundle at the same time as serving the respondent's notice on the persons required to be served in accordance with rule 52.5(6).

7.13 The respondent's notice and any skeleton argument must be served in accordance with the time limits set out in rule 52.5(6) except [where] this requirement is modified by paragraph 7.7.

APPEALS TO THE HIGH COURT

8.1
(Appeal from a county court)

Re-hearings

9.1 The hearing of an appeal will not be a re-hearing (as opposed to a review of the decision of the lower court) unless it is required by any enactment or rule or the appeal is from the decision of a minister, person or other body and the minister, person or other body-
(1) did not hold a hearing to come to that decision; or
(2) held a hearing to come to that decision, but the procedure adopted did not provide for the consideration of evidence.

Appeals Transferred to the Court of Appeal

10.1 Where an appeal is transferred to the Court of Appeal under rule 52.14 the Court of Appeal may give such additional directions as are considered appropriate.

Applications

11.1 Where a party to an appeal makes an application whether in an appeal notice or by Part 23 application notice, the provisions of Part 23 will apply.

11.2 The applicant must file the following documents with the notice
(1) one additional copy of the application notice for the appeal court and one copy for each of the respondents;
(2) where applicable a sealed copy of the order which is the subject of the main appeal;
(3) a bundle of documents in support which should include:
  (*a*) the Part 23 application notice
  (*b*) any witness statements and affidavits filed in support of the application notice
  (*c*) the documents specified in paragraph 5.6 (6) [*5.6 (7)*]above in so far as they have not already been filed with the appellant's notice.

DISPOSING OF APPLICATIONS OR APPEALS BY CONSENT

Dismissal of applications or appeals by consent

12.1 These paragraphs do not apply where any party to the proceedings is a child or patient.

12.2 Where an appellant does not wish to pursue an application or an appeal, he may request the appeal court for an order that his application or appeal be dismissed. Such a request must contain a statement that the appellant is not a child or patient. If such a request is granted it will usually be on the basis that the appellant pays the costs of the application or appeal.

12.3 If the appellant wishes to have the application or appeal dismissed without costs, his request must be accompanied by a consent signed by the respondent or his legal representative stating that the respondent is not a child or patient and consents to the dismissal of the application or appeal without costs.

12.4 Where a settlement has been reached disposing of the application or appeal, the parties may make a joint request to the court stating that none of them is a child or patient, and asking that the application or appeal be dismissed by consent. If the request is granted the application or appeal will be dismissed.

Allowing unopposed appeals or applications on paper

13.1 The appeal court will not make an order allowing an application or appeal unless satisfied that the decision of the lower court was wrong. Where the appeal court is requested by all parties to allow an application or an appeal the court may consider the request on the papers. The request should state that none of the parties is a child or patient and set out the relevant history of the proceedings and the matters relied on as justifying the proposed order and be accompanied by a copy of the proposed order.

Procedure for Structured settlements and consent orders involving a child or patient

13.2 Settlements relating to appeals and applications where one of the parties is a child or a patient; and structured settlements which are agreed upon at the appeal stage require the court's approval.

Child

13.3 In cases involving a child a copy of the proposed order signed by the parties' solicitors should be sent to the appeal court, together with an opinion from the advocate acting on behalf of the child.

Patient

13.4 Where a party is a patient the same procedure will be adopted, but the documents filed should also include any relevant reports prepared for the Court of Protection and a document evidencing formal approval by that court where required.

Structured settlements

13.5 Where a structured settlement has been negotiated in a case which is under appeal the documents filed should include those which would be required in the case of a structured settlement dealt with at first instance. Details can be found in the Practice Direction which supplements CPR Part 40.

SUMMARY ASSESSMENT OF COSTS

14.1 Costs are likely to be assessed by way of summary assessment at the following hearings:
(1) contested directions hearings;
(2) applications for permission to appeal at which the respondent is present;
(3) dismissal list hearings in the Court of Appeal at which the respondent is present;
(4) appeals from case management decisions; and
(5) appeals listed for less than one day.

14.2 Parties attending any of the hearings referred to in paragraph 13.1 should be prepared to deal with the summary assessment.

OTHER SPECIAL PROVISIONS REGARDING THE COURT OF APPEAL

15.1–15.14

SECTION II – GENERAL PROVISIONS ABOUT STATUTORY APPEALS AND APPEALS BY WAY OF CASE STATED

16.1 This section of this practice direction contains general provisions about statutory appeals (paragraphs 16.1-16.6) and appeals by way of case stated (paragraphs 17.1–17.20).

16.2 Where any of the provisions in this section provide for documents to be filed at the appeal court, these documents are in addition to any documents required under Part 52 or section I of this practice direction.

STATUTORY APPEALS

17.1 This part of this section-
(1) applies where under any enactment an appeal (other than by way of case stated) lies to the court from a Minister of State, government department, tribunal or other person ("statutory appeals"); and
(2) is subject to any provision about a specific category of appeal in any enactment or Section III of this practice direction.

Part 52

17.2 Part 52 applies to statutory appeals with the following amendments:

Filing of appellant's notice

17.3 The appellant must file the appellant's notice at the appeal court within 28 days after the date of the decision of the lower court he wishes to appeal.

17.4 Where a statement of the reasons for a decision is given later than the notice of that decision, the period for filing the appellant's notice is calculated from the date on which the statement is received by the appellant.

Service of appellant's notice

17.5 In addition to the respondents to the appeal, the appellant must serve the appellant's notice in accordance with rule 52.4(3) on the chairman of the tribunal, Minister of State, government department or other person from whose decision the appeal is brought.

Right of Minister etc. to be heard on the appeal

17.6 Where the appeal is from an order or decision of a Minister of State or government department, the Minister or department, as the case may be, is entitled to attend the hearing and to make representations to the court.

APPEALS BY WAY OF CASE STATED

18.1 This part of this section-
(1) applies where under any enactment-

(*a*) an appeal lies to the court by way of case stated; or
(*b*) a question of law may be referred to the court by way of case stated; and
(2) is subject to any provision about [*to*] a specific category of appeal in any enactment or Section III of this practice direction.

Part 52

18.2 Part 52 applies to appeals by way of case stated subject to the following amendments.

Case stated by Crown Court or Magistrates' Court

Application to state a case

18.3 The procedure for applying to the Crown Court or a Magistrates' Court to have a case stated for the opinion of the High Court is set out in the Crown Court Rules 1982 and the Magistrates' Courts Rules 1981 respectively.

Filing of appellant's notice

18.4 The appellant must file the appellant's notice at the appeal court within 10 days after he receives the stated case.

Documents to be lodged

18.5 The appellant must lodge the following documents with his appellant's notice:
(1) the stated case;
(2) a copy of the judgment, order or decision in respect of which the case has been stated; and
(3) where the judgment, order or decision in respect of which the case has been stated was itself given or made on appeal, a copy of the judgment, order or decision appealed from.

Service of appellant's notice

18.6 The appellant must serve the appellant's notice and accompanying documents on all respondents within 4 days after they are filed or lodged at the appeal court.

Case stated by Minister, government department, tribunal or other person

18.7–18.20

Extradition

19.1 Paragraphs 18.3 to 18.6 apply to appeals by case stated under-
(1) section 7 of the Criminal Justice Act 1988; and
(2) section 7A of the Fugitive Offenders Act 1967,
and references in those paragraphs to appellant and respondent shall be construed as references to the requesting state and the person whose surrender is sought respectively.

19.2 An application for an order under either of the sections mentioned in paragraph 19.1 or under section 2A of the Backing of Warrants (Republic of Ireland) Act 1965 requiring a court to state a case must be made in accordance with paragraphs 18.17 to 18.20 and the references in those paragraphs to a tribunal and the secretary of a tribunal shall be construed as references to the court and the clerk of the court respectively.

SECTION III – PROVISIONS ABOUT SPECIFIC APPEALS[1]

20.1–20.3

---

1. None of the appeals specified relate to the jurisdiction of magistrates.

APPEALS TO THE COURT OF APPEAL[1]

21.1–21.10

---

1. None of the provisions specified relate to the jurisdiction of magistrates.

APPEALS TO THE HIGH COURT – QUEEN'S BENCH AND CHANCERY DIVISIONS

22.1–23.9

---

1. None of the provisions specified relate to the jurisdiction of magistrates.

APPEALS TO THE HIGH COURT – CHANCERY DIVISION

24.1

---

1. None of the provisions specified relate to the jurisdiction of magistrates.

PART 54[1]

I JUDICIAL REVIEW AND STATUTORY REVIEW

1–6563X   54.1. Scope and interpretation.   (1) This Section of this Part contains rules about judicial review.

(2) In this Section—

(a) a "claim for judicial review" means a claim to review the lawfulness of—

  (i) an enactment; or

  (ii) a decision, action or failure to act in relation to the exercise of a public function.

(b) (*revoked*)

(c) (*revoked*)

(d) (*revoked*)

(e) "the judicial review procedure" means the Part 8 procedure as modified by this Section;

(f) "interested party" means any person (other than the claimant and defendant) who is directly affected by the claim; and

(g) "court" means the High Court, unless otherwise stated.

(Rule 8.1(6)(*b*) provides that a rule or practice direction may, in relation to a specified type of proceedings, disapply or modify any of the rules set out in Part 8 as they apply to those proceedings).

---

1. The Practice Direction supplementing Part 54 is reproduced in this PART, post.

1–6563Y   54.2. When this Section must be used.   The judicial review procedure must be used in a claim for judicial review where the claimant is seeking—

(a) a mandatory order;

(b) a prohibiting order;

(c) a quashing order; or

(d) an injunction under section 30 of the Supreme Court Act 1981 (restraining a person from acting in any office in which he is not entitled to act).

1–6563Z   54.3. When this Section may be used.   (1) The judicial review procedure may be used in a claim for judicial review where the claimant is seeking—

(a) a declaration; or

(b) an injunction.

(Section 31(2) of the Supreme Court Act 1981 sets out the circumstances in which the court may grant a declaration or injunction in a claim for judicial review)

(Where the claimant is seeking a declaration or injunction in addition to one of the remedies listed in rule 54.2, the judicial review procedure must be used)

(2) A claim for judicial review may include a claim for damages, restitution or the recovery of a sum due but may not seek such a remedy alone.

(Section 31(4) of the Supreme Court Act 1981 sets out the circumstances in which the court may award damages, restitution or the recovery of a sum due on a claim for judicial review)

1–6563ZA   54.4. Permission required.   The court's permission to proceed is required in a claim for judicial review whether started under this Section or transferred to the Administrative Court.

1–6563ZB   54.5. Time limit for filing claim form.   (1) The claim form must be filed—

(a) promptly; and

(b) in any event not later than 3 months after the grounds to make the claim first arose.

(2) The time limit in this rule may not be extended by agreement between the parties.

(3) This rule does not apply when any other enactment specifies a shorter time limit for making the claim for judicial review.

1–6563ZC   54.6. Claim form.   (1) In addition to the matters set out in rule 8.2 (contents of the claim form) the claimant must also state—

(a) the name and address of any person he considers to be an interested party;

(b) that he is requesting permission to proceed with a claim for judicial review; and

(c) any remedy (including any interim remedy) he is claiming.

(Part 25 sets out how to apply for an interim remedy)

(2) The claim form must be accompanied by the documents required by the relevant practice direction.

1–6563ZD   54.7. Service of claim form.   The claim form must be served on—

(a) the defendant; and

(b) unless the court otherwise directs, any person the claimant considers to be an interested party,

within 7 days after the date of issue.

1–6563ZE   54.8. Acknowledgement of service.   (1) Any person served with the claim form who wishes to take part in the judicial review must file an acknowledgement of service in the relevant practice form in accordance with the following provisions of this rule.

(2) Any acknowledgement of service must be—

(*a*) filed not more than 21 days after service of the claim form; and

(*b*) served on—

    (i) the claimant; and

    (ii) subject to any direction under rule 54.7(*b*), any other person named in the claim form,

as soon as practicable and, in any event, not later than 7 days after it is filed.

(3) The time limits under this rule may not be extended by agreement between the parties.

(4) The acknowledgement of service—

(*a*) must—

    (i) where the person filing it intends to contest the claim, set out a summary of his grounds for doing so; and

    (ii) state the name and address of any person the person filing it considers to be an interested party; and

(*b*) may include or be accompanied by an application for directions.

(5) Rule 10.3(2) does not apply.

1–6563ZF   54.9. Failure to file acknowledgement of service.   (1) Where a person served with the claim form has failed to file an acknowledgement of service in accordance with rule 54.8, he—

(*a*) may not take part in a hearing to decide whether permission should be given unless the court allows him to do so; but

(*b*) provided he complies with rule 54.14 or any other direction of the court regarding the filing and service of—

    (i) detailed grounds for contesting the claim or supporting it on additional grounds; and

    (ii) any written evidence,

may take part in the hearing of the judicial review.

(2) Where that person takes part in the hearing of the judicial review, the court may take his failure to file an acknowledgement of service into account when deciding what order to make about costs.

(3) Rule 8.4 does not apply.

1–6563ZG   54.10. Permission given.   (1) Where permission to proceed is given the court may also give directions.

(2) Directions under paragraph (1) may include a stay of proceedings to which the claim relates.

(Rule 3.7 provides a sanction for the non-payment of the fee payable when permission to proceed has been given)

---

1. The grant of permission whether made on the papers or after oral argument, will be deemed to contain an order that costs be costs in the case: *Practice Note (Administrative Court)* [2004] 2 All ER 994.

1–6563ZH   54.11. Service of order giving or refusing permission.   The court will serve—

(*a*) the order giving or refusing permission; and

(*b*) any directions,

on—

    (i) the claimant;

    (ii) the defendant; and

    (iii) any other person who filed an acknowledgement of service.

1–6563ZI   54.12. Permission decision without a hearing.   (1) This rule applies where the court, without a hearing—

(*a*) refuses permission to proceed; or

(*b*) gives permission to proceed—

    (i) subject to conditions; or

    (ii) on certain grounds only.

(2) The court will serve its reasons for making the decision when it serves the order giving or refusing permission in accordance with rule 54.11.

(3) The claimant may not appeal but may request the decision to be reconsidered at a hearing.

(4) A request under paragraph (3) must be filed within 7 days after service of the reasons under paragraph (2).

(5) The claimant, defendant and any other person who has filed an acknowledgement of service will be given at least 2 days' notice of the hearing date.

1–6563ZJ   54.13. Defendant etc may not apply to set aside.   Neither the defendant nor any other person served with the claim form may apply to set aside an order giving permission to proceed.

1–6563ZK   54.14. Response.   (1) A defendant and any other person served with the claim form who wishes to contest the claim or support it on additional grounds must file and serve—

    (*a*)   detailed grounds for contesting the claim or supporting it on additional grounds; and

    (*b*)   any written evidence,

within 35 days after service of the order giving permission.

    (2) The following rules do not apply—

    (*a*)   rule 8.5(3) and 8.5(4) (defendant to file and serve written evidence at the same time as acknowledgement of service); and

    (*b*)   rule 8.5(5) and 8.5(6) (claimant to file and serve any reply within 14 days).

1–6563ZL   54.15. Where claimant seeks to rely on additional grounds.   The court's permission is required if a claimant seeks to rely on grounds other than those for which he has been given permission to proceed.

1–6563ZM   54.16. Evidence.   (1) Rule 8.6 does not apply.

    (2) No written evidence may be relied on unless—

    (*a*)   it has been served in accordance with any—

        (i)   rule under this Section; or

        (ii)   direction of the court; or

    (*b*)   the court gives permission.

1–6563ZN   54.17. Court's powers to hear any person.   (1) Any person may apply for permission—

    (*a*)   to file evidence; or

    (*b*)   make representations at the hearing of the judicial review.

    (2) An application under paragraph (1) should be made promptly.

1–6563ZO   54.18. Judicial review may be decided without a hearing.   The court may decide the claim for judicial review without a hearing where all the parties agree.

1–6563ZP   54.19. Court's powers in respect of quashing orders.   (1) This rule applies where the court makes a quashing order in respect of the decision to which the claim relates.

    (2) The court may—

    (*a*)   remit the matter to the decision-maker; and

    (*b*)   direct it to reconsider the matter and reach a decision in accordance with the judgment of the court.

    (3) Where the court considers that there is no purpose to be served in remitting the matter to the decision-maker it may, subject to any statutory provision, take the decision itself.

    (Where a statutory power is given to a tribunal, person or other body it may be the case that the court cannot take the decision itself)

1–6563ZQ   54.20. Transfer.   The court may—

    (*a*)   order a claim to continue as if it had not been started under this Section; and

    (*b*)   where it does so, give directions about the future management of the claim.

    (Part 30 (transfer) applies to transfers to and from the Administrative Court)

II Sᴛᴀᴛᴜᴛᴏᴋᴘ Rᴇᴠᴉᴇᴡ ᴜɴᴅᴇᴋ ᴛʜᴇ Nᴀᴛɪᴏɴᴀʟɪᴛʏ, Iᴍᴍɪɢʀᴀᴛɪᴏɴ ᴀɴᴅ Aѕʏʟᴜᴍ Aᴄᴛ 2002

STATUTORY REVIEW UNDER THE NATIONALITY, IMMIGRATION AND ASYLUM ACT 2002

III APPLICATIONS FOR STATUTORY REVIEW UNDER SECTION 103A OF THE NATIONALITY, IMMIGRATION AND ASYLUM ACT 2002

PRACTICE DIRECTION – JUDICIAL REVIEW

THIS PRACTICE DIRECTION SUPPLEMENTS PART 54.

1–6563ZR   1.1 In addition to Part 54 and this practice direction attention is drawn to:

    section 31 of the Supreme Court Act 1981; and

    the Human Rights Act 1998

THE COURT

    2.1 Part 54 claims for judicial review are dealt with in the Administrative Court.

    2.2 Where the claim is proceeding in the Administrative Court in London, documents must be filed at the Administrative Court Office, the Royal Courts of Justice, Strand, London, WC2A 2LL.

    2.3 Where the claim is proceeding in the Administrative Court in Wales (see paragraph 3.1), documents must be filed at the Law Courts, Cathays Park, Cardiff, CF10 3PG.

Urgent applications

    2.4 Where urgency makes it necessary for the claim for judicial review to be made outside London or Cardiff, the Administrative Court Office in London should be consulted (if necessary, by telephone) prior to filing the claim form.

JUDICIAL REVIEW CLAIMS IN WALES

3.1 A claim for judicial review may be brought in the Administrative Court in Wales where the claim or any remedy sought involves:

(1) a devolution issue arising out of the Government of Wales Act 1998; or

(2) an issue concerning the National Assembly for Wales, the Welsh executive, or any Welsh public body (including a Welsh local authority) (whether or not it involves a devolution issue).

3.2 Such claims may also be brought in the Administrative Court at the Royal Courts of Justice.

RULE 54.5 – TIME LIMIT FOR FILING CLAIM FORM

4.1 Where the claim is for a quashing order in respect of a judgment, order or conviction, the date when the grounds to make the claim first arose, for the purposes of rule 54.5(1)(*b*), is the date of that judgment, order or conviction.

RULE 54.6 – CLAIM FORM

Interested parties

5.1 Where the claim for judicial review relates to proceedings in a court or tribunal, any other parties to those proceedings must be named in the claim form as interested parties under rule 54.6(1)(*a*) (and therefore served with the claim form under rule 54.7(*b*)).

5.2 For example, in a claim by a defendant in a criminal case in the Magistrates or Crown Court for judicial review of a decision in that case, the prosecution must always be named as an interested party.

Human rights

5.3 Where the claimant is seeking to raise any issue under the Human Rights Act 1998, or seeks a remedy available under that Act, the claim form must include the information required by paragraph 16 of the practice direction supplementing Part 16.

Devolution issues

5.4 Where the claimant intends to raise a devolution issue, the claim form must:

(1) specify that the applicant wishes to raise a devolution issue and identify the relevant provisions of the Government of Wales Act 1998, the Northern Ireland Act 1998 or the Scotland Act 1998; and

(2) contain a summary of the facts, circumstances and points of law on the basis of which it is alleged that a devolution issue arises.

5.5 In this practice direction "devolution issue" has the same meaning as in paragraph 1, schedule 8 to the Government of Wales Act 1998; paragraph 1, schedule 10 to the Northern Ireland Act 1998; and paragraph 1, schedule 6 of the Scotland Act 1998.

Claim form

5.6 The claim form must include or be accompanied by-

(1) a detailed statement of the claimant's grounds for bringing the claim for judicial review;

(2) a statement of the facts relied on;

(3) any application to extend the time limit for filing the claim form;

(4) any application for directions; and

(5) a time estimate for the hearing.

5.7 In addition, the claim form must be accompanied by

(1) any written evidence in support of the claim or application to extend time;

(2) a copy of any order that the claimant seeks to have quashed;

(3) where the claim for judicial review relates to a decision of a court or tribunal, an approved copy of the reasons for reaching that decision;

(4) copies of any documents on which the claimant proposes to rely;

(5) copies of any relevant statutory material;

(6) a list of essential documents for advance reading by the court (with page references to the passages relied on); and

5.8 Where it is not possible to file all the above documents, the claimant must indicate which documents have not been filed and the reasons why they are not currently available.

Bundle of documents

5.9 The claimant must file two copies of a paginated and indexed bundle containing all the documents referred to in paragraphs 4.6 and 4.7.

5.10 Attention is drawn to rules 8.5(1) and 8.5(7).

RULE 54.7 – SERVICE OF CLAIM FORM

6.1 Except as required by rules 54.11 or 54.12(2), the Administrative Court will not serve documents and service must be effected by the parties.

RULE 54.8 – ACKNOWLEDGMENT OF SERVICE

7.1 Attention is drawn to rule 8.3(2) and the relevant practice direction and to rule 10.5.

RULE 54.10 – PERMISSION GIVEN

Directions

8.1 Case management directions under rule 54.10(1) may include directions about serving the claim form and any evidence on other persons.

8.2 Where a claim is made under the Human Rights Act 1998, a direction may be made for giving notice to the Crown or joining the Crown as a party. Attention is drawn to rule 19.4A and paragraph 6 of the Practice Direction supplementing Section I of Part 19.

8.3 A direction may be made for the hearing of the claim for judicial review to be held outside London or Cardiff. Before making any such direction the judge will consult the judge in charge of the Administrative Court as to its feasibility.

Permission without a hearing

8.4 The court will generally, in the first instance, consider the question of permission without a hearing.

Permission hearing

8.5 Neither the defendant nor any other interested party need attend a hearing on the question of permission unless the court directs otherwise.

8.6 Where the defendant or any party does attend a hearing, the court will not generally make an order for costs against the claimant.

RULE 54.11 – SERVICE OF ORDER GIVING OR REFUSING PERMISSION

9.1 An order refusing permission or giving it subject to conditions or on certain grounds only must set out or be accompanied by the court's reasons for coming to that decision.

RULE 54.14 – RESPONSE

10.1 Where the party filing the detailed grounds intends to rely on documents not already filed, he must file a paginated bundle of those documents when he files the detailed grounds.

RULE 54.15 – WHERE CLAIMANT SEEKS TO RELY ON ADDITIONAL GROUNDS

11.1 Where the claimant intends to apply to rely on additional grounds at the hearing of the claim for judicial review, he must give notice to the court and to any other person served with the claim form no later than 7 clear days before the hearing (or the warned date where appropriate).

RULE 54.16 – EVIDENCE

12.1 Disclosure is not required unless the court orders otherwise.

RULE 54.17 – COURT'S POWERS TO HEAR ANY PERSON

13.1 Where all the parties consent, the court may deal with an application under rule 54.17 without a hearing.

13.2 Where the court gives permission for a person to file evidence or make representations at the hearing of the claim for judicial review, it may do so on conditions and may give case management directions.

RULE 54.20 – TRANSFER

14.1 Attention is drawn to rule 30.5.

14.2 In deciding whether a claim is suitable for transfer to the Administrative Court, the court will consider whether it raises issues of public law to which Part 54 should apply.

Skeleton arguments

15.1 The claimant must file and serve a skeleton argument not less than 21 working days before the date of the hearing of the judicial review (or the warned date).

15.2 The defendant and any other party wishing to make representations at the hearing of the judicial review must file and serve a skeleton argument not less than 14 working days before the date of the hearing of the judicial review (or the warned date).

15.3 Skeleton arguments must contain:

(1) a time estimate for the complete hearing, including delivery of judgment;

(2) a list of issues;

(3) a list of the legal points to be taken (together with any relevant authorities with page references to the passages relied on);

(4) a chronology of events (with page references to the bundle of documents (see paragraph 16.1);

(5) a list of essential documents for the advance reading of the court (with page references to

the passages relied on) (if different from that filed with the claim form) and a time estimate for that reading; and

(6) a list of persons referred to.

Bundle of documents to be filed

16.1 The claimant must file a paginated and indexed bundle of all relevant documents required for the hearing of the judicial review when he files his skeleton argument.

16.2 The bundle must also include those documents required by the defendant and any other party who is to make representations at the hearing.

Agreed final order

17.1 If the parties agree about the final order to be made in a claim for judicial review, the claimant must file at the court a document (with 2 copies) signed by all the parties setting out the terms of the proposed agreed order together with a short statement of the matters relied on as justifying the proposed agreed order and copies of any authorities or statutory provisions relied on.

17.2 The court will consider the documents referred to in paragraph 17.1 and will make the order if satisfied that the order should be made.

17.3 If the court is not satisfied that the order should be made, a hearing date will be set.

17.4 Where the agreement relates to an order for costs only, the parties need only file a document signed by all the parties setting out the terms of the proposed order.

SCHEDULE 1

RSC ORDER 54[1]
APPLICATIONS FOR WRIT OF HABEAS CORPUS

1–6564 1. Application for writ of habeas corpus ad subjiciendum. (1) Subject to rule 11, an application for a writ of habeas corpus ad subjiciendum shall be made to a judge in court, except that—

(a) it shall be made to a Divisional Court of the Queen's Bench Division if the Court so directs;
(b) it may be made to a judge otherwise than in court at any time when no judge is sitting in court; and
(c) any application on behalf of a minor must be made in the first instance to a judge otherwise than in court.

(2) An application for such writ may be made ex parte and, subject to paragraph (3), must be supported by an affidavit by the person restrained showing that it is made at his instance and setting out the nature of the restraint.

(3) Where the person restrained is unable for any reason to make the affidavit required by paragraph (2), the affidavit may be made by some other person on his behalf and that affidavit must state that the person restrained is unable to make the affidavit himself and for what reason.

---

1. Order 54 is printed as amended by SI 1971/1269 and SI 1980/2000.

1–6564A 2. Power of Court to whom ex parte application made. (1) The Court or judge to whom an application under rule 1 is made ex parte may make an order forthwith for the writ to issue, or may—

(a) where the application is made to a judge otherwise than in court, direct that an originating summons for the writ be issued, or that an application therefor be made by originating motion to a Divisional Court or to a judge in court;
(b) where the application is made to a judge in court, adjourn the application so that notice thereof may be given, or direct that an application be made by originating motion to a Divisional Court;
(c) where the application is made to a Divisional Court, adjourn the application so that notice thereof may be given.

(2) The summons or notice of the motion must be served on the person against whom the issue of the writ is sought and on such other persons as the Court or judge may direct, and, unless the Court or judge otherwise directs, there must be at least 8 clear days between the service of the summons or notice and the date named therein for the hearing of the application.

1–6564B 3. Copies of affidavits to be supplied. Every party to an application under rule 1 must supply to every other party on demand and on payment of the proper charges copies of the affidavits which he proposes to use at the hearing of the application.

1–6564C 4. Power to order release of person restrained. (1) Without prejudice to rule 2(1), the Court or judge hearing an application for a writ of habeas corpus ad subjiciendum may in its or his discretion order that the person restrained be released, and such order shall be a sufficient warrant to any governor of a prison, constable or other person for the release of the person under restraint.

(2) Where such an application in a criminal cause or matter is heard by a judge and the judge does not order the release of the person restrained, he shall direct that the application be made by originating motion to a Divisional Court of the Queen's Bench Division.

1–6564D 5. Directions as to return to writ. Where a writ of habeas corpus ad subjiciendum is ordered to issue, the Court or judge by whom the order is made shall give directions as to the Court or judge before whom, and the date on which, the writ is returnable.

1–6564E 6. Service of writ and notice. (1) Subject to paragraphs (2) and (3), a writ of habeas corpus ad subjiciendum must be served personally on the person to whom it is directed.

(2) If it is not possible to serve such writ personally, or if it is directed to a governor of a prison or other public official, it must be served by leaving it with a servant or agent of the person to whom the writ is directed at the place where the person restrained is confined or restrained.

(3) If the writ is directed to more than one person, the writ must be served in manner provided by this rule

on the person first named in the writ, and copies must be served on each of the other persons in the same manner as the writ.

(4) There must be served with the writ a notice (in Form No 90 in Appendix A) stating the Court or judge before whom and the date on which the person restrained is to be brought and that in default of obedience proceedings for committal of the party disobeying will be taken.

1–6564F 7. Return to the writ. (1) The return to a writ of habeas corpus ad subjiciendum must be indorsed on or annexed to the writ and must state all the causes of the detainer of the person restrained.

(2) The return may be amended, or another return substituted therefor, by leave of the Court or judge before whom the writ is returnable.

1–6564G 8. Procedure at hearing of writ. When a return to a writ of habeas corpus ad subjiciendum is made, the return shall first be read, and motion then made for discharging or remanding the person restrained or amending or quashing the return, and where that person is brought up in accordance with the writ, his counsel shall be heard first, then the counsel for the Crown, and then one counsel for the person restrained in reply.

1–6564H 9. Bringing up prisoner to give evidence, etc. (1) An application for a writ of habeas corpus ad testificandum or of habeas corpus ad respondendum must be made on affidavit to a judge in chambers.

(2) An application for an order to bring up a prisoner, otherwise than by writ of habeas corpus, to give evidence in any cause or matter, civil or criminal, before any court, tribunal or justice must be made on affidavit to a judge in chambers.

1–6564I 10. Form of writ. A writ of habeas corpus must be in Form No 89, 91 or 92 in Appendix A, whichever is appropriate.

1–6564J 11. Applications relative to the custody, etc, of minors. An application by a parent or guardian of a minor for a writ of habeas corpus ad subjiciendum relative to the custody, care or control of the minor must be made in the Family Division, and this Order shall accordingly apply to such applications with the appropriate modifications.

1–6564JA
]
                                Form No 87
                              [(Royal Arms)
        Notice of motion for writ of habeas corpus ad subjiciendum
        (O 54 r 2)
        In the High Court of Justice19No

        Queen's Bench Division [(or Family Division as the case may be)].

        In the matter of A.B.
        and
        In the matter of an application for a writ
of habeas corpus ad subjiciendum
        Take notice that pursuant to the direction of the Honourable Mr. Justice(or a Divisional Court), the Queen's Bench Division [(or Family Division as the case may be)] of the High Court of Justice will be moved on the   day of   19   , or so soon thereafter as counsel can be heard on behalf of A.B. for an order that a writ of habeas corpus do issue directed toto have the body of the said A.B. before the Queen's Bench Division [(or Family Division as the case may be)] of the High Court of Justice at such time as the Court or judge may direct upon the grounds set out in the affidavits of the said A.B. and   and the exhibits therein respectively referred to used on the application to the Honourable Mr. Justice   (or the Divisional Court) for such order, copies of which affidavits and exhibits are served herewith.
        And that the costs of and occasioned by this motion be the applicant's to be taxed and paid by the respondents to the applicant.
        And take notice that on the hearing of this motion the said A.B. will use the affidavits of himself and the said and the exhibits therein referred to.
        Dated the   day of   19   .
          (Signed)
            of
          Solicitor for
        To
        Solicitor for

                              RSC ORDER 79[1]
                           CRIMINAL PROCEEDINGS

1–6564K 9. Bail. (1) Subject to the provisions of this rule, every application to the High Court in respect of bail in any criminal proceedings—

(a) where the defendant is in custody, must be made by summons before a judge in chambers to show cause why the defendant should not be granted bail;

(b) where the defendant has been granted bail, must be made by summons before a judge in chambers to show cause why the variation in the arrangements for bail proposed by the applicant should not be made.

(2) Subject to paragraph (5), the summons (in Form No 97 or 97A in Appendix A) must, at least 24 hours before the day named therein for the hearing, be served—

(a) where the application was made by the defendant, on the prosecutor and on the Director of Public Prosecutions, if the prosecution is being carried on by him;

(b) where the application was made by the prosecutor or a constable under section 3(8) of the Bail Act 1976, on the defendant;

and Order 32, rule 5, shall apply in relation to the summons.

(3) Subject to paragraph (5), every application must be supported by affidavit[2].

(4) Where a defendant in custody who desires to apply for bail is unable through lack of means to instruct a solicitor, he may give notice in writing to the judge in chambers stating his desire to apply for bail and

requesting that the official solicitor shall act for him in the application, and the judge may, if he thinks fit, assign the official solicitor to act for the applicant accordingly.

(5) Where the official solicitor has been so assigned the judge may, if he thinks fit, dispense with the requirements of paragraphs (1) to (3) and deal with the application in a summary manner.

(6) Where the judge in chambers by whom an application for bail in criminal proceedings is heard grants the defendant bail, the order must be in Form No 98 in Appendix A and a copy of the order shall be transmitted forthwith—

(*a*) where the proceedings in respect of the defendant have been transferred to the Crown Court for trial or where the defendant has been committed to the Crown Court to be sentenced or otherwise dealt with, to the appropriate officer of the Crown Court;

(*b*) in any other case, to the clerk of the court which committed the defendant.

(6A) The recognizance of any surety required as a condition of bail granted as aforesaid may, where the defendant is in a prison or other place of detention, be entered into before the governor or keeper of the prison or place as well as before the persons specified in section 8(4) of the Bail Act 1976.

(6B) Where under section 3(5) or (6) of the Bail Act 1976 a judge in chambers imposes a requirement to be complied with before a person's release on bail, the judge may give directions as to the manner in which and the person or persons before whom the requirement may be complied with.

(7) A person who in pursuance of an order for the grant of bail made by a judge under this rule proposes to enter into a recognizance or give security must, unless the judge otherwise directs, give notice (in Form No 100 in Appendix A) to the prosecutor at least 24 hours before he enters into the recognizance or complies with the requirement as aforesaid.

(8) Where in pursuance of such an order as aforesaid a recognizance is entered into or requirement complied with before any person, it shall be the duty of that person to cause the recognizance or, as the case may be, a statement of the requirement complied with to be transmitted forthwith—

(*a*) where the proceedings in respect of the defendant have been transferred to the Crown Court for trial or where the defendant has been committed to the Crown Court to be sentenced or otherwise dealt with, to the appropriate officer of the Crown Court;

(*b*) in any other case, to the clerk of the court which committed the defendant;

and a copy of such recognizance or statement shall at the same time be sent to the governor or keeper of the prison or other place of detention in which the defendant is detained, unless the recognizance was entered into or the requirement complied with before such governor or keeper.

(9) *Revoked.*

(10) An order by the judge in chambers varying the arrangements under which the defendant has been granted bail shall be in Form 98A in Appendix A and a copy of the order shall be transmitted forthwith—

(*a*) where the proceedings in respect of the defendant have been transferred to the Crown Court for trial or where the defendant has been committed to the Crown Court to be sentenced or otherwise dealt with, to the appropriate officer of the Crown Court;

(*b*) in any other case, to the clerk of the court which committed the defendant.

(11) Where in pursuance of an order of a judge in chambers or of the Crown Court a person is released on bail in any criminal proceeding pending the determination of an appeal to the High Court or House of Lords or an application for an order of certiorari, then, upon the abandonment of the appeal or application, or upon the decision of the High Court or House of Lords being given, any justice (being a justice acting for the same petty sessions area as the magistrates' court by which that person was convicted or sentenced) may issue process for enforcing the decision in respect of which such appeal or application was brought or, as the case may be, the decision of the High Court or House of Lords.

(12) If an applicant to the High Court in any criminal proceedings is refused bail by a judge in chambers, the applicant shall not be entitled to make a fresh application for bail to any other judge or to a Divisional Court[3].

(13) The record required by section 5 of the Bail Act 1976 to be made by the High Court shall be made by including in the file relating to the case in question a copy of the relevant order of the Court and shall contain the particulars set out in Form No 98 or 98A in Appendix A, whichever is appropriate, except that in the case of a decision to withhold bail the record shall be made by inserting a statement of the decision on the Court's copy of the relevant summons and including it in the file relating to the case in question.

(14) In the case of a person whose return is sought under the Fugitive Offenders Act 1967 or whose surrender is sought under Part I of the Criminal Justice Act 1988, this rule shall apply as if references to the defendant were references to that person and references to the prosecutor were references to the state seeking the return or surrender of that person.

---

1. Order 79 is printed as amended by SI 1967/1809, SI 1971/1955, SI 1978/251, SI 1989/1307 and SI 1995/2206.

2. See title Evidence in PART IX: PRECEDENTS AND FORMS, post. This will be sworn by anyone with knowledge of the case; where the defendant was represented by a solicitor on the unsuccessful bail application, that solicitor could appropriately do this in his own name, especially where the defendant is in a prison some distance away. Whichever of the following matters are relevant and known should be included: (i) present and anticipated charge(s); (ii) likely plea and any mitigation; (iii) defendant's personal circumstances and antecedents including previous convictions; (iv) complete history with dates of the proceedings so far; (v) statement of prosecution objections to bail and defendant's answers; (vi) defendant's proposals if released on bail including names and addresses of proposed sureties.

3. Rule 9(12) does not bar the exercise by a Crown Court judge of the Crown Court's jurisdiction in respect of bail under s 81(1) of the Supreme Court Act 1981, this PART, ante (*R v Crown Court at Reading, ex p Malik* [1981] QB 451, [1981] 1 All ER 249).

1–6564L

No 97
Summons to grant bail

[(Royal Arms)]
In the High Court of Justice,
Queen's Bench Division.
Let all parties concerned attend the judge in chambers on   the day of   19   at   o'clock on the hearing of an application on behalf of A.B. to be granted bail as to his commitment on the   day of   by a magistrates' court sitting at   (or by the Crown Court at   ) (or by the High Court).
Dated the   day of   19   .
This summons was taken out by   of   (agent for   of   ) solicitor for the said A.B.

1–6564M

No 97A

Summons to vary arrangements for bail in a criminal proceeding

(O 79 r 9)

[(Royal Arms)

]

In the High Court of Justice,

Queen's Bench Division.

Let all parties concerned attend the judge in chambers on the   day of   19   at   o'clock on the hearing of an application (on behalf of A.B.) (by   ) that the terms on which A.B. was granted bail by   on should be varied as follows—

Terms on which A.B. was granted bail—

Proposed variation—

Dated the   day of   19   .

This summons was taken out by (of   (agent for   of   ) solicitor for the said A.B.) ((as prosecutor) (a constable of   Police Force)).

No 98

Order of judge in chambers to release prisoner on bail

No 98A

Order of judge in chambers varying arrangements for bail

No 99

Order of Court of Appeal to admit prisoner to bail (*a*)

No 100

Notice of bail

---

1. This is under Ord 59 r 20 which relates to the release on bail of a person imprisoned for contempt of court, and makes provision for the taking of sureties by a Justice of the Peace.

RSC ORDER 109[1]

THE ADMINISTRATION OF JUSTICE ACT 1960

1–6564N   2. Appeals under s 13 of Act. (1) An appeal to a Divisional Court of the High Court under section 13 of the Administration of Justice Act 1960[2] shall be heard and determined by a Divisional Court of the Queen's Bench Division.

(2) *Revoked.*

(3) Order 55, rules 4(2) and 5, shall not apply in relation to an appeal to a Divisional Court under the said section 13.

(4) Unless the Court gives leave to the contrary, there shall be not more than 4 clear days between the date on which the order or decision appealed against was made and the day named in the notice of the originating motion for the hearing of the appeal.

(5) The notice must be served, and the appeal entered, not less than one clear day before the day named in the notice for the hearing of the appeal.

---

1. Order 109 is printed as amended by SI 1982/1111, amended by SI 1991/1884.
2. Section 13 relates to appeal in cases of contempt of court.

1–6564O   3. Release of appellant on bail. (1) Where, in the case of an appeal under section 13 of the Administration of Justice Act 1960 to a Divisional Court or to the House of Lords from a Divisional Court, the appellant is in custody, the High Court may order his release on his giving security (whether by recognizance, with or without sureties, or otherwise and for such reasonable sum as the Court may fix) for his appearance, within 10 days after the judgment of the Divisional Court, or, as the case may be, of the House of Lords, on the appeal shall have been given, before the court from whose order or decision the appeal is brought unless the order or decision is reversed by that judgment.

(2) Order 79, rule 9(1) to (6) and (8) shall apply in relation to an application to the High Court for bail pending an appeal under the said section 13 to which this rule applies, and to the admission of a person to bail in pursuance of an order made on the application, as they apply in relation to an application to that Court for bail in criminal proceedings, and to the admission of a person to bail in pursuance of an order made on the application, but with the substitution, for references to the defendant, of references to the appellant, and, for references to the prosecutor, of references to the proper officer of the court from whose order or decision the appeal is brought and to the parties to the proceedings in that court who are directly affected by the appeal.

RSC ORDER 115[1]

CONFISCATION AND FORFEITURE IN CONNECTION WITH CRIMINAL PROCEEDINGS

I. DRUG TRAFFICKING ACT 1994 AND THE CRIMINAL JUSTICE (INTERNATIONAL CO-OPERATION) ACT 1990

Interpretation

1–6564P   1. (1) In this Part of this Order, ''the Act'' means the Drug Trafficking Act 1994 and a section referred to by number means the section so numbered in the Act.

(2) Expressions used in this Part of this Order which are used in the Act have the same meanings in this Part of this Order as in the Act and include any extended meaning given by the Criminal Justice (Confiscation) (Northern Ireland) Order 1990.

---

1. This order was inserted into the Rules by SI 1986/2289 and has been amended by SI 1988/298, SI 1989/386 and 1307, SI 1991/184, SI 1995/2206 and 3316 amended by SI 2001/1388. Rules 15–34, except r 20, 21, 22(*c*) (so far as that rule enables the court to give directions and make declarations) and 23(*b*), only apply to proceedings to which Pt I of the Drug Trafficking Act 1994 applies.

Assignment of proceedings

1–6564Q   2. Subject to rule 12 the jurisdiction of the High Court under the Act shall be exercised by a judge of the Chancery Division or of the Queen's Bench Division in chambers.

Title of proceedings

1–6564R   2A. An originating process under this Part of this Order shall be entitled in the matter of the defendant, naming him, and in the matter of the Act, and all subsequent documents in the matter shall be so entitled.

Application for confiscation order

1–6564S 2B. (1) An application by the prosecutor for a confiscation order under section 19 shall be made by summons, where there have been proceedings against the defendant in the High Court, and shall otherwise be made by originating motion.

(2) The application shall be supported by an affidavit giving full particulars of the following matters—

(a) the grounds for believing that the defendant has died or absconded;

(b) the date or approximate date on which the defendant died or absconded;

(c) where the application is made under section 19(2), the offence or offences of which the defendant was convicted, and the date and place of conviction;

(d) where the application is made under section 19(4), the proceedings which have been initiated against the defendant (including particulars of the offence and the date and place of institution of those proceedings); and

(e) where the defendant is alleged to have absconded, the steps taken to contact him.

(3) The prosecutor's statement under section 11 shall be exhibited to the affidavit and shall include the following particulars—

(a) the name of the defendant;

(b) the name of the person by whom the statement is given;

(c) such information known to the prosecutor as is relevant to the determination whether the defendant has benefited from drug trafficking and to the assessment of the value of his proceeds of drug trafficking.

(4) Unless the Court otherwise orders, an affidavit under paragraph (2) may contain statements of information and belief, with their sources and grounds.

(5) The application and the affidavit in support shall be served not less than 7 days before the date fixed for the hearing of the application on—

(a) the defendant (or on the personal representatives of a deceased defendant);

(b) any person who the prosecutor reasonably believes is likely to be affected by the making of a confiscation order; and

(c) the receiver, where one has been appointed in the matter.

Application for restraint order or charging order

1–6564T 3. (1) An application for a restraint order under section 26 or for a charging order under section 27 (to either of which may be joined an application for the appointment of a receiver) may be made by the prosecutor ex parte by originating motion.

(2) An application under paragraph (1) shall be supported by an affidavit, which shall—

(a) give the grounds for the application; and

(b) to the best of the deponent's ability, give full particulars of the realisable property in respect of which the order is sought and specify the person or persons holding such property.

(3) Unless the Court otherwise directs, an affidavit under paragraph (2) may contain statements of information or belief with the sources and grounds thereof.

Restraint order and charging order

1–6564U 4. (1) A restraint order may be made subject to conditions and exceptions, including but not limited to conditions relating to the indemnifying of third parties against expenses incurred in complying with the order, and exceptions relating to living expenses and legal expenses of the defendant, but the prosecutor shall not be required to give an undertaking to abide by any order as to damages sustained by the defendant as a result of the restraint order.

(2) Unless the Court otherwise directs, a restraint order made ex parte shall have effect until a day which shall be fixed for the hearing inter partes of the application and a charging order shall be an order to show cause, imposing the charge until such day.

(3) Where a restraint order is made the prosecutor shall serve copies of the order and of the affidavit in support on the defendant and on all other named persons restrained by the order and shall notify all other persons or bodies affected by the order of its terms.

(4) Where a charging order is made the prosecutor shall, unless the Court otherwise directs, serve copies of the order and of the affidavit in support on the defendant and, where the property to which the order relates is held by another person, on that person and shall serve a copy of the order on such of the persons or bodies specified[1] in Order 50, rule 2(1)(b) to (d) as shall be appropriate.

---

1. That is:

2(1)

(b) where the order relates to securities other than securities in court, copies of the order shall also be served—

(i) in the case of government stock for which the Bank of England keeps the register, on the Bank of England;

(ii) in the case of government stock to which (i) does not apply, on the keeper of the register;

(iii) in the case of stock of any body incorporated within England and Wales, on that body, or, where the register is kept by the Bank of England, on the Bank of England;

(iv) in the case of stock of any body incorporated outside England and Wales or of any state or territory outside the United Kingdom, being stock registered in a register kept in England and Wales, on the keeper of the register;

(v) in the case of units of any unit trust in respect of which a register of the unit holders is kept in England and Wales, on the keeper of the register;

(c) where the order relates to a fund in court, a copy of the order shall be served on the Accountant General at the Court Funds Office; and

(d) where the order relates to an interest under a trust, copies of the order shall be served on such of the trustees as the Court may direct.

Discharge or variation of order

1–6564V 5. (1) Any person or body on whom a restraint order or a charging order is served or who is notified of such an order may apply by summons to discharge or vary the order.

(2) The summons and any affidavit in support shall be lodged with the court and served on the prosecutor and, where he is not the applicant, on the defendant, not less than two clear days before the date fixed for the hearing of the summons.

(3) Upon the court being notified that proceedings for the offences have been concluded or that the amount payment of which is secured by a charging order has been paid into court, any restraint or charging order, as the case may be, shall be discharged.

(4) The Court may also discharge a restraint order or a charging order upon receiving notice from the prosecutor that it is no longer appropriate for the restraint order or the charging order to remain in place.

Further application by prosecutor

1–6564W   **6.** (1) Where a restraint order or a charging order has been made the prosecutor may apply by summons or, where the case is one of urgency or the giving of notice would cause a reasonable apprehension of dissipation of assets, ex parte—

(a)   to vary such order, or

(b)   for a restraint order or a charging order in respect of other realisable property, or

(c)   for the appointment of a receiver.

(2) An application under paragraph (1) shall be supported by an affidavit which, where the application is for a restraint order or a charging order, shall to the best of the deponent's ability give full particulars of the realisable property in respect of which the order is sought and specify the person or persons holding such property.

(3) The summons and affidavit in support shall be lodged with the court and served on the defendant and, where one has been appointed in the matter, on the receiver, not less than two clear days before the date fixed for the hearing of the summons.

(4) Rule 4(3) and (4) shall apply to the service of restraint orders and charging orders respectively made under this rule on persons other than the defendant.

Realisation of property

1–6564X   **7.** (1) An application by the prosecutor under section 29 shall, where there have been proceedings against the defendant in the High Court, be made by summons and shall otherwise be made by originating motion.

(2) The summons or originating motion, as the case may be, shall be served with the evidence in support not less than 7 days before the date fixed for the hearing of the summons on—

(a)   the defendant,

(b)   any person holding any interest in the realisable property to which the application relates, and

(c)   the receiver, where one has been appointed in the matter.

(3) The application shall be supported by an affidavit, which shall, to the best of the deponent's ability, give full particulars of the realisable property to which it relates and specify the person or persons holding such property, and a copy of the confiscation order, of any certificate issued by the Crown Court under section 5(2) and of any charging order made in the matter shall be exhibited to such affidavit.

(4) The Court may, on an application under section 29—

(a)   exercise the power conferred by section 30(2) to direct the making of payments by a receiver;

(b)   give directions in respect of the property interests to which the application relates; and

(c)   make declarations in respect of those interests.

Receivers

1–6564Y   **8.** (1) Subject to the provisions of this rule, the provisions[1] of Order 30, rules 2 to 8 shall apply where a receiver is appointed in pursuance of a charging order or under section 26 or 29.

(2) Where the receiver proposed to be appointed has been appointed receiver in other proceedings under the Act, it shall not be necessary for an affidavit of fitness to be sworn or for the receiver to give security, unless the Court otherwise orders.

(3) Where a receiver has fully paid the amount payable under the confiscation order and any sums remain in his hands, he shall apply by summons for directions as to the distribution of such sums.

(4) A summons under paragraph (3) shall be served with any evidence in support not less than 7 days before the date fixed for the hearing of the summons on—

(a)   the defendant, and

(b)   any other person who held property realised by the receiver.

(5) A receiver may apply for an order to discharge him from his office by making an application, which shall be served, together with any evidence in support, on all persons affected by his appointment not less than 7 days before the day fixed for the hearing of the application.

---

1. These provisions relate to the giving of securities by receivers, remuneration of receivers, service of order appointing receiver, receiver's accounts, payments into court by receivers, default by receivers and directions to receivers.

Certificate of inadequacy

1–6564Z   **9.** (1) The defendant or a receiver appointed under section 26 or 29 or in pursuance of a charging order may apply by summons for a certificate under section 17(1).

(2) A summons under paragraph (1) shall be served with any supporting evidence not less than 7 days before the date fixed for the hearing of the summons on the prosecutor and, as the case may be, on either the defendant or the receiver (where one has been appointed).

Certificate under section 16

1–6564ZA   **9A.** An application under section 16(2) (increase in realisable property) shall be served with any supporting evidence not less than 7 days before the date fixed for the hearing of the application on the defendant and, as the case may be, on either the prosecutor or (where one has been appointed in the matter) on the receiver.

Compensation

1–6564ZB   **10.** An application for an order under section 18 shall be made by summons, which shall be served, with any supporting evidence, on the person alleged to be in default and on the relevant authority under section 18(5) not less than 7 days before the date fixed for the hearing of the summons.

Disclosure of information

1–6564ZC   **11.** (1) An application by the prosecutor under section 59 shall be made by summons, which shall state the nature of the order sought and whether material sought to be disclosed is to be disclosed to a receiver appointed under section 26 or 29 or in pursuance of a charging order or to a person mentioned in section 59(8).

(2) The summons and affidavit in support shall be served on the authorised Government Department in accordance with Order 77, rule 4 not less than 7 days before the date fixed for the hearing of the summons.

(3) The affidavit in support of an application under paragraph (1) shall state the grounds for believing that the conditions in section 59(4) and, if appropriate, section 59(7) are fulfilled.

Compensation for, discharge and variation of compensation orders

1–6564ZD   **11A.** (1) An application under section 21, 22 or 23 shall be made by summons which, together with any evidence in support, shall be lodged with the Court and served on the prosecutor not less than 7 days before the day fixed for the hearing of the summons.

(2) Notice shall also be served on any receiver appointed in pursuance of a charging order or under section 26 or 29.

(3) An application for an order under section 22 shall be supported by an affidavit giving details of—

(a) the confiscation order made under section 19(4);
(b) the acquittal of the defendant;
(c) the realisable property held by the defendant; and
(d) the loss suffered by the applicant as a result of the confiscation order.

(4) An application for an order under section 23 shall be supported by an affidavit giving details of—

(a) the confiscation order made under section 19(4);
(b) the date on which the defendant ceased to be an absconder;
(c) the date on which proceedings against the defendant were instituted and a summary of the steps taken in the proceedings since then; and
(d) any indication given by the prosecutor that he does not intend to proceed against the defendant.

(5) An application made under section 21 shall be supported by an affidavit giving details of—

(a) the confiscation order made under section 19(4);
(b) the circumstances in which the defendant ceased to be an absconder; and
(c) the amounts referred to in section 21(2).

(6) Where an application is made for an order under section 23(3) or 24(2)(b), the affidavit shall also include—

(a) details of the realisable property to which the application relates; and
(b) details of the loss suffered by the applicant as a result of the confiscation order.

(7) Unless the Court otherwise orders, an affidavit under paragraphs (3) to (6) may contain statements of information and belief, with the sources and grounds thereof.

Exercise of powers under sections 37 and 40

1–6564ZE   **12.** The powers conferred on the High Court by sections 37 and 40 may be exercised by a judge in chambers and a master of the Queen's Bench Division.

Application for registration

1–6564ZF   **13.** An application for registration of an order specified in an Order in Council made under section 37 or of an external confiscation order under section 40(1) may be made ex parte.

Evidence in support of application under section 37

1–6564ZG   **14.** An application for registration of an order specified in an Order in Council made under section 37 must be supported by an affidavit—

(i) exhibiting the order or a certified copy thereof, and
(ii) stating, to the best of the deponent's knowledge, particulars of what property the person against whom the order was made holds in England and Wales, giving the source of the deponent's knowledge.

Evidence in support of application under section 40(1)

1–6564ZH   **15.** (1) An application for registration of an external confiscation order must be supported by an affidavit—

(a) exhibiting the order or a verified or certified or otherwise duly authenticated copy thereof and, where the order is not in the English language, a translation thereof into English certified by a notary public or authenticated by affidavit, and
(b) stating—

(i) that the order is in force and is not subject to appeal,
(ii) where the person against whom the order was made did not appear in the proceedings, that he received notice thereof in sufficient time to enable him to defend them,
(iii) in the case of money, either that at the date of the application the sum payable under the order has not been paid or the amount which remains unpaid, as may be appropriate, or, in the case of other property, the property which has not been recovered, and
(iv) to the best of the deponent's knowledge, particulars of what property the person against whom the order was made holds in England and Wales, giving the source of the deponent's knowledge.

(2) Unless the Court otherwise directs, an affidavit for the purposes of this rule may contain statements of information or belief with the sources and grounds thereof.

Register of orders

1–6564ZI   **16.** (1) There shall be kept in the Central Office under the direction of the Master of the Crown Office a register of the orders registered under the Act.

(2) There shall be included in such register particulars of any variation or setting aside of a registration and of any execution issued on a registered order.

Notice of registration

1–6564ZJ   **17.** (1) Notice of the registration of an order must be served on the person against whom it was obtained by delivering it to him personally or by sending it to him at his usual or last known address or place of business or in such other manner as the Court may direct.

(2) Service of such a notice out of the jurisdiction is permissible without leave, and Order 11, rules 5, 6 and 8 shall apply in relation to such a notice as they apply in relation to a writ.

(3) *Revoked.*

Application to vary or set aside registration

1–6564ZK   **18.** An application by the person against whom an order was made to vary or set aside the registration of an order must be made to a judge by summons supported by affidavit.

Enforcement of order

1–6564ZL   **19.** (1) *Revoked.*

(2) If an application is made under rule 18, an order shall not be enforced until after such application is determined.

Variation, satisfaction and discharge of registered order

1–6564ZM   **20.** Upon the court being notified by the applicant for registration that an order which has been registered has been varied, satisfied or discharged, particulars of the variation, satisfaction or discharge, as the case may be, shall be entered in the register.

Rules to have effect subject to Orders in Council

1–6564ZN   **21.** Rules 12 to 20 shall have effect subject to the provisions of the Order in Council made under section 37 or, as the case may be, of the Order in Council made under section 39.

Criminal Justice (International Co-operation) Act 1990: external forfeiture orders

1–6564ZO   **21A.** The provisions of this Part of this Order shall, with such modifications as are necessary and subject to the provisions of any Order in Council made under section 9 of the Criminal Justice (International Co-operation) Act 1990, apply to proceedings for the registration and enforcement of external forfeiture orders as they apply to such proceedings in relation to external confiscation orders.

For the purposes of this rule, an external forfeiture order is an order made by a court in a country or territory outside the United Kingdom which is enforceable in the United Kingdom by virtue of any such Order in Council.

II. PART VI OF THE CRIMINAL JUSTICE ACT 1988

Interpretation

1–6564ZP   **22.** (1) In this Part of this Order, "the 1988 Act" means the Criminal Justice Act 1988 and a section referred to by number means the section so numbered in that Act.

(2) Expressions which are used in this Part of this Order which are used in the 1988 Act have the same meanings in this Part of this Order as in the 1988 Act and include any extended meaning given by the Criminal Justice (Confiscation) (Northern Ireland) Order 1990.

Application of Part I of Order 115

1–6564ZQ   **23.** Part I of Order 115 (except rule 11) shall apply for the purposes of proceedings under Part VI of the 1988 Act with the necessary modifications and, in particular,—

(a) references to drug trafficking offences and to drug trafficking shall be construed as references to offences to which Part VI of the 1988 Act applies and to committing such an offence;

(b) references to the Drug Trafficking Act 1994 shall be construed as references to the 1988 Act and references to sections 5(2), 26, 27, 29, 30(2), 17(1), 18, 18(5), 39 and 40 of the 1994 Act shall be construed as references to sections 73(6), 77, 78, 80, 81(1), 83(1), 89, 89(5), 96 and 97 of the 1988 Act respectively;

(c) rule 3(2) shall have effect as if the following sub-paragraphs were substituted for sub-paragraphs (a) and (b)—

"(a) state, as the case may be, either that proceedings have been instituted against the defendant for an offence to which Part VI of the 1988 Act applies (giving particulars of the offence) and that they have not been concluded or that, whether by the laying of an information or otherwise, a person is to be charged with such an offence;

(b) state, as the case may be, either that a confiscation order has been made or the grounds for believing that such an order may be made;" and

(d) rule 7(3) shall have effect as if the words "certificate issued by a magistrates' court or the Crown Court" were substituted for the words "certificate issued by the Crown Court".

(e) rule 8 shall have effect as if the following paragraph were added at the end—

"(6) Where a receiver applies for the variation of a confiscation order, the application shall be made by summons, which shall be served, with any supporting evidence, on the defendant and any other person who may be affected by the making of an order under section 83 of the 1988 Act, not less than 7 days before the date fixed for the hearing of the summons.";

(f) rule 11 shall apply with the necessary modifications where an application is made under section 93J of the 1988 Act for disclosure of information held by government departments.

III. PREVENTION OF TERRORISM (TEMPORARY PROVISIONS) ACT 1989

Interpretation

1-6564ZR   24. In this Part of this Order—

(a) "the Act" means the Prevention of Terrorism (Temporary Provisions) Act 1989;
(b) "Schedule 4" means Schedule 4 to the Act; and
(c) expressions used have the same meanings as they have in Part III of, and Schedule 4 to, the Act.

Assignment of proceedings

1-6564ZS   25. (1) Subject to paragraph (2), the jurisdiction of the High Court under the Act shall be exercised by a judge of the Queen's Bench Division or of the Chancery Division in chambers.

(2) The jurisdiction conferred on the High Court by paragraph 9 of Schedule 4 may also be exercised by a master of the Queen's Bench Division.

Application for restraint order

1-6564ZT   26. (1) An application for a restraint order under paragraphs 3 and 4 of Schedule 4 may be made by the prosecutor ex parte by originating motion.

(2) An application under paragraph (1) shall be supported by an affidavit, which shall—

(a) state, as the case may be, either—

(i) that proceedings have been instituted against a person for an offence under any of sections 15 to 18 of the Act and that they have not been concluded; or
(ii) that a criminal investigation has been started in England and Wales with regard to such an offence,

and in either case give details of the alleged or suspected offence and of the defendant's involvement;

(b) where proceedings have been instituted, state, as the case may be, that a forfeiture order has been made in the proceedings or the grounds for believing that such an order may be made;

(ba) where proceedings have not been instituted—

(i) indicate the state of progress of the investigation and when it is anticipated that a decision will be taken on whether to institute proceedings against the defendant;
(ii) state the grounds for believing that a forfeiture order may be made in any proceedings against the defendant; and
(iii) verify that the prosecutor is to have the conduct of any such proceedings;

(c) to the best of the deponent's ability, give full particulars of the property in respect of which the order is sought and specify the person or persons holding such property and any other persons having an interest in it.

(3) An originating motion under paragraph (1) shall be entitled in the matter of the defendant, naming him, and in the matter of the Act, and all subsequent documents in the matter shall be so entitled.

(4) Unless the Court otherwise directs, an affidavit under paragraph (2) may contain statements of information or belief with the sources and grounds thereof.

Restraint order

1-6564ZU   27. (1) A restraint order may be made subject to conditions and exceptions, including but not limited to conditions relating to the indemnifying of third parties against expenses incurred in complying with the order, and exceptions relating to living expenses and legal expenses of the defendant, but the prosecutor shall not be required to give an undertaking to abide by any order as to damages sustained by the defendant as a result of the restraint order.

(2) Unless the Court otherwise directs, a restraint order made ex parte shall have effect until a day which shall be fixed for the hearing inter partes of the application.

(3) Where a restraint order is made the prosecutor shall serve copies of the order and, unless the court otherwise orders, of the affidavit in support on the defendant and on all other persons affected by the order.

Discharge or variation of order

1-6564ZV   28. (1) Subject to paragraph (2), an application to discharge or vary a restraint order shall be made by summons.

(2) Where the case is one of urgency, an application under this rule by the prosecutor may be made ex parte.

(3) The application and any affidavit in support shall be lodged with the court and, where the application is made by summons, shall be served on the following persons (other than the applicant)—

(a) the prosecutor;
(b) the defendant; and
(c) all other persons restrained or otherwise affected by the order;

not less than two clear days before the date fixed for the hearing of the summons.

(4) Where a restraint order has been made and has not been discharged, the prosecutor shall notify the court when proceedings for the offence have been concluded, and the court shall thereupon discharge the restraint order.

(5) Where an order is made discharging or varying a restraint order, the applicant shall serve copies of the order of discharge or variation on all persons restrained by the earlier order and shall notify all other persons affected of the terms of the order of discharge or variation.

Compensation

1-6564ZW   29. An application for an order under paragraph 7 of Schedule 4 shall be made by summons, which shall be served, with any supporting evidence, on the person alleged to be in default and on the relevant authority under paragraph 7(5) not less than 7 days before the date fixed for the hearing of the summons.

Application for registration

1-6564ZX   30. An application for registration of a Scottish order, a Northern Ireland order or an Islands order may be made ex parte.

Evidence in support of application

1–6564ZY 31. (1) An application for registration of any such order as is mentioned in rule 30 must be supported by an affidavit—

  (*a*) exhibiting the order or a certified copy thereof, and

  (*b*) which shall, to the best of the deponent's ability, give particulars of such property in respect of which the order was made as is in England and Wales, and specify the person or persons holding such property.

(2) Unless the Court otherwise directs, an affidavit for the purposes of this rule may contain statements of information or belief with the sources and grounds thereof.

Register of orders

1–6564ZZ 32. (1) There shall be kept in the Central Office under the direction of the Master of the Crown Office a register of the orders registered under the Act.

(2) There shall be included in such register particulars of any variation or setting aside of a registration, and of any execution issued on a registered order.

Notice of registration

1–6564ZZA 33. (1) Notice of the registration of an order must be served on the person or persons holding the property referred to in rule 31(*b*) and any other persons appearing to have an interest in that property.

(2) Service of such a notice out of the jurisdiction is permissible without leave, and Order 11, rules 5, 6 and 8 shall apply in relation to such a notice as they apply in relation to a writ.

(3) *Revoked.*

Application to vary or set aside registration

1–6564ZZB 34. An application to vary or set aside the registration of an order must be made to a judge by summons supported by affidavit.

This rule does not apply to a variation or cancellation under rule 36.

Enforcement of order

1–6564ZZC 35. (1) *Revoked.*

(2) If an application is made under rule 34, an order shall not be enforced until after such application is determined.

(3) This rule does not apply to the taking of steps under paragraph 5 or 6 of Schedule 4, as applied by paragraph 9(6) of that Schedule.

Variation and cancellation of registration

1–6564ZZD 36. If effect has been given (whether in England and Wales or elsewhere) to a Scottish, Northern Ireland or Islands order, or if the order has been varied or discharged by the court by which it was made, the applicant for registration shall inform the court and—

  (*a*) if such effect has been given in respect of all the money or other property to which the order applies, or if the order has been discharged by the court by which it was made, registration of the order shall be cancelled;

  (*b*) if such effect has been given in respect of only part of the money or other property, or if the order has been varied by the court by which it was made, registration of the order shall be varied accordingly.

ORDER 116[1]
THE CRIMINAL PROCEDURE AND INVESTIGATIONS ACT 1996

Application

1–6564ZZE 1. This Order shall apply in relation to acquittals in respect of offences alleged to be committed on or after 15th April 1997.

---

1. Order 116 was inserted by SI 1998/1898.

Interpretation

1–6564ZZF 2. In this Order, unless the context otherwise requires—

"the Act" means the Criminal Procedure and Investigations Act 1996;

"acquitted person" means a person whose acquittal of an offence is the subject of a certification under section 54(2) of the Act, and "acquittal" means the acquittal of that person of that offence;

"deponent" means a deponent to an affidavit filed under rule 5, 7, 8 or 9;

"magistrates' court" has the same meaning as in section 148 of the Magistrates' Courts Act 1980;

"prosecutor" means the individual or body which acted as prosecutor in the proceedings which led to the acquittal;

"record of court proceedings" means—

  (*a*) (where the proceedings took place in the Crown Court) a transcript of the evidence, or

  (*b*) a note of the evidence made by the justices' clerk,

in the proceedings which led to the conviction for the administration of justice offence referred to in section 54(1)(*b*) of the Act or, as the case may be, the proceedings which led to the acquittal;

"single judge" means a judge of the Queen's Bench Division.

Assignment of proceedings

1–6564ZZG 3. The jurisdiction of the High Court under section 54(3) of the Act shall be exercised by a single judge and, subject to rule 10(13), that jurisdiction shall be exercised in chambers.

Time limit for making application

1–6564ZZH   **4.** An application under section 54(3) of the Act shall be made not later than 28 days after—

(a) the expiry of the period allowed for appealing (whether by case stated or otherwise), or making an application for leave to appeal, against the conviction referred to in section 54(1)(b) of the Act; or

(b) where notice of appeal or application for leave to appeal against the conviction is given, the determination of the appeal or application for leave to appeal and, for this purpose, "determination" includes abandonment (within the meaning of rule 10 of the Criminal Appeal Rules 1968 or, as the case may be, rule 11 of the Crown Court Rules 1982).

Application

1–6564ZZI   **5.** (1) An application under section 54(3) of the Act shall be made by originating motion which shall be issued out of the Crown Office by the prosecutor.

(2) The application shall be accompanied by—

(a) an affidavit which deals with the conditions in section 55(1), (2), and (4) of the Act and which exhibits any relevant documents (which may include a copy of any record of court proceedings);

(b) a copy of the certification under section 54(2) of the Act.

Notice to the acquitted person

1–6564ZZJ   **6.** (1) The prosecutor shall, within 4 days of the issue of the application, serve written notice on the acquitted person that the application has been issued.

(2) The notice given under paragraph (1) shall—

(a) specify the date on which the application was issued;

(b) be accompanied by a copy of the application and of the documents which accompanied it;

(c) inform the acquitted person that—

(i) the result of the application may be the making of an order by the High Court quashing the acquittal, and

(ii) if he wishes to respond to the application, he must, within 28 days of the date of service on him of the notice, file in the Crown Office any affidavit on which he intends to rely.

Affidavit of service on an acquitted person

1–6564ZZK   **7.** The prosecutor shall, as soon as practicable after service of the notice under rule 6, lodge with the Crown Office an affidavit of service which exhibits a copy of the notice.

Response of acquitted person

1–6564ZZL   **8.** (1) If the acquitted person wishes to respond to the application, he shall, within 28 days of service on him of notice under rule 6, file in the Crown Office an affidavit which—

(a) deals with the conditions in section 55(1), (2), and (4) of the Act; and

(b) exhibits any relevant documents (which may include a copy of any record of court proceedings).

(2) The acquitted person shall, within 4 days of the filing of the documents mentioned in paragraph (1), serve copies of them on the prosecutor.

Evidence

1–6564ZZM   **9.** (1) An affidavit filed under rule 5, 7, 8 or this rule may contain statements of information or belief with the sources and grounds thereof.

(2) The prosecutor may, not later than 10 days after expiry of the period allowed under rule 8(1), apply ex parte for an order granting leave to file further affidavit evidence.

(3) If the single judge grants leave, the order shall specify a period within which further affidavit evidence or records are to be filed, and the Crown Office shall serve a copy of the order on the prosecutor and on the acquitted person.

(4) The prosecutor shall, within 4 days of filing further evidence in the Crown Office, serve a copy of that evidence on the acquitted person.

Determination of the application

1–6564ZZN   **10.** (1) Subject to paragraph (3), the single judge shall determine whether or not to make an order under section 54(3) of the Act on the basis of the written material provided under rules 5, 7, 8 and 9 in the absence of the prosecutor, the acquitted person, or of any deponent.

(2) The determination shall not be made, and any hearing under paragraph (3) shall not take place, before the expiry of—

(a) 10 days after the expiry of the period allowed under rule 8(1), or

(b) 10 days after the expiry of the period allowed by any order made under rule 9(3).

(3) The single judge may, of his own motion or on the application of the prosecutor or acquitted person, order a hearing of the application if he thinks fit.

(4) An application under paragraph (3) shall state whether a hearing is desired in order for a deponent for the other party to attend and be cross-examined, and, if so, the reasons for wishing the deponent to attend.

(5) An application under paragraph (3) shall be made no later than 7 days after the expiry of the period allowed—

(a) under rule 8(1) or

(b) by any order made under rule 9(3).

(6) Where a hearing is ordered, the single judge may, of his own motion or on the application of the prosecutor or acquitted person, order a deponent to attend in order to be cross-examined.

(7) The prosecutor or the acquitted person, as the case may be, shall within 4 days after lodging the application under paragraph (3), serve a copy of it on the other party, and file in the Crown Office an affidavit of service.

(8) A party served under paragraph (7) shall, within 5 days of service, file any representations he wishes to make as to whether or not a hearing should be ordered.

(9) Subject to paragraph (10) below—

(a) the single judge shall not determine an application for a hearing under paragraph (3) unless—

  (i) an affidavit of service has been filed as required by paragraph (7), and
  (ii) the period for filing representations allowed under paragraph (8) has elapsed; or
  (iii) representations have been filed under paragraph (8);

(b) the requirements imposed by sub-paragraph (a)(i) and (iii) are satisfied even though the affidavit of service or, as the case may be, the representations are filed outside the time limits allowed.

(10) Where after an application for a hearing has been made—

(a) no affidavit of service has been filed and
(b) no representations under paragraph (8) have been received after the expiry of 7 days from the lodging of the application,

the single judge may reject the application.

(11) Where after a hearing is ordered, either the prosecutor or the acquitted person desires a deponent for the other party to attend the hearing in order to be cross-examined, he must apply ex parte, for an order under paragraph (5) giving his reasons.

(12) The Crown Office shall serve notice on the prosecutor and the acquitted person of any order made under the foregoing paragraphs of this rule and, where a hearing is ordered, the notice shall—

(a) set out the date, time and place of the hearing, and
(b) give details of any deponent ordered to attend for cross-examination.

(13) A hearing ordered under paragraph (3) above shall be in open court unless the single judge otherwise directs.

(14) The Crown Office shall serve notice of any order made under section 54(3) of the Act quashing the acquittal or of a decision not to make such an order on the prosecutor, the acquitted person and—

(a) where the court before which the acquittal or conviction occurred was a magistrates' court, on the justices' clerk;
(b) where the court before which the acquittal or conviction occurred was the Crown Court, on the appropriate officer of the Crown Court sitting at the place where the acquittal or conviction occurred.

Judicial Committee (Devolution Issues) Rules Order 1999
(SI 1999/665 amended by SI 2003/1880 and SI 2005/1138)

1–6574   **1.** This Order may be cited as the Judicial Committee (Devolution Issues) Rules Order 1999 and shall come into force as provided in article 4.

1–6575   **2.** The Rules set out in the Schedule to this Order shall have effect and may be cited as the Judicial Committee (Devolution Issues) Rules 1999.

1–6576   **3.** The Judicial Committee (General Appellate Jurisdiction) Rules shall not apply to matters falling within the scope of the Rules scheduled to this Order.

1–6577   **4.** This Order shall come into force as follows—

(a) Parts II and III of the Schedule on 6th May 1999;
(b) Part IV of the Schedule on the day appointed for the commencement of Parts II and III of the Northern Ireland Act 1998;
(c) articles 2 and 3 and Parts I and V of the Schedule on the same day as Parts II and III of the Schedule, or on the same day as Part IV, whichever is the earlier;
(d) save as aforesaid, on the day it is made.

SCHEDULE
THE JUDICIAL COMMITTEE (DEVOLUTION ISSUES) RULES 1999

1–6578

CONTENTS

PART I
GENERAL

PART II
PROCEEDINGS UNDER THE SCOTLAND ACT 1998

PART III
PROCEEDINGS UNDER THE GOVERNMENT OF WALES ACT 1998

PART IV
PROCEEDINGS UNDER THE NORTHERN IRELAND ACT 1998

PART V
COMMON RULES

CHAPTER 1
SPECIAL LEAVE TO APPEAL

CHAPTER 2
APPEALS

CHAPTER 3
REFERENCES

CHAPTER 4
MISCELLANEOUS

PART I
GENERAL

1–6579   Application   1.1. (1) These rules apply to proceedings in the Judicial Committee of the Privy Council as follows.

(2) Parts I, II and V apply to proceedings under the Scotland Act 1998.

(3) Parts I, III and V apply to proceedings under the Government of Wales Act 1998.

(4) Parts I, IV and V apply to proceedings under the Northern Ireland Act 1998.

1–6580   Interpretation   1.2. (1) In these rules, unless the context otherwise requires—

"appendix" means an appendix prepared pursuant to rules 5.21, 5.22 and 5.57;

"Board" means a Board of the Judicial Committee comprising a quorum (or more) of members of the Committee;

"Case" means a succinct written statement of a party's argument prepared in accordance with rules 5.30, 5.31 and 5.56;

"counsel", in relation to any proceedings, includes any person with a right of audience before the Judicial Committee in those proceedings;

"court" includes a tribunal;

"judgment" includes decree, order, sentence, decision, determination or declaration of any court, judge or judicial officer;

"Judicial Committee" means the Judicial Committee of the Privy Council;

"Law Officer" means the Attorney General, the Lord Advocate, the Advocate General for Scotland or the Attorney General for Northern Ireland;

"Registrar" means the Registrar of the Privy Council;
"Registry" means the Registry of the Judicial Committee, Downing Street, London SW1;
"solicitor" includes a London agent;
"statement" means a statement of facts and issues prepared pursuant to rule 5.20.

(2) Where by these rules any step is required to be taken in connection with proceedings in the Judicial Committee, whether in the way of lodging a document, entering an appearance, lodging security, or otherwise, such step shall be taken in the Registry.

(3) Where a party is acting in person in any proceedings references in these rules to that party's counsel or solicitor shall, except in rule 5.14(2), be construed as references to that party in person.

1–6581 Lodgement and service 1.3. (1) Documents need not be lodged personally but may not be lodged by facsimile transfer ("fax"), nor may service on a party be effected by fax unless and then only to the extent that that party has indicated that he is willing to accept service by that means. Notifications sent by fax should be followed by dispatch of the original to the recipient.

(2) Where under these rules a petition or reference is to be lodged and served on another party the original petition or reference that is lodged shall be endorsed with a signed certificate of service or accompanied by an affidavit of service.

1–6582 Conduct of litigation in the Judicial Committee 1.4. (1) Notwithstanding the Order in Council of 6th March 1896 relating to the admission of proctors, solicitors and agents to practise before the Privy Council, any person who has a right to conduct litigation in any of the superior courts of England and Wales, Scotland or Northern Ireland may conduct litigation in the Judicial Committee and no declaration or enrolment shall be required.

(2) Solicitors outside London may appoint London agents. Any additional costs incurred as a result of a decision not to do so may be disallowed on taxation.

1–6583 Mode of addressing petitions and references 1.5. All petitions, references and notices of motion shall be addressed to the Judicial Committee.

1–6584 Appearance by petitioner 1.6. A person who lodges a reference or a petition of appeal shall also lodge a completed appearance form but shall not be required to pay any separate fee therefor.

PART II
PROCEEDINGS UNDER THE SCOTLAND ACT 1998

PART III
PROCEEDINGS UNDER THE GOVERNMENT OF WALES ACT 1998

1–6585 Interpretation of Part III 3.1. In this Part, except where the context otherwise requires, references by number to paragraphs are references to the paragraphs so numbered in Schedule 8 to the Government of Wales Act 1998.

1–6586 References under paragraph 31(1) 3.2. (1) A reference by the Attorney General or the Assembly of a devolution issue to the Judicial Committee under paragraph 31(1) shall be made by lodging the reference and serving a copy on the other ("the respondent").

(2) The reference shall state the question to be determined.

(3) In a case to which paragraph 31(2) applies the reference shall be accompanied by a certificate that paragraph 31(2)(a) has been complied with.

1–6587 3.3. The respondent shall within 14 days either—

(a) if he intends to participate in the proceedings, enter an appearance; or
(b) if not, give notice to the Registry to that effect;

and notify the originating party accordingly.

1–6588 3.4. (1) The originating party and (if participating in the proceedings) the respondent shall each lodge a Case with respect to the question referred.

(2) The originating party shall lodge his Case within two months of lodging the reference and the respondent shall lodge his Case within two months of entering an appearance.

1–6589 References by courts 3.5. (1) A reference to the Judicial Committee under paragraph 10, 18, 19, 27, 29 or 30 shall be made by lodging the reference in the Registry.

(2) The court lodging the reference shall serve a copy of it on—

(a) the parties;
(b) the Assembly, if it is not already a party; and
(c) the relevant Law Officer, if he is not already a party.

(3) In this rule and in rules 3.7, 3.8 and 3.9 "relevant Law Officer" means—

(a) where the reference or appeal is from a court in England and Wales or from the House of Lords in proceedings that originated in England and Wales, the Attorney General;
(b) where the reference or appeal is from a court in Scotland or from the House of Lords in Scottish proceedings, the Advocate General for Scotland;
(c) where the reference or appeal is from a court in Northern Ireland or from the House of Lords in proceedings that originated in Northern Ireland, the Attorney General for Northern Ireland.

1–6590 **3.6.** (1) The reference shall set out the following:

   (*a*) the question referred;
   (*b*) the addresses of the parties;
   (*c*) the name and address of the person who applied for or required the reference to be made;
   (*d*) a concise statement of the background to the matter including—

      (i) the facts of the case, including any relevant findings of fact by the referring court or lower courts; and
      (ii) the main issues in the case and the contentions of the parties with regard to them;

   (*e*) the relevant law, including the relevant provisions of the Government of Wales Act 1998;
   (*f*) the reasons why an answer to the question is considered necessary for the purpose of disposing of the proceedings.

(2) All judgments already given in the proceedings shall be annexed to the reference.

1–6591 **3.7.** (1) Any party to the proceedings in the court making the reference who intends to participate in the proceedings in the Judicial Committee shall within 14 days of service of the copy reference on him—

   (*a*) enter an appearance; and
   (*b*) give notice to the other parties that he has done so.

(2) Any party who does not intend to participate shall give notice in writing to the Registry and the other parties accordingly.
(3) Where notice has to be given under this rule, it shall also be given to the relevant Law Officer and the Assembly even if they are not parties.

1–6592 **3.8.** (1) Unless they are already parties to the proceedings, the Assembly and the relevant Law Officer may intervene in the proceedings on the reference in accordance with this rule; and he shall thereupon become a party to the proceedings on the reference.
(2) The intervener shall within 14 days of service of the copy reference on him—

   (*a*) enter an appearance; and
   (*b*) give notice of the fact to the parties, the other person who may intervene under this rule and, in the case of a reference under paragraph 30, the court making the reference.

1–6593 **Appeals** **3.9.** (1) A person who desires to appeal to the Judicial Committee—

   (*a*) under paragraph 20, or
   (*b*) having obtained leave to appeal from the court appealed from, under paragraphs 11, 21 or 28,

shall lodge a petition of appeal within six weeks of the date on which the order appealed from was made or leave to appeal was granted, as the case may be.
(2) A person who desires to appeal to the Judicial Committee under paragraphs 11, 21 or 28, having obtained special leave to appeal from the Judicial Committee, shall lodge a petition of appeal within 14 days of the grant of special leave.
(3) The appellant shall serve a copy of the petition on all the other parties and, if not already a party, on the Assembly and the relevant Law Officer.
(4) Unless already a party to the proceedings, the Assembly and the relevant Law Officer may intervene in the proceedings on the appeal in the Judicial Committee if within 14 days of service of the petition on him he enters an appearance and gives notice of the fact to the parties and the other person with a right to intervene under this rule; and he shall thereupon become a respondent to the appeal.

PART IV
PROCEEDINGS UNDER THE NORTHERN IRELAND ACT 1998

PART V
COMMON RULES

CHAPTER 1
SPECIAL LEAVE TO APPEAL

CHAPTER 2
APPEALS

1–6594 **Anonymity and reporting restrictions** **5.15.** (1) In any appeal where in the courts below the title used for the proceedings has been such as to conceal the identity of any person, this fact should be clearly drawn to the attention of the Registry at the time the appeal is lodged.
(2) Where in relation to any appeal the Judicial Committee has power to make an order restricting reporting of the appeal, parties should also consider whether it would be appropriate for the power to be exercised and must in any event inform the Registry if such an order has been made by a court below. A request for such an order should be made in writing, preferably on behalf of all parties to the appeal, as soon as possible after the appeal has been presented and not later than 14 days before the commencement of the hearing, citing the power under which it may be made.

1–6595 **Appearance by respondent** **5.18.** (1) A respondent who intends to participate in the proceedings before the Judicial Committee should enter an appearance to an appeal within 14 days of receiving service of the petition of appeal and notify the appellant in writing that he has done so.
(2) A respondent who intends to take no part in the proceedings before the Judicial Committee should notify the Registry in writing of that fact.
(3) Communications concerning the appeal will be sent by the Registry only to those respondents who have entered an appearance.

1–6596 **Appendix** **5.21.** (1) The appellant shall also prepare and lodge an appendix containing documents used in evidence or recording proceedings in the courts below.
(2) The contents of the appendix shall if possible be agreed between the parties before lodgement.

1–6597 **Contents of appendix** **5.22.** (1) The appendix should contain only such documents, or such extracts from documents, as are clearly necessary for the support and understanding of the argument of the appeal.

(2) The appendix should not include—

(*a*) any document which was not used in evidence or does not record proceedings relevant to the action in the court below; or

(*b*) transcripts of arguments in the courts below unless and to the extent that—

(i) any party relies on remarks by a judge; or

(ii) the arguments refer to facts which are admitted by all parties and as to which no evidence was called.

(3) The appendix may consist of one or two parts. Part I should contain—

(*a*) formal originating documents;

(*b*) case stated (if any);

(*c*) judgments of the courts at first instance and on appeal together with copies of the orders of all courts;

(*d*) the relevant legislation;

(*e*) any crucial document on which the action is founded, such as a will, contract, map, plan etc., or the relevant extract from such a document.

(4) Other documents should be included in Part II of the appendix.

1–6598 Documents in readiness at hearing 5.23. Any documents disputed between the parties, and any documents that are not included in the appendix but that may be required at the hearing, should be held in readiness and, subject to leave being given, may be introduced at an appropriate moment. Five copies are required. The other parties must be given notice of any documents that will be held in readiness at the hearing.

1–6599 Respondent's additional documents 5.24. (1) Where the appellant declines to include in the appendix any documents which the respondent considers necessary for their argument of the appeal, the respondent shall prepare and reproduce them (at his own cost, subject to any subsequent order for costs).

(2) The respondent's additional documents shall be produced in the same form as, and paginated consecutively with, the appendix.

1–6600 Scottish Record 5.25. Appellants in Scottish appeals should include in Part I of the appendix—

(*a*) in civil appeals the Record and Interlocutors; and

(*b*) in criminal appeals the indictment or complaint and Interlocutors.

1–6601 Time limit for lodging statement and appendix 5.26. The statement and appendix shall be lodged by the appellant within 28 days of lodging the petition of appeal.

1–6602 Lodgement 5.27. (1) The appellant shall deposit in the Judicial Committee seven copies of the statement, seven copies of Part I of the appendix and 17 copies of Part II of the appendix (if any).

(2) The respondent must also (where applicable) lodge seven copies of his additional documents if supplementary to Part I of the appendix (17 copies if supplementary to Part II of the appendix).

1–6603 Allocation of time 5.29. (1) Within seven days of the setting down of the appeal each party shall notify the Registry of the time, in hours, that counsel consider necessary for each address which it is proposed should be made on behalf of that party.

(2) Subject to any directions that may be given at or before the hearing counsel will be expected to confine their submissions to the time indicated in their estimates.

(3) Amended estimates should be communicated to the Registry at once.

1–6604 Appellant's and respondent's Cases 5.30. (1) Within 28 days after the setting down of the appeal, the parties shall each lodge seven copies of their Cases and give notice of having done so to the other parties.

(2) A Case should be a succinct statement of a party's argument in the appeal, omitting (though if necessary referring to) material contained in the statement of facts and issues and the appendix and confined to the heads of argument which counsel propose to submit at the hearing. It should consist of paragraphs numbered consecutively; and references by page and line to the relevant portions of the statement of facts and issues and the appendix shall as far as practicable be reproduced in the margin.

(3) If a party intends to invite the Judicial Committee to depart from one of its own decisions this intention must be clearly stated in a separate paragraph of the Case, to which special attention must be drawn. A respondent who wishes to contend that a decision of the court below should be affirmed on grounds other than those relied on by that court must set out the grounds for that contention in the Case.

(4) All Cases shall conclude with a numbered summary of the reasons upon which the argument is founded, and must bear the signature of at least one counsel who has appeared in the court below or who will be briefed for the hearing before the Judicial Committee.

(5) Two or more appellants or respondents may, at their own risk as to costs, lodge separate Cases in the same appeal.

(6) No party to an appeal shall be entitled to be heard by the Judicial Committee unless he has previously lodged his Case in accordance with this rule.

1–6605 Exchange of Cases 5.32. As soon as all the Cases have been lodged, all parties shall exchange Cases. The number of Cases provided should be sufficient to meet the reasonable requirements of the other parties.

1–6606 Bound volumes 5.33. (1) As soon as Cases have been exchanged, and in any event no later than 14 days before the proposed date of hearing, the appellant must lodge (in addition to the documents earlier lodged) ten bound volumes. Each should contain:—

(*a*) the petition of appeal;

(*b*) the petition of cross appeal (if any);

(*c*) the statement of facts and issues;

(*d*) the appellant's and respondent's Cases;

(*e*) Part I of the appendix;

(*f*) respondent's additional documents (if any and if supplementary to Part I of the appendix).

(2) To enable the appellant to lodge the bound volumes, the respondent must provide him with ten further copies of his Case and, where applicable, with ten further copies of the additional documents.

(3) The respondent should arrange with the appellant for the binding of such volumes as the respondent's counsel and solicitor may require.

1-6607 Notice of Hearing etc 5.34. (1) Once an appeal has been set down it may be called on at any time, possibly at short notice.

(2) The Registry must be informed as early as possible of the names of counsel briefed.

(3) Unless otherwise ordered upon application before or at the hearing, only two counsel shall be admitted to be heard on behalf of each party or intervenor.

1-6608 Authorities 5.35. (1) At least 7 days before the hearing of the appeal solicitors for all parties should lodge a list or photocopies of the authorities and legislative texts (other than those included in Part I of the appendix) to be cited at the hearing.

(2) Lists should indicate by reference and photocopies by highlighting those particular passages of the authorities and legislative texts on which counsel rely.

(3) Where a case is not reported in the Law Reports or Session Cases, references to or copies of other recognised reports should be provided.

1-6609 Submissions as to costs 5.36. (1) If counsel wish to seek an order other than that costs be awarded to the successful party, submissions to that effect should be made at the hearing immediately after the conclusion of the argument.

(2) *Revoked.*

(3) Where one party is legally aided and where, in the event of proceedings being decided in favour of the unassisted party, the unassisted party intends to apply for costs he shall—

(a) make a submission to that effect under this rule; and

(b) give the authority responsible for the grant of legal aid not less than seven days' notice of his intention to do so.

1-6610 Judgment 5.37. (1) Where judgment is reserved, the Registrar shall in due course notify the parties of the day appointed for the delivery of judgment.

(2) One junior only of counsel for each party or group of parties who have lodged a Case is required to attend when judgment is delivered.

1-6611 Bills of costs 5.38. Bills of costs for taxation shall be lodged within three months from the date of the final judgment or the decision of the Judicial Committee.

1-6612 Taxation of costs 5.39. (1) All bills of costs under the orders of the Judicial Committee shall be taxed by the Registrar, or such other person as the Judicial Committee may appoint.

(2) The amount of costs which a party shall be entitled to recover shall be the amount allowed after taxation on the standard basis unless the Judicial Committee has expressly awarded costs on the indemnity basis.

(3) In no case will costs be allowed which have been unreasonably incurred or are unreasonable in amount.

(4) On a taxation on the standard basis costs will only be allowed if they are reasonable and proportionate to the matters in issue and any doubt as to whether costs were reasonably incurred or are reasonable and proportionate in amount shall be resolved in favour of the party against whom the award of costs has been made ("the paying party").

(5) On a taxation on the indemnity basis, any doubt as to whether costs were reasonably incurred or are reasonable in amount shall be resolved in favour of the party to whom costs have been awarded ("the receiving party").

1-6612A 5.39A. (1) The Registrar shall, as soon as possible after the Judicial Committee have given their decision as to the costs of an appeal, petition or other matter, issue to the receiving party an order to tax and a notice requiring him within three months of the date of the notice (or such other period as the Registrar may specify) to lodge his bill of costs and serve a copy on the paying party; and the Registrar shall send a copy of the order and notice to the paying party.

(2) Together with the bill of costs the receiving party shall lodge counsel's receipted fee notes and written evidence of any other disbursement that is claimed and that exceeds £250.

(3) Within 21 days after service of the bill upon him, the paying party may lodge points of dispute, to which the receiving party may lodge a response.

(4) As soon as possible after the expiry of 21 days after the bill of costs has been lodged the Registrar shall issue a notice to all parties specifying the day and hour appointed by him for taxation.

(5) A copy of every document lodged by a party under this rule must at the same time be served on the opposite party, and the Registry must be notified in writing that such service has been effected.

1-6612B 5.39B. (1) Any party who is dissatisfied with all or part of a taxation may within 14 days after the taxation appeal to the Judicial Committee by lodging a petition setting out the items objected to and stating concisely in each case the nature and grounds of the objections.

(2) Any party to whom a copy of the petition is delivered may within 14 days after such delivery lodge a response to the grounds of appeal stating concisely the reasons why they are opposed.

(3) A petition lodged under paragraph (1) above and a response lodged under paragraph (2) above must be served on all other parties who attended the taxation and on any other party to whom the Registrar directs that a copy should be delivered.

(4) The petition shall in the first instance be considered by a Board of the Judicial Committee which may—

(a) allow or dismiss the appeal without a hearing;

(b) invite any or all of the parties to lodge submissions or further submissions in writing on such matters connected with the appeal as may be specified;

(c) direct that the appeal be referred for an oral hearing.

CHAPTER 3
REFERENCES

1-6613 Presentation of reference 5.41. (1) A reference lodged in the Registry under these rules shall consist of numbered paragraphs and be endorsed with the title of the reference and the name and address of the person or court making the reference.

(2) The original reference must be—

(a) signed by the person making the reference or his counsel or solicitor, or, where the reference is by a court, by a judge or proper officer of the court; and
(b) lodged in the Registry together with—

(i) for references from courts, seven copies;
(ii) for other references, 17 copies.

1–6614 Service of reference 5.42. Where the reference is by a court, service of the reference on the parties may be effected in any manner authorised by the rules of that court.

1–6615 Lodgement of Cases 5.43. (1) Each party must lodge the following number of copies of his Case—

(a) where the reference is from a court, seven copies;
(b) for other references, 17 copies.

(2) Where the reference is by a court, the parties shall lodge their Cases within 28 days after the appendix has been lodged.

1–6616 Setting down for hearing 5.44. A reference shall be automatically set down for hearing when all the parties have lodged their Cases.

1–6617 Automatic remission to referring court after judgment 5.45. Unless the Judicial Committee directs otherwise, once a final judgment has been given on a reference by a court the proceedings shall stand remitted to the court from which the reference came without further order, subject to the disposal of any outstanding issues as to the costs of the reference.

1–6618 Application of other provisions of this Part 5.46. (1) Rules 5.18(3), 5.29, 5.30(2) to (6), 5.32, 5.34, 5.35, 5.37 and Chapter 4 shall apply, so far as applicable and with such modifications as are necessary, to references and documents originating references as they apply to appeals and petitions of appeal.
(2) In rules applied by this rule the term "appellant" shall be construed to mean the person making the reference or, as the case may be, the person who applied for or required the reference to be made.
(3) Where the reference is by a court—

(a) rules 5.15, 5.21 to 5.27, 5.33, 5.36, 5.38 and 5.39 shall in addition likewise apply;
(b) the appendix shall not include any material contained in the reference or its annex;
(c) the terms "courts below" and "lower courts" and similar expressions shall be construed as meaning the court making the reference and the courts (if any) below that court.

CHAPTER 4
MISCELLANEOUS

1–6619 Legal aid 5.47. (1) A party to whom a legal aid certificate has been issued for the appeal must immediately lodge the certificate, or a copy of it, in the Registry.
(2) Where applicable an emergency certificate, and subsequent amendments, and the authority for leading counsel, must also be lodged.
(3) Where a prospective petitioner or appellant has applied for legal aid, the Registry and the other parties to the proposed petition or appeal must be informed in writing within the original time limit for lodging the petition. The period within which a petition may be lodged will then be extended to 28 days after the final determination of the legal aid application.
(4) Where a respondent to an appeal has applied for legal aid, the Registry must be informed within the original time limit for lodging the statement and appendix. That time limit will then be extended to six weeks after the final determination of the legal aid application.
(5) The person applying for legal aid must inform the Registry and the other parties in writing immediately the application is finally determined indicating the date of the determination.
(6) Where a legal aid certificate is granted, the date of final determination is the date of issue of the certificate. Where legal aid is refused the date of final determination is the date of issue of the letter of refusal.

1–6620 Cross-appeals 5.48. (1) A petition of cross-appeal must be presented within six weeks of the presentation of the original appeal.
(2) Argument in respect of a cross-appeal must be included by each party in their Case in the original appeal. Such an inclusive Case must clearly state that it is lodged in respect of both the original and cross-appeals.
(3) Documents in respect of both the original appeal and the cross-appeal should be included in one appendix. Lodgement of the statement and appendix, and setting down for hearing, are the responsibility of the original appellant.

1–6621 References to the European Court of Justice 5.49. (1) An order by the Judicial Committee referring a question to the Court of Justice of the European Communities ("the European Court") for a preliminary ruling may be made on its own motion at any stage of proceedings or on the application of a party by notice of motion before the hearing.
(2) The proceedings in which an order is made shall, unless the Judicial Committee otherwise orders, be stayed until the European Court has given a preliminary ruling on the question referred to it or the reference is withdrawn.

1–6622 Consolidation and conjoinder 5.50. (1) Where the issues in two or more appeals are similar, they may be consolidated or conjoined to avoid, wherever possible, separate representations by counsel or any duplication in the submissions made.
(2) Applications to consolidate or to conjoin appeals and other incidental applications must be made by petition.
(3) The petition should be signed by all the petitioners or their solicitors and must be submitted to the solicitors for all the other parties who have entered appearance for the endorsement of their consent. If consent is refused, the petition must be endorsed with a certificate that it has been served on the solicitors in question.
(4) If all parties consent to or join in the petition, one copy only of the petition should be lodged. If any party refuses consent, rule 5.52 shall apply.

1–6623   **Withdrawal of petitions and appeals**   **5.51.** (1) Subject to the provisions of this rule—

   (*a*)   a petition for special leave to appeal; or
   (*b*)   an appeal;

may be withdrawn by giving notice in writing to the Registrar, copied to the respondent.

   (2) Where the parties are agreed as to the terms on which the petition or appeal is to be withdrawn—

   (*a*)   the notice to the Registrar should briefly indicate the terms of the agreement; and
   (*b*)   the respondent shall confirm his agreement to the Registrar in writing.

   (3) Subject to paragraph (4) below and to any agreement between the parties, the petitioner or appellant shall be liable to pay the respondent's costs on the standard basis.

   (4) Any party who wishes to oppose the withdrawal of the appeal or petition, or who seeks terms for the withdrawal other than those provided for in this rule, may lodge a petition seeking some other order.

1–6624   **Incidental petitions and motions**   **5.52.** (1) Unless the Registrar directs otherwise, incidental petitions (including any interlocutory petition which relates to a petition of appeal) shall be referred to a Board.

   (2) The original and six copies of the petition must be lodged and a copy served on the other party.

   (3) If an oral hearing is ordered the parties may apply to the Registrar to lodge affidavits and such other documents as they may wish. In addition to the original, six copies will be required. Copies of such documents must be served on the other parties not less than seven days before the hearing.

   (4) This rule shall apply, with appropriate modifications, to notices of motion as it applies to incidental petitions.

1–6625   **New submissions**   **5.53.** If, after the conclusion of the argument of an appeal, a party wishes to bring to the notice of the Judicial Committee new circumstances which have arisen and which might affect the decision or order of the Judicial Committee, application must be made forthwith to the Registrar for leave to make new submissions. The application should indicate the circumstances and the submissions it is desired to make, and a copy must be sent to the other parties to the appeal.

1–6626   **Interveners**   **5.54.** (1) Except as otherwise provided by these rules, leave to intervene in proceedings is required and must be applied for by petition. The petition should be certified with the consent of the parties in the Case or, if consent is refused, the petition should be endorsed with a certificate of service on the parties. All petitions for leave to intervene, whether opposed by the parties or not, will be referred to a Board.

   (2) References in these rules to a party and to a respondent shall be deemed to include a person intervening.

1–6627   **Preparation of documents**   **5.55.** (1) Documents which are not clearly legible or which are not produced in the form specified will not be accepted by the Registry.

   (2) All formal documents should be produced on good quality A4 paper, bound down the left hand edge and using both sides of the paper.

1–6628   **Form of statement and Case**   **5.56.** (1) The statement and Case should be produced with letters down the inside margin. The outside margin should carry references to the relevant pages of the appendix.

   (2) The front page of the statement should carry the references of every law report of the cause in the courts below. A head-note summary should be given, whether or not the cause has been reported.

   (3) The front page of the statement should carry an indication of the time occupied by the cause in each court below.

   (4) The statement should be signed by counsel on both sides, and their names clearly indicated. Where the statement is not agreed to by all parties it should be signed by counsel for the appellant and should indicate that the respondent has been given an opportunity to join in the statement.

   (5) Each party's Case should be signed by his counsel above their printed names.

1–6629   **Form of appendix**   **5.57.** (1) The appendix should be bound with plastic comb binding, in limp board covers.

   (2) All documents must be numbered and each part of the appendix must contain a list of its contents.

   (3) Documents of an unsuitable size or form for binding with the other documents, such as maps or booklets, should be inserted in pockets at the back of the appropriate volume.

1–6630   **Form of bound volumes**   **5.58.** The bound volumes should be bound in the same manner as the appendix. They should contain cut out indices for each of the items listed in rule 5.33(1), tabbed with the name of the document on the front sheet of each. The front cover should carry a list of the contents and the names of the solicitors for all parties. The short title of the cause and (if there is more than one volume) the volume number should be given on a strip affixed to the plastic spine. Each volume should include a few blank pages at either end.

1–6631   **Power to give directions and excuse compliance with rules**   **5.59.** (1) The Registrar may give such directions in matters of practice and procedure as may be just and expedient and may for sufficient cause shown—

   (*a*)   extend or abridge any time limit laid down by these rules;
   (*b*)   excuse the parties from compliance with any of the requirements of these rules.

   (2) If in the opinion of the Registrar it is desirable that any application for such direction or excusal should be dealt with by the Judicial Committee in open court he may direct the applicant to lodge, and to serve the opposite party with, a notice of motion returnable before the Committee.

   (3) The Registrar may give directions as to the total length of time allowed for a hearing or the length of time each party shall be allowed for his oral argument. Parties will be expected to complete their submissions within the time allowed.

   (4) Any party aggrieved by a decision by the Registrar to exercise or refuse to exercise his powers under these rules may appeal, by notice of motion, to the Judicial Committee.

1–6632   **Amendment of documents**   **5.60.** (1) Any document lodged in connection with an appeal, petition or other matter pending before the Judicial Committee may be amended by leave of the Registrar.

   (2) If the Registrar is of opinion that an application for leave to amend should be dealt with by the Committee

in open court, he may direct the applicant to lodge in the Registry, and to serve the opposite party with a notice of motion returnable before the Committee.

1–6633 Fees 5.61. (1) The Council Office fees to be taken in proceedings to which these rules apply are set out in the Table below.

(2) The Registrar may direct that—

(a) the payment of any fee shall be remitted on grounds of hardship;
(b) the appropriate fee must be paid at the time a chargeable step is taken.

Table of Fees

1–6634

	£
1 Lodging—	
(a) a petition for special leave to appeal	120.00
(b) a petition of appeal	100.00
(c) any other petition or motion	75.00
(d) a reference by a court	nil
(e) any other reference	100.00
2 Entering appearance—	
(a) in the case of a reference by a court	75.00
(b) in any other case	30.00
3 Lodging Case	300.00
4 Lodging affidavit	25.00
5 Original Order of the Judicial Committee	30.00
6 Office Copy of Committee Order	10.00
7 Certificate delivered to the parties	25.00
8 Taxing fee (including certificate)	5% of the sum allowed.

Prosecution of Offences Act 1985 (Specified Proceedings) Order 1999
(SI 1999/904)

1–6635 1. This Order may be cited as the Prosecution of Offences Act 1985 (Specified Proceedings) Order 1999 and shall come into operation on 4th May 1999.

1–6636 2. The Prosecution of Offences Act 1985 (Specified Proceedings) Order 1985 is hereby revoked.

1–6637 3. (1) Subject to paragraphs (2) and (3) below, proceedings for the offences mentioned in the Schedule to this Order are hereby specified for the purposes of section 3 of the Prosecution of Offences Act 1985 (which, amongst other things, places a duty on the Director of Public Prosecutions to take over the conduct of all criminal proceedings, other than specified proceedings, instituted on behalf of a police force).

(2) Where a summons has been issued in respect of an offence mentioned in the Schedule to this Order, proceedings for that offence cease to be specified when the summons is served on the accused unless the documents described in section 12(3)(b) of the Magistrates' Courts Act 1980 (pleading guilty by post etc) are served upon the accused with the summons.

(3) Proceedings for an offence cease to be specified if at any time a magistrates' court begins to receive evidence in those proceedings; and for the purpose of this paragraph nothing read out before the court under section 12(7) of the Magistrates' Courts Act 1980 shall be regarded as evidence.

Practice Note (Devolution issues: Wales)[1]

SUPREME COURT—LORD BINGHAM OF CORNHILL CJ, OTTON AND ROBERT WALKER LJJ 30—JUNE 1999

---

1. [1999] 3 All ER 466, [2000] 1 Cr App Rep 101.

PRACTICE—DEVOLUTION ISSUES—WALES—DIRECTIONS—NOTICE TO ATTORNEY GENERAL AND ASSEMBLY—REFERENCE OF DEVOLUTION ISSUE BY ONE COURT TO ANOTHER COURT—REFERENCE OF DEVOLUTION ISSUE TO JUDICIAL COMMITTEE OF PRIVY COUNCIL—JUDICIAL REVIEW PROCEEDINGS—FAMILY PROCEEDINGS—CIVIL PROCEEDINGS—CRIMINAL PROCEEDINGS—APPEALS—GOVERNMENT OF WALES ACT 1998, SCH 8.

Lord Bingham of Cornhill CJ gave the following direction at the sitting of the court.

1–6638 This practice direction applies to proceedings in England and Wales in the Court of Appeal (Civil and Criminal Divisions), the High Court, the Crown Court, the county courts and the magistrates' courts.

It is made: (i) by the Lord Chief Justice as President of the Criminal Division of the Court of Appeal and President of the Queen's Bench Division of the High Court; (ii) by the Master of the Rolls as President of the Court of Appeal (Civil Division); (iii) by the President of the Family Division of the High Court; (iv) by the Vice-Chancellor as Vice-President of the Chancery Division of the High Court; and (v) by the Vice-Chancellor, on behalf of the Lord Chancellor, pursuant to s 5 of the Civil Procedure Act 1997.

This Practice Direction is divided into four parts: Part I Introduction; Part II Directions applicable to all proceedings; Part III Directions applicable to specific proceedings (paras 14.2 and 14.3 deal with Crown Office applications in Wales); and Part IV Appeals

PART I INTRODUCTION
Definitions

1–6639 1. In this Practice Direction: 'the Assembly' means the National Assembly for Wales or Cynulliad Cenedlaethol Cymru; 'the GWA' means the Government of Wales Act 1998; 'the NIA' means the Northern Ireland Act 1998; 'the SA' means the Scotland Act 1998; 'the Acts' mean the GWA, the NIA and the SA; 'the Judicial Committee' means the Judicial Committee of the Privy Council; 'the CPR' means the Civil Procedure Rules 1998; 'the FPR' means the Family Proceedings Rules 1991,SI 1991/1247; 'the FPC' means the Family Proceedings Courts (Children Act 1989) Rules 1991, SI 1991/1395; 'devolution issue' has the same meaning as in para 1, Sch 8 to the GWA; para 1, Sch 10 to the NIA; and para 1, Sch 6 of the SA; 'devolution issue notice' means a notice that a devolution issue has arisen in proceedings.

Scope

1–6640 2.1. This Practice Direction supplements the provisions dealing with devolution issues in the Acts. It deals specifically with the position if a devolution issue arises under the GWA. If a devolution issue arises under the NIA or the SA the procedure laid down in this Practice Direction should be adapted as required.

2.2. This Practice Direction also deals with Crown Office applications in Wales (see paras 14.2 and 14.3).

The devolution legislation

1–6641 3.1. Schedule 8 to the GWA contains provisions dealing with devolution issues arising out of the GWA; Sch 10 to the NIA contains provisions dealing with devolution issues arising out of the NIA; and Sch 6 to the SA contains provisions dealing with devolution issues arising out of the SA.

3.2. Broadly a devolution issue will involve a question whether a devolved body has acted or proposes to act within its powers (which includes not acting incompatibly with Convention rights[1] and Community law[2]) or has failed to comply with a duty imposed on it. Reference should be made to the Acts where 'devolution issue' is defined.

3.3. (1) If a devolution issue under the GWA arises in proceedings, the court must order notice of it to be given to the Attorney General and the Assembly if they are not already a party. They have a right to take part as a party in the proceedings so far as they relate to a devolution issue, if they are not already a party (para 5, Sch 8 to the GWA.) If they do take part, they may require the court to refer the devolution issue to the Judicial Committee (para30, Sch 8 to the GWA)[3].

(2) There are similar provisions in the NIA and the SA although the persons to be notified are different (paras 13, 14, and 33, Sch 10 to the NIA; paras 16, 17 and 33, Sch 6 to the SA).

3.4. Under all the Acts the court may refer a devolution issue to another court as follows.

(1) A magistrates' court may refer a devolution issue arising in civil or summary proceedings to the High Court (paras 6 and 9, Sch 8 to the GWA; paras 15 and 18, Sch 10 to the NIA; and paras 18 and 21, Sch 6 to the SA).

(2) The Crown Court may refer a devolution issue arising in summary proceedings to the High Court and a devolution issue arising in proceedings on indictment to the Court of Appeal (para 9, Sch 8 to the GWA; para 18, Sch 10 to the NIA; para 21, Sch 6 to the SA).

(3) A county court, the High Court (unless the devolution issue has been referred to the High Court)[4], and the Crown Court[5] may refer a devolution issue arising in civil proceedings to the Court of Appeal (para 7, Sch 8 to the GWA; para 16, Sch 10 to the NIA; para 19, Sch 6 to the SA).

(4) A tribunal from which there is no appeal must, and any other tribunal may, refer a devolution issue to the Court of Appeal (para 8, Sch 8 to the GWA; para 17, Sch 10 to the NIA; para 20, Sch 6 to the SA).

(5) The Court of Appeal may refer a devolution issue to the Judicial Committee, unless the devolution issue was referred to it by another court (para 10, Sch 8 to the GWA; para 19, Sch 10 to the NIA; para 22, Sch 6 to the SA).

(6) An appeal against the determination of a devolution issue by the High Court or the Court of Appeal on a reference lies to the Judicial Committee with the leave of the court concerned, or, failing such leave, with special leave of the Judicial Committee (para 11, Sch 8 to the GWA; para 20, Sch 10 to the NIA; para 23, Sch 6 to the SA).

3.5. A court may take into account additional expense which the court considers that a party has incurred as a result of the participation of the Attorney General or the Assembly in deciding any question as to costs (para 35, Sch 8 to the GWA).

---

1. The rights and fundamental freedoms set out in: (*a*) arts 2 to 12 and 14 of the European Convention on Human Rights (the ECHR), (*b*) arts 1 to 3 of the First Protocol (agreed at Paris on 20 March 1952), and (*c*) arts 1 and 2 of the Sixth Protocol (agreed at Strasbourg on 11 May 1994), as read with arts 16 and 18 of the ECHR (s 1 of the Human Rights Act 1998; s 107(1) and (5) GWA; ss 6(2), 24(1) and 98(1) NIA; ss 29(2), 57(2) and 126(1) SA).
2. All the rights, powers, liabilities, obligations and restrictions from time to time created or arising by or under the Community Treaties; and all the remedies and procedures from time to time provided for by or under the Community Treaties (ss 106(7) and 155(1), GWA; ss 6(2), 24(1) and 98(1), NIA; ss 29(2), 57(2) and 126(9) SA).

3. If the Attorney General or the Assembly had become a party to the original proceedings but did not exercise their right to require the devolution issue to be referred to the Judicial Committee and the court decided the case, they would have the same rights of appeal as parties. These would not allow them to appeal a decision made in proceedings on indictment, although the Attorney General has a power under s 36 of the Criminal Justice Act 1972 to refer a point of law to the Court of Appeal where the defendant has been acquitted in a trial on indictment.

4. If an appeal by way of case stated in criminal proceedings goes to the Divisional Court there appears to be no power for the Divisional Court to refer a devolution issue to the Court of Appeal.

5. Eg in appeals from a magistrates' court in a licensing matter.

PART II DIRECTIONS APPLICABLE TO ALL PROCEEDINGS

Scope

1–6642 **4.** Paragraphs 5 to 13 apply to proceedings in England and Wales in the magistrates' courts, the county courts, the Crown Court, the High Court and the Court of Appeal (Civil and Criminal Division). Paragraph 10 also applies to the form and procedure for a reference to the Court of Appeal by a tribunal.

Raising the question as to whether a devolution issue arises

1–6643 **5.1.** Where a party to any form of proceedings wishes to raise an issue which may be a devolution issue whether as a claim (or part of a claim) to enforce or establish a legal right or to seek a remedy or as a defence (or part of a defence), the provisions of this Practice Direction apply in addition to the rules of procedure applicable to the proceedings in which the issue arises.

5.2. A court may, of its own volition, require the question of whether a devolution issue arises to be considered, if the materials put before the court indicate such an issue may arise, even if the parties have not used the term 'devolution issue'.

Determination by a court of whether a devolution issue arises

1–6644 **6.1.** The court may give such directions as it considers appropriate to obtain clarification or additional information to establish whether a devolution issue arises.

6.2. In determining whether a devolution issue arises the court, notwithstanding the contention of a party to the proceedings, may decide that a devolution issue shall *not* be taken to arise if the contention appears to the court to be frivolous or vexatious (para 2 of Sch 8 to the GWA).

6.3. If the court determines that a devolution issue arises it must state what that devolution issue is clearly and concisely.

Notice of devolution issue to the Attorney General and the Assembly

1–6645 **7.1.** If a court determines that a devolution issue arises in the proceedings, it must order a devolution issue notice substantially in the form numbered 'DI 1' in Annex 1 to be given to the Attorney General and the Assembly unless they are already a party to the proceedings (para 5(1), Sch 8 to the GWA).

7.2. A court receiving a reference does not have to serve a devolution issue notice unless it determines that a devolution issue that was not identified by the court making the reference has arisen. In that case the court receiving the reference must serve a devolution issue notice which must: (1) state what devolution issue has been referred to it; (2) state what further devolution issue has arisen; and (3) identify the referring court.

7.3. If the devolution issue has arisen in criminal proceedings, the devolution issue notice must state: (1) whether the proceedings have been adjourned; (2) whether the defendant is remanded in custody; and (3) if the defendant has been remanded in custody and his trial has not commenced, when the custody time limit expires[1].

7.4. If the devolution issue arises in an appeal, the devolution issue notice must: (1) state that the devolution issue arises in an appeal; (2) identify the court whose decision is being appealed; and (3) state whether the devolution issue is raised for the first time on appeal; or, if it is not, state that the devolution issue was raised in the court whose decision is being appealed, what decision was reached by that court, and the date of the previous notice to the Attorney General and the Assembly.

7.5. The devolution issue notice will specify a date which will be 14 days, or such longer period as the court may direct (see below), after the date of the devolution issue notice as the date by which the Attorney General or the Assembly must notify the court that he or it wishes to take part as a party to the proceedings, so far as they relate to a devolution issue.

7.6. The court may, in exceptional circumstances, specify a date longer than 14 days after the date of the devolution issue notice as the date by which the Attorney General and the Assembly must notify the court that he or it wishes to take part as a party to the proceedings. The court may do this before the notice is given, or before or after the expiry of the period given in the notice.

7.7. (1) On the date of the devolution issue notice, (a) the devolution issue notice for the Attorney General must be faxed to him by the court[2]; and (b) the devolution issue notice for the Assembly must be faxed by the court to the Counsel General for the Assembly.

(2) On the same day as a fax is sent a copy of the devolution issue notice must be sent by the court by first class post to the Attorney General and the Counsel General for the Assembly.

7.8. The court may, on such terms as it considers appropriate, order such additional documents to be served (eg in civil proceedings, the claim form) or additional information to be supplied with the devolution issue notice.

7.9. (1) When a court orders a devolution issue notice to be given the court may make such further orders as it thinks fit in relation to any adjournment, stay, continuance of the proceedings, or interim measures, during the period within which the Attorney General and the Assembly have to notify the court if they intend to take part as a party to the proceedings.

(2) Before ordering an adjournment in criminal proceedings, the court will consider all material circumstances, including whether it would involve delay that might extend beyond the custody time limits if the defendant is remanded in custody and his trial has not commenced.

7.10. If neither the Attorney General nor the Assembly notify the court within the specified time that he or it wishes to take part as a party to the proceedings: (1) the proceedings should immediately continue on expiry of the period within which they had to notify the court; and (2) the court has no duty to inform them of the outcome of the proceedings apart from the duty to notify them if the court decides to refer the devolution issue to another court (see para 10.3(5))[3].

---

1. Custody time limits are imposed by the Prosecution of Offences (Custody Time Limits) Regulations 1987, SI 1987/299, as amended.
2. See Annex 2 for information about fax numbers and addresses.
3. If there is an appeal, the appeal court will serve a devolution issue notice on the Attorney General and the Assembly (see para 7.4).

Adding the Attorney General or the Assembly to the proceedings and their right to require referral of a devolution issue to the Judicial Committee

1–6646 8.1. If the Attorney General or the Assembly wishes to take part as a party to the proceedings so far as they relate to a devolution issue, he or it must send to the court and the other parties (and to each other if only one of them has become a party) a notice substantially in the form numbered 'DI 2' shown in Annex 1 within the time specified in the devolution issue notice.

8.2. On receipt of this form the court may give such consequential directions as it considers necessary.

8.3. If the Attorney General or the Assembly is a party to the proceedings, and either of them wishes to require the court to refer the devolution issue to the Judicial Committee, he or it must as soon as practicable send to the court and the other parties (and to each other if only one of them has become a party) a notice substantially in the form numbered 'DI 3' shown in Annex 1.

Determination by the court of whether or not to make a reference of a devolution issue if the Attorney General or the Assembly do not require a reference

1–6647 9.1. If the court is not required to refer the devolution issue to the Judicial Committee, the court will decide whether it should refer the devolution issue to the relevant court as specified in para 3.4.

9.2. Before deciding whether to make a reference the court may hold a directions hearing or give written directions as to the making of submissions on the question of whether to make a reference.

9.3. The court may make a decision on the basis of written submissions if its procedures permit this and it wishes to do so, or the court may have a hearing before making a decision.

9.4. In exercising its discretion as to whether to make a reference, the court will have regard to all relevant circumstances and in particular to: (1) the importance of the devolution issue to the public in general; (2) the importance of the devolution issue to the original parties to the proceedings; (3) whether a decision on the reference of the devolution issue will be decisive of the matters in dispute between the parties; (4) whether all the relevant findings of fact have been made (a devolution issue will not, unless there are exceptional circumstances, be suitable for a reference if it has to be referred on the basis of assumed facts); (5) the delay that a reference would entail particularly in cases involving children and criminal cases (including whether the reference is likely to involve delay that would extend beyond the expiry of the custody time limits if the defendant is remanded in custody and his trial has not commenced); and (6) additional costs that a reference might involve[1].

9.5. The court should state its reasons for making or declining to make a reference.

9.6. If the court decides not to refer the case, it will give directions for the future conduct of the action, which will include directions as to the participation of the Attorney General and the Assembly if they are parties.

---

1. In criminal cases s 16 of the Prosecution of Offences Act 1985 does not enable a court receiving a reference to make a defendant's costs order. If the defendant is subsequently acquitted by the court who made the reference that court can make a defendant's costs order. However it would not cover the costs of the reference as 'proceedings' is defined in s 21 as including proceedings in any court below but makes no mention of proceedings on a reference.

Form and procedure for references

1–6648 10.1. If the court or tribunal is required by the Attorney General or the Assembly (in relation to any proceedings before the court to which he or it is a party) to refer the devolution issue to the Judicial Committee: (1) the court or tribunal will make the reference as soon as practicable after receiving the notice from the Attorney General or the Assembly substantially in the form numbered 'DI 3' shown in Annex 1, and follow the procedure for references in the Judicial Committee (Devolution Issues) Rules Order 1999, SI 1999/665; and (2) the court or tribunal may order the parties, or any of them, to draft the reference.

10.2. If the Court of Appeal decides to refer the devolution issue to the Judicial Committee: (1)

it will follow the procedure in the Judicial Committee (Devolution Issues) Rules Order 1999; and (2) the court may order the parties, or any of them, to draft the reference.

10.3. If any other court or tribunal decides, or if a tribunal is required, to refer the devolution issue to another court:

(1) The reference must be substantially in the form numbered 'DI 4' shown in Annex 1 and must set out the following: (*a*) the question referred; (*b*) the addresses of the parties, except in the case of family proceedings, for which see paras 15.2–4; (*c*) a concise statement of the background of the matter including—(i) the facts of the case, including any relevant findings of fact by the referring court or lower courts; and (ii) the main issues in the case and the contentions of the parties with regard to them; (*d*) the relevant law, including the relevant provisions of the GWA; (*e*) the reasons why an answer to the question is considered necessary for the purpose of disposing of the proceedings.

(2) All judgments already given in the proceedings will be annexed to the reference.

(3) The court may order the parties, or any of them, to draft the reference.

(4) The court or tribunal will transmit the reference to: (*a*) the Civil Appeals Office Registry if the reference is to the Court of Appeal from a county court, the High Court or the Crown Court in civil proceedings, or from a tribunal; (*b*) the Registrar of Criminal Appeals if the reference is to the Court of Appeal from the Crown Court in proceedings on indictment; and (*c*) the Crown Office if the reference is to the High Court from a magistrates' court in civil or summary proceedings or from the Crown Court in summary proceedings[1]. If the reference is transmitted to Cardiff an additional copy of the reference must be filed so that it can be retained by the Cardiff Office. The original reference will be forwarded to the Crown Office in London.

(5) At the same time as the reference is transmitted to the court receiving the reference a copy of the reference will be sent by first class post to: (*a*) the parties; (*b*) the Attorney General if he is not already a party; and (*c*) the Assembly if it is not already a party.

(6) Each person on whom a copy of the reference is served must within 21 days notify the court to which the reference is transmitted and the other persons on whom the reference is served whether they wish to be heard on the reference.

(7) The court receiving the reference (either the Court of Appeal or the High Court) will give directions for the conduct of the reference, including the lodging of cases or skeleton arguments; and transmit a copy of the determination on the reference to the referring court.

(8) If there has been an appeal to the Judicial Committee against a decision of the High Court or the Court of Appeal on a reference, and a copy of the Judicial Committee's decision on that appeal has been sent to the High Court or Court of Appeal (as the case may be), that court will send a copy to the court which referred the devolution issue to it.

10.4. When a court receives notification of the decision on a reference, it will determine how to proceed with the remainder of the case.

---

1. See Annex 2 for the relevant addresses. It shows The Law Courts, Cathays Park, Cardiff CF10 3PG and the Royal Courts of Justice, Strand, London WC2A 2LL as alternative addresses for transmitting documents to the Crown Office. If the order is transmitted to Cardiff, the additional copy will be forwarded by the Cardiff Office to the Crown Office in London.

Power of the court to deal with pending proceedings if a reference is made (whether by the Attorney General, the Assembly or the court).

1–6649 11. If a reference is made the court will adjourn or stay the proceedings in which the devolution issue arose, unless it otherwise orders; and will make such further orders as it thinks fit in relation to any adjournment or stay.

The Welsh language

12.1. If any party wishes to put forward a contention in relation to a devolution issue that involves comparison of the Welsh and English texts of any Assembly subordinate legislation, that party must give notice to the court as soon as possible.

12.2. Upon receipt of the notification, the court will consider the appropriate means of determining the issue, including, if necessary, the appointment of a Welsh speaking judicial assessor to assist the court.

12.3. Parties to any proceedings in which the Welsh language may be used must also comply with the [*Practice Direction (criminal: consolidated)* [2002] 3 All ER 904, [2002] 1 WLR 2870[1]] and the Practice Direction of 26 April 1999 (relating to civil proceedings). These Practice Directions apply, as appropriate, to proceedings involving a devolution issue in which the Welsh language may be used.

---

1. Paragraphs III.22, III.23 in this Part, post.

Crown Proceedings Act 1947 (s 19)

1–6650 13. Where the court has determined that a devolution issue arises, the Attorney General will give any necessary consent to: (1) the proceedings being transferred to The Law Courts, Cathays Park, Cardiff CF10 3PG, or to such other district registry as shall (exceptionally) be directed by the court; and (2) to the trial taking place at Cardiff or at such other trial location as shall (exceptionally) be directed by the court.

PART III DIRECTIONS APPLICABLE TO SPECIFIC PROCEEDINGS

Judicial review proceedings; Crown Office applications in Wales

1–6651 **14.1.** RSC Ord 53, Sch 1 to the CPR contains the procedure to be followed in applications for judicial review.

14.2. Notwithstanding Queen's Bench Practice Direction 23 and prescribed Forms 86A and 86B[1] facilities will be available for applications for judicial review to be lodged at The Law Courts, Cathays Park, Cardiff CF10 3PG if the relief sought or the grounds of the application involve either or both of the following: (1) a devolution issue arising out of the GWA; (2) an issue concerning the Welsh Assembly, the Welsh executive, or any Welsh public body (including a Welsh local authority) even if it does not involve a devolution issue. Such applications may continue be lodged at the Crown Office in London, if the applicant prefers to do that.

14.3. If applications are lodged at Cardiff an additional copy of the application must be filed so that it can be retained by the Cardiff Office. The original application will be forwarded to the Crown Office in London.

14.4. If a party intends to raise a devolution issue, the application notice must (in addition to the matters listed in RSC Ord 53, r 3(2)(*a*)): (1) specify that the applicant wishes to raise a devolution issue and identify the relevant provisions of the GWA; and (2) contain a summary of the facts and circumstances and points of law on the basis of which it is alleged that a devolution issue arises in sufficient detail to enable the court to determine whether a devolution issue arises.

---

1. Queen's Bench Practice Direction 23 2C(2) provides that wherever practicable proceedings should be commenced in London, although applications can be made outside London in cases of urgency. Prescribed Forms 86A and 86B give the address for delivery of the forms as the Crown Office, Royal Courts of Justice, Strand, London WC2A 2LL. It is hoped that these forms will be amended to give The Law Courts, Cathays Park, Cardiff CF10 3PG as an alternative address for the Crown Office.

Family proceedings in the magistrates' courts, the county courts and the High Court

1–6652 **15.1.** In any proceedings in which any question with respect to the upbringing of a child arises, the court shall have regard to the general principle that any delay in determining the question is likely to prejudice the welfare of the child[1].

15.2. If the FPR apply, the court will comply with r 10.21[2].

15.3. If Pt IV of the FPR applies, the court will comply with r 4.23[3].

15.4. If the FPC apply, the court will comply with rr 23 and 33A[4].

15.5. If the proceedings are listed in column (i) of App 3 to the FPR or Sch 2 to the FPC, a copy of any notice to be given to the parties must also be given to the persons set out in column (iv) of App 3 or Sch 2 as the case may be.

15.6. A party wishing to raise a devolution issue must, wherever possible, raise it (giving full particulars of the provisions relied on) in the application or answer or at the first directions hearing where appropriate.

15.7. If a party has not raised a devolution issue as above, the party must seek the permission of the court to raise it at a later stage.

15.8. Where a court has referred the devolution issue to another court and has received notification of the decision on the reference, the matter should so far as is practicable be placed before the same judge or magistrates who dealt with the case before the reference.

---

1. Section 1(2) of the Children Act 1989.
2. Rule 10.21 states: "(1) Subject to rule 2.3 [of the FPR] nothing in these rules shall be construed as requiring any party to reveal the address of their private residence (or that of any child) save by order of the court".
3. Rule 4.23 states: "(1) Notwithstanding any rule of court to the contrary, no document, other than a record of an order, held by the court and relating to proceedings to which [Pt IV] applies shall be disclosed, other than to—(a) a party, (b) the legal representative of a party (c) the guardian ad litem, (d) the Legal Aid Board, or (e) a welfare officer, without the leave of the judge or the district judge".
4. Rule 23 states: "(1) No document, other than a record of an order, held by the court and relating to relevant proceedings shall be disclosed, other than to—(a) a party, (b) the legal representative of a party, (c) the guardian ad litem, (d) the Legal Aid Board, or (e) a welfare officer, without leave of the justices' clerk or the court".

Civil proceedings in the county courts and the High Court

Criminal proceedings in the Crown Court

1–6653 **17.** If the defendant wishes to raise a devolution issue he should do so at the plea and directions hearing.

Criminal and civil proceedings in the magistrates' courts

1–6654 **18.1.** (1) Where a defendant, who has been charged or has had an information laid against him in respect of a criminal offence and has entered a plea of 'Not guilty', wishes to raise a devolution issue he should, wherever possible, give full particulars of the provisions relied on by notice in writing.

(2) Where a party to a complaint, or applicant for a licence wishes to raise a devolution issue he should, wherever possible, give full particulars of the provisions relied on by notice in writing.

(3) Such notice should be given to the prosecution (and other party if any) and the court as soon as practicable after the 'Not guilty' plea is entered or the complaint or application is made as the case may be.

18.2. Where proceedings are to be committed or transferred to the Crown Court by the magistrates, the question as to whether a devolution issue arises shall be a matter for the Crown Court.

PART IV APPEALS

Appeals to the Court of Appeal (Civil and Criminal Division)

Appeals to the Crown Court

1–6655   20. A notice of appeal from a decision of the magistrates' courts to the Crown Court must specify whether the devolution issue was considered in the court below and if so, provide details of the decision. If it was not so considered, the notice should specify: (1) that the appeal raises a devolution issue and the relevant provisions of the GWA; and (2) the facts and circumstances and points of law on the basis of which it is alleged that a devolution issue arises in sufficient detail to enable the court to determine whether a devolution issue arises.

ANNEX 1

DI 1

DEVOLUTION ISSUES

Notice of Devolution Issue to Attorney General and the National Assembly for Wales

[NAME OF CASE]

1–6656   Take notice that the above mentioned case has raised a devolution issue as defined by Schedule 8 to the Government of Wales Act 1998. Details of the devolution issue are given in the attached Schedule.

This notice meets the notification requirements under paragraph 5(1) of Schedule 8 to the Government of Wales Act 1998. You may take part as a party to these proceedings, so far as they relate to a devolution issue (paragraph 5(2) of Schedule 8). If you want to do this you must notify the court by completing the attached form, and returning it to the court at [address] by [date].

DATED

To: The Attorney General
             The National Assembly for Wales
             Other parties (where appropriate)

DI 2

DEVOLUTION ISSUES

Notice of intention of Attorney General or the National Assembly for Wales to become party to proceedings, so far as they relate to a devolution issue, under paragraph 5(2) Schedule 8 to the Government of Wales Act 1998

IN THE [NAME OF COURT]

[CASE NAME]

1–6657   Take notice that the [Attorney General the National Assembly for Wales] intends to take part as a party to proceedings so far as they relate to a devolution issue as permitted by paragraph 5(2) of Schedule 8 to the Government of Wales Act 1998 in relation to the devolution issue raised by [ ] which notice was received by the [Attorney General] [Assembly] on [ ].

[The [ ] also gives notice that it [requires the matter to be referred to is still considering whether to require the matter to be referred to] the Judicial Committee of the Privy Council under paragraph 30 of Schedule 8 to the Government of Wales Act 1998.]

[DATE]

On behalf of the [Attorney General]
[National Assembly for Wales]
To: The clerk of the court at [ ]
             The parties to the case
             [Attorney General] [National Assembly for Wales]

DI 3

DEVOLUTION ISSUES

Notice by Attorney General or National Assembly for Wales that they require devolution issue to be referred to the Judicial Committee of the Privy Council

IN THE [COURT]

[CASE NAME]

1–6658 The [Attorney General] [National Assembly for Wales] gives notice that the devolution issue, which has been raised in the above case and to which [he] [it] is a party, must be referred to the Judicial Committee of the Privy Council under paragraph 30 of Schedule 8 to the Government of Wales Act 1998.
[DATE]

On behalf of the [Attorney General
National Assembly for Wales]
To: The clerk of the court at [ ]
                The parties to the case
                [Attorney General] [National Assembly for Wales]

DI 4

DEVOLUTION ISSUES

*Reference by the court or tribunal of devolution issue to
[High Court] [Court of Appeal] [Judicial Committee of the Privy Council]*

IN THE [COURT]

[CASE NAME]

1–6659 It is ordered that the devolution issue(s) set out in the Sch be referred to the [High Court] [Court of Appeal] [Judicial Committee of the Privy Council] for determination in accordance with paragraph [ ] of Schedule 8 to the Government of Wales Act 1998.
   It is further ordered that the proceedings be stayed until the [High Court] [Court of Appeal] [Judicial Committee of the Privy Council] determine the devolution issue[s] or until further order.
DATED

Judge/clerk to the magistrates court
Chairman of the Tribunal
[Address]

SKELETON REFERENCE TO BE ATTACHED TO FORM DI 4

IN THE [COURT]

[CASE NAME]

1–6660 (*a*) [The question referred.]
       (*b*) [The addresses of the parties]
       (*c*) [A concise statement of the background to the matters including—i. The facts of the case including any relevant findings of fact by the referring court or lower courts; and ii. The main issues in the case and the contentions of the parties with regard to them;]
       (*d*) [the relevant law including the relevant provisions of the Government of Wales Act 1998]
       (*e*) [the reasons why an answer to the question is considered necessary for the purpose of disposing of the proceedings.]
       [All judgments already given in the proceedings are annexed to this reference.]

ANNEX 2

ADDRESSES

1–6661 1 Notices to the National Assembly for Wales (*Cynulliad Cenedlaethol Cymru*) must be sent to the Counsel General to the National Assembly for Wales, Crown Buildings, Cathays Park, Cardiff CF99 INA. Fax number: [ ].
   2 Notices to the Attorney General must be sent to the Attorney General's Chambers, 9 Buckingham Gate, London SW1E 6JP. Fax number [ ].
   3 References to the Crown Office under paragraph 9.3(1)c of the Practice Direction may be sent to the Crown Office, Royal Courts of Justice, Strand, London WC2A 2LL; or the Law Courts, Cathays Park, Cardiff CF 10 3PG (2 copies).

EXPLANATORY NOTE

   4 The addresses and fax numbers above are the best information available, however it is possible that these (particularly the fax numbers and address for Notices to the Assembly) may change, it would therefore be advisable to confirm the numbers before sending information.

Magistrates' Courts Warrants (Specification of Provisions) Order 2000[1]

(SI 2000/3278 amended by SI 2004/1835)

1–6800   1. Citation and commencement.   This Order may be cited as the Magistrates' Courts Warrants (Specification of Provisions) Order 2000 and shall come into force on 8th January 2001.

---

1. Made by the Lord Chancellor under s 125A(3) of the Magistrates' Courts Act 1980.

1–6801   2. Specified provisions.   The following provisions are specified for the purposes of section 125A(3) of the Magistrates' Courts Act 1980—

(a) paragraph 7(2) of Schedule 7 to the Powers of Criminal Courts (Sentencing) Act 2000;
(aa) section 7(1) of the Bail Act 1976;
(b) in the Magistrates' Court Act 1980—

    (i)   section 1;
    (ii)   section 13;
    (iii) section 76;
    (iv)   section 83(1) and (2);
    (v)   section 86(4);
    (vi)   section 93(5);
    (vii) section 97;
    (viii) section 97A;
    (ix)   section 136;

(c) section 40 of the Child Support Act 1991;
(d) paragraph 4 of Schedule 3 to the Crime and Disorder Act 1998;
(e) in the Powers of Criminal Courts (Sentencing) Act 2000:

    (i)   section 104(1);
    (ii)   section 123(1);
    (iii) paragraph 3(1)(b) of Schedule 3;
    (iv)   paragraph 1(1) of Schedule 5;
    (v)   paragraph 6(2) of Schedule 8 (but only where an application is made under paragraph 2(1) of that Schedule);

(f) regulations 41(1) and 42(5)(b) of the Community Charges (Administration and Enforcement) Regulations 1989;
(g) regulations 16(3)(a) and 17(5)(b) of the Non-Domestic Rating (Collection and Enforcement) (Local Lists) Regulations 1989;
(h) regulations 47(3)(a) and 48(5)(b) of the Council Tax (Administration and Enforcement) Regulations 1992.

Justices and Justices' Clerks (Costs) Regulations 2001[1]

(SI 2001/1296)

1–6920   1. Citation and commencement.   These Regulations may be cited as the Justices and Justices' Clerks (Costs) Regulations 2001 and shall come into force on the second day after the day on which the Regulations are made.

---

1. Made by the Lord Chancellor in exercise of the powers conferred on him by s 53A(4) of the Justices of the Peace Act 1997. These rules are continued in force and have effect as if made under s 34(4) of the Courts Act 2003 by the Courts Act 2003 (Transitional Provisions, Savings and Consequential Provisions) Order 2005, SI 2005/911.

1–6921   2. Interpretation.   In these Regulations—

"claim" means a claim for costs made by the receiving party;
"costs judge" means a taxing master of the Supreme Court;
"order" means an order of the court made under section 53A(3) of the Justices of the Peace Act 1997 that the Lord Chancellor make a payment in respect of the costs of a person in the proceedings;
"proceedings" means proceedings in respect of any act or omission of a justice of the peace or a justices' clerk in the execution (or purported execution) of his duty—

    (i)   as a single justice; or
    (ii) as a justices' clerk exercising, by virtue of any statutory provision, any of the functions of a single justice;

"receiving party" means the person in whose favour the order is made.

1–6922   3. The payment of costs by the Lord Chancellor.   No order shall be made under section 53A(3) of the Justices of the Peace Act 1997 in favour of—

(a) a public authority; or
(b) a person acting—

    (i)   on behalf of a public authority, or
    (ii) in his capacity as an official appointed by a public authority.

1–6923   4. Determination of costs. Where the court makes an order, the amount of costs payable by the Lord Chancellor shall be determined in accordance with these Regulations.

1–6924   5. Court order and determination of costs by the court. (1) Except as provided for in paragraph (2), when making the order the court shall—

    (a) determine such an amount as it considers sufficient reasonably to compensate the receiving party for any costs properly incurred by him in the proceedings, and
    (b) specify that amount in the order.

    (2) The amount of costs shall be determined by a costs judge in accordance with regulations 6 and 7 where—

    (a) the hearing has lasted more than one day or there is insufficient time for the court to determine the costs on the day of the hearing, or
    (b) the court considers that there is other good reason for the costs judge to determine the amount of costs.

    (3) The court shall serve the order on the receiving party and on the Lord Chancellor together with, where paragraph (2) applies, notification that costs will be determined by a costs judge.

1–6925   6. Determination of costs by a costs judge. (1) Where the amount of costs is to be determined by a costs judge, the receiving party shall, no later than three months from (but excluding) the date on which the order was made, file his claim and a copy of the order in the Supreme Court Costs Office and serve a copy of the claim on the Lord Chancellor.

    (2) On the application of the receiving party to the Supreme Court Costs Office, the costs judge may, in exceptional circumstances, extend the period of three months.

    (3) A claim shall—

    (a) summarise the items of work done by a legal representative or the receiving party as a litigant in person, as appropriate;
    (b) state, where appropriate, the dates on which items of work were done, the time taken and the sums claimed; and
    (c) specify any disbursements claimed, including counsel's fees, the circumstances in which they were incurred and the amounts claimed in respect of them,

and shall be accompanied by receipts or other evidence of the receiving party's payment of the costs claimed, and any receipts or other documents in support of any disbursements claimed.

    (4) If the receiving party wishes to draw any special circumstances to the attention of the costs judge, he shall specify those circumstances in his claim.

    (5) If the Lord Chancellor wishes to make any written representations in respect of the claim he shall, no later than one month from (but excluding) the date on which the Lord Chancellor received the claim from the receiving party, file any written representations at the Supreme Court Costs Office and serve a copy of them on the receiving party.

    (6) The costs judge may make directions in respect of—

    (a) the claim;
    (b) any written representations;
    (c) the filing and serving of any further particulars or documents; and
    (d) ensuring that the determination of costs is dealt with justly.

    (7) Where the costs judge considers it appropriate, the claim shall be listed for a hearing before him, and the Supreme Court Costs Office shall serve on the receiving party and on the Lord Chancellor notification of the place, date and time of the hearing.

1–6926   7. (1) The costs judge shall consider the claim and shall allow such costs in respect of—

    (a) such work as appears to him to have been actually and reasonably done; and
    (b) such disbursements as appear to him to have been actually and reasonably incurred,

as he considers sufficient reasonably to compensate the receiving party for any expenses properly incurred by him in the proceedings.

    (2) In determining costs under paragraph (1) the costs judge shall take into account all the relevant circumstances of the case including the nature, importance, complexity or difficulty of the work and the time involved.

    (3) When determining costs for the purposes of this regulation, there shall be allowed a reasonable amount in respect of all costs reasonably incurred and any doubts which the costs judge may have as to whether the costs were reasonably incurred or were reasonable in amount shall be resolved against the receiving party.

    (4) When the costs judge has determined the amount of costs payable to the receiving party, the Supreme Court Costs Office shall notify the receiving party and the Lord Chancellor of the amount of costs payable.

Magistrates' Courts (International Criminal Court) (Forms) Rules 2001[1]

(SI 2001/2600)

1–6930   1. These Rules may be cited as the Magistrates' Courts (International Criminal Court) (Forms) Rules 2001 and shall come into force on 1st September 2001.

1. Made by the Secretary of State in exercise of the powers conferred on him by s 49 of the International Criminal Court Act 2001.

1–6931 2. In these Rules:

"the Act" means the International Criminal Court Act 2001;

"competent court" has the same meaning as it has in the Act; and

"the International Criminal Court" means the International Criminal Court established by the Statute of the International Criminal Court, done at Rome on 17th July 1998.

1–6932 3. The provisions of the Magistrates' Courts Rules 1981 shall have effect subject to the provisions of these Rules.

1–6933 4. Consent to surrender given under section 7 of the Act (consent to surrender) must be in writing in form 1 set out in the Schedule to these Rules or a form to the like effect.

1–6934 5. Waiver given under section 13 of the Act (waiver of the right to review) must be in writing in form 2 set out in the Schedule to these Rules or a form to the like effect.

Rules 4 and 5   SCHEDULE
                                                                      FORMS
1–6935

FORM 1
NOTICE OF CONSENT TO SURRENDER (INTERNATIONAL CRIMINAL COURT ACT 2001, SECTION 7)

(a) Whereas on the   day of   20   , I was arrested in pursuance of a warrant under section 2 of the International Criminal Court Act 2001 with a view to a delivery order being made providing for me to be delivered up into the custody of the International Criminal Court.

or

(b) Whereas on the   day of   20   , I was convicted by the International Criminal Court and on the   day of   20   , I was arrested in pursuance of a warrant under section 2 of the International Criminal Court Act 2001 with a view to a delivery order being made providing for me to be delivered up into the custody of [the International Criminal Court] [the state of enforcement (*insert name of the state of enforcement*)].

And whereas I understand that, unless I consent to my delivery, I shall have the right:

(a) to make representations at delivery proceedings as to the matters of which the competent court is to be satisfied before making a delivery order, and

(b) to make an application to the competent court at the time of the delivery proceedings for the determination of whether I was lawfully arrested in pursuance of the warrant and whether my rights have been respected, and

(c) if a delivery order is made, to seek a review of the delivery order, and

(d) to make an application for habeas corpus, and

(e) not to have the delivery order executed against me until after the end of the period of 15 days beginning with the date on which the order is made, or (if later), while any habeas corpus proceedings are still pending.

I therefore give notice of my consent to surrender to be delivered up into the custody of the International Criminal Court or into the custody of the state of enforcement (*insert name of the state of enforcement*), whichever is appropriate. I understand that by consenting to my surrender I waive my right to seek a review of the delivery order under section 12 of the International Criminal Court Act 2001 and I consent to the Secretary of State giving directions for the execution of the delivery order before the period of 15 days has expired.

(Signed by the person to be delivered)

Print name and sign

or where it is inappropriate to act for themselves under section 7(2)(b) of the International Criminal Court Act 2001.

(Signed on their behalf)

Print name and sign

This notification was signed by the above-mentioned person in my presence on the   day of 20   .

(Justice of the Peace for   )

1–6936

FORM 2
NOTICE OF WAIVER OF THE RIGHT TO REVIEW (INTERNATIONAL CRIMINAL COURT ACT 2001, SECTION 13)

(a) Whereas on the   day of   20   , a competent court made a delivery order providing for me to be delivered up into the custody of the International Criminal Court.

or

(b) Whereas on the   day of   20   , a competent court made a delivery order providing for me to be delivered up into the custody of the state of enforcement (*insert name of the state of enforcement*).

And whereas I understand that, unless I waive my right to seek a review of the delivery order I have the right:

(a) for the delivery order to be reviewed, and

(b) to make an application for habeas corpus, and

(c) not to have the delivery order executed against me until after the end of the period of 15 days beginning with the date on which the order is made, or (if later), while any habeas corpus proceedings are still pending.

I therefore give notice that I waive my right to seek a review of the delivery order and I consent to the

Secretary of State giving directions for the execution of the delivery order before the period of 15 days has expired.
(Signed by the person to be delivered)
(Print and sign name)
    or where it is inappropriate to act for themselves under section 13(2)(b) of the International Criminal Court Act 2001.
(Signed on their behalf)
(Print and sign name)
    This notification was signed by the above-mentioned person in my presence on the   day of
20   .
    (Justice of the Peace for   )

Magistrates' Courts (Detention and Forfeiture of Terrorist Cash) (No 2) Rules 2001[1]

(SI 2001/4013 amended by SI 2003/1236)

1-6940   1. Citation and commencement. These Rules may be cited as the Magistrates' Courts (Detention and Forfeiture of Terrorist Cash) (No 2) Rules 2001 and shall come into force on 20th December 2001.

---

1. Made by the Lord Chancellor in exercise of the powers conferred on him by s 144 of the Magistrates' Courts Act 1980 and after consultation with the Rule Committee appointed under that s 144.

1-6941   2. Revocation. The Magistrates' Courts (Detention and Forfeiture of Terrorist Cash) Rules 2001 are hereby revoked.

1-6942   3. Interpretation. In these Rules—

(a) "the Act" means the "Anti-terrorism, Crime and Security Act 2001";
(b) words and expressions used have the same meaning as in Schedule 1 to the Act;
(c) a reference to a paragraph of Schedule 1 by number alone is a reference to a paragraph so numbered in Schedule 1 to the Act; and
(d) a reference to a form is a reference to a form set out in the Schedule to these Rules.

1-6943   4. First application for continued detention of seized cash. (1) The first application under paragraph 3(5) of Schedule 1 for an order under paragraph 3(2) of Schedule 1 for continued detention of cash seized under paragraph 2 of Schedule 1 shall be made in Form A and may be sent to the justices' clerk for the petty sessions area in which the cash was seized.
    (2) A copy of the written application and notification of the hearing of the application shall be given by the applicant to the person from whom the cash was seized.
    (3) Where seized cash is found in a letter, parcel, container or other means of unattended dispatch, the reference in paragraph (2) to the person from whom the cash was seized shall be read as a reference to the sender and intended recipient of the letter, parcel, container or other means of unattended dispatch.
    (4) Where paragraph (3) applies, the court shall not decline to hear an application solely on the ground that it has not been proved that the sender and intended recipient have received a copy of the written application and notification of hearing.
    (5) *Revoked.*
    (6) The justices' clerk shall give—

(a) notice of the order, and
(b) a copy of the order,

to the person from whom the cash was seized and to any other person who is affected by the order.

1-6944   5. Further applications for continued detention of seized cash. (1) An application under paragraph 3(5) of Schedule 1 for a further order under paragraph 3(2) of Schedule 1 for the continued detention of cash shall be in Form A and may be sent to the justices' clerk referred to in rule 4(1).
    (2) The applicant shall send a copy of the application to every person to whom notice of previous orders made under paragraph 3(2) of Schedule 1 has been given.
    (3) The justices' clerk shall fix a date for the hearing of the application, which, unless he directs otherwise, shall not be earlier than seven days from the date on which it is fixed, and he shall notify the applicant and every person to whom notice of the previous orders has been given of that date.
    (4) *Revoked.*
    (5) The justices' clerk shall give a copy of the order to every person to whom notice of the previous orders has been given.

(6) The justices' clerks shall also give—

(a)   notice of the order, and

(b)   a copy of the order,

to any other person other than one referred to in paragraph (5) who is affected by the order.

1–6945   6. Applications for release of detained cash.   (1) An application under paragraph 5(2) or paragraph 9(1) of Schedule 1 for the release of detained cash shall be made in writing to the justices' clerk referred to in rule 4(1), and shall specify the grounds on which it is made.

(2)   The justices' clerk shall send a copy of the application to the authorised officer who seized the cash and to every person to whom notice of an order made under paragraph 3(2) of Schedule 1 has been given.

(3)   The justices' clerk shall fix a date for the hearing of the application, which, unless he directs otherwise, shall not be earlier than seven days from the date on which it is fixed, and shall notify the applicant, the authorised officer who seized the cash and every person to whom notice of an order made under paragraph 3(2) of Schedule 1 has been given of that date.

(4)   At a hearing of an application under paragraph 9(1) of Schedule 1, the court may, if it thinks fit, order that the applicant shall be joined as a party to all the proceedings in relation to the detained cash.

(5)   A direction under paragraph 5(2) of Schedule 1 for the release of detained cash shall provide for the release of the cash within seven days of the date of the making of the direction or such longer period as with the agreement of the applicant may be specified in the direction, except that the cash shall not be released whilst paragraph 5(4) of Schedule 1 applies.

(6)   An order under paragraph 9(3) of Schedule 1 for the release of detained cash shall provide for the release of the cash within seven days of the date of the making of the order or such longer period as with the agreement of the applicant may be specified in the order.

1–6946   7. Application for forfeiture of detained cash.   (1) An application under paragraph 6(1) of Schedule 1 for the forfeiture of detained cash shall be in Form F and may be sent to the justices' clerk referred to in rule 4(1).

(2)   The applicant shall send a copy of the application to every person to whom notice of an order made under paragraph 3(2) of Schedule 1 has been given.

(3)   The justices' clerk shall fix a date for the hearing of the application, which unless he directs otherwise, shall not be earlier than seven days from the date on which it is fixed, and shall notify the applicant and every person to whom notice of an order made under paragraph 3(2) of Schedule 1 has been given of that date.

(4)   An order for the forfeiture of detained cash under paragraph 6(2) of Schedule 1 and a copy of the order shall be given by the justices' clerk to every person to whom notice of an order made under paragraph 3(2) of Schedule 1 has been given.

1–6947   8. Application for compensation.   (1) An application under paragraph 10(1) of Schedule 1 for compensation shall be made in writing to the justices' clerk referred to in rule 4(1), and shall specify the grounds on which it is made.

(2)   The justices' clerk shall send a copy of the application to—

(a)   the Commissioners of Customs and Excise, if the cash which is the subject of the application was seized by a customs officer;

(b)   the police force to which the constable belongs, if the cash which is the subject of the application was seized by a constable;

(c)   the Secretary of State, if the cash which is the subject of the application was seized by an immigration officer.

(3)   The justices' clerk shall fix a date for the hearing of the application, which, unless he directs otherwise, shall not be earlier than seven days from the date on which it is fixed, and shall notify the applicant and the person referred to in paragraph (2) of that date.

1–6948   9. Notice.   Any notice or copy of any order required to be given to any person under these Rules may be given by post to his last known address.

1–6949   10. Procedure at hearings.   (1) At the hearing of an application under Schedule 1 to the Act, any person to whom notice of the application has been given may attend and be heard on the question of whether the application should be granted, but the fact that any such person does not attend shall not prevent the court from hearing the application.

(2)   Subject to the foregoing provisions of these Rules, proceedings on such an application shall be regulated in the same manner as proceedings on a complaint, and accordingly for the purposes of these Rules, the application shall be deemed to be a complaint, the applicant a complainant, the respondents to be defendants and any notice given by the justices' clerk under rules 5(3), 6(3), 7(3) or 8(3) to be a summons: but nothing in this rule shall be construed as enabling a warrant of arrest to be issued for failure to appear in answer to any such notice.

(3)   At the hearing of an application under Schedule 1 to the Act, the court shall require the matters contained in the application to be sworn by the applicant under oath, may require the applicant to answer any questions under oath and may require any response from the respondent to the application to be made under oath.

(4)   The court shall record or cause to be recorded in writing the substance of any statements made under oath which are not already recorded in the written application.

SCHEDULE

1–6950

FORM A

First/Further** application for continued detention of seized cash
(Paragraph 3(5) of Schedule 1 to the Anti-terrorism, Crime and Security Act 2001; MC (Detention and Forfeiture of Terrorist Cash) (No 2) Rules 2001 rr 4(1), 5(1))
Magistrates' Court
(Code   )
Date
Name of person from whom cash seized*
Address*
Names and addresses of any other persons likely to be affected by an order for detention of the cash (if known)
Amount seized (estimated**)
Date of seizure
Time of seizure
Place of seizure
Date of latest order for continued detention of seized cash (if any)
Amount detained under latest order for continued detention (if any)
Amounts released since the latest order for continued detention (if any)
I,
of
(official address and position of applicant)
Authorised Officer/Commissioner of Customs and Excise**, apply for an order under paragraph 3(2) of Schedule 1 to the Anti-terrorism, Crime and Security Act 2001 authorising the continued detention of cash in the sum of   and will state upon oath that one of the three grounds below is satisfied:
**1 There are reasonable grounds for suspecting that the cash is intended to be used for the purposes of terrorism and that either—

(a) its continued detention is justified while its intended use is further investigated or consideration is given to bringing (in the United Kingdom or elsewhere) proceedings against any person for an offence with which the cash is connected, or
(b) proceedings against any person for an offence with which the cash is connected have been started and have not been concluded.

**2 There are reasonable grounds for suspecting that the cash consists of resources of an organisation which is a proscribed organisation and that either—

(a) its continued detention is justified while investigation is made into whether or not it consists of such resources or consideration is given to bringing (in the United Kingdom or elsewhere) proceedings against any person for an offence with which the cash is connected, or
(b) proceedings against any person for an offence with which the cash is connected have been started and have not been concluded.

**3 There are reasonable grounds for suspecting that the cash is property earmarked as terrorist property and that either—

(a) its continued detention is justified while its derivation is further investigated or consideration is given to bringing (in the United Kingdom or elsewhere) proceedings against any person for an offence with which the cash is connected, or
(b) proceedings against any person for an offence with which the cash is connected have been started and have not been concluded.

(state grounds)
Signed
To: The Clerk to the Justices

Magistrates' Court

Notes to the Applicant—
First Application—You must give a copy of this application and notification of the hearing of it to the person from whom the cash was seized.
Further Application—This application must wherever possible be submitted to the Justices' Clerk at least seven days before the expiry of the last period of detention that was ordered by the court. You must send a copy of this application to the person from whom the cash was seized and any other person specified in any order made under paragraph 3(2) of Schedule 1.
*In the case of a letter, parcel, container or other means of unattended dispatch, insert names and addresses, if known, of sender and intended recipient.
**Delete as appropriate

1–6951 *Forms B–E revoked.*

1–6955

FORM F

Application for forfeiture of detained cash
(Paragraph 6(1) of Schedule 1 to the Anti-terrorism, Crime and Security Act 2001; MC (Detention and Forfeiture of Terrorist Cash (No 2) Rules 2001 r 7(1))
Magistrates' Court
(Code)
Date
Name of person from whom cash seized*
Address*
Names and addresses of any other persons identified by the Court as being affected by this order
Amount seized (estimated**)
Date of seizure

Time of seizure
Place of seizure
Date of latest order for continued detention of seized cash (if any)
Amount detained under latest order for continued detention (if any)
Amounts released since the latest order for continued detention (if any)
I,
of
(official address and position of applicant)
Authorised Officer/Commissioner of Customs and Excise**, apply for an order under paragraph 6 of Schedule 1 to the Anti-terrorism, Crime and Security Act 2001 for the forfeiture of cash in the sum of   together with any interest accruing thereon pursuant to paragraph 4(1) of Schedule 1 to that Act, on the grounds that the said cash

**1 is intended to be used for the purposes of terrorism
**2 consists of the resources of an organisation which is a proscribed organisation
**3 is or represents property obtained through terrorism (ie is property earmarked as terrorist property within the meaning of Part 5 of Schedule 1 to that Act)

(state grounds)
To: The Clerk to the Justices

Magistrates' Court

Note to the Applicant—You must send a copy of this application to the person from whom the cash was seized and any other person specified in any order made under paragraph 3(2) of Schedule 1.

*In the case of a letter, parcel, container or other means of unattended dispatch, insert names and addresses, if known, of sender and an intended recipient.
**Delete as appropriate.

1–6956   *Form G revoked.*

1–6970

Practice Direction (criminal: consolidated)[1]

Court of Appeal, Criminal Division
Lord Woolf CJ
8 July 2002 as amended 29 July 2004

Practice – Criminal proceedings – Consolidation of existing practice directions, practice statements and practice notes.

This is a consolidation, with some amendments, of existing Practice Directions, Practice Statements and Practice Notes as they affect proceedings in the Court of Appeal (Criminal Division), the Crown Court and the magistrates' courts, with the exception of the Practice Directions which relate to costs. Practice Directions relating to costs are consolidated in the Practice Direction on Costs in Criminal Proceedings, handed down on 18 May 2004.

---

1. [2002] 3 All ER 904, [2002] 1 WLR 2870 consolidated with amendments and reissued on 29 July 2004 and amended by the following: *Forms for use in criminal proceedings* [2005] 2 All ER 916, [2005] 2 Cr App R 17, *Jury Service* [2005] 3 All ER 89, [2005] 1 WLR 1361, [2005] 2 Cr App R 16 (not reproduced in this work), *Case Management* [2005] 3 All ER 91, [2005] 1 WLR 1491, [2005] 2 Cr App R 18, *Crown Court: Classification and Allocation of Business* [2005] 1 WLR 2215, [2005] 2 Cr App R 33; *Forms for use in criminal proceedings* [2006] 3 All ER 484, [2006] 1 WLR 1152, [2006] 2 Cr App R 22. Previous amending directions to *the Consolidated Criminal Practice Direction* were: (No 1) (Support For Witnesses Giving Evidence By Live Television Link); (No 2) (Appeals Against Sentence – the Provision of Notice to the Prosecution) 10 October 2003 [2003] 4 All ER 665; (No 3) (Bail: Failure to Surrender and Trials in Absence) 22 January 2004, [2004] 1 Cr App R 28; (No 4) (Guidance to Jurors) 23 February 2004, [2004] 2 Cr App R 1; (No 5) (Listing of Appeals against Conviction and Sentence in the Court of Appeal Criminal Division) 8 March 2004, [2004] 2 Cr App R 2; (No 7) (Explanations for the Imposition of Custodial Sentences) [2004] 2 Cr App R 25; (No 8) (Mandatory Life Sentences) 2 August 2004, [2005] 1 Cr App R 8. The following direction was revoked: *Life Sentences – Procedure for passing a mandatory life sentence* [2004] 1 WLR 1874; [2004] 2 Cr App R 24.

PART I
DIRECTIONS OF GENERAL APPLICATION
I.1 Court dress

I.1.1 In magistrates' courts, advocates appear without robes or wigs. In all other courts, Queen's Counsel wear a short wig and a silk (or stuff) gown over a court coat with bands, junior counsel wear a short wig and stuff gown with bands, and solicitors and other advocates authorised under the Courts and Legal Services Act 1990 wear a black stuff gown with bands.

I.2 Unofficial tape recording of proceedings

I.2.1 Section 9 of the Contempt of Court Act 1981 contains provisions governing the unofficial use of tape recorders in court. Section 9(1) provides that it is a contempt of court: (a) to use in court, or bring into court for use, any tape recorder or other instrument for recording sound, except with the leave of the court; (b) to publish a recording of legal proceedings made by means of any such instrument, or any recording derived directly or indirectly from it, by playing it in the hearing of the public or any section of the public, or to dispose of it or any recording so derived, with a view to such publication; (c) to use any such recording in contravention of any conditions of leave granted under para (a). These provisions do not apply to the making or use of sound recordings for purposes of official transcripts of the proceedings, upon which the Act imposes no restriction whatever.

I.2.2 The discretion given to the court to grant, withhold or withdraw leave to use tape recorders or to impose conditions as to the use of the recording is unlimited, but the following factors may be relevant to its exercise: (a) the existence of any reasonable need on the part of the applicant for leave, whether a litigant or a person connected with the press or broadcasting, for the recording to be made; (b) the risk that the recording could be used for the purpose of briefing witnesses out of court; (c) any possibility that the use of the recorder would disturb the proceedings or distract or worry any witnesses or other participants.

I.2.3 Consideration should always be given whether conditions as to the use of a recording made pursuant to leave should be imposed. The identity and role of the applicant for leave and the nature of the subject matter of the proceedings may be relevant to this.

I.2.4 The particular restriction imposed by s 9(1)(b) applies in every case, but may not be present to the mind of every applicant to whom leave is given. It may therefore be desirable on occasion for this provision to be drawn to the attention of those to whom leave is given.

I.2.5 The transcript of a permitted recording is intended for the use of the person given leave to make it and is not intended to be used as, or to compete with, the official transcript mentioned in s 9(4).

I.3 Restrictions on reporting proceedings

I.3.1 Under s 4(2) of the Contempt of Court Act 1981 a court may, where it appears necessary for avoiding a substantial risk of prejudice to the administration of justice in the proceedings before it or in any others pending or imminent, order that publication of any report of the proceedings or part thereof be postponed for such time as the court thinks necessary for that purpose. Section 11 of the 1981 Act provides that a court may prohibit the publication of any name or other matter in connection with the proceedings before it which it has allowed to be withheld from the public.

I.3.2 When considering whether to make such an order there is nothing which precludes the court from hearing a representative of the press. Indeed it is likely that the court will wish to do so.

I.3.3 It is necessary to keep a permanent record of such orders for later reference. For this purpose all orders made under s 4(2) must be formulated in precise terms having regard to the decision in *R v Horsham Justices, ex p Farquharson* [1982] QB 762, [1982] 2 All ER 269, 76 Cr App Rep 87, and orders under both sections must be committed to writing either by the judge personally or by the clerk of the court under the judge's directions. An order must state (a) its precise scope, (b) the time at which it shall cease to have effect, if appropriate, and (c) the specific purpose of making the order. Courts will normally give notice to the press in some form that an order has been made under either section of the 1981 Act and the court staff should be prepared to answer any inquiry about a specific case, but it is, and will remain, the responsibility of those reporting cases, and their editors, to ensure that no breach of any orders occurs and the onus rests on them to make inquiry in any case of doubt.

I.4 Availability of judgments given in the Court of Appeal and the High Court

I.4.1 Reference should be made to para 9 of *Practice Direction* (*Court of Appeal (Civil Division)*) [1999] 2 All ER 490, [1999] 1 WLR 1027.

I.5 Wards of court

I.5.1 Where a child has been interviewed by the police in connection with contemplated criminal proceedings and the child subsequently becomes a ward of court, no leave of the wardship court is required for the child to be called as a witness in those proceedings. Where, however, the police desire to interview a child who is already a ward of court, application must, other than in the exceptional cases referred to in para I.5.3, be made to the wardship court, on summons and on notice to all parties, for leave for the police to do so. Where, however, a party may become the subject of a criminal investigation and it is considered necessary for the ward to be interviewed without that party knowing that the police are making inquiries, the application for leave may be made ex parte to a judge without notice to that party. Notice, should, where practicable, be given to the reporting officer.

I.5.2 Where leave is given the order should, unless some special reason requires the contrary, give leave for any number of interviews which may be required by the prosecution or the police. If it is desired to conduct any interview beyond what has been permitted by the order, a further application should be made.

I.5.3 The exceptional cases are those where the police need to deal with complaints or alleged offences concerning wards and it is appropriate, if not essential, for action to be taken straight away without the prior leave of the wardship court. Typical examples may be: (a) serious offences against the ward, such as rape, where medical examination and the collection of scientific evidence ought to be carried out promptly; (b) where the ward is suspected by the police of having committed a criminal act and the police wish to interview him about it; (c) where the police wish to interview the ward as a potential witness. The list is not exhaustive; there will inevitably be other instances where immediate action is appropriate. In such cases the police should notify the parent or foster parent with whom the ward is living or other 'appropriate adult' within the *Code of Practice for the Detention, Treatment and Questioning of Persons by Police Officers*, so that that adult has the opportunity of being present when the police interview the child. Additionally, if practicable, the reporting officer (if one has been appointed) should be notified and invited to attend the police interview or to nominate a third party to attend on his behalf. A record of the interview or a copy of any statement made by the ward should be supplied to the reporting officer.

Where the ward has been interviewed without the reporting officer's knowledge, he should be informed at the earliest opportunity. So too, if it be the case that the police wish to conduct further interviews. The wardship court should be appraised of the situation at the earliest possible opportunity thereafter by the reporting officer, the parent, foster parent (through the local authority) or other responsible adult.

I.5.4 No evidence or documents in the wardship proceedings or information about the proceedings should be disclosed in the criminal proceedings without leave of the wardship court.

I.6 Spent convictions

I.6.1 The effect of s 4(1) of the Rehabilitation of Offenders Act 1974 is that a person who has become a rehabilitated person for the purpose of the Act in respect of a conviction (known as a 'spent' conviction) shall be treated for all purposes in law as a person who has not committed or been charged with or prosecuted for or convicted of or sentenced for the offence or offences which were the subject of that conviction.

I.6.2 Section 4(1) of the 1974 Act does not apply, however, to evidence given in criminal proceedings (see s 7(2)(a)). Convictions are often disclosed in such criminal proceedings. When the Bill was before the House of Commons on 28 June 1974 the hope was expressed that the Lord Chief Justice would issue a practice direction for the guidance of the Crown Court with a view to reducing disclosure of spent convictions to a minimum and securing uniformity of approach. The direction is set out in the following paragraphs. The same approach should be adopted in all courts of criminal jurisdiction.

I.6.3 During the trial of a criminal charge, reference to previous convictions (and therefore to spent convictions) can arise in a number of ways. The most common is when the character of the accused or a witness is sought to be attacked by reference to his criminal record, but there are, of course, cases where previous convictions are relevant and admissible as, for instance, to prove system.

I.6.4 It is not possible to give general directions which will govern all these different situations, but it is recommended that both court and advocates should give effect to the general intention of Parliament by never referring to a spent conviction when such reference can reasonably be avoided.

I.6.5 After a verdict of guilty the court must be provided with a statement of the defendant's record for the purposes of sentence. The record supplied should contain all previous convictions, but those which are spent should, so far as practicable, be marked as such.

I.6.6 No one should refer in open court to a spent conviction without the authority of the judge, which authority should not be given unless the interests of justice so require.

I.6.7 When passing sentence the judge should make no reference to a spent conviction unless it is necessary to do so for the purpose of explaining the sentence to be passed.

I. 7 Explanations for the imposition of custodial sentences

I.7.1 The practical effect of custodial sentences imposed by the courts is almost entirely governed by statutory provisions. Those statutory provisions, changed by Parliament from time to time, are not widely understood by the general public. It is desirable that when sentence is passed the practical effect of the sentence should be understood by the defendant, any victim and any member of the public who is present in court or reads a full report of the proceedings.

I.7.2 Whenever a custodial sentence is imposed on an offender the court should explain the practical effect of the sentence in addition to complying with existing statutory requirements. This will be no more than an explanation; the sentence will be that pronounced by the court.

I.7.3 Sentencers should give the explanation in terms of their own choosing, taking care to ensure that the explanation is clear and accurate. No form of words is prescribed. Annexed to this Practice Direction are short statements which may, adapted as necessary, be of value as models (see Annex C). These statements are based on the statutory provisions in force on 1 January 1998 and will, of course, require modification if those provisions are materially amended.

I.7.4 Sentencers will continue to give such explanation as they judge necessary of ancillary orders relating to matters such as disqualification, compensation, confiscation, costs and so on.

I.7.5 The power of the Secretary of State to release a prisoner early under supervision is not part of the sentence. The judge is therefore not required in his sentencing remarks to provide an explanation of this power. However, in explaining the effect of custodial sentences the judge should not say anything which conflicts with the existence of this power.

I.8 Words to be used when passing sentence

I.8.1 Where a court passes on a defendant more than one term of imprisonment the court should state in the presence of the defendant whether the terms are to be concurrent or consecutive. Should this not be done the court clerk should ask the court, before the defendant leaves court, to do so.

I.8.2 If a prisoner is, at the time of sentence, already serving two or more consecutive terms of imprisonment and the court intends to increase the total period of imprisonment, it should use the expression 'consecutive to the total period of imprisonment to which you are already subject' rather than 'at the expiration of the term of imprisonment you are now serving', lest the prisoner be not then serving the last of the terms to which he is already subject.

I.9 Substitution of suspended sentences for immediate custodial sentences

I.9.1 Where an appellate court substitutes a suspended sentence of imprisonment for one having immediate effect, the court should have in mind any period the appellant has spent in custody. If the court is of the opinion that it would be fair to do so, an approximate adjustment to the term of the suspended sentence should be made. Whether or not the court makes such adjustment, it should state that it had that period in mind. The court should further indicate that the operational period of suspension runs from the date the court passes the suspended sentence.

I.10 References to the Court of Justice of the European Communities

I.10.1 These are the subject of *Practice Direction (ECJ references: procedure)* [1999] 1 WLR 260, [1999] 1 Cr App R 452, to which reference should be made.

I.11 Devolution issues

I.11.1 These are the subject of *Practice Note (devolution issues: Wales)* [1999] 3 All ER 466, [1999] 1 WLR 1592, [1999] 2 Cr App R 486, to which reference should be made.

I.12 Preparation of judgments: neutral citation

I.12.1 Since 11 January 2001 every judgment of the Court of Appeal, and of the Administrative Court, and since 14 January 2002 every judgment of the High Court, has been prepared and issued as approved with single spacing, paragraph numbering (in the margins) and no page numbers. In courts with more than one judge the paragraph numbering continues sequentially through each judgment and does not start again at the beginning of each judgment. Indented paragraphs are not numbered. A unique reference number is given to each judgment. For judgments of the Court of Appeal this number is given by the official shorthand writers. For judgments of the High Court it is provided by the Mechanical Recording Department at the Royal Courts of Justice. Such a number will also be furnished, on request to the Mechanical Recording Department, Royal Courts of Justice, Strand, London WC2A 2LL (Tel: 020 7947 7771), to High Court judgments delivered outside London.

I.12.2 Each Court of Appeal judgment starts with the year, followed by EW (for England and Wales), then CA (for Court of Appeal), followed by Civ or Crim and finally the sequential number. For example *Smith v Jones* [2001] EWCA Civ 10.

I.12.3 In the High Court, represented by HC, the number comes before the divisional abbreviation and, unlike Court of Appeal judgments, the latter is bracketed: (Ch), (Pat), (QB), (Admin), (Comm), (Admlty), (TCC) or (Fam) as appropriate. For example, [2002] EWHC 123 (Fam) or [2002] EWHC 124 (QB) or [2002] EWHC 125 (Ch).

I.12.4 This 'neutral citation', as it is called, is the official number attributed to the judgment and must always be used at least once when the judgment is cited in a later judgment. Once the judgment is reported this neutral citation appears in front of the familiar citation from the law reports series. Thus: *Smith v Jones* [2001] EWCA Civ 10, [2001] QB 124, [2001] 2 All ER 364, etc.

I.12.5 Paragraph numbers are referred to in square brackets. When citing a paragraph from a High Court judgment it is unnecessary to include the descriptive word in brackets: (Admin), (QB) or whatever. When citing a paragraph from a Court of Appeal judgment, however, Civ or Crim is included. If it is desired to cite more than one paragraph of a judgment each numbered paragraph should be enclosed with a square bracket. Thus para 59 in *Green v White* [2002] EWHC 124 (QB) would be cited: *Green v White* [2002] EWHC 124 at [59], paras 30–35 in *Smith v Jones* would be *Smith v Jones* [2001] EWCA Civ 10 at [30]–[35]; similarly, where a number of paragraphs are cited: *Smith v Jones* [2001] EWCA Civ 10 at [30], [35] and [40]–[43].

I.12.6 If a judgment is cited more than once in a later judgment it is helpful if only one abbreviation is used, eg *Smith v Jones* or *Smith's* case, but preferably not both (in the same judgment).

I.13 Bail: Failure to Surrender and Trials in Absence

I.13.1 The following directions take effect immediately[1].

I.13.2 The failure of the defendants to comply with the terms witnesses of their bail by not surrendering can undermine the administration of justice. It can disrupt proceedings. The resulting delays impact on victims, and other court users and also waste costs. A defendant's failure to surrender affects not only the case with which he is concerned, but also the courts' ability to administer justice more generally by damaging the confidence of victims, witnesses and the public in the effectiveness of the court system and the judiciary. It is, therefore most important that defendants who are granted bail appreciate the significance of the obligation to surrender to custody in accordance with the terms of their bail and that courts take appropriate action if they fail to do so.

I.13.3 There are at least three courses of action for the courts to consider taking:-

[A] imposing penalties for the failure to surrender;
[B] revoking bail or imposing more stringent bail conditions; and
[C] conducting trials in the absence of the defendant.

PENALTIES FOR FAILURE TO SURRENDER

I.13.4 A defendant who commits a section 6(1) or section 6(2) Bail Act 1976 offence commits an offence that stands apart from the proceedings in respect of which bail was granted. The seriousness of the offence can be reflected by an appropriate penalty being imposed for the Bail Act offence.

I.13.5 The common practice at present of courts automatically deferring disposal of a section 6(1) or section 6(2) Bail Act 1976 offence (failure to surrender) until the conclusion of the proceedings in respect of which bail was granted should no longer be followed. Instead, courts should now deal with defendants as soon as is practicable. In deciding what is practicable, the Court must take into account when the proceedings in respect of which bail was granted are expected to conclude, the seriousness of the offence for which the defendant is already being prosecuted, the type of penalty that might be imposed for the breach of bail and the original offence as well as any other relevant circumstances. If there is no good reason for postponing dealing with the breach until after the trial, the breach should be dealt with as soon as practicable. If the disposal of the breach of bail is deferred, then it is still necessary to consider imposing a separate penalty at the trial and the sentence for the breach of the bail should usually be custodial and consecutive to any other custodial sentence (as to which see I.13.13). In addition, bail should usually be revoked in the meantime (see I.13.14 to 16). In the case of offences which cannot, or are unlikely to, result in a custodial sentence, trial in the absence of the defendant may be a pragmatic sensible response to the situation (see I.13.17 to I.13.19). This is not a penalty for the Bail Act offence and a penalty may also be imposed for the Bail Act offence.

Initiating proceedings – bail granted by a police officer

I.13.6   When a person has been granted bail by a police officer to attend court and subsequently fails to surrender to custody, the decision whether to initiate proceedings for a section 6(1) or section 6(2) offence will be for the police/prosecutor.

I.13.7   The offence in this form is a summary offence and should be initiated as soon as practicable after the offence arises in view of the six month time limit running from the failure to surrender. It should be dealt with on the first appearance after arrest, unless an adjournment is necessary, as it will be relevant in considering whether to grant bail again.

Initiating proceedings – bail granted by a court

I.13.8   When a person has been granted bail by a court and subsequently fails to surrender to custody, on arrest that person should normally be brought as soon as appropriate before the court at which the proceedings in respect of which bail was granted are to be heard. (The six months time limit does not apply where bail was granted by the court). Should the defendant commit another offence outside the jurisdiction of the bail court, the Bail Act offence should, where practicable, be dealt with by the new court at the same time as the new offence. If impracticable, the defendant may, if this is appropriate, be released formally on bail by the new court so that the warrant may be executed for his attendance before the first court in respect of the substantive and Bail Act offences.

I.13.9   Given that bail was granted by a court, it is more appropriate that the court itself should initiate the proceedings by its own motion. The court will be invited to take proceedings by the prosecutor, if the prosecutor considers proceedings are appropriate.

Conduct of Proceedings

I.13.10   Proceedings under section 6 Bail Act 1976 may be conducted either as a summary offence or as a criminal contempt of court. Where the court is invited to take proceedings by the prosecutor, the prosecutor will conduct the proceedings and, if the matter is contested, call the evidence. Where the court initiates proceedings without such an invitation the same role can be played by the prosecutor at the request of the court, where this is practicable.

I.13.11   The burden of proof is on the defendant to prove that he had reasonable cause for his failure to surrender to custody (s 6(3) Bail Act 1976).

Proceedings to be progressed to disposal as soon as is practicable

I.13.12 If the court decides to proceed, the section 6 Bail Act offence should be concluded as soon as practicable.

Sentencing for a Bail Act offence

I.13.13   In principle, a custodial sentence for the offence of failing to surrender should be ordered to be served consecutively to any other sentence imposed at the same time for another offence unless there are circumstances that make this inappropriate (see *White* & *McKinnon*).

RELATIONSHIP BETWEEN THE BAIL ACT OFFENCE AND FURTHER REMANDS ON BAIL OR IN CUSTODY

I.13.14   When a defendant has been convicted of a Bail Act offence, the court should review the remand status of the defendant, including the conditions of that bail, in respect of the main proceedings for which bail had been granted.

I.13.15   Failure by the defendant to surrender or a conviction for failing to surrender to bail in connection with the main proceedings will be significant factors weighing against the re-granting of bail or, in the case of offences which do not normally give rise to a custodial sentence, in favour of trial in the absence of the offender.

I.13.16   Whether or not an immediate custodial sentence has been imposed for the Bail Act offence, the court may, having reviewed the defendant's remand status, also remand the defendant in custody in the main proceedings.

TRIALS IN ABSENCE

I.13.17   A defendant has a right, in general, to be present and to be represented at his trial. However, a defendant may choose not to exercise those rights by voluntarily absenting himself and failing to instruct his lawyers adequately so that they can represent him and, in the case of proceedings before the magistrates' court, there is an express statutory power to hear trials in the defendant's absence (s 11 of the Magistrates' Courts Act 1980). In such circumstances, the court has discretion whether the trial should take place in his/her absence.

I.13.18   The court must exercise its discretion to proceed in the absence of the defendant with the utmost care and caution. The overriding concern must be to ensure that such a trial is as fair as circumstances permit and leads to a just outcome.

I.13.19   Due regard should be had to the judgment of Lord Bingham in *R v Jones* [2003] AC 1, [2002] 2 All ER 113 in which Lord Bingham identified circumstances to be taken into account before proceeding, which include: the conduct of the defendant, the disadvantage to the defendant, public interest, the effect of any delay and whether the attendance of the defendant could be secured at a later hearing. Other relevant considerations are the seriousness of the offence and likely outcome if the defendant is found guilty. If the defendant is only likely to be fined for a summary offence this can be relevant since the costs that a defendant might otherwise be ordered to pay as a result of an adjournment could be disproportionate. In the case of summary proceedings the fact that there can be an appeal that is a complete rehearing is also relevant, as is the power to re-open the case under s 142 of the Magistrates' Court Act 1980.

---

1. The introduction to Amendment No 3 to the *Consolidated Criminal Practice Direction (Bail: Failure to Surrender and Trials in Absence)* 22 January 2004 which inserted paras I.13.1 to I.13.19 states:

> An additional section, set out below, is added to Part I of the Consolidated Practice Direction. This replaces section V.56 (Failure to Surrender) and takes into account the judgment of the Court of Appeal (Criminal Division) in *R v Andrew Ross White and R v Neil McKinnon* [2002] EWCA Crim 2952, [2003] 2 Cr App R (S) 29, 5 December 2002 and the judgment of the House of Lords in *R v Jones* [2003] AC 1, [2002] 2 All ER 113, 20 February 2002. The direction applies to persons released on bail in all criminal proceedings, including appeals to the Court of Appeal Criminal Division.

I.14 Forms

1.14.1 This Practice Direction supplements Part 5 (forms) of the Criminal Procedure Rules.

1.14.2 The forms set out in Annex D, or forms to that effect, are to be used in the criminal courts on or after 4 April 2005, when the Criminal Procedure Rules come into force. Almost all are identical to those in use before that date, and accordingly a form in use before that date which corresponds with one set out in Annex D may still be used in connection with the rule to which it applies.

1.14.3 The table at the beginning of Annex D lists the forms set out in that Annex and—

- shows the rule in connection with which each form applies
- describes each form
- in the case of a form in use before the Criminal Procedure Rules came into force, shows the legislation by which the form was prescribed and by what number (if any) it was known.

PART II
FURTHER DIRECTIONS APPLYING IN THE COURT OF APPEAL (CRIMINAL DIVISION)

II.1–II.20

PART III
FURTHER DIRECTIONS APPLYING IN THE CROWN COURT AND MAGISTRATES' COURTS

III.21.1 Classification of Crown Court business and allocation to Crown Court centres

Classification

III.21.2 For the purposes of trial in the Crown Court offences are classified as follows:

Class 1: (a) misprision of treason and treason felony; (b) murder; (c) genocide; (d) torture, hostage-taking and offences under the War Crimes Act 1991; (e) an offence under the Official Secrets Acts; (f) soliciting, incitement, attempt or conspiracy to commit any of the above offences.

Class 2: (a) manslaughter; (b) infanticide; (c) child destruction; (d) abortion (s 58 of the Offences against the Person Act 1861); (e) rape; (f) sexual intercourse with a girl under 13; (g) incest with girl under 13; (h) sedition; (i) an offence under s 1 of the Geneva Conventions Act 1957; (j) mutiny; (k) piracy; (l) soliciting, incitement, attempt or conspiracy to commit any of the above offences.

Class 3: (a) all offences triable only on indictment other than those in classes 1, 2 and 4; (b) soliciting, incitement, attempt or conspiracy to commit any of the above offences.

Class 4: (a) wounding or causing grievous bodily harm with intent (s 18 of the Offences against the Person Act 1861); (b) robbery or assault with intent to rob (s 8 of the Theft Act 1968); (c) soliciting, incitement or attempt to commit any of the above offences; (d) conspiracy at common law, or conspiracy to commit any offence other than those included in classes 1, 2 and 3; (e) all offences which are triable either way.

Cases committed, transferred or sent for trial

III.21.3 Save as provided in para III.21.4, for certain offences in class 2 and offences in class 3(a), the magistrates' court, upon either committing a person for trial under s 6 of the Magistrates' Courts Act 1980, transferring a person under either s 4 of the Criminal Justice Act 1987 or s 53 of the Criminal Justice Act 1991 or sending a person under s 51 of the Crime and Disorder Act 1998, shall, if the offence or any of the offences is included in classes 1 or 2, specify the most convenient location of the Crown Court where a High Court judge, or, where the case is included in class 1, where a circuit judge duly approved for that purpose by the Lord Chief Justice regularly sits. These courts will be identified by the presiding judges on each circuit. Where an offence is in class 4 the magistrates' court shall specify the most convenient location of the Crown Court.

III.21.4 Where a presiding judge has directed that cases of rape, sexual intercourse with a girl under 13, incest with a girl under 13 or soliciting, incitement, attempt or conspiracy to commit any of these offences (all of which are within class 2) or class 3 offences, may be committed, transferred or sent from a specified magistrates' court or courts to a specified location of the Crown Court at which a High Court judge does not regularly sit, the magistrates' court shall specify that location.

III.21.5 In selecting the most convenient location of the Crown Court the justices shall have regard to the considerations referred to in s 7 of the Magistrates' Courts Act 1980 and s 51(10) of the Crime and Disorder Act 1998 and the location or locations of the Crown Court designated by a presiding judge as the location to which cases should normally be committed from their petty sessions area.

III.21.6 Where on one occasion a person is committed in respect of a number of offences all the committals shall be to the same location of the Crown Court and that location shall be the one where a High Court judge regularly sits if such a location is appropriate for any of the offences.

Committals for sentence or to be dealt with

III.21.7. Where a community rehabilitation order, an order for conditional discharge or a community punishment order has been made, or suspended sentence has been passed, and the offender is committed to be dealt with for the original offence or in respect of the suspended sentence, he shall be committed in accordance with paras III.21.8–III.21.11.

III.21.8 If the order was made or the sentence was passed by the Crown Court he shall be committed to the location of the Crown Court where the order was made or suspended sentence was passed unless it is inconvenient or impracticable to do so.

III.21.9 If he is not so committed and the order was made by a High Court judge he shall be committed to the most convenient location of the Crown Court where a High Court judge regularly sits.

III.21.10 In all other cases where a person is committed for sentence or to be dealt with he shall be committed to the most convenient location of the Crown Court.

III.21.11 In selecting the most convenient location of the Crown Court the justices shall have regard to the locations of the Crown Court designated by a presiding judge as the locations to which cases should normally be committed from their petty sessions area.

Notice of transfer in cases of serious or complex fraud

III.21.12 Where a notice of transfer is served under s 4 of the Criminal Justice Act 1987 (cases of serious or complex fraud) the proposed place of trial to be specified in the notice shall be one of the following Crown Court centres: (a) Midland Circuit: Birmingham (also sitting at West Midlands trial centre), Leicester, Northampton, Nottingham, Wolverhampton (also sitting at West Midlands trial centre); (b) North Eastern: Bradford, Leeds, Newcastle, Sheffield, Teesside; (c) Northern: Liverpool, Manchester; (d) South Eastern: Central Criminal Court, Chelmsford, Harrow, Kingston, Knightsbridge, Luton, Maidstone, Middlesex Guildhall, Norwich, Oxford, Reading, Snaresbrook, Southwark, Wood Green; (e) Wales and Chester: Cardiff, Chester, Mold, Swansea, Warrington; (f) Western: Bristol, Plymouth, Portsmouth, Truro, Winchester.

Notice of transfer in child witness cases

III.21.13 Where a notice of transfer is served under s 53 of the Criminal Justice Act 1991 (child witness cases) the proposed place of trial to be specified in accordance with para 1(1) of Sch 6 to the 1991 Act shall be a Crown Court centre which is equipped with live television link facilities. The following Crown Court centres are so equipped: Birmingham, Bradford, Bristol, Caernarfon, Cardiff, Carlisle, Central Criminal Court, Chelmsford, Croydon, Exeter, Gloucester, Grimsby, Guildford, Harrow, Hull, Leeds, Leicester, Lewes, Lincoln, Liverpool, Maidstone, Manchester, Mold, Newcastle, Northampton, Norwich, Nottingham, Plymouth, Portsmouth, Preston, Reading, Sheffield, Southwark, St Albans, Stafford, Swansea, Teesside, Truro, Winchester, Wolverhampton.

III.22 Applications for evidence to be given in Welsh

III.22.1 If a defendant in a court in England asks to give or call evidence in the Welsh language the case should not be transferred to Wales. In ordinary circumstances interpreters can be provided on request.

III.23 Use of the Welsh language in courts in Wales

III.23.1 The purpose of this direction is to reflect the principle of the Welsh Language Act 1993 that in the administration of justice in Wales the English and Welsh languages should be treated on a basis of equality.

General

III.23.2 It is the responsibility of the legal representatives in every case in which the Welsh language may be used by any witness or party or in any document which may be placed before the court to inform the court of that fact so that appropriate arrangements can be made for the listing of the case.

III.23.3 If the possible use of the Welsh language is known at the time of committal, transfer or appeal to the Crown Court, the court should be informed immediately after committal or transfer or when the notice of appeal is lodged. Otherwise the court should be informed as soon as possible use of the Welsh language becomes known.

III.23.4 If costs are incurred as a result of failure to comply with these directions, a wasted costs order may be made against the defaulting party and/or his legal representatives.

III.23.5 The law does not permit the selection of jurors in a manner which enables the court to discover whether a juror does or does not speak Welsh or to secure a jury whose members are bilingual to try a case in which the Welsh language may be used.

Plea and directions hearings

III.23.6 An advocate in a case in which the Welsh language may be used must raise that matter at the plea and directions hearing and endorse details of it on the judge's questionnaire so that appropriate directions may be given for the progress of the case.

Listing

III.23.7 The listing officer, in consultation with the resident judge, should ensure that a case in which the Welsh language may be used is listed (a) wherever practicable before a Welsh speaking judge, and (b) in a court in Wales with simultaneous translation facilities.

Interpreters

III.23.8. Whenever an interpreter is needed to translate evidence from English into Welsh or from Welsh into English, the court manager in whose court the case is to be heard shall ensure that the attendance is secured of an interpreter whose name is included in the list of approved court interpreters.

Jurors

III.23.9. The jury bailiff when addressing the jurors at the start of their period of jury service shall inform them that each juror may take an oath or affirm in Welsh or English as he wishes.

III.23.10 After the jury has been selected to try a case, and before it is sworn, the court officer swearing in the jury shall inform the jurors in open court that each juror may take an oath or affirm in Welsh or English as he wishes.

Witnesses

III.23.11 When each witness is called the court officer administering the oath or affirmation shall inform the witness that he may be sworn or affirm Welsh or English as he wishes.

Opening/closing of courts

III.23.12 Unless it is not reasonably practicable to do so, the opening and closing of the court should be performed in Welsh and English.

Role of liaison judge

III.23.13 If any question or problem arises concerning the implementation of paras III.23.1–III.23.12, contact should in the first place be made with the liaison judge for Welsh language matters on circuit.

III.24 Evidence by written statement

III.24.1 Where the prosecution proposes to tender written statements in evidence either under ss 5A and 5B of the Magistrates' Courts Act 1980 or s 9 of the Criminal Justice Act 1967 it will frequently be not only proper, but also necessary for the orderly presentation of the evidence, for certain statements to be edited. This will occur either because a witness has made more than one statement whose contents should conveniently be reduced into a single, comprehensive statement or where a statement contains inadmissible, prejudicial or irrelevant material. Editing of statements should in all circumstances be done by a Crown Prosecutor (or by a legal representative, if any, of the prosecutor if the case is not being conducted by the Crown Prosecution Service) and not by a police officer.

Composite statements

III.24.2 A composite statement giving the combined effect of two or more earlier statements or settled by a person referred to in para 24.1 must be prepared in compliance with the requirements of ss 5A and 5B of the 1980 Act or s 9 of the 1967 Act as appropriate and must then be signed by the witness.

Editing single statements

III.24.3 There are two acceptable methods of editing single statements.

(a) By marking *copies* of the statement in a way which indicates the passages on which the prosecution will not rely. This merely indicates that the prosecution will not seek to adduce the evidence so marked. The *original signed statement* to be tendered to the court is not marked in any way. The marking on the copy statement is done by lightly striking out the passages to be edited so that what appears beneath can still be read, or by bracketing, or by a combination of both. It is not permissible to produce a photocopy with the deleted material obliterated, since this would be contrary to the requirement that the defence and the court should be served with copies of the signed original statement. Whenever the striking out/bracketing method is used, it will assist if the following words appear at the foot of the frontispiece or index to any bundle of copy statements to be tendered:

'The prosecution does not propose to adduce evidence of those passages of the attached copy statements which have been struck out and/or bracketed (nor will it seek to do so at the trial unless a notice of further evidence is served).'

(b) By obtaining a fresh statement, signed by the witness, which omits the offending material, applying the procedure in para III.24.2.

III.24.4 In most cases where a single statement is to be edited, the striking out/bracketing method will be the more appropriate, but the taking of a fresh statement is preferable in the following circumstances. (a) When a police (or other investigating) officer's statement contains details of interviews with more suspects than are eventually charged, a fresh statement should be prepared and signed omitting all details of interview with those not charged except, in so far as it is relevant, for the bald fact that a certain named person was interviewed at a particular time, date and place. (b) When a suspect is interviewed about more offences than are eventually made the subject of committal charges, a fresh statement should be prepared and signed omitting all questions and answers about the uncharged offences unless either they might appropriately be taken into consideration or evidence about those offences is admissible on the charges preferred, such as evidence of system. It may, however, be desirable to replace the omitted questions and answers with a phrase such as: 'After referring to some other matters, I then said . . .', so as to make it clear that part of the interview has been omitted. (c) A fresh statement should normally be prepared and signed if the only part of the original on which the prosecution is relying is only a small proportion of the whole, although it remains desirable to use the alternative method if there is reason to believe that the defence might itself wish to rely, in mitigation or for any other purpose, on at least some of those parts which the prosecution does not propose to adduce. (d) When the passages contain material which the prosecution is entitled to withhold from disclosure to the defence.

III.24.5 Prosecutors should also be aware that, where statements are to be tendered under s 9 of the 1967 Act in the course of *summary* proceedings, there will be a need to prepare fresh statements excluding inadmissible or prejudicial material rather than using the striking out or bracketing method.

III.24.6 None of the above principles applies, in respect of committal proceedings, to documents which are exhibited (including statements under caution and signed contemporaneous notes). Nor do they apply to oral statements of a defendant which are recorded in the witness statements of interviewing police officers, except in the circumstances referred to in para III.24.4(b). All this material should remain in its original state in the committal bundles, any editing being left to prosecuting counsel at the Crown Court (after discussion with defence counsel and, if appropriate, the trial judge).

III.24.7 Whenever a fresh statement is taken from a witness, a copy of the earlier, unedited statement(s) of that witness will be given to the defence in accordance with the Attorney General's guidelines on the disclosure of unused material (*Practice Note (criminal evidence: unused material)*/[1982] 1 All ER 734, (1982) 74 Cr App R 302) unless there are grounds under para 6 of the guidelines for withholding such disclosure.

III.25 Bail during trial

III.25.1 Paragraphs III.25.2– III.25.5. are to be read subject to the Bail Act 1976, especially s 4.

III.25.2 Once a trial has begun the further grant of bail, whether during the short adjournment or overnight, is in the discretion of the trial judge. It may be a proper exercise of this discretion to refuse bail during the short adjournment if the accused cannot otherwise be segregated from witnesses and jurors.

III.25.3 An accused who was on bail while on remand should not be refused overnight bail during the trial unless in the opinion of the judge there are positive reasons to justify this refusal. Such reasons are likely to be: (a) that a point has been reached where there is a real danger that the accused will abscond, either because the case is going badly for him, or for any other reason; (b) that there is a real danger that he may interfere with witnesses or jurors.

III.25.4 There is no universal rule of practice that bail shall not be renewed when the summing-up has begun. Each case must be decided in the light of its own circumstances and having regard to the judge's assessment from time to time of the risks involved.

III.25.5 Once the jury has returned a verdict a further renewal of bail should be decided in the light of the gravity of the offence and the likely sentence to be passed in all the circumstances of the case.

III.26 Facts to be stated on pleas of guilty

III.26.1 To enable the press and the public to know the circumstances of an offence of which an accused has been convicted and for which he is to be sentenced, in relation to each offence to which an accused has pleaded guilty the prosecution shall state those facts in open court before sentence is imposed.

III.27 Antecedents

Standard for the provision of information of antecedents in the Crown Court and magistrates' courts

III.27.1 In the Crown Court the police will provide brief details of the circumstances of the last three similar convictions and/or of convictions likely to be of interest to the court, the latter being judged on a case-by-case basis. This information should be provided separately and attached to the antecedents as set out below.

III.27.2 Where the current alleged offence could constitute a breach of an existing community order, eg community rehabilitation order, and it is known that that order is still in force then, to enable the court to consider the possibility of revoking that order, details of the circumstances of the offence leading to the community order should be included in the antecedents as set out below.

Preparation of antecedents and standard formats to be used

III.27.3 In magistrates' courts and the Crown Court: personal details and summary of convictions and cautions—Police National Computer [PNC] court/defence/probation summary sheet; previous convictions—PNC court/defence/probation printout, supplemented by Form MG 16 if the police force holds convictions not shown on PNC; recorded cautions—PNC court/defence/probation printout, supplemented by Form MG 17 if the police force holds cautions not shown on PNC; and, in addition, in the Crown Court: circumstances of the last three similar convictions; circumstances of offence leading to a community order still in force; Form MG(c). The detail should be brief and include the date of the offence.

Provision of antecedents to the court and parties
Crown Court

III.27.4 The Crown Court antecedents will be prepared by the police immediately following committal proceedings, including committals for sentence, transfers under s 4 of the Criminal

Justice Act 1987 or s 53 of the Criminal Justice Act 1991 or upon receipt of a notice of appeal, excluding non-imprisonable motoring offences.

III.27.5　Seven copies of the antecedents will be prepared in respect of each defendant. Two copies are to be provided to the Crown Prosecution Service (CPS) direct, the remaining five to be sent to the Crown Court. The court will send one copy to the defence and one to the Probation Service. The remaining copies are for the court's use. Where following conviction a custodial order is made one copy is to be attached to the order sent to the prison.

III.27.6　The antecedents must be provided, as above, within 21 days of committal or transfer in each case. Any points arising from them are to be raised with the police by the defence solicitor as soon as possible and, where there is time, at least seven days before the hearing date so that the matter can be resolved prior to that hearing.

III.27.7　Seven days before the hearing date the police will check the record of convictions. Details of any additional convictions will be provided using the standard format above. These will be provided as above and attached to the documents already supplied. Details of any additional outstanding cases will also be provided at this stage.

Magistrates' courts

III.27.8　The magistrates' court antecedents will be prepared by the police and submitted to the CPS with the case file.

III.27.9　Five copies of the antecedents will be prepared in respect of each defendant and provided to the CPS who will be responsible for distributing them to others at the sentencing hearing. Normally two copies will be provided to the court, one to the defence and one to the Probation Service when appropriate. Where following conviction a custodial order is made, one of the court's copies is to be attached to the order sent to the prison.

III.27.10　In instances where antecedents have been provided to the court some time before the hearing the police will, if requested to do so by the CPS, check the record of convictions. Details of any additional convictions will be provided using the standard format above. These will be provided as above and attached to the documents already supplied. Details of any additional outstanding cases will also be provided at this stage.

III.27.11　The above arrangements whereby the police provide the antecedents to the CPS for passing on to others will apply unless there is a local agreement between the CPS and the court that alters that arrangement.

III.28　Personal statements of victims

III.28.1　This section draws attention to a scheme, which started on 1 October 2001, to give victims a more formal opportunity to say how a crime has affected them. It may help to identify whether they have a particular need for information, support and protection. It will also enable the court to take the statement into account when determining sentence.

III.28.2　When a police officer takes a statement from a victim the victim will be told about the scheme and given the chance to make a victim personal statement. A victim personal statement may be made or updated at any time prior to the disposal of the case. The decision about whether or not to make a victim personal statement is entirely for the victim. If the court is presented with a victim personal statement the following approach should be adopted. (a) The victim personal statement and any evidence in support should be considered and taken into account by the court prior to passing sentence. (b) Evidence of the effects of an offence on the victim contained in the victim personal statement or other statement, must be in proper form, that is a witness statement made under s 9 of the Criminal Justice Act 1967 or an expert's report, and served upon the defendant's solicitor or the defendant, if he is not represented, prior to sentence. Except where inferences can properly be drawn from the nature of or circumstances surrounding the offence, a sentencer must not make assumptions unsupported by evidence about the effects of an offence on the victim. (c) The court must pass what it judges to be the appropriate sentence having regard to the circumstances of the offence and of the offender, taking into account, so far as the court considers it appropriate, the consequences to the victim. The opinions of the victim or the victim's close relatives as to what the sentence should be are therefore not relevant, unlike the consequence of the offence on them. Victims should be advised of this. If, despite the advice, opinions as to sentence are included in the statement, the court should pay no attention to them. (d) The court should consider whether it is desirable in its sentencing remarks to refer to the evidence provided on behalf of the victim.

III.29　Support for witnesses giving evidence by live television link

III.29.1　This section of the Practice Direction is made pursuant to r 7 of the Crown Court (Special Measures Directions and Directions Prohibiting Cross-examination) Rules 2002, SI 2002/1688, and r 7 of the Magistrates' Courts (Special Measures Directions) Rules 2002, SI 2002/1687, and supersedes previous guidance given by the senior presiding judges, Watkins LJ in 1991 and Auld LJ in 1998.

III.29.2　An increased degree of flexibility is now appropriate as to who can act as supporter of a witness giving evidence by live television link. Where a special measures direction is made enabling a vulnerable, intimidated or child witness to give evidence by means of a live television link, the trial judge will make a direction as to the identity of the witness supporter. Where practical, the direction will be made before the trial commences. In giving the direction, the trial judge will balance all relevant interests—see para 1.11 of the guidance *Achieving Best Evidence*. The witness supporter should be completely independent of the witness and his or her family and have no previous knowledge of or personal involvement in the case. The supporter should also be suitably trained so as to understand the obligations of, and comply with, the national standards relating to witness supporters. Providing these criteria are met, the witness supporter need not be an usher or court official. Thus, for example, the functions of the witness supporter may be performed by a representative of the Witness Service.

III.29.3 Where the witness supporter is someone other than the court usher, the usher should continue to be available both to assist the witness and the witness supporter, and to ensure that the judge's requirements are properly complied with in the CCTV room.

III.30 Treatment of vulnerable defendants

III.30.1 This direction applies to proceedings in the Crown Court and in magistrates' courts on the trial, sentencing or (in the Crown Court) appeal of (a) children and young persons under 18 or (b) adults who suffer from a mental disorder within the meaning of the Mental Health Act 1983 or who have any other significant impairment of intelligence and social function. In this direction such defendants are referred to collectively as "vulnerable defendants". The purpose of this direction is to extend to proceedings in relation to such persons in the adult courts procedures analogous to those in use in youth courts.

III.30.2 The steps which should be taken to comply with paragraphs III.30.3 to III.30.17 should be judged, in any given case, taking account of the age, maturity and development (intellectual, social and emotional) of the defendant concerned and all other circumstances of the case.

The overriding principle

III.30.3 A defendant may be young and immature or may have a mental disorder within the meaning of the Mental Health Act 1983 or some other significant impairment of intelligence and social function such as to inhibit his understanding of and participation in the proceedings. The purpose of criminal proceedings is to determine guilt, if that is in issue, and decide on the appropriate sentence if the defendant pleads guilty or is convicted. All possible steps should be taken to assist a vulnerable defendant to understand and participate in those proceedings. The ordinary trial process should, so far as necessary, be adapted to meet those ends. Regard should be had to the welfare of a young defendant as required by section 44 of the Children and Young Persons Act 1933, and generally to Parts 1 and 3 of the Criminal Procedure Rules (the overriding objective and the court's powers of case management).

Before the trial, sentencing or appeal

III.30.4 If a vulnerable defendant, especially one who is young, is to be tried jointly with one who is not, the court should consider at the plea and case management hearing, or at a case management hearing in a magistrates' court, whether the vulnerable defendant should be tried on his own and should so order unless of the opinion that a joint trial would be in accordance with Part 1 of the Criminal Procedure Rules (the overriding objective) and in the interests of justice. If a vulnerable defendant is tried jointly with one who is not, the court should consider whether any of the modifications set out in this direction should apply in the circumstances of the joint trial and so far as practicable make orders to give effect to any such modifications.

III.30.5 At the plea and case management hearing, or at a case management hearing in a magistrates' court, the court should consider and so far as practicable give directions on the matters covered in paragraphs III.30.9 to III.30.17.

III.30.6 It may be appropriate to arrange that a vulnerable defendant should visit, out of court hours and before the trial, sentencing or appeal hearing, the courtroom in which that hearing is to take place so that he can familiarise himself with it.

III.30.7 If any case against a vulnerable defendant has attracted or may attract widespread public or media interest, the assistance of the police should be enlisted to try and ensure that the defendant is not, when attending the court, exposed to intimidation, vilification or abuse. Section 41 of the Criminal Justice Act 1925 prohibits the taking of photographs of defendants and witnesses (among others) in the court building or in its precincts, or when entering or leaving those precincts. A direction informing media representatives that the prohibition will be enforced may be appropriate.

III.30.8 The court should be ready at this stage, if it has not already done so, where relevant to make a reporting restriction under section 39 of the Children and Young Persons Act 1933 or, on an appeal to the Crown Court from a youth court, to remind media representatives of the application of section 49 of that Act. Any such order, once made, should be reduced to writing and copies should on request be made available to anyone affected or potentially affected by it.

The trial, sentencing or appeal hearing

III.30.9 Subject to the need for appropriate security arrangements the proceedings should, if practicable, be held in a courtroom in which all the participants are on the same or almost the same level.

III.30.10 A vulnerable defendant, especially if he is young, should normally, if he wishes, be free to sit with members of his family or others in a like relationship, and with some other suitable supporting adult such as a social worker, and in a place which permits easy, informal communication with his legal representatives. The court should ensure that a suitable supporting adult is available throughout the course of the proceedings.

III.30.11 At the beginning of the proceedings the court should ensure that what is to take place has been explained to a vulnerable defendant in terms he can understand, and at trial in the Crown Court it should ensure in particular that the role of the jury has been explained. It should remind those representing the vulnerable defendant and the supporting adult of their responsibility to explain each step as it takes place, and at trial to explain the possible consequences of a guilty verdict. Throughout the trial the court should continue to ensure, by any appropriate means, that the defendant understands what is happening and what has been said by those on the bench, the advocates and witnesses.

III.30.12 A trial should be conducted according to a timetable which takes full account of a vulnerable defendant's ability to concentrate. Frequent and regular breaks will often be appropriate. The court should ensure, so far as practicable, that the trial is conducted in simple, clear language that the defendant can understand and that cross-examination is conducted by questions that are short and clear.

III.30.13 A vulnerable defendant who wishes to give evidence by live link in accordance with section 33A of the Youth Justice and Criminal Evidence Act 1999 may apply for a direction to that effect. Before making such a direction the court must be satisfied that it is in the interests of justice to do so, and that the use of a live link would enable the defendant to participate more effectively as a witness in the proceedings. The direction will need to deal with the practical arrangements to be made, including the room from which the defendant will give evidence, the identity of the person or persons who will accompany him, and how it will be arranged for him to be seen and heard by the court.

III.30.14 In the Crown Court robes and wigs should not be worn unless the court for good reason orders that they should. It may be appropriate for the court to be robed for sentencing in a grave case even though it has sat without robes for trial. It is generally desirable that those responsible for the security of a vulnerable defendant who is in custody, especially if he is young, should not be in uniform, and that there should be no recognisable police presence in the courtroom save for good reason.

III.30.15 The court should be prepared to restrict attendance by members of the public in the court room to a small number, perhaps limited to those with an immediate and direct interest in the outcome. The court should rule on any challenged claim to attend.

III.30.16 Facilities for reporting the proceedings (subject to any restrictions under section 39 or 49 of the Children and Young Persons Act 1933) must be provided. But the court may restrict the number of reporters attending in the courtroom to such number as is judged practicable and desirable. In ruling on any challenged claim to attend in the court room for the purpose of reporting the court should be mindful of the public's general right to be informed about the administration of justice.

III.30.17 Where it has been decided to limit access to the courtroom, whether by reporters or generally, arrangements should be made for the proceedings to be relayed, audibly and if possible visually, to another room in the same court complex to which the media and the public have access if it appears that there will be a need for such additional facilities. Those making use of such a facility should be reminded that it is to be treated as an extension of the court room and that they are required to conduct themselves accordingly.

III.30.18 Where the court is called upon to exercise its discretion in relation to any procedural matter falling within the scope of this practice direction but not the subject of specific reference, such discretion should be exercised having regard to the principles in paragraph III.30.3.

PART IV
FURTHER DIRECTIONS APPLYING IN THE CROWN COURT

IV.30 Modes of address and titles of judges
Mode of address

IV.30.1 The following judges, when sitting in court, should be addressed as 'My Lord' or 'My Lady', as the case may be, whatever their personal status: (a) any circuit judge sitting as a judge of the High Court under s 9(1) of the Supreme Court Act 1981; (b) any judge sitting at the Central Criminal Court; (c) any senior circuit judge who is the honorary recorder of the city in which he sits.

IV.30.2 Subject to para IV.30.1, circuit judges, recorders and deputy circuit judges should be addressed as 'Your Honour' when sitting in court.

Description

IV.30.3 In cause lists, forms and orders members of the judiciary should be described as follows: (d) circuit judges, as 'His [or Her] Honour Judge A' (when the judge is sitting as a judge of the High Court under s 9(1) of the Supreme Court Act 1981 the words 'sitting as a judge of the High Court' should be added); (e) recorders, as 'Mr [or Mrs] Recorder B'. This style is appropriate irrespective of any honour or title which the recorder might possess, but if in any case it is desired to include an honour or title the alternative description 'Sir CD, Recorder' or 'The Lord D, Recorder' may be used; (f) deputy circuit judges, as 'His [or Her] Honour EF, sitting as a Deputy Circuit Judge'.

IV.31 Transfer of cases from one circuit to another

IV.31.1–3 An application that a case be transferred from one circuit to another should not be granted unless the judge is satisfied that: (a) the approval of the presiding judges and circuit administrator for each circuit has been obtained, or (b) the case may be transferred under general arrangements approved by the presiding judges and circuit administrators.

IV.32 Transfer of proceedings between locations of the Crown Court

IV.32.1 Without prejudice to the provisions of s 76 of the Supreme Court Act 1981 (committal for trial: alteration of place of trial) directions may be given for the transfer from one location of the Crown Court to another of: (a) appeals; (b) proceedings on committal for sentence or to be dealt with.

IV.32.2 Such directions may be given in a particular case by an officer of the Crown Court, or generally, in relation to a class or classes of case, by the presiding judge or a judge acting on his behalf.

IV.32.3 If dissatisfied with such directions given by an officer of the Crown Court, any party to the proceedings may apply to a judge of the Crown Court who may hear the application in chambers.

IV.33 Allocation of business within the Crown Court

General

IV.33.1 Cases in class 1 are to be tried by a High Court judge. A case of murder or soliciting, incitement, attempt or conspiracy to commit murder, may be released, by or on the authority of a presiding judge, for trial by a deputy High Court judge, a circuit judge or a deputy circuit judge approved for the purpose by the Lord Chief Justice.

IV.33.2 Cases in class 2 are to be tried by a High Court judge unless a particular case is released by or on the authority of a presiding judge for trial by a deputy High Court judge, circuit judge or a deputy circuit judge. A case of rape, or of a serious sexual offence of any class, may be released by a presiding judge for trial only by a circuit judge, deputy circuit judge or recorder approved for the purpose by the senior presiding judge with the concurrence of the Lord Chief Justice.

IV.33.3 Cases in class 3 may be tried by a High Court judge or, in accordance with general or particular directions given by a presiding judge, by a circuit judge, a deputy circuit judge or a recorder who has attended a Judicial Studies Board Continuation Seminar and has been duly authorised by a presiding judge.

IV.33.4 Cases in class 4 may be tried by a High Court judge, a deputy High Court judge, a circuit judge, a deputy circuit judge or a recorder. A case in class 4 shall not be listed for trial by a High Court judge except with the consent of that judge or of a presiding judge.

IV.33.5 Appeals from decisions of magistrates shall be heard by: (a) a resident judge, or (b) a circuit judge, nominated by the resident judge, who regularly sits at the Crown Court centre, or (c) an experienced recorder specifically approved by the presiding judges for the purpose, or (d) where no circuit judge or recorder satisfying the requirements above is available and it is not practicable to obtain the approval of the presiding judges, by a circuit judge or recorder selected by the resident judge to hear a specific case or cases.

IV.33.6 With the exception of courts operating the plea and directions scheme referred to in paras IV.41.1ff, the following arrangements for pre-trial proceedings shall apply. (a) Applications or matters arising before trial (including those relating to bail) should be listed where possible before the judge by whom the case is expected to be tried. Where a case is to be tried by a High Court judge who is not available the application or matter should be listed before any other High Court judge then sitting at the Crown Court centre at which the matter has arisen, before a presiding judge, before the resident judge for the centre, or, with the consent of the presiding judge, before a circuit judge nominated for the purpose. (b) In other cases, if the circuit judge or recorder who is expected to try the case is not available, the matter shall be referred to the resident judge or, if he is not available, to any judge or recorder then sitting at the centre.

IV.33.7 Matters to be dealt with (eg in which a community rehabilitation order has been made or a suspended sentence passed) should, where possible, be listed before the judge who originally dealt with the matter, or, if not, before a judge of the same or higher status.

Allocation of proceedings to a court comprising lay justices

IV.33.8 In addition to the classes of case specified in s 74 of the Supreme Court Act 1981 (appeals), any other proceedings, apart from cases listed for pleas of not guilty which, in accordance with these directions are listed for hearing by a circuit judge or recorder, are suitable for allocation to a court comprising Justices of the Peace.

Absence of resident judge

IV.33.9 When a resident judge is absent from his centre, the presiding judges may authorise another judge who sits regularly at the same centre to exercise his responsibility.

Applications for removal of a driving disqualification

IV.33.10 Application should be made to the location of the Crown Court where the order of disqualification was made.

Presiding judges' directions

IV.33.11 For the just, speedy and economical disposal of the business of a circuit, presiding judges shall, with the approval of the senior presiding judge, issue directions as to the need, where appropriate, to reserve a case for trial by a High Court judge (or Deputy High Court judge) and as to the allocation of work between circuit judges, (deputy circuit judges) and recorders and where necessary the devolved responsibility of resident judges for such allocation. In such directions specific provision should be made for cases in the following categories. (a) Cases where death or serious risk to life, or the infliction of grave injury is involved, including motoring cases of this category arising from dangerous driving and/or excess alcohol. (b) Cases where loaded firearms are alleged to have been used. (c) Cases of arson or criminal damage with intent to endanger life. (d) Cases of defrauding government departments or local authorities or other public bodies of amounts in excess of £25,000. (e) Offences under the Forgery and Counterfeiting Act 1981 where the amount of money or the value of goods exceeds £10,000. (f) Offences involving violence to a police officer which result in the officer being unfit for duty for more than 28 days. (g) Any offence involving loss to any person or body of a sum in excess of £100,000. (h) Cases where there is a risk of substantial political or racial feeling being excited by the offence or the trial. (i) Cases which have given rise to widespread public concern. (j) Cases of robbery or assault with intent to rob where gross violence was used, or serious injury was caused, or where the accused was armed with a dangerous weapon for the purpose of the robbery, or where the theft was intended to be from a bank, a building society or a post office. (k) Cases involving the manufacture or distribution of substantial quantities of drugs. (l) Cases the trial of which is likely to last more than ten days. (m) Cases involving the trial of more than five defendants. (n) Cases in which the accused holds a senior public office, or is a member of a profession or other person carrying a special duty or responsibility to the public, including a police officer when acting as such. (o) Cases where a difficult issue of law is likely to be involved or a prosecution for the offence is rare or novel.

IV.33.12 With the approval of the senior presiding judge, general directions may be given by the presiding judges of the South Eastern Circuit concerning the distribution and allocation of business of all classes at the Central Criminal Court.

IV.34 Settling the indictment

IV.34.1 Where an indictment contains counts which differ materially from, or are additional to, the charges on which an accused was committed for trial, the CPS shall notify the accused of the fact and shall, in any event, send a copy of the indictment to the accused.

IV.34.2 There is no rule of law or practice which prohibits two indictments being in existence at the same time for the same offence against the same person on the same facts. But the court will not allow the prosecution to proceed on both such indictments. They cannot in law be tried together and the court will insist that the prosecution elect the one on which the trial shall proceed. Where different persons have been separately committed for trial for offences which can lawfully be charged in the same indictment it is permissible to join in one indictment the counts founded on the separate committals despite the fact that an indictment in respect of one of those committals has already been signed.

IV.34.3 It is undesirable that a large number of counts should be contained in one indictment. Where defendants on trial have a variety of offences alleged against them the prosecution should be put to their election and compelled to proceed on a certain number only, leaving a decision to be taken later whether to try any of the remainder. Where an indictment contains substantive counts and one or more related conspiracy counts the judge should require the prosecution to justify the joinder. Failing justification the Crown should be required to elect whether to proceed on the substantive counts or the conspiracy counts. A joinder is justified for this purpose if the judge considers that the interests of justice demand it. In either event, if there is a conviction, the other count(s) can remain on the file marked 'Not to be proceeded with without leave of the court'. Should such conviction(s) be quashed, the others can be tried. It is possible to split an indictment and put some counts into another indictment.

IV.35 Voluntary bills of indictment

IV.35.1 Section 2(2)(b) of the Administration of Justice (Miscellaneous Provisions) Act 1933 allows the preferment of a bill of indictment by the direction or with the consent of a judge of the High Court. Bills so preferred are known as voluntary bills.

IV.35.2 Applications for such consent must not only comply with each paragraph of the Indictments (Procedure) Rules 1971, SI 1971/2084, but must also be accompanied by: (a) a copy of any charges on which the defendant has been committed for trial; (b) a copy of any charges on which his committal for trial was refused by the magistrates' court; (c) a copy of any existing indictment which has been preferred in consequence of his committal; (d) a summary of the evidence or other document which (i) identifies the counts in the proposed indictment on which he has been committed for trial (or which are substantially the same as charges on which he has been so committed), and (ii) in relation to each other count in the proposed indictment, identifies the pages in the accompanying statements and exhibits where the essential evidence said to support that count is to be found; (e) marginal markings of the relevant passages on the pages of the statements and exhibits identified under (d)(ii). These requirements should be complied with in relation to each defendant named in the indictment for which consent is sought, whether or not it is proposed to prefer any new count against him.

IV.35.3 The preferment of a voluntary bill is an exceptional procedure. Consent should only be granted where good reason to depart from the normal procedure is clearly shown and only where the interests of justice, rather than considerations of administrative convenience, require it.

IV.35.4 Neither the 1933 Act nor the 1971 rules expressly require a prosecuting authority applying for consent to the preferment of a voluntary bill to give notice of the application to the prospective defendant or to serve on him a copy of documents delivered to the judge; nor is it expressly required that the prospective defendant have any opportunity to make any submissions to the judge, whether in writing or orally.

IV.35.5 The prosecuting authorities for England and Wales have issued revised guidance to prosecutors on the procedures to be adopted in seeking judicial consent to the preferment of voluntary bills. These procedures direct prosecutors: (a) on the making of application for consent to preferment of a voluntary bill, forthwith to give notice to the prospective defendant that such application has been made; (b) at about the same time, to serve on the prospective defendant a copy of all the documents delivered to the judge (save to the extent that these have already been served on him); (c) to inform the prospective defendant that he may make submissions in writing to the judge, provided that he does so within nine working days of the giving of notice under (a) above. Prosecutors will be directed that these procedures should be followed unless there are good grounds for not doing so, in which case prosecutors will inform the judge that the procedures have not been followed and seek his leave to dispense with all or any of them. Judges should not give leave to dispense unless good grounds are shown.

IV.35.6 A judge to whom application for consent to the preferment of a voluntary bill is made will, of course, wish to consider carefully the documents submitted by the prosecutor and any written submissions timeously made by the prospective defendant, and may properly seek any necessary amplification. The judge may invite oral submissions from either party, or accede to a request for an opportunity to make such oral submissions, if the judge considers it necessary or desirable to receive such oral submissions in order to make a sound and fair decision on the application. Any such oral submissions should be made on notice to the other party, who should be allowed to attend.

IV.36 Abuse of process stay applications

IV.36.1 In all cases where a defendant in the Crown Court proposes to make an application to stay an indictment on the grounds of abuse of process, written notice of such application must be given to the prosecuting authority and to any co-defendant not later than 14 days before the date fixed or warned for trial (the relevant date). Such notice must: (a) give the name of the case and the indictment number; (b) state the fixed date or the warned date as appropriate; (c) specify the nature of the application; (d) set out in numbered subparagraphs the grounds upon which the application is to be made; (e) be copied to the chief listing officer at the court centre where the case is due to be heard.

IV.36.2 Any co-defendant who wishes to make a like application must give a like notice not later than seven days before the relevant date, setting out any additional grounds relied upon.

IV.36.3 In relation to such applications, the following automatic directions shall apply. (a) the advocate for the applicant(s) must lodge with the court and serve on all other parties a skeleton argument in support of the application at least five clear working days before the relevant date. If reference is to be made to any document not in the existing trial documents, a paginated and indexed bundle of such documents is to be provided with the skeleton argument. (b) The advocate for the prosecution must lodge with the court and serve on all other parties a responsive skeleton argument at least two clear working days before the relevant date, together with a supplementary bundle if appropriate.

IV.36.4 All skeleton arguments must specify any propositions of law to be advanced (together with the authorities relied upon in support, with page references to passages relied upon) and, where appropriate, include a chronology of events and a list of dramatis personae. In all instances where reference is made to a document, the reference in the trial documents or supplementary bundle is to be given.

IV.36.5 The above time limits are minimum time limits. In appropriate cases the court will order longer lead times. To this end in all cases where defence advocates are, at the time of the plea and directions hearing, considering the possibility of an abuse of process application, this must be raised with the judge dealing with the matter, who will order a different timetable if appropriate, and may wish, in any event, to give additional directions about the conduct of the application.

IV.37 Citation of Hansard

IV.37.1 Where any party intends to refer to the reports of Parliamentary proceedings as reported in the Official Reports of either House of Parliament ('Hansard') in support of any such argument as is permitted by the decisions in *Pepper (Inspector of Taxes) v Hart* 1993] AC 593, [1993] 1 All ER 42 and *Pickstone v Freemans plc* [1989] AC 66, [1988] 2 All ER 803 or otherwise must, unless the court otherwise directs, serve upon all other parties and the court copies of any such extract together with a brief summary of the argument intended to be based upon such extract. No other report of Parliamentary proceedings may be cited.

IV.37.2 Unless the court otherwise directs, service of the extract and summary of the argument shall be effected not less than five clear working days before the first day of the hearing, whether or not it has a fixed date. Advocates must keep themselves informed as to the state of the lists where no fixed date has been given. Service on the court shall be effected by sending three copies to the chief clerk of the relevant Crown Court centre. If any party fails to do so the court may make such order (relating to costs or otherwise) as is in all the circumstances appropriate.

IV.38 Applications for representation orders

IV.38.1 Applications for representation by a Queen's Counsel alone or by more than one advocate under Pt IV of the Criminal Defence Service (General) (No 2) Regulations 2001, SI 2001/1437, made to the Crown Court shall be placed before the resident judge of that Crown Court (or, in his absence, a judge nominated for that purpose by a presiding judge of the circuit) who shall determine the application, save that, where the application relates to a case which is to be heard before a named High Court judge or a named circuit judge, he should refer the application to the named judge for determination.

IV.38.2 This does not apply where an application is made in the course of a trial or of a preliminary hearing, pre-trial review, or plea and directions hearing by the judge presiding at that trial or hearing.

IV.38.3 In the event of any doubt as to the proper application of this direction, reference shall be made by the judge concerned to a presiding judge of the circuit, who shall give such directions as he thinks fit.

IV.39 Trial of children and young persons

IV.39.1 This direction applies to trials of children and young persons in the Crown Court. In it children and young persons are together called 'young defendants'.

IV.39.2 The steps which should be taken to comply with paras IV.39.3– IV.39.17 should be judged, in any given case, taking account of the age, maturity and development (intellectual and emotional) of the young defendant on trial and all other circumstances of the case.

The overriding principle

IV.39.3 Some young defendants accused of committing serious crimes may be very young and very immature when standing trial in the Crown Court. The purpose of such trial is to determine guilt (if that is in issue) and decide the appropriate sentence if the young defendant pleads guilty or is convicted. The trial process should not itself expose the young defendant to avoidable intimidation, humiliation or distress. All possible steps should be taken to assist the young defendant to understand and participate in the proceedings. The ordinary trial process should, so far as necessary, be adapted to meet those ends. Regard should be had to the welfare of the young defendant as required by s 44 of the Children and Young Persons Act 1933.

Before trial

IV.39.4 If a young defendant is indicted jointly with an adult defendant, the court should consider at the plea and directions hearing whether the young defendant should be tried on his own and should ordinarily so order unless of opinion that a joint trial would be in the interests of justice and would not be unduly prejudicial to the welfare of the young defendant. If a young defendant is tried jointly with an adult the ordinary procedures will apply subject to such modifications (if any) as the court may see fit to order.

IV.39.5 At the plea and directions hearing before trial of a young defendant, the court should consider and so far as practicable give directions on the matters covered in paras IV.39.9–IV.39.15.

IV.39.6 It may be appropriate to arrange that a young defendant should visit, out of court hours and before the trial, the courtroom in which the trial is to be held so that he can familiarise himself with it.

IV.39.7 If any case against a young defendant has attracted or may attract widespread public or media interest, the assistance of the police should be enlisted to try and ensure that a young defendant is not, when attending for the trial, exposed to intimidation, vilification or abuse.

IV.39.8 The court should be ready at this stage (if it has not already done so) to give a direction under s 39 of the 1933 Act or, as the case may be, s 45 of the Youth Justice and Criminal Evidence Act 1999. Any such order, once made, should be reduced to writing and copies should on request be made available to anyone affected or potentially affected by it.

The trial

IV.39.9 The trial should, if practicable, be held in a courtroom in which all the participants are on the same or almost the same level.

IV.39.10 A young defendant should normally, if he wishes, be free to sit with members of his family or others in a like relationship and in a place which permits easy, informal communication with his legal representatives and others with whom he wants or needs to communicate.

IV.39.11 The court should explain the course of proceedings to a young defendant in terms he can understand, should remind those representing a young defendant of their continuing duty to explain each step of the trial to him and should ensure, so far as practicable, that the trial is conducted in language which the young defendant can understand.

IV.39.12 The trial should be conducted according to a timetable which takes full account of a young defendant's inability to concentrate for long periods. Frequent and regular breaks will often be appropriate.

IV.39.13 Robes and wigs should not be worn unless the young defendant asks that they should or the court for good reason orders that they should. Any person responsible for the security of a young defendant who is in custody should not be in uniform. There should be no recognisable police presence in the courtroom save for good reason.

IV.39.14 The court should be prepared to restrict attendance at the trial to a small number, perhaps limited to some of those with an immediate and direct interest in the outcome of the trial. The court should rule on any challenged claim to attend.

IV.39.15 Facilities for reporting the trial (subject to any direction given under s 39 of the 1933 Act or s 45 of the 1999 Act) must be provided. But the court may restrict the number of those attending in the courtroom to report the trial to such number as is judged practicable and desirable. In ruling on any challenged claim to attend the courtroom for the purpose of reporting the trial the court should be mindful of the public's general right to be informed about the administration of justice in the Crown Court. Where access to the courtroom by reporters is restricted, arrangements should be made for the proceedings to be relayed, audibly and if possible visually, to another room in the same court complex to which the media have free access if it appears that there will be a need for such additional facilities.

IV.39.16 Where the court is called upon to exercise its discretion in relation to any procedural matter failing within the scope of this practice direction but not the subject of specific reference, such discretion should be exercised having regard to the principles in para IV.39.3.

Appeal and committals for sentence

IV.39.17 This practice direction does not in terms apply to appeals and committals for sentence, but regard should be paid to the effect of it if the arrangements for hearing any appeal or committal might otherwise be prejudicial to the welfare of a young defendant.

IV.40 Video recorded evidence-in-chief

IV.40.1 The procedure for making application for leave to adduce a video recording of testimony from a witness under s 27 of the Youth Justice and Criminal Evidence Act 1999 is laid down in r 8 of the Crown Court (Special Measures Directions and Directions Prohibiting Cross-Examination) Rules 2002, SI 2002/1688.

IV.40.2 Where a court, on application by a party to the proceedings or of its own motion, grants leave to admit a video recording in evidence under s 27(1) of the 1999 Act it may direct that any part of the recording be excluded (s 27(2) and (3)). When such direction is given, the party who made application to admit the video recording must edit the recording in accordance with the judge's directions and send a copy of the edited recording to the appropriate officer of the Crown Court and to every other party to the proceedings.

IV.40.3 Where a video recording is to be adduced during proceedings before the Crown Court, it should be produced and proved by the interviewer, or any other person who was present at the interview with the witness at which the recording was made. The applicant should ensure that such a person will be available for this purpose, unless the parties have agreed to accept a written statement in lieu of attendance by that person.

IV.40.4 Once a trial has begun if, by reason of faulty or inadequate preparation or for some other cause, the procedures set out above have not been properly complied with and an application is made to edit the video recording, thereby making necessary an adjournment for the work to be carried out, the court may make at its discretion an appropriate award of costs.

IV.41 Management of cases to be heard in the Crown Court

IV.41.1 This section of the practice direction supplements the rules in Part 3 of the Criminal Procedure Rules as they apply to the management of cases to be heard in the Crown Court. Where time limits or other directions in the Consolidated Criminal Practice Direction appear inconsistent with this section, the directions in this section take precedence.

IV.41.2 The case details form set out in annex E should be completed by the Crown Court case progression officer in all cases to be tried on indictment.

Cases sent for trial

IV.41.3 A preliminary hearing ("PH") is not required in every case sent for trial under s 51 of the Crime and Disorder Act 1998: see rule 12.2 (which altered the Crown Court rule from which it derived). A PH should normally only be ordered by the magistrates' court or by the Crown Court where:

(i)   there are case management issues which call for such a hearing;
(ii)   the case is likely to last for more than 4 weeks;
(iii)   it would be desirable to set an early trial date;
(iv)   the defendant is a child or young person;
(v)   there is likely to be a guilty plea and the defendant could be sentenced at the preliminary hearing; or
(vi)   it seems to the court that it is a case suitable for a preparatory hearing in the Crown Court (see ss 7 and 9 of the Criminal Justice Act 1987 and ss 29–32 of the Criminal Procedure and Investigations Act 1996).

A PH, if there is one, should be held about 14 days after sending.

IV.41.4 The case progression form to be used in the magistrates' court and the PH form to be used in the Crown Court are set out in annex E with guidance notes. The forms provide a detailed timetable to enable the subsequent plea and case management hearing ("PCMH") to be effective.

IV.41.5 Where the magistrates' court does not order a PH it should order a PCMH to be held within about 14 weeks after sending for trial where a defendant is in custody and within about 17 weeks after sending for trial where a defendant is on bail. Those periods accommodate the periods fixed by the relevant rules for the service of the prosecution case papers and for making all potential preparatory applications. Where the parties realistically expect to have completed their preparation for the PCMH in less time than that then the magistrates' court should order it to be held earlier. But it will not normally be appropriate to order that the PCMH be held on a date before the expiry of at least 4 weeks from the date on which the prosecutor expects to serve the prosecution case papers, to allow the defence a proper opportunity to consider them. To order that a PCMH be held before the parties have had a reasonable opportunity to complete their preparation in accordance with the Criminal Procedure Rules risks compromising the effectiveness of this most important pre-trial hearing and risks wasting their time and that of the court.

Cases committed for trial

IV.41.6 For cases committed to the Crown Court for trial under s 6 of the Magistrates' Courts Act 1980 the case progression form to be used in the magistrates' court is set out in annex E with guidance notes. A PCMH should be ordered by the magistrates' court in every case, to be held within about 7 weeks after committal. That period accommodates the periods fixed by the relevant rules for making all potential preparatory applications. Where the parties realistically expect to have completed their preparation for the PCMH in less time than that then the magistrates' court should order it to be held earlier. However, to order that a PCMH be held before the parties have had a reasonable opportunity to complete their preparation in accordance with the Criminal Procedure Rules risks compromising the effectiveness of this most important pre-trial hearing and risks wasting their time and that of the court.

Cases transferred for trial

IV.41.7 In a case transferred to the Crown Court for trial under s 4(1) of the Criminal Justice Act 1987 or under s 53(1) of the Criminal Justice Act 1991 the directions contained in the case progression form used in cases for committal for trial apply as if the case had been committed on the date of the notice of transfer. A PMCH should be listed by the Crown Court to be held within about 7 weeks after transfer. That period accommodates the periods fixed by the relevant rules for making all potential preparatory applications. Where the parties realistically expect to have completed their preparation for the PCMH in less time than that then the magistrates' court should order it to be held earlier. However, to order that a PCMH be held before the parties have had a reasonable opportunity to complete their preparation in accordance with the Criminal Procedure Rules risks compromising the effectiveness of this most important pre-trial hearing and risks wasting their time and that of the court.

Plea and case management hearing

IV.41.8 Active case management at the PCMH is essential to reduce the number of ineffective and cracked trials and delays during the trial to resolve legal issues. The effectiveness of a PCMH hearing in a contested case depends in large measure upon preparation by all concerned and upon the presence of the trial advocate or an advocate who is able to make decisions and give the court the assistance which the trial advocate could be expected to give. Resident Judges in setting the listing policy should ensure that list officers fix cases as far as possible to enable the trial advocate to conduct the PCMH and the trial.

IV.41.9 In Class 1 and Class 2 cases, and in all cases involving a serious sexual offence against a child, the PCMH must be conducted by a High Court judge; by a circuit judge or by a recorder to whom the case has been assigned in accordance with paragraph IV.33 (allocation of business within the Crown Court); or by a judge authorised by the Presiding Judges to conduct such hearings. In the event of a guilty plea before such an authorised judge, the case will be adjourned for sentencing by a High Court judge or by a circuit judge or recorder to whom the case has been assigned.

Use of the PCMH form

IV.41.10 The PCMH form as set out in annex E must be used in accordance with the guidance notes.

Further pre-trial hearings after the PCMH

IV.41.11 Additional pre-trial hearings should be held only if needed for some compelling reason. Such hearings – often described informally as 'mentions' – are expensive and should actively be discouraged. Where necessary the power to give, vary or revoke a direction without a hearing should be used. Rule 3.9(3) of the Criminal Procedure Rules enables the Court to require the parties' case progression officers to inform the Crown Court case progression officer that the case is ready for trial, that it will proceed as a trial on the date fixed and will take no more or less time than that previously ordered.

IV.42 Juries

IV.43 Evidence of tape recorded interviews

IV.43.1 Where a suspect is to be interviewed by the police, the *Code of Practice on Tape Recording of Interviews with Suspects* effective from 10 April 1995 and issued under s 60 of the Police and Criminal Evidence Act 1984 applies. Where a record of the interview is to be prepared this should be in accordance with the national guidelines approved by the Secretary of State, as envisaged by note E:5A of the Code.

IV.43.2 Where the prosecution intends to adduce evidence of the interview- in-evidence, and agreement between the parties has not been reached about the record, sufficient notice must be given to allow consideration of any amendment to the record or the preparation of any transcript of the interview or any editing of a tape for the purpose of playing it back in court. To that end, the following practice should be followed. (a) Where the defence is unable to agree a record of interview or transcript (where one is already available) the prosecution should be notified no more than 21 days from the date of committal or date of transfer, or at the PDH if earlier, with a view to securing agreement to amend. The notice should specify the part to which objection is taken or the part omitted which the defence consider should be included. A copy of the notice should be supplied to the court within the period specified above. (b) If agreement is not reached and it is proposed that the tape or part of it be played in court, notice should be given to the prosecution by the defence no more than 14 days after the expiry of the period in (a), or as ordered at the PDH, in order that counsel for the parties may agree those parts of the tape that should not be adduced and that arrangements may be made, by editing or in some other way, to exclude that material. A copy of the notice should be supplied to the court within the period specified above. (c) Notice of any agreement reached under (a) or (b) should be supplied to the court by the prosecution as soon as is practicable. (d) Alternatively, if, in any event, prosecuting counsel proposes to play the tape or part of it, the prosecution should, within 28 days of the date of committal or date of transfer or, if earlier, at the PDH, notify the defence and the court. The defence should notify the prosecution and the court within 14 days of receiving the notice if they object to the production of the tape on the basis that a part of it should be excluded. If the objections raised by the defence are accepted, the prosecution should prepare an edited tape or make other arrangements to exclude the material part and should notify the court of the arrangements made. (e) Whenever editing or amendment of a record of interview or of a tape or of a transcript takes place, the following general principles should be followed: (i) where a defendant has made a statement which includes an admission of one or more other offences, the portion relating to other offences should be omitted unless it is or becomes admissible in evidence; (ii) where the statement of one defendant contains a portion which is partly in his favour and partly implicatory of a co-defendant in the trial, the defendant making the statement has the right to insist that everything relevant which is in his favour goes before the jury. In such a case the judge must be consulted about how best to protect the position of the co-defendant.

IV.43.3 If there is a failure to agree between counsel under para IV.43.2(a)–(e), or there is a challenge to the integrity of the master tape, notice and particulars should be given to the court and to the prosecution by the defence as soon as is practicable. The court may then, at its discretion, order a pre-trial review or give such other directions as may be appropriate.

IV.43.4 If a tape is to be adduced during proceedings before the Crown Court it should be produced and proved by the interviewing officer or any other officer who was present at the interview at which the recording was made. The prosecution should ensure that such an officer will be available for this purpose.

IV.43.5 Where such an officer is unable to act as the tape machine operator it is for the prosecution to make some other arrangement.

IV.43.6 In order to avoid the necessity for the court to listen to lengthy or irrelevant material before the relevant part of a tape recording is reached, counsel shall indicate to the tape machine operator those parts of a recording which it may be necessary to play. Such an indication should, so far as possible, be expressed in terms of the time track or other identifying process used by the interviewing police force and should be given in time for the operator to have located those parts by the appropriate point in the trial.

IV.43.7 Once a trial has begun, if, by reason of faulty preparation or for some other cause, the procedures above have not been properly complied with, and an application is made to amend the record of interview or transcript or to edit the tape, as the case may be, thereby making necessary an adjournment for the work to be carried out, the court may make at its discretion an appropriate award of costs.

IV.43.8 Where a case is listed for hearing on a date which falls within the time limits set out above, it is the responsibility of the parties to ensure that all the necessary steps are taken to comply with this practice direction within such shorter period as is available.

IV.43.9 In para IV.43.2(a) and (d), 'date of transfer' is the date on which notice of transfer is given in accordance with the provisions of s 4(1)(c) of the Criminal Justice Act 1987.

IV.43.10 This direction should be read in conjunction with the *Code of Practice on Tape Recording* referred to in para IV.43.1 and with Home Office circular 26/1995.

IV.44 Defendant's right to give or not to give evidence

IV.44.1 At the conclusion of the evidence for the prosecution, s 35(2) of the Criminal Justice and Public Order Act 1994 requires the court to satisfy itself that the accused is aware that the stage has been reached at which evidence can be given for the defence and that he can, if he wishes, give evidence and that, if he chooses not to give evidence, or having been sworn, without good cause refuses to answer any question, it will be permissible for the jury to draw such inferences as appear proper from his failure to give evidence or his refusal, without good cause, to answer any question.

If the accused is legally represented

IV.44.2 Section 35(1) provides that s 35(2) does not apply if at the conclusion of the evidence for the prosecution the accused's legal representative informs the court that the accused will give evidence. This should be done in the presence of the jury. If the representative indicates that the accused will give evidence the case should proceed in the usual way.

IV.44.3 If the court is not so informed, or if the court is informed that the accused does not intend to give evidence, the judge should in the presence of the jury inquire of the representative in these terms:

'Have you advised your client that the stage has now been reached at which he may give evidence and, if he chooses not to do so or, having been sworn, without good cause refuses to answer any question, the jury may draw such inferences as appear proper from his failure to do so?'

IV.44.4 If the representative replies to the judge that the accused has been so advised, then the case shall proceed. If counsel replies that the accused has not been so advised, then the judge shall direct the representative to advise his client of the consequences set out in para IV.44.3 and should adjourn briefly for this purpose before proceeding further.

If the accused is not legally represented

IV.44.5 If the accused is not represented, the judge shall at the conclusion of the evidence for the prosecution and in the presence of the jury say to the accused:

'You have heard the evidence against you. Now is the time for you to make your defence. You may give evidence on oath, and be cross-examined like any other witness. If you do not give evidence or, having been sworn, without good cause refuse to answer any question the jury may draw such inferences as appear proper. That means they may hold it against you. You may also call any witness or witnesses whom you have arranged to attend court. Afterwards you may also, if you wish, address the jury by arguing your case from the dock. But you cannot at that stage give evidence. Do you now intend to give evidence?'

IV.45 Discussions about sentence

IV.46 Majority verdicts

IV.47 Imposition of discretionary life sentences

IV.48 Life Sentences for juveniles convicted of murder

IV.49 Life sentences

IV.50 Bail pending appeal

PART V
FURTHER DIRECTIONS APPLYING IN THE MAGISTRATES' COURTS
V.51 Mode of trial

V.51.1 The purpose of these guidelines is to help magistrates decide whether or not to commit defendants charged with 'either way' offences for trial in the Crown Court. Their object is to provide guidance not direction. They are not intended to impinge on a magistrate's duty to consider each case individually and on its own particular facts. These guidelines apply to all defendants aged 18 and above.

General mode of trial considerations

V.51.2 Section 19 of the Magistrates' Courts Act 1980 requires magistrates to have regard to the following matters in deciding whether an offence is more suitable for summary trial or trial on indictment: (a) the nature of the case; (b) whether the circumstances make the offence one of a serious character; (c) whether the punishment which a magistrates' court would have power to inflict for it would be adequate; (d) any other circumstances which appear to the court to make it more suitable for the offence to be tried in one way rather than the other; (e) any representations made by the prosecution or the defence.

V.51.3 Certain general observations can be made: (f) the court should never make its decision on the grounds of convenience or expedition; (g) the court should assume for the purpose of deciding mode of trial that the prosecution version of the facts is correct; (h) the fact that the offences are alleged to be specimens is a relevant consideration (although, it has to be borne in mind that difficulties can arise in sentencing in relation to specimen counts, see *R v Clark* [1996] 2 Cr App Rep (S) 351 and *R v Kidd, R v Canavan, R v Shaw* [1998] 1 All ER 42, [1998] 1 Cr App Rep (S) 243); the fact that the defendant will be asking for other offences to be taken into consideration, if convicted, is not; (i) where cases involve complex questions of fact or difficult questions of law, including difficult issues of disclosure of sensitive material, the court should consider committal for trial; (j) where two or more defendants are jointly charged with an offence each has an individual right to elect his mode of trial; k) in general, except where otherwise stated, either way offences should be tried summarily unless the court considers that the particular case has one or more of the features set out in paras V.51.4– V.51.18 and that its sentencing powers are insufficient; (l) the court should also consider its power to commit an offender for sentence under ss 3 and 4 of the Powers of Criminal Courts (Sentencing) Act 2000, if information emerges during the course of the hearing which leads it to conclude that the offence is so serious, or the offender such a risk to the public, that its powers to sentence him are inadequate. This means that committal for sentence is no longer determined by reference to the character and antecedents of the offender.

Features relevant to individual offences

V.51.4 Where reference is made in these guidelines to property or damage of 'high value' it means a figure equal to at least twice the amount of the limit (currently £5,000) imposed by statute on a magistrates' court when making a compensation order.

Burglary: dwelling house

V.51.5 Cases should be tried summarily unless the court considers that one or more of the following features is present in the case *and* that its sentencing powers are insufficient. Magistrates should take account of their powers under ss 3 and 4 of the Powers of Criminal Courts (Sentencing) Act 2000 to commit for sentence, see para V.51.3(g): (m) entry in the daytime when the occupier (or another) is present; (n) entry at night of a house which is normally occupied, whether or not the occupier (or another) is present; (o) the offence is alleged to be one of a series of similar offences; (p) when soiling, ransacking, damage or vandalism occurs; (q) the offence has professional hallmarks; (r) the unrecovered property is of high value: see para V.51.4 for definition of high value; (s) the offence is racially motivated.

Note: attention is drawn to para 28(c) of Sch 1 to the Magistrates' Courts Act 1980 by which offences of burglary in a dwelling cannot be tried summarily if any person in the dwelling was subjected to violence or the threat of violence.

Burglary: non-dwelling

V.51.6 Cases should be tried summarily unless the court considers that one or more of the following features is present in the case and that its sentencing powers are insufficient. Magistrates should take account of their powers under ss 3 and 4 of the 2000 Act to commit for sentence, see para V.51.3(g): (t) entry of a pharmacy or doctor's surgery; (u) fear is caused or violence is done to anyone lawfully on the premises (eg night-watchman, security guard); (v) the offence has professional hallmarks; (w) vandalism on a substantial scale; (x) the unrecovered property is of high value: see para V.51.4 for definition of high value; (y) the offence is racially motivated.

Theft and fraud

V.51.7 Cases should be tried summarily unless the court considers that one or more of the following features is present in the case *and* that its sentencing powers are insufficient. Magistrates should take account of their powers under ss 3 and 4 of the 2000 Act to commit for sentence, see para V.51.3(z): (a) breach of trust by a person in a position of substantial authority, or in whom a high degree of trust is placed; (aa) theft or fraud which has been committed or disguised in a sophisticated manner; (bb) theft or fraud committed by an organised gang; (cc) the victim is particularly vulnerable to theft or fraud, eg the elderly or infirm; (dd) the unrecovered property is of high value: see para V.51.4 for definition of high value.

Handling

V.51.8 Cases should be tried summarily unless the court considers that one or more of the following features is present in the case and that its sentencing powers are insufficient. Magistrates should take account of their powers under ss 3 and 4 of the 2000 Act to commit for sentence, see para V.51.3(g): (ee) dishonest handling of stolen property by a receiver who has commissioned the theft; (ff) the offence has professional hallmarks; (gg) the property is of high value: see para V.51.4 for definition of high value.

Social security frauds

V.51.9 Cases should be tried summarily unless the court considers that one or more of the following features is present in the case and that its sentencing powers are insufficient. Magistrates should take account of their powers under ss 3 and 4 of the 2000 Act to commit for sentence, see para V.51.3(g): (hh) organised fraud on a large scale; (ii) the frauds are substantial and carried out over a long period of time.

Violence (ss 20 and 47 of the Offences against the Person Act 1861)

V.51.10 Cases should be tried summarily unless the court considers that one or more of the following features is present in the case *and* that its sentencing powers are insufficient. Magistrates should take account of their powers under ss 3 and 4 of the 2000 Act to commit for sentence, see para V.51.3(g): (jj) the use of a weapon of a kind likely to cause serious injury; (kk) a weapon is used and serious injury is caused; (ll) more than minor injury is caused by kicking or head-butting; (mm) serious violence is caused to those whose work has to be done in contact with the public or are likely to face violence in the course of their work; (nn) violence to vulnerable people, eg the elderly and infirm; (oo) the offence has clear racial motivation.

Note: the same considerations apply to cases of domestic violence.

Public Order Act offences

V.51.11 Cases should be tried summarily unless the court considers that one or more of the following features is present in the case and that its sentencing powers are insufficient. Magistrates should take account of their powers under ss 3 and 4 of the 2000 Act to commit for sentence, see para V.51.3(g): (pp) cases of violent disorder should generally be committed for trial; (qq) affray; (i) organised violence or use of weapons; (ii) significant injury or substantial damage; (iii) the offence has clear racial motivation; (iv) an attack on police officers, ambulance staff, fire-fighters and the like.

Violence to and neglect of children

V.51.12 Cases should be tried summarily unless the court considers that one or more of the following features is present in the case *and* that its sentencing powers are insufficient. Magistrates should take account of their powers under ss 3 and 4 of the 2000 Act to commit for sentence, see para V.51.3(g): (rr) substantial injury; (ss) repeated violence or serious neglect, even if the physical harm is slight; (tt) sadistic violence, eg deliberate burning or scalding.

Indecent assault

V.51.13 Cases should be tried summarily unless the court considers that one or more of the following features is present in the case *and* that its sentencing powers are insufficient. Magistrates should take account of their powers under ss 3 and 4 of the 2000 Act to commit for sentence, see para V.51.3(g): (uu) substantial disparity in age between victim and defendant, and a more serious assault; (vv) violence or threats of violence; (www) relationship of trust or responsibility between defendant and victim; (xx) several more serious similar offences; (yy) the victim is particularly vulnerable; (zz) serious nature of the assault.

Unlawful sexual intercourse

V.51.14 Cases should be tried summarily unless the court considers that one or more of the following features is present in the case and that its sentencing powers are insufficient. Magistrates should take account of their powers under ss 3 and 4 of the 2000 Act to commit for sentence, see para V.51.3(g): (aaa) wide disparity of age; (bbb) breach of position of trust; (ccc) the victim is particularly vulnerable.

Note: unlawful sexual intercourse with a girl *under 13* is triable only on indictment.

Drugs

V.51.15 Class A: (ddd) supply; possession with intent to supply: these cases should be committed for trial; (eee) possession: should be committed for trial unless the amount is consistent only with personal use.

V.51.16 Class B: (fff) supply; possession with intent to supply: should be committed for trial unless there is only small scale supply for no payment: (ggg) possession: should be committed for trial when the quantity is substantial and not consistent only with personal use.

Dangerous driving and aggravated vehicle taking

V.51.17 Cases should be tried summarily unless the court considers that one or more of the following features is present in the case *and* that its sentencing powers are insufficient. Magistrates should take account of their powers under ss 3 and 4 of the 2000 Act to commit for sentence, see para V.51.3(g): (hhh) alcohol or drugs contributing to the dangerous driving; (iii) grossly excessive speed; (jjj) racing; (kkk) prolonged course of dangerous driving; (lll) other related offences; (mmm) significant injury or damage sustained.

Criminal damage

V.51.18 Cases should be tried summarily unless the court considers that one or more of the following features is present in the case and that its sentencing powers are insufficient. Magistrates should take account of their powers under ss 3 and 4 of the 2000 Act to commit for sentence, see para V.51.3(g): (nnn) deliberate fire-raising; (ooo) committed by a group; (ppp) damage of a high value; (qqq) the offence has clear racial motivation.

Note: offences set out in Sch 2 to the Magistrates' Courts Act 1980 (which includes offences of criminal damage which do not amount to arson) *must* be tried summarily if the value of the property damaged or destroyed is £5,000 or less.

V.52 Committal for sentence and appeals to Crown Court

V.52.1 Any case notes should be sent to the Crown Court when there is an appeal, thereby making them available to the judge if the judge requires them in order to decide before the hearing questions of listing or representation or the like. They will also be available to the court during the hearing if it becomes necessary or desirable for the court to see what happened in the lower court. On a committal for sentence or an appeal, any reasons given by the magistrates for their decision should be included with the notes.

V.53 Bail before committal for trial

V.53.1 Rules 19 and 20 of the Crown Court Rules 1982, SI 1982/1109, apply to these applications.

V.53.2 Before the Crown Court can deal with an application it must be satisfied that the magistrates' court has issued a certificate under s 5(6A) of the Bail Act 1976 that it heard full argument on the application for bail before it refused the application. A copy of the certificate will be issued to the applicant and not sent directly to the Crown Court. It will therefore be necessary for the applicant's solicitors to attach a copy of the certificate to the bail application form. If the certificate is not enclosed with the application form it will be difficult to avoid some delay in listing.

Venue

V.53.3 Applications should be made to the court to which the defendant will be or would have been committed for trial. In the event of an application in a purely summary case, it should be made to the Crown Court centre which normally receives class 4 work. The hearing will be listed as a chambers matter unless a judge has directed otherwise.

V.54 Contempt in the face of the magistrates' court

General

V.54.1 Section 12 of the Contempt of Court Act 1981 gives magistrates' courts the power to detain until the court rises, someone, whether a defendant or another person present in court, who wilfully insults anyone specified in s 12 or who interrupts proceedings. In any such case, the court may order any officer of the court, or any constable, to take the offender into custody and detain him until the rising of the court; and the court may, if it thinks fit, commit the offender to custody for a specified period not exceeding one month or impose a fine not exceeding level 4 on the standard scale or both. This power can be used to stop disruption of their proceedings. Detention is until the person can be conveniently dealt with without disruption of the proceedings. Prior to the court using the power the offender should be warned to desist or face the prospect of being detained.

V.54.2 Magistrates' courts also have the power to commit to custody any person attending or brought before a magistrates' court who refuses without just cause to be sworn or to give evidence under s 97(4) of the Magistrates' Courts Act 1980, until the expiration of such period not exceeding one month as may be specified in the warrant or until he sooner gives evidence or produces the document or thing, or impose on him a fine not exceeding £2,500, or both.

V.54.3 In the exercise of any of these powers, as soon as is practical, and in any event prior to an offender being proceeded against, an offender should be told of the conduct which it is alleged to constitute his offending in clear terms. When making an order under s 12 the justices should state their findings of fact as to the contempt.

V.54.4 Exceptional situations require exceptional treatment. While this direction deals with the generality of situations, there will be a minority of situations where the application of the direction will not be consistent with achieving justice in the special circumstances of the particular case. Where this is the situation, the compliance with the direction should be modified so far as is necessary so as to accord with the interests of justice.

V.54.5 The power to bind persons over to be of good behaviour in respect of their conduct in court should cease to be exercised.

Contempt consisting of wilfully insulting anyone specified in s 12 or interrupting proceedings

V.54.6 In the case of someone who wilfully insults anyone specified in s 12 of the 1981 Act or interrupts proceedings, if an offender expresses a willingness to apologise for his misconduct, he should be brought back before the court at the earliest convenient moment in order to make the apology and to give undertakings to the court to refrain from further misbehaviour.

V.54.7 In the majority of cases, an apology and a promise as to future conduct should be sufficient for justices to order an offender's release. However, there are likely to be certain cases where the nature and seriousness of the misconduct requires the justices to consider using their powers under s 12(2) of the 1981 Act either to fine or to order the offender's committal to custody.

Where an offender is detained for contempt of court

V.54.8 Anyone detained under either of these provisions in paras V.54.1 or V.54.2 should be seen by the duty solicitor or another legal representative and be represented in proceedings if they so wish. Public funding should generally be granted to cover representation. The offender must be afforded adequate time and facilities in order to prepare his case. The matter should be resolved the same day if at all possible.

V.54.9 The offender should be brought back before the court before the justices conclude their daily business. The justices should ensure that he understands the nature of the proceedings, including his opportunity to apologise or give evidence and the alternative of them exercising their powers.

V.54.10 Having heard from the offender's solicitor, the justices should decide whether to take further action.

Sentencing of an offender who admits being in contempt

V.54.11 If an offence of contempt is admitted the justices should consider whether they are able to proceed on the day or whether to adjourn to allow further reflection. The matter should be dealt with on the same day if at all possible. If the justices are of the view to adjourn they should generally grant the offender bail unless one or more of the exceptions to the right to bail in the Bail Act 1976 are made out.

V.54.12 When they come to sentence the offender where the offence has been admitted, the justices should first ask the offender if he has any objection to them dealing with the matter. If there is any objection to the justices dealing with the matter a differently-constituted panel should hear the proceedings. If the offender's conduct was directed to the justices, it will not be appropriate for the same bench to deal with the matter.

V.54.13 The justices should consider whether an order for the offender's discharge is appropriate, taking into account any time spent on remand, whether the offence was admitted and the seriousness of the contempt. Any period of committal should be for the shortest time commensurate with the interests of preserving good order in the administration of justice.

Trial of the issue where the contempt is not admitted

V.54.14 Where the contempt is not admitted the justices' powers are limited to making arrangements for a trial to take place. They should not at this stage make findings against the offender.

V.54.15 In the case of a contested contempt the trial should take place at the earliest opportunity and should be before a bench of justices other than those before whom the alleged contempt took place. If a trial of the issue can take place on the day such arrangements should be made taking into account the offender's rights under art 6 of the European Convention for the Protection of Human Rights and Fundamental Freedoms 1950 (Rome, 4 November 1950; TS 71 (1953); Cmd 8969) [as set out in Sch 1 to the Human Rights Act 1998]. If the trial cannot take place that day the justices should again bail the offender unless there are grounds under the 1976 Act to remand him in custody.

V.54.16 The offender is entitled to call and examine witnesses where evidence is relevant. If the offender is found by the court to have committed contempt the court should again consider first whether an order for his discharge from custody is sufficient to bring proceedings to an end. The justices should also allow the offender a further opportunity to apologise for his contempt or to make representations. If the justices are of the view that they must exercise their powers to commit to custody under s 12(2) of the 1981 Act, they must take into account any time spent on remand and the nature and seriousness of the contempt. Any period of committal should be for the shortest period of time commensurate with the interests of preserving good order in the administration of justice.

V.55 Clerk retiring with justices

V.55.1 A justices' clerk is responsible for: (a) the legal advice tendered to the justices within the area; (b) the performance of any of the functions set out below by any member of his staff acting as legal adviser; (c) ensuring that competent advice is available to justices when the justices' clerk is not personally present in court; and (d) the effective delivery of case management and the reduction of unnecessary delay.

V.55.2 Where a person other than the justices' clerk (a 'legal adviser'), who is authorised to do so, performs any of the functions referred to in this direction he will have the same responsibilities as the justices' clerk. The legal adviser may consult the justices' clerk or other person authorised by the justices' clerk for that purpose before tendering advice to the bench. If the justices' clerk or that person gives any advice directly to the bench, he should give the parties or their advocates an opportunity of repeating any relevant submissions prior to the advice being given.

V.55.3 It shall be the responsibility of the legal adviser to provide the justices with any advice they require properly to perform their functions, whether or not the justices have requested that advice, on: (a) questions of law (including European Court of Human Rights jurisprudence and those matters set out in s 2(1) of the Human Rights Act 1998); (b) questions of mixed law and fact; (c) matters of practice and procedure; (d) the range of penalties available; (e) any relevant decisions of the superior courts or other guidelines; (f) other issues relevant to the matter before the court; and (g) the appropriate decision-making structure to be applied in any given case. In addition to advising the justices it shall be the legal adviser's responsibility to assist the court, where appropriate, as to the formulation of reasons and the recording of those reasons.

V.55.4 A justices' clerk or legal adviser must not play any part in making findings of fact, but may assist the bench by reminding them of the evidence, using any notes of the proceedings for this purpose.

V.55.5 A justices' clerk or legal adviser may ask questions of witnesses and the parties in order to clarify the evidence and any issues in the case. A legal adviser has a duty to ensure that every case is conducted fairly.

V.55.6 When advising the justices, the justices' clerk or legal adviser, whether or not previously in court, should: (a) ensure that he is aware of the relevant facts; and (b) provide the parties with the information necessary to enable the parties to make any representations they wish as to the advice before it is given.

V.55.7 At any time justices are entitled to receive advice to assist them in discharging their responsibilities. If they are in any doubt as to the evidence which has been given, they should seek the aid of their legal adviser, referring to his notes as appropriate. This should ordinarily be done in open court. Where the justices request their adviser to join them in the retiring room, this request should be made in the presence of the parties in court. Any legal advice given to the justices other than in open court should be clearly stated to be provisional and the adviser should subsequently repeat the substance of the advice in open court and give the parties an opportunity to make any representations they wish on that provisional advice. The legal adviser should then state in open court whether the provisional advice is confirmed or if it is varied the nature of the variation.

V.55.8 The performance of a legal adviser may be appraised by a person authorised by the magistrates' courts committee to do so. For that purpose the appraiser may be present in the justices' retiring room. The content of the appraisal is confidential, but the fact that an appraisal has taken place, and the presence of the appraiser in the retiring room, should be briefly explained in open court.

V.55.9 The legal adviser is under a duty to assist unrepresented parties to present their case, but must do so without appearing to become an advocate for the party concerned.

V.55.10 The role of legal advisers in fine default proceedings or any other proceedings for the enforcement of financial orders, obligations or penalties is to assist the court. They must not act in an adversarial or partisan manner. With the agreement of the justices a legal adviser may ask questions of the defaulter to elicit information which the justices will require to make an adjudication, for example to facilitate his explanation for the default. A legal adviser may also advise the justices in the normal way as to the options open to them in dealing with the case. It would be inappropriate for the legal adviser to set out to establish wilful refusal or neglect or any other type of culpable behaviour, to offer an opinion on the facts, or to urge a particular course of action upon the justices. The duty of impartiality is the paramount consideration for the legal adviser at all times, and this takes precedence over any role he may have as a collecting officer. The appointment of other staff to 'prosecute' the case for the collecting officer is not essential to ensure compliance with the law, including the Human Rights Act 1998. Whether to make such appointments is a matter for the justices' chief executive.

V.56 Case management in magistrates' courts

V.56.1 This section of the practice direction supplements the rules in Part 3 of the Criminal Procedure Rules as they apply to the management of cases in magistrates' courts. Where time limits or other directions in the Consolidated Criminal Practice Direction appear inconsistent with this section, the directions in this section take precedence. To avoid unnecessary and wasted hearings the parties should be allowed adequate time to prepare the case, having regard to the time limits for applications and notices set by the Criminal Procedure Rules and by other legislation. When those time limits have expired the parties will be expected to be fully prepared.

Cases to be tried summarily by the magistrates' court

V.56.2 The case progression form to be used is set out in annex E with guidance notes. The form, read with the notes, constitutes a case progression timetable for the effective preparation of a case.

Cases sent, committed or transferred to the Crown Court for trial

V.56.3 The case progression forms set out in annex E with guidance notes are to be used in connection with cases that are sent to the Crown Court for trial under section 51 of the Crime and Disorder Act 1998 and cases that are committed to the Crown Court for trial under section 6 of the Magistrates' Courts Act 1980. In a case transferred to the Crown Court for trial under section 4(1) of the Criminal Justice Act 1987 or under section 53(1) of the Criminal Justice Act 1991 the directions contained in the case progression form used for committal for trial apply as if the case had been committed on the date of the notice of transfer.

V.56.4 A preliminary hearing ('PH') is not required in every case sent for trial under section 51 of the Crime and Disorder Act 1998: see rule 12.2 (which altered the Crown Court rule from which it derived). A PH should be ordered only where such a hearing is considered necessary. The PH should be held about 14 days after sending.

V.56.5 Whether or not a magistrates' court orders a PH, a plea and case management hearing ('PCMH') should be ordered in every case sent or committed to the Crown Court for trial. The PCMH should be held within about 7 weeks after committal for trial, within about 14 weeks after sending for trial where a defendant is in custody and within about 17 weeks after sending for trial where a defendant is on bail.

Use of the forms: directions that apply by default

V.56.6 The case progression forms to be used in magistrates' courts contain directions some of which are determined by Criminal Procedure Rules or by other legislation and some of which are discretionary, as explained in the guidance notes. All those directions apply in every case unless the court otherwise orders.

List of Practice Directions, Practice Notes and Practice Statements included in this consolidation

List of Practice Directions, Practice Notes and Practice Statements not included in this consolidation, but no longer applicable in criminal proceedings

Explanations for the imposition of custodial sentences: forms of words

The following forms may need to be adapted in the light of such provisions or practices as are in force affecting possible earlier release.

Forms of words are provided for use where the offender (a) will be a short-term prisoner not subject to licence; (b) will be a short-term prisoner subject to licence; (c) will be a long-term prisoner; (d) will be subject to a discretionary sentence of life imprisonment.

Sentencers will bear in mind that where an offender is sentenced to terms which are consecutive, or wholly or partly concurrent, they are to be treated as a single term: s 51(2) of the Criminal Justice Act 1991.

(a) Total term less than 12 months:

'The sentence is (. . .) months.'

'You will serve half that sentence in prison/a young offender institution. After that time you will be released.'

'Your release will not bring this sentence to an end. If after your release and before the end of the period covered by the sentence you commit any further offence, you may be ordered to return to custody to serve the balance of the original sentence outstanding at the date of the further offence, as well as being punished for that new offence.'

'Any time you have spent on remand in custody in connection with the offence(s) for which you are now being sentenced will count as part of the sentence to be served, unless it has already been counted.'

(b) Total term of 12 months and less than four years:

'The sentence is (. . .) (months/years).'

'You will serve half that sentence in a prison/a young offender institution. After that time you will be released.'

'Your release will not bring this sentence to an end. If after your release and before the end of the period covered by the sentence you commit any further offence you may be ordered to return to custody to serve the balance of the original sentence outstanding at the date of the further offence, as well as being punished for that new offence.'

'Any time you have spent on remand in custody in connection with the offence(s) for which you are now being sentenced will count as part of the sentence to be served, unless it has already been counted.'

'After your release you will also be subject to supervision on licence until the end of three-quarters of the total sentence. (If an order has been made under s 85 of the Powers of Criminal Courts (Sentencing) Act 2000: After your release you will also be subject to supervision on licence for the remainder of the licence period.) If you fail to comply with any of the requirements of your licence then again you may be brought before a court which will have power to suspend your licence and order your return to custody.'

(c) Total term of four years or more:

'The sentence is (. . .) (years/months).'

'Your case will not be considered by the Parole Board until you have served at least half that period in custody. Unless the Parole Board recommends earlier release, you will not be released until you have served two-thirds of that sentence.'

'Your release will not bring the sentence to an end. If after your release and before the end of the period covered by the sentence you commit any further offence you may be ordered to return to custody to serve the balance of the original sentence outstanding at the date of the new offence, as well as being punished for that new offence.'

'Any time you have spent in custody on remand in connection with the offence(s) for which you are now being sentenced will count as part of the sentence to be served, unless it has already been counted.'

'After your release you will also be subject to supervision on licence until the end of three-quarters of the total sentence. (If an order has been made under s 85 of the Powers of Criminal Courts (Sentencing) Act 2000: After your release you will also be subject to supervision on licence for the remainder of the licence period.) You will be liable to be recalled to prison if your licence is revoked, either on the recommendation of the Parole Board, or, if it is thought expedient in the public interest, by the Secretary of State.'

(d) Discretionary life sentence:

'The sentence of the court is life imprisonment/custody for life/detention for life under s 91 of the Powers of Criminal Courts (Sentencing) Act 2000. For the purposes of s 82A of that Act the court specifies a period of (x) years. That means that your case will not be considered by the Parole Board until you have served at least (x) years in custody. After that time the Parole Board will be entitled to consider your release. When it is satisfied that you need no longer be confined in custody for the protection of the public it will be able to direct your release. Until it is so satisfied you will remain in custody.'

'If you are released, it will be on terms that you are subject to a licence for the rest of your life and liable to be recalled to prison at any time if your licence is revoked, either on the recommendation of the Parole Board, or, if it is thought expedient in the public interest, by the Secretary of State.'

ANNEX D

Forms for use in criminal proceedings[1]

---

1. The forms referred to in Annex D are available on HM Court Service website: http://www.hmcourts-service.gov.uk – go to Forms and Guidance and in 'Work Type' select Criminal Procedure Rules.

Rule in connection with which the form is to be used	Description of form	Former Rule which prescribed the form	Former number of the form
Part 7: Commencing proceedings in a magistrates' court			
	Information	Magistrates' Courts (Forms) Rules 1981, Sch 2	Form 1
	Information on commission of further offence during probation period	Magistrates' Courts (Forms) Rules 1981, Sch 2	Form 77
	Information on commission of further offence during operation period of suspended sentence under s 123(1) of the Powers of Criminal Courts (Sentencing) Act 2000	Magistrates' Courts (Forms) Rules 1981, Sch 2	Form 84
	Information for failure to comply with requirements of probation, community service or combination order under para 3, Part 2 of Sch 3 to the Powers of Criminal Courts (Sentencing) Act 2000	Magistrates' Courts (Forms) Rules 1981, Sch 2	Form 92I
	Information for failure to comply with requirements of attendance centre order or on breach of Attendance Centre Rules under para 1 of Sch 5 to the Powers of Criminal Courts (Sentencing) Act 2000	Magistrates' Courts (Children and Young Persons) Rules 1992, Sch 2.	Form 7
	Information for search warrant under s 32 of the Children and Young Persons Act 1969	Magistrates' Courts (Children and Young Persons) Rules 1992, Sch 2.	Form 10
	Statutory Declaration under s 72(2) of the Road Traffic Offenders Act 1988	Magistrates' Courts (Forms) Rules 1981, Sch 2	Form 160
	Statutory Declaration under s 73(2) of the Road Traffic Offenders Act 1988	Magistrates' Courts (Forms) Rules 1981, Sch 2	Form 161
Part 10: Committal for trial			
Rule 10.5(1)(*f*)	List of exhibits	Magistrates' Courts (Forms) Rules 1981, Sch 2	Form 26
Part 13: Dismissal of charges sent or transferred to the Crown Court			
Part 15: Preparatory hearings in cases of serious fraud and other complex and lengthy cases in the Crown Court			
Part 16: Restrictions on reporting and public access			
Rule 16.1(1)	Application for a reporting direction under s 46 Youth Justice and Criminal Evidence Act 1999	Magistrates' Courts (Reports Relating to Adult Witnesses) Rules 2004, r 2; Crown Court (Reports Relating to Adult Witnesses) Rules 2004, r 2	Form A
Rule 16.4(4)	Application for an excepting direction under s 46(9) Youth Justice and Criminal Evidence Act 1999	Magistrates' Courts (Reports Relating to Adult Witnesses) Rules 2004, r 2; Crown Court (Reports Relating to Adult Witnesses) Rules 2004, r 5	Form B

Rule in connection with which the form is to be used	Description of form	Former Rule which prescribed the form	Former number of the form
Part 17: Extradition [Note: These forms should be used only in proceedings where the request for extradition was received by the relevant authority in the United Kingdom on or before 31st December 2003].			
Rule 17.2(1)	Simplified procedure: notice of waiver	Magistrates' Courts (Extradition) Rules, r 5(1)	Form 1
Rule 17.3(2)	Notice of consent to committal for return under s 14 of the Extradition Act 1989	Magistrates' Courts (Extradition) Rules, r 6(2).	Form 2
Rule 17.4(2)	Notice of consent to committal for return under s 14A of the Extradition Act 1989	Magistrates' Courts (Extradition) Rules, r 7(2).	Form 3
Rule 17.11(1)	Endorsement of warrant of arrest under s 1 of the Backing of Warrants (Republic of Ireland) Act 1965	Magistrates' Courts (Backing of Warrants) Rules 1965, Schedule.	Form 1
Rule 17.11(1)	Provisional warrant of arrest under s 4 of the Backing of Warrants (Republic of Ireland) Act 1965	Magistrates' Courts (Backing of Warrants) Rules 1965, Schedule.	Form 3
Rule 17.11(1)	Warrant of arrest on failure to surrender to bail under s 5(4) of the Backing of Warrants (Republic of Ireland) Act 1965	Magistrates' Courts (Backing of Warrants) Rules 1965, Schedule.	Form 9
Rule 17.5 Rule 17.11(1)	Consent to Earlier Return under s 3(1)(a) of the Backing of Warrants (Republic of Ireland) Act 1965	Magistrates' Courts (Backing of Warrants) Rules 1965, Schedule.	Form 2
	Warrant of commitment of person ordered to be delivered up under the Backing of Warrants (Republic of Ireland) Act 1965	Magistrates' Courts (Backing of Warrants) Rules 1965, Schedule.	Form 4
	Warrant of commitment awaiting Irish warrant under the Backing of Warrants (Republic of Ireland) Act 1965	Magistrates' Courts (Backing of Warrants) Rules 1965, Schedule.	Form 5
	Warrant of commitment: recognizance to be taken later under the Backing of Warrants (Republic of Ireland) Act 1965	Magistrates' Courts (Backing of Warrants) Rules 1965, Schedule.	Form 6
	Recognizance under the Backing of Warrants (Republic of Ireland) Act 1965	Magistrates' Courts (Backing of Warrants) Rules 1965, Schedule.	Form 7
	Warrant of delivery up of person bailed under the Backing of Warrants (Republic of Ireland) Act 1965	Magistrates' Courts (Backing of Warrants) Rules 1965, Schedule.	Form 8
	Notice of consent to surrender under s 7 of the International Criminal Court Act 2001	Magistrates' Courts (International Criminal Court) (Forms) Rules 2001, r 4	Form 1
	Notice of waiver of the right to review under s 13 of the International Criminal Court Act 2001	Magistrates' Courts (International Criminal Court) (Forms) Rules 2001, r 5	Form 2
Part 18: Warrants			
	Warrant to enter and search premises under s 15 of the Police and Criminal Evidence Act 1984 *(Welsh language version available)*	Magistrates' Courts (Forms) Rules 1981, Sch 2	Form 156
Part 19: Bail in magistrates' courts and the Crown Court			
Rule 19.17(2)	Notice of Appeal by the Prosecution under s 1 of the Bail (Amendment) Act 1993 against the Granting of Bail	Crown Court Rules 1982, r 11A(2)	

Rule in connection with which the form is to be used	Description of form	Former Rule which prescribed the form	Former number of the form
Rule 19.17(6)	Notice of Abandonment of Appeal under s 1 of the Bail (Amendment) Act 1993 Against the Granting of Bail	Crown Court Rules 1982, r 11A(6)	
Rule 19.18(4)	Form of notice of application relating to bail in the Crown Court	Crown Court Rules 1982, r 19(4).	
Part 27: Witness statements			
Rule 27.1(1)	Statement of witness *(Welsh language version available)*	Magistrates' Courts Rules 1981, r 70	Form 13
Rule 27.1(2) *[check]*	Notice to defendant: proof by written statement *(Welsh language version available)*	Magistrates' Courts Rules 1981, r 70; Magistrates' Courts (Forms) Rules 1981, Sch 2	Form 14
Part 29: Special measures directions			
Rule 29.1(1) Rule 29.1(2)	Form of application for a special measures direction under s 19 Youth Justice and Criminal Evidence Act 1999	Magistrates' Courts (Special Measures Directions) Rules 2002, r 2 Crown Court (Special Measures Directions and Directions Prohibiting Cross-examination) Rules 2002, r 2	
Part 30: Use of live television link other than for vulnerable witness			
Part 34: Hearsay evidence			
Rule 34.2 Rule 68.20(1)	Notice of intention to introduce hearsay evidence under s 114 Criminal Justice Act 2003		
Rule 34.5 Rule 68.20(1)	Notice of opposition to the introduction of hearsay evidence under s 114 Criminal Justice Act 2003		
Part 35: Evidence of bad character			
Rule 35.2 Rule 68.21	Application for leave to adduce non-defendant's bad character		
Rule 35.4(1) Rule 68.21	Notice of intention to adduce defendant's bad character		
Rule 35.6 Rule 68.21	Application to exclude evidence of the defendant's bad character		
Part 37: Summary trial			
	Notice of intention to cite previous convictions under s 104 Magistrates' Courts Act 1980 *(Welsh language version available)*	Magistrates' Courts (Forms) Rules 1981, Sch 2	Form 29
	Notice of intention to cite previous convictions for offences involving obligatory or discretionary disqualification from driving under s 13 Road Traffic Offenders Act 1988 *(Welsh language version available)*	Magistrates' Courts (Forms) Rules 1981, Sch 2	Form 30
Part 40: Tainted acquittals			
Part 41: Retrial following acquittal for serious offence			
Part 48: Community penalties			
Rule 48.1(2) and (3)	Notice of curfew order with an Electronic monitoring requirement	Crown Court Rules 1982, r 37	
Rule 48.1(2) and (3)	Notice of community rehabilitation order with curfew and electronic monitoring requirements	Crown Court Rules 1982, r 37A	

Rule in connection with which the form is to be used	Description of form	Former Rule which prescribed the form	Former number of the form
Part 50: Civil orders made in criminal proceedings			
Rule 50.1(1)	Sexual Offences Prevention Order under s 104 Sexual Offences Act 2003	Magistrates' Courts (Sexual Offences Prevention Orders) Rules 2004, r 4(3)	
Rule 50.1(2)	Interim Sexual Offences Prevention Order under s 109 Sexual Offences Act 2003	Magistrates' Courts (Sexual Offences Prevention Orders) Rules 2004, r 4(4)	
Rule 50.2(1)	Parenting Order under s 8 Crime and Disorder Act 1998	Magistrates' Courts (Parenting Orders) Rules 2004, r 7	
Rule 50.2(2)	Parenting Order under para 9D, Sch 1, Powers of Criminal Courts (Sentencing) Act 2000	Magistrates' Courts (Parenting Orders) Rules 2004, rule 8	
Rule 50.4	Anti-Social Behaviour Order made on Conviction under s 1C Crime and Disorder Act 1998	Crown Court Rules 1982, rule 38	
Part 64: Appeal to the High Court by way of case stated			
	Recognizance to prosecute on appeal before the High Court on case stated and for bail pending appeal under s 114 of the Magistrates' Courts Act 1980 *(Welsh language version available)*	Magistrates' Courts (Forms) Rules 1981, Sch 2	Form 121
	Case Stated under s 111 of the Magistrates' Courts Act 1980	Magistrates' Courts (Forms) Rules 1981, Sch 2	Form 155
Part 65: Appeal to the Court of Appeal against ruling in preparatory hearing			
Part 66: Appeal to the Court of Appeal against ruling adverse to prosecution			
Part 67: Appeal to the Court of Appeal regarding reporting or public access			
Part 68: Appeal to the Court of Appeal against conviction or sentence			
Rule 68.2(1)	Judge's certificate	Criminal Appeal Rules 1968, r 1	Form 1
Rule 68.3(1) and (2)	Notice and grounds of appeal or application for leave to appeal	Criminal Appeal Rules 1968, r 2	Form NG (2 & 3)
Rule 68.3(1A), and (2)	Notice of grounds of appeal or application for leave to appeal against life sentence minimum term		
Rule 68.5(2)	Application for determination by Court of Appeal	Criminal Appeal Rules 1968, rr 11 and 12	Form 15
Rule 68.7(1)	Notice of Application for Bail	Criminal Appeal Rules 1968, r 3.	Form 4
Rule 68.8(2)	Recognizance of appellant's surety	Criminal Appeal Rules 1968, r 4.	Form 8
Rule 68.8(2)	Recognizance of appellant's surety pending retrial	Criminal Appeal Rules 1968, r 4(2).	Form 10
Rule 68.8(5)	Certificate by Registrar of grant and of conditions of bail	Criminal Appeal Rules 1968, r 4(5) and (8).	Form 11
Rule 68.15(1)	Notice of application for witness order and/or leave to call a witness	Criminal Appeal Rules 1968, r 3	Form 6
Rule 68.16(1)	Witness Order	Criminal Appeal Rules 1968, r 9.	Form 13
Rule 68.22(1)	Notice of abandonment of proceedings	Criminal Appeal Rules, r 10	Form 14
Rule 68.26(1)	Notice of application for leave to be present	Criminal Appeal Rules, r 3	Form 5

Rule in connection with which the form is to be used	Description of form	Former Rule which prescribed the form	Former number of the form
Rule 68.28	Warrant directing conveyance of appellant to hospital	Criminal Appeal Rules 1968, r 14	Form 16
Rule 68.31	Notice of application for leave to arraign/to set aside order for retrial	Criminal Appeal Rules, rule 2A	Form 3A
Part 71: Appeal to the Court of Appeal under POCA 2002 – general rules			
Part 72: Appeal to the Court of Appeal under POCA 2002 - prosecutor's appeal regarding confiscation			
Part 73: Appeal to the Court of Appeal under POCA 2002 –restraint and receivership orders			
Part 74: Appeal to the House of Lords			

ANNEX E

Forms to facilitate case management

MAGISTRATES' COURT CASE PROGRESSION[1]
Case committed for trial to the Crown Court under section 6 of the Magistrates' Courts Act 1980
Case sent to the Crown Court under section 51 of the Crime and Disorder Act 1998
Case to be tried in the magistrates' court

---

1. See PART IX: PRECEDENTS AND FORMS, post for these forms.

Travel Restriction Order (Prescribed Removal Powers) Order 2002[1]
(SI 2002/313 amended by SI 2006/1003)

1-7100 1. Citation and commencement. This Order may be cited as the Travel Restriction Order (Prescribed Removal Powers) Order 2002 and shall come into force on 1st April 2002.

---

1. Made by the Secretary of State in exercise of powers under s 37(4) of the Criminal Justice and Police Act 2001.

1-7101 2. Prescribed removal powers. Each of the powers set out in the Schedule to this Order is designated as a prescribed removal power for the purposes of section 37 of the Criminal Justice and Police Act 2001.

SCHEDULE

1-7102

Colonial Prisoners Removal Act 1884 (c 31)	Section 3(1)
United Nations Act 1946 (c 45)	Powers to order or direct the removal of a person from the United Kingdom conferred by Orders in Council made in exercise of the power contained in section 1(1)
Backing of Warrants (Republic of Ireland) Act 1965 (c 45)	Section 2(1)
Immigration Act 1971 (c 77)	Section 5(1); Schedule 2, paragraphs 8, 9, 10, 12, 13 and 14; Schedule 3, paragraph 1
Mental Health Act 1983 (c 20)	Section 86(2)(*a*) and (*b*)
Repatriation of Prisoners Act 1984 (c 47)	Sections 1(1), 2 and 4(1)
Extradition Act 1989 (c 33)	Section 12(1) and Schedule 1, paragraph 8(2)
Criminal Justice (International Co-operation) Act 1990 (c 5)	Section 5
Immigration and Asylum Act 1999 (c 33)	Section 10
Immigration (European Economic Area) Regulations 2000	Regulation 19(3)
International Criminal Court Act 2001 (c 17)	Sections 5, 7, 15, 21, 32 and 43

Police (Retention and Disposal of Items Seized) Regulations 2002
(SI 2002/1372)

1-7150 1. Citation and commencement. These Regulations may be cited as the Police (Retention and Disposal of Items Seized) Regulations 2002 and shall come into force on 10th June 2002.

1-7151 2. Extent. These Regulations extend to England and Wales only.

1-7152 3. Revocation. The Police (Retention and Disposal of Items seized under section 60 of the Criminal Justice and Public Order Act 1994) Regulations 1999 are hereby revoked in relation to England and Wales.

1–7153 4. Interpretation.   In these Regulations—

"owner" in relation to an item to which regulation 5 below applies means the person from whom it was seized, and "ownership" shall be construed accordingly;

"relevant officer" means the chief officer of the police force of which the constable by whom an item was seized is a member or, where the constable concerned is not a member of a police force, the person who has the direction and control of the body of constables in question;

"the 1994 Act" means the Criminal Justice and Public Order Act 1994.

1–7154 5. Detention and safe-keeping.   (1) This regulation applies to any item which has been seized by a constable under section 60 or 60AA of the 1994 Act, unless it is an item of property to which the Police (Property) Regulations 1997 apply.

(2) An item to which this regulation applies shall be retained by, or in accordance with arrangements made by the relevant officer for the period set out in paragraph (3) below from the date on which it was seized unless, before the end of that period, the owner of the item has been ascertained and has made an application under regulation 6 below which has been successful.

(3) The period referred to in paragraph (2) above shall be 2 months in the case of an item seized under section 60AA(2)(b) of the 1994 Act (items worn to conceal identity) and 6 months in the case of an item seized under section 60(6) of that Act (dangerous instruments and offensive weapons).

(4) Any item to which this regulation applies and which is for the time being retained under paragraph (2) shall be kept safely and, so far as possible, in the same condition as when it was seized.

1–7155 6. Disposal to the owner.   (1) The owner of an item to which regulation 5 above applies may, at any time within the period set out in paragraph (3) of that regulation, apply to the relevant officer for the item to be released to him.

(2) An application under this regulation shall be made orally or in writing and shall be accompanied by evidence of ownership by the applicant.

(3) Where the relevant officer is satisfied that the applicant is the owner of the item concerned and that further retention of the item is not necessary for the purposes of any criminal proceedings he shall arrange for the item concerned to be returned to the applicant.

1–7156 7. Disposal otherwise than to the owner and destruction.   (1) After the expiration of the period set out in regulation 5(3) above or the determination of an unsuccessful application under regulation 6 above, whichever is the later, an item to which regulation 5 above applies shall, subject to paragraph (2) below, be destroyed or otherwise disposed of in accordance with the directions of the relevant officer.

(2) Where further retention of such an item is, in the opinion of the relevant officer, necessary for the purposes of criminal proceedings, the item shall be retained until he is satisfied that retention is no longer necessary and then destroyed or otherwise disposed of in accordance with his directions.

Magistrates' Courts (Anti-Social Behaviour Orders) Rules 2002[1]
(SI 2002/2784 as amended by SI 2003/1236)

1–7220 2. Citation, interpretation and commencement.   (1) These Rules may be cited as the Magistrates' Courts (Anti-Social Behaviour Orders) Rules 2002 and shall come into force on 2nd December 2002.

(2) In these Rules any reference to a numbered section is a reference to the section so numbered in the Crime and Disorder Act 1998, any reference to a "form" includes a form to like effect, and, unless otherwise stated, reference to a "Schedule" is a reference to a Schedule hereto.

---

1. Made by the Lord Chancellor, in exercise of the powers conferred by the Magistrates' Courts Act 1980, and after consultation with the Rule Committee appointed under that s 144.

1–7221 3. Transitional Provisions.   After these Rules come into force, rules 6 and 7 of, and Schedules 5 and 6 to the Magistrates' Courts (Sex Offender and Anti-Social Behaviour Orders) Rules 1998 shall (notwithstanding their revocation) continue to apply to proceedings commenced prior to the commencement of these Rules.

1–7222 4. Forms.   (1) An application for an anti-social behaviour order may be in the form set out in Schedule 1.

(2) *Revoked.*

(3) *Revoked.*

(4) *Revoked.*

(5) An application for an interim anti-social behaviour order made under section 1D may be in the form set out in Schedule 5.

(6) *Revoked.*

1–7223 5. Interim Orders. (1) An application for an interim order under section 1D, may, with leave of the justices' clerk, be made without notice being given to the defendant.

(2) The justices' clerk shall only grant leave under paragraph (1) of this rule if he is satisfied that it is necessary¹ for the application to be made without notice being given to the defendant.

(3) If an application made under paragraph (2) is granted, then the interim order and the application for an anti-social behaviour order under section 1 (together with a summons giving a date for the defendant to attend court) shall be served on the defendant in person as soon as practicable after the making of the interim order.

(4) An interim order which is made at the hearing of an application without notice shall not take effect until it has been served on the defendant.

(5) If such an interim order made without notice is not served on the defendant within seven days of being made, then it shall cease to have effect.

(6) An interim order shall cease to have effect if the application for an anti-social behaviour order is withdrawn.

(7) Where the court refuses to make an interim order without notice being given to the defendant it may direct that the application be made on notice.

(8) If an interim order is made without notice being given to the defendant, and the defendant subsequently applies to the court for the order to be discharged or varied, his application shall not be dismissed without the opportunity for him to make oral representations to the court.

---

1. The test to be applied is not whether it is just to make the interim order but whether it is necessary for the application to be made without notice, a less stringent test. The following, non-exhaustive factors should be considered:

1 The likely response of the defendant upon receiving notice of such application.
2 Whether such response was liable to prejudice the complainant having regard to the complainant's vulnerability.
3 The gravity of the conduct complained of within the scope of conduct tackled by anti-social behaviour orders in general as opposed to the particular locality.
4 The urgency of the matter.
5 The nature of the prohibitions sought in the interim anti-social order.
6 The right of the defendant to know about the proceedings against him.
7 The counter-balancing protections for the rights of the defendant, namely: (a) the ineffectiveness of the order until served; (b) the limited period of time the order was effective; (c) the defendant's right of application to vary or discharge (*R (on the application of Manchester City Council) v Manchester City Magistrates' Court* [2005] EWHC 253 (Admin), (2005) Times, 8 March).

1–7224 6. Application for variation or discharge. (1) This rule applies to the making of an application for the variation or discharge of an order made under section 1, 1C or, subject to rule 5(8) above, 1D.

(2) An application to which this rule applies shall be made in writing to the magistrates' court which made the order, or in the case of an application under section 1C to any magistrates' court in the same petty sessions area, and shall specify the reason why the applicant for variation or discharge believes the court should vary or discharge the order, as the case may be.

(3) Subject to rule 5(8) above, where the court considers that there are no grounds upon which it might conclude that the order should be varied or discharged, as the case may be, it may determine the application without hearing representations from the applicant for variation or discharge or from any other person.

(4) Where the court considers that there are grounds upon which it might conclude that the order should be varied or discharged, as the case may be, the justices' chief executive shall, unless the application is withdrawn, issue a summons giving not less than 14 days' notice in writing of the date, time and place appointed for the hearing.

(5) The justices' chief executive shall send with the summons under paragraph 4 above a copy of the application for variation or discharge of the anti-social behaviour order.

1–7225 7. Service. (1) Subject to rule 5(3), any summons, or copy of an order or application required to be sent under these Rules to the defendant shall be either given to him in person or sent by post to the last known address, and, if so given or sent, shall be deemed to have been received by him unless he proves otherwise.

(2) Any summons, copy of an order or application required to be sent to the defendant under these Rules shall also be sent by the justices' chief executive to the applicant authority, and to any relevant authority whom the applicant is required by section 1E to have consulted before making the application and, where appropriate, shall invite them to make observations and advise them of their right to be heard at the hearing.

1–7226 8. Delegation by justices' clerk. (1) In this rule, "employed as a clerk of the court" has the same meaning as in rule 2(1) of the Justices' Clerks (Qualifications of Assistants) Rules 1979.

(2) Anything authorised to be done by, to or before a justices' clerk under these Rules, may be done instead by, to or before a person employed as a clerk of the court where that person is appointed by the magistrates' courts committee to assist him and where that person has been specifically authorised by the justices' clerk for that purpose.

(3) Any authorisation by the justices' clerk under paragraph (2) shall be recorded in writing at the time the authority is given or as soon as practicable thereafter.

1–7227

Rule 4(1)

SCHEDULE 1

FORM

Application for Anti-social Behaviour Order (Crime and Disorder Act 1998, s 1(1))

.... **Magistrates' Court**

(Code)

Date: ....

Defendant: ....

Address: ....

....

Applicant Authority: ....

Relevant authorities ....

consulted: ....

And it is alleged

    (a) that the defendant has acted on . . [dates(s)] at [place(s)] in an anti-social manner, that is to say, in a manner that caused or was likely to cause harassment, alarm or distress to one or more persons not of the same household as himself; and

    (b) that an anti-social behaviour order is necessary to protect relevant persons from further anti-social acts by him, and accordingly application is made for an anti-social behaviour order containing the following prohibition(s):—

Short description of acts: ....

....

The complaint of: ....

Name of Applicant Authority: ....

Address of Applicant Authority: ....

who [upon oath] states that the defendant was responsible for the acts of which particulars are given above, in respect of which this complaint is made.

Taken [and sworn] before me

Justice of the Peace
[By order of the clerk of the court]

1–7228   *Schedule 2 revoked.*

1–7229   *Schedule 3 revoked.*

1–7230   *Schedule 4 revoked.*

1–7231

Rule 4(5)

SCHEDULE 5

FORM

Application for an Interim Order (Crime and Disorder Act 1998, s 1D)

.... Magistrates' Court

(Code)

Date: ....

Defendant: ....

Address: ....

....

Applicant Authority: ....

Relevant Authorities Consulted: ....

....

....

Reasons for applying for an interim ....

order: ....

....

Do you wish this application to be heard: [] without notice being given to the defendant

    [] with notice being given to the defendant

If you wish the application to be heard without notice state reasons:—

....

....

The complaint of: ....

Address of Applicant Authority: ....

Who [upon oath] states that the information given above is correct.

Taken [and sworn] before me.

Justice of the Peace

[By order of the clerk of the court]

NOTE: This application must be accompanied by an application for an anti-social behaviour order (Crime and Disorder Act 1998, s 1).

1–7232

SCHEDULE 6

Revoked.

Magistrates' Courts (Detention and Forfeiture of Cash) Rules 2002[1]

(SI 2002/2998 amended by SI 2003/1236, SI 2005/617 and SI 2006/594)

1–7240   1. Citation and commencement.   These Rules may be cited as the Magistrates' Courts (Detention and Forfeiture of Cash) Rules 2002 and shall come into force on 30th December 2002.

---

1. Made by the Lord Chancellor, in exercise of the powers conferred by the Magistrates' Courts Act 1980, and after consultation with the Rule Committee appointed under that s 144.

1–7241   2. Interpretation.   In these Rules—

  (a) "the Act" means the Proceeds of Crime Act 2002;
  (b) "justices' clerk" means the justices' clerk for the justices who are to hear or have heard an application;
  (c) words and expressions used have the same meaning as in Chapter 3 of Part 5 of the Act;
  (d) a reference to a form is a reference to a form set out in the Schedule to these Rules or a form with the same effect.

1–7242   3. Prior approval of searches for cash.   (1) An application to a justice of the peace under section 290(1) of the Act for prior approval of a search for cash under section 289 of the Act may be made without notice.

(2) A justice of the peace may grant such an application without a hearing and may conduct any hearing in private.

1–7243   4. First application for the continued detention of seized cash.   (1) The first application under section 295(4) of the Act for an order under section 295(2) of the Act for the continued detention of cash seized under section 294 of the Act may be made in form A and may be sent to the designated officer for the local justice area of the court before which the applicant wishes to make the application.

(2) But where the reasonable grounds for suspicion which led to the seizure of cash to which an application under section 295(4) of the Act relates are connected to the reasonable grounds for suspicion which led to the seizure of other cash to which a previous order made under section 295(2) of the Act relates, then the application may be sent to the designated officer for the local justice area of the court which made the previous order.

(3) Except where paragraph (4) or paragraph (7) applies, a copy of the written application and notification of the hearing of the application shall be given by the applicant to the person from whom the cash was seized.

(4) Where seized cash is found in a means of unattended dispatch, such as an unattended letter, parcel or container, copies of the written application and notification of the hearing of the application shall be sent by the applicant to the sender and intended recipient of the means of unattended dispatch.

(5) But where paragraph (4) applies the applicant is not required to send copies of the written application and notification of the hearing to a sender or intended recipient who cannot be identified.

(6) Where paragraph (4) applies, the court shall not decline to hear an application solely on the ground that it has not been proved that the sender and intended recipient have been given a copy of the written application and notification of the hearing.

(7) Where unattended cash is seized (other than where the cash is found in a means of unattended dispatch) the applicant need not give a copy of the written application and notification of the hearing to any person.

(8) *Revoked.*

(9) The designated officer shall give—

  (a) notice of the order, and
  (b) a copy of the order,

to the person from whom the cash was seized and to any other person known to be affected by the order.

1–7244   5. Further applications for the continued detention of seized cash.   (1) An application under section 295(4) of the Act for a further order under section 295(2) of the Act for the continued detention of cash may be made in Form A and may be sent to the designated officer to whom the first application under section 295(4) of the Act was sent.

(2) The applicant shall send a copy of the application to every person to whom notice of previous related orders made under section 295(2) of the Act has been given.

(3) The justices' clerk shall fix a date for the hearing of the application, which, unless he directs otherwise, shall not be earlier than seven days from the date on which it is fixed, and the justices' chief executive shall notify that date to the applicant and every person to whom notice of the previous orders has been given.

(4) *Revoked.*

(5) The designated officer shall give a copy of the order to every person to whom notice of the previous related orders has been given.

(6) designated officer shall also give—

  (a) notice of the order, and

(b) a copy of the order,

to any person other than one referred to in paragraph (5) known to be affected by the order.

1–7245 6. Applications for the release of detained cash. (1) An application under section 297(3) or 301(1) of the Act for the release of detained cash shall be made in writing and sent to the designated officer for the local justice area of the court before which the applicant wishes to make the application.

(2) But if the applicant has been given notice of an order under section 295(2) of the Act in respect of the detained cash, then the application shall be sent to the designated officer who sent him that notice.

(3) The designated officer shall send a copy of the application to—

(a) the Commissioners of Customs and Excise, if the cash which is the subject of the application was seized by a customs officer;

(ab) the Director General of the Serious Organised Crime Agency if the cash which is the subject of the application was seized by a member of the staff of that Agency who is designated under section 43 of the Serious Organised Crime and Police Act 2005;

(b) the chief officer of the police force to which the constable belongs, if the cash which is the subject of the application was seized by a constable; and

(c) every person to whom notice of the order made under section 295(2) of the Act has been given.

(4) The justices' clerk shall fix a date for the hearing of the application, which, unless he directs otherwise, shall not be earlier than seven days from the date on which it is fixed, and the designated officer shall notify that date to the applicant and to every person to whom a copy of the application is required to be sent under paragraph (3).

(5) At the hearing of an application under section 301(1) of the Act, the court may, if it thinks fit, order that the applicant shall be joined as a party to all the proceedings in relation to the detained cash.

(6) *Revoked.*

(7) A direction under section 297(2) of the Act and an order under section 301(3) or (4) of the Act shall provide for the release of the cash within seven days of the date of the making of the order or direction, or such longer period as, with the agreement of the applicant, may be specified, except that cash shall not be released whilst section 298(4) of the Act applies.

1–7246 7. Application for forfeiture of detained cash. (1) An application under section 298(1) of the Act for the forfeiture of detained cash may be in Form G and may be sent to the designated officer to whom applications for the continued detention of the cash under section 295(4) of the Act have been sent.

(2) Where no applications in respect of the cash have been made under section 295(4) of the Act, the application shall be sent to—

(a) the designated officer for the local justice area of the court before which the applicant wishes to make the application; or

(b) where the reasonable grounds for suspicion which led to the seizure of cash to which the application for forfeiture relates are connected to the reasonable grounds for suspicion which led to the seizure of cash to which an order made under section 295(2) of the Act relates, to the justices' chief executive for the petty sessions area of the court which made the order under section 295(2).

(3) The applicant shall send a copy of the application to every person to whom notice of an order made under section 295(2) of the Act in respect of the detained cash has been given and to any other person identified by the court as being affected by the application.

(4) The justices' clerk shall set a date for a directions hearing, which, unless he directs otherwise, shall not be earlier than seven days from the date on which it is fixed, and the designated officer shall notify that date to the applicant and to every person to whom a copy of the application is required to be sent under paragraph (3).

(5) At the directions hearing, the court may give directions relating to the management of the proceedings, including directions as to the date for the hearing of the application.

(6) If neither the person from whom the cash was seized, nor any other person who is affected by the detention of the cash, seeks to contest the application, the court may decide the application at the directions hearing.

(7) An order for the forfeiture of detained cash under section 298(2) of the Act and a copy of the order shall be given by the designated officer to every person to whom notice of an order made under section 295(2) of the Act in respect of the detained cash has been given and to any other person known to be affected by the order.

1–7247 8. Application for compensation. (1) An application under section 302(1) for compensation shall be made in writing and sent to the designated officer for the local justicearea of the court before which the applicant wishes to make the application.

(2) But if the applicant has been given notice of an order under section 295(2) of the Act in respect of the cash which is the subject of the application, then the application shall be sent to the designated officer who sent him that notice.

(3) The designated officer shall send a copy of the application to—

(a) the Commissioners of Customs and Excise, if the cash which is the subject of the application was seized by a customs officer;

(ab) the Director General of the Serious Organised Crime Agency if the cash which is the subject of the application was seized by a member of the staff of that Agency who is designated under section 43 of the Serious Organised Crime and Police Act 2005;

(b) the chief officer of the police force to which the constable belongs, if the cash which is the subject of the application was seized by a constable.

The justices' clerk shall fix a date for the hearing of the application, which, unless he directs otherwise, shall not be earlier than seven days from the date on which it is fixed, and the designated officer shall notify the applicant and the person referred to in paragraph (3) of that date.

1-7248   9. Notice.   Any notification or document required to be given or sent to any person under these Rules may be given by post or by facsimile to his last known address, or to any other address given by that person for the purpose of service of documents under these Rules.

1-7249   10. Transfer of proceedings.   (1) Any person who is a party to, or affected by, proceedings under Chapter 3 of Part 5 of the Act may, at any time, make an application to the court dealing with the matter for the proceedings to be transferred to a different local justice area.

(2) Any such application shall be made in writing and sent to the designated officer for the local justice area in which the proceedings are being dealt with and shall specify the grounds on which it is made.

(3) The designated officer shall send a copy of the application to the parties to the proceedings and any other person affected by the proceedings.

(4) The justices' clerk shall fix a date for the hearing of the application, which, unless he directs otherwise, shall not be earlier than seven days from the date on which it is fixed, and the designated officer for the local justice shall notify the date to the applicant and every person to whom a copy of the application is required to be sent under paragraph (3).

(5) The court may grant the application if it is satisfied that it would be more convenient or fairer for proceedings to be transferred to a different local justice area.

(6) If the application is granted—

(a) the designated officer shall give a copy of the order to the parties to the proceedings and any other person affected by the proceedings;

(b) the designated officer shall send all relevant papers to the justices' chief executive for the petty sessions area to which proceedings are transferred;

(c) any further proceedings under Chapter 3 of Part 5 of the Act in respect of the cash to which the proceedings relate shall be dealt with in the local justice area to which proceedings are transferred;

(d) any requirement under these Rules to make an application to a designated officerofficer shall be read as a requirement to make an application to the designated officer for the local justice area to which proceedings are transferred.

1-7250   11. Procedure at hearings.   (1) At the hearing of an application under Chapter 3 of Part 5 of the Act, any person to whom notice of the application has been given may attend and be heard on the question of whether the application should be granted, but the fact that any such person does not attend shall not prevent the court from hearing the application.

(2) Subject to the foregoing provisions of these Rules, proceedings on such an application shall be regulated in the same manner as proceedings on a complaint, and accordingly for the purposes of these Rules, the application shall be deemed to be a complaint, the applicant a complainant, the respondents to be defendants and any notice given by the designated officer under rules 5(3), 6(4), 7(4), 8(4) or 10(4) to be a summons: but nothing in this rule shall be construed as enabling a warrant of arrest to be issued for failure to appear in answer to any such notice.

(3) At the hearing of an application under Chapter 3 of Part 5 of the Act, the court shall require the matters contained in the application to be sworn by the applicant under oath, may require the applicant to answer any questions under oath and may require any response from the respondent to the application to be made under oath.

(4) The court shall record or cause to be recorded the substance of any statements made under oath which are not already recorded in the written application.

1-7251

SCHEDULE

Form A

Rules 4(1) and 5(1) and Rule 2

First/Further** application for continued detention of seized cash
(Section 295(4) Proceeds of Crime Act 2002; MC (Detention and Forfeiture of Cash) Rules 2002 rr 4(1), 5(1)
Magistrates' Court
(Code)
Date
Name of person from whom cash seized
Address*
Names and addresses of any other persons likely to be affected by an order for detention of the cash (if known)
Amount seized/Estimated amount seized (only in the case of a first application for continued detention) **
Amount to which reasonable grounds of suspicion apply/Estimated amount to which reasonable grounds for

suspicion apply (only in the case of a first application for continued detention) ** where it is not reasonably practicable to detain only that part

    Date of seizure
    Time of seizure
    Place of seizure
    Date of latest order for continued detention of seized cash (if any)
    Amount detained under latest order for continued detention (if any)
    Amounts released since the latest order for continued detention (if any)
I,
of
(official address and position of applicant)
Constable/Customs Officer **, apply for an order under section 295(2) of the Proceeds of Crime Act 2002 authorising the continued detention of cash in the sum of .... and will state upon oath that one of the two grounds below is satisfied in relation to all of the cash/ the sum of but it is not reasonably practicable to detain only that part of the cash **;

1. There are reasonable grounds for suspecting that the cash is recoverable property and that either—

  (a) its continued detention is justified while its derivation is further investigated or consideration is given to bringing (in the United Kingdom or elsewhere) proceedings against any person for an offence with which the cash is connected, or
  (b) proceedings against any person for an offence with which the cash is connected have been started and have not been concluded.

2. There are reasonable grounds for suspecting that the cash is intended to be used in unlawful conduct and that either—

  (a) its continued detention is justified while its intended use is further investigated or consideration is given to bringing (in the United Kingdom or elsewhere) proceedings against any person for an offence with which the cash is connected, or
  (b) proceedings against any person for an offence with which the cash is connected have been started and have not been concluded.
(state grounds)

Signed
To: The Designated Officer
Magistrates' Court
Notes to the Applicant—
First Application—You must give a copy of this application and notification of the hearing of it to the person from whom the cash was seized ***.
Further Application—This application must wherever possible be submitted to the designated officer at least seven days before the expiry of the last period of detention that was ordered by the court. You must give a copy of this application to the person from whom the cash was seized and any other person specified in any order made under section 295(2) of the Proceeds of Crime Act 2002 ***.
*In the case of a means of unattended dispatch such as a letter, parcel or container, insert names and addresses, if known, of sender and intended recipient. In the case of any other unattended cash, state that you believe the cash was unattended and explain your grounds for believing that the cash was unattended.
**Delete as appropriate
*** In the case of a means of unattended dispatch such as a letter, parcel or container, the copy application and, if applicable, notification of hearing should be given to the sender and intended recipient (if known), rather than the person from whom the cash was seized. In the case of any other unattended cash, there is no requirement to give the copy application and, if applicable, notification of hearing to the person from whom the cash was seized.

FORMS B–F

Revoked.

FORM G

Rule 7(1)

    Application for forfeiture of detained cash
    (Section 298(1) of the Proceeds of Crime Act 2002; MC (Detention and Forfeiture of Cash) Rules 2002 r 7(1))
    Magistrates' Court
    (Code)
    Date
    Name of person from whom cash seized*
    Address*
    Names and addresses of any other persons identified by the court as being affected by this application
    Amount seized
    Date of seizure
    Time of seizure
    Place of seizure
    Date of latest order for continued detention of seized cash (if any)
    Amount detained under latest order for continued detention (if any)
    Amounts released since the latest order for continued detention (if any)
I
of
(official address and position of applicant)
Constable/Customs Officer**, apply for an order under 298(2) of the Proceeds of Crime Act 2002 for the forfeiture of cash in the sum of together with any interest accruing thereon pursuant to section 296(1) of that Act, on the grounds that the cash is recoverable property or is intended by any person for use in unlawful conduct.
(state grounds)
To: The Designated Officer
Magistrates' Court
Note to the Applicant—You must send a copy of this application to the person from whom the cash was

seized and any other person specified in any order made under section 295(2) of the Proceeds of Crime Act 2002***.

Note to copy recipients—If you are not the person from whom the cash was seized but the cash belongs to you and the court decides not to make a forfeiture order, you may apply to the court under section 301(4) of the Proceeds of Crime Act 2002 for the cash to be released to you. You can make an application before the court makes its decision on forfeiture. However, the court will not be able to release the cash to you until the forfeiture proceedings are finished.

*In the case of a means of unattended dispatch such as a letter, parcel or container, insert names and addresses, if known, of sender and intended recipient. In the case of any other unattended cash, state that you believe the cash was unattended and explain your grounds for believing that the cash was unattended.

**Delete as appropriate

*** In the case of a means of unattended dispatch such as a letter, parcel or container, the copy application and, if applicable, notification of hearing should be given to the sender and intended recipient (if known), rather than the person from whom the cash was seized. In the case of any other unattended cash, there is no requirement to give the copy application and, if applicable, notification of hearing to the person from whom the cash was seized.

FORM H

Revoked.

Magistrates' Courts (Forfeiture of Political Donations) Rules 2003[1]
(SI 2003/1645)

1-7270   1. Citation, commencement and interpretation.   (1) These Rules may be cited as the Magistrates' Courts (Forfeiture of Political Donations) Rules 2003 and shall come into force on 24th July 2003.

(2) In these Rules—

(a)   a reference to a section by number alone or reference to a schedule by number alone is a reference to the section so numbered or schedule so numbered respectively in the Political Parties, Elections and Referendums Act 2000;

(b)   any reference to a form is a reference to a form set out in the Schedule to these Rules or a form to like effect.

(c)   "applicant" means the Commission.

(d)   "forfeiture order" means an order pursuant to section 58(2) and includes orders made under section 58(2) as applied by—

(i)   paragraph 8 of Schedule 7;
(ii)   paragraph 7 of Schedule 11;
(iii)   paragraph 7 of Schedule 15; and
(iv)   paragraph 7 of Schedule 2A to the Representation of the People Act 1983; or
(v)   an order made under section 65(6); or
(vi)   an order made under paragraph 12(4) of Schedule 7.

(e)   "respondent" means the registered party, regulated donee, recognised third party, permitted participant or candidate or election agent (as appropriate) respectively, against whom a forfeiture order is sought.

(f)   "relevant petty sessions area" means the petty sessions area within which the Commission's principal office is situated.

---

1. Made by the Lord Chancellor, in exercise of the powers conferred upon him by ss 144 and 145(1)(g) of the Magistrates' Courts Act 1980 and s 60(1) of the Political Parties, Elections and Referendums Act 2000, after consultation with the Rule Committee appointed under s 144.

1-7271   2. Application for forfeiture.   (1) An application for a forfeiture order shall be in Form A, A1, A2, A3, A4, B, or B1 as appropriate, and shall be addressed to the justices' chief executive for the relevant petty sessions area.

(2) The justices' clerk shall, as soon as reasonably practicable, fix a date for the hearing, give notice in writing to the applicant of it and give notice in writing to the respondent of the application and of the date, time and place fixed for the hearing.

1-7272   3. Transfer.   (1) The court may, of its own initiative or on the application of any party to the proceedings, order that the hearing be transferred to the court of another petty sessions area having regard to—

(a)   whether it would be more convenient or fair for the hearing to be held in some other court;
(b)   the importance of the outcome of the hearing to the public in general;
(c)   the facilities available at the court where the application for a forfeiture order was lodged and whether they may be inadequate because of—

(i)   any disability of any party to the proceedings or representative of any such party (as appropriate) or any potential witness;
(ii)   press and public interest;

(d)   any other matters that may affect the just disposal of the hearing.

(2) If the court makes an order under paragraph (1) the justices' chief executive shall give notice to the parties to the proceedings.

(3) Any order of the court made before the transfer of proceedings shall not be affected by the order for transfer.

1–7273   4. Joinder.   (1) The court may order that any person who is not already a party to the proceedings ("the joined party") be made one, if it thinks it is desirable to do so.

(2) The court may make an order under paragraph (1), on the application of an existing party to the proceedings, or otherwise, including of its own initiative.

(3) If the court makes an order under paragraph (1) the justices' chief executive shall give notice to the parties to the proceedings.

(4) The court may give such further directions as to the joinder of the joined party as it thinks fit.

(5) If the court makes an order under paragraph (4) the justices' chief executive shall give notice to the other parties to the proceedings.

1–7274   5. Procedure at hearing.   (1) Any person—

(a)   to whom notice of the application has been given; or

(b)   who has been joined as a party to the proceedings under rule 4;

may attend and be heard on the question of whether a forfeiture order should be made.

(2) If any person referred to in paragraph (1) fails to attend or to be represented at the hearing of which he has been duly notified the court may unless it is satisfied that there is good and sufficient reason for such absence—

(a)   hear and determine the proceedings in the absence of the party to the proceedings or his representative, or

(b)   postpone or adjourn the hearing.

(3) Before deciding to hear and determine any proceedings in the absence of a party to the proceedings or his representative, the court shall—

(a)   consider any representations in writing; or

(b)   otherwise submitted by or on behalf of that party in response to the notice of the hearing; and

(c)   shall give any party to the proceedings present at the hearing an opportunity to be heard in regard to those representations.

(4) The justices' chief executive shall, as soon as reasonably practicable after the hearing, send a copy of any order made at the hearing to any person referred to in paragraph (1) who has failed to attend or to be represented at the hearing.

(5) Subject to the foregoing provisions of these Rules—

(a)   proceedings on an application for a forfeiture order shall be regulated in the same manner as proceedings on complaint; and

(b)   accordingly, for the purpose of this rule—

(i)   the application shall be deemed to be a complaint;

(ii)   the applicant to be the complainant;

(iii)   the respondent to be the defendant; and

(iv)   any notice given under rule 2(2) of these Rules to be a summons;

but nothing in this rule shall be construed as enabling a warrant of arrest to be issued for failure to appear in answer to any such notice.

1–7275

Rule 2

SCHEDULE

FORM A

Application for Forfeiture Pursuant to section 58(2)—Registered Party

...............................Magistrates' Court

.... Code

Date ....

.... (name of applicant) of .... (address of applicant) applies for an order for forfeiture pursuant to section 58(2) of the Political Parties, Elections and Referendums Act 2000, against ...... (name of registered party) of ...... (address of registered party) of an amount equal to the value of the donation made on .... and accepted by the registered party on.., on the following grounds:

To: The Justices' Chief Executive

......................Magistrates' Court

FORM **A1**

Application for Forfeiture Pursuant to Section 58(2)—Regulated Donee

...............................Magistrates' Court

.... Code

Date ....

.... (name of applicant) of .... (address of applicant) applies for an order for forfeiture pursuant to section 58(2) of the Political Parties, Elections and Referendums Act 2000, as applied by paragraph 8 of Schedule 7 to that Act against............ (name of regulated donee) of ....(address of regulated donee) of an amount equal to the value of the controlled donation made on ....and accepted by the regulated donee on ...., on the following grounds:

To: The Justices' Chief Executive

......................Magistrates' Court

FORM A2

Application for Forfeiture Pursuant to Section 58(2)—Recognised Third Party

....Magistrates' Court
.... Code

Date ....
.... (name of applicant) of .... (address of applicant)
applies for an order for forfeiture pursuant to section 58(2) of the Political Parties, Elections and Referendums
Act 2000, as applied by paragraph 7 of Schedule 11 to that Act, against ..... (name of recognised third party)
of ....(address of recognised third party) of an amount equal to the value of the relevant
donation made on .... and accepted by the recognised third party on ...., on the
following grounds:

To: The Justices' Chief Executive
.....................Magistrates' Court

FORM A3

Application for Forfeiture Pursuant to Section 58(2)—Permitted Participants

....Magistrates' Court
.... Code

Date ....
.... (name of applicant) of .... (address of applicant)
applies for an order for forfeiture pursuant to section 58(2) of the Political Parties, Elections and Referendums
Act 2000, as applied by paragraph 7 of Schedule 15 to that Act, against .... (name of permitted
participant) of .... (address of permitted participant) of an amount equal to the value of the
relevant donation made on .... and accepted by the permitted participant on ...., on the
following grounds:

To: The Justices' Chief Executive
.....................Magistrates' Court

FORM A4

Application for Forfeiture Pursuant to Section 58(2)—Candidates or Election Agents

....Magistrates' Court
.... Code

Date ....
.... (name of applicant) of .... (address of applicant)
applies for an order for forfeiture pursuant to section 58(2) of the Political Parties, Elections and Referendums
Act 2000, as applied by paragraph 7 of Schedule 2A to the Representation of the People Act 1983,
against .... (name of candidate/election agent as appropriate)
of ....(address of candidate/election agent as appropriate) of an amount equal to the value
of the relevant donation made on .... and accepted by the candidate/election agent (delete
as appropriate) on ...., on the following grounds:
To: The Justices' Chief Executive
.....................Magistrates' Court

FORM B

Application for Forfeiture Pursuant to Section 65(6)—Registered Party

....Magistrates' Court
.... Code

Date ....
.... (name of applicant) of .... (address of applicant)
applies for an order for forfeiture pursuant to section 65(6) of the Political Parties, Elections and Referendums
Act 2000, against .... (name of registered party) of .... (address of registered party)
of an amount equal to the value of the donation made on .... and accepted by the registered
party on..............., on the following grounds:
To: The Justices' Chief Executive
.....................Magistrates' Court

FORM B1

Application for Forfeiture Pursuant to Paragraph 12(4) of Schedule 7—regulated Donee

....Magistrates' Court
.... Code

Date ....
.... (name of applicant) of .... (address of applicant)
applies for an order for forfeiture pursuant to paragraph 12(4) of Schedule 7 to the Political Parties, Elections
and Referendums Act 2000, against .... (name of regulated donee) of .... (address
of regulated donee) of an amount equal to the value of the controlled donation made on .... and
accepted by the regulated donee on ...., on the following grounds:
To: The Justices' Chief Executive
.....................Magistrates' Court
This reflects the wording used in section 33A of the Youth Justice and Criminal Evidence Act 1999, as inserted
by section 47 of the Police and Justice Act 2006.

Magistrates' Courts (Parenting Orders) Rules 2004[1]
(SI 2004/247 amended by the Courts Act 2004, Sch 8)

1–7330 1. Citation, interpretation and commencement. These Rules may be cited as the Magistrates' Courts (Parenting Orders) Rules 2004 and shall come into force on 27th February 2004.

1–7331 2. In these Rules the "2003 Act" means the Anti-social Behaviour Act 2003.

1–7332 3. Parenting Orders under the Anti-social Behaviour Act 2003. An application for a parenting order made under section 20 of the 2003 Act shall be made by complaint and in the form set out at Schedule 1 or a form to like effect.

1–7333 4. A parenting order made under section 20 of the 2003 Act shall be in the form set out at Schedule 2 or a form to like effect.

1–7334 5. An application for a parenting order made under section 26 of the 2003 Act shall be made by complaint and in the form set out at Schedule 3 or a form to like effect.

1–7335 6. A parenting order made under section 26 of the 2003 Act shall be in the form set out at Schedule 4 or a form to like effect.

1–7336 7. Parenting Orders under the Crime and Disorder Act 1998. *Revoked.*

1–7337 8. Parenting Orders under the Powers of Criminal Courts (Sentencing) Act 2000. *Revoked.*

1–7338 9. Application for variation or discharge. An application for the variation or discharge of an order made under section 20(3) or section 26(3) of the 2003 Act, or under paragraph 9D of Schedule 1 to the Powers of Criminal Courts (Sentencing) Act 2000 shall be made by complaint to the magistrates' court which made the order, and shall specify the reason why the applicant for variation or discharge believes the court should vary or discharge the order, as the case may be.[1]

---

1. Revoked in so far as relates to criminal proceedings, see the Criminal Procedure Rules 2005, Part 50 in this PART, post.

1–7339

Rule 3

SCHEDULE 1

APPLICATION FOR PARENTING ORDER (ANTI-SOCIAL BEHAVIOUR ACT 2003, SECTION 20)

.... Magistrates' Court
.... Code

Date:..
Child or young person:...
Child or young person's address: ....
....
Child or young person's age: ....
Parent:...
Parent's address:..
....
which is in the area of [   ] Local Education Authority
Parent:...
Parent's address:..
....
which is in the area of [   ] Local Education Authority
Applicant Local Education Authority:.............................
It is alleged that:

(*a*) the child or young person has been excluded from school on disciplinary grounds; and
(*b*) the prescribed conditions are satisfied in that [insert details].

[The parent(s) entered into a parenting contract on [date].] [It is alleged that the parent(s) have failed to comply with the parenting contract, a copy of which is attached to this application form.
Short description of alleged failure to comply with parenting contract:
Evidence of this alleged failure to comply is attached.]
[It is alleged that the parent(s) have refused to enter into a parenting contract.]
[The child or young person is under 16. Information as to the family circumstances of the child or young person is attached.]
[It is alleged that:

(*a*) the attendance of the parent at a residential course is likely to be more effective than their attendance at a non-residential course in improving the child's or young person's behaviour; and
(*b*) any interference with family life which is likely to result from the attendance of the parent at a residential course is proportionate in all the circumstances.

The court is requested to order that the counselling or guidance programme may include a residential element.]
Short description of the counselling/guidance programme to be attended by the parent(s):
Further requirements to be included in the order:

1–7340

Rule 4

SCHEDULE 2
PARENTING ORDER (ANTI-SOCIAL BEHAVIOUR ACT 2003, SECTION 20)

....Magistrates' Court
.... Code

Date:..
Person(s) named in order:...
Age(s):..years (if under 18)
....years (if under 18)
Address(es): ....
....
....
Applicant Local Education Authority:..
Responsible officer: ....
[*insert child's/young person's name*] of [*insert address*] who is believed to have been born on [*insert date of birth*], has been excluded from [details of school at which the child or young person is registered] and that the prescribed conditions are met in that [insert details].

Decision: In exercise of its powers under section 20(3) of the Anti-social Behaviour Act 2003 (the "2003 Act") and having complied with its duties under that section[, and having complied with its duty under section 21(1) of the 2003 Act in considering the failure of the persons named above to [enter into][comply with] a parenting contract], the court has decided to impose a parenting order on the person(s) named above being parent(s) of the pupil because the court considers that the order would be desirable in the interests of improving the behaviour of the pupil.

The requirements of the order are as follows:

[*insert person's name*] shall for a period of [*insert length of requirement*] beginning with the date of the order comply with such requirements as are listed in the Schedule to the order.

[*insert person's name*] shall for a concurrent period of [*insert length of requirement*] not exceeding three months attend a counselling or guidance programme as directed by the responsible officer.

[The court is satisfied that the requirements of section 20(7) and (8) of the 2003 Act have been met and the counselling or guidance programme may be or include a residential course.]

[(*In the event that the child/young person is under 16.*) The court has complied with its duties under section 21(2) of the 2003 Act and has obtained and considered information about the child's/young person's family circumstances, and the likely effect of the order on those circumstances.]

The court has complied with its duties under section 21(3) of the 2003 Act, and has explained to the person(s) named above the effect of the order and its requirements, what may happen if he/she/they fail(s) to comply with these requirements (as set out in section 9(7) of the Crime and Disorder Act 1998), and that the court has power (under section 9(5) of the Crime and Disorder Act 1998) to review the order on the application of the person(s) named above or the responsible officer.

Justice of the Peace
[or By order of the Court,
Clerk of the Court]

SCHEDULE

Any requirement(s) imposed by the court under section 20(4)(*a*) and (*b*) of the 2003 Act should be listed here.

1–7341

Rule 5

SCHEDULE 3
APPLICATION FOR PARENTING ORDER (ANTI-SOCIAL BEHAVIOUR ACT 2003, SECTION 26)

....Magistrates' Court
.... Code

Date:..
Child or young person:..
Child or young person's address: ....
....
Child or young person's age: ....
Parent/Guardian: ....
Parent/Guardian's address:...
....
Parent/Guardian: ....
Parent/Guardian's address:...
....
Applicant:...
Responsible officer: ....
It is alleged that:

(*a*) the child or young person has acted on [*insert date(s)*] at [*insert place(s)*] in an anti-social manner, that is to say, in a manner that caused or was likely to cause harassment, alarm or distress to one or more persons not of the same household as himself; or

(*b*) the child or young person has on [*insert date(s)*] at [*insert place(s)*] engaged in criminal conduct.

Short description of acts:
[Evidence of these acts is attached.]
[The parent(s)/guardian(s) entered into a parenting contract on [*insert date*].] [It is alleged that the parent(s)/guardian(s) have failed to comply with the parenting contract, a copy of which is attached to this application form.

Short description of alleged failure to comply with parenting contract:
Evidence of this alleged failure to comply is attached.]
[It is alleged that the parent(s)/guardian(s) have refused to enter into a parenting contract.]
[The child or young person is under 16. Information as to the family circumstances of the child or young person is attached.]
[It is alleged that:

(*a*) the attendance of the parent(s)/guardian(s) at a residential course is likely to be more effective than their attendance at a non-residential course in preventing the child or young person from engaging in further criminal conduct or anti-social behaviour; and

(*b*) any interference with family life which is likely to result from the attendance of the parent(s)/guardian(s) at a residential course is proportionate in all the circumstances.

The court is requested to order that the counselling or guidance programme may [include][consist of] a residential course.

Evidence to support the request for a residential requirement is attached.]

Short description of the counselling/guidance programme to be attended by the parent(s)/guardian(s):

Further requirements to be included in the order:

1–7342

Rule 6

SCHEDULE 4

PARENTING ORDER (ANTI-SOCIAL BEHAVIOUR ACT 2003, SECTION 26)

.... Magistrates' Court

.... Code

Date:..

Person(s) named in order:..

Age(s):.....................................years (if under 18)

.....................................years (if under 18)

Address(es): ....

....

....

Applicant Youth Offending Team:..

Responsible officer: ....

[*insert child's/young person's name*] of [*insert address*], who is believed to have been born on [*insert date of birth*], has [behaved in a manner which is anti-social, that is to say, in a manner that caused or was likely to cause harassment, alarm or distress to one or more persons not of the same household as himself] [engaged in criminal conduct] [*delete as applicable*].

Decision: In exercise of its powers under section 26(3) of the Anti-social Behaviour Act 2003 (the "2003 Act") and having complied with its duties under that section[, and having complied with its duty under section 27(1) of the 2003 Act in considering the failure of the persons named above to [enter into][comply with] a parenting contract], the court has decided to impose a parenting order on the person(s) named above because the court considers that the order would be desirable in the interests of preventing the child or young person from engaging in further [anti-social behaviour] [criminal conduct] [*delete as applicable*].

The requirements of the order are as follows:

[*insert person's name*] shall for a period of [*insert length of requirement*] beginning with the date of the order comply with such requirements as are listed in the Schedule to the order.

[*insert person's name*] shall for a concurrent period of [*insert length of requirement*] not exceeding three months attend a counselling or guidance programme as directed by the responsible officer.

[[*insert person's name*] shall on [*insert dates*] attend a residential course at [*insert address*] as directed by the responsible officer. The court is satisfied that the requirements of section 26(7) and (8) of the 2003 Act have been met.]

[(*In the event that the child/young person is under 16*.) The court has complied with its duties under section 27(2) of the 2003 Act and has obtained and considered information about the child's/young person's family circumstances, and the likely effect of the order on those circumstances.]

The court has complied with its duties under section 27(3) of the 2003 Act, and has explained to the person(s) named above the effect of the order and its requirements, what may happen if he/she/they fail(s) to comply with these requirements (as set out in section 9(7) of the Crime and Disorder Act 1998), and that the court has power (under section 9(5) of the Crime and Disorder Act 1998) to review the order on the application of the person(s) named above or the responsible officer.

Justice of the Peace

[or By order of the Court,

Clerk of the Court]

SCHEDULE

Any requirement(s) imposed by the court under section 26(4)(*a*) and (*b*) of the 2003 Act should be listed here.

1–7343

Rule 7

SCHEDULE 5

PARENTING ORDER (CRIME AND DISORDER ACT 1998, SECTION 8)

.... Family Proceedings][[Youth][Magistrates'] Court

.... (Code)

Date:..

Person(s) named in order:..

Age(s):.....................................years (if under 18)

.....................................years (if under 18)

Address(es): ....

....

....

Responsible officer: ....

[[*insert child's/young person's name*] of [*insert address*] who is believed to have been born on [*insert date of birth*], has been [made subject to a [child safety order][anti-social behaviour order][sex offender order]][found guilty of an offence, namely, [brief details of offence and statute]]]. [The above named has been convicted of an offence under [section 443][section 444] of the Education Act 1996] [*delete as applicable*].

Decision: In exercise of its powers under section 8 of the Crime and Disorder Act 1998 (the "1998 Act") and having complied with its duties under [section 9(1) and (2)] [section 9(2) and (2A) (*in the case of a referral order*)] of the 1998 Act, the court has decided to impose a parenting order on the person(s) named above because the court considers that the order would be desirable in the interests of preventing [a repetition of the kind of behaviour which led to the imposition of a [child safety order][anti-social behaviour order][sex offender order]][the commission of further offences by the child or young person][the commission of further offences under [section 443][section 444] of the Education Act 1996] *[delete as applicable]*.

The requirements of the order are as follows:

[*insert person's name*] shall for a period of [*insert length of requirement*] beginning with the date of the order comply with such requirements as are listed in the Schedule to the order.

[*insert person's name*] shall, for a concurrent period of [*insert length of requirement*] not exceeding three months attend a counselling or guidance programme as directed by the responsible officer.

[[*insert person's name*] shall, on [*insert dates*] attend a residential course at [*insert address*] as directed by the responsible officer. The court is satisfied that the requirements of section 8(7A) of the 1998 Act have been met.]

[(*In the event that the child/young person is under 16.*) The court has complied with its duties under section 9(2) of the 1998 Act and has obtained and considered information about the child's/young person's family circumstances, and the likely effect of the order on those circumstances.]

The court has complied with its duties under section 9(3) to 9(7) of the 1998 Act, and has explained to the person(s) named above the effect of the order and its requirements, what may happen if he/she/they fail(s) to comply with these requirements, and that the court has power to review the order on the application of the person(s) named above or the responsible officer.

Justice of the Peace
[or By order of the Court,
Clerk of the Court]

SCHEDULE

Any requirement(s) imposed by the court under section 8(4)(*a*) and (*b*) of the 1998 Act should be listed here.

1-7344　　　　　　　　　SCHEDULE 6
PARENTING ORDER (POWERS OF CRIMINAL COURTS (SENTENCING) ACT 2000, SCHEDULE 1, PARAGRAPH 9D)

Revoked.

Magistrates' Courts (Foreign Travel Orders) Rules 2004[1]
(SI 2004/1051)

1-7350　1. Citation, commencement and interpretation. These Rules may be cited as the Magistrates' Courts (Foreign Travel Orders) Rules 2004 and shall come into force on 1 May 2004.

---

1. Made by the Lord Chancellor, in exercise of the power conferred on him by s 144 of the Magistrates' Courts Act 1980, after consultation with the rule committee appointed under the said s 144.

1-7351　2. In these Rules—

(*a*) a reference to a numbered section is a reference to the section so numbered in the Sexual Offences Act 2003[1]; and

(*b*) a reference to a Schedule is a reference to a Schedule to these Rules.

---

1. In PART VIII, title SEXUAL OFFENCES, post.

1-7352　3. Foreign travel orders. (1) An application for a foreign travel order under section 114(1) may be in the form set out in Schedule 1.

(2) A summons directed to the defendant requiring him to appear before a magistrates' court to answer an application referred to in paragraph (1) may be in the form set out in Schedule 2.

(3) A foreign travel order shall be in the form set out in Schedule 3.

(4) As soon as reasonably practicable after a foreign travel order has been made, the Justices' Chief Executive shall serve a copy of that order on the defendant. Any copy of an order required to be sent under these Rules to the defendant shall be either given to him in person or sent by post to his last known address and, if so given or sent, shall be deemed to have been received by him, unless the defendant proves that it was not received by him.

1-7353　4. Time limit for service of a notice under section 116(6). If the defendant wishes to serve on the applicant a notice under section 116(6), he must do so no later than 3 days before the hearing date for the application for the foreign travel order.

1-7354
Rule 3(1)　　　　　　　　　SCHEDULE 1
FORM—APPLICATION FOR [FOREIGN TRAVEL ORDER]
(SEXUAL OFFENCES ACT 2003), s[114(1)]

Application for [Foreign Travel Order]

(SEXUAL OFFENCES ACT 2003, s[114(1)])

.... Magistrates' Court
.... (*Code*)

Date:...
Defendant:.....................................
Address:..
....

The defendant is a qualifying offender by virtue of the following facts:
Offence:...

If committed abroad, the corresponding offence this would have constituted had the act been done in the United Kingdom:

Date of [conviction] [finding] [caution]...
Court / Police Station...
[And it is alleged that the defendant has since the date (or the first date) of the above conviction, finding or caution, acted in such as way as to give reasonable cause to believe that a foreign travel order under section 114(1) of the Sexual Offences Act 2003 is necessary to protect children generally or any particular child from serious sexual harm from the defendant outside the United Kingdom
Short description of acts, including date(s) and further comments:
....
....
....

Accordingly application is made for a foreign travel order
prohibiting travel [to this country / these countries][to this region / these regions] [abroad more generally]:—]
....
....
Short description of acts:...
....
The complaint of ....
Address:...
....

who [upon oath] states that the facts given in this form are true to the best of his knowledge and belief.
Taken [and sworn] before me

Justice of the Peace
[Justices' Clerk]

1–7355

Rule 3(2)   SCHEDULE 2
FORM—SUMMONS ON APPLICATION FOR [FOREIGN TRAVEL ORDER] (SEXUAL OFFENCES ACT 2003) [s 114]

....Magistrates' Court
....(Code)

Date:...
To the defendant:..
Address:...
....

You are hereby summonsed to appear on..
(date)
at... [time] before the Magistrates' Court at ....
to answer to an application for a foreign travel order, which application is attached to this summons.
Copied to the applicant:...

Justice of the Peace
[Justices' Clerk]

NOTE:

Where the court is satisfied that this summons was served on you within what appears to the court to be a reasonable time before the hearing or adjourned hearing, it may issue a warrant for your arrest or proceed in your absence.

If a foreign travel order is made against you, you will be subject to the prohibitions made in it. You will also be subject to the foreign travel notification regulations made under section 86 of the Sexual Offences Act 2003, which oblige you to notify the police of any plans you have to travel abroad for a period of 3 days or longer. If details are known to you 7 days before you travel you must inform the police 7 days before you travel. Otherwise you must inform the police no less than 24 hours in advance of travel.

If, without reasonable excuse, you do anything you are prohibited from doing by the order, or if you fail to comply with the foreign travel notification regulations made under section 86 of the Sexual Offences Act 2003 you shall be liable on conviction to imprisonment for a term not exceeding 5 years.

1–7356

Rule 3(3)   SCHEDULE 3
FORM—FOREIGN TRAVEL ORDERS (SEXUAL OFFENCES ACT 2003, s 114)

Foreign Travel Orders (Sexual Offences Act 2003, s 114)

....Magistrates' Court
....(Code)

Date:...
Defendant:...
Address:...
....
On the complaint of—
Complainant:...
Address:...

It is adjudged that the defendant is a qualifying offender by reason of the following:
Offence:...
If committed abroad, corresponding offence had the act been done in the UK:
....
Date of [conviction] [finding] [caution]:...
[Court] [Police station]:..

And it is adjudged that the defendant's behaviour, since the date (or first date) of the above conviction, finding or caution, makes it necessary to make a foreign travel order under section 114(1) of the Sexual Offences Act 2003 to protect children generally or any child from serious sexual harm from the defendant outside the United Kingdom.

Short description of acts (including date(s)) and further comments:

....

....

And it is ordered that the defendant is prohibited from travel [to this country / these countries] [to this region / these regions] [abroad more generally]:—

....

....

Until .... [*date not more than six months from date of order*]

And while this order (as renewed from time to time) has effect, the defendant shall be subject to section 86 of the Sexual Offences Act 2003

[OR *where the defendant is already subject to the notification requirements on the making of this order*.

And the defendant, who was a relevant offender within the meaning of Part 2 of the Sexual Offences Act 2003 immediately before the making of this order, but who would otherwise cease to be subject to the notification requirements of the said Part 2 while this order has effect, shall remain subject to the foreign travel notification requirements of section 86 for the duration of this order as renewed from time to time.].

Justice of the Peace
[Justices' Clerk]

NOTE:
For the period of this order, you are subject to the foreign travel notification regulations made under section 86 of the Sexual Offences Act 2003, which oblige you to notify the police of any plans you have to travel abroad for a period of 3 days or longer. If details are known to you 7 days before you travel you must inform the police 7 days before you travel. Otherwise you must inform the police no less than 24 hours in advance.

Your local Police Service Headquarters will be able to explain these conditions in more detail.

The restrictions in this order apply throughout the United Kingdom (England and Wales, Scotland and Northern Ireland).

If, without reasonable excuse, you do anything you are prohibited from doing by this order or you fail to comply with the notification requirements of Part 2 of the Sexual Offences Act 2003 you shall be liable on conviction to imprisonment for a term not exceeding 5 years.

Magistrates' Courts (Notification Orders) Rules 2004[1]
(SI 2004/1052)

1–7360   1. Citation, commencement, interpretation.   These Rules may be cited as the Magistrates' Courts (Notification Orders) Rules 2004 and shall come into force on 1 May 2004.

---

1. Made by the Lord Chancellor, in exercise of the power conferred on him by s 144 of the Magistrates' Courts Act 1980, after consultation with the rule committee appointed under the said s 44.

1–7361   2.   In these Rules—

    (*a*) a reference to a numbered section is a reference to a section so numbered in the Sexual Offences Act 2003[1]; and

    (*b*) a reference to a Schedule is a reference to a Schedule to these Rules except where it is made clear that it refers to a Schedule to the Sexual Offences Act 2003.

---

1. In PART VIII, title SEXUAL OFFENCES, post.

1–7362   3. Notification orders and interim notification orders.   (1) An application for—

    (*a*) a notification order made under section 97(1), or

    (*b*) an interim notification order made under section 100(2)

may be in the form set out in Schedule 1.

(2) A summons directed to the defendant requiring him to appear before a magistrates' court to answer an application referred to in paragraph (1) may be in the form set out in Schedule 2.

(3) A notification order shall be in the form set out in Schedule 3.

(4) An interim notification order shall be in the form set out in Schedule 4.

(5) As soon as reasonably practicable after a notification order or an interim notification order has been made, the Justices' Chief Executive shall serve a copy of that order on the defendant. Any copy of an order required to be sent under these Rules to the defendant shall be either given to him in person or sent by post to his last known address and, if so given or sent, shall be deemed to have been received by him, unless the defendant proves that it was not received by him.

1–7363   4. Time limit for service of a notice under section 99(3).   If a defendant wishes to serve on the applicant a notice under section 99(3), he must do so no later than 3 days before the hearing date for the application for the notification order.

1–7364

Rule 3(1)

SCHEDULE 1

FORM—APPLICATION FOR NOTIFICATION ORDER AND INTERIM NOTIFICATION ORDER SEXUAL OFFENCES ACT 2003 (SOA 2003) SECTIONS 97 AND 100

Application for Notification Order and Interim Notification Order] Sexual Offences Act 2003 (SOA 2003) sections 97 and 100]

.... Magistrates' Court

.... [*Code*]

Date..

Defendant ....

Address..

....

It appears that the defendant

[resides in the ....

.... police area]

[is in or is intending to come to the ....

.... police area because

....

It appears that the defendant on .... [*date*(s)]

at .... [*court/police station*]

in .... [*country outside the United Kingdom*]

and under the law in force in that country outside the United Kingdom,

[was convicted of a relevant offence (as defined in section 99 of the SOA 2003)]

[in respect of a relevant offence, was made subject to a finding equivalent to a finding that he was not guilty by reason of insanity]

[in respect of a relevant offence, was made subject to a finding equivalent to a finding that he was under a disability and did the act charged]

[was cautioned in respect of a relevant offence].

The offence as described in the law in force in the country outside the United Kingdom:

....

The offence, listed in Schedule 3 to the SOA 2003, that this would have constituted had the act been done in any part of the United Kingdom:

....

Where the above conviction, finding or caution above occurred before 1st September 1997, it appears that [the defendant was dealt with in relation to the offence or finding on or after that date or has yet to be dealt with]

[the defendant, in respect of that offence or finding, was, under the law in force in the country concerned, subject to detention, supervision or any other disposal as referred to in section 97(3)(*c*) of the SOA 2003.]

It further appears that the notification period that would have applied under section 82 of the SOA 2003 had the conviction, finding or caution taken place in the United Kingdom has not expired.

[Additional information relating to an application for an interim notification order:

....]

Accordingly application is made for

[a notification order]

[an interim notification order]

[a notification order and an interim notification order]

which will make the defendant subject to the notification requirements in Part 2 of the SOA 2003.

The complaint of ....

Address..

....

Who [upon oath] states that the facts given in this form are true to the best of his knowledge and belief.

Taken [and sworn] before me

Justice of the Peace
[Justices' Clerk]

Address. . . . .

Who [upon oath] states that the facts given in this form are true to the best of his knowledge and belief.

Taken [and sworn] before me

Justice of the Peace
[Justices' Clerk]

1–7365

Rule 3(2)

SCHEDULE 2

FORM—SUMMONS ON APPLICATION FOR [A NOTIFICATION ORDER [AND] AN INTERIM NOTIFICATION ORDER] (SEXUAL OFFENCES ACT 2003) [S 97] [AND] [S 100])

.... Magistrates' Court

.... [*Code*]

Date: ....

To the defendant: ....

Address: ....

You are hereby summonsed to appear on .... [*date*]

at .... [*time*] before the ....Magistrates' Court

to answer an application for a [notification order] [interim notification order], which application is attached to this summons.

Justice of the Peace
[Justices' Clerk]

NOTE:

Where the court is satisfied that this summons was served on you within what appears to the court to be a reasonable time before the hearing or adjourned hearing, it may issue a warrant for your arrest or proceed in your absence.

If a notification order is made against you, you will be subject to the notification requirements of Part 2 of the Sexual Offences Act 2003, which include obligations on you to notify the police of:

—your name, home address, date of birth and national insurance number within 3 days;

—any changes to your name or home address (within 3 days of the change);

—any address you stay at or plan to stay at in addition to your home address for a period of longer than 7 days within a twelve month period (within 3 days);

—any plans you have to travel abroad for a period of 3 days or longer (if details are known to you 7 days before you travel you must inform the police 7 days before you travel. Otherwise you must inform the police no less than 24 hours in advance).

If, without reasonable excuse, you fail to comply with the notification requirements of Part 2 of the Sexual Offences Act 2003 you shall be liable on conviction to imprisonment for a term not exceeding five years.

1-7366
Rule 3(3)

SCHEDULE 3
FORM—NOTIFICATION ORDER (SEXUAL OFFENCES ACT 2003, s 97)

Notification Order (Sexual Offences Act 2003, s 97)

....Magistrates' Court
....[*Code*]

Date:...
Defendant:..
Address:..
....

On the complaint of
Complainant:..
Address:..
....

It is adjudged that the following facts have been made out and therefore the conditions are met for a notification order to be made against the above defendant.

1. On.. [*date(s)*]
at... [*court/police station*]
in... [*country outside the United Kingdom*]
and under the law in force in that country outside the United Kingdom, the defendant
[was convicted of a relevant offence (as defined in section 99 of the SOA 2003)]
[in respect of a relevant offence, was made subject to a finding equivalent to a finding that he was not guilty by reason of insanity]
[in respect of a relevant offence, was made subject to a finding equivalent to a finding that he was under a disability and did the act charged]
[was cautioned in respect of a relevant offence].
The offence as described in the law in force in the country outside the United Kingdom:
....
The offence, listed in Schedule 3 to the SOA 2003, that this would have constituted had the act been done in any part of the United Kingdom:

2. [The above conviction, finding or caution occurred on or after 1st September 1997]
[Where the above conviction or finding took place before 1st September 1997,]
[the defendant was dealt with in relation to the offence or finding on or after that date or has yet to be dealt with]
[the defendant, in respect of that offence or finding, was, under the law in force in the country concerned, subject to .... [*details of detention, supervision or other disposal as referred to in section 97(3)(c) of the SOA 2003.*]]
3. The notification period that would have applied under section 82 of the SOA 2003 had the conviction, finding or caution taken place in the United Kingdom has not expired.

It is ordered that the defendant must comply with the notification requirements of Part 2 of the Sexual Offences Act 2003 subject to the modifications set out in section 98 of that Act. In particular, the defendant's initial notification to the police must be made within 3 days of the service of this order.

The defendant must comply with the notification requirements for the period set out in section 82 of the Sexual Offences Act 2003. That is for [the period of his conditional discharge or equivalent][two years][five years][seven years][ten years][an indefinite period] starting from:
.... [*the date of conviction, finding or caution in the country outside the United Kingdom*]

Justice of the Peace
[Justices' Clerk]

NOTE:
The requirement of a notification order is that you (the defendant) will be subject to the notification requirements of Part 2 of the Sexual Offences Act 2003 as modified in section 98 of that Act. The requirements of that Act include an obligation on you to report to a prescribed police station within 3 days of the service of this order and to notify the police of your name(s), home address, date of birth and national insurance number. Thereafter you are obliged to notify the police of:

—any changes to your name or home address (within 3 days of the change);
—any address you stay at or plan to stay at in addition to your home address for a period of longer than 7 days within a twelve month period (within 3 days);
—any plans you have to travel abroad for a period of 3 days or longer (if details are known to you 7 days before you travel you must inform the police 7 days before you travel. Otherwise you must inform the police no less than 24 hours in advance).

Your local Police Service Headquarters will be able to explain these conditions in more detail—in particular, the information you must bring with you when you make your initial notification—and tell you at which local police station you should attend.

The restrictions in this order apply throughout the United Kingdom (England and Wales, Scotland and Northern Ireland).

If, without reasonable excuse, you fail to comply with the notification requirements of Part 2 of the Sexual Offences Act 2003 you shall be liable on conviction to imprisonment for a term not exceeding 5 years.

1–7367

Rule 3(4)   SCHEDULE 4

FORM—INTERIM NOTIFICATION ORDER (SEXUAL OFFENCES ACT 2003 s 100)

Interim Notification Order (Sexual Offences Act 2003 s 100)

.... Magistrates' Court
....*[Code]*
Date:...
Defendant:..
Address:...
....

On the complaint of
Complainant:...
Address:...
....

An application for a notification order has been made by the complainant and that application has not yet been determined.

The court considers it is just to make an interim notification order.

It is ordered that the defendant is subject to the notification requirements of Part 2 of the Sexual Offences Act 2003, subject to the modification that the relevant date (within the meaning of that Part) means the date of service of this order.

This interim notification order will last until

.... *[date]*
and will cease to have effect, if it has not already done so, on determination of the main application.

Justice of the Peace
[Justices' Clerk]

NOTE:

The requirement of an interim notification order is that you (the defendant) will be subject to the notification requirements of Part 2 of the Sexual Offences Act 2003 as modified in section 100(6) of that Act, namely that the "relevant date" means the date of service of the order. The requirements of that Act include an obligation on you to report to a prescribed police station within 3 days of the service of this order and to notify the police of your name(s), home address, date of birth and national insurance number. Thereafter you are obliged to notify the police of:

—any changes to your name or home address (within 3 days of the change);
—any address you stay at or plan to stay at in addition to your home address for a period of longer than 7 days within a twelve month period (within 3 days);
—any plans you have to travel abroad for a period of 3 days or longer (if details are known to you 7 days before you travel you must inform the police 7 days before you travel. Otherwise you must inform the police no less than 24 hours in advance).

Your local Police Service Headquarters will be able to explain these conditions in more detail—in particular the information you must bring with you when you make your initial notification—and tell you at which local police station you should attend.

The restrictions in this order apply throughout the United Kingdom (England and Wales, Scotland and Northern Ireland).

If, without reasonable excuse, you fail to comply with the notification requirements of Part 2 of the Sexual Offences Act 2003 you shall be liable on conviction to imprisonment for a term not exceeding 5 years.

Magistrates' Courts (Risk of Sexual Harm Orders) Rules 2004[1]
(SI 2004/1053)

1–7370 1. Citation, commencement and interpretation.   These Rules may be cited as the Magistrates' Courts (Risk of Sexual Harm Orders) Rules 2004 and shall come into force on 1st May 2004.

1. Made by the Lord Chancellor, in exercise of the power conferred on him by s 144 of the Magistrates' Courts Act 1980, after consultation with the rule committee appointed under the said s 144.

1–7371 2.   In these Rules—

(a) a reference to a numbered section is a reference to the section so numbered in the Sexual Offences Act 2003[1]; and
(b) a reference to a Schedule is a reference to a Schedule to these Rules.

1. In PART VIII, title SEXUAL OFFENCES, post.

1–7372 3. Risk of sexual harm orders and interim risk of sexual harm orders.   (1) An application for

(a) a risk of sexual harm order made under section 123(1), or
(b) an interim risk of sexual harm order made under section 126(2)

may be in the form set out in Schedule 1.

(2) A summons directed to the defendant requiring him to appear before a magistrates' court to answer an application referred to in paragraph (1) may be in the form set out in Schedule 2.

(3) A risk of sexual harm order shall be in the form set out in Schedule 3.

(4) An interim risk of sexual harm order shall be in the form set out in Schedule 4.

(5) As soon as reasonably practicable after a risk of sexual harm order or an interim risk of sexual harm order has been made, the Justices' Chief Executive shall serve a copy of that order on the defendant. Any copy of an order required to be sent under these Rules to the defendant

shall be either given to him in person or sent by post to his last known address and, if so given or sent, shall be deemed to have been received by him, unless the defendant proves that it was not received by him.

1–7373

Rule 3(1)   SCHEDULE 1

FORM—RULE 3(1) APPLICATION FOR [RISK OF SEXUAL HARM ORDER] [AND] [INTERIM RISK OF SEXUAL HARM ORDER] (SEXUAL OFFENCES ACT 2003 s[s][123] [AND] [126]).

Rule 3(1) Application for [Risk of Sexual Harm Order] [and] [Interim Risk of Sexual Harm Order] (Sexual Offences Act 2003 s[s][123] [and] [126]).

.... Magistrates' Court
.... [*Code*]

Date:..
Defendant:...
Address:...

It is alleged that the defendant has on at least two occasions done an act within section 123(3) of the Sexual Offences Act 2003 (the "2003 Act"), as a result of which there is reasonable cause to believe that an order under section 123 of the 2003 Act is necessary to protect children generally or any child from harm from the defendant.

Short description of acts, including date(s):

....
....
....

[Additional information relating to an application for an interim risk of sexual harm order:

....
....]

Accordingly application is made for
[a risk of sexual harm order]
[an interim risk of sexual harm order]
[a risk of sexual harm order and an interim risk of sexual harm order] containing the following prohibition(s):—

....
....

The complaint of ....
Address:...

who [upon oath] states that the facts given in this form are true to the best of his knowledge and belief.
Taken [and sworn] before me

Justice of the Peace
[Justices' Clerk]

1–7374

Rule 3(2)   SCHEDULE 2

FORM—SUMMONS ON APPLICATION FOR [RISK OF SEXUAL HARM ORDER] [AND] [INTERIM RISK OF SEXUAL HARM ORDER] (SEXUAL OFFENCES ACT 2003 s[s] [123] [AND] [126]).

Summons on Application for [Risk of Sexual Harm Order] [and] [Interim Risk of Sexual Harm Order] (Sexual Offences Act 2003 s[s] [123] [and] [126]).

.... Magistrates' Court
.... [*Code*]

Date:..
To the defendant: ....
Address:...

You are hereby summonsed to appear on.. [*date*]
at.. [*time*] before the Magistrates' Court at ....
to answer to an application for [a risk of sexual harm order] [and] [an interim risk of sexual harm order], which application is attached to this summons.

Justice of the Peace
[Justices' Clerk]

NOTE:

Where the court is satisfied that this summons was served on you within what appears to the court to be a reasonable time before the hearing or adjourned hearing, it may issue a warrant for your arrest or proceed in your absence.

If a risk of sexual harm order or an interim risk of sexual harm order is made against you, you will be subject to the prohibitions set out in the order. If, without reasonable excuse, you do anything you are prohibited from doing by such an order you shall be liable on conviction to imprisonment for a term not exceeding five years and you will become subject to the notification requirements of Part 2 of the Sexual Offences Act 2003 (commonly known as the "sex offenders register").

1–7375

Rule 3(3)   SCHEDULE 3

FORM—RISK OF SEXUAL HARM ORDER (SEXUAL OFFENCES ACT 2003 s 123)

Risk of Sexual Harm Order (Sexual Offences Act 2003 s 123)

.... Magistrates' Court
.... [*Code*]

Date:..
Defendant:...
Address: ....

On the complaint of
Complainant...

Address:..

It is adjudged that the defendant has on at least two occasions done an act within section 123(3) of the Sexual Offences Act 2003 (the "2003 Act") and that it is necessary to make a risk of sexual harm order under section 123 of the 2003 for the purpose of protecting children generally or any child from harm from him.
Description of relevant acts and any further comments:
....
....

And it is ordered that the defendant is prohibited from:
....
....

until... *[date, not less than 2 years from date of order]* or until further order.

Justice of the Peace
[Justices' Clerk]

NOTE:
If, without reasonable excuse, you do anything you are prohibited from doing by a risk of sexual harm order, you shall be liable on conviction to imprisonment for a term not exceeding five years and you will become subject to the notification requirements of Part 2 of the Sexual Offences Act 2003 (commonly known as "the sex offenders register").

1–7376

Rule 3(4)

SCHEDULE 4
FORM—INTERIM RISK OF SEXUAL HARM ORDER (SEXUAL OFFENCES ACT 2003 s 126)

Interim Risk of Sexual Harm Order (Sexual Offences Act 2003 s 126)

.... Magistrates' Court
.... *[Code]*

Date:..
Defendant:...
Address:...

On the complaint of
Complainant...
Address:...

An application for a risk of sexual harm order, under section 123 of the Sexual Offences Act 2003 has been made and that application has not yet been determined.
The court considers it just to make an interim risk of sexual harm order.
Reasons:
....
....

It is ordered that the defendant is prohibited from:
....
....

This interim risk of sexual harm order will last until
.... *[date]*
and will cease to have effect, if it has not already done so, on determination of the main application.

Justice of the Peace
[Justices' Clerk]

NOTE:
If, without reasonable excuse, you do anything you are prohibited from doing by an interim risk of sexual harm order, you shall be liable on conviction to imprisonment for a term not exceeding five years and you will become subject to the notification requirements of Part 2 of the Sexual Offences Act 2003 (commonly known as the "sex offenders register").

Magistrates' Courts (Sexual Offences Prevention Orders) Rules 2004[1]
(SI 2004/1054 amended by the Courts Act 2003, Sch 8)

1–7380 1. Citation and commencement.   These Rules may be cited as the Magistrates' Courts (Sexual Offences Prevention Orders) Rules 2004 and shall come into force on 1 May 2004.

1. Made by the Lord Chancellor, in exercise of the power conferred on him by s 144 of the Magistrates' Courts Act 1980, after consultation with the rule committee appointed under the said s 144.

1–7381 2.   In these Rules—
  (a) a reference to a numbered section is a reference to the section so numbered in the Sexual Offences Act 2003[1]; and
  (b) a reference to a Schedule is a reference to a Schedule to these Rules.

1. In PART VIII, title SEXUAL OFFENCES, post.

1–7382 3. Revocation.   These Rules hereby revoke—
  (a) the Magistrates' Courts (Sex Offender Orders) Rules 2002; and
  (b) Rules 85 to 87 of the Magistrates' Courts (Miscellaneous Amendments) Rules 2003.

1–7383 4. Sexual Offences Prevention Orders and Interim Sexual Offences Prevention Orders.
Revoked.

1-7384 5. Time limit for service of a notice under section 106(11). If the defendant wishes to serve on the applicant a notice under section 106(11), he must do so no later than 3 days before the hearing date for the application for the sexual offences prevention order.

1-7385

Rule 4(1)   **SCHEDULE 1**

FORM—APPLICATION FOR [SEXUAL OFFENCES PREVENTION ORDER] [AND] [INTERIM SEXUAL OFFENCES PREVENTION ORDER] (SEXUAL OFFENCES ACT 2003 [s 104] [AND] [s 109])

.... Magistrates' Court

.... (*Code*)

Date:..

Defendant:..

Address:..

The defendant is a qualifying offender by virtue of the following facts:

Offence:..

If committed abroad, the corresponding offence this would have constituted had the act been done in the United Kingdom:

Date of [conviction] [finding] [caution]:...

Court/Police Station: ....

[And it is alleged that the defendant has since the date (or the first date) of the above conviction, finding or caution, acted in such as way as to give reasonable cause to believe that a sexual offences prevention order under section 104(1) of the Sexual Offences Act 2003 is necessary to protect the public or any particular members of the public from serious sexual harm from him. Short description of acts, including date(s) and further comments:

....

....]

[Information relating to an application for an interim sexual offences prevention order:

[*Where application is made for interim order only:*

Date of application for sexual offences prevention order: ....]

Accordingly application is made for

[a sexual offences prevention order]

[an interim sexual offences prevention order]

[a sexual offences prevention order and an interim sexual offences prevention order] containing the following prohibition(s):—

....

....

The complaint of ....

Address:..

who [upon oath] states that the facts given in this form are true to the best of his knowledge and belief.

Taken [and sworn] before me

                                 Justice of the Peace

                                 [Justices' Clerk]

1-7386

Rule 4(2)   **SCHEDULE 2**

FORM—SUMMONS ON APPLICATION FOR [SEXUAL OFFENCES PREVENTION ORDER] [AND] [INTERIM SEXUAL OFFENCES PREVENTION ORDER] (SEXUAL OFFENCES ACT 2003 [s 104] [AND] [s 109])

.... Magistrates' Court

.... (*Code*)

Date:..

To the defendant: ....

Address: ....

You are hereby summonsed to appear on .... [*date*]

at.. [*time*] before the Magistrates' Court at .

to answer to an application for [a sexual offences prevention order] [and] [an interim sexual offences prevention order], which application is attached to this summons.

Copied to the applicant: ....

                                 Justice of the Peace

                                 [Justices' Clerk]

NOTE: Where the court is satisfied that this summons was served on you within what appears to the court to be a reasonable time before the hearing or adjourned hearing, it may issue a warrant for your arrest or proceed in your absence.

If a sexual offences prevention order is made against you, you will be subject to the prohibitions made in it. You will also be subject to the notification requirements of Part 2 of the Sexual Offences Act 2003 (commonly known as the 'sex offenders' register'). These include obligations on you to notify the police of:

    your name(s), home address, date of birth and national insurance number (within 3 days of service of the order);

    any changes to your name or home address (within 3 days of the change)

    any address you stay at or plan to stay at in addition to your home address for a period of 7 days or more within a twelve month period (within 3 days)

    any plans you have to travel abroad for a period of 3 days or longer (if you know the details 7 days or more before you travel you must inform the police no less than 7 days in advance. Otherwise you must inform the police no less than 24 hours in advance).

If, without reasonable excuse, you do anything you are prohibited from doing by the order or you fail to comply with the notification requirements of Part 2 of the Sexual Offences Act 2003 you shall be liable on conviction to imprisonment for a term not exceeding 5 years.

1–7387

Rule 4(3)

SCHEDULE 3

FORM—SEXUAL OFFENCES PREVENTION ORDER (SEXUAL OFFENCES ACT 2003 S 104)

.... Magistrates' Court

.... *(Code)*

Date:..

Defendant:..

Address:..

On the complaint of—

Complainant:...

Address:..

It is adjudged that the defendant is a qualifying offender by reason of the following:

Offence:...

If committed abroad, corresponding offence had the act been done in the UK:

Date of [conviction] [finding] [caution]:...

[Court] [Police station]:..

And it is adjudged that the defendant's behaviour, since the date (or first date) of the above conviction, finding or caution, makes it necessary to make a sexual offences prevention order under section 104(1) of the Sexual Offences Act 2003 to protect the public or any particular members of the public from serious sexual harm from him.

Short description of acts (including date(s)) and further comments:

....

It is ordered that the defendant is prohibited from:

....

until.. [*date not less than 5 years from date of order*]

or until further order.

And while this order (as renewed from time to time) has effect, the defendant shall be subject to the notification requirements of Part 2 of the Sexual Offences Act 2003 and the 'relevant date' within the meaning of that Part is the date of service of this order.

[*OR where the defendant is already subject to the notification requirements on the making of this order*:

And the defendant, who was a relevant offender within the meaning of Part 2 of the Sexual Offences Act 2003 immediately before the making of this order, but who would otherwise cease to be subject to the notification requirements of the said Part 2 while this order has effect, shall remain subject to the notification requirements for the duration of this order as renewed from time to time.]

Justice of the Peace

[Justices' Clerk]

NOTE: One of the requirements of a sexual offences prevention order is that you (the defendant) will be subject to the notification requirements of Part 2 of the Sexual Offences Act 2003. (Unless you are already subject to these requirements and have complied), these requirements include an obligation on you to report to a prescribed police station within 3 days of the service of this order and to notify the police of your name(s), home address, date of birth and National Insurance number. Thereafter you are obliged to notify the police of:

any changes to your name or home address (within 3 days of the change)

any address you stay at or plan to stay at in addition to your home address for a period of 7 days or more within a twelve month period (within 3 days)

any plans you have to travel abroad for a period of 3 days or longer (if you know the details 7 days or more before you travel you must inform the police no less than 7 days in advance. Otherwise you must inform the police no less than 24 hours in advance).

Your local Police Service Headquarters will be able to explain these conditions in more detail—in particular the information you must bring with you when you make your initial notification—and tell you at which local police station you should attend.

The restrictions in this order apply throughout the United Kingdom (England and Wales, Scotland and Northern Ireland).

If, without reasonable excuse, you do anything you are prohibited from doing by this order or you fail to comply with the notification requirements of Part 2 of the Sexual Offences Act 2003 you shall be liable on conviction to imprisonment for a term not exceeding 5 years.

1–7388

Rule 4(4)

SCHEDULE 4

FORM—INTERIM SEXUAL OFFENCES PREVENTION ORDER (SEXUAL OFFENCES ACT 2003 S 109)

.... Magistrates' Court

.... *(Code)*

Date:..

Defendant:..

Address:..

On the complaint of

Complainant:...

Address:..

An application for a sexual offences prevention order under section 104 of the Sexual Offences Act 2003 has been made and that application has not yet been determined.

The court considers it just to make an interim sexual offences prevention order.

Reasons:

....

It is ordered that the defendant is prohibited from:

....

This interim risk of sexual harm order will last until

.... *[date]*

and will cease to have effect, if it has not already done so, on determination of the main application.

And while this order has effect, the defendant shall be subject to the notification requirements of Part 2 of the Sexual Offences Act 2003 and the 'relevant date' within the meaning of that Part is the date of service of this order.

[*OR where the defendant is already subject to the notification requirements on the making of this order:*

And the defendant, who was a relevant offender within the meaning of Part 2 of the Sexual Offences Act 2003 immediately before the making of this order, but who would cease to be subject to the notification requirements of the said Part 2 while this order has effect, shall remain subject to the notification requirements for the duration of this order.]

Justice of the Peace
[Justices' Clerk]

NOTE: One of the requirements of an interim sexual offences prevention order is that you (the defendant) will be subject to the notification requirements of Part 2 of the Sexual Offences Act 2003. (Unless you are already subject to these requirements and have complied), these requirements include an obligation on you to report to a prescribed police station within 3 days of the service of this order and to notify the police of your name(s), home address, date of birth and National Insurance number. Thereafter you are obliged to notify the police of:

any changes to your name or home address (within 3 days of the change)

any address you stay at or plan to stay at in addition to your home address for a period of 7 days or more within a twelve month period (within 3 days)

any plans you have to travel abroad for a period of 3 days or longer (if you know the details 7 days or more before you travel you must inform the police no less than 7 days in advance. Otherwise you must inform the police no less than 24 hours in advance).

Your local Police Service Headquarters will be able to explain these conditions in more detail—in particular the information you must bring with you when you make your initial notification—and tell you at which local police station you should attend.

The restrictions in this order apply throughout the United Kingdom (England and Wales, Scotland and Northern Ireland).

If, without reasonable excuse, you do anything you are prohibited from doing by this order or you fail to comply with the notification requirements of Part 2 of the Sexual Offences Act 2003 you shall be liable on conviction to imprisonment for a term not exceeding 5 years.

Practice Direction (Costs: Criminal Proceedings)[1]

---

1. [2004] 2 All ER 1070, [2004] 1 WLR 2657, [2004] 2 Cr App R 395.

18 May 2004. LORD WOOLF CJ gave the following direction at the sitting of the court:

1–7390 CONTENTS

1–7391

Part I: Introduction

Scope

I.1. I.1.1 This direction shall have effect in magistrates courts, the Crown Court, the Administrative Court and the Court of Appeal (Criminal Division) where the court, in the exercise of its discretion, considers an award of costs in criminal proceedings or deals with criminal defence service funded work and recovery of defence costs orders. The provisions in this practice direction will take effect from 18 May 2004.

The power to award costs

I.2. I.2.1 The powers enabling the court to award costs in criminal proceedings are primarily contained in Pt II of the Prosecution of Offences Act 1985 (ss 16, 17 and 18) (POA 1985), the Access to Justice Act 1999 (in relation to funded clients) and in regulations made under those Acts including the Costs in Criminal Cases (General) Regulations 1986, SI 1986/1335 (as amended). References in this direction are to the POA 1985 and those regulations unless otherwise stated. Schedule 1 sets out details of the relevant regulations.

I.2.2 Section 16 of the Act makes provision for the award of defence costs out of central funds. Section 17 provides for an award of costs to a private prosecutor out of central funds. Section 18 gives power to order a convicted defendant or unsuccessful appellant to pay costs to the prosecutor. Section 19(1) of the Act and reg 3 of the 1986 regulations provide for awards of costs between parties and s 19A provides for the court to disallow or order a legal or other representative of a party to the proceedings to meet wasted costs.

I.2.3 The Supreme Court also has the power under its inherent jurisdiction over officers of the court to order a solicitor personally to pay costs thrown away. It may also give directions relating to CDS funded costs and recovery of defence costs orders.

Extent of orders for costs from central funds

I.3. I.3.1 Where a court orders that the costs of a defendant, appellant or private prosecutor should be paid from central funds, the order will be for such amount as the court considers sufficient reasonably to compensate the party for expenses incurred by him in the proceedings. This will include the costs incurred in the proceedings in the lower courts unless for good reason the court directs that such costs are not included in the order, but it cannot include expenses incurred which do not directly relate to the proceedings themselves, such as loss of earnings. Where the party in whose favour the costs order is made is CDS-funded, he will only recover his personal costs (see s 21(4A)(*a*)). Schedule 2 sets out the extent of availability of costs from central funds and the relevant statutory authority.

Amount of costs to be paid

I.4. I.4.1 Except where the court has directed, in an order for costs out of central funds, that only a specified sum shall be paid, the amount of costs to be paid shall be determined by the appropriate officer of the court. The court may however order the disallowance of costs out of central funds not properly incurred or direct the determining officer to consider whether or not specific items have been properly incurred. The court may also make observations regarding CDS funded costs. The procedures to be followed when such circumstances arise are set out in this direction.

I.4.2 Where the court orders an offender to pay costs to the prosecutor, orders one party to pay costs to another party, disallows or orders a legal or other representative to meet any wasted costs, the order for costs must specify the sum to be paid or disallowed.

I.4.3 Where the court is required to specify the amount of costs to be paid it cannot delegate the decision. Wherever practicable those instructing advocates should provide the advocate with details of costs incurred at each stage in the proceedings. The court may however require the appropriate officer of the court to make inquiries to inform the court as to the costs incurred and may adjourn the proceedings for inquiries to be made if necessary. Special provisions apply in relation to recovery of defence costs orders as to which see Pt XI, below.

1-7392

PART II: DEFENCE COSTS FROM CENTRAL FUNDS

In a magistrates' court

II.1

II.1.1 Where an information laid before a justice of the peace charging a person with an offence is not proceeded with, a magistrates' court inquiring into an indictable offence as examining justices determines not to commit the accused for trial, or a magistrates' court dealing summarily with an offence dismisses the information, the court may make a defendant's costs order. An order under s 16 of the Act may also be made in relation to breach of bind-over proceedings in a magistrates' court or the Crown Court (see reg 14(4) of 1986 regulations). As is the case with the Crown Court (see below) such an order should normally be made unless there are positive reasons for not doing so. For example, where the defendant's own conduct has brought suspicion on himself and has misled the prosecution into thinking that the case against him was stronger than it was, the defendant can be left to pay his own costs. In the case of a partial acquittal the court may make a part order (details are at paras II.2.1 and II.2.2, below).

II.1.2 Whether to make such an award is a matter in the discretion of the court in the light of the circumstances of each particular case.

In the Crown Court

II.2. II.2.1 Where a person is not tried for an offence for which he has been indicted, or in respect of which proceedings against him have been sent for trial or transferred for trial, or has been acquitted on any count in the indictment, the court may make a defendant's costs order in his favour. Such an order should normally be made whether or not an order for costs between the parties is made, unless there are positive reasons for not doing so. For example, where the defendant's own conduct has brought suspicion on himself and has misled the prosecution into thinking that the case against him was stronger than it was, the defendant can be left to pay his own costs. The court when declining to make a costs order should explain, in open court, that the reason for not making an order does not involve any suggestion that the defendant is guilty of any criminal conduct but the order is refused because of the positive reason that should be identified.

II.2.2 Where a person is convicted of some count(s) in the indictment and acquitted on other(s) the court may exercise its discretion to make a defendant's costs order but may order that only part of the costs incurred be paid. The court should make whatever order seems just having regard to the relative importance of the two charges and the conduct of the parties generally. Where the court considers that it would be inappropriate that the defendant should recover all of the costs properly incurred, the amount must be specified in the order.

II.2.3 The Crown Court may make a defendant's costs order in favour of a successful appellant (see s 16(3) of the Act).

In the Administrative Court

II.3. II.3.1 The court may make a defendant's costs order on determining proceedings in a criminal cause or matter.

II.4

In the Court of Appeal, Criminal Division

1-7393

PART III: PRIVATE PROSECUTOR'S COSTS FROM CENTRAL FUNDS

III.1. III.1.1 There is no power to order the payment of costs out of central funds of any prosecutor who is a public authority, a person acting on behalf of a public authority, or acting as an official appointed by a public authority as defined in the Act. In the limited number of cases in which a prosecutor's costs may be awarded out of central funds, an application is to be made by the prosecution in each case. An order should be made save where there is good reason for not doing so, for example, where proceedings have been instituted or continued without good cause. This provision applies to proceedings in respect of an indictable offence or proceedings before the Administrative Court in respect of a summary offence. Regulation 14(1) of the 1986 regulations extends it to certain committals for sentence from a magistrates' court.

1-7394

PART IV: COSTS OF WITNESS, INTERPRETER OR MEDICAL EVIDENCE

IV.1. IV.1 The costs of attendance of a witness required by the accused, a private prosecutor or the court, or of an interpreter required because of the accused's lack of English or of an oral report by a medical practitioner are allowed out of central funds unless the court directs otherwise (see s 19(3) of the POA 1985 and reg 16(1) of the 1986 regulations). If, and only if, the court makes such a direction can the expense of the witness be claimed as a disbursement out of CDS funds. A witness includes any person properly attending to give evidence whether or not he gives evidence or is called, but it does not include a character witness unless the court has certified that the interests of justice require his attendance.

IV.2 The Crown Court may order the payment out of central funds of such sums as appear to be sufficient reasonably to compensate any medical practitioner for the expenses, trouble or loss of time properly incurred in preparing and making a report on the mental condition of a person accused of murder (see s 34(5) of the Mental Health (Amendment) Act 1982).

1–7395

PART V: DISALLOWANCE OF COSTS OUT OF CENTRAL FUNDS

V.1. V.1.1 Where the court makes an order for costs out of central funds, it must: (*a*) direct the appropriate authority to disallow the costs incurred in respect of any items if it is plain that those costs were not properly incurred; such costs are not payable under ss 16(6) and 17(1) of the Act, and it may: (*b*) direct the appropriate authority to consider or investigate on determination any items which may have been improperly incurred. Costs not properly incurred include costs in respect of work unreasonably done, eg, if the case has been conducted unreasonably so as to incur unjustified expense, or costs have been wasted by failure to conduct proceedings with reasonable competence and expedition. In a plain case it will usually be more appropriate to make a wasted costs order under s 19A of the Act (see Pt VIII, below). The precise terms of the order for costs and of any direction must be entered in the court record.

V.1.2 Where the court has in mind that a direction in accordance with para V.1.1(*a*) or (*b*) might be given it must inform any party whose costs might be affected, or his legal representative, of the precise terms thereof and give a reasonable opportunity to show cause why no direction should be given.

If a direction is given under para V.1.1(*b*) the court should inform the party concerned of his rights to make representations to the appropriate authority.

V.1.3 The appropriate authority may consult the court on any matter touching upon the allowance or disallowance of costs. It is not appropriate for the court to make a direction under para V.1.1(*a*) when so consulted.

1–7396

PART VI: AWARD OF COSTS AGAINST OFFENDERS AND APPELLANTS

VI.1. VI.1.1 A magistrates' court or the Crown Court may make an order for costs against a person convicted of an offence before it or in dealing with it in respect of certain orders as to sentence specified in reg 14(3) of the 1986 regulations. The Crown Court may make an order against an unsuccessful appellant and against a person committed by a magistrates' court in respect of the proceedings specified in reg 14(1) and (2). The court may make such order payable to the prosecutor as it considers just and reasonable (s 18(1) of the Act).

VI.1.2 In a magistrates' court where the defendant is ordered to pay a sum not exceeding £5 by way of fine, penalty, forfeiture or compensation the court must not make a costs order unless in the particular circumstances of the case it considers it right to do so (s 18(4) of the Act). Where the defendant is under 18 the amount of any costs awarded against him by a magistrates' court shall not exceed the amount of any fine imposed on him (s 18(5)).

VI.1.3 The Court of Appeal Criminal Division may order an unsuccessful appellant to pay costs to such person as may be named in the order. Such costs may include the costs of any transcript obtained for the proceedings in the Court of Appeal (s 18(2), (6) of the Act).

VI.1.4 An order should be made where the court is satisfied that the offender or appellant has the means and the ability to pay.

VI.1.5 The amount must be specified in the order by the court.

VI.1.6 The Administrative Court is not covered by s 18 of the Act but it has complete discretion over all costs between the parties in relation to proceedings before it.

VI.1.7 An order under s 18 of the Act includes Legal Services Commission (LSC)-funded costs (see s 21(4A)(*b*) of the Act).

1–7397

PART VII: AWARD OF COSTS BETWEEN THE PARTIES

Costs incurred as a result of unnecessary or improper act or omission

VII.1. VII.1.1 A magistrates' court, the Crown Court and the Court of Appeal Criminal Division may order the payment of any costs incurred as a result of any unnecessary or improper act or omission by or on behalf of any party to the proceedings as distinct from his legal representative (s 19 of the Act and reg 3 of the 1986 regulations).

VII.1.2 The court must hear the parties and may then order that all or part of the costs so incurred by one party shall be paid to him by the other party.

VII.1.3 Before making such an order the court must take into account any other order as to costs and the order must specify the amount of the costs to be paid. The court is entitled to take such an order into account when making any other order as to costs in the proceedings (see regs 3(2)–(4) of the 1986 regulations). The order can extend to LSC costs incurred on behalf of any party (s 21 (4A)(*b*) of the Act).

VII.1.4 In a magistrates' court no order may be made which requires a convicted person under 17 to pay an amount by way of costs which exceeds the amount of any fine imposed upon him (see reg 3(5) of the 1986 regulations).

VII.1.5 Such an order is appropriate only where the failure is that of the defendant or of the prosecutor. Where the failure is that of the legal representative(s) Pts VIII and IX (below) apply.

Costs in restraint, confiscation or receivership proceedings
VII.2

Award of costs against third parties

VII.3. VII.3.1 The magistrates' court, the Crown Court and the Court of Appeal may make a third-party costs order if there has been serious misconduct (whether or not constituting a contempt of court) by a third party and the court considers it appropriate, having regard to that misconduct, to make a third-party costs order against him. A 'third party costs order' is an order as to the payment of costs incurred by a party to criminal proceedings by a person who is not a party to those proceedings (the third party) (see s 19B of the POA 1985 as inserted by s 93 of the Courts Act 2003).

VII.3.2 The Lord Chancellor may make regulations: (*a*) specifying types of conduct in respect of which a third party costs order may not be made; (*b*) allowing the making of a third-party costs order at any time; (*c*) making provision for any other order as to costs which has been made in respect of the proceedings to be varied on, or taken account of in, the making of a third-party costs order; (*d*) making provision for account to be taken of any third-party costs order in the making of any other order as to costs in respect of the proceedings.

VII.3.4 Regulations will provide that the third party may appeal to the Crown Court against a third-party costs order made by a magistrates' court and to the Court of Appeal against a third-party costs order made by the Crown Court.

VII.3.5 These provisions came into force on 1 February 2004.

1-7398

PART VIII: COSTS AGAINST LEGAL REPRESENTATIVES—WASTED COSTS

VIII.1. VIII.1.1 Section 19A of the Act allows a magistrates' court, the Crown Court or the Court of Appeal Criminal Division to disallow or order the legal or other representative to meet the whole or any part of the wasted costs. The order can be made against any person exercising a right of audience or a right to conduct litigation (in the sense of acting for a party to the proceedings). 'Wasted costs' are costs incurred by a party (which includes an LSC-funded party) as a result of any improper, unreasonable or negligent act or omission on the part of any representative or his employee, or which, in the light of any such act or omission occurring after they were incurred, the court considers it unreasonable to expect that party to pay (s 19A(3) of the POA 1985; s 89(8) of the Proceeds of Crime Act 2002).

VIII.1.2 The judge has a much greater and more direct responsibility for costs in criminal proceedings than in civil and should keep the question of costs in the forefront of his mind at every stage of the case and ought to be prepared to take the initiative himself without any prompting from the parties.

VIII.1.3 Regulation 3B of the 1986 regulations requires the court to specify the amount of the wasted costs and before making the order to allow the legal or other representative and any party to the proceedings to make representations. In making the order the court must take into account any other orders for costs and must take the wasted costs order into account when making any other order as to costs. The court should also give reasons for making the order and must notify any interested party (which includes the CDS fund and central funds determining authorities) of the order and the amount.

VIII.1.4 Judges contemplating making a wasted costs order should bear in mind the guidance given by the Court of Appeal in *Re a barrister (wasted costs order)(No 1 of 1991)*[1992] 3 All ER 429, [1993] QB 293. The guidance, which is set out below, is to be considered together with all the statutory and other rules and recommendations set out by Parliament and in this practice direction: (i) There is a clear need for any judge or court intending to exercise the wasted costs jurisdiction to formulate carefully and concisely the complaint and grounds upon which such an order may be sought. These measures are draconian and, as in contempt proceedings, the grounds must be clear and particular. (ii) Where necessary a transcript of the relevant part of the proceedings under discussion should be available and in accordance with the rules a transcript of any wasted cost hearing must be made. (iii) A defendant involved in a case where such proceedings are contemplated should be present if, after discussion with counsel, it is thought that his interest may be affected and he should certainly be present and represented if the matter might affect the course of his trial. Regulation 3B(2) of the Costs in Criminal Cases (General) (Amendment) Regulations 1991, SI 1991/789 furthermore requires that before a wasted costs order is made 'the court shall allow the legal or other representative and any party to the proceedings to make representations'. There may be cases where it may be appropriate for counsel for the Crown to be present. (iv) A three-stage test or approach is recommended when a wasted costs order is contemplated: (*a*) Has there been an improper, unreasonable or negligent act or omission? (*b*) As a result have any costs been incurred by a party? (*c*) If the answers to (*a*) and (*b*) are 'yes', should the court exercise its discretion to disallow or order the representative to meet the whole or any part of the relevant costs, and if so what specific sum is involved? (v) It is inappropriate to propose any settlement that the representative might forego fees. The complaint should be formally stated by the judge and the representative invited to make his own comments. After any other party has been heard the judge should give his formal ruling. Discursive conservations may be unfair and should certainly not take place. (vi) The judge must specify the sum to be allowed or ordered. Alternatively the relevant available procedure should be substituted should it be impossible to fix the sum (see para VIII.1.7, below).

VIII.1.5 The Court of Appeal has given further guidance in *Re P (a barrister)* [2001] EWCA Crim 1728, [2002] 1 Cr App R 207 (Court of Appeal) as follows: (i) The primary object is not to punish but to compensate, albeit as the order is sought against a non-party, it can from that perspective be regarded as penal. (ii) The jurisdiction is a summary jurisdiction to be exercised by the court which has 'tried the case in the course of which the misconduct was committed'. (iii) Fairness is assured if the lawyer alleged to be at fault has sufficient notice of the complaint made against him and a proper opportunity to respond to it. (iv) Because of the penal element a mere mistake is not sufficient to justify an order there must be a more serious error. (v) Although the trial judge can decline to consider an application in respect of costs, for example on the ground that he or she is personally embarrassed by an appearance of bias, it will only be in exceptional circumstances that it will be appropriate to pass the matter to another judge, and the fact that, in the proper exercise of his judicial function, a judge has expressed views in relation to the conduct of a lawyer against whom an order is sought, does not of itself normally constitute bias or the appearance of bias so as to necessitate a transfer. (vi) If the allegation is one of serious misconduct or crime the standard of proof will be higher but otherwise it will be the normal civil standard of proof.

VIII.1.6 Though the court cannot delegate its decision to the appropriate authority, it may require the appropriate officer of the court to make inquiries and inform the court as to the likely amount of costs incurred.

VIII.1.7 The court may postpone the making of a wasted costs order to the end of the case if it appears more appropriate to do so, for example, because the likely amount is not readily available, there is a possibility of conflict between the legal representatives as to the apportionment of blame, or the legal representative concerned is unable to make full representations because of a possible conflict with the duty to the client.

VIII.1.8 A wasted costs order should normally be made regardless of the fact that the client of the legal representative concerned is CDS-funded. However where the court is minded to disallow substantial costs out of the CDS fund, it may, instead of making a wasted costs order, make observations to the determining authority that work may have been unreasonably done (see para X.1.1, below). This practice should only be adopted where the extent and amount of the costs wasted is not entirely clear.

The Administrative Court

VIII.2

1–7399

PART IX: AWARDS OF COSTS AGAINST SOLICITORS UNDER THE COURTS INHERENT JURISDICTION

1–7400

PART X: CDS-FUNDED COSTS

1–7401

PART XI: RECOVERY OF DEFENCE COSTS ORDERS

1–7402

PART XII: ADVICE ON APPEAL TO THE COURT OF APPEAL CRIMINAL DIVISION

1–7403

PART XIII: APPEALS TO A COSTS JUDGE AND TO THE HIGH COURT PURSUANT TO THE COSTS IN CRIMINAL CASES (GENERAL) REGULATIONS 1986, THE LEGAL AID IN CRIMINAL AND CARE PROCEEDINGS (COSTS) REGULATIONS 1989, THE CROWN COURT RULES 1982 AND THE CRIMINAL DEFENCE SERVICE (FUNDING) ORDER 2001

1–7404

PART XIV: VAT

XIV.1. XIV.1.1 Every taxable person as defined by the Value Added Tax Act 1994 must be registered and in general terms (subject to the exceptions set out in the Act) whenever a taxable person supplies goods or services in the United Kingdom in the course of business a liability to Value Added Tax (VAT) arises.

XIV.1.2 Responsibility for making a charge to VAT in a proper case and for accounting to HM Customs & Excise for the proper amount of VAT is totally that of the registered person concerned or the person required to be registered.

XIV.1.3 The following directions will apply to all bills of costs lodged for determination or assessment after the date hereof.

VAT registration number

XIV.2. XIV.2.1 The number allocated by HM Customs and Excise to every person registered under the Act (except a government department) must appear in a prominent place at the head of every bill of costs, fee sheet, account or voucher on which VAT is being included as part of a claim for costs.

Action before taxation

XIV.3. XIV.3.1 VAT should not be included in a claim for costs in a between-the-parties bill of costs if the receiving party is able to recover the VAT as input tax. Where the receiving party is able to obtain credit from HM Customs and Excise for a proportion of the VAT as input tax only that proportion which is not eligible for credit should be claimed in the bill.

XIV.3.2 The responsibility for ensuring that VAT is claimed in a between-the-parties bill of costs only when the receiving party is unable to recover the VAT or a proportion thereof as input tax, is upon the receiving party. On an assessment of costs payable out of public funds the costs officer or determining officer as the case may be must continue to satisfy himself as to the tax position.

XIV.3.3 Where there is a dispute as to whether VAT is properly claimed in a between-the-parties bill of costs the receiving party must provide a certificate signed by the solicitors or the auditors of the receiving party in the form in Sch 4. Where the receiving party is a litigant in person who is claiming VAT, reference should be made by him to HM Customs and Excise and whenever possible a statement to similar effect produced on assessment.

XIV.3.4 Where there is a dispute as to whether any service in respect of which a charge is proposed to be made in the bill is zero rated or exempt, reference should be made to HM Customs and Excise and wherever possible the view of HM Customs and Excise obtained and made known on assessment. In the case of a between the parties bill such application should be made by the receiving party. In the case of a bill from a solicitor to his own client such application should be made by the client.

Form of bill of costs where VAT is included as part of the costs claimed

Form of bill of costs where VAT rate changes

XIV.4. XIV.4.1 Where there is a change in the rate of VAT, suppliers of goods and services are entitled by s 88(1) and (2) of the 1994 Act in most circumstances to elect whether the new or the old rate of VAT should apply to a supply where the basic and actual tax points span a period during which there has been a change in VAT rates.

XIV.4.2 It will be assumed, unless a contrary indication is given in writing, that an election to take advantage of the provisions mentioned in para XIV.4.1, above, and to charge VAT at the lower rate has been made. In any case in which an election to charge at the lower rate is not made, such a decision must be justified in accordance with the principles of assessment which are applicable to the basis upon which the costs are ordered to be assessed.

Apportionment

XIV.5. XIV.5.1 All bills of costs, fees and disbursements on which VAT is included must be divided into separate parts so as to show work done before, on and after the date or dates from which any change in the rate of VAT takes effect. Where a lump sum charge is made for work which spans a period during which there has been a change in VAT rates, and paras XIV.4.1 and XIV.4.2, above, do not apply, reference should be made to paras 30.9 and 30.10 of HM Customs and Excise Notice 700 (April 2002 edition) (or any revised edition of that notice), a copy of which is in the possession of every registered trader. If necessary, the lump sum should be apportioned.

Disbursements

XIV.6. XIV.6.1 VAT attributable to any disbursement eg an expert's report, must (except in the case of a between-the-parties bill where VAT is not claimed) be shown as a separate item in the receipt or voucher.

XIV.6.2 (1) Petty (or general) disbursements such as postage, fares etc which are normally treated as part of a solicitor's overheads and included in his profit costs should be charged with VAT even though they bear no tax when the solicitor incurs them. The costs of travel by public transport on a specific journey for a particular client where it forms part of the service rendered by a solicitor to his client eg charged in his bill of costs attract VAT. (2) With effect from 3 January 1978 VAT is added to sheriff's fees (see the Sheriffs' Fees (Amendment No 2) Order 1977, SI 1977/2111).

XIV.6.3 Reference is made to the criteria set out in the VAT Guide (HM Customs and Excise Notice 700 (April 2002 edn) para 25.1, or any revised edition of that notice), as to expenses which are not subject to VAT. Charges for the cost of travel by public transport, postage, telephone calls and telegraphic transfers where these form part of the service rendered by the solicitor to his client are examples of charges which do not satisfy these criteria and are thus liable to VAT at the standard rate.

CDS funding

XIV.7. XIV.7.1 VAT will be payable in respect of every supply made pursuant to a criminal contract or otherwise with the benefit of CDS Funding where it is made by a taxable person and the assisted person belongs in the UK or other member state of the European Union and is a private individual or receives the supply for non-business purposes. The place where a person belongs is determined by s 9 of the 1994 Act.

Tax invoice

XIV.8. XIV.8.1 Where costs are payable out of the LSC fund or central funds pursuant to any authority the tax invoice in the case of counsel will consist of his fee note and in the case of a solicitor his bill of costs as determined or assessed together with the payment advice supplied by the court as to the fees allowed on determination or assessment.

Appeal

XIV.9. XIV.9.1 Where the fees or costs as determined or assessed are varied on appeal the VAT charged will be amended as appropriate by the costs officer or determining officer as the case may be.

Vouchers

XIV.10. XIV.10.1 Where receipted accounts for disbursements made by the solicitor or his client are retained as tax invoices a photostat copy of any such receipted account may be produced and will be accepted as sufficient evidence of payment when disbursements are vouched.

Solicitors and other litigants acting in person

XIV.11. XIV.11.1 Where a litigant acts in litigation on his own behalf he is not treated for the purposes of VAT as having supplied services and therefore no VAT is chargeable on that litigant's between-the-parties bill of costs unless VAT has been charged on disbursements when the normal rules will apply.

XIV.11.2 Similarly, where a solicitor acts in litigation on his own behalf even on a matter arising out of his practice he is not treated for the purposes of VAT as having supplied services and therefore no VAT is chargeable on the bill of that solicitor.

XIV.11.3 Consequently where such a bill as is described in the preceding two paragraphs is presented for agreement, determination or assessment VAT should not be claimed and will not be allowed on determination or assessment unless tax has been paid on disbursements.

Government departments

XIV.12. XIV.12.1 On an assessment between the parties where costs are being paid to a government department in respect of services rendered by its legal staff, VAT should not be added since such services do not attract VAT.

1–7405

PART XV: REVOCATIONS

Discharge of Fines by Unpaid Work (Pilot Schemes) Order 2004
(SI 2004/2198 as amended by SI 2005/563 and 617 and 2006/502)

1–7406   **1.**   This Order may be cited as the Discharge of Fines by Unpaid Work (Pilot Schemes) Order 2004 and shall come into force on 21st September 2004.

1–7407   **2.**   Schedule 6 to the Courts Act 2003 (Discharge of Fines by Unpaid Work) is to have effect in relation to the local justice areas specified in the Schedule to this Order for the period beginning on 21st September 2004 and ending on 31st March 2007.

1–7408

SCHEDULE
PILOT SCHEME AREAS

Local Justice Areas in Cambridgeshire:
Peterborough
Huntingdon
Wisbech
Local Justice Areas in South Yorkshire:
Sheffield
Barnsley
Local Justice Areas in Cheshire:
Halton
Warrington
Local Justice Areas in Cumbria:
Kendal (South Lakeland)
Barrow (Furness and District)
Local Justice Areas in Devon and Cornwall:
South Devon
Central Devon
East Cornwall
West Cornwall
Local Justice Areas in Gloucestershire:
Gloucester
Stroud
Forest of Dean

Penalties for Disorderly Behaviour (Amendment etc) Order 2004[1]
(SI 2004/3166)

1–7410   **1. Citation, commencement and interpretation.**   (1) This Order may be cited as the Penalties for Disorderly Behaviour (Amendment of Minimum Age) Order 2004 and shall come into force on the twenty fourth day after the day on which it is made.

(2) In this Order—

"chief officer of police" in relation to any penalty notice means the chief officer of police for the police area in which the offence to which the notice relates is alleged to have been committed or, if the penalty notice was given by a member of the British Transport Police, the Chief Constable of the British Transport Police;

"guardian" means a person who has for the time being the care of a young penalty recipient and includes a local authority who have parental responsibility for a young penalty recipient who is in their care or is provided with accommodation by them in the exercise of any social services functions;

"local authority" and "parental responsibility" have the same meanings as in the Children Act 1989;

"social services functions" in relation to a local authority has the meaning given by section 1A of the Local Authority Social Services Act 1970;

"young penalty recipient" means a person under the age of 16 who is given a penalty notice;

"the 2001 Act" means the Criminal Justice and Police Act 2001.

---

1. Made by the Secretary of State, in exercise of the powers conferred upon him by s 2(6), (7) and (9) of the Criminal Justice and Police Act 2001.

1–7411 2. Amendment of section 2 of the Criminal Justice and Police Act 2001. In section 2(1) of the 2001 Act, for "16" there is substituted "10".

1–7412 3. Notification of parent or guardian. (1) The chief officer of police must notify such parent or guardian of a young penalty recipient as he thinks fit of the giving of the penalty notice concerned.

(2) A notification under paragraph (1) must be in writing and must include a copy of the penalty notice.

(3) A notification under paragraph (1) may be served—

(a) by giving it to the parent or guardian personally; or

(b) by sending it to the parent or guardian at his usual or last-known address by first-class post.

(4) A notification under paragraph (1) must be served before the end of the period of 28 days beginning with the date on which the penalty notice was given.

(5) Where a notification under paragraph (1) is sent to the parent or guardian by first-class post, service shall be deemed to have been effected on the second day after posting.

1–7413 4. Re-issue of notification. (1) This article applies if a notification is served under article 3(1) and—

(a) the chief officer of police decides that the notification should have been served on some other parent or guardian of the young penalty recipient; or

(b) the chief officer of police discovers that the person on whom the notification was served is not a parent or guardian of the young penalty recipient.

(2) The chief officer of police may cancel the original notification at any time before the end of the period of 21 days beginning with the date on which it is served.

(3) If the chief officer of police cancels the original notification under paragraph (2), he must—

(a) as soon as reasonably practicable inform the recipient of the original notification in writing that the original notification has been cancelled; and

(b) notify such other person who is a parent or guardian of the young penalty recipient as he thinks fit of the giving of the penalty notice.

(4) A notification under paragraph (3)(b) must be served before the end of the period of 14 days beginning with the date on which the original notification was cancelled.

(5) Paragraphs (2), (3) and (5) of article 3 apply to a notification under paragraph (3)(b) as they apply to a notification under article 3(1).

1–7414 5. Liability of parent or guardian to pay penalty. Where a parent or guardian of a young penalty recipient is notified—

(a) under article 3(1) of the giving of a penalty notice and the notification is not cancelled under article 4(2); or

(b) under article 4(3)(b) of the giving of a penalty notice,

that parent or guardian is liable to pay the penalty under the notice.

1–7415 6. Modifications of the Criminal Justice and Police Act 2001. (1) In its application to a young penalty recipient, Chapter 1 of Part 1 of the 2001 Act is to have effect with the following modifications and those modifications are to be construed in accordance with this Order.

(2) Section 4(5) is to have effect as if for "against A as a fine" there were substituted "as a fine against the parent or guardian of A who has been notified of the giving of the penalty notice under article 3(1) or 4(3)(b) of the Penalties for Disorderly Behaviour (Amendment of Minimum Age) Order 2004".

(3) Section 5(1) is to have effect as if for "beginning with the date on which the notice was given" there were substituted "beginning with the date on which notification under article 3(1) of the Penalties for Disorderly Behaviour (Amendment of Minimum Age) Order 2004 was served on the parent or guardian of the person to whom the penalty notice was given or, if a notification under article 3(1) of that Order is cancelled under article 4(2) of that Order, beginning with the date on which notification under article 4(3)(b) of that Order was served on the parent or guardian of the person to whom the penalty notice was given".

(4) Section 7(1) is to have effect as if for "a person to whom a penalty notice is given" there were substituted "a parent or guardian who has been notified of the giving of a penalty notice under article 3(1) or 4(3)(*b*) of the Penalties for Disorderly Behaviour (Amendment of Minimum Age) Order 2004".

(5) Section 10 is to have effect as if for subsection (2) there were substituted—

"(2) Subsection (3) applies if, in any proceedings, the defaulter claims that—

(*a*) he is not a parent or guardian of the person to whom the penalty notice concerned was issued;

(*b*) he was not properly notified of the giving of the penalty notice concerned under article 3(1) or 4(3)(*b*) of the Penalties for Disorderly Behaviour (Amendment of Minimum Age) Order 2004."

(6) Section 10(4) is to have effect as if for "that he was the recipient of the penalty notice" there were substituted "to be incorrect".

Criminal Procedure Rules 2005[1]

(SI 2005/384 as amended by SI 2006/353 and 2636 and SI 2007/699)

1. Made by the Criminal Procedure Rule Committee in accordance with s 69 of the Courts Act 2003.

1–7420

ARRANGEMENT OF RULES

1–7421

PART 1
THE OVERRIDING OBJECTIVE

1.1. The overriding objective. (1) The overriding objective of this new code is that criminal cases be dealt with justly.

(2) Dealing with a criminal case justly includes—

(a) acquitting the innocent and convicting the guilty;

(b) dealing with the prosecution and the defence fairly;

(c) recognising the rights of a defendant, particularly those under Article 6 of the European Convention on Human Rights;

(d) respecting the interests of witnesses, victims and jurors and keeping them informed of the progress of the case;

(e) dealing with the case efficiently and expeditiously;

(f) ensuring that appropriate information is available to the court when bail and sentence are considered; and

(g) dealing with the case in ways that take into account—

(i) the gravity of the offence alleged,

(ii) the complexity of what is in issue,
(iii) the severity of the consequences for the defendant and others affected, and
(iv) the needs of other cases.

1.2. The duty of the participants in a criminal case. (1) Each participant, in the conduct of each case, must—

(a) prepare and conduct the case in accordance with the overriding objective;
(b) comply with these Rules, practice directions and directions made by the court; and
(c) at once inform the court and all parties of any significant failure (whether or not that participant is responsible for that failure) to take any procedural step required by these Rules, any practice direction or any direction of the court. A failure is significant if it might hinder the court in furthering the overriding objective.

(2) Anyone involved in any way with a criminal case is a participant in its conduct for the purposes of this rule.

1.3. The application by the court of the overriding objective. The court must further the overriding objective in particular when—

(a) exercising any power given to it by legislation (including these Rules);
(b) applying any practice direction; or
(c) interpreting any rule or practice direction.

1-7422

Part 2
Understanding and Applying the Rules

2.1. When the Rules apply. (1) In general, the Criminal Procedure Rules apply—

(a) in all criminal cases in magistrates' courts and in the Crown Court; and
(b) in all cases in the criminal division of the Court of Appeal.

(2) If a rule applies only in one or two of those courts, the rule makes that clear.
(3) The Rules apply on and after 4th April, 2005, but do not affect any right or duty existing under the rules of court revoked by the coming into force of these Rules.
(4) The rules in Part 33 apply in all cases in which the defendant is charged on or after 6 November 2006 and in other cases if the court so orders.
(5) The rules in Part 14 apply in cases in which one of the events listed in sub-paragraphs (a) to (d) of rule 14.1(1) takes place on or after 2nd April 2007. In other cases the rules of court replaced by those rules apply.
(6) The rules in Part 28 apply in cases in which an application under rule 28.3 is made on or after 2nd April 2007. In other cases the rules replaced by those rules apply.

2.2. Definitions. (1) In these Rules, unless the context makes it clear that something different is meant:

"court" means a tribunal with jurisdiction over criminal cases. It includes a judge, recorder, District Judge (Magistrates' Courts), lay justice and, when exercising their judicial powers, the Registrar of Criminal Appeals, a justices' clerk or assistant clerk;
"court officer" means the appropriate member of the staff of a court; and
"Practice Direction" means the Lord Chief Justice's Consolidated Criminal Practice Direction[1], as amended.

(2) Definitions of some other expressions are in the rules in which they apply.

2.3. References to Acts of Parliament and to Statutory Instruments. In these Rules, where a rule refers to an Act of Parliament or to subordinate legislation by title and year, subsequent references to that Act or to that legislation in the rule are shortened: so, for example, after a reference to the Criminal Procedure and Investigations Act 1996 that Act is called "the 1996 Act"; and after a reference to the Criminal Procedure and Investigations Act 1996 (Defence Disclosure Time Limits) Regulations 1997 those Regulations are called "the 1997 Regulations".

2.4. The glossary. The glossary at the end of the Rules is a guide to the meaning of certain legal expressions used in them.

---

1. See para **1-6970**, ante.

1-7423

Part 3
Case Management

3.1. The scope of this Part. This Part applies to the management of each case in a magistrates' court and in the Crown Court (including an appeal to the Crown Court) until the conclusion of that case.

3.2. The duty of the court.　(1) The court must further the overriding objective by actively managing the case.

(2) Active case management includes—

(a)　the early identification of the real issues;

(b)　the early identification of the needs of witnesses;

(c)　achieving certainty as to what must be done, by whom, and when, in particular by the early setting of a timetable for the progress of the case;

(d)　monitoring the progress of the case and compliance with directions;

(e)　ensuring that evidence, whether disputed or not, is presented in the shortest and clearest way;

(f)　discouraging delay, dealing with as many aspects of the case as possible on the same occasion, and avoiding unnecessary hearings;

(g)　encouraging the participants to co-operate in the progression of the case; and

(h)　making use of technology.

(3) The court must actively manage the case by giving any direction appropriate to the needs of that case as early as possible.

3.3. The duty of the parties.　Each party must—

(a)　actively assist the court in fulfilling its duty under rule 3.2, without or if necessary with a direction; and

(b)　apply for a direction if needed to further the overriding objective.

3.4. Case progression officers and their duties.　(1) At the beginning of the case each party must, unless the court otherwise directs—

(a)　nominate an individual responsible for progressing that case; and

(b)　tell other parties and the court who he is and how to contact him.

(2) In fulfilling its duty under rule 3.2, the court must where appropriate—

(a)　nominate a court officer responsible for progressing the case; and

(b)　make sure the parties know who he is and how to contact him.

(3) In this Part a person nominated under this rule is called a case progression officer.

(4) A case progression officer must—

(a)　monitor compliance with directions;

(b)　make sure that the court is kept informed of events that may affect the progress of that case;

(c)　make sure that he can be contacted promptly about the case during ordinary business hours;

(d)　act promptly and reasonably in response to communications about the case; and

(e)　if he will be unavailable, appoint a substitute to fulfil his duties and inform the other case progression officers.

3.5. The court's case management powers.　(1) In fulfilling its duty under rule 3.2 the court may give any direction and take any step actively to manage a case unless that direction or step would be inconsistent with legislation, including these Rules.

(2) In particular, the court may—

(a)　nominate a judge, magistrate, justices' clerk or assistant to a justices' clerk to manage the case;

(b)　give a direction on its own initiative or on application by a party;

(c)　ask or allow a party to propose a direction;

(d)　for the purpose of giving directions, receive applications and representations by letter, by telephone or by any other means of electronic communication, and conduct a hearing by such means;

(e)　give a direction without a hearing;

(f)　fix, postpone, bring forward, extend or cancel a hearing;

(g)　shorten or extend (even after it has expired) a time limit fixed by a direction;

(h)　require that issues in the case should be determined separately, and decide in what order they will be determined; and

(i)　specify the consequences of failing to comply with a direction.

(3) A magistrates' court may give a direction that will apply in the Crown Court if the case is to continue there.

(4) The Crown Court may give a direction that will apply in a magistrates' court if the case is to continue there.

(5) Any power to give a direction under this Part includes a power to vary or revoke that direction.

3.6. Application to vary a direction.　(1) A party may apply to vary a direction if—

(a)　the court gave it without a hearing;

(b)　the court gave it at a hearing in his absence; or

(c)　circumstances have changed.

(2) A party who applies to vary a direction must—

(a)　apply as soon as practicable after he becomes aware of the grounds for doing so; and

(b) give as much notice to the other parties as the nature and urgency of his application permits.

3.7. Agreement to vary a time limit fixed by a direction. (1) The parties may agree to vary a time limit fixed by a direction, but only if—

   (a) the variation will not—

     (i) affect the date of any hearing that has been fixed, or

     (ii) significantly affect the progress of the case in any other way;

   (b) the court has not prohibited variation by agreement; and

   (c) the court's case progression officer is promptly informed.

(2) The court's case progression officer must refer the agreement to the court if he doubts the condition in paragraph (1)(a) is satisfied.

3.8. Case preparation and progression. (1) At every hearing, if a case cannot be concluded there and then the court must give directions so that it can be concluded at the next hearing or as soon as possible after that.

(2) At every hearing the court must, where relevant—

   (a) if the defendant is absent, decide whether to proceed nonetheless;

   (b) take the defendant's plea (unless already done) or if no plea can be taken then find out whether the defendant is likely to plead guilty or not guilty;

   (c) set, follow or revise a timetable for the progress of the case, which may include a timetable for any hearing including the trial or (in the Crown Court) the appeal;

   (d) in giving directions, ensure continuity in relation to the court and to the parties' representatives where that is appropriate and practicable; and

   (e) where a direction has not been complied with, find out why, identify who was responsible, and take appropriate action.

3.9. Readiness for trial or appeal. (1) This rule applies to a party's preparation for trial or (in the Crown Court) appeal, and in this rule and rule 3.10 trial includes any hearing at which evidence will be introduced.

(2) In fulfilling his duty under rule 3.3, each party must—

   (a) comply with directions given by the court;

   (b) take every reasonable step to make sure his witnesses will attend when they are needed;

   (c) make appropriate arrangements to present any written or other material; and

   (d) promptly inform the court and the other parties of anything that may—

     (i) affect the date or duration of the trial or appeal, or

     (ii) significantly affect the progress of the case in any other way.

(3) The court may require a party to give a certificate of readiness.

3.10. Conduct of a trial or an appeal. In order to manage the trial or (in the Crown Court) appeal, the court may require a party to identify—

   (a) which witnesses he intends to give oral evidence;

   (b) the order in which he intends those witnesses to give their evidence;

   (c) whether he requires an order compelling the attendance of a witness;

   (d) what arrangements, if any, he proposes to facilitate the giving of evidence by a witness;

   (e) what arrangements, if any, he proposes to facilitate the participation of any other person, including the defendant;

   (f) what written evidence he intends to introduce;

   (g) what other material, if any, he intends to make available to the court in the presentation of the case;

   (h) whether he intends to raise any point of law that could affect the conduct of the trial or appeal; and

   (i) what timetable he proposes and expects to follow.

3.11. Case management forms and records. (1) The case management forms set out in the Practice Direction must be used, and where there is no form then no specific formality is required.

(2) The court must make available to the parties a record of directions given.

1–7424

PART 4
SERVICE OF DOCUMENTS

4.1. When this Part applies. The rules in this Part apply to the service of every document in a case to which these Rules apply, subject to any special rules in other legislation (including other Parts of these Rules) or in the Practice Direction.

4.2. Methods of service. A document may[1] be served by any of the methods described in rules 4.3 to 4.6 (subject to rule 4.7), or in rule 4.8.

4.3. Service by handing over a document. (1) A document may be served[2] on—

   (a) an individual by handing it to him or her;

(b) a corporation by handing it to a person holding a senior position in that corporation;
(c) an individual or corporation who is legally represented in the case by handing it to that representative;
(d) the prosecution by handing it to the prosecutor or to the prosecution representative;
(e) the court officer by handing it to a court officer with authority to accept it at the relevant court office; and
(f) the Registrar of Criminal Appeals by handing it to a court officer with authority to accept it at the Criminal Appeal Office.

(2) If an individual is 17 or under, a copy of a document served under paragraph (1)(a) must be handed to his or her parent, or another appropriate adult, unless no such person is readily available.

4.4. Service by leaving or posting a document. (1) A document may be served by leaving it at the appropriate address for service under this rule or by sending it to that address by first class post or by the equivalent of first class post.
(2) The address for service under this rule on—

(a) an individual is an address where it is reasonably believed that he or she will receive it;
(b) a corporation is its principal office in England and Wales, and if there is no readily identifiable principal office then any place in England and Wales where it carries on its activities or business;
(c) an individual or corporation who is legally represented in the case is that representative's office;
(d) the prosecution is the prosecutor's office;
(e) the court officer is the relevant court office; and
(f) the Registrar of Criminal Appeals is the Criminal Appeal Office, Royal Courts of Justice, Strand, London WC2A 2LL.

4.5. Service through a document exchange. A document may be served by document exchange (DX) where—

(a) the writing paper of the person to be served gives a DX box number; and
(b) that person has not refused to accept service by DX.

4.6. Service by fax, e-mail or other electronic means. (1) A document may be served by fax, e-mail or other electronic means where—

(a) the person to be served has given a fax, e-mail or other electronic address; and
(b) that person has not refused to accept service by that means.

(2) Where a document is served under this rule the person serving it need not provide a paper copy as well.

4.7. Documents that must be served only by handing them over, leaving or posting them. (1) The documents listed in this rule may be served—

(a) on an individual only under rule 4.3(1)(a) or rule 4.4(1) and (2)(a); and
(b) on a corporation only under rule 4.3(1)(b) or rule 4.4(1) and (2)(b).

(2) Those documents are—

(a) a summons, requisition or witness summons;
(b) notice of an order under section 25 of the Road Traffic Offenders Act 1988;
(c) a notice of registration under section 71(6) of that Act;
(d) a notice of discontinuance under section 23(4) of the Prosecution of Offences Act 1985;
(e) notice under rule 37.3(1) of the date, time and place to which the trial of an information has been adjourned, where it was adjourned in the defendant's absence;
(f) a notice of fine or forfeited recognizance required by rule 52.1(1);
(g) notice under section 86 of the Magistrates' Courts Act 1980 of a revised date to attend a means inquiry;
(h) notice of a hearing to review the postponement of the issue of a warrant of commitment under section 77(6) of the Magistrates' Courts Act 1980;
(i) a copy of the minute of a magistrates' court order required by rule 52.7(1);
(j) an invitation to make observations or attend a hearing under rule 53.1(2) on the review of a compensation order under section 133 of the Powers of Criminal Courts (Sentencing) Act 2000;
(k) any notice or document served under Part 19.

4.8. Service by person in custody. (1) A person in custody may serve a document by handing it to the custodian addressed to the person to be served.
(2) The custodian must—

(a) endorse it with the time and date of receipt;
(b) record its receipt; and
(c) forward it promptly to the addressee.

4.9. Service by another method. (1) The court may allow service of a document by a method other than those described in rules 4.3 to 4.6 and in rule 4.8.
(2) An order allowing service by another method must specify—

(*a*)   the method to be used; and
(*b*)   the date on which the document will be served.

4.10. Date of service.   (1) A document served under rule 4.3 or rule 4.8 is served on the day it is handed over.

(2) Unless something different is shown, a document served on a person by any other method is served—

(*a*)   in the case of a document left at an address, on the next business day after the day on which it was left;

(*b*)   in the case of a document sent by first class post or by the equivalent of first class post, on the second business day after the day on which it was posted or despatched;

(*c*)   in the case of a document served by document exchange, on the second business day after the day on which it was left at the addressee's DX or at a correspondent DX;

(*d*)   in the case of a document transmitted by fax, e-mail or other electronic means, on the next business day after it was transmitted; and

(*e*)   in any case, on the day on which the addressee responds to it if that is earlier.

(3) Unless something different is shown, a document produced by a court computer system is to be taken as having been sent by first class post or by the equivalent of first class post to the addressee on the business day after the day on which it was produced.

(4) In this Part "business day" means any day except Saturday, Sunday, Christmas Day, Boxing Day, Good Friday, Easter Monday or a bank holiday.

(5) Where a document is served on or by the court officer, "business day" does not include a day on which the court office is closed.

4.11. Proof of service.   The person who serves a document may prove that by signing a certificate[1] explaining how and when it was served[2].

4.12. Court's power to give directions about service.   (1) The court may specify the time as well as the date by which a document must be—

(*a*)   served under rule 4.3 or rule 4.8; or
(*b*)   transmitted by fax, e-mail or other electronic means if it is served under rule 4.6.

(2) The court may treat a document as served if the addressee responds to it even if it was not served in accordance with the rules in this Part.

---

1. For manner of proving service, see r 4.11, post.
2. The use of the word "may" connotes that the prosecution has a choice of one of the methods of fulfilling the obligation it has of serving the summons; the court has no power to require the prosecution to choose one of the three methods in the rule (*R (on the application of Durham County Council) v North Durham Justices* [2004] EWHC 1073 (Admin), 168 JP 269).
3. A summons requiring a person charged with an offence to appear before a court in England or Wales may be served on him without endorsement in Scotland or Northern Ireland (Criminal Law Act 1977, s 39, ante).

1–7425

PART 5
FORMS

5.1. Forms.   The forms set out in the Practice Direction shall be used as appropriate in connection with the rules to which they apply.

5.2. Magistrates' court forms in Welsh.   (1) Subject to the provisions of this rule, the Welsh language forms set out in the Practice Direction or forms to the like effect may be used in connection with proceedings in magistrates' courts in Wales.

(2) Both a Welsh form and an English form may be used in the same document.

(3) When only a Welsh form set out in the Practice Direction accompanying this rule, or only the corresponding English form, is used in connection with proceedings in magistrates' courts in Wales, there shall be added the following words in Welsh and English:

"Darperir y ddogfen hon yn Gymraeg/Saesneg os bydd arnoch ei heisiau. Dylech wneud cais yn ddi-oed i (Glerc Llys yr Ynadon) (rhodder yma'r cyfeiriad) . . . .
This document will be provided in Welsh/English if you require it. You should apply immediately to (the Justices' Clerk to the Magistrates' Court) (address). . . . .
If a person other than a justices' clerk is responsible for sending or giving the document, insert that person's name."

(4) The justices' clerk or other person responsible for the service of a form bearing the additional words set out in paragraph (3) above shall, if any person upon whom the form is served so requests, provide him with the corresponding English or Welsh form.

(5) In this rule any reference to serving a document shall include the sending, giving or other delivery of it.

(6) In the case of a discrepancy between an English and Welsh text the English text shall prevail.

5.3. Signature of magistrates' court forms by justices' clerk.   (1) Subject to paragraph (2) below, where any form prescribed by these Rules contains provision for signature by a justice of the peace only, the form shall have effect as if it contained provision in the alternative for signature by the justices' clerk.

(2) This rule shall not apply to any form of information, complaint, statutory declaration or warrant, other than a warrant of commitment or of distress.

(3) In this rule where a signature is required on a form or warrant other than an arrest, remand or commitment warrant, an electronic signature incorporated into the document will satisfy this requirement.

1-7426

PART 6
COURT RECORDS

6.1. Magistrates' court register. (1) A magistrates' court officer shall keep a register in which there shall be entered—

(a) a minute or memorandum[1] of every adjudication[2] of the court; and

(b) a minute or memorandum of every other proceeding or thing required by these Rules or any other enactment to be so entered.

(2) The register may be stored in electronic form on the court computer system and entries in the register shall include, where relevant, the following particulars—

(a) the name of the informant, complainant or applicant;
(b) the name and date of birth (if known) of the defendant or respondent;
(c) the nature of offence, matter of complaint or details of the application;
(d) the date of offence or matter of complaint;
(e) the plea or consent to order; and
(f) the minute of adjudication.

(3) Particulars of any entry relating to a decision about bail or the reasons for any such decisions or the particulars of any certificate granted under section 5(6A) of the Bail Act 1976 may be made in a book separate from that in which the entry recording the decision itself is made, but any such separate book shall be regarded as forming part of the register.

(4) Where, by virtue of section 128(3A) of the Magistrates' Courts Act 1980, an accused gives his consent to the hearing and determination in his absence of any application for his remand on an adjournment of the case under sections 5, 10(1) or 18(4) of that Act, the court shall cause the consent of the accused, and the date on which it was notified to the court, to be entered in the register.

(5) Where any consent mentioned in paragraph (4) is withdrawn, the court shall cause the withdrawal of the consent and the date on which it was notified to the court to be entered in the register.

(6) On the summary trial of an information the accused's plea shall be entered in the register.

(7) Where a court tries any person summarily in any case in which he may be tried summarily only with his consent, the court shall cause his consent to be entered in the register and, if the consent is signified by a person representing him in his absence, the court shall cause that fact also to be entered in the register.

(8) Where a person is charged before a magistrates' court with an offence triable either way the court shall cause the entry in the register to show whether he was present when the proceedings for determining the mode of trial were conducted and, if they were conducted in his absence, whether they were so conducted by virtue of section 18(3) of the 1980 Act (disorderly conduct on his part) or by virtue of section 23(1) of that Act (consent signified by person representing him).

(9) In any case to which section 22 of the 1980 Act (certain offences triable either way to be tried summarily if value involved is small) applies, the court shall cause its decision as to the value involved or, as the case may be, the fact that it is unable to reach such a decision to be entered in the register.

(10) Where a court has power under section 53(3) of the 1980 Act to make an order with the consent of the defendant without hearing evidence, the court shall cause any consent of the defendant to the making of the order to be entered in the register.

(11) In the case of conviction or dismissal, the register shall clearly show the nature of the offence of which the accused is convicted or, as the case may be, the nature of the offence charged in the information that is dismissed.

(12) An entry of a conviction in the register shall state the date of the offence.

(13) Where a court is required under section 130(3) of the Powers of Criminal Courts (Sentencing) Act 2000 to give reasons for not making a compensation order the court shall cause the reasons given to be entered in the register.

(14) Where a court passes a custodial sentence, the court shall cause a statement of whether it obtained and considered a pre-sentence report before passing sentence to be entered in the register.

(15) Every register shall be open to inspection during reasonable hours by any justice of the peace, or any person authorised in that behalf by a justice of the peace or the Lord Chancellor.

(16) A record of summary conviction or order made on complaint required for an appeal or other legal purpose may be in the form of certified extract from the court register.

(17) Such part of the register as relates to proceedings in a youth court may be recorded separately and stored in electronic form on the court computer system.

---

1. For admissibility in evidence of a certified extract from the register, see 6.4, *post*.
2. It is not the entry in the register which makes or contributes to the making of the conviction or order. That

has already been done (*R v Manchester Justices, ex p Lever* [1937] 2 KB 96, [1937] 3 All ER 4, 101 JP 407). The clerk's duty relating to entries in the register was considered in *R v Huntingdon Justices, ex p Simpkin and Coombes* (1959) 123 JP 166; a verbal inaccuracy in an entry in the register may be corrected by the clerk within the scope of his duty. If the court convicts of part only of the offence charged, e.g. theft of one only of a number of articles charged, the adjudication should show what the defendant has been convicted of (*Machent v Quinn* [1970] 2 All ER 255, 134 JP 501).

6.2. Registration of endorsement of licence under section 57 of the Road Traffic Offenders Act 1988. A magistrates' court officer or justices' clerk who, as a fixed penalty clerk within the meaning of section 69(4) of the Road Traffic Offenders Act 1988, endorses a driving licence under section 57(3) or (4) of that Act (endorsement of licences without hearing) shall register the particulars of the endorsement in a book separate from the register kept under rule 6.1 but any such book shall be regarded as forming part of the register.

6.3. Registration of certificate issued under section 70 of the Road Traffic Offenders Act 1988. A magistrates' court officer shall register receipt of a registration certificate issued under section 70 of the Road Traffic Offenders Act 1988 (sum payable in default of fixed penalty to be enforced as a fine) in a book separate from the register kept under rule 6.1 but any such book shall be regarded as forming part of the register.

6.4. Proof of proceedings in magistrates' courts. The register of a magistrates' court, or an extract from the register certified by the magistrates' court officer as a true extract, shall be admissible in any legal proceedings as evidence of the proceedings of the court entered in the register.

1–7427

PART 7
COMMENCING PROCEEDINGS IN MAGISTRATES' COURTS

7.1. Information and complaint. (1) An information may be laid or complaint made by the prosecutor[1] or complainant in person or by his counsel or solicitor or other person authorised in that behalf.

(2) Subject to any provision of the Magistrates' Courts Act 1980 and any other enactment, an information or complaint need not be in writing or on oath.

---

1. Unless the information is required by statute to be laid by any particular person any person may lay it where the offence is not an individual grievance, but a matter of public policy and utility, and concerns the public morals (*Cole v Coulton* (1860) 24 JP 596; *Back v Holmes* (1887) 51 JP 693; *Giebler v Manning* [1906] 1 KB 709, 70 JP 181; *Lake v Smith* (1911) 76 JP 71). In modern language the test may be restated by identifying a requirement that the prosecution establish a public interest and benefit, as opposed to a purely private interest in criminal proceedings. Accordingly, prosecutions are commonly brought by bodies to protect copyright and animal welfare. Also, subject to vires, bus or train companies which seek to protect their staff from violence are entitled to commence a prosecution in the event of the police declining to do so. Where a chief executive of a company was alleged to have been assaulted by a shareholder at the annual general meeting, the company, subject to its having relevant authority to do so was entitled to institute criminal proceedings (which it did through an individual informant), there being sufficient public interest in the management of company meetings of this type (*R (Gladstone plc) v Manchester City Magistrates' Court* [2004] EWHC 2806 (Admin), [2005] 2 All ER 56, [2005] 1 WLR 1987). In the case of a police prosecution, the information should be laid by the officer reporting the offence, the chief constable, or some other member of the force who is authorised to lay an information (*Rubin v DPP* [1989] 2 All ER 241, 153 JP 289, DC).

7.2. Statement of offence. (1) Every written charge issued by a public prosecutor and every information, summons or warrant laid in or issued by a magistrates' court shall be sufficient if it—

(a) describes the offence with which the accused is charged, or of which he is convicted, in ordinary language avoiding as far as possible the use of technical[1] terms; and
(b) gives such particulars[2] as may be necessary to provide reasonable information about the nature of the charge.

(2) It shall not be necessary for any of those documents to—

(a) state all the elements[3] of the offence; or
(b) negative[4] any matter upon which the accused may rely[5].

(3) If the offence charged is one created by or under any Act, the description of the offence shall contain a reference to the section[6] of the Act, or, as the case may be, the rule, order, regulation, bylaw or other instrument creating the offence.

---

1. Such expressions as "knowingly" and "wilfully" are technical and need not appear in the particulars (*Lomas v Peek* [1947] 2 All ER 574, 112 JP 12); but see *Waring v Wheatley* (1951) 115 JP 630, where the omission of the word "wilful" from the information invalidated a conviction.
2. Such particulars as may be necessary for giving reasonable information as to the nature of the charge must be included; if the particulars given are insufficient, the court should require better particulars to be given. See *Robertson v Rosenberg* (1951) 115 JP 128; *Atterton v Browne* [1945] KB 122, 109 JP 25; *Simmons v Fowler* (1950) 48 LGR 623; and *Stephenson v Johnson* [1954] 1 All ER 369, 118 JP 199; and *R v Gregory* [1972] 2 All ER 861, 136 JP 569. Application for reasonable particulars of the nature of a charge may be made at any time after the charge is preferred (*R v Aylesbury Justices, ex p Wisbey* [1965] 1 All ER 602, 129 JP 175, *Dacre Son & Hartley Ltd v North Yorkshire Trading Standards* [2004] EWHC 2783 (Admin), 169 JP 59).
A person charged with an offence under s 1 of the Protection of Animals Act 1911 is entitled to know what act or omission is alleged to have caused the unnecessary suffering, and if a charge is specified in this way

problems of duplicity will often fall away since it will be obvious whether separate acts or omissions constituting separate offences are being charged; however, the absence of such particularity does not render the proceedings a nullity or a conviction unsafe provided the requisite information is given to the defendant in good time for him/her to be able fairly to meet the case against him/her: *Nash v Birmingham Crown Court* [2005] EWHC Admin 338, (2005) 169 JP 157.

3. For instance, it need not negative any statutory exception, exemption, proviso, excuse or qualification (see Magistrates' Courts Act, 1980, s 101, ante).

4. Where a statute requires for instance, that a business shall not be carried on without registration, it is unnecessary for the negative clause to be specified in the information, and, even if specified, it need not be proved by the prosecution (*Buckman v Button* [1943] KB 405, [1943] 2 All ER 82, 107 JP 153; *R v Oliver* [1944] KB 68, [1943] 2 All ER 800, 108 JP 30). The onus of proving that a licensed person holds a proper licence rests with him (*Apothecaries' Co v Bentley* (1824) Ry & M 159; *Turner v Johnston* (1886) 51 JP 22; *Williams v Russell* (1933) 97 JP 128; *R v Scott* (1921) 86 JP 69); but the proof that such a person allowed prostitutes to remain on his premises longer than necessary to obtain refreshments is upon the informant (*Miller v Dudley Justices* (1898) 46 WR 606). See *Buckman v Button* [1943] KB 405, [1943] 2 All ER 82, 107 JP 152; *R v Oliver* [1944] KB 63, [1943] 2 All ER 800, 108 JP 30.

5. Such as an exception, exemption, proviso, excuse or qualification and precisely the same meaning as exception or proviso can be conferred by the word "unless" (*Roche v Willis* (1934) 98 JP 227, [1934] All ER Rep 613).

6. The omission to state the section, or to state it incorrectly, may be fatal (*Atterton v Browne* [1945] KB 122, 109 JP 25; *Hunter v Coombs* [1962] 1 All ER 904, 126 JP 300).

7.3. Information or written charge to be for one offence only.
(1) Subject to any Act passed after[1] 2nd October 1848, a magistrates' court shall not proceed to the trial of an information or written charge that charges more than one[2] offence.

(2) Nothing in this rule shall prohibit two or more informations or written charges being set out in one document[3].

(3) If, notwithstanding paragraph (1), it appears to the court at any stage in the trial of an information that the information or written charge charges more than one offence, the court shall call upon the prosecutor to elect on which offence he desires the court to proceed, whereupon the offence or offences on which the prosecutor does not wish to proceed shall be struck out of the information or written charge; and the court shall then proceed to try that information or written charge afresh.

(4) If a prosecutor who is called upon to make an election under paragraph (3) fails to do so, the court shall dismiss the information or written charge.

(5) Where, after an offence has or offences have been struck out of the information or written charge under paragraph (3), the accused requests an adjournment and it appears to the court that he has been unfairly prejudiced, it shall adjourn the trial.

---

1. See Children and Young Persons Act, 1933, s 14(2), in PART V: YOUTH COURTS, post, for an exception to this rule in a post-1848 statute.

2. All persons alleged to have joined committing the same offence may be named in the same information; and it will be for the court to determine whether the cases shall be heard together or separately (see *R v Cridland* (1857) 21 JP 404; *Ex p Brown* (1852) 16 JP 69; *R v Lipscombe, ex p Biggins* (1861) 25 JP 726; *R v Littlechild* (1871) LR 6 QB 293, 35 JP 661). And see *R v Wood, ex p Farwell* (1918) 82 JP 268, and *R v Chambers* (1939) 83 Sol Jo 439.

Where a penalty was prescribed for emitting smoke or steam from an engine on the highway, justices were right in overruling an objection to an information that it disclosed two offences, in charging that smoke *and* steam were emitted (*Davis v Loach* (1886) 51 JP 118). But where a penalty was created under bye-laws of a tramway company for emitting smoke or steam so as to constitute a reasonable ground of complaint "to the public *or* the passengers", a conviction was bad for not specifying against which class the offence had been committed (*Cottrell v Lempriere* (1890) 24 QBD 634, 54 JP 583). Sending forth black smoke from several unconnected chimneys on the same premises may be charged as one complaint as creating only one offence (*Barnes v Norris* (1876) 41 JP 150). Where appellant was convicted for neglecting to comply with a notice specifying certain matters in respect of which the laying out *or* construction of certain streets was in contravention of bye-laws relating thereto, the conviction was quashed for uncertainty and for including two offences (*R v Slater, ex p Bowler* (1903) 67 JP 299). See also *R v Wells, etc Justices, ex p Clifford* (1904) 68 JP 392; *R v Surrey Justices, ex p Witherick* [1932] 1 KB 450, 95 JP 219; *Jones v Sherwood* [1942] 1 KB 127, 106 JP 65; *Bastin v Davies* [1950] 2 KB 579, [1950] 1 All ER 1095, 114 JP 302, and cf *R v Jones, ex p Thomas* [1921] 1 KB 632, 85 JP 112.

A charge of being in charge of a motor vehicle "while under the influence of drink or drug" is not bad for uncertainty, for the essence of the offence is being in charge of the motor vehicle while in a state of self-induced incapacity (*Thompson v Knights* [1947] KB 336, [1947] 1 All ER 112, 111 JP 43): applied in *R v Clow* [1965] 1 QB 598, [1963] 2 All ER 216, 127 JP 371, where it was held that an indictment charging driving "at a speed and in a manner dangerous to the public" was not bad for duplicity; and in *Newton Ltd v Smith, Standerwick Ltd v Smith* [1962] 2 QB 278, [1962] 2 All ER 19, 126 JP 324, in which a charge that a defendant "wilfully or negligently" failed to observe conditions was not bad for duplicity. See also, on a similar point, *Ware v Fox; Fox v Dingley* [1967] 1 All ER 100, 131 JP 113; *Jemmison v Priddle* [1972] 1 QB 489, [1972] 1 All ER 539, 136 JP 230, and as to several counts on an indictment, *R v Wilson* (1979) 69 Cr App Rep 83. The earlier cases were distinguished in *Mallon v Allon* [1964] 1 QB 385, [1963] 3 All ER 843, 128 JP 81, where it was held that a requirement that "no person shall be admitted to or allowed to remain on certain premises" referred to two separate acts or incidents. An information charging the offences conjunctively, ie "did admit and allow to remain" was bad for duplicity. If an enactment forbids the doing of act A or B, it creates two offences; but if it creates a duty to do either act A or B, to constitute an offence there must be a failure to do both acts (*Field v Hopkinson* [1944] KB 42, 108 JP 21); cf *North v Gerrish* (1959) 123 JP 313, in Part VII: Transport title Road Traffic, post.

In breach proceedings, where two separate kinds of breach are alleged – for example, failing to keep in touch and failing to reside where directed – there is a need to lay separate informations in respect of each of the kinds of breach, though within each kind there is no need to allege each of the instances separately (*S v Doncaster Youth Offending Team* [2003] EWHC 1128 (Admin), (2003) 167 JP 381).

3. A single summons may set out separately several informations or complaints (see r 7.7, post).

7.4. Duty of court officer receiving statutory declaration under section 14(1) of the Magistrates' Courts Act 1980. Where a magistrates' court officer receives a statutory declaration which complies with section 14(1) of the Magistrates' Courts Act 1980 (accused did not know of proceedings), he shall—

(*a*)   note the receipt of the declaration in the register; and

(*b*)   inform the prosecutor and, if the prosecutor is not a constable, the chief officer of police of the receipt of the declaration.

7.5. Notice of order under section 25 of the Road Traffic Offenders Act 1988. (1) Where a magistrates' court makes an order under section 25 of the Road Traffic Offenders Act 1988 that an offender shall inform the court of his date of birth or sex or both and the offender is not present in court, the court officer shall serve notice in writing of the order on the offender.

(2) *Revoked.*

7.6. Statutory declaration under section 72 and 73 of the Road Traffic Offenders Act 1988. Where a magistrates' court officer receives a statutory declaration under section 72 and 73 of the Road Traffic Offenders Act 1988 (fixed penalty notice or notice fixed to vehicle invalid) he shall send a copy of it to the appropriate chief officer of police.

7.7. Form of summons or requisition. (1) A summons or requisition must state the name of the justice[1] or public prosecutor responsible for issuing it.

(2) A summons or requisition requiring a person to appear before a magistrates' court to answer to an information, written charge or complaint shall state shortly the matter of the information, written charge or complaint and shall state the time and place at which the defendant is required by the summons or requisition to appear.

(3) A single summons or requisition may be issued against a person in respect of several informations, written charges or complaints; but the summons or requisition shall state the matter of each information, written charge or complaint separately and shall have effect as several summonses or requisitions, each issued in respect of one information, written charge or complaint.

(4) In this rule where a signature is required, an electronic signature incorporated into the document shall satisfy this requirement.

---

1. Or justices' clerk acting under the Justices' Clerks Rules 2005, post. For the justices' clerk's power to delegate his functions under the Justices' Clerks Rules 2005 to a person appointed by a magistrates' courts committee to assist him, see the 2005 Rules, r 3, this Part, ante. Although a summons must be authorised individually by a justice or by the justices' clerk (or a person appointed to assist him) and must bear the signature of the person who issued it the task can be lightened by batches of informations or complaints having similar characteristics being assembled and placed before a single individual, and the task of stating the name can be performed vicariously by the use of a facsimile signature on a rubber stamp.

7.8. Summons or warrant to secure attendance of a parent or guardian at a youth court. Where a child or young person is charged with an offence, or is for any other reason brought before a court, a summons or warrant may be issued by a court to enforce the attendance of a parent or guardian under section 34A of the Children and Young Persons Act 1933, in the same manner as if an information were laid upon which a summons or warrant could be issued against a defendant under the Magistrates' Courts Act 1980 and a summons to the child or young person may include a summons to the parent or guardian to enforce his attendance for the said purpose.

7.9. Magistrates' court officer to have copies of documents sent to accused under section 12(1) of the Magistrates' Courts Act 1980. Where the prosecutor notifies a magistrates' court officer that the documents mentioned in section 12(1)(*a*) and 12(1)(*b*) of the Magistrates' Courts Act 1980 have been served upon the accused, the prosecutor shall send to the court officer a copy of the document mentioned in section 12(1)(*b*).

1–7428

PART 8
OBJECTING TO THE DISCONTINUANCE OF PROCEEDINGS IN A MAGISTRATES' COURT

8.1. Time for objecting. The period within which an accused person may give notice under section 23(7) of the Prosecution of Offences Act 1985 that he wants proceedings against him to continue is 35 days from the date when the proceedings were discontinued under that section.

8.2. Form of notice. Notice under section 23(3), (4) or (7) of the Prosecution of Offences Act 1985 shall be given in writing and shall contain sufficient particulars to identify the particular offence to which it relates.

8.3. Duty of Director of Public Prosecutions. On giving notice under section 23(3) or (4) of the Prosecution of Offences Act 1985 the Director of Public Prosecutions shall inform any person who is detaining the accused person for the offence in relation to which the notice is given that he has given such notice and of the effect of the notice.

8.4. Duty of magistrates' court. On being given notice under section 23(3) of the Prosecution of

Offences Act 1985 in relation to an offence for which the accused person has been granted bail by a court, a magistrates' court officer shall inform—

(*a*) any sureties of the accused; and
(*b*) any persons responsible for securing the accused's compliance with any conditions of bail

that he has been given such notice and of the effect of the notice.

1–7429

PART 9
PRE-TRIAL HEARINGS IN MAGISTRATES' COURTS[1]

1. There are currently no rules in this Part.

1–7430

PART 10
COMMITTAL FOR TRIAL

10.1. Restrictions on reports of committal proceedings. (1) Except in a case where evidence is, with the consent of the accused, to be tendered in his absence under section 4(4)(*b*) of the Magistrates' Courts Act 1980 (absence caused by ill health), a magistrates' court acting as examining justices shall before admitting any evidence explain to the accused the restrictions on reports of committal proceedings imposed by section 8 of that Act and inform him of his right to apply[1] to the court for an order removing those restrictions.

(2) Where a magistrates' court has made an order under section 8(2) of the 1980 Act removing restrictions on the reports of committal proceedings, such order shall be entered in the register.

(3) Where the court adjourns any such proceedings to another day, the court shall, at the beginning of any adjourned hearing, state that the order has been made.

1. If an accused is absent through ill-health, it will be open to his legal representative to make such an application.

10.2. Committal for trial without consideration of the evidence. (1) This rule[1] applies to committal proceedings where the accused has a solicitor acting for him in the case and where the court has been informed that all the evidence falls within section 5A(2) of the Magistrates' Courts Act 1980.

(2) A magistrates' court inquiring into an offence in committal proceedings to which this rule applies shall cause the charge to be written down, if this has not already been done, and read to the accused and shall then ascertain whether he wishes to submit that there is insufficient evidence to put him on trial by jury for the offence with which he is charged.

(3) If the court is satisfied that the accused or, as the case may be, each of the accused does not wish to make such a submission as is referred to in paragraph (2) it shall, after receiving any written evidence falling within section 5A(3) of the 1980 Act, determine whether or not to commit the accused for trial without consideration of the evidence, and where it determines not to so commit the accused it shall proceed in accordance with rule 10.3.

1. This rule prescribes the procedure to be adopted when a defendant is committed for trial without consideration of the evidence in accordance with s 6 of the Magistrates' Courts Act 1980.

10.3. Consideration of evidence at committal proceedings. (1) This rule does not apply to committal proceedings where under section 6(2) of the Magistrates' Courts Act of 1980 a magistrates' court commits a person for trial without consideration of the evidence[1].

(2) A magistrates' court inquiring into an offence as examining justices, having ascertained—

(*a*) that the accused has no legal representative acting for him in the case; or
(*b*) that the accused's legal representative has requested the court to consider a submission that there is insufficient evidence to put the accused on trial by jury for the offence with which he is charged, as the case may be,

shall permit the prosecutor to make an opening address to the court, if he so wishes, before any evidence is tendered.

(3) After such opening address, if any, the court shall cause evidence to be tendered in accordance with sections 5B(4), 5C(4), 5D(5) and 5E(3) of the 1980 Act, that is to say by being read out aloud, except where the court otherwise directs or to the extent that it directs that an oral account be given of any of the evidence.

(4) The court may view any exhibits produced before the court and may take possession of them.

(5) After the evidence has been tendered the court shall hear any submission which the accused may wish to make as to whether there is sufficient evidence to put him on trial by jury for any indictable offence.

(6) The court shall permit the prosecutor to make a submission—

(*a*) in reply to any submission made by the accused in pursuance of paragraph (5); or
(*b*) where the accused has not made any such submission but the court is nevertheless minded not to commit him for trial.

(7) After hearing any submission made in pursuance of paragraph (5) or (6) the court shall, unless it decides not to commit the accused for trial, cause the charge to be written down, if this

has not already been done, and, if the accused is not represented by counsel or a solicitor, shall read the charge to him and explain it in ordinary language.

---

1. The relevant rule in such cases is r 6, supra.

10.4. Court's reminder to a defendant of right to object to evidence being read at trial without further proof. A magistrates' court which commits a person for trial shall forthwith remind him of his right to object, by written notification to the prosecutor and the Crown Court within 14 days of being committed unless that court in its discretion permits such an objection to be made outside that period, to a statement or deposition being read as evidence at the trial without oral evidence being given by the person who made the statement or deposition, and without the opportunity to cross-examine that person.

10.5. Material to be sent to court of trial[1]. (1) As soon as practicable after the committal of any person for trial, and in any case within 4 days from the date of his committal (not counting Saturdays, Sundays, Good Friday, Christmas Day or Bank Holidays), the magistrates' court officer shall, subject to the provisions of section 7 of the Prosecution of Offences Act 1985 (which relates to the sending of documents and things to the Director of Public Prosecutions), send to the Crown Court officer—

(a) the information, if it is in writing;

(b)
   (i) the evidence tendered in accordance with section 5A of the Magistrates' Courts Act 1980 and, where any of that evidence consists of a copy of a deposition or documentary exhibit which is in the possession of the court, any such deposition or documentary exhibit, and
   (ii) a certificate to the effect that that evidence was so tendered;

(c) any notification by the prosecutor under section 5D(2) of the 1980 Act regarding the admissibility of a statement under section 23 or 24 of the Criminal Justice Act 1988 (first hand hearsay; business documents);

(d) a copy of the record made in pursuance of section 5 of the Bail Act 1976 relating to the grant or withholding of bail in respect of the accused on the occasion of the committal;

(e) any recognizance entered into by any person as surety for the accused together with a statement of any enlargement thereof under section 129(4) of the 1980 Act;

(f) a list of the exhibits produced in evidence before the justices or treated as so produced[2];

(g) such of the exhibits referred to in paragraph (1)(f) as have been retained by the justices[3];

(h) the names and addresses of any interpreters engaged for the defendant for the purposes of the committal proceedings, together with any telephone numbers at which they can be readily contacted, and details of the languages or dialects in connection with which they have been so engaged;

(i) if the committal was under section 6(2) of the 1980 Act (committal for trial without consideration of the evidence), a statement to that effect;

(j) if the magistrates' court has made an order under section 8(2) of the 1980 Act (removal of restrictions on reports of committal proceedings), a statement to that effect;

(k) the certificate of the examining justices as to the costs of the prosecution under the Costs in Criminal Cases (General) Regulations 1986;

(l) if any person under the age of 18 is concerned in the committal proceedings, a statement whether the magistrates' court has given a direction under section 39 of the Children and Young Persons Act 1933 (prohibition of publication of certain matter in newspapers);

(m) a copy of any representation order previously made in the case;

(n) a copy of any application for a representation order previously made in the case which has been refused; and

(o) any documents relating to an appeal by the prosecution against the granting of bail.

(2) The period of 4 days specified in paragraph (1) may be extended in relation to any committal for so long as the Crown Court officer directs, having regard to the length of any document mentioned in that paragraph or any other relevant circumstances.

---

1. Where a person is charged before a magistrates' court with murder, manslaughter or infanticide or an offence under s 1 of the Road Traffic Act 1988 (causing death by reckless driving) or an offence under s 2(1) of the Suicide Act 1961, consisting of aiding, abetting, counselling or procuring the suicide of another, the justices' chief executive for the magistrates' court shall inform the coroner who is responsible for holding an inquest of the making of the charge and of the result of the proceedings (Coroners Act 1988, s 17, in PART VIII—title CORONERS, post).

2. See s 102 of the Magistrates' Courts Act, 1980.

3. Articles (other than articles produced by a witness subject to a conditional witness order, see para (1)) may have been retained which, by reason of their bulky or perishable nature, would not usefully be sent to the officer of the court of trial, and might well be retained in safe custody by the court: for instance, the bath exhibited in *R v Smith* (1915) 80 JP 31, would be unlikely to be required in advance of the trial. In cases of doubt, we recommend that the proper officer of the court of trial should be invited to say whether he desires a particular exhibit to be sent to him. The court has the responsibility of preserving and retaining exhibits in a criminal case: generally it entrusts the prosecution (1) to take all proper care to preserve the exhibits safe from loss or damage, (2) to co-operate with the defence in order to allow them reasonable access to the exhibits for the purpose of inspection and examination, and (3) to produce the exhibits at the trial. The prosecution may allow exhibits to be sent to a court in another country and need not seek the English court's permission first. The prosecution may need to make an application in respect of exhibits to the Crown Court where they are

deteriorating or there is a dispute with the defence over tests on an exhibit (*R v Lambeth Metropolitan Stipendiary Magistrate, ex p McComb* [1983] QB 551, [1983] 1 All ER 321).

1–7431

PART 11
TRANSFER FOR TRIAL OF SERIOUS FRAUD CASES OR CASES INVOLVING CHILDREN

11.1. Interpretation of this Part. (1) In this Part:

"notice of transfer" means a notice referred to in section 4(1) of the Criminal Justice Act 1987 or section 53(1) of the Criminal Justice Act 1991.

(2) Where this Part requires a document to be given or sent, or a notice to be communicated in writing, it may, with the consent of the addressee, be sent by electronic communication.

(3) Electronic communication means a communication transmitted (whether from one person to another, from one device to another or from a person to a device or vice versa)—

    (a) by means of an electronic communications network (within the meaning of the Communications Act 2003); or

    (b) by other means but while in an electronic form.

11.2. Transfer on bail. (1) Where a person in respect of whom notice of transfer has been given—

    (a) is granted bail under section 5(3) or (7A) of the Criminal Justice Act 1987 by the magistrates' court to which notice of transfer was given; or

    (b) is granted bail under paragraph 2(1) or (7) of Schedule 6 to the Criminal Justice Act 1991 by the magistrates' court to which notice of transfer was given,

the magistrates' court officer shall give notice thereof in writing to the governor of the prison or remand centre to which the said person would have been committed by that court if he had been committed in custody for trial.

(2) Where notice of transfer is given under section 4(1) of the 1987 Act in respect of a corporation the magistrates' court officer shall give notice thereof to the governor of the prison to which would be committed a male over 21 committed by that court in custody for trial.

11.3. Notice where person removed to hospital. Where a transfer direction has been given by the Secretary of State under section 47 or 48 of the Mental Health Act 1983 in respect of a person remanded in custody by a magistrates' court and, before the direction ceases to have effect, notice of transfer is given in respect of that person, the magistrates' court officer shall give notice thereof in writing—

    (a) to the governor of the prison to which that person would have been committed by that court if he had been committed in custody for trial; and

    (b) to the managers of the hospital where he is detained.

11.4. Variation of arrangements for bail. (1) A person who intends to make an application to a magistrates' court under section 3(8) of the Bail Act 1976 as that subsection has effect under section 3(8A) of that Act shall give notice thereof in writing to the magistrates' court officer, and to the designated authority or the defendant, as the case may be, and to any sureties concerned.

(2) Where, on an application referred to in paragraph (1), a magistrates' court varies or imposes any conditions of bail, the magistrates' court officer shall send to the Crown Court officer a copy of the record made in pursuance of section 5 of the 1976 Act relating to such variation or imposition of conditions.

11.5. Documents etc to be sent to Crown Court. As soon as practicable after a magistrates' court to which notice of transfer has been given has discharged the functions reserved to it under section 4(1) of the Criminal Justice Act 1987 or section 53(3) of the Criminal Justice Act 1991, the magistrates' court officer shall send to the Crown Court officer—

    (a) a list of the names, addresses and occupations of the witnesses;

    (b) a copy of the record made in pursuance of section 5 of the Bail Act 1976 relating to the grant of withholding of bail in respect of the accused;

    (c) any recognizance entered into by any person as surety for the accused together with a statement of any enlargement thereof;

    (d) a copy of any representation order previously made in the case; and

    (e) a copy of any application for a representation order previously made in the case which has been refused.

1–7432

PART 12
SENDING FOR TRIAL

12.1. Documents to be sent to the Crown Court. (1) As soon as practicable after any person is sent for trial (pursuant to section 51 of the Crime and Disorder Act 1998), and in any event within 4 days from the date on which he is sent (not counting Saturdays, Sundays, Good Friday, Christmas Day or Bank Holidays), the magistrates' court officer shall, subject to section 7 of the Prosecution of Offences Act 1985 (which relates to the sending of documents and things to the Director of Public Prosecutions), send to the Crown Court officer—

- (a) the information, if it is in writing;
- (b) the notice required by section 51(7) of the 1998 Act;
- (c) a copy of the record made in pursuance of section 5 of the Bail Act 1976 relating to the granting or withholding of bail in respect of the accused on the occasion of the sending;
- (d) any recognizance entered into by any person as surety for the accused together with any enlargement thereof under section 129(4) of the Magistrates' Courts Act 1980;
- (e) the names and addresses of any interpreters engaged for the defendant for the purposes of the appearance in the magistrates' court, together with any telephone numbers at which they can be readily contacted, and details of the languages or dialects in connection with which they have been so engaged;
- (f) if any person under the age of 18 is concerned in the proceedings, a statement whether the magistrates' court has given a direction under section 39 of the Children and Young Persons Act 1933 (prohibition of publication of certain matter in newspapers);
- (g) a copy of any representation order previously made in the case;
- (h) a copy of any application for a representation order previously made in the case which has been refused; and
- (i) any documents relating to an appeal by the prosecution against the granting of bail.

(2) The period of 4 days specified in paragraph (1) may be extended in relation to any sending for trial for so long as the Crown Court officer directs, having regard to any relevant circumstances.

12.2. Time for first appearance of accused sent for trial. A Crown Court officer to whom notice has been given under section 51(7) of the Crime and Disorder Act 1998, shall list the first Crown Court appearance of the person to whom the notice relates in accordance with any directions given by the magistrates' court.

1–7433

PART 13
DISMISSAL OF CHARGES TRANSFERRED OR SENT TO THE CROWN COURT

13.1. Interpretation of this Part. In this Part:

"notice of transfer" means a notice referred to in section 4(1) of the Criminal Justice Act 1987 or section 53(1) of the Criminal Justice Act 1991; and

"the prosecution" means the authority by or on behalf of whom notice of transfer was given under the 1987 or 1991 Acts, or the authority by or on behalf of whom documents were served under paragraph 1 of Schedule 3 to the Crime and Disorder Act 1998.

13.2. Written notice of oral application for dismissal. (1) Where notice of transfer has been given under the Criminal Justice Act 1987 or the Criminal Justice Act 1991, or a person has been sent for trial under the Crime and Disorder Act 1998, and the person concerned proposes to apply orally—

- (a) under section 6(1) of the 1987 Act;
- (b) under paragraph 5(1) of Schedule 6 to the 1991 Act; or
- (c) under paragraph 2(1) of Schedule 3 to the 1998 Act

for any charge in the case to be dismissed, he shall give notice of his intention in writing to the Crown Court officer at the place specified by the notice of transfer under the 1987 or 1991 Acts or the notice given under section 51(7) of the 1998 Act as the proposed place of trial. Notice of intention to make an application under the 1987 or 1991 Acts shall be in the form set out in the Practice Direction.

(2) Notice of intention to make an application shall be given—

- (a) in the case of an application to dismiss charges transferred under the 1987 Act, not later than 28 days after the day on which notice of transfer was given;
- (b) in the case of an application to dismiss charges transferred under the 1991 Act, not later than 14 days after the day on which notice of transfer was given; and
- (c) in the case of an application to dismiss charges sent under the 1998 Act, not later than 14 days after the day on which the documents were served under paragraph 1 of Schedule 3 to that Act,

and a copy of the notice shall be given at the same time to the prosecution and to any person to whom the notice of transfer relates or with whom the applicant for dismissal is jointly charged.

(3) The time for giving notice may be extended, either before or after it expires, by the Crown Court, on an application made in accordance with paragraph (4).

(4) An application for an extension of time for giving notice shall be made in writing to the Crown Court officer, and a copy thereof shall be given at the same time to the prosecution and to any other person to whom the notice of transfer relates or with whom the applicant for dismissal is jointly charged. Such an application made in proceedings under the 1987 or 1991 Acts shall be in the form set out in the Practice Direction.

(5) The Crown Court officer shall give notice in the form set out in the Practice Direction of the judge's decision on an application under paragraph (3)—

- (a) to the applicant for dismissal;
- (b) to the prosecution; and
- (c) to any other person to whom the notice of transfer relates or with whom the applicant for dismissal is jointly charged.

(6) A notice of intention to make an application under section 6(1) of the 1987 Act, paragraph

5(1) of Schedule 6 to the 1991 Act or paragraph 2(1) of Schedule 3 to the 1998 Act shall be accompanied by a copy of any material on which the applicant relies and shall—

(*a*)   specify the charge or charges to which it relates;

(*b*)   state whether the leave of the judge is sought under section 6(3) of the 1987 Act, paragraph 5(4) of Schedule 6 to the 1991 Act or paragraph 2(4) of Schedule 3 to the 1998 Act to adduce oral evidence on the application, indicating what witnesses it is proposed to call at the hearing; and

(*c*)   in the case of a transfer under the 1991 Act, confirm in relation to each such witness that he is not a child to whom paragraph 5(5) of Schedule 6 to that Act applies.

(7)   Where leave is sought from the judge for oral evidence to be given on an application, notice of his decision, indicating what witnesses are to be called if leave is granted, shall be given in writing by the Crown Court officer to the applicant for dismissal, the prosecution and to any other person to whom the notice of transfer relates or with whom the applicant for dismissal is jointly charged. Notice of a decision in proceedings under the 1987 or 1991 Acts shall be in the form set out in the Practice Direction.

(8)   Where an application for dismissal under section 6(1) of the 1987 Act, paragraph 5(1) of Schedule 6 to the 1991 Act or paragraph 2(1) of Schedule 3 to the 1998 Act is to be made orally, the Crown Court officer shall list the application for hearing before a judge of the Crown Court and the prosecution shall be given the opportunity to be represented at the hearing.

13.3. Written application for dismissal.   (1) Application may be made for dismissal under section 6(1) of the Criminal Justice Act 1987, paragraph 5(1) of Schedule 6 to the Criminal Justice Act 1991 or paragraph 2(1) of Schedule 3 to the Crime and Disorder Act 1998 without an oral hearing. Such an application shall be in writing, and in proceedings under the 1987 or 1991 Acts shall be in the form set out in the Practice Direction.

(2)   The application shall be sent to the Crown Court officer and shall be accompanied by a copy of any statement or other document, and identify any article, on which the applicant for dismissal relies.

(3)   A copy of the application and of any accompanying documents shall be given at the same time to the prosecution and to any other person to whom the notice of transfer relates or with whom the applicant for dismissal is jointly charged.

(4)   A written application for dismissal shall be made—

(*a*)   not later than 28 days after the day on which notice of transfer was given under the 1987 Act;

(*b*)   not later than 14 days after the day on which notice of transfer was given under the 1991 Act; or

(*c*)   not later than 14 days after the day on which documents required by paragraph 1 of Schedule 3 to the 1998 Act were served

unless the time for making the application is extended, either before or after it expires, by the Crown Court; and rule 13.2(4) and (5) shall apply for the purposes of this paragraph as if references therein to giving notice of intention to make an oral application were references to making a written application under this rule.

13.4. Prosecution reply.   (1) Not later than seven days from the date of service of notice of intention to apply orally for the dismissal of any charge contained in a notice of transfer or based on documents served under paragraph 1 of Schedule 3 to the Crime and Disorder Act 1998, the prosecution may apply to the Crown Court under section 6(3) of the Criminal Justice Act 1987, paragraph 5(4) of Schedule 6 to the Criminal Justice Act 1991 or paragraph 2(4) of Schedule 3 to the 1998 Act for leave to adduce oral evidence at the hearing of the application, indicating what witnesses it is proposed to call.

(2)   Not later than seven days from the date of receiving a copy of an application for dismissal under rule 13.3, the prosecution may apply to the Crown Court for an oral hearing of the application.

(3)   An application under paragraph (1) or (2) shall be served on the Crown Court officer in writing and, in the case of an application under paragraph (2), shall state whether the leave of the judge is sought to adduce oral evidence and, if so, shall indicate what witnesses it is proposed to call. Where leave is sought to adduce oral evidence under paragraph 5(4) of Schedule 6 to the 1991 Act, the application should confirm in relation to each such witness that he is not a child to whom paragraph 5(5) of that Schedule applies. Such an application in proceedings under the 1987 or 1991 Acts shall be in the form set out in the Practice Direction.

(4)   Notice of the judge's determination upon an application under paragraph (1) or (2), indicating what witnesses (if any) are to be called shall be served in writing by the Crown Court officer on the prosecution, on the applicant for dismissal and on any other party to whom the notice of transfer relates or with whom the applicant for dismissal is jointly charged. Such a notice in proceedings under the 1987 or 1991 Acts shall be in the form set out in the Practice Direction.

(5)   Where, having received the material specified in rule 13.2 or, as the case may be, rule 13.3, the prosecution proposes to adduce in reply thereto any written comments or any further evidence, the prosecution shall serve any such comments, copies of the statements or other documents outlining the evidence of any proposed witnesses, copies of any further documents and, in the case of an application to dismiss charges transferred under the 1991 Act, copies of any video recordings which it is proposed to tender in evidence, on the Crown Court officer not later than 14 days from the date of receiving the said material, and shall at the same time serve

copies thereof on the applicant for dismissal and any other person to whom the notice of transfer relates or with whom the applicant is jointly charged. In the case of a defendant acting in person, copies of video recordings need not be served but shall be made available for viewing by him.

(6) The time for—

(*a*) making an application under paragraph (1) or (2) above; or
(*b*) serving any material on the Crown Court officer under paragraph (5) above

may be extended, either before or after it expires, by the Crown Court, on an application made in accordance with paragraph (7) below.

(7) An application for an extension of time under paragraph (6) above shall be made in writing and shall be served on the Crown Court officer, and a copy thereof shall be served at the same time on to the applicant for dismissal and on any other person to whom the notice of transfer relates or with whom the applicant for dismissal is jointly charged. Such an application in proceedings under the 1987 or 1991 Acts shall be in the form set out in the Practice Direction.

13.5. Determination of applications for dismissal—procedural matters. (1) A judge may grant leave for a witness to give oral evidence on an application for dismissal notwithstanding that notice of intention to call the witness has not been given in accordance with the foregoing provisions of this Part.

(2) Where an application for dismissal is determined otherwise than at an oral hearing, the Crown Court officer shall as soon as practicable, send to all the parties to the case written notice of the outcome of the application. Such a notice in proceedings under the 1987 and 1991 Acts shall be in the form set out in the Practice Direction.

13.6. Service of documents. *Revoked*

1–7434

PART 14
THE INDICTMENT

14.1. Signature and service of indictment. (1) The prosecutor must serve a draft indictment on the Crown Court officer not more than 28 days after—

(*a*) service on the defendant and on the Crown Court officer of copies of the documents containing the evidence on which the charge or charges are based, in a case where the defendant is sent for trial;
(*b*) a High Court judge gives permission to serve a draft indictment;
(*c*) the Court of Appeal orders a retrial; or
(*d*) the committal or transfer of the defendant for trial.

(2) The Crown Court may extend the time limit, even after it has expired.
(3) Unless the Crown Court otherwise directs, the court officer must—

(*a*) sign and date the draft, which then becomes an indictment; and
(*b*) serve a copy of the indictment on all parties.

14.2. Form and content of indictment. (1) An indictment must be in one of the forms set out in the Practice Direction and must contain, in a paragraph called a "count"—

(*a*) a statement of the offence charged that—
   (i) describes the offence in ordinary language, and
   (ii) identifies any legislation that creates it; and
(*b*) such particulars of the conduct constituting the commission of the offence as to make clear what the prosecutor alleges against the defendant.

(2) More than one incident of the commission of the offence may be included in a count if those incidents taken together amount to a course of conduct having regard to the time, place or purpose of commission.

(3) An indictment may contain more than one count if all the offences charged—

(*a*) are founded on the same facts; or
(*b*) form or are a part of a series of offences of the same or a similar character.

(4) The counts must be numbered consecutively.
(5) An indictment may contain—

(*a*) any count charging substantially the same offence as one—
   (i) specified in the notice of the offence or offences for which the defendant was sent for trial,
   (ii) on which the defendant was committed for trial, or
   (iii) specified in the notice of transfer given by the prosecutor; and
(*b*) any other count based on the prosecution evidence already served which the Crown Court may try.

1–7435

PART 15
PREPARATORY HEARINGS IN CASES OF SERIOUS FRAUD AND OTHER COMPLEX, SERIOUS OR LENGTHY CASES IN
THE CROWN COURT

15.1. Application for a preparatory hearing. (1) A party who wants the court to order a preparatory hearing under section 7(2) of the Criminal Justice Act 1987 or under section 29(4) of the Criminal Procedure and Investigations Act 1996 must—

(a) apply in the form set out in the Practice Direction;
(b) include a short explanation of the reasons for applying; and
(c) serve the application on the court officer and all other parties.

(2) A prosecutor who wants the court to order that—

(a) the trial will be conducted without a jury under section 43 or section 44 of the Criminal Justice Act 2003; or
(b) the trial of some of the counts included in the indictment will be conducted without a jury under section 17 of the Domestic Violence, Crime and Victims Act 2004,

must apply under this rule for a preparatory hearing, whether or not the defendant has applied for one.

15.2. Time for applying for a preparatory hearing. (1) A party who applies under rule 15.1 must do so not more than 28 days after—

(a) the committal of the defendant;
(b) the consent to the preferment of a bill of indictment in relation to the case;
(c) the service of a notice of transfer; or
(d) where a person is sent for trial, the service of copies of the documents containing the evidence on which the charge or charges are based.

(2) A prosecutor who applies under rule 15.1 because he wants the court to order a trial without a jury under section 44 of the Criminal Justice Act 2003 (jury tampering) must do so as soon as reasonably practicable where the reasons do not arise until after that time limit has expired.

(3) The court may extend the time limit, even after it has expired.

15.3. Representations concerning an application. (1) A party who wants to make written representations concerning an application made under rule 15.1 must—

(a) do so within 7 days of receiving a copy of that application; and
(b) serve those representations on the court officer and all other parties.

(2) A defendant who wants to oppose an application for an order that the trial will be conducted without a jury under section 43 or section 44 of the Criminal Justice Act 2003 must serve written representations under this rule, including a short explanation of the reasons for opposing that application.

15.4. Determination of an application. (1) Where an application has been made under rule 15.1(2), the court must hold a preparatory hearing[1].

(2) Other applications made under rule 15.1 should normally be determined without a hearing.

(3) The court officer must serve on the parties in the case, in the form set out in the Practice Direction—

(a) notice of the determination of an application made under rule 15.1; and
(b) an order for a preparatory hearing made by the court of its own initiative, including one that the court is required to make.

---

1. The case management powers of the court include the power to deal with matters preliminary to trial exclusively by means of written submissions and to specify the length of such submissions. Defendants should be provided with copies of the submissions as should representatives of the media present at the hearing. The court is not bound to allow oral submissions and is entitled to put a time limit on them: *R v K (Note)* [2006] EWCA Crim 724, [2006] 2 All ER 552, [2006] Crim LR 1012.

15.5. Disclosure of prosecution case. (1) Any disclosure order under section 9 of the Criminal Justice Act 1987, or section 31 of the Criminal Procedure and Investigations Act 1996, must identify any documents that are required to be prepared and served by the prosecutor under that order.

(2) A disclosure order under either of those sections does not require a defendant to disclose who will give evidence, except to the extent that disclosure is required—

(a) by section 6A(2) of the 1996 Act (disclosure of alibi); or
(b) by Part 24 of these Rules (disclosure of expert evidence).

(3) The court officer must serve notice of the order, in the relevant form set out in the Practice Direction, on the parties.

15.6. Service. *Revoked.*

1–7436

PART 16
RESTRICTIONS ON REPORTING AND PUBLIC ACCESS

16.1. Application for a reporting direction under section 46(6) of the Youth Justice and Criminal Evidence Act 1999. (1) An application for a reporting direction made by a party to any criminal proceedings, in relation to a witness in those proceedings, must be made in the form set out in the Practice Direction or orally under rule 16.3.

(2) If an application for a reporting direction is made in writing, the applicant shall send that application to the court officer and copies shall be sent at the same time to every other party to those proceedings.

16.2. Opposing an application for a reporting direction under section 46(6) of the Youth Justice and Criminal Evidence Act 1999. (1) If an application for a reporting direction is made in writing, any party to the proceedings who wishes to oppose that application must notify the applicant and the court officer in writing of his opposition and give reasons for it.

(2) A person opposing an application must state in the written notification whether he disputes that the—

(*a*) witness is eligible for protection under section 46 of the Youth Justice and Criminal Evidence Act 1999; or

(*b*) granting of protection would be likely to improve the quality of the evidence given by the witness or the level of co-operation given by the witness to any party to the proceedings in connection with that party's preparation of its case.

(3) The notification under paragraph (1) must be given within five business days of the date the application was served on him unless an extension of time is granted under rule 16.6.

16.3. Urgent action on an application under section 46(6) of the Youth Justice and Criminal Evidence Act 1999. (1) The court may give a reporting direction under section 46 of the Youth Justice and Criminal Evidence Act 1999 in relation to a witness in those proceedings, notwithstanding that the five business days specified in rule 16.2(3) have not expired if—

(*a*) an application is made to it for the purposes of this rule; and

(*b*) it is satisfied that, due to exceptional circumstances, it is appropriate to do so.

(2) Any party to the proceedings may make the application under paragraph (1) whether or not an application has already been made under rule 16.1.

(3) An application under paragraph (1) may be made orally or in writing.

(4) If an application is made orally, the court may hear and take into account representations made to it by any person who in the court's view has a legitimate interest in the application before it.

(5) The application must specify the exceptional circumstances on which the applicant relies.

16.4. Excepting direction under section 46(9) of the Youth Justice and Criminal Evidence Act 1999. (1) An application for an excepting direction under section 46(9) of the Youth Justice and Criminal Evidence Act 1999 (a direction dispensing with restrictions imposed by a reporting direction) may be made by—

(*a*) any party to those proceedings; or

(*b*) any person who, although not a party to the proceedings, is directly affected by a reporting direction given in relation to a witness in those proceedings.

(2) If an application for an excepting direction is made, the applicant must state why—

(*a*) the effect of a reporting direction imposed places a substantial and unreasonable restriction on the reporting of the proceedings; and

(*b*) it is in the public interest to remove or relax those restrictions.

(3) An application for an excepting direction may be made in writing, pursuant to paragraph (4), at any time after the commencement of the proceedings in the court or orally at a hearing of an application for a reporting direction.

(4) If the application for an excepting direction is made in writing it must be in the form set out in the Practice Direction and the applicant shall send that application to the court officer and copies shall be sent at the same time to every party to those proceedings.

(5) Any person served with a copy of an application for an excepting direction who wishes to oppose it, must notify the applicant and the court officer in writing of his opposition and give reasons for it.

(6) The notification under paragraph (5) must be given within five business days of the date the application was served on him unless an extension of time is granted under rule 16.6.

16.5. Variation or revocation of a reporting or excepting direction under section 46 of the Youth Justice and Criminal Evidence Act 1999. (1) An application for the court to—

(*a*) revoke a reporting direction; or

(*b*) vary or revoke an excepting direction,

may be made to the court at any time after the commencement of the proceedings in the court.

(2) An application under paragraph (1) may be made by a party to the proceedings in which the direction was issued, or by a person who, although not a party to those proceedings, is in the opinion of the court directly affected by the direction.

(3) An application under paragraph (1) must be made in writing and the applicant shall send that application to the officer of the court in which the proceedings commenced, and at the same time copies of the application shall be sent to every party or, as the case may be, every party to the proceedings.

(4) The applicant must set out in his application the reasons why he seeks to have the direction varied or, as the case may be, revoked.

(5) Any person served with a copy of an application who wishes to oppose it, must notify the applicant and the court officer in writing of his opposition and give reasons for it.

(6) The notification under paragraph (5) must be given within five business days of the date the application was served on him unless an extension of time is granted under rule 16.6.

16.6. Application for an extension of time in proceedings under section 46 of the Youth Justice and Criminal Evidence Act 1999. (1) An application may be made in writing to extend the period of time for notification under rule 16.2(3), rule 16.4(6) or rule 16.5(6) before that period has expired.

(2) An application must be accompanied by a statement setting out the reasons why the applicant is unable to give notification within that period.

(3) An application must be sent to the court officer and a copy of the application must be sent at the same time to the applicant.

16.7. Decision of the court on an application under section 46 of the Youth Justice and Criminal Evidence Act 1999.   (1) The court may—

(a)   determine any application made under rules 16.1 and rules 16.3 to 16.6 without a hearing; or

(b)   direct a hearing of any application.

(2) The court officer shall notify all the parties of the court's decision as soon as reasonably practicable.

(3) If a hearing of an application is to take place, the court officer shall notify each party to the proceedings of the time and place of the hearing.

(4) A court may hear and take into account representations made to it by any person who in the court's view has a legitimate interest in the application before it.

16.8. Proceedings sent or transferred to the Crown Court with direction under section 46 of the Youth Justice and Criminal Evidence Act 1999 in force.   Where proceedings in which reporting directions or excepting directions have been ordered are sent or transferred from a magistrates' court to the Crown Court, the magistrates' court officer shall forward copies of all relevant directions to the Crown Court officer at the place to which the proceedings are sent or transferred.

16.9. Hearings in camera and applications under section 46 of the Youth Justice and Criminal Evidence Act 1999.   If in any proceedings, a prosecutor or defendant has served notice under rule 16.10 of his intention to apply for an order that all or part of a trial be held in camera, any application under this Part relating to a witness in those proceedings need not identify the witness by name and date of birth.

16.10. Application to hold a Crown Court trial in camera.   (1) Where a prosecutor or a defendant intends to apply for an order that all or part of a trial be held in camera for reasons of national security or for the protection of the identity of a witness or any other person, he shall not less than 7 days before the date on which the trial is expected to begin serve a notice in writing to that effect on the Crown Court officer and the prosecutor or the defendant as the case may be.

(2) On receiving such notice, the court officer shall forthwith cause a copy thereof to be displayed in a prominent place within the precincts of the Court.

(3) An application by a prosecutor or a defendant who has served such a notice for an order that all or part of a trial be heard in camera shall, unless the Court orders otherwise, be made in camera, after the defendant has been arraigned but before the jury has been sworn and, if such an order is made, the trial shall be adjourned until whichever of the following shall be appropriate—

(a)   24 hours after the making of the order, where no application for leave to appeal from the order is made; or

(b)   after the determination of an application for leave to appeal, where the application is dismissed; or

(c)   after the determination of the appeal, where leave to appeal is granted.

16.11. Crown Court hearings in chambers.   (1) The criminal jurisdiction of the Crown Court specified in the following paragraph may be exercised by a judge of the Crown Court sitting in chambers.

(2) The said jurisdiction is—

(a)   hearing applications for bail;

(b)   issuing a summons or warrant;

(c)   hearing any application relating to procedural matters preliminary or incidental to criminal proceedings in the Crown Court, including applications relating to legal aid;

(d)   jurisdiction under rules 12.2 (listing first appearance of accused sent for trial), 28.3 (application for witness summons), 63.2(5) (extending time for appeal against decision of magistrates' court), and 64.7 (application to state case for consideration of High Court);

(e)   hearing an application under section 41(2) of the Youth Justice and Criminal Evidence Act 1999 (evidence of complainant's previous sexual history);

(f)   hearing applications under section 22(3) of the Prosecution of Offences Act 1985 (extension or further extension of custody time limit imposed by regulations made under section 22(1) of that Act);

(g)   hearing an appeal brought by an accused under section 22(7) of the 1985 Act against a decision of a magistrates' court to extend, or further extend, such a time limit, or brought by the prosecution under section 22(8) of the same Act against a decision of a magistrates' court to refuse to extend, or further extend, such a time limit;

(h)   hearing appeals under section 1 of the Bail (Amendment) Act 1993 (against grant of bail by magistrates' court); and

(i)   hearing appeals under section 16 of the Criminal Justice Act 2003 (against condition of bail imposed by magistrates' court).

PART 17
EXTRADITION

17.1. Refusal to make an order of committal[1]. (1) Where a magistrates' court refuses to make an order of committal in relation to a person in respect of the offence or, as the case may be, any of the offences to which the authority to proceed relates and the state, country or colony seeking the surrender of that person immediately informs the court that it intends to make an application to the court to state a case for the opinion of the High Court, if the magistrates' court makes an order in accordance with section 10(2) of the Extradition Act 1989 releasing that person on bail, the court officer shall forthwith send a copy of that order to the Administrative Court Office.

(2) Where a magistrates' court refuses to make an order of committal in relation to a person in respect of the offence or, as the case may be, any of the offences to which the authority to proceed relates and the state, country or colony seeking his surrender wishes to apply to the court to state a case for the opinion of the High Court under section 10(1) of the 1989 Act, such application must be made to the magistrates' court within the period of 21 days following the day on which the court refuses to make the order of committal unless the court grants a longer period within which the application is to be made.

(3) Such an application shall be made in writing and shall identify the question or questions of law on which the opinion of the High Court is sought.

(4) Within 21 days after receipt of an application to state a case under section 10(1) of the 1989 Act, the magistrates' court officer shall send a draft case to the solicitor for the state, country or colony and to the person whose surrender is sought or his solicitor and shall allow each party 21 days within which to make representations thereon; within 21 days after the latest day on which such representations may be made the court of committal shall, after considering any such representations and making such adjustments, if any, to the draft case as it thinks fit, state and sign the case which the court officer shall forthwith send to the solicitor for the state, country or colony.

---

1. Rules 17.1 to 17.11 have effect only in proceedings where the request for extradition was received by the relevant authority in the United Kingdom on or before 31 December 2003.

17.2. Notice of waiver. (1) A notice given under section 14 of, or paragraph 9 of Schedule 1 to, the Extradition Act 1989 (notice of waiver under the simplified procedure) shall be in the form set out in the Practice Direction or a form to the like effect.

(2) Such a notice shall be signed in the presence of the Senior District Judge (Chief Magistrate) or another District Judge (Magistrates' Courts) designated by him for the purposes of the Act, a justice of the peace or a justices' clerk.

(3) Any such notice given by a person in custody shall be delivered to the Governor of the prison in whose custody he is.

(4) If a person on bail gives such notice he shall deliver it to, or send it by post in a registered letter or by recorded delivery service addressed to, the Under Secretary of State, Home Office, London SW1H 9AT.

17.3. Notice of consent. (1) A person arrested in pursuance of a warrant under section 8 of or paragraph 5 of Schedule 1 to the Extradition Act 1989 may at any time consent to his return; and where such consent is given in accordance with the following provisions of this rule, the Senior District Judge (Chief Magistrate) or another District Judge (Magistrates' Courts) designated by him for the purposes of the Act may order the committal for return of that person in accordance with section 14(2) of that Act or, as the case may be, paragraph 9(2) of Schedule 1 to the Act.

(2) A notice of consent for the purposes of this rule shall be given in the form set out in the Practice Direction and shall be signed in the presence of the Senior District Judge (Chief Magistrate) or another District Judge (Magistrates' Courts) designated by him for the purposes of the 1989 Act.

17.4. Notice of consent (parties to 1995 Convention). (1) This rule applies as between the United Kingdom and states other than the Republic of Ireland that are parties to the Convention drawn up on the basis of Article 31 of the Treaty on European Union on Simplified Extradition Procedures between the Member States of the European Union, in relation to which section 14A of the Extradition Act 1989 applies by virtue of section 34A and Schedule 1A of that Act.

(2) Notice of consent for the purposes of section 14A(3) of the 1989 Act shall be given in the form set out in the Practice Direction and shall be signed in the presence of the Senior District Judge (Chief Magistrate) or another District Judge (Magistrates' Courts) designated by him for the purposes of that Act.

(3) A Senior District Judge (Chief Magistrate) or another District Judge (Magistrates' Courts) designated by him for the purposes of the Act may order the committal for return of a person if he gives consent under section 14A of the 1989 Act in accordance with paragraph (2) above before he is committed under section 9 of that Act.

17.5. Consent to early removal to Republic of Ireland. (1) A notice given under section 3(1)(*a*) of the Backing of Warrants (Republic of Ireland) Act 1965 (consent to surrender earlier than is otherwise permitted) shall be signed in the presence of a justice of the peace or a justices' clerk.

(2) Any such notice given by a person in custody shall be delivered to the Governor of the prison in whose custody he is.

(3) If a person on bail gives such notice, he shall deliver it to, or send it by post in a registered letter or by recorded delivery service addressed to, the police officer in charge of the police station specified in his recognizance.

(4) Any such notice shall be attached to the warrant ordering the surrender of that person.

17.6. Bail pending removal to Republic of Ireland. (1) The person taking the recognizance of a person remanded on bail under section 2(1) or 4(3) of the Backing of Warrants (Republic of Ireland) Act 1965 shall furnish a copy of the recognizance to the police officer in charge of the police station specified in the recognizance.

(2) The court officer for a magistrates' court which ordered a person to be surrendered and remanded him on bail shall deliver to, or send by post in a registered letter or by recorded delivery service addressed to, the police officer in charge of the police station specified in the recognizance the warrant ordering the person to be surrendered.

(3) The court officer for a magistrates' court which refused to order a person to be delivered under section 2 of the 1965 Act but made an order in accordance with section 2A(2) of that Act releasing that person on bail, upon the chief officer of police immediately informing the court that he intended to make an application to the court to state a case for the opinion of the High Court, shall forthwith send a copy of that order to the Administrative Court Office.

17.7. Delivery of warrant issued in Republic of Ireland. (1) The court officer for a magistrates' court which ordered a person to be surrendered under section 2(1) of the Backing of Warrants (Republic of Ireland) Act 1965 shall deliver to, or send by post in a registered letter or by recorded delivery service addressed to—

(a) if he is remanded in custody under section 5(1)(a) of the 1965 Act, the prison Governor to whose custody he is committed;

(b) if he is remanded on bail under section 5(1)(b) of the 1965 Act, the police officer in charge of the police station specified in the recognizance; or

(c) if he is committed to the custody of a constable pending the taking from him of a recognizance under section 5(1) of the 1965 Act, the police officer in charge of the police station specified in the warrant of commitment,

the warrant of arrest issued by a judicial authority in the Republic of Ireland and endorsed in accordance with section 1 of the 1965 Act.

(2) The Governor or police officer to whom the said warrant of arrest is delivered or sent shall arrange for it to be given to the member of the police force of the Republic into whose custody the person is delivered when the person is so delivered.

17.8. Verification of warrant etc issued in Republic of Ireland. (1) A document purporting to be a warrant issued by a judicial authority in the Republic of Ireland shall, for the purposes of section 7(a) of the Backing of Warrants (Republic of Ireland) Act 1965, be verified by a certificate purporting to be signed by a judicial authority, a clerk of a court or a member of the police force of the Republic and certifying that the document is a warrant and is issued by a judge or justice of a court or a peace commissioner.

(2) A document purporting to be a copy of a summons issued by a judicial authority in the Republic shall, for the purposes of section 7(a) of the 1965 Act, be verified by a certificate purporting to be signed by a judicial authority, a clerk of a court or a member of the police force of the Republic and certifying that the document is a true copy of such a summons.

(3) A deposition purporting to have been made in the Republic, or affidavit or written statement purporting to have been sworn therein, shall, for the purposes of section 7(c) of the 1965 Act, be verified by a certificate purporting to be signed by the person before whom it was sworn and certifying that it was so sworn.

17.9. Application to state a case where court declines to order removal to Republic of Ireland. (1) Where a magistrates' court refuses to make an order in relation to a person under section 2 of the Backing of Warrants (Republic of Ireland) Act 1965, any application to the court under section 2A(1) of that Act to state a case for the opinion of the High Court on any question of law arising in the proceedings must be made to the court by the chief officer of police within the period of 21 days following the day on which the order was refused, unless the court grants a longer period within which the application is to be made.

(2) Such an application shall be made in writing and shall identify the question or questions of law on which the opinion of the High Court is sought.

17.10. Draft case where court declines to order removal to Republic of Ireland. Within 21 days after receipt of an application to state a case under section 2A(1) of the Backing of Warrants (Republic of Ireland) Act 1965, the magistrates' court officer shall send a draft case to the applicant or his solicitor and to the person to whom the warrant relates or his solicitor and shall allow each party 21 days within which to make representations thereon; within 21 days after the latest day on which such representations may be made the court shall, after considering such representations and making such adjustments, if any, to the draft case as it thinks fit, state and sign the case which the court officer shall forthwith send to the applicant or his solicitor.

17.11. Forms for proceedings for removal to Republic of Ireland. Where a requirement is imposed by the Backing of Warrants (Republic of Ireland) Act 1965 for the use of a form, and an appropriate form is contained in the Practice Direction, that form shall be used.

PART 18
WARRANTS

18.1. Scope of this Part and interpretation. (1) This Part applies to any warrant issued by a justice of the peace.

(2) Where a rule applies to some of those warrants and not others, it says so.

(3) In this Part, the "relevant person" is the person against whom the warrant is issued.

18.2. Warrants must be signed. Every warrant under the Magistrates' Courts Act 1980 must be signed by the justice issuing it, unless rule 5.3 permits the justices' clerk to sign it.

18.3. Warrants issued when the court office is closed. (1) If a warrant is issued when the court office is closed, the applicant must—

(a) serve on the court officer any information on which that warrant is issued; and
(b) do so within 72 hours of that warrant being issued.

(2) In this rule, the court office is the office for the local justice area in which the justice is acting when he issues the warrant.

18.4. Commitment to custody must be by warrant. A justice of the peace must issue a warrant of commitment when committing a person to—

(a) a prison;
(b) a young offender institution;
(c) a remand centre;
(d) detention at a police station under section 128(7) of the Magistrates' Courts Act 1980; or
(e) customs detention under section 152 of the Criminal Justice Act 1988.

18.5. Terms of a warrant of arrest. A warrant[1] of arrest must require the persons to whom it is directed to arrest the relevant person.

---

1. For backing of an English warrant for execution in the Isles of Man, Guernsey, Jersey, Alderney or Sark and *vice versa*, see Indictable Offences Act 1848, s 13 in PART VIII: title EXTRADITION etc, post. For the execution of a warrant of arrest in Scotland or Northern Ireland, see the Criminal Justice and Public Order Act 1994, Pt X, this Part, post.

18.6. Terms of a warrant of commitment or detention: general rules. (1) A warrant of commitment or detention must require—

(a) the persons to whom it is directed to—
  (i) arrest the relevant person, if he is at large,
  (ii) take him to the prison or place specified in the warrant, and
  (iii) deliver him with the warrant to the governor or keeper of that prison or place; and
(b) the governor or keeper to keep the relevant person in custody at that prison or place—
  (i) for as long as the warrant requires, or
  (ii) until he is delivered, in accordance with the law, to the court or other proper place or person.

(2) Where the justice issuing a warrant of commitment or detention is aware that the relevant person is already detained in a prison or other place of detention, the warrant must be delivered to the governor or keeper of that prison or place.

18.7. Terms of a warrant committing a person to customs detention. (1) A warrant committing a person to customs detention under section 152 of the 1988 Act must—

(a) be directed to the officers of Her Majesty's Revenue and Customs; and
(b) require those officers to keep the person committed in their custody, unless in the meantime he be otherwise delivered, in accordance with the law, to the court or other proper place or person, for a period (not exceeding 192 hours) specified in the warrant.

(2) Rules 18.6(1), 18.10 and 18.12 do not apply where this rule applies.

18.8. Form of warrant where male aged 15 or 16 is committed. (1) This rule applies where a male aged 15 or 16 years is remanded or committed to—

(a) local authority accommodation, with a requirement that he be placed and kept in secure accommodation;
(b) a remand centre; or
(c) a prison.

(2) The court must include in the warrant of commitment a statement of any declaration that is required in connection with that remand or committal.

18.9. Information to be included in a warrant. A warrant of arrest, commitment or detention must contain the following information—

(a) the name or a description of the relevant person; and
(b) either—

    (i) a statement of the offence with which the relevant person is charged,

    (ii) a statement of the offence[1] of which the person to be committed or detained was convicted; or

    (iii) any other ground on which the warrant is issued.

---

1. Where the warrant is issued on committal for trial, it may set out a number of offences and will be treated as several and distinct warrants for all the offences (*R v Phillips, R v Quayle* [1939] 1 KB 63, [1938] 3 All ER 674).

18.10. Persons who may execute a warrant. A warrant of arrest, commitment or detention may be executed by—

(a) the persons to whom it is directed; or

(b) by any of the following persons, whether or not it was directed to them—

    (i) a constable for any police area in England and Wales, acting in his own police area, and

    (ii) any person authorised under section 125A (civilian enforcement officers) or section 125B (approved enforcement agencies) of the Magistrates' Courts Act 1980.

18.11. Making an arrest under a warrant. (1) The person executing a warrant of arrest, commitment or detention must, when arresting the relevant person—

(a) either—

    (i) show the warrant (if he has it with him) to the relevant person, or

    (ii) tell the relevant person where the warrant is and what arrangements can be made to let that person inspect it;

(b) explain, in ordinary language, the charge and the reason for the arrest; and

(c) (unless he is a constable in uniform) show documentary proof of his identity.

(2) If the person executing the warrant is one of the persons referred to in rule 18.10(b)(ii) (civilian enforcement officers or approved enforcement agencies), he must also show the relevant person a written statement under section 125A(4) or section 125B(4) of the Magistrates' Courts Act 1980, as appropriate.

18.12. Place of detention. (1) This rule applies to any warrant of commitment or detention.

(2) The person executing the warrant is required to take the relevant person to the prison or place of detention specified in the warrant.

(3) But where it is not immediately practicable to do so, or where there is some other good reason, the relevant person may be taken to any prison or place where he may be lawfully detained until such time when he can be taken to the prison or place specified in the warrant.

(4) If (and for as long as) the relevant person is detained in a place other than the one specified in the warrant, the warrant will have effect as if it specified the place where he is in fact being detained.

(5) The court must be kept informed of the prison or place where the relevant person is in fact being detained.

(6) The governor or keeper of the prison or place, to which the relevant person is delivered, must give a receipt on delivery.

18.13. Duration of detention where bail is granted subject to pre-release conditions. (1) This rule applies where a magistrates' court—

(a) grants bail to a person subject to conditions which must be met prior to release on bail; and

(b) commits that person to custody until those conditions are satisfied.

(2) The warrant of commitment must require the governor or keeper of the prison or place of detention to bring the relevant person to court either before or at the end of a period of 8 clear days from the date the warrant was issued, unless section 128(3A) or section 128A of the Magistrates' Courts Act 1980 applies to permit a longer period.

18.14. Validity of warrants that contain errors. A warrant of commitment or detention will not be invalidated[1] on the ground that it contains an error, provided that the warrant—

(a) is issued in relation to a valid—

    (i) conviction, or

    (ii) order requiring the relevant person to do, or to abstain from doing, something; and

(b) it states that it is issued in relation to that conviction or order.

---

1. The issue of a warrant of commitment is a judicial act, and if the power to issue it is dependent on a sum of money not having been paid, *certiorari* will lie to quash a warrant issued in error after payment of the money (*R v Doherty, ex p Isaacs* (1910) 74 JP 304).

18.15. Circumstances in which a warrant will cease to have effect. (1) A warrant issued under any of the provisions listed in paragraph (2) will cease to have effect when—

(a) the sum in respect of which the warrant is issued (together with the costs and charges of commitment, if any) is paid to the person who is executing the warrant;

(b) that sum is offered to, but refused by, the person who is executing the warrant; or

(c) a receipt for that sum given by—

  (i) the court officer for the court which issued the warrant, or
  (ii) the charging or billing authority,

is produced to the person who is executing the warrant.

(2) Those provisions are—

(a) section 76 (warrant to enforce fines and other sums);
(b) section 83(1) and (2) (warrant to secure attendance of offender for purposes of section 82);
(c) section 86(4) (warrant to arrest offender following failure to appear on day fixed for means inquiry);
(d) section 136 (committal to custody overnight at police station), of the Magistrates' Courts Act 1980.

(3) No person may execute, or continue to execute, a warrant that ceases to have effect under this rule.

18.16. Warrant endorsed for bail (record to be kept). A person executing a warrant of arrest that is endorsed for bail under section 117 of the Magistrates' Courts Act 1980 must—

(a) make a record stating—

  (i) the name of the person arrested,
  (ii) the charge and the reason for the arrest,
  (iii) the fact that the person is to be released on bail,
  (iv) the date, time and place at which the person is required to appear before the court, and
  (v) any other details which he considers to be relevant; and

(b) after making the record—

  (i) sign the record,
  (ii) invite the person arrested to sign the record and, if they refuse, make a note of that refusal on the record,
  (iii) make a copy of the record and give it to the person arrested, and
  (iv) send the original record to the court officer for the court which issued the warrant

1-7439

PART 19
BAIL IN MAGISTRATES' COURTS AND THE CROWN COURT

19.1. Application to a magistrates' court to vary conditions of police bail. (1) An application under section 43B(1) of the Magistrates' Courts Act of 1980 or section 47(1E) of the Police and Criminal Evidence Act 1984 shall—

(a) be made in writing;
(b) contain a statement of the grounds upon which it is made;
(c) specify the offence with which the applicant was charged before his release on bail;
(d) where the applicant has been bailed following charge, specify the offence with which he was charged and, in any other case, specify the offence under investigation; and
(e) specify the name and address of any surety provided by the applicant before his release on bail to secure his surrender to custody.

(2) Any such application shall be sent to the court officer for—

(a) the magistrates' court appointed by the custody officer as the court before which the applicant has a duty to appear; or

(b) if no such court has been appointed, a magistrates' court acting for the local justice area in which the police station at which the applicant was granted bail or at which the conditions of his bail were varied, as the case may be, is situated.

(3) The court officer to whom an application is sent under paragraph (2) above shall serve notice in writing of the date, time and place fixed for the hearing of the application on—

(a) the applicant;
(b) the prosecutor or, if the applicant has not been charged, the chief officer of police or other investigator, together with a copy of the application; and
(c) any surety in connection with bail in criminal proceedings granted to, or the conditions of which were varied by a custody officer in relation to, the applicant.

(4) The time fixed for the hearing shall be not later than 72 hours after receipt of the application. In reckoning for the purposes of this paragraph any period of 72 hours, no account shall be taken of Christmas Day, Boxing Day, Good Friday, any bank holiday, or any Saturday or Sunday.

(5) *Revoked.*

(6) If the magistrates' court hearing an application under section 43B(1) of the 1980 Act or section 47(1E) of the 1984 Act discharges or enlarges any recognizance entered into by any surety or increases or reduces the amount in which that person is bound, the court officer shall forthwith give notice thereof to the applicant and to any such surety.

(7) In this rule, "the applicant" means the person making an application under section 43B(1) of the 1980 Act or section 47(1E) of the 1984 Act.

19.2. Application to a magistrates' court to reconsider grant of police bail. (1) The appropriate court for the purposes of section 5B of the Bail Act 1976 in relation to the decision of a constable to grant bail shall be—

(a) the magistrates' court appointed by the custody officer as the court before which the person to whom bail was granted has a duty to appear; or

(b) if no such court has been appointed, a magistrates' court acting for the local justice area in which the police station at which bail was granted is situated.

(2) An application under section 5B(1) of the 1976 Act shall—

(a) be made in writing;

(b) contain a statement of the grounds on which it is made;

(c) specify the offence which the proceedings in which bail was granted were connected with, or for;

(d) specify the decision to be reconsidered (including any conditions of bail which have been imposed and why they have been imposed);

(e) specify the name and address of any surety provided by the person to whom the application relates to secure his surrender to custody; and

(f) contain notice of the powers available to the court under section 5B of the 1976 Act.

(3) The court officer to whom an application is sent under paragraph (2) above shall serve notice in writing of the date, time and place fixed for the hearing of the application on—

(a) the prosecutor who made the application;

(b) the person to whom bail was granted, together with a copy of the application; and

(c) any surety specified in the application.

(4) The time fixed for the hearing shall be not later than 72 hours after receipt of the application. In reckoning for the purpose of this paragraph any period of 72 hours, no account shall be taken of Christmas Day, Good Friday, any bank holiday or any Sunday.

(5) *Revoked.*

(6) At the hearing of an application under section 5B of the 1976 Act the court shall consider any representations made by the person affected (whether in writing or orally) before taking any decision under that section with respect to him; and, where the person affected does not appear before the court, the court shall not take such a decision unless it is proved to the satisfaction of the court, on oath or in the manner set out by rule 4.2(1), that the notice required to be given under paragraph (3) of this rule was served on him before the hearing.

(7) Where the court proceeds in the absence of the person affected in accordance with paragraph (6)—

(a) if the decision of the court is to vary the conditions of bail or impose conditions in respect of bail which has been granted unconditionally, the court officer shall notify the person affected;

(b) if the decision of the court is to withhold bail, the order of the court under section 5B(5)(b) of the 1976 Act (surrender to custody) shall be signed by the justice issuing it or state his name and be authenticated by the signature of the clerk of the court.

(8) *Revoked.*

19.3. Notice of change of time for appearance before magistrates' court. Where—

(a) a person has been granted bail under the Police and Criminal Evidence Act 1984 subject to a duty to appear before a magistrates' court and the court before which he is to appear appoints a later time at which he is to appear; or

(b) a magistrates' court further remands a person on bail under section 129 of the Magistrates' Courts Act 1980 in his absence,

it shall give him and his sureties, if any, notice thereof.

19.4. Directions by a magistrates' court as to security, etc. Where a magistrates' court, under section 3(5) or (6) of the Bail Act 1976, imposes any requirement to be complied with before a person's release on bail, the court may give directions as to the manner in which and the person or persons before whom the requirement may be complied with.

19.5. Requirements to be complied with before release on bail granted by a magistrates' court.
(1) Where a magistrates' court has fixed the amount¹ in which a person (including any surety) is to be bound by a recognizance, the recognizance may be entered into—

(a) in the case of a surety where the accused is in a prison or other place of detention, before the governor or keeper of the prison or place as well as before the persons mentioned in section 8(4)(a) of the Bail Act 1976;

(b) in any other case, before a justice of the peace, a justices' clerk, a magistrates' court officer, a police officer who either is of the rank of inspector or above or is in charge of a police station or, if the person to be bound is in a prison or other place of detention, before the governor or keeper of the prison or place; or

(c) where a person other than a police officer is authorised under section 125A or 125B of the Magistrates' Courts Act 1980 to execute a warrant of arrest providing for a recognizance to be entered into by the person arrested (but not by any other person), before the person executing the warrant.

(2) The court officer for a magistrates' court which has fixed the amount in which a person (including any surety) is to be bound by a recognizance or, under section 3(5), (6) or (6A) of the 1976 Act imposed any requirement to be complied with before a person's release on bail or any condition of bail shall issue a certificate showing the amount and conditions, if any, of the

recognizance, or as the case may be, containing a statement of the requirement or condition of bail; and a person authorised to take the recognizance or do anything in relation to the compliance with such requirement or condition of bail shall not be required to take or do it without production of such a certificate as aforesaid.

(3) If any person proposed as a surety for a person committed to custody by a magistrates' court produces to the governor or keeper of the prison or other place of detention in which the person so committed is detained a certificate to the effect that he is acceptable as a surety, signed by any of the justices composing the court or the clerk of the court and signed in the margin by the person proposed as surety, the governor or keeper shall take the recognizance of the person so proposed.

(4) Where the recognizance of any person committed to custody by a magistrates' court or of any surety of such a person is taken by any person other than the court which committed the first-mentioned person to custody, the person taking the recognizance shall send it to the court officer for that court:

Provided that, in the case of a surety, if the person committed has been committed to the Crown Court for trial or under any of the enactments mentioned in rule 43.1(1), the person taking the recognizance shall send it to the Crown Court officer.

---

1. The power to fix the amount where recognizances are to be entered into later is contained in the Magistrates' Courts Act 1980, s 119, ante.

19.6. Notice to governor of prison, etc, where release from custody is ordered by a magistrates' court. Where a magistrates' court has, with a view to the release on bail of a person in custody, fixed the amount in which he or any surety of such a person shall be bound or, under section 3(5), (6) or (6A) of the Bail Act 1976, imposed any requirement to be complied with before his release or any condition of bail—

- (a) the magistrates' court officer shall give notice thereof to the governor or keeper of the prison or place where that person is detained by sending him such a certificate as is mentioned in rule 19.5(2); and
- (b) any person authorised to take the recognizance of a surety or do anything in relation to the compliance with such requirement shall, on taking or doing it, send notice thereof by post to the said governor or keeper and, in the case of a recognizance of a surety, shall give a copy of the notice to the surety.

19.7. Release when notice received by governor of prison that recognizances have been taken or requirements complied with. Where a magistrates' court has, with a view to the release on bail of a person in custody, fixed the amount in which he or any surety of such a person shall be bound or, under section 3(5) or (6) of the Bail Act 1976, imposed any requirement to be complied with before his release and given notice thereof in accordance with this Part to the governor or keeper of the prison or place where that person is detained, the governor or keeper shall, when satisfied that the recognizances of all sureties required have been taken and that all such requirements have been complied with, and unless he is in custody for some other cause, release him.

19.8. Notice from a magistrates' court of enlargement of recognizances. (1) If a magistrates' court before which any person is bound by a recognizance to appear enlarges the recognizance to a later time under section 129 of the Magistrates' Courts Act 1980 in his absence, it shall give him and his sureties, if any, notice thereof.

(2) If a magistrates' court, under section 129(4) of the 1980 Act, enlarges the recognizance of a surety for a person committed for trial on bail, it shall give the surety notice thereof.

19.9. Further remand of minors by a youth court. Where a child or young person has been remanded, and the period of remand is extended in his absence in accordance with section 48 of the Children and Young Persons Act 1933, notice shall be given to him and his sureties (if any) of the date at which he will be required to appear before the court.

19.10. Notes of argument in magistrates' court bail hearings. Where a magistrates' court hears full argument as to bail, the clerk of the court shall take a note of that argument.

19.11. Bail records to be entered in register of magistrates' court. Any record required by section 5 of the Bail Act 1976 to be made by a magistrates' court (together with any note of reasons required by section 5(4) to be included and the particulars set out in any certificate granted under section 5(6A)) shall be made by way of an entry in the register.

19.12. Notification of bail decision by magistrate after arrest while on bail. Where a person who has been released on bail and is under a duty to surrender into the custody of a court is brought under section 7(4)(a) of the Bail Act 1976 before a justice of the peace, the justice shall cause a copy of the record made in pursuance of section 5 of that Act relating to his decision under section 7(5) of that Act in respect of that person to be sent to the court officer for that court:

Provided that this rule shall not apply where the court is a magistrates' court acting for the same local justice area as that for which the justice acts.

19.13. Transfer of remand hearings. (1) Where a magistrates' court, under section 130(1) of the

Magistrates' Courts Act 1980, orders that an accused who has been remanded in custody be brought up for any subsequent remands before an alternate magistrates' court, the court officer for the first-mentioned court shall, as soon as practicable after the making of the order and in any case within 2 days thereafter (not counting Sundays, Good Friday, Christmas Day or bank holidays), send to the court officer for the alternate court—

(a) a statement indicating the offence or offences charged;
(b) a copy of the record made by the first-mentioned court in pursuance of section 5 of the Bail Act 1976 relating to the withholding of bail in respect of the accused when he was last remanded in custody;
(c) a copy of any representation order previously made in the same case;
(d) a copy of any application for a representation order;
(e) if the first-mentioned court has made an order under section 8(2) of the 1980 Act (removal of restrictions on reports of committal proceedings), a statement to that effect.
(f) a statement indicating whether or not the accused has a solicitor acting for him in the case and has consented to the hearing and determination in his absence of any application for his remand on an adjournment of the case under sections 5, 10(1) and 18(4) of the 1980 Act together with a statement indicating whether or not that consent has been withdrawn;
(g) a statement indicating the occasions, if any, on which the accused has been remanded under section 128(3A) of the 1980 Act without being brought before the first-mentioned court; and
(h) if the first-mentioned court remands the accused under section 128A of the 1980 Act on the occasion upon which it makes the order under section 130(1) of that Act, a statement indicating the date set under section 128A(2) of that Act.

(2) Where the first-mentioned court is satisfied as mentioned in section 128(3A) of the 1980 Act, paragraph (1) shall have effect as if for the words "an accused who has been remanded in custody be brought up for any subsequent remands before" there were substituted the words "applications for any subsequent remands of the accused be made to".

(3) The court officer for an alternate magistrates' court before which an accused who has been remanded in custody is brought up for any subsequent remands in pursuance of an order made as aforesaid shall, as soon as practicable after the order ceases to be in force and in any case within 2 days thereafter (not counting Sundays, Good Friday, Christmas Day or bank holidays), send to the court officer for the magistrates' court which made the order—

(a) a copy of the record made by the alternate court in pursuance of section 5 of the 1976 Act relating to the grant or withholding of bail in respect of the accused when he was last remanded in custody or on bail;
(b) a copy of any representation order made by the alternate court;
(c) a copy of any application for a representation order made to the alternate court;
(d) if the alternate court has made an order under section 8(2) of the 1980 Act (removal of restrictions on reports of committal proceedings), a statement to that effect;
(e) a statement indicating whether or not the accused has a solicitor acting for him in the case and has consented to the hearing and determination in his absence of any application for his remand on an adjournment of the case under sections 5, 10(1) and 18(4) of the 1980 Act together with a statement indicating whether or not that consent has been withdrawn; and
(f) a statement indicating the occasions, if any, on which the accused has been remanded by the alternate court under section 128(3A) of the 1980 Act without being brought before that court.

(4) Where the alternate court is satisfied as mentioned in section 128(3A) of the 1980 Act paragraph (2) above shall have effect as if for the words "an accused who has been remanded in custody is brought up for any subsequent remands" there shall be substituted the words "applications for the further remand of the accused are to be made".

19.14. Notice of further remand in certain cases. Where a transfer direction has been given by the Secretary of State under section 47 of the Mental Health Act 1983 in respect of a person remanded in custody by a magistrates' court and the direction has not ceased to have effect, the court officer shall give notice in writing to the managers of the hospital where he is detained of any further remand under section 128 of the Magistrates' Courts Act 1980.

19.15. Cessation of transfer direction. Where a magistrates' court directs, under section 52(5) of the Mental Health Act 1983, that a transfer direction given by the Secretary of State under section 48 of that Act in respect of a person remanded in custody by a magistrates' court shall cease to have effect, the court officer shall give notice in writing of the court's direction to the managers of the hospital specified in the Secretary of State's direction and, where the period of remand has not expired or the person has been committed to the Crown Court for trial or to be otherwise dealt with, to the Governor of the prison to which persons of the sex of that person are committed by the court if remanded in custody or committed in custody for trial.

19.16. Lodging an appeal against a grant of bail by a magistrates' court. (1) Where the prosecution wishes to exercise the right of appeal, under section 1 of the Bail (Amendment) Act 1993, to a judge of the Crown Court against a decision to grant bail, the oral notice[1] of appeal must be given to the justices' clerk and to the person concerned, at the conclusion of the proceedings in which such bail was granted and before the release of the person concerned.

(2) When oral notice of appeal is given, the justices' clerk shall announce in open court the time at which such notice was given.

(3) A record of the prosecution's decision to appeal and the time the oral notice of appeal was given shall be made in the register and shall contain the particulars set out.

(4) Where an oral notice of appeal has been given the court shall remand the person concerned in custody by a warrant of commitment.

(5) On receipt of the written notice of appeal required by section 1(5) of the 1993 Act, the court shall remand the person concerned in custody by a warrant of commitment, until the appeal is determined or otherwise disposed of.

(6) A record of the receipt of the written notice of appeal shall be made in the same manner as that of the oral notice of appeal under paragraph (3).

(7) If, having given oral notice of appeal, the prosecution fails to serve a written notice of appeal within the two hour period referred to in section 1(5) of the 1993 Act the justices' clerk shall, as soon as practicable, by way of written notice (served by a court officer) to the persons in whose custody the person concerned is, direct the release of the person concerned on bail as granted by the magistrates' court and subject to any conditions which it imposed.

(8) If the prosecution serves notice of abandonment of appeal on a court officer, the justices' clerk shall, forthwith, by way of written notice (served by the court officer) to the governor of the prison where the person concerned is being held, or the person responsible for any other establishment where such a person is being held, direct his release on bail as granted by the magistrates' court and subject to any conditions which it imposed.

(9) A court officer shall record the prosecution's failure to serve a written notice of appeal, or its service of a notice of abandonments.

(10) Where a written notice of appeal has been served on a magistrates' court officer, he shall provide as soon as practicable to a Crown Court officer a copy of that written notice, together with—

    (a) the notes of argument made by the court officer for the court under rule 19.10; and
    (b) a note of the date, or dates, when the person concerned is next due to appear in the magistrates' court, whether he is released on bail or remanded in custody by the Crown Court.

(11) References in this rule to "the person concerned" are references to such a person within the meaning of section 1 of the 1993 Act.

---

1. Oral notice which was given to the justices' chief executive for the court 5 minutes after the conclusion of the proceedings and after the justices had left the court building was held to be valid (*R v Isleworth Crown Court, ex p Clarke* [1998] 1 Cr App Rep 257).

19.17. Crown Court procedure on appeal against grant of bail by a magistrates' court. (1) This rule shall apply where the prosecution appeals under section 1 of the Bail (Amendment) Act 1993 against a decision of a magistrates' court granting bail and in this rule "the person concerned" has the same meaning as in that Act.

(2) The written notice of appeal required by section 1(5) of the 1993 Act shall be in the form set out in the Practice Direction and shall be served on—

    (a) the magistrates' court officer; and
    (b) the person concerned.

(3) The Crown Court officer shall enter the appeal and give notice of the time and place of the hearing to—

    (a) the prosecution;
    (b) the person concerned or his legal representative; and
    (c) the magistrates' court officer.

(4) The person concerned shall not be entitled to be present at the hearing of the appeal unless he is acting in person or, in any other case of an exceptional nature, a judge of the Crown Court is of the opinion that the interests of justice require his to be present and gives him leave to be so.

(5) Where a person concerned has not been able to instruct a solicitor to represent him at the appeal, he may give notice to the Crown Court requesting that the Official Solicitor shall represent him at the appeal, and the court may, if it thinks fit, assign the Official Solicitor to act for the person concerned accordingly.

(6) At any time after the service of written notice of appeal under pagraph (2), the prosecution may abandon the appeal by giving notice in writing in the form set out in the Practice Direction.

(7) The notice of abandonment required by the preceding paragraph shall be served on—

    (a) the person concerned or his legal representative;
    (b) the magistrates' court officer; and
    (c) the Crown Court officer.

(8) Any record required by section 5 of the Bail Act 1976 (together with any note of reasons required by subsection (4) of that section to be included) shall be made by way of an entry in the file relating to the case in question and the record shall include the following particulars, namely—

    (a) the effect of the decision;
    (b) a statement of any condition imposed in respect of bail, indicating whether it is to be complied with before or after release on bail; and
    (c) where bail is withheld, a statement of the relevant exception to the right to bail (as provided in Schedule 1 to the 1976 Act) on which the decision is based.

(9) The Crown Court officer shall, as soon as practicable after the hearing of the appeal, give notice of the decision and of the matters required by the preceding paragraph to be recorded to—

(a) the person concerned or his legal representative;
(b) the prosecution;
(c) the police;
(d) the magistrates' officer; and
(e) the governor of the prison or person responsible for the establishment where the person concerned is being held.

(10) Where the judge hearing the appeal grants bail to the person concerned, the provisions of rule 19.18(9) (informing the Court of any earlier application for bail) and rule 19.22 (conditions attached to bail granted by the Crown Court) shall apply as if that person had applied to the Crown Court for bail.

(11) The notices required by paragraphs (3), (5), (7) and (9) of this rule may be served under rule 4.6 (service by fax, e-mail or other electronic means) and the notice required by paragraph (3) may be given by telephone.

19.18. Applications to Crown Court relating to bail. (1) This rule applies where an application to the Crown Court relating to bail is made otherwise than during the hearing of proceedings in the Crown Court.

(2) Subject to paragraph (7) below, notice in writing of intention to make such an application to the Crown Court shall, at least 24 hours before it is made, be given to the prosecutor and if the prosecution is being carried on by the Crown Prosecution Service, to the appropriate Crown Prosecutor or, if the application is to be made by the prosecutor or a constable under section 3(8) of the Bail Act 1976, to the person to whom bail was granted.

(3) On receiving notice under paragraph (2), the prosecutor or appropriate Crown Public Prosecutor or, as the case may be, the person to whom bail was granted shall—

(a) notify the Crown Court officer and the applicant that he wishes to be represented at the hearing of the application;
(b) notify the Crown Court officer and the applicant that he does not oppose the application; or
(c) give to the Crown Court officer, for the consideration of the Crown Court, a written statement of his reasons for opposing the application, at the same time sending a copy of the statement to the applicant.

(4) A notice under paragraph (2) shall be in the form set out in the Practice Direction or a form to the like effect, and the applicant shall give a copy of the notice to the Crown Court officer.

(5) Except in the case of an application made by the prosecutor or a constable under section 3(8) of the 1976 Act, the applicant shall not be entitled to be present on the hearing of his application unless the Crown Court gives him leave to be present[1].

(6) Where a person who is in custody or has been released on bail desires to make an application relating to bail and has not been able to instruct a solicitor to apply on his behalf under the preceding paragraphs of this rule, he may give notice in writing to the Crown Court of his desire to make an application relating to bail, requesting that the Official Solicitor shall act for him in the application, and the Court may, if it thinks fit, assign the Official Solicitor to act for the applicant accordingly.

(7) Where the Official Solicitor has been so assigned the Crown Court may, if it thinks fit, dispense with the requirements of paragraph (2) and deal with the application in a summary manner.

(8) Any record required by section 5 of the 1976 Act (together with any note of reasons required by section 5(4) to be included) shall be made by way of an entry in the file relating to the case in question and the record shall include the following particulars, namely—

(a) the effect of the decision;
(b) a statement of any condition imposed in respect of bail, indicating whether it is to be complied with before or after release on bail;
(c) where conditions of bail are varied, a statement of the conditions as varied; and
(d) where bail is withheld, a statement of the relevant exception to the right to bail (as provided in Schedule 1 to the 1976 Act) on which the decision is based.

(9) Every person who makes an application to the Crown Court relating to bail shall inform the Court of any earlier application to the High Court or the Crown Court relating to bail in the course of the same proceedings.

---

1. This may be incompatible with art 5(3) of the European Convention on Human Rights. The case law of the European Court of Human Rights suggests that art 5 generally requires that the accused and his legal representative be present at an oral hearing for the determination of bail: *Keus v Netherlands* (1990) 13 EHRR 700 and *Farmakopoulos v Belgium* (1992) 16 EHRR 187.

19.19. Notice to governor of prison of committal on bail. (1) Where the accused is committed or sent for trial on bail, a magistrates' court officer shall give notice thereof in writing to the governor of the prison to which persons of the sex of the person committed or sent are committed or sent by that court if committed or sent in custody for trial and also, if the person committed or sent is under 21, to the governor of the remand centre to which he would have been committed or sent if the court had refused him bail.

(2) Where a corporation is committed or sent for trial, a magistrates' court officer shall give

notice thereof to the governor of the prison to which would be committed or sent a man committed or sent by that court in custody for trial.

19.20. Notices on committal of person subject to transfer direction. Where a transfer direction has been given by the Secretary of State under section 48 of the Mental Health Act 1983 in respect of a person remanded in custody by a magistrates' court and, before the direction ceases to have effect, that person is committed or sent for trial, a magistrates' court officer shall give notice—

 (*a*) to the governor of the prison to which persons of the sex of that person are committed or sent by that court if committed or sent in custody for trial; and

 (*b*) to the managers of the hospital where he is detained.

19.21. Variation of arrangements for bail on committal to Crown Court. Where a magistrates' court has committed or sent a person on bail to the Crown Court for trial or under any of the enactments mentioned in rule 43.1(1) and subsequently varies any conditions of the bail or imposes any conditions in respect of the bail, the magistrates' court officer shall send to the Crown Court officer a copy of the record made in pursuance of section 5 of the Bail Act 1976 relating to such variation or imposition of conditions.

19.22. Conditions attached to bail granted by the Crown Court. (1) Where the Crown Court grants bail, the recognizance of any surety required as a condition of bail may be entered into before an officer of the Crown Court or, where the person who has been granted bail is in a prison or other place of detention, before the governor or keeper of the prison or place as well as before the persons specified in section 8(4) of the Bail Act 1976.

(2) Where the Crown Court under section 3(5) or (6) of the 1976 Act imposes a requirement to be complied with before a person's release on bail, the Court may give directions as to the manner in which and the person or persons before whom the requirement may be complied with.

(3) A person who, in pursuance of an order made by the Crown Court for the grant of bail, proposes to enter into a recognizance or give security must, unless the Crown Court otherwise directs, give notice to the prosecutor at least 24 hours before he enters into the recognizance or gives security as aforesaid.

(4) Where, in pursuance of an order of the Crown Court, a recognizance is entered into or any requirement imposed under section 3(5) or (6) of the 1976 Act is complied with (being a requirement to be complied with before a person's release on bail) before any person, it shall be his duty to cause the recognizance or, as the case may be, a statement of the requirement to be transmitted forthwith to the court officer; and a copy of the recognizance or statement shall at the same time be sent to the governor or keeper of the prison or other place of detention in which the person named in the order is detained, unless the recognizance was entered into or the requirement was complied with before such governor or keeper.

(5) Where, in pursuance of section 3(5) of the 1976 Act, security has been given in respect of a person granted bail with a duty to surrender to the custody of the Crown Court and either—

 (*a*) that person surrenders to the custody of the Court; or

 (*b*) that person having failed to surrender to the custody of the Court, the Court decides not to order the forfeiture of the security,

the court officer shall as soon as practicable give notice of the surrender to custody or, as the case may be, of the decision not to forfeit the security to the person before whom the security was given.

19.23. Estreat of recognizances in respect of person bailed to appear before the Crown Court. (1) Where a recognizance has been entered into in respect of a person granted bail to appear before the Crown Court and it appears to the Court that a default[1] has been made in performing the conditions of the recognizance, other than by failing to appear before the Court in accordance with any such condition, the Court may order the recognizance to be estreated.

(2) Where the Crown Court is to consider making an order under paragraph (1) for a recognizance to be estreated, the court officer shall give notice to that effect to the person by whom the recognizance was entered into indicating the time and place at which the matter will be considered; and no such order shall be made before the expiry of 7 days after the notice required by this paragraph has been given.

---

1. "Default" means "failure" and does not indicate that there must be established some fault on the part of the defendant or surety before the court can consider estreating a recognizance (*R v Crown Court at Warwick, ex p Smalley* [1987] 1 WLR 237, 84 Cr App Rep 51). The power of the Crown Court to order a recognizance to be estreated is subject to the right of the person concerned to apply under s 31(1) of the Powers of Criminal Courts Act 1973, in Part III: Sentencing post, for time for payment or for payment by instalments, or for the discharge of the recognizance or a reduction of the amount due under it. For consideration of these provisions, see *R v Crown Court at Wood Green, ex p Howe* [1992] 3 All ER 366, [1992] 1 WLR 702.

19.24. Forfeiture of recognizances in respect of person bailed to appear before the Crown Court. (1) Where a recognizance is conditioned for the appearance of an accused before the Crown Court and the accused fails to appear in accordance with the condition, the Court shall declare the recognizance to be forfeited.

(2) Where the Crown Court declares a recognizance to be forfeited under paragraph (1), the court officer shall issue a summons to the person by whom the recognizance was entered into

requiring him to appear before the Court at a time and place specified in the summons to show cause why the Court should not order the recognizance to be estreated.

(3) At the time specified in the summons the Court may proceed in the absence of the person by whom the recognizance was entered into if it is satisfied that he has been served with the summons.

1–7440

PART 20
CUSTODY TIME LIMITS

20.1. Appeal to the Crown Court against a decision of a magistrates' court in respect of a custody time limit. (1) This rule applies—

- (a) to any appeal brought by an accused, under section 22(7) of the Prosecution of Offences Act 1985, against a decision of a magistrates' court to extend, or further extend, a custody time limit imposed by regulations made under section 22(1) of the 1985 Act; and
- (b) to any appeal brought by the prosecution, under section 22(8) of the 1985 Act, against a decision of a magistrates' court to refuse to extend, or further extend, such a time limit.

(2) An appeal to which this rule applies shall be commenced by the appellant's giving notice in writing of appeal—

- (a) to the court officer for the magistrates' court which took the decision;
- (b) if the appeal is brought by the accused, to the prosecutor and, if the prosecution is to be carried on by the Crown Prosecution Service, to the appropriate Crown Prosecutor;
- (c) if the appeal is brought by the prosecution, to the accused; and
- (d) to the Crown Court officer.

(3) The notice of an appeal to which this rule applies shall state the date on which the custody time limit applicable to the case is due to expire and, if the appeal is brought by the accused under section 22(7) of the 1985 Act, the date on which the custody time limit would have expired had the court decided not to extend or further extend that time limit.

(4) On receiving notice of an appeal to which this rule applies, the Crown Court officer shall enter the appeal and give notice of the time and place of the hearing to—

- (a) the appellant;
- (b) the other party to the appeal; and
- (c) the court officer for the magistrates' court which took the decision.

(5) Without prejudice to the power of the Crown Court to give leave for an appeal to be abandoned, an appellant may abandon an appeal to which this rule applies by giving notice in writing to any person to whom notice of the appeal was required to be given by paragraph (2) of this rule not later than the third day preceding the day fixed for the hearing of the appeal:

Provided that, for the purpose of determining whether notice was properly given in accordance with this paragraph, there shall be disregarded any Saturday and Sunday and any day which is specified to be a bank holiday in England and Wales under section 1(1) of the Banking and Financial Dealings Act 1971.

1–7441

PART 21
ADVANCE INFORMATION

21.1. Scope of procedure for furnishing advance information. This Part applies in respect of proceedings against any person ("the accused") for an offence triable either way[1].

---

1. These provisions may be incompatible with the European Convention on Human Rights. There is a general requirement under art 6 of the Convention that "all material evidence for or against the accused" be disclosed before trial: see *Edwards v United Kingdom* (1992) 15 EHRR 417 at para 36. In *Jespers v Belgium* (1981) 27 DR 61 the European Commission of Human Rights held that the "equality of arms" principle imposed on prosecuting and investigating authorities an obligation to disclose any material in their possession, or to which they could gain access, which may assist the accused in exonerating himself or in obtaining a reduction in sentence. Where disclosure is not made, the court must assess the impact of non-disclosure on the fairness of the trial as a whole: see *ex p Imbert* [1999] 2 Cr App Rep 276. But, it is submitted, there is nothing to prevent a magistrates' court ordering disclosure where fairness dictates that such a step be taken.

21.2. Notice to accused regarding advance information. As soon as practicable after a person has been charged with an offence in proceedings in respect of which this Part applies or a summons has been served on a person in connection with such an offence, the prosecutor shall provide him with a notice in writing explaining the effect of rule 21.3 and setting out the address at which a request under that section may be made.

21.3. Request for advance information. (1) If, in any proceedings in respect of which this Part applies, either before the magistrates' court considers whether the offence appears to be more suitable for summary trial or trial on indictment or, where the accused has not attained the age of 18 years when he appears or is brought before a magistrates' court, before he is asked whether he pleads guilty or not guilty, the accused or a person representing the accused requests the prosecutor to furnish him with advance information, the prosecutor shall, subject to rule 21.4, furnish him as soon as practicable with either—

(a)   a copy of those parts of every written statement which contain information as to the facts and matters of which the prosecutor proposes to adduce evidence in the proceedings; or

(b)   a summary of the facts and matters of which the prosecutor proposes to adduce evidence in the proceedings[1].

(2) In paragraph (1) above, "written statement" means a statement made by a person on whose evidence the prosecutor proposes to rely in the proceedings and, where such a person has made more than one written statement one of which contains information as to all the facts and matters in relation to which the prosecutor proposes to rely on the evidence of that person, only that statement is a written statement for purposes of paragraph (1) above.

(3) Where in any part of a written statement or in a summary furnished under paragraph (1) above reference is made to a document[2] on which the prosecutor proposes to rely, the prosecutor shall, subject to rule 21.4, when furnishing the part of the written statement or the summary, also furnish either a copy of the document or such information as may be necessary to enable the person making the request under paragraph (1) above to inspect the document or a copy thereof.

---

1. The prosecution cannot be required under r 4 to provide the defence with copies of allegedly pornographic material seized from the defendant; recourse, however, may be made to an adjournment in such a case for the purpose of allowing fuller disclosure (*R v Dunmow Justices, ex p Nash* (1993) 157 JP 1153). In relation to proceedings for a sexual offence, access to material relating to a victim is restricted by the Sexual Offences (Protected Material) Act 1997, in Part VIII: title Sexual Offences, post.

2. "Document" here includes a video and where a video (constituting *the* identification evidence) is referred to in the advance information furnished to the accused he is entitled to an adjournment to view it: *R v Calderdale Magistrates' Court, ex p Donahue and Cutler* [2001] Crim LR 141, DC. However, a simple reference in a case summary, supplied under the 1985 Rules, to DNA profiles cannot be said to be a reference to a "document" within the meaning of r 4 and the prosecution is not obliged to provide further information about the DNA profiling; furthermore, the decision in *R v Calderdale Magistrates' Court* (supra) was founded upon a concession that a video was a document, and the matter may fall to be decided in a subsequent case where the concession is not made: *R (on the application of the DPP) v Croydon Magistrates' Court* [2001] EWHC Admin 552.

21.4. Refusal of request for advance information.   (1) If the prosecutor is of the opinion that the disclosure of any particular fact or matter in compliance with the requirements imposed by rule 21.3 might lead to any person on whose evidence he proposes to rely in the proceedings being intimidated, to an attempt to intimidate him being made or otherwise to the course of justice being interfered with, he shall not be obliged to comply with those requirements in relation to that fact or matter.

(2) Where, in accordance with paragraph (1) above, the prosecutor considers that he is not obliged to comply with the requirements imposed by rule 21.3 in relation to any particular fact or matter, he shall give notice in writing to the person who made the request under that section to the effect that certain advance information is being withheld by virtue of that paragraph.

21.5. Duty of court regarding advance information.   (1) Subject to paragraph (2), where an accused appears or is brought before a magistrates' court in proceedings in respect of which this Part applies, the court shall, before it considers whether the offence appears to be more suitable for summary trial or trial on indictment, satisfy itself that the accused is aware of the requirements which may be imposed on the prosecutor under rule 21.3.

(2) Where the accused has not attained the age of 18 years when he appears or is brought before a magistrates' court in proceedings in respect of which this rule applies, the court shall, before the accused is asked whether he pleads guilty or not guilty, satisfy itself that the accused is aware of the requirements which may be imposed on the prosecutor under rule 21.3.

21.6. Adjournment pending furnishing of advance information.   (1) If, in any proceedings in respect of which this Part applies, the court is satisfied that, a request under rule 21.3 having been made to the prosecutor by or on behalf of the accused, a requirement imposed on the prosecutor by that section has not been complied with[1], the court shall adjourn the proceedings pending compliance with the requirement unless the court is satisfied that the conduct of the case for the accused will not be substantially prejudiced by non-compliance with the requirement.

(2) Where, in the circumstances set out in paragraph (1) above, the court decides not to adjourn the proceedings, a record of that decision and of the reasons why the court was satisfied that the conduct of the case for the accused would not be substantially prejudiced by non-compliance with the requirement shall be entered in the register kept under rule 6.1.

---

1. The sanction for breach is in the rules themselves and it is appropriate to dismiss a case as an abuse of process on the ground of breach of the rules only in exceptional cases (*King v Kucharz* (1989) 153 JP 336). Therefore the court should not state, on granting an adjournment for disclosure, that failure to do so will entail dismissal of the case. Even if this is said, no legitimate expectation on behalf of the defendant will have been created as such dismissal would not be lawful (*R (on the application of AP, MD and JS) v Leeds Youth Court* [2001] EWHC Admin 215, 165 JP 684).

PART 22
DISCLOSURE BY THE PROSECUTION[1]

---

1. There are currently no rules in this Part.

1–7443

PART 23
DISCLOSURE BY THE DEFENCE[1]

___

1. There are currently no rules in this Part.

1–7444

PART 24
DISCLOSURE OF EXPERT EVIDENCE

24.1. Requirement to disclose expert evidence. (1) Following—

- (a) a plea of not guilty by any person to an alleged offence in respect of which a magistrates' court proceeds to summary trial;
- (b) the committal for trial of any person;
- (c) the transfer to the Crown Court of any proceedings for the trial of a person by virtue of a notice of transfer given under section 4 of the Criminal Justice Act 1987;
- (d) the transfer to the Crown Court of any proceedings for the trial of a person by virtue of a notice of transfer served on a magistrates' court under section 53 of the Criminal Justice Act 1991;
- (e) the sending of any person for trial under section 51 of the Crime and Disorder Act 1998;
- (f) the preferring of a bill of indictment charging a person with an offence under the authority of section 2(2)(b) of the Administration of Justice (Miscellaneous Provisions) Act 1933; or
- (g) the making of an order for the retrial of any person,

if any party[1] to the proceedings proposes to adduce expert evidence (whether of fact or opinion) in the proceedings (otherwise than in relation to sentence) he shall as soon as practicable, unless in relation to the evidence in question he has already done so or the evidence is the subject of an application for leave to adduce such evidence in accordance with section 41 of the Youth Justice and Criminal Evidence Act 1999—

- (i) furnish the other party or parties and the court with a statement in writing of any finding or opinion which he proposes to adduce by way of such evidence and notify the expert of this disclosure, and
- (ii) where a request in writing is made to him in that behalf by any other party, provide that party also with a copy of (or if it appears to the party proposing to adduce the evidence to be more practicable, a reasonable opportunity to examine) the record of any observation, test, calculation or other procedure on which such finding or opinion is based and any document or other thing or substance in respect of which any such procedure has been carried out.

(2) A party may by notice in writing waive his right to be furnished with any of the matters mentioned in paragraph (1) and, in particular, may agree that the statement mentioned in paragraph (1)(a) may be furnished to him orally and not in writing.

(3) In paragraph (1), "document" means anything in which information of any description is recorded.

___

1. These rules are not an exhaustive statement of the prosecutor's duty; see *R v Ward* [1993] 2 All ER 577, [1993] 1 WLR 619, 96 Cr App Rep 1, CA.

24.2. Withholding evidence. (1) If a party has reasonable grounds for believing that the disclosure of any evidence in compliance with the requirements imposed by rule 24.1 might lead to the intimidation, or attempted intimidation, of any person on whose evidence he intends to rely in the proceedings, or otherwise to the course of justice being interfered with, he shall not be obliged to comply with those requirements in relation to that evidence.

(2) Where, in accordance with paragraph (1), a party considers that he is not obliged to comply with the requirements imposed by rule 24.1 with regard to any evidence in relation to any other party, he shall give notice in writing to that party to the effect that the evidence is being withheld and the grounds for doing so.

24.3. Effect of failure to disclose. A party who seeks to adduce expert evidence in any proceedings and who fails to comply with rule 24.1 shall not adduce that evidence in those proceedings without the leave of the court[1].

___

1. The court is entitled not to allow cross examination of expert witnesses on behalf of defendants who have not served a statement of those experts' evidence on the prosecutor or to take the evidence of those experts into account when considering the cases of those defendants: *Skinner v DPP* [2004] EWHC 2914 (Admin), [2005] RTR 17.

1–7445

PART 25
APPLICATIONS FOR PUBLIC INTEREST IMMUNITY AND SPECIFIC DISCLOSURE

25.1. Public interest: application by prosecutor. (1) This rule applies to the making of an application by the prosecutor under section 3(6), 7A(8) or 8(5) of the Criminal Procedure and Investigations Act 1996.

(2) Notice of such an application shall be served on the court officer and shall specify the nature of the material to which the application relates.

(3) Subject to paragraphs (4) and (5) below, a copy of the notice of application shall be served on the accused by the prosecutor.

(4) Where the prosecutor has reason to believe that to reveal to the accused the nature of the material to which the application relates would have the effect of disclosing that which the prosecutor contends should not in the public interest be disclosed, paragraph (3) above shall not apply but the prosecutor shall notify the accused that an application to which this rule applies has been made.

(5) Where the prosecutor has reason to believe that to reveal to the accused the fact that an application is being made would have the effect of disclosing that which the prosecutor contends should not in the public interest be disclosed, paragraph (3) above shall not apply.

(6) Where an application is made in the Crown Court to which paragraph (5) above applies, notice of the application may be served on the trial judge or, if the application is made before the start of the trial, on the judge, if any, who has been designated to conduct the trial instead of on the court officer.

25.2. Public interest: hearing of application by prosecutor. (1) This rule applies to the hearing of an application by the prosecutor under section 3(6), 7A(8) or 8(5) of the Criminal Procedure and Investigations Act 1996.

(2) Where notice of such an application is served on the Crown Court officer, the officer shall on receiving it refer it—

(*a*) if the trial has started, to the trial judge; or
(*b*) if the application is received before the start of the trial either—

  (i) to the judge who has been designated to conduct the trial, or
  (ii) if no judge has been designated for that purpose, to such judge as may be designated for the purposes of hearing the application.

(3) Where such an application is made and a copy of the notice of application has been served on the accused in accordance with rule 25.1(3), then subject to paragraphs (4) and (5) below—

(*a*) the court officer shall on receiving notice of the application give notice to—

  (i) the prosecutor,
  (ii) the accused, and
  (iii) any person claiming to have an interest in the material to which the application relates who has applied under section 16(*b*) of the 1996 Act to be heard by the court,

of the date and time when and the place where the hearing will take place and, unless the court orders otherwise, such notice shall be given in writing;

(*b*) the hearing shall be inter partes; and
(*c*) the prosecutor and the accused shall be entitled to make representations to the court.

(4) Where the prosecutor applies to the court for leave to make representations in the absence of the accused, the court may for that purpose sit in the absence of the accused and any legal representative of his.

(5) Subject to rule 25.5(4) (interested party entitled to make representations), where a copy of the notice of application has not been served on the accused in accordance with rule 25.1(3)—

(*a*) the hearing shall be ex parte;
(*b*) only the prosecutor shall be entitled to make representations to the court;
(*c*) the accused shall not be given notice as specified in paragraph (3)(*a*)(ii) of this rule; and
(*d*) where notice of the application has been served in the Crown Court in pursuance of rule 25.1(6), the judge on whom it is served shall take such steps as he considers appropriate to ensure that notice is given as required by paragraph (3)(*a*)(i) and (iii) of this rule.

25.3. Public interest: non-disclosure order. (1) This rule applies to an order under section 3(6), 7A(8) or 8(5) of the Criminal Procedure and Investigations Act 1996.

(2) On making an order to which this rule applies, the court shall state its reasons for doing so. Where such an order is made in the Crown Court, a record shall be made of the statement of the court's reasons.

(3) In a case where such an order is made following—

(*a*) an application to which rule 25.1(4) (nature of material not to be revealed) applies; or
(*b*) an application notice of which has been served on the accused in accordance with rule 25.1(3) but the accused has not appeared or been represented at the hearing of that application,

the court officer shall notify the accused that an order has been made. No notification shall be given in a case where an order is made following an application to which rule 25.1(5) (fact of application not to be revealed) applies.

25.4. Review of non-disclosure order: application by accused. (1) This rule applies to an application by the accused under section 14(2) or section 15(4) of the Criminal Procedure and Investigations Act 1996.

(2) Such an application shall be made by notice in writing to the court officer for the court that made the order under section 3(6), 7A(8) or 8(5) of the 1996 Act and shall specify the reason why

the accused believes the court should review the question whether it is still not in the public interest to disclose the material affected by the order.

(3) A copy of the notice referred to in paragraph (2) shall be served on the prosecutor at the same time as it is sent to the court officer.

(4) Where such an application is made in a magistrates' court, the court officer shall take such steps as he thinks fit to ensure that the court has before it any document or other material which was available to the court which made the order mentioned in section 14(2) of the 1996 Act.

(5) Where such an application is made in the Crown Court, the court officer shall refer it—

(a) if the trial has started, to the trial judge; or
(b) if the application is received before the start of the trial either—

  (i) to the judge who has been designated to conduct the trial, or
  (ii) if no judge has been designated for that purpose, to the judge who made the order to which the application relates.

(6) The judge to whom such an application has been referred under paragraph (5) shall consider whether the application may be determined without a hearing and, subject to paragraph (7), may so determine it if he thinks fit.

(7) No application to which this rule applies shall be determined by the Crown Court without a hearing if it appears to the judge that there are grounds on which the court might conclude that it is in the public interest to disclose material to any extent.

(8) Where a magistrates' court considers that there are no grounds on which it might conclude that it is in the public interest to disclose material to any extent it may determine an application to which this rule applies without hearing representations from the accused, the prosecutor or any person claiming to have an interest in the material to which the application relates.

(9) Subject to paragraphs (10) and (11) of this rule and to rule 25.5(4) (interested party entitled to make representations), the hearing of an application to which this rule applies shall be inter partes and the accused and the prosecutor shall be entitled to make representations to the court.

(10) Where after hearing the accused's representations the prosecutor applies to the court for leave to make representations in the absence of the accused, the court may for that purpose sit in the absence of the accused and any legal representative of his.

(11) Subject to rule 25.5(4), where the order to which the application relates was made following an application of which the accused was not notified under rule 25.1(3) or (4), the hearing shall be ex parte and only the prosecutor shall be entitled to make representations to the court.

(12) The court officer shall give notice in writing to—

(a) the prosecutor;
(b) except where a hearing takes place in accordance with paragraph (11), the accused; and
(c) any person claiming to have an interest in the material to which the application relates who has applied under section 16(b) of the 1996 Act to be heard by the court,

of the date and time when and the place where the hearing of an application to which this rule applies will take place and of any order which is made by the court following its determination of the application.

(13) Where such an application is determined without a hearing in pursuance of paragraph (6), the court officer shall give notice in writing in accordance with paragraph (12) of any order which is made by the judge following his determination of the application.

25.5. Public interest applications: interested persons. (1) Where the prosecutor has reason to believe that a person who was involved (whether alone or with others and whether directly or indirectly) in the prosecutor's attention being brought to any material to which an application under section 3(6), 7A(8), 8(5), 14(2) or 15(4) of the Criminal Procedure and Investigations Act 1996 relates may claim to have an interest in that material, the prosecutor shall—

(a) in the case of an application under section 3(6), 7A(8) or 8(5) of the 1996 Act, at the same time as notice of the application is served under rule 25.1(2) or (6); or
(b) in the case of an application under section 14(2) or 15(4) of the 1996 Act, when he receives a copy of the notice referred to in rule 25.4(2),

give notice in writing to—

  (i) the person concerned of the application, and
  (ii) the court officer or, as the case may require, the judge of his belief and the grounds for it.

(2) An application under section 16(b) of the 1996 Act shall be made by notice in writing to the court officer or, as the case may require, the judge as soon as is reasonably practicable after receipt of notice under paragraph (1)(i) above or, if no such notice is received, after the person concerned becomes aware of the application referred to in that sub-paragraph and shall specify the nature of the applicant's interest in the material and his involvement in bringing the material to the prosecutor's attention.

(3) A copy of the notice referred to in paragraph (2) shall be served on the prosecutor at the same time as it is sent to the court officer or the judge as the case may require.

(4) At the hearing of an application under section 3(6), 7A(8), 8(5), 14(2) or 15(4) of the 1996 Act a person who has made an application under section 16(b) in accordance with paragraph (2) of this rule shall be entitled to make representations to the court.

25.6. Disclosure: application by accused and order of court. (1) This rule applies to an application by the accused under section 8(2) of the Criminal Procedure and Investigations Act 1996.

(2) Such an application shall be made by notice in writing to the court officer and shall specify—

(a) the material to which the application relates;

(b) that the material has not been disclosed to the accused;

(c) the reason why the material might be expected to assist the applicant's defence as disclosed by the defence statement given under section 5 or 6 of the 1996 Act; and

(d) the date of service of a copy of the notice on the prosecutor in accordance with paragraph (3).

(3) A copy of the notice referred to in paragraph (2) shall be served on the prosecutor at the same time as it is sent to the court officer.

(4) Where such an application is made in the Crown Court, the court officer shall refer it—

(a) if the trial has started, to the trial judge, or

(b) if the application is received before the start of the trial—

    (i) to the judge who has been designated to conduct the trial, or

    (ii) if no judge has been designated for that purpose, to such judge as may be designated for the purposes of determining the application.

(5) A prosecutor receiving notice under paragraph (3) of an application to which this rule applies shall give notice in writing to the court officer within 14 days of service of the notice that—

(a) he wishes to make representations to the court concerning the material to which the application relates; or

(b) if he does not so wish, that he is willing to disclose that material,

and a notice under paragraph 5(a) shall specify the substance of the representations he wishes to make.

(6) A court may determine an application to which this rule applies without hearing representations from the applicant or the prosecutor unless—

(a) the prosecutor has given notice under paragraph (5)(a) and the court considers that the representations should be made at a hearing; or

(b) the court considers it necessary to hear representations from the applicant or the prosecutor in the interests of justice for the purposes of determining the application.

(7) Subject to paragraph (8), where a hearing is held in pursuance of this rule—

(a) the court officer shall give notice in writing to the prosecutor and the applicant of the date and time when and the place where the hearing will take place;

(b) the hearing shall be inter partes; and

(c) the prosecutor and the applicant shall be entitled to make representations to the court.

(8) Where the prosecutor applies to the court for leave to make representations in the absence of the accused, the court may for that purpose sit in the absence of the accused and any legal representative of his.

(9) A copy of any order under section 8(2) of the 1996 Act shall be served on the prosecutor and the applicant.

25.7. Disclosure: application for extension of time limit and order of the court. (1) This rule applies to an application under regulation 3(2) of the Criminal Procedure and Investigations Act 1996 (Defence Disclosure Time Limits) Regulations 1997, including that regulation as applied by regulation 4(2).

(2) An application to which this rule applies shall be made by notice in writing to the court officer and shall, in addition to the matters referred to in regulation 3(3)(a) to (c) of the 1997 Regulations, specify the date of service of a copy of the notice on the prosecutor in accordance with paragraph (3) of this rule.

(3) A copy of the notice referred to in paragraph (2) of this rule shall be served on the prosecutor at the same time as it is sent to the court officer.

(4) The prosecutor may make representations to the court concerning the application and if he wishes to do so he shall do so in writing within 14 days of service of a notice under paragraph (3) of this rule.

(5) On receipt of representations under paragraph (4) above, or on the expiration of the period specified in that paragraph if no such representations are received within that period, the court shall consider the application and may, if it wishes, do so at a hearing.

(6) Where a hearing is held in pursuance of this rule—

(a) the court officer shall give notice in writing to the prosecutor and the applicant of the date and time when and the place where the hearing will take place;

(b) the hearing shall be inter partes; and

(c) the prosecutor and the applicant shall be entitled to make representations to the court.

(7) A copy of any order under regulation 3(1) or 4(1) of the 1997 Regulations shall be served on the prosecutor and the applicant.

25.8. Public interest and disclosure applications: general. (1) Any hearing held under this Part may be adjourned from time to time.

(2) Any hearing referred to in paragraph (1) other than one held under rule 25.7 may be held in private.

(3) Where a Crown Court hearing, or any part thereof, is held in private under paragraph (2),

the court may specify conditions subject to which the record of its statement of reasons made in pursuance of rule 25.3(2) is to be kept.

(4) Where an application or order to which any provision of this rule applies is made after the start of a trial in the Crown Court, the trial judge may direct that any provision of this rule requiring notice of the application or order to be given to any person shall not have effect and may give such direction as to the giving of notice in relation to that application or order as he thinks fit.

1–7446

PART 26

CONFIDENTIAL MATERIAL

26.1. Application for permission to use or disclose object or information. (1) This rule applies to an application under section 17(4) of the Criminal Procedure and Investigations Act 1996.

(2) Such an application shall be made by notice in writing to the court officer for the court which conducted or is conducting the proceedings for whose purposes the applicant was given, or allowed to inspect, the object to which the application relates.

(3) The notice of application shall—

(a) specify the object which the applicant seeks to use or disclose and the proceedings for whose purposes he was given, or allowed to inspect, it;

(b) where the applicant seeks to use or disclose any information recorded in the object specified in pursuance of paragraph (3)(a), specify that information;

(c) specify the reason why the applicant seeks permission to use or disclose the object specified in pursuance of paragraph (3)(a) or any information specified in pursuance of paragraph (3)(b);

(d) describe any proceedings in connection with which the applicant seeks to use or disclose the object or information referred to in paragraph (3)(c); and

(e) specify the name and address of any person to whom the applicant seeks to disclose the object or information referred to in paragraph (3)(c).

(4) Where the court officer receives an application to which this rule applies, the court officer or the clerk of the magistrates' court shall fix a date and time for the hearing of the application.

(5) The court officer shall give the applicant and the prosecutor at least 28 days' notice of the date fixed in pursuance of paragraph (4) and shall at the same time send to the prosecutor a copy of the notice given to him in pursuance of paragraph (2).

(6) Where the prosecutor has reason to believe that a person may claim to have an interest in the object specified in a notice of application in pursuance of paragraph (3)(a), or in any information so specified in pursuance of paragraph (3)(b), he shall, as soon as reasonably practicable after receipt of a copy of that notice under paragraph (5), send a copy of the notice to that person and inform him of the date fixed in pursuance of paragraph (4).

26.2. Prosecutor or interested party wishing to be heard. (1) This rule applies to an application under section 17(6)(b) of the Criminal Procedure and Investigations Act 1996.

(2) An application to which this rule applies shall be made by notice in writing to the court officer of the court referred to in rule 26.1(2) not less than 7 days before the date fixed in pursuance of rule 26.1(4).

(3) The applicant shall at the same time send to the person whose application under section 17(4) of the 1996 Act is concerned a copy of the notice given in pursuance of paragraph (2).

26.3. Decision on application for use or disclosure. (1) Where no application to which rule 26.2 applies is made in accordance with paragraph (2) of that rule, the court shall consider whether the application under section 17(4) of the Criminal Procedure and Investigations Act 1996 may be determined without hearing representations from the accused, the prosecutor or any person claiming to have an interest in the object or information to which the application relates, and may so determine it if the court thinks fit.

(2) Where an application to which rule 26.1 applies is determined without hearing any such representations the court officer shall give notice in writing to the person who made the application and to the prosecutor of any order made under section 17(4) of the 1996 Act or, as the case may be, that no such order has been made.

26.4. Unauthorised use or disclosure. (1) This rule applies to proceedings to deal with a contempt of court under section 18 of the Criminal Procedure and Investigations Act 1996.

(2) In such proceedings before a magistrates' court the Magistrates' Courts Act 1980 shall have effect subject to the modifications contained in paragraphs (3) to (7) (being provisions equivalent to those in Schedule 3 to the Contempt of Court Act 1981 subject to modifications which the Lord Chancellor considered appropriate after consultation with the rule committee for magistrates' courts).

(3) Where proceedings to which this rule applies are taken of the court's own motion the provisions of the 1980 Act listed in paragraph (4) shall apply as if a complaint had been made against the person against whom the proceedings are taken and subject to the modifications specified in paragraphs (5) and (6).

(4) The provisions referred to in paragraph (3) are—

(a) section 51 (issue of summons);

(b) section 53(1) and (2) (procedure on hearing);

(c) section 54 (adjournment);

(*d*)   section 55 (non-appearance of defendant);
(*e*)   section 97(1) (summons to witness);
(*f*)   section 101 (onus of proving exceptions etc);
(*g*)   section 121(1) and (3)(*a*) (constitution and place of sitting of court); and
(*h*)   section 123 (defect in process).

(5)   In—

(*a*)   section 55(1) for the words "the complainant appears but the defendant does not" there shall be substituted the words "the defendant does not appear"; and
(*b*)   section 55(2) the words "if the complaint has been substantiated on oath, and" shall be omitted.

(6)   In section 123(1) and (2) the words "adduced on behalf of the prosecutor or complainant" shall be omitted.

(7)   Where proceedings to which this rule applies are taken by way of complaint for an order—

(*a*)   section 127 of the 1980 Act (limitation of time) shall not apply to the complaint;
(*b*)   the complaint may be made by the prosecutor or by any other person claiming to have an interest in the object, or in any information recorded in an object, the use or disclosure of which is alleged to contravene section 17 of the 1996 Act; and
(*c*)   the complaint shall be made to the magistrates' court officer for the magistrates' court which conducted or is conducting the proceedings for whose purposes the object mentioned in paragraph (7)(*b*) was given or inspected.

(8)   An application to the Crown Court for an order of committal or for the imposition of a fine in proceedings to which this rule applies may be made by the prosecutor or by any other person claiming to have an interest in the object, or in any information recorded in an object, the use or disclosure of which is alleged to contravene section 17 of the 1996 Act. Such an application shall be made in accordance with paragraphs (9) to (20).

(9)   An application such as is referred to in paragraph (8) shall be made by notice in writing to the court officer at the same place as that in which the Crown Court sat or is sitting to conduct the proceedings for whose purposes the object mentioned in paragraph (2) was given or inspected.

(10)   The notice referred to in paragraph (9) shall set out the name and a description of the applicant, the name, description and address of the person sought to be committed or fined and the grounds on which his committal or the imposition of a fine is sought and shall be supported by an affidavit verifying the facts.

(11)   Subject to paragraph (12), the notice referred to in paragraph (9), accompanied by a copy of the affidavit in support of the application, shall be served personally on the person sought to be committed or fined.

(12)   The court may dispense with service of the notice under this rule if it is of the opinion that it is necessary to do so in order to protect the applicant or for another purpose identified by the court.

(13)   Nothing in the foregoing provisions of this rule shall be taken as affecting the power of the Crown Court to make an order of committal or impose a fine of its own motion against a person guilty of a contempt under section 18 of the 1996 Act.

(14)   Subject to paragraph (15), proceedings to which this rule applies shall be heard in open court.

(15)   Proceedings to which this rule applies may be heard in private where—

(*a*)   the object, the use or disclosure of which is alleged to contravene section 17 of the 1996 Act, is; or
(*b*)   the information, the use or disclosure of which is alleged to contravene that section, is recorded in,

an object which is, or forms part of, material in respect of which an application was made under section 3(6), 7A(8) or 8(5) of the 1996 Act, whether or not the court made an order that the material be not disclosed:

Provided that where the court hears the proceedings in private it shall nevertheless, if it commits any person to custody or imposes a fine on him in pursuance of section 18(3) of the 1996 Act, state in open court the name of that person, the period specified in the order of committal or, as the case may be, the amount of the fine imposed, or both such period and such amount where both are ordered.

(16)   Except with the leave of the court hearing an application for an order of committal or for the imposition of a fine no grounds shall be relied upon at the hearing except the grounds set out in the notice referred to in paragraph (9).

(17)   If on the hearing of the application the person sought to be committed or fined expresses a wish to give oral evidence on his own behalf, he shall be entitled to do so.

(18)   The court by whom an order of committal is made may by order direct that the execution of the order of committal shall be suspended for such period or on such terms or conditions as it may specify.

(19)   Where execution of an order of committal is suspended by an order under paragraph (18), the applicant for the order of committal must, unless the court otherwise directs, serve on the person against whom it was made a notice informing him of the making and terms of the order under that paragraph.

(20)   The court may, on the application of any person committed to custody for a contempt under section 18 of the 1996 Act, discharge him.

26.5. Forfeiture of object used or disclosed without authority.   (1) Where the Crown Court finds a person guilty of contempt under section 18 of the Criminal Procedure and Investigations Act 1996 and proposes to make an order under section 18(4) or (7), the court may adjourn the proceedings.

(2) Where the court adjourns the proceedings under paragraph (1), the court officer shall give notice to the person found guilty and to the prosecutor—

(a) that the court proposes to make such an order and that, if an application is made in accordance with paragraph (5), it will before doing so hear any representations made by the person found guilty, or by any person in respect of whom the prosecutor gives notice to the court under paragraph (3); and

(b) of the time and date of the adjourned hearing.

(3) Where the prosecutor has reason to believe that a person may claim to have an interest in the object which has been used or disclosed in contravention of section 17 of the 1996 Act he shall, on receipt of notice under paragraph (2), give notice of that person's name and address to the court office for the court which made the finding of guilt.

(4) Where the court officer receives a notice under paragraph (3), he shall, within 7 days of the finding of guilt, notify the person specified in that notice—

(a) that the court has made a finding of guilt under section 18 of the 1996 Act, that it proposes to make an order under section 18(4) or, as the case may be, 18(7) and that, if an application is made in accordance with paragraph (5), it will before doing so hear any representations made by him; and

(b) of the time and date of the adjourned hearing.

(5) An application under section 18(6) of the 1996 Act shall be made by notice in writing to the court officer not less than 24 hours before the time set for the adjourned hearing.

1–7447

PART 27
WITNESS STATEMENTS

27.1. Witness statements in magistrates' courts. (1) Written statements to be tendered in evidence in accordance with section 5B of the Magistrates' Courts Act 1980 or section 9 of the Criminal Justice Act 1967 shall be in the form set out in the Practice Direction.

(2) When a copy of any of the following evidence, namely—

(a) evidence tendered in accordance with section 5A of the 1980 Act (committal for trial); or

(b) a written statement tendered in evidence under section 9 of the 1967 Act (proceedings other than committal for trial),

is given to or served on any party to the proceedings a copy of the evidence in question shall be given to the court officer as soon as practicable thereafter, and where a copy of any such statement as is referred to in sub-paragraph (b) is given or served by or on behalf of the prosecutor, the accused shall be given notice by or on behalf of the prosecutor of his right to object to the statement being tendered in evidence.

(3) Where—

(a) a statement or deposition to be tendered in evidence in accordance with section 5A of the 1980 Act; or

(b) a written statement to be tendered in evidence under section 9 of the 1967 Act,

refers to any document or object as an exhibit, that document or object shall wherever possible be identified by means of a label or other mark of identification signed by the maker of the statement or deposition, and before a magistrates' court treats any document or object referred to as an exhibit in such a statement or deposition as an exhibit produced and identified in court by the maker of the statement or deposition, the court shall be satisfied that the document or object is sufficiently described in the statement or deposition for it to be identified.

(4) If it appears to a magistrates' court that any part of any evidence tendered in accordance with section 5A of the 1980 Act or a written statement tendered in evidence under section 9 of the 1967 Act is inadmissible there shall be written against that part—

(a) in the case of any evidence tendered in accordance with section 5A of the 1980 Act, but subject to paragraph (5) of this rule, the words "Treated as inadmissible" together with the signature and name of the examining justice or, where there is more than one examining justice, the signature and name of one of the examining justices by whom the evidence is so treated;

(b) in the case of a written statement tendered in evidence under section 9 of the 1967 Act the words "Ruled inadmissible" together with the signature and name of one of the justices who ruled the statement to be inadmissible.

(5) Where the nature of the evidence referred to in paragraph (4)(a) is such that it is not possible to write on it, the words set out in that sub-paragraph shall instead be written on a label or other mark of identification which clearly identifies the part of the evidence to which the words relate and contains the signature and name of an examining justice in accordance with that sub-paragraph.

(6) Where, before a magistrates' court—

(a) a statement or deposition is tendered in evidence in accordance with section 5A of the 1980 Act; or

(b) a written statement is tendered in accordance with section 9 of the 1967 Act, the name of the maker of the statement or deposition shall be read aloud unless the court otherwise directs.

(7) Where—

(a) under section 5B(4), 5C(4), 5D(5) or 5E(3) of the 1980 Act; or

(b) under section 9(6) of the 1967 Act,

in any proceedings before a magistrates' court any part of the evidence has to be read out aloud, or an account has to be given orally of so much of any evidence as is not read out aloud, the evidence shall be read or the account given by or on behalf of the party which has tendered the evidence.

(8) Statements and depositions tendered in evidence in accordance with section 5A of the 1980 Act before a magistrates' court acting as examining justices shall be authenticated by a certificate[1] signed by one of the examining justices.

(9) Where, before a magistrates' court—

(a) evidence is tendered as indicated in paragraph (2)(a) of this rule, retained by the court, and not sent to the Crown Court under rule 10.5; or

(b) a written statement is tendered in evidence as indicated in paragraph (2)(b) of this rule and not sent to the Crown Court under rule 43.1 or 43.2,

all such evidence shall, subject to any direction of the court in respect of non-documentary exhibits falling within paragraph (9)(a), be preserved for a period of three years by the magistrates' court officer for the magistrates' court.

---

1. The fact that an examining justice has failed to sign the certificate does not render the committal proceedings invalid (*R v Carey* (1982) 76 Cr App Rep 152).

27.2. Right to object to evidence being read in Crown Court trial. (1) The prosecutor shall, when he serves on any other party a copy of the evidence to be tendered in committal proceedings, notify that party that if he is committed for trial he has the right to object, by written notification to the prosecutor and the Crown Court within 14 days of being so committed unless the court in its discretion permits such an objection to be made outside that period, to a statement or deposition being read as evidence at the trial without oral evidence being given by the person who made the statement or deposition and without the opportunity to cross-examine that person.

(2) The prosecutor shall, on notifying a party as indicated in paragraph (1), send a copy of such notification to the magistrates' court officer.

(3) Any objection under paragraph 1(3)(c) or paragraph 2(3)(c) of Schedule 2 to the Criminal Procedure and Investigations Act 1996 to the reading out at the trial of a statement or deposition without further evidence shall be made in writing to the prosecutor and the Crown Court within 14 days of the accused being committed for trial unless the court at its discretion permits such an objection to be made outside that period.

1–7448

PART 28

WITNESS SUMMONSES, WARRANTS AND ORDERS

28.1. When this Part applies. (1) This Part applies in magistrates' courts and in the Crown Court where—

(a) a party wants the court to issue a witness summons, warrant or order under—

    (i) section 97 of the Magistrates' Courts Act 1980,

    (ii) section 2 of the Criminal Procedure (Attendance of Witnesses) Act 1965, or

    (iii) section 7 of the Bankers' Books Evidence Act 1879;

(b) the court considers the issue of such a summons, warrant or order on its own initiative as if a party had applied; or

(c) one of those listed in rule 28.7 wants the court to withdraw such a summons, warrant or order.

(2) A reference to a 'witness' in this Part is a reference to a person to whom such a summons, warrant or order is directed.

28.2. Issue etc of summons, warrant or order with or without a hearing. (1) The court may issue or withdraw a witness summons, warrant or order with or without a hearing.

(2) A hearing under this Part must be in private unless the court otherwise directs.

28.3. Application for summons, warrant or order: general rules. (1) A party who wants the court to issue a witness summons, warrant or order must apply as soon as practicable after becoming aware of the grounds for doing so.

(2) The party applying must—

(a) identify the proposed witness;

(b) explain—

    (i) what evidence the proposed witness can give or produce,

    (ii) why it is likely to be material evidence, and

    (iii) why it would be in the interests of justice to issue a summons, order or warrant as appropriate.

(3) The application may be made orally unless—

(a)   rule 28.5 applies; or
(b)   the court otherwise directs.

28.4. Written application: form and service.   (1) An application in writing under rule 28.3 must be in the form set out in the Practice Direction, containing the same declaration of truth as a witness statement.
(2) The party applying must serve the application—

(a)   in every case, on the court officer and as directed by the court; and
(b)   as required by rule 28.5, if that rule applies.

28.5. Application for summons to produce a document, etc: special rules.   (1) This rule applies to an application under rule 28.3 for a witness summons requiring the proposed witness—

(a)   to produce in evidence a document or thing; or
(b)   to give evidence about information apparently held in confidence,

that relates to another person.
(2) The application must be in writing in the form required by rule 28.4.
(3) The party applying must serve the application—

(a)   on the proposed witness, unless the court otherwise directs; and
(b)   on one or more of the following, if the court so directs—

     (i)   a person to whom the proposed evidence relates,
     (ii)   another party.

(4) The court must not issue a witness summons where this rule applies unless—

(a)   everyone served with the application has had at least 14 days in which to make representations, including representations about whether there should be a hearing of the application before the summons is issued; and
(b)   the court is satisfied that it has been able to take adequate account of the duties and rights, including rights of confidentiality, of the proposed witness and of any person to whom the proposed evidence relates.

(5) This rule does not apply to an application for an order to produce in evidence a copy of an entry in a banker's book.

28.6. Application for summons to produce a document, etc: court's assessment of relevance and confidentiality.   (1) This rule applies where a person served with an application for a witness summons requiring the proposed witness to produce in evidence a document or thing objects to its production on the ground that—

(a)   it is not likely to be material evidence; or
(b)   even if it is likely to be material evidence, the duties or rights, including rights of confidentiality, of the proposed witness or of any person to whom the document or thing relates outweigh the reasons for issuing a summons.

(2) The court may require the proposed witness to make the document or thing available for the objection to be assessed.
(3) The court may invite—

(a)   the proposed witness or any representative of the proposed witness; or
(b)   a person to whom the document or thing relates or any representative of such a person,

to help the court assess the objection.

28.7. Application to withdraw a summons, warrant or order.   (1) The court may withdraw a witness summons, warrant or order if one of the following applies for it to be withdrawn—

(a)   the party who applied for it, on the ground that it no longer is needed;
(b)   the witness, on the grounds that—

     (i)   he was not aware of any application for it, and
     (ii)   he cannot give or produce evidence likely to be material evidence, or
     (iii)   even if he can, his duties or rights, including rights of confidentiality, or those of any person to whom the evidence relates outweigh the reasons for the issue of the summons, warrant or order; or

(c)   any person to whom the proposed evidence relates, on the grounds that—

     (i)   he was not aware of any application for it, and
     (ii)   that evidence is not likely to be material evidence, or
     (iii)   even if it is, his duties or rights, including rights of confidentiality, or those of the witness outweigh the reasons for the issue of the summons, warrant or order.

(2) A person applying under the rule must—

(a)   apply in writing as soon as practicable after becoming aware of the grounds for doing so, explaining why he wants the summons, warrant or order to be withdrawn; and
(b)   serve the application on the court officer and as appropriate on—

     (i)   the witness,
     (ii)   the party who applied for the summons, warrant or order, and

(iii) any other person who he knows was served with the application for the summons, warrant or order.

(3) Rule 28.6 applies to an application under this rule that concerns a document or thing to be produced in evidence.

28.8. Court's power to vary requirements under this Part. (1) The court may—

(*a*) shorten or extend (even after it has expired) a time limit under this Part; and
(*b*) where a rule or direction requires an application under this Part to be in writing, allow that application to be made orally instead.

(2) Someone who wants the court to allow an application to be made orally under paragraph (1)(*b*) of this rule must—

(*a*) give as much notice as the urgency of his application permits to those on whom he would otherwise have served an application in writing; and
(*b*) in doing so explain the reasons for the application and for wanting the court to consider it orally.

1–7449

PART 29
SPECIAL MEASURES DIRECTIONS

29.1. Application for special measures directions. (1) An application by a party in criminal proceedings for a magistrates' court or the Crown Court to give a special measures direction under section 19 of the Youth Justice and Criminal Evidence Act 1999 must be made in writing in the form set out in the Practice Direction.

(2) If the application is for a special measures direction—

(*a*) enabling a witness to give evidence by means of a live link, the information sought in Part B of that form must be provided;
(*b*) providing for any examination of a witness to be conducted through an intermediary, the information sought in Part C of that form must be provided; or
(*c*) enabling a video recording of an interview of a witness to be admitted as evidence in chief of the witness, the information sought in Part D of that form must be provided.

(3) The application under paragraph (1) above must be sent to the court officer and at the same time a copy thereof must be sent by the applicant to every other party to the proceedings.

(4) The court officer must receive the application—

(*a*) in the case of an application to a youth court, within 28 days of the date on which the defendant first appears or is brought before the court in connection with the offence;
(*b*) in the case of an application to a magistrates' court, within 14 days of the defendant indicating his intention to plead not guilty to any charge brought against him and in relation to which a special measures direction may be sought; and
(*c*) in the case of an application to the Crown Court, within 28 days of

(i) the committal of the defendant, or
(ii) the consent to the preferment of a bill of indictment in relation to the case, or
(iii) the service of a notice of transfer under section 53 of the Criminal Justice Act 1991, or
(iv) where a person is sent for trial under section 51 of the Crime and Disorder Act 1998, the service of copies of the documents containing the evidence on which the charge or charges are based under paragraph 1 of Schedule 3 to that Act, or
(v) the service of a Notice of Appeal from a decision of a youth court or a magistrates' court.

(5) A party to whom an application is sent in accordance with paragraph (3) may oppose the application for a special measures direction in respect of any, or any particular, measure available in relation to the witness, whether or not the question whether the witness is eligible for assistance by virtue of section 16 or 17 of the 1999 Act is in issue.

(6) A party who wishes to oppose the application must, within 14 days of the date the application was served on him, notify the applicant and the court officer, as the case may be, in writing of his opposition and give reasons for it.

(7) Paragraphs (5) and (6) do not apply in respect of an application for a special measures direction enabling a child witness in need of special protection to give evidence by means of a live link if the opposition is that the special measures direction is not likely to maximise the quality of the witness's evidence.

(8) In order to comply with paragraph (6)—

(*a*) a party must in the written notification state whether he—

(i) disputes that the witness is eligible for assistance by virtue of section 16 or 17 of the 1999 Act,
(ii) disputes that any of the special measures available would be likely to improve the quality of evidence given by the witness or that such measures (or a combination of them) would be likely to maximise the quality of that evidence, and
(iii) opposes the granting of a special measures direction; and

(*b*) where the application relates to the admission of a video recording, a party who receives a recording must provide the information required by rule 29.7(7) below.

(9) Except where notice is received in accordance with paragraph (6), the court (including, in the case of an application to a magistrates' court, a single justice of the peace) may—

(a) determine the application in favour of the applicant without a hearing; or
(b) direct a hearing.

(10) Where a party to the proceedings notifies the court in accordance with paragraph (6) of his opposition to the application, the justices' clerk or the Crown Court must direct a hearing of the application.

(11) Where a hearing of the application is to take place in accordance with paragraph (9) or (10) above, the court officer shall notify each party to the proceedings of the time and place of the hearing.

(12) A party notified in accordance with paragraph (11) may be present at the hearing and be heard.

(13) The court officer must, within 3 days of the decision of the court in relation to an application under paragraph (1) being made, notify all the parties of the decision, and if the application was made for a direction enabling a video recording of an interview of a witness to be admitted as evidence in chief of that witness, the notification must state whether the whole or specified parts only of the video recording or recordings disclosed are to be admitted in evidence.

(14) In this Part:

"an intermediary" has the same meaning as in section 29 of the 1999 Act; and
"child witness in need of protection" shall be construed in accordance with section 21(1) of the 1999 Act.

29.2. Application for an extension of time. (1) An application may be made in writing for the period of 14 days or, as the case may be, 28 days specified in rule 29.1(4) to be extended.

(2) The application may be made either before or after that period has expired.

(3) The application must be accompanied by a statement setting out the reasons why the applicant is or was unable to make the application within that period and a copy of the application and the statement must be sent to every other party to the proceedings.

(4) An application for an extension of time under this rule shall be determined by a single justice of the peace or a judge of the Crown Court without a hearing unless the justice or the judge otherwise directs.

(5) The court officer shall notify all the parties of the court's decision.

29.3. Late applications. (1) Notwithstanding the requirements of rule 29.1—

(a) an application may be made for a special measures direction orally at the trial; or
(b) a magistrates' court or the Crown Court may of its own motion raise the issue whether a special measures direction should be given.

(2) Where an application is made in accordance with paragraph (1)(a)—

(a) the applicant must state the reasons for the late application; and
(b) the court must be satisfied that the applicant was unable to make the application in accordance with rule 29.1.

(3) The court shall determine before making a special measures direction—

(a) whether to allow other parties to the proceedings to make representations on the question;
(b) the time allowed for making such representations (if any); and
(c) whether the question should be determined following a hearing at which the parties to the proceedings may be heard.

(4) Paragraphs (2) and (3) do not apply in respect of an application made orally at the trial for a special measures direction—

(a) enabling a child witness in need of special protection to give evidence by means of a live link; or
(b) enabling a video recording of such a child to be admitted as evidence in chief of the witness,

if the opposition is that the special measures direction will not maximise the quality of the witness's evidence.

29.4. Discharge or variation of a special measures direction. (1) An application to a magistrates' court or the Crown Court to discharge or vary a special measures direction under section 20(2) of the Youth Justice and Criminal Evidence Act 1999 must be in writing and each material change of circumstances which the applicant alleges has occurred since the direction was made must be set out.

(2) An application under paragraph (1) must be sent to the court officer as soon as reasonably practicable after the change of circumstances occurs.

(3) The applicant must also send copies of the application to each party to the proceedings at the same time as the application is sent to the court officer.

(4) A party to whom an application is sent in accordance with paragraph (3) may oppose the application on the ground that it discloses no material change of circumstances.

(5) Rule 29.1(6) to (13) shall apply to an application to discharge or vary a special measures direction as it applies to an application for a direction.

29.5. Renewal application following a material change of circumstances. (1) Where an application for a special measures direction has been refused by a magistrates' court or the Crown Court, the application may only be renewed ("renewal application") where there has been a material change of circumstances since the court refused the application.

(2) The applicant must—

(a) identify in the renewal application each material change of circumstances which is alleged to have occurred; and

(b) send the renewal application to the court officer as soon as reasonably practicable after the change occurs.

(3) The applicant must also send copies of the renewal application to each of the parties to the proceedings at the same time as the application is sent to the court officer.

(4) A party to whom the renewal application is sent in accordance with paragraph (3) above may oppose the application on the ground that it discloses no material change of circumstances.

(5) Rules 29.1(6) to (13), 29.6 and 29.7 apply to a renewal application as they apply to the application which was refused.

29.6. Application for special measures direction for witness to give evidence by means of a live television link. (1) Where the application for a special measures direction is made, in accordance with rule 29.1(2)(a), for a witness to give evidence by means of a live link, the following provisions of this rule shall also apply.

(2) A party who seeks to oppose an application for a child witness to give evidence by means of a live link must, in order to comply with rule 29.1(5), state why in his view the giving of a special measures direction would not be likely to maximise the quality of the witness's evidence.

(3) However, paragraph (2) does not apply in relation to a child witness in need of special protection.

(4) Where a special measures direction is made enabling a witness to give evidence by means of a live link, the witness shall be accompanied at the live link only by persons acceptable to the court.

(5) If the special measures directions combine provisions for a witness to give evidence by means of a live link with provision for the examination of the witness to be conducted through an intermediary, the witness shall be accompanied at the live link only by—

(a) the intermediary; and

(b) such other persons as may be acceptable to the court.

29.7. Video recording of testimony from witnesses. (1) Where an application is made to a magistrates' court or the Crown Court for a special measures direction enabling a video recording of an interview of a witness to be admitted as evidence in chief of the witness, the following provisions of this rule shall also apply.

(2) The application made in accordance with rule 29.1(1) must be accompanied by the video recording which it is proposed to tender in evidence and must include—

(a) the name of the defendant and the offence to be charged;

(b) the name and date of birth of the witness in respect of whom the application is made;

(c) the date on which the video recording was made;

(d) a statement as to whether, and if so at what point in the video recording, an oath was administered to, or a solemn declaration made by, the witness;

(e) a statement that, in the opinion of the applicant, either—

(i) the witness is available for cross-examination, or

(ii) the witness is not available for cross-examination and the parties have agreed that there is no need for the witness to be so available;

(f) a statement of the circumstances in which the video recording was made which complies with paragraph (4) of this rule; and

(g) the date on which the video recording was disclosed to the other party or parties.

(3) Where it is proposed to tender part only of a video recording of an interview with the witness, the application must specify that part and be accompanied by a video recording of the entire interview, including those parts which it is not proposed to tender in evidence, and by a statement of the circumstances in which the video recording of the entire interview was made which complies with paragraph (4) of this rule.

(4) The statement of the circumstances in which the video recording was made referred to in paragraphs (2)(f) and (3) of this rule shall include the following information, except in so far as it is contained in the recording itself—

(a) the times at which the recording commenced and finished, including details of interruptions;

(b) the location at which the recording was made and the usual function of the premises;

(c) in relation to each person present at any point during, or immediately before, the recording—

(i) their name, age and occupation,

(ii) the time for which each person was present, and

(iii) the relationship, if any, of each person to the witness and to the defendant;

(d) in relation to the equipment used for the recording—

(i) a description of the equipment,

(ii) the number of cameras used,

(iii) whether the cameras were fixed or mobile,

      (iv) the number and location of the microphones,

      (v) the video format used; and

      (vi) whether it offered single or multiple recording facilities and, if so, which were used; and

  (e) the location of the mastertape if the video recording is a copy and details of when and by whom the copy was made.

  (5) If the special measures directions enabling a video recording of an interview of a witness to be admitted as evidence in chief of the witness with provision for the examination of the witness to be conducted through an intermediary, the information to be provided under paragraph (4)(c) shall be the same as that for other persons present at the recording but with the addition of details of the declaration made by the intermediary under rule 29.9.

  (6) If the special measures directions enabling a video recording of an interview of a witness to be admitted as evidence in chief of the witness with provision for the witness, in accordance with section 30 of the Youth Justice and Criminal Evidence Act 1999, to be provided with a device as an aid to communication during the video recording of the interview the information to be included under paragraph (4)(d) shall include also details of any such device used for the purposes of recording.

  (7) A party who receives a recording under paragraph (2) must within 14 days of its receipt, notify the applicant and the court officer, in writing—

  (a) whether he objects to the admission under section 27 of the 1999 Act of any part of the video recording or recordings disclosed, giving his reasons why it would not be in the interests of justice for the recording or any part of it to be admitted;

  (b) whether he would agree to the admission of part of the video recording or recordings and, if so, which part or parts; and

  (c) whether he wishes to be represented at any hearing of the application.

  (8) A party who seeks to oppose an application for a special measures direction enabling a video recording of an interview of a child witness to be admitted as evidence in chief of the witness must, in order to comply with rule 29.1(6), state why in his view the giving of a special measures direction would not be likely to maximise the quality of the witness's evidence.

  (9) However, paragraph (8) does not apply if the witness is a child witness in need of special protection.

  (10) Notwithstanding the provisions of rule 29.1 and this rule, any video recording which the defendant proposes to tender in evidence need not be sent to the prosecution until the close of the prosecution case at the trial.

  (11) The court may determine an application by the defendant to tender in evidence a video recording even though the recording has not, in accordance with paragraph (10), been served upon the prosecution.

  (12) Where a video recording which is the subject of a special measures direction is sent to the prosecution after the direction has been made, the prosecutor may apply to the court for the direction to be varied or discharged.

  (13) An application under paragraph (12) may be made orally to the court.

  (14) A prosecutor who makes an application under paragraph (12) must state—

  (a) why he objects to the admission under section 27 of the 1999 Act of any part of the video recording or recordings disclosed, giving his reasons why it would not be in the interests of justice for the recording or any part of it to be admitted; and

  (b) whether he would agree to the admission of part of the video recording or recordings and, if so, which part or parts.

  (15) The court must, before determining the application—

  (a) direct a hearing of the application; and

  (b) allow all the parties to the proceedings to be present and be heard on the application.

  (16) The court officer must notify all parties to the proceedings of the decision of the court as soon as may be reasonable after the decision is given.

  (17) Any decision varying a special measures direction must state whether the whole or specified parts of the video recording or recordings subject to the application are to be admitted in evidence.

29.8. Expert evidence in connection with special measures directions. Any party to proceedings in a magistrates' court or the Crown Court who proposes to adduce expert evidence (whether of fact or opinion) in connection with an application or renewal application for, or for varying or discharging, a special measures direction must, not less than 14 days before the date set for the trial to begin—

  (a) furnish the other party or parties and the court with a statement in writing of any finding or opinion which he proposes to adduce by way of such evidence and notify the expert of this disclosure; and

  (b) where a request is made to him in that behalf by any other party to those proceedings, provide that party also with a copy of (or if it appears to the party proposing to adduce the evidence to be more practicable, a reasonable opportunity to examine) the record of any observation, test, calculation or other procedure on which such finding or opinion is based and any document or other thing or substance in respect of which any such procedure has been carried out.

29.9. Intermediaries. The declaration required to be made by an intermediary in accordance with section 29(5) of the Youth Justice and Criminal Evidence Act 1999 shall be in the following form:

"I solemnly, sincerely and truly declare that I will well and faithfully communicate questions and answers and make true explanation of all matters and things as shall be required of me according to the best of my skill and understanding."

1–7450

PART 30
USE OF LIVE TELEVISION LINK OTHER THAN FOR VULNERABLE WITNESSES

30.1. Evidence by live television link in the Crown Court where witness is outside the United Kingdom. (1) Any party may apply for leave under section 32(1) of the Criminal Justice Act 1988 for evidence to be given through a live television link by a witness who is outside the United Kingdom.

(2) An application under paragraph (1), and any matter relating thereto which, by virtue of the following provisions of this rule, falls to be determined by the Crown Court, may be dealt with in chambers by any judge of the Crown Court.

(3) An application under paragraph (1) shall be made by giving notice in writing, which shall be in the form set out in the Practice Direction.

(4) An application under paragraph (1) shall be made within 28 days after the date of the committal of the defendant or, as the case may be, of the giving of a notice of transfer under section 4(1)(c) of the Criminal Justice Act 1987, or of the service of copies of the documents containing the evidence on which the charge or charges are based under paragraph 1 of Schedule 3 to the Crime and Disorder Act 1998, or of the preferring of a bill of indictment in relation to the case.

(5) The period of 28 days in paragraph (4) may be extended by the Crown Court, either before or after it expires, on an application made in writing, specifying the grounds of the application. The court officer shall notify all the parties of the decision of the Crown Court.

(6) The notice under paragraph (3) or any application under paragraph (5) shall be sent to the court officer and at the same time a copy thereof shall be sent by the applicant to every other party to the proceedings.

(7) A party who receives a copy of a notice under paragraph (3) shall, within 28 days of the date of the notice, notify the applicant and the court officer, in writing—

(a) whether or not he opposes the application, giving his reasons for any such opposition; and
(b) whether or not he wishes to be represented at any hearing of the application.

(8) After the expiry of the period referred to in paragraph (7), the Crown Court shall determine whether an application under paragraph (1) is to be dealt with—

(a) without a hearing; or
(b) at a hearing at which the applicant and such other party or parties as the court may direct may be represented;
(c) and the court officer shall notify the applicant and, where necessary, the other party or parties, of the time and place of any such hearing.

(9) The court officer shall notify all the parties of the decision of the Crown Court in relation to an application under paragraph (1) and, where leave is granted, the notification shall state—

(a) the country in which the witness will give evidence;
(b) if known, the place where the witness will give evidence;
(c) where the witness is to give evidence on behalf of the prosecutor, or where disclosure is required by section 5(7) of the Criminal Procedure and Investigations Act 1996 (alibi) or by rules under section 81 of the Police and Criminal Evidence Act 1984 (expert evidence), the name of the witness;
(d) the location of the Crown Court at which the trial should take place; and
(e) any conditions specified by the Crown Court in accordance with paragraph (10).

(10) The Crown Court dealing with an application under paragraph (1) may specify that as a condition of the grant of leave the witness should give the evidence in the presence of a specified person who is able and willing to answer under oath or affirmation any questions the trial judge may put as to the circumstances in which the evidence is given, including questions about any persons who are present when the evidence is given and any matters which may affect the giving of the evidence.

1–7451

PART 31
RESTRICTION ON CROSS-EXAMINATION BY A DEFENDANT ACTING IN PERSON

31.1. Restrictions on cross-examination of witness. (1) This rule and rules 31.2 and 31.3 apply where an accused is prevented from cross-examining a witness in person by virtue of section 34, 35 or 36 of the Youth Justice and Criminal Evidence Act 1999.

(2) The court shall explain to the accused as early in the proceedings as is reasonably practicable that he—

(a) is prevented from cross-examining a witness in person; and
(b) should arrange for a legal representative to act for him for the purpose of cross-examining the witness.

(3) The accused shall notify the court officer within 7 days of the court giving its explanation, or within such other period as the court may in any particular case allow, of the action, if any, he has taken.

(4) Where he has arranged for a legal representative to act for him, the notification shall include details of the name and address of the representative.

(5) The notification shall be in writing.

(6) The court officer shall notify all other parties to the proceedings of the name and address of the person, if any, appointed to act for the accused.

(7) Where the court gives its explanation under paragraph (2) to the accused either within 7 days of the day set for the commencement of any hearing at which a witness in respect of whom a prohibition under section 34, 35 or 36 of the 1999 Act applies may be cross-examined or after such a hearing has commenced, the period of 7 days shall be reduced in accordance with any directions issued by the court.

(8) Where at the end of the period of 7 days or such other period as the court has allowed, the court has received no notification from the accused it may grant the accused an extension of time, whether on its own motion or on the application of the accused.

(9) Before granting an extension of time, the court may hold a hearing at which all parties to the proceedings may attend and be heard.

(10) Any extension of time shall be of such period as the court considers appropriate in the circumstances of the case.

(11) The decision of the court as to whether to grant the accused an extension of time shall be notified to all parties to the proceedings by the court officer.

31.2. Appointment of legal representative. (1) Where the court decides, in accordance with section 38(4) of the Youth Justice and Criminal Evidence Act 1999, to appoint a qualified legal representative, the court officer shall notify all parties to the proceedings of the name and address of the representative.

(2) An appointment made by the court under section 38(4) of the 1999 Act shall, except to such extent as the court may in any particular case determine, terminate at the conclusion of the cross-examination of the witness or witnesses in respect of whom a prohibition under section 34, 35 or 36 of the 1999 Act applies.

31.3. Appointment arranged by the accused. (1) The accused may arrange for the qualified legal representative, appointed by the court under section 38(4) of the Youth Justice and Criminal Evidence Act 1999, to be appointed to act for him for the purpose of cross-examining any witness in respect of whom a prohibition under section 34, 35 or 36 of the 1999 Act applies.

(2) Where such an appointment is made—

(a) both the accused and the qualified legal representative appointed shall notify the court of the appointment; and

(b) the qualified legal representative shall, from the time of his appointment, act for the accused as though the arrangement had been made under section 38(2)(a) of the 1999 Act and shall cease to be the representative of the court under section 38(4).

(3) Where the court receives notification of the appointment either from the qualified legal representative or from the accused but not from both, the court shall investigate whether the appointment has been made, and if it concludes that the appointment has not been made, paragraph (2)(b) shall not apply.

(4) An accused may, notwithstanding an appointment by the court under section 38(4) of the 1999 Act, arrange for a legal representative to act for him for the purpose of cross-examining any witness in respect of whom a prohibition under section 34, 35 or 36 of the 1999 Act applies.

(5) Where the accused arranges for, or informs the court of his intention to arrange for, a legal representative to act for him, he shall notify the court, within such period as the court may allow, of the name and address of any person appointed to act for him.

(6) Where the court is notified within the time allowed that such an appointment has been made, any qualified legal representative appointed by the court in accordance with section 38(4) of the 1999 Act shall be discharged.

(7) The court officer shall, as soon as reasonably practicable after the court receives notification of an appointment under this rule or, where paragraph (3) applies, after the court is satisfied that the appointment has been made, notify all the parties to the proceedings—

(a) that the appointment has been made;

(b) where paragraph (4) applies, of the name and address of the person appointed; and

(c) that the person appointed by the court under section 38(4) of the 1999 Act has been discharged or has ceased to act for the court.

31.4. Prohibition on cross-examination of witness. (1) An application by the prosecutor for the court to give a direction under section 36 of the Youth Justice and Criminal Evidence Act 1999 in relation to any witness must be sent to the court officer and at the same time a copy thereof must be sent by the applicant to every other party to the proceedings.

(2) In his application the prosecutor must state why, in his opinion—

(a) the evidence given by the witness is likely to be diminished if cross-examination is undertaken by the accused in person;

(b) the evidence would be improved if a direction were given under section 36(2) of the 1999 Act; and

(c) it would not be contrary to the interests of justice to give such a direction.

(a) details of the request in respect of which the notice under section 30(3) of the 2003 Act was given;
(b) the date on which, and place at which, the proceedings under Part 1 of Schedule 2 to that Act in respect of that request took place;
(c) the technical conditions, such as the type of equipment used, under which the proceedings took place;
(d) the name of the witness who gave evidence;
(e) the name of any person who took part in the proceedings as a legal representative or an interpreter; and
(f) the language in which the evidence was given.

(3) As soon as practicable after the proceedings under Part 1 of Schedule 2 to the 2003 Act took place, the justices' clerk or Crown Court officer shall send to the external authority that made the request a copy of an extract of so much of the overseas record as relates to the proceedings in respect of that request.

32.8. Record of telephone link hearing before a nominated court. (1) This rule applies where a court is nominated under section 31(4) of the Crime (International Co-operation) Act 2003.
(2) The justices' clerk or Crown Court officer shall enter in an overseas record—

(a) details of the request in respect of which the notice under section 31(4) of the 2003 Act was given;
(b) the date, time and place at which the proceedings under Part 2 of Schedule 2 to the 2003 Act took place;
(c) the name of the witness who gave evidence;
(d) the name of any interpreter who acted at the proceedings; and
(e) the language in which the evidence was given.

32.9. Overseas record. (1) The overseas records of a magistrates' court shall be part of the register (within the meaning of section 150(1) of the Magistrates' Courts Act 1980) and shall be kept in a separate book.
(2) The overseas records of any court shall not be open to inspection by any person except—

(a) as authorised by the Secretary of State; or
(b) with the leave of the court.

PART 33
EXPERT EVIDENCE

33.1. Reference to expert. A reference to an 'expert' in this Part is a reference to a person who is required to give or prepare expert evidence for the purpose of criminal proceedings, including evidence required to determine fitness to plead or for the purpose of sentencing.

33.2. Expert's duty to the court. (1) An expert must help the court to achieve the overriding objective by giving objective, unbiased opinion on matters within his expertise.
(2) This duty overrides any obligation to the person from whom he receives instructions or by whom he is paid.
(3) This duty includes an obligation to inform all parties and the court if the expert's opinion changes from that contained in a report served as evidence or given in a statement under Part 24 or Part 29.

33.3. Content of expert's report. (1) An expert's report must—

(a) give details of the expert's qualifications, relevant experience and accreditation;
(b) give details of any literature or other information which the expert has relied on in making the report;
(c) contain a statement setting out the substance of all facts given to the expert which are material to the opinions expressed in the report or upon which those opinions are based;
(d) make clear which of the facts stated in the report are within the expert's own knowledge;
(e) say who carried out any examination, measurement, test or experiment which the expert has used for the report and—

  (i) give the qualifications, relevant experience and accreditation of that person,
  (ii) say whether or not the examination, measurement, test or experiment was carried out under the expert's supervision, and
  (iii) summarise the findings on which the expert relies;

(f) where there is a range of opinion on the matters dealt with in the report—

  (i) summarise the range of opinion, and
  (ii) give reasons for his own opinion;

(g) if the expert is not able to give his opinion without qualification, state the qualification;
(h) contain a summary of the conclusions reached;
(i) contain a statement that the expert understands his duty to the court, and has complied and will continue to comply with that duty; and
(j) contain the same declaration of truth as a witness statement.

(2) Only sub-paragraphs (i) and (j) of rule 33.3(1) apply to a summary by an expert of his conclusions served in advance of that expert's report.

33.4. Expert to be informed of service of report.　A party who serves on another party or on the court a report by an expert must, at once, inform that expert of that fact.

33.5. Pre-hearing discussion of expert evidence.　(1) This rule applies where more than one party wants to introduce expert evidence.

(2) The court may direct the experts to—

(a) discuss the expert issues in the proceedings; and
(b) prepare a statement for the court of the matters on which they agree and disagree, giving their reasons.

(3) Except for that statement, the content of that discussion must not be referred to without the court's permission.

33.6. Failure to comply with directions.　A party may not introduce expert evidence without the court's permission if the expert has not complied with a direction under rule 33.5.

33.7. Court's power to direct that evidence is to be given by a single joint expert.　(1) Where more than one defendant wants to introduce expert evidence on an issue at trial, the court may direct that the evidence on that issue is to be given by one expert only.

(2) Where the co-defendants cannot agree who should be the expert, the court may—

(a) select the expert from a list prepared or identified by them; or
(b) direct that the expert be selected in such other manner as the court may direct.

33.8. Instructions to a single joint expert.　(1) Where the court gives a direction under rule 33.7 for a single joint expert to be used, each of the co-defendants may give instructions to the expert.

(2) When a co-defendant gives instructions to the expert he must, at the same time, send a copy of the instructions to the other co-defendant(s).

(3) The court may give directions about—

(a) the payment of the expert's fees and expenses; and
(b) any examination, measurement, test or experiment which the expert wishes to carry out.

(4) The court may, before an expert is instructed, limit the amount that can be paid by way of fees and expenses to the expert.

(5) Unless the court otherwise directs, the instructing co-defendants are jointly and severally liable for the payment of the expert's fees and expenses.

1-7454

PART 34
HEARSAY EVIDENCE

34.1. When this Part applies.　This Part applies in a magistrates' court and in the Crown Court where a party wants to introduce evidence on one or more of the grounds set out in section 114(1)(d) , section 116, section 117 and section 121 of the Criminal Justice Act 2003, and in this Part that evidence is called "hearsay evidence".

34.2. Notice of hearsay evidence.　The party who wants to introduce hearsay evidence must give notice in the form set out in the Practice Direction to the court officer and all other parties.

34.3. When the prosecutor must give notice of hearsay evidence.　The prosecutor must give notice of hearsay evidence—

(a) in a magistrates' court, at the same time as he complies or purports to comply with section 3 of the Criminal Procedure and Investigations Act 1996 (disclosure by prosecutor); or
(b) in the Crown Court, not more than 14 days after—

(i) the committal of the defendant, or
(ii) the consent to the preferment of a bill of indictment in relation to the case, or
(iii) the service of a notice of transfer under section 4 of the Criminal Justice Act 1987 (serious fraud cases) or under section 53 of the Criminal Justice Act 1991 (certain cases involving children), or
(iv) where a person is sent for trial under section 51 of the Crime and Disorder Act 1998 (indictable-only offences sent for trial), the service of copies of the documents containing the evidence on which the charge or charges are based under paragraph 1 of Schedule 3 to the 1998 Act.

34.4. When a defendant must give notice of hearsay evidence.　A defendant must give notice of hearsay evidence not more than 14 days after the prosecutor has complied with or purported to comply with section 3 of the Criminal Procedure and Investigations Act 1996 (disclosure by prosecutor).

34.5. Opposing the introduction of hearsay evidence.　A party who receives a notice of hearsay evidence may oppose it by giving notice within 14 days in the form set out in the Practice Direction to the court officer and all other parties.

34.6. Methods of giving notice. *Revoked.*

34.7. Court's power to vary requirements under this Part. The court may—

(a) dispense with the requirement to give notice of hearsay evidence;

(b) allow notice to be given in a different form, or orally; or

(c) shorten a time limit or extend it (even after it has expired).

34.8. Waiving the requirement to give a notice of hearsay evidence. A party entitled to receive a notice of hearsay evidence may waive his entitlement by so informing the court and the party who would have given the notice.

1–7455

PART 35
EVIDENCE OF BAD CHARACTER

35.1. When this Part applies. This Part applies in a magistrates' court and in the Crown Court when a party wants to introduce evidence of bad character as defined in section 98 of the Criminal Justice Act 2003.

35.2. Introducing evidence of non-defendant's bad character. A party who wants to introduce evidence of a non-defendant's bad character or who wants to cross-examine a witness with a view to eliciting that evidence, under section 100 of the Criminal Justice Act 2003 must apply in the form set out in the Practice Direction and the application must be received by the court officer and all other parties to the proceedings—

(a) not more than 14 days after the prosecutor has—

(i) complied or purported to comply with section 3 of the Criminal Procedure and Investigations Act 1996 (disclosure by the prosecutor); or

(ii) disclosed the previous convictions of that non-defendant; or

(b) as soon as reasonably practicable, where the application concerns a non-defendant who is to be invited to give (or has given) evidence for a defendant.

35.3. Opposing introduction of evidence of non-defendant's bad character. A party who receives a copy of an application under rule 35.2 may oppose that application by giving notice in writing to the court officer and all other parties to the proceedings not more than 14 days after receiving that application.

35.4. Prosecutor introducing evidence of defendant's bad character. (1) A prosecutor who wants to introduce evidence of a defendant's bad character or who wants to cross-examine a witness with a view to eliciting that evidence, under section 101 of the Criminal Justice Act 2003 must give notice in the form set out in the Practice Direction to the court officer and all other parties to the proceedings.

(2) Notice under paragraph (1) must be given—

(a) in a case to be tried in a magistrates' court, at the same time as the prosecutor complies or purports to comply with section 3 of the Criminal Procedure and Investigations Act 1996; and

(b) in a case to be tried in the Crown Court, not more than 14 days after—

(i) the committal of the defendant, or

(ii) the consent to the preferment of a bill of indictment in relation to the case, or

(iii) the service of notice of transfer under section 4(1) of the Criminal Justice Act 1987 (notices of transfer) or under section 53(1) of the Criminal Justice Act 1991 (notices of transfer in certain cases involving children), or

(iv) where a person is sent for trial under section 51 of the Crime and Disorder Act 1998 (sending cases to the Crown Court) the service of copies of the documents containing the evidence on which the charge or charges are based under paragraph 1 of Schedule 3 to that Act.

35.5. Co-defendant introducing evidence of defendant's bad character. A co-defendant who wants to introduce evidence of a defendant's bad character or who wants to cross-examine a witness with a view to eliciting that evidence under section 101 of the Criminal Justice Act 2003 must give notice in the form set out in the Practice Direction to the court officer and all other parties to the proceedings not more than 14 days after the prosecutor has complied or purported to comply with section 3 of the Criminal Procedure and Investigations Act 1996.

35.6. Defendant applying to exclude evidence of his own bad character. A defendant's application to exclude bad character evidence must be in the form set out in the Practice Direction and received by the court officer and all other parties to the proceedings not more than 14 days after receiving a notice given under rules 35.4 or 35.5.

35.7. Methods of giving notice. *Revoked.*

35.8. Court's power to vary requirements under this Part. The court may—

(a) allow a notice or application required under this rule to be given in a different form, or orally; or

(b) shorten a time-limit under this rule or extend it even after it has expired.

35.9. Defendant waiving right to receive notice. A defendant entitled to receive a notice under this Part may waive his entitlement by so informing the court and the party who would have given the notice.

1-7456

PART 36
EVIDENCE ABOUT A COMPLAINANT'S SEXUAL BEHAVIOUR

36.1. When this Part applies. This Part applies in magistrates' courts and in the Crown Court where a defendant wants to—

(a) introduce evidence; or

(b) cross-examine a witness

about a complainant's sexual behaviour despite the prohibition in section 41 of the Youth Justice and Criminal Evidence Act 1999.

36.2. Application for permission to introduce evidence or cross-examine. The defendant must apply for permission to do so—

(a) in writing; and

(b) not more than 28 days after the prosecutor has complied or purported to comply with section 3 of the Criminal Procedure and Investigations Act 1996 (disclosure by prosecutor).

36.3. Content of application. The application must—

(a) identify the issue to which the defendant says the complainant's sexual behaviour is relevant;

(b) give particulars of—

(i) any evidence that the defendant wants to introduce, and

(ii) any questions that the defendant wants to ask;

(c) identify the exception to the prohibition in section 41 of the Youth Justice and Criminal Evidence Act 1999 on which the defendant relies; and

(d) give the name and date of birth of any witness whose evidence about the complainant's sexual behaviour the defendant wants to introduce.

36.4. Service of application. The defendant must serve the application on the court officer and all other parties.

36.5. Reply to application. A party who wants to make representations about an application under rule 36.2 must—

(a) do so in writing not more than 14 days after receiving it; and

(b) serve those representations on the court officer and all other parties.

36.6. Application for special measures. If the court allows an application under rule 36.2 then—

(a) a party may apply not more than 14 days later for a special measures direction or for the variation of an existing special measures direction; and

(b) the court may shorten the time for opposing that application.

36.7. Court's power to vary requirements under this Part. The court may shorten or extend (even after it has expired) a time limit under this Part.

1-7457

PART 37
SUMMARY TRIAL

37.1. Order of evidence and speeches: information[1]. (1) On the summary trial of an information, where the accused does not plead guilty, the prosecutor shall call the evidence for the prosecution, and before doing so may address the court.

(2) At the conclusion of the evidence for the prosecution, the accused may address the court, whether or not he afterwards calls evidence.

(3) At the conclusion of the evidence, if any, for the defence, the prosecutor may call evidence to rebut[2] that evidence.

(4) At the conclusion of the evidence for the defence and the evidence, if any, in rebuttal, the accused may address the court if he has not already done so.

(5) Either party may, with the leave of the court, address the court a second time, but where the court grants leave to one party it shall not refuse leave to the other[3].

(6) Where both parties address the court twice the prosecutor shall address the court for the second time before the accused does so.

1. This rule deals only with the order of the proceedings and does not prevent the justices, in their discretion, from permitting the clerk to examine witnesses on behalf of an unrepresented party who is not competent nor desirous of doing so (*Simms v Moore* [1970] 2 QB 327, [1970] 3 All ER 1, 134 JP 573). There is a general discretion in a magistrates' court to permit the calling of evidence by the prosecution after the close of its case up to the time when the Bench retires. Before exercising that discretion, the justices should look carefully at the interests of justice overall, and in particular, the risk of any prejudice whatsoever to the defendant (*Jolly v DPP* [2000] Crim LR 471, DC). If the matter is one of substance, the prosecution might not be allowed to reopen its case but where the matter is one of technicality, such as proof of a statutory rule or order, the court shall allow the prosecution to proceed (*Price v Humphries* [1958] 2 QB 353, [1958] 2 All ER 725, [1958] 3 WLR 304; *Hammond v Wilkinson* (2001) 165 JP 786, [2001] Crim LR 323, DC (proof of statutory instrument)). See also *Cook v DPP* [2001] Crim LR 321, DC where, in a Crown Court appeal against conviction, the prosecution omitted to adduce evidence under s 69 of PACE (since repealed) of the proper functioning of an Intoximeter device and sought leave to do so after the defence had begun it closing speech; held once the judge had decided that the evidence was admissible by way of recall the only lawful way he could exercise his discretion was to grant the application; and *Hughes v DPP* [2003] EWHC 2470 (Admin), (2003) 167 JP 589, in which it was stated that when a point without merit arises out of an omission or oversight on the part of the prosecutor and is taken in a trial, justices should use their discretion to allow the relevant witness to be recalled to give further evidence, particularly where that evidence will be uncontroversial and any eventual conviction would be unmeritorious.

2. "Rebutting evidence" must be confined to a matter which arises unexpectedly in the course of the defence (*R v Whelan* (1881) 14 Cox CC 595). It is only proper for the prosecution to call rebutting evidence if during the defendant's case some matter has arisen *ex improviso* which no human ingenuity could foresee (*R v Harris* [1927] 2 KB 587, 91 JP 152; *R v Liddle* (1928) 21 Cr App Rep 3; *R v McMahon* (1933) 24 Cr App Rep 95; *R v Day* [1940] 1 All ER 402, 104 JP 181; *R v Browne* (1943) 29 Cr App Rep 106); *Price v Humphries* [1958] 2 QB 353, [1958] 2 All ER 725, 122 JP 423.

3. The terms of para (5) are such that the prosecutor may be allowed to address the court a second time even if the accused does not wish to do so.

37.2. Procedure on information where accused is not legally represented. (1) The court shall explain to an accused who is not legally represented the substance of the charge in simple language.

(2) If an accused who is not legally represented, instead of asking a witness in support of the charge questions by way of cross-examination, makes assertions, the court shall then put to the witness such questions as it thinks necessary on behalf of the accused and may for this purpose question the accused in order to bring out or clear up any point arising out of such assertions.

37.3. Adjournment of trial of information. (1) Where in the absence of the accused a magistrates' court adjourns the trial of an information, the court officer shall give to the accused notice in writing of the time and place at which the trial is to be resumed.

(2) *Revoked.*

37.4. Formal admissions. Where under section 10 of the Criminal Justice Act 1967 a fact is admitted orally in court by or on behalf of the prosecutor or defendant for the purposes of the summary trial of an offence the court shall cause the admission to be written down and signed by or on behalf of the party making the admission.

37.5. Notice of intention to cite previous convictions. Service on any person of a notice of intention to cite previous convictions under section 104 of the Magistrates' Courts Act 1980 or section 13 of the Road Traffic Offenders Act 1988 may be effected by delivering it to him or by sending it by post in a registered letter or by recorded delivery service, or by first class post addressed to him at his last known or usual place of abode.

37.6. Preservation of depositions where offence triable either way is dealt with summarily. The magistrates' court officer for the magistrates' court by which any person charged with an offence triable either way has been tried summarily shall preserve for a period of three years such depositions as have been taken.

37.7. Order of evidence and speeches: complaint. (1) On the hearing of a complaint, except where the court determines under section 53(3) of the Magistrates' Courts Act 1980 to make the order with the consent of the defendant without hearing evidence, the complainant shall call his evidence, and before doing so may address the court.

(2) At the conclusion of the evidence for the complainant the defendant may address the court, whether or not he afterwards calls evidence.

(3) At the conclusion of the evidence, if any, for the defence, the complainant may call evidence to rebut that evidence.

(4) At the conclusion of the evidence for the defence and the evidence, if any, in rebuttal, the defendant may address the court if he has not already done so.

(5) Either party may, with the leave of the court, address the court a second time, but where the court grants leave to one party it shall not refuse leave to the other[1].

(6) Where the defendant obtains leave to address the court for a second time his second address shall be made before the second address, if any, of the complainant.

---

1. The terms of para (5) are such that the complainant may be allowed to address the court a second time even if the defendant does not wish to do so.

PART 38
TRIAL OF CHILDREN AND YOUNG PERSONS

38.1. Application of this Part. (1) This Part applies, subject to paragraph (3) of this rule, where proceedings to which paragraph (2) applies are brought in a magistrates' court in respect of a child or young person ("the relevant minor").

(2) This paragraph applies to proceedings in which the relevant minor is charged with an offence, and, where he appears or is brought before the court, to proceedings under—

    (a) Paragraphs 1, 2, 5 and 6 of Schedule 7 to the Powers of Criminal Courts (Sentencing) Act 2000 (breach, revocation and amendment of supervision orders);

    (b) Part II, III or IV of Schedule 3 to the 2000 Act (breach, revocation and amendment of certain community orders);

    (c) Paragraphs 4, 5, 6 and 7 of Schedule 5 to the 2000 Act (breach, revocation and amendment of attendance centre orders); and

    (d) Schedule 8 to the 2000 Act (breach, revocation and amendment of action plan orders and reparation orders).

(3) Where the court is inquiring into an offence as examining justices, only rules 38.2, 38.3 and 38.5(3) apply, and where the proceedings are of a kind mentioned in paragraph (2)(a), (b) or (c) rule 38.4 does not apply.

38.2. Assistance in conducting case. (1) Except where the relevant minor is legally represented, the magistrates' court shall allow his parent or guardian to assist him in conducting his case.

(2) Where the parent or guardian cannot be found or cannot in the opinion of the court reasonably be required to attend, the court may allow any relative or other responsible person to take the place of the parent or guardian for the purposes of this Part.

38.3. Duty of court to explain nature of proceedings etc. (1) The magistrates' court shall explain to the relevant minor the nature of the proceedings and, where he is charged with an offence, the substance[1] of the charge.

(2) The explanation shall be given in simple language suitable to his age and understanding.

---

  1. It was held in a case decided in respect of earlier Rules in which identical words were used that there need be no elaboration or detailed explanation of the constituents of the offence: it is enough that the child or young person sufficiently understands the charge to which he is asked to plead (*R v Blandford Justices, ex p G (an infant)* [1967] 1 QB 82, [1966] 1 All ER 1021, 130 JP 260).

38.4. Duty of court to take plea to charge. Where the relevant minor is charged with an offence the magistrates' court shall, after giving the explanation required by rule 38.3, ask him whether he pleads guilty or not guilty to the charge.

38.5. Evidence in support of charge. (1) Where—

    (a) the relevant minor is charged with an offence and does not plead guilty, or

    (b) the proceedings are of a kind mentioned in rule 38.1(2)(a), (b) or (c),

the magistrates' court shall hear the witnesses in support of the charge or, as the case may be, the application.

(2) Except where—

    (a) the proceedings are of a kind mentioned in rule 38.1(2)(a), (b) or (c), and

    (b) the relevant minor is the applicant,

each witness may at the close of his evidence-in-chief be cross-examined by or on behalf of the relevant minor.

(3) If in any case where the relevant minor is not legally represented or assisted as provided by rule 38.2, the relevant minor, instead of asking questions by way of cross-examination, makes assertions, the court shall then put to the witness such questions as it thinks necessary on behalf of the relevant minor and may for this purpose question the relevant minor in order to bring out or clear up any point arising out of any such assertions.

38.6. Evidence in reply. If it appears to the magistrates' court after hearing the evidence in support of the charge or application that a prima facie case is made out, the relevant minor shall, if he is not the applicant and is not legally represented, be told that he may give evidence or address the court, and the evidence of any witnesses shall be heard.

1–7459

PART 39

TRIAL ON INDICTMENT

1–7460

PART 40

TAINTED ACQUITTALS

40.1. Time of certification. Where a person is convicted of an offence as referred to in section 54(1)(b) of the Criminal Procedure and Investigations Act 1996 and it appears to the court before which the conviction has taken place that the provisions of section 54(2) are satisfied, the court shall make the certification referred to in section 54(2) at any time following conviction but no later than—

    (a) immediately after the court sentences or otherwise deals with that person in respect of the offence; or (*b*) where the court, being a magistrates' court, commits that person to the Crown Court, or remits him to another magistrates' court, to be dealt with in respect of the offence, immediately after he is so committed or remitted, as the case may be; or

(*c*) where that person is a child or young person and the court, being the Crown Court, remits him to a youth court to be dealt with in respect of the offence, immediately after he is so remitted.

40.2. Form of certification in the Crown Court. A certification referred to in section 54(2) of the Criminal Procedure and Investigations Act 1996 by the Crown Court shall be drawn up in the form set out in the Practice Direction.

40.3. Service of a copy of the certification. (1) Where a magistrates' court or the Crown Court makes a certification as referred to in section 54(2) of the Criminal Procedure and Investigations Act 1996, the court officer shall, as soon as practicable after the drawing up of the form, serve a copy on the acquitted person referred to in the certification, on the prosecutor in the proceedings which led to the acquittal, and, where the acquittal has taken place before a court other than, or at a different place to, the court where the certification has been made, on—

(*a*) the clerk of the magistrates' court before which the acquittal has taken place; or

(*b*) the Crown Court officer at the place where the acquittal has taken place.

(2) *Revoked.*

(3) *Revoked.*

(4) *Revoked.*

40.4. Entry in register or records in relation to the conviction which occasioned certification. A clerk of a magistrates' court or an officer of a Crown Court which has made a certification under section 54(2) of the Criminal Procedure and Investigations Act 1996 shall enter in the register or records, in relation to the conviction which occasioned the certification, a note of the fact that certification has been made, the date of certification, the name of the acquitted person referred to in the certification, a description of the offence of which the acquitted person has been acquitted, the date of the acquittal, and the name of the court before which the acquittal has taken place.

40.5. Entry in the register or records in relation to the acquittal. The court officer of the court before which an acquittal has taken place shall, as soon as practicable after receipt of a copy of a form recording a certification under section 54(2) of the Criminal Procedure and Investigations Act 1996 relating to the acquittal, enter in the register or records a note that the certification has been made, the date of the certification, the name of the court which has made the certification, the name of the person whose conviction occasioned the making of the certification, and a description of the offence of which that person has been convicted. Where the certification has been made by the same court as the court before which the acquittal has occurred, sitting at the same place, the entry shall be made as soon as practicable after the making of the certification. In the case of an acquittal before a magistrates' court the entry in the register shall be signed by the clerk of the court.

40.6. Display of copy certification form. (1) Where a court makes a certification as referred to in section 54(2) of the Criminal Procedure and Investigations Act 1996, the court officer shall, as soon as practicable after the drawing up of the form, display a copy of that form at a prominent place within court premises to which place the public has access.

(2) Where an acquittal has taken place before a court other than, or at a different place to, the court which has made the certification under section 54(2) of the 1996 Act in relation to the acquittal, the court officer at the court where the acquittal has taken place shall, as soon as practicable after receipt of a copy of the form recording the certification, display a copy of it at a prominent place within court premises to which place the public has access.

(3) The copy of the form referred to in paragraph (1), or the copy referred to in paragraph (2), shall continue to be displayed as referred to, respectively, in those paragraphs at least until the expiry of 28 days from, in the case of paragraph (1), the day on which the certification was made, or, in the case of paragraph (2), the day on which the copy form was received at the court.

40.7. Entry in the register or records in relation to decision of High Court. (1) The court officer at the court where an acquittal has taken place shall, on receipt from the Administrative Court Office of notice of an order made under section 54(3) of the Criminal Procedure and Investigations Act 1996 quashing the acquittal, or of a decision not to make such an order, enter in the register or records, in relation to the acquittal, a note of the fact that the acquittal has been quashed by the said order, or that a decision has been made not to make such an order, as the case may be.

(2) The court officer of the court which has made a certification under section 54(2) of the 1996 Act shall, on receipt from the Administrative Court Office of notice of an order made under section 54(3) of that Act quashing the acquittal referred to in the certification, or of a decision not to make such an order, enter in the register or records, in relation to the conviction which occasioned the certification, a note that the acquittal has been quashed by the said order, or that a decision has been made not to make such an order, as the case may be.

(3) The entries in the register of a magistrates' court referred to, respectively, in paragraphs (1) and (2) above shall be signed by the magistrates' court officer.

40.8. Display of copy of notice received from High Court. (1) Where the court officer of a court which has made a certification under section 54(2) of the Criminal Procedure and Investigations Act 1996 or before which an acquittal has occurred to which such a certification refers, receives from the Administrative Court Office notice of an order quashing the acquittal concerned, or notice of a decision not to make such an order, he shall, as soon as practicable after receiving the notice, display a copy of it at a prominent place within court premises to which place the public has access.

(2) The copy notice referred to in paragraph (1) shall continue to be displayed as referred to in that paragraph at least until the expiry of 28 days from the day on which the notice was received at the court.

1–7461
PART 41
RETRIAL FOLLOWING ACQUITTAL FOR SERIOUS OFFENCE

1–7462
PART 42
REMITTAL FROM ONE MAGISTRATES' COURT TO ANOTHER FOR SENTENCE

42.1. Remittal for sentence. (1) Where a magistrates' court remits an offender to some other magistrates' court under section 10 of the Powers of Criminal Courts (Sentencing) Act 2000 after convicting him of an offence, the court officer for the convicting court shall send to the court officer for the other court—

- (a) a copy signed by the court officer for the convicting court of the minute or memorandum of the conviction and remittal entered in the register;
- (b) a copy of any note of the evidence given at the trial of the offender, any written statement tendered in evidence and any deposition;
- (c) such documents and articles produced in evidence before the convicting court as have been retained by that court;
- (d) any report relating to the offender considered by the convicting court;
- (e) if the offender is remitted on bail, a copy of the record made by the convicting court in pursuance of section 5 of the Bail Act 1976 relating to such bail and also any recognizance entered into by any person as his surety;
- (f) if the convicting court makes an order under section 148 of the 2000 Act (restitution orders), a copy signed by the court officer for the convicting court of the minute or memorandum of the order entered in the register;
- (g) a copy of any representation order previously made in the same case; and
- (h) a copy of any application for a representation order.

(2) Where a magistrates' court remits an offender to some other magistrates' court as aforesaid and the other court remits him back to the convicting court under section 10(5) of the 2000 Act, the court officer for the other court shall send to the court officer for the convicting court—

- (a) a copy signed by the court officer for the other court of the minute or memorandum of the remittal back entered in the register;
- (b) if the offender is remitted back on bail, a copy of the record made by the other court in pursuance of section 5 of the Bail Act 1976 relating to such bail and also any recognizance entered into by any person as his surety; and
- (c) all documents and articles sent in pursuance of paragraph (1) of this rule.

(3) In this rule "the offender", "the convicting court" and "the other court" have the same meanings as in section 10 of the 2000 Act.

1–7463
PART 43
COMMITTAL TO THE CROWN COURT FOR SENTENCE

43.1. Committals for sentence, etc. (1) Where a magistrates' court commits an offender to the Crown Court under the Vagrancy Act 1824[1], sections 3, 6, 116(3)(b) or 120(2)(a) of the Powers of Criminal Courts (Sentencing) Act 2000 or section 6 of the Bail Act 1976 after convicting him of an offence, the magistrates' court officer shall send[2] to the Crown Court officer—

- (a) a copy signed by the magistrates' court officer of the minute or memorandum of the conviction entered in the register;
- (b) copy of any note of the evidence given at the trial of the offender, any written statement tendered in evidence and any deposition;
- (c) such documents and articles produced in evidence before the court as have been retained by the court;
- (d) any report relating to the offender considered by the court;
- (e) if the offender is committed on bail, a copy of the record made in pursuance of section 5 of the 1976 Act relating to such bail and also any recognizance entered into by any person as his surety;
- (f) if the court imposes under section 26 of the Road Traffic Offenders Act 1988 an interim disqualification for holding or obtaining a licence under Part III of the Road Traffic Act 1988, a statement of the date of birth and sex of the offender;
- (g) if the court makes an order under section 148 of the 2000 Act (restitution orders), a copy signed by the clerk of the convicting court of the minute or memorandum of the order entered in the register; and

(h) any documents relating to an appeal by the prosecution against the granting of bail.

(2) Where a magistrates' court commits an offender to the Crown Court under the Vagrancy Act 1824 or sections 3, 6 or 120(2) of the 2000 Act and the magistrates' court on that occasion imposes, under section 26 of the Road Traffic Offenders Act 1988, an interim disqualification for holding or obtaining a licence under Part III of the Road Traffic Act 1988, the magistrates' court officer shall give notice of the interim disqualification to the Crown Court officer.

(3) Where a magistrates' court commits a person on bail to the Crown Court under any of the enactments mentioned in paragraph (2) of this rule or under section 6 of the Bail Act 1976 the magistrates' court officer shall give notice thereof in writing to the governor of the prison to which persons of the sex of the person committed are committed by that court if committed in custody for trial and also, if the person committed is under the age of 21, to the governor of the remand centre to which he would have been committed if the court had refused him bail.

---

1. Committal to Crown Court of an incorrigible rogue.

2. Where the charge is for breach of a probation order, the probation order and a statement of the breach in respect of which the charge is brought should be sent (*R v Maber* [1954] 1 All ER 666, 118 JP 259). The documents specified should be forwarded, despite the fact that the accused has appealed against conviction (*R v Dorset Quarter Sessions, ex p O'Brien* [1956] 1 QB 452n, [1956] 1 All ER 449, 120 JP 132). Note also the documents to be forwarded under the Criminal Defence Service (General) (No 2) Regulations 2001, reg 18, ante.

Where the justices determine a factual issue which is relevant to sentence, and thereafter commit the defendant for sentence, the justices must ensure that the Crown Court is informed of the facts found; see *Munroe v Crown Prosecution Service* [1988] Crim LR 823, DC.

43.2. Committal to Crown Court for order restricting discharge, etc. Where a magistrates' court commits an offender to the Crown Court either—

(a) under section 43 of the Mental Health Act 1983 with a view to the making of a hospital order with an order restricting his discharge; or

(b) under section 3 of the Powers of Criminal Courts (Sentencing) Act 2000, as modified by section 43(4) of the 1983 Act, with a view to the passing of a more severe sentence than the magistrates' court has power to inflict if such an order is not made,

The magistrates' court officer shall send to the Crown Court officer—

(i) the copies, documents and articles specified in rule 43.1,

(ii) any written evidence about the offender given by a medical practitioner under section 37 of the 1983 Act or a copy of a note of any oral evidence so given,

(iii) the name and address of the hospital the managers of which have agreed to admit the offender if a hospital order is made, and

(iv) if the offender has been admitted to a hospital under section 37 of the 1983 Act, the name and address of that hospital.

1–7464

PART 44

SENTENCING CHILDREN AND YOUNG PERSONS

44.1. Procedure after finding against minor in a magistrates' court. (1) This rule applies where—

(a) the relevant minor (as defined in rule 38.1) is found guilty by a magistrates' court of an offence, whether after a plea of guilty or otherwise; or

(b) in proceedings of a kind mentioned in rule 38.1(2)(a), (b) or (c) the court is satisfied that the case for the applicant—

(i) if the relevant minor is not the applicant, has been made out, or

(ii) if he is the applicant, has not been made out.

(2) Where this rule applies—

(a) the relevant minor and his parent or guardian, if present, shall be given an opportunity of making a statement;

(b) the court shall take into consideration all available information as to the general conduct, home surroundings, school record and medical history of the relevant minor and, in particular, shall take into consideration such information as aforesaid which is provided in pursuance of section 9 of the Children and Young Persons Act 1969;

(c) if such information as aforesaid is not fully available, the court shall consider the desirability of adjourning the proceedings for such inquiry as may be necessary;

(d) any written report of a probation officer, local authority, local education authority, educational establishment or registered medical practitioner may be received and considered by the court without being read aloud; and

(e) if the court considers it necessary in the interests of the relevant minor, it may require him or his parent or guardian, if present, to withdraw from the court.

(3) The court shall arrange for copies of any written report before the court to be made available to—

(a) the legal representative, if any, of the relevant minor;

(b) any parent or guardian of the relevant minor who is present at the hearing; and

(c) the relevant minor, except where the court otherwise directs on the ground that it appears to it impracticable to disclose the report having regard to his age and understanding or undesirable to do so having regard to potential serious harm which might thereby be suffered by him.

(4) In any case in which the relevant minor is not legally represented and where a report which has not been made available to him in accordance with a direction under paragraph (3)(*c*) has been considered without being read aloud in pursuance of paragraph (2)(*d*) or where he or his parent or guardian has been required to withdraw from the court in pursuance of paragraph (2)(*e*), then—

(*a*) the relevant minor shall be told the substance of any part of the information given to the court bearing on his character or conduct which the court considers to be material to the manner in which the case should be dealt with unless it appears to it impracticable so to do having regard to his age and understanding; and

(*b*) the parent or guardian of the relevant minor, if present, shall be told the substance of any part of such information which the court considers to be material as aforesaid and which has reference to his character or conduct or to the character, conduct, home surroundings or health of the relevant minors, and if such a person, having been told the substance of any part of such information, desires to produce further evidence with reference thereto, the court, if it thinks the further evidence would be material, shall adjourn the proceedings for the production thereof and shall, if necessary in the case of a report, require the attendance at the adjourned hearing of the person who made the report.

44.2. Duty of magistrates' court to explain manner in which it proposes to deal with case and effect of order. (1) Before finally disposing of the case or before remitting the case to another court in pursuance of section 8 of the Powers of Criminal Courts (Sentencing) Act 2000, the magistrates' court shall inform the relevant minor and his parent or guardian, if present, or any person assisting him in his case, of the manner in which it proposes to deal with the case and allow any of those persons so informed to make representations; but the relevant minor shall not be informed as aforesaid if the court considers it undesirable so to do.

(2) On making any order, the court shall explain to the relevant minor the general nature and effect of the order unless, in the case of an order requiring his parent or guardian to enter into a recognizance, it appears to it undesirable so to do.

1–7465

PART 45
DEFERRED SENTENCE

1–7466

PART 46
CUSTODIAL SENTENCES[1]

---

[1] There are currently no rules in this Part.

1–7467

PART 47
SUSPENDED SENTENCES OF IMPRISONMENT

47.1. Entries in magistrates' court register in respect of suspended sentences. (1) Where under section 119 of the Powers of Criminal Courts (Sentencing) Act 2000 a magistrates' court deals with a person in respect of a suspended sentence otherwise than by making an order under section 119(1)(*a*), the court shall cause to be entered in the register its reasons for its opinion that it would be unjust to make such an order.

(2) Where an offender is dealt with under section 119 of the 2000 Act in respect of a suspended sentence passed by a magistrates' court, the court officer shall note this in the register, or where the suspended sentence was not passed by that court, shall notify the court officer for the court by which it was passed who shall note it in the register.

47.2. Suspended sentence supervision orders. (1) Where a magistrates' court makes an order under section 119(1)(*a*) or (*b*) of the Powers of Criminal Courts (Sentencing) Act 2000 in respect of a person who is subject to a suspended sentence supervision order, the court officer shall note this in the register, or where that order was not made by that court, shall—

(*a*) if the order was made by another magistrates' court, notify the court officer for that court who shall note the court register accordingly; or

(*b*) if the order was made by the Crown Court, notify the Crown Court officer.

(2) Where a magistrates' court discharges a suspended sentence supervision order under section 124(1) of the 2000 Act, the court officer shall note this in the register, or where that order was not made by that court, shall—

(*a*) if the order was made by another magistrates' court, notify the court officer for that court who shall note the court register accordingly; or

(*b*) if the order was made by the Crown Court, notify the Crown Court officer.

(3) Where a magistrates' court fines a person under section 123 of the 2000 Act for breach of the requirements of a suspended sentence supervision order which was not made by that court, the court officer shall—

(a) if the order was made by another magistrates' court, notify the court officer for that court; or

(b) if the order was made by the Crown Court, notify the Crown Court officer.

1–7468

PART 48
COMMUNITY PENALTIES

48.1. Curfew order or requirement with electronic monitoring requirement. (1) This rule applies where the Crown Court makes—

(a) a curfew order with an electronic monitoring requirement under section 35 of the Crime (Sentences) Act 1997 or under sections 37 and 36B of the Powers of Criminal Courts (Sentencing) Act 2000; or

(b) a community rehabilitation order with curfew and electronic monitoring requirements under section 41 of and paragraph 7 of Schedule 2 to the 2000 Act.

(2) The court officer shall serve notice of the order on the person in respect of whom it is made by way of pages 1 and 2 of the form set out in the Practice Direction.

(3) The court officer shall serve notice of the order on the person responsible for electronically monitoring compliance with it by way of the form set out in the Practice Direction.

(4) Where any community order additional to the curfew order has been made in respect of the offender, the court officer shall serve a copy of the notice required by paragraph (3) on the local probation board or Youth Offending Team responsible for the offender.

1–7469

PART 49
HOSPITAL AND GUARDIANSHIP ORDERS

49.1. Remand by magistrates' court for medical inquiries. On exercising the powers conferred by section 11 of the Powers of Criminal Courts (Sentencing) Act 2000 a magistrates' court shall—

(a) where the accused is remanded in custody, send to the institution or place to which he is committed; or

(b) where the accused is remanded on bail, send to the institution or place at which, or the person by whom, he is to be examined,

a statement of the reasons why the court is of opinion that an inquiry ought to be made into his physical or mental condition and of any information before the court about his physical or mental condition.

49.2. Hospital or guardianship order imposed by a magistrates' court. (1) The magistrates' court by which a hospital order is made under section 37 of the Mental Health Act 1983 shall send to the hospital named in the order such information in the possession of the court as it considers likely to be of assistance in dealing with the patient to whom the order relates, and in particular such information about the mental condition, character and antecedents of the patient and the nature of the offence.

(2) The magistrates' court by which a guardianship order is made under section 37 of the 1983 Act shall send to the local health authority named therein as guardian or, as the case may be, the local health authority for the area in which the person so named resides, such information in the possession of the court as it considers likely to be of assistance in dealing with the patient to whom the order relates and in particular such information about the mental condition, character and antecedents of the patient and the nature of the offence.

(3) The magistrates' court by which an offender is ordered to be admitted to hospital under section 44 of the 1983 Act shall send to the hospital such information in the possession of the court as it considers likely to assist in the treatment of the offender until his case is dealt with by the Crown Court.

1–7470

PART 50
SUPPLEMENTARY ORDERS MADE ON CONVICTION

50.1. Sexual offences prevention orders made by a magistrates' court on conviction. (1) A sexual offences prevention order made by a magistrates' court under section 104 of the Sexual Offences Act 2003 shall be in the form set out in the Practice Direction.

(2) An interim sexual offences prevention order made by a magistrates' court under section 109 of the 2003 Act shall be in the form set out in the Practice Direction.

(3) As soon as reasonably practicable after a sexual offences prevention order or an interim sexual offences prevention order has been made, the court officer shall serve a copy of that order on the defendant. Any copy of an order required to be sent under this rule to the defendant shall be either given to him in person or sent by post to his last known address and, if so given or sent, shall be deemed to have been received by him, unless the defendant proves that it was not received by him.

50.2. Parenting orders made by a magistrates' court on conviction. (1) A parenting order made by a magistrates' court under section 8 of the Crime and Disorder Act 1998 shall be in the form set out in the Practice Direction.

(2) A parenting order made by a magistrates' court under paragraph 9D of Schedule 1 to the

Powers of Criminal Courts (Sentencing) Act 2000 shall be in the form set out in the Practice Direction.

50.3. Variation of certain orders by a magistrates' court. (1) An application to a magistrates' court for variation or discharge of any of the following orders shall be by complaint:

   (a) A parenting order made under section 9(5) of the Crime and Disorder Act 1998;

   (b) A parenting order made under paragraph 9D of Schedule 1 to the Powers of Criminal Courts (Sentencing) Act 2000;

   (c) a reparation order, under paragraph 5 of Schedule 8 to the Powers of Criminal Courts (Sentencing) Act 2000; or

   (d) an action plan order, under that paragraph.

(2) An application under paragraph (1)(b) above shall be made to the magistrates' court which made the order, and shall specify the reason why the applicant for variation or discharge believes the court should vary or discharge the order, as the case may be.

50.4. Anti-social behaviour orders made by the Crown Court on conviction. An order made by the Crown Court under section 1C of the Crime and Disorder Act 1998 on conviction in criminal proceedings shall be in the form set out in the Practice Direction.

1–7471

PART 51
FINES[1]

_____

[1] There are currently no rules in this Part.

1–7472

PART 52
ENFORCEMENT OF FINES

52.1. Notice to defendant of fine or forfeited recognizance. (1) Where under section 140(1) of the Powers of Criminal Courts (Sentencing) Act 2000 or section 67(2) of the Criminal Justice Act 1988 a magistrates' court is required to enforce payment of a fine imposed or recognizance forfeited by the Crown Court or where a magistrates' court allows time for payment of a sum adjudged to be paid by a summary conviction, or directs that the sum be paid by instalments, or where the offender is absent when a sum is adjudged to be paid by a summary conviction, the magistrates' court officer shall serve on the offender notice[1] in writing stating the amount of the sum and, if it is to be paid by instalments, the amount of the instalments, the date on which the sum, or each of the instalments, is to be paid and the places and times at which payment[2] may be made; and a warrant of distress or commitment shall not be issued until the preceding provisions of this rule have been complied with.

   (2) *Revoked.*

_____

[1] Where further time is allowed or an order for payment by instalments is made on adjourning a means inquiry hearing, service of a notice under this Rule is mandatory, (*R v Farnham Justices, ex p Hunt* (1976) 140 JP Jo 453).

2. For restrictions on the amount that can be offered in coin ("legal tender"), see the Coinage Act 1971, s 2 in Part VIII, title Currency, post.

52.2. Payment of fine to be made to magistrates' court officer. (1) A person adjudged by the conviction of a magistrates' court to pay any sum shall, unless the court otherwise directs, pay that sum, or any instalment of that sum, to the court officer.

(2) Where payment of any sum or instalment of any sum adjudged to be paid by the conviction or order of a magistrates' court is made to any person[1] other than the court officer, that person, unless he is the person to whom the court has directed payment to be made or, in the case of a child, is the person with whom the child has his home, shall, as soon as may be, account for and, if the court officer so requires, pay over the sum or instalment to the court officer.

(3) Where payment of any sum adjudged to be paid by the conviction or order of a magistrates' court, or any instalment of such a sum, is directed to be made to the court officer for another court, the court officer for the court that adjudged the sum to be paid shall pay over any sums received by him on account of the said sum or instalment to the court officer for that other court.

_____

1. For instance, the person exercising supervision under the Magistrates' Courts Act 1980, s 88, ante.

52.3. Duty of magistrates' court officer to give receipt. The court officer for a magistrates' court shall give or send a receipt to any person who makes a payment to him in pursuance of a conviction or order of a magistrates' court and who asks for a receipt.

52.4. Application to magistrates' court for further time. An application under section 75(2) of the Magistrates' Courts Act 1980 (further time to pay) may, unless the court requires the applicant to attend, be made in writing.

52.5. Notice of date of hearing of means inquiry, etc in magistrates' court. *Revoked.*

52.6. Review of terms of postponement of warrant of commitment by magistrates' court. An application under section 77(5) of the Magistrates' Courts Act 1980 may be made in writing or in person.

52.7. Notice to defendant before enforcing magistrates' court order. (1) A warrant of commitment shall not be issued for disobedience to an order of a magistrates' court unless the defendant has been previously served with a copy of the minute of the order, or the order was made in his presence and the warrant is issued on that occasion:

Provided that this paragraph shall not apply to an order to pay money.

(2) *Revoked.*

52.8. Execution of magistrates' court distress warrant. (1) A warrant of distress issued for the purpose of levying a sum[1] adjudged to be paid by a summary conviction or order—

(a) shall name or otherwise describe the person against whom the distress is to be levied;

(b) shall be directed to the constables of the police area in which the warrant is issued or to the civilian enforcement officers for the area in which they are employed, or to a person named in the warrant and shall, subject to, and in accordance with, the provisions of this rule, require them to levy the said sum by distress and sale of the goods[2] belonging to the said person;

(c) may where it is directed to the constables of a police area, instead of being executed by any of those constables, be executed by any person under the direction of a constable.

(2) The warrant shall authorise the person charged with the execution of it to take as well any money as any goods of the person against whom the distress is levied; and any money so taken shall be treated as if it were the proceeds of the sale of goods taken under the warrant.

(3) The warrant shall require the person charged with the execution to pay the sum to be levied to the court officer for the court that issued the warrant.

(4) A warrant to which this rule applies may be executed by the persons to whom it was directed or by any of the following persons, whether or not the warrant was directed to them—

(a) A constable for any police area in England and Wales, acting in his own police area;

(b) where the warrant is one to which section 125A of the Magistrates' Courts Act 1980 applies, a civilian enforcement officer within the meaning of section 125A of the 1980 Act; and

(c) where the warrant is one to which section 125A of the 1980 Act applies, any of the individuals described in section 125B(1) of the 1980 Act;

and in this rule any reference to the person charged with the execution of a warrant includes any of the above persons who is for the time being authorised to execute the warrant, whether or not they have the warrant in their possession at the time.

(5) A person executing a warrant of distress shall—

(a) either—

(i) if he has the warrant with him, show it to the person against whom the distress is levied, or

(ii) otherwise, state where the warrant is and what arrangements may be made to allow the person against whom distress is levied to inspect it;

(b) explain, in ordinary language, the sum for which distress is levied and the reason for the distress;

(c) where the person executing the warrant is one of the persons referred to in paragraph (4)(b) or (c) above, show the person against whom distress is levied a written statement under section 125A(4) or 125B(4) as appropriate; and

(d) in any case, show documentary proof of his identity.

(6) There shall not be taken under the warrant the clothing or bedding of any person or his family or the tools, books, vehicles or other equipment which he personally needs to use in his employment, business or vocation, provided that in this paragraph the word "person" shall not include a corporation.

(7) The distress levied under any such warrant as aforesaid shall be sold within such period beginning not earlier than the 6th day after the making of the distress as may be specified in the warrant, or if no period is specified in the warrant, within a period beginning on the 6th day and ending on the 14th day after the making of the distress:

Provided that with the consent in writing of the person against whom the distress is levied the distress may be sold before the beginning of the said period.

(8) The clerk of the court which issued the warrant may, on the application of the person charged with the execution of it, extend the period within which the distress must be sold by any number of days not exceeding 60; but following the grant of such an application there shall be no further variation or extension of that period.

(9) The said distress shall be sold by public auction or in such other manner as the person against whom the distress is levied may in writing allow.

(10) Notwithstanding anything in the preceding provisions of this rule, the said distress shall not be sold if the sum for which the warrant was issued and the charges of taking and keeping the distress have been paid.

(11) Subject to any direction to the contrary in the warrant, where the distress is levied on household goods, the goods shall not, without the consent in writing of the person against whom the distress is levied, be removed from the house until the day of sale; and so much of the goods

shall be impounded as is in the opinion of the person executing the warrant sufficient to satisfy the distress, by affixing to the articles impounded a conspicuous mark[3].

(12) The person charged with the execution of any such warrant as aforesaid shall cause the distress to be sold, and may deduct out of the amount realised by the sale all costs and charges incurred in effecting the sale; and he shall return to the owner the balance, if any, after retaining the amount of the sum for which the warrant was issued and the proper costs and charges of the execution of the warrant.

(13) The person charged with the execution of any such warrant as aforesaid shall as soon as practicable send to the court officer for the court that issued it a written account of the costs and charges incurred in executing it; and the court officer shall allow the person against whom the distress was levied to inspect the account within one month after the levy of the distress at any reasonable time to be appointed by the court.

(14) If any person pays or tenders to the person charged with the execution of any such warrant as aforesaid the sum mentioned in the warrant, or produces a receipt for that sum given by the court officer for the court that issued the warrant, and also pays the amount of the costs and charges[4] of the distress up to the time of the payment or tender or the production of the receipt, the person as aforesaid shall not execute the warrant, or shall cease to execute it, as the case may be.

---

1. Where the fine and costs are not to exceed a fixed sum, the further costs of enforcing payment by distress warrant may be added (*Cook v Plaskett* (1882) 47 JP 265).

2. Goods seized by a constable under a distress warrant are in *custodia legis*, and a landlord has no right to distrain or make a claim upon them. The Landlord and Tenant Act 1709, s 1, which requires the sheriff to pay the landlord his arrears of rent before the removal of goods under an execution, has no application to goods seized by a constable in the execution of a justice's warrant of distress (*Potts v Hickman* [1941] AC 2112, [1940] 4 All ER 491, 105 JP 26). Water fittings let for hire are not the subject of distress (Water Act 1945, s 35(2)); nor are gas fittings let for hire and marked with a sufficient mark indicating ownership of a public gas supplier (Gas Act 1986, Sch 5, para 19, in PART VIII: title ENERGY, post). Similar protection is given to electrical plant etc belonging to a public electricity supplier (Electricity Act 1989, Sch 6, para 9, in PART VIII: title ENERGY, post).

3. For offence of removing goods so marked, or defacing or removing the mark, see Magistrates' Courts Act 1980, s 78(4), ante.

4. For offence of exacting excessive costs and charges, see Magistrates' Courts Act 1980, s 78(5), ante.

52.9. Payment after imprisonment imposed by magistrates' court. (1) The persons authorised for the purposes of section 79(2) of the Magistrates' Courts Act 1980 to receive a part payment are—

(a) unless there has been issued a warrant of distress or commitment, the court officer for the court enforcing payment of the sum, or any person appointed under section 88 of that Act to supervise the offender;

(b) where the issue of a warrant of commitment has been suspended on conditions which provide for payment to be made to the court officer for another magistrates' court, that court officer;

(c) any constable holding a warrant of distress or commitment or, where the warrant is directed to some other person, that person; and

(d) the governor or keeper of the prison or place in which the defaulter is detained, or other person having lawful custody of the defaulter:

Provided that—

(i) the said governor or keeper shall not be required to accept any sum tendered in part payment under the said section 79(2) of the 1980 Act except on a week-day between 9 o'clock in the morning and 5 o'clock in the afternoon, and

(ii) no person shall be required to receive in part payment under the said subsection (2) an amount which, or so much of an amount as, will not procure a reduction of the period for which the defaulter is committed or ordered to be detained.

(2) Where a person having custody of a defaulter receives payment of any sum he shall note receipt of the sum on the warrant of commitment.

(3) Where the magistrates' court officer for a court other than the court enforcing payment of the sums receives payment of any sum he shall inform the magistrates' court officer for the other court.

(4) Where a person appointed under section 88 of the 1980 Act to supervise an offender receives payment of any sum, he shall send it forthwith to the magistrates' court officer for the court which appointed him.

52.10. Order for supervision made by magistrates' court. (1) Unless an order under section 88(1) of the Magistrates' Courts Act 1980 is made in the offender's presence, the court officer for the court making the order shall deliver to the offender, or serve on him by post, notice in writing of the order.

(2) It shall be the duty of any person for the time being appointed under the said section to advise and befriend the offender with a view to inducing him to pay the sum adjudged to be paid and thereby avoid committal to custody and to give any information required by a magistrates' court about the offender's conduct and means.

52.11. Transfer of magistrates' court fine order. (1) The court officer for a magistrates' court which has made a transfer of fine order under section 89 or 90 or section 90 as applied by section

91 of the Magistrates' Courts Act 1980 shall send to the clerk of the court having jurisdiction under the order a copy of the order.

(2) Where a magistrates' court has made a transfer of fine order in respect of a sum adjudged to be paid by a court in Scotland or in Northern Ireland the court officer shall send a copy of the order to the clerk of the Scottish court or to the clerk of the Northern Irish court, as the case may be.

(3) Where a court officer receives a copy of a transfer of fine order (whether made in England and Wales, or in Scotland or in Northern Ireland) specifying his court as the court by which payment of the sum in question is to be enforceable, he shall thereupon, if possible, deliver or send by post to the offender notice in writing.

(4) Where under a transfer of fine order a sum adjudged to be paid by a Scottish court or by a Northern Irish court is enforceable by a magistrates' court—

(a) if the sum is paid, the court officer shall send it to the clerk of the Scottish court or to the clerk of the Northern Irish court, as the case may be; or

(b) if the sum is not paid, the court officer shall inform the clerk of the Scottish court or the clerk of the Northern Irish court, as the case may be, of the manner in which the adjudication has been satisfied or that the sum, or any balance thereof, appears to be irrecoverable.

52.12. Directions by magistrates' court that money found on defaulter shall not be applied in satisfaction of debt. Where the defaulter is committed to, or ordered to be detained in, a prison or other place of detention, any direction given under section 80(2) of the Magistrates' Courts Act 1980 shall be endorsed on the warrant of commitment.

52.13. Particulars of fine enforcement to be entered in magistrates' court register. (1) Where the court on the occasion of convicting an offender of an offence issues a warrant of commitment for a default in paying a sum adjudged to be paid by the conviction or, having power to issue such a warrant, fixes a term of imprisonment under section 77(2) of the Magistrates' Courts Act 1980, the reasons for the court's action shall be entered in the register, or any separate record kept for the purpose of recording particulars of fine enforcement.

(2) There shall be entered in the register, or any such record, particulars of any—

(a) means inquiry under section 82 of the 1980 Act;

(b) hearing under subsection (5) of the said section 82;

(c) allowance of further time for the payment of a sum adjudged to be paid by a conviction;

(d) direction that such a sum shall be paid by instalments including any direction varying the number of instalments payable, the amount of any instalments payable and the date on which any instalment becomes payable;

(e) distress for the enforcement of such a sum;

(f) attachment of earnings order for the enforcement of such a sum;

(g) decision of the Secretary of State to make deductions from income support under section 24 of the Criminal Justice Act 1991;

(h) order under the 1980 Act placing a person under supervision pending payment of such a sum;

(i) order under section 85(1) of the 1980 Act remitting the whole or any part of a fine;

(j) order under section 120(4) of the 1980 Act remitting the whole or any part of any sum enforceable under that section (forfeiture of recognizance);

(k) authority granted under section 87(3) of the 1980 Act authorising the taking of proceedings in the High Court or county court for the recovery of any sum adjudged to be paid by a conviction;

(l) transfer of fine order made by the court;

(m) order transferring a fine to the court;

(n) order under section 140(1) of the Powers of Criminal Courts (Sentencing) Act 2000 specifying the court for the purpose of enforcing a fine imposed or a recognizance forfeited by the Crown Court; and

(o) any fine imposed or recognizance forfeited by a coroner which has to be treated as imposed or forfeited by the court;

(p) reference by a justice of the peace of an application under section 77(5) of the 1980 Act for a review of the terms on which a warrant of commitment is postponed; or

(q) order under section 77(3) of the 1980 Act varying the time for which or the conditions subject to which a warrant of commitment is postponed.

52.14. Attendance Centre Order imposed by magistrates' court in default of payment of a financial penalty. (1) Where any person is ordered, under section 60 of the Powers of Criminal Courts (Sentencing) Act 2000, to attend at an attendance centre in default of payment of a sum of money, payment may thereafter be made—

(a) of the whole of the said sum, to the court officer for the magistrates' court which made the order, or

(b) of the whole or, subject to paragraph (2), any part of the said sum, to the officer in charge of the attendance centre specified in the order ("the officer in charge").

(2) The officer in charge may not accept a part payment that would not secure the reduction by one or more complete hours of the period of attendance specified in the order.

(3) On receiving a payment under paragraph (1) the court officer shall forthwith notify the officer in charge.

(4) The officer in charge shall pay any money received by him under paragraph (1) above to

the court officer and shall note the receipt of the money in the register maintained at the attendance centre.

1–7473

PART 53
COMPENSATION ORDERS

53.1. Review of compensation order made by a magistrates' court. (1) An application under section 133 of the Powers of Criminal Courts (Sentencing) Act 2000 for the review of a compensation order shall be by complaint.

(2) The court officer for the magistrates' court to which the complaint is made shall send a letter to the person for whose benefit the compensation order was made, inviting him to make observations and to attend any hearing of the complaint and advising him of his right to be heard.

1–7474

PART 54
CONDITIONAL DISCHARGE

54.1. Further offence committed after offender conditionally discharged by a magistrates' court. (1) Where a magistrates' court deals with a person under section 13 of the Powers of Criminal Courts (Sentencing) Act 2000 in relation to an order for conditional discharge which was not made by that court the court officer shall give notice of the result of the proceedings to the court officer for the court by which the order was made.

(2) The court officer for a magistrates' court receiving a notice under this rule shall note the decision of the other court in the register.

1–7475

PART 55
ROAD TRAFFIC PENALTIES

55.1. Endorsement of driving licence by magistrates' court. (1) Where a magistrates' court convicts a person of an offence and, under section 44 of the Road Traffic Offenders Act 1988 orders that particulars of the conviction, and, if the court orders him to be disqualified, particulars of the disqualification, shall be endorsed on any licence held by him, the particulars to be endorsed shall include—

(a) the name of the local justice area for which the court is acting;
(b) the date of the conviction and the date on which sentence was passed (if different);
(c) particulars of the offence including the date on which it was committed; and
(d) particulars of the sentence of the court (including the period of disqualification, if any).

(2) Where a magistrates' court orders that the licence of an offender be endorsed as mentioned in paragraph (1) or imposes an interim disqualification as mentioned in rule 43.1(1)(f) and the court officer knows or is informed of the date of birth and sex of the offender, the court officer shall send the information to the licensing authority which granted the licence.

55.2. Application to magistrates' court for removal of disqualification. (1) n application under section 42 of the Road Traffic Offenders Act 1988 or paragraph 7 of Schedule 4 to the Road Traffic (Consequential Provisions) Act 1988 for an order removing a disqualification or disqualifications for holding or obtaining a licence shall be by complaint.

(2) The justice to whom the complaint is made shall issue a summons directed to the chief officer of police[1] requiring him to appear before a magistrates' court to show cause why an order should not be made on the complaint.

(3) Where a magistrates' court makes an order under either of the provisions mentioned in paragraph (1) the court shall cause notice of the making of the order and a copy of the particulars of the order endorsed on the licence, if any, previously held by the applicant for the order to be sent to the licensing authority to which notice of the applicant's disqualification was sent.

---

1. Chief Officer of Police is not defined in these rules or in the principal Act, but in s 101(1) of the Police Act 1996 is defined as meaning, with the exception of the metropolis, the chief constable.

55.3. Application to magistrates' court for review of course organiser's refusal to issue certificate of satisfactory completion of driving course. (1) An application to the supervising court under section 34B(6) or (7) of the Road Traffic Offenders Act 1988 shall be served on the court officer within 28 days after the date specified in an order under section 34A(2) of the1988 Act, where that date falls on or after 24th May 1993.

(2) An application under section 34B(6) of the 1988 Act shall be accompanied by the notice under section 34B(5) of the 1988 Act.

(3) Where such an application is served on the court officer—

(a) he shall fix a date and time for the hearing of the application; and
(b) he shall—

(i)   serve a copy of the application on the course organiser, and
(ii) serve notice of the hearing on the applicant and course organiser.

(4) If the course organiser fails to appear or be represented at the hearing of the application without reasonable excuse, the court may proceed to decide the application in his absence.

(5) In this rule, "course organiser" and "supervising court" have the meanings assigned to them in England and Wales by section 34C of the 1988 Act.

55.4. Notice of registration to defaulter under section 71(6) of the Road Traffic Offenders Act 1988. *Revoked.*

1–7476

CONFISCATION PROCEEDINGS UNDER THE CRIMINAL JUSTICE ACT 1988 AND THE DRUG TRAFFICKING ACT 1994

56.1. Statements etc, relevant to making confiscation orders. (1) Where a prosecutor or defendant—

(a) tenders to a magistrates' court any statement or other document under section 73 of the Criminal Justice Act 1988 in any proceedings in respect of an offence listed in Schedule 4 to that Act; or

(b) tenders to the Crown Court any statement or other document under section 11 of the Drug Trafficking Act 1994 or section 73 of the 1988 Act in any proceedings in respect of a drug trafficking offence or in respect of an offence to which Part VI of the 1988 Act applies,

he must serve a copy as soon as practicable on the defendant or the prosecutor, as the case may be.

(2) Any statement tendered by the prosecutor to the magistrates' court under section 73 of the 1988 Act or to the Crown Court under section 11(1) of the 1994 Act or section 73(1A) of the 1988 Act shall include the following particular—

(a) the name of the defendant;

(b) the name of the person by whom the statement is made and the date on which it was made;

(c) where the statement is not tendered immediately after the defendant has been convicted, the date on which and the place where the relevant conviction occurred; and

(d) such information known to the prosecutor as is relevant to the determination as to whether or not the defendant has benefited from drug trafficking or relevant criminal conduct and to the assessment of the value of his proceeds of drug trafficking or, as the case may be, benefit from relevant criminal conduct.

(3) Where, in accordance with section 11(7) of the 1994 Act or section 73(1C) of the 1988 Act, the defendant indicates the extent to which he accepts any allegation contained within the prosecutor's statement, if he indicates the same in writing to the prosecutor, he must serve a copy of that reply on the court officer.

(4) Expressions used in this rule shall have the same meanings as in the 1994 Act or, where appropriate, the 1988 Act.

56.2. Postponed determinations. (1) Where an application is made by the defendant or the prosecutor—

(a) to a magistrates' court under section 72A(5)(a) of the Criminal Justice Act 1988 asking the court to exercise its powers under section 72A(4) of that Act; or

(b) to the Crown Court under section 3(5)(a) of the Drug Trafficking Act 1994 asking the Court to exercise its powers under section 3(4) of that Act, or under section 72A(5)(a) of the 1988 Act asking the court to exercise its powers under section 72A(4) of the 1988 Act,

the application must be made in writing and a copy must be served on the prosecutor or the defendant, as the case may be.

(2) A party served with a copy of an application under paragraph (1) shall, within 28 days of the date of service, notify the applicant and the court officer, in writing, whether or not he proposes to oppose the application, giving his reasons for any opposition.

(3) After the expiry of the period referred to in paragraph (2), the court shall determine whether an application under paragraph (1) is to be dealt with—

(a) without a hearing; or

(b) at a hearing at which the parties may be represented.

56.3. Confiscation orders—revised assessments. (1) Where the prosecutor makes an application under section 13, 14 or 15 of the Drug Trafficking Act 1994 or section 74A, 74B or 74C of the Criminal Justice Act 1988, the application must be in writing and a copy must be served on the defendant.

(2) The application must include the following particulars—

(a) the name of the defendant;

(b) the date on which and the place where any relevant conviction occurred;

(c) the date on which and the place where any relevant confiscation order was made or, as the case may be, varied;

(d) the grounds on which the application is made; and

(e) an indication of the evidence available to support the application.

56.4. Application to Crown Court to discharge or vary order to make material available. (1) Where an order under section 93H of the Criminal Justice Act 1988 (order to make material available), section 55 of the Drug Trafficking Act 1994 (order to make material available), or section 345 of the Proceeds of Crime Act 2002 (production orders) has been made by the Crown

Court, any person affected by it may apply in writing to the court officer for the order to be discharged or varied, and on hearing such an application a circuit judge or, in the case of an order under the 2002 Act, a judge entitled to exercise the jurisdiction of the Crown Court may discharge the order or make such variations to it as he thinks fit.

(2) Subject to paragraph (3), where a person proposes to make an application under paragraph (1) for the discharge or variation of an order, he shall give a copy of the application, not later than 48 hours before the making of the application—

(a) to a constable at the police station specified in the order; or

(b) where the application for the order was made under the 2002 Act and was not made by a constable, to the office of the appropriate officer who made the application, as specified in the order,

in either case together with a notice indicating the time and place at which the application for discharge or variation is to be made.

(3) A circuit judge or, in the case of an order under the 2002 Act, a judge entitled to exercise the jurisdiction of the Crown Court may direct that paragraph (2) need not be complied with if he is satisfied that the person making the application has good reason to seek a discharge or variation of the order as soon as possible and it is not practicable to comply with that paragraph.

(4) In this rule:

"appropriate officer" has the meaning given to it by section 378 of the 2002 Act;

"constable" includes a person commissioned by the Commissioners of Customs and Excise;

"police station" includes a place for the time being occupied by Her Majesty's Customs and Excise.

56.5. Application to Crown Court for increase in term of imprisonment in default of payment of a confiscation order. (1) This rule applies to applications made, or that have effect as made, to the Crown Court under section 10 of the Drug Trafficking Act 1994 and section 75A of the Criminal Justice Act 1988 (interest on sums unpaid under confiscation orders).

(2) Notice of an application to which this rule applies to increase the term of imprisonment or detention fixed in default of payment of a confiscation order by a person ("the defendant") shall be made by the prosecutor in writing to the court officer.

(3) A notice under paragraph (2) shall—

(a) state the name and address of the defendant;

(b) specify the grounds for the application;

(c) give details of the enforcement measures taken, if any; and

(d) include a copy of the confiscation order.

(4) On receiving a notice under paragraph (2), the court officer shall—

(a) forthwith send to the defendant and the magistrates' court required to enforce payment of the confiscation order under section 140(1) of the Powers of Criminal Courts (Sentencing) Act 2000, a copy of the said notice; and

(b) notify in writing the applicant and the defendant of the date, time and place appointed for the hearing of the application.

(5) Where the Crown Court makes an order pursuant to an application mentioned in paragraph (1) above, the court officer shall send forthwith a copy of the order—

(a) to the applicant;

(b) to the defendant;

(c) where the defendant is at the time of the making of the order in custody, to the person having custody of him; and

(d) to the magistrates' court mentioned in paragraph (4)(a).

56.6. Drug trafficking—compensation on acquittal in Crown Court. Where a Crown Court cancels a confiscation order under section 22(2) of the Drug Trafficking Act 1994, the court officer shall serve notice to that effect on the High Court and on the magistrates' court which has responsibility for enforcing the order.

1–7477

PART 57
PROCEEDS OF CRIME ACT 2002—RULES APPLICABLE TO ALL PROCEEDINGS

1–7478

PART 58
PROCEEDS OF CRIME ACT 2002—RULES APPLICABLE ONLY TO CONFISCATION PROCEEDINGS

Contents of this Part

58.6. Application by magistrates' court officer to discharge confiscation order. (1) This rule applies where a magistrates' court officer makes an application under section 24 or 25 of the Proceeds of Crime Act 2002 for the discharge of a confiscation order.

(2) The application must be in writing and give details of—

(a) the confiscation order;
(b) the amount outstanding under the order; and
(c) the grounds for the application.

(3) The application must be served on—

(a) the defendant;
(b) the prosecutor; and
(c) any receiver appointed under section 50 of the 2002 Act.

(4) The Crown Court may determine the application without a hearing unless a person listed in paragraph (3) indicates, within seven days after the application was served on him, that he would like to make representations.

(5) If the Crown Court makes an order discharging the confiscation order, the court must, at once, send a copy of the order to—

(a) the magistrates' court officer who applied for the order;
(b) the defendant;
(c) the prosecutor; and
(d) any receiver appointed under section 50 of the 2002 Act.

58.8. Application for discharge of confiscation order made against an absconder. (1) This rule applies if the defendant makes an application under section 30 of the Proceeds of Crime Act 2002 for the discharge of a confiscation order.

(2) The application must be in writing and supported by a witness statement which must give details of—

(a) the confiscation order made under section 28 of the 2002 Act;
(b) the date on which the defendant ceased to be an absconder;
(c) the acquittal of the defendant if he has been acquitted of the offence concerned; and
(d) if the defendant has not been acquitted of the offence concerned—

(i) the date on which the defendant ceased to be an absconder,
(ii) the date on which the proceedings taken against the defendant were instituted and a summary of steps taken in the proceedings since then, and
(iii) any indication given by the prosecutor that he does not intend to proceed against the defendant.

(3) The application and witness statement must be lodged with the Crown Court.

(4) The application and witness statement must be served on the prosecutor or, if the Director is appointed as the enforcement authority under section 34 of the 2002 Act, the Director at least seven days before the date fixed by the court for hearing the application, unless the Crown Court specifies a shorter period.

(5) If the Crown Court orders the discharge of the confiscation order, the court must serve notice on the magistrates' court responsible for enforcing the order if the Director has not been appointed as the enforcement authority under section 34 of the 2002 Act.

58.9. Application for increase in term of imprisonment in default. (1) This rule applies where the prosecutor or the Director makes an application under section 39(5) of the Proceeds of Crime Act 2002 to increase the term of imprisonment in default of payment of a confiscation order.

(2) The application must be made in writing and give details of—

(a) the name and address of the defendant;
(b) the confiscation order;
(c) the grounds for the application; and
(d) the enforcement measures taken, if any.

(3) On receipt of the application, the court must—

(a) at once, send to the defendant and, if the Director has not been appointed as the enforcement authority under section 34 of the 2002 Act, the magistrates' court responsible for enforcing the order, a copy of the application; and
(b) fix a time, date and place for the hearing and notify the applicant and the defendant of that time, date and place.

(4) If the Crown Court makes an order increasing the term of imprisonment in default, the court must, at once, send a copy of the order to—

(a) the applicant;
(b) the defendant;
(c) where the defendant is in custody at the time of the making of the order, the person having custody of the defendant; and

(d) if the Director has not been appointed as the enforcement authority under section 34 of the 2002 Act, the magistrates' court responsible for enforcing the order.

58.12. Payment of money in bank or building society account in satisfaction of confiscation order. (1) An order under section 67 of the Proceeds of Crime Act 2002 requiring a bank or building society to pay money to a magistrates' court officer ("a payment order") shall—

(a) be directed to the bank or building society in respect of which the payment order is made;
(b) name the person against whom the confiscation order has been made;
(c) state the amount which remains to be paid under the confiscation order;
(d) state the name and address of the branch at which the account in which the money ordered to be paid is held and the sort code of that branch, if the sort code is known;
(e) state the name in which the account in which the money ordered to be paid is held and the account number of that account, if the account number is known;
(f) state the amount which the bank or building society is required to pay to the court officer under the payment order;
(g) give the name and address of the court officer to whom payment is to be made; and
(h) require the bank or building society to make payment within a period of seven days beginning on the day on which the payment order is made, unless it appears to the court that a longer or shorter period would be appropriate in the particular circumstances.

(2) The payment order shall be served on the bank or building society in respect of which it is made by leaving it at, or sending it by first class post to, the principal office of the bank or building society.

(3) A payment order which is served by first class post shall, unless the contrary is proved, be deemed to have been served on the second business day after posting.

(4) In this rule "confiscation order" has the meaning given to it by section 88(6) of the Proceeds of Crime Act 2002.

1-7479

PART 59
PROCEEDS OF CRIME ACT 2002—RULES APPLICABLE ONLY TO RESTRAINT PROCEEDINGS

1-7480

PART 60
PROCEEDS OF CRIME ACT 2002—RULES APPLICABLE ONLY TO RECEIVERSHIP PROCEEDINGS

1-7481

PART 61
PROCEEDS OF CRIME ACT 2002—RULES APPLICABLE TO RESTRAINT AND RECEIVERSHIP PROCEEDINGS

1-7482

PART 62
PROCEEDS OF CRIME ACT 2002—RULES APPLICABLE TO INVESTIGATIONS

62.1. Account monitoring orders under the Terrorism Act 2000 and the Proceeds of Crime Act 2002. (1) Where a circuit judge makes an account monitoring order under paragraph 2(1) of Schedule 6A to the Terrorism Act 2000 the court officer shall give a copy of the order to the financial institution specified in the application for the order.

(2) Where any person other than the person who applied for the account monitoring order proposes to make an application under paragraph 4(1) of Schedule 6A to the 2000 Act or section 375(2) of the Proceeds of Crime Act 2002 for the discharge or variation of an account monitoring order he shall give a copy of the proposed application, not later than 48 hours before the application is to be made—

(a) to a police officer at the police station specified in the account monitoring order; or
(b) where the application for the account monitoring order was made under the 2002 Act and was not made by a constable, to the office of the appropriate officer who made the application, as specified in the account monitoring order,

in either case together with a notice indicating the time and place at which the application for discharge or variation is to be made.

(3) In this rule:

"appropriate officer" has the meaning given to it by section 378 of the 2002 Act; and
references to the person who applied for an account monitoring order must be construed in accordance with section 375(4) and (5) of the 2002 Act.

62.2. Customer information orders under the Proceeds of Crime Act 2002. (1) Where any person other than the person who applied for the customer information order proposes to make an application under section 369(3) of the Proceeds of Crime Act 2002 for the discharge or variation of a customer information order, he shall, not later than 48 hours before the application is to be made, give a copy of the proposed application—

(a) to a police officer at the police station specified in the customer information order; or
(b) where the application for the customer information order was not made by a constable, to the office of the appropriate officer who made the application, as specified in the customer information order,

in either case together with a notice indicating the time and place at which the application for a discharge or variation is to be made.

(2) In this rule:

"appropriate officer" has the meaning given to it by section 378 of the 2002 Act; and references to the person who applied for the customer information order must be construed in accordance with section 369(5) and (6) of the 2002 Act.

62.3. Proof of identity and accreditation.   (1) This rule applies where—

(a) an appropriate officer makes an application under section 345 (production orders), section 363 (customer information orders) or section 370 (account monitoring orders) of the Proceeds of Crime Act 2002 for the purposes of a confiscation investigation or a money laundering investigation; or

(b) the Director of the Assets Recovery Agency makes an application under section 357 of the 2002 Act (disclosure orders) for the purposes of a confiscation investigation.

(2) Subject to section 449 of the 2002 Act (which makes provision for members of staff of the Assets Recovery Agency to use pseudonyms), the appropriate officer or the Director of the Assets Recovery Agency, as the case may be, must provide the judge with proof of his identity and, if he is an accredited financial investigator, his accreditation under section 3 of the 2002 Act.

(3) In this rule:

"appropriate officer" has the meaning given to it by section 378 of the 2002 Act; and "confiscation investigation" and "money laundering investigation" have the meanings given to them by section 341 of the 2002 Act.

1–7483

PART 63

APPEAL TO THE CROWN COURT AGAINST CONVICTION OR SENTENCE

63.1. Application of this Part.   This Part shall apply to any appeal under section 108(1) of the Magistrates' Courts Act 1980 (conviction and sentence), section 45(1) of the Mental Health Act 1983 (hospital or guardianship order in the absence of conviction) and paragraph 11 of Schedule 3 to the Powers of Criminal Courts (Sentencing) Act 2000 (re-sentencing on failure to comply with supervision order).

63.2. Notice of appeal.   (1) An appeal shall be commenced by the appellant's giving notice of appeal in accordance with the following provisions of this rule.

(2) The notice required by the preceding paragraph shall be in writing and shall be given to a court officer for the magistrates' court and to any other party to the appeal.

(3) Notice of appeal shall be given not later than 21 days after the day on which the decision appealed against is given and, for this purpose, where the court has adjourned the trial of an information after conviction, that day shall be the day on which the court sentences or otherwise deals with the offender:

Provided that, where a court exercises its power to defer sentence under section 1(1) of the Powers of Criminal Courts (Sentencing) Act 2000, that day shall, for the purposes of an appeal against conviction, be the day on which the court exercises that power.

(4) A notice of appeal shall state the grounds of appeal.

(5) The time for giving notice of appeal may be extended[1], either before or after it expires, by the Crown Court, on an application made in accordance with paragraph (6).

(6) An application for an extension of time shall be made in writing, specifying the grounds of the application and sent to a Crown Court officer.

(7) Where the Crown Court extends the time for giving notice of appeal, the Crown Court officer shall give notice[2] of the extension to—

(a) the appellant; and

(b) the magistrates' court officer,

and the appellant shall give notice of the extension to any other party to the appeal.

---

1. It would appear that the Crown Court may extend the time either in relation to a notice previously given (though out of time) or in relation to a notice not yet given. The clerk of a magistrates' court should accept any notice of appeal notwithstanding that it is out of time. It will be good practice for him to notify the appellant of his right to apply for an extension of time to the Crown Court. Where the Crown Court refuses an extension of time, it should give a brief statement why (*Re Worth (application for judicial review)* (1979) 1 FLR 159).

2. It is submitted that a notice of appeal given out of time requires an extension of time by the Crown Court to perfect its validity; therefore, until notice of the extension has been received by the clerk of the magistrates' court, there does not arise the courts' power to release the appellant from custody under the Magistrates' Courts Act 1980, s 113, ante.

63.3. Documents to be sent to Crown Court.   (1) The magistrates' court officer shall as soon as practicable[1] send to the Crown Court officer any notice of appeal[2] to the Crown Court given to the magistrates' court officer.

(2) The magistrates' court officer shall send to the Crown Court officer, with the notice of appeal[3], a copy of the extract of the magistrates' court register relating to that decision[4] and of the last known or usual place of abode of the parties to the appeal.

(3) Where any person, having given notice of appeal to the Crown Court, has been granted bail[5] for the purposes of the appeal the magistrates' court officer for the court from whose

decision the appeal is brought shall before the day fixed for the hearing of the appeal send to the Crown Court officer a copy of the record made in pursuance of section 5 of the Bail Act 1976.

(4) Where a notice of appeal is given in respect of a hospital order or guardianship order made under section 37 of the Mental Health Act 1983 (powers of courts to order hospital admission or guardianship), a magistrates' court officer for the court from which the appeal is brought shall send with the notice to the Crown Court officer any written evidence considered by the court under section 37(2) of the 1983 Act.

(5) Where a notice of appeal is given in respect of an appeal against conviction by a magistrates' court the magistrates' court officer shall send with the notice to the Crown Court officer any admission of facts made for the purposes of the summary trial under section 10 of the Criminal Justice Act 1967 (proof by formal admission).

(6) Where a notice of appeal is given in respect of an appeal against sentence by a magistrates' court, and where that sentence was a custodial sentence, the magistrates' court officer shall send with the notice to the Crown Court officer a statement of whether the magistrates' court obtained and considered a pre-sentence report before passing such sentence.

---

1. The requirements of this rule should be complied with even where the notice of appeal is given after twenty-one days have expired; it will be for the Crown Court to decide whether or not to extend the time for appealing (see Crown Court Rules 1982, r 7, post).

2. In a case where the provisions of the Road Traffic (New Drivers) Act 1995 apply, notice of the appeal must be given by the magistrates' court to the Secretary of State for Transport in accordance with the New Drivers (Appeals Procedure) Regulations 1997, in PART VII, TRANSPORT, title ROAD TRAFFIC, post.

3. Note also the documents to be forwarded under the Criminal Defence Service (General) (No 2) Regulations 2001, reg 18 in this Part, ante.

4. On appeal against conviction, notes of evidence should be forwarded to the appropriate officer of the Crown Court. This will assist the administration of the court's business and, in the proper case, the court may be referred to the notes in order to ascertain what transpired in the court below (*Practice Direction (criminal: consolidated)* [2002] para V.52, in this Part, post, explaining *R v Recorder of Grimsby, ex p Fuller* [1956] 1 QB 36, [1955] 3 All ER 300, 119 JP 560). In the light of the decision in *Dutta v Westcott* [1987] QB 291, [1986] 3 All ER 381, [1987] RTR 173, which says that where an appeal in a traffic case is successful, the Crown Court may deal with other traffic cases heard by the justices at the same time and order penalty points thereon even though there has been no formal appeal relating to them, the clerk should clearly include in the statement of the decision details of those other traffic offences.

5. See the Magistrates' Courts Act 1980, s 113, this Part, ante.

63.4. Entry of appeal and notice of hearing.   On receiving notice of appeal, the Crown Court officer shall enter the appeal and give notice of the time and place of the hearing to—

   (a) the appellant;
   (b) any other party to the appeal; and
   (c) the magistrates' court officer.

63.5. Abandonment of appeal—notice.   (1) Without prejudice to the power of the Crown Court to give leave for an appeal to be abandoned, an appellant may abandon an appeal by giving notice in writing, in accordance with the following provisions of this rule, not later than the third day before the day fixed for hearing the appeal.

(2) The notice required by the preceding paragraph shall be given—

   (a) to the magistrates' court officer;
   (b) to the Crown Court officer; and
   (c) to any other party to the appeal.

(3) For the purposes of determining whether notice of abandonment was given in time there shall be disregarded any Saturday, Sunday and any day which is specified to be a bank holiday in England and Wales under section 1(1) of the Banking and Financial Dealings Act 1971.

63.6. Abandonment of appeal—bail.   Where notice to abandon an appeal has been given by the appellant, any recognizance conditioned for the appearance of the appellant at the hearing of the appeal shall have effect as if conditioned for the appearance of the appellant before the court from whose decision the appeal was brought at a time and place to be notified to the appellant by the court officer for that court.

63.7. Number and qualification of justices—appeals from youth courts.   Subject to the provisions of rule 63.8 and to any directions under section 74(4) of the Supreme Court Act 1981 (directions disapplying the set out number and qualifications of justices), on the hearing of an appeal from a youth court the Crown Court shall consist of a judge sitting with two justices each of whom is a member of a youth court panel and who are chosen so that the Court shall include a man and a woman.

63.8. Number and qualification of justices—dispensation for special circumstances.   (1) The Crown Court may enter on any appeal notwithstanding that the Court is not constituted as required by section 74(1) of the Supreme Court Act 1981 or rule 63.7 if it appears to the judge that the Court could not be constituted without unreasonable delay and the Court includes one justice who is a member of a youth court panel.

(2) The Crown Court may at any stage continue with any proceedings with a Court from which any one or more of the justices initially comprising the Court has withdrawn, or is absent for any reason.

63.9. Disqualifications. A justice of the peace shall not sit in the Crown Court on the hearing of an appeal in a matter on which he adjudicated[1].

---

1. The prohibition contained in this rule is not exhaustive in the context of a justice's disqualification from sitting, and it does not imply that there are no other circumstances where a justice is also disqualified on the basis of a previous connection with the case; see *R v Crown Court at Bristol, ex p Cooper* [1990] 2 All ER 193, [1990] 1 WLR 1031, CA.

1–7484

PART 64

APPEAL TO THE HIGH COURT BY WAY OF CASE STATED

64.1. Application to a magistrates' court to state a case. (1) An application under section 111(1) of the Magistrates' Courts Act 1980 shall be made in writing and signed by or on behalf of the applicant and shall identify the question or questions of law or jurisdiction on which the opinion of the High Court is sought.

(2) Where one of the questions on which the opinion of the High Court is sought is whether there was evidence on which the magistrates' court could come to its decision, the particular finding of fact made by the magistrates' court which it is claimed cannot be supported by the evidence before the magistrates' court shall be specified in such application.

(3) Any such application shall be sent to a court officer for the magistrates' court whose decision is questioned.

64.2. Consideration of a draft case by a magistrates' court. (1) Within 21 days after receipt of an application made in accordance with rule 64.1, a court officer for the magistrates' court whose decision is questioned shall, unless the justices refuse to state a case under section 111(5) of the Magistrates' Courts Act 1980, send a draft case in which are stated the matters required under rule 64.6 (content of case stated) to the applicant or his legal representative and shall send a copy thereof to the respondent or his legal representative.

(2) Within 21 days after receipt of the draft case under paragraph (1), each party may make representations thereon. Any such representations shall be in writing and signed by or on behalf of the party making them and shall be sent to the magistrates' court officer.

(3) Where the justices refuse to state a case under section 111(5) of the 1980 Act and they are required by a mandatory order of the High Court under section 111(6) to do so, this rule shall apply as if in paragraph (1)—

    (a) for the words "receipt of an application made in accordance with rule 64.1" there were substituted the words "the date on which a mandatory order under section 111(6) of the 1980 Act is made"; and

    (b) the words "unless the justices refuse to state a case under section 111(5) of the 1980 Act" were omitted.

64.3. Preparation and submission of final case to a magistrates' court. (1) Within 21 days after the latest day on which representations may be made under rule 64.2, the justices whose decision is questioned shall make such adjustments, if any, to the draft case prepared for the purposes of that rule as they think fit, after considering any such representations, and shall state and sign the case.

(2) A case may be stated on behalf of the justices whose decision is questioned by any 2 or more of them and may, if the justices so direct, be signed on their behalf by the justices' clerk.

(3) Forthwith after the case has been stated and signed a court officer for the court shall send it to the applicant or his legal representative, together with any statement required by rule 64.4.

64.4. Extension of time limits by a magistrates' court. (1) If a magistrates' court officer is unable to send to the applicant a draft case under rule 64.2(1) within the time required by that paragraph, he shall do so as soon as practicable thereafter and the provisions of that rule shall apply accordingly; but in that event a court officer shall attach to the draft case, and to the final case when it is sent to the applicant or his legal representative under rule 64.3(3), a statement of the delay and the reasons for it.

(2) If a magistrates' court officer receives an application in writing from or on behalf of the applicant or the respondent for an extension of the time within which representations on the draft case may be made under rule 64.2(2), together with reasons in writing for it, the justices' clerk may, by notice in writing sent to the applicant, or respondent as the case may be, by the magistrates' court officer, extend the time and the provisions of that paragraph and of rule 64.3 shall apply accordingly; but in that event the court officer shall attach to the final case, when it is sent to the applicant or his legal representative under rule 64.3(3), a statement of the extension and the reasons for it.

(3) If the justices are unable to state a case within the time required by rule 64.3(1), they shall do so as soon as practicable thereafter and the provisions of that rule shall apply accordingly; but in that event a court officer shall attach to the final case, when it is sent to the applicant or his legal representative under rule 64.3(3), a statement of the delay and the reasons for it.

64.5. Service of documents where application made to a magistrates' court. *Revoked.*

64.6. Content of case stated by a magistrates' courts. (1) A case stated by the magistrates' court shall state the facts found by the court and the question or questions of law or jurisdiction on which the opinion of the High Court is sought.

(2) Where one of the questions on which the opinion of the High Court is sought is whether there was evidence on which the magistrates' court could come to its decision, the particular finding of fact which it is claimed cannot be supported by the evidence before the magistrates' court shall be specified in the case.

(3) Unless one of the questions on which the opinion of the High Court is sought is whether there was evidence on which the magistrates' court could come to its decision, the case shall not contain a statement of evidence[1].

---

1. Save where the condition set out in r 81(3) is satisfied, a statement of the evidence should not be included. Moreover, the High Court is not competent to receive with the case stated notes of evidence; see *Cotgreave and Cotgreave v Cheshire County Council* (1992) 157 JP 85.

64.7. Application to the Crown Court to state a case. (1) An application under section 28 of the Supreme Court Act 1981 to the Crown Court to state a case for the opinion of the High Court shall be made in writing to a court officer within 21 days after the date of the decision in respect of which the application is made.

(2) The application shall state the ground on which the decision of the Crown Court is questioned.

(3) After making the application, the applicant shall forthwith send a copy of it to the parties to the proceedings in the Crown Court.

(4) On receipt of the application, the Crown Court officer shall forthwith send it to the judge who presided at the proceedings in which the decision was made.

(5) On receipt of the application, the judge shall inform the Crown Court officer as to whether or not he has decided to state a case and that officer shall give notice in writing to the applicant of the judge's decision.

(6) If the judge considers that the application is frivolous, he may refuse to state a case and shall in that case, if the applicant so requires, cause a certificate stating the reasons for the refusal to be given to him.

(7) If the judge decides to state a case, the procedure to be followed shall, unless the judge in a particular case otherwise directs, be the procedure set out in paragraphs (8) to (12) of this rule.

(8) The applicant shall, within 21 days of receiving the notice referred to in paragraph (5), draft a case and send a copy of it to the Crown Court officer and to the parties to the proceedings in the Crown Court.

(9) Each party to the proceedings in the Crown Court shall, within 21 days of receiving a copy of the draft case under paragraph (8), either—

(a) give notice in writing to the applicant and the Crown Court officer that he does not intend to take part in the proceedings before the High Court;

(b) indicate in writing on the copy of the draft case that he agrees with it and send the copy to a court officer; or

(c) draft an alternative case and send it, together with the copy of the applicant's case, to the Crown Court officer.

(10) The judge shall consider the applicant's draft case and any alternative draft case sent to the Crown Court officer under paragraph (9)(c).

(11) If the Crown Court so orders, the applicant shall, before the case is stated and delivered to him, enter before the Crown Court officer into a recognizance, with or without sureties and in such sum as the Crown Court considers proper, having regard to the means of the applicant, conditioned to prosecute the appeal without delay.

(12) The judge shall state and sign a case within 14 days after either—

(a) the receipt of all the documents required to be sent to a court officer under paragraph (9); or

(b) the expiration of the period of 21 days referred to in that paragraph,

whichever is the sooner.

(13) A case stated by the Crown Court shall state the facts found by the Crown Court, the submissions of the parties (including any authorities relied on by the parties during the course of those submissions), the decision of the Crown Court in respect of which the application is made and the question on which the opinion of the High Court is sought.

(14) Any time limit referred to in this rule may be extended[1] either before or after it expires by the Crown Court.

(15) If the judge decides not to state a case but the stating of a case is subsequently required by a mandatory order of the High Court, paragraphs (7) to (14) shall apply to the stating of the case save that—

(a) in paragraph (7) the words "If the judge decides to state a case" shall be omitted; and

(b) in paragraph (8) for the words "receiving the notice referred to in paragraph (5)" there shall be substituted the words "the day on which the mandatory order was made".

---

1. The use of the expression "Crown Court" rather than "judge" reflects the possibility, not that the justices have to be involved, but that a judge other than the one who had heard the appeal may consider the relevant application. Where following an acquittal in the Crown Court on appeal from a magistrates' court, the prosecution seek an extension of the 21 day time limit in r 26(1) in which they may apply to the Court for a case to be stated, the Crown Court should not grant the extension without giving the defendant the opportunity to make representations on the subject (*DPP v Coleman* [1998] 1 All ER 912, [1998] 2 Cr App Rep 7).

1–7485

PART 65
APPEAL TO THE COURT OF APPEAL AGAINST RULING IN PREPARATORY HEARING

1–7486

PART 66
APPEAL TO THE COURT OF APPEAL AGAINST RULING ADVERSE TO PROSECUTION

1–7487

PART 67
APPEAL TO THE COURT OF APPEAL AGAINST ORDER RESTRICTING REPORTING OR PUBLIC ACCESS

1–7488

PART 68
APPEAL TO THE COURT OF APPEAL AGAINST CONVICTION OR SENTENCE

1–7489

PART 69
REFERENCE TO THE COURT OF APPEAL OF POINT OF LAW

1–7490

PART 70
REFERENCE TO THE COURT OF APPEAL OF UNDULY LENIENT SENTENCE

1–7491

PART 71
APPEAL TO THE COURT OF APPEAL UNDER THE PROCEEDS OF CRIME ACT 2002 — GENERAL RULES

1–7492

PART 72
APPEAL TO THE COURT OF APPEAL UNDER PROCEEDS OF CRIME ACT 2002 — PROSECUTOR'S APPEAL REGARDING CONFISCATION

1–7493

PART 73
APPEAL TO THE COURT OF APPEAL UNDER POCA 2002 — RESTRAINT OR RECEIVERSHIP ORDERS

1–7494

PART 74
APPEAL TO THE HOUSE OF LORDS

1–7495

PART 75
REFERENCE TO THE EUROPEAN COURT

75.1. Reference to the European Court. (1) In this rule "order" means an order referring a question to the European Court for a preliminary ruling under Article 234 of the Treaty establishing the European Community, Article 150 of the Treaty establishing Euratom or Article 41 of the Treaty establishing the Coal and Steel Community.

(2) An order may be made—

(a) by the Crown Court of its own motion or on application by a party to proceedings in the Crown Court; or

(b) by the Court of Appeal, on application or otherwise, at any time before the determination of an appeal or application for leave to appeal under Part I of the Criminal Appeal Act 1968.

(3) An order shall set out in a schedule the request for the preliminary ruling of the European Court, and the court making the order may give directions as to the manner and form in which the schedule is to be prepared.

(4) When an order has been made, a copy shall be sent to the senior master of the Supreme Court (Queen's Bench Division) for transmission to the Registrar of the European Court.

(5) The Crown Court proceedings in which an order is made shall, unless the Crown Court otherwise determines, be adjourned until the European Court has given a preliminary ruling on the question referred to it.

(6) Nothing in paragraph (5) above shall be taken as preventing the Crown Court from deciding any preliminary or incidental question that may arise in the proceedings after an order is made and before a preliminary ruling is given by the European Court.

(7) No appeal or application for leave to appeal, in the course of which an order is made, shall, unless the Court of Appeal otherwise orders, be determined until the European Court has given a preliminary ruling on the question referred to it.

1–7496

PART 76
REPRESENTATION ORDERS[1]

---

1. There are currently no rules in this Part.

1–7497

PART 77
RECOVERY OF DEFENCE COSTS ORDERS[1]

1. There are currently no rules in this Part.

1–7498

PART 78
COSTS ORDERS AGAINST THE PARTIES

78.1. Crown Court's jurisdiction to award costs in appeal from magistrates' court. (1) Subject to the provisions of section 109(1) of the Magistrates' Courts Act 1980 (power of magistrates' courts to award costs on abandonment of appeals from magistrates' courts), no party shall be entitled to recover any costs of any proceedings in the Crown Court from any other party to the proceedings except under an order of the Court.

(2) Subject to the following provisions of this rule, the Crown Court may make such order for costs as it thinks just.

(3) No order for costs shall be made on the abandonment of an appeal from a magistrates' court by giving notice under rule 63.5.

(4) Without prejudice to the generality of paragraph (2), the Crown Court may make an order for costs on dismissing an appeal where the appellant has failed to proceed with the appeal or on the abandonment of an appeal not being an appeal to which paragraph (3) applies.

78.2. Crown Court's jurisdiction to award costs in magistrates' court proceedings from which appeal is brought. Where an appeal is brought to the Crown Court from the decision of a magistrates' court and the appeal is successful, the Crown Court may make any order as to the costs of the proceedings in the magistrates' court which that court had power to make.

78.3. Taxation of Crown Court costs. (1) Where under these Rules the Crown Court has made an order for the costs of any proceedings to be paid by a party and the Court has not fixed a sum, the amount of the costs to be paid shall be ascertained as soon as practicable by the Crown Court officer (hereinafter referred to as the taxing authority).

(2) On a taxation under the preceding paragraph there shall be allowed the costs reasonably incurred in or about the prosecution and conviction or the defence, as the case may be.

78.4. Review of Crown Court costs by taxing authority. (1) Any party dissatisfied with the taxation of any costs by the taxing authority under rule 78.3 may apply to the taxing authority to review his decision.

(2) The application shall be made by giving notice to the taxing authority and to any other party to the taxation within 14 days of the taxation, specifying the items in respect of which the application is made and the grounds of objection.

(3) Any party to whom notice is given under the preceding paragraph may within 14 days of the service of the notice deliver to the taxing authority answers in writing to the objections specified in that notice to the taxing authority and, if he does, shall send copies to the applicant for the review and to any other party to the taxation.

(4) The taxing authority shall reconsider his taxation in the light of the objections and answers, if any, of the parties and any oral representations made by or on their behalf and shall notify them of the result of his review.

78.5. Further review of Crown Court costs by Taxing Master. (1) Any party dissatisfied with the result of a review of taxation under rule 78.4 may, within 14 days of receiving notification thereof, request the taxing authority to supply him with reasons in writing for his decision and may within 14 days of the receipt of such reasons apply to the Chief Taxing Master for a further review and shall, in that case, give notice of the application to the taxing authority and to any other party to the taxation, to whom he shall also give a copy of the reasons given by the taxing authority.

(2) Such application shall state whether the application wishes to appear or be represented, or whether he will accept a decision given in his absence and shall be accompanied by a copy of the notice given under rule 78.4, of any answer which may have been given under paragraph (3) thereof and of the reasons given by the taxing authority for his decision, together with the bill of costs and full supporting documents.

(3) A party to the taxation who receives notice of an application under this rule shall inform the Chief Taxing Master whether he wishes to appear or be represented at a further review, or whether he will accept a decision given in his absence.

(4) The further review shall be conducted by a Taxing Master and if the applicant or any other party to the taxation has given notice of his intention to appear or be represented, the Taxing Master shall inform the parties (or their agents) of the date on which the further review will take place.

(5) Before reaching his decision the Taxing Master may consult the judge who made the order for costs and the taxing authority and, unless the Taxing Master otherwise directs, no further evidence shall be received on the hearing of the further review; and no ground of objection shall be valid which was not raised on the review under rule 78.4.

(6) In making his review, the Taxing Master may alter the assessment of the taxing authority in respect of any sum allowed, whether by increase or decrease.

(7) The Taxing Master shall communicate the result of the further review to the parties and to the taxing authority.

78.6. Appeal to High Court judge after review of Crown Court costs. (1) Any party dissatisfied with the result of a further review under rule 78.5 may, within 14 days of receiving notification thereof, appeal by originating summons to a judge of the Queen's Bench Division of the High Court if, and only if, the Taxing Master certifies that the question to be decided involves a point of principle of general importance.

(2) On the hearing of the appeal the judge may reverse, affirm or amend the decision appealed against or make such other order as he thinks appropriate.

78.7. Supplementary provisions on Crown Court costs. (1) On a further review or an appeal to a judge of the High Court the Taxing Master or judge may make such order as he thinks just in respect of the costs of the hearing of the further review or the appeal, as the case may be.

(2) The time set out by rules 78.4, 78.5 and 78.6 may be extended by the taxing authority, Taxing Master or judge of the High Court on such terms as he thinks just.

1–7499
GLOSSARY

This glossary is a guide to the meaning of certain legal expressions as used in these rules.

Expression	Meaning
Account monitoring order	an order requiring certain types of financial institution to provide certain information held by them relating to a customer for the purposes of an investigation
Action plan order	a type of community sentence requiring a child or young person to comply with a three month plan relating to his actions and whereabouts and to comply with the directions of a responsible officer (eg probation officer)
Admission of evidence	acceptance by the court of the evidence into proceedings (not all evidence tendered by the parties may be allowable in court)
to adduce	to put forward (in evidence)
to adjourn	to suspend or delay the hearing of a case until another day
Advance information	information about the case against an accused, to which the accused may be entitled before he or she enters a plea
Affidavit	a written, sworn statement of evidence
Affirmation	a non-religious alternative to the oath sworn by someone about to give evidence in court or swearing a statement
Appellant	person who is appealing against a decision of the court
to arraign	to put charges to the defendant in open court in the Crown Court
Arraignment	the formal process of putting charges to the defendant in the Crown Court which consists of three parts: (1) calling him to the bar by name, (2) putting the charges to him by reading from the indictment and (3) asking him whether he pleads guilty or not guilty
Authorities	judicial decisions or opinions of authors of repute used as grounds of statements of law
bill of indictment	a written accusation of a crime against one or more persons—a criminal trial in the Crown Court cannot start without a valid indictment
in camera (trial)	proceedings which are held in private
Case stated	an appeal to the High Court against the decision of a magistrates court on the basis that the decision was wrong in law or in excess of the magistrates' jurisdiction
in chambers	proceedings which may be held in private
child safety order	an order made by a magistrates' court placing a child under the supervision of a responsible officer where the child has committed acts which could, had he been over 10 years old at the time, have constituted an offence or which have or are likely to cause harassment, alarm or distress
Committal	sending someone to a court (usually from a magistrates' court to the Crown court) or to prison
Committal for sentence	procedure whereby a person convicted in a magistrates' court is sent to the Crown Court for sentencing when the sentencing powers of the magistrates' court are not considered sufficient

Expression	Meaning
Committal proceedings	preliminary hearing in a magistrates' court before a case is sent to be tried before a jury in the Crown Court
Compellable witness	a witness who can be forced to give evidence against an accused (not all witnesses are compellable)
Compensation order	an order that a convicted person must pay compensation for loss or damage caused by the convicted person
Complainant	a person who makes a formal complaint—in relation to an offence of rape or other sexual offences the complainant is the person against whom the offence is alleged to have been committed
Complaint	document used to start certain types of proceedings in a magistrates' court, or the process of using such a document to start proceedings
Conditional discharge	an order which does not impose any immediate punishment on a person convicted of an offence, subject to the condition that he does not commit an offence in a specified period
Confiscation order	an order that private property be taken into possession by the state
Convention right	a right under the European Convention on Human Rights
Costs	the expenses involved in a court case, including the fees of the solicitors and barristers and of the court
Counsel	a barrister
Cross examination	questioning of a witness by a party other than the party who called the witness
Custody time limit	the maximum period, as set down in statute, for which a person may be kept in custody before being brought to trial—these maximum periods may only be extended by an order of the judge
Customer information order	an order requiring a financial institution to provide certain information held by them relating to a customer for the purposes of an investigation into the proceeds of crime
Declaration of incompatibility	a declaration by a court that a piece of UK legislation is incompatible with the provisions of the European Convention of Human Rights
Deferred sentence	a sentence which is determined after a delay to allow the court to assess any change in the person's conduct or circumstances after his or her conviction
Deposition	written record of a witness' written evidence
Estreatment (of recognizance)	Forfeiture
Evidence in chief	the evidence given by a witness for the party who called him
Examining justice	a magistrate carrying out his or her function of checking that a case appears on the face of the prosecution case papers to exist against an accused before the case is put forward for trial in the Crown Court—see committal and sending for trial
Exhibit	a document or thing presented as evidence in court
ex parte	a hearing where only one party is allowed to attend and make submissions
Forfeiture by peaceable re-entry	the re-possession by a landlord of premises occupied by tenants
Guardianship order	an order appointing someone to take charge of a child's affairs and property
Hearsay evidence	oral or written statements made by someone who is not a witness in the case but which the court is asked to accept as proving what they say—this expression is defined further by rule 34.1 for the purposes of Part 34, and by rule 57.1 for the purposes of Parts 57–61
Hospital order	an order that an offender be admitted to and detained in a specified hospital

Expression	Meaning
Indictment	the document containing the formal charges against a defendant—a trial in the Crown Court cannot start without this
Informant	someone who lays an information
Information	statement by which a magistrate is informed of the offence for which a summons or warrant is required—the procedure by which this statement is brought to the magistrates' attention is known as laying an information
Interested party	a person or organisation who is not the prosecutor or defendant but who has some other legal interest in a criminal case—this expression is defined further in rule 66.1, for the purposes of Part 66 only
Intermediary	a person who asks a witness (particularly a child) questions posed by the cross-examining legal representative
inter partes	a hearing where both parties attend and can make submissions
Justice of the peace	a lay magistrate or District Judge (Magistrates' Courts);
Justices' clerk	post in the magistrates' court of person who has various powers and duties in a magistrates' court, including giving advice to the magistrates on law and procedure
Leave of the court	permission granted by the court
Leave to appeal	permission granted to appeal the decision of a court
Letter of request	letter issued to a foreign court asking a judge to take the evidence of some person within that court's jurisdiction
to levy distress	to seize property from a debtor or a wrongdoer
live link	audio and/or video equipment set up in order to enable evidence to be given from outside the court room in which a case is being heard
local justice area	an area established for the purposes of the administration of magistrates' courts
mandatory order	order from the divisional Court of the Queen's Bench Division ordering a body (such as a magistrates' court) to do something (such as rehear a case)
nominated court	a court nominated to take evidence pursuant to a request by a foreign court
notice of transfer	procedure used in cases of serious and complex fraud, and in certain cases involving child witnesses, whereby the prosecution can, without seeking judicial approval, have the case sent direct to the Crown Court without the need to have the accused committed for trial
offence triable only summarily	an offence which can be tried only in a magistrates' court
offence triable either way	an offence which may be tried either in the magistrates' court or in the Crown Court
offence triable only on indictment	an offence which can be tried only in the Crown Court
in open court	in a courtroom which is open to the public
order of committal	an order sending someone to prison for contempt of court
order restricting discharge	an order restricting the discharge from hospital of patients who have been sent there for psychiatric treatment
parenting order	an order which can be made in certain circumstances where a child has been convicted of an offence which may require parents of the offender to comply with certain requirements including attendance of counselling or guidance sessions
party	a person or organisation directly involved in a criminal case, either as prosecutor or defendant
practice direction	direction relating to the practice and procedure of the courts
to prefer, preferment	to bring or lay a charge or indictment
preparatory hearing	a hearing forming part of the trial sometimes used in long and complex cases to settle various issues without requiring the jury to attend

Expression	Meaning
prima facie case	a prosecution case which is strong enough to require the defendant to answer it
primary legislation	Acts of Parliament
realisable property	property which can be sold for money
receiver	a person appointed with certain powers in respect of the property and affairs of a person who has obtained such property in the course of criminal conduct and who has been convicted of an offence—there are various types of receiver (management receiver, director's receiver, enforcement receiver)
receivership order	an order that a person's assets be put into the hands of an official with certain powers and duties to deal with that property
recognizance	formal undertaking to pay the crown a specified sum if an accused fails to surrender to custody
register	the formal records kept by a magistrates' court
to remand	to send a person away when a case is adjourned until another date—the person may be remanded on bail (when he can leave, subject to conditions) or in custody
reparation order	an order made against a child or young person who has been convicted of an offence, requiring him or her to make specific reparations to the victim or to the community at large
representation order	an order authorising payment of legal aid for a defendant
requisition	a document issued under section 29 of the Criminal Justice Act 2003 requiring a person to appear before a magistrates' court to answer a written charge
respondent	the other party (to the appellant) in a case which is the subject of an appeal
restraint order	an order prohibiting a person from dealing with any realisable property held by him
seal	a formal mark which the court puts on a document to indicate that the document has been issued by the court
security	money deposited to ensure that the defendant attends court
sending for trial	procedure whereby indictable offences are transferred to the Crown Court without the need for a committal hearing in the magistrates' court
skeleton argument	a document prepared by a party or their legal representative setting out the basis of the party's argument, including any arguments based on law—the court may require such documents to be served on the court and on the other party prior to a trial
special measures	measures which can be put in place to provide protection and/ or anonymity to a witness (eg a screen separating witness from the accused)
statutory declaration	a declaration made before a Commissioner for Oaths in a prescribed form
to stay	to halt proceedings, apart from taking any steps allowed by the Rules or the terms of the stay—proceedings may be continued if a stay is lifted
summons	a document signed by a magistrate after an information is laid before him which sets out the basis of the accusation against the accused and the time and place when he must appear
surety	a person who guarantees that a defendant will attend court
suspended sentence	sentence which takes effect only if the offender commits another offence punishable with imprisonment within the specified period
supervision order	an order placing a person who has been given a suspended sentence under the supervision of a local officer
tainted acquittal	an acquittal affected by interference with a witness or a juror
taxation of costs	the assessment of the expenses involved in a court case

Expression	Meaning
taxing authority	a body which assesses costs
Taxing Master	a judge who assesses costs
territorial authority	the UK authority which has power to do certain things in connection with co-operation with other countries and international organisations in relation to the collection of or hearing of evidence etc
transfer direction (mental health)	a direction that a person who is serving a sentence of imprisonment who is suffering from a mental disorder be transferred to a hospital and be detained there for treatment
warrant of arrest	court order to arrest a person
warrant of commitment	court order sending someone to prison
warrant of distress	court order giving the power to seize goods from a debtor to pay his debts
warrant of detention	a court order authorising someone's detention
wasted costs order	an order that a barrister or solicitor is not to be paid fees that they would normally be paid by the Legal Services Commission
witness	a person who gives evidence, either by way of a written statement or orally in court
witness summons	a document served on a witness requiring him or her to attend court to give evidence
writ of venire de novo	an order directing a new trial after a mistrial involving a fundamental irregularity
written charge	a document issued by a public prosecutor under section 29 of the Criminal Justice Act 2003 which institutes criminal proceedings by charging a person with an offence
youth court	magistrates' courts exercising jurisdiction over offences committed by and other matters related to, children and young persons.

Justices' Clerks Rules 2005[1]

(SI 2005/545 as amended by SI 2005/2796 and SI 2006/2493)

1–7500 1. These Rules may be cited as the Justices' Clerks Rules 2005 and shall come into force on 1 April 2005.

---

1. Made by the Lord Chancellor, in exercise of the powers conferred upon him by s 144 of the Magistrates' Courts Act 1980 and s 28 of the Courts Act 2003, after consultation with the Criminal Procedure Rule Committee, the Family Procedure Rule Committee and the Magistrates' Courts Rule Committee.

1–7501 2. The things specified in the Schedule to these Rules, being authorised to be done by, to or before a single justice of the peace, may be done by, to or before a justices' clerk[1].

---

1. Where the justices' clerk exercises his discretion in refusing some application, the justices' clerk cannot be required to reconsider the matter; also he could not give reasons for his decision but it is neither usual nor obligatory to do so (*R v Worthing Justices, ex p Norvell* [1981] 1 WLR 413). For the power to authorise a person appointed to assist a justices' clerk to exercise these functions see r 3 below.

1–7502 3. (1) The things specified in paragraphs 1 to 36 and 44 to 71[1] in the Schedule to these Rules, being authorised to be done by, to or before a justices' clerk, may be done by, to or before an assistant clerk, provided that that person has been specifically authorised by the justices' clerk for that purpose, and any reference in the Schedule to a justices' clerk shall be taken to include such a person.

(2) The powers authorised to be exercised by a justices' clerk at an early administrative hearing under section 50 of the Crime and Disorder Act 1998 may be exercised instead by an assistant clerk who has been specifically authorised by the justices' clerk for that purpose.

(3) Any authorisation by the justices' clerk under paragraph (1) or (2) above shall be recorded in writing at the time the authority is given or as soon as practicable thereafter.

---

1. For power of a justices' clerk to authorise a person, employed as a clerk in court to assist him, to exercise the powers under paras 37–43 of the Schedule, see r 32 of, and Sch 3 to, the Family Proceedings Courts (Children Act 1989) Rules 1991, SI 1991/1395 and r 15 of, and Sch 2 to, the Family Proceedings Courts (Matrimonial Proceedings etc) Rules 1991, SI 1991/1991 in PART IV, post.

1–7503   **4.** The Justices' Clerks Rules 1999 are hereby revoked.

1–7503A   **5.** Until the commencement of paragraph 125 of Schedule 32 to the Criminal Justice Act 2003—

   (*a*) paragraph 25 of the Schedule shall have effect as if the words "paragraph 18" were substituted for the words "paragraph 15"; and

   (*b*) paragraph 27 of the Schedule shall have effect as if the words "paragraph 4(5)" were substituted for the words "paragraph 4(6)".

1–7504   SCHEDULE

1. The laying of an information or the making of a complaint, other than an information or complaint substantiated on oath[1].

---

1. A written information or complaint is laid or made when it is received at the office of the clerk to the justices. The delivery and receipt of such an information or complaint is ministerial, and it can sensibly be inferred that any member of the staff in the office of the clerk to the justices authorised to handle incoming post has authority to receive it (*R v Manchester Stipendiary Magistrate, ex p Hill* [1983] 1 AC 328, [1982] 2 All ER 963, 146 JP 348, HL).

2. The issue of any summons, including a witness summons.

3. The issue of a warrant of arrest, whether or not endorsed for bail, for failure to surrender to the court, where there is no objection on behalf of the accused.

4. The marking of an information as withdrawn.

5. The dismissing of an information, or the discharging of an accused in respect of an information, or the discharging of an accused in respect of an information, where no evidence is offered by the prosecution.

6. The making of an order for the payment of defence costs out of central funds.

7. The adjournment of the hearing of a complaint if the parties to the complaint consent to the complaint being adjourned.

8. The extending of bail on the same conditions as those (if any) previously imposed, or, with the consent of the prosecutor and the accused, the imposing or varying of conditions of bail.

9. The further adjournment of criminal proceedings with the consent of the prosecutor and the accused, if but only if,

   (*a*) the accused, not having been remanded on the previous adjournment, is not remanded on the further adjournment; or

   (*b*) the accused, having been remanded on bail on the previous adjournment, is remanded on bail on the like terms and conditions, or, with the consent of the prosecutor and the accused, on other terms and conditions.

10. (1) The further adjournment of criminal proceedings, where there has been no objection by the prosecutor, where the accused, having been remanded on bail on the previous adjournment, is remanded on bail on the like terms and conditions in his absence.

(2) The remand of the accused on bail in his absence at the time of further adjourning the proceedings in pursuance of sub-paragraph (1) above.

11. (1) The appointment of a later time at which a person, who has been granted bail under the Police and Criminal Evidence Act 1984 subject to a duty to appear before a magistrates' court, is to appear, and the enlargement of any sureties for that person at that time, in accordance with section 43(1) of the Magistrates' Courts Act 1980, provided there is no objection by the prosecutor.

(2) Where a person has been granted police bail to appear at a magistrates' court, the appointment of an earlier time for his appearance.

12. The committal of a person for trial on bail in accordance with section 6(2) and (3)(*b*) of the Magistrates' Courts Act 1980 where, having been remanded on bail on the previous adjournment, he is released on bail on the like terms and conditions.

13. *Revoked.*

14. The asking of an accused whether he pleads guilty or not guilty to a charge, after having stated to him the substance of the information laid against him.

15. The fixing or setting aside of a date, time and place for the trial of an information.

16. The making of a direction in accordance with rule 93A(7) or (8) of the Magistrates' Courts Rules 1981.

17. The giving, variation or revocation of directions for the conduct of a criminal trial, including directions as to the following matters, namely—

   the timetable for proceedings;

   the attendance of the parties;

   the service of documents (including summaries of any legal arguments relied on by the parties);

   the manner in which evidence is to be given.

18. With the consent of the parties, the giving, variation or revocation of orders for separate or joint trials in the case of two or more accused or two or more informations.

19. The extension, with the consent of the accused, of an overall time limit under section 22 of the Prosecution of Offences Act 1985.

Sentences etc   **20.** The request of a pre-sentence report following a plea of guilty[1].

21. The request of a medical report and, for that purpose, the remand of an accused on bail on the same conditions as those (if any) previously imposed, or, with the consent of the prosecutor and the accused, on other conditions.

22. The remitting of an offender to another court for sentence.

23. Where an accused has been convicted of an offence, the making of an order for him to produce his driving licence.

24. The giving of consent for another magistrates' court to deal with an offender for an earlier offence in respect of which, after the offender had attained the age of eighteen years, a court had made an order for conditional discharge, where the justices' clerk is the clerk of the court which made the order, or in the case of a community rehabilitation order, of that court or the supervising court.

25. The amending, in accordance with paragraph 15 of Schedule 3 to the Powers of Criminal Courts (Sentencing) Act 2000, of a community rehabilitation order or community punishment order by substituting for the local justice area specified in the order the other area in which the offender proposes to reside or is residing.

26. The varying, in accordance with paragraph 5(1) of Schedule 5 to the Powers of Criminal Courts (Sentencing) Act 2000, of an attendance centre order by—

(a) varying the day or hour specified in the order for the offender's first attendance at the relevant attendance centre; or

(b) substituting for the relevant attendance centre an attendance centre which the justices' clerk is satisfied is reasonably accessible to the offender, having regard to his age, the means of access available to him and any other circumstances.

27. The signing of a certificate given to the Crown Court under paragraph 4(6) of Schedule 3 to the Powers of Criminal Courts (Sentencing) Act 2000 as to non-compliance with a community order.

28. The acceptance under section 14 of the Magistrates Courts Act 1980 of service of such a statutory declaration as is mentioned in subsection (3) of that section.

---

1. When requesting a pre-sentence report a justices' clerk is not permitted to give an indication of seriousness: Crime and Disorder Act 1998, s 49(3), in this PART, ante.

Fines 29. The issue of a warrant of distress.

30. The allowing of further time for payment of a sum enforceable by a magistrates' court.

31. The varying of the number of instalments payable, the amount of any instalment payable and the date on which any instalment becomes payable where a magistrates' court has ordered that a sum adjudged to be paid shall be paid by instalments.

32. The making of a transfer of fine order under section 89 of the Magistrates' Courts Act 1980.

33. The making of an order before an enquiry into the means of a person under section 82 of the Magistrates' Courts Act 1980 that that person shall furnish to the court a statement of his means under section 84 of that Act.

34. The fixing under section 86(3) of the Magistrates' Courts Act 1980 of a later day in substitution for a day previously fixed for the appearance of an offender to enable an enquiry into his means to be made under section 82 of that Act or to enable a hearing required by section 82(5) of that Act to be held.

35. The making or withdrawal of an application to the Secretary of State, pursuant to the Fines (Deductions from Income Support) Regulations 1992, for deductions to be made from an offender's income support.

36. The doing of such other things as are required or permitted to be done by a magistrates' court under the Fines (Deductions from Income Support) Regulations 1992.

Family etc 37. The transfer of proceedings in accordance with any order made by the Lord Chancellor under Part I of Schedule 11 to the Children Act 1989.

38. The appointment of a children's guardian or solicitor for a child under section 41 of the Children Act 1989.

39. The giving, variation or revocation of directions in accordance with rule 6 of the Family Proceedings Courts (Matrimonial Proceedings etc) Rules 1991 or rule 14 of the Family Proceedings Courts (Children Act 1989) Rules 1991.

40. The making of an order, in accordance with rule 28 of the Family Proceedings Courts (Children Act 1989) Rules 1991, under sections 11(3) or 38(1) of the Children Act 1989.

41. By virtue of rule 33 of the Family Proceedings Courts (Children Act 1989) Rules 1991, the issuing of a witness summons under section 97 of the Magistrates' Courts Act 1980 in relevant proceedings within the meaning of section 93(3) of the Children Act 1989.

42. The request of a welfare report under section 7 of the Children Act 1989.

43. By virtue of rule 16(2) of the Family Proceedings Courts (Matrimonial Proceedings etc) Rules 1991, the issuing of a witness summons under section 97 of the Magistrates' Courts Act 1980 in proceedings under the Domestic Proceedings and Magistrates' Courts Act 1978 or Schedule 6 to the Civil Partnership Act 2004.

44. The determination that a complaint for the revocation, discharge, revival, alteration, variation or enforcement of a magistrates' court maintenance order be dealt with by a magistrates' court acting for another local justice area in accordance with the provisions of rule 41 or 59 of the Magistrates' Courts Rules 1981.

45. The fixing or setting aside of a date, time and place for any hearing or directions hearing in connection with an application made in accordance with the Family Procedure (Adoption) Rules 2005 ("the Adoption Rules").

46. The exercising of the case management powers in accordance with rule 12(2)(a) to (c), (e), (g), (i), (j), (m) and (n), and, if exercised of own initiative, in accordance with rule 13(1) to (4) and (6) of the Adoption Rules.

47. The taking of a step instead of a court officer in accordance with rule 14(b) of the Adoption Rules.

48. (1) The giving, variation or revocation of directions in accordance with—

(a) rules 20(3), 21(1) and (2), 23(4), 24(4), 25, 26(1), (4) and (5), 27(4)(b)(ii), 32(4) and (7), 34(b), 35(3), 36(1)(b), 37(4) and (5), 39, 55(3) and (5), 57(2), 63(1), 64(2)(a) and (b), 65(1), (3) and (4)(a), 66(2)(b)(ii), 72(4), 74(1) and (3)(a), 77, 78(1)(b), 83, 85(1)(a), 86(4)(c), 92(c), 93(2), 97(3), 99(4), 103(3), 104(2), 107(1)(b), 112(1) and (4), 113(2), 126(2) and (3), 131(3) and (4), 138(3) and (8), 139(2), 149(2), 158, 160(1) and (3)(b), 161(3), 162(1), 165, 167(2) and (3), 168(3), 169(2)(a) and (3)(a) and 170(2) and (3)(a) of the Adoption Rules and, with the consent of the parties, rules 23(2) and (3) and 24(3)(a) of those Rules;

(b) paragraph 2.3 of the practice direction supplementing Part 2, rule 9(4) of those Rules;

(c) paragraph 1 of the practice direction supplementing Part 5, rule 24(1)(b)(ii) of those Rules;

(d) paragraph 1.2 of the practice direction supplementing Part 8, rule 78 of those Rules;

(e) paragraphs 2.5, 2.6, 2.9, 4, 5.1, 8.2, 8.4, 8.5 and 8.6 of the practice direction supplementing Part 9 of those Rules;

(f)(f) paragraphs 4.1, 4.2 and 5.5 of the practice direction supplementing Part 10 of those Rules;

(g) paragraphs 15.4 and 25.1, and annex 3, of the practice direction supplementing Part 15 of those Rules; and

(h) paragraph 4 of the practice direction supplementing Part 17 of those Rules.

(2) Where the justices' clerk considers, for whatever reason, that it is inappropriate to give a direction on a particular matter, he shall refer the matter to the court which may give any appropriate direction.

49. (1) The request for any relevant forms of consent to be filed in accordance with rule 24(2)(a)(i) or (b)(i) or (3)(b).

(2) The request for a statement made under section 20(4)(a) or (b) to be filed in accordance with rule 24(2)(b)(ii) or (iii).

50. The request for a report on the suitability of the prospective adopters to be prepared in accordance with rule 24(2)(a)(ii) or (b)(iv).

51. The monitoring of compliance with the court's timetable and directions by the parties in accordance with rule 26(7) of the Adoption Rules.

52. The appointment of a children's guardian for a child in accordance with rule 59 of the Adoption Rules.

53. The giving of permission for a children's guardian to have legal representation in accordance with rule 64(2)(c) of the Adoption Rules.

54. (1) The recording of reasons for—

(a) refusing to appoint a children's guardian in accordance with rule 60(1)(a) of the Adoption Rules;

(b) terminating the appointment of a children's guardian in accordance with rule 61(2); or

(c) terminating the appointment of a solicitor for a child in accordance with rule 68(5), of those Rules.

(2) The recording of the appointment of a solicitor for a child or refusal to make such an appointment in accordance with rule 68(6) of those Rules.

55. The appointment of a reporting officer in accordance with rule 69 of the Adoption Rules.

56. The request for a welfare report in accordance with rule 73(1) of the Adoption Rules.

57. The request for a further report from the local authority or adoption agency or for assistance in accordance with rule 29(4) of the Adoption Rules.

58. The giving of permission for any of the orders referred to in section 41(2) (recovery orders) of the Adoption and Children Act 2002 to be made without notice.

59. The choosing of which method of service to use in accordance with rule 36(2) of the Adoption Rules.

60. For the purposes of the law relating to contempt of court, the giving of permission for information relating to proceedings held in private to be communicated in accordance with rule 78(1)(a) of the Adoption Rules.

61. The removal of protected information from a document before it is disclosed to an adopted adult in accordance with rule 84(2) of the Adoption Rules.

62. The dispensing with the requirement to file an application notice in accordance with rule 87(2)(b) of the Adoption Rules.

63. The giving of permission to make an application without serving a copy of the application notice on the respondents in accordance with rule 88(2)(c) of the Adoption Rules.

64. The giving of an extension of time to file and serve evidence under rule 102 of the Adoption Rules or the giving of permission to file and serve additional evidence before the hearing in accordance with rule 103(1)(b) of those Rules.

65. The giving of permission for—

(a) a notice of making or refusal of a final order to be sent to any other person in accordance with rule 112(1)(f)(f) of the Adoption Rules;

(b) a copy of a final order to be sent to any other person in accordance with rule 112(3) of those Rules.

66. The giving of permission to call an expert or put in evidence an expert's report in accordance with rule 157(1) of the Adoption Rules.

67. The giving of permission with regard to the written questions that can be put to an expert in accordance with rule 159(2)(c)(i) of the Adoption Rules.

68. The selection of an expert in accordance with rule 160(3)(a) of the Adoption Rules.

69. The giving of permission for a document to be taken out of the court office in which it was filed or lodged, or is held in accordance with paragraph 2.4 of the practice direction supplementing Part 2, rule 9(4) of the Adoption Rules.

70. The taking of a note of proceedings in accordance with paragraph 7 of the practice direction supplementing Part 9 of the Adoption Rules.

71. The issuing of a witness summons under section 97 of the Magistrates' Courts Act 1980 in proceedings under the Adoption and Children Act 2002.

Magistrates' Courts Fees Order 2005[1]

(SI 2005/3444 amended by SI 2006/715)

1–7510   1. Citation and commencement.   This Order may be cited as the Magistrates' Courts Fees Order 2005 and shall come into force on 10th January 2006.

---

1. Made by the Lord Chancellor in exercise of the powers conferred by ss 92 and 108(6) of the Courts Act 2003.

1–7511   2. Fees to be taken.   The fees set out in column 2 of the Schedule to this Order shall be taken in magistrates' courts in respect of the items described in column 1 in accordance with and subject to the directions specified in column 1.

1–7512   3.   (1) No fees shall be taken in respect of—

(a) criminal matters (except for the supply of a document prepared for use in connection with a criminal matter but which is for use in connection with a matter which is not a criminal matter);

(b) any summons, warrant, notice or order issued, given or made under sections 83(1) or (2), 88, 89 or 136 of the Magistrates' Courts Act 1980, or under any rule made for the purpose of those provisions; or

(c) binding over proceedings.

(2) In this article, "binding over proceedings" means any proceedings instituted (whether by way of complaint under section 115 of the Magistrates' Courts Act 1980 or otherwise) with a view to obtaining from a magistrates' court an order requiring a person to enter into a recognizance to keep the peace or to be of good behaviour.

1–7513   4. Exemptions and remissions.   No fee shall be payable under this Order by a party who, at the time when a fee would otherwise become payable,—

(*a*) is in receipt of—

(i) legal advice and assistance under Part II or Part III of the Legal Aid Act 1988 in connection with the matter to which the proceedings relate; or

(ii) representation under Part IV of the Legal Aid Act 1988 for the purposes of the proceedings;

(*b*) is receiving services funded by the Legal Services Commission as part of the Community Legal Service; or

(*c*) is in receipt of—

(i) income support under the Social Security Contributions and Benefits Act 1992;

(ii) income-based jobseeker's allowance under the Jobseekers Act 1995;

(iii) guarantee credit under the State Pension Credit Act 2002;

(iv) any element of child tax credit, under the Tax Credits Act 2002, other than the family element; or

(v) working tax credit under the Tax Credits Act 2002.

1–7514 5. The Lord Chancellor may on the ground of financial hardship or for other reasonable cause remit in whole or in part any fee prescribed by this Order.

1–7515 6 Consequential amendment. In regulation 7(1)(*b*) of the Register of Fines Regulations 2003 for "Part 1 of Schedule 6 to the Magistrates' Courts Act 1980" substitute "an Order made under section 92 of the Courts Act 2003 (fees)".

1–7516

Article 2   **SCHEDULE**
                                    FEES TO BE TAKEN

Column 1 Number and description of fee	Column 2 Amount of fee
1 Attendance	
1.1 On a justice of the peace, to view deserted premises in order to affix notice or to give possession thereof, or to view a highway, bridge or nuisance	£44
2 Case for the opinion of High Court	
2.1 On an application to state a case for the opinion of the High Court under section 111 Magistrates' Courts Act 1980: drawing of case, copies, taking recognizance as required by section 114 of that Act and enlargement and renewal of such recognizance	£382
2.2 On a request for a certificate of refusal to state a case	£8
3 Certificate	
3.1 On a request for a certificate not otherwise charged	£25
4 Register of Judgments, Orders and Fines	
4.1 On a request for a certificate of satisfaction	£15
5 Council tax and rates	
5.1 On an application for a liability order (each defendant)	£3
Commitment	
5.2 On a complaint (or application) and the issue of a summons or a warrant of arrest without issuing a summons	£25
5.3 On the issue of a warrant of arrest if the summons is not obeyed	£25
5.4 On the making of a commitment order	£40
6 Copy Documents	
6.1 On a request for a copy of any document	
(a) for the first page (except the first page of a subsequent copy of the same document supplied at the same time)	£1.10
(b) per page in any other case	
Where a fee has been paid for a summons, order or warrant no fee shall be charged for a copy of that document.	55p
(c) each additional copy	10p
7 Duplicate	
7.1 For the duplicate of any document	£5
8 Proceedings under the Domestic Proceedings and Magistrates' Courts Act 1978	
8.1 On an application for an order for financial provision (excluding an application to vary or revoke such an order or in respect of an application for an order made to the benefit of, or against, a person residing outside the United Kingdom)	£175
9 Proceedings under the Family Law Act 1986	
9.1 On an application for a declaration of parentage (each child)	£130
10 Proceedings under the Children Act 1989	
10.1 On an application or request for permission under the following provisions of the Children Act 1989—	
(a) section 4(1)(c) or (3) or 4A(1)(b) or (3) (parental responsibility)	£175
(b) section 5(1) or 6(7) (guardians)	£175
(c) section 10(1) or (2) (section 8 orders)	£175
(d) section 13(1) (change of child's surname or removal from jurisdiction while residence order in force)	£175
(e) section 14A(3) or (6)(a), 14C(3) or 14D(1) (special guardianship orders)	£140
(f) section 31 (care or supervision order)	£150
For the purposes of fee 10.1(f) a care order does not include an interim care order, and a supervision order does not include an interim supervision order.	
(g) section 33(7) (change of child's surname or removal from jurisdiction while care order in force)	£150
(h) section 34 (contact with a child in care)	£150

Column 1 Number and description of fee	Column 2 Amount of fee
(i) section 36 (education supervision order)	£150
(j) section 43 (child assessment order)	£150
(k) Part XA (affecting the registration of a child minder or day carer including appeals against cancellation or varying the conditions of the registration)	£150
(l) paragraph 1(1), 2(1), 6(5) or 14(1) of Schedule 1 (financial provision)	£175
(m) paragraph 8(1) of Schedule 8 (appeals concerning foster parenting)	£150
10.2 On an application to vary, extend or discharge an order relating to provisions to which the following fees apply—	
(a) fees 10.1(a) to (d) and (l)	£175
(b) fees 10.1(f) to (j)	£150
Where an application requires the permission of the court, the relevant fee applies where permission is sought but no further fee may be charged if permission is granted and the application is made.	
Where an application is made or filed or permission is sought under or relating to provisions of the Children Act 1989 which are listed in two or more different numbered fees, only the highest fee shall be payable.	
Where an application is made or filed or permission is sought under or relating to two or more provisions of the Children Act 1989 which are listed in the same numbered fee, that fee shall be payable only once.	
Where the same application is made or filed or permission is sought in respect of two or more children at the same time, only one fee shall be payable in respect of each numbered fee.	
11 Proceedings under the Human Fertilisation and Embryology Act 1990	
11.1 On an application under section 30 (parental order)	£175
12 Proceedings under the Child Support Act 1991	
12.1 On an application for a liability order	£40
12.2 On commencing an appeal under section 20	£130
12.3 On commencing an appeal against deduction from earnings order	£80
12.4 On a complaint (or application), the issue of a summons and/or a warrant of arrest, and the making of a commitment order (combined fee)	£90
13 Proceedings under the Adoption and Children Act 2002	
13.1 On an application or request for permission under Part 1 of the Adoption and Children Act 2002 including applications to vary or revoke an order	£140
Where an application requires the permission of the court, the relevant fee applies where permission is sought but no further fee may be charged if permission is granted and the application is made.	
14 Proceedings under Schedule 6 to the Civil Partnership Act 2004	
14.1 On an application for an order for financial provision (excluding an application to vary or revoke such an order or in respect of an application for an order made to the benefit of, or against, a person residing outside the United Kingdom)	£175
15 Proceedings to vary, extend or revoke an order made in family proceedings	
15.1 On an application to vary, extend or revoke an order not otherwise charged	£20
16 Licences	
16.1 For every licence, consent or authority not otherwise provided for, to include registration when necessary	£8
16.2 On an application for the revocation of a licence not otherwise provided for	£30
17 Oaths	
17.1 On the attestation of constable	£8
17.2 For every oath, affirmation or solemn declaration not otherwise charged (no fee is payable for the swearing in of witnesses in civil proceedings or in any case where an Act directs that no fee shall be taken)	£8
18 Other civil proceedings	
18.1 On a complaint (or application)	£25
18.2 On the issue of a summons and copy	£25
18.3 On the issue of a warrant and copy	£25
18.4 On the making of an order and copy	£25
19 Warrant of Entry	
19.1 On the application for a warrant of entry	£3
Note: Only one fee is payable where more than one document is issued in relation to a partnership.]	

Register of Judgments, Orders and Fines Regulations 2005[1]
(SI 2005/3595)

1–7530   1. Citation, commencement and duration.   These Regulations may be cited as the Register of Judgments, Orders and Fines Regulations 2005.

---

1. Made by the Lord Chancellor in exercise of the powers conferred upon him by section 98(1), (2) and (3) and section 108(6) of the Courts Act 2003.

1–7531   2.   These Regulations shall come into force—

(a) for the purposes of this regulation and regulations 1 and 4, on the day after the day on which these Regulations are made; and

(b) for all other purposes, on 6th April 2006.

1–7532   3. Interpretation.   In these Regulations—

"the 1998 Rules" means the Civil Procedure Rules 1998;

"the Act" means the Courts Act 2003;

"Administrative Court" has the same meaning as in Part 54 of the 1998 Rules;

"amendment notice" means the notice given to the Registrar in accordance with regulation 21;

"applicable charge" means the charge fixed by the Lord Chancellor in accordance with section 98(4) of the Act, or in accordance with section 98(4) as applied by section 98(7)(*b*) of the Act;

"appropriate officer" means—

(*a*) in the case of the High Court or a county court, an officer of the court in which the judgment is entered;

(*b*) in the case of a registration under paragraph 38(1)(*b*) of Schedule 5 to the Act—

(i) where a fines officer exercises the power to register following service of a notice under paragraph 37(6)(*b*) of that Schedule, that officer; or

(ii) where a court exercises the power to register by virtue of paragraph 39(3) or (4) of that Schedule, an officer of that court;

(*c*) in respect of a liability order designated for the purposes of section 33(5) of the Child Support Act 1991, the Secretary of State;

"appropriate fee" means the fee prescribed under section 92(1) of the Act;

"certificate of satisfaction" means the certificate applied for under regulation 17;

"data protection principles" means the principles set out in Part 1 of Schedule 1 to the Data Protection Act 1998, as read subject to Part 2 of that Schedule and section 27(1) of that Act;

"debt" means the sum of money owed by virtue of a judgment, administration order or fine, and "debtor" means the individual, incorporated or unincorporated body liable to pay that sum;

"family proceedings" has the same meaning as in section 63 (interpretation) of the Family Law Act 1996;

"judgment" means any judgment or order of the court for a sum of money and, in respect of a county court, includes a liability order designated by the Secretary of State for the purposes of section 33(5) of the Child Support Act 1991;

"Local Justice Area" means the area specified in an order made under section 8(2) of the Act;

"Registrar" means—

(*a*) where the Register is kept by a body corporate in accordance with section 98(6) of the Act, that body corporate; or

(*b*) otherwise, the Lord Chancellor;

"the Register" means the register kept in accordance with section 98(1) of the Act;

"satisfied", in relation to a debt, means that the debt has been paid in full, and "satisfaction" is to be construed accordingly;

"Technology and Construction Court" has the same meaning as in Part 60 of the 1998 Rules.

1–7533 4. *Amends the Register of Fines Regulations 2003.*

1–7534 5. Performance of steps under these Regulations. Any step to be taken under these Regulations by the appropriate officer or the Registrar shall be taken—

(*a*) in respect of—

(i) the registration of judgments to which regulation 8(1)(*a*) applies; and

(ii) the registration of administration orders to which regulation 8(1)(*b*) applies,

within one working day;

(*b*) in respect of the registration of sums to which regulation 8(1)(*c*) applies, as soon as may be reasonably practicable.

1–7535 6, 7. *Keeping of the register by the Registrar.*

1–7537 8. Registration of judgments, administration orders and fines. (1) The appropriate officer shall send to the Registrar a return of—

(*a*) subject to regulation 9, every judgment entered in—

(i) the High Court; and

(ii) a county court;

(*b*) every administration order made under section 112 of the County Courts Act 1984 (power of county courts to make administration orders);

(*c*) every sum to be registered by virtue of paragraph 38(1)(*b*) of Schedule 5 to the Act (further steps available against defaulters).

(2) Following receipt of a return sent in accordance with paragraph (1), the Registrar shall record the details of the return as an entry in the Register.

1–7538 9. *Requirements of reg 8(1)(a) not to apply to certain judgments of the High Court and county courts.*

1–7539 10. Information contained in the appropriate officer's return. The return sent by virtue of regulation 8(1) shall contain details of—

(*a*) the full name and address of the debtor in respect of whom the entry in the Register is to be made;

(b) if the entry is to be in respect of an individual, that individual's date of birth (where known);
(c) the amount of the debt;
(d) the case number;
(e) in respect of a return sent by virtue of regulation 8(1)(a) regarding a liability order designated under section 33(5) of the Child Support Act 1991, the date of the judgment;
(f) in respect of all other returns sent by virtue of regulation 8(1)(a)—

  (i) the name of the court which made the judgment; and
  (ii) the date of the judgment;

(g) in respect of a return sent by virtue of regulation 8(1)(b)—

  (i) the name of the court which made the administration order; and
  (ii) the date of the order;

(h) in respect of a return sent by virtue of regulation 8(1)(c)—

  (i) the Local Justice Area which imposed the fine; and
  (ii) the date of conviction.

1–7540 11, 12. *Cancellation or endorsement of entries relating to judgments of the High Court or a county court and endorsement of entries relating to county court administration orders.*

1–7542 13 Cancellation or endorsement of entries relating to fines. (1) This regulation applies where an entry in the Register is one to which regulation 8(1)(c) applies (fines subject to registration under Schedule 5 to the Act).
(2) Where it comes to the attention of the appropriate officer that—

(a) the debt to which the entry relates has been satisfied one month or less from the date on which the fine was registered;
(b) the conviction for which the fine was imposed has been set aside or reversed; or
(c) the fine has been remitted in full,

that officer shall send a request to the Registrar to cancel the entry.
(3) Where it comes to the attention of the appropriate officer that the debt has been satisfied more than one month from the date on which the fine was registered, that officer shall send a request to the Registrar to endorse the entry as to the satisfaction of the debt.

1–7543 14 Cancellation of entries in the Register—additional provisions. Where an entry in the Register is endorsed in accordance with regulations 11(3) or 13(3) and the appropriate officer is later of the opinion that the debt was satisfied one month or less from—

(a) the date of the judgment or administration order; or
(b) the date on which the fine was registered,

that officer shall send a request to the Registrar to cancel the relevant entry.

1–7544 15. Where—

(a) it comes to the attention of the appropriate officer that an administrative error has been made; and
(b) he is of the opinion that the error is such to require the cancellation of an entry in the Register,

that officer shall send a request to the Registrar to cancel the relevant entry.

1–7545 16 Cancellation and endorsement of entries in the Register by the Registrar. Following receipt of a request under—

(a) regulation 11(2), 13(2), 14 or 15 (debt due satisfied in one month or less, etc), the Registrar shall cancel the relevant entry;
(b) regulation 11(3) or 13(3) (debt due satisfied in more than one month), the Registrar shall endorse the relevant entry as to the satisfaction of the debt;
(c) regulation 12(2) (administration order has been varied, revoked or debt has been satisfied), the Registrar shall endorse the relevant entry accordingly.

1–7546 17. Application for, and issue of, a certificate of satisfaction. (1) A registered debtor may apply to the appropriate officer for a certificate ("certificate of satisfaction") as to the satisfaction of the debt.
(2) An application under paragraph (1) shall be—

(a) made in writing; and
(b) accompanied by the appropriate fee.

1–7547 18. *Documents required to substantiate application under s 17(1) in relation to judgments entered in the High Court or a county court.*

1–7548 19. Where an application has been made under regulation 17(1) and—

(a) the appropriate officer is of the opinion that the debt has been satisfied; or
(b) a notice has been sent in accordance with regulation 18(3) and the creditor has not responded within the time limit provided,

the appropriate officer shall issue a certificate of satisfaction to the registered debtor.

1–7549   20. Amendment of the Register in respect of the amount registered.   (1) Where it comes to the attention of the appropriate officer that the amount liable to be paid differs from the amount entered in the Register, due to—

(a)   the issue of a final costs certificate; or

(b)   an increase in the amount of the debt,

the appropriate officer shall send a return to the Registrar to amend the Register to reflect the revised amount.

(2) The return sent in accordance with paragraph (1) shall contain the same information as prescribed by regulation 10 in respect of the return sent in accordance with regulation 8(1).

(3) Following receipt of a return sent in accordance with this regulation, the Registrar shall amend the Register accordingly.

1–7550   21. Correction of registered details of the judgment, administration order or fine.   (1) Where it comes to the attention of a registered debtor that the entry in the Register relating to his debt is inaccurate with respect to the details of the judgment, administration order or fine, that debtor may give notice to the Registrar requiring an amendment to be made ("amendment notice").

(2) The amendment notice shall—

(a)   identify the entry which is alleged to be inaccurate; and

(b)   state the amendment which is required.

1–7551   22.   Following receipt of an amendment notice in respect of an entry in the Register, the Registrar shall request that the appropriate officer verify the details of that entry.

1–7552   23.   Following receipt of a request for verification under regulation 22, the appropriate officer shall—

(a)   check the information contained in the entry against the official records; and

(b)   reply to the request, where applicable stating any necessary amendment.

1–7553   24.   (1) Where the appropriate officer informs the Registrar that the entry is inaccurate and requests an amendment, the Registrar shall amend the Register to rectify the inaccuracy.

(2) Following an amendment to the Register in accordance with paragraph (1), the Registrar shall inform the registered debtor of the action taken and the reasons for having taken that action.

1–7554   25.   Where the appropriate officer informs the Registrar that the entry is accurate, the Registrar shall inform the registered debtor that no action is to be taken and the reasons for not taking any action.

1–7555   Removal of entries in the Register26.   The Registrar shall remove any entry in the Register registered—

(a)   by virtue of regulation 8(1)(a) or (b), six years from the date of the judgment;

(b)   by virtue of regulation 8(1)(c), five years from the date of conviction.

1–7556   Searches of the Register

27.   (1) Subject to regulation 29, searches of a section of the Register may be carried out on payment of the applicable charge relevant to the type and method of search.

(2) The types of search which may be carried out are—

(a)   at a stated address, against a named individual or unincorporated body;

(b)   against a named incorporated body;

(c)   a periodical search—

(i)   relating to a named court;

(ii)   within a named county; or

(iii)   with the agreement of the Registrar, against such other criteria as may be requested.

1–7557   28. Certified copies.   On receipt of—

(a)   a written request for a certified copy of an entry in the Register; and

(b)   the applicable charge for such a request,

the Registrar shall provide a copy of that entry, certified by him as a true and complete copy of the entry in the Register.

1–7558   29. Refusal of access to the Register and appeals.   (1) The Registrar may—

(a)   refuse a person access to the Register, or to a part of the Register; and

(b)   refuse to carry out a search of the Register,

if he believes that the purpose for which access has been requested or for which the results of the search will be used contravenes—

(i)   any of the data protection principles; or

(ii)   the provisions of any other enactment.

(2) Where a refusal is made under paragraph (1), the person who has been denied access to, or has been denied a search of, the Register may appeal to a county court against the decision of the Registrar.

Practice Direction (Magistrates' Courts: Anti-Social Behaviour Orders: Composition of Benches)[1]

1. [2006] 1 All ER 886, [2006] 1 WLR 636, 170 JP 173.
24 February 2006. Sir Igor Judge P circulated the following direction with the agreement of Sir Anthony Clarke MR:

1–7559   **[1].** Where there is an application to a magistrates' court for an anti-social behaviour order under s 1 of the Crime and Disorder Act 1998, or an application to a magistrates' court for an anti-social behaviour order to be varied or discharged under s 1(8) of the Act, and the person against whom the order is sought is under 18, the justices constituting the court should normally be qualified to sit in the youth court.

     [2]. Applications for interim orders under s 1D of the Act, including those made without notice, may be listed before justices who are not so qualified.

     [3]. If it is not practicable to constitute a bench in accordance with para [1], in particular where to do so would result in a delayed hearing, this direction does not apply.

Fines Collection Regulations 2006[1]
(SI 2006/501)

PART 1
INTRODUCTION

1–7560   **1. Citation, commencement, extent and interpretation.**   (1) These Regulations may be cited as the Fines Collection Regulations 2006 and shall come into force on the 27th March 2006.

     (2) These Regulations extend to England and Wales only.

     (3) In these Regulations—

"attachable earnings" has the same meaning as it has in paragraph 3 of Schedule 3 to the Attachment of Earnings Act 1971;

"authorised person" means a person who is employed by the contractor and is authorised to carry out or direct and supervise the clamping, release from clamping, removal and release from storage, of vehicles.

"charges due" means any charge to payable to the contractor by P in addition to the sum due—

     (a) when payment is made to an authorised person so that the vehicle is not clamped,

     (b) as a condition of the release of the vehicle from clamping, and

     (c) as a condition of the removal, storage and release of the vehicle from storage,

     within the range approved by the Lord Chancellor for such charges;

"clamp" means an immobilisation device and related expressions shall be construed accordingly;

"clamping contractor" means a person authorised to undertake the clamping, removal and storage of vehicles by and in accordance with a contract with the Lord Chancellor or the designated officer for a court, "the contractor" means the clamping contractor;

"clamping notice" means a notice affixed to a car to inform the owner that their car is clamped;

"earnings" has the same meaning as it has in section 24 of the Attachment of Earnings Act 1971;

"pay-day" has the same meaning as it has in paragraph 2 of Schedule 3 to the Attachment of Earnings Act 1971;

"Schedule 5" means Schedule 5 to the Courts Act 2003;

"vehicle" means a motor vehicle,

"working day" means a day other than a Saturday, Sunday, Christmas Day, Good Friday or bank holiday,

and, save where the context requires otherwise, a reference to clamping or storage includes release from clamping or, as the case may be, release from storage.

1. Made by the Lord Chancellor in exercise of the powers conferred on him by s 108(6) of, and paragraphs 38(2)(b), 41, 42(3), 42A(4), 43, 44, 45 and 46 of Schedule 5 to, the Courts Act 2003.

PART 2
FINE INCREASE, DELIVERY AND SUMMONS

1–7561   **2. Increase in fine.**   The increase in the fine under paragraph 42A of Schedule 5 shall be 50% of the fine.

1–7562   **3. Delivery of further steps notice.**   A further steps notice issued under paragraph 37 of Schedule 5 may be delivered by hand or be sent by post to P's last known address.

1–7563   **4. Summons for ensuring attendance of P before the court.**   A fines officer may for the purpose of ensuring that P attends a magistrates' court to which he has referred P's case under paragraph 37 or 42 of Schedule 5, issue a summons requiring P to appear before the court at the time and place appointed in the summons.

PART 3
ATTACHMENT OF EARNINGS

1–7564 5 Tables and calculation method for attachment of earnings orders. In the case of an attachment of earnings order made under Schedule 5, the employer shall make deductions from P's earnings in accordance with the following tables and regulations 6 to 15—

Tables of Periodical Deductions from Earnings

Table A
Deductions from Weekly Earnings

(1) Attachable Earnings	(2) Percentage deduction rate
Not exceeding £55	0
Exceeding £55 but not exceeding £100	3
Exceeding £100 but not exceeding £135	5
Exceeding £135 but not exceeding £165	7
Exceeding £165 but not exceeding £260	12
Exceeding £260 but not exceeding £370	17
Exceeding £370	17 in respect of the first £370 and 50 in respect of the remainder.

Table B
Deductions from Monthly Earnings

(1) Attachable Earnings	(2) Percentage deduction rate
Not exceeding £220	0
Exceeding £220 but not exceeding £400	3
Exceeding £400 but not exceeding £540	5
Exceeding £540 but not exceeding £660	7
Exceeding £660 but not exceeding £1,040	12
Exceeding £1,040 but not exceeding £,1480	17
Exceeding £1,480	17 in respect of the first £1,480 and 50 in respect of the remainder.

Table C
Deductions from Daily Earnings

(1) Attachable Earnings	(2) Percentage deduction rate
Not exceeding £8	0
Exceeding £8 but not exceeding £15	3
Exceeding £15 but not exceeding £20	5
Exceeding £20 but not exceeding £24	7
Exceeding £24 but not exceeding £38	12
Exceeding £38 but not exceeding £53	17
Exceeding £53	17 in respect of the first £53 and 50 in respect of the remainder.

1–7565 6. Subject to regulations 7 and 8, the sum to be deducted by an employer under an attachment of earnings order on any pay-day shall be—

(a) where P's earnings from the employer are payable weekly, a sum equal to the appropriate percentage of the attachable earnings otherwise payable on that pay-day; and for this purpose the appropriate percentage is the percentage (or percentages) specified in column 2 of Table A in regulation 5 in relation to the band in column 1 of that Table within which the attachable earnings fall;

(b) where his earnings from the employer are payable monthly, a sum equal to the appropriate percentage of the attachable earnings otherwise payable on that pay-day; and for this purpose the appropriate percentage is the percentage (or percentages) specified in column 2 of Table B in regulation 5 in relation to the band in column 1 of that Table within which the attachable earnings fall; and

(c) where his earnings from the employer are payable at regular intervals of a whole number of weeks or months, the sum arrived at by—

(i) calculating what would be his weekly or monthly attachable earnings (the "notional attachable earnings") by dividing the attachable earnings payable to him by the employer on the pay-day by that whole number of weeks or months, as the case may be,

(ii) ascertaining the percentage (or percentages) specified in column 2 of Table A (if the whole number is of weeks) or of Table B (if the whole number is of months) in regulation 5 in relation to the band in column 1 of that Table within which the notional attachable earnings calculated under paragraph (i) fall, and

(iii) calculating the sum which equals the appropriate percentage (or percentages) of the notional attachable earnings for any of those weeks or months and multiplying that sum by the whole number of weeks or months, as appropriate.

1–7566   **7.** Where regulation 6 applies and the amount to be paid to P on any pay-day includes an advance in respect of future pay, the sum to be deducted on that pay-day shall be the aggregate of the amount which would otherwise fall to be deducted under regulation 6 and—

    (*a*)   where the amount advanced would otherwise have been paid on a single pay-day, the sum which would have been deducted on that pay-day in accordance with regulation 6 if the amount advanced had been the amount of attachable earnings on that day; or

    (*b*)   where the amount advanced would otherwise have been paid on more than one pay-day, the sums which would have been deducted on each of the relevant pay-days in accordance with regulation 6 if—

        (i)   an equal proportion of the amount advanced had been paid on each of those days; and

        (ii) the attachable earnings of P on each of those days had been an amount equal to that proportion.

1–7567   **8.** Where the amount payable to P on any pay-day is reduced by reason of an earlier advance of pay, the attachable earnings of P on that day shall, for the purposes of regulation 6, be the attachable earnings less the amount of that deduction.

1–7568   **9.** Subject to regulations 10 and 11, where P's earnings from the employer are payable at regular intervals other than at intervals to which regulation 6 applies, the sum to be deducted on any pay-day shall be arrived at by—

    (*a*)   calculating what would be his daily attachable earnings (the "notional daily attachable earnings") by dividing the attachable earnings payable to him by the employer on the pay-day by the number of days in the interval,

    (*b*)   ascertaining the percentage (or percentages) specified in column 2 of Table C in regulation 5 in relation to the band in column 1 of that Table within which the notional daily attachable earnings calculated under sub-paragraph (*a*) fall, and

    (*c*)   calculating the sum which equals the appropriate percentage (or percentages) of the notional daily attachable earnings and multiplying that sum by the number of days in the interval.

1–7569   **10.** Where P's earnings are payable as mentioned in regulation 9, and the amount to be paid to P on any pay-day includes an amount advanced in respect of future pay, the amount of P's notional daily attachable earnings under paragraph (*a*) of that regulation shall be calculated in accordance with the formula—

$$(A + B) / (C + D)$$

where:

  A is the amount of attachable earnings payable to him on that pay-day (exclusive of the amount advanced);

  B is the amount advanced;

  C is the number of days in the period for which the amount of attachable earnings is payable; and

  D is the number of days in the period for which, but for the agreement to pay in advance, the amount advanced would have been payable.

1–7570   **11.** Regulation 8 applies in relation to regulation 9 as it applies in relation to regulation 6.

1–7571   **12.** Where earnings are payable to P by the employer by 2 or more series of payments at regular intervals—

    (*a*)   if some or all of the intervals are of different lengths—

        (i)   for the purpose of arriving at the sum to be deducted, whichever of regulations 6, 7, 8, 9, 10 and 11 is appropriate shall apply to the series with the shortest interval (or, if there is more than one series with the shortest interval, such one of those series as the employer may choose), and

        (ii) in relation to the earnings payable in every other series, the sum to be deducted shall be 20 per cent of the attachable earnings or, where on any pay-day an amount advanced is also paid, 20 per cent of the aggregate of the attachable earnings and the amount advanced;

    (*b*)   if all of the intervals are of the same length, whichever of regulations 6, 7, 8, 9, 10 and 11 is appropriate shall apply to such series as the employer may choose and paragraph (*a*)(ii) shall apply to every other series,

and regulation 8 shall apply in relation to paragraph (*a*)(ii) as it applies in relation to regulation 6.

1–7572   **13.** Subject to regulations 14 and 15, where P's earnings from the employer are payable at irregular intervals, the sums to be deducted on any pay-day shall be arrived at by—

    (*a*)   calculating what would be his daily attachable earnings by dividing the attachable earnings payable to him by the employer on the pay-day—

        (i)   by the number of days since earnings were last payable by the employer to him, or

        (ii) if the earnings are the first earnings to be payable by the employer to him with respect to the employment in question, by the number of days since he began the employment;

(*b*) ascertaining the percentage (or percentages) specified in column 2 of Table C in regulation 5 in relation to the band in column 1 of that Table within which the notional attachable earnings calculated under paragraph (*a*) fall; and

(*c*) calculating the sum which equals the appropriate percentage (or percentages) of the daily attachable earnings and multiplying that sum by the same number as that of the divisor for the purposes of the calculation mentioned in paragraph (*a*).

1–7573 **14.** Where on the same pay-day there are payable to P by the employer both earnings payable at regular intervals and earnings payable at irregular intervals, for the purpose of arriving at the sum to be deducted on the pay-day under the foregoing paragraphs all the earnings shall be aggregated and treated as earnings payable at the regular interval.

1–7574 **15.** Where there are earnings payable to P by the employer at regular intervals on one pay-day, and earnings are payable by the employer to him at irregular intervals on a different pay-day, the sum to be deducted on each of the pay-days on which the earnings which are payable at irregular intervals are so payable shall be 20 per cent of the attachable earnings payable to him on the day.

PART 4

CLAMPING OF MOTOR VEHICLES

1–7575 **16. Requirements with respect to the making of a clamping order.** Before a clamping order is made by the court under paragraph 39(3)(*b*) or 42(2)(*c*), or by the fines officer under paragraph 40, of Schedule 5 the court or, as the case may be, the fines officer must be satisfied—

(*a*) that P has the means to pay the sum due; and

(*b*) that the value of the vehicle or vehicles to be clamped, if sold, would be likely to exceed the amount of the sum due, the amount of the likely charges due and the likely costs of the sale.

1–7576 **17. Matters to be included in a clamping order.** A clamping order must specify—

(*a*) P's full name, address and date of birth;

(*b*) details—

(i) of P's conviction (including date and nature) for which the liability to pay the sum due was imposed,

(ii) of the amount of the sum due,

(iii) of the collection order,

(iv) of the further steps notice, and

(v) of the vehicle or vehicles to be clamped;

(*c*) the date after which the order must be executed if the sum due is not paid;

(*d*) the name, official address and telephone number of the fines officer and the court; and

(*e*) how the sum due may be paid.

1–7577 **18. Procedure on making a clamping order.** (1) On the making of a clamping order by the court or the fines officer, the fines officer must send a copy of the order to a clamping contractor who, if the sum due is not paid, must execute the order in accordance with these Regulations on or after the date specified in the order.

(2) The copy of the clamping order sent to the clamping contractor must be accompanied by details of P's last known address, the vehicle or vehicles to be clamped and, if known, the likely whereabouts of the vehicle or vehicles to be clamped.

1–7578 **19. Places where vehicles may be clamped.** (1) Vehicles may be clamped at any place (including on any highway or road) to which the public has access.

(2) Vehicles may be clamped on any private land to which access may be had at the time of clamping, without opening or removing any door, gate or other barrier.

(3) Authorised persons and other employees of the contractor entering land in accordance with paragraph (2) may enter such private land with their equipment and with or without a vehicle or vehicles for the purpose of clamping a vehicle on the land, releasing it from a clamp or removing it to secure storage.

1–7579 **20. Vehicles which must not be clamped.** The following vehicles must not be clamped—

(*a*) a vehicle not registered in P's name under the Vehicle Excise and Registration Act 1994;

(*b*) a vehicle on which a current disabled person's badge is displayed or in relation to which there are reasonable grounds for believing that it is used for the carriage of a disabled person;

(*c*) a vehicle used for police, fire or ambulance purposes; and

(*d*) a vehicle being used by a doctor on call away from his usual place of work which is displaying a British Medical Association badge or other health emergency badge showing the doctor's address.

1–7580 **21. Defect in clamping order or irregularity in its execution.** (1) A clamping order made for the purpose of enforcing payment of a sum adjudged to be paid, as mentioned in paragraph 1 of Schedule 5, shall not be held void by reason of any defect in the order.

(2) A person acting in the execution of a clamping order shall not be deemed to be a trespasser by reason only of any irregularity in the execution of the order.

(3) Nothing in this regulation shall prejudice the claim of any person for special damages in respect of any loss caused by a defect in the order or irregularity in its execution.

1–7581   22. Clamping a vehicle.   (1) If a vehicle to be clamped is so positioned that, while the vehicle is clamped in that position there would be at any time a contravention of any prohibition or restriction imposed by or under any enactment, the authorised person must before the vehicle is clamped, have it repositioned to the nearest place where there would be no such contravention while it is clamped there.

(2) If a repositioned vehicle is not visible from the place in which it was originally positioned, the authorised person must ensure that a notice is placed at or near the original position of the vehicle indicating that the vehicle has been clamped as required by the clamping order, where the vehicle may be found and giving a telephone number available during all reasonable hours for enquires by P or a person acting on his behalf.

(3) No extra charge may be required in respect of the repositioning of the vehicle.

(4) On clamping a vehicle the authorised person must affix in a prominent position on the vehicle a clamping notice specifying—

  (*a*) that the vehicle has been clamped and that it is an offence under paragraph 49 of Schedule 5 to remove or attempt to remove the clamp or the notice;

  (*b*) details of the clamping order;

  (*c*) how to secure the release of the vehicle;

  (*d*) the amount of the sum due and charges payable for the release of the vehicle;

  (*e*) a telephone number and address for enquires;

  (*f*) the name and address of the clamping contractor;

  (*g*) the name, official address and telephone number of the fines officer and the court;

  (*h*) the opening hours of the contractor and the court; and

  (*i*) how to apply under regulations 27 and 28 for the release of a vehicle wrongly clamped.

1–7582   23. Release of vehicle on payment of charges and sum due.   (1) The office of the contractor where payment of the sum due and charge or charges due may be made must be readily accessible from the place where the vehicle is clamped during all hours when the contractor undertakes clamping and for a least 2 hours thereafter.

(2) Payment of, or towards the payment of, the sum due and the charge or charges due can be made to the authorised person, as well as at the contractor's office, or at the court office specified in the clamping notice. A reasonable method of payment must be accepted by the contractor or authorised person.

(3) A vehicle in respect of which the sum due and charge or charges due have been paid in full must be released from clamping or, as the case may be, storage within—

  (*a*) 4 hours of the time of payment if payment is made at or to the contractor's office or the court; or

  (*b*) 2 hours of the time of payment if payment is made to an authorised person.

(4) If any payment made by P or a person acting on his behalf is less than the amount of the sum due and charge or charges due, it must first be applied to meet the charge or charges and any balance remaining must then be applied towards payment of the sum due.

(5) On payment by P or a person acting on his behalf of, or towards the payment of, the sum due and charge or charges due, the contractor or the authorised person must issue a receipt which includes the following information—

  (*a*) the contractor's name, address, telephone number, and value added tax registered number;

  (*b*) the registration mark of the vehicle;

  (*c*) the date of the clamping order requiring the vehicle to be clamped;

  (*d*) the name, official address and telephone number of the fines officer and the court;

  (*e*) if applicable, the date and time of clamping;

  (*f*) the name of P and, if payment is made by a person acting on his behalf, of that person;

  (*g*) the name or identification number, or both, of the member of the contractor's staff issuing the receipt;

  (*h*) the amount, date and time of the payment;

  (*i*) how to apply under regulations 27 and 28 for the release of a vehicle wrongly clamped;

  (*j*) if applicable, the place where the vehicle is clamped; and

  (*k*) the serial number of the receipt.

1–7583   24. Removal of vehicle for storage.   (1) A vehicle clamped under a clamping order must, unless released from clamping under regulation 23, 27 or 28, remain clamped where it is positioned or repositioned for the period of not less than 24 hours from the time of clamping.

(2) When the period referred to in paragraph (1) has expired, if—

  (*a*) the sum due and charge or charges due have not been paid in full;

  (*b*) there is no application under regulations 27 or 28 outstanding; and

  (*c*) the case has not been referred to the court under paragraph 42(1) of Schedule 5,

the contractor must have the vehicle removed by, or under the direction and supervision of, an authorised person to secure premises for storage.

(3) When a vehicle is removed to storage the contractor must send by post to P at his last

known address or have delivered to him by hand, with a copy to the fines officer, a written notice specifying—

   (a) the contractor's name, address and telephone number;
   (b) his value added tax registered number;
   (c) the registration mark of the clamped vehicle;
   (d) the date, time and place of clamping;
   (e) that the vehicle was clamped under the clamping order;
   (f) the date of the clamping order and the name, official address and telephone number of the fines officer and the court;
   (g) that since the sum due and charges due have not been paid in full the vehicle has been removed for storage;
   (h) the date of removal of the vehicle and the address, telephone number for, and hours of opening of, the storage premises;
   (i) the daily or weekly storage charge payable;
   (j) that the vehicle will be released on payment of the amount of the sum due and charges due in full with a statement of how the amount is made up;
   (k) how to pay the sum due and charges due;
   (l) how to apply under regulations 27 and 28 for the release of a vehicle wrongly clamped; and
   (m) a serial number of the notice.

1–7584 **25. Storage of vehicle.** (1) A vehicle removed to storage must remain in storage, unless released on payment of the sum due and charges due in full or pursuant to a decision under regulation 27 or an order under regulation 28(6), or sold or otherwise disposed of by order of the court under paragraph 41(2) of Schedule 5.

   (2) The clamping contractor may subcontract the storage of vehicles to another person or storage may be undertaken by another person under a contract with the Lord Chancellor and, in any such case, references in these Regulations to the "clamping contractor", except in this paragraph, and "the contractor", so far as applicable to the storage of vehicles under these Regulation, shall be construed as references to that other person.

   (3) Premises used for the storage of vehicles must be secure and such as to protect the vehicles from damage or deterioration.

1–7585 **26. Sale of clamped vehicles.** (1) The period referred to in paragraph 41(1)(b) (power to order sale of clamped vehicle) of Schedule 5 for the sale of a vehicle shall be the period of 1 month from the date on which the vehicle was clamped.

   (2) If the sum due has not been paid in full before the expiry of the period of 10 clear working days from the date the vehicle was clamped the fines officer must apply in writing to the court for an order for sale of the vehicle under paragraph 41(2) of Schedule 5. A copy of the application must be sent to P by post at his last known address.

   (3) The hearing for the sale of a vehicle must not be listed before the expiry of the period of 21 days from the date the vehicle was clamped.

   (4) When the application under paragraph (2) is listed for hearing the court must notify P in writing—

   (a) of the date, time and place of the hearing;
   (b) that he may attend, and be represented at, the hearing and may submit written representations;
   (c) that the court has the power to order the sale of the vehicle if the sum due has not been paid in full before the expiry of the period of 1 month from the date the vehicle was clamped; and
   (d) of the amount of the sum due and charges payable to secure the release of the vehicle,

and must notify the fines officer of the date and time of the hearing.

   (5) The fines officer must make himself available for the hearing but only for the purpose of answering the court's questions and providing relevant information.

   (6) If at the hearing the court decides that it will order the vehicle to be sold on the expiry of the period of 1 month from the date the vehicle was clamped if the sum due is not paid in full before the expiry of that period, the fines officer must so notify P in writing.

   (7) If at the hearing the court decides that the vehicle should not be sold it may direct that the vehicle be released to P with or without payment of the charges due.

   (8) In considering whether or not to order the sale of the vehicle the court must consider the history of P's case, in particular whether the clamping order was justified, reasonable and proportionate.

   (9) After the court's decision on the application the case remains with the fines officer under the collection order.

   (10) If the court makes an order for sale the fines officer must send a copy of the order for sale to the contractor who must arrange for the vehicle or vehicles to be sold by an agent or by auction.

   (11) On the sale of a vehicle pursuant to an order under paragraph 41(2) of Schedule 5 the ownership of the vehicle shall vest in the purchaser and the contractor must secure the registration of the vehicle in the name of the purchaser under the Vehicle Excise and Registration Act 1994.

   (12) When the vehicle has been sold the contractor must first deduct from the net proceeds of sale an amount equal to the charges due and must then transmit the remaining balance to the fines officer.

(13) The fines officer, receiving the remaining balance from the contractor, must deduct an amount sufficient to discharge P's liability in respect of the sum due, and send payment of any remaining balance to P within 10 working days of the date of the sale of the vehicle, accompanied by a written statement of account.

(14) If when a vehicle is sold, the net proceeds of sale are not sufficient to meet the amount of the sum due and charges due, the net proceeds of sale must first be applied towards meeting the charges due and then, if a balance remains, towards discharging P's liability in respect of the sum due.

(15) Where the balance is not sufficient to satisfy payment of the sum due the fines officer must then seek to recover the outstanding amount of the sum due under the collection order and the powers conferred by Schedule 5, including his power to refer the case to the court under paragraph 42 of that Schedule.

1–7586   27. Release of vehicle wrongly clamped.   (1) Where a vehicle is clamped, removed or stored in breach of any provision of this Part of these Regulations, a person may apply for the release and, where appropriate, the return of the vehicle in accordance with this regulation and regulation 28.

(2) Before making an application to the court under regulation 28, a request for the release and, where appropriate, return of the vehicle must be made to—

(a) the fines officer, if the breach relates to the content or making of the clamping order, or
(b) the contractor, if the breach relates to the execution of the clamping order, removal or storage of a vehicle.

(3) If a request is made to—

(a) the contractor in a case where an alleged breach concerns the content or making of the clamping order, he must refer that request to the fines officer; and
(b) to the fines officer in a case where an alleged breach concerns the execution of the clamping order, removal or storage, he must refer that request to the contractor.

(4) The fines officer or, as the case may be, the contractor must send to that person written notice of his decision within 7 working days of the date on which that request was made.

(5) If the decision is to accept the request, arrangements must immediately be made for the release and, where appropriate, return of the vehicle without charge.

1–7587   28.   (1) A person may apply to the court for the release and, where appropriate, the return of the vehicle if, having made a request under regulation 27—

(a) the request was refused; or
(b) there was a failure to make a decision on that request within the period referred to in regulation 27(4).

(2) An application must be made in writing, within 10 workings days (or such further time as the court may allow) of the date when—

(a) the applicant received notice of the decision on his request under regulation 27; or
(b) if there was a failure to make a decision, the expiry of the period referred to in regulation 27(4).

(3) An application must be listed for an expedited hearing.
(4) The designated officer of the court must notify—

(a) the applicant and the fines officer or, as the case may be, the contractor, of the date time and place of the hearing; and
(b) the applicant that he may attend, and be represented at, the hearing and submit written representations.

(5) The fines officer or, as the case may be, a senior manager of the contractor, must be available for the hearing but only for the purpose of answering the court's questions and to provide relevant information, including the decision letter on the initial application.

(6) On an application, the court may—

(a) order the release and, where appropriate the return, of the vehicle with or without payment of the charges due; or
(b) dismiss the application.

PART 5
APPLICATION OF ENACTMENTS WITH MODIFICATIONS

1–7588   29. Purpose of the application of enactments.   The application of enactments with modifications in this Part is for the purpose of giving effect to Schedule 5 and section 97 of the Courts Act 2003 so far as it relates to that Schedule.

1–7589   30. Application with modifications of the Magistrates' Courts (Attachment of Earnings) Rules 1971.   In the case of a person aged 18 or over liable to pay a sum to which Schedule 5 applies, the Magistrates' Courts (Attachment of Earnings) Rules 1971 shall apply to attachments of earnings orders made under that Schedule as they apply to such orders made under the Attachment of Earnings Act 1971 but with the following modifications—

(a) omit—
    (i)   rule 2(6) (interpretation of references to attachment of earnings order); and

     (ii) rule 4 (jurisdiction as respects complaints for an attachment of earnings order);

 (*b*) in rule 6 (service of orders and notices)—

     (i) in paragraphs (1) and (2) after "magistrates' court" insert "or a fines officer, as the case may be,";

     (ii) in paragraph (2), for "8 or 11" substitute "8(5)"; and

     (iii) in paragraph (3)—

          (*aa*) omit sub-paragraphs (*a*) and (*b*); and

          (*bb*) in sub-paragraph (*c*) for the words from "65(2)" to the end of that sub-paragraph substitute "77(2) of the Magistrates' Courts Act 1980 (postponement of issue of warrant)".

 (*c*) omit—

     (i) rule 8 (notice of application for appropriate variation order);

     (ii) rule 9 (jurisdiction as respects complaints for the discharge and variation of attachment of earnings orders);

     (iii) rule 10 (complaints for variation or discharge of attachment of earnings orders against persons outside United Kingdom); and

     (iv) rule 11 (complaints by debtors for variation or discharge of attachment of earnings orders against persons who cannot be found);

 (*d*) in rule 12 (variation of attachment of earnings order on change of employment)—

     (i) after "magistrates' court" insert "or a fines officer, as the case may be,";

     (ii) after both occurrences of "the court" insert "or the fines officer, as the case may be,"; and

     (iii) after "its" insert "or his".

 (*e*) in rule 13 (discharge of attachment of earnings order by court of its own motion)—

     (i) in paragraph (1)—

          (*aa*) after "a magistrates' court" insert "or a fines officer, as the case may be,";

          (*bb*) after "the magistrates' court" and after "the court", in each place insert "or the fines officer, as the case may be,";

          (*cc*) after "its" insert "or his";

     (ii) omit paragraph (2); and

     (iii) in the heading to the rule, for "of its" substitute "or fines officer of its or his".

 (*f*) omit rule 14 (temporary variation of protected earnings rate);

 (*g*) in rule 15 (consolidated attachment orders)—

     (i) in paragraph (1), after the first occurrence of "a magistrates' court" insert "or a fines officer, as the case may be,";

     (ii) in paragraph (2),—

          (*aa*) after "a magistrates' court" insert "or a fines officer, as the case may be,"; and

          (*bb*) after "it" insert "or he";

     (iii) in paragraph (3)—

          (*aa*) after "a magistrates' court" insert "or a fines officer, as the case may be,";

          (*bb*) after "any magistrates' court" insert "or fines officer"; and

          (*cc*) after "the court" insert "or the fines officer, as the case may be,";

     (iv) in paragraph (4)—

          (*aa*) after "magistrates' courts" insert "or fines officers";

          (*bb*) after "a magistrates' court" insert "or a fines officer, as the case may be,"; and

          (*cc*) after "those courts" insert "or one of those fines officers, as the case may be,";

     (v) in paragraph (5), after "debtor" insert "but a fines officer may exercise the powers conferred under paragraphs (2) to (4) of this Rule of his own motion only";

     (vi) omit paragraph (8);

     (vii) in paragraph (9)—

          (*aa*) after both occurrences of "magistrates' court" insert "or a fines officer, as the case may be,";

          (*bb*) after the first occurrence of the "first mentioned court" insert "or the first mentioned fines officer, as the case may be,";

          (*cc*) after "second mentioned court" insert "or the court for which the second mentioned fines officer made the relevant attachment of earnings order";

          (*dd*) after the second occurrence of the "first mentioned court" insert "or the court for which the first mentioned fines officer is to make the consolidated attachment order"; and

          (*ee*) for the words from "72 of the Magistrates' Courts Act 1952" to "(transfer of enforcement of legal aid contribution orders)" substitute "89 of the Magistrates' Courts Act 1980 (transfer of fine order)";

     (viii)for paragraph (10) substitute—

"(10) Where a magistrates' court or, as the case may be, a fines officer makes a consolidated attachment order, the order shall specify the percentage deduction rate in accordance with the Fines Collection Regulations 2006.

(11) Paragraph (10) applies irrespective of whether the orders to be consolidated include any order made—

    (a) (before 27th March 2006) under section 1(3)(*b*) of the Act, to secure the payment of a sum adjudged to be paid by a conviction or treated as so adjudged to be paid; or

    (b) under section 1(3)(*c*) of the Act, to secure the payment of a sum required to be paid under section 17(2) of the Access to Justice Act 1999 (recovery of criminal defence costs in publicly funded cases)."

  (h) in rule 16 (transfer of fines etc with view to making consolidated attachment order)—

    (i) in paragraph (1)—

      (aa)after both occurrences of "a magistrates' court", insert "or a fines officer, as the case may be,";

      (bb)after "first mentioned court" insert "or the first mentioned fines officer, as the case may be,"; and

      (cc)after "second mentioned court" insert "or the second mentioned fines officer, as the case may be,";

    (ii) in paragraph (2)—

      (aa)after "the court", insert "or, as the case may be, the fines officer"; and

      (bb)after "a court", insert "or a fines officer"; and

    (iii) in paragraph (3), for the words from "72" to the end of that paragraph substitute "89 (transfer of fine order) or section 90 (transfer of fines to Scotland or Northern Ireland) of the Magistrates' Courts Act 1980";

  (i) in rule 18 (method of making payment under attachment of earnings order)—

    (i) in paragraph (1), omit "and the person entitled to receive payments under the related maintenance order"; and

    (ii) omit paragraph (3); and

  (j) omit—

    (i) rule 19 (payments under attachment of earnings order after imprisonment imposed);

    (ii) in rule 22 (justices' clerks), in paragraph (2), sub-paragraphs (*b*), (*c*) and (*e*); and

    (iii) rule 23 (application of these Rules to attachment of earnings orders in respect of fines etc).

1–7590 31. Application with modifications of the Fines (Deductions from Income Support) Regulations 1992. In the case of a person aged 18 or over liable to pay a sum to which Schedule 5 applies, the Fines (Deductions from Income Support) Regulations 1992 apply to applications for benefit deductions made under that Schedule, as they apply to such applications made under those Regulations but with the following modifications—

  (a) in regulation 1 (citation, commencement and interpretation), in paragraph (2)—

    (i) in the definition of "application", for "made under regulation 2" substitute "for benefit deductions made under Schedule 5 to the Courts Act 2003";

    (ii) after the definition of "court" insert—

""in default on a collection order" has the same meaning as it has under paragraph 24A of Schedule 5 to the Courts Act 2003;

"existing defaulter" has the same meaning as it has under paragraph 3 of Schedule 5 to the Courts Act 2003;

"the fines officer", in relation to a person subject to a collection order made under Schedule 5 to the Courts Act 2003, means any fines officer working at the fines office specified in that order;";

    (iii) after the definition of "state pension credit" insert—

""sum due" has the same meaning as it has in paragraph 2 of Schedule 5 to the Courts Act 2003";".

  (b) in regulation 2 (application for deductions from income support, state pension credit or jobseeker's allowance)—

    (i) omit paragraph (1); and

    (ii) in paragraph (2), after "court" insert "or the fines officer, as the case may be,";

  (c) in regulation 2A (information that the court may require) in paragraph (1)—

    (i) after "court" insert "or the fines officer, as the case may be,"; and

    (ii) in the heading to the regulation, after "court" insert "or fines officer";

  (d) In regulation 3 (contents of application)—

    (i) in paragraph (1)—

      (aa)in sub-paragraphs (*b*) and (*c*) for "compensation order" substitute "order requiring payment of the sum due";

      (bb)in sub-paragraph (*d*) for the words from "fine" to the end of that sub-paragraph substitute "sum due"; and

      (cc)for sub-paragraph (*g*) substitute—

"(g) whether the offender—

(i) is an existing defaulter and his existing default cannot be disregarded;
(ii) has consented to the making of the application; or
(iii) is in default on a collection order";
(ii) in paragraph (2) after "court" insert "or a fines officer, as the case may be,"; and
(iii) in paragraph (3)—

(*aa*)after "a court" insert "or a fines officer, as the case may be,"; and
(*bb*)after "the court" insert "or the fines officer, as the case may be,";

(*e*) in regulation 4 (deductions from offender's income support, state pension credit or jobseeker's allowance), in paragraphs (1) and (2)—

(i)   after "a court" insert "or a fines officer, as the case may be,";
(ii) after "the court" insert "by or for which the application was made"; and
(iii) for "fine or the sum required to be paid by compensation order" substitute "sum due";

(*f*) in regulation 7 (circumstances, time of making and termination of deductions)—

(i) omit paragraph (2)(*c*);
(ii) in paragraph (4)(*c*)—

(*aa*)after "a court" insert "or a fines officer, as the case may be,"; and
(*bb*)after "its" insert "or his";

(iii) in paragraph (4)(*d*) for "fine or under the compensation order as the case may be" substitute "sum due"; and
(iv) in paragraph (7) after "the court" insert "or the fines officer, as the case may be,"; and

(*g*) in regulation 8 (withdrawal of application), after "court" insert "or a fines officer, as the case may be,".

PART 6
REVOCATIONS AND TRANSITIONAL PROVISION

1–7591 32. Revocations. The following Regulations are revoked—

(*a*) The Fines Collection Regulations 2004;
(*b*) The Fines Collection (Amendment) Regulations 2004; and
(*c*) The Fines Collection (Amendment) Regulations 2005.

1–7592 33. Transitional provision and savings. (1) Subject to paragraph (2), these Regulations apply to any order made under Schedule 5, notwithstanding that the order may have been made before these Regulations come into force.
(2) Where a clamping order is made before 27th March 2006, Part 4 of the Fines Collection Regulations 2004 shall continue to have effect in relation to that order, as if these Regulations had not been brought into force.

Codes of Practice and Guidelines

Criminal Procedure and Investigations Act 1996
Code of Practice under Part II[1]

1–7700
Preamble
This code of practice is issued under Part II of the Criminal Procedure and Investigations Act 1996 ('the Act'). It sets out the manner in which police officers are to record, retain and reveal to the prosecutor material obtained in a criminal investigation and which may be relevant to the investigation, and related matters.

---
1. This Code, a draft of which was laid before Parliament on 21 February 2005 was brought into force on 4 April 2005 by the Criminal Procedure and Investigations Act 1996 (Code of Practice) Order 2005, SI 2005/985.

Introduction
1.1. This code of practice applies in respect of criminal investigations conducted by police officers which begin on or after the day on which this code comes into effect. Persons other than police officers who are charged with the duty of conducting an investigation as defined in the Act are to have regard to the relevant provisions of the code, and should take these into account in applying their own operating procedures.
1.2. This code does not apply to persons who are not charged with the duty of conducting an investigation as defined in the Act.
1.3. Nothing in this code applies to material intercepted in obedience to a warrant issued under section 2 of the Interception of Communications Act 1985 or section 5 of the Regulation of Investigatory Powers Act 2000, or to any copy of that material as defined in section 10 of the 1985 Act or section 15 of the 2000 Act.
1.4. This code extends only to England and Wales.

Definitions

1–7701 **2.1.** In this code:

— *a criminal investigation* is an investigation conducted by police officers with a view to it being ascertained whether a person should be charged with an offence, or whether a person charged with an offence is guilty of it. This will include:

  — investigations into crimes that have been committed;
  — investigations whose purpose is to ascertain whether a crime has been committed, with a view to the possible institution of criminal proceedings; and
  — investigations which begin in the belief that a crime may be committed, for example when the police keep premises or individuals under observation for a period of time, with a view to the possible institution of criminal proceedings;

— charging a person with an offence includes prosecution by way of summons;
— *an investigator* is any police officer involved in the conduct of a criminal investigation. All investigators have a responsibility for carrying out the duties imposed on them under this code, including in particular recording information, and retaining records of information and other material;
— the *officer in charge of an investigation* is the police officer responsible for directing a criminal investigation. He is also responsible for ensuring that proper procedures are in place for recording information, and retaining records of information and other material, in the investigation;
— the *disclosure officer* is the person responsible for examining material retained by the police during the investigation; revealing material to the prosecutor during the investigation and any criminal proceedings resulting from it, and certifying that he has done this; and disclosing material to the accused at the request of the prosecutor;
— the *prosecutor* is the authority responsible for the conduct, on behalf of the Crown, of criminal proceedings resulting from a specific criminal investigation;
— *material* is material of any kind, including information and objects, which is obtained in the course of a criminal investigation and which may be relevant to the investigation. This includes not only material coming into the possession of the investigator (such as documents seized in the course of searching premises) but also material generated by him (such as interview records);
— material may be *relevant to an investigation* if it appears to an investigator, or to the officer in charge of an investigation, or to the disclosure officer, that it has some bearing on any offence under investigation or any person being investigated, or on the surrounding circumstances of the case, unless it is incapable of having any impact on the case;
— *sensitive material* is material, the disclosure of which, the disclosure officer believes, would give rise to a real risk of serious prejudice to an important public interest;
— references to *prosecution disclosure* are to the duty of the prosecutor under sections 3 and 7A of the Act to disclose material which is in his possession or which he has inspected in pursuance of this code, and which might reasonably be considered capable of undermining the case against the accused, or of assisting the case for the accused;
— references to the disclosure of material to a person accused of an offence include references to the disclosure of material to his legal representative;
— references to police officers and to the chief officer of police include those employed in a police force as defined in section 3(3) of the Prosecution of Offences Act 1985.

General responsibilities

1–7702 **3.1.** The functions of the investigator, the officer in charge of an investigation and the disclosure officer are separate. Whether they are undertaken by one, two or more persons will depend on the complexity of the case and the administrative arrangements within each police force. Where they are undertaken by more than one person, close consultation between them is essential to the effective performance of the duties imposed by this code. 3.2 In any criminal investigation, one or more deputy disclosure officers may be appointed to assist the disclosure officer, and a deputy disclosure officer may perform any function of a disclosure officer as defined in paragraph 2.1.

  3.3. The chief officer of police for each police force is responsible for putting in place arrangements to ensure that in every investigation the identity of the officer in charge of an investigation and the disclosure officer is recorded. The chief officer of police for each police force shall ensure that disclosure officers and deputy disclosure officers have sufficient skills and authority, commensurate with the complexity of the investigation, to discharge their functions effectively. An individual must not be appointed as disclosure officer, or continue in that role, if that is likely to result in a conflict of interest, for instance, if the disclosure officer is the victim of the alleged crime which is the subject of the investigation. The advice of a more senior officer must always be sought if there is doubt as to whether a conflict of interest precludes an individual acting as disclosure officer. If thereafter the doubt remains, the advice of a prosecutor should be sought.

  3.4. The officer in charge of an investigation may delegate tasks to another investigator, to civilians employed by the police force, or to other persons participating in the investigation under arrangements for joint investigations, but he remains responsible for ensuring that these have been carried out and for accounting for any general policies followed in the investigation. In particular, it is an essential part of his duties to ensure that all material which may be relevant to an investigation is retained, and either made available to the disclosure officer or (in exceptional circumstances) revealed directly to the prosecutor.

3.5. In conducting an investigation, the investigator should pursue all reasonable lines of inquiry, whether these point towards or away from the suspect. What is reasonable in each case will depend on the particular circumstances. For example, where material is held on computer, it is a matter for the investigator to decide which material on the computer it is reasonable to inquire into, and in what manner.

3.6. If the officer in charge of an investigation believes that other persons may be in possession of material that may be relevant to the investigation, and if this has not been obtained under paragraph 3.5 above, he should ask the disclosure officer to inform them of the existence of the investigation and to invite them to retain the material in case they receive a request for its disclosure. The disclosure officer should inform the prosecutor that they may have such material. However, the officer in charge of an investigation is not required to make speculative enquiries of other persons; there must be some reason to believe that they may have relevant material. That reason may come from information provided to the police by the accused or from other inquiries made or from some other source.

3.7. If, during a criminal investigation, the officer in charge of an investigation or disclosure officer for any reason no longer has responsibility for the functions falling to him, either his supervisor or the police officer in charge of criminal investigations for the police force concerned must assign someone else to assume that responsibility. That person's identity must be recorded, as with those initially responsible for these functions in each investigation.

Recording of information

1–7703 **4.1.** If material which may be relevant to the investigation consists of information which is not recorded in any form, the officer in charge of an investigation must ensure that it is recorded in a durable or retrievable form (whether in writing, on video or audio tape, or on computer disk).

4.2. Where it is not practicable to retain the initial record of information because it forms part of a larger record which is to be destroyed, its contents should be transferred as a true record to a durable and more easily-stored form before that happens.

4.3. Negative information is often relevant to an investigation. If it may be relevant it must be recorded. An example might be a number of people present in a particular place at a particular time who state that they saw nothing unusual.

4.4. Where information which may be relevant is obtained, it must be recorded at the time it is obtained or as soon as practicable after that time. This includes, for example, information obtained in house-to-house enquiries, although the requirement to record information promptly does not require an investigator to take a statement from a potential witness where it would not otherwise be taken.

Retention of material
(a) Duty to retain material

1–7704 **5.1.** The investigator must retain material obtained in a criminal investigation which may be relevant to the investigation. Material may be photographed, video-recorded, captured digitally or otherwise retained in the form of a copy rather than the original at any time, if the original is perishable; the original was supplied to the investigator rather than generated by him and is to be returned to its owner; or the retention of a copy rather than the original is reasonable in all the circumstances.

5.2. Where material has been seized in the exercise of the powers of seizure conferred by the Police and Criminal Evidence Act 1984, the duty to retain it under this code is subject to the provisions on the retention of seized material in section 22 of that Act.

5.3. If the officer in charge of an investigation becomes aware as a result of developments in the case that material previously examined but not retained (because it was not thought to be relevant) may now be relevant to the investigation, he should, wherever practicable, take steps to obtain it or ensure that it is retained for further inspection or for production in court if required.

5.4. The duty to retain material includes in particular the duty to retain material falling into the following categories, where it may be relevant to the investigation:

— crime reports (including crime report forms, relevant parts of incident report books or police officer's notebooks);
— custody records;
— records which are derived from tapes of telephone messages (for example, 999 calls) containing descriptions of an alleged offence or offender;
— final versions of witness statements (and draft versions where their content differs from the final version), including any exhibits mentioned (unless these have been returned to their owner on the understanding that they will be produced in court if required);
— interview records (written records, or audio or video tapes, of interviews with actual or potential witnesses or suspects);
— communications between the police and experts such as forensic scientists, reports of work carried out by experts, and schedules of scientific material prepared by the expert for the investigator, for the purposes of criminal proceedings;
— records of the first description of a suspect by each potential witness who purports to identify or describe the suspect, whether or not the description differs from that of subsequent descriptions by that or other witnesses;
— any material casting doubt on the reliability of a witness.

5.5. The duty to retain material, where it may be relevant to the investigation, also includes in particular the duty to retain material which may satisfy the test for prosecution disclosure in the Act, such as:

— information provided by an accused person which indicates an explanation for the offence with which he has been charged;
— any material casting doubt on the reliability of a confession;
— any material casting doubt on the reliability of a prosecution witness.

5.6. The duty to retain material falling into these categories does not extend to items which are purely ancillary to such material and possess no independent significance (for example, duplicate copies of records or reports).

(b) *Length of time for which material is to be retained.*

5.7. All material which may be relevant to the investigation must be retained until a decision is taken whether to institute proceedings against a person for an offence. 5.8 If a criminal investigation results in proceedings being instituted, all material which may be relevant must be retained at least until the accused is acquitted or convicted or the prosecutor decides not to proceed with the case.

5.9. Where the accused is convicted, all material which may be relevant must be retained at least until:

— the convicted person is released from custody, or discharged from hospital, in cases where the court imposes a custodial sentence or a hospital order;
— six months from the date of conviction, in all other cases.

If the court imposes a custodial sentence or hospital order and the convicted person is released from custody or discharged from hospital earlier than six months from the date of conviction, all material which may be relevant must be retained at least until six months from the date of conviction.

5.10. If an appeal against conviction is in progress when the release or discharge occurs, or at the end of the period of six months specified in paragraph 5.9, all material which may be relevant must be retained until the appeal is determined. Similarly, if the Criminal Cases Review Commission is considering an application at that point in time, all material which may be relevant must be retained at least until the Commission decides not to refer the case to the Court

Preparation of material for prosecutor

(a) *Introduction*

1-7705 **6.1.** The officer in charge of the investigation, the disclosure officer or an investigator may seek advice from the prosecutor about whether any particular item of material may be relevant to the investigation.

6.2. Material which may be relevant to an investigation, which has been retained in accordance with this code, and which the disclosure officer believes will not form part of the prosecution case, must be listed on a schedule.

6.3. Material which the disclosure officer does not believe is sensitive must be listed on a schedule of non-sensitive material. The schedule must include a statement that the disclosure officer does not believe the material is sensitive.

6.4. Any material which is believed to be sensitive must be either listed on a schedule of sensitive material or, in exceptional circumstances, revealed to the prosecutor separately. If there is no sensitive material, the disclosure officer must record this fact on a schedule of sensitive material. 6.5 Paragraphs 6.6 to 6.11 below apply to both sensitive and non-sensitive material. Paragraphs 6.12 to 6.14 apply to sensitive material only.

(b) *Circumstances in which a schedule is to be prepared*

6.6. The disclosure officer must ensure that a schedule is prepared in the following circumstances:

— the accused is charged with an offence which is triable only on indictment;
— the accused is charged with an offence which is triable either way, and it is considered either that the case is likely to be tried on indictment or that the accused is likely to plead not guilty at a summary trial;
— the accused is charged with a summary offence, and it is considered that he is likely to plead not guilty.

6.7. In respect of either way and summary offences, a schedule may not be needed if a person has admitted the offence, or if a police officer witnessed the offence and that person has not denied it. 6.8 If it is believed that the accused is likely to plead guilty at a summary trial, it is not necessary to prepare a schedule in advance. If, contrary to this belief, the accused pleads not guilty at a summary trial, or the offence is to be tried on indictment, the disclosure officer must ensure that a schedule is prepared as soon as is reasonably practicable after that happens.

(c) *Way in which material is to be listed on schedule*

6.9. The disclosure officer should ensure that each item of material is listed separately on the schedule, and is numbered consecutively. The description of each item should make clear the nature of the item and should contain sufficient detail to enable the prosecutor to inspect the material before deciding whether or not it should be disclosed.

6.10. In some enquiries it may not be practicable to list each item of material separately. For example, there may be many items of a similar or repetitive nature. These may be listed in a block and described by quantity and generic title.

6.11. Even if some material is listed in a block, the disclosure officer must ensure that any items among that material which might satisfy the test for prosecution disclosure are listed and described individually.

(d) Treatment of sensitive material

6.12. Subject to paragraph 6.13 below, the disclosure officer must list on a sensitive schedule any material, the disclosure of which he believes would give rise to a real risk of serious prejudice to an important public interest, and the reason for that belief. The schedule must include a statement that the disclosure officer believes the material is sensitive. Depending on the circumstances, examples of such material may include the following among others:

— material relating to national security;
— material received from the intelligence and security agencies;
— material relating to intelligence from foreign sources which reveals sensitive intelligence gathering methods;
— material given in confidence;
— material relating to the identity or activities of informants, or undercover police officers, or witnesses, or other persons supplying information to the police who may be in danger if their identities are revealed;
— material revealing the location of any premises or other place used for police surveillance, or the identity of any person allowing a police officer to use them for surveillance;
— material revealing, either directly or indirectly, techniques and methods relied upon by a police officer in the course of a criminal investigation, for example covert surveillance techniques, or other methods of detecting crime;
— material whose disclosure might facilitate the commission of other offences or hinder the prevention and detection of crime;
— material upon the strength of which search warrants were obtained;
— material containing details of persons taking part in identification parades;
— material supplied to an investigator during a criminal investigation which has been generated by an official of a body concerned with the regulation or supervision of bodies corporate or of persons engaged in financial activities, or which has been generated by a person retained by such a body;
— material supplied to an investigator during a criminal investigation which relates to a child or young person and which has been generated by a local authority social services department, an Area Child Protection Committee or other party contacted by an investigator during the investigation;
— material relating to the private life of a witness.

6.13. In exceptional circumstances, where an investigator considers that material is so sensitive that its revelation to the prosecutor by means of an entry on the sensitive schedule is inappropriate, the existence of the material must be revealed to the prosecutor separately. This will apply only where compromising the material would be likely to lead directly to the loss of life, or directly threaten national security.

6.14. In such circumstances, the responsibility for informing the prosecutor lies with the investigator who knows the detail of the sensitive material. The investigator should act as soon as is reasonably practicable after the file containing the prosecution case is sent to the prosecutor. The investigator must also ensure that the prosecutor is able to inspect the material so that he can assess whether it is disclosable and, if so, whether it needs to be brought before a court for a ruling on disclosure.

Revelation of material to prosecutor

1–7706   **7.1.** The disclosure officer must give the schedules to the prosecutor. Wherever practicable this should be at the same time as he gives him the file containing the material for the prosecution case (or as soon as is reasonably practicable after the decision on mode of trial or the plea, in cases to which paragraph 6.8 applies).

7.2. The disclosure officer should draw the attention of the prosecutor to any material an investigator has retained (including material to which paragraph 6.13 applies) which may satisfy the test for prosecution disclosure in the Act, and should explain why he has come to that view. 7.3 At the same time as complying with the duties in paragraphs 7.1 and 7.2, the disclosure officer must give the prosecutor a copy of any material which falls into the following categories (unless such material has already been given to the prosecutor as part of the file containing the material for the prosecution case):

— information provided by an accused person which indicates an explanation for the offence with which he has been charged;
— any material casting doubt on the reliability of a confession;
— any material casting doubt on the reliability of a prosecution witness;
— any other material which the investigator believes may satisfy the test for prosecution disclosure in the Act.

7.4. If the prosecutor asks to inspect material which has not already been copied to him, the disclosure officer must allow him to inspect it. If the prosecutor asks for a copy of material which has not already been copied to him, the disclosure officer must give him a copy. However, this does not apply where the disclosure officer believes, having consulted the officer in charge of the investigation, that the material is too sensitive to be copied and can only be inspected. 7.5 If material consists of information which is recorded other than in writing, whether it should be given to the prosecutor in its original form as a whole, or by way of relevant extracts recorded in the same form, or in the form of a transcript, is a matter for agreement between the disclosure officer and the prosecutor.

Subsequent action by disclosure officer

1–7707 **8.1.** At the time a schedule of non-sensitive material is prepared, the disclosure officer may not know exactly what material will form the case against the accused, and the prosecutor may not have given advice about the likely relevance of particular items of material. Once these matters have been determined, the disclosure officer must give the prosecutor, where necessary, an amended schedule listing any additional material:

— which may be relevant to the investigation,
— which does not form part of the case against the accused,
— which is not already listed on the schedule, and
— which he believes is not sensitive,

unless he is informed in writing by the prosecutor that the prosecutor intends to disclose the material to the defence. 8.2 Section 7A of the Act imposes a continuing duty on the prosecutor, for the duration of criminal proceedings against the accused, to disclose material which satisfies the test for disclosure (subject to public interest considerations). To enable him to do this, any new material coming to light should be treated in the same way as the earlier material.

8.3. In particular, after a defence statement has been given, the disclosure officer must look again at the material which has been retained and must draw the attention of the prosecutor to any material which might reasonably be considered capable of undermining the case for the prosecution against the accused or of assisting the case for the accused; and he must reveal it to him in accordance with paragraphs 7.4 and 7.5 above.

Certification by disclosure officer

1–7708 **9.1.** The disclosure officer must certify to the prosecutor that to the best of his knowledge and belief, all relevant material which has been retained and made available to him has been revealed to the prosecutor in accordance with this code. He must sign and date the certificate. It will be necessary to certify not only at the time when the schedule and accompanying material is submitted to the prosecutor, and when relevant material which has been retained is reconsidered after the accused has given a defence statement, but also whenever a schedule is otherwise given or material is otherwise revealed to the prosecutor.

Disclosure of material to accused

1–7709 **10.1.** If material has not already been copied to the prosecutor, and he requests its disclosure to the accused on the ground that:

— it satisfies the test for prosecution disclosure, **or**
— the court has ordered its disclosure after considering an application from the accused,

the disclosure officer must disclose it to the accused.

10.2. If material has been copied to the prosecutor, and it is to be disclosed, whether it is disclosed by the prosecutor or the disclosure officer is a matter of agreement between the two of them.

10.3. The disclosure officer must disclose material to the accused either by giving him a copy or by allowing him to inspect it. If the accused person asks for a copy of any material which he has been allowed to inspect, the disclosure officer must give it to him, unless in the opinion of the disclosure officer that is either not practicable (for example because the material consists of an object which cannot be copied, or because the volume of material is so great), or not desirable (for example because the material is a statement by a child witness in relation to a sexual offence). 10.4 If material which the accused has been allowed to inspect consists of information which is recorded other than in writing, whether it should be given to the accused in its original form or in the form of a transcript is matter for the discretion of the disclosure officer. If the material is transcribed, the disclosure officer must ensure that the transcript is certified to the accused as a true record of the material which has been transcribed.

10.5. If a court concludes that an item of sensitive material satisfies the prosecution disclosure test and that the interests of the defence outweigh the public interest in withholding disclosure, it will be necessary to disclose the material if the case is to proceed. This does not mean that sensitive documents must always be disclosed in their original form: for example, the court may agree that sensitive details still requiring protection should be blocked out, or that documents may be summarised, or that the prosecutor may make an admission about the substance of the material under section 10 of the Criminal Justice Act 1967.

Code for Crown Prosecutors[1]

1–7720 **1. Introduction.** 1.1 The decision to prosecute an individual is a serious step. Fair and effective prosecution is essential to the maintenance of law and order. But even in a small case, a prosecution has serious implications for all involved – the victim, a witness and a defendant. The Crown Prosecution Service applies the Code for Crown Prosecutors so that it can make fair and consistent decisions about prosecutions.

1.2 The Code contains information that is important to police officers, to others who work in the criminal justice system and to the general public. It helps the Crown Prosecution Service to play its part in making sure that justice is done.

1.3 The Code is also designed to make sure that everyone knows the principles that the Crown Prosecution Service applies when carrying out its work. By applying the same principles, everyone involved in the system is helping to treat victims fairly and to prosecute fairly but effectively.

---

1. This code was published in 2000 and replaces all earlier versions.

2. General Principles. 2.1 Each case is unique and must be considered on its own, but there are general principles that apply in all cases.

2.2 The duty of the Crown Prosecution Service is to make sure that the right person is prosecuted for the right offence and that all relevant facts are given to the court.

2.3 Crown Prosecutors must be fair, independent and objective. They must not let their personal views of the ethnic or national origin, sex, religious beliefs, political views or sexual preference of the offender, victim or witness influence their decisions. They must also not be affected by improper or undue pressure from any source.

3. Review. 3.1 Proceedings are usually started by the police. Sometimes they may consult the Crown Prosecution Service before charging a defendant. Each case that the police send to the Crown Prosecution Service is reviewed by a Crown Prosecutor to make sure that it meets the tests set out in this Code. Crown Prosecutors may decide to continue with the original charges, to change the charges or sometimes to stop the proceedings.

3.2 Review, however, is a continuing process so that Crown Prosecutors can take into account any change in circumstances. Wherever possible, they talk to the police first if they are thinking about changing the charges or stopping the proceedings. This gives the police the chance to provide more information that may affect the decision. The Crown Prosecution Service and the police work closely together to reach the right decision, but the final responsibility for the decision rests with the Crown Prosecution Service.

4. The Code Tests. 4.1 There are two stages in the decision to prosecute. The first stage is **the evidential test**. If the case does not pass the evidential test, it must not go ahead, no matter how important or serious it may be. If the case does pass the evidential test, Crown Prosecutors must decide if a prosecution is needed in the public interest.

4.2 This second stage is **the public interest test**. The Crown Prosecution Service will only start or continue with a prosecution when the case has passed both tests. The evidential test is explained in s 5 and the public interest test is explained in s 6.

5. The Evidential Test. 5.1 Crown Prosecutors must be satisfied that there is enough evidence to provide a 'realistic prospect of conviction' against each defendant on each charge. They must consider what the defence case may be and how that is likely to affect the prosecution case.

5.2 A realistic prospect of conviction is an objective test. It means that a jury or bench of magistrates, properly directed in accordance with the law, is more likely than not to convict the defendant of the charge alleged.

5.3 When deciding whether there is enough evidence to prosecute, Crown Prosecutors must consider whether the evidence can be used and is reliable. There will be many cases in which the evidence does not give any cause for concern. But there will also be cases in which the evidence may not be as strong as it first appears. Crown Prosecutors must ask themselves the following questions:

Can the evidence be used in court?

(*a*) Is it likely that the evidence will be excluded by the court? There are certain legal rules which might mean that evidence which seems relevant cannot be given at a trial. For example, is it likely that the evidence will be excluded because of the way in which it was gathered or because of the rule against using hearsay as evidence? If so, is there enough other evidence for a realistic prospect of conviction?

Is the evidence reliable?

(*b*) Is there evidence which might support or detract from the reliability of a confession? Is the reliability affected by factors such as the defendant's age, intelligence or level of understanding?

(*c*) What explanation has the defendant given? Is a court likely to find it credible in the light of the evidence as a whole? Does it support an innocent explanation?

(*d*) If the identity of the defendant is likely to be questioned, is the evidence about this strong enough?

(*e*) Is the witness's background likely to weaken the prosecution case? For example, does the witness have any motive that may affect his or her attitude to the case, or a relevant previous conviction?

(*f*) Are there concerns over the accuracy or credibility of a witness? Are these concerns based on evidence or simply information with nothing to support it? Is there further evidence which the police should be asked to seek out which may support or detract from the account of the witness?

6. The Public Interest Test. 6.1 In 1951, Lord Shawcross, who was Attorney-General, made the classic statement on public interest, which has been supported by Attorneys-General ever since:'It has never been the rule in this country – I hope it never will be – that suspected criminal offences must automatically be the subject of prosecution'.(House of Commons Debates, Vol. 483, col. 681, 29 January 1951.)

6.2 The public interest must be considered in each case where there is enough evidence to provide a realistic prospect of conviction. A prosecution will usually take place unless there are public interest factors tending against prosecution which clearly outweigh those tending in favour. Although there may be public interest factors against prosecution in a particular case, often the prosecution should go ahead and those factors should be put to the court for consideration when sentence is being passed.

6.3 Crown Prosecutors must balance factors for and against prosecution carefully and fairly. Public interest factors that can affect the decision to prosecute usually depend on the seriousness of the offence or the circumstances of the suspect. Some factors may increase the need to prosecute but others may suggest that another course of action would be better.

The following lists of some common public interest factors, both for and against prosecution, are not exhaustive. The factors that apply will depend on the facts in each case.

Some common public interest factors in favour of prosecution.

6.4 The more serious the offence, the more likely it is that a prosecution will be needed in the public interest. A prosecution is likely to be needed if:

(a) a conviction is likely to result in a significant sentence;
(b) a weapon was used or violence was threatened during the commission of the offence;
(c) the offence was committed against a person serving the public (for example, a police or prison officer, or a nurse);
(d) the defendant was in a position of authority or trust;
(e) the evidence shows that the defendant was a ringleader or an organiser of the offence;
(f) there is evidence that the offence was premeditated;
(g) there is evidence that the offence was carried out by a group;
(h) the victim of the offence was vulnerable, has been put in considerable fear, or suffered personal attack, damage or disturbance;
(i) the offence was motivated by any form of discrimination against the victim's ethnic or national origin, sex, religious beliefs, political views or sexual orientation, or the suspect demonstrated hostility towards the victim based on any of those characteristics;
(j) there is a marked difference between the actual or mental ages of the defendant and the victim, or if there is any element of corruption;
(k) the defendant's previous convictions or cautions are relevant to the present offence;
(l) the defendant is alleged to have committed the offence whilst under an order of the court;
(m) there are grounds for believing that the offence is likely to be continued or repeated, for example, by a history of recurring conduct; or
(n) the offence, although not serious in itself, is widespread in the area where it was committed.

Some common public interest factors against prosecution

6.5 A prosecution is less likely to be needed if:

(a) the court is likely to impose a nominal penalty;
(b) the defendant has already been made the subject of a sentence and any further conviction would be unlikely to result in the imposition of an additional sentence or order, unless the nature of the particular offence requires a prosecution;
(c) the offence was committed as a result of a genuine mistake or misunderstanding (these factors must be balanced against the seriousness of the offence);
(d) the loss or harm can be described as minor and was the result of a single incident, particularly if it was caused by a misjudgement;
(e) there has been a long delay between the offence taking place and the date of the trial, unless:

the offence is serious;
the delay has been caused in part by the defendant;
the offence has only recently come to light; or
the complexity of the offence has meant that there has been a long investigation;

(f) a prosecution is likely to have a bad effect on the victim's physical or mental health, always bearing in mind the seriousness of the offence;
(g) the defendant is elderly or is, or was at the time of the offence, suffering from significant mental or physical ill health, unless the offence is serious or there is a real possibility that it may be repeated. The Crown Prosecution Service, where necessary, applies Home Office guidelines about how to deal with mentally disordered offenders. Crown Prosecutors must balance the desirability of diverting a defendant who is suffering from significant mental or physical ill health with the need to safeguard the general public;
(h) the defendant has put right the loss or harm that was caused (but defendants must not avoid prosecution solely because they pay compensation); or
(i) details may be made public that could harm sources of information, international relations or national security;

6.6 Deciding on the public interest is not simply a matter of adding up the number of factors on each side. Crown Prosecutors must decide how important each factor is in the circumstances of each case and go on to make an overall assessment.

The relationship between the victim and the public interest

6.7 The Crown Prosecution Service prosecutes cases on behalf of the public at large and not just in the interests of any particular individual. However, when considering the public interest test Crown Prosecutors should always take into account the consequences for the victim of the decision whether or not to prosecute, and any views expressed by the victim or the victim's family.

6.8 It is important that a victim is told about a decision which makes a significant difference to the case in which he or she is involved. Crown Prosecutors should ensure that they follow any agreed procedures.

Youths

6.9 Crown Prosecutors must consider the interests of a youth when deciding whether it is in the public interest to prosecute. However Crown Prosecutors should not avoid prosecuting simply because of the defendant's age. The seriousness of the offence or the youth's past behaviour is very important.

6.10 Cases involving youths are usually only referred to the Crown Prosecution Service for prosecution if the youth has already received a reprimand and final warning, unless the offence is so serious that neither of these were appropriate. Reprimands and final warnings are intended to prevent re-offending and the fact that a further offence has occurred indicates that attempts to divert the youth from the court system have not been effective. So the public interest will usually require a prosecution in such cases, unless there are clear public interest factors against prosecution.

Police Cautions

6.11 These are only for adults. The police make the decision to caution an offender in accordance with Home Office guidelines.

6.12 When deciding whether a case should be prosecuted in the courts, Crown Prosecutors should consider the alternatives to prosecution. This will include a police caution. Again the Home Office guidelines should be applied. Where it is felt that a caution is appropriate, Crown Prosecutors must inform the police so that they can caution the suspect. If the caution is not administered because the suspect refuses to accept it or the police do not wish to offer it, then the Crown Prosecutor may review the case again.

7. Charges. 7.1 Crown Prosecutors should select charges which:

(a) reflect the seriousness of the offending;
(b) give the court adequate sentencing powers; and
(c) enable the case to be presented in a clear and simple way.

This means that Crown Prosecutors may not always continue with the most serious charge where there is a choice. Further, Crown Prosecutors should not continue with more charges than are necessary.

7.2 Crown Prosecutors should never go ahead with more charges than are necessary just to encourage a defendant to plead guilty to a few. In the same way, they should never go ahead with a more serious charge just to encourage a defendant to plead guilty to a less serious one.

7.3 Crown Prosecutors should not change the charge simply because of the decision made by the court or the defendant about where the case will be heard.

8. Mode of Trial. 8.1 The Crown Prosecution Service applies the current guidelines for magistrates who have to decide whether cases should be tried in the Crown Court when the offence gives the option.(See the 'National Mode of Trial Guidelines' issued by the Lord Chief Justice.) Crown Prosecutors should recommend Crown Court trial when they are satisfied that the guidelines require them to do so.

8.2 Speed must never be the only reason for asking for a case to stay in the magistrates' courts. But Crown Prosecutors should consider the effect of any likely delay if they send a case to the Crown Court, and any possible stress on victims and witnesses if the case is delayed.

9. Accepting Guilty Pleas. 9.1 Defendants may want to plead guilty to some, but not all, of the charges. Or they may want to plead guilty to a different, possibly less serious, charge because they are admitting only part of the crime. Crown Prosecutors should only accept the defendant's plea if they think the court is able to pass a sentence that matches the seriousness of the offending. Crown Prosecutors must never accept a guilty plea just because it is convenient.

10. Re-starting a Prosecution. 10.1 People should be able to rely on decisions taken by the Crown Prosecution Service. Normally, if the Crown Prosecution Service tells a suspect or defendant that there will not be a prosecution, or that the prosecution has been stopped, that is the end of the matter and the case will not start again. But occasionally there are special reasons why the Crown Prosecution Service will re-start the prosecution, particularly if the case is serious.

10.2 These reasons include:

(a) rare cases where a new look at the original decision shows that it was clearly wrong and should not be allowed to stand;
(b) cases which are stopped so that more evidence which is likely to become available in the fairly near future can be collected and prepared. In these cases, the Crown Prosecutor will tell the defendant that the prosecution may well start again;
(c) cases which are stopped because of a lack of evidence but where more significant evidence is discovered later.

Further copies may be obtained from:

Crown Prosecution Service
Communications Branch
50 Ludgate Hill
London
EC4M 7EX
Telephone: 020 7796 8442
Fax: 020 7796 8351
Email: commsdept@cps.gov.uk

Translations into other languages are available and audio or braille copies are available. Please contact CPS Communications Branch (above) for details.

Code of Practice for Constables and Customs Officers under the Proceeds of Crime Act 2002

INTRODUCTION

1-7730   1. This code of practice is made in connection with the exercise by a customs officer and (in relation to England and Wales and Northern Ireland only) a constable of the search powers conferred by s 289 of the Proceeds of Crime Act 2002 ("the Act"). The code is made under s 292 of the Act. There is a separate code of practice for constables exercising their powers in relation to Scotland, made under s 293 of the Act by Scottish Ministers.

2. The code does not apply to searches carried out under any other legislation, including searches at the borders by customs officers undertaken under existing powers, or searches under Part 8 of this Act. If searches conducted under other legislation result in cash being seized under s 294, the provisions of this code do not apply.

3. The code should be available at all police stations for consultation by the police and members of the public. It should also be available at police offices at ports where the powers are, or are likely, to be used. The code should also form part of the published instructions or guidance for customs officers. If the provisions of this code are not observed, the magistrate or sheriff may draw into question the legality of any search for cash seized.

4. In this code:

reference to a person's rank includes a person acting temporarily in that rank.

"officer" includes a customs officer or constable unless otherwise specified.

cash means notes and coins in any currency, postal orders, cheques of any kind (including travellers' cheques), bankers' drafts and bearer bonds and bearer shares found at any place in the United Kingdom. The definition of 'cash' can be amended by an order made by the Secretary of State under s 289(7) – officers should be made aware of any such order made. The power of search does not extend to any other property (eg jewellery, pieces of art etc.)

GENERAL

5. The right to respect for private life and home –and the right to peaceful enjoyment of possessions –are both safeguarded by the Human Rights Act 1998. Powers of search may involve significant interference with the privacy of those whose premises and persons are searched and therefore need to be fully and clearly justified before they are used. In particular, officers should consider at every stage whether the necessary objectives can be achieved by less intrusive means. In all cases officers should exercise their powers courteously and with respect for the persons and property of those concerned. The possibility of using reasonable force to give effect to the power of detention of a person and search of a person or premises should only be considered where this is necessary and proportionate in all the circumstances.

6. Powers to detain and search a person must be used fairly, responsibly, with respect for people being searched and without unlawful discrimination. The Race Relations Act 1976 as amended makes it unlawful for police officers to discriminate on the grounds of race, colour, or ethnic origin when using their powers.

Scope of the search powers

7. The Act provides power for officers to search for cash where:

   (a) the officer is lawfully on any premises and has reasonable grounds for suspecting that there is on the premises cash which satisfies the conditions below; or

   (b) the officer has reasonable grounds for suspecting that a person is carrying cash which satisfies the conditions below.

8. The conditions are that:

- the cash is recoverable property (ie it is obtained through unlawful conduct or represents property obtained through unlawful conduct) or the cash is intended for use in unlawful conduct; (conduct occurring in any part of the United Kingdom is 'unlawful conduct' if it is unlawful under the criminal law of that part. Conduct which occurs in a country outside the United Kingdom and is unlawful under the criminal law in that country, and if it occurred in a part of the United Kingdom, would be unlawful under the criminal law of that part is also 'unlawful conduct') and

- the cash does not amount to less than the minimum amount specified under the Act (currently £10,000 – this amount can be amended by an order made by the Secretary of State under s 303 – officers should be made aware of any such order made)

9. Where the power to search a person is exercised the Act requires that the officer or constable may require the person – so far as he thinks necessary or expedient – to permit:

   (a) a search of any article he has with him; or

   (b) a search of his person.

THE OFFICER MAY DETAIN THE PERSON FOR SO LONG AS IS NECESSARY TO CARRY OUT THE SEARCH.

10. The powers conferred are civil in nature and exercisable only so far as reasonably required for the purposes of finding cash. The powers do not include the power to enter premises. They are exercisable by a customs officer only if he has reasonable grounds for suspecting that the unlawful conduct that makes the cash recoverable property or intended for use in unlawful conduct relates to an assigned matter within the meaning of the Customs and Excise Management Act 1979. Assigned matters are matters in relation to which the Commissioners for Customs and

Excise are required, in pursuance of any enactment, to perform any duties. Unlawful conduct that can be prosecuted by customs officers currently includes:

drug trafficking;

money laundering,;

evasion of VAT, excise and other indirect taxes and duties; and

evasion of a wide range of import and export prohibitions and restrictions.

REASONABLE GROUNDS FOR SUSPICION

11. In order to exercise the search power an officer must have reasonable grounds for suspecting that cash meeting the conditions set out in para 8 will be found.

12. Whether there are reasonable grounds for suspicion will depend on the circumstances in each case. There must be some objective basis for that suspicion based on facts, information and/or intelligence. The officer should take into account such factors as how the individual or premises were identified, previous intelligence on persons or premises, previous involvement with the persons or premises, and suspected links with criminal activities, whether here or overseas.

13. Reasonable suspicion can never be supported on the basis of personal factors alone without reliable supporting intelligence or information or some specific behaviour by the person concerned. For example, a person's race, age, appearance, or the fact that the person is know to have a previous conviction, cannot be used alone or in combination with each other as the reason for searching that person. Reasonable suspicion cannot be based on generalisations or stereotypical images of certain groups or categories of people being more likely to be involved in criminal activity. It should normally be linked to accurate and current intelligence or information

AUTHORITY TO SEARCH FOR CASH

14. Any decision to search for cash under the Act must, if practicable, be approved by a justice of the peace, or a sheriff in Scotland. Judicial approval is only likely to be impractical because of the immediacy of the circumstances of the case. This is more likely to be the case in relation to the search of a person than the search of premises. But officers must assess each case on its merits. There can be no assumption that judicial approval is impracticable for all searches of a person – officers must carefully consider any decision not to obtain such approval.

15. In order to obtain approval from a justice of the peace or sheriff an officer will need to make contact with the clerk of a magistrates' court or sheriff's court, to arrange a hearing which can be held without notice and in private. The usual reason to hold an application without notice and in private would be so not to alert persons connected to the cash that such action is contemplated. This may have the effect of the person moving the cash and thereby frustrating the operation of the scheme. However, if there is no concern that the cash would be removed the respondent should normally be notified of the intention of making an application for prior approval to search for cash. Annexed are a model application and draft order. The officer will need to:

- identify himself to the magistrate or sheriff (giving name, rank, any warrant or other identifying number, and home station or place of work);
- lodge his written application;
- explain to the justice or sheriff the reasonable grounds he or she has for undertaking the search;
- answer any questions that the justice or sheriff may have.

16. If judicial approval for a search is impracticable, a senior officer should provide approval as follows:

- where a search is undertaken by a constable, by a police officer of the rank of Inspector or above;
- where a search is undertaken by a customs officer, by a Customs Officer Pay Band 7 or above.

17. If an application for an authority is refused (either by the judicial or senior officer process) the officer must not make a fresh application for a search of the same person or premises unless he has new information.

18. Authorisation to search should be obtained prior to the actual search itself where practicable.

The officer should explain to the senior officer the reasonable grounds he or she has for undertaking the search. The authority should only be given where the senior officer is satisfied that the necessary grounds exist. The senior officer should take a written record of such reasons. Oral authorisation should be supported by written authorisation as soon as that is reasonably practicable.

19. If approval by a senior officer for a search is impracticable, a search may be conducted without approval. It is unlikely that senior officer approval will be impracticable unless there is some problem in making contact. However if a search is conducted without any prior approval, the officer must give an explanation of the reasons for the search to a senior officer as soon as that is reasonably practicable. The senior officer should take a written record of these reasons.

REPORTS TO THE "APPOINTED PERSON"

20. If a search is conducted without prior judicial approval - whether with or without senior officer approval the officer is legally required to prepare a report in the following circumstances:

- if the search does not result in the seizure of cash, or
- if cash is released before the matter proceeds to a detention hearing, or
- if the court at a detention hearing does not authorise the detention of the seized cash for more than 48 hours after it was initially seized.

Cash may not be detained for more than 48 hours except by order of a magistrate or sheriff, the application for an order is commonly known as a 'detention hearing'.

21. This report must set out why it was not practicable to obtain judicial prior approval and why circumstances led him to believe that the search powers were exercisable. These factors could include why the officer was on the premises where the search took place, what aroused his/her suspicion and why there was a need for an immediate search. If the prior approval of a senior officer was obtained, the report should state this, with the senior officer's reasons for approval, if practicable.

22. The report must be submitted to the independent person appointed by the Secretary of State.

23. The report should normally be submitted as soon as practicable and in no event any later than 14 days of the exercise of the search powers. Following the submission of his report, the reporting officer must also submit, to the appointed person referred to in para 22, any supplementary information which the appointed person reasonably requires him to submit.

STEPS PRIOR TO SEARCH OF A PERSON

24. If the officer suspects that the person has cash concealed on his or her person, the officer must take the following steps:

- inform the person that he has reasonable grounds for suspecting that he or she has cash on their person which is not less than the minimum amount and is recoverable property or is intended by any person in unlawful conduct;
- inform the person that he has the power to search them under s 289 of the Proceeds of Crime Act 2002 for the purposes of finding such cash;
- produce any document authorising the search (if applicable);
- ask the person to confirm or deny whether they have cash on their person; and
- allow the person the opportunity to produce and hand over the cash.

These steps do not necessarily have to be followed in the order presented. The officer will have flexibility depending on the circumstances of an individual case, but that all the steps must be undertaken.

25. Before any search for cash takes place the officer must take reasonable steps to give the person to be searched the following information:

- the officer's name (unless the officer reasonably believes that giving his or her name might put him or her in danger, in which case a warrant card number or other identification should be given which proves their status as a constable or customs officer but not their name);
- the fact that the search is being carried out under s 289 of the Proceeds of Crime Act 2002; and
- a clear explanation of:
  - (i) the purpose of the search; and
  - (ii) the grounds for the reasonable suspicion

26. Officers not in uniform should show their warrant cards or other suitable form of identification.

27. Before the search takes place the officer must inform the person (or occupier) of his entitlement to a copy of the record of the search.

28. If the person to be searched does not appear to understand what is being said or the officer has doubts as to the person's ability to speak and/or understand English or that the person is deaf or has difficulty with hearing or speaking, the officer should take reasonable steps to ensure that the person understands. Where desirable and practicable someone who can act as an interpreter should be identified, but if no such person can be identified, the search should still be allowed to proceed.

SEARCH OF A PERSON

29. The minimum amount of cash that may be seized is currently £10,000. This is set out in a statutory instrument [The Proceeds of Crime Act 2002 (Recovery of Cash in Summary Proceedings: Minimum Amount) Order 2002]. The statutory instrument should be available with the code. This amount can be amended by a statutory instrument made by the Secretary of State under s 303 – officers should be made aware of any such order made and it should be made available with the code. There is no maximum amount of cash that may be seized.

30. All searches should be carried out with courtesy, consideration and respect for the person concerned. An officer of the same sex as the person being searched should attend the search as a witness wherever practicable. The co-operation of the person to be searched must be sought in every case, even if the person initially objects to the search. A forcible search may be made only if it has been established that the person is unwilling to co-operate. Officers might want to consider the possibility of using reasonable force as a last resort if this appears to be the only way in which to give effect to their power of detention and search.

31. The length of time for which a person may be detained must be reasonable and kept to a minimum. The thoroughness and extent of a search must depend on what type and amount of cash is suspected of being carried.

32. This search power does not extend to requiring a person to undergo an intimate or strip search. An intimate search is one involving a physical - and not just visual – examination of a person's body orifices. A strip search is any search that involves the removal of an article of clothing that:

- is being worn (wholly or partly) on the trunk and
- is being so worn either next to the skin or next to an article of underwear.

If a search reveals an item suspected of containing cash which is next to the skin (eg a money belt) an officer can only request the person to remove it.

33. A person must not be asked to remove any clothing in public other than an outer coat, jacket or gloves. A search in public of a person's clothing that has not been removed must be restricted to superficial examination of outer garments. This does not, however, prevent an officer from placing his hand inside the pockets of the outer clothing, or feeling round the inside of collars, socks and shoes if this is reasonable or necessary in the circumstances. Particular sensitivity should be exercised where the person being searched is wearing items of clothing which he or she says are of religious significance.

34. If on reasonable grounds it is considered necessary to conduct a more thorough search this must be done out of public view. Any search involving the removal of more than an outer coat, jacket, gloves, headgear or footwear may only be made by an officer of the same sex as the person searched. It may not be made in the presence of anyone of the opposite sex unless the person being searched specifically requests it.

35. If the officer discovers cash during a search he or she should give the person who has possession of it an opportunity to provide an explanation of its ownership, origins, purpose and destination. If, in a particular case, questioning which covers whether the person has committed an offence, is likely to constitute questions that require a caution – under the Police and Criminal Evidence Act 1984 Code C in England and Wales.

SEARCH OF PREMISES

GENERAL

36. No right of entry is conferred by s 289 of the Proceeds of Crime Act 2002. In order to search for cash on premises an officer must be lawfully on premises. This would include a search of premises undertaken with the consent of a person entitled to grant entry to the premises. It would also include a search carried out when an officer has exercised a power of entry conferred by a search warrant granted in some other connection or power of entry conferred under some other legislation such as the Police and Criminal Evidence Act 1984 or Customs and Excise Management Act 1979 and circumstances subsequently lead him to believe that there is cash on the premises. 'Premises' includes any place and, in particular, include any vehicle. A search must be made at a reasonable hour – ie in the case of domestic premises outside normal sleeping hours and in the case of business premises during normal business hours - unless this might frustrate the purpose of the search.

37. If it is proposed to search premises with the consent of a person entitled to grant entry to the premises the consent must, if practicable, be given in writing before the search takes place. The officer must make any necessary enquiries in order to be satisfied that the person is in a position to give such consent.

38. Before seeking consent the officer in charge of the search shall state the purpose of the proposed search and its extent. This information must be as specific as possible. The person concerned must be clearly informed that they are not obliged to consent.

39. An officer cannot enter and search premises or continue to search premises if the consent has been given under duress or is withdrawn before the search is completed.

CONDUCT OF SEARCHES

40. Premises may be searched only to the extent necessary to achieve the object of the search. A search may not continue once the object of the search has been found - and no search may continue once the officer in charge of the search is satisfied that whatever is sought is not on the premises. (This does not prevent a further search if new information comes to light justifying such a search.)

41. Searches must be conducted with due consideration for the property and privacy of the occupier of the premises searched and with no more disturbance than necessary.

42. The occupier shall be asked whether they wish a friend neighbour or other person to witness the search. That person must be allowed to do so unless the officer in charge of the search has reasonable grounds for believing that the presence of the person asked for would seriously hinder the investigation or endanger the officers concerned or other people. A search need not be unreasonably delayed for this purpose. A record of the action taken under this paragraph, including the grounds for refusing a request from the occupier, shall be made on the premises search record. Where a search is being conducted with the consent of the occupier, the occupier is entitled to refuse consent until a friend or neighbour arrives.

RECORDING REQUIREMENTS – SEARCHES OF A PERSON

43. An officer who has carried out a search in the exercise of any power to which this Code applies must make a written record of it at the time, unless there are exceptional circumstances that would make this wholly impracticable – such as when the officer's presence is urgently required elsewhere. If a record is not made at the time the officer must do so as soon as practicable afterwards. There may be situations in which it is not practicable to obtain the

information necessary to complete a record, but the officer must make every reasonable effort to do so.

44. A copy of a record made at the time must be given immediately to the person who has been searched. If a record is not made at the time the person must be told how they can apply for a copy of the record once made. The officer must ask for the name, address and date of birth of the person searched, but there is no obligation on a person to provide these details and no power of detention if the person is unwilling to do so.

45. The following information must always be included in the record of a search even if the person does not wish to provide any personal details:

- the name of the person searched, or (if it is not given) a description;
- a note of the person's self defined ethnic background (if provided);
- the date, time and place that the person was first detained;
- the date, time and place the person was searched (if different);
- the grounds for making it (and of any necessary authorisation if given). If a search is conducted without judicial prior approval, the reason for not obtaining such;
- its outcome (eg seizure of cash, no further action);
- a note of any injury or damage to property resulting from it;
- the identity of the officer making the search (subject to para 25).

46. A record is required for each person searched, if more than one person is searched at the same time. The record of the grounds for making a search must, briefly but informatively, explain the reasons for suspecting the person concerned, by reference to the person's behaviour and/or other circumstances. If a person is detained with a view to performing a search, but the search is not carried out due to the grounds for suspicion being eliminated as a result of questioning the person, a record must still be made.

RECORDING REQUIREMENTS – SEARCH OF PREMISES

47. Where premises have been searched in circumstances to which this Code applies the officer in charge of the search shall make or have made a record of the search on returning to his normal place of work. The record shall include:

- the address of the premises searched (and if relevant and possible the part of those premises searched);
- the date, time and duration of the search;
- the authority under which the search was made, including whether prior judicial or senior officer approval was obtained;
- the name of the officer in charge of the search and the names of all other officers who conducted the search;
- the names of any people on the premises if they are known;
- any grounds for refusing the occupier's request to have someone present during the search;
- details of any damage caused during the search and the circumstances in which it was caused;
- whether any cash was seized.

48. In the case of searches undertaken by police officers the record of the search made in accordance with paragraphs 45 and 47 shall be made, copied or referred to in the search register. In the case of searches undertaken by customs officers the record of the search shall be maintained in a suitable form.

IN THE MAGISTRATES COURT AT

[insert name of the court]

PROCEEDS OF CRIME ACT 2002

AUTHORITY FOR A SEARCH UNDER SECTION 289

1. This is an authority for a search made by *[name of the JP]* on the application of *[]* of the *[]*. The Justice has heard the applicant and is satisfied there are reasonable grounds to suspect that there is on *[name of premises and/or person]* cash which is recoverable property or is intended by any person for use in unlawful conduct, and the amount of which is not less than the minimum amount.

2. The Justice has authorised [name of officer] to search [name and address of the premises/ name of persons] for cash found there which is reasonably suspected to be recoverable property or is intended by any person for use in unlawful conduct, and the amount of which is not less than the minimum amount.

3. This authority continues in force until the end of the period of one month starting with the day on which it was issued.

4. This authority is valid for one search.

EXCEPTIONS TO THE AUTHORITY

5. This authority does not provide the authority to enter any premises. It does not require a person to submit to an intimate search or strip search.

.... Signature of justice

.... Name of justice

[court stamp]

.... Date

PROCEEDS OF CRIME ACT 2002

INFORMATION IN SUPPORT OF AN APPLICATION FOR AN AUTHORITY FOR A SEARCH

The information of *[Officer]*
of the *[Name and address of unit/agency]*
Who upon oath/affirmation states:

1. I apply for an authority to search for the purposes of finding cash which is recoverable property or is intended by any person for use in unlawful conduct, and the amount of which is not less than the minimum amount in respect of persons *[named]* and/or premises at *[address]*.

2. I make this application because I have reasonable grounds for suspecting that on the identified premises and/or persons there is cash which is recoverable property or is intended by any person for use in unlawful conduct, and the amount of which is not less than the minimum amount. These grounds are *[insert reasons, attaching any relevant documentation]*.

Signature ....

Name ....

Date..

Conditional Cautioning: Code of Practice

Criminal Justice Act 2003, ss 22–27

Draft of 18 February 2004

1–7740

Introduction

1.1 This Code of Practice has been approved by Parliament and brought into force by statutory instrument (ref). It extends to England and Wales. The Code governs the use of conditional cautions under Part 3 of the Criminal Justice Act 2003 ("the Act"). The text of the relevant provisions of the Act is attached at Annex A.

1.2 Conditional cautioning enables offenders to be given a suitable disposal without the involvement of the usual court processes. Where rehabilitative or reparative conditions (or both) are considered preferable to prosecution, conditional cautioning provides a statutory means of enforcing them through prosecution for the original offence in the event of non-compliance. The key to determining whether a conditional caution should be given – instead of prosecution or a simple caution – is that the imposition of specified conditions will be an appropriate and effective means of addressing an offender's behaviour or making reparation for the effects of the offence on the victim or the community.

1.3 The Act defines a conditional caution as 'a caution which is given in respect of an offence committed by the offender and which has conditions attached to it'. If an offender fails without reasonable excuse to comply with the conditions attached to a conditional caution the Act provides for criminal proceedings to be instituted and the caution cancelled.

1.4 Such a caution may only be given by an authorised person, defined as a constable; a person designated as an investigating officer under s 38 of the Police Reform Act 2002; or a person authorised for the purpose by a relevant prosecutor. The authorised person should be suitably trained.

1.5 A relevant prosecutor is defined as –

(*a*) the Attorney General,
(*b*) the Director of the Serious Fraud Office,
(*c*) the Director of Public Prosecutions,
(*d*) a Secretary of State,
(*e*) the Commissioners of Inland Revenue,
(*f*) the Commissioners of Customs and Excise, or
(*g*) a person specified as a relevant prosecutor in an order made by the Secretary of State for the purposes of this Part of the Act.

1.6 Although this Code is expressed largely in terms of the police and CPS, it applies equally to conditional cautions given on the authority of other relevant prosecutors, who should ensure that their procedures (with any necessary adaptations) comply with the relevant provisions of the Code.

Conditional cautioning as a disposal

2.1 A conditional caution is a statutory development of the non-statutory police caution ('simple caution') which has long been available, at the discretion of the police and CPS, as an alternative to prosecution in suitable cases. The basic criteria for a conditional caution – ie those which must be satisfied before this disposal can be considered – are:

- that the offender is 18 or over[1];
- that the offender admits the offence to the authorised person; and
- that there is, in the opinion of the relevant prosecutor, evidence sufficient to charge the offender with the offence[2].

2.2 In cases where these criteria are satisfied, a conditional caution may be considered as an alternative to charge, taking into account the factors outlined in section 3 of this Code. The simple caution will remain available as a disposal, and may be appropriate in cases where no suitable conditions readily suggest themselves, or where prosecution would not be in the public interest, or where the suspect has forestalled what would otherwise have been a suitable condition by (for example) paying compensation to the victim (and can establish that he has done so). For those offences for which there is the option of issuing a fixed penalty notice, that will generally be the appropriate disposal unless such a notice has already been issued to the offender, in which case a conditional caution might be more suitable.

2.3 The issue of simple cautions and penalty notices will continue to be a matter for the police. The discretion of the police in respect of decisions whether to charge has been reduced with the introduction of the arrangements in Sch 2 to the Criminal Justice Act 2003, whereby the Director of Public Prosecutions is empowered to issue guidance about how custody officers should proceed in cases where they consider that there would be sufficient evidence to prosecute. The effect of the guidance[3] which the DPP has issued pursuant to s 37A of the Police and Criminal Evidence Act 1984 is that it is for the CPS to decide whether or not a suspect should be charged and to determine which charge should be brought, although the police retain the discretion to charge in minor, routine cases.

2.4 But the police have no such discretion in respect of conditional cautions, which may be given only where the prosecutor considers that it is appropriate to do so, even in cases where it would have been open to the police to charge without reference. It follows that, where it appears to the police that the statutory requirements are met and that a conditional caution might be appropriate, it is for the prosecutor to decide that a conditional caution is the right disposal and what condition(s) would be suitable. It is also open to the prosecutor to take the view that a conditional caution is an appropriate disposal without this having been suggested by the police.

2.5 The necessary consultation should be carried out as quickly as possible, either face-to-face with a Crown Prosecutor located in the police station, by telephone, or using any arrangements whereby advice may be sought out of hours. It is acknowledged that Restorative Justice processes will involve consultation with the parties at the outset. This process should be carefully managed to balance the benefits of using restorative methods against the desirability of early disposal. Where, exceptionally, the necessary reference to the CPS cannot be done on the spot, the suspect should be bailed under s37(7)(a) of the Police and Criminal Evidence Act 1984 for a sufficient period to enable the CPS to decide whether prosecution or a conditional caution would be appropriate.

2.6 Where the decision of the CPS is that a caution would be appropriate if acceptable conditions can be agreed at a mediation meeting with the victim, the suspect should be bailed under s37(7)(a) for a period that will allow such a meeting to take place before the resulting conditions are approved by the prosecutor and the offer of a caution made to the offender.

2.7 Where several related or similar offences are admitted they may be grouped and dealt with by a single conditional caution; breach of any of the conditions would make the offender liable for prosecution for all of the offences.

2.8 A conditional caution is a statutory disposal and may be cited in any subsequent court proceedings.

---

1. For offenders under 18, simple cautions were replaced with reprimands and final warnings under s 65 of the Crime and Disorder Act 1998; for further details, see Final Warning Scheme: Guidance for the Police and Youth Offending Teams (Home Office, November 2002, available at www.homeoffice.gov.uk).
2. Note that the person to whom the admissions are made may be a police officer but the decision as to sufficiency of evidence must be taken by a prosecutor.
3. *Guidance to Police Officers and Crown Prosecutors in respect of the making of charging decisions.*

Deciding when a conditional caution may be appropriate

3.1 Guidance about existing cautions advises the police that, in considering whether an offender should be charged or cautioned, they should have regard to the seriousness of the offence and to the offender's criminal record. The same considerations will apply to conditional cautions, and authorised persons as well as relevant prosecutors should apply the principles of the Code for Crown Prosecutors and take into consideration the latest Home Office Circular in relation to cautions, when deciding whether an offence may be suitable for a conditional caution. Careful account should be taken of special guidance in relation to domestic violence and hate crime including homophobic crime and crime involving a racist element.

3.2 Conditions attached to cautions must either facilitate the rehabilitation of the offender or ensure that the offender makes reparation for the offence, or both. Where the circumstances of a particular case or offender readily suggest conditions of this type, and where such conditions will provide a proportionate response to the offence bearing in mind the public interest, a conditional caution will usually be appropriate. It must be remembered that the offender must consent to the conditions as a pre-requisite to imposing them1.

3.3 It is not intended to establish a progression so that a conditional caution is regarded as the logical next step for an offender who has received a simple caution. Indeed a person who has recently been cautioned for a similar offence should not be given a conditional caution, unless exceptionally it is believed that the condition would be effective in breaking the pattern of offending. Previous cautions (or indeed convictions) for quite dissimilar offences may be disregarded, however, as may cautions or convictions more than 5 years old. Failure to comply with a previous conditional caution would normally rule out the issue of another.

---

1. Where the proposed conditions would involve a restorative justice mediation process, this might affect the time of administering a conditional caution; see related guidance on the use of restorative justice.

The requirements set out in the Act

4.1 The following requirements must be complied with:

(i)   The authorised person has evidence that the offender has committed an offence.

> This will be the evidence on the basis of which the suspect would otherwise fall to be charged, which must include an admission made under caution in interview and any witness statements. In order to avoid any suggestion that an admission has been obtained by offering an inducement, the prospect of a conditional caution should on no account be mentioned until the suspect has made a clear and reliable admission under a cautioned interview to all the elements of the offence.

(ii)   The relevant prosecutor decides –

> (a) that there is sufficient evidence to charge the offender with the offence, and
> (b) that a conditional caution should be given to the offender in respect of that offence.

> The relevant prosecutor will apply the evidential test in the usual way according to the Code for Crown Prosecutors – ie that there would be a realistic prospect of conviction if the offender were to be prosecuted. The prosecutor must also conclude that the public interest would be served by the offender receiving a conditional caution, if he accepts it and subject to his performing the agreed conditions. In addition, since the fall-back is that the offender will be prosecuted if he either does not accept or fails to perform the conditions, the prosecutor must be satisfied that prosecution would be in the public interest in those contingencies.

(iii)   The offender admits to the authorised person that he committed the offence.

> In addition to the admission made in interview (see (i) above), it is necessary that at the time the conditional caution is administered the offender admits to the authorised person that he committed the offence. Offenders should be advised at that point of their right to seek legal advice[1] to ensure they give informed consent to accepting both the caution and to the conditions.

(iv)   The authorised person explains the effect of the conditional caution to the offender and warns him that failure to comply with any of the conditions attached to the caution is likely to result in the offender being prosecuted for the original offence.

> The implications of the caution should be explained, including that there are circumstances in which it may be disclosed (such as to certain potential employers, and to a court in any future criminal proceedings) and, where the offence is listed in Sch 1 to the Sex Offenders Act 1997, that accepting a caution will result in the offender being required to notify the police of their name and address and certain other details. There should not be any negotiation with the offender over the conditions: if he does not accept them in full, he should be prosecuted.

> It should be made clear in explaining the consequences of non-compliance that the conditions are to be performed within the agreed time. It must be explained clearly that failure to comply will prompt a reconsideration of the case and usually result in the offender being prosecuted for the original offence.

(v)   The offender signs a document which contains –

> (a) details of the offence,
> (b) an admission by him that he committed the offence,
> (c) *his consent to being given the conditional caution,*
> (d) an agreement to comply with the conditions attached to the caution, which must be set out on the face of the document, and
> (e) an explanation of the implications referred to in (iv) above.

> After the offender has admitted to the offence and, having heard the explanation referred to above, has agreed to the conditions, he must sign a pro-forma to this effect. A standard form is available and must be used by all forces. This document will contain details of the offence, the offender's admission, and the conditions and timescale for completing them to which he has agreed. It must be explained to the offender before the form is signed that it will be admissible as evidence in court if the offender is subsequently prosecuted for the original offence in the event of non-compliance.

---

1. Advice is available either from a Duty Solicitor or own solicitor free of charge, although in some circumstances this may be limited to telephone advice only.

Types of condition

5.1 Conditions attached to a caution must be –

- *Proportionate* to the offence. The offender is unlikely to agree to a condition that is more onerous than the punishment that would probably be given if the case were taken to court. On the other hand, conditions that amount to far less than the punishment that would be probably be given by a court are unlikely to satisfy the victims or the public interest.

- *Achievable*: the conditions must be clearly defined in terms of what must be done and within what period of time. Conditions must be realistic and should take account of the particular offender's physical and mental capacity, so that he could reasonably be expected to achieve them within the time set; otherwise the only result will be a delayed prosecution.

- *Appropriate:* the conditions should be relevant to the offence or the offender.

5.2   The Act requires that conditions should fall into one or both of two categories: rehabilitation and reparation.

- *Rehabilitation*: this might include taking part in treatment for drug or alcohol dependency (eg self-help groups such as Alcoholics Anonymous or attendance on a drug awareness and education programme including assessment of personal needs and appropriate onward referral), anger management courses, or driving rectification classes and the like, or involvement in a restorative justice process (which may lead to reparation). The offender would be expected to pay reasonable costs, if there are any, and a requirement to do so should be one of the conditions. The fact that provision of some sorts of course may be subject to resource implications (and possibly a waiting list) will need to be taken into account, bearing in mind that completion of any conditions should be swift and achievable within a reasonable time (see section 6 below).
- *Reparation*: this might include repairing or otherwise making good any damage caused to property (eg by cleaning graffiti), restoring stolen goods, paying modest financial compensation, or in some cases a simple apology to the victim.

Compensation may be paid to an individual or to the community in the form of an appropriate charity.

5.3   Offenders should be required as standard to comply with a condition not to commit further offences during the period specified for the performance of the conditions[1].

5.4   Specific conditions such as that the offender should avoid a particular street or public house may be included, but consideration should also be given as to whether alternatives such as Anti-Social Behaviour Orders or Restriction Orders etc would be more appropriate or timely.

5.5   The police, CPS and National Probation Service (NPS) should take steps at local level (eg through the Local Criminal Justice Board or Crime and Disorder Reduction Partnership) to identify agencies, groups or organizations, voluntary or statutory, which provide courses or other activities that might form part of a conditional caution, and which it may be appropriate to consult when deciding whether a case is suitable for a conditional caution. The NPS should be approached in appropriate cases to assist in determining whether certain offenders are suitable for a conditional caution, for example where there are concerns about the health, behaviour or background of the offender.

5.6   When conditions are imposed that require the performance of some task other than the simple payment of compensation or the attendance on a course supervised by an organization responsible for monitoring attendance, careful thought should be given to how performance will be measured and who will be the appropriate person to give assurances that the condition has been completed. This should be documented as part of the description of the condition, in order that the relevant prosecutor and the offender are in no doubt as to the conditions and the measurement of performance. (See also section 10.1.)

---

1.   It will be for the CPS to decide whether the alleged further offending is such as to require the conditional caution to be cancelled and the original offence prosecuted.

Time limits

6.1   The deadline for the completion of conditions should not be too long. This is particularly important in relation to summary offences, for most of which there is a time limit of six months within which a prosecution must commence; for these offences the deadline set should leave enough time for a prosecution to proceed in the event of noncompliance.

6.2   Where the condition is for an offender to go on a course of treatment for behaviour/substance abuse, which may take longer than six months to deliver, the relevant prosecutor will need to consider whether this is appropriate, depending on the attitude of the offender and the likelihood of compliance. There is no reason why undertaking a course of longer duration should not be a condition, provided that (to satisfy the reasonableness test) the offender is only required under the terms of the conditional caution to attend for part of it. For example, a course may last 12 months to achieve best results. In such a case, the offender might agree, under the conditions of his caution, to attend for 4 months, and thereafter it will be up to him to continue the treatment for his own benefit, rather than under any legal compulsion.

Involvement of victims

7.1   In the course of interviewing the victim about the offence, it would be important to ascertain whether any resulting loss, damage or injury is such that it could readily be made good; what the victim's attitude would be towards an offer of reparation from the offender, should one be made; and whether they would be content for such reparation to be made the condition of a caution. Where a caution (simple or conditional) is at that stage regarded as a possibility, the fact may be mentioned to the victim in order to ascertain their views, but it is vital not to give the impression that the victim's views (if any) will be conclusive as to the outcome, which (it should be explained) is at the discretion of the CPS. In some circumstances the relevant prosecutor may consider that further conditions to those the victim would accept are needed to ensure that cases are met with overall conditions proportionate to the level of offence. In such circumstances prosecutors will consider whether some explanation to this effect will be helpful to the victim or to the offender.

7.2   The Victim Personal Statement (VPS) scheme provides victims with the opportunity to describe the effects of the crime and to have these effects taken into account as the case progresses through the criminal justice system. If it is subsequently proposed to approach the victim for an interview specifically about conditional cautioning, the contents of the VPS (if he or she has made one) should be considered beforehand, but it should not be considered sufficient, on its own, to inform a decision to pursue a restorative justice route.

7.3 Further information and guidance on the victim personal statement scheme can be found on the Home Office website at: http://www.homeoffice.gov.uk/justice/victims/personal/index.html

Restorative justice

8.1 Restorative justice processes bring victims and offenders, and sometimes community members, into contact, either face to face or indirectly, to focus on the impact of a particular crime, and together to agree what can be done to repair the harm caused by that crime. Such processes must always be voluntary for both the victim and the offender. Any person delivering a restorative process, including preparatory work with victims and offenders, must be trained in restorative justice and must meet the required standards. See guidance on this at www.homeoffice.gov.uk/justice/victims/restorative/index.html

8.2 Restorative justice processes can be used as a condition of the caution (where the contact with the victim, direct or indirect, is itself the condition) if both victim and offender consent to this. Alternatively, they can be used as the decision-making process whereby conditions, such as compensation, rehabilitative activities, or other kinds of reparation, are agreed. It should be noted that in this second case, the 'outcome agreement' arising from the process forms a basis for conditions to be approved or formulated by the prosecutor. Notwithstanding the outcome agreement, the prosecutor retains a duty to ensure that the conditions are proportionate to the offending and meet the public interest requirements of the case. Depending on the views of the victim, and any other conditions attached to the caution, the CPS/police will need to take a view as to which use of restorative justice is appropriate in a particular case.

8.3 It is desirable that, where RJ-trained personnel are available and a case with a personal victim is being considered for a conditional caution, the victim should be contacted (unless there are exceptional reasons not to do so) to ask for their views on reparation as a condition of the caution, or (if the offender has already indicated they are willing) whether they would like to be involved in a direct or indirect restorative justice process. Restorative justice processes may also be appropriate for crimes with a corporate victim, or crimes where the community as a whole has suffered. In these cases, or in cases where a personal victim has chosen to have no involvement, officers may still wish to deliver the caution, and decide any conditions of the caution, in a restorative manner.

Places where cautions may be given

9.1 Conditional cautions will usually be given at the local police station, but there is the option of selecting a location appropriate to the offence; eg there may be value in giving it at the place where vandalism has occurred. It will be for the authorised person to determine the venue for administering the caution. However, it is not suitable for conditional cautions to be delivered on the street, or in the offender's home. Where restorative justice forms part of the conditional caution, it may be that the local community centre would be more accessible and less threatening for the victim and others attending a restorative conference than the police station.

Monitoring and compliance

10.1 It is essential that there should be robust monitoring of compliance with the conditions of a caution. The onus is on the offender to show that the conditions have been met, and the conditions should be expressed in a way that makes clear to the offender what is to be done, by when, and what will be acceptable as evidence that it has been done. For example, an offender who agrees to attend a course might be required to produce a letter from the organiser confirming that he has done so. Depending on the nature of the condition, it may be appropriate for other agencies[1] managing the conditional caution to monitor performance and report to the relevant prosecutor any failure fully to comply. At the end of the process the offender will sign a form that will include a declaration that the conditions have been met.

10.2 Failure to comply with any of the conditions means that the offender may be prosecuted for the original offence. The offender will be required as a standard condition to report any failure to comply and explain whether there are circumstances that might amount to a reasonable excuse. Where the offender fails to report and give reasons, a prosecution may (following a prompt CPS review) be commenced, usually by the issue of a summons.

---

1. Monitoring may be carried out by any appropriate agency nominated by the authorised person. This might include the use of Community Support Officers or Neighbourhood Wardens, where available, who could check on the completion of a condition which includes public work in the community.

ANNEX A

CRIMINAL JUSTICE ACT 2003

PART 3

CONDITIONAL CAUTIONS

Attorney General's Guidelines on Disclosure[1]

DISCLOSURE OF UNUSED MATERIAL IN CRIMINAL PROCEEDINGS

---

1. Published April 2005.

1–7750

INTRODUCTION

1 Every accused person has a right to a fair trial, a right long embodied in our law and guaranteed under art 6 of the European Convention on Human Rights (ECHR). A fair trial is the proper object and expectation of all participants in the trial process. Fair disclosure to an accused is an inseparable part of a fair trial.

2 What must be clear is that a fair trial consists of an examination not just of all the evidence the parties wish to rely on but also all other relevant subject matter. A fair trial should not require consideration of irrelevant material and should not involve spurious applications or arguments which serve to divert the trial process from examining the real issues before the court.

3 The scheme set out in the Criminal Procedure and Investigations Act 1996 (as amended by the Criminal Justice Act 2003) (the Act) is designed to ensure that there is fair disclosure of material which may be relevant to an investigation and which does not form part of the prosecution case. Disclosure under the Act should assist the accused in the timely preparation and presentation of their case and assist the court to focus on all the relevant issues in the trial. Disclosure which does not meet these objectives risks preventing a fair trial taking place.

4 This means that the disclosure regime set out in the Act must be scrupulously followed. These Guidelines build upon the existing law to help to ensure that the legislation is operated more effectively, consistently and fairly.

5 Disclosure must not be an open ended trawl of unused material. A critical element to fair and proper disclosure is that the defence play their role to ensure that the prosecution are directed to material which might reasonably be considered capable of undermining the prosecution case or assisting the case for the accused. This process is key to ensuring prosecutors make informed determinations about disclosure of unused material.

6 Fairness does recognise that there are other interests that need to be protected, including those of victims and witnesses who might otherwise be exposed to harm. The scheme of the Act protects those interests. It should also ensure that material is not disclosed which overburdens the participants in the trial process, diverts attention from the relevant issues, leads to unjustifiable delay, and is wasteful of resources.

7 Whilst it is acknowledged that these Guidelines have been drafted with a focus on Crown Court proceedings the spirit of the Guidelines must be followed where they apply to proceedings in the magistrates' court.

GENERAL PRINCIPLES

8 Disclosure refers to providing the defence with copies of, or access to, any material which might reasonably be considered capable of undermining the case for the prosecution against the accused, or of assisting the case for the accused, and which has not previously been disclosed.

9 Prosecutors will only be expected to anticipate what material might weaken their case or strengthen the defence in the light of information available at the time of the disclosure decision, and this may include information revealed during questioning.

10 Generally, material which can reasonably be considered capable of undermining the prosecution case against the accused or assisting the defence case will include anything that tends to show a fact inconsistent with the elements of the case that must be proved by the prosecution. Material can fulfil the disclosure test:

    (a) by the use to be made of it in cross-examination; or

    (b) by its capacity to support submissions that could lead to:

        (i) the exclusion of evidence; or

        (ii) a stay of proceedings; or

        (iii) a court or tribunal finding that any public authority had acted incompatibly with the accused 's rights under the ECHR, or

    (c) by its capacity to suggest an explanation or partial explanation of the accused's actions.

11 In deciding whether material may fall to be disclosed under para 10, especially (b)(ii), prosecutors must consider whether disclosure is required in order for a proper application to be made. The purpose of this para is not to allow enquiries to support speculative arguments or for the manufacture of defences.

12 Examples of material that might reasonably be considered capable of undermining the prosecution case or of assisting the case for the accused are:

    i.   Any material casting doubt upon the accuracy of any prosecution evidence.

    ii.   Any material which may point to another person, whether charged or not (including a co-accused) having involvement in the commission of the offence.

    iii. Any material which may cast doubt upon the reliability of a confession.

    iv. Any material that might go to the credibility of a prosecution witness.

    v.   Any material that might support a defence that is either raised by the defence or apparent from the prosecution papers.

    vi. Any material which may have a bearing on the admissibility of any prosecution evidence.

13 It should also be borne in mind that while items of material viewed in isolation may not be reasonably considered to be capable of undermining the prosecution case or assisting the accused, several items together can have that effect.

14 Material relating to the accused's mental or physical health, intellectual capacity, or to any ill treatment which the accused may have suffered when in the investigator's custody is likely to fall within the test for disclosure set out in para 8 above.

DEFENCE STATEMENTS

15 A defence statement must comply with the requirements of s 6A of the Act. A comprehensive defence statement assists the participants in the trial to ensure that it is fair. The trial process is not well served if the defence make general and unspecified allegations and then seek far-reaching disclosure in the hope that material may turn up to make them good. The more detail a defence statement contains the more likely it is that the prosecutor will make an informed decision about whether any remaining undisclosed material might reasonably be considered capable of undermining the prosecution case or of assisting the case for the accused, or whether to advise the investigator to undertake further enquiries. It also helps in the management of the trial by narrowing down and focussing on the issues in dispute. It may result in the prosecution discontinuing the case. Defence practitioners should be aware of these considerations when advising their clients.

16 Whenever a defence solicitor provides a defence statement on behalf of the accused it will be deemed to be given with the authority of the solicitor's client.

CONTINUING DUTY OF PROSECUTOR TO DISCLOSE

17 Section 7A of the Act imposes a continuing duty upon the prosecutor to keep under review at all times the question of whether there is any unused material which might reasonably be considered capable of undermining the prosecution case against the accused or assisting the case for the accused and which has not previously been disclosed. This duty arises after the prosecutor has complied with the duty of initial disclosure or purported to comply with it and before the accused is acquitted or convicted or the prosecutor decides not to proceed with the case. If such material is identified, then the prosecutor must disclose it to the accused as soon as is reasonably practicable.

18 As part of their continuing duty of disclosure, prosecutors should be open, alert and promptly responsive to requests for disclosure of material supported by a comprehensive defence statement. Conversely, if no defence statement has been served or if the prosecutor considers that the defence statement is lacking specificity or otherwise does not meet the requirements of s 6A of the Act, a letter should be sent to the defence indicating this. If the position is not resolved satisfactorily, the prosecutor should consider raising the issue at a hearing for directions to enable the court to give a warning or appropriate directions.

19 When defence practitioners are dissatisfied with disclosure decisions by the prosecution and consider that they are entitled to further disclosure, applications to the court should be made pursuant to s 8 of the Act and in accordance with the procedures set out in the Criminal Procedure Rules. Applications for further disclosure should not be made as ad hoc applications but dealt with under the proper procedures.

APPLICATIONS FOR NON-DISCLOSURE IN THE PUBLIC INTEREST

20 Before making an application to the court to withhold material which would otherwise fall to be disclosed, on the basis that to disclose would give rise to a real risk of serious prejudice to an important public interest, prosecutors should aim to disclose as much of the material as they properly can (for example, by giving the defence redacted or edited copies or summaries). Neutral material or material damaging to the defendant need not be disclosed and must *not* be brought to the attention of the court. It is only in truly borderline cases that the prosecution should seek a judicial ruling on the disclosability of material in its possession.

21 Prior to or at the hearing, the court must be provided with full and accurate information. Prior to the hearing the prosecutor and the prosecution advocate must examine all material, which is the subject matter of the application and make any necessary enquiries of the investigator. The prosecutor (or representative) and/or investigator should attend such applications.

22 The principles set out at para 36 of *R v H and C* should be rigorously applied firstly by the prosecutor and then by the court considering the material. It is essential that these principles are scrupulously attended to to ensure that the procedure for examination of material in the absence of the accused is compliant with art 6 of ECHR.

RESPONSIBILITIES

INVESTIGATORS AND DISCLOSURE OFFICERS

23 Investigators and disclosure officers must be fair and objective and must work together with prosecutors to ensure that disclosure obligations are met. A failure to take action leading to inadequate disclosure may result in a wrongful conviction. It may alternatively lead to a successful abuse of process argument, an acquittal against the weight of the evidence or the appellate courts may find that a conviction is unsafe and quash it.

24 Officers appointed as disclosure officers must have the requisite experience, skills, competence and resources to undertake their vital role. In discharging their obligations under the Act, code, common law and any operational instructions, investigators should always err on the side of recording and retaining material where they have any doubt as to whether it may be relevant.

25 An individual must not be appointed as disclosure officer, or continue in that role, if that is likely to result in a conflict of interest, for instance, if the disclosure officer is the victim of the alleged crime which is the subject of investigation. The advice of a more senior investigator must always be sought if there is doubt as to whether a conflict of interest precludes an individual acting as the disclosure officer. If thereafter a doubt remains, the advice of a prosecutor should be sought.

26 There may be a number of disclosure officers, especially in large and complex cases. However, there must be a lead disclosure officer who is the focus for enquiries and whose responsibility it is to ensure that the investigator's disclosure obligations are complied with. Disclosure officers, or their deputies, must inspect, view or listen to all relevant material that has been retained by the investigator, and the disclosure officer must provide a personal declaration to the effect that this task has been undertaken.

27 Generally this will mean that such material must be examined in detail by the disclosure officer or the deputy, but exceptionally the extent and manner of inspecting, viewing or listening will depend on the nature of material and its form. For example, it might be reasonable to examine digital material by using software search tools, or to establish the contents of large volumes of material by dip sampling. If such material is not examined in detail, it must nonetheless be described on the disclosure schedules accurately and as clearly as possible. The extent and manner of its examination must also be described together with justification for such action.

28 Investigators must retain material that may be relevant to the investigation. However, it may become apparent to the investigator that some material obtained in the course of an investigation because it was considered potentially relevant, is in fact incapable of impact. It need not then be retained or dealt with in accordance with these Guidelines, although the investigator should err on the side of caution in coming to this conclusion and seek the advice of the prosecutor as appropriate.

29 In meeting the obligations in para 6.9 and 8.1 of the Code, it is crucial that descriptions by disclosure officers in non-sensitive schedules are detailed, clear and accurate. The descriptions may require a summary of the contents of the retained material to assist the prosecutor to make an informed decision on disclosure. Sensitive schedules must contain sufficient information to enable the prosecutor to make an informed decision as to whether or not the material itself should be viewed, to the extent possible without compromising the confidentiality of the information.

30 Disclosure officers must specifically draw material to the attention of the prosecutor for consideration where they have any doubt as to whether it might reasonably be considered capable of undermining the prosecution case or of assisting the case for the accused.

31 Disclosure officers must seek the advice and assistance of prosecutors when in doubt as to their responsibility as early as possible. They must deal expeditiously with requests by the prosecutor for further information on material, which may lead to disclosure.

Prosecutors

32 Prosecutors must do all that they can to facilitate proper disclosure, as part of their general and personal professional responsibility to act fairly and impartially, in the interests of justice and in accordance with the law. Prosecutors must also be alert to the need to provide advice to, and where necessary probe actions taken by, disclosure officers to ensure that disclosure obligations are met.

33 Prosecutors must review schedules prepared by disclosure officers thoroughly and must be alert to the possibility that relevant material may exist which has not been revealed to them or material included which should not have been. If no schedules have been provided, or there are apparent omissions from the schedules, or documents or other items are inadequately described or are unclear, the prosecutor must at once take action to obtain properly completed schedules. Likewise schedules should be returned for amendment if irrelevant items are included. If prosecutors remain dissatisfied with the quality or content of the schedules they must raise the matter with a senior investigator, and if necessary, persist, with a view to resolving the matter satisfactorily.

34 Where prosecutors have reason to believe that the disclosure officer has not discharged the obligation in para 26 to inspect, view or listen to relevant material, they must at once raise the matter with the disclosure officer and, if it is believed that the officer has not inspected, viewed or listened to the material, request that it be done.

35 When prosecutors or disclosure officers believe that material might reasonably be considered capable of undermining the prosecution case or assisting the case for the accused, prosecutors must always inspect, view or listen to the material and satisfy themselves that the prosecution can properly be continued having regard to the disclosability of the material reviewed. Their judgement as to what other material to inspect, view or listen to will depend on the circumstances of each case.

36 Prosecutors should copy the defence statement to the disclosure officer and investigator as soon as reasonably practicable and prosecutors should advise the investigator if, in their view, reasonable and relevant lines of further enquiry should be pursued.

37 Prosecutors cannot comment upon, or invite inferences to be drawn from, failures in defence disclosure otherwise than in accordance with s 11 of the Act. Prosecutors may cross-examine the accused on differences between the defence case put at trial and that set out in his or her defence statement. In doing so, it may be appropriate to apply to the judge under s 6E of the Act for copies of the statement to be given to a jury, edited if necessary to remove inadmissible material. Prosecutors should examine the defence statement to see whether it points to other lines of enquiry. If the defence statement does point to other reasonable lines of inquiry further investigation is required and evidence obtained as a result of these enquiries may be used as part of the prosecution case or to rebut the defence.

38 Once initial disclosure is completed and a defence statement has been served requests for disclosure should ordinarily only be answered if the request is in accordance with and relevant

to the defence statement. If it is not, then a further or amended defence statement should be sought and obtained before considering the request for further disclosure.

39 Prosecutors must ensure that they record in writing all actions and decisions they make in discharging their disclosure responsibilities, and this information is to be made available to the prosecution advocate if requested or if relevant to an issue.

40 If the material does not fulfil the disclosure test there is no requirement to disclose it. For this purpose, the parties' respective cases should not be restrictively analysed but must be carefully analysed to ascertain the specific facts the prosecution seek to establish and the specific grounds on which the charges are resisted. Neutral material or material damaging to the defendant need not be disclosed and must not be brought to the attention of the court. Only in truly borderline cases should the prosecution seek a judicial ruling on the disclosability of material in its hands.

41 If prosecutors are satisfied that a fair trial cannot take place where material which satisfies the disclosure test cannot be disclosed, and that this cannot or will not be remedied including by, for example, making formal admissions, amending the charges or presenting the case in a different way so as to ensure fairness or in other ways, they must not continue with the case.

PROSECUTION ADVOCATES

42 Prosecution advocates should ensure that all material that ought to be disclosed under the Act is disclosed to the defence. However, prosecution advocates cannot be expected to disclose material if they are not aware of its existence. As far as is possible, prosecution advocates must place themselves in a fully informed position to enable them to make decisions on disclosure.

43 Upon receipt of instructions, prosecution advocates should consider as a priority all the information provided regarding disclosure of material. Prosecution advocates should consider, in every case, whether they can be satisfied that they are in possession of all relevant documentation and that they have been instructed fully regarding disclosure matters. Decisions already made regarding disclosure should be reviewed. If as a result, the advocate considers that further information or action is required, written advice should be promptly provided setting out the aspects that need clarification or action. Prosecution advocates must advise on disclosure in accordance with the Act. If necessary and where appropriate a conference should be held to determine what is required.

44 The prosecution advocate must keep decisions regarding disclosure under review until the conclusion of the trial. The prosecution advocate must in every case specifically consider whether he or she can satisfactorily discharge the duty of continuing review on the basis of the material supplied already, or whether it is necessary to inspect further material or to reconsider material already inspected. Prosecution advocates must not abrogate their responsibility under the Act by disclosing material which could not be considered capable of undermining the prosecution case or of assisting the case for the accused.

45 Prior to the commencement of a trial, the prosecuting advocate should always make decisions on disclosure in consultation with those instructing him or her and the disclosure officer. After a trial has started, it is recognised that in practice consultation on disclosure issues may not be practicable; it continues to be desirable, however, whenever this can be achieved without affecting unduly the conduct of the trial.

46 There is no basis in law or practice for disclosure on a "counsel to counsel" basis.

INVOLVEMENT OF OTHER AGENCIES

MATERIAL HELD BY GOVERNMENT DEPARTMENTS OR OTHER CROWN BODIES

47 Where it appears to an investigator, disclosure officer or prosecutor that a Government department or other Crown body has material that may be relevant to an issue in the case, reasonable steps should be taken to identify and consider such material. Although what is reasonable will vary from case to case, the prosecution should inform the department or other body of the nature of its case and of relevant issues in the case in respect of which the department or body might possess material, and ask whether it has any such material.

48 It should be remembered that investigators, disclosure officers and prosecutors cannot be regarded to be in constructive possession of material held by Government departments or Crown bodies simply by virtue of their status as Government departments or Crown bodies.

49 Departments in England and Wales should have identified personnel as established Enquiry Points to deal with issues concerning the disclosure of information in criminal proceedings.

50 Where, after reasonable steps have been taken to secure access to such material, access is denied the investigator, disclosure officer or prosecutor should consider what if any further steps might be taken to obtain the material or inform the defence.

MATERIAL HELD BY OTHER AGENCIES

51 There may be cases where the investigator, disclosure officer or prosecutor believes that a third party (for example, a local authority, a social services department, a hospital, a doctor, a school, a provider of forensic services) has material or information which might be relevant to the prosecution case. In such cases, if the material or information might reasonably be considered capable of undermining the prosecution case or of assisting the case for the accused prosecutors should take what steps they regard as appropriate in the particular case to obtain it.

52 If the investigator, disclosure officer or prosecutor seeks access to the material or information but the third party declines or refuses to allow access to it, the matter should not be left. If despite any reasons offered by the third party it is still believed that it is reasonable to seek

production of the material or information, and the requirements of s 2 of the Criminal Procedure (Attendance of Witnesses) Act 1965 or as appropriate s 97 of the Magistrates Courts Act 1980[1] are satisfied, then the prosecutor or investigator should apply for a witness summons causing a representative of the third party to produce the material to the Court.

53 Relevant information which comes to the knowledge of investigators or prosecutors as a result of liaison with third parties should be recorded by the investigator or prosecutor in a durable or retrievable form (for example potentially relevant information revealed in discussions at a child protection conference attended by police officers).

54 Where information comes into the possession of the prosecution in the circumstances set out in paragraphs 51-53 above, consultation with the other agency should take place before disclosure is made: there may be public interest reasons which justify withholding disclosure and which would require the issue of disclosure of the information to be placed before the court.

---

1. The equivalent legislation in Northern Ireland is s 51A of the Judicature (Northern Ireland) Act 1978 and art 118 of the Magistrates' Courts (Northern Ireland) Order 1981.

OTHER DISCLOSURE

DISCLOSURE PRIOR TO INITIAL DISCLOSURE

55 Investigators must always be alive to the potential need to reveal and prosecutors to the potential need to disclose material, in the interests of justice and fairness in the particular circumstances of any case, after the commencement of proceedings but before their duty arises under the Act. For instance, disclosure ought to be made of significant information that might affect a bail decision or that might enable the defence to contest the committal proceedings.

56 Where the need for such disclosure is not apparent to the prosecutor, any disclosure will depend on what the accused chooses to reveal about the defence. Clearly, such disclosure will not exceed that which is obtainable after the statutory duties of disclosure arise.

SUMMARY TRIAL

57 The prosecutor should, in addition to complying with the obligations under the Act, provide to the defence all evidence upon which the Crown proposes to rely in a summary trial. Such provision should allow the accused and their legal advisers sufficient time properly to consider the evidence before it is called.

MATERIAL RELEVANT TO SENTENCE

58 In all cases the prosecutor must consider disclosing in the interests of justice any material, which is relevant to sentence (eg information which might mitigate the seriousness of the offence or assist the accused to lay blame in part upon a co-accused or another person).

POST-CONVICTION

59 The interests of justice will also mean that where material comes to light after the conclusion of the proceedings, which might cast doubt upon the safety of the conviction, there is a duty to consider disclosure. Any such material should be brought immediately to the attention of line management.

60 Disclosure of any material that is made outside the ambit of Act will attract confidentiality by virtue of *Taylor v SFO* (1998).

APPLICABILITY OF THESE GUIDELINES

61 Although the relevant obligations in relation to unused material and disclosure imposed on the prosecutor and the accused are determined by the date on which the investigation began, these Guidelines should be adopted with immediate effect in relation to all cases submitted to the prosecuting authorities in receipt of these Guidelines save where they specifically refer to the statutory or Code provisions of the Criminal Justice Act 2003 that do not yet apply to the particular case.

1–7760

Criminal Case Management Framework
Second Edition

CONTENTS

---

1. Page references in the Route Maps refer to the Framework as originally published by the DCA.

FOREWORD

The Right Honourable The Lord Woolf, The Lord Chief Justice of England and Wales

Foreword to the 1st Edition

The just determination of criminal cases requires methodical and thorough preparation. Where a trial is needed, there must be a fair opportunity for the prosecution and the defence to present their evidence in a manner which is consistent with the interests of justice.

The newly appointed Criminal Procedure Rules Committee met for the first time on 29 June 2004 and, as soon as practicable, after its rule making powers are brought into force, the Committee will produce a modern procedural code for the criminal courts. This Framework is published in advance of the Rules, but is consistent with the overall objective of the Rules; its purpose is to provide guidance to those who are engaged in any criminal case, as to their functions and as to what the court will expect of them at the various stages of a case. Compliance with the principles of the Framework may involve a change in culture on behalf of some of those engaged in the preparation and conduct of trials, but this is necessary if the modern procedural code is to take effect quickly.

The Framework is based on practices developed by the police, Crown Prosecution Service, lawyers and the courts. It is supported in decisions of the Court of Appeal Criminal Division and supplemented by the work of the Effective Trial Management Team established by the DCA, the Attorney General and Home Office. Its drafting has been a considerable task in which the judiciary have been actively involved.

I am very encouraged to learn that at the same time as the drafting work has been proceeding, work has been done in developing an IT specification for a case progression system to support the Framework. It will be essential to the operation of the Framework that such an IT system is provided as soon as possible.

It is hoped that the Framework will lead to a clearer understanding of what should be done so that cases are prepared appropriately and can be brought to a conclusion with efficiency, the minimum of delay and without adjournments.

The key to the success of the Framework and the new procedural code will be the co-operation of the different agencies involved in the criminal justice system and of the legal profession and the acceptance of (*a*) active pre-trial case management by the court, (*b*) listing suited to local conditions and (*c*) tight control of the conduct of the trial itself. The prosecution, the defence and the public will benefit from this.

The principles upon which the judiciary will approach these issues can be summarised as follows:

A. Pre-trial case management

1. The court, with the assistance of the prosecution and the defence, will actively manage all criminal cases and apply the relevant statutes, rules, and practice directions.
2. The court will expect the participants to prepare and conduct each case properly and in accordance with the relevant statutes, rules, and practice directions.
3. At each hearing the participants must expect, and be prepared for, the court to:
   (*a*) enquire into the progress of the case and compliance with orders or directions of the court and make appropriate orders in relation to any failure to prepare or conduct the case properly;
   (*b*) set a timetable for the preparation, trial and completion of the case;
   (*c*) enquire into and take action in relation to any hearing which is wholly or partly ineffective or unnecessary;
   (*d*) make orders and directions in accordance with its duty actively to manage the case (such orders and directions may add to or differ from the steps for which this Framework provides);
   (*e*) enquire whether the prosecution has reviewed the charges and are satisfied that they remain appropriate and that the defendant has been properly advised in relation to credit for pleas of guilty and the consequences of failing to attend court when required to do so;
   (*f*) direct the issue of a bench warrant not backed for bail if the defendant does not attend;
   (*g*) continue with the hearing in the absence of the defendant where appropriate;
   (*h*) deal summarily with issues arising under s 6 of the Bail Act 1976.
4. Between each hearing the participants must be prepared for the court to monitor the progress of the case and to call any party to account (by listing the case for hearing or otherwise) for any failure to comply with any order, direction, statute, rule, or practice direction or any other failure to prepare or conduct the case properly.
5. Participants must expect the court to deal with any failure to prepare or conduct the case properly by the imposition of such sanction, costs order, or penalty as permitted by statute, rule, or practice direction.
6. Subject to statute, rule, or practice direction currently in force, the pre-trial procedure at a Crown Court will be decided by the Resident Judge at that court and from April 2005 the pre-trial procedure at a magistrates' court will be decided by the judicial members of the Justices' Issues Group (or until its establishment by the Chairman of the Bench and the Justices' Clerk).
7. Nothing in these principles affects the obligation of the participants actively to co-operate with each other and with the court in the efficient and effective management and conduct of cases.

B. Listing

8. The Resident Judge at each Crown Court and the judicial members of the Justices Issues Group for each magistrates' court within its area will respectively determine the listing practices for that court or area and direct, in liaison with the listing officer, the listing so as to ensure that, as far as possible, all cases are brought to a hearing or trial with the minimum of delay and in accordance with the interests of justice, heard by an appropriate judge or bench and that the available judiciary is fully and effectively deployed, consistent with the needs of the witnesses of the prosecution and the defence.

9. The Resident Judge and the Justices Issues Group will ensure that interested parties have an opportunity to make representations about listing practices and will take into account any representations which may from time to time be made.

C. Trial Management

10. The court will actively manage all criminal trials.

11. The judiciary is entitled to expect that all persons in custody will be produced at court sufficiently in advance of the hearing. At each trial the advocates must expect, and be prepared for, the court to:

    (a) start the case promptly without the advocates needing time to take instructions or confer with each other (as this must be done beforehand);
    (b) ensure that defendants in custody and on bail arrive at the court on time;
    (c) investigate any failure to comply with pre-trial directions;
    (d) require, no later than the outset of the trial, the identification of the issues in the case;
    (e) focus the conduct of the trial on the issues in the case;
    (f) require for consideration by the court, where appropriate, a timetable for the case until its conclusion;
    (g) require prompt notification of any changes in the timetable;
    (h) make the participants adhere to the timetable approved by the court (subject to any issues that may arise) and to take such action as may be necessary to ensure that the trial is conducted so that it concludes within the time allowed;
    (i) require the provision of skeleton arguments for any points of law in advance of the hearing and to ensure that any oral submissions are made with economy;
    (j) curtail any examination or cross-examination submission or speech that is protracted or repetitive or oppressive.

12. "Court" in these principles and in the Framework means judges, recorders, magistrates, district judges, and legal advisers exercising delegated powers.

I earnestly hope that everyone will embrace the principles which underpin this guidance. They will greatly improve the criminal justice process and encourage the more constructive involvement of those involved, for the benefit of the whole community.

Foreword to the 2nd Edition

The purpose of the Framework is to provide a clearer understanding of what should be done at each stage of the trial process, so that cases are prepared appropriately and can be brought to a conclusion with efficiency, the minimum of delay and without adjournments.

The Framework complements Part 3 of the Criminal Procedure Rules on case management. The first edition of the Framework, which I jointly issued with the Attorney General, Lord Falconer and Baroness Scotland in July 2004, was produced with the Rules in mind and this revision has been updated to reflect the changes arising from the introduction of the Rules on 4 April 2005.

The Rules introduce a new set of case management forms, which are set out in my Practice Direction on Criminal Case Management. This direction and the case progression forms to which this direction refers are the product of work carried out over several months by a group of Committee members and others chaired by Lord Justice Hooper (a team who owe an enormous debt of gratitude to the late Lord Justice Kay).

The Rules represent a blueprint for transforming our venerable Criminal Justice System that has served us for centuries, into a system which is appropriate for the 21st century. Their implementation has required a vast amount of effort and co-operation from all those engaged in the CJS including the Department for Constitutional Affairs, the Home Office, the Attorney General's Office, practitioners from both sides of the profession and all those who are concerned with the welfare of victims and witnesses of crime.

The new Criminal Procedure Rules make it explicit that the judiciary are to be responsible for case management and, for the first time, gave the judiciary the necessary powers which apply to the Crown Court and the magistrates' court.

Case Management is already an established part of the civil and criminal justice systems. However, the extent to which cases were managed previously in the criminal part of the system has very much depended upon the individual judge. From 4 April 2005 this changed, Judges are now required to exercise an extensive managerial role at the Plea and Case Management Hearing (PCMH) which is to take place in every case.

In addition to the introduction of the Rules the section of the Crown Court Manual dealing with listing in the Crown and magistrates' courts has been revised and updated. The changes made emphasise the fact that the Judge will make firm arrangements for the listing of cases at the Plea and Case Management Hearing and that the parties must comply with the directions and timetable then set so that cases are ready to be heard in accordance with that timetable. This helps to support the Rules and the new case management regime.

I earnestly hope that everyone will embrace the principles that underpin this guidance and the new case management regime. I hope they will greatly improve the criminal justice process and encourage the more constructive involvement of all those involved.

Secretary of State for Constitutional Affairs and Lord Chancellor, Attorney General and Fiona Mactaggart

The aim of the Criminal Justice System (CJS) is to convict the guilty and acquit the innocent and through doing this to reduce the number of victims. This requires thorough investigations, accurate charging decisions, effective prosecutions and defence services, and robust case management.

We have made good progress in improving performance in these areas, for example:

— CPS Duty Prosecutors have been placed in police stations throughout England and Wales to make sure that accurate charging decisions are made;

— we have introduced dedicated Witness Care Units through the No Witness No Justice Project which bring together police and the CPS to meet the needs of individual victims and witnesses and;

— the Criminal Procedure Rules 2005, along with the Lord Chief Justice's Consolidated Criminal Practice Direction, set out new measures to manage cases more effectively through the system.

This revised Framework brings together these initiatives in one document. Developed by practitioners, with local practitioners in mind, it provides local areas with operational guidance on case management good practice. We encourage each criminal justice area to consider the contents of this issue and make what further changes consistent with the Framework are required to their locally produced frameworks.

We believe this Framework will promote the spread of national practice across areas, provide court users with more consistency and higher levels of service. We commend it to you.

INTRODUCTION

1. Outlined below is important information for those using this Framework. It explains what the Framework *is* and equally important what it *isn't*. It describes how the Framework has been produced and updated and who was involved in these processes. Overall, it provides the necessary context for someone to use the Framework.

What is the "Criminal Case Management Framework"?

2. Put simply the Framework is a guide. It provides operational practitioners with guidance on how cases might be managed most effectively and efficiently from pre-charge through to conclusion. It describes case management procedures and the roles and responsibilities of administrative staff operating those procedures, and of the defence. It also sets out the expectations of the judiciary.

3. The Framework has been produced to complement the commencement of the Criminal Procedure Rules on 4 April 2005. Part 3 of the Rules for the first time gives courts explicit powers to manage the progression of criminal cases and the Rules are complemented by this Framework. The Framework was first issued on 21 July 2004, and has now been updated to take account of the Rules. The Rules also introduce provisions set out in the Criminal Justice Act 2003 and the Courts Act 2003 – namely new provisions for prosecution appeals, bad character, hearsay, and binding rulings in the magistrates' courts.

4. To be comprehensive, the Framework also includes references to Statutory Charging and for witness management that are being delivered through the Criminal Case Management Programme.

5. The Framework covers **adult cases** only. **It does not cover cases involving youth offenders**.

6. The first edition of the Framework applied only to those cases that were prosecuted by the CPS; however, this revision covers **all adult prosecutions** in the magistrates' and Crown Court, as set out in the Criminal Procedure Rules 2005[1]. A separate Framework dedicated to the Youth Court is currently being produced and will be available in Spring 2006.

7. The Framework does not cover every possible activity needed for a case to achieve a just and efficient outcome. First, the Framework addresses issues of case management only. So, for example, the Framework covers the case management role of advocates but does not cover the advocacy process itself. The same can be said for the roles of other practitioners. Secondly, where there is an established existing source of guidance this is not replicated in the Framework but instead a reference is made. So the Framework must be read in conjunction with, and does not replace, other professional standards (eg the Bar's Code of Conduct, Farquharson Guidelines), and other national and local guidelines (eg guidance on the prioritisation of cases involving child witnesses).

8. For completeness, appeals to the Court of Appeal are included in the route map, although they are not described in the detail of the Framework.

---

1. Criminal Procedure Rules 2005, Part 2.1(1)(*a*).

---

9. The Framework has not been designed to be read from cover to cover. On first glance the Framework might appear quite repetitive. This is because each section has been designed to stand alone, to allow the reader to see the full picture at each part of the process, without having to cross reference to other sections.

10. Where the Framework refers to 'he' or 'him' this should be read as meaning 'he or she' or 'him or her'.

What are the main changes in this revision?
11. This edition of the Framework incorporates the following changes:

(a) A new Part A on 'Pre-charge consideration (diversion from prosecution)'[1], which sets out the preliminary process by which prosecutors consider diversion from prosecution as an alternative to charging (a process known as Conditional Cautioning).
(b) Changes in procedure as a result of the introduction of the Criminal Procedure Rules 2005, including Part 3 of the Rules on case management. Extracts from the Rules have been replicated in full (in blue text) for the assistance and information of practitioners.
(c) Developments in Statutory Charging and No Witness No Justice.
(d) Additional developing policy areas, such as bail and defendant attendance recommendations arising from the OCJR Defendant Attendance Steering Group.
(e) Principles relating to the listing of cases in the magistrates' and Crown Court. Annex A contains an extract from Section 14 of the Crown Court Manual on the 'Listing of Cases' which is issued under and with the authority of the Lord Chief Justice.

How was the first Framework produced?
12. A criminal justice group has brought together a wide range of personal experience and practice from local areas, including lessons learned from the early test areas for the Effective Trial Management Programme, and documented this in the Criminal Case Management Framework.
13. To ensure that the views of all those involved in case management are considered, the criminal justice group had a wide membership including operational practitioners, defence, judiciary, (Crown Court and Magistrates' Association), Justices' Clerks Society, Criminal Justice Act Implementation Team, Criminal Procedure Rules Committee Secretariat, and officials from the Department for Constitutional Affairs, CPS and Home Office. The senior judiciary has been regularly consulted and the Framework has been reviewed with them.

---

1. Conditional Cautioning was introduced in the Criminal Justice Act 2003, ss 22–27 and at present is operational in a limited number of early implementation sites.

How has the second edition been produced?
14. For the second edition of the Framework, the criminal justice group and the senior judiciary have again been consulted on the updates and additions that have been included in this revision.
15. The Lord Chief Justice and the Attorney General, Lord Falconer and Fiona Mactaggart have welcomed the Criminal Case Management Framework; their support is underlined in the Foreword to this document.

How will the Framework be used?
16. The Framework can be used by individual practitioners who are encouraged to consider its guidance and to adopt those practices that they consider would help to improve performance.
17. Additionally, each local criminal justice area will be asked to compare their locally produced Frameworks against the revisions contained in this edition of the Framework and make what further changes consistent with the Framework are required to the local case management and other practices of the defence, criminal justice agencies and other participants. Local areas will have already started this work in their consideration of the implementation of those provisions of the Criminal Justice Act 2003, the Criminal Procedure Rules 2005 and the supporting Practice Direction. Resident Judges and magistrates will locally decide, within the parameters set by the Criminal Procedure Rules and the Consolidated Criminal Practice Direction, whether changes should be made to court practices and, if so, what they should be. In doing so they will consider the Framework and representations from the defence, criminal justice agencies and other participants to help inform their decisions. The Effective Trial Management Programme (ETMP) Team has provided support to each criminal justice area during the planning and customisation stages through a range of activities eg by providing guidance, facilitating local workshops and discussions. All areas have commenced their implementation and ETMP Area Co-ordinators will continue their support through this and the evaluation stages, which in addition, will include providing advice on good practice and emerging developments from other areas.

How does the Framework work?
18. The Framework follows case management through the whole of the criminal justice process. It starts with pre-charge consideration, where prosecutors have the opportunity to consider a diversion from Prosecution, where appropriate. It then sets out pre-charge activities, the charge, the magistrates' courts and Crown Court process and concludes with the sentence or other outcome. It is recognised that some residual action may take place, eg drug trafficking and proceeds of crime hearings.
19. The Framework consists of:

— **a route map**, which highlights the key steps in the case management process:
  • Each key step in the process is represented by a box on the route map and given a page number that relates to the relevant section of the detailed guidance itself.
  • Each step outlines the activity to be undertaken and completed up to and including that point. Cases should not proceed to the next step in the process until this work is completed. The route map is not intended to reflect the length of time between each step of the process, eg although trial and sentence are shown as separate processes, they can occur on the same day.

- For ease of reference there are three separate route maps, one each for guilty plea and not guilty plea non traffic cases and one for traffic cases.
- **detailed guidance** on each key step describing:
  - The overall goal for that step in the criminal justice process.
  - Objectives – these set out what separate outcomes are expected in order to achieve the goal for that step.
  - Actions – these set out what needs to be done in order to achieve the objectives and the goal for each step. Each action is then separately identified and the detail of what has to be delivered to complete the action is set out below the relevant section.
  - Case Progression Roles and Responsibilities – this section sets out the roles and responsibilities of administrative staff and of the defence and advocates.

These are not listed in chronological order and can be used as a checklist by practitioners.

20. A practitioner can use the route map or the table of contents quickly to find the part of the detail that he or she requires.

Case Progression

21. The Criminal Procedure Rules[1] sets out the duties of Case Progression Officers:

1. At the beginning of the case each party must, unless the court otherwise directs:
   (a) nominate an individual responsible for progressing that case; and
   (b) tell other parties and the court who he is and how to contact him.

2. In fulfilling its duty under rule 3.2, the court must where appropriate:
   (a) nominate a court officer responsible for progressing the case; and
   (b) make sure the parties know who he is and how to contact him.

3. In this Part a person nominated under this rule is called a case progression officer.

4. A case progression officer must:
   (i) monitor compliance with directions;
   (ii) make sure that the court is kept informed of events that may affect the progress of that case;
   (iii) make sure that he can be contacted promptly about the case during ordinary business hours;
   (iv) act promptly and reasonably in response to communications about the case; and
   (v) if he will be unavailable, appoint a substitute to fulfill his duties and inform the other case progression officers.

22. Further guidance on the role of Case Progression officers can be obtained by contacting your local ETMP Area Co-ordinator and found in section 2 of the ETMP Implementation and Evaluation Toolkit, 'Case Progression Officers and Human Resource Activities'. The Toolkit is issued by ETMP to assist local areas and gives practical examples of tasks that Case Progression Officers should be undertaking as part of their everyday duties.

Further information

23. An electronic version of the Framework and details on who should be contacted for information about it are available on www.cjsonline.gov.uk/framework

---

1. Criminal Procedure Rules 2005 rule 3.4.

Abbreviations and definitions

Advance Information Further detail on the provision of advance information can be found in the Manual of Guidance

Bail Bail in all criminal proceedings is to be granted in accordance with the Bail Act 1976 as amended. At the point of charge the defendant should be given a leaflet entitled 'So you got bail' which sets out the importance of complying with bail conditions and the consequences of failing to do so.

Bench warrants For guidance on the issue and execution of warrants please refer to GDC9 (Guidance on How to Report the New FTA Warrant Enforcement Targets), GDC10 (Clarification on How to measure out of area FTA Warrants) and GDC11 (Failure to Appear Warrant Enforcement Standard) – copies available upon request from FTAWarrants@cjs.gsi.gov.uk

Contact Directory The Contact Directory will outline a range of options that will be used by the Witness Care Officers

Cautions Alternatives to prosecution for adult suspects include a simple caution and a Conditional Caution

Simple caution – A simple caution should only be given if the public interest justifies it and in accordance with Home Office guidelines. Where it is felt that such a caution is appropriate, crown prosecutors must inform the police so they can caution the suspect. If the caution is not administered, because the suspect refuses to accept it, a crown prosecutor may review the case again

Conditional Caution – Conditional Cautions are a new disposal introduced in the Criminal Justice Act 2003. A Conditional Caution may be appropriate where a crown prosecutor considers that while the public interest justifies a prosecution, the interests of the suspect, victim and community may be better served by the suspect complying with suitable conditions aimed at rehabilitation or reparation. These may include restorative processes

CC Crown Court

Conditional Cautioning Conditional Cautioning was introduced in the Criminal Justice Act 2003, ss 22–27 and at present is operational in a limited number of early implementation sites

CPS/PSR pack CPS/PSR pack will normally consist of the charge sheet or summons (MG4), the case summary, if appropriate (MG5), previous behaviour whilst on bail (MG8), relevant witness statements (MG11), records of interviews (MG15) or short descriptive notes (MG15), TIC sheets, if available (MG18) and previous convictions where appropriate

Committal hearing A procedure in the magistrates' court where, in eitherway cases, the defendant is committed to stand his or her trial in the Crown Court, provided the court is satisfied on the evidence that the defendant has a case to answer

CJS Criminal justice system

CPIA Criminal Procedure and Investigations Act 1996

CPO Case progression officer

Conclusion The conclusion of a case whether a defendant is convicted or acquitted

Criminal Case Management Programme The Criminal Case Management Programme brings together three major elements of Criminal Justice reform: Statutory Charging, the Effective Trial Management Programme and No Witness, No Justice

Crown prosecutor Crown prosecutors are responsible for reviewing and, where appropriate, prosecuting criminal cases following investigation by the police. They also advise the police on matters relating to criminal cases. In each case reviewed the prosecutor will consider whether there is sufficient evidence and, if so, whether the public interest requires a prosecution. Although crown prosecutors work closely with the police they are responsible to The Crown Prosecution Service, an independent governmental organisation

Disclosure (Prosecution) Authorities relating to disclosure for the prosecution are:

— Part 1, Criminal Procedure and Investigations Act 1996 and for investigations begun on or after 4th April 2005 the 1996 Act as amended by the relevant provisions in Part 5 of Criminal Justice Act 2003
— Attorney General's Guidelines on Disclosure 2005
— Police-CPS Joint Operational Instructions on disclosure

Disclosure (Defence) Authorities relating to disclosure for the defence are:

— Part 1 Criminal Procedure and Investigations Act 1996 and for investigations begun on or after 4 April 2005, the 1996 Act as amended by the relevant provisions of Part 5, Criminal Justice Act 2003, CPI Act 1996 (Defence Disclosure Time Limits) Regulations 1997 (SI 1997 No 684)
— Attorney General's Guidelines on Disclosure 2005

DCW Designated caseworker. DCWs are CPS staff, who are not lawyers, but who are permitted to undertake all work in magistrates' courts other than trials, proofs in absence in either-way cases, committals and sendings, pre-trial reviews, Newton hearings and contested bail hearings

Director's Guidance on Charging Issued by the Director of Public Prosecutions under section 37 A (1) (*a*) of the Police and Criminal Evidence Act 1984, as inserted by the Criminal Justice Act 2003, and being brought into effect on an area basis

DNA Guidance The DNA Guidance is available locally and on the ACPO and CPS intranets

Duty Prosecutor CPS deploy Duty Prosecutors to operational police units. They provide guidance and advice to investigators and make charging decisions. In addition, an out of hours service will operate nationally through CPS Direct. A Duty Prosecutor is not defined in law but is anyone fulfilling the charging duties as set out in the DPP Guidance on Charging

EAH Early Administrative Hearing. The first hearing of a case in the magistrates' court in which a not guilty plea is anticipated, or the case is indictable and must be sent immediately to the Crown Court

EFH Early First Hearing. The first hearing of a case in the magistrates' court in which a guilty plea is anticipated

Either-way cases Offences that can be tried either in the magistrates' court or the Crown Court

Evidential file Please see Annex B, Content of Expedited and Evidential Charging Decision Reports and Case File

Evidential requirements The Threshold Test requires crown prosecutors to decide whether there is at least a reasonable suspicion that the suspect has committed an offence, and if there is, whether it is in the public interest to charge that suspect. The Threshold Test is applied to those cases in which it would not be appropriate to release a suspect on bail after charge, but the evidence to apply the Full Code Test is not yet available

Expedited file Please see Annex B, Content of Expedited and Evidential Charging Decision Reports and Case File

Full Code Test The Full Code Test has two stages. The first stage is consideration of the evidence. If the case does not pass the evidential stage it must not go ahead no matter how important or serious it may be. If the case does pass the evidential stage, crown prosecutors must proceed to the second stage and decide if a prosecution is needed in the public interest

Full file Please see Annex B, Content of Expedited and Evidential Charging Decision Reports and Case File

G Guilty plea

Indictable-only cases Offences which can only be tried in the Crown Court

Manual of Guidance Information on the contents of case files can be found in Section 1 of the Manual of Guidance – A Guide to Case Building

MC Magistrates' court

MOT Mode of Trial. A procedure in the magistrates' court where, in either-way cases a not guilty plea or no plea is indicated, a decision is made as to whether the trial is to take place in the magistrates' court or Crown Court, depending upon seriousness

Newton hearing (NH) This is held when a defendant admits his or her guilt but disputes the prosecution version of events and the court needs to determine the basis on which the defendant is to be sentenced. In the Crown Court, Newton hearings are held by a judge alone

NG Not guilty plea

Non-specified offences Those traffic offences not included in The Prosecution of Offences Act 1985 (Specified Proceedings) Order 1999, SI 1999/904 made under the provisions of s 3(3) Prosecution of Offences Act 1985

PCMH Plea and case management hearing. A procedure in the Crown Court at which a defendant is required to enter his or her plea and the judge may makes directions as to the progress of the case

PBV Plea before venue. A procedure in the magistrates' court where, in an either-way case, a defendant is given the opportunity to indicate his or her likely plea

Preliminary hearing Where the court so determines, this may be the first hearing of an indictable only case prior to the PCMH at the Crown Court

Prosecution rights of appeal Prosecution rights of appeal only apply to cases tried on indictment. The prosecution may appeal a ruling by a judge in relation to a trial, that is made at any time until the start of the judge's summing up and the ruling relates to one or more offences in the indictment. An appeal may be made against a ruling which in effect terminates the proceedings for that offence. When considering any such appeal, prosecutors must follow the CPS Legal Guidance

PYO Persistent Young Offender. This is a young person aged 10–17 years who has been sentenced by any criminal court in the UK on three or more occasions for one or more recordable offences and within three years of the last sentencing occasion is subsequently arrested or has an information laid against him or her for a further recordable offence

s 6(1) readout committal A magistrates' court enquiry into an offence as examining justices on consideration of the evidence

s 11(2) Magistrates' Courts Act 1980 The provision whereby a court can proceed in the absence of an accused when a summons has been issued and duly served and such service can be proved

s 12 Magistrates' Courts Act 1980 Cases are those cases in which the prosecution decide to invoke the "guilty plea by post" procedure under s 12 Magistrates' Court Act 1980

s 51 Indictable only cases sent from the magistrates' court directly to the Crown Court under s 51 of the Crime and Disorder Act 1998

Special measures Measures which can be put in place to provide protection and/or anonymity to a witness (eg a screen separating witness from the accused)

Specified offences Specified offences are those so specified in the Prosecution of Offences Act 1985 (Specified Proceedings) Order 1999, SI 1999/904 made under the provisions of s 3(3) Prosecution of Offences Act 1985

SR – Special reasons Where a defendant wishes to argue that there are 'special reasons' why he or she should not be disqualified from driving or why his or her driving licence or record should not be endorsed with penalty points. In the Crown Court, special reasons hearings are held by a judge alone

Summary cases Offences that can only be tried in the magistrates' courts

Transfer Cases under s 53 Criminal Justice Act 1991 involving charges of sexual offences and offences involving violence or cruelty concerning children, whereby the DPP has served a notice of Transfer at which stage the functions of the magistrates cease save in relation to bail and reporting restrictions and public funding (formerly known as 'legal aid') . Section 53 Criminal Justice Act 1991 will be repealed by ss. 41 and 332, Schedule 3 para 62(1) and (2) of the Criminal Justice Act 2003 (**when commenced**) (allocation/sending of cases) and transfers under s 4 Criminal Justice Act 1987. All transfer proceedings will be replaced by the unified sending procedure under schedule 3 Criminal Justice Act 2003

Threshold Test The Threshold Test requires crown prosecutors to decide whether there is at least a reasonable suspicion that the suspect has committed an offence, and if there is, whether it is in the public interest to charge that suspect. The Threshold Test is applied to those cases in which it would not be appropriate to release a suspect on bail after charge, but the evidence to apply the Full Code Test is not yet available

Trial by Crown Court judge alone Provisions for trial by Crown Court judge alone are contained within the Criminal Justice Act 2003 (in relation to certain cases of fraud and jury intimidation) and in the Domestic Violence, Crime and Victims Act 2004 (in relation to counts which are samples of other counts upon which a jury has convicted)

Witness Care Units Where Witness Care Units are not established the roles and responsibilities will be delivered by the prosecution team, subject to local agreement

1-7762 Key to page numbers used in the Route Maps

The Route Map – Guilty plea cases (non-traffic)

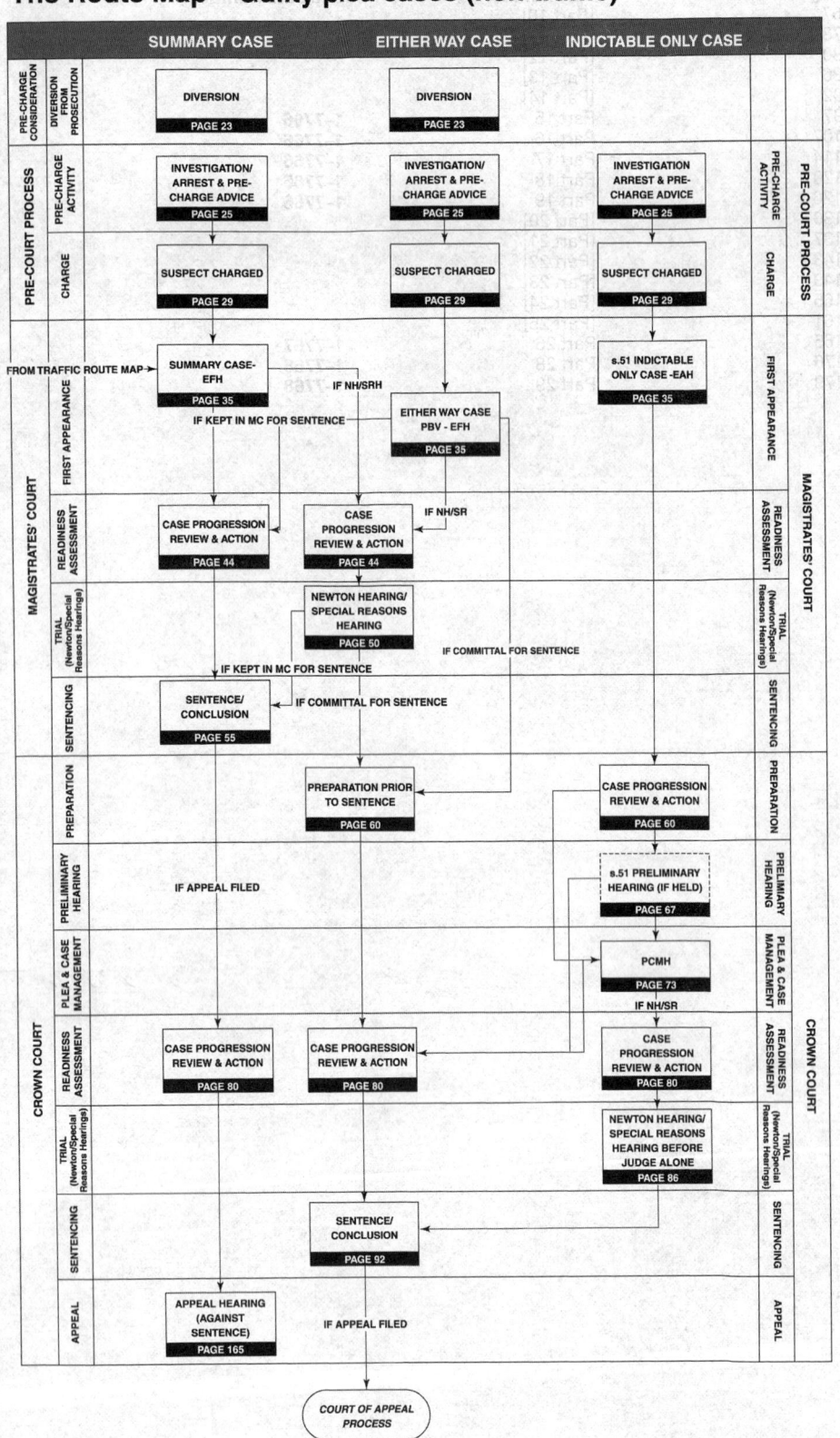

The Route Map – Not guilty plea cases (non-traffic)

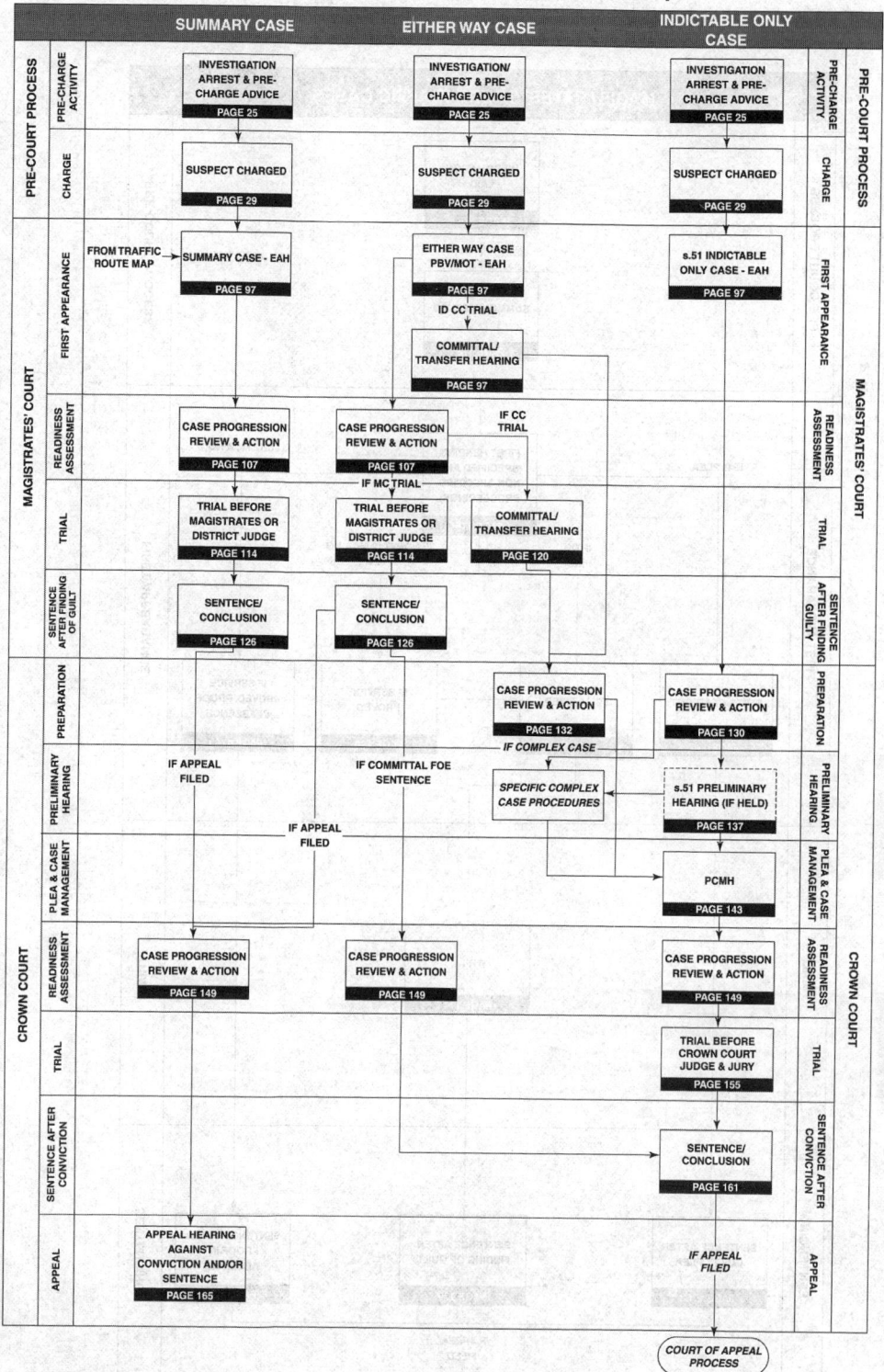

NOTE: PLEAS MAY CHANGE TO GUILTY AT ANY STAGE IN WHICH CASE REFER TO APPROPRIATE STEP OF THE GUILTY PLEA ROUTE MAP

The Route Map – Traffic cases

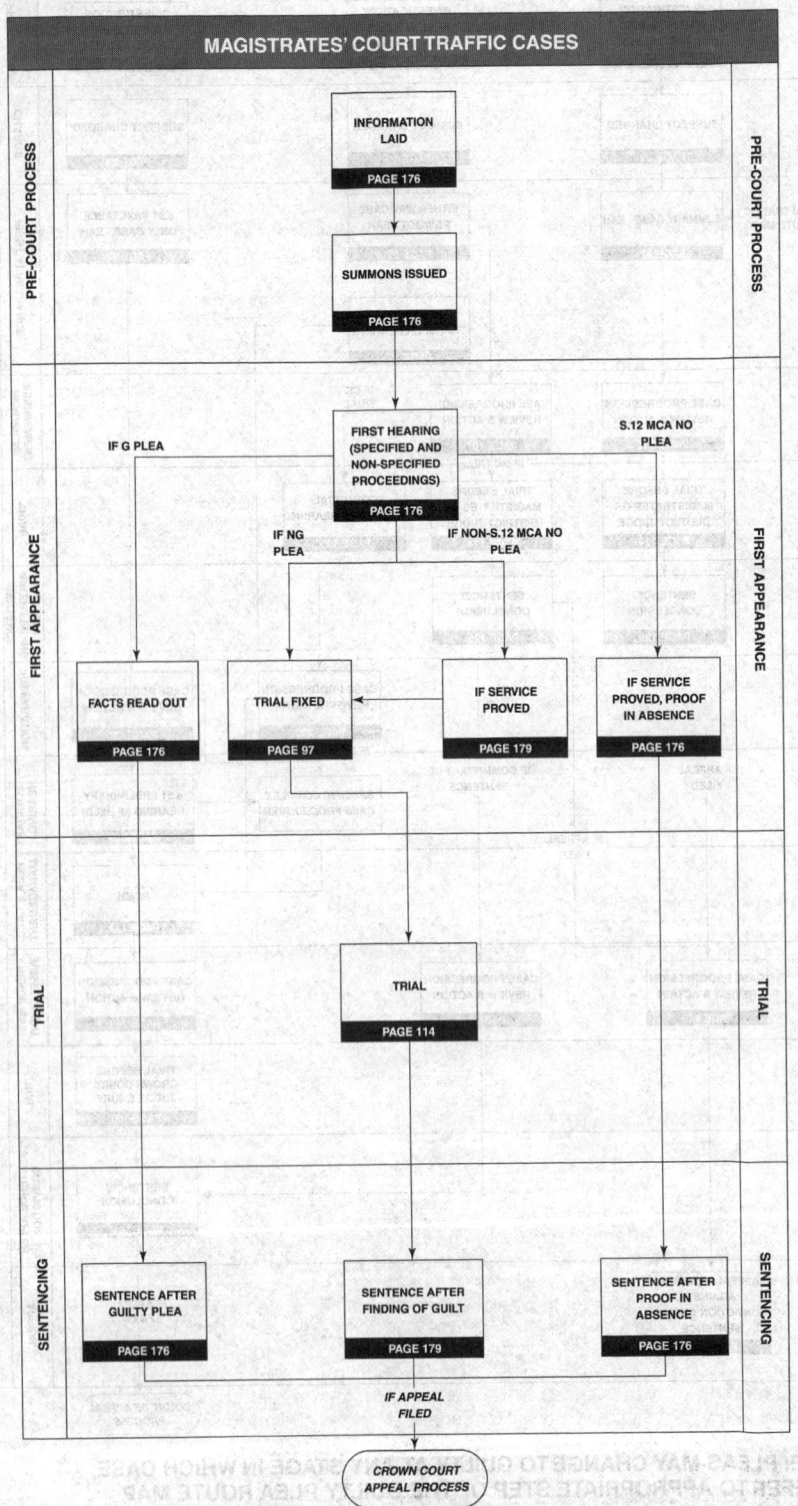

MAGISTRATES' COURT TRAFFIC CASES

PRE-COURT PROCESS

INFORMATION LAID
PAGE 176

SUMMONS ISSUED
PAGE 176

FIRST APPEARANCE

FIRST HEARING (SPECIFIED AND NON-SPECIFIED PROCEEDINGS)
PAGE 176

IF G PLEA

S.12 MCA NO PLEA

IF NG PLEA

IF NON-S.12 MCA NO PLEA

FACTS READ OUT
PAGE 176

TRIAL FIXED
PAGE 97

IF SERVICE PROVED
PAGE 179

IF SERVICE PROVED, PROOF IN ABSENCE
PAGE 176

TRIAL

TRIAL
PAGE 114

SENTENCING

SENTENCE AFTER GUILTY PLEA
PAGE 176

SENTENCE AFTER FINDING OF GUILT
PAGE 179

SENTENCE AFTER PROOF IN ABSENCE
PAGE 176

IF APPEAL FILED

CROWN COURT APPEAL PROCESS

1–7763

PRE-CHARGE CONSIDERATION

PART A PRE-CHARGE CONSIDERATION (DIVERSION FROM PROSECUTION)

The preliminary process by which custody officers and crown prosecutors consider diversion from prosecution as an alternative to charging

Objective

A.1 (a) To ensure the early identification and consideration of diversion from prosecution is undertaken in all appropriate cases in accordance with the Home Office Circular on Cautioning and The Director's Guidance on Conditional Cautioning

Action – bail cases

A.2 Investigation and arrest Wherever possible, investigation will be undertaken prior to, or soon after, arrest to ensure that the evidential requirements will be met when the case is considered for diversion

A.3 Consideration of diversion by custody officer In all cases where the threshold test is met, the custody officer will consider the appropriateness of diversion from prosecution, prior to referring the case to a prosecutor for a charging decision, or proceeding to charge

A.4 Referral to a crown prosecutor where Conditional Cautioning is to be considered Where an indictable only case appears suitable for a simple caution, or where a Conditional Caution appears appropriate, the case will be referred to a prosecutor in accordance with The Director's Guidance on Conditional Cautioning

A.5 Diversion Where the custody officer considers the case suitable for a simple caution (case which is not indictable only), he will proceed to make arrangements for the caution to be administered. Where a crown prosecutor notifies a custody officer that a case is suitable for a Conditional Caution and confirms the conditions to be complied with, the custody officer will make arrangements for the Conditional Caution to be administered

A.6 Failure to comply

(a) Where it appears to a custody officer or authorised person[1], that the conditions of any Conditional Caution have not been complied with, the case will be referred back to a crown prosecutor who will decide (in accordance with The Director's Guidance on Charging and the Code for Crown Prosecutors) whether or not the person is to be charged for the original offence

(b) Where a person declines a caution (simple or Conditional) or does not attend to be cautioned the case will be referred back to a crown prosecutor who will decide (in accordance with The Director's Guidance on Charging and the Code for Crown Prosecutors) whether or not the person is to be charged for the original offence

Case progression roles and responsibilities

A.7 Prosecution Team (a) Following charge the case will progress in accordance with Part 5 of this Framework

---

1. Section 22 Criminal Justice Act 2003 and para 12.2 of The Director's Guidance on Conditional Cautioning – the authorised person is the person who administers the caution and is defined by the Act. It can be a police officer or any other person authorised by the Director of Public Prosecutions.

1–7764

PRE-COURT PROCESS

PART 1 PRE-CHARGE ACTIVITY (CHARGING DECISIONS MADE BY CROWN PROSECUTORS)

The preparatory process by crown prosecutors to consider the evidence and the appropriate charge

Objectives

1.1

(a) To ensure that an effective early advice resource is available to investigators through the deployment of duty prosecutors and through the allocation of individual or specialist prosecutors in appropriate cases

(b) To ensure that charging decisions are made in accordance with The Director's Guidance on Charging and the Code for Crown Prosecutors

(c) To utilise a period of pre-charge bail in appropriate cases to gather the evidence required to meet the full test set out in the Code for Crown Prosecutors

(d) To ensure the early identification and termination of non-viable cases

(e) To consider victims' and witnesses' needs at the earliest opportunity

Actions

1.2 Investigation and arrest Wherever possible, investigation will be undertaken prior to, or soon after, arrest to ensure that the evidential requirements of the report to the crown prosecutor can be met where the suspect is in custody

1.3 Early consultation with Crown Prosecution Service (CPS) Early consultations, in cases referable to crown prosecutors for charging decisions, will be undertaken to identify those cases likely to proceed and to form an early view as to the appropriate charges and the evidence that will be required to support them or whether the case is suitable for caution or Conditional Caution

1.4 Case building on pre-charge bail Following early consultations a period of pre-charge bail with/without conditions will be utilised to obtain the evidence specified in the MG3 Action Plan. The case will then be referred to the prosecutor for a charging decision. Where it is clear from the outset that the defendant will contest the allegations, a Manual of Guidance full file will be completed where possible for the first hearing

1.5 Charging decision Charging decisions will be made following a review of evidence in cases and will be in accordance with The Director's Guidance on Charging and applying the appropriate test set out in the Code for Crown Prosecutors

Case Progression Roles and Responsibilities

1.6 Prosecution Team

(a) Whenever an arrest occurs or an investigation commences, the police will ensure that where the charging decision is one that must be undertaken by a crown prosecutor, an early consultation with a duty prosecutor will take place

(b) CPS will ensure that investigators have access to duty prosecutors or individual allocated or specialist prosecutors in appropriate cases

(c) Ensure that third party material is properly considered as part of the investigation

(d) Appoint a CPIA disclosure officer in the case to consider all disclosure issues including third party material

(e) Consider any expert evidence required

(f) Where it is clear that a case will proceed to a prosecution and will be contested, the police will commence preparation of the required full prosecution file from the outset and where possible complete it in time for the first hearing

(g) Fully complete the MG11, witness statement form, including the witness needs assessment and ensure that the risk assessment is completed

(h) The police will identify special measures needs[1] and ensure the opportunity to provide a victim personal statement[2] has been offered[3]

(i) Ensure that charging decisions are made following a review of evidence and that the charges are appropriate to the case and in accordance with the Code for Crown Prosecutors

(j) The prosecutor will discuss victim and witness issues with the police officer and trigger any relevant support requirements, eg referrals to Victim Support (including the Witness Service) in accordance with existing referral agreements

(k) The prosecutor will consider all victim and witness issues when making charging decisions

---

1. Part 2 Chapter 1 Youth Justice and Criminal Evidence Act 1999
2. Practice Directions (Criminal Proceedings: Consolidation) para 28 [2002]1 WLR. 2870 as amended 22nd March 2005
3. In domestic violence cases many victims do not want the defendant to know how badly they or the wider family have been affected by his or her actions. Where however a victim has withdrawn support for the prosecution, a VPS can provide them with the opportunity to tell the defendant and the court how they feel and how certain disposals might assist the victim and/or their family in any ongoing relationship with the defendant. This can support the course of the prosecution and contribute to the future safety of the victim and any others involved

---

PART 2 PRE-CHARGE ACTIVITY (CHARGING DECISIONS MADE BY THE POLICE)

The preparatory process by the police to consider the evidence and appropriate charge

Objectives

2.1

(a) To ensure the charge is supported by the evidence and appropriate for the circumstances of the case

(b) To ensure the decision is in compliance with The Director's Guidance on Charging and the Code for Crown Prosecutors

(c) To ensure the early identification and termination of non-viable cases

(d) In appropriate cases, to consider victim and witness needs at the earliest opportunity

Actions

2.2 Investigation and arrest Wherever possible, investigation will be undertaken prior to, or soon after arrest, to ensure that the evidential requirements can be met where the suspect is in custody

2.3 Charging decision

(a) A charging decision will be made following a review of the evidence and in accordance with The Director's Guidance on Charging and appropriate test set out in the Code for Crown Prosecutors

(b) If, after such a review, the appropriate police officer is of the view that the case may be suitable for a Conditional Caution, he or she must refer the case to a crown prosecutor for a decision as to the appropriate course of action

Case Progression Roles and Responsibilities

2.4 Prosecution Team
Police

(a) Court proceedings will not be commenced until the police have the material required to progress the case at the first appearance unless justified by the nature of the case

(b) Fully complete the MG11, witness statement form, including the witness needs assessment, and ensure that the risk assessment is completed

(c) Identify special measures needs[1] and ensure the opportunity to provide a victim personal statement[2] has been offered[3]

(d) Commence file preparation and ensure that due consideration is given to CPIA disclosure, third party disclosure and expert evidence

---

1. Part 2 Chapter 1 Youth Justice and Criminal Evidence Act 1999.
2. *Practice Direction (Criminal Proceedings: Consolidation)* para 28 [2002] 1 WLR 2870 as amended 22 March 2005
3. In domestic violence cases many victims do not want the defendant to know how badly they or the wider family have been affected by his or her actions. Where however a victim has withdrawn support for the prosecution, a VPS can provide them with the opportunity to tell the defendant and the court how they feel and how certain disposals might assist the victim and/or their family in any ongoing relationship with the defendant. This can support the course of the prosecution and contribute to the future safety of the victim and any others involved.

PART 3 CHARGE (CHARGING DECISIONS MADE BY CROWN PROSECUTORS)

The accused is charged with the correct charge in accordance with the evidence and the case is ready to proceed

Objective

3.1

(a) To charge the alleged offender with the right offence based on the evidence in accordance with the Code for Crown Prosecutors

(b) To remand the defendant on bail or in custody to the correct court (EAH or EFH)

(c) To contact victims and witnesses at the earliest opportunity

(d) To identify cases to be transferred to the Crown Court under s 53 Criminal Justice Act 1991 and s 4 Criminal Justice Act 1987

Action – Bail cases

3.2 Charge defendant

(a) At the time of charge the defendant will be given a leaflet, 'Going to court – information for you' available in several different languages, which can be viewed online at www.cjsonline.gov.uk. This leaflet provides information on the court process including his or her obligations to the court, the location/set up of the court and advice on instructing a solicitor. The leaflet informs the defendant that he or she will generally be given credit for an early guilty plea. The defendant should also be advised of the information available to defendants on www.cjsonline.gov.uk/defendants/ walkthrough. Areas may display posters in police stations and court waiting areas giving details of these leaflets and the website

(b) Following charge, in addition to the leaflet, a reminder card may be issued giving date of first hearing, setting out key messages (eg credit for guilty pleas, attending solicitor to give instructions and attending court when required otherwise the case may proceed in his or her absence)

(c) The defendant's legal representative should, wherever practicable, apply for a representation order prior to the first appearance

(d) The police will send a fully completed charge sheet and bail sheet to court including where practicable the defendant's address and telephone number

(e) Where a remand in custody or conditional bail is sought, MG7 evidence and supporting evidence should be completed by the police and forwarded to the CPS

(f) The police will ensure that the file is available to CPS advocate for presentation at court

3.3 Provide letter from prosecution team to defence solicitor, where known, to seek early involvement Upon completion of the full file the prosecution team will send a letter to defence solicitors, where known, setting out the issues identified by the prosecution and with the intention of securing agreement to s 9 evidence and s 10 admissions. The prosecution team DNA Guidance includes a template letter to the defence solicitor

3.4 Prosecution Team provide advance information file as appropriate The advance information file will contain the evidence upon which the charging decision has been made and any CPIA material, if appropriate

3.5 Allocate case to appropriate first hearing court The Justices' Issues Group (judicial membership) will decide on local listing practice.[1] Generally, this will provide that anticipated guilty plea cases suitable for designated case worker[2] presentation will be allocated to an EFH court and all other cases will be allocated to an EAH court

3.6 Contact victims and prosecution witnesses Where practicable, the Witness Care Unit (where established) will contact the victims and witnesses, by their preferred method at the point of charge to provide a case update

Case Progression Roles and Responsibilities

3.7 Prosecution Team

(a) Provide advance information for the defence, as soon as practicable following charging of defendant, or to be made available on the morning of the court hearing

(b) Where the prosecution team are in a position to proceed to committal or transfer at the first appearance, they will endeavour to serve papers on the defence in advance of the hearing. The file will include CPIA disclosure, details of all expert evidence and third party material where possible

(c) Be in a position to deal with the plea before venue procedure at the first hearing

(d) In all cases involving DNA information, and some fingerprint cases, ensure compliance with the prosecution team DNA Guidance regarding staged report

(e) Where a full file is made available in advance of the first hearing, a draft indictment will be provided, where appropriate

(f) Ensure that witness availability has been received

(g) Where available, ensure that the victim personal statement is taken into account when considering victim issues eg appropriate special measures applications[3]

(h) Keep victims and witnesses informed of bail decisions

(i) If required, notify any witnesses of hearing date

(j) Ensure prosecution file contains material on which CPIA disclosure decision can be made if required, eg third party material, expert evidence and CPIA disclosure

Case Progression Function

(k) Act as a single point of contact for the prosecution team

(l) After the point of charge and prior to the first hearing date, the prosecution case progression officer or the person identified to carry out this role will ensure that advance information has been served on a defendant's solicitors, where known, or is available to be served at court

(m) Ensure that the prosecution file is made available to the advocate to undertake the hearing and that it is fit for purpose in accordance with the Manual of Guidance

Witness Care Unit (where established)

(n) Ensure initial contact is made with victims and witnesses and any action required is undertaken

3.8 Defence Case Progression Function

(a) Make early application for representation order, where appropriate

(b) Contact the prosecution case progression officer or the person identified to carry out this role to obtain the advance information

(c) Obtain information, where appropriate, on defendant's previous convictions

(d) Check that the defendant has been advised of the possible discount in sentence for an early guilty plea

(e) Consider letter from prosecution regarding agreement of s 9 statements and s 10 admissions, particularly in cases involving DNA or fingerprint material

Custody cases and cases involving persistent young offenders

3.9 In cases where it is proposed to withhold bail following charge, the charging decision will be made applying the Threshold test, as set out in the Code for Crown Prosecutors and The Director's Guidance on Charging

3.10 Charging decisions concerning persistent young offenders will be made in accordance with The Director's Guidance on Charging. Cases will be managed between arrest and charging using a period of pre-charge bail, where appropriate and having regard to the 71 day target applicable to those cases

---

1. Principles of Listing are attached at Annex A
2. The Extended Remit of Crown Prosecution Service Designated Caseworkers April 2004
3. Part 2 Chapter 1 Youth Justice and Criminal Evidence Act 1999

PART 4 CHARGE (CHARGING DECISIONS MADE BY THE POLICE)

The accused is charged with the correct charge in accordance with the evidence and the case is ready to proceed

Objective

4.1

(a) To charge the alleged offender with the right offence based on the evidence

(b) To remand the defendant on bail or in custody to the correct court (EAH or EFH)

(c) To contact victims and witnesses at the earliest opportunity

Action – bail cases

4.2 Charge defendant

(a) At the time of charge the defendant will be given a leaflet, 'Going to court – information to you' available in several different languages, which can be viewed online at www.cjsonline.gov.uk. This leaflet provides information on the court process including his or her obligations to the court, the location/set up of the court and advice on instructing a solicitor. The leaflet informs the defendant that he or she will generally be given credit for an early guilty plea. The defendant should also be advised of the information available to defendants on www.cjsonline.gov.uk/defendants/walkthrough. Areas may display posters in police stations and court waiting areas giving details of these leaflets and the website.

(b) Following charge, in addition to the leaflet, a reminder card may be issued giving date of first hearing, setting out key messages (eg credit for guilty pleas, attending solicitor to give instructions and attending court when required otherwise the case may proceed in his or her absence)

(c) The defendant's legal representative should, wherever practicable, apply for a representation order prior to the first appearance

(d) A fully completed charge sheet and bail sheet will be sent to the court including where practicable the defendants address and telephone number

(e) Where a remand in custody or conditional bail is sought, MG7 evidence and supporting evidence should be completed by the police and forwarded to the CPS or other prosecutor

(f) The police will ensure the file is available to CPS advocate or other prosecutor for presentation at court

4.3 Police provide advance information file as appropriate

(a) The advance information file will contain the evidence upon which the charging decision has been made

(b) Where a not guilty plea is anticipated, the police will provide the CPS with CPIA disclosure, details of all expert evidence and third party material

(c) In cases involving DNA or fingerprints material, refer to the prosecution team DNA Guidance

4.4 Allocate case to appropriate first hearing court The Justices' Issues Group (judicial membership) will decide on local listing practice.[1] Generally, this will provide that anticipated guilty plea cases suitable for designated case worker presentation will be allocated to the EFH court and all other cases will be allocated to an EAH court

4.5 Contact prosecution victims and witnesses Where practicable, the Witness Care Unit (where established) will contact victims and witnesses by their preferred method at the point of charge to provide a case update

Case Progression Roles and Responsibilities
4.6 Prosecution Team

(a) Provide advance information for the defence, as soon as practicable following charging of defendant or to be made available on the morning of the court hearing

(b) Provide prosecution file in accordance with Manual of Guidance

(c) In all cases involving DNA information, and some fingerprint cases, ensure compliance with the prosecution team DNA Guidance regarding staged report

(d) Ensure that witness availability has been received

(e) Where available, ensure that the victim personal statement is taken into account when considering victim issues, eg appropriate special measures application[2]

(f) Keep victims informed of bail decisions

(g) If required, notify any witnesses of hearing date

Case Progression Function

(h) Act as a single point of contact for the prosecution team

(i) After the point of charge and prior to the first hearing date, the prosecution case progression officer or the person identified to carry out this role will ensure that advance information has been served on a defendant's solicitors, where known, or is available to be served at court

(j) Ensure that the prosecution file is made available to the advocate to undertake the hearing and that it is fit for purpose in accordance with the Manual of Guidance

(k) Ensure prosecution file contains material on which CPIA disclosure decision can be made if required, eg third party material, expert evidence and CPIA disclosure

Witness Care Unit (where established)

(l) Ensure that the victim personal statement is passed to the prosecution team for inclusion on the file

(m) Ensure initial contact is made with victims and witnesses and any action required is undertaken

4.7 Defence Case Progression Function

(a) Make early application for representation order, where appropriate

(b) Contact the prosecution case progression officer or the person identified to carry out this role to obtain the advance information

(c) Check that the defendant has been advised of the possible discount in sentence for an early guilty plea

(d) Obtain information, where appropriate, on defendant's previous convictions

(e) Consider letter from prosecution regarding agreement of s 9 statements and s 10 admissions, particularly in cases involving DNA or fingerprint material

Custody cases and cases involving persistent young offenders

4.8 In cases where it is proposed to withhold bail following charge, the charging decision will be made applying the Threshold test, as set out in the Code for Crown Prosecutors and The Director's Guidance on Charging

4.9 Charging decisions concerning persistent young offenders will be made in accordance with The Director's Guidance on Charging. Cases will be managed between arrest and charging using a period of pre-charge bail, where appropriate and having regard to the 71 day target applicable to those cases

---

1. Principles of Listing are attached at Annex A
2. Part 2 Chapter 1 Youth Justice and Criminal Evidence Act 1999

1–7765

MAGISTRATES' COURT GUILTY PLEA CASES

PART 5 FIRST APPEARANCE

This will ordinarily be a hearing before the court. The aim of the parties is to be ready to proceed to sentence in cases where it is appropriate

Objective

5.1

(a) To ascertain the plea and enter that plea where appropriate
(b) To ensure that summary and either-way cases progress to an effective sentence hearing
(c) To prepare for indictable-only cases to be sent directly to the Crown Court at the first hearing
(d) To avoid unnecessary hearings by being prepared for sentencing on the same day where appropriate
(e) To continue to keep victims and witnesses informed of progress

Action

5.2 Representation¹

(a) If the defendant wishes to be represented by a solicitor he should be encouraged to do so as soon as possible or see the duty solicitor on the day
(b) The court administration will consider determining all applications for legal representation on the day of submission and where applications are handed to the legal adviser in court the expectation is that they will be considered there and then
(c) Where it is not known who is representing the defendant until the matter comes to court for the first time, then subject to the information provided, the length of any adjournment will be a matter for the court who may, where appropriate, deal with the case later in that day's list²
(d) Where the defendant has been unable to instruct a representative prior to the first hearing and where it is practicable, the court administration will try to provide facilities for defence representatives to take meaningful instructions at court on the first occasion

5.3 Plea and plea before venue³

(a) The Justices' Issues Group (judicial membership) will decide on local listing practice. Generally, this will provide that expected guilty pleas will be allocated to the EFH court. In the event of a not guilty plea being entered, cases will be transferred to the EAH court

Summary cases only

(b) The defendant will be asked to enter a plea at the first appearance. In the event of guilty pleas being entered all participants should be prepared for the case to proceed to sentence where appropriate

Either-way offences only⁴

(c) Prosecution and defence should be in a position to deal with the plea before venue procedure, with the defence having sufficient instructions for an indication of plea to be given where appropriate
(d) It is for the court to decide the appropriate venue for sentence⁵
(e) If committed to the Crown Court, it is for the court to fix a date for the sentence hearing in the Crown Court. It is for the court to identify cases requiring the benefit of a pre-sentence report or other reports and request those be prepared in readiness for the hearing in the Crown Court where appropriate

5.4 Indictable-only cases (s 51)⁶

(a) The case will be sent to the Crown Court under s 51 procedure
(b) The defendant may be requested to give an indication of plea in the magistrates' court
(c) Where a guilty plea is indicated, the court may fix a date for the formal entry of plea in the Crown Court and give appropriate directions⁷ for the service of papers, the preferment of the indictment if not already preferred, preparation of pre-sentence report(s) and any other necessary orders to enable sentencing of the defendant on the date fixed, subject to any direction of the Resident Judge
(d) If there is then known to be an issue as to the basis or acceptability of a guilty plea, the parties may be asked whether a preliminary hearing in the Crown Court is necessary or desirable
(e) Where the court orders that a preliminary hearing should take place, a date will be fixed for the hearing and the court may give directions⁸

5.5 Sentence and committal for sentence[9]

(a) If the defendant wants other offences to be taken into consideration, those offences should be set out in writing and put before the court

(b) On conclusion of the prosecution case and following representation by the defence, where the court is considering a custodial or community sentence, the case may be adjourned for reports to be prepared

(c) Where the court is considering a specific sentence, the responsible probation officer will conduct enquiries and produce a pre-sentence report on the same day unless further enquiries are required or there is a need for a fuller report[10]

5.6 Defendant information

(a) Where the defendant has been given a reminder card this should be completed if there is to be a further hearing

(b) The defence representative will inform the defendant of the next hearing date in advance and should, where appropriate remind him or her of it. Where agreed locally, the court administration may offer an additional reminder service, including by telephone where appropriate

5.7 Case progression activity

(a) At the beginning of each case, each party must, unless the court otherwise directs: nominate an individual responsible for progressing the case; and tell the other parties and the court who he is and how to contact him[11]

(b) The court must where appropriate nominate a court officer responsible for progressing the case; and make sure that the parties know who he is and how to contact him

(c) A case progression officer must:[12]

   (i) monitor compliance with directions

   (ii) make sure that the court is kept informed of events that may affect the progress of the case

   (iii) make sure that he can be contacted promptly about the case during ordinary business hours

   (iv) act promptly and reasonably in response to communications about the case

   (v) if he will be unavailable, appoint a substitute to fulfil his duties and inform the other case progression officers

The Court

5.8 The Criminal Procedure Rules 2005 provide that at every hearing, if a case cannot be concluded there and then the court must give directions so that it can be concluded at the next hearing or as soon as possible after that.[13]

At every hearing the court must, where relevant:

(a) if the defendant is absent, decide whether to proceed nonetheless[14]

(b) take the defendant's plea (unless already done) or if no plea can be taken then find out whether the defendant is likely to plead guilty or not guilty

(c) set, follow or revise a timetable for the progress of the case, which may include a timetable for any hearing including the trial or (in the Crown Court) the appeal

(d) in giving directions, ensure continuity in relation to the court and the parties' representatives where that is appropriate and practicable

(e) where a direction has not been complied with, find out why, identify who was responsible, and take appropriate action

5.9 In addition, the participants must expect the court actively to manage the case in accordance with the Criminal Procedure Rules 2005 and, where appropriate, to:

(a) pass sentence

(b) give directions so that all outstanding issues concerning sentence (including any relating to the basis of plea or special reasons) are determined and sentence passed on next occasion

(c) decide whether any further reports are needed

(d) fix the date for determining outstanding issues and passing sentence

(e) require the parties to give accurate, carefully considered time estimates

(f) consider bail[15]

(g) announce the next hearing

(h) enquire into and take action in relation to any hearing which is wholly or partly ineffective or unnecessary

5.10 It is for the court to decide the appropriate venue for sentence[16]

Case Progression Roles and Responsibilities

5.11 Each party must prepare and conduct the case in accordance with the Criminal Procedure Rules 2005 and actively assist the court in fulfilling its duty under those Rules, and must:[17]

(a) comply with directions given by the court

(b) take every reasonable step to make sure his witnesses will attend when they are needed

(c) make appropriate arrangements to present any written or other material

(d) promptly inform the court and the other parties of anything that may:

   (i) affect the date or duration of the trial or appeal, or

   (ii) significantly affect the progress of the case in any other way

There are also additional responsibilities for advocates, administrative staff and the defence as follows:

5.12 Prosecution Advocate

(a) Be in a position to deal with the plea before venue procedure
(b) Be in a position to deal with sentence where appropriate
(c) Ensure all relevant information including up to date antecedents is before the court to make any orders ancillary to sentence, eg costs, compensation
(d) If a pre-sentence report is requested, if so instructed and where practicable, ensure the CPS/PSR pack is given to the probation service officer at court on the same day to enable preparation of reports
(e) Record next date of hearing or sentence and record directions made, eg in readiness for Newton hearing or sentence
(f) Ensure that any requests or actions are brought to the attention of the prosecution team
(g) Be prepared to provide copies of documents which need to be drawn to the court's attention

5.13 Defence Advocate

(a) Be in a position to deal with the plea before venue procedure, having sufficient instructions for a plea to be indicated
(b) Be in a position to deal with sentence where appropriate
(c) Confirm to the court[18] if required that:

   (i) the defendant is aware of the importance of giving instructions and/ or attending appointments with his or her solicitor or representative and attending court when required
   (ii) in the event of non-attendance, the defendant had been made aware of the hearing date and the consequences of non-attendance
   (iii) the defendant has been advised of the importance of attending probation appointments where a pre-sentence report is requested

(d) Be prepared to provide copies of documents which need to be drawn to the court's attention
(e) Record next date of hearing or sentence and record directions made, eg in readiness for Newton hearing or sentence
(f) Ensure that any requests or actions are brought to the attention of the defence representative

5.14 Magistrates' Court Administration Court Office

(a) Deal with applications for representation on the day of receipt, where possible
(b) Promptly prepare warrants on the day of hearing
(c) In s 51 cases, promptly send papers to the Crown Court

Case Progression Officer

(d) Notify the parties of the name and contact details of the nominated individual responsible for progressing the case
(e) Record the name of the case progression officers for the prosecution team and the defence
(f) Record next date of hearing or sentence, and record and monitor directions made, eg in readiness for Newton hearing or sentence and ensure compliance by the due date
(g) Check defendant's representation status
(h) In the event of non-compliance with directions, ascertain from parties why the directions have not been complied with and take appropriate action, including use of delegated powers and/or referral to the court
(i) Set up such further hearings as necessary including progression hearings
(j) Ensure that required reports and information are ready for sentence hearing, if the required reports are not ready, make further enquiries and refer to the court to list for hearing if required
(k) Ensure all other relevant information is available, eg DVLA printout
(l) Ensure that confidential communications eg about possible pleas, are not passed to the court or other parties without agreement
(m) Ensure that case progression forms are sent to the Crown Court

5.15 Prosecution Team

(a) The police and where appropriate court civilian enforcement officers to use every effort to execute bench warrants promptly
(b) The police to ensure that the prosecution file is completed and submitted in accordance with the Manual of Guidance and any order of the court

Case Progression Function

(c) Notify the parties of the name and contact details of the nominated individual responsible for progressing the case
(d) Record the name of the case progression officers for the court and the defence
(e) Ensure that the prosecution file is made available to the advocate to undertake the hearing and that it is fit for purpose in accordance with the Manual of Guidance
(f) In all cases involving DNA information, and some fingerprint cases, ensure compliance with the prosecution team DNA Guidance regarding staged report
(g) Record next date of hearing or sentence, and record and monitor directions made, eg in readiness for Newton hearing or sentence and ensure compliance by the due date

(h) If a pre-sentence report is requested and the CPS/PSR pack is not provided in court, ensure the same is provided for the Probation Service within locally agreed time limits

(i) Ensure any actions required are brought to the attention of the appropriate lawyer

(j) If unable to comply with directions to refer to the magistrates' court case progression officer forthwith

(k) Receive and action requests arising or received from the prosecution advocate or the court administration

(l) Ensure that consideration is given to the involvement of the Witness Service

(m) Ensure any witnesses are available for Newton hearing or special reasons

(n) Ensure that details are available to enable compensation to be considered at the earliest opportunity

(o) Ensure that appropriate, applications prior to trial of issues or ancillary to sentence have been made, eg special measures, hearsay and bad character, and that responses have been made to any such applications received, where appropriate. Ensure also that consideration has been given to applying for any ruling to be made binding. If not, to bring this to the attention of the appropriate lawyer

(p) Inform the court forthwith of anything which might compromise the effectiveness of the next hearing

(q) Make any application for an adjournment immediately after the grounds for doing so are known and support such application with the appropriate necessary evidence

Witness Care Unit (where established)

(r) If required, notify victims and witnesses of hearing date

(s) Inform victims and witnesses of the outcome of the hearing

5.16 Defence Case Progression Function

(a) Notify the parties of the name and contact details of the individual responsible for progressing the case

(b) Record the name of the case progression officers for the court and the prosecution team

(c) Record next date of hearing or sentence, and record and monitor directions made, eg in readiness for Newton hearing or sentence and ensure compliance by the due date

(d) If unable to comply with directions to refer to the magistrates' court case progression officer forthwith

(e) Inform the defendant of the time and date of the next hearing and where appropriate, provide a further reminder of the hearing date

(f) Inform the court forthwith of anything which might compromise the effectiveness of the next hearing, including a lack of instructions from the defendant[19]

(g) Make any application for an adjournment immediately after the grounds for doing so are known and support such application with the appropriate necessary evidence

(h) Ensure funding is in place including making timely application for public funding (formerly known as 'legal aid') to fund expert witnesses, where appropriate

(i) Consider letter from prosecution regarding agreement of s 9 statements and s 10 admissions, particularly in cases involving DNA or fingerprint material

(j) If witnesses are unable to attend, notify the magistrates' court case progression officer as soon as possible

(k) Ensure that appropriate applications prior to trial of issues or ancillary to sentence have been made, eg special measures, hearsay and bad character, and that responses have been made to any such applications received, where appropriate. Ensure also that consideration has been given to applying for any ruling to be made binding

(l) Ensure that consideration is given to the involvement of the Witness Service

(m) Receive and action requests arising or received from the defence advocate or the court administration

5.17 National Offender Management Service – Productions from Prison Custody

(a) The PECS contractor, or in the case of Category A prisoners the Prison Service, to ensure that all persons in custody are produced at the court when required and taken to each courtroom promptly in accordance with PECS and Prison Service contracts

(b) The PECS contractor, or Prison Service in respect of Category A prisoner movements, to notify the court administration immediately of any problems anticipated or arising in respect of the production of persons in custody

5.18 National Offender Management Service – Probation Service

(a) Ensure the probation service officer obtains relevant information from the prosecution advocate or team to prepare a pre-sentence report

(b) Reports to be made available in accordance with National Standards

(c) Comply with the directions of the court

(d) Provide the court, prosecution and defence with information about the defendant, where relevant and appropriate

---

1. Section 50 Crime and Disorder Act 1998, Legal Aid Act 1988 and Legal Advice and Assistance Regulations (& Scope) Regulations 1989, Access to Justice Act 1999 and Criminal Defence Service (General) (No 2) Regulations 2001

2. Applications to transfer representation will be determined in accordance with Regulation 16 and 16A of Criminal Defence Service (General) (No 2) Regs 2001 as amended by Criminal Defence Service (General) (No 2) (Amendment) Regs 2004

3. Sections 17A–17C and Sch 1 MCA 1980, Magistrates' Court (Advance Information) Rules 1985, Part 6 and

Sch 3 Criminal Justice Act 2003 (**when commenced**) (committals for sentence/allocation/ sending of either-way cases/advance indication of sentence), Consolidated Criminal Practice Direction (Case Management) V56 Case Management in Magistrates' Courts

4. Section 19, 20 and 21 Magistrates' Courts Act 1980, as amended by Pt 6 and Schedule 3 Criminal Justice Act 2003 (**when commenced**), (allocation and sending of cases)

5. Part 12 Chapter 5 Criminal Justice Act 2003 Chapter 44

6. Section 51 Crime and Disorder Act 1998 as amended by Pt 6 and Schedule 3 Criminal Justice Act 2003 (**when commenced**)(sending of cases to the Crown Court), Criminal Procedure Rules Part 12

7. Criminal Procedure Rules 3.5(3) – "A magistrates' court may give a direction that will apply in the Crown Court if the case is to continue there" and Consolidated Criminal Practice Direction (Case Management) as amended 22 March 2005, case progression forms and accompanying guidance notes

8. Criminal Procedure Rules 2005 Part 3.5(3) (as above) and 3.11 Consolidated Criminal Practice Direction (Case Management) v56 Case Management in the Magistrates' Court as amended 22 March 2005

9. Sections 3, 6, 81 and 152 PCC(s)A 2000, ss 144 (reduction in sentences for guilty pleas and committals for sentence) and 154 (**when commenced**) (increase in magistrates' sentencing powers) CJA 2003

10. Probation Service National Standard B5

11. Criminal Procedure Rules 2005 Part 3.4(1)

12. Criminal Procedure Rules 2005 Part 3.4(4)

13. Criminal Procedure Rules 2005 rule 3.8

14. *Practice Direction (Criminal Proceedings:Consolidation)* para.1.13 [2004] 1 WLR 589

15. Amendment No 3 to the Consolidated Criminal Practice Direction (Bail: Failure to Surrender and Trials in Absence) sets out 'The failure of defendants to comply with the terms of their bail by not surrendering can undermine the administration of justice . . . It is therefore most important that defendants who are granted bail appreciate the significance of the obligation to surrender to custody in accordance with the terms of their bail and that courts take appropriate action if they fail to do so. There are at least three courses of action for the courts to consider taking:- [A] imposing penalties for the failure to surrender; [B] revoking bail or imposing more stringent bail conditions; and [C] conducting trials in absence of the defendant'.

16. Part 12 Chapter 5 Criminal Justice Act 2003 Chapter 44

17. Criminal Procedure Rules 2005 rule 3.9(2)

18. Further guidance on this subject may be issued

19. A solicitor is not required to disclose any matters or information which comes to him or her in privileged circumstances as defined in s 10 Police and Criminal Evidence Act 1984

PART 6   READINESS ASSESSMENT

This is generally an out of court process requiring compliance by the parties to inform the court of readiness for the next hearing; a hearing before the court may take place if there is a material failure likely to affect the proper progress of the case

Objectives

6.1

(a)   To ensure the case is ready for sentence
(b)   To ensure that the victims, witnesses and the defendant are informed of the hearing date
(c)   To ensure that all reports are completed and available to all parties
(d)   To continue to keep victims and witnesses informed of progress
(e)   To ensure that any case listed for trial of issues ancillary to sentence is ready to proceed

Action

6.2 Case progression activity A case progression officer must:[1]

(i)   monitor compliance with directions
(ii)   make sure that the court is kept informed of events that may affect the progress of the case
(iii)   make sure that he can be contacted promptly about the case during ordinary business hours
(iv)   act promptly and reasonably in response to communications about the case
(v)   if he will be unavailable, appoint a substitute to fulfil his duties and inform the other case progression officers

6.3 Defendant information

(a)   Where the readiness assessment is conducted in the presence of the defendant, the reminder card should be completed if there is to be a further hearing
(b)   The defence representative will inform the defendant of the next hearing date in advance and should, where appropriate remind him or her of it. Where agreed locally, the court administration may offer an additional reminder service, including by telephone where appropriate

The Court

6.4 The Criminal Procedure Rules 2005 provide that at every hearing, if a case cannot be concluded there and then the court must give directions so that it can be concluded at the next hearing or as soon as possible after that.[2] At every hearing the court must, where relevant:

(a)   if the defendant is absent, decide whether to proceed nonetheless[3]
(b)   take the defendant's plea (unless already done) or if no plea can be taken then find out whether the defendant is likely to plead guilty or not guilty
(c)   set, follow or revise a timetable for the progress of the case, which may include a timetable for any hearing including the trial or (in the Crown Court) the appeal
(d)   in giving directions, ensure continuity in relation to the court and the parties' representatives where that is appropriate and practicable

(e) where a direction has not been complied with, find out why, identify who was responsible, and take appropriate action

6.5 In addition, the participants must expect the court actively to manage the case in accordance with the Criminal Procedure Rules 2005 and, where appropriate, to:

(a) list the case for further directions if it appears that the case may not be ready for hearing in time
(b) enquire into and take action in relation to any hearing which is wholly or partly ineffective or unnecessary
(c) give further directions so that all outstanding issues (including any relating to the basis of plea and special reasons) are determined and sentence passed on one occasion
(d) decide whether any further reports are needed
(e) fix the date for determining outstanding issues and passing sentence
(f) whether directions are made in the course of oral hearings or by some other procedure is for the court to decide, both generally and in particular cases
(g) consider bail[4]
(h) announce the date of the next hearing

6.6 It is for the court to decide the appropriate venue for sentence[5]

Case Progression Roles and Responsibilities

6.7 Each party must prepare and conduct the case in accordance with the Criminal Procedure Rules 2005 and actively assist the court in fulfilling its duty under those Rules, and must:[6]

(a) comply with directions given by the court
(b) take every reasonable step to make sure his witnesses will attend when they are needed
(c) make appropriate arrangements to present any written or other material
(d) promptly inform the court and the other parties of anything that may:
(i) affect the date or duration of the trial or appeal, or
(ii) significantly affect the progress of the case in any other way

There are also additional responsibilities for advocates, administrative staff and the defence as follows:

6.8 Prosecution Advocate

(a) Where a trial of issues hearing will take place, provide all relevant information to the prosecution team to enable compliance with provisions for notification of readiness within the time specified by the court
(b) Where there is a hearing, ensure that any requests or actions are brought to the attention of the prosecution team for action

6.9 Defence Advocate

(a) Where there is a hearing, confirm to the court[7] if required that in the event of non-attendance, the defendant had been made aware of the hearing date and the consequences of non-attendance
(b) Where a trial of issues hearing will take place, provide all relevant information to defence representative to enable compliance with provisions for notification of readiness within the time specified by the court
(c) Where there is a hearing, ensure that any requests or actions are brought to the attention of the defence representative for action

6.10 Magistrates' Court Administration
Case Progression Officer

(a) Check defendant's representation status if appropriate
(b) Check that the case is ready to proceed at the hearing. If not, take appropriate action and refer to the court
(c) In the event of non-compliance with directions, ascertain from parties why directions have not been complied with and then refer to the court
(d) Send out certificate of readiness forms (if used) to the parties for completion, or other procedure specified by the court where required (Newton hearing)
(e) Where agreed locally, remind the defendant of the hearing time and date
(f) Ensure that required reports and information are ready for sentence hearing. If the required reports are not ready, make further enquiries and refer to the court to list for hearing if required
(g) Ensure that, where notified by the prosecution and/or defence, the facilities to play video and/or audio recordings are available
(h) Ensure all other relevant information is available, eg DVLA printout
(i) Ensure that confidential communications eg about possible pleas, are not passed to the court or other parties without agreement

6.11 Prosecution Team
Case Progression Function

(a) Where a trial of issues will take place, identify the nominated person for future contact on case progression matters
(b) Provide the magistrates' court case progression officer with information about relevant applications and all other information relating to readiness for the next hearing
(c) Provide the prosecution advocate with details of up-to-date antecedents and offences to be taken into consideration, if appropriate

(d) Ensure that all the relevant material, including reports or other documents, is ready and has been copied for the court

(e) Ensure that all relevant exhibits are at court and that the court administration has been notified that the facilities to play video and/or audio recordings will be required, where appropriate

(f) Ensure that consideration is given to the involvement of the Witness Service

(g) Ensure that appropriate applications prior to trial of issues or ancillary to sentence have been made, eg special measures, hearsay and bad character, and that responses have been made to any such applications received, where appropriate. Ensure also that consideration has been given to applying for any ruling to be made binding. If not, to bring this to the attention of the appropriate lawyer

(h) In all cases involving DNA information, and some fingerprint cases, ensure compliance with the prosecution team DNA Guidance regarding staged report

(i) Ensure that the court administration is notified of any special requirements, other than special measures, of victims and witnesses

(j) Ensure all relevant papers have been filed with the court administration prior to hearing and if not, take appropriate action

(k) Ensure that the prosecution file is made available to the advocate to undertake any hearing and that it is fit for purpose in accordance with the Manual of Guidance

(l) Receive and action requests arising or received from the prosecution advocate or the court administration

(m) Ensure that any compensation details and/or victim personal statements are available to the court

(n) Comply with provisions for notification of readiness within the time specified by the court

(o) Inform the court forthwith of anything which might compromise the effectiveness of the next hearing

(p) Make any application for an adjournment immediately after the grounds for doing so are known and support such application with the appropriate necessary evidence

Witness Care Unit (where established)

(q) Ensure victims have been notified of the sentence hearing date or, where appropriate, the trial of issues ancillary to sentence hearing date, and whether they are required to attend court

(r) If required arrange for relevant victims and witnesses to be in attendance at the sentence hearing date. Conduct a needs assessment and provide tailored support for those required to attend court

(s) Ensure that the court administration is notified of any special requirements, other than special measures, of victims and witnesses

(t) Share information about victims and witnesses with prosecution team

6.12 Defence Case Progression Function

(a) Where a trial of issues hearing will take place, identify the nominated person for future contact on case progression matters

(b) Ensure that all the relevant material, including reports or other documents, is ready and has been copied for the court

(c) Consider letter from prosecution regarding agreement of s 9 statements and s 10 admissions, particularly in cases involving DNA or fingerprint material

(d) Inform the defendant of the time and date of the next hearing and, where appropriate, provide a further reminder

(e) Inform the court forthwith of anything which might compromise the effectiveness of the next hearing, including a lack of instructions from the defendant[8]

(f) Make any application for an adjournment immediately after the grounds for doing so are known and support such application with the appropriate necessary evidence

(g) Notify the magistrates' court case progression officer of any difficulties having an impact on the effectiveness of the next hearing forthwith

(h) Endeavour, if appropriate, to ensure character witnesses are available for the sentence

(i) Endeavour, if appropriate, to ensure any defence witnesses are available for Newton hearing or special reasons

(j) Ensure that appropriate applications prior to trial of issues or ancillary to sentence have been made, eg special measures, hearsay and bad character, and that responses have been made to any such applications received, where appropriate. Ensure also that consideration has been given to applying for any ruling to be made binding. If not, to make such application

(k) Endeavour where appropriate to inform the court administration of any special requirements of witnesses, other than special measures, together with those of the defendant and that consideration is given to the involvement of the Witness Service

(l) Ensure that the court administration has been notified that the facilities to play video and/or audio recordings will be required, where appropriate

(m) Provide the magistrates' court case progression officer with information about relevant applications and all other information relating to readiness for the next hearing

(n) Receive and action requests arising from the defence advocate or the court administration

(o) Comply with provisions for notification of readiness within the time specified by the court

6.13 Witness Service

(a) Provide pre-court visits for witnesses to familiarise themselves with the courtroom when referred in advance of court attendance and where resources allow

(b) Share information about victims and witnesses with the prosecution team

6.14 National Offender Management Service – Productions from Prison Custody

(a) The PECS contractor, or in the case of Category A prisoners the Prison Service, to ensure that all persons in custody are produced at the court when required and taken to each courtroom promptly in accordance with PECS and Prison Service contracts

(b) The PECS contractor, or Prison Service in respect of Category A prisoner movements, to notify the court administration immediately of any problems anticipated or arising in respect of the production of persons in custody

---

1. Criminal Procedure Rules 2005 rule 3.4(4)
2. Criminal Procedure Rules 2005 rule 3.8
3. *Practice Direction (Criminal Proceedings: Consolidation)* para.1.13 [2004] 1 WLR 589
4. Amendment No 3 to the Consolidated Criminal Practice Direction (Bail: Failure to Surrender and Trials in Absence) sets out 'The failure of defendants to comply with the terms of their bail by not surrendering can undermine the administration of justice . . . It is therefore most important that defendants who are granted bail appreciate the significance of the obligation to surrender to custody in accordance with the terms of their bail and that courts take appropriate action if they fail to do so. There are at least three courses of action for the courts to consider taking: [A] imposing penalties for the failure to surrender; [B] revoking bail or imposing more stringent bail conditions; and [C] conducting trials in absence of the defendant'.
5. Part 12 Chapter 5 Criminal Justice Act 2003 Chapter 44
6. Criminal Procedure Rules 2005 rule 3.9(2)
7. Further guidance on this subject may be issued
8. A solicitor is not required to disclose any matters or information which comes to him or her in privileged circumstances as defined in s 10 Police and Criminal Evidence Act 1984

PART 7 TRIAL OF ISSUES ANCILLARY TO SENTENCE (SUCH AS NEWTON HEARINGS)

This is a hearing to determine issues ancillary to sentence

Objectives

7.1

(a) To ensure that hearings will be effective and proceed when and where listed

(b) To avoid unnecessary hearings by being prepared for sentencing on the same day where appropriate

(c) The parties to arrange the attendance of witnesses so as to present evidence clearly and in a helpful order, making full use of court time and avoiding unnecessary waiting

(d) To provide victims and witnesses for the prosecution and defence with support

Action

7.2 Case progression activity A case progression officer must:[1]

(i) monitor compliance with directions

(ii) make sure that the court is kept informed of events that may affect the progress of the case

(iii) make sure that he can be contacted promptly about the case during ordinary business hours

(iv) act promptly and reasonably in response to communications about the case

(v) if he will be unavailable, appoint a substitute to fulfil his duties and inform the other case progression officers

7.3 Sentence and committal for sentence[2]

(a) Communicate decision of findings

(b) Case concluded

(c) Committal to Crown Court for sentence

7.4 Defendant information

(a) Where the defendant has been given a reminder card this should be completed if there is to be a further hearing

(b) The defence representative will inform the defendant of the next hearing date in advance and should, where appropriate remind him or her of it. Where agreed locally, the court administration may offer an additional reminder service, including by telephone where appropriate

The Court

7.5 The Criminal Procedure Rules 2005 provide that at every hearing, if a case cannot be concluded there and then the court must give directions so that it can be concluded at the next hearing or as soon as possible after that.[3]

At every hearing the court must, where relevant:

(a) if the defendant is absent, decide whether to proceed nonetheless[4]

(b) take the defendant's plea (unless already done) or if no plea can be taken then find out whether the defendant is likely to plead guilty or not guilty

(c) set, follow or revise a timetable for the progress of the case, which may include a timetable for any hearing including the trial or (in the Crown Court) the appeal

(d) in giving directions, ensure continuity in relation to the court and the parties' representatives where that is appropriate and practicable

(e) where a direction has not been complied with, find out why, identify who was responsible, and take appropriate action

7.6 In addition, the participants must expect the court actively to manage the case in accordance with the Criminal Procedure Rules 2005 and, where appropriate, to:

(a) give further directions so that all outstanding issues are determined and sentence passed on one occasion
(b) decide whether any further reports are needed
(c) fix the date for determining outstanding issues and passing sentence
(d) enquire into and take action in relation to any hearing which is wholly or partly ineffective or unnecessary
(e) pass sentence

7.7 It is for the court to decide the appropriate venue for sentence[5]

Case Progression Roles and Responsibilities

7.8 Each party must prepare and conduct the case in accordance with the Criminal Procedure Rules 2005 and actively assist the court in fulfilling its duty under those Rules, and must:[6]

(a) comply with directions given by the court
(b) take every reasonable step to make sure his witnesses will attend when they are needed
(c) make appropriate arrangements to present any written or other material
(d) promptly inform the court and the other parties of anything that may:

   (i) affect the date or duration of the trial or appeal, or
   (ii) significantly affect the progress of the case in any other way

There are also additional responsibilities for advocates, administrative staff and the defence as follows:

7.9 Prosecution Advocate

(a) If the hearing is ineffective, complete the form recording the reason for this and place the form before the magistrates for their consideration before leaving the court
(b) Provide the court with details of up-to-date antecedents and offences to be taken into consideration if appropriate
(c) Ensure that any requests or actions are brought to the attention of the prosecution team for action
(d) If a pre-sentence report is requested, if so instructed and where practicable, ensure the CPS/PSR pack is given to the probation service officer at court on the same day to enable preparation of reports

7.10 Defence Advocate

(a) Confirm to the court,[7] if required, that:

   (i) in the event of non-attendance, the defendant had been made aware of the hearing date and the consequences of non-attendance
   (ii) the defendant has been advised of the importance of attending probation appointments where a pre-sentence report is requested

(b) If the hearing is ineffective, complete the form recording the reason for this and place the form before the magistrates for their consideration before leaving the court

7.11 Magistrates' Court Administration
Court Office

(a) Promptly prepare warrants on the day of hearing
(b) If the hearing is ineffective, ensure that a form is completed by advocates to record the reasons for this and place the form before the magistrates for their consideration before the advocates leave the court.[8] Thereafter take appropriate action to ensure the next hearing is effective

Case Progression Officer

(c) Where agreed locally, remind the defendant of the date and time of the next hearing, including by telephone where appropriate
(d) Ensure that confidential communications eg about possible pleas, are not passed to the court or other parties without agreement

7.12 Prosecution Team

(a) The police and where appropriate court civilian enforcement officers to use every effort to execute bench warrants promptly
(b) The police to ensure any evidential material required to resolve any issues ancillary to sentence, as ordered by the court, is provided to the prosecution

Case Progression Function

(c) Ensure that the prosecution file is made available to the advocate to undertake the hearing and that it is fit for purpose in accordance with the Manual of Guidance
(d) In all cases involving DNA information, and some fingerprint cases, ensure compliance with the prosecution team DNA Guidance regarding staged report
(e) Receive and action requests arising or received from the prosecution advocate or the court administration
(f) If a pre-sentence report is requested and the CPS/PSR pack is not provided in court, ensure it is provided for the Probation Service within time limits agreed locally

(g) Inform the court forthwith of anything which might compromise the effectiveness of the next hearing

(h) Make enquiries as to the whereabouts of prosecution witnesses should they fail to attend in good time and supply the information to the prosecution advocate, so that the court can be properly informed at the hearing

(i) Make any application for an adjournment immediately after the grounds for doing so are known and support such application with the appropriate necessary evidence

Witness Care Unit (where established)

(j) Notify victims and witnesses of outcome of hearing and thank them for their contribution

7.13 Defence Case Progression Function

(a) Consider letter from prosecution regarding agreement of s 9 statements and s 10 admissions, particularly in cases involving DNA or fingerprint material

(b) Inform the defendant of the date and time of the next hearing and, if appropriate, provide a further reminder

(c) Inform the court forthwith of anything which might compromise the effectiveness of the next hearing, including a lack of instructions from the defendant[9]

(d) Make any application for an adjournment immediately after the grounds for doing so are known and support such application with the appropriate necessary evidence

(e) Make enquiries as to the whereabouts of defence witnesses should they fail to attend in good time and supply the information to the defence advocate, so that the court can be properly informed at the hearing

(f) Receive and action requests arising or received from the defence advocate or the court administration

7.14 Witness Service

(a) Provide support to witnesses during the day and if necessary accompany witnesses to courtroom when referred in advance of court attendance and where resources allow

(b) Share information about victims and witnesses with the prosecution team

7.15 National Offender Management Service – Productions from Prison Custody

(a) The PECS contractor, or in the case of Category A prisoners the Prison Service, to ensure that all persons in custody are produced at the court when required and taken to each courtroom promptly in accordance with PECS and Prison Service contracts

(b) The PECS contractor, or Prison Service in respect of Category A prisoner movements, to notify the court administration immediately of any problems anticipated or arising in respect of the production of persons in custody

7.16 National Offender Management Service – Probation Service

(a) Ensure the probation service officer obtains relevant information from the prosecution advocate or team to prepare a pre-sentence report

(b) Reports to be made available in accordance with National Standards

(c) Comply with the directions of the court

(d) Provide the court, prosecution and defence with information about the defendant, where relevant and appropriate

---

1. Criminal Procedure Rules 2005 rule 3.4(4)
2. Sections 3, 6 and 152 Powers of Criminal Courts (Sentencing) Act 2000, s 144 Criminal Justice Act 2003 (reduction in sentences for guilty plea and committal for sentence)
3. Criminal Procedure Rules 2005 rule 3.8
4. *Practice Direction (Criminal Proceedings: Consolidation)* para.1.13 [2004] 1 WLR 589
5. Part 12 Chapter 5 Criminal Justice Act 2003 Chapter 44
6. Criminal Procedure Rules 2005 rule 3.9(2)
7. Further guidance on this subject may be issued
8. Effective, Cracked, Ineffective and Vacated Trials in Magistrates' Courts: Operational Guidance for Monitoring Scheme
9. A solicitor is not required to disclose any matters or information which comes to him or her in privileged circumstances as defined in s 10 Police and Criminal Evidence Act 1984

PART 8 SENTENCING

A hearing at which sentence will be passed

Objectives

8.1

(a) To ensure that the sentencing hearing can go ahead on the date, at the time and in the location fixed and the court has the requisite information to sentence offender justly

(b) To provide outcome information to all victims and witnesses

Action

8.2 Case progression activity A case progression officer must:[1]

(i) monitor compliance with directions

(ii) make sure that the court is kept informed of events that may affect the progress of the case

(iii) make sure that he can be contacted promptly about the case during ordinary business hours

(iv) act promptly and reasonably in response to communications about the case

(v) if he will be unavailable, appoint a substitute to fulfil his duties and inform the other case progression officers

8.3 Sentence and committal for sentence[2] If the case is committed to the Crown Court for sentence, a date for sentence can be fixed where directions have been given by the Resident Judge

The Court

8.4 The Criminal Procedure Rules 2005 provide that at every hearing, if a case cannot be concluded there and then the court must give directions so that it can be concluded at the next hearing or as soon as possible after that.[3] At every hearing the court must, where relevant:

(a) if the defendant is absent, decide whether to proceed nonetheless[4]
(b) take the defendant's plea (unless already done) or if no plea can be taken then find out whether the defendant is likely to plead guilty or not guilty
(c) set, follow or revise a timetable for the progress of the case, which may include a timetable for any hearing including the trial or (in the Crown Court) the appeal
(d) in giving directions, ensure continuity in relation to the court and the parties' representatives where that is appropriate and practicable
(e) where a direction has not been complied with, find out why, identify who was responsible, and take appropriate action

8.5 In addition, the participants must expect the court actively to manage the case in accordance with the Criminal Procedure Rules 2005 and, where appropriate, to:

(a) pass sentence
(b) enquire into and take action in relation to any hearing which is wholly or partly ineffective or unnecessary

8.6 It is for the court to decide the appropriate venue for sentence[5]

Case Progression Roles and Responsibilities

8.7 Each party must:[6]

(a) comply with directions given by the court
(b) take every reasonable step to make sure his witnesses will attend when they are needed
(c) make appropriate arrangements to present any written or other material
(d) promptly inform the court and the other parties of anything that may:

(i) affect the date or duration of the trial or appeal or
(ii) significantly affect the progress of the case in any other way

There are also additional responsibilities for advocates, administrative staff and the defence as follows:

8.8 Prosecution Advocate

(a) Review the statutory provisions relevant to the court's sentencing powers and any relevant Sentencing Guidelines Council guidance and guideline cases and consider, where appropriate, drawing them to the attention of the court
(b) Review the statutory provisions relating to any ancillary orders (such as anti-social behaviour orders) that might be relevant and consider, where appropriate, drawing them to the court's attention; provide, when necessary, drafts of such orders
(c) Provide the court with details of up-to-date antecedents and offences to be taken into consideration if appropriate
(d) Be prepared to provide copies of documents which need to be drawn to the court's attention
(e) Record date of sentence and any directions made
(f) Be prepared to tell the sentencing court at what stage in the proceedings a guilty plea was entered and this should include whether there was an indication of a willingness to plead guilty before the first court appearance, such as during the police interview
(g) Ensure that any requests or actions are brought to the attention of the prosecution team for action

8.9 Defence Advocate

(a) Confirm to the court[7] if required that in the event of non-attendance, the defendant had been made aware of the hearing date and the consequences of non-attendance
(b) Be prepared to provide copies of documents which need to be drawn to the court's attention
(c) Ensure that any requests or actions are brought to the attention of the defence representative for action
(d) Record date of sentence and any directions made

8.10 Magistrates' Court Administration
Court Office

(a) Promptly prepare warrants on the day of hearing

Case Progression Officer

(b) Check appropriate reports have been prepared
(c) Monitor the progress of a case until conclusion and ensure that all reports and information which are required for sentencing are available to the court
(d) Where agreed locally, remind the defendant of the date and time of the next hearing, including by telephone where appropriate

(e) Ensure that confidential communications are not passed to the court or other parties without agreement

8.11 Prosecution Team

(a) The police and where appropriate court civilian enforcement officers to use every effort to execute bench warrants promptly
(b) The police to ensure that the prosecution file is completed and submitted in accordance with the Manual of Guidance and any order of the court

Case Progression Function

(c) Ensure the court administration has all relevant papers for the court
(d) Ensure that the prosecution file is made available to the advocate to undertake the hearing and that it is fit for purpose in accordance with the Manual of Guidance
(e) In all cases involving DNA information, and some fingerprint cases, ensure compliance with the prosecution team DNA Guidance regarding staged report
(f) Receive and action requests arising or received from the prosecution advocate or the court administration
(g) If the hearing is ineffective, take appropriate action to ensure future conclusion can take place
(h) Inform the court forthwith of anything which might compromise the effectiveness of the next hearing
(i) Make any application for an adjournment immediately after the grounds for doing so are known and support such application with the appropriate necessary evidence

Witness Care Unit (where established)

(j) Provide outcome information to all victims and witnesses and thank them for their contribution

8.12 Defence Case Progression Function

(a) Inform the defendant of the time and date of any future hearing and, where appropriate, provide a further reminder
(b) Inform the court forthwith of anything which might compromise the effectiveness of the next hearing, including a lack of instructions from the defendant[8]
(c) Make any application for an adjournment immediately after the grounds for doing so are known and support such application with the appropriate necessary evidence
(d) If the hearing is ineffective, take appropriate action to ensure future conclusion can take place
(e) Receive and action requests arising or received from the defence advocate or the court administration
(f) Consider letter from prosecution regarding agreement of s 9 statements and s 10 admissions, particularly in cases involving DNA or fingerprint material

8.13 National Offender Management Service – Productions from Prison Custody

(a) The PECS contractor, or in the case of Category A prisoners the Prison Service, to ensure that all persons in custody are produced at the court when required and taken to each courtroom promptly in accordance with PECS and Prison Service contracts
(b) The PECS contractor, or Prison Service in respect of Category A prisoner movements, to notify the court administration immediately of any problems anticipated or arising in respect of the production of persons in custody

8.14 National Offender Management Service – Probation Service

Reports to be made available in accordance with National Standards

---

1. Criminal Procedure Rules 2005 rule 3.4(4)
2. Sections 3, 6 and 152 Powers of Criminal Courts (Sentencing) Act 2000, s 144 Criminal Justice Act 2003 (reduction in sentences for guilty pleas and committals for sentence)
3. Criminal Procedure Rules 2005 rule 3.8
4. *Practice Direction (Criminal Proceedings: Consolidation)* para.1.13 [2004] 1 WLR 589
5. Part 12 Chapter 5 Criminal Justice Act 2003 Chapter 44
6. Criminal Procedure Rules 2005 rule 3.9(2)
7. Further guidance on this subject may be issued
8. A solicitor is not required to disclose any matters or information which comes to him or her in privileged circumstances as defined in s 10 Police and Criminal Evidence Act 1984

CROWN COURT – GUILTY PLEA CASES

PART 9 PREPARATION PRIOR TO FIRST HEARING IN THE CROWN COURT

PART 10 PRELIMINARY HEARING (INDICTABLE-ONLY CASES)

PART 11 PLEA AND CASE MANAGEMENT HEARING

PART 12 READINESS ASSESSMENT

PART 13 TRIAL OF ISSUES ANCILLARY TO SENTENCE (SUCH AS NEWTON HEARINGS)

PART 14 SENTENCING

1–7766

MAGISTRATES' COURT – NOT GUILTY CASES

PART 15 FIRST APPEARANCE

A hearing at which the court will determine the future timetable of the case, including if appropriate, fixing a trial date

Objectives

15.1

(a) To ascertain plea, and if guilty transfer case to EFH court
(b) To prepare for indictable-only cases to be sent directly to the Crown Court at the first hearing
(c) To ensure that the parties prepare the case properly and are ready for trial when the case is listed
(d) To continue to keep victims and witnesses informed of progress

Action

15.2 Representation[1]

(a) If the defendant wishes to be represented by a solicitor he or she should be encouraged to do so as soon as possible or see the duty solicitor on the day
(b) The court administration will consider undertaking to determine all applications for legal representation on the day of submission and where applications are handed to the legal adviser in court the expectation is that they will be considered there and then
(c) Where it is not known who is representing the defendant until the matter comes to court for the first time, then, subject to the volume of information provided, the length of any adjournment will be a matter for the court who may, where appropriate, deal with the case later in that day's list[2]
(d) Where the defendant has been unable to instruct a representative prior to the first hearing and where it is practicable, the court administration will try to provide facilities for defence representatives to take meaningful instructions at court on the first occasion

15.3 Plea and plea before venue[3]

(a) The Justices' Issues Group (judicial membership) will decide on local listing practice. Generally, this will provide that expected not guilty pleas will be allocated to the EAH court. In the event of a guilty plea being entered, cases will be transferred to EFH court
(b) The defendant may be asked to enter a plea (summary cases only)
(c) The defendant may be asked to indicate his or her plea. If not guilty or no indication is given, it is for the court to determine venue (either-way cases only)

15.4 Indictable-only (s 51)[4]

(a) The defence may be requested to give an indication of plea at the magistrates' court
(b) If a not guilty plea is indicated or no indication is given, the parties may be asked whether a preliminary hearing in the Crown Court is necessary or desirable[5]
(c) Where the court orders that a preliminary hearing should take place a date may be fixed for the hearing and the court may give directions[6]
(d) Where the court does not order a preliminary hearing to take place, a date for the plea and case management hearing should normally be fixed and directions given for the service of papers and the future progress of the case[6]

15.5 Mode of trial, election and s 53 Criminal Justice Act 1991 – either-way only[7] Where the court declines jurisdiction or where the defendant elects Crown Court trial, the case may be adjourned for a committal hearing or transfer unless the prosecution are in a position to proceed on the day or at the first hearing

15.6 Committal to Crown Court for trial where appropriate Where the prosecution are in a position to proceed to committal at the first hearing, the case may be committed to Crown Court for trial. The prosecution file will contain the evidence on which the prosecution intend to rely, exhibits, CPIA disclosure, expert evidence, and details of any third party material
Please refer to part 18 for detail on committal process
15.7 Summary trial progression[8]
Trial date

(a) Where a progression hearing is not required the court may immediately fix the trial date and order the parties to lodge a certificate of readiness or other procedure specified by the court within the time specified by the court
(b) Where a progression hearing is required, the trial date and any progression hearing date may be fixed at the same time

Directions for the future progress of case

(c) The court may give directions timetabling the future progression of the case. The court may also require a party to identify matters relating to the attendance of witnesses, written evidence and points of law to be addressed prior to the trial[9]
(d) Where a progression hearing is required, the court may adjourn for a period according to the needs of the individual case. The parties should expect the court, wherever possible, to conduct a progression hearing or pre-trial review and fix the trial date at the first hearing

(e) Alternatively, the parties may be provided with forms and given directions for the exchange of completed forms on paper

(f) Where a trial date has been fixed, the court administration may provide the parties with a certificate of readiness for trial form for completion or other procedure specified by the court

15.8 Defendant information

(a) Where the defendant has been given a reminder card this should be completed if there is to be a further hearing

(b) The defence representative will inform the defendant of the next hearing date in advance and should, where appropriate remind him or her of it. Where agreed locally, the court administration may offer an additional reminder service, including by telephone where appropriate

(c) Where a defendant who has previous convictions is unrepresented, the legal adviser will inform him or her of the implications of the bad character provisions of the Criminal Justice Act 2003

15.9 Case progression activity

(a) At the beginning of each case, each party must, unless the court otherwise directs: nominate an individual responsible for progressing the case; and tell the other parties and the court who he is and how to contact him[10]

(b) The court must where appropriate nominate a court officer responsible for progressing the case; and make sure that the parties know who he is and how to contact him

(c) A case progression officer must:[11]

   (i) monitor compliance with directions

   (ii) make sure that the court is kept informed of events that may affect the progress of the case

   (iii) make sure that he can be contacted promptly about the case during ordinary business hours

   (iv) act promptly and reasonably in response to communications about the case

   (v) if he will be unavailable, appoint a substitute to fulfil his duties and inform the other case progression officers

The Court

15.10 The form, content and frequency of further pre-trial procedures is for the court to decide

15.11 The Criminal Procedure Rules 2005 provide that at every hearing, if a case cannot be concluded there and then the court must give directions so that it can be concluded at the next hearing or as soon as possible after that.[12] At every hearing the court must, where relevant:

(a) if the defendant is absent, decide whether to proceed nonetheless[13]

(b) take the defendant's plea (unless already done) or if no plea can be taken then find out whether the defendant is likely to plead guilty or not guilty

(c) set, follow or revise a timetable for the progress of the case, which may include a timetable for any hearing including the trial or (in the Crown Court) the appeal

(d) in giving directions, ensure continuity in relation to the court and the parties' representatives where that is appropriate and practicable

(e) where a direction has not been complied with, find out why, identify who was responsible, and take appropriate action

15.12 In addition, the participants must expect the court actively to manage the case in accordance with the Criminal Procedure Rules 2005 and, where appropriate, to:

(a) list the case for further directions if it appears that the case may not be ready for hearing in time

(b) enquire into and take action in relation to any hearing which is wholly or partly ineffective or unnecessary

(c) fix the date for determining outstanding pre-trial issues

(d) consider whether a binding ruling may be appropriate[14]

(e) consider bail[15]

(f) announce the date of the next hearing

(g) if requested, consider either hearing the case later the same day to enable appropriate instructions to be taken or adjourning for the shortest possible period

(h) set a committal hearing date for matters to be committed to the Crown Court for trial

Case Progression Roles and Responsibilities

15.13 Each party must prepare and conduct the case in accordance with the Criminal Procedure Rules 2005 and actively assist the court in fulfilling its duty under those Rules, and must:[16]

(a) comply with directions given by the court

(b) take every reasonable step to make sure his witnesses will attend when they are needed

(c) make appropriate arrangements to present any written or other material

(d) promptly inform the court and the other parties of anything that may:

   (i) affect the date or duration of the trial or appeal or

   (ii) significantly affect the progress of the case in any other way

There are also additional responsibilities for advocates, administrative staff and the defence as follows:

15.14 Prosecution Advocate

(a) Be in a position to deal with the plea before venue procedure
(b) Prepare for committal hearing and serve all required papers on defence
(c) Where appropriate be prepared for the case to be committed to the Crown Court for trial
(d) Record next date of hearing, trial or committal hearing and directions made by the court
(e) Ensure that any requests or actions are brought to the attention of the prosecution team for action

15.15 Defence Advocate

(a) Be in a position to deal with the plea before venue procedure, having sufficient instructions for a plea to be indicated
(b) Where the prosecution have served committal papers in advance, be in a position to proceed with committal
(c) Confirm to the court[17] if required that:
  (i) the defendant is aware of the importance of giving instructions and/or attending appointments with his or her solicitor or representative and attending court when required
  (ii) in the event of non-attendance, the defendant had been made aware of the hearing date and the consequences of non-attendance
  (iii) the defendant has been advised of the possible discount in sentence for an early guilty plea
(d) Record next date of hearing, trial or committal hearing, and directions made by the court
(e) Ensure that any requests or actions are brought to the attention of the defence representative for action where appropriate

15.16 Magistrates' Court Administration

(a) Promptly prepare warrants on the day of hearing

Case Progression Officer

(b) Notify the parties of the name and contact details of the nominated individual responsible for progressing the case
(c) Record the name of the case progression officers for the prosecution and the defence
(d) Record next date of hearing or trial, and record for case progression purposes and monitor directions made by the court
(e) Check defendant's representation status
(f) In the event of non-compliance with directions, ascertain from parties the reasons for non-compliance and refer to the court as appropriate
(g) Set up such further hearings as necessary to include progression hearings or pre-trial reviews
(h) Ensure that, where notified by the prosecution and/or defence, the facilities to play video and/or audio recordings are available
(i) Ensure that confidential communications eg about possible pleas, are not passed to the court or other parties without agreement
(j) Ensure that case progression forms are sent to the Crown Court in indictable-only cases

15.17 Prosecution Team

(a) The police and where appropriate court civilian enforcement officers to use every effort to execute bench warrants promptly
(b) The police to ensure that the prosecution file is completed and submitted to the CPS or other prosecutor in accordance with the Manual of Guidance provisions and any orders of the court

Case Progression Function

(c) Notify the parties of the name and contact details of the nominated individual responsible for progressing the case
(d) Record the name of the case progression officers for the prosecution team and the defence
(e) Ensure that the prosecution file is made available to the advocate to undertake the hearing and that it is fit for purpose in accordance with the Manual of Guidance
(f) In all cases involving DNA information, and some fingerprint cases, ensure compliance with the prosecution team DNA Guidance regarding staged report
(g) Ensure service of CPIA disclosure has taken place
(h) Identify any outstanding evidence (expert or otherwise) or CPIA disclosure material (including third party material) and chase such documentation from appropriate person
(i) Ensure that all relevant exhibits are at court and that the court administration has been notified that the facilities to play video and/or audio recordings will be required, where appropriate
(j) Record next date of hearing or trial, and directions made by the court, for case progression purposes
(k) Ensure that appropriate pre-trial applications have been made, eg special measures, hearsay and bad character, and that responses have been made to any such applications received, where appropriate. Ensure also that consideration has been given to applying for any ruling to be made binding. If not, to bring this to the attention of the appropriate lawyer
(l) Action any requests or directions from the court
(m) If unable to comply with directions to refer to the magistrates' court case progression officer forthwith

(n) Ensure that consideration is given to the involvement of the Witness Service
(o) Keep Witness Care Unit informed of action and progress, particularly where progression takes place outside of courtroom
(p) Comply with provisions for notification of readiness within the time specified by the court
(q) Obtain details to enable compensation to be considered at the earliest opportunity
(r) Receive and action requests arising or received from the prosecution advocate or the court administration
(s) Ensure that all the relevant material, including reports or other documents, is ready and has been copied for the court
(t) Inform the court forthwith of anything which might compromise the effectiveness of the next hearing
(u) Make any application for an adjournment immediately after the grounds for doing so are known and support such application with the appropriate necessary evidence

Witness Care Unit (where established)

(v) Notify victims and witnesses of the outcome of the hearing where required
(w) Ensure victims and witnesses have been notified of hearing date
(x) Ensure that the court administration is notified of any special requirements, other than special measures, of victims and witnesses
(y) Share information about victims and witnesses with the prosecution team

15.18 Defence Case Progression Function

(a) Notify the parties of the name and contact details of the nominated individual responsible for progressing the case
(b) Record the name of the case progression officers for the court and prosecution team
(c) Record next date of hearing or trial and directions made by the court for case progression purposes
(d) Action any requests or directions from the court
(e) Receive and action requests from the defence advocate or the court administration
(f) Ensure that all the relevant material, including reports or other documents, is ready and has been copied for the court
(g) Where the prosecution has served CPIA disclosure prepare and serve defence statement within the required time limit, if appropriate
(h) Inform the defendant of the time and date of the next hearing and, where appropriate, provide a further reminder
(i) Inform the court forthwith of anything which might compromise the effectiveness of the next hearing, including a lack of instructions from the defendant[18]
(j) Make any application for an adjournment immediately after the grounds for doing so are known and support such application with the appropriate necessary evidence
(k) Ensure funding is in place including making timely application for public funding (formerly known as 'legal aid') to fund expert witnesses, where appropriate
(l) Ensure that there are no outstanding CPIA disclosure issues or issues regarding expert evidence or third party material
(m) Endeavour to ensure any defence witnesses are available for trial date and ensure that consideration is given to the involvement of the Witness Service
(n) Ensure that appropriate pre-trial applications have been made, eg special measures, hearsay and bad character, and that responses have been made to any such applications received, where appropriate. Ensure also that consideration has been given to applying for any ruling to be made binding. If not, to make such application
(o) If unable to comply with directions to refer to the magistrates' court case progression officer forthwith
(p) Comply with provisions for notification of readiness within the time specified by the court
(q) Consider letter from prosecution regarding agreement of s 9 statements and s 10 admissions, particularly in cases involving DNA or fingerprint material

15.19 National Offender Management Service – Productions from Prison Custody

(a) The PECS contractor, or in the case of Category A prisoners the Prison Service, to ensure that all persons in custody are produced at the court when required and taken to each courtroom promptly in accordance with PECS and Prison Service contracts
(b) The PECS contractor, or Prison Service in respect of Category A prisoner movements, to notify the court administration immediately of any problems anticipated or arising in respect of the production of persons in custody

---

1. Section 50 Crime and Disorder Act 1998, Legal Aid Act 1988 and Legal Advice and Assistance Regulations (& Scope) Regulations 1988, Access to Justice Act 1999 and Criminal Defence Service (General) (No 2) Regulations 2001
2. Applications to transfer representation will be determined in accordance with Regulation 16 and 16A of Criminal Defence Service (General) (No 2) Regs 2001 as amended by Criminal Defence Service (General) (No 2) (Amendment) Regs 2004
3. Section 17A–17C and Schedule 1 Magistrates' Court Act 1980, Magistrates' Court (Advance Information) Rules 1985 Part 6 and sch 3 Criminal Justice Act 2003 (committals for sentence/allocation/sending of either-way cases/advance indication of sentence) (**when commenced)**
4. Section 51 Crime and Disorder Act 1998 as amended by pt 6 and Schedule 3 Criminal Justice Act 2003 (when commenced) sending of cases to Crown Court
5. Criminal Procedure Rules 2005 rule 12
6. Criminal Procedure Rules 2005 rule 3.5(3) – "A magistrates' court may give a direction that will apply in the Crown Court if the case is to continue there" and 3.11 " (1) The case management forms set out in the

Practice Direction must be used, and where there is no form then no specific formality is required (2) The court must make available to the parties a record of directions given."

   7. Section 53 Criminal Justice Act 1991 will be repealed by ss 41 and 332, Schedule 3 para 62(1) and (2) and Schedule 37 Part 4 and ss 17–20 Magistrates' Court Act 1980 inclusive will be amended by s 41 and Schedule 3, paras 1 and 3 CJA 2003. (**when commenced**) (allocation/sending of cases)

   8. Section 45 and Schedule 3 of The Courts Act 2003 (binding pre-trial rulings)

   9. Criminal Procedure Rules 2005 part 3.10

  10. Criminal Procedure Rules 2005 rule 3.4(1)

  11. Criminal Procedure Rules 2005 rule 3.4(4)

  12. Criminal Procedure Rules 2005 rule 3.8

  13. *Practice Direction (Criminal Proceedings: Consolidation)* para.1.13 [2004] 1 WLR 589

  14. Section 45 and Schedule 3 Courts Act 2003 (pre-trial binding rulings)

  15. Amendment No 3 to the Consolidated Criminal Practice Direction (Bail: Failure to Surrender and Trials in Absence) sets out "The failure of defendants to comply with the terms of their bail by not surrendering can undermine the administration of justice . . . It is therefore most important that defendants who are granted bail appreciate the significance of the obligation to surrender to custody in accordance with the terms of their bail and that courts take appropriate action if they fail to do so. There are at least three courses of action for the courts to consider taking: [A] imposing penalties for the failure to surrender; [B] revoking bail or imposing more stringent bail conditions; and [C] conducting trials in absence of the defendant".

  16. Criminal Procedure Rules 2005 rule 3.9(2)

  17. Further guidance on this subject may be issued

  18. A solicitor is not required to disclose any matters or information which comes to him or her in privileged circumstances as defined in s 10 Police and Criminal Evidence Act 1984

PART 16 READINESS ASSESSMENT (FOR TRIAL, COMMITTAL OR TRANSFER)

This is generally an out of court process requiring compliance by the parties to inform the court of readiness for trial; a hearing before the court may take place if there is a material failure likely to affect the proper progress of the case

Objectives

16.1

  (a) To ensure that the case is ready for an effective trial, committal or transfer and that the parties are fully prepared

  (b) To identify and address any further risks to the effectiveness of the trial, committal or transfer

  (c) To identify victim and witness needs and provide tailored interventions to ensure attendance at court

  (d) To continue to keep victims and witnesses informed of progress

Action

16.2 Compliance with directions

  (a) The defence and prosecution will comply with the procedure for notifying the magistrates' court case progression officer as to compliance with directions made

  (b) The prosecution team case progression officer or person identified to carry out this role, and the person within the defence nominated to carry out this role, will attempt to resolve any problems by discussion. Where this is unsuccessful, the parties will inform the magistrates' court case progression officer forthwith

  (c) The magistrates' court case progression officer will identify any problems and attempt to resolve them by discussion with the parties, failing which the case may be referred to the court. The case may then be either listed for a further hearing or directions given out of court

  (d) Where there has been non-compliance or there is a request for a change in the directions any party can request a hearing

  (e) The court may make or vary directions without the need for a hearing at the request of the parties or otherwise. Either party may apply to have such directions or variations reconsidered at a hearing

16.3 Pre-trial readiness check The court will decide readiness on the basis of the papers before it

16.4 Pre-committal or transfer readiness check The prosecution should ensure that the committal papers have been served and that CPIA disclosure (including third party material information) has been prepared, or in the case of a transfer, that the transfer papers and CPIA disclosure (including third party material information) have been served

16.5 Defendant information

  (a) Where the readiness assessment is conducted in the presence of the defendant, the reminder card should be completed if there is to be a further hearing

  (b) The defence representative will inform the defendant of the next hearing date in advance and should, where appropriate remind him or her of it. Where agreed locally the court administration may offer an additional reminder service, including by telephone where appropriate

16.6 Case progression activity A case progression officer must:[1]

  (i)   monitor compliance with directions

  (ii) make sure that the court is kept informed of events that may affect the progress of the case

  (iii) make sure that he can be contacted promptly about the case during ordinary business hours

(iv) act promptly and reasonably in response to communications about the case
(v) if he will be unavailable, appoint a substitute to fulfil his duties and inform the other case progression officers

The Court

16.7 The Criminal Procedure Rules 2005 provide that at every hearing, if a case cannot be concluded there and then the court must give directions so that it can be concluded at the next hearing or as soon as possible after that.[2] At every hearing the court must, where relevant:

(a) if the defendant is absent, decide whether to proceed nonetheless[3]
(b) take the defendant's plea (unless already done) or if no plea can be taken then find out whether the defendant is likely to plead guilty or not guilty
(c) set, follow or revise a timetable for the progress of the case, which may include a timetable for any hearing including the trial or (in the Crown Court) the appeal
(d) in giving directions, ensure continuity in relation to the court and the parties' representatives where that is appropriate and practicable
(e) where a direction has not been complied with, find out why, identify who was responsible, and take appropriate action

16.8 In addition, the participants must expect the court actively to manage the case in accordance with the Criminal Procedure Rules 2005 and, where appropriate, to:

(a) list the case for further directions if it appears that ready for hearing in time
(b) make further directions including in relation to appropriate
(c) enquire into and take action in relation to any hearing or partly ineffective or unnecessary
(d) fix the date for determining outstanding pre-trial
(e) consider bail[4]
(f) announce the date of the next hearing

Case Progression Roles and Responsibilities

16.9 Each party must prepare and conduct the case in accordance with the Criminal Procedure Rules 2005 and actively assist the court in fulfilling its duty under those Rules, and must:[5]

(a) comply with directions given by the court
(b) take every reasonable step to make sure his witnesses will attend when they are needed
(c) make appropriate arrangements to present any written or other material
(d) promptly inform the court and the other parties of anything that may:

(i) affect the date or duration of the trial or appeal or
(ii) significantly affect the progress of the case in any other way

There are also additional responsibilities for advocates, administrative staff and the defence as follows:

16.10 Prosecution Advocate

(a) Provide all relevant information to the prosecution team case progression officer, or the person identified to carry out this role, to enable compliance with provisions for notification of readiness within the time specified by the court
(b) Where there is a hearing, ensure that any requests or actions are brought to the attention of the prosecution team for action

16.11 Defence Advocate

(a) Where there is a hearing, confirm to the court[6] if required that in the event of non-attendance, the defendant had been made aware of the hearing date and the consequences of non-attendance
(b) Provide all relevant information to the defence representative to enable compliance with provisions for notification of readiness within the time specified by the court
(c) Where there is a hearing, ensure that any requests or actions are brought to the attention of the defence representative for action, where appropriate

16.12 Magistrates' Court Administration

(a) Where there is a hearing, promptly prepare warrants on the day

Case Progression Officer

(b) Check defendant's representation status if appropriate
(c) Check that the case is ready to proceed at the trial, committal or transfer, and if not take appropriate action
(d) If the court is notified by the defence that a s 6(1) readout committal is required, liaise with the parties to fix an appropriate date for this hearing to take place
(e) Where agreed locally, remind the defendant of the hearing time and date
(f) Send out certificate of readiness forms (if used) to the parties for completion
(g) Ensure that, where notified by the prosecution and/or defence, the facilities to play video and/or audio recordings are available
(h) Ensure that confidential communications eg about possible pleas, are not passed to the court or other parties without agreement

16.13 Prosecution Team

(a) Where there is a hearing, the police and where appropriate court civilian enforcement officers to use every effort to execute bench warrants promptly

(b) The police to ensure that the prosecution file is completed and submitted to the CPS or other prosecutor in accordance with the Manual of Guidance provisions and any orders of the court

Case Progression Function

(c) Identify the nominated person for future contact on case progression matters
(d) If unable to proceed to committal, notify the court administration and defence in advance of the hearing
(e) If notified that a s 6(1) readout committal is required, liaise with the magistrates' court case progression officer for appropriate hearing date and ensure the file is in a fit state for the hearing to take place on the date fixed
(f) Ensure that the prosecution file is made available to the advocate to undertake the hearing and that it is fit for purpose in accordance with the Manual of Guidance
(g) In all cases involving DNA information, and some fingerprint cases, ensure compliance with the prosecution team DNA Guidance regarding staged report
(h) Ensure service of CPIA disclosure has taken place and that there are no outstanding issues regarding expert evidence or third party material
(i) Ensure that consideration is given to the involvement of the Witness Service
(j) Ensure that appropriate pre-trial applications have been made, eg special measures, hearsay and bad character, and that responses have been made to any such applications received, where appropriate. Ensure also that consideration has been given to applying for any ruling to be made binding. If not, to bring this to the attention of the appropriate lawyer
(k) Provide the magistrates' court case progression officer with information about relevant applications and all other information relating to readiness for the next hearing
(l) Ensure that all relevant exhibits are at court and that the court administration has been notified that the facilities to play video and/or audio recordings will be required, where appropriate
(m) Ensure all relevant papers have been filed with the court prior to trial and if not, take appropriate action
(n) Ensure that all relevant material, including reports or other documents, is ready and has been copied for the court
(o) Comply with provisions for notification of readiness within the time specified by the court
(p) Receive and action requests arising or received from the prosecution advocate or the court administration
(q) Inform the court forthwith of anything which might compromise the effectiveness of the next hearing
(r) Make any application for an adjournment immediately after the grounds for doing so are known and support such application with the appropriate necessary evidence

Witness Care Unit (where established)

(s) Maintain contact with victims and witnesses and confirm their availability for hearing
(t) Utilise the needs assessment to identify victim and witness needs
(u) Utilise the Contact Directory to provide tailored interventions to ensure attendance at court
(v) Ensure that the court administration is notified of any special requirements, other than special measures, of victims and witnesses
(w) Provide the Witness Service with information on witnesses attending court and special measures if granted and continue to provide updates of any change in circumstances
(x) Provide victims and witnesses with updates on special measures
(y) Share information about victims and witnesses with the prosecution team

16.14 Defence Case Progression Function

(a) Identify the nominated person for future contact on case progression matters
(b) Ensure that all the relevant material, including reports or other documents, is ready and has been copied for the court
(c) Consider CPIA disclosure and prepare and serve defence statement within the requisite time, if appropriate
(d) Inform the defendant of the time and date of the next hearing and where appropriate, provide a further reminder
(e) Inform the court forthwith of anything which might compromise the effectiveness of the next hearing, including a lack of instructions from the defendant[6]
(f) Make any application for an adjournment immediately after the grounds for doing so are known and support such application with the appropriate necessary evidence
(g) If unable to proceed to committal, notify court administration and prosecution in advance of the hearing
(h) Notify the court administration and the prosecution if s 6(1) readout committal is required and liaise with the court case progression officer to fix an appropriate hearing date
(i) Endeavour to ensure defence witnesses are available for trial
(j) Ensure that the court administration has been notified that the facilities to play video and/ or audio recordings will be required, where appropriate
(k) Receive and action requests arising from the defence advocate or the court administration
(l) Comply with provisions for notification of readiness within the time specified by the court
(m) Provide the magistrates' court case progression officer with information about relevant applications and all other information relating to readiness for the next hearing
(n) Endeavour where appropriate to inform the court administration of any special requirements, other than special measures, of witnesses together with those of the defendant and that consideration is given to the involvement of the Witness Service

(o) Ensure that appropriate pre-trial applications have been made, eg special measures, hearsay and bad character, and that responses have been made to any such applications received, where appropriate. Ensure also that consideration has been given to applying for any ruling to be made binding. If not, to make such application

(p) Consider letter from prosecution regarding agreement of s 9 statements and s 10 admissions, particularly in cases involving DNA or fingerprint material

16.15 Witness Service

(a) Provide pre-court visits for witnesses to familiarise themselves with the courtroom when referred in advance of court attendance and where resources allow

(b) Share information about victims and witnesses with the prosecution team

16.16 National Offender Management Service – Productions from Prison Custody

(a) The PECS contractor, or in the case of Category A prisoners the Prison Service, to ensure that all persons in custody are produced at the court when required and taken to each courtroom promptly in accordance with PECS and Prison Service contracts

(b) The PECS contractor, or Prison Service in respect of Category A prisoner movements, to notify the court administration immediately of any problems anticipated or arising in respect of the production of persons in custody

---

1. Criminal Procedure Rules 2005 rule 3.4(4)
2. Criminal Procedure Rules 2005 rule 3.8
3. Practice Direction *(Criminal Proceedings: Consolidation)* para.1.13 [2004] 1 WLR 589
4. Amendment No 3 to the Consolidated Criminal Practice Direction (Bail: Failure to Surrender and Trials in Absence) sets out "The failure of defendants to comply with the terms of their bail by not surrendering can undermine the administration of justice ... It is therefore most important that defendants who are granted bail appreciate the significance of the obligation to surrender to custody in accordance with the terms of their bail and that courts take appropriate action if they fail to do so. There are at least three courses of action for the courts to consider taking: [A] imposing penalties for the failure to surrender; [B] revoking bail or imposing more stringent bail conditions; and [C] conducting trials in absence of the defendant".
5. Criminal Procedure Rules 2005 rule 3.9(2)
6. Further guidance on this subject may be issued
7. A solicitor is not required to disclose any matters or information which comes to him or her in privileged circumstances as defined in s 10 Police and Criminal Evidence Act 1984

PART 17 TRIAL

A hearing at which the court determines the outcome of the defendant's case

Objectives

17.1

(a) To ensure that trials are effective and proceed when listed

(b) The parties to arrange the attendance of witnesses so as to present evidence clearly and in a helpful order, making full use of court time and avoiding unnecessary waiting

(c) To ensure that victims and witnesses for the prosecution and defence are given appropriate support

Action

17.2 Summary trial hearing Conduct summary trial in accordance with Magistrates' Court Rules

17.3 Witness attendance enforced where not forthcoming Where every effort has been made to enable witness attendance, to enforce witness attendance where not forthcoming, including consideration of issuing and serving a witness summons

17.4 Sentence and/or make ancillary orders where appropriate Case concludes

17.5 Case progression activity A case progression officer must:[1]

(i) monitor compliance with directions

(ii) make sure that the court is kept informed of events that may affect the progress of the case

(iii) make sure that he can be contacted promptly about the case during ordinary business hours

(iv) act promptly and reasonably in response to communications about the case

(v) if he will be unavailable, appoint a substitute to fulfil his duties and inform the other case progression officers

17.6 Defendant information

(a) Where the defendant has been given a reminder card this should be completed if there is to be a further hearing

(b) The defence representative will inform the defendant of the next hearing date in advance and should, where appropriate, remind him or her of it.

Where agreed locally, the court administration may offer an additional reminder service, including by telephone where appropriate

The Court

17.7 The Criminal Procedure Rules 2005 provide that at every hearing, if a case cannot be concluded there and then the court must give directions so that it can be concluded at the next hearing or as soon as possible after that.[2]

At every hearing the court must, where relevant:

    (a) if the defendant is absent, decide whether to proceed nonetheless[3]

    (b) take the defendant's plea (unless already done) or if no plea can be taken then find out whether the defendant is likely to plead guilty or not guilty

    (c) set, follow or revise a timetable for the progress of the case, which may include a timetable for any hearing including the trial or (in the Crown Court) the appeal

    (d) in giving directions, ensure continuity in relation to the court and the parties' representatives where that is appropriate and practicable

    (e) where a direction has not been complied with, find out why, identify who was responsible, and take appropriate action

17.8 In addition, the participants must expect the court actively to manage the case in accordance with the Criminal Procedure Rules 2005 and, where appropriate, to:

    (a) enquire into, and take action in relation to, any hearing which is wholly or partly ineffective or unnecessary

    (b) require a full explanation if a witness is required to attend and either is not called or is asked no relevant questions by the party requiring his or her attendance

    (c) if the defendant is convicted, decide as to the appropriate venue for sentence[4]

    (d) if the defendant is convicted, to pass sentence

    (e) if the defendant is acquitted, to make such orders as the court considers appropriate including a defendant's costs order in a specific sum

    (f) consider making ancillary orders

Case Progression Roles and Responsibilities

17.9 Each party must prepare and conduct the case in accordance with the Criminal Procedure Rules 2005 and actively assist the court in fulfilling its duty under those Rules, and must:[5]

    (a) comply with directions given by the court

    (b) take every reasonable step to make sure his witnesses will attend when they are needed

    (c) make appropriate arrangements to present any written or other material

    (d) promptly inform the court and the other parties of anything that may:

        (i) affect the date or duration of the trial or appeal or

        (ii) significantly affect the progress of the case in any other way

There are also additional responsibilities for advocates, administrative staff and the defence as follows:

17.10 Prosecution Advocate

    (a) Introduce himself or herself to prosecution witnesses and ensure that all prosecution witnesses are present

    (b) Where witness(es) do not attend, consider using the victim personal statement where available in support of an application for a witness summons or for an application to admit a written statement as evidence of fact in the absence of any direct oral evidence[6]

    (c) Record next date of hearing or sentence and record any directions made

    (d) Ensure that any requests or actions are brought to the attention of the prosecution team for action

    (e) In the event of conviction, if a pre-sentence report is requested, if so instructed and where practicable, ensure the CPS/PSR pack is given to the probation service officer at court on the same day to enable preparation of reports

    (f) If the hearing is ineffective, complete the form recording the reason for this and place the form before the magistrates for their consideration before leaving the court

17.11 Defence Advocate

    (a) Introduce himself or herself to defendant and defence witnesses and ensure that all witnesses are present

    (b) Confirm to the court[7] if required that:

        (i) in the event of non-attendance, the defendant has been made aware of the hearing date and the consequences of non-attendance

        (ii) In the event of a conviction, that the defendant has been advised of the importance of attending probation appointments where a presentence report has been requested

    (c) Record next date of hearing or sentence and record any directions made

    (d) Ensure that any requests or actions are brought to the attention of the defence representative for action

    (e) If the hearing is ineffective, complete the form recording the reason for this and place the form before the magistrates for their consideration before leaving the court

17.12 Magistrates' Court Administration

    (a) Promptly prepare warrants on the day of hearing

    (b) If the hearing is ineffective, ensure that a form is completed by advocates to record the reasons for this and place the form before the magistrates for their consideration before the advocates leave the court[8]

Case Progression Officer

    (c) Where agreed locally, remind the defendant of the date and time of the next hearing, including by telephone where appropriate

    (d) Monitor the progress of a case until conclusion and take appropriate action to ensure the next hearing is effective

(e) Ensure that all reports and information which are required before sentencing are available to the court

(f) Ensure that confidential communications eg about possible pleas, are not passed to the court or other parties without agreement

17.13 Prosecution Team

(a) The police and where appropriate court civilian enforcement officers to use every effort to execute bench warrants promptly

(b) The police to ensure that the prosecution file is completed and submitted in accordance with the Manual of Guidance and any order of the court

Case Progression Function

(c) Ensure that the prosecution file is made available to the advocate to undertake the hearing and that it is fit for purpose in accordance with the Manual of Guidance

(d) In all cases involving DNA information, and some fingerprint cases, ensure compliance with the prosecution team DNA Guidance regarding staged report

(e) Ensure that all the relevant material, including reports or other documents, is ready and has been copied for the court

(f) Make enquiries as to the whereabouts of prosecution witnesses should they fail to attend in good time and supply the information to the prosecution advocate, so that the court can be properly informed at the hearing

(g) Provide the prosecution advocate with details of up-to-date antecedents if appropriate

(h) Receive and action requests arising or received from the prosecution advocate or the court administration

(i) In the event of a conviction, if a pre-sentence report is requested and the CPS/PSR pack has not been provided to the probation service officer in court, ensure the same is provided for the Probation Service within locally agreed time limits

(j) Inform the court forthwith of anything which might compromise the effectiveness of the next hearing

(k) Make any application for an adjournment immediately after the grounds for doing so are known and support such application with the appropriate necessary evidence

Witness Care Unit (where established)

(l) Ensure the tailored interventions provided to secure victim and witness attendance at court have been successful

(m) Ensure victims and witnesses have been notified of any future hearing date (eg for sentence) and are informed of the outcome of the hearing

(n) Thank victims and witnesses for their participation

17.14 Defence Case Progression Function

(a) Ensure that all the relevant material, including reports or other documents, is ready and has been copied for the court

(b) Inform the defendant of the time and date of the next hearing and, where appropriate, provide a further reminder

(c) Inform the court forthwith of anything which might compromise the effectiveness of the next hearing, including a lack of instructions from the defendant[9]

(d) Make any application for an adjournment immediately after the grounds for doing so are known and support such application with the appropriate necessary evidence

(e) Make enquiries as to the whereabouts of defence witnesses should they fail to attend in good time and supply the information to the defence advocate, so that the court can be properly informed at the hearing

(f) Receive and action requests arising or received from the defence advocate or the court administration

(g) Consider letter from prosecution regarding agreement of s 9 statements and s 10 admissions, particularly in cases involving DNA or fingerprint material

17.15 Witness Service

(a) Provide support to witnesses during the day and if necessary accompany witnesses to the courtroom when referred in advance of court attendance and where resources allow

(b) Share information about victims and witnesses with the prosecution team

(c) Bring to the attention of the relevant advocate needs for special measures not identified elsewhere

17.16 National Offender Management Service – Productions from Prison Custody

(a) The PECS contractor, or in the case of Category A prisoners the Prison Service, to ensure that all persons in custody are produced at the court when required and taken to each courtroom promptly in accordance with PECS and Prison Service contracts

(b) The PECS contractor, or Prison Service in respect of Category A prisoner movements, to notify the court administration immediately of any problems anticipated or arising in respect of the production of persons in custody

17.17 National Offender Management Service – Probation Service

(a) In the event of a conviction, ensure the probation service officer obtains relevant information from the prosecution advocate or team to prepare a pre-sentence report

(b) Reports to be made available in accordance with National Standards

(c) Comply with the directions of the court

(*d*) Provide the court, prosecution and defence with information about the defendant, where relevant and appropriate

---

1. Criminal Procedure Rules 2005 rule 3.4(4)
2. Criminal Procedure Rules 2005 rule 3.8
3. *Practice Direction (Criminal Proceedings: Consolidation)* para.1.13 [2004] 1 WLR 589
4. Part 12 Chapter 5 Criminal Justice Act 2003 Chapter 44
5. Criminal Procedure Rules 2005 rule 3.9(2)
6. Section 116 Criminal Justice Act 2003
7. Further guidance on this subject may be issued
8. Effective, Cracked, Ineffective and Vacated Trials in Magistrates' Courts: Operational Guidance for Monitoring scheme
9. A solicitor is not required to disclose any matters or information which comes to him or her in privileged circumstances as defined in s 10 Police and Criminal Evidence Act 1984

PART 18 COMMITTAL OR TRANSFER TO THE CROWN COURT FOR TRIAL

A hearing for committal to the Crown Court except where the case proceeds by way of transfer

Objectives

18.1

(*a*) To commit the case to the Crown Court for trial on indictment
(*b*) To transfer appropriate cases to the Crown Court for trial as expeditiously as possible

Action

18.2 Case progression activity

A case progression officer must:[1]

(i) monitor compliance with directions
(ii) make sure that the court is kept informed of events that may affect the progress of the case
(iii) make sure that he can be contacted promptly about the case during ordinary business hours
(iv) act promptly and reasonably in response to communications about the case
(v) if he will be unavailable, appoint a substitute to fulfil his duties and inform the other case progression officers

18.3 Committal for trial hearing[2]

Where a case is committed to the Crown Court a date for plea and case management hearing may be fixed by the magistrates' court and committal papers and draft indictment forwarded to the Crown Court in accordance with directions given by the Resident Judge

18.4 Issue of automatic directions

(*a*) On committal, automatic directions may be given in the magistrates' court in accordance with directions given by the Resident Judge at the Crown Court. The court may identify case issues and direct orders to be complied with by the parties in readiness for the plea and case management hearing at the Crown Court. The parties may be provided with directions and timetables for resolving outstanding casework issues
(*b*) Any application to vary the directions must be made in writing to the Crown Court prior to the expiration of the date for compliance

18.5 Transfer of case[3]

(*a*) The prosecution will serve a notice of transfer and draft indictment upon the court. The case will be automatically transferred to the Crown Court for trial where a date will be set for the plea and case management hearing
(*b*) Once the notice of transfer is served, there will be no further hearing of the case before the magistrates' court and the functions will cease, subject to certain exceptions

18.6 Defendant information

(*a*) Where the defendant has been given a reminder card this should be completed if there is to be a further hearing
(*b*) The defence representative will inform the defendant of the next hearing date in advance and should, where appropriate remind him or her of it. Where agreed locally, the court administration may offer an additional reminder service, including by telephone where appropriate

The Court

18.7 The Criminal Procedure Rules 2005 provide that at every hearing, if a case cannot be concluded there and then the court must give directions so that it can be concluded at the next hearing or as soon as possible after that.[4]

At every hearing the court must, where relevant:

(*a*) if the defendant is absent, decide whether to proceed nonetheless[5]
(*b*) take the defendant's plea (unless already done) or if no plea can be taken then find out whether the defendant is likely to plead guilty or not guilty
(*c*) set, follow or revise a timetable for the progress of the case, which may include a timetable for any hearing including the trial or (in the Crown Court) the appeal
(*d*) in giving directions, ensure continuity in relation to the court and the parties' representatives where that is appropriate and practicable

(e) where a direction has not been complied with, find out why, identify who was responsible, and take appropriate action

18.8 The participants must expect the court actively to manage the case in accordance with the Criminal Procedure Rules 2005 and, where appropriate, to:

(a) commit the case to the Crown Court for trial and set a date for the plea and case management hearing
(b) list the case for further directions if it appears that the case may not be ready for hearing in time
(c) enquire into and take action in relation to any hearing which is wholly or partly ineffective or unnecessary and fix the date for determining outstanding pre-trial issues
(d) consider bail[6]
(e) announce the date of the next hearing
(f) consider making ancillary orders

Case Progression Roles and Responsibilities

18.9 Each party must prepare and conduct the case in accordance with the Criminal Procedure Rules 2005 and actively assist the court in fulfilling its duty under those Rules, and must:[7]

(a) comply with directions given by the court
(b) take every reasonable step to make sure his witnesses will attend when they are needed
(c) make appropriate arrangements to present any written or other material
(d) promptly inform the court and the other parties of anything that may:

    (i) affect the date or duration of the trial or appeal or
    (ii) significantly affect the progress of the case in any other way

There are also additional responsibilities for advocates, administrative staff and the defence as follows:

18.10 Prosecution Advocate

(a) Ensure that the date of the plea and case management hearing is noted on the prosecution papers
(b) Ensure that any requests or actions are brought to the attention of the prosecution team for action
(c) Ensure that, where available, CPIA disclosure is served upon the defence advocate

18.11 Defence Advocate

(a) Ensure that the date of the plea and case management hearing is noted on the defence papers
(b) Ensure that any requests or actions are brought to the attention of the defence representative for action
(c) Confirm to the court[8] if required that in the event of non-attendance, the defendant had been made aware of the hearing date and the consequences of non-attendance

18.12 Magistrates' Court Administration

(a) Promptly prepare warrants on the day of hearing
(b) Ensure that all committal papers are sent to the Crown Court[9]
(c) Ensure that the notice of transfer and all relevant papers are sent to the Crown Court[10]
(d) Ensure that confidential communications eg about possible pleas, are not passed to the court or other parties without agreement
(e) Ensure that case progression forms are sent to the Crown Court

18.13 Prosecution Team

(a) The police and where appropriate court civilian enforcement officers to use every effort to execute bench warrants promptly
(b) The police to ensure that the prosecution file is completed and submitted to the CPS in accordance with the Manual of Guidance provisions and any orders of the court

Case Progression Function

(c) Ensure that the prosecution file is made available to the advocate to undertake the hearing and that it is fit for purpose in accordance with the Manual of Guidance
(d) In all cases involving DNA information, and some fingerprint cases, ensure compliance with the prosecution team DNA Guidance regarding staged report
(e) Receive and action requests arising or received from the prosecution advocate or the court administration
(f) Ensure CPIA disclosure is served and consideration given to expert evidence and third party disclosure
(g) In transfer cases, ensure that all required transfer papers are served on the defence and the Crown Court within the requisite time
(h) Where the defence have served a defence statement, prepare and serve further CPIA disclosure as appropriate
(i) Consider whether a witness summons is appropriate
(j) Ensure that, where an application is made for video evidence to be played as evidence in chief, the visual recordings are copied and that either records of visual interviews (ROVIs), or where needed, transcripts are obtained and that copies of the visual recordings and the ROVIs transcripts are supplied to the court, defence and prosecution advocate, as required

(k) Ensure that appropriate pre-trial applications have been made, eg special measures, hearsay and bad character, and that responses have been made to any such applications received, where appropriate. Ensure also that consideration has been given to applying for any ruling to be made binding. If not, to bring this to the attention of the appropriate lawyer

(l) Ensure that all the relevant material, including reports or other documents, is ready and has been copied for the court

(m) Inform the court forthwith of anything which might compromise the effectiveness of the next hearing

(n) Make any application for an adjournment immediately after the grounds for doing so are known and support such application with the appropriate necessary evidence

Witness Care Unit (where established)

(o) Ensure victims and witnesses have been notified of hearing date

(p) Ensure that the court administration is notified of any special requirements, other than special measures, of victims and witnesses

(q) Provide the Witness Service with information on witnesses attending court and special measures, if granted, and continue to provide updates of any change in circumstances

(r) Provide victims and witnesses with updates on special measures

(s) Share information about victims and witnesses with the prosecution team

18.14 Defence Case Progression Function

(a) Ensure that all the relevant material, including reports or other documents, is ready and has been copied for the court

(b) Inform the defendant of the time and date of the next hearing and, where appropriate, provide a further reminder

(c) Inform the court forthwith of anything which might compromise the effectiveness of the next hearing, including a lack of instructions from the defendant[11]

(d) Make any application for an adjournment immediately after the grounds for doing so are known and support such application with the appropriate necessary evidence

(e) Where the prosecution have served CPIA disclosure, prepare and serve the defence statement within the required time limit

(f) Ensure that there are no outstanding issues regarding expert evidence or third party material

(g) Where the prosecution have served video evidence in advance, ensure that this has been considered

(h) Receive and action requests arising or received from the defence advocate or the court administration

(i) Ensure that appropriate pre-trial applications have been made, eg special measures, hearsay and bad character, and that responses have been made to any such applications received, where appropriate. Ensure also that consideration has been given to applying for any ruling to be made binding. If not, to make such application

(j) Consider letter from prosecution regarding agreement of s 9 statements and s 10 admissions, particularly in cases involving DNA or fingerprint material

18.15 Witness Service

(a) Provide pre-court visits for witnesses to familiarise themselves with the courtroom when referred in advance of court attendance and where resources allow

(b) Share information about victims and witnesses with the prosecution team

18.16 National Offender Management Service – Productions from Prison Custody

(a) The PECS contractor, or in the case of Category A prisoners the Prison Service, to ensure that all persons in custody are produced at the court when required and taken to each courtroom promptly in accordance with PECS and Prison Service contracts

(b) The PECS contractor, or Prison Service in respect of Category A prisoner movements, to notify the court administration immediately of any problems anticipated or arising in respect of the production of persons in custody

---

1. Section 6 Magistrates' Court Act 1980, as amended by part 6 and Schedule 3 Criminal Justice Act 2003 (**when commenced**) (allocation/sending of either-way cases)

2. Section 53 Criminal Justice Act 1991 will be repealed by ss 41 and 332, Schedule 3 para 62(1) and (2) and Schedule 37 Pt 4 CJA 2003. (**when commenced**) (allocation/sending of cases)

3. Criminal Procedure Rules 2005 rule 3.4(4)

4. Criminal Procedure Rules 2005 rule 3.8

5. *Practice Direction (Criminal Proceedings: Consolidation)* para.1.13 [2004] 1 WLR 589

6. Amendment No 3 to the Consolidated Criminal Practice Direction (Bail: Failure to Surrender and Trials in Absence) sets out "The failure of defendants to comply with the terms of their bail by not surrendering can undermine the administration of justice . . . It is therefore most important that defendants who are granted bail appreciate the significance of the obligation to surrender to custody in accordance with the terms of their bail and that courts take appropriate action if they fail to do so. There are at least three courses of action for the courts to consider taking: [A] imposing penalties for the failure to surrender; [B] revoking bail or imposing more stringent bail conditions; and [C] conducting trials in absence of the defendant".

7. Criminal Procedure Rules 2005 rule 3.9(2)

8. Further guidance on this subject may be issued

9. In accordance with Magistrates' Court Rules 1981 r 11

10. In accordance with Magistrates' Courts (Notices of Transfer) Rules 1988 r 7

11. A solicitor is not required to disclose any matters or information which comes to him or her in privileged circumstances as defined in s 10 Police and Criminal Evidence Act 1984

PART 19 SENTENCE AFTER FINDING OF GUILT

A hearing at which sentence will be passed

Objective

19.1

(a) To ensure that the sentencing hearing will go ahead on the date, at the time and in the location fixed and the court has the requisite information to sentence offender justly

(b) To provide outcome information to all victims and witnesses

Action

19.2 Case progression activity A case progression officer must:[1]

(i) monitor compliance with directions

(ii) make sure that the court is kept informed of events that may affect the progress of the case

(iii) make sure that he can be contacted promptly about the case during ordinary business hours

(iv) act promptly and reasonably in response to communications about the case

(v) if he will be unavailable, appoint a substitute to fulfil his duties and inform the other case progression officers

19.3 Sentence and committal for sentence[2] Case concludes in the magistrates' court

The Court

19.4 The Criminal Procedure Rules 2005 provide that at every hearing, if a case cannot be concluded there and then the court must give directions so that it can be concluded at the next hearing or as soon as possible after that.[3]

At every hearing the court must, where relevant:

(a) if the defendant is absent, decide whether to proceed nonetheless[4]

(b) take the defendant's plea (unless already done) or if no plea can be taken then find out whether the defendant is likely to plead guilty or not guilty

(c) set, follow or revise a timetable for the progress of the case, which may include a timetable for any hearing including the trial or (in the Crown Court) the appeal

(d) in giving directions, ensure continuity in relation to the court and the parties' representatives where that is appropriate and practicable

(e) where a direction has not been complied with, find out why, identify who was responsible, and take appropriate action

19.5 In addition, the participants must expect the court actively to manage the case and, where appropriate, to:

(a) enquire into and take action in relation to any hearing which is wholly or partly ineffective or unnecessary

(b) decide as to the appropriate venue for sentence[5]

(c) pass sentence

(d) consider making ancillary orders

Case Progression Roles and Responsibilities

19.6 Each party must prepare and conduct the case in accordance with the Criminal Procedure Rules 2005 and actively assist the court in fulfilling its duty under those Rules, and must:[6]

(a) comply with directions given by the court

(b) take every reasonable step to make sure his witnesses will attend when they are needed

(c) make appropriate arrangements to present any written or other material

(d) promptly inform the court and the other parties of anything that may:

(i) affect the date or duration of the trial or appeal or

(ii) significantly affect the progress of the case in any other way

There are also additional responsibilities for advocates, administrative staff and the defence as follows:

19.7 Prosecution Advocate

(a) Review the statutory provisions relevant to the court's sentencing powers and any relevant Sentencing Guidelines Council guidance and guideline cases and consider, where appropriate, drawing them to the attention of the court

(b) Review the statutory provisions relating to any ancillary orders (such as anti-social behaviour orders) that might be relevant and consider, where appropriate, drawing them to the court's attention; provide, when necessary, drafts of such orders

(c) Ensure that any requests or actions are brought to the attention of the prosecution team for action

(d) Be prepared to provide copies of documents which need to be drawn to the court's attention

19.8 Defence Advocate

(a) Confirm to the court,[7] if required, that in the event of non-attendance, the defendant had been made aware of the hearing date and the consequences of non-attendance

(b) Be prepared to provide copies of documents which need to be drawn to the court's attention

(c) Ensure that any requests or actions are brought to the attention of the defence representative for action

19.9 Magistrates' Court Administration

(a) Promptly prepare warrants on the day of hearing

Case Progression Officer

(b) Where agreed locally, remind the defendant of the date and time of the next hearing, including by telephone where appropriate
(c) Check appropriate reports have been prepared and received
(d) Monitor a case until conclusion and ensure that all reports and information (eg DVLA printout) which are required for sentencing are available to the court
(e) Ensure that confidential communications are not passed to the court or other parties without agreement

19.10 Prosecution Team

(a) The police and where appropriate court civilian enforcement officers to use every effort to execute bench warrants promptly
(b) The police to ensure any evidential material required to resolve any issues ancillary to sentence, as ordered by the court, is provided to the prosecution

Case Progression Function

(c) Ensure that the prosecution file is made available to the advocate to undertake the hearing and that it is fit for purpose in accordance with the Manual of Guidance
(d) Ensure all relevant information is before the court to enable the court to make any orders ancillary to sentence
(e) Ensure that all the relevant material, including reports or other documents, is ready and has been copied for the court
(f) Ensure the court administration has all relevant papers for the court
(g) Receive and action requests arising or received from the prosecution advocate or the court administration
(h) Provide prosecution advocate with up-to-date antecedents, if appropriate
(i) Inform the court forthwith of anything which might compromise the effectiveness of the next hearing
(j) Make any application for an adjournment immediately after the grounds for doing so are known and support such application with the appropriate necessary evidence

Witness Care Unit (where established)

(k) Provide outcome information to all victims and witnesses and thank them for their contribution

19.11 Defence Case Progression Function

(a) Inform the defendant of the time and date of the next hearing and, where appropriate, provide a further reminder
(b) Inform the court forthwith of anything which might compromise the effectiveness of the next hearing, including a lack of instructions from the defendant[8]
(c) Make any application for an adjournment immediately after the grounds for doing so are known and support such application with the appropriate necessary evidence
(d) Ensure that all the relevant material, including reports or other documents, is ready and has been copied for the court
(e) Receive and action requests arising or received from the defence advocate or the court administration
(f) Consider letter from prosecution regarding agreement of s 9 statements and s 10 admissions, particularly in cases involving DNA or fingerprint material

19.12 National Offender Management Service – Productions from Prison Custody

(a) The PECS contractor, or in the case of Category A prisoners the Prison Service, to ensure that all persons in custody are produced at the court when required and taken to each courtroom promptly in accordance with PECS and Prison Service contracts
(b) The PECS contractor, or Prison Service in respect of Category A prisoner movements, to notify the court administration immediately of any problems anticipated or arising in respect of the production of persons in custody

19.13 National Offender Management Service – Probation Service Reports to be made available in accordance with National Standards

1. Criminal Procedure Rules 2005 rule 3.4(4)
2. Sections 3, 6 and 152 Powers of Criminal Courts (Sentencing) Act 2000, s 144 Criminal Justice Act 2003 (reduction in sentences for guilty pleas and committals for sentence)
3. Criminal Procedure Rules 2005 rule 3.8
4. *Practice Direction (Criminal Proceedings: Consolidation)* para.1.13 [2004] 1 WLR 589
5. Part 12 Chapter 5 Criminal Justice Act 2003 Chapter 44
6. Criminal Procedure Rules 2005 rule 3.9(2)
7. Further guidance on this subject may be issued
8. A solicitor is not required to disclose any matters or information which comes to him or her in privileged circumstances as defined in s 10 Police and Criminal Evidence Act 1984

CROWN COURT – NOT GUILTY CASES

PART 20 PREPARATION PRIOR TO FIRST HEARING IN THE CROWN COURT

PART 21 PRELIMINARY HEARING

PART 22 PLEA AND CASE MANAGEMENT HEARING

PART 23 READINESS ASSESSMENT (FOR TRIAL)

PART 24 TRIAL

PART 25 SENTENCE AFTER CONVICTION

1–7767

CROWN COURT – APPEALS FROM THE MAGISTRATES' COURT

PART 26 READINESS ASSESSMENT

This is generally an out of court process requiring compliance by the parties to inform the court of readiness for the next hearing; a hearing before the court may take place if there is a material failure likely to affect the proper progress of the case

Objectives

26.1 Appeal against conviction and/or sentence

(a) To ensure that the case is ready for an effective hearing and that the parties are fully prepared

(b) To identify and address any risks to the effectiveness of the hearing

(c) To ensure that victims or complainants and witnesses are made aware of the hearing date

Action

26.2 Case progression activity

(a) The court may ascertain the readiness for hearing of a case through the lodging of a certificate of readiness or through another procedure specified by the court within the time specified by the court

(b) At the beginning of each case each party and the court must, unless the court otherwise directs, nominate an individual responsible for progressing the case and tell the other parties and the court who he is and how to contact him[1]

(c) A case progression officer must:[2]

  (i) monitor compliance with directions

  (ii) make sure that the court is kept informed of events that may affect the progress of the case

  (iii) make sure that he can be contacted promptly about the case during ordinary business hours

  (iv) act promptly and reasonably in response to communications about the case

  (v) if he will be unavailable, appoint a substitute to fulfil his duties and inform the other case progression officers

The Court

26.3 The Criminal Procedure Rules 2005 provide that at every hearing, if a case cannot be concluded there and then the court must give directions so that it can be concluded at the next hearing or as soon as possible after that.[3]

At every hearing the court must, where relevant:

(a) if the defendant is absent, decide whether to proceed nonetheless[4]

(b) take the defendant's plea (unless already done) or if no plea can be taken then find out whether the defendant is likely to plead guilty or not guilty

(c) set, follow or revise a timetable for the progress of the case, which may include a timetable for any hearing including the trial or (in the Crown Court) the appeal

(d) in giving directions, ensure continuity in relation to the court and the parties' representatives where that is appropriate and practicable

(e) where a direction has not been complied with, find out why, identify who was responsible, and take appropriate action

26.4 In addition, the participants must expect the court actively to manage the case in accordance with the Criminal Procedure Rules 2005 and, where appropriate, to:

(a) list the case for hearing at the earliest opportunity where a custodial sentence has been imposed at the magistrates' court

(b) list the case for further directions if it appears that the case may not be ready for hearing in time

(c) enquire into and take action in relation to any hearing which is wholly or partly ineffective or unnecessary

Case Progression Roles and Responsibilities

26.5 Each party must prepare and conduct the case in accordance with the Criminal Procedure Rules 2005 and actively assist the court in fulfilling its duty under those Rules, and must:[5]

(a) comply with directions given by the court
(b) take every reasonable step to make sure his witnesses will attend when they are needed
(c) make appropriate arrangements to present any written or other material
(d) promptly inform the court and the other parties of anything that may:

    (i) affect the date or duration of the trial or appeal or
    (ii) significantly affect the progress of the case in any other way

There are also additional responsibilities for advocates, administrative staff and the defence as follows:

26.6 Respondent Advocate
Where there is a hearing, ensure that any requests or actions are brought to the attention of the respondent team for action

26.7 Appellant Advocate
(a) Where there is a hearing and if required, confirm to the court[6] that:

    (i) the appellant is aware of the importance of giving instructions and/or attending appointments with his or her solicitor or representative and attending court when required
    (ii) in the event of non-attendance, the appellant had been made aware of the hearing date and the consequences of non-attendance

(b) Where there is a hearing, ensure that any requests or actions are brought to the attention of the appellant's representative for action

26.8 Crown Court Administration
(a) On receipt of a notice of appeal against conviction or sentence send a copy of the notice of appeal to the respondent team

Case Progression Officer
(b) Ensure that the parties have been notified of the name and contact details of the nominated individual responsible for progressing the case
(c) Record the name of the case progression officers for the respondent team and the appellant
(d) Check that the case is ready to proceed at the hearing and if not, to take appropriate action
(e) Where agreed locally, remind the appellant of the hearing time and date
(f) Ensure that, where notified by the appellant and/or respondent team, the facilities to play video and/or audio recordings are available if required
(g) Check appropriate reports have been prepared
(h) Ensure that confidential communications eg about possible pleas, are not passed to the court or other parties without agreement

26.9 Respondent Team
(a) Notify the parties of the name and contact details of the nominated individual responsible for progressing the case
(b) Record the name of the case progression officers for the court and the appellant
(c) Advise the Crown Court administration within the time specified by the court after the sending of the copy of the notice of appeal, of the names of the witnesses in the case
(d) Ensure the list of witnesses identifies separately:

    (i) those who gave oral evidence in the magistrates' court and
    (ii) those whose statements were read

(e) Obtain witness availability and ensure it is notified to the Crown Court administration within the time specified by the court
(f) Ensure that the file is made available to the advocate to undertake the hearing and that it is fit for purpose in accordance with the Manual of Guidance[7]
(g) In all cases involving DNA information, and some fingerprint cases, ensure compliance with the prosecution team DNA Guidance regarding staged report
(h) Provide the Crown Court case progression officer with information about relevant applications and all other information relating to readiness for the next hearing
(i) Ensure that all relevant exhibits are at court and that the court administration has been notified that the facilities to play video and/or audio recordings will be required where appropriate
(j) Ensure any victim/complainant and respondent witnesses required have been notified of the hearing date
(k) Ensure that consideration is given to the involvement of the Witness Service
(l) Ensure that all relevant papers are filed with the court prior to the hearing
(m) Receive and action requests arising or received from the respondent advocate or the court administration
(n) Ensure that appropriate, pre-trial applications have been made, eg special measures, hearsay and bad character, and consideration has been given to applying for any ruling to be made binding. If not, to bring this to the attention of the appropriate lawyer
(o) Comply with provisions for notification of readiness within the time specified by the court
(p) Inform the court forthwith of anything which might compromise the effectiveness of the next hearing
(q) Make any application for an adjournment immediately after the grounds for doing so are known and support such application with the appropriate necessary evidence
(r) Ensure that all the relevant material including reports, or other documents is ready, and has been copied for the court

Witness Care Unit (where established)

(s) Ensure victim/complainant and witnesses have been notified of hearing date and are able to attend court if required
(t) Utilise the needs assessment to identify victim and witness needs
(u) Utilise the Contact Directory to provide tailored interventions to ensure attendance
(v) Ensure that the court administration is notified of any special requirements, other than special measures, of victims and witnesses
(w) Provide Witness Service with information on witnesses attending court and special measures if granted and continue to provide updates of any change in circumstances
(x) Provide victims or complainants and witnesses with updates on special measures
(y) Share information about victims and witnesses with the respondent team

26.10 Appellant Case Progression Function

(a) Notify the parties of the name and contact details of the nominated individual responsible for progressing the case
(b) Record the name of the case progression officers for the court and the respondent
(c) Ensure that all the relevant material, including reports or other documents, is ready and has been copied for the court
(d) Inform appellant of date and time of next hearing and where appropriate, provide a further reminder
(e) Inform the court forthwith of anything which might compromise the effectiveness of the next hearing, including a lack of instructions from the appellant[8]
(f) Make any application for an adjournment immediately after the grounds for doing so are known and support such application with the appropriate necessary evidence
(g) Obtain witness availability and ensure it is notified to the Crown Court administration within the time specified by the court
(h) Ensure that appropriate, pre-trial applications have been made, eg special measures, hearsay and bad character, and consideration has been given to applying for any ruling to be made binding. If not, to make such an application
(i) Endeavour where appropriate to inform the court administration of any special requirements, other than special measures, of witnesses together with those of the appellant and that consideration is given to the involvement of the Witness Service
(j) Comply with provisions for notification of readiness within the time specified by the court
(k) Provide the Crown Court case progression officer with information about relevant applications and all other information relating to readiness for the next hearing
(l) Ensure that the court administration has been notified that the facilities to play video and/or audio recordings will be required where appropriate
(m) Endeavour to ensure that any witnesses required by the appellant have been notified of the hearing date and are available to attend
(n) Receive and action requests arising or received from the appellant advocate or the court administration

26.11 Witness Service

(a) Provide pre-court visits for witnesses to familiarise themselves with the courtroom when referred in advance of court attendance and where resources allow
(b) Share information about victims and witnesses with the prosecution team

26.12 National Offender Management Service – Productions from Prison Custody

(a) The PECS contractor, or in the case of Category A prisoners the Prison Service, to ensure that all persons in custody are produced at the court when required and taken to each courtroom promptly in accordance with PECS and Prison Service contracts
(b) The PECS contractor, or Prison Service in respect of Category A prisoner movements, to notify the court administration immediately of any problems anticipated or arising in respect of the production of persons in custody

---

1. Criminal Procedure Rules 2005 rule 3.4(1)
2. Criminal Procedure Rules 2005 rule 3.4(4)
3. Criminal Procedure Rules 2005 rule 3.8
4. *Practice Direction (Criminal Proceedings: Consolidation)* para.1.13 [2004] 1 WLR 589
5. Criminal Procedure Rules 2005 rule 3.9(2)
6. Further guidance may be issued on this subject
7. Manual of Guidance for the Preparation of Prosecution Case Files
8. A solicitor is not required to disclose any matters or information which comes to him or her in privileged circumstances as defined in s 10 Police and Criminal Evidence Act 1984

PART 27 DETERMINATION

A hearing to determine whether appeal should be allowed or dismissed

Objectives

27.1

(a) To ensure that hearings[1] are effective and proceed to conclusion when listed
(b) To continue to keep victims and witnesses informed of progress

Action

27.2 Case progression activity A case progression officer must:[2]

(i)   monitor compliance with directions
(ii)   make sure that the court is kept informed of events that may affect the progress of the case
(iii)   make sure that he can be contacted promptly about the case during ordinary business hours
(iv)   act promptly and reasonably in response to communications about the case
(v)   if he will be unavailable, appoint a substitute to fulfil his duties and inform the other case progression officers

27.3 Notify magistrates' court of outcome Copy orders to be sent to each party and the magistrates' court

The Court

27.4 The Criminal Procedure Rules 2005 provide that at every hearing, if a case cannot be concluded there and then the court must give directions so that it can be concluded at the next hearing or as soon as possible after that.[3]

At every hearing the court must, where relevant:

(i)   if the defendant is absent, decide whether to proceed nonetheless[4]
(ii)   take the defendant's plea (unless already done) or if no plea can be taken then find out whether the defendant is likely to plead guilty or not guilty
(iii)   set, follow or revise a timetable for the progress of the case, which may include a timetable for any hearing including the trial or (in the Crown Court) the appeal
(iv)   in giving directions, ensure continuity in relation to the court and the parties' representatives where that is appropriate and practicable
(v)   where a direction has not been complied with, find out why, identify who was responsible, and take appropriate action

27.5 In addition, the participants must expect the court actively to manage the case in accordance with the Criminal Procedure Rules 2005 and where appropriate, to:

(*a*)   enquire into and take action in relation to any hearing which is wholly or partly ineffective or unnecessary
(*b*)   if the appeal is dismissed, consider the sentence and costs
(*c*)   if the appeal is allowed, consider costs

Case Progression Roles and Responsibilities

27.6 Each party must prepare and conduct the case in accordance with the Criminal Procedure Rules 2005 and actively assist the court in fulfilling its duty under those Rules, and must:[5]

(*a*)   comply with directions given by the court
(*b*)   take every reasonable step to make sure his witnesses will attend when they are needed
(*c*)   make appropriate arrangements to present any written or other material
(*d*)   promptly inform the court and the other parties of anything that may:

    (i)   affect the date or duration of the trial or appeal or
    (ii)   significantly affect the progress of the case in any other way

There are also additional responsibilities for advocates, administrative staff and the defence as follows:

27.7 Respondent Advocate

(*a*)   Ensure that any requests or actions are brought to the attention of the respondent team for action, eg costs, compensation orders
(*b*)   Review the statutory provisions relevant to the court's sentencing powers and any relevant Sentencing Guidelines Council guidance and guideline cases and consider, where appropriate, drawing them to the attention of the court
(*c*)   Review the statutory provisions relating to any ancillary orders (such as anti-social behaviour orders) that might be relevant and consider, where appropriate, drawing them to the court's attention; provide, when necessary, drafts of such orders
(*d*)   Ensure court has all information for sentence/ancillary orders
(*e*)   In the event of a pre-sentence report being requested, ensure that the CPS/PSR pack is provided to the probation service officer, if practicable and if instructed to do so, to enable preparation of reports
(*f*)   If the hearing is ineffective, complete the form recording the reason for this and place the form before the judge for his or her consideration before leaving the court
(*g*)   Be prepared to provide copies of documents which need to be drawn to the court's attention

If appeal against conviction allowed

(*h*)   Case concludes and no further role

27.8 Appellant's Advocate

(*a*)   Confirm to the court[6] if required that in the event of non-attendance, the appellant had been made aware of the hearing date and the consequences of non-attendance
(*b*)   Ensure the court has all information for sentence/ancillary orders
(*c*)   Advise the appellant of the importance of attending probation appointments where a pre-sentence report is requested

(d) If the hearing is ineffective, complete the form recording the reason for this and place the form before the judge for his or her consideration before leaving the court

(e) Be prepared to provide copies of documents which need to be drawn to the court's attention

(f) Ensure that any requests or actions are brought to the attention of the appellant representative for action

If appeal against conviction allowed

(g) Case concludes and no further role

27.9 Crown Court Administration

(a) If the hearing is ineffective, ensure that a form is completed by advocates to record the reasons for this and hand the form to the judge to sign prior to the advocates leaving the court. Thereafter take appropriate action to ensure the next hearing is effective

Case Progression Officer

(b) Where agreed locally, remind the appellant of the date and time of the next hearing, including by telephone where appropriate

(c) Check appropriate reports have been prepared

If appeal against conviction allowed

(d) Case concludes and no further role

(e) Ensure that confidential communications eg about possible pleas, are not passed to the court or other parties without agreement

27.10 Respondent Team

Case Progression Function

(a) Ensure that the file is made available to the advocate to undertake the hearing and that it is fit for purpose in accordance with the Manual of Guidance

(b) In all cases involving DNA information, and some fingerprint cases, ensure compliance with the prosecution team DNA Guidance regarding staged report

(c) Provide Respondent advocate with up to date antecedents if appropriate

(d) Ensure that relevant information is available to enable the court to make any orders ancillary to sentence

(e) Ensure the court has all relevant papers

(f) Receive and action requests arising or received from the respondent advocate or the court administration

(g) Make enquiries as to the whereabouts of respondent witnesses should they fail to attend in good time and supply the information to the respondent advocate, so that the court can be properly informed at the hearing

If appeal against conviction allowed

(h) Case concludes and no further role

Witness Care Unit (where established)

(i) Provide outcome information to all victims and witnesses and thank them for their contribution

27.11 Appellant Case Progression Function

(a) Inform the appellant of the time and date of the next hearing and, where appropriate, provide a further reminder

(b) Receive and action requests arising or received from the appellant advocate or the court administration

(c) Make enquiries as to the whereabouts of appellant's witnesses should they fail to attend in good time and supply the information to the appellant advocate, so that the court can be properly informed at the hearing

If appeal against conviction allowed

(d) Case concludes and no further role

27.12 Witness Service

(a) Provide support to witnesses during the day and, if necessary, accompany witnesses to the courtroom

(b) Share information about victims and witnesses with the prosecution team

(c) Bring to the attention of the relevant advocate needs for special measures not identified elsewhere

27.13 National Offender Management Service – Productions from Prison Custody

(a) The PECS contractor, or in the case of Category A prisoners the Prison Service, to ensure that all persons in custody are produced at the court when required and taken to each courtroom promptly in accordance with PECS and Prison Service contracts

(b) The PECS contractor, or Prison Service in respect of Category A prisoner movements, to notify the court administration immediately of any problems anticipated or arising in respect of the production of persons in custody

27.14 National Offender Management Service – Probation Service

(a) Ensure the probation service officer obtains relevant information from the respondent advocate or team to prepare a pre-sentence report

(b) Reports to be prepared in accordance with National Standards and generally provided wherever possible to the court the day before the next hearing
(c) Comply with the directions of the court
(d) Provide the court, prosecution and defence with information about the defendant, where relevant and appropriate

---

1. The Consolidated Criminal Practice Direction 2004 Part IV. 39. 17
2. Criminal Procedure Rules 2005 rule 3.4(4)
3. Criminal Procedure Rules 2005 rule 3.8
4. *Practice Direction (Criminal Proceedings: Consolidation)* para.1.13 [2004] 1 WLR 589
5. Criminal Procedure Rules 2005 rule 3.9(2)
6. Further guidance on this subject may be issued

1–7768

MAGISTRATES' COURT – TRAFFIC CASES

PART 28 SPECIFIED AND NON-SPECIFIED CASES TO WHICH S 11(2) AND S 12 MAGISTRATES' COURTS ACT 1980 (GUILTY/PROOF IN ABSENCE) PROCEDURE HAS BEEN APPLIED

A hearing at which the court may determine the outcome of the defendant's case and pass sentence where appropriate

Objectives
28.1
(a) To commence proceedings for correct offences at the earliest opportunity and in all cases within time limits
(b) To comply with s 12 Magistrates' Court Act procedure in all appropriate cases
(c) To avoid unnecessary hearings by being prepared for sentencing on the same day where appropriate
(d) Where proceedings are not served, they should be reissued for service on not more than two occasions

Actions
28.2 Plea
(a) The Justices' Issues Group (judicial membership) will decide on local listing practice.[1] Generally this will provide that these cases, where possible, will be listed in a designated traffic court or otherwise treated as an EFH
(b) The court administration should obtain an up to date DVLA printout where required prior to the initial hearing

28.3 Proof in absence where no plea received
(a) If the court proceeds to deal with the defendant in absence a CPS prosecutor will be required
(b) Where proceedings are not served, they should be reissued for service on not more than two occasions. Generally, if the defendant is not served after the second attempt, the prosecution should consider withdrawing the proceedings

28.4 Reissue proceedings The police will reissue and re-serve proceedings as soon as possible after notification from the court of ineffective service
28.5 Sentence or conclusion Case concluded

The Court
28.6 The Criminal Procedure Rules 2005 provide that at every hearing, if a case cannot be concluded there and then the court must give directions so that it can be concluded at the next hearing or as soon as possible after that.[2]
At every hearing the court must, where relevant:
(a) if the defendant is absent, decide whether to proceed nonetheless[3]
(b) take the defendant's plea (unless already done) or if no plea can be taken then find out whether the defendant is likely to plead guilty or not guilty
(c) set, follow or revise a timetable for the progress of the case, which may include a timetable for any hearing including the trial or (in the Crown Court) the appeal
(d) in giving directions, ensure continuity in relation to the court and the parties' representatives where that is appropriate and practicable
(e) where a direction has not been complied with, find out why, identify who was responsible, and take appropriate action

28.7 In addition, the participants must expect the court actively to manage the case in accordance with the Criminal Procedure Rules 2005 and, where appropriate, to:
(a) proceed to sentence where a guilty plea is entered or where the case has been proved in absence
(b) proceed to deal with the case at the earliest possible opportunity and where appropriate within three hearings
(c) adjourn the case if the defendant's driving licence or DVLA printout is not available

Case Progression Roles and Responsibilities

28.8 Each party must prepare and conduct the case in accordance with the Criminal Procedure Rules 2005 and actively assist the court in fulfilling its duty under those Rules, and must:[4]

(a) comply with directions given by the court
(b) take every reasonable step to make sure his witnesses will attend when they are needed
(c) make appropriate arrangements to present any written or other material
(d) promptly inform the court and the other parties of anything that may:
(i) affect the date or duration of the trial or appeal or
(ii) significantly affect the progress of the case in any other way

There are also additional responsibilities for advocates, administrative staff and the defence as follows:

28.9 Prosecution Team

Police

(a) Put all appropriate cases through the s 12 MCA procedure, serving evidence and documentation prior to the first hearing
(b) Provide evidence of service, together with the papers, to the court to enable the case to proceed at the first hearing
(c) When required, to reissue and re-serve documentation expeditiously and then comply with 28.3(b) above

CPS

(d) Ensure that a prosecutor is available to deal with cases that have to be proved in absence

28.10 Magistrates' Court Administration

(a) Where possible list in designated traffic court without a CPS prosecutor subject to local listing practice
(b) Deal with case in accordance with s 12 MCA procedure, in the absence of a prosecutor (Legal Adviser role)
(c) Move to a CPS prosecutor court and provide file to enable case to be proved in absence, when required
(d) In the event of non service, to ensure that the police are notified at the earliest possible opportunity
(e) Ensure that confidential communications eg about possible pleas, are not passed to the court or other parties without agreement

---

1. Principles of Listing are attached at Annex A
2. Criminal Procedure Rules 2005 rule 3.8
3. *Practice Direction (Criminal Proceedings: Consolidation)* para.1.13 [2004] 1 WLR 589
4. Criminal Procedure Rules 2005 rule 3.9(2)

PART 29 SPECIFIED AND NON-SPECIFIED CASES INCLUDING THOSE WHERE s 12 MAGISTRATES' COURTS ACT PROCEDURE APPLIES – NOT GUILTY PLEAS

A hearing at which the court determines the outcome of the defendant's case

Objective

29.1 To ensure that the case progresses to an effective hearing and where appropriate is concluded at the second listing

Action

29.2 Plea The Justices' Issues Group (judicial membership)[1] will decide on local listing practice. Generally this will provide that these cases, where possible, may be listed in a designated traffic court. However, where this is not possible, the case may be treated as an Early Administrative Hearing (EAH)

29.3 Trial[2] Cases where a not guilty plea is entered will follow the not guilty route
see Part 15 onwards for details
29.4 Sentence or conclusion Case concluded

The Court

29.5 The Criminal Procedure Rules 2005 provide that at every hearing, if a case cannot be concluded there and then the court must give directions so that it can be concluded at the next hearing or as soon as possible after that.**236**
At every hearing the court must, where relevant:

(a) if the defendant is absent, decide whether to proceed nonetheless237
(b) take the defendant's plea (unless already done) or if no plea can be taken then find out whether the defendant is likely to plead guilty or not guilty
(c) set, follow or revise a timetable for the progress of the case, which may include a timetable for any hearing including the trial or (in the Crown Court) the appeal
(d) in giving directions, ensure continuity in relation to the court and the parties' representatives where that is appropriate and practicable
(e) where a direction has not been complied with, find out why, identify who was responsible, and take appropriate action

29.6 In addition, the participants must expect the court actively to manage the case in accordance with the Criminal Procedure Rules 2005 and, where appropriate, to:

(a) order that a plea be taken at the first hearing after service of documentation on accused has been proved
(b) fix a trial date at the first hearing
(c) list the case for a pre-trial review in complex cases
(d) pass sentence

Case Progression Roles and Responsibilities

29.7 Each party must prepare and conduct the case in accordance with the Criminal Procedure Rules 2005 and actively assist the court in fulfilling its duty under those Rules, and must:[5]

(a) comply with directions given by the court
(b) take every reasonable step to make sure his witnesses will attend when they are needed
(c) make appropriate arrangements to present any written or other material
(d) promptly inform the court and the other parties of anything that may:

    (i) affect the date or duration of the trial or appeal or
    (ii) significantly affect the progress of the case in any other way

There are also additional responsibilities for advocates, administrative staff and the defence as follows:

29.8 Prosecution Team
Police
(a) Put all appropriate cases through the s 12 MCA procedure, serving evidence and documentation prior to the first hearing
(b) In non s 12 MCA cases to provide file to the prosecution team to enable prosecutor to present case at the first hearing
(c) Provide the prosecution team with witness availability
(d) Where a not guilty plea is entered send evidence to the prosecution team

CPS
(e) Ensure the file is provided to the prosecution advocate in readiness for first and any subsequent hearings
(f) Ensure that in the event of a trial, the file is in a fit state for that purpose
(g) Warn witnesses in readiness for trial and ensure witnesses are able to attend

29.9 Magistrates' Court Administration
(a) Where possible, list in designated traffic court as appropriate, subject to local listing practice
(b) Ensure that confidential communications eg about possible pleas, are not passed to the court or other parties without agreement

---

1. Principles of Listing are attached at Annex A
2. Section 45 and sch 3 Courts Act 2003 (binding pre-trial rulings)
3. Criminal Procedure Rules 2005 rule 3.8
4. *Practice Direction (Criminal Proceedings: Consolidation)* para.1.13 [2004] 1 WLR 589
5. Criminal Procedure Rules 2005 rule 3.9(2)

PART 30   NON-SPECIFIED OFFENCES TO WHICH s 12 MAGISTRATES' COURT ACT 1980 PROCEDURE HAS NOT BEEN APPLIED: GUILTY PLEAS

A hearing at which sentence will be passed

Objective
30.1
(a) To lay information for correct offences at the earliest opportunity and in all cases within time limits
(b) To list for conclusion as an EFH case
(c) To avoid unnecessary hearings by being prepared for sentencing on the same day where appropriate

Action
30.2 Plea If a guilty plea is entered all participants should be prepared for the case to proceed to sentence. The court administration will obtain up to date DVLA printout prior to the initial hearing

The Court
30.3 The Criminal Procedure Rules 2005 provide that at every hearing, if a case cannot be concluded there and then the court must give directions so that it can be concluded at the next hearing or as soon as possible after that.[1]
At every hearing the court must, where relevant:

(a) if the defendant is absent, decide whether to proceed nonetheless[2]
(b) take the defendant's plea (unless already done) or if no plea can be taken then find out whether the defendant is likely to plead guilty or not guilty

(c) set, follow or revise a timetable for the progress of the case, which may include a timetable for any hearing including the trial or (in the Crown Court) the appeal

(d) in giving directions, ensure continuity in relation to the court and the parties' representatives where that is appropriate and practicable

(e) where a direction has not been complied with, find out why, identify who was responsible, and take appropriate action

30.4 In addition, the participants must expect the court actively to manage the case in accordance with the Criminal Procedure Rules 2005 and, where appropriate, to pass sentence

Case Progression Roles and Responsibilities

30.5 Each party must prepare and conduct the case in accordance with the Criminal Procedure Rules 2005 and actively assist the court in fulfilling its duty under those Rules, and must:[3]

(a) comply with directions given by the court

(b) take every reasonable step to make sure his witnesses will attend when they are needed

(c) make appropriate arrangements to present any written or other material

(d) promptly inform the court and the other parties of anything that may:

    (i) affect the date or duration of the trial or appeal or

    (ii) significantly affect the progress of the case in any other way

There are also additional responsibilities for advocates, administrative staff and the defence as follows:

30.6 Magistrates' Court Administration

(a) List for conclusion in EFH court subject to local listing practice

(b) Ensure that confidential communications eg about possible pleas, are not passed to the court or other parties without agreement

30.7 Prosecution Team

Police

Provide EFH file to prosecutor

---

1. Criminal Procedure Rules 2005 rule 3.8
2. *Practice Direction (Criminal Proceedings: Consolidation)* para.1.13 [2004] 1 WLR 589
3. Criminal Procedure Rules 2005 rule 3.9(2)

1–7769

ANNEX A

SECTION 14 OF THE CROWN COURT MANUAL – LISTING OF CASES

This section of the Crown Court Manual is issued under and with the authority of the Lord Chief Justice.

— It sets out the principles applicable to listing in the Crown and magistrates' courts.

— It supports the Criminal Procedure Rules which introduce new principles of case management to criminal cases. The changes made emphasise the fact:

— that judges will be required to make firm arrangements for the listing of cases at the Plea and Case Management Hearing (or earlier)

— that parties must comply with the directions and timetable then set so that cases are ready to be heard in accordance with that timetable

— that cases commence promptly at the appointed hour in accordance with that timetable.

— It sets out the new arrangements for the assignment of judges to cases.

— It emphasises the importance, recently stressed by the Court of Appeal, of ensuring that no short hearings in other cases interrupt the prompt commencement or continuation of trials each day at the time appointed

Contents

1. Introduction Listing is a judicial responsibility and function. The overall purpose is to ensure that, as far as possible, all cases are brought to a hearing or trial in accordance with the interests of justice, that the resources available for criminal justice are deployed as effectively as possible, and that, consistent with the needs of the victims, witnesses of the prosecution and the defence and defendants, cases are heard by an appropriate judge or bench with the minimum of delay.

The Concordat[1] states that judges are responsible for deciding on the assignment of cases to particular courts and the listing of those cases before particular judges, working with HMCS. Therefore:

(a) The Presiding Judges of the Circuit have the overall responsibility for listing on each Circuit/Region. As set out at paragraph 4(2) below, certain cases in the Crown Court must be referred to the Presiding Judges for directions; the Presiding Judges will be supported by a Regional Listing co-ordinator.

(b) In the Crown Court, subject to the supervision of the Presiding Judges, the Resident Judge at each Crown Court is responsible for listing at his/her Crown Court centre; the Resident Judge is responsible (following guidance or directions issued by the Lord Chief Justice and by the Senior Presiding Judge and Presiding Judges under paragraph IV 33 of the

Consolidated Practice Direction) for determining the Listing Practice to be followed at that centre, for prioritising the needs of one case against another and deciding upon which date a case is listed and before which judge.

(c) The Listing Officer in the Crown Court is responsible for carrying out the day-to-day operation of Listing Practice under the direction of the Resident Judge. The Listing Officer at each Crown Court centre has one of the most important functions at that Crown Court and makes a vital contribution to the efficient running of that Crown Court and to the efficient operation of the administration of criminal justice.

(d) In the magistrates' court, the judicial members of the Justices Issues Group for each Area are responsible for determining the Listing Practice in that Area. The day-to-day operation of that Listing Practice is the responsibility of the Justices Clerk with the assistance of the Listing Officer.

(e) The Local Criminal Justice Board in each CJS Area is responsible for delivering the policies and aims of the National Criminal Justice Board by:

— Improving the performance of the local criminal justice agencies
— Improving provisions for victims, witnesses and others involved
— Improving public confidence

2. Principles of listing Lord Steyn summarised the guiding principle which must be followed:[2]

"There must be fairness to all sides. In a criminal case this requires the court to consider a triangulation of interests. It involves taking into account the position of the accused, the victim and his or her family, and the public."

When setting the Listing Practice, the Resident Judge or the judicial members of the Justices Issues Group should, in addition to following any directions given by the Lord Chief Justice, the Head of Criminal Justice, the Senior Presiding Judge and the Presiding Judges, take into account the overall purpose of listing as set out above and, in addition, the following principles; these are not listed in order of priority or importance.

(a) Meeting the needs of victims and witnesses; each of whom may have differing needs – the young and the vulnerable require particular attention.

(b) Ensuring the timely trial of cases so that justice is not delayed.

— In general, each case should be tried within as short a time of its arrival in the court as is consistent with the interests of justice, the needs of victims and witnesses, and with the proper preparation by the prosecution and defence of their cases in accordance with the directions and timetable set before or at the Plea and Case Management Hearing.
— Priority should be accorded to the trial of young defendants, and cases where there are vulnerable or young witnesses.
— Custody time limits should be observed.
— Priority may also be accorded to other types of case.

(c) Providing for certainty, and/or as much advance notice as possible, as to the trial date.

(d) Seeing that a judge or bench with any necessary authorisation and of appropriate experience is available to try each case and, wherever desirable, there is judicial continuity.

(e) Taking into account the position of the defendant as to whether he/she is in custody or on bail.

(f) Striking a balance in the use of resources, by taking account of:

— The efficient deployment of the judiciary in the Crown Court, and in the magistrates' court the proper and efficient deployment of the judiciary as is consonant with the need for magistrates' competences to be maintained and the Venne criteria to be followed.
— The proper use of the courtrooms available at the court.
— The provision in long cases for adequate reading time for the judiciary.
— The facilities in the available courtrooms, including the security needs (such as a secure dock), size and equipment, such as video link facilities.
— The desirability of timing Plea and Case Management Hearings so that the trial advocates can attend.
— The proper use of those who attend the Crown Court as jurors.
— The need to return those sentenced to custody as soon as possible after the sentence is passed, and to facilitate the efficient operation of the prison escort contract.

(g) Providing:

— the defendant and the prosecution with the advocate of their choice where this does not result in undue delay to the trial of the case.[3]
— for the efficient deployment of advocates, lawyers and designated case workers of the Crown Prosecution Service, and other prosecuting authorities, and of the resources available to the independent legal profession, for example by trying to group certain cases together.

(h) Meeting the need for special security measures for category A and other high-risk defendants.

(i) Taking into account the impact of policies, targets and initiatives of:

— Her Majesty's Government and its agencies.
— Local Authorities, the Criminal Justice Board for the Area, the Chief Constable or Chief Crown Prosecutor for the Area and other local bodies.

Although the Listing Practice at each court centre will take into account these principles, the practice adopted will vary from court to court depending particularly on:
- The number of court rooms and the facilities available
- Location
- Workload – its volume and type
- The available number of advocates and lawyers
- The proximity of the prison, particularly for women, juveniles, and young offenders
- The surrounding geography and public transport facilities
- The effective trial rate, after allowing for cracked, ineffective and vacated trials

What is plain is that a Listing Practice that will operate successfully in a small two-court centre is unlikely to suit the needs of a metropolitan multi-court centre and vice versa. It may also mean that on occasions the Listing Practice set may result in the judge working in chambers on his judicial work.

3. Setting the listing practice at each court centre

(a) Determination

(i) The Resident Judge at each Crown Court and the judicial members of the Justices Issues Group in each Area will, in relation to the Crown Court and magistrates' courts respectively, set overall Listing Practice in a local area in accordance with the objectives and considerations set out above.

(ii) The Resident Judge, or the judicial members of the Justices Issues Group, as the case may be, will consider representations made by local criminal justice agencies and representatives of the defence and witnesses, in the setting of the Listing Practice and in the periodic reviews of that Listing Practice. Consultation with Local Criminal Justice Boards regarding local listing issues and the impact on cracked and ineffective trials should also take place.

(iii) It will be for the Resident Judge, or the judicial members of the Justices Issues Group, to consider whether to do this by seeking comments in writing on the draft Listing Practice, or by convening a special meeting, or by discussing the issues at the court users' meetings referred to below, or otherwise conducting the consultation in the manner he or they consider best.

(b) Monthly analysis of the performance

(i) The Court Manager, Listing Officer and/or Case Progression Officer should each month, or at such other period as may be specified by the Resident Judge or Bench Chairman and Justices Clerk:

- Review the causes of ineffective, cracked and vacated trials and provide to the Resident Judge (or the Bench Chairman and Justices' Clerk and District Judge, as the case may be) an analysis of each case or specified categories of case and the lessons to be learnt.

- In the Crown Court, provide to and discuss with the Resident Judge the list of any outstanding cases which are older than 20 weeks, or such other shorter period as is specified by the Resident Judge. This list can be provided by the Crest RAGE report.

(ii) Monthly (or other periodic) meetings should be also arranged between the Court Manager, Listing Officer or Case Progression Officer and local court users (including the CPS, Witness Care Unit, the Witness Service, police and defence solicitors (where possible)) and representatives of the Local Criminal Justice Board to discuss:

- The analysis of cracked, ineffective and vacated trials (based on enquiry into the matters disclosed by the form completed after the enquiry conducted by the judge or the chairman presiding over the court for that case).

- The action that might be taken to address any similar problems in advance of the trial and to improve the provisions for witnesses.

The discussion of the analysis of the reasons for cracked, ineffective and vacated trials should be minuted, and copies of the minutes should be sent to all the parties to the cases discussed. The outcome of these discussions may provide information for the Resident Judge and judicial members of the Justices Issues Group respectively to contribute to his/her/their review of Listing Practice.

(c) User Meetings

(i) The Resident Judge or the representatives of the Justices Issues Group respectively (such as the Justices' Clerk and/or legal advisers) will hold periodic court user meetings with representatives of local prosecutors or other criminal justice agencies and representatives of the defence.

(ii) One of the agenda items will normally be the operation of the Listing Practice.

(d) Resolution of difficulties

(i) Where difficulties arise, whether around listing generally or regarding specific cases, which cannot be resolved by the Listing Officer, the matter should be referred for consideration:

- In the Crown Court, to the Resident Judge or the judge assigned to a specific case.

— In the magistrates' courts, to the Justices' Clerk, if it relates to a specific case, or, if it relates to more general issues, to the judicial members of the Justices Issues Group and then, if necessary, to the Area Judicial Forum.

(ii) Where resolution of disagreement, either in relation to the Crown Court or magistrates' courts cannot be reached locally, as set out in sub-paragraph (i), the issue should be referred without delay to the Presiding Judges or the Senior Presiding Judge.

---

1. The agreement reached between the Lord Chief Justice and the Secretary of State for Constitutional Affairs and Lord Chancellor set out in statement to the House of Lords on 26 January 2004.
2. House of Lords – *A-G's Reference (No 3 of 1999)* [2001] 2 AC 91.
3. This does not in any way affect applications for changes in representation orders. For that, see the ruling of HH Judge Wakerley QC (as he then was) in *Asghar Ali* which has been circulated by the JSB.

ANNEX B

CONTENT OF EXPEDITED AND EVIDENTIAL CHARGING DECISION REPORTS AND CASE FILE

Straightforward and 'Guilty Plea' cases

Pre-charge Expedited Report For charging decision – to custody officer or Duty Prosecutor	Post-charge Expedited File For EFH court hearing
MG 3 – Report to crown prosecutor (for offences where CPS decide charge) **MG 11(s)*** – Key witness statement(s) or Index (if visually recorded) (if witnessed by police, use MG 11 of one officer)	**MG 1** – File front sheet **MG 4** – Charge sheet **MG 5** – Case file summary (unless the statements cover all elements of the case)
MG 15 – SDN or verbal summary of admissions. (SDN can be written on officer's MG11)	**MG 6** – Case file information (if there is information for the investigator to record)
Phoenix print (suspect pre-cons, cautions, etc)	**MG 10** – Witness non-availability (PYO only) **MG 11(s)*** – Key witness statement(s) or Index (if visually recorded) **SDN** – may be written on MG15, MG5 or MG11 of officer **Phoenix print** (suspect pre-cons, cautions, etc.) **Where applicable, include the following:** **MG 2** – Initial witness assessment
Once a charging decision has been made, the 'Pre-charge Expedited Report' becomes the 'Post-charge Expedited File' for court.	**MG 3** – Report to crown prosecutor (for offences where CPS decide charge) **MG 3A** – Further report to crown prosecutor **MG 4A** – Conditional bail form **MG 4B** – Request to vary police conditional bail **MG 4C** – Security/Surety **MG 7** – Remand application
Further Upgrading? Not required if the case is disposed of at the first court appearance. If a 'not-guilty' plea is entered or the defendant elects Crown Court, prepare a Full File.	**MG 8** – Breach of bail conditions **MG 11** – Other witness statements already taken **MG 13** – Application for order on conviction **MG 18** – Offences taken into consideration (TIC) **MG 19** – Compensation form (plus supporting documents)
***Include details of pre-cons for witnesses who have provided 'Key' MG11s if case involves a remand in custody**	**Copy of documentary exhibits/photos** **Police racist incident form/crime report (in racist incident cases)**

Contested or Crown Court cases

Pre-charge Evidential Report For charging decision – to Custody Officer or Duty Prosecutor	Post-charge Evidential File For EAH court hearing	Upgrade to Full File For Crown Court or contested cases
MG 3 – Report to crown prosecutor (suggest charges)	MG 1 – File front sheet	MG 6C – Schedule of Non-sensitive unused materials
MG 5 – Case summary (unless the statements cover all elements of the case)	MG 3 – Report to crown prosecutor	MG 6D – Schedule of sensitive material
MG 6 – Case file information	MG 4 – Charge sheet	MG 6E – Disclosure officer's report
MG 11(s) – Key witness statement(s) or Index (if visually recorded). If witnessed by police, use MG11 of one officer, summarise evidence of others	MG 5 – Case file summary (unless MG11(s) cover all elements of case)	MG 9 – Witness list
MG12 – Exhibits list	MG 6 – Case file information (if there is information for the investigator to record)	MG11 – All other statements
MG15 – Interview record: SDN / ROTI / ROVI (SDN can be on MG5, officer's MG11 or MG15)	MG 10 – Witness non-availability	Custody record
Crime report and incident log	MG 11(s) – Key witness statement(s) or Index (if visually recorded)	Where applicable, include the following:
Any unused material which might undermine the case (disclosure schedules not required at this stage)	MG 12 – Exhibits list	MG 2 – Initial witness assessment
Copies of Key documentary exhibits	Copies of Key exhibits/photos	MG 6B – police officer's disciplinary record
Phoenix print (suspect pre-cons, cautions, etc.)	MG 15 – Interview record – SDN / ROTI / ROVI (SDN can be on MG5, officer's MG11 or MG15)	Phoenix print (witness pre-cons, cautions, etc see the JOPI)
	Phoenix print (suspect pre-cons, cautions, etc.)	
	Where they are applicable, include the following:	
	MG 2 – Initial witness assessment	
Once a charging decision has been made, the 'Pre-charge Evidential Report' becomes the 'Post-charge Evidential File' for court.	MG 3A – Further report to crown prosecutor	
	MG 4A/B/C – Bail/security/surety	
	MG 7 – Remand application	
Further Upgrading? Where it is clear that the case will be heard in the Crown Court, or a not guilty plea is likely, a Full File should be prepared and submitted with the MG3.	MG 11 – Other witness statements already taken	
	MG 13 – Application for order on conviction	
	MG 18 – Offences TIC	
	MG 19 – Compensation form plus supporting documents	
	Police racist incident form / crime report (in racist incident cases)	

PART II
EVIDENCE

INTRODUCTION AND CONTENTS

2–1 Part II of this manual deals principally with the law of evidence. The narrative sets out the law on a number of topics such as the nature of evidence, witnesses, relevance and admissibility, etc. Finally, we set out shortly some of the basic rules concerning the interpretation of legislation.

The basic statement of principle or authority is set out first, followed by a commentary, statement of secondary principles, illustrations, procedures and exceptions or variations in smaller type. This text, rather than the footnotes to statutes, should generally be used for comprehensive information on matters of evidence and interpretation. Finally, we reproduce the text of statutes and statutory instruments on evidence and interpretation, including the Codes of Practice under the Police and Criminal Evidence Act 1984, arranged chronologically and annotated.

General principles of the law of evidence
RELEVANCE AND ADMISSIBILITY

2-20　Evidence is relevant if it is logically probative or disprobative of some matter which requires proof[1]. Evidence is generally admissible if it relates to the facts directly in issue. It may also be admissible of other facts, often referred to as "circumstantial evidence", which render the facts in issue probable or improbable[2]. Common law or statutory provisions exclude some facts which would otherwise seem logically relevant; these are discussed later in succeeding paragraphs. Sometimes whole issues may be precluded from presentation before the court by rules as to estoppel, res judicata, autrefois convict, autrefois acquit[3].

Where the complainant had made allegations of sexual abuse against three individuals who were not acting in concert, the evidence that two of the abusers had admitted the abuse and that she had been telling the truth in those cases was not logically relevant to case of the third. It was merely a form of 'oath helping' and as it was not relevant, it was not admissible[4].

　　1.　*DPP v Kilbourne* [1973] 1 All ER 440, *per* Lord Simon of Glaisdale.
　　2.　*Dowling v Dowling* (1860) 10 ICLR 236.
　　3.　See para **1–448 Res judicata, estoppel; autrefois convict/acquit; functus officio** in PART I: MAGISTRATES' COURTS, PROCEDURE, ante.
　　4.　*R v T* [2006] EWCA Crim 2006, [2007] 1 Cr App R 4, [2007] Crim LR 165.

2-21　No fact can be proved with absolute certainty. All that can be done is to adduce such evidence of facts that the court is satisfied that the fact is so. This may be done by direct evidence or by inference from facts[1] but the matter must not be left to rest in surmise, conjecture, or guess[2]. Justices should not proceed upon their knowledge gained in other proceedings without first giving the party affected thereby an opportunity of dealing with such matters and any inference to be drawn therefrom[3].

　　1.　See for example *Hampson v Powell* [1970] 1 All ER 929, 134 JP 321.
　　2.　*Hawkins v Powells Tillery Steam Coal Co Ltd* [1911] 1 KB 988; but obviously allowing for opinion from expert witnesses, *Lewis v Port of London Authority* (1914) 111 LT 776.
　　3.　*Thomas v Thomas* [1961] 1 All ER 19, [1961] 1 WLR 1, 125 JP 95; *Brinkley v Brinkley* [1965] P 75, [1963] 1 All ER 493, 107 Sol Jo 77.

THE PRINCIPLE OF ORALITY

2-22　The law of evidence has its origins in trial before a jury where the assumption was that oral evidence was to be given by a witness of facts which he himself had observed. There was concern that the relaying of the testimony of witnesses who were not present in court and could not be cross-examined could impair the reliability of evidence. The only other "direct" evidence available to the court was that of things or objects which the court could see or examine for itself. The admissibility of the latter form of evidence, "real evidence"[1], has given rise to little difficulty in practice. Distinguishing direct oral evidence from the mere relaying of a statement from another person and whether such evidence, "hearsay evidence", is admissible has proved more complex. Apart from determining whether a second hand statement is to be admitted as evidence of the facts which it describes (in which case it is hearsay), or merely that it was said at all to establish, for example, that the hearing of this statement was the reason why the witness acted as he did (not hearsay), a strict application of the hearsay rule would frustrate the administration of justice. For example, a printed statute would be admissible as real evidence, ie as an object consisting of ink and paper. But if the intention were to admit the meaning of the text, this would be hearsay. Accordingly, the Common Law developed a number of exceptions to the rule against the admission of hearsay evidence, such as that in relation to public documents[2] or where the circumstances were such that the possibility of concoction or distortion could be disregarded, as in "res gestae"[3]. The "rule against hearsay" was the main constituent of the law of evidence until recently. However, the Civil Evidence Act 1995 has for practical purposes, abolished the hearsay rule in civil proceedings, subject to certain procedural safeguards[4]. In criminal proceedings, the Criminal Justice Act 2003, whilst specifically preserving former common law exceptions, has fundamentally recast the approach to the admission of hearsay evidence with a view to making such evidence more readily admissible[5].

　　1.　See para **2–60 Documents and material objects as evidence**, post.
　　2.　See para **2–63 Public documents**, post.
　　3.　See para **2–264 Res gestae**, post.
　　4.　See para **2–340 Hearsay in civil proceedings**, post.
　　5.　See para **2–250 Admission of hearsay evidence in criminal proceedings**, post.

EVIDENCE OF FACT AND EVIDENCE OF OPINION

2-23　The opinion of a witness is generally inadmissible; he is there to relate observed facts[1]. Expert witnesses may however be called upon to state their opinion on a matter within their special knowledge or skill, where the court itself cannot form an opinion, special study, skill or experience being required[2]. A non-expert witness may give admissible evidence whether a person was drunk[3] (but not whether he was fit to drive), whether an estimate as to the value of damage to a window was accurate[4].

1. *Carter v Boehm* (1766) 3 Burr 1905, *Hollington v Hewthorne* [1943] 2 All ER 35, *R v Davies* [1962] 3 All ER 97.
2. *Folkes v Chadd* (1782) 3 Doug KB 157.
3. *R v Davies* [1962] 3 All ER 97, [1962] 1 WLR 1111.
4. *R v Beckett* (1913) 29 TLR 332.

CORROBORATION AND WEIGHT OF EVIDENCE

2–24 "Corroboration is therefore nothing other than evidence which confirms or supports or strengthens other evidence. It is, in short, evidence which renders other evidence more probable"[1].

By English common law, the evidence of one competent witness is enough to support a verdict in either civil or criminal proceedings. There are exceptions.

1. Some statutes require that the absence of corroboration must lead to an acquittal[2].
2. Where a rule of practice having the force of a rule of law provides for corroboration, for example in the case of persons of admittedly bad character, or where the witness can reasonably be suggested to have some purpose of his own to serve in giving false evidence; thus a court should recognise it is always really dangerous to convict on the evidence of particular witnesses, unless corroborated in a material particular by independent testimony, implicating the accused or confirming disputed items in the case[3].

To the extent that it needs corroboration, evidence to which this rule applies is suspect. It must, however, be sufficient, satisfactory and credible in itself; corroboration cannot make good anything lacking in this respect[4].

3. In matrimonial proceedings, by rule of practice, "justices should remind themselves, as they proceed to adjudication, of the desirability of corroboration, not least where on the face of the complainant's evidence it is available, just as they should remind themselves of the onus and standard of proof"[5]. The court may act on the uncorroborated evidence of a spouse, if it is in no doubt where the truth lies, but if the appellate court is convinced that the trial court proceeded oblivious of the rule of practice, it will intervene, especially where the case involves allegations of sexual misconduct.

The requirement whereby at a trial on indictment it was obligatory for the court to give the jury a warning about convicting the accused on the uncorroborated evidence of a person merely because that person was

(a) an alleged accomplice of the accused, or
(b) where the offence charged was a sexual offence, the person in respect of whom it was alleged to have been committed,

has been abolished, as has any similar requirement applicable on the summary trial of a person for an offence[6]. In such cases it is a matter for the judge's discretion what, if any, warning he considers appropriate in respect of such a witness. Whether the judge chooses to give a warning and in what terms will depend on the circumstances of the case, the issues raised, the content and quality of the witness's evidence and whether there is an evidential basis for suggesting that the evidence of the witness may be unreliable[7].

The broad discretion to give a warning about a witness and its terms, extends to cases of "cell confessions" ie the confession by one prisoner to another. The points which may require consideration will depend on the circumstances of the particular case and may include the fact that such confessions are often easy to concoct and difficult to prove; that prisoners may have many motives to lie and whether such an issue is raised on the evidence; and whether the informant has a significant criminal record or history of lying[8].

---

1. LORD SIMON OF GLAISDALE in *DPP v Kilbourne* [1973] AC 729, [1973] 1 All ER 440, 137 JP 193.
2. See for example Perjury Act 1911, s 13, Representation of the People Act 1983, s 168(5) (personation); Road Traffic Regulation Act 1984, s 89 (speeding).
3. *R v Baskerville* [1916] 2 KB 658, 80 JP 446; *R v Beebe* (1925) 89 JP 175; *DPP v Kilbourne*, supra and cf *R v Sidhu* (1976) 63 Cr App Rep 24 (affray cases); and see *R v Reeves* (1978) 68 Cr App Rep 331, [1979] Crim LR 459 and *R v Stewart* [1986] Crim LR 805.
4. *A-G of Hong Kong v Wong Muk Ping* [1987] AC 501, [1987] 2 All ER 488.
5. Sir Jocelyn Simon P in *Alli v Alli* [1965] 3 All ER 480, 130 JP 6.
6. Criminal Justice and Public Order Act 1994, s 32, this PART, post.
7. *R v Makanjuola* [1995] 3 All ER 730, [1995] 1 WLR 1348, [1995] 2 Cr App Rep 469, CA.
8. *R v Stone* [2005] EWCA Crim 105, [2005] Crim LR 569.

Matters that can be assumed without evidence

JUDICIAL NOTICE

2–40 When a court takes judicial notice of a fact, it finds that the fact exists although it has not been established by evidence.

Facts of which the court will take judicial notice include statutes[1], the ordinary course of nature[2], time[3], the ordinary meaning of English words[4], although reference may be made in relation to such matters to legal or medical text books, almanacs, dictionaries, expert treatises[5]. Other facts of which the court may take judicial notice include the status of a foreign government after inquiry of a

Secretary of State[6], the existence of a state of war[7], custom[8], or the ordinary processes of arrest, charge and bail within its jurisdiction[9].

1. See post **2–63 Public documents**.
2. *R v Luffe* (1807) 8 East 193; *McQuaker v Goddard* [1940] 1 KB 687, [1940] 1 All ER 471.
3. *Walker v Stretton* (1896) 60 JP 313.
4. *Chapman v Kirke* [1948] 2 KB 450, [1948] 2 All ER 556.
5. See for example *McCarthy v The Melita (Owners)* (1923) 130 LT 445; *Page v Faucet* (1591) Cro Eliz 227; *Walker v Stretton*, supra; *East London Rly Co v Thames Conservators* (1904) 68 JP 302.
6. *Duff Development Co Ltd v Kelanton Government* [1924] AC 797 and see *Foster v Globe Venture Syndicate Ltd* [1900] 1 Ch 811 and cf *Re Amand* [1941] 2 KB 239; *Re Amand (No 2)* [1942] 1 KB 445, [1942] 1 All ER 236.
7. *R v Bottrill, ex p Kuechenmeister* [1947] 1 KB 41, [1946] 2 All ER 434.
8. *Brandao v Barnett* (1846) 12 Cl & Fin 787.
9. See *Allen v Ireland* [1984] 1 WLR 903, 148 JP 545.

JUSTICES' LOCAL OR SPECIALIST KNOWLEDGE

2–41   Justices may not act on personal knowledge of facts, and the courts must be cautious not to treat a factual conclusion as obvious even though the man in the street would unhesitatingly hold it so[1]. Nevertheless, justices may take into consideration matters which they know of their own knowledge, particularly matters in regard to the locality[2], but such knowledge must be properly applied and within reasonable limits[3].

The knowledge should be of a general nature, not the type of knowledge that may be varied by the specific individual characteristics of the particular case[4]. Further, the knowledge which the justices propose to bring into consideration should be brought to the notice of the parties so that they may if they wish call evidence or make representations dealing with it[5]. A justice having specialist knowledge may draw on it when interpreting the evidence, but must not, as it were, give evidence in contradiction of what he has heard in court[6]. For example it is wrong for magistrates to perform their own private tests on defective tyres with a tyre tread gauge in the retiring room[7].

Justices have a discretion to view the scene of an alleged offence, but before doing so should inform the parties that they propose to view the scene. It is undesirable for justices to have a view unaccompanied by the parties or their representatives. As a general rule they should be so accompanied because matters may arise upon which the parties may wish to comment[8]. The reasoning behind this principle, so far as the accused is concerned, is that he might be able to point out some important matter of which his legal adviser was unaware or which the justices were making a mistake about[9]. Care must be taken over the travel arrangements to view the scene of an alleged offence; the prosecutor should not travel with the justices otherwise a reasonable person would suspect that a fair trial was not possible[9]. Where an irregularity occurs whereby one of the justices adjudicating pays a personal and unofficial visit to the scene of the alleged offence, the justices may take into account the wishes and representations of the parties in deciding whether they should continue with the trial[10].

1. *Carter v Eastbourne Borough Council* (2000) 164 JP 273. However, justices may use, and should be encouraged to use, their common sense and local and general knowledge, and are entitled to take judicial notice that birds as common as goldfinches are 'ordinarily resident in or visitors to Great Britain' (*Hughes v DPP* [2003] EWHC Admin 2470, (2003) 167 JP 167).
2. *Ingram v Percival* [1969] 1 QB 548, [1968] 3 All ER 657, 133 JP 1; *Borthwick v Vickers* [1973] Crim LR 317; *Chesson v Jordan* [1981] Crim LR 333; *Kent v Stamps* [1982] RTR 273.
3. *Keane v Mount Vernon Colliery Co Ltd* [1933] AC 309.
4. *Reynolds v Llanelly Associated Tinplate Co Ltd* [1948] 1 All ER 140.
5. *Church v Church* (1933) 97 JP 91; *Thomas v Thomas* [1961] 1 All ER 19, [1961] 1 WLR 1, 121 JP 95.
6. *Wetherall v Harrison* [1976] QB 773, [1976] 1 All ER 241, 140 JP 143. See also *Hill v Baxter* [1958] 1 QB 277, [1958] 1 All ER 193, 122 JP 134; *Bensley v Smith* [1972] RTR 221.
7. *R v Tiverton Justices, ex p Smith* (1981) 145 JP 177.
8. *Parry v Boyle* (1986) 83 Cr App Rep 310, [1986] Crim LR 551.
9. *R v Ely Justices, ex p Burgess* [1992] 157 JP 484, [1992] Crim LR 888.
10. *Telfer and Telfer v DPP* (1994) 160 JP 512.

PRESUMPTIONS[1]

2–42   Courts may draw a particular inference from a particular fact or from particular evidence unless the truth of the inference is disproved.

1. Legality and accuracy: there is a presumption that things have been done and operate in a regular and lawful manner, for example that a police officer has been formally appointed[2], a solicitor admitted[3], a limited company incorporated[4], a highway used publicly for 20 years is a dedicated right of way[5], machinery works accurately[6]; that a police officer requiring a breath test from a motorist was in uniform[7].
2. Documents: a private document 20 years old produced from proper custody is presumed to be genuine[8], documents are presumed to have been made on the date they bear, a signed deed to have been sealed and delivered[9], a properly addressed, prepaid, posted letter to have arrived in the ordinary course of post[10].
3. Legitimacy, marriage, death: a child conceived or born in wedlock is presumed legitimate where the spouses were not legally separated at the time of conception[11]; evidence of a ceremony of marriage presumes a valid marriage[12] as does cohabitation[13]; a person who has

not been heard of for seven years or more by those who would be likely to hear of him, is presumed dead[14].

4. Sale of motor vehicles: for the purposes of both criminal and civil proceedings, certain presumptions enable a valid title to be obtained to a motor vehicle which is sold when still subject to a bailment, hire purchase or conditional sale agreement[15].

---

1. As to the meaning of the word "presumption" see **2–43**, post.
2. *R v Gordon* (1789) 1 Leach 515.
3. *Berryman v Wise* (1791) 4 Term Rep 366.
4. *R v Langton* (1876) 2 QBD 296.
5. Highways Act 1980, s 31(1) in PART VII: TRANSPORT title HIGHWAYS, post.
6. *Tingle Jacobs & Co v Kennedy* [1964] 1 All ER 888n, [1964] 1 WLR 638n, CA (traffic lights); *Nicholas v Penny* [1950] 2 All ER 89 (speedometer).
7. *Gage v Jones* [1983] RTR 508.
8. Evidence Act 1938, s 4, post.
9. *Hall v Bainbridge and Enderby* (1848) 12 QB 699, 17 LJQB 317. A deed need now only be signed, witnessed and delivered; it must be clear it is intended to be a deed but does not require to be written on any particular substance, nor a seal, nor authority to deliver an instrument as a deed to be given by deed (Law of Property (Miscellaneous Provisions) Act 1989 s 1).
10. Interpretation Act 1978, s 7 (service), but see Magistrates' Courts Rules 1981, r 99, Criminal Procedure Rules 2005, Part 4, (service of summons) in PART I: MAGISTRATES' COURTS, PROCEDURE, ante.
11. *Banbury Peerage Case* (1811) 1 Sim & St 153; *Head v Head* (1823) 1 Sim & St 150 and see *R v Hemmings* [1939] 1 All ER 417; *Francis v Francis* [1960] P 17, [1959] 3 All ER 206 and *Knowles v Knowles* [1962] 1 All ER 659 and as to rebuttal, Family Law Reform Act 1969, s 26 in PART IV: FAMILY LAW post. See also *Re Overbury, Sheppard v Matthews* [1955] Ch 122, [1954] 3 All ER 308 (conflicting presumptions on early remarriage).
12. *Piers v Piers* (1849) 2 HL Cas 331; *Mahadervan v Mahadervan* [1964] P 233, [1962] 3 All ER 1108.
13. *Re Taplin* [1937] 3 All ER 105.
14. *Chipchase v Chipchase* [1939] 3 All ER 895; *Chard v Chard* [1956] P 259, [1955] 3 All ER 721, and note Offences Against the Person Act 1861, s 57 (bigamy) and Matrimonial Causes Act 1973, s 19.
15. See the Hire Purchase Act 1964, ss 27, 28 substituted by the Consumer Credit Act 1974, Sch 4, para 22.

2–43   The word "presumption" is commonly used with several distinct meanings.

1. A presumption of law properly means a rebuttable proposition of law, and it is in this sense that the word "presumption" is used above. There are however other uses of the word.
2. A presumption of fact may mean that provisional conclusions are to be drawn from circumstantial evidence, for example; that a person in possession of stolen property soon after the theft is the thief or handler if the defendant offers no explanation for the possession of the property or the court is sure any explanation he gives is untrue[1].
3. A presumption of law may in fact mean an irrebuttable rule of law, for example that a child under the age of ten cannot be guilty of an offence[2].
4. A presumption of law may actually be another way of expressing the burden of proof, for example that a person is presumed innocent until proved guilty, that proof that a person had an article made or adapted for use in committing burglary, theft or cheat is evidence that he had it with him for such use[3].

Where presumptions conflict, they are treated as cancelling one another out and the issue is decided henceforward without reference to either[4].

Where the conduct in the litigation of a party to it is such as to lead to the reasonable inference or presumption that he disbelieves in his own case, it may be proved and used in evidence against him[5].

---

1. *R v Aves* [1950] 2 All ER 330, 114 JP 402; *R v Smith* (1984) 148 JP 215.
2. Children and Young Persons Act 1933, s 50 in PART V: YOUTH COURTS, post.
3. Theft Act 1968, s 25(3) in PART VIII: THEFT, post.
4. *R v Willshire* (1881) 6 QBD 366.
5. *R v Watt* (1905) 70 JP 29.

FORMAL ADMISSIONS

2–44   Any fact of which oral evidence may be given in criminal proceedings may be admitted by or on behalf of the prosecutor or defendant as conclusive evidence against the person making it[1]. If the admission is made orally in court, the court shall cause the admission to be written down and signed by or on behalf of the party making it[2]. If it is made out of court it shall be in writing[1].

An admission made by an individual in criminal proceedings must be made by his counsel or solicitor (if made in court) or approved by him (if made out of court). If made by a body corporate it must be signed by a director, manager, secretary, clerk or similar officer[1]. The admission may be withdrawn with the leave of the court[1]. Leave is unlikely to be given unless the court receives evidence from the accused and those advising him that the admissions have been made by a matter of mistake or misunderstanding[3]. A person may make a written admission in relation to certain road traffic offences that he was the driver of a particular vehicle on a particular occasion[4].

In civil proceedings any party can make admissions without giving evidence. The terms of s 53(2) of the Magistrates' Courts Act 1980 do not require the court to hear evidence of the elements necessary to prove the complaint but rather provide that the court shall hear such evidence *as is necessary to be called* to prove the complaint: thus it is possible for the court to make an order where the complainant's solicitor outlines the facts and the defendant's solicitor admits the relevant facts, does not call any witnesses and addresses the court on his client's behalf[5].

Because the clerk is under a duty to supply a note of evidence in the event of an appeal in matrimonial and guardianship cases, it is normal to require some formal evidence, however brief, in these cases.

1. Criminal Justice Act 1967, s 10 in PART I: MAGISTRATES' COURTS, PROCEDURE, ante.
2. Criminal Procedure Rules 2005, Part 37, in PART I: MAGISTRATES' COURTS, PROCEDURE, ante.
3. *R v Kolton* [2000] Crim LR 761, CA.
4. See the Road Traffic Offenders Act 1988, s 12 in PART IV: ROAD TRAFFIC, post.
5. *Berkhamsted RDC v Duerdin-Dutton* (1964) 108 Sol Jo 157 (complaint for a nuisance order under Public Health Act 1936, s 94); *R v King's Lynn Magistrates' Court, ex p M* [1988] FCR 436, [1988] 2 FLR 79, (admission of defendant in affiliation proceedings that he was the father and that he consented to the making of an affiliation order held gave the court jurisdiction to make the order without hearing evidence).

Sources of evidence: documents and objects
DOCUMENTS AND MATERIAL OBJECTS AS EVIDENCE

2–60 Evidence may be presented to the court otherwise than by straightforward oral testimony by a witness as to facts observed. This other kind of evidence includes formal admissions, written statements, public and private documents[1], bankers' books, maps and plans, sound and video recordings, trade and business records, depositions, certificates and declarations, and material objects such as fingerprints, weapons and other articles which are sometimes called "real evidence".

Each has rules and procedures which must be observed if it is to be admitted in evidence. Some documents are allowed to speak for themselves, others need to be presented by a witness before becoming receivable in evidence.

1. As to what comprises a document, see para **2–61**, post; as to presumptions which may apply to certain documents, see para **2–42 Presumptions**, ante.

2–61 Documents as real evidence. The presence of a document at a particular location together with the writing or words on it may be of evidential value and may be admissible provided the evidence is not unduly prejudicial. A document which falls into this category is often referred to as "real" evidence. Such a document does not constitute an exception to the hearsay rule because it is not put in to prove the truth of its contents, but as itself a fact which affords circumstantial evidence upon which the court may draw an inference[1].

For a document to be admissible as "real" evidence, there must be established a link between the document and the defendant. Accordingly, there must be prima facie evidence that the defendant was the author of the document, that he was in control or in possession of it, that he knew of the document or that he was in some other way connected with it[1].

It is essential in all cases where it is desired to introduce a document as "real" evidence to identify the issue or issues to which the document or some feature connected with it is or are alleged to have probative force and their relevance or potential relevance to the charge[2].

1. See *R v Lydon* (1986) 85 Cr App Rep 221; see also *Howey v Bradley* [1970] Crim LR 223; *R v Horne* [1992] Crim LR 304.
2. *R v Balogun* [1997] Crim LR 500 (letter showing previous drug-related association held to be inadmissible where there was no evidence of a connection between that association and an alleged offence of importation of cocaine).

2–62 Witness statements. In criminal proceedings a written statement by any person may be admissible as evidence to the like extent as oral evidence to the like effect by that person, subject to specific procedural requirements being followed[1].

The statement will usually be read aloud at the hearing, and an oral account given of any part that is not read aloud[1].

1. See the Criminal Justice Act 1967, s 9 in PART I: MAGISTRATES' COURTS, PROCEDURE, ante.

2–63 Public documents[1]. A document made by a public officer for the purpose of the public making use of it and being able to refer to it[2] is receivable in evidence provided it purports to be sealed, stamped or signed as may be required by any Act applying to it, without further proof[3]. It is usually produced by way of an examined or certified copy[4], although judicial notice may be taken of some documents otherwise produced.

1. The admissibility of public information of this sort was preserved by the Criminal Justice Act 2003, s 118(1). See this PART, post.
2. *Sturla v Freccia* (1880) 5 App Cas 623, 44 JP 812; *Lilley v Pettit* [1946] KB 401, [1946] 1 All ER 593, 110 JP 218, and see *Mercer v Denne* [1904] 2 Ch 584, 68 JP 479; affd [1905] 2 Ch 538, 70 JP 65, CA.
3. Evidence Act 1845, s 1, post.
4. Evidence Act 1851, s 14, post.

2–64   Specific provision is made for the production in evidence of a great number of different public documents. Those likely to be required in magistrates' courts are as follows.

1.   *Acts of Parliament*: public Acts are to be judicially noticed[1], private and local personal Acts are to be admitted without proof if printed by the Queen's Printer or under HMSO superintendence or authority[2].

2.   *Proclamations, orders or regulations* by the Queen, or Privy Council, or Government Department (statutory instruments) may be admitted as *prima facie* evidence by production of a copy of the Gazette, or a copy printed by the Government printer or under HMSO superintendence or authority[3].

3.   *Acts, ordinances and statutes* by the legislature of any British Possession, and orders, regulations and other instruments issued thereunder may be admitted without proof if they purport to be printed by the Government printer[4].

4.   *Evidence of any judgment, decision, declaration or opinion* of the European Court of Human Rights, the European Commission of Human Rights or the Committee of Ministers of which account may have to be taken under s 2(1) of the Human Rights Act 1998 is to be given in proceedings before any court or tribunal in such manner as may be provided by rules made under the Act[5].

5.   A *local government byelaw* may be produced in the form of a printed copy endorsed by a certificate purporting to be signed by the proper officer of the authority stating that it was made by the authority, that the copy is a true copy, and the dates of confirmation or despatch to the Secretary of State and of commencement; this is *prima facie* evidence of those facts[6]. A byelaw will be treated as valid unless it is so uncertain in its language as to have no ascertainable meaning, or so unclear in its effect as to be incapable of certain application in any case. So long as in certain circumstances an offence would undoubtedly be committed, byelaws should (subject to any issue of severance) be upheld and to that extent enforced; if that test is not met they should be struck down for uncertainty[7]. A magistrates' court has jurisdiction to determine the validity of a local government or other byelaw, and it is inappropriate for the proceedings before magistrates to be adjourned so that the validity of the byelaw can be determined in the High Court by way of judicial review[8]. A defendant is not precluded from raising in a criminal prosecution the contention that a byelaw or an administrative act undertaken pursuant to it was ultra vires and unlawful, and in that regard there is no distinction to be drawn between substantive and procedural error[9]. When determining whether a byelaw that is bad in part may be severed so as to be upheld and enforced in part, it is essential that the part to be upheld and enforced should be substantially severable, ie that the substance of what remains should be essentially unchanged in its legislative purpose, operation and effect[10]. Where a properly constituted criminal court has ruled that byelaws on which a prosecution has been based are invalid, the authority responsible for promulgating those byelaws must have regard to that decision in its dealings with others who were not parties to those proceedings and if it fails to do so it may be acting *Wednesbury* unreasonably even if it is not bound by judicial precedent such as where the decision declaring the byelaw invalid is that of a magistrates' court or the Crown Court. If however there are serious doubts about the correctness of the criminal court's decision as to the validity of the byelaws, and there are serious reasons of public safety or security which require the retention of the byelaws pending an appeal, a case might be made for retaining them, provided an appeal is pursued with expedition, or other means found urgently to establish their validity in a court[11].

6.   *European Economic Community treaties, the Official Journal, and European Court decisions and opinions* are to be judicially noticed; evidence of Community instruments, documents, European Court judgments or orders may be given by production of an EEC certified true copy; evidence of Community instruments may also be given by production of a Queen's Printer's Copy or a copy certified by an authorised officer of a Government department having custody of the instrument[12].

7.   A *Supreme Court document* (ie document of the Court of Appeal, High Court or Crown Court) purporting to be sealed or stamped with the seal or stamp of the Supreme Court shall be received in evidence without further proof[13]; an office copy is admissible to the same extent as the original[14]. Courts take judicial notice of the signatures of judges of the Court of Appeal or the High Court when attached to a judicial or official document[15].

8.   *Previous convictions* may be proved by a certified copy of the court record, together with evidence of identity[16]: proof of identity does not mean conclusive proof but undisputed evidence of fact so strong that the court may find that identity has been proved[17]. In civil proceedings, proof that a person has been convicted is proof that he committed the offence unless the contrary is proved[18]. A previous conviction may be proved in criminal proceedings by producing an appropriate certificate with a copy of the person's fingerprints[19]. A magistrates' court convicting a person of a summary offence may take account of previous summary convictions stated in a notice proved to have been served on that person not less than seven days previously[20].

9.   *Magistrates' court proceedings* may be admitted in evidence by production of the register or (more usually) by a document purporting to be an extract from the register certified by the Clerk to the Justices as a true extract[21].

10. *County Court proceedings* are recorded in books or documents kept by the Registrar: these, or a copy purporting to be signed and certified as a true copy by the Registrar, shall be admitted as evidence of the entry and proceeding without further proof[22].

11. *Courts of justice in any foreign state or British colony*: any judgment, decree, order or other judicial proceeding or legal document of such a court is admissible if an authenticated copy purporting to be sealed by the court or signed by a judge and stating that the court has no seal is produced[23]. Proof that the defendant is the person referred to in the certificate of conviction may be given in ways similar to a domestic conviction[24].

12. *Foreign, dominion and colonial courts* (including Isle of Man and Channel Islands), register entries may be admitted by means of a certificate purporting to be signed and authenticated in the manner specified in an applicable Order in Council[25].

13. *Insolvency*: a statement of affairs prepared for the purposes of a provision of the Insolvency Act 1986 or any other statement made in pursuance of a requirement under the Act may be used in evidence against any person making or concurring in making the statement[26].

14. A *certificate of incorporation* of a company is conclusive evidence that the requirements of the Companies Act 1985 as to registration have been complied with, that the company is authorised to be registered and is duly registered, and if it is stated to be a public company, that it is such[27].

15. *Consent of a Law Officer of the Crown or the Director*: any document purporting to be such a consent for, or to, the institution of criminal proceedings, and signed by the Law Officer, Director or a Crown Prosecutor, is admissible as *prima facie* evidence without further proof[28].

16. *Births, deaths and marriages* may be proved by a certified copy of an entry purporting to be sealed or stamped with the seal of the General Register Office, provided that the entry as to birth or death purports to be signed by such informant as might be required to give the registrar that information[29]. Such a certified copy is *prima facie* evidence of all matters required to be registered and as to the truth of which the registrar has a duty to satisfy himself[30]. Accordingly a certified copy of a birth is some evidence not only of the date of birth but also of the marriage of the persons registered as the parents[31]. Evidence of identification of a child with that named in the certificate should be given[32]. The age of a child may be proved by any other legal means[33]. A certified copy as to a death is no evidence of the cause of death as the registrar does not have to satisfy himself as to the accuracy of the information either by a medical certificate or a coroner's inquest[34]. An entry in a registrar's district register may be proved by a certified copy under the hand of the Deputy Superintendent Registrar who also certifies that the register book is in his lawful custody[35].

---

1. Interpretation Act 1978, s 3, post.
2. Evidence Act 1845, s 3; Documentary Evidence Act 1882, s 2, post.
3. Documentary Evidence Act 1868, s 2; Documentary Evidence Act 1882, s 2, post. See also Statutory Instruments Act 1946 and Interpretation Act 1978, post.
4. Evidence (Colonial Statutes) Act 1907, s 1, post.
5. Human Rights Act 1998, s 2(2) in PART VIII: HUMAN RIGHTS, post.
6. Local Government Act 1972, s 238 in PART VIII: LOCAL GOVERNMENT, post.
7. *Percy v Hall* [1996] 4 All ER 523, [1997] 3 WLR 573, CA.
8. *R v Crown Court at Reading, ex p Hutchinson* [1988] QB 384, [1988] 1 All ER 333, 87 Cr App Rep 36.
9. *Boddington v British Transport Police* [1998] 2 All ER 203, 2 WLR 639, 162 JP 455.
10. *DPP v Hutchinson* [1990] 2 AC 783, [1990] 2 All ER 836, 155 JP 71, HL.
11. See the remarks of Carnwath J in *Secretary of State for Defence v Percy* [1999] 1 All ER 732, Ch D (a case concerning byelaws made under s 14 of the Military Lands Act 1892).
12. European Communities Act 1972, s 3, in PART I: MAGISTRATES' COURTS, PROCEDURE, ante.
13. Supreme Court Act 1981, s 132, and as to divorce court orders see also Supreme Court of Judicature (Consolidation) Act 1925, s 200(2).
14. Rules of the Supreme Court 1965, Ord 38, r 10.
15. Evidence Act 1845, s 2, post.
16. Previous convictions may of course be admitted, *R v Turner* (1924) 18 Cr App Rep 161. *Practice Direction (criminal: consolidated)* [2002] para III.27, in PART I: MAGISTRATES' COURTS, PROCEDURE, ante, makes arrangements for the provision of information of antecedents in the Crown Court and in the magistrates' courts. As to proof of conviction, see the Police and Criminal Evidence Act 1984, ss 73–75, post.
17. *Martin v White* [1910] 1 KB 665, 74 JP 106. See also *R v Derwentside Magistrates' Court, ex p Heaviside* (1995) 160 JP 317, [1996] RTR 384; considered in *R v Derwentside Magistrates' Court, ex p Swift* (1995) 160 JP 468, [1997] RTR 89; *R v DPP, ex p Mansfield* (1995) 160 JP 472, [1997] RTR 96.
18. See Civil Evidence Act 1968, s 11, post.
19. See Criminal Justice Act 1948, s 39 in PART I: MAGISTRATES' COURTS, PROCEDURE, ante, and see also post para **2–84 Certificates and declarations**.
20. Magistrates' Courts Act 1980, s 104 in PART I: MAGISTRATES' COURTS, PROCEDURE, ante.
21. Magistrates' Courts Rules 1981, r 68, Criminal Procedure Rules 2005, Part 6, in PART I: MAGISTRATES' COURTS, PROCEDURE, ante.
22. County Courts Act 1984, s 12.
23. Evidence Act 1851, s 7, post: and for acts of State, proclamations, treaties.
24. See *R v Mauricia* [2002] EWCA Crim 676, [2002] 2 Cr App Rep 27, [2002] Crim LR 655 and see the Police and Criminal Evidence Act 1984, ss 73–75 and notes thereto, in this PART, post.
25. Evidence (Foreign, Dominion and Colonial Documents) Act 1933, s 1 and Oaths and Evidence (Overseas Authorities and Countries) Act 1963, s 5, post. Note also the special provisions of the Maintenance Orders (Reciprocal Enforcement) Act 1972 ss 13, 15, 36 in PART IV: FAMILY LAW, post
26. Insolvency Act 1986, s 433, in PART VIII, title INSOLVENCY, post.
27. Companies Act 1985, s 13.
28. Prosecution of Offences Act 1985 s 26 in PART I, MAGISTRATES' COURTS, PROCEDURE, ante.

29. Births and Deaths Registration Act 1953, s 34, in PART VIII, title BIRTHS AND DEATHS, post, Marriage Act 1949, s 65(3).
30. *Doe d, France v Andrews* (1850) 15 QB 756; *Re Goodrich's Estate, Payne v Bennett* [1904] P 138; *Brierley v Brierley and Williams* [1918] P 257.
31. *Re Stollery, Weir v Treasury Solicitor* [1926] Ch 284, 90 JP 90.
32. *R v Rogers* (1914) 79 JP 16.
33. *R v Cox* (1884) 48 JP 440.
34. *Bird v Keep* [1918] 2 KB 692.
35. *R v Weaver* (1873) LR 2 CCR 85, 38 JP 102.

2–65 Documents which are not admissible in evidence or do not constitute prima facie evidence.   There are a number of document in common circulation to which special attention should be drawn because they are either not admissible in evidence or do not constitute *prima facie* evidence.

1. *Circulars from government departments* are not admissible in evidence[1] and those departments have no power in law to bind themselves as servants of the Crown by pronouncements[2].
2. A *motor vehicle registration book* is not admissible evidence of its contents[3].
3. *Regimental records* are not public documents because they are not documents to which the public can have access, and are not kept for the use and information of the public but of the Crown and the executive, therefore they are not available as *prima facie* evidence in criminal proceedings[4], but they are so admissible in civil proceedings (eg affiliation)[5].

---

1. *Peagram v Peagram* [1926] 2 KB 165, 90 JP 136.
2. *A-G v Lewis and Burrows Ltd* [1932] 1 KB 538, 96 JP 25.
3. *R v Sealby* [1965] 1 All ER 701.
4. *Lilley v Pettit* [1946] KB 401, [1946] 1 All ER 593, 110 JP 218.
5. *Andrews v Cordiner* [1947] KB 655, [1947] 1 All ER 777, 111 JP 308.

2–66 Proof of statements in documents.   Where a statement in a document is admissible as evidence in criminal proceedings, the statement may be proved by either producing the document or, whether or not the document exists, a copy of the document or the material part of it, authenticated in whatever way the court may approve[1].

In civil proceedings where a statement contained in a document is admissible as evidence it may be proved—

(a) by the production of that document, or

(b) whether or not that document is still in existence, by the production of a copy of that document or of the material part of it,

authenticated in such manner as the court may approve[2]. It is immaterial for this purpose how many removes there are between a copy and the original[3].

A document which is shown to form part of the records of a business or public authority may be received in evidence in civil proceedings without further proof. A document shall be taken to form part of the records of a business or public authority if there is produced to the court a certificate to that effect signed by an officer of the business or authority to which the records belong[4].

---

1. Criminal Justice Act 2003, s 133. See this PART, post.
2. Civil Evidence Act 1995, s 8(1), this PART, post.
3. Civil Evidence Act 1995, s 8(2), this PART, post.
4. Civil Evidence Act 1995, s 9(1), (2), this PART, post.

2–67   Secondary evidence of a private document by means of a copy or the oral evidence of a witness who can remember the original may be given when a proper explanation is given of the absence of better evidence[1], and one sort of secondary evidence is not intrinsically better than another sort[2]; this may include an examined copy of a copy[3]. The old rule that a party must produce the best evidence that the nature of the case would allow, no longer applies except where the original document is available in that party's hands[4].

Secondary evidence of a document may be given in the following circumstances.

1. Where the opposite party has the document and refuses to produce it after proper notice to produce[5]. Objection for want of notice must be taken at the time the evidence is tendered[6]. Generally speaking, a defendant in a criminal case cannot and should not be required to produce evidence against himself[7].
2. Where a third person has the document and refuses to produce it for example because of privilege, but not where he has been summoned and can be compelled to produce it[8].
3. Where the original is lost or destroyed, if a proper search has been made for it[9].
4. Where the original is not physically or conveniently removable or may not be lawfully moved[10].

If a document is attested but is not required by law to be attested in order to be valid, it may be proved in some other way than by calling the attesting witness[11]. Where an attesting witness is called, he is the witness of the court and can be cross-examined by the party calling him[12].

Where documents found in the possession of the accused are relevant to prove any part of the case for the prosecution, they should be produced by the officer who found them, and evidence should be given as to how they came into existence and how they got into his possession[13].

---

1. *Lucas v Williams & Sons* [1892] 2 QB 113.
2. *Brown v Woodman* (1834) 6 C & P 206; *Hall v Ball* (1841) 3 Man & G 242.
3. *R v Collins* (1960) 44 Cr App Rep 170.
4. *Kajala v Noble* (1982) 75 Cr App Rep 149, [1982] Crim LR 433; *R v Wayte* (1982) 76 Cr App Rep 110 (photocopies).
5. *Read v Brookman* (1788) 3 TR 151; *Dwyer v Collins* (1852) 7 Exch 639; *R v Nowaz* [1976] 3 All ER 5, [1976] 1 WLR 830, 140 JP 512.
6. *R v Sanders* [1919] 1 KB 550; *James v Audigier* (1932) 49 TLR 36.
7. *R v Worsenham* (1701) 1 Ld Raym 705; *Trust Houses Ltd v Postlethwaite* (1944) 109 JP 12, but see *Spokes v Grosvenor Hotel Co* [1897] 2 QB 124.
8. *Mills v Oddy* (1834) 6 C & P 728; and see *R v Llanfaethly Inhabitants* (1853) 2 E & B 940, 18 JP 8, also *R v Nowaz*, supra.
9. *Read v Brookman*, supra; *Brewster v Sewell* (1820) 3 B & Ald 296; see also *R v Wayte*, supra (photocopies).
10. *Mortimer v M'Callan* (1840) 6 M & W 58; *Owner v Bee Hive Spinning Co Ltd* [1914] 1 KB 105, 78 JP 15.
11. Criminal Procedure Act 1868, s 7, post.
12. *Oakes v Uzzell* [1932] P 19.
13. *R v Treacy* [1944] 2 All ER 229.

2–68 Handwriting. Handwriting may be proved by the evidence of someone who has knowledge of it, having seen the person write at least once[1], or corresponded regularly with him or acted upon such correspondence[2]. Comparison of a disputed writing with any writing proved to be genuine shall be permitted to be made by witnesses[3]. In criminal cases the evidence of an expert is desirable[4].

A person is a handwriting expert when he has adequate knowledge and skill as to handwriting, whether acquired in the course of his business or not[5]. Someone who has acquired information on the subject only in the course of the case is not entitled to give evidence as an expert[4]. Justices should have vividly in mind that, in the absence of expert evidence, they are themselves not qualified to make comparisons[6].

---

1. *R v McCartney and Hansen* (1928) 20 Cr App Rep 179.
2. *Goulds v Jones* (1762) 1 Wm Bl 384; *Harrington v Fry* (1824) Ry & M 90; *R v Slaney* (1832) 5 C & P 213; *R v O'Brien* (1911) 7 Cr App Rep 29.
3. Criminal Procedure Act 1865, s 8, post, in PART I: MAGISTRATES' COURTS, PROCEDURE, ante.
4. *R v Rickard* (1918) 82 JP 256, 13 Cr App Rep 140.
5. *R v Silverlock* [1894] 2 QB 766, 58 JP 788.
6. *R v O'Sullivan* [1969] 2 All ER 237, [1969] 1 WLR 497, 133 JP 338.

2–69 Bankers' books. *Prima facie* evidence of an entry in a banker's book may be given by means of an examined copy of the entry, proved either orally or by way of affidavit to be correct and of an entry made in one of the ordinary books of the bank in that bank's custody or control and in the usual and ordinary course of business[1]. The bank may not be compelled to produce the books themselves except by special order of a judge[2], but a magistrates' court may order that a party to legal proceedings be at liberty to inspect and take copies of entries for the purpose of proceedings[3].

---

1. Bankers' Books Evidence Act 1879, ss 3–5, post.
2. Bankers' Books Evidence Act 1879, s 6, post.
3. Bankers' Books Evidence Act 1879, s 7, post; *R v Kinghorn* [1908] 2 KB 949, 72 JP 478.

2–80 An order to inspect bankers books and take copies may be made either with or without summoning the bank or any other party, and shall be served on the bank three clear days before the proposed inspection unless the court otherwise orders[1]. Great care should be exercised in criminal proceedings: the justices should be satisfied that proceedings have been properly begun and not started merely to enable the application to be made, and that the prosecution have other evidence to support the charge preferred and are not using the application as a fishing expedition for evidence[2]. The High Court has concurrent jurisdiction and justices should decline to make an order if they feel the application is more appropriate for the High Court because of its difficulty[2]. Where the High Court has dealt with such an application there is no appeal to the Court of Appeal[3].

Although an application can be made *ex parte*, there is much to be said for notice being given[4]. An order can be made relating to the banking account of a person not a party to the proceedings where the court is satisfied that the account is in fact though not in name that of a party to the proceedings, or that party has control over it and used it for his own purposes so that the entries will be admissible in evidence, but such jurisdiction should be exercised with great caution and only after notice to such person and the defendant[5]. The fact that the entries would incriminate the defendant is no reason for refusing an order before the hearing[2], although it should not be made before the hearing if the defendant swears that the entries are irrelevant[6].

The mere fact that the defendant says he intends to plead guilty is not a proper reason for the court refusing to make an order[7], but justices should take care that the person whose bank account is to be inspected is not oppressed, that the prosecution are not using their powers for ulterior motives, and that the period of disclosure is limited to that relevant to the charge[7]. The gravity of the charge and the public interest may lead to an extension of the period of search[8].

1. Bankers' Books Evidence Act 1879, s 7, post; *R v Kinghorn* [1908] 2 KB 949, 72 JP 478.
2. *Williams v Summerfield* [1972] 2 QB 512, [1972] 2 All ER 1334, 136 JP 616; *R v Nottingham Justices, ex p Lynn* (1984) 79 Cr App Rep 238.
3. *Bonalumi v Secretary of State for the Home Department* [1985] QB 675, [1985] 1 All ER 797, CA.
4. *R v Marlborough Street Metropolitan Stipendiary Magistrate, ex p Simpson* (1980) 70 Cr App Rep 291.
5. *South Staffordshire Tramways Co v Ebbsmith* [1895] 2 QB 669; *Pollock v Garle* [1898] 1 Ch 1; *Ironmonger & Co v Dyne* (1928) 44 TLR 579; *R v Andover Justices, ex p Rhodes* [1980] Crim LR 644; *R v Grossman* (1981) 73 Cr App Rep 302, [1981] Crim LR 396.
6. *South Staffordshire Tramways Co v Ebbsmith*, supra.
7. *Owen v Sambrook* [1981] Crim LR 329.
8. *R v Nottingham Justices, ex p Lynn*, supra.

2–81   Medical records.   Medical evidence is admissible to show that a witness suffers from some disease or defect or abnormality of mind that affects his reliability as a witness[1], but a witness summons to produce medical records should be issued only where it is shown that there are substantial grounds for believing that the records contain such relevant matters, and then the records should be produced to the court and not to the prosecution or defence until the court has decided whether they should be disclosed[2]. The contents of a document may be proved by the production of an enlargement of a microfilm copy of the document[3].

1. *Toohey v Metropolitan Police Comr* [1965] AC 595, [1965] 1 All ER 506, 129 JP 191.
2. *R v Westacott* [1983] Crim LR 545.
3. Police and Criminal Evidence Act 1984, s 71, post.

2–82   Sound and video recordings.   The term "document" means anything in which information of any description is recorded[1]. Accordingly, this will include sound and video recordings.
As evidence of identity.   Where identification of the offender depends on the evidence of a witness describing what he saw either on a visual display unit or on a video recording, that evidence is necessarily subject to the directions as to identification laid down in *R v Turnbull*[2], and justices must direct themselves accordingly[3]. It is wrong to use a video after committal proceedings to try to improve a quality of a witness's evidence of identification[4].
Evidence of a video tape recording of a robbery and evidence of police officers, who had viewed the video in a police station, of the purported recognition of suspects, is prima facie admissible, subject to the discretion of the court to exclude it[5]. Where a police witness has by lengthy and studious application acquired special knowledge that the court does not possess, he may be entitled to give opinion evidence of identification as an "expert ad hoc"; such evidence is no more secondary evidence than is any oral identification made from a photograph[6].
Facial mapping by way of video superimposition is a species of real evidence to which no special rules apply. If such evidence is not sufficiently intelligible to the court without help, an expert should be called to assist with the interpretation of the evidence[7].
In *A-G's Reference (No 2 of 2002)*[8], it was held that, on the authorities, there were at least 4 circumstances in which, subject to the trial judge's discretion, evidence was admissible from which the jury, provided appropriate directions were given, could be invited to conclude that the defendant committed an offence on the basis of video footage of a crime scene. Those were: (*a*) where the image was sufficiently clear for the jury to be able to compare it with the defendant in the dock; (*b*) if the witness who had recognised the defendant had known him sufficiently well, he or she could give evidence even if the video footage was no longer available; (*c*) where a witness who did not know the defendant had spent time viewing the video and, consequently, had acquired a special knowledge that the jury did not have, he could give evidence in relation to the video and a reasonable contemporary photograph of the defendant, provided that the video and photograph were available to the jury; and (*d*) a suitably qualified expert in facial mapping skills could give evidence in relation to a video and a contemporary photograph of the defendant provided that the video and photograph were available to the jury. Therefore, other than in cases in which a witness did not know the defendant but had acquired special skills in relation to a video as a result of frequent playing and analysis of it, a witness was not generally required to possess any special skills, abilities, experiences or knowledge that the jury did not have.
In English law there is generally nothing unlawful about a breach of privacy and therefore, subject to the discretion of the court to exclude evidence under s 78 of PACE 1984, evidence of private conversations in a domestic house obtained by a bugging device is admissible[9].
As evidence in chief.   Video recordings of testimony from child witnesses in cases of sexual offences and offences involving cruelty or violence may be admissible in certain prescribed circumstances[10]. Guidance on the adducing of tape recorded interviews is given in the *Practice Direction (criminal: consolidated)* [2002][11].
When the relevant provisions come into force, subject to various conditions the court may direct that a video recording of an account of a witness (other than the defendant) that was given when the relevant events were fresh in the witness' memory shall be admitted as evidence in chief of the witness[12].

1. Criminal Justice Act 2003, s 134(1). See this PART, post. As to proof of statements in documents, see para **2–289**, ante
2. As to *R v Turnbull* [1977] QB 224, [1976] 3 All ER 549, 40 JP 648, CA, see para **2–312 Identification: Turnbull guidelines**, post.

3. *Taylor v Chief Constable of Cheshire* [1987] 1 All ER 225, [1986] 1 WLR 1479, 151 JP 103. See also para **2–85 Photographs and sketches,** post.
4. *R v Smith and Doe* (1986) 85 Cr App Rep 197, CA.
5. *R v Caldwell* [1993] Crim LR 862.
6. *R v Clare and Peach* (1955) 159 JP 412, [1995] 2 Cr App Rep 333, CA.
7. *R v Clarke* [1995] 2 Cr App Rep 425, CA.
8. [2002] EWCA Crim 2373, [2003] Crim LR 192.
9. *R v Khan (Sultan)* [1996] 3 All ER 289, [1996] 3 WLR 162, [1996] 2 Cr App Rep 440, HL.
10. Youth Justice and Criminal Evidence Act 1999, ss 27, 28, in this PART, post.
11. Paragraph 43, in PART I: MAGISTRATES' COURTS, PROCEDURE, ante.
12. Criminal Justice Act 2003, ss 137 and 138: see this PART, post.

2–83 Depositions.   Depositions are statements of witnesses taken before a judicial authority which is responsible for authenticating them. They may thereafter be admissible in court proceedings.

The principal kinds of depositions are as follows.

1. Deposition of a child or young person, whose attendance at court to give evidence in relation to an offence against him under the First Schedule to the Children and Young Persons Act 1933 would involve serious danger to his life or health, is admissible in evidence subject to conditions[1].
2. Deposition of a witness before a justice or magistrate in the dominions, or any British consular officer elsewhere is admissible in civil or criminal proceedings subject to conditions[2]; evidence may be taken abroad in the case of offences at sea[3].
3. Deposition duly authenticated of evidence taken in a court outside the United Kingdom is admissible in proceedings for a maintenance order[4].
4. The evidence taken before a coroner's jury and the facts found by them are not generally admissible even in civil actions[5], but statements or depositions of the defendant before the coroner are admissible if properly proved, that is by a person who was present at the inquest and who can swear that the deposition is in the coroner's handwriting, was read over to the prisoner and was afterwards signed by him[6]. A witness cannot be asked in cross-examination what he said before the coroner, but his deposition may be put into his hands for him to read over to himself and refresh his memory[7]. If the witness has died or is ill or insane, his deposition if duly signed by him and the coroner[8] excluding any inadmissible evidence, is admissible[9]. A statement made in depositions before a coroner may be used when a witness proves adverse[10].

---

1. Children and Young Persons Act 1933, ss 42 and 43 in PART V: YOUTH COURTS, post.
2. Merchant Shipping Act 1995, s 286 in PART VII: TRANSPORT, title MERCHANT SHIPPING, post.
3. Merchant Shipping Act 1995, s 283, in PART VII: TRANSPORT, title MERCHANT SHIPPING, post.
4. Maintenance Orders (Facilities for Enforcement) Act 1920, ss 8 and 9, Maintenance Orders (Reciprocal Enforcement) Act 1972, s 13 in PART VI: FAMILY LAW, post.
5. *Bird v Keep* [1918] 2 KB 692; *Re Pitts, Cox v Kilsby* [1931] 1 Ch 546.
6. *R v Marriott* (1911) 75 JP 288, 22 Cox CC 211.
7. *R v Barnet* (1850) 4 Cox CC 269.
8. *R v Butcher* (1900) 64 JP 808.
9. *R v Cowle* (1907) 71 JP 152; *R v Black* (1910) 74 JP 71.
10. See the Criminal Procedure Act 1865, ss 3–5, in PART I: MAGISTRATES' COURTS, PROCEDURE, ante.

2–84 Certificates and declarations.   Provision is made for the admissibility in evidence of certain certificates[1] and declarations for particular purposes.

Those most commonly encountered in magistrates' courts include the following: reference should be made to the statutory provisions for detailed requirements to be followed before these certificates are used or accepted in evidence.

1. The service of documents required in proceedings may be proved by a solemn declaration or, in appropriate circumstances, by a certificate by the person effecting service[2].
2. An extract from the court register certified by the Clerk is admissible in any legal proceedings as evidence of proceedings in that court[3].
3. A certificate of the clerk of a magistrates' court is evidence that a magistrates' court maintenance order is in force[4].
4. A certificate of a constable that a specified person stated on a particular occasion that a particular motor vehicle was being driven or used by or belonged to that person or was used by or belonged to a firm in which that person was a partner or a corporation of which he was a director, officer or employee, is admissible in evidence in relation to certain offences[5].
5. A statutory declaration as to the despatch or receipt of goods or a posted packet, or failure to arrive or condition on despatch or receipt may be admissible in proceedings for theft of anything in the course of transmission for handling stolen goods from such a theft[6].
6. Records kept by the Driver and Vehicle Licensing Agency as to driving or vehicle licences and duly authenticated are admissible to the same extent that oral evidence would be admissible: where the proceedings relate to an offence involving discretionary or obligatory disqualification and the defendant is absent, then provided the requisite notice has been served on him, previous convictions and orders stated in the notice are treated as having been admitted by him[7].
7. A certificate showing the proportion of alcohol in a specimen or breath or the proportion of alcohol or any drug found in a specimen of blood or urine is admissible if served on and

accepted by a defendant[8] in proceedings for driving or being in charge when under the influence of drink or drugs or with alcohol concentration above the prescribed limit.

8. In proceedings relating to Social Security offences, provision is made for the conclusive determination of questions by the Secretary of State, and evidence thereof as well as of non-payment and previous offences, by certificate[9].

1. See also ante, **2–64** for public documents which may be admissible.
2. Magistrates' Courts Rules 1981, r 67, Criminal Procedure Rules 2005, Part 4, in PART I: MAGISTRATES' COURTS, PROCEDURE, ante.
3. Magistrates' Courts Rules 1981, r 68, Criminal Procedure Rules 2005, Part 6, in PART I: MAGISTRATES' COURTS, PROCEDURE, ante. See also ante para **2–64** *Previous convictions*.
4. Magistrates' Courts Rules 1981, r 69 in PART I: MAGISTRATES' COURTS, PROCEDURE, ante.
5. Road Traffic Offenders Act 1988, s 11 in PART IV: ROAD TRAFFIC, post. See also s 12 as to admission of driving.
6. Theft Act 1968, s 27 in PART VIII: THEFT, post.
7. Road Traffic Offenders Act 1988, s 13 and see also Vehicle Excise and Registration Act 1994, s 51 in PART IV: ROAD TRAFFIC, post.
8. Road Traffic Offenders Act 1988, s 16 in PART IV: ROAD TRAFFIC, post.
9. Social Security Administration Act 1992, s 116 et seq in PART VIII: title SOCIAL SECURITY, post.

2–85 Photographs and sketches.   The Criminal Justice Act 2003 reformulated the law on hearsay evidence in criminal proceedings. Section 115 of the Act defines "statement" as "any representation of fact or opinion made by a person by whatever means; and it includes a representation made in a sketch, photofit or other pictorial form". We reproduce below the narrative that appeared in the previous edition of this work, but it should be read subject to the new provisions which are summarised at para **2–260** et seq, post.

Photographs have been admitted in evidence in relation to identity[1], the appearance of land[2], indecent practices of the accused[3]. It is not necessary for the original of a film to be produced[4]. Evidence of what was seen by witnesses on a video film may be admitted, notwithstanding that the tape has since been inadvertently erased, provided the court carefully assesses the weight and reliability of that evidence[5]. The Civil Evidence Act 1968, ss 1–10 which *inter alia* makes provision for the admissibility of photographs as documents, is not in force in relation to magistrates' courts.

A police officer's sketch made under the direction of a witness who had seen the accused has been admitted as part of that witness's evidence[6]. Similarly, a photofit picture of a defendant is admissible at his trial as part of a witness's evidence and does not constitute a breach of either the hearsay rule or the rule against the admission of earlier consistent statements[7].

Where photographs taken of the defendants during the commission of an offence are used to identify the accused in the dock, the court should exercise particular caution, taking account of factors such as the quality of the photographs, the extent of the exposure of the facial features of the person photographed, evidence (or the absence of it) of a change in a defendant's appearance, and the opportunity the court has had to look at the accused in the dock and over what period of time, before concluding that it was safe to regard the man in the dock as being the man in the photograph[8].

1. *R v Tolson*, supra; *Hill v Hill and Easton* (1915) 31 TLR 541; *C v C and C* [1972] 3 All ER 577, [1972] 1 WLR 1335, 136 JP 775; *R v Dodson, R v Williams* [1984] 1 WLR 971, (security camera in building society office); and see also PART I: MAGISTRATES' COURTS, PROCEDURE, ante para **1–227 Identification by witnesses, fingerprints, photographs, body samples**.
2. *Hindson v Ashby*, supra; *R v United Kingdom Electric Telegraph Co* (1862) 3 F & F 73.
3. *R v Twiss* [1918] 2 KB 853, 83 JP 23.
4. *Kajala v Noble* (1982) 75 Cr App Rep 149, [1982] Crim LR 433.
5. *Taylor v Chief Constable of Cheshire* [1987] 1 All ER 225, [1986] 1 WLR 1479, 151 JP 103.
6. *R v Percy Smith* [1976] Crim LR 511.
7. *R v Cook* [1987] QB 417, [1987] 1 All ER 1049, CA. See also *R v Constantinou* (1989) 153 JP 619, 91 Cr App Rep 76, CA.
8. See *R v Dodson, R v Williams*, supra.

2–86 Maps and plans[1].   Maps, including ordnance survey maps, and plans are admissible but only as part of the evidence of the person who made them[2] or, in our view, to the extent that they have been personally verified by the witness producing them. Evidence of the relative position of things may be given in criminal proceedings by the production of a plan or drawing by a constable, an architect, chartered surveyor, civil or municipal engineer or land agent, accompanied by the requisite certificate[3].

Admiralty plans and charts, ordnance survey maps, deposited plans and other maps and surveys have been admitted in limited circumstances, for example to prove general geographic facts, general names applied to districts, the relative position of towns or countries or other places[4].

A map or plan prepared for the trial and containing any references to occurrences which are the subject-matter of the investigation, but which did not exist when the survey was made, is inadmissible if objection is taken to it[5]; for example in a road traffic case a skid mark visible at the time of the survey may be shown but not the alleged position of a car which had been moved by the time the survey was begun.

1. The admissibility of public information of this sort was preserved by the Criminal Justice Act 2003, s 118(1). See this PART, post.
2. *R v Milton* (1843) 1 Car & Kir 58.

3. See the provisions of the Criminal Justice Act 1948, s 41 to which are noted the Evidence by Certificate Rules 1961, in PART I: MAGISTRATES' COURTS, PROCEDURE, ante.

4. *Birrell v Dryer* (1884) 9 App Cas 345; *Mercer v Denne* [1904] 2 Ch 534, 68 JP 479; affd [1905] 2 Ch 538, 70 JP 65; *A-G v Antrobus* [1905] 2 Ch 188, 69 JP 141; *A-G v Meyrick and Jones* (1915) 79 JP 515.

5. *R v Mitchell* (1852) 6 Cox CC 82.

2–87   Fingerprints and palmprints. The taking of fingerprints and of intimate and other samples is governed by the Police and Criminal Evidence Act and the Code of Practice thereunder[1]. Fingerprints or palmprints of an accused are admissible, even when the accused had not been cautioned when asked to provide the prints[2]; identification by a fingerprints expert may be sufficient by itself[3]. An accused person's identity with a person who has previously been convicted may be established by fingerprint evidence[4].

Fingerprint evidence is admissible as a matter of law if it tends to prove the guilt of the accused. It may so tend, even if there are only a few similar ridge characteristics but it may, in such a case, have little weight. It may be excluded in the exercise of judicial discretion, if its prejudicial effect outweighs its probative value. When the prosecution seek to rely on fingerprint evidence, it will usually be necessary to consider two questions: the first, a question of fact, is whether the control print from the accused has ridge characteristics, and if so how many, similar to those of the print on the item relied on. The second, a question of expert opinion, is whether the print on the item relied on was made by the accused. This opinion will usually be based on the number of similar ridge characteristics in the context of other findings made on comparison of the two prints[5].

If there are fewer than eight similar ridge characteristics, it is highly unlikely that a court will exercise its discretion to admit such evidence and, save in wholly exceptional circumstances, the prosecution should not seek to adduce such evidence. If there are eight or more similar ridge characteristics, a court may or may not exercise its discretion in favour of admitting the evidence. How the discretion is exercised will depend on all the circumstances of the case, including in particular:

1. the experience and expertise of the witness;
2. the number of similar ridge characteristics;
3. whether there are dissimilar characteristics;
4. the size of the print relied on, in that the same number of similar ridge characteristics may be more compelling in a fragment of print than in an entire print; and
5. the quality and clarity of the print on the item relied on, which may involve, for example consideration of possible injury to the person who left the print, as well as factors such as smearing or contamination[5].

1. See the Police and Criminal Evidence Act 1984, ss 61–65, in PART I: MAGISTRATES' COURTS, PROCEDURE, ante, and the Code of Practice for the Identification of Persons by Police Officers, this PART, post.
2. *Callis v Gunn* [1964] 1 QB 495, [1963] 3 All ER 677, 48 Cr App Rep 36.
3. *R v Castleton* (1909) 3 Cr App Rep 74; *R v Bacon* (1915) 11 Cr App Rep 90, but see *R v Court* (1960) 44 Cr App Rep 242.
4. Criminal Justice Act 1948, s 39 in PART I: MAGISTRATES' COURTS, PROCEDURE, ante.
5. *R v Buckley* (1999) 163 JP 561, CA.

2–88   Appearance of persons. A person's appearance may constitute evidence, for example by way of disproof of his statement as to age[1], or that liquor was sold to someone who appeared to the court to be under eighteen[2]. A resemblance between a child and its alleged parent is admissible as evidence of parentage, although it is regarded as unsafe and conjectural[3].

1. *R v Viasani* (1867) 31 JP 260; *R v Turner* [1910] 1 KB 346, 74 JP 81.
2. *Wallworth v Balmer* [1965] 3 All ER 721, [1966] 1 WLR 16.
3. *C v C and C* [1972] 3 All ER 577, [1972] 1 WLR 1335, 136 JP 775.

2–89   Evidence of tracker dogs. Evidence of the reactions of a tracker dog can be admitted provided the dog handler can establish by detailed evidence that the dog was properly trained and that over a period of time the dog's reactions showed it was a reliable pointer to the existence of the scent of some particular individual[1].

It is important to lay a proper foundation for the admission of such evidence by detailed evidence establishing the reliability of the dog in question. The judge, in directing the jury, should alert them to the care they need to take and to look with circumspection at the evidence of tracker dogs, having regard to the fact that the dog may not always be reliable and cannot be cross-examined[1].

1. *R v Pieterson* [1995] 1 WLR 293, [1995] 2 Cr App Rep 11, [1995] Crim LR 402.

Sources of evidence: witnesses

2–100   Privilege: witness protected by public policy and generally. No action lies against a witness for anything he says when giving evidence in a court of law[1] nor against an advocate for what he says in the course of his duty as such[2] nor against a justice of the peace for what he says when acting judicially or for what he does when acting within his jurisdiction[3].

A witness may not be required to state facts or to produce documents the disclosure of which would harm the public interest[4], or disclose the channels through which criminal information has been obtained unless disclosure is necessary to establish innocence[5].

Statements made "without prejudice" are excluded from being given in evidence in civil proceedings[6].

A witness is protected by privilege in both civil and criminal proceedings where the answer to a question or the production of a document would tend to expose the witness to a criminal charge[7], but not if it would expose to civil proceedings[8] or some forfeiture[9]. The privilege also extends in civil proceedings to questions tending to expose the witness' spouse to proceedings for a criminal offence or for the recovery of a penalty[10]. In criminal proceedings, there is no privilege for a witness in respect of questions tending to incriminate his or her spouse[11].

A witness in a court of justice is privileged in what he says though actuated by express malice and not testifying *bona fides*[12], but the words must be spoken with reference to the subject of inquiry[13].

A witness in criminal proceedings who is not a party cannot be compelled to produce any deed or other document relating to his title to land[14].

The general discretion not to compel the disclosure of sources of information can include not identifying premises from which surveillance took place[15]. A person who gives information about child abuse to a local authority or to the NSPCC enjoys an immunity from disclosure of his identity in legal proceedings similar to that which the law accords to police informers[16]. However, the law has moved on especially in the light of the European Convention on Human Rights and, with regard to revealing the identity of informers, the court will proceed on a more case-specific approach to balance the competing public interests in the protection of an informer and in doing justice. Considerable weight will be given to the protection of informers but in civil proceedings, where the liberty of the subject is not at stake, the pressure for disclosure will be less compelling[17].

A letter written "without prejudice" to the legal rights of the writer protects the whole of the correspondence of which it forms part[6]: the intention is to encourage the settlement of disputes. Marking letters "private and confidential" does not impose any condition as to the way in which they may be used[18].

A witness claiming privilege against self-incrimination should claim it after being sworn and the question put[19], although it is the practice for the court to intervene and warn him of the dangers of answering. The danger of incrimination must be real and appreciable; it is for the court to decide whether the danger exists, it is not sufficient that the witness states that the answer might incriminate him[20]. In any proceedings a witness may be required to answer a question tending to show he has committed adultery[21] provided the evidence is relevant and admissible[22].

There is no privilege in respect of communications between husband and wife[23].

---

1. *Dawkins v Lord Rokeby* (1875) LR 7 HL, 744, 40 JP 20; *Roy v Prior* [1971] AC 470, [1970] 2 All ER 729; see also *Trapp v Mackie* [1979] 1 All ER 489, [1979] 1 WLR 377.

2. *Munster v Lamb* (1883) 11 QBD 588, 47 JP 805.

3. See ante para **1–41 Protection and indemnification of justices and justices' clerks**, and the Courts Act 2003, ss 31–35 in PART I: MAGISTRATES' COURTS, PROCEDURE.

4. *Duncan v Cammell Laird & Co Ltd* [1942] AC 264, [1942] 1 All ER 587; *Conway v Rimmer* [1968] 1 All ER 874; see also *R v Lewes Justices, ex p the Gaming Board of Great Britain* [1971] 2 All ER 1126; *Rogers v Secretary of State for the Home Department* [1973] AC 388, [1972] 2 All ER 1057.

5. *Marks v Beyfus* (1890) 25 QBD 494 (strictly applicable only in *public* prosecutions); applied in *R v Agar* [1990] 2 All ER 442, 154 JP 89, CA, and see *R v Langford* [1990] Crim LR 653.

6. *Paddock v Forester* (1842) 3 Man & G 903; *Cory v Bretton* (1830) 4 C & P 462; *Walker v Wilsher* (1889) 23 QBD 335.

7. See eg *Redfern v Redfern* [1891] P 139, [1886–90] All ER Rep 524 and *Re Westinghouse Electric Corpn Uranium Contract Litigation MDL Docket No 235* [1977] 3 All ER 703; Evidence Act 1851, s 3, post; Civil Evidence Act 1968, s 14, post; see also para **2–126 Competency of parties and their spouses**, post.

8. Witnesses Act 1806, s 1, post.

9. Civil Evidence Act 1968, s 16(1).

10. Civil Evidence Act 1968, s 14(1)(b), in this PART, post.

11. See *R v Pitt* [1983] QB 25, [1982] 3 All ER 63, and para **2–127**, post.

12. *Dawkins v Rokeby*, supra.

13. *Seaman v Netherclift* (1876) 2 CPD 53, 41 JP 389.

14. *Doe d Earl of Egremont v Date* (1842) 3 QB 609, 11 LJQB 220; *Pickering v Noyes* (1823) 1 B & C 262, 1 LJ OS KB 110. As to civil proceedings see the Civil Evidence Act 1968, s 16(1), post.

15. *R v Rankine* [1986] QB 861, [1986] 2 All ER 566, CA. See also *R v Brown* (1987) 87 Cr App Rep 52, [1988] Crim LR 239, CA, *R v Johnson* [1989] 1 All ER 121, [1988] 1 WLR 1377 (guidance given by Court of Appeal on requirements for excluding evidence which would reveal address and identity of occupiers of private premises used as police observation posts), and *Blake and Austin v DPP* (1993) 97 Cr App Rep 169, [1993] Crim LR 283 (evidence of identity of observation post not disclosed because occupier, who was vulnerable, would be in danger of at least harassment).

16. *D v National Society for the Prevention of Cruelty to Children* [1978] AC 171, [1977] 1 All ER 589, 141 JP 157.

17. *Chief Constable of the Greater Manchester Police v McNally* [2002] EWCA Civ 14, [2002] Crim LR 832.

18. *Kitcat v Sharp* (1882) 48 LT 63.

19. *Boyle v Wiseman* (1855) 10 Exch 647.

20. *R v Boyes* (1861) 25 JP 789.

Where a witness who has been summoned to give a deposition under para 4 of Sch 3 to the Crime and Disorder Act 1998 to make a deposition refuses to answer questions on the ground of self-incrimination that claim must be the subject of a proper investigation by the justices in respect of every question for which it is claimed and before acceding to such a claim the court should satisfy itself, from the circumstances of the case and the nature of the evidence which the witness is called to give, that there is a real and appreciable danger to the witness with reference to the ordinary operation of the law in the ordinary course of things, and not a danger of an imaginary or insubstantial character; reliance by a witness on legal advice is not capable without more of amounting to just excuse for a claim to privilege: *R (Crown Prosecution Service) v Bolton Magistrates' Court* [2003] EWHC 2697 (Admin), [2004] 1 WLR 835, [2004] 1 Cr App R 438.

21. See *Blunt v Park Lane Hotel Ltd* [1942] 2 KB 253, [1942] 2 All ER 187; Civil Evidence Act 1968, s 16(5), post.
22. *Clifford v Clifford* [1961] 3 All ER 231 (cross-examination as to credit).
23. See the Civil Evidence Act 1968, s 16(3), and the Police and Criminal Evidence Act 1984, s 80(9), post.

2–101   **Professional privilege.**   A witness cannot be compelled to disclose confidential communications between legal adviser and client or information obtained for the purposes of litigation. Legal professional privilege is not just an ordinary rule of evidence but a fundamental condition on which the administration of justice as a whole rests. It is based on the principle that a client should be able to consult his lawyer in confidence and without fear that his communications will be revealed without his consent, because otherwise he may hold back half the truth[1].

Statements made by the parties in a matrimonial case in the presence of a probation officer with a view to effecting a reconciliation should not be received in evidence, nor should communications with a marriage guidance counsellor[2]. Similarly, in children's cases, statements made by one or other of the parties in the course of meetings held or communications made for the purpose of conciliation may not, save in the exceptional case, be given in evidence in proceedings under the Children Act 1989[3].

It is not the case that legal professional privilege does no more than entitle the client to require his lawyer to withhold privileged documents in judicial or quasi-judicial proceedings, leaving the question of whether such documents may be disclosed on other occasions to the implied duty of confidence subsisting between solicitor and client; the policy of legal professional privilege requires that the client should be secure in the knowledge that protected documents and information will not be disclosed at all; and any statutory obligation to disclose documents cannot override legal professional privilege unless it does so expressly or by necessary implication[4].

Legal professional privilege is that of the client who alone can waive it[5]. It extends to communications, statements, reports etc made or procured for taking professional advice in proceedings pending or threatened or even anticipated[6], and to confidential communications between solicitors and expert witnesses, but not to documents upon which the expert bases his opinion[7]. Legal professional privilege does not attach to a solicitor's record time on an attendance note, time sheet, or fee note as they do not record anything passing between solicitor and client and are not connected with the obtaining of legal advice[8] nor to evidence from a solicitor as to the identity of a person he represented in court on an earlier occasion[9]. Where within a communication there was the commission of a criminal offence (a threat over the telephone), that freed the communication from the cloak of legal professional privilege[10].

Privilege does not apply to disclosures to clergymen[11], doctors (although a court would have an overriding discretion to allow a doctor not to answer a question[12], a psychiatrist[13], a surveyor reporting prior to a dispute, on the state of some property[14], a journalist[15].

There is no privilege for statements made to a doctor who is examining a defendant or suspect[16]. If a defendant makes admissions to a doctor during an examination, he does not have the protection afforded to him when interviewed by the police[17]. The doctor is, however, in the same position as a prisoner or prison officer called to give evidence of admissions made to him. The admission or otherwise of the evidence is a matter for the discretion of the court[18].

Even legal professional communications may not be privileged in special circumstances, for example communications made by a client to his solicitor to enable him to obtain advice in furtherance of a criminal design[19], or a note in the defendant's handwriting to his counsel admitting perjury[20], or a statement made by the defendant to his solicitors when the statement is sent, without the defendant's knowledge or consent, to the prosecutor in an attempt to persuade the prosecutor to drop the case[21]. A solicitor is not however in a better position than his client, who cannot prevent the seizure of incriminating material by handing it over to his solicitor[22].

There is no reason in principle why an accused should not be cross-examined on a letter written by his solicitors containing a proposal as to plea if it is inconsistent with his testimony and, thus, goes to his credibility, and the same applies to an alibi notice or defence case statement if it becomes similarly relevant during the trial[23].

The privilege in matrimonial cases is the privilege of the parties and can be waived, for example by the parties giving conflicting evidence of what occurred so as to make the probation officer's evidence admissible[24]: the privilege may be waived either in whole or in part[25]. The privilege extends to an exchange of letters between a husband and a probation officer[26], interviews and correspondence with third parties solely to effect a reconciliation between the parties[27] and may extend to conversations between the parties conducted on the like basis[28]. A conversation between a social worker and the putative father about the possibility of adopting the child has been held to be not privileged[29].

---

1. *R v Derby Magistrates' Court, ex p B* [1995] 4 All ER 526, [1995] 3 WLR 681, HL.
2. See Domestic Proceedings and Magistrates' Courts Act 1978, s 26(2) in PART VI: FAMILY LAW, post.
3. In *Re D (minors) (Conciliation: Disclosure of Information* [1993] 2 WLR 721, [1993] 1 FLR 932, [1993] 1 FCR 877. See also the Children Act 1989, s 7, and notes thereto in PART IV, post.
4. *R (on the application of Morgan Grenfell & Co Ltd) v Special Commissioner of Income Tax* [2002] UKHL 21, [2003] 1 AC 563, [2002] 3 All ER 1.
5. *Wilson v Rostall* (1792) 4 Term Rep 753.
6. *Ogden v London Electric Rly Co* (1933) 149 LT 476.
7. *R v King* [1983] 1 All ER 929, [1983] 1 WLR 441, 147 JP 65. However, the court is not additionally entitled to have the opinion of an expert which is based on material which is privileged and which is provided to the expert in privileged circumstances; thus, when the defence instructed a psychiatrist in a murder case, but decided not to call him as a witness, the solicitor's instructions and what the defendant said to the psychiatrist were both privileged communications and the opinion of the psychiatrist was, therefore, based on privileged material and was not admissible for the prosecution (*R v*

Davies [2002] EWCA Crim 85, (2002) 166 JP 243). See also *R v R* [1994] 4 All ER 260, [1994] 1 WLR 758, (1995) Cr App Rep 183, CA, which is referred to in para **1–2704**, ante.
    8. *R v Crown Court at Manchester, ex p Rogers* [1999] 4 All ER 35, [1999] 1 WLR 832, [1999] 2 Cr Rep 267. See also *C v C (evidence: privilege)* [2001] EWCA Civ 469, [2001] 3 WLR 446, [2001] 1 FCR 756, [2002] Fam 42, [2001] 2 FLR 184.
    9. *R (Howe) v South Durham Magistrates' Court* [2004] EWHC 362 (Admin), 168 JP 424, [2004] Crim LR 963.
    10. *C v C (evidence: privilege)* (supra).
    11. *Normanshaw v Normanshaw and Neasham* (1893) 69 LT 468; *Wheeler v Le Marchant* (1881) 17 Ch D 675, 45 JP 728.
    12. *Hunter v Mann* [1974] QB 767, [1974] 2 All ER 414.
    13. *R v Stanley Smith* [1979] 3 All ER 605, 144 JP 53.
    14. *Wheeler v Le Marchant*, supra.
    15. *A-G v Mulholland, A-G v Foster* [1963] 2 QB 420, [1963] 1 All ER 767; *A-G v Clough* [1963] 1 QB 773, [1963] 1 All ER 420.
    16. *R v Smith* (1979) 69 Cr App Rep 378, CA.
    17. *R v McDonald* [1991] Crim LR 122, CA.
    18. *R v Gayle* [1994] Crim LR 679, CA.
    19. *R v Cox and Railton* (1885) 14 QBD 153, 49 JP 374; *R v Smith* (1915) 80 JP 31, but see *Butler v Board of Trade* [1971] Ch 680, [1970] 3 All ER 593 (warning against course of conduct). See also *R (Hallinan Blackburn Gittings & Nott (a firm)) v Crown Court at Middlesex Guildhall* [2004] EWHC 2726 (Admin), [2005] 1 WLR 766 (witness statement taken by defending solicitors from person claiming to be present at defendant's arrest – evidence coming to light of conspiracy to pervert the course of justice involving the defendant, the statement maker and another, which was freestanding and independent in the sense it did not require a judgment to be made in relation to the issues in the trial – judge entitled to conclude that the statement (and other associated items) were not covered by legal professional privilege).
    20. *R v Tomkins* (1977) 67 Cr App Rep 181.
    21. *R v Cottrill* [1997] Crim LR 56.
    22. *R v Peterborough Justices, ex p Hicks* [1978] 1 All ER 225, [1977] 1 WLR 1371.
    23. *R v Hayes* [2004] EWCA Crim 2844, [2005] 1 Cr App R 33.
    24. *McTaggart v McTaggart* [1949] P 94, [1948] 2 All ER 754.
    25. *Pais v Pais* [1971] P 119, [1970] 3 All ER 491 (marriage guidance counsellors).
    26. *Mole v Mole* [1951] P 21, [1950] 2 All ER 328.
    27. *Pool v Pool* [1951] P 470, [1951] 2 All ER 563; *Henley v Henley* [1955] P 202, [1955] 1 All ER 590, 119 JP 215.
    28. *Theodoropoulos v Theodoropoulos* [1964] P 311, [1963] 2 All ER 772.
    29. *R v Nottingham County Justices, ex p Bostock* [1970] 2 All ER 641, 134 JP 535.

2–102 Persons who are deaf and without speech[1]. A person who is deaf and without speech is a competent witness if he can understand the nature of an oath. This may be established, either by signs, or through an interpreter, or in writing. But the evidence of a deaf witness unable to express himself intelligently and in a way which can be faithfully interpreted, must be excluded altogether[2].

    1. Note the definition of "oral evidence" in s 134 of the Criminal Justice Act 2003 (in this PART, post) includes non verbal evidence.
    2. *R v Imrie* (1917) 12 Cr App Rep 282.

2–103 *Matters on which expert evidence may be called.* Expert opinion may be called to assist the court in matters of legitimacy as to whether periods of gestation could be too long or too short[1]; a psychologist may give evidence of the respective personalities of defendants based on commonly-employed clinical tests[2]; that the expert has not personally examined the witness is not determinative that his evidence be not admitted as to the weight to be attached to the witness' evidence[3]; a medical witness may express an opinion whether wounds on a body he had not seen could have been self-inflicted, assuming the facts described by another witness who had seen the body were true[4]; a police officer with fifteen years' experience in a traffic division who had attended a course of accident investigation and attended to more than 400 fatal road accidents, can give expert evidence of his theories and conclusions on an accident[5]. Voice identification is a field where expert opinion is admissible, even though it is not an exact science[6] but no prosecution should be brought in which one of the planks is voice identification given by an expert which is solely confined to auditory analysis, there should also be expert evidence of acoustic analysis which includes formant analysis except: where voices of are of a known group and the issue is which voice has spoken which words; where there are rare characteristics which render a speaker identifiable; or the issue relates to the accent or dialect of a speaker[7]. An expert in the production of high quality sound recordings may give evidence as to voice identity, having based his opinion on a comparative tape recording which he had prepared[8]. The evidence of a skilled lip reader may be admissible as evidence of what was being said in a CCTV recording although the court should warn itself of the potential limitations of such evidence, the risk of mistake and why the witness might be mistaken and the way in which a convincing, authoritative and truthful witness might yet be a mistaken witness. The court should consider the particular strengths and weaknesses of the material in the case and that the quality of the evidence would be affected by such matters as the lighting at the scene, the angle of the view in relation to those speaking, the distances involved, whether anything interfered with the observation, familiarity on the part of the lip-reader with the language spoken, the extent of the use of single syllable words, any awareness on the part of the expert witness of the context of the speech and whether the probative value of the evidence depends on isolated words or phrases or the general impact of long passages of conversation[9].

Evidence of a doctor, both of fact and opinion, may be admitted if—

(i)   it is relevant to an issue in the case;
(ii) it is not hearsay;
(iii) in so far as it is evidence of opinion, it is not founded on hearsay, and
(iv) in so far as it is evidence of opinion, it relates to matters outside the knowledge and experience of the tribunal of fact[10].

There are no special rules where medical experts are concerned, and no single test that can provide a threshold for admissibility; developments in scientific thinking should not be kept from the court merely because they are at the stage of hypothesis[11].

The opinion of a witness is admissible to ascertain foreign law including Scottish law[12], and colonial law except in the Privy Council[13], but he must in all cases be a professional lawyer or a holder of an office requiring and implying legal knowledge[14]. Where evidence is conflicting or obscure, the court itself will consider the passage cited and attempt to determine its proper meaning[15].

Expert opinion is necessary only when the expert can furnish the court with scientific information likely to be outside its experience; for example a psychiatrist is not necessary to say how an ordinary person who is not suffering from mental illness is likely to react to the stresses and strains of life[16]; or the effects of cocaine and its various methods of ingestion[17]; expert evidence on whether material is obscene is probably admissible only where a special audience is in contemplation[18].

An expert may refer to professional treatises, tables, reports etc to refresh his memory, but it is his evidence and not that material which is admissible[19]. When an expert witness is asked to express his opinion on a question, the primary facts on which that opinion is based must be proved by admissible evidence given either by the expert himself or some other competent witness. However once such facts are proved, the expert witness is then entitled to draw on the work (including unpublished work) of others in his field of expertise as part of the process of arriving at his conclusion, provided he refers to that material in his evidence so that the cogency and probative value of his conclusion can be tested by reference to that material. Reliance on the work of others and reference to it in evidence does not infringe the hearsay rule in these circumstances[20].

---

1. *Gaskill v Gaskill* [1921] P 425, [1921] All ER Rep 365; *Preston-Jones v Preston-Jones* [1951] AC 391, [1951] 1 All ER 124.
2. *Lowery v R* [1973] 3 All ER 662, PC. See also *R v Ward* (1993) 96 Cr App Rep 1; *R v O'Brien* [2000] Crim LR 676, CA.
3. *R v Pinfold* [2003] EWCA Crim 3643, [2004] 2 Cr App R 5.
4. *R v Mason* (1911) 76 JP 184.
5. *R v Oakley* [1979] RTR 417.
6. *R v Robb* [1991] Crim LR 539, CA.
7. *R v O'Docherty* [2003] 1 Cr App R 5 (Northern Ireland).
8. *R v Bentum* (1989) 153 JP 538, CA.
9. *R v Lutrell* [2004] EWCA Crim 1344, [2004] 2 Cr App R 520, [2004] Crim LR 939.
10. *Wood v DPP* (1988) 153 JP 20.
11. *R v Harris*, [2005] EWCA Crim 1980, [2006] 1 Cr App Rep 55.
12. *R v Povey* (1852) Dears CC 32, 16 JP 745, except in the House of Lords, *Cooper v Cooper* (1888) 13 App Cas 88.
13. *Mostyn v Fabrigas* (1775) 1 Cowp 161.
14. *R v Moscovitch* (1927) 138 LT 183; *R v Naguib* [1917] 1 KB 359, 81 JP 116.
15. *De Beeche v South American Stores (Gath and Chaves) Ltd and Chilian Stores (Gath and Chaves) Ltd* [1935] AC 148; *R v Secretary of State for India, ex p Ezekiel* [1941] 2 KB 169, [1941] 2 All ER 546.
16. *R v Turner* [1975] 1 All ER 70; *R v Weightman* (1990) 92 Cr App Rep 291.
17. *R v Skirving, R v Grossman* [1985] QB 819, [1985] 2 All ER 705, CA.
18. *DPP v Jordan* [1977] AC 699, [1976] 3 All ER 775.
19. *Fenwick v Bell* (1844) 1 Car & Kir 312; *R v Somers* [1963] 3 All ER 808, [1963] 1 WLR 1306.
20. *R v Abadom* [1983] 1 All ER 364, [1983] 1 WLR 126, 76 Cr App Rep 48, CA. See also *R v Hodges* [2003] EWCA Crim 290, [2003] 2 Cr App R 15, where police officers, after the relevant primary facts were established by admissible evidence, were allowed to testify as to normal methods of supply of unlawful drugs, street values and quantities for personal use on the basis information that have come to them from various sources during their substantial experience in the investigation of drugs offences.

2–104   *Duties of an expert witness in a criminal trial.*   In *R v B (T)*[1] the Court of Appeal held as follows:

(1)   The duties of an expert witness in a criminal trial were owed to the court and overrode any obligation to the person from whom the expert had received instructions or by whom the expert was paid.

(2)   Expert reports should include details of the expert's relevant academic and professional qualifications and range and extent of the expertise; a statement setting out the substance of all the instructions received, questions upon which an opinion was sought and evidence material to the opinions expressed or upon which the opinions were based; information as to who had carried out tests, etc, and whether such tests were carried out under the expert's supervision; where there was a range of opinion on matters dealt with in the report, any material facts which detracted from the expert's opinion should be set out; relevant extracts of literature or any other material which might assist the court; a statement to the effect that the expert had complied with his/her duty to the court to provide independent assistance by way of objective, unbiased opinion and an acknowledgement that the expert would inform all parties if his/her opinion changed on any material issues; further or supplemental reports must also comply with these guidelines.

1. [2006] EWCA Crim 417, [2006] 2 Cr.App.R.3, [2006] Crim LR 745. This guidance was expressed to be additional to the specific factors referred to by Cresswell J in *The Ikarian Reefer* [1993] 2 Lloyds Rep 68.

2–105   Expert reports. An expert report is admissible as evidence in criminal proceedings, whether or not the person making it attends to give oral evidence in those proceedings. If the person making the report does not give oral evidence, the report shall only be admissible with leave of the court. An expert report, when admitted, shall be evidence of any fact or opinion of which the person making it could have given oral evidence[1].

For the purpose of determining whether to give leave the court shall have regard—

   (*a*)   to the contents of the report;
   (*b*)   to the reasons why it is proposed that the person making the report shall not give oral evidence;
   (*c*)   to any risk that its admission or exclusion will result in unfairness to the accused; and
   (*d*)   to any other circumstances that appear to the court to be relevant[2].

1. Criminal Justice Act 1988, s 30, this PART, post.
2. Criminal Justice Act 1988, s 30(3), this PART, post. This is a summary of the factors to which the court shall have regard; s 30 should be read in detail before being used.

Evidence in criminal proceedings

INTRODUCTION

2–120   Facts which suggest motive, preparation, intention are admissible, such as expressions of ill will[1], threats[2], unexplained acts of violence to the prosecutor[3], and other acts of violence or threats can be admissible as justification in self-defence[4]. However in relation to a trial of an offence of strict liability, evidence which goes beyond establishing the specified elements of the offence: proof of motive, intention, knowledge and so on is not relevant and therefore inadmissible especially where such evidence serves no purpose other than to incline the court to think badly of that defendant[5]. These principles also apply to offences involving mens rea; as a general rule, the prosecution is entitled to adduce evidence that is sufficiently relevant to an issue in the case as advanced by the prosecution[6], but all that is irrelevant or not sufficiently relevant to the case as put should, generally speaking, be excluded.

The mere fact that evidence is indecent is no objection to it being received where it is necessary to a decision[7].

The fact of a previous acquittal is normally irrelevant[8], as are the facts of a previous conviction[9] so far as evidence for determining the facts in issue are concerned. In general evidence given in another case may not be taken into account[10]. The principle of double jeopardy does not render inadmissible relevant evidence merely because that evidence shows or tends to show that the defendant was, in fact, guilty of an offence of which he had earlier been acquitted provided it is to be led not for the purpose of punishing the accused for the offence of which he had been acquitted, but in order to prove that he is guilty of the subsequent offence for which he is being tried[11]. An acquittal is not conclusive evidence of innocence and does not mean that all relevant issues have been resolved in favour of the defendant and provided there is no unfairness to an accused, the prosecution may seek to contradict a previous acquittal for the purpose of proving a different offence[12].

1. *R v Clewes* (1830) 4 C & P 221.
2. *R v Mason* (1912) 8 Cr App Rep 121.
3. *R v Mobbs* (1853) 117 JP 713.
4. *R v Hopkins* (1866) 31 JP 105; *R v Weston* (1879) 14 Cox CC 346.
5. *R v Sandhu* [1997] Crim LR 288, CA.
6. *R v Byrne* [2002] EWCA Crim 632, [2002] 2 Cr App Rep 21, [2002] Crim LR 487.
7. *Da Costa v Jones* (1778) 2 Cowp 729.
8. *Maxwell v DPP* [1935] AC 309, 98 JP 387.
9. *R v Shepherd* [1980] Crim LR 428.
10. *Taylor's Central Garages (Exeter) Ltd v Roper* (1951) 115 JP 445, but see post **2–265 Confessions**.
11. *R v Z* [2000] 3 All ER 385, [2000] 3 WLR 117, [2000] 2 Cr App R 281, HL.
12. *R v Terry* [2005] 2 Cr App R 7 (on the issue whether the accused was in a certain motor vehicle at the time, the offering of no evidence on other counts, did not act as a bar to proceedings on other counts).

Confessions and the exclusion of unfairly obtained evidence

CONFESSIONS

2–121   In *criminal proceedings* a confession made by an accused person may be given in evidence against him so far as it is relevant to any matter in issue in the proceedings. If however it is represented that the confession was or may have been obtained by oppression or in consequence of anything said or done which was likely, in the circumstances existing at the time, to render it unreliable, the court shall not allow it to be given in evidence except in so far as the prosecution prove to the court beyond reasonable doubt that it was not so obtained[1].

"Oppression" includes torture, inhuman or degrading treatment and the use or threat of violence[1].

For the purpose of determining in a summary trial whether to allow evidence of a confession to be given against the accused after it has been represented it was obtained by oppression or other improper process, the justices shall hold a trial within a trial[2].

A fact discovered as the result of a confession wholly excluded, or as the result of an excluded part of a confession can still be given in evidence, but the fact that it was discovered as the result of the statement of an accused person may not, unless such evidence is given by him or on his behalf[3].

Criminal proceedings includes proceedings before examining justices[4]. "Confession" includes any statement wholly or partly adverse to the person who made it, whether made to a person in authority or not and whether made in words or otherwise[5]. There is a special need for caution where the confession was made by a mentally handicapped person[6].

A confession made by a defendant to a probation officer who was interviewing him for the purpose of preparing a pre sentence report can be admitted in evidence in a trial; but the importance of candour in such an interview is such that the prosecution should think carefully about whether it is right to rely on evidence so produced and should only rely on it if it is in the public interest so to do[7]. If the prosecution does decide to rely on such evidence the court still has a discretion under s 78 of PACE to ensure that no injustice occurs[8].

Where a mixed statement is before the court, that is, one including admissions and excuses, the court must consider the whole statement, even though it may have to give different weight to each part[9]. This principle applies to all mixed statements tendered by the Crown and not just to mixed statements made to the police, but does not apply to wholly exculpatory and self-serving statements by a defendant which are not evidence of any fact asserted[10]. However, where the defendant does not testify, but relies on the exculpatory parts of a mixed statement, the court is entitled to give less weight to those parts of the statement which have not been tested by cross-examination[11].

In a joint trial of two defendants where an admission of one defendant is not adduced in evidence by the prosecution, it may put in evidence by the co-accused where it is relevant to his defence and was not obtained in a manner which would have made it inadmissible at the instance of the prosecution under s 76(2) of the Police and Criminal Evidence Act 1984. The admission may be put either to witnesses to whom the confession was made or to the co-accused by way of cross-examination, and may be relevant both as to credibility and as to the facts in issue[9]. While an excluded, under 76 of PACE, confession by one co-accused cannot be put in evidence by another co-accused, if the former gives evidence the latter may cross-examine him upon that confession[12].

Where there are co-defendants and the case against one of them depends on the court being satisfied as to the guilt of the other, and the prosecution relies on out of court admissions by the latter to establish his (the latter's) guilt, then if the court finds the latter guilty it is entitled to rely on that conviction when considering the case against the former; provided the admissions are not used to confront any part of the former's defence this does not infringe the rule that out of court admissions made by one co-defendant in the absence of the other are inadmissible as against that other[13].

1. Police and Criminal Evidence Act 1984, s 76, this PART, post. A "confession" under s 76 does not include a statement intended by the maker to be exculpatory or neutral and which appears to be so on its face, but which becomes damaging to him at trial because, for example, of its inconsistency with his evidence: *R v Hasan* [2005] UKHL 22, [2005] 4 All ER 685.
2. See para **1–567 Summary criminal trial**—in PART I: MAGISTRATES' COURTS, PROCEDURE, ante and para **2–1357**.
3. Police and Criminal Evidence Act 1984, s 76(4), (5), this PART, post.
4. *R v Oxford City Justices, ex p Berry* [1988] QB 507, [1987] 1 All ER 1244, 151 JP 505.
5. Police and Criminal Evidence Act 1984, s 82(1), this PART, post.
6. Police and Criminal Evidence Act 1984, s 77, this PART, post.
7. *R v Elleray* [2003] EWCA Crim 553, (2003) 167 JP 325, [2003] 2 Cr App R 165.
8. *R v Elleray*, supra.
9. *R v Sharp* [1988] 1 All ER 65, [1988] 1 WLR 7, 152 JP 164, HL; see also *Western v DPP* [1997] 1 Cr App Rep 474.
10. *R v Aziz* [1995] 3 All ER 149, [1995] 3 WLR 53, [1995] 2 Cr App Rep 478, HL.
11. *R v Myers* [1997] 4 All ER 314, [1997] 3 WLR 552, [1998] 1 Cr App Rep 153, HL.
12. *R v Corelli* [2001] EWCA Crim 974, [2001] Crim LR 913.
13. *R v Hayter* [2003] EWCA Crim 1048, [2003] 1 WLR 1910, [2003] Crim LR 887.

ADMISSIONS AND THE PRIVILEGE AGAINST SELF-INCRIMINATION

2–122   While the overall fairness of a criminal trial cannot be compromised, the constituent rights comprised expressly or impliedly within art 6 are not themselves absolute. Limited qualification of the right against self-incrimination is acceptable if it is reasonably directed towards a clear and proper objective and represents no greater qualification than the situation requires. There is a clear public interest in enforcing road traffic legislation and s 172 of the Road Traffic Act 1988 (which imposes a duty to give information as to the identity of the driver, etc, in certain circumstances), properly applied, does not represent a disproportionate response to the high incidence of vehicle related death and injury on the roads. Section 172 provides for the putting of a single, simple question and the answer cannot in itself incriminate the suspect since it is not without more an offence to drive a car; the section does not sanction prolonged questioning about facts alleged to give rise to criminal offences and the penalty for declining to answer is moderate. Accordingly, it does not infringe a defendant's rights under art 6 for the prosecution to lead evidence of an admission obtained under s 172(2)(a)[1].

1. *Brown v Stott (Procurator Fiscal, Dunfermline)* [2003] 1 AC 681, [2001] 2 All ER 97, [2001] 2 WLR 817, [2001] RTR 121, PC. (See, however, *Heaney and McGuinnes v Ireland* [2001] Crim LR 481, ECtHR, where it was held that the requirement under s 52 of the Offences Against the State Act 1939 to give a full account to the police of, inter alia, movements and actions within a specified period upon pain of a penalty of up to 6 months' imprisonment violated art 6(1) and art 6(2)).

THE EXCLUSION OF UNFAIRLY OBTAINED EVIDENCE

2–123   Where a confession itself has been excluded as inadmissible, there remains the question of evidence of facts revealed by it; the rule is that such evidence remains admissible "for a fact . . . must exist invariably in the same manner whether the confession from which it derives be in other respects true or false . . . Facts thus obtained, however, must be fully and satisfactorily proved without calling in the aid of any part of the confession from which they may have been derived"[1]. Nor does the illegality of the means through which evidence has been obtained render it inadmissible[2]; it is admissible even though obtained by an illegal search[3], through theft[4].

In any criminal proceedings the court may refuse to allow evidence on which the prosecution proposes to rely to be given if it appears to the court that, having regard to all the circumstances, including the circumstances in which the evidence was obtained, the admission of the evidence would have such an adverse effect on the fairness of the proceedings that the court ought not to admit it[5].

Section 78 of the Police and Criminal Evidence Act 1984 has not altered the substantive rule of law that entrapment or the use of an *agent provocateur* do not *per se* afford a defence in law to a criminal charge. Therefore, the fact that evidence has been obtained by such a means does not of itself require the court to exclude it, but the court, in exercising its discretion, in accordance with s 78, must have regard to the adverse effect which admission of the evidence would have on the fairness of the proceedings[6]. However, where investigating officers use a suspect to make contact with others, in ways which might incriminate the suspect, as a result of inducements and without warning the suspect that whatever happened might be used as evidence not only against others but against himself, then they do so at the price of not being able to use the evidence against the suspect; ie as against the suspect the evidence should be excluded under s 78 of PACE[7].

The power under s 78 of the 1984 Act is sufficiently wide for the court to exercise it on its own motion; it is a power to be exercised whenever an issue appears as to whether the court could conclude that evidence should not be admitted. The burden of proof does not enter into play; each side will seek to persuade the court as to the impact that admission would have on the fairness of the proceedings[8].

Issues of fairness may also arise under Article 6(1) of the European Convention on Human Rights[9]. Domestic law recognises that it would be deeply offensive to ordinary notions of fairness if a defendant were to be convicted and punished for committing a crime which he only committed because he had been incited, persuaded, pressurised or wheedled into committing it by a law enforcement officer. On the other hand, it has been recognised that law enforcement agencies have a general duty to the public to enforce the law and it has been regarded as unobjectionable if a law enforcement officer gives a defendant an opportunity to break the law, of which the defendant freely takes advantage, in circumstances where it appears that the defendant would have behaved in the same way if the opportunity had been offered by anyone else. When applying these principles and exercising the judicial discretion conferred by s 78 of the 1984 Act, justices may and should have regard to the European Convention on Human Rights[10].

Where the accused makes an application for unfair evidence to be excluded, he has no right to have that application determined as a preliminary issue. Nevertheless, the justices are under a duty to deal with the application when it arises, or leave the decision until the end of the hearing, with the objective of securing that the trial is fair and just to both sides[11].

In most trials in a magistrates' court, the better course will be for the whole of the prosecution case to be heard, including the disputed evidence, before any trial within a trial is held. For the purpose of deciding what course to take the court is entitled to ask the accused the extent of the issues which would be addressed by the evidence of the accused in the trial within a trial. If the issues are limited to the circumstances in which the evidence was obtained, there will in most cases be no apparent reason why the accused should not be heard on a *voire dire*. If the accused intends to give evidence in contradiction of some part of the prosecution's account of "all the circumstances", upon which he can properly be cross-examined in the *voire dire*, it will be open to the court to conclude that the proceedings on the *voire dire* may be protracted and will introduce issues which will have to be re-examined in the remaining stages of the trial if a prima facie case is held to have been established. In that event, the court may decide that the securing of a just trial to both sides does not require the holding of a trial within a trial[12].

1. *R v Warwickshall* (1783) 1 Leach 298.
2. This is subject to the requirements of the European Convention on Human Rights. Evidence obtained by mistreatment can never be relied upon: *Austria v Italy* (1963) 6 Yearbook 740. Otherwise, the use of unlawfully obtained evidence is not ruled out under the Convention, subject to a number of safeguards. In *Schenk v Switzerland* (1988) 13 EHRR 242 the European Court of Human Rights found no breach of art 6(1) of the Convention where evidence of telephone calls which had been unlawfully obtained were admitted in evidence. In that case, the evidence in question was not the only evidence on which the applicant's conviction was based. See also *Khan v United Kingdom* (2000) 8 BHRC 310, [2000] Crim LR 684 where the evidence obtained against the accused through a listening device was admitted, although in breach of art 8 and the sole or main evidence was not *contrary* to the then domestic law and there was no contention that the evidence was unreliable or unauthentic. Also *Chalkley v United Kingdom* [2003] Crim LR 51 ECtHR

where the police had arrested the defendant, made a copy of his house key and used the period of his arrest to install a recording device. Although art 8 rights had been breached, the refusal of the trial judge to exclude evidence of the recording did not mean the proceedings were unfair. In *R v Bailey* [2001] EWCA Crim 733 the point was made that an authentic recording by an undercover officer and an accurate transcription of it provided the best possible evidence of what was said and, if the tape recordings were excluded, the officers would still be entitled to depose to what was said and to refresh their memories from the recordings; therefore, it is not unfair to admit the most reliable and undisputed evidence of what happened when less certain evidence of that would be admissible.

    3. *Jones v Owen* (1870) 34 JP 759; *Kuruma Son of Kaniu v R* [1955] AC 197, [1955] 1 All ER 236, 119 JP 157; *Jeffrey v Black* [1978] 1 All ER 555, 142 JP 122.

    4. *R v Leathem* (1861) 8 Cox CC 498.

    5. Police and Criminal Evidence Act 1984, s 78, this PART, post.

    6. *R v Smurthwaite and R v Gill* [1994] 1 All ER 898, 98 Cr App Rep 437, 158 JP 165. See also *Ealing London Borough v Woolworths plc* [1995] Crim LR 68.

    7. *R v De Silva* [2002] EWCA Crim 2673, [2003] Cr App R 5, [2003] Crim LR 474.

    8. *Re Saifi* [2001] 4 All ER 168, [2001] 1 WLR 1134.

    9. See *Teixeira de Castro v Portugal* (1998) 28 EHRR 101 considered in *Nottingham City Council v Amin* [2000] 2 All ER 946, [2000] 1 WLR 1071, [2000] Crim LR 174, [2000] 1 Cr App Rep 426, CA.

    10. *Nottingham City Council v Amin* [2000] 2 All ER 946, [2000] 1 WLR 1071, [2000] Crim LR 174, [2000] 1 Cr App Rep 426, CA.

    11. *Vel v Owen* [1987] Crim LR 49, 151 JP 510.

    12. *Halawa v Federation Against Copyright Theft* (1994) 159 JP 816, [1995] 1 Cr App Rep 21.

Witnesses in criminal proceedings

PROPERTY IN A WITNESS

2-124   So far as witnesses of fact are concerned, neither side in proceedings has exclusive property. Neither can prohibit the other side from seeing a witness of fact, from getting the facts from him and from calling him to give evidence or issuing him with a witness summons. Nor is there property in an expert witness as to the facts he has observed and his own independent opinion on them[1].

    A witness who has already given a statement to one side and who is to be called to give evidence would, it seems to us, be able to refuse to be interviewed by the other side. It seems to us that a Chief Constable cannot refuse to allow a police officer of his force to be interviewed by the defence, even when that officer is going to give evidence, but the relationship between the officer and his Chief Constable may inhibit the former from agreeing to be interviewed when he knows that is contrary to the latter's wishes.

    1. See *Harmony Co SA v Saudi Europe Line Ltd* [1979] 3 All ER 117, [1979] 1 WLR 1380.

COMPETENCE AND COMPELLABILITY TO GIVE EVIDENCE

2-125   The general rule is that at every stage in criminal proceedings all persons are (whatever their age) competent to give evidence[1]. Exceptions to this general rule are

    (a) if it appears to the court that he is not a person who is able to—

        (i) understand questions put to him as a witness, and

        (ii) give answers to them which can be understood[2]; and

    (b) a person charged in criminal proceedings is not competent to give evidence in the proceedings for the prosecution (whether he is the only person, or is one of two or more persons, charged in the proceedings[3]).

However a person "charged in criminal proceedings" does not include a person who is not, or is no longer, liable to be convicted of any offence in the proceedings (whether as a result of pleading guilty or for any other reason)[4]. It is for the court to determine whether a witness in criminal proceedings is competent to give evidence in the proceedings[5] and it is for the party calling the witness to satisfy the court that, on the balance of probabilities, the witness is competent to give evidence in the proceedings[6]. In determining whether the witness is competent, the court must treat the witness as having the benefit of any special measures direction which the court has given or proposes to give, in relation to the witness[7] and may receive expert evidence on the question[8]. Any questioning of the witness (where the court considers that necessary) must be conducted by the court in the presence of the parties[9].

    Someone who is competent to give evidence is usually compellable as well, but a rule of law may render them non-compellable, for example members of diplomatic missions[10], judges of the High Court and inferior courts[11] (but not magistrates or their clerks[12], accused persons and their spouses in certain circumstances[13].

    If a witness refuses without just cause to be sworn or give evidence or produce a document or thing, he may be fined or committed to custody[14]. If a witness becomes incapable of giving further evidence, the court has a discretion to allow the trial to continue on the basis of evidence already given[15].

    The beginning of the trial is the appropriate time to raise and determine an issue as to competence and compellability[16]. Once the issue of competence of a prosecution witness is raised, it is for the prosecution to prove that the person is competent to testify, conditions of admissibility to be proved beyond reasonable doubt[16]. Whether the issue can be properly considered in the absence of oral evidence from at least the witness whose competence is challenged, will depend on the circumstances affecting that person[16]. A person having been previously convicted of any crime or offence, or having an interest in the matter in question, is not thereby prevented from giving evidence[17].

It is essential in the case of a young child witness to interview him appropriately and promptly as young children do not have the ability to lay down memory in a manner comparable to adults. Efforts should be made to fast track such cases and it is not an option to wait weeks, for example, for forensic evidence[18].

---

1. Youth Justice and Criminal Evidence Act 1999, s 53(1), in this PART, post.
2. Youth Justice and Criminal Evidence Act 1999, s 53(3), in this PART, post.
3. Youth Justice and Criminal Evidence Act 1999, s 53(4), in this PART, post.
4. Youth Justice and Criminal Evidence Act 1999, s 53(5), in this PART, post.
5. Youth Justice and Criminal Evidence Act 1999, s 54(1), in this PART, post.
6. Youth Justice and Criminal Evidence Act 1999, s 54(2), in this PART, post.
7. Youth Justice and Criminal Evidence Act 1999, s 54(3), in this PART, post.
8. Youth Justice and Criminal Evidence Act 1999, s 54(5), in this PART, post.
9. Youth Justice and Criminal Evidence Act 1999, s 54(6), in this PART, post.
10. See ante para **1–462 Diplomatic immunity and parliamentary privilege**, in PART I: MAGISTRATES' COURTS, PROCEDURE.
11. *Warren v Warren* [1997] 1 FCR 237, CA.
12. *Re McC (a minor)* [1985] AC 528, [1984] 3 WLR 1227, sub nom *McC v Mullan* [1984] 3 All ER 908, HL and see *McKinley v McKinley* [1960] 1 All ER 476, [1960] 1 WLR 120, 124 JP 171.
13. See post para **2–126 Competency of parties and their spouses**.
14. Magistrates' Courts Act 1980, s 97(4) in PART I: MAGISTRATES' COURTS PROCEDURE, ante.
15. See *R v Stretton* (1986) 86 Cr App Rep 7, CA.
16. *R v Yacob* (1981) 72 Cr App Rep 313, [1981] Crim LR 248.
17. Evidence Act 1843, s 1, post.
18. *R v Powell* [2006] EWCA Crim 3, [2006] 1 Cr App R 31, [2006] Crim LR 781 (conviction of indecent assault on child of three and a half quashed where witness not interviewed until nine weeks after the incident and the trial did not take place for another seven months). See also *R v McPherson* [2005] EWCA Crim 3605, [2006] 1 Cr App R 30.

2–126 Competency of parties and their spouses[1].   A person charged in criminal proceedings shall not be called as a witness in the proceedings except on his own application[4]. The failure of the accused to give evidence shall not be made the subject of any comment by the prosecution[4]. By "any comment", it is meant that there should be no comment whatsoever by the prosecution, whether favourable or unfavourable[5].

Marriage partners are competent to give evidence to the same extent as other witnesses. The wife or husband of the person charged is compellable to give evidence:

(a)   on behalf of that person

(b)   on behalf of any other person charged in the proceedings but only in respect of any specified offence with which the person is charged; or

(c)   for the prosecution but only in respect of any specified offence with which any person is charged in the proceedings.

An offence is specified for the purposes of (a) or (b) above if:

(i)   it involves an assault on, or injury or a threat of injury to, the wife or husband of a person who was at the material time under the age of 16;

(ii)   it is a sexual offence alleged to have been committed in respect of a person who was at the material time under that age; or

(iii)   it consists of attempting or conspiring to commit, or of aiding, abetting, counselling or procuring or inciting the commission of, an offence falling within (i) or (ii) above. Except where he or she is charged in any proceedings[6].

---

1. Any enactment or rule of law relating to the giving of evidence by a spouse applies in relation to a civil partner as it applies in relation to the spouse: see s 84 of the Civil Partnerships Act 2004 in PART VI: FAMILY LAW, post.
4. Criminal Evidence Act 1898, s 1, post.
5. *R v Riley and Everitt* (1989) 154 JP 637, CA.
6. Police and Criminal Evidence Act 1984, s 80 in this PART, post.

2–127   An accused person enjoys protection from cross-examination as to previous convictions or as to bad character[1], but may otherwise be asked any question notwithstanding that it would tend to criminate him as to the offence charged[2]. An unrepresented defendant should have his right to give evidence explained to him[3]. Whilst the prosecution must not comment on the failure of the accused to give evidence, it would seem that the court itself may, with care, comment to explain some point which has arisen in the trial, but not to suggest that it took that failure to mean that the accused had no defence and was guilty because he had failed to give evidence[4].

When the decision is taken by the defendant not to give evidence, it should be the invariable practice of his legal representative to have that decision recorded and to cause the defendant to sign the record, giving a clear indication that (i) he has by his own will decided not to give evidence and (ii) that he has so decided bearing in mind the advice, if any, given to him by the legal representative[5].

The failure of the wife or husband of the accused to give evidence shall not be made the subject of any comment by the prosecution[6], but it would seem that an inadvertent comment by the prosecution does not make the trial a nullity where it is disregarded by the court[7].

A person who has been but is no longer married to the accused is competent and compellable to give evidence as if they had never been married to one another[8]. There is no longer any prohibition on compelling disclosure of communications made during a marriage[9]. Public policy considerations do not entitle the prosecution to seek injunctive relief to prevent the Registrar General complying with his statutory duty to issue a certificate which has the effect of allowing a prisoner to marry a prosecution witness and thereby take advantage of s 80 of the 1984 Act[10].

In circumstances where she is not a compellable witness, a wife's choice of giving evidence or refusing to do so exists up to the moment she enters the witness box; once started however, she must complete her evidence in the ordinary way and may be liable to be treated as a hostile witness; before she takes the oath the court should explain to her that she has the right to refuse to give evidence against her husband, but if she chooses to give evidence against him she will be treated like any other witness and may be treated as a hostile witness[11]. Where the prosecutor has information that a spouse is unwilling to give evidence against her husband, the prosecutor must disclose the information to the defence and notify the court before seeking to call the witness. The court must then warn the spouse that she is not obliged to give evidence[12].

---

1. Criminal Justice Act 2003, s 101, post.
2. See the Criminal Evidence Act 1898, s 1(2) post, and para **2–210** et seq, post.
3. *R v Warren* (1909) 2 Cr App Rep 194, and when dealing with a defendant who is a minor, see Criminal Procedure Rules 2005, Part 38.
4. Based on comments relating to trial on indictment in *R v Rhodes* [1899] 1 QB 77, 62 JP 774; *R v Smith* (1915) 80 JP 31; *R v Bernard* (1908) 1 Cr App Rep 218; *Waugh v R* [1950] AC 203; *R v Bathurst* [1968] 2 QB 99, [1968] 1 All ER 1175; *R v Sparrow* [1973] 2 All ER 129, 137 JP 449; *R v Gallagher* [1974] 3 All ER 118.
5. *R v Bevan* (1993) 157 JP 1121, 98 Cr App Rep 354.
6. Police and Criminal Evidence Act 1984, s 80A, this PART, post.
7. *R v Dickman* (1910) 74 JP 449, 5 Cr App Rep 135, CCA.
8. Police and Criminal Evidence Act 1984, s 80(5) this PART, post.
9. The Criminal Evidence Act 1898, s 1(d) and the Evidence Amendment Act 1853, s 3 have been repealed.
10. *R (CPS) v Registrar General of Births, Deaths and Marriages* [2002] EWCA Civ 1661, [2003] 1 All ER 540, [2003] 1 FCR 109.
11. *R v Pitt* [1983] QB 25, [1982] 3 All ER 63.
12. *R v Birmingham Magistrates' Court, ex p Shields* (1994) 158 JP 845.

2–128   Co-defendants.   A co-defendant, as a person charged in criminal proceedings, shall not be called as a witness in the proceedings except upon his own application[1].

A co-defendant who has pleaded guilty is a competent and compellable witness for the prosecution or the defence in the trial of his former co-accused[2], as is a co-defendant who has been acquitted[3]. It is otherwise not proper for the prosecution to call as witnesses persons who are themselves concerned in the charge being tried[4], but this rule does not apply to an accomplice who has been separately charged and tried[5]. The discretion to exclude evidence whose prejudicial effect outweighs its probative value is confined to evidence on which the prosecution seeks to rely. Therefore there is no discretion to exclude the exculpatory part of a mixed statement containing admissions notwithstanding the exculpatory material is prejudicial to a co-accused[6].

---

1. Criminal Evidence Act 1898, s 1, post.
2. *R v Gallagher* (1875), 39 JP 502, 13 Cox CC 61.
3. *R v Rowland* (1826) Ry & M 401 and see *R v Boal* [1965] 1 QB 402, [1964] 3 All ER 269, 128 JP 573; *R v Conti* (1974) 58 Cr App Rep 387.
4. *R v Grant* [1944] 2 All ER 311; *R v Sharrock* [1948] 1 All ER 145, 112 JP 162; *R v Pipe* (1967) 51 Cr App Rep 17.
5. *R v Palmer* (1993) 158 JP 138, 99 Cr App Rep 83, [1994] Crim LR 122.
6. *Lobban v R* [1995] 2 All ER 602, [1995] 1 WLR 877, [1995] 2 Cr App Rep 573.

2–129   A co-defendant may give evidence on his own behalf or that of his co-defendant and may be cross-examined as to his guilt[1] or that of his co-defendant[2]. If a defendant refuses to answer questions incriminating other persons, the court is not bound to receive his evidence[3]. In a joint trial of two or more defendants for a joint offence the court is entitled to consider first the case in respect of defendant A which is solely based on his own out of court admissions and then to use its findings of A's guilt and the role A played as a fact to be used evidentially in respect of co-defendant B; where proof of A's guilt is necessary for there to be a case to answer against B, there is a case to answer against B at the close of the prosecution case where the only evidence of A's guilt is his own out of court admissions[4]. An acquitted person called as a witness by an accused may be cross-examined by co-accused if the evidence tends to incriminate them[5]. A plea of guilty by a co-accused is not evidence against an accused[6]. Acts and statements by one of several joint offenders or conspirators or other persons engaged in any common transaction, involving mutual legal responsibility, are parts of such common transaction and are evidence against the other party or parties thereto, as if they were done or made by him or them, so far as they were in the execution or furtherance of their common purpose, but not otherwise[7]. Statements made by joint offenders in the absence of each other may be admissible evidence, not in proof of what they contain but to prove that the makers of the statements were acting in concert[8].

---

1. *R v Rowland* [1910] 1 KB 458, 74 JP 144.
2. *R v McDonell (or McDonald)* (1909) 73 JP 490 and see *R v Paul, R v McFarlane* [1920] 2 KB 183, 84 JP 144.
3. *R v Minihane* (1921) 16 Cr App Rep 38.
4. *R v Hayter* [2005] UKHL 6, [2005] 2 Cr App 3, [2005] Crim LR 720.
5. *R v Burdett* (1855) Dears CC 431, 19 JP 87. However, questioning intended to show that a non-defendant (as a formerly acquitted defendant would be) was or was jointly responsible for the misconduct charged may be caught by the restrictions on admitting evidence of a non-defendant's bad character contained in s 100 of the Criminal Justice Act 2003

(see this PART, post), and thus need to meet the test prescribed by that section (see, particularly, s 100(3)(*d*)) and be granted leave.
  6. *R v Smith* (1984) 148 JP 215.
  7. *R v Blake* (1844) 6 QB 126. See also *R v Gray* (1994) 138 Sol Jo LB 199, [1994] 39 LS Gaz R 38, CA.
  8. *Mawaz Khan v R* [1967] AC 454, [1967] 1 All ER 80. See para **2–269 Common enterprise**, post.

2–140　Accomplices.　There is no formal definition of the term "accomplice" in the authorities, but the House of Lords[1] has recognised the following, being called as witnesses for the prosecution, as being accomplices.

    1.　Persons who are participants in the actual crime charged, whether as principals[2] or accessories (the natural and primary meaning of the term "accomplice").
    2.　A receiver of stolen goods in the trial of the actual thief.
    3.　Parties to crimes, identical in type to the offence charged, evidence of which has been admitted as proving system and intent and negativing accident.

The view was expressed[1] that the term "accomplice" should not be extended beyond these three classes.
  An accomplice who has been separately committed for trial and has pleaded guilty may be called to give evidence against a defendant, both in the committal proceedings and at the trial, without the accomplice first having been sentenced[3].
  Whilst nothing in the European Convention on Human Rights prevents a court from relying on accomplice evidence, safeguards will be needed where an accomplice has been offered immunity from prosecution[4].

  1.　In *Davies v DPP* [1954] AC 378, [1954] 1 All ER 507, 118 JP 222.
  2.　See ante in PART I: MAGISTRATES' COURTS, PROCEDURE, para **1–321 Aid, abet, counsel or procure**, and para **1–389** *Duplicity*. As to the competence of accomplices, see *R v Turner Shervill* [1975] Crim LR 415.
  3.　*R v Palmer* (1993) 158 JP 138, [1994] Crim LR 122.
  4.　*X v United Kingdom* (1976) 7 DR 115.

2–141　The requirement whereby at a trial on indictment it was obligatory for the court to give the jury a warning about convicting the accused on the uncorroborated evidence of a person merely because that person was an alleged accomplice has been abolished, as has any similar requirement applicable on the summary trial of a person for an offence[1]. The matter is now for the discretion of the court. Where one defendant gave evidence blaming the other defendant, evidence from the first defendant's wife was capable of corroborating it, provided it was recognised that there was a danger in relying on her evidence as she had an interest to serve[2]. An accomplice's wife giving evidence against his co-defendants where he himself gave no evidence has been treated as an independent witness[3]. A police spy, informer or *agent provocateur* is not treated as an accomplice[4]. A justice has no power to make a promise of pardon to an accomplice[5], but it may be appropriate to consider the privilege of a witness against self-incrimination[6]. Where one accomplice gives evidence for the prosecution his previous convictions should normally be disclosed by the prosecution to the court at the outset of the trial unless the defence has indicated otherwise[7].

  1.　Criminal Justice and Public Order Act 1994, s 32, this PART, post.
  2.　*R v Allen, R v Evans* [1965] 2 QB 295, [1964] 3 All ER 401, 129 JP 7.
  3.　*R v Willis* [1916] 1 KB 933, 80 JP 279.
  4.　*R v Bickley* (1909) 73 JP 239; *Sneddon v Stevenson* [1967] 2 All ER 1272, 131 JP 441 and see also *R v Mealey* (1975) 60 Cr App Rep 59 (*agent provocateur*, "entrapment") and *R v Willis* [1976] Crim LR 127; *R v Sang* [1979] 2 All ER 46, 143 JP 352 ("entrapment", unfair evidence).
  5.　See *R v Turner* (1975) 61 Cr App Rep 67 (undertakings of immunity from prosecution by police and the DPP).
  6.　See ante para **2–100 Privilege: witness protected by public policy and generally**.
  7.　*R v Taylor* [1999] 2 Cr Rep 163, 163 JP 168, [1999] Crim LR 407, CA.

MEASURES FOR PROTECTING AND ENHANCING THE EVIDENCE OF WITNESSES

2–142　Preparation of witnesses.　The training or coaching of witnesses is prohibited. However, this principle does not preclude pre-trial arrangements to familiarise a witness with the layout of the court, the likely sequence of events when the witness is giving evidence and a balanced appraisal of the different responsibilities of the various participants. None of which involves discussions about proposed or intended evidence. Normally such arrangements are made by the Witness Service but where they are made by an outside organization the Crown Prosecution Service should be informed in the case of prosecution witnesses of the proposed familiarisation process which should be reduced into writing. In the case of defence witnesses, counsel's advice should be sought on the proposals and these should be in writing. The process should be supervised preferably by an accredited organization or by a solicitor or barrister or responsible person with knowledge of the criminal justice process but without any personal knowledge of the matters in issue. A record should be kept[1].

  1.　*R v Momodou* [2005] EWCA Crim 177, [2005] 2 All ER 571, [2005] 2 Cr App R 6, 169 JP 186.

2–143   Special measures directions in case of vulnerable and intimidated witnesses[1].   In the case of certain witnesses in criminal proceedings (other than the accused[2]) a court may make a special measures direction[3] for the purpose of improving the quality of a witness's evidence.

Special measures[4] are:

— screening the witness from the accused[5];
— the giving of evidence by live link[6];
— the giving of evidence in private[7];
— removal of wigs and gowns[8];
— video recorded evidence in chief[9];
— video recorded cross-examination and re-examination[10];
— examination of the witness through an intermediary[11];
— aids to communication[12].

Other protection offered to witnesses includes:

— protection from cross-examination by the accused in person[13];
— restriction on evidence and questions about the complainant's sexual behaviour[14];
— restrictions on reporting[15].

Inherent powers to protect a witness (including the accused) continue to apply:

— provision of interpreter;
— use of screens.

Under the law as it was before the introduction of special measures it was possible 'in rare and exceptional circumstances' for a witness to give evidence out of sight of the defendant, eg behind a screen. In considering an application the court would have regard to the following factors in the exercise of its discretion:

(*a*)   are there real grounds for fear of the consequences if the evidence were given and the identity of the witness revealed;

(*b*)   the evidence must be sufficiently relevant and important to make it unfair to make the Crown proceed without it;

(*c*)   the Crown must satisfy the court that the creditworthiness of the witness has been fully investigated and disclosed;

(*d*)   the court must be satisfied that there would be no undue prejudice to the accused;

(*e*)   the court should balance the need for protection of the witness, including the extent of that protection, against unfairness or the appearance of unfairness[16].

Eligibility for assistance A witness is eligible for assistance if he is under 17 years or the quality of his evidence is likely to be diminished because he is suffering from a mental disorder or has a physical disability or disorder[17]; or by reason of the witness's fear or distress[18]. A person under 17 years is always eligible for assistance; a complainant in respect of a sexual case is presumed to be eligible for assistance unless the witness notifies the court that he does not wish to be so eligible[19]; and in the case of other witnesses the court must take into account the witnesses' own views as to their eligibility.

Quality of evidence Special measures may only be authorised where the court considers they would improve the quality of the witness's evidence ie quality in terms of completeness, coherence and accuracy. Coherence refers to a witness's ability in giving evidence to give answers which address the questions put to the witness and can be understood both individually and collectively[20].

Admissibility of evidence Where a statement made by a witness in criminal proceedings is, in accordance with a special measures direction, not made by the witness in direct oral testimony in court, the statement is treated as if it were made by the witness in direct oral testimony in court and accordingly:

(a)   it is admissible evidence of any fact of which such testimony from the witness would be admissible;

(b)   is not capable of corroborating any other evidence given by the witness[21].

This applies also where video recorded evidence is not made by the witness on oath even though it would have been required to be made on oath if made by the witness in direct oral testimony in court[22]. In estimating the weight (if any) to be attached to the statement, the court must have regard to all the circumstances from which an inference can reasonably be drawn (as to the accuracy of the statement or otherwise)[23].

False statements will attract penalties under the Perjury Act 1911 if made on oath and otherwise under the Youth Justice and Criminal Evidence Act 1999[24].

---

1. See generally *Achieving Best Evidence in Criminal Proceedings: Guidance for Vulnerable or Intimidated Witnesses, including Children* (Home Office et al January 2002 – www.homeoffice.gov.uk) particularly in respect of procedures for the interviewing of children and vulnerable witnesses. Although those provisions of the Youth Justice and Criminal Evidence Act 1998 which introduce special measures are now in force with the exception of s 28 (video recorded cross-examination or re-examination), the availability of special measures is subject to notification by the Secretary of State. Magistrates' courts were notified by Home Office letter dated 10 July 2002 that the following special measures would be available to all magistrates' courts from 24 July 2002 but only in respect of child witnesses in cases involving sexual offences, violence (including threats and cruelty): evidence by live link; video recorded evidence in chief. Courts in Merseyside were notified by Home Office Letter dated 13 February 2004 that as from 23 February 2004, s 29 of the 1999 Act may be made available for s 16 witnesses in Liverpool Crown Court and Magistrates' Courts and Youth Courts in Merseyside and that s 30 may be made available for such witnesses in Magistrates' Courts and Youth Courts in Merseyside. Magistrates' courts were notified by Home Office Letter dated 20 May 2004 that the following provisions were available

to all magistrates' courts and youth courts from 3 June 2004: for ss 16 and 17 witness, s 23 (screening witness from the accused), s 25 (evidence given in private); and for s 16 witnesses, s 30 (aids to communication). By Criminal Justice Performance Directorate Letter dated 1 September 2004, West London Magistrates' Court was notified that s 24 (evidence by live link) was available additionally for s 17 witnesses from 1 September 2004. Magistrates' courts were notified by Office for Criminal Justice Reform Letter dated 3 August 2005 that the s 24 (evidence by live link) was available for all ss 16 and 17 witness in magistrates' courts in England and Wales as from 3 October 2005. Availability of special measures in magistrates' courts is set out in the table below:

Magistrates' courts (as at 3 October 2005 (HOC 39/2005)	Section 16 witnesses (children & vulnerable adults)	Section 17 witnesses (intimidated/fear or distress)
Section 23 screening witness from accused	Full availability	Full availability
Section 24 evidence by live link	Full availability	Full availability
Section 25 evidence given in private	Full availability	Full availability
Section 26 removal of wigs and gowns	*Not applicable*	*Not applicable*
Section 27 video recorded evidence in chief	Partial availability – for child witnesses in need of special protection *only*)	NOT available
Section 28 video recorded cross-examination/re-examination	NOT available	NOT available
Section 29 examination through an intermediary	Partial availability – *pilot areas*	*Not applicable*
Section 30 aids to communication	Full availability	*Not applicable*

Since Parliament has decided that the normal practice will be for children under 17 years to give evidence by live link, there will have to be special reasons for departing from that practice; there is nothing inconsistent in the special measures provisions with art 6 of the ECHR, since the accused has every opportunity to challenge and question the prosecutions witnesses at the trial itself and the only thing missing is a face-to-face confrontation which the ECHR does not guarantee: *R v Camberwell Green Youth Court, ex p D (a minor), R v Camberwell Green Youth Court, ex p G* [2005] UKHL 4, [2005] 1 All ER 999, [2005] 1 WLR 393, (2005) 169 JP 105.

There may be an inherent power to allow a defendant to give evidence by live link, though the need for this will rarely arise: *R v Camberwell Green Youth Court, ex p D (a minor), R v Camberwell Green Youth Court, ex p G*, supra (doubting the correctness of *R (on the application of S) v Waltham Forest Youth Court* [2004] EWHC 715 (Admin), (2004) 168 JP 293). In any event, provision is now made for the evidence of certain accused to be given by live link: 1999 Act, Chapter 1A, ss 33A–33C, post.

2. For special measures in respect of an accused, see para **2–168 Use of live links for certain accused persons**. Before the amendment of the 1999 Act by the Police and Justice Act 2006, it had been held that the provision that the statutory "special measures" regime did not apply to an accused (or co-accused) was compatible with art 6 of the European Convention on Human Rights (*R (S) v Waltham Forest Youth Court* [2004] EWHC 715 (Admin), [2004] 2 Cr App R 21, 168 JP 293) (but doubts were expressed on the correctness of this decision in *R v Camberwell Youth Court, ex p D (a minor)*, supra.

3. Youth Justice and Criminal Evidence Act 1999, s 19, 33, in this PART, post.
4. Youth Justice and Criminal Evidence Act 1999, s 18, 33, in this PART, post.
5. Youth Justice and Criminal Evidence Act 1999, s 23, in this PART, post.
6. Youth Justice and Criminal Evidence Act 1999, s 24, in this PART, post.
7. Youth Justice and Criminal Evidence Act 1999, s 25, in this PART, post.
8. Youth Justice and Criminal Evidence Act 1999, s 26, in this PART, post.
9. Youth Justice and Criminal Evidence Act 1999, s 27, in this PART, post.
10. Youth Justice and Criminal Evidence Act 1999, s 28, in this PART, post.
11. Youth Justice and Criminal Evidence Act 1999, s 29, in this PART, post.
12. Youth Justice and Criminal Evidence Act 1999, s 30, in this PART, post.
13. Youth Justice and Criminal Evidence Act 1999, ss 34–38, in this PART, post.
14. Youth Justice and Criminal Evidence Act 1999, s 41, in this PART, post.
15. Youth Justice and Criminal Evidence Act 1999, s 44-48, in this PART, post.
16. See *R v Taylor (Gary)* (1994) Times, 17 August, CA, *R v DIX, SCY, GCZ* (1989) 91 Cr App Rep 36, sub nom *R v X, R v Y, R v Z* [1990] Crim LR 515, CA.
17. Youth Justice and Criminal Evidence Act 1999, s 16, in this PART, post.
18. Youth Justice and Criminal Evidence Act 1999, s 17, in this PART, post. Note examination of a witness through an intermediary and use of a communication aid are not available to a witness eligible only on the ground of fear or distress.
19. Youth Justice and Criminal Evidence Act 1999, s 17(4), in this PART, post.
20. Youth Justice and Criminal Evidence Act 1999, s 16(5), in this PART, post.
21. Youth Justice and Criminal Evidence Act 1999, s 31(1), (2), in this PART, post.
22. Youth Justice and Criminal Evidence Act 1999, s 31(3), in this PART, post.
23. Youth Justice and Criminal Evidence Act 1999, s 31(4), in this PART, post.
24. Youth Justice and Criminal Evidence Act 1999 s 31(6), (7),

2–144 *Witnesses eligible for assistance on grounds of age or incapacity.*   A witness in criminal proceedings (other than the accused) is eligible for assistance:

(a) if under the age of 17 at the time when it falls to the court to decide whether to make a special measures direction in relation to the witness; or

(b) if the court considers that the quality of evidence given by the witness is likely to be diminished by reasons of any of the following circumstances namely that the witness:

— suffers from mental disorder within the meaning of the Mental Health Act 1983; otherwise has a significant impairment of intelligence and social functioning; or

— having considered any views of the witness has a physical disability or is suffering from a physical disorder[1].

References to the quality of a witness's evidence are to its quality in terms of completeness, coherence and accuracy; and for this purpose "coherence" refers to a witness's ability in giving evidence to give answers which address the questions put to the witness and can be understood both individually and collectively[2].

---

1. Youth Justice and Criminal Evidence Act 1999, s 16, in this PART, post.
2. Youth Justice and Criminal Evidence Act 1999, s 16(5), 33(1).

2–145   *Witnesses eligible for assistance on grounds of fear or distress about testifying.* A witness in criminal proceedings (other than the accused) is eligible for assistance if the court is satisfied that the quality of evidence given by the witness is likely to be diminished by reason of fear or distress on the part of the witness in testifying in the proceedings[1]. The court must take into account in particular:

(*a*)   the nature and alleged circumstances of the offence to which the proceedings relate;

(*b*)   the age of the witness;

(*c*)   such of the following matters as appear to the court to be relevant:

(i)   the social and cultural background and ethnic origins of the witness;

(ii)   the domestic and employment circumstances of the witness;

(iii)   any religious beliefs or political opinions of the witness;

(*d*)   any behaviour towards the witness on the part of:

(i)   the accused

(ii)   members of the family or associates of the accused, or

(iii)   any other person who is likely to be an accused or a witness in the proceedings[2].

The court must in addition consider any views expressed by the witness[3].

A witness who is the complainant in respect of a sexual offence is eligible for assistance unless the witness has informed the court of the witness's wish not to be so eligible[4].

---

1. Youth Justice and Criminal Evidence Act 1999, s 17(1), in this PART, post.
2. Youth Justice and Criminal Evidence Act 1999, s 17(2), in this PART, post.
3. Youth Justice and Criminal Evidence Act 1999, s 17(3), in this PART, post.
4. Youth Justice and Criminal Evidence Act 1999, s 17(5), in this PART, post.

2–146   Special measures directions. Where in criminal proceedings, a party to the proceedings makes an application for a special measures direction in relation to a witness other than the accused, or the court of its own motion raises the issue whether such a direction should be given and the court determines that the witness is eligible for assistance, the court must:

(*a*)   determine whether any of the special measures available in relation to the witness (or any combination of them) would be likely to improve the quality of evidence given by the witness; and

(*b*)   if so,

(i)   determine which of these measures (or combination of them) would be likely to maximise so far as practicable the quality of such evidence; and

(ii)   give a direction providing for the measure or measures to apply to evidence given by the witness[1].

In determining whether any special measure or measures would or would not be likely to improve, or to maximise so far as practicable, the quality of evidence given by the witness, the court must consider all the circumstances of the case, including in particular:

(*a*)   any views expressed by the witness; and

(*b*)   whether the measure or measures might tend to inhibit such evidence being effectively tested by a party to the proceedings[2].

A special measure is not to be taken to be available in relation to a witness unless the court has been notified by the Secretary of State that relevant arrangements may be made available in the area in which it appears to the court that the proceedings will take place[3]. A special measures direction has binding effect from the time it is made until the proceedings are determined (by acquittal, conviction or otherwise), or are abandoned[4]. The court, on application by a party to the proceedings where there has been a material change of circumstances or if its own motion, may discharge or vary a special measures direction if it appears to the court to be in the interests of justice to do so[5]. The court must state in open court its reasons for giving or varying or refusing an application for, or for the variation or discharge of, or discharging a special measures direction and in the case of a magistrates' court records such reasons in the court register[6]. Restrictions apply to the reporting of the making of a special measures direction (or an order that a defendant may not cross-examine in person a particular witness)[7].

In determining whether to admit video recorded evidence in chief which had been taken in breach of the guidelines the starting point is the words of the statute. The Youth Justice and Criminal Evidence Act 1999 makes it clear that there is a strong presumption in favour of the use of special measures. In proceedings in the Crown Court it has been held that the appropriate test is "Could a reasonable jury properly directed be sure that the witness has given a credible and accurate account on the video tape, notwithstanding any breaches?" If "Yes", it was a matter for the jury. If "No", the interview would be inadmissible. The test could also be expressed in this way: "Were the breaches such that a reasonable jury properly directed could not be sure that the witness gave a credible and accurate account in the video interview". The prime consideration is the reliability of the videoed evidence, which would normally be assessed by reference to the interview itself, the conditions under which it was held, the age of the child, and the nature and extent of any breach of the code. There might be cases in which other evidence in the case demonstrated that the breaches had not had the effect of undermining the credibility or accuracy of the video interview. But any reference to other evidence should be undertaken with considerable caution, since it might not be often that it could assist as to the credibility, accuracy and completeness of a video interview[8].

1. Youth Justice and Criminal Evidence Act 1999, s 19(1), (2), in this PART, post.
2. Youth Justice and Criminal Evidence Act 1999, s 19(3), in this PART, post.
3. Youth Justice and Criminal Evidence Act 1999, s 18(2), in this PART, post.
4. Youth Justice and Criminal Evidence Act 1999, s 20(1), in this PART, post.
5. Youth Justice and Criminal Evidence Act 1999, s 20(2), in this PART, post.
6. Youth Justice and Criminal Evidence Act 1999, s 20(5), in this PART, post.
7. Youth Justice and Criminal Evidence Act 1999, s 47, in this PART, post.
8. *R v K* [2006] EWCA Crim 472, [2006] 2 Cr App R 10, 170 JP 558.

2–147 *Special provisions relating to child witnesses.* Where a court in making a determination whether a witness is eligible for special assistance, determines that a witness in criminal proceedings is a child witness, ie is under the age of 17 years[1], the court must first have regard to the following.

The primary rule is that the court must give a special measures direction which complies with the following requirements:

(*a*) it must provide for a video recording of an interview of the witness to be admitted as evidence in chief; and

(*b*) any evidence of the witness which is not given by means of a video recording is to be given by means of a live link[2].

It is assumed[3] that these measures will improve the quality of the child's evidence, however the primary rule (for children other than those in need of 'special protection') is subject to the following limitations:

(*a*) the availability of the special measure;

(*b*) where the court is of the opinion that it would not be in the interests of justice that the video recording or part of it should be admitted in evidence; and

(*c*) to the extent that the court is satisfied that compliance with the primary rule would not be likely to maximise the quality of the witness's evidence so far as practicable[4].

A child witness is in need of ***special protection*** if the offence (or any of the offences) to which the proceedings relate is an offence under Part I of the Sexual Offences Act 2003[5], kidnapping, false imprisonment or an offence under s 1 or 2 of the Child Abduction Act 1984; any offence under s 1 of the Children and Young Persons Act 1933; any offence which involves an assault on, or injury or a threat of injury to, any person[6].

In the case of a child witness in need of special protection 'the primary rule' is strengthened in that (subject to the availability of the measure):

— (sexual cases) any special measures direction given by the court, in relation to such a child, must in addition provide for video recorded cross-examination or re-examination to apply to any cross-examination of the witness otherwise than by the accused in person and any subsequent re-examination subject to the availability of this special measure and provided the witness has not informed the court that he does not want that special measure to apply to him[7].

— (sexual and violence cases etc) it is conclusively presumed that the use of video recorded evidence in chief and evidence given by live link will maximise the quality of the witness's evidence[8].

The primary rule for child witnesses including those in need of special protection, is a *minimum* level of protection and, where the necessary criteria are satisfied, the court may make other additional, special measures including video-recorded cross-examination where this is not within the primary rule.

Wards of court Where the child to be interviewed is a ward of court, leave of the wardship court is generally required except in the circumstances in the *Practice Direction (crime: consolidation)* [2002][9].

1. Youth Justice and Criminal Evidence Act 1999, s 21(1)(*a*), in this PART, post.
2. Youth Justice and Criminal Evidence Act 1999, s 21(3), in this PART, post.
3. Youth Justice and Criminal Evidence Act 1999, s 19(2), in this PART, post.
4. Youth Justice and Criminal Evidence Act 1999, s 21(4), in this PART, post.
5. Also offences under the following repealed provisions: the Sexual Offences Act 1956; the Indecency with Children Act 1960; the Sexual Offences Act 1967; s 54 of the Criminal Law Act 1977, or the Protection of Children Act 1978.
6. Youth Justice and Criminal Evidence Act 1999, s 21(1)(*b*), in this PART, post.
7. Youth Justice and Criminal Evidence Act 1999, s 21(6), (7), in this PART, post.
8. Youth Justice and Criminal Evidence Act 1999, s 22(5), in this PART, post.
9. Paragraph 27 in PART I: MAGISTRATES' COURTS, PROCEDURE, ante. See also *Re K (minors) (Wardship: Criminal Proceedings)* [1988] Fam 1, [1988] 1 All ER 214, 152 JP 185, *Re A (A Minor) (Wardship: Police Caution)* [1989] Fam 103,

[1989] 3 All ER 610 (when applying for leave to interview a ward, consent to a caution being administered to the ward, depending the circumstances, may be sought at the same time).

2–148 *Extension of special provisions to certain witnesses over 17 years.* The special provisions applicable to a child witness and a child witness who is in need of special protection apply with modifications to a "qualifying witness" and a "qualifying witness in need of special protection". A "qualifying witness" is a witness in criminal proceedings (other than the accused) who:

— is not a witness eligible for special measures at the time of the hearing, but
— was under the age of 17 when a relevant recording was made[1].

A 'relevant recording' is a video recording of an interview of the witness made with a view to its admission in chief of the witness[2].

1. Youth Justice and Criminal Evidence Act 1999, s 22(1)(*a*), (*b*), in this PART, post.
2. Youth Justice and Criminal Evidence Act 1999, s 22(1)(*c*), in this PART, post.

2–149 **Special measures.** The following special measures are available in relation to a witness eligible for assistance on the grounds of age or incapacity or on grounds of fear or distress about testifying:

2–160 *Screening witness from accused.* Provision may be made for the witness, while giving testimony or being sworn in court to be prevented by means of a screen or other arrangement from seeing the accused provided that the arrangement must not prevent the witness from being able to see and to be seen by the justices, legal representatives acting in the proceedings and any interpreter or other person appointed to assist the witness[1].

1. Youth Justice and Criminal Evidence Act 1999, s 23, in this PART, post.

2–161 *Evidence by live link.* A witness may give evidence by means of a live television link or other arrangement whereby a witness, while absence from the courtroom is able to see and hear a person there and to be seen and heard by the justices, legal representatives acting in the proceedings and any interpreter or other person appointed to assist the witness[1]. In proceedings before a magistrates' court where suitable live link facilities are not available at any petty sessional court-house in which that court can sit, the court may sit at a place where those facilities are available and which has been appointed for this purpose by the justices[2]. The court may make a direction as to who may act as a witness supporter and sit in the live link room with the witness balancing all the relevant interests. The witness supporter should be completely independent of the witness and his family and have no previous knowledge of or personal involvement in the case and should be suitably trained. A witness supporter may often be a representative of the Witness Service[3].

1. Youth Justice and Criminal Evidence Act 1999, s 24(1), (8), in this PART, post.
2. Youth Justice and Criminal Evidence Act 1999, s 24(4), in this PART, post.
3. Guidance on the provision of support for witnesses giving evidence by live television link is given in the *Practice Direction (criminal: consolidated)* [2002] para III.29 in PART I: MAGISTRATES' COURTS, PROCEDURE, ante.

2–162 *Evidence given in private.* During the giving of the witness's evidence, persons of any description specified in a special measures direction may be excluded from the court[1]. The persons who may be excluded do not include:

— the accused,
— legal representatives acting in the proceedings, or
— any interpreter or other person appointed to assist the witness[2].

Any special measures direction providing for representatives of news gathering or reporting organisations to be excluded must be expressed not to apply to one named individual who is a representative of such an organisation and has been nominated for the purpose by one or more such organisations unless it appears to the court that no such nomination has been made[3].

A special measures direction may only provide for the exclusion of persons where:

(a) the proceedings relate to a sexual offence; or
(b) it appears to the court that there are reasonable grounds for believing that any person other than the accused has sought, or will seek, to intimidate the witness in connection with testifying in the proceedings[4].

1. Youth Justice and Criminal Evidence Act 1999, s 25(1) in this PART, post.
2. Youth Justice and Criminal Evidence Act 1999, s 25(2), in this PART, post.
3. Youth Justice and Criminal Evidence Act 1999, s 25(3), in this PART, post.
4. Youth Justice and Criminal Evidence Act 1999, s 25(4), in this PART, post.

2–163 *Removal of wigs and gowns.* In the superior courts, a special measures direction may provide for the wearing of wigs or gowns to be dispensed with during the giving of the witness's evidence[1].

1. Youth Justice and Criminal Evidence Act 1999, s 26, in this PART, post.

2–164   ***Video recorded evidence in chief.***   A video recording of an interview of the witness may be admitted as evidence in chief of the witness except where the court is of the opinion, having regard to all the circumstances of the case, that in the interests of justice the recording, or that part of it, should not be so admitted[1]. The court must consider whether any prejudice to the accused which might result from that part being so admitted is outweighed by the desirability of showing the whole, or substantially the whole, of the recorded interview[2].

Where a special measures direction provides for a recording to be admitted, the court may nevertheless subsequently direct that it is not to be so admitted if:

(*a*)   it appears to the court that:

    (i)   the witness will not be available for cross-examination (whether conducted in the ordinary way or in accordance with any special measures direction), and

    (ii)   the parties to the proceedings have not agreed that there is no need for the witness to be so available; or

(*b*)   any rules of court requiring disclosure of the circumstances in which the recording was made have not been complied with to the satisfaction of the court[3].

Where a video recording is admitted under this provision, the witness must be called by the party tendering the video in evidence unless a special measures direction provides for the witness's evidence on cross-examination to be given otherwise than by testimony in court or the parties have agreed that there is no need for the witness to be available for cross-examination[4]. The witness may not give evidence in chief otherwise than by means of the recording as to any matter which in the opinion of the court has been dealt with adequately in the witness's recorded testimony or, without the permission of the court, as to any other matter which in the opinion of the court, is dealt with in that testimony[5]. Permission may be granted if it appears to the court to be in the interests of justice to do so and the court may direct that such evidence is given by the witness by means of a live link[6]. Examining justices may consider a video recording in relation to which it is proposed to apply for a special measures direction providing for it to be admitted at the trial[7].

---

1. Youth Justice and Criminal Evidence Act 1999, s 27(1), (2), in this PART, post.
2. Youth Justice and Criminal Evidence Act 1999, s 27(3), in this PART, post.
3. Youth Justice and Criminal Evidence Act 1999, s 27(4), in this PART, post.
4. Youth Justice and Criminal Evidence Act 1999, s 27(5), in this PART, post.
5. Youth Justice and Criminal Evidence Act 1999, s 27(5), in this PART, post.
6. Youth Justice and Criminal Evidence Act 1999, s 27(6), in this PART, post.
7. Youth Justice and Criminal Evidence Act 1999, s 27(10), in this PART, post.

2–165   ***Video recorded cross-examination or re-examination.***   Where a special measures direction provides for a video recording to be admitted as evidence in chief of the witness, the direction may also provide for any cross-examination and re-examination to be video-recorded and for such a recording to be admitted as evidence of the witness[1]. Such a recording must be in the presence of such persons as rules of court or the direction may provide and in the absence of the accused but in circumstances where the judge or justices and legal representatives are able to see and hear the examination of the witness and to communicate with the persons in whose presence the recording is being made and the accused is able to see and hear (except to the extent that the person is unable to see or hear by reason of any impairment of eyesight or hearing[2]) any such examination and to communicate with any legal representative acting for him[3]. The court may subsequently direct that such evidence is not to be admitted if any of the requirements has not been complied with to the satisfaction of the court[4]. Where a recording has been made of any examination of the witness, the witness may not be subsequently cross-examined or re-examined in respect of any evidence given by the witness in the proceedings unless the court gives a further special measures direction for the examination to be video-recorded in relation to any subsequent cross-examination or re-examination, of the witness and the court may only give such a further direction if the proposed cross-examination is a result of the party subsequently becoming aware of a matter which that party could not with reasonable diligence have ascertained since the time of the original recording or where for any other reason it is in the interests of justice to give the further direction[5]. But none of these provisions applies in relation to any cross-examination of the witness by the accused in person (in a case where he is able to do so)[6].

---

1. Youth Justice and Criminal Evidence Act 1999, s 28(1), in this PART, post.
2. Youth Justice and Criminal Evidence Act 1999, s 33(3), in this PART, post.
3. Youth Justice and Criminal Evidence Act 1999, s 28(2), in this PART, post.
4. Youth Justice and Criminal Evidence Act 1999, s 28(4), in this PART, post.
5. Youth Justice and Criminal Evidence Act 1999, s 28(5), (6), in this PART, post.
6. Youth Justice and Criminal Evidence Act 1999, s 28(7) and see Chapter II, ss 34–40 (Protection of witnesses from cross-examination by accused in person) in this PART, post.

2–166   ***Examination of witness through intermediary.***   A special measures direction may provide for any examination of the witness (however and whenever conducted) to be conducted through an interpreter or other person approved by the court ("an intermediary")[1]. The function of an intermediary is to communicate:

(*a*) to the witness, questions put to the witness, and

(*b*) to any person asking such questions, the answers given by the witness in reply to them,

and to explain such questions or answers so far as necessary to enable them to be understood by the witness or person in question[2].

Any examination of the witness must take place in the presence of such persons as rules of court or the direction may provide, but in circumstances in which the judge or justices and legal representatives acting in the proceedings are able to see and hear[3] the examination of the witness and to communicate with the intermediary[4].

A person may not act as an intermediary in a particular case except after making a declaration, in such form as may be prescribed by rules of court, that he will faithfully perform his function as intermediary and section 1 of the Perjury Act 1911 will apply to such a person[5]. An intermediary may be used, with the court's prior permission, for the purposes of an interview with a witness which is video recorded with a view to its admission as evidence in chief of the witness[6].

---

1. Youth Justice and Criminal Evidence Act 1999, s 29(1), in this PART, post.
2. Youth Justice and Criminal Evidence Act 1999, s 29(2), in this PART, post
3. For "see and hear" see s 33(3), in this PART, post.
4. Youth Justice and Criminal Evidence Act 1999, s 29(3), in this PART, post.
5. Youth Justice and Criminal Evidence Act 1999, s 29(5), in this PART, post.
6. Youth Justice and Criminal Evidence Act 1999, s 29(6), in this PART, post.

2–167 *Aids to communication.* A special measures direction may provide for a witness, while giving evidence (whether by testimony in court or otherwise), to be provided with such device as the court considers appropriate with a view to enabling questions or answers to be communicated to or by the witness despite any disability or disorder or other impairment which the witness has or suffers from[1].

---

1. Youth Justice and Criminal Evidence Act 1999, s 30, in this PART, post.

2–168 Use of live links for certain accused persons. The court may, on the application of an accused, give a direction for his evidence to be given by live link[1] ie an arrangement by which he is absent from the court room but is able to see and hear a person there and to be seen and heard by the judge or magistrates, any co-accused, any legal representative and any interpreter[2]. The accused must either be:

— under 18 years and his ability to participate in the proceedings in court as a witness is compromised by his level of intellectual ability or social functioning; or

— 18 years and over and suffering from a mental disorder or otherwise have a significant impairment of intelligence and social function so that he is unable to participate effectively as a witness giving oral evidence in court; and (in either case)

— use of a live link would enable him to participate more effectively as a witness[3].

The court must be satisfied that it is in the interests of justice for the accused to give evidence through live link[4]. A live link direction is that any oral evidence to be given by the accused is to be given through a live link and, while the direction is in force, not otherwise[5]. A direction may be discharged by the court of its own motion or on application by a party at any time, if it appears to be in the interests of justice to do so[6]. The court must give reasons for giving, discharging or refusing an application to give or discharge a live link direction, and enter such reasons in the register[7].

---

1. Youth Justice and Criminal Evidence Act 1999, s 33A(2), in this PART: STATUTES ON EVIDENCE, post..
2. Youth Justice and Criminal Evidence Act 1999, s 33B(1), (2), in this PART: STATUTES ON EVIDENCE, post..
3. Youth Justice and Criminal Evidence Act 1999, s 33A(4), (5), in this PART: STATUTES ON EVIDENCE, post..
4. Youth Justice and Criminal Evidence Act 1999, s 33A(2)(b), in this PART: STATUTES ON EVIDENCE, post..
5. Youth Justice and Criminal Evidence Act 1999, s 33A(3), (6), in this PART: STATUTES ON EVIDENCE, post.
6. Youth Justice and Criminal Evidence Act 1999, s 33A(7), in this PART: STATUTES ON EVIDENCE, post.
7. Youth Justice and Criminal Evidence Act 1999, s 33A(8), in this PART: STATUTES ON EVIDENCE, post.

2–169 Witness anonymity. The following principles were stated in *R v Davis; R v Ellis*[1] in relation to fair trials and witness anonymity. The Convention rights of witnesses include, where necessary, the preservation of their anonymity. The concealment of the identity of witnesses is not inconsistent with the right to a fair trial, provided that the need for anonymity is clearly established; that cross-examination of the witness by an advocate for the defendant is permitted; and that the trial is fair. A trial will not inevitably be considered unfair, and a conviction unsafe, simply because the evidence of anonymous witnesses may be decisive to the outcome. The potential disadvantages to a defendant require the court to examine the application for witness anonymity with scrupulous care to ensure that it is necessary and that the witness is indeed in genuine and justified fear of serious consequences if his true identity becomes known to the defendant or his associates. The court should be alert to potential or actual disadvantages faced by a defendant in consequence of any anonymity ruling and should ensure that necessary and appropriate precautions are taken to ensure that the trial itself will be fair. Provided that appropriate safeguards are applied, and the judge is satisfied that a fair trial can take place, it can proceed. If not, the judge should not permit anonymity.

---

1. [2006] EWCA Crim 1155, [2006] 4 All ER 648, [2006] 1 WLR 3130.

2–180 Protection of witnesses from cross-examination by accused in person. No person charged with a sexual offence may in any criminal proceedings cross-examine in person a witness who is the complainant, either:

(a) in connection with that offence, or

(b) in connection with any other offence (of whatever nature) with which that person is charged in the proceedings[1].

Nor may a person charged with one of the following offences:

(i) any offence under Part I of the Sexual Offences Act 2003[2];

(ii) Kidnapping, false imprisonment or an offence under s 1 or 2 of the Child Abduction Act 1984;

(iii) any offence under s 1 of the Children and Young Persons Act 1933;

(iv) any offence which involves an assault on, or injury or a threat of injury to, any person;

cross-examine in person a protected witness, either:

(a) in connection with that offence, or

(b) in connection with any other offence (of whatever nature) in which that person is charged in the proceedings[3].

A "*protected witness*" is a witness who either is the complainant or is alleged to have been a witness to the commission of the offence and is either a child or falls to be cross-examined after giving evidence in chief (whether wholly or in part) by means of a video recording made at a time when the witness was a child or in any other way at any such time[4]. A child means a person under the age of 17 years (for the purpose of the offences listed at (i) above, and a person under the age of 14 years for the purposes of offences listed at (ii)–(iii) above)[5]. A "witness" also includes a witness who is charged with an offence in the proceedings[6].

Where neither of the above provisions operate to prevent an accused in any criminal proceedings from cross-examining a witness in person and either on application the prosecutor of where the court raises the issue of its own motion, if it appears to the court:

(a) that the quality of evidence given by the witness on cross-examination

   (i) is likely to be diminished if the cross-examination (or further cross-examination) is conducted by the accused in person, and

   (ii) would be likely to be improved if a direction were given prohibiting the accused from cross-examining in person a particular witness, and

(b) that it would not be contrary to the interests of justice to give such a direction[7].

In determining whether the quality of the witness's evidence is likely to be diminished if he is cross-examined by the accused in person, the court must have regard, in particular, to:

(a) any views expressed by the witness as to whether or not the witness is content to be cross-examined by the accused in person;

(b) the nature of the questions likely to be asked, having regard to the issues in the proceedings and the defence case advanced so far (if any);

(c) any behaviour on the part of the accused at any stage of the proceedings, both generally and in relation to the witness;

(d) any relationship (of whatever nature) between the witness and the accused;

(e) whether any person (other than the accused), is or has at any time been charged in the proceedings with a sexual offence or an offence to which the provisions relating to child complainants and other child witnesses apply, and if so whether any of the provisions relating to these witnesses and complainants in proceedings for sexual offences operates or would have operated to prevent that person from cross-examining the witness in person;

(f) any special measures direction which the court has given, or proposes to give, in relation to the witness[8].

Where an accused is prevented from cross-examining a witness in person the court must invite the accused to arrange for a legal representative to act for him for the purpose of cross-examining the witness. If the accused fails to do so within the time specified by the court and in accordance with rules of court, the court must consider whether it is in the interests of justice for the witness to be cross-examined by a legal representative appointed to represent the interests of the accused (but who is not responsible to the accused)[9].

A direction has binding effect from the time it is made until the witness to whom it applies is discharged[10]. The court may in accordance with rules of court discharge a direction if it appears to the court to be in the interests of justice to do so either on application by a party to the proceedings, if there has been a material change in circumstances since the direction was made, or of its own motion[11]. The court must state in open court its reasons for giving, refusing an application for, or the discharge of, or discharging a direction and, if it is a magistrates' court, must cause them to be entered in the court register[12].

---

1. Youth Justice and Criminal Evidence Act 1999, s 34, in this PART, post.
2. Also offences under the following repealed provisions: the Sexual Offences Act 1956; the Indecency with Children Act 1960; the Sexual Offences Act 1967; s 54 of the Criminal Law Act 1977, or the Protection of Children Act 1978.
3. Youth Justice and Criminal Evidence Act 1999, s 35, in this PART, post.
4. Youth Justice and Criminal Evidence Act 1999, s 35(2), in this PART, post.

5. Youth Justice and Criminal Evidence Act 1999, s 35(4), in this PART, post.
6. Youth Justice and Criminal Evidence Act 1999, s 35(5), in this PART, post.
7. Youth Justice and Criminal Evidence Act 1999, s 36(1), (2), in this PART, post.
8. Youth Justice and Criminal Evidence Act 1999, s 36(3), in this PART, post.
9. Youth Justice and Criminal Evidence Act 1999, s 38, in this PART, post.
10. Youth Justice and Criminal Evidence Act 1999, s 37(1), in this PART, post.
11. Youth Justice and Criminal Evidence Act 1999, s 37(2), in this PART, post.
12. Youth Justice and Criminal Evidence Act 1999, s 37(4), in this PART, post.

2–181   Protection of complainants in proceedings for sexual offences.   If at a trial a person is charged with a sexual offence, then, except with the leave of the court:

(a)   no evidence may be adduced, and

(b)   no question may be asked in cross-examination, by or on behalf of the accused at the trial, about any sexual behaviour of the complainant[1].

The court may give leave only on application made by or on behalf of an accused, and may not give such leave unless it is satisfied:

(a)   that the evidence or question relates to a relevant issue in the case and that that issue is not an issue of consent or is an issue of consent and the sexual behaviour of the complainant to which the evidence or question relates is alleged

(i)   to have taken place at or about the same time as the event which is the subject matter of the charge; or

(ii)   to have been, in any respect, so similar to any sexual behaviour of the complainant which took place as part of the event or to any other sexual behaviour of the complainant which took place at or about the that the similarity cannot reasonably be explained as a coincidence (but no evidence or question shall be regarded as relating to a relevant issue in the case if it appears to the court to be reasonable to assume that its purpose (or main purpose) is to establish or elicit material for impugning the credibility of the complainant as a witness); or

(b)   that the evidence or question relates to any evidence adduced by the prosecution about any sexual behaviour of the complainant; and in the opinion of the court, would go no further than is necessary to enable the evidence adduced by the prosecution to be rebutted or explained by or on behalf of the accused[2].

This restriction applies also to the following proceedings as they apply to a trial: proceedings before examining justices; a hearing held, between conviction and sentencing, for the purpose of determining matters relevant to the court's decision as to how the accused is to be dealt with (a "*Newton*" hearing) and applications, to the Crown Court to discharge matters transferred or sent for trial[3]. Where this restriction applies in relation to a trial by virtue of the fact that one or more of a number of defendants charged in the proceedings is or are charged with a sexual offence, it shall cease to apply if the charge against that person or persons is not proceeded with by the prosecutor, but it does not cease to apply in the event of that person or persons pleading guilty to or being convicted of the charge[4].

An application for leave must be heard in private and in the absence of the complainant. The court must state in open court its reasons for giving or refusing leave and, if it gives leave, the extent to which evidence may be adduced or questions asked in pursuance of the leave, and a magistrates' court must cause those matters to be entered in the register of its proceedings[5].

Rules of court may make provision for applications for leave to provide specified particulars and information for the court and for the manner in which sensitive information is to be handled[6].

1. Youth Justice and Criminal Evidence Act 1999, s 41(1), in this PART, post.
2. Youth Justice and Criminal Evidence Act 1999, s 41(2)–(6), in this PART, post.
3. Youth Justice and Criminal Evidence Act 1999, s 42(3), in this PART, post.
4. Youth Justice and Criminal Evidence Act 1999, s 41(7), in this PART, post.
5. Youth Justice and Criminal Evidence Act 1999, s 43(1), (2), in this PART, post.
6. Youth Justice and Criminal Evidence Act 1999, s 43(3), in this PART, post and see the Criminal Procedure Rules 2005, Part 36, in PART I: MAGISTRATES' COURTS, PROCEDURE, ante.

2–182   Power to restrict reports about certain adult witnesses in criminal proceedings.   Where in any criminal proceedings in any court a party to the proceedings makes an application for the court to give a reporting direction in relation to a witness in the proceedings (other than the accused) who has attained the age of 18, if the court determines:

(a)   that the witness is eligible for protection, and

(b)   that giving a reporting direction in relation to the witness is likely to improve:

(i)   the quality of evidence given by the witness, or

(ii)   the level of co-operation given by the witness to any party to the proceedings in connection with that party's preparation of its case,

the court may give a reporting direction in relation to the witness[1].

A witness is eligible for protection if the court is satisfied:

(a)   that the quality of evidence given by the witness, or

(b)   the level of co-operation given by the witness to any party to the proceedings in connection with that party's preparation of its case, is likely to be diminished by reason of fear or distress on the part of the witness in connection with being identified by members of the public as a witness in the proceedings[2]. In determining whether a witness is eligible for protection, the court must take into account, in particular:

(a) the nature and alleged circumstances of the offence to which the proceedings relate;

(b) the age of the witness;

(c) such of the following matters as appear to the court to be relevant, namely:

    (i) the social and cultural background and ethnic origins of the witness,

    (ii) the domestic and employment circumstances of the witness, and

    (iii) any religious beliefs or political opinions of the witness;

(d) any behaviour towards the witness on the part of

    (i) the accused,

    (ii) members of the family or associates of the accused, or

    (iii) any other person who is likely to be an accused or a witness in the proceedings[3].

The court must in addition consider any views of the witness[4].

A 'reporting direction' is a direction that no matter relating to the witness shall during the witness's lifetime be included in any publication if it is likely to lead members of the public to identify him as being a witness in the proceedings[5]. The matters in relation to which the restrictions apply include in particular:

(a) the witness's name,

(b) the witness's address,

(c) the identity of any educational establishment attended by the witness,

(d) the identity of any place of work, and

(e) any still or moving picture of the witness[6].

In determining whether to give a reporting direction or to make an "excepting direction" to dispense with any of the restrictions imposed by a reporting direction, the court must consider:

(a) whether it would be in the interests of justice to do so, and:

(b) the public interest in avoiding the imposition of a substantial and unreasonable restriction on the reporting of the proceedings[7].

Procedure The procedure for making an application for a restriction order or an exception order is prescribed by rules of court[8].

---

1. Youth Justice and Criminal Evidence Act 1999, s 46(1), (2), in this PART, post.
2. Youth Justice and Criminal Evidence Act 1999, s 46(3), in this PART, post.
3. Youth Justice and Criminal Evidence Act 1999, s 46(4), in this PART, post.
4. Youth Justice and Criminal Evidence Act 1999, s 46(5), in this PART, post.
5. Youth Justice and Criminal Evidence Act 1999, s 46(6), in this PART, post.
6. Youth Justice and Criminal Evidence Act 1999, s 46(7), in this PART, post.
7. Youth Justice and Criminal Evidence Act 1999, s 46(8), in this PART, post.
8. See the Criminal Procedure Rules 2005, Part 16, in PART I: MAGISTRATES' COURTS, PROCEDURE, ante.

Evidence of bad character

APPROACH TO THE ADMISSIBILITY OF EVIDENCE OF BAD CHARACTER

2–200   The circumstances in which a party is permitted to adduce evidence in the course of a trial of the bad character of an accused or a person other than an accused are prescribed by the provisions of Part 11, Chapter 1 of the Criminal Justice Act 2003[1]. The common law rules governing the admissibility of bad character in criminal proceedings have been abolished[2]. The 2003 Act completely reverses the pre-existing rule. Evidence of bad character is now admissible if it satisfies certain criteria and the approach is no longer one of inadmissibility subject to exceptions. The new law does not use terms such as "enhanced probative value" or other terms applicable to the former common law for the admission of "similar fact evidence". An "enhanced relevance" test applies in relation to s 100 of the Act (bad character of a non-defendant) but if a defendant's bad character is relevant to an important issue between the prosecution and the defence, then, unless there is an application to exclude the evidence, it is admissible. Leave is not required. The former common law test one stage test which balanced probative value against prejudicial effect is obsolete[3].

In the application of the bad character provisions of the 2003 Act, the court will often have to exercise its judgment in the specific factual context of the individual case, or exercise its judicial discretion. The Court of Appeal (Criminal Division) has emphasised that the context in which a decision is made is usually the critical ingredient of the decision. Accordingly, the creation and subsequent citation of "authority", which in reality represents no more than observations on a fact-specific decision of the court at first instance, is unnecessary and may be counter-productive. Responsibility for application of the principles is for the court of trial[4].

---

1. In this PART, post.
2. Criminal Justice Act 2003, s 99, in this PART, post.
3. *R v Weir* [2005] EWCA Crim 2866, [2006] 2 All ER 570, [2006] 1 WLR 1885, [2006] 1 Cr App R 19.
4. *R v Renda* [2005] EWCA Crim 2826, [2006] 2 All ER 553, [2006] 1 Cr App R 24, [2006] Crim LR 534.

DEFINITION OF BAD CHARACTER

2–201   "Bad character" is defined as "misconduct" or a "disposition towards misconduct"[1]. "Misconduct is defined as "the commission of any offence or other reprehensible behaviour"[2].

Excluded from its definition of bad character are – (*a*) misconduct which has to do with the alleged facts of the charge which the defendant faces; and (*b*) misconduct in connection with the investigation or prosecution of that offence[3].

The word "reprehensible" carries with it some element of culpability or blameworthiness. But the fact that the defendant was found not fit to plead and received an absolute discharge 18 months after an apparent incident of gratuitous violence occurred does not mean that it was not reprehensible behaviour[4].

The common law rules governing the admissibility of bad character in criminal proceedings have been abolished[5].

In the provisions below that refer to the relevance of evidence or its probative value, when making any such assessment the court is to assume that the evidence is true[6], unless on the basis of any material before the court (including any evidence it decides to hear on the matter) no court or jury could reasonable find it to be true[7].

There is no reason in principle why evidence relating to allegations that have never been tried, because of a stay of proceedings for abuse of process, should not be admissible[8]. Whilst the making of an allegation may not be capable of being evidence of a *non-defendant's* bad character, since if the allegation were not to be admitted there would have to be an investigation of relevant matters, those considerations do not apply to evidence of a *defendant's* bad character since the relevance or probative value of such evidence depends on the assumption that it is true; whether or not the allegations are ultimately found to be true is a matter for the court or jury[8].

Where the court makes a relevant ruling it must state its reasons for doing so and, it is a magistrate's court, it must cause the ruling and the reasons for it to be entered in the court register[9]. A "relevant ruling", for this purpose, is a ruling: (*a*) on whether an item of evidence is evidence of a person's bad character; (*b*) on whether an item of evidence is admissible under one of the gateways; or (*c*) (Crown Court trial only) a ruling on whether to stop proceedings[10].

---

1.   Section 98 of the Criminal Justice Act 2003. See this PART, post.
2.   Criminal Justice Act 2003, s 112(1).
3.   Criminal Justice Act 2003, s 98.
4.   *R v Renda* [2005] EWCA Crim 2826, [2006] 2 All ER 553, [2006] 1 Cr App R 24, [2006] Crim LR 534.
5.   Criminal Justice Act 2003, s 99.
6.   Criminal Justice Act 2003, s 109(1).
7.   Criminal Justice Act 2003, s 109(2).
8.   *R v Edwards (Stewart), R v McLean, R v Smith (David), R v Enright* [2005] EWCA Crim 3244, [2006] 3 All ER 882, [2006] 1 WLR 1524, (2006) 2 Cr App R 4 in which it was stated: "Whilst we note the observation of Rose LJ in *R v Bovell, R v Dowds* [2005] EWCA Crim 1091 at [21], [2005] 2 Cr App R 27 (p 401) at [21] that the court entertained considerable doubt whether the mere making of an allegation is capable of being evidence within s 100(1), we are persuaded that it so capable, at any rate when considering the effect of s 109 in relation to an issue under s 101(1)(*d*). This is an area, however, in which it is important to guard against satellite litigation (see *R v Bovell* [2005] 2 Cr App R 27 at [22]). Further, it is appropriate to proceed with caution and with due regard to the judge's discretion to exclude evidence (para 1 vii)." See further para **2–214**, post.
9.   Criminal Justice Act 2003, s 110(1).
10. Criminal Justice Act 2003, s 110(2). As to stopping proceedings, see para **2–217**, post.

2–202   "Misconduct" is not limited to previous convictions, nor to cautions. It can extend to behaviour which may not have given rise to either a conviction or a caution[1].

Where a defendant was accused of robbery and alleged that the victim had offered to supply him with drugs and that the victim had taken an ecstasy tablet, this was misconduct which had to do with the alleged facts of the charge with which the defendant faced and was not therefore evidence of bad character[2].

---

1.   *R v S* [2006] EWCA Crim 756, 170 JP 434.
2.   *R v Machado* [2006] EWCA Crim 837, 170 JP 400.

Evidence of bad character of the defendant

GATEWAYS FOR THE ADMISSIBILITY OF EVIDENCE OF DEFENDANT'S BAD CHARACTER

2–210   There are seven gateways[1]. In criminal proceedings evidence of the defendant's bad character is admissible if, but only if:

(1)   all parties to the proceedings agree that it is admissible;
(2)   the evidence is adduced by the defendant himself or is given in answer to a question asked by him in cross-examination and intended to elicit it;
(3)   it is important explanatory evidence[2];
(4)   it is relevant to an important matter in issue between the defendant and the prosecution[3];
(5)   it has substantial probative value in relation to an important matter in issue between the defendant and a co-defendant[4];

(6) it is evidence to correct a false impression given by the defendant[5]; or

(7) the defendant has made an attack on another person's character[6].

1. These are listed in s 101(1)(a)–(g) of the Criminal Justice Act 2003. See this Part, post.
2. See para **2–212**, post.
3. See para **2–213**, post.
4. See para **2–214**, post.
5. See para **2–215**, post.
6. See para **2–216**, post.

2–211 Duty to exclude such evidence in certain circumstances . The court must not admit evidence under (4) or (6) above if, on an application by the defendant to exclude it, it appears to the court that the admission of the evidence would have such an adverse effect on the fairness of the proceedings that the court ought not to admit it[1]. When the court is considering this matter, the provision that multiple charges in the same proceedings are to be treated as if each offence were charged in separate proceedings does not apply[2]. On the making of such an application to exclude the court must have regard, in particular, to the length of time between the matters to which the evidence relates and the matters which form to the subject of the offence charged[3]. These provisions only apply to two of the gateways but where they do not apply, the provisions of s 78 of the Police and Criminal Evidence Act 1984, should be considered[4].

In proceedings for an offence committed or allegedly committed by the defendant after he attained 21, evidence of an offence committed by him when he was aged under 14 is not admissible unless both of the offences are triable only on indictment and the court is satisfied that the interests of justice require the evidence to be admissible[5]. These requirements are additional to those set out above[6].

The effect of admitting any conviction is prejudicial to the defence but Parliament has permitted it. But the judge is expressly required to consider the prejudicial effect and must not admit it if it would have such an adverse effect on the fairness on the proceedings that it ought not to be admitted. Accordingly, in a case of robbery, admission of a large number of convictions for different offences of dishonesty is bound to be more prejudicial than a limited number of a more specific type[7].

1. Criminal Justice Act 2003, s 101(3).
2. Criminal Justice Act 2003, s 112(3).
3. Criminal Justice Act 2003, s 101(4).
4. *R v Highton* [2005] EWCA Crim 1985, [2005] 1 WLR 3472, *R v Weir* [2005] EWCA Crim 2866, [2006] 2 All ER 570, [2006] 1 WLR 1885, [2006] 1 Cr App R 19.
5. Criminal Justice Act 2003, s 108(2).
6. Criminal Justice Act 2003, s 108(3).
7. *R v Tully* [2006] EWCA Crim 2270, 171 JP 25.

2–212 Meaning of "important explanatory evidence". Evidence is important explanatory evidence if, without it, the court or jury would find it impossible or difficult to understand other evidence in the case, and its value for understanding the evidence as a whole is substantial[1].

1. Section 102 of the Criminal Justice Act 2003. See this Part, post.

2–213 Meaning of "important matter" and "matter in issue between the defendant and the prosecution". Only prosecution evidence[1] is admissible under this gateway.

"Important matter" means a matter of substantial importance in the context of the case as a whole[2]. The matters in issue, for the purpose of this gateway, include –

(1) the question whether the defendant has a propensity to commit offences of the kind with which he is charged, except where his having such a propensity makes it no more likely that he is guilty of the offence; and

(2) the question whether the defendant has a propensity to be untruthful, except where it is not suggested that the defendant's case is untruthful in any respect[3].

Where (1) above applies, one of the ways in which propensity may be established is by evidence of a conviction for an offence of the same description[4], or within the same category[5], as the current offence, but this does not apply if the court is satisfied, by reason of the passage of time since the conviction, that it would be unjust for it to apply[6].

A defendant's propensity to commit offences of the kind with which he is charged can be proved in ways other than by evidence that he has been convicted of an offence of the same description or an offence of the same category. The statutory provision allows for the admission of, for example, the fact that the defendant has previously asked to have taken into consideration offences of the kind with which he is now charged or has been cautioned[7]. Convictions sought to be relied on to show propensity are not confined to offences that pre-date the offence charged in the instant proceedings[8]. Moreover, the mere making of an allegation is capable of being evidence within s 100(1), at any rate when considering the effect of s 109 (assumption of truth) in relation to an issue under s 101(1)(d)[9]. This is an area, however, in which it is important to guard against satellite litigation; further, it is appropriate to proceed with caution and with due regard to the judge's discretion to exclude evidence[9].

1. Defined in s 112(1) of the Criminal Justice Act 2003. See this Part, post.
2. Criminal Justice Act 2003, s 112(1).
3. Criminal Justice Act 2003, s 103(1). The question of propensity to tell untruths should be considered separately from

propensity to commit the current offence before the accused is cross-examined on the former basis: *R v Atkinson* [2006] EWCA Crim 1424, (2006) 170 JP 605.

4. Defined in s 103(4)(*a*), ibid, to mean that the statement of offence would be in the same terms in a written charge or indictment. Section 112, ibid, defines "written charge".

5. Section 103(4)(*b*) provides that two offences are of the same category as each other if they belong to the same category of offences prescribed for these purposes by an order made by the Secretary of State. The Criminal Justice Act 2003 (Categories of Offences) Order, SI 2004/3346, has been made.

6. Criminal Justice Act 2003, s 103(3).

7. *R v Weir* [2005] EWCA Crim 2866, [2006] 2 All ER 570, [2006] 1 WLR 1885, [2006] 1 Cr App R 19.

8. *R v Adenusi* [2006] EWCA Crim 1059, [2006] Crim LR 929.

9. *R v Edwards (Stewart), R v McLean, R v Smith (David), R v Enright* [2005] EWCA Crim 3244, [2006] 3 All ER 882, [2006] 1 WLR 1524 (cf the observations of Rose LJ in *R v Bovell* [2005] EWCA Crim 1091, [2005] 2 Cr App R 401, at para 21).

2–214 "Matter in issue between the defendant and a co-defendant" – restrictions. Only evidence which has been or is to be adduced by the co-defendant or which a witness has given or is to be invited to give in cross-examination by the co-defendant is admissible under this gateway[1].

Evidence which is relevant to the question whether the defendant has a propensity to be untruthful is admissible on that basis under this gateway only if the nature or conduct of his defence is such as to undermine the co-defendant's defence[2].

The Court of Appeal has given the following general guidance in relation to co-defendant applications to admit bad character evidence:

"(v) Simply because an application to admit evidence of bad character is made by a co-defendant, the judge is not bound to admit it. The gateway in s 101(1)(*e*) must be gone through. Sections 101(1)(*d*) and (*e*) give rise to different considerations. In determining an application under s 101(1)(*e*) analysis with a fine tooth comb is unlikely to be helpful; it is the context of the case as a whole that matters. Section 112 makes this clear by its definition of what amounts to an important matter in issue.

(vi) There are a number of other points about the position of co-defendants:

(*a*) the gateways under ss 101(1)(*d*), (*f*) and (*g*) are not open to them as only prosecution evidence, as defined in s 112, is admissible: see ss 103(6), 105(7) and 106(3);

(*b*) section 104(1) is not exhaustive of the scope of s 101(1)(*e*). It limits evidence relevant to a defendant's propensity to be untruthful.

(*c*) whether a defendant's stance amounts to no more than a denial of participation (see *R v Varley* (1982) 75 Cr App R 242), or gives rise to an important matter in issue between a defendant and a co-defendant, will inevitably turn on the facts of the individual case."[3]

1. Section 104(2) of the Criminal Justice Act 2003. See this PART, post.
2. Criminal Justice Act 2003, s 104(1).
3. *R v Edwards and Rowlands, R v McLean, R v Smith (David), R v Enright and Gray* [2005] EWCA Crim 3244, [2006] 2 Cr App R 62.

2–215 "Evidence to correct a false impression". Only prosecution evidence[1] is admissible under this gateway[2]; and evidence is admissible only if it goes no further than to correct the false impression[3].

For the purposes of this gateway the defendant gives a false impression if he is responsible for the making of an express or implied assertion which is apt to give the court or jury a false or misleading impression about him; and evidence to correct such an impression is evidence which has probative value in correcting it[4]. A simple denial of the offence or offences alleged cannot, for the purposes of s 101(1)(*f*), be treated as a false impression given by the defendant. But it is otherwise where the defendant puts himself forward not only as not having any previous convictions but as enjoying a good reputation as for, example, a priest. The former common law rule that character was indivisible is reversed now that evidence is admissible under this gateway "only if it goes no further than is necessary to correct the false impression"[5].

A defendant is treated as responsible for making an assertion if –

(1) he makes the assertion, whether or not in the course of testifying;

(2) he makes the assertion during a caution interview before being charged with the current offence, or on being charged with the current offence or being officially warned of possible prosecution for it;

(3) a defence witness makes the assertion;

(4) the assertion is made by any witness in cross-examination in response to a question asked by the defendant that was intended, or was likely, to elicit it; or

(5) the assertion was made by any person out of court and the defendant adduces evidence of it in the proceedings[6].

A defendant who would otherwise be treated as responsible for making an assertion shall not be so treated if, or to the extent that, he withdraws it or disassociates himself from it[7]. A concession extracted in cross-examination that the defendant was not telling the truth in part of his examination-in-chief will not normally amount to a withdrawal or disassociation from the original assertion for the purpose of s 105(3)[8].

Where it appears to the court that a defendant by means of his conduct (other than the giving of evidence) in the proceedings is seeking to give the court or jury a false or misleading impression about himself, the court may if it appears just to do so treat the defendant as being responsible for the making of an assertion which is apt to give that impression[9]. "Conduct", here, includes appearance or dress[10].

---

1. Defined in s 112(1) of the Criminal Justice Act 2003. See this PART, post.
2. Criminal Justice Act 2003, s 105(7).
3. Criminal Justice Act 2003, s 105(6).
4. Criminal Justice Act 2003, s 105(1).
5. *R v Weir* [2005] EWCA Crim 2866, [2006] 2 All ER 570, [2006] 1 WLR 1885, [2006] 1 Cr App R 19.
6. Criminal Justice Act 2003, s 105(2).
7. Criminal Justice Act 2003, s 105(3).
8. *R v Renda* [2005] EWCA Crim 2826, [2006] 2 All ER 553, [2006] 1 Cr App R 24, [2006] Crim LR 534.
9. Criminal Justice Act 2003, s 105(4).
10. Criminal Justice Act 2003, s 105(5).

2–216   "**Attack on another person's character**".   Only prosecution evidence[1] is admissible under this gateway[2].

"Evidence attacking the other person's character" means evidence to the effect that the other person has committed an offence or has behaved or is disposed to behave in a reprehensible way; and 'imputation about the other person' means an assertion to that effect[3].

A defendant makes an attack on another person's character if –

(a)   he adduces evidence attacking that person's character;

(b)   he (or any legal representative appointed under s 38(4) of the Youth Justice and Criminal Evidence Act 1999 to cross-examine a witness) asks questions in cross-examination that are intended to elicit such evidence or are likely to do so; or

(c)   evidence is given of an imputation made about that person by the defendant during a caution interview before he was charged with the current offence, or on being charged with the current offence or being officially informed he might be prosecuted for it[4].

---

1. Defined in s 112(1) of the Criminal Justice Act 2003. See this PART, post.
2. Criminal Justice Act 2003, s 106(3).
3. Criminal Justice Act 2003, s 106(2).
4. Criminal Justice Act 2003, s 106(1)(*a*)–(*c*).

2–217   **Stopping proceedings where admitted evidence of a defendant's bad character has become contaminated.**   This applies only to jury trial either to determine guilt or to determine under the Criminal Procedure Insanity Act 1964 whether or not the defendant did the act or made the omission charged[1]. Where, during such a hearing, evidence of the defendant's bad character has been admitted under any of gateways (3)–(7) specified in para **2–210**, ante, and the evidence has become contaminated[2] and the court is satisfied that the contamination is such that, considering the importance of the evidence to the case against the defendant, his conviction of the offence would be unsafe, the court must either direct an acquittal or a retrial before a different jury[3].

These provisions were considered by the Court of Appeal in *R v C*[4]. It was held:

"For the purposes of s 107, contamination may result from deliberate collusion, or the exercise of improper pressure, but it may equally arise innocently, or through inadvertence. Moreover, contamination issues extend to evidence of bad character in the broad sense, as well as to unequivocal evidence of bad character arising from unchallenged, and usually unchallengeable, evidence of previous convictions. The direct concern is not the admissibility of bad character evidence . . . but rather the consequences of its admission. Strikingly, the unusual feature of s 107 is that after the admission of evidence a duty is imposed on the judge to make what is in truth a finding of fact. Plainly if the case goes to the jury issues such as contamination and collusion will be left to them in the familiar way, with appropriate directions and warnings. But the decision at the end of the prosecution case, or indeed at any later stage in the trial, whether the evidence of a witness is false, or misleading, or different from what it would have been if it had not been contaminated, requires that the judge should form his own assessment, or judgment, of matters traditionally regarded as questions of fact for the exclusive decision of the jury. . . The effect of s 107 is to reduce the risk of a conviction based on over-reliance on evidence of previous misconduct and acknowledges the potential danger that, where the evidence is contaminated, the evidence of bad character may have a disproportionate impact on the evaluation of the case by the jury. In other words the dangers inherent in contamination may be obscured by the evidence of the defendant's bad character."

Their Lordships further stated that, where there was a distinct possibility of witness contamination, the decision on whether to admit the evidence of bad character would be better deferred until the relevant witnesses had given their evidence.

---

1. Section 107(1) and (3), respectively, of the Criminal Justice Act 2003. See this Part, post.
2. As defined in Criminal Justice Act 2003, s 107(5).
3. Criminal Justice Act 2003, s 107(1) and (3), respectively.
4. [2006] EWCA Crim 1079, [2006] 3 All ER 689, [2006] 1 WLR 2994, [2006] 2 Cr App R 28, (2007) 171 JP 108.

2–218   **Means of adducing previous convictions.**   Where it is only the fact of the conviction that is relied on, a memorandum of conviction adduced under ss 73 and 74 of PACE, reciting the same details of name and date of birth the defendant's, may constitute proof that the conviction relates to the defendant, but the ultimate decision as to whether the evidence amounts to conclusive proof is a matter for the court[1].

Where the prosecution sought to adduce evidence of the appellant's previous convictions under s 101(1)(d) and 117 of the Criminal Justice Act 2003, (although the normal way (ss 73 and 74 of PACE) could have been used), they relied on a written statement of a police officer that set out the *modus operandi* of the offences in question. Since the information had come from the complainant, she was the relevant person within the meaning of s 117(2)(b) and as she had not supplied the information on the form (the officer had done that) the information giving details of the methods used was inadmissible. The prosecution needs to determine if it needs more evidence than the mere fact of the conviction to achieve the purpose for which it wants the evidence to be adduced. If more evidence is required than that which could be established relying on PACE, the prosecution has to ensure that it had available the necessary evidence. This would normally require the availability of either a statement by the complainant relating to the previous convictions in a sexual case or the complainant to be available to give first-hand evidence of what had happened, though "care must be exercised to ensure that it is necessary to go to the lengths of requiring the complainant in a sexual case which has occurred in the past to be brought before the court"[2]. However, there can be cases where the matter is simply too complicated to be dealt with in this way; whatever the complainant might have said in a statement at the time or might say now in evidence to the court, it might be that the defendant had been sentenced on a different basis as a result of a basis of plea accepted by the prosecution and the judge[3].

Foreign convictions are no longer subject to the rule in *Hollington v Hewthorne*[4] which has been abolished by the Criminal Justice Act 2003, s 99. Such convictions may be proved under the Evidence Act 1851[5].

---

1. *R v Burns* [2006] EWCA Crim 617, [2006] 1 WLR 1273, (2006) 170 JP 428, [2006] 2 Cr App R 16 (their lordships added that if the defendant had an extremely common name and there was a discrepancy as to the date of birth it might well be that the memorandum would not be properly admissible as capable of proving identity). Section 117 of the Criminal Justice Act 2003 was not under consideration in *Burns*, where the process of admitting evidence of this kind was referred to a matter of fact rather than law; having regard to that provision it may well that the admissibility of a business record is a matter of law solely for the determination of the judge: *R v Lewendon Practice Note* [2006] EWCA Crim 648, [2006] 1 WLR 1278.
2. *R v Humpris* [2005] EWCA Crim 2030, (2005) 169 JP 441, at para [26].
3. *R v Ainscough* [2006] EWCA Crim 694, (2006) 170 JP 517, [2006] Crim LR 635 where it was held that it was not enough for the prosecution simply to rely on the details recorded on the police national computer. For further discussion on this topic, see para **2–219,** post.
4. [1943] 1 KB 587.
5. In this PART, post.

GUIDANCE FROM THE COURT OF APPEAL ON THE BAD CHARACTER PROVISIONS OF THE CRIMINAL JUSTICE ACT 2003

2–219   In *R v Hanson, R v Pickstone & R v Gilmore*[1] the Court of Appeal gave the following guidance on the bad character provisions of the CJA 2003. Though the guidance is directed towards jury trial, it is submitted that it is equally relevant to summary trial.

(1) The starting point should be for judges and practitioners to bear in mind that Parliament's purpose in the legislation was to assist in the evidence-based conviction of the guilty, without putting those who are not guilty at risk of conviction by prejudice. It is accordingly to be hoped that prosecution applications to adduce such evidence will not be made routinely, simply because a defendant has previous convictions, but will be based on the particular circumstances of each case.

(2) Where propensity to commit the offence is relied upon by reference to s 101(1)(d) and s 103(1)(a), there are essentially three questions to be considered: (i) whether the history of conviction(s) establishes a propensity to commit offences of the kind charged; (ii) whether that propensity makes it more likely that the defendant committed the offence charged; and (iii) whether it is unjust to rely on the conviction(s) of the same description or category and, in any event, whether the proceedings will be unfair if they are admitted. In referring to the offences of the same description or category, s 103(2) is not exhaustive of the types of conviction which might be relied upon to show evidence of propensity to commit offences of the kind charged. Nor, however, is it necessarily sufficient in order to show such propensity that a conviction should be of the same description or type as that charged. There is no minimum number of events necessary to demonstrate such a propensity. The fewer the number of convictions, the weaker is likely to be the evidence of propensity. A single previous conviction for an offence of the same description or category will often not show propensity. But it may do so where, for example, it shows a tendency to unusual behaviour, or where its circumstances demonstrate probative force in relation to the offence charged. Circumstances demonstrating probative force are not confined to those sharing striking similarity. But if the modus operandi has significant features shared by the offence charged, it may show propensity. When considering what is just under s 103(3) and the fairness of the proceedings under s 101(3), the judge may, along with other factors, take into consideration the degree of similarity between the previous conviction and the offence charged (albeit that they are both within the same description or prescribed category). This does not however mean that what used to be referred to as striking similarity must be shown before convictions become admissible. The judge may also take into consideration the respective gravity of the past and present offences. He or she must also consider the strength of the

prosecution case. If there is no, or very little, other evidence against a defendant, it is unlikely to be just to admit his previous convictions, whatever they are. In principle, if there is a substantial gap between the dates of the commission of and conviction for the earlier offence(s), the date of commission is, generally, to be regarded as being of more significance than the date of admissibility when assessing admissibility. Old convictions with no special features shared with the offence charged are likely seriously to affect the fairness of the proceedings adversely, unless, despite their age, it can properly be said that they show a continuing propensity. It will often be necessary, before determining admissibility, and even when considering offences of the same description or category, to examine each individual conviction rather than merely to look at the nature of the offence or at the defendant's record as a whole. The sentence passed will not normally be probative or admissible at the behest of the Crown. Where past events are disputed, the judge must take care not to permit the trial unreasonably to be diverted into an investigation of matters not charged on the indictment.

(3) Where propensity to untruthfulness is relied upon by reference to s 101(1)(*d*) and s 103(1)(*b*), propensity to untruthfulness is not the same as propensity to dishonesty. Previous convictions, whether for offences of dishonesty or otherwise, are therefore only likely to be capable of showing a propensity to be truthful where, in the present case, truthfulness is in issue and, in the earlier case, either there was a plea of not guilty and the defendant gave an account (on arrest, in interview or in evidence) which the jury must have disbelieved, or the way in which the offence was committed shows a propensity for untruthfulness, for example by the making of false representations. The observations made above as to the number of previous convictions apply equally.

(4) Where an attack by a defendant on the character of another person is relied upon by reference to s 101(1)(g), pre-2003 Act authorities will continue to apply when assessing whether an attack has been made on another person's character, to the extent that they are compatible with s 106.

(5) If a judge has directed himself correctly, the Court of Appeal will be very slow to interfere with a ruling either as to admissibility or as to the consequences of non-compliance with the regulations for the giving of notice of intention to rely on bad character evidence. It will not interfere unless the judge's judgment as to the capacity of prior events to establish propensity is plainly wrong, or discretion has been exercised unreasonably in a *Wednesbury* sense. Furthermore, if, following a ruling that evidence of bad character is admissible, a defendant pleads guilty, it is highly unlikely that an appeal against conviction will be entertained.

(6) The Crown needs to have decided, at the time of giving notice of the application, whether it proposes to rely simply on the fact of conviction or also upon the circumstances of it. It is to be expected that the relevant circumstances of previous convictions will, generally, be capable of agreement, and that, subject to the trial judge's ruling as to admissibility, they will be put before the jury by way of admission. Even where the circumstances are genuinely in dispute, it is to be expected that the minimum indisputable facts will thus be admitted. It will be very rare indeed for it to be necessary for the judge to hear evidence before ruling on admissibility under the Act.

(7) In any case in which evidence of bad character is admitted to show propensity, whether to commit offences or to be untruthful, the judge in summing up should warn the jury clearly against placing undue reliance on previous convictions. Evidence of bad character cannot be used simply to bolster a weak case or to prejudice the minds of the jury against the defendant. Without purporting to frame a specimen direction, in particular, a jury should be directed: (i) that they should not conclude that a defendant is guilty or untruthful merely because he has these convictions; (ii) that, although the convictions might show a propensity, this does not mean that he committed this offence or has been untruthful in this case; (iii) that whether they in fact show a propensity is for them to decide; (iv) that they must take into account what a defendant has said about his previous convictions; and (v) that, although they are entitled, if they find propensity is shown, to take this into account when determining guilt, propensity is only one relevant factor and they must assess its significance in the light of all the other evidence in the case.

Where two convictions arise from a single incident (eg the simultaneous possession of two types of Class A drugs) this should be treated as one offence for the purpose of determining propensity to commit the current offence[2].

The thrust of the guidance in *Hanson* is that the court should only admit convictions which have some probative force by reason of their similarity to the offence charged. Accordingly, on a charge of robbery, it was casting the net too widely to admit evidence of a propensity to obtain other people's property by some means or another, instead of restricting the evidence to that of previous robberies as there must be a degree of similarity, even if they did not need to be striking in the way that 'similar fact' evidence had to be under the former law. The fact that the convictions are for offences of the same description or category does not automatically mean that they should be admitted[3].

Although untruthfulness is not synonymous with dishonesty and a previous conviction for an offence of dishonesty will not necessarily be capable of establishing a propensity for untruthfulness, it does not follow however, that previous convictions, which do not involve the making of false statements or the giving of false evidence, are incapable of having substantial probative value in relation to credibility of a defendant, when he has given evidence which undermines the defence of a co-accused. The degree of caution which is applied to a Crown application against a defendant who is on trial when considering relevance or discretion should not be applied when what is at stake is a defendant's right to deploy relevant material to defend himself against a criminal charge. A co-defendant should be able to deploy evidence against another co-accused whose history of criminal behaviour or other misconduct is such as to be capable of showing him to be unscrupulous and/or otherwise unreliable. This may be shown by widely differing conduct which does not involve an offence of untruthfulness e.g. from large scale drug or people trafficking via housebreaking to criminal violence[4].

1. [2005] EWCA Crim 824, [2005] 1 WLR 3169, (2005) 169 JP 250, [2005] 2 Cr App R 21.
2. *R v Atkinson* [2006] EWCA Crim 1424, (2006) 170 JP 605.
3. *R v Tully* [2006] EWCA Crim 2270, 171 JP 25.
4. *R v Lawson* [2006] EWCA Crim 2572, [2007] 1 Cr App R 11, 171 JP 43, [2007] Crim LR 232.

USE TO WHICH BAD CHARACTER EVIDENCE MAY BE PUT

2–220 Once admitted under one of the gateways, the question arises is the purpose for which the evidence can be used confined to the terms of the gateway through which it passed? In *R v Highton, R v Van Nguyen & R v Carp*[1], the Court of Appeal held:

"10. We therefore conclude that a distinction must be drawn between the admissibility of evidence of bad character, which depends upon it getting through one of the gateways, and the use to which it may be put once it is admitted. The use to which it may be put depends upon the matters to which it is relevant rather than upon the gateway through which it was admitted. It is true that the reasoning that leads to the admission of evidence under gateway 101(1)(*d*) may also determine the matters to which the evidence is relevant or primarily relevant once admitted. That is not true, however, of all the gateways. In the case of gateway 101(1)(*g*), for example, admissibility depends on the defendant having made an attack on another person's character, but once the evidence is admitted, it may, depending on the particular facts, be relevant not only to credibility but also to propensity to commit offences of the kind with which the defendant is charged.

11. This approach underlines the importance of the guidance that was given in *R v Hanson* [2005] 1 WLR 3169 to the care that the judge must exercise to give the jury appropriate warnings when summing up. (We refer in particular to para 18 of that judgment and para 3 of the judgment of *R v Edwards* [2005] EWCA Crim 1813 and its commendation of the summing up of Judge Mort in R v Chohan). In *R v Edwards* Rose LJ said, at para 3:

'What the summing up must contain is a clear warning to the jury against placing undue reliance on previous convictions, which cannot, by themselves, prove guilt. It should be explained why the jury has heard the evidence and the ways in which it is *relevant* to and may help their decision. Bearing in mind that *relevance* will depend primarily, though not always exclusively, on the gateway in section 101(1) of the Criminal Justice Act 2003, through which the evidence has been admitted. For example, some evidence admitted through gateway (*g*), because of an attack on another person's character, may be relevant or irrelevant to propensity, so as to require a direction on this aspect.' (Emphasis added.)

12. Protection is also provided for the defendant at the stage of admissibility by the terms of section 101(3) if the admission of the evidence could cause unfairness, and by the reference in section 103(3) to convictions which it would be unjust to admit as evidence of a propensity to commit offences of the kind with which he is charged because the court is satisfied, "by reason of the length of time since the conviction or for any other reason" that it would be unjust for subsection 103(2) to apply. In this context, there is a very close relationship between the requirements of fairness and the general requirement of the rules of evidence that, unless evidence is relevant, it should not be admitted.

13. Those provisions protect against unfairness arising out of the admission of bad character evidence under section 101(1)(*d*) or (*g*). The question also arises as to whether reliance can be placed on section 78 of the Police and Criminal Evidence Act 1984. The application of section 78 does not call directly for decision in this case. We, therefore, do not propose to express any concluded view as to the relevance of section 78. However, it is right that we should say that, without having heard full argument, our inclination is to say that section 78 provides an additional protection to a defendant. In light of this preliminary view as to the effect of section 78, judges may consider that it is a sensible precaution, when making rulings as to the use of evidence of bad character, to apply the provisions of section 78 and exclude evidence where it would be appropriate to do so under section 78, pending a definitive ruling to the contrary. Adopting this course will avoid any risk of injustice to the defendant.

14. In addition, as section 78 serves a very similar purpose to article 6 of the Convention for the Protection of Human Rights and Fundamental Freedoms, following the course we have recommended should avoid any risk of the court failing to comply with article 6. To apply section 78 should also be consistent with the result to which the court would come if it complied with its obligation under section 3 of the Human Rights Act 1998 to construe sections 101 and 103 of the 2003 Act in accordance with the Convention."

1. [2005] EWCA Crim 1985, [2005] 1 WLR 3472, [2006] 1 Cr App R 7, [2006] Crim LR 52.

2–221 **Weight to be given to previous convictions.** In *R v Edwards, R v Fysh, R v Duggan R v Chohan*[1] the Court of Appeal held that judges must give a clear warning to the jury against placing undue reliance on previous convictions, which cannot, by themselves, prove guilt. It should be explained why the jury has heard the evidence and the ways in which it is relevant to and may help their decision, bearing in mind that relevance will depend primarily, though not always exclusively, on the gateway in s 101(1) of the Criminal Justice Act 2003, through which the evidence has been admitted. For example, some evidence admitted through gateway (*g*), because of an attack on another person's character, may be relevant or irrelevant to propensity, so as to require a direction on this aspect. Provided the judge gives such a clear warning, explanation and guidance as to use, the terms in which he or she does so can properly differ. There is no rigid formula to be adhered to. That said, the summing up in one of the cases under appeal, which is reproduced in part below, was described by the court as "almost impeccable".

> "You have to decide to what extent, if at all, his character helps you when you are considering whether or not he is guilty. You must not convict simply because of his convictions, nor mainly because of them. The propensity or tendency amounts to some additional evidence pointing to guilt, but please bear in mind, even if he did have such a tendency, it does not necessarily prove that he would commit further offences or that he has committed these offences.
>
> You are also entitled to consider the evidence of (D's) previous convictions in the following way. If you think it right, you may take it into account, when deciding whether or not his evidence to you was truthful, because a person with convictions for dishonesty may be less likely to tell the truth, but it does not follow that he is not capable of telling the truth. Indeed, (D) says, 'The fact that on the previous occasions I have been arrested and I have always held my hands up means that, when I plead not guilty, I am likely to be telling the truth' and you decide to what extent his character helps you when judging his evidence. So that is the extent to which the evidence of his previous convictions may be used for the particular purposes I have just indicated, if you find it helpful."

---

1. [2005] EWCA Crim 1813, [2006] 1 Cr App R 31.

Bad character of non defendants

2–230 The common law rules governing the admissibility of bad character in criminal proceedings have been abolished[1].

In criminal proceedings evidence of the bad character of a person other than the defendant is admissible if, and only if – (*a*) it is important explanatory evidence[2]; or (*b*) it has substantial probative value[3] in relation to a matter which (i) is a matter in issue in the proceedings, and (ii) is of substantial importance in the context of the case as a whole; or (*c*) all parties to the proceedings agree to the evidence being admissible[4]. Although couched in different terms from the provisions relating to the introduction of the defendant's bad character, the provision of s 100(1) cover matters of credibility[5]. The evidence may also be adduced to show the complainant had a propensity to act in the way asserted by the defendant[6].

Except where (*c*) above applies, the evidence must not be given without the leave of the court[7].

"Bad character" is defined as "misconduct" or a "disposition towards" misconduct[8]. "Misconduct" means "the commission of any offence or other reprehensible behaviour"[9].

Excluded from the definition of bad character are – (*a*) misconduct which has to do with the alleged facts of the charge which the defendant faces; and (*b*) misconduct in connection with the investigation or prosecution of that offence[10].

In the provisions of Chapter 11 of the Criminal Justice Act 2003 that refer to the relevance of evidence or its probative value, when making any such assessment the court is to assume that the evidence is true[11], unless on the basis of any material before the court (including any evidence it decides to hear on the matter) no court or jury could reasonably find it to be true[12].

Where the court makes a relevant ruling it must state its reasons for doing so and, it is a magistrate's court, it must cause the ruling and the reasons for it to be entered in the court register[13]. A "relevant ruling", for this purpose, is a ruling: (*a*) on whether an item of evidence is evidence of a person's bad character; (*b*) on whether an item of evidence is admissible under one of the gateways; or (Crown Court trial only) a ruling on whether to stop proceedings[14].

Where a witness is lawfully questioned as to whether he has been convicted of any offence, and he either denies or does not admit that fact or fails to answer, it is lawful for the cross-examining party to prove that conviction[15].

As to the finality of a witness' answer when cross-examined as to credit, see para **1–666** cross-examination as to credit, ante.

---

1. The Criminal Justice Act 2003, s 99. See this PART, post.
2. Defined in Criminal Justice Act 2003, s 100(2).
3. In assessing the probative value of evidence the court must have regard to the matters specified in s 100(3), ibid, and to any other matters it considers relevant.
4. Criminal Justice Act 2003, s 100(1).
5. *R v Weir* [2005] EWCA Crim 2866, [2006] 2 All ER 570, [2006] 1 WLR 1885, [2006] 1 Cr App R 19.
6. *R v S* [2006] EWCA Crim 1303, [2006] 2 Cr App R 31, [2006] Crim LR 181 (previous convictions for dishonesty did not show propensity to untruthfulness but did show that she would cry rape when her additional demands for money were not met).
7. Criminal Justice Act 2003, s 100(4).

8. Criminal Justice Act 2003, s 98.
9. Criminal Justice Act 2003, s 112(1).
10. Criminal Justice Act 2003, s 98.
11. Criminal Justice Act 2003, s 109(1).
12. Criminal Justice Act 2003, s 109(2).
13. Criminal Justice Act 2003, s 110(1).
14. Criminal Justice Act 2003, s 110(2).
15. Criminal Procedure Act 1865, s 6. See this PART, post.

Relevance of good character to credibility and propensity

2–240   In the Crown Court the judge is under a duty to give a direction as to the relevance of the defendant's good character and we would suggest that magistrates should similarly remind themselves of the relevance of good character.

A direction as to the relevance of his good character to a defendant's credibility is to be given where he has testified or made pre-trial answers or statements. A direction is also to be given as to the relevance of his good character to the likelihood of his having committed the offence charged, whether or not he has testified, or made pre-trial answers or statements[1]. A direction as to the relevance of the defendant's good character to the credibility of his evidence must also be given notwithstanding that the defendant is shown to have told lies in interview with the police[2], or that he has pleaded guilty to another offence in an indictment arising out of the same incident on the same occasion[3] but not on the basis that the history of bad character has been held to be inadmissible under the Criminal Justice Act 2003 as not being capable of having substantial probative value on the issue of his truthfulness or credibility[4]. However, the trial judge has a residual discretion to decline to give any character directions in the case of a defendant without previous convictions if the judge considers it an insult to common sense to give such directions, eg where the defendant although he has no previous convictions, is shown beyond doubt to have been guilty of serious criminal behaviour similar to the offence charged[5]. In deciding whether to give a character direction, the fact that the defendant has been cautioned for a criminal offence is a matter which the trial judge is entitled to take into account and to dispense with that part of the character direction relating to propensity[6].

On a review of the above authorities it has been held that[7]: (i) the primary rule is that a person of previous good character must be given a full direction covering both credibility and propensity: where there are no further facts to complicate the position, such a direction is mandatory and should be unqualified; (ii) if a defendant has a previous conviction which, either because of its age or its nature, may entitle him to be treated as of effective good character, the court has a discretion so to treat him, and if it does so treat him the defendant is entitled to a full good character direction: where the previous conviction can only be regarded as irrelevant or of no significance in relation to the offence charged, that discretion ought to be exercised in favour of treating the defendant as of good character; (iii) where there is room for uncertainty as to how a defendant of effective good character should be treated or where a defendant, of either absolute or effective good character, has been shown at trial, whether by admission or otherwise, to be guilty of criminal conduct, the prima facie rule of practice is to give a modified good character direction, not to withhold it altogether; (iv) there remains a narrowly circumscribed residual discretion to withhold a good character direction, in whole or part, where it would make no sense, or would be meaningless, or absurd or an insult to common sense, to do otherwise: however, even in the context of serious crime it may be crucial that a critical intent separated the admitted criminality from that charged; (v) a direction should never be misleading: where therefore a defendant has withheld something of his record, the court may forfeit the more ample, if qualified, direction which it may otherwise have been able to give.

In the Crown Court it has been held that once the judge has formed the view that a previous conviction should not be held against the accused, it was insufficient that he direct the jury of this but he should also have the benefit of a good character direction[8].

---

1. *R v Vye* [1993] 3 All ER 241, [1993] 1 WLR 471; followed in *R v Aziz* [1995] 3 All ER 149, [1995] 3 WLR 53, HL.
2. *R v Kabariti* (1990) 92 Cr App Rep 362, CA.
3. *R v Teasdale* [1993] 4 All ER 290, CA.
4. *R v Lawson* [2006] EWCA Crim 2572, [2007] 1 Cr App R 11, 171 JP 43, [2007] Crim LR 232.
5. *R v Aziz* [1995] 3 All ER 149, [1995] 3 WLR 53, [1995] 2 Cr App Rep 478, HL.
6. *R v Martin* (1999) 164 JP 174, CA.
7. *R v Gray* [2004] EWCA (Crim) 1074, [2004] Cr App R 30.
8. *R v Payton* [2006] EWCA Crim 1226, [2006] Crim LR 997.

Admission of hearsay evidence in criminal proceedings
HEARSAY AND THE EUROPEAN CONVENTION ON HUMAN RIGHTS

2–250   Hearsay in criminal proceedings is governed by the provisions of Chapter 2 of Part 11 of the Criminal Justice Act 2003[1]. Certain common law categories of hearsay were preserved[2], but the law was otherwise reformulated.

In applying the new provisions, courts must have regard to the fair trial requirements of the European Convention on Human Rights. Article 6(3)(*d*) specifically provides that everyone charged with a criminal offence shall be entitled to "examine or have examined witnesses against him". From this the European Court and Commission of Human Rights have derived the following general principles[3]:

(*a*) all the evidence should be produced in the presence of the accused;
(*b*) the hearing of witnesses should be adversarial; and
(*c*) the accused should be given an adequate and proper opportunity to challenge and question a witness against him, either at the time the witness was making a statement or at some later stage of the proceedings.

However, these are general principles. They form the framework within which evidential issues fall to be determined, but they are not inviolable[3].

Nothing in art 6(3)(*d*) prevents a court from relying on hearsay evidence, but only if there are counterbalancing factors which preserve the rights of the defence[4]. In practice, this means that the European Court and Commission of Human Rights will balance the reasons advanced by the authorities for relying on hearsay evidence against the inevitable infringement of the accused's right to challenge and question all the witnesses against him. Relevant factors in this balancing exercise include the opportunities (if any) the defence had to challenge the evidence in question prior to trial, whether the defence requested the attendance of the witness in question and the impact of the evidence on the trial. Although the context is always important, as a general rule, any conviction based solely or mainly on hearsay evidence is likely to violate art 6(3)(*d*)[4]. The admissibility of evidence is, however, primarily a matter for regulation by national law[5].

---

1. In this PART, post. Narrative on the new provisions will be found at para **2–260** et seq.
2. Criminal Justice Act 2003, s 118.
3. *Barberà, Messegué and Jabardo v Spain* (1988) 11 EHRR 360.
4. *Kostovski v Netherlands* (1989) 12 EHRR 434. In domestic law it has been held that art 6(3)(*d*) is designed to secure equality of arms. As the hearsay provisions of the Criminal Justice Act 2003 apply equally to prosecution and defence, there is no inherent inequality of arms arising out of those provisions. It does not give a defendant an absolute right to examine every witness whose testimony is adduced against him. The touchstone is whether fairness of the trial so requires. Thus, in a case where almost all the hearsay evidence derived directly or indirectly from the complainant and she was available for examination there was no breach of art 6(3)(*d*): *R v Xhabri* [2005] EWCA Crim 3135, [2006] 1 All ER 776. Where a witness who is the sole witness of a crime has made a statement to be used in its prosecution and has since died, there may be a strong public interest in the admission of the statement in evidence so that the prosecution may proceed; this must not be allowed to override the defendant's right to a fair trial, but the provision in art 6(3)(*d*) that a person charged should be able to have witnesses against him examined was one specific aspect of a fair trial and if the opportunity to examine a witness was not provided the question was whether the proceedings as a whole, including the way in which the evidence was taken, were fair; thus, in a case where the only direct witness (the complainant) to an alleged sexual assault had died before trial, but the appellant had been able to attack the accuracy of her statement by exploring the inconsistencies between it and evidence of recent complaints made by her, and through expert evidence, and the trial judge had adequately directed the jury as to the difficulties which the admission of the statement might provide for the appellant, the proceedings as a whole had not been unfair: *R v Al-Khawaja* [2005] EWCA Crim 2697, [2006] 1 All ER 543, [2006] 1 WLR 1078.
5. See, for example, *Doorson v Netherlands* (1996) 22 EHRR 330.

Hearsay under the Criminal Justice Act 2003

2–260 In criminal proceedings[1], a statement[2] not made in oral evidence in the proceedings is admissible as evidence of any matter stated[2] if, but only if:

(*a*) any provision of Chapter 2 of Part 11 of the Criminal Justice Act 2003 makes it admissible,
(*b*) any rule of law preserved by s 118 of the Criminal Justice Act 2003 makes it admissible,
(*c*) all parties to the proceedings agree to it being admissible, or
(*d*) the court is satisfied that it is in the interests of justice for it to be admissible[3].

In deciding whether a statement should be admitted under (*d*) above, the court must have regard to the following factors and to any others it considers relevant:

(*a*) how much probative value the statement has (assuming it is true) in relation to a matter in issue in the proceedings, or how valuable it is for the understanding of other evidence in the case;
(*b*) what other evidence has been, or can be, given on the matter of evidence mentioned in (*a*) above;
(*c*) how important the matter or evidence mentioned in (*a*) above is in the context of the case as a whole;
(*d*) the circumstances in which the statement was made;
(*e*) how reliable the maker of the statement appears to be;
(*f*) how reliable the evidence of the making of the statement appears to be;
(*g*) whether oral evidence of the matter stated can be given and, if not, why it cannot;

(*h*) the amount of difficulty involved in challenging the statement;
(*i*) the extent to which that difficulty would be likely to prejudice the party facing it[4].

In deciding whether it is in the interests of justice to admit hearsay evidence, there is no obligation on the court to embark on an investigation in order to reach a conclusion established by reference to each of the nine factors (a)–(i) above. What is required of the court is the exercise of judgment, in the light of these factors. The court is not required to reach a specific conclusion in relation to each or any of them. Consideration must be given to those identified factors and any others which the court considers relevant. The significance of those factors both in relation to each other and having regard to such weight as they bear individually and in relation to each other. The court will then be able to reach a proper conclusion as to whether or not the evidence should be admitted[5].

Nothing in Chapter 2 of Part 11 of the Criminal Justice Act 2003 affects any non-hearsay exclusionary rule of evidence[6].

The provisions of the Criminal Justice Act 2003 abolish the common law rules against the admission of hearsay evidence with the exception of those which are expressly preserved. The new rule against the admission of hearsay does not extend to implied assertions[7].

---

1. This means criminal proceedings to which the strict rules of evidence apply: Criminal Justice Act 2003, s 134(1).
2. These terms are defined in Criminal Justice Act 2003, s 115.
3. Criminal Justice Act 2003, s 114(1).
4. Criminal Justice Act 2003, s 114(2).
5. *R v Taylor* [2006] EWCA Crim 260, [2006] 2 Cr App R 14, 170 JP 353, [2006] Crim LR 639.
6. Criminal Justice Act 2003, s 114(3).
7. *R v Singh* [2006] EWCA Crim 660, [2006] 1 WLR 1564, [2006] 2 Cr App R 12, 170 JP 222.

CASES WHERE A WITNESS IS UNAVAILABLE

2-261 In criminal proceedings[1] a statement[2] not made in oral evidence in the proceedings is admissible as evidence of any matter stated[2] if:

(*a*) oral evidence by the maker of the statement ('the relevant person') would be admissible as evidence of that matter,
(*b*) the relevant person is identified to the court's satisfaction, and
(*c*) any of the following conditions is satisfied:

  (i) the relevant person is dead;
  (ii) the relevant person is unfit to be a witness because of his bodily or mental condition;
  (iii) the relevant person is outside the UK and it is not reasonably practicable[3] to secure his attendance;
  (iv) the relevant person cannot be found although such steps as it is reasonable practicable to take to find him have been taken;
  (v) through fear[4] the relevant person does not give (or does not continue to give) oral evidence in the proceedings, either at all or in connection with the subject matter of the statement, and the court gives leave for the statement to be given in evidence[5].

However, a condition set out in (i)–(v) above which is in fact satisfied is to be treated as not satisfied if it is shown that the relevant circumstance is caused by the person in support of whose case it is sought to give the statement in evidence, or by a person acting on his behalf, to prevent the relevant person giving evidence in the proceedings[6].

Leave may be given under (*c*) (v) above only if the court considers that the statement ought to be admitted in the interests of justice, having regard to:

(*a*) the statement's contents,
(*b*) to any risk that its admission or exclusion will result in unfairness to any party to the proceedings (and in particular to how difficult it will be to challenge the statement if the relevant person does not give oral evidence),
(*c*) in appropriate cases, to the fact that special measures for the given of evidence by fearful witnesses[7] could be made in relation to the relevant person, and
(*d*) to any other relevant circumstance[8].

An application under section 116(2)(e), may commonly be made in cases of alleged domestic violence where the complainant having made the initial complaint and a statement, then makes a second statement that she does not wish to give evidence through fear of the defendant. In *R (Robinson) v Sutton Coldfield Magistrates' Court*[9] the justices were entitled to consider the following factors in the case before them in deciding to admit in evidence the original statement of the complainant:

– the evidence of her fear in her second statement;
– the serious nature of the case as the interests of justice require that serious assaults in which injury is caused are resolved by a trial where it is possible to hold a trial that is fair to both sides;

- the presence of photographic evidence showing that the complainant had injuries consistent with the assault in her statement;
- admissions in interview of presence alone with the complainant at the time of the alleged assault;
- the opportunity for the defendant to comment on the prosecution case in interview;
- concessions in interview about the truthfulness of the complainant;
- whether the defendant specifically denied the offence;
- there is no principle that where evidence represents the sole substantial evidence in the case, it should never be admissible in the form of admissible hearsay and that it led automatically to a defendant's right to a fair trial under art 6 of the Human Rights Convention being infringed.

Nothing set out above makes a statement admissible as evidence if the relevant person did not have the required capability at the time when he made the statement[10].

As for the admissibility of evidence going to the credibility of the maker of the statement and the court's general discretion to exclude evidence and proof of statements in documents see post[11].

---

1. This means criminal proceedings to which the strict rules of evidence apply: Criminal Justice Act 2003, s 134(1).
2. This term are defined in the Criminal Justice Act 2003, s 115.
3. "Reasonably practicable" must be judged on the basis of the steps taken, or not taken, by the party seeking to secure the attendance of the witness, but that is only the first stage. The court must also consider whether to exercise its powers under s 126 of the 2003 Act (see para **2–287**, post), or under s 78 of PACE. Whether it is fair to admit a statement depends in part on what efforts should reasonably be made to secure the attendance of the witness, or, at least, to arrange a procedure whereby the contents of the statements could be clarified and challenged: *R v C and K* [2006] EWCA Crim 197, [2006] Crim LR 637.
4. "Fear" is to be widely construed and (for example) includes fear of the death or injury of another person or of financial loss: Criminal Justice Act 2003, s 116(3). Whether it is fair to admit a statement depends in part on what efforts should reasonably be made to secure the attendance of the witness, or, at least, to arrange a procedure whereby the contents of the statements could be clarified and challenged: *R v C and K* [2006] EWCA Crim 197, [2006] Crim LR 637. Where there is a statement from the witness which states that he is in fear and explains why, and there is no reason to doubt the statement, the condition is satisfied. Whether fear is objectively justified, however, is a matter which can be considered as part of the question of unfairness under s 166(4): *R v Doherty* [2006] EWCA Crim 2716, (2007) 171 JP 79.
5. Criminal Justice Act 2003, s 116(1) and (2).
6. Criminal Justice Act 2003, s 166(5)
7. See para **2–145**, ante.
8. Criminal Justice Act 2003, s 116(4). Applying these considerations is an evaluative and fact-sensitive exercise of the sort the trial court is best placed to perform; the Court of Appeal will only interfere if it is satisfied that the judge's decision was plainly wrong or was perverse or unreasonable: *R v Doherty*, supra.
9. [2006] EWHC 307 (Admin), [2006] 4 All ER 1029, [2006] 2 Cr App R 13, 170 JP 336.
10. Criminal Justice Act 2003, s 123(1). "The required capability" is defined in s 123(3), ibid. As to the procedure for determining required capability and the standard of proof, see s 123(4), ibid.
11. Respectively, paras **2–285** and **2–287**, post.

BUSINESS AND OTHER DOCUMENTS

2–262   In criminal proceedings[1] a statement[2] contained in a document[3] is admissible as evidence of any matter stated[2] if:

(*a*)   oral evidence given in the proceedings would be admissible as evidence of that matter,
(*b*)   the first set of requirements set our below are satisfied, and
(*c*)   the second set of requirements set out below are also satisfied in cases where they are required to be[4]

The first set of requirements are:

(*a*)   the document or the part containing the statement was created or received by a person in the course of a trade, business, profession or other occupation, or as the holder of a paid or unpaid office,
(*b*)   the supplier of the information contained in the statement had or might reasonably be supposed to have had personal knowledge of the matters dealt with, and
(*c*)   Each person (if any) though whom the information was supplied from the original source to the end maker or receiver of the document or the part of it containing the statement received the information in the course of a trade, etc, as mentioned in (*a*) above[5].

The second set of requirements must additionally be satisfied if the statement was prepared for the purposes of pending or contemplated criminal proceedings, but was not obtained pursuant to a request under s 7 of the Criminal (International Cooperation) Act 2003[6] or an order (relating to overseas evidence). The second set of requirements are:

(1)   any of the five conditions set out in para **2–261** *Cases where a witness is unavailable* at (*c*) (i)–(v), or
(2)   the relevant person cannot reasonably be expected to have any recollection of the matters dealt with in the statement (having regard to the length of time since he supplied the information and all other circumstances)[7].

However, if the court is satisfied that the statement's reliability as evidence for the purpose for which it is tendered is doubtful in view of:

(a)   its contents,
(b)   the source of the information contained in it,
(c)   the way in which or the circumstances in which the information was supplied or received, or
(d)   the way in which or the circumstances in which the document concerned was created or received

the court may make a direction and if it does so the statement will not be admissible under this head[8].

Nothing set out above makes a statement admissible as evidence if any of the persons referred to in the first set of requirements above as a person who must at any time have supplied or received the information concerned or created or received the document or part concerned:

(a)   did not have the required capability at that time, or
(b)   cannot be identified but cannot reasonably be assumed to have had the required capability at that time[9].

As for the admissibility of evidence going to the credibility of the maker of the statement and the court's general discretion to exclude evidence and proof of statement in documents see post[10].

---

1. This means criminal proceedings to which the strict rules of evidence apply: Criminal Justice Act 2003, s 134(1).
2. These terms are defined in the Criminal Justice Act 2003, s 115.
3. Defined in s 134(1), ibid, as anything in which information of any description is recorded.
4. Criminal Justice Act 2003, s 117(1).
5. Thus, where A gave details of a car registration to motorist B, who then gave those details to the police, this requirement was not satisfied; each person in the line along which the information was transmitted must have received it in the course of a trade, etc, and that was not the case in relation to B, though this illustrates that the sweeping up provisions regarding multiple hearsay – s 121, post – should be applied with common sense and reason: *Maher v DPP* [2006] EWHC 1271 (Admin), (2006) 170 JP 441.
6. See para **1–4185**, ante.
7. Criminal Justice Act 2003, s 117(5).
8. Criminal Justice Act 2003, s 117(6) and (7).
9. Criminal Justice Act 2003, s 123(2). "The required capability" is defined in CJA 2003, s 123(3). As to the procedure for determining required capability and the standard of proof, see CJA 2003, s 123(4).
10. Respectively, paras **2–285, 2–287** and **2–289**, post.

PRESERVED COMMON LAW CATEGORIES

2–263   The preserved categories are:

(1)   Public information etc[1];
(2)   Reputation as to character;
(3)   Reputation or family tradition,
(4)   Res gestae[2];
(5)   Confessions etc[3];
(6)   Admissions by agents etc[4];
(7)   Common enterprise; and
(8)   Expert evidence[5].

Save as preserved above, the common law rules governing the admissibility of hearsay evidence in criminal proceedings are abolished[6].

---

1. See para **2–63**, ante.
2. See para **2–264**, post.
3. See paras **2–265, 2–266**,post.
4. See para **2–268**, post.
5. See para **2–103**, ante.
6. Criminal Justice Act 2003, s 118(2).

2–264   Res gestae.   The Criminal Justice Act 2003 preserved "any rule of law under which in criminal proceedings a statement is admissible as evidence of any matter stated if –

(a)   the statement was made by a person so emotionally overpowered by an event that the possibility of concoction or distortion can be disregarded,
(b)   the statement accompanies an act which can be properly evaluated as evidence only if considered in conjunction with the statement, or
(c)   the statement relates to a physical sensation or a mental state (such as intention or emotion)"[1].

Actions, statements and incidents which are connected with and occur at the same time as the facts in issue, so as to be part of the same story, are admissible in evidence; they are often referred to as being part of the *res gestae*. Thus a court is enabled to define when a situation began and ended, for example, considering what happened before a gun was fired or a knife inserted; it may hear what words were spoken (as distinct from accepting the truth of what they convey); it may hear what would otherwise be a statement excluded under the hearsay rule, because it was clearly made in circumstances of spontaneity or involvement in the event, and being approximately contemporaneous with that event the possibility of concoction or fabrication can be disregarded, for example a statement made by the victim of an attack or by a bystander indicating the identity of the attacker[2].

Where the victim of an attack, who was grievously wounded, informed witnesses within minutes of the attack of what had occurred in such circumstances as to satisfy the court that the event was so unusual or startling or dramatic as to dominate the thoughts of the victim so as to exclude the possibility of concoction or distortion and the statement was made in conditions of approximate but not exact contemporaneity, evidence of what the victim said was held to be admissible as to the truth of the facts recited as an exception to the hearsay rule[3].

However, where the prosecution did not regard a witness as likely to tell the truth and, therefore, did not call her but sought to rely on the evidence of others as to what she said at the time of the alleged offence under the res gestae exception to the hearsay rule, the evidence was admissible but the judge should have been willing to entertain a defence application to exclude it under s 78 of PACE; as a general principle, it could not be right that the Crown should be permitted to rely only on such part of a victim's evidence as they considered reliable, without being prepared to tender the victim to the defence[4].

---

1. Section 118, in this PART, post.
2. *Ratten v R* [1972] AC 378, [1971] 3 All ER 801, 136 JP 27, PC; *R v Turnbull* (1984) 80 Cr App Rep 104, [1984] LS Gaz R 2142.
3. *R v Andrews* [1987] AC 281, [1987] 1 All ER 513, 151 JP 548, HL (victim, mortally attacked with knives, making statement to police within 10–15 minutes of attack; victim kept alive on life support machine but died 2 months after attack).
4. *A-G's Reference (No 1 of 2003)* [2003] 2 Cr App R 29.

2–265 Confessions. In both civil and criminal cases, statements against their own interests are admissible against the parties who made them. In civil cases they are called "informal admissions" and in criminal cases "confessions".

In *criminal proceedings* a confession made by an accused person may be given in evidence against him so far as it is relevant to any matter in issue in the proceedings. If however it is represented that the confession was or may have been obtained by oppression or in consequence of anything said or done which was likely, in the circumstances existing at the time, to render it unreliable, the court shall not allow it to be given in evidence except in so far as the prosecution prove to the court beyond reasonable doubt that it was not so obtained[1].

"Oppression" includes torture, inhuman or degrading treatment and the use or threat of violence[1]. For the purpose of determining in a summary trial whether to allow evidence of a confession to be given against the accused after it has been represented it was obtained by oppression or other improper process, the justices shall hold a trial within a trial[2].

A fact discovered as the result of a confession wholly excluded, or as the result of an excluded part of a confession can still be given in evidence, but the fact that it was discovered as the result of the statement of an accused person may not, unless such evidence is given by him or on his behalf[3].

Criminal proceedings includes proceedings before examining justices[4]. "Confession" includes any statement wholly or partly adverse to the person who made it, whether made to a person in authority or not and whether made in words or otherwise[5]. There is a special need for caution where the confession was made by a mentally handicapped person[6].

A confession made by a defendant to a probation officer who was interviewing him for the purpose of preparing a pre sentence report can be admitted in evidence in a trial; but the importance of candour in such an interview is such that the prosecution should think carefully about whether it is right to rely on evidence so produced and should only rely on it if it is in the public interest so to do[7]. If the prosecution does decide to rely on such evidence the court still has a discretion under s 78 of PACE to ensure that no injustice occurs[8].

Where a mixed statement is before the court, that is, one including admissions and excuses, the court must consider the whole statement, even though it may have to give different weight to each part[9]. This principle applies to all mixed statements tendered by the Crown and not just to mixed statements made to the police, but does not apply to wholly exculpatory and self-serving statements by a defendant which are not evidence of any fact asserted[10]. However, where the defendant does not testify, but relies on the exculpatory parts of a mixed statement, the court is entitled to give less weight to those parts of the statement which have not been tested by cross-examination[11].

In a joint trial of two defendants where an admission of one defendant is not adduced in evidence by the prosecution, it may put in evidence by the co-accused where it is relevant to his defence and was not obtained in a manner which would have made it inadmissible at the instance of the prosecution under s 76(2) of the Police and Criminal Evidence Act 1984. The admission may be put either to witnesses to whom the confession was made or to the co-accused by way of cross-examination, and may be relevant both as to credibility and as to the facts in issue[9]. While an excluded, under 76 of PACE, confession by one co-accused cannot be put in evidence by another co-accused, if the former gives evidence the latter may cross-examine him upon that confession[12].

Where there are co-defendants and the case against one of them depends on the court being satisfied as to the guilt of the other, and the prosecution relies on out of court admissions by the latter to establish his (the latter's) guilt, then if the court finds the latter guilty it is entitled to rely on that conviction when considering the case against the former; provided the admissions are not used to confront any part of the former's defence this does not infringe the rule that out of court admissions made by one co-defendant in the absence of the other are inadmissible as against that other[13].

---

1. Police and Criminal Evidence Act 1984, s 76, this PART, post. A "confession" under s 76 does not include a statement intended by the maker to be exculpatory or neutral and which appears to be so on its face, but which becomes damaging to him at trial because, for example, of its inconsistency with his evidence: *R v Hasan* [2005] UKHL 22, [2005] 4 All ER 685.

2. See para **1–567 Summary criminal trial**—in PART I: MAGISTRATES' COURTS, PROCEDURE, ante and para **2–1357**.
3. Police and Criminal Evidence Act 1984, s 76(4), (5), this PART, post.
4. *R v Oxford City Justices, ex p Berry* [1988] QB 507, [1987] 1 All ER 1244, 151 JP 505.
5. Police and Criminal Evidence Act 1984, s 82(1), this PART, post.
6. Police and Criminal Evidence Act 1984, s 77, this PART, post.
7. *R v Elleray* [2003] EWCA Crim 553, (2003) 167 JP 325, [2003] Cr App R 11.
8. *R v Elleray*, supra.
9. *R v Sharp* [1988] 1 All ER 65, [1988] 1 WLR 7, 152 JP 164, HL; see also *Western v DPP* [1997] 1 Cr App Rep 474.
10. *R v Aziz* [1995] 3 All ER 149, [1995] 3 WLR 53, [1995] 2 Cr App Rep 478, HL.
11. *R v Myers* [1997] 4 All ER 314, [1997] 3 WLR 552, [1998] 1 Cr App Rep 153, HL.
12. *R v Corelli* [2001] EWCA Crim 974, [2001] Crim LR 913.
13. *R v Hayter* [2003] EWCA Crim 1048, [2003] 1 WLR 1910, [2003] Crim LR 887.

2–266 Statements made in the presence of a party. Relevant statements made in the presence and hearing of a party are in principle admissible in both civil and criminal proceedings. However, the "rule of law undoubtedly is that a statement made in the presence of an accused person even upon an occasion which should be expected reasonably to call for some explanation or denial from him, is not evidence against him of the facts stated save so far as he accepts the statement, so as to make it, in effect, his own. If he accepts the statement in part alone, then to that extent alone does it become his statement. He may accept the statement by word or conduct, action or demeanour, and it is the function of the [justices] . . . . to determine whether his words, action, conduct or demeanour at the time when a statement was made amounts to an acceptance of it in whole or in part. It by no means follows . . . that a mere denial by the accused of the facts mentioned in the statement necessarily renders the statement inadmissible, because he may deny the statement in such a manner and under such circumstances as may lead [the justices] to disbelieve him, and constitute evidence from which an acknowledgment may be inferred by them"[1]. In deciding whether to admit such evidence, the court should consider: is it a proper conclusion that the defendant adopted the statement in question; if so is the matter of sufficient relevance to justify its admission in evidence; and if so would its admission have such an adverse effect on the fairness of the proceedings that the court ought not to admit it[2].

In very exceptional circumstances an inference may be drawn from a failure to give an explanation or a disclaimer, but silence alone cannot give rise to an inference that the accused person accepts the truth of the statement[3], except possibly where the accused person remains silent in the face of an accusation made among persons speaking on even terms[4]. As a matter of practice if the court is satisfied that an acknowledgment cannot reasonably be inferred, it should exclude the evidence[5].

The same principles are applicable in relation to an untruthful statement made by a companion in answer to a question from the police addressed to both the defendant and his companion and the issue arises as to whether the defendant has joined in the answer; the court is entitled to consider whether the defendant's reaction to that question and answer could amount to his adoption of that answer, provided it directs itself first to consider the question as to whether in all the circumstances, the question called for some response from the defendant and secondly whether by his reaction, the defendant adopted the answer made[6].

1. *Per* Lord Atkinson in *R v Christie* [1914] AC 545, 78 JP 321, with references to "the justices" substituted for those to "the jury".
2. *R v Osborne* [2005] TLR 525, CA.
3. *Hall v R* [1971] 1 All ER 322, 135 JP 141.
4. *Parkes v R* [1976] 3 All ER 380, 140 JP 634.
5. *R v Christie* [1914] AC 545, 78 JP 321.
6. *R v Collins, R v Keep* [2004] EWCA Crim 83, [2004] 1 WLR 1705.

2–267 A relevant statement made in the hearing but not the presence of a plaintiff was held admissible[1], but statements out of the hearing of a party are usually excluded[2] unless they come within one of the exceptions to the hearsay rule[3]. A statement handed to or read to the accused during interrogation will be admissible only in the unlikely event of its evidential value outweighing its prejudicial nature[4].

Failure to deny a formal charge made by the police does not entitle the court to infer an admission[5]. Evidence of the defendant's conduct on arrest may be admissible as being inconsistent with the reactions of an innocent person[6].

1. *Neile v Jakle* (1849) 2 Car & Kir 709.
2. *R v Gibson* (1887) 18 QBD 537, 51 JP 742.
3. See para **2–250 Hearsay**.
4. *R v Thompson* [1910] 1 KB 640, 74 JP 176; *R v Christie* [1914] AC 545, 78 JP 321; *R v Taylor* [1978] Crim LR 92, and see Rule V of the Judges' Rules.
5. *R v Whitehead* [1929] 1 KB 99, 92 JP 197.
6. *Preece v Parry* [1983] Crim LR 170.

2–268 Admissions by agents etc . Where a principal has constituted an agent as his representative in the transaction of his business, the acts of the agent and the agents' representations, declarations and admissions in the course of that business, will bind the principal, provided the existence of the agency is first proved[1].

Where an employee is not constituted an agent, it is not within the scope of his authority to make admissions as to matters that have happened[2], but an offence by an incorporated body must be committed by its employee, and his explanation may be accepted as the employer's statement[3]. A statement made by a person who described himself as a depot manager was *prima facie* admissible in evidence in proceedings against his employing company[4].

---

1. See *G (a) v G (T)* [1970] 2 QB 643, [1970] 3 All ER 546.
2. *Great Western Rly Co v Willis* (1865) 18 CBNS 748; *Johnson v Lindsay* (1889) 53 JP 599.
3. *Edwards' Creameries Ltd v Smith* (1922) 86 JP 155.
4. *Edwards v Brookes (Milk) Ltd* [1963] 3 All ER 62, [1963] 1 WLR 795, 127 JP 497.

2–269   Common enterprise.   Acts and statements by one of several joint offenders or conspirators or other persons engaged in any common transaction, involving mutual legal responsibility, are parts of such common transaction and are evidence against the other party or parties thereto, as if they were done or made by him or them, so far as they were in the execution or furtherance of their common purpose, but not otherwise[1]. Statements made by joint offenders in the absence of each other may be admissible evidence, not in proof of what they contain but to prove that the makers of the statements were acting in concert[2].

---

1. *R v Blake* (1844) 6 QB 126. See also *R v Gray* (1994) 138 Sol Jo LB 199, [1994] 39 LS Gaz R 38, CA.
2. *Mawaz Khan v R* [1967] AC 454, [1967] 1 All ER 80.

2–280   Expert evidence.   The admission of expert evidence is discussed above[1].

---

1. See para **2–103 Matters on which expert evidence may be called**, ante.

PREVIOUS STATEMENTS BY A WITNESS

2–281   Inconsistent statements.   If in criminal proceedings[1] a person gives oral evidence and he admits making a previous inconsistent statement, or a previous inconsistent statement is proved by virtue of section 3, 4 or 5 of the Criminal Procedure Act 1865[2], the statement is admissible of any matter stated[3] of which oral evidence by him would be admissible[4].

If in criminal proceedings[1] evidence of an inconsistent statement by any person is given in relation to that person's credibility[5], that statement is admissible as evidence of any matter stated[3] in it of which oral evidence by that person would be admissible[6].

---

1. Defined in s 134(1) of the Criminal Justice Act 2003.
2. See this Part, post.
3. Defined in Criminal Justice Act 2003, s 115(3).
4. Criminal Justice Act 2003, s 119(1).
5. As to the credibility of the first mentioned person: see para **2–282**, post.
6. Criminal Justice Act 2003, s 119(2).

2–282   Other previous statements of a witness.   If a previous statement of a witness called to give evidence in criminal proceedings[1] is admitted as evidence to rebut a suggestion that his oral evidence has been fabricated, that statement is admissible of any matter of which oral evidence by the witness would be admissible[2].

A statement by a witness in a document[3] which he uses to refresh his memory while giving evidence, on which he is cross-examined and which as a consequence is received in evidence in the proceedings, is admissible as evidence of any matter stated[4] in it of which oral evidence by him would be admissible[5].

A previous statement by a witness is admissible of any matter stated[4] of which oral evidence by him would be admissible if any of the following conditions is satisfied:

(*a*)   the statement identifies or describes a person, object or place,
(*b*)   the statement was made by the witness when the matters stated[4] were fresh in his memory but he does not remember them, and cannot reasonably be expected to remember them, well enough to given oral evidence of them in the proceedings,
(*c*)   the witness claims to be the victim of the offence in question, and:

    (i)   the statement consists of a complaint by the witness (whether to a person in authority or not) about conduct which, if proved, would constitute the offence or part of the offence,
    (ii)   the complaint was made as soon as could reasonably be expected after the alleged conduct, and
    (iii)   before the statement is adduced the witness gives oral evidence in connection with its subject matter[6]

and, while giving evidence the witness indicates that to the best of his belief he made the statement, and that to the best of his belief it states the truth[7].

These provisions are not limited, as was the earlier common law exception relating to recent complaint to sexual cases. The statutory provisions are freestanding and provide their own criteria and should not be regarded as importing various restrictions from the old law[8]. Accordingly, where the conditions in (c) were complied with and it was expected that the complainant would give evidence, a judge was right to make a pre-trial ruling that other witnesses could give evidence of what the complainant had told them about the treatment she was receiving[9]. These provisions allow the admission of more than one hearsay statement and any statement is admissible to prove the truth of the matter stated and not merely to demonstrate consistency[8].

Nothing in this paragraph or **2–281** above makes a statement admissible as evidence if it was made by a person who did not have the required capacity at the time when he made the statement[10].

As to the court's general discretion to exclude evidence and proof of statement in documents see post[11].

---

1. Defined in Criminal Justice Act 2003, s 134(1).
2. Criminal Justice Act 2003, s 120(2).
3. Defined in Criminal Justice Act 2003, s 134(1).
4. Defined in Criminal Justice Act 2003, s 115(3).
5. Criminal Justice Act 2003, s 120(3).
6. For the purposes of (c), the fact that the complaint was elicited (for example, by a leading question) is irrelevant unless a threat or promise was made: Criminal Justice Act 2003, s 120(8).
7. Criminal Justice Act 2003, s 120(4).
8. *R v O* [2006] EWCA Crim 556, [2006] 2 Cr App R 27, [2006] Crim LR 918.
9. *R v Xhabri* [2006] EWCA Crim 3135, [2006] 1 All ER 776, [2006] 1 Cr App R 26 (in any event, such evidence would have been admitted in the interests of justice, see post.).
10. Criminal Justice Act 2003, s 123(1). As to the test of capability, see s 123(3), ibid. As to the procedure for determining capability and the standard of proof, see s 123(4), ibid.
11. Respectively, paras **2–287** and **2–289**, post.

2–283 *Hearsay statements admitted in the interests of justice.* Where the victim of false imprisonment, rape and threats to kill made communications to various persons including her mother and others, it was held that it was in the interests of justice to allow her to give evidence of the content of those communications not merely as evidence of how she was reacting but as evidence of the truth of the statements that she was making as to her predicament. The jury would wish to know whether she had sought to communicate with the outside world and in what terms. Similarly, hearsay evidence given by other witnesses of what the complainant said was admitted on the same basis[1].

---

1. *R v Xhabri* [2006] EWCA Crim 3135, [2006] 1 All ER 776, [2006] 1 Cr App R 26.

ADDITIONAL REQUIREMENTS FOR MULTIPLE HEARSAY

2–284 A hearsay statement is not admissible to prove the fact that an earlier hearsay statement has been made unless:

(a) either of the statements is admissible under para **2–262 *Business and other documents***, or para **2–282 *Previous statements by a witness***, ante;
(b) all parties to the proceedings so agree; or
(c) the court is satisfied that the value of the evidence in question, taking into account how reliable the statements appear to be, is so high that the interests of justice require the later statement to be admissible for that purpose[1].

For these purposes, "hearsay statement" means a statement, not made in oral evidence, that is relied on as evidence of a matter stated[2] in it[3].

---

1. Section 121(1) of the Criminal Justice Act 2003. It was held in *Maher v DPP* [2006] EWHC 1271 (Admin), (2006) 170 JP 441, that in the circumstances of that case – registration details of a car passed in note form (since lost) by A to B and by B (by telephone) to the police – that the provisions about the interests of justice should have been considered cumulatively with the interests of justice criteria in s 114(2), ante (which provided on the facts of the case an overwhelming case why the evidence should be admitted).
2. Defined in Criminal Justice Act 2003, s 115(3).
3. Criminal Justice Act 2003, s 121(2).

IMPUGNING THE CREDIBILITY OF THE MAKER OF A HEARSAY STATEMENT

2–285 If, in criminal proceedings[1] a statement[2] not made in oral evidence is admitted as evidence of any matter stated[2] and the maker of the statement does not give oral evidence in connection with the subject matter of the statement:

(a) any evidence which (if he had given evidence) would have been admissible as relevant to his credibility as a witness is so admissible in the proceedings;
(b) evidence may with the court's leave be given of any matter which (if he had given such evidence) could have been put to him in cross-examination as relevant to his credibility as a witness but of which evidence could not have been adduced by the cross-examining party;
(c) evidence tending to prove that he made (at whatever time) any other statement inconsistent with the statement admitted as evidence is admissible for the purpose of showing that he contradicted himself[3].

If as a result of evidence admitted under this head an allegation is made against the maker of a statement, the court may permit a party to lead additional evidence of such description as the court may specify for the purposes of denying or answering the allegation[4].

In the case of a statement in a document[5] which is admitted under para **2–262 Business and other documents** above, each person who, in order for the statement to be admissible, must have supplied or received the information concerned or created or received the document or part concerned is to be treated as the maker of the statement for the above purposes[6].

---

1. Defined in s 134(1) of the Criminal Justice Act 2003.
2. Defined in Criminal Justice Act 2003, s 115.
3. Section 124(1) and (2). In relation to (c), the previous inconsistent statement is admissible as evidence of any matter stated in it of which oral evidence by that person would be admissible: s 119(2).
4. Criminal Justice Act 2003, s 124(3).
5. Defined in Criminal Justice Act 2003, s 134(1).
6. Criminal Justice Act 2003, s 124(4).

STOPPING THE CASE WHERE HEARSAY EVIDENCE IS FOUND TO BE UNCONVINCING

2–286   This applies only to trial on indictment and it requires the judge to stop the trial and acquit the defendant or order a retrial if hearsay evidence has been admitted but has then transpired to be unconvincing, and its importance to the case against the defendant is such that his conviction of the offence would be unsafe[1].

---

1. Section 125 of the Criminal Justice Act 2003.

COURT'S GENERAL DISCRETION TO EXCLUDE EVIDENCE

2–287   In criminal proceedings[1] the court may refuse to admit a statement[2] as evidence of a matter stated[2] if:

(a)   the statement was made otherwise than in oral evidence in the proceedings, and
(b)   the court is satisfied that the case for excluding the statement, taking account of the danger that to admit it would result in undue waste of time, substantially outweighs the case for admitting it, taking account of the value of the evidence[3].

The above is without prejudice to the court's power to exclude evidence under s 78 of PACE or to any other power to exclude evidence at the court's discretion[4].

---

1. Defined in s 134(1) of the Criminal Justice Act 2003.
2. Defined in Criminal Justice Act 2003, s 115.
3. Criminal Justice Act 2003, s 126(1). As to the broad approach that is being taken to the interpretation of this provision, see *R v C and K* [2006] EWCA Crim 197, [2006] Crim LR 637, and the commentary thereon.
4. Criminal Justice Act 2003, s 126(2).

EVIDENCE FROM COMPUTERS OR MACHINES

2–288   Where a representation of any fact is made otherwise than by a person, but depends for its accuracy on information supplied (directly or indirectly) by a person, the representation is not admissible in criminal proceedings[1] as evidence of the fact unless it is proved that the information was accurate[2]. This does not affect the operation of the presumption that a mechanical device has been properly set or calibrated[3].

---

1. Defined in s 134(1) of the Criminal Justice Act 2003.
2. Criminal Justice Act 2003, s 129(1).
3. Criminal Justice Act 2003, s 129(2).

PROOF OF STATEMENTS IN DOCUMENTS

2–289   Where a statement[1] in a document[2] is admissible as evidence in criminal proceedings, the statement may be proved by producing either:

(a)   the document, or
(b)   (whether or not the document exists) a copy of the document or of the material part of it,

authenticated in whatever way the court may approve.

---

1. Defined in s 115 of the Criminal Justice Act 2003.
2. Defined in s 134(1).

PROCEDURE FOR TENDERING HEARSAY EVIDENCE

2-300 Part 34 of the Criminal Procedure Rules 2005 provides that in the magistrates' court:

(*a*) the prosecutor must give notice of hearsay evidence at the same time as he complies or purports to comply with the duty of primary disclosure under s 3 of the Criminal Procedure Act 1996, and

(*b*) the defendant must give notice of hearsay evidence not more than 14 days after the prosecutor has complied or purported to comply with the above duty.

A party who receives a notice of hearsay evidence may oppose it by given notice with 14 days in the prescribed form.

A notice under this Part may, with the consent of the addressee, be sent by fax or other electronic means.

The court may dispense with the above requirement to give notice, or allow notice to be given in a different form or orally, or shorten a time limit or extend it (even after it has expired)

A party entitled to receive a notice of hearsay evidence may waive his entitlement by so informing the court and the party who would have given the notice.

Special rules of evidence in criminal proceedings

IDENTIFICATION

2-310 In criminal proceedings the court will need to be satisfied as to the identity of the accused as the person who it is said committed the offence. This will not become an issue where, for example, the accused pleads guilty, or identity is otherwise admitted, but in all other cases sufficient evidence of identity should be an element of the prosecution case.

Identification of the accused by a witness for the first time in court at the trial is an unsatisfactory method and should be avoided if possible[1]. The police should have arranged an identity parade or the use of photographs where this was clearly necessary; they should not point out a suspect and ask the witness if that was the alleged offender[2]. Nevertheless, dock identifications are customary in the magistrates' court and are necessary to deal with the problem of defendants, such as those charged with motoring offences, who having made no statement to the police, are entitled to sit back and, in the absence of identification, submit that it has not been proven that they were the driver[3].

A prosecutor with a duty to prosecute summary non-arrestable offences may be hampered by the lack of power to invoke identity procedures under the Police and Criminal Evidence Act 1984 without the co-operation of the defendant. However, the prosecution may not seek to rely on that lack of power to press for a dock identification[4].

Paragraph 2.3 of CODE D of the Police and Criminal Evidence Act 1984 (whenever a suspect disputes an identification an identification parade shall be held if the suspect consents) is mandatory and applies (subject to the exceptions stated therein) even where there has previously been a "fully satisfactory" or "actual and complete" or "unequivocal" identification of the suspect by the relevant witness; however, paragraph 2.3 should not be construed to cover all possible situations (eg an eye witness makes it plain to the police that he cannot identify the culprit, or the case is one of pure recognition of somebody well known to the witness)[5]. An informal street identification shortly after an alleged assault, by the victim of the alleged assailant, is permissible; but if it takes place in unsatisfactory circumstances (no written record made of the victim's first description of the assailant, where there was no information to suggest that that was impracticable, and the suspect was in a police van at the time) and the suspect continues to dispute identification but no ID parade is held, it will be unsafe for justices to convict in reliance on that identification evidence[6].

Where a witness's statement refers to the accused's name, in the absence of any contrary suggestion it may be assumed that he is referring to the accused and not to someone else with the same name[7].

Identification may be by handwriting[8], by voice[9], or by video recording[10].

There is no objection in principle to the admissibility of ear print identification evidence, but it is essential that expert evidence going to issues of identity should be carefully scrutinised; evidence from an expert in ear print comparison can be flawed just as the evidence of a fingerprint evidence expert can be flawed, and the probative value of such evidence depends on the reliability of the scientific technique[11].

"Partial" or "non" identification evidence may be admissible: a failure to make a positive identification is no bar to describing either the event or the offender[12]. There are at least two situations where a qualified identification may in the appropriate circumstances be both relevant and probative: first, where, it supports or at least is consistent with other evidence which indicates that the defendant committed the crime, and, secondly, the explanation for a non- or qualified identification may help to place the non- or qualified identification in its proper context and so, eg, show that the other evidence given by the witness may still be correct[13].

---

1. *R v John* [1973] Crim LR 113.
2. *R v Smith and Evans* (1908) 1 Cr App Rep 203; *R v Dickman* (1910) 74 JP 449; *R v Chapman* (1911) 7 Cr App Rep 53, 28 TLR 81.

3. *Barnes v Chief Constable of Durham* [1997] 2 Cr App Rep 505, 162 JP 126. See also *Karia v DPP* [2002] EWHC 2175 (Admin), (2002) 166 JP 753, where it was held that it was permissible for the prosecution to seek and to rely on a dock identification where there had been no prior notification that identification was in issue, and it did not breach art 6 to require a defendant to indicate before trial that identification as the driver of a motor vehicle was in issue.
4. *North Yorkshire Trading Standards Department v Williams* (1994) 159 JP 383.
5. *R v Forbes* [2001] 1 All ER 686, [2001] 2 WLR 1, [2001] 1 Cr App Rep 430, HL.
6. *Ryan v DPP* CO/1315/2000, DC.
7. *Ellis v Jones* [1973] 2 All ER 893.
8. See ante **2–68 Handwriting**.
9. *R v Keating* (1909) 2 Cr App Rep 61, 73 JP 112. As to voice identification parade and direction to a jury, see *R v Hersey* [1998] Crim LR 281, and commentary thereto.
10. See ante para **2–82 Sound and video recordings**.
11. *R v Dallagher* [2002] EWCA Crim 1903, [2003] 1 Cr App R 12.
12. *R v George* [2002] EWCA Crim 1923, [2003] Crim LR 282.
13. *R v George*, supra.

2–311 Where witnesses fail to remember whether it was the accused they identified at an identification parade, their evidence may be supplemented by a police officer who can confirm that they did identify the accused[1]. Where a constable or traffic warden obtains a person's name and address from a driving licence produced by them and is later unable to identify them in court, there is nevertheless evidence of identity on which the justices may act[2], and this applies equally where the driver does not produce a licence but states his name and address and appears by counsel in answer to a summons[3]. Failure to hold an identification parade in accordance with Code D of the Police and Criminal Evidence Act 1984 is not necessarily fatal to a prosecution in particular where proof of guilt depends on deducing the identity of the accused from the primary facts rather than the disputed visual identification evidence of individual witnesses[4]. Identification by voice involves particular dangers particularly that of a stranger even where there is a good opportunity to listen to the voice and the court must be alert to the dangers of such evidence which may be more acute even than in the case of visual evidence[5].

1. *R v Osbourne* [1973] 1 QB 678, [1973] 1 All ER 649, 137 JP 287.
2. *Marshall v Ford* (1908) 72 JP 480; *Cooke v McCann* [1974] RTR 131, [1973] Crim LR 522.
3. *Creed v Scott* [1976] RTR 485, [1976] Crim LR 381.
4. *R v Kelly* (1998) 162 JP 231, CA.
5. *R v Roberts* [2000] Crim LR 183, CA.

TURNBULL GUIDELINES

2–312 Guidance has been given by the Court of Appeal to judges when summing up in disputed identity cases[1]. In our view, the clerk in a magistrates' court should advise justices of these guidelines in appropriate cases so they may be applied. The guidelines are as follows.

Where the case against the accused depends wholly or substantially on the correctness of one or more identifications, the judge should

1. warn the jury of the special need for caution in relying on correctness of identification;
2. make some reference to the possibility that a mistaken witness could be convincing and that a number of witnesses could all be mistaken;
3. direct the jury to examine closely the circumstances of the identification; how long seen, how far away, in what light, was observation impeded, had the witness seen the accused before and if so how often, if only seen occasionally had he any special reason for remembering the accused, how long was there between the original observation and the subsequent identification to the police, was there any material discrepancy between the witness's description of the accused given to the police and the accused's actual appearance; if the prosecution have reason to believe in any case that there is a material discrepancy between the witness's description and the accused's actual appearance they should supply the accused or his legal advisers with the original description, and in all cases such descriptions should be supplied to the defence on request, both in summary trials and trials on indictment;
4. remind the jury of any specific weakness in the identification evidence; recognition might be more reliable than the identification of a stranger but the jury should be reminded that mistakes in recognising close friends and relatives are sometimes made.

These matters all go to the quality of the evidence. If the quality is good, for example identification made over a long period of observation or in satisfactory conditions by a relative, neighbour, close friend, workmate and the like, the jury may be left to assess the value of the identifying evidence even though there was no other evidence to support it. However, if in the judgment of the judge, the quality of evidence is poor, for example a fleeting glance, or longer observation in difficult conditions, then he should withdraw the case from the jury unless there is other evidence supporting the correctness of the identification. It is not sufficient, however, simply to ask whether the evidence was a "fleeting glance", the key question is what is the quality of that evidence[2]. The supporting evidence need not necessarily be corroboration but should be such that its effect is to make the jury sure that there has been no mistaken identification. The judge should identify to the jury the evidence he adjudges capable of supporting the evidence of identification. Further, if there was any evidence or circumstances such as the accused electing not to give evidence which a jury might think supported identity evidence but which did not have that quality, the judge should say so.

Where the identity of the accused is at issue and the accused admits that he was present at the scene of the offence but denies participation in it a *Turnbull* direction is necessary[3]. In such circumstances, however, it is the possibility of a mistake which is the necessary prerequisite for an identification issue to arise such as to require a *Turnbull* direction; where there is no basis for such a mistake but what is in question is what the accused has done, the issue is not one of identification[4]. Similarly, where there is strong evidence that the accused was with another person at the relevant time, a purported identification of that other person should, as a rule, be the subject of a *Turnbull* direction[5]. A *Turnbull* direction is not required in respect of identification of a motor car[6]. Where the accused is identified by victims of different offences and similar fact evidence is adduced in support of the identification, evidence other than similarity of facts must establish that the defendant has committed one offence before similar fact evidence can support identification on the remaining offences[7].

In identification cases a photograph of the accused and the crime report should be routinely forwarded by the police to the Crown Prosecution Service in order that they may be disclosed to the defence[8].

1. *R v Turnbull* [1977] QB 224, [1976] 3 All ER 549, 140 JP 648, and see *R v Weeder* (1980) 71 Cr App Rep 228 1; *McShane v Northumbria Chief Constable* (1979) 72 Cr App Rep 208 and *Mills v R* [1995] 3 All ER 865, [1995] 1 WLR 511, [1995] Crim LR 884, CA.
2. *R v Williams (John)* (1994) Times, 7 October, CA.
3. *R v Thornton* [1995] 1 Cr App Rep 578, (1994) 158 JP 1155, CA.
4. *R v Slater* [1995] 1 Cr App Rep 584, [1995] Crim LR 244, CA.
5. See *R v Both* (1990) 154 JP 849, [1990] Crim LR 716, CA.
6. *R v Browning* (1991) 94 Cr App Rep 109, CA.
7. *R v McGranaghan* [1995] 1 Cr App Rep 559, note.
8. *R v F (a Juvenile)* (1993) 158 JP 49.

EVIDENCE FROM OBJECTS AT THE SCENE

2–313 Material objects discovered when following up an inadmissible confession or during an unlawful search are admissible if relevant[1].

To make property found in the prisoner's possession admissible in evidence, there must be some link between the property and the crime alleged[2]. The property of a murdered person found in a place visited by the alleged murderer is admissible against him[3].

Paper with a name written on it found near a gun on a grass verge one mile from the scene of a robbery has been ruled admissible[4].

1. *R v Leatham* (1861) 3 E & E 658, 25 JP 468; *Kuruma Son of Kaniu v R* [1955] AC 197, [1955] 1 All ER 236.
2. *R v Taylor* (1923) 87 JP 104.
3. *R v Palmer* (1911) 6 Cr App Rep 237; and see *R v Podmore* (1930) 46 TLR 365.
4. *R v Sean Lydon* [1987] Crim LR 407, CA.

DNA PROFILES

2–314 When a criminal leaves a stain of blood or semen at the scene of the crime it may prove possible to extract from that crime stain sufficient sections of DNA to enable a comparison to be made with the same sections extracted from a sample of blood provided by the suspect. The Court of Appeal has given guidance about DNA testing and the conclusions that can properly be drawn from such testing[1].

The following procedures should be adopted where DNA evidence is involved—

(a) The scientist should adduce the evidence of the DNA comparisons between the crime stain and the defendant's sample together with his calculations of the random occurrence ration.

(b) Whenever DNA evidence is to be adduced the Crown should serve on the defence details as to how the calculations have been carried out which are sufficient to enable the defence to scrutinise the basis of the calculations.

(c) The Forensic Science Service should make available to a defence expert, if requested, the databases upon which the calculations have been based.

(d) Any issue of expert evidence should be identified and, if possible, resolved before trial. This area should be explored by the court in the pre-trial review[1].

(e) In the absence of special features, expert evidence should not be admitted to induce juries to attach mathematical values to probabilities arising from non-scientific evidence adduced at the trial[2].

1. *R v Doheny and Adams* [1997] 1 Cr App Rep 369.
2. *R v Denis Adams (No 2)* [1998] 1 Cr App Rep 377.

DRAWING INFERENCES FROM THE ACCUSED'S SILENCE

2–315 **Effect of accused's failure to mention facts when questioned or charged**[1]. Justices may draw such inferences as appear proper from a failure by the accused to mention facts when questioned or charged[2]. No inference may be drawn however, if the accused had not been allowed an opportunity to consult a solicitor prior to being questioned or charged[3]. In a magistrates' court the inferences may be drawn when inquiring into an offence as examining justices, when determining whether there is a case to answer, or in determining whether the accused is guilty of the offence charged[4]. An inference may be drawn, adverse to the accused, even if he does not give evidence[5].

An inference may be drawn where, in any proceedings against a person for an offence, evidence is given that the accused—

   (a)   at any time before he was charged with the offence, on being questioned under caution by a constable trying to discover whether or by whom the offence had been committed[6], failed to mention any fact relied on in his defence[7] in those proceedings; or

   (b)   on being charged[8] with the offence or officially informed that he might be prosecuted for it, failed to mention any such fact,

being a fact which in the circumstances existing at the time the accused could reasonably have been expected to mention when so questioned, charged or informed, as the case may be[9].

A person shall not have the proceedings against him committed to the Crown Court for trial, have a case to answer or be convicted of an offence solely on an inference drawn from a failure to mention any fact when questioned or charged[10].

Subject to any directions by the court, evidence tending to establish the failure may be given before or after the evidence tending to establish the fact which the accused is alleged to have failed to mention[11].

These provisions apply in relation to questioning by persons, other than constables, who are charged with the duty of investigating offences or charging offenders[12].

It is expressly stated by s 34 of the Criminal Justice and Public Order Act 1994 that the provisions of the section do not—

   (a)   prejudice the admissibility in evidence of the silence or other reaction of the accused in the face of anything said in his presence relating to the conduct in respect of which he is charged, in so far as evidence thereof would be admissible apart from that section; or

   (b)   preclude the drawing of any inference from any such silence or other reaction of the accused which could properly be drawn apart from that section[13].

There are six conditions which should be met before the court may draw an inference from a failure by the accused to mention facts when questioned or charged—

   (i)   there must be proceedings against a person for an offence;

   (ii)   the alleged failure must occur before the accused is charged;

   (iii) the alleged failure must occur during questioning under caution by a constable or other investigating officer;

   (iv) the constable's or other officer's questioning must be directed to trying to discover whether or by whom the alleged offence had been committed;

   (v)   the alleged failure by the accused must be to mention any fact relied on in his defence in those proceedings;

   (vi) the accused failed to mention a fact which in the circumstances existing at the time the accused could reasonably have been expected to mention when so questioned[14].

Where a suspect refuses to leave his cell for interview, an adverse inference cannot be drawn because the silence is not in the face of questioning[15].

A defendant is entitled to give evidence of the conversation he had with his solicitor prior to the interview, in which he offered no comment, to rebut any allegation of post-interview fabrication[16].

If, in the course of pre-trial questioning by the police, a suspect goes beyond saying that he declines to answer on legal advice and he or his solicitor explains the basis on which he has been advised, a waiver of professional privilege is involved. But where, during the pre-trial questioning, the suspect or his solicitor states that the suspect declines to answer questions on legal advice and prosecution evidence called at trial is limited to reporting that statement, then there is no waiver of privilege[17].

If at trial, the defendant or his solicitor gives evidence not merely of the defendant's refusal to answer pre-trial questions on legal advice, but also of the grounds on which such advice was given, or if the defence elicit evidence at trial of a statement made by a defendant or his solicitor pre-trial of the grounds on which legal advice had been given to answer no questions, the defendant voluntarily withdraws the veil of privilege which would otherwise protect confidential communications between his legal adviser and himself, and having done so he cannot resist questioning directed to the nature of that advice and the factual premises on which it had been based[18].

Where a suspect accused of assault gave a no comment interview on legal advice, stating the reason to be that there was no written statement from the complainant, and then ran self defence at his trial, the judge was entitled to direct the jury that an inference could be drawn under s 34; even if the solicitor had given evidence at the trial an inference would still have been possible because adequate oral disclosure of the complaint had been made and there was, therefore, no objectively sound reason for the advice; reasonable circumstances might include mental disability, confusion, intoxication and shock[19].

It is not the purpose of s 34 to prevent an inference from being drawn where the defendant genuinely or reasonably believed that, regardless of his guilt or innocence, he was entitled to take advantage of legal advice to remain silent to impede the prosecution against him, in which case the advice was not the only reason for failing to mention facts later relied on; belief in the entitlement to remain silent and the reasons for exercising it are different things, and while the belief in the right might be genuine it did not follow that the reason for exercising it was; the question for the court is whether regardless of advice, genuinely given and accepted, a defendant remained silent not because of the advice but because he had no or no satisfactory explanation to give[20].

The word "fact" should be given a broad and not a narrow or pedantic meaning. The word covers any alleged fact which is in issue and is put forward as part of the defence case: if the defendant advances at trial any pure fact or exculpatory explanation or account which, if it were true, he could reasonably have been expected to advance earlier, s 34 is potentially applicable. A defendant relies on a fact or matter in his defence not only when he gives or adduces evidence of it but also when counsel, acting on his instructions, puts a specific and positive case to prosecution witnesses, as opposed to asking questions intended to probe or test the prosecution case, whether or not the prosecution witness accepts the suggestion put[21].

A "fact" is not confined only to events or acts and may include an explanation tailored by the defendant to fit the prosecution case which the defendant did not believe would stand up to scrutiny at the time[16] but not to matters mentioned in answer to cross-examination which are more in the way of an explanation, a theory or a possibility[22]. Where in an interview a defendant hands to the police a prepared statement and then responds to all questions with "no comment", it is not open to the court to draw adverse inferences from his failure to answer questions where he does not rely at his trial on any new fact not covered by his statement[23]. The practice of submitting a pre-prepared statement and declining to answer questions might prove dangerous for an innocent person who subsequently discovers at his trial that something significant has been omitted from his statement. Where there are differences between what is in a pre-prepared statement and what is said at trial, the court may be better, depending on the circumstances, to consider a difference as constituting a previous lie rather than as a foundation for a s 34 inference[24]. However, it has been held that there is nothing in the language of the section that requires the s 34 issue to be capable of resolution as a separate (ie from the main) issue in the case[25].

A fact may be "relied on" within the meaning of s 34 whether it is adduced in evidence in the course of the prosecution case or defence case; the section expressly contemplates that a fact may be relied on even though it is not put in evidence on the defendant's behalf[26].

1. Under the Human Rights Act 1998, the Criminal Justice and Public Order Act 1994, s 34, so far as it is possible to do so, must be read and given effect in a way which is compatible with the Convention rights. See para **2–319**, post.

2. Criminal Justice and Public Order Act 1994, s 34, this PART, post.

3. Criminal Justice and Public Order Act 1994, s 34(2A), this PART, post.

4. Criminal Justice and Public Order Act 1994, s 34(2), this PART, post.

5. *R v Bowers, Taylor and Millau* (1998) 163 JP 33.

6. An adverse inference may be drawn even though the defendant's "no comment" stance had no bearing on the decision whether or not he would be prosecuted since the interviewing officer was of the opinion that there was already sufficient evidence to bring charges; whether "an offence had been committed" for the purposes of s 34 depends as much on the available of defences as it depends on proof of the elements of the offence (*R v Elliott* [2002] EWCA Crim 931, [2002] All ER (D) 221 (Apr)).

7. There is a distinction between admitting part of the prosecution case and asserting a fact; thus, if a defendant admits at trial for the first time that a fingerprint found at the scene is his, but offers no explanation for it being found where it was, he is not relying on a fact: *R v Betts and Hall* [2001] EWCA Crim 224, [2001] 2 Cr App Rep 257.

8. It is open to a judge (subject to a review of all the considerations that may point to unfairness) to direct a jury that an inference may be drawn from failure to mention at the time of charge facts later relied on by the defendant in his defence even though no inference can be drawn from silence at interview (because the interview was ruled inadmissible) (*R v Dervish* [2001] EWCA Crim 2789, [2002] 2 Cr App Rep 6).

9. Criminal Justice and Public Order Act 1994, s 34(1), this PART, post. It is particularly important that a jury should not be left at liberty to draw an adverse inference notwithstanding that it may be satisfied with the plausibility of the defendant's explanation for his silence: see *Condron v United Kingdom* (2000) 31 EHRR 1; *R v Betts and Hall*, supra; *R v Daly*, infra.

10. Criminal Justice and Public Order Act 1994, s 38(3), this PART, post.

11. Criminal Justice and Public Order Act 1994, s 34(3), this PART, post.

12. Criminal Justice and Public Order Act 1994, s 34(4), this PART, post.

13. Criminal Justice and Public Order Act 1994, s 34(5), this PART, post.

14. *R v Argent* (1996) 161 JP 190, [1997] 2 Cr App Rep 27, [1997] Crim LR 346.

15. *R v Johnson* [2005] EWCA Crim 971, [2006] Crim LR 253.

16. *R v Daniel* (1998) 162 JP 578.

17. *R v Bowden* [1999] 4 All ER 43, [1999] 1 WLR 823, 163 JP 337, [1999] 2 Cr App Rep 176, CA.

18. *R v Milford* [2001] Crim LR 330, CA.

19. *R v Howell* [2003] EWCA Crim 01, [2005] 1 Cr App R 1, [2003] Crim LR 405.

20. *R v Hoare* [2004] EWCA Crim 784, [2005] 1 WLR 1804, [2005] 1 Cr App R 22, [2005] Crim LR 567. *Hoare* and other authorities were considered in *R v Beckles* [2004] EWCA Crim 2766, [2005] 1 All ER 705, [2005] 1 WLR 2829, [2005] 1 Cr App R 23. It was held that, where a solicitor's advice was relied upon by the defendant, the ultimate question for the jury remained under s 34 whether the facts relied on at the trial were facts which the defendant could reasonably have been expected to mention at interview. If they were not, that was the end of the matter. If the jury consider that the defendant genuinely relied on the advice that was not necessarily the end of the matter. It might still not have been reasonable for him to rely on the advice, or the advice might not have been the true explanation for his silence. Where, however, it is concluded that the defendant genuinely and reasonably acted on advice to remain silent, and this was his reason for doing so, an inference should not be drawn. See also *R v Bresa* [2005] EWCA Crim 1414, [2006] Crim LR 179.

21. *R v Webber* [2004] UKHL 1, [2004] 1 All ER 770, [2004] 1 WLR 404, [2004] 1 Cr App R 40.

22. *R v Nickolson* [1999] Crim LR 61, CA.

23. *R v McGarry* [1999] 1 WLR 1500, [1999] 1 Cr App Rep 377, [1999] Crim LR 316, CA; *R v Knight* [2003] EWCA Crim 1977, [2004] 1 WLR 340, [2004] 1 Cr App R 9, [2003] Crim LR 799.

24. *R v Turner* [2003] EWCA Crim 3108, [2004] 1 All ER 1025, [2004] 1 Cr App R 24.

25. *R v Daly* [2001] EWCA Crim 2643, [2002] 2 Cr App Rep 14, [2002] Crim LR 237. See also *R v Hearn & Colman* (unreported: decided May 4, 2000) and *R v Gowland-Wynn* [2001] EWCA Crim 2715, [2002] 1 Cr App Rep 41, [2002] Crim LR 210.

26. *R v Chenia* [2002] EWCA Crim 2345, [2004] 1 All ER 543, [2003] 2 Cr App R 6.

2–316   **Effect of accused's silence at trial[1].**   On the trial of any person, the justices, in determining whether the accused is guilty of the offence charged, may draw such inferences as appear proper from the failure of the accused to give evidence or his refusal, without good cause, to answer any question[2].

At the conclusion of the evidence for the prosecution, s 35(2) of the Criminal Justice and Public Order Act 1994[3] requires the court to satisfy itself[4] that the accused is aware that the stage has been reached at which evidence can be given for the defence and that he can, if he wishes, give evidence and that, if he chooses not to give evidence, or having been sworn, without good cause refuses to answer any question, it will be permissible for the court to draw such inferences as appear proper from his failure to give evidence or his refusal, without good cause, to answer any question. This requirement, however, does not apply if at the conclusion of the evidence of the prosecution, the accused's legal representative informs the court that the accused will give evidence or, where he is unrepresented, the court ascertains from him that he will give evidence[5].

A person shall not be convicted of an offence solely on an inference drawn from a failure to give evidence or a refusal, without good cause, to answer any question[6]. A person who, having been sworn, refuses to answer any question shall be taken to do so without good cause unless—

> (a)   he is entitled to refuse to answer the question by virtue of any enactment, whenever passed or made, or on the ground of privilege; or
>
> (b)   the court in the exercise of its general discretion excuses him from answering it[7].

These provisions of s 35 of the Criminal Justice and Public Order Act 1994 do not render the accused compellable to give evidence on his own behalf, and accordingly he shall not be guilty of contempt of court by reason of a failure to do so[8]. Moreover, s 35 has no application if the accused's guilt is not in issue, or it appears to the court that the physical or mental condition of the accused makes it undesirable for him to give evidence[9].

If the accused is legally represented, but the court is not informed at the conclusion of the evidence for the prosecution that the accused will give evidence, or if the court is informed that the accused does *not* intend to give evidence, the court should inquire of the legal representative in these terms:

> "Have you advised your client that the stage has now been reached at which he may give evidence and, if he chooses not to do so or, having been sworn, without good cause refuses to answer any question, the court may draw such inferences as appear proper from his failure to do so?"

If the representative replies to the court that the accused has been so advised, then the case shall proceed. If the representative replies that the accused has not been so advised then the court shall direct the representative to advise his client of the consequences of a failure to give evidence or a refusal, without good cause, to answer any question, and should adjourn briefly for this purpose before proceeding further[10].

If the accused is not legally represented, the court at the conclusion of the evidence for the prosecution should say to the accused[11]:

> "You have heard the evidence against you. Now is the time for you to make your defence. You may give evidence on oath, and be cross-examined like any other witness. If you do not give evidence or, having been sworn, without good cause refuse to answer any question the court may draw such inferences as appear proper. That means they may hold it against you. You may also call any witness or witnesses whom you have arranged to attend court. Afterwards you may also, if you wish, address the court by arguing your case from the dock. But you cannot at that stage give evidence. Do you now intend to give evidence?"

Failure by the court to give a warning to a defendant as to the consequences of his not giving evidence whether he is represented or not constitutes an irregularity in the proceedings rendering them liable to be quashed by judicial review[12].

The effect of s 35 of the Criminal Justice and Public Order Act 1994 is that the court may regard the inference from failure to testify as, in effect, a further evidential factor in support of the prosecution's case. However, it cannot be the only factor to justify a conviction, and the totality of the evidence must prove guilt beyond reasonable doubt[13]. The Court of Appeal has given guidance on the essentials which must be highlighted when directing a jury with regard to the application of s 35, and we would suggest that the following factors should also be included in the advice given to justices:

> (i)   The burden of proof remains on the prosecution throughout, and the prosecution must prove guilt beyond reasonable doubt.
>
> (ii)   The defendant is entitled to remain silent. That is his right and his choice. The right of silence remains.
>
> (iii)   An inference from failure to give evidence cannot on its own prove guilt; that is expressly stated in s 38(3) of the 1994 Act.
>
> (iv)   The court must be satisfied that the prosecution has established a case to answer *before* drawing any inferences from silence.
>
> (v)   If an accused person gives as a reason for not answering questions that he had been advised by his solicitor not to do so, that advice does not amount to a waiver of privilege, but that bare assertion is not likely of itself to be regarded as a sufficient reason for not mentioning matters relevant to the defence[13].
>
> (vi)   If, despite any evidence relied on to explain his silence or in the absence of any such evidence, the court concludes the silence can only sensibly be attributed to the defendant's having no

answer, or none that would stand up to cross-examination, the court may draw an adverse inference[13].

The rule against advocates giving evidence dressed up as a submission applies in the context of applying s 35. It is not proper for a defence advocate to give to the justices reasons for his client's silence at trial in the absence of evidence to support such reasons[14].

It has been held in relation to a trial on indictment that it will only be in very rare cases that a judge will have to consider whether it is undesirable for an accused to give evidence on account of his mental condition, as opposed, to his being unfit to plead[15]. Although the court has a wide discretion, there has to be an evidential basis for any determination about whether an accused's mental condition makes it undesirable for him to give evidence. A statement or submission of an advocate is insufficient Also that he might have difficulty in giving evidence does not make it undesirable for him to give evidence. Such difficulty can be taken into account by the tribunal of fact and goes to the weight of the evidence not as to the decision whether or not it is undesirable for him to give evidence[16].

1. Under the Human Rights Act 1998, the Criminal Justice and Public Order Act 1994, s 35, so far as it is possible to do so, must be read and given effect in a way which is compatible with the Convention rights. See para **2–319**, post.

2. Criminal Justice and Public Order Act 1994, s 35, this PART, post.

3. See this PART, post.

4. If the defendant is absent at that stage of the trial the court cannot be so satisfied and an adverse inference is not, therefore, permissible: *R v Gough* (2001) 165 JPN 895.

5. Criminal Justice and Public Order Act 1994, s 35(1), this PART, post.

6. Criminal Justice and Public Order Act 1994, s 38(3), this PART, post.

7. Criminal Justice and Public Order Act 1994, s 35(5), this PART, post.

8. Criminal Justice and Public Order Act 1994, s 35(4), this PART, post.

9. Criminal Justice and Public Order Act 1994, s 35(1), this PART, post.

10. *Practice Direction (criminal: consolidated)* [2002] para IV.44, in PART I: MAGISTRATES' COURTS, PROCEDURE, ante.

11. This text is taken from para IV.44 of *Practice Direction (criminal: consolidated)* in PART I: MAGISTRATES' COURTS, PROCEDURE, ante, but modified for use in magistrates' courts by the substitution of the word "court" for "jury".

12. *Radford v Kent County Council* (1998) 162 JP 697, DC (on the facts where the defendant was legally represented, the justices had correctly applied the burden and standard of proof and had drawn no adverse inference from the accused's failure to give evidence, the failure did not amount to a material irregularity).

13. *R v Cowan* [1995] 4 All ER 939, [1996] 1 Cr App Rep 1, 160 JP 165, CA. In *R v Becouarn* [2005] UKHL 55, [2005] 4 All ER 673, [2005] 1 WLR 2589, [2006] 1 Cr App R 2 the House of Lords considered the position where the silence of the accused might be due, not to him having no answer to the charge or one that would stand up to cross-examination, but to the risk that he might be cross-examined in relation to previous convictions (a matter then governed by s 1 of the Criminal Evidence Act 1898), and concluded that, where testifying would render a defendant liable to "loss of his shield", a judge could direct the jury in accordance with the standard JSB direction or an appropriate adaptation thereof and did not have to direct a jury as to this possible motive for failing to testify. However, a judge had an overriding discretion to decline to allow inferences to be drawn where he thought fairness so dictated in the circumstances of the particular case.

Their lordships noted that the problems arising in the appeal would generally cease to be material in view of the commencement of s 101 of the Criminal Justice Act 2003, but declined to express a view as to the possible effect of that provision on inferences from failure to testify.

14. *R v Condron* [1997] 1 WLR 827, [1997] Crim LR 215.

15. *R v Friend* [1997] 1 WLR 1433, [1997] 2 Cr App Rep 231, CA (defendant aged 14½, with a mental age of 9 or 10—held an inference could be drawn from his failure to give evidence).

16. *DPP v Kavanagh* [2005] EWHC 820 (Admin), [2006] Crim LR 370.

2–317 Effect of accused's failure or refusal to account for objects, substances or marks[1]. Justices may draw such inferences as appear proper from a failure or refusal of the accused to account for any object, substance or mark which is on him or in his possession when he is arrested[2]. No inference may be drawn however, if the accused had not been allowed an opportunity to consult a solicitor prior to being questioned or charged[3]. In a magistrates' court the inferences may be drawn when inquiring into an offence as examining justices, in determining whether the accused is guilty of the offence charged[4].

Section 36 of the Criminal Justice and Public Order Act 1994[5] provides that where—

(a) a person is arrested by a constable, and there is—

    (i) on his person; or

    (ii) in or on his clothing or footwear; or

    (iii) otherwise in his possession; or

    (iv) in any place in which he is at the time of his arrest, any object, substance or mark, or there is any mark on any such object; and

(b) that or another constable investigating the case reasonably believes that the presence of the object, substance or mark may be attributable to the participation of the person arrested in the commission of an offence specified by the constable; and

(c) the constable informs the person arrested that he so believes, and requests him to account for the presence of the object, substance or mark; and

(d) the person fails or refuses to do so,

then if, in any proceedings against the person for the offence so specified, evidence of those matters is given, the court may draw such inferences from the failure or refusal as appear proper.

These provisions do not apply unless the accused was told in ordinary language by the constable when making the request in paragraph (c) above what the effect of s 36 would be if he failed or refused to comply with the request[6]. The provisions apply in relation to officers of customs and excise as they apply to constables[7]. They also apply to the condition of clothing or footwear as they apply to a substance or mark thereon[8].

A person shall not have the proceedings against him committed to the Crown Court for trial, have a case to answer or be convicted of an offence solely on an inference drawn from a failure or a refusal for the purposes of s 36(2)[9].

Section 36 does not preclude the drawing of any inference from a failure or refusal of the accused to account for the presence of an object, substance or mark or from the condition of clothing or footwear which could properly be drawn apart from that section[10].

---

1. Under the Human Rights Act 1998, the Criminal Justice and Public Order Act 1994, s 36, so far as it is possible to do so, must be read and given effect in a way which is compatible with the Convention rights. See para **2–319**, post.
2. Criminal Justice and Public Order Act 1994, s 36, this PART, post.
3. Criminal Justice and Public Order Act 1994, s 34(2A), this PART, post.
4. Criminal Justice and Public Order Act 1994, s 36(2), this PART, post.
5. See this PART, post.
6. Criminal Justice and Public Order Act 1994, s 36(4), this PART, post.
7. Criminal Justice and Public Order Act 1994, s 36(5), this PART, post.
8. Criminal Justice and Public Order Act 1994, s 36(3), this PART, post.
9. Criminal Justice and Public Order Act 1994, s 38(3), this PART, post.
10. Criminal Justice and Public Order Act 1994, s 36(6), this PART, post.

2–318   Effect of accused's failure or refusal to account for presence at a particular place[1].
Justices may draw such inferences as appear proper from a failure or refusal of the accused to account for his presence at a particular place[2]. No inference may be drawn however, if the accused had not been allowed an opportunity to consult a solicitor prior to being questioned or charged[3]. In a magistrates' court the inferences may be drawn when inquiring into an offence as examining justices, in determining whether there is a case to answer, or in determining whether the accused is guilty of the offence charged[4].

Section 37 of the Criminal Justice and Public Order Act 1994[5] provides that where—

(a) a person arrested by a constable was found by him at a place at or about the time the offence for which he was arrested is alleged to have been committed; and

(b) that or another constable investigating the offence reasonably believes that the presence of the person at that place and at that time may be attributable to his participation in the commission of the offence; and

(c) the constable informs the person that he so believes, and requests him to account for that presence; and

(d) the person fails or refuses to do so,

then if, in any proceedings against the person for the offence, evidence of those matters is given, the court may draw such inferences from the failure or refusal as appear proper.

These provisions do not apply unless the accused was told in ordinary language by the constable when making the request in paragraph (c) above what the effect of s 37 would be if he failed or refused to comply with the request[6]. The provisions apply in relation to officers of customs and excise as they apply in relation to constables[7].

A person shall not have the proceedings against him committed to the Crown Court for trial, have a case to answer or be convicted of an offence solely on an inference drawn from a failure or a refusal for the purposes of s 37(2)[8].

Section 37 does not preclude the drawing of any inference from a failure or refusal of the accused to account for his presence at a place which could properly be drawn apart from that section[9].

For the purposes of s 37, "place" includes any building or part of a building, any vehicle, vessel, aircraft or hovercraft and any other place whatsoever[10].

---

1. Under the Human Rights Act 1998, the Criminal Justice and Public Order Act 1994, s 37, so far as it is possible to do so, must be read and given effect in a way which is compatible with the Convention rights. See para **2–319**, post.
2. Criminal Justice and Public Order Act 1994, s 37, this PART, post.
3. Criminal Justice and Public Order Act 1994, s 34(2A), this PART, post.
4. Criminal Justice and Public Order Act 1994, s 37(2), this PART, post.
5. See this PART, post.
6. Criminal Justice and Public Order Act 1994, s 37(3), this PART, post.
7. Criminal Justice and Public Order Act 1994, s 37(4), this PART, post.
8. Criminal Justice and Public Order Act 1994, s 38(3), this PART, post.
9. Criminal Justice and Public Order Act 1994, s 37(5), this PART, post.
10. Criminal Justice and Public Order Act 1994, s 38(1), this PART, post.

2–319   Drawing adverse inferences: the position under the European Convention on Human Rights. The European Court of Human Rights has implied a right of silence into Article 6 of the European Convention on Human Rights. The essence of the right is that the accused should be protected from improper compulsion by the authorities[1]. Where it applies, the rule against compulsion extends not only to the answering of questions but also to the imposition of a requirement, on pain of criminal sanctions, to produce documentation which would furnish evidence of offences which the authorities believe the individual has committed[2]. However, the right to silence under the Convention is not absolute; in some circumstances a court might legitimately draw inferences from silence[3]. A conviction should not be based solely or mainly on the silence of the accused, either during questioning or at trial[4]. However, immunity from self-incrimination does not prevent the silence of the accused being taken into account in circumstances where the facts call out for an explanation from him[5]. Safeguards such as a reason for drawing adverse inferences may also be important[6].

Fairness would seem to require that the court should not draw an adverse inference if it believes that the accused's silence at interview was for good reason based on the advice of his solicitor and that the silence could not be sensibly attributed to his having no answer to the questions, or none that would stand up to cross-examination[7].

1. *Murray v United Kingdom* (1996) 22 EHRR 29.
2. *Funke v France* (1993) 16 EHRR 297; *Saunders v United Kingdom* (1996) 23 EHRR 313. However, see *L v United Kingdom* [2000] 2 FCR 145, [2000] 2 FLR 322, ECtHR; and *A-G's Reference (No 7 of 2000)* [2001] EWCA Crim 888, [2001] 2 Cr App Rep 286.
3. *Murray v United Kingdom* (1996) 22 EHRR 29.
4. *Murray v United Kingdom* (1996) 22 EHRR 29. See also *Telfner v Austria* [2001] Crim LR 821, ECtHR.
5. *Murray v United Kingdom* (1996) 22 EHRR 29. See also; *Averill v United Kingdom* (2000) 8 BHRC 430, ECtHR. See also *R v Betts and Hall* [2001] EWCA Crim 224, [2001] 2 Cr App Rep 257.
6. *Murray v United Kingdom* (1996) 22 EHRR 29 at paras 51 and 52.
7. *Condron v United Kingdom* (2000) 8 BHRC 290, [2000] Crim LR 679 ECtHR; *Averill v United Kingdom* (2000) 8 BHRC 430, ECtHR. See also *R v Betts and Hall* [2001] EWCA Crim 224, [2001] 2 Cr App Rep 257.

DRAWING INFERENCES FROM THE ACCUSED'S LIES

2–330   Statements made out of court, for example statements to the police, which are proved and admitted to be false, may in certain circumstances amount to corroboration. The lie must first of all have been deliberate; secondly it must relate to a material issue; thirdly the motive must be a realisation of guilt and a fear of the truth; fourthly the statement must clearly be shown to be a lie by evidence other than that of the accomplice who is to be corroborated, that is by admission or by evidence from an independent witness[1]. Lies told in court may similarly provide corroboration provided they fulfil these four criteria[2]. Where the person is accused of two offences, assault and rape, his lie could only be corroboration if the court was satisfied that he was trying to lie his way out of the particular offence in question[17]. In general there is no conflict between the principles governing the drawing of adverse inferences from lies told out of court and those governing the inferences to be drawn under s 35 of the Criminal Justice and Public Order Act 1994[3] where the accused fails to give evidence. If the court is satisfied there is an innocent explanation for any of the lies, it will not hold that against him whether or not he gives evidence. If on the other hand, the court is satisfied that the failure to give evidence is to be explained only on the basis that the defendant cannot give an innocent explanation for the lies, it may draw an adverse inference[4].

1. *R v Lucas* [1981] QB 720, [1981] 2 All ER 1008, 145 JP 471.
2. *R v West* [1984] Crim LR 236.
3. In this PART, post.
4. *R v Napper* (1995) 161 JP 16, CA.

Evidence in civil proceedings

HEARSAY IN CIVIL PROCEEDINGS

2–340   In civil proceedings evidence shall not be excluded on the ground that it is hearsay[1]. Except in the case of hearsay evidence which is otherwise admissible, safeguards, laid down by the Civil Evidence Act 1995, in relation to the admission of such evidence must be observed[2].

1. Civil Evidence Act 1995, s 1, this PART, post.
2. Civil Evidence Act 1995, ss 2–4, this PART, post.

HEARSAY: CHILD CASES

2–341   The general rule that hearsay evidence is not admissible applies in civil proceedings involving children, unless the proceedings are of a kind prescribed by order[1] made by the Lord Chancellor under s 96 of the Children Act 1989. Subject to this exception, hearsay evidence of children cannot be admitted to prove the truth of the facts alleged, except by agreement, or pursuant to the provisions of the Civil Evidence Act 1968, which cannot apply to children too young to give sworn evidence, in cases involving custody or access[2]. It should be noted that the Civil Evidence Act 1968 Part I[3], relating to hearsay evidence, has not been brought into force in respect of proceedings before magistrates' courts, and instead reference should be made to the Evidence Act 1938[3]. The strict rules of evidence do not, however, apply in the wardship jurisdiction, and the High Court may admit hearsay evidence of children in wardship cases[4].

The Children (Admissibility of Hearsay Evidence) Order 1993 provides that in civil proceedings before the High Court or a county court and in family proceedings in a magistrates' court, evidence given in connection with the upbringing, maintenance or welfare of a child shall be admissible notwithstanding any rule of law relating to hearsay.

A further exception to the hearsay rule in child cases applies in relation to statements made to the court welfare officer and contained in his written report or in oral evidence to the court[5]. The reliance to be placed upon the report and the weight to be attached to information contained in it will be a matter for the court.

---

1. Children (Admissibility of Hearsay Evidence) Order 1993, SI 1993/621, in PART VI: FAMILY LAW, post.
2. *H v H, K v K (Child Abuse: Evidence)* [1990] Fam 86, [1989] 3 All ER 740, [1989] FCR 356, CA.
3. See this title, post.
4. See *Re K (Infants)* [1965] AC 201, [1963] 3 All ER 191, HL; and *H v H, K v K (Child Abuse: Evidence)* [1990] Fam 86, [1989] 3 All ER 740, [1989] FCR 356, CA.
5. See the Domestic Proceedings and Magistrates' Courts Act 1978, s 12(6), in PART VI: title FAMILY LAW, post. See also *Thompson v Thompson* (1975) [1986] 1 FLR 212n, CA.

Interpretation of statutes and statutory instruments

STATUTES AND STATUTORY INSTRUMENTS

2–350   General principles for the interpretation of Acts of Parliament and subordinate legislation and the meaning of many expressions commonly used in them, are established by case law and by the Interpretation Act 1978, post. Some further provision is made by the European Communities Act 1972, post for European Economic Community legislation.

Under the Human Rights Act 1998, all legislation (primary, subordinate and whenever enacted) must, if possible, be interpreted so as to be compatible with the European Convention on Human Rights[1]. This is a new rule of construction which is of general application[2].

Besides the public general Acts of Parliament (chapter number in large arabic numerals) there are local Acts (for example those promoted by local authorities or nationalised undertakings, chapter number in small roman numerals) and personal Acts (for example to disentail lands settled by Act of Parliament, chapter number in small italicised arabic numerals). They are all deemed "public Acts" and shall be judicially noticed as such[3].

The word "enactment" is to be distinguished from the word "Act"; the latter means "Act of Parliament" but the former can include something other than an Act, for example a regulation[4].

---

1. Human Rights Act 1998, s 3(1) in PART VIII: title HUMAN RIGHTS, post.
2. See para **2–353**, this PART post.
3. Interpretation Act 1978, s 3: as to statutory instruments, see the Statutory Instruments Act 1946, post.
4. See *DPP v Lamb* [1941] 2 KB 89, [1941] 2 All ER 499, 105 JP 251.

PARTS OF THE STATUTE

2–351   The title and preamble[1] can help in ascertaining the scope of the statute and supply the key to the meaning of doubtful or ambiguous expressions; if however the meaning is clear, it must not be restricted or contradicted by references to the long title[2].

Headings, cross-headings, side notes, punctuation and brackets are not treated as parts of the statute and must not be given the same weight as the words of the section themselves, nor be allowed to control them. A cross-heading may help to resolve ambiguities and act as a pointer towards Parliament's intention, but a side-note or punctuation may only rarely be so used[3].

A proviso makes an exception within the ambit only of its own section; it should be construed with the enacting part, and may indeed remove doubt as to its scope[4]. A schedule is completely part of the Act but in the event of a discrepancy between it and a section, the section must prevail[5].

The long title is the part beginning "An Act to . . .", stating the function of the Act, and should be distinguished from the short title which normally appears near the end of the sections and states "This Act may be cited as . . ." The short title is for identification, not description, and should not be used for the purpose of interpretation[6]. Public general Acts in modern times do not normally have preambles.

---

1. *A-G v HRH Prince Ernest Augustus of Hanover* [1957] AC 436, [1957] 1 All ER 49.
2. *Sage v Eichholz* [1919] All ER Rep 424 at 428; *R v Bates* [1952] 2 All ER 842, [1953] 1 WLR 77, CCA; *Fisher v Raven* [1964] AC 210, [1963] 2 All ER 389, 127 JP 383; *Ward v Holman* [1964] 2 QB 580, [1964] 2 All ER 729; *Brown v Brown* [1964] 2 All ER 828.
3. *Duke of Devonshire v O'Connor* (1890) 24 QBD 468, 54 JP 740; *R v Bates*, supra; *IRC v Hinchy* [1960] AC 748, [1960] 1 All ER 505; *DPP v Schildkamp* [1971] AC 1, [1969] 3 All ER 1640.
4. *West Derby Union v Metropolitan Life Assurance Society* [1897] AC 647, 61 JP 820.
5. *Re Baines* (1840) 1 Cr & Ph 31.
6. *Vacher & Sons v London Society of Compositors* [1913] AC 107.

OPERATION OF THE STATUTE

2–352   Acts of Parliament are cited by reference to the short title plus chapter number and calendar year or, prior to 1963, by the regnal year[1]. They come into force at the beginning of the day provided for commencement or when no such provision is made, at the beginning of the day on which they receive Royal Assent[2]. Statutes are not to be construed as having retrospective operation unless such a construction is plainly indicated by the particular Act or arises by necessary implication. Where an enactment relates to procedure then ordinarily it affects proceedings after its commencement even though they may relate to events before its commencement[3].

Repeal does not revive earlier repealed enactments nor will it affect existing matters which have arisen under the repealed enactment such as rights, obligations, penalties unless the repeal provision says so, and provision is made for unbroken progression between repeal and re-enactment[4]. An enactment may be repealed by express words in a later statute—for which no particular form of words is necessary—and that later statute often re-enact or consolidates earlier provisions, or repeal may be inferred in the case of irreconcilable conflict between two Acts, where it has been found impossible to construe the provisions so as to give effect to both[5]. The presumption in the case of a consolidating Act is that the legislature intended to reproduce the existing position[6]. Where an Act incorporates part of an earlier statute which is then repealed, that repeal will not take away the effect of the incorporated words in the later Act[7].

The declaration in s 16(1) of the Interpretation Act 1978 that the repeal of an enactment does not affect any "obligation or liability acquired" under the repealed enactment applies to criminal as well as civil proceedings[8].

Where HM Customs and Excise erroneously applied for forfeiture of cash under s 26 of the Criminal Justice (International Co-operation) Act 1990 and the magistrates' court made a forfeiture order under that provision when it had in fact already been repealed, it was held that, since the defendant had not been misled or prejudiced by reference to the wrong statute instead of its re-enacted successor, the maxim *falso demonstratio non nocet* should apply to save the application for forfeiture mistakenly made under the repealed s 26[9].

Courts lean strongly against interpreting criminal legislation as retrospective; the retrospective application of increased penalties to offences already completed is prohibited by the European Convention on Human Rights, Article 7 and the UN Covenant on Civil and Political Rights, Article 15[10]. The Divisional Court has looked disapprovingly at a court adjourning a case to the following day as it considered a change in the law coming into force then would enable it to do better justice[11].

The Crown Court will hear a case committed to it even though a change in the law has made the offence triable summarily only[12].

Where an Act provides for commencement on a date to be appointed by some person, it may require that he shall make his appointment by a certain date. Where no such provision is made, the Secretary of State has a power not a duty to appoint a day. The power is to be exercised to bring sections into force when it is appropriate to do so[13].

1. See the Acts of Parliament Numbering and Citation Act 1962.
2. Interpretation Act 1978, s 4, this PART, post.
3. *R v Chandra Dharma* [1905] 2 KB 335, 69 JP 198 (time for commencing prosecution); *National Real Estate and Finance Co Ltd v Hassan* [1939] 2 KB 61, [1939] 2 All ER 154 (service of counter-notice in landlord and tenant proceedings); *DPP v Lamb* [1941] 2 KB 39, [1941] 2 All ER 499, 105 JP 251 (higher penalty).
4. See the Interpretation Act 1978, ss 15–17, this PART, post.
5. *Hill v Hall* (1876) 1 Ex D 411, 41 JP 183.
6. *Gilbert v Gilbert and Boucher* [1928] P 1.
7. *R v Smith* (1873) LR 8 QB 146, 37 JP 214; *Jenkins v Great Central Rly Co* [1912] 1 KB 1.
8. *Aitken v South Hams District Council* [1995] 1 AC 262, [1994] 3 All ER 400, 159 JP 25, HL (notice served under s 58(1) of the Control of Pollution Act 1974 held to remain effective and to be enforceable notwithstanding the repeal of that Act).
9. *R v Dover Magistrates' Court, ex p Webb* (1998) 162 JP 295.
10. See *Waddington v Miah* [1974] 2 All ER 377, 138 JP 497; *Thomson Yellow Pages Ltd v Pugh* (1974) 119 Sol Jo 233; *R v Deery* [1977] Crim LR 550; *R v Penrith Justices, ex p Hay* [1979] LS Gaz R 847.
11. *R v Walsall Justices, ex p W* [1990] 1 QB 253, [1989] 3 All ER 460, 153 JP 624.
12. *R v Crown Court at Leeds, ex p Wood* (1989) Times, 17 July, DC.
13. *R v Secretary of State for the Home Department, ex p Fire Brigades Union* [1995] 2 AC 513, [1995] 2 All ER 244, [1995] NLJR 521, HL.

CONSTRUCTION GENERALLY

2–353 Under the Human Rights Act 1998, so far as it is possible to do so, primary legislation and subordinate legislation must be read and given effect in a way which is compatible with the rights protected by the European Convention on Human Rights[1]. This applies to all legislation, whenever enacted. Courts must strive to find a construction consistent with the intentions of Parliament and the wording of legislation which is nearest to the Convention rights protected under the Act[2]. Courts should proceed on the basis that Parliament is deemed to have intended its statutes to be compatible with the Convention to which the UK is bound: the only basis for courts concluding that Parliament has failed to carry that intention into effect is where it is impossible to construe a statute so as to be compatible with the Convention[3].

This rule of construction applies to past as well as to future legislation. To the extent that it affects the meaning of a legislative provision, courts will not be bound by previous interpretations. They will be able to build a new body of case law taking into account the Convention rights[4].

For legislation passed after the Human Rights Act 1998 becomes law, the Act provides that the minister in charge of a Bill in either House of Parliament must make and publish a written statement to the effect either that in his view the provisions of the Bill are compatible with Convention rights or that although he is unable to make such a statement the Government nevertheless wishes the House to proceed with the Bill[5].

Where it simply is not possible to interpret primary legislation so as to be compatible with the Convention, the courts have no power to strike it down. However, the House of Lords, Judicial Committee of the Privy Council, Court of Appeal and the High (and the High Court of Justiciary in

Scotland) have power to make a "declaration of incompatibility" which is intended to prompt government action. Such a declaration does not affect the validity, continuing operation or enforcement of the provision in respect of which it is made[6]. Nor does it bind the parties to the proceedings in which it is made[7].

When the court is considering the compatibility of primary legislation with Convention rights, it must identify the policy objective of the legislation and assess whether the means employed to achieve that objective were proportionate to any adverse effects of the legislation; in doing so the court is entitled, if necessary, to have regard to relevant background material, including ministerial statements and explanatory departmental notes when the Bill was proceeding through Parliament; it is not for courts, however, to consider the quality or sufficiency of Parliament's reasons for passing a particular enactment; the aforementioned sources may be considered, but for the strictly limited purpose of assessing the compatibility of the legislation with Convention rights, which is an exercise that the court may wish to perform to determine, for example, whether the aim of the legislation is legitimate one[8].

Where it simply is not possible to interpret subordinate legislation so as to be compatible with the Convention, the courts have power to disapply it. The only exception is where primary legislation prevents the removal of any incompatibility[9].

Where no question of compatibility with Convention rights arises, other rules of construction prevail. Acts of Parliament are to be construed according to the intention of Parliament, which is to be sought only in the words used in the Act unless they are imprecise and ambiguous[10]. The grammatical, ordinary and natural sense of all the words, read in the context of the statute in which they appear, is to be used. Where the meaning is plain, then it must be adopted, however inconvenient that may seem. Where the words are ambiguous, then the meaning which avoids being unreasonable, inconvenient, absurd or inconsistent within the statute should be adopted[11]. If a statute enlarges or restricts the ordinary meaning by way of definition, that will govern what is proposed, authorised or done under or by reference to that statute[12].

Where once words in an Act of Parliament have received a judicial construction in one of the superior courts and the legislature has repeated them without any alteration in a subsequent statute, the legislature must be taken to have used them according to the meaning thus given them[13], but this rule of interpretation is to be regarded as a valuable presumption only[14].

Where two or more Acts are by express provision to be read together, or construed as one, every part of each of them must be construed as if it had been contained in one Act, unless there is some manifest discrepancy[15]: a provision that they may be cited together has not the same effect[16].

A court considering the ordinary meaning of words may take into account decisions on their meaning in other statutes. If the words have special meanings or definitions, then only statutes dealing with the same specific subject matter may be called in aid[17].

Penal statutes are construed according to the letter, but where a literal reading produces an unintelligible result, the court can seek an alternative, intelligible meaning, even if it is detrimental to the defendant[18], subject to the provisions of the Human Rights Act 1998. If two meanings are possible, the more lenient one should be adopted[19]. Specific provision is made to prevent punishment twice for the same offence[20].

Masculine includes feminine, singular includes plural, and vice versa in each case[21].

Where general words follow particular ones the rule is to construe them as applicable only to objects *eiusdem generis* with those previously stated[22].

Subject to the provisions of the Human Rights Act 1998, where the meaning of an Act is in doubt, one should adopt the meaning which best leads to the suppression of the mischief and the advancement of the remedy which the legislature had in view[23]. The grammatical and ordinary sense of words may be modified so as to avoid absurdity and inconsistence but no further[24]; given a choice a court will adopt the interpretation not leading to absurdity, but it has nothing to do with the policy of an Act which it may be called upon to interpret, even where difficulties, extravagant results or even most fantastic results are produced[25].

Where the draftsman failed to use language apt to achieve the clear intention of the legislature, it is permissible for the court to use its interpretative powers to read words into the relevant provisions to give effect to that intention[26].

Applying the *eiusdem generis* rule, "all signals, warning signposts, direction posts, signs or other devices" did not include a painted line[27], the sentence "in all times of public processions, rejoicings or illuminations, and in any case when the streets are liable to be obstructed" did not entitle a local authority to create a six-month one-way traffic system[28]; the rule did not apply to the phrase "no theatre or other place of public entertainment"[29], "quay or other place"[30], "all parochial or other rates"[31], "pieces of coal and other obstructions"[32]. The rule will always give way to the clearly ascertained intention of Parliament in the enactment in question.

Subject to any question of Parliamentary privilege, a court may make reference to Parliamentary materials, such as Hansard, where (*a*) legislation is ambiguous or obscure, or leads to an absurdity; (*b*) the material relied upon consists of one or more statements by a minister or other promoter of the Bill together, if necessary, with such other Parliamentary material as is necessary to understand such statements and their effect; and (*c*) the statements relied upon are clear[33]. However, it is questionable to use this material in criminal proceedings as it is arguable that if a criminal statute is ambiguous, the defendant should have the benefit of the ambiguity[34]. In construing a statutory instrument it is also legitimate for a court for the purpose of ascertaining the intention of Parliament to take into account the terms in which the draft regulations were presented by the responsible minister and which formed the basis of its acceptance[35].

Reports of commissioners, including law commissioners, and white papers may be looked at for the purpose solely of ascertaining the mischief which the statute is intended to cure but not for the purpose of discovering the meaning of the words used by Parliament to effect such cure[36]. From the 1998-1999 Parliamentary session, Explanatory Notes have been published with public bills and revised as the bill proceeds through its legislative stages. These notes may be referred to by courts as an aid to the construction of provisions of the Act. Insofar as they cast light on the objective setting or contextual scene of the statute, and the mischief at which it is aimed, they are admissible as aids to construction. However, it is impermissible to treat the wishes and desires of the Government about the scope of the statutory language as reflecting the will of Parliament. The object is to see what is the intention expressed by the words enacted[37].

1. Human Rights Act 1998, s 3(1) in PART VIII: title HUMAN RIGHTS, post.
2. Lord Chancellor. HL Official Report, col 535, 18 November.
3. Lord Chancellor. HL Official Report, col 535, 18 November.
4. White Paper: *Rights Brought Home: The Human Rights Bill* (1997, Cm 7382) para 3.2.
5. Human Rights Act, s 19 in PART VIII: title HUMAN RIGHTS, post.
6. Human Rights Act, s 4(6)(*a*) in PART VIII: title HUMAN RIGHTS, post.
7. Human Rights Act, s 4(6)(*b*) in PART VIII: title HUMAN RIGHTS, post.
8. *Wilson v First County Trust Ltd (No 2)* [2003] UKHL 40, [2004] 1 AC 816, [2003] 3 WLR 568.
9. Human Rights Act, s 4(4)(*b*) in PART VIII: title HUMAN RIGHTS, post.
10. *Sussex Peerage Case* (1844) 11 Cl & Fin 85.
11. *Grey v Pearson* [1843–60] All ER Rep 21 at 36.
12. *Wyre Forest District Council v Secretary of State for the Environment* [1990] 2 AC 357, [1990] 1 All ER 780, HL.
13. Per James LJ in *Re Cathcart, ex p Campbell* (1870) 5 Ch App 703; cf *Young v Gentle* [1915] 2 KB 661, 79 JP 347; *Trebanog Working Men's Club and Institute Ltd v Macdonald* [1940] 1 KB 576, [1940] 1 All ER 454, 104 JP 171.
14. *Barras v Aberdeen Steam Trawling and Fishing Co Ltd* [1933] AC 402, HL.
15. *Canada Southern Rly Co v International Bridge Co* (1883) 8 App Cas 723; *Hart v Hudson Bros Ltd* [1928] 2 KB 629, 92 JP 170.
16. *Vacher & Sons Ltd v London Society of Compositors* [1913] AC 107.
17. See eg *Goodman v J Eban Ltd* [1954] 1 QB 550, [1954] 1 All ER 763 ("sign"); *Goldsmith's Co v Wyatt* [1907] 1 KB 95 ("plate"); *J M Knowles Ltd v Rand* [1962] 2 All ER 926, [1962] 1 WLR 893, 126 JP 442 ("agriculture").
18. *R v Oakes* [1959] 2 QB 350, [1959] 2 All ER 92, 123 JP 290; *Kennedy v Spratt* [1972] AC 83, [1971] 2 All ER 805.
19. *Re HPC Productions Ltd* [1962] Ch 466, [1962] 1 All ER 37.
20. Interpretation Act 1978, s 18, this PART, post.
21. Interpretation Act 1978, s 6, this PART, post.
22. *Sandiman v Breach* (1827) 7 B & C 96.
23. *Warburton v Loveland* (1832) 6 Bli NS 1.
24. *Grey v Pearson*, supra.
25. *Vacher & Sons Ltd v London Society of Compositors*, supra; *Barnard v Gorman* [1941] AC 378, [1941] 3 All ER 45, JP 379; *IRC v Hinchy* [1960] 1 All ER 505 at 512; *Hewison v Skegness UDC* [1963] 1 QB 584, [1963] 1 All ER 205, 127 JP 118.
26. *Inco Europe Ltd v First Choice Distribution (a firm)* [2000] 2 All ER 109, [2000] 1 WLR 586). See also *R (on the application of the Crown Prosecution Service) v Bow Street Magistrates' Court (James and others, interested parties)* [2006] EWHC 1763 (Admin), [2006] 4 All ER 1342, [2007] 1 WLR 291.
27. *Evans v Cross* [1938] 1 KB 694, [1938] 1 All ER 751.
28. *Brownsea Haven Properties Ltd v Poole Corpn* [1958] Ch 574, [1958] 1 All ER 205, 122 JP 97.
29. *Allen v Emmerson* [1944] KB 362, [1944] 1 All ER 344, 108 JP 220.
30. *Roe v Hemmings* [1951] 1 KB 676, [1951] 1 All ER 389, 115 JP 126.
31. *Re Ellwood* [1927] 1 Ch 455.
32. *Alexander v Tredegar Iron and Coal Co Ltd* [1945] AC 286, [1945] 2 All ER 275.
33. *Pepper v Hart* [1993] AC 593, [1993] 1 All ER 42, HL. See also *Practice Directions: (Hansard extracts)* (1994) Times, 31 December, CA. See also *Wilson v First County Trust Ltd (No 2)*, supra, in which Lord Hope, at para 113, explained that the purpose of the decision in *Pepper v Hart* "(was) to prevent the executive seeking to place a meaning on words used in legislation which (was) different from that which ministers attributed to those words when promoting the legislation in Parliament ... the exception thus stated has commanded broad acceptance where it has operated as a kind of quasi-estoppel against the executive"; it is not for the courts to consider the quality or sufficiency of Parliament's reasons for passing a particular enactment, but the court may consider a variety of sources of information for the strictly limited purpose of considering the compatibility of legislation with Convention rights, which is an exercise the court may wish to perform to determine, for example, whether the aim of the legislation is a legitimate one. At para 66, Lord Nicholls stated: "I expect that occasions when resort to Hansard is necessary as part of the statutory 'compatibility' exercise will seldom arise".
34. *Soe Thet v DPP* 19 October 2006, unreported, Admin, per Lord Phillips, LCJ.
35. *Pickstone v Freemans plc* [1989] AC 66, HL.
36. *Eastman Photographic Materials Co Ltd v Comptroller-General of Patents, Designs and Trademarks* [1898] AC 571 HL(E); *Assam Railways and Trading Co Ltd v IRC* [1935] AC 445 HL(E).
37. See *R (on the application of Westminster City Council) v National Asylum Support Service* [2002] UKHL 38, [2002] 4 All ER 654, [2002] 1 WLR 2956, per Lord Steyn and see the article by R Munday at 170 JPN 124.

PARTICULAR WORDS

2–354 Many words and expressions are defined by the Interpretation Act 1978[1], it is also unusual for any Act of Parliament these days not to have a definition section either for the entire Act or for each Part, or even for a single section or for all of these[2]. In appropriate circumstances the meaning of words having an especial significance throughout a statute or group of statutes is discussed in this work in an introductory note[3].

"And" in ordinary language is conjunctive and "or" is disjunctive but they may exchange functions in certain contexts[4].

"Shall" and "must" in ordinary language are imperative; "may" is permissive. Where the context of particular statutes has required it, however, the courts have often departed from this rule in respect of these and similar expression[5]. Enabling words become compulsory when the power conferred thereby is coupled with a duty to exercise it[6].

The distinction between felony and misdemeanour has been abolished and the law relating to the latter applied to the former; the word "offence" is now to be read for both[7].

---

1. See Interpretation Act 1978, ss 5–11 and Sch 1, this PART, post.
2. In general in this Manual we print all the relevant parts of definition sections.
3. See for example the general notes to PART VI: FAMILY LAW, and PART IV: ROAD TRAFFIC, post.
4. See for disjunctive "and", *R v Oakes* [1959] 2 QB 350, [1959] 2 All ER 92, 123 JP 290; *John G Stein & Co Ltd v O'Hanlon* [1965] AC 890, [1965] 1 All ER 547, and for conjunctive "or" see *Re Mills, ex p Bankrupt v Official Receiver* [1966] 1 All ER 516; *Vernon v Paddon* [1973] 3 All ER 302, 137 JP 758; *Federal Steam Navigation Co Ltd v Department of Trade and Industry* [1974] 2 All ER 97 ("the owner or master shall be guilty of an offence" meant both could be prosecuted).
5. *Re Newport Bridge* (1859) 2 E & E 377, 24 JP 133 ("shall and may be lawful"); *Julius v Lord Bishop of Oxford* (1860) 5 App Cas 214, 44 JP 600 ("it shall be lawful"); *R v Mitchell, ex p Livesey* [1913] 1 KB 561, 77 JP 148 ("may"); *R v Spelthorne Justices, ex p Freeman* (1928) 92 JP Jo 362 ("may").
6. *R v Roberts* [1901] 2 KB 117, 65 JP 359; *Dawson v Dawson* (1929) 93 JP 187; *Sheffield Corpn v Luxford* [1929] 2 KB 180, 93 JP 235; *R v Worcestershire Justices, ex p Lower Avon Navigation Co Ltd* (1939) 103 JP 223.
7. Criminal Law Act 1967, s 1 in PART I: MAGISTRATES' COURTS, PROCEDURE, ante.

TIME

2–355 An expression of time in an Act means, in the absence of contrary statement, Greenwich mean time[1]; summer time is one hour in advance of that and during that period references to time must be so taken to mean that[2], with savings for astronomy, meteorology and navigation[2].

The word "year" may be used in a statute to mean either the calendar year January 1st to December 31st or some other period of 365 days; its meaning is a matter of construction for the courts[3]. The word "month" means a calendar month[4], although in pre-1851 statutes the term "lunar month" may be found, meaning a period of twenty-eight days. The word "week" may mean the calendar week beginning on Sunday and ending on Saturday, or any period of seven days; the court must construe the word according to the statute. A day normally runs from midnight to midnight, but in certain contexts can mean a period of twenty-four hours, or the period between sunrise and sunset. Sunrise and sunset are expressions of fact which vary according to the locality and the court should hear evidence thereon[5], but it would appear that the court can take judicial notice of such times by perusal of an almanac[6] although in borderline cases the inference which can be drawn from such a perusal may be insufficient to satisfy the court[7].

The running of a statutory period often excludes the first day and includes the last day[8], but a number of phrases and words have been construed as meaning clear days, thus excluding the day of the commencing event and the day of the resulting happening[9]. The days in any period of time are consecutive days and include Sundays, unless the statute says otherwise[10] but the term "weekdays" does not include Sunday[11]. Courts take notice of fractions of a day only to show which was the first of two acts[12] or to resolve conflicting rights[13]. Judicial acts relate back to the earliest moment of the day on which they are performed; they will therefore be given precedence over non-judicial acts which in point of time they follow[14].

Where an Act requires something to be done "immediately" or "forthwith", according to the context and the circumstances it means any reasonable time thereafter; the two words mean the same[15] and what is reasonable is a matter for the court to decide in all the circumstances[16]. When the time within which a person is required to act is fixed by reference to a period of months or calendar months from a particular date, the specified period elapses on the corresponding day of the month of expiry, and no account should be taken of the fact that some months are longer or shorter than others; thus a three month notice given on 30th April will expire on 30th July; but if the relevant calendar month in which a period expires is too short to provide a corresponding date, the period expires on the last day of that month: thus a three month notice given on 31st January will expire on 30th April[17].

Civil and criminal cases are treated the same as to computation of time[18].

---

1. Interpretation Act 1978, s 9, this PART, post.
2. See the Summer Time Act 1972, ss 1, 3 and the period which may be stated by Order thereunder.
3. Note however the Interpretation Act 1978, Sch 1 (financial year).
4. Interpretation Act 1978, Sch 1; see also the Prison Act 1952, s 24(1).
5. *Gordon v Cann* (1899) 68 LJQB 434, 63 JP 32, and see 62 JP Jo 484 and 80 JP Jo 110.
6. Compare *Walker v Stretton* (1896) 60 JP 313.
7. See commentary in *R v Crush* [1978] Crim LR 357. For special definitions see the Night Poaching Act 1828, s 12 ("night"), the Game Act 1831, s 34 ("daytime"), in PART VIII: title GAME, post.
8. Note especially the making of a complaint for an order (*Radcliffe v Bartholomew* [1892] 1 QB 161 "within one calendar month" approved as a general principle in *Marren v Dawson Bentley & Co Ltd* [1961] 2 QB 135, [1961] 2 All ER 270 "after the expiration of"; see also *Cartwright v MacCormack* [1963] 1 All ER 11 "the duration of this cover note shall not be more than Fifteen Days from the date of commencement of insurance stated herein"; in *Trow v Ind Coope (West Midlands) Ltd* [1967] 2 QB 899, [1967] 2 All ER 900 the phrase "beginning with the date" included the first day in a limitation period for service of a writ.
9. For example see *R v Long* [1960] 1 QB 681, [1959] 3 All ER 559 "at least three days"; *R v Turner* [1910] 1 KB 346, 74 JP 81 "not less than seven days notice"; *Warr v Warr* [1975] Fam 25, [1975] 1 All ER 85 "continuous period of at least two years immediately preceding the presentation of the petition".

10. *Peacock v R* (1858) 4 CBNS 264; *Ex p Simpkin* (1859) 9 E & E 392, 24 JP 262; *Woodhouse v Woods* (1859) 23 JP 759; *R v Greville* (1929) 21 Cr App Rep 108. "Daily" includes Sunday (*LCC v South Metropolitan Gas Co* [1904] 1 Ch 76, 68 JP 102).

11. *LCC v Gainsborough* [1923] 2 KB 301, 87 JP 102. As to "income tax weeks" see eg definition in s 99 of the Social Security Act 1973.

12. *Campbell v Strangeways* (1877) 3 CPD 105, 42 JP 39 (person who bought a dog licence at 1 p.m. convicted of keeping dog without licence at noon).

13. *Tomlinson v Bullock* (1879) 4 QBD 230, 43 JP 508; *Kruhlak v Kruhlak (No 2)* [1958] 2 All ER 294, 122 JP 360, compare *Clarke v Bradlaugh* (1881) 7 QBD 151, 46 JP 118.

14. *Re Warren, ex p Wheeler v Trustee in Bankruptcy* [1938] Ch 725, [1938] 2 All ER 331, and see also *Kruhlak v Kruhlak*, supra.

15. Per COCKBURN LCJ in *R v Berkshire Justices* (1879) 4 QBD 469, 43 JP 607.

16. In *Hillingdon London Borough v Cutler* [1968] 1 QB 124, [1967] 2 All ER 361, 131 JP 361 a delay of over six months was held to be reasonable whereas in *Re Muscovitch, ex p Muscovitch* [1939] Ch 694, [1939] 1 All ER 135 a delay of seven days was not. In *R v Immigration Appeal Tribunal, ex p Samaraweera* [1974] 2 All ER 171, [1974] 1 WLR 487 the Divisional Court considered the meaning of "as soon as practicable".

17. *Dodds v Walker* [1981] 2 All ER 609, [1981] 1 WLR 1027, HL.

18. See *Radcliffe v Bartholomew* and *Marren v Dawson Bentley & Co Ltd*, supra.

Statutes on Evidence and Interpretation

Witnesses Act 1806[1]
(46 Geo 3 c 37)

2–760   1. Witnesses cannot refuse to answer questions tending to establish their indebtedness, etc.   A witness cannot by law refuse to answer a question[2] relevant to the matter in issue, the answering of which has no tendency to accuse himself or to expose him to penalty or forfeiture of any nature whatsoever, by reason only or on the sole ground that the answering of such question may establish or tend to establish that he owes a debt, or is otherwise subject to a civil suit either at the instance of his Majesty or of any other person or persons.
[Witnesses Act 1806, s 1.]

---

1. The Short Titles Act 1896 provided for this Act to be cited with other Acts as the Evidence Acts 1806 to 1895; those other Acts which are printed in this Manual are the Evidence Act 1843, the Evidence Act 1845, the Evidence Act 1851, the Evidence Amendment Act 1853, the Documentary Evidence Act 1868, the Documentary Evidence Act 1882.

2. Read this provision together with the Civil Evidence Act 1968, ss 14(1) and 16(1), this PART, post.

Statutory Declarations Act 1835[1]
(5 & 6 Will 4 c 62)

2–770   7. Oaths in courts of justice, etc, still to be taken.   Provided also, . . . that nothing in this Act contained shall extend or apply to any oath, solemn affirmation, or affidavit, which now is or hereafter may be made or taken, or be required to be made or taken, in any judicial proceeding in any court of justice, or in any proceeding for or by way of summary conviction before any justice or justices of the peace; but all such oaths, affirmations, and affidavits shall continue to be required, and to be administered, taken, and made, as well and in the same manner as if this Act had not been passed.
[Statutory Declarations Act 1835, s 7, as amended by the Statute Law Revision (No 2) Act 1888.]

---

1. Only those provisions of the Act which are relevant to justices of the peace and the work of magistrates' courts are included in this manual.

2–771   13. Justices, etc, not to administer oaths, etc, touching matters whereof they have no jurisdiction by statute—Proviso as to certain oaths.   . . . It shall not be lawful[1] for any justice of the peace[2] or other person to administer or cause to allow to be administered, or to receive or cause or allow to be received, any oath, affidavit, or solemn affirmation touching any matter or thing whereof such justice or other person hath not jurisdiction or cognisance by some statute in force at the time being: Provided always, that nothing herein contained shall be construed to extend to any oath, affidavit, or solemn affirmation before any justice in any matter or thing touching the preservation of the peace, or the prosecution, trial, or punishment of offences, or touching any proceedings before either of the Houses of Parliament or any committee thereof respectively, nor to any oath, affidavit, or affirmation which may be required by the laws of any foreign country to give validity to instruments in writing designed to be used in such foreign countries respectively.
[Statutory Declarations Act 1835, s 13, as amended by the Statute Law Revision Act 1890.]

---

1. An offence consisting in contravention of this section is triable either way (Magistrates' Courts Act 1980, Sch 1, in PART I: MAGISTRATES' COURTS, PROCEDURE, ante). For procedure in respect of an offence which is triable either way, see the Magistrates' Courts Act 1980, ss 17A–21, in PART I: MAGISTRATES' COURTS, PROCEDURE, ante.

2. See also ss 15 and 18 post as to the power of justices and other persons to receive declarations.

2–772   **15. Declarations substituted for oaths and affidavits required by 5 Geo 2 c 7, and 54 Geo 3 c 15.** . . . In any action or suit . . . brought or intended to be brought in any court of law or equity within any of the territories, plantations, colonies, or dependencies abroad, being within and part of his Majesty's dominions, for or relating to any debt or account, wherein any person residing in Great Britain and Ireland shall be a party, or for or relating to any lands, tenements, or hereditaments or other property situate, lying, and being in the said places respectively, it shall and may be lawful to and for the plaintiff or defendant, and also to and for any witness to be examined or made use of in such action or suit, to verify or prove any matter or thing relating thereto by solemn declaration or declarations in writing in the form in the schedule hereunto annexed, made before any justice of the peace, notary public, or other officer now by law authorised to administer an oath, and certified and transmitted under the signature and seal of any such justice, notary public duly admitted and practising, or other officer; which declaration, and every declaration relative to such matter or thing as aforesaid, in any foreign kingdom or state, or to the voyage of any ship or vessel, every such justice of the peace, notary public, or other officer shall be and he is hereby authorised and empowered to administer or receive; and every declaration so made, certified, and transmitted, shall in all such actions and suits be allowed to be of the same force and effect, as if the person or persons making the same had appeared and sworn or affirmed the matters contained in such declaration viva voce in open court, or upon a commission issued for the examination of witnesses or of any party in such action or suit respectively; provided that in every such declaration there shall be expressed the addition of the party making such declaration and the particular place of his or her abode.
[Statutory Declarations Act 1835, s 15, as amended by the Statute Law Revision Act 1890 and the Statute Law Revision Act 1892.]

2–773   **16. Declaration in writing sufficient to prove execution of any will, codicil, etc.** . . . It shall and may be lawful to and for any attesting witness to the execution of any will or codicil, deed or instrument in writing, and to and for any other competent person, to verify and prove the signing, sealing, publication, or delivery of any such will, codicil, deed, or instrument in writing, by such declaration in writing made as aforesaid; and every such justice, notary, or other officer shall be and is hereby authorised and empowered to administer or receive such declaration.
[Statutory Declarations Act 1835, s 16, as amended by the Statute Law Revision (No 2) Act 1888.]

2–774   **18. Voluntary declaration in the form in the schedule may be taken—Making false declaration a misdemeanor[1].** . . . It shall and may be lawful for any justice of the peace, notary public, or other officer now by law authorised to administer an oath, to take and receive the declaration of any person voluntarily making the same before him in the form in the schedule to this Act annexed . . .
[Statutory Declarations Act 1835, s 18, as amended by the Statute Law Revision (No 2) Act 1890 and the Perjury Act 1911, ss 17, 18 and Sch.]

---

1. This offence is now contained in the Perjury Act 1911, s 5, in PART VIII: title PERJURY, post.

2–775   **19. Fees payable on oath shall be paid on declarations substituted in lieu thereof.** . . . Whenever any declaration shall be made and subscribed by any person or persons under or in pursuance of the provisions of this Act or any of them, all and every such fees or fee as would have been due and payable on the taking or making any legal oath, solemn affirmation, or affidavit shall be in like manner due and payable upon making and subscribing such declaration.
[Statutory Declarations Act 1835, s 19, as amended by the Statute Law Revision (No 2) Act 1888.]

2–776   **20. Declarations to be in the form prescribed in schedule[1].** . . . In all cases where a declaration in lieu of an oath shall have been substituted by this Act, or by virtue of any power or authority hereby given, or where a declaration is directed or authorised to be made and subscribed under the authority of this Act, or of any power hereby given, although the same be not substituted in lieu of an oath heretofore legally taken, such declaration, unless otherwise directed under the powers hereby given, shall be in the form prescribed in the schedule hereunto annexed.
[Statutory Declarations Act 1835, s 20, as amended by the Statute Law Revision (No 2) Act 1888.]

---

1. For the prescribed form of statutory declaration, see PART IX: PRECEDENTS AND FORMS, EVIDENCE, post.

2–777   SCHEDULE
Prescribed form of statutory declaration[1]

---

1. For the prescribed form of statutory declaration, see PART IX: PRECEDENTS AND FORMS, EVIDENCE, post.

Evidence Act 1845
(8 & 9 Vict c 113)

2–790   **1. Certain documents purporting to be sealed, signed, etc, to be received in evidence without proof of seal or signature etc, of person signing the same, where the original record could have been received.**   Whenever by any Act now in force or hereafter to be in force any certificate, official or public document[1], or document or proceeding of any corporation or joint

stock or other company, or any certified copy of any document, bye law, entry in any register or other book, or of any other proceeding, shall be receivable in evidence of any particular in any court of justice, or before any legal tribunal, or either House of Parliament, or any committee of either House, or in any judicial proceeding, the same shall respectively be admitted in evidence, provided they respectively purport to be sealed or impressed with a stamp or sealed and signed, or signed alone, as required, or impressed with a stamp and signed, as directed by the respective Acts made or to be hereafter made, without any proof of the seal or stamp, where a seal or stamp is necessary, or of the signature or of the official character of the person appearing to have signed the same, and without any further proof thereof, in every case in which the original record could have been received in evidence.
[Evidence Act 1845, s 1.]

1. A public document is a document made by a public officer for the purpose of the public making use of it and being able to refer to it (*Sturla v Freccia* (1880) 5 App Cas 623; *Lilley v Pettit* [1946] KB 401, [1946] 1 All ER 593. A document made for a temporary purpose is not a public document (*Mercer v Denne* [1905] 2 Ch 538, 70 JP 65).

2–791   2. Courts, etc, to take judicial notice of signatures of judges attached to decrees, etc.
All courts, judges, masters in chancery, masters of courts, commissioners judicially acting, and other judicial officers, shall henceforth take judicial notice of the signature of any of the judges of the High Court and Court of Appeal, provided such signature be attached or appended to any decree, order, certificate, or other judicial or official document.
[Evidence Act 1845, s 2, as amended by the Statute Law Revision Act 1891 and the Supreme Court of Judicature (Consolidation) Act 1925, s 224(1).]

2–792   3. Queen's printers' copies of private Acts etc, admissible.   All copies of private and local and personal Acts of Parliament not public Acts[1] if purporting to be printed by the Queen's printers[2], and all copies of the journals of either House of Parliament, and of royal proclamations, purporting to be printed by the printers to the crown or by the printers to either House of Parliament, or by any or either of them, shall be admitted as evidence thereof by all courts, judges, justices, and others without any proof being given that such copies were so printed.
[Evidence Act 1845, s 3, as amended by the Statute Law Revision Act 1891.]

1. Public Acts are to be judicially noticed by virtue of the Interpretation Act 1978, s 3, post.
2. This provision is applied to HMSO by the Documentary Evidence Act 1882, s 2, post.

Evidence Act 1851
(14 & 15 Vict c 99)

2–810   2. Parties to be admissible witnesses.   On the trial of any issue joined, or of any matter or question, or on any inquiry arising in any suit, action or other proceeding in any court of justice, or before any person having by law, or by consent of parties, authority to hear, receive, and examine evidence, the parties thereto and the persons in whose behalf any such suit, action, or other proceeding may be brought or defended, shall, except as hereinafter excepted, be competent and compellable to give evidence, either viva voce or by deposition, according to the practice of the court, on behalf of either or any of the parties to the said suit, action, or other proceeding.
[Evidence Act 1851, s 2.]

2–811   3. Saving as to criminal proceedings.   But nothing herein contained shall render any person who in any criminal proceeding is charged with the commission of any indictable offence, or any offence punishable on summary conviction, competent or compellable to give evidence for or against himself or herself, or shall render any person compellable to answer any question tending to criminate himself or herself or shall in any criminal proceeding render any husband competent or compellable to give evidence for or against his wife, or any wife competent or compellable to give evidence for or against her husband.
[Evidence Act 1851, s 3.]

2–812   7. Proof of foreign and colonial acts of state, judgments, etc[1].   All proclamations, treaties and other acts of state of any foreign state or of any British colony, and all judgments, decrees, orders, and other judicial proceedings of any court of justice in any foreign state or in any British colony, and all affidavits, pleadings, and other legal documents filed or deposited in any such court, may be proved in any court of justice, or before any person having by law or by consent of parties authority to hear, receive and examine evidence, either by examined copies or by copies authenticated as hereinafter mentioned; that is to say, if the document sought to be proved be a proclamation, treaty, or other act of state, the authenticated copy to be admissible in evidence must purport to be sealed with the seal of the foreign state or British colony to which the original document belongs; and if the document sought to be proved be a judgment, decree, order, or other judicial proceeding of any foreign or colonial court, or an affidavit, pleading, or other legal document filed or deposited in any such court, the authenticated copy to be admissible in evidence must purport either to be sealed with the seal of the foreign or colonial court to which the original document belongs, or, in the event of such court having no seal, to be signed by the judge, or, if there be more than one judge, by any one

of the judges of the said court; and such judge shall attach to his signature a statement in writing on the said copy that the court whereof he is a judge has no seal; but if any of the aforesaid authenticated copies shall purport to be sealed or signed as herein before respectively directed, the same shall respectively be admitted in evidence in every case in which the original document could have been received in evidence, without any proof of the seal where a seal is necessary, or of the signature, or of the truth of the statement attached thereto, where such signature and statement are necessary, or of the judicial character of the person appearing to have made such signature and statement.
[Evidence Act 1851, s 7.]

1. For proof that the person referred to in any certificate of conviction is the defendant, see *R v Mauricia* [2002] EWCA Crim 676, [2002] 2 Cr App Rep 27 and see the Police and Criminal Evidence Act 1984, ss 73–75 and notes thereto, in this PART, post.

2–813   14. Examined or certified copies or extracts of public documents to be admissible in evidence.   Whenever any book or other document is of such a public nature as to be admissible in evidence on its mere production from the proper custody, and no Statute exists which renders its contents provable by means of a copy, any copy thereof or extract therefrom shall be admissible in evidence in any court of justice, or before any person now or hereafter having by law or by consent of parties authority to hear, receive, and examine evidence, provided it be proved to be an examined copy or extract or provided it purport to be signed and certified as a true copy or extract by the officer to whose custody the original is intrusted, and which officer is hereby required to furnish such certified copy or extract to any person applying at a reasonable time for the same, upon payment of a reasonable sum for the same, not exceeding fourpence for every folio of ninety words.
[Evidence Act 1851, s 14.]

2–814   15. Penalty for falsely certifying documents.   If any officer authorised or required by this Act to furnish any certified copies or extracts shall wilfully certify any document as being a true copy or extract, knowing that the same is not a true copy or extract. as the case may be, he shall be guilty of a misdemeanour, and be liable, upon conviction, to imprisonment for any term not exceeding eighteen months.
[Evidence Act 1851, s 15.]

2–815   16. Administration of oaths.   Every court, judge, justice, officer, commissioner, arbitrator, or other person, now or hereafter having by law or by consent of parties authority to hear, receive, and examine evidence, is hereby empowered to administer an oath to all such witnesses as are legally called before them respectively.
[Evidence Act 1851, s 16.]

2–816   19. Interpretation of "British Colony".   The words "British Colony" as used in this Act shall apply . . . to the islands of Guernsey, Jersey, Alderney, Sark, and Man, and to all other possessions of the British Crown, wheresoever and whatsoever.
[Evidence Act 1851, s 19.]

Evidence Amendment Act 1853
(16 & 17 Vict c 83)

2–830   1. Husbands and wives of parties to be admissible witnesses.   On the trial of any issue joined, or of any matter or question, or on any inquiry arising in any suit, action, or other proceeding in any court of justice, or before any person having by law or by consent of parties authority to hear, receive, and examine evidence, the husbands and wives of the parties thereto, and of the persons in whose behalf any such suit, action, or other proceeding may be brought or instituted, or opposed or defended, shall, except as hereinafter excepted, be competent and compellable to give evidence, either viva voce or by deposition, according to the practice of the court, on behalf of either or any of the parties to the said suit, action or other proceeding.
[Evidence Amendment Act 1853, s 1.]

2–831   2. Saving as to criminal cases.   Nothing herein shall render any husband[1] competent or compellable to give evidence for or against his wife, or any wife[1] competent or compellable to give evidence for or against her husband, in any criminal proceeding.
[Evidence Amendments Act 1853, s 2, as amended by the Evidence Further Amendment Act 1869, s 1.]

1. This includes a former spouse in respect of things done during the marriage, and applies to a "spouse" of a voidable marriage which has been annulled between the things done and the prosecution (*R v Algar* [1954] 1 QB 279, [1953] 2 All ER 1381).

Documentary Evidence Act 1868
(31 & 32 Vict c 37)

2–870   2. Mode of proving certain documents.   Prima facie evidence of any proclamation, order, or regulation issued before or after the passing of this Act by Her Majesty, or by the Privy Council, also of any proclamation, order, or regulation issued before or after the passing of this Act by or under the authority of any such department of the Government or officer or office-holder in the Scottish Administration as is mentioned in the first column of the schedule hereto[1], may be given in all courts of justice, and in all legal proceedings whatsoever, in all or any of modes hereinafter mentioned; that is to say:

(1) By the production of a copy of the Gazette purporting to contain such proclamation, order, or regulation.

(2) By the production of a copy of such proclamation, order, or regulation, purporting to be printed by the Government printer[2], or [*colonies*].

(3) By the production, in the case of any proclamation, order, or regulation issued by Her Majesty or by the Privy Council, of a copy or extract purporting to be certified to be true by the clerk of the Privy Council, or by any one of the lords or others of the Privy Council, and, in the case of any proclamation, order, or regulation issued by or under the authority of any of the said departments or officers or office-holders, by the production of a copy or extract purporting to be certified to be true by the person or persons specified in the second column of the said schedule in connexion with such department or officer or office-holder.

Any copy or extract made in pursuance of this Act may be in print or in writing, or partly in print and partly in writing.

No proof shall be required of the handwriting or official position of any person certifying, in pursuance of this Act, to the truth of any copy of or extract from any proclamation, order, or regulation.

[Documentary Evidence Act 1868, s 2 as amended by SI 1999/1042, Sch 1.]

---

1. This Schedule is not printed here; it sets out the Departments of State as well as other authorities such as the Commissioners of Customs and Excise, the Forestry Commissioners, the Charity Commissioners.

2. This provision is applied to Her Majesty's Stationery Office by the Documentary Evidence Act 1882, s 2, post.

Prevention of Crimes Act 1871
(34 & 35 Vict c 112)

2–880 18. Evidence of previous conviction. A previous conviction may be proved in any legal proceeding whatever against any person by producing a record or extract of such conviction, and by giving proof of the identity of the person against whom the conviction is sought to be proved with the person appearing in the record or extract of conviction to have been convicted.

A record or extract of a conviction shall in the case of an indictable offence consist of a certificate containing the substance and effect only (omitting the formal part of the indictment and conviction), and purporting to be signed by the proper officer of the court by which such conviction was made; and in the case of a summary conviction shall consist of a copy of such conviction purporting to be signed by any justice of the peace having jurisdiction over the offence in respect of which such conviction was made, or to be signed by the proper officer of the court by which such conviction was made, or by the proper officer of any court to which such conviction has been returned.

A record or extract of any conviction made in pursuance of this section shall be admissible in evidence without proof of the signature or official character of the person appearing to have signed the same.★

A previous conviction in any one part of the United Kingdom[1] may be proved[2] against a prisoner in any other part of the United Kingdom.

A fee not exceeding 25p may be charged for a record of a conviction given in pursuance of this section.
The mode of proving a previous conviction authorized by this section shall be in addition to and not in exclusion of any other authorized mode of proving such conviction. ★

In this section "proper officer" means—

(*a*) in relation to a magistrates' court in England and Wales, the designated officer for the court; and

(*b*) in relation to any other court, the clerk of the court or other officer having the custody of the records of the court, or the deputy of such clerk or other officer.

[Prevention of Crimes Act 1871, s 18 as amended by the Decimal Currency Act 1969, s 10(1), Statute Law (Repeals) Act 1981, the Police and Criminal Evidence Act 1984, Sch 7, SI 1985/1934, the Access to Justice Act 1999, Sch 13 and the Courts Act 2003, Sch 8.]

★Underlined words repealed, in relation to criminal proceedings only, by the Police and Criminal Evidence Act 1984, s 119, Sch 7, Pt IV and SI 1985/1934, arts 2, 3(c), Schedule.

1. This still includes the Republic of Ireland (Irish Free State (Consequential Adaptation of Enactments) Order 1923).

2. As to proof of conviction, see the Police and Criminal Evidence Act 1984, ss 73–75, post, the Criminal Justice Act 1948, s 39 (fingerprints) and the Criminal Procedure Rules 2005, Part 6 (court register or extract).

Bankers' Books Evidence Act 1879
(42 & 43 Vict c 11)

2–890 3. Mode of proof of entries in bankers' books. Subject to the provisions of this Act, a copy of any entry in a banker's book[1] shall in all legal proceedings be received as prima facie evidence[2] of such entry, and of the matters, transactions, and accounts therein recorded.

[Bankers' Books Evidence Act 1879, s 3.]

1. The Act covers entries kept on microfilm, magnetic tape and other forms of mechanical or electronic data retrieval mechanism: see s 9(2), post and *Barker v Wilson* [1980] 2 All ER 81, [1980] 1 WLR 884, 144 JP 425.
2. This applies only to entries which, by the general law of evidence, would be *prima facie* evidence (*Harding v Williams* (1880) 14 Ch D 197).

2–891   4. Proof that book is a banker's book.   A copy of an entry in a banker's book shall not be received in evidence under this Act unless it be first proved that the book was at the time of the making of the entry one of the ordinary books of the bank, and that the entry was made in the usual and ordinary course of business[1], and that the book is in the custody or control of the bank.

Such proof may be given by a partner or officer of the bank, and may be given orally or by an affidavit sworn before any commissioner or person authorised to take affidavits.

Where the proceedings concerned are proceedings before a magistrates' court inquiring into an offence as examining justices, this section shall have effect with the omission of the words "orally or". [Bankers' Books Evidence Act 1879, s 4 as amended by the Criminal Procedure and Investigations Act 1996, Sch 1.]

1. A book is used in the ordinary business of the bank, although not in daily use, if it is kept by the bank so that it may be referred to when required (*Idiots Asylum v Handysides* (1906) 22 TLR 573).

2–892   5. Verification of copy.   A copy of an entry in a banker's book shall not be received in evidence under this Act unless it be further proved that the copy has been examined with the original entry and is correct.

Such proof shall be given by some person who has examined the copy with the original entry[1], and may be given either orally or by an affidavit sworn before any commissioner or person authorised to take affidavits.

Where the proceedings concerned are proceedings before a magistrates' court inquiring into an offence as examining justices, this section shall have effect with the omission of the words "either orally or". [Bankers' Books Evidence Act 1879, s 5 as amended by the Criminal Procedure and Investigations Act 1996, Sch 1.]

1. Copies may be verified by someone other than a partner or officer of the bank (*R v Albutt* (1910) 75 JP 112, 6 Cr App Rep 55, CCA).

2–893   6. Case in which banker, etc, not compellable to produce book, etc.   A banker or officer of a bank shall not, in any legal proceeding to which the bank is not a party, be compellable to produce any banker's book the contents of which can be proved under this Act, or under the Civil Evidence (Scotland) Act 1988 or Schedule 8 to the Criminal Procedure (Scotland) Act 1995, or to appear as a witness to prove the matters, transactions, and accounts therein recorded, unless by order of a judge made for special cause. [Bankers' Books Evidence Act 1879, s 6 as amended by the Civil Evidence (Scotland) Act 1988, s 7, and the Criminal Procedure (Consequential Provisions) (Scotland) Act 1995, Sch 4.]

2–894   7. Court or judge may order inspection, etc[1].   On the application of any party to a legal proceeding a court or judge may order that such party be at liberty to inspect and take copies of any entries in a banker's book for any of the purposes of such proceedings. An order under this section may be made either with or without summoning the bank or any other party, and shall be served on the bank three clear days before the same is to be obeyed, unless the court or judge otherwise directs. [Bankers' Books Evidence Act 1879, s 7.]

1. For notes on the application of s 7 see para **2–198**, ante.

2–895   8. Costs.   The costs of any application to a court or judge under or for the purposes of this Act, and the costs of anything done or to be done under an order of a court or judge made under or for the purposes of this Act shall be in the discretion of the court or judge, who may order the same or any part thereof to be paid to any party by the bank where the same have been occasioned by any default or delay on the part of the bank. Any such order against a bank may be enforced as if the bank was a party to the proceeding. [Bankers' Books Evidence Act 1879, s 8.]

2–896   9. Interpretation of "bank," "banker," and "bankers' books".   (1) In this Act the expressions "bank" and "banker" mean—

(*a*)   a deposit-taker;
(*b*)   *Repealed*;
(*c*)   the National Savings Bank;
(*d*)   *Repealed*.

(1A)   "Deposit taker" means—

(*a*)   a person who has permission under Part 4 of the Financial Services and Markets Act 2000 to accept deposits; or

(b)   an EEA firm of the kind mentioned in paragraph 5(*b*) of Schedule 3 to that Act which has permission under paragraph 15 of that Schedule (as a result of qualifying for authorisation under paragraph 12(1) of that Schedule) to accept deposits or other repayable funds from the public.

(1B)   But a person is not a deposit-taker if he has permission to accept deposits only for the purpose of carrying on another regulated activity in accordance with that permission.

(1C)   Subsections (1A) and (1B) must be read with—

(a)   section 22 of the Financial Services and Markets Act 2000;
(b)   any relevant order under that section; and
(c)   Schedule 2 to that Act.

(2)   Expressions in this Act relating to "bankers' books" include ledgers, day books, cash books, account books and other records[2] used in the ordinary business of the bank, whether those records are in written form or are kept on microfilm, magnetic tape or any other form of mechanical or electronic data retrieval mechanism.

[Banker's Books Evidence Act 1879, s 9, as substituted by the Banking Act 1979, Sch 6, amended by the Trustee Savings Bank Act 1981, Sch 6, the Trustee Savings Bank Act 1985, Sch 4, the Building Societies Act 1986, Sch 18, the Banking Act 1987, Sch 6, SI 2001/1149 and SI 2001/3649.]

---

1.   As to authorised institutions under the Banking Act 1987, see ss 8–18 of that Act, in PART VII: title BANK AND BANKING, post. Subsection (1)(*a*), as substituted by the Banking Act 1987, Sch 6, shall not affect the operation of this Act in relation to any entry in any banker's book made or transaction carried out before this substituted provision came into force (Banking Act 1987, Sch 6, para 1(2)).

2.   Cheques and paying-in slips are not within the definition (*Williams v Williams* [1988] QB 161, [1987] 3 All ER 257).

2–897   10. Interpretation of "legal proceeding," "court," "judge".   In this Act—

The expression "legal proceeding" means any civil or criminal proceeding or inquiry in which evidence is or may be given, and includes

(a)   an arbitration;
(b)   an application to, or an inquiry or other proceeding before, the Solicitors Disciplinary Tribunal or any body exercising functions in relation to solicitors in Scotland or Northern Ireland corresponding to the functions of that Tribunal; and
(c)   an investigation, consideration or determination of a complaint by a member of the panel of ombudsmen for the purposes of the ombudsman scheme within the meaning of the Financial Services and Markets Act 2000;

The expression "the court" means the court, judge, arbitrator, persons or person before whom a legal proceeding is held or taken;

The expression "a judge" means with respect to England a judge of the High Court, and with respect to Scotland a lord ordinary of the Outer House of the Court of Session, and with respect to Ireland a judge of the High Court in Ireland;

The judge of a county court may with respect to any action in such court exercise the powers of a judge under this Act.

[Bankers' Books Evidence Act, 1879, s 10, as amended by the Statute Law Reform Act 1898 and the Solicitors Act 1974, s 86 and SI 2001/3649.]

Documentary Evidence Act 1882
(45 & 46 Vict c 9)

2–910   2. Documents printed under superintendence of Stationery Office receivable in evidence.   Where any enactment, whether passed before or after the passing of this Act, provides that a copy of any Act of Parliament, proclamation, order, regulation, rule, warrant, circular, list, gazette, or document shall be conclusive evidence, or be evidence, or have any other effect, when purporting to be printed by the Government Printer, or the Queen's Printer, or the Queen's Printer for Scotland, or a printer authorised by Her Majesty, or otherwise under Her Majesty's authority, whatever may be the precise expression used, such copy shall also be conclusive evidence, or evidence, or have the said effect (as the case may be) if it purports to be printed under the superintendence or authority of Her Majesty's Stationery Office.

[Documentary Evidence Act 1882, s 2 as amended by SI 1999/1042, art 1.]

Criminal Evidence Act 1898
(61 and 62 Vict c 36)

2–920   1. Competency of witnesses in criminal cases[1].   Every person charged with an offence, shall be a competent witness for the defence at every stage of the proceedings, whether the person so charged is charged solely or jointly with any other person. Provided as follows:

(a)   A person so charged shall not be called as a witness in pursuance of this Act except upon his own application;
(b)–(d)   *Repealed;*

(*e*) Subject to section 101 of the Criminal Justice Act 2003 (admissibility of eveidence of defendant's bad character), a person charged and being a witness in pursuance of this Act may be asked any question in[2] cross-examination notwithstanding that it would tend to criminate him as to the offence charged;

(*f*) A person charged and called as a witness in pursuance of this Act shall not be asked, and if asked shall not be required to answer, any question tending to show that he has committed or been convicted of or been charged with any offence other than that wherewith he is then charged, or is of bad character, unless—

   (i) the proof that he has committed or been convicted of such other offence is admissible evidence to show that he is guilty of the offence wherewith he is then charged; or

   (ii) he has personally or by his advocate asked questions of the witnesses for the prosecution with a view to establish his own good character, or has given evidence of his good character, or the nature or conduct of the defence is such as to involve imputations on the character of the prosecutor or the witnesses[3] for the prosecution the deceased victim of the alleged crime; or

   (iii) he has given evidence[4] against any other person charged in the same proceedings.

(*g*) Every person called as a witness in pursuance of this Act shall[5], unless otherwise ordered by the court, give his evidence from the witness box or other place from which the other witnesses give their evidence;

(*h*) *Repealed.**

[Criminal Evidence Act 1898, s 1, as amended by the Criminal Evidence Act 1979, s 1, the Criminal Justice Act 1982, Sch 16, the Police and Criminal Evidence Act 1984, Sch 7 and the Criminal Justice and Public Order Act 1994, s 31 and Schs 10 and 11.]

---

*Section 1 is amended by the Youth Justice and Criminal Evidence Act 1999, Sch 4, when in force.
1. For notes on the application of s 1 see ante **2–332 Competency of parties and their spouses**; **2–334 Co-defendants**; **2–478 Cross-examination of the accused as to character**.
2. See ante **2–334 Co-defendants**.
3. "Witness" is not confined to a witness who gives oral testimony. A witness is a person who has material evidence to give and includes a witness whose evidence is read at a trial under, for example, s 9 of the Criminal Justice Act 1967 or s 23 of the Criminal Justice Act 1988 (*R v Miller* [1997] 2 Cr App Rep 178, CA).
4. The giving of evidence by the defendant against a co-defendant is essential if paragraph (*f*) is to be applied, cross-examination that damages a co-defendant is insufficient (*R v Knutton* [1993] Crim LR 208).
5. A defendant has a right to give evidence from the witness box, and justices do not have a discretion to direct where evidence shall be given. However, in exceptional circumstances such as misconduct, the court may order the evidence to be given from the dock; see *R v Farnham Justices, ex p Gibson* (1991) 155 JP 792, [1991] Crim LR 642, DC.

2–921 2. Evidence of person charged. Where the only witness to the facts of the case called by the defence is the person charged, he shall be called as a witness immediately[1] after the close of the evidence for the prosecution.
[Criminal Evidence Act 1898, s 2.]

---

1. Notwithstanding this section, the order of speeches where a person is charged with an offence before a magistrates' court is prescribed in the Criminal Procedure Rules 2005, Part 37.

2–922 3. Right of reply. The fact that the person charged has been called as a witness shall not of itself confer on the prosecution the right of reply.
[Criminal Evidence Act 1898, s 3, amended by Criminal Procedure (Right of Reply) Act 1964, s 1(2).]

2–923 6. Provision as to previous Acts. (1) This Act shall apply to all criminal proceedings, including proceedings in courts-martial under the Army Act 1955 and the Air Force Act 1955, and proceedings in courts-martial under the Naval Discipline Act 1957 and in Standing Civilian Courts established under the Armed Forces Act 1976.
(2) *Repealed.*
[Criminal Evidence Act 1898, s 6, as amended by the Revision of the Army and Air Force Acts (Transitional Provisions) Act 1955, s 3, the Armed Forces Act 1971, s 49(3), the Armed Forces Act 1976, Sch 9, the Statute Law (Repeals) Act 1981, Sch 1, Part I, the Police and Criminal Evidence Act 1984, Sch 7 and the Armed Forces Act 2001, Sch 7.]

Evidence (Colonial Statutes) Act 1907
(7 Edw 7 c 16)

2–940 1. Proof of statutes of British possessions. (1) Copies of Acts, ordinances, and statutes passed (whether before or after the passing of this Act) by the Legislature of any British possession, and of orders, regulations and other instruments issued or made, whether before or after the passing of this Act, under the authority of any such Act, ordinance, or statute, if purporting to be printed by the Government printer, shall be received in evidence by all courts of justice in the United Kingdom without any proof being given that the copies were so printed.
(3) In this Act—

The expression "Government printer" means, as respects any British possession, the printer purporting to be the printer authorised to print the Acts, ordinances, or statutes of the Legislature of that possession, or otherwise to be the Government printer of that possession:

The expression "British possession" means any part of His Majesty's dominions exclusive of the United Kingdom, and, where parts of those dominions are under both a central and a local Legislature, shall include both all parts under the central Legislature and each part under a local Legislature.

[Evidence (Colonial Statutes) Act 1907, s 1(1) and (3).]

Evidence (Foreign, Dominion and Colonial Documents) Act 1933
(23 & 24 Geo 5 c 4)

2–950 1. Proof and effect of foreign, dominion and colonial registers and certain official certificates. (1) *Repealed.*

(2) An Order in Council made under section 5 of the Oaths and Evidence (Overseas Authorities and Countries) Act 1963 may provide that in all parts of the United Kingdom—

(a) a register of the country to which the Order relates, being such a register as is specified in the Order, shall be deemed to be a public register kept under the authority of the law of that country and recognised by the courts thereof as an authentic record, and to be a document of such a public nature as to be admissible as evidence of the matters regularly recorded therein;

(b) such matters as may be specified in the Order shall, if recorded in such a register, be deemed until the contrary is proved, to be regularly recorded therein;

(c) subject to any conditions specified in the Order and to any requirements of rules of court a document purporting to be issued in the country to which the Order relates as an official copy of an entry in such a register as is so specified, and purporting to be authenticated as such in the manner specified in the Order as appropriate in the case of such a register, shall, without evidence as to the custody of the register or of inability to produce it and without any further or other proof, be received as evidence that the register contains such an entry;

(d) subject as aforesaid a certificate purporting to be given in the country to which the Order relates as an official certificate of any such class as is specified in the Order, and purporting to be signed by the officer, and to be authenticated in the manner specified in the Order as appropriate in the case of a certificate of that class, shall be received as evidence of the facts stated in the certificate;

(e) no official document issued in the country to which the Order relates as proof of any matters for the proof of which provision is made by the Order shall, if otherwise admissible in evidence, be inadmissible by reason only that it is not authenticated by the process known as legalisation.

(3) Official books of record preserved in a central registry and containing entries copied from original registers may, if those entries were copied by officials in the course of their duty, themselves be treated for the purposes of this section as registers.

(4) In this section the expression "country" means a Dominion, the Isle of Man, any of the Channel Islands, a British colony or protectorate, a foreign country, a colony or protectorate of a foreign country, or any mandated territory:

Provided that where a part of a country is under both a local and a central legislature, an Order under this section may be made as well with respect to that part, as with respect to all the parts under that central legislature.

[Evidence (Foreign Dominion and Colonial Documents) Act 1933, s 1, as amended by the Oaths and Evidence (Overseas Authorities and Countries) Act 1963, s 5(2).]

Evidence Act 1938
(1938 c 28)

2–962 3. Proof of instrument to validity of which attestation is necessary. Subject as hereinafter provided, in any proceedings, whether civil or criminal, an instrument to the validity of which attestation is requisite may, instead of being proved by an attesting witness, be proved in the manner in which it might be proved if no attesting witness were alive[1].

Provided that nothing in this section shall apply to the proof of wills or other testamentary documents.

[Evidence Act 1938, s 3.]

---

1. See also the Criminal Procedure Act 1865, s 7, ante.

2–963 4. Presumptions as to documents twenty years old. In any proceedings, whether civil or criminal, there shall, in the case of a document[1] proved, or purporting, to be not less than twenty years old, be made any presumption which immediately before the commencement of this Act would

have been made in the case of a document of like character proved, or purporting, to be not less than thirty years old.
[Evidence Act 1938, s 4.]

___

1. "Document" includes books, maps, plans, drawings and photographs (s 6).

Statutory Instruments Act 1946
(9 & 10 Geo 6 c 36)

2–1000   1. Definition of "Statutory Instrument".   (1) Where by this Act or any Act passed after the commencement of this Act[1] power to make, confirm or approve orders, rules, regulations or other subordinate legislation is conferred on His Majesty in Council or on any Minister of the Crown then, if the power is expressed—

    (a)   in the case of a power conferred on His Majesty, to be exercisable by Order in Council;

    (b)   in the case of a power conferred on a Minister of the Crown, to be exercisable by statutory instrument,

any document by which that power is exercised shall be known as a "statutory instrument" and the provisions of this Act shall apply thereto accordingly.

(1A) The references in subsection (1) to a Minister of the Crown shall be construed as including references to the National Assembly for Wales.*

(2) Where by any Act passed before the commencement of this Act power to make statutory rules within the meaning of the Rules Publication Act, 1893[2] was conferred on any rule-making authority within the meaning of that Act, any document by which that power is exercised after the commencement of this Act shall, save as is otherwise provided by regulations made under this Act, be known as a "statutory instrument"[3] and the provisions of this Act shall apply thereto accordingly. [Statutory Instruments Act 1946, s 1, as amended by the Government of Wales Act 1998, Sch 12.]

___

*Substituted by the Government of Wales Act 2006, Sch 10 immediately after the ordinary election (under the Government of Wales Act 1998, s 3) held in 2007.

1. 1st January 1948.

2. Statutory Rules under this Act mean rules, regulations, or byelaws made under any Act of Parliament which (i) related to any Court in the United Kingdom or to the practice, procedure, costs or fees therein, or to any fees or matters applying generally throughout England, Scotland or Ireland, or (ii) were made by the Queen in Council, the Judicial Committee, the Treasury, the Lord Chancellor, a Secretary of State, the Admiralty, the Board of Trade, or any other Government Department.

3. The provisions of the Interpretation Act 1978, post apply generally to statutory instruments, but note that the instrument itself (or its enabling statute) will have to make specific provision for judicial notice (see Interpretation Act 1978, s 23—in practice generally done by providing for the 1978 Act to apply to the instrument as if it were an Act of Parliament) and unless s 17(2)(b) of the 1978 Act applies (repeal and re-enactment) or there is an express saving, the repeal of an Act terminates instruments made under it; (*Watson v Winch* [1916] 1 KB 688, 80 JP 149; *Wicks v DPP* [1947] AC 362, [1947] 1 All ER 205).

2–1001   3. Supplementary provisions as to publication[1].   (1) Regulations made for the purposes of this Act shall make provision for the publication by His Majesty's Stationery Office of lists showing the date upon which every statutory instrument printed and sold by or under the authority of the King's printer of Acts of Parliament was first issued by or under the authority of that office; and in any legal proceedings a copy of any list so published shall be received in evidence as a true copy, and in entry therein shall be conclusive evidence of the date on which any statutory instrument was first issued by His Majesty's Stationery Office.

(2) In any proceedings against any person for an offence consisting of a contravention of any such statutory instrument, it shall be a defence to prove that the instrument had not been issued by or under the authority of His Majesty's Stationery Office at the date of the alleged contravention unless it is proved that at that date reasonable steps had been taken for the purpose of bringing the purport of the instrument to the notice of the public, or of persons likely to be affected by it, or of the person charged[2].

(3) Save as therein otherwise expressly provided, nothing in this section shall affect any enactment or rule of law relating to the time at which any statutory instrument comes into operation. [Statutory Instruments Act 1946, s 3 as amended by the Statutory Instruments (Production and Sale) Act 1996, s 1.]

___

1. Section 3 was amended by the Statutory Instruments (Production and Sale) Act 1996 to provide for sale or issue under the authority of the King's printer and dispensing with the requirement in sub-s(1) to bear the imprint of the King's printer. These amendments have retrospective effect except in relation to proceedings commenced before 21 June 1996.

2. These provisions were considered and applied in *Defiant Cycle Co Ltd v Newell* [1953] 2 All ER 38, 117 JP 324 and in *R v Sheet Metalcraft Ltd* [1954] 1 QB 586, [1954] 1 All ER 542, 118 JP 190.

Oaths and Evidence (Overseas Authorities and Countries) Act 1963
(1963 c 27)

2–1020   5. Amendment of [the Evidence (Foreign, Dominion and Colonial Documents) Act 1933].   (1) If Her Majesty in Council is satisfied as respects any country that—

(a) there exist in that country public registers kept under the authority of the law of that country and recognised by the courts of that country as authentic records, and

(b) that the registers are regularly and properly kept,

Her Majesty may by Order in Council¹ make in respect of that country and all or any of those registers such provision as is specified in subsection (2) of section 1 of the Evidence (Foreign, Dominion and Colonial Documents) Act 1933.
[Oaths and Evidence (Overseas Authorities and Countries) Act 1963, s 5(1).]

---

1. Orders in Council have been made for the following countries: Aden, Antigua, Australia, Bahamas, Barbados, Basutoland, Bechuanaland Protectorate, Belgium, Bermuda, British Antarctic Territory, British Guiana, British Honduras, Canada (certain provinces only, see SI 1962 No 2606), Cayman Islands, Denmark, Dominica, France, Falkland Islands, Fiji, Germany (Federal Republic), Gibraltar, Grenada, Hong Kong, Ireland (Republic of), Italy, Kenya, Luxembourg, Mauritius, Montserrat, Netherlands, New Zealand, St Helena, Saint Lucia, Sarawak, Seychelles, Sierra Leone, Swaziland, Tanganyika, Turks and Caicos Island, Uganda, United States of America, Zanzibar.

Civil Evidence Act 1968
(1968 c 64)

PART II
MISCELLANEOUS AND GENERAL
Convictions, etc, as evidence in civil proceedings

2–1040 **11. Convictions as evidence in civil proceedings.** (1) In any civil proceedings the fact that a person has been convicted of an offence by or before any court in the United Kingdom or by a court-martial there or elsewhere shall (subject to subsection (3) below) be admissible in evidence for the purpose of proving, where to do so is relevant to any issue in those proceedings, that he committed that offence, whether he was so convicted upon a plea of guilty or otherwise and whether or not he is a party to the civil proceedings; but no conviction other than a subsisting¹ one shall be admissible in evidence by virtue of this section.

(2) In any civil proceedings in which by virtue of this section a person is proved to have been convicted of an offence by or before any court in the United Kingdom or by a court-martial there or elsewhere—

(a) he shall be taken to have committed that offence unless the contrary is proved; and

(b) without prejudice to the reception of any other admissible evidence for the purpose of identifying the facts on which the conviction was based, the contents of any document which is admissible as evidence of the conviction, and the contents of the information, complaint, indictment or charge-sheet on which the person in question was convicted, shall be admissible in evidence for that purpose.

(3) Nothing in this section shall prejudice the operation of section 13 of this Act or any other enactment whereby a conviction or a finding of fact in any criminal proceedings is for the purposes of any other proceedings made conclusive evidence of any fact.

(4) Where in any civil proceedings the contents of any document are admissible in evidence by virtue of subsection (2) above, a copy of that document, or of the material part thereof, purporting to be certified or otherwise authenticated by or on behalf of the court or authority having custody of that document shall be admissible in evidence and shall be taken to be a true copy of that document or part unless the contrary is shown.

(5) Nothing in any of the following enactments, that is to say—

(a) section 14 of the Powers of Criminal Courts (Sentencing) Act 2000 (under which a conviction leading to discharge is to be disregarded except as therein mentioned);

(b) section 9 of the Criminal Justice (Scotland) Act 1949 (which makes similar provision in respect of convictions on indictment in Scotland); and

(c) section 8 of the Probation Act (Northern Ireland) 1950 (which corresponds to the said section 12) or any corresponding enactment of the Parliament of Northern Ireland for the time being in force,

shall affect the operation of this section; and for the purposes of this section any order made by a court of summary jurisdiction in Scotland under section 1 or section 2 of the said Act of 1949 shall be treated as a conviction.

(6) In this section "court-martial" means a court-martial constituted under the Army Act 1955, the Air Force Act 1955, or the Naval Discipline Act, and in relation to a court-martial "conviction" means a finding of guilty which is, or falls to be treated as, the finding of the court, and "convicted" shall be construed accordingly.
[Civil Evidence Act 1968, s 11, as amended by the Powers of Criminal Courts Act 1973, Sch 5, the Criminal Justice Act 1991, Sch 11, the Armed Forces Act 1996, Schs 1 and 7, the Powers of Criminal Courts (Sentencing) Act 2000, Sch 9 and the Armed Forces Act 2001, Sch 7.]

---

1. This includes a conviction subject to appeal, but civil proceedings should be adjourned until the appeal is determined (*Re Raphael, Raphael v d'Antin* [1973] 3 All ER 19).

2–1041   **12. Findings of adultery and paternity as evidence in civil proceedings.**   (1) In any civil proceedings—

    (a)   the fact that a person has been found guilty of adultery in any matrimonial proceedings; and
    (b)   the fact that a person has been found to be the father of a child in relevant proceedings before any court in England and Wales or Northern Ireland or has been adjudged to be the father of a child in affiliation proceedings before any court in the United Kingdom;

shall (subject to subsection (3) below) be admissible in evidence for the purpose of proving, where to do so is relevant to any issue in those civil proceedings, that he committed the adultery to which the finding relates or, as the case may be, is (or was) the father of that child, whether or not he offered any defence to the allegation of adultery or paternity and whether or not he is a party to the civil proceedings; but no finding or adjudication other than a subsisting one shall be admissible in evidence by virtue of this section.

(2) In any civil proceedings in which by virtue of this section a person is proved to have been found guilty of adultery as mentioned in subsection (1)(a) above or to have been found or adjudged to be the father of a child as mentioned in subsection (1)(b) above—

    (a)   he shall be taken to have committed the adultery to which the finding relates or, as the case may be, to be (or have been) the father of that child, unless the contrary is proved; and
    (b)   without prejudice to the reception of any other admissible evidence for the purpose of identifying the facts on which the finding or adjudication was based, the contents of any document which was before the court, or which contains any pronouncement of the court, in the other proceedings in question shall be admissible in evidence for that purpose.

(3) Nothing in this section shall prejudice the operation of any enactment whereby a finding of fact in any matrimonial or affiliation proceedings is for the purposes of any other proceedings made conclusive evidence of any fact.

(4) Subsection (4) of section 11 of this Act shall apply for the purposes of this section as if the reference to subsection (2) were a reference to subsection (2) of this section.

(5) In this section—

"matrimonial proceedings" means any matrimonial cause in the High Court or a county court in England and Wales or in the High Court in Northern Ireland, any consistorial action in Scotland, or any appeal arising out of any such cause or action;
"relevant proceedings" means—

    (a)   proceedings on a complaint under section 42 of the National Assistance Act 1948 or section 26 of the Social Security Act 1986;
    (b)   proceedings under the Children Act 1989;
    (c)   proceedings which would have been relevant proceedings for the purposes of this section in the form in which it was in force before the passing of the Children Act 1989;
    (d)   *Repealed*;
    (e)   proceedings which are relevant proceedings as defined in section 8(5) of the Civil Evidence Act (Northern Ireland) 1971.

"affiliation proceedings" means, in relation to Scotland, any action of affiliation and aliment;

and in this subsection "consistorial action" does not include an action of aliment only between husband and wife raised in the Court of Session or an action of interim aliment raised in the sheriff court.

[Civil Evidence Act 1968, s 12, as amended by the Family Law Reform Act 1987, s 29, the Courts and Legal Services Act 1990, Sch 16, the Child Support Act 1991, s 27, SI 1995/756 and the Child Support, Pensions and Social Security Act 2000, Sch 9.]

2–1042   **13. Conclusiveness of convictions for purposes of defamation actions.**   (1) In an action for libel or slander in which the question whether the plaintiff did or did not commit a criminal offence is relevant to an issue arising in the action, proof that, at the time when that issue falls to be determined, he stands convicted of that offence shall be conclusive evidence that he committed that offence; and his conviction thereof shall be admissible in evidence accordingly.

(2) In any such action as aforesaid in which by virtue of this section the plaintiff is proved to have been convicted of an offence, the contents of any document which is admissible as evidence of the conviction, and the contents of the information, complaint, indictment or charge-sheet on which he was convicted, shall, without prejudice to the reception of any other admissible evidence for the purpose of identifying the facts on which the conviction was based, be admissible in evidence for the purpose of identifying those facts.

(2A) In the case of an action for libel or slander in which there is more than one plaintiff—

    (a)   the references in subsections (1) and (2) above to the plaintiff shall be construed as references to any of the plaintiffs, and
    (b)   proof that any of the plaintiffs stands convicted of an offence shall be conclusive evidence that he committed that offence so far as that fact is relevant to any issue arising in relation to his cause of action or that of any other plaintiff.

(3) For the purposes of this section a person shall be taken to stand convicted of an offence if but only if there subsists against him a conviction of that offence by or before a court in the United Kingdom or by a court-martial there or elsewhere.

(4) Subsections (4) to (6) of section 11 of this Act shall apply for the purposes of this section as they apply for the purposes of that section, but as if in the said subsection (4) the reference to subsection (2) were a reference to subsection (2) of this section.

(5) The foregoing provisions of this section shall apply for the purposes of any action begun after the passing of this Act, whenever the cause of action arose, but shall not apply for the purposes of any action begun before the passing of this Act or any appeal or other proceedings arising out of any such action.

[Civil Evidence Act 1968, s 13 as amended by the Defamation Act 1996, s 12.]

Privilege

2–1043 14. Privilege against incrimination[1] of self or spouse. (1) The right of a person in any legal proceedings other than criminal proceedings to refuse to answer any question or produce any document or thing if to do so would tend to expose that person to proceedings for an offence or for the recovery of a penalty—

(a) shall apply only as regards criminal offences under the law of any part of the United Kingdom and penalties provided for by such law; and

(b) shall include a like right to refuse to answer any question or produce any document or thing if to do so would tend to expose the husband or wife of that person to proceedings for any such criminal offence or for the recovery of any such penalty.

(2) In so far as any existing enactment conferring (in whatever words) powers of inspection or investigation confers on a person (in whatever words) any right otherwise than in criminal proceedings to refuse to answer any question or give any evidence tending to incriminate that person, subsection (1) above shall apply to that right as it applies to the right described in that subsection; and every such existing enactment shall be construed accordingly.

(3) In so far as any existing enactment provides (in whatever words) that in any proceedings other than criminal proceedings a person shall not be excused from answering any question or giving any evidence on the ground that to do so may incriminate that person, that enactment shall be construed as providing also that in such proceedings a person shall not be excused from answering any question or giving any evidence on the ground that to do so may incriminate the husband or wife of that person.

(4) Where any existing enactment (however worded) that—

(a) confers powers of inspection or investigation; or

(b) provides as mentioned in subsection (3) above,

further provides (in whatever words) that any answer or evidence given by a person shall not be admissible in evidence against that person in any proceedings or class of proceedings (however described, and whether criminal or not), that enactment shall be construed as providing also that any answer or evidence given by that person shall not be admissible in evidence against the husband or wife of that person in the proceedings or class of proceedings in question.

(5) In this section "existing enactment" means any enactment passed before this Act; and the references to giving evidence are references to giving evidence in any manner, whether by furnishing information, making discovery, producing documents or otherwise.

[Civil Evidence Act 1968, s 14.]

---

1. This section was considered in conjunction with the Theft Act 1968, s 31(1) and possible proceedings under the Copyright Act 1956, s 21, in *Rank Film Distributors Ltd v Video Information Centre* [1982] AC 380, [1981] 2 All ER 76 (discovery of documents and answers to interrogatories required of "pirate" film dealers).

2–1044 15. Privilege for certain communications relating to patent proceedings. (1) This section applies to any communication made for the purpose of any pending or contemplated proceedings under the Patents Act 1949, before the comptroller or the Appeal Tribunal, being either—

(a) a communication between the patent agent of a party to those proceedings and that party or any other person; or

(b) a communication between a party to those proceedings and a person other than his patent agent made for the purpose of obtaining, or in response to a request for, information which that party is seeking for the purpose of submitting it to his patent agent.

For the purposes of this subsection a communication made by or to a person acting—

(i) on behalf of a patent agent; or

(ii) on behalf of a party to any pending or contemplated proceedings,

shall be treated as made by or to that patent agent or party, as the case may be.

(2) In any legal proceedings other than criminal proceedings a communication to which this section applies shall be privileged from disclosure in like manner as if the proceedings mentioned in the foregoing subsection had been proceedings before the High Court and the patent agent in question had been the solicitor of the party concerned.

(3) For the purposes of this section a communication made for the purposes of a pending or contemplated application for a patent or any other pending or contemplated proceeding under the Patents Act 1949, shall be treated as made for the purpose of contemplated proceedings under that Act before the comptroller or the Appeal Tribunal of every kind to which a proceeding of that

description may give rise, whether or not any such proceedings are actually contemplated when the communication is made.

(4) in this section—

"the comptroller" and "the Appeal Tribunal" have the same meanings as in the Patents Act 1949; "patent agent" means a person registered as a patent agent in the register of patent agents maintained pursuant to the Patents Act 1949, or a company lawfully practising as a patent agent in the United Kingdom or the Isle of Man; and

"party", in relation to any contemplated proceedings, means a prospective party thereto.
[Civil Evidence Act 1968, s 15.]

2–1045   16. Abolition of certain privileges.   (1) The following rules of law are hereby abrogated except in relation to criminal proceedings, that is to say—

(a)   the rule whereby, in any legal proceedings, a person cannot be compelled to answer any question or produce any document or thing if to do so would tend to expose him to a forfeiture; and

(b)   the rule whereby, in any legal proceedings, a person other than a party to the proceedings cannot be compelled to produce any deed or other document relating to his title to any land.

(2) The rule of law whereby, in any civil proceedings, a party to the proceedings cannot be compelled to produce any document relating solely to his own case and in no way tending to impeach that case or support the case of any opposing party is hereby abrogated.

(3) *Spent.*

(4) In section 43(1) of the Matrimonial Causes Act 1965 (under which the evidence of a husband or wife is admissible in any proceedings to prove that marital intercourse did or did not take place between them during any period, but a husband or wife is not compellable in any proceedings to give evidence of the matters aforesaid), the words from "but a husband or wife" to the end of the subsection shall cease to have effect except in relation to criminal proceedings.

(5) A witness in any proceedings instituted in consequence of adultery, whether a party to the proceedings or not, shall not be excused from answering any question by reason that it tends to show that he or she has been guilty of adultery; and accordingly the proviso to section 3 of the Evidence Further Amendment Act 1869, and, in section 43(2) of the Matrimonial Causes Act 1965, the words from "but" to the end of the subsection shall cease to have effect.
[Civil Evidence Act 1968, s 16.]

2–1046   17. Consequential amendments relating to privilege.   (1) In relation to England and Wales—

(a)   repealed

(b)   section 8(5) of the Parliamentary Commissioner Act 1967 (which provides that, subject as there mentioned, no person shall be compelled for the purposes of an investigation under that Act to give any evidence or produce any document which he could not be compelled to give or produce in proceedings before the High Court) shall have effect as if before the word "proceedings" there were inserted the word "civil";

and, so far as it applies to England and Wales, any other existing enactment, however framed or worded, which in relation to any tribunal, investigation or inquiry (however described) confers on persons required to answer questions or give evidence any privilege described by reference to the privileges of witnesses in proceedings before any court shall, unless the contrary intention appears, be construed as referring to the privileges of witnesses in civil proceedings before that court.

(3) Without prejudice to the generality of subsections (2) to (4) of section 14 of this Act, the enactments mentioned in the Schedule to this Act shall have effect subject to the amendments provided for by that Schedule (being verbal amendments to bring those enactments into conformity with the provisions of that section).

(4) Subsection (5) of section 14 of this Act shall apply for the purposes of this section as it applies for the purposes of that section.
[Civil Evidence Act 1968, s 17, as amended by the Evidence (Proceedings in Other Jurisdictions) Act 1975, Sch 2 and the Inquiries Act 2005, Sch 3.]

General

2–1047   18. General interpretation, and savings.   (1) In this Act "civil proceedings" includes, in addition to civil proceedings in any of the ordinary courts of law—

(a)   civil proceedings before any other tribunal, being proceedings in relation to which the strict rules of evidence apply; and

(b)   an arbitration or reference, whether under an enactment or not,

but does not include civil proceedings in relation to which the strict rules of evidence do not apply.

(2) In this Act—

"court" does not include a court-martial, and, in relation to an arbitration or reference, means the arbitrator or umpire and, in relation to proceedings before a tribunal (not being one of the ordinary courts of law), means the tribunal;

"legal proceedings" includes an arbitration or reference, whether under an enactment or not;

and for the avoidance of doubt it is hereby declared that in this Act, and in any amendment made by this Act in any other enactment, references to a person's husband or wife do not include references to a person who is no longer married to that person.

(3) Any reference in this Act to any other enactment is a reference thereto as amended, and includes a reference thereto as applied, by or under any other enactment.

(4) Nothing in this Act shall prejudice the operation of any enactment which provides (in whatever words) that any answer or evidence given by a person in specified circumstances shall not be admissible in evidence against him or some other person in any proceedings or class of proceedings (however described).

In this subsection the reference to giving evidence is a reference to giving evidence in any manner, whether by furnishing information, making discovery, producing documents or otherwise.

(5) Nothing in this Act shall prejudice—

(a) any power of a court, in any legal proceedings, to exclude evidence (whether by preventing questions from being put or otherwise) at its discretion; or

(b) the operation of an agreement (whenever made) between the parties to any legal proceedings as to the evidence which is to be admissible (whether generally or for any particular purpose) in those proceedings.

(6) It is hereby declared that where, by reason of any defect of speech or hearing from which he is suffering, a person called as a witness in any legal proceedings gives his evidence in writing or by signs, that evidence is to be treated for the purposes of this Act as being given orally.
[Civil Evidence Act 1968, s 18.]

Civil Evidence Act 1972
(1972 c 30)

2–1151   **2.** *Rules of Court.*

2–1152   **3. Admissibility of expert opinion and certain expressions of non-expert opinion.**
(1) Subject to any rules of court made in pursuance of this Act, where a person is called as a witness in any civil proceedings, his opinion on any relevant matter on which he is qualified to give expert evidence shall be admissible in evidence.

(2) It is hereby declared that where a person is called as a witness in any civil proceedings, a statement of opinion by him on any relevant matter on which he is not qualified to give expert evidence, if made as a way of conveying relevant facts personally perceived by him, is admissible as evidence of what he perceived.

(3) In this section "relevant matter" includes an issue in the proceedings in question.
[Civil Evidence Act 1972, s 3 as amended by the Civil Evidence Act 1995, Sch 2.]

2–1153   **4. Evidence of foreign law.** (1) It is hereby declared that in civil proceedings a person who is suitably qualified to do so on account of his knowledge or experience is competent to give expert evidence as to the law of any country or territory outside the United Kingdom, or of any part of the United Kingdom other than England and Wales, irrespective of whether he has acted or is entitled to act as a legal practitioner there.

(2) Where any question as to the law of any country or territory outside the United Kingdom, or of any part of the United Kingdom other than England and Wales, with respect to any matter has been determined (whether before or after the passing of this Act) in any such proceedings as are mentioned in subsection (4) below, then in any civil proceedings (not being proceedings before a court which can take judicial notice of the law of that country, territory or part with respect to that matter)—

(a) any finding made or decision given on that question in the first-mentioned proceedings shall, if reported or recorded in citable form, be admissible in evidence for the purpose of proving the law of that country, territory or part with respect to that matter; and

(b) if that finding or decision, as so reported or recorded, is adduced for that purpose, the law of that country, territory or part with respect to that matter shall be taken to be in accordance with that finding or decision unless the contrary is proved:

Provided that paragraph (b) above shall not apply in the case of a finding or decision which conflicts with another finding or decision on the same question adduced by virtue of this subsection in the same proceedings.

(3) Except with the leave of the court, a party to any civil proceedings shall not be permitted to adduce any such finding or decision as is mentioned in subsection (2) above by virtue of that subsection unless he has in accordance with rules of court given to every other party to the proceedings notice that he intends to do so.

(4) The proceedings referred to in subsection (2) above are the following, whether civil or criminal, namely—

(a) proceedings at first instance in any of the following courts, namely the High Court, the Crown Court, a court of quarter sessions, the Court of Chancery of the county palatine of Lancaster and the Court of Chancery of the county palatine of Durham;

(b) appeals arising out of any such proceedings as are mentioned in paragraph (a) above;

(c) proceedings before the Judicial Committee of the Privy Council on appeal (whether to Her Majesty in Council or to the Judicial Committee as such) from any decision of any court outside the United Kingdom.

(5) For the purposes of this section a finding or decision on any such question as is mentioned in subsection (2) above shall be taken to be reported or recorded in citable form if, but only if, it is reported or recorded in writing in a report, transcript or other document which, if that question had been a question as to the law of England and Wales, could be cited as an authority in legal proceedings in England and Wales.
[Civil Evidence Act 1972, s 4.]

2–1154   5. Interpretation and savings. (1) In this Act "civil proceedings" means civil proceedings, before any tribunal, in relation to which the strict rules of evidence apply, whether as a matter of law or by agreement of the parties; and references to "the court" shall be construed accordingly.

(2) *Tribunals.*

(3) Nothing in this Act shall prejudice—

(a) any power of a court, in any civil proceedings, to exclude evidence (whether by preventing questions from being put or otherwise) at its discretion; or

(b) the operation of any agreement (whenever made) between the parties to any civil proceedings as to the evidence which is to be admissible (whether generally or for any particular purpose) in those proceedings.
[Civil Evidence Act 1972, s 5, as amended by the Civil Evidence Act 1995, Sch 1.]

Oaths Act 1978
(1978 c 19)

2–1190   1. Manner of administration of oaths. (1) Any oath may be administered[1] and taken in England, Wales or Northern Ireland in the following form and manner—
The person taking the oath shall hold the New Testament, or in the case of a Jew, the Old Testament, in his uplifted hand, and say or repeat after the officer administering the oath the words "I swear by Almighty God that . . .", followed by the words of the oath prescribed by law[2].

(2) The officer shall (unless the person about to take the oath voluntarily objects thereto, or is physically incapable of so taking the oath) administer the oath in the form and manner aforesaid without question.

(3) In the case of a person who is neither a Christian nor a Jew, the oath shall be administered in any lawful manner.

(4) In this section "officer" means any person duly authorised to administer oaths.
[Oaths Act 1978, s 1.]

---

1. The Evidence Act 1851, s 16 ante states who shall be empowered to administer an oath.
2. These words are directive so that although they should be complied with, failure to do so does not necessarily invalidate the taking of the oath (*R v Chapman* [1980] Crim LR 42).

PART II
UNITED KINGDOM
Oaths

2–1191   3. Swearing with uplifted hands. If any person to whom an oath is administered desires to swear with uplifted hand, in the form and manner in which an oath is usually administered in Scotland, he shall be permitted so to do, and the oath shall be administered to him in such form and manner without further question.
[Oaths Act 1978, s 3.]

2–1192   4. Validity of oaths. (1) In any case in which an oath may lawfully be and has been administered to any person, if it has been administered in a form and manner other than that prescribed by law, he is bound by it if it has been administered in such form and with such ceremonies as he may have declared to be binding.

(2) Where an oath has been duly administered and taken, the fact that the person to whom it was administered had, at the time of taking it, no religious belief, shall not for any purpose effect the validity of the oath.
[Oaths Act 1978, s 4.]

Solemn affirmations

2–1193   5. Making of solemn affirmations. (1) Any person who objects to being sworn shall be permitted to make his solemn affirmation instead of taking an oath[1].

(2) Subsection (1) above shall apply in relation to a person to whom it is not reasonably practicable without inconvenience or delay to administer an oath in the manner appropriate to his religious belief as it applies in relation to a person objecting to be sworn.

(3) A person who may be permitted under subsection (2) above to make his solemn affirmation may also be required to do so.

(4) A solemn affirmation shall be of the same force and effect as an oath.
[Oaths Act 1978, s 5.]

---

1. It is generally impermissible for a witness to be cross-examined about his reason for not taking an oath on a holy book unless the ground has properly been laid for an expectation that the witness would normally take the oath (*R v Mehrban* [2001] EWCA Crim 2627, [2002] 1 Cr App Rep 40, [2002] Crim LR 439).

2–1194 6. Form of affirmation. (1) Subject to subsection (2) below, every affirmation shall be as follows—

"I, ... do solemnly, sincerely and truly declare and affirm,"
and then proceed with the words of the oath prescribed by law, omitting any words of imprecation or calling to witness.

(2) Every affirmation in writing shall commence—

"I, ... of . . . . do, solemnly and sincerely affirm,"
and the form in lieu of jurat shall be "Affirmed at . . . . this
day of . . . . 19 . . . , Before me."
[Oaths Act 1978, s 6.]

Interpretation Act 1978
(1978 c 30)

General provisions as to enactment and operation

2–1210 1. Words of enactment. Every section of an Act takes effect as a substantive enactment without introductory words.
[Interpretation Act 1978, s 1.]

2–1211 2. Amendment or repeal in same Session. Any Act may be amended or repealed in the Session of Parliament in which it is passed.
[Interpretation Act 1978, s 2.]

2–1212 3. Judicial notice. Every Act is a public Act to be judicially noticed as such, unless the contrary is expressly provided by the Act.
[Interpretation Act 1978, s 3.]

2–1213 4. Time of commencement. An Act or provision of an Act comes into force—

(a) where provision is made for it to come into force on a particular day[1], at the beginning of that day;
(b) where no provision is made for its coming into force, at the beginning of the day on which the Act receives the Royal Assent.
[Interpretation Act 1978, s 4.]

---

1. When commencement is "at the expiration of one month beginning with the date on which it is passed", a statute which receives the Royal Assent on 29 July comes into force at midnight on 28/29 August (*Hare v Gocher* [1962] 2 QB 641, [1962] 2 All ER 763, 126 JP 395). Section 13 of the 1978 Act enables powers to make subordinate legislation to be exercised before commencement, and operative from commencement.

Where the Executive has taken action on new legislation in the period between Royal Assent and promulgation of the Act, the availability of judicial review may remedy any unfairness and any contravention of the principles of acting in accordance with the law and legal certainty in the European Convention on Human Rights: *R (L) v Secretary of State for the Home Department* [2003] EWCA Civ 25, [2003] 1 All ER 1062, [2003] 1 WLR 1230.

Interpretation and construction

2–1214 5. Definitions. In any Act, unless the contrary intention appears, words and expressions listed in Schedule 1 to this Act are to be construed according to that Schedule.
[Interpretation Act 1978, s 5.]

2–1215 6. Gender and number. In any Act, unless the contrary intention appears—

(a) words importing the masculine gender include the feminine;
(b) words importing the feminine gender include the masculine;
(c) words in the singular include[1] the plural and words in the plural include the singular.
[Interpretation Act 1978, s 6.]

---

1. To "include" the plural does not mean that the word must discard its singularity. Subject to the context, the Act authorises a process of selective pluralising (*No 20 Cannon Street Ltd v Singer and Friedlander Ltd* [1974] 2 All ER 577).

2–1216 7. References to service by post. Where an Act authorises or requires any document to be served by post (whether the expression "serve" or the expression "give" or "send"[1] or any other expression is used) then, unless the contrary intention appears, the service is deemed to be effected

by properly addressing, pre-paying and posting a letter containing the document and, unless the contrary is proved, to have been effected at the time at which the letter would be delivered in the ordinary course of post[2].
[Interpretation Act 1978, s 7.]

1. The ordinary meaning of "send" is dispatch, unless it is used with other words which make it clear that "delivery" is intended (*Retail Dairy Co Ltd v Clarke* [1912] 2 KB 388, 76 JP 282).

Section 7 is in two parts. The first part provides that the dispatch of a document in the manner laid down shall be deemed to be service thereof. The second part provides that, unless the contrary is proved, service is effected on the day when in the ordinary course of post the document would be delivered. The second part comes into play only where the Act provides that a document has to be received by a certain time (*per* PARKER LJ in *R v London Quarter Sessions Appeals Committee, ex p Rossi* [1956] 1 QB 682, [1956] 1 All ER 670, 120 JP 239). In that case, a notice of hearing was returned undelivered; that negatived the presumption of effected service; similarly with a notice of intended prosecution under the Road Traffic Act (*Beer v Davies* [1958] 2 QB 187, [1958] 2 All ER 255, 122 JP 344). On the other hand, receipt by the accused's wife at his house has sufficed (*Burt v Kirkcaldy* [1965] 1 All ER 741, 129 JP 190) and even when he was in hospital and was not told of the notice although he could have dealt with it himself (*Hosier v Goodall* [1962] 2 QB 401, [1962] 1 All ER 30, 126 JP 52). See now, however, the Road Traffic Offenders Act 1988, s 1, in PART IV: TRANSPORT, title ROAD TRAFFIC, post, which makes special provision for notices of intended prosecution.

In *Moody v Godstone RDC* [1966] 2 All ER 696, 130 JP 332, it was stated that the second part of what was s 26 of the Interpretation Act 1889 could not enable a defendant to show that he had not received a registered letter containing an enforcement notice under the Town and Country Planning Act; the situation was however different where there was evidence of the letter being returned marked "gone away" (*Maltglade Ltd v St Albans RDC* [1972] 3 All ER 129). Refusal of a registered letter containing a notice to quit did not prevent good service (*Van Grutten v Trevenen* [1902] 2 KB 82).

The *Practice Direction* [1985] 1 All ER 889, [1985] 1 WLR 489, provides that it will be taken, subject to proof to the contrary, that delivery in the ordinary course of post was effected in the case of first class mail, on the second working day after posting, and in the case of second class mail, on the fourth working day after posting. "Working days" are Monday to Friday, excluding any Bank Holiday.

2. See service provisions in the Magistrates' Courts Rules 1981, rr 67 and 99 and the Criminal Procedure Rules 2005, Part 4, in PART I: MAGISTRATES' COURTS, PROCEDURE, ante.

2–1217 8. References to distance. In the measurement of any distance for the purposes of an Act, that distance shall, unless the contrary intention appears, be measured in a straight line on a horizontal plane[1].
[Interpretation Act 1978, s 8.]

1. See *Langley v Wilson* [1943] 2 All ER 213.

2–1218 9. References to time of day. Subject to section 3 of the Summer Time Act 1972[1] (construction of references to points of time during the period of summer time), whenever an expression of time occurs in an Act, the time referred to shall, unless it is otherwise specifically stated, be held to be Greenwich mean time.
[Interpretation Act 1978, s 9.]

1. See para **2–744 Time** ante.

2–1219 10. References to the Sovereign. In any Act a reference to the Sovereign reigning at the time of the passing of the Act is to be construed, unless the contrary intention appears, as a reference to the Sovereign for the time being.
[Interpretation Act 1978, s 10.]

2–1220 11. Construction of subordinate legislation. Where an Act confers power to make subordinate legislation, expressions used in that legislation have, unless the contrary intention appears, the meaning which they bear in the Act.
[Interpretation Act 1978, s 11.]

Statutory powers and duties

2–1221 12. Continuity of powers and duties. (1) Where an Act confers a power or imposes a duty it is implied, unless the contrary intention appears, that the power may be exercised, or the duty is to be performed, from time to time as occasion requires.

(2) Where an Act confers a power or imposes a duty on the holder of an office as such, it is implied, unless the contrary intention appears, that the power may be exercised, or the duty is to be performed, by the holder for the time being of the office.
[Interpretation Act 1978, s 12.]

2–1222 13. Anticipatory exercise of powers. Where an Act which (or any provision of which) does not come into force immediately on its passing confers power to make subordinate legislation, or to make appointments, give notices, prescribe forms or do any other thing for the purposes of the Act, then, unless the contrary intention appears, the power may be exercised, and any instrument made thereunder may be made so as to come into force, at any time after the passing of the Act so far as may be necessary or expedient for the purpose—

(*a*) of bringing the Act or any provision of the Act into force; or
(*b*) of giving full effect to the Act or any such provision at or after the time when it comes into force.
[Interpretation Act 1978, s 13.]

2–1223 14. Implied power to amend. Where an Act confers power to make—

(*a*) rules, regulations or byelaws; or

(*b*) Orders in Council, orders or other subordinate legislation to be made by statutory instrument,

it implies, unless the contrary intention appears, a power, exercisable in the same manner and subject to the same conditions or limitations, to revoke, amend or re-enact any instrument made under the power.
[Interpretation Act 1978, s 14.]

Repealing enactments

2–1224 15. Repeal of repeal. Where an Act repeals a repealing enactment, the repeal does not revive any enactment previously repealed unless words are added reviving it.
[Interpretation Act 1978, s 15.]

2–1225 16. General savings. (1) Without prejudice to section 15, where an Act repeals an enactment, the repeal does not, unless the contrary intention[1] appears—

(*a*) revive anything not in force or existing at the time at which the repeal takes effect;

(*b*) affect the previous operation of the enactment repealed or anything duly done or suffered under that enactment;

(*c*) affect any right, privilege, obligation or liability[2] acquired, accrued or incurred under that enactment;

(*d*) affect any penalty, forfeiture or punishment incurred in respect of any offence committed against that enactment;

(*e*) affect any investigation, legal proceeding or remedy in respect of any such right, privilege, obligation, liability, penalty, forfeiture or punishment;

and any such investigation, legal proceeding or remedy may be instituted, continued or enforced, and any such penalty, forfeiture or punishment may be imposed, as if the repealing Act had not been passed.

(2) This section applies to the expiry of a temporary enactment as if it were repealed by an Act.
[Interpretation Act 1978, s 16.]

---

1. It is the repealing Act, not the one that is being repealed, which must manifest a contrary intention so as to exclude the operation of s 16 (*Aitken v South Hams District Council* [1994] 3 All ER 400, [1994] 3 WLR 333, 159 JP 25, HL). An enactment which effects a repeal not by using the word "repeal" but by providing that the repealed provision "shall cease to have effect" does not indicate a "contrary intention" within the meaning of s 16 (*Metropolitan Police Comr v Simeon* [1982] 2 All ER 813, 146 JP 286).

2. The words "obligation or liability" apply to criminal as well as civil enforcement (*Aitken v South Hams District Council* [1995] 1 AC 262, [1994] 3 All ER 400, 159 JP 25, HL).

2–1226 17. Repeal and re-enactment. (1) Where an Act repeals a previous enactment and substitutes provisions for the enactment repealed, the repealed enactment remains in force until the substituted provisions come into force.

(2) Where an Act repeals and re-enacts, with or without modification, a previous enactment then, unless the contrary intention appears—

(*a*) any reference in any other enactment to the enactment so repealed shall be construed as a reference to the provision re-enacted;

(*b*) in so far as any subordinate legislation made or other thing done under the enactment so repealed, or having effect as if so made or done, could have been made or done under the provision re-enacted, it shall have effect as if made or done under that provision.
[Interpretation Act 1978, s 17.]

Miscellaneous

2–1227 18. Duplicated offences. Where an act or omission constitutes an offence under two or more Acts, or both under an Act and at common law, the offender shall, unless the contrary intention appears, be liable to be prosecuted and punished under either or any of those Acts or at common law, but shall not be liable to be punished more than once for the same offence.
[Interpretation Act 1978, s 18.]

2–1228 19. Citation of other Acts. (1) Where an Act cites another Act by year, statute, session or chapter, or a section or other portion of another Act by number or letter, the reference shall, unless the contrary intention appears, be read as referring—

(*a*) in the case of Acts included in any revised edition of the statutes printed by authority, to that edition;

(*b*) in the case of Acts not so included but included in the edition prepared under the direction of the Record Commission, to that edition;

(*c*) in any other case, to the Acts printed by the Queen's Printer, or under the superintendence or authority of Her Majesty's Stationery Office.

(2) An Act may continue to be cited by the short title authorised by any enactment notwithstanding the repeal of that enactment.
[Interpretation Act 1978, s 19.]

2–1229　20. References to other enactments.　(1) Where an Act describes or cites a portion of an enactment by referring to words, sections or other parts from or to which (or from and to which) the portion extends, the portion described or cited includes the words, sections or other parts referred to unless the contrary intention appears.

(2) Where an Act refers to an enactment, the reference, unless the contrary intention appears, is a reference to that enactment as amended, and includes a reference thereto as extended or applied, by or under any other enactment, including any other provision of that Act.

[Interpretation Act 1978, s 20.]

2–1229A　20A. References to Community instruments.　Where an Act passed after the commencement of this section refers to a Community instrument that has been amended, extended or applied by another such instrument, the reference, unless the contrary intention appears, is a reference to that instrument as so amended, extended or applied.

[Interpretation Act 1978, s 20 as inserted by the Legislative and Regulatory Reform Act 2006, s 25.]

Supplementary

2–1240　21. Interpretation etc.　(1) In this Act "Act" includes a local and personal or private Act; and "subordinate legislation" means Orders in Council, orders, rules, regulations, schemes, warrants, byelaws and other instruments made or to be made under any Act.

(2) This Act binds the Crown.

[Interpretation Act 1978, s 21.]

2–1241　22. Application to Acts and Measures.　(1) This Act applies to itself, to any Act passed after the commencement of this Act (subject, in the case of section 20A, to the provision made in that section) and, to the extent specified in Part I of Schedule 2, to Acts passed before the commencement of this Act.

(2) In any of the foregoing provisions of this Act a reference to an Act is a reference to an Act to which that provision applies; but this does not affect the generality of references to enactments or of the references in section 19(1) to other Acts.

(3) [General Synod.]

[Interpretation Act 1978, s 22 as amended by the Legislative and Regulatory Reform Act 2006, s 25.]

2–1242　23. Application to other instruments.　(1) The provisions of this Act, except sections 1 to 3 and 4 (*b*), apply, so far as applicable and unless the contrary intention appears, to subordinate legislation made after the commencement of this Act and, to the extent specified in Part II of Schedule 2, to subordinate legislation made before the commencement of this Act, as they apply to Acts.

(2) In the application of this Act to Acts passed or subordinate legislation made after the commencement of this Act, all references to an enactment include an enactment comprised in subordinate legislation whenever made, and references to the passing or repeal of an enactment are to be construed accordingly.

(3) Sections 9 and 19(1) also apply to deeds and other instruments and documents as they apply to Acts and subordinate legislation; and in the application of section 17(2)(*a*) to Acts passed or subordinate legislation made after the commencement of this Act, the reference to any other enactment includes any deed or other instrument or document.

(4) Subsections (1) and (2) of this section do not apply to Orders in Council made under section 5 of the Statutory Instruments Act 1946, section 1(3) of the Northern Ireland (Temporary Provisions) Act 1972 or Schedule 1 to the Northern Ireland Act 1974.

[Interpretation Act 1978, s 23.]

2–1242A　23A. Acts of the Scottish Parliament etc.　(1) This Act applies in relation to an Act of the Scottish Parliament and an instrument made under such an Act only to the extent provided in this section.

(2) Except as provided in subsection (3) below, sections 15 to 18 apply to—

(*a*)　an Act of the Scottish Parliament as they apply to an Act,

(*b*)　an instrument made under an Act of the Scottish Parliament as they apply to subordinate legislation.

(3) In the application of those sections to an Act and to subordinate legislation—

(*a*)　references to an enactment include an enactment comprised in, or in an instrument made under, an Act of the Scottish Parliament, and

(*b*)　the reference in section 17(2)(*b*) to subordinate legislation includes an instrument made under an Act of the Scottish Parliament.

(4) In the application of section 20 to an Act and to subordinate legislation, references to an enactment include an enactment comprised in, or in an instrument made under, an Act of the Scottish Parliament.*

[Interpretation Act 1978, s 23A as inserted by the Scotland Act 1998, Sch 8.]

---

*New s 23B inserted by the Government of Wales Act 2006, Sch 10 immediately after the ordinary election (under the Government of Wales Act 1998, s 3) held in 2007.

2–1243   25. Repeals and savings.   (1) *Repeals.*

(2) Without prejudice to section 17(2)(*a*), a reference to the Interpretation Act 1889, to any provision of that Act or to any other enactment repealed by this Act[1], whether occurring in another Act, in subordinate legislation, in Northern Ireland legislation or in any deed or other instrument or document, shall be construed as referring to this Act, or to the corresponding provision of this Act, as it applies to Acts passed at the time of the reference.

(3) The provisions of this Act relating to Acts passed after any particular time do not affect the construction of Acts passed before that time, though continued or amended by Acts passed thereafter.
[Interpretation Act 1978, s 25.]

---

1. The 1978 Act came into force on 1 January 1979.

Section 5   SCHEDULE 1[1]
                                    WORDS AND EXPRESSIONS DEFINED

(*As amended by the Nurses, Midwives and Health Visitors Act 1979, Sch 7, the Magistrates' Courts Act 1980, Sch 7, the British Nationality Act 1981, Sch 9, the Medical Act 1983, Sch 5, the County Courts Act 1984, Sch 2, the Building Act 1984, Sch 6, the Finance Act, 1987, Sch 15, the Family Law Reform Act 1987, Sch 2, the Criminal Justice Act 1988, Sch 15, the Water Act 1989, Sch 25, the Children Act 1989, Sch 15, the Water Consolidation (Consequential Provisions) Act 1991, Sch 1, the Local Government Act 1992, Sch 3, the Local Government (Wales) Act 1994, Sch 2, the Police Act 1996, Sch 7, the Trusts of Land and Appointment of Trustees Act 1996, Sch 3, the Scotland Act 1998, Sch 8, SI 2002/253, the Criminal Justice Act 2003, Sch 3, the Civil Partnership Act 2004, Sch 27 and the Immigration, Asylum and Nationality Act 2006, s 64.*)*

2–1244   *Note:* The years or dates which follow certain entries in this Schedule are relevant for the purposes of paragraph 4 of Schedule 2 (application to existing enactments).

Definitions

"Act" means an Act of Parliament.

"Associated state" means a territory maintaining a status of association with the United Kingdom in accordance with the West Indies Act 1967. [16th February 1967]

"British Islands" means the United Kingdom, the Channel Islands and the Isle of Man. [1889]

"British overseas territory" has the same meaning as in the British Nationality Act 1981;

"British possession" means any part of Her Majesty's dominions outside the United Kingdom; and where parts of such dominions are under both a central and a local legislature, all parts under the central legislature are deemed, for the purposes of this definition, to be one British possession. [1889]

"Building regulations", in relation to England and Wales, has the meaning given by section 122 of the Building Act 1984.

"Central funds", in an enactment providing in relation to England and Wales for the payment of costs out of central funds, means money provided by Parliament.*

"Civil partnership" means a civil partnership which exists under or by virtue of the Civil Partnership Act 2004 (and any reference to a civil partnership is to be read accordingly).

"Colony" means any part of Her Majesty's dominions outside the British Islands except—

    (*a*)   countries having fully responsible status within the Commonwealth;
    (*b*)   territories for whose external relations a country other than the United Kingdom is responsible;
    (*c*)   associated states;

and where parts of such dominions are under both a central and a local legislature, all parts under the central legislature are deemed for the purposes of this definition to be one colony. [1889]

"Commencement", in relation to an Act or enactment, means the time when the Act or enactment comes into force.

"Committed for trial" means—

    (*a*)   in relation to England and Wales, committed in custody or on bail by a magistrates' court pursuant to section 6 of the Magistrates' Courts Act 1980, or by any judge or other authority having power to do so, with a view to trial before a judge and jury; [1889]*
    (*b*)   [*Northern Ireland.*] [1st January 1979]

"The Communities", "the Treaties" or "the Community Treaties" and other expressions defined by section 1 of and Schedule 1 to the European Communities Act 1972 have the meanings prescribed by that Act.

"The Corporation Tax Acts" means the enactments relating to the taxation of the income and chargeable gains of companies and of company distributions (including provisions relating to income tax);

"County court" means—

    (*a*)   in relation to England and Wales, a court held for a district under the County Courts Act 1984; [1846]
    (*b*)   [*Northern Ireland.*] [1889]

"Court of Appeal" means—

    (*a*)   in relation to England and Wales, Her Majesty's Court of Appeal in England;
    (*b*)   [*Northern Ireland.*]

"Crown Court" means—

    (*a*)   in relation to England and Wales, the Crown Court constituted by section 4 of the Courts Act 1971;
    (*b*)   [*Northern Ireland.*]

"Enactment" does not include an enactment comprised in, or an instrument made under, an Act of the Scottish Parliament.

"England" means, subject to any alteration of boundaries under Part IV of the Local Government Act 1972, the area consisting of the counties established by section 1 of that Act, Greater London and the Isles of Scilly. [1st April 1974]

"Financial year" means, in relation to matters relating to the Consolidated Fund, the National Loans Fund, or moneys provided by Parliament, or to the Exchequer or to central taxes or finance, the twelve months ending with 31st March. [1889]

"High Court" means—

    (a) in relation to England and Wales, Her Majesty's High Court of Justice in England;
    (b) [*Northern Ireland.*]

"The Immigration Acts" has the meaning given by section 64 of the Immigration, Asylum and Nationality Act 2006.

"The Income Tax Acts" means all enactments relating to income tax, including any provisions of the Corporation Tax Acts which relate to income tax.

"Land" includes buildings and other structures, land covered with water, and any estate, interest, easement, servitude or right in or over land. [1st January 1979][2].

"London borough" means a borough described in Schedule 1 to the London Government Act 1963, "inner London borough" means one of the boroughs so described and numbered from 1 to 12 and "outer London borough" means one of the boroughs so described and numbered from 13 to 32, subject (in each case) to any alterations made under Part IV of the Local Government Act 1972 or Part II of the Local Government Act 1992.

"Lord Chancellor" means the Lord High Chancellor of Great Britain.

"Magistrates' court" has the meaning assigned to it—

    (a) in relation to England and Wales, by section 148 of the Magistrates' Courts Act 1980;
    (b) [Northern Ireland.]

"Month" means calendar month. [1850]

"Oath" and "affidavit" include affirmation and declaration, and "swear" includes affirm and declare.

"Ordnance Map" means a map made under powers conferred by the Ordnance Survey Act 1841 or the Boundary Survey (Ireland) Act 1854.

"Parliamentary Election" means the election of a Member to serve in Parliament for a constituency. [1889]

"PAYE income" has the meaning given by section 683 of the Income Tax (Earnings and Pensions) Act 2003.

"PAYE regulations" means regulations under section 684 of that Act.

"Person" includes a body of persons corporate or unincorporate. [1889][3]

"Police area", "police authority" and other expressions relating to the police have the meaning or effect described—

    (a) in relation to England and Wales, by section 101(1) of the Police Act 1996;
    (b) in relation to Scotland, by sections 50 and 51(4) of the Police (Scotland) Act 1967.

"Registered" in relation to nurses, midwives and health visitors, means registered in the register maintained under article 5 of the Nursing and Midwifery Order 2001 by virtue of qualifications in nursing, midwifery or health visiting, as the case may be.

"Registered medical practitioner" means a fully registered person within the meaning of the Medical Act 1983, [1st January 1979]**

"Rules of Court" in relation to any court means rules made by the authority having power to make rules or orders regulating the practice and procedure of that court, and in Scotland includes Acts of Adjournal and Acts of Sederunt; and the power of the authority to make rules of court (as above defined) includes power to make such rules for the purpose of any Act which directs or authorises anything to be done by rules of court. [1889]

"Secretary of State" means one of Her Majesty's Principal Secretaries of State.***

"Sent for trial" means, in relation to England and Wales, sent by a magistrates' court to the Crown Court for trial pursuant to section 51 or 51A of the Crime and Disorder Act 1998.

"Sewerage undertaker", in relation to England and Wales, shall be construed in accordance with section 6 of the Water Industry Act 1991.

"The standard scale", with reference to a fine or penalty for an offence triable only summarily,—

    (a) in relation to England and Wales, has the meaning given by section 37 of the Criminal Justice Act 1982;
    (b)–(c) *Scotland; Northern Ireland.*

"Statutory declaration" means a declaration made by virtue of the Statutory Declarations Act 1835[4].

"Statutory maximum", with reference to a fine or penalty on summary conviction for an offence,—

    (a) in relation to England and Wales, means the prescribed sum within the meaning of section 32 of the Magistrates' Courts Act 1980;
    (b)–(c) *Scotland; Northern Ireland.*

"Supreme Court" means—

    (a) in relation to England and Wales, the Court of Appeal and the High Court together with the Crown Court;

(b) *[Northern Ireland.]*★★★

"The Tax Acts" means the Income Tax Acts and the Corporation Tax Acts.

"United Kingdom" means Great Britain and Northern Ireland. [12th April 1927]

"Wales" means the combined areas of the counties which were created by section 20 of the Local Government Act 1972, as originally enacted, but subject to any alteration made under section 73 of that Act (consequential alteration of boundary following alteration of watercourse).

"Water undertaker", in relation to England and Wales, shall be construed in accordance with section 6 of the Water Industry Act 1991.

"Writing" includes typing, printing, lithography, photography and other modes of representing or reproducing words in a visible form, and expressions referring to writing are construed accordingly.

Construction of certain expressions relating to offences

In relation to England and Wales—

(a) "indictable offence" means an offence which, if committed by an adult, is triable on indictment, whether it is exclusively so triable or triable either way;

(b) "summary offence" means an offence which, if committed by an adult, is triable only summarily;

(c) "offence triable either way" means an offence, other than an offence triable on indictment only by virtue of Part V of the Criminal Justice Act 1988[5] which, if committed by an adult, is triable either on indictment or summarily;

and the terms "indictable", "summary" and "triable either way", in their application to offences, are to be construed accordingly.

In the above definitions references to the way or ways in which an offence is triable are to be construed without regard to the effect, if any, of section 22 of the Magistrates' Courts Act 1980 on the mode of trial in a particular case.

Construction of certain references to relationships

In relation to England and Wales—

(a) references (however expressed) to any relationship between two persons;

(b) references to a person whose father and mother were or were not married to each other at the time of his birth; and

(c) references cognate with references falling within paragraph (b) above, shall be construed in accordance with section 1 of the Family Law Reform Act 1987. [The date of the coming into force of that section.]

---

*Repealed by the Criminal Justice Act 2003, Sch 3 from a date to be appointed.
**Definition substituted by SI 2002/3135 from a date to be notified in the London, Edinburgh and Belfast Gazettes.
***Definition "Senior Courts" inserted and definition "Supreme Court" substituted by the Constitutional Reform Act 2005, Sch 11 from a date to be appointed.

1. The following definitions are not reproduced in this manual: "Bank of England", "Bank of Ireland", "Charity Commissioners", "Church Commissioners", "Colonial legislature", "Comptroller and Auditor General", "Consular Officer", "Court of Summary Jurisdiction" (etc, Northern Ireland), "Crown Estate Commissioners", "Governor-General", "Her Majesty's Revenue and Customs", "Lands Clauses Acts", "Local land charges register", "National Debt Commissioners", "Northern Ireland legislation", "Officer of Revenue and Customs", "The Privy Council", "Sheriff", "The Treasury", "Trust of Land" and "trustees of land".

2. But see Sch 2, para 5(b), post.

3. A contrary intention is inferred in a case involving personal violence (*Pharmaceutical Society v London and Provincial Supply Association* (1880) 5 App Cas 857, 45 JP 20; *R v Great North of England Rly Co* (1846) 9 QB 315, 11 JP 21. What is now the Magistrates' Courts Act 1980, Sch 3, ante, is merely machinery and does not alter the substantive law (*R v Cory Bros & Co* [1927] 1 KB 810).

4. See Precedent No 167 in Part IX: Precedents and Forms, post.

5. See Part I: Magistrates' Courts, Procedure, ante.

Sections 22, 23   SCHEDULE 2
Application of Act to Existing Enactments

(As amended by the British Nationality Act 1981, Sch 9, the Family Law Reform Act 1987, Schs 2 and 4 and the Health Authorities Act 1995, Sch 3.)

Part I
Acts

2–1245   1. The following provisions of this Act apply to Acts whenever passed:

Section 6(a) and (c) so far as applicable to enactments relating to offences punishable on indictment or on summary conviction
Section 9
Section 10
Section 11 so far as it relates to subordinate legislation made after the year 1889
Section 18
Section 19(2).

2. The following apply to Acts passed after the year 1850:

Section 1
Section 2
Section 3
Section 6(a) and (c) so far as not applicable to such Acts by virtue of paragraph 1
Section 15
Section 17(1).

3. The following apply to Acts passed after the year 1889:

Section 4
Section 7
Section 8
Section 12
Section 13
Section 14 so far as it relates to rules, regulations or byelaws
Section 16(1)
Section 17(2)(*a*)
Section 19(1)
Section 20(1).

4. (1) Subject to the following provisions of this paragraph—

(*a*) paragraphs of Schedule 1 at the end of which a year or date is specified or described apply, so far as applicable, to Acts passed on or after the date, or after the year, so specified or described; and
(*b*) paragraphs of that Schedule at the end of which no year or date is specified or described apply, so far as applicable, to Acts passed at any time.

(2) The definition of "British Islands", in its application to Acts passed after the establishment of the Irish Free State but before the commencement of this Act, includes the Republic of Ireland.

(3) The definition of "colony", in its application to an Act passed at any time before the commencement of this Act, includes—

(*a*) any colony within the meaning of section 18(3) of the Interpretation Act 1889 which was excluded, but in relation only to Acts passed at a later time, by any enactment repealed by this Act;
(*b*) any country or territory which ceased after that time to be part of Her Majesty's dominions but subject to a provision for the continuation of existing law as if it had not so ceased;

and paragraph (*b*) of the definition does not apply.

(4) The definition of "Lord Chancellor" does not apply to Acts passed before 1st October 1921 in which that expression was used in relation to Ireland only.

(5) The definition of "person", so far as it includes bodies corporate, applies to any provision of an Act whenever passed relating to an offence punishable on indictment or on summary conviction.

(6) This paragraph applies to the Water Act 1973 as if they were passed after 1st April 1974.

5. The following definitions shall be treated as included in Schedule 1 for the purposes specified in this paragraph—

(*a*) in any Act passed before 1st April 1974, a reference to England includes Berwick upon Tweed and Monmouthshire and, in the case of an Act passed before the Welsh Language Act 1967, Wales;
(*b*) in any Act passed before the commencement of this Act and after the year 1850, "land" includes messuages, tenements and hereditaments, houses and buildings of any tenure;
(*c*) in any Act passed before the commencement of the Criminal Procedure (Scotland) Act 1975, "the Summary Jurisdiction (Scotland) Acts" means Part II of that Act.

PART II
SUBORDINATE LEGISLATION

6. Sections 4(*a*), 9 and 19(1), and so much of Schedule 1 as defines the following expressions, namely—

England;
Local land charges register and appropriate local land charges register;
Police area (and related expressions) in relation to Scotland;
United Kingdom;
Wales,

apply to subordinate legislation made at any time before the commencement of this Act as they apply to Acts passed at that time.

7. The definition in Schedule 1 of "county court", in relation to England and Wales, applies to Orders in Council made after the year 1846.

Police and Criminal Evidence Act 1984

(1984 c 60)

PART VII[1]
DOCUMENTARY[2] EVIDENCE IN CRIMINAL PROCEEDINGS

2–1352   71. Microfilm copies. In any proceedings the contents of a document may (whether or not the document is still in existence) be proved by the production of an enlargement of a microfilm copy of that document or of the material part of it, authenticated in such manner as the court may approve.

Where the proceedings concerned are proceedings before a magistrates' court inquiring into an offence as examining justices this section shall have effect with the omission of the words "authenticated in such manner as the court may approve".

[Police and Criminal Evidence Act 1984, s 71, as amended by the Criminal Procedure and Investigations Act 1996, Sch 1.]

2–1353   72. Part VII—supplementary. (1) In this Part of this Act—

"copy", in relation to a document, means anything onto which information recorded in the document has been copied, by whatever means and whether directly or indirectly, and "statement" means any representation of fact, however made; and "proceedings" means criminal proceedings, including—[*inclusion of courts-martial etc.*]

(2) Nothing in this Part of this Act shall prejudice any power of a court to exclude evidence (whether by preventing questions from being put or otherwise) at its discretion.
[Police and Criminal Evidence Act 1984, s 72 as amended by the Civil Evidence Act 1995, Sch 1 and the Armed Forces Act 1996, Sch 1.]

PART VIII[1]
EVIDENCE IN CRIMINAL PROCEEDINGS—GENERAL

Convictions and acquittals

2–1354   **73. Proof of convictions and acquittals.**   (1) Where in any proceedings the fact that a person has in the United Kingdom been convicted or acquitted of an offence otherwise than by a Service court is admissible in evidence, it may be proved by producing a certificate of conviction or, as the case may be, of acquittal relating to that offence, and proving that the person named in the certificate as having been convicted or acquitted of the offence is the person whose conviction or acquittal of the offence is to be proved[2].

(2) For the purposes of this section a certificate of conviction or of acquittal—

(*a*)   shall, as regards a conviction or acquittal on indictment, consist of a certificate, signed by the proper officer of the court where the conviction or acquittal took place, giving the substance and effect (omitting the formal parts) of the indictment and of the conviction or acquittal; and

(*b*)   shall, as regards a conviction or acquittal on a summary trial, consist of a copy of the conviction or of the dismissal of the information, signed by the proper officer of the court where the conviction or acquittal took place or by the proper officer of the court, if any, to which a memorandum of the conviction or acquittal was sent;

and a document purporting to be a duly signed certificate of conviction or acquittal under this section shall be taken to be such a certificate unless the contrary is proved.

(3) In subsection (2) above "proper officer" means—

(*a*)   in relation to a magistrates' court in England and Wales, the designated officer for the court; and

(*b*)   in relation to any other court, the clerk of the court, his deputy or any other person having custody of the court record.

(4) The method of proving a conviction or acquittal authorised by this section shall be in addition to and not to the exclusion of any other authorised manner of proving a conviction or acquittal.
[Police and Criminal Evidence Act 1984, s 73, as amended by the Access to Justice Act 1999, Sch 13 and the Courts Act 2003, Sch 8.]

---

1. Part VIII contains ss 73–82.
2. Proof of a conviction pursuant to this section involves two requirements. First, production of a certificate of conviction and, secondly, proof that the person named in the certificate, as having been convicted, is one and the same person (*R v Derwentside Magistrates' Court, ex p Heaviside* (1995) 160 JP 317, [1996] RTR 384). It is a matter for the justices in each case to determine on the evidence presented to them whether they are satisfied so they are sure that the defendant actually is the individual to whom the previous conviction refers (*R v Derwentside Magistrates' Court, ex p Swift* (1995) 160 JP 468, [1997] RTR 89; *R v DPP, ex p Mansfield* (1995) 160 JP 472, [1997] RTR 96); an informal admission to the police when charged is sufficient, it is not necessary to have a formal admission under s 10 of the Criminal Justice Act 1967 (*DPP v Mooney* [1997] RTR 434, [1997] Crim LR 137, DC—defendant "pleaded" guilty to driving whilst disqualified to the police when charged). A judge was fully entitled to reach the conclusion of the identity of the accused and the conviction by reference to the appellant's uncommon name, date of birth and addresses on the Isle of Wight. The confusion with another person was minimal: *R v Lewendon* [2006] EWCA Crim 648, [2006] 1 WLR 1278, [2006] Cr App R 19.
   Foreign convictions are admissible in accordance with s 7 of the Evidence Act 1851, in this PART, ante, and may be proved by any evidence in the ordinary way. Evidence of fingerprints may be admitted although foreign convictions are not within the provisions of the Criminal Evidence Act 1948 (*R v Mauricia* [2002] EWCA Crim 676, [2002] 2 Cr App Rep 27).

2–1355   **74. Conviction as evidence of commission of offence.**   (1) In any proceedings the fact that a person other than the accused has been convicted[1] of an offence by or before any court in the United Kingdom or by a Service court outside the United Kingdom shall be admissible in evidence for the purpose of proving that that person committed that offence, where evidence of his having done so is admissible is given.[2]

(2) In any proceedings in which by virtue of this section a person other than the accused is proved to have been convicted of an offence by or before any court in the United Kingdom or by a Service court outside the United Kingdom, he shall be taken to have committed that offence unless the contrary is proved.

(3) In any proceedings where evidence is admissible of the fact that the accused has committed an offence[3], if the accused is proved to have been convicted of the offence—

(*a*)   by or before any court in the United Kingdom; or

(*b*)   by a Service court outside the United Kingdom,

he shall be taken to have committed that offence unless the contrary is proved.

(4) Nothing in this section shall prejudice—

(*a*)   the admissibility in evidence of any conviction which would be admissible apart from this section; or

(b)   the operation of any enactment whereby a conviction or a finding of fact in any proceedings is for the purposes of any other proceedings made conclusive evidence of any fact.
[Police and Criminal Evidence Act 1984, s 74 as amended by the Criminal Justice Act 2003, Sch 36.]

1. "Convicted" can mean a plea of guilty or a formal finding of guilt as well as a final disposal of the case (*R v Robertson* [1987] QB 920, [1987] 3 All ER 231, CA); whether or not that person has been sentenced is irrelevant (*R v Golder* [1987] QB 920, [1987] 3 All ER 231).
2. It is understood that there is a drafting error in sub-s (1), in that words "is given" should have been included in the substitution made by the Criminal Justice Act 2003, s 331, Sch 36, Pt 5, para 85(1), (2). We await government clarification.
3. Section 74(3) does not define, or enlarge, the circumstances in which evidence of the commission of the earlier offence is admissible: *R v Harris* [2001] Crim LR 227, CA.

2–1356   75. Provisions supplementary to section 74.   (1) Where evidence that a person has been convicted of an offence is admissible by virtue of section 74 above, then without prejudice to the reception of any other admissible evidence for the purpose of identifying the facts on which the conviction was based—

(a)   the contents of any document which is admissible as evidence of the conviction; and
(b)   the contents of the information, complaint, indictment or charge-sheet on which the person in question was convicted,

shall be admissible in evidence for that purpose.

(2)   Where in any proceedings the contents of any document are admissible in evidence by virtue of subsection (1) above, a copy of that document, or of the material part of it, purporting to be certified or otherwise authenticated by or on behalf of the court or authority having custody of that document shall be admissible in evidence and shall be taken to be a true copy of that document or part unless the contrary is shown.

(3)   Nothing in any of the following—

(a)   section 14 of the Powers of Criminal Courts (Sentencing) Act 2000 (under which a conviction leading to probation or discharge is to be disregarded except as mentioned in that section);
(b)   section 247 of the Criminal Procedure (Scotland) Act 1995 (which makes similar provision in respect of convictions on indictment in Scotland); and
(c)   section 8 of the Probation Act (Northern Ireland) 1950 (which corresponds to section 13 of the Powers of Criminal Courts Act 1973) or any legislation which is in force in Northern Ireland for the time being and corresponds to that section,

shall affect the operation of section 74 above; and for the purposes of that section any order made by a court of summary jurisdiction in Scotland under section 228 or section 246(3) of the said Act of 1995 shall be treated as a conviction.

(4)   Nothing in section 74 above shall be construed as rendering admissible in any proceedings evidence of any conviction other than a subsisting one.
[Police and Criminal Evidence Act 1984, s 75 as amended by the Criminal Procedure (Consequential Provisions) (Scotland) Act 1995, Sch 4 and the Powers of Criminal Courts (Sentencing) Act 2000, Sch 9.]

Confessions

2–1357   76. Confessions[1].   (1) In any proceedings a confession made by an accused person may be given in evidence[2] against him in so far as it is relevant to any matter in issue in the proceedings and is not excluded by the court in pursuance of this section.

(2)   If, in any proceedings[3] where the prosecution proposes to give in evidence a confession made by an accused person, it is represented[4] to the court[5] that the confession was or may have been obtained—

(a)   by oppression[6] of the person who made it; or
(b)   in consequence of anything said or done[7] which was likely, in the circumstances[8] existing at the time, to render unreliable[9] any confession which might be made by him[10] in consequence thereof,

the court shall not allow[11] the confession to be given in evidence against him except in so far as the prosecution proves to the court beyond reasonable doubt that the confession (notwithstanding that it may be true) was not obtained as aforesaid[12].

(3)   In any proceedings where the prosecution proposes to give in evidence a confession made by an accused person, the court may of its own motion require the prosecution, as a condition of allowing it to do so, to prove that the confession was not obtained as mentioned in subsection (2) above.

(4)   The fact that a confession is wholly or partly excluded in pursuance of this section shall not affect the admissibility in evidence—

(a)   of any facts discovered as a result of the confession; or
(b)   where the confession is relevant as showing that the accused speaks, writes or expresses himself in a particular way, of so much of the confession as is necessary to show that he does so.

(5)   Evidence that a fact to which this subsection applies was discovered as a result of a statement made by an accused person shall not be admissible[13] unless evidence of how it was discovered is given by him or on his behalf.

(6) Subsection (5) above applies—

(*a*) to any fact discovered as a result of a confession which is wholly excluded in pursuance of this section; and

(*b*) to any fact discovered as a result of a confession which is partly so excluded, if the fact is discovered as a result of the excluded part of the confession.

(7) Nothing in Part VII of this Act shall prejudice the admissibility of a confession made by an accused person.

(8) In this section "oppression" includes torture, inhuman or degrading treatment, and the use or threat of violence (whether or not amounting to torture).

(9) Where the proceedings mentioned in subsection (1) above are proceedings before a magistrates' court inquiring into an offence as examining justices this section shall have effect with the omission of—

(*a*) in subsection (1) the words "and is not excluded by the court in pursuance of this section", and

(*b*) subsections (2) to (6) and (8).

[Police and Criminal Evidence Act 1984, s 76 as amended by the Criminal Procedure and Investigations Act 1996, Sch 1.]

---

1. "Confession" is defined in s 82 below.

2. Of course, a court must go on to decide what weight to give to evidence that has been found admissible.

3. This includes committal proceedings—see sub-s (9), post.

4. "Representation" is not the same as, nor does it include, cross-examination. If no such representation is made before the close of the prosecution case, the defendant is at liberty to raise admissibility or weight of the confession at any subsequent stage of the trial, see *R v Liverpool Juvenile Court, ex p R* [1988] QB 1, [1987] 2 All ER 668, 151 JP 516.

5. Compare "it appears to the court" in s 78(1), post: it would seem that the accused does not bear even an evidential burden under s 76(2) but may simply "represent" in order to put the prosecution to proof.

6. "Oppression" should be given its ordinary dictionary meaning, and denotes the exercise of authority or power in a burdensome, harsh or wrongful manner, or unjust or cruel treatment or the imposition of unreasonable or unjust burdens, in circumstances which would almost always entail some impropriety on the part of the interrogator (*R v Fulling* [1987] QB 476, [1987] 2 All ER 65, CA). A confession obtained after repeatedly shouting questions at an accused who was borderline mentally handicapped has been held to be unreliable by reason of oppression (*R v Paris* (1992) 97 Cr App Rep 99).

7. The words "said or done" do not include anything said or done by the person making the confession, but are limited to something external to that person and to something which is likely to have some influence on him (*R v Goldenberg* (1988) 152 JP 557, [1988] Crim LR 678, CA). The test to be applied is an objective one. Therefore, where the accused has a mental condition, it is not what the police officers may have thought about the accused's mental condition which is material, but what is subsequently ascertained from medical evidence to have been the state of the mental condition (*R v Everett* [1988] Crim LR 826). Similarly where a pregnant teenager of limited intelligence was denied access to a solicitor (*R v McGovern* (1990) 92 Cr App Rep 228, CA). Advice properly given to the defendant by a solicitor does not normally provide a basis for excluding a subsequent confession under s 76(2). One of the duties of a legal adviser is to give the client realistic advice. That does not mean the advice must be directed to "getting the client off", or simply make life difficult for the prosecution. The advice may and sometime ought to be robust (*R v Wahab* [2002] EWCA Crim 1570, [2003] 1 Cr App Rep 232).

8. The defendant's mental condition may be a "circumstance" which the court must take into account where relevant to do so, and includes mental impairment, impairment of intelligence or social functioning, or personality disorder. It would seem that the mental state of a drug addict who has just taken a fix or who is in withdrawal may be a potentially relevant circumstance, see *R v Crampton* [1991] Crim LR 277 and *R v Walker* [1998] Crim LR 211, CA, but see *R v Goldenberg*, supra, where the fact that the defendant was an addict in need of a fix was discounted and the interview admitted.

9. Where there was a breach of the Code of Practice in respect of a person with an IQ of about 80, it was held that in view of the sub-normal mentality of the defendant it was particularly important that the Code should have been observed; accordingly since there was a possibility of an unreliable confession the conviction was quashed (*R v Delaney* (1988) 153 JP 103, 88 Cr App Rep 338, [1989] Crim LR 139, CA). Whether or not someone who is a drug addict is fit to be interviewed, in the sense that his answers can be relied upon as being truthful, is a matter for judgment of those present at the time, see *R v Crampton* (1990) 92 Cr App Rep 369, CA.

10. Note that it is not the actual confession which was made, but *any* confession which *might* be made, a more speculative requirement.

11. The time to make a submission that the confession be excluded is before it is put in evidence, not afterwards (*R v Sat-Bhambra* (1988) 152 JP 365). For the purpose of determining on summary trial whether to allow evidence of the confession to be given, the justices shall hold a trial within a trial (*R v Liverpool Juvenile Court, ex p R* [1988] QB 1, [1987] 2 All ER 668, 151 JP 516). For principles to be applied, see para **1–567** in PART I: MAGISTRATES' COURTS, PROCEDURE, ante (for the respective roles of the judge and jury in the Crown Court, see *R v Mushtaq* [2005] UKHL 25, [2005] 3 All ER 885, [2005] 1 WLR 1513, [2005] 2 Cr App R 32). The code does not prevent a police officer from asking questions at or near the scene of a suspected crime, and admissions then made are prima facie admissible even though resulting from giving the opportunity to offer an innocent explanation (*R v Maguire* (1989) 90 Cr App Rep 115, [1989] Crim LR 815, CA; however, such informal questioning is limited and may lead to what may properly be regarded as an interview to which Code C applies (*R v Weekes* (1993) 97 Cr App Rep 222, CA). In such circumstances, although a contemporaneous record of the interview is no longer possible, a record should be made as soon as practicable of the earlier questions and answers, the reason for the absence of a contemporaneous note should be recorded and the suspect should be given the opportunity to check the record (*R v Park* (1993) 158 JP 144, [1994] Crim LR 285).

12. Regard may be had to the Codes of Practice: see s 67(11), in PART I: MAGISTRATES' COURTS, PROCEDURE, ante and the Codes of Practice are set out in this PART, post.

13. Taken with sub-s (6), this ensures that an inadmissible confession is not later introduced in evidence. The meaning of sub-ss (4)–(6) is that a fact discovered as the result of a confession (or part of a confession) which has been excluded can still be given in evidence, but the fact that it was discovered as the result of a statement by the accused may not unless such evidence is given by him or on his behalf.

2–1357A   **76A. Confessions may be given in evidence for co-accused.**   (1) In any proceedings a confession made by an accused person may be given in evidence for another person charged in the same proceedings (a co-accused) in so far as it is relevant to any matter in issue in the proceedings and is not excluded by the court in pursuance of this section.

(2) If, in any proceedings where a co-accused proposes to give in evidence a confession made by an accused person, it is represented to the court that the confession was or may have been obtained—

   (*a*) by oppression of the person who made it; or

   (*b*) in consequence of anything said or done which was likely, in the circumstances existing at the time, to render unreliable any confession which might be made by him in consequence thereof,

the court shall not allow the confession to be given in evidence for the co-accused except in so far as it is proved to the court on the balance of probabilities that the confession (notwithstanding that it may be true) was not so obtained.

(3) Before allowing a confession made by an accused person to be given in evidence for a co-accused in any proceedings, the court may of its own motion require the fact that the confession was not obtained as mentioned in subsection (2) above to be proved in the proceedings on the balance of probabilities.

(4) The fact that a confession is wholly or partly excluded in pursuance of this section shall not affect the admissibility in evidence—

   (*a*) of any facts discovered as a result of the confession; or

   (*b*) where the confession is relevant as showing that the accused speaks, writes or expresses himself in a particular way, of so much of the confession as is necessary to show that he does so.

(5) Evidence that a fact to which this subsection applies was discovered as a result of a statement made by an accused person shall not be admissible unless evidence of how it was discovered is given by him or on his behalf.

(6) Subsection (5) above applies—

   (*a*) to any fact discovered as a result of a confession which is wholly excluded in pursuance of this section; and

   (*b*) to any fact discovered as a result of a confession which is partly so excluded, if the fact is discovered as a result of the excluded part of the confession.

(7) In this section "oppression" includes torture, inhuman or degrading treatment, and the use or threat of violence (whether or not amounting to torture).

[Police and Criminal Evidence Act 1984, s 76A as inserted by the Criminal Justice Act 2003, s 128.]

2–1358 **77. Confessions[1] by mentally handicapped persons.**   (1) Without prejudice to the general duty of the court at a trial on indictment with a jury to direct the jury on any matter on which it appears to the court appropriate to do so, where at such a trial—

   (*a*) the case against the accused depends wholly or substantially on a confession by him; and

   (*b*) the court is satisfied—

      (i) that he is mentally handicapped; and

      (ii) that the confession was not made in the presence of an independent person,

the court shall[2] warn the jury that there is special need for caution before convicting the accused in reliance on the confession, and shall explain that the need arises because of the circumstances mentioned in paragraphs (*a*) and (*b*) above.

(2) In any case where at the summary trial of a person for an offence it appears to the court that a warning under subsection (1) above would be required if the trial were on indictment with a jury, the court shall treat the case as one in which there is a special need for caution before convicting the accused on his confession.

(2A) In any case where at the trial on indictment without a jury of a person for an offence it appears to the court that a warning under subsection (1) above would be required if the trial were with a jury, the court shall treat the case as one in which there is a special need for caution before convicting the accused on his confession.

(3) In this section—

"independent person" does not include a police officer or a person employed for, or engaged on, police purposes[3];

"mentally handicapped", in relation to a person, means that he is in a state of arrested or incomplete development of mind which includes significant impairment of intelligence and social functioning; and

"police purposes" has the meaning assigned to it by section 101(2) of the Police Act 1996.

[Police and Criminal Evidence Act 1984, s 77 as amended by the Police Act 1996, Sch 7 and the Criminal Justice Act 2003, Sch 36.]

---

   1. "Confession" is defined in s 82 below.

   2. See *R v Lamont* [1989] Crim LR 813, CA.

   3. Accordingly for these purposes, "independent person" may include the accused's own solicitor (*R v Lewis (Martin)* [1996] Crim LR 260, CA).

Miscellaneous

2–1359 **78. Exclusion of unfair evidence.**   (1) In any proceedings[1] the court may refuse[2] to allow evidence[3] on which the prosecution[4] proposes to rely to be given if it appears to the court[5] that, having regard to all the circumstances, including the circumstances in which the evidence was obtained, the admission of the evidence would have such an adverse effect on the fairness[6] of the proceedings[7] that the court ought not to admit it.

(2) Nothing in this section shall prejudice any rule of law requiring a court to exclude evidence.

(3) This section shall not apply in the case of proceedings before a magistrates' court inquiring into an offence as examining justices.

[Police and Criminal Evidence Act 1984, s 78, as amended by the Criminal Procedure and Investigations Act 1996, Sch 1.]

---

1. This section does not apply to committal proceedings—see sub-s (3), post. Sections 76 and 78 of PACE continue to have potential relevance to extradition proceedings subsequent to the amendments made to s 9(8) by the Criminal Justice and Public Order Act 1994. However, where a district judge is concerned in extradition proceedings with the fairness of admitting evidence he must have regard to the extradition context in which the issue arises; his decision is in, and solely for the purpose of, his determination on the issue of extradition and he should only exclude evidence where to admit it would outrage civilised values: *R v Bow Street Magistrates' Court, ex p Proulx* [2001] 1 All ER 57, DC. See also *Re Saifi* [2001] 4 All ER 168, [2001] 1 WLR 1134.

2. Even where the breach adversely affects the fairness of the proceedings, exclusion is not automatic (*R v Walsh* (1989) 91 Cr App Rep 161, [1989] Crim LR 822, CA). Justices should not use the discretion under s 78 to deny themselves the opportunity of coming to a conclusion on an essential element in the prosecution case, even where as a result of scientific examination, material evidence has been irretrievably altered before examination by a defence expert; see *DPP v British Telecommunications plc* (1990) 155 JP 869, [1991] Crim LR 532.

3. "Evidence" includes all evidence, including a confession, which may be introduced by the prosecution at a trial; accordingly a confession may be excluded under this section regardless of whether its admissibility falls to be considered under s 76(2), ante (*R v Mason* [1987] 3 All ER 481, 151 JP 747, CA). Section 78 may be applied to evidence of breath test procedures under the Road Traffic Acts (*Hudson v DPP* (1991) 156 JP 168).

4. The discretion to exclude evidence does not extend to evidence of one co-accused which implicates the other even though such evidence has been tendered by the prosecution where the prosecution does not seek to rely on it, see *Lobban v R* [1995] 2 All ER 602, [1995] 1 WLR 877, [1995] 2 Cr App Rep 573 (mixed statement of one accused tendered by the prosecution, the exculpatory part of which implicated the co-accused).

5. Unlike s 76(2) ante, the burden of proof does not enter into play and facts do not need to be established or proved to any particular standard; each side will seek to persuade the court as to the impact that admission would have on the fairness of the proceedings: *Re Saifi* [2001] 4 All ER 168, [2001] 1 WLR 1134. Where the accused makes an application for unfair evidence to be excluded, he has no right to have the exclusion of that evidence determined as a preliminary issue by means of a trial within a trial. Accordingly, it will be for the justices to decide whether to deal with the application to exclude the evidence when it arises or before the end of the prosecution case, or to leave the decision until the end of the hearing (*Vel v Owen* [1987] Crim LR 496, and see commentary thereto).

6. The determination under s 78 of the fairness of evidence is distinct from the exercise of discretion on an application for a stay of criminal proceedings as an abuse of process, since the latter might involve not only consideration of the potential fairness of a trial, but also the balancing of the interest of prosecuting a criminal to conviction against that of discouraging abuse of power; see *R v Chalkley* [1998] 2 All ER 155.

7. *Fairness of police investigation* It would seem that the court is not called on to decide the fairness of prosecution enquiries; the approach in *R v Sang* [1980] AC 402, [1979] 2 All ER 46, 143 JP 352, CA of considering whether the prejudicial nature of the evidence itself outweighs its probative value will continue to be appropriate. Where the police obtained evidence through trick or deceit as part of an undercover operation, it was held that before deciding whether that evidence should be excluded the court should consider the whole operation including other evidence available, such as the obtaining of fingerprints; see *R v Christou* [1992] QB 979, [1992] 4 All ER 559, [1992] Crim LR 729, CA. See also *R v Bryce* [1992] 4 All ER 567, [1992] Crim LR 728 (evidence of off-the-record confession and conversation between defendant and undercover police officer), *R v Bailey* [1993] 3 All ER 513, 97 Cr App Rep 365, [1993] Crim LR 681 (evidence of secretly taped conversations between two co-accused who had been placed in the same cell while on remand as the result of a police subterfuge was held to be admissible); *Williams v DPP* [1993] 3 All ER 365, 98 Cr App Rep 209 (police officers parked an insecure and unattended van containing an apparently valuable load of cartons of cigarettes which were in fact dummy cartons—held that the police had done nothing to force, persuade, encourage or coerce the defendants to interfere with the vehicle and that in those circumstances the prosecution evidence was properly admitted). Also, a court must consider what weight to give to any evidence which has been admitted. Before deciding to admit tape recordings of a conversation between the defendant and an undercover police officer, the court does not have to ascertain what passed between the defendant and a police informer and it is the admissibility of the undercover officer's evidence that falls to be determined and not the hypothetical evidence of an informant not intended to be called and not said to have been solicited (*R v Mann, R v Dixon* [1995] Crim LR 647). As to confessions, see s 76, ante.

Interviews Where there have been significant and substantial breaches of the "verballing" provisions of Code C of the Codes of Practice, the evidence so obtained should frequently be excluded; see *R v Keenan* [1990] 2 QB 54, [1989] 3 All ER 598, 90 Cr App Rep 1, CA; similarly where there were substantial breaches (failure to caution and to keep proper record) even though these were not deliberate or flagrant (*R v Sparks* [1991] Crim LR 128). Code C: Code of Practice for the Detention Treatment and Questioning of Persons by Police Officers (see this PART, post) requires, *inter alia*, that records must be made of interviews, and that any comments made by a suspect, including unsolicited comments, made outside the context of an interview but which might be relevant to an offence, must also be recorded with an opportunity provided to the suspect, when practicable, to read that record and sign it; where, however, Code C was breached in relation to a pre-caution admission of driving by a suspect who was subsequent charged with a drink driving offence, but there was no bad faith and the suspect had ample opportunities subsequently to put forward his apparently different version of events, the justices were entitled not to exclude the evidence of the admission: *Watson v DPP* [2003] EWHC Admin 1466, (2004) 168 JP 116. The fact, however, that a person is seen to drive out of a public house car park does not in itself give rise to grounds to suspect a drink driving offence; accordingly, to question such a person about whether he has been drinking does not engage paras 10 and 11 of Code C and, therefore, a prior caution is unnecessary: *Sneyd v DPP* [2006] EWHC 560 (Admin), (2006) 170 JP 545, [2007] RTR 7. Code C applies to "Hansard" interviews carried out by officers of the Inland Revenue and such interviews should, accordingly, be carried out under caution and recorded; however, the purpose of para 10.1 of Code is to ensure that the suspect does not make admissions unless he wishes to and that he is aware of the consequences if he does, and not to prevent suspects from telling lies; therefore, depending on the facts, evidence of such lies may be admissible notwithstanding non-compliance with Code C (*R v Gill* [2003] EWCA Crim 2256, [2003] 4 All ER 681, [2004] 1 WLR 469, [2003] Crim LR 883, [2004] Cr App R 20). Code C para 10.1 and art 5(2) of the European Convention for the Protection of Human Rights and Fundamental Freedom oblige the police where, having made an arrest, they propose to question a suspect or to question him further in relation to an offence which is more serious than the offence in respect of which the arrest was made, before questioning or questioning further, either to charge the suspect with the more serious offence or at least ensure that he is aware of the true nature of the investigation (*R v Kirk* [1999] 4 All ER 698, [2000] 1 WLR 567, [2000] 1 Cr App Rep 400, CA). Evidence was also excluded where the Code of Practice as to identification of a driver was breached (*Powell v DPP* (1991) 157 JP 700). Where customs officers should have cautioned travellers because they were seen assisting each other with a suitcase which was heavy with drugs, although the breach of Code C was significant and substantial, fairness did not require the exclusion of the questions and answers. There was no surprise or unfairness as the questions were of a type which any traveller, and certainly one involved in drug-smuggling, must expect to face upon entry to the country. They were not ones which the defendants might not have expected and which they would not be ready to answer without the presence of a solicitor. Nor was there any issue dispute over the content of the questions and answers (*R v Senior* [2004] EWCA Crim 454, [2004] 3 All ER 9, [2004] 2 Cr App R 12, [2004] Crim LR 749; and see also *R v Rehman* [2006] EWCA Crim 1900, [2007] Crim LR 101).

Identification Although para 3.12 of Code of Practice D requires that an identification procedure shall be held and is mandatory (subject to the conditions and exceptions stated therein), failure to comply with that paragraph may not result in the exclusion under s 78 of a street identification: *R v Forbes* [2001] 1 All ER 626, [2001] 2 WLR 1, [2001] 1 Cr App Rep 430, HL. Police officers involved in a surveillance operation, who did not know the defendant but had been supplied with a photograph of him, could give evidence of identification by reference to the photograph; and failure to hold an identification parade in these circumstances did not render the trial or the admission of the photograph unfair: *R v Chapman* (2000) 165 JPN 950, CA (decided before *Forbes*, supra, but considered to remain correct as to no grounds for excluding the evidence). An informal street identification shortly after an alleged assault, by the victim of the alleged assailant, is permissible; but if it takes place in unsatisfactory circumstances (no written record made of the victim's first description of the assailant, where there was no information to suggest that that was impracticable, and the suspect was in a police van at the time) and the suspect continues to dispute identification but no ID parade is held, it will be unsafe for justices to convict in reliance on that identification and, accordingly, it should be excluded under s 78: *Ryan v DPP* CO/1315/2000, DC. Unfairness is less likely where the evidence is a material object there for all to see (*R v Stewart* [1995] Crim LR 500, CA (a static diversionary apparatus used for abstraction of electricity)).

Conviction of co-accused Where a defendant was charged with conspiracy to obtain property, it was held, in the circumstances, that evidence of the conviction of a co-accused, which was otherwise admissible under s 74(1), ante, should have been excluded under this section (*R v O'Connor* [1987] Crim LR 260, CA). All the circumstances of the evidence should be considered, even in the absence of impropriety (*R v O'Leary* [1988] Crim LR 827).

Entrapment Entrapment is not a defence; the essential question is whether the admission of evidence will so prejudice a fair trial that it should not be admitted (*Williams and O'Hare v DPP* [1993] Crim LR 775). For the position under the European Convention on Human Rights see *Teixeira de Castro v Portugal* (1998) 28 EHRR 101. The fact that evidence has been obtained by entrapment or by an agent provocateur or by a trick does not of itself require the judge to exclude it. It should be excluded if in all the circumstances there would be an adverse effect on the fairness of the proceedings. The court may take into account the following: (1) Was the officer enticing the defendant to commit an offence he would not otherwise have committed? (2) What was the nature of the entrapment? (3) Does the evidence consist of admission to a completed offence or does it consist of the actual commission of an offence? (4) How active or passive was the officer's role in obtaining evidence? (5) Is there an unassailable record of what occurred or is it strongly corroborated? (6) Has an undercover officer abused his role to ask questions which ought properly to have been asked as a police officer in accordance with the Code of Practice under the Act? (*R v Smurthwaite, R v Gill* [1994] 1 All ER 898, 158 JP 165, 98 Cr App Rep 437.) The issue is whether the fairness of the proceedings would be adversely affected by admitting the evidence of the agent provocateur or evidence which is available as the result of his action or actions. A judge might readily conclude that such evidence should be excluded if there is good reason to question the credibility of the evidence and that question is not susceptible of being properly or fairly resolved in the course of the proceedings from available, admissible and untainted evidence. But if the 'unfairness' is no more than a visceral reaction that it is in principle unfair as a matter of policy, or wrong as a matter of law, for a person to be prosecuted for a crime which he would not have committed without the incitement or encouragement of others, that is insufficient, unless the behaviour of the police, someone acting on behalf of the police or the prosecuting authority has been such as to justify a stay on the ground of abuse of process (*R v Shannon* [2001] 1 WLR 51, [2001] 1 Cr App Rep 12, [2000] Crim LR 1001, CA). The above authorities were reviewed and approved. A guide to whether police conduct was acceptable is to consider whether the police did no more than present the defendant with an unexceptional opportunity to commit a crime; ie did no more than might have been expected from others in the circumstances. But as the technique is intrusive its use should be proportionate and not random. In considering whether police conduct was improper relevant circumstances include: whether the nature of the offence require more proactive techniques; is there good reason for the police operation; the nature and extent of police participation in a crime. A defendant's criminal record is unlikely to be relevant unless linked to other factors grounding reasonable suspicion. The discretion in s 78 is not amended by art 6 of the European Convention on Human Rights (*R v Looseley* [2001] UKHL 53, [2001] 4 All ER 897, [2001] 1 WLR 2060.)

Details of pre-trial plea bargaining, etc There is no reason in principle or fairness why an accused should not be cross examined on a letter written by his solicitors containing a proposal as to plea if it is inconsistent with his testimony and, thus, goes to his credibility, and the same applies to an alibi notice or defence case statement if it becomes similarly relevant during the trial (*R v Hayes* [2004] EWCA Crim 2844, [2005] 1 Cr App R 33.)

Customs and Excise Code of Practice C applies to Customs Officers interviewing a suspected person. They must either administer a caution and follow the Code of Practice or, if they wish to see whether the suspect will lead them to others involved in drug trafficking, they must avoid asking questions in relation to the offence (*R v Okafor* [1994] 3 All ER 741, CA).

Retention of fingerprints and samples It was held in *A-G's Reference (No 3 of 1999)* [2001] 2 AC 91, [2001] 2 WLR 56 that the prohibition contained in s 64 of PACE on the retention of fingerprints and samples did not make evidence obtained as a result of failure to comply with it inadmissible, but left it to the discretion of the court whether or not to exclude the evidence under s 78 of PACE. For an example where evidence relating to a defendant's DNA profile ought to have been excluded see *R v Nathaniel* (1995) 159 JP 419, [1995] 2 Cr App Rep 565, CA. As to the retention of fingerprints and samples that should have been destroyed prior to the coming into effect on 11 May 2001 of the changes made to s 64 by the Criminal Justice and Police Act 2001, and as to the use information derived from such samples, see the Criminal Justice and Police Act, s 82(6), PART I, ante.

Road traffic – evidence of specimens for analysis For the exercise of the discretion under s 78 to exclude evidence of the analysis of specimens, see the notes to s 7 of the Road Traffic Act 1988, in PART VII: TRANSPORT, post.

2–1360   79. Time for taking accused's evidence. If at the trial of any person for an offence—

    (*a*)   the defence intends to call two or more witnesses to the facts of the case; and

    (*b*)   those witnesses include the accused,

the accused shall be called before the other witness or witnesses unless the court in its discretion otherwise directs.

[Police and Criminal Evidence Act 1984, s 79.]

2–1361   80. Compellability of accused's spouse[1] or civil partner. (1) *Repealed.*

    (2) In any proceedings the spouse or civil partner of a person charged in the proceedings shall, subject to subsection (4) below, be compellable to give evidence on behalf of that person.

(2A) In any proceedings the spouse or civil partner of a person charged in the proceedings shall, subject to subsection (4) below, be compellable—

(a) to give evidence on behalf of any other person charged in the proceedings but only in respect of any specified offence with which that other person is charged; or

(b) to give evidence for the prosecution but only in respect of any specified offence with which any person is charged in the proceedings.

(3) In relation to the spouse[2] or civil partner[2] of a person charged in any proceedings, an offence is a specified offence for the purposes of subsection (2A) above if—

(a) it involves an assault on, or injury or a threat of injury to, the spouse or civil partner or a person who was at the material time under the age of 16;

(b) it is a sexual offence alleged to have been committed in respect of a person who was at the material time under that age; or

(c) it consists of attempting or conspiring to commit, or of aiding, abetting, counselling, procuring or inciting the commission of, an offence falling within paragraph (a) or (b) above.

(4) No person who is charged in any proceedings shall be compellable by virtue of subsection (2) or (2A) above to give evidence in the proceedings.

(4A) References in this section to a person charged in any proceedings do not include a person who is not, or is no longer, liable to be convicted of any offence in the proceedings (whether as a result of pleading guilty or for any other reason).

(5) In any proceedings[3] a person who has been but is no longer married to the accused shall be compellable to give evidence as if that person and the accused had never been married.

(5A) In any proceedings a person who has been but is no longer the civil partner of the accused shall be compellable to give evidence as if that person and the accused had never been civil partners.

(6) Where in any proceedings the age of any person at any time is material for the purposes of subsection (3) above, his age at the material time shall for the purposes of that provision be deemed to be or to have been that which appears to the court to be or to have been his age at that time.

(7) In subsection (3)(b) above "sexual offence" means an offence under the Sexual Offences Act 1956, the Indecency with Children Act 1960, the Protection of Children Act 1978 or Part 1 of the Sexual Offences Act 2003.

(8) *Repealed.*

(9) *Repealed.*

[Police and Criminal Evidence Act 1984, s 80 as amended by the Youth Justice and Criminal Evidence Act 1999, s 67, the Sexual Offences Act 2003, Sch 6 and the Civil Partnership Act 2004, Sch 27.]

---

1. For the competence and compellability of spouses and civil partners see para **2–332 Competency of parties and their spouses,** ante.

2. The provision that wives and husbands are only compellable in certain circumstances is not extended to those in the position of a spouse but not married to the accused nor is there anything in art 8(1) of the European Convention on Human Rights that such a concession has to be made to those in the position of a husband and wife (*R v Pearce* [2002] EWCA Crim 2834, [2002] 1 WLR 1553, [2002] 1 Cr App Rep 39, 166 JP 103).

3. This means "in any proceedings" which take place after s 80(5) came into force on 1 January 1986 (*R v Cruttenden* [1991] 2 QB 66, [1991] 3 All ER 242, CA).

2–1361A 80A. Rule where accused's spouse or civil partner not compellable. The failure of the spouse or civil partner of a person charged in any proceedings to give evidence in the proceedings shall not be made the subject of any comment by the prosecution.

[Police and Criminal Evidence Act 1984, s 80A as inserted by the Youth Justice and Criminal Evidence Act 1999, s 67(1) and amended by the Civil Partnership Act 2004, Sch 27.]

2–1362 81. Advance notice of expert evidence in Crown Court. *Criminal Procedure Rules*[1] *may make provision.*

---

1. See the Criminal Procedure Rules 2005, Part 24, in PART I: MAGISTRATES' COURTS, PROCEDURE, ante.

Part VIII—supplementary

2–1363 82. Part VIII—interpretation. (1) In this Part of this Act—

"confession" includes any statement[1] wholly or partly adverse to the person who made it, whether made to a person in authority or not and whether made in words or otherwise;

"court-martial" means a court-martial constituted under the Army Act 1955, the Air Force Act 1955 or the Naval Discipline Act 1957 or a disciplinary court constituted under section 52G of the said Act of 1957*;

proceedings" means criminal proceedings, including—

(a) proceedings in the United Kingdom or elsewhere before a court-martial constituted under the Army Act 1955, the Air Force Act 1955 or the Naval Discipline Act 1957**;

(b) proceedings in the United Kingdom or elsewhere before the Courts-Martial Appeal Court—

(i) on an appeal from a court-martial so constituted**; or

(ii) on a reference under section 34 of the Courts-Martial (Appeals) Act 1968; and

(c) proceedings before a Standing Civilian Court; and

"Service court" means a court-martial or a Standing Civilian Court.

(2) In this Part of this Act references to conviction before a Service court are references to a finding of guilty which is, or falls to be treated as, the finding of the court; and "convicted" shall be construed accordingly.

(3) Nothing in this Part of this Act shall prejudice any power of a court to exclude evidence (whether by preventing questions from being put or otherwise) at its discretion.

[Police and Criminal Evidence Act 1984, s 82, as amended by the Armed Forces Act 1996, Schs 1 and 6.]

---

*Repealed by the Armed Forces Act 2001, Sch 7, from a date to be appointed.
**Repealed by the Youth Justice and Criminal Evidence Act 1999, Sch 6, from a date to be appointed.

1. A statement is to be interpreted in the light of the circumstances when it was made. Therefore a statement that was wholly exculpatory when it was made does not become a 'confession' because it is later used by the prosecution to contradict or cast doubt on other statements of the accused. The accused is not without a remedy given the availability of the discretion to exclude evidence (including a purely exculpatory statement) in s 78. Accordingly s 76 and 82(1) are compatible with art 6 of the European Convention: *R v Z* [2005] UKHL 22, *[2005] 2 AC 467*, [2005] 2 WLR 709, sub nom *R v Hasan* [2005] 4 All ER 685, [2006] Crim LR 142.

Section 70   SCHEDULE
                                                            SCHEDULE 3
                              PROVISIONS SUPPLEMENTARY TO SECTIONS 68 AND 69[1]

(As amended by the Criminal Justice Act 1988, Sch 16, the Statute Law (Repeals) Act 1993, Sch 1 and the Criminal Procedure and Investigations Act 1996, Sch 1.)

PART I
PROVISIONS SUPPLEMENTARY TO SECTION 68

2–1364   **1–7.** *Repealed.*

PART II
PROVISIONS SUPPLEMENTARY TO SECTION 69

8. In any proceedings where it is desired to give a statement in evidence in accordance with section 69 above, a certificate—

(a) identifying the document containing the statement and describing the manner in which it was produced;
(b) giving such particulars of any device involved in the production of that document as may be appropriate for the purpose of showing that the document was produced by a computer;
(c) dealing with any of the matters mentioned in subsection (1) of section 69 above; and
(d) purporting to be signed by a person occupying a responsible position in relation to the operation of the computer,

shall be evidence of anything stated in it; and for the purposes of this paragraph it shall be sufficient for a matter to be stated to the best of the knowledge and belief of the person stating it.

9. Notwithstanding paragraph 8 above, a court may require oral evidence to be given of anything of which evidence could be given by a certificate under that paragraph; but the preceding provisions of this paragraph shall not apply where the court is a magistrates' court inquiring into an offence as examining justices.

10. Any person who in a certificate tendered under paragraph 8 above in a magistrates' court, the Crown Court or the Court of Appeal makes a statement which he knows to be false or does not believe to be true shall be guilty of an offence and liable[2]—

(a) on conviction on indictment to imprisonment for a term not exceeding two years or to a fine or to both;
(b) on summary conviction to imprisonment for a term not exceeding six months or to a fine not exceeding the statutory maximum or to both.

11. In estimating the weight, if any, to be attached to a statement regard shall be had to all the circumstances from which any inference can reasonably be drawn as to the accuracy or otherwise of the statement and, in particular—

(a) to the question whether or not the information which the information contained in the statement reproduces or is derived from was supplied to the relevant computer, or recorded for the purpose of being supplied to it, contemporaneously with the occurrence or existence of the facts dealt with in that information; and
(b) to the question whether or not any person concerned with the supply of information to that computer, or with the operation of that computer or any equipment by means of which the document containing the statement was produced by it, had any incentive to conceal or misrepresent the facts.

12. For the purposes of paragraph 11 above information shall be taken to be supplied to a computer whether it is supplied directly or (with or without human intervention) by means of any appropriate equipment.*

PART III
PROVISIONS SUPPLEMENTARY TO SECTIONS 68 AND 69

13. *Repealed.*

14. For the purpose of deciding whether or not a statement is so admissible the court may draw any reasonable inference—

(a) from the circumstances in which the statement was made or otherwise came into being; or
(b) from any other circumstances, including the form and contents of the document in which the statement is contained.

15. Provision may be made by rules of court for supplementing the provisions of section 68 or 69 above or this Schedule.*

*Repealed by the Youth Justice and Criminal Evidence Act 1999, Sch 6, when in force.
1. See definition of "document" noted to the heading to Pt VII of this Act, above.
2. For procedure in respect of an offence triable either way, see Magistrates' Courts Act 1980, ss 17A–21 in PART I: MAGISTRATES' COURTS, PROCEDURE, ante.

Criminal Justice Act 1988[1]
(1988 c 33)

PART II[2]
DOCUMENTARY EVIDENCE IN CRIMINAL PROCEEDINGS

2–1470   **23. First-hand hearsay.**   *Repealed.*[3]

     1. For other provisions of the Criminal Justice Act 1988, see PART I: MAGISTRATES' COURTS, PROCEDURE, ante; see also PART VIII: titles OFFENSIVE WEAPONS, PERSONS, OFFENCES AGAINST and SEXUAL OFFENCES, post.
     2. Part II contains ss 23–28. The provisions of sections 23–26 are not contrary to art 6 of the European Convention on Human Rights as the question which arises under art 6 is whether the proceedings considered as a whole are fair. Further ss 23–26 require a balancing exercise so that it is not unfair to the accused to admit a statement under these provisions (*R v Thomas* [1998] Crim LR 887, CA). But see *R v Radak* [1999] 1 Cr App Rep 187, [1999] Crim LR 223, CA where the prosecution had the opportunity but failed to obtain evidence from a witness in the United States by commission pursuant to s 3 of the Criminal Justice (International Cooperation) Act 1990 and thereby unfairly deprived the defendant of the opportunity to cross examine the witness.
     3. Sections 23–28 and Schedule 2 repealed by the Criminal Justice Act 2003, Sch 37, except in relation to criminal proceedings which began before 4 April 2005.

2–1471   **24. Business etc documents**[1]**.**   *Repealed.*

2–1472   **25. Principles to be followed by court**[1]**.**   *Repealed.*

2–1473   **26. Statements in documents that appear to have been prepared for purposes of criminal proceedings or investigations.**   *Repealed.*

2–1474   **27. Proof of statements contained in documents.**   *Repealed.*

2–1475   **28. Documentary evidence—supplementary.**   *Repealed.*

PART III[1]
OTHER PROVISIONS ABOUT EVIDENCE IN CRIMINAL PROCEEDINGS

2–1476   **30. Expert reports.**   (1) An expert report shall be admissible as evidence in criminal proceedings, whether or not the person making it attends to give oral evidence in those proceedings.
     (2) If it is proposed that the person making the report shall not give oral evidence, the report shall only be admissible with the leave of the court.
     (3) For the purpose of determining whether to give leave the court shall have regard—

     (*a*)   to the contents of the report;
     (*b*)   to the reasons why it is proposed that the person making the report shall not give oral evidence;
     (*c*)   to any risk, having regard in particular to whether it is likely to be possible to controvert statements in the report if the person making it does not attend to give oral evidence in the proceedings, that its admission or exclusion will result in unfairness to the accused or, if there is more than one, to any of them; and
     (*d*)   to any other circumstances that appear to the court to be relevant.

     (4) An expert report, when admitted, shall be evidence of any fact or opinion of which the person making it could have given oral evidence.
     (4A) Where the proceedings mentioned in subsection (1) above are proceedings before a magistrates' court inquiring into an offence as examining justices this section shall have effect with the omission of—

     (*a*)   in subsection (1) the words "whether or not the person making it attends to give oral evidence in those proceedings", and
     (*b*)   subsections (2) to (4).

     (5) In this section "expert report" means a written report by a person dealing wholly or mainly with matters on which he is (or would if living be) qualified to give expert evidence[2].
[Criminal Justice Act 1988, s 30, as amended by the Criminal Procedure and Investigations Act 1996, Sch 1.]

     1. Part III contains ss 29–34.
     2. See generally commentary in para **2–343 Expert opinion**, ante.

2–1477   **31. Form of evidence and glossaries.**   For the purpose of helping members of juries to understand complicated issues of fact or technical terms Criminal Procedure Rules may make provision—

(*a*) as to the furnishing of evidence in any form, notwithstanding the existence of admissible material from which the evidence to be given in that form would be derived; and

(*b*) as to the furnishing of glossaries for such purposes as may be specified;

in any case where the court gives leave for, or requires, evidence or a glossary to be so furnished.
[Criminal Justice Act 1988, s 31, as amended by SI 2004/2035.]

2–1478 32. Evidence through television links[1]. (1) A person other than the accused may give evidence through a live television link in proceedings to which subsection (1A) below applies if—

(*a*) the witness is outside the United Kingdom;

(*b*) *repealed**

but evidence may not be so given without the leave of the court.

(1A) This subsection applies—

(*a*) to trials on indictment, appeals to the criminal division of the Court of Appeal and hearings of references under section 9 of the Criminal Appeal Act 1995; and

(*b*) to proceedings in youth courts, appeals to the Crown Court arising out of such proceedings and hearings of references under section 11 of the Criminal Appeal Act 1995 so arising.

(2) *Repealed.*

(3) A statement made on oath by a witness outside the United Kingdom and given in evidence through a link by virtue of this section shall be treated for the purposes of section 1 of the Perjury Act 1911 as having been made in the proceedings in which it is given in evidence.

(3A)–(3E) *Repealed.*

(4) Without prejudice to the generality of any enactment conferring power to make Criminal Procedure Rules such rules may make such provision as appears to the Criminal Procedure Rule Committee to be necessary or expedient for the purposes of this section.

(5), (6) *Repealed.*

[Criminal Justice Act 1988, s 32 as amended by the Criminal Justice Act 1991, s 55, the Criminal Justice and Public Order Act 1994, Sch 9, the Criminal Appeal Act 1995, Sch 2 and the Sexual Offences Act 2003, Sch 6, the Youth Justice and Criminal Evidence Act 1999, Schs 6 and 7 and SI 2004/2035.]

---

1. Applied to Service Courts, with modifications, by the Criminal Justice Act 1988 (Application to Service Courts) (Evidence) Order 2006, SI 2006/2890.

2–1479 32A. Video recordings of testimony from child witnesses. *Repealed.*

2–1480 33. Evidence of persons under 14 in committal proceedings. *Amendment of the Magistrates' Courts Act 1980 by the substitution of a new s 103[1].*

---

1. For the substituted s 103, see the Magistrates' Courts Act 1980 in PART I: MAGISTRATES' COURTS, PROCEDURE, ante.

2–1481 33A. *Repealed.*

2–1482 34. Abolition of requirement of corroboration for unsworn evidence of children.
(1) *Repealed.*

(2) Any requirement whereby at a trial on indictment it is obligatory for the court to give the jury a warning about convicting the accused on the uncorroborated evidence of a child is abrogated.

(3) Unsworn evidence admitted by virtue of section 56 of the Youth Justice and Criminal Evidence Act 1999 may corroborate evidence (sworn or unsworn) given by any other person.

[Criminal Justice Act 1988, s 34 as amended by the Criminal Justice Act 1991, Schs 11 and 13, the Criminal Justice and Public Order Act 1994, s 32 and Sch 11 and the Youth Justice and Criminal Evidence Act 1999, Sch 4.]

2–1483 34A. Cross-examination of alleged child victims. *Repealed.*

Section 28   SCHEDULE 2
                          DOCUMENTARY EVIDENCE—SUPPLEMENTARY

2–1484 [*Repealed by the Criminal Justice Act 2003, Sch 37, except in relation to criminal proceedings which began before 4 April 2005.*]

Welsh Language Act 1993
(1993 c 38)

PART III[1]
MISCELLANEOUS
Welsh in legal proceedings

2–1485 22. Use of Welsh in legal proceedings. (1) In any legal proceedings[2] in Wales the Welsh language may be spoken by any party, witness or other person who desires to use it, subject in the case of proceedings in a court other than a magistrates' court to such prior notice as may be required by rules of court; and any necessary provision for interpretation shall be made accordingly.

(2) Any power to make rules[3] of court includes power to make provision as to the use, in proceedings in or having a connection with Wales, of documents in the Welsh language.
[Welsh Language Act 1993, s 22.]

1. Part III contains ss 22–37.
2. For use of the Welsh language in proceedings before courts in Wales, see *Practice Direction (criminal: consolidated)* [2002] para III.23, in PART I: MAGISTRATES' COURTS, PROCEDURE, ante.
3. The Magistrates' Courts (Welsh Forms) Rules 1986, SI 1986/1079, and the Magistrates' Courts (Children and Young Persons) (Welsh Forms) Rules 1973, SI 1973/1119, have been made.

2-1486   23. Oaths and affirmations.   (1) The Lord Chancellor may, after consulting the Lord Chief Justice of England and Wales, make rules prescribing a translation in the Welsh language of any form for the time being prescribed by law as the form of any oath or affirmation to be administered and taken or made by any person in any court, and an oath or affirmation administered and taken or made in any court in Wales in the translation prescribed by such rules shall, without interpretation, be of the like effect as if it had been administered and taken or made in the English language.

(2) The Lord Chief Justice may nominate a judicial office holder (as defined in section 109(4) of the Constitutional Reform Act 2005) to exercise his functions under this section.
[Welsh Language Act 1993, s 23 as amended by the Constitutional Reform Act 2005, Sch 4.]

1. See note 2 to s 22(2), ante.

2-1487   24. Provision of interpreters.   (1) The Lord Chancellor may make rules as to the provision and employment of interpreters of the Welsh and English languages for the purposes of proceedings before courts in Wales.

(2) The interpreters shall be paid, out of the same fund as the expenses of the court are payable, such remuneration in respect of their services as the Lord Chancellor may determine.

(3) The Lord Chancellor's powers under this section shall be exercised with the consent of the Treasury.
[Welsh Language Act 1993, s 24.]

Statutory names, forms etc

2-1488   25. Powers to give Welsh names to statutory bodies etc.   (1) Where a name is conferred by an Act of Parliament on any body, office or place, the appropriate Minister may by order confer on the body, office or place an alternative name in Welsh.

(2) Where an Act of Parliament gives power, exercisable by statutory instrument, to confer a name on any body, office or place, the power shall include power to confer alternative names in English and Welsh.

(3) Subsection (1) above does not apply in relation to a name conferred on any area or local authority by the Local Government Act 1972.
[Welsh Language Act 1993, s 25 as amended by the Local Government (Wales) Act 1994, Sch 16.]

2-1489   26. Powers to prescribe Welsh forms.   (1) This section applies where an Act of Parliament specifies, or confers power to specify,—

(a)   the form of any document, or
(b)   any form of words,

which is to be or may be used for an official or public purpose or for any other purpose where the consequences in law of any act depend on the form used.

(2) Where the Act itself specifies the form of the document or the form of words, the appropriate Minister may by order prescribe—

(a)   a form of the document in Welsh, or partly in Welsh and partly in English or, as the case may be,
(b)   a form of words in Welsh,

for use in such circumstances and subject to such conditions as may be prescribed by the order.

(3) Where the Act confers a power[1] to specify the form of the document or the form of words, the power shall include power to prescribe—

(a)   separate forms of the document, or separate forms of words, in Welsh and in English, and
(b)   in the case of a document, a form partly in Welsh and partly in English,

for use in such circumstances and subject to such conditions as may be prescribed by the instrument by which the power is exercised.

(4) Where the powers conferred by this section are exercised in relation to the form of a document or a form of words, a reference in an Act or instrument to the form shall, so far as may be necessary, be construed as (or as including) a reference to the form prescribed under or by virtue of this section.

(5) This section shall not apply in relation to a provision which—

(a)   confers, or gives power to confer, a name on any body, office or place, or
(b)   requires specified words to be included in the name of any body, office or place.
[Welsh Language Act 1993, s 26.]

1. The Companies (Welsh Language Forms and Documents) Regulations 1994, SI 1994/117 have been made in respect of requirements under the Companies Act 1985, ss 287, 288, 363, 710B and 744. The Attestation of Constables (Welsh Language) Order 2002, SI 2002/2312 has also been made.

2–1490 27. Provisions supplementary to sections 25 and 26. (1) Anything done in Welsh by virtue of section 26 above shall have the like effect as if done in English.

(2) Any provision authorising—

(*a*) the use of a document or words to the like effect as a document or words of which another version is prescribed by virtue of section 26 above, or

(*b*) the adaptation of a document or words of which another version is so prescribed,

shall apply in relation to both versions.

(3) The powers to make orders under sections 25(1) and 26(2) above shall be exercisable by statutory instrument, which shall be laid before Parliament after being made.

(4) References in sections 25 and 26 above to an Act of Parliament include references to Acts passed after this Act; and in those sections "the appropriate Minister" in relation to any Act means—

(*a*) in the case of provisions for the execution of which in Wales a Minister other than the Secretary of State is responsible, that Minister, and

(*b*) in any other case, the Secretary of State.

(5) Any question arising under paragraphs (*a*) and (*b*) of subsection (4) above shall be determined by the Treasury; and in that subsection "Minister" includes the Treasury, the Commissioners of Customs and Excise and the Commissioners of Inland Revenue.
[Welsh Language Act 1993, s 27.]

Criminal Justice and Public Order Act 1994[1]
(1994 c 33)

PART III[2]
COURSE OF JUSTICE: EVIDENCE, PROCEDURE, ETC
Corroboration

2–1492 32. Abolition of corroboration rules. (1) Any requirement whereby at a trial on indictment it is obligatory for the court to give the jury a warning about convicting the accused on the uncorroborated evidence of a person merely because that person is—

(*a*) an alleged accomplice of the accused, or

(*b*) where the offence charged is a sexual offence, the person in respect of whom it is alleged to have been committed,

is hereby abrogated.

(2) *Amendment of s 34(2) of Criminal Justice Act 1988.*

(3) Any requirement that—

(*a*) is applicable at the summary trial of a person for an offence, and

(*b*) corresponds to the requirement mentioned in subsection (1) above or that mentioned in section 34(2) of the Criminal Justice Act 1988,

is hereby abrogated.

(4) Nothing in this section applies in relation to—

(*a*) any trial, or

(*b*) any proceedings before a magistrates' court as examining justices,

which began before the commencement of this section.
[Criminal Justice and Public Order Act 1994, s 32.]

1. The Criminal Justice and Public Order Act 1994 is printed partly in PART II and partly in PARTS I, V and VIII of this Manual. All the provisions printed in this PART have been brought into force.
2. Part III contains ss 31–53.

2–1493 33. *Abolition of corroboration requirements under Sexual Offences Act 1956.*

Inferences from accused's silence[1]

2–1494 34. Effect of accused's failure to mention facts when questioned or charged.
(1) Where, in any proceedings against a person for an offence, evidence is given that the accused—

(*a*) at any time before he was charged with the offence, on being questioned under caution by a constable trying to discover whether or by whom the offence had been committed, failed to mention any fact relied on in his defence in those proceedings; or

(*b*) on being charged with the offence or officially informed that he might be prosecuted for it, failed to mention any such fact,

being a fact which in the circumstances existing at the time the accused could reasonably have been expected to mention when so questioned, charged or informed, as the case may be, subsection (2) below applies.

(2) Where this subsection applies—

(a) a magistrates' court inquiring into the offence as examining justices;

(b) a judge, in deciding whether to grant an application made by the accused under—

   (i) section 6 of the Criminal Justice Act 1987 (application for dismissal of charge of serious fraud in respect of which notice of transfer has been given under section 4 of that Act); or

   (ii) paragraph 5 of Schedule 6 to the Criminal Justice Act 1991 (application for dismissal of charge of violent or sexual offence involving child in respect of which notice of transfer has been given under section 53 of that Act);

(c) the court, in determining whether there is a case to answer; and

(d) the court or jury, in determining whether the accused is guilty of the offence charged,

may draw such inferences from the failure as appear proper.

(2A) Where the accused was at an authorised place of detention at the time of the failure, subsections (1) and (2) above do not apply if he had not been allowed an opportunity to consult a solicitor prior to being questioned, charged or informed as mentioned in subsection (1) above.[2]

(3) Subject to any directions by the court, evidence tending to establish the failure may be given before or after evidence tending to establish the fact which the accused is alleged to have failed to mention.

(4) This section applies in relation to questioning by persons (other than constables) charged with the duty of investigating offences or charging offenders as it applies in relation to questioning by constables; and in subsection (1) above "officially informed" means informed by a constable or any such person.

(5) This section does not—

(a) prejudice the admissibility in evidence of the silence or other reaction of the accused in the face of anything said in his presence relating to the conduct in respect of which he is charged, in so far as evidence thereof would be admissible apart from this section; or

(b) preclude the drawing of any inference from any such silence or other reaction of the accused which could properly be drawn apart from this section.

(6) This section does not apply in relation to a failure to mention a fact if the failure occurred before the commencement[3] of this section.

(7) *Repealed.*

[Criminal Justice and Public Order Act 1994, s 34 as amended by the Criminal Procedure and Investigations Act 1996, s 44 and the Youth Justice and Criminal Evidence Act 1999, s 58.]

---

1. For consideration of ss 34–38 of this Act, see paras **2–496** to **2–499**, ante.
2. Section 34(2A) is inserted in relation to proceedings instituted on or after 1 April 2003, whether the relevant failure or refusal on the part of the accused took place before or after that date.
3. Section 34 came into force on 10 April 1995 (SI 1995/721).

2–1495 **35. Effect of accused's silence at trial.** (1) At the trial of any person for an offence, subsections (2) and (3) below apply unless—

(a) the accused's guilt is not in issue; or

(b) it appears to the court that the physical or mental condition of the accused makes it undesirable for him to give evidence;

but subsection (2) below does not apply if, at the conclusion of the evidence for the prosecution, his legal representative informs the court that the accused will give evidence or, where he is unrepresented, the court ascertains from him that he will give evidence.

(2) Where this subsection applies, the court shall, at the conclusion of the evidence for the prosecution, satisfy itself[1] (in the case of proceedings on indictment with a jury, in the presence of the jury) that the accused is aware that the stage has been reached at which evidence can be given for the defence and that he can, if he wishes, give evidence and that, if he chooses not to give evidence, or having been sworn, without good cause refuses to answer any question, it will be permissible for the court or jury to draw such inferences as appear proper from his failure to give evidence or his refusal, without good cause, to answer any question.

(3) Where this subsection applies, the court or jury, in determining whether the accused is guilty of the offence charged, may draw such inferences as appear proper from the failure of the accused to give evidence or his refusal, without good cause, to answer any question.

(4) This section does not render the accused compellable to give evidence on his own behalf, and he shall accordingly not be guilty of contempt of court by reason of a failure to do so.

(5) For the purposes of this section a person who, having been sworn, refuses to answer any question shall be taken to do so without good cause unless—

(a) he is entitled to refuse to answer the question by virtue of any enactment, whenever passed or made, or on the ground of privilege; or

(b) the court in the exercise of its general discretion excuses him from answering it.

(6) *Repealed.*

(7) This section applies—

(a) in relation to proceedings on indictment for an offence, only if the person charged with the offence is arraigned on or after the commencement[2] of this section;

(b) in relation to proceedings in a magistrates' court, only if the time when the court begins to receive evidence in the proceedings falls after the commencement[2] of this section.

[Criminal Justice and Public Order Act 1994, s 35 as amended by the Crime and Disorder Act 1998, s 35 and Sch 10, and the Criminal Justice Act 2003, Sch 36.]

---

1. If the defendant is absent at that stage of the trial the court cannot be so satisfied and an adverse inference is not, therefore, permissible: *R v Gough* [2001] EWCA Crim. 2545, [2002] 2 Cr App Rep 8, [2002] Crim LR 526.

2. Section 35 came into force on 10 April 1995 (SI 1995/721).

2–1496 **36. Effect of accused's failure or refusal to account for objects, substances or marks.**

(1) Where—

(a) a person is arrested by a constable, and there is—

(i) on his person; or

(ii) in or on his clothing or footwear; or

(iii) otherwise in his possession; or

(iv) in any place in which he is at the time of his arrest,

any object, substance or mark, or there is any mark on any such object; and

(b) that or another constable investigating the case reasonably believes that the presence of the object, substance or mark may be attributable to the participation of the person arrested in the commission of an offence specified by the constable; and

(c) the constable informs the person arrested that he so believes, and requests him to account for the presence of the object, substance or mark; and

(d) the person fails or refuses to do so,

then if, in any proceedings against the person for the offence so specified, evidence of those matters is given, subsection (2) below applies.

(2) Where this subsection applies—

(a) a magistrates' court inquiring into the offence as examining justices;

(b) a judge, in deciding whether to grant an application made by the accused under—

(i) section 6 of the Criminal Justice Act 1987 (application for dismissal of charge of serious fraud in respect of which notice of transfer has been given under section 4 of that Act); or

(ii) paragraph 5 of Schedule 6 to the Criminal Justice Act 1991 (application for dismissal of charge of violent or sexual offence involving child in respect of which notice of transfer has been given under section 53 of that Act);

(c) the court, in determining whether there is a case to answer; and

(d) the court or jury, in determining whether the accused is guilty of the offence charged,

may draw such inferences from the failure or refusal as appear proper.

(3) Subsections (1) and (2) above apply to the condition of clothing or footwear as they apply to a substance or mark thereon.

(4) Subsections (1) and (2) above do not apply unless the accused was told in ordinary language by the constable when making the request mentioned in subsection (1)(c) above what the effect of this section would be if he failed or refused to comply with the request.

(4A) Where the accused was at an authorised place of detention at the time of the failure or refusal, subsections (1) and (2) above do not apply if he had not been allowed an opportunity to consult a solicitor prior to the request being made.[1]

(5) This section applies in relation to officers of customs and excise as it applies in relation to constables.

(6) This section does not preclude the drawing of any inference from a failure or refusal of the accused to account for the presence of an object, substance or mark or from the condition of clothing or footwear which could properly be drawn apart from this section.

(7) This section does not apply in relation to a failure or refusal which occurred before the commencement[2] of this section.

(8) *Repealed.*

[Criminal Justice and Public Order Act 1994, s 36 as amended by the Criminal Procedure and Investigations Act 1996, s 44 and the Youth Justice and Criminal Evidence Act 1999, 58.]

---

1. Section 36(4A) is inserted in relation to proceedings instituted on or after 1 April 2003, whether the relevant failure or refusal on the part of the accused took place before or after that date.

2. Section 36 came into force on 10 April 1995 (SI 1995/721).

2–1497 **37. Effect of accused's failure or refusal to account for presence at a particular place.** (1) Where—

(a) a person arrested by a constable was found by him at a place at or about the time the offence for which he was arrested is alleged to have been committed; and (*b*)   that or another constable investigating the offence reasonably believes that the presence of the person at that place and at that time may be attributable to his participation in the commission of the offence; and

(*c*)   the constable informs the person that he so believes, and requests him to account for that presence; and

(*d*)   the person fails or refuses to do so,

then if, in any proceedings against the person for the offence, evidence of those matters is given, subsection (2) below applies.

(2) Where this subsection applies—

(*a*)   a magistrates' court inquiring into the offence as examining justices;

(*b*)   a judge, in deciding whether to grant an application made by the accused under—

   (i)   section 6 of the Criminal Justice Act 1987 (application for dismissal of charge of serious fraud in respect of which notice of transfer has been given under section 4 of that Act); or

   (ii)   paragraph 5 of Schedule 6 to the Criminal Justice Act 1991 (application for dismissal of charge of violent or sexual offence involving child in respect of which notice of transfer has been given under section 53 of that Act);

(*c*)   the court, in determining whether there is a case to answer; and

(*d*)   the court or jury, in determining whether the accused is guilty of the offence charged,

may draw such inferences from the failure or refusal as appear proper.

(3) Subsections (1) and (2) do not apply unless the accused was told in ordinary language by the constable when making the request mentioned in subsection (1)(*c*) above what the effect of this section would be if he failed or refused to comply with the request.

(3A) Where the accused was at an authorised place of detention at the time of the failure or refusal, subsections (1) and (2) do not apply if he had not been allowed an opportunity to consult a solicitor prior to the request being made.[1]

(4) This section applies in relation to officers of customs and excise as it applies in relation to constables.

(5) This section does not preclude the drawing of any inference from a failure or refusal of the accused to account for his presence at a place which could properly be drawn apart from this section.

(6) This section does not apply in relation to a failure or refusal which occurred before the commencement[2] of this section.

(7) *Repealed.*

[Criminal Justice and Public Order Act 1994, s 37 as amended by the Criminal Procedure and Investigations Act 1996, s 44 and the Youth Justice and Criminal Evidence Act 1999, s 58.]

---

1. Section 37(3A) is inserted in relation to proceedings instituted on or after 1 April 2003, whether the relevant failure or refusal on the part of the accused took place before or after that date.
2. Section 37 came into force on 10 April 1995 (SI 1995/721).

2–1498   38. Interpretation and savings for sections 34, 35, 36 and 37. (1) In sections 34, 35, 36 and 37 of this Act—

"legal representative" means an authorised advocate or authorised litigator, as defined by section 119(1) of the Courts and Legal Services Act 1990; and

"place" includes any building or part of a building, any vehicle, vessel, aircraft or hovercraft and any other place whatsoever.

(2) In sections 34(2), 35(3), 36(2) and 37(2), references to an offence charged include references to any other offence of which the accused could lawfully be convicted on that charge.

(2A) In each of sections 34(2A), 36(4A) and 37(3A) "authorised place of detention" means—

(*a*)   a police station; or

(*b*)   any other place prescribed for the purposes of that provision by order made by the Secretary of State;

and the power to make an order under this subsection shall be exercisable by statutory instrument which shall be subject to annulment in pursuance of a resolution of either House of Parliament.[1]

(3) A person shall not have the proceedings against him transferred to the Crown Court for trial, have a case to answer or be convicted of an offence solely on an inference drawn from such a failure or refusal as is mentioned in section 34(2), 35(3), 36(2) or 37(2).

(4) A judge shall not refuse to grant such an application as is mentioned in section 34(2)(*b*), 36(2)(*b*) and 37(2)(*b*) solely on an inference drawn from such a failure as is mentioned in section 34(2), 36(2) or 37(2).

(5) Nothing in sections 34, 35, 36 or 37 prejudices the operation of a provision of any enactment which provides (in whatever words) that any answer or evidence given by a person in specified circumstances shall not be admissible in evidence against him or some other person in any proceedings or class of proceedings (however described, and whether civil or criminal).

In this subsection, the reference to giving evidence is a reference to giving evidence in any manner, whether by furnishing information, making discovery, producing documents or otherwise.

(6) Nothing in sections 34, 35, 36 or 37 prejudices any power of a court, in any proceedings, to exclude evidence (whether by preventing questions being put or otherwise) at its discretion.

[Criminal Justice and Public Order Act 1994, s 38, as amended by the Youth Justice and Criminal Evidence Act 1999, s 58.]

---

1. Section 38(2A) is inserted in relation to proceedings instituted on or after 1 April 2003, whether the relevant failure or refusal on the part of the accused took place before or after that date.

2–1499   39. *Power to apply sections 34 to 38 to armed forces.*

Civil Evidence Act 1995[1]
(1995 c 38)

Admissibility of hearsay evidence

2–1501   1. Admissibility of hearsay evidence.   (1) In civil proceedings evidence shall not be excluded on the ground that it is hearsay.

(2) In this Act—

(a)   "hearsay" means a statement made otherwise than by a person while giving oral evidence in the proceedings which is tendered as evidence of the matters stated; and

(b)   references to hearsay include hearsay of whatever degree.

(3) Nothing in this Act affects the admissibility of evidence admissible apart from this section.

(4) The provisions of sections 2 to 6 (safeguards and supplementary provisions relating to hearsay evidence) do not apply in relation to hearsay evidence admissible apart from this section, notwithstanding that it may also be admissible by virtue of this section.

[Civil Evidence Act 1995, s 1.]

---

1. This Act provides for the admissibility of hearsay evidence and the proof of certain documentary evidence in civil proceedings.

The Civil Evidence Act 1995 is to be brought into force in accordance with s 16, post. Except for ss 10 and 16(5) all provisions of the Civil Evidence Act 1995 came into force on 31 January 1997 (SI 1996/3217).

Safeguards in relation to hearsay evidence

2–1502   2. Notice of proposal to adduce hearsay evidence.   (1) A party proposing to adduce hearsay evidence in civil proceedings shall, subject to the following provisions of this section, give to the other party or parties to the proceedings—

(a)   such notice (if any) of that fact, and

(b)   on request, such particulars of or relating to the evidence,

as is reasonable and practicable in the circumstances for the purpose of enabling him or them to deal with any matters arising from its being hearsay.

(2) Provision may be made by rules[1] of court—

(a)   specifying classes of proceedings or evidence in relation to which subsection (1) does not apply, and

(b)   as to the manner in which (including the time within which) the duties imposed by that subsection are to be complied with in the cases where it does apply.

(3) Subsection (1) may also be excluded by agreement of the parties; and compliance with the duty to give notice may in any case be waived by the person to whom notice is required to be given.

(4) A failure to comply with subsection (1), or with rules under subsection (2)(b), does not affect the admissibility of the evidence but may be taken into account by the court—

(a)   in considering the exercise of its powers with respect to the course of proceedings and costs, and

(b)   as a matter adversely affecting the weight to be given to the evidence in accordance with section 4.

[Civil Evidence Act 1995, s 2.]

---

1. See the Magistrates' Courts (Hearsay Evidence in Civil Proceedings) Rules 1999, in this PART, post.

2–1503   3. Power to call witness for cross-examination on hearsay statement.   Rules[1] of court may provide that where a party to civil proceedings adduces hearsay evidence of a statement made by a person and does not call that person as a witness, any other party to the proceedings may, with the leave of the court, call that person as a witness and cross-examine him on the statement as if he had been called by the first-mentioned party and as if the hearsay statement were his evidence in chief.

[Civil Evidence Act 1995, s 3.]

---

1. See the Magistrates' Courts (Hearsay Evidence in Civil Proceedings) Rules 1999, in this PART, post.

2–1504   4. Considerations relevant to weighing of hearsay evidence.   (1) In estimating the weight (if any) to be given to hearsay evidence in civil proceedings the court shall have regard to any circumstances from which any inference can reasonably be drawn as to the reliability or otherwise of the evidence.

(2) Regard may be had, in particular, to the following—

(a) whether it would have been reasonable and practicable for the party by whom the evidence was adduced to have produced the maker of the original statement as a witness;

(b) whether the original statement was made contemporaneously with the occurrence or existence of the matters stated;

(c) whether the evidence involves multiple hearsay;

(d) whether any person involved had any motive to conceal or misrepresent matters;

(e) whether the original statement was an edited account, or was made in collaboration with another or for a particular purpose;

(f) whether the circumstances in which the evidence is adduced as hearsay are such as to suggest an attempt to prevent proper evaluation of its weight.

[Civil Evidence Act 1995, s 4.]

Supplementary provisions as to hearsay evidence

2–1505　5. Competence and credibility.　(1) Hearsay evidence shall not be admitted in civil proceedings if or to the extent that it is shown to consist of, or to be proved by means of, a statement made by a person who at the time he made the statement was not competent as a witness.

For this purpose "not competent as a witness" means suffering from such mental or physical infirmity, or lack of understanding, as would render a person incompetent as a witness in civil proceedings; but a child shall be treated as competent as a witness if he satisfies the requirements of section 96(2)(a) and (b) of the Children Act 1989 (conditions for reception of unsworn evidence of child).

(2) Where in civil proceedings hearsay evidence is adduced and the maker of the original statement, or of any statement relied upon to prove another statement, is not called as a witness—

(a) evidence which if he had been so called would be admissible for the purpose of attacking or supporting his credibility as a witness is admissible[1] for that purpose in the proceedings; and

(b) evidence tending to prove that, whether before or after he made the statement, he made any other statement inconsistent with it is admissible[1] for the purpose of showing that he had contradicted himself.

Provided that evidence may not be given of any matter of which, if he had been called as a witness and had denied that matter in cross-examination, evidence could not have been adduced by the cross-examining party.

[Civil Evidence Act 1995, s 5.]

---

1. See the Magistrates' Courts (Hearsay Evidence in Civil Proceedings) Rules 1999, in this Part, post for the requirement to give notice to the other party of the intention to attack the credibility of the person who made the statement or allege that he has made another statement inconsistent with it.

2–1506　6. Previous statements of witnesses.　(1) Subject as follows, the provisions of this Act as to hearsay evidence in civil proceedings apply equally (but with any necessary modifications) in relation to a previous statement made by a person called as a witness in the proceedings.

(2) A party who has called or intends to call a person as a witness in civil proceedings may not in those proceedings adduce evidence of a previous statement made by that person, except—

(a) with the leave of the court, or

(b) for the purpose of rebutting a suggestion that his evidence has been fabricated.

This shall not be construed as preventing a witness statement (that is, a written statement of oral evidence which a party to the proceedings intends to lead) from being adopted by a witness in giving evidence or treated as his evidence.

(3) Where in the case of civil proceedings section 3, 4 or 5 of the Criminal Procedure Act 1865 applies, which make provision as to—

(a) how far a witness may be discredited by the party producing him,

(b) the proof of contradictory statements made by a witness, and

(c) cross-examination as to previous statements in writing,

this Act does not authorise the adducing of evidence of a previous inconsistent or contradictory statement otherwise than in accordance with those sections.

This is without prejudice to any provision made by rules of court under section 3 above (power to call witness for cross-examination on hearsay statement).

(4) Nothing in this Act affects any of the rules of law as to the circumstances in which, where a person called as a witness in civil proceedings is cross-examined on a document used by him to refresh his memory, that document may be made evidence in the proceedings.

(5) Nothing in this section shall be construed as preventing a statement of any description referred to above from being admissible by virtue of section 1 as evidence of the matters stated.

[Civil Evidence Act 1995, s 6.]

2–1507　7. Evidence formerly admissible at common law.　(1) The common law rule effectively preserved by section 9(1) and (2)(a) of the Civil Evidence Act 1968 (admissibility of admissions adverse to a party) is superseded by the provisions of this Act.

(2) The common law rules effectively preserved by section 9(1) and (2)(*b*) to (*d*) of the Civil Evidence Act 1968, that is, any rule of law whereby in civil proceedings—

(*a*) published works dealing with matters of a public nature (for example, histories, scientific works, dictionaries and maps) are admissible as evidence of facts of a public nature stated in them,

(*b*) public documents (for example, public registers, and returns made under public authority with respect to matters of public interest) are admissible as evidence of facts stated in them, or

(*c*) records (for example, the records of certain courts, treaties, Crown grants, pardons and commissions) are admissible as evidence of facts stated in them,

shall continue to have effect.

(3) The common law rules effectively preserved by section 9(3) and (4) of the Civil Evidence Act 1968, that is, any rule of law whereby in civil proceedings—

(*a*) evidence of a person's reputation is admissible for the purpose of proving his good or bad character, or

(*b*) evidence of reputation or family tradition is admissible—

(i) for the purpose of proving or disproving pedigree or the existence of a marriage, or

(ii) for the purpose of proving or disproving the existence of any public or general right or of identifying any person or thing,

shall continue to have effect in so far as they authorise the court to treat such evidence as proving or disproving that matter.

Where any such rule applies, reputation or family tradition shall be treated for the purposes of this Act as a fact and not as a statement or multiplicity of statements about the matter in question.

(4) The words in which a rule of law mentioned in this section is described are intended only to identify the rule and shall not be construed as altering it in any way.

[Civil Evidence Act 1995, s 7.]

Other matters

2–1508 8. Proof of statements contained in documents.   (1) Where a statement contained in a document is admissible as evidence in civil proceedings, it may be proved—

(*a*) by the production of that document, or

(*b*) whether or not that document is still in existence, by the production of a copy of that document or of the material part of it,

authenticated in such manner as the court may approve.

(2) It is immaterial for this purpose how many removes there are between a copy and the original.

[Civil Evidence Act 1995, s 8.]

2–1509 9. Proof of records of business or public authority.   (1) A document which is shown to form part of the records of a business or public authority may be received in evidence in civil proceedings without further proof.

(2) A document shall be taken to form part of the records of a business or public authority if there is produced to the court a certificate to that effect signed by an officer of the business or authority to which the records belong.

For this purpose—

(*a*) a document purporting to be a certificate signed by an officer of a business or public authority shall be deemed to have been duly given by such an officer and signed by him; and

(*b*) a certificate shall be treated as signed by a person if it purports to bear a facsimile of his signature.

(3) The absence of an entry in the records of a business or public authority may be proved in civil proceedings by affidavit of an officer of the business or authority to which the records belong.

(4) In this section—

"records" means records in whatever form;

"business" includes any activity regularly carried on over a period of time, whether for profit or not, by any body (whether corporate or not) or by an individual;

"officer" includes any person occupying a responsible position in relation to the relevant activities of the business or public authority or in relation to its records; and

"public authority" includes any public or statutory undertaking, any government department and any person holding office under Her Majesty.

(5) The court may, having regard to the circumstances of the case, direct that all or any of the above provisions of this section do not apply in relation to a particular document or record, or description of documents or records.

[Civil Evidence Act 1995, s 9.]

2–1510 10. *Admissibility and proof of Ogden Tables.*

General

2–1511   11. Meaning of "civil proceedings".   In this Act "civil proceedings" means civil proceedings, before any tribunal, in relation to which the strict rules of evidence apply, whether as a matter of law or by agreement of the parties.

References to "the court" and "rules of court" shall be construed accordingly.

[Civil Evidence Act 1995, s 11.]

2–1512   12. Provisions as to rules of court[1].   (1) Any power to make rules of court regulating the practice or procedure of the court in relation to civil proceedings includes power to make such provision as may be necessary or expedient for carrying into effect the provisions of this Act.

(2) Any rules of court made for the purposes of this Act as it applies in relation to proceedings in the High Court apply, except in so far as their operation is excluded by agreement, to arbitration proceedings to which this Act applies, subject to such modifications as may be appropriate.

Any question arising as to what modifications are appropriate shall be determined, in default of agreement, by the arbitrator or umpire, as the case may be.

[Civil Evidence Act 1995, s 12.]

---

1. See the Magistrates' Courts (Hearsay Evidence in Civil Proceedings) Rules 1999, in this PART, post.

2–1513   13. Interpretation.   In this Act—

"civil proceedings" has the meaning given by section 11 and "court" and "rules of court" shall be construed in accordance with that section;

"document" means anything in which information of any description is recorded, and "copy", in relation to a document, means anything onto which information recorded in the document has been copied, by whatever means and whether directly or indirectly;

"hearsay" shall be construed in accordance with section 1(2);

"oral evidence" includes evidence which, by reason of a defect of speech or hearing, a person called as a witness gives in writing or by signs;

"the original statement", in relation to hearsay evidence, means the underlying statement (if any) by—

(a)   in the case of evidence of fact, a person having personal knowledge of that fact, or

(b)   in the case of evidence of opinion, the person whose opinion it is; and

"statement" means any representation of fact or opinion, however made.

[Civil Evidence Act 1995, s 13.]

2–1514   14. Savings.   (1) Nothing in this Act affects the exclusion of evidence on grounds other than that it is hearsay.

This applies whether the evidence falls to be excluded in pursuance of any enactment or rule of law, for failure to comply with rules of court or an order of the court, or otherwise.

(2) Nothing in this Act affects the proof of documents by means other than those specified in section 8 or 9.

(3) Nothing in this Act affects the operation of the following enactments—

(a)   section 2 of the Documentary Evidence Act 1868 (mode of proving certain official documents);

(b)   section 2 of the Documentary Evidence Act 1882 (documents printed under the superintendence of Stationery Office);

(c)   section 1 of the Evidence (Colonial Statutes) Act 1907 (proof of statutes of certain legislatures);

(d)   section 1 of the Evidence (Foreign, Dominion and Colonial Documents) Act 1933 (proof and effect of registers and official certificates of certain countries);

(e)   section 5 of the Oaths and Evidence (Overseas Authorities and Countries) Act 1963 (provision in respect of public registers of other countries).

[Civil Evidence Act 1995, s 14.]

2–1515   15. *Consequential amendments and repeals*

2–1516   16. Short title, commencement and extent.   (1) This Act may be cited as the Civil Evidence Act 1995.

(2) The provisions of this Act come into force on such day as the Lord Chancellor may appoint by order[1] made by statutory instrument, and different days may be appointed for different provisions and for different purposes.

(3) Subject to subsection (3A), the provisions of this Act shall not apply in relation to proceedings begun before commencement.

(3A) Transitional provisions for the application of the provisions of this Act to proceedings begun before commencement may be made by rules of court or practice directions.

(4) This Act extends to England and Wales.

(5) *Northern Ireland.*

(6) The provisions of Schedules 1 and 2 (consequential amendments and repeals) have the same extent as the enactments respectively amended or repealed.

[Civil Evidence Act 1995, s 16, as amended by SI 1999/1217.]

1. The Civil Evidence Act 1995 (Commencement No 1) Order 1996, SI 1996/3217, except for ss 10 and 16(5), brought all provisions of the Act into force on 31 January 1997.

Youth Justice and Criminal Evidence Act 1999
(1999 c 23)

PART II[1]

GIVING OF EVIDENCE OR INFORMATION FOR PURPOSES OF CRIMINAL PROCEEDINGS

CHAPTER I[2]

SPECIAL MEASURES DIRECTIONS IN CASE OF VULNERABLE AND INTIMIDATED WITNESSES

Preliminary

2–1517   16. Witnesses eligible for assistance on grounds of age or incapacity. (1) For the purposes of this Chapter a witness in criminal proceedings (other than the accused) is eligible for assistance by virtue of this section—

   (*a*) if under the age of 17 at the time of the hearing; or
   (*b*) if the court considers that the quality of evidence given by the witness is likely to be diminished by reason of any circumstances falling within subsection (2).

   (2) The circumstances falling within this subsection are—

   (*a*) that the witness—

     (i) suffers from mental disorder within the meaning of the Mental Health Act 1983, or
     (ii) otherwise has a significant impairment of intelligence and social functioning;

   (*b*) that the witness has a physical disability or is suffering from a physical disorder.

   (3) In subsection (1)(*a*) "the time of the hearing", in relation to a witness, means the time when it falls to the court to make a determination for the purposes of section 19(2) in relation to the witness.
   (4) In determining whether a witness falls within subsection (1)(*b*) the court must consider any views expressed by the witness.
   (5) In this Chapter references to the quality of a witness's evidence are to its quality in terms of completeness, coherence and accuracy; and for this purpose "coherence" refers to a witness's ability in giving evidence to give answers which address the questions put to the witness and can be understood both individually and collectively.
[Youth Justice and Criminal Evidence Act 1999, s 16.]

---

1. Part II contains ss 16–63 and Schs 2 and 3. This Act is to be brought into force in accordance with the provisions of s 68 and orders made thereunder. The following provisions came into force on the passing of the Act (17 July 1999): s 6(4), Chapters I–IV of Part II for the purpose only of making rules of court, s 40(1), ss 58(5) and 61(2) for the purpose only of the exercise of any power to make an order, s 61(1) and (3) and ss 62–66 and 68. At the date of going to press, the following commencement orders had been made: (No 1) SI 1999/3427; (No 2) SI 2000/1034; (No 3) SI 2000/1587; (No 4) SI 2000/2091; (No 5) SI 2000/3075, which brought into force the following provisions: ss 34 and 35, ss 38–40, ss 41–43 and s 67 (partially) and Schs 4 (partially), Sch 5, Sch 6 (partially) and Sch 7 (partially); (No 7) SI 2002/1739 which brought into force, in so far as they were not already in force, inter alia ss 16–27, 30, 31–33, 36–37, 47, 53–57 on 24 July 2002; (No 8) SI 2003/707 which brought into force s 58 and Sch 7 para 8 on 1 April 2003; (No 9) SI 2004/299 which brought into force s 29 on 23 February 2004; (No 10) SI 2004/2428 (ss 46, 48(*b*), (*d*), 49–52, Sch 2 paras 4, 6-14, Sch 6 (part), Sch 7 para 6 on 7 October 2004; (No 12) SI 2006/2885 (s 61(2), s 67(3) (partially), Sch 6 (part)). However, the availability of special measures to courts is subject to the receipt of notification from the Home Office, see note to s 18, post. (Part I of the 1999 Act was repealed and replaced by the Powers of Criminal Courts (Sentencing) Act 2000 in PART III: SENTENCING, ante).
2. See para **2–345A**, ante. This chapter is concerned not to restrict the rights of defendants but to augment the protection available for other witnesses. Accordingly there is no power under these provisions to make special measures directions in respect of defendants or co-defendants nor is there any inherent or common law power to make such orders involving video or live link evidence although there are some 'special measures' such as use of screens, which are available at common law. Furthermore the statutory regime in this chapter is compatible with art 6 of the European Convention on Human Rights (*R (S) v Waltham Forest Youth Court* [2004] EWHC 715 (Admin), 168 JP 293) (but see also the doubts expressed on the correctness of this decision that the court had no inherent discretion to afford special measures to a defendant in *R v Camberwell Youth Court, ex p D (a minor)*, supra).

2–1518   17. Witnesses eligible for assistance on grounds of fear or distress about testifying.
(1) For the purposes of this Chapter a witness in criminal proceedings (other than the accused) is eligible for assistance by virtue of this subsection if the court is satisfied that the quality of evidence given by the witness is likely to be diminished by reason of fear or distress on the part of the witness in connection with testifying in the proceedings.
   (2) In determining whether a witness falls within subsection (1) the court must take into account, in particular—

   (*a*) the nature and alleged circumstances of the offence to which the proceedings relate;
   (*b*) the age of the witness;
   (*c*) such of the following matters as appear to the court to be relevant, namely—

     (i) the social and cultural background and ethnic origins of the witness,
     (ii) the domestic and employment circumstances of the witness, and
     (iii) any religious beliefs or political opinions of the witness;

(*d*) any behaviour towards the witness on the part of—

    (i) the accused,

    (ii) members of the family or associates of the accused, or

    (iii) any other person who is likely to be an accused or a witness in the proceedings.

(3) In determining that question the court must in addition consider any views expressed by the witness.

(4) Where the complainant in respect of a sexual offence is a witness in proceedings relating to that offence (or to that offence and any other offences), the witness is eligible for assistance in relation to those proceedings by virtue of this subsection unless the witness has informed the court of the witness' wish not to be so eligible by virtue of this subsection.

[Youth Justice and Criminal Evidence Act 1999, s 17.]

2–1519 18. Special measures available to eligible witnesses. (1) For the purposes of this Chapter—

(*a*) the provision which may be made by a special measures direction by virtue of each of sections 23 to 30 is a special measure available in relation to a witness eligible for assistance by virtue of section 16; and

(*b*) the provision which may be made by such a direction by virtue of each of sections 23 to 28 is a special measure available in relation to a witness eligible for assistance by virtue of section 17;

but this subsection has effect subject to subsection (2).

(2) Where (apart from this subsection) a special measure would, in accordance with subsection (1)(*a*) or (*b*), be available in relation to a witness in any proceedings, it shall not be taken by a court to be available in relation to the witness unless—

(*a*) the court has been notified[1] by the Secretary of State that relevant arrangements may be made available in the area in which it appears to the court that the proceedings will take place, and

(*b*) the notice has not been withdrawn.

(3) In subsection (2) "relevant arrangements" means arrangements for implementing the measure in question which cover the witness and the proceedings in question.

(4) The withdrawal of a notice under that subsection relating to a special measure shall not affect the availability of that measure in relation to a witness if a special measures direction providing for that measure to apply to the witness's evidence has been made by the court before the notice is withdrawn.

(5) The Secretary of State may by order make such amendments of this Chapter as he considers appropriate for altering the special measures which, in accordance with subsection (1)(*a*) or (*b*), are available in relation to a witness eligible for assistance by virtue of section 16 or (as the case may be) section 17, whether—

(*a*) by modifying the provisions relating to any measure for the time being available in relation to such a witness,

(*b*) by the addition—

    (i) (with or without modifications) of any measure which is for the time being available in relation to a witness eligible for assistance by virtue of the other of those sections, or

    (ii) of any new measure, or

(*c*) by the removal of any measure.

[Youth Justice and Criminal Evidence Act 1999, s 18.]

---

1. For notifications and availability of special measures, see note to para **2–345A Special measure directions in case of vulnerable and intimidated witnesses**, ante.

Special measures directions

2–1520 19. Special measures direction relating to eligible witness. (1) This section applies where in any criminal proceedings—

(*a*) a party to the proceedings makes an application for the court to give a direction under this section in relation to a witness in the proceedings other than the accused, or

(*b*) the court of its own motion raises the issue whether such a direction should be given.

(2) Where the court determines that the witness is eligible for assistance by virtue of section 16 or 17, the court must then—

(*a*) determine whether any of the special measures available in relation to the witness (or any combination of them) would, in its opinion, be likely to improve the quality of evidence given by the witness; and

(*b*) if so—

    (i) determine which of those measures (or combination of them) would, in its opinion, be likely to maximise so far as practicable the quality of such evidence; and

    (ii) give a direction under this section providing for the measure or measures so determined to apply to evidence given by the witness.

(3) In determining for the purposes of this Chapter whether any special measure or measures would or would not be likely to improve, or to maximise so far as practicable, the quality of evidence given by the witness, the court must consider all the circumstances of the case, including in particular—

(*a*) any views expressed by the witness; and

(*b*) whether the measure or measures might tend to inhibit such evidence being effectively tested by a party to the proceedings.

(4) A special measures direction must specify particulars of the provision made by the direction in respect of each special measure which is to apply to the witness's evidence.

(5) In this Chapter "special measures direction" means a direction under this section.

(6) Nothing in this Chapter is to be regarded as affecting any power of a court to make an order or give leave of any description (in the exercise of its inherent jurisdiction or otherwise)—

(*a*) in relation to a witness who is not an eligible witness, or

(*b*) in relation to an eligible witness where (as, for example, in a case where a foreign language interpreter is to be provided) the order is made or the leave is given otherwise than by reason of the fact that the witness is an eligible witness.

[Youth Justice and Criminal Evidence Act 1999, s 19.]

2–1521 **20. Further provisions about directions: general.** (1) Subject to subsection (2) and section 21(8), a special measures direction has binding effect from the time it is made until the proceedings for the purposes of which it is made are either—

(*a*) determined (by acquittal, conviction or otherwise), or

(*b*) abandoned,

in relation to the accused or (if there is more than one) in relation to each of the accused.

(2) The court may discharge or vary (or further vary) a special measures direction if it appears to the court to be in the interests of justice to do so, and may do so either—

(*a*) on an application made by a party to the proceedings, if there has been a material change of circumstances since the relevant time, or

(*b*) of its own motion.

(3) In subsection (2) "the relevant time" means—

(*a*) the time when the direction was given, or

(*b*) if a previous application has been made under that subsection, the time when the application (or last application) was made.

(4) Nothing in section 24(2) and (3), 27(4) to (7) or 28(4) to (6) is to be regarded as affecting the power of the court to vary or discharge a special measures direction under subsection (2).

(5) The court must state in open court its reasons for—

(*a*) giving or varying,

(*b*) refusing an application for, or for the variation or discharge of, or

(*c*) discharging,

a special measures direction and, if it is a magistrates' court, must cause them to be entered in the register of its proceedings.

(6) Criminal Procedure Rules[1] of court may make provision—

(*a*) for uncontested applications to be determined by the court without a hearing;

(*b*) for preventing the renewal of an unsuccessful application for a special measures direction except where there has been a material change of circumstances;

(*c*) for expert evidence to be given in connection with an application for, or for varying or discharging, such a direction;

(*d*) for the manner in which confidential or sensitive information is to be treated in connection with such an application and in particular as to its being disclosed to, or withheld from, a party to the proceedings.

[Youth Justice and Criminal Evidence Act 1999, s 20 as amended by the Courts Act 2003, Sch 8.]

---

1. See the Criminal Procedure Rules 2005, Part 29, in PART I: MAGISTRATES' COURTS, PROCEDURE, ante.

2–1522 **21. Special provisions relating to child witnesses.** (1) For the purposes of this section—

(*a*) a witness in criminal proceedings is a "child witness" if he is an eligible witness by reason of section 16(1)(*a*) (whether or not he is an eligible witness by reason of any other provision of section 16 or 17);

(*b*) a child witness is "in need of special protection" if the offence (or any of the offences) to which the proceedings relate is—

(i) an offence falling within section 35(3)(*a*) (sexual offences etc), or

(ii) an offence falling within section 35(3)(*b*), (*c*) or (*d*) (kidnapping, assaults etc); and

(*c*) a "relevant recording", in relation to a child witness, is a video recording of an interview of the witness made with a view to its admission as evidence in chief of the witness.

(2) Where the court, in making a determination for the purposes of section 19(2), determines that a witness in criminal proceedings is a child witness, the court must—

(a) first have regard to subsections (3) to (7) below; and

(b) then have regard to section 19(2);

and for the purposes of section 19(2), as it then applies to the witness, any special measures required to be applied in relation to him by virtue of this section shall be treated as if they were measures determined by the court, pursuant to section 19(2)(a) and (b)(i), to be ones that (whether on their own or with any other special measures) would be likely to maximise, so far as practicable, the quality of his evidence.

(3) The primary rule in the case of a child witness is that the court must give a special measures direction in relation to the witness which complies with the following requirements—

(a) it must provide for any relevant recording to be admitted under section 27 (video recorded evidence in chief); and

(b) it must provide for any evidence given by the witness in the proceedings which is not given by means of a video recording (whether in chief or otherwise) to be given by means of a live link in accordance with section 24.

(4) The primary rule is subject to the following limitations—

(a) the requirement contained in subsection (3)(a) or (b) has effect subject to the availability (within the meaning of section 18(2)) of the special measure in question in relation to the witness;

(b) the requirement contained in subsection (3)(a) also has effect subject to section 27(2); and

(c) the rule does not apply to the extent that the court is satisfied that compliance with it would not be likely to maximise the quality of the witness's evidence so far as practicable (whether because the application to that evidence of one or more other special measures available in relation to the witness would have that result or for any other reason).

(5) However, subsection (4)(c) does not apply in relation to a child witness in need of special protection.

(6) Where a child witness is in need of special protection by virtue of subsection (1)(b)(i), any special measures direction given by the court which complies with the requirement contained in subsection (3)(a) must in addition provide for the special measure available under section 28 (video recorded cross-examination or re-examination) to apply in relation to—

(a) any cross-examination of the witness otherwise than by the accused in person, and

(b) any subsequent re-examination.

(7) The requirement contained in subsection (6) has effect subject to the following limitations—

(a) it has effect subject to the availability (within the meaning of section 18(2)) of that special measure in relation to the witness; and

(b) it does not apply if the witness has informed the court that he does not want that special measure to apply in relation to him.

(8) Where a special measures direction is given in relation to a child witness who is an eligible witness by reason only of section 16(1)(a), then—

(a) subject to subsection (9) below, and

(b) except where the witness has already begun to give evidence in the proceedings,

the direction shall cease to have effect at the time when the witness attains the age of 17.

(9) Where a special measures direction is given in relation to a child witness who is an eligible witness by reason only of section 16(1)(a) and—

(a) the direction provides—

(i) for any relevant recording to be admitted under section 27 as evidence in chief of the witness, or

(ii) for the special measure available under section 28 to apply in relation to the witness, and

(b) if it provides for that special measure to so apply, the witness is still under the age of 17 when the video recording is made for the purposes of section 28,

then, so far as it provides as mentioned in paragraph (a)(i) or (ii) above, the direction shall continue to have effect in accordance with section 20(1) even though the witness subsequently attains that age. [Youth Justice and Criminal Evidence Act 1999, s 21.]

2–1523 22. Extension of provisions of section 21 to certain witnesses over 17. (1) For the purposes of this section—

(a) a witness in criminal proceedings (other than the accused) is a "qualifying witness" if he—

(i) is not an eligible witness at the time of the hearing (as defined by section 16(3)), but

(ii) was under the age of 17 when a relevant recording was made;

(b) a qualifying witness is "in need of special protection" if the offence (or any of the offences) to which the proceedings relate is—

(i) an offence falling within section 35(3)(a) (sexual offences etc), or

(ii) an offence falling within section 35(3)(b), (c) or (d) (kidnapping, assaults etc); and

(c)   a "relevant recording", in relation to a witness, is a video recording of an interview of the witness made with a view to its admission as evidence in chief of the witness.

(2)   Subsections (2) to (7) of section 21 shall apply as follows in relation to a qualifying witness—

(a)   subsections (2) to (4), so far as relating to the giving of a direction complying with the requirement contained in subsection (3)(a), shall apply to a qualifying witness in respect of the relevant recording as they apply to a child witness (within the meaning of that section);

(b)   subsection (5), so far as relating to the giving of such a direction, shall apply to a qualifying witness in need of special protection as it applies to a child witness in need of special protection (within the meaning of that section); and

(c)   subsections (6) and (7) shall apply to a qualifying witness in need of special protection by virtue of subsection (1)(b)(i) above as they apply to such a child witness as is mentioned in subsection (6).

[Youth Justice and Criminal Evidence Act 1999, s 22.]

Special measures

2–1524   **23. Screening witness from accused.**   (1) A special measures direction may provide for the witness, while giving testimony or being sworn in court, to be prevented by means of a screen or other arrangement from seeing the accused.

(2)   But the screen or other arrangement must not prevent the witness from being able to see, and to be seen by—

(a)   the judge or justices (or both) and the jury (if there is one);

(b)   legal representatives acting in the proceedings; and

(c)   any interpreter or other person appointed (in pursuance of the direction or otherwise) to assist the witness.

(3)   Where two or more legal representatives are acting for a party to the proceedings, subsection (2)(b) is to be regarded as satisfied in relation to those representatives if the witness is able at all material times to see and be seen by at least one of them.

[Youth Justice and Criminal Evidence Act 1999, s 23.]

2–1525   **24. Evidence by live link.**   (1) A special measures direction may provide for the witness to give evidence by means of a live link.

(2)   Where a direction provides for the witness to give evidence by means of a live link, the witness may not give evidence in any other way without the permission of the court.

(3)   The court may give permission for the purposes of subsection (2) if it appears to the court to be in the interests of justice to do so, and may do so either—

(a)   on an application by a party to the proceedings, if there has been a material change of circumstances since the relevant time, or

(b)   of its own motion.

(4)   In subsection (3) "the relevant time" means—

(a)   the time when the direction was given, or

(b)   if a previous application has been made under that subsection, the time when the application (or last application) was made.

(5)–(7)   *Repealed.*

(8)   In this Chapter "live link" means a live television link or other arrangement whereby a witness, while absent from the courtroom or other place where the proceedings are being held, is able to see and hear a person there and to be seen and heard by the persons specified in section 23(2)(a) to (c).

[Youth Justice and Criminal Evidence Act 1999, s 24 as amended by the Courts Act 2003, Sch 8.]

2–1526   **25. Evidence given in private.**   (1) A special measures direction may provide for the exclusion from the court, during the giving of the witness's evidence, of persons of any description specified in the direction.

(2)   The persons who may be so excluded do not include—

(a)   the accused,

(b)   legal representatives acting in the proceedings, or

(c)   any interpreter or other person appointed (in pursuance of the direction or otherwise) to assist the witness.

(3)   A special measures direction providing for representatives of news gathering or reporting organisations to be so excluded shall be expressed not to apply to one named person who—

(a)   is a representative of such an organisation, and

(b)   has been nominated for the purpose by one or more such organisations,

unless it appears to the court that no such nomination has been made.

(4)   A special measures direction may only provide for the exclusion of persons under this section where—

(a)   the proceedings relate to a sexual offence; or

(*b*) it appears to the court that there are reasonable grounds for believing that any person other than the accused has sought, or will seek, to intimidate the witness in connection with testifying in the proceedings.

(5) Any proceedings from which persons are excluded under this section (whether or not those persons include representatives of news gathering or reporting organisations) shall nevertheless be taken to be held in public for the purposes of any privilege or exemption from liability available in respect of fair, accurate and contemporaneous reports of legal proceedings held in public.
[Youth Justice and Criminal Evidence Act 1999, s 25.]

2-1527   26. Removal of wigs and gowns. A special measures direction may provide for the wearing of wigs or gowns to be dispensed with during the giving of the witness's evidence.
[Youth Justice and Criminal Evidence Act 1999, s 26.]

2-1528   27. Video recorded evidence in chief¹. (1) A special measures direction may provide for a video recording of an interview of the witness to be admitted as evidence in chief of the witness.

(2) A special measures direction may, however, not provide for a video recording, or a part of such a recording, to be admitted under this section if the court is of the opinion, having regard to all the circumstances of the case, that in the interests of justice the recording, or that part of it, should not be so admitted.

(3) In considering for the purposes of subsection (2) whether any part of a recording should not be admitted under this section, the court must consider whether any prejudice to the accused which might result from that part being so admitted is outweighed by the desirability² of showing the whole, or substantially the whole, of the recorded interview.

(4) Where a special measures direction provides for a recording to be admitted under this section, the court may nevertheless subsequently direct that it is not to be so admitted if—

(*a*) it appears to the court that—

    (i) the witness will not be available for cross-examination (whether conducted in the ordinary way or in accordance with any such direction), and

    (ii) the parties to the proceedings have not agreed that there is no need for the witness to be so available; or

(*b*) any Criminal Procedure Rules requiring disclosure of the circumstances in which the recording was made have not been complied with to the satisfaction of the court.

(5) Where a recording is admitted under this section—

(*a*) the witness must be called by the party tendering it in evidence, unless—

    (i) a special measures direction provides for the witness's evidence on cross-examination to be given otherwise than by testimony in court, or

    (ii) the parties to the proceedings have agreed as mentioned in subsection (4)(*a*)(ii); and

(*b*) the witness may not give evidence in chief otherwise than by means of the recording—

    (i) as to any matter which, in the opinion of the court, has been dealt with adequately in the witness's recorded testimony, or

    (ii) without the permission of the court, as to any other matter which, in the opinion of the court, is dealt with in that testimony.

(6) Where in accordance with subsection (2) a special measures direction provides for part only of a recording to be admitted under this section, references in subsections (4) and (5) to the recording or to the witness's recorded testimony are references to the part of the recording or testimony which is to be so admitted.

(7) The court may give permission for the purposes of subsection (5)(*b*)(ii) if it appears to the court to be in the interests of justice to do so, and may do so either—

(*a*) on an application by a party to the proceedings, if there has been a material change of circumstances since the relevant time, or

(*b*) of its own motion.

(8) In subsection (7) "the relevant time" means—

(*a*) the time when the direction was given, or

(*b*) if a previous application has been made under that subsection, the time when the application (or last application) was made.

(9) The court may, in giving permission for the purposes of subsection (5)(*b*)(ii), direct that the evidence in question is to be given by the witness by means of a live link; and, if the court so directs, subsections (5) to (7) of section 24 shall apply in relation to that evidence as they apply in relation to evidence which is to be given in accordance with a special measures direction.

(10) A magistrates' court inquiring into an offence as examining justices under section 6 of the Magistrates' Courts Act 1980 may consider any video recording in relation to which it is proposed to apply for a special measures direction providing for it to be admitted at the trial in accordance with this section.

(11) Nothing in this section affects the admissibility of any video recording which would be admissible apart from this section.
[Youth Justice and Criminal Evidence Act 1999, s 27 as amended by the Courts Act 2003, Sch 8.]

1. For editing and production of video evidence-in-chief, see *Practice Direction (criminal: consolidated)* [2002] para IV.40, in PART I: MAGISTRATES' COURTS, PROCEDURE, ante.

2. The word "desirability" in s 27(3) does not operate to extend the common law rules on the admissibility of evidence; to hold otherwise would admit inadmissible evidence simply because it was given by way of video and would ignore s 31(5) (*R (on the application of the Crown Prosecution Service, Harrow) v Brentford Youth Court* [2003] EWHC 2409 (Admin), (2003) 167 JP 614, [2004] Crim LR 159). The legislative purpose of s 27(3) was: (i) to resolve in favour of video evidence its question of relative worth in relation to live evidence; and (ii) to tackle the problem of the unusual case in which the evidence of a child or a disabled person could not be given without referring to inadmissible matters, e.g. where a disabled child was unable to give evidence without referring to matters that could be excluded from an adult's evidence by appropriate questioning. In those circumstances, if the evidence could not be understood without the whole of it being played, and it is desirable that the whole should be played, then the judge should direct himself or the jury to ignore the inadmissible material (*R (on the application of the Crown Prosecution Service, Harrow) v Brentford Youth Court*, supra).

2–1528A   28. Video recorded cross-examination or re-examination.   (1) Where a special measures direction provides for a video recording[1] to be admitted under section 27 as evidence in chief of the witness, the direction may also provide—

(a)   for any cross-examination of the witness, and any re-examination, to be recorded by means of a video recording; and

(b)   for such a recording to be admitted, so far as it relates to any such cross-examination or re-examination, as evidence of the witness under cross-examination or on re-examination, as the case may be.

(2)   Such a recording must be made in the presence of such persons as Criminal Procedure Rules or the direction may provide and in the absence of the accused, but in circumstances in which—

(a)   the judge or justices (or both) and legal representatives acting in the proceedings are able to see and hear the examination of the witness and to communicate with the persons in whose presence the recording is being made, and

(b)   the accused is able to see and hear any such examination and to communicate with any legal representative acting for him.

(3)   Where two or more legal representatives are acting for a party to the proceedings, subsection (2)(a) and (b) are to be regarded as satisfied in relation to those representatives if at all material times they are satisfied in relation to at least one of them.

(4)   Where a special measures direction provides for a recording to be admitted under this section, the court may nevertheless subsequently direct that it is not to be so admitted if any requirement of subsection (2) or Criminal Procedure Rules or the direction has not been complied with to the satisfaction of the court.

(5)   Where in pursuance of subsection (1) a recording has been made of any examination of the witness, the witness may not be subsequently cross-examined or re-examined in respect of any evidence given by the witness in the proceedings (whether in any recording admissible under section 27 or this section or otherwise than in such a recording) unless the court gives a further special measures direction making such provision as is mentioned in subsection (1)(a) and (b) in relation to any subsequent cross-examination, and re-examination, of the witness.

(6)   The court may only give such a further direction if it appears to the court—

(a)   that the proposed cross-examination is sought by a party to the proceedings as a result of that party having become aware, since the time when the original recording was made in pursuance of subsection (1), of a matter which that party could not with reasonable diligence have ascertained by then, or

(b)   that for any other reason it is in the interests of justice to give the further direction.

(7)   Nothing in this section shall be read as applying in relation to any cross-examination of the witness by the accused in person (in a case where the accused is to be able to conduct any such cross-examination).

[Youth Justice and Criminal Evidence Act 1999, s 28 as amended by the Courts Act 2003, Sch 8.]

1. As s 28 covers the situation where cross-examination is to be video recorded, there is no need for a general rule that where evidence is given by means of video recorded evidence in chief and cross examination by live link, such cross examination should be recorded so that if the evidence in chief is replayed to the jury, the cross examination may also be replayed (*R v Mullen* [2004] EWCA Crim 602, [2004] 2 Cr App R 18, [2005] Crim LR 76).

2–1529   29. Examination of witness through intermediary.   (1) A special measures direction may provide for any examination of the witness (however and wherever conducted) to be conducted through an interpreter or other person approved by the court for the purposes of this section ("an intermediary").

(2)   The function of an intermediary is to communicate—

(a)   to the witness, questions put to the witness, and

(b)   to any person asking such questions, the answers given by the witness in reply to them,

and to explain such questions or answers so far as necessary to enable them to be understood by the witness or person in question.

(3)   Any examination of the witness in pursuance of subsection (1) must take place in the presence of such persons as Criminal Procedure Rules or the direction may provide, but in circumstances in which—

(a) the judge or justices (or both) and legal representatives acting in the proceedings are able to see and hear the examination of the witness and to communicate with the intermediary, and

(b) (except in the case of a video recorded examination) the jury (if there is one) are able to see and hear the examination of the witness.

(4) Where two or more legal representatives are acting for a party to the proceedings, subsection (3)(a) is to be regarded as satisfied in relation to those representatives if at all material times it is satisfied in relation to at least one of them.

(5) A person may not act as an intermediary in a particular case except after making a declaration, in such form as may be prescribed by Criminal Procedure Rules[1], that he will faithfully perform his function as intermediary.

(6) Subsection (1) does not apply to an interview of the witness which is recorded by means of a video recording with a view to its admission as evidence in chief of the witness; but a special measures direction may provide for such a recording to be admitted under section 27 if the interview was conducted through an intermediary and—

(a) that person complied with subsection (5) before the interview began, and

(b) the court's approval for the purposes of this section is given before the direction is given.

(7) Section 1 of the Perjury Act 1911 (perjury) shall apply in relation to a person acting as an intermediary as it applies in relation to a person lawfully sworn as an interpreter in a judicial proceeding; and for this purpose, where a person acts as an intermediary in any proceeding which is not a judicial proceeding for the purposes of that section, that proceeding shall be taken to be part of the judicial proceeding in which the witness's evidence is given.
[Youth Justice and Criminal Evidence Act 1999, s 29 as amended by the Courts Act 2003, Sch 8.]

---

1. See the Criminal Procedure Rules 2005, Part 29, in PART I: MAGISTRATES' COURTS, PROCEDURE, ante.

2–1530   30. Aids to communication. A special measures direction may provide for the witness, while giving evidence (whether by testimony in court or otherwise), to be provided with such device as the court considers appropriate with a view to enabling questions or answers to be communicated to or by the witness despite any disability or disorder or other impairment which the witness has or suffers from.
[Youth Justice and Criminal Evidence Act 1999, s 30.]

Supplementary

2–1531   31. Status of evidence given under Chapter I. (1) Subsections (2) to (4) apply to a statement made by a witness in criminal proceedings which, in accordance with a special measures direction, is not made by the witness in direct oral testimony in court but forms part of the witness's evidence in those proceedings.

(2) The statement shall be treated as if made by the witness in direct oral testimony in court; and accordingly—

(a) it is admissible evidence of any fact of which such testimony from the witness would be admissible;

(b) it is not capable of corroborating any other evidence given by the witness.

(3) Subsection (2) applies to a statement admitted under section 27 or 28 which is not made by the witness on oath even though it would have been required to be made on oath if made by the witness in direct oral testimony in court.

(4) In estimating the weight (if any) to be attached to the statement, the court must have regard to all the circumstances from which an inference can reasonably be drawn (as to the accuracy of the statement or otherwise).

(5) Nothing in this Chapter (apart from subsection (3)) affects the operation of any rule of law relating to evidence in criminal proceedings.

(6) Where any statement made by a person on oath in any proceeding which is not a judicial proceeding for the purposes of section 1 of the Perjury Act 1911 (perjury) is received in evidence in pursuance of a special measures direction, that proceeding shall be taken for the purposes of that section to be part of the judicial proceeding in which the statement is so received in evidence.

(7) Where in any proceeding which is not a judicial proceeding for the purposes of that Act—

(a) a person wilfully makes a false statement otherwise than on oath which is subsequently received in evidence in pursuance of a special measures direction, and

(b) the statement is made in such circumstances that had it been given on oath in any such judicial proceeding that person would have been guilty of perjury,

he shall be guilty of an offence and liable to any punishment which might be imposed on conviction of an offence under section 57(2) (giving of false unsworn evidence in criminal proceedings).

(8) In this section "statement" includes any representation of fact, whether made in words or otherwise.
[Youth Justice and Criminal Evidence Act 1999, s 31.]

2–1532   32. Warning to jury. Where on a trial on indictment with a jury evidence has been given in accordance with a special measures direction, the judge must give the jury such warning (if any)

as the judge considers necessary to ensure that the fact that the direction was given in relation to the witness does not prejudice the accused.
[Youth Justice and Criminal Evidence Act 1999, s 32 as amended by the Criminal Justice Act 2003, Sch 36.]

2–1533   33. Interpretation etc of Chapter I.   (1) In this Chapter—

"eligible witness" means a witness eligible for assistance by virtue of section 16 or 17;

"live link" has the meaning given by section 24(8);

"quality", in relation to the evidence of a witness, shall be construed in accordance with section 16(5);

"special measures direction" means (in accordance with section 19(5)) a direction under section 19.

(2) In this Chapter references to the special measures available in relation to a witness shall be construed in accordance with section 18.

(3) In this Chapter references to a person being able to see or hear, or be seen or heard by, another person are to be read as not applying to the extent that either of them is unable to see or hear by reason of any impairment of eyesight or hearing.

(4) In the case of any proceedings in which there is more than one accused—

(a) any reference to the accused in sections 23 to 28 may be taken by a court, in connection with the giving of a special measures direction, as a reference to all or any of the accused, as the court may determine, and

(b) any such direction may be given on the basis of any such determination.

[Youth Justice and Criminal Evidence Act 1999, s 33.]

CHAPTER 1A
USE OF LIVE LINK FOR EVIDENCE OF CERTAIN ACCUSED PERSONS

2–1533A   33A. Live link directions.   (1) This section applies to any proceedings (whether in a magistrates' court or before the Crown Court) against a person for an offence.

(2) The court may, on the application of the accused, give a live link direction if it is satisfied—

(a) that the conditions in subsection (4) or, as the case may be, subsection (5) are met in relation to the accused, and

(b) that it is in the interests of justice for the accused to give evidence through a live link.

(3) A live link direction is a direction that any oral evidence to be given before the court by the accused is to be given through a live link.

(4) Where the accused is aged under 18 when the application is made, the conditions are that—

(a) his ability to participate effectively in the proceedings as a witness giving oral evidence in court is compromised by his level of intellectual ability or social functioning, and

(b) use of a live link would enable him to participate more effectively in the proceedings as a witness (whether by improving the quality of his evidence or otherwise).

(5) Where the accused has attained the age of 18 at that time, the conditions are that—

(a) he suffers from a mental disorder (within the meaning of the Mental Health Act 1983) or otherwise has a significant impairment of intelligence and social function,

(b) he is for that reason unable to participate effectively in the proceedings as a witness giving oral evidence in court, and

(c) use of a live link would enable him to participate more effectively in the proceedings as a witness (whether by improving the quality of his evidence or otherwise).

(6) While a live link direction has effect the accused may not give oral evidence before the court in the proceedings otherwise than through a live link.

(7) The court may discharge a live link direction at any time before or during any hearing to which it applies if it appears to the court to be in the interests of justice to do so (but this does not affect the power to give a further live link direction in relation to the accused).

The court may exercise this power of its own motion or on an application by a party.

(8) The court must state in open court its reasons for—

(a) giving or discharging a live link direction, or

(b) refusing an application for or for the discharge of a live link direction,

and, if it is a magistrates' court, it must cause those reasons to be entered in the register of its proceedings.

[Youth Justice and Criminal Evidence Act 1999, s 33A as inserted by the Police and Justice Act 2006, s 47.]

2–1533B   33B. Section 33A: meaning of "live link".   (1) In section 33A "live link" means an arrangement by which the accused, while absent from the place where the proceedings are being held, is able—

(a) to see and hear a person there, and

(b) to be seen and heard by the persons mentioned in subsection (2),

and for this purpose any impairment of eyesight or hearing is to be disregarded.

(2) The persons are—

(a) the judge or justices (or both) and the jury (if there is one),
(b) where there are two or more accused in the proceedings, each of the other accused,
(c) legal representatives acting in the proceedings, and
(d) any interpreter or other person appointed by the court to assist the accused.
[Youth Justice and Criminal Evidence Act 1999, s 33B as inserted by the Police and Justice Act 2006, s 47.]

2–1533C 33C. Saving. Nothing in this Chapter affects—

(a) any power of a court to make an order, give directions or give leave of any description in relation to any witness (including an accused), or
(b) the operation of any rule of law relating to evidence in criminal proceedings.
[Youth Justice and Criminal Evidence Act 1999, s 33C as inserted by the Police and Justice Act 2006, s 47.]

CHAPTER II
PROTECTION OF WITNESSES FROM CROSS-EXAMINATION BY ACCUSED IN PERSON
General prohibitions

2–1534 34. Complainants in proceedings for sexual offences. No person charged with a sexual offence may in any criminal proceedings cross-examine in person a witness who is the complainant, either—

(a) in connection with that offence, or
(b) in connection with any other offence (of whatever nature) with which that person is charged in the proceedings.
[Youth Justice and Criminal Evidence Act 1999, s 34.]

2–1535 35. Child complainants and other child witnesses. (1) No person charged with an offence to which this section applies may in any criminal proceedings cross-examine in person a protected witness, either—

(a) in connection with that offence, or
(b) in connection with any other offence (of whatever nature) with which that person is charged in the proceedings.

(2) For the purposes of subsection (1) a "protected witness" is a witness who—

(a) either is the complainant or is alleged to have been a witness to the commission of the offence to which this section applies, and
(b) either is a child or falls to be cross-examined after giving evidence in chief (whether wholly or in part)—

    (i) by means of a video recording made (for the purposes of section 27) at a time when the witness was a child, or
    (ii) in any other way at any such time.

(3) The offences to which this section applies are—

(a) any offence under—

    (i) *revoked*
    (ii) *revoked*
    (iii) *revoked*
    (iv) *revoked*
    (v) the Protection of Children Act 1978; or
    (vi) Part 1 of the Sexual Offences Act 2003

(b) kidnapping, false imprisonment or an offence under section 1 or 2 of the Child Abduction Act 1984;
(c) any offence under section 1 of the Children and Young Persons Act 1933;
(d) any offence (not within any of the preceding paragraphs) which involves an assault on, or injury or a threat of injury to, any person.

(4) In this section "child" means—

(a) where the offence falls within subsection (3)(a), a person under the age of 17; or
(b) where the offence falls within subsection (3)(b), (c) or (d), a person under the age of 14.

(5) For the purposes of this section "witness" includes a witness who is charged with an offence in the proceedings.
[Youth Justice and Criminal Evidence Act 1999, s 35 as amended by the Sexual Offences Act 2003, Schs 6 and 7.]

Prohibition imposed by court

2–1536 36. Direction prohibiting accused from cross-examining particular witness.
(1) This section applies where, in a case where neither of sections 34 and 35 operates to prevent an accused in any criminal proceedings from cross-examining a witness in person—

(a) the prosecutor makes an application for the court to give a direction under this section in relation to the witness, or
(b) the court of its own motion raises the issue whether such a direction should be given.

(2) If it appears to the court—

(a) that the quality of evidence given by the witness on cross-examination—

    (i) is likely to be diminished if the cross-examination (or further cross-examination) is conducted by the accused in person, and

    (ii) would be likely to be improved if a direction were given under this section, and

(b) that it would not be contrary to the interests of justice to give such a direction,

the court may give a direction prohibiting the accused from cross-examining (or further cross-examining) the witness in person.

(3) In determining whether subsection (2)(a) applies in the case of a witness the court must have regard, in particular, to—

(a) any views expressed by the witness as to whether or not the witness is content to be cross-examined by the accused in person;

(b) the nature of the questions likely to be asked, having regard to the issues in the proceedings and the defence case advanced so far (if any);

(c) any behaviour on the part of the accused at any stage of the proceedings, both generally and in relation to the witness;

(d) any relationship (of whatever nature) between the witness and the accused;

(e) whether any person (other than the accused) is or has at any time been charged in the proceedings with a sexual offence or an offence to which section 35 applies, and (if so) whether section 34 or 35 operates or would have operated to prevent that person from cross-examining the witness in person;

(f) any direction under section 19 which the court has given, or proposes to give, in relation to the witness.

(4) For the purposes of this section—

(a) "witness", in relation to an accused, does not include any other person who is charged with an offence in the proceedings; and

(b) any reference to the quality of a witness's evidence shall be construed in accordance with section 16(5).

[Youth Justice and Criminal Evidence Act 1999, s 36.]

2–1537 **37. Further provisions about directions under section 36.** (1) Subject to subsection (2), a direction has binding effect from the time it is made until the witness to whom it applies is discharged.

In this section "direction" means a direction under section 36.

(2) The court may discharge a direction if it appears to the court to be in the interests of justice to do so, and may do so either—

(a) on an application made by a party to the proceedings, if there has been a material change of circumstances since the relevant time, or

(b) of its own motion.

(3) In subsection (2) "the relevant time" means—

(a) the time when the direction was given, or

(b) if a previous application has been made under that subsection, the time when the application (or last application) was made.

(4) The court must state in open court its reasons for—

(a) giving, or

(b) refusing an application for, or for the discharge of, or

(c) discharging,

a direction and, if it is a magistrates' court, must cause them to be entered in the register of its proceedings.

(5) Criminal Procedure Rules[1] may make provision—

(a) for uncontested applications to be determined by the court without a hearing;

(b) for preventing the renewal of an unsuccessful application for a direction except where there has been a material change of circumstances;

(c) for expert evidence to be given in connection with an application for, or for discharging, a direction;

(d) for the manner in which confidential or sensitive information is to be treated in connection with such an application and in particular as to its being disclosed to, or withheld from, a party to the proceedings.

[Youth Justice and Criminal Evidence Act 1999, s 37 as amended by the Courts Act 2003, Sch 8.]

---

1. See the Criminal Procedure Rules 2005, Part 29, in PART I: MAGISTRATES' COURTS, PROCEDURE, *ante*.

Cross-examination on behalf of accused

2–1538 **38. Defence representation for purposes of cross-examination.** (1) This section applies where an accused is prevented from cross-examining a witness in person by virtue of section 34, 35 or 36.

(2) Where it appears to the court that this section applies, it must—

(a) invite the accused to arrange for a legal representative to act for him for the purpose of cross-examining the witness; and

(b) require the accused to notify the court, by the end of such period as it may specify, whether a legal representative is to act for him for that purpose.

(3) If by the end of the period mentioned in subsection (2)(b) either—

(a) the accused has notified the court that no legal representative is to act for him for the purpose of cross-examining the witness, or

(b) no notification has been received by the court and it appears to the court that no legal representative is to so act,

the court must consider whether it is necessary in the interests of justice for the witness to be cross-examined by a legal representative appointed to represent the interests of the accused.

(4) If the court decides that it is necessary in the interests of justice for the witness to be so cross-examined, the court must appoint a qualified legal representative (chosen by the court) to cross-examine the witness in the interests of the accused.

(5) A person so appointed shall not be responsible to the accused.

(6) Criminal Procedure Rules[1] may make provision—

(a) as to the time when, and the manner in which, subsection (2) is to be complied with;

(b) in connection with the appointment of a legal representative under subsection (4), and in particular for securing that a person so appointed is provided with evidence or other material relating to the proceedings.

(7) Criminal Procedure Rules made in pursuance of subsection (6)(b) may make provision for the application, with such modifications as are specified in the rules, of any of the provisions of—

(a) Part I of the Criminal Procedure and Investigations Act 1996 (disclosure of material in connection with criminal proceedings), or

(b) the Sexual Offences (Protected Material) Act 1997.

(8) For the purposes of this section—

(a) any reference to cross-examination includes (in a case where a direction is given under section 36 after the accused has begun cross-examining the witness) a reference to further cross-examination; and

(b) "qualified legal representative" means a legal representative who has a right of audience (within the meaning of the Courts and Legal Services Act 1990) in relation to the proceedings before the court.

[Youth Justice and Criminal Evidence Act 1999, s 38 as amended by the Courts Act 2003, Sch 8.]

---

1. See the Criminal Procedure Rules 2005, Part 29, in PART I: MAGISTRATES' COURTS, PROCEDURE, ante.

2-1539 39. Warning to jury. (1) Where on a trial on indictment with a jury an accused is prevented from cross-examining a witness in person by virtue of section 34, 35 or 36, the judge must give the jury such warning (if any) as the judge considers necessary to ensure that the accused is not prejudiced—

(a) by any inferences that might be drawn from the fact that the accused has been prevented from cross-examining the witness in person;

(b) where the witness has been cross-examined by a legal representative appointed under section 38(4), by the fact that the cross-examination was carried out by such a legal representative and not by a person acting as the accused's own legal representative.

(2) Subsection (8)(a) of section 38 applies for the purposes of this section as it applies for the purposes of section 38.

[Youth Justice and Criminal Evidence Act 1999, s 39 as amended by the Criminal Justice Act 2003, Sch 36.]

2-1540 40. Funding of defence representation. (1) In section 19(3) of the Prosecution of Offences Act 1985 (regulations authorising payments out of central funds), after paragraph (d) there shall be inserted—

"(e) to cover the proper fee or costs of a legal representative appointed under section 38(4) of the Youth Justice and Criminal Evidence Act 1999 (defence representation for purposes of cross-examination) and any expenses properly incurred in providing such a person with evidence or other material in connection with his appointment."

(2) In section 21(3) of the Legal Aid Act 1988 (cases where, subject to means, representation must be granted), after paragraph (d) there shall be inserted—

"(e) where a person is prevented from conducting any cross-examination as mentioned in section 38(1) of the Youth Justice and Criminal Evidence Act 1999 (defence representation for purposes of cross-examination), for conducting the cross-examination on behalf of that person (otherwise than as a person appointed under section 38(4) of that Act)."

[Youth Justice and Criminal Evidence Act 1999, s 40.]

CHAPTER III
PROTECTION OF COMPLAINANTS IN PROCEEDINGS FOR SEXUAL OFFENCES

2–1541   41. Restriction on evidence or questions about complainant's sexual history. (1) If at a trial a person is charged with a sexual offence, then, except with the leave of the court—

    (*a*) no evidence may be adduced, and
    (*b*) no question may be asked in cross-examination,

by or on behalf of any accused at the trial, about any sexual behaviour[1] of the complainant.

(2) The court may[2] give leave in relation to any evidence or question only on an application[3] made by or on behalf of an accused, and may not give such leave unless it is satisfied—

    (*a*) that subsection (3) or (5) applies, and
    (*b*) that a refusal of leave might have the result of rendering unsafe a conclusion of the jury or (as the case may be) the court on any relevant issue in the case.

(3) This subsection applies if the evidence or question relates to a relevant issue in the case and either—

    (*a*) that issue is not an issue of consent; or
    (*b*) it is an issue of consent and the sexual behaviour of the complainant to which the evidence or question relates is alleged to have taken place at or about the same time as the event which is the subject matter of the charge against the accused; or
    (*c*) it is an issue of consent and the sexual behaviour of the complainant to which the evidence or question relates is alleged to have been, in any respect, so similar—

        (i) to any sexual behaviour of the complainant which (according to evidence adduced or to be adduced by or on behalf of the accused) took place as part of the event which is the subject matter of the charge against the accused, or
        (ii) to any other sexual behaviour of the complainant which (according to such evidence) took place at or about the same time as that event,

    that the similarity cannot reasonably be explained as a coincidence[4].

(4) For the purposes of subsection (3) no evidence or question shall be regarded as relating to a relevant issue in the case if it appears to the court to be reasonable to assume that the purpose (or main purpose) for which it would be adduced or asked is to establish or elicit material for impugning the credibility of the complainant as a witness.

(5) This subsection applies if the evidence or question—

    (*a*) relates to any evidence adduced by the prosecution about any sexual behaviour of the complainant; and
    (*b*) in the opinion of the court, would go no further than is necessary to enable the evidence adduced by the prosecution to be rebutted or explained by or on behalf of the accused.

(6) For the purposes of subsections (3) and (5) the evidence or question must relate to a specific instance (or specific instances) of alleged sexual behaviour on the part of the complainant (and accordingly nothing in those subsections is capable of applying in relation to the evidence or question to the extent that it does not so relate).

(7) Where this section applies in relation to a trial by virtue of the fact that one or more of a number of persons charged in the proceedings is or are charged with a sexual offence—

    (*a*) it shall cease to apply in relation to the trial if the prosecutor decides not to proceed with the case against that person or those persons in respect of that charge; but
    (*b*) it shall not cease to do so in the event of that person or those persons pleading guilty to, or being convicted of, that charge.

(8) Nothing in this section authorises any evidence to be adduced or any question to be asked which cannot be adduced or asked apart from this section.
[Youth Justice and Criminal Evidence Act 1999, s 41.]

---

1. Questions or evidence about false statements in the past by a complainant about sexual assaults, or such questions or evidence about a failure to complain about the alleged assault which is the subject matter of the charge, are not questions or evidence about any "sexual behaviour" of the complainant and they are not, therefore, caught by s 41; however, questions about alleged sexual abuse of the complainant by other parties, where there is no material to justify a claim that the allegations were false, do relate to the complainant's sexual behaviour and, therefore, fall within the prohibition of s 41: *R v T* [2001] EWCA Crim 1877, [2002] 1 All ER 683, [2002] 1 WLR 632, [2002] Crim LR 73; *R v C* [2003] EWCA 29, [2003] All ER (D) 247 (Jan), (2003) 167 JPN 83; *R v H* [2003] EWCA Crim 2367 [2003] All ER (D) 332 (Jul); *R v Garaxo* [2005] EWCA Crim 1170, [2005] Crim LR 883.

Once the criteria (see below) for admissibility are established all the evidence in relation to the issue can be adduced; if the evidence is relevant and admissible the court has to discretion to exclude it or limit it: *R v F* [2005] EWCA Crim 493, [2005] 2 Cr App R 13, [2005] Crim LR 564.

It is professional improper for the defendant's representative to put such a question without a proper evidential basis for asserting that such a previous statement was made and was untrue: *R v T* (supra).

It is irrelevant that the complainant is too young to have an understanding of sexual matters; the issue is what is in normal English a sexual experience and that does not depend on the perception of the complainant: *R v E* [2004] EWCA Crim 1313, [2005] Crim LR 227. Similarly, the prohibition in this section applies where the defence wish to rely on statements by the complainant as evidence on which the defendant's belief in consent was based even where the defence are not asserting either the truth or falsity of the statements: *R v W* [2004] EWCA Crim 3103, [2005] Crim LR 965. Article 6 "equality of arms" considerations did not apply where the prosecution adduced evidence that the complainant had previously had sexual intercourse on one occasion to bolster her evidence that she had deliberately lied when she told her assailant that she was a virgin (*R v Norova* [2006] EWCA Crim 1884, [2007] Crim LR 165).

2. Section 41 calls for the making of a judgement rather than the exercise of a discretion: "It is sometimes loosely suggested that the operation of s 41 involves the exercise of judicial discretion. In reality, the trial judge is making a judgment whether to admit, or refuse to admit evidence which is relevant, or asserted by the defence to be relevant. If the evidence is not relevant, on elementary principles, it is not admissible. If it is relevant, then subject to s 41(4) and assuming that the criteria for admitting the evidence are established, in our judgment the court lacks any discretion to refuse to admit it, or to limit relevant evidence which is properly admissible. In short, once the criteria for admissibility are established, all the evidence relevant to the issues may be adduced. As part of his control over the case, the judge is required to ensure that a complainant is not unnecessarily humiliated or cross-examined with inappropriate aggression, or treated otherwise than with proper courtesy. All that is elementary, but his obligation to see that the complainant's interests are protected throughout the trial process does not permit him, by way of a general discretion, to prevent the proper deployment of evidence which falls within the ambit permitted by the statute merely because, as here, it comes in a stark, uncompromising form": *R v F* [2005] EWCA Crim 493, [2005] 1 WLR 2848, per Judge LJ at para 29.

3. For procedure, see the Criminal Procedure Rules 2005, Part 36, in PART I: MAGISTRATES' COURTS, PROCEDURE, ante..

4. Section 41(3)(*b*) and (*c*) apply where the issue is consent, not belief in consent. As to whether this contravenes the defendant's right to a fair trial under art 6, it was held in *R v A (No 2)* [2001] UKHL 25, [2001] 3 All ER, 165 JP 609 that these provisions are very restrictive, but the latter (ie s 41(3)(*c*) could be read down under s 3 of the Human Rights Act 1998 "to subordinate the niceties of the language, in particular the touchstone of coincidence, to broader considerations of relevance judged by logical and commonsense criteria of time and circumstances ... under s 41(3)(*c*) of the 1999 Act, construed where necessary by applying the interpretative obligation under s 3 of the 1998 Act, and due regard always being paid to the importance of seeking to protect the complainant from indignity and humiliating questions, the test of admissibility is whether the evidence (and questions relating to it) is nevertheless so relevant to the issue of consent that to exclude it would endanger the fairness of the trial under art 6 of the Convention. If this test is satisfied the evidence should not be excluded" (per Lord Steyn at paras 45–6).

2-1542   42. Interpretation and application of section 41.   (1) In section 41—

(*a*) "relevant issue in the case" means any issue falling to be proved by the prosecution or defence in the trial of the accused;

(*b*) "issue of consent" means any issue whether the complainant in fact consented to the conduct constituting the offence with which the accused is charged (and accordingly does not include any issue as to the belief of the accused that the complainant so consented);

(*c*) "sexual behaviour" means any sexual behaviour or other sexual experience, whether or not involving any accused or other person, but excluding (except in section 41(3)(*c*)(i) and (5)(*a*)) anything alleged to have taken place as part of the event which is the subject matter of the charge against the accused; and

(*d*) subject to any order made under subsection (2), "sexual offence" shall be construed in accordance with section 62.

(2) The Secretary of State may by order make such provision as he considers appropriate for adding or removing, for the purposes of section 41, any offence to or from the offences which are sexual offences for the purposes of this Act by virtue of section 62.

(3) Section 41 applies in relation to the following proceedings as it applies to a trial, namely—

(*a*) proceedings before a magistrates' court inquiring into an offence as examining justices,

(*b*) the hearing of an application under paragraph 5(1) of Schedule 6 to the Criminal Justice Act 1991 (application to dismiss charge following notice of transfer of case to Crown Court),

(*c*) the hearing of an application under paragraph 2(1) of Schedule 3 to the Crime and Disorder Act 1998 (application to dismiss charge by person sent for trial under section 51 of that Act),

(*d*) any hearing held, between conviction and sentencing, for the purpose of determining matters relevant to the court's decision as to how the accused is to be dealt with, and

(*e*) the hearing of an appeal,

and references (in section 41 or this section) to a person charged with an offence accordingly include a person convicted of an offence.

[Youth Justice and Criminal Evidence Act 1999, s 42.]

2-1543   43. Procedure on applications under section 41.   (1) An application for leave shall be heard in private and in the absence of the complainant.

In this section "leave" means leave under section 41.

(2) Where such an application has been determined, the court must state in open court (but in the absence of the jury, if there is one)—

(*a*) its reasons for giving, or refusing, leave, and

(*b*) if it gives leave, the extent to which evidence may be adduced or questions asked in pursuance of the leave,

and, if it is a magistrates' court, must cause those matters to be entered in the register of its proceedings.

(3) Criminal Procedure Rules may make provision—

(*a*) requiring applications for leave to specify, in relation to each item of evidence or question to which they relate, particulars of the grounds on which it is asserted that leave should be given by virtue of subsection (3) or (5) of section 41;

(*b*) enabling the court to request a party to the proceedings to provide the court with information which it considers would assist it in determining an application for leave;

(c) for the manner in which confidential or sensitive information is to be treated in connection with such an application, and in particular as to its being disclosed to, or withheld from, parties to the proceedings.

[Youth Justice and Criminal Evidence Act 1999, s 43 as amended by the Courts Act 2003, Sch 8.]

CHAPTER IV
REPORTING RESTRICTIONS
Reports relating to persons under 18

2–1544 **44. Restrictions on reporting alleged offences involving persons under 18.** (1) This section applies (subject to subsection (3)) where a criminal investigation has begun in respect of—

(a) an alleged offence against the law of—

    (i) England and Wales, or
    (ii) Northern Ireland; or

(b) an alleged civil offence (other than an offence falling within paragraph (a)) committed (whether or not in the United Kingdom) by a person subject to service law.

(2) No matter relating to any person involved in the offence shall while he is under the age of 18 be included in any publication if it is likely to lead members of the public to identify him as a person involved in the offence.

(3) The restrictions imposed by subsection (2) cease to apply once there are proceedings in a court (whether a court in England and Wales, a service court or a court in Northern Ireland) in respect of the offence.

(4) For the purposes of subsection (2) any reference to a person involved in the offence is to—

(a) a person by whom the offence is alleged to have been committed; or
(b) if this paragraph applies to the publication in question by virtue of subsection (5)—

    (i) a person against or in respect of whom the offence is alleged to have been committed, or
    (ii) a person who is alleged to have been a witness to the commission of the offence;

except that paragraph (b)(i) does not include a person in relation to whom section 1 of the Sexual Offences (Amendment) Act 1992 (anonymity of victims of certain sexual offences) applies in connection with the offence.

(5) Subsection (4)(b) applies to a publication if—

(a) where it is a relevant programme, it is transmitted, or
(b) in the case of any other publication, it is published,

on or after such date as may be specified in an order made by the Secretary of State.

(6) The matters relating to a person in relation to which the restrictions imposed by subsection (2) apply (if their inclusion in any publication is likely to have the result mentioned in that subsection) include in particular—

(a) his name,
(b) his address,
(c) the identity of any school or other educational establishment attended by him,
(d) the identity of any place of work, and
(e) any still or moving picture of him.

(7) Any appropriate criminal court may by order dispense, to any extent specified in the order, with the restrictions imposed by subsection (2) in relation to a person if it is satisfied that it is necessary in the interests of justice to do so.

(8) However, when deciding whether to make such an order dispensing (to any extent) with the restrictions imposed by subsection (2) in relation to a person, the court shall have regard to the welfare of that person.

(9) In subsection (7) "appropriate criminal court" means—

(a) in a case where this section applies by virtue of subsection (1)(a)(i) or (ii), any court in England and Wales or (as the case may be) in Northern Ireland which has any jurisdiction in, or in relation to, any criminal proceedings (but not a service court unless the offence is alleged to have been committed by a person subject to service law);
(b) in a case where this section applies by virtue of subsection (1)(b), any court falling within paragraph (a) or a service court.

(10) The power under subsection (7) of a magistrates' court in England and Wales may be exercised by a single justice.

(11) In the case of a decision of a magistrates' court in England and Wales, or a court of summary jurisdiction in Northern Ireland, to make or refuse to make an order under subsection (7), the following persons, namely—

(a) any person who was a party to the proceedings on the application for the order, and
(b) with the leave of the Crown Court*, any other person,

may, in accordance with Criminal Procedure Rules in Engalnd and Wals, or rules of court in Northern Ireland, appeal to the Crown Court against that decision or appear or be represented at the hearing of such an appeal.

(12) On such an appeal the Crown Court*—

(a) may make such order as is necessary to give effect to its determination of the appeal; and

(b) may also make such incidental or consequential orders as appear to it to be just.

(13) In this section—

(a) "civil offence" means an act or omission which, if committed in England and Wales, would be an offence against the law of England and Wales;

(b) any reference to a criminal investigation, in relation to an alleged offence, is to an investigation conducted by police officers, or other persons charged with the duty of investigating offences, with a view to it being ascertained whether a person should be charged with the offence;

(c) any reference to a person subject to service law is to—

(i) a person subject to military law, air-force law or the Naval Discipline Act 1957, or

(ii) any other person to whom provisions of Part II of the Army Act 1955, Part II of the Air Force Act 1955 or Parts I and II of the Naval Discipline Act 1957 apply (whether with or without any modifications).

[Youth Justice and Criminal Evidence Act 1999, s 44 as amended by the Courts Act 2003, Sch 8.]

---

*Amended in relation to Northern Ireland by SI 2003/1247 from a date to be appointed.

2–1545   45. Power to restrict reporting of criminal proceedings involving persons under 18.

(1) This section applies (subject to subsection (2)) in relation to—

(a) any criminal proceedings in any court (other than a service court) in England and Wales or Northern Ireland; and

(b) any proceedings (whether in the United Kingdom or elsewhere) in any service court.

(2) This section does not apply in relation to any proceedings to which section 49 of the Children and Young Persons Act 1933 applies.

(3) The court may direct that no matter relating to any person concerned in the proceedings shall while he is under the age of 18 be included in any publication if it is likely to lead members of the public to identify him as a person concerned in the proceedings.

(4) The court or an appellate court may by direction ("an excepting direction") dispense, to any extent specified in the excepting direction, with the restrictions imposed by a direction under subsection (3) if it is satisfied that it is necessary in the interests of justice to do so.

(5) The court or an appellate court may also by direction ("an excepting direction") dispense, to any extent specified in the excepting direction, with the restrictions imposed by a direction under subsection (3) if it is satisfied—

(a) that their effect is to impose a substantial and unreasonable restriction on the reporting of the proceedings, and

(b) that it is in the public interest to remove or relax that restriction;

but no excepting direction shall be given under this subsection by reason only of the fact that the proceedings have been determined in any way or have been abandoned.

(6) When deciding whether to make—

(a) a direction under subsection (3) in relation to a person, or

(b) an excepting direction under subsection (4) or (5) by virtue of which the restrictions imposed by a direction under subsection (3) would be dispensed with (to any extent) in relation to a person,

the court or (as the case may be) the appellate court shall have regard to the welfare of that person.

(7) For the purposes of subsection (3) any reference to a person concerned in the proceedings is to a person—

(a) against or in respect of whom the proceedings are taken, or

(b) who is a witness in the proceedings.

(8) The matters relating to a person in relation to which the restrictions imposed by a direction under subsection (3) apply (if their inclusion in any publication is likely to have the result mentioned in that subsection) include in particular—

(a) his name,

(b) his address,

(c) the identity of any school or other educational establishment attended by him,

(d) the identity of any place of work, and

(e) any still or moving picture of him.

(9) A direction under subsection (3) may be revoked by the court or an appellate court.

(10) An excepting direction—

(a) may be given at the time the direction under subsection (3) is given or subsequently; and

(b) may be varied or revoked by the court or an appellate court.

(11) In this section "appellate court", in relation to any proceedings in a court, means a court dealing with an appeal (including an appeal by way of case stated) arising out of the proceedings or with any further appeal.

[Youth Justice and Criminal Evidence Act 1999, s 45.]

2–1546   **46. Power to restrict reports about certain adult witnesses in criminal proceedings.**

(1) This section applies where—

(a) in any criminal proceedings in any court (other than a service court) in England and Wales or Northern Ireland, or

(b) in any proceedings (whether in the United Kingdom or elsewhere) in any service court,

a party to the proceedings makes an application[1] for the court to give a reporting direction in relation to a witness in the proceedings (other than the accused) who has attained the age of 18.

In this section "reporting direction" has the meaning given by subsection (6).

(2) If the court determines—

(a) that the witness is eligible for protection, and

(b) that giving a reporting direction in relation to the witness is likely to improve—

(i) the quality of evidence given by the witness, or

(ii) the level of co-operation given by the witness to any party to the proceedings in connection with that party's preparation of its case,

the court may give a reporting direction in relation to the witness.

(3) For the purposes of this section a witness is eligible for protection if the court is satisfied—

(a) that the quality of evidence given by the witness, or

(b) the level of co-operation given by the witness to any party to the proceedings in connection with that party's preparation of its case,

is likely to be diminished by reason of fear or distress on the part of the witness in connection with being identified by members of the public as a witness in the proceedings.

(4) In determining whether a witness is eligible for protection the court must take into account, in particular—

(a) the nature and alleged circumstances of the offence to which the proceedings relate;

(b) the age of the witness;

(c) such of the following matters as appear to the court to be relevant, namely—

(i) the social and cultural background and ethnic origins of the witness,

(ii) the domestic and employment circumstances of the witness, and

(iii) any religious beliefs or political opinions of the witness;

(d) any behaviour towards the witness on the part of—

(i) the accused,

(ii) members of the family or associates of the accused, or

(iii) any other person who is likely to be an accused or a witness in the proceedings.

(5) In determining that question the court must in addition consider any views expressed by the witness.

(6) For the purposes of this section a reporting direction in relation to a witness is a direction that no matter relating to the witness shall during the witness's lifetime be included in any publication if it is likely to lead members of the public to identify him as being a witness in the proceedings.

(7) The matters relating to a witness in relation to which the restrictions imposed by a reporting direction apply (if their inclusion in any publication is likely to have the result mentioned in subsection (6)) include in particular—

(a) the witness's name,

(b) the witness's address,

(c) the identity of any educational establishment attended by the witness,

(d) the identity of any place of work, and

(e) any still or moving picture of the witness.

(8) In determining whether to give a reporting direction the court shall consider—

(a) whether it would be in the interests of justice to do so, and

(b) the public interest in avoiding the imposition of a substantial and unreasonable restriction on the reporting of the proceedings.

(9) The court or an appellate court may by direction ("an excepting direction") dispense, to any extent specified in the excepting direction, with the restrictions imposed by a reporting direction if—

(a) it is satisfied that it is necessary in the interests of justice to do so, or

(b) it is satisfied—

(i) that the effect of those restrictions is to impose a substantial and unreasonable restriction on the reporting of the proceedings, and

(ii) that it is in the public interest to remove or relax that restriction;

but no excepting direction shall be given under paragraph (b) by reason only of the fact that the proceedings have been determined in any way or have been abandoned.

(10) A reporting direction may be revoked by the court or an appellate court.

(11) An excepting direction—

(a) may be given at the time the reporting direction is given or subsequently; and

(b) may be varied or revoked by the court or an appellate court.

(12) In this section—

(a) "appellate court", in relation to any proceedings in a court, means a court dealing with an appeal (including an appeal by way of case stated) arising out of the proceedings or with any further appeal;

(b) references to the quality of a witness's evidence are to its quality in terms of completeness, coherence and accuracy (and for this purpose "coherence" refers to a witness's ability in giving evidence to give answers which address the questions put to the witness and can be understood both individually and collectively);

(c) references to the preparation of the case of a party to any proceedings include, where the party is the prosecution, the carrying out of investigations into any offence at any time charged in the proceedings.

[Youth Justice and Criminal Evidence Act 1999, s 46.]

---

1. For commentary on this provision, see para **2–182** and for the procedure for making applications under this section, see the Criminal Procedure Rules 2005, Part 16, in PART I: MAGISTRATES' COURTS, PROCEDURE, ante.

Reports relating to directions under Chapter I or II

2-1547 47. Restrictions on reporting directions under Chapter I or II. (1) Except as provided by this section, no publication shall include a report of a matter falling within subsection (2).

(2) The matters falling within this subsection are—

(a) a direction under section 19 or 36 or an order discharging, or (in the case of a direction under section 19) varying, such a direction;

(aa) a direction under Article 7 or 24 of the Criminal Evidence (Northern Ireland) Order 1999 or an order discharging, or (in the case of a direction under Article 7) varying, such a direction;

(b) proceedings—

(i) on an application for such a direction or order, or

(ii) where the court acts of its own motion to determine whether to give or make any such direction or order.

(3) The court dealing with a matter falling within subsection (2) may order that subsection (1) is not to apply, or is not to apply to a specified extent, to a report of that matter.

(4) Where—

(a) there is only one accused in the relevant proceedings, and

(b) he objects to the making of an order under subsection (3),

the court shall make the order if (and only if) satisfied after hearing the representations of the accused that it is in the interests of justice to do so; and if the order is made it shall not apply to the extent that a report deals with any such objections or representations.

(5) Where—

(a) there are two or more accused in the relevant proceedings, and

(b) one or more of them object to the making of an order under subsection (3),

the court shall make the order if (and only if) satisfied after hearing the representations of each of the accused that it is in the interests of justice to do so; and if the order is made it shall not apply to the extent that a report deals with any such objections or representations.

(6) Subsection (1) does not apply to the inclusion in a publication of a report of matters after the relevant proceedings are either—

(a) determined (by acquittal, conviction or otherwise), or

(b) abandoned,

in relation to the accused or (if there is more than one) in relation to each of the accused.

(7) In this section "the relevant proceedings" means the proceedings to which any such direction as is mentioned in subsection (2) relates or would relate.

(8) Nothing in this section affects any prohibition or restriction by virtue of any other enactment on the inclusion of matter in a publication.

[Youth Justice and Criminal Evidence Act 1999, s 47.]

Other restrictions

2-1548 48. *Amendments relating to other reporting restrictions*

Offences

2-1549 49. Offences under Chapter IV. (1) This section applies if a publication—

(a) includes any matter in contravention of section 44(2) or of a direction under section 45(3) or 46(2); or

(b) includes a report in contravention of section 47.

(2) Where the publication is a newspaper or periodical, any proprietor, any editor and any publisher of the newspaper or periodical is guilty of an offence.

(3) Where the publication is a relevant programme—

(a) any body corporate or Scottish partnership engaged in providing the programme service in which the programme is included, and

(b) any person having functions in relation to the programme corresponding to those of an editor of a newspaper,

is guilty of an offence.

(4) In the case of any other publication, any person publishing it is guilty of an offence.

(5) A person guilty of an offence under this section is liable on summary conviction to a fine not exceeding level 5 on the standard scale.

(6) Proceedings for an offence under this section in respect of a publication falling within subsection (1)(b) may not be instituted—

(a) in England and Wales otherwise than by or with the consent of the Attorney General, or

(b) in Northern Ireland otherwise than by or with the consent of the Attorney General for Northern Ireland.

[Youth Justice and Criminal Evidence Act 1999, s 49.]

2–1550　50. Defences. (1) Where a person is charged with an offence under section 49 it shall be a defence to prove that at the time of the alleged offence he was not aware, and neither suspected nor had reason to suspect, that the publication included the matter or report in question.

(2) Where—

(a) a person is charged with an offence under section 49, and

(b) the offence relates to the inclusion of any matter in a publication in contravention of section 44(2),

it shall be a defence to prove that at the time of the alleged offence he was not aware, and neither suspected nor had reason to suspect, that the criminal investigation in question had begun.

(3) Where—

(a) paragraphs (a) and (b) of subsection (2) apply, and

(b) the contravention of section 44(2) does not relate to either—

(i) the person by whom the offence mentioned in that provision is alleged to have been committed, or

(ii) (where that offence is one in relation to which section 1 of the Sexual Offences (Amendment) Act 1992 applies) a person who is alleged to be a witness to the commission of the offence,

it shall be a defence to show to the satisfaction of the court that the inclusion in the publication of the matter in question was in the public interest on the ground that, to the extent that they operated to prevent that matter from being so included, the effect of the restrictions imposed by section 44(2) was to impose a substantial and unreasonable restriction on the reporting of matters connected with that offence.

(4) Subsection (5) applies where—

(a) paragraphs (a) and (b) of subsection (2) apply, and

(b) the contravention of section 44(2) relates to a person ("the protected person") who is neither—

(i) the person mentioned in subsection (3)(b)(i), nor

(ii) a person within subsection (3)(b)(ii) who is under the age of 16.

(5) In such a case it shall be a defence, subject to subsection (6), to prove that written consent to the inclusion of the matter in question in the publication had been given—

(a) by an appropriate person, if at the time when the consent was given the protected person was under the age of 16, or

(b) by the protected person, if that person was aged 16 or 17 at that time,

and (where the consent was given by an appropriate person) that written notice had been previously given to that person drawing to his attention the need to consider the welfare of the protected person when deciding whether to give consent.

(6) The defence provided by subsection (5) is not available if—

(a) (where the consent was given by an appropriate person) it is proved that written or other notice withdrawing the consent—

(i) was given to the appropriate recipient by any other appropriate person or by the protected person, and

(ii) was so given in sufficient time to enable the inclusion in the publication of the matter in question to be prevented; or

(b) subsection (8) applies.

(7) Where—

(a) a person is charged with an offence under section 49, and

(b) the offence relates to the inclusion of any matter in a publication in contravention of a direction under section 46(2), it shall be a defence, unless subsection (8) applies, to prove that the person in relation to whom the direction was given had given written consent to the inclusion of that matter in the publication.

(8) Written consent is not a defence if it is proved that any person interfered—

(a) with the peace or comfort of the person giving the consent, or
(b) (where the consent was given by an appropriate person) with the peace or comfort of either that person or the protected person,

with intent to obtain the consent.

(9) In this section—

"an appropriate person" means (subject to subsections (10) to (12))—

(a) in England and Wales or Northern Ireland, a person who is a parent or guardian of the protected person, or
(b) in Scotland, a person who has parental responsibilities (within the meaning of section 1(3) of the Children (Scotland) Act 1995) in relation to the protected person;

"guardian", in relation to the protected person, means any person who is not a parent of the protected person but who has parental responsibility for the protected person within the meaning of—

(a) (in England and Wales) the Children Act 1989, or
(b) (in Northern Ireland) the Children (Northern Ireland) Order 1995.

(10) Where the protected person is (within the meaning of the Children Act 1989) a child who is looked after by a local authority, "an appropriate person" means a person who is—

(a) a representative of that authority, or
(b) a parent or guardian of the protected person with whom the protected person is allowed to live.

(11) Where the protected person is (within the meaning of the Children (Northern Ireland) Order 1995) a child who is looked after by an authority, "an appropriate person" means a person who is—

(a) an officer of that authority, or
(b) a parent or guardian of the protected person with whom the protected person is allowed to live.

(12) Where the protected person is (within the meaning of section 17(6) of the Children (Scotland) Act 1995) a child who is looked after by a local authority, "an appropriate person" means a person who is—

(a) a representative of that authority, or
(b) a person who has parental responsibilities (within the meaning of section 1(3) of that Act) in relation to the protected person and with whom the protected person is allowed to live.

(13) However, no person by whom the offence mentioned in section 44(2) is alleged to have been committed is, by virtue of subsections (9) to (12), an appropriate person for the purposes of this section.

(14) In this section "the appropriate recipient", in relation to a notice under subsection (6)(a), means—

(a) the person to whom the notice giving consent was given,
(b) (if different) the person by whom the matter in question was published, or
(c) any other person exercising, on behalf of the person mentioned in paragraph (b), any responsibility in relation to the publication of that matter;

and for this purpose "person" includes a body of persons and a partnership.
[Youth Justice and Criminal Evidence Act 1999, s 50.]

2-1551   51. Offences committed by bodies corporate or Scottish partnerships. (1) If an offence under section 49 committed by a body corporate is proved—

(a) to have been committed with the consent or connivance of, or
(b) to be attributable to any neglect on the part of,

an officer, the officer as well as the body corporate is guilty of the offence and liable to be proceeded against and punished accordingly.

(2) In subsection (1) "officer" means a director, manager, secretary or other similar officer of the body, or a person purporting to act in any such capacity.

(3) If the affairs of a body corporate are managed by its members, "director" in subsection (2) means a member of that body.

(4) Where an offence under section 49 is committed by a Scottish partnership and is proved to have been committed with the consent or connivance of a partner, he as well as the partnership shall be guilty of the offence and shall be liable to be proceeded against and punished accordingly.
[Youth Justice and Criminal Evidence Act 1999, s 51.]

Supplementary

2-1552   52. Decisions as to public interest for purposes of Chapter IV. (1) Where for the purposes of any provision of this Chapter it falls to a court to determine whether anything is (or, as the case may be, was) in the public interest, the court must have regard, in particular, to the matters referred to in subsection (2) (so far as relevant).

(2) Those matters are—

(a) the interest in each of the following—

(i) the open reporting of crime,
(ii) the open reporting of matters relating to human health or safety, and
(iii) the prevention and exposure of miscarriages of justice;

(b) the welfare of any person in relation to whom the relevant restrictions imposed by or under this Chapter apply or would apply (or, as the case may be, applied); and

(c) any views expressed—

(i) by an appropriate person on behalf of a person within paragraph (b) who is under the age of 16 ("the protected person"), or
(ii) by a person within that paragraph who has attained that age.

(3) In subsection (2) "an appropriate person", in relation to the protected person, has the same meaning as it has for the purposes of section 50.
[Youth Justice and Criminal Evidence Act 1999, s 52.]

CHAPTER V
COMPETENCE OF WITNESSES AND CAPACITY TO BE SWORN
Competence of witnesses

2–1553 53. Competence of witnesses to give evidence. (1) At every stage in criminal proceedings all persons are (whatever their age) competent to give evidence.

(2) Subsection (1) has effect subject to subsections (3) and (4).

(3) A person is not competent to give evidence in criminal proceedings if it appears to the court that he is not a person who is able to—

(a) understand questions put to him as a witness, and
(b) give answers to them which can be understood[1].

(4) A person charged in criminal proceedings is not competent to give evidence in the proceedings for the prosecution (whether he is the only person, or is one of two or more persons, charged in the proceedings).

(5) In subsection (4) the reference to a person charged in criminal proceedings does not include a person who is not, or is no longer, liable to be convicted of any offence in the proceedings (whether as a result of pleading guilty or for any other reason).
[Youth Justice and Criminal Evidence Act 1999, s 53.]

---

1. It may not always require 100 per cent, or near, mutual understanding between questioner and questioned as a precondition of competence. The court should also make allowance for the fact that the witness's performance and command of the detail may vary according to the importance to him of the subject matter of the question, how recent it was and any strong feelings that it may have engendered. It is for the court to determine the question of competence almost as a matter of feel, taking into account the effect of the potential witness's performance as a whole, whether there is a common and comprehensible thread in his responses to the questions, however patchy (*R v Sed* [2004] EWCA Crim 1294, [2004] 1 WLR 3218, [2005] 1 Cr App R 4).

2–1554 54. Determining competence of witnesses. (1) Any question whether a witness in criminal proceedings is competent to give evidence in the proceedings, whether raised—

(a) by a party to the proceedings, or
(b) by the court of its own motion,

shall be determined by the court in accordance with this section.

(2) It is for the party calling the witness to satisfy the court that, on a balance of probabilities, the witness is competent to give evidence in the proceedings.

(3) In determining the question mentioned in subsection (1) the court shall treat the witness as having the benefit of any directions under section 19 which the court has given, or proposes to give, in relation to the witness.

(4) Any proceedings held for the determination of the question shall take place in the absence of the jury (if there is one).

(5) Expert evidence may be received on the question.

(6) Any questioning of the witness (where the court considers that necessary) shall be conducted by the court in the presence of the parties.
[Youth Justice and Criminal Evidence Act 1999, s 54.]

Giving of sworn or unsworn evidence

2–1555 55. Determining whether witness to be sworn. (1) Any question whether a witness in criminal proceedings may be sworn for the purpose of giving evidence on oath, whether raised—

(a) by a party to the proceedings, or
(b) by the court of its own motion,

shall be determined by the court in accordance with this section.

(2) The witness may not be sworn for that purpose unless—

(a) he has attained the age of 14, and

(b) he has a sufficient appreciation of the solemnity of the occasion and of the particular responsibility to tell the truth which is involved in taking an oath.

(3) The witness shall, if he is able to give intelligible testimony, be presumed to have a sufficient appreciation of those matters if no evidence tending to show the contrary is adduced (by any party).

(4) If any such evidence is adduced, it is for the party seeking to have the witness sworn to satisfy the court that, on a balance of probabilities, the witness has attained the age of 14 and has a sufficient appreciation of the matters mentioned in subsection (2)(b).

(5) Any proceedings held for the determination of the question mentioned in subsection (1) shall take place in the absence of the jury (if there is one).

(6) Expert evidence may be received on the question.

(7) Any questioning of the witness (where the court considers that necessary) shall be conducted by the court in the presence of the parties.

(8) For the purposes of this section a person is able to give intelligible testimony if he is able to—

(a) understand questions put to him as a witness, and

(b) give answers to them which can be understood.

[Youth Justice and Criminal Evidence Act 1999, s 55.]

2–1556   56. Reception of unsworn evidence. (1) Subsections (2) and (3) apply to a person (of any age) who—

(a) is competent to give evidence in criminal proceedings, but

(b) (by virtue of section 55(2)) is not permitted to be sworn for the purpose of giving evidence on oath in such proceedings.

(2) The evidence in criminal proceedings of a person to whom this subsection applies shall be given unsworn.

(3) A deposition of unsworn evidence given by a person to whom this subsection applies may be taken for the purposes of criminal proceedings as if that evidence had been given on oath.

(4) A court in criminal proceedings shall accordingly receive in evidence any evidence given unsworn in pursuance of subsection (2) or (3).

(5) Where a person ("the witness") who is competent to give evidence in criminal proceedings gives evidence in such proceedings unsworn, no conviction, verdict or finding in those proceedings shall be taken to be unsafe for the purposes of any of sections 2(1), 13(1) and 16(1) of the Criminal Appeal Act 1968 (grounds for allowing appeals) by reason only that it appears to the Court of Appeal that the witness was a person falling within section 55(2) (and should accordingly have given his evidence on oath).

[Youth Justice and Criminal Evidence Act 1999, s 56.]

2–1557   57. Penalty for giving false unsworn evidence. (1) This section applies where a person gives unsworn evidence in criminal proceedings in pursuance of section 56(2) or (3).

(2) If such a person wilfully gives false evidence in such circumstances that, had the evidence been given on oath, he would have been guilty of perjury, he shall be guilty of an offence and liable on summary conviction to—

(a) imprisonment for a term not exceeding 6 months, or

(b) a fine not exceeding £1,000,

or both.

(3) In relation to a person under the age of 14, subsection (2) shall have effect as if for the words following "on summary conviction" there were substituted "to a fine not exceeding £250".

[Youth Justice and Criminal Evidence Act 1999, s 57.]

CHAPTER VII

GENERAL

2–1557A

     61 Application of Part II to service courts   (1) The Secretary of State may by order[1] direct that any provision of—

(a) Chapters I to III and V, or

(b) sections 62, 63 and 65 so far as having effect for the purposes of any of those Chapters,

shall apply, subject to such modifications as he may specify, to any proceedings before a service court.

(2) Chapter IV (and sections 62, 63 and 65 so far as having effect for the purposes of that Chapter) shall have effect for the purposes of proceedings before a service court subject to any modifications which the Secretary of State may by order specify.

(3) The power to make an order under section 39 of the Criminal Justice and Public Order Act 1994 (power to apply sections 34 to 38 to the armed forces) in relation to any provision of sections 34 to 38 of that Act shall be exercisable in relation to any provision of those sections as amended by section 58 above.

[Youth Justice and Criminal Evidence Act 1999, s 61.]

1. The following Youth Justice and Criminal Evidence Act 1999 orders have been made: Application to Courts-Martial SI 2006/2886; Application to Courts-Martial Appeal Court SI 2006/2887; Application to Standing Civilian Courts SI 2006/2888.

2–1558   62. Meaning of "sexual offence" and other references to offences.   (1) In this Part "sexual offence" means any offence under Part 1 of the Sexual Offences Act 2003.

(2) In this Part any reference (including a reference having effect by virtue of this subsection) to an offence of any description ("the substantive offence") is to be taken to include a reference to an offence which consists of attempting or conspiring to commit, or of aiding, abetting, counselling, procuring or inciting the commission of, the substantive offence.

[Youth Justice and Criminal Evidence Act 1999, s 62 as amended by the Sexual Offences Act 2003, Sch 6.]

2–1559   63. General interpretation etc of Part II.   (1) In this Part (except where the context otherwise requires)—

"accused", in relation to any criminal proceedings, means any person charged with an offence to which the proceedings relate (whether or not he has been convicted);

"the complainant", in relation to any offence (or alleged offence), means a person against or in relation to whom the offence was (or is alleged to have been) committed;

"court" (except in Chapter IV or V or subsection (2)) means a magistrates' court, the Crown Court or the criminal division of the Court of Appeal;

"legal representative" means any authorised advocate or authorised litigator (as defined by section 119(1) of the Courts and Legal Services Act 1990);

"picture" includes a likeness however produced;

"the prosecutor" means any person acting as prosecutor, whether an individual or body;

"publication" includes any speech, writing, relevant programme or other communication in whatever form, which is addressed to the public at large or any section of the public (and for this purpose every relevant programme shall be taken to be so addressed), but does not include an indictment or other document prepared for use in particular legal proceedings;

"relevant programme" means a programme included in a programme service, within the meaning of the Broadcasting Act 1990;

"service court" means—

(a) a court-martial constituted under the Army Act 1955, the Air Force Act 1955 or the Naval Discipline Act 1957,

(b) the Courts-Martial Appeal Court, or

(c) a Standing Civilian Court;

"video recording" means any recording, on any medium, from which a moving image may by any means be produced, and includes the accompanying sound-track;

"witness", in relation to any criminal proceedings, means any person called, or proposed to be called, to give evidence in the proceedings.

(2) Nothing in this Part shall affect any power of a court to exclude evidence at its discretion (whether by preventing questions being put or otherwise) which is exercisable apart from this Part.

[Youth Justice and Criminal Evidence Act 1999, s 63, as amended by the Armed Forces Act 2001, Sch 7.]

PART III[1]
FINAL PROVISIONS

2–1560   68. Short title, commencement and extent.   (1) This Act may be cited as the Youth Justice and Criminal Evidence Act 1999.

(2) *Scotland.*

(3) Subject to subsection (4), this Act shall not come into force until such day as the Secretary of State may by order appoint; and different days may be appointed for different purposes or different areas.

(4) The following provisions come into force on the day on which this Act is passed—

(a) section 6(4);

(b) the provisions of Chapters I to IV of Part II for the purpose only of the exercise of any power to make rules of court;

(c) section 40(1);

(d) sections 58(5) and 61(2) for the purpose only of the exercise of any power to make an order;

(e) section 61(1) and (3), sections 62 to 66 and this section.

(5)–(10) *Extent.*

[Youth Justice and Criminal Evidence Act 1999, s 68.]

1. Part III contains ss 64–68 and Schs 4–7.

Criminal Justice Act 2003
(2003 c 44)

PART 111
EVIDENCE
CHAPTER 1[2]
EVIDENCE OF BAD CHARACTER
Introductory

2–1561   98. Bad character.   References in this Chapter to evidence of a person's "bad character" are to evidence of, or of a disposition towards, misconduct on his part, other than evidence which—

   (*a*)   has to do with the alleged facts of the offence with which the defendant is charged, or

   (*b*)   is evidence of misconduct in connection with the investigation or prosecution of that offence.

[Criminal Justice Act 2003, s 98.]

1. Part 11 contains ss 98–141. Sections 139–141 came into force on 5 April 2004: see the Criminal Justice Act (Commencement No 3 and Transitional Provisions) Order 2004, SI 2004/929. Sections 98–110 and 112 came into force on 15 December 2004: see the Criminal Justice Act 2003 (Commencement No 6 and Transitional Provisions) Order 2004, SI 2004/3033. For narrative on these provisions see paras **2–249A** to **I** and **K–M** (bad character of defendants), ante.

2. Chapter 1 contains ss 98–113.

2–1562   99. Abolition of common law rules.   (1) The common law rules governing the admissibility of evidence of bad character in criminal proceedings are abolished[1].

(2) Subsection (1) is subject to section 118(1) in so far as it preserves the rule under which in criminal proceedings a person's reputation is admissible for the purposes of proving his bad character.

[Criminal Justice Act 2003, s 99.]

1. This includes the rule in *Hollington v Hewthorne* [1943] 1 KB 587 in relation to foreign convictions (having been previously abolished in relation to domestic convictions by the Police and Criminal Evidence Act 1984, s 73). Such convictions may be proved under the Evidence Act 1851, in this PART, ante: *R v Kordasinski* [2006] EWCA Crim 2894, (2006) Times 16 November.

Persons other than defendants

2–1563   100. Non-defendant's bad character.   (1) In criminal proceedings evidence of the bad character of a person other than the defendant is admissible if and only if—

   (*a*)   it is important explanatory evidence,

   (*b*)   it has substantial probative value in relation to a matter which—

     (i)   is a matter in issue in the proceedings, and

     (ii)   is of substantial importance in the context of the case as a whole, or

   (*c*)   all parties to the proceedings agree to the evidence being admissible.

(2) For the purposes of subsection (1)(a) evidence is important explanatory evidence if—

   (*a*)   without it, the court or jury would find it impossible or difficult properly to understand other evidence in the case, and

   (*b*)   its value for understanding the case as a whole is substantial.

(3) In assessing the probative value of evidence for the purposes of subsection (1)(b) the court must have regard to the following factors (and to any others it considers relevant)—

   (*a*)   the nature and number of the events, or other things, to which the evidence relates;

   (*b*)   when those events or things are alleged to have happened or existed;

   (*c*)   where—

     (i)   the evidence is evidence of a person's misconduct, and

     (ii)   it is suggested that the evidence has probative value by reason of similarity between that misconduct and other alleged misconduct,

the nature and extent of the similarities and the dissimilarities between each of the alleged instances of misconduct;

   (*d*)   where—

     (i)   the evidence is evidence of a person's misconduct,

     (ii)   it is suggested that that person is also responsible for the misconduct charged, and

     (iii)   the identity of the person responsible for the misconduct charged is disputed,

the extent to which the evidence shows or tends to show that the same person was responsible each time.

(4) Except where subsection (1)(c) applies, evidence of the bad character of a person other than the defendant must not be given without leave of the court[1].

[Criminal Justice Act 2003, s 100.]

1. For procedure, see the Criminal Procedure Rules 2005, Part 35, in PART I: MAGISTRATES' COURTS, PROCEDURE, ante at para **1–7455.**

Defendants

2–1564 **101. Defendant's bad character**[1]. (1) In criminal proceedings evidence of the defendant's bad character is admissible if, but only if—

(a) all parties to the proceedings agree to the evidence being admissible,

(b) the evidence is adduced by the defendant himself or is given in answer to a question asked by him in cross-examination and intended to elicit it,

(c) it is important explanatory evidence,

(d) it is relevant to an important matter in issue between the defendant and the prosecution,

(e) it has substantial probative value in relation to an important matter in issue between the defendant and a co-defendant,

(f) it is evidence to correct a false impression given by the defendant, or

(g) the defendant has made an attack on another person's character.

(2) Sections 102 to 106 contain provision supplementing subsection (1).

(3) The court must not admit evidence under subsection (1)(d) or (g) if, on an application by the defendant to exclude it, it appears to the court that the admission of the evidence would have such an adverse effect on the fairness of the proceedings that the court ought not to admit it.

(4) On an application to exclude evidence under subsection (3) the court must have regard, in particular, to the length of time between the matters to which that evidence relates and the matters which form the subject of the offence charged.

[Criminal Justice Act 2003, s 101.]

---

1. For procedure for where prosecutor or co-accused seeks to adduce evidence of defendant's bad character and where defendant opposes adducing of his bad character, see see the Criminal Procedure Rules 2005, Part 35, in PART I: MAGISTRATES' COURTS, PROCEDURE, ante at para 1–7455.

2–1565 **102. Important explanatory evidence.** For the purposes of section 101(1)(c) evidence is important explanatory evidence if—

(a) without it, the court or jury would find it impossible or difficult properly to understand other evidence in the case, and

(b) its value for understanding the case as a whole is substantial.

[Criminal Justice Act 2003, s 102.]

2–1566 **103. Matter in issue between the defendant and the prosecution.** (1) For the purposes of section 101(1)(d) the matters in issue between the defendant and the prosecution include—

(a) the question whether the defendant has a propensity to commit offences of the kind with which he is charged, except where his having such a propensity makes it no more likely that he is guilty of the offence;

(b) the question whether the defendant has a propensity to be untruthful, except where it is not suggested that the defendant's case is untruthful in any respect.

(2) Where subsection (1)(a) applies, a defendant's propensity to commit offences of the kind with which he is charged may (without prejudice to any other way of doing so) be established by evidence that he has been convicted of—

(a) an offence of the same description as the one with which he is charged, or

(b) an offence of the same category as the one with which he is charged.

(3) Subsection (2) does not apply in the case of a particular defendant if the court is satisfied, by reason of the length of time since the conviction or for any other reason, that it would be unjust for it to apply in his case.

(4) For the purposes of subsection (2)—

(a) two offences are of the same description as each other if the statement of the offence in a written charge or indictment would, in each case, be in the same terms;

(b) two offences are of the same category as each other if they belong to the same category of offences prescribed for the purposes of this section by an order[1] made by the Secretary of State.

(5) A category prescribed by an order under subsection (4)(b) must consist of offences of the same type.

(6) Only prosecution evidence is admissible under section 101(1)(d).

[Criminal Justice Act 2003, s 103.]

---

1. The Criminal Justice Act 2003 (Categories of Offences) Order 2004, SI 2004/3346 has been made in this PART, post.

2–1567 **104. Matter in issue between the defendant and a co-defendant.** (1) Evidence which is relevant to the question whether the defendant has a propensity to be untruthful is admissible on that basis under section 101(1)(e) only if the nature or conduct of his defence is such as to undermine the co-defendant's defence.

(2) Only evidence—

(*a*) which is to be (or has been) adduced by the co-defendant, or
(*b*) which a witness is to be invited to give (or has given) in cross-examination by the co-defendant,

is admissible under section 101(1)(*e*).
[Criminal Justice Act 2003, s 104.]

2–1568   105. Evidence to correct a false impression.   (1) For the purposes of section 101(1)(*f*)—

(*a*) the defendant gives a false impression if he is responsible for the making of an express or implied assertion which is apt to give the court or jury a false or misleading impression about the defendant;
(*b*) evidence to correct such an impression is evidence which has probative value in correcting it.

(2) A defendant is treated as being responsible for the making of an assertion if—

(*a*) the assertion is made by the defendant in the proceedings (whether or not in evidence given by him),
(*b*) the assertion was made by the defendant—

(i) on being questioned under caution, before charge, about the offence with which he is charged, or
(ii) on being charged with the offence or officially informed that he might be prosecuted for it,

and evidence of the assertion is given in the proceedings,

(*c*) the assertion is made by a witness called by the defendant,
(*d*) the assertion is made by any witness in cross-examination in response to a question asked by the defendant that is intended to elicit it, or is likely to do so, or
(*e*) the assertion was made by any person out of court, and the defendant adduces evidence of it in the proceedings.

(3) A defendant who would otherwise be treated as responsible for the making of an assertion shall not be so treated if, or to the extent that, he withdraws it or disassociates himself from it.
(4) Where it appears to the court that a defendant, by means of his conduct (other than the giving of evidence) in the proceedings, is seeking to give the court or jury an impression about himself that is false or misleading, the court may if it appears just to do so treat the defendant as being responsible for the making of an assertion which is apt to give that impression.
(5) In subsection (4) "conduct" includes appearance or dress.
(6) Evidence is admissible under section 101(1)(*f*) only if it goes no further than is necessary to correct the false impression.
(7) Only prosecution evidence is admissible under section 101(1)(*f*).
[Criminal Justice Act 2003, s 105.]

2–1569   106. Attack on another person's character.   (1) For the purposes of section 101(1)(*g*) a defendant makes an attack on another person's character if—

(*a*) he adduces evidence attacking the other person's character,
(*b*) he (or any legal representative appointed under section 38(4) of the Youth Justice and Criminal Evidence Act 1999 (c 23) to cross-examine a witness in his interests) asks questions in cross-examination that are intended to elicit such evidence, or are likely to do so, or
(*c*) evidence is given of an imputation about the other person made by the defendant—

(i) on being questioned under caution, before charge, about the offence with which he is charged, or
(ii) on being charged with the offence or officially informed that he might be prosecuted for it.

(2) In subsection (1) "evidence attacking the other person's character" means evidence to the effect that the other person—

(*a*) has committed an offence (whether a different offence from the one with which the defendant is charged or the same one), or
(*b*) has behaved, or is disposed to behave, in a reprehensible way;

and "imputation about the other person" means an assertion to that effect.
(3) Only prosecution evidence is admissible under section 101(1)(*g*).
[Criminal Justice Act 2003, s 106.]

2–1570   107. Stopping the case where evidence contaminated[1].   (1) If on a defendant's trial before a judge and jury for an offence—

(*a*) evidence of his bad character has been admitted under any of paragraphs (*c*) to (*g*) of section 101(1), and
(*b*) the court is satisfied at any time after the close of the case for the prosecution that—

(i) the evidence is contaminated, and
(ii) the contamination is such that, considering the importance of the evidence to the case against the defendant, his conviction of the offence would be unsafe,

the court must either direct the jury to acquit the defendant of the offence or, if it considers that there ought to be a retrial, discharge the jury.

(2) Where—

(a) a jury is directed under subsection (1) to acquit a defendant of an offence, and
(b) the circumstances are such that, apart from this subsection, the defendant could if acquitted of that offence be found guilty of another offence,

the defendant may not be found guilty of that other offence if the court is satisfied as mentioned in subsection (1)(b) in respect of it.

(3) If—

(a) a jury is required to determine under section 4A(2) of the Criminal Procedure (Insanity) Act 1964 (c 84) whether a person charged on an indictment with an offence did the act or made the omission charged,
(b) evidence of the person's bad character has been admitted under any of paragraphs (c) to (g) of section 101(1), and
(c) the court is satisfied at any time after the close of the case for the prosecution that—

   (i) the evidence is contaminated, and
   (ii) the contamination is such that, considering the importance of the evidence to the case against the person, a finding that he did the act or made the omission would be unsafe,

the court must either direct the jury to acquit the defendant of the offence or, if it considers that there ought to be a rehearing, discharge the jury.

(4) This section does not prejudice any other power a court may have to direct a jury to acquit a person of an offence or to discharge a jury.

(5) For the purposes of this section a person's evidence is contaminated where—

(a) as a result of an agreement or understanding between the person and one or more others, or
(b) as a result of the person being aware of anything alleged by one or more others whose evidence may be, or has been, given in the proceedings,

the evidence is false or misleading in any respect, or is different from what it would otherwise have been.

[Criminal Justice Act 2003, s 107.]

---

1. For guidance as to the operation of s 107 and the relevant principles, see *R v C* [2006] EWCA Crim 1079, [2006] 3 All ER 689, [2006] 2 Cr App R 28.

2–1571   108. Offences committed by defendant when a child. (1) Section 16(2) and (3) of the Children and Young Persons Act 1963 (c 37) (offences committed by person under 14 disregarded for purposes of evidence relating to previous convictions) shall cease to have effect.

(2) In proceedings for an offence committed or alleged to have been committed by the defendant when aged 21 or over, evidence of his conviction for an offence when under the age of 14 is not admissible unless—

(a) both of the offences are triable only on indictment, and
(b) the court is satisfied that the interests of justice require the evidence to be admissible.

(3) Subsection (2) applies in addition to section 101.

[Criminal Justice Act 2003, s 108.]

General

2–1572   109. Assumption of truth in assessment of relevance or probative value. (1) Subject to subsection (2), a reference in this Chapter to the relevance or probative value of evidence is a reference to its relevance or probative value on the assumption that it is true.

(2) In assessing the relevance or probative value of an item of evidence for any purpose of this Chapter, a court need not assume that the evidence is true if it appears, on the basis of any material before the court (including any evidence it decides to hear on the matter), that no court or jury could reasonably find it to be true.

[Criminal Justice Act 2003, s 109.]

2–1573   110. Court's duty to give reasons for rulings. (1) Where the court makes a relevant ruling—

(a) it must state in open court (but in the absence of the jury, if there is one) its reasons for the ruling;
(b) if it is a magistrates' court, it must cause the ruling and the reasons for it to be entered in the register of the court's proceedings.

(2) In this section "relevant ruling" means—

(a) a ruling on whether an item of evidence is evidence of a person's bad character;

(*b*)   a ruling on whether an item of such evidence is admissible under section 100 or 101 (including a ruling on an application under section 101(3));

.(*c*)   a ruling under section 107.

[Criminal Justice Act 2003, s 110.]

2–1574   111. Rules of court.   (1) Rules[1] of court may make such provision as appears to the appropriate authority to be necessary or expedient for the purposes of this Act; and the appropriate authority is the authority entitled to make the rules.

(2) The rules may, and, where the party in question is the prosecution, must, contain provision requiring a party who—

(*a*)   proposes to adduce evidence of a defendant's bad character, or

(*b*)   proposes to cross-examine a witness with a view to eliciting such evidence,

to serve on the defendant such notice, and such particulars of or relating to the evidence, as may be prescribed[1].

(3) The rules may provide that the court or the defendant may, in such circumstances as may be prescribed, dispense with a requirement imposed by virtue of subsection (2).

(4) In considering the exercise of its powers with respect to costs, the court may take into account any failure by a party to comply with a requirement imposed by virtue of subsection (2) and not dispensed with by virtue of subsection (3).

(5) The rules[1] may—

(*a*)   limit the application of any provision of the rules to prescribed circumstances;

(*b*)   subject any provision of the rules to prescribed exceptions;

(*c*)   make different provision for different cases or circumstances.

(6) Nothing in this section prejudices the generality of any enactment conferring power to make rules of court; and no particular provision of this section prejudices any general provision of it.

(7) In this section—

"prescribed" means prescribed by rules of court;

"rules of court" means—

(*a*)   Crown Court Rules;

(*b*)   Criminal Appeal Rules;

(*c*)   rules under section 144 of the Magistrates' Courts Act 1980 (c 43).

[Criminal Justice Act 2003, s 111.]

---

1. See the Criminal Procedure Rules 2005, Part 35, in PART I: MAGISTRATES' COURTS, PROCEDURE, ante which prescribes the procedure for the admission of evidence of bad character; and for prescribed forms of application, see Annex D to the *Practice Direction (crime: consolidated)*.

2–1575   112. Interpretation of Chapter 1.   (1) In this Chapter—

"bad character" is to be read in accordance with section 98;

"criminal proceedings" means criminal proceedings in relation to which the strict rules of evidence apply;

"defendant", in relation to criminal proceedings, means a person charged with an offence in those proceedings; and "co-defendant", in relation to a defendant, means a person charged with an offence in the same proceedings;

"important matter" means a matter of substantial importance in the context of the case as a whole;

"misconduct" means the commission of an offence or other reprehensible behaviour;

"offence" includes a service offence;

"probative value", and "relevant" (in relation to an item of evidence), are to be read in accordance with section 109;

"prosecution evidence" means evidence which is to be (or has been) adduced by the prosecution, or which a witness is to be invited to give (or has given) in cross-examination by the prosecution;

"service offence" means an offence under the Army Act 1955 (3 & 4 Eliz 2 c 18), the Air Force Act 1955 (3 & 4 Eliz 2 c 19) or the Naval Discipline Act 1957 (c 53);

"written charge" has the same meaning as in section 29 and also includes an information.

(2) Where a defendant is charged with two or more offences in the same criminal proceedings, this Chapter (except section 101(3)) has effect as if each offence were charged in separate proceedings; and references to the offence with which the defendant is charged are to be read accordingly.

(3) Nothing in this Chapter affects the exclusion of evidence—

(*a*)   under the rule in section 3 of the Criminal Procedure Act 1865 (c 18) against a party impeaching the credit of his own witness by general evidence of bad character,

(*b*)   under section 41 of the Youth Justice and Criminal Evidence Act 1999 (c 23) (restriction on evidence or questions about complainant's sexual history), or

(*c*)   on grounds other than the fact that it is evidence of a person's bad character.

[Criminal Justice Act 2003, s 112.]

2–1576   113. *Armed forces*

CHAPTER 2[1]
HEARSAY EVIDENCE

Hearsay: main provisions

2–1577 114. Admissibility of hearsay evidence. (1) In criminal proceedings a statement not made in oral evidence in the proceedings is admissible as evidence of any matter stated if, but only if—

(a) any provision of this Chapter or any other statutory provision makes it admissible,
(b) any rule of law preserved by section 118 makes it admissible,
(c) all parties to the proceedings agree to it being admissible, or
(d) the court is satisfied that it is in the interests of justice for it to be admissible.

(2) In deciding whether a statement not made in oral evidence should be admitted under subsection (1)(d), the court must have regard to the following factors (and to any others it considers relevant)—

(a) how much probative value the statement has (assuming it to be true) in relation to a matter in issue in the proceedings, or how valuable it is for the understanding of other evidence in the case;
(b) what other evidence has been, or can be, given on the matter or evidence mentioned in paragraph (a);
(c) how important the matter or evidence mentioned in paragraph (a) is in the context of the case as a whole;
(d) the circumstances in which the statement was made;
(e) how reliable the maker of the statement appears to be;
(f) how reliable the evidence of the making of the statement appears to be;
(g) whether oral evidence of the matter stated can be given and, if not, why it cannot;
(h) the amount of difficulty involved in challenging the statement;
(i) the extent to which that difficulty would be likely to prejudice the party facing it.

(3) Nothing in this Chapter affects the exclusion of evidence of a statement on grounds other than the fact that it is a statement not made in oral evidence in the proceedings.
[Criminal Justice Act 2003, s 114.]

---

1. Chapter 2 contains ss 114–136. For procedure, see the Criminal Procedure Rules 2005, Part 34, in PART I: MAGISTRATES' COURTS, PROCEDURE, ante at para **1–7454**. Narrative on the new provisions will be found at para **2–375A**, et seq.

2–1578 115. Statements and matters stated. (1) In this Chapter references to a statement or to a matter stated are to be read as follows.
(2) A statement is any representation of fact or opinion made by a person by whatever means; and it includes a representation made in a sketch, photofit or other pictorial form.
(3) A matter stated is one to which this Chapter applies if (and only if) the purpose, or one of the purposes, of the person making the statement appears to the court to have been—

(a) to cause another person to believe the matter, or[1]
(b) to cause another person to act or a machine to operate on the basis that the matter is as stated.
[Criminal Justice Act 2003, s 115.]

---

1. As to whether the mention of a name in a telephone call made by person (who could not subsequently be traced) falls within this definition, see *R v Isichei* [2006] EWCA Crim 1815, (2006) 170 JP 753 (the court concluded that that the judge might have been wrong in deciding it had not been a statement within s 115(3), but the evidence had in any event been admissible under s 114)).

Principal categories of admissibility

2–1579 116. Cases where a witness is unavailable. (1) In criminal proceedings a statement not made in oral evidence in the proceedings is admissible as evidence of any matter stated if—

(a) oral evidence given in the proceedings by the person who made the statement would be admissible as evidence of that matter,
(b) the person who made the statement (the relevant person) is identified to the court's satisfaction, and
(c) any of the five conditions mentioned in subsection (2) is satisfied.

(2) The conditions are—

(a) that the relevant person is dead;
(b) that the relevant person is unfit to be a witness because of his bodily or mental condition;
(c) that the relevant person is outside the United Kingdom and it is not reasonably practicable to secure his attendance;

(*d*) that the relevant person cannot be found although such steps as it is reasonably practicable to take to find him have been taken;

(*e*) that through fear the relevant person does not give (or does not continue to give) oral evidence in the proceedings, either at all or in connection with the subject matter of the statement, and the court gives leave for the statement to be given in evidence.

(3) For the purposes of subsection (2)(*e*) "fear" is to be widely construed and (for example) includes fear of the death or injury of another person or of financial loss.

(4) Leave may be given under subsection (2)(*e*) only if the court considers that the statement ought to be admitted in the interests of justice, having regard—

(*a*) to the statement's contents,

(*b*) to any risk that its admission or exclusion will result in unfairness to any party to the proceedings (and in particular to how difficult it will be to challenge the statement if the relevant person does not give oral evidence),

(*c*) in appropriate cases, to the fact that a direction under section 19 of the Youth Justice and Criminal Evidence Act 1999 (c 23) (special measures for the giving of evidence by fearful witnesses etc) could be made in relation to the relevant person, and

(*d*) to any other relevant circumstances.

(5) A condition set out in any paragraph of subsection (2) which is in fact satisfied is to be treated as not satisfied if it is shown that the circumstances described in that paragraph are caused—

(*a*) by the person in support of whose case it is sought to give the statement in evidence, or

(*b*) by a person acting on his behalf,

in order to prevent the relevant person giving oral evidence in the proceedings (whether at all or in connection with the subject matter of the statement).
[Criminal Justice Act 2003, s 116.]

2–1580 117. Business and other documents. (1) In criminal proceedings a statement contained in a document is admissible as evidence of any matter stated if—

(*a*) oral evidence given in the proceedings would be admissible as evidence of that matter,

(*b*) the requirements of subsection (2) are satisfied, and

(*c*) the requirements of subsection (5) are satisfied, in a case where subsection (4) requires them to be.

(2) The requirements of this subsection are satisfied if—

(*a*) the document or the part containing the statement was created or received by a person in the course of a trade, business, profession or other occupation, or as the holder of a paid or unpaid office,

(*b*) the person who supplied the information contained in the statement (the relevant person) had or may reasonably be supposed to have had personal knowledge of the matters dealt with, and

(*c*) each person (if any) through whom the information was supplied from the relevant person to the person mentioned in paragraph (*a*) received the information in the course of a trade, business, profession or other occupation, or as the holder of a paid or unpaid office.

(3) The persons mentioned in paragraphs (*a*) and (*b*) of subsection (2) may be the same person.

(4) The additional requirements of subsection (5) must be satisfied if the statement—

(*a*) was prepared for the purposes of pending or contemplated criminal proceedings, or for a criminal investigation, but

(*b*) was not obtained pursuant to a request under section 7 of the Crime (International Co-operation) Act 2003 (c 32) or an order under paragraph 6 of Schedule 13 to the Criminal Justice Act 1988 (c 33) (which relate to overseas evidence).

(5) The requirements of this subsection are satisfied if—

(*a*) any of the five conditions mentioned in section 116(2) is satisfied (absence of relevant person etc), or

(*b*) the relevant person cannot reasonably be expected to have any recollection of the matters dealt with in the statement (having regard to the length of time since he supplied the information and all other circumstances).

(6) A statement is not admissible under this section if the court makes a direction to that effect under subsection (7).

(7) The court may make a direction under this subsection if satisfied that the statement's reliability as evidence for the purpose for which it is tendered is doubtful in view of—

(*a*) its contents,

(*b*) the source of the information contained in it,

(*c*) the way in which or the circumstances in which the information was supplied or received, or

(*d*) the way in which or the circumstances in which the document concerned was created or received.
[Criminal Justice Act 2003, s 117.]

2–1581   **118. Preservation of certain common law categories of admissibility.** (1) The following rules of law are preserved.

Public information etc		
1	Any rule of law under which in criminal proceedings—	
		(*a*) published works dealing with matters of a public nature (such as histories, scientific works, dictionaries and maps) are admissible as evidence of facts of a public nature stated in them,
		(*b*) public documents (such as public registers, and returns made under public authority with respect to matters of public interest) are admissible as evidence of facts stated in them,
		(*c*) records (such as the records of certain courts, treaties, Crown grants, pardons and commissions) are admissible as evidence of facts stated in them, or
		(*d*) evidence relating to a person's age or date or place of birth may be given by a person without personal knowledge of the matter.
Reputation as to character		
2	Any rule of law under which in criminal proceedings evidence of a person's reputation is admissible for the purpose of proving his good or bad character. Note The rule is preserved only so far as it allows the court to treat such evidence as proving the matter concerned.	
Reputation or family tradition		
3	Any rule of law under which in criminal proceedings evidence of reputation or family tradition is admissible for the purpose of proving or disproving—	
		(*a*) pedigree or the existence of a marriage,
		(*b*) the existence of any public or general right, or
		(*c*) the identity of any person or thing.
	Note	
	The rule is preserved only so far as it allows the court to treat such evidence as proving or disproving the matter concerned.	
Res gestae		
4	Any rule of law under which in criminal proceedings a statement is admissible as evidence of any matter stated if—	
		(*a*) the statement was made by a person so emotionally overpowered by an event that the possibility of concoction or distortion can be disregarded,
		(*b*) the statement accompanied an act which can be properly evaluated as evidence only if considered in conjunction with the statement, or
		(*c*) the statement relates to a physical sensation or a mental state (such as intention or emotion).
Confessions etc		
5	Any rule of law relating to the admissibility of confessions or mixed statements in criminal proceedings.	
Admissions by agents etc		
6	Any rule of law under which in criminal proceedings—	
		(*a*) an admission made by an agent of a defendant is admissible against the defendant as evidence of any matter stated, or
		(*b*) a statement made by a person to whom a defendant refers a person for information is admissible against the defendant as evidence of any matter stated.

Common enterprise	
7	Any rule of law under which in criminal proceedings a statement made by a party to a common enterprise is admissible against another party to the enterprise as evidence of any matter stated.
Expert evidence	
8	Any rule of law under which in criminal proceedings an expert witness may draw on the body of expertise relevant to his field.

(2) With the exception of the rules preserved by this section, the common law rules governing the admissibility of hearsay evidence in criminal proceedings are abolished.
[Criminal Justice Act 2003, s 118.]

2–1582   119. Inconsistent statements.   (1) If in criminal proceedings a person gives oral evidence and—

(*a*)   he admits making a previous inconsistent statement, or

(*b*)   a previous inconsistent statement made by him is proved by virtue of section 3, 4 or 5 of the Criminal Procedure Act 1865 (c 18),

the statement is admissible as evidence of any matter stated of which oral evidence by him would be admissible.

(2) If in criminal proceedings evidence of an inconsistent statement by any person is given under section 124(2)(*c*), the statement is admissible as evidence of any matter stated in it of which oral evidence by that person would be admissible.
[Criminal Justice Act 2003, s 119.]

2–1583   120. Other previous statements of witnesses.   (1) This section applies where a person (the witness) is called to give evidence in criminal proceedings.

(2) If a previous statement by the witness is admitted as evidence to rebut a suggestion that his oral evidence has been fabricated, that statement is admissible as evidence of any matter stated of which oral evidence by the witness would be admissible.

(3) A statement made by the witness in a document—

(*a*)   which is used by him to refresh his memory while giving evidence,

(*b*)   on which he is cross-examined, and

(*c*)   which as a consequence is received in evidence in the proceedings,

is admissible as evidence of any matter stated of which oral evidence by him would be admissible.

(4) A previous statement by the witness is admissible as evidence of any matter stated of which oral evidence by him would be admissible, if—

(*a*)   any of the following three conditions is satisfied, and

(*b*)   while giving evidence the witness indicates that to the best of his belief he made the statement, and that to the best of his belief it states the truth.

(5) The first condition is that the statement identifies or describes a person, object or place.

(6) The second condition is that the statement was made by the witness when the matters stated were fresh in his memory but he does not remember them, and cannot reasonably be expected to remember them, well enough to give oral evidence of them in the proceedings.

(7) The third condition is that—

(*a*)   the witness claims to be a person against whom an offence has been committed,

(*b*)   the offence is one to which the proceedings relate,

(*c*)   the statement consists of a complaint made by the witness (whether to a person in authority or not) about conduct which would, if proved, constitute the offence or part of the offence,

(*d*)   the complaint was made as soon as could reasonably be expected after the alleged conduct,

(*e*)   the complaint was not made as a result of a threat or a promise, and

(*f*)   before the statement is adduced the witness gives oral evidence in connection with its subject matter.

(8) For the purposes of subsection (7) the fact that the complaint was elicited (for example, by a leading question) is irrelevant unless a threat or a promise was involved.
[Criminal Justice Act 2003, s 120.]

Supplementary

2–1584   121. Additional requirement for admissibility of multiple hearsay.   (1) A hearsay statement is not admissible to prove the fact that an earlier hearsay statement was made unless—

(*a*)   either of the statements is admissible under section 117, 119 or 120,

(*b*)   all parties to the proceedings so agree, or

(*c*)   the court is satisfied that the value of the evidence in question, taking into account how reliable the statements appear to be, is so high that the interests of justice require the later statement to be admissible for that purpose.

(2) In this section "hearsay statement" means a statement, not made in oral evidence, that is relied on as evidence of a matter stated in it.
[Criminal Justice Act 2003, s 121.]

2–1585   122. Documents produced as exhibits.   (1) This section applies if on a trial before a judge and jury for an offence—

(*a*)   a statement made in a document is admitted in evidence under section 119 or 120, and
(*b*)   the document or a copy of it is produced as an exhibit.

(2) The exhibit must not accompany the jury when they retire to consider their verdict unless—

(*a*)   the court considers it appropriate, or
(*b*)   all the parties to the proceedings agree that it should accompany the jury.
[Criminal Justice Act 2003, s 122.]

2–1586   123. Capability to make statement.   (1) Nothing in section 116, 119 or 120 makes a statement admissible as evidence if it was made by a person who did not have the required capability at the time when he made the statement.

(2) Nothing in section 117 makes a statement admissible as evidence if any person who, in order for the requirements of section 117(2) to be satisfied, must at any time have supplied or received the information concerned or created or received the document or part concerned—

(*a*)   did not have the required capability at that time, or
(*b*)   cannot be identified but cannot reasonably be assumed to have had the required capability at that time.

(3) For the purposes of this section a person has the required capability if he is capable of—

(*a*)   understanding questions put to him about the matters stated, and
(*b*)   giving answers to such questions which can be understood.

(4) Where by reason of this section there is an issue as to whether a person had the required capability when he made a statement—

(*a*)   proceedings held for the determination of the issue must take place in the absence of the jury (if there is one);
(*b*)   in determining the issue the court may receive expert evidence and evidence from any person to whom the statement in question was made;
(*c*)   the burden of proof on the issue lies on the party seeking to adduce the statement, and the standard of proof is the balance of probabilities.
[Criminal Justice Act 2003, s 123.]

2–1587   124. Credibility.   (1) This section applies if in criminal proceedings—

(*a*)   a statement not made in oral evidence in the proceedings is admitted as evidence of a matter stated, and
(*b*)   the maker of the statement does not give oral evidence in connection with the subject matter of the statement.

(2) In such a case—

(*a*)   any evidence which (if he had given such evidence) would have been admissible as relevant to his credibility as a witness is so admissible in the proceedings;
(*b*)   evidence may with the court's leave be given of any matter which (if he had given such evidence) could have been put to him in cross-examination as relevant to his credibility as a witness but of which evidence could not have been adduced by the cross-examining party;
(*c*)   evidence tending to prove that he made (at whatever time) any other statement inconsistent with the statement admitted as evidence is admissible for the purpose of showing that he contradicted himself.

(3) If as a result of evidence admitted under this section an allegation is made against the maker of a statement, the court may permit a party to lead additional evidence of such description as the court may specify for the purposes of denying or answering the allegation.

(4) In the case of a statement in a document which is admitted as evidence under section 117 each person who, in order for the statement to be admissible, must have supplied or received the information concerned or created or received the document or part concerned is to be treated as the maker of the statement for the purposes of subsections (1) to (3) above.
[Criminal Justice Act 2003, s 124.]

2–1588   125. Stopping the case where evidence is unconvincing.   (1) If on a defendant's trial before a judge and jury for an offence the court is satisfied at any time after the close of the case for the prosecution that—

(*a*)   the case against the defendant is based wholly or partly on a statement not made in oral evidence in the proceedings, and
(*b*)   the evidence provided by the statement is so unconvincing that, considering its importance to the case against the defendant, his conviction of the offence would be unsafe,

the court must either direct the jury to acquit the defendant of the offence or, if it considers that there ought to be a retrial, discharge the jury.

(2) Where—

(a) a jury is directed under subsection (1) to acquit a defendant of an offence, and

(b) the circumstances are such that, apart from this subsection, the defendant could if acquitted of that offence be found guilty of another offence,

the defendant may not be found guilty of that other offence if the court is satisfied as mentioned in subsection (1) in respect of it.

(3) If—

(a) a jury is required to determine under section 4A(2) of the Criminal Procedure (Insanity) Act 1964 (c 84) whether a person charged on an indictment with an offence did the act or made the omission charged, and

(b) the court is satisfied as mentioned in subsection (1) above at any time after the close of the case for the prosecution that—

(i) the case against the defendant is based wholly or partly on a statement not made in oral evidence in the proceedings, and

(ii) the evidence provided by the statement is so unconvincing that, considering its importance to the case against the person, a finding that he did the act or made the omission would be unsafe,

the court must either direct the jury to acquit the defendant of the offence or, if it considers that there ought to be a rehearing, discharge the jury.

(4) This section does not prejudice any other power a court may have to direct a jury to acquit a person of an offence or to discharge a jury.

[Criminal Justice Act 2003, s 125.]

2–1589   126. Court's general discretion to exclude evidence.   (1) In criminal proceedings the court may refuse to admit a statement as evidence of a matter stated if—

(a) the statement was made otherwise than in oral evidence in the proceedings, and

(b) the court is satisfied that the case for excluding the statement, taking account of the danger that to admit it would result in undue waste of time, substantially outweighs the case for admitting it, taking account of the value of the evidence.

(2) Nothing in this Chapter prejudices—

(a) any power of a court to exclude evidence under section 78 of the Police and Criminal Evidence Act 1984 (c 60) (exclusion of unfair evidence), or

(b) any other power of a court to exclude evidence at its discretion (whether by preventing questions from being put or otherwise).

[Criminal Justice Act 2003, s 126.]

Miscellaneous

2–1590   127. Expert evidence: preparatory work.   (1) This section applies if—

(a) a statement has been prepared for the purposes of criminal proceedings,

(b) the person who prepared the statement had or may reasonably be supposed to have had personal knowledge of the matters stated,

(c) notice is given under the appropriate rules that another person (the expert) will in evidence given in the proceedings orally or under section 9 of the Criminal Justice Act 1967 (c 80) base an opinion or inference on the statement, and

(d) the notice gives the name of the person who prepared the statement and the nature of the matters stated.

(2) In evidence given in the proceedings the expert may base an opinion or inference on the statement.

(3) If evidence based on the statement is given under subsection (2) the statement is to be treated as evidence of what it states.

(4) This section does not apply if the court, on an application by a party to the proceedings, orders that it is not in the interests of justice that it should apply.

(5) The matters to be considered by the court in deciding whether to make an order under subsection (4) include—

(a) the expense of calling as a witness the person who prepared the statement;

(b) whether relevant evidence could be given by that person which could not be given by the expert;

(c) whether that person can reasonably be expected to remember the matters stated well enough to give oral evidence of them.

(6) Subsections (1) to (5) apply to a statement prepared for the purposes of a criminal investigation as they apply to a statement prepared for the purposes of criminal proceedings, and in such a case references to the proceedings are to criminal proceedings arising from the investigation.

(7) The appropriate rules are rules made—

(a) under section 81 of the Police and Criminal Evidence Act 1984 (advance notice of expert evidence in Crown Court), or

(b) under section 144 of the Magistrates' Courts Act 1980 (c 43) by virtue of section 20(3) of the Criminal Procedure and Investigations Act 1996 (c 25) (advance notice of expert evidence in magistrates' courts).

[Criminal Justice Act 2003, s 127.]

2–1591 128. Confessions. *Inserts s 76A into the Police and Criminal Evidence Act 1984.*

2–1592 129. Representations other than by a person. (1) Where a representation of any fact—

(a) is made otherwise than by a person, but

(b) depends for its accuracy on information supplied (directly or indirectly) by a person,

the representation is not admissible in criminal proceedings as evidence of the fact unless it is proved that the information was accurate.

(2) Subsection (1) does not affect the operation of the presumption that a mechanical device has been properly set or calibrated.

[Criminal Justice Act 2003, s 129.]

2–1593 130. Depositions. In Schedule 3 to the Crime and Disorder Act 1998 (c 37), sub-paragraph (4) of paragraph 5 is omitted (power of the court to overrule an objection to a deposition being read as evidence by virtue of that paragraph).

[Criminal Justice Act 2003, s 130.]

2–1594 131. Evidence at retrial

General

2–1595 132. Rules of court. (1) Rules of court may make such provision as appears to the appropriate authority to be necessary or expedient for the purposes of this Chapter; and the appropriate authority is the authority entitled to make the rules.

(2) The rules may make provision about the procedure to be followed and other conditions to be fulfilled by a party proposing to tender a statement in evidence under any provision of this Chapter.

(3) The rules may require a party proposing to tender the evidence to serve on each party to the proceedings such notice, and such particulars of or relating to the evidence, as may be prescribed.

(4) The rules may provide that the evidence is to be treated as admissible by agreement of the parties if—

(a) a notice has been served in accordance with provision made under subsection (3), and

(b) no counter-notice in the prescribed form objecting to the admission of the evidence has been served by a party.

(5) If a party proposing to tender evidence fails to comply with a prescribed requirement applicable to it—

(a) the evidence is not admissible except with the court's leave;

(b) where leave is given the court or jury may draw such inferences from the failure as appear proper;

(c) the failure may be taken into account by the court in considering the exercise of its powers with respect to costs.

(6) In considering whether or how to exercise any of its powers under subsection (5) the court shall have regard to whether there is any justification for the failure to comply with the requirement.

(7) A person shall not be convicted of an offence solely on an inference drawn under subsection (5)(b).

(8) Rules under this section may—

(a) limit the application of any provision of the rules to prescribed circumstances;

(b) subject any provision of the rules to prescribed exceptions;

(c) make different provision for different cases or circumstances.

(9) Nothing in this section prejudices the generality of any enactment conferring power to make rules of court; and no particular provision of this section prejudices any general provision of it.

(10) In this section—

"prescribed" means prescribed by rules of court;

"rules of court" means—

(a) Crown Court Rules;

(b) Criminal Appeal Rules;

(c) rules under section 144 of the Magistrates' Courts Act 1980 (c 43).

[Criminal Justice Act 2003, s 132.]

2–1596 133. Proof of statements in documents. Where a statement in a document is admissible as evidence in criminal proceedings, the statement may be proved by producing either—

(a) the document, or

(b) (whether or not the document exists) a copy of the document or of the material part of it,

authenticated in whatever way the court may approve.
[Criminal Justice Act 2003, s 133.]

2–1597   134. Interpretation of Chapter 2.   (1) In this Chapter—

"copy", in relation to a document, means anything on to which information recorded in the
document has been copied, by whatever means and whether directly or indirectly;

"criminal proceedings" means criminal proceedings in relation to which the strict rules of evidence
apply;

"defendant", in relation to criminal proceedings, means a person charged with an offence in those
proceedings;

"document" means anything in which information of any description is recorded;

"oral evidence" includes evidence which, by reason of any disability, disorder or other impairment,
a person called as a witness gives in writing or by signs or by way of any device;

"statutory provision" means any provision contained in, or in an instrument made under, this or
any other Act, including any Act passed after this Act.

(2) Section 115 (statements and matters stated) contains other general interpretative provisions.

(3) Where a defendant is charged with two or more offences in the same criminal proceedings,
this Chapter has effect as if each offence were charged in separate proceedings.
[Criminal Justice Act 2003, s 134.]

2–1598   135. Armed forces

2–1599   136. Repeals etc.   In the Criminal Justice Act 1988 (c 33), the following provisions (which
are to some extent superseded by provisions of this Chapter) are repealed—

(*a*) Part 2 and Schedule 2 (which relate to documentary evidence);

(*b*) in Schedule 13, paragraphs 2 to 5 (which relate to documentary evidence in service courts
etc).
[Criminal Justice Act 2003, s 136.]

CHAPTER 3[1]
Miscellaneous and Supplemental

2–1600   137. Evidence by video recording[2].   (1) This section applies where—

(*a*) a person is called as a witness in proceedings for an offence triable only on indictment, or for
a prescribed offence triable either way,

(*b*) the person claims to have witnessed (whether visually or in any other way)—

(i) events alleged by the prosecution to include conduct constituting the offence or part of
the offence, or

(ii) events closely connected with such events,

(*c*) he has previously given an account of the events in question (whether in response to questions
asked or otherwise),

(*d*) the account was given at a time when those events were fresh in the person's memory (or
would have been, assuming the truth of the claim mentioned in paragraph (*b*)),

(*e*) a video recording was made of the account,

(*f*) the court has made a direction that the recording should be admitted as evidence in chief of
the witness, and the direction has not been rescinded, and

(*g*) the recording is played in the proceedings in accordance with the direction.

(2) If, or to the extent that, the witness in his oral evidence in the proceedings asserts the truth of
the statements made by him in the recorded account, they shall be treated as if made by him in that
evidence.

(3) A direction under subsection (1)(*f*)—

(*a*) may not be made in relation to a recorded account given by the defendant;

(*b*) may be made only if it appears to the court that—

(i) the witness's recollection of the events in question is likely to have been significantly better
when he gave the recorded account than it will be when he gives oral evidence in the
proceedings, and

(ii) it is in the interests of justice for the recording to be admitted, having regard in particular
to the matters mentioned in subsection (4).

(4) Those matters are—

(*a*) the interval between the time of the events in question and the time when the recorded account
was made;

(*b*) any other factors that might affect the reliability of what the witness said in that account;

(*c*) the quality of the recording;

(*d*) any views of the witness as to whether his evidence in chief should be given orally or by means
of the recording.

(5) For the purposes of subsection (2) it does not matter if the statements in the recorded account
were not made on oath.

(6) In this section "prescribed" means of a description specified in an order made by the Secretary of State.

[Criminal Justice Act 2003, s 137.]

---

1. Chapter 3 contains ss 137–141.
2. At the time of going to press this section had not come into force.

2–1601   138. Video evidence: further provisions[1]. (1) Where a video recording is admitted under section 137, the witness may not give evidence in chief otherwise than by means of the recording as to any matter which, in the opinion of the court, has been dealt with adequately in the recorded account.

(2) The reference in subsection (1)(*f*) of section 137 to the admission of a recording includes a reference to the admission of part of the recording; and references in that section and this one to the video recording or to the witness's recorded account shall, where appropriate, be read accordingly.

(3) In considering whether any part of a recording should be not admitted under section 137, the court must consider—

(*a*) whether admitting that part would carry a risk of prejudice to the defendant, and

(*b*) if so, whether the interests of justice nevertheless require it to be admitted in view of the desirability of showing the whole, or substantially the whole, of the recorded interview.

(4) A court may not make a direction under section 137(1)(*f*) in relation to any proceedings unless—

(*a*) the Secretary of State has notified the court that arrangements can be made, in the area in which it appears to the court that the proceedings will take place, for implementing directions under that section, and

(*b*) the notice has not been withdrawn.

(5) Nothing in section 137 affects the admissibility of any video recording which would be admissible apart from that section.

[Criminal Justice Act 2003, s 138.]

---

1. At the time of going to press this section had not come into force.

2–1602   139. Use of documents to refresh memory[1]. (1) A person giving oral evidence in criminal proceedings about any matter may, at any stage in the course of doing so, refresh his memory of it from a document made or verified by him at an earlier time if—

(*a*) he states in his oral evidence that the document records his recollection of the matter at that earlier time, and

(*b*) his recollection of the matter is likely to have been significantly better at that time than it is at the time of his oral evidence.

(2) Where—

(*a*) a person giving oral evidence in criminal proceedings about any matter has previously given an oral account, of which a sound recording was made, and he states in that evidence that the account represented his recollection of the matter at that time,

(*b*) his recollection of the matter is likely to have been significantly better at the time of the previous account than it is at the time of his oral evidence, and

(*c*) a transcript has been made of the sound recording,

he may, at any stage in the course of giving his evidence, refresh his memory of the matter from that transcript.

[Criminal Justice Act 2003, s 139.]

---

1. Sections 139–141 came into force on 5 April 2004: see the Criminal Justice Act (Commencement No 3 and Transitional Provisions) Order 2004, SI 2004/929.

2–1603   140. Interpretation of Chapter 3.   In this Chapter—

"criminal proceedings" means criminal proceedings in relation to which the strict rules of evidence apply;

"defendant", in relation to criminal proceedings, means a person charged with an offence in those proceedings;

"document" means anything in which information of any description is recorded, but not including any recording of sounds or moving images;

"oral evidence" includes evidence which, by reason of any disability, disorder or other impairment, a person called as a witness gives in writing or by signs or by way of any device;

"video recording" means any recording, on any medium, from which a moving image may by any means be produced, and includes the accompanying sound-track.

[Criminal Justice Act 2003, s 140.]

2–1604   141. Saving.   No provision of this Part has effect in relation to criminal proceedings begun before the commencement of that provision.

[Criminal Justice Act 2003, s 141.]

Statutory Instruments, Codes of Practice and Practice Directions on Evidence

Police and Criminal Evidence Act 1984 Codes of Practice

---

1. These Codes of Practice are issued under ss 66 and 67 (and, in respect of Code E, s 60(1) and, in respect of Code F, s 60A) of the Police and Criminal Evidence Act 1984; they are admissible in evidence, and account may be taken by the court of any relevant provision. Each provides that the Annexes are provisions of the code but that notes for guidance are not.

2–1902

CONTENTS

Notes for guidance
4   Entry without warrant – particular powers

   (a)   Making an arrest etc
   (b)   Search of premises where arrest takes place or the arrested person was immediately before arrest
   (c)   Search of premises occupied or controlled by the arrested person

5   Search with consent
Notes for guidance
6   Searching premises – general considerations

   (a)   Time of searches
   (b)   Entry other than with consent
   (c)   Notices of Powers and Rights
   (d)   Conduct of searches
   (e)   Leaving premises
   (f)   Searches under PACE Schedule 1 or the Terrorism Act 2000, Schedule 5

Notes for guidance
7   Seizure and retention of property

   (a)   Seizure
   (b)   Criminal Justice and Police Act 2001: Specific procedures for seize and sift powers
   (c)   Retention
   (d)   Rights of owners etc

Notes for guidance
8   Action after searches
9   Search registers
Note for guidance

C   CODE OF PRACTICE FOR THE DETENTION, TREATMENT AND QUESTIONING OF PERSONS BY POLICE OFFICERS

1   General
Notes for guidance
2   Custody records
Note for guidance
3   Initial action

   (a)   Detained persons – normal procedure
   (b)   Detained persons – special groups
   (c)   Persons attending a police station voluntarily
   (d)   Documentation
   (e)   Persons answering street bail

Notes for guidance
4   Detainee's property

   (a)   Action
   (b)   Documentation

Notes for guidance
5   Right not to be held incommunicado

   (a)   Action
   (b)   Documentation

Notes for guidance
6   Right to legal advice

   (a)   Action
   (b)   Documentation

Notes for guidance
7   Citizens of independent Commonwealth countries or foreign nationals

   (a)   Action
   (b)   Documentation

Note for guidance
8   Conditions of detention

   (a)   Action
   (b)   Documentation

Notes for guidance
9   Care and treatment of detained persons

   (a)   General
   (b)   Clinical treatment and attention
   (c)   Documentation

Notes for guidance
10 Cautions

    (a) When a caution must be given
    (b) Terms of the cautions
    (c) Special warnings under the Criminal Justice and Public Order Act 1994, sections 36 and 37
    (d) Juveniles and persons who are mentally disordered or otherwise mentally vulnerable
    (e) Documentation

Notes for guidance
11 Interviews – general

    (a) Action
    (b) Interview records
    (c) Juveniles and mentally disordered or otherwise mentally vulnerable people
    (d) Vulnerable suspects – urgent interviews at police stations

Notes for guidance
12 Interviews in police stations

    (a) Action
    (b) Documentation

Notes for guidance
13 Interpreters

    (a) General
    (b) Foreign languages
    (c) Deaf people and people with speech difficulties
    (d) Additional rules for detained persons
    (e) Documentation

14 Questioning – special restrictions
Note for guidance
15 Reviews and extensions of detention

    (a) Persons detained under PACE
    (b) Persons detained under the Terrorism Act 2000
    (c) Telephone review of detention
    (d) Documentation

Notes for guidance
16 Charging detained persons

    (a) Action
    (b) Documentation

Notes for guidance
17 Testing persons for the presence of specified Class A drugs

    (a) Action
    (b) Documentation
    (c) General

Notes for guidance
ANNEX A – INTIMATE AND STRIP SEARCHES
ANNEX B – DELAY IN NOTIFYING ARREST OR ALLOWING ACCESS TO LEGAL ADVICE
ANNEX C – RESTRICTION ON DRAWING ADVERSE INFERENCES FROM SILENCE AND TERMS OF THE CAUTION WHEN THE RESTRICTION APPLIES
ANNEX D – WRITTEN STATEMENTS UNDER CAUTION
ANNEX E – SUMMARY OF PROVISIONS RELATING TO MENTALLY DISORDERED AND OTHERWISE MENTALLY VULNERABLE PEOPLE
ANNEX F – COUNTRIES WITH WHICH BILATERAL CONSULAR CONVENTIONS OR AGREEMENTS REQUIRING NOTIFICATION OF THE ARREST AND DETENTION OF THEIR NATIONALS ARE IN FORCE AS AT 1 APRIL 2003
ANNEX G – FITNESS TO BE INTERVIEWED
ANNEX H – DETAINED PERSON: OBSERVATION LIST
ANNEX I – POLICE AREAS WHERE THE POWER TO TEST PERSONS AGED 18 AND OVER FOR SPECIFIED CLASS A DRUGS UNDER SECTION 63B OF PACE HAS BEEN BROUGHT INTO FORCE
ANNEX J – POLICE AREAS WHERE THE POWER TO TEST PERSONS AGED 14 AND OVER FOR SPECIFIED CLASS A DRUGS UNDER SECTION 63B OF PACE (AS AMENDED BY SECTION 5 OF THE CRIMINAL JUSTICE ACT 2003) HAS BEEN BROUGHT INTO FORCE

---

1. The list of contents is not reproduced here, for the text of Code H, see post.

2–1903

A CODE OF PRACTICE FOR THE EXERCISE BY:
POLICE OFFICERS OF STATUTORY POWERS OF STOP AND SEARCH
POLICE OFFICERS AND POLICE STAFF OF REQUIREMENTS TO RECORD PUBLIC ENCOUNTERS[1]

COMMENCEMENT – TRANSITIONAL ARRANGEMENTS

This code applies to any search by a police officer and the requirement to record public encounters taking place after midnight on 31 December 2005.

---

1. This Code of Practice (draft code laid before Parliament on 8 November 2005) is issued under ss 66 and 67 of the Police and Criminal Evidence Act 1984; it is admissible thereunder in evidence and account may be taken by the court of any relevant provision. the Police and Criminal Evidence At 1984 (Codes of Practice) Order 2005, SI 2005/3503 applies to any search by a police officer on or after 1 January 2005. Code A was revised by the Police and Criminal Evidence Act 1984 (Codes of Practice) (Revisions to Code A) Order 2006, SI 2006/2165 which appointed 31 August 2006 as the date on which revisions to Code of Practice A laid in draft before Parliament on 10 August 2006 came into operation.

GENERAL

This code of practice must be readily available at all police stations for consultation by police officers, police staff, detained persons and members of the public.

The notes for guidance included are not provisions of this code, but are guidance to police officers and others about its application and interpretation. Provisions in the annexes to the code are provisions of this code.

This code governs the exercise by police officers of statutory powers to search a person or a vehicle without first making an arrest. The main stop and search powers to which this code applies are set out in Annex A, but that list should not be regarded as definitive. [See Note 1] In addition, it covers requirements on police officers and police staff to record encounters not governed by statutory powers. This code does not apply to:

(a) the powers of stop and search under;

    (i) Aviation Security Act 1982, section 27(2);

    (ii) Police and Criminal Evidence Act 1984, section 6(1) (which relates specifically to powers of constables employed by statutory undertakers on the premises of the statutory undertakers).

(b) searches carried out for the purposes of examination under Schedule 7 to the Terrorism Act 2000 and to which the Code of Practice issued under paragraph 6 of Schedule 14 to the Terrorism Act 2000 applies.

1 PRINCIPLES GOVERNING STOP AND SEARCH

1.1 Powers to stop and search must be used fairly, responsibly, with respect for people being searched and without unlawful discrimination. The Race Relations (Amendment) Act 2000 makes it unlawful for police officers to discriminate on the grounds of race, colour, ethnic origin, nationality or national origins when using their powers.

1.2 The intrusion on the liberty of the person stopped or searched must be brief and detention for the purposes of a search must take place at or near the location of the stop.

1.3 If these fundamental principles are not observed the use of powers to stop and search may be drawn into question. Failure to use the powers in the proper manner reduces their effectiveness. Stop and search can play an important role in the detection and prevention of crime, and using the powers fairly makes them more effective.

1.4 The primary purpose of stop and search powers is to enable officers to allay or confirm suspicions about individuals without exercising their power of arrest. Officers may be required to justify the use or authorisation of such powers, in relation both to individual searches and the overall pattern of their activity in this regard, to their supervisory officers or in court. Any misuse of the powers is likely to be harmful to policing and lead to mistrust of the police. Officers must also be able to explain their actions to the member of the public searched. The misuse of these powers can lead to disciplinary action.

1.5 An officer must not search a person, even with his or her consent, where no power to search is applicable. Even where a person is prepared to submit to a search voluntarily, the person must not be searched unless the necessary legal power exists, and the search must be in accordance with the relevant power and the provisions of this Code. The only exception, where an officer does not require a specific power, applies to searches of persons entering sports grounds or other premises carried out with their consent given as a condition of entry.

2 EXPLANATION OF POWERS TO STOP AND SEARCH

2.1 This code applies to powers of stop and search as follows:

(a) powers which require reasonable grounds for suspicion, before they may be exercised; that articles unlawfully obtained or possessed are being carried, or under Section 43 of the Terrorism Act 2000 that a person is a terrorist;

(b) authorised under section 60 of the Criminal Justice and Public Order Act 1994, based upon a reasonable belief that incidents involving serious violence may take place or that people are carrying dangerous instruments or offensive weapons within any locality in the police area;

(c) authorised under section 44(1) and (2) of the Terrorism Act 2000 based upon a consideration that the exercise of one or both powers is expedient for the prevention of acts of terrorism;

(d) powers to search a person who has not been arrested in the exercise of a power to search premises (see Code B paragraph 2.4).

Searches requiring reasonable grounds for suspicion

2.2 Reasonable grounds for suspicion depend on the circumstances in each case. There must be an objective basis for that suspicion based on facts, information, and/or intelligence which are relevant to the likelihood of finding an article of a certain kind or, in the case of searches under section 43 of the Terrorism Act 2000, to the likelihood that the person is a terrorist. Reasonable suspicion can never be supported on the basis of personal factors alone without reliable supporting intelligence or information or some specific behaviour by the person concerned. For example, a person's race, age, appearance, or the fact that the person is known to have a previous conviction, cannot be used alone or in combination with each other as the reason for searching that person. Reasonable suspicion cannot be based on generalisations or stereotypical images of certain groups or categories of people as more likely to be involved in criminal activity. A person's religion cannot be considered as reasonable grounds for suspicion and should never be considered as a reason to stop or stop and search an individual.

2.3 Reasonable suspicion can sometimes exist without specific information or intelligence and on the basis of some level of generalisation stemming from the behaviour of a person. For example, if an officer encounters someone on the street at night who is obviously trying to hide something, the officer may (depending on the other surrounding circumstances) base such suspicion on the fact that this kind of behaviour is often linked to stolen or prohibited articles being carried. Similarly, for the purposes of section 43 of the Terrorism Act 2000, suspicion that a person is a terrorist may arise from the person's behaviour at or near a location which has been identified as a potential target for terrorists.

2.4 However, reasonable suspicion should normally be linked to accurate and current intelligence or information, such as information describing an article being carried, a suspected offender, or a person who has been seen carrying a type of article known to have been stolen recently from premises in the area. Searches based on accurate and current intelligence or information are more likely to be effective. Targeting searches in a particular area at specified crime problems increases their effectiveness and minimises inconvenience to law-abiding members of the public. It also helps in justifying the use of searches both to those who are searched and to the public. This does not however prevent stop and search powers being exercised in other locations where such powers may be exercised and reasonable suspicion exists.

2.5 Searches are more likely to be effective, legitimate, and secure public confidence when reasonable suspicion is based on a range of factors. The overall use of these powers is more likely to be effective when up to date and accurate intelligence or information is communicated to officers and they are well-informed about local crime patterns.

2.6 Where there is reliable information or intelligence that members of a group or gang habitually carry knives unlawfully or weapons or controlled drugs, and wear a distinctive item of clothing or other means of identification to indicate their membership of the group or gang, that distinctive item of clothing or other means of identification may provide reasonable grounds to stop and search a person. [See Note 9]

2.7 A police officer may have reasonable grounds to suspect that a person is in innocent possession of a stolen or prohibited article or other item for which he or she is empowered to search. In that case the officer may stop and search the person even though there would be no power of arrest.

2.8 Under section 43(1) of the Terrorism Act 2000 a constable may stop and search a person whom the officer reasonably suspects to be a terrorist to discover whether the person is in possession of anything which may constitute evidence that the person is a terrorist. These searches may only be carried out by an officer of the same sex as the person searched.

2.9 An officer who has reasonable grounds for suspicion may detain the person concerned in order to carry out a search. Before carrying out a search the officer may ask questions about the person's behaviour or presence in circumstances which gave rise to the suspicion. As a result of questioning the detained person, the reasonable grounds for suspicion necessary to detain that person may be confirmed or, because of a satisfactory explanation, be eliminated. [See Notes 2 and 3] Questioning may also reveal reasonable grounds to suspect the possession of a different kind of unlawful article from that originally suspected. Reasonable grounds for suspicion however cannot be provided retrospectively by such questioning during a person's detention or by refusal to answer any questions put.

2.10 If, as a result of questioning before a search, or other circumstances which come to the attention of the officer, there cease to be reasonable grounds for suspecting that an article is being carried of a kind for which there is a power to stop and search, no search may take place. [See Note 3] In the absence of any other lawful power to detain, the person is free to leave at will and must be so informed.

2.11 There is no power to stop or detain a person in order to find grounds for a search. Police officers have many encounters with members of the public which do not involve detaining people against their will. If reasonable grounds for suspicion emerge during such an encounter, the officer may search the person, even though no grounds existed when the encounter began. If an officer is detaining someone for the purpose of a search, he or she should inform the person as soon as detention begins.

Searches authorised under section 60 of the Criminal Justice and Public Order Act 1994
2.12 Authority for a constable in uniform to stop and search under section 60 of the Criminal Justice and Public Order Act 1994 may be given if the authorising officer reasonably believes:

(a) that incidents involving serious violence may take place in any locality in the officer's police area, and it is expedient to use these powers to prevent their occurrence, or

(b) that persons are carrying dangerous instruments or offensive weapons without good reason in any locality in the officer's police area.

2.13 An authorisation under section 60 may only be given by an officer of the rank of inspector or above, in writing, specifying the grounds on which it was given, the locality in which the powers may be exercised and the period of time for which they are in force. The period authorised shall be no longer than appears reasonably necessary to prevent, or seek to prevent incidents of serious violence, or to deal with the problem of carrying dangerous instruments or offensive weapons. It may not exceed 24 hours. [See Notes 10-13]

2.14 If an inspector gives an authorisation, he or she must, as soon as practicable, inform an officer of or above the rank of superintendent. This officer may direct that the authorisation shall be extended for a further 24 hours, if violence or the carrying of dangerous instruments or offensive weapons has occurred, or is suspected to have occurred, and the continued use of the powers is considered necessary to prevent or deal with further such activity. That direction must also be given in writing at the time or as soon as practicable afterwards. [See Note 12]

Powers to require removal of face coverings

2.15 Section 60AA of the Criminal Justice and Public Order Act 1994 also provides a power to demand the removal of disguises. The officer exercising the power must reasonably believe that someone is wearing an item wholly or mainly for the purpose of concealing identity. There is also a power to seize such items where the officer believes that a person intends to wear them for this purpose. There is no power to stop and search for disguises. An officer may seize any such item which is discovered when exercising a power of search for something else, or which is being carried, and which the officer reasonably believes is intended to be used for concealing anyone's identity. This power can only be used if an authorisation under section 60 or an authorisation under section 60AA is in force.

2.16 Authority for a constable in uniform to require the removal of disguises and to seize them under section 60AA may be given if the authorising officer reasonably believes that activities may take place in any locality in the officer's police area that are likely to involve the commission of offences and it is expedient to use these powers to prevent or control these activities.

2.17 An authorisation under section 60AA may only be given by an officer of the rank of inspector or above, in writing, specifying the grounds on which it was given, the locality in which the powers may be exercised and the period of time for which they are in force. The period authorised shall be no longer than appears reasonably necessary to prevent, or seek to prevent the commission of offences. It may not exceed 24 hours. [See Notes 10-13]

2.18 If an inspector gives an authorisation, he or she must, as soon as practicable, inform an officer of or above the rank of superintendent. This officer may direct that the authorisation shall be extended for a further 24 hours, if crimes have been committed, or is suspected to have been committed, and the continued use of the powers is considered necessary to prevent or deal with further such activity. This direction must also be given in writing at the time or as soon as practicable afterwards. [See Note 12]

Searches authorised under section 44 of the Terrorism Act 2000

2.19 An officer of the rank of assistant chief constable (or equivalent) or above, may give authority for the following powers of stop and search under section 44 of the Terrorism Act 2000 to be exercised in the whole or part of his or her police area if the officer considers it is expedient for the prevention of acts of terrorism:

(a) under section 44(1) of the Terrorism Act 2000, to give a constable in uniform power to stop and search any vehicle, its driver, any passenger in the vehicle and anything in or on the vehicle or carried by the driver or any passenger; and

(b) under section 44(2) of the Terrorism Act 2000, to give a constable in uniform power to stop and search any pedestrian and anything carried by the pedestrian.

An authorisation under section 44(1) may be combined with one under section 44(2).

2.20 If an authorisation is given orally at first, it must be confirmed in writing by the officer who gave it as soon as reasonably practicable.

2.21 When giving an authorisation, the officer must specify the geographical area in which the power may be used, and the time and date that the authorisation ends (up to a maximum of 28 days from the time the authorisation was given). [See Notes 12 and 13]

2.22 The officer giving an authorisation under section 44(1) or (2) must cause the Secretary of State to be informed, as soon as reasonably practicable, that such an authorisation has been given. An authorisation which is not confirmed by the Secretary of State within 48 hours of its having been given, shall have effect up until the end of that 48 hour period or the end of the period specified in the authorisation (whichever is the earlier). [See Note 14]

2.23 Following notification of the authorisation, the Secretary of State may:

(i) cancel the authorisation with immediate effect or with effect from such other time as he or she may direct;

(ii) confirm it but for a shorter period than that specified in the authorisation; or

(iii) confirm the authorisation as given.

2.24 When an authorisation under section 44 is given, a constable in uniform may exercise the powers:

(a) only for the purpose of searching for articles of a kind which could be used in connection with terrorism (see paragraph 2.25);

(b) whether or not there are any grounds for suspecting the presence of such articles.

2.24A When a Community Support Officer on duty and in uniform has been conferred powers under Section 44 of the Terrorism Act 2000 by a Chief Officer of their force, the exercise of this power must comply with the requirements of this Code of Practice, including the recording requirements.

2.25 The selection of persons stopped under section 44 of Terrorism Act 2000 should reflect an objective assessment of the threat posed by the various terrorist groups active in Great Britain. The powers must not be used to stop and search for reasons unconnected with terrorism. Officers must take particular care not to discriminate against members of minority ethnic groups in the exercise of these powers. There may be circumstances, however, where it is appropriate for officers to take account of a person's ethnic origin in selecting persons to be stopped in response to a specific terrorist threat (for example, some international terrorist groups are associated with particular ethnic identities). [See Notes 12 and 13]

2.26 The powers under sections 43 and 44 of the Terrorism Act 2000 allow a constable to search only for articles which could be used for terrorist purposes. However, this would not prevent a search being carried out under other powers if, in the course of exercising these powers, the officer formed reasonable grounds for suspicion.

Powers to search in the exercise of a power to search premises

2.27 The following powers to search premises also authorise the search of a person, not under arrest, who is found on the premises during the course of the search:

(a) section 139B of the Criminal Justice Act 1988 under which a constable may enter school premises and search the premises and any person on those premises for any bladed or pointed article or offensive weapon; and

(b) under a warrant issued under section s.23(3) of the Misuse of Drugs Act 1971 to search premises for drugs or documents but only if the warrant specifically authorises the search of persons found on the premises.

2.28 Before the power under section 139B of the Criminal Justice Act 1988 may be exercised, the constable must have reasonable grounds to believe that an offence under section 139A of the Criminal Justice Act 1988 (having a bladed or pointed article or offensive weapon on school premises) has been or is being committed. A warrant to search premises and persons found therein may be issued under section s.23(3) of the Misuse of Drugs Act 1971 if there are reasonable grounds to suspect that controlled drugs or certain documents are in the possession of a person on the premises.

2.29 The powers in paragraph 2.27(a) or (b) do not require prior specific grounds to suspect that the person to be searched is in possession of an item for which there is an existing power to search. However, it is still necessary to ensure that the selection and treatment of those searched under these powers is based upon objective factors connected with the search of the premises, and not upon personal prejudice.

3 CONDUCT OF SEARCHES

3.1 All stops and searches must be carried out with courtesy, consideration and respect for the person concerned. This has a significant impact on public confidence in the police. Every reasonable effort must be made to minimise the embarrassment that a person being searched may experience. [See Note 4]

3.2 The co-operation of the person to be searched must be sought in every case, even if the person initially objects to the search. A forcible search may be made only if it has been established that the person is unwilling to co-operate or resists. Reasonable force may be used as a last resort if necessary to conduct a search or to detain a person or vehicle for the purposes of a search.

3.3 The length of time for which a person or vehicle may be detained must be reasonable and kept to a minimum. Where the exercise of the power requires reasonable suspicion, the thoroughness and extent of a search must depend on what is suspected of being carried, and by whom. If the suspicion relates to a particular article which is seen to be slipped into a person's pocket, then, in the absence of other grounds for suspicion or an opportunity for the article to be moved elsewhere, the search must be confined to that pocket. In the case of a small article which can readily be concealed, such as a drug, and which might be concealed anywhere on the person, a more extensive search may be necessary. In the case of searches mentioned in paragraph 2.1(b), (c), and (d), which do not require reasonable grounds for suspicion, officers may make any reasonable search to look for items for which they are empowered to search. [See Note 5]

3.4 The search must be carried out at or near the place where the person or vehicle was first detained. [See Note 6]

3.5 There is no power to require a person to remove any clothing in public other than an outer coat, jacket or gloves except under section 45(3) of the Terrorism Act 2000 (which empowers a constable conducting a search under section 44(1) or 44(2) of that Act to require a person to remove headgear and footwear in public) and under section 60AA of the Criminal Justice and Public Order Act 1994 (which empowers a constable to require a person to remove any item worn to conceal identity). [See Notes 4 and 6] A search in public of a person's clothing which has not been removed must be restricted to superficial examination of outer garments. This does not, however, prevent an officer from placing his or her hand inside the pockets of the outer clothing, or feeling round the inside of collars, socks and shoes if this is reasonably necessary in the circumstances to look for the object of the search or to remove and examine any item reasonably suspected to be the object of the search. For the same reasons, subject to the restrictions on the removal of headgear, a person's hair may also be searched in public (see paragraphs 3.1 and 3.3).

3.6 Where on reasonable grounds it is considered necessary to conduct a more thorough search (eg by requiring a person to take off a T-shirt), this must be done out of public view, for example, in a police van unless paragraph 3.7 applies, or police station if there is one nearby. [See Note 6] Any search involving the removal of more than an outer coat, jacket, gloves, headgear or footwear, or any other item concealing identity, may only be made by an officer of the same sex as the person searched and may not be made in the presence of anyone of the opposite sex unless the person being searched specifically requests it. [See Notes 4, 7 and 8]

3.7 Searches involving exposure of intimate parts of the body must not be conducted as a routine extension of a less thorough search, simply because nothing is found in the course of the initial search. Searches involving exposure of intimate parts of the body may be carried out only at a nearby police station or other nearby location which is out of public view (but not a police vehicle). These searches must be conducted in accordance with paragraph 11 of Annex A to Code C except that an intimate search mentioned in paragraph 11(f) of Annex A to Code C may not be authorised or carried out under any stop and search powers. The other provisions of Code C do not apply to the conduct and recording of searches of persons detained at police stations in the exercise of stop and search powers. [See Note 7]

Steps to be taken prior to a search

3.8 Before any search of a detained person or attended vehicle takes place the officer must take reasonable steps to give the person to be searched or in charge of the vehicle the following information:

(a) that they are being detained for the purposes of a search

(b) the officer's name (except in the case of enquiries linked to the investigation of terrorism, or otherwise where the officer reasonably believes that giving his or her name might put him or her in danger, in which case a warrant or other identification number shall be given) and the name of the police station to which the officer is attached;

(c) the legal search power which is being exercised; and

(d) a clear explanation of:

  (i)   the purpose of the search in terms of the article or articles for which there is a power to search; and

  (ii) in the case of powers requiring reasonable suspicion (see paragraph 2.1(a)), the grounds for that suspicion; or

  (iii) in the case of powers which do not require reasonable suspicion (see paragraph 2.1(b), and (c)), the nature of the power and of any necessary authorisation and the fact that it has been given.

3.9 Officers not in uniform must show their warrant cards. Stops and searches under the powers mentioned in paragraphs 2.1(b), and (c) may be undertaken only by a constable in uniform.

3.10 Before the search takes place the officer must inform the person (or the owner or person in charge of the vehicle that is to be searched) of his or her entitlement to a copy of the record of the search, including his entitlement to a record of the search if an application is made within 12 months, if it is wholly impracticable to make a record at the time. If a record is not made at the time the person should also be told how a copy can be obtained (see section 4). The person should also be given information about police powers to stop and search and the individual's rights in these circumstances.

3.11 If the person to be searched, or in charge of a vehicle to be searched, does not appear to understand what is being said, or there is any doubt about the person's ability to understand English, the officer must take reasonable steps to bring information regarding the person's rights and any relevant provisions of this Code to his or her attention. If the person is deaf or cannot understand English and is accompanied by someone, then the officer must try to establish whether that person can interpret or otherwise help the officer to give the required information.

4 RECORDING REQUIREMENTS

4.1 An officer who has carried out a search in the exercise of any power to which this Code applies, must make a record of it at the time, unless there are exceptional circumstances which would make this wholly impracticable (eg in situations involving public disorder or when the officer's presence is urgently required elsewhere). If a record is not made at the time, the officer must do so as soon as practicable afterwards. There may be situations in which it is not practicable to obtain the information necessary to complete a record, but the officer should make every reasonable effort to do so. [See Note 21]

4.2 A copy of a record made at the time must be given immediately to the person who has been searched. The officer must ask for the name, address and date of birth of the person searched, but there is no obligation on a person to provide these details and no power of detention if the person is unwilling to do so.

4.3 The following information must always be included in the record of a search even if the person does not wish to provide any personal details:

(i)   the name of the person searched, or (if it is withheld) a description;

(ii)   a note of the person's self-defined ethnic background; [See Note 18]

(iii)   when a vehicle is searched, its registration number; [See Note 16]

(iv)   the date, time, and place that the person or vehicle was first detained;

(v)   the date, time and place the person or vehicle was searched (if different from (iv));

(vi)   the purpose of the search;

(vii) the grounds for making it, or in the case of those searches mentioned in paragraph 2.1(b) and (c), the nature of the power and of any necessary authorisation and the fact that it has been given; [See Note 17]

(viii)its outcome (eg arrest or no further action);

(ix)   a note of any injury or damage to property resulting from it;

(x)   subject to paragraph 3.8(b), the identity of the officer making the search. [See Note 15]

4.4 Nothing in paragraph 4.3 (x) or 4.10A requires the names of police officers to be shown on the search record or any other record required to be made under this code in the case of enquiries linked to the investigation of terrorism or otherwise where an officer reasonably believes that recording names might endanger the officers. In such cases the record must show the officers' warrant or other identification number and duty station.

4.5 A record is required for each person and each vehicle searched. However, if a person is in a vehicle and both are searched, and the object and grounds of the search are the same, only one record need be completed. If more than one person in a vehicle is searched, separate records for each search of a person must be made. If only a vehicle is searched, the name of the driver and his or her self-defined ethnic background must be recorded, unless the vehicle is unattended.

4.6 The record of the grounds for making a search must, briefly but informatively, explain the reason for suspecting the person concerned, by reference to the person's behaviour and/or other circumstances.

4.7 Where officers detain an individual with a view to performing a search, but the search is not carried out due to the grounds for suspicion being eliminated as a result of questioning the person detained, a record must still be made in accordance with the procedure outlined in Paragraph 4.12

4.8 After searching an unattended vehicle, or anything in or on it, an officer must leave a notice in it (or on it, if things on it have been searched without opening it) recording the fact that it has been searched.

4.9 The notice must include the name of the police station to which the officer concerned is attached and state where a copy of the record of the search may be obtained and where any application for compensation should be directed.

4.10 The vehicle must if practicable be left secure.

4.10A When an officer makes a record of the stop electronically and is unable to produce a copy of the form at the time, the officer must explain how the person can obtain a full copy of the record of the stop or search and give the person a receipt which contains:

•   a unique reference number and guidance on how to obtain a full copy of the stop or search;

•   the name of the officer who carried out the stop or search (unless paragraph 4.4 applies); and

•   the power used to stop and search them. [See Note 21]

Recording of encounters not governed by Statutory Powers

4.11 *Not used*

4.12 When an officer requests a person in a public place to account for themselves, i.e. their actions, behaviour, presence in an area or possession of anything, a record of the encounter must be completed at the time and a copy given to the person who has been questioned. The record must identify the name of the officer who has made the stop and conducted the encounter. This does not apply under the exceptional circumstances outlined in paragraph 4.1 of this code.

4.13 This requirement does not apply to general conversations such as when giving directions to a place, or when seeking witnesses. It also does not include occasions on which an officer is seeking general information or questioning people to establish background to incidents which have required officers to intervene to keep the peace or resolve a dispute.

4.14 A separate record need not be completed when:

- stopping a person in a vehicle when an HORT/1 form, a Vehicle Defect Rectification Scheme Notice, or a Fixed Penalty Notice is issued. It also does not apply when a specimen of breath is required under Section 6 of the Road Traffic Act 1988.
- stopping a person when a Penalty Notice is issued for an offence.

4.15 Officers must inform the person of their entitlement to a copy of a record of the encounter.

4.16 The provisions of paragraph 4.4 of this code apply equally when the encounters described in 4.12 and 4.13 are recorded.

4.17 The following information must be included in the record

(i) the date, time and place of the encounter;
(ii) if the person is in a vehicle, the registration number;
(iii) the reason why the officer questioned that person; [See Note 17]
(iv) a note of the person's self-defined ethnic background; [See Note 18]
(v) the outcome of the encounter.

4.18 There is no power to require the person questioned to provide personal details. If a person refuses to give their self-defined ethnic background, a form must still be completed, which includes a description of the person's ethnic background. [See Note 18]

4.19 A record of an encounter must always be made when the criteria set out in 4.12 have been met.If the criteria are not met but the person requests a record, the officer should provide a copy of the form but record on it that the encounter did not meet the criteria. The officer can refuse to issue the form if he or she reasonably believes that the purpose of the request is deliberately aimed at frustrating or delaying legitimate police activity. [See Note 20].

4.20 All references to officers in this section include police staff designated as Community Support Officers under section 38 of the Police Reform Act 2002.

5 MONITORING AND SUPERVISING THE USE OF STOP AND SEARCH POWERS

5.1 Supervising officers must monitor the use of stop and search powers and should consider in particular whether there is any evidence that they are being exercised on the basis of stereotyped images or inappropriate generalisations. Supervising officers should satisfy themselves that the practice of officers under their supervision in stopping, searching and recording is fully in accordance with this Code. Supervisors must also examine whether the records reveal any trends or patterns which give cause for concern, and if so take appropriate action to address this

5.2 Senior officers with area or force-wide responsibilities must also monitor the broader use of stop and search powers and, where necessary, take action at the relevant level.

5.3 Supervision and monitoring must be supported by the compilation of comprehensive statistical records of stops and searches at force, area and local level. Any apparently disproportionate use of the powers by particular officers or groups of officers or in relation to specific sections of the community should be identified and investigated.

5.4 In order to promote public confidence in the use of the powers, forces in consultation with police authorities must make arrangements for the records to be scrutinised by representatives of the community, and to explain the use of the powers at a local level. [See Note 19].

Notes for Guidance
Officers exercising stop and search powers

1 This code does not affect the ability of an officer to speak to or question a person in the ordinary course of the officer's duties without detaining the person or exercising any element of compulsion. It is not the purpose of the code to prohibit such encounters between the police and the community with the co-operation of the person concerned and neither does it affect the principle that all citizens have a duty to help police officers to prevent crime and discover offenders. This is a civic rather than a legal duty; but when a police officer is trying to discover whether, or by whom, an offence has been committed he or she may question any person from whom useful information might be obtained, subject to the restrictions imposed by Code C. A person's unwillingness to reply does not alter this entitlement, but in the absence of a power to arrest, or to detain in order to search, the person is free to leave at will and cannot be compelled to remain with the officer.

2 In some circumstances preparatory questioning may be unnecessary, but in general a brief conversation or exchange will be desirable not only as a means of avoiding unsuccessful searches, but to explain the grounds for the stop/search, to gain cooperation and reduce any tension there might be surrounding the stop/search.

3 Where a person is lawfully detained for the purpose of a search, but no search in the event takes place, the detention will not thereby have been rendered unlawful.

4 Many people customarily cover their heads or faces for religious reasons – for example, Muslim women, Sikh men, Sikh or Hindu women, or Rastafarian men or women. A police officer cannot order the removal of a head or face covering except where there is reason to believe that the item is being worn by the individual wholly or mainly for the purpose of disguising identity, not simply because it disguises identity. Where there may be religious sensitivities about ordering the removal of such an item, the officer should permit the item to be removed out of public view. Where practicable, the item should be removed in the presence of an officer of the same sex as the person and out of sight of anyone of the opposite sex .

5 A search of a person in public should be completed as soon as possible.

6 A person may be detained under a stop and search power at a place other than where the person was first detained, only if that place, be it a police station or elsewhere, is nearby. Such a place should be located within a reasonable travelling distance using whatever mode of travel (on foot or by car) is appropriate. This applies to all searches under stop and search powers, whether or not they involve the removal of clothing or exposure of intimate parts of the body (see paragraphs 3.6 and 3.7) or take place in or out of public view. It means, for example, that a search under the stop and search power in section 23 of the Misuse of Drugs Act 1971 which involves the compulsory removal of more than a person's outer coat, jacket or gloves cannot be carried out unless a place which is both nearby the place they were first detained and out of public view, is available. If a search involves exposure of intimate parts of the body and a police station is not nearby, particular care must be taken to ensure that the location is suitable in that it enables the search to be conducted in accordance with the requirements of paragraph 11 of Annex A to Code C.

7 A search in the street itself should be regarded as being in public for the purposes of paragraphs 3.6 and 3.7 above, even though it may be empty at the time a search begins. Although there is no power to require a person to do so, there is nothing to prevent an officer from asking a person voluntarily to remove more than an outer coat, jacket or gloves (and headgear or footwear under section 45(3) of the Terrorism Act 2000) in public.

8 Where there may be religious sensitivities about asking someone to remove headgear using a power under section 45(3) of the Terrorism Act 2000, the police officer should offer to carry out the search out of public view (for example, in a police van or police station if there is one nearby).

9 Other means of identification might include jewellery, insignias, tattoos or other features which are known to identify members of the particular gang or group.

Authorising officers

10 The powers under section 60 are separate from and additional to the normal stop and search powers which require reasonable grounds to suspect an individual of carrying an offensive weapon (or other article). Their overall purpose is to prevent serious violence and the widespread carrying of weapons which might lead to persons being seriously injured by disarming potential offenders in circumstances where other powers would not be sufficient. They should not therefore be used to replace or circumvent the normal powers for dealing with routine crime problems. The purpose of the powers under section 60AA is to prevent those involved in intimidatory or violent protests using face coverings to disguise identity.

11 Authorisations under section 60 require a reasonable belief on the part of the authorising officer. This must have an objective basis, for example: intelligence or relevant information such as a history of antagonism and violence between particular groups; previous incidents of violence at, or connected with, particular events or locations; a significant increase in knife-point robberies in a limited area; reports that individuals are regularly carrying weapons in a particular locality; or in the case of section 60AA previous incidents of crimes being committed while wearing face coverings to conceal identity.

12 It is for the authorising officer to determine the period of time during which the powers mentioned in paragraph 2.1 (b) and (c) may be exercised. The officer should set the minimum period he or she considers necessary to deal with the risk of violence, the carrying of knives or offensive weapons, or terrorism. A direction to extend the period authorised under the powers mentioned in paragraph 2.1(b) may be given only once. Thereafter further use of the powers requires a new authorisation. There is no provision to extend an authorisation of the powers mentioned in paragraph 2.1(c); further use of the powers requires a new authorisation.

13 It is for the authorising officer to determine the geographical area in which the use of the powers is to be authorised. In doing so the officer may wish to take into account factors such as the nature and venue of the anticipated incident, the number of people who may be in the immediate area of any possible incident, their access to surrounding areas and the anticipated level of violence. The officer should not set a geographical area which is wider than that he or she believes necessary for the purpose of preventing anticipated violence, the carrying of knives or offensive weapons, acts of terrorism, or, in the case of section 60AA, the prevention of commission of offences. It is particularly important to ensure that constables exercising such powers are fully aware of where they may be used. If the area

specified is smaller than the whole force area, the officer giving the authorisation should specify either the streets which form the boundary of the area or a divisional boundary within the force area. If the power is to be used in response to a threat or incident that straddles police force areas, an officer from each of the forces concerned will need to give an authorisation.

14 An officer who has authorised the use of powers under section 44 of the Terrorism Act 2000 must take immediate steps to send a copy of the authorisation to the National Joint Unit, Metropolitan Police Special Branch, who will forward it to the Secretary of State. The Secretary of State should be informed of the reasons for the authorisation. The National Joint Unit will inform the force concerned, within 48 hours of the authorisation being made, whether the Secretary of State has confirmed or cancelled or altered the authorisation.

Recording

15 Where a stop and search is conducted by more than one officer the identity of all the officers engaged in the search must be recorded on the record. Nothing prevents an officer who is present but not directly involved in searching from completing the record during the course of the encounter.

16 Where a vehicle has not been allocated a registration number (eg a rally car or a trials motorbike) that part of the requirement under 4.3(iii) does not apply.

17 It is important for monitoring purposes to specify whether the authority for exercising a stop and search power was given under section 60 of the Criminal Justice and Public Order Act 1994, or under section 44(1) or 44(2) of the Terrorism Act 2000.

18 Officers should record the self-defined ethnicity of every person stopped according to the categories used in the 2001 census question listed in Annex B. Respondents should be asked to select one of the five main categories representing broad ethnic groups and then a more specific cultural background from within this group. The ethnic classification should be coded for recording purposes using the coding system in Annex B. An additional "Not stated" box is available but should not be offered to respondents explicitly. Officers should be aware and explain to members of the public, especially where concerns are raised, that this information is required to obtain a true picture of stop and search activity and to help improve ethnic monitoring, tackle discriminatory practice, and promote effective use of the powers. If the person gives what appears to the officer to be an "incorrect" answer (eg a person who appears to be white states that they are black), the officer should record the response that has been given. Officers should also record their own perception of the ethnic background of every person stopped and this must be done by using the PNC/Phoenix classification system. If the "Not stated" category is used the reason for this must be recorded on the form.

19 Arrangements for public scrutiny of records should take account of the right to confidentiality of those stopped and searched. Anonymised forms and/or statistics generated from records should be the focus of the examinations by members of the public.

20 Where an officer engages in conversation which is not pertinent to the actions or whereabouts of the individual (eg does not relate to why the person is there, what they are doing or where they have been or are going) then issuing a form would not meet the criteria set out in paragraph 4.12. Situations designed to impede police activity may arise, for example, in public order situations where individuals engage in dialogue with the officer but the officer does not initiate or engage in contact about the person's individual circumstances.

21 In situations where it is not practicable to provide a written record of the stop or stop and search at that time, the officer should consider providing the person with details of the station to which the person may attend for a record. This may take the form of a simple business card, adding the date of the stop or stop and search.

Annex A Summary of Main Stop and Search Powers

This table relates to stop and search powers only. Individual statutes below may contain other police powers of entry, search and seizure.

Power	Object of Search	Extent of Search	Where Exercisable
Unlawful articles general			
1. Public Stores Act 1875, s6	HM Stores stolen or unlawfully obtained	Persons, vehicles and vessels	Anywhere where the constabulary powers are exercisable
2. Firearms Act 1968, s 47	Firearms	Persons and vehicles	A public place, or anywhere in the case of reasonable suspicion of offences of carrying firearms with criminal intent or trespassing with firearms

Power	Object of Search	Extent of Search	Where Exercisable
3. Misuse of Drugs Act 1971, 23	Controlled drugs	Persons and vehicles	Anywhere
4. Customs and Excise Management Act 1979, s163	Goods: (*a*) on which duty has not been paid; (*b*) being unlawfully removed, imported or exported; (*c*) otherwise liable to forfeiture to HM Customs and Excise	Vehicles and vessels only	Anywhere
5. Aviation Security Act 1982, s 27(1)	Stolen or unlawfully obtained goods	Airport employees and vehicles carrying airport employees or aircraft or any vehicle in a cargo area whether or not carrying an employee	Any designated airport
6. Police and Criminal Evidence Act 1984, s1	Stolen goods; articles for use in certain Theft Act offences; offensive weapons, including bladed or sharply-pointed articles (except folding pocket knives with a bladed cutting edge not exceeding 3 inches); prohibited possession of a category 4 (display grade) firework, any person under 18 in possession of an adult firework in a public place.	Persons and vehicles	Where there is public access
	Criminal Damage: Articles made, adapted or intended for use in destroying or damaging property	Persons and vehicles	Where there is public access
Police and Criminal Evidence Act 1984, s 6(3) (by a constable of the United Kingdom Atomic Energy Authority Constabulary in respect of property owned or controlled by British Nuclear Fuels plc)	HM Stores (in the form of goods and chattels belonging to British Nuclear Fuels plc)	Persons, vehicles and vessels	Anywhere where the constabulary powers are exercisable
7. Sporting events (Control of Alcohol etc.) Act 1985, s7	Intoxicating liquor	Persons, coaches and trains	Designated sports grounds or coaches and trains travelling to or from a designated sporting event

Power	Object of Search	Extent of Search	Where Exercisable
8. Crossbows Act 1987, s4	Crossbows or parts of crossbows (except crossbows with a draw weight of less than 1.4 kilograms)	Persons and vehicles	Anywhere except dwellings
9. Criminal Justice Act 1988, s 139B	Offensive weapons, bladed or sharply pointed article	Persons	School premises
Evidence of game and wildlife offences			
10. Poaching Prevention Act 1862, s2	Game or poaching equipment	Persons and vehicles	A public place
11. Deer Act 1991, s12	Evidence of offences under the Act	Persons and vehicles	Anywhere except dwellings
12. Conservation of Seals Act 1970, s 4	Seals or hunting equipment	Vehicles only	Anywhere
13. Badgers Act 1992, s 11	Evidence of offences under the Act	Persons and vehicles	Anywhere
14. Wildlife and Countryside Act 1981, s 19	Evidence of wildlife offences	Persons and vehicles	Anywhere except dwellings
Other			
15. Terrorism Act 2000, s 43	Evidence of liability to arrest under section 14 of the Act	Persons	Anywhere
16. Terrorism Act 2000, s 44(1)	Articles which could be used for a purpose connected with the commission, preparation or instigation of acts of terrorism	Vehicles, driver and passengers	Anywhere within the area or locality authorized under subsection (1)
17. Terrorism Act 2000, s 44(2)	Articles which could be used for a purpose connected with the commission, preparation or instigation of acts of terrorism	Pedestrians	Anywhere within the area of locality authorised
18. Paragraphs 7 and 8 of Schedule 7 to the Terrorism Act 2000	Anything relevant to determining if a person being examined falls within paragraph 2(1)(a) to (c) of Schedule 5	Persons, vehicles, vessels etc.	Ports and airports
19. Section 60 Criminal Justice and Public Order Act 1994, as amended by s 8 of the Knives Act 1997	Offensive weapons or dangerous instruments to prevent incidents of serious violence or to deal with the carrying of such items	Persons and vehicles	Anywhere within a locality authorised under subsection (1)

ANNEX B SELF-DEFINED ETHNIC CLASSIFICATION CATEGORIES

White W

A. White – British W1
B. White – Irish W2

C. Any other White background W9

Mixed M
D. White and Black Caribbean M1
E. White and Black African M2
F. White and Asian M3
G. Any other Mixed Background M9

Asian/Asian – British A
H. Asian – Indian A1
I. Asian – Pakistani A2
J. Asian – Bangladeshi A3
K. Any other Asian background A9

Black/Black – British B
L. Black – Caribbean B1
M. Black African B2
N. Any other Black background B9

Other O
O. Chinese O1
P. Any other O9

Not Stated NS

ANNEX C SUMMARY OF POWERS OF COMMUNITY SUPPORT OFFICERS TO SEARCH AND SEIZE

The following is a summary of the search and seizure powers that may be exercised by a community support officer (CSO) who has been designated with the relevant powers in accordance with Part 4 of the Police Reform Act 2002.

When exercising any of these powers, a CSO must have regard to any relevant provisions of this Code, including section 3 governing the conduct of searches and the steps to be taken prior to a search.

1. Power to stop and search not requiring consent

Designation	Power conferred	Object of Search	Extent of Search	Where Exercisable
Police Reform Act 2002, Schedule 4, paragraph 15	(a) Terrorism Act 2000, s.44(1)(a) and (d), and 45(2);	Items intended to be used in connection with terrorism.	(a) Vehicles or anything carried in or on the vehicle and anything carried by driver or passenger	Anywhere within area of in locality authorised and in the company and under the supervision of a constable.
	(b) Terrorism Act 2000, s.44 (2)(b) and 45(2).		(b) Anything carried by a pedestrian.	

2. Powers to search requiring the consent of the person and seizure
A CSO may detain a person using reasonable force where necessary as set out in Part 1 of Schedule 4 to the Police Reform Act 2002. If the person has been lawfully detained, the CSO may search the person provided that person gives consent to such a search in relation to the following:

Designation	Powers conferred	Object of Search	Extent of Search	Where Exercisable
Police Reform Act 2002, Schedule 4, paragraph 7A	(a) Criminal Justice and Police Act 2001, s 12(2)	a) Alcohol or a container for alcohol	a) Persons	a) Designated public place
	(b) Confiscation of Alcohol (Young Persons) Act 1997, s1	b) Alcohol	b) Persons under 18 years old	b) Public place

Designation	Powers conferred	Object of Search	Extent of Search	Where Exercisable
(c) Children and Young Persons Act 1933, section 7(3)	(c) Tobacco or cigarette papers	(c) Persons under 16 years old found smoking	c) Public place

3. Powers to search not requiring the consent of the person and seizure

A CSO may detain a person using reasonable force where necessary as set out in Part 1 of Schedule 4 to the Police Reform Act 2002. If the person has been lawfully detained, the CSO may search the person without the need for that person's consent in relation to the following:

Designation	Powers conferred	Object of Search	Extent of Search	Where Exercisable
Police Reform Act 2002, Schedule 4, paragraph 2A	Police and Criminal Evidence Act 1984, s.32	a) Objects that might be used to cause physical injury to the person or the CSO.	Persons made subject to a requirement to wait.	Any place where the requirement to wait has been made.
		b) Items that might be used to assist escape.		

4. Powers to seize without consent

This power applies when drugs are found in the course of any search mentioned above.

Designation	Powers conferred	Object of Seizure	Where Exercisable
Police Reform Act 2002, Schedule 4, paragraph 7B	*Police Reform Act 2002, Schedule 4, paragraph 7B*	Controlled drugs in a person's possession.	Any place where the person is in possession of the drug.

2–1908

B CODE OF PRACTICE FOR SEARCHES OF PREMISES BY POLICE OFFICERS AND THE SEIZURE OF PROPERTY FOUND BY POLICE OFFICERS ON PERSONS OR PREMISES[1]

COMMENCEMENT – TRANSITIONAL ARRANGEMENTS

This Code applies to applications for warrants made after midnight on 31 December 2005and to searches and seizures taking place after midnight on 31 December 2005.

1. This Code of Practice (draft code laid before Parliament on 8 November 2005) is issued under ss 66 and 67 of the Police and Criminal Evidence Act 1984; it is admissible thereunder in evidence and account may be taken by the court of any relevant provision. The Police and Criminal Evidence At 1984 (Codes of Practice) Order 2005, SI 2005/3503 applies to (a) any application for a warrant to search premises made after 31st December 2005; and (b) to any search of premises or seizure of property taking place after midnight on 31st December 2005, notwithstanding that the search or seizure in question may have taken place in pursuance of a warrant granted or applied for before that time.

1 INTRODUCTION

1.1 This Code of Practice deals with police powers to:

- search premises
- seize and retain property found on premises and persons

1.1A These powers may be used to find:

- property and material relating to a crime
- wanted persons
- children who abscond from local authority accommodation where they have been remanded or committed by a court

1.2 A justice of the peace may issue a search warrant granting powers of entry, search and seizure, eg warrants to search for stolen property, drugs, firearms and evidence of serious offences. Police also have powers without a search warrant. The main ones provided by the Police and Criminal Evidence Act 1984 (PACE) include powers to search premises:

- to make an arrest
- after an arrest

1.3 The right to privacy and respect for personal property are key principles of the Human Rights Act 1998. Powers of entry, search and seizure should be fully and clearly justified before use because they may significantly interfere with the occupier's privacy. Officers should consider if the necessary objectives can be met by less intrusive means.

1.4 In all cases, police should:

- exercise their powers courteously and with respect for persons and property
- only use reasonable force when this is considered necessary and proportionate to the circumstances

1.5 If the provisions of PACE and this Code are not observed, evidence obtained from a search may be open to question.

2 GENERAL

2.1 This Code must be readily available at all police stations for consultation by:

- police officers
- police staff
- detained persons
- members of the public

2.2 The Notes for Guidance included are not provisions of this Code.

2.3 This Code applies[1] to searches of premises:

(a) by police for the purposes of an investigation into an alleged offence, with the occupier's[2] consent, other than:

- routine[2] scene of crime searches;
- calls to a fire or burglary made by or on behalf of an occupier or searches following the activation of fire or burglar alarms or discovery of insecure premises;
- searches when paragraph 5.4 applies;
- bomb threat calls;

(b) under powers conferred on police officers by PACE, sections 17, 18 and 32;

(c) undertaken in pursuance of search warrants issued to and executed by constables in accordance with PACE, sections 15 and 16. See Note 2A;

(d) subject to paragraph 2.6, under any other power given to police to enter premises with or without a search warrant for any purpose connected with the investigation into an alleged or suspected offence. See Note 2B.

For the purposes of this Code, 'premises' as defined in PACE, section 23, includes any place, vehicle, vessel, aircraft, hovercraft, tent or movable structure and any offshore installation as defined in the Mineral Workings (Offshore Installations) Act 1971, section 1. See Note 2D

2.4 A person who has not been arrested but is searched during a search of premises should be searched in accordance with Code A. See Note 2C

2.5 This Code does not apply to the exercise of a statutory power to enter premises or to inspect goods, equipment or procedures if the exercise of that power is not dependent on the existence of grounds for suspecting that an offence may have been committed and the person exercising the power has no reasonable grounds for such suspicion.

2.6 This Code does not affect any directions of a search warrant or order, lawfully executed in England or Wales that any item or evidence seized under that warrant or order be handed over to a police force, court, tribunal, or other authority outside England or Wales. For example, warrants and orders issued in Scotland or Northern Ireland, see Note 2B(f) and search warrants issued under the Criminal Justice (International Co-operation) Act 1990, section 7.

2.7 When this Code requires the prior authority or agreement of an officer of at least inspector or superintendent rank, that authority may be given by a sergeant or chief inspector authorised to perform the functions of the higher rank under PACE, section 107.

2.8 Written records required under this Code not made in the search record shall, unless otherwise specified, be made:

- in the recording officer's pocket book ('pocket book' includes any official report book issued to police officers) or
- on forms provided for the purpose

2.9 Nothing in this Code requires the identity of officers, or anyone accompanying them during a search of premises, to be recorded or disclosed:

(a) in the case of enquiries linked to the investigation of terrorism; or

(b) if officers reasonably believe recording or disclosing their names might put them in danger.

In these cases officers should use warrant or other identification numbers and the name of their police station. Police staff should use any identification number provided to them by the police force. See Note 2E

2.10 The 'officer in charge of the search' means the officer assigned specific duties and responsibilities under this Code.Whenever there is a search of premises to which this Code applies one officer must act as the officer in charge of the search. See Note 2F

2.11 In this Code:

(a) 'designated person' means a person other than a police officer, designated under the Police Reform Act 2002, Part 4 who has specified powers and duties of police officers conferred or imposed on them. See Note 2G

(b) any reference to a police officer includes a designated person acting in the exercise or performance of the powers and duties conferred or imposed on them by their designation.

(c) a person authorised to accompany police officers or designated persons in the execution of a warrant has the same powers as a constable in the execution of the warrant and the search and seizure of anything related to the warrant. These powers must be exercised in the company and under the supervision of a police officer. See Note 3C

2.12 If a power conferred on a designated person:

(a) allows reasonable force to be used when exercised by a police officer, a designated person exercising that power has the same entitlement to use force;

(b) includes power to use force to enter any premises, that power is not exercisable by that designated person except:

(i) in the company and under the supervision of a police officer; or

(ii) for the purpose of:

- saving life or limb; or
- preventing serious damage to property.

2.13 Designated persons must have regard to any relevant provisions of the Codes of Practice.

---

1. Subject to the qualification in para 2.5 (formerly 1.3B) below, this Code of Practice applies to trading standards officers who have reasonable grounds for suspecting the commission of an offence and who exercise powers of search and seizure under s 29 of the Consumer Protection Act 1987, in PART VIII: title CONSUMER PROTECTION; see *Dudley Metropolitan Borough Council v Debenhams plc* (1994) 159 JP 18 (which was decided on the wording of this code before the insertion of paragraph 2.5 (formerly 1.3B).

2. The Code applies generally to the search of premises and the occupier of the premises is not deprived of the protection of the Code because at the time he is being viewed by the police as a witness rather than as a suspect. Accordingly his consent should be obtained. Nor can a search which involves prolonged occupation of premises to carry out various activities including forensic investigation be characterised as a "routine scene of crime search" (*R v Sanghera* [2001] 1 Cr App Rep 299, [2001] Crim LR 480, CA).

Notes for guidance

2A PACE sections 15 and 16 apply to all search warrants issued to and executed by constables under any enactment, eg search warrants issued by a:

(a) justice of the peace under the:

- Theft Act 1968, section 26 – stolen property;
- Misuse of Drugs Act 1971, section 23 – controlled drugs;
- PACE, section 8 – evidence of an indictable offence;
- Terrorism Act 2000, Schedule 5, paragraph 1;

(b) judge of the High Court, a Circuit judge, a Recorder or a District Judge under the:

- PACE, Schedule 1;
- Terrorism Act 2000, Schedule 5, paragraph 11.

2B Examples of the other powers in paragraph 2.3(d) include:

(a) Road Traffic Act 1988, section 6E(1) giving police power to enter premises under section 6E(1) to:

(i) under section 4(7) to:

- arrest a person for driving or being in charge of a vehicle when unfit;

(ii) under section 6(6) to:

- require a person to provide a specimen of breath; or
- arrest a person following:

– a positive breath test;
– failure to provide a specimen of breath;

(b) Transport and Works Act 1992, section 30(4) giving police powers to enter premises mirroring the powers in (a) in relation to specified persons working on transport systems to which the Act applies;

(c) Criminal Justice Act 1988, section 139B giving police power to enter and search school premises for offensive weapons, bladed or pointed articles;

(d) Terrorism Act 2000, Schedule 5, paragraphs 3 and 15 empowering a superintendent in urgent cases to give written authority for police to enter and search premises for the purposes of a terrorist investigation;

(e) Explosives Act 1875, section 73(b) empowering a superintendent to give written authority for police to enter premises, examine and search them for explosives;

(f) search warrants and production orders or the equivalent issued in Scotland or Northern Ireland endorsed under the Summary Jurisdiction (Process) Act 1881 or the Petty Sessions (Ireland) Act 1851 respectively for execution in England and Wales.

2C The Criminal Justice Act 1988, section 139B provides that a constable who has reasonable grounds to believe an offence under the Criminal Justice Act 1988, section 139A has or is being committed may enter school premises and search the premises and any persons on the premises for any bladed or pointed article or offensive weapon. Persons may be searched under a warrant issued under the Misuse of Drugs Act 1971, section 23(3) to search premises for drugs or documents only if the warrant specifically authorises the search of persons on the premises.

2D The Immigration Act 1971, Part III and Schedule 2 gives immigration officers powers to enter and search premises, seize and retain property, with and without a search warrant. These are similar to the powers available to police under search warrants issued by a justice of the peace and without a warrant under PACE, sections 17, 18, 19 and 32 except they only apply to specified offences under the Immigration Act 1971 and immigration control powers. For certain types of investigations and enquiries these powers avoid the need for the Immigration Service to rely on police officers becoming directly involved. When exercising these powers, immigration officers are required by the Immigration and Asylum Act 1999, section 145 to have regard to this Code's corresponding provisions. When immigration officers are dealing with persons or property at police stations, police officers should give appropriate assistance to help them discharge their specific duties and responsibilities.

2E The purpose of paragraph 2.9(b) is to protect those involved in serious organised crime investigations or arrests of particularly violent suspects when there is reliable information that those arrested or their associates may threaten or cause harm to the officers or anyone accompanying them during a search of premises. In cases of doubt, an officer of inspector rank or above should be consulted.

2F For the purposes of paragraph 2.10, the officer in charge of the search should normally be the most senior officer present. Some exceptions are:

(a) a supervising officer who attends or assists at the scene of a premises search may appoint an officer of lower rank as officer in charge of the search if that officer is:

  • more conversant with the facts;
  • a more appropriate officer to be in charge of the search;

(b) when all officers in a premises search are the same rank. The supervising officer if available must make sure one of them is appointed officer in charge of the search, otherwise the officers themselves must nominate one of their number as the officer in charge;

(c) a senior officer assisting in a specialist role. This officer need not be regarded as having a general supervisory role over the conduct of the search or be appointed or expected to act as the officer in charge of the search.

Except in (c), nothing in this Note diminishes the role and responsibilities of a supervisory officer who is present at the search or knows of a search taking place.

2G An officer of the rank of inspector or above may direct a designated investigating officer not to wear a uniform for the purposes of a specific operation.

3 SEARCH WARRANTS AND PRODUCTION ORDERS

(a) Before making an application

3.1 When information appears to justify an application, the officer must take reasonable steps to check the information is accurate, recent and not provided maliciously or irresponsibly. An application may not be made on the basis of information from an anonymous source if corroboration has not been sought. See Note 3A

3.2 The officer shall ascertain as specifically as possible the nature of the articles concerned and their location.

3.3 The officer shall make reasonable enquiries to:

(i) establish if:

  • anything is known about the likely occupier of the premises and the nature of the premises themselves;
  • the premises have been searched previously and how recently;

(ii) obtain any other relevant information.

3.4 An application:

(a) to a justice of the peace for a search warrant or to a judge of the High Court, a Circuit judge, a Recorder or a District Judge for a search warrant or production order under

PACE, Schedule 1 must be supported by a signed written authority from an officer of inspector rank or above:

Note: If the case is an urgent application to a justice of the peace and an inspector or above is not readily available, the next most senior officer on duty can give the written authority.

(b) to a circuit judge under the Terrorism Act 2000, Schedule 5 for

- a production order;
- search warrant; or
- an order requiring an explanation of material seized or produced under such a warrant or production order must be supported by a signed written authority from an officer of superintendent rank or above.

3.5 Except in a case of urgency, if there is reason to believe a search might have an adverse effect on relations between the police and the community, the officer in charge shall consult the local police/community liaison officer:

- before the search; or
- in urgent cases, as soon as practicable after the search

(b) Making an application

3.6 A search warrant application must be supported in writing, specifying:

(a) the enactment under which the application is made, see Note 2A;

(b)

  (i) whether the warrant is to authorise entry and search of:

- one set of premises; or
- if the application is under PACE section 8, or Schedule 1, paragraph 12, more than one set of specified premises or all premises occupied or controlled by a specified person, and

  (ii) the premises to be searched;"

(c) the object of the search, see Note 3B;

(d) the grounds for the application, including, when the purpose of the proposed search is to find evidence of an alleged offence, an indication of how the evidence relates to the investigation;

(da) where the application is under PACE section 8, or Schedule 1, paragraph 12 for a single warrant to enter and search:

  (i) more than one set of specified premises, the officer must specify each set of premises which it is desired to enter and search

  (ii) all premises occupied or controlled by a specified person, the officer must specify;

- as many sets of premises which it is desired to enter and search as it is reasonably practicable to specify
- the person who is in occupation or control of those premises and any others which it is desired to search
- why it is necessary to search more premises than those which can be specified
- why it is not reasonably practicable to specify all the premises which it is desired to enter and search

(db) whether an application under PACE section 8 is for a warrant authorising entry and search on more than one occasion, and if so, the officer must state the grounds for this and whether the desired number of entries authorised is unlimited or a specified maximum.

(e) there are no reasonable grounds to believe the material to be sought, when making application to a:

  (i) justice of the peace or a judge of the High Court, a Circuit judge, a Recorder or a District Judge, consists of or includes items subject to legal privilege;

  (ii) justice of the peace, consists of or includes excluded material or special procedure material;

Note: this does not affect the additional powers of seizure in the Criminal Justice and Police Act 2001, Part 2 covered in paragraph 7.7, see Note 3B;

(f) if applicable, a request for the warrant to authorise a person or persons to accompany the officer who executes the warrant, see Note 3C.

3.7 A search warrant application under PACE, Schedule 1, paragraph 12(a), shall if appropriate indicate why it is believed service of notice of an application for a production order may seriously prejudice the investigation. Applications for search warrants under the Terrorism Act 2000, Schedule 5, paragraph 11 must indicate why a production order would not be appropriate.

3.8 If a search warrant application is refused, a further application may not be made for those premises unless supported by additional grounds.

Notes for guidance

3A The identity of an informant need not be disclosed when making an application, but the officer should be prepared to answer any questions the magistrate or judge may have about:

- the accuracy of previous information from that source
- any other related matters

3B The information supporting a search warrant application should be as specific as possible, particularly in relation to the articles or persons being sought and where in the premises it is suspected they may be found. The meaning of 'items subject to legal privilege', 'excluded material' and 'special procedure material' are defined by PACE, sections 10, 11 and 14 respectively.

3C Under PACE, section 16(2), a search warrant may authorise persons other than police officers to accompany the constable who executes the warrant. This includes, eg any suitably qualified or skilled person or an expert in a particular field whose presence is needed to help accurately identify the material sought or to advise where certain evidence is most likely to be found and how it should be dealt with. It does not give them any right to force entry, but it gives them the right to be on the premises during the search and to search for or seize property without the occupier's permission.

4 ENTRY WITHOUT WARRANT – PARTICULAR POWERS

(a) Making an arrest etc
4.1 The conditions under which an officer may enter and search premises without a warrant are set out in PACE, section 17. It should be noted that this section does not create or confer any powers of arrest. See other powers in Note 2B(a).

(b) Search of premises where arrest takes place or the arrested person was immediately before arrest
4.2 When a person has been arrested for an indictable offence, a police officer has power under PACE, section 32 to search the premises where the person was arrested or where the person was immediately before being arrested.

(c) Search of premises occupied or controlled by the arrested person
4.3 The specific powers to search premises occupied or controlled by a person arrested for an indictable offence are set out in PACE, section 18. They may not be exercised, except if section 18 (5) applies, unless an officer of inspector rank or above has given written authority. That authority should only be given when the authorising officer is satisfied the necessary grounds exist. If possible the authorising officer should record the authority on the Notice of Powers and Rights and, subject to paragraph 2.9, sign the Notice. The record of the grounds for the search and the nature of the evidence sought as required by section 18(7) of the Act should be made in:

- the custody record if there is one, otherwise
- the officer's pocket book, or
- the search record

5 SEARCH WITH CONSENT

5.1 Subject to paragraph 5.4, if it is proposed to search premises with the consent of a person entitled to grant entry the consent must, if practicable, be given in writing on the Notice of Powers and Rights before the search. The officer must make any necessary enquiries to be satisfied the person is in a position to give such consent. See Notes 5A and 5B

5.2 Before seeking consent the officer in charge of the search shall state the purpose of the proposed search and its extent. This information must be as specific as possible, particularly regarding the articles or persons being sought and the parts of the premises to be searched. The person concerned must be clearly informed they are not obliged to consent and anything seized may be produced in evidence. If at the time the person is not suspected of an offence, the officer shall say this when stating the purpose of the search.

5.3 An officer cannot enter and search or continue to search premises under paragraph 5.1 if consent is given under duress or withdrawn before the search is completed.

5.4 It is unnecessary to seek consent under paragraphs 5.1 and 5.2 if this would cause disproportionate inconvenience to the person concerned. See Note 5C

Notes for guidance
5A In a lodging house or similar accommodation, every reasonable effort should be made to obtain the consent of the tenant, lodger or occupier. A search should not be made solely on the basis of the landlord's consent unless the tenant, lodger or occupier is unavailable and the matter is urgent.

5B If the intention is to search premises under the authority of a warrant or a power of entry and search without warrant, and the occupier of the premises co-operates in accordance with paragraph 6.4, there is no need to obtain written consent.

5C Paragraph 5.4 is intended to apply when it is reasonable to assume innocent occupiers would agree to, and expect, police to take the proposed action, eg if:

- a suspect has fled the scene of a crime or to evade arrest and it is necessary quickly to check surrounding gardens and readily accessible places to see if the suspect is hiding
- police have arrested someone in the night after a pursuit and it is necessary to make a brief check of gardens along the pursuit route to see if stolen or incriminating articles have been discarded

6 SEARCHING PREMISES – GENERAL CONSIDERATIONS

(a) Time of searches

6.1 Searches made under warrant must be made within three calendar months of the date of the warrant's issue.

6.2 Searches must be made at a reasonable hour unless this might frustrate the purpose of the search.

6.3 When the extent or complexity of a search mean it is likely to take a long time, the officer in charge of the search may consider using the seize and sift powers referred to in section 7.

6.3A A warrant under PACE, section 8 may authorise entry to and search of premises on more than one occasion if, on the application, the justice of the peace is satisfied that it is necessary to authorise multiple entries in order to achieve the purpose for which the warrant is issued. No premises may be entered or searched on any subsequent occasions without the prior written authority of an officer of the rank of inspector who is not involved in the investigation. All other warrants authorise entry on one occasion only.

6.3B Where a warrant under PACE section 8, or Schedule 1, paragraph 12 authorises entry to and search of all premises occupied or controlled by a specified person, no premises which are not specified in the warrant may be entered and searched without the prior written authority of an officer of the rank of inspector who is not involved in the investigation.

(b) Entry other than with consent

6.4 The officer in charge of the search shall first try to communicate with the occupier, or any other person entitled to grant access to the premises, explain the authority under which entry is sought and ask the occupier to allow entry, unless:

(i) the search premises are unoccupied;
(ii) the occupier and any other person entitled to grant access are absent;
(iii) there are reasonable grounds for believing that alerting the occupier or any other person entitled to grant access would frustrate the object of the search or endanger officers or other people.

6.5 Unless sub-paragraph 6.4(iii) applies, if the premises are occupied the officer, subject to paragraph 2.9, shall, before the search begins:

(i) identify him or herself, show their warrant card (if not in uniform) and state the purpose of and grounds for their search;
(ii) identify and introduce any person accompanying the officer on the search (such persons should carry identification for production on request) and briefly describe that person's role in the process.

6.6 Reasonable and proportionate force may be used if necessary to enter premises if the officer in charge of the search is satisfied the premises are those specified in any warrant, or in exercise of the powers described in paragraphs 4.1 to 4.3, and if:

(i) the occupier or any other person entitled to grant access has refused entry;
(ii) it is impossible to communicate with the occupier or any other person entitled to grant access; or
(iii) any of the provisions of paragraph 6.4 apply.

(c) Notice of Powers and Rights

6.7 If an officer conducts a search to which this Code applies the officer shall, unless it is impracticable to do so, provide the occupier with a copy of a Notice in a standard format:

(i) specifying if the search is made under warrant, with consent, or in the exercise of the powers described in paragraphs 4.1 to 4.3. Note: the notice format shall provide for authority or consent to be indicated, see paragraphs 4.3 and 5.1;
(ii) summarising the extent of the powers of search and seizure conferred by PACE;
(iii) explaining the rights of the occupier, and the owner of the property seized;
(iv) explaining compensation may be payable in appropriate cases for damages caused entering and searching premises, and giving the address to send a compensation application, see Note 6A;

(v)   stating this Code is available at any police station.

6.8   If the occupier is:

- present, copies of the Notice and warrant shall, if practicable, be given to them before the search begins, unless the officer in charge of the search reasonably believes this would frustrate the object of the search or endanger officers or other people
- not present, copies of the Notice and warrant shall be left in a prominent place on the premises or appropriate part of the premises and endorsed, subject to paragraph 2.9 with the name of the officer in charge of the search, the date and time of the search

The warrant shall be endorsed to show this has been done.

(d)   Conduct of searches

6.9   Premises may be searched only to the extent necessary to achieve the object of the search, having regard to the size and nature of whatever is sought.

6.9A   A search may not continue under:

- a warrant's authority once all the things specified in that warrant have been found
- any other power once the object of that search has been achieved

6.9B   No search may continue once the officer in charge of the search is satisfied whatever is being sought is not on the premises. See Note 6B. This does not prevent a further search of the same premises if additional grounds come to light supporting a further application for a search warrant or exercise or further exercise of another power. For example, when, as a result of new information, it is believed articles previously not found or additional articles are on the premises.

6.10   Searches must be conducted with due consideration for the property and privacy of the occupier and with no more disturbance than necessary. Reasonable force may be used only when necessary and proportionate because the co-operation of the occupier cannot be obtained or is insufficient for the purpose. See Note 6C

6.11   A friend, neighbour or other person must be allowed to witness the search if the occupier wishes unless the officer in charge of the search has reasonable grounds for believing the presence of the person asked for would seriously hinder the investigation or endanger officers or other people. A search need not be unreasonably delayed for this purpose. A record of the action taken should be made on the premises search record including the grounds for refusing the occupier's request.

6.12   A person is not required to be cautioned prior to being asked questions that are solely necessary for the purpose of furthering the proper and effective conduct of a search, see Code C, paragraph 10.1(c). For example, questions to discover the occupier of specified premises, to find a key to open a locked drawer or cupboard or to otherwise seek co-operation during the search or to determine if a particular item is liable to be seized.

6.12A   If questioning goes beyond what is necessary for the purpose of the exemption in Code C, the exchange is likely to constitute an interview as defined by Code C, paragraph 11.1A and would require the associated safeguards included in Code C, section 10.

(e)   Leaving premises

6.13   If premises have been entered by force, before leaving the officer in charge of the search must make sure they are secure by:

- arranging for the occupier or their agent to be present
- any other appropriate means

(f)   Searches under PACE Schedule 1 or the Terrorism Act 2000, Schedule 5

6.14   An officer shall be appointed as the officer in charge of the search, see paragraph 2.10, in respect of any search made under a warrant issued under PACE Act 1984, Schedule 1 or the Terrorism Act 2000, Schedule 5. They are responsible for making sure the search is conducted with discretion and in a manner that causes the least possible disruption to any business or other activities carried out on the premises.

6.15   Once the officer in charge of the search is satisfied material may not be taken from the premises without their knowledge, they shall ask for the documents or other records concerned. The officer in charge of the search may also ask to see the index to files held on the premises, and the officers conducting the search may inspect any files which, according to the index, appear to contain the material sought. A more extensive search of the premises may be made only if:

- the person responsible for them refuses to:
  - produce the material sought, or
  - allow access to the index
- it appears the index is:
  - inaccurate, or
  - incomplete
- for any other reason the officer in charge of the search has reasonable grounds for believing such a search is necessary in order to find the material sought

Notes for guidance

6A Whether compensation is appropriate depends on the circumstances in each case. Compensation for damage caused when effecting entry is unlikely to be appropriate if the search was lawful, and the force used can be shown to be reasonable, proportionate and necessary to effect entry. If the wrong premises are searched by mistake everything possible should be done at the earliest opportunity to allay any sense of grievance and there should normally be a strong presumption in favour of paying compensation.

6B It is important that, when possible, all those involved in a search are fully briefed about any powers to be exercised and the extent and limits within which it should be conducted.

6C In all cases the number of officers and other persons involved in executing the warrant should be determined by what is reasonable and necessary according to the particular circumstances.

7 SEIZURE AND RETENTION OF PROPERTY

(a) Seizure

7.1 Subject to paragraph 7.2, an officer who is searching any person or premises under any statutory power or with the consent of the occupier may seize anything:

(a) covered by a warrant

(b) the officer has reasonable grounds for believing is evidence of an offence or has been obtained in consequence of the commission of an offence but only if seizure is necessary to prevent the items being concealed, lost, disposed of, altered, damaged, destroyed or tampered with

(c) covered by the powers in the Criminal Justice and Police Act 2001, Part 2 allowing an officer to seize property from persons or premises and retain it for sifting or examination elsewhere See Note 7B

7.2 No item may be seized which an officer has reasonable grounds for believing to be subject to legal privilege, as defined in PACE, section 10, other than under the Criminal Justice and Police Act 2001, Part 2.

7.3 Officers must be aware of the provisions in the Criminal Justice and Police Act 2001, section 59, allowing for applications to a judicial authority for the return of property seized and the subsequent duty to secure in section 60, see paragraph 7.12(iii).

7.4 An officer may decide it is not appropriate to seize property because of an explanation from the person holding it but may nevertheless have reasonable grounds for believing it was obtained in consequence of an offence by some person. In these circumstances, the officer should identify the property to the holder, inform the holder of their suspicions and explain the holder may be liable to civil or criminal proceedings if they dispose of, alter or destroy the property.

7.5 An officer may arrange to photograph, image or copy, any document or other article they have the power to seize in accordance with paragraph 7.1. This is subject to specific restrictions on the examination, imaging or copying of certain property seized under the Criminal Justice and Police Act 2001, Part 2. An officer must have regard to their statutory obligation to retain an original document or other article only when a photograph or copy is not sufficient.

7.6 If an officer considers information stored in any electronic form and accessible from the premises could be used in evidence, they may require the information to be produced in a form:

• which can be taken away and in which it is visible and legible; or
• from which it can readily be produced in a visible and legible form

(b) Criminal Justice and Police Act 2001: Specific procedures for seize and sift powers

7.7 The Criminal Justice and Police Act 2001, Part 2 gives officers limited powers to seize property from premises or persons so they can sift or examine it elsewhere. Officers must be careful they only exercise these powers when it is essential and they do not remove any more material than necessary. The removal of large volumes of material, much of which may not ultimately be retainable, may have serious implications for the owners, particularly when they are involved in business or activities such as journalism or the provision of medical services. Officers must carefully consider if removing copies or images of relevant material or data would be a satisfactory alternative to removing originals. When originals are taken, officers must be prepared to facilitate the provision of copies or images for the owners when reasonably practicable. See Note 7C

7.8 Property seized under the Criminal Justice and Police Act 2001, sections 50 or 51 must be kept securely and separately from any material seized under other powers. An examination under section 53 to determine which elements may be retained must be carried out at the earliest practicable time, having due regard to the desirability of allowing the person from whom the property was seized, or a person with an interest in the property, an opportunity of being present or represented at the examination.

7.8A All reasonable steps should be taken to accommodate an interested person's request to be present, provided the request is reasonable and subject to the need to prevent harm to, interference with, or unreasonable delay to the investigatory process. If an examination proceeds in the absence of an interested person who asked to attend or their representative, the officer who exercised the relevant seizure power must give that person a written notice of why the examination was carried out in those circumstances. If it is necessary for security reasons or to maintain confidentiality officers may exclude interested persons from decryption or other processes which facilitate the examination but do not form part of it. See Note 7D

7.9　It is the responsibility of the officer in charge of the investigation to make sure property is returned in accordance with sections 53 to 55. Material which there is no power to retain must be:

- separated from the rest of the seized property
- returned as soon as reasonably practicable after examination of all the seized property

7.9A　Delay is only warranted if very clear and compelling reasons exist, eg the:

- unavailability of the person to whom the material is to be returned
- need to agree a convenient time to return a large volume of material

7.9B　Legally privileged, excluded or special procedure material which cannot be retained must be returned:

- as soon as reasonably practicable
- without waiting for the whole examination

7.9C　As set out in section 58, material must be returned to the person from whom it was seized, except when it is clear some other person has a better right to it. See Note 7E

7.10　When an officer involved in the investigation has reasonable grounds to believe a person with a relevant interest in property seized under section 50 or 51 intends to make an application under section 59 for the return of any legally privileged, special procedure or excluded material, the officer in charge of the investigation should be informed as soon as practicable and the material seized should be kept secure in accordance with section 61. See Note 7C

7.11　The officer in charge of the investigation is responsible for making sure property is properly secured. Securing involves making sure the property is not examined, copied, imaged or put to any other use except at the request, or with the consent, of the applicant or in accordance with the directions of the appropriate judicial authority. Any request, consent or directions must be recorded in writing and signed by both the initiator and the officer in charge of the investigation. See Notes 7F and 7G

7.12　When an officer exercises a power of seizure conferred by sections 50 or 51 they shall provide the occupier of the premises or the person from whom the property is being seized with a written notice:

(i)　specifying what has been seized under the powers conferred by that section;
(ii)　specifying the grounds for those powers;
(iii)　setting out the effect of sections 59 to 61 covering the grounds for a person with a relevant interest in seized property to apply to a judicial authority for its return and the duty of officers to secure property in certain circumstances when an application is made;
(iv)　specifying the name and address of the person to whom:

- notice of an application to the appropriate judicial authority in respect of any of the seized property must be given;
- an application may be made to allow attendance at the initial examination of the property.

7.13　If the occupier is not present but there is someone in charge of the premises, the notice shall be given to them. If no suitable person is available, so the notice will easily be found it should either be:

- left in a prominent place on the premises
- attached to the exterior of the premises

(c) Retention

7.14　Subject to paragraph 7.15, anything seized in accordance with the above provisions may be retained only for as long as is necessary. It may be retained, among other purposes:

(i)　for use as evidence at a trial for an offence;
(ii)　to facilitate the use in any investigation or proceedings of anything to which it is inextricably linked, see Note 7H;
(iii)　for forensic examination or other investigation in connection with an offence;
(iv)　in order to establish its lawful owner when there are reasonable grounds for believing it has been stolen or obtained by the commission of an offence.

7.15　Property shall not be retained under paragraph 7.14(i), (ii) or (iii) if a copy or image would be sufficient.

(d) Rights of owners etc

7.16 If property is retained, the person who had custody or control of it immediately before seizure must, on request, be provided with a list or description of the property within a reasonable time.

7.17 That person or their representative must be allowed supervised access to the property to examine it or have it photographed or copied, or must be provided with a photograph or copy, in either case within a reasonable time of any request and at their own expense, unless the officer in charge of an investigation has reasonable grounds for believing this would:

(i)   prejudice the investigation of any offence or criminal proceedings; or
(ii)   lead to the commission of an offence by providing access to unlawful material such as pornography;

A record of the grounds shall be made when access is denied.

Notes for guidance

7A   Any person claiming property seized by the police may apply to a magistrates' court under the Police (Property) Act 1897 for its possession and should, if appropriate, be advised of this procedure.

7B   The powers of seizure conferred by PACE, sections 18(2) and 19(3) extend to the seizure of the whole premises when it is physically possible to seize and retain the premises in their totality and practical considerations make seizure desirable. For example, police may remove premises such as tents, vehicles or caravans to a police station for the purpose of preserving evidence.

7C   Officers should consider reaching agreement with owners and/or other interested parties on the procedures for examining a specific set of property, rather than awaiting the judicial authority's determination. Agreement can sometimes give a quicker and more satisfactory route for all concerned and minimise costs and legal complexities.

7D   What constitutes a relevant interest in specific material may depend on the nature of that material and the circumstances in which it is seized. Anyone with a reasonable claim to ownership of the material and anyone entrusted with its safe keeping by the owner should be considered.

7E   Requirements to secure and return property apply equally to all copies, images or other material created because of seizure of the original property.

7F   The mechanics of securing property vary according to the circumstances; "bagging up", i.e. placing material in sealed bags or containers and strict subsequent control of access is the appropriate procedure in many cases.

7G   When material is seized under the powers of seizure conferred by PACE, the duty to retain it under the Code of Practice issued under the Criminal Procedure and Investigations Act 1996 is subject to the provisions on retention of seized material in PACE, section 22.

7H   Paragraph 7.14 (ii) applies if inextricably linked material is seized under the Criminal Justice and Police Act 2001, sections 50 or 51. Inextricably linked material is material it is not reasonably practicable to separate from other linked material without prejudicing the use of that other material in any investigation or proceedings. For example, it may not be possible to separate items of data held on computer disk without damaging their evidential integrity. Inextricably linked material must not be examined, imaged, copied or used for any purpose other than for proving the source and/or integrity of the linked material.

8 ACTION AFTER SEARCHES

8.1 If premises are searched in circumstances where this Code applies, unless the exceptions in paragraph 2.3(a) apply, on arrival at a police station the officer in charge of the search shall make or have made a record of the search, to include:

(i)   the address of the searched premises;
(ii)   the date, time and duration of the search;
(iii)   the authority used for the search:

-   if the search was made in exercise of a statutory power to search premises without warrant, the power which was used for the search:
-   if the search was made under a warrant or with written consent;

     – a copy of the warrant and the written authority to apply for it, see paragraph 3.4; or
     – the written consent;

     shall be appended to the record or the record shall show the location of the copy warrant or consent.

(iv)   subject to paragraph 2.9, the names of:

-   the officer(s) in charge of the search;
-   all other officers and any authorised persons who conducted the search;

(v)   the names of any people on the premises if they are known;
(vi)   any grounds for refusing the occupier's request to have someone present during the search, see paragraph 6.11;

(vii) a list of any articles seized or the location of a list and, if not covered by a warrant, the grounds for their seizure;

(viii) whether force was used, and the reason;

(ix) details of any damage caused during the search, and the circumstances;

(x) if applicable, the reason it was not practicable;

    (a) to give the occupier a copy of the Notice of Powers and Rights, see paragraph 6.7;

    (b) before the search to give the occupier a copy of the Notice, see paragraph 6.8;

(xi) when the occupier was not present, the place where copies of the Notice of Powers and Rights and search warrant were left on the premises, see paragraph 6.8.

8.2 On each occasion when premises are searched under warrant, the warrant authorising the search on that occasion shall be endorsed to show:

(i) if any articles specified in the warrant were found and the address where found;

(ii) if any other articles were seized;

(iii) the date and time it was executed and if present, the name of the occupier or if the occupier is not present the name of the person in charge of the premises;

(iv) subject to paragraph 2.9, the names of the officers who executed it and any authorised persons who accompanied them;

(v) if a copy, together with a copy of the Notice of Powers and Rights was:

- handed to the occupier; or
- endorsed as required by paragraph 6.8; and left on the premises and where.

8.3 Any warrant shall be returned within three calendar months of its issue or sooner on completion of the search(es) authorised by that warrant, if it was issued by a:

- justice of the peace, to the designated officer for the local justice area in which the justice was acting when issuing the warrant; or
- judge, to the appropriate officer of the court concerned

9 SEARCH REGISTERS

9.1 A search register will be maintained at each sub-divisional or equivalent police station. All search records required under paragraph 8.1 shall be made, copied, or referred to in the register. See Note 9A

Note for guidance

9A Paragraph 9.1 also applies to search records made by immigration officers. In these cases, a search register must also be maintained at an immigration office. See also Note 2D

2–1916

CODE C CODE OF PRACTICE FOR THE DETENTION, TREATMENT AND QUESTIONING OF PERSONS BY POLICE OFFICERS[1]

COMMENCEMENT – TRANSITIONAL ARRANGEMENTS

This Code applies to people in police detention after midnight on 24 July 2006, notwithstanding that their period of detention may have commenced before that time.

---

1. This Code of Practice (draft code laid before Parliament on 14 June 2006) is issued under ss 66 and 67 of the Police and Criminal Evidence Act 1984; it is admissible thereunder in evidence and account may be taken by the court of any relevant provision. The Police and Criminal Evidence Act 1984 (Code of Practice C and Code of Practice H) Order 2006, SI 2006/1938 applies to any person in police detention, other than someone in police detention following arrest under s 41 of the Terrorism Act 2000, after midnight on 24 July 2006, notwithstanding that his period of detention may have commenced before that time .

1 GENERAL

1.1 All persons in custody must be dealt with expeditiously, and released as soon as the need for detention no longer applies.

1.1A A custody officer must perform the functions in this Code as soon as practicable. A custody officer will not be in breach of this Code if delay is justifiable and reasonable steps are taken to prevent unnecessary delay. The custody record shall show when a delay has occurred and the reason. See *Note 1H*

1.2 This Code of Practice must be readily available at all police stations for consultation by:

- police officers
- police staff
- detained persons
- members of the public.

1.3 The provisions of this Code:

- include the *Annexes*
- do not include the *Notes for Guidance*.

1.4 If an officer has any suspicion, or is told in good faith, that a person of any age may be mentally disordered or otherwise mentally vulnerable, in the absence of clear evidence to dispel that suspicion, the person shall be treated as such for the purposes of this Code. See *Note 1G*

1.5 If anyone appears to be under 17, they shall be treated as a juvenile for the purposes of this Code in the absence of clear evidence that they are older.

1.6 If a person appears to be blind, seriously visually impaired, deaf, unable to read or speak or has difficulty orally because of a speech impediment, they shall be treated as such for the purposes of this Code in the absence of clear evidence to the contrary.

1.7 'The appropriate adult' means, in the case of a:

(a) juvenile:

    (i) the parent, guardian or, if the juvenile is in local authority or voluntary organisation care, or is otherwise being looked after under the Children Act 1989, a person representing that authority or organisation;

    (ii) a social worker of a local authority social services department;

    (iii) failing these, some other responsible adult aged 18 or over who is not a police officer or employed by the police.

(b) person who is mentally disordered or mentally vulnerable: See Note 1D

    (iv) a relative, guardian or other person responsible for their care or custody;

    (v) someone experienced in dealing with mentally disordered or mentally vulnerable people but who is not a police officer or employed by the police;

    (vi) failing these, some other responsible adult aged 18 or over who is not a police officer or employed by the police.

1.8 If this Code requires a person be given certain information, they do not have to be given it if at the time they are incapable of understanding what is said, are violent or may become violent or in urgent need of medical attention, but they must be given it as soon as practicable.

1.9 References to a custody officer include any:

- police officer; or
- designated staff custody officer acting in the exercise or performance of the powers and duties conferred or imposed on them by their designation,

performing the functions of a custody officer. See *Note 1J*.

1.9A When this Code requires the prior authority or agreement of an officer of at least inspector or superintendent rank, that authority may be given by a sergeant or chief inspector authorised to perform the functions of the higher rank under the Police and Criminal Evidence Act 1984 (PACE), section 107.

1.10 Subject to *paragraph 1.12*, this Code applies to people in custody at police stations in England and Wales, whether or not they have been arrested, and to those removed to a police station as a place of safety under the Mental Health Act 1983, sections 135 and 136. *Section 15* applies solely to people in police detention, e.g. those brought to a police station under arrest or arrested at a police station for an offence after going there voluntarily.

1.11 People detained under the Terrorism Act 2000, Schedule 8 and section 41 and other provisions of that Act are not subject to any part of this Code. Such persons are subject to the Code of Practice for detention, treatment and questioning of persons by police officers detained under that Act.

1.12 This Code's provisions do not apply to people in custody:

(i) arrested on warrants issued in Scotland by officers under the Criminal Justice and Public Order Act 1994, section 136(2), or arrested or detained without warrant by officers from a police force in Scotland under section 137(2). In these cases, police powers and duties and the person's rights and entitlements whilst at a police station in England or Wales are the same as those in Scotland;

(ii) arrested under the Immigration and Asylum Act 1999, section 142(3) in order to have their fingerprints taken;

(iii) whose detention is authorised by an immigration officer under the Immigration Act 1971;

(iv) who are convicted or remanded prisoners held in police cells on behalf of the Prison Service under the Imprisonment (Temporary Provisions) Act 1980;

(v) not used

(vi) detained for searches under stop and search powers except as required by Code A.

The provisions on conditions of detention and treatment in *sections 8* and *9* must be considered as the minimum standards of treatment for such detainees.

1.13 In this Code:

(a) 'designated person' means a person other than a police officer, designated under the Police Reform Act 2002, Part 4 who has specified powers and duties of police officers conferred or imposed on them;

(*b*) reference to a police officer includes a designated person acting in the exercise or performance of the powers and duties conferred or imposed on them by their designation.

1.14 Designated persons are entitled to use reasonable force as follows:-

(*a*) when exercising a power conferred on them which allows a police officer exercising that power to use reasonable force, a designated person has the same entitlement to use force; and

(*b*) at other times when carrying out duties conferred or imposed on them that also entitle them to use reasonable force, for example:

- when at a police station carrying out the duty to keep detainees for whom they are responsible under control and to assist any other police officer or designated person to keep any detainee under control and to prevent their escape.
- when securing, or assisting any other police officer or designated person in securing, the detention of a person at a police station.
- when escorting, or assisting any other police officer or designated person in escorting, a detainee within a police station.
- for the purpose of saving life or limb; or
- preventing serious damage to property.

1.15 Nothing in this Code prevents the custody officer, or other officer given custody of the detainee, from allowing police staff who are not designated persons to carry out individual procedures or tasks at the police station if the law allows. However, the officer remains responsible for making sure the procedures and tasks are carried out correctly in accordance with the Codes of Practice. Any such person must be:

(*a*) a person employed by a police authority maintaining a police force and under the control and direction of the Chief Officer of that force;

(*b*) employed by a person with whom a police authority has a contract for the provision of services relating to persons arrested or otherwise in custody.

1.16 Designated persons and other police staff must have regard to any relevant provisions of the Codes of Practice.

1.17 References to pocket books include any official report book issued to police officers or other police staff.

Notes for guidance

1A Although certain sections of this Code apply specifically to people in custody at police stations, those there voluntarily to assist with an investigation should be treated with no less consideration, e.g. offered refreshments at appropriate times, and enjoy an absolute right to obtain legal advice or communicate with anyone outside the police station.

1B A person, including a parent or guardian, should not be an appropriate adult if they:

- *are*
  - *suspected of involvement in the offence*
  - *the victim*
  - *a witness*
  - *involved in the investigation*

- *received admissions prior to attending to act as the appropriate adult.*

Note: If a juvenile's parent is estranged from the juvenile, they should not be asked to act as the appropriate adult if the juvenile expressly and specifically objects to their presence.

1C If a juvenile admits an offence to, or in the presence of, a social worker or member of a youth offending team other than during the time that person is acting as the juvenile's appropriate adult, another appropriate adult should be appointed in the interest of fairness.

1D In the case of people who are mentally disordered or otherwise mentally vulnerable, it may be more satisfactory if the appropriate adult is someone experienced or trained in their care rather than a relative lacking such qualifications. But if the detainee prefers a relative to a better qualified stranger or objects to a particular person their wishes should, if practicable, be respected.

1E A detainee should always be given an opportunity, when an appropriate adult is called to the police station, to consult privately with a solicitor in the appropriate adult's absence if they want. An appropriate adult is not subject to legal privilege.

1F A solicitor or independent custody visitor (formerly a lay visitor) present at the police station in that capacity may not be the appropriate adult.

1G 'Mentally vulnerable' applies to any detainee who, because of their mental state or capacity, may not understand the significance of what is said, of questions or of their replies. 'Mental disorder' is defined in the Mental Health Act 1983, section 1(2) as 'mental illness, arrested or incomplete development of mind, psychopathic disorder and any other disorder or disability of mind'. When the custody officer has any doubt about the mental state or capacity of a detainee, that detainee should be treated as mentally vulnerable and an appropriate adult called.

1H Paragraph 1.1A is intended to cover delays which may occur in processing detainees e.g. if:

- a large number of suspects are brought into the station simultaneously to be placed in custody;
- interview rooms are all being used;
- there are difficulties contacting an appropriate adult, solicitor or interpreter.

1I The custody officer must remind the appropriate adult and detainee about the right to legal advice and record any reasons for waiving it in accordance with section 6.

1J The designation of police staff custody officers applies only in police areas where an order commencing the provisions of the Police Reform Act 2002, section 38 and Schedule 4A, for designating police staff custody officers is in effect.

1K This Code does not affect the principle that all citizens have a duty to help police officers to prevent crime and discover offenders. This is a civic rather than a legal duty; but when a police officer is trying to discover whether, or by whom, an offence has been committed he is entitled to question any person from whom he thinks useful information can be obtained, subject to the restrictions imposed by this Code. A person's declaration that he is unwilling to reply does not alter this entitlement.

2 CUSTODY RECORDS

2.1A When a person is brought to a police station:

- under arrest
- is arrested at the police station having attended there voluntarily or
- attends a police station to answer bail

they should be brought before the custody officer as soon as practicable after their arrival at the station or, if appropriate, following arrest after attending the police station voluntarily. This applies to designated and non-designated police stations. A person is deemed to be "at a police station" for these purposes if they are within the boundary of any building or enclosed yard which forms part of that police station.

2.1 A separate custody record must be opened as soon as practicable for each person brought to a police station under arrest or arrested at the station having gone there voluntarily or attending a police station in answer to street bail. All information recorded under this Code must be recorded as soon as practicable in the custody record unless otherwise specified. Any audio or video recording made in the custody area is not part of the custody record.

2.2 If any action requires the authority of an officer of a specified rank, subject to *paragraph 2.6A*, their name and rank must be noted in the custody record.

2.3 The custody officer is responsible for the custody record's accuracy and completeness and for making sure the record or copy of the record accompanies a detainee if they are transferred to another police station. The record shall show the:

- time and reason for transfer;
- time a person is released from detention.

2.4 A solicitor or appropriate adult must be permitted to consult a detainee's custody record as soon as practicable after their arrival at the station and at any other time whilst the person is detained. Arrangements for this access must be agreed with the custody officer and may not unreasonably interfere with the custody officer's duties.

2.4A When a detainee leaves police detention or is taken before a court they, their legal representative or appropriate adult shall be given, on request, a copy of the custody record as soon as practicable. This entitlement lasts for 12 months after release.

2.5 The detainee, appropriate adult or legal representative shall be permitted to inspect the original custody record after the detainee has left police detention provided they give reasonable notice of their request. Any such inspection shall be noted in the custody record.

2.6 Subject to *paragraph 2.6A*, all entries in custody records must be timed and signed by the maker. Records entered on computer shall be timed and contain the operator's identification.

2.6A Nothing in this Code requires the identity of officers or other police staff to be recorded or disclosed:

(*a*) not used;
(*b*) if the officer or police staff reasonably believe recording or disclosing their name might put them in danger.

In these cases, they shall use their warrant or other identification numbers and the name of their police station. See *Note 2A*

2.7 The fact and time of any detainee's refusal to sign a custody record, when asked in accordance with this Code, must be recorded.

Note for guidance

2A The purpose of paragraph 2.6A(b) is to protect those involved in serious organised crime investigations or arrests of particularly violent suspects when there is reliable information that those arrested or their associates may threaten or cause harm to those involved. In cases of doubt, an officer of inspector rank or above should be consulted.

3 INITIAL ACTION

(a) Detained persons – normal procedure

3.1 When a person is brought to a police station under arrest or arrested at the station having gone there voluntarily, the custody officer must make sure the person is told clearly about the following continuing rights which may be exercised at any stage during the period in custody:

(i)   the right to have someone informed of their arrest as in *section 5*;
(ii)   the right to consult privately with a solicitor and that free independent legal advice is available;
(iii) the right to consult these Codes of Practice. See *Note 3D*

3.2 The detainee must also be given:

- a written notice setting out:
  - the above three rights;
  - the arrangements for obtaining legal advice;
  - the right to a copy of the custody record as in *paragraph 2.4A*;
  - the caution in the terms prescribed in *section 10*.

- an additional written notice briefly setting out their entitlements while in custody, see *Notes 3A* and *3B*.

Note: The detainee shall be asked to sign the custody record to acknowledge receipt of these notices. Any refusal must be recorded on the custody record.

3.3 A citizen of an independent Commonwealth country or a national of a foreign country, including the Republic of Ireland, must be informed as practicable about their rights of communication with their High Commission, Embassy or Consulate. See *section 7*

3.4 The custody officer shall:

- record the offence(s) that the detainee has been arrested for and the reason(s) for the arrest on the custody record. See *paragraph 10.3* and *Code G paragraphs 2.2* and *4.3*.
- note on the custody record any comment the detainee makes in relation to the arresting officer's account but shall not invite comment. If the arresting officer is not physically present when the detainee is brought to a police station, the arresting officer's account must be made available to the custody officer remotely or by a third party on the arresting officer's behalf. If the custody officer authorises a person's detention the detainee must be informed of the grounds as soon as practicable and before they are questioned about any offence;
- note any comment the detainee makes in respect of the decision to detain them but shall not invite comment;
- not put specific questions to the detainee regarding their involvement in any offence, nor in respect of any comments they may make in response to the arresting officer's account or the decision to place them in detention. Such an exchange is likely to constitute an interview as in *paragraph 11.1A* and require the associated safeguards in *section 11*.

See *paragraph 11.13* in respect of unsolicited comments.

3.5 The custody officer shall:

(a) ask the detainee, whether at this time, they:

(i)   would like legal advice, see *paragraph 6.5*;
(iii)   want someone informed of their detention, see *section 5*;

(b) ask the detainee to sign the custody record to confirm their decisions in respect of (a);

(c) determine whether the detainee:

(iii)   is, or might be, in need of medical treatment or attention, see *section 9*;
(iv)   requires:

- an appropriate adult;
- help to check documentation;
- an interpreter;

(d) record the decision in respect of (c).

3.6 When determining these needs the custody officer is responsible for initiating an assessment to consider whether the detainee is likely to present specific risks to custody staff or themselves. Such assessments should always include a check on the Police National Computer, to be carried out as soon as practicable, to identify any risks highlighted in relation to the detainee. Although such assessments are primarily the custody officer's responsibility, it may be necessary for them to consult and involve others, e.g. the arresting officer or an appropriate health care professional, see *paragraph 9.13*. Reasons for delaying the initiation or completion of the assessment must be recorded.

3.7 Chief Officers should ensure that arrangements for proper and effective risk assessments required by *paragraph 3.6* are implemented in respect of all detainees at police stations in their area.

3.8 Risk assessments must follow a structured process which clearly defines the categories of risk to be considered and the results must be incorporated in the detainee's custody record. The custody officer is responsible for making sure those responsible for the detainee's custody are appropriately briefed about the risks. If no specific risks are identified by the assessment, that should be noted in the custody record. See *Note 3E* and *paragraph 9.14*

3.9 The custody officer is responsible for implementing the response to any specific risk assessment, e.g.:

- reducing opportunities for self harm;
- calling a health care professional;
- increasing levels of monitoring or observation.

3.10 Risk assessment is an ongoing process and assessments must always be subject to review if circumstances change.

3.11 If video cameras are installed in the custody area, notices shall be prominently displayed showing cameras are in use. Any request to have video cameras switched off shall be refused.

(b) Detained persons – special groups

3.12 If the detainee appears deaf or there is doubt about their hearing or speaking ability or ability to understand English, and the custody officer cannot establish effective communication, the custody officer must, as soon as practicable, call an interpreter for assistance in the action under *paragraphs 3.1–3.5*. See *section 13*

3.13 If the detainee is a juvenile, the custody officer must, if it is practicable, ascertain the identity of a person responsible for their welfare. That person:

- may be:
  - the parent or guardian;
  - if the juvenile is in local authority or voluntary organisation care, or is otherwise being looked after under the Children Act 1989, a person appointed by that authority or organisation to have responsibility for the juvenile's welfare;
  - any other person who has, for the time being, assumed responsibility for the juvenile's welfare.
- must be informed as soon as practicable that the juvenile has been arrested, why they have been arrested and where they are detained. This right is in addition to the juvenile's right in *section 5* not to be held incommunicado. See *Note 3C*

3.14 If a juvenile is known to be subject to a court order under which a person or organisation is given any degree of statutory responsibility to supervise or otherwise monitor them, reasonable steps must also be taken to notify that person or organisation (the 'responsible officer'). The responsible officer will normally be a member of a Youth Offending Team, except for a curfew order which involves electronic monitoring when the contractor providing the monitoring will normally be the responsible officer.

3.15 If the detainee is a juvenile, mentally disordered or otherwise mentally vulnerable, the custody officer must, as soon as practicable:

- inform the appropriate adult, who in the case of a juvenile may or may not be a person responsible for their welfare, as in *paragraph 3.13*, of:
  - the grounds for their detention;
  - their whereabouts.
- ask the adult to come to the police station to see the detainee.

3.16 It is imperative that a mentally disordered or otherwise mentally vulnerable person, detained under the Mental Health Act 1983, section 136, be assessed as soon as possible. If that assessment is to take place at the police station, an approved social worker and a registered medical practitioner shall be called to the station as soon as possible in order to interview and examine the detainee. Once the detainee has been interviewed, examined and suitable arrangements made for their treatment or care, they can no longer be detained under section 136. A detainee must be immediately discharged from detention under section 136 if a registered medical practitioner, having examined them, concludes they are not mentally disordered within the meaning of the Act.

3.17 If the appropriate adult is:

- already at the police station, the provisions of *paragraphs 3.1 to 3.5* must be complied with in the appropriate adult's presence;
- not at the station when these provisions are complied with, they must be complied with again in the presence of the appropriate adult when they arrive.

3.18 The detainee shall be advised that:

- the duties of the appropriate adult include giving advice and assistance;
- they can consult privately with the appropriate adult at any time.

3.19 If the detainee, or appropriate adult on the detainee's behalf, asks for a solicitor to be called to give legal advice, the provisions of *section 6* apply.

3.20 If the detainee is blind, seriously visually impaired or unable to read, the custody officer shall make sure their solicitor, relative, appropriate adult or some other person likely to take an interest in them and not involved in the investigation is available to help check any documentation. When this Code requires written consent or signing the person assisting may be asked to sign instead, if the detainee prefers. This paragraph does not require an appropriate adult to be called solely to assist in checking and signing documentation for a person who is not a juvenile, or mentally disordered or otherwise mentally vulnerable (see *paragraph 3.15*).

(c) Persons attending a police station voluntarily
3.21 Anybody attending a police station voluntarily to assist with an investigation may leave at will unless arrested. See *Note 1K*. If it is decided they shall not be allowed to leave, they must be informed at once that they are under arrest and brought before the custody officer, who is responsible for making sure they are notified of their rights in the same way as other detainees. If they are not arrested but are cautioned as in *section 10*, the person who gives the caution must, at the same time, inform them they are not under arrest, they are not obliged to remain at the station but if they remain at the station they may obtain free and independent legal advice if they want. They shall be told the right to legal advice includes the right to speak with a solicitor on the telephone and be asked if they want to do so.

3.22 If a person attending the police station voluntarily asks about their entitlement to legal advice, they shall be given a copy of the notice explaining the arrangements for obtaining legal advice. See *paragraph 3.2*

(d) Documentation
3.23 The grounds for a person's detention shall be recorded, in the person's presence if practicable.

3.24 Action taken under *paragraphs 3.12* to *3.20* shall be recorded.

(e) Persons answering street bail
3.25 When a person is answering street bail, the custody officer should link any documentation held in relation to arrest with the custody record. Any further action shall be recorded on the custody record in accordance with paragraphs 3.23 and 3.24 above.

Notes for guidance
3A The notice of entitlements should:

- *list the entitlements in this Code, including:*

  - *visits and contact with outside parties, including special provisions for Commonwealth citizens and foreign nationals;*
  - *reasonable standards of physical comfort;*
  - *adequate food and drink;*
  - *access to toilets and washing facilities, clothing, medical attention, and exercise when practicable.*

- *mention the:*

  - *provisions relating to the conduct of interviews;*
  - *circumstances in which an appropriate adult should be available to assist the detainee and their statutory rights to make representation whenever the period of their detention is reviewed.*

3B In addition to notices in English, translations should be available in Welsh, the main minority ethnic languages and the principal European languages, whenever they are likely to be helpful. Audio versions of the notice should also be made available.

3C If the juvenile is in local authority or voluntary organisation care but living with their parents or other adults responsible for their welfare, although there is no legal obligation to inform them, they should normally be contacted, as well as the authority or organisation unless suspected of involvement in the offence concerned. Even if the juvenile is not living with their parents, consideration should be given to informing them.

3D The right to consult the Codes of Practice does not entitle the person concerned to delay unreasonably any necessary investigative or administrative action whilst they do so. Examples of action which need not be delayed unreasonably include:

- *procedures requiring the provision of breath, blood or urine specimens under the Road Traffic Act 1988 or the Transport and Works Act 1992;*

- searching detainees at the police station;
- taking fingerprints, footwear impressions or non-intimate samples without consent for evidential purposes.

3E Home Office Circular 32/2000 provides more detailed guidance on risk assessments and identifies key risk areas which should always be considered.

4 DETAINEE'S PROPERTY

(a) Action

4.1 The custody officer is responsible for:

(a) ascertaining what property a detainee:

(i) has with them when they come to the police station, whether on:

- arrest or re-detention on answering to bail;
- commitment to prison custody on the order or sentence of a court;
- lodgement at the police station with a view to their production in court from prison custody;
- transfer from detention at another station or hospital;
- detention under the Mental Health Act 1983, section 135 or 136;
- remand into police custody on the authority of a court

(ii) might have acquired for an unlawful or harmful purpose while in custody;

(b) the safekeeping of any property taken from a detainee which remains at the police station.

The custody officer may search the detainee or authorise their being searched to the extent they consider necessary, provided a search of intimate parts of the body or involving the removal of more than outer clothing is only made as in *Annex A*. A search may only be carried out by an officer of the same sex as the detainee. See *Note 4A*

4.2 Detainees may retain clothing and personal effects at their own risk unless the custody officer considers they may use them to cause harm to themselves or others, interfere with evidence, damage property, effect an escape or they are needed as evidence. In this event the custody officer may withhold such articles as they consider necessary and must tell the detainee why.

4.3 Personal effects are those items a detainee may lawfully need, use or refer to while in detention but do not include cash and other items of value.

(b) Documentation

4.4 It is a matter for the custody officer to determine whether a record should be made of the property a detained person has with him or had taken from him on arrest. Any record made is not required to be kept as part of the custody record but the custody record should be noted as to where such a record exists. Whenever a record is made the detainee shall be allowed to check and sign the record of property as correct. Any refusal to sign shall be recorded.

4.5 If a detainee is not allowed to keep any article of clothing or personal effects, the reason must be recorded.

Notes for guidance

4A PACE, Section 54(1) and paragraph 4.1 require a detainee to be searched when it is clear the custody officer will have continuing duties in relation to that detainee or when that detainee's behaviour or offence makes an inventory appropriate. They do not require every detainee to be searched, e.g. if it is clear a person will only be detained for a short period and is not to be placed in a cell, the custody officer may decide not to search them. In such a case the custody record will be endorsed 'not searched', paragraph 4.4 will not apply, and the detainee will be invited to sign the entry. If the detainee refuses, the custody officer will be obliged to ascertain what property they have in accordance with paragraph 4.1.

4B Paragraph 4.4 does not require the custody officer to record on the custody record property in the detainee's possession on arrest if, by virtue of its nature, quantity or size, it is not practicable to remove it to the police station.

4C Paragraph 4.4 does not require items of clothing worn by the person be recorded unless withheld by the custody officer as in paragraph 4.2.

5 RIGHT NOT TO BE HELD INCOMMUNICADO

(a) Action

5.1 Any person arrested and held in custody at a police station or other premises may, on request, have one person known to them or likely to take an interest in their welfare informed at public expense of their whereabouts as soon as practicable. If the person cannot be contacted the detainee may choose up to two alternatives. If they cannot be contacted, the person in charge of detention or the investigation has discretion to allow further attempts until the information has been conveyed. See *Notes 5C* and *5D*

5.2 The exercise of the above right in respect of each person nominated may be delayed only in accordance with *Annex B*.

5.3 The above right may be exercised each time a detainee is taken to another police station.

5.4 The detainee may receive visits at the custody officer's discretion. See *Note 5B*

5.5 If a friend, relative or person with an interest in the detainee's welfare enquires about their whereabouts, this information shall be given if the suspect agrees and *Annex B* does not apply. See *Note 5D*

5.6 The detainee shall be given writing materials, on request, and allowed to telephone one person for a reasonable time, see *Notes 5A* and *5E*. Either or both these privileges may be denied or delayed if an officer of inspector rank or above considers sending a letter or making a telephone call may result in any of the consequences in:

(a) *Annex B paragraphs 1* and *2* and the person is detained in connection with an indictable offence;

(b) *Not used*

Nothing in this paragraph permits the restriction or denial of the rights in *paragraphs 5.1* and *6.1*.

5.7 Before any letter or message is sent, or telephone call made, the detainee shall be informed that what they say in any letter, call or message (other than in a communication to a solicitor) may be read or listened to and may be given in evidence. A telephone call may be terminated if it is being abused. The costs can be at public expense at the custody officer's discretion.

5.7A Any delay or denial of the rights in this section should be proportionate and should last no longer than necessary.

(b) *Documentation*

5.8 A record must be kept of any:

(a) request made under this section and the action taken;

(b) letters, messages or telephone calls made or received or visit received;

(c) refusal by the detainee to have information about them given to an outside enquirer. The detainee must be asked to countersign the record accordingly and any refusal recorded.

Notes for guidance

5A A person may request an interpreter to interpret a telephone call or translate a letter.

5B At the custody officer's discretion, visits should be allowed when possible, subject to having sufficient personnel to supervise a visit and any possible hindrance to the investigation.

5C If the detainee does not know anyone to contact for advice or support or cannot contact a friend or relative, the custody officer should bear in mind any local voluntary bodies or other organisations who might be able to help. Paragraph 6.1 applies if legal advice is required.

5D In some circumstances it may not be appropriate to use the telephone to disclose information under paragraphs 5.1 and 5.5.

5E The telephone call at paragraph 5.6 is in addition to any communication under paragraphs 5.1 and 6.1.

6 RIGHT TO LEGAL ADVICE

(a) *Action*

6.1 Unless *Annex B* applies, all detainees must be informed that they may at any time consult and communicate privately with a solicitor, whether in person, in writing or by telephone, and that free independent legal advice is available from the duty solicitor. See *paragraph 3.1, Note 6B* and *Note 6J*

6.2 Not Used

6.3 A poster advertising the right to legal advice must be prominently displayed in the charging area of every police station. See *Note 6H*

6.4 No police officer should, at any time, do or say anything with the intention of dissuading a detainee from obtaining legal advice.

6.5 The exercise of the right of access to legal advice may be delayed only as in *Annex B*. Whenever legal advice is requested, and unless *Annex B* applies, the custody officer must act without delay to secure the provision of such advice. If, on being informed or reminded of this right, the detainee declines to speak to a solicitor in person, the officer should point out that the right includes the right to speak with a solicitor on the telephone. If the detainee continues to waive this right the officer should ask them why and any reasons should be recorded on the custody record or the interview record as appropriate. Reminders of the right to legal advice must be given as in *paragraphs 3.5, 11.2, 15.4, 16.4, 2B of Annex A, 3 of Annex K* and *16.5* and *Code D, paragraphs 3.17(ii)* and *6.3*. Once it is clear a detainee does not want to speak to a solicitor in person or by telephone they should cease to be asked their reasons. See *Note 6K*.

6.5A In the case of a juvenile, an appropriate adult should consider whether legal advice from a solicitor is required. If the juvenile indicates that they do not want legal advice, the appropriate adult has the right to ask for a solicitor to attend if this would be in the best interests of the person. However, the detained person cannot be forced to see the solicitor if he is adamant that he does not wish to do so.

6.6 A detainee who wants legal advice may not be interviewed or continue to be interviewed until they have received such advice unless:

(a) *Annex B* applies, when the restriction on drawing adverse inferences from silence in *Annex C* will apply because the detainee is not allowed an opportunity to consult a solicitor; or

(b) an officer of superintendent rank or above has reasonable grounds for believing that:

   (i) the consequent delay might:

- lead to interference with, or harm to, evidence connected with an offence;
- lead to interference with, or physical harm to, other people;
- lead to serious loss of, or damage to, property;
- lead to alerting other people suspected of having committed an offence but not yet arrested for it;
- hinder the recovery of property obtained in consequence of the commission of an offence.

   (ii) when a solicitor, including a duty solicitor, has been contacted and has agreed to attend, awaiting their arrival would cause unreasonable delay to the process of investigation.

Note: In these cases the restriction on drawing adverse inferences from silence in *Annex C* will apply because the detainee is not allowed an opportunity to consult a solicitor.

(c) the solicitor the detainee has nominated or selected from a list:

   (i) cannot be contacted;

   (ii) has previously indicated they do not wish to be contacted; or

   (iii) having been contacted, has declined to attend; and

   the detainee has been advised of the Duty Solicitor Scheme but has declined to ask for the duty solicitor.

In these circumstances the interview may be started or continued without further delay provided an officer of inspector rank or above has agreed to the interview proceeding.

Note: The restriction on drawing adverse inferences from silence in Annex C will not apply because the detainee is allowed an opportunity to consult the duty solicitor;

(d) the detainee changes their mind, about wanting legal advice.

In these circumstances the interview may be started or continued without delay provided that:

   (i) the detainee agrees to do so, in writing or on the interview record made in accordance with Code E or F; and

   (ii) an officer of inspector rank or above has inquired about the detainee's reasons for their change of mind and gives authority for the interview to proceed.

Confirmation of the detainee's agreement, their change of mind, the reasons for it if given and, subject to *paragraph 2.6A,* the name of the authorising officer shall be recorded in the written interview record or the interview record made in accordance with Code E or F. See *Note 6I.* Note: In these circumstances the restriction on drawing adverse inferences from silence in *Annex C* will not apply because the detainee is allowed an opportunity to consult a solicitor if they wish.

6.7 If *paragraph 6.6(b)(i)* applies, once sufficient information has been obtained to avert the risk, questioning must cease until the detainee has received legal advice unless *paragraph 6.6(a), (b)(ii), (c)* or *(d)* applies.

6.8 A detainee who has been permitted to consult a solicitor shall be entitled on request to have the solicitor present when they are interviewed unless one of the exceptions in *paragraph 6.6* applies.

6.9 The solicitor may only be required to leave the interview if their conduct is such that the interviewer is unable properly to put questions to the suspect. See *Notes 6D and 6E*

6.10 If the interviewer considers a solicitor is acting in such a way, they will stop the interview and consult an officer not below superintendent rank, if one is readily available, and otherwise an officer not below inspector rank not connected with the investigation. After speaking to the solicitor, the officer consulted will decide if the interview should continue in the presence of that solicitor. If they decide it should not, the suspect will be given the opportunity to consult another solicitor before the interview continues and that solicitor given an opportunity to be present at the interview. See *Note 6E*

6.11 The removal of a solicitor from an interview is a serious step and, if it occurs, the officer of superintendent rank or above who took the decision will consider if the incident should be reported to the Law Society. If the decision to remove the solicitor has been taken by an officer below superintendent rank, the facts must be reported to an officer of superintendent rank or above who will similarly consider whether a report to the Law Society would be appropriate. When the solicitor concerned is a duty solicitor, the report should be both to the Law Society and to the Legal Services Commission.

6.12 'Solicitor' in this Code means:

- a solicitor who holds a current practising certificate
- an accredited or probationary representative included on the register of representatives maintained by the Legal Services Commission.

6.12A An accredited or probationary representative sent to provide advice by, and on behalf of, a solicitor shall be admitted to the police station for this purpose unless an officer of inspector rank or above considers such a visit will hinder the investigation and directs otherwise. Hindering the investigation does not include giving proper legal advice to a detainee as in *Note 6D*. Once admitted to the police station, *paragraphs 6.6 to 6.10* apply.

6.13 In exercising their discretion under *paragraph 6.12A*, the officer should take into account in particular:

- whether:
  - the identity and status of an accredited or probationary representative have been satisfactorily established;
  - they are of suitable character to provide legal advice, e.g. a person with a criminal record is unlikely to be suitable unless the conviction was for a minor offence and not recent.
- any other matters in any written letter of authorisation provided by the solicitor on whose behalf the person is attending the police station. See *Note 6F*

6.14 If the inspector refuses access to an accredited or probationary representative or a decision is taken that such a person should not be permitted to remain at an interview, the inspector must notify the solicitor on whose behalf the representative was acting and give them an opportunity to make alternative arrangements. The detainee must be informed and the custody record noted.

6.15 If a solicitor arrives at the station to see a particular person, that person must, unless *Annex B* applies, be so informed whether or not they are being interviewed and asked if they would like to see the solicitor. This applies even if the detainee has declined legal advice or, having requested it, subsequently agreed to be interviewed without receiving advice. The solicitor's attendance and the detainee's decision must be noted in the custody record.

(b) Documentation

6.16 Any request for legal advice and the action taken shall be recorded.

6.17 A record shall be made in the interview record if a detainee asks for legal advice and an interview is begun either in the absence of a solicitor or their representative, or they have been required to leave an interview.

Notes for guidance

6A In considering if paragraph 6.6(b) applies, the officer should, if practicable, ask the solicitor for an estimate of how long it will take to come to the station and relate this to the time detention is permitted, the time of day (i.e. whether the rest period under paragraph 12.2 is imminent) and the requirements of other investigations. If the solicitor is on their way or is to set off immediately, it will not normally be appropriate to begin an interview before they arrive. If it appears necessary to begin an interview before the solicitor's arrival, they should be given an indication of how long the police would be able to wait before 6.6(b) applies so there is an opportunity to make arrangements for someone else to provide legal advice.

6B A detainee who asks for legal advice should be given an opportunity to consult a specific solicitor or another solicitor from that solicitor's firm or the duty solicitor. If advice is not available by these means, or they do not want to consult the duty solicitor, the detainee should be given an opportunity to choose a solicitor from a list of those willing to provide legal advice. If this solicitor is unavailable, they may choose up to two alternatives. If these attempts are unsuccessful, the custody officer has discretion to allow further attempts until a solicitor has been contacted and agrees to provide legal advice. Apart from carrying out these duties, an officer must not advise the suspect about any particular firm of solicitors.

6C Not Used

6D A detainee has a right to free legal advice and to be represented by a solicitor. The solicitor's only role in the police station is to protect and advance the legal rights of their client. On occasions this may require the solicitor to give advice which has the effect of the client avoiding giving evidence which strengthens a prosecution case. The solicitor may intervene in order to seek clarification, challenge an improper question to their client or the manner in which it is put, advise their client not to reply to particular questions, or if they wish to give their client further legal advice. Paragraph 6.9 only applies if the solicitor's approach or conduct prevents or unreasonably obstructs proper questions being put to the suspect or the suspect's response being recorded. Examples of unacceptable conduct include answering questions on a suspect's behalf or providing written replies for the suspect to quote.

6E An officer who takes the decision to exclude a solicitor must be in a position to satisfy the court the decision was properly made. In order to do this they may need to witness what is happening.

6F If an officer of at least inspector rank considers a particular solicitor or firm of solicitors is persistently sending probationary representatives who are unsuited to provide legal advice, they should inform an officer of at least superintendent rank, who may wish to take the matter up with the Law Society.

6G Subject to the constraints of Annex B, a solicitor may advise more than one client in an investigation if they wish. Any question of a conflict of interest is for the solicitor under their professional code of conduct. If, however, waiting for a solicitor to give advice to one client may lead to unreasonable delay to the interview with another, the provisions of paragraph 6.6(b) may apply.

6H In addition to a poster in English, a poster or posters containing translations into Welsh, the main minority ethnic languages and the principal European languages should be displayed wherever they are likely to be helpful and it is practicable to do so.

6I Paragraph 6.6(d) requires the authorisation of an officer of inspector rank or above to the continuation of an interview when a detainee who wanted legal advice changes their mind. It is permissible for such authorisation to be given over the telephone, if the authorising officer is able to satisfy themselves about the reason for the detainee's change of mind and is satisfied it is proper to continue the interview in those circumstances.

6J Whenever a detainee exercises their right to legal advice by consulting or communicating with a solicitor, they must be allowed to do so in private. This right to consult or communicate in private is fundamental. If the requirement for privacy is compromised because what is said or written by the detainee or solicitor for the purpose of giving and receiving legal advice is overheard, listened to, or read by others without the informed consent of the detainee, the right will effectively have been denied. When a detainee chooses to speak to a solicitor on the telephone, they should be allowed to do so in private unless this is impractical because of the design and layout of the custody area or the location of telephones. However, the normal expectation should be that facilities will be available, unless they are being used, at all police stations to enable detainees to speak in private to a solicitor either face to face or over the telephone.

6K A detainee is not obliged to give reasons for declining legal advice and should not be pressed to do so.

7 CITIZENS OF INDEPENDENT COMMONWEALTH COUNTRIES OR FOREIGN NATIONALS

(a) Action

7.1 Any citizen of an independent Commonwealth country or a national of a foreign country, including the Republic of Ireland, may communicate at any time with the appropriate High Commission, Embassy or Consulate. The detainee must be informed as soon as practicable of:

- this right;
- their right, upon request, to have their High Commission, Embassy or Consulate told of their whereabouts and the grounds for their detention. Such a request should be acted upon as soon as practicable.

7.2 If a detainee is a citizen of a country with which a bilateral consular convention or agreement is in force requiring notification of arrest, the appropriate High Commission, Embassy or Consulate shall be informed as soon as practicable, subject to *paragraph 7.4*. The countries to which this applies as at 1 April 2003 are listed in *Annex F*.

7.3 Consular officers may visit one of their nationals in police detention to talk to them and, if required, to arrange for legal advice. Such visits shall take place out of the hearing of a police officer.

7.4 Notwithstanding the provisions of consular conventions, if the detainee is a political refugee whether for reasons of race, nationality, political opinion or religion, or is seeking political asylum, consular officers shall not be informed of the arrest of one of their nationals or given access or information about them except at the detainee's express request.

(b) Documentation

7.5 A record shall be made when a detainee is informed of their rights under this section and of any communications with a High Commission, Embassy or Consulate.

Note for guidance

7A The exercise of the rights in this section may not be interfered with even though Annex B applies.

8 CONDITIONS OF DETENTION

(a) Action

8.1 So far as it is practicable, not more than one detainee should be detained in each cell.

8.2 Cells in use must be adequately heated, cleaned and ventilated. They must be adequately lit, subject to such dimming as is compatible with safety and security to allow people detained overnight to sleep. No additional restraints shall be used within a locked cell unless absolutely necessary and then only restraint equipment, approved for use in that force by the Chief Officer, which is reasonable and necessary in the circumstances having regard to the detainee's demeanour and with a view to ensuring their safety and the safety of others. If a detainee is deaf, mentally disordered or otherwise mentally vulnerable, particular care must be taken when deciding whether to use any form of approved restraints.

8.3 Blankets, mattresses, pillows and other bedding supplied shall be of a reasonable standard and in a clean and sanitary condition. See *Note 8A*

8.4 Access to toilet and washing facilities must be provided.

8.5 If it is necessary to remove a detainee's clothes for the purposes of investigation, for hygiene, health reasons or cleaning, replacement clothing of a reasonable standard of comfort and cleanliness shall be provided. A detainee may not be interviewed unless adequate clothing has been offered.

8.6 At least two light meals and one main meal should be offered in any 24 hour period. See *Note 8B*. Drinks should be provided at meal times and upon reasonable request between meals. Whenever necessary, advice shall be sought from the appropriate health care professional, see *Note 9A*, on medical and dietary matters. As far as practicable, meals provided shall offer a varied diet and meet any specific dietary needs or religious beliefs the detainee may have. The detainee may, at the custody officer's discretion, have meals supplied by their family or friends at their expense. See *Note 8A*

8.7 Brief outdoor exercise shall be offered daily if practicable.

8.8 A juvenile shall not be placed in a police cell unless no other secure accommodation is available and the custody officer considers it is not practicable to supervise them if they are not placed in a cell or that a cell provides more comfortable accommodation than other secure accommodation in the station. A juvenile may not be placed in a cell with a detained adult.

(b) Documentation

8.9 A record must be kept of replacement clothing and meals offered.

8.10 If a juvenile is placed in a cell, the reason must be recorded.

8.11 The use of any restraints on a detainee whilst in a cell, the reasons for it and, if appropriate, the arrangements for enhanced supervision of the detainee whilst so restrained, shall be recorded. See *paragraph 3.9*

Notes for guidance

8A The provisions in paragraph 8.3 and 8.6 respectively are of particular importance in the case of a person likely to be detained for an extended period. In deciding whether to allow meals to be supplied by family or friends, the custody officer is entitled to take account of the risk of items being concealed in any food or package and the officer's duties and responsibilities under food handling legislation.

8B Meals should, so far as practicable, be offered at recognised meal times, or at other times that take account of when the detainee last had a meal.

9 CARE AND TREATMENT OF DETAINED PERSONS

(a) General

9.1 Nothing in this section prevents the police from calling the police surgeon or, if appropriate, some other health care professional, to examine a detainee for the purposes of obtaining evidence relating to any offence in which the detainee is suspected of being involved. See *Note 9A*

9.2 If a complaint is made by, or on behalf of, a detainee about their treatment since their arrest, or it comes to notice that a detainee may have been treated improperly, a report must be made as soon as practicable to an officer of inspector rank or above not connected with the investigation. If the matter concerns a possible assault or the possibility of the unnecessary or unreasonable use of force, an appropriate health care professional must also be called as soon as practicable.

9.3 Detainees should be visited at least every hour. If no reasonably foreseeable risk was identified in a risk assessment, see *paragraphs 3.6 – 3.10*, there is no need to wake a sleeping detainee. Those suspected of being intoxicated through drink or drugs or having swallowed drugs, see *Note 9CA*, or whose level of consciousness causes concern must, subject to any clinical directions given by the appropriate health care professional, see *paragraph 9.13*:

- be visited and roused at least every half hour
- have their condition assessed as in *Annex H*
- and clinical treatment arranged if appropriate

See *Notes 9B, 9C* and *9H*

9.4 When arrangements are made to secure clinical attention for a detainee, the custody officer must make sure all relevant information which might assist in the treatment of the detainee's condition is made available to the responsible health care professional. This applies whether or not the health care professional asks for such information. Any officer or police staff with relevant information must inform the custody officer as soon as practicable.

(b) Clinical treatment and attention

9.5 The custody officer must make sure a detainee receives appropriate clinical attention as soon as reasonably practicable if the person:

(a) appears to be suffering from physical illness; or
(b) is injured; or
(c) appears to be suffering from a mental disorder; or
(d) appears to need clinical attention

9.5A This applies even if the detainee makes no request for clinical attention and whether or not they have already received clinical attention elsewhere. If the need for attention appears urgent, e.g. when indicated as in *Annex H*, the nearest available health care professional or an ambulance must be called immediately.

9.5B The custody officer must also consider the need for clinical attention as set out in Note for Guidance 9C in relation to those suffering the effects of alcohol or drugs.

9.6 *Paragraph 9.5* is not meant to prevent or delay the transfer to a hospital if necessary of a person detained under the Mental Health Act 1983, section 136. See *Note 9D.* When an assessment under that Act takes place at a police station, see *paragraph 3.16*, the custody officer must consider whether an appropriate health care professional should be called to conduct an initial clinical check on the detainee. This applies particularly when there is likely to be any significant delay in the arrival of a suitably qualified medical practitioner.

9.7 If it appears to the custody officer, or they are told, that a person brought to a station under arrest may be suffering from an infectious disease or condition, the custody officer must take reasonable steps to safeguard the health of the detainee and others at the station. In deciding what action to take, advice must be sought from an appropriate health care professional. See *Note 9E.* The custody officer has discretion to isolate the person and their property until clinical directions have been obtained.

9.8 If a detainee requests a clinical examination, an appropriate health care professional must be called as soon as practicable to assess the detainee's clinical needs. If a safe and appropriate care plan cannot be provided, the police surgeon's advice must be sought. The detainee may also be examined by a medical practitioner of their choice at their expense.

9.9 If a detainee is required to take or apply any medication in compliance with clinical directions prescribed before their detention, the custody officer must consult the appropriate health care professional before the use of the medication. Subject to the restrictions in *paragraph 9.10,* the custody officer is responsible for the safekeeping of any medication and for making sure the detainee is given the opportunity to take or apply prescribed or approved medication. Any such consultation and its outcome shall be noted in the custody record.

9.10 No police officer may administer or supervise the self-administration of medically prescribed controlled drugs of the types and forms listed in the Misuse of Drugs Regulations 2001, Schedule 2 or 3. A detainee may only self-administer such drugs under the personal supervision of the registered medical practitioner authorising their use. Drugs listed in Schedule 4 or 5 may be distributed by the custody officer for self- administration if they have consulted the registered medical practitioner authorising their use, this may be done by telephone, and both parties are satisfied self-administration will not expose the detainee, police officers or anyone else to the risk of harm or injury.

9.11 When appropriate health care professionals administer drugs or other medications, or supervise their self-administration, it must be within current medicines legislation and the scope of practice as determined by their relevant professional body.

9.12 If a detainee has in their possession, or claims to need, medication relating to a heart condition, diabetes, epilepsy or a condition of comparable potential seriousness then, even though *paragraph 9.5* may not apply, the advice of the appropriate health care professional must be obtained.

9.13 Whenever the appropriate health care professional is called in accordance with this section to examine or treat a detainee, the custody officer shall ask for their opinion about:

- any risks or problems which police need to take into account when making decisions about the detainee's continued detention;
- when to carry out an interview if applicable; and
- the need for safeguards.

9.14 When clinical directions are given by the appropriate health care professional, whether orally or in writing, and the custody officer has any doubts or is in any way uncertain about any aspect of the directions, the custody officer shall ask for clarification. It is particularly important that directions concerning the frequency of visits are clear, precise and capable of being implemented. See *Note 9F*.

(c) Documentation

9.15 A record must be made in the custody record of:

(a) the arrangements made for an examination by an appropriate health care professional under *paragraph 9.2* and of any complaint reported under that paragraph together with any relevant remarks by the custody officer;

(b) any arrangements made in accordance with *paragraph 9.5*;

(c) any request for a clinical examination under *paragraph 9.8* and any arrangements made in response;

(d) the injury, ailment, condition or other reason which made it necessary to make the arrangements in (a) to (c), *see Note 9G*;

(e) any clinical directions and advice, including any further clarifications, given to police by a health care professional concerning the care and treatment of the detainee in connection with any of the arrangements made in (a) to (c), *see Note 9F*;

(f) if applicable, the responses received when attempting to rouse a person using the procedure in *Annex H*, *see Note 9H*.

9.16 If a health care professional does not record their clinical findings in the custody record, the record must show where they are recorded. See *Note 9G*. However, information which is necessary to custody staff to ensure the effective ongoing care and well being of the detainee must be recorded openly in the custody record, see *paragraph 3.8* and *Annex G, paragraph 7*.

9.17 Subject to the requirements of *Section 4*, the custody record shall include:

- a record of all medication a detainee has in their possession on arrival at the police station;
- a note of any such medication they claim to need but do not have with them.

Notes for guidance

9A A 'health care professional' means a clinically qualified person working within the scope of practice as determined by their relevant professional body. Whether a health care professional is 'appropriate' depends on the circumstances of the duties they carry out at the time.

9B Whenever possible juveniles and mentally vulnerable detainees should be visited more frequently.

9C A detainee who appears drunk or behaves abnormally may be suffering from illness, the effects of drugs or may have sustained injury, particularly a head injury which is not apparent. A detainee needing or dependent on certain drugs, including alcohol, may experience harmful effects within a short time of being deprived of their supply. In these circumstances, when there is any doubt, police should always act urgently to call an appropriate health care professional or an ambulance. Paragraph 9.5 does not apply to minor ailments or injuries which do not need attention. However, all such ailments or injuries must be recorded in the custody record and any doubt must be resolved in favour of calling the appropriate health care professional.

9CA Paragraph 9.3 would apply to a person in police custody by order of a magistrates' court under the Criminal Justice Act 1988, section 152 (as amended by the Drugs Act 2005, section 8) to facilitate the recovery of evidence after being charged with drug possession or drug trafficking and suspected of having swallowed drugs. In the case of the healthcare needs of a person who has swallowed drugs, the custody officer subject to any clinical directions, should consider the necessity for rousing every half hour. This does not negate the need for regular visiting of the suspect in the cell.

9D Whenever practicable, arrangements should be made for persons detained for assessment under the Mental Health Act 1983, section 136 to be taken to a hospital. There is no power under that Act to transfer a person detained under section 136 from one place of safety to another place of safety for assessment.

9E It is important to respect a person's right to privacy and information about their health must be kept confidential and only disclosed with their consent or in accordance with clinical advice when it is necessary to protect the detainee's health or that of others who come into contact with them.

9F The custody officer should always seek to clarify directions that the detainee requires constant observation or supervision and should ask the appropriate health care professional to explain precisely what action needs to be taken to implement such directions.

9G Paragraphs 9.15 and 9.16 do not require any information about the cause of any injury, ailment or condition to be recorded on the custody record if it appears capable of providing evidence of an offence.

9H The purpose of recording a person's responses when attempting to rouse them using the procedure in Annex H is to enable any change in the individual's consciousness level to be noted and clinical treatment arranged if appropriate.

10 CAUTIONS

(a) When a caution must be given

10.1 A person whom there are grounds to suspect of an offence, see *Note 10A*, must be cautioned before any questions about an offence, or further questions if the answers provide the grounds for suspicion, are put to them if either the suspect's answers or silence, (i.e. failure or refusal to answer or answer satisfactorily) may be given in evidence to a court in a prosecution. A person need not be cautioned if questions are for other necessary purposes, e.g.:

(a)   solely to establish their identity or ownership of any vehicle;

(b)   to obtain information in accordance with any relevant statutory requirement, see *paragraph 10.9*;

(c)   in furtherance of the proper and effective conduct of a search, e.g. to determine the need to search in the exercise of powers of stop and search or to seek cooperation while carrying out a search;

(d)   to seek verification of a written record as in *paragraph 11.13*;

(e)   Not used

10.2 Whenever a person not under arrest is initially cautioned, or reminded they are under caution, that person must at the same time be told they are not under arrest and are free to leave if they want to. See *Note 10C*

10.3 A person who is arrested, or further arrested, must be informed at the time, or as soon as practicable thereafter, that they are under arrest and the grounds for their arrest, see paragraph 3.4, *Note 10B* and *Code G, paragraphs 2.2 and 4.3.*.

10.4 As per *Code G, section 3*, a person who is arrested, or further arrested, must also be cautioned unless:

(a)   it is impracticable to do so by reason of their condition or behaviour at the time;

(b)   they have already been cautioned immediately prior to arrest as in *paragraph 10.1*.

(b) Terms of the cautions

10.5 The caution which must be given on:

(a)   arrest;

(b)   all other occasions before a person is charged or informed they may be prosecuted, see *section 16*,

should, unless the restriction on drawing adverse inferences from silence applies, see *Annex C*, be in the following terms:

"You do not have to say anything. But it may harm your defence if you do not mention when questioned something which you later rely on in Court. Anything you do say may be given in evidence."

See *Note 10G*

10.6 *Annex C, paragraph 2* sets out the alternative terms of the caution to be used when the restriction on drawing adverse inferences from silence applies.

10.7 Minor deviations from the words of any caution given in accordance with this Code do not constitute a breach of this Code, provided the sense of the relevant caution is preserved. See *Note 10D*

10.8 After any break in questioning under caution, the person being questioned must be made aware they remain under caution. If there is any doubt the relevant caution should be given again in full when the interview resumes. See *Note 10E*

10.9 When, despite being cautioned, a person fails to co-operate or to answer particular questions which may affect their immediate treatment, the person should be informed of any relevant consequences and that those consequences are not affected by the caution. Examples are when a person's refusal to provide:

•   their name and address when charged may make them liable to detention;

•   particulars and information in accordance with a statutory requirement, e.g. under the Road Traffic Act 1988, may amount to an offence or may make the person liable to a further arrest.

(c) Special warnings under the Criminal Justice and Public Order Act 1994, sections 36 and 37

10.10 When a suspect interviewed at a police station or authorised place of detention after arrest fails or refuses to answer certain questions, or to answer satisfactorily, after due warning, see *Note 10F*, a court or jury may draw such inferences as appear proper under the Criminal Justice and Public Order Act 1994, sections 36 and 37. Such inferences may only be drawn when:

(a) the restriction on drawing adverse inferences from silence, see *Annex C*, does not apply; and

(b) the suspect is arrested by a constable and fails or refuses to account for any objects, marks or substances, or marks on such objects found:

- on their person;
- in or on their clothing or footwear;
- otherwise in their possession; or
- in the place they were arrested;

(c) the arrested suspect was found by a constable at a place at or about the time the offence for which that officer has arrested them is alleged to have been committed, and the suspect fails or refuses to account for their presence there.

When the restriction on drawing adverse inferences from silence applies, the suspect may still be asked to account for any of the matters in (b) or (c) but the special warning described in *paragraph 10.11* will not apply and must not be given.

10.11 For an inference to be drawn when a suspect fails or refuses to answer a question about one of these matters or to answer it satisfactorily, the suspect must first be told in ordinary language:

(a) what offence is being investigated;
(b) what fact they are being asked to account for;
(c) this fact may be due to them taking part in the commission of the offence;
(d) a court may draw a proper inference if they fail or refuse to account for this fact;
(e) a record is being made of the interview and it may be given in evidence if they are brought to trial.

(d) Juveniles and persons who are mentally disordered or otherwise mentally vulnerable

10.12 If a juvenile or a person who is mentally disordered or otherwise mentally vulnerable is cautioned in the absence of the appropriate adult, the caution must be repeated in the adult's presence.

(e) Documentation

10.13 A record shall be made when a caution is given under this section, either in the interviewer's pocket book or in the interview record.

Notes for guidance

10A There must be some reasonable, objective grounds for the suspicion, based on known facts or information which are relevant to the likelihood the offence has been committed and the person to be questioned committed it.

10B An arrested person must be given sufficient information to enable them to understand that they have been deprived of their liberty and the reason they have been arrested, e.g. when a person is arrested on suspicion of committing an offence they must be informed of the suspected offence's nature, when and where it was committed. The suspect must also be informed of the reason or reasons why the arrest is considered necessary. Vague or technical language should be avoided.

10C The restriction on drawing inferences from silence, see Annex C, paragraph 1, does not apply to a person who has not been detained and who therefore cannot be prevented from seeking legal advice if they want, see paragraph 3.21.

10D If it appears a person does not understand the caution, the person giving it should explain it in their own words.

10E It may be necessary to show to the court that nothing occurred during an interview break or between interviews which influenced the suspect's recorded evidence. After a break in an interview or at the beginning of a subsequent interview, the interviewing officer should summarise the reason for the break and confirm this with the suspect.

10F The Criminal Justice and Public Order Act 1994, sections 36 and 37 apply only to suspects who have been arrested by a constable or Customs and Excise officer and are given the relevant warning by the police or customs officer who made the arrest or who is investigating the offence. They do not apply to any interviews with suspects who have not been arrested.

10G Nothing in this Code requires a caution to be given or repeated when informing a person not under arrest they may be prosecuted for an offence. However, a court will not be able to draw any inferences under the Criminal Justice and Public Order Act 1994, section 34, if the person was not cautioned.

11 INTERVIEWS – GENERAL

(a) Action

11.1A An interview is the questioning of a person regarding their involvement or suspected involvement in a criminal offence or offences which, under *paragraph 10.1*, must be carried out under caution. Whenever a person is interviewed they must be informed of the nature of the offence, or further offence. Procedures under the Road Traffic Act 1988, section 7 or the Transport and Works Act 1992, section 31 do not constitute interviewing for the purpose of this Code.

11.1 Following a decision to arrest a suspect, they must not be interviewed about the relevant offence except at a police station or other authorised place of detention, unless the consequent delay would be likely to:

(a) lead to:

- interference with, or harm to, evidence connected with an offence;
- interference with, or physical harm to, other people; or
- serious loss of, or damage to, property;

(b) lead to alerting other people suspected of committing an offence but not yet arrested for it; or

(c) hinder the recovery of property obtained in consequence of the commission of an offence.

Interviewing in any of these circumstances shall cease once the relevant risk has been averted or the necessary questions have been put in order to attempt to avert that risk.

11.2 Immediately prior to the commencement or re-commencement of any interview at a police station or other authorised place of detention, the interviewer should remind the suspect of their entitlement to free legal advice and that the interview can be delayed for legal advice to be obtained, unless one of the exceptions in *paragraph 6.6* applies. It is the interviewer's responsibility to make sure all reminders are recorded in the interview record.

11.3 Not Used

11.4 At the beginning of an interview the interviewer, after cautioning the suspect, see *section 10*, shall put to them any significant statement or silence which occurred in the presence and hearing of a police officer or other police staff before the start of the interview and which have not been put to the suspect in the course of a previous interview. See *Note 11A*. The interviewer shall ask the suspect whether they confirm or deny that earlier statement or silence and if they want to add anything.

11.4A A significant statement is one which appears capable of being used in evidence against the suspect, in particular a direct admission of guilt. A significant silence is a failure or refusal to answer a question or answer satisfactorily when under caution, which might, allowing for the restriction on drawing adverse inferences from silence, see *Annex C*, give rise to an inference under the Criminal Justice and Public Order Act 1994, Part III.

11.5 No interviewer may try to obtain answers or elicit a statement by the use of oppression. Except as in *paragraph 10.9*, no interviewer shall indicate, except to answer a direct question, what action will be taken by the police if the person being questioned answers questions, makes a statement or refuses to do either. If the person asks directly what action will be taken if they answer questions, make a statement or refuse to do either, the interviewer may inform them what action the police propose to take provided that action is itself proper and warranted.

11.6 The interview or further interview of a person about an offence with which that person has not been charged or for which they have not been informed they may be prosecuted, must cease when:

(a) the officer in charge of the investigation is satisfied all the questions they consider relevant to obtaining accurate and reliable information about the offence have been put to the suspect, this includes allowing the suspect an opportunity to give an innocent explanation and asking questions to test if the explanation is accurate and reliable, e.g. to clear up ambiguities or clarify what the suspect said;

(b) the officer in charge of the investigation has taken account of any other available evidence; and

(c) the officer in charge of the investigation, or in the case of a detained suspect, the custody officer, see *paragraph 16.1*, reasonably believes there is sufficient evidence to provide a realistic prospect of conviction for that offence. See *Note 11B*

This paragraph does not prevent officers in revenue cases or acting under the confiscation provisions of the Criminal Justice Act 1988 or the Drug Trafficking Act 1994 from inviting suspects to complete a formal question and answer record after the interview is concluded.

(b) Interview records

11.7 (a) An accurate record must be made of each interview, whether or not the interview takes place at a police station

(b) The record must state the place of interview, the time it begins and ends, any interview breaks and, subject to *paragraph 2.6A*, the names of all those present; and must be made on the forms provided for this purpose or in the interviewer's pocket book or in accordance with the Codes of Practice E or F;

(c) Any written record must be made and completed during the interview, unless this would not be practicable or would interfere with the conduct of the interview, and must constitute either a verbatim record of what has been said or, failing this, an account of the interview which adequately and accurately summarises it.

11.8 If a written record is not made during the interview it must be made as soon as practicable after its completion.

11.9 Written interview records must be timed and signed by the maker.

11.10 If a written record is not completed during the interview the reason must be recorded in the interview record.

11.11 Unless it is impracticable, the person interviewed shall be given the opportunity to read the interview record and to sign it as correct or to indicate how they consider it inaccurate. If the person interviewed cannot read or refuses to read the record or sign it, the senior interviewer present shall read it to them and ask whether they would like to sign it as correct or make their mark or to indicate how they consider it inaccurate. The interviewer shall certify on the interview record itself what has occurred. See *Note 11E*

11.12 If the appropriate adult or the person's solicitor is present during the interview, they should also be given an opportunity to read and sign the interview record or any written statement taken down during the interview.

11.13 A written record shall be made of any comments made by a suspect, including unsolicited comments, which are outside the context of an interview but which might be relevant to the offence. Any such record must be timed and signed by the maker. When practicable the suspect shall be given the opportunity to read that record and to sign it as correct or to indicate how they consider it inaccurate. See *Note 11E*

11.14 Any refusal by a person to sign an interview record when asked in accordance with this

Code must itself be recorded.

(c) Juveniles and mentally disordered or otherwise mentally vulnerable people

11.15 A juvenile or person who is mentally disordered or otherwise mentally vulnerable must not be interviewed regarding their involvement or suspected involvement in a criminal offence or offences, or asked to provide or sign a written statement under caution or record of interview, in the absence of the appropriate adult unless *paragraphs 11.1, 11.18* to *11.20* apply. See *Note 11C*

11.16 Juveniles may only be interviewed at their place of education in exceptional circumstances and only when the principal or their nominee agrees. Every effort should be made to notify the parent(s) or other person responsible for the juvenile's welfare and the appropriate adult, if this is a different person, that the police want to interview the juvenile and reasonable time should be allowed to enable the appropriate adult to be present at the interview. If awaiting the appropriate adult would cause unreasonable delay, and unless the juvenile is suspected of an offence against the educational establishment, the principal or their nominee can act as the appropriate adult for the purposes of the interview.

11.17 If an appropriate adult is present at an interview, they shall be informed:

- they are not expected to act simply as an observer; and
- the purpose of their presence is to:
    - advise the person being interviewed;
    - observe whether the interview is being conducted properly and fairly;
    - facilitate communication with the person being interviewed.

(d) Vulnerable suspects – urgent interviews at police stations

11.18 The following persons may not be interviewed unless an officer of superintendent rank or above considers delay will lead to the consequences in *paragraph 11.1(a)* to *(c)*, and is satisfied the interview would not significantly harm the person's physical or mental state (see Annex G):

(a) a juvenile or person who is mentally disordered or otherwise mentally vulnerable if at the time of the interview the appropriate adult is not present;

(b) anyone other than in (a) who at the time of the interview appears unable to:
- appreciate the significance of questions and their answers; or
- understand what is happening because of the effects of drink, drugs or any illness, ailment or condition;

(c) a person who has difficulty understanding English or has a hearing disability, if at the time of the interview an interpreter is not present.

11.19 These interviews may not continue once sufficient information has been obtained to avert the consequences in *paragraph 11.1(a)* to *(c)*.

11.20 A record shall be made of the grounds for any decision to interview a person under *paragraph 11.18*.

Notes for guidance

11A Paragraph 11.4 does not prevent the interviewer from putting significant statements and silences to a suspect again at a later stage or a further interview.

11B The Criminal Procedure and Investigations Act 1996 Code of Practice, paragraph 3.4 states 'In conducting an investigation, the investigator should pursue all reasonable lines of enquiry, whether these point towards or away from the suspect. What is reasonable will depend on the particular circumstances.' *Interviewers should keep this in mind when deciding what questions to ask in an interview.*

11C Although juveniles or people who are mentally disordered or otherwise mentally vulnerable are often capable of providing reliable evidence, they may, without knowing or wishing to do so, be particularly prone in certain circumstances to provide information that may be unreliable, misleading or self-incriminating. Special care should always be taken when questioning such a person, and the appropriate adult should be involved if there is any doubt about a person's age, mental state or capacity. Because of the risk of unreliable evidence it is also important to obtain corroboration of any facts admitted whenever possible.

11D Juveniles should not be arrested at their place of education unless this is unavoidable. When a juvenile is arrested at their place of education, the principal or their nominee must be informed.

11E Significant statements described in paragraph 11.4 will always be relevant to the offence and must be recorded. When a suspect agrees to read records of interviews and other comments and sign them as correct, they should be asked to endorse the record with, e.g. 'I agree that this is a correct record of what was said' and add their signature. If the suspect does not agree with the record, the interviewer should record the details of any disagreement and ask the suspect to read these details and sign them to the effect that they accurately reflect their disagreement. Any refusal to sign should be recorded.

12 INTERVIEWS IN POLICE STATIONS

(a) Action

12.1 If a police officer wants to interview or conduct enquiries which require the presence of a detainee, the custody officer is responsible for deciding whether to deliver the detainee into the officer's custody.

12.2 Except as below, in any period of 24 hours a detainee must be allowed a continuous period of at least 8 hours for rest, free from questioning, travel or any interruption in connection with the investigation concerned. This period should normally be at night or other appropriate time which takes account of when the detainee last slept or rested. If a detainee is arrested at a police station after going there voluntarily, the period of 24 hours runs from the time of their arrest and not the time of arrival at the police station. The period may not be interrupted or delayed, except:

   (a) when there are reasonable grounds for believing not delaying or interrupting the period would:

      (i)   involve a risk of harm to people or serious loss of, or damage to, property;
      (iii) delay unnecessarily the person's release from custody;
      (iii) otherwise prejudice the outcome of the investigation;

   (b) at the request of the detainee, their appropriate adult or legal representative;
   (c) when a delay or interruption is necessary in order to:

      (i)   comply with the legal obligations and duties arising under *section 15*;
      (ii) to take action required under *section 9* or in accordance with medical advice.

If the period is interrupted in accordance with *(a)*, a fresh period must be allowed. Interruptions under *(b)* and *(c)*, do not require a fresh period to be allowed.

12.3 Before a detainee is interviewed the custody officer, in consultation with the officer in charge of the investigation and appropriate health care professionals as necessary, shall assess whether the detainee is fit enough to be interviewed. This means determining and considering the risks to the detainee's physical and mental state if the interview took place and determining what safeguards are needed to allow the interview to take place. See *Annex G*. The custody officer shall not allow a detainee to be interviewed if the custody officer considers it would cause significant harm to the detainee's physical or mental state. Vulnerable suspects listed at *paragraph 11.18* shall be treated as always being at some risk during an interview and these persons may not be interviewed except in accordance with *paragraphs 11.18* to *11.20*.

12.4 As far as practicable interviews shall take place in interview rooms which are adequately heated, lit and ventilated.

12.5 A suspect whose detention without charge has been authorised under PACE, because the detention is necessary for an interview to obtain evidence of the offence for which they have been arrested, may choose not to answer questions but police do not require the suspect's consent or agreement to interview them for this purpose. If a suspect takes steps to prevent themselves being questioned or further questioned, e.g. by refusing to leave their cell to go to a suitable interview room or by trying to leave the interview room, they shall be advised their consent or agreement to interview is not required. The suspect shall be cautioned as in *section 10*, and informed if they fail or refuse to co-operate, the interview may take place in the cell and that their failure or refusal to cooperate may be given in evidence. The suspect shall then be invited to co-operate and go into the interview room.

12.6 People being questioned or making statements shall not be required to stand.

12.7 Before the interview commences each interviewer shall, subject to *paragraph 2.6A*, identify themselves and any other persons present to the interviewee.

12.8 Breaks from interviewing should be made at recognised meal times or at other times that take account of when an interviewee last had a meal. Short refreshment breaks shall be provided at approximately two hour intervals, subject to the interviewer's discretion to delay a break if there are reasonable grounds for believing it would:

(i) involve a:

- risk of harm to people;
- serious loss of, or damage to, property;

(ii) unnecessarily delay the detainee's release;

(iii) otherwise prejudice the outcome of the investigation.

See *Note 12B*

12.9 If during the interview a complaint is made by or on behalf of the interviewee concerning the provisions of this Code, the interviewer should:

(i) record it in the interview record;

(ii) inform the custody officer, who is then responsible for dealing with it as in *section 9*.

(b) Documentation

12.10 A record must be made of the:

- time a detainee is not in the custody of the custody officer, and why
- reason for any refusal to deliver the detainee out of that custody

12.11 A record shall be made of:

(a) the reasons it was not practicable to use an interview room; and

(b) any action taken as in *paragraph 12.5*.

The record shall be made on the custody record or in the interview record for action taken whilst an interview record is being kept, with a brief reference to this effect in the custody record.

12.12 Any decision to delay a break in an interview must be recorded, with reasons, in the interview record.

12.13 All written statements made at police stations under caution shall be written on forms provided for the purpose.

12.14 All written statements made under caution shall be taken in accordance with *Annex D*. Before a person makes a written statement under caution at a police station they shall be reminded about the right to legal advice. See *Note 12A*

Notes for guidance

12A It is not normally necessary to ask for a written statement if the interview was recorded in writing and the record signed in accordance with paragraph 11.11 or audibly or visually recorded in accordance with Code E or F. Statements under caution should normally be taken in these circumstances only at the person's express wish. A person may however be asked if they want to make such a statement.

12B Meal breaks should normally last at least 45 minutes and shorter breaks after two hours should last at least 15 minutes. If the interviewer delays a break in accordance with paragraph 12.8 and prolongs the interview, a longer break should be provided. If there is a short interview, and another short interview is contemplated, the length of the break may be reduced if there are reasonable grounds to believe this is necessary to avoid any of the consequences in paragraph 12.8(i) to (iii).

13 INTERPRETERS

(a) General

13.1 Chief officers are responsible for making sure appropriate arrangements are in place for provision of suitably qualified interpreters for people who:

- are deaf;
- do not understand English.

Whenever possible, interpreters should be drawn from the National Register of Public Service Interpreters (NRPSI) or the Council for the Advancement of Communication with Deaf People (CADCP) Directory of British Sign Language/English Interpreters.

(b) Foreign languages

13.2 Unless *paragraphs 11.1, 11.18* to *11.20* apply, a person must not be interviewed in the absence of a person capable of interpreting if:

(a) they have difficulty understanding English;

(b) the interviewer cannot speak the person's own language;

(c) the person wants an interpreter present.

13.3 The interviewer shall make sure the interpreter makes a note of the interview at the time in the person's language for use in the event of the interpreter being called to give evidence, and certifies its accuracy. The interviewer should allow sufficient time for the interpreter to note each question and answer after each is put, given and interpreted. The person should be allowed to read the record or have it read to them and sign it as correct or indicate the respects in which they consider it inaccurate. If the interview is audibly recorded or visually recorded, the arrangements in Code E or F apply.

13.4 In the case of a person making a statement to a police officer or other police staff other than in English:

- (a) the interpreter shall record the statement in the language it is made;
- (b) the person shall be invited to sign it;
- (c) an official English translation shall be made in due course.

(c) Deaf people and people with speech difficulties

13.5 If a person appears to be deaf or there is doubt about their hearing or speaking ability, they must not be interviewed in the absence of an interpreter unless they agree in writing to being interviewed without one or *paragraphs 11.1, 11.18* to *11.20* apply.

13.6 An interpreter should also be called if a juvenile is interviewed and the parent or guardian present as the appropriate adult appears to be deaf or there is doubt about their hearing or speaking ability, unless they agree in writing to the interview proceeding without one or *paragraphs 11.1, 11.18* to *11.20* apply.

13.7 The interviewer shall make sure the interpreter is allowed to read the interview record and certify its accuracy in the event of the interpreter being called to give evidence. If the interview is audibly recorded or visually recorded, the arrangements in Code E or F apply.

(d) Additional rules for detained persons

13.8 All reasonable attempts should be made to make the detainee understand that interpreters will be provided at public expense.

13.9 If *paragraph 6.1* applies and the detainee cannot communicate with the solicitor because of language, hearing or speech difficulties, an interpreter must be called. The interpreter may not be a police officer or any other police staff when interpretation is needed for the purposes of obtaining legal advice. In all other cases a police officer or other police staff may only interpret if the detainee and the appropriate adult, if applicable, give their agreement in writing or if the interview is audibly recorded or visually recorded as in Code E or F.

13.10 When the custody officer cannot establish effective communication with a person charged with an offence who appears deaf or there is doubt about their ability to hear, speak or to understand English, arrangements must be made as soon as practicable for an interpreter to explain the offence and any other information given by the custody officer.

(e) Documentation

13.11 Action taken to call an interpreter under this section and any agreement to be interviewed in the absence of an interpreter must be recorded.

14 QUESTIONING – SPECIAL RESTRICTIONS

14.1 If a person is arrested by one police force on behalf of another and the lawful period of detention in respect of that offence has not yet commenced in accordance with PACE, section 41 no questions may be put to them about the offence while they are in transit between the forces except to clarify any voluntary statement they make.

14.2 If a person is in police detention at a hospital they may not be questioned without the agreement of a responsible doctor. See *Note 14A*

Note for guidance

14A If questioning takes place at a hospital under paragraph 14.2, or on the way to or from a hospital, the period of questioning concerned counts towards the total period of detention permitted.

15 REVIEWS AND EXTENSIONS OF DETENTION

(a) Persons detained under PACE

15.1 The review officer is responsible under PACE, section 40 for periodically determining if a person's detention, before or after charge, continues to be necessary. This requirement continues throughout the detention period and except as in *paragraph 15.10*, the review officer must be present at the police station holding the detainee. See *Notes 15A* and 15B

15.2 Under PACE, section 42, an officer of superintendent rank or above who is responsible for the station holding the detainee may give authority any time after the second review to extend the maximum period the person may be detained without charge by up to 12 hours. Further detention without charge may be authorised only by a magistrates' court in accordance with PACE, sections 43 and 44. See *Notes 15C, 15D* and 15E

15.2A Section 42(1) of PACE as amended extends the maximum period of detention for indictable offences from 24 hours to 36 hours. Detaining a juvenile or mentally vulnerable person for longer than 24 hours will be dependent on the circumstances of the case and with regard to the person's:

(*a*) special vulnerability;
(*b*) the legal obligation to provide an opportunity for representations to be made prior to a decision about extending detention;
(*c*) the need to consult and consider the views of any appropriate adult; and
(*d*) any alternatives to police custody.

15.3 Before deciding whether to authorise continued detention the officer responsible under *paragraphs 15.1* or *15.2* shall give an opportunity to make representations about the detention to:

(*a*) the detainee, unless in the case of a review as in *paragraph 15.1*, the detainee is asleep;
(*b*) the detainee's solicitor if available at the time; and
(*c*) the appropriate adult if available at the time.

15.3A Other people having an interest in the detainee's welfare may also make representations at the authorising officer's discretion.

15.3B Subject to *paragraph 15.10*, the representations may be made orally in person or by telephone or in writing. The authorising officer may, however, refuse to hear oral representations from the detainee if the officer considers them unfit to make representations because of their condition or behaviour. See *Note 15C*

15.3C The decision on whether the review takes place in person or by telephone or by video conferencing (see Note 15G) is a matter for the review officer. In determining the form the review may take, the review officer must always take full account of the needs of the person in custody. The benefits of carrying out a review in person should always be considered, based on the individual circumstances of each case with specific additional consideration if the person is:

(*a*) a juvenile (and the age of the juvenile); or
(*b*) mentally vulnerable; or
(*c*) has been subject to medical attention for other than routine minor ailments; or
(*d*) there are presentational or community issues around the person's detention.

15.4 Before conducting a review or determining whether to extend the maximum period of detention without charge, the officer responsible must make sure the detainee is reminded of their entitlement to free legal advice, see *paragraph 6.5,* unless in the case of a review the person is asleep.

15.5 If, after considering any representations, the officer decides to keep the detainee in detention or extend the maximum period they may be detained without charge, any comment made by the detainee shall be recorded. If applicable, the officer responsible under *paragraph 15.1* or *15.2* shall be informed of the comment as soon as practicable. See also *paragraphs 11.4* and *11.13*

15.6 No officer shall put specific questions to the detainee:

• regarding their involvement in any offence; or
• in respect of any comments they may make:

– when given the opportunity to make representations; or
– in response to a decision to keep them in detention or extend the maximum period of detention.

Such an exchange could constitute an interview as in *paragraph 11.1A* and would be subject to the associated safeguards in *section 11* and, in respect of a person who has been charged, *paragraph 16.5*. See also *paragraph 11.13*

15.7 A detainee who is asleep at a review, see *paragraph 15.1*, and whose continued detention is authorised must be informed about the decision and reason as soon as practicable after waking.

15.8 Not used

(b) Telephone review of detention

15.9 PACE, section 40A provides that the officer responsible under section 40 for reviewing the detention of a person who has not been charged, need not attend the police station holding the detainee and may carry out the review by telephone.

15.9A PACE, section 45A(2) provides that the officer responsible under section 40 for reviewing the detention of a person who has not been charged, need not attend the police station holding the detainee and may carry out the review by video conferencing facilities (See *Note 15G*).

15.9B A telephone review is not permitted where facilities for review by video conferencing exist and it is practicable to use them.

15.9C The review officer can decide at any stage that a telephone review or review by video conferencing should be terminated and that the review will be conducted in person. The reasons for doing so should be noted in the custody record. See *Note 15F*

15.10 When a telephone review is carried out, an officer at the station holding the detainee shall be required by the review officer to fulfil that officer's obligations under PACE section 40 or this Code by:

(a) making any record connected with the review in the detainee's custody record;
(b) if applicable, making a record in (a) in the presence of the detainee; and
(c) giving the detainee information about the review.

15.11 When a telephone review is carried out, the requirement in *paragraph 15.3* will be satisfied:

(a) if facilities exist for the immediate transmission of written representations to the review officer, e.g. fax or email message, by giving the detainee an opportunity to make representations:

(i) orally by telephone; or
(ii) in writing using those facilities; and

(b) in all other cases, by giving the detainee an opportunity to make their representations orally by telephone.

(c) Documentation

15.12 It is the officer's responsibility to make sure all reminders given under *paragraph 15.4* are noted in the custody record.

15.13 The grounds for, and extent of, any delay in conducting a review shall be recorded.

15.14 When a telephone review is carried out, a record shall be made of:

(a) the reason the review officer did not attend the station holding the detainee;
(b) the place the review officer was;
(c) the method representations, oral or written, were made to the review officer, see *paragraph 15.11*.

15.15 Any written representations shall be retained.

15.16 A record shall be made as soon as practicable about the outcome of each review or determination whether to extend the maximum detention period without charge or an application for a warrant of further detention or its extension. If *paragraph 15.7* applies, a record shall also be made of when the person was informed and by whom. If an authorisation is given under PACE, section 42, the record shall state the number of hours and minutes by which the detention period is extended or further extended. If a warrant for further detention, or extension, is granted under section 43 or 44, the record shall state the detention period authorised by the warrant and the date and time it was granted.

Notes for guidance
15A Review officer for the purposes of:

- PACE, sections 40 and 40A means, in the case of a person arrested but not charged, an officer of at least inspector rank not directly involved in the investigation and, if a person has been arrested and charged, the custody officer;

15B The detention of persons in police custody not subject to the statutory review requirement in paragraph 15.1 should still be reviewed periodically as a matter of good practice. Such reviews can be carried out by an officer of the rank of sergeant or above. The purpose of such reviews is to check the particular power under which a detainee is held continues to apply, any associated conditions are complied with and to make sure appropriate action is taken to deal with any changes. This includes the detainee's prompt release when the power no longer applies, or their transfer if the power requires the detainee be taken elsewhere as soon as the necessary arrangements are made. Examples include persons:

(a) *arrested on warrant because they failed to answer bail to appear at court;*
(b) *arrested under the Bail Act 1976, section 7(3) for breaching a condition of bail granted after charge;*
(c) *in police custody for specific purposes and periods under the Crime (Sentences) Act 1997, Schedule 1;*
(d) *convicted, or remand prisoners, held in police stations on behalf of the Prison Service under the Imprisonment (Temporary Provisions) Act 1980, section 6;*
(e) *being detained to prevent them causing a breach of the peace;*
(f) *detained at police stations on behalf of the Immigration Service.*
(g) *detained by order of a magistrates' court under the Criminal Justice Act 1988, section 152 (as amended by the Drugs Act 2005, section 8) to facilitate the recovery of evidence after being charged with drug possession or drug trafficking and suspected of having swallowed drugs.*

The detention of persons remanded into police detention by order of a court under the

Magistrates' Courts Act 1980, section 128 is subject to a statutory requirement to review that detention. This is to make sure the detainee is taken back to court no later than the end of the period authorised by the court or when the need for their detention by police ceases, whichever is the sooner.

15C *In the case of a review of detention, but not an extension, the detainee need not be woken for the review. However, if the detainee is likely to be asleep, e.g. during a period of rest allowed as in paragraph 12.2, at the latest time a review or authorisation to extend detention may take place, the officer should, if the legal obligations and time constraints permit, bring forward the procedure to allow the detainee to make representations. A detainee not asleep during the review must be present when the grounds for their continued detention are recorded and must at the same time be informed of those grounds unless the review officer considers the person is incapable of understanding what is said, violent or likely to become violent or in urgent need of medical attention.*

15D *An application to a Magistrates' Court under PACE, sections 43 or 44 for a warrant of further detention or its extension should be made between 10am and 9pm, and if possible during normal court hours. It will not usually be practicable to arrange for a court to sit specially outside the hours of 10am to 9pm. If it appears a special sitting may be needed outside normal court hours but between 10am and 9pm, the clerk to the justices should be given notice and informed of this possibility, while the court is sitting if possible.*

15E *In paragraph 15.2, the officer responsible for the station holding the detainee includes a superintendent or above who, in accordance with their force operational policy or police regulations, is given that responsibility on a temporary basis whilst the appointed long-term holder is off duty or otherwise unavailable.*

15F *The provisions of PACE, section 40A allowing telephone reviews do not apply to reviews of detention after charge by the custody officer When video conferencing is not required, they allow the use of a telephone to carry out a review of detention before charge. The procedure under PACE, section 42 must be done in person.*

15G *The use of video conferencing facilities for decisions about detention under section 45A of PACE is subject to the introduction of regulations by the Secretary of State.*

16   CHARGING DETAINED PERSONS

(a) Action

16.1   When the officer in charge of the investigation reasonably believes there is sufficient evidence to provide a realistic prospect of conviction for the offence (see *paragraph 11.6*), they shall without delay, and subject to the following qualification, inform the custody officer who will be responsible for considering whether the detainee should be charged. See *Notes 11B* and *16A*. When a person is detained in respect of more than one offence it is permissible to delay informing the custody officer until the above conditions are satisfied in respect of all the offences, but see *paragraph 11.6*. If the detainee is a juvenile, mentally disordered or otherwise mentally vulnerable, any resulting action shall be taken in the presence of the appropriate adult if they are present at the time. See *Notes 16B* and *16C*.

16.1A   Where guidance issued by the Director of Public Prosecutions under section 37A is in force the custody officer must comply with that Guidance in deciding how to act in dealing with the detainee. See *Notes 16AA* and *16AB*.

16.1B   Where in compliance with the DPP's Guidance the custody officer decides that the case should be immediately referred to the CPS to make the charging decision, consultation should take place with a Crown Prosecutor as soon as is reasonably practicable. Where the Crown Prosecutor is unable to make the charging decision on the information available at that time, the detainee may be released without charge and on bail (with conditions if necessary) under section 37(7)(a). In such circumstances, the detainee should be informed that they are being released to enable the Director of Public Prosecutions to make a decision under section 37B.

16.2   When a detainee is charged with or informed they may be prosecuted for an offence, see *Note 16B*, they shall, unless the restriction on drawing adverse inferences from silence applies, see *Annex C*, be cautioned as follows:

'You do not have to say anything. But it may harm your defence if you do not mention now something which you later rely on in court. Anything you do say may be given in evidence.'

Annex C, paragraph 2 sets out the alternative terms of the caution to be used when the restriction on drawing adverse inferences from silence applies.

16.3   When a detainee is charged they shall be given a written notice showing particulars of the offence and, subject to *paragraph 2.6A*, the officer's name and the case reference number. As far as possible the particulars of the charge shall be stated in simple terms, but they shall also show the precise offence in law with which the detainee is charged. The notice shall begin:

'You are charged with the offence(s) shown below.' Followed by the caution.

If the detainee is a juvenile, mentally disordered or otherwise mentally vulnerable, the notice should be given to the appropriate adult.

16.4   If, after a detainee has been charged with or informed they may be prosecuted for an offence, an officer wants to tell them about any written statement or interview with another person relating to such an offence, the detainee shall either be handed a true copy of the written statement or the content of the interview record brought to their attention. Nothing shall be done to invite any reply or comment except to:

(a) caution the detainee, *'You do not have to say anything, but anything you do say may be given in evidence.'*; and
(b) remind the detainee about their right to legal advice.

16.4A If the detainee:

- cannot read, the document may be read to them
- is a juvenile, mentally disordered or otherwise mentally vulnerable, the appropriate adult shall also be given a copy, or the interview record shall be brought to their attention

16.5 A detainee may not be interviewed about an offence after they have been charged with, or informed they may be prosecuted for it, unless the interview is necessary:

- to prevent or minimise harm or loss to some other person, or the public
- to clear up an ambiguity in a previous answer or statement
- in the interests of justice for the detainee to have put to them, and have an opportunity to comment on, information concerning the offence which has come to light since they were charged or informed they might be prosecuted

Before any such interview, the interviewer shall:

(a) caution the detainee, *'You do not have to say anything, but anything you do say may be given in evidence.'*;
(b) remind the detainee about their right to legal advice.

See *Note 16B*

16.6 The provisions of *paragraphs 16.2* to *16.5* must be complied with in the appropriate adult's presence if they are already at the police station. If they are not at the police station then these provisions must be complied with again in their presence when they arrive unless the detainee has been released.

See *Note 16C*

16.7 When a juvenile is charged with an offence and the custody officer authorises their continued detention after charge, the custody officer must try to make arrangements for the juvenile to be taken into the care of a local authority to be detained pending appearance in court unless the custody officer certifies it is impracticable to do so or, in the case of a juvenile of at least 12 years old, no secure accommodation is available and there is a risk to the public of serious harm from that juvenile, in accordance with PACE, section 38(6). See *Note 16D*

(b) Documentation

16.8 A record shall be made of anything a detainee says when charged.

16.9 Any questions put in an interview after charge and answers given relating to the offence shall be recorded in full during the interview on forms for that purpose and the record signed by the detainee or, if they refuse, by the interviewer and any third parties present. If the questions are audibly recorded or visually recorded the arrangements in Code E or F apply.

16.10 If it is not practicable to make arrangements for a juvenile's transfer into local authority care as in *paragraph 16.7*, the custody officer must record the reasons and complete a certificate to be produced before the court with the juvenile. See *Note 16D*

Notes for guidance

16A The custody officer must take into account alternatives to prosecution under the *Crime and Disorder Act 1998*, reprimands and warning applicable to persons under 18, and in national guidance on the cautioning of offenders, for persons aged 18 and over.

16AA When a person is arrested under the provisions of the *Criminal Justice Act 2003* which allow a person to be re-tried after being acquitted of a serious offence which is a qualifying offence specified in Schedule 5 to that Act and not precluded from further prosecution by virtue of section 75(3) of that Act the detention provisions of PACE are modified and make an officer of the rank of superintendent or above who has not been directly involved in the investigation responsible for determining whether the evidence is sufficient to charge.

16AB Where Guidance issued by the Director of Public Prosecutions under section 37B is in force, a custody officer who determines in accordance with that Guidance that there is sufficient evidence to charge the detainee, may detain that person for no longer than is reasonably necessary to decide how that person is to be dealt with under PACE, section 37(7)(a) to (d), including, where appropriate, consultation with the Duty Prosecutor. The period is subject to the maximum period of detention before charge determined by PACE, sections 41 to 44. Where in accordance with the Guidance the case is referred to the CPS for decision, the custody officer should ensure that an officer involved in the investigation sends to the CPS such information as is specified in the Guidance.

16B The giving of a warning or the service of the Notice of Intended Prosecution required by the Road Traffic Offenders Act 1988, section 1 does not amount to informing a detainee they may be prosecuted for an offence and so does not preclude further questioning in relation to that offence.

16C There is no power under PACE to detain a person and delay action under paragraphs 16.2 to 16.5 solely to await the arrival of the appropriate adult. After charge, bail cannot be refused, or release on bail delayed, simply because an appropriate adult is not available, unless the absence of that adult provides the custody officer with the necessary grounds to authorise detention after charge under PACE, section 38.

16D Except as in paragraph 16.7, neither a juvenile's behaviour nor the nature of the offence provides grounds for the custody officer to decide it is impracticable to arrange the juvenile's transfer to local authority care. Similarly, the lack of secure local authority accommodation does not make it impracticable to transfer the juvenile. The availability of secure accommodation is only a factor in relation to a juvenile aged 12 or over when the local authority accommodation would not be adequate to protect the public from serious harm from them. The obligation to transfer a juvenile to local authority accommodation applies as much to a juvenile charged during the daytime as to a juvenile to be held overnight, subject to a requirement to bring the juvenile before a court under PACE, section 46.

17 TESTING PERSONS FOR THE PRESENCE OF SPECIFIED CLASS A DRUGS

(a) Action

17.1 This section of Code C applies only in selected police stations in police areas where the provisions for drug testing under section 63B of PACE (as amended by section 5 of the Criminal Justice Act 2003 and section 7 of the Drugs Act 2005) are in force and in respect of which the Secretary of State has given a notification to the relevant chief officer of police that arrangements for the taking of samples have been made. Such a notification will cover either a police area as a whole or particular stations within a police area. The notification indicates whether the testing applies to those arrested or charged or under the age of 18 as the case may be and testing can only take place in respect of the persons so indicated in the notification. Testing cannot be carried out unless the relevant notification has been given and has not been withdrawn. See *Note 17F*

17.2 A sample of urine or a non-intimate sample may be taken from a person in police detention for the purpose of ascertaining whether he has any specified Class A drug in his body only where they have been brought before the custody officer and:

(a) either the arrest condition, see *paragraph 17.3*, or the charge condition, see *paragraph 17.4* is met;
(b) the age condition see *paragraph 17.5*, is met;
(c) the notification condition is met in relation to the arrest condition, the charge condition, or the age condition, as the case may be. (Testing on charge and/or arrest must be specifically provided for in the notification for the power to apply. In addition, the fact that testing of under 18s is authorised must be expressly provided for in the notification before the power to test such persons applies.). See *paragraph 17.1*; and
(d) a police officer has requested the person concerned to give the sample (the request condition).

17.3 The arrest condition is met where the detainee:

(a) has been arrested for a trigger offence, see *Note 17E*, but not charged with that offence; or
(b) has been arrested for any other offence but not charged with that offence and a police officer of inspector rank or above, who has reasonable grounds for suspecting that their misuse of any specified Class A drug caused or contributed to the offence, has authorised the sample to be taken.

17.4 The charge condition is met where the detainee:

(a) has been charged with a trigger offence, or
(b) has been charged with any other offence and a police officer of inspector rank or above, who has reasonable grounds for suspecting that the detainee's misuse of any specified Class A drug caused or contributed to the offence, has authorised the sample to be taken.

17.5 The age condition is met where:

(a) in the case of a detainee who has been arrested but not charged as in *paragraph 17.3*, they are aged 18 or over;
(b) in the case of a detainee who has been charged as in *paragraph 17.4*, they are aged 14 or over.

17.6 Before requesting a sample from the person concerned, an officer must:

(a) inform them that the purpose of taking the sample is for drug testing under PACE. This is to ascertain whether they have a specified Class A drug present in their body;

(b) warn them that if, when so requested, they fail without good cause to provide a sample they may be liable to prosecution;

(c) where the taking of the sample has been authorised by an inspector or above in accordance with *paragraph 17.3(b)* or *17.4(b)* above, inform them that the authorisation has been given and the grounds for giving it;

(d) remind them of the following rights, which may be exercised at any stage during the period in custody:

  (i)   the right to have someone informed of their arrest [see section 5];
  (ii) the right to consult privately with a solicitor and that free independent legal advice is available [see section 6]; and
  (iii) the right to consult these Codes of Practice [see section 3].

17.7 In the case of a person who has not attained the age of 17 —

(a) the making of the request for a sample under *paragraph 17.2(d)* above;
(b) the giving of the warning and the information under *paragraph 17.6* above; and
(c) the taking of the sample,

may not take place except in the presence of an appropriate adult. (see Note 17G)

17.8 Authorisation by an officer of the rank of inspector or above within *paragraph 17.3(b)* or *17.4(b)* may be given orally or in writing but, if it is given orally, it must be confirmed in writing as soon as practicable.

17.9 If a sample is taken from a detainee who has been arrested for an offence but not charged with that offence as in *paragraph 17.3*, no further sample may be taken during the same continuous period of detention. If during that same period the charge condition is also met in respect of that detainee, the sample which has been taken shall be treated as being taken by virtue of the charge condition, see *paragraph 17.4*, being met.

17.10 A detainee from whom a sample may be taken may be detained for up to six hours from the time of charge if the custody officer reasonably believes the detention is necessary to enable a sample to be taken. Where the arrest condition is met, a detainee whom the custody officer has decided to release on bail without charge may continue to be detained, but not beyond 24 hours from the relevant time (as defined in section 41(2) of PACE), to enable a sample to be taken.

17.11 A detainee in respect of whom the arrest condition is met, but not the charge condition, see *paragraphs 17.3* and *17.4*, and whose release would be required before a sample can be taken had they not continued to be detained as a result of being arrested for a further offence which does not satisfy the arrest condition, may have a sample taken at any time within 24 hours after the arrest for the offence that satisfies the arrest condition.

(b) Documentation

17.12 The following must be recorded in the custody record:

(a) if a sample is taken following authorisation by an officer of the rank of inspector or above, the authorisation and the grounds for suspicion;
(b) the giving of a warning of the consequences of failure to provide a sample;
(c) the time at which the sample was given; and
(d) the time of charge or, where the arrest condition is being relied upon, the time of arrest and, where applicable, the fact that a sample taken after arrest but before charge is to be treated as being taken by virtue of the charge condition, where that is met in the same period of continuous detention. See *paragraph 17.9*

(c) General

17.13 A sample may only be taken by a prescribed person. See *Note 17C*.

17.14 Force may not be used to take any sample for the purpose of drug testing.

17.15 The terms "Class A drug" and "misuse" have the same meanings as in the Misuse of Drugs Act 1971. "Specified" (in relation to a Class A drug) and "trigger offence" have the same meanings as in Part III of the Criminal Justice and Court Services Act 2000.

17.16 Any sample taken:

(a) may not be used for any purpose other than to ascertain whether the person concerned has a specified Class A drug present in his body; and
(b) must be retained until the person concerned has made their first appearance before the court.

(d) Assessment of misuse of drugs

17.17 Under the provisions of Part 3 of the Drugs Act 2005, where a detainee has tested positive for a specified Class A drug under section 63B of PACE a police officer may, at any time before the person's release from the police station, impose a requirement for them to attend an initial assessment of their drug misuse by a suitably qualified person and to remain for its duration. The requirement may only be imposed on a person if:

(*a*) they have reached the age of 18
(*b*) notification has been given by the Secretary of State to the relevant chief officer of police that arrangements for conducting initial assessments have been made for those from whom samples for testing have been taken at the police station where the detainee is in custody.

17.18 When imposing a requirement to attend an initial assessment the police officer must:

(*a*) inform the person of the time and place at which the initial assessment is to take place;
(*b*) explain that this information will be confirmed in writing; and
(*c*) warn the person that he may be liable to prosecution if he fails without good cause to attend the initial assessment and remain for it's duration

17.19 Where a police officer has imposed a requirement to attend an initial assessment in accordance with *paragraph 17.17*, he must, before the person is released from detention, give the person notice in writing which:

(*a*) confirms that he is required to attend and remain for the duration of an initial assessment; and
(*b*) confirms the information and repeats the warning referred to in *paragraph 17.18*.

17.20 The following must be recorded in the custody record:

(*a*) that the requirement to attend an initial assessment has been imposed; and
(*b*) the information, explanation, warning and notice given in accordance with *paragraphs 17.17* and *17.19*.

17.21 Where a notice is given in accordance with *paragraph 17.19*, a police officer can give the person a further notice in writing which informs the person of any change to the time or place at which the initial assessment is to take place and which repeats the warning referred to in *paragraph 17.18(c)*.

17.22 Part 3 of the Drugs Act 2005 also requires police officers to have regard to any guidance issued by the Secretary of State in respect of the assessment provisions.

Notes for guidance

17A When warning a person who is asked to provide a urine or non-intimate sample in accordance with paragraph 17.6(b), the following form of words may be used:
"You do not have to provide a sample, but I must warn you that if you fail or refuse without good cause to do so, you will commit an offence for which you may be imprisoned, or fined, or both".

17B A sample has to be sufficient and suitable. A sufficient sample is sufficient in quantity and quality to enable drug-testing analysis to take place. A suitable sample is one which by its nature, is suitable for a particular form of drug analysis.

17C A prescribed person in paragraph 17.13 is one who is prescribed in regulations made by the Secretary of State under section 63B(6) of the Police and Criminal Evidence Act 1984. [The regulations are currently contained in regulation SI 2001 No. 2645, the Police and Criminal Evidence Act 1984 (Drug Testing Persons in Police Detention) (Prescribed Persons) Regulations 2001.]

17D The retention of the sample in paragraph 17.16(b) allows for the sample to be sent for confirmatory testing and analysis if the detainee disputes the test. But such samples, and the information derived from them, may not be subsequently used in the investigation of any offence or in evidence against the persons from whom they were taken.

17E Trigger offences are:

1. *Offences under the following provisions of the Theft Act 1968:*

section 1	(theft)
section 8	(robbery)
section 9	(burglary)
section 10	(aggravated burglary)
section 12	(taking a motor vehicle or other conveyance without authority)
section 12A	(aggravated vehicle-taking)
section 15	(obtaining property by deception)
section 22	(handling stolen goods)
section 25	(going equipped for stealing etc.)

2. Offences under the following provisions of the Misuse of Drugs Act 1971, if committed in respect of a specified Class A drug:–

section 4	*(restriction on production and supply of controlled drugs)*
section 5(2)	(possession of a controlled drug)
section 5(3)	(possession of a controlled drug with intent to supply)

3. *An offence under section 1(1) of the Criminal Attempts Act 1981 if committed in respect of an offence under any of the following provisions of the Theft Act 1968:*

section 1	(theft)
section 8	(robbery)
section 9	(burglary)
section 15	(obtaining property by deception)
section 22	(handling stolen goods)

4. Offences under the following provisions of the Vagrancy Act 1824:

| section 3 | (begging) |
| section 4 | (persistent begging) |

17F *The power to take samples is subject to notification by the Secretary of State that appropriate arrangements for the taking of samples have been made for the police area as a whole or for the particular police station concerned for whichever of the following is specified in the notification:*

(a) persons in respect of whom the arrest condition is met;
(b) persons in respect of whom the charge condition is met;
(c) persons who have not attained the age of 18.

Note: Notification is treated as having been given for the purposes of the charge condition in relation to a police area, if testing (on charge) under section 63B(2) of PACE was in force immediately before section 7 of the Drugs Act 2005 was brought into force; and for the purposes of the age condition, in relation to a police area or police station, if immediately before that day, notification that arrangements had been made for the taking of samples from persons under the age of 18 (those aged 14-17) had been given and had not been withdrawn.

17G Appropriate adult in paragraph 17.7 means the person's –

(a) parent or guardian or, if they are in the care of a local authority or voluntary organisation, a person representing that authority or organisation; or
(b) a social worker of, in England, a local authority or, in Wales, a local authority social services department; or
(c) if no person falling within (a) or (b) above is available, any responsible person aged 18 or over who is not a police officer or a person employed by the police.

ANNEX A – INTIMATE AND STRIP SEARCHES

A Intimate search

1. An intimate search consists of the physical examination of a person's body orifices other than the mouth. The intrusive nature of such searches means the actual and potential risks associated with intimate searches must never be underestimated.

(a) Action

2. Body orifices other than the mouth may be searched only:

(a) if authorised by an officer of inspector rank or above who has reasonable grounds for believing that the person may have concealed on themselves:

(i) anything which they could and might use to cause physical injury to themselves or others at the station; or
(ii) a Class A drug which they intended to supply to another or to export;

and the officer has reasonable grounds for believing that an intimate search is the only means of removing those items; and

(b) if the search is under *paragraph 2(a)(ii)* (a drug offence search), the detainee's appropriate consent has been given in writing.

2A. Before the search begins, a police officer, designated detention officer or staff custody officer, must tell the detainee:

(a) that the authority to carry out the search has been given;
(b) the grounds for giving the authorisation and for believing that the article cannot be removed without an intimate search.

2B Before a detainee is asked to give appropriate consent to a search under *paragraph 2(a)(ii)* (a drug offence search) they must be warned that if they refuse without good cause their refusal may harm their case if it comes to trial, see *Note A6.* This warning may be given by a police officer or member of police staff. A detainee who is not legally represented must be reminded of their entitlement to have free legal advice, see Code C, *paragraph 6.5*, and the reminder noted in the custody record.

3. An intimate search may only be carried out by a registered medical practitioner or registered nurse, unless an officer of at least inspector rank considers this is not practicable and the search is to take place under *paragraph 2(a)(i)*, in which case a police officer may carry out the search. See *Notes A1 to A5*

3A. Any proposal for a search under *paragraph 2(a)(i)* to be carried out by someone other than a registered medical practitioner or registered nurse must only be considered as a last resort and when the authorising officer is satisfied the risks associated with allowing the item to remain with the detainee outweigh the risks associated with removing it. See *Notes A1 to A5*

4. An intimate search under:

- *paragraph 2(a)(i)* may take place only at a hospital, surgery, other medical premises or police station
- *paragraph 2(a)(ii)* may take place only at a hospital, surgery or other medical premises and must be carried out by a registered medical practitioner or a registered nurse

5. An intimate search at a police station of a juvenile or mentally disordered or otherwise mentally vulnerable person may take place only in the presence of an appropriate adult of the same sex, unless the detainee specifically requests a particular adult of the opposite sex who is readily available. In the case of a juvenile the search may take place in the absence of the appropriate adult only if the juvenile signifies in the presence of the appropriate adult they do not want the adult present during the search and the adult agrees. A record shall be made of the juvenile's decision and signed by the appropriate adult.

6. When an intimate search under *paragraph 2(a)(i)* is carried out by a police officer, the officer must be of the same sex as the detainee. A minimum of two people, other than the detainee, must be present during the search. Subject to *paragraph 5*, no person of the opposite sex who is not a medical practitioner or nurse shall be present, nor shall anyone whose presence is unnecessary. The search shall be conducted with proper regard to the sensitivity and vulnerability of the detainee.

(b) Documentation

7. In the case of an intimate search, the following shall be recorded as soon as practicable, in the detainee's custody record:

(a) for searches under *paragraphs 2(a)(i)* and *(ii)*;

- the authorisation to carry out the search;
- the grounds for giving the authorisation;
- the grounds for believing the article could not be removed without an intimate search
- which parts of the detainee's body were searched
- who carried out the search
- who was present
- the result.

(b) for searches under paragraph 2(a)(ii):

- the giving of the warning required by *paragraph 2B*;
- the fact that the appropriate consent was given or (as the case may be) refused, and if refused, the reason given for the refusal (if any).

8. If an intimate search is carried out by a police officer, the reason why it was impracticable for a registered medical practitioner or registered nurse to conduct it must be recorded.

B Strip search

9. A strip search is a search involving the removal of more than outer clothing. In this Code, outer clothing includes shoes and socks.

(a) Action

10. A strip search may take place only if it is considered necessary to remove an article which a detainee would not be allowed to keep, and the officer reasonably considers the detainee might have concealed such an article. Strip searches shall not be routinely carried out if there is no reason to consider that articles are concealed.

The conduct of strip searches

11. When strip searches are conducted:

(a) a police officer carrying out a strip search must be the same sex as the detainee;

(b) the search shall take place in an area where the detainee cannot be seen by anyone who does not need to be present, nor by a member of the opposite sex except an appropriate adult who has been specifically requested by the detainee;

(c) except in cases of urgency, where there is risk of serious harm to the detainee or to others, whenever a strip search involves exposure of intimate body parts, there must be at least two people present other than the detainee, and if the search is of a juvenile or mentally disordered or otherwise mentally vulnerable person, one of the people must be the appropriate adult. Except in urgent cases as above, a search of a juvenile may take place in the absence of the appropriate adult only if the juvenile signifies in the presence of the appropriate adult that they do not want the adult to be present during the search and the adult agrees. A record shall be made of the juvenile's decision and signed by the appropriate adult. The presence of more than two people, other than an appropriate adult, shall be permitted only in the most exceptional circumstances;

(d) the search shall be conducted with proper regard to the sensitivity and vulnerability of the detainee in these circumstances and every reasonable effort shall be made to secure the detainee's co-operation and minimise embarrassment. Detainees who are searched shall not normally be required to remove all their clothes at the same time, e.g. a person should be allowed to remove clothing above the waist and redress before removing further clothing;

(e) if necessary to assist the search, the detainee may be required to hold their arms in the air or to stand with their legs apart and bend forward so a visual examination may be made of the genital and anal areas provided no physical contact is made with any body orifice;

(f) if articles are found, the detainee shall be asked to hand them over. If articles are found within any body orifice other than the mouth, and the detainee refuses to hand them over, their removal would constitute an intimate search, which must be carried out as in *Part A*;

(g) a strip search shall be conducted as quickly as possible, and the detainee allowed to dress as soon as the procedure is complete.

(b) Documentation

12. A record shall be made on the custody record of a strip search including the reason it was considered necessary, those present and any result.

Notes for guidance

A1 Before authorising any intimate search, the authorising officer must make every reasonable effort to persuade the detainee to hand the article over without a search. If the detainee agrees, a registered medical practitioner or registered nurse should whenever possible be asked to assess the risks involved and, if necessary, attend to assist the detainee.

A2 If the detainee does not agree to hand the article over without a search, the authorising officer must carefully review all the relevant factors before authorising an intimate search. In particular, the officer must consider whether the grounds for believing an article may be concealed are reasonable.

A3 If authority is given for a search under paragraph 2(a)(i), a registered medical practitioner or registered nurse shall be consulted whenever possible. The presumption should be that the search will be conducted by the registered medical practitioner or registered nurse and the authorising officer must make every reasonable effort to persuade the detainee to allow the medical practitioner or nurse to conduct the search.

A4 A constable should only be authorised to carry out a search as a last resort and when all other approaches have failed. In these circumstances, the authorising officer must be satisfied the detainee might use the article for one or more of the purposes in paragraph 2(a)(i) and the physical injury likely to be caused is sufficiently severe to justify authorising a constable to carry out the search.

A5 If an officer has any doubts whether to authorise an intimate search by a constable, the officer should seek advice from an officer of superintendent rank or above.

A6 In warning a detainee who is asked to consent to an intimate drug offence search, as in paragraph 2B, the following form of words may be used:

"You do not have to allow yourself to be searched, but I must warn you that if you refuse without good cause, your refusal may harm your case if it comes to trial."

ANNEX B – DELAY IN NOTIFYING ARREST OR ALLOWING ACCESS TO LEGAL ADVICE

A Persons detained under PACE

1. The exercise of the rights in *Section 5* or *Section 6*, or both, may be delayed if the person is in police detention, as in PACE, section 118(2), in connection with an indictable offence, has not yet been charged with an offence and an officer of superintendent rank or above, or inspector rank or above only for the rights in *Section 5*, has reasonable grounds for believing their exercise will:

(i) lead to:

- interference with, or harm to, evidence connected with an indictable offence; or
- interference with, or physical harm to, other people; or

(ii) lead to alerting other people suspected of having committed an indictable offence but not yet arrested for it; or

(iii) hinder the recovery of property obtained in consequence of the commission of such an offence.

2. These rights may also be delayed if the officer has reasonable grounds to believe that:

(i) the person detained for an indictable offence has benefited from their criminal conduct (decided in accordance with Part 2 of the Proceeds of Crime Act 2002); and

(ii) the recovery of the value of the property constituting that benefit will be hindered by the exercise of either right.

3. Authority to delay a detainee's right to consult privately with a solicitor may be given only if the authorising officer has reasonable grounds to believe the solicitor the detainee wants to consult will, inadvertently or otherwise, pass on a message from the detainee or act in some other way which will have any of the consequences specified under *paragraphs 1 or 2*. In these circumstances the detainee must be allowed to choose another solicitor. See *Note B3*

4. If the detainee wishes to see a solicitor, access to that solicitor may not be delayed on the grounds they might advise the detainee not to answer questions or the solicitor was initially asked to attend the police station by someone else. In the latter case the detainee must be told the solicitor has come to the police station at another person's request, and must be asked to sign the custody record to signify whether they want to see the solicitor.

5. The fact the grounds for delaying notification of arrest may be satisfied does not automatically mean the grounds for delaying access to legal advice will also be satisfied.

6. These rights may be delayed only for as long as grounds exist and in no case beyond 36 hours after the relevant time as in PACE, section 41. If the grounds cease to apply within this time, the detainee must, as soon as practicable, be asked if they want to exercise either right, the custody record must be noted accordingly, and action taken in accordance with the relevant section of the Code.

7. A detained person must be permitted to consult a solicitor for a reasonable time before any court hearing.

B Not used

C Documentation
13. The grounds for action under this Annex shall be recorded and the detainee informed of them as soon as practicable.

14. Any reply given by a detainee under *paragraphs 6 or 11* must be recorded and the detainee asked to endorse the record in relation to whether they want to receive legal advice at this point.

D Cautions and special warnings
15. When a suspect detained at a police station is interviewed during any period for which access to legal advice has been delayed under this Annex, the court or jury may not draw adverse inferences from their silence.

Notes for guidance
B1 Even if Annex B applies in the case of a juvenile, or a person who is mentally disordered or otherwise mentally vulnerable, action to inform the appropriate adult and the person responsible for a juvenile's welfare if that is a different person, must nevertheless be taken as in paragraph 3.13 and 3.15.

B2 In the case of Commonwealth citizens and foreign nationals, see Note 7A.

B3 A decision to delay access to a specific solicitor is likely to be a rare occurrence and only when it can be shown the suspect is capable of misleading that particular solicitor and there is more than a substantial risk that the suspect will succeed in causing information to be conveyed which will lead to one or more of the specified consequences.

ANNEX C – RESTRICTION ON DRAWING ADVERSE INFERENCES FROM SILENCE AND TERMS OF THE CAUTION WHEN THE RESTRICTION APPLIES

(a) The restriction on drawing adverse inferences from silence
1. The Criminal Justice and Public Order Act 1994, sections 34, 36 and 37 as amended by the Youth Justice and Criminal Evidence Act 1999, section 58 describe the conditions under which adverse inferences may be drawn from a person's failure or refusal to say anything about their involvement in the offence when interviewed, after being charged or informed they may be prosecuted. These provisions are subject to an overriding restriction on the ability of a court or jury to draw adverse inferences from a person's silence. This restriction applies:

   (a) to any detainee at a police station, see Note 10C who, before being interviewed, see *section 11* or being charged or informed they may be prosecuted, see section 16, has:

      (i) asked for legal advice, see *section 6, paragraph 6.1*;

      (ii) not been allowed an opportunity to consult a solicitor, including the duty solicitor, as in this Code; and

      (iii) not changed their mind about wanting legal advice, see *section 6, paragraph 6.6(d)*

Note the condition in (ii) will
- apply when a detainee who has asked for legal advice is interviewed before speaking to a solicitor as in *section 6, paragraph 6.6(a)* or *(b)*.
- not apply if the detained person declines to ask for the duty solicitor, see *section 6, paragraphs 6.6(c)* and *(d)*;

(b) to any person charged with, or informed they may be prosecuted for, an offence who:

(i) has had brought to their notice a written statement made by another person or the content of an interview with another person which relates to that offence, see *section 16, paragraph 16.4*;

(ii) is interviewed about that offence, see *section 16, paragraph 16.5*; or

(iii) makes a written statement about that offence, see *Annex D paragraphs 4* and *9*.

(b) Terms of the caution when the restriction applies

2. When a requirement to caution arises at a time when the restriction on drawing adverse inferences from silence applies, the caution shall be:

'You do not have to say anything, but anything you do say may be given in evidence.'

3. Whenever the restriction either begins to apply or ceases to apply after a caution has already been given, the person shall be re-cautioned in the appropriate terms. The changed position on drawing inferences and that the previous caution no longer applies shall also be explained to the detainee in ordinary language. See *Note C2*

Notes for guidance

C1 The restriction on drawing inferences from silence does not apply to a person who has not been detained and who therefore cannot be prevented from seeking legal advice if they want to, see paragraphs 10.2 and 3.15.

C2 The following is suggested as a framework to help explain changes in the position on drawing adverse inferences if the restriction on drawing adverse inferences from silence:

(a) begins to apply:

'The caution you were previously given no longer applies. This is because after that caution:

(i) you asked to speak to a solicitor but have not yet been allowed an opportunity to speak to a solicitor. See paragraph 1(a); or

(ii) you have been charged with/informed you may be prosecuted. See paragraph 1(b).

'This means that from now on, adverse inferences cannot be drawn at court and your defence will not be harmed just because you choose to say nothing. Please listen carefully to the caution I am about to give you because it will apply from now on. You will see that it does not say anything about your defence being harmed.'

(b) ceases to apply before or at the time the person is charged or informed they may be prosecuted, see paragraph 1(a);

'The caution you were previously given no longer applies. This is because after that caution you have been allowed an opportunity to speak to a solicitor. Please listen carefully to the caution I am about to give you because it will apply from now on. It explains how your defence at court may be affected if you choose to say nothing.'

ANNEX D – WRITTEN STATEMENTS UNDER CAUTION

(a) Written by a person under caution

(a) Written by a person under caution

1. A person shall always be invited to write down what they want to say.

2. A person who has not been charged with, or informed they may be prosecuted for, any offence to which the statement they want to write relates, shall:

(a) unless the statement is made at a time when the restriction on drawing adverse inferences from silence applies, see Annex C, be asked to write out and sign the following before writing what they want to say:

'I make this statement of my own free will. I understand that I do not have to say anything but that it may harm my defence if I do not mention when questioned something which I later rely on in court. This statement may be given in evidence.';

(b) if the statement is made at a time when the restriction on drawing adverse inferences from silence applies, be asked to write out and sign the following before writing what they want to say;

'I make this statement of my own free will. I understand that I do not have to say anything. This statement may be given in evidence.'

3. When a person, on the occasion of being charged with or informed they may be prosecuted for any offence, asks to make a statement which relates to any such offence and wants to write it they shall:

(a) unless the restriction on drawing adverse inferences from silence, see *Annex C*, applied when they were so charged or informed they may be prosecuted, be asked to write out and sign the following before writing what they want to say:

'I make this statement of my own free will. I understand that I do not have to say anything but that it may harm my defence if I do not mention when questioned something which I later rely on in court. This statement may be given in evidence.';

(b) if the restriction on drawing adverse inferences from silence applied when they were so charged or informed they may be prosecuted, be asked to write out and sign the following before writing what they want to say:

'I make this statement of my own free will. I understand that I do not have to say anything. This statement may be given in evidence.'

4. When a person, who has already been charged with or informed they may be prosecuted for any offence, asks to make a statement which relates to any such offence and wants to write it they shall be asked to write out and sign the following before writing what they want to say:

'I make this statement of my own free will. I understand that I do not have to say anything. This statement may be given in evidence.';

5. Any person writing their own statement shall be allowed to do so without any prompting except a police officer or other police staff may indicate to them which matters are material or question any ambiguity in the statement.

(b) Written by a police officer or other police staff

6. If a person says they would like someone to write the statement for them, a police officer, or other police staff shall write the statement.

7. If the person has not been charged with, or informed they may be prosecuted for, any offence to which the statement they want to make relates they shall, before starting, be asked to sign, or make their mark, to the following:

(a) unless the statement is made at a time when the restriction on drawing adverse inferences from silence applies, see Annex C:

'I, ..., wish to make a statement. I want someone to write down what I say. I understand that I do not have to say anything but that it may harm my defence if I do not mention when questioned something which I later rely on in court. This statement may be given in evidence.';

(b) if the statement is made at a time when the restriction on drawing adverse inferences from silence applies:

'I, ..., wish to make a statement. I want someone to write down what I say. I understand that I do not have to say anything. This statement may be given in evidence.'

8. If, on the occasion of being charged with or informed they may be prosecuted for any offence, the person asks to make a statement which relates to any such offence they shall before starting be asked to sign, or make their mark to, the following:

(a) unless the restriction on drawing adverse inferences from silence applied, see Annex C, when they were so charged or informed they may be prosecuted:

'I, ..., wish to make a statement. I want someone to write down what I say. I understand that I do not have to say anything but that it may harm my defence if I do not mention when questioned something which I later rely on in court. This statement may be given in evidence.';

(b) if the restriction on drawing adverse inferences from silence applied when they were so charged or informed they may be prosecuted:

'I, ..., wish to make a statement. I want someone to write down what I say. I understand that I do not have to say anything. This statement may be given in evidence.'

9. If, having already been charged with or informed they may be prosecuted for any offence, a person asks to make a statement which relates to any such offence they shall before starting, be asked to sign, or make their mark to:

'I, ..., wish to make a statement. I want someone to write down what I say. I understand that I do not have to say anything. This statement may be given in evidence.'

10. The person writing the statement must take down the exact words spoken by the person making it and must not edit or paraphrase it. Any questions that are necessary, e.g. to make it more intelligible, and the answers given must be recorded at the same time on the statement form.

11. When the writing of a statement is finished the person making it shall be asked to read it and to make any corrections, alterations or additions they want. When they have

finished reading they shall be asked to write and sign or make their mark on the following certificate at the end of the statement:

'I have read the above statement, and I have been able to correct, alter or add anything I wish. This statement is true. I have made it of my own free will.'

12. If the person making the statement cannot read, or refuses to read it, or to write the above mentioned certificate at the end of it or to sign it, the person taking the statement shall read it to them and ask them if they would like to correct, alter or add anything and to put their signature or make their mark at the end. The person taking the statement shall certify on the statement itself what has occurred.

ANNEX E – SUMMARY OF PROVISIONS RELATING TO MENTALLY DISORDERED AND OTHERWISE MENTALLY VULNERABLE PEOPLE

1. If an officer has any suspicion, or is told in good faith, that a person of any age may be mentally disordered or otherwise mentally vulnerable, or mentally incapable of understanding the significance of questions or their replies that person shall be treated as mentally disordered or otherwise mentally vulnerable for the purposes of this Code. See *paragraph 1.4*

2. In the case of a person who is mentally disordered or otherwise mentally vulnerable, 'the appropriate adult' means:

    (a) a relative, guardian or other person responsible for their care or custody;
    (b) someone experienced in dealing with mentally disordered or mentally vulnerable people but who is not a police officer or employed by the police;
    (c) failing these, some other responsible adult aged 18 or over who is not a police officer or employed by the police.

See *paragraph 1.7(b) and Note 1D*

3. If the custody officer authorises the detention of a person who is mentally vulnerable or appears to be suffering from a mental disorder, the custody officer must as soon as practicable inform the appropriate adult of the grounds for detention and the person's whereabouts, and ask the adult to come to the police station to see them. If the appropriate adult:

- is already at the station when information is given as in *paragraphs 3.1 to 3.5* the information must be given in their presence
- is not at the station when the provisions of *paragraph 3.1 to 3.5* are complied with these provisions must be complied with again in their presence once they arrive.

See *paragraphs 3.15 to 3.17*

4. If the appropriate adult, having been informed of the right to legal advice, considers legal advice should be taken, the provisions of *section 6* apply as if the mentally disordered or otherwise mentally vulnerable person had requested access to legal advice. See *paragraph 3.19* and *Note E1*.

5. The custody officer must make sure a person receives appropriate clinical attention as soon as reasonably practicable if the person appears to be suffering from a mental disorder or in urgent cases immediately call the nearest health care professional or an ambulance. It is not intended these provisions delay the transfer of a detainee to a place of safety under the Mental Health Act 1983, section 136 if that is applicable. If an assessment under that Act is to take place at a police station, the custody officer must consider whether an appropriate health care professional should be called to conduct an initial clinical check on the detainee. See *paragraph 9.5* and *9.6*

6. It is imperative a mentally disordered or otherwise mentally vulnerable person detained under the Mental Health Act 1983, section 136 be assessed as soon as possible. If that assessment is to take place at the police station, an approved social worker and registered medical practitioner shall be called to the station as soon as possible in order to interview and examine the detainee. Once the detainee has been interviewed, examined and suitable arrangements been made for their treatment or care, they can no longer be detained under section 136. A detainee should be immediately discharged from detention if a registered medical practitioner having examined them, concludes they are not mentally disordered within the meaning of the Act. See *paragraph 3.16*

7. If a mentally disordered or otherwise mentally vulnerable person is cautioned in the absence of the appropriate adult, the caution must be repeated in the appropriate adult's presence. See *paragraph 10.12*

8. A mentally disordered or otherwise mentally vulnerable person must not be interviewed or asked to provide or sign a written statement in the absence of the appropriate adult unless the provisions of *paragraphs 11.1* or *11.18* to *11.20* apply. Questioning in these circumstances may not continue in the absence of the appropriate adult once sufficient information to avert the risk has been obtained. A record shall be made of the grounds for any decision to begin an interview in these circumstances. See *paragraphs 11.1, 11.15* and *11.18* to *11.20*

9. If the appropriate adult is present at an interview, they shall be informed they are not expected to act simply as an observer and the purposes of their presence are to:

- advise the interviewee
- observe whether or not the interview is being conducted properly and fairly
- facilitate communication with the interviewee

See *paragraph 11.17*

10. If the detention of a mentally disordered or otherwise mentally vulnerable person is reviewed by a review officer or a superintendent, the appropriate adult must, if available at the time, be given an opportunity to make representations to the officer about the need for continuing detention. See *paragraph 15.3*

11. If the custody officer charges a mentally disordered or otherwise mentally vulnerable person with an offence or takes such other action as is appropriate when there is sufficient evidence for a prosecution this must be done in the presence of the appropriate adult. The written notice embodying any charge must be given to the appropriate adult. See *paragraphs 16.1 to 16.4A*

12. An intimate or strip search of a mentally disordered or otherwise mentally vulnerable person may take place only in the presence of the appropriate adult of the same sex, unless the detainee specifically requests the presence of a particular adult of the opposite sex. A strip search may take place in the absence of an appropriate adult only in cases of urgency when there is a risk of serious harm to the detainee or others. See *Annex A, paragraphs 5 and 11(c)*

13. Particular care must be taken when deciding whether to use any form of approved restraints on a mentally disordered or otherwise mentally vulnerable person in a locked cell. See *paragraph 8.2*

Notes for guidance

E1 The purpose of the provision at paragraph 3.19 is to protect the rights of a mentally disordered or otherwise mentally vulnerable detained person who does not understand the significance of what is said to them. If the detained person wants to exercise the right to legal advice, the appropriate action should be taken and not delayed until the appropriate adult arrives. A mentally disordered or otherwise mentally vulnerable detained person should always be given an opportunity, when an appropriate adult is called to the police station, to consult privately with a solicitor in the absence of the appropriate adult if they want.

E2 Although people who are mentally disordered or otherwise mentally vulnerable are often capable of providing reliable evidence, they may, without knowing or wanting to do so, be particularly prone in certain circumstances to provide information that may be unreliable, misleading or self-incriminating. Special care should always be taken when questioning such a person, and the appropriate adult should be involved if there is any doubt about a person's mental state or capacity. Because of the risk of unreliable evidence, it is important to obtain corroboration of any facts admitted whenever possible.

E3 Because of the risks referred to in Note E2, which the presence of the appropriate adult is intended to minimise, officers of superintendent rank or above should exercise their discretion to authorise the commencement of an interview in the appropriate adult's absence only in exceptional cases, if it is necessary to avert an immediate risk of serious harm. See paragraphs 11.1, 11.18 to 11.20

ANNEX F – COUNTRIES WITH WHICH BILATERAL CONSULAR CONVENTIONS OR AGREEMENTS REQUIRING NOTIFICATION OF THE ARREST AND DETENTION OF THEIR NATIONALS ARE IN FORCE AS AT 1 APRIL 2003

Armenia	Kazakhstan
Austria	Macedonia
Azerbaijan	Mexico
Belarus	Moldova
Belgium	Mongolia
Bosnia-Herzegovina	Norway
Bulgaria	Poland
China*	Romania
Croatia	Russia
Cuba	Slovak Republic
Czech Republic	Slovenia
Denmark	Spain
Egypt	Sweden
France	Tajikistan
Georgia	Turkmenistan
German Federal Republic	Ukraine
Greece	USA
Hungary	Uzbekistan
Italy	Yugoslavia
Japan	

* Police are required to inform Chinese officials of arrest/detention in the Manchester consular district only. This comprises Derbyshire, Durham, Greater Manchester, Lancashire, Merseyside, North South and West Yorkshire, and Tyne and Wear.

ANNEX G – FITNESS TO BE INTERVIEWED

1. This Annex contains general guidance to help police officers and health care professionals assess whether a detainee might be at risk in an interview.

2. A detainee may be at risk in a interview if it is considered that:

(*a*) conducting the interview could significantly harm the detainee's physical or mental state;

(*b*) anything the detainee says in the interview about their involvement or suspected involvement in the offence about which they are being interviewed **might** be considered unreliable in subsequent court proceedings because of their physical or mental state.

3. In assessing whether the detainee should be interviewed, the following must be considered:

(*a*) how the detainee's physical or mental state might affect their ability to understand the nature and purpose of the interview, to comprehend what is being asked and to appreciate the significance of any answers given and make rational decisions about whether they want to say anything;

(*b*) the extent to which the detainee's replies may be affected by their physical or mental condition rather than representing a rational and accurate explanation of their involvement in the offence;

(*c*) how the nature of the interview, which could include particularly probing questions, might affect the detainee.

4. It is essential health care professionals who are consulted consider the functional ability of the detainee rather than simply relying on a medical diagnosis, e.g. it is possible for a person with severe mental illness to be fit for interview.

5. Health care professionals should advise on the need for an appropriate adult to be present, whether reassessment of the person's fitness for interview may be necessary if the interview lasts beyond a specified time, and whether a further specialist opinion may be required.

6. When health care professionals identify risks they should be asked to quantify the risks. They should inform the custody officer:

• whether the person's condition:

  – is likely to improve

  – will require or be amenable to treatment; and

• indicate how long it may take for such improvement to take effect

7. The role of the health care professional is to consider the risks and advise the custody officer of the outcome of that consideration. The health care professional's determination and any advice or recommendations should be made in writing and form part of the custody record.

8. Once the health care professional has provided that information, it is a matter for the custody officer to decide whether or not to allow the interview to go ahead and if the interview is to proceed, to determine what safeguards are needed. Nothing prevents safeguards being provided in addition to those required under the Code. An example might be to have an appropriate health care professional present during the interview, in addition to an appropriate adult, in order constantly to monitor the person's condition and how it is being affected by the interview.

ANNEX H – DETAINED PERSON: OBSERVATION LIST

1. If any detainee fails to meet any of the following criteria, an appropriate health care professional or an ambulance must be called.

2. When assessing the level of rousability, consider:

Rousability – can they be woken?

• go into the cell
• call their name
• shake gently

Response to questions – can they give appropriate answers to questions such as:

• What's your name?
• Where do you live?
• Where do you think you are?

Response to commands – can they respond appropriately to commands such as:

- Open your eyes!
- Lift one arm, now the other arm!

3. Remember to take into account the possibility or presence of other illnesses, injury, or mental condition, a person who is drowsy and smells of alcohol may also have the following:

- Diabetes
- Epilepsy
- Head injury
- Drug intoxication or overdose
- Stroke

ANNEX I

Not used.

ANNEX J

Not used.

ANNEX K – X-RAYS AND ULTRASOUND SCANS

(a) **Action**

1. PACE, section 55A allows a person who has been arrested and is in police detention to have an X-ray taken of them or an ultrasound scan to be carried out on them (or both) if:

(*a*) authorised by an officer of inspector rank or above who has reasonable grounds for believing that the detainee:

(i) may have swallowed a Class A drug; and

(ii) was in possession of that Class A drug with the intention of supplying it to another or to export; and

(*b*) the detainee's appropriate consent has been given in writing.

2. Before an x-ray is taken or an ultrasound scan carried out, a police officer, designated detention officer or staff custody officer must tell the detainee:

(*a*) that the authority has been given; and

(*b*) the grounds for giving the authorisation.

3. Before a detainee is asked to give appropriate consent to an x-ray or an ultrasound scan, they must be warned that if they refuse without good cause their refusal may harm their case if it comes to trial, see *Notes K1* and *K2*. This warning may be given by a police officer or member of police staff. A detainee who is not legally represented must be reminded of their entitlement to have free legal advice, see Code C, *paragraph 6.5*, and the reminder noted in the custody record.

4. An x-ray may be taken, or an ultrasound scan may be carried out, only by a registered medical practitioner or registered nurse, and only at a hospital, surgery or other medical premises.

(b) **Documentation**

5. The following shall be recorded as soon as practicable in the detainee's custody record:

(*a*) the authorisation to take the x-ray or carry out the ultrasound scan (or both);

(*b*) the grounds for giving the authorisation;

(*c*) the giving of the warning required by *paragraph 3*; and

(*d*) the fact that the appropriate consent was given or (as the case may be) refused, and if refused, the reason given for the refusal (if any); and

(*e*) if an x-ray is taken or an ultrasound scan carried out:

- where it was taken or carried out
- who took it or carried it out
- who was present
- the result

6 Paragraphs 1.4 – 1.7 of this Code apply and an appropriate adult should be present when consent is sought to any procedure under this Annex.

Notes for guidance

K1 If authority is given for an x-ray to be taken or an ultrasound scan to be carried out (or both), consideration should be given to asking a registered medical practitioner or registered nurse to explain to the detainee what is involved and to allay any concerns the detainee might have about the effect which taking an x-ray or carrying out an ultrasound scan might have on them. If appropriate consent is not given, evidence of the explanation may, if the case comes to trial, be relevant to determining whether the detainee had a good cause for refusing.

K2 In warning a detainee who is asked to consent to an X-ray being taken or an ultrasound scan being carried out (or both), as in paragraph 3, the following form of words may be used:

> "You do not have to allow an x-ray of you to be taken or an ultrasound scan to be carried out on you, but I must warn you that if you refuse without good cause, your refusal may harm your case if it comes to trial."

2–1938

D CODE OF PRACTICE FOR THE IDENTIFICATION OF PERSONS BY POLICE OFFICERS

COMMENCEMENT – TRANSITIONAL ARRANGEMENTS

This code has effect in relation to any identification procedure carried out after midnight on 31 December 2005

---

1. This Code of Practice (draft code laid before Parliament on 8 November 2005) is issued under ss 66 and 67 of the Police and Criminal Evidence Act 1984; it is admissible thereunder in evidence and account may be taken by the court of any relevant provision. the Police and Criminal Evidence Act 1984 (Codes of Practice) Order 2005, SI 2005/3503 has effect in relation to any identification procedure carried out on or after 1 January 2005.

1 INTRODUCTION

1.1 This Code of Practice concerns the principal methods used by police to identify people in connection with the investigation of offences and the keeping of accurate and reliable criminal records.

1.2 Identification by witnesses arises, eg, if the offender is seen committing the crime and a witness is given an opportunity to identify the suspect in a video identification, identification parade or similar procedure. The procedures are designed to:

- test the witness' ability to identify the person they saw on a previous occasion
- provide safeguards against mistaken identification.

While this Code concentrates on visual identification procedures, it does not preclude the police making use of aural identification procedures such as a "voice identification parade", where they judge that appropriate.

1.3 Identification by fingerprints applies when a person's fingerprints are taken to:

- compare with fingerprints found at the scene of a crime
- check and prove convictions
- help to ascertain a person's identity.

1.3A Identification using footwear impressions applies when a person's footwear impressions are taken to compare with impressions found at the scene of a crime.

1.4 Identification by body samples and impressions includes taking samples such as blood or hair to generate a DNA profile for comparison with material obtained from the scene of a crime, or a victim.

1.5 Taking photographs of arrested people applies to recording and checking identity and locating and tracing persons who:

- are wanted for offences
- fail to answer their bail.

1.6 Another method of identification involves searching and examining detained suspects to find, eg, marks such as tattoos or scars which may help establish their identity or whether they have been involved in committing an offence.

1.7 The provisions of the Police and Criminal Evidence Act 1984 (PACE) and this Code are designed to make sure fingerprints, samples, impressions and photographs are taken, used and retained, and identification procedures carried out, only when justified and necessary for preventing, detecting or investigating crime. If these provisions are not observed, the application of the relevant procedures in particular cases may be open to question.

2 GENERAL

2.1 This Code must be readily available at all police stations for consultation by:

- police officers and police staff
- detained persons
- members of the public

2.2 The provisions of this Code:

- include the Annexes
- do not include the Notes for guidance.

2.3 Code C, paragraph 1.4, regarding a person who may be mentally disordered or otherwise mentally vulnerable and the Notes for guidance applicable to those provisions apply to this Code.

2.4 Code C, paragraph 1.5, regarding a person who appears to be under the age of 17 applies to this Code.

2.5 Code C, paragraph 1.6, regarding a person who appears blind, seriously visually impaired, deaf, unable to read or speak or has difficulty orally because of a speech impediment applies to this Code.

2.6 In this Code:

- 'appropriate adult' means the same as in Code C, paragraph 1.7,
- 'solicitor' means the same as in Code C, paragraph 6.12

and the Notes for guidance applicable to those provisions apply to this Code.

2.7 References to custody officers include those performing the functions of custody officer, see paragraph 1.9 of Code C.

2.8 When a record of any action requiring the authority of an officer of a specified rank is made under this Code, subject to paragraph 2.18, the officer's name and rank must be recorded.

2.9 When this Code requires the prior authority or agreement of an officer of at least inspector or superintendent rank, that authority may be given by a sergeant or chief inspector who has been authorised to perform the functions of the higher rank under PACE, section 107.

2.10 Subject to paragraph 2.18, all records must be timed and signed by the maker.

2.11 Records must be made in the custody record, unless otherwise specified. References to 'pocket book' include any official report book issued to police officers or police staff.

2.12 If any procedure in this Code requires a person's consent, the consent of a:

- mentally disordered or otherwise mentally vulnerable person is only valid if given in the presence of the appropriate adult
- juvenile, is only valid if their parent's or guardian's consent is also obtained unless the juvenile is under 14, when their parent's or guardian's consent is sufficient in its own right. If the only obstacle to an identification procedure in section 3 is that a juvenile's parent or guardian refuses consent or reasonable efforts to obtain it have failed, the identification officer may apply the provisions of paragraph 3.21. See Note 2A.

2.13 If a person is blind, seriously visually impaired or unable to read, the custody officer or identification officer shall make sure their solicitor, relative, appropriate adult or some other person likely to take an interest in them and not involved in the investigation is available to help check any documentation. When this Code requires written consent or signing, the person assisting may be asked to sign instead, if the detainee prefers. This paragraph does not require an appropriate adult to be called solely to assist in checking and signing documentation for a person who is not a juvenile, or mentally disordered or otherwise mentally vulnerable (see Note 2B and Code C paragraph 3.15).

2.14 If any procedure in this Code requires information to be given to or sought from a suspect, it must be given or sought in the appropriate adult's presence if the suspect is mentally disordered, otherwise mentally vulnerable or a juvenile. If the appropriate adult is not present when the information is first given or sought, the procedure must be repeated in the presence of the appropriate adult when they arrive. If the suspect appears deaf or there is doubt about their hearing or speaking ability or ability to understand English, and effective communication cannot be established, the information must be given or sought through an interpreter.

2.15 Any procedure in this Code involving the participation of a suspect who is mentally disordered, otherwise mentally vulnerable or a juvenile must take place in the presence of the appropriate adult. See Code C paragraph 1.4.

2.15A Any procedure in this Code involving the participation of a witness who is or appears to be mentally disordered, otherwise mentally vulnerable or a juvenile should take place in the presence of a pre-trial support person. However, the support-person must not be allowed to prompt any identification of a suspect by a witness. See note 2AB.

2.16 References to:

- 'taking a photograph', include the use of any process to produce a single, still or moving, visual image
- 'photographing a person', should be construed accordingly
- 'photographs', 'films', 'negatives' and 'copies' include relevant visual images recorded, stored, or reproduced through any medium
- 'destruction' includes the deletion of computer data relating to such images or making access to that data impossible.

2.17 Except as described, nothing in this Code affects the powers and procedures:

(i) for requiring and taking samples of breath, blood and urine in relation to driving offences, etc, when under the influence of drink, drugs or excess alcohol under the:

- Road Traffic Act 1988, sections 4 to 11
- Road Traffic Offenders Act 1988, sections 15 and 16
- Transport and Works Act 1992, sections 26 to 38;

(ii) under the Immigration Act 1971, Schedule 2, paragraph 18, for taking photographs and fingerprints from persons detained under that Act, Schedule 2, paragraph 16 (Administrative Controls as to Control on Entry etc.); for taking fingerprints in accordance with the Immigration and Asylum Act 1999; sections 141 and 142(3), or other methods for collecting information about a person's external physical characteristics provided for by regulations made under that Act, section 144;

(iii) under the Terrorism Act 2000, Schedule 8, for taking photographs, fingerprints, skin impressions, body samples or impressions from people:

- arrested under that Act, section 41,
- detained for the purposes of examination under that Act, Schedule 7, and to whom the Code of Practice issued under that Act, Schedule 14, paragraph 6, applies ('the terrorism provisions') See Note 2C;

(iv) for taking photographs, fingerprints, skin impressions, body samples or impressions from people who have been:

- arrested on warrants issued in Scotland, by officers exercising powers under the Criminal Justice and Public Order Act 1994, section 136(2)
- arrested or detained without warrant by officers from a police force in Scotland exercising their powers of arrest or detention under the Criminal Justice and Public Order Act 1994, section 137(2), (Cross Border powers of arrest etc.).

Note: In these cases, police powers and duties and the person's rights and entitlements whilst at a police station in England and Wales are the same as if the person had been arrested in Scotland by a Scottish police officer.

2.18 Nothing in this Code requires the identity of officers or police staff to be recorded or disclosed:

(a) in the case of enquiries linked to the investigation of terrorism;
(b) if the officers or police staff reasonably believe recording or disclosing their names might put them in danger.

In these cases, they shall use warrant or other identification numbers and the name of their police station. See Note 2D

2.19 In this Code:

(a) 'designated person' means a person other than a police officer, designated under the Police Reform Act 2002, Part 4, who has specified powers and duties of police officers conferred or imposed on them;
(b) any reference to a police officer includes a designated person acting in the exercise or performance of the powers and duties conferred or imposed on them by their designation.

2.20 If a power conferred on a designated person:

(a) allows reasonable force to be used when exercised by a police officer, a designated person exercising that power has the same entitlement to use force;
(b) includes power to use force to enter any premises, that power is not exercisable by that designated person except:

(i) in the company, and under the supervision, of a police officer; or
(ii) for the purpose of:

- saving life or limb; or
- preventing serious damage to property.

2.21 Nothing in this Code prevents the custody officer, or other officer given custody of the detainee, from allowing police staff who are not designated persons to carry out individual procedures or tasks at the police station if the law allows. However, the officer remains responsible for making sure the procedures and tasks are carried out correctly in accordance with the Codes of Practice. Any such person must be:

(a) a person employed by a police authority maintaining a police force and under the control and direction of the Chief Officer of that force;
(b) employed by a person with whom a police authority has a contract for the provision of services relating to persons arrested or otherwise in custody.

2.22 Designated persons and other police staff must have regard to any relevant provisions of the Codes of Practice.

Notes for guidance

2A For the purposes of paragraph 2.12, the consent required from a parent or guardian may, for a juvenile in the care of a local authority or voluntary organisation, be given by that authority or organisation. In the case of a juvenile, nothing in paragraph 2.12 requires the parent, guardian or representative of a local authority or voluntary organisation to be present to give their consent, unless they are acting as the appropriate adult under paragraphs 2.14 or 2.15. However, it is important that a parent or guardian not present is fully informed before being asked to consent. They must be given the same information about the procedure and the juvenile's suspected involvement in the offence as the juvenile and appropriate adult. The parent or guardian must also be allowed to speak to the juvenile and the appropriate adult if they wish. Provided the consent is fully informed and is not withdrawn, it may be obtained at any time before the procedure takes place.

2AB The Youth Justice and Criminal Evidence Act 1999 guidance "Achieving Best Evidence in Criminal Proceedings" indicates that a pre-trial support person should accompany a vulnerable witness during any identification procedure. It states that this support person should not be (or not likely to be) a witness in the investigation.

2B People who are seriously visually impaired or unable to read may be unwilling to sign police documents. The alternative, i.e. their representative signing on their behalf, seeks to protect the interests of both police and suspects.

2C Photographs, fingerprints, samples and impressions may be taken from a person detained under the terrorism provisions to help determine whether they are, or have been, involved in terrorism, as well as when there are reasonable grounds for suspecting their involvement in a particular offence.

2D The purpose of paragraph 2.18(b) is to protect those involved in serious organised crime investigations or arrests of particularly violent suspects when there is reliable information that those arrested or their associates may threaten or cause harm to the officers. In cases of doubt, an officer of inspector rank or above should be consulted.

3 IDENTIFICATION BY WITNESSES

3.1 A record shall be made of the suspect's description as first given by a potential witness. This record must:

(a) be made and kept in a form which enables details of that description to be accurately produced from it, in a visible and legible form, which can be given to the suspect or the suspect's solicitor in accordance with this Code; and

(b) unless otherwise specified, be made before the witness takes part in any identification procedures under paragraphs 3.5 to 3.10, 3.21 or 3.23. A copy of the record shall where practicable, be given to the suspect or their solicitor before any procedures under paragraphs 3.5 to 3.10, 3.21 or 3.23 are carried out. See Note 3E

(a) Cases when the suspect's identity is not known

3.2 In cases when the suspect's identity is not known, a witness may be taken to a particular neighbourhood or place to see whether they can identify the person they saw. Although the number, age, sex, race, general description and style of clothing of other people present at the location and the way in which any identification is made cannot be controlled, the principles applicable to the formal procedures under paragraphs 3.5 to 3.10 shall be followed as far as practicable. For example:

(a) where it is practicable to do so, a record should be made of the witness' description of the suspect, as in paragraph 3.1(a), before asking the witness to make an identification;

(b) care must be taken not to direct the witness' attention to any individual unless, taking into account all the circumstances, this cannot be avoided. However, this does not prevent a witness being asked to look carefully at the people around at the time or to look towards a group or in a particular direction, if this appears necessary to make sure that the witness does not overlook a possible suspect simply because the witness is looking in the opposite direction and also to enable the witness to make comparisons between any suspect and others who are in the area; See Note 3F

(c) where there is more than one witness, every effort should be made to keep them separate and witnesses should be taken to see whether they can identify a person independently;

(d) once there is sufficient information to justify the arrest of a particular individual for suspected involvement in the offence, eg, after a witness makes a positive identification, the provisions set out from paragraph 3.4 onwards shall apply for any other witnesses in relation to that individual. Subject to paragraphs 3.12 and 3.13, it is not necessary for the witness who makes such a positive identification to take part in a further procedure;

(e) the officer or police staff accompanying the witness must record, in their pocket book, the action taken as soon as, and in as much detail, as possible. The record should include: the date, time and place of the relevant occasion the witness claims to have previously seen the suspect; where any identification was made; how it was made and the conditions at the time (eg, the distance the witness was from the suspect, the weather and light); if the witness's attention was drawn to the suspect; the reason for this; and anything said by the witness or the suspect about the identification or the conduct of the procedure.

3.3 A witness must not be shown photographs, computerised or artist's composite likenesses or similar likenesses or pictures (including 'E-fit' images) if the identity of the suspect is known to the police and the suspect is available to take part in a video identification, an identification parade or a group identification. If the suspect's identity is not known, the showing of such images to a witness to obtain identification evidence must be done in accordance with Annex E.

(b) Cases when the suspect is known and available[1]

3.4 If the suspect's identity is known to the police and they are available, the identification procedures set out in paragraphs 3.5 to 3.10 may be used. References in this section to a suspect being 'known' mean there is sufficient information known to the police to justify the arrest of a particular person for suspected involvement in the offence. A suspect being 'available' means they are immediately available or will be within a reasonably short time and willing to take an effective part in at least one of the following which it is practicable to arrange:

- video identification;
- identification parade; or
- group identification.

1. Section 3.4 (formerly 2.1) pre-supposes that a witness has identified a suspect, that the identity of the suspect is known to the police, and that the evidence in question is disputed. Accordingly, the viewing of a video tape taken subsequent to the alleged offence as part of the investigative process does not constitute a procedure governed by Code D; see *R v Jones (MA)* (1993) 158 JP 293.

Video identification

3.5 A 'video identification' is when the witness is shown moving images of a known suspect, together with similar images of others who resemble the suspect. Moving images must be used unless:

- the suspect is known but not available (see paragraph 3.21 of this Code); or
- in accordance with paragraph 2A of Annex A of this Code, the identification officer does not consider that replication of a physical feature can be achieved or that it is not possible to conceal the location of the feature on the image of the suspect.

The identification officer may then decide to make use of video identification but using still images
3.6 Video identifications must be carried out in accordance with Annex A.

Identification parade

3.7 An 'identification parade' is when the witness sees the suspect in a line of others who resemble the suspect.
3.8 Identification parades must be carried out in accordance with Annex B.

Group identification

3.9 A 'group identification' is when the witness sees the suspect in an informal group of people.
3.10 Group identifications must be carried out in accordance with Annex C.

Arranging identification procedures
3.11 Except for the provisions in paragraph 3.19, the arrangements for, and conduct of, the identification procedures in paragraphs 3.5 to 3.10 and circumstances in which an identification procedure must be held shall be the responsibility of an officer not below inspector rank who is not involved[1] with the investigation, 'the identification officer'. Unless otherwise specified, the identification officer may allow another officer or police staff, see paragraph 2.21, to make arrangements for, and conduct, any of these identification procedures. In delegating these procedures, the identification officer must be able to supervise effectively and either intervene or be contacted for advice. No officer or any other person involved with the investigation of the case against the suspect, beyond the extent required by these procedures, may take any part in these procedures or act as the identification officer. This does not prevent the identification officer from consulting the officer in charge of the investigation to determine which procedure to use. When an identification procedure is required, in the interest of fairness to suspects and witnesses, it must be held as soon as practicable.

1. Where an investigating officer, although not taking any part in the arrangements for a parade, nevertheless went into the parade room, looked at the parade, had an opportunity of talking to the witness, and then the witness was introduced into the parade, it was held that the investigating officer was taking part in the conduct of the parade and, accordingly, that the evidence of the identification parade should be excluded (*R v Gall* (1989) 90 Cr App Rep 64, CA). But it would seem that taking a suspect to the parade is outside the administration of the parade itself; see *R v Jones (Terrence)* [1992] Crim LR 365, CA.

Circumstances in which an identification procedure must be held
3.12 Whenever:
(i) a witness has identified a suspect or purported to have identified them prior to any identification procedure set out in paragraphs 3.5 to 3.10 having been held; or
(ii) there is a witness available, who expresses an ability to identify the suspect, or where there is a reasonable chance of the witness being able to do so, and they have not been given an opportunity to identify the suspect in any of the procedures set out in paragraphs 3.5 to 3.10, and the suspect disputes being the person the witness claims to have seen, an identification procedure shall be held unless it is not practicable[1] or

it would serve no useful purpose[2] in proving or disproving whether the suspect was involved in committing the offence. For example, when it is not disputed that the suspect is already well known to the witness who claims to have seen them commit the crime.

3.13 Such a procedure may also be held if the officer in charge of the investigation considers it would be useful.

---

1. Where the practicability of holding a parade is in issue, the defence should require the attendance of the relevant police officer so his opinion can be tested (*R v Penny* (1991) 94 Cr App Rep 354, CA).

2. Where a witness can give only a general description of a person observed, including what that person was wearing, but is not able positively to identify the person because he cannot describe that person's facial features, no purpose would be served by holding an identification parade; see *R v Gayle* [1999] 2 Cr App Rep 130. There has to have been a purported visual identification by a witness before the terms of Code D 2.3 come into operation. Therefore the police were not required to hold an identity parade where the sole witness stated he could not identify the accused and could not either give a description or only a description of such generality that there is no reason to think that an identification parade would take the matter any further (whether in terms of recognition or elimination (*R v Nicholson* [2000] 1 Cr App Rep 182, CA).

Selecting an identification procedure

3.14 If, because of paragraph 3.12, an identification procedure is to be held, the suspect shall initially be offered a video identification unless:

(a) a video identification is not practicable; or
(b) an identification parade is both practicable and more suitable than a video identification; or
(c) paragraph 3.16 applies.

The identification officer and the officer in charge of the investigation shall consult each other to determine which option is to be offered. An identification parade may not be practicable because of factors relating to the witnesses, such as their number, state of health, availability and travelling requirements. A video identification would normally be more suitable if it could be arranged and completed sooner than an identification parade.

3.15 A suspect who refuses the identification procedure first offered shall be asked to state their reason for refusing and may get advice from their solicitor and/or if present, their appropriate adult. The suspect, solicitor and/or appropriate adult shall be allowed to make representations about why another procedure should be used. A record should be made of the reasons for refusal and any representations made. After considering any reasons given, and representations made, the identification officer shall, if appropriate, arrange for the suspect to be offered an alternative which the officer considers suitable and practicable. If the officer decides it is not suitable and practicable to offer an alternative identification procedure, the reasons for that decision shall be recorded.

3.16 A group identification may initially be offered if the officer in charge of the investigation considers it is more suitable than a video identification or an identification parade and the identification officer considers it practicable to arrange.

Notice to suspect

3.17 Unless paragraph 3.20 applies, before a video identification, an identification parade or group identification[1] is arranged, the following shall be explained to the suspect:

(i) the purposes of the video identification, identification parade or group identification;
(ii) their entitlement to free legal advice; see Code C, paragraph 6.5;
(iii) the procedures for holding it, including their right to have a solicitor or friend present;
(iv) that they do not have to consent to or co-operate in a video identification, identification parade or group identification;
(v) that if they do not consent to, and co-operate in, a video identification, identification parade or group identification, their refusal may be given in evidence in any subsequent trial and police may proceed covertly without their consent or make other arrangements to test whether a witness can identify them, see paragraph 3.21;
(vi) whether, for the purposes of the video identification procedure, images of them have previously been obtained, see paragraph 3.20, and if so, that they may co-operate in providing further, suitable images to be used instead;
(vii) if appropriate, the special arrangements for juveniles;
(viii) if appropriate, the special arrangements for mentally disordered or otherwise mentally vulnerable people;
(ix) that if they significantly alter their appearance between being offered an identification procedure and any attempt to hold an identification procedure, this may be given in evidence if the case comes to trial, and the identification officer may then consider other forms of identification, see paragraph 3.21 and Note 3C;
(x) that a moving image or photograph may be taken of them when they attend for any identification procedure;
(xi) whether, before their identity became known, the witness was shown photographs, a computerised or artist's composite likeness or similar likeness or image by the police, see Note 3B;

(xii) that if they change their appearance before an identification parade, it may not be practicable to arrange one on the day or subsequently and, because of the appearance change, the identification officer may consider alternative methods of identification, see Note 3C;

(xiii) that they or their solicitor will be provided with details of the description of the suspect as first given by any witnesses who are to attend the video identification, identification parade, group identification or confrontation, see paragraph 3.1.

3.18 This information must also be recorded in a written notice handed to the suspect. The suspect must be given a reasonable opportunity to read the notice, after which, they should be asked to sign a second copy to indicate if they are willing to co-operate with the making of a video or take part in the identification parade or group identification. The signed copy shall be retained by the identification officer.

3.19 The duties of the identification officer under paragraphs 3.17 and 3.18 may be performed by the custody officer or other officer not involved in the investigation if:

(a) it is proposed to release the suspect in order that an identification procedure can be arranged and carried out and an inspector is not available to act as the identification officer, see paragraph 3.11, before the suspect leaves the station; or

(b) it is proposed to keep the suspect in police detention whilst the procedure is arranged and carried out and waiting for an inspector to act as the identification officer, see paragraph 3.11, would cause unreasonable delay to the investigation.

The officer concerned shall inform the identification officer of the action taken and give them the signed copy of the notice. See Note 3C

3.20 If the identification officer and officer in charge of the investigation suspect, on reasonable grounds that if the suspect was given the information and notice as in paragraphs 3.17 and 3.18, they would then take steps to avoid being seen by a witness in any identification procedure, the identification officer may arrange for images of the suspect suitable for use in a video identification procedure to be obtained before giving the information and notice. If suspect's images are obtained in these circumstances, the suspect may, for the purposes of a video identification procedure, co-operate in providing suitable new images to be used instead, see paragraph 3.17(vi).

---

1. Where a breach of the procedure under section 3.14 (formerly 2.7) relating to group identification occurred, but no unfairness resulted from that breach, it was held that the court in the exercise of its discretion had properly admitted evidence of the identification (*R v Grannell* (1989) 90 Cr App Rep 149, CA).

(c) Cases when the suspect is known but not available

3.21 When a known suspect is not available or has ceased to be available, see paragraph 3.4, the identification officer may make arrangements for a video identification (see Annex A). If necessary, the identification officer may follow the video identification procedures but using still images. Any suitable moving or still images may be used and these may be obtained covertly if necessary. Alternatively, the identification officer may make arrangements for a group identification. See Note 3D. These provisions may also be applied to juveniles where the consent of their parent or guardian is either refused or reasonable efforts to obtain that consent have failed (see paragraph 2.12).

3.22 Any covert activity should be strictly limited to that necessary to test the ability of the witness to identify the suspect.

3.23 The identification officer may arrange for the suspect to be confronted by the witness if none of the options referred to in paragraphs 3.5 to 3.10 or 3.21 are practicable. A "confrontation" is when the suspect is directly confronted by the witness. A confrontation does not require the suspect's consent. Confrontations must be carried out in accordance with Annex D.

3.24 Requirements for information to be given to, or sought from, a suspect or for the suspect to be given an opportunity to view images before they are shown to a witness, do not apply if the suspect's lack of co-operation prevents the necessary action.

(d) Documentation

3.25 A record shall be made of the video identification, identification parade, group identification or confrontation on forms provided for the purpose.

3.26 If the identification officer considers it is not practicable to hold a video identification or identification parade requested by the suspect, the reasons shall be recorded and explained to the suspect.

3.27 A record shall be made of a person's failure or refusal to co-operate in a video identification, identification parade or group identification and, if applicable, of the grounds for obtaining images in accordance with paragraph 3.20.

(e) Showing films and photographs of incidents and information released to the media

3.28 Nothing in this Code inhibits showing films or photographs to the public through the national or local media, or to police officers for the purposes of recognition and tracing suspects. However, when such material is shown to potential witnesses, including police officers, see Note 3A, to obtain identification evidence, it shall be shown on an individual basis to avoid any possibility of collusion, and, as far as possible, the showing shall follow the principles for video identification if the suspect is known, see Annex A, or identification by photographs if the suspect is not known, see Annex E.

3.29 When a broadcast or publication is made, see paragraph 3.28, a copy of the relevant material released to the media for the purposes of recognising or tracing the suspect, shall be kept. The suspect or their solicitor shall be allowed to view such material before any procedures under paragraphs 3.5 to 3.10, 3.21 or 3.23 are carried out, provided it is practicable and would not unreasonably delay the investigation. Each witness involved in the procedure shall be asked, after they have taken part, whether they have seen any broadcast or published films or photographs relating to the offence or any description of the suspect and their replies shall be recorded. This paragraph does not affect any separate requirement under the Criminal Procedure and Investigations Act 1996 to retain material in connection with criminal investigations.

(f) Destruction and retention of photographs taken or used in identification procedures
3.30 PACE, section 64A, see paragraph 5.12, provides powers to take photographs of suspects and allows these photographs to be used or disclosed only for purposes related to the prevention or detection of crime, the investigation of offences or the conduct of prosecutions by, or on behalf of, police or other law enforcement and prosecuting authorities inside and outside the United Kingdom or the enforcement of a sentence. After being so used or disclosed, they may be retained but can only be used or disclosed for the same purposes.

3.31 Subject to paragraph 3.33, the photographs (and all negatives and copies), of suspects not taken in accordance with the provisions in paragraph 5.12 which are taken for the purposes of, or in connection with, the identification procedures in paragraphs 3.5 to 3.10, 3.21 or 3.23 must be destroyed unless the suspect:

(a) is charged with, or informed they may be prosecuted for, a recordable offence;
(b) is prosecuted for a recordable offence;
(c) is cautioned for a recordable offence or given a warning or reprimand in accordance with the Crime and Disorder Act 1998 for a recordable offence; or
(d) gives informed consent, in writing, for the photograph or images to be retained for purposes described in paragraph 3.30.

3.32 When paragraph 3.31 requires the destruction of any photograph, the person must be given an opportunity to witness the destruction or to have a certificate confirming the destruction if they request one within five days of being informed that the destruction is required.

3.33 Nothing in paragraph 3.31 affects any separate requirement under the Criminal Procedure and Investigations Act 1996 to retain material in connection with criminal investigations.

Notes for guidance
3A Except for the provisions of Annex E, paragraph 1, a police officer who is a witness for the purposes of this part of the Code is subject to the same principles and procedures as a civilian witness.

3B When a witness attending an identification procedure has previously been shown photographs, or been shown or provided with computerised or artist's composite likenesses, or similar likenesses or pictures, it is the officer in charge of the investigation's responsibility to make the identification officer aware of this.

3C The purpose of paragraph 3.19 is to avoid or reduce delay in arranging identification procedures by enabling the required information and warnings, see sub-paragraphs 3.17(ix) and 3.17(xii), to be given at the earliest opportunity.

3D Paragraph 3.21 would apply when a known suspect deliberately makes themself 'unavailable' in order to delay or frustrate arrangements for obtaining identification evidence. It also applies when a suspect refuses or fails to take part in a video identification, an identification parade or a group identification, or refuses or fails to take part in the only practicable options from that list. It enables any suitable images of the suspect, moving or still, which are available or can be obtained, to be used in an identification procedure. Examples include images from custody and other CCTV systems and from visually recorded interview records, see Code F Note for Guidance 2D.

3E When it is proposed to show photographs to a witness in accordance with Annex E, it is the responsibility of the officer in charge of the investigation to confirm to the officer responsible for supervising and directing the showing, that the first description of the suspect given by that witness has been recorded. If this description has not been recorded, the procedure under Annex E must be postponed. See Annex E paragraph 2

3F The admissibility and value of identification evidence obtained when carrying out the procedure under paragraph 3.2 may be compromised if:

(a) before a person is identified, the witness' attention is specifically drawn to that person; or
(b) the suspect's identity becomes known before the procedure.

4 IDENTIFICATION BY FINGERPRINTS AND FOOTWEAR IMPRESSIONS

(A) Taking fingerprints in connection with a criminal investigation

(a) General

4.1 References to 'fingerprints' means any record, produced by any method, of the skin pattern and other physical characteristics or features of a person's:

(i)   fingers; or
(ii) palms.

(b) Action

4.2 A person's fingerprints may be taken in connection with the investigation of an offence only with their consent or if paragraph 4.3 applies. If the person is at a police station consent must be in writing.

4.3 PACE, section 61, provides powers to take fingerprints without consent from any person over the age of ten years:

(a) under section 61(3), from a person detained at a police station in consequence of being arrested for a recordable offence, see Note 4A, if they have not had their fingerprints taken in the course of the investigation of the offence unless those previously taken fingerprints are not a complete set or some or all of those fingerprints are not of sufficient quality to allow satisfactory analysis, comparison or matching.

(b) under section 61(4), from a person detained at a police station who has been charged with a recordable offence, see Note 4A, or informed they will be reported for such an offence if they have not had their fingerprints taken in the course of the investigation of the offence unless those previously taken fingerprints are not a complete set or some or all of those fingerprints are not of sufficient quality to allow satisfactory analysis, comparison or matching.

(c) under section 61(4A), from a person who has been bailed to appear at a court or police station if the person:

(i)   has answered to bail for a person whose fingerprints were taken previously and there are reasonable grounds for believing they are not the same person; or
(ii) who has answered to bail claims to be a different person from a person whose fingerprints were previously taken;
and in either case, the court or an officer of inspector rank or above, authorises the fingerprints to be taken at the court or police station;

(d) under section 61(6), from a person who has been:

(i)   convicted of a recordable offence;
(ii) given a caution in respect of a recordable offence which, at the time of the caution, the person admitted; or
(iii) warned or reprimanded under the Crime and Disorder Act 1998, section 65, for a recordable offence.

4.4 PACE, section 27, provides power to:

(a) require the person as in paragraph 4.3(d) to attend a police station to have their fingerprints taken if the:

(i)   person has not been in police detention for the offence and has not had their fingerprints taken in the course of the investigation of that offence; or
(ii) fingerprints that were taken from the person in the course of the investigation of that offence, do not constitute a complete set or some, or all, of the fingerprints are not of sufficient quality to allow satisfactory analysis, comparison or matching; and

(b) arrest, without warrant, a person who fails to comply with the requirement.

Note: The requirement must be made within one month of the date the person is convicted, cautioned, warned or reprimanded and the person must be given a period of at least 7 days within which to attend. This 7 day period need not fall during the month allowed for making the requirement.

4.5 A person's fingerprints may be taken, as above, electronically.

4.6 Reasonable force may be used, if necessary, to take a person's fingerprints without their consent under the powers as in paragraphs 4.3 and 4.4.

4.7 Before any fingerprints are taken with, or without, consent as above, the person must be informed:

(a) of the reason their fingerprints are to be taken;
(b) of the grounds on which the relevant authority has been given if the power mentioned in paragraph 4.3 (c) applies;
(c) that their fingerprints may be retained and may be subject of a speculative search against other fingerprints, see Note 4B, unless destruction of the fingerprints is required in accordance with Annex F, Part (a); and

(d) that if their fingerprints are required to be destroyed, they may witness their destruction as provided for in Annex F, Part (a).

(c) Documentation

4.8 A record must be made as soon as possible, of the reason for taking a person's fingerprints without consent. If force is used, a record shall be made of the circumstances and those present.

4.9 A record shall be made when a person has been informed under the terms of paragraph 4.7(c), of the possibility that their fingerprints may be subject of a speculative search.

(B) Taking fingerprints in connection with immigration enquiries

Action

4.10 A person's fingerprints may be taken for the purposes of Immigration Service enquiries in accordance with powers and procedures other than under PACE and for which the Immigration Service (not the police) are responsible, only with the person's consent in writing or if paragraph 4.11 applies.

4.11 Powers to take fingerprints for these purposes without consent are given to police and immigration officers under the:

(a) Immigration Act 1971, Schedule 2, paragraph 18(2), when it is reasonably necessary for the purposes of identifying a person detained under the Immigration Act 1971, Schedule 2, paragraph 16 (Detention of person liable to examination or removal);

(b) Immigration and Asylum Act 1999, section 141(7)(a), from a person who fails to produce, on arrival, a valid passport with a photograph or some other document satisfactorily establishing their identity and nationality if an immigration officer does not consider the person has a reasonable excuse for the failure;

(c) Immigration and Asylum Act 1999, section 141(7)(b), from a person who has been refused entry to the UK but has been temporarily admitted if an immigration officer reasonably suspects the person might break a condition imposed on them relating to residence or reporting to a police or immigration officer, and their decision is confirmed by a chief immigration officer;

(d) Immigration and Asylum Act 1999, section 141(7)(c), when directions are given to remove a person:

- as an illegal entrant,
- liable to removal under the Immigration and Asylum Act 1999, section 10,
- who is the subject of a deportation order from the UK;

(e) Immigration and Asylum Act 1999, section 141(7)(d), from a person arrested under UK immigration laws under the Immigration Act 1971, Schedule 2, paragraph 17;

(f) Immigration and Asylum Act 1999, section 141(7)(e), from a person who has made a claim:

- for asylum
- under Article 3 of the European Convention on Human Rights; or

(g) Immigration and Asylum Act 1999, section 141(7)(f), from a person who is a dependant of someone who falls into (b) to (f) above.

4.12 The Immigration and Asylum Act 1999, section 142(3), gives a police and immigration officer power to arrest, without warrant, a person who fails to comply with a requirement imposed by the Secretary of State to attend a specified place for fingerprinting.

4.13 Before any fingerprints are taken, with or without consent, the person must be informed:

(a) of the reason their fingerprints are to be taken;

(b) the fingerprints, and all copies of them, will be destroyed in accordance with Annex F, Part B.

4.14 Reasonable force may be used, if necessary, to take a person's fingerprints without their consent under powers as in paragraph 4.11.

4.15 Paragraphs 4.1 and 4.8 apply.

(C) Taking footwear impressions in connection with a criminal investigation

(a) Action

4.16 Impressions of a person's footwear may be taken in connection with the investigation of an offence only with their consent or if paragraph 4.17 applies. If the person is at a police station consent must be in writing.

4.17 PACE, section 61A, provides power for a police officer to take footwear impressions without consent from any person over the age of ten years who is detained at a police station:

(a) in consequence of being arrested for a recordable offence, see Note 4A; or if the detainee has been charged with a recordable offence, or informed they will be reported for such an offence; and

(b) the detainee has not had an impression of their footwear taken in the course of the investigation of the offence unless the previously taken impression is not complete or is not of sufficient quality to allow satisfactory analysis, comparison or matching (whether in the case in question or generally).

4.18 Reasonable force may be used, if necessary, to take a footwear impression from a detainee without consent under the power in paragraph 4.17.

4.19 Before any footwear impression is taken with, or without, consent as above, the person must be informed:

(a) of the reason the impression is to be taken;

(b) that the impression may be retained and may be subject of a speculative search against other impressions, see Note 4B, unless destruction of the impression is required in accordance with Annex F, Part (a); and

(c) that if their footwear impressions are required to be destroyed, they may witness their destruction as provided for in Annex F, Part (a).

(b) Documentation

4.20 A record must be made as soon as possible, of the reason for taking a person's footwear impressions without consent. If force is used, a record shall be made of the circumstances and those present.

4.21 A record shall be made when a person has been informed under the terms of paragraph 4.19(b), of the possibility that their footwear impressions may be subject of a speculative search.

Notes for guidance

4A References to 'recordable offences' in this Code relate to those offences for which convictions, cautions, reprimands and warnings may be recorded in national police records. See PACE, section 27(4). The recordable offences current at the time when this Code was prepared, are any offences which carry a sentence of imprisonment on conviction (irrespective of the period, or the age of the offender or actual sentence passed) as well as the non-imprisonable offences under the Vagrancy as amended Act 1824 sections 3 and 4 (begging and persistent begging), the Street Offences Act 1959, section 1 (loitering or soliciting for purposes of prostitution), the Road Traffic Act 1988, section 25 (tampering with motor vehicles) the Criminal Justice and Public Order Act 1994, section 167 (touting for hire car services) and others listed in the National Police Records (Recordable Offences) Regulations 2000.

4B Fingerprints, footwear impressions or a DNA sample (and the information derived from it) taken from a person arrested on suspicion of being involved in a recordable offence, or charged with such an offence, or informed they will be reported for such an offence, may be subject of a speculative search. This means the fingerprints, footwear impressions or DNA sample may be checked against other fingerprints, footwear impressions and DNA records held by, or on behalf of, the police and other law enforcement authorities in, or outside, the UK, or held in connection with, or as a result of, an investigation of an offence inside or outside the UK. Fingerprints, footwear impressions and samples taken from a person suspected of committing a recordable offence but not arrested, charged or informed they will be reported for it, may be subject to a speculative search only if the person consents in writing. The following is an example of a basic form of words:

"I consent to my fingerprints, footwear impressions and DNA sample and information derived from it being retained and used only for purposes related to the prevention and detection of a crime, the investigation of an offence or the conduct of a prosecution either nationally or internationally.

I understand that my fingerprints, footwear impressions or DNA sample may be checked against other fingerprint and DNA records held by or on behalf of relevant law enforcement authorities, either nationally or internationally. I understand that once I have given my consent for my fingerprints, footwear impressions or DNA sample to be retained and used I cannot withdraw this consent."

See Annex F regarding the retention and use of fingerprints, footwear impressions taken with consent for elimination purposes.

5 EXAMINATIONS TO ESTABLISH IDENTITY AND THE TAKING OF PHOTOGRAPHS

(A) Detainees at police stations

(a) Searching or examination of detainees at police stations

5.1 PACE, section 54A (1), allows a detainee at a police station to be searched or examined or both, to establish:

(a) whether they have any marks, features or injuries that would tend to identify them as a person involved in the commission of an offence and to photograph any identifying marks, see paragraph 5.5; or

(b) their identity, see Note 5A.

A person detained at a police station to be searched under a stop and search power, see Code A, is not a detainee for the purposes of these powers.

5.2 A search and/or examination to find marks under section 54A(1)(a) may be carried out without the detainee's consent, see paragraph 2.12, only if authorised by an officer of at least inspector rank when consent has been withheld or it is not practicable to obtain consent, see Note 5D.

5.3 A search or examination to establish a suspect's identity under section 54A(1)(b) may be carried out without the detainee's consent, see paragraph 2.12, only if authorised by an officer of at least inspector rank when the detainee has refused to identify themselves or the authorising officer has reasonable grounds for suspecting the person is not who they claim to be.

5.4 Any marks that assist in establishing the detainee's identity, or their identification as a person involved in the commission of an offence, are identifying marks. Such marks may be photographed with the detainee's consent, see paragraph 2.12; or without their consent if it is withheld or it is not practicable to obtain it, see Note 5D.

5.5 A detainee may only be searched, examined and photographed under section 54A, by a police officer of the same sex.

5.6 Any photographs of identifying marks, taken under section 54A, may be used or disclosed only for purposes related to the prevention or detection of crime, the investigation of offences or the conduct of prosecutions by, or on behalf of, police or other law enforcement and prosecuting authorities inside, and outside, the UK. After being so used or disclosed, the photograph may be retained but must not be used or disclosed except for these purposes, see Note 5B.

5.7 The powers, as in paragraph 5.1, do not affect any separate requirement under the Criminal Procedure and Investigations Act 1996 to retain material in connection with criminal investigations.

5.8 Authority for the search and/or examination for the purposes of paragraphs 5.2 and 5.3 may be given orally or in writing. If given orally, the authorising officer must confirm it in writing as soon as practicable. A separate authority is required for each purpose which applies.

5.9 If it is established a person is unwilling to co-operate sufficiently to enable a search and/or examination to take place or a suitable photograph to be taken, an officer may use reasonable force to:

(a) search and/or examine a detainee without their consent; and

(b) photograph any identifying marks without their consent.

5.10 The thoroughness and extent of any search or examination carried out in accordance with the powers in section 54A must be no more than the officer considers necessary to achieve the required purpose. Any search or examination which involves the removal of more than the person's outer clothing shall be conducted in accordance with Code C, Annex A, paragraph 11.

5.11 An intimate search may not be carried out under the powers in section 54A.

(b) Photographing detainees at police stations and other persons elsewhere than at a police station

5.12 Under PACE, section 64A, an officer may photograph:

(a) any person whilst they are detained at a police station; and

(b) any person who is elsewhere than at a police station and who has been:-

(i) arrested by a constable for an offence;

(ii) taken into custody by a constable after being arrested for an offence by a person other than a constable;

(iii) made subject to a requirement to wait with a community support officer under paragraph 2(3) or (3B) of Schedule 4 to the Police Reform Act 2002;

(iv) given a penalty notice by a constable in uniform under Chapter 1 of Part 1 of the Criminal Justice and Police Act 2001, a penalty notice by a constable under section 444A of the Education Act 1996, or a fixed penalty notice by a constable in uniform under section 54 of the Road Traffic Offenders Act 1988;

(v) given a notice in relation to a relevant fixed penalty offence (within the meaning of paragraph 1 of Schedule 4 to the Police Reform Act 2002) by a community support officer by virtue of a designation applying that paragraph to him; or

(vi) given a notice in relation to a relevant fixed penalty offence (within the meaning of paragraph 1 of Schedule 5 to the Police Reform Act 2002) by an accredited person by virtue of accreditation specifying that that paragraph applies to him.

5.12A Photographs taken under PACE, section 64A:

(a) may be taken with the person's consent, or without their consent if consent is withheld or it is not practicable to obtain their consent, see Note 5E; and

(b) may be used or disclosed only for purposes related to the prevention or detection of crime, the investigation of offences or the conduct of prosecutions by, or on behalf of, police or other law enforcement and prosecuting authorities inside and outside the United Kingdom or the enforcement of any sentence or order made by a court when dealing with an offence. After being so used or disclosed, they may be retained but can only be used or disclosed for the same purposes. See Note 5B.

5.13 The officer proposing to take a detainee's photograph may, for this purpose, require the person to remove any item or substance worn on, or over, all, or any part of, their head or face. If they do not comply with such a requirement, the officer may remove the item or substance.

5.14 If it is established the detainee is unwilling to co-operate sufficiently to enable a suitable photograph to be taken and it is not reasonably practicable to take the photograph covertly, an officer may use reasonable force, see Note 5F:

(a) to take their photograph without their consent; and

(b) for the purpose of taking the photograph, remove any item or substance worn on, or over, all, or any part of, the person's head or face which they have failed to remove when asked.

5.15 For the purposes of this Code, a photograph may be obtained without the person's consent by making a copy of an image of them taken at any time on a camera system installed anywhere in the police station.

(c) Information to be given

5.16 When a person is searched, examined or photographed under the provisions as in paragraph 5.1 and 5.12, or their photograph obtained as in paragraph 5.15, they must be informed of the:

(a) purpose of the search, examination or photograph;

(b) grounds on which the relevant authority, if applicable, has been given; and

(c) purposes for which the photograph may be used, disclosed or retained.

This information must be given before the search or examination commences or the photograph is taken, except if the photograph is:

(i) to be taken covertly;

(ii) obtained as in paragraph 5.15, in which case the person must be informed as soon as practicable after the photograph is taken or obtained.

(d) Documentation

5.17 A record must be made when a detainee is searched, examined, or a photograph of the person, or any identifying marks found on them, are taken. The record must include the:

(a) identity, subject to paragraph 2.18, of the officer carrying out the search, examination or taking the photograph;

(b) purpose of the search, examination or photograph and the outcome;

(c) detainee's consent to the search, examination or photograph, or the reason the person was searched, examined or photographed without consent;

(d) giving of any authority as in paragraphs 5.2 and 5.3, the grounds for giving it and the authorising officer.

5.18 If force is used when searching, examining or taking a photograph in accordance with this section, a record shall be made of the circumstances and those present.

(B) Persons at police stations not detained

5.19 When there are reasonable grounds for suspecting the involvement of a person in a criminal offence, but that person is at a police station voluntarily and not detained, the provisions of paragraphs 5.1 to 5.18 should apply, subject to the modifications in the following paragraphs.

5.20 References to the 'person being detained' and to the powers mentioned in paragraph 5.1 which apply only to detainees at police stations shall be omitted.

5.21 Force may not be used to:

(a) search and/or examine the person to:

(i) discover whether they have any marks that would tend to identify them as a person involved in the commission of an offence; or

(ii) establish their identity, see Note 5A;

(b) take photographs of any identifying marks, see paragraph 5.4; or

(c) take a photograph of the person.

5.22 Subject to paragraph 5.24, the photographs, of persons, or of their identifying marks which are not taken in accordance with the provisions mentioned in paragraphs 5.1 or 5.12, must be destroyed (together with any negatives and copies) unless the person:

(a)　is charged with, or informed they may be prosecuted for, a recordable offence;
(b)　is prosecuted for a recordable offence;
(c)　is cautioned for a recordable offence or given a warning or reprimand in accordance with the Crime and Disorder Act 1998 for a recordable offence; or
(d)　gives informed consent, in writing, for the photograph or image to be retained as in paragraph 5.6.

5.23　When paragraph 5.22 requires the destruction of any photograph, the person must be given an opportunity to witness the destruction or to have a certificate confirming the destruction provided they so request the certificate within five days of being informed the destruction is required.

5.24　Nothing in paragraph 5.22 affects any separate requirement under the Criminal Procedure and Investigations Act 1996 to retain material in connection with criminal investigations.

Notes for guidance

5A　The conditions under which fingerprints may be taken to assist in establishing a person's identity, are described in Section 4.

5B　Examples of purposes related to the prevention or detection of crime, the investigation of offences or the conduct of prosecutions include:

(a)　checking the photograph against other photographs held in records or in connection with, or as a result of, an investigation of an offence to establish whether the person is liable to arrest for other offences;
(b)　when the person is arrested at the same time as other people, or at a time when it is likely that other people will be arrested, using the photograph to help establish who was arrested, at what time and where;
(c)　when the real identity of the person is not known and cannot be readily ascertained or there are reasonable grounds for doubting a name and other personal details given by the person, are their real name and personal details. In these circumstances, using or disclosing the photograph to help to establish or verify their real identity or determine whether they are liable to arrest for some other offence, eg by checking it against other photographs held in records or in connection with, or as a result of, an investigation of an offence;
(d)　when it appears any identification procedure in section 3 may need to be arranged for which the person's photograph would assist;
(e)　when the person's release without charge may be required, and if the release is:
　　(i)　on bail to appear at a police station, using the photograph to help verify the person's identity when they answer their bail and if the person does not answer their bail, to assist in arresting them; or
　　(ii)　without bail, using the photograph to help verify their identity or assist in locating them for the purposes of serving them with a summons to appear at court in criminal proceedings;
(f)　when the person has answered to bail at a police station and there are reasonable grounds for doubting they are the person who was previously granted bail, using the photograph to help establish or verify their identity;
(g)　when the person arrested on a warrant claims to be a different person from the person named on the warrant and a photograph would help to confirm or disprove their claim;
(h)　when the person has been charged with, reported for, or convicted of, a recordable offence and their photograph is not already on record as a result of (a) to (f) or their photograph is on record but their appearance has changed since it was taken and the person has not yet been released or brought before a court.

5C　There is no power to arrest a person convicted of a recordable offence solely to take their photograph. The power to take photographs in this section applies only where the person is in custody as a result of the exercise of another power, eg arrest for fingerprinting under PACE, section 27.

5D　Examples of when it would not be practicable to obtain a detainee's consent, see paragraph 2.12, to a search, examination or the taking of a photograph of an identifying mark include:

(a)　when the person is drunk or otherwise unfit to give consent;
(b)　when there are reasonable grounds to suspect that if the person became aware a search or examination was to take place or an identifying mark was to be photographed, they would take steps to prevent this happening, eg by violently resisting, covering or concealing the mark etc and it would not otherwise be possible to carry out the search or examination or to photograph any identifying mark;
(c)　in the case of a juvenile, if the parent or guardian cannot be contacted in sufficient time to allow the search or examination to be carried out or the photograph to be taken.

5E　Examples of when it would not be practicable to obtain the person's consent, see paragraph 2.12, to a photograph being taken include:

(a) when the person is drunk or otherwise unfit to give consent;
(b) when there are reasonable grounds to suspect that if the person became aware a photograph, suitable to be used or disclosed for the use and disclosure described in paragraph 5.6, was to be taken, they would take steps to prevent it being taken, eg by violently resisting, covering or distorting their face etc, and it would not otherwise be possible to take a suitable photograph;
(c) when, in order to obtain a suitable photograph, it is necessary to take it covertly; and
(d) in the case of a juvenile, if the parent or guardian cannot be contacted in sufficient time to allow the photograph to be taken.

5F The use of reasonable force to take the photograph of a suspect elsewhere than at a police station must be carefully considered. In order to obtain a suspect's consent and co-operation to remove an item of religious headwear to take their photograph, a constable should consider whether in the circumstances of the situation the removal of the headwear and the taking of the photograph should be by an officer of the same sex as the person. It would be appropriate for these actions to be conducted out of public view

6 IDENTIFICATION BY BODY SAMPLES AND IMPRESSIONS

(A) General

6.1 References to:

(a) an 'intimate sample' mean a dental impression or sample of blood, semen or any other tissue fluid, urine, or pubic hair, or a swab taken from any part of a person's genitals or from a person's body orifice other than the mouth;
(b) a 'non-intimate sample' means:

(i) a sample of hair, other than pubic hair, which includes hair plucked with the root, see Note 6A;
(ii) a sample taken from a nail or from under a nail;
(iii) a swab taken from any part of a person's body other than a part from which a swab taken would be an intimate sample;
(iv) saliva;
(v) a skin impression which means any record, other than a fingerprint, which is a record, in any form and produced by any method, of the skin pattern and other physical characteristics or features of the whole, or any part of, a person's foot or of any other part of their body.

(B) Action

(a) Intimate samples

6.2 PACE, section 62, provides that intimate samples may be taken under:

(a) section 62(1), from a person in police detention only:

(i) if a police officer of inspector rank or above has reasonable grounds to believe such an impression or sample will tend to confirm or disprove the suspect's involvement in a recordable offence, see Note 4A, and gives authorisation for a sample to be taken; and
(ii) with the suspect's written consent;

(b) section 62(1A), from a person not in police detention but from whom two or more non-intimate samples have been taken in the course of an investigation of an offence and the samples, though suitable, have proved insufficient if:

(i) a police officer of inspector rank or above authorises it to be taken; and
(ii) the person concerned gives their written consent. See Notes 6B and 6C

6.3 Before a suspect is asked to provide an intimate sample, they must be warned that if they refuse without good cause, their refusal may harm their case if it comes to trial, see Note 6D. If the suspect is in police detention and not legally represented, they must also be reminded of their entitlement to have free legal advice, see Code C, paragraph 6.5, and the reminder noted in the custody record. If paragraph 6.2(b) applies and the person is attending a station voluntarily, their entitlement to free legal advice as in Code C, paragraph 3.21 shall be explained to them.

6.4 Dental impressions may only be taken by a registered dentist. Other intimate samples, except for samples of urine, may only be taken by a registered medical practitioner or registered nurse or registered paramedic.

(b) Non-intimate samples

6.5 A non-intimate sample may be taken from a detainee only with their written consent or if paragraph 6.6 applies.

6.6

(a) under section 63, a non-intimate sample may not be taken from a person without consent and the consent must be in writing (aa) A non-intimate sample may be taken from a person without the appropriate consent in the following circumstances:

  (i) under section 63(2A) where the person is in police detention as a consequence of his arrest for a recordable offence and he has not had a non-intimate sample of the same type and from the same part of the body taken in the course of the investigation of the offence by the police or he has had such a sample taken but it proved insufficient.

  (ii) Under section 63(3) (a) where he is being held in custody by the police on the authority of a court and an officer of at least the rank of inspector authorises it to be taken.

(b) under section 63(3A), from a person charged with a recordable offence or informed they will be reported for such an offence: and

  (i) that person has not had a non-intimate sample taken from them in the course of the investigation; or

  (ii) if they have had a sample taken, it proved unsuitable or insufficient for the same form of analysis, see Note 6B; or

(c) under section 63(3B), from a person convicted of a recordable offence after the date on which that provision came into effect. PACE, section 63A, describes the circumstances in which a police officer may require a person convicted of a recordable offence to attend a police station for a non-intimate sample to be taken.

6.7 Reasonable force may be used, if necessary, to take a non-intimate sample from a person without their consent under the powers mentioned in paragraph 6.6.

6.8 Before any intimate sample is taken with consent or non-intimate sample is taken with, or without, consent, the person must be informed:

(a) of the reason for taking the sample;

(b) of the grounds on which the relevant authority has been given;

(c) that the sample or information derived from the sample may be retained and subject of a speculative search, see Note 6E, unless their destruction is required as in Annex F, Part A.

6.9 When clothing needs to be removed in circumstances likely to cause embarrassment to the person, no person of the opposite sex who is not a registered medical practitioner or registered health care professional shall be present, (unless in the case of a juvenile, mentally disordered or mentally vulnerable person, that person specifically requests the presence of an appropriate adult of the opposite sex who is readily available) nor shall anyone whose presence is unnecessary. However, in the case of a juvenile, this is subject to the overriding proviso that such a removal of clothing may take place in the absence of the appropriate adult only if the juvenile signifies, in their presence, that they prefer the adult's absence and they agree.

(c) Documentation

6.10 A record of the reasons for taking a sample or impression and, if applicable, of its destruction must be made as soon as practicable. If force is used, a record shall be made of the circumstances and those present. If written consent is given to the taking of a sample or impression, the fact must be recorded in writing.

6.11 A record must be made of a warning given as required by paragraph 6.3.

6.12 A record shall be made of the fact that a person has been informed as in paragraph 6.8(c) that samples may be subject of a speculative search.

Notes for guidance

6A When hair samples are taken for the purpose of DNA analysis (rather than for other purposes such as making a visual match), the suspect should be permitted a reasonable choice as to what part of the body the hairs are taken from. When hairs are plucked, they should be plucked individually, unless the suspect prefers otherwise and no more should be plucked than the person taking them reasonably considers necessary for a sufficient sample.

6B

(a) An insufficient sample is one which is not sufficient either in quantity or quality to provide information for a particular form of analysis, such as DNA analysis. A sample may also be insufficient if enough information cannot be obtained from it by analysis because of loss, destruction, damage or contamination of the sample or as a result of an earlier, unsuccessful attempt at analysis.

(b) An unsuitable sample is one which, by its nature, is not suitable for a particular form of analysis.

6C Nothing in paragraph 6.2 prevents intimate samples being taken for elimination purposes with the consent of the person concerned but the provisions of paragraph 2.12 relating to the role of the appropriate adult, should be applied. Paragraph 6.2(b) does not, however, apply where the non-intimate samples were previously taken under the Terrorism Act 2000, Schedule 8, paragraph 10.

6D In warning a person who is asked to provide an intimate sample as in paragraph 6.3, the following form of words may be used:

"You do not have to provide this sample/allow this swab or impression to be taken, but I must warn you that if you refuse without good cause, your refusal may harm your case if it comes to trial."

6E Fingerprints or a DNA sample and the information derived from it taken from a person arrested on suspicion of being involved in a recordable offence, or charged with such an offence, or informed they will be reported for such an offence, may be subject of a speculative search. This means they may be checked against other fingerprints and DNA records held by, or on behalf of, the police and other law enforcement authorities in or outside the UK or held in connection with, or as a result of, an investigation of an offence inside or outside the UK. Fingerprints and samples taken from any other person, eg a person suspected of committing a recordable offence but who has not been arrested, charged or informed they will be reported for it, may be subject to a speculative search only if the person consents in writing to their fingerprints being subject of such a search. The following is an example of a basic form of words:

"I consent to my fingerprints/DNA sample and information derived from it being retained and used only for purposes related to the prevention and detection of a crime, the investigation of an offence or the conduct of a prosecution either nationally or internationally.

I understand that this sample may be checked against other fingerprint/DNA records held by or on behalf of relevant law enforcement authorities, either nationally or internationally.

I understand that once I have given my consent for the sample to be retained and used I cannot withdraw this consent."

See Annex F regarding the retention and use of fingerprints and samples taken with consent for elimination purposes.

6F Samples of urine and non-intimate samples taken in accordance with sections 63B and 63C of PACE may not be used for identification purposes in accordance with this Code. See Code C note for guidance 17D.

ANNEX A – VIDEO IDENTIFICATION

(a) General

1. The arrangements for obtaining and ensuring the availability of a suitable set of images to be used in a video identification must be the responsibility of an identification officer, who has no direct involvement with the case.

2. The set of images must include the suspect and at least eight other people who, so far as possible, resemble the suspect in age, general appearance and position in life. Only one suspect shall appear in any set unless there are two suspects of roughly similar appearance, in which case they may be shown together with at least twelve other people.

2A. If the suspect has an unusual physical feature, eg, a facial scar, tattoo or distinctive hairstyle or hair colour which does not appear on the images of the other people that are available to be used, steps may be taken to:

(a) conceal the location of the feature on the images of the suspect and the other people; or

(b) replicate that feature on the images of the other people.

For these purposes, the feature may be concealed or replicated electronically or by any other method which it is practicable to use to ensure that the images of the suspect and other people resemble each other. The identification officer has discretion to choose whether to conceal or replicate the feature and the method to be used. If an unusual physical feature has been described by the witness, the identification officer should, if practicable, have that feature replicated. If it has not been described, concealment may be more appropriate.

2B. If the identification officer decides that a feature should be concealed or replicated, the reason for the decision and whether the feature was concealed or replicated in the images shown to any witness shall be recorded.

2C. If the witness requests to view an image where an unusual physical feature has been concealed or replicated without the feature being concealed or replicated, the witness may be allowed to do so.

3. The images used to conduct a video identification shall, as far as possible, show the suspect and other people in the same positions or carrying out the same sequence of movements. They shall also show the suspect and other people under identical conditions unless the identification officer reasonably believes:

(a) because of the suspect's failure or refusal to co-operate or other reasons, it is not practicable for the conditions to be identical; and

(b) any difference in the conditions would not direct a witness' attention to any individual image.

4. The reasons identical conditions are not practicable shall be recorded on forms provided for the purpose.

5. Provision must be made for each person shown to be identified by number.

6. If police officers are shown, any numerals or other identifying badges must be concealed. If a prison inmate is shown, either as a suspect or not, then either all, or none of, the people shown should be in prison clothing.

7. The suspect or their solicitor, friend, or appropriate adult must be given a reasonable opportunity to see the complete set of images before it is shown to any witness. If the suspect has a reasonable objection to the set of images or any of the participants, the suspect shall be asked to state the reasons for the objection. Steps shall, if practicable, be taken to remove the grounds for objection. If this is not practicable, the suspect and/or their representative shall be told why their objections cannot be met and the objection, the reason given for it and why it cannot be met shall be recorded on forms provided for the purpose.

8. Before the images are shown in accordance with paragraph 7, the suspect or their solicitor shall be provided with details of the first description of the suspect by any witnesses who are to attend the video identification. When a broadcast or publication is made, as in paragraph 3.28, the suspect or their solicitor must also be allowed to view any material released to the media by the police for the purpose of recognising or tracing the suspect, provided it is practicable and would not unreasonably delay the investigation.

9. The suspect's solicitor, if practicable, shall be given reasonable notification of the time and place the video identification is to be conducted so a representative may attend on behalf of the suspect. If a solicitor has not been instructed, this information shall be given to the suspect. The suspect may not be present when the images are shown to the witness(es). In the absence of the suspect's representative, the viewing itself shall be recorded on video. No unauthorised people may be present.

(b) Conducting the video identification

10. The identification officer is responsible for making the appropriate arrangements to make sure, before they see the set of images, witnesses are not able to communicate with each other about the case, see any of the images which are to be shown, see, or be reminded of, any photograph or description of the suspect or be given any other indication as to the suspect's identity, or overhear a witness who has already seen the material. There must be no discussion with the witness about the composition of the set of images and they must not be told whether a previous witness has made any identification.

11. Only one witness may see the set of images at a time. Immediately before the images are shown, the witness shall be told that the person they saw on a specified earlier occasion may, or may not, appear in the images they are shown and that if they cannot make a positive identification, they should say so. The witness shall be advised that at any point, they may ask to see a particular part of the set of images or to have a particular image frozen for them to study. Furthermore, it should be pointed out to the witness that there is no limit on how many times they can view the whole set of images or any part of them. However, they should be asked not to make any decision as to whether the person they saw is on the set of images until they have seen the whole set at least twice.

12. Once the witness has seen the whole set of images at least twice and has indicated that they do not want to view the images, or any part of them, again, the witness shall be asked to say whether the individual they saw in person on a specified earlier occasion has been shown and, if so, to identify them by number of the image. The witness will then be shown that image to confirm the identification, see paragraph 17.

13. Care must be taken not to direct the witness' attention to any one individual image or give any indication of the suspect's identity. Where a witness has previously made an identification by photographs, or a computerised or artist's composite or similar likeness, the witness must not be reminded of such a photograph or composite likeness once a suspect is available for identification by other means in accordance with this Code. Nor must the witness be reminded of any description of the suspect.

14. After the procedure, each witness shall be asked whether they have seen any broadcast or published films or photographs, or any descriptions of suspects relating to the offence and their reply shall be recorded.

(c) Image security and destruction

15. Arrangements shall be made for all relevant material containing sets of images used for specific identification procedures to be kept securely and their movements accounted for. In particular, no-one involved in the investigation shall be permitted to view the material prior to it being shown to any witness.

16. As appropriate, paragraph 3.30 or 3.31 applies to the destruction or retention of relevant sets of images.

(d) Documentation

17. A record must be made of all those participating in, or seeing, the set of images whose names are known to the police.

18. A record of the conduct of the video identification must be made on forms provided for the purpose. This shall include anything said by the witness about any identifications or the conduct of the procedure and any reasons it was not practicable to comply with any of the provisions of this Code governing the conduct of video identifications.

ANNEX B – IDENTIFICATION PARADES

(a) General

1. A suspect must be given a reasonable opportunity to have a solicitor or friend present, and the suspect shall be asked to indicate on a second copy of the notice whether or not they wish to do so.

2. An identification parade may take place either in a normal room or one equipped with a screen permitting witnesses to see members of the identification parade without being seen. The procedures for the composition and conduct of the identification parade are the same in both cases, subject to paragraph 8 (except that an identification parade involving a screen may take place only when the suspect's solicitor, friend or appropriate adult is present or the identification parade is recorded on video).

3. Before the identification parade takes place, the suspect or their solicitor shall be provided with details of the first description of the suspect by any witnesses who are attending the identification parade. When a broadcast or publication is made as in paragraph 3.28, the suspect or their solicitor should also be allowed to view any material released to the media by the police for the purpose of recognising or tracing the suspect, provided it is practicable to do so and would not unreasonably delay the investigation.

(b) Identification parades involving prison inmates

4. If a prison inmate is required for identification, and there are no security problems about the person leaving the establishment, they may be asked to participate in an identification parade or video identification.

5. An identification parade may be held in a Prison Department establishment but shall be conducted, as far as practicable under normal identification parade rules. Members of the public shall make up the identification parade unless there are serious security, or control, objections to their admission to the establishment. In such cases, or if a group or video identification is arranged within the establishment, other inmates may participate. If an inmate is the suspect, they are not required to wear prison clothing for the identification parade unless the other people taking part are other inmates in similar clothing, or are members of the public who are prepared to wear prison clothing for the occasion.

(c) Conduct of the identification parade

6. Immediately before the identification parade, the suspect must be reminded of the procedures governing its conduct and cautioned in the terms of Code C, paragraphs 10.5 or 10.6, as appropriate.

7. All unauthorised people must be excluded from the place where the identification parade is held.

8. Once the identification parade has been formed, everything afterwards, in respect of it, shall take place in the presence and hearing of the suspect and any interpreter, solicitor, friend or appropriate adult who is present (unless the identification parade involves a screen, in which case everything said to, or by, any witness at the place where the identification parade is held, must be said in the hearing and presence of the suspect's solicitor, friend or appropriate adult or be recorded on video).

9. The identification parade shall consist of at least eight people (in addition to the suspect) who, so far as possible, resemble the suspect in age, height, general appearance and position in life. Only one suspect shall be included in an identification parade unless there are two suspects of roughly similar appearance, in which case they may be paraded together with at least twelve other people. In no circumstances shall more than two suspects be included in one identification parade and where there are separate identification parades, they shall be made up of different people.

10. If the suspect has an unusual physical feature, eg, a facial scar, tattoo or distinctive hairstyle or hair colour which cannot be replicated on other members of the identification parade, steps may be taken to conceal the location of that feature on the suspect and the other members of the identification parade if the suspect and their solicitor, or appropriate adult, agree. For example, by use of a plaster or a hat, so that all members of the identification parade resemble each other in general appearance[1].

11. When all members of a similar group are possible suspects, separate identification parades shall be held for each unless there are two suspects of similar appearance when they may appear on the same identification parade with at least twelve other members of

the group who are not suspects. When police officers in uniform form an identification parade any numerals or other identifying badges shall be concealed.

12. When the suspect is brought to the place where the identification parade is to be held, they shall be asked if they have any objection to the arrangements for the identification parade or to any of the other participants in it and to state the reasons for the objection. The suspect may obtain advice from their solicitor or friend, if present, before the identification parade proceeds. If the suspect has a reasonable objection to the arrangements or any of the participants, steps shall, if practicable, be taken to remove the grounds for objection. When it is not practicable to do so, the suspect shall be told why their objections cannot be met and the objection, the reason given for it and why it cannot be met, shall be recorded on forms provided for the purpose.

13. The suspect may select their own position in the line, but may not otherwise interfere with the order of the people forming the line. When there is more than one witness, the suspect must be told, after each witness has left the room, that they can, if they wish, change position in the line. Each position in the line must be clearly numbered, whether by means of a number laid on the floor in front of each identification parade member or by other means.

14. Appropriate arrangements must be made to make sure, before witnesses attend the identification parade, they are not able to:

(i) communicate with each other about the case or overhear a witness who has already seen the identification parade;

(ii) see any member of the identification parade;

(iii) see, or be reminded of, any photograph or description of the suspect or be given any other indication as to the suspect's identity; or

(iv) see the suspect before or after the identification parade.

15. The person conducting a witness to an identification parade must not discuss with them the composition of the identification parade and, in particular, must not disclose whether a previous witness has made any identification.

16. Witnesses shall be brought in one at a time. Immediately before the witness inspects the identification parade, they shall be told the person they saw on a specified earlier occasion may, or may not, be present and if they cannot make a positive identification, they should say so. The witness must also be told they should not make any decision about whether the person they saw is on the identification parade until they have looked at each member at least twice.

17. When the officer or police staff (see paragraph 3.11) conducting the identification procedure is satisfied the witness has properly looked at each member of the identification parade, they shall ask the witness whether the person they saw on a specified earlier occasion is on the identification parade and, if so, to indicate the number[2] of the person concerned, see paragraph 28.

18. If the witness wishes to hear any identification parade member speak, adopt any specified posture or move, they shall first be asked whether they can identify any person(s) on the identification parade on the basis of appearance only. When the request is to hear members of the identification parade speak, the witness shall be reminded that the participants in the identification parade have been chosen on the basis of physical appearance only. Members of the identification parade may then be asked to comply with the witness' request to hear them speak, see them move or adopt any specified posture.

19. If the witness requests that the person they have indicated remove anything used for the purposes of paragraph 10 to conceal the location of an unusual physical feature, that person may be asked to remove it.

20. If the witness makes an identification after the identification parade has ended, the suspect and, if present, their solicitor, interpreter or friend shall be informed. When this occurs, consideration should be given to allowing the witness a second opportunity to identify the suspect.

21. After the procedure, each witness shall be asked whether they have seen any broadcast or published films or photographs or any descriptions of suspects relating to the offence and their reply shall be recorded.

22. When the last witness has left, the suspect shall be asked whether they wish to make any comments on the conduct of the identification parade.

---

1. Police may take steps, in good faith, such as the use of make up, to make volunteers on an identity parade resemble the suspect (*R v Marrin* (2002) Times, 5 March, CA).

2. Where the witness, who had watched the parade from behind a screen, subsequently forgot the number of the suspect's position, a police inspector's evidence of the witness's identification was admissible (*R v McCay* [1990] 1 WLR 645; but see commentary in [1990] Crim LR 341).

(d) Documentation

23. A video recording must normally be taken of the identification parade. If that is impracticable, a colour photograph must be taken. A copy of the video recording or photograph shall be supplied, on request, to the suspect or their solicitor within a reasonable time.

24. As appropriate, paragraph 3.30 or 3.31, should apply to any photograph or video taken as in paragraph 23.

25. If any person is asked to leave an identification parade because they are interfering with its conduct, the circumstances shall be recorded.

26. A record must be made of all those present at an identification parade whose names are known to the police.

27. If prison inmates make up an identification parade, the circumstances must be recorded.

28. A record of the conduct of any identification parade must be made on forms provided for the purpose. This shall include anything said by the witness or the suspect about any identifications or the conduct of the procedure, and any reasons it was not practicable to comply with any of this Code's provisions.

ANNEX C – GROUP IDENTIFICATION

(a) General

1. The purpose of this Annex is to make sure, as far as possible, group identifications follow the principles and procedures for identification parades so the conditions are fair to the suspect in the way they test the witness' ability to make an identification.

2. Group identifications may take place either with the suspect's consent and cooperation or covertly without their consent.

3. The location of the group identification is a matter for the identification officer, although the officer may take into account any representations made by the suspect, appropriate adult, their solicitor or friend.

4. The place where the group identification is held should be one where other people are either passing by or waiting around informally, in groups such that the suspect is able to join them and be capable of being seen by the witness at the same time as others in the group. For example people leaving an escalator, pedestrians walking through a shopping centre, passengers on railway and bus stations, waiting in queues or groups or where people are standing or sitting in groups in other public places[1].

5. If the group identification is to be held covertly, the choice of locations will be limited by the places where the suspect can be found and the number of other people present at that time. In these cases, suitable locations might be along regular routes travelled by the suspect, including buses or trains or public places frequented by the suspect.

6. Although the number, age, sex, race and general description and style of clothing of other people present at the location cannot be controlled by the identification officer, in selecting the location the officer must consider the general appearance and numbers of people likely to be present. In particular, the officer must reasonably expect that over the period the witness observes the group, they will be able to see, from time to time, a number of others whose appearance is broadly similar to that of the suspect.

7. A group identification need not be held if the identification officer believes, because of the unusual appearance of the suspect, none of the locations it would be practicable to use satisfy the requirements of paragraph 6 necessary to make the identification fair.

8. Immediately after a group identification procedure has taken place (with or without the suspect's consent), a colour photograph or video should be taken of the general scene, if practicable, to give a general impression of the scene and the number of people present. Alternatively, if it is practicable, the group identification may be video recorded.

9. If it is not practicable to take the photograph or video in accordance with paragraph 8, a photograph or film of the scene should be taken later at a time determined by the identification officer if the officer considers it practicable to do so.

10. An identification carried out in accordance with this Code remains a group identification even though, at the time of being seen by the witness, the suspect was on their own rather than in a group.

11. Before the group identification takes place, the suspect or their solicitor shall be provided with details of the first description of the suspect by any witnesses who are to attend the identification. When a broadcast or publication is made, as in paragraph 3.28, the suspect or their solicitor should also be allowed to view any material released by the police to the media for the purposes of recognising or tracing the suspect, provided that it is practicable and would not unreasonably delay the investigation.

12. After the procedure, each witness shall be asked whether they have seen any broadcast or published films or photographs or any descriptions of suspects relating to the offence and their reply recorded.

---

1. The foyer of a magistrates' court might be appropriate for a group identification where there is likely to be a greater coming and going of a greater variety of people than at a police station (*R v Tiplady* (1995) 159 JP 548, [1995] Crim LR 651).

(b) Identification with the consent of the suspect

13. A suspect must be given a reasonable opportunity to have a solicitor or friend present. They shall be asked to indicate on a second copy of the notice whether or not they wish to do so.

14. The witness, the person carrying out the procedure and the suspect's solicitor, appropriate adult, friend or any interpreter for the witness, may be concealed from the sight of the individuals in the group they are observing, if the person carrying out the procedure considers this assists the conduct of the identification.

15. The person conducting a witness to a group identification must not discuss with them the forthcoming group identification and, in particular, must not disclose whether a previous witness has made any identification.

16. Anything said to, or by, the witness during the procedure about the identification should be said in the presence and hearing of those present at the procedure.

17. Appropriate arrangements must be made to make sure, before witnesses attend the group identification, they are not able to:

(i) communicate with each other about the case or overhear a witness who has already been given an opportunity to see the suspect in the group;

(ii) see the suspect; or

(iii) see, or be reminded of, any photographs or description of the suspect or be given any other indication of the suspect's identity.

18. Witnesses shall be brought one at a time to the place where they are to observe the group. Immediately before the witness is asked to look at the group, the person conducting the procedure shall tell them that the person they saw may, or may not, be in the group and that if they cannot make a positive identification, they should say so. The witness shall be asked to observe the group in which the suspect is to appear. The way in which the witness should do this will depend on whether the group is moving or stationary.

Moving group

19. When the group in which the suspect is to appear is moving, eg leaving an escalator, the provisions of paragraphs 20 to 24 should be followed.

20. If two or more suspects consent to a group identification, each should be the subject of separate identification procedures. These may be conducted consecutively on the same occasion.

21. The person conducting the procedure shall tell the witness to observe the group and ask them to point out any person they think they saw on the specified earlier occasion.

22. Once the witness has been informed as in paragraph 21 the suspect should be allowed to take whatever position in the group they wish.

23. When the witness points out a person as in paragraph 21 they shall, if practicable, be asked to take a closer look at the person to confirm the identification. If this is not practicable, or they cannot confirm the identification, they shall be asked how sure they are that the person they have indicated is the relevant person.

24. The witness should continue to observe the group for the period which the person conducting the procedure reasonably believes is necessary in the circumstances for them to be able to make comparisons between the suspect and other individuals of broadly similar appearance to the suspect as in paragraph 6.

Stationary groups

25. When the group in which the suspect is to appear is stationary, eg people waiting in a queue, the provisions of paragraphs 26 to 29 should be followed.

26. If two or more suspects consent to a group identification, each should be subject to separate identification procedures unless they are of broadly similar appearance when they may appear in the same group. When separate group identifications are held, the groups must be made up of different people.

27. The suspect may take whatever position in the group they wish. If there is more than one witness, the suspect must be told, out of the sight and hearing of any witness, that they can, if they wish, change their position in the group.

28. The witness shall be asked to pass along, or amongst, the group and to look at each person in the group at least twice, taking as much care and time as possible according to the circumstances, before making an identification. Once the witness has done this, they shall be asked whether the person they saw on the specified earlier occasion is in the group and to indicate any such person by whatever means the person conducting the procedure considers appropriate in the circumstances. If this is not practicable, the witness shall be asked to point out any person they think they saw on the earlier occasion.

29. When the witness makes an indication as in paragraph 28, arrangements shall be made, if practicable, for the witness to take a closer look at the person to confirm the identification. If this is not practicable, or the witness is unable to confirm the identification, they shall be asked how sure they are that the person they have indicated is the relevant person.

All cases

30. If the suspect unreasonably delays joining the group, or having joined the group, deliberately conceals themselves from the sight of the witness, this may be treated as a refusal to co-operate in a group identification.

31. If the witness identifies a person other than the suspect, that person should be

informed what has happened and asked if they are prepared to give their name and address. There is no obligation upon any member of the public to give these details. There shall be no duty to record any details of any other member of the public present in the group or at the place where the procedure is conducted.

32. When the group identification has been completed, the suspect shall be asked whether they wish to make any comments on the conduct of the procedure.

33. If the suspect has not been previously informed, they shall be told of any identifications made by the witnesses.

(c) Identification without the suspect's consent

34. Group identifications held covertly without the suspect's consent should, as far as practicable, follow the rules for conduct of group identification by consent.

35. A suspect has no right to have a solicitor, appropriate adult or friend present as the identification will take place without the knowledge of the suspect.

36. Any number of suspects may be identified at the same time.

(d) Identifications in police stations

37. Group identifications should only take place in police stations for reasons of safety, security or because it is not practicable to hold them elsewhere.

38. The group identification may take place either in a room equipped with a screen permitting witnesses to see members of the group without being seen, or anywhere else in the police station that the identification officer considers appropriate.

39. Any of the additional safeguards applicable to identification parades should be followed if the identification officer considers it is practicable to do so in the circumstances.

(e) Identifications involving prison inmates

40. A group identification involving a prison inmate may only be arranged in the prison or at a police station.

41. When a group identification takes place involving a prison inmate, whether in a prison or in a police station, the arrangements should follow those in paragraphs 37 to 39. If a group identification takes place within a prison, other inmates may participate. If an inmate is the suspect, they do not have to wear prison clothing for the group identification unless the other participants are wearing the same clothing.

(f) Documentation

42. When a photograph or video is taken as in paragraph 8 or 9, a copy of the photograph or video shall be supplied on request to the suspect or their solicitor within a reasonable time.

43. Paragraph 3.30 or 3.31, as appropriate, shall apply when the photograph or film taken in accordance with paragraph 8 or 9 includes the suspect.

44. A record of the conduct of any group identification must be made on forms provided for the purpose. This shall include anything said by the witness or suspect about any identifications or the conduct of the procedure and any reasons why it was not practicable to comply with any of the provisions of this Code governing the conduct of group identifications.

ANNEX D – CONFRONTATION BY A WITNESS

1. Before the confrontation takes place, the witness must be told that the person they saw may, or may not, be the person they are to confront and that if they are not that person, then the witness should say so.

2. Before the confrontation takes place the suspect or their solicitor shall be provided with details of the first description of the suspect given by any witness who is to attend. When a broadcast or publication is made, as in paragraph 3.28, the suspect or their solicitor should also be allowed to view any material released to the media for the purposes of recognising or tracing the suspect, provided it is practicable to do so and would not unreasonably delay the investigation.

3. Force may not be used to make the suspect's face visible to the witness.

4. Confrontation must take place in the presence of the suspect's solicitor, interpreter or friend unless this would cause unreasonable delay.

5. The suspect shall be confronted independently by each witness, who shall be asked "Is this the person?". If the witness identifies the person but is unable to confirm the identification, they shall be asked how sure they are that the person is the one they saw on the earlier occasion.

6. The confrontation should normally take place in the police station, either in a normal room or one equipped with a screen permitting a witness to see the suspect without being seen. In both cases, the procedures are the same except that a room equipped with a screen may be used only when the suspect's solicitor, friend or appropriate adult is present or the confrontation is recorded on video.

7. After the procedure, each witness shall be asked whether they have seen any broadcast

or published films or photographs or any descriptions of suspects relating to the offence and their reply shall be recorded.

ANNEX E – SHOWING PHOTOGRAPHS

(a) Action

1. An officer of sergeant rank or above shall be responsible for supervising and directing the showing of photographs. The actual showing may be done by another officer or police staff, see paragraph 3.11.

2. The supervising officer must confirm the first description of the suspect given by the witness has been recorded before they are shown the photographs. If the supervising officer is unable to confirm the description has been recorded they shall postpone showing the photographs.

3. Only one witness shall be shown photographs at any one time. Each witness shall be given as much privacy as practicable and shall not be allowed to communicate with any other witness in the case.

4. The witness shall be shown not less than twelve photographs at a time, which shall, as far as possible, all be of a similar type.

5. When the witness is shown the photographs, they shall be told the photograph of the person they saw may, or may not, be amongst them and if they cannot make a positive identification, they should say so. The witness shall also be told they should not make a decision until they have viewed at least twelve photographs. The witness shall not be prompted or guided in any way but shall be left to make any selection without help.

6. If a witness makes a positive identification from photographs, unless the person identified is otherwise eliminated from enquiries or is not available, other witnesses shall not be shown photographs. But both they, and the witness who has made the identification, shall be asked to attend a video identification, an identification parade or group identification unless there is no dispute about the suspect's identification.

7. If the witness makes a selection but is unable to confirm the identification, the person showing the photographs shall ask them how sure they are that the photograph they have indicated is the person they saw on the specified earlier occasion.

8. When the use of a computerised or artist's composite or similar likeness has led to there being a known suspect who can be asked to participate in a video identification, appear on an identification parade or participate in a group identification, that likeness shall not be shown to other potential witnesses.

9. When a witness attending a video identification, an identification parade or group identification has previously been shown photographs or computerised or artist's composite or similar likeness (and it is the responsibility of the officer in charge of the investigation to make the identification officer aware that this is the case), the suspect and their solicitor must be informed of this fact before the identification procedure takes place.

10. None of the photographs shown shall be destroyed, whether or not an identification is made, since they may be required for production in court. The photographs shall be numbered and a separate photograph taken of the frame or part of the album from which the witness made an identification as an aid to reconstituting it.

(b) Documentation

11. Whether or not an identification is made, a record shall be kept of the showing of photographs on forms provided for the purpose. This shall include anything said by the witness about any identification or the conduct of the procedure, any reasons it was not practicable to comply with any of the provisions of this Code governing the showing of photographs and the name and rank of the supervising officer.

12. The supervising officer shall inspect and sign the record as soon as practicable.

ANNEX F – FINGERPRINTS, FOOTWEAR IMPRESSIONS AND SAMPLES – DESTRUCTION AND SPECULATIVE SEARCHES

(a) Fingerprints, footwear impressions and samples taken in connection with a criminal investigation

1. When fingerprints, footwear impressions or DNA samples are taken from a person in connection with an investigation and the person is not suspected of having committed the offence, see Note F1, they must be destroyed as soon as they have fulfilled the purpose for which they were taken unless:

    (a) they were taken for the purposes of an investigation of an offence for which a person has been convicted; and

    (b) fingerprints, footwear impressions or samples were also taken from the convicted person for the purposes of that investigation.

However, subject to paragraph 2, the fingerprints, footwear impressions and samples, and the information derived from samples, may not be used in the investigation of any offence or in evidence against the person who is, or would be, entitled to the destruction of the fingerprints, footwear impressions and samples, see Note F2.

2. The requirement to destroy fingerprints, footwear impressions and DNA samples, and information derived from samples, and restrictions on their retention and use in paragraph 1 do not apply if the person gives their written consent for their fingerprints, footwear impressions or sample to be retained and used after they have fulfilled the purpose for which they were taken, see Note F1.

3. When a person's fingerprints, footwear impressions or sample are to be destroyed:

(a) any copies of the fingerprints and footwear impressions must also be destroyed;
(b) the person may witness the destruction of their fingerprints, footwear impressions or copies if they ask to do so within five days of being informed destruction is required;
(c) access to relevant computer fingerprint data shall be made impossible as soon as it is practicable to do so and the person shall be given a certificate to this effect within three months of asking; and
(d) neither the fingerprints, footwear impressions, the sample, or any information derived from the sample, may be used in the investigation of any offence or in evidence against the person who is, or would be, entitled to its destruction.

4. Fingerprints, footwear impressions or samples, and the information derived from samples, taken in connection with the investigation of an offence which are not required to be destroyed, may be retained after they have fulfilled the purposes for which they were taken but may be used only for purposes related to the prevention or detection of crime, the investigation of an offence or the conduct of a prosecution in, as well as outside, the UK and may also be subject to a speculative search. This includes checking them against other fingerprints, footwear impressions and DNA records held by, or on behalf of, the police and other law enforcement authorities in, as well as outside, the UK.

(b) Fingerprints taken in connection with Immigration Service enquiries

5. Fingerprints taken for Immigration Service enquiries in accordance with powers and procedures other than under PACE and for which the Immigration Service, not the police, are responsible, must be destroyed as follows:

(a) fingerprints and all copies must be destroyed as soon as practicable if the person from whom they were taken proves they are a British or Commonwealth citizen who has the right of abode in the UK under the Immigration Act 1971, section 2(1)(b);
(b) fingerprints taken under the power as in paragraph 4.11(g) from a dependant of a person in 4.11 (b) to (f) must be destroyed when that person's fingerprints are to be destroyed;
(c) fingerprints taken from a person under any power as in paragraph 4.11 or with the person's consent which have not already been destroyed as above, must be destroyed within ten years of being taken or within such period specified by the Secretary of State under the Immigration and Asylum Act 1999, section 143(5).

Notes for guidance

F1 Fingerprints, footwear impressions and samples given voluntarily for the purposes of elimination play an important part in many police investigations. It is, therefore, important to make sure innocent volunteers are not deterred from participating and their consent to their fingerprints, footwear impressions and DNA being used for the purposes of a specific investigation is fully informed and voluntary. If the police or volunteer seek to have the fingerprints, footwear impressions or samples retained for use after the specific investigation ends, it is important the volunteer's consent to this is also fully informed and voluntary. Examples of consent for:

• DNA/fingerprints/footwear impressions – to be used only for the purposes of a specific investigation;
• DNA/fingerprints/footwear impressions – to be used in the specific investigation and retained by the police for future use.

To minimise the risk of confusion, each consent should be physically separate and the volunteer should be asked to sign each consent.

(a) DNA:

(i) DNA sample taken for the purposes of elimination or as part of an intelligence-led screening and to be used only for the purposes of that investigation and destroyed afterwards:

"I consent to my DNA/mouth swab being taken for forensic analysis. I understand that the sample will be destroyed at the end of the case and that my profile will only be compared to the crime stain profile from this enquiry. I have been advised that the person taking the sample may be required to give evidence and/or provide a written statement to the police in relation to the taking of it".

(ii) DNA sample to be retained on the National DNA database and used in the future:

"I consent to my DNA sample and information derived from it being retained and used only for purposes related to the prevention and detection of a crime, the investigation of an offence or the conduct of a prosecution either nationally or internationally."

"I understand that this sample may be checked against other DNA records held by, or on behalf of, relevant law enforcement authorities, either nationally or internationally".

"I understand that once I have given my consent for the sample to be retained and used I cannot withdraw this consent."

(b) Fingerprints:

(i) Fingerprints taken for the purposes of elimination or as part of an intelligence-led screening and to be used only for the purposes of that investigation and destroyed afterwards:

"I consent to my fingerprints being taken for elimination purposes. I understand that the fingerprints will be destroyed at the end of the case and that my fingerprints will only be compared to the fingerprints from this enquiry. I have been advised that the person taking the fingerprints may be required to give evidence and/or provide a written statement to the police in relation to the taking of it."

(ii) Fingerprints to be retained for future use:

"I consent to my fingerprints being retained and used only for purposes related to the prevention and detection of a crime, the investigation of an offence or the conduct of a prosecution either nationally or internationally".

"I understand that my fingerprints may be checked against other records held by, or on behalf of, relevant law enforcement authorities, either nationally or internationally."

"I understand that once I have given my consent for my fingerprints to be retained and used I cannot withdraw this consent."

(c) Footwear impressions:

(i) Footwear impressions taken for the purposes of elimination or as part of an intelligence-led screening and to be used only for the purposes of that investigation and destroyed afterwards:

"I consent to my footwear impressions being taken for elimination purposes. I understand that the footwear impressions will be destroyed at the end of the case and that my footwear impressions will only be compared to the footwear impressions from this enquiry. I have been advised that the person taking the footwear impressions may be required to give evidence and/or provide a written statement to the police in relation to the taking of it."

(ii) Footwear impressions to be retained for future use:

"I consent to my footwear impressions being retained and used only for purposes related to the prevention and detection of a crime, the investigation of an offence or the conduct of a prosecution either nationally or internationally".

"I understand that my footwear impressions may be checked against other records held by, or on behalf of, relevant law enforcement authorities, either nationally or internationally."

"I understand that once I have given my consent for my footwear impressions to be retained and used I cannot withdraw this consent."

F2 The provisions for the retention of fingerprints, footwear impressions and samples in paragraph 1 allow for all fingerprints, footwear impressions and samples in a case to be available for any subsequent miscarriage of justice investigation.

2–1948

E CODE OF PRACTICE ON AUDIO RECORDING INTERVIEWS WITH SUSPECTS[1]

COMMENCEMENT – TRANSITIONAL ARRANGEMENTS

This code applies to interviews carried out after midnight on 31 December 2005, notwithstanding that the interview may have commenced before that time.

---

1. This Code of Practice (draft code laid before Parliament on 8 November 2005) is issued under ss 60 and 67 of the Police and Criminal Evidence Act 1984; it is admissible thereunder in evidence and account may be taken by the court of any relevant provision. the Police and Criminal Evidence At 1984 (Codes of Practice) Order 2005, SI 2005/3503 has effect in relation to interviews carried on or after 1 January 2005 notwithstanding the interview may have commenced before that time.

1 GENERAL

1.1 This Code of Practice must be readily available for consultation by:

- police officers
- police staff
- detained persons
- members of the public.

1.2 The Notes for Guidance included are not provisions of this Code.

1.3 Nothing in this Code shall detract from the requirements of Code C, the Code of Practice for the detention, treatment and questioning of persons by police officers.

1.4 This Code does not apply to those people listed in Code C, paragraph 1.12.

1.5 The term:

- 'appropriate adult' has the same meaning as in Code C, paragraph 1.7
- 'solicitor' has the same meaning as in Code C, paragraph 6.12.

1.6 In this Code:

(aa) 'recording media' means any removable, physical audio recording medium (such as magnetic type, optical disc or solid state memory) which can be played and copied;

(a) 'designated person' means a person other than a police officer, designated under the Police Reform Act 2002, Part 4 who has specified powers and duties of police officers conferred or imposed on them;(b)any reference to a police officer includes a designated person acting in the exercise or performance of the powers and duties conferred or imposed on them by their designation.

1.7 If a power conferred on a designated person:

(a) allows reasonable force to be used when exercised by a police officer, a designated person exercising that power has the same entitlement to use force;

(b) includes power to use force to enter any premises, that power is not exercisable by that designated person except:

  (i) in the company, and under the supervision, of a police officer; or
  (ii) for the purpose of:

   - saving life or limb; or
   - preventing serious damage to property.

1.8 Nothing in this Code prevents the custody officer, or other officer given custody of the detainee, from allowing police staff who are not designated persons to carry out individual procedures or tasks at the police station if the law allows. However, the officer remains responsible for making sure the procedures and tasks are carried out correctly in accordance with these Codes. Any such civilian must be:

(a) a person employed by a police authority maintaining a police force and under the control and direction of the Chief Officer of that force; or

(b) employed by a person with whom a police authority has a contract for the provision of services relating to persons arrested or otherwise in custody.

1.9 Designated persons and other police staff must have regard to any relevant provisions of the Codes of Practice.

1.10 References to pocket book include any official report book issued to police officers or police staff.

1.11 References to a custody officer include those performing the functions of a custody officer as in paragraph 1.9 of Code C..

2 RECORDING AND SEALING MASTER RECORDINGS

2.1 Recording of interviews shall be carried out openly to instil confidence in its reliability as an impartial and accurate record of the interview.

2.2 One recording, the master recording, will be sealed in the suspect's presence. A second recording will be used as a working copy. The master recording is either of the two recordings used in a twin deck machine or the only recording in a single deck machine. The working copy is either the second/third /drive used in a twin/triple deck/drive machine or a copy of the master tape made by a single deck machine. See Notes 2A and 2B

2.3 Nothing in this Code requires the identity of officers or police staff conducting interviews to be recorded or disclosed:

(a) in the case of enquiries linked to the investigation of terrorism; or

(b) if the interviewer reasonably believes recording or disclosing their name might put them in danger.

In these cases interviewers should use warrant or other identification numbers and the name of their police station. See Note 2C.

Notes for guidance

2A The purpose of sealing the master tape in the suspect's presence is to show the tape's integrity is preserved. If a single deck machine is used the working copy of the master tape must be made in the suspect's presence and without the master tape leaving their sight. The working copy shall be used for making further copies if needed.

2B *Not used.*

2C The purpose of paragraph 2.3(b) is to protect those involved in serious organised crime investigations or arrests of particularly violent suspects when there is reliable information that those arrested or their associates may threaten or cause harm to those involved. In cases of doubt, an officer of inspector rank or above should be consulted.

3 INTERVIEWS TO BE AUDIO RECORDED

3.1 Subject to paragraphs 3.3 and 3.4, audio recording shall be used at police stations for any interview:

(a) with a person cautioned under Code C, section 10 in respect of any indictable offence, including an offence triable either way; see Note 3A
(b) which takes place as a result of an interviewer exceptionally putting further questions to a suspect about an offence described in paragraph 3.1(a) after they have been charged with, or told they may be prosecuted for, that offence, see Code C, paragraph 16.5
(c) when an interviewer wants to tell a person, after they have been charged with, or informed they may be prosecuted for, an offence described in paragraph 3.1(a), about any written statement or interview with another person, see Code C, paragraph 16.4.

3.2 The Terrorism Act 2000 makes separate provision for a Code of Practice for the audio recording of interviews of those arrested under Section 41 or detained under Schedule 7 of the Act. The provisions of this Code do not apply to such interviews.

3.3 The custody officer may authorise the interviewer not to audio record the interview when it is:

(a) not reasonably practicable because of equipment failure or the unavailability of a suitable interview room or recorder and the authorising officer considers, on reasonable grounds, that the interview should not be delayed; or
(b) clear from the outset there will not be a prosecution.

Note: In these cases the interview should be recorded in writing in accordance with Code C, section 11. In all cases the custody officer shall record the specific reasons for not audio recording. See Note 3B

3.4 If a person refuses to go into or remain in a suitable interview room, see Code C paragraph 12.5, and the custody officer considers, on reasonable grounds, that the interview should not be delayed the interview may, at the custody officer's discretion, be conducted in a cell using portable recording equipment or, if none is available, recorded in writing as in Code C, section 11. The reasons for this shall be recorded.

3.5 The whole of each interview shall be audio recorded, including the taking and reading back of any statement.

Notes for guidance
3A Nothing in this Code is intended to preclude audio recording at police discretion of interviews at police stations with people cautioned in respect of offences not covered by paragraph 3.1, or responses made by persons after they have been charged with, or told they may be prosecuted for, an offence, provided this Code is complied with. 3B A decision not to audio record an interview for any reason may be the subject of comment in court. The authorising officer should be prepared to justify that decision.

4 THE INTERVIEW

(a) General
4.1 The provisions of Code C:

• sections 10 and 11, and the applicable Notes for Guidance apply to the conduct of interviews to which this Code applies
• paragraphs 11.7 to 11.14 apply only when a written record is needed.

4.2 Code C, *paragraphs 10.10, 10.11* and Annex C describe the restriction on drawing adverse inferences from a suspect's failure or refusal to say anything about their involvement in the offence when interviewed or after being charged or informed they may be prosecuted, and how it affects the terms of the caution and determines if and by whom a special warning under sections 36 and 37 can be given.

(b) Commencement of interviews
4.3 When the suspect is brought into the interview room the interviewer shall, without delay but in the suspect's sight, load the recorder with new recoding media and set it to record. The recording media must be unwrapped or opened in the suspect's presence.

4.4 The interviewer should tell the suspect about the recording process.. The interviewer shall:

(a) say the interview is being audibly recorded
(b) subject to paragraph 2.3, give their name and rank and that of any other interviewer present
(c) ask the suspect and any other party present, eg a solicitor, to identify themselves
(d) state the date, time of commencement and place of the interview
(e) state the suspect will be given a notice about what will happen to the copies of the recording.

See Note 4A

4.5 The interviewer shall:

- caution the suspect, see Code C, section 10
- remind the suspect of their entitlement to free legal advice, see Code C, paragraph 11.2.

4.6 The interviewer shall put to the suspect any significant statement or silence; see Code C, paragraph 11.4.

(c) Interviews with deaf persons
4.7 If the suspect is deaf or is suspected of having impaired hearing, the interviewer shall make a written note of the interview in accordance with Code C, at the same time as audio recording it in accordance with this Code. See Notes 4B and 4C

(d) Objections and complaints by the suspect
4.8 If the suspect objects to the interview being audibly recorded at the outset, during the interview or during a break, the interviewer shall explain that the interview is being tape recorded and that this Code requires the suspect's objections to be recorded on the audio recording. When any objections have been tape recorded or the suspect has refused to have their objections recorded, the interviewer shall say they are turning off the recorder, give their reasons and turn it off. The interviewer shall then make a written record of the interview as in Code C, section 11. If, however, the interviewer reasonably considers they may proceed to question the suspect with the audio recording still on, the interviewer may do so. This procedure also applies in cases where the suspect has previously objected to the interview being visually recorded, see Code F 4.8, and the investigating officer has decided to audibly record the interview. See Note 4D.

4.9 If in the course of an interview a complaint is made by or on behalf of the person being questioned concerning the provisions of this Code or Code C, the interviewer shall act as in Code C, paragraph 12.9. See Notes 4E and 4F

4.10 If the suspect indicates they want to tell the interviewer about matters not directly connected with the offence and they are unwilling for these matters to be audio recorded, the suspect should be given the opportunity to tell the interviewer at the end of the formal interview.

(e) Changing recording media
4.11 When the recorder shows the recording media only has a short time left, the interviewer shall tell the suspect the recording media are coming to an end and round off that part of the interview. If the interviewer leaves the room for a second set of recording media, the suspect shall not be left unattended. The interviewer will remove the recording media from the recorder and insert the new recording media which shall be unwrapped or opened in the suspect's presence. The recorder should be set to record on the new media. To avoid confusion between the recording media, the interviewer shall mark the media with an identification number immediately after they are removed from the recorder.

(f) Taking a break during interview
4.12 When a break is taken, the fact that a break is to be taken, the reason for it and the time shall be recorded on the audio recording.

4.12A When the break is taken and the interview room vacated by the suspect, the recording media shall be removed from the recorder and the procedures for the conclusion of an interview followed; see paragraph 4.18.

4.13 When a break is a short one and both the suspect and an interviewer remain in the interview room, the recording may be stopped. There is no need to remove the recording media and when the interview recommences the recording should continue on the same recording media. The time the interview recommences shall be recorded on the audio recording.

4.14 After any break in the interview the interviewer must, before resuming the interview, remind the person being questioned that they remain under caution or, if there is any doubt, give the caution in full again. See Note 4G

(g) Failure of recording equipment
4.15 If there is an equipment failure which can be rectified quickly, eg by inserting new recording media, the interviewer shall follow the appropriate procedures as in paragraph 4.11. When the recording is resumed the interviewer shall explain what happened and record the time the interview recommences. If, however, it will not be possible to continue recording on that recorder and no replacement recorder is readily available, the interview may continue without being audibly recorded. If this happens, the interviewer shall seek the custody officer's authority as in paragraph 3.3. See Note 4H

(h) Removing recording media from the recorder
4.16 When recording media removed from the recorder during the interview, they shall be retained and the procedures in paragraph 4.18 followed.

(i) Conclusion of interview

4.17 At the conclusion of the interview, the suspect shall be offered the opportunity to clarify anything he or she has said and asked if there is anything they want to add.

4.18 At the conclusion of the interview, including the taking and reading back of any written statement, the time shall be recorded and the recording shall be stopped. The interviewer shall seal the master recording with a master recording label and treat it as an exhibit in accordance with force standing orders. The interviewer shall sign the label and ask the suspect and any third party present during the interview to sign it. If the suspect or third party refuse to sign the label an officer of at least inspector rank, or if not available the custody officer, shall be called into the interview room and asked, subject to paragraph 2.3, to sign it.

4.19 The suspect shall be handed a notice which explains:

- how the audio recording will be used
- the arrangements for access to it
- that if the person is charged or informed they will be prosecuted, a copy of the audio recording will be supplied as soon as practicable or as otherwise agreed between the suspect and the police.

Notes for guidance

4A For the purpose of voice identification the interviewer should ask the suspect and any other people present to identify themselves.

4B This provision is to give a person who is deaf or has impaired hearing equivalent rights of access to the full interview record as far as this is possible using audio recording.

4C The provisions of Code C, section 13 on interpreters for deaf persons or for interviews with suspects who have difficulty understanding English continue to apply. However, in an audibly recorded interview the requirement on the interviewer to make sure the interpreter makes a separate note of the interview applies only to paragraph 4.7 (interviews with deaf persons).

4D The interviewer should remember that a decision to continue recording against the wishes of the suspect may be the subject of comment in court.

4E If the custody officer is called to deal with the complaint, the recorder should, if possible, be left on until the custody officer has entered the room and spoken to the person being interviewed. Continuation or termination of the interview should be at the interviewer's discretion pending action by an inspector under Code C, paragraph 9.2.

4F If the complaint is about a matter not connected with this Code or Code C, the decision to continue is at the interviewer's discretion. When the interviewer decides to continue the interview, they shall tell the suspect the complaint will be brought to the custody officer's attention at the conclusion of the interview. When the interview is concluded the interviewer must, as soon as practicable, inform the custody officer about the existence and nature of the complaint made.

4G The interviewer should remember that it may be necessary to show to the court that nothing occurred during a break or between interviews which influenced the suspect's recorded evidence. After a break or at the beginning of a subsequent interview, the interviewer should consider summarising on the record the reason for the break and confirming this with the suspect..

4H Where the interview is being recorded and the media or the recording equipment fails the officer conducting the interview should stop the interview immediately. Where part of the interview is unaffected by the error and is still accessible on the media, that media shall be copied and sealed in the suspect's presence and the interview recommenced using new equipment/media as required. Where the content of the interview has been lost in its entirety the media should be sealed in the suspect's presence and the interview begun again. If the recording equipment cannot be fixed or no replacement is immediately available the interview should be recorded in accordance with Code C, section 11.

5 AFTER THE INTERVIEW

5.1 The interviewer shall make a note in their pocket book that the interview has taken place, was audibly recorded, duration and date and the master recording's identification number.

5.2 If no proceedings follow in respect of the person whose interview was recorded, the recording media must be kept securely as in paragraph 6.1 and Note 6A.

Note for guidance

5A Any written record of an audibly recorded interview should be made in accordance with national guidelines approved by the Secretary of State.

6 MEDIA SECURITY

6.1 The officer in charge of each police station at which interviews with suspects are recorded shall make arrangements for master recordings to be kept securely and their movements accounted for on the same basis as material which may be used for evidential purposes, in accordance with force standing orders. See Note 6A

6.2 A police officer has no authority to break the seal on a master recording required for criminal trial or appeal proceedings. If it is necessary to gain access to the master recording, the police officer shall arrange for its seal to be broken in the presence of a representative of the Crown Prosecution Service. The defendant or their legal adviser should be informed and given a reasonable opportunity to be present. If the defendant or their legal representative is present they shall be invited to reseal and sign the master recording. If either refuses or neither is present this should be done by the representative of the Crown Prosecution Service. See Notes 6B and 6C.

6.3 If no criminal proceedings result or the criminal trial result and, if applicable, appeal proceedings to which the interview relates have been concluded, the chief officer of police is responsible for establishing arrangements for breaking the seal on the master recording, if necessary.

6.4 When the master recording seal is broken, a record must be made of the procedure followed, including the date, time, place and persons present.

Notes for guidance

6A This section is concerned with the security of the master recording sealed at the conclusion of the interview. Care must be taken of working copies of recordings because their loss or destruction may lead to the need to access master recordings.

6B If the recording has been delivered to the crown court for their keeping after committal for trial the crown prosecutor will apply to the chief clerk of the crown court centre for the release of the recording for unsealing by the crown prosecutor.

6C Reference to the Crown Prosecution Service or to the crown prosecutor in this part of the Code should be taken to include any other body or person with a statutory responsibility for prosecution for whom the police conduct any audibly recorded interviews.

2–1960

F CODE OF PRACTICE ON VISUAL RECORDING WITH SOUND OF INTERVIEWS WITH SUSPECTS[1]

COMMENCEMENT – TRANSITIONAL ARRANGEMENTS

The contents of this code should be considered if an interviewing officer decides to make a visual recording with sound of an interview with a suspect after midnight on 31 October 2005. There is no statutory requirement to visually record interviews

---

1. This Code of Practice (draft code laid before Parliament on 8 November 2005) is issued under ss 66 and 67 of the Police and Criminal Evidence Act 1984; it is admissible thereunder in evidence and account may be taken by the court of any relevant provision. the Police and Criminal Evidence At 1984 (Codes of Practice) Order 2005, SI 2005/3503 has effect in relation to interviews carried on or after 1 January 2005 notwithstanding the interview may have commenced before that time.

1 GENERAL

1.1 This code of practice must be readily available for consultation by police officers and other police staff, detained persons and members of the public.

1.2 The notes for guidance included are not provisions of this code. They form guidance to police officers and others about its application and interpretation.

1.3 Nothing in this code shall be taken as detracting in any way from the requirements of the Code of Practice for the Detention, Treatment and Questioning of Persons by Police Officers (Code C). [See Note 1A].

1.4 The interviews to which this Code applies are set out in paragraphs 3.1 - 3.3.

1.5 In this code, the term "appropriate adult", "solicitor" and "interview" have the same meaning as those set out in Code C. The corresponding provisions and Notes for Guidance in Code C applicable to those terms shall also apply where appropriate.

1.6 Any reference in this code to visual recording shall be taken to mean visual recording with sound.

1.7 References to "pocket book" in this Code include any official report book issued to police officers.

Note for Guidance

1A As in paragraph 1.9 of Code C, references to custody officers include those carrying out the functions of a custody officer.

2 RECORDING AND SEALING OF MASTER TAPES

2.1 The visual recording of interviews shall be carried out openly to instil confidence in its reliability as an impartial and accurate record of the interview. [See Note 2A].

2.2 The camera(s) shall be placed in the interview room so as to ensure coverage of as much of the room as is practicably possible whilst the interviews are taking place.

2.3 The certified recording medium will be of a high quality, new and previously unused. When the certified recording medium is placed in the recorder and switched on to record, the correct date and time, in hours, minutes and seconds, will be superimposed automatically, second by second, during the whole recording. [See Note 2B].

2.4 One copy of the certified recording medium, referred to in this code as the master copy, will be sealed before it leaves the presence of the suspect. A second copy will be used as a working copy. [See Note 2C and 2D].

2.5 Nothing in this code requires the identity of an officer to be recorded or disclosed if:

(a) the interview or record relates to a person detained under the Terrorism Act 2000; or
(b) otherwise where the officer reasonably believes that recording or disclosing their name might put them in danger.

In these cases, the officer will have their back to the camera and shall use their warrant or other identification number and the name of the police station to which they are attached. Such instances and the reasons for them shall be recorded in the custody record. [See Note 2E]

Notes for Guidance

2A Interviewing officers will wish to arrange that, as far as possible, visual recording arrangements are unobtrusive. It must be clear to the suspect, however, that there is no opportunity to interfere with the recording equipment or the recording media.

2B In this context, the certified recording media will be of either a VHS or digital CD format and should be capable of having an image of the date and time superimposed upon them as they record the interview.

2C The purpose of sealing the master copy before it leaves the presence of the suspect is to establish their confidence that the integrity of the copy is preserved.

2D The recording of the interview may be used for identification procedures in accordance with paragraph 3.21 or Annex E of Code D.

2E The purpose of the paragraph 2.5 is to protect police officers and others involved in the investigation of serious organised crime or the arrest of particularly violent suspects when there is reliable information that those arrested or their associates may threaten or cause harm to the officers, their families or their personal property.

3 INTERVIEWS TO BE VISUALLY RECORDED

3.1 Subject to paragraph 3.2 below, if an interviewing officer decides to make a visual recording these are the areas where it might be appropriate:

(a) with a suspect in respect of an indictable offence (including an offence triable either way) [see Notes 3A and 3B];
(b) which takes place as a result of an interviewer exceptionally putting further questions to a suspect about an offence described in sub-paragraph (a) above after they have been charged with, or informed they may be prosecuted for, that offence [see Note 3C];
(c) in which an interviewer wishes to bring to the notice of a person, after that person has been charged with, or informed they may be prosecuted for an offence described in sub-paragraph (a) above, any written statement made by another person, or the content of an interview with another person [see Note 3D]
(d) with, or in the presence of, a deaf or deaf/blind or speech impaired person who uses sign language to communicate;
(e) with, or in the presence of anyone who requires an "appropriate adult"; or
(f) in any case where the suspect or their representative requests that the interview be recorded visually.

3.2 The Terrorism Act 2000 makes separate provision for a code of practice for the video recording of interviews in a police station of those detained under Schedule 7 or section 41 of the Act. The provisions of this code do not therefore apply to such interviews [see Note 3E].

3.3 The custody officer may authorise the interviewing officer not to record the interview visually:

(a) where it is not reasonably practicable to do so because of failure of the equipment, or the non-availability of a suitable interview room, or recorder, and the authorising officer considers on reasonable grounds that the interview should not be delayed until the failure has been rectified or a suitable room or recorder becomes available. In such cases the custody officer may authorise the interviewing officer to audio record the interview in accordance with the guidance set out in Code E;
(b) where it is clear from the outset that no prosecution will ensue; or
(c) where it is not practicable to do so because at the time the person resists being taken to a suitable interview room or other location which would enable the interview to be recorded, or otherwise fails or refuses to go into such a room or location, and the authorising officer considers on reasonable grounds that the interview should not be delayed until these conditions cease to apply. In all cases the custody officer shall make a note in the custody records of the reasons for not taking a visual record. [See Note 3F].

3.4 When a person who is voluntarily attending the police station is required to be cautioned in accordance with Code C prior to being interviewed, the subsequent interview shall be recorded, unless the custody officer gives authority in accordance with the provisions of paragraph 3.3 above for the interview not to be so recorded.

3.5 The whole of each interview shall be recorded visually, including the taking and reading back of any statement.

3.6 A visible illuminated sign or indicator will light and remain on at all times when the recording equipment is activated or capable of recording or transmitting any signal or information

Notes for Guidance

3A Nothing in the code is intended to preclude visual recording at police discretion of interviews at police stations with people cautioned in respect of offences not covered by paragraph 3.1, or responses made by interviewees after they have been charged with, or informed they may be prosecuted for, an offence, provided that this code is complied with.

3B Attention is drawn to the provisions set out in Code C about the matters to be considered when deciding whether a detained person is fit to be interviewed. 3C Code C sets out the circumstances in which a suspect may be questioned about an offence after being charged with it.

3D Code C sets out the procedures to be followed when a person's attention is drawn after charge, to a statement made by another person. One method of bringing the content of an interview with another person to the notice of a suspect may be to play him a recording of that interview.

3E When it only becomes clear during the course of an interview which is being visually recorded that the interviewee may have committed an offence to which paragraph 3.2 applies, the interviewing officer should turn off the recording equipment and the interview should continue in accordance with the provisions of the Terrorism Act 2000.

3F A decision not to record an interview visually for any reason may be the subject of comment in court. The authorising officer should therefore be prepared to justify their decision in each case.

4 The Interview

(a) General

4.1 The provisions of Code C in relation to cautions and interviews and the Notes for Guidance applicable to those provisions shall apply to the conduct of interviews to which this Code applies.

4.2 Particular attention is drawn to those parts of Code C that describe the restrictions on drawing adverse inferences from a suspect's failure or refusal to say anything about their involvement in the offence when interviewed, or after being charged or informed they may be prosecuted and how those restrictions affect the terms of the caution and determine whether a special warning under Sections 36 and 37 of the Criminal Justice and Public Order Act 1994 can be given.

(b) Commencement of interviews

4.3 When the suspect is brought into the interview room the interviewer shall without delay, but in sight of the suspect, load the recording equipment and set it to record. The recording media must be unwrapped or otherwise opened in the presence of the suspect. [See Note 4A]

4.4 The interviewer shall then tell the suspect formally about the visual recording. The interviewer shall:

(a) explain the interview is being visually recorded;
(b) subject to paragraph 2.5, give his or her name and rank, and that of any other interviewer present;
(c) ask the suspect and any other party present (eg his solicitor) to identify themselves.
(d) state the date, time of commencement and place of the interview; and
(e) state that the suspect will be given a notice about what will happen to the recording.

4.5 The interviewer shall then caution the suspect, which should follow that set out in Code C, and remind the suspect of their entitlement to free and independent legal advice and that they can speak to a solicitor on the telephone.

4.6 The interviewer shall then put to the suspect any significant statement or silence (i.e. failure or refusal to answer a question or to answer it satisfactorily) which occurred before the start of the interview, and shall ask the suspect whether they wish to confirm or deny that earlier statement or silence or whether they wish to add anything. The definition of a "significant" statement or silence is the same as that set out in Code C.

(c) Interviews with the deaf

4.7 If the suspect is deaf or there is doubt about their hearing ability, the provisions of Code C on interpreters for the deaf or for interviews with suspects who have difficulty in understanding English continue to apply.

(d) Objections and complaints by the suspect

4.8 If the suspect raises objections to the interview being visually recorded either at the outset or during the interview or during a break in the interview, the interviewer shall explain the fact that the interview is being visually recorded and that the provisions of this code require that the suspect's objections shall be recorded on the visual recording. When any objections have been visually recorded or the suspect has refused to have their objections recorded, the interviewer shall say that they are turning off the recording equipment, give their reasons and turn it off. If a separate audio recording is being maintained, the officer shall ask the person to record the the reasons for refusing to agree to visual recording of the interview. Paragraph 4.8 of Code E will apply if the person objects to audio recording of the interview. If the interviewer reasonably considers they may proceed to question the suspect with the visual recording still on, the interviewer may do so. See Note 4G.

4.9 If in the course of an interview a complaint is made by the person being questioned, or on their behalf, concerning the provisions of this code or of Code C, then the interviewer shall act in accordance with Code C, record it in the interview record and inform the custody officer. [See 4B and 4C].

4.10 If the suspect indicates that they wish to tell the interviewer about matters not directly connected with the offence of which they are suspected and that they are unwilling for these matters to be recorded, the suspect shall be given the opportunity to tell the interviewer about these matters after the conclusion of the formal interview.

(e) Changing the recording media

4.11 In instances where the recording medium is not of sufficient length to record all of the interview with the suspect, further certified recording medium will be used. When the recording equipment indicates that the recording medium has only a short time left to run, the interviewer shall advise the suspect and round off that part of the interview. If the interviewer wishes to continue the interview but does not already have further certified recording media with him, they shall obtain a set. The suspect should not be left unattended in the interview room. The interviewer will remove the recording media from the recording equipment and insert the new ones which have been unwrapped or otherwise opened in the suspect's presence. The recording equipment shall then be set to record. Care must be taken, particularly when a number of sets of recording media have been used, to ensure that there is no confusion between them. This could be achieved by marking the sets of recording media with consecutive identification numbers.

(f) Taking a break during the interview

4.12 When a break is to be taken during the course of an interview and the interview room is to be vacated by the suspect, the fact that a break is to be taken, the reason for it and the time shall be recorded. The recording equipment must be turned off and the recording media removed. The procedures for the conclusion of an interview set out in paragraph 4.19, below, should be followed.

4.13 When a break is to be a short one, and both the suspect and a police officer are to remain in the interview room, the fact that a break is to be taken, the reasons for it and the time shall be recorded on the recording media. The recording equipment may be turned off, but there is no need to remove the recording media. When the interview is recommenced the recording shall continue on the same recording media and the time at which the interview recommences shall be recorded.

4.14 When there is a break in questioning under caution, the interviewing officer must ensure that the person being questioned is aware that they remain under caution. If there is any doubt, the caution must be given again in full when the interview resumes. [See Notes 4D and 4E].

(g) Failure of recording equipment

4.15 If there is a failure of equipment which can be rectified quickly, the appropriate procedures set out in paragraph 4.12 shall be followed. When the recording is resumed the interviewer shall explain what has happened and record the time the interview recommences. If, however, it is not possible to continue recording on that particular recorder and no alternative equipment is readily available, the interview may continue without being recorded visually. In such circumstances, the procedures set out in paragraph 3.3 of this code for seeking the authority of the custody officer will be followed. [See Note 4F].

(h) Removing used recording media from recording equipment

4.16 Where used recording media are removed from the recording equipment during the course of an interview, they shall be retained and the procedures set out in paragraph 4.18 below followed.

(i) Conclusion of interview

4.17 Before the conclusion of the interview, the suspect shall be offered the opportunity to clarify anything he or she has said and asked if there is anything that they wish to add.

4.18 At the conclusion of the interview, including the taking and reading back of any written statement, the time shall be recorded and the recording equipment switched off. The master tape or CD shall be removed from the recording equipment, sealed with a master copy label and treated as an exhibit in accordance with the force standing orders. The interviewer shall sign the label and also ask the suspect and any appropriate adults or other third party present during the interview to sign it. If the suspect or third party refuses to sign the label, an officer of at least the rank of inspector, or if one is not available, the custody officer, shall be called into the interview room and asked to sign it.

4.19 The suspect shall be handed a notice which explains the use which will be made of the recording and the arrangements for access to it. The notice will also advise the suspect that a copy of the tape shall be supplied as soon as practicable if the person is charged or informed that he will be prosecuted.

Notes for Guidance

4A The interviewer should attempt to estimate the likely length of the interview and ensure that an appropriate quantity of certified recording media and labels with which to seal the master copies are available in the interview room.

4B Where the custody officer is called immediately to deal with the complaint, wherever possible the recording equipment should be left to run until the custody officer has entered the interview room and spoken to the person being interviewed. Continuation or termination of the interview should be at the discretion of the interviewing officer pending action by an inspector as set out in Code C.

4C Where the complaint is about a matter not connected with this code of practice or Code C, the decision to continue with the interview is at the discretion of the interviewing officer. Where the interviewing officer decides to continue with the interview, the person being interviewed shall be told that the complaint will be brought to the attention of the custody officer at the conclusion of the interview. When the interview is concluded, the interviewing officer must, as soon as practicable, inform the custody officer of the existence and nature of the complaint made.

4D In considering whether to caution again after a break, the officer should bear in mind that he may have to satisfy a court that the person understood that he was still under caution when the interview resumed.

4E The officer should bear in mind that it may be necessary to satisfy the court that nothing occurred during a break in an interview or between interviews which influenced the suspect's recorded evidence. On the re-commencement of an interview, the officer should consider summarising on the tape or CD the reason for the break and confirming this with the suspect.

4F If any part of the recording media breaks or is otherwise damaged during the interview, it should be sealed as a master copy in the presence of the suspect and the interview resumed where it left off. The undamaged part should be copied and the original sealed as a master tape in the suspect's presence, if necessary after the interview. If equipment for copying is not readily available, both parts should be sealed in the suspect's presence and the interview begun again.

4G The interviewer should be aware that a decision to continue recording against the wishes of the suspect may be the subject of comment in court.

5 After the Interview

5.1 The interviewer shall make a note in his or her pocket book of the fact that the interview has taken place and has been recorded, its time, duration and date and the identification number of the master copy of the recording media.

5.2 Where no proceedings follow in respect of the person whose interview was recorded, the recording media must nevertheless be kept securely in accordance with paragraph 6.1 and Note 6A.

Note for Guidance

5A Any written record of a recorded interview shall be made in accordance with national guidelines approved by the Secretary of State, and with regard to the advice contained in the Manual of Guidance for the preparation, processing and submission of files.

6 Master Copy Security

(a) General

6.1 The officer in charge of the police station at which interviews with suspects are recorded shall make arrangements for the master copies to be kept securely and their movements accounted for on the same basis as other material which may be used for evidential purposes, in accordance with force standing orders [See Note 6A].

(b) Breaking master copy seal for criminal proceedings

6.2 A police officer has no authority to break the seal on a master copy which is required for criminal trial or appeal proceedings. If it is necessary to gain access to the master copy, the police officer shall arrange for its seal to be broken in the presence of a representative of the Crown Prosecution Service. The defendant or their legal adviser shall be informed and given a reasonable opportunity to be present. If the defendant or their legal representative is present they shall be invited to reseal and sign the master copy. If either refuses or neither is present, this shall be done by the representative of the Crown Prosecution Service. [See Notes 6B and 6C].

(c) Breaking master copy seal: other cases

6.3 The chief officer of police is responsible for establishing arrangements for breaking the seal of the master copy where no criminal proceedings result, or the criminal proceedings, to which the interview relates, have been concluded and it becomes necessary to break the seal. These arrangements should be those which the chief officer considers are reasonably necessary to demonstrate to the person interviewed and any other party who may wish to use or refer to the interview record that the master copy has not been tampered with and that the interview record remains accurate. [See Note 6D]

6.4 Subject to paragraph 6.6, a representative of each party must be given a reasonable opportunity to be present when the seal is broken, the master copy copied and resealed.

6.5 If one or more of the parties is not present when the master copy seal is broken because they cannot be contacted or refuse to attend or paragraph 6.6 applies, arrangements should be made for an independent person such as a custody visitor, to be present. Alternatively, or as an additional safeguard, arrangement should be made for a film or photographs to be taken of the procedure.

6.6 Paragraph 6.5 does not require a person to be given an opportunity to be present when:

(a) it is necessary to break the master copy seal for the proper and effective further investigation of the original offence or the investigation of some other offence; and

(b) the officer in charge of the investigation has reasonable grounds to suspect that allowing an opportunity might prejudice any such an investigation or criminal proceedings which may be brought as a result or endanger any person. [See Note 6E]

(d) Documentation

6.7 When the master copy seal is broken, copied and re-sealed, a record must be made of the procedure followed, including the date time and place and persons present.

Notes for Guidance

6A This section is concerned with the security of the master copy which will have been sealed at the conclusion of the interview. Care should, however, be taken of working copies since their loss or destruction may lead unnecessarily to the need to have access to master copies.

6B If the master copy has been delivered to the Crown Court for their keeping after committal for trial the Crown Prosecutor will apply to the Chief Clerk of the Crown Court Centre for its release for unsealing by the Crown Prosecutor.

6C Reference to the Crown Prosecution Service or to the Crown Prosecutor in this part of the code shall be taken to include any other body or person with a statutory responsibility for prosecution for whom the police conduct any recorded interviews.

6D The most common reasons for needing access to master copies that are not required for criminal proceedings arise from civil actions and complaints against police and civil actions between individuals arising out of allegations of crime investigated by police.

6E Paragraph 6.6 could apply, for example, when one or more of the outcomes or likely outcomes of the investigation might be: (i) the prosecution of one or more of the original suspects, (ii) the prosecution of someone previously not suspected, including someone who was originally a witness; and (iii) any original suspect being treated as a prosecution witness and when premature disclosure of any police action, particularly through contact with any parties involved, could lead to a real risk of compromising the investigation and endangering witnesses.

2-1970

G CODE OF PRACTICE FOR THE STATUTORY POWER OF ARREST BY POLICE OFFICERS[1]

COMMENCEMENT

This Code applies to any arrest made by a police officer after midnight on 31 December 2005

---

1. This Code of Practice (draft code laid before Parliament on 8 November 2005) is issued under ss 66 and 67 of the Police and Criminal Evidence Act 1984; it is admissible thereunder in evidence and account may be taken by the court of any relevant provision. the Police and Criminal Evidence At 1984 (Codes of Practice) Order 2005, SI 2005/3503 has effect in relation to arrests carried on or after 1 January 2005.

1 INTRODUCTION

1.1 This Code of Practice deals with statutory power of police to arrest persons suspected of involvement in a criminal offence.

1.2 The right to liberty is a key principle of the Human Rights Act 1998. The exercise of the power of arrest represents an obvious and significant interference with that right.

1.3 The use of the power must be fully justified and officers exercising the power should consider if the necessary objectives can be met by other, less intrusive means. Arrest must never be used simply because it can be used. Absence of justification for exercising the powers of arrest may lead to challenges should the case proceed to court. When the power of arrest is exercised it is essential that it is exercised in a nondiscriminatory and proportionate manner.

1.4 Section 24 of the Police and Criminal Evidence Act 1984 (as substituted by section 110 of the Serious Organised Crime and Police Act 2005) provides the statutory power of arrest. If the provisions of the Act and this Code are not observed, both the arrest and the conduct of any subsequent investigation may be open to question.

1.5 This code of practice must be readily available at all police stations for consultation by police officers and police staff, detained persons and members of the public.

1.6 The notes for guidance are not provisions of this code.

2 ELEMENTS OF ARREST UNDER SECTION 24 PACE

2.1 A lawful arrest requires two elements:

A person's involvement or suspected involvement or attempted involvement in the commission of a criminal offence;

AND

Reasonable grounds for believing that the person's arrest is necessary.

2.2 Arresting officers are required to inform the person arrested that they have been arrested, even if this fact is obvious, and of the relevant circumstances of the arrest in relation to both elements and to inform the custody officer of these on arrival at the police station. See Code C paragraph 3.4.

Involvement in the commission of an offence'

2.3 A constable may arrest without warrant in relation to any offence, except for the single exception listed in Note for Guidance 1. A constable may arrest anyone:

- who is about to commit an offence or is in the act of committing an offence
- whom the officer has reasonable grounds for suspecting is about to commit an offence or to be committing an offence
- whom the officer has reasonable grounds to suspect of being guilty of an offence which he or she has reasonable grounds for suspecting has been committed
- anyone who is guilty of an offence which has been committed or anyone whom the officer has reasonable grounds for suspecting to be guilty of that offence.

Necessity criteria

2.4 The power of arrest is only exercisable if the constable has reasonable grounds for believing that it is necessary to arrest the person. The criteria for what may constitute necessity are set out in paragraph 2.9. It remains an operational decision at the discretion of the arresting officer as to:

- what action he or she may take at the point of contact with the individual;
- the necessity criterion or criteria (if any) which applies to the individual; and
- whether to arrest, report for summons, grant street bail, issue a fixed penalty notice or take any other action that is open to the officer.

2.5 In applying the criteria, the arresting officer has to be satisfied that at least one of the reasons supporting the need for arrest is satisfied.

2.6 Extending the power of arrest to all offences provides a constable with the ability to use that power to deal with any situation. However applying the necessity criteria requires the constable to examine and justify the reason or reasons why a person needs to be taken to a police station for the custody officer to decide whether the person should be placed in police detention.

2.7 The criteria below are set out in section 24 of PACE as substituted by section 110 of the Serious Organised Crime and Police Act 2005. The criteria are exhaustive. However, the circumstances that may satisfy those criteria remain a matter for the operational discretion of individual officers. Some examples are given below of what those circumstances may be.

2.8 In considering the individual circumstances, the constable must take into account the situation of the victim, the nature of the offence, the circumstances of the suspect and the needs of the investigative process.

2.9 The criteria are that the arrest is necessary:

(a) to enable the name of the person in question to be ascertained (in the case where the constable does not know, and cannot readily ascertain, the person's name, or has reasonable grounds for doubting whether a name given by the person as his name is his real name)

(b) correspondingly as regards the person's address

an address is a satisfactory address for service of summons if the person will be at it for a sufficiently long period for it to be possible to serve him or her with a summons; or, that some other person at that address specified by the person will accept service of the summons on their behalf.

(c) to prevent the person in question –

   (i) causing physical injury to himself or any other person;
   (ii) suffering physical injury ;
   (iii) causing loss or damage to property;
   (iv) committing an offence against public decency (only applies where members of the public going about their normal business cannot reasonably be expected to avoid the person in question); or
   (v) causing an unlawful obstruction of the highway;

(d) to protect a child or other vulnerable person from the person in question

(e) to allow the prompt and effective investigation of the offence or of the conduct of the person in question.

This may include cases such as:

   (i) Where there are reasonable grounds to believe that the person:

- has made false statements;
- has made statements which cannot be readily verified;
- has presented false evidence;
- may steal or destroy evidence;
- may make contact with co-suspects or conspirators;
- may intimidate or threaten or make contact with witnesses;
- where it is necessary to obtain evidence by questioning; or

   (ii) when considering arrest in connection with an indictable offence, there is a need to:

- enter and search any premises occupied or controlled by a person
- search the person
- prevent contact with others
- take fingerprints, footwear impressions, samples or photographs of the suspect

   (iii) ensuring compliance with statutory drug testing requirements.

(f) to prevent any prosecution for the offence from being hindered by the disappearance of the person in question.

(g) This may arise if there are reasonable grounds for believing that

- if the person is not arrested he or she will fail to attend court
- street bail after arrest would be insufficient to deter the suspect from trying to evade prosecution

3 INFORMATION TO BE GIVEN ON ARREST

(a) Cautions – when a caution must be given (taken from Code C section 10)

3.1 A person whom there are grounds to suspect of an offence (see Note 2) must be cautioned before any questions about an offence, or further questions if the answers provide the grounds for suspicion, are put to them if either the suspect's answers or silence, (i.e. failure or refusal to answer or answer satisfactorily) may be given in evidence to a court in a prosecution. A person need not be cautioned if questions are for other necessary purposes eg:

(a) solely to establish their identity or ownership of any vehicle;
(b) to obtain information in accordance with any relevant statutory requirement;
(c) in furtherance of the proper and effective conduct of a search, eg to determine the need to search in the exercise of powers of stop and search or to seek cooperation while carrying out a search;
(d) to seek verification of a written record as in Code C paragraph 11.13;
(e) when examining a person in accordance with the Terrorism Act 2000, Schedule 7 and the Code of Practice for Examining Officers issued under that Act, Schedule 14, paragraph 6.

3.2 Whenever a person not under arrest is initially cautioned, or reminded they are under caution, that person must at the same time be told they are not under arrest and are free to leave if they want to.

3.3 A person who is arrested, or further arrested, must be informed at the time, or as soon as practicable thereafter, that they are under arrest and the grounds for their arrest, see Note 3.

3.4 A person who is arrested, or further arrested, must also be cautioned unless:

(a) it is impracticable to do so by reason of their condition or behaviour at the time;
(b) they have already been cautioned immediately prior to arrest as in paragraph 3.1.
(c) Terms of the caution (Taken from Code C section 10)

3.5 The caution, which must be given on arrest, should be in the following terms:
"You do not have to say anything. But it may harm your defence if you do not mention when questioned something which you later rely on in Court. Anything you do say may be given in evidence."
See Note 5

3.6 Minor deviations from the words of any caution given in accordance with this Code do not constitute a breach of this Code, provided the sense of the relevant caution is preserved. See Note 6

3.7 When, despite being cautioned, a person fails to co-operate or to answer particular questions which may affect their immediate treatment, the person should be informed of any relevant consequences and that those consequences are not affected by the caution. Examples are when a person's refusal to provide:

- their name and address when charged may make them liable to detention;
- particulars and information in accordance with a statutory requirement, eg under the Road Traffic Act 1988, may amount to an offence or may make the person liable to a further arrest.

4 RECORDS OF ARREST

(a) General

4.1 The arresting officer is required to record in his pocket book or by other methods used
for recording information:

- the nature and circumstances of the offence leading to the arrest
- the reason or reasons why arrest was necessary
- the giving of the caution
- anything said by the person at the time of arrest

4.2 Such a record should be made at the time of the arrest unless impracticable to do. If not made at that time, the record should then be completed as soon as possible thereafter.

4.3 On arrival at the police station, the custody officer shall open the custody record (see paragraph 1.1A and section 2 of Code C). The information given by the arresting officer on the circumstances and reason or reasons for arrest shall be recorded as part of the custody record. Alternatively, a copy of the record made by the officer in accordance with paragraph 4.1 above shall be attached as part of the custody record. See paragraph 2.2 and Code C paragraphs 3.4 and 10.3.

4.4 The custody record will serve as a record of the arrest. Copies of the custody record will be provided in accordance with paragraphs 2.4 and 2.4A of Code C and access for inspection of the original record in accordance with paragraph 2.5 of Code C.

(b) Interviews and arrests

4.5 Records of interview, significant statements or silences will be treated in the same way as set out in sections 10 and 11 of Code C and in Code E (tape recording of interviews).

Notes for guidance

1 The powers of arrest for offences under sections 4(1) and 5(1) of the Criminal Law Act 1967 require that the offences to which they relate must carry a sentence fixed by law or one in which a first time offender aged 18 or over could be sentenced to 5 years or more imprisonment

2 There must be some reasonable, objective grounds for the suspicion, based on known facts or information which are relevant to the likelihood the offence has been committed and the person to be questioned committed it.

3 An arrested person must be given sufficient information to enable them to understand they have been deprived of their liberty and the reason they have been arrested, eg when a person is arrested on suspicion of committing an offence they must be informed of the suspected offence's nature, when and where it was committed. The suspect must also be informed of the reason or reasons why arrest is considered necessary. Vague or technical language should be avoided.

4 Nothing in this Code requires a caution to be given or repeated when informing a person not under arrest they may be prosecuted for an offence. However, a court will not be able to draw any inferences under the Criminal Justice and Public Order Act 1994, section 34, if the person was not cautioned.

5 If it appears a person does not understand the caution, the people giving it should explain it in their own words.

6 The powers available to an officer as the result of an arrest – for example, entry and

search of premises, holding a person incommunicado, setting up road blocks – are only available in respect of indictable offences and are subject to the specific requirements on authorisation as set out in the 1984 Act and relevant PACE Code of Practice.

2–1980

CODE H CODE OF PRACTICE IN CONNECTION WITH THE DETENTION, TREATMENT AND QUESTIONING BY POLICE OFFICERS OF PERSONS UNDER SECTION 41 OF, AND SCHEDULE 8 TO, THE TERRORISM ACT 2000[1]

COMMENCEMENT – TRANSITIONAL ARRANGEMENTS

This Code applies to people in police detention following their arrest under section 41 of the Terrorism Act 2000, after midnight (on 24 July 2006), notwithstanding that they may have been arrested before that time.

N. This Code of Practice (draft code laid before Parliament on 14 June 2006) is issued under ss 66 and 67 of the Police and Criminal Evidence Act 1984; it is admissible thereunder in evidence and account may be taken by the court of any relevant provision. The Police and Criminal Evidence Act 1984 (Code of Practice C and Code of Practice H) Order 2006, SI 2006/1938 applies to any person arrested under section 41 of the Terrorism Act 2000 and who is in police detention after midnight on 24th July 2006, notwithstanding that he may have been arrested before that time.

1 GENERAL

1.1 This Code of Practice applies to, and only to, persons arrested under section 41 of the Terrorism Act 2000 (TACT) and detained in police custody under those provisions and Schedule 8 of the Act. References to detention under this provision that were previously included in PACE Code C – Code for the Detention, Treatment, and Questioning of Persons by Police Officers, no longer apply.

1.2 The Code ceases to apply at any point that a detainee is:

(a) charged with an offence
(b) released without charge, or
(c) transferred to a prison see *section 14.5*

1.3 References to an offence in this Code include being concerned in the commission, preparation or instigation of acts of terrorism.

1.4 This Code's provisions do not apply to detention of individuals under any other terrorism legislation. This Code does not apply to people:

(i) detained under section 5(1) of the Prevention of Terrorism Act 2005.
(ii) detained for examination under TACT Schedule 7 and to whom the Code of Practice issued under that Act, Schedule 14, paragraph 6 applies;
(iii) detained for searches under stop and search powers.

The provisions for the detention, treatment and questioning by police officers of persons other than those in police detention following arrest under section 41 of TACT, are set out in Code C issued under section 66(1) of the Police & Criminal Evidence Act (PACE)1984 (PACE Code C).

1.5 All persons in custody must be dealt with expeditiously, and released as soon as the need for detention no longer applies.

1.6 There is no provision for bail under TACT prior to charge.

1.7 An officer must perform the assigned duties in this Code as soon as practicable. An officer will not be in breach of this Code if delay is justifiable and reasonable steps are taken to prevent unnecessary delay. The custody record shall show when a delay has occurred and the reason. See *Note 1H*

1.8 This Code of Practice must be readily available at all police stations for consultation by:

• police officers
• police staff
• detained persons
• members of the public.

1.9 The provisions of this Code:

• include the *Annexes*
• do not include the *Notes for Guidance*.

1.10 If an officer has any suspicion, or is told in good faith, that a person of any age may be mentally disordered or otherwise mentally vulnerable, in the absence of clear evidence to dispel that suspicion, the person shall be treated as such for the purposes of this Code. See *Note 1G*

1.11 For the purposes of this Code, a juvenile is any person under the age of 17. If anyone appears to be under 17, and there is no clear evidence that they are 17 or over, they shall be treated as a juvenile for the purposes of this Code.

1.12 If a person appears to be blind, seriously visually impaired, deaf, unable to read or speak or has difficulty orally because of a speech impediment, they shall be treated as such for the purposes of this Code in the absence of clear evidence to the contrary.

1.13 'The appropriate adult' means, in the case of a:

(a) juvenile:

  (i) the parent, guardian or, if the juvenile is in local authority or voluntary organisation care, or is otherwise being looked after under the Children Act 1989, a person representing that authority or organisation;

  (ii) a social worker of a local authority social services department;

  (iii) failing these, some other responsible adult aged 18 or over who is not a police officer or employed by the police.

(b) person who is mentally disordered or mentally vulnerable: See *Note 1D*

  (i) a relative, guardian or other person responsible for their care or custody;

  (ii) someone experienced in dealing with mentally disordered or mentally vulnerable people but who is not a police officer or employed by the police;

  (iii) failing these, some other responsible adult aged 18 or over who is not a police officer or employed by the police.

1.14 If this Code requires a person be given certain information, they do not have to be given it if at the time they are incapable of understanding what is said, are violent or may become violent or in urgent need of medical attention, but they must be given it as soon as practicable.

1.15 References to a custody officer include any:-

* police officer; or
* designated staff custody officer acting in the exercise or performance of the powers and duties conferred or imposed on them by their designation,

performing the functions of a custody officer. See *Note 1J*.

1.16 When this Code requires the prior authority or agreement of an officer of at least inspector or superintendent rank, that authority may be given by a sergeant or chief inspector authorised by section 107 of PACE to perform the functions of the higher rank under TACT.

1.17 In this Code:

(a) 'designated person' means a person other than a police officer, designated under the Police Reform Act 2002, Part 4 who has specified powers and duties of police officers conferred or imposed on them;

(b) reference to a police officer includes a designated person acting in the exercise or performance of the powers and duties conferred or imposed on them by their designation.

1.18 Designated persons are entitled to use reasonable force as follows:-

(a) when exercising a power conferred on them which allows a police officer exercising that power to use reasonable force, a designated person has the same entitlement to use force; and

(b) at other times when carrying out duties conferred or imposed on them that also entitle them to use reasonable force, for example:

* when at a police station carrying out the duty to keep detainees for whom they are responsible under control and to assist any other police officer or designated person to keep any detainee under control and to prevent their escape.
* when securing, or assisting any other police officer or designated person in securing, the detention of a person at a police station.
* when escorting, or assisting any other police officer or designated person in escorting, a detainee within a police station.
* for the purpose of saving life or limb; or
* preventing serious damage to property.

1.19 Nothing in this Code prevents the custody officer, or other officer given custody of the detainee, from allowing police staff who are not designated persons to carry out individual procedures or tasks at the police station if the law allows. However, the officer remains responsible for making sure the procedures and tasks are carried out correctly in accordance with the Codes of Practice. Any such person must be:

(a) a person employed by a police authority maintaining a police force and under the control and direction of the Chief Officer of that force;

(b) employed by a person with whom a police authority has a contract for the provision of services relating to persons arrested or otherwise in custody.

1.20 Designated persons and other police staff must have regard to any relevant provisions of this Code.

1.21 References to pocket books include any official report book issued to police officers or other police staff.

Notes for guidance

1A   Although certain sections of this Code apply specifically to people in custody at police stations, those there voluntarily to assist with an investigation should be treated with no less consideration, e.g. offered refreshments at appropriate times, and enjoy an absolute right to obtain legal advice or communicate with anyone outside the police station.

1B   A person, including a parent or guardian, should not be an appropriate adult if they:

- *are*
  - *suspected of involvement in the offence or involvement in the commission, preparation or instigation of acts of terrorism*
  - *the victim*
  - *a witness*
  - *involved in the investigation*
- *received admissions prior to attending to act as the appropriate adult.*

Note: If a juvenile's parent is estranged from the juvenile, they should not be asked to act as the appropriate adult if the juvenile expressly and specifically objects to their presence.

1C   If a juvenile admits an offence to, or in the presence of, a social worker or member of a youth offending team other than during the time that person is acting as the juvenile's appropriate adult, another appropriate adult should be appointed in the interest of fairness.

1D   In the case of people who are mentally disordered or otherwise mentally vulnerable, it may be more satisfactory if the appropriate adult is someone experienced or trained in their care rather than a relative lacking such qualifications. But if the detainee prefers a relative to a better qualified stranger or objects to a particular person their wishes should, if practicable, be respected.

1E   A detainee should always be given an opportunity, when an appropriate adult is called to the police station, to consult privately with a solicitor in the appropriate adult's absence if they want. An appropriate adult is not subject to legal privilege.

1F   A solicitor or independent custody visitor (formerly a lay visitor) present at the police station in that capacity may not be the appropriate adult.

1G   'Mentally vulnerable' applies to any detainee who, because of their mental state or capacity, may not understand the significance of what is said, of questions or of their replies. 'Mental disorder' is defined in the Mental Health Act 1983, section 1(2) as 'mental illness, arrested or incomplete development of mind, psychopathic disorder and any other disorder or disability of mind'. When the custody officer has any doubt about the mental state or capacity of a detainee, that detainee should be treated as mentally vulnerable and an appropriate adult called.

1H   Paragraph 1.7 is intended to cover delays which may occur in processing detainees eg if:

- *a large number of suspects are brought into the station simultaneously to be placed in custody;*
- *interview rooms are all being used;*
- *there are difficulties contacting an appropriate adult, solicitor or interpreter.*

1I   The custody officer must remind the appropriate adult and detainee about the right to legal advice and record any reasons for waiving it in accordance with section 6.

1J   The designation of police staff custody officers applies only in police areas where an order commencing the provisions of the Police Reform Act 2002, section 38 and Schedule 4A, for designating police staff custody officers is in effect.

1K   This Code does not affect the principle that all citizens have a duty to help police officers to prevent crime and discover offenders. This is a civic rather than a legal duty; but when a police officer is trying to discover whether, or by whom, an offence has been committed he is entitled to question any person from whom he thinks useful information can be obtained, subject to the restrictions imposed by this Code. A person's declaration that he is unwilling to reply does not alter this entitlement.

1L   If a person is moved from a police station to receive medical treatment, or for any other reason, the period of detention is still calculated from the time of arrest under section 41 of TACT (or, if a person was being detained under TACT Schedule 7 when arrested, from the time at which the examination under Schedule 7 began).

1M   Under Paragraph 1 of Schedule 8 to TACT, all police stations are designated for detention of persons arrested under section 41 of TACT. Paragraph 4 of Schedule 8 requires that the constable who arrests a person under section 41 takes him as soon as practicable to the police station which he considers is "most appropriate".

2 CUSTODY RECORDS

2.1   When a person is brought to a police station:

- under TACT section 41 arrest, or
- is arrested under TACT section 41 at the police station having attended there voluntarily,

they should be brought before the custody officer as soon as practicable after their arrival at the station or, if appropriate, following arrest after attending the police station voluntarily *see Note 3H.* A person is deemed to be "at a police station" for these purposes if they are within the boundary of any building or enclosed yard which forms part of that police station.

2.2 A separate custody record must be opened as soon as practicable for each person brought to a police station under arrest or arrested at the station having gone there voluntarily. All information recorded under this Code must be recorded as soon as practicable in the custody record unless otherwise specified. Any audio or video recording made in the custody area is not part of the custody record.

2.3 If any action requires the authority of an officer of a specified rank, this must be noted in the custody record, subject to paragraph 2.8.

2.4 The custody officer is responsible for the custody record's accuracy and completeness and for making sure the record or copy of the record accompanies a detainee if they are transferred to another police station. The record shall show the:

- time and reason for transfer;
- time a person is released from detention.

2.5 A solicitor or appropriate adult must be permitted to consult a detainee's custody record as soon as practicable after their arrival at the station and at any other time whilst the person is detained. Arrangements for this access must be agreed with the custody officer and may not unreasonably interfere with the custody officer's duties or the justifiable needs of the investigation.

2.6 When a detainee leaves police detention or is taken before a court they, their legal representative or appropriate adult shall be given, on request, a copy of the custody record as soon as practicable. This entitlement lasts for 12 months after release.

2.7 The detainee, appropriate adult or legal representative shall be permitted to inspect the original custody record once the detained person is no longer held under the provisions of TACT section 41 and Schedule 8, provided they give reasonable notice of their request. Any such inspection shall be noted in the custody record.

2.8 All entries in custody records must be timed and identified by the maker. Nothing in this Code requires the identity of officers or other police staff to be recorded or disclosed in the case of enquiries linked to the investigation of terrorism. In these cases, they shall use their warrant or other identification numbers and the name of their police station *see Note 2A.* If records are entered on computer these shall also be timed and contain the operator's identification.

2.9 The fact and time of any detainee's refusal to sign a custody record, when asked in accordance with this Code, must be recorded.

Note for guidance

2A The purpose of paragraph 2.8 is to protect those involved in terrorist investigations or arrests of terrorist suspects from the possibility that those arrested, their associates or other individuals or groups may threaten or cause harm to those involved.

3 INITIAL ACTION

(a) Detained persons – normal procedure

3.1 When a person is brought to a police station under arrest or arrested at the station having gone there voluntarily, the custody officer must make sure the person is told clearly about the following continuing rights which may be exercised at any stage during the period in custody:

(i)   the right to have someone informed of their arrest as in *section 5;*
(ii) the right to consult privately with a solicitor and that free independent legal advice is available;
(iii) the right to consult this Code of Practice. See *Note 3D*

3.2 The detainee must also be given:

- a written notice setting out:

  - the above three rights;
  - the arrangements for obtaining legal advice;
  - the right to a copy of the custody record as in *paragraph 2.6;*
  - the caution in the terms prescribed in *section 10.*

- an additional written notice briefly setting out their entitlements while in custody, see *Notes 3A* and *3B.*

Note: The detainee shall be asked to sign the custody record to acknowledge receipt of these notices. Any refusal must be recorded on the custody record.

3.3 A citizen of an independent Commonwealth country or a national of a foreign country, including the Republic of Ireland, must be informed as soon as practicable about their rights of communication with their High Commission, Embassy or Consulate. See *section 7*

3.4 The custody officer shall:

- record that the person was arrested under section 41 of TACT and the reason(s) for the arrest on the custody record. See *paragraph 10.2 and Note for Guidance 3G.*

- note on the custody record any comment the detainee makes in relation to the arresting officer's account but shall not invite comment. If the arresting officer is not physically present when the detainee is brought to a police station, the arresting officer's account must be made available to the custody officer remotely or by a third party on the arresting officer's behalf;
- note any comment the detainee makes in respect of the decision to detain them but shall not invite comment;
- not put specific questions to the detainee regarding their involvement in any offence, nor in respect of any comments they may make in response to the arresting officer's account or the decision to place them in detention *See paragraphs 14.1* and *14.2* and *Notes for Guidance 3H, 14A* and *14B*. Such an exchange is likely to constitute an interview as in *paragraph 11.1* and require the associated safeguards in *section 11*.

See *paragraph 5.9 of the Code of Practice issued under TACT Schedule 8 Paragraph 3* in respect of unsolicited comments.

If the first review of detention is carried out at this time, see paragraphs 14.1 and 14.2, and Part II of Schedule 8 to the Terrorism Act 2000 in respect of action by the review officer.

3.5 The custody officer shall:

(a) ask the detainee, whether at this time, they:

(vii) would like legal advice, see *section 6*;

(viii) want someone informed of their detention, see *section 5*;

(b) ask the detainee to sign the custody record to confirm their decisions in respect of (*a*);

(c) determine whether the detainee:

(i) is, or might be, in need of medical treatment or attention, see *section 9*;

(ii) requires:

- an appropriate adult;
- help to check documentation;
- an interpreter;

(d) record the decision in respect of (*c*).

3.6 When determining these needs the custody officer is responsible for initiating an assessment to consider whether the detainee is likely to present specific risks to custody staff, any individual who may have contact with detainee (e.g. legal advisers, medical staff), or themselves. Such assessments should always include a check on the Police National Computer, to be carried out as soon as practicable, to identify any risks highlighted in relation to the detainee. Although such assessments are primarily the custody officer's responsibility, it will be necessary to obtain information from other sources, especially the investigation team *See Note 3E*, the arresting officer or an appropriate health care professional, see *paragraph 9.15*. Reasons for delaying the initiation or completion of the assessment must be recorded.

3.7 Chief Officers should ensure that arrangements for proper and effective risk assessments required by *paragraph 3.6* are implemented in respect of all detainees at police stations in their area.

3.8 Risk assessments must follow a structured process which clearly defines the categories of risk to be considered and the results must be incorporated in the detainee's custody record. The custody officer is responsible for making sure those responsible for the detainee's custody are appropriately briefed about the risks. The content of any risk assessment and any analysis of the level of risk relating to the person's detention is not required to be shown or provided to the detainee or any person acting on behalf of the detainee. If no specific risks are identified by the assessment, that should be noted in the custody record. See *Note 3F* and *paragraph 9.15*

3.9 Custody officers are responsible for implementing the response to any specific risk assessment, which should include for example:

- reducing opportunities for self harm;
- calling a health care professional;
- increasing levels of monitoring or observation;
- reducing the risk to those who come into contact with the detainee.

See Note for Guidance 3F

3.10 Risk assessment is an ongoing process and assessments must always be subject to review if circumstances change.

3.11 If video cameras are installed in the custody area, notices shall be prominently displayed showing cameras are in use. Any request to have video cameras switched off shall be refused.

3.12 A constable, prison officer or other person authorised by the Secretary of State may take any steps which are reasonably necessary for

(a) photographing the detained person

(b) measuring him, or

(c) identifying him.

3.13 Paragraph 3.12 concerns the power in TACT Schedule 8 Paragraph 2. The power in

TACT Schedule 8 Paragraph 2 does not cover the taking of fingerprints, intimate samples or non-intimate samples, which is covered in TACT Schedule 8 paragraphs 10-15.

(b) Detained persons – special groups
3.14 If the detainee appears deaf or there is doubt about their hearing or speaking ability or ability to understand English, and the custody officer cannot establish effective communication, the custody officer must, as soon as practicable, call an interpreter for assistance in the action under *paragraphs 3.1–3.5*. See *section 13*
3.15 If the detainee is a juvenile, the custody officer must, if it is practicable, ascertain the identity of a person responsible for their welfare. That person:

* may be:
  - the parent or guardian;
  - if the juvenile is in local authority or voluntary organisation care, or is otherwise being looked after under the Children Act 1989, a person appointed by that authority or organisation to have responsibility for the juvenile's welfare;
  - any other person who has, for the time being, assumed responsibility for the juvenile's welfare.

* must be informed as soon as practicable that the juvenile has been arrested, why they have been arrested and where they are detained. This right is in addition to the juvenile's right in *section 5* not to be held incommunicado. See *Note 3C*

3.16 If a juvenile is known to be subject to a court order under which a person or organisation is given any degree of statutory responsibility to supervise or otherwise monitor them, reasonable steps must also be taken to notify that person or organisation (the 'responsible officer'). The responsible officer will normally be a member of a Youth Offending Team, except for a curfew order which involves electronic monitoring when the contractor providing the monitoring will normally be the responsible officer.
3.17 If the detainee is a juvenile, mentally disordered or otherwise mentally vulnerable, the custody officer must, as soon as practicable:

* inform the appropriate adult, who in the case of a juvenile may or may not be a person responsible for their welfare, as in *paragraph 3.15,* of:
  - the grounds for their detention;
  - their whereabouts.
* ask the adult to come to the police station to see the detainee.

3.18 If the appropriate adult is:

* already at the police station, the provisions of *paragraphs 3.1* to *3.5* must be complied with in the appropriate adult's presence;
* not at the station when these provisions are complied with, they must be complied with again in the presence of the appropriate adult when they arrive.

3.19 The detainee shall be advised that:

* the duties of the appropriate adult include giving advice and assistance;
* they can consult privately with the appropriate adult at any time.

3.20 If the detainee, or appropriate adult on the detainee's behalf, asks for a solicitor to be called to give legal advice, the provisions of *section 6* apply.
3.21 If the detainee is blind, seriously visually impaired or unable to read, the custody officer shall make sure their solicitor, relative, appropriate adult or some other person likely to take an interest in them and not involved in the investigation is available to help check any documentation. When this Code requires written consent or signing the person assisting may be asked to sign instead, if the detainee prefers. This paragraph does not require an appropriate adult to be called solely to assist in checking and signing documentation for a person who is not a juvenile, or mentally disordered or otherwise mentally vulnerable (see *paragraph 3.17*).

(c) Documentation
3.22 The grounds for a person's detention shall be recorded, in the person's presence if practicable.
3.23 Action taken under *paragraphs 3.14* to *3.22* shall be recorded.

Notes for guidance
3A The notice of entitlements should:

* *list the entitlements in this Code, including:*
  - *visits and contact with outside parties where practicable, including special provisions for Commonwealth citizens and foreign nationals;*
  - *reasonable standards of physical comfort;*
  - *adequate food and drink;*
  - *access to toilets and washing facilities, clothing, medical attention, and exercise when practicable.*

- mention the:
  - provisions relating to the conduct of interviews;
  - circumstances in which an appropriate adult should be available to assist the detainee and their statutory rights to make representation whenever the period of their detention is reviewed.

3B In addition to notices in English, translations should be available in Welsh, the main minority ethnic languages and the principal European languages whenever they are likely to be helpful. Audio versions of the notice should also be made available.

3C If the juvenile is in local authority or voluntary organisation care but living with their parents or other adults responsible for their welfare, although there is no legal obligation to inform them, they should normally be contacted, as well as the authority or organisation unless suspected of involvement in the offence concerned. Even if the juvenile is not living with their parents, consideration should be given to informing them.

3D The right to consult this or other relevant Codes of Practice does not entitle the person concerned to delay unreasonably any necessary investigative or administrative action whilst they do so. Examples of action which need not be delayed unreasonably include:

- searching detainees at the police station;
- taking fingerprints or non-intimate samples without consent for evidential purposes.

3E The investigation team will include any officer involved in questioning a suspect, gathering or analysing evidence in relation to the offences of which the detainee is suspected of having committed. Should a custody officer require information from the investigation team, the first point of contact should be the officer in charge of the investigation.

3F Home Office Circular 32/2000 provides more detailed guidance on risk assessments and identifies key risk areas which should always be considered. This should be read with the Guidance on Safer Detention & Handling of Persons in Police Custody issued by the National Centre for Policing Excellence in conjunction with the Home Office and Association of Chief Police Officers.

3G Arrests under TACT section 41 can only be made where an officer has reasonable grounds to suspect that the individual concerned is a "terrorist". This differs from the PACE power of arrest in that it need not be linked to a specific offence. There may also be circumstances where an arrest under TACT is made on the grounds of sensitive information which can not be disclosed. In such circumstances, the grounds for arrest may be given in terms of the interpretation of a "terrorist" set out in TACT sections 40(1)(a) or 40(1)(b).

3H For the purpose of arrests under TACT section 41, the review officer is responsible for authorising detention (see Paragraphs 14.1 and 14.2, and Notes for Guidance 14A and 14B). The review officer's role is explained in TACT Schedule 8 Part II. A person may be detained after arrest pending the first review, which must take place as soon as practicable after the person's arrest.

4 DETAINEE'S PROPERTY

(a) Action

4.1 The custody officer is responsible for:

(a) ascertaining what property a detainee:

  (i) has with them when they come to the police station, either on first arrival at the police station or any subsequent arrivals at a police station in connection with that detention.

  (ii) might have acquired for an unlawful or harmful purpose while in custody;

(b) the safekeeping of any property taken from a detainee which remains at the police station.

The custody officer may search the detainee or authorise their being searched to the extent they consider necessary, provided a search of intimate parts of the body or involving the removal of more than outer clothing is only made as in *Annex A*. A search may only be carried out by an officer of the same sex as the detainee. See *Note 4A*

4.2 Detainees may retain clothing and personal effects at their own risk unless the custody officer considers they may use them to cause harm to themselves or others, interfere with evidence, damage property, effect an escape or they are needed as evidence. In this event the custody officer may withhold such articles as they consider necessary and must tell the detainee why.

4.3 Personal effects are those items a detainee may lawfully need, use or refer to while in detention but do not include cash and other items of value.

(b) Documentation

4.4 It is a matter for the custody officer to determine whether a record should be made of the property a detained person has with him or had taken from him on arrest (see *Note for Guidance 4D*). Any record made is not required to be kept as part of the custody record but the custody record should be noted as to where such a record exists. Whenever a record is made the detainee shall be allowed to check and sign the record of property as correct. Any refusal to sign shall be recorded.

4.5 If a detainee is not allowed to keep any article of clothing or personal effects, the reason must be recorded.

Notes for guidance

4A PACE, Section 54(1) and paragraph 4.1 require a detainee to be searched when it is clear the custody officer will have continuing duties in relation to that detainee or when that detainee's behaviour or offence makes an inventory appropriate. They do not require every detainee to be searched, e.g. if it is clear a person will only be detained for a short period and is not to be placed in a cell, the custody officer may decide not to search them. In such a case the custody record will be endorsed 'not searched', paragraph 4.4 will not apply, and the detainee will be invited to sign the entry. If the detainee refuses, the custody officer will be obliged to ascertain what property they have in accordance with paragraph 4.1.

4B Paragraph 4.4 does not require the custody officer to record on the custody record property in the detainee's possession on arrest if, by virtue of its nature, quantity or size, it is not practicable to remove it to the police station.

4C Paragraph 4.4 does not require items of clothing worn by the person be recorded unless withheld by the custody officer as in paragraph 4.2.

4D Section 43(2) of TACT allows a constable to search a person who has been arrested under section 41 to discover whether he has anything in his possession that may constitute evidence that he is a terrorist.

5 RIGHT NOT TO BE HELD INCOMMUNICADO

(a) Action

5.1 Any person arrested and held in custody at a police station or other premises may, on request, have one named person who is a friend, relative or a person known to them who is likely to take an interest in their welfare informed at public expense of their whereabouts as soon as practicable. If the person cannot be contacted the detainee may choose up to two alternatives. If they cannot be contacted, the person in charge of detention or the investigation has discretion to allow further attempts until the information has been conveyed. See *Notes 5D* and *5E*.

5.2 The exercise of the above right in respect of each person nominated may be delayed only in accordance with *Annex B*.

5.3 The above right may be exercised each time a detainee is taken to another police station or returned to a police station having been previously transferred to prison. This Code does not afford such a right to a person on transfer to a prison, where a detainee's rights will be governed by Prison Rules *see paragraph 14.8*.

5.4 If the detainee agrees, they may receive visits from friends, family or others likely to take an interest in their welfare, at the custody officer's discretion. Custody Officers should liaise closely with the investigation team (see *Note 3E*) to allow risk assessments to be made where particular visitors have been requested by the detainee or identified themselves to police. In circumstances where the nature of the investigation means that such requests can not be met, consideration should be given, in conjunction with a representative of the relevant scheme, to increasing the frequency of visits from independent visitor schemes. See *Notes 5B* and *5C*.

5.5 If a friend, relative or person with an interest in the detainee's welfare enquires about their whereabouts, this information shall be given if the suspect agrees and *Annex B* does not apply. See *Note 5E*.

5.6 The detainee shall be given writing materials, on request, and allowed to telephone one person for a reasonable time, see *Notes 5A* and *5F*. Either or both these privileges may be denied or delayed if an officer of inspector rank or above considers sending a letter or making a telephone call may result in any of the consequences in *Annex B paragraphs 1* and *2*, particularly in relation to the making of a telephone call in a language which an officer listening to the call (see paragraph 5.7) does not understand. See *note 5G*.

Nothing in this paragraph permits the restriction or denial of the rights in *paragraphs 5.1* and *6.1*.

5.7 Before any letter or message is sent, or telephone call made, the detainee shall be informed that what they say in any letter, call or message (other than in a communication to a solicitor) may be read or listened to and may be given in evidence. A telephone call may be terminated if it is being abused *see Note 5G*. The costs can be at public expense at the custody officer's discretion.

5.8 Any delay or denial of the rights in this section should be proportionate and should last no longer than necessary.

(b) Documentation

5.9 A record must be kept of any:

(a) request made under this section and the action taken;

(b) letters, messages or telephone calls made or received or visit received;

(c) refusal by the detainee to have information about them given to an outside enquirer, or any refusal to see a visitor. The detainee must be asked to countersign the record accordingly and any refusal recorded.

Notes for guidance

5A A person may request an interpreter to interpret a telephone call or translate a letter.

5B At the custody officer's discretion (and subject to the detainee's consent), visits from friends, family or others likely to take an interest in the detainee's welfare, should be allowed when possible, subject to sufficient personnel being available to supervise a visit and any possible hindrance to the investigation. Custody Officers should bear in mind the exceptional nature of prolonged TACT detention and consider the potential benefits that visits may bring to the health and welfare of detainees who are held for extended periods.

5C Official visitors should be given access following consultation with the officer who has overall responsibility for the investigation provided the detainee consents, and they do not compromise safety or security or unduly delay or interfere with the progress of an investigation. Official visitors should still be required to provide appropriate identification and subject to any screening process in place at the place of detention. Official visitors may include:

- *An accredited faith representative*
- *Members of either House of Parliament*
- *Public officials needing to interview the prisoner in the course of their duties*
- *Other persons visiting with the approval of the officer who has overall responsibility for the investigation*
- *Consular officials visiting a detainee who is a national of the country they represent subject to Annex F.*

Visits from appropriate members of the Independent Custody Visitors Scheme should be dealt with in accordance with the separate Code of Practice on Independent Custody Visiting.

5D If the detainee does not know anyone to contact for advice or support or cannot contact a friend or relative, the custody officer should bear in mind any local voluntary bodies or other organisations that might be able to help. Paragraph 6.1 applies if legal advice is required.

5E In some circumstances it may not be appropriate to use the telephone to disclose information under paragraphs 5.1 and 5.5.

5F The telephone call at paragraph 5.6 is in addition to any communication under paragraphs 5.1 and 6.1. Further calls may be made at the custody officer's discretion.

5G The nature of terrorism investigations means that officers should have particular regard to the possibility of suspects attempting to pass information which may be detrimental to public safety, or to an investigation.

6 RIGHT TO LEGAL ADVICE

(a) Action

6.1 Unless *Annex B* applies, all detainees must be informed that they may at any time consult and communicate privately with a solicitor, whether in person, in writing or by telephone, and that free independent legal advice is available from the duty solicitor. Where an appropriate adult is in attendance, they must also be informed of this right. See *paragraph 3.1, Note 1I, Note 6B* and *Note 6I*

6.2 A poster advertising the right to legal advice must be prominently displayed in the charging area of every police station. See *Note 6G*

6.3 No police officer should, at any time, do or say anything with the intention of dissuading a detainee from obtaining legal advice.

6.4 The exercise of the right of access to legal advice may be delayed exceptionally only as in *Annex B*. Whenever legal advice is requested, and unless *Annex B* applies, the custody officer must act without delay to secure the provision of such advice. If, on being informed or reminded of this right, the detainee declines to speak to a solicitor in person, the officer should point out that the right includes the right to speak with a solicitor on the telephone (see *paragraph 5.6*). If the detainee continues to waive this right the officer should ask them why and any reasons should be recorded on the custody record or the interview record as appropriate. Reminders of the right to legal advice must be given as in *paragraphs 3.5, 11.3*, and the PACE Code D on the Identification of Persons by Police Officers (PACE Code D), *paragraphs 3.19(ii)* and *6.2*. Once it is clear a detainee does not want to speak to a solicitor in person or by telephone they should cease to be asked their reasons. See *Note 6J*.

6.5 An officer of the rank of Commander or Assistant Chief Constable may give a direction under TACT Schedule 8 paragraph 9 that a detainee may only consult a solicitor within the sight and hearing of a qualified officer. Such a direction may only be given if the officer has reasonable grounds to believe that if it were not, it may result in one of the consequences set out in TACT Schedule 8 paragraphs 8(4) or 8(5)(c). See *Annex B paragraph 3* and *Note 6I*. A "qualified officer" means a police officer who:

(a)   is at least the rank of inspector;

(b)   is of the uniformed branch of the force of which the officer giving the direction is a member, and

(c)   in the opinion of the officer giving the direction, has no connection with the detained person's case

Officers considering the use of this power should first refer to Home Office Circular 40/2003.

6.6   In the case of a juvenile, an appropriate adult should consider whether legal advice from a solicitor is required. If the juvenile indicates that they do not want legal advice, the appropriate adult has the right to ask for a solicitor to attend if this would be in the best interests of the person. However, the detained person cannot be forced to see the solicitor if he is adamant that he does not wish to do so.

6.7   A detainee who wants legal advice may not be interviewed or continue to be interviewed until they have received such advice unless:

(a)   *Annex B* applies, when the restriction on drawing adverse inferences from silence in *Annex C* will apply because the detainee is not allowed an opportunity to consult a solicitor; or

(b)   an officer of superintendent rank or above has reasonable grounds for believing that:

    (i)   the consequent delay might:

- lead to interference with, or harm to, evidence connected with an offence;
- lead to interference with, or physical harm to, other people;
- lead to serious loss of, or damage to, property;
- lead to alerting other people suspected of having committed an offence but not yet arrested for it;
- hinder the recovery of property obtained in consequence of the commission of an offence.

    (ii)   when a solicitor, including a duty solicitor, has been contacted and has agreed to attend, awaiting their arrival would cause unreasonable delay to the process of investigation.

Note: In these cases the restriction on drawing adverse inferences from silence in *Annex C* will apply because the detainee is not allowed an opportunity to consult a solicitor.

(c)   the solicitor the detainee has nominated or selected from a list:

    (i)   cannot be contacted;

    (ii)   has previously indicated they do not wish to be contacted; or

    (iii)   having been contacted, has declined to attend; and

the detainee has been advised of the Duty Solicitor Scheme but has declined to ask for the duty solicitor.

    In these circumstances the interview may be started or continued without further delay provided an officer of inspector rank or above has agreed to the interview proceeding.

    Note: The restriction on drawing adverse inferences from silence in *Annex C* will not apply because the detainee is allowed an opportunity to consult the duty solicitor;

(d)   the detainee changes their mind, about wanting legal advice.

    In these circumstances the interview may be started or continued without delay provided that:

    (i)   the detainee agrees to do so, in writing or on the interview record made in accordance with the Code of Practice issued under TACT Schedule 8 Paragraph 3; and

    (ii)   an officer of inspector rank or above has inquired about the detainee's reasons for their change of mind and gives authority for the interview to proceed.

Confirmation of the detainee's agreement, their change of mind, the reasons for it if given and, subject to *paragraph 2.8,* the name of the authorising officer shall be recorded in the written interview record or the interview record made in accordance with the Code of Practice issued under Paragraph 3 of Schedule 8 to the Terrorism Act. See *Note 6H.* Note: In these circumstances the restriction on drawing adverse inferences from silence in *Annex C* will not apply because the detainee is allowed an opportunity to consult a solicitor if they wish.

6.8   If *paragraph 6.7(a)* applies, where the reason for authorising the delay ceases to apply, there may be no further delay in permitting the exercise of the right in the absence of a further authorisation unless *paragraph 6.7 (b), (c)* or *(d)* applies.

6.9   A detainee who has been permitted to consult a solicitor shall be entitled on request to have the solicitor present when they are interviewed unless one of the exceptions in *paragraph 6.7* applies.

6.10   The solicitor may only be required to leave the interview if their conduct is such that the interviewer is unable properly to put questions to the suspect. See *Notes 6C* and *6D*

6.11 If the interviewer considers a solicitor is acting in such a way, they will stop the interview and consult an officer not below superintendent rank, if one is readily available, and otherwise an officer not below inspector rank not connected with the investigation. After speaking to the solicitor, the officer consulted will decide if the interview should continue in the presence of that solicitor. If they decide it should not, the suspect will be given the opportunity to consult another solicitor before the interview continues and that solicitor given an opportunity to be present at the interview. See *Note 6D*

6.12 The removal of a solicitor from an interview is a serious step and, if it occurs, the officer of superintendent rank or above who took the decision will consider if the incident should be reported to the Law Society. If the decision to remove the solicitor has been taken by an officer below superintendent rank, the facts must be reported to an officer of superintendent rank or above who will similarly consider whether a report to the Law Society would be appropriate. When the solicitor concerned is a duty solicitor, the report should be both to the Law Society and to the Legal Services Commission.

6.13 'Solicitor' in this Code means:

- a solicitor who holds a current practising certificate
- an accredited or probationary representative included on the register of representatives maintained by the Legal Services Commission.

6.14 An accredited or probationary representative sent to provide advice by, and on behalf of, a solicitor shall be admitted to the police station for this purpose unless an officer of inspector rank or above considers such a visit will hinder the investigation and directs otherwise. Hindering the investigation does not include giving proper legal advice to a detainee as in *Note 6C*. Once admitted to the police station, *paragraphs 6.7* to *6.11* apply.

6.15 In exercising their discretion under *paragraph 6.14*, the officer should take into account in particular:

- whether:
  - the identity and status of an accredited or probationary representative have been satisfactorily established;
  - they are of suitable character to provide legal advice,
  - any other matters in any written letter of authorisation provided by the solicitor on whose behalf the person is attending the police station. See *Note 6E*

6.16 If the inspector refuses access to an accredited or probationary representative or a decision is taken that such a person should not be permitted to remain at an interview, the inspector must notify the solicitor on whose behalf the representative was acting and give them an opportunity to make alternative arrangements. The detainee must be informed and the custody record noted.

6.17 If a solicitor arrives at the station to see a particular person, that person must, unless *Annex B* applies, be so informed whether or not they are being interviewed and asked if they would like to see the solicitor. This applies even if the detainee has declined legal advice or, having requested it, subsequently agreed to be interviewed without receiving advice. The solicitor's attendance and the detainee's decision must be noted in the custody record.

(b) Documentation

6.18 Any request for legal advice and the action taken shall be recorded.

6.19 A record shall be made in the interview record if a detainee asks for legal advice and an interview is begun either in the absence of a solicitor or their representative, or they have been required to leave an interview.

Notes for guidance

6A If paragraph 6.7(b) applies, the officer should, if practicable, ask the solicitor for an estimate of how long it will take to come to the station and relate this to the time detention is permitted, the time of day (i.e. whether the rest period under paragraph 12.2 is imminent) and the requirements of other investigations. If the solicitor is on their way or is to set off immediately, it will not normally be appropriate to begin an interview before they arrive. If it appears necessary to begin an interview before the solicitor's arrival, they should be given an indication of how long the police would be able to wait so there is an opportunity to make arrangements for someone else to provide legal advice. Nothing within this section is intended to prevent police from ascertaining immediately after the arrest of an individual whether a threat to public safety exists (see paragraph 11.2).

6B A detainee who asks for legal advice should be given an opportunity to consult a specific solicitor or another solicitor from that solicitor's firm or the duty solicitor. If advice is not available by these means, or they do not want to consult the duty solicitor, the detainee should be given an opportunity to choose a solicitor from a list of those willing to provide legal advice. If this solicitor is unavailable, they may choose up to two alternatives. If these attempts are unsuccessful, the custody officer has discretion to allow further attempts until a solicitor has been contacted and agrees to provide legal advice. Apart from carrying out these duties, an officer must not advise the suspect about any particular firm of solicitors.

6C A detainee has a right to free legal advice and to be represented by a solicitor. The solicitor's only role in the police station is to protect and advance the legal rights of their client. On occasions this may require the solicitor to give advice which has the effect of the client avoiding giving evidence which strengthens a prosecution case. The solicitor may intervene in order to seek clarification, challenge an improper question to their client or the manner in which it is put, advise their client not to reply to particular questions, or if they wish to give their client further legal advice. Paragraph 6.9 only applies if the solicitor's approach or conduct prevents or unreasonably obstructs proper questions being put to the suspect or the suspect's response being recorded. Examples of unacceptable conduct include answering questions on a suspect's behalf or providing written replies for the suspect to quote.

6D An officer who takes the decision to exclude a solicitor must be in a position to satisfy the court the decision was properly made. In order to do this they may need to witness what is happening.

6E If an officer of at least inspector rank considers a particular solicitor or firm of solicitors is persistently sending probationary representatives who are unsuited to provide legal advice, they should inform an officer of at least superintendent rank, who may wish to take the matter up with the Law Society.

6F Subject to the constraints of Annex B, a solicitor may advise more than one client in an investigation if they wish. Any question of a conflict of interest is for the solicitor under their professional code of conduct. If, however, waiting for a solicitor to give advice to one client may lead to unreasonable delay to the interview with another, the provisions of paragraph 6.7(b) may apply.

6G In addition to a poster in English, a poster or posters containing translations into Welsh, the main minority ethnic languages and the principal European languages should be displayed wherever they are likely to be helpful and it is practicable to do so.

6H Paragraph 6.7(d) requires the authorisation of an officer of inspector rank or above to the continuation of an interview when a detainee who wanted legal advice changes their mind. It is permissible for such authorisation to be given over the telephone, if the authorising officer is able to satisfy themselves about the reason for the detainee's change of mind and is satisfied it is proper to continue the interview in those circumstances.

6I Whenever a detainee exercises their right to legal advice by consulting or communicating with a solicitor, they must be allowed to do so in private. This right to consult or communicate in private is fundamental. Except as allowed by the Terrorism Act 2000, Schedule 8, paragraph 9, if the requirement for privacy is compromised because what is said or written by the detainee or solicitor for the purpose of giving and receiving legal advice is overheard, listened to, or read by others without the informed consent of the detainee, the right will effectively have been denied. When a detainee chooses to speak to a solicitor on the telephone, they should be allowed to do so in private unless a direction under Schedule 8, paragraph 9 of the Terrorism Act 2000 has been given or this is impractical because of the design and layout of the custody area, or the location of telephones. However, the normal expectation should be that facilities will be available, unless they are being used, at all police stations to enable detainees to speak in private to a solicitor either face to face or over the telephone.

6J A detainee is not obliged to give reasons for declining legal advice and should not be pressed to do so.

7 CITIZENS OF INDEPENDENT COMMONWEALTH COUNTRIES OR FOREIGN NATIONALS

(a) Action

7.1 Any citizen of an independent Commonwealth country or a national of a foreign country, including the Republic of Ireland, may communicate at any time with the appropriate High Commission, Embassy or Consulate. The detainee must be informed as soon as practicable of:

- this right;
- their right, upon request, to have their High Commission, Embassy or Consulate told of their whereabouts and the grounds for their detention. Such a request should be acted upon as soon as practicable.

7.2 If a detainee is a citizen of a country with which a bilateral consular convention or agreement is in force requiring notification of arrest, the appropriate High Commission, Embassy or Consulate shall be informed as soon as practicable, subject to *paragraph 7.4*. The countries to which this applies as at 1 April 2003 are listed in *Annex F*.

7.3 Consular officers may visit one of their nationals in police detention to talk to them and, if required, to arrange for legal advice. Such visits shall take place out of the hearing of a police officer.

7.4 Notwithstanding the provisions of consular conventions, if the detainee is a political refugee whether for reasons of race, nationality, political opinion or religion, or is seeking political asylum, consular officers shall not be informed of the arrest of one of their nationals or given access or information about them except at the detainee's express request.

(b) Documentation
7.5 A record shall be made when a detainee is informed of their rights under this section and of any communications with a High Commission, Embassy or Consulate.

Note for guidance
7A The exercise of the rights in this section may not be interfered with even though Annex B applies.

8 CONDITIONS OF DETENTION

(a) Action
8.1 So far as it is practicable, not more than one detainee should be detained in each cell.
8.2 Cells in use must be adequately heated, cleaned and ventilated. They must be adequately lit, subject to such dimming as is compatible with safety and security to allow people detained overnight to sleep. No additional restraints shall be used within a locked cell unless absolutely necessary and then only restraint equipment, approved for use in that force by the Chief Officer, which is reasonable and necessary in the circumstances having regard to the detainee's demeanour and with a view to ensuring their safety and the safety of others. If a detainee is deaf, mentally disordered or otherwise mentally vulnerable, particular care must be taken when deciding whether to use any form of approved restraints.
8.3 Blankets, mattresses, pillows and other bedding supplied shall be of a reasonable standard and in a clean and sanitary condition.
8.4 Access to toilet and washing facilities must be provided.
8.5 If it is necessary to remove a detainee's clothes for the purposes of investigation, for hygiene, health reasons or cleaning, replacement clothing of a reasonable standard of comfort and cleanliness shall be provided. A detainee may not be interviewed unless adequate clothing has been offered.
8.6 At least two light meals and one main meal should be offered in any 24 hour period. See *Note 8B*. Drinks should be provided at meal times and upon reasonable request between meals. Whenever necessary, advice shall be sought from the appropriate health care professional, see *Note 9A*, on medical and dietary matters. As far as practicable, meals provided shall offer a varied diet and meet any specific dietary needs or religious beliefs the detainee may have. Detainees should also be made aware that the meals offered meet such needs. The detainee may, at the custody officer's discretion, have meals supplied by their family or friends at their expense. See *Note 8A*
8.7 Brief outdoor exercise shall be offered daily if practicable. Where facilities exist, indoor exercise shall be offered as an alternative if outside conditions are such that a detainee can not be reasonably expected to take outdoor exercise (e.g., in cold or wet weather) or if requested by the detainee or for reasons of security, see *Note 8C*.
8.8 Where practicable, provision should be made for detainees to practice religious observance. Consideration should be given to providing a separate room which can be used as a prayer room. The supply of appropriate food and clothing, and suitable provision for prayer facilities, such as uncontaminated copies of religious books, should also be considered. See *Note 8D*.
8.9 A juvenile shall not be placed in a cell unless no other secure accommodation is available and the custody officer considers it is not practicable to supervise them if they are not placed in a cell or that cell provides more comfortable accommodation than other secure accommodation in the station. A juvenile may not be placed in a cell with a detained adult.
8.10 Police stations should keep a reasonable supply of reading material available for detainees, including but not limited to, the main religious texts. See *Note 8D*. Detainees should be made aware that such material is available and reasonable requests for such material should be met as soon as practicable unless to do so would:

(i)   interfere with the investigation; or
(ii) prevent or delay an officer from discharging his statutory duties, or those in this Code.

If such a request is refused on the grounds of (i) or (ii) above, this should be noted in the custody record and met as soon as possible after those grounds cease to apply.

(b) Documentation
8.11 A record must be kept of replacement clothing and meals offered.
8.12 The use of any restraints on a detainee whilst in a cell, the reasons for it and, if appropriate, the arrangements for enhanced supervision of the detainee whilst so restrained, shall be recorded. See *paragraph 3.9*

Notes for guidance
8A In deciding whether to allow meals to be supplied by family or friends, the custody officer is entitled to take account of the risk of items being concealed in any food or package and the officer's duties and responsibilities under food handling legislation. If an officer needs to examine food or other items supplied by family and friends before deciding

whether they can be given to the detainee, he should inform the person who has brought the item to the police station of this and the reasons for doing so.

8B Meals should, so far as practicable, be offered at recognised meal times, or at other times that take account of when the detainee last had a meal.

8C In light of the potential for detaining individuals for extended periods of time, the overriding principle should be to accommodate a period of exercise, except where to do so would hinder the investigation, delay the detainee's release or charge, or it is declined by the detainee.

8D Police forces should consult with representatives of the main religious communities to ensure the provision for religious observance is adequate, and to seek advice on the appropriate storage and handling of religious texts or other religious items.

9 CARE AND TREATMENT OF DETAINED PERSONS

(a) General

9.1 Notwithstanding other requirements for medical attention as set out in this section, detainees who are held for more than 96 hours must be visited by a healthcare professional at least once every 24 hours.

9.2 Nothing in this section prevents the police from calling the police surgeon or, if appropriate, some other health care professional, to examine a detainee for the purposes of obtaining evidence relating to any offence in which the detainee is suspected of being involved. See *Note 9A*

9.3 If a complaint is made by, or on behalf of, a detainee about their treatment since their arrest, or it comes to notice that a detainee may have been treated improperly, a report must be made as soon as practicable to an officer of inspector rank or above not connected with the investigation. If the matter concerns a possible assault or the possibility of the unnecessary or unreasonable use of force, an appropriate health care professional must also be called as soon as practicable.

9.4 Detainees should be visited at least every hour. If no reasonably foreseeable risk was identified in a risk assessment, see *paragraphs 3.6 – 3.10*, there is no need to wake a sleeping detainee. Those suspected of being intoxicated through drink or drugs or having swallowed drugs, see *Note 9C*, or whose level of consciousness causes concern must, subject to any clinical directions given by the appropriate health care professional, see *paragraph 9.15*:

- be visited and roused at least every half hour
- have their condition assessed as in *Annex H*
- and clinical treatment arranged if appropriate

See *Notes 9B, 9C* and *9G*

9.5 When arrangements are made to secure clinical attention for a detainee, the custody officer must make sure all relevant information which might assist in the treatment of the detainee's condition is made available to the responsible health care professional. This applies whether or not the health care professional asks for such information. Any officer or police staff with relevant information must inform the custody officer as soon as practicable.

(b) Clinical treatment and attention

9.6 The custody officer must make sure a detainee receives appropriate clinical attention as soon as reasonably practicable if the person:

(a) appears to be suffering from physical illness; or
(b) is injured; or
(c) appears to be suffering from a mental disorder; or
(d) appears to need clinical attention

9.7 This applies even if the detainee makes no request for clinical attention and whether or not they have already received clinical attention elsewhere. If the need for attention appears urgent, e.g. when indicated as in *Annex H*, the nearest available health care professional or an ambulance must be called immediately.

9.8 The custody officer must also consider the need for clinical attention as set out in *Note* 9C in relation to those suffering the effects of alcohol or drugs.

9.9 If it appears to the custody officer, or they are told, that a person brought to a station under arrest may be suffering from an infectious disease or condition, the custody officer must take reasonable steps to safeguard the health of the detainee and others at the station. In deciding what action to take, advice must be sought from an appropriate health care professional. See *Note 9D*. The custody officer has discretion to isolate the person and their property until clinical directions have been obtained.

9.10 If a detainee requests a clinical examination, an appropriate health care professional must be called as soon as practicable to assess the detainee's clinical needs. If a safe and appropriate care plan cannot be provided, the police surgeon's advice must be sought. The detainee may also be examined by a medical practitioner of their choice at their expense.

9.11 If a detainee is required to take or apply any medication in compliance with clinical directions prescribed before their detention, the custody officer must consult the appropriate health care professional before the use of the medication. Subject to the restrictions in *paragraph 9.12*, the custody officer is responsible for the safekeeping of any medication and for making sure the detainee is given the opportunity to take or apply prescribed or approved medication. Any such consultation and its outcome shall be noted in the custody record.

9.12 No police officer may administer or supervise the self-administration of medically prescribed controlled drugs of the types and forms listed in the Misuse of Drugs Regulations 2001, Schedule 2 or 3. A detainee may only self-administer such drugs under the personal supervision of the registered medical practitioner authorising their use. Drugs listed in Schedule 4 or 5 may be distributed by the custody officer for self- administration if they have consulted the registered medical practitioner authorising their use, this may be done by telephone, and both parties are satisfied self-administration will not expose the detainee, police officers or anyone else to the risk of harm or injury.

9.13 When appropriate health care professionals administer drugs or other medications, or supervise their self-administration, it must be within current medicines legislation and the scope of practice as determined by their relevant professional body.

9.14 If a detainee has in their possession, or claims to need, medication relating to a heart condition, diabetes, epilepsy or a condition of comparable potential seriousness then, even though *paragraph 9.6* may not apply, the advice of the appropriate health care professional must be obtained.

9.15 Whenever the appropriate health care professional is called in accordance with this section to examine or treat a detainee, the custody officer shall ask for their opinion about:

- any risks or problems which police need to take into account when making decisions about the detainee's continued detention;
- when to carry out an interview if applicable; and
- the need for safeguards.

9.16 When clinical directions are given by the appropriate health care professional, whether orally or in writing, and the custody officer has any doubts or is in any way uncertain about any aspect of the directions, the custody officer shall ask for clarification. It is particularly important that directions concerning the frequency of visits are clear, precise and capable of being implemented. See *Note 9E*.

(c) Documentation

9.17 A record must be made in the custody record of:

(a) the arrangements made for an examination by an appropriate health care professional under *paragraph 9.3* and of any complaint reported under that paragraph together with any relevant remarks by the custody officer;
(b) any arrangements made in accordance with *paragraph 9.6*;
(c) any request for a clinical examination under *paragraph 9.10* and any arrangements made in response;
(d) the injury, ailment, condition or other reason which made it necessary to make the arrangements in (a) to (c), see *Note 9F*;
(e) any clinical directions and advice, including any further clarifications, given to police by a health care professional concerning the care and treatment of the detainee in connection with any of the arrangements made in (a) to (c), see *Note 9E*;
(f) if applicable, the responses received when attempting to rouse a person using the procedure in *Annex H,* see *Note 9G*.

9.18 If a health care professional does not record their clinical findings in the custody record, the record must show where they are recorded. See *Note 9F*. However, information which is necessary to custody staff to ensure the effective ongoing care and well being of the detainee must be recorded openly in the custody record, see *paragraph 3.8* and *Annex G, paragraph 7*.

9.19 Subject to the requirements of *Section 4*, the custody record shall include:

- a record of all medication a detainee has in their possession on arrival at the police station;
- a note of any such medication they claim to need but do not have with them.

Notes for guidance

9A A 'health care professional' means a clinically qualified person working within the scope of practice as determined by their relevant professional body. Whether a health care professional is 'appropriate' depends on the circumstances of the duties they carry out at the time.

9B Whenever possible juveniles and mentally vulnerable detainees should be visited more frequently.

9C A detainee who appears drunk or behaves abnormally may be suffering from illness, the effects of drugs or may have sustained injury, particularly a head injury which is not apparent. A detainee needing or dependent on certain drugs, including alcohol, may experience harmful effects within a short time of being deprived of their supply. In these circumstances, when there is any doubt, police should always act urgently to call an appropriate health care professional or an ambulance. Paragraph 9.6 does not apply to minor ailments or injuries which do not need attention. However, all such ailments or injuries must be recorded in the custody record and any doubt must be resolved in favour of calling the appropriate health care professional.

9D It is important to respect a person's right to privacy and information about their health must be kept confidential and only disclosed with their consent or in accordance with clinical advice when it is necessary to protect the detainee's health or that of others who come into contact with them.

9E The custody officer should always seek to clarify directions that the detainee requires constant observation or supervision and should ask the appropriate health care professional to explain precisely what action needs to be taken to implement such directions.

9F Paragraphs 9.17 and 9.18 do not require any information about the cause of any injury, ailment or condition to be recorded on the custody record if it appears capable of providing evidence of an offence.

9G The purpose of recording a person's responses when attempting to rouse them using the procedure in Annex H is to enable any change in the individual's consciousness level to be noted and clinical treatment arranged if appropriate.

10 CAUTIONS

(a) When a caution must be given

10.1 A person whom there are grounds to suspect of an offence, see *Note 10A,* must be cautioned before any questions about an offence, or further questions if the answers provide the grounds for suspicion, are put to them if either the suspect's answers or silence, (i.e. failure or refusal to answer or answer satisfactorily) may be given in evidence to a court in a prosecution.

10.2 A person who is arrested, or further arrested, must be informed at the time, or as soon as practicable thereafter, that they are under arrest and the grounds for their arrest, see paragraph 3.4, *Note 3G* and *Note 10B.*

10.3 As per *section 3* of PACE Code G, a person who is arrested, or further arrested, must also be cautioned unless:

(a) it is impracticable to do so by reason of their condition or behaviour at the time;
(b) they have already been cautioned immediately prior to arrest as in *paragraph 10.1.*

(b) Terms of the cautions

10.4 The caution which must be given on:

(a) arrest;
(b) all other occasions before a person is charged or informed they may be prosecuted, see *PACE Code C,* section 16.

should, unless the restriction on drawing adverse inferences from silence applies, see *Annex C,* be in the following terms:

"You do not have to say anything. But it may harm your defence if you do not mention when questioned something which you later rely on in Court. Anything you do say may be given in evidence."
See *Note 10F*

10.5 *Annex C, paragraph 2* sets out the alternative terms of the caution to be used when the restriction on drawing adverse inferences from silence applies.

10.6 Minor deviations from the words of any caution given in accordance with this Code do not constitute a breach of this Code, provided the sense of the relevant caution is preserved. See *Note 10C*

10.7 After any break in questioning under caution, the person being questioned must be made aware they remain under caution. If there is any doubt the relevant caution should be given again in full when the interview resumes. See *Note 10D*

10.8 When, despite being cautioned, a person fails to co-operate or to answer particular questions which may affect their immediate treatment, the person should be informed of any relevant consequences and that those consequences are not affected by the caution. Examples are when a person's refusal to provide:

•   their name and address when charged may make them liable to detention;
•   particulars and information in accordance with a statutory requirement

(c) Special warnings under the Criminal Justice and Public Order Act 1994, sections 36 and 37

10.9 When a suspect interviewed at a police station or authorised place of detention after arrest fails or refuses to answer certain questions, or to answer satisfactorily, after due warning, see *Note 10E,* a court or jury may draw such inferences as appear proper under the Criminal Justice and Public Order Act 1994, sections 36 and 37. Such inferences may only be drawn when:

(a) the restriction on drawing adverse inferences from silence, see *Annex C,* does not apply; and

(b) the suspect is arrested by a constable and fails or refuses to account for any objects, marks or substances, or marks on such objects found:

- on their person;
- in or on their clothing or footwear;
- otherwise in their possession; or
- in the place they were arrested;

(c) the arrested suspect was found by a constable at a place at or about the time the offence for which that officer has arrested them is alleged to have been committed, and the suspect fails or refuses to account for their presence there.

When the restriction on drawing adverse inferences from silence applies, the suspect may still be asked to account for any of the matters in (*b*) or (*c*) but the special warning described in *paragraph 10.10* will not apply and must not be given.

10.10 For an inference to be drawn when a suspect fails or refuses to answer a question about one of these matters or to answer it satisfactorily, the suspect must first be told in ordinary language:

(a) what offence is being investigated;
(b) what fact they are being asked to account for;
(c) this fact may be due to them taking part in the commission of the offence;
(d) a court may draw a proper inference if they fail or refuse to account for this fact;
(e) a record is being made of the interview and it may be given in evidence if they are brought to trial.

(d) Juveniles and persons who are mentally disordered or otherwise mentally vulnerable

10.11 If a juvenile or a person who is mentally disordered or otherwise mentally vulnerable is cautioned in the absence of the appropriate adult, the caution must be repeated in the adult's presence.

(e) Documentation

10.12 A record shall be made when a caution is given under this section, either in the interviewer's pocket book or in the interview record.

Notes for guidance

10A There must be some reasonable, objective grounds for the suspicion, based on known facts or information which are relevant to the likelihood the offence has been committed and the person to be questioned committed it.

10B An arrested person must be given sufficient information to enable them to understand that they have been deprived of their liberty and the reason they have been arrested, e.g. when a person is arrested on suspicion of committing an offence they must be informed of the suspected offence's nature, when and where it was committed see Note 3G. The suspect must also be informed of the reason or reasons why the arrest is considered necessary. Vague or technical language should be avoided.

10C If it appears a person does not understand the caution, the person giving it should explain it in their own words.

10D It may be necessary to show to the court that nothing occurred during an interview break or between interviews which influenced the suspect's recorded evidence. After a break in an interview or at the beginning of a subsequent interview, the interviewing officer should summarise the reason for the break and confirm this with the suspect.

10E The Criminal Justice and Public Order Act 1994, sections 36 and 37 apply only to suspects who have been arrested by a constable or Customs and Excise officer and are given the relevant warning by the police or customs officer who made the arrest or who is investigating the offence. They do not apply to any interviews with suspects who have not been arrested.

10F Nothing in this Code requires a caution to be given or repeated when informing a person not under arrest they may be prosecuted for an offence. However, a court will not be able to draw any inferences under the Criminal Justice and Public Order Act 1994, section 34, if the person was not cautioned.

11 INTERVIEWS – GENERAL

(a) Action

11.1 An interview in this Code is the questioning of a person arrested on suspicion of being a terrorist which, under *paragraph 10.1,* must be carried out under caution. Whenever a person is interviewed they must be informed of the grounds for arrest *see Note 3G.*

11.2 Following a decision to arrest a suspect, they must not be interviewed about the relevant offence except at a place designated for detention under Schedule 8 paragraph 1 of the Terrorism Act 2000, unless the consequent delay would be likely to:

(a) lead to:
- interference with, or harm to, evidence connected with an offence;
- interference with, or physical harm to, other people; or
- serious loss of, or damage to, property;

(b) lead to alerting other people suspected of committing an offence but not yet arrested for it; or

(c) hinder the recovery of property obtained in consequence of the commission of an offence.

Interviewing in any of these circumstances shall cease once the relevant risk has been averted or the necessary questions have been put in order to attempt to avert that risk.

11.3 Immediately prior to the commencement or re-commencement of any interview at a designated place of detention, the interviewer should remind the suspect of their entitlement to free legal advice and that the interview can be delayed for legal advice to be obtained, unless one of the exceptions in *paragraph 6.7* applies. It is the interviewer's responsibility to make sure all reminders are recorded in the interview record.

11.4 At the beginning of an interview the interviewer, after cautioning the suspect, see *section 10*, shall put to them any significant statement or silence which occurred in the presence and hearing of a police officer or other police staff before the start of the interview and which have not been put to the suspect in the course of a previous interview. See *Note 11A*. The interviewer shall ask the suspect whether they confirm or deny that earlier statement or silence and if they want to add anything.

11.5 A significant statement is one which appears capable of being used in evidence against the suspect, in particular a direct admission of guilt. A significant silence is a failure or refusal to answer a question or answer satisfactorily when under caution, which might, allowing for the restriction on drawing adverse inferences from silence, see *Annex C*, give rise to an inference under the Criminal Justice and Public Order Act 1994, Part III.

11.6 No interviewer may try to obtain answers or elicit a statement by the use of oppression. Except as in *paragraph 10.8*, no interviewer shall indicate, except to answer a direct question, what action will be taken by the police if the person being questioned answers questions, makes a statement or refuses to do either. If the person asks directly what action will be taken if they answer questions, make a statement or refuse to do either, the interviewer may inform them what action the police propose to take provided that action is itself proper and warranted.

11.7 The interview or further interview of a person about an offence with which that person has not been charged or for which they have not been informed they may be prosecuted, must cease when:

(a) the officer in charge of the investigation is satisfied all the questions they consider relevant to obtaining accurate and reliable information about the offence have been put to the suspect, this includes allowing the suspect an opportunity to give an innocent explanation and asking questions to test if the explanation is accurate and reliable, e.g. to clear up ambiguities or clarify what the suspect said;

(b) the officer in charge of the investigation has taken account of any other available evidence; and

(c) the officer in charge of the investigation, or in the case of a detained suspect, the custody officer, see *PACE Code C paragraph 16.1*, reasonably believes there is sufficient evidence to provide a realistic prospect of conviction for that offence. See *Note 11B*.

(b) Interview records

11.8 Interview records should be made in accordance with the Code of Practice issued under Schedule 8 Paragraph 3 to the Terrorism Act where the interview takes place at a designated place of detention.

(c) Juveniles and mentally disordered or otherwise mentally vulnerable people

11.9 A juvenile or person who is mentally disordered or otherwise mentally vulnerable must not be interviewed regarding their involvement or suspected involvement in a criminal offence or offences, or asked to provide or sign a written statement under caution or record of interview, in the absence of the appropriate adult unless *paragraphs 11.2, 11.11 to 11.13* apply. See *Note 11C*.

11.10 If an appropriate adult is present at an interview, they shall be informed:
- they are not expected to act simply as an observer; and
- the purpose of their presence is to:
  - advise the person being interviewed;
  - observe whether the interview is being conducted properly and fairly;
  - facilitate communication with the person being interviewed.

The appropriate adult may be required to leave the interview if their conduct is such that the interviewer is unable properly to put questions to the suspect. This will include situations where the appropriate adult's approach or conduct prevents or unreasonably obstructs proper questions being put to the suspect or the suspect's responses being recorded. If the interviewer considers an appropriate adult is acting in such a way, they will stop the interview and consult an officer not below superintendent rank, if one is readily available, and otherwise an officer not below inspector rank not connected with the investigation. After speaking to the appropriate adult, the officer consulted will decide if the interview should continue without the attendance of that appropriate adult. If they decide it should not, another appropriate adult should be obtained before the interview continues, unless the provisions of paragraph 11.11 below apply.

(d) Vulnerable suspects – urgent interviews at police stations

11.11 The following persons may not be interviewed unless an officer of superintendent rank or above considers delay will lead to the consequences in *paragraph 11.2(a) to (c)*, and is satisfied the interview would not significantly harm the person's physical or mental state (see Annex G):

(a) a juvenile or person who is mentally disordered or otherwise mentally vulnerable if at the time of the interview the appropriate adult is not present;

(b) anyone other than in (*a*) who at the time of the interview appears unable to:

  • appreciate the significance of questions and their answers; or
  • understand what is happening because of the effects of drink, drugs or any illness, ailment or condition;

(c) a person who has difficulty understanding English or has a hearing disability, if at the time of the interview an interpreter is not present.

11.12 These interviews may not continue once sufficient information has been obtained to avert the consequences in *paragraph 11.2(a) to (c)*.

11.13 A record shall be made of the grounds for any decision to interview a person under *paragraph 11.11*.

Notes for guidance

11A Paragraph 11.4 does not prevent the interviewer from putting significant statements and silences to a suspect again at a later stage or a further interview.

11B The Criminal Procedure and Investigations Act 1996 Code of Practice, paragraph 3.4 states 'In conducting an investigation, the investigator should pursue all reasonable lines of enquiry, whether these point towards or away from the suspect. What is reasonable will depend on the particular circumstances.' Interviewers should keep this in mind when deciding what questions to ask in an interview.

11C Although juveniles or people who are mentally disordered or otherwise mentally vulnerable are often capable of providing reliable evidence, they may, without knowing or wishing to do so, be particularly prone in certain circumstances to provide information that may be unreliable, misleading or self-incriminating. Special care should always be taken when questioning such a person, and the appropriate adult should be involved if there is any doubt about a person's age, mental state or capacity. Because of the risk of unreliable evidence it is also important to obtain corroboration of any facts admitted whenever possible.

11D Consideration should be given to the effect of extended detention on a detainee and any subsequent information they provide, especially if it relates to information on matters that they have failed to provide previously in response to similar questioning see Annex G.

11E Significant statements described in paragraph 11.4 will always be relevant to the offence and must be recorded. When a suspect agrees to read records of interviews and other comments and sign them as correct, they should be asked to endorse the record with, e.g. 'I agree that this is a correct record of what was said' and add their signature. If the suspect does not agree with the record, the interviewer should record the details of any disagreement and ask the suspect to read these details and sign them to the effect that they accurately reflect their disagreement. Any refusal to sign should be recorded.

12 INTERVIEWS IN POLICE STATIONS

(a) Action

12.1 If a police officer wants to interview or conduct enquiries which require the presence of a detainee, the custody officer is responsible for deciding whether to deliver the detainee into the officer's custody.

12.2 Except as below, in any period of 24 hours a detainee must be allowed a continuous period of at least 8 hours for rest, free from questioning, travel or any interruption in connection with the investigation concerned. This period should normally be at night or other appropriate time which takes account of when the detainee last slept or rested. If a detainee is arrested at a police station after going there voluntarily, the period of 24 hours runs from the time of their arrest (or, if a person was being detained under TACT Schedule 7 when arrested, from the time at which the examination under Schedule 7 began) and not the time of arrival at the police station. The period may not be interrupted or delayed, except:

(a) when there are reasonable grounds for believing not delaying or interrupting the period would:

   (i) involve a risk of harm to people or serious loss of, or damage to, property;
   (ii) delay unnecessarily the person's release from custody;
   (iii) otherwise prejudice the outcome of the investigation;

(b) at the request of the detainee, their appropriate adult or legal representative;
(c) when a delay or interruption is necessary in order to:

   (i) comply with the legal obligations and duties arising under *section 14*;
   (ii) to take action required under *section 9* or in accordance with medical advice.

If the period is interrupted in accordance with *(a)*, a fresh period must be allowed. Interruptions under *(b)* and *(c)*, do not require a fresh period to be allowed.

12.3 Before a detainee is interviewed the custody officer, in consultation with the officer in charge of the investigation and appropriate health care professionals as necessary, shall assess whether the detainee is fit enough to be interviewed. This means determining and considering the risks to the detainee's physical and mental state if the interview took place and determining what safeguards are needed to allow the interview to take place. The custody officer shall not allow a detainee to be interviewed if the custody officer considers it would cause significant harm to the detainee's physical or mental state. Vulnerable suspects listed at *paragraph 11.11* shall be treated as always being at some risk during an interview and these persons may not be interviewed except in accordance with *paragraphs 11.11* to *11.13*.

12.4 As far as practicable interviews shall take place in interview rooms which are adequately heated, lit and ventilated.

12.5 A suspect whose detention without charge has been authorised under TACT Schedule 8, because the detention is necessary for an interview to obtain evidence of the offence for which they have been arrested, may choose not to answer questions but police do not require the suspect's consent or agreement to interview them for this purpose. If a suspect takes steps to prevent themselves being questioned or further questioned, e.g. by refusing to leave their cell to go to a suitable interview room or by trying to leave the interview room, they shall be advised their consent or agreement to interview is not required. The suspect shall be cautioned as in *section 10*, and informed if they fail or refuse to co-operate, the interview may take place in the cell and that their failure or refusal to co-operate may be given in evidence. The suspect shall then be invited to co-operate and go into the interview room.

12.6 People being questioned or making statements shall not be required to stand.

12.7 Before the interview commences each interviewer shall, subject to the qualification at *paragraph 2.8,* identify themselves and any other persons present to the interviewee.

12.8 Breaks from interviewing should be made at recognised meal times or at other times that take account of when an interviewee last had a meal. Short refreshment breaks shall be provided at approximately two hour intervals, subject to the interviewer's discretion to delay a break if there are reasonable grounds for believing it would:

(i) involve a:

   • risk of harm to people;
   • serious loss of, or damage to, property;

(ii) unnecessarily delay the detainee's release;
(iii) otherwise prejudice the outcome of the investigation.

See *Note 12B*

12.9 During extended periods where no interviews take place, because of the need to gather further evidence or analyse existing evidence, detainees and their legal representative shall be informed that the investigation into the relevant offence remains ongoing. If practicable, the detainee and legal representative should also be made aware in general terms of any reasons for long gaps between interviews. Consideration should be given to allowing visits, more frequent exercise, or for reading or writing materials to be offered *see paragraph 5.4, section 8* and *Note 12C*.

12.10 If during the interview a complaint is made by or on behalf of the interviewee concerning the provisions of this Code, the interviewer should:

(i) record it in the interview record;
(ii) inform the custody officer, who is then responsible for dealing with it as in *section 9*.

(b) Documentation

12.11 A record must be made of the:

   • time a detainee is not in the custody of the custody officer, and why
   • reason for any refusal to deliver the detainee out of that custody

12.12 A record shall be made of:

(a) the reasons it was not practicable to use an interview room; and
(b) any action taken as in *paragraph 12.5*.

The record shall be made on the custody record or in the interview record for action taken whilst an interview record is being kept, with a brief reference to this effect in the custody record.

12.13 Any decision to delay a break in an interview must be recorded, with reasons, in the interview record.

12.14 All written statements made at police stations under caution shall be written on forms provided for the purpose.

12.15 All written statements made under caution shall be taken in accordance with *Annex D*. Before a person makes a written statement under caution at a police station they shall be reminded about the right to legal advice. See *Note 12A*

Notes for guidance
12A It is not normally necessary to ask for a written statement if the interview was recorded in writing and the record signed in accordance with the Code of Practice issued under TACT Schedule 8 Paragraph 3. Statements under caution should normally be taken in these circumstances only at the person's express wish. A person may however be asked if they want to make such a statement.

12B Meal breaks should normally last at least 45 minutes and shorter breaks after two hours should last at least 15 minutes. If the interviewer delays a break in accordance with paragraph 12.8 and prolongs the interview, a longer break should be provided. If there is a short interview, and another short interview is contemplated, the length of the break may be reduced if there are reasonable grounds to believe this is necessary to avoid any of the consequences in paragraph 12.8(i) to (iii).

12C Consideration should be given to the matters referred to in paragraph 12.9 after a period of over 24 hours without questioning. This is to ensure that extended periods of detention without an indication that the investigation remains ongoing do not contribute to a deterioration of the detainee's well-being.

13 INTERPRETERS

(a) General
13.1 Chief officers are responsible for making sure appropriate arrangements are in place for provision of suitably qualified interpreters for people who:

• are deaf;
• do not understand English.

Whenever possible, interpreters should be drawn from the National Register of Public Service Interpreters (NRPSI) or the Council for the Advancement of Communication with Deaf People (CACDP) Directory of British Sign Language/English Interpreters.

(b) Foreign languages
13.2 Unless *paragraphs 11.2, 11.11* to *11.13* apply, a person must not be interviewed in the absence of a person capable of interpreting if:

(a) they have difficulty understanding English;
(b) the interviewer cannot speak the person's own language;
(c) the person wants an interpreter present.

13.3 The interviewer shall make sure the interpreter makes a note of the interview at the time in the person's language for use in the event of the interpreter being called to give evidence, and certifies its accuracy. The interviewer should allow sufficient time for the interpreter to note each question and answer after each is put, given and interpreted. The person should be allowed to read the record or have it read to them and sign it as correct or indicate the respects in which they consider it inaccurate. If the interview is audibly recorded or visually recorded with sound, the Code of Practice issued under paragraph 3 of Schedule 8 to the Terrorism Act 2000 will apply.

13.4 In the case of a person making a statement to a police officer or other police staff other than in English:

(a) the interpreter shall record the statement in the language it is made;
(b) the person shall be invited to sign it;
(c) an official English translation shall be made in due course.

(c) Deaf people and people with speech difficulties
13.5 If a person appears to be deaf or there is doubt about their hearing or speaking ability, they must not be interviewed in the absence of an interpreter unless they agree in writing to being interviewed without one or *paragraphs 11.2, 11.11* to *11.13* apply.

13.6 An interpreter should also be called if a juvenile is interviewed and the parent or guardian present as the appropriate adult appears to be deaf or there is doubt about their hearing or speaking ability, unless they agree in writing to the interview proceeding without one or *paragraphs 11.2, 11.11* to *11.13* apply.

13.7 The interviewer shall make sure the interpreter is allowed to read the interview record and certify its accuracy in the event of the interpreter being called to give evidence. If the interview is audibly recorded or visually recorded, the Code of Practice issued under TACT Schedule 8 Paragraph 3 will apply.

(d) Additional rules for detained persons

13.8 All reasonable attempts should be made to make the detainee understand that interpreters will be provided at public expense.

13.9 If *paragraph 6.1* applies and the detainee cannot communicate with the solicitor because of language, hearing or speech difficulties, an interpreter must be called. The interpreter may not be a police officer or any other police staff when interpretation is needed for the purposes of obtaining legal advice. In all other cases a police officer or other police staff may only interpret if the detainee and the appropriate adult, if applicable, give their agreement in writing or if the interview is audibly recorded or visually recorded as in the Code of Practice issued under TACT Schedule 8 Paragraph 3.

13.10 When the custody officer cannot establish effective communication with a person charged with an offence who appears deaf or there is doubt about their ability to hear, speak or to understand English, arrangements must be made as soon as practicable for an interpreter to explain the offence and any other information given by the custody officer.

(e) Documentation

13.11 Action taken to call an interpreter under this section and any agreement to be interviewed in the absence of an interpreter must be recorded.

14 REVIEWS AND EXTENSIONS OF DETENTION

(a) Reviews and Extensions of Detention

14.1 The powers and duties of the review officer are in the Terrorism Act 2000, Schedule 8, Part II. See *Notes 14A* and *14B*. A review officer should carry out his duties at the police station where the detainee is held, and be allowed such access to the detainee as is necessary for him to exercise those duties.

14.2 For the purposes of reviewing a person's detention, no officer shall put specific questions to the detainee:

- regarding their involvement in any offence; or
- in respect of any comments they may make:
  - when given the opportunity to make representations; or
  - in response to a decision to keep them in detention or extend the maximum period of detention.

Such an exchange could constitute an interview as in *paragraph 11.1* and would be subject to the associated safeguards in *section 11* and, in respect of a person who has been charged see *PACE Code C Section 16.8.*

14.3 If detention is necessary for longer than 48 hours, a police officer of at least superintendent rank, or a Crown Prosecutor may apply for warrants of further detention under the Terrorism Act 2000, Schedule 8, Part III.

14.4 When an application for a warrant of further or extended detention is sought under Paragraph 29 or 36 of Schedule 8, the detained person and their representative must be informed of their rights in respect of the application. These include:

a) the right to a written or oral notice of the warrant See *Note 14G.*
b) the right to make oral or written representations to the judicial authority about the application.
c) the right to be present and legally represented at the hearing of the application, unless specifically excluded by the judicial authority.
d) their right to free legal advice (see section 6 of this Code).

(b) Transfer of detained persons to Prison

14.5 Where a warrant is issued which authorises detention beyond a period of 14 days from the time of arrest (or if a person was being detained under TACT Schedule 7, from the time at which the examination under Schedule 7 began), the detainee must be transferred from detention in a police station to detention in a designated prison as soon as is practicable, unless:

a) the detainee specifically requests to remain in detention at a police station and that request can be accommodated, or
b) there are reasonable grounds to believe that transferring a person to a prison would:
   i) significantly hinder a terrorism investigation;
   ii) delay charging of the detainee or his release from custody, or
   iii) otherwise prevent the investigation from being conducted diligently and expeditiously.

If any of the grounds in (b)(i) to (iii) above are relied upon, these must be presented to the judicial authority as part of the application for the warrant that would extend detention beyond a period of 14 days from the time of arrest (or if a person was being detained under TACT Schedule 7, from the time at which the examination under Schedule 7 began) *See Note 14J.*

14.6 If a person remains in detention at a police station under a warrant of further detention as described at section 14.5, they must be transferred to a prison as soon as practicable after the grounds at (b)(i) to (iii) of that section cease to apply.

14.7 Police should maintain an agreement with the National Offender Management Service (NOMS) that stipulates named prisons to which individuals may be transferred under this section. This should be made with regard to ensuring detainees are moved to the most suitable prison for the purposes of the investigation and their welfare, and should include provision for the transfer of male, female and juvenile detainees. Police should ensure that the Governor of a prison to which they intend to transfer a detainee is given reasonable notice of this. Where practicable, this should be no later than the point at which a warrant is applied for that would take the period of detention beyond 14 days.

14.8 Following a detained person's transfer to a designated prison, their detention will be governed by the terms of Schedule 8 and Prison Rules, and this Code of Practice will not apply during any period that the person remains in prison detention. The Code will once more apply if a detained person is transferred back from prison detention to police detention. In order to enable the Governor to arrange for the production of the detainee back into police custody, police should give notice to the Governor of the relevant prison as soon as possible of any decision to transfer a detainee from prison back to a police station. Any transfer between a prison and a police station should be conducted by police, and this Code will be applicable during the period of transit See *Note 14K*. A detainee should only remain in police custody having been transferred back from a prison, for as long as is necessary for the purpose of the investigation.

14.9 The investigating team and custody officer should provide as much information as necessary to enable the relevant prison authorities to provide appropriate facilities to detain an individual. This should include, but not be limited to:

i)   medical assessments
ii) security and risk assessments
iii) details of the detained person's legal representatives
iv) details of any individuals from whom the detained person has requested visits, or who have requested to visit the detained person.

14.10 Where a detainee is to be transferred to prison, the custody officer should inform the detainee's legal adviser beforehand that the transfer is to take place (including the name of the prison). The custody officer should also make all reasonable attempts to inform:

• family or friends who have been informed previously of the detainee's detention; and
• the person who was initially informed of the detainee's detention as at *paragraph 5.1.*

(c) Documentation

14.11 It is the responsibility of the officer who gives any reminders as at *paragraph 14.4,* to ensure that these are noted in the custody record, as well any comments made by the detained person upon being told of those rights.

14.12 The grounds for, and extent of, any delay in conducting a review shall be recorded.

14.13 Any written representations shall be retained.

14.14 A record shall be made as soon as practicable about the outcome of each review or determination whether to extend the maximum detention period without charge or an application for a warrant of further detention or its extension.

14.15 Any decision not to transfer a detained person to a designated prison under paragraph *14.5,* must be recorded, along with the reasons for this decision. If a request under paragraph *14.5(a)* is not accommodated, the reasons for this should also be recorded.

Notes for guidance

14A TACT Schedule 8 Part II sets out the procedures for review of detention up to 48 hours from the time of arrest under TACT section 41 (or if a person was being detained under TACT Schedule 7, from the time at which the examination under Schedule 7 began). These include provisions for the requirement to review detention, postponing a review, grounds for continued detention, designating a review officer, representations, rights of the detained person and keeping a record. The review officer's role ends after a warrant has been issued for extension of detention under Part III of Schedule 8.

14B Section 24(1) of the Terrorism Act 2006, amended the grounds contained within the 2000 Act on which a review officer may authorise continued detention. Continued detention may be authorised if it is necessary-

a) to obtain relevant evidence whether by questioning him or otherwise
b) to preserve relevant evidence
c) while awaiting the result of an examination or analysis of relevant evidence

d)   for the examination or analysis of anything with a view to obtaining relevant evidence
e)   pending a decision to apply to the Secretary of State for a deportation notice to be served on the detainee, the making of any such application, or the consideration of any such application by the Secretary of State
f)   pending a decision to charge the detainee with an offence.

14C Applications for warrants to extend detention beyond 48 hours, may be made for periods of 7 days at a time (initially under TACT Schedule 8 paragraph 29, and extensions thereafter under TACT Schedule 8, Paragraph 36), up to a maximum period of 28 days from the time of arrest (or if a person was being detained under TACT Schedule 7, from the time at which the examination under Schedule 7 began). Applications may be made for shorter periods than 7 days, which must be specified. The judicial authority may also substitute a shorter period if he feels a period of 7 days is inappropriate.

14D Unless Note 14F applies, applications for warrants that would take the total period of detention up to 14 days or less should be made to a judicial authority, meaning a District Judge (Magistrates' Court) designated by the Lord Chancellor to hear such applications.

14E Any application for a warrant which would take the period of detention beyond 14 days from the time of arrest (or if a person was being detained under TACT Schedule 7, from the time at which the examination under Schedule 7 began), must be made to a High Court Judge.

14F If an application has been made to a High Court judge for a warrant which would take detention beyond 14 days, and the High Court judge instead issues a warrant for a period of time which would not take detention beyond 14 days, further applications for extension of detention must also be made to a High Court judge, regardless of the period of time to which they refer.

14G TACT Schedule 8 Paragraph 31 requires a notice to be given to the detained person if a warrant is sought for further detention. This must be provided before the judicial hearing of the application for that warrant and must include:

a)   notification that the application for a warrant has been made
b)   the time at which the application was made
c)   the time at which the application is to be heard
d)   the grounds on which further detention is sought.

A notice must also be provided each time an application is made to extend an existing warrant

14H An officer applying for an order under TACT Schedule 8 Paragraph 34 to withhold specified information on which he intends to rely when applying for a warrant of further detention, may make the application for the order orally or in writing. The most appropriate method of application will depend on the circumstances of the case and the need to ensure fairness to the detainee.

14I Where facilities exist, hearings relating to extension of detention under Part III of Schedule 8 may take place using video conferencing facilities provided that the requirements set out in Schedule 8 are still met. However, if the judicial authority requires the detained person to be physically present at any hearing, this should be complied with as soon as practicable. Paragraphs 33(4) to 33(9) of TACT Schedule 8 govern the relevant conduct of hearings.

14J Transfer to prison is intended to ensure that individuals who are detained for extended periods of time are held in a place designed for longer periods of detention than police stations. Prison will provide detainees with a greater range of facilities more appropriate to longer detention periods.

14K The Code will only apply as is appropriate to the conditions of detention during the period of transit. There is obviously no requirement to provide such things as bed linen or reading materials for the journey between prison and police station.

15 CHARGING
15.1 Charging of detained persons is covered by PACE and guidance issued under PACE by the Director of Public Prosecutions. General guidance on charging can be found in section 16 of PACE Code C.

16 TESTING PERSONS FOR THE PRESENCE OF SPECIFIED CLASS A DRUGS
16.1 The provisions for drug testing under section 63B of PACE (as amended by section 5 of the Criminal Justice Act 2003 and section 7 of the Drugs Act 2005), do not apply to detention under TACT section 41 and Schedule 8. Guidance on these provisions can be found in section 17 of PACE Code C.

ANNEX A – INTIMATE AND STRIP SEARCHES

A Intimate search
1. An intimate search consists of the physical examination of a person's body orifices other than the mouth. The intrusive nature of such searches means the actual and potential risks associated with intimate searches must never be underestimated.

(a) Action

2. Body orifices other than the mouth may be searched only if authorised by an officer of inspector rank or above who has reasonable grounds for believing that the person may have concealed on themselves anything which they could and might use to cause physical injury to themselves or others at the station and the officer has reasonable grounds for believing that an intimate search is the only means of removing those items.

3. Before the search begins, a police officer, designated detention officer or staff custody officer, must tell the detainee:-

(a) that the authority to carry out the search has been given;
(b) the grounds for giving the authorisation and for believing that the article cannot be removed without an intimate search.

4. An intimate search may only be carried out by a registered medical practitioner or registered nurse, unless an officer of at least inspector rank considers this is not practicable, in which case a police officer may carry out the search. See *Notes A1 to A5*

5. Any proposal for a search under *paragraph 2* to be carried out by someone other than a registered medical practitioner or registered nurse must only be considered as a last resort and when the authorising officer is satisfied the risks associated with allowing the item to remain with the detainee outweigh the risks associated with removing it. See *Notes A1 to A5*

6. An intimate search at a police station of a juvenile or mentally disordered or otherwise mentally vulnerable person may take place only in the presence of an appropriate adult of the same sex, unless the detainee specifically requests a particular adult of the opposite sex who is readily available. In the case of a juvenile the search may take place in the absence of the appropriate adult only if the juvenile signifies in the presence of the appropriate adult they do not want the adult present during the search and the adult agrees. A record shall be made of the juvenile's decision and signed by the appropriate adult.

7. When an intimate search under *paragraph 2* is carried out by a police officer, the officer must be of the same sex as the detainee. A minimum of two people, other than the detainee, must be present during the search. Subject to *paragraph 6*, no person of the opposite sex who is not a medical practitioner or nurse shall be present, nor shall anyone whose presence is unnecessary. The search shall be conducted with proper regard to the sensitivity and vulnerability of the detainee.

(b) Documentation

8. In the case of an intimate search under paragraph 2, the following shall be recorded as soon as practicable, in the detainee's custody record:

* the authorisation to carry out the search;
* the grounds for giving the authorisation;
* the grounds for believing the article could not be removed without an intimate search
* which parts of the detainee's body were searched
* who carried out the search
* who was present
* the result.

9. If an intimate search is carried out by a police officer, the reason why it was impracticable for a registered medical practitioner or registered nurse to conduct it must be recorded.

B Strip search

10. A strip search is a search involving the removal of more than outer clothing. In this Code,outer clothing includes shoes and socks.

(a) Action

11. A strip search may take place only if it is considered necessary to remove an article which a detainee would not be allowed to keep, and the officer reasonably considers the detainee might have concealed such an article. Strip searches shall not be routinely carried out if there is no reason to consider that articles are concealed.

The conduct of strip searches

12. When strip searches are conducted:

(a) a police officer carrying out a strip search must be the same sex as the detainee;
(b) the search shall take place in an area where the detainee cannot be seen by anyone who does not need to be present, nor by a member of the opposite sex except an appropriate adult who has been specifically requested by the detainee;
(c) except in cases of urgency, where there is risk of serious harm to the detainee or to others, whenever a strip search involves exposure of intimate body parts, there must be at least two people present other than the detainee, and if the search is of a juvenile or mentally disordered or otherwise mentally vulnerable person, one of the people must be the appropriate adult. Except in urgent cases as above, a search of a juvenile may take place in the absence of the appropriate adult only if the juvenile

signifies in the presence of the appropriate adult that they do not want the adult to be present during the search and the adult agrees. A record shall be made of the juvenile's decision and signed by the appropriate adult. The presence of more than two people, other than an appropriate adult, shall be permitted only in the most exceptional circumstances;

(d) the search shall be conducted with proper regard to the sensitivity and vulnerability of the detainee in these circumstances and every reasonable effort shall be made to secure the detainee's co-operation and minimise embarrassment. Detainees who are searched shall not normally be required to remove all their clothes at the same time, e.g. a person should be allowed to remove clothing above the waist and redress before removing further clothing;

(e) if necessary to assist the search, the detainee may be required to hold their arms in the air or to stand with their legs apart and bend forward so a visual examination may be made of the genital and anal areas provided no physical contact is made with any body orifice;

(f) if articles are found, the detainee shall be asked to hand them over. If articles are found within any body orifice other than the mouth, and the detainee refuses to hand them over, their removal would constitute an intimate search, which must be carried out as in *Part A*;

(g) a strip search shall be conducted as quickly as possible, and the detainee allowed to dress as soon as the procedure is complete.

(b) Documentation

13. A record shall be made on the custody record of a strip search including the reason it was considered necessary, those present and any result.

Notes for guidance

A1   *Before authorising any intimate search, the authorising officer must make every reasonable effort to persuade the detainee to hand the article over without a search. If the detainee agrees, a registered medical practitioner or registered nurse should whenever possible be asked to assess the risks involved and, if necessary, attend to assist the detainee.*

A2   *If the detainee does not agree to hand the article over without a search, the authorising officer must carefully review all the relevant factors before authorising an intimate search. In particular, the officer must consider whether the grounds for believing an article may be concealed are reasonable.*

A3   *If authority is given for a search under paragraph 2, a registered medical practitioner or registered nurse shall be consulted whenever possible. The presumption should be that the search will be conducted by the registered medical practitioner or registered nurse and the authorising officer must make every reasonable effort to persuade the detainee to allow the medical practitioner or nurse to conduct the search.*

A4   *A constable should only be authorised to carry out a search as a last resort and when all other approaches have failed. In these circumstances, the authorising officer must be satisfied the detainee might use the article for one or more of the purposes in paragraph 2 and the physical injury likely to be caused is sufficiently severe to justify authorising a constable to carry out the search.*

A5   *If an officer has any doubts whether to authorise an intimate search by a constable, the officer should seek advice from an officer of superintendent rank or above.*

ANNEX B – DELAY IN NOTIFYING ARREST OR ALLOWING ACCESS TO LEGAL ADVICE FOR PERSONS DETAINED UNDER THE TERRORISM ACT 2000.

A Delays under TACT Schedule 8

1. The rights as in *sections 5* or *6,* may be delayed if the person is detained under the Terrorism Act 2000, section 41, has not yet been charged with an offence and an officer of superintendent rank or above has reasonable grounds for believing the exercise of either right will have one of the following consequences:

(a) interference with or harm to evidence of a serious offence,

(b) interference with or physical injury to any person,

(c) the alerting of persons who are suspected of having committed a serious offence but who have not been arrested for it,

(d) the hindering of the recovery of property obtained as a result of a serious offence or in respect of which a forfeiture order could be made under section 23,

(e) interference with the gathering of information about the commission, preparation or instigation of acts of terrorism,

(f) the alerting of a person and thereby making it more difficult to prevent an act of terrorism, or

(g) the alerting of a person and thereby making it more difficult to secure a person's apprehension, prosecution or conviction in connection with the commission, preparation or instigation of an act of terrorism.

2. These rights may also be delayed if the officer has reasonable grounds for believing that:

(a) the detained person has benefited from his criminal conduct (to be decided in accordance with Part 2 of the Proceeds of Crime Act 2002), and

(b) the recovery of the value of the property constituting the benefit will be hindered by—

(i) informing the named person of the detained person's detention (in the case of an authorisation under Paragraph 8(1)(a) of Schedule 8 to TACT, or

(ii) the exercise of the right under paragraph 7 (in the case of an authorisation under Paragraph 8(1)(b) of Schedule 8 to TACT.

3. Authority to delay a detainee's right to consult privately with a solicitor may be given only if the authorising officer has reasonable grounds to believe the solicitor the detainee wants to consult will, inadvertently or otherwise, pass on a message from the detainee or act in some other way which will have any of the consequences specified under *paragraph 8 of Schedule 8 to the Terrorism Act 2000*. In these circumstances the detainee must be allowed to choose another solicitor. See *Note B3*

4. If the detainee wishes to see a solicitor, access to that solicitor may not be delayed on the grounds they might advise the detainee not to answer questions or the solicitor was initially asked to attend the police station by someone else. In the latter case the detainee must be told the solicitor has come to the police station at another person's request, and must be asked to sign the custody record to signify whether they want to see the solicitor.

5. The fact the grounds for delaying notification of arrest may be satisfied does not automatically mean the grounds for delaying access to legal advice will also be satisfied.

6. These rights may be delayed only for as long as is necessary but not beyond 48 hours from the time of arrest (or if a person was being detained under TACT Schedule 7, from the time at which the examination under Schedule 7 began). If the above grounds cease to apply within this time the detainee must as soon as practicable be asked if they wish to exercise either right, the custody record noted accordingly, and action taken in accordance with the relevant section of this Code.

7. A person must be allowed to consult a solicitor for a reasonable time before any court hearing.

B Documentation

8. The grounds for action under this Annex shall be recorded and the detainee informed of them as soon as practicable.

9. Any reply given by a detainee under *paragraph 6* must be recorded and the detainee asked to endorse the record in relation to whether they want to receive legal advice at this point.

C Cautions and special warnings

10. When a suspect detained at a police station is interviewed during any period for which access to legal advice has been delayed under this Annex, the court or jury may not draw adverse inferences from their silence.

Notes for guidance

B1 Even if Annex B applies in the case of a juvenile, or a person who is mentally disordered or otherwise mentally vulnerable, action to inform the appropriate adult and the person responsible for a juvenile's welfare if that is a different person, must nevertheless be taken as in paragraph 3.15 and 3.17.

B2 In the case of Commonwealth citizens and foreign nationals, see Note 7A.

B3 A decision to delay access to a specific solicitor is likely to be a rare occurrence and only when it can be shown the suspect is capable of misleading that particular solicitor and there is more than a substantial risk that the suspect will succeed in causing information to be conveyed which will lead to one or more of the specified consequences.

ANNEX C – RESTRICTION ON DRAWING ADVERSE INFERENCES FROM SILENCE AND TERMS OF THE CAUTION WHEN THE RESTRICTION APPLIES

(a) The restriction on drawing adverse inferences from silence

1. The Criminal Justice and Public Order Act 1994, sections 34, 36 and 37 as amended by the Youth Justice and Criminal Evidence Act 1999, section 58 describe the conditions under which adverse inferences may be drawn from a person's failure or refusal to say anything about their involvement in the offence when interviewed, after being charged or informed they may be prosecuted. These provisions are subject to an overriding restriction on the

ability of a court or jury to draw adverse inferences from a person's silence. This restriction applies:

(a) to any detainee at a police station who, before being interviewed, see *section 11* or being charged or informed they may be prosecuted, see *section 15,* has:

   (i)   asked for legal advice, see *section 6, paragraph 6.1;*
   (ii) not been allowed an opportunity to consult a solicitor, including the duty solicitor, as in this Code; and
   (iii) not changed their mind about wanting legal advice, see *section 6, paragraph 6.7(c)*

   Note the condition in (ii) will

   – apply when a detainee who has asked for legal advice is interviewed before speaking to a solicitor as in *section 6, paragraph 6.6(a)* or *(b).*
   – not apply if the detained person declines to ask for the duty solicitor, see *section 6, paragraphs 6.7(b)* and *(c);*

(b) to any person charged with, or informed they may be prosecuted for, an offence who:

   (i)   has had brought to their notice a written statement made by another person or the content of an interview with another person which relates to that offence, see PACE Code C *section 16, paragraph 16.6;*
   (ii) is interviewed about that offence, see PACE Code C *section 16, paragraph 16.8;* or
   (iii) makes a written statement about that offence, see *Annex D paragraphs 4* and *9.*

(b) Terms of the caution when the restriction applies

2. When a requirement to caution arises at a time when the restriction on drawing adverse inferences from silence applies, the caution shall be:

   'You do not have to say anything, but anything you do say may be given in evidence.'

3. Whenever the restriction either begins to apply or ceases to apply after a caution has already been given, the person shall be re-cautioned in the appropriate terms. The changed position on drawing inferences and that the previous caution no longer applies shall also be explained to the detainee in ordinary language. See *Note C1*

Notes for guidance

C1 The following is suggested as a framework to help explain changes in the position on drawing adverse inferences if the restriction on drawing adverse inferences from silence:

   (a) begins to apply:

      'The caution you were previously given no longer applies. This is because after that caution:
      (i) you asked to speak to a solicitor but have not yet been allowed an opportunity to speak to a solicitor. See paragraph 1(a); or
      (ii) you have been charged with/informed you may be prosecuted. See paragraph 1(b).
      'This means that from now on, adverse inferences cannot be drawn at court and your defence will not be harmed just because you choose to say nothing. Please listen carefully to the caution I am about to give you because it will apply from now on. You will see that it does not say anything about your defence being harmed.'

   (b) ceases to apply before or at the time the person is charged or informed they may be prosecuted, see paragraph 1(a);

      'The caution you were previously given no longer applies. This is because after that caution you have been allowed an opportunity to speak to a solicitor. Please listen carefully to the caution I am about to give you because it will apply from now on. It explains how your defence at court may be affected if you choose to say nothing.'

ANNEX D – WRITTEN STATEMENTS UNDER CAUTION

(a) Written by a person under caution

1. A person shall always be invited to write down what they want to say.

2. A person who has not been charged with, or informed they may be prosecuted for, any offence to which the statement they want to write relates, shall:

(a) unless the statement is made at a time when the restriction on drawing adverse inferences from silence applies, see Annex C, be asked to write out and sign the following before writing what they want to say:

'*I make this statement of my own free will. I understand that I do not have to say anything but that it may harm my defence if I do not mention when questioned something which I later rely on in court. This statement may be given in evidence.*';

(b) if the statement is made at a time when the restriction on drawing adverse inferences from silence applies, be asked to write out and sign the following before writing what they want to say;

'*I make this statement of my own free will. I understand that I do not have to say anything. This statement may be given in evidence.*'

3. When a person, on the occasion of being charged with or informed they may be prosecuted for any offence, asks to make a statement which relates to any such offence and wants to write it they shall:

(a) unless the restriction on drawing adverse inferences from silence, see *Annex C*, applied when they were so charged or informed they may be prosecuted, be asked to write out and sign the following before writing what they want to say:

'*I make this statement of my own free will. I understand that I do not have to say anything but that it may harm my defence if I do not mention when questioned something which I later rely on in court. This statement may be given in evidence.*';

(b) if the restriction on drawing adverse inferences from silence applied when they were so charged or informed they may be prosecuted, be asked to write out and sign the following before writing what they want to say:

'*I make this statement of my own free will. I understand that I do not have to say anything. This statement may be given in evidence.*'

4. When a person, who has already been charged with or informed they may be prosecuted for any offence, asks to make a statement which relates to any such offence and wants to write it they shall be asked to write out and sign the following before writing what they want to say:

'*I make this statement of my own free will. I understand that I do not have to say anything. This statement may be given in evidence.*';

5. Any person writing their own statement shall be allowed to do so without any prompting except a police officer or other police staff may indicate to them which matters are material or question any ambiguity in the statement.

(b) Written by a police officer or other police staff

6. If a person says they would like someone to write the statement for them, a police officer, or other police staff shall write the statement.

7. If the person has not been charged with, or informed they may be prosecuted for, any offence to which the statement they want to make relates they shall, before starting, be asked to sign, or make their mark, to the following:

(a) unless the statement is made at a time when the restriction on drawing adverse inferences from silence applies, see *Annex C*:

'*I, ... , wish to make a statement. I want someone to write down what I say. I understand that I do not have to say anything but that it may harm my defence if I do not mention when questioned something which I later rely on in court. This statement may be given in evidence.*';

(b) if the statement is made at a time when the restriction on drawing adverse inferences from silence applies:

'*I, ... , wish to make a statement. I want someone to write down what I say. I understand that I do not have to say anything. This statement may be given in evidence.*'

8. If, on the occasion of being charged with or informed they may be prosecuted for any offence, the person asks to make a statement which relates to any such offence they shall before starting be asked to sign, or make their mark to, the following:

(a) unless the restriction on drawing adverse inferences from silence applied, see *Annex C*, when they were so charged or informed they may be prosecuted:

'*I, ... , wish to make a statement. I want someone to write down what I say. I understand that I do not have to say anything but that it may harm my defence if I do not mention when questioned something which I later rely on in court. This statement may be given in evidence.*';

(b) if the restriction on drawing adverse inferences from silence applied when they were so charged or informed they may be prosecuted:

'*I, ... , wish to make a statement. I want someone to write down what I say. I understand that I do not have to say anything. This statement may be given in evidence.*'

9. If, having already been charged with or informed they may be prosecuted for any offence, a person asks to make a statement which relates to any such offence they shall before starting, be asked to sign, or make their mark to:

'*I, ..., wish to make a statement. I want someone to write down what I* say. I understand that I do not have to say anything. This statement may be given in evidence.'

10. The person writing the statement must take down the exact words spoken by the person making it and must not edit or paraphrase it. Any questions that are necessary, e.g. to make it more intelligible, and the answers given must be recorded at the same time on the statement form.

11. When the writing of a statement is finished the person making it shall be asked to read it and to make any corrections, alterations or additions they want. When they have finished reading they shall be asked to write and sign or make their mark on the following certificate at the end of the statement:

'I have read the above statement, and I have been able to correct, alter or add anything I wish. This statement is true. I have made it of my own free will.'

12. If the person making the statement cannot read, or refuses to read it, or to write the above mentioned certificate at the end of it or to sign it, the person taking the statement shall read it to them and ask them if they would like to correct, alter or add anything and to put their signature or make their mark at the end. The person taking the statement shall certify on the statement itself what has occurred.

ANNEX E – SUMMARY OF PROVISIONS RELATING TO MENTALLY DISORDERED AND OTHERWISE MENTALLY VULNERABLE PEOPLE

1. If an officer has any suspicion, or is told in good faith, that a person of any age may be mentally disordered or otherwise mentally vulnerable, or mentally incapable of understanding the significance of questions or their replies that person shall be treated as mentally disordered or otherwise mentally vulnerable for the purposes of this Code. See *paragraph 1.10*

2. In the case of a person who is mentally disordered or otherwise mentally vulnerable, 'the appropriate adult' means:

(a) a relative, guardian or other person responsible for their care or custody;
(b) someone experienced in dealing with mentally disordered or mentally vulnerable people but who is not a police officer or employed by the police;
(c) failing these, some other responsible adult aged 18 or over who is not a police officer or employed by the police.

See *paragraph 1.13(b) and Note 1D*

3. If the detention of a person who is mentally vulnerable or appears to be suffering from a mental disorder is authorised by the review officer (see *paragraphs 14.1* and *14.2* and *Notes for Guidance 14A* and *14B*), the custody officer must as soon as practicable inform the appropriate adult of the grounds for detention and the person's whereabouts, and ask the adult to come to the police station to see them. If the appropriate adult:

- is already at the station when information is given as in *paragraphs 3.1* to *3.5* the information must be given in their presence
- is not at the station when the provisions of *paragraph 3.1* to *3.5* are complied with these provisions must be complied with again in their presence once they arrive.

See *paragraphs 3.15* to *3.16*

4. If the appropriate adult, having been informed of the right to legal advice, considers legal advice should be taken, the provisions of *section 6* apply as if the mentally disordered or otherwise mentally vulnerable person had requested access to legal advice. See *paragraph 3.20* and *Note E1.*

5. The custody officer must make sure a person receives appropriate clinical attention as soon as reasonably practicable if the person appears to be suffering from a mental disorder or in urgent cases immediately call the nearest health care professional or an ambulance. It is not intended these provisions delay the transfer of a detainee to a place of safety under the Mental Health Act 1983, section 136 if that is applicable. If an assessment under that Act is to take place at a police station, the custody officer must consider whether an appropriate health care professional should be called to conduct an initial clinical check on the detainee. See *paragraph 9.6* and *9.8*

6. If a mentally disordered or otherwise mentally vulnerable person is cautioned in the absence of the appropriate adult, the caution must be repeated in the appropriate adult's presence. See *paragraph 10.11*

7. A mentally disordered or otherwise mentally vulnerable person must not be interviewed or asked to provide or sign a written statement in the absence of the appropriate adult unless the provisions of *paragraphs 11.2* or *11.11* to *11.13* apply. Questioning in these circumstances may not continue in the absence of the appropriate adult once sufficient information to avert the risk has been obtained. A record shall be made of the grounds for any decision to begin an interview in these circumstances. See *paragraphs 11.2, 11.9* and *11.11* to *11.13*

8. If the appropriate adult is present at an interview, they shall be informed they are not expected to act simply as an observer and the purposes of their presence are to:

- advise the interviewee
- observe whether or not the interview is being conducted properly and fairly
- facilitate communication with the interviewee

See *paragraph 11.10*

9. If the custody officer charges a mentally disordered or otherwise mentally vulnerable person with an offence or takes such other action as is appropriate when there is sufficient evidence for a prosecution this must be done in the presence of the appropriate adult. The written notice embodying any charge must be given to the appropriate adult. See *paragraphs PACE Code C Section 16.*

10. An intimate or strip search of a mentally disordered or otherwise mentally vulnerable person may take place only in the presence of the appropriate adult of the same sex, unless the detainee specifically requests the presence of a particular adult of the opposite sex. A strip search may take place in the absence of an appropriate adult only in cases of urgency when there is a risk of serious harm to the detainee or others. See *Annex A, paragraphs 6 and 12(c)*

11. Particular care must be taken when deciding whether to use any form of approved restraints on a mentally disordered or otherwise mentally vulnerable person in a locked cell. See *paragraph 8.2*

Notes for guidance

E1 *The purpose of the provision at paragraph 3.20 is to protect the rights of a mentally disordered or otherwise mentally vulnerable detained person who does not understand the significance of what is said to them. If the detained person wants to exercise the right to legal advice, the appropriate action should be taken and not delayed until the appropriate adult arrives. A mentally disordered or otherwise mentally vulnerable detained person should always be given an opportunity, when an appropriate adult is called to the police station, to consult privately with a solicitor in the absence of the appropriate adult if they want.*

E2 *Although people who are mentally disordered or otherwise mentally vulnerable are often capable of providing reliable evidence, they may, without knowing or wanting to do so, be particularly prone in certain circumstances to provide information that may be unreliable, misleading or self-incriminating. Special care should always be taken when questioning such a person, and the appropriate adult should be involved if there is any doubt about a person's mental state or capacity. Because of the risk of unreliable evidence, it is important to obtain corroboration of any facts admitted whenever possible.*

E3 *Because of the risks referred to in Note E2, which the presence of the appropriate adult is intended to minimise, officers of superintendent rank or above should exercise their discretion to authorise the commencement of an interview in the appropriate adult's absence only in exceptional cases, if it is necessary to avert an immediate risk of serious harm. See paragraphs 11.2, 11.11 to 11.13*

ANNEX F – COUNTRIES WITH WHICH BILATERAL CONSULAR CONVENTIONS OR AGREEMENTS REQUIRING NOTIFICATION OF THE ARREST AND DETENTION OF THEIR NATIONALS ARE IN FORCE.

Armenia	Kazakhstan
Austria	Macedonia
Azerbaijan	Mexico
Belarus	Moldova
Belgium	Mongolia
Bosnia-Herzegovina	Norway
Bulgaria	Poland
China*	Romania
Croatia	Russia
Cuba	Slovak Republic
Czech Republic	Slovenia
Denmark	Spain
Egypt	Sweden
France	Tajikistan
Georgia	Turkmenistan
German Federal Republic	Ukraine
Greece	USA
Hungary	Uzbekistan
Italy	Yugoslavia
Japan	

*   Police are required to inform Chinese officials of arrest/detention in the Manchester consular district only. This comprises Derbyshire, Durham, Greater Manchester, Lancashire, Merseyside, North South and West Yorkshire, and Tyne and Wear.

ANNEX G – FITNESS TO BE INTERVIEWED

1. This Annex contains general guidance to help police officers and health care professionals assess whether a detainee might be at risk in an interview.

2. A detainee may be at risk in a interview if it is considered that:

(a) conducting the interview could significantly harm the detainee's physical or mental state;

(b) anything the detainee says in the interview about their involvement or suspected involvement in the offence about which they are being interviewed **might** be considered unreliable in subsequent court proceedings because of their physical or mental state.

3. In assessing whether the detainee should be interviewed, the following must be considered:

(a) how the detainee's physical or mental state might affect their ability to understand the nature and purpose of the interview, to comprehend what is being asked and to appreciate the significance of any answers given and make rational decisions about whether they want to say anything;

(b) the extent to which the detainee's replies may be affected by their physical or mental condition rather than representing a rational and accurate explanation of their involvement in the offence;

(c) how the nature of the interview, which could include particularly probing questions, might affect the detainee.

4. It is essential health care professionals who are consulted consider the functional ability of the detainee rather than simply relying on a medical diagnosis, e.g. it is possible for a person with severe mental illness to be fit for interview.

5. Health care professionals should advise on the need for an appropriate adult to be present, whether reassessment of the person's fitness for interview may be necessary if the interview lasts beyond a specified time, and whether a further specialist opinion may be required.

6. When health care professionals identify risks they should be asked to quantify the risks. They should inform the custody officer:

- whether the person's condition:

  - is likely to improve
  - will require or be amenable to treatment; and

- indicate how long it may take for such improvement to take effect

7. The role of the health care professional is to consider the risks and advise the custody officer of the outcome of that consideration. The health care professional's determination and any advice or recommendations should be made in writing and form part of the custody record.

8. Once the health care professional has provided that information, it is a matter for the custody officer to decide whether or not to allow the interview to go ahead and if the interview is to proceed, to determine what safeguards are needed. Nothing prevents safeguards being provided in addition to those required under the Code. An example might be to have an appropriate health care professional present during the interview, in addition to an appropriate adult, in order constantly to monitor the person's condition and how it is being affected by the interview.

Annex H – Detained Person: Observation List

1. If any detainee fails to meet any of the following criteria, an appropriate health care professional or an ambulance must be called.

2. When assessing the level of rousability, consider:

Rousability – can they be woken?

- go into the cell
- call their name
- shake gently

Response to questions – can they give appropriate answers to questions such as:

- What's your name?
- Where do you live?
- Where do you think you are?

Response to commands – can they respond appropriately to commands such as:

- Open your eyes!
- Lift one arm, now the other arm!

3. Remember to take into account the possibility or presence of other illnesses, injury, or mental condition, a person who is drowsy and smells of alcohol may also have the following:

- Diabetes
- Epilepsy
- Head injury
- Drug intoxication or overdose
- Stroke

Magistrates' Courts (Hearsay Evidence in Civil Proceedings) Rules 1999[1]
(SI 1999/681 amended by SI 2001/615)

2–2334 1. Citation and commencement. These Rules may be cited as the Magistrates' Courts (Hearsay Evidence in Civil Proceedings) Rules 1999 and shall come into force on 1st April 1999.

---

1. Made by the Lord Chancellor in exercise of the powers conferred upon him by s 144 of the Magistrates' Courts Act 1980 and ss 2 (2) , 3 and 12 of the Civil Evidence Act 1995.

2–2336 2. Application and interpretation. (1) In these Rules, the "1995 Act" means the Civil Evidence Act 1995.

(2) In these Rules—

"hearsay evidence" means evidence consisting of hearsay within the meaning of section 1(2) of the 1995 Act;

"hearsay notice" means a notice under section 2 of the 1995 Act.

(3) These Rules shall apply to hearsay evidence in civil proceedings in magistrates' courts.

2–2337 3. Hearsay notices. (1) Subject to paragraphs (2) and (3), a party who desires to give hearsay evidence at the hearing must, not less than 21 days before the date fixed for the hearing, serve a hearsay notice on every other party and file a copy in the court by serving it on the justices' chief executive.

(2) Subject to paragraph (3), the court or the justices' clerk may make a direction substituting a different period of time for the service of the hearsay notice under paragraph (1) on the application of a party to the proceedings.

(3) The court may make a direction under paragraph (2) of its own motion.

(4) A hearsay notice must—

(a) state that it is a hearsay notice;

(b) identify the proceedings in which the hearsay evidence is to be given;

(c) state that the party proposes to adduce hearsay evidence;

(d) identify the hearsay evidence;

(e) identify the person who made the statement which is to be given in evidence; and

(f) state why that person will not be called to give oral evidence.

(5) A single hearsay notice may deal with the hearsay evidence of more than one witness.

2–2338 4. Power to call witness for cross-examination on hearsay evidence. (1) Where a party tenders as hearsay evidence a statement made by a person but does not propose to call the person who made the statement to give evidence, the court may, on application, allow another party to call and cross-examine the person who made the statement on its contents.

(2) An application under paragraph (1) must—

(a) be served on the justices' chief executive with sufficient copies for all other parties;

(b) unless the court otherwise directs, be made not later than 7 days after service of the hearsay notice; and

(c) give reasons why the person who made the statement should be cross-examined on its contents.

(3) On receipt of an application under paragraph (1)—

(a) the justices' clerk must—

(i) unless the court otherwise directs, allow sufficient time for the applicant to comply with paragraph (4); and

(ii) fix the date, time and place of the hearing; and

(b) the justices' chief executive must—

(i) endorse the date, time and place of the hearing on the copies of the application filed by the applicant; and

(ii) return the copies to the applicant forthwith.

(4) Subject to paragraphs (5) and (6), on receipt of the copies from the justices' chief executive under paragraph (3)(c), the applicant must serve a copy on every other party giving not less than 3 days' notice of the hearing of the application.

(5) The court or the justices' chief executive may give directions as to the manner in which service under paragraph (4) is to be effected and may, subject to giving notice to the applicant, alter or dispense with the notice requirement under paragraph (4) if the court or the justices' clerk, as the case may be, considers it is in the interests of justice to do so.

(6) The court may hear an application under paragraph (1) *ex parte* if it considers it is in the interests of justice to do so.

(7) Subject to paragraphs (5) and (6), where an application under paragraph (1) is made, the applicant must file with the court a statement at or before the hearing of the application that service of a copy of the application has been effected on all other parties and the statement must indicate the manner, date, time and address at which the document was served.

(8) The court must notify all parties of its decision on an application under paragraph (1).

2–2339   5. Credibility and previous inconsistent statements.   (1) If—

(*a*)   a party tenders as hearsay evidence a statement made by a person but does not call the person who made the statement to give oral evidence, and

(*b*)   another party wishes to attack the credibility of the person who made the statement or allege that the person who made the statement made any other statement inconsistent with it,

that other party must notify the party tendering the hearsay evidence of his intention.

(2) Unless the court or the justices' clerk otherwise directs, a notice under paragraph (1) must be given not later than 7 days after service of the hearsay notice and, in addition to the requirements in paragraph (1), must be served on every other party and a copy filed in the court.

(3) If, on receipt of a notice under paragraph (1), the party referred to in paragraph (1)(*a*) calls the person who made the statement to be tendered as hearsay evidence to give oral evidence, he must, unless the court otherwise directs, notify the court and all other parties of his intention.

(4) Unless the court or the justices' clerk otherwise directs, a notice under paragraph (3) must be given not later than 7 days after the service of the notice under paragraph (1).

2–2340   6. Service.   (1) Where service of a document is required by these Rules it may be effected, unless the contrary is indicated—

(*a*)   if the person to be served is not known by the person serving to be acting by solicitor—

   (i)   by delivering it to him personally, or

   (ii)   by delivering at, or by sending it by first-class post to, his residence or his last known residence, or

(*b*)   if the person to be served is known by the person serving to be acting by solicitor—

   (i)   by delivering the document at, or sending it by first-class post to, the solicitor's address for service,

   (ii)   where the solicitor's address for service includes a numbered box at a document exchange, by leaving the document at that document exchange or at a document exchange which transmits documents on every business day to that document exchange, or

   (iii)   by sending a legible copy of the document by facsimile transmission to the solicitor's office.

(2) In this rule, "first-class post" means first-class post which has been pre-paid or in respect of which pre-payment is not required.

(3) A document shall, unless the contrary is proved, be deemed to have been served—

(*a*)   in the case of service by first-class post, on the second business day after posting,

(*b*)   in the case of service in accordance with paragraph (1)(*b*)(ii), on the second business day after the day on which it is left at the document exchange, and

(*c*)   in the case of service in accordance with paragraph (1)(*b*)(iii), where it is transmitted on a business day before 4 pm, on that day and in any other case, on the next business day.

(4) In this rule, "business day" means any day other than—

(*a*)   a Saturday, Sunday, Christmas Day or Good Friday; or

(*b*)   a bank holiday under the Banking and Financial Dealings Act 1971, in England and Wales.

2–2341   7. *Amendment to the Justices' Clerks Rules 1970*

Criminal Justice Act 2003 (Categories of Offences) Order 2004
(SI 2004/3346)

2–2350   1. (1) This Order may be cited as the Criminal Justice Act 2003 (Categories of Offences) Order 2004 and shall come into force 14 days after the day on which it is made or on the day that sections 98 to 110 of the 2003 Act (Evidence of Bad Character) come into force, whichever is later.

(2) In this Order "the 2003 Act" means the Criminal Justice Act 2003.

---

1. Made by the Secretary of State, in exercise of the powers conferred upon him by s 103(4)(*b*) of the Criminal Justice Act 2003.

2–2351   2. (1) The categories of offences set out in Parts 1 and 2 of the Schedule to this Order are hereby prescribed for the purposes of section 103(4)(b) of the 2003 Act.

(2) Two offences are of the same category as each other if they are included in the same Part of the Schedule.

2–2352

Article 2

SCHEDULE
PRESCRIBED CATEGORIES OF OFFENCES

PART 1
THEFT CATEGORY

1. An offence under section 1 of the Theft Act 1968 (theft).
2. An offence under section 8 of that Act (robbery).
3. An offence under section 9(1)(a) of that Act (burglary) if it was committed with intent to commit an offence of stealing anything in the building or part of a building in question.
4. An offence under section 9(1)(b) of that Act (burglary) if the offender stole or attempted to steal anything in the building or that part of it.
5. An offence under section 10 of that Act (aggravated burglary) if the offender committed a burglary described in paragraph 3 or 4 of this Part of the Schedule.
6. An offence under section 12 of that Act (taking motor vehicle or other conveyance without authority).
7. An offence under section 12A of that Act (aggravated vehicle-taking).
8. An offence under section 22 of that Act (handling stolen goods).
9. An offence under section 25 of that Act (going equipped for stealing).
10. An offence under section 3 of the Theft Act 1978 (making off without payment).
11. An offence of—

(a) aiding, abetting, counselling, procuring or inciting the commission of an offence specified in this Part of this Schedule; or
(b) attempting to commit an offence so specified.

PART 2
SEXUAL OFFENCES (PERSONS UNDER THE AGE OF 16) CATEGORY

1. An offence under section 1 of the Sexual Offences Act 1956 (rape) if it was committed in relation to a person under the age of 16.
2. An offence under section 5 of the Sexual Offences Act 1956 (intercourse with a girl under thirteen).
3. An offence under section 6 of that Act (intercourse with a girl under sixteen).
4. An offence under section 7 of that Act (intercourse with a defective) if it was committed in relation to a person under the age of 16.
5. An offence under section 10 of that Act (incest by a man) if it was committed in relation to a person under the age of 16.
6. An offence under section 11 of that Act (incest by a woman) if it was committed in relation to a person under the age of 16.
7. An offence under section 12 of that Act (buggery) if it was committed in relation to a person under the age of 16.
8. An offence under section 13 of that Act (indecency between men) if it was committed in relation to a person under the age of 16.
9. An offence under section 14 of that Act (indecent assault on a woman) if it was committed in relation to a person under the age of 16.
10. An offence under section 15 of that Act (indecent assault on a man) if it was committed in relation to a person under the age of 16.
11. An offence under section 128 of the Mental Health Act 1959 (sexual intercourse with patients) if it was committed in relation to a person under the age of 16.
12. An offence under section 1 of the Indecency with Children Act 1960 (indecent conduct towards young child).
13. An offence under section 54 of the Criminal Law Act 1977 (inciting a girl under 16 to have incestuous sexual intercourse).
14. An offence under section 3 of the Sexual Offences (Amendment) Act 2000 (abuse of a position of trust) if it was committed in relation to a person under the age of 16.
15. An offence under section 1 of the Sexual Offences Act 2003 (rape) if it was committed in relation to a person under the age of 16.
16. An offence under section 2 of that Act (assault by penetration) if it was committed in relation to a person under the age of 16.
17. An offence under section 3 of that Act (sexual assault) if it was committed in relation to a person under the age of 16.
18. An offence under section 4 of that Act (causing a person to engage in sexual activity without consent) if it was committed in relation to a person under the age of 16.
19. An offence under section 5 of the Sexual Offences Act 2003 (rape of a child under 13).
20. An offence under section 6 of that Act (assault of a child under 13 by penetration).
21. An offence under section 7 of that Act (sexual assault of a child under 13).
22. An offence under section 8 of that Act (causing or inciting a child under 13 to engage in sexual activity).
23. An offence under section 9 of that Act (sexual activity with a child).
24
An offence under section 10 of that Act (causing or inciting a child to engage in sexual activity).
25. An offence under section 14 of that Act if doing it will involve the commission of an offence under sections 9 and 10 of that Act (arranging or facilitating the commission of a child sex offence).
26. An offence under section 16 of that Act (abuse of position of trust: sexual activity with a child) if it was committed in relation to a person under the age of 16.
27. An offence under section 17 of that Act (abuse of position of trust: causing or inciting a child to engage in sexual activity) if it was committed in relation to a person under the age of 16.
28. An offence under section 25 of that Act (sexual activity with a child family member) if it was committed in relation to a person under the age of 16.
29. An offence under section 26 of that Act (inciting a child family member to engage in sexual activity) if it was committed in relation to a person under the age of 16.
30. An offence under section 30 of that Act (sexual activity with a person with a mental disorder impeding choice) if it was committed in relation to a person under the age of 16.

31. An offence under section 31 of that Act (causing or inciting a person with a mental disorder impeding choice to engage in sexual activity) if it was committed in relation to a person under the age of 16.

32. An offence under section 34 of that Act (inducement, threat, or deception to procure activity with a person with a mental disorder) if it was committed in relation to a person under the age of 16.

33. An offence under section 35 of that Act (causing a person with a mental disorder to engage in or agree to engage in sexual activity by inducement, threat or deception) if it was committed in relation to a person under the age of 16.

34. An offence under section 38 of that Act (care workers: sexual activity with a person with a mental disorder) if it was committed in relation to a person under the age of 16.

35. An offence under section 39 of that Act (care workers: causing or inciting sexual activity) if it was committed in relation to a person under the age of 16.

36. An offence of—

(a) aiding, abetting, counselling, procuring or inciting the commission of an offence specified in this Part of this Schedule; or

(b) attempting to commit an offence so specified.

Introduction: sentencing practice

SENTENCING PURPOSES AND GUIDELINES

3–10   ***The purposes of sentencing.***   Any court dealing with an offender in respect of his offence must have regard to the following purposes of sentencing—

- (a) the punishment of offenders,
- (b) the reduction of crime (including its reduction by deterrence),
- (c) the reform and rehabilitation of offenders,
- (d) the protection of the public, and
- (e) the making of reparation by offenders to persons affected by their offences[1].

Duty to have regard to sentencing guidelines.   Every court must, in sentencing an offender or in exercising any other function relating thereto, have regard to any relevant guidelines issued by the Sentencing Guidelines Council[2]. Whilst it is not open to sentencers to disregard guidelines issued by the Council, it does not follow that the guidelines have to followed in every case, but the sentencer must explain why he is not going to follow a relevant guideline[3].

1. Criminal Justice Act 2003, s 140. See this PART, post. This duty does not apply in relation to an offender aged under 18 at the time of conviction, minimum sentences for certain firearms offences, required custodial sentences for dangerous offender, or in relation to the making of a hospital order with or without a restriction order: CJA 2003, s 140(2). As to the principle of sentencing, see paras **3-70** to **3-77**, post.
2. CJA 2003, s 172. As to the constitution and functions of the Sentencing Guidelines Council and the Sentencing Advisory Panel, see CJA 2003, ss 167-171.
3. See *R v Oosthuizen* [2005] EWCA Crim 1978, [2006] 1 Cr App R (S) 73; *R v Bowering* [2005] EWCA Crim 3215, [2006] 2 Cr App R (S) 10, [2006] Crim LR 361; and *R v Gisbourne* [2005] EWCA Crim 2491, [2006] Crim LR 363. All the sentences were reduced because there had been no discounts for pleading guilty, contrary to the Council's guidance; it was held the fact that the offenders had been caught "red-handed" was no longer a reason for withholding credit. See further para **3-74**, post.

REASONS FOR AND EXPLANATION OF SENTENCES

3-20   A court when passing sentence must state in open court, in ordinary language and in general terms, its reasons for choosing that particular sentence, its effect, the effect of non compliance with any requirements it may contain, any power to vary or review the sentence on the application of the offender or any other person, and, in the case of a fine, the effect of failure to pay[1].

Where the sentence is of a different kind, or outside the range indicated by guidelines issued by the Sentencing Guidelines Council, the court must state the reason for the departure[2].

The court must state any aggravating or mitigating or aggravating factors that it has regarded as being of particular importance[3], and if it has reduced the sentence on account of a guilty plea it must state that fact[4].

If the sentence is a custodial sentence or a community sentence the court must usually state why it is of the opinion required for the imposition of such a sentence[5]. Model explanations for the imposition of custodial sentences have been provided[6].

1. Criminal Justice Act 2003, s 174. See this PART, post.
2. CJA 2003, s 174(2)(a).
3. CJA 2003, s 174(2)(e).
4. CJA 2003, s 174(d).
5. CJA 2003, s 174(2)(b) and (c).
6. See *Practice Direction (criminal: consolidated)* [2002] paras 1.7, 1.8, Annex C, in PART 1: MAGISTRATES' COURTS, PROCEDURE, ante.

DEALING WITH ALL ELEMENTS TOGETHER

3-30   It is bad sentencing practice to deal on different occasions with different elements in the disposal of an offence[1]. The terms of s 10 of the Magistrates' Courts Act 1980 prevent the court from adjourning if it has partially sentenced an offender. However, a youth court is specifically not required to adjourn proceedings by reason only of the fact that the court commits the accused for trial on another offence or because the accused is charged with another offence[2].

1. *R v Payne* [1950] 1 All ER 102, 114 JP 68; *R v Talgarth Justices, ex p Bithell* [1973] 2 All ER 717, [1973] 1 WLR 1327, 137 JP 666; cf *R v Annesley* [1976] 1 All ER 589, 140 JP 207 (Crown Court).
2. Magistrates' Courts Act 1980, s 10(3A) in PART I: MAGISTRATES' COURTS, PROCEDURE, ante.

SENTENCING CO-DEFENDANTS

3-31   All those concerned with the same offence or group of offences should appear at the same court at the same time[1] and be dealt with in an even-handed fashion.

Complete consistency is impossible when dealing with co-defendants, and it is right to consider all the circumstances in respect of each offender separately, including the different statutory provisions governing defendants of different ages[2]. A minor should generally be dealt with by a youth court acting for the area where he resides[3], which may mean separating defendants. Where a participant in the same or related offences receives an unduly lenient sentence, the other defendants may expect to have their disparate sentences reduced on appeal, even if they were not in themselves excessive[4]. Appeal courts with whom the question of disparity of sentence is raised will ask not only whether the appellants labour under a sense of grievance but also whether there is justification for that grievance, and will uphold apparently disparate sentences which are otherwise correct in principle[5]. When dealing with offences arising out of the criminal behaviour of a group of people, not all of whom are before the court, it is no mitigation for the one or more who have been apprehended to say that others were equally to blame[6]; for example the one motorist stopped out of several who were speeding. It is however important for the court to distinguish carefully between the criminal conduct of the offender before the court, and the criminal conduct of a group of people involved in an incident; for example the proven criminal damage caused by a football hooligan to a road sign, as against broken windows, destroyed walls, stolen property and personal injury caused by the crowd. Although there may be cases in which it is desirable that one co-defendant should be sentenced before another co-defendant, in general it is better to postpone sentence of those who have pleaded guilty until the court has heard all the evidence relating to the charge out of which the plea of guilty arises[7]. Furthermore, it is not desirable to sentence a defendant who has pleaded guilty before the end of the trial of co-defendants if it is proposed to call him as a witness on behalf of a co-defendant[7]. Similarly, it is the general practice not to sentence an accomplice who has been separately charged and who has pleaded guilty until the conclusion of all the proceedings in the case, in order that the court can get the flavour of the case and look at it in the round at the conclusion of all the evidence[8].

A difference in sex is not a good reason for drawing a distinction between a man and a woman when passing sentence[9]. In sentencing a defendant who has pleaded guilty, the court may take account of facts advanced on the trial of other co-defendants, provided he has the opportunity of commenting on those facts[10].

1. *R v Stroud* [1978] Crim LR 173; *R v Weekes* (1980) 2 Cr App Rep (S) 377.
2. *R v Midgley* [1975] Crim LR 469. See also *R v Harper* (1994) 16 Cr App Rep (S) 639.
3. Powers of Criminal Courts (Sentencing) Act 2000, s 6, in this PART, post.
4. *R v Hair and Singh* [1978] Crim LR 698; *R v Weekes, Hellier, Mann, Turner* (1982) 74 Cr App Rep 161.
5. *R v Potter* [1977] Crim LR 112; *R v Lowe* (1989) Times, 14 November, CA.
6. *R v Johnson* [1975] Crim LR 470.
7. *R v Coffey* (1982) 74 Cr App Rep 168.
8. See *R v Palmer* (1993) 158 JP 138, [1994] Crim LR 122 and *Chan Wai-Keung v R* [1995] 2 All ER 438, [1995] 1 WLR 251, [1995] 2 Cr App Rep 194, [1995] Crim LR 566.
9. *R v Okuya* (1984) 6 Cr App Rep (S) 253, [1984] Crim LR 766.
10. *R v Patrick Smith* (1988) 10 Cr App Rep (S) 271.

REMITTING AN OFFENDER TO ANOTHER COURT

3–32 A court may remit an offender to another magistrates' court to be dealt with in the following circumstances—

(1) the offender has attained the age of 18,
(2) the offence is punishable with imprisonment or driving disqualification, and the court has convicted him of it,
(3) the other magistrates' court has convicted him of another such offence but has not yet dealt with him by way of sentence or otherwise,
(4) the other magistrates' court consents to the offender being remitted to it for this offence[1].

This can be a convenient and appropriate means of ensuring that an offender is dealt with at one time for all outstanding matters against him. The remitting court will leave all sentencing considerations to the other court, with the exception of any restitution order, which is specifically empowered to make[3]. The court to which he is remitted has full powers, including the power itself to remit the case under this section[2].

A child or young person should be dealt with by a youth court acting either for the same place as the remitting court, or for the place where he habitually resides; except in a case of homicide, other courts are bound to remit an offender to such a court unless they are satisfied that it would be undesirable to do so[3].

An adult court dealing with a child or young person (for example jointly charged with adult offenders) possesses only limited sentencing powers[4].

1. Powers of Criminal Courts (Sentencing) Act 2000, s 10 in this PART, post.
2. Powers of Criminal Courts (Sentencing) Act 2000, s 10(7) in this PART, post.
3. Powers of Criminal Courts (Sentencing) Act 2000, ss 6 and 8(6) in this PART, post.
4. See para **5–10**, post.

3–33 Sentencing hearing by live link. Where a live link direction is in force at a preliminary hearing at which the accused is convicted[1], or in any other case where the accused is convicted and it is likely that he is to be held in custody during any sentencing hearing, the court may proceed to sentence by the existing live link direction or the court may, of its own motion or on application by a party, make a live link direction in relation to all or specified sentencing hearings in those proceedings. The accused must consent and the court must be satisfied that it is not contrary to the interests of justice to proceed in this way. However, the accused may not give oral evidence by live link unless he consents and it is not contrary to the interests of justice for him to give it in that way[2].

The court must give its reasons for refusing an application for, or for the rescission of a live link direction[3].

1. See para **1–424A Use of live link at preliminary hearings where accused is in custody**, ante.
2. Crime and Disorder Act 1998, ss 57D and 57E, in PART I: MAGISTRATES' COURTS, PROCEDURE, ANTE.
3. Crime and Disorder Act 1998, s 57E(8), in PART I: MAGISTRATES' COURTS, PROCEDURE, ANTE.

PREVIOUS CONVICTIONS

3–34 Justices should announce publicly their decision to convict before inquiring into previous convictions[1]. Thereafter, we suggest the following practice—

(1) the defendant's full record should be produced;

(2) "spent" convictions[2] should be marked; all other previous convictions should be read from the record by the person giving antecedents to the court;

(3) but the following should not be read out,

    (a) convictions of an entirely different nature from the offence(s) presently under consideration,

    (b) relevant convictions five or more years old unless there were more than one or two,

    (c) where the defendant is aged 21 or over, any findings of guilt made when he was under 14[3];

(4) the written record should always be available to the court;

(5) the court should ask the defendant if he agrees that the record given to the court is his record, and accurate.

In considering the seriousness of an offence committed by an offender who has one or more previous convictions, the court must treat each previous conviction by a court within the United Kingdom or a previous finding of guilt in service disciplinary proceedings as an aggravating factor if the court considers that it can reasonably be so treated having regard to the nature of the offence to which it relates, its relevance to the current offence and the time that has elapsed since the conviction[4]. A previous conviction by a court outside the United Kingdom may be treated as an aggravating factor if the court considers it appropriate to do so[5].

Both the justices and the clerk of the court should have the opportunity of looking at the full record.

The defendant should be given the opportunity of challenging or explaining previous convictions[6].

In passing sentence the court should refer to a "spent" conviction only when it is necessary to explain the sentence to be passed[7].

1. *Davies v Griffiths* [1937] 2 All ER 671, 101 JP 247.
2. See the Rehabilitation of Offenders Act 1974, this PART, post, and Home Office Circulars 98/1975 and 130/1975.
3. Children and Young Persons Act 1963, s 16(2) in PART V: YOUTH COURTS, post.
4. Criminal Justice Act 2003, s 143(2) and (4). See this PART, post.
5. Criminal Justice Act 2003, s 143(5).
6. *Hastings v Ostle* (1930) 94 JP 209; *Hill v Tothill* (1936) 80 Sol Jo 572; *R v East Kerrier Justices, ex p Munday* [1952] 2 QB 719, [1952] 2 All ER 144, 116 JP 339. For methods of proving previous convictions, see PART II: EVIDENCE, para **2–193**, ante.
7. See *Practice Direction (criminal: consolidated)* [2002] para I.6, in PART I: MAGISTRATES' COURTS, PROCEDURE, ante, and Home Office Circulars 98/1975 and 130/1975.

OFFENCES TAKEN INTO CONSIDERATION

3–35 When deciding sentence, justices[1] may take into consideration other offences admitted by the defendant but with which he has not been charged. Such admitted offence may be an offence "associated with another" for the purposes of the Powers of Criminal Courts (Sentencing) Act 2000[2]. We suggest the following practice—

(1) the prosecution should prepare a written list showing the date, place and nature of each offence[3] which the accused should read and sign;

(2) in court the list should be put to the accused personally either by reading out each offence, or by reference to a copy of the list which the accused should have been given, and he should be asked if he admits each one, and whether he wishes the court to take it into consideration;

(3) in announcing sentence, the justices should refer specifically to the fact that they have taken each further offence into consideration, and this should be recorded in the court register.

The express and unequivocal consent of the offender is necessary, by way of a statement of admission and desire to have the further offences taken into consideration[4]. The consent of the prosecution is also necessary, but should not be withheld except on good grounds[5]. The request that offences be taken into consideration should be made by the accused himself, and no pressure should be brought to bear to encourage him to take this course[6]. If the offender is committed for sentence, the procedure should be repeated in the Crown Court[7].

Offences which a magistrates' court would have no jurisdiction to try should be excluded[8]. A charge where conviction involves any disqualification, for example driving when under the influence of drink, is not appropriate to be taken into consideration when passing sentence for another class of offence, for example dishonesty[9]. If however the principal offence carries disqualification, another offence also involving disqualification may be taken into consideration[10]. A breach of a probation (now community) order should not be taken into consideration, but should be made the subject of a separate sentence[11].

As for the meaning of the term "taken into consideration" the Court of Appeal[12] has given the following guidance. A sentence is intended to reflect a defendant's overall criminality. It is an essential prerequisite that offences cannot be taken into consideration without the express agreement of the defendant. If they are to be taken into account (and the court is not obliged to take them into account), they have relevance to the overall criminality. When assessing the significance of "TICs" of course the court is likely to attach weight to the demonstrable fact that the defendant has assisted the police, particularly if they enabled the police to clear up offences which might not otherwise have been brought to justice. It is also true that co-operative behaviour of that kind will often provide its own very early indication of guilt, and usually means that no further proceedings at all need be started. They might also serve to demonstrate a genuine determination by the offender to "wipe the slate clean" so that when he emerges from whatever sentence is imposed on him he can put his past completely behind him, without having worry or concern that offences might be revealed, and that he is then returned to court. As in so many aspects of sentencing, the way in which the court deals with offences to be taken into consideration depends on context. In some cases, the offences taken into consideration will end up by adding nothing, or nothing very much, to the sentence which the court would otherwise impose. On the other hand, offences taken into consideration might aggravate the sentence and lead to a substantial increase in it. For example, the offences might show a pattern of criminal activity that suggests careful planning or deliberate rather than casual involvement in a crime. They might show an offence or offences committed on bail, after an earlier arrest. They might show a return to crime immediately after the offender has been before the court and given a chance that, by committing the crime, he has immediately rejected. There are many situations in which similar issues might arise. One advantage to the defendant is that if an offence is taken into consideration, there is no likely risk of any further prosecution for it; if, on the other hand, it is not, that risk remains. In short, offences taken into consideration are indeed taken into consideration. They are not ignored or expunged or disregarded.

1. *R v Marquis* (1951) 115 JP 329.
2. Powers of Criminal Courts (Sentencing) Act 2000, s 161(1), this PART, post.
3. *R v Hicks* (1924) 88 JP 68.
4. *DPP v Anderson* [1978] AC 964, [1978] 2 All ER 512, 142 JP 391.
5. *R v McLean* [1911] 1 KB 332, 75 JP 127; *R v Syres* (1908) 73 JP 13; *R v Smith* (1921) 85 JP 224.
6. *R v Davis* [1943] KB 274, [1943] 1 All ER 305, 107 JP 75; *R v Marquis*, supra; *R v Nelson* [1967] 1 All ER 358n, [1967] 1 WLR 449, 131 JP 229, CA.
7. *R v Davies* (1980) 72 Cr App Rep 262.
8. *R v Warn* [1937] 4 All ER 327, 102 JP 46.
9. *R v Collins* [1947] KB 560, [1947] 1 All ER 147, 111 JP 154; *R v Simons* [1953] 2 All ER 599, [1953] 1 WLR 1014, 117 JP 422, CCA.
10. *R v Jones* [1970] 3 All ER 815, 135 JP 36.
11. *R v Webb* [1953] 2 QB 390, [1953] 1 All ER 1156, 117 JP 319.
12. *R v Miles* [2006] EWCA Crim 256, (2006) 170 JPN 204.

Information for sentencing

GENERAL CONSIDERATIONS

3–50 After conviction or finding of guilt, the court will look to the prosecution and the defence in turn for information enabling it to decide sentence. The prosecution must state the facts in open court to enable the press and the public to know the circumstances of the offences for which the defendant is to be sentenced[1]. Consideration of pre-sentence reports should precede any address in mitigation[2]. Information from prosecution or defence is presented in the form of unsworn statements, although either side may call evidence after conviction in order to clarify issues of fact which have not been resolved by the plea and which are relevant to the determination of sentence, and the court itself may likewise call for evidence[3]. The other side should always be given the opportunity of challenging any statement made[4]; the procedure then is for the person making the statement to be sworn following which he may then be questioned[5].

Information after conviction or finding of guilt is not based strictly on the law of evidence. The prosecution will in general limit itself to informing the court of the circumstances of the offence and the character and antecedents of the offender. As to the offence, it will inform the court of any factors making the offence unusually serious, but will also reveal any mitigating circumstances which are known[6]. If evidence is to be introduced which would tend to aggravate the offence and which would be disputed, then it should be notified in advance to the defence[7]. The prosecution should not address the court as to sentence, except where a technicality is involved, such as the maximum sentence permitted by law[8]. Unless there are different local arrangements, the police will be responsible for preparing five copies of the antecedents of which two will be for the court, one for the defence and one for the probation service. Where a custodial sentence is imposed, one of the court's copies is to be attached to the order sent to the prison[9].

The defendant is entitled to give evidence in mitigation[10] and will be liable to prosecution for perjury if he gives false material evidence[11]. A heavier sentence should not however be imposed for an offence because the court thinks a defendant has committed perjury[12]. Where a defendant puts forward mitigation which is quite inconsistent with other information before the court, it is for the defendant to indicate that he wishes to make good that submission and he takes the chance if he does not offer to call evidence to the fact in question; accordingly, if he elects not to call evidence, the justices are not obliged, before passing sentence, to tell the defendant that they do not accept his mitigation[13]. It is our view that free scope should not be given for attacks on third parties who are not in court. There may be occasions where sworn evidence should be looked for, and an opportunity given to third parties to respond. Where there is a difference in the accounts of the facts of an offence by the offender and by the child victim of a sexual offence, the court, for the purposes of sentencing, should disregard the allegations of the victim unless they are corroborated in respect of the points of difference[14].

In appropriate cases the court may reduce a sentence by reason of the assistance which the offender gives to the police leading to the conviction of other offenders[15]. Guidance as to the proper principles to be followed by the court when considering a written confidential report made by a police officer which indicates that the defendant has given information to the police, has been given by the Court of Appeal[16].

The court itself may ask for such information as it requires[17], but it should not seek to inquire into other offences which are denied; these should be properly charged and tried[18]. Where the court is inclined to take a view on a question of fact relevant to sentence which has not been clearly resolved, the defendant should be given the opportunity of addressing the court on the matter[19].

The factual basis of a sentence must be clear. Where a defendant, charged with an offence triable either way, makes an unequivocal guilty plea and upon the facts advanced by the prosecution it is indicated that the plea involves a clear admission to the whole of the ingredients of the offence, the justices are obliged to accept that plea and record it[20].

As for cases where a plea of guilty is tendered on a basis of fact substantially different from that tendered by the prosecution, see para **1–581**, ante.

The clerk of the court must not be a party to the decision as to the sentence to be imposed, but will advise as to the law and will provide information so as to assist consistency in sentencing[21].

Sentencers are obliged to pay attention to guidance given by the Court of Appeal when determining sentence[22].

See, further, paragraphs 1.1.15–1.1.17 of the guidance issued by the Sentencing Guidelines Council in relation to the sentencing framework contained in the Criminal Justice Act 2003, para **3–117**, post.

Guidelines have been issued as to seeking an advance sentencing indication in advance of plea, but these currently apply only to the Crown Court[23].

1. See *Practice Direction (criminal: consolidated)* [2002] para III.26, in PART I: MAGISTRATES' COURTS, PROCEDURE, ante.
2. *R v Kirkham* (1968) 112 Sol Jo 151.
3. *R v Gravell* (1978) and commentary thereon in Crim LR 438.
4. *R v Campbell* (1911) 75 JP Jo 88; *R v Metcalfe* (1913) 9 Cr App Rep 7.
5. *R v Butterwasser* [1948] 1 KB 4, [1947] 2 All ER 415, 111 JP 527.
6. *R v Van Pelz* [1943] KB 157, [1943] 1 All ER 36, 107 JP 24.
7. *R v Robinson* (1969) 53 Cr App Rep 314.
8. *R v Atkinson* [1978] 2 All ER 460, [1978] 1 WLR 425, 142 JP 378. See discussion of the prosecutor's role at [1979] Crim LR 480 et seq.
9. See *Practice Direction (criminal: consolidated)* [2002] para III.27, ibid.
10. *R v Cross* [1975] Crim LR 591; *R v Billericay Justices, ex p Rumsey* [1978] Crim LR 305.
11. *R v Wheeler* [1917] 1 KB 283, 81 JP 75.
12. *R v Quinn* (1932) 23 Cr App Rep 196.
13. *Gross v O'Toole* (1982) 4 Cr App Rep (S) 283.
14. *R v Long* [1980] Crim LR 315.
15. *R v King* (1985) 82 Cr App Rep 120, [1985] Crim LR 748.
16. *See R v X* [1999] 2 Cr App Rep 125, [1999] Crim LR 678, CA. See also this PART para **3–172** Mitigation for assistance post.
17. *R v Van Pelz*, supra.
18. *R v Huchison* [1972] 1 All ER 936, [1972] 1 WLR 398, 136 JP 304; *R v Morgan* [1981] Crim LR 56.
19. See *R v Lester* (1976) 63 Cr App Rep 144.
20. *R v Telford Magistrates' Court, ex p Darlington* (1987) 152 JP 215.
21. See ante PART I: MAGISTRATES' COURTS, para **1–25 Justices' clerks**.
22. *R v Johnson* (1994) 15 Cr App Rep (S) 827, [1994] Crim LR 537.
23. *R v Goodyear Practice Note* [2005] EWCA Crim 888, [2005] 3 All ER 117, [2005] 1 WLR 2532, [2005] 2 Cr App R 20.

VICTIM PERSONAL STATEMENTS

3–51 Where an investigating police officer takes a statement from a victim he will be informed that he may, if he wishes, make a victim personal statement which should be considered by the court before passing sentence. The procedure and use to be made of such statements are set out in the *Practice Direction (criminal: consolidated)* [2002] para I.6[1].

1. PART I: MAGISTRATES' COURTS, PROCEDURE, ante.

POWER TO ADJOURN FOR PRE-SENTENCE INQUIRIES

3–52 After conviction, the court may adjourn for up to four weeks at a time (three weeks if the defendant is kept in custody) to enable inquiries to be made and to determine the most suitable method of dealing with the case[1]. The defendant shall be granted bail unless the offence is imprisonable and one of the general exceptions to the right to bail contained in the Bail Act 1976, Sch 1, Part I, paras 2–6, applies, or that it would be impracticable to complete the inquiries or make the report without keeping the defendant in custody[2]. In the case of a non-imprisonable offence, bail may only be withheld if one of the exceptions specified in paras 2–5 of Part II of Sch 1 to the Bail Act 1976 applies.

The commonest source of information is the pre-sentence report. In the case of an offender aged 18 or over the report will be prepared by a probation officer[3]. In respect of younger offenders the report will be prepared by a probation officer, social worker or member of a youth offending team[4].

If, when adjourning a case for sentence, the court requests a pre-sentence report and releases the defendant on bail, there is no obligation on the court to indicate to the defendant that he is still liable to be sentenced to prison once the pre-sentence report has been obtained[5]. Nevertheless, it is usually the better practice for the court to give such an indication[6]. Since a pre-sentence report is required by virtue of the provisions of s 81(1) of the Powers of Criminal Courts (Sentencing) Act 2000 (see now s 156(3)(*a*) of the Criminal Justice Act 2003), a defendant is not entitled to believe that, because a pre-sentence report has been ordered, a non-custodial sentence will be passed[5]. See further *Express or implied indications limiting future sentencing options*, para **3–53**, post.

---

1. Magistrates' Courts Act 1980, s 10(3) in PART I: MAGISTRATES' COURTS, PROCEDURE, ante.
2. Bail Act 1976, Sch 1, para 7 in PART I: MAGISTRATES' COURTS, PROCEDURE, ante.
3. Criminal Justice Act 2003, s 158(2)(*a*). See this PART, post.
4. Criminal Justice Act 2003, s 158(2)(*b*).
5. *R v Woodin* (1993) 15 Cr App Rep (S) 307, [1994] Crim LR 72.
6. *R v Renan* (1994) 158 JP 621, 15 Cr App Rep (S) 722, [1994] Crim LR 379.

EXPRESS OR IMPLIED INDICATIONS LIMITING FUTURE SENTENCING OPTIONS

3–53   Under the line of authorities commencing with *R v Gillam*[1] it was held, prior to the implementation of the Criminal Justice Act 1991, that where a court postponed sentence so that an alternative to custody could be examined, and that alternative was found to be a satisfactory one in all respects, the sentencer ought to adopt the alternative since a feeling of injustice might otherwise be aroused. Although a community sentence is not to be regarded as an alternative to a custodial sentence, the principle underlying *Gillam* still applies[2]; accordingly, where a court adjourns for a pre-sentence report and gives a provisional indication that it is considering a community sentence, it should not subsequently pass a custodial sentence if the pre-sentence report suggests that a community sentence would be a suitable method of dealing with the offender. Moreover, where the court adjourns for a further assessment and investigation, the defendant should invariably be told in clear terms that he must not assume from the fact that the court is ordering a further adjournment that he is likely to receive any particular form of sentence or that a custodial sentence is ruled out, whatever the further inquiry may reveal[2]. It would appear that a sentencer must also ensure that neither his comments nor his conduct during the sentencing hearing raise the expectation that a custodial sentence will not be imposed[3].

---

1. *R v Gillam* [1981] Crim LR 55; *R v Millwood* (1982) 4 Cr App Rep (S) 281, explained in *R v Moss* [1983] Crim LR 751; and see *R v Wilkinson* (1987) 9 Cr App Rep (S) 469, *R v McMillan* (1988) 10 Cr App Rep (S) 205 and *R v Chamberlain* (1994) 16 Cr App Rep (S) 473, [1995] Crim LR 85; *R v Inner London Crown Court, ex p Mentesh* [2001] 1 Cr App Rep (S) 94.
2. *R v Chamberlain* (1994) 16 Cr App Rep (S) 473, [1995] Crim LR 85, CA.
3. *R v Jackson* [1996] Crim LR 355, [1996] 2 Cr App Rep (S) 175.

PRE-SENTENCE REPORTS

3–54   A pre-sentence report is a report in writing which, with a view to assisting the court in determining the most suitable method of dealing with an offender, is submitted by a probation officer or, if the offender is aged under 18, by a social worker of a local authority social services department or a member of a youth offending team, and contains information on prescribed matters presented in a prescribed manner.

There is a statutory duty on the court to obtain and consider a pre-sentence report before it can form an opinion which may lead to a custodial sentence unless the court is of the opinion that it is unnecessary to obtain a pre-sentence report[1]. A court may conclude that it is unnecessary to obtain a pre-sentence report before imposing a custodial sentence where the court is prepared to make every possible assumption in favour of the offender[2].

Similarly, unless in the circumstances of the case the court is of the opinion that it is unnecessary to obtain a pre-sentence report, the court must obtain and consider a pre-sentence report before forming an opinion as to whether the case is sufficiently serious for a community sentence or an opinion as to any restrictions on liberty to be included within such a sentence; likewise the court must have the assistance of a report before forming an opinion as to the suitability for the offender of any particular requirements to be included in such an order[3].

Where a child or young person is found guilty of an offence, the youth court shall take into consideration such information as to the general conduct, home surroundings, school record and medical history of the child or young person as may be necessary to enable it to deal with the case in his best interests; if such information is not fully available it should consider remanding for reports[4].

The demands of a drug treatment and testing order and the need for the offender to be susceptible to treatment mean that a reasoned assessment should always be made, save in the most exceptional circumstances, of the offender's suitability for the order; and the court should be slow to act against the conclusions of a reasoned probation service assessment unless it has cogent reasons for doing so[5].

Whilst a probation officer may not state his view of the seriousness of the offence he may include in his report what an offender has said in the course of interview even where what is said is not in the defendant's favour[6]. It is for the court to decide whether the report actually available to the court is adequate for sentencing purposes and complies with the statutory duty[7]. The court is not obliged to ensure that every detail of information put before the court by the defendant is checked and confirmed in a further pre-sentence report or by way of addendum[7].

When a report by a probation officer is presented to the adult court, a copy shall be given by the court to the offender or his counsel or solicitor, but where the offender is under 18 years of age, the copy report need not be given to him but must be given to his parent or guardian if present in court[8]. The court shall also give a copy of the report to the prosecutor[8] except that if the prosecutor is not of a prescribed[9] description a copy need not be given to the prosecutor if the court considers that it would be inappropriate for him to be given it[10]. The prosecutor shall not use or disclose any information disclosed in the report otherwise than for the purpose of making representations to the court about matters contained in the report. The report should not be read out aloud[11].

Where second-hand information and opinion appear in a report, the officer making the report should endeavour to make this clear and indicate its source and his own reasons, if any, for agreeing with it[12]. When a report by a social worker of a local authority social services department is presented to the adult court, we would suggest, if the parties agree, that the report should be presented to the court in the same manner as if it were a report by a probation officer.

When the report is presented in the youth court, it may be received and considered without being read out aloud. However, if the minor is not legally represented and the report has not been made available to him, or if the offender or his parent or guardian had been required to withdraw, the court must tell them the substance of the material parts of the report[13].

In both adult and youth court, an offender wishing to challenge material matters contained in a report should be given the opportunity of questioning the officer making the report, who will be sworn for this purpose, and of calling further material evidence.

---

1. Criminal Justice Act 2003, s 156(3) and (4). See this PART, post. Where the court is considering the imposition of a first custodial sentence, other than perhaps for a very short period of time, it should be the inevitable practice first to obtain a pre sentence report: *R v Stephenson* [2001] EWCA Crim 1360, (2001) 165 JPN 435.
2. *R v Armsaramah* (2000) 164 JP 709, [2000] Crim LR 1033, [2001] 1 Cr App Rep (S) 467, CA.
3. Criminal Justice Act 2003, s 156(3)(b).
4. Criminal Procedure Rules 2005, Part 44, in PART I: MAGISTRATES' COURTS, PROCEDURE, ante.
5. *R (on the application of Inner London Probation Service) v Tower Bridge Magistrates' Court* [2001] EWCH Admin 401, [2002] 1 Cr App Rep (S) 179.
6. *R v Salisbury Magistrates' Court, ex p Gray* (1999) 163 JP 732, [2000] 1 Cr App Rep (S) 267, DC.
7. *R v Okinikan* [1993] 2 All ER 5, [1993] 1 WLR 173.
8. Criminal Justice Act 2003, s 156(2). If the offender is aged under 18 and it appears to the court that disclosure to him or any parent or guardian of any information contained in the report would be likely to create a risk of significant harm to the offender, a complete copy of the report need not be given to offender or, as the case may be, to that parent or guardian: CJA 2003, s 156(3).
9. The Pre-Sentence Report Disclosure (Prescription of Prosecutors) Order 1998, SI 1998/191 has been made. For those prosecutors who have been prescribed, see the note to s 50 of the Crime (Sentences) Act 1997, in this PART, post.
10. Criminal Justice Act 2003, s 159(4).
11. *R v Smith* [1968] Crim LR 33.
12. *Thompson v Thompson* (1975) [1986] 1 FLR 212n, CA.
13. Criminal Procedure Rules 2005, Part 44, in PART I: MAGISTRATES' COURTS, PROCEDURE, ante.

MEDICAL REPORTS

3–55 A medical report may be asked for where the court is satisfied that the accused did the act or made the omission charged, but is of opinion that an inquiry ought to be made into his physical or mental condition before the method of dealing with him is determined[1].

Where the offender is or appears to be mentally disordered[2], the court must obtain and consider a medical report before passing a custodial sentence unless, in the circumstances of the case, the court is of the opinion that it is unnecessary to obtain such a report[3]. This requirement is additional to any requirement also to obtain a pre sentence report[4]. "Medical report" here means a report as to an offender's mental condition made or submitted orally or in writing by a registered medical practitioner who is approved for the purposes of s 12 of the Mental Health Act 1983 by the Secretary of State as having special experience in the diagnosis or treatment of a mental disorder[5].

The court is required to send to the place where he is committed or is to be examined, a statement of the reasons why it is of opinion that the inquiry ought to be made, and also any information it already has about the accused's physical and mental condition[6].

A written report purporting to be signed by a medical practitioner may be received in evidence without proof of the signature or qualifications of the practitioner, but the court may in any case require the practitioner to give oral evidence. A copy of the report is given to counsel or solicitor for the accused. If he is not represented, the substance of the report shall be disclosed to him or, where he is a child or young person, to his parent or guardian if in court. In all cases the accused has the right to require the practitioner to be called to give oral evidence, and to call evidence in rebuttal of what is said in the report[7].

A doctor who is instructed by the defendant himself to prepare a medical report for use at the sentencing hearing is not in breach of his duty of confidence to the defendant by disclosing the report to the prosecution, if there is a stronger public interest that the report should be disclosed because the defendant is a danger to the public[8].

1. Powers of Criminal Courts (Sentencing) Act 2000, s 11, this PART, post.
2. Ie suffering from a mental disorder within the meaning of the Mental Health Act 1983: Criminal Justice Act 2003, s 157(5). See this PART, post.
3. CJA 2003, s 157(1) and (2).
4. CJA 2003, s 157(7).
5. CJA 2003, s 157(6).
6. Magistrates' Courts Rules 1981, r 24.
7. Mental Health Act 1983, s 54(2) and (3) in PART VIII: title MENTAL HEALTH, post.
8. *R v Crozier* (1990) 12 Cr App Rep (S) 206, [1991] Crim LR 138, CA.

SOLDIERS APPEARING BEFORE MAGISTRATES' COURTS

3–56 Generally an officer from a soldier's unit stationed in the United Kingdom will attend court with him when he appears. This will depend on the seriousness of the offence and the distance of the unit from the court. The officer will be able to tell the court about the soldier's general character, his length of service, net rate of pay with details of deductions, present employment or trade, any particular domestic problems, and particulars of conviction by a court-martial (except minor offences of a purely military character). He will also (if asked) tell the court that a sentence of imprisonment (including a suspended sentence) will almost certainly require discharge of the soldier from the Army; he will be able to say whether there are exceptional grounds for recommending the soldier's retention[1]. The officer will arrange to pay any fine, penalty, damages, compensation or costs out of the unit's imprest account unless the money could not be recovered from the soldier's account within three months, or his earlier discharge or transfer to the Regular Reserve[2].

Except when on duty under arms, Service male personnel are not to wear their headdress while the judge or magistrate is present in court[3].

1. Queen's Regulations for the Army 1975, reg 6.174.
2. See also the Army Act 1955, s 146, in PART VIII, title ARMED FORCES, post.
3. Queen's Regulations for the Army 1975, reg 7.025.

DEFERRING SENTENCE

3–57 Section 278 of, and Sch 23 to, the Criminal Justice Act 2003 substituted new ss 1–1D for ss 1 and 2 of the Powers of Criminal Courts (Sentencing) Act 2000. These provisions empower the court, without prejudice to any other power to defer passing sentence for any other purpose, to defer passing sentence for up to 6 months for the purpose of enabling the court which will pass sentence to have regard to the defendant's conduct after conviction, including, where appropriate, the making by him of any reparation for the offence, or any change in his circumstances[1]. The eventual sentencing court may also have regard to the extent to which the offender has complied with any requirements imposed by the court which deferred sentence[2].

Sentence may not be deferred unless: (*a*) the offender consents; (*b*) the offender undertakes to comply with any requirements as to his conduct during the period of deferment that the court considers it appropriate to impose; and (*c*) the court is satisfied, having regard to the nature of the offence and the character and circumstances of the offender, that it would be in the interests of justice to defer sentence[3].

Sentence may not be deferred more than once[4]. Copies of the order, including any requirements, must be served forthwith on the offender and any person appointed to supervise him during the period of deferment; the latter may be a probation officer or any other person whom the court thinks appropriate to supervise him and who consents so to act[5].

When the court defers sentence it must not, on the same occasion, remand the offender[6].

If the offender fails to appear on the date to which sentence was deferred the court may issue a summons or warrant[7].

Where the person appointed to supervise the offender has reported that the offender has failed to comply with one or more of the requirements imposed by the deferring court, the court may issue a summons or warrant to bring him before the court, and if the court is satisfied as to the non-compliance it may deal with the offender before the end of the period of deferment[8].

If the offender is convicted in Great Britain of any offence during the period of deferment, the court which deferred sentence may deal him before the end of the period of deferment and may issue a summons or warrant to secure the attendance of the offender for that purpose[9]. Where a court has deferred sentencing for an offence and the offender is convicted of any other offence during the period of deferment, the court which passes sentence for the new offence may also deal with him for the deferred sentence offence, except that this power must not be exercised by a magistrates' court if the deferring court was the Crown Court[10].

The power of the court sentencing for the deferred offence, under whichever of the above means that power arises, includes the power to deal with the offender in any way in which the original court could have dealt with him if it had not deferred sentence, and in the case of a magistrates' court this includes committing the offender to the Crown Court for sentence under s 3 of the Powers of Criminal Courts (Sentencing) Act 2000[11].

Where it falls upon a magistrates' court to determine sentence at the end of the period of deferment, or to determine before the end of the period of deferment whether or not there has been non-compliance with a requirement made of the offender, and a justice of the peace is satisfied that the person appointed to supervise the offender during the period of deferment is likely to be able to give evidence that may assist the court in relation to either of these determinations and that that person will not voluntarily attend as a witness, the justice of the peace may issue a summons to require the supervisor's attendance[12].

The Sentencing Guidelines Council has issued guidance on the use of deferred sentences[13].

1. Powers of Criminal Courts (Sentencing) Act 2000, s 1, this PART, post.
2. PCC(S)A 2000, s 1(2).
3. PCC(S)A 2000, s 1(3). The requirements may include a requirement of residence: ibid, s 1A(1).
4. PCC(S)A 2000, s 1(4).
5. PCC(S)A 2000, s 1(5). As to the appointment of a supervisor, and his duties to monitor the offender and to provide information to the court, see PCC(S)A 2000, s 1A.
6. PCC(S)A 2000, s 1(6).
7. PCC(S)A 2000, s 1(7).
8. PCC(S)A 2000, s 1B.
9. PCC(S)A 2000, s 1C(1), (4).
10. PCC(S)A 2000, s 1C(3).
11. PCC(S)A 2000, s 1D(2).
12. PCC(S)A 2000, s 1D(4)–(6).
13. See para **3–58**, below.

GUIDANCE OF THE SENTENCING GUIDELINES COUNCIL ON DEFERRED SENTENCES

3–58 The following guidance on deferred sentences has been given by the Sentencing Guidelines Council as part of its guidance in relation to the sentencing framework contained in the Criminal Justice Act 2003.

'SECTION 1 PART 2 – DEFERRED SENTENCES

A Statutory Provisions.

1.2.1 Under the existing legislation[1], a court can defer a sentence for up to six months, provided the offender consents and the court considers that deferring the sentence is in the interests of justice.

1.2.2 The new provisions[2] continue to require the consent of the offender and that the court be satisfied that the making of such a decision is in the interests of justice. However, it is also stated that the power to defer sentence can only be exercised where:

"the offender undertakes to comply with any requirements as to his conduct during the period of the deferment that the court considers it appropriate to impose;"[3]

1.2.3 This enables the court to impose a wide variety of conditions (including a residence requirement)[4]. The Act allows the court to appoint the probation service or other responsible person to oversee the offender's conduct during this period and prepare a report for the court at the point of sentence i.e. the end of the deferment period.

1.2.4 As under the existing legislation, if the offender commits another offence during the deferment period the court may have the power to sentence for both the original and the new offence at once. Sentence cannot be deferred for more than six months and, in most circumstances, no more than one period of deferment can be granted[5].

1.2.5 A significant change is the provision enabling a court to deal with an offender before the end of the period of deferment[6]. For example if the court is satisfied that the offender has failed to comply with one or more requirements imposed in connection with the deferment, the offender can be brought back before the court and the court can proceed to sentence.

B Use of Deferred Sentences.

1.2.6 Under the new framework, there is a wider range of sentencing options open to the courts, including the increased availability of suspended sentences, and deferred sentences are likely to be used in very limited circumstances. A deferred sentence enables the court to review the conduct of the defendant before passing sentence, having first prescribed certain requirements. It also provides several opportunities for an offender to have some influence as to the sentence passed –

(a) it tests the commitment of the offender not to re-offend;
(b) it gives the offender an opportunity to do something where progress can be shown within a short period;
(c) it provides the offender with an opportunity to behave or refrain from behaving in a particular way that will be relevant to sentence.

1.2.7 Given the new power to require undertakings and the ability to enforce those undertakings before the end of the period of deferral, the decision to defer sentence should be predominantly for a small group of cases at either the custody threshold or the community sentence threshold where the sentencer feels that there would be particular value in giving the offender the opportunities listed because, if the offender complies with the requirements, a different sentence will be justified at the end of the deferment period. This could be a community sentence instead of a custodial sentence or a fine or discharge instead of a community sentence. It may, rarely, enable a custodial sentence to be suspended rather than imposed immediately.

The use of deferred sentences should be predominantly for a small group of cases close to a significant threshold where, should the defendant be prepared to adapt his behaviour in a way clearly specified by the sentencer, the court may be prepared to impose a lesser sentence.

1.2.8 A court may impose any conditions during the period of deferment that it considers appropriate[7]. These could be specific requirements as set out in the provisions for community sentences[21], or requirements that are drawn more widely. These should be specific, measurable conditions so that the offender knows exactly what is required and the court can assess compliance; the restriction on liberty should be limited to ensure that the offender has a reasonable expectation of being able to comply whilst maintaining his or her social responsibilities.

1.2.9 Given the need for clarity in the mind of the offender and the possibility of sentence by another court, the court should give a clear indication (and make a written record) of the type of sentence it would be minded to impose if it had not decided to defer and ensure that the offender understands the consequences of failure to comply with the court's wishes during the deferral period.

When deferring sentence, the sentencer must make clear the consequence of not complying with any requirements and should indicate the type of sentence it would be minded to impose. Sentencers should impose specific, measurable conditions that do not involve a serious restriction on liberty.'

1. Powers of Criminal Courts (Sentencing) Act 2000, ss 1 and 2.
2. Criminal Justice Act 2003, Sch 23 repealing and replacing ss 1 and 2 of the 2000 Act.
3. Criminal Justice Act 2003, new s 1(3)(b) as inserted by Sch 23 to the Criminal Justice Act 2003.
4. Criminal Justice Act 2003, new s 1A(1).
5. Criminal Justice Act 2003, new s 1(4).
6. Criminal Justice Act 2003, new s 1B.
7. Criminal Justice Act 2003, new s 1(3)(b) as inserted by sch 23 to the Criminal Justice Act 2003.

Principles of sentencing

OVERARCHING PRINCIPLES – THE GUIDANCE OF THE SENTENCING GUIDELINES COUNCIL ON SERIOUSNESS AND THE SENTENCING THRESHOLDS

3–70 The Sentencing Guidelines Council has issued the following guidelines.

'A Statutory Provisions.

1.1 In every case where the offender is aged 18 or over at the time of conviction, the court must have regard to the five purposes of sentencing contained in section 142(1) Criminal Justice Act 2003:

(a) the punishment of offenders
(b) the reduction of crime (including its reduction by deterrence)
(c) the reform and rehabilitation of offenders
(d) the protection of the public
(e) the making of reparation by offenders to persons affected by their offence

1.2 The Act does not indicate that any one purpose should be more important than any other and in practice they may all be relevant to a greater or lesser degree in any individual case – the sentencer has the task of determining the manner in which they apply.

1.3 The sentencer must start by considering the seriousness of the offence, the assessment of which will:

- determine which of the sentencing thresholds has been crossed;
- indicate whether a custodial, community or other sentence is the most appropriate;
- be the key factor in deciding the length of a custodial sentence, the onerousness of requirements to be incorporated in a community sentence and the amount of any fine imposed.

1.4 A court is required to pass a sentence that is commensurate with the seriousness of the offence. The seriousness of an offence is determined by two main parameters; the culpability of the offender and the harm caused or risked being caused by the offence.

1.5 Section 143(1) Criminal Justice Act 2003 provides:

"In considering the seriousness of any offence, the court must consider the offender's culpability in committing the offence and any harm which the offence caused, was intended to cause or might foreseeably have caused."

B Culpability.

1.6 Four levels of criminal culpability can be identified for sentencing purposes:

1.7 Where the offender;

(i) has the intention to cause harm, with the highest culpability when an offence is planned. The worse the harm intended, the greater the seriousness.

(ii) is reckless as to whether harm is caused, that is, where the offender appreciates at least some harm would be caused but proceeds giving no thought to the consequences even though the extent of the risk would be obvious to most people.

(iii) has knowledge of the specific risks entailed by his actions even though he does not intend to cause the harm that results.

(iv) is guilty of negligence.

Note: There are offences where liability is strict and no culpability need be proved for the purposes of obtaining a conviction, but the degree of culpability is still important when deciding sentence. The extent to which recklessness, knowledge or negligence are involved in a particular offence will vary.

C Harm.

1.8 The relevant provision is widely drafted so that it encompasses those offences where harm is caused but also those where neither individuals nor the community suffer harm but a risk of harm is present.

To individual victims

1.9 The types of harm caused or risked by different types of criminal activity are diverse and victims may suffer physical injury, sexual violation, financial loss, damage to health or psychological distress. There are gradations of harm within all of these categories.

1.10 The nature of harm will depend on personal characteristics and circumstances of the victim and the court's assessment of harm will be an effective and important way of taking into consideration the impact of a particular crime on the victim.

1.11 In some cases no actual harm may have resulted and the court will be concerned with assessing the relative dangerousness of the offender's conduct; it will consider the likelihood of harm occurring and the gravity of the harm that could have resulted.

To the community

1.12 Some offences cause harm to the community at large (instead of or as well as to an individual victim) and may include economic loss, harm to public health, or interference with the administration of justice.

Other types of harm

1.13 There are other types of harm that are more difficult to define or categorise. For example, cruelty to animals certainly causes significant harm to the animal but there may also be a human victim who also suffers psychological distress and/or financial loss.

1.14 Some conduct is criminalised purely by reference to public feeling or social mores. In addition, public concern about the damage caused by some behaviour, both to individuals and to society as a whole, can influence public perception of the harm caused, for example, by the supply of prohibited drugs.

D The Assessment of Culpability and Harm.

1.15 Section 143(1) makes clear that the assessment of the seriousness of any individual offence must take account not only of any harm actually caused by the offence, but also of any harm that was intended to be caused or might foreseeably be caused by the offence.

1.16 Assessing seriousness is a difficult task, particularly where there is an imbalance between culpability and harm:

- sometimes the harm that actually results is greater than the harm intended by the offender;
- in other circumstances, the offender's culpability may be at a higher level than the harm resulting from the offence.

1.17 Harm must always be judged in the light of culpability. The precise level of culpability will be determined by such factors as motivation, whether the offence was planned or spontaneous or whether the offender was in a position of trust.

Culpability will be greater if:

- an offender deliberately causes more harm than is necessary for the commission of the offence, or
- where an offender targets a vulnerable victim (because of their old age or youth, disability or by virtue of the job they do).

1.18 Where unusually serious harm results and was unintended and beyond the control of the offender, culpability will be significantly influenced by the extent to which the harm could have been foreseen.

1.19 If much more harm, or much less harm has been caused by the offence than the offender intended or foresaw, the culpability of the offender, depending on the circumstances, may be regarded as carrying greater or lesser weight as appropriate.

The culpability of the offender in the particular circumstances of an individual case should be the initial factor in determining the seriousness of an offence.

(i) Aggravating Factors

1.20 Sentencing guidelines for a particular offence will normally include a list of aggravating features which, if present in an individual instance of the offence, would indicate either a higher than usual level of culpability on the part of the offender, or a greater than usual degree of harm caused by the offence (or sometimes both).

1.21 The lists below bring together the most important aggravating features with potential application to more than one offence or class of offences. They include some factors (such as the vulnerability of victims or abuse of trust) which are integral features of certain offences; in such cases, the presence of the aggravating factor is already reflected in the penalty for the offence and cannot be used as justification for increasing the sentence further. The lists are not intended to be comprehensive and the aggravating factors are not listed in any particular order of priority. On occasions, two or more of the factors listed will describe the same feature of the offence and care needs to be taken to avoid "double-counting". Those factors starred with an asterisk are statutory aggravating factors where the statutory provisions are in force. Those marked with a hash are yet to be brought into force but as factors in an individual case are still relevant and should be taken into account.

1.22 Factors indicating higher culpability:

- Offence committed whilst on bail for other offences
- Failure to respond to previous sentences
- Offence was racially or religiously aggravated
- Offence motivated by, or demonstrating, hostility to the victim based on his or her sexual orientation (or presumed sexual orientation)
- Offence motivated by, or demonstrating, hostility based on the victim's disability (or presumed disability)
- Previous conviction(s), particularly where a pattern of repeat offending is disclosed
- Planning of an offence
- An intention to commit more serious harm than actually resulted from the offence
- Offenders operating in groups or gangs
- "Professional" offending
- Commission of the offence for financial gain (where this is not inherent in the offence itself)
- High level of profit from the offence
- An attempt to conceal or dispose of evidence
- Failure to respond to warnings or concerns expressed by others about the offender's behaviour
- Offence committed whilst on licence
- Offence motivated by hostility towards a minority group, or a member or members of it
- Deliberate targeting of vulnerable victim(s)
- Commission of an offence while under the influence of alcohol or drugs
- Use of a weapon to frighten or injure victim
- Deliberate and gratuitous violence or damage to property, over and above what is needed to carry out the offence
- Abuse of power
- Abuse of a position of trust

1.23 Factors indicating a more than usually serious degree of harm:

- Multiple victims
- An especially serious physical or psychological effect on the victim, even if unintended
- A sustained assault or repeated assaults on the same victim
- Victim is particularly vulnerable
- Location of the offence (for example, in an isolated place)
- Offence is committed against those working in the public sector or providing a service to the public
- Presence of others e.g. relatives, especially children or partner of the victim
- Additional degradation of the victim (e.g. taking photographs of a victim as part of a sexual offence)
- In property offences, high value (including sentimental value) of property to the victim, or substantial consequential loss e.g. where the theft of equipment causes serious disruption to a victim's life or business)

(ii) Mitigating factors

1.24 Some factors may indicate that an offender's culpability is unusually low, or that the harm caused by an offence is less than usually serious.

1.25 Factors indicating significantly lower culpability:

- A greater degree of provocation than normally expected
- Mental illness or disability
- Youth or age, where it affects the responsibility of the individual defendant
- The fact that the offender played only a minor role in the offence

(iii) Personal mitigation

1.26 Section 166(1) Criminal Justice Act 2003 makes provision for a sentencer to take account of any matters that 'in the opinion of the court, are relevant in mitigation of sentence'.

1.27 When the court has formed an initial assessment of the seriousness of the offence, then it should consider any offender mitigation. The issue of remorse should be taken into account at this point along with other mitigating features such as admissions to the police in interview.

(iv) Reduction for a guilty plea

1.28 Sentencers will normally reduce the severity of a sentence to reflect an early guilty plea. This subject is covered by a separate guideline and provides a sliding scale reduction with a normal maximum one-third reduction being given to offenders who enter a guilty plea at the first reasonable opportunity.

1.29 Credit may also be given for ready co-operation with the authorities. This will depend on the particular circumstances of the individual case.

E The Sentencing Thresholds.

1.30 Assessing the seriousness of an offence is only the first step in the process of determining the appropriate sentence in an individual case. Matching the offence to a type and level of sentence is a separate and complex exercise assisted by the application of the respective threshold tests for custodial and community sentences.

The Custody Threshold

1.31 Section 152(2) Criminal Justice Act 2003 provides:

> "The court must not pass a custodial sentence unless it is of the opinion that the offence, or the combination of the offence and one or more offences associated with it, was so serious that neither a fine alone nor a community sentence can be justified for the offence."

1.32 In applying the threshold test, sentencers should note:

- the clear intention of the threshold test is to reserve prison as a punishment for the most serious offences;
- it is impossible to determine definitively which features of a particular offence make it serious enough to merit a custodial sentence;
- passing the custody threshold does not mean that a custodial sentence should be deemed inevitable, and custody can still be avoided in the light of personal mitigation or where there is a suitable intervention in the community which provides sufficient restriction (by way of punishment) while addressing the rehabilitation of the offender to prevent future crime. For example, a prolific offender who currently could expect a short custodial sentence (which, in advance of custody plus, would have no provision for supervision on release) might more appropriately receive a suitable community sentence.

1.33 The approach to the imposition of a custodial sentence under the new framework should be as follows:

- (a) has the custody threshold been passed?
- (b) if so, is it unavoidable that a custodial sentence be imposed?
- (c) if so, can that sentence be suspended? (sentencers should be clear that they would have imposed a custodial sentence if the power to suspend had not been available)
- (d) if not, can the sentence be served intermittently?
- (e) if not, impose a sentence which takes immediate effect for the term commensurate with the seriousness of the offence.

The Threshold for Community Sentences

1.34 Section 148(1) Criminal Justice Act 2003 provides:

> "A court must not pass a community sentence on an offender unless it is of the opinion that the offence, or the combination of the offence and one or more offences associated with it, was serious enough to warrant such a sentence."

1.35 In addition, the threshold for a community sentence can be crossed even though the seriousness criterion is not met. Section 151 Criminal Justice Act 2003 provides that, in relation to an offender aged 16 or over on whom, on 3 or more previous occasions, sentences had been passed consisting only of a fine, a community sentence may be imposed (if it is in the interests of justice) despite the fact that the seriousness of the current offence (and others associated with it) might not warrant such a sentence.

1.36 Sentencers should consider all of the disposals available (within or below the threshold passed) at the time of sentence before reaching the provisional decision to make a community sentence, so that, even where the threshold for a community sentence has been passed, a financial penalty or discharge may still be an appropriate penalty.

Summary

1.37 It would not be feasible to provide a form of words or to devise any formula that would provide a general solution to the problem of where the custody threshold lies. Factors vary too widely between offences for this to be done. It is the task of guidelines for individual offences to provide more detailed guidance on what features within that offence point to a custodial sentence, and also to deal with issues such as sentence length, the appropriate requirements for a community sentence or the use of appropriate ancillary orders.

Having assessed the seriousness of an individual offence, sentencers must consult the sentencing guidelines for an offence of that type for guidance on the facts that are likely to indicate whether a custodial sentence or other disposal is most likely to be appropriate.

F Prevalence.

1.38 The seriousness of an individual case should be judged on its own dimensions of harm and culpability rather than as part of a collective social harm. It is legitimate for the overall approach to sentencing levels for particular offences to be guided by their cumulative effect. However, it would be wrong to further penalise individual offenders by increasing sentence length for committing an individual offence of that type.

1.39 There may be exceptional local circumstances that arise which may lead a court to decide that prevalence should influence sentencing levels. The pivotal issue in such cases will be the harm being caused to the community. It is essential that sentencers both have supporting evidence from an external source (for example the local Criminal Justice Board) to justify claims that a particular crime is prevalent in their area and are satisfied that there is a compelling need to treat the offence more seriously than elsewhere.

The key factor in determining whether sentencing levels should be enhanced in response to prevalence will be the level of harm being caused in the locality. Enhanced sentences should be exceptional and in response to exceptional circumstances. Sentencers must sentence within the sentencing guidelines once the prevalence has been addressed.'

RACIAL AND RELIGIOUS AGGRAVATION

3–71 *Offences which are specifically racially or religiously aggravated (ss 29–32 of the Crime and Disorder Act 1998).* The principles stated below are derived from cases that were concerned with racial aggravation, but it is submitted that they are equally applicable to cases of religious aggravation.

Since Parliament has increased the maximum sentence of 5 years for assault occasioning actual bodily harm to 7 years where that offence is racially aggravated, it will generally be appropriate, following a trial, that a period of up to 2 years' imprisonment should be added to the term of imprisonment otherwise appropriate for the offence, had it not been racially aggravated. Accordingly, it will often be helpful if the sentencer first considers, though he need not express it, the appropriate sentence for the offence in the absence of racial aggravation and then adds a further term for the racial element so that the total sentence reflects the overall criminality[1]. In some cases, however, where the racial aggravation is so inherent and integral to the offence itself it is not sensible to assess the overall criminality involved in such a discrete way[2].

The level of sentence for a racially aggravated offence, having regard to the possible maximum addition, will depend on all the circumstances of the particular case. Relevant factors will include the nature of the hostile demonstration, whether by language, gestures or weapons; its length; its location and the number of those demonstrating and those demonstrated against[1].

The increase from 5 to 7 years of the maximum terms for racially aggravated assault occasioning actual bodily harm and maliciously wounding/grievous bodily harm does not set a maximum for the term that should be added for other offences involving racial aggravation; the appropriate amount to add in other cases will depend upon all the circumstances[3].

The offence of racially aggravated threatening, abusive or insulting words, created by s 31 of the Crime and Disorder Act 1998, which is punishable as an either way offence with a term of imprisonment up to 2 years, reflects the seriousness with which Parliament regards racial aggravation. In bad examples of the offence, the sentence needs to be severe to reflect public concern about conduct which damages good race relations within the community[4].

Offences other than those which are specifically racially aggravated. Where the court is considering the seriousness of an offence other than one which is specifically racially aggravated under ss 29–32 of the Crime and Disorder Act 1998, and the court finds that the offence was racially or religiously aggravated as those terms are defined by s 28 of the above Act, it shall treat that fact as an aggravating factor and shall state in open court that the offence was so aggravated[5]. However, where an allegation of racial or religious aggravation is withdrawn by agreement between the parties at the start of the trial, that reduces the ambit of the offence on which the defendant is liable to be sentenced and convicted; the judge cannot introduce racial or religious aggravation at the stage of sentencing[6].

Where the racial aggravation comprises only a racist remark, but it is unclear which of several defendants made that remark, it is not open to the court to make all the members of the group criminally liable for the remark; therefore, the sentence should not be increased on account of racial aggravation[7].

---

1. *R v Saunders* [2000] 1 Cr App Rep 458, [2000] 2 Cr App Rep (S) 71, [2000] Crim LR 314, CA. See also *R v Foster* [2001] 1 Cr App Rep (S) 383; *R v Beglin* [2002] EWCA 1887, [2003] 1 Cr App Rep (S) 21.
2. *R v Fitzgerald* [2003] EWCA Crim 2875, [2004] 12 Cr App R (S) 74.
3. *R v Morrison* [2001] 1 Cr App Rep (S) 12, [2000] Crim LR 605 (where the circumstances justified an increase of 2 years for a burglary that was racially aggravated).
4. *R v Miller* [1999] 2 Cr App Rep (S) 392, [1999] Crim LR 590, CA (sentence of 18 months' imprisonment upheld for offence of racially aggravated threatening words and behaviour directed to a conductor of a train). See also *R v Clark* [2003] EWCA Crim 3143, [2004] 2 Cr App R (S) 1 (sentence reduced from 21 to 12 months' imprisonment where, on the underground, the defendant committed racially aggravated harassment causing fear of violence, first towards a female passenger and then towards an off duty police officer, but he had pleaded guilty and had been attending counselling for alcohol addiction while in custody; *R v Gaunt* [2003] EWCA Crim 3925, [2004] 2 Cr App R (S) 37 (manager failing to prevent the racially aggravated harassment of one of his employees by three other employees: sentence reduced from 18 to 6 months' imprisonment because the defendant was aware only of a small part of the conduct that had taken place); and *R v Barrie* [2005] EWCA Crim 1318, [2006] 1 Cr App R (S) 40 (6 months' imprisonment following a trial on a charge of religiously aggravated intention harassment upheld where the appellant addressed abusive remarks to 2 television licensing enquiry agents on the basis of their religion).
5. Criminal Justice Act 2003, s 144: see this PART, post.
6. *G and T v DPP* [2004] EWHC Admin 183, (2004) 168 JP 313. See also *R v McGillivray* [2005] EWCA Crim 604, [2005] 2 Cr App R (S) 60.
7. *R v Davies* [2003] EWCA Crim 3700, [2004] Crim LR 677.

AGGRAVATION RELATED TO DISABILITY OR SEXUAL ORIENTATION

3–72 If, at the time of committing the offence or immediately before or after doing so, the offender demonstrated towards the victim of the offence hostility based (whether wholly or only partly) on the latter's sexual or presumed sexual orientation or a disability or presumed disability, or the offence is motivated (whether wholly or partly) by hostility towards persons who are of a particular sexual orientation or towards persons who have a disability or a particular disability, the court must treat the fact that the offence was committed in any of those circumstances as an aggravating factor and must state in open court that the offence was committed in such circumstances[1].

---

1. Criminal Justice Act 2003, s 146: see this PART, post.

3–73   Other statutory aggravating factors: offences committed while on bail. In considering the seriousness of any offence committed while the offender was on bail, the court must treat the fact that it was committed in those circumstances as an aggravating factor[1].

---

1. Criminal Justice Act 2003, s 143(4): see this PART, POST.

CREDIT FOR PLEADING GUILTY – THE GUIDANCE OF THE SENTENCING GUIDELINES COUNCIL

3–74   Reduction in sentence for a guilty plea. The following guidelines have been issued by the Sentencing Guidelines Council. '1.1 This guideline applies whether a case is dealt with in a magistrates' court or in the Crown Court and whenever practicable in the youth court (taking into account legislative restrictions such as those relevant to the length of Detention and Training orders).

1.2 (Offence of murder)

1.3 This guideline can also be found at www.sentencing-guidelines.gov.uk or can be obtained from the Council's Secretariat at Room G11, Allington Towers, 19 Allington Street, London SW1E 5EB.

B Statement of Purpose.

2.1 A reduction in sentence is appropriate because a guilty plea avoids the need for a trial (thus enabling other cases to be disposed of more expeditiously), shortens the gap between charge and sentence, saves considerable cost, and, in the case of an early plea, saves victims and witnesses from the concern about having to give evidence.

2.2 It is a separate issue from aggravation and mitigation generally.

2.3 The sentencer should address the issue of remorse, together with any other mitigating features present, such as admissions to the police in interview, separately, when deciding the most appropriate length of sentence before calculating the reduction for the guilty plea.

2.4 The implications of other offences that an offender has asked to be taken into consideration should also be reflected in the sentence before the reduction for guilty plea has been applied.

2.5 A reduction in sentence should be applied to any of the punitive elements of a penalty. The guilty plea reduction has no impact on sentencing decisions in relation to ancillary orders.

2.6 Where an offence crosses the threshold for imposition of a community or custodial sentence, application of the reduction principle may properly form the basis for imposing a fine or discharge rather than a community sentence, or an alternative to an immediate custodial sentence. Where the reduction is applied in this way, the actual sentence imposed incorporates the reduction.

C Application of the Reduction Principle.

3.1 Recommended Approach

(The following is shown in the guidelines In flow diagram form):

(i)   The court decides sentence for the offences taking into account TICs.

(ii)   The court selects the amount of the reducing by reference to the sliding scale.

(iii) The Court applies a reduction to the sentence decided on.

(iv) When pronouncing sentence the court should usually state what the sentence would have been if there had been no reduction as a result of the guilty plea.)

D Determining the Level of Reduction.

4.1 The level of reduction should be a proportion of the total sentence imposed, with the proportion based upon the stage in the proceedings at which the guilty plea was entered.

4.2 Save where section 152(3) of the Posers of Criminal Courts (Sentencing) Act 2000 applies (this provision will be superseded by s 144(2) of the Criminal Justice Act 2003 Act) the level of the reduction will be gauged on a sliding scale ranging from a maximum of one third (where the guilty plea was entered at the first reasonable opportunity in relation to the offence for which sentence is being imposed), reducing to a maximum of one quarter (where a trial date has been set) and to a maximum of one tenth (for a guilty plea entered at the 'door of the court' or after the trial has begun) (this is illustrated pictorially in the guidelines)

4.3 The level of reduction should reflect the stage at which the offender indicated a willingness to admit guilt to the offence for which he is eventually sentenced.

(i)   The maximum reduction will be given only where the offender indicated willingness to admit guilt at the first reasonable opportunity. When this occurs will vary from case to case. See Annex 2 for illustrative examples.

(ii)   Where the admission of guilt comes later than the first reasonable opportunity, the reduction for guilty plea will be less than one third.

(iii) Where the plea of guilty comes very late, it is still appropriate to give some reduction.
(iv) If after pleading guilty there is a Newton hearing and the offender's version of the circumstances of the offence is rejected, this should be taken into account in determining the level of reduction.
(v) If the not guilty plea was entered and maintained for tactical reasons (such as to retain privileges whilst on remand), a late guilty plea should attract very little, if any, discount.

E Withholding a Reduction.

On the basis of dangerousness
5.1 Where the court has determined that a longer than commensurate, extended, or indeterminate sentence is required for the protection of the public, the minimum custodial term but not the protection of public element of the sentence should be reduced to reflect the plea.
Where an offender is caught "red-handed"
5.2 Since the purpose of giving credit is to encourage those who are guilty to plead at the earliest opportunity, there is no reason why credit should be withheld or reduced on these grounds alone. The normal sliding scale should apply.
Where the maximum penalty for the offence is thought to be too low
5.3 The sentencer is bound to sentence for the offence with which the offender has been charged, and to which he has pleaded guilty. The sentencer cannot remedy perceived defects (for example an inadequate charge or maximum penalty) by refusal of the appropriate discount.
Where jurisdictional issues arise
(i) Where two or more summary only offences are to be sentenced
5.4 In circumstances where the maximum sentence available is six months imprisonment and the sentence for each offence should be reduced to reflect the guilty plea, it may be appropriate for the sentences to be ordered to run consecutively to each other. The overall sentence would not undermine the general principle that the maximum sentence should not be imposed following a guilty plea, since the decision whether or not to make the individual sentences concurrent or consecutive will follow the normal principles that apply to that decision. However, the totality of the sentence should make some allowance for the entry of a guilty plea.
(ii) Where a maximum sentence might still be imposed
5.5 Despite a guilty plea being entered which would normally attract a reduction in sentence, a magistrates' court may impose a sentence of imprisonment of 6 months for a single either-way offence where that offence would have attracted a sentence of in the region of 9 months if it had been committed to the Crown Court.
5.6 Similarly, a detention and training order of 24 months may be imposed on an offender aged under 18 if the offence is one which would but for the plea have ttracted a sentence of long-term detention in excess of 24 months under the Powers of Criminal Courts (Sentencing) Act 2000, section 91.

F (Application to Sentencing for Murder).
ANNEX 1 CRIMINAL JUSTICE ACT 2003.
(Reproduces the relevant provisions of the Criminal Justice Act 2003.)
ANNEX 2 FIRST REASONABLE OPPORTUNITY.   1. The critical time for determining the maximum reduction for a guilty plea is the first reasonable opportunity for the defendant to have indicated a willingness to plead guilty. This opportunity will vary with a wide range of factors and the Court will need to make a judgement on the particular facts of the case before it.
2. The key principle is that the purpose of giving a reduction is to recognise the benefits that come from a guilty plea both for those directly involved in the case in question but also in enabling Courts more quickly to deal with other outstanding cases.
3. This Annex seeks to help Courts to adopt a consistent approach by giving examples of circumstances where a determination will have to be made.
(*a*) the first reasonable opportunity may be the first time that a defendant appears before the court and has the opportunity to plead guilty.
(*b*) but the court may consider that it would be reasonable to have expected an indication of willingness even earlier, perhaps whilst under interview.
Note: For (a) and (b) to apply, the Court will need to be satisfied that the defendant (and any legal adviser) would have had sufficient information about the allegations
(*c*) where an offence triable either way is committed to the Crown Court for trial and the defendant pleads guilty at the first hearing in that Court, the reduction will be less than if there had been an indication of a guilty plea given to the magistrates' court (maximum reduction of one third) but more than if the plea had been entered after a trial date had been set (maximum reduction of one quarter), and is likely to be in the region of 30%.
(*d*) where a defendant is convicted after pleading guilty to an alternative (lesser) charge to that to which he/she had pleaded not guilty, the extent of any reduction will have to be judged against the earliness of any indication of willingness to plead guilty to the lesser charge and the reason why that lesser charge was proceeded with in preference to the original charge.'

CHILDREN AND YOUNG PERSONS

3–75 Every court in dealing with a child or young person shall have regard to the welfare of the child or young person, and shall in a proper case take steps for removing him from undesirable surroundings and for securing that proper provision is made for his education and training[1]. The words "conviction" and "sentence" are not to be used in relation to children and young persons dealt with summarily[2].

---

1. Children and Young Persons Act 1933, s 44 in PART V: YOUTH COURTS, post.
2. Children and Young Persons Act 1933, s 59 in PART V: YOUTH COURTS, post.

EFFECT OF SUBSTANTIAL DELAY BETWEEN OFFENCE AND CONVICTION

3–76 Where there is a substantial interval between the offence and the conviction, the court must first consider what sentence the defendant would have received if he had been dealt with at the time that the offences had occurred; once that has been determined it must be treated as a powerful indication in deciding the proper sentence at the present time[1].

---

1. See *R v Fowler* [2002] EWCA Crim 620, [2002] 2 Cr App Rep (S) 463, [2002] Crim LR 521 and the commentary thereon. See also *R v Bowers* [1999] 2 Cr App Rep (S) 97; *R v Cuddington* (1994) 16 Cr App Rep (S) 246; and *R v Dashwood* (1994) 16 Cr App Rep (S) 733. See also *R v Ghafoor* [2002] EWCA Crim 1857, [2003] 1 Cr App Rep (S) 84, [2002] Crim LR 739 (offender who attained 18 between the date of offence and the date of conviction should have received the same term of detention as would have been imposed if he had not attained that age); and *R v LM* [2002] EWCA Crim 3407, [2003] 2 Cr App Rep (S) 26 (offender who attained 15 between the date of offence and the date of conviction should normally receive the same sentence as he would have received on the former date).

OTHER EXCEPTIONAL, PERSONAL FACTORS

3–77 Asperger's Syndrome (which is a form of, or is related to, autism), which can give rise to major problems with social relationships and unusual behaviour, combined with a very high risk of suicide in the event of a prison sentence, may persuade the court to take an exceptional course[1]. Interference with studies may merit a reduction in the sentence normally appropriate for the offence[2]. A short life expectancy may persuade the court to reduce the sentence it would otherwise impose[3].

---

1. *R v Gibson* [2001] EWCA Crim 656, (2001) 165 JPN 656 (6 counts relating to burglary and disinterring bodies in a cemetery – sentence reduced from 18 months to 6 months to enable the defendant's immediate release).
2. *R v Orr* [2001] EWCA Crim 673 (over £9000 dishonestly obtained, but sentence reduced from 9 to 6 months as the defendant was studying to go to university later that year).
3. *R v Lewis* [2001] EWCA Crim 935, (2001) 165 JPN 295 (perverting the course of justice – the court would have substituted 18 months, but in the light of the defendant's short life expectancy the sentence was reduced to 12 months).

THE TOTALITY PRINCIPLE

3–78 Where a court is dealing with an offender in respect of several offences and has carefully calculated the sentence in relation to each offence, it should then review the aggregate sentence and decide whether the total sentence is just and appropriate[1]. However, when considering custodial and community sentences the requirement to assess the seriousness of the offence, or the offence and one or more offences associated with it, needs to be borne in mind at the outset[2]. Where an offender pleads guilty to offences which the prosecution puts forward as specimen counts, but does not admit any other allegation or ask for any other offences to be taken into consideration, he must be sentenced solely on the basis of the offences of which he has been convicted[3].

A whole series of short consecutive sentences should be avoided, but equally a series of comparable concurrent sentences would be wrong where the offences ranged from the serious to the trivial; a fair course is to impose the "total" sentence in respect of the most grave offence, and lesser concurrent sentences for the others[4]. It is inadvisable to impose a succession of non-custodial sentences on an offender so that he becomes liable to the simultaneous enforcement of a number of different sentences if a further conviction occurs[5]. Where a court imposes a custodial sentence on a serving prisoner and orders the new sentence to run consecutively to the existing sentence the totality of the combined sentence should be considered and the later sentence should be adjusted if the aggregate is unjust[6].

---

1. *R v Hewitt* [1980] Crim LR 116.
2. Powers of Criminal Courts (Sentencing) Act 2000, ss 35(1), 79(2)
3. *R v Perkins* (1993) 15 Cr App Rep (S) 402; *R v Kidd* [1998] 1 All ER 42, [1998] 1 WLR 604 sub nom *R v Canavan* [1998] 1 Cr App Rep 79, 161 JP 709, [1998] 1 Cr App Rep (S) 243.
4. *R v Smith* [1975] Crim LR 468.
5. *R v Docker* (1979) 1 Cr App Rep (S) 151.
6. *R v Jones* [1996] 1 Cr App Rep (S) 153, CA; *R v Stevens* [1997] 2 Cr App Rep (S) 180.

ORDERS OF NO SEPARATE PENALTY WHEN DEALING WITH MULTIPLE OFFENCES

3–79 Where an offender has been found guilty of a number of offences, the court may deal with some of the offences by ordering *no separate penalty*[1]. The occasions in the magistrates' court when such an order will be made are likely to be comparatively rare and confined to cases where no additional penalty is deemed appropriate because of the number and nature of offences, or because the principal sentence passed is not available to the court for all the offences being dealt with[1]. If the court is dealing with an offence for which the penalty is in part fixed by law (eg ordering endorsement of driving licence or disqualification from driving a motor vehicle), it would seem that the court must make the order which the law stipulates, and that it may not circumvent that requirement by ordering *no separate penalty*.

On appeal, the Crown Court may confirm, reverse or vary any part of the decision appealed against, including a determination not to impose a separate penalty in respect of an offence[2].

---

1. See for example *R v Fairhurst* [1987] 1 All ER 46, [1986] 1 WLR 1374, CA (when imposing detention under s 91 of the Powers of Criminal Courts (Sentencing) Act 2000 it may be appropriate to impose no separate penalty for the offences for which s 91 detention is not available). It is submitted that where the court is dealing with offences committed on either side of the commencement on 4 April 2005, of the sentencing framework of the Criminal Justice Act 2003, one option would be for the court to deal with the pre-commencement offences by way of no separate penalty so as to avoid possible difficulties arising from the differences between the two sentencing regimes, especially as to powers in the event of breach.
2. Supreme Court Act 1981, s 48(2)(*a*), in PART I: MAGISTRATES' COURTS, PROCEDURE, ante.

Non-custodial orders available for offenders aged 18 and above

SUMMARY

3–90 Sentences available to magistrates' courts in dealing with an adult (age 21 or over) and a young offender (age 18–20) are as follows[1].

Absolute and conditional discharge, Powers of Criminal Courts (Sentencing) Act 2000, ss 12–15;

Compensation, Powers of Criminal Courts (Sentencing) Act 2000, ss 130–134;

Fine, Magistrates' Courts Act 1980, s 32; every statute creating a summary offence;

Attendance centre (under 21 only), Powers of Criminal Courts (Sentencing) Act 2000, ss 60–62;

In relation to offences committed before 4 April 2005:

Probation, Powers of Criminal Courts (Sentencing) Act 2000, ss 41–45; Community service, Powers of Criminal Courts (Sentencing) Act 2000, ss 46–50; Combination order (Powers of Criminal Courts (Sentencing) Act 2000, s 51); and Curfew order (Powers of Criminal Courts (Sentencing) Act 2000, ss 37–40);

In relation to offences committed on or after 4 April 2005:

a community sentence consisting of one or more community orders, the Criminal Justice Act 2003, ss 177–180, ss 199–223.

Short local detention, Magistrates' Courts Act 1980, s 135;

Detention in a young offender institution (under 21 only), Powers of Criminal Courts (Sentencing) Act 2000, ss 76–84, 96–98;

Imprisonment[2], (various provision of the Powers of Criminal Courts (Sentencing) Act 2000 and the Criminal Justice Act 2003).

---

1. See also para **3–320**, ante: **Orders in respect of mentally disordered offenders**, para **3–170**, ante et seq: **Ancillary orders**; para **3–360**, **Binding over, recognizances** and para **3–154**, ante: **Committal to the Crown Court for sentence** and see PART V: YOUTH COURTS, post, for Orders in respect of Minors (which includes a note on the powers of an adult court to deal with a minor).
2. Including suspended sentences of imprisonment, intermittent custody (though the pilots for this have ceased and it seems unlikely that this form of custody will be implemented in the foreseeable future and "custody plus" (when the relevant provisions of the Criminal Justice Act 2003 come into force).

ORDERS OF ABSOLUTE AND CONDITIONAL DISCHARGE

3–91 Where a court is of opinion, having regard to the circumstances including the nature of the offence and the character of the offender, that it is inexpedient to inflict punishment and that a probation order is not appropriate, it may make an order discharging him absolutely or alternatively discharging him subject to the condition that he commits no offence during such period, not exceeding three years from the date of the order, as may be specified therein[1].

Before making an order for conditional discharge, the court must explain to the offender in ordinary language that if he commits another offence during the period of the conditional discharge, he will be liable to be sentenced for the original offence[1]; it is usual for the court to fulfil this mandatory duty itself, although it may for reasons of justice and convenience delegate the task of explanation to another[2].

For the one offence, a fine may not be imposed in addition to an order of discharge,[3] nor may the court impose a deprivation order[4]. Magistrates' courts should refrain in normal circumstances from making an order of discharge in respect of an offence committed during the operational period of a suspended sentence imposed by the Crown Court; the proper course is to commit the defendant to the Crown Court so that all matters may be dealt with together[5]. The court, on making an order for conditional discharge, may allow any person who consents to do so, to give security for the good behaviour of the offender, if it thinks it expedient for the purpose of the reformation of the offender[6].

1. Powers of Criminal Courts (Sentencing) Act 2000, s 12, this PART, post.
2. *R v Wehner* [1977] 3 All ER 553, [1977] 1 WLR 1143.
3. *R v McClelland* [1951] 1 All ER 557, 115 JP 179.
4. *R v Hunt* [1978] Crim LR 697.
5. *R v Tarry* [1970] 2 QB 560, [1970] 2 All ER 185; *R v Moore* [1995] QB 353, [1995] 4 All ER 843, [1995] 2 WLR 728, CA.
6. Powers of Criminal Courts (Sentencing) Act 2000, s 12(6), this PART, post

3–92   Commission of further offence during operational period of discharge.   Where a person is proved to have committed *an offence during a period of conditional discharge*, the court may deal with him in any way it could have done for the original offence[1]. Crown Court orders must be dealt with by the Crown Court[1], the offender being committed in custody or on bail to the Crown Court. Magistrates' courts orders are dealt with either by the court which made the order or, with the consent of that court, by a magistrates' court convicting the offender of another offence[1], or by the Crown Court[1]. Special provision is made where the order for conditional discharge was made by a magistrates' court in the case of an offender under the age of 18 years in respect of an offence triable only on indictment in the case of an adult[2].

The subsequent convictions should be put to the offender and, if disputed, the court should decide whether a further offence has been committed within the terms of the section[3]. The original offence should not be "taken into consideration" in dealing with the subsequent offence, but should be made the subject of a separate sentence which, if imprisonment, should be consecutive to any existing term, and more than nominal[4], although in a proper case for example where a sentence of borstal training is imposed for the further offence, there may be a nominal sentence[5]. An order for damages or compensation made with the original conditional discharge will continue in force[6]. The Criminal Justice Act 1967, s 56(2) refers only to a "probationer" which implies that if the magistrates' court wishes to commit the offender to the Crown Court for his latest offences it may only commit for sentence (see post) and not under s 56. Nevertheless, it has been held[7] that the power to commit under s 56 *is* available when an offender subject to a conditional discharge is committed to the Crown Court under the Criminal Justice Act 1991, s 1B(5).

1. Powers of Criminal Courts (Sentencing) Act 2000, s 13, this PART, post.
2. Powers of Criminal Courts (Sentencing) Act 2000, s 13(9), this PART, post.
3. *R v Devine* [1956] 1 All ER 548, 120 JP 238; *R v Long* [1960] 1 QB 681, [1959] 3 All ER 559, 124 JP 4.
4. *R v Webb* [1953] 2 QB 390, [1953] 1 All ER 1156, 117 JP 319; *R v Stuart* [1964] 3 All ER 672, 129 JP 35.
5. *R v Fry* [1955] 1 All ER 21, 119 JP 75.
6. *R v Evans* [1963] 1 QB 979, [1961] 1 All ER 313, 125 JP 134.
7. See *R v Penfold* (1995) 16 Cr App Rep (S) 1016, [1995] Crim LR 666 and commentary.

COMPENSATION AS A COMPLETE SENTENCE

3–93   A court by or before which an offender is convicted of an offence, instead of or in addition to dealing with him in any other way, may, on an application or otherwise, make a order requiring him to pay compensation for any personal injury, loss of damage resulting from that offence or any other offence which is taken into consideration by the court in determining sentence; or may make an order requiring him to make payments for funeral expenses or bereavement in respect of a death resulting from any such offence other than a death arising out of a road traffic accident[1].

Where the court considers that it would be appropriate both to impose a fine and to make a compensation order, but the offender has insufficient means to pay both an appropriate fine and appropriate compensation, the court must give preference to compensation (though it may impose a fine as well)[2].

1. Powers of Criminal Courts (Sentencing) Act 2000, s 130(1), in this PART, post. An order may not, however, be made *instead of* another sentence in respect of an offence for which the sentence is fixed by law or falls to be imposed under certain enactments that stipulate a minimum, mandatory sentence: see s 130(2).
As to the appropriateness of an order and the assessment of the amount to be paid, see para **3–172**, post.
2. Powers of Criminal Courts Act 2000, s 130(12).

FINES: GENERAL PRINCIPLES

3–94   Every criminal offence triable by magistrates has a maximum fine fixed by statute or subordinate instrument. Fines for summary offences in statutes are fixed as to maxima by reference to levels on the **standard scale**[1], and similar provision has been made with respect to subordinate legislation[2].

Subject to certain exceptions, the maximum fine for an offence triable either way is **the prescribed sum** unless a larger sum is specified[3].

The amount of any fine fixed by the court shall be such as, in the opinion of the court, reflects the seriousness of the offence[4]. In fixing the amount of any fine, the court must take into account the circumstances of the case including, among other things, the financial circumstances of the offender (whether an individual or other person) so far as they are known, or appear, to the court[5].

Before fixing the amount of any fine to be imposed on an offender who is an individual, the court must inquire into his financial circumstances[6]. Where a person has been convicted of an offence, the court may, before sentencing him, make a financial circumstances order with respect to him[7]. This means an order requiring the offender to give to the court, within such period as may be specified, such statement of his financial circumstances as the court may require[8]. There are penal provisions for failure to comply with a financial circumstances order, or for knowingly/recklessly furnishing a false statement or knowingly failing to disclose a material fact[9]. The offender is also under a statutory duty to furnish a statement of his financial circumstances in response to an official request; again, there are offences relating to non-compliance, false statements and non-disclosure[10].

Where an offender has been convicted in his absence and he has failed to furnish a statement of his financial circumstances, or has failed to comply with a financial circumstances order, or has otherwise failed to co-operate with the court in its inquiry into his financial circumstances, and the court considers that it has insufficient information to make a proper determination of his financial circumstances, it may make such a determination as it thinks fit[11].

In determining the amount of a fine in respect of a person who has spent some time in custody, some credit should normally be given for the period spent in custody. The amount of credit given will depend on the circumstances and is in the discretion of the court[12].

If the defendant cannot pay a fine then, if that were the appropriate type of penalty, it would be wrong in principle to impose a more severe type of sentence, for example suspended imprisonment[13].

It was not possible to impose in respect of the same offence a fine with what were probation and community service orders, and we are of the opinion that this principle is unaffected by the replacement of these orders with community sentences; a fine may similarly not be combined with an order of discharge for the same offence[14].

It has been held in relation to "old-style" suspended prison sentences[15] that a court may combine such a sentence with a fine; this adds a sting to what might otherwise be thought by the convicted person to be a "let-off"[16], but it is wrong to impose a fine and a conditional discharge for the same offence[17].

---

1. Criminal Justice Act 1982, s 37, this PART, post.
2. See the Criminal Justice Act 1988, ss 51–59, in PART I: MAGISTRATES' COURTS, PROCEDURE, ante.
3. Magistrates' Courts Act 1980, s 32 in Part I: Magistrates' Courts, Procedure, ante.
4. Criminal Justice Act 2003, s 164(2): see this PART, post.
5. Criminal Justice Act 2003, s 164(3).
6. Criminal Justice Act 2003, s 164(1).
7. Criminal Justice Act 2003, s 162.
8. Criminal Justice Act 2003, s 162(3).
9. Criminal Justice Act 2003, s 162(3) and (4).
10. Criminal Justice Act 1991, s 20A(1A), see this PART, post.
11. Criminal Justice Act 2003, s 164(5). The court may later remit the fine in whole or in part if on a subsequent means inquiry the court is satisfied that if that information had been available at the time of sentence the could would not have fined or fined a smaller amount, as the case may be: CJA 2003, s 165.
12. *R v Warden* (1996) 2 Cr App Rep (S) 269, 160 JP 363, [1996] Crim LR 443, CA.
13. *R v McGowan* [1975] Crim LR 113.
14. *R v Carnwell* [1979] Crim LR 59; *R v McClelland* [1951] 1 All ER 557, 115 JP 179; *R v Parry* [1951] 1 KB 590, [1950] 2 All ER 1179.
15. Ie those imposed for offences committed before 4 April 2005. (The suspended sentence provisions of the Criminal Justice Act 2003, this PART, post, apply to subsequent offences.)
16. *R v King* [1970] 2 All ER 249, 134 JP 537.
17. *R v Sanck* (1990) 12 Cr App Rep (S) 155.

FINES: CORPORATE DEFENDANTS

3–95   The principle that a fine should reflect not only the gravity of the offence but also the means of the offender applies just as much to corporate defendants as to any other. The starting point in assessing a corporate defendant's means is its annual accounts. If a defendant company wishes to make any submission to the court about its ability to pay a fine, it should supply copies of its accounts and any other financial information, on which it intends to rely, in good time before the hearing both to the court and to the prosecution. Where accounts or other financial information are deliberately not supplied, the court will be entitled to conclude that the company is in a position to pay any financial penalty it is minded to impose[1].

While with a personal defendant there are arguments for keeping the period over which a fine is to be paid within bounds, those arguments are much weaker when one is considering a corporate defendant. Therefore, it is acceptable on proper facts and in appropriate circumstances for a fine to be payable by a company over a substantially longer period than might be appropriate in the case of an individual[2].

In the case of a small company where the directors are likely to be shareholders, and therefore the main losers if a severe sanction is imposed on the company, the court must be alert to make sure that it is not in effect imposing a double punishment on the company and the directors. Nevertheless, it is important in many cases that fines should be imposed which make it clear that there is a personal responsibility to the corporation of which they are directors[3].

For commercial crimes under the Trade Descriptions Act 1968, such as offences contrary to s 13 of the Act, if fines imposed are to be effective they must be realistic. The Court of Appeal has given guidance that the level of penalties imposed by magistrates' courts are too low and should be increased[3].

Fisheries offences of underdeclaring catches, particularly if they involve persistent breaches, call for fines that are real deterrents[4].

1. *R v F Howe and Son (Engineers) Ltd* [1999] 2 All ER 249, 163 JP 359, [1999] 2 Cr App Rep (S) 37, [1999] Crim LR 238, CA applied in *R v Cappagh Public Works Ltd* [1999] 2 Cr App Rep (S) 301, CA and *R v Rimac Ltd* [2000] 1 Cr App Rep (S) 468, CA. See also, for reductions of fines wholly or partly on account of the means of the company: *R v Patchett Engineering Ltd* [2001] 1 Cr App Rep (S) 138 (£75,000 to £20,000); *R v Supremeplan Ltd* [2001] 1 Cr App Rep (S) 244 (£25,000 to £2,500, though compensation increased from £3,000 to £7,500); and *R v Cardiff City Transport* [2001] 1 Cr App Rep (S) 141 (£75,000 to £40,000).
2. *R v Rollco Screw and Rivet Co Ltd* [1999] 2 Cr App Rep (S) 436, CA.
3. *R v Docklands Estates Ltd* [2001] 1 Cr App Rep (S) 270, (2000) 164 JP 505 (fines of £7,500 for each of 3 offences under s 13 of the Trade Descriptions Act 1968 imposed on a company with a modest turnover reduced on appeal to £2,000 for each offence having regard to the seriousness of the offence and the means of the company).
4. See *Anglo-Spanish Fisheries Ltd* [2001] 1 Cr App R (S) 73; *R v Ramosa Ltd* [2004] EWCA Crim 2171, [2005] 1 Cr App R (S) 77.

FINES FOR HEALTH AND SAFETY OFFENCES

3–96   When dealing with a breach of the health and safety legislation and determining the level of fine and costs to impose on a corporate defendant, the court should have regard to the following propositions[1]:

(a)   In assessing the gravity of the breach, the court should consider how far short of the appropriate standard the defendant fell in failing to meet the reasonably practicable test.

(b)   Generally, where death is the consequence[2] of a criminal act, it is regarded as an aggravating feature of the offence – the penalty should reflect public disquiet at the unnecessary loss of life.

(c)   The size of a company and its financial strength or weakness cannot affect the degree of care that is required in matters of safety.

(d)   Particular aggravating factors will include:

(i)   a failure to heed warnings;
(ii)   deliberately profiting financially from a failure to take necessary health and safety steps or specifically running a risk in order to save money.

(e)   Particular mitigating factors will include:

(i)   prompt admission of responsibility and a timely guilty plea;
(ii)   steps to remedy deficiencies after they are drawn to the defendant's attention;
(iii) a good safety record.

(f)   Where a defendant company is in a position to pay the whole of the prosecution costs in addition to the fine, there is no reason in principle for the court not to make an order accordingly – the costs do not need to be scaled down so as not to exceed the fine[1].

The Court of Appeal has recommended that when the Health and Safety Executive commences proceedings, it should list in writing for the assistance of the court not merely the facts of the case, but the aggravating features, as set out in *R v F Howe and Son (Engineers) Ltd*[1], which it says exist in the particular case. That document should be served upon the court and upon the defendants for the latter to consider. If the defendants plead guilty they should submit a similar document outlining the mitigating features that the court is to take into account. If by the time the matter comes to court there is agreement between the parties as to which are the relevant mitigating and aggravating factors that the court should take into account, and the plea is upon an agreed basis, that agreed basis should be put into writing so that there is no doubt what is the proper basis upon which the court should pass sentence[3].

Health and safety offences are not directly analogous to environmental offences since health and safety offences inevitably present at least a threat of personal injury or death, whereas environmental offences may, but need not, do so. Nevertheless, there is a general perception in relation to both health and safety and environmental offences that the general level of sentencing has been too low. Many of the propositions set out above in *R v F Howe and Son (Engineers) Ltd*[1] will also be relevant to sentencing a corporate defendant for an environmental offence[4].

In relation to offences involving safety at sea the court must have regard to the level of culpability, the financial circumstances of the defendant company and the consequences and potential consequences to others of the breach of safety which the court is examining[5].

---

1. *R v F Howe and Son (Engineers) Ltd* [1999] 2 All ER 249, 163 JP 359, [1999] 2 Cr App Rep (S) 37, [1999] Crim LR 238, CA.
The following examples illustrate the approach of the Court of Appeal: *R v Avon Lippiatt Hobbs (Contractors) Ltd* [2003] EWCA Crim 627, [2003] 2 Cr App R (S) 71 (fines totalling £250,000 reduced to £150,000 where, in the course of tunnelling under a road using an impact mole, gas pipes were struck and there was an explosion some hours later that destroyed a house and badly burned an employee); *R v Yorkshire Sheeting and Insulation Ltd* [2003] EWCA Crim 458, [2003] 2 Cr App R (S) 93 (£100,000 fine reduced to £55,000 where inadequate safety precautions resulted in a roof sheeter falling through an unprotected roof light, but none of the aggravating factors identified in *Howe*, save death, was present); *R v P & O (Irish Sea Ltd)* [2004] EWCA Crim 3236, [2005] 2 Cr App R (S) 21 (fines totalling £300,000 reduced to £225,000 where pedestrian employee killed by driver of a stacker truck during unloading from a ferry, but apart from this there were no significant aggravating factors and there were numerous mitigating factors); *R v Jarvis Facilities Ltd* [2005] EWCA Crim 1409, [2006] 1 Cr App R (S) 44 (fine reduced from £400,000 to £275,000 where a rail junction with a speed limit of 25 mph should have been physically closed due to the removal of a section of rail on a diversionary route through the junction, but the signaller had no means of knowing this, a freight train was diverted down the route and it derailed, though remained upright; while public service cases would often be treated more seriously, the sentencer had overestimated the actual risk generated); and *R v Transco plc* [2006] EWCA Crim 838, [2006] 2 Cr App R (S) 111 (fine

reduced from £1m to £250,000 where the company pleaded guilty to failing to discharge a duty of care under s 3 of the Health and Safety at Work Act 1974; it had been called to a building after a leak from a fractured gas main escaped causing gas to enter the building; it identified the source of the leak and, dealt with the fracture and ventilated the building; it then allowed residents to return, but, half an hour later, one resident lit a cigarette which ignited gas and he died of his injuries a few days later; it transpired that a void 2m high above his ceiling had filled with gas which had seeped into the room after it had been ventilated; however, the flats were unusually constructed and, apparently, in breach of building regulations; the case did not involve systematic fault but merely a mistake by one or more individuals handling an emergency; the guilty plea was promptly entered; and there was no question of cost cutting or profit motives, and the company's safety record was generally good).

2. Conversely, where the health and safety failings were due to ignorance and did not cause or contribute to the death, attention should focus on the extent to which the breach jeopardised general safety aspects: *R v Wilson & Mainprize* [2004] EWCA Crim 2086, [2005] 1 Cr App R (S) 64.

3. *R v Friskies Petcare (UK) Ltd* [2000] 2 Cr App Rep (S) 401, CA.

4. *R v Milford Haven Port Authority* [2000] 2 Cr App Rep (S) 423, CA. See also *R v Anglian Water Services [2003] EWCA Crim* 2243, [2004] 1 Cr App R (S) 62 (river polluted by discharge of 200 tonnes of sewage – a 2 kilometre stretch was badly affected and much damage was done to the fish and wildlife living it, but the river recovered within 24 hours due to the prompt remedial action taken by the defendant company – £200,000 fine reduced to £60,000).

5. *R v Armana Ltd* [2004] EWCA Crim 1069, [2005] 1 Cr App R (S) 7 (£40,000 fine reduced to £15,000 where the company had a clear safety record, had co-operated fully with the investigation, the breach did not arise from any operational failure of safety measures and the company had lost more than £400,000 in its last trading year).

IMPRISONMENT/DETENTION IN DEFAULT OF IMMEDIATE PAYMENT

3–97   A magistrates' court shall not on the occasion of convicting an offender of an offence issue a warrant in default of paying a sum adjudged to be paid by the conviction unless:

(*a*)   in the case of an offence punishable with imprisonment, he appears to have sufficient means to pay the sum forthwith;

(*b*)   it appears to the court that he is unlikely to remain long enough at a place of abode in the UK to enable payment of the sum to be enforced by other methods[1]; or

(*c*)   on the occasion of that conviction the court sentences him to immediate imprisonment or detention in a young offender institution for that or another offence or he is already serving such a sentence[2].

The same restrictions apply to fixing, at the time of conviction, a term of imprisonment which is to be served in the event of a future default (a postponed warrant of commitment)[3].

However, the court has an unrestricted power to impose short local detention in default of immediate payment[4].

As to the duty/power to make attachment of earnings or benefit orders where the court does not order immediate payment of a sum adjudged to be paid by a conviction, see para **3–99 Dispensing with immediate payment and collection orders**, post.

---

1. However, see para **3–99 Dispensing with immediate payment and collection orders**, post.

2. Magistrates' Courts Act 1980, s 1(1), in PART 1: MAGISTRATES' COURTS, PROCEDURE, ante. As to release from custody and reduction of detention on payment, see Magistrates' Courts Act 1980, s 79. As to the power to order the search of an offender and to apply any money found on him in payment of the fine, etc, see Magistrates' Courts Act 1980, s 80.

3. Magistrates' Courts Act 1980, s 82(2). As to postponing the issue of a warrant, see Magistrates' Courts Act 1980, s 77.

4. Magistrates' Courts Act 1980, s 135: see para **1–2218**, post.

FINES IN RESPECT OF SERVING PRISONERS

3–98   Where the court does not on the occasion of the offender's conviction issue a warrant of commitment of imprisonment/detention for default in paying a sum adjudged to be paid by a conviction or fix a term of imprisonment/detention to be served in the event of a future default (see para **3–97 Imprisonment/detention in default of immediate payment**, ante), it may thereafter issue a warrant of imprisonment/detention[1], where the defaulter is serving a sentence of custody for life, or a term of imprisonment, detention under section 108 of the Powers of Criminal Courts (Sentencing) Act 2000 or detention in a young offender institution[2]. Before issuing a warrant of commitment in these circumstances the court must give the defaulter prior notice of its intention to do so, and an opportunity to make representations to the court[3]. It may also be necessary to give notice of hearing to a party who has a direct interest in the proceeds of the sum adjudged to be paid[4]. Where the outstanding sum is a confiscation order under s 2 of the Drug Trafficking Act 1994, the prosecutor should be given an opportunity of being heard[5]. Although in such circumstances the court is not required to hold a means inquiry it should have regard to any assets of the defaulter which may be available for distress[4], or realisable by other methods of recovery[5].

An offender is already serving a term of imprisonment from the moment that the sentence is pronounced; accordingly, provided the offender is given an opportunity to make representations against the issue of such a warrant, the court may issue a warrant of commitment in the same proceedings, subsequent to the imposition of the custodial sentence[6].

---

1. Detention applies where the defaulter is aged 18–20: see Powers of Criminal Courts (Sentencing) Act 2000, s 108, this PART, post.

2. Magistrates' Courts Act 1980, s 82(3), in PART I: MAGISTRATES' COURTS, PROCEDURE, ante.

3. Magistrates' Courts Act 1980, s 82, in PART I: MAGISTRATES' COURTS, PROCEDURE, ante. [4]See *R v Clacton Justices, ex p Customs and Excise Comrs* (1987) 152 JP 129.

5. *R v Harrow Justices, ex p DPP* [1991] 3 All ER 873, [1991] 1 WLR 395; *R v Liverpool Magistrates' Court, ex p Ansen* [1998] 1 All ER 692, DC.

6. *R v Grimsby and Cleethorpes Justices, ex p Walters* [1997] 1 WLR 89, 161 JP 25.

DISPENSING WITH IMMEDIATE PAYMENT AND COLLECTION ORDERS

3-99 **Powers of search.** The court may order the offender to be searched, and any money found on him applied towards payment of the fine, and the balance, if any, returned to him; the money shall not however be so applied if the court is satisfied that the money does not belong to him or that its loss would be more injurious to his family than would be his detention[1].

Special cases: serving soldiers and foreign lorry drivers. Where the defendant is in the Armed Forces, arrangements may be made for payment out of his unit's imprest account provided it can be recovered in turn from him within three months or his earlier discharge or transfer to Regular Reserve[2]. If the defendant is a foreign lorry driver from a European country which is party to bilateral agreements with the United Kingdom on road transport, as an alternative to committal in default, the court may allow time for payment, warning the defendant of the possible consequences for him and his employer under the agreements should the fine not be paid[3].

Usual cases. Having decided the amount of the fine, the court must then consider how payment is to be made. The court may, instead of requiring immediate payment, allow time for payment, or order payment by instalments[4]. Where this occurs, and the sum due consists of or includes a compensation order, the court must make an attachment of earnings or order or an application for benefit deductions unless it is impracticable or inappropriate to do to so[5]. In any other case, the court may make such an order at this stage, but only if the payer ("P") consents[6].

Whether or not the court makes an attachment order or an application for benefit deductions at this stage, the court must make a collection order relating to the sum due, unless it appears to the court that it is impracticable or inappropriate to make the order. If P is subject to a collection order, the powers of any court to deal with his liability are subject to certain provisions and regulations[7]. If the court has not made an attachment order, the collection order must state the terms of payments[8]. If the court has made an attachment order or application for benefit deductions, the collection order must state the reserve terms, which are the terms of payment to take effect if the attachment order or application fails[9].

Other options. If it allows time for payment, or orders payment by instalments, it may in the defendant's presence fix a day on which, if any part of the sum, or any instalment which has fallen due, remains unpaid, the defendant must appear before the court again[10]. It may make a money payments supervision order[11]; or it may issue a warrant of distress where default is made in paying forthwith, or direct its issue but postponed on conditions[12]. The convicting court may make a transfer of fine order where the defendant lives in another court's area (including Scotland), and that court will then collect and enforce the fine[13].

---

1. Magistrates' Courts Act 1980, s 80.
2. See eg the Queen's Regulations for the Army 1975, reg 6.174.
3. If, in such circumstances, a fine is not paid within the time allowed, the court should send details of the case (personal particulars of the offender and of his employer, offence, amount of fine and the date by which payment was due) to:—
Freight Policy and Road Haulage Division, Room S16/09, Department of Transport, 2 Marsham Street, London, SW1P 3EB (Home Office Circular 1/1987, dated 12 January 1987).
4. Magistrates' Courts Act 1980, s 75.
5. Courts Act 2003, Sch 5, para 7A: in PART I: MAGISTRATES' COURTS, PROCEDURE, ante.
6. Courts Act 2003, Sch 5, para 9. As to the deduction rate from earnings, see the Fines Collection Regulations 2006, in PART I: STATUTORY INSTRUMENTS AND PRACTICE DIRECTIONS ON PROCEDURE, ante
7. Ie Courts Act 2003, Sch 5 and the Fines Collection Regulations 2006: see Sch 5, para 12.
8. Courts Act 2003, Sch 5, para 14. As to the variation of these terms, see Sch 5, para 6.
9. Courts Act 2003, Sch 5, para 15. See paras 16 and 17 for the meaning of "fails".
10. Magistrates' Courts Act 1980, s 86. This will be inappropriate if the court has made an attachment order or an application for deduction from benefits and/or a collection order.
11. Magistrates' Courts Act 1980, s 88; Criminal Procedure Rules 2005, Part 52, in PART I: MAGISTRATES' COURTS, PROCEDURE, ante.
12. Magistrates' Courts Act 1980, ss 76 and 77.
13. Magistrates' Courts Act 1980, ss 89 and 90; Criminal Procedure Rules 2005, Part 52, in PART I: MAGISTRATES' COURTS, PROCEDURE, ante.

ENFORCEMENT OF FINES AFTER CONVICTION: POWERS OF FINES
OFFICERS

3-110 The following applies on the first occasion on which the payer ("P") is in default on a collection order containing payment terms and there is no pending application, appeal or reference of a specified kind[1]. The fines officer must make an attachment of earnings order or application for benefit deductions if it appear to him that P is, respectively, working or entitled to a relevant benefit, unless it is impracticable or inappropriate to make such an order or application[2]. If it appears that P is both working and receiving a relevant benefit, the fines officer must either make an attachment order or apply for benefit deductions[3].

If a collection order contains reserve terms and the attachment of earnings order or application for benefit deductions fails[4], the fines officer must deliver to P a notice informing him of the failure and that the reserve terms have come into effect, what he must do to comply with those terms and of his right to apply to the fines officer to vary the reserve terms. P may then apply to the fines officer to vary those terms, provided he is not in default on the collection order[5].

If P is in default on a collection order, the provisions stated above concerning the making of an attachment of earnings order or application for deduction of benefits on the occasion of the first default on a collection order do not apply, and there is no pending application, appeal of reference of a specified kind[1], the fines officer must refer P's case to the magistrates' court or deliver to him a "further steps notice", in writing and dated, describing the further steps he intends to take. Within 10 working days[6] of the date of the further steps notice P may appeal against it to the magistrates' court[7]. The further steps are: the issue of a warrant of distress; registering the sum in the register of judgements and orders required to be kept under s 98 of the Courts Act 2003; making an attachment of earnings order or an application for benefit deductions; a clamping order; and taking proceedings by virtue of the Magistrates' Courts Act 1980, s 87(1) to enforce payment by the High Court or county court[8], provided that the fines officer has made enquiries into the defaulter's means and it appears to the fines officer that the defaulter has sufficient means to pay the sum forthwith[9]. If P does not appeal within 10 days, or he does so but the further steps notice is confirmed or varied, any of the step specified in the notice (or the notice as varied) may be taken[10].

The fines officer may also refer a case to the magistrates' court at any time while a collection order is in force and the whole or part of the sum due remains outstanding[11].

To ensure that P attends the magistrates' court pursuant to either kind of reference described above, the fines officer may issue a summons[12].

1. Ie as specified in Courts Act 2003, Sch 5, para 25.
2. Courts Act 2003, Sch 5, para 26(1) and (2).
3. Courts Act 2003, Sch 5, para 26(3).
4. "Fails" is defined in Courts Act 2003, Sch 5, paras 16 and 17.
5. Courts Act 2003, Sch 5, para 31(1). For the relevant criteria, procedure, powers of the fines officer and right of appeal, see paras 31(2)–(4) and 32.
6. Defined in Courts Act 2003, Sch 5, Para 52.
7. Courts Act 2003, Sch 5, para 37.
8. Courts Act 2003, Sch 5, para 38. A vehicle cannot be clamped unless it is registered in P's name under the Vehicle Excise and Registration Act 1994: para 38(3). For the power to order the sale of a clamped vehicle, see para 41 and the Fines Collections Regulations in PART I: STATUTORY INSTRUMENTS AND PRACTICE DIRECTIONS ON PROCEDURE, ANTE.
9. Magistrates' Courts Act 1980, s 87(3A).
10. Courts Act 2003, Sch 5, para 40.
11. Courts Act 2003, Sch 5, para 42.
12. Regulation 4 of the Fines Collection Regulations 2006 in PART I: STATUTORY INSTRUMENTS AND PRACTICE DIRECTIONS ON PROCEDURE, ANTE.

ENFORCEMENT AFTER CONVICTION: POWERS OF THE COURT (OTHER THAN IMPRISONMENT)

3–111   Where the fines officer refers a default on a collection order to the magistrates' court, the court may vary the payment terms or the reserve terms; take any of the further steps described in para **3–110**, ante; or discharge the order and exercise any of its standard powers in relation to persons liable to pay fines or other sum[1]. On an appeal against a further steps notice, the court may vary or quash the notice; vary it so as to specify any of the further steps described in para **3–110**, ante; vary the payment terms or reserve terms; or discharge the order and exercise any of its standard powers[2].

Where the fines officer refers a case to the magistrates' court otherwise than in consequence of a default, where there is a collection order in force and the whole or part of the sum due is outstanding, the court may confirm or vary the payment terms or reserve terms; exercise any of its standard powers in respect of persons liable to pay fines or other sums, in which case it may also discharge the order; or exercise any power it could exercise under any other paragraph of Sch 5 to the Courts Act 2003[3].

Increase in fine.   Where P is in default on a collection order, the sum due consists of or includes a fine, and the fines officer has referred the default to a magistrates' court either as an alternative to the issue of a further steps notice or after taking any of the further steps described in para **3–110**, ante, if the court is satisfied that the default is due to P's wilful refusal or culpable neglect it may increase the fine (but not any other sum which is due) by 50%[4].

The standard powers of magistrates' courts in relation to a defaulter, except imprisonment and detention

(a) Remission: a fine (but only a fine) may be remitted in whole or in part if the court thinks it is just to do so having regard to a change in circumstances which has occurred since the conviction[5]. A magistrates' court may not, however, remit the whole or any part of a fine imposed by, or sum due under a recognizance forfeited by, the Crown Court or Court of Appeal or House of Lords, without the consent of the Crown Court[6].
(b) Money payment supervision order[7].
(c) Distress warrant: a distress warrant may be issued for the purposes of distraining on the defaulter's money and goods; the issue of the warrant may be postponed on conditions[8].

(d) Attendance centre order: such an order may be made only where a centre is available and the defaulter is aged under 25[9].

(e) Curfew and community service orders: where the court has power to issue a warrant of commitment, it may instead make a community service or curfew order provided it has been notified by the secretary of state that arrangements for implementing the order are available in the relevant area[10].

---

1. Courts Act 2003, Sch 5, para 39(3): in PART I: STATUTES ON PROCEDURE, ante.
2. Courts Act 2003, Sch 5, para 39(4). "Standard powers" means any power that the court would have had if P had not been subject to a collection order but had been liable to pay the sum due: Sch 5, para 50.
3. Courts Act 2003, Sch 5, para 42(2).
4. Courts Act 2003, Sch 5, para 42A and reg 3 of the Fines Collections Regulations in PART I: STATUTORY INSTRUMENTS AND PRACTICE DIRECTIONS ON PROCEDURE, ante.
5. Magistrates' Courts Act 1980, s 85: in PART I: STATUTES ON PROCEDURE, ante. This will require alteration of any period of community service, number of days of a curfew order, or term of detention or imprisonment that has already been fixed in default of payment.
6. The Powers of Criminal Courts (Sentencing) Act 2000, s 140(5), in this PART, post.
7. Magistrates' Courts Act 1980, s 88 in PART I: STATUTES ON PROCEDURE, ante; Criminal Procedure Rules 2005, Part 52, in PART I: STATUTORY INSTRUMENTS AND PRACTICE DIRECTIONS ON PROCEDURE, ante.
8. Magistrates' Courts Act 1980, ss 76–78 in PART I: STATUTES ON PROCEDURE, ante; Criminal Procedure Rules 2005, Part 52 in PART I: STATUTORY INSTRUMENTS AND PRACTICE DIRECTIONS ON PROCEDURE, ante.
9. Powers of Criminal Courts (Sentencing) Act 2000, s 60, in this PART, post. This is prospectively repealed in part by Part 7 of Sch 37 to the Criminal Justice Act 2003 to reduce the maximum age to 20.
10. Crime (Sentences) Act 1997, s 35, in this PART, post. These powers are prospectively repealed and replaced, respectively, by Part 7 of Sch 37 to, and s 300 of, the Criminal Justice Act 2003.

PROCEDURE AND RESTRICTIONS ON THE IMPOSITION OF IMPRISONMENT OR DETENTION FOR DEFAULT

3–112 Imprisonment, or in the case of defaulters aged 18 to 20 detention[1], may be used where the court has, since the conviction, inquired into the defaulter's means in his presence on at least one occasion and it may issue a warrant of commitment if—

(i) in the case of an offence punishable with imprisonment, the defaulter appears to the court to have sufficient means to pay the sum forthwith[2], or

(ii) the court is satisfied that the default is due to the defaulter's wilful refusal or culpable neglect *and* the court has considered or tried all other methods of enforcing payment of the sum and it appears to the court that they are inappropriate or unsuccessful[2].

For the purpose of securing the attendance of an offender at a means inquiry, the court may issue a summons or a warrant of arrest and, either before or on inquiring into a person's means, a justice may order him to furnish to the court within a period specified in the order such statement of his means as the court may require[3]. A means inquiry is not a formality and the defendant should be examined in detail[4], in particular the court should inquire into:

(1) Income
(2) Capital or savings
(3) Expenditure
(4) Circumstances of the original failure to pay sums as they come due
(5) Failure to pay in accordance with any terms subsequently set by the court
(6) Likelihood of paying in the future

Where possible the defendant should be required to substantiate his account with documentary evidence. The attention of the court should be drawn to all relevant information relating to the defendant's ability to pay, eg correspondence on the file[5].

Wilful or culpable neglect. A causal connection must be established between the behaviour of the defaulter and failure to pay which is in some way blameworthy[6]. Wilful refusal or culpable neglect must be established on the criminal standard of proof[7]. "Wilful refusal" means a deliberate defiance of a court order and is apt to cover the situation where the offender says or demonstrates by his actions that he is not prepared to pay the fine as a point of principle; "culpable neglect" means a reckless disregard of a court order and is apt to cover the situation where the offender frivolously applies any available income to non-essential items rather than payment of the fine[8]. Where a person claims income support on behalf of himself and his cohabitee, the money received by him is for the support of both of them and the cohabitee is entitled to a share of the money from which to meet her financial obligations. If in such circumstances the cohabitee defaults in payment of a fine the court may find culpable neglect, because the claimant does not have sole entitlement to determine the use of the money[9].

Duty to consider other methods. Even where the court has inquired sufficiently into the defaulter's means, it is obliged to consider or try all other methods of enforcing the sum. Accordingly even where it was demonstrated that the defaulter had the means to pay, a commitment warrant will be quashed where the court cannot demonstrate that it has considered non-custodial alternatives.

There is no discretion in the court; it must *consider* or *try* all the other methods of enforcing payment before issuing a warrant of commitment[10], and this must include considering the suitability of a money payments supervision order[11].

Committal is not an appropriate course in a case involving a single mother with very little income who was trying her best to balance her financial obligations, although not always succeeding to give priority to the most important ones; moreover, such imprisonment would interfere to a serious degree with her children's right to family life under art 8 and it, therefore, had to be justified as pursuing a legitimate aim and as being necessary in a democratic society, and while it was not possible to say that committal as a last resort would never be sufficiently necessary to override the rights of the children to be cared for by their mother at home it was not possible to justify a committal without even trying out a money payment supervision order[12].

In ruling out any of these non custodial options the court must exercise its discretion judicially and on sufficient evidence so that, for example, where there is evidence that a defaulter has assets with which he can pay the sum owed, a distress warrant should be issued[13]. The court should take care that the defaulter is given a proper opportunity to put his case and that all relevant factors have been taken into account before reaching a finding that there has been "culpable neglect" to pay[14]. "Considering" other methods of enforcement may involve not only consideration when retired having heard the evidence, but in a case where the defaulter gives evidence canvassing issues raised with him[15].

Immediate and postponed warrants of commitment. Where the court decides under (i) or (ii) (above in this paragraph) to impose imprisonment or order detention in default, it may issue the warrant of commitment forthwith or postpone the issue until such time and on such conditions, if any, as it thinks just[16]. Before immediately issuing a warrant of commitment, consideration should be given to postponing the warrant[17]. If the issue of the warrant of commitment is postponed, it cannot subsequently be issued at a hearing at which the offender is not present without first giving the offender notice in writing stating that the court intends to hold a hearing to consider whether to issue the warrant and giving the reason why the court so intends[18].

Varying the terms of a postponed warrant of commitment. The court has the power to direct the further postponement of the warrant of commitment or to vary the conditions on which the issue of the warrant was previously postponed, but only if it thinks it just to do so having regard to a change of circumstances since the relevant time, namely the date when the issue of the warrant was postponed or any previous direction with respect to the postponement or conditions of postponement[19]. Without prejudice to the generality of the aforementioned power, if on an application by an offender in respect of whom the issue of a warrant has been postponed, it appears to a justice of the peace acting in the local justice area in which the warrant has been or would have been issued that there has been a change in circumstances since the relevant time (as defined above) which would make it just for the court to exercise its powers of variation, the application must be referred to the court and the applicant must be given notice of the time and place when it will be heard[20]. If the warrant is issued before the hearing of the application, the court has the power to order that it shall cease to have effect and to order that the offender shall be released if he has already been arrested, but it may only do so if it is satisfied that that the change of circumstances on which the applicant relies was not put before the court when it was determining whether to issue the warrant[21].

Reasons for decision. When the court issues a warrant of commitment it shall state on which of the grounds in (i) or (ii) (above in this paragraph) the warrant is issued, and that ground shall be specified in the warrant[22]. In the case of offenders under the age of 21 years (but not older offenders), the court is also obliged to state reasons why no other method is considered appropriate for dealing with the offender[23] and should set out seriatim why it has rejected each of the non custodial means of enforcement[24]. These reasons should be set out in the warrant of commitment; failure to do so will make the warrant liable to be quashed by judicial review[25].

---

1. Powers of Criminal Courts (Sentencing) Act 2000, s 108, this Part, post.

2. Magistrates' Courts Act 1980, s 82(3) and (4), in PART I: MAGISTRATES' COURTS, PROCEDURE, ante. THE SPECIFIED METHODS FOR THIS PURPOSE ARE: A WARRANT OF DISTRESS; AN APPLICATION TO THE HIGH COURT OR COUNTY COURT FOR ENFORCEMENT; A MONEY PAYMENT SUPERVISION ORDER; AN ATTACHMENT OF EARNINGS ORDER; AND, IF THE OFFENDER IS AGED UNDER 25, AN ATTENDANCE CENTRE ORDER: S 82(4A).

3. Magistrates' Courts Act 1980, s 84, in PART I: MAGISTRATES' COURTS, PROCEDURE,, ANTE.

4. See, for example, *R v York City Justices, ex p Farmery* (1988) 153 JP 257.

5. See, for example, *R v Newport Pagnell Justices, ex p Smith* (1988) 152 JP 475 (decided under s 82(5A) of the Magistrates' Courts Act 1980, in PART I: MAGISTRATES' COURTS, PROCEDURE,, ANTE).

6. *R v Manchester City Magistrates' Court, ex p Davies* [1989] QB 631, [1989] 1 All ER 90, [1988] 3 WLR 1357, CA.

7. *R v South Tyneside Justices, ex p Martin* (1995) Independent, 20 September.

8. *R v Luton Magistrates' Court, ex p Sullivan* [1992] 2 FLR 196, [1992] 1 FCR 475.

9. *Alcott v DPP* (1996) 161 JP 53.

10. *R v Norwich Magistrates' Court, ex p Lilly* (1987) 151 JP 766.

11. *R v Exeter City Magistrates' Court, ex p Sugar* (1992) 157 JP 766.

12. *R (on the application of Stokes) v Gwent Magistrates' Court* [2001] EWHC Admin 569, (2001) 165 JP 766.

13. See *R v Clacton Justices, ex p Customs and Excise Comrs* (1987) 152 JP 129.

14. *R v York Magistrates' Court, ex p Grimes* (1997) 161 JP 550, DC.

15. *Uberoi v Middlesex Justices* (2 November 1995, unreported) and see (1996) 160 JPB 863.

16. *R v Slough Justices, ex p Lindsay* [1997] 2 FCR 636, [1997] 1 FLR 695, DC.

17. Magistrates' Courts Act 1980, s 77, in PART I: MAGISTRATES' COURTS, PROCEDURE, ante.

18. Magistrates' Courts Act 1980, s 82(5A)–(5F), in PART I: MAGISTRATES' COURTS, PROCEDURE, ante. The notice must state the time and place appointed for the hearing, which must be at least 21 days after the issue of the notice or, where the notice was given at the same time as the court exercised its power to fixed the suspended term, any date after the expiry of the period for which the warrant was postponed (subss (5D) and (5E)). The notice must also inform the offender that he may make representations to the court in person or in writing (subs (5C(*b*)).

19. Magistrates' Courts Act 1980, s 77(3) and (4), in PART I: MAGISTRATES' COURTS, PROCEDURE, ANTE

20. Magistrates' Courts Act 1980, s 77(5), (6).

21. Magistrates' Courts Act 1980, s 77(8).

22. Magistrates' Courts Act 1980, s 82(6).
23. *R v Stockport Justices, ex p Conlon* [1997] 2 All ER 204, 161 JP 81.
24. Powers of Criminal Courts (Sentencing) Act 2000, s 108, this Part, post.
25. *R v Oldham Justices, ex p Cawley* [1996] 1 All ER 464, [1996] 2 WLR 681, sub nom *Re Cawley* 160 JP 133.

ENFORCEMENT OF CROWN COURT FINES

3–113 Fine: enforcement of a fine imposed by the Crown Court. A fine imposed or a recognizance forfeited by the Crown Court is to be treated for the purposes of collection, enforcement and remission of the fine or other sum as having been imposed or forfeited by the magistrates' court specified in an order made by the Crown Court or if no order is made, by the magistrates' court by which the offender was committed to the Crown Court to be tried or dealt with, and in the case of a fine as having been so imposed on conviction by the magistrates' court in question[1]. If the Crown Court imposes a fine on any person or forfeits his recognizance, the court may make an order allowing time for payment of the amount due or direct payment of that amount by instalments of such amounts and on such dates respectively as may be specified[2]. The Crown Court shall also make an order fixing a term of imprisonment or of detention under s 108 of the Powers of Criminal Courts (Sentencing) Act 2000 which he is to undergo if any fine or forfeited recognizance which he is liable to pay is not duly paid or recovered[3]. These provisions are also applied to a confiscation order made by the Crown Court, eg a confiscation order made under Part VI of the Criminal Justice Act 1988[4] or an order made under Part I of the Drug Trafficking Act 1994[5].

While the Crown Court may allow time for payment, or payment by instalments, of costs and compensation[6], it does not have power to fix a term of imprisonment or detention in default of payment. Any term in default of payment must be fixed by the magistrates' court responsible for the collection and enforcement of the costs and compensation[7].

The magistrates' court should approach enforcement of a Crown Court fine, recognizance or confiscation order as if it had fixed a term of imprisonment in default, just as the Crown Court has done, and as if it had postponed the issue of the warrant for the period of time that the Crown Court has set for the sum to be paid. Accordingly, if in such circumstances the defendant defaults in payment of the sum ordered by the Crown Court, there is no requirement under s 82(3) of the Magistrates' Courts Act 1980 to hold a means inquiry before issuing the commitment warrant[8]. However, the magistrates' court may not issue the warrant of commitment at a hearing at which the offender is not present unless the clerk of the court has served on the offender a notice in writing stating that the court intends to hold a hearing to consider whether to issue the warrant[9].

In proceedings to enforce a confiscation order the justices are entitled to hear representations from the prosecution regarding the background circumstances of the case[10].

---

1. Powers of Criminal Courts (Sentencing) Act 2000, s 140(1), this PART, post.
2. Powers of Criminal Courts (Sentencing) Act 2000, s 139(1), this PART, post.
3. Powers of Criminal Courts (Sentencing) Act 2000, s 139(2), this PART, post.
4. Criminal Justice Act 1988, s 75(1), in PART I: MAGISTRATES' COURTS, PROCEDURE, ante.
5. Drug Trafficking Act 1994, s 9, in PART VIII: MEDICINE AND PHARMACY, post.
6. Powers of Criminal Courts (Sentencing) Act 2000, s 141, this PART, post.
7. Administration of Justice Act 1970, s 41, in PART I: MAGISTRATES' COURTS, PROCEDURE, ante.
8. *R v Hastings and Rother Justices, ex p Anscombe* (1998) 162 JP 340.
9. Magistrates' Courts Act 1980, s 82(5), in PART I: MAGISTRATES' COURTS, PROCEDURE, ante.
10. See *R v Harrow Justices, ex p DPP* [1991] 1 WLR 395, (1991) 155 JP 979; and *R v Hastings and Rother Justices, ex p Anscombe* (1998) 162 JP 340.

EFFECT OF WINDING UP OR BANKRUPTCY

3–114 In bankruptcy any fine[1] imposed for an offence, and in winding up or bankruptcy any obligation arising under a confiscation order made under the Drug Trafficking Offences Act 1986, s 1[2] is not provable[3]. Similarly, it would seem that a fine should not be included in an administration order[4]. Where an interim order under s 253 of the Insolvency Act 1986[5] has been made pending a proposal for an individual voluntary arrangement, there is no obligation on justices to stay proceedings in the magistrates' court for enforcement of a fine[6].

A fine for this purpose includes a pecuniary forfeiture or compensation payable under a conviction[7], and would also seem to extend to a forfeiture of a recognisance[8] and an order for payment of back duty arising from the keeping of an unlicensed mechanically propelled vehicle[9]. However, the meaning of "fine" does not extend to include an order for costs adjudged to be paid on conviction, nor does it apply to an order for the payment of arrears of contributions to which the Social Security Act 1975 applies[10].

In the case of companies, magistrates' courts will have a discretion whether or not to prove for a fine in winding up. In the case of provable debts, other than "fines", which have been adjudged to be paid on conviction, we would expect persons to whom such debts were payable themselves to prove in winding up or bankruptcy.

If the money and goods of a company are insufficient to satisfy a fine by means of distress, the clerk of a magistrates' court may make an application in relation to the company for an administration order or winding-up[11].

Reference should be made to the Insolvency Act 1986 and the Insolvency Rules 1986,

SI 1986/1925, as amended, for the law and procedure relating to company insolvency and individual insolvency, but the following provisions are of general relevance and should be noted.

Winding up.   In a winding up by the court, any disposition of the company's property made after the commencement of the winding up is, unless the court otherwise orders, void[12]. Where a company registered in England and Wales is being wound up by the court, any attachment, sequestration, distress or execution put in force against the effects of the company after the commencement of the winding up is void[13]. At any time after the presentation of the winding up petition, and before the winding up order has been made, the company, or any creditor or contributory, may apply to the court having jurisdiction to wind up the company, to restrain further proceedings in any action or proceeding which is pending in any court against the company[14].

Administration.   Where an administration order is made in relation to a company under section 8 of the Insolvency Act 1986, no proceedings or other legal process may be commenced or continued, and no distress may be levied, against the company or its property except with the consent of the administrator or the leave of the court[15].

Bankruptcy.   Proceedings for recovery of a debt which is provable in bankruptcy[16] shall not be commenced by a creditor against a person who has been adjudged bankrupt except with leave of the court to which the bankruptcy proceedings have been allocated[17]. Any court in which proceedings are pending against any person may, on proof that a bankruptcy petition has been presented in respect of that person or that he is an undischarged bankrupt, either stay the proceedings or allow them to continue on such terms as it thinks fit[18].

Where any person is adjudged bankrupt, any disposition of property, including a payment in cash or otherwise, made by that person during the period beginning with the presentation of the bankruptcy petition and ending with the vesting of the bankrupt's estate in a trustee, is void unless made with the consent of the court to which the bankruptcy proceedings have been allocated. Any such payment which is thereby rendered void shall be held by the person paid for the bankrupt as part of his estate[19]. After the vesting in the trustee of the bankrupt's estate, the trustee may claim, subject to certain exceptions, any property which has been acquired by, or has devolved upon, the bankrupt since the commencement of the bankruptcy[20]. If the court administering the bankruptcy, on application of the trustee, makes an income payments order, it may discharge or vary any attachment of earnings order that is for the time being in force to secure payments by the bankrupt[21].

The discharge of an individual from bankruptcy does not release the bankrupt from any liability in respect of a fine or from any liability under a recognisance except, in the case of a penalty imposed for an offence under an enactment relating to the public revenue or of a recognisance, with the consent of the Treasury[22].

---

1. "Fine" has the meaning given by s 281(8) of the Insolvency Act 1986 which applies s 150(1) of the Magistrates' Courts Act 1980, in Part I: Magistrates Courts, Procedure, ante (Insolvency Rules 1986, r 12.3, SI 1986/1925 as amended.
2. See title Medicine and Pharmacy, in Part VIII, post.
3. Insolvency Rules 1986, r 12.3.
4. As to administration orders, see the County Courts Act 1984, ss 112, 112A and 112B. See also an opinion of the Justices' Clerks' Society – Inclusion of unpaid fines in administration orders – JCS News sheet 96/5, dated 6 February 1996.
5. As to individual voluntary arrangements, see the Insolvency Act 1986, ss 252–263.
6. *R v Barnet Magistrates' Court, ex p Phillipou* (unreported) (1996) CO/3535/94.
7. Magistrates' Courts Act 1980, s 150(1), in Part I: Magistrates' Courts, Procedure, ante.
8. See the Magistrates' Courts Act 1980, s 120(4), in Part I: Magistrates' Courts, Procedure, ante.
9. See the Vehicle Excise and Registration Act 1994, s 32(2), (3) in Part VII: Transport, title Road Traffic, post.
10. See the Social Security Administration Act 1992, s 121(4), title Social Security, in Part VIII, post.
11. Magistrates' Courts Act 1980, s 87A, in Part I: Magistrates' Courts, Procedure, ante.
12. Insolvency Act 1986, s 127.
13. Insolvency Act 1986, s 128.
14. Insolvency Act 1986, s 126.
15. Insolvency Act 1986, s 11(3).
16. For the meaning of "bankruptcy debt", see the Insolvency Act 1986, s 382, and as to provable debts, see the Insolvency Rules 1986, r 12.3.
17. Insolvency Act 1986, s 285(3), in Part VIII: Insolvency, post.
18. Insolvency Act 1986, s 285(2), in Part VIII: Insolvency, post.
19. Insolvency Act 1986, s 284, in Part VIII: Insolvency, post.
20. Insolvency Act 1986, s 307.
21. Insolvency Act 1986, s 310.
22. Insolvency Act 1986, s 281(4), in Part VIII: Insolvency, post.

COMMUNITY SENTENCES GENERALLY

3–115   Community sentences lie between financial penalties and imprisonment. The Criminal Justice Act 2003 introduced a new community sentence defined as a community order containing one or more of a total of 12 requirements[1]. In relation to offenders aged 18 and above, the new sentence applies to offences committed on or after 4 April 2005; in relation to offenders aged 16 and 17 the relevant date is 4 April 2009[2].

There are different powers of breach for "old" and "new" community sentences. Generally speaking[3], in relation to the former the court can impose a fine not exceeding £1,000; or revoke the order and, if it was made by a magistrates' court, re-sentence the offender or, if it was made by the Crown Court, commit him to the Crown Court for re-sentencing. In relation to the latter, the court must either: (*a*) amend the terms of the community order so as to impose more onerous requirements which the court could include if it were then making the order; or, (*b*) if the order was made by a magistrates' court, re-sentence the offender in any way in which the court could deal with him if he had just been convicted of the offence[4] or, (*c*) if it was made by the Crown Court, commit him to the Crown Court for re-sentencing.

A further, significant difference is that, in relation to "new" orders only, the court may exercise powers (b) and (c) above if the offender is convicted of a further offence during the currency of the order[5].

Where the court is dealing with offences that straddle the above commencement date, it is submitted that it permissible in principle, and desirable in practice, to sentence under one of the regimes only and to mark those offences which would come under the other regime "no separate penalty".

For narrative on the former community sentences, readers should refer to para **3–211** et seq of the 2005 edition of this work.

---

1. Listed in s 177 of the Criminal Justice Act 2003: see this PART, post.
2. See the Criminal Justice Act 2003 (Commencement No 8 and Transitional and Saving Provisions) Order 2005, SI 2005/950, as amended by SI 2007/391.
3. There are other options in relation to community punishment orders and combination orders, and curfew and community rehabilitation orders for offenders under the age of 21.
4. This includes the power to impose a custodial sentence for a non-imprisonable offence if the offenders is aged 18 or over and has persistently failed to comply with the terms of the order: see Criminal Justice Act 2003, Sch 8, para 9(1)(c).

DRUG REHABILITATION REQUIREMENT

3–116 A community sentence containing a drug rehabilitation requirement is the successor to "drug treatment and testing" orders, in relation to which the Court of Appeal gave the following guidance, which, it is submitted, continues to apply.

In *R v Woods and Collins*[1] the Court of Appeal summarised as follows the general approach to be derived from the authorities on drug treatment and testing orders.

(1) A drug-treatment and testing order was designed for repeat offenders whose offending was driven by drug dependence. Such offenders would often be those who would otherwise be sent to prison for a significant period. A drug-treatment and testing order was not a soft option. It imposed significant obligations on the offender and the court retained intensive supervision of his progress if he failed.

(2) The fact that the defendant had been a prolific offender did not necessarily mean that a drug-treatment and testing order would not be appropriate. There were plainly cases in which the nature of the offence or the scale of offending was such that only a custodial sentence was justified.

(3) A drug-treatment and testing order was an expensive order. It was not in the interests of the public or of the offender for such an order to be made where there were no reasonable prospects of its success. That would divert scarce resources from other cases. However, a 100 per cent success rate could not be expected.

(4) It followed that the judge had difficult balancing decisions to make at two stages. The first was, did the case warrant adjournment for a report on the possible availability of such an order? The second was, if there was such a report and it was favourable, was a drug-treatment and testing order the right disposal?

(5) The court would underline that a judge was not under an obligation to adjourn for a report in every case in which it was represented that the cause of the defendant's offending was drug dependence, and that the defendant would welcome a drug-treatment and testing order. It would be wasteful to adjourn for a report if there was no prospect of such an order being made and it would unjustifiably raise false expectations in the defendant.

(6) Experienced trial judges sitting in criminal cases had considerable knowledge of drug-treatment and testing orders because they supervised their working. At the stage of considering whether or not to seek a report they knew to look for possible signs that such an order might be effective. Generally they would have the assistance of the standard pre-sentence report. They were likely to look for indications that the defendant was likely to engage with the order and that he had sufficient stability in his home life to provide reasonable prospects of its succeeding. They were right at that stage to consider the nature of his offending. The other offences or the personal characteristics of the defendant, such as repeated breaches of community orders, might demonstrate that a drug treatment and testing order would plainly be inappropriate. They should not, however, reject the possibility of a drug-treatment and testing order simply on the ground that the defendant was a repeat thief or burglar for whom otherwise a custodial sentence would be inevitable.

(7) If a report was obtained, the judge had a second, often very difficult, decision to make. The decision was that of the judge, not the probation officer. It was the judge who had to weigh in the balance the public interest as well as the interests of the defendant. It was the judge who had to assess the criminality of the defendant as well as the desirability and prospects of rehabilitation. A drug-treatment and testing order might give excessive weight to the issue of rehabilitation.

(8) If at either stage the judge had properly addressed the issue before him and exercised his judgment, the court considered that it would be relatively rare for the Court of Appeal to say that he had arrived at a decision which erred in principle.

---

1. [2005] EWCA Crim 2065, [2006] 1 Cr App R (S) 83, [2005] Crim LR 982.

GUIDANCE OF THE SENTENCING GUIDELINES COUNCIL ON COMMUNITY SENTENCES

3–117   The following is an extract from the guidance of the Sentencing Guidelines Council in relation to the sentencing framework contained in the Criminal Justice Act 2003.
'Section 1 Part 1 – Community Sentences

A Statutory Provisions (i) The Thresholds for Community Sentences.
1.1.1 Seriousness – Section 148 Criminal Justice Act 2003:
(1) A court must not pass a community sentence on an offender unless it is of the opinion that the offence, or the combination of the offence and one or more offences associated with it, was serious enough to warrant such a sentence.
1.1.2 Persistent Offenders – Section 151 Criminal Justice Act 2003:
(1) Subsection (2) applies where—

(a)   a person aged 16 or over is convicted of an offence ("the current offence"),
(b)   on three or more previous occasions he has, on conviction by a court in the United Kingdom of any offence committed by him after attaining the age of 16, had passed on him a sentence consisting only of a fine, and
(c)   despite the effect of section 143(2), the court would not (apart from this section) regard the current offence, or the combination of the current offence and one or more offences associated with it, as being serious enough to warrant a community sentence.

(2) The court may make a community order in respect of the current offence instead of imposing a fine if it considers that, having regard to all the circumstances including the matters mentioned in subsection (3), it would be in the interests of justice to make such an order.
(ii) The Sentences Available
1.1.3 Meaning of Community Sentence – Section 147 Criminal Justice Act 2003
(1) In this Part "community sentence" means a sentence which consists of or includes –

(a)   a community order (as defined by section 177), or
(b)   one or more youth community orders.

1.1.4 Offenders aged 16* or over – Section 177 Criminal Justice Act 2003:
(1) Where a person aged 16* or over is convicted of an offence, the court by or before which he is convicted may make an order (in this Part referred to as a "community order") imposing on him any one or more of the following requirements –

(a)   an unpaid work requirement (as defined by section 199),
(b)   an activity requirement (as defined by section 201),
(c)   a programme requirement (as defined by section 202),
(d)   a prohibited activity requirement (as defined by section 203),
(e)   a curfew requirement (as defined by section 204),
(f)   an exclusion requirement (as defined by section 205),
(g)   a residence requirement (as defined by section 206),
(h)   a mental health treatment requirement (as defined by section 207),
(i)   a drug rehabilitation requirement (as defined by section 209),
(j)   an alcohol treatment requirement (as defined by section 212),
(k)   a supervision requirement (as defined by section 213), and
(l)   in a case where the offender is aged under 25, an attendance centre requirement (as defined by section 214).

(2) Subsection (1) has effect subject to sections 150 and 218 and to the following provisions of Chapter 4 relating to particular requirements –

(a)   section 199(3) (unpaid work requirement),
(b)   section 201(3) and (4) (activity requirement),
(c)   section 202(4) and (5) (programme requirement),
(d)   section 203(2) (prohibited activity requirement),
(e)   section 207(3) (mental health treatment requirement),
(f)   section 209(2) (drug rehabilitation requirement), and
(g)   section 212(2) and (3) (alcohol treatment requirement).

(3) Where the court makes a community order imposing a curfew requirement or an exclusion requirement, the court must also impose an electronic monitoring requirement (as defined by section 215) unless –

(*a*) it is prevented from doing so by section 215(2) or 218(4), or
(*b*) in the particular circumstances of the case, it considers it inappropriate to do so.

(4) Where the court makes a community order imposing an unpaid work requirement, an activity requirement, a programme requirement, a prohibited activity requirement, a residence requirement, a mental health treatment requirement, a drug rehabilitation requirement, an alcohol treatment requirement, a supervision requirement or an attendance centre requirement, the court may also impose an electronic monitoring requirement unless prevented from doing so by section 215(2) or 218(4).

(iii) Determining Which Orders to make & Requirements to Include
1.1.5 Suitability – Section 148 Criminal Justice Act 2003
(2) Where a court passes a community sentence which consists of or includes a community order –

(*a*) the particular requirement or requirements forming part of the community order must be such as, in the opinion of the court, is, or taken together are, the most suitable for the offender, and
(*b*) the restrictions on liberty imposed by the order must be such as in the opinion of the court are commensurate with the seriousness of the offence, or the combination of the offence and one or more offences associated with it.

1.1.6 Restrictions on liberty – Section 149 Criminal Justice Act 2003
(1) In determining the restrictions on liberty to be imposed by a community order or youth community order in respect of an offence, the court may have regard to any period for which the offender has been remanded in custody in connection with the offence or any other offence the charge for which was founded on the same facts or evidence.
1.1.7 Compatibility – Section 177 Criminal Justice Act 2003
(2) Before making a community order imposing two or more different requirements falling within subsection (1), the court must consider whether, in the circumstances of the case, the requirements are compatible with each other.
(iv) Electronic Monitoring
1.1.8 Section 177 Criminal Justice Act 2003
(3) Where the court makes a community order imposing a curfew requirement or an exclusion requirement, the court must also impose an electronic monitoring requirement (as defined by section 215) unless –

(*a*) it is prevented from doing so by section 215(2) or 218(4), or
(*b*) in the particular circumstances of the case, it considers it inappropriate to do so.

(4) Where the court makes a community order imposing an unpaid work requirement, an activity requirement, a programme requirement, a prohibited activity requirement, a residence requirement, a mental health treatment requirement, a drug rehabilitation requirement, an alcohol treatment requirement, a supervision requirement or an attendance centre requirement, the court may also impose an electronic monitoring requirement unless prevented from doing so by section 215(2) or 218(4).

B Imposing a Community Sentence – The Approach.
1.1.9 On pages 8 and 9 of the Seriousness guideline (see para 3–70, ante) the two thresholds for the imposition of a community sentence are considered. Sentencers must consider all of the disposals available (within or below the threshold passed) at the time of sentence, and reject them before reaching the provisional decision to make a community sentence, so that even where the threshold for a community sentence has been passed a financial penalty or discharge may still be an appropriate penalty. Where an offender has a low risk of reoffending, particular care needs to be taken in the light of evidence that indicates that there are circumstances where inappropriate intervention can increase the risk of re-offending rather than decrease it. In addition, recent improvements in enforcement of financial penalties make them a more viable sentence in a wider range of cases.
1.1.10 Where an offender is being sentenced for a non-imprisonable offence or offences, great care will be needed in assessing whether a community sentence is appropriate since failure to comply could result in a custodial sentence.
1.1.11 Having decided (in consultation with the Probation Service where appropriate) that a community sentence is justified, the court must decide which requirements should be included in the community order. The requirements or orders imposed will have the effect of restricting the offender's liberty, whilst providing punishment in the community, rehabilitation for the offender, and/or ensuring that the offender engages in reparative activities.
The key issues arising are:

(i)   which requirements to impose;
(ii)   how to make allowance for time spent in custody; and
(iii) how to deal with breaches.

(i) Requirements
1.1.12 When deciding which requirements to include, the court must be satisfied on three matters–

(i)   that the restriction on liberty is commensurate with the seriousness of the offence(s);[1]
(ii)   that the requirements are the most suitable for the offender;[2] and
(iii) that, where there are two or more requirements included, they are compatible with each other[3].

1.1.13 Sentencers should have the possibility of breach firmly in mind when passing sentence for the original offence. If a court is to reflect the seriousness of an offence, there is little value in setting requirements as part of a community sentence that are not demanding enough for an offender. On the other hand, there is equally little value in imposing requirements that would 'set an offender up to fail' and almost inevitably lead to sanctions for a breach.

In community sentences, the guiding principles are proportionality and suitability. Once a court has decided that the offence has crossed the community sentence threshold and that a community sentence is justified, the *initial* factor in defining which requirements to include in a community sentence should be the seriousness of the offence.

1.1.14 This means that "seriousness" is an important factor in deciding whether the Court chooses the low, medium or high range (see below) but, having taken that decision, selection of the content of the order within the range will be determined by a much wider range of factors.

- Sentencing ranges must remain flexible enough to take account of the suitability of the offender, his or her ability to comply with particular requirements and their availability in the local area.
- The justification for imposing a community sentence in response to persistent petty offending is the persistence of the offending behaviour rather than the seriousness of the offences being committed. The requirements imposed should ensure that the restriction on liberty is proportionate to the seriousness of the offending, to reflect the fact that the offences, of themselves, are not sufficiently serious to merit a community sentence.

(a) Information for Sentencers

1.1.15 In many cases, a pre-sentence report[4] will be pivotal in helping a sentencer decide whether to impose a custodial sentence or whether to impose a community sentence and, if so, whether particular requirements, or combinations of requirements, are suitable for an individual offender. The court must always ensure (especially where here are multiple requirements) that the restriction on liberty placed on the offender is proportionate to the seriousness of the offence committed[5]. The court must also consider the likely effect of one requirement on another, and that they do not place conflicting demands upon the offender[6].

1.1.16 The Council supports the approach proposed by the Panel at paragraph 78 of its Advice that, having reached the provisional view that a community sentence is the most appropriate disposal, the sentencer should request a pre-sentence report, indicating which of the three sentencing ranges is relevant and the purpose(s) of sentencing that the package of requirements is required to fulfil. Usually the most helpful way for the court to do this would be to produce a written note for the report writer, copied on the court file. If it is known that the same tribunal and defence advocate will be present at the sentencing hearing and a probation officer is present in court when the request for a report is made, it may not be necessary to commit details of the request to writing. However, events may change during the period of an adjournment and it is good practice to ensure that there is a clear record of the request for the court. These two factors will guide the Probation Service in determining the nature and combination of requirements that may be appropriate and the onerousness and intensity of those requirements. A similar procedure should apply when ordering a pre-sentence report when a custodial sentence is being considered.

1.1.17 There will be occasions when any type of report may be unnecessary despite the intention to pass a community sentence though this is likely to be infrequent. A court could consider dispensing with the need to obtain a pre-sentence report for adult offenders –

- where the offence falls within the LOW range of seriousness and
- where the sentencer was minded to impose a single requirement, such as an exclusion requirement (where the circumstances of the case mean that this would be an appropriate disposal without electronic monitoring) and
- where the sentence will not require the involvement of the Probation Service, for example an electronically monitored curfew (subject to the court being satisfied that there is an appropriate address at which the curfew can operate).

(b) Ranges of Sentence Within the Community Sentence Band

1.1.18 To enable the court to benefit from the flexibility that community sentences provide and also to meet its statutory obligations, any structure governing the use of community requirements must allow the courts to choose the most appropriate sentence for each individual offender.

1.1.19 Sentencers have a statutory obligation to pass sentences that are commensurate with the seriousness of an offence. However, within the range of sentence justified by the seriousness of the offence(s), courts will quite properly consider those factors that heighten the risk of the offender committing further offences or causing further harm with a view to lessening that risk. The extent to which requirements are imposed must be capable of being varied to ensure that the restriction on liberty is commensurate with the seriousness of the offence.

1.1.20 The Council recognises that it would be helpful for sentencers to have a framework to help them decide on the most appropriate use of the new community sentence. While there is no single guiding principle, the seriousness of the offence that has been committed is an important factor. Three sentencing ranges (low, medium and high) within the community sentence band can be identified. It is not possible to position particular types of offence at firm points within the three ranges because the seriousness level of an offence is largely dependent upon the culpability of the offender and this is uniquely variable. The difficulty is particularly acute in relation to the medium range where it is clear that requirements will need to be tailored across a relatively wide range of offending behaviour.

1.1.21 In general terms, the lowest range of community sentence would be for those offenders whose offence was relatively minor within the community sentence band and would include persistent petty offenders whose offences only merit a community sentence by virtue of failing to respond to the previous imposition of fines. Such offenders would merit a 'light touch' approach, for example, normally a single requirement such as a short period of unpaid work, or a curfew, or a prohibited activity requirement or an exclusion requirement (where the circumstances of the case mean that this would be an appropriate disposal without electronic monitoring).

1.1.22 The top range would be for those offenders who have only just fallen short of a custodial sentence and for those who have passed the threshold but for whom a community sentence is deemed appropriate.

1.1.23 In all three ranges there must be sufficient flexibility to allow the sentence to be varied to take account of the suitability of particular requirements for the individual offender and whether a particular requirement or package of requirements might be more effective at reducing any identified risk of re-offending. It will fall to the sentencer to ensure that the sentence strikes the right balance between proportionality and suitability.

There should be three sentencing ranges (low, medium and high) within the community sentence band based upon seriousness.

It is not intended that an offender necessarily progress from one range to the next on each sentencing occasion. The decision as to the appropriate range each time is based upon the seriousness of the new offence(s). The decision on the nature and severity of the requirements to be included in a community sentence should be guided by:

(i)   the assessment of offence seriousness (LOW, MEDIUM OR HIGH);
(ii) the purpose(s) of sentencing the court wishes to achieve;
(iii) the risk of re-offending;
(iv) the ability of the offender to comply, and
(v)   the availability of requirements in the local area.

The resulting restriction on liberty must be a proportionate response to the offence that was committed.

1.1.24 Below we set out a non-exhaustive description of examples of requirements that might be appropriate in the three sentencing ranges. These examples focus on punishment in the community, although it is recognised that not all packages will necessarily need to include a punitive requirement. There will clearly be other requirements of a rehabilitative nature, such as a treatment requirement or an accredited programme, which may be appropriate depending on the specific needs of the offender and assessment of suitability. Given the intensity of such interventions, it is expected that these would normally only be appropriate at medium and high levels of seriousness, and where assessed as having a medium or high risk of re-offending. In addition, when passing sentence in any one of the three ranges, the court should consider whether a rehabilitative intervention such as a programme requirement, or a restorative justice intervention might be suitable as an additional or alternative part of the sentence.

LOW

1.1.25 For offences only just crossing the community sentence threshold (such as persistent petty offending, some public order offences, some thefts from shops, or interference with a motor vehicle, where the seriousness of the offence or the nature of the offender's record means that a discharge or fine is inappropriate).

1.1.26 Suitable requirements might include:

•   40 to 80 hours of unpaid work or
•   a curfew requirement within the lowest range (e.g. up to 12 hours per day for a few weeks) or
•   an exclusion requirement (where the circumstances of the case mean that this would be an appropriate disposal without electronic monitoring) lasting a few months or
•   a prohibited activity requirement or
•   an attendance centre requirement (where available).

1.1.27 Since the restriction on liberty must be commensurate with the seriousness of the offence, particular care needs to be taken with this band to ensure that this obligation is complied with. In most cases, only one requirement will be appropriate and the length may be curtailed if additional requirements are necessary.

MEDIUM

1.1.28 For offences that obviously fall within the community sentence band such as handling stolen goods worth less than £1000 acquired for resale or somewhat more valuable goods acquired for the handler's own use, some cases of burglary in commercial premises, some cases of taking a motor vehicle without consent, or some cases of obtaining property by deception.

1.1.29 Suitable requirements might include:

•   a greater number (e.g. 80 to 150) of hours of unpaid work or
•   an activity requirement in the middle range (20 to 30 days) or
•   a curfew requirement within the middle range (e.g. up to 12 hours for 2–3 months) or
•   an exclusion requirement lasting in the region of 6 months or
•   a prohibited activity requirement.

1.1.30 Since the restriction on liberty must be commensurate with the seriousness of the offence, particular care needs to be taken with this band to ensure that this obligation is complied with.

HIGH

1.1.31 For offences that only just fall below the custody threshold or where the custody threshold is crossed but a community sentence is more appropriate in all the circumstances, for example some cases displaying the features of a standard domestic burglary committed by a first-time offender.

1.1.32 More intensive sentences which combine two or more requirements may be appropriate at this level. Suitable requirements might include an unpaid work order of between 150 and 300 hours; an activity requirement up to the maximum 60 days; an exclusion order lasting in the region of 12 months; a curfew requirement of up to 12 hours a day for 4–6 months.

(c) Electronic Monitoring

1.1.33 The court must also consider whether an electronic monitoring requirement[7] should be imposed which is mandatory[8] in some circumstances.

Electronic monitoring should be used with the primary purpose of promoting and monitoring compliance with other requirements, in circumstances where the punishment of the offender and/or the need to safeguard the public and prevent re-offending are the most important concerns.

(d) Recording the Sentence Imposed

1.1.34 Under the new framework there is only one (generic) community sentence provided by statute. This does not mean that offenders who have completed a community sentence and have then re-offended should be regarded as ineligible for a second community sentence on the basis that this has been tried and failed. Further community sentences, perhaps with different requirements, may well be justified.

1.1.35 Those imposing sentence will wish to be clear about the 'purposes' that the community sentence is designed to achieve when setting the requirements. Sharing those purposes with the offender and Probation Service will enable them to be clear about the goals that are to be achieved.

1.1.36 Any future sentencer must have full information about the requirements that were inserted by the court into the previous community sentence imposed on the offender (including whether it was a low/medium/high level order) and also about the offender's response. This will enable the court to consider the merits of imposing the same or different requirements as part of another community sentence. The requirements should be recorded in such a way as to ensure that they can be made available to another court if another offence is committed.

When an offender is required to serve a community sentence, the court records should be clearly annotated to show which particular requirements have been imposed.

(ii) Time Spent on Remand

1.1.37 The court will need to consider whether to give any credit for time spent in custody on remand[9]. (For further detail from the Panel's Advice, see Annex A)

The court should seek to give credit for time spent on remand (in custody or equivalent status) in all cases. It should make clear, when announcing sentence, whether or not credit for time on remand has been given (bearing in mind that there will be no automatic reduction in sentence once section 67 of the Criminal Justice Act 1967 is repealed) and should explain its reasons for not giving credit when it considers either that this is not justified, would not be practical, or would not be in the best interests of the offender.

1.1.38 Where an offender has spent a period of time in custody on remand, there will be occasions where a custodial sentence is warranted but the length of the sentence justified by the seriousness of the offence would mean that the offender would be released immediately. Under the present framework, it may be more appropriate to pass a community sentence since that will ensure supervision on release.

1.1.39 However, given the changes in the content of the second part of a custodial sentence of 12 months or longer, a court in this situation where the custodial sentence would be 12 months or more should, under the new framework, pass a custodial sentence in the knowledge that licence requirements will be imposed on release from custody. This will ensure that the sentence imposed properly reflects the seriousness of the offence.

1.1.40 Recommendations made by the court at the point of sentence will be of particular importance in influencing the content of the licence. This will properly reflect the gravity of the offence(s) committed.

(iii) Breaches

1.1.41 Where an offender fails, without reasonable excuse, to comply with one or more requirements, the "responsible officer"[10] can either give a warning or initiate breach proceedings. Where the offender fails to comply without reasonable excuse for the second time within a 12-month period, the 'responsible officer' must initiate proceedings.

1.1.42 In such proceedings the court must[11] either increase the severity of the existing sentence (i.e. impose more onerous conditions including requirements aimed at enforcement, such as a curfew or supervision requirement) or revoke the existing sentence and proceed as though sentencing for the original offence. The court is required to take account of the circumstances of the breach[12], which will inevitably have an impact on its response.

1.1.43 In certain circumstances (where an offender has wilfully and persistently failed to comply with an order made in respect of an offence that is not itself punishable by imprisonment), the court can impose a maximum of 51 weeks custody[13].

1.1.44 When increasing the onerousness of requirements, the court must consider the impact on the offender's ability to comply and the possibility of precipitating a custodial sentence for further breach. For that reason, and particularly where the breach occurs towards the end of the sentence, the court should take account of compliance to date and may consider that extending the supervision or operational periods will be more sensible; in other cases it might choose to add punitive or rehabilitative requirements instead. In making these changes the court must be mindful of the legislative restrictions on the overall length of community sentences and on the supervision and operational periods allowed for each type of requirement.

1.1.45 The court dealing with breach of a community sentence should have as its primary objective ensuring that the requirements of the sentence are finished, and this is important if the court is to have regard to the statutory purposes of sentencing. A court that imposes a custodial sentence for breach without giving adequate consideration to alternatives is in danger of imposing a sentence that is not commensurate with the seriousness of the original offence and is solely a punishment for breach. This risks undermining the purposes it has identified as being important. Nonetheless, courts will need to be vigilant to ensure that there is a realistic prospect of the purposes of the order being achieved.

Having decided that a community sentence is commensurate with the seriousness of the offence, the primary objective when sentencing for breach of requirements is to ensure that those requirements are completed.

1.1.46 A court sentencing for breach must take account of the extent to which the offender has complied with the requirements of the community order, the reasons for breach and the point at which the breach has occurred. Where a breach takes place towards the end of the operational period and the court is satisfied that the offender's appearance before the court is likely to be sufficient in itself to ensure future compliance, then given that it is not open to the court to make no order, an approach that the court might wish to adopt could be to re-sentence in a way that enables the original order to be completed properly – for example, a differently constructed community sentence that aims to secure compliance with the purposes of the original sentence.

1.1.47 If the court decides to increase the onerousness of an order, it must give careful consideration, with advice from the Probation Service, to the offender's ability to comply. A custodial sentence should be the last resort, where all reasonable efforts to ensure that an offender completes a community sentence have failed.

The Act allows for a custodial sentence to be imposed in response to breach of a community sentence. Custody should be the last resort, reserved for those cases of deliberate and repeated breach where all reasonable efforts to ensure that the offender complies have failed.

Before increasing the onerousness of requirements, sentencers should take account of the offender's ability to comply and should avoid precipitating further breach by overloading the offender with too many or conflicting requirements.

There may be cases where the court will need to consider re-sentencing to a differently constructed community sentence in order to secure compliance with the purposes of the original sentence, perhaps where there has already been partial compliance or where events since the sentence was imposed have shown that a different course of action is likely to be effective.'

* *The orders in respect of 16 and 17 year-olds are due to come into effect on April 4, 2007: see the Criminal Justice Act 2003 (Commencement No 8 and Transitional and Savings Provisions) Order 2005, SI 2005/950, art 2(2). Pending this, the provisions of ss 41-58 of, and Schs 2 and 4 to, the Powers of Criminal Courts Act 2000 continue to have effect (subject to any necessary modification): see SI 2005/950, Sch 2, para 8.*

1. Criminal Justice Act 2003, s 148(2).
2. Criminal Justice Act 2003, s 148(2)(a).
3. Criminal Justice Act 2003, s 177(6).
4. Under the Act, a pre-sentence report includes a full report following adjournment, a specific sentence report, a short format report or an oral report. The type of report supplied will depend on the level of information requested. Whenever it appears, the term "pre-sentence report" includes all these types of report.
5. Criminal Justice Act 2003, s 148(2).
6. Criminal Justice Act 2003, s 177(6).
7. Criminal Justice Act 2003, s 177(3) and (4).
8. Unless the necessary facilities are not avoidable or, in the particular circumstances of the case, the court considers it inappropriate.
9. Criminal Justice Act 2003, s 149.
10. Criminal Justice Act 2003, Sch 8, paras 5–6.
11. Criminal Justice Act 2003, Sch 8, paras 9–10.
12. Criminal Justice Act 2003, Sch 8, para 9(2).
13. Criminal Justice Act 2003, Sch 8, para 9(1)(c).

Custodial sentences

GENERAL RESTRICTIONS AND PRINCIPLES

3–130 Introduction. The Criminal Justice Act 2003 substantially changed the law on sentencing. At the date at which this volume states the law, not all of these reforms were in force. Moreover, of those which have been brought into effect many apply only to offences committed on or after a specified date, and many have been implemented with transitional arrangements pending the commencement of other provisions[1]. To avoid confusion, the narrative below reflects the law as in force at the time of going to press and as applicable to offences committed on or after 4 April 2005. For offences committed before this date, readers should consult the 2005 edition of this work.

General restrictions on custodial sentences. The following restrictions or principles apply to sentences of imprisonment for offences other than those for which a custodial sentence is fixed by law or is obligatory[2]:

(a) the court must be of the opinion that the offence, or the combination of the offence and one or more offences associated with it, is so serious[3] that neither a fine alone not a community sentence can be justified for it, unless the offender expresses his unwillingness to comply with a requirement in a community order for which an expression of such willingness is necessary[4];

(b) before forming the opinion referred to in (a) above, the court must obtain and consider a pre sentence report unless the court is of the opinion that it is unnecessary to obtain such a report[5];

(c) where the offender is or appears to be mentally disordered the court must obtain a medical report unless the court is of the opinion that it is unnecessary to obtain such a report[6];

(d) the defendant must be present[7];

(e) the defendant must be legally represented, unless he was granted a right to legal representation but this was withdrawn through his conduct or he has refused or failed to apply for a right to legal representation[8];

(f) the sentence must be for the shortest term that in the opinion of the court is commensurate with the seriousness of the offence and one or more offences associated with it[9] and

(g) the court must give its reasons for, and explain the effect of, the sentence[10] and the reasons must be specified in the warrant of commitment and entered in the court register[11].

Guidance on the imposition of discretionary sentences of imprisonment. In recent years, the Court of Appeal has made various pronouncements of a general nature in relation to discretionary sentences of imprisonment. We set out some of these below, though it must be borne in mind that they pre-date the, as yet incomplete, implementation of the sentencing framework of the Criminal Justice Act 2003. Of particular note, the 2003 Act, for the first time, put the purposes of sentencing on a statutory footing[12], and increased the range and potential severity of community orders. See, also, the Sentencing Guidelines Council's guidance on the sentencing thresholds[3].

In response to the sharp rise in the female prison population since 1993 the Lord Chief Justice has stated that where an offence involving dishonesty, but not the use of violence, is committed by a mother responsible for the care of her children and of previous good character, she should not be sentenced to imprisonment where an alternative is available[13]. More generally, the Lord Chief Justice has stated that sentencers must take into account the impact on the prison system of the numbers that prisoners are currently required to accommodate; only those who need to be in prison should be sent there, and the terms should be no longer than are necessary[14].

The Court of Appeal has declined to lay down prescriptive rules as to the kinds of offence which fall within the description "so serious that only such a sentence can be justified for the offence". However, the Court of Appeal has said[15] that in approaching cases which are on or near the custody threshold courts will usually find it helpful to begin by considering the nature and extent of the defendant's criminal intention and the nature and extent of any injury or damage caused to the victim. Other things being equal, an offence which is deliberate and premeditated will usually be more serious than one which is spontaneous and unpremeditated or which involves an excessive response to provocation; an offence which inflicts personal injury or mental trauma, particularly if permanent, will usually be more serious than one which inflicts financial loss only. In considering the seriousness of any offence the court may take into account any previous convictions of the offender or any failure to respond to previous sentences and must treat it as an aggravating factor if the offence was committed while the offender was on bail.

In deciding whether to impose a custodial sentence in borderline cases the sentencing court will ordinarily take account of matters relating to the offender:

(1) The court will have regard to the offender's admission of responsibility for the offence, particularly if reflected in a plea of guilty tendered at the earliest opportunity and accompanied by hard evidence of genuine remorse, as shown for example, by an expression of regret to the victim and an offer of compensation.

(2) Where offending has been fuelled by addiction to drink or drugs, the court will be inclined to look more favourably on an offender who has already demonstrated, by taking practical steps to that end, a genuine, self-motivated determination to address his addiction.

(3) Youth and immaturity, while affording no defence, will often justify a less rigorous penalty than would be appropriate for an adult.

(4) Some measure of leniency will ordinarily be extended to offenders of previous good character, the more so if there is evidence of positive good character, such as a solid employment record or faithful discharge of family duties, as opposed to a mere absence of previous convictions. It will sometimes be appropriate to take account of family responsibilities, or physical or mental disability.

(5) While the court will never impose a custodial sentence unless satisfied that it is necessary to do so, there will be an even greater reluctance to impose a custodial sentence on an offender who has never before served such a sentence.

The prevalence of a particular class of offence and public concern about them are relevant to seriousness[16]. Nevertheless, the court is still required to consider whether a custodial sentence is appropriate having regard to mitigating factors available and relevant to the offender, as opposed to such factors as are relevant to the offence[17].

Once an offender qualifies for a custodial sentence, the court is not precluded from passing on the same occasion custodial sentences for offences which themselves do not satisfy the statutory requirements in s 148 of the Criminal Justice Act 2003. However, it will usually be inappropriate in such circumstances for consecutive sentences to be passed for offences which do not themselves meet that test[18].

Where an offender has been sentenced to a term of imprisonment and it is intended to proceed further against him for offences previously committed and which are then known to the police, it is the duty of the responsible authorities to make up their minds at once whether any and, if so, what steps are to be taken. It is not fair either to the convicted person or to the public to leave him in prison to serve his term and after release commence for the first time proceedings against him for an offence committed before the term of imprisonment began[19].

The fact that an offender may have to serve his sentence in isolation or will otherwise find prison difficult to cope with is irrelevant[20]. However, responsibility for complying with article 3 of the European Convention on Human Rights may, in some cases, require the court to make inquiry of the conditions under which the defendant is to be held[21].

Courts should not adjust prison terms for offences according to whether or not the offender might be eligible for early release on home detention curfew; this is far too speculative anarea and basis on which sentencers should proceed[22].

---

1. See the Criminal Justice Act 2003 (Commencement No 8 and Transitional and Saving Provisions) Order 2005, SI 2005/950 and the Criminal Justice Act 2003 (Sentencing) (Transitory Provisions) Order 2005, SI 2005/643.
2. Ie murder; and sentences that fall to be imposed under s 51A(2) of the Firearms Act 1968 (minimum terms of 3 and 5 years for certain firearms offences), ss 110(2) or 111(2) of the Powers of Criminal Courts (Sentencing) Act 2000 (minimum terms of 7 years and 3 years for a third conviction for, respectively, class A drug trafficking and burglary), or ss 225–228 of the Criminal Justice Act 2003 (certain violent or sexual offences).
3. See the guidance of the Sentencing Guidelines Council at para **3–70 *E The Sentencing Thresholds***, ante.
4. Criminal Justice Act 2003, s 152(1) and (3): see this PART, post.
5. CJA 2003, s 156(3). However, failure to obtain and consider such a report will not invalidate the sentence: CJA 2003, s 156(6).
6. CJA 2003, s 157(1) and (2). However, failure to obtain and consider such a report will not invalidate the sentence: CJA 2003, s 157(4).
7. Magistrates' Courts Act 1980, s 11(3)
8. Powers of Criminal Courts (Sentencing) Act 2000, s 83: see this PART, post.
9. Criminal Justice Act 2003, s 153(2).
10. CJA 2003, s 174. Model explanations for the imposition of custodial sentences have been provided: see *Practice Direction (criminal: consolidated)* [2002] paras 1.7, 1.8, Annex C, in PART 1: MAGISTRATES' COURTS, PROCEDURE, ante.
11. CJA 2003, s 174(5).
12. See para **3–10**, ante.
13. *R v Mills* [2002] EWCA Crim 26, [2002] 2 Cr App Rep (S) 51, [2002] Crim LR 331.
14. *R v Kefford* [2002] EWCA Crim 519, [2002] 2 Cr App Rep (S) 495, [2002] Crim LR 432. See also *A-G's Reference (No 11 of 2006) (Thomas Richard Edwin Scarth)* [2006] EWCA Crim 856, [2006] 2 Cr App R (S) 108, where it was held that prison overcrowding might be a relevant factor where the sentencer's decision was on the cusp; prison overcrowding would also make it all the more important that the sentencer complied with the requirements of ss 152 and 154 of the Criminal Justice Act 2003. The observations on the need to avoid custodial sentences were subject to the exception that courts should not be deterred from imprisoning those for appropriate periods those who committed offences involving violence or intimidation other grave crimes.
15. *R v Howells* [1999] 1 All ER 50, [1999] 1 Cr App Rep 98, 162 JP 731.
16. *R v Cox* [1993] 2 All ER 19, [1993] 1 WLR 188; *R v Cunningham* [1993] 2 All ER 15, [1993] 1 WLR 183.
17. Criminal Justice Act 2003, s 166, this PART, post; *R v Cox* [1993] 2 All ER 19, [1993] 1 WLR 188, this PART, post.
18. *R v Oliver* [1993] 2 All ER 9, [1993] 1 WLR 177.
19. *R v Silverman* (1986) 25 Cr App Rep 101; *R v Fairfield* (1987) 9 Cr App Rep (S) 49.
20. *R v Parker* (1996) 2 Cr App Rep (S) 275, [1996] Crim LR 445.
21. See *Price v United Kingdom* [2001] Crim LR 916 (severely disabled defendant subjected to degrading treatment when kept in unsuitable conditions).
22. *R v Abdullah Al-Buhairi* [2003] EWCA Crim 2922, [2004] 1 CrApp R (S) 83.

SHORT LOCAL DETENTION

3–131   A magistrates' court may, instead of imposing imprisonment on a person, order him to be detained within the precincts of the court house or at any police station until 8 pm, or such earlier time as will give him a reasonable opportunity of returning to his abode that day[1].

This is not imprisonment, and hence is free from the restrictions which apply to imprisonment, whether as a primary sentence or in default of paying a fine. Accordingly, these powers are available in the case of offenders aged 18–20.

---

1. Magistrates' Courts Act 1980, s 135: see Part I: Magistrates' Courts, Procedure, ante.

DETENTION IN A YOUNG OFFENDER INSTITUTION[1]

3–132   Where an offender aged 18, 19 or 20[2] is convicted of an offence which is punishable with imprisonment in the case of a person aged 21 or over, the court may pass a sentence of detention in a young offender institution[3]. It is the date of conviction which is relevant for the purpose of determining the age of the offender[3]. Sentences of detention up to the maximum permitted period of imprisonment for an adult convicted of the offence in question may be passed[4]. However, a magistrates' court shall not pass a sentence of detention in a young offender institution which exceeds six months for any one offence[5]. The minimum term of detention will be 21 days[6].

Where an offender is convicted of more than one offence for which he is liable to a sentence of detention in a young offender institution, or an offender who is serving such a sentence is convicted of one or more further offences for which he is liable to such a sentence, the court has the same power to pass consecutive sentences of detention as if they were sentences of imprisonment[3]. Where an offender who is serving a sentence of detention in a young offender institution, and is aged over 21 years, is convicted of one or more further offences for which he is liable to imprisonment, the court has power to pass one or more sentences of imprisonment to run consecutively upon the sentence of detention in a young offender institution[7].

An offender sentenced to detention in a young offender institution must be released as soon as he has served one half of the sentence[8]. He shall be under the supervision of a probation officer or a social worker of a local authority social services department for a period usually of three months[9]. Since the period under supervision is an integral part of the sentence, courts are recommended to inform the offender at the time of sentencing that the sentence comprises a period in custody followed by a period under supervision, and that while under supervision he must comply with such requirements as may be specified in a notice from the Secretary of State. Failure to comply with such a requirement is an offence punishable on summary conviction by a fine not exceeding **level 3** on the standard scale or to an appropriate custodial sentence for a period not exceeding **30 days**[9].

Young adults sentenced to detention shall be taken to an allocation unit for assessment and onward transfer to an appropriate young offender institution.

1. As to custodial sentences generally, see para **3–130**. Detention in a young offender institute for offenders aged 18–20 is prospectively abolished by the Criminal Justice and Courts Services Act 2002: see PART I, MAGISTRATES' COURTS, PROCEDURE, ante.
2. For offenders under 18 see para **5–60** post.
3. Powers of Criminal Courts (Sentencing) Act 2000, s 96, this PART, post.
4. Powers of Criminal Courts (Sentencing) Act 2000, s 97(1), this PART, post.
5. Powers of Criminal Courts (Sentencing) Act 2000, s 78(1), this PART, post.
6. Powers of Criminal Courts (Sentencing) Act 2000, s 97(2), this PART, post.
7. Powers of Criminal Courts (Sentencing) Act 2000, s 97(5), this PART, post.
8. Criminal Justice Act 1991, s 33.
9. Criminal Justice Act 1991, s 65, this PART, post. As to the requirements that may be included, see s 65(5A) and (5B).

IMPRISONMENT[1]

3–133 The following paragraphs state the law following the partial implementation of the custody provisions of the Criminal Justice Act 2003. Of particular note, "custody plus", a new form of sentence introduced by that Act, has not been brought into effect.

1. As to custodial sentences generally, see para **3–130**, ante.

3–134 Maximum terms and principles governing consecutive terms. (*a*) Maximum terms
Pending further implementation of the sentencing provisions of the Criminal Justice Act 2003, the maximum term of imprisonment that can be passed in the magistrates' court for any single offence is 6 months[1]. Consecutive terms can be imposed in respect of 2 or more offences with an aggregate maximum of 12 months where the court is dealing with 2 or more either way offences, or 6 months in any other case[2]. The restriction on aggregate terms applies, however, only to sentences imposed on the same occasion[3].

(*b*) Principles governing consecutive sentences
The general principle is that consecutive sentences should not be passed in respect of two or more offences arising out of the same facts and involving the same criminality, for example obtaining goods and obtaining pecuniary advantage by deception in the course of the same transaction[4], or almost simultaneous indecent assault and assault occasioning actual bodily harm[5], or multiple deaths arising out of the same incident of dangerous driving[6], but in special circumstances where for example a defendant persistently drove while disqualified and when he had had too much to drink, the practice of passing concurrent sentences for two offences arising out of the same facts could not apply, otherwise the defendant would have a licence to drive with excess alcohol without any added penalty[7]. Where a defendant had been charged with an offence and while on bail for the offence had committed another offence of the same character, the sentences in respect of each offence should be served consecutively[8]. A custodial sentence imposed for failure to answer bail should in principle be ordered to be served consecutively to any sentence imposed for the substantive offence for which the offender is before the court[9]. Likewise, where following arrest a defendant had assaulted the police, the sentence for that assault should be consecutive to that for the offence for which he had been arrested[8]. If the offender is already subject to two or more consecutive terms of imprisonment, any new consecutive sentence should be announced as "consecutive to the total period of imprisonment to which you are already subject"[9]. One prison term cannot be made partly consecutive to another[10].

It is wrong to impose a disproportionate sentence in order to defeat the operation of the Rehabilitation of Offenders Act 1974[11]. On the other hand, the court should not shut its eyes to the injustice which a consecutive term of imprisonment may have if the offender is put into a different early release category[12]. Where the imposition of a consecutive term of imprisonment in default of payment of a fine may have such effect, unless there are good reasons for concluding that the fine should be wiped off by a concurrent term of imprisonment, the appropriate course may be not to deal with the default until the offender has served his sentence on existing matters and has been released[13].

---

1. Powers of Criminal Courts (Sentencing) Act 2000, this PART, post.
2. Magistrates' Courts Act 1980, s 133: see PART I: MAGISTRATES' COURTS, PROCEDURE, ante. The restrictions in s 133 do not apply to activating suspended sentences or ordering the return to prison of an offender under the Powers of Criminal Courts (Sentencing) Act 2000; see the footnotes to s 133.
3. *R v Metropolitan Stipendiary Magistrate for South Westminster, ex p Green* [1977] 1 All ER 353, 141 JP 151; *Re Forrest* [1981] AC 1038, [1981] 2 All ER 71.
4. *R v Torr* [1966] 1 All ER 178, [1966] 1 WLR 52, 130 JP 139.
5. *R v Stabler* (1984) 6 Cr App Rep (S) 129. But offences committed in close temporal proximity and against the same factual background may justify consecutive sentences: *R v Partridge* (2001) 165 JPN 915 (related domestic assaults – the first against the defendant's wife's lover and the second against the wife herself).
6. *R v Noble* [2002] EWCA Crim 1713, [2002] Crim LR 676.
7. *R v Wheatley* [1984] RTR 273, [1984] Crim LR 183; followed in *R v Dillon* [1984] RTR 270 and *R v Matthews* (1988) 9 Cr App Rep (S) 367, [1988] Crim LR 128, CA. See also *R v Dent* [2001] EWCA Crim 935, (2001) 165 JPN 254 (6 months' imprisonment for driving while disqualified consecutive to 15 months for dangerous driving upheld).
8. *R v White; R v McKinnon* (2002) 146 Sol Jo LB 281.
9. *R v David Hill* (1983) 5 Cr App Rep (S) 214, CA.
10. *R v Gregory and Mills* [1969] 2 All ER 174, [1969] 1 WLR 455, 133 JP 731.
11. *R v Jeffcoate* [1980] Crim LR 61.
12. *R v Burnley Magistrates' Court, ex p Halstead* (1990) 155 JP 288, 12 Cr App Rep (S) 468 (defendant serving a sentence of 12 months' detention ordered to serve a further 14 days' detention for an unpaid fine whereby she became eligible for only one-third remission rather than one-half, thus increasing the total term of detention to be served by 74 days; on appeal additional term of 14 days quashed) and see *R v Waite* (1992) 13 Cr App Rep (S) 26; *R v Ensley* [1996] 1 Cr App Rep (S) 294 and *R v Cozens* (1996) 2 Cr App Rep (S) 321, [1996] Crim LR 522.
13. *R v Ipswich Justices, ex p Smith* (1992) 156 JP 787.

3–135   Duration of the sentence.   A sentence of imprisonment for "one calendar month" expires at the first moment of the corresponding day in the succeeding month; but if, owing to the shortness of the month, there is no such corresponding day, then it ends at the last moment of the last day of the succeeding month[1]. The imprisonment under the order of a magistrates' court runs from the date of reception at the prison; where a prisoner cannot be taken to the prison on the same day, an express order ought to be inserted in the commitment that the sentence is to be reckoned from the date on which it is passed[2]. Warrants of commitment in which the word "month" is used are construed as meaning calendar months unless the contrary is expressed[3]. The prisoner may be conveyed either to the prison mentioned in the warrant of commitment or to any other prison[4].

---

1. *Migotti v Colvill* (1879) 4 CPD 233, 43 JP 620 (31 October–30 November).
2. *Henderson v Preston* (1888) 21 QBD 362, 52 JP 820 (arrest 24 August, taken to prison for seven days 25 August, released 1 September). See 56 JP 568.
3. Prison Act 1952, s 24.
4. Criminal Procedure Rules 2005, Part 18, in PART I: MAGISTRATES' COURTS, PROCEDURE, ante.

3–136   Imprisonment combined with financial orders.   Although many statutes make the maximum penalty both imprisonment and a fine, it is not usually appropriate to impose a fine (or to order costs) at the same time as imposing an immediate sentence of imprisonment, on the principle that on release from prison the defendant will need such money as he earns in order to get started in life again. A fine or costs may, however, be ordered in special circumstances where, for example, the defendant has private capital[1]. A similar principle applies in the case of compensation, but it may be reasonable to order a restricted amount of compensation to be paid after release if the defendant can be expected to be earning[2]. If the offender has no means, the question of his ability to find work on release from prison should be taken into account[3].

---

1. *R v Judd* [1971] 1 All ER 127n and *R v Gaston* [1971] 1 All ER 128n
2. *R v Bradburn* (1973) 57 Cr App Rep 948; *R v Wylie* [1975] RTR 94.
3. *R v McIntosh* [1973] Crim LR 378.

3–137   Enforcing fines at the same time as imposing imprisonment.   Where a magistrates' court on the one occasion imposes imprisonment and a fine for the *same* offence (and throughout "fine" includes costs, damages and compensation[1]), it may exceed in aggregate the normal limits of 6 months total for summary offences, 12 months for offences triable either way if it then or later imposes an alternative imprisonment in default of paying the fine[2].

Where a magistrates' court on the one occasion imposes imprisonment and a fine for *different* offences, it may not on that occasion impose alternative imprisonment in default so that in aggregate the total imprisonment exceeds the aforementioned maximum overall terms. If however the court on the one occasion imposes imprisonment and a fine for *different* offences, and then on a *later* occasion deals with the fine by way of enforcement, it may then impose imprisonment in default of payment of the fine consecutive to imprisonment being served which in the aggregate exceeds the aforementioned maximum overall terms[3].

If the court is dealing on one occasion with several fines and imposes imprisonment in default of payment, the aggregate may not exceed the aforementioned maximum overall terms[4].

Where a court on the one occasion imposes imprisonment for an offence and then imposes imprisonment in default of payment of a fine imposed on a previous occasion, it may not exceed the aforementioned maximum overall terms[5].

1. *R v Raisis* [1969] 3 All ER 455, 133 JP 731.
2. Magistrates' Courts Act 1980, s 150(3).
3. Magistrates' Courts Act 1980, s 133(4).
4. *R v Metropolitan Stipendiary Magistrate for South Westminster, ex p Green* [1977] 1 All ER 353, 141 JP 151; *Re Forrest* [1981] AC 1038, [1981] 2 All ER 711.
5. Magistrates' Courts Act 1980, s 133(1), (2), (5).

3–138   Early release and licence.

(*a*) Release from sentences of less than 12 months

Pending the implementation of the "custody plus" provisions of the Criminal Justice Act 2003, the early release and licence provisions of that Act are of no effect in relation to any sentence of imprisonment of less than 12 months[1]. Persons subject to such sentences continue to be dealt with in accordance with the Criminal Justice Act 1991 and must be released unconditionally when they have served one half of the term[2]. If such an offender, after his release but before the end of his sentence, commits a further imprisonable offence the court can order his return to prison to serve the whole or part of the unexpired term of the original sentence[3].

(*b*) Release from longer determinate sentences

Persons sentenced to determinate terms of imprisonment, other than "dangerous offenders"[4], must be released at the halfway point of the sentence *if the sentence was imposed for an offence committed on or after 4 April 2005*[5]. In relation to *earlier* offences, the early release provisions, and consequential repeals, of the Criminal Justice Act 2003 are of no effect[6] and such persons will continue to be subject to the early release provisions of the Criminal Justice Act 1991 at the halfway point of the sentence if it was for less than 4 years, no later that the two-thirds point in any other case[7]. The Sentencing Guidelines Council has issued guidance in relation to custodial sentences of 12 months or more[8].

Release on licence.   For the time being, the early release and licence provisions of the Criminal Justice Act 2003 are of no effect in relation to prison sentences of less than 12 months[6]. In respect of determinate sentences of at least 12 months *imposed for offences committed on or after 4 April 2005*, other than extended sentences for imposed under the dangerous offender provisions, the Secretary of State must release an offender on licence no later when he has reached the halfway point of the sentence, and earlier release is possible within certain limits[9]. The licence runs for the remainder of the sentence[10]. As to recall for offences committed before 4 April 2005, and the duration of the period of licence following release from such recall, see s 254 of the Criminal Justice Act 2003 and the note thereto[11].

In relation of offences committed on or after 4 April 2005, a court which sentences an offender to a term of imprisonment of at least 12 months for an offence may recommend to the Secretary of State particular conditions to be included[12]. The Sentencing Guidelines Council has issued guidance as to the use of this power[13].

1. See para 14 of Sch 2 to the Criminal Justice Act 2003 (Commencement No 8 and Transitional and Savings Provisions) Order, SI 2005/950.
2. Criminal Justice Act 1991, s 33. As for earlier release on home detention curfew, see CJA 1991, s 34A et seq.
3. Under the Powers of Criminal Courts (Sentencing) Act 2000, s 116, the repeal of which is of no effect in relation to sentences of less than 12 months, whenever the offence was committed, or longer sentences for offences committed prior to 4 April 2005: see para 29 of Sch 2 to the Criminal Justice Act 2003 (Commencement No 8 and Transitional and Saving Provisions) Order 2005.
4. See para **3–153**, ante.
5. Criminal Justice Act 2003, s 244.
6. See para 19 of Sch 2 to the Criminal Justice Act 2003 (Commencement No 8 and Transitional and Savings Provisions) Order, SI 2005/950.
7. See the Criminal Justice Act 1991, ss 33 et seq.
8. See para **3–153** at 2.1.1, post.
9. See CJA 2003, ss 244–246. As to the operation of early release in relation to intermittent custody see, CJA 2003, s 245.
10. CJA 2003, s 249.
11. In this Part, post, at para **3–2041.**
12. CJA 2003, s 238.
13. See para **3–153** at 2.1.11, post.

3–139   Credit for time on remand.   Again, the provisions of the Criminal Justice Act 2003 as to the crediting of periods of remand[1] apply only to offences committed on or after 4 April 2005[2]. The new provisions require the court to direct that the number of days for which the offender was remanded in custody[3] in connection with the offence or a related offence[4] must count towards the sentence as time served, expect to the extent that rules[5] otherwise provide or the court is of the opinion that it is just in all the circumstances not to given such a direction. Where the court is of the aforementioned opinion it must state why it is giving no credit or reduced credit in respect of the period on remand[6]. The Sentencing Guidelines Council has given guidance in relation to the treatment of time spent on remand[7]. The Court of Appeal has also given general guidance and held that where a sentencer is considering making no direction it is good practice to state this in advance so that defence counsel can address the issue and seek to persuade him otherwise[8]. The 2003 Act provisions on credit for time on remand apply to any sentence of imprisonment, whether it is: an

original sentence of imprisonment, one imposed for breach of a community order, one imposed by way of activation of a suspended sentence, one imposed in default of payment of a sum adjudged to be paid by way of a conviction, one imposed for want of sufficient distress to satisfy any sum of money, or one imposed for failure to do or abstain from doing anything required to be done or left undone[9].

The provisions of s 67 of the Criminal Justice Act 1967 continue to apply to offences committed before 4 April 2005[10].

1. Criminal Justice Act 2003, s 240.
2. CJA 2003, s 240(1)(*a*).
3. Defined in CJA 2003, s 242(2).
4. Defined in CJA 2003,s 240(1)(*b*).
5. See the Remand in Custody (Effect of Concurrent and Consecutive Sentences of Imprisonment) Rules 2005, SI 2995/2954 in this part, post.
6. CJA 2003, s 240(4), (6).
7. See para **3–117** at 1.1.37, post.
8. *R v Dean Badredan Barber* [2006] EWCA Crim 162, [2006] 2 Cr App R (S) 81, [2006] Crim LR 549.
9. See the definition of 'sentence of imprisonment' in CJA 2003, s 305 as modified for these purposes by s 242(1).
10. See the Crime (Sentences) Act 1997 (Commencement No 4) Order 2005, SI 2005/932. As to the scope of s 67, readers should refer to para **3–244** of the 2005 edition of this work.

3–150 Order for return following commission of further offence. Where an offender has been released from prison in respect of a prison sentence *of at least 12 months* imposed for an offence committed before 4 April 2005, or in respect of a prison sentence of less than 12 months imposed for an offence whenever committed, a court dealing with a subsequent offence can make an order under s 116 of the Powers of Criminal Courts (Sentencing) Act 2000 returning the offender to custody for the relevant period, and order that the sentence for the subsequent offence shall run consecutively to that period[1].

1. The repeal of s 116 is of no effect in relation to sentences of less than 12 months, whenever the offence was committed, or longer sentences for offences committed prior to 4 April 2005: see para 29 of Sch 2 to the Criminal Justice Act 2003 (Commencement No 8 and Transitional and Saving Provisions) Order 2005, SI 2005/950. See also *R v Ian Lloyd Howell* [2006] EWCA Crim 860, [2006] 2 Cr App R (S) 115, [2006] Crim LR 763
As to the principles governing orders of return, readers should refer to the footnotes to s 116 at page 1752 of the 2005 edition of this work.

SUSPENDED PRISON SENTENCES OF IMPRISONMENT

3–151 (a) *Offences committed before 4 April 2005.* The provisions of the Criminal Justice Act 2005 in relation to suspended sentence of imprisonment are of no effect in relation to these offences[1]. Accordingly, suspended sentences for such offences continue to be governed by the former provision[2].
(b) *Offences committed on or after 4 April 2005.* The Criminal Justice Act 2003 makes provision for suspended sentences[3]. As currently modified[4], these provision enable the court to suspend a sentence of imprisonment, or, in the case of offender aged 18–20, a sentence of detention in a young offender institute, of at least 14 days and not more than 12 months, in the case of the Crown Court, or 6 months in the case of the magistrates' court. The Sentencing Guidelines Council has issued guidance in relation to the suspended sentence provisions of the 2003 Act, which includes a full description of the requirements for, content of and powers in the event of breach of such a sentence[5].

In summary, a suspended sentence order must include one or more of the requirements that can be included in a community order and any such requirement must be complied with during the "supervision period" which will be not less than 6 months or more than 2 years. The order must also specify an "operational period" which will be again be for not less than 6 months or more than 2 years. The "supervision" and "operational" periods can be different, but the former may not exceed the latter. The sentence of imprisonment will not take effect unless during the supervision period the offender fails to comply with a requirement of the order or during the operational period the offender commits a further imprisonable offence in the UK.

A community sentence cannot be passed at the same time as a suspended sentence[6].

For the purpose of crediting periods of remand in custody a suspended sentence is to be treated as a sentence of imprisonment when it is activated and as being imposed by the order that so activates it[7].

There is power to provide for periodic review of suspended sentence orders[8].

There are provisions dealing with the breach or amendment of suspended sentence orders and the effect of a further conviction[9].

1. See para 14 of Sch 2 to the Criminal Justice Act 2003 (Commencement No 8 and Transitional and Savings Provisions) Order 2005, SI 2005/950.
2. As to which, see paras **3–247** and **3–248** of the 2005 edition of this work.
3. In ss 189–194 and Sch 12.
4. By the Criminal Justice Act 2003 (Sentencing) (Transitory Provisions) Order 2005.
5. See para **3–117**, Section 2, Part 2, post.
6. Criminal Justice Act 2003, s 189(5).
7. Criminal Justice Act 2003, s 240(7).
8. Criminal Justice Act 2003, ss 191 & 192.
9. Criminal Justice Act 2003, Sch 12.

GUIDANCE OF THE SENTENCING GUIDELINES COUNCIL ON
SUSPENDED SENTENCES

3–152 The following is an extract from the guidance of the Sentencing Guidelines Council on new sentences under the Criminal Justice Act 2003.

'*Section 2 Part 2 – Suspended Sentences of Imprisonment*

A Statutory Provisions. 2.2.1 Section 189 Criminal Justice Act 2003

(1) A court which passes a sentence of imprisonment for a term of at least 28 weeks but not more than 51 weeks[1] in accordance with section 181 may –

(a) order the offender to comply during a period specified for the purposes of this paragraph in the order (in this Chapter referred to as "the supervision period") with one or more requirements falling within section 190(1)and specified in the order, and

(b) order that the sentence of imprisonment is not to take effect unless either—

(i) during the supervision period the offender fails to comply with a requirement imposed under paragraph (a), or

(ii) during a period specified in the order for the purposes of this subparagraph (in this Chapter referred to as "the operational period") the offender commits in the United Kingdom another offence (whether or not punishable with imprisonment), and (in either case) a court having power to do so subsequently orders under paragraph 8 of Schedule 12 that the original sentence is to take effect.

(2) Where two or more sentences imposed on the same occasion are to be served consecutively, the power conferred by subsection (1) is not exercisable in relation to any of them unless the aggregate of the terms of the sentences does not exceed 65 weeks.

(3) The supervision period and the operational period must each be a period of not less than six months and not more than two years beginning with the date of the order.

(4) The supervision period must not end later than the operational period.

(5) A court which passes a suspended sentence on any person for an offence may not impose a community sentence in his case in respect of that offence or any other offence of which he is convicted by or before the court or for which he is dealt with by the court.

(6) Subject to any provision to the contrary contained in the Criminal Justice Act 1967 (c 80), the Sentencing Act or any other enactment passed or instrument made under any enactment after 31st December 1967,a suspended sentence which has not taken effect under paragraph 8 of Schedule 12 is to be treated as a sentence of imprisonment for the purposes of all enactments and instruments made under enactments.

(7) In this Part –

(a) "suspended sentence order " means an order under subsection (1),

(b) "suspended sentence" means a sentence to which a suspended sentence order relates, and

(c) "community requirement", in relation to a suspended sentence order, means a requirement imposed under subsection (1)(a).

2.2.2 Imposition of requirements – Section 190 Criminal Justice Act 2003

(1) The requirements falling within this subsection are—

(a) unpaid work requirement (as defined by section 199),

(b) an activity requirement (as defined by section 201),

(c) a programme requirement (as defined by section 202),

(d) a prohibited activity requirement (as defined by section 203),

(e) a curfew requirement (as defined by section 204),

(f) an exclusion requirement (as defined by section 205),

(g) a residence requirement (as defined by section 206),

(h) a mental health treatment requirement (as defined by section 207),

(i) a drug rehabilitation requirement (as defined by section 209),

(j) an alcohol treatment requirement (as defined by section 212),

(k) a supervision requirement (as defined by section 213), and

(l) in a case where the offender is aged under 25, an attendance centre requirement (as defined by section 214).

(2) Section 189(1)(a) has effect subject to section 218 and to the following provisions of Chapter 4 relating to particular requirements-

(a) section 199(3) (unpaid work requirement)

(b) section 201(3)and (4) (activity requirement),

(c) section 202(4)and (5) (programme requirement),

(d) section 203(2) (prohibited activity requirement),

(e) section 207(3) (mental health treatment requirement),

(f) section 209(2) (drug rehabilitation requirement), and

(g) section 212(2) and (3) (alcohol treatment requirement).

(3) Where the court makes a suspended sentence order imposing a curfew requirement or an

exclusion requirement, it must also impose an electronic monitoring requirement (as defined by section 215) unless—

    (a) the court is prevented from doing so by section 215(2) or 218(4), or

    (b) in the particular circumstances of the case, it considers it inappropriate to do so.

(4) Where the court makes a suspended sentence order imposing an unpaid work requirement, an activity requirement, a programme requirement, a prohibited activity requirement, a residence requirement, a mental health treatment requirement, a drug rehabilitation requirement, an alcohol treatment requirement, a supervision requirement or an attendance centre requirement, the court may also impose an electronic monitoring requirement unless the court is prevented from doing so by section 215(2) or 218(4).

(5) Before making a suspended sentence order imposing two or more different requirements falling within subsection (1), the court must consider whether, in the circumstances of the case, the requirements are compatible with each other.

2.2.3 Power to provide for review – Section 191 Criminal Justice Act 2003

(1) A suspended sentence order may –

    (a) provide for the order to be reviewed periodically at specified intervals,

    (b) provide for each review to be made, subject to section 192(4), at a hearing held for the purpose by the court responsible for the order (a "review hearing"),

    (c) require the offender to attend each review hearing, and

    (d) provide for the responsible officer to make to the court responsible for the order, before each review, a report on the offender's progress in complying with the community requirements of the order.

(2) Subsection (1) does not apply in the case of an order imposing a drug rehabilitation requirement (provision for such a requirement to be subject to review being made by section 210).

(3) In this section references to the court responsible for a suspended sentence order are references—

    (a) where a court is specified in the order in accordance with subsection (4), to that court;

    (b) in any other case, to the court by which the order is made.

(4) Where the area specified in a suspended sentence order made by a magistrates' court is not the area for which the court acts, the court may, if it thinks fit, include in the order provision specifying for the purpose of subsection (3) a magistrates' court which acts for the area specified in the order.

(5) Where a suspended sentence order has been made on an appeal brought from the Crown Court or from the criminal division of the Court of Appeal, it is to be taken for the purposes of subsection (3)(b) to have been made by the Crown Court.

2.2.4 Periodic reviews – Section 192 Criminal Justice Act 2003

(1) At a review hearing (within the meaning of subsection (1) of section 191) the court may, after considering the responsible officer's report referred to in that subsection, amend the community requirements of the suspended sentence order, or any provision of the order which relates to those requirements.

(2) The court—

    (a) may not amend the community requirements of the order so as to impose a requirement of a different kind unless the offender expresses his willingness to comply with that requirement,

    (b) may not amend a mental health treatment requirement, a drug rehabilitation requirement or an alcohol treatment requirement unless the offender expresses his willingness to comply with the requirement as amended,

    (c) may amend the supervision period only if the period as amended complies with section 189(3) and (4),

    (d) may not amend the operational period of the suspended sentence, and

    (e) except with the consent of the offender, may not amend the order while an appeal against the order is pending.

(3) For the purposes of subsection (2)(a)—

    (a) a community requirement falling within any paragraph of section 190(1) is of the same kind as any other community requirement falling within that paragraph, and

    (b) an electronic monitoring requirement is a community requirement of the same kind as any requirement falling within section 190(1) to which it relates.

(4) If before a review hearing is held at any review the court, after considering the responsible officer's report, is of the opinion that the offender's progress in complying with the community requirements of the order is satisfactory, it may order that no review hearing is to be held at that review; and if before a review hearing is held at any review, or at a review hearing, the court, after considering that report, is of that opinion, it may amend the suspended sentence order so as to provide for each subsequent review to be held without a hearing.

(5) If at a review held without a hearing the court, after considering the responsible officer's report, is of the opinion that the offender's progress under the order is no longer satisfactory, the court may require the offender to attend a hearing of the court at a specified time and place.

(6) If at a review the court is of the opinion that the offender has without reasonable excuse failed to comply with any of the community requirements of the order, the court may adjourn the hearing for the purpose of dealing with the case under paragraph 8 of Schedule 12.

(7) At a review hearing the court may amend the suspended sentence order so as to vary the intervals specified under section 191(1).

(8) In this section any reference to the court, in relation to a review without a hearing is to be read –

   (*a*) in the case of the Crown Court, as a reference to a judge of the court, and

   (*b*) in the case of a magistrates ' court, as a reference to a justice of the peace acting for the commission area for which the court acts.

2.2.5 Breach, revocation or amendment of orders, and effect of further conviction—
Section 193 Criminal Justice Act 2003

Schedule 12 (which relates to the breach, revocation or amendment of the community requirements of suspended sentence orders, and to the effect of any further conviction) shall have effect.

B Imposing a Suspended Sentence.

2.2.6 A suspended sentence is a sentence of imprisonment. It is subject to the same criteria as a sentence of imprisonment which is to commence immediately. In particular, this requires a court to be satisfied that the custody threshold has been passed and that the length of the term is the shortest term commensurate with the seriousness of the offence.

2.2.7 A court which passes a prison sentence of less than 12 months may suspend it for between 6 months and 2 years (the operational period)[2]. During that period, the court can impose one or more requirements for the offender to undertake in the community. The requirements are identical to those available for the new community sentence.

2.2.8 The period during which the offender undertakes community requirements is "the supervision period" when the offender will be under the supervision of a "responsible officer"; this period may be shorter than the operational period. The court may periodically review the progress of the offender in complying with the requirements and the reviews will be informed by a report from the responsible officer.

2.2.9 If the offender fails to comply with a requirement during the supervision period, or commits a further offence during the operational period, the suspended sentence can be activated in full or in part or the terms of the supervision made more onerous. There is a presumption that the suspended sentence will be activated either in full or in part.

(i) The decision to suspend

2.2.10 There are many similarities between the suspended sentence and the community sentence. In both cases, requirements can be imposed during the supervision period and the court can respond to breach by sending the offender to custody. The crucial difference is that the suspended sentence is a prison sentence and is appropriate only for an offence that passes the custody threshold and for which imprisonment is the only option. A community sentence may also be imposed for an offence that passes the custody threshold where the court considers that to be appropriate.

2.2.11 The full decision making process for imposition of custodial sentences under the new framework (including the custody threshold test) is set out in paragraphs 1.31–1.33 of the Seriousness guideline. For the purposes of suspended sentences the relevant steps are:

   (*a*) has the custody threshold been passed?

   (*b*) if so, is it unavoidable that a custodial sentence be imposed?

   (*c*) if so, can that sentence be suspended? (sentencers should be clear that they would have imposed a custodial sentence if the power to suspend had not been available)

   (*d*) if not, can the sentence be served intermittently?

   (*e*) if not, impose a sentence which takes immediate effect for the term commensurate with the seriousness of the offence.

(ii) Length of sentence

2.2.12 Before making the decision to suspend sentence, the court must already have decided that a prison sentence is justified and should also have decided the length of sentence that would be the shortest term commensurate with the seriousness of the offence if it were to be imposed immediately. The decision to suspend the sentence should not lead to a longer term being imposed than if the sentence were to take effect immediately.

A prison sentence that is suspended should be for the same term that would have applied if the offender were being sentenced to immediate custody.

2.2.13 When assessing the length of the operational period of a suspended sentence, the court should have in mind the relatively short length of the sentence being suspended and the advantages to be gained by retaining the opportunity to extend the operational period at a later stage (see below).

The operational period of a suspended sentence should reflect the length of the sentence being suspended. As an approximate guide, an operational period of up to 12 months might normally be appropriate for a suspended sentence of up to 6 months and an operational period of up to 18 months might normally be appropriate for a suspended sentence of up to 12 months.

(iii) Requirements

2.2.14 The court will set the requirements to be complied with during the supervision period. Whilst the offence for which a suspended sentence is imposed is generally likely to be more serious than one for which a community sentence is imposed, the imposition of the custodial sentence is a clear punishment and deterrent. In order to ensure that the overall terms of the sentence are commensurate with the seriousness of the offence, it is likely that the requirements to be undertaken during the supervision period would be less onerous than if a community sentence had been imposed. These requirements will need to ensure that they properly address those factors that are most likely to reduce the risk of re-offending.

Because of the very clear deterrent threat involved in a suspended sentence, requirements imposed as part of that sentence should generally be less onerous than those imposed as part of a community sentence. A court wishing to impose onerous or intensive requirements on an offender should reconsider its decision to suspend sentence and consider whether a community sentence might be more appropriate.

C Breaches.

2.2.15 The essence of a suspended sentence is to make it abundantly clear to an offender that failure to comply with the requirements of the order or commission of another offence will almost certainly result in a custodial sentence. Where an offender has breached any of the requirements without reasonable excuse for the first time, the responsible officer must either give a warning or initiate breach proceedings[3]. Where there is a further breach within a twelve-month period, breach proceedings must be initiated[4].

2.2.16 Where proceedings are brought the court has several options, including extending the operational period. However, the presumption (which also applies where breach is by virtue of the commission of a further offence) is that the suspended prison sentence will be activated (either with its original custodial term or a lesser term) unless the court takes the view that this would, in all the circumstances, be unjust. In reaching that decision, the court may take into account both the extent to which the offender has complied with the requirements and the facts of the new offence[5].

2.2.17 Where a court considers that the sentence needs to be activated, it may activate it in full or with a reduced term. Again, the extent to which the requirements have been complied with will be very relevant to this decision.

2.2.18 If a court amends the order rather than activating the suspended prison sentence, it must either make the requirements more onerous, or extend the supervision or operational periods (provided that these remain within the limits defined by the Act)[6]. In such cases, the court must state its reasons for not activating the prison sentence[7], which could include the extent to which the offender has complied with requirements or the facts of the subsequent offence.

2.2.19 If an offender near the end of an operational period (having complied with the requirements imposed) commits another offence, it may be more appropriate to amend the order rather than activate it.

2.2.20 If a new offence committed is of a less serious nature than the offence for which the suspended sentence was passed, it may justify activating the sentence with a reduced term or amending the terms of the order.

2.2.21 It is expected that any activated suspended sentence will be consecutive to the sentence imposed for the new offence.

2.2.22 If the new offence is non-imprisonable, the sentencer should consider whether it is appropriate to activate the suspended sentence at all.

Where the court decides to amend a suspended sentence order rather than activate the custodial sentence, it should give serious consideration to extending the supervision or operational periods (within statutory limits) rather than making the requirements more onerous.'

---

1. Since "custody plus" is not expected to be brought into force until a later date, it is likely that transitional provisions will provide for this power to be used for any sentence of imprisonment of less than 12 months.
2. The power to suspend a sentence is expected to come into force earlier than the provisions implementing "custody plus" and transitional provisions are expected to enable any sentence of imprisonment of under 12 months to be suspended. This guidelines therefore is written in the language of the expected transitional provisions.
3. Criminal Justice Act 2003, Sch 12, para 4.
4. Criminal Justice Act 2003, Sch 12, para 5.
5. Criminal Justice Act 2003, Sch 12, para 8(4).
6. Criminal Justice Act 2003, s 189(3) and (4).
7. Criminal Justice Act 2003, Sch 12, para 8(3)

DANGEROUS OFFENDERS

3–153   *Offences committed before 4 April 2005.*   For violent or sexual offences committed before the above date, readers should refer to para **3–241B** of the 2005 edition of this work.

Offences committed on or after 4 April 2005.   The provisions of Chapter 5 of Part 12 of the Criminal Justice Act 2003[1] apply to specified violent and sexual offences, which are listed, respectively, in Parts 1 and 2 of Schedule 15 to the Act. Such offences are "serious" where they carry, in the case of a person aged 18 or over, imprisonment (or, pending its abolition, detention in a young offender institute) for life or for a determinate period of at least 10 years.

Where a person aged at least 18 is convicted of a *serious* offence, for which the court would not otherwise impose a life sentence, and the court is of the opinion that there is a significant risk to members of the public of serious harm[2] occasioned by the commission by him of further specified offences, it must impose a sentence of imprisonment (or detention) for public protection, which is a sentence for an indeterminate period[3]. There are correlative provisions in relation to offenders aged under 18[4].

Where a person aged at least 18 is convicted of a specified offence which is *not* a serious offence, and the court considers that there is a significant risk to members of the public of serious harm[2] occasioned by the commission by him of further specified offences, it must impose a sentence comprising a custodial term of at least 12 months (but no greater than the maximum term permitted for the offence) and a further period (the extension period) of up to 5 years in the case of a specified violence or 8 years for a specified sexual offence for which the offender will be on licence[5]. Subject to the aforementioned maxima, the extension period will be of such length as the court considers necessary for the purpose of protecting members of the public from serious harm[2] occasioned by the commission by him of further specified offences[6]. Again, there are correlative provisions for offenders aged under 18[7].

The assessment of dangerousness

(a) Offenders who have not previously been convicted of a relevant offence[8] (or are aged under 18)

In making the required assessment the court must take into account information about the offence, and may take into account any information about any pattern of behaviour of which it forms part; the court may also take into account any information about the offender[9].

(b) Offenders aged at least 18 who have previously been convicted in any part of the UK of a relevant offence[8].

In making the required the required assessment the court *must assume* that the relevant risk exists unless, after taking into account the information referred to in a) above the court considers it would be unreasonable to conclude that there is such a risk[10].

Judicial guidance on assessing significant risk. In *R v Lang and other appeals*[11] the Court of Appeal held as follows:

"(14) The following factors had to be borne in mind when a court was assessing significant risk.

(a) The risk had to be significant. That was a higher threshold than a mere possibility of occurrence, and could be taken to mean 'noteworthy, of considerable amount or importance'.

(b) In assessing the risk of further offences being committed, the court had to take into account the nature and circumstances of the instant offence; the defendant's history of offending, including not just the kind of offence, but its circumstances and the sentence passed (details of which the prosecution had to have available) and whether the defendant demonstrated any pattern; social and economic factors in relation to the defendant including accommodation, employability, education, associates, relationships and drug or alcohol abuse; and the defendant's thinking, attitude towards offending and supervision and emotional state. Information in relation to those matters would most readily (though not exclusively) come from antecedents and pre-sentence and medical reports. The court would be guided, but not bound by, the assessment of risk, in such reports. A judge who might contemplate differing from the assessment should give counsel the opportunity of addressing the point.

(c) Where the foreseen specified offence was serious, there would clearly be some cases, though not by any means all, in which there might be a significant risk of serious harm. For example, robbery was a serious offence, but could be committed in a wide variety of ways, many of which did not give rise to a significant risk of serious harm. Accordingly, the court had to guard against assuming that there was a significant risk of serious harm, merely because the foreseen specified offence was serious. A pre-sentence report should usually be obtained before any sentence was passed which was based upon significant risk of harm. In a small number of cases, where the circumstances of the current offence, or the history of the defendant, suggested mental abnormality on his part, a medical report might be necessary before risk could properly be assessed.

(d) Where the foreseen specified offence was not serious, there would be comparatively few cases in which a risk of serious harm would properly be regarded as significant. The huge variety of offences in Sch 15 included many which in themselves were not suggestive of serious harm. Violent or sexual offending at a relatively low level, without serious harm, would not of itself give rise to a significant risk of serious harm in the future[12]. There might, in such cases, be some risk of future victims becoming more adversely affected that past victims, but that, of itself, did not give risk to a significant risk of serious harm.

(e) In respect of the rebuttable presumption to which s 229(3) gave rise, the court was accorded a discretion where, in the light of information about the current offence, the defendant, and his previous offences, it would be unreasonable to conclude that there was a significant risk. The exercise of such a discretion was historically at the very heart of judicial sentencing, and the language of the statute indicated that judges were expected, albeit starting from the assumption, to exercise their ability to reach a reasonable conclusion in the light of the information before them. It was to be noted that the assumption would be rebutted, if at all, as an exercise of judgment: the statute included no reference to the burden or standard of proof. However, it would usually be unreasonable to conclude that the assumption applied unless information as to the offences, pattern of behaviour, and defendant showed a significant risk of serious harm from further offences.

(f) In relation to defendants under 18 and adults with no relevant previous convictions at the time the specified offence was committed, the court's discretion under s 229(2) was not constrained by any initial assumption such as, under s 229(3), applied to adults with previous convictions. It was still necessary, when sentencing young offenders, to bear in mind that, within a shorter time than adults, they might change and develop. That factor, and their level of maturity might be highly pertinent when assessing what their future conduct might be, and whether it might give rise to a significant risk of serious harm.

(g) In relation to particularly young offenders, an indeterminate sentence might be inappropriate even where a serious offence had been committed and there was a significant risk of serious harm from further offences.

(h) It could not have been Parliament's intention, in a statute dealing with the liberty of a subject, to require the imposition of indeterminate sentences for the commission of relatively minor offences. On the contrary, Parliament's repeatedly expressed intention was to protect the public from serious harm. However, depending on the circumstances of the case, an escalation of risk of serious harm could properly be inferred from a multiplicity of relatively minor offences.

(i) Courts should usually and in accordance with s 174(1)(a) give reasons for their conclusions, in particular: that there was or was not a significant risk of further offences or serious harm and, where the assumption under s 229 (3) arose, for making or not making the assumption, or for not imposing an extended sentence. Courts should, in giving reasons, identify the information which they had taken into account.

(15) The risk to be assessed was to 'members of the public', an all-embracing term which was wider than 'others' (which would exclude the defendant himself). There was no reason to construe it so as to exclude any particular group, for example, prison officers or staff at mental hospitals, all of whom, like the defendant, were members of the public. In some cases, particular members of the public might be more at risk than members of the public generally, for example where a defendant had a history of violence to cohabitees or of sexually abusing the children of cohabitees, or as in one of the instant cases, where the defendant had a particular problem relating to a particular woman.

(16) Where defendants were to be sentenced for several offences, only some of which were serious or specified, a court which imposed an indeterminate sentence under ss 225 or 226, or an extended sentence under ss 227 or 228 for the principal offences, should generally impose a shorter concurrent term for the other offences. In the case of a specified offence where there was a risk of serious harm, the sentence for some other offence had to be an extended sentence where the principal offence was a serious offence. It would not usually be appropriate to impose consecutive extended sentences where the principle offence was serious or merely specified.

(17) Care should be taken to ensure that a continuing offence which straddled the commencement date should be indicted so that sentences could be imposed on either the new or old provisions.

(18) Where, in relation to a dangerous offender, the requirements of the Mental Health Act 1983 were satisfied, the court could dispose of the case under those provisions (s 37 of the 1983 Act as amended by the 2003 Act)."

The guidance given in *R v Lang* was considered by the Court of Appeal in *R v Johnson, R v Lawton, R v Hamilton, R v Gordon A-G's Reference (No 64 of 2006) Practice Note* [2006] EWCA Crim 2486, [2007] 1 WLR 585, and Sir Igor Judge P added this.

"Much of the argument in *R v Lang* itself, and many of the submissions in grounds of appeal and arguments coming to this court, on the issue of dangerousness were and are focussed on section 229(3), and whether, and if so in what circumstances the assumption of dangerousness should be disapplied. *R v Lang* was particularly focussed on this issue, and nothing in this judgment is intended to undermine the guidance provided by *R v Lang*.

10 We can now address a number of specific issues. (i) Just as the absence of previous convictions does not preclude a finding of dangerousness, the existence of previous convictions for specified offences does not compel such a finding. There is a presumption that it does so, which may be rebutted. (ii) If a finding of dangerousness can be made against an offender without previous specified convictions, it also follows that previous offences, not in fact specified for the purposes of section 229, are not disqualified from consideration. Thus, for example, as indeed the statute recognises, a pattern of minor previous offences of gradually escalating seriousness may be significant. In other words, it is not right, as many of the submissions made to us suggested, that unless the previous offences were specified offences they were irrelevant. (iii) Where the facts of the instant offence, or indeed any specified offences for the purposes of section 229(3) are examined, it may emerge that no harm actually occurred. That may be advantageous to the offender, and some of the cases examined in *R v Lang* exemplify the point. Another such example is *R v Isa* [2005] EWCA Crim 3330, [2006] Crim LR 356. On the other hand the absence of harm may be entirely fortuitous. A victim cowering away from an armed assailant may avoid direct physical injury or serious psychological harm. Faced with such a case, the sentencer considering dangerousness may wish to reflect, for example, on the likely response of the offender if his victim, instead of surrendering, resolutely defended himself. It does not automatically follow from the absence of actual harm caused by the offender to date, that the risk that he will cause serious harm in the future is negligible. Nothing in the decision in *R v Shaffi* [2006] EWCA Crim 418, [2006] 2 Cr App Rep (S) 606, which was relied on before us, suggests the contrary. Giving the judgment of the court, at para 11, Sir Richard Curtis summarised the various submissions made on behalf of the appellant. One of them was that the appellant's previous convictions demonstrated that although the appellant was carrying a knife and a screwdriver in two of the cases, no harm was actually occasioned. The court accepted the force of the overall submission made by counsel that the sentencer was wrong to find that there was a risk of serious harm, and the court was unable to find significant evidence of such harm caused during the commission of the appellant's previous offences. However the conclusion represented a finding of fact in the

particular case. *R v Shaffi* is not authority for the proposition that as a matter of law offences which did not result in harm to the victim should be treated as irrelevant. Indeed if that is what *R v Shaffi* decided, it would, in effect, have rewritten the statute. (iv) We considered arguments based on the inadequacy, suggestibility, or vulnerability of the offender, and how these and similar characteristics may bear on dangerousness. Such characteristics may serve to mitigate the offender's culpability. In the final analysis however they may also serve to produce or reinforce the conclusion that the offender is dangerous. In one of the instant cases it was suggested that the sentence was wrong because an inadequate offender had suffered what was described as an "aberrant moment". But, as experience shows, aberrant moments may be productive of catastrophe. The sentencer is right to be alert to such risks of aberrant moments in the future, and their consequences. (v) In *R v Lang*, Rose LJ suggested that the prosecution should be in a position to describe the facts of previous specified offences. This is plainly desirable, (see also *R v Isa*) but this is not always practicable. There is no reason why the prosecution's failure to comply with this good practice, even when it can and should, should either make an adjournment obligatory, or indeed preclude the imposition of the sentence, when appropriate. In any such case, counsel for the defendant should be in a position to explain the circumstances, on the basis of his instructions. If the Crown is not in a position to challenge those instructions, then the court may proceed on the information it has. Equally, there are some situations in which the sentence imposed by the court dealing with earlier specified offences may enable the sentencer to draw inferences about its seriousness, or otherwise. In short, failure to comply with best practice on this point should be discouraged, but it does not normally preclude the imposition of the sentence. (vi) The effect of the 2003 Act, and *R v Lang*, has been examined in a number of cases. It is not obligatory for the sentencer to spell out all the details of the earlier specified offences. To the extent that a judge is minded to rely upon a disputed fact in reaching a finding of dangerousness, he should not rely on that fact unless the dispute can fairly be resolved adversely to the defendant. In the end, the requirement is that the sentencing remarks should explain the reasoning which has led the sentencer to the conclusion.

11 At the risk of stating the obvious, the final consideration to which we draw attention, is that this court will not normally interfere with the conclusions reached by a sentencer who has accurately identified the relevant principles, and applied his mind to the relevant facts."

Examples of the application of the above principles: (a) cases not involving the rebuttable presumption of dangerousness (ie the accused had no previous convictions for "relevant" offences)

In a case where the offender (19) was convicted of assault occasioning actual bodily harm, and the case was appalling in terms of the length and general ferocity of the attack, but the consequential harm fell short of "serious personal injury", the only previous conviction was for an offence of battery and the two offences stood as essentially isolated incidents, it was not open to the judge to find that the strict criteria of s 227 had been met[13].

The gravity of the current offence may justify the conclusion that anyone committing such an offence would be likely to do so again, notwithstanding the lack of previous convictions and the absence of psychiatric evidence pointing to a likelihood of re-offending[14].

The sentencing court is entitled to form its own view about the presence or absence of risk, without having expert evidence and without being bound to follow the assessment made in the PSR[15].

(b) cases where, by virtue of past offences, the rebuttable assumption applies

Robbery

In a case where the offender (18) pleaded guilty to being one of a group of people that carried out a violent robbery (the victim was punched and kicked to the ground) in a subway in the early hours of the morning, and his previous record, in chronological order, comprised two convictions for possessing offensive weapons, possessing a bladed article and assault occasioning actual harm, violent disorder and, finally, robbery, the assumption raised by s 229(3) was not rebutted and a term of custody for public protection was correctly imposed[16]. However, where the accused had a previous conviction for robbery, but his record did not indicate that serious harm had been occasioned, even when he had a screwdriver or knife as a weapon, and the assumption was found to be rebutted[17]. It was also found to be rebutted where the current offence was robbery by snatching a handbag and there were previous convictions, most seriously under s 20 of the Offences Against the Person Act 1861; while there was a risk of further specified offences the judge had been wrong to find a risk of significant harm[18]. A different conclusion was reached, however, where 2 defendants robbed a bookmaker's shop, their records included convictions for robbery which, in the case of the first defendant, included robbery of a similar kind and the use of non-robbery-related violence and, while the second defendant did not have a record of actual violence or harm, it could be inferred that this was only because nobody had previous sought to confront him[19].

Sexual offences

However, where an offender pleaded guilty to 3 offences of having sexual activity with a child, and his only previous conviction was some 30 years earlier for an offence of indecent assault for which he was fined, the earlier offence was not such as of itself to give rise to a significant risk of serious harm (however, the index alone justified a sentence of imprisonment for public protection)[20].

Dangerous offenders and committal for trial/sentence

Magistrates' courts cannot impose indeterminate or extended sentences for dangerous offenders.

At the date at which this volume states the law the substituted s 3 and the new s 3A of the Powers of Criminal Courts (Sentencing) Act 2000 which deal, respectively, with "committal for sentence on indication of guilty plea to serious offence triable either way" and "committal for sentence of dangerous young offenders" had not been brought into force (cf committal for sentence of dangerous young offenders). Consequently, it is be necessary to have recourse to s 3[21] in its existing form to commit offenders to the Crown Court

Pending the implementation of the new committal for sentence provisions, magistrates' courts are not required to carry out an assessment as to whether or not an offender is dangerous, they must merely decide whether or not their powers are adequate; it follows that where a magistrates' court purports to carry out this assessment and arrives at a negative conclusion, this does not give rise to a legitimate expectation that an extended sentence may or may not be imposed[22].

---

1. See this PART, post.
2. "Serious harm" means death or serious personal injury, whether physical or psychological: Criminal Justice Act 2003, s 224(3).
3. CJA 2003, s 225(1)–(4).
4. CJA 2003, s 226.
5. CJA 2003, s 227.
6. CJA 2003, s 227(2).
7. CJA 2003, s 228.
8. Defined to include "specified" offences and the offences listed in the Criminal Justice Act 2003, Schs 16 (Scottish offences) and 17 (Northern Irish offences).
9. CJA 2003, s 229(2). This includes information gather for the purpose of making an application for an anti-social behaviour order: *R v Hillman* [2006] EWCA Crim 690, [2006] Crim LR 662 (though see the commentary on the case).
10. CJA 2003, s 229(3).
11. [2005] EWCA Crim 2864, [2006] 1 WLR 2509, [2006] 2 Cr App R (S) 3
12. See, for example, *R v Isa* [2005] EWCA Crim 3330, [2006] 2 Cr App R (S) 29, [2006] Crim LR 356 in which it was held that neither the previous convictions nor the present offence provided a basis for inferring that any further offences would result in serious harm; the offender was (merely) a persistent, low-level sexual offender. See also the examples given in subparagraph (*a*), infra.
13. *R v Timothy Bailey* [2006] EWCA Crim 144, [2006] 2 Cr App R (S) 50.
14. *R v Betteridge* [2006] EWCA Crim 400, [2006] Crim LR 563 (which concerned the rape of a 14-year-old girl). However, see also *R v Monks* [2006] EWCA Crim 54. [2006] Crim LR 447 (criteria not met in the case of a man guilty of 9 offences of having sexual activity with boys aged 15)..
15. *R v Samuel B* [2006] EWCA Crim 400, [2006] 2 Cr App R (S) 71.
16. *R v Christopher Malcolm Davies* [2006] EWCA Crim 428, [2006] 2 Cr App R (S) 73.
17. *R v Shaffi* [2006] EWCA Crim 418, [2006] Crim LR 665.
18. *R v McGrady* [2006] EWCA Crim 1547, [2006] Crim LR 940.
19. *R v Bryan and Bryan* [2006] EWCA Crim 1660, [2006] Crim LR 942.
20. *R v Horace Llewellyn Greaves* [2006] EWCA Crim 641, [2006] 2 Cr App R (S) 89.
21. At para 3–1555, this PART, post.
22. *R v S, Burt* [2005] EWCA Crim 3616, [2006] 2 Cr App R (S) 35.

COMMITTAL TO THE CROWN COURT FOR SENTENCE*

3-154   On conviction of an offence triable either way, the offender may be committed in custody or on bail to the Crown Court for sentence[1]. In the case of a corporation, the question of custody or bail will not arise. The court must be of opinion that the offence or the combination of the offence and one or more offences associated with it was so serious that greater punishment should be inflicted for the offence than the court has power to inflictor, in the case of a violent or sexual offence committed by a person who is not less than 21 years old, that a sentence of imprisonment for term longer than the court has power to impose is necessary to protect the public from serious harm[2].. Where the court is minded to commit the offender for sentence it should first invite representations from the defence and, if it proceeds to commit, it should make clear its opinion when doing so, although this is not binding on the Crown Court.

Where an offender, or his representative, indicates, in accordance with s 17A(6) of the Magistrates' Courts Act 1980[3], that he would plead guilty if the offence were to proceed to trial the offender may be committed to the Crown Court for sentence if the court is of such opinion as is referred to above[4]. However, if the court does not form such an opinion but nevertheless commits the offender to the Crown Court for trial for one or more *related offences*, it may in accordance with s 6 of the Powers of Criminal Courts (Sentencing) Act 2000 also commit him to the Crown Court to be dealt with in accordance with the provisions of s 5 of the Powers of Criminal Courts (Sentencing) Act 2000[5]. Where the court does commit the offender to the Crown Court to be dealt with, but it does not state that, in its opinion, it does have power so to commit him under s 3(2) of the Powers of Criminal Courts (Sentencing) Act 2000, the provisions of s 5 of the 2000 Act will not apply unless he is convicted before the Crown Court of one or more of the *related offences*[6]. Where the provisions of s 5 do not apply, the Crown Court will have power to deal with the offender in respect of the offence in any manner in which the magistrates' court might have dealt with him[7].

The opinion that the offence or offences are so serious as to require committal to the Crown Court may be formed after jurisdiction has been accepted and, it would seem, that opinion is not dependent on information showing the offence or offences to be more serious than they were originally thought to be being received after the decision to try the case summarily was made[8]. Nevertheless, justices must still apply their minds to the matters which they are required by s 19(3) of the Magistrates' Courts Act 1980 to consider before deciding to accept summary jurisdiction[9]. Justices may commit a defendant to the Crown Court for sentence if they are of the opinion that, while imprisonment would not be appropriate, the offence was so serious that a larger fine is merited that they have power to impose[10]. A defendant may not be committed for sentence where he has been given a legitimate expectation that the case will be dealt with summarily[11].

For the purposes of a committal for sentence on the indication of a guilty plea under s 4 of the 2000 Act, one offence is related to another if, were they both to be prosecuted on indictment, the charges for them could be joined in the same indictment[12]. Charges for any offences may be joined in the same indictment if those charges are founded on the same facts, or form or are a part of a series of offences of the same or a similar character[13]. Where the magistrates' court makes a mistake and instead of committing under s 3(2) commits under s 4 in circumstances where there are no related offences and does not state that it had power to commit under s 3(2) of the 2000 Act, the powers of the Crown Court are limited to those of the magistrates' court[14].

In most cases where a plea of guilty is made at the plea before venue, it will not be usual to alter the position as regards bail or custody. In the usual case, when a person who has been on bail pleads at the plea before venue, the practice should normally be to continue bail, even if it is anticipated that a custodial sentence will be imposed by the Crown Court, unless there are good reasons for remanding the defendant in custody. If the defendant is in custody, then after entering a plea of guilty at the plea before venue, it will be unusual, if the reasons for remanding in custody remain unchanged, to alter the position[15]. Where following plea before venue an offender is committed to the Crown Court for sentence, but before he is sentenced it is discovered that the decision to commit for sentence was taken on the wrong view of the facts, the proper approach will be to allow the offender to make an application to change his plea. If such an application is allowed, the Crown Court may then remit the case to the magistrates' court so that the matter may be considered on a proper view of the facts for the purposes of s 3 of the Powers of Criminal Courts (Sentencing) Act 2000[16].

Other powers of committal to the Crown Court for sentence arise under the following: Vagrancy Act 1824 (incorrigible rogue[17]); Powers of Criminal Courts (Sentencing) Act 2000, ss 13(5) (conditionally discharged person convicted of further offence), s 116(3)(b) (offender convicted of offence committed during currency of original sentence), s 120(2) offender convicted during operational period of suspended sentence). In relation to these powers as well as the major power to commit for sentence, if the magistrates' court commits to the Crown Court for sentence, then if the offence on which it commits is an indictable offence, it may also commit the offender to be dealt with in respect of any other offence whatsoever in respect of which it has itself power to deal with him. If the offence is on the other hand a summary offence, it may also commit him for sentence if that offence is imprisonable or disqualifiable, or it may commit him in respect of any suspended sentence of imprisonment which it would itself have power to deal with. The committing court must not itself exercise any sentencing powers or duties but must leave them to the Crown Court; it may however impose an interim driving disqualification if that is appropriate[18]. If the court considers that a restriction order under the Mental Health Act 1983 is appropriate, it will commit the offender for trial or sentence to the Crown Court as it does not itself possess this power[19].

In considering the seriousness of any offence for this purpose, the court may take into account any previous convictions of the offender or any failure of his to respond to previous sentences. If such offence was committed while the offender was on bail, the court must treat the fact that it was committed in those circumstances as an aggravating factor[20].

There may be no committal for sentence with respect to offences of criminal damage if the value involved is small[21].

A further power of committal to the Crown Court for sentence arises[22] where a court convicts a person who, having been released on bail in criminal proceedings fails without reasonable cause to surrender to custody, and the court thinks that the circumstances of the offence are such that greater punishment should be inflicted for that offence than the court has power to inflict.

The Crown Court will deal with the offender as if he had just been convicted on indictment; it is not limited to a sentence exceeding 6 months only by an excess justified by reference to the offender's record[23].

Where a case was erroneously committed to the Crown Court for sentence (the prior consent of the DPP, which was a prerequisite to the prosecution, had not been obtained by that stage, though it was given subsequently), it was unnecessary for the judge to use s 66 of the Courts Act 2003 to exercise the powers of district judge and re-commit the offender; the judge should instead have considered whether it was Parliament's intention that such a failure rendered the proceedings a nullity (however, the judge had been entitled to use his powers under s 66)[24].

---

*This paragraph states the law pending the commencement of the substituted s 3 and new s 3A of the Powers of Criminal Courts (Sentencing) Act 2000. Until these provisions come into force, recourse must be had to the existing s 3 to commit "dangerous" offenders for indeterminate or extended sentences. See further para 3–153, ante.

1. Powers of Criminal Courts (Sentencing) Act 2000, s 3, this PART, post. It is unnecessary for justices to state their reasons for committing for sentence since the person so committed will have an opportunity to make full representations to the sentencing court: *R v Wirral Magistrates' Court, ex p Jermyn* [2001] 1 Cr App Rep (S) 485, [2001] Crim LR 47, DC. See notes in para 1–2067, ante, as to the need for justices to forward to the Crown Court their findings on factual issues relevant to sentence; as to making an application to the Crown Court to change a plea of guilty, and as to resolving disagreement between the prosecution version of the facts and that of the defence.

2. Powers of Criminal Courts (Sentencing) Act 2000, s 3, this PART, post. The terms "associated with it", "violent offence", "sexual offence", "serious harm" are all defined in s 161 of the Powers of Criminal Courts (Sentencing) Act 2000, this PART, post.

3. See PART I: MAGISTRATES' COURTS, PROCEDURE, ante.

4. Powers of Criminal Courts (Sentencing) Act 2000, s 3(2), this PART, post. See also *R v Warley Magistrates' Court, ex p DPP* [1998] 2 Cr App Rep 307, 162 JP 559, [1998] Crim LR 684, CA, and commentary at para 1–508 GUIDANCE ON WHETHER TO COMMIT FOR SENTENCE, ante.

5. Powers of Criminal Courts (Sentencing) Act 2000, s 4(2), this PART, post.

6. Powers of Criminal Courts (Sentencing) Act 2000, s 4(4), this PART, post.

7. Powers of Criminal Courts (Sentencing) Act 2000, s 4(5), this PART, post.
8. *R v Sheffield Crown Court and Sheffield Stipendiary Magistrate, ex p DPP* (1994) 158 JP 334, 15 Cr App Rep (S) 768, [1994] Crim LR 470; *R v Dover Magistrates' Court, ex p Pamment* (1994) 158 JP 665, 15 Cr App Rep (S) 778, [1994] Crim LR 471; *R v North Sefton Magistrates' Court, ex p Marsh* [1994] Crim LR 865, 159 JP 9, (1994) 16 Cr App Rep (S) 401.
9. *R v Flax Bourton Magistrates, ex p Customs and Excise Comrs* (1996) 160 JP 481, [1996] Crim LR 907.
10. *R v North Essex Justices, ex p Lloyd* (2000) 165 JP 117, DC.
11. See para **1–508 GUIDANCE ON WHETHER TO COMMIT FOR SENTENCE**, in PART I: MAGISTRATES' COURTS, PROCEDURE, ante.
12. Powers of Criminal Courts (Sentencing) Act 2000, s 4(7), this PART, post.
13. Criminal Procedure Rules 2005, r 14.2 in PART I: MAGISTRATES' COURTS, PROCEDURE, ante.
14. Powers of Criminal Courts (Sentencing) Act 2000, s 5(2) and see *R v Sallis* [2003] EWCA Crim 233, [2003] 2 Cr App Rep (s) 394.
15. *R v Rafferty* [1999] 1 Cr App Rep 235, (1998) 162 JP 353, [1998] Crim LR 433.
16. *R v Crown Court at Isleworth, ex p Buda* [2000] Crim LR 111, [2000] 1 Cr App Rep (S) 538.
17. See PART VIII: VAGRANTS, post.
18. Road Traffic Offenders Act 1988, s 26(1) in PART VII: TRANSPORT, post.
19. See para **3–322**, ante.
20. Powers of Criminal Courts (Sentencing) Act 2000, s 151(2), this Part, post.
21. Magistrates' Courts Act 1980, s 33(1), in PART I, ante.
22. See the Bail Act 1976, s 6(6), PART I, ante.
23. Powers of Criminal Courts (Sentencing) Act 2000, s 5, this PART, post; *R v Lowes* (1998) 10 Cr App Rep (S) 175, CA.
24. *R v Ashton, R v Draz, R v. O'Reilly* [2006] EWCA Crim 794, [2006] Crim App R 15.

GUIDANCE OF THE SENTENCING GUIDELINES COUNCIL ON CUSTODIAL SENTENCES OF 12 MONTHS OR MORE

3–155 The following guidance on custodial sentences of 12 months or more has been given by the Sentencing Guidelines Council as part of its guidance in relation to the sentencing framework contained in the Criminal Justice Act 2003.

'**SECTION 2 – CUSTODIAL SENTENCES**
PART 1 – CUSTODIAL SENTENCES OF 12 MONTHS OR MORE

A Statutory Provisions.
2.1.1 Under existing legislation:

- an adult offender receiving a custodial sentence of at least 12 months and below 4 years will automatically be released at the halfway point and will then be supervised under licence until the three-quarter point of the sentence. [For some, the actual release date may be earlier as a result of release on Home Detention Curfew (HDC).]
- an adult offender receiving a determinate sentence of 4 years or above will be eligible for release from the halfway point and, if not released before, will automatically be released at the two-thirds point. After release, the offender will be supervised under licence until the three-quarter point of the sentence.

2.1.2 Under the new framework, the impact of a custodial sentence will be more severe since the period in custody and under supervision will be for the whole of the sentence term set by the court. Additionally, separate provisions for the protection of the public will be introduced for those offenders designated as "dangerous" under the Act which are designed to ensure that release only occurs when it is considered safe to do so.

2.1.3 Where a prison sentence of 12 months or more is imposed on an offender who is not classified as "dangerous", that offender will be entitled to be released from custody after completing half of the sentence. The whole of the second half of the sentence will be subject to licence requirements. These requirements will be set shortly before release by the Secretary of State (with advice from the Governor responsible for authorising the prisoner's release in consultation with the Probation Service) but a court will be able to make recommendations at the sentencing stage on the content of those requirements[1]. The conditions that the Secretary of State may attach to a licence are to be prescribed by order[2].

2.1.4 The Act requires that a custodial sentence for a fixed term should be for the shortest term that is commensurate with the seriousness of the offence[3].

B Imposition of Custodial Sentences of 12 Months or more.
(i) Length of Sentence
2.1.5 The requirement that the second half of a prison sentence will be served in the community subject to conditions imposed prior to release is a major new development and will require offenders to be under supervision for the full duration of the sentence prescribed by the court. The Probation Service will be able to impose a number of complementary requirements on the offender during the second half of a custodial sentence and these are expected to be more demanding and involve a greater restriction on liberty than current licence conditions.

2.1.6 As well as restricting liberty to a greater extent, the new requirements will last until the very end of the sentence, rather than to the three-quarter point as at present, potentially making a custodial sentence significantly more demanding than under existing legislation.

Breach of these requirements at any stage is likely to result in the offender being returned to custody and this risk continues, therefore, for longer under the new framework than under the existing legislation.

Transitional arrangements.

2.1.7 In general, a fixed term custodial sentence of 12 months or more under the new framework will increase the sentence actually served (whether in custody or in the community) since it continues to the end of the term imposed. Existing guidelines issued since 1991 have been based on a different framework and so, in order to maintain consistency between the lengths of sentence under the current and the new framework, there will need to be some adjustment to the starting points for custodial sentences contained in those guidelines (subject to the special sentences under the 2003 Act where the offender is a "dangerous" offender).

2.1.8 This aspect of the guideline will be temporary to overcome the short-term situation where sentencing guidelines (issued since implementation of the reforms to custodial sentences introduced by the Criminal Justice Act 1991) are based on a different framework and the new framework has made those sentences more demanding. As new guidelines are issued they will take into account the new framework in providing starting points and ranges of appropriate sentence lengths for offences and an adjustment will not be necessary.

2.1.9 Since there are so many factors that will vary, it is difficult to calculate precisely how much more demanding a sentence under the new framework will be. The Council's conclusion is that the sentencer should seek to achieve the best match between a sentence under the new framework and its equivalent under the old framework so as to maintain the same level of punishment. As a guide, the Council suggests the sentence length should be reduced by in the region of 15%.

2.1.10 The changes in the nature of a custodial sentence will require changes in the way the sentence is announced. Sentencers will need to continue[4] to spell out the practical implications of the sentence being imposed so that offenders, victims and the public alike all understand that the sentence does not end when the offender is released from custody. The fact that a breach of the requirements imposed in the second half of the sentence is likely to result in a return to custody should also be made very clear at the point of sentence.

- When imposing a fixed term custodial sentence of 12 months or more under the new provisions, courts should consider reducing the overall length of the sentence that would have been imposed under the current provisions by in the region of 15%.
- When announcing sentence, sentencers should explain the way in which the sentence has been calculated, how it will be served and the implications of non-compliance with licence requirements. In particular, it needs to be stated clearly that the sentence is in two parts, one in custody and one under supervision in the community.
- This proposal does not apply to sentences for dangerous offenders, for which separate provision has been made in the Act.

(ii) Licence conditions

2.1.11 Under the Act, a court imposing a prison sentence of 12 months or more may recommend conditions that should be imposed by the Secretary of State (with advice from the Governor responsible for authorising the prisoner's release in consultation with the Probation Service) on release from custody[5]. Recommendations do not form part of the sentence and they are not binding on the Secretary of State[6].

2.1.12 When passing such a sentence, the court will not know with any certainty to what extent the offender's behaviour may have been addressed in custody or what the offender's health and other personal circumstances might be on release and so it will be extremely difficult, especially in the case of longer custodial sentences, for sentencers to make an informed judgement about the most appropriate licence conditions to be imposed on release. However, in most cases, it would be extremely helpful for sentencers to indicate areas of an offender's behaviour about which they have the most concern and to make suggestions about the types of intervention whether this, in practice, takes place in prison or in the community.

2.1.13 The involvement of the Probation Service at the pre-sentence stage will clearly be pivotal. A recommendation on the likely post-release requirements included in a presentence report will assist the court with the decision on overall sentence length, although any recommendation would still have to be open to review when release is being considered. A curfew, exclusion requirement or prohibited activity requirement might be suitable conditions to recommend for the licence period. A court might also wish to suggest that the offender should complete a rehabilitation programme, for example for drug abuse, anger management, or improving skills such as literacy and could recommend that this should be considered as a licence requirement if the programme has not been undertaken or completed in custody.

2.1.14 The Governor responsible for authorising the prisoner's release, in consultation with the Probation Service, is best placed to make recommendations at the point of release; this is the case at present and continues to be provided for in the Act. Specific court recommendations will only generally be appropriate in the context of relatively short sentences, where it would not be unreasonable for the sentencer to anticipate the relevance of particular requirements at the point of release. Making recommendations in relation to longer sentences (other than suggestions about the types of intervention that might be appropriate at some point during the sentence) would be unrealistic. The Governor and Probation Service should have due regard to any recommendations made by the sentencing court and the final recommendation to the Secretary of State on licence conditions will need to build upon any interventions during the custodial period and any other changes in the offender's circumstances.

- A court may sensibly suggest interventions that could be useful when passing sentence, but should only make specific recommendations about the requirements to be imposed on licence when announcing short sentences and where it is reasonable to anticipate their relevance at the point of release. The Governor and Probation Service should have due regard to any recommendations made by the sentencing court but its decision should be contingent upon any changed circumstances during the custodial period.

- The court should make it clear, at the point of sentence, that the requirements to be imposed on licence will ultimately be the responsibility of the Governor and Probation Service and that they are entitled to review any recommendations made by the court in the light of any changed circumstances.'

---

1. Criminal Justice Act 2003, s 238(1).
2. Criminal Justice Act 2003, s 250.
3. Criminal Justice Act 2003, s 153(2).
4. Having reference to the *Consolidated Criminal Practice Direction* [2002] 2 Cr App R 533, Annex C, as suitably amended.
5. Criminal Justice Act 2003, s 238(1).
6. Criminal Justice Act 2003, s 250.

Ancillary orders

3–170   Ancillary orders are available to a court when passing sentence. These orders do not stand alone, but may be made at the same time as other sentences are passed for the same offence. They may be used by any court including an adult court dealing with a juvenile by means of a discharge or fine or by requiring a recognizance from the parent or guardian[1]. Subject to certain exceptions, ancillary orders are deemed to form part of the sentence for the purposes of any appeal against sentence to the Crown Court[2]. Ancillary orders most commonly made by courts when passing sentence are as follows—

Compensation, Powers of Criminal Courts (Sentencing) Act 2000, s 130;
Restitution, Powers of Criminal Courts (Sentencing) Act 2000, s 148;
Deprivation, Powers of Criminal Courts (Sentencing) Act 2000, s 143;
Costs, Prosecution of Offences Act 1985, s 18;
Driving disqualification for any offence, Powers of Criminal Courts (Sentencing) Act 2000, s 146;
Driving disqualification, Road Traffic Offenders Act 1988, ss 34–36;
Endorsement of driving licence, Road Traffic Offenders Act 1988, s 44;
Recommendation for deportation, Immigration Act 1971, s 6;
Anti-social behaviour; Crime and Disorder Act 1998, s 1C.

In addition, offenders convicted of certain sexual offences, or, if found to be under a disability, found to have done the act, or cautioned may be subject to the notification requirements of the Sexual Offences Act 2003[3].

---

1. Powers of Criminal Courts (Sentencing) Act 2000, s 8(6), this PART, post.
2. See para **1–760** and the Magistrates' Courts Act 1980, s 108(3), in PART I, ante.
3. See PART VIII: title SEXUAL OFFENCES, post.

COMPENSATION

3–171   A magistrates' court by or before which a person is convicted of an offence may instead of or in addition to dealing with him in any other way order him to pay up to a total of £5,000 compensation for any personal injury, loss or damage resulting from that offence or any other offence which is taken into consideration by the court when determining sentence, or to make payments for funeral expenses or bereavement in respect of a death resulting from any such offence, other than a death due to an accident arising out of the presence of a motor vehicle on a road1. If the court does not make a compensation order in a case where it is empowered to do so, it shall give reasons for not doing so on passing sentence[1].

A compensation order may only be made in respect of injury, loss or damage (other than loss suffered by a person's dependants in consequence of his death) which was due to an accident arising out of the presence of a motor vehicle on a road, if—

(a)   it is in respect of damage which is treated by virtue of s 130(5) of the Powers of Criminal Courts (Sentencing) Act 2000 as resulting from an offence under the Theft Act 1968; or

(b)   it is in respect of injury, loss or damage as respects which—

(i)   the offender is uninsured in relation to the use of the vehicle; and

(ii)   compensation is not payable under any arrangements to which the Secretary of State is a party[2].

If the court considers that it would be appropriate both to impose a fine and to make a compensation order, but the offender has insufficient means to pay both an appropriate fine and appropriate compensation, preference shall be given to compensation[3].

It is inappropriate to make a compensation order in a modest amount to a small child who has been sexually abused and such an order is capable of being misunderstood[4].

1. Powers of Criminal Courts (Sentencing) Act 2000, ss 130, 131, this PART, post.
2. Powers of Criminal Courts (Sentencing) Act 2000, s 130(6), this PART, post.
3. Powers of Criminal Courts (Sentencing) Act 2000, s 130(12), this PART, post.
4. *A-G's Reference (No 35 of 1994)* (1995) 16 Cr App R (S) 635. See also *A-G's Reference (No 70 of 2003)* [2004] EWCA Crim 163, [2004] 2 Cr App R (S) 49.

3–172   Compensation order: when appropriate and assessing the amount.   A compensation order is merely a means which is available to the criminal court of giving effect to a victim's legitimate civil claim and it is not, therefore, a sufficient way in which to deal with a grave offence of wounding with intent to cause grievous bodily harm[1]. A compensation order should not be made when deferring sentence[2], although the court could make it one of the requirements of the deferment that the offender save money towards the making of a compensation order at the time he is sentenced. A compensation order should not be made when committing to the Crown Court for sentence[3]. It is rarely appropriate to add a compensation order to a custodial sentence as this may tempt the offender to commit further offences on his release[4]. The amounts which a magistrates' court can order for one offence, and for any offences taken into consideration with it, must not aggregate more than £5,000[5]. There is no such limit in the Crown Court.

A compensation order may only be made in respect of injury, loss or damage which was due to an accident arising out of the presence of a motor vehicle on a road, if:

(*a*)   it is in respect of damage which is treated as resulting from an offence under the Theft Act 1968; or

(*b*)   it is in respect of injury, loss or damage as respects which the offender is uninsured in relation to the use of the vehicle; and compensation is not payable under the agreement between the Secretary of State and the Motor Insurers' Bureau[6].

Since the Motor Insurers' Bureau will not pay out in respect of the first £300 of any claim, it will always be the case that compensation under the agreement is not payable in respect of that amount; accordingly, the court may award compensation but only up to that figure[7].

An order must relate to a specific offence and to a specific loser[8]. A compensation order may not be made in respect of loss or damage arising from admitted offences which have not been charged or formally taken into consideration[9]. The order must specify the amount and any instalments[10]. Compensation ordered shall be of such amount as the court considers appropriate having regard to any evidence and to any representations that are made by or on behalf of the accused or the prosecutor[11]. This means that the court can make assessments and approximations where the evidence is scanty or incomplete and make such order as is "appropriate". But where the defendant challenges the basis on which any compensation order could be made and real issues are raised whether the claimants have suffered any, and if so what loss, evidence must be received to establish the defendant's liability to pay compensation[12]. Where a complete reconciliation between the parties as to the proper amount of compensation would present a difficult and complex task, but the calculation of the minimum loss arising is a comparatively simple matter, the court should make a compensation order in the latter amount rather than decline to make any order on the ground of complexity[13].

The court is not bound to apply the strict concepts of causation in tort, but there must be evidence of causation before a compensation order can be made[14]. This may involve a chain of events[15]. An order can be made to compensate for terror and distress directly occasioned by the offence[16], but any order made should be on the basis of a proper assessment of the amount payable in respect of the victim's experience[17]. A compensation order may properly be made against an offender convicted of violent disorder in respect of injuries inflicted by another person, if the offender participated in the violent disorder in the course of which the injuries were inflicted[18]. Before ordering compensation to a witness to an offence, the court must first have some evidence that the witness did experience distress[19]. The law does not require an application to be made by the victim[20]. The existence of a civil liability is not a condition precedent to the making of a valid compensation order[21]. A court has power to order payment of compensation, notwithstanding the death of the victim[22].

Where a substantial sum of compensation is contemplated in respect of personal injury there should be up to date and detailed information before the court as to the extent of the injury, such as medical reports and photographs. The proper course in such a case is to leave the matter to the county court where the extent of the injuries can be investigated[23], although if the sum likely to be awarded is not very great and the criminal court has enough information about the assault and its consequences, it may be appropriate to make an order[24].

When assessing compensation under s 35 of the Powers of Criminal Courts Act 1973 in respect of an offence of statutory nuisance by a landlord under s 82 of the Environment Protection Act 1990[25], the court should take into account only the injury, loss or damage caused by the continuation of the nuisance from the date when the period stated in the complainant's s 82(6) notice expired to the date of hearing[26].

In special circumstances, for example where there has been the loss of use of a banknote, and the sum was large and the period long, the court may consider awarding interest on the compensation[27].

A joint and several order against two or more offenders is possible but should not be made if substantial justice can be achieved by an order made severally, ie requiring each offender to pay the appropriate proportion[28]. The amount should in general be awarded in equal proportions; distinction should be made only where it can be shown that one of the convicted persons was more responsible than the other or where the ability or inability to pay is markedly different[29].

The Home Office has issued guidance to the courts on the use of compensation orders, including the level of compensation in personal injury cases and advises the courts of the basis on which awards are currently made by the Criminal Injuries Compensation Authority[30].

1. *A-G's Reference (No 10 of 1992)* (1993) 15 Cr App Rep (S) 1.
2. See the wording of ss 1(1) and 130(1) of the Powers of Criminal Courts (Sentencing) Act 2000 in this Part, post.
3. See *R v Brogan* [1975] 1 All ER 879, 139 JP 296; Criminal Justice Act 1967, s 56(5) in Part I: Magistrates' Courts, Procedure, ante.
4. *R v Wilkinson* (1979) 1 Cr App Rep (S) 69; *R v Shenton* (1979) 1 Cr App Rep (S) 81.
5. Powers of Criminal Courts (Sentencing) Act 2000, s 131(1), this Part, post.
6. Powers of Criminal Courts (Sentencing) Act 2000, s 130(6)-(7), this Part, post.
7. *DPP v Scott* [1995] RTR 40, 159 JP 261. See also *R v Austin* (1995) 2 Cr App Rep (S) 191, [1996] Crim LR 446, [1996] RTR 414.
8. *R v Oddy* [1974] 2 All ER 666, [1974] 1 WLR 1212, 138 JP 515, CA.
9. *R v Crutchley and Tonks* (1993) 15 Cr App Rep (S) 627, [1994] Crim LR 309; *R v Hose* (1994) 16 Cr App Rep (S) 682, [1995] Crim LR 259.
10. *R v Miller* [1976] Crim LR 694.
11. Powers of Criminal Courts (Sentencing) Act 2000, s 130(4), this Part, post.
12. *R v Horsham, ex p Richards* [1985] 2 All ER 1114, [1985] 1 WLR 986, 145 JP 567.
13. *R v James* [2003] EWCA Crim 811, [2003] 2 Cr App R (S) 97.
14. *R v Derby* (1990) 12 Cr App Rep (S) 502.
15. *R v Taylor* (1993) 14 Cr App Rep (S) 276, [1993] Crim LR 317.
16. *Bond v Chief Constable of Kent* [1983] 1 All ER 456, [1983] 1 WLR 40, 147 JP 107.
17. *R v Godfrey* (1994) 15 Cr App Rep (S) 536.
18. *R v Geurtjens* (1992) 14 Cr App Rep (S) 280; *R v Denness* [1996] 1 Cr App Rep (S) 159, [1995] Crim LR 750.
19. *R v Vaughan* (1990) 12 Cr App Rep (S) 46, CA.
20. Powers of Criminal Courts (Sentencing) Act 2000, s 130(1), this Part, post.
21. *R v Chappel* (1984) 80 Cr App Rep 31, [1984] Crim LR 574.
22. *Holt v DPP* [1996] 2 Cr App Rep (S) 314, [1996] Crim LR 524.
23. *R v Cooper* [1982] Crim LR 308.
24. *R v Welch* (1984) 6 Cr App Rep (S) 13.
25. See title Public Health, in Part VIII, post.
26. *R v Crown Court at Liverpool, ex p Cooke* [1996] 4 All ER 589, [1997] 1 WLR 700, [1997] 1 Cr App Rep (S) 7, DC.
27. *R v Schofield* [1978] 2 All ER 705, [1978] 1 WLR 979, 142 JP 426.
28. *R v Grundy* [1974] 1 All ER 292, [1974] 1 WLR 139, 138 JP 242, CA.
29. *R v Amey* [1983] 1 All ER 865, [1983] 1 WLR 345, 147 JP 124, CA. See also *R v Beddow* (1987) 9 Cr App Rep (S) 235, [1987] Crim LR 833, CA.
30. See Home Office Circulars 85/1988, dated 19 September 1988, and 53/1993, dated 23 November 1993; see in particular the annex to the latter circular which updates guidance on compensation in personal injury cases.

3–173 Compensation: relevance of the offender's means. The order must be precise in its terms[1]. In determining whether to make an order and any amount, the court shall have regard to the offender's means[2]. There must be a scrupulous inquiry into the offender's financial circumstances, and a compensation order must not be made on the basis of pure speculation as to his future prospects[3]. It cannot claim to have such a regard when instalments over a long period eg six years are ordered[4]. There is, however, no reason in principle why an order should not extend for two or even three years[5]. When considering the defendant's means, the court may have regard to potential income[6]. There is no general principle that a compensation order should not be made if it forced the offender to sell his matrimonial home[7]. With an offender reluctant to disclose means, the court could indicate a provisional figure of compensation and then require the offender to show that his means are such that the figure cannot be met if he wishes to avoid that order[8]. Where there are several claimants and the offenders' means are insufficient to meet all the claims, the course to be adopted as a general rule is apportionment commensurate with the total liability. But the court has an inherent power to see that justice is done, and it may, if there are strong grounds for doing so, depart from the normal pro rata basis to make such adjustment as is reasonable[9].

Compensation orders were not introduced to enable the convicted to buy themselves out of the penalties for crime, but as a convenient and rapid means of avoiding the expense of resort to civil litigation when the offender clearly has means which would allow compensation to be paid[10]. A compensation order made by the court of trial can be extremely beneficial as long as it is confined to simple, straightforward cases and generally cases where no great amount is at stake[11].

For the purpose of payment of compensation, including payment by the parent of a youth, and for enforcement, compensation is treated exactly like a fine[12].

1. *R v Scott (formerly Lutta)* (1986) 150 JP 286, CA "to be paid as quickly as possible" wrong.
2. Powers of Criminal Courts (Sentencing) Act 2000, s 130(11); *R v Oddy* [1974] 2 All ER 666, 138 JP 515 (£1,200 at £3.50 a week plus £37.40 a week inappropriate).
3. *R v Ellis* (1993) 158 JP 386.
4. *R v Daly* [1974] 1 All ER 290, 138 JP 245; *R v Meeks* (1975) 139 JP Jo 532 (£6,500 payable over 20 years inappropriate); *R v Miller* [1976] Crim LR 694; *R v Webb and Davis* (1979) 1 Cr App Rep (S) 16; *R v Making* [1982] Crim LR 613 (order for payments over 71/2 years reduced to 2 years).
5. *R v Olliver and Olliver* (1989) 153 JP 369, [1989] Crim LR 387, CA; applied in *R v Yehou* [1997] 2 Cr App Rep (S) 48 (compensation order for £9,110 reduced to £3,900 to be paid at £25 per week over 3 years).
6. *R v Ford* [1977] Crim LR 114.
7. *R v McGuire* (1992) 13 Cr App Rep (S) 332.
8. *R v Phillips* [1989] Crim LR 160. NB The offender is under a statutory duty to furnish a statement of his financial circumstances, and he commits an offence punishable with a fine not exceeding level 2 if he fails to do so: Criminal Justice Act 1991, s 20A(1A), see this Part, post. The court is also empowered to make a "financial circumstances order" in

relation to an offender, non-compliance with which constitutes an offence punishable with a fine not exceeding level 3: Criminal Justice Act 2003, s 162, see this PART, post.
   9. *R v Amey* [1983] 1 All ER 865, [1983] 1 WLR 345, 147 JP 124.
   10. Per Scarman LJ in *R v Inwood* (1974) 60 Cr App Rep 70.
   11. See *R v Daly* [1974] 1 All ER 290, 138 JP 245; *R v Kneeshaw* [1975] QB 57 [1974] 1 All ER 896, 138 JP 291; *R v Donovan* [1982] RTR 126; *R v Inwood* (1974) 60 Cr App Rep 70; *Hyde v Emery* (1984) 6 Cr App Rep (S) 206 (compensation order in respect of unemployment benefit obtained by false representation).
   12. Magistrates' Courts Act 1980, s 150(1): see also paras **3–99** and **5–13**, et seq, post.

3–174   Criminal injuries compensation scheme. In appropriate cases, courts will wish to draw the attention of victims of violence to the criminal injuries compensation scheme administered by the Criminal Injuries Compensation Authority, Tay House, 300 Bath Street, Glasgow G2 4JR. The nature of the claims which the Authority will entertain, and information on procedure are contained in a guide to Criminal Injuries Compensation – The Tariff Scheme effective from 1 April 1994[1]. It should be observed that the Authority will not make awards of less than a specified amount, set at £1,000 at 1 April 1994[1]; thus courts should pay especial attention to their powers to compensate for moderate injuries. Council Directive 2004/80/EC of 29 April 2004 (OJ No L 261, 6.8.2004, p 15) relating to compensation to crime victims sets up a system of co-operation to facilitate access to compensation to victims of violent intentional crimes in cases where the crime was committed in a Member State other than that where the victim is habitually resident. Domestic effect to the Directive is made by the Victims of Violent Intentional Crime (Arrangements for Compensation) (European Communities) Regulations 2005, SI 2005/3396 in relation to applicants for compensation whose injuries result from violent intentional crime committed on or after 1 July 2005.

   1. The Tariff Scheme, Issue No 2 (4/94) issued by the Criminal Injuries Compensation Authority.

RESTITUTION

3–175 The court by or before which an offender is convicted may on the conviction make an order for the restitution of goods[1]. Such an order may be made where—

(1) goods have been stolen or obtained by deception or blackmail; and
(2) the offender is convicted of any offence with reference to the theft, whether or not stealing is the gist of his offence; or
(3) the offender is convicted of any other offence but an offence under (2) is taken into consideration; and
(4) in the court's opinion the relevant facts sufficiently appear from evidence given at the trial or from the available documents (that is, admissible written statements or admissions).

The court may exercise any of the following powers—

(1) order anyone having possession or control of the goods to restore them to any person entitled to recover them from him;
(2) order the delivery or transfer of goods representing the proceeds of any disposal or realisation of the stolen goods on the application of the person entitled to the goods;
(3) order that a sum not exceeding the value of the stolen goods be paid out of money taken from the offender on his apprehension to the person entitled to recovery of the goods;
(4) order that there be paid out of money taken from the offender on his apprehension an amount paid for the purchase of the goods or lent on the security of them in good faith to the purchaser or lender.

Orders may be made under both (2) and (3) provided that a person does not recover more than the value of the goods.
   The conviction of an offender does not in itself affect the title to goods stolen or obtained by fraud or other wrongful means[2]. Where goods have been recovered, an order under (3) should not be made in respect of goods which were not the subject of the charge[3]. Restitution orders should not be made if there is any doubt at all whether the money or goods in question belong to a third party[4]. With regard to disputes, or the disposal of property in police possession, recourse may be necessary to the civil courts, or to procedures under the Police (Property) Act 1897[5]. Where the court commits the offender to the Crown Court for sentence, it does not have power to make a restitution order because that right or duty becomes vested in the Crown Court[6].
   It should be noted that although the court need not require an application to be made to it under (1), (3) and (4), under (2) an application is necessary. Furthermore there is no power to order the sale of articles and distribution of the proceeds[7].

   1. Powers of Criminal Courts (Sentencing) Act 2000, s 148, this PART, post.
   2. Theft Act 1968, s 31(2).
   3. *R v Parker* [1970] 2 All ER 458, 134 JP 497.
   4. *Stamp v United Dominions Trust (Commercial) Ltd* [1967] 1 QB 418, [1967] 1 All ER 251, 131 JP 177; *R v Ferguson* [1970] 2 All ER 820, 134 JP 608.
   5. PART VIII.
   6. *R v Blackpool Justices, ex p Charleson and Gregory* [1972] 3 All ER 854, 137 JP 25.
   7. *R v Thibeault* (1982) 147 JP 173, 76 Cr App Rep 201, [1983] Crim LR 102.

DEPRIVATION

3–176   Where a person is convicted of an offence and—

(*a*) the court is satisfied that any property which has been lawfully seized from him or which was in his possession or under his control at the time when he was apprehended for the offence or when a summons in respect of it was issued—

    (i) has been used for the purpose of committing, or facilitating the commission of, any offence; or

    (ii) was intended by him to be used for that purpose; or

(*b*) the offence, or an offence which the court has taken into consideration in determining his sentence, consists of unlawful possession of property which—

    (i) has been lawfully seized from him; or

    (ii) was in his possession or under his control at the time when he was apprehended for the offence of which he has been convicted or when a summons in respect of that offence was issued,

the court may make an order depriving him of his rights, if any, in the property[1].

A deprivation order may be made whether or not the court also deals with the offender in respect of the offence in any other way. In considering whether to make such an order the court shall have regard to the value of the property, and to the likely financial and other effects on the offender of the making of the order, together with any other order the court contemplates making[1]. A deprivation order should be considered as part of the overall penalty for the offence and the other sentence should be adjusted accordingly[2]. If the effect of the order, taken together with any other sentences or orders made, would create an excessive criminal penalty, the deprivation order should not be made[3].

Numerous other statutes provide for courts to order forfeiture of particular objects, for example anything relating to the misuse of drugs[4], firearms[5], fish and fishing tackle[6], alcohol[7], obscene articles[8], offensive weapons[9], wireless telegraphy apparatus[10]. Reference should be made to each statute individually as the circumstances in which an order may be made will vary considerably.

The effect of the order is to place the property in police possession; thereafter an application under the Police (Property) Act 1897 may, with limits, be made. It is not for the court making the deprivation order to determine any question of ownership[11]. Where the offender is committed to the Crown Court for sentence, the making of any deprivation order should be left to that court[12]. A deprivation order may be combined with an order of absolute or conditional discharge[13].

A deprivation order is appropriate only in simple cases where it will not be difficult to implement[14]. It is incumbent on the court to look for proof of the circumstances which would justify an order; a simple prosecution request for a forfeiture order is not sufficient[15].

---

1. Powers of Criminal Courts (Sentencing) Act 2000, s 143, this PART, post.
2. *R v Joyce* [1991] RTR 241, 11 Cr App Rep (S) 253, CA; *R v Priestly* (1996) 2 Cr App Rep (S) 144, [1996] Crim LR 356.
3. *R v Highbury Corner Stipendiary Magistrate, ex p Di Matteo* [1992] 1 All ER 102, [1991] 1 WLR 1374, 156 JP 61.
4. Misuse of Drugs Act 1971, s 27, in PART VIII: title MEDICINE AND PHARMACY, post.
5. Firearms Act 1968, s 52 in PART VIII: title FIREARMS, post, Deer Act 1963, s 6, Game Laws (Amendment) Act 1960, s 3 in PART VIII: title GAME, post.
6. Salmon and Freshwater Fisheries Act 1975, Sch 4 para 5 in PART VIII: title FISHERIES, post.
7. Licensing Act 2003, ss 136–138, 144 in PART VIII: title LOCAL GOVERNMENT, post.
8. Obscene Publications Act, 1959, s 3 in PART VIII: title OBSCENE AND HARMFUL PUBLICATIONS, post.
9. Prevention of Crime Act, 1953, s 1 in PART VIII: title OFFENSIVE WEAPONS, post.
10. Wireless Telegraphy Act 2006, s 103 and Sch 5, post in PART VIII: title TELECOMMUNICATIONS AND BROADCASTING, post.
11. See *R v Chester Justices, ex p Smith* (1977) 67 Cr App Rep 133, [1978] Crim LR 226.
12. Powers of Criminal Courts (Sentencing) Act 2000, s 7(1), this PART, post.
13. Powers of Criminal Courts (Sentencing) Act 2000, ss 12(7), this PART, post.
14. *R v Troth* [1980] Crim LR 249 (jointly owned vehicle).
15. *R v Pemberton* (1983) 4 Cr App Rep (S) 328, [1983] Crim LR 121.

COSTS

3–177   The following orders for the payment of costs may be made by a magistrates' court:

(1) defence costs from central funds when an information is not proceeded with, or examining justices determine not to commit for trial, or an information is dismissed on summary trial ("defendant's costs order")[1];

(2) private prosecutor's costs in respect of an indictable offence from central funds[2];

(3) prosecution "just and reasonable" costs to be paid by the accused on conviction[3];

(4) either party to pay to the other, costs incurred as a result of an unnecessary or improper act or omission[4];

(5) to compensate a witness or person attending to give evidence, an interpreter, or a medical practitioner making an oral or written report, from central funds[4];

The court may also disallow, or (as the case may be) order the legal or other representative to meet, the whole or part of wasted costs[5].

Costs to be paid by an accused person on conviction must be specified in the order, payable to a specified person, and be of a just and reasonable amount; in particular where a fine, penalty, forfeiture or compensation does not exceed £5 then the court should not order payment of costs unless in the particular circumstances it considers it right to do so; also where the accused is under 17 years of age, costs shall not exceed the amount of any fine imposed. Costs ordered may include costs of the prosecuting authority in carrying out investigations with a view to the prosecution of a defendant where a prosecution results and the defendant is convicted[6]. The prosecution should serve on the defence, at the earliest time, full details of its costs, so as to give the defence a proper opportunity to consider them and make representations on them[6]

Where the prosecutor adopts the procedure contained in s 12 of the Magistrates' Courts Act 1980, enabling the defendant to plead guilty without appearing before the court, a claim for costs by the prosecutor against the defendant may be notified to the defendant in the same document as contains the statement of facts, although the claim will not form part of the statement. A claim for costs so notified shall be brought to the attention of the court at the hearing by the justices' clerk so that the justices may decide whether to order the defendant to pay the costs[7].

Costs ordered to be paid by the defendant under the above provisions shall be treated for the purposes of collection and enforcement as if they had been adjudged to be paid on conviction[8], and therefore are recoverable in the same manner as a fine.

Costs ordered to be paid by a defendant on conviction should be kept in step with any fine imposed, but if the defendant has the means to pay it is not wrong in principle to make an order for costs which substantially exceeds the amount of the fine[9]. Any order for costs should be within the means of the offender so that it can be paid off in a reasonable time, within about 12 months[10]. It is unlawful for justices to make an order for costs which the defendant has no realistic prospect of paying, or in the hope or expectation that it will be paid by a third party[11]. Costs should be ordered only after an investigation of the offender's means, and if the offender is sentenced to custody, only if there are assets out of which the order can be paid[12].

The principles to be applied in determining the amount of costs to be paid by a defendant were considered in *R v Northallerton Magistrates' Court, ex p Dove*[13]:

(1) An order to pay costs to the prosecutor should never exceed the sum which, having regard to the defendant's means and any other financial order imposed upon him, the defendant is able to pay and which is reasonable to order the defendant to pay.

(2) Such an order should never exceed the sum which the prosecutor has actually and reasonably incurred.

(3) Where the defendant has, by his conduct, put the prosecutor to avoidable expense, he may, subject to his means, be ordered to pay some or all of that sum to the prosecutor. But he is not to be punished for exercising a constitutional right to defend himself.

(4) The costs ordered to be paid should not, in the ordinary way, be grossly disproportionate to the fine.

(5) It is for the defendant facing a financial penalty, by way of a fine or an order for costs, to disclose to the justices such data relevant to his financial position as will enable the justices to assess what he can reasonably afford to pay. In the absence of such disclosure, the justices may draw reasonable inferences as to the defendant's means from evidence they have heard and from all the circumstances of the case.

(6) It is incumbent on any court, which proposes to make any financial order against a defendant, to give the defendant a fair opportunity to adduce any relevant financial information and make any appropriate submissions. If the court has it in mind to make any unusual or unconventional order potentially adverse to a defendant, it should alert the defendant and his advisers to that possibility.

Where there are several accused it will *usually* be appropriate when making an order for costs to look to see what would be a reasonable estimate of costs if each defendant were tried alone. However, this is not a test to be applied in all cases, and in others where the principal offender stood to gain financially from the offences and has the means to pay, it may be appropriate to order him to bear the full costs of the prosecution[14].

Where an offender ought to have been dealt with in the magistrates' court for an offence to which he was willing to plead guilty, it is wrong for the Crown Court to order payment of costs at the level appropriate to that court, but instead it should make an order to pay costs at the rate which would have been incurred in the magistrates' court[15]. Where an offender faced a charge of careless driving, but a charge of driving a motor vehicle on a footpath was substituted and the offender would have paid a fixed penalty for that offence if he had been offered that option, it was incumbent upon the justices either not to order payment of prosecution costs or to give reasons why costs should be paid in the face of the fact that the offender would have paid a fixed penalty[16].

---

1. See Prosecution of Offences Act 1985, s 16, in PART I: MAGISTRATES' COURTS, PROCEDURE, ante and commentary in para **1–800 Costs**, ante.

2. Prosecution of Offences Act 1985, s 17 in PART I: MAGISTRATES' COURTS, PROCEDURE, ante, and commentary in para **1–801 Costs**, ante.

3. Prosecution of Offences Act 1985, s 18 in Part I: Magistrates' Courts, Procedure, ante. See also *R v Bye* [2005] EWCA Crim 1230, [2006] 1 Cr App R (S) 27 (offender convicted of an offence of affray arising from a road rage incident and sentenced to 8 months' imprisonment, 12 months' disqualification under s 146 of the Powers of Criminal Courts (Sentencing) Act 2003 (see para **3–178**, post) and deprived of his rights in his motor car with an order that £15,000 of the sale proceeds should be paid to the victim as compensation: latter order quashed on the grounds that the rest of the sentence was an adequate penalty and £15,000 was manifestly excessive where the complainant had suffered no significant injury).

4. Prosecution of Offences Act 1985, s 19 and see the Costs in Criminal Cases (General) Regulations in PART I: MAGISTRATES' COURTS, PROCEDURE, ante.

5. Prosecution of Offences Act 1985, s 19A and see the Costs in Criminal Cases (General) Regulations 1986 in PART I: MAGISTRATES' COURTS, PROCEDURE, ante.

6. *R v Associated Octel Ltd* [1997] Crim LR 144.

7. *R v Coventry Magistrates' Court, ex p DPP* (1990) 154 JP 765, [1990] RTR 193.

8. Administration of Justice Act 1970, s 41 and Sch 9, in PART I: MAGISTRATES' COURTS, PROCEDURE, ante. For the meaning of the expression "sum adjudged to be paid by a conviction", see the Magistrates' Courts Act 1980, s 150(3), in PART I: MAGISTRATES' COURTS, PROCEDURE, ante.

9. *R v Boyle* (1995) 16 Cr App Rep (S) 927, [1995] Crim LR 514, CA.

10. *R v Nottingham Magistrates' Court, ex p Fohmann* (1986) 151 JP 49, 84 Cr App Rep 316. See also *R v Jones* [1988] Crim LR 390.

11. *R v Barnet Magistrates' Court, ex p Cantor* [1998] 2 All ER 333, 162 JP 137, [1999] 1 WLR 334.

12. *R v Baker* (1992) 14 Cr App Rep (S) 242.

13. (1999) 163 JP 657, [1999] Crim LR 760, [2000] 1 Cr App Rep (S) 136, DC.

14. *R v Harrison* (1992) 14 Cr App Rep (S) 419. See also *R v Fresha Bakeries* [2002] EWCA Crim 1451, [2002] All ER (D) 408 (May), [2003] 1 Cr App Rep (S) 202, [2002]JPN 479: a sentencing court is entitled to order any defendant to pay a contribution to prosecution costs that exceeds those costs that relate to him alone where he was more responsible for the criminal conduct that led to the convictions than his co-defendants.

15. *R v Joel* (1993) 15 Cr App Rep (S) 5; *R v Sentonco* [1996] 1 Cr App Rep (S) 174, [1995] Crim LR 665.

16. *Ritson v Durham Magistrates' Court* [2001] EWHC Admin 519, (2001) 166 JP 218.

DRIVING DISQUALIFICATION FOR ANY OFFENCE

3–178 Where a court convicts a person of an offence it may, instead of (except certain offences where the penalty is fixed or mandatory) or in addition to dealing with him in any other way, order him to be disqualified for such period as it thinks fit, for holding or obtaining a driving licence[1]. Where such an order of disqualification is made the court must require the defendant to produce any driving licence held by him together with its counterpart; or his Community licence and counterpart (if any)[2].

This power is available in respect of any offence. HOC 59/2003 envisages possible uses of this power to combat anti-social behaviour and in particular in respect of convictions for offences such as: kerb crawling[3]; misuse of vehicles off-road[4]; abandoned vehicles[5]. Where an offender was arrested for proving a positive roadside breath test, but escaped from lawful custody before an evidential breath test could be carried 18 months' disqualification was entirely merited[6]. Disqualification under this provision is also appropriate for an offence of affray arising out of a road rage incident[7].

Disqualification under this provision does not result in endorsement of the licence but the court will return the licence to the DVLA with the accompanying notification using offence code NE98. After the expiry of the disqualification the licence will not be returned to the driver (except for foreign licences); the offender will need to apply for return of their licence.

1. Powers of Criminal Courts (Sentencing) Act 2000, s 146(1), in this PART, post.
2. Powers of Criminal Courts (Sentencing) Act 2000, s 146(4), in this PART, post.
3. Sexual Offences Act 1985, s 1, in PART VIII: title SEXUAL OFFENCES, post.
4. Road Traffic Act 1988, s 34, in PART IV: title ROAD TRAFFIC, post.
5. Refuse Disposal (Amenity) Act 1978, in PART VIII: title PUBLIC HEALTH, post.
6. *R v Waring* [2005] EWCA Crim 1080, [2006] 1 Crim App R (S) 9.
7. *R v Bye* [2005] EWCA Crim 1230, [2006] 1 Cr App R (S) 27 (12 months' disqualification upheld).

3–179 Driving disqualification where vehicle used for purposes of crime. The Crown Court may disqualify an offender convicted before it (or committed for sentence by a magistrates' court under s 3 of the Powers of Criminal Courts (Sentencing) Act 2000) of an offence punishable by a term of two years imprisonment or more[1]. Any court may also use this power to disqualify for such period as it thinks fit where a person is convicted of common assault or of any other offence involving an assault (including an offence of aiding, abetting, counselling or procuring, or inciting to the commission of, an offence) where the court is satisfied that the assault was committed by driving a motor vehicle[2].

Where such an order of disqualification is made the court must require the defendant to produce any driving licence held by him together with its counterpart; or his Community licence and counterpart (if any)[3].

1. Powers of Criminal Courts (Sentencing) Act 2000, s 147(1), in this PART, post.
2. Powers of Criminal Courts (Sentencing) Act 2000, s 147(2), in this PART, post.
3. Powers of Criminal Courts (Sentencing) Act 2000, s 147(5), in this PART, post.

DRIVING DISQUALIFICATION UNDER THE ROAD TRAFFIC OFFENDERS 1988

3–190 The most serious driving offences carry obligatory, minimum disqualification and endorsement. Less serious offences carry obligatory endorsement and discretionary disualification or penalty points of numbers of ranges of numbers that vary according to the offence. The points system provides that where 12 or more penalty points are to be taken into account the court must generally disqualify the offender for the minimum period.

The rules and principles governing disqualification and endorsement are summarised in paras **4–17** to **4–25**, in PART IV: ROAD TRAFFIC, post.

RECOMMENDATION FOR DEPORTATION

3–191 Recommendation for deportation may be ordered only in the circumstances set out in the Immigration Act 1971, s 6[1].

---

1. In PART VIII: title IMMIGRATION, post. For a full discussion of recommendations for deportation, see the notes to s 6. As to the impact here of the Human Rights Act 1998 and EC Directive 2004/38/EC (which gave EC citizens and their families enhanced rights to reside within the territory of member states), see *R v Nelson Carmona* [2006] EWCA Crim 508, 2 Cr App R (S) 102, [2006] Crim LR 657.

Ancillary orders imposing restrictions or obligations

ANTI-SOCIAL BEHAVIOUR ORDERS ON CONVICTION

3–210 Where an offender is convicted of an offence committed on or after 2 December 2002[1] and the court considers

- that the offender has acted, at any time since 1 April 1999[2], in a manner that caused or was likely to cause harassment, alarm or distress to one or more persons not of the same household as himself, and
- that an anti-social order made on conviction is necessary[3] to protect persons in any place in England and Wales from further anti-social acts by him

the court by or before which he is convicted, whether or not an application has been made for such an order, may make an anti-social order which prohibits the offender from doing anything described in the order[4]. Where the offender is committed to the Crown Court for sentence, the making of any such order will be a matter for the Crown Court[5].

Such an order may only be made in addition to a sentence imposed or conditional discharge made, in respect of the offence of which he has been convicted[6]. The order takes effect for a period (not less than two years[7]) specified in the order or until further order and takes effect on the day on which it is made although the court may provide for the suspension of those requirements in the order specified by the court, during any period when the offender is in custody[8].

Breach of any requirements of the order is an offence triable either way for which, on conviction, the court may not make a conditional discharge[9].

An offender made the subject of an order may apply to the court which made the order or, where the order was made by a magistrates' court, any magistrates' court acting for the same petty sessions area as that court, to vary or discharge the order, but no application for discharge may be made before the end of the period of two years beginning with the day on which the order takes effect[10].

---

1. Ie the commencement date of s 1C of the Crime and Disorder Act 1998, see s 1C(10) in PART I: MAGISTRATES' COURTS, PROCEDURE, ante and SI 2002/2750.
2. Ie the commencement date of s 1 of the Crime and Disorder Act 1998, see s 1C(10) in PART I: MAGISTRATES' COURTS, PROCEDURE, ante and SI 1998/3263.
3. See para **3–211**, post.
4. Crime and Disorder Act 1998, s 1C(1)–(3), in PART I: MAGISTRATES' COURTS, PROCEDURE The Magistrates' Courts (Anti-Social Behaviour Orders) Rules 2002, this PART, post, provide forms in relation to orders under s 1C and make provision for applications to vary or discharge such orders.
5. Crime and Disorder Act 1998, s 1C(10), in PART I: MAGISTRATES' COURTS, PROCEDURE.
6. Crime and Disorder Act 1998, s 1C(4), in PART I: MAGISTRATES' COURTS, PROCEDURE.
7. Just because the *order* shall have effect for not less than two years, it does not follow that each and every prohibition within a particular order must endure for the life of the order: *Lonergan (Ashley) v (1) Lewes Crown Court (2) Brighton & Hove City Council & Secretary of State for the Home Department (Interested Party)* [2005] EWHC 457 (Admin), [2005] 2 All ER 362, [2005] 1 WLR 2570 approved in *R v Boness, R v Bebbington* (see para **3–211**, post).
8. Crime and Disorder Act 1998, s 1C(5), (9), s 1(7) in PART I: MAGISTRATES' COURTS, PROCEDURE. Where custodial sentences in excess of a few months are passed and offenders are liable to be released on licence (and therefore subject to recall) the circumstances in which there will be a demonstrable necessity to make a suspended anti-social behaviour order, to take effect on release, will be limited, although there will be cases in which geographical restraints can properly supplement licence conditions: *R v P* [2004] All ER (D) 32 (Feb).
9. Crime and Disorder Act 1998, ss 1C(9), 1(10)–(11), in PART I: MAGISTRATES' COURTS, PROCEDURE.
10. Crime and Disorder Act 1998, s 1C(6)–(8), in PART I: MAGISTRATES' COURTS, PROCEDURE.

3–211 Guidance on the making and terms of ASBOs. In *R v Boness, R v Bebbington*[1] the Court of Appeal gave the following guidance:

(1) An ASBO had to be precise and capable of being understood by the offender. It followed that the court should ask itself, before making an order, whether the terms of the order were clear so that the defendant would know precisely what it was that he was prohibited from doing[2].

(2) Following a finding that the defendant had acted in an anti-social manner (whether or not the act constituted a criminal offence), the test for making an order that prohibited the offender from doing something was one of necessity[3]. Each separate order prohibiting a person from doing a specified thing had to be necessary to protect persons from further anti-social acts by

him. Accordingly, any order had to be tailor-made for the individual defendant, not designed on a word processor for use in every case.

(3) Given the requirement that the order had to be necessary to protect persons from further anti-social acts by the defendant, the purpose of an ASBO was not to punish. It followed that the use of an ASBO to punish a defendant was unlawful.

A court should not allow itself to be diverted by a defendant's representative's seeking the imposition of an ASBO at the sentencing stage in the hope that the court might make such an order as an alternative to prison or other sanction. It might be better for the court to decide the appropriate sentence and then move on to consider whether an ASBO should be made or not after sentence had been passed, albeit at the same hearing.

(4) It followed from the requirement that the order had to be necessary to protect persons from further anti-social acts by him, that the court should not impose an order which prohibited a defendant from committing a specified criminal offence, if the sentence which could be passed following conviction for the offence should be a sufficient deterrent.

Were the defendant to be liable, following conviction for the offence, to imprisonment, then an ASBO would add nothing other than to increase the sentence if the sentence for the offence was less than five years' imprisonment. However, if the defendant was not going to be deterred from committing the offence by a sentence of imprisonment for that offence, the ASBO was not likely, it might be thought, further to deter, and was therefore not necessary. The test for making an order was not whether the defendant needed reminding that certain matters constitute criminal conduct, but whether it was necessary. An ASBO should not be used merely to increase the sentence of imprisonment which a defendant was liable to receive[4]. Whilst different considerations might apply where the maximum sentence was a fine, the court had still to go through all the steps to ensure that the order was necessary.

(5) A court should be reluctant to impose an order which prohibited a defendant from committing a specified criminal offence. The aim of an ASBO was to prevent anti-social behaviour, by enabling them to take action before the anti-social behaviour it was designed to prevent was to take place[5].

(6) Not only had the court to consider whether an order was necessary to protect persons from further anti-social acts by him, the terms of the order had to be proportionate in the sense that they had to be commensurate with the risk to be guarded against[6]. That was particularly important where an order might interfere with a defendant's right under the European Convention on Human Rights as protected under the Human Rights Act 1998.

In *R (on the application of W) v Acton Youth Court*[7] it was held that proceedings under s 1C were civil in nature; and hearsay evidence was admissible; the first criterion, namely that the defendant has acted in an anti-social manner, attracted the criminal standard of proof, but the second criterion, namely was an order necessary to protect persons from further anti-social acts, was not a matter of standard of proof but involved an exercise of judgment; the requirements of procedural fairness must be scrupulously followed, but a challenge by way of judicial review, as opposed to an appeal to the court, would succeed only if the proceedings before the magistrates were so flawed that the making of an order amounted to an excess of jurisdiction; where the allegations were far wider than the facts of the instant case or previous convictions the defendant must be given adequate time to prepared to meet those allegations, but justices were entitled to expect that if there were a need for an adjournment an application would be made; drafting points were important, but did not justify judicial review of the order; and justices should give reasons in some form.

There are no rules regarding the service and use of hearsay evidence in the Crown Court, but hearsay evidence is nonetheless admissible under the Civil Evidence Act 1995 and the principles set out in the Magistrates' Courts Rules 1981 should be followed; further, the prosecution should identify the particular facts said to constitute anti-social behaviour and, if not accepted, those facts should be proved to the criminal standard before being acted upon by the judge[8].

---

1. [2005] EWCA Crim 2395, (2005) 169 JP 621, [2006] 1 Cr App R (S) 120.

2. *R v P* [2004] All ER (D) 32 (Feb) applied. See also *P (Shane Tony)* [2004] EWCA Crim 287; [2004] 2 Cr App R (S) 63 (at para 34) in which it was held, inter alia, that the terms of the order must be precise and capable of being understood by offender; the findings of fact giving rise to the making of the order must be recorded; the order must be explained to the offender; the exact terms of the order must be pronounced in open court; and the written order must accurately reflect the order as pronounced.

3. See also *R v Rush* [2005] EWCA Crim 1316, [2006] 1 Cr App R (S) 35, where it was held that an order should not be part of the normal sentencing process, particularly in cases which did not themselves specifically involve intimidation and harassment; ; and *R (on the application of Mills) v Birmingham Magistrates' Court* [2005] EWHC 2732 (Admin), (2006) 170 JP 237, in which it was held that whilst the circumstances of some thefts and shoplifting might fall within the relevant words of the statute, where the offender had done nothing to cause harassment, alarm or distress there was no evidence of anti-social behaviour and to make an ABSO had been perverse. See further *R v H, Stevens and Lovegrove* [2006] EWCA Crim 255, [2006] 2 Cr App R (S) 68, where there was no evidence that the appellant's offences (thefts) created the kind of conditions that were the normal prerequisite to the making of the order and the ASBO was quashed.

4. Following *R v Kirby* [2005] EWCA Crim 1228, [2006] 1 Cr App R (S) 26, in which it was held that where the underlying objective was to give the court higher sentencing powers in the event of future similar offending, it was not a use of the power which should normally be exercised, and *Williams* [2005] EWCA Crim 1796. [2006] 1 Cr App R (S) 56; and declining to follow *R v Hall* [2004] EWCA Crim 2671, [2004] 1 Cr App R (S) 118, [2005] Crim LR 153. See further *R v Lawson* [2005] EWCA Crim 1840, [2006] 1 Cr App R (S) 59.

5. The court gave the example of an offender who caused criminal damage by spraying graffiti. The order should be aimed at facilitating action to be taken to prevent graffiti spraying by him and/or his associates before it took place. An order in clear and simple terms preventing the offender from being in possession of a can of spray paint in a public place gave the police or others responsible for protecting the property an opportunity to take action in advance of the actual

spraying and made it clear to the offender that he had lost the right to carry such a can for the duration of the order. Similarly, if a court wished to make an order prohibiting a group of youngsters from racing cars or motor bikes on an estate or driving at excessive speed (anti-social behaviour for those living on the estate), then the order should not (normally) prohibit driving whilst disqualified. It should prohibit, for example, the offender whilst on the estate from taking part in, or encouraging, racing or driving at excessive speed. It might also prevent the group from congregating with named others in a particular area of the estate. Such an order gave those responsible for enforcing order on the estate the opportunity to take action to prevent the anti-social conduct, it is to be hoped, before it takes place. Neighbours could alert the police who would not have to wait for the commission of a particular criminal offence.

There is no absolute bar, however, on terms that prohibit specific acts that would have amounted to a criminal offence; it all depends on the whether the particular prohibition is really necessary to protect members of the public from anti-social behaviour by the person who is the subject of the order: *Hills v Chief Constable of Essex* [2006] EWHC 2633 (Admin), (2007) 171 JP 14 (which was in fact concerned with a prohibition on carrying knives that was intended to cover behaviour not caught by the criminal law, ie carrying penknives that might be less than 3 inches long).

6. See, for example, *R v McGrath* [2005] EWCA Crim 353, [2005] 2 Cr App R (S) 85. Most of the appellant's offending related to thefts from cars parked in railway station car parks. Therefore, it was appropriate to prohibit him from entering such car parks. However, a restriction on entering any car park within 3 specified counties was too wide, since it would prevent him even from entering a supermarket car park as a passenger in a car. Similarly, a prohibition on possessing tools or implements that could be used to break into cars was too wide, and it overlapped with the offence of going equipped for theft.

7. [2005] EWHC Admin 954, [2006] 170 JP 31.

8. *R v W; R v F* [2006] EWCA Crim 686, (2006) 170 JP 406, [2006] 2 Cr App R (S) 110.

Ancillary orders on conviction of sex offenders

NOTIFICATION REQUIREMENTS

3–230   A chief officer of police may apply by complaint to a magistrates' court for a notification order in respect of a defendant dealt with for a relevant offence by a court in an overseas jurisdiction which has a similar effect to a notification requirement in respect of a domestic offence[1]. An interim order may be applied for where an application for such an order has not been determined[2]. An appeal from an order made by a magistrates' court is to the Crown Court[3]. Failure, without reasonable excuse, to comply with the notification requirements is an offence triable either way[4].

---

1. Sexual Offences Act 2003, s 97, in PART VIII: title SEXUAL OFFENCES, post
2. Sexual Offences Act 2003, s 100, in PART VIII: title SEXUAL OFFENCES, post.
3. Sexual Offences Act 2003, s 101, in PART VIII: title SEXUAL OFFENCES, post.
4. Sexual Offences Act 2003, ss 91 and 98, in Part VIII: title Sexual Offences, post.

SEXUAL OFFENCES PREVENTION ORDER

3–240   This order may be made by a court where it deals with an offender in respect of certain offences listed in Schedules 3 or 5 of the Sexual Offences Act 2003 or where a chief officer of police has made an application to the court by way of complaint.

A court may make a sexual offences prevention order if:

–   the offence is one listed in Schs 3 or 5 of the Sexual Offences Act 2003;
–   it is satisfied that it is necessary to make such an order, for the purpose of protecting the public or any particular members of the public from serious sexual harm from the defendant[1].

The person specified in the order does not need to be the victim of the instant offence or the likely target of further Sch 3 offences, provided there is a risk that further Sch 3 offences will be committed and that the person in question will suffer serious psychological harm in consequence and it is necessary to make the order[2].

If it appears to a chief officer of police that the following conditions are fulfilled with respect to any person in his police area, namely—

(*a*)   that the person is a qualifying offender; and
(*b*)   that the person has acted, since the appropriate date, in such a way as to give reasonable cause to believe that it necessary for such an order to be made,

the chief officer of police may apply for an order to be made in respect of the person[3]. Such an application must be made by way of complaint to the magistrates' court whose commission area includes any place where it is alleged that the defendant acted so as to give cause for the complaint[4].

If it is proved[5] that the defendant's behaviour since the appropriate date makes it necessary to make such an order, for the purpose of protecting the public or any particular members of the public from serious sexual harm from the defendant, the court may make an order which prohibits the defendant from doing anything described in the order and the prohibitions that may be imposed are those necessary for the purpose of protecting the public from serious sexual harm from the defendant[6]. A sex offender order shall have effect for a period, not less than 5 years specified in the order or until further order, and, while such order is in force, the notification requirements under Part 2 of the Sexual Offences Act 2003 shall have effect[7].

For these purposes "a qualifying offender" includes a person who has been convicted of a sexual offence to which Schs 3 or 5 applies, as well as other categories of person[10] and offenders who have committed certain offences overseas[8]. "The appropriate date" in relation to a sex offender means the date or, as the case may be, the first date on which he has been convicted, found, cautioned or punished of a relevant offence[9].

An application may be made to a court to vary, renew or discharge a sexual offences prevention order and an interim order may be applied for where an application for such an order has not been determined[10]. An appeal from an order made by a magistrates' court is to the Crown Court[11].

If without reasonable excuse a person does anything which he is prohibited from doing by a sexual offences prevention order, he shall be guilty of an offence which is triable either way[12].

It is not appropriate for a sentence to be reduced to limit the extent of an offender's obligation to register under the Sexual Offences Act 2003[13].

---

1. Sexual Offences Act 2003, s 104(1)(b), in PART VIII: title SEXUAL OFFENCES, post. This provision focuses on the risk of further offences and the court has to conduct a risk assessment and to satisfy itself that it is necessary (which imports a higher threshold than "desirable") to make an order because of the likelihood of the defendant committing further, relevant offences, not necessarily against the person to be protected by the order but with that person being likely to suffer serious harm, which may be psychological harm, as a result (in the present case, a sibling of the abused child); although there are powers to vary orders under s 108, they may be invoked only by the persons specified in s 108(2) and if the order prevents contact with a family member who is not qualified to invoke s 108 it may contain a provision that the jurisdiction of the family courts can be invoked: *R v D (Sexual Offences: Prevention Order)* [2005] EWCA Crim 3660, [2006] 2 All ER 726, [2006] 1 WLR 1088.
2. *R v D* [2005] EWCA Crim 3660, [2006] 1 FLR 943, [2006] 2 Cr App R (S) 32, [2006] Crim LR 364 (where the offences were against the defendant's daughter and the order prohibited any contact or communication not only with her but also with the defendant's psychologically disturbed son; however, the order was amended so that the family jurisdiction could be invoked to lift the prohibition).
3. Sexual Offences Act 2003, s 104(5), in PART VIII: title SEXUAL OFFENCES, post.
4. Sexual Offences Act 2003, s 104(6), in PART VIII: title SEXUAL OFFENCES, post.
5. In *B v Chief Constable of the Avon and Somerset Constabulary* [2001] 1 All ER 562, DC (a decision under s 2 of the Crime and Disorder Act 1998) it was held that magistrates are not obliged to apply the criminal standard of proof; proceedings under what is now s 104 are civil rather than criminal in character. However, a bare balance of probability is not to be applied; in relation to what is now the s 104(4)(b) condition, the civil standard to apply should for all practical purposes be indistinguishable from the criminal standard and, in relation to the s 104(1)(a) condition, the civil standard should be applied with the strictness appropriate to the seriousness of the matters to be proved and the implications of proving them.
6. Sexual Offences Act 2003, s 104(1)(a), in PART VIII: title SEXUAL OFFENCES, post. An order should be in clear, simple terms so as to be readily understandable even by those who are not very bright, and the order must not be wider than necessary for the purpose of protecting the public from serious harm: *B v Chief Constable of the Avon and Somerset Constabulary* (supra).
7. Sexual Offences Act 2003, s 107, in PART VIII: title SEXUAL OFFENCES, post.
8. Sexual Offences Act 2003, s 106(5)–(7), in PART VIII: title SEXUAL OFFENCES, post.
9. Sexual Offences Act 2003, s 106(8), in PART VIII: title SEXUAL OFFENCES, post.
10. Sexual Offences Act 2003, ss 108 and 109, in PART VIII: title SEXUAL OFFENCES, post.
11. Sexual Offences Act 2003, s 110, in PART VIII: title SEXUAL OFFENCES, post.
12. Sexual Offences Act 2003, s 113, in PART VIII: title SEXUAL OFFENCES, post.
13. *Re A-G's reference (No 50 of 1997)* [1998] 2 Cr App R (S) 155.

Sentencing guidelines and examples of sentencing for particular offences

3–260 Offences involving violence. Offenders who commit acts of serious *violence* must expect custodial sentences[1] and immediate custodial sentences must be expected by persons who deliberately use violence to impede the police in maintaining public order[2], as in dealing with football hooliganism[3]. A proven racial element in an offence of violence is a gravely aggravating feature justifying an increase in sentence[4]. Although courts will not tolerate violence as a means of retaliation or revenge, where victims of racial abuse are provoked into violence the racial element may be taken into account as a mitigating factor[5]. Substantial sentences of detention will be imposed for offences of violence accompanied by violent, racialist language—5 months' youth custody upheld on a man aged 20 who assaulted a restaurant proprietor with a jack handle following a dispute[6]. Kicking a victim on the ground and, even worse, stamping on his head, is the kind of conduct which must be visited, save in the most exceptional and unusual circumstances, by a custodial sentence[7]. Although head-butting does not technically involve the use of a weapon, the head is nonetheless a dangerous and effective substitute for a weapon and a very serious view is taken of using the head in this way[8].

Racism is evil and cannot coexist with fairness and justice. The courts must do all they can to convey that message clearly by the sentences which they pass in relation to racially aggravated offences. Those who indulge in racially aggravated violence must expect to be punished severely, in order to discourage the repetition of that behaviour, by them or others[9]. On the other hand, where offences of violence, albeit serious, are committed against a background of extreme racial tension with the some of the defendants themselves being the victims of racially aggravated assaults, the normal penalty may be mitigated[10].

There is no logical basis for treating cases involving motorists more leniently than other cases of assault occasioning actual bodily harm[11]. Incidents involving a violent attack on a motorist, arising in the course of parking or other motoring altercations, are on the increase and courts must indicate that they are not to be tolerated. Custody is almost inevitable and where any significant injury is caused, the period in question will be months rather than weeks, even if the offender was a person of previous good character[12]. Violence arising out of driving encounters must be visited with a custodial sentence, but the sentences should be as short as reasonably possible for men of good character[13].

To "glass" someone is a dangerous crime which would inevitably receive a custodial sentence[14]. Nevertheless, for such offences of wounding under s 20 of the Offences Against the Person Act 1861, courts should look with some care at sentences over 2 years' imprisonment to see whether in truth there is a real justification for a sentence of that length on the facts of the particular case[15]. Anyone attacking a member of the public who intervenes to defend a person in danger of being injured must expect severe punishment[16]. Minor assaults which unexpectedly result in serious injuries may attract custodial sentences[17].

An offence of assault occasioning actual bodily harm which consisted of an unprovoked gratuitous drunken attack on an innocent man in a public place causing a cut to the eyebrow which required stitches and bruising to the face and jaw, was held to be so serious that only a custodial sentence could be justified[18]. Also held to be so serious that only a custodial sentence could be justified was an assault occasioning actual bodily harm where the Court of Appeal said that it was a case where a short sharp sentence was all that was required to mark the court's attitude to a vicious assault[19], and a common assault, which was held to have been a very reckless act, whereby the defendant threw a car battery through the window of a vehicle in which the victim was sitting[20]. When dealing with an offence of common assault the court is entitled to take into account any injuries inflicted[21].

Police officers face a difficult task when dealing with incidents of disorder, but they must not resort to gratuitous violence either by initiating attacks without justification or using excessive force in self defence or to make arrests[22].

Where an assault occasioning bodily harm is committed by "stalking" the offence is so serious only a custodial sentence is justified[23].

School teachers are in a particularly vulnerable position and are entitled to look to the courts for protection for themselves and punishment of offenders who commit acts of violence on them[24].

Taxi drivers and others who carry out public service duties deserve the protection of the court from those who assault; where such assaults cause actual bodily harm the custody threshold is crossed, and where the assault is aggravated by racial abuse against the victim it is even clearer that custody must follow[25].

An exclusion order under the Licensed Premises (Exclusion of Certain Persons) Act 1980[26] is designed for and justified in cases of those who might shortly be described as making a nuisance of themselves in public houses and as therefore qualifying to be debarred from going in to the annoyance of other customers and possible danger to the licensee[27]. The court may make a licensed premises exclusion order of its own volition[28]. It is not wrong in principle for an exclusion order to specify a large number of public houses in an area where the offender might go to drink[29].

Inflicting burns, albeit minor, in the course of a domestic argument crosses the custody threshold, but where the offender is of good character and pleads guilty a very short term of imprisonment is sufficient[30].

---

1. See *R v Sergeant* (1974) 60 Cr App Rep 74 and *R v Thompson* [1974] Crim LR 720.
2. *R v Coleman* [1975] Crim LR 349.
3. *R v Johnson* [1975] Crim LR 470; *R v Bruce* (1977) 65 Cr App Rep 148. See also *R v H* [2001] EWCA Crim 1349, (2001) 165 JPN 415; *R v Broyd* [2001] EWCA Crim 1437, [2002] 1 Cr App Rep (S) 197.
4. *A-G's References (Nos 29, 30 and 31 of 1994) (R v Ribbans)* (1994) 16 Cr App Rep (S) 698, [1995] Crim LR 258, CA; *R v Craney and Corbett* [1996] 2 Cr App Rep (S) 336, [1996] Crim LR 525.
5. *R v Wadha* [1996] 2 Cr App Rep (S) 216, [1996] Crim LR 358.
6. *R v English* (1985) 7 Cr App Rep (S) 65.
7. *A-G's Reference (No 10 of 1992)* (1993) 15 Cr App Rep (S) 1.
8. *R v Rigg* (1997) Times, 4 July, CA.
9. *R v Saunders* [2000] 1 Cr App Rep 458, [2000] 2 Cr App Rep (S) 71, [2000] Crim LR 314, CA (3 ½ years' imprisonment upheld for offence of assault occasioning actual bodily harm, which was aggravated by racial abuse, causing a cut lip, grazing, bruising and tenderness to face and shoulder). See also *R v Salihu* [2001] EWCA Crim 483, (2001) 165 JPN 214, (6 months upheld for racially aggravated assault by beating of a traffic warden; and *R v Kim Joyce* [2001] EWCA Crim 2433, [2002] 1 Cr App Rep (S) 582 (15 months' imprisonment reduced to 7 (without the racial element it would have been 4) where the defendant, who had been excluded from a department store, entered that store, was racially abusive to a security guard and punched him in the face as she was being escorted out).
10. *R v H* [2001] EWCA Crim 1349, (2001) 165 JPN 775 (defendants were members of an Asian gang that attacked a lone white youth; during the attack an iron bar was used and the victim sustained fractures to his jaw and arm — detention and training orders reduced from 18 to 10 months on account of the background, personal mitigation and guilty pleas).
11. *R v Doyle* [1999] 1 Cr App Rep (S) 383 (12 months' imprisonment upheld for an assault occasioning actual bodily harm committed by one driver on another following a traffic incident — defendant punched the other driver 5 or 6 times and kicked him 5 times on the legs as he lay on the ground).
12. *R v Sharpe* [2000] 1 Cr App Rep (S) 1 (8 months' imprisonment for assault occasioning actual bodily harm in which the defendant head-butted the victim so as to cause a broken nose in an incident involving a parking space).
13. *R v Ord and Ord* (1990) 12 Cr App Rep (S) 12, CA 8 weeks for punch which fractured nose; *R v Atkins* (1992) 14 Cr App Rep (S) 146 (6 weeks' imprisonment for single blow following traffic incident); *R v Jarvis* (1993) 15 Cr App Rep (S) 83 (12 months' imprisonment on motorist upheld for inflicting grievous bodily harm on a pedestrian causing him to fall to the ground and break his wrist; *R v Fenton* (1994) 15 Cr App Rep (S) 682, [1994] Crim LR 464 (7 days' imprisonment for common assault — defendant stopped his car, went back to another motorist and pushed him in the chest; *R v Emmin* (1994) 16 Cr App Rep (S) 63 (assault by one motorist on another after a driving incident where the defendant broke a car window, punched the driver and then dragged him out of the vehicle and continued to assault him — 6 months' imprisonment reduced to 3 months); *R v Charlton* (1994) 16 Cr App Rep (S) 703 (6 months' imprisonment upheld for an assault occasioning actual bodily harm on a traffic warden by driving a van at him to frighten him but unintentionally causing injury); *R v Bayes* (1994) 16 Cr App Rep (S) 290 (driving incident in which an offender with previous convictions for violence unlawfully wounded another motorist by hitting him with a hammer causing superficial cuts and bruises—15 months' imprisonment); *R v Arnold* [1996] 1 Cr App Rep (S) 115 (6 months' imprisonment upheld for a motorist who seized and butted another motorist in the face, causing a broken nose); *R v Maben* [1997] 2 Cr App Rep (S) 341 (9 months' imprisonment upheld for assault occasioning actual bodily harm by punching another driver 3 times in a road rage incident causing corneal bleeding and lacerations to the eye); and *R v Aylett* [2005] EWCA Crim 1297, [2006] 1 Cr App R (S) 34 (12 months' imprisonment for racially aggravated common assault following a trial reduced to 9 (including 3 months for racial aggravation) where, in a road rage incident, the appellant, without provocation and with accompanying racial abuse, punched a man in the face and spat at him).

14. *R v Stewart* (1990) 12 Cr App Rep (S) 15, CA, see *R v Liggett* (1990) 12 Cr App Rep (S) 53, CA, *R v Ronaldson* (1990) 12 Cr App Rep (S) 91, CA; *R v Bottasso* (1993) 15 Cr App Rep (S) 39; *R v Marsden* (1993) 15 Cr App Rep (S) 177 *and A-G's Reference (No 20 of 1993)* (1994) 15 Cr App Rep (S) 797, CA.

15. *R v Robertson* [1998] 1 Cr App Rep (S) 21 (30 months' imprisonment for unlawful wounding by "glassing" a man in a public house reduced to 2 years).

16. *R v Gardiner* (1994) 15 Cr App Rep (S) 747, [1994] Crim LR 539, CA (offender punched intervening member of the public in the nose causing fracture, laceration and swelling—sentence reduced to 18 months' imprisonment on appeal).

17. See *R v Collyer* [1996] 2 Cr App Rep (S) 238 (18 months' imprisonment reduced to 10 months for inflicting grievous bodily harm where the victim stepped back to avoid a punch and fell under a lorry suffering grave injuries), *R v Barr* [1996] 2 Cr App Rep (S) 294 (4 years' imprisonment reduced to 30 months where the victim was kicked by his brother as he was going upstairs causing him to fall and suffer spinal injuries) and *R v Clarke* [1999] 2 Cr App Rep (S) 400 (18 months' detention in a young offender institution for maliciously inflicting grievous bodily harm, where the defendant unintentionally caused serious injuries by a single fist blow, reduced to six months). However, for an example of a case were a community penalty was held to be appropriate see *R v Peters* [2001] Crim 1952, (2001) 165 JPN 735 (scuffle in a pub left the victim with a minor cut, but this was not a case of "glassing" and the defendant was a young man of ability with no previous convictions – community punishment order substituted for prison term).

18. *R v Audit*, (1993) 15 Cr App Rep (S) 36, [1993] Crim LR 627 (sentence reduced to 3 months' imprisonment on appeal). See *R v Mellor* (1995) 16 Cr App Rep (S) 230 (assault occasioning actual bodily harm involving an unprovoked attack where the victim suffered a number of blows knocking his glasses off causing bruises and cuts which required stitches—6 months' imprisonment upheld).

19. *R v Graham* [1993] Crim LR 628 (defendant convicted of assault occasioning actual bodily harm—struck the victim 2 blows causing fracture and swelling to nose, and black eyes—28 days' imprisonment substituted).

20. *R v Ross* (1993) 15 Cr App Rep (S) 384, [1994] Crim LR 78 (reduced to 4 months' imprisonment on appeal).

21. *R v Crown Court at Nottingham, ex p DPP* (1995) 160 JP 78, [1996] 1 Cr App Rep (S) 283, [1995] Crim LR 902.

22. *R v Mathew Dunn* [2003] EWCA Crim 709, [2003] 2 Cr App R (S) 90 (3 months' imprisonment upheld for common assault by a police officer who twice kicked a man on the ground while other officers were restraining that man).

23. *R v Smith* [1997] Crim LR 614, [1998] 1 Cr App Rep (S) 138 (30 months' imprisonment reduced to 21 months where, after the end of a relationship, the defendant "stalked" the complainant for over four years causing her to become clinically depressed); *R v Notice* [2000] 1 Cr App Rep (S) 75 (2 years' imprisonment for assault occasioning actual bodily harm in the form of "stalking" reduced to 15 months –victim caused considerable upset and distress over many months which led to psychiatric injury to her and required her in part to change her lifestyle and move her place of work –nevertheless, the case could be distinguished from *R v Smith, supra*).

24. *R v Byrne* [2000] 1 Cr App Rep (S) 282 (15 months' imprisonment imposed on a parent who pleaded guilty to assault occasioning actual bodily harm on a teacher ,who he mistakenly believed had assaulted his son, reduced to 9 months).

25. *R v Alexander* [2004] EWCA Crim 3398, [2005] 2 Cr App R (S) 49 (15 months' imprisonment, imposed after a trial on a 21-year-old man of good character, upheld).

26. See THIS PART, post.

27. *R v Grady* (1990) 12 Cr App Rep (S) 152, CA.

28. *R v Penn* [1996] 2 Cr App Rep (S) 214, [1996] Crim LR 360.

29. *R v Arrowsmith* [2003] EWCA Crim 701, [2003] 2 Cr App R (S) 46.

30. *R v Hinds* [2001] EWCA Crim 1774, (2001) 165 JPN 715 (3 months reduced to 28 days where defendant threw some hot porridge at the back of his girlfriend's head after she had asked him to leave).

3–261　Football and other sports related violence. Football hooligans who are 17 years and older should expect to lose their liberty if they are convicted of offences of violence which cause injury to other people or criminal damage which can fairly be called vandalism[1]. The following guidelines have been given by the Court of Appeal as to sentencing in such cases. Unless there are exceptional mitigating circumstances, youths between the ages of 17 and 21 who are convicted of any offence involving violence towards police officers, or others trying to maintain order or to spectators who are not themselves involved in the violence, should be made the subject of a short term of detention in a young offender institution; but if any weapon has been used or a disabling injury was caused or there is evidence that the convicted youth is addicted to the use of violence, a longer term of detention in a young offender institution would be appropriate. If the injury should be such as to amount to grievous bodily harm, as is likely to arise from stabbing, a longish sentence may be necessary. These guidelines may not be appropriate for youths under 18, but a youth court should consider the need for deterring the disorderly young as well as for reforming them. Applying the above guidelines to disorderly youths who have done violence to one another may be inappropriate because much will depend in each case upon what happened and why it happened[2].

In relation to public order offences involving one set of supporters attacking another, the court should not confine itself to looking at the individual roles of the defendants but should look at the whole picture[3].

An immediate custodial sentence will be appropriate for a deliberate act of violence committed by one player on another during a football match[4].

---

1. *R v Motley* (1978) 66 Cr App Rep 274.

2. *R v Wood* (1984) 6 Cr App Rep (S) 2.

3. *R v Fox and Hicks* [2005] EWCA Crim 1122, [2006] 1 Crim App R (S) 17 (defendants aged 35 and 25 pleaded guilty to affray committed during a serious disturbance following a football match: 12 months upheld for the younger offender, who had previous convictions for threatening behaviour; sentence reduced to 8 months for the older offender, who was of previous good character and had played a lesser role in events).

4. *R v Birkin* (1988) 10 Cr App Rep (S) 303, [1988] Crim LR 854 (6 months' imprisonment for assault occasioning actual bodily harm whereby offender struck another player a blow which broke his jaw in two places); *R v Lloyd* (1989) 11 Cr App Rep (S) 36 (18 months' imprisonment for deliberately kicking a player in the face during a game of rugby football, fractured cheek bone); *R v Shervill* (1989) 11 Cr App Rep (S) 284, CA (2 months' imprisonment for kicking another player in the mouth, causing a wound which required stitching); *R v Davies* [1991] Crim LR 70 (6 months' imprisonment upheld for an unprovoked blow, causing a fractured cheekbone, on the face of an opposing player committed on the field but not in the course of play); *R v Chapman* (1989) 11 Cr App Rep (S) 93, CA (18 months' imprisonment, with 12 months to serve and the balance suspended, for defendant who pleaded guilty to unlawful wounding in course of football match whereby he kicked victim on the head as he lay on the ground, causing swelling and laceration); *R v Rogers* (1993)

15 Cr App Rep (S) 393 (4 months' imprisonment for inflicting grievous bodily harm during dispute in soccer match—defendant butted an opposing player so as to cause a displaced fracture of the cheek bone); *A-G's Reference (No 27 of 1993)* (1994) 15 Cr App Rep (S) 737, CA (probation order varied to 6 months' imprisonment where offender butted opposing player in "off the ball" incident causing shattered cheekbone and eye socket, a trapped nerve and laceration to the face); *R v Goodwin* (1995) 16 Cr App Rep (S) 885, CA (6 months' imprisonment reduced to 4 months for unnecessarily but deliberately striking an opposing player with an elbow in the face during the course of play inflicting grievous bodily harm); *R v Calton* [1999] 2 Cr App Rep (S) 64 (12 months' detention in a young offender institution for inflicting grievous bodily harm in the course of a school rugby match reduced to 3 months—defendant kicked player on opposing side on the right side of the head causing a fracture); *R v David James Bowyer* [2001] EWCA Crim 1853, [2002] 1 Cr App Rep (S) 448 (8 months' imprisonment following a trial "severe" but not "manifestly excessive" where, in the course of a rugby match, the defendant struck an opposing player breaking his jaw in 2 places); *R v Jason John Tasker* [2001] EWCA Crim 2213, [2002] 1 Cr App Rep (S) 515 (12 months' imprisonment reduced to 6 where, in a football game, the victim was pulled to the ground (but not by the defendant) and the defendant came across the field and kicked him in the face, causing a fracture of the lower eye socket and a possible fracture of the cheekbone); and *R v Bobby Ahmed* [2002] EWCA Crim 779, [2002] 2 Cr App Rep (S) 535 (total of 34 months' imprisonment upheld where, in a football game, the defendant assaulted an opponent breaking his nose, then assaulted the referee after he had been sent off, and then assaulted the first victim again as he was lying on the ground defenceless causing a broken jaw and eye socket).

3–262   Assaults on police officers.   Where violence is used against a uniformed police officer in the course of his duty it is inappropriate to impose a very short custodial sentence under the "clang of the prison gates" principle[1].

Police officers who are performing a difficult public duty, in circumstances where they are only too likely to encounter bad temper and unreasonableness deserve such protection as the courts can give[2]. Any attack on a police officer, particularly one dealing with a difficult situation is a serious matter and will lead to a custodial sentence[3]. A frenzied attack on a police officer involving repeated punches will justify a much longer sentence[4].

When police officers in the course of their duty have to go to deal with a disturbance, the last thing they need is young men intervening to try and save somebody who is being arrested. Even less do they need to be exposed to physical violence. In such cases the courts must mark their very real displeasure at those who behave in that way[5]. Deterrent sentences are necessary when attacks are made on police officers by mobs of youths inflamed by drink[6].

---

1. *R v Crimes* (1983) 5 Cr App Rep (S) 358 (6 months' imprisonment upheld – defendant pleaded guilty to assault on a police officer, occasioning actual bodily harm and driving while disqualified – defendant stopped in his car after a chase and then tried to escape on foot after the officer took hold of him; the defendant hit the officer in the chest with his fists, knocking him to the ground, then as both officer and the defendant were struggling on the ground, kicked him on the knees causing cuts).

2. *R v Fletcher* [1998] 1 Cr App Rep (S) 7 (9 months' imprisonment upheld for assault occasioning actual bodily harm on a police officer who was attempting to remove an illegally parked vehicle).

3. *R v Elliott* [2000] 1 Cr App Rep (S) 264 (sentence of 12 months' imprisonment reduced to 8 months for an assault on a police officer who was attempting to arrest the defendant – officer was struck twice on the back of the head, with the effect of dazing him and resulting in bruises. See also *R v Michael Paul Broyd* [2001] EWCA Crim 1437, [2002] 1 Cr App Rep (S) 197 (9 months' imprisonment following a guilty plea upheld where the defendant, who had been arrested after a struggle, had head butted the arresting officer causing a split lip and a chipped tooth).

4. *R v Casey* [2000] 1 Cr App Rep (S) 221 (sentence of 3 years' imprisonment for assault occasioning actual bodily harm and common assault reduced to 2 years 3 months – frenzied attack on police officer involving 5 or 6 punches to the head causing the officer to fall to the ground; defendant then sat astride him and continued to punch the officer repeatedly to the face; defendant pleaded guilty – held the taking of drugs, a combination of cocaine and steroids, was no excuse).

5. *R v McGrath* (1990) 12 Cr App Rep (S) 204 (3 months' imprisonment upheld on a young man of previous good character for an assault occasioning actual bodily harm to a police officer who was in the course of arresting a friend of the defendant – fighting broke out at a discoteque to which police were called – defendant butted officer on the right side of the head and punched him in the eye).

6. *R v Nawrot* (1988) 10 Cr App Rep (S) 239 (2 years' imprisonment upheld on defendant, aged 21, who was one of a group of 20 youths who attacked a police officer kicking him on the legs and body – defendant ran at the officer and punched him n the jaw, knocking him unconscious).

3–263   Assaults on hospital staff.   The public are rightly concerned about violence towards those employed in hospitals. Doctors, nurses and auxiliary staff often work long hours in difficult circumstances, which may be emotionally draining and are often marked by pressure of many kinds. In a civilised society, such people are entitled to whatever protection the courts can give, and those who use physical violence against them should expect a sentence of immediate imprisonment. The length of that sentence, however, must depend on the circumstances of the particular case. Aggravating features will include the striking of repeated blows, the use of a weapon or feet or headbutting, the infliction of serious or lasting injury and the use of violence to more than one person. Mitigating features will include immediate and genuine remorse, a plea of guilty, previous good character and the personal circumstances of the offender, particularly those relevant to his state of mind at the time[1].

---

1. *R v McNally* [2000] 1 Cr App Rep (S) 535 (sentence of 12 months' imprisonment for assault occasioning actual bodily harm on a doctor at a hospital reduced to 6 months—defendant, who pleaded guilty, had gone to the hospital where his 15 month old son was a patient—after approaching a staff nurse with an inquiry about an appointment with a doctor an argument developed—eventually the defendant struck the doctor in the face causing him to lose his balance and fall backwards).

3–264   Domestic violence.   The Sentencing Guidelines Council has produced the following definitive guidelines.

'DOMESTIC VIOLENCE

A Definition of Domestic Violence.

1.1 There is no specific offence of domestic violence and conduct amounting to domestic violence is covered by a number of statutory provisions. For the purposes of this guideline, wherever such offending occurs, domestic violence is: "Any incident of threatening behaviour, violence or abuse [psychological, physical, sexual, financial or emotional] between adults who are or have been intimate partners or family members, regardless of gender or sexuality."[1]

1.2 Most incidents of domestic violence can be charged as one of a wide range of offences including physical assault (with or without a weapon), harassment, threats to cause injury or to kill, destroying or damaging property, false imprisonment (locking the victim in a room or preventing that person from leaving the house), and sexual offences.

1.3 This guideline covers issues which are relevant across the range of offences that might be committed in a domestic context. Under the above definition, the domestic context includes relationships involving intimate partners who are living together, intimate partners who do not live together and former intimate partners. It is also wide enough to include relationships between family members, for example between a father and a daughter, or a mother and a daughter, perhaps where the daughter is the mother's carer.

B Assessing Seriousness.

2.1 As a starting point for sentence, offences committed in a domestic context should be regarded as being no less serious than offences committed in a nondomestic context.

2.2 Thus, the starting point for sentencing should be the same irrespective of whether the offender and the victim are known to each other (whether by virtue of being current or former intimate partners, family members, friends or acquaintances) or unknown to each other.

2.3 A number of aggravating factors may commonly arise by virtue of the offence being committed in a domestic context and these will increase the seriousness of such offences. These are described in more detail in C below.

C Aggravating and Mitigating Factors.

3.1 Since domestic violence takes place within the context of a current or past relationship, the history of the relationship will often be relevant in assessing the gravity of the offence. Therefore, a court is entitled to take into account anything occurring within the relationship as a whole, which may reveal relevant aggravating or mitigating factors.

3.2 The following aggravating and mitigating factors (which are not intended to be exhaustive) are of particular relevance to offences committed in a domestic context, and should be read alongside the general factors set out in the Council guideline Overarching Principles: Seriousness.[2]

Aggravating Factors

(i) Abuse of trust and abuse of power

3.3 The guideline Overarching Principles: Seriousness identifies abuse of a position of trust and abuse of power as factors that indicate higher culpability. Within the nature of relationship required to meet the definition of domestic violence set out above, trust implies a mutual expectation of conduct that shows consideration, honesty, care and responsibility. In some such relationships, one of the parties will have the power to exert considerable control over the other.

3.4 In the context of domestic violence:

- an abuse of trust, whether through direct violence or emotional abuse, represents a violation of this understanding;
- an abuse of power in a relationship involves restricting another individual's autonomy which is sometimes a specific characteristic of domestic violence. This involves the exercise of control over an individual by means which may be psychological, physical, sexual, financial or emotional.

3.5 Where an abuse of trust or abuse of power is present, it will aggravate the seriousness of an offence. These factors are likely to exist in many offences of violence within a domestic context.

3.6 However, the breadth of the definition of domestic violence (set out in 1.1 above) encompasses offences committed by a former spouse or partner. Accordingly, there will be circumstances where the abuse of trust or abuse of power may be a very minor feature of an offence or may be deemed no longer to exist – for example, where the offender and victim have been separated for a long period of time.

(ii) Victim is particularly vulnerable

3.7 For cultural, religious, language, financial or any other reasons, some victims of domestic violence may be more vulnerable than others, not least because these issues may make it almost impossible for the victim to leave a violent relationship.

3.8 Where a perpetrator has exploited a victim's vulnerability (for instance, when the circumstances have been used by the perpetrator to prevent the victim from seeking and obtaining help), an offence will warrant a higher penalty.

3.9 Age, disability or the fact that the victim was pregnant or had recently given birth at the time of the offence may make a victim particularly vulnerable.

3.10 Any steps taken to prevent the victim reporting an incident or obtaining assistance will usually aggravate the offence.

(iii) Impact on children

3.11 Exposure of children to an offence (either directly or indirectly) is an aggravating factor.

3.12 Children are likely to be adversely affected by directly witnessing violence or other abuse and by being aware of it taking place while they are elsewhere in the home.[3]

(iv) Using contact arrangements with a child to instigate an offence

3.13 An offence will be aggravated where an offender exploits contact arrangements with a child in order to commit an offence.

(v) A proven history of violence or threats by the offender in a domestic setting

3.14 It is important that an assessment of the seriousness of an offence recognises the cumulative effect of a series of violent incidents or threats over a prolonged period, where such conduct has been proved or accepted.

3.15 Where an offender has previously been convicted of an offence involving domestic violence either against the same or a different partner, this is likely to be a statutory aggravating factor.[4]

(vi) A history of disobedience to court orders

3.16 A breach of an order that has been imposed for the purpose of protecting a victim can cause significant harm or anxiety. Where an offender's history of disobedience has had this effect, it will be an aggravating factor.

3.17 Commission of the offence in breach of a non-molestation order imposed in civil proceedings, in breach of a sentence (such as a conditional discharge) imposed for similar offending, or while subject to an ancillary order, such as a restraining order, will aggravate the seriousness of the offence.

3.18 The appropriate response to breach of a civil order is dealt with in a separate guideline Breach of a Protective Order.

(vii) Victim forced to leave home

3.19 An offence will be aggravated if, as a consequence, the victim is forced to leave home.

Mitigating Factors

(i) Positive good character

3.20 As a general principle of sentencing, a court will take account of an offender's positive good character. However, it is recognised that one of the factors that can allow domestic violence to continue unnoticed for lengthy periods is the ability of the perpetrator to have two personae. In respect of an offence of violence in a domestic context, an offender's good character in relation to conduct outside the home should generally be of no relevance where there is a proven pattern of behaviour.

3.21 Positive good character is of greater relevance in the rare case where the court is satisfied that the offence was an isolated incident.

(ii) Provocation

3.22 It may be asserted that the offence, at least in part, has been provoked by the conduct of the victim. Such assertions need to be treated with great care, both in determining whether they have a factual basis and in considering whether in the circumstances the alleged conduct amounts to provocation sufficient to mitigate the seriousness of the offence.

3.23 For provocation to be a mitigating factor, it will usually involve actual or anticipated violence including psychological bullying. Provocation is likely to have more of an effect as mitigation if it has taken place over a significant period of time.

D *Other factors influencing sentence.*

Wishes of the victim and effect of the sentence

4.1 As a matter of general principle, a sentence imposed for an offence of violence should be determined by the seriousness of the offence, not by the expressed wishes of the victim.

4.2 There are a number of reasons why it may be particularly important that this principle is observed in a case of domestic violence:

- it is undesirable that a victim should feel a responsibility for the sentence imposed;
- there is a risk that a plea for mercy made by a victim will be induced by threats made by, or by a fear of, the offender;

- the risk of such threats will be increased if it is generally believed that the severity of the sentence may be affected by the wishes of the victim.

4.3 Nonetheless, there may be circumstances in which the court can properly mitigate a sentence to give effect to the expressed wish of the victim that the relationship be permitted to continue. The court must, however, be confident that such a wish is genuine, and that giving effect to it will not expose the victim to a real risk of further violence. Critical conditions are likely to be the seriousness of the offence and the history of the relationship. It is vitally important that the court has up-to-date information in a pre-sentence report and victim personal statement. 4.4 Either the offender or the victim (or both) may ask the court to take into consideration the interests of any children and to impose a less severe sentence. The court will wish to have regard not only to the effect on the children if the relationship is disrupted but also to the likely effect on the children of any further incidents of domestic violence.

E *Factors to Take into Consideration.*

The following points of principle should be considered by a court when imposing sentence for any offence of violence committed in domestic context.

1. Offences committed in a domestic context should be regarded as being no less serious than offences committed in a non-domestic context.

2. Many offences of violence in a domestic context are dealt with in a magistrates' court as an offence of common assault or assault occasioning actual bodily harm because the injuries sustained are relatively minor. Offences involving serious violence will warrant a custodial sentence in the majority of cases.

3. Some offences will be specified offences for the purposes of the dangerous offender provisions.[5]

In such circumstances, consideration will need to be given to whether there is a significant risk of serious harm to members of the public, which include, of course, family members. If so, the court will be required to impose a life sentence, imprisonment for public protection or an extended sentence.

4. Where the custody threshold is only just crossed, so that if a custodial sentence is imposed it will be a short sentence, the court will wish to consider whether the better option is a suspended sentence order or a community order, including in either case a requirement to attend an accredited domestic violence programme. Such an option will only be appropriate where the court is satisfied that the offender genuinely intends to reform his or her behaviour and that there is a real prospect of rehabilitation being successful. Such a situation is unlikely to arise where there has been a pattern of abuse.'

---

1. This is the Government definition of domestic violence agreed in 2004. It is taken from Policy on Prosecuting cases of Domestic Violence, Crown Prosecution Service, 2005.
2. See para **3–70**, ante.
3. The definition of "harm" in s 31(9) of the Children Act 1989 as amended by s 120 of the Adoption and Children Act 2002 includes "impairment suffered from seeing or hearing the ill-treatment of another".
4. Criminal Justice Act 2003, s 143(2).
5. Criminal Justice Act 2003, Part 12, Chapter 5.

OFFENCES UNDER THE PUBLIC ORDER ACT 1986

3–265 *Violent disorder.* Where a large group of youths congregate together and engage in fighting in the street, the court has a duty to punish the wrong-doers properly and make it clear how such offenders can expect to be dealt with, especially if conduct of that kind is rife in the area[1]. Longer terms of imprisonment will be upheld where the violent disorder has elements of racial abuse[2]. To assault a police officer in the context of violent disorder makes the offence much more serious[3]. Where the violent disorder is in the form of a retaliatory attack, an immediate custodial sentence is inevitable and it must be seen not only to punish the offender but also to deter others[4]. It is important to consider the individual acts of the offender but this must be viewed in the context of the fear caused in the general public by the whole incident[5].

---

1. *R v Cotter and Farrell* (1989) 11 Cr App Rep (S) 102, CA (for offence of violent disorder, contrary to s 2 of the Public Order Act 1986, sentences reduced to 4 months' imprisonment and 3 months' detention for offenders who had been concerned in an incident in which a large number of youths fought in the street).
2. *R v Alderson* (1989) 11 Cr App Rep (S) 301 (30 months' imprisonment for taking part in a violent attack in a cafe which had racial elements, and caused £500 worth of damage).
3. *R v Coote* (1992) 14 Cr App Rep (S) 40 (12 months' imprisonment upheld for violent disorder on the basis that the defendant attacked a police officer who was trying to assist his friend).
4. *R v Betts* (1994) 16 Cr App Rep (S) 436.
5. *R v Tomlinson* (1993) 157 JP 695. See also *R v Abyado* (2001) 165 JPN 795 (acts of any individual had to be viewed in the context of the overall violence).

3–266 *Affray.* An immediate custodial sentence will be justified for an offence of affray if it is a serious case of its kind, notwithstanding that it consisted of a spontaneous fight[1].

---

1. *R v Charles and Jones* (1989) 11 Cr App Rep (S) 125, CA (3 months' imprisonment for 2 men of previous good character who pleaded guilty to affray which consisted of a spontaneous fight in a restaurant, during which chairs were broken and used as weapons); *R v Gulliver* (1991) 12 Cr App Rep (S) 769 (6 months' imprisonment for participating in a fight in a public house); *R v Williams* [1997] 2 Cr App Rep (S) 97 (21 months' imprisonment reduced to 12 months where a man of previous good character pleaded guilty at the earliest opportunity to an affray which involved an incident outside a corner shop in which bottles were thrown and threatening and racist remarks were made about the occupants of the shop); *R v Byrne* [1998] 1 Cr App Rep (S) 105 (6 months' imprisonment upheld for affray and 9 months substituted for unlawful wounding to which the offender pleaded guilty, offences consisted of picking up a bar stool and throwing it across the bar, the stool struck a member of staff knocking her unconscious and causing a wound on her head that required stitches); *R v Miller* [1998] 2 Cr App Rep (S) 398 (21 months' detention in a young offender institution upheld for affray in the form of a racially motivated unprovoked attack, defendant pleaded guilty and was one of a number of youths who attacked a black man who was walking home along a street); *R v Pollinger and Pearson* [1999] 1 Cr App Rep (S) 128 (4 months' imprisonment upheld for an affray in the course of a disturbance at a football match); *R v Elder* [2001] EWCA Crim 39, (2001) 165 JPN 95 (6 months reduced to 3 where the defendant with her boyfriend visited her mother and disabled stepfather, whom the defendant had not seen for 10 years, in their caravan, a quarrel broke out instigated by the defendant, her boyfriend became violent towards her stepfather throwing him to the floor, the defendant sat astride her stepfather and beat him with her fists and, when the defendant's mother tried to pull her off, the defendant clawed her face and pulled her hair, and after the defendant was finally forced out she threatened to 'torch' the caravan); and *R v Bradley* [2005] EWCA Crim 1461, [2006] 1 Cr App R (S) 42 (12 months' detention upheld on guilty pleas where the appellants – man of 21 and 2 women aged 19 and 18 – were involved in prolonged, sporadic street fighting following verbal exchanges in a club and outside a chip shop between 2 groups of young people).

THREATS TO KILL

3–267 The range of criminality embraced by this offence is very wide indeed. Aggravating features of an offence may be if the threat to kill was accompanied by the flourish of a weapon[1], or the extent to which the victims were literally in fear of their lives, when the background generally to the offence, such as obscene telephone calls to the victims will be of relevance[2].

Threatening to kill may be a "violent offence" for the purposes of the Powers of Criminal Courts

(Sentencing) Act 2000, s 79(2)(*b*), and a longer than normal sentence may be necessary to protect the victim[3].

Serious offences committed in the domestic context may attract sentences of 6 years or more[4].

Threats to kill made to a police officer by a defendant, who was still agitated following his release from custody, while not of the most serious kind, were exacerbated by the fact that the threats were not merely made to the police officer but to members of his family[5].

---

1. *R v Mason* (1995) 16 Cr App Rep (S) 804 (total of 4 years' imprisonment upheld for 2 counts of threatening to kill, of affray and one of criminal damage; defendant threatened to kill a friend with a rifle by pushing the friend to the ground, pressing the rifle against his forehead and cocking the rifle).
2. *R v Walker* [1996] 1 Cr App Rep (S) 180 (4 years' imprisonment upheld for making threats to kill by telephone to 2 women against the background of a previous conviction for obscene telephone calls to the women).
3. *R v Wilson* [1998] 1 Cr App Rep (S) 341 (4 years' imprisonment upheld for 4 counts of threatening to kill offender's wife).
4. *A-G's Reference (No 52 of 1996)* [1997] 2 Cr App Rep (S) 230 (defendant assaulted woman with whom he had lived and forced her and their son to get into her car which the defendant then drove towards a river, threatening to drive the car into the river and kill the woman and their son: total sentences of 18 months' imprisonment varied to 3½ years). *R v Healy* [1998] 1 Cr App Rep (S) 107 (5 years' imprisonment reduced to 3 years for threatening to kill a woman after the breakdown of their relationship which had lasted 10 years; after receiving telephone calls during the night and other abuse, defendant entered her home carrying a knife and threatened to kill her, she activated an alarm and managed to escape).
5. *R v Choudhury* [1997] 2 Cr App Rep (S) 300 (2 years' imprisonment substituted on appeal). See also *R v Orivin* [1999] 1 Cr App Rep (S) 103 (18 months' imprisonment for threats to kill police officers in a domestic dispute in which the defendant claimed to have a shotgun which he, in fact, did not have).

HARASSMENT[1]

3–268 In determining the appropriate sentence for a defendant who has committed an offence under the Protection from Harassment Act 1997, the court should consider:

(1) whether the offence is one of harassment contrary to s 2 of the Act or harassment causing fear of violence contrary to s 4;

(2) whether there is a history of disobedience to court orders, whether orders under the Act or civil orders;

(3) the seriousness of the defendant's conduct which can range from actual violence through to threats and down to letters expressing affection rather than any wish to harm the victim;

(4) whether there has been persistent misconduct or a solitary instance of misbehaviour;

(5) the physical and psychological effect upon the victim, whether the victim requires protection, and the level of risk that the defendant poses to the victim or to the victim's children or family;

(6) the defendant's mental health and whether he is ready to undergo treatment or receive the necessary help from the probation service; and

(7) the defendant's reaction to the court proceedings particularly whether he has pleaded guilty, whether there is remorse and whether there is recognition of the need for help[2].

For a first offence, a short sharp sentence may be appropriate, though much will depend on the factors of repetition, and breach of court orders, and the nature of the misconduct[3]. For a second offence longer sentences of about 15 months on a plea of guilty will be an appropriate starting point[2]. Where the victim is a young girl at a vulnerable stage in her life who was frightened by the defendant's actions a sentence of imprisonment is necessary[4].

It is proper to regard the power to impose a sentence by way of punishment in respect of harassment and the protection which a restraining order under s 5 of the Act provides for the victim as complementary provisions. The sentencer should do the best he can to assess what form of punishment and length of sentence is most likely to lead to the defendant behaving and not breaching the restraining order[5].

The following principles apply to the making of restraining orders under s 5.

(1) The purpose is to prohibit particular conduct with a view to protecting the victim or victims and to prevent further offences under ss 2 or 4.

(2) The order must be drafted in clear and precise terms.

(3) Orders should be framed in practical terms; a radius order will not necessarily be invalid, and if necessary a map should be prepared.

(4) In considering the terms and extent of an order the court should have regard to issues of proportionality. The power to vary or discharge orders is an important safeguard; an order will be unlikely to be varied on appeal if an application to vary or discharge is in the circumstances the appropriate course[6].

---

1. For breach of restraining orders, see para **3–308**, post.
2. *R v Liddle* [1999] 3 All ER 816, [2000] 1 Cr App Rep (S) 131, CA; followed in *R v Sutton* [2001] EWCA Crim 291, [2001] 2 Cr App Rep (S) 414 (3 years reduced to 1 year in respect of a man of good character who made a number of telephone calls in which he uttered threats and demanded money).
3. See, for example, *R v Tully* [2002] EWCA Crim 1660, [2003] 1 Cr App R (S) where 8 months was upheld for an offence involving persistent harassment and sustained threats.
4. *R v Hill* [2000] 1 Cr App Rep (S) 8 (12 months' imprisonment for an offence contrary to s 4 committed by a man aged 24 who persistently telephoned a girl aged 13 and made sexual threats including a threat to rape her—as a consequence the girl became very frightened and was afraid to leave the house).
5. *R v Mohbub Miah* [2000] 2 Cr App Rep (S) 439, CA.
6. *R v Debnath* [2005] EWCA Crim 3472, [2006] 2 Cr App R (S) 25, [2006] Crim LR 451.

OFFENSIVE WEAPONS

3–269 In *R v Poulton and R v Celaire*[1], the Court of Appeal, following consultation with the SAP, gave the following sentencing guidelines in relation to the possession of offensive weapons.

Where a weapons offence was committed in conjunction with another offence, the usual totality principle applied. A concurrent sentence was appropriate if the weapons offence was ancillary to a more serious offence, but not if the former was distinct and independent from any other offence. In determining sentence, a balance had to be struck between the fact that the offence did not involve physical injury and the public's concern that carrying weapons encouraged violence and might encourage more serious criminal behaviour. It was often helpful to have regard to the sort of questions covered in the case of *R v Avis* (firearms).

A number of factors might aggravate an offence; for example, if there was a specific plan to use the weapon to commit or threaten violence or intimidate others, if the offence was motivated by hostility towards a minority individual or group, and if the defendant was under the influence of drink or drugs at the time. Other aggravating factors might include the vulnerable nature of the premises[2]; for example, schools, hospitals, and other places where vulnerable persons might be present; or that the offence was committed at a large public gathering, particularly if there was a risk of disorder; or that it was committed on public transport, licensed premises, or other premises where public services were carried out, such as doctors' surgeries and social security offices. It would also aggravate the offence if the defendant were on bail. The nature of the weapon was not the primary, determinative factor because relatively less serious weapons could be used to create fear, and more dangerous weapons might be carried for self defence (with no intent to use them). However, the carrying of certain weapons, for example flick or butterfly knives, might shed light on the defendant's intention.

Mitigating factors might include carrying the weapon only briefly, co-operation with the police and a timely plea of guilty.

Previous convictions for violence and for carrying particularly dangerous weapons with the intent of causing fear or injury justified a sentence at or near the statutory maximum. Generally, previous convictions for violence justified a longer sentence. The custody threshold would invariably be crossed in the case of an adult defendant if the weapon were used to threaten or cause fear. Custody might still be appropriate[3] without threatening use, but the threshold might not be crossed in cases that lacked aggravating features and where the weapon was not particularly dangerous. In such cases, a high community penalty was justified.

Courts also had to accord to certain statutory duties, including the prevention of crime by young people and the interests of children. In cases involving young offenders a PSR should be obtained before sentence.

---

1. [2002] EWCA Crim 2487, [2003] 1 Cr App R (S) 116, [2003] Crim LR 124.
2. For example, airports. In *R v Charles* [2004] EWCA Crim 1977, [2005] 1 Cr App R (S) 56 the court upheld a sentence of 2 months' imprisonment, despite considerable mitigation, where the defendant had unintentionally included within his luggage a cosh, CS gas canister and lock knife.
3. See, for example, *R v Brookes, R v McIntosh* [2004] EWCA Crim 288, [2004] 2 Cr. App R (S) 65 (sentences reduced to 3 months where 1 defendant had a flick knife, the other had a 5-inch knife, they had previous convictions for violence but neither knew that the other was armed (a seriously aggravating factor) and the personal mitigation justified the exceptional course of reducing the sentences to 3 months' imprisonment).

OFFENCES INVOLVING VIOLENCE TO, OR NEGLECT OF, CHILDREN

3–280 When sentencing for offences of violence committed towards children it is necessary for the court to punish the offender who has committed the offence, it is necessary to provide some sort of expiation of the offence for the offender, it is necessary to satisfy public conscience, and it is necessary to deter others from committing this sort of behaviour by making it clear that condign punishment will be the result[1].

It is important to distinguish between cases of wilful ill treatment and cases of neglect. If the defendant pleads guilty on the latter basis the court should not sentence on the former basis without first conducting a "Newton" hearing. Where two defendants blame each other the court must resolve the conflict by hearing evidence or it must sentence each defendant on the basis of his or her plea, notwithstanding that one is inconsistent with the other[2].

An immediate sentence of imprisonment may be the only appropriate sentence for an offence of *wilful neglect to a child* where the child has suffered very considerably from the neglect: 9 months' imprisonment upheld on a woman, aged 27 with no previous convictions, who neglected her two children, aged 4 and almost 2, to the extent that they had suffered an unusually high number of injuries and bruises, and who rejected all attempts by the social services and the NSPCC to assist her[3]. Anyone who assaults a child by striking him and throwing him about the room and then forcing the child's head into a toilet basin and flushing the toilet can expect to lose his liberty. When the violence is prolonged and where it is fuelled by a drunken rage, then a substantial period of imprisonment can be expected.[4] Imprisonment may also be appropriate where the wilful neglect has involved leaving a 3 year old child on her own all day[5] or failing to obtain medical assistance after a baby has been injured[6]. Similarly, imprisonment may be the appropriate sentence for assault occasioning actual bodily harm on a baby[7]. However, in the case of a mother suffering from post-natal depression after a difficult pregnancy and birth, a sentence beyond a short custodial sentence will be inappropriate[8]. Moreover, in the ordinary way a custodial sentence would not be necessary for a single, albeit wilful, act of neglect[9]; or for an isolated incident of violence consisting of a slap on the face of an 11-month-old child by her father, a man of good character, which did not cause her lasting injury and which occurred at a time when he was depressed and subject to panic attacks[10]. The position is different, however, where a significant injury is deliberately inflicted to a small child[11].

Where the offence consists of inappropriate forms of punishment and chastisement, it is less serious than inflicting pain gratuitously or out of malice and a custodial sentence may not automatically be called for[12].

In proceedings alleging cruelty to a child under 16 years of age, although the defence of duress may have been rejected by the court, evidence that the mother of the child was subject to a condition known as "learned helplessness" or "battered woman syndrome" in which she was unable to resist or stand up to the father of her child and protect the child from violence, as a result of his treatment to her, is relevant to mitigation[13].

Custodial sentences of 9 months and 6 months have been upheld on the parents and grandparents of a child who had been removed from the jurisdiction to frustrate care proceedings[14].

---

1. *R v Durkin* (1989) 11 Cr App Rep (S) 313, [1989] Crim LR 922, CA (18 months' imprisonment for a father aged 21 of previous good character who pleaded guilty to inflicting grievous bodily harm on his son aged 19 months; child hyperactive and difficult; father lost temper and held child over bath filled with very hot water so that the child's feet were badly scalded). *R v Dawson* (1989) 11 Cr App Rep (S) 338, [1989] Crim LR 922, CA, (12 months' imprisonment upheld on a father aged 34 of previous good character who pleaded guilty to inflicting grievous bodily harm on his baby aged 15 days: baby had been suffering from colic—father under stress—when baby did not stop crying he struck her on the head with his hand causing a fractured skull); *R v Todd* (1990) 12 Cr App Rep (S) 14, CA (4 months imprisonment for actual bodily harm on 3-year-old by slapping her hard twice on face with open hand, bruises showing imprint of hand); *R v Barnes* (1992) 14 Cr App Rep (S) 547 (28 days' imprisonment for assault occasioning actual bodily harm to a 10-month-old baby by slapping her on the face so as to cause bruises—held to be so serious that only a custodial sentence could be justified); *R v Mason* (1994) 15 Cr App Rep (S) 745 (2 years' imprisonment upheld for inflicting grievous bodily harm on a 10 week old baby by striking him twice with fist on side of head causing fractured skull); *R v David* (1994) 15 Cr App Rep (S) 867 (4 years' imprisonment reduced to 3 years for cruelty to a 6-month-old baby by violent acts over a period of 2–4 months causing injuries); *R v Moore* (1994) 16 Cr App Rep (S) 65 (cruelty to a child by failure to secure medical treatment for an accidental burn—6 months' imprisonment correct in principle but reduced to 4 months' because a long period of time had elapsed since the commission of the offence); *R v Burtenshaw* (1994) 16 Cr App Rep (S) 227 (infliction of grievous bodily harm to a five-month-old child resulting in a spiral fracture of the humerus, fractures to the ribs and ankles and head injuries—3 years' imprisonment reduced to 2 years; *R v Scott* (1994) 16 Cr App Rep (S) 451 (2 years' imprisonment reduced to 12 months for inflicting grievous bodily harm on a baby by shaking it so as to cause brain damage; *R v Lewis* (1996) 2 Cr App Rep (S) 431 (15 months' imprisonment upheld for cruelty to child involving the infliction of a hairline fracture); *R v Lavell* (1996) 2 Cr App Rep (S) 91 (16 months' imprisonment upheld for deliberately scalding a child's arm and failing to obtain medical assistance); *R v S, M J* [1999] 1 Cr App Rep (S) 67 (three months' imprisonment on the father of a four-month-old child who unintentionally hurt the child by shaking him and then delayed obtaining medical help for an hour); *R v J H* [2000] 1 Cr App Rep (S) 551 (4 years' imprisonment for inflicting grievous bodily harm by shaking a 3-month-old baby and then accidentally dropping it on its head, reduced to 2 years); *R v Sujan Ali* [2001] EWCA Crim 884, [2002] 2 Cr App Rep (S) 542 (assault by father on his 3-year-old daughter with a cane that supported a house plant, the attack being sustained and causing numerous superficial injuries, 18 months' imprisonment reduced to 12 months); *R v O* [2004] EWCA Crim 1750, [2005] 1 Cr App R (S) 47 (defendant did nothing to prevent her boyfriend from regularly beating her 6-year-old daughter, causing bruising all over the child's body and face: 2 years reduced to 18 months because of early guilty plea and prolonged delay before sentencing).
2. *R v J & M* [2004] EWCA Crim 2002, [2005] 1 Cr App R (S) 63.
3. *R v Harris* (1988) 10 Cr App Rep (S) 164, CA.
4. *R v O'Gorman* [1999] 2 Cr App Rep (S) 280 (30 months' imprisonment imposed on a man for cruelty and assault occasioning actual bodily harm to the 8-year-old son of his co-habitee reduced to 21 months).
5. *R v Colwell* (1993) 15 Cr App Rep (S) 323. See also *R v Banu and Ali* (1994) 16 Cr App Rep (S) 656 (3 years' imprisonment upheld where a young child was starved and neglected for a period of about 4 months).
6. *R v Edwards* [1999] 1 Cr App Rep (S) 301 (12 months' imprisonment upheld on the father of an 11 day old baby who failed to obtain medical assistance after the baby had been caused injury apparently by burning with a cigarette); *R v Taggart* [1999] 2 Cr App Rep (S) 68 (½ years' imprisonment for cruelty to a child by allowing her to be accidentally scalded and then failing to get medical assistance until the following day reduced to 2½ years).
7. *R v Jeffrey* (1989) 11 Cr App Rep (S) 265, CA (9 months' imprisonment for father, aged 22, of previous good character, who struck his 3-month-old baby at least 2 blows, causing her a black eye and bruising).
8. *R v Isaac* [1998] 1 Cr App Rep (S) 266 (sentence of 3 years' imprisonment imposed on a woman suffering from post-natal depression for cruelty to a baby aged 6 weeks varied to a probation order).
9. *R v Caroline Ann Laut* [2001] Crim 2474, [2002] 2 Cr App Rep (S) 21 (where a mother was guilty of wilful neglect in a manner likely to cause unnecessary suffering by asking her 7-year-old son to hold a broken door of a washing machine closed so that the machine would work, he slipped and his arm went into the machine causing multiple fractures; because a health visitor had previously warned her against this a custodial sentence was justified, but the term was reduced from 4 months to 12 weeks).
10. *R v Ahmed* [2003] EWCA Crim 1398, [2003] 1 Cr App R (S) 40 (if sentencing originally the Court would have imposed a community penalty).
11. *R v P* [2003] EWCA Crim 3774, [2004] 2 Cr App R (S) 32 (mother of 4 children, who was inadequate and isolated, applied a hot iron to the shin of her 4-year-old son to teach him a lesson because he had been naughty: 8 months' imprisonment upheld).
12. *A-G's Reference No 105 of 2004* [2004] EWCA Crim 3295, [2005] 2 Cr App R (S) 42.
13. *R v Emery* (1992) 14 Cr App Rep (S) 394 (mother convicted of cruelty to a child who died at age of 11 months—mother failed to protect child from violence by father—sentence reduced on appeal to 30 months).
14. *R v JA* [2001] EWCA Crim 1974, [2002] 1 Cr App Rep (S) 473.

FIREARMS OFFENCES

3–281   The appropriate level of sentence for a firearms offence will depend on all the facts and circumstances relevant to the offence and the offender. It will usually be appropriate for the sentencing court to ask itself a series of questions:

(1) What sort of weapon is involved? Genuine firearms are more dangerous than imitation firearms. Loaded firearms are more dangerous than unloaded firearms. Unloaded firearms for which ammunition is available are more dangerous than firearms for which no ammunition is available. Possession of a firearm which has no lawful use (such as a sawn-off shotgun) will be viewed even more seriously than possession of a firearm which is capable of lawful use.

(2) What (if any) use has been made of the firearm? It is necessary for the court, as with any other offence, to take account of all circumstances surrounding any use made of the firearm—the more prolonged and premeditated and violent the use, the more serious the offence is likely to be.

(3) With what intention (if any) did the defendant possess or use the firearm? Generally speaking, the most serious offences under the Act are those which require proof of a specific criminal intent (to endanger life, to cause fear of violence, to resist arrest, to commit an indictable offence). The more serious the act intended, the more serious the offence.

(4) What is the defendant's record? The seriousness of any firearms offence is inevitably increased if the offender has an established record of committing firearms offences or crimes of violence[1].

The Court of Appeal has said that given the clear public need to discourage the unlawful possession and use of firearms, both real and imitation, and the intention of Parliament expressed in a continuing increase in maximum penalties, the courts should treat any offence against the provisions of the Firearms Act 1968, as amended, as serious. Some of the sentences imposed for these offences in the past have failed to reflect the seriousness of such offences and the justifiable public concern which they arouse. Save for minor infringements which may be and are properly dealt with summarily, offences against these provisions will almost invariably merit terms of custody, even on a plea of guilty and in the case of an offender with no previous record. Where there are breaches of sections 4, 5, 16, 16A, 17(1) and (2), 18(1), 19 or 21, of the 1968 Act the custodial term is likely to be of considerable length, and where the four suggestions above yield answers adverse to the offender, terms at or approaching the maximum may in a contested case be appropriate. An indeterminate sentence should however be imposed only where the established criteria for imposing such a sentence are met.

Shortened shot guns can have no legal use. Those who involve themselves with them even if only as minders or caretakers, must expect to receive sentences which contain a deterrent element. A sentence of $2\frac{1}{2}$ years' imprisonment for such an offence, even where there are no aggravating features, is not either wrong in principle or manifestly excessive[2].

---

1. *R v Avis* [1998] 1 Cr App Rep 420, [1998] 2 Cr App Rep (S) 178, [1998] Crim LR 428. See also *R v Wright* [2000] 1 Cr App Rep (S) 109 (4 years' imprisonment for possessing a short barrelled revolver and ammunition reduced to 2 years—held, considering *R v Avis*, supra, that although the weapon was loaded, it had not been used and the defendant had had it only for a short time—there was no allegation of an intention to use the weapon), and *R v Hair* [2000] 1 Cr App Rep (S) 118 (2 years' imprisonment upheld in the case of a woman who looked after a short-barrelled revolver and 104 rounds of live ammunition on behalf of her stepson). For possession of a BB gun in a public place, see *R v Rattigan* [2005] EWCA Crim 162, [2005] 2 Cr App R (S) 61 (sentenced reduced to 10 months on a guilty plea where the possession was for a short time only and the gun was not waved about).

2. *R v Ashman* [1997] 1 Cr App Rep (S) 241 ($2\frac{1}{2}$ years' imprisonment upheld for possessing a shortened shotgun without a certificate—sawn-off shotgun and some cartridges found in the boot of the defendant's car); *R v Holmes* [1999] 2 Cr App Rep (S) 383 ($2\frac{1}{2}$ years' imprisonment upheld for possessing a shortened shotgun which the defendant acquired with a view to suicide—gun left readily visible to a passing member of the public in an unsecured car).

THEFT AND OTHER OFFENCES INVOLVING DISHONESTY

3-282 The Court of Appeal has given the following guidance on sentencing in cases of *theft from shops*. In relation to thefts by organised gangs, where this occurs repeatedly or on a large scale sentences in the order of 4 years may be appropriate even on a plea of guilty; where such thefts are followed by violence to a shopkeeper sentences in excess of 4 years are appropriate.

In relation thefts by isolated individuals not involving violence or threats of violence the following principles are appropriate:

(1) Custody should be the last resort and would almost never be appropriate for a first offence. A surviving exception to the latter are cases involving the use of a child in the theft. A community penalty may in some cases be appropriate on a plea by a first-time offender, even when other adults are involved and the offence was organised.

(2) Where the offence is attributable to drug addiction and a drug treatment testing order may be appropriate.

(3) A short custodial term not exceeding one month may be appropriate for a persistent offender on a minor scale; if the persistence also involved preparing equipment to facilitate the offence two months may be called for.

(4) Even where a defendant falls to be sentenced for a large number of offences, or there is a history of similar offending on a large scale, it will rarely be appropriate to sentence to more than 2 years on a plea of guilty and the offences will often merit no more than 12 to 18 months[1].

The *handling* of goods of substantial value by a man of previous good character was appropriately dealt with by two months' imprisonment[2].

For offences of *theft or fraud in breach of trust* by employees and professional persons, a term of immediate imprisonment is generally inevitable save in very exceptional circumstances or where the amount of money obtained was small[3]. The Court of Appeal has given the following guidelines to assist courts dealing with such cases—

(1) Despite the great punishment that offenders of this sort bring upon themselves, the court should nevertheless pass a sufficiently substantial term of imprisonment to mark publicly the gravity of the offence.

(2) The sum involved is obviously not the only factor to be considered, but it may in many cases provide a useful guide. Where the amount is not small, but is less than £17,500, terms of imprisonment from the very short up to 21 months will be appropriate; cases involving sums between £17,500 and £100,000 will merit 2 to 3 years; cases involving sums between £100,000 and £250,000 will merit 3 to 4 years; cases involving between £250,000 and £1 million will merit between 5 and 9 years; cases involving £1 million or more, will merit 10 years or more (*R v Clark* [1998] Crim LR 227, [1998] 2 Cr App Rep (S) 95, [1998] 2 Cr App Rep 137).

(3) The terms suggested are appropriate where the case was contested: in any case where there is a plea of guilty the court should give the appropriate discount. It will not usually be appropriate in cases of serious breach of trust to suspend any part of the sentence.

(4) Where the sums involved are exceptionally large, and not stolen on a single occasion, or the dishonesty is directed at more than one victim or groups of victims, consecutive sentences may be called for.

(5) While the circumstances will vary infinitely, the court will wish to pay regard to the following matters in determining what the proper level of sentence should be: the quality and degree of trust reposed in the offender, including his rank: the period over which the fraud or thefts had been perpetrated: the use to which the money or property dishonestly taken had been put: the effect on the victim: the impact of the offences on the public and public confidence: the effect on fellow employees or partners: the effect on the offender himself: his own history: those matters of mitigation special to himself, such as illness, being placed under great strain by excessive responsibility: long delay, say over two years, between his being confronted with his dishonesty and the start of the trial: and any help given by him to the police[4].

Employees of security companies can expect to be treated more harshly because of their particular supervisory role[5]. *Theft by a warehouse assistant,* which involved a systematic breach of trust over a period of weeks and a double fraud on the employers, was held to be so serious that only a custodial sentence could be justified[6].

Offences of theft and false accounting involving a total of £1,700 committed over a period of several months by a sales assistant of previous good character in the course of her employment, were held to merit two months' immediate imprisonment[7]. When sentencing for persistent *thefts by baggage handlers* at airports consideration should be given to a starting point of 3 years' imprisonment[8].

Offences involving *stock-market dishonesty* are easy to commit, very expensive and difficult to detect and prove, and can be very lucrative for the perpetrator. The Court of Appeal has said that people who indulge in such offences or any other sort of cheating connected with the Stock Market should be on notice that it was not only their assets which were at risk but also their liberty[9]. A custodial sentence will also be justified for *theft from an insurance company*[10].

Theft of furniture from an elderly person, even though the value of the property stolen is low, may be so serious that only a custodial sentence can be justified, if the victim was intimidated in his own home[11]. *Theft of small sums of money from elderly persons,* amounting to a substantial sum in total, is so serious that only a custodial sentence can be justified[12]. Elderly people are easy prey, and courts will be failing in their duty if they do not impose deterrent sentences[13].

Theft by a care assistant from a disabled person who is incapable of looking after himself and obtaining a substantial sum of money from the victim is a serious breach of trust and may well justify a sentence of imprisonment substantially greater than that suggested in the case of *Barrick*[14].

Obtaining by deception involving unauthorised use of a credit card justifies a custodial sentence of more than very short duration where the offending, though opportunistic at the start, was persisted in for some time and the total value of the goods obtained was substantial[15].

Inciting others to commit offences contrary to s 3 of the Computer Misuse Act 1990 did not cross the custody threshold where the basis of plea was that the defendant supplied 20 devices that enabled subscribers to cable television companies to gain access to all the channels provided by the companies regardless of the number of channels or programmes for which the subscribers had paid; but the defendant was of good character, he earned only a small sum from the scheme and shortly afterwards the cable companies developed technology to protect themselves from this particular form of dishonesty[16]. However, the manufacture and distribution of cable cubes which allowed subscribers to cable services to view channels to which they had not subscribed, producing a profit to the defendants of about £6,000, did cross the custody threshold[17].

Imprisonment is appropriate for offences of *fraudulent trading* even in circumstances which are not described as long term frauds. Part of the purpose of imprisonment in such cases is to deter other businessmen who fall into financial difficulties from resorting to dishonest borrowing in order to fund a shortfall in their liquidity[18]. For long term frauds the offender can expect to receive a longer term of imprisonment[19].

---

1. *R v Page* [2004] EWCA Crim 3358, [2005] 2 Cr App R (S) 37.
2. *R v Wilson* (1980) 2 Cr App Rep (S) 196 and *R v Caroline S* [1996] 2 Cr App Rep (S) 256 (12 months' imprisonment

for neglecting three children by going away on holiday and leaving them alone approved in principle but reduced to 5 months in view of the adverse effect of the sentence on the children themselves).

3. See, for example, *R (on the application of Sogbesan) v Inner London Crown Court* [2002] EWHC 1581, [2002] Crim LR 748 (custody threshold not crossed where goods and cash worth in total £216 were obtained by an 18-year-old employee in breach of trust).

4. *R v Barrick* (1985) 149 JP 705, 81 Cr App Rep 78, [1985] Crim LR 602; as updated in *R v Clark* [1998] 2 Cr App Rep 137, [1998] 2 Cr App Rep (S) 95, [1998] Crim LR 227.

Cases where the guidelines in *R v Barrick* (but prior to the updating in *R v Clark*) have been applied include *R v Chatfield* (1985) 7 Cr App Rep (S) 262, [1986] Crim LR 71 (theft of £350 over period of 21/2 years by honorary secretary of community centre: 4 months' imprisonment upheld); *R v Colley* (1985) 7 Cr App Rep (S) 264, [1986] Crim LR 72 (theft of £1,000 by accounts clerk: 6 months' imprisonment upheld); *R v Mossop* (1985) 7 Cr App Rep (S) 283, [1986] Crim LR 72 (criminal deception by dentist on National Health Service to an amount of £6,826: 9 months' imprisonment upheld); *R v Poulter* (1985) 7 Cr App Rep (S) 260, [1986] Crim LR 73 (theft from mail by postman, 26 other offences to be considered, total amount stolen £100: 18 months' imprisonment reduced to 12 months); *R v Boggs* (1990) 12 Cr App Rep (S) 39, CA (theft of £438 by an employee at kiosk with responsibility for banking takings—6 months' imprisonment reduced to 2 months' suspended); *R v Robinson* (1993) 14 Cr App Rep (S) 559, (exceptionally theft and false accounting by a sub-postmistress involving £4,500, 4 months' imprisonment reduced to 2 months); *R v McCormick* [1994] Crim LR 612, (1994) 16 Cr App Rep (S) 134, CA (ticket clerk for ferry company kept 4 fares (£1 each) obtained by the reissue of used tickets and was found in possession of other tickets which would have produced a further £13—custodial sentence correct in principle but sentence of 28 days' imprisonment reduced to allow for immediate release after 5 days). See also *R v Griffiths* [2000] 1 Cr App Rep (S) 240 (sentence reduced to 12 months' imprisonment on a club treasurer who stole a total of about £7,300 from the club over a period of about 7 years and attempted to conceal the thefts by falsifying documents – credit given for defendant's admission and early plea); *R v James* [2000] 1 Cr App Rep (S) 285 (14 months' imprisonment for theft of £5,318 by a post office counter clerk reduced to 9 months—defendant ,who stole money from her till on 2 occasions, pleaded guilty); and *R v Beard* [2001[EWCA Crim 1774, (2001) 165 JPN 715 (4 months reduced to 2 where a store supervisor was convicted, after a trial, of theft by enabling a customer, her partner, to leave the store with £260 worth of unpaid for goods).

5. *R v Colley and Marples* (1989) 11 Cr App Rep (S) 462, CA.

6. *R v Hill* (1993) 14 Cr App Rep (S) 556 (3 months' detention held to be correct in principle for offender aged 18, employed as a warehouse assistant, who stole goods valued at a total of £15,000 belonging to his employer and then obtained money by deception by taking them back).

7. *R v Bagnall* (1985) 7 Cr App Rep (S) 40.

8. *R v Dhunay* (1986) 8 Cr App Rep (S) 107, CA.

9. *R v Best* (1987) Times, 6 October. See also *R v Griffiths* (1989) 11 Cr App Rep (S) 216, CA.

10. *R v Dover* (1994) 16 Cr App Rep (S) 61 (chairman of a property management company obtained £4,000 from an insurance company by fraudulently inflating a claim for storm damage—5 months' imprisonment upheld, but described as "lenient"; *R v Bedding* (1994) 16 Cr App Rep (S) 101 (12 months' imprisonment upheld for conspiring to obtain £16,500 by arranging a fake burglary and making a false insurance claim); *R v Thomas* (1994) 16 Cr App Rep (S) 539 (6 months' imprisonment reduced to 4 months for defrauding an insurance company of £900 by dishonestly inflating a claim following a burglary).

11. *R v Flynn* (1993) 14 Cr App Rep (S) 422 (defendants stole furniture valued £30 from elderly couple aged 82 and 77 with a view to persuading them to buy replacements—sentences reduced to 3 and 4 months respectively on appeal).

12. *R v Hemingway* (1993) 15 Cr App Rep (S) 67 (15 months' imprisonment for a series of thefts of modest amounts of money from elderly persons, amounting in total to over £2,000).

13. *R v Dolphy* [1999] 1 Cr App Rep (S) 73 (4 years' imprisonment upheld for theft of £287 in cash from a lady aged 68 who had just collected her pension at a post office by a man with a long record of offences of dishonesty).

14. *R v Ross-Goulding* [1997] 2 Cr App Rep (S) 348 (15 months' imprisonment upheld for the theft of £8,000 and forgery by a care assistant from a disabled person whom the defendant was meant to be helping when performing her duties; no previous convictions; defendant married with 3 young children).

15. *R v Wallace* [2001] EWCA Crim 1405, (2001) 165 JPN 715 (the defendant received a credit card by mistake and then used it on 137 occasions, obtaining goods worth £8,677 – 8 months not manifestly excessive).

16. *R v Maxwell-King* [2001] 2 Cr App Rep (S) 136, (2001) Times, January 2.

17. *R v Moore & Crumblehulme* [2002] EWCA Crim 1907, [2003] 1 Cr App R (S) 83 (though the sentences were reduced from seven months to four on account of personal mitigation).

18. *R v Thobani* [1998] 1 Cr App Rep (S) 227 (9 months' imprisonment upheld on a man of previous good character who pleaded guilty to fraudulent trading, the defendant successfully managed a small company for a number of years, but when it ran into financial difficulties he continued to obtain goods on credit and eventually the company was wound up with a loss to creditors of about £79,000).

19. *R v Elcock* [1998] 2 Cr App Rep (S) 126 (21 months' imprisonment upheld for fraudulent trading in the form of a long term fraud over a period of 6 months, selling goods supplied by the duped suppliers quickly at under cost price, providing false references, not keeping any records and running a cash only business, total losses £56,000).

HANDLING STOLEN GOODS

3–283 In *R v Webbe* [2001] EWCA Crim 1217, [2002] 1 Cr App Rep (S) 82 the Court of Appeal considered the proposals of the Sentencing Advisory Panel (with which it largely agreed) and, while acknowledging the wide variety of circumstances that handling stolen goods can involve, gave the following guidance:

"[15] ... Paragraph 11 of (the panel's advice), with which we agree, is in these terms:

The relative seriousness of a particular case of handling depends upon the interplay of a different factors. One important issue is whether the handler has had advance knowledge of the original offence; or has directly or indirectly made known his willingness to receive the proceeds of the original offence, as compared with a handler who has had no connection with the original offence but who has dishonestly accepted the stolen goods at an undervalue. Where the handler has had knowledge of the original offence, the seriousness of the handling is inevitably linked to the seriousness of that original offence. The link to the original offence explains the need for the high maximum penalty of 14 years' imprisonment for handling, which might otherwise look anomalous. Sentences approaching the maximum should clearly be reserved for the most serious and unusual cases where the handler had previous knowledge of a very serious offence such as an armed robbery, which itself carries life imprisonment as its maximum.

[16] Paragraph 12, with the terms of which we also agree, says as follows:

The replacement value of the goods involved is often a helpful indication of the seriousness of the offence. (In this context the Mode of Trial guidelines suggest that cases of handling should normally be dealt with in the magistrates' court, and hence attract a maximum sentence of six months' imprisonment, if the value of the property is under £10,000.) We do not, however, believe that monetary value in itself should be regarded as the determining factor."

[17] We interpose the comment that it is important for sentencers to bear in mind that value would not be regarded as prescriptive. There is an obvious difference, for example, between the gravity of receiving in a public house £100 worth of stolen television sets, and the gravity of receiving £100 in cash from the proceeds of a robbery which has taken place in the receiver's presence. Furthermore, accurate values in relation to the property received may very often be extremely difficult to ascertain.

[18] The panel, in para 12 of their advice, go on to identify other factors significantly affecting the relative seriousness of the handling offence, namely the level of sophistication of the handler, the ultimate designation of the goods, the criminal origin of the goods, the impact on the victim, the level of profit made or expected by the handler, and, especially in cases of actual or intended disposal of goods, the precise role played by the handler. In our judgment, those factors are rightly identified.

[19] We also agree, in relation to para 13 of the panel's advice, that handling cases at or towards the lower end of the scale are characterised by the handler having no connection with the original offence, an absence of sophistication on the part of the handler, the less serious nature of the original offence, the relatively low value of the goods and the absence of any significant profit.

[20] The sentencing panel, in para 14, go on to identify nine factors, which may be regarded as aggravating the offence. With each of those factors we agree. They are as follows:

(1) The closeness of the handler to the primary offence. (We add that closeness may be geographical, arising from presence at or near the primary offence when it was committed, or temporal, where the handler instigated or encouraged the primary offence beforehand, or, soon after, provided a safe haven or route for disposal).
(2) Particular seriousness in the primary offence.
(3) High value of the goods to the loser, including sentimental value.
(4) The fact that the goods were the proceeds of a domestic burglary.
(5) Sophistication in relation to the handling.
(6) A high level of profit made or expected by the handler.
(7) The provision by the handler of a regular outlet for stolen goods.
(8) Threats of violence or abuse of power by the handler over others, for example, an adult commissioning criminal activity by children, or a drug dealer pressurizing addicts to steal in order to pay for their habit.
(9) As is statutorily provided by s 151(2) of the Powers of Criminal Courts (Sentencing) Act 2000, the commission of an offence while on bail.

[21] We also agree with the mitigating factors identified as being among those relevant by the sentencing panel: namely, low monetary value of the goods, the fact that the offence was a one-off offence, committed by an otherwise honest defendant, the fact that there is little or no benefit to the defendant, and the fact of voluntary restitution to the victim.

[22] We also agree with the panel that other factors to be taken into account include personal mitigation, ready co-operation with the police, previous convictions, especially for offences of dishonesty and, as statutorily provided by s 152 of the Powers of Criminal Courts (Sentencing) Act 2000, a timely plea of guilty.

[23] The panel, in para 21 of their advice, helpfully identify four possible levels of seriousness of the offence. They suggest that a distinction can be drawn between offences first, for which a fine or a discharge is appropriate; second, for which a community sentence is appropriate; third, for those which cross the custody threshold and, fourth, more serious offences.

[24] We agree that offences do fall into those four categories. We do not, however, take the view that it is always possible to draw a distinction between the first two categories of offence with quite the clarity which the panel suggest.

[25] In our judgment, the panel are right to say that, where the property handled is of low monetary value and was acquired for the receiver's own use, the starting point should generally be a moderate fine or, in some cases (particularly, of course, if a fine cannot be paid by a particular defendant) a discharge. Such an outcome would, in our judgment be appropriate in relation to someone of previous good character handling low value domestic goods for his own use. By low value we mean less than four figures.

[26] We agree that, irrespective of value, the presence of any one of the aggravating features to which we have referred is likely to result in a community sentence rather than a fine or discharge. We agree that a community sentence may be appropriate where property worth less than four figures is acquired for resale, or where more valuable goods are acquired for the handler's own use. Such a sentence may well be appropriate in relation to a young offender with little criminal experience, playing a peripheral role. But adult defendants with a record of dishonesty are likely to attract a custodial sentence.

[27] Thus far, as we have indicated, we agree with the factors which the panel identifies in relation to the sentencing process for less serious offences. But we do not believe that a clear dividing line is capable of being drawn between those offences which, appropriately attract, on the one hand, a discharge or fine and, on the other, a community sentence.

[28] So far as the custody threshold is concerned, we agree that a defendant either with a record of offences of dishonesty, or who engages in sophisticated law breaking, will attract a custodial sentence. It is in relation to the length of that sentence that the aggravating and mitigating features which we have earlier identified will come into play, as will the personal mitigation of the offender, who may appropriately, in accordance with *R v Ollerenshaw* [1999] 1 Cr App Rep (S) 65, be dealt with by a somewhat shorter sentence than might, at first blush, otherwise have seemed appropriate.

[29] We also agree with the panel that, in relation to more serious offences, there will be some for which a sentence within the range of 12 months to 4 years will be appropriate and there will be others for which a sentence of considerably more than 4 years, up to the maximum, may be appropriate. In this regard, the factors to be taken into consideration will include whether an offence is committed in the context of a business, whether the offender is acting as an organiser or distributor of the proceeds of crime and whether the offender has made himself available to other criminals as willing to handle the proceeds of thefts or burglaries.

[30] In all of these more serious cases, according to the other circumstances, sentences in the range of 12 months to 4 years are likely to be appropriate if the value of the goods involved is up to around £100,000. Where the value of the goods is in excess of £100,000, or where the offence is highly organised and bears the hallmarks of a professional commercial operation, a sentence of 4 years and upwards is likely to be appropriate, and it will be the higher where the source of the handled property is known by the handler to be a serious violent offence such as armed robbery. As we have earlier indicated, sentences significantly higher than 4 years also may be appropriate where a professional handler, over a substantial period of time, demonstrated by his record or otherwise, has promoted and encouraged, albeit indirectly, criminal activity by others.

[31] The sentences which we have indicated will, of course, be subject to discount in appropriate cases for a plea of guilty.

[32] We should also add that a court passing sentence in handling cases should always have in mind the power to make restitution orders under ss 148 and 149 of the Powers of Criminal Courts (Sentencing) Act 2000, to make compensation orders under s 130 of the Powers of Criminal Court (Sentencing) Act 2000, and to make confiscation orders in relation to profits, under the Criminal Justice Act 1988 and the Proceeds of Crime Act 1995. A Magistrates' Court cannot, of course, make a confiscation order in a case of handling. But it is open to magistrates, in such a case, where appropriate, to commit to the Crown Court for sentence."

BURGLARY

3–284 **Domestic burglary.** In *R v McInerney and R v Keating*[1], Lord Woolf CJ, following consultation with the SAP, gave the following guidance to apply directly only to cases of trespass accompanied by theft or an intention to steal.

'The observations in *R v Brewster* (infra) as to the seriousness of offences of domestic burglary remain highly relevant.

The following guidance is subject to the need to have regard to the particular circumstances of the offence, its effect on the victim and the record of the offender.

A degree of caution must be exercised when using the results of public opinion surveys (the SAP had commissioned such research, which, in any event, did not indicate any clear desire for heavier sentences). When the Court framed or revised guidelines, the need to promote public confidence in the criminal justice system was only one of the considerations the Court had to have regard to. The Court also had to consider the cost of different sentences and their relative effectiveness in preventing re-offending. There was an extremely high level of re-offending by those released from prison for offences such as burglary.

Section 111 of the Powers of Criminal Courts (Sentencing) Act 2000 required the court to impose a sentence of at least 3 years for a third or subsequent burglary conviction, unless there were specific circumstances that made that sentence unjust. Such a sentence might be unjust if 2 of the offences were committed many years earlier than the 3rd, or the offender had made real efforts to reform or to conquer his drug addiction but some personal tragedy had triggered the 3rd offence, or if the first 2 offences were committed when the offender was aged under 16. Section 111 gave the sentencer a fairly substantial degree of discretion as to the categories of situations where the presumption of a minimum sentence could be rebutted (see *R v Offen*[2]).

A standard burglary This had the features: (*a*) it was committed by a repeat offender; (*b*) it involved the theft of electrical goods or personal items such as jewellery; (*c*) damage caused by the break-in itself; (*d*) some turmoil in the house or damage to items; (*e*) no injury or violence, but some trauma to the victim. Not all these features need be present to bring an offence into this category.

Aggravating and mitigating features The following factors should now apply, though they were examples and not an exhaustive list and there could be overlap between the categories.

The high-level aggravating factors were: (*a*) force used or threatened against the victim; (*b*) an especially traumatic effect on the victim; (*c*) professional planning, organisation or execution; (*d*) vandalism of the premises; (*e*) racial aggravation; (*f*) targeting of a vulnerable victim, including cases of deception or distraction of the elderly.

The medium-level aggravating features were: (*a*) vulnerable victim, though not targeted as such; (*b*) victim at home, whether the burglary was in daytime or at night; (*c*) goods of high value, either financially or sentimentally; (*d*) the burglars worked in a group.

The number of offences might indicate that the offender was a professional burglar, which would be a high-level aggravating factor but, even if they did not, the number could still be at least a medium-level aggravating factor. The fact that the offender was on bail or licence at the time could also be an aggravating factor.

The SAP, rightly, did not seek to indicate the percentage uplift that should result from the presence of any of the above high or medium-level factors, but the Court agreed with the SAP that it was appropriate for the sentencer to reflect the degree of harm done, including the impact of the burglary on the victim, whether foreseen by the offender or not. If the offender foresaw a result of the offending behaviour then that increased the seriousness of the offence.

The SAP identified mitigating features, again not as an exhaustive list, as: (*a*) first offence; (*b*) nothing or only property of very low value stolen; (*c*) offender played only a minor part in the offence; and (*d*) no damage or disturbance to the property. If the offence was committed on impulse that could also be a mitigating factor.

If the offence was committed at night it would be more likely that the premises would be occupied. Additionally, an intrusion into an occupied home would be more frightening to the occupants if they found they had intruders at a time when it was dark, particularly if they were awoken from their sleep. A confrontation of the householder by the burglar could amount to an aggravating feature.

Other relevant mitigating factors were: (*a*) timely plea of guilty; (*b*) offender's age or state of health, both physical and mental; (*c*) evidence of genuine remorse; (*d*) response to previous sentences; (*e*) ready co-operation with the police.

An offender's criminal record was significant. The type and number of past offences had to be considered, and efforts made by the offender to rehabilitate himself were important. Where the offence was driven by alcohol or drug addiction, while the taking of drink or drugs was no mitigation, the sentencer must recognise the fact of the addiction and the importance of breaking the drink or drug problem. When an offender was making or was prepared to make real efforts to break his addiction, it was important for the sentencer to make allowances if the process of rehabilitation proved to be irregular. What might be important was the overall progress.

More than 3 years might be appropriate for some first-time offences; conversely, there were some 3rd or subsequent offences that might justify sentences of less the 3 years. It had to be borne in mind, in relation to s 111, that a single domestic burglary would accrue a qualifying conviction. Totality was also important; an offender convicted on one occasion of a number of burglaries, or asking for further burglaries to be taken into account, would also only accrue one qualifying conviction.

The SAP's suggested starting points For a completed offence, not taking into account any aggravating features or personal mitigation or the discount for pleading guilty, the SAP recommended:

(*a*) for a low-level burglary committed by a first-time domestic burglar or some second-time offenders where there was no damage to property and no property or property of only low value was stolen, the starting point should be a community sentence. This applied also to thefts, provided they were of low value, from attached garages or from vacant property. The Court endorsed these recommendations

(*b*) for a standard domestic burglary committed by a first-time domestic burglar, the starting point should be 9 months, making such cases suitable to be heard in magistrates' courts if the offender pleaded guilty. That rose to 18 months for a second-time domestic burglar, or 3 years for a third or subsequent conviction. The Court adopted a different approach: see below

(*c*) in the case of a standard domestic burglary that additionally displayed any one of the medium-level aggravating features, but committed by a first-time domestic burglar, the starting point should be 12 months. For a second-time domestic burglar that rose to 2 years, or $3\frac{1}{2}$ years for a third or subsequent conviction. The Court adopted a different approach: see below

(*d*) In the case of a standard domestic burglary that additionally displayed any one of the high-level aggravating features, but was committed by a first-time domestic burglar, the starting point should be 18 months, rising to 3 years for a second-time offender, or $4\frac{1}{2}$ years for a third or subsequent conviction. The presence of more than one of the high-level aggravating features could bring the sentence significantly above these starting points. The Court endorsed these recommendations

The Court's starting points as to (b) and (c) An unqualified approach under (*b*) and (*c*) would reinforce the flaws of present sentencing policies. Its effect on the pattern of re-offending would be limited. There were cases where the clang of the prison gates could have a deterrent effect on a first-time offender, but their numbers would not be substantial. If a first prison sentence failed to deter it would be even less likely that a moderately longer sentence, that gave no opportunity for tackling offending behaviour, would achieve anything.

The Court had not forgotten the importance of maintaining public confidence. On the contrary, the Court intended that its guidance should provide greater protection than was provided at present. As a result of prison overcrowding, the Prison Service could not achieve the limited assistance that could otherwise be provided during a short sentence. Meanwhile, there was positive evidence emerging as to what could be achieved by punishment in the community.

The Court's guidance Instead of the approach suggested by the SAP at (*b*) and (*c*) above in cases in which the court would otherwise be looking at starting points of up to 18 months, the initial approach should be to impose a community sentence, subject to conditions to ensure it was an effective punishment and offered action on the part of the Probation Service to tackle offending behaviour and, when appropriate, underlying problems such as drug addiction. If, and only if, the offender had demonstrated by his or her behaviour that punishment in the community was not practicable, should the court resort to custody. Factors that indicated that a community disposal was not a practical option might relate to the effect of the offence on the victim, the nature of the offence or the offender's record. The ability of this community sentence approach to provide better protection for the public would be increased when the Criminal Justice Bill was passed and made more sentencing options available. If an offender failed to comply with a community sentence, particularly if he committed further offences during its currency, he should be re-sentenced, and the non-compliance would be a strong indicator that a custodial sentence, possibly of substantial length, was necessary.

Where a custodial sentence was necessary, it should be no longer than it needed to be. In the case of repeat and aggravated offences long sentences would still be necessary as indicated in (*b*)–(*d*) above. As to incremental increases, these should slow significantly after the third conviction to reflect the need to maintain proportionality between burglary and other serious offences.

In relation to juveniles, it was important that they should be dealt with in the youth court and not the Crown Court.

When appropriate, compensation and restitution orders should always be made.'

We set out below the former guidance of the Court of Appeal, and some other earlier decisions of the Court, which continue to have some relevance, albeit no longer as to starting points

In *R v Brewster* Lord Bingham CJ made the following observations:

(*a*) Domestic burglary is, and always has been, regarded as a very serious offence. It may involve considerable loss to the victim. Even when it does not, the victim may lose possessions of particular value to him or her. To those who are insured, the receipt of financial compensation does not replace what is lost. But many victims are uninsured; because they may have fewer possessions, they are the more seriously injured by the loss of those they do have.

(*b*) The loss of material possessions is, however, only part (and often a minor part) of the reason why domestic burglary is a serious offence. Most people, perfectly legitimately, attach importance to the privacy and security of their own homes. That an intruder should break in or enter, for his own dishonest purposes, leaves the victim with a sense of violation and insecurity. Even where the victim is unaware, at the time, that the burglar is in the house, it can be a frightening experience to learn that a burglary has taken place; and it is all the more frightening if the victim confronts or hears the burglar. Generally speaking, it is more frightening if the victim is in the house when the burglary takes place, and if the intrusion takes place at night; but that does not mean that the offence is not serious if the victim returns to an empty house during the daytime to find that it has been burgled.

(*c*) The seriousness of the offence can vary almost infinitely from case to case. It may involve an impulsive act involving an object of little value (reaching through a window to take a bottle of milk, or stealing a can of petrol from an outhouse). At the other end of the spectrum it may involve a professional, planned organisation, directed at objects of high value. Or the offence may be deliberately directed at the elderly, the disabled or the sick, and it may involve repeated burglaries of the same premises. It may sometimes be accompanied by acts of wanton vandalism.

(*d*) The record of the offender is of more significance in the case of domestic burglary than in the case of some other crimes. There are some professional burglars whose records show that from an early age they have behaved as predators preying on their fellow citizens, returning to their trade almost as soon as each prison sentence has been served. Such defendants must continue to receive substantial terms of imprisonment. There are, however, other domestic burglars whose activities are of a different character, and whose careers may lack any element of persistence or deliberation. They are entitled to more lenient treatment.

(*e*) It is common knowledge that many domestic burglars are drug addicts who burgle and steal in order to raise money to satisfy their craving for drugs. This is often an expensive craving, and it is not uncommon to learn that addicts commit a burglary, or even several burglaries, each day, often preying on houses in less affluent areas of the country. But to the victim of burglary the motivation of the burglar may well be of secondary interest. Self-induced addiction cannot be relied on as mitigation. The courts will not be easily persuaded that an addicted offender is genuinely determined and able to conquer his addiction.

(*f*) Generally speaking, domestic burglaries are the more serious if they are of occupied houses at night; if they are the result of professional planning, organisation or execution; if they are targeted at the elderly, the disabled and the sick; if there are repeated visits to the same premises; if they are committed by persistent offenders; if they are accompanied by vandalism or any wanton injury to the victim; if they are shown to have a seriously traumatic effect on the victim; if the offender operates as one of a group; if goods of high value (whether actual or sentimental) are targeted or taken; if force is used or threatened; if there is a pattern of repeat offending. It mitigates the seriousness of an offence if the offender pleads guilty, particularly if the plea is indicated at an early stage and there is hard evidence of genuine regret and remorse.

(g) Earlier cases showed:

(i) that burglary of a dwelling-house, occupied or unoccupied, is not necessarily and in all cases an offence of such seriousness that a non-custodial sentence cannot be justified;

(ii) that the decision whether a custodial sentence is required, and if so the length of such sentence, is heavily dependent on the aggravating and mitigating features mentioned above and, usually to a lesser extent, the personal circumstances of the offender;

(iii) that the courts, particularly the higher courts, have generally reflected in their sentences the abhorrence with which the public regard those who burgle the houses of others[1].

In an earlier case, the Court of Appeal said that a judge dealing with an offence of burglary or attempted burglary, committed at the dead of night in a residential area, is fully entitled to regard that offence as so serious that only a custodial sentence can be justified. Indeed, a judge would be failing in his duty if he did not consider whether or not to impose a custodial sentence[4]. Burglary of occupied premises carried out by two people who had set out together with implements was held to be so serious that only a custodial sentence could be justified[5].

However, burglary from the communal area of a block of flats is not dwelling-house burglary in the true sense and, in some circumstances at least, may not cross the custody threshold[6].

Burglary of commercial premises. Burglaries of commercial premises vary in their gravity and where the offence was well planned and targeted a substantial sentence is required[7]. For burglary of shop premises by a persistent offender for the purpose of stealing substantial quantities of goods for disposal to the criminal underworld, a sentence of 18 months' imprisonment was held to be appropriate[8]; but a shorter term of imprisonment for such an offence may be sufficient in a case where the offender is not the originator or planner[9]. Similarly, burglary of a shop where entry was gained by removing bricks from a wall and property worth £600 was stolen has been held to be so serious that only a custodial sentence could be justified[10]. A "ram raid" burglary where a JCB digger was used in an attempt to remove an automatic cash machine from the wall of a building society branch office has been held to be a particularly serious offence which transcends the ordinary type of theft or attempted theft[11]. However, burglary of club premises, in which nothing was stolen, was held not to be so serious that only a custodial sentence could be justified[12].

---

1. [2002] EWCA Crim 3003, [2003] 2 Cr App R (S) 39.
2. [2001] 2 All ER 154, [2001] 1 WLR 253.
3. *R v Brewster* [1997] Crim LR 690, [1998] 1 Cr App Rep 220, [1998] 1 Cr App Rep (S) 181.
4. *R v Nicholson* (1993) 15 Cr App Rep (S) 226. See also *R v Middlemiss* [1999] 1 Cr App Rep (S) 62 (three years' imprisonment upheld for burglary by night of occupied house while the owners were asleep – owners disturbed and caused a considerable degree of distress).
5. *R v Russell and Hadjithemistou* (1993) 15 Cr App Rep (S) 41 (9 months' imprisonment upheld for burglary of a flat by day by 2 women equipped with housebreaking implements—both detained by the occupier and nothing was stolen).
6. See *R v Doyle* [2001] 2 Cr App Rep (S) 8, CA (only a pot plant was stolen, the defendant was effectively of good character and the PSR stated she was in fear and under the influence of her heroin addicted co-accused).
7. *R v Cole* (1996) 1 Cr App Rep (S) 193 (5 years' imprisonment upheld for a carefully planned burglary of commercial premises in which a total of £6,500 in cash and some cheques were stolen).
8. *R v Eastlake* (1980) 71 Cr App Rep 363.
9. *R v Ingham* (1980) 71 Cr App Rep 377.
10. *R v Dorries* (1993) 14 Cr App Rep (S) 608 (two defendants found in possession after the burglary of a hammer, a crowbar, gloves, a torch, pliers and a radio scanner to intercept police messages—one aged 28 sentenced to 21 months' imprisonment (including offence of reckless driving in an attempt to avoid arrest), and the other aged 21, sentenced to 6 months' detention).
11. *R v Byrne* (1994) 16 Cr App Rep (S) 140.
12. *R v Tetteh* (1993) 15 Cr App Rep (S) 46.

FRAUDULENT EVASION OF EXCISE DUTY

3–285 In *R v Czyzewski, Bryan, Mitchell, Diafi and Ward*[1] the Court of Appeal issued revised guidelines for cases of fraudulent evasion of payment of duty on tobacco or alcohol, modifying the sentencing levels proposed in *R v Dosanjh*[2]. The guidelines follow closely the recommendations of the Sentencing Advisory Panel, which took into account various matters since the decision in *Dosanjh*, including the decision in *R v Kefford*[3] in which the Court emphasised the need for sentencers to take into account the size of the prison population so that only those that needed to be sent to prison were sent there.

Seriousness

The principal factors are the level of duty evaded; the complexity and sophistication of the organisation involved; the function of the defendant within the organisation and the amount of profit he personally made.

The following factors aggravate the offence:

(1) playing an organisational role;

(2) making repeated importations, particularly in the face of warnings from the authorities;

(3) professional smuggling, evidence of which will include – complex organisation with many involved; accounts or budgets; obtaining from different sources; integrating freight movements with commercial organisations; sophisticated methods of concealment; varying methods and routes; links with overseas organisations; and the value of the goods involved (as a guide 1/2 million cigarettes or duty evaded of £75,000 potentially indicates professional smuggling);

(4)   using a legitimate business as a front;
(5)   abusing a position of privilege, eg as a customs officer or as an employee of a security firm;
(6)   using children or vulnerable adults;
(7)   threatening violence to the law enforcement agencies;
(8)   dealing in goods that carry an additional health risk due to possible contamination; or
(9)   disposing of goods to under age purchasers.

Offending on bail or having previous convictions are statutory aggravating factors.

Mitigating factors
These will include a prompt plea of guilty; co-operation with the authorities, particularly in providing information about the organisation; and, to a limited extent, previous good character. Pressure from others may, depending on the circumstances, afford good mitigation.

Starting points
For an offender of good character and disregarding any personal mitigation:

(1)   where the duty evaded is under £1000 and the level of personal profit is small, a moderate; or, if the personal mitigation is particularly strong and there has been no earlier warning, a conditional discharge may be appropriate;
(2)   where the duty evaded by a first time offender is not more than £10,000 (about 65,000 cigarettes), or the defendant's offending is at a low level, either within an organisation or persistently as an individual, a community sentence or curfew order enforced by tagging, or a higher level of fine; the custody threshold is likely to be crossed if any of the above aggravating factors are present;
(3)   where the duty evaded is between £10,000 and £100,000, for a defendant operating individually or at a low level within an organisation, up to 9 months' imprisonment; some cases may be appropriately heard by magistrates, but others, particularly if any of the above aggravating factors are present, should be dealt with by the Crown Court;
(4)   where the duty evaded exceeds £100,000 the length of imprisonment will depend, mainly, on the professionalism of the defendant and whether or not any other aggravating factors are present; subject to that, where the duty evaded is up to £500,000, 9 months–3 years; £500,000 - £1m, 3–5 years; more than £1m, 5–7 years, though in exceptional cases it may be appropriate to charge cheating the public revenue, which carries a maximum sentence of life imprisonment.

Sentencers should also bear in mind their powers to making orders of confiscation of assets, compensation, deprivation and disqualification from driving where a vehicle was used.

---

1.   [2003] EWCA Crim 2139, [2004] 3 All ER 135, (2003) 167 JP 409, [2004] 1 Cr App R (S) 49.
2.   [1998] 3 All ER 618, [1999] 1 Cr App Rep (S) 107.
3.   [2002] EWCA Crim 519, [2002] 2 Cr App Rep (S) 495.

DRUGS OFFENCES

3–286   Importation of drugs.   *Class 'A' drugs*: There are inherent difficulties in valuing drugs and the Court of Appeal has said that a better way to measure the relative significance of any seizure of class 'A' drugs is by weight rather than by street value[1]. Accordingly, in cases of importation of *heroin or cocaine*, the sentence should be related to the weight of pure drug imported, rather than the estimated street value of the consignment. Where the weight of the drugs at 100% purity is of the order of 500 grammes or more, sentences of 10 years and upwards will be appropriate. Where the weight at 100% purity is of the order of 5 kilogrammes or more, sentences of 14 years and upwards will be appropriate[1].

Ecstasy (MDA), is a synthetic amphetamine derivative capable of causing convulsions, collapse and other dangerous consequences. Ecstasy is normally supplied in tablet form, each tablet containing 100 mg of the active constituent. The tariff in regard to offences concerning Ecstasy should be maintained substantially at the same levels as in relation to other class 'A' drugs. Therefore, in general for 5,000 tablets or more of Ecstasy the appropriate sentence will be of the order of 10 years and upwards; for 50,000 tablets or more, 14 years and upwards. If analysis shows a substantially different content in an individual case, then the weight of the constituent will be the determinative factor so far as this particular criterion is concerned[2].

No distinction is to be drawn between the various categories of class A drugs, and any idea that those who import or deal in cocaine or LSD should be treated more leniently than those who import or deal in heroin is entirely wrong[3].

Class 'B' drugs: Importation of very small amounts of *cannabis* for personal use can be dealt with as if it were simple possession. Otherwise importation of amounts up to 20 kilogrammes of cannabis resin and cannabis or the equivalent in cannabis oil, will, save in the most exceptional cases, attract sentences of between 18 months and 3 years, with the lowest ranges reserved for pleas of guilty in cases where there has been small profit to the offender. The good character of the courier (as he usually is) is of less importance than the good character of the defendant in other cases. Medium quantities over 20 kilogrammes will attract sentences of 3 to 6 years' imprisonment, depending upon the amount involved, and all the other circumstances of the case[4]. The importation of 100 kilogrammes by persons playing more than a subordinate role, following a trial, should attract sentences of 7 to 8 years. 10 years is appropriate as a starting point, following a trial, for importations of 500 kg or more, by such persons[5].

There are two significant differences between cannabis and *amphetamine*. Notwithstanding a decline in the street value of amphetamine, weight for weight it remains vastly more valuable than cannabis. Secondly, it is the practice to retail amphetamine to consumers in a highly adulterated form. While goods seized at the point of importation may contain a high percentage of amphetamine, at a retail level the purity may well be no more than 10% to 12% or even less. Accordingly with amphetamine, levels of sentence should depend not on market value, but, subject to other considerations, on the quantity of the amphetamine in question, calculated on the basis of 100% pure amphetamine base (ie the maximum theoretical purity of 73% amphetamine base in amphetamine sulphate, the remaining 27% being the sulphate).

On conviction for importing *amphetamine* following a contested trial, a custodial sentence will almost invariably be called for save in exceptional circumstances or where the quantity of the drug is so small as to be compatible only with personal consumption by the importer. The ordinary level of sentence on conviction following a contested trial (subject to all other considerations, and on quantities calculated on the basis of 100% pure amphetamine base) should be:

(1) Up to 500 grammes: up to 2 years' imprisonment;
(2) More than 500 grammes but less than 2.5 kilos: 2–4 years;
(3) More than 2.5 kilos but less than 10 kilos: 4–7 years;
(4) More than 10 but less than 15 kilos: 7–10 years;
(5) More than 15 kilos: upwards of 10 years, subject to the statutory maximum of 14 years[6].

It is particularly important that persons concerned with the importation of drugs into the United Kingdom should be encouraged by the sentencing policy of the courts to give information to the police. An immediate confession of guilt, coupled with considerable assistance to the police, may properly be marked by a substantial reduction in what would otherwise be the proper sentence[7].

---

1. *R v Aranguren* (1994) 16 Cr App Rep (S) 211.
2. *R v Warren and Beeley* [1996] 1 Cr App Rep (S) 233.
3. *R v Martinez* (1984) 6 Cr App Rep (S) 364. See also *R v De Brito* [2000] 2 Cr App Rep (S) 255 (2 years' imprisonment upheld for importing 2 small quantities of cocaine by post for personal use—one envelope contained 21.5 grammes at 26% purity, equivalent to 5.59 grammes at 100% purity; the other contained 21.5 grammes at 23% purity, equivalent to 4.94 grammes at 100% purity).
4. *R v Aramah* (1983) 147 JP 217, 76 Cr App Rep 190 (6 years' imprisonment for importing 59 kg of herbal cannabis by a man with a previous conviction for a similar offence); *R v Daly* (1987) 9 Cr App Rep (S) 519, [1988] Crim LR 258, CA (4 years' imprisonment for attempting to import 15 kg of cannabis—held guidelines in *Aramah* still effective in relation to offences involving cannabis); *R v Adewoye* (1988) 10 Cr App Rep (S) 226 (18 months' imprisonment for importing 3.37 kilogrammes of herbal cannabis with a view to sale on man aged 53 with no previous convictions—held that a court was not expected necessarily to make a minute comparison of the precise amounts and values of the Cannabis imported with sentences imposed in other cases); *R v Hedley* (1989) 90 Cr App Rep 70, 11 Cr App Rep (S) 298, CA, [1989] Crim LR 842 (2 years' imprisonment for possession of cannabis resin (valued at £8,000/£10,000) with intent to supply, with confiscation order in sum of £8,000—*Aramah* guidelines still in force so far as cannabis is concerned); *R v Daly* (1989) 11 Cr App Rep (S) 243, CA (30 months' imprisonment for possession of 450 grammes of cannabis with intent to supply). See also *R v Elder and Pyle* (1994) 15 Cr App Rep (S) 514 (importation of small quantities of cannabis (200 grammes of cannabis resin and 700 grammes of herbal cannabis) for personal use by persons with no previous convictions for drug offences did not cross the custody threshold—9 months' imprisonment, suspended, substituted with a community service order for 180 hours); *R v Bell* (1994) 16 Cr App Rep (S) 93 (8 years' imprisonment upheld for importing 387 grammes of cocaine concealed in soap); *R v Holloway* (1994) 16 Cr App Rep (S) 220 (3 months' imprisonment upheld where an offender smuggled diazepam tablets with intent to supply them to a friend in prison); *R v Blyth* [1996] 1 Cr App Rep (S) 388 (2 years' imprisonment upheld for importing 16 kilogrammes of cannabis resin as a courier); *R v Astbury* (1996) 2 Cr App Rep (S) 93 (9 months' imprisonment reduced to 3 months for importing 1100 grammes of herbal cannabis for personal use).
5. *R v Ronchetti* [1998] 2 Cr App Rep (S) 100.
6. *R v Wijs* [1998] Crim LR 587, [1998] 2 Cr App Rep 436, [1999] 1 Cr App Rep (S) 181.
7. *R v Afzal* (1989) Times 14 October.

3–287   Supplying controlled drugs.   *Class A drugs* : The sentence for supplying a Class A drug will largely depend on the degree of involvement, the amount of trafficking and the weight of pure drug being handled. It is seldom that a sentence of less than three years will be justified and the nearer the source of supply the defendant is shown to be, the heavier the sentence. There may be cases of supplying class A drugs where sentences similar to those appropriate to large scale importers will be necessary[1]. The guideline that a sentence of less than three years will seldom be justified does not mean that a sentence of more than three years cannot be justified, and the guidelines suggested in *Aramah* for small scale dealing in heroin should be raised[2]. The view expressed in *Aranguren* that estimated retail value should not be the primary guide for measuring the significance of any seizure of class 'A' drugs, but instead the weight and purity of the drug should be relied upon, applies also to the supply of controlled drugs[3].

Although the quantity of *LSD* is not an irrelevant measure, there are difficulties in using the quantity of LSD as a guide because the quantity of LSD involved is often minute. Where a court is dealing with impregnated squares, the number of impregnated squares provides the best guide. The sentence should normally be based on the number of squares to be marketed, assuming an LSD content of about 50 microgrammes of LSD per square, plus or minus 10 microgrammes, but with discretion in the sentencer to vary the sentence upwards or downwards where there is any more significant variation. With a quantity of 25,000 or more squares or dosage units, the sentence should in the ordinary case be 10 years or more. Where LSD is seized in the form of tablets or crystals, the number of 50 microgrammes dosage units which can be produced should be calculated, so as to achieve equivalence with the sentences in the above guideline[3].

Ecstasy[4] is a drug in the same category as heroin and cocaine and the normal starting point for possession of such a drug with intent to supply is 5 years[5]. There is no authority for stating that Ecstasy should be treated as more serious than the supply of other Class A drugs[6]. Nevertheless, possession on behalf of others is more serious than possession on behalf of oneself, and possession of Ecstasy with a view to getting a much used drug into a nightclub and evading the security check at the door for the purpose is also more serious than possession in more straightforward circumstances[7].

Magic Mushrooms: These have a powerful hallucinogenic effect similar to that of LSD, and once a "trip" has started it cannot be controlled; accordingly, this drug should not be treated differently from other Class A drugs[8].

Supply of class A or indeed any drugs to a *serving prisoner* is a most serious offence for which a lengthy custodial sentence is required[9].

Supply to school children: it is against the public interest that children at school should be targeted in the supply of drugs, particularly with a hallucinatory drug such as LSD, or for that matter any class A drug. The gravamen in such cases is the supply to school children and the corrupting of the young and unaddicted. Deterrent sentences should be passed, and where the court is dealing with offences committed by young offenders detention under s 53(2) of the Children and Young Persons Act 1933 may be appropriate[10].

Class B drugs: The supply of massive quantities of cannabis will justify sentences in the region of 10 years for those playing anything more than a subordinate role. Otherwise the bracket should be between one to four years' imprisonment, depending upon the scale of the operation. Supplying a number of small sellers comes at the top of the bracket. At the lower end will be the retailer of a small amount to a consumer. Where there is no commercial motive (for example, where cannabis is supplied at a party), the offence may well be serious enough to justify a short custodial sentence[11]. The re-classification of cannabis as a Class C drug has not affected the sentencing guidelines since the maximum penalty for supplying a Class C drug rose from 5 years to 14 years, meaning the maximum for supplying cannabis remained the same; possession of cannabis with intent to supply thus continues almost inevitably to attract a custodial sentence[12].

Possession of *cannabis* with intent to supply where the offender agrees to store the drug on behalf of another person will attract a custodial sentence in accordance with *Aramah,* although the court may take into account the extent to which the offender was involved in supplying that drug. Nevertheless, warehousing a quantity of drugs is a considerable service to the dealer, and persons who accede to such a request to do so must appreciate that they will face a substantial sentence when caught[13].

Possession of *amphetamine sulphate* with intent to supply will also attract a custodial sentence in accordance with *Aramah*[14].

Supply to *serving prisoners*: the taking of drugs into a prison is a serious matter, because drugs inside prison have much greater value than they have on the streets. Drugs have become the main currency in prison. The trouble that drugs can cause in prison is obvious: injury to persons, particularly prison staff and damage to property can easily follow from the taking of drugs in a prison setting. Such offences are all too prevalent and require the courts to impose deterrent sentences. These are not offences for which a nominal period of imprisonment is appropriate, despite the mitigation which may exist for the individual defendant. In most cases the defendant will be a person of good character, and have available other points of mitigation[15].

Prisoners who become involved in dealing with drugs, particularly Class A drugs, whilst in prison can expect lengthy additions to their sentences. The fact that a prisoner was minding drugs for another and was not a dealer himself does not necessarily mean that he should receive a shorter sentence because those who minded drugs prevented the real dealers from being caught. Therefore, where a minder has protected the dealer, he can expect no mercy from the court. It is very different if the person who has been minding the drugs names the dealer concerned[16].

Supply of Viagra without prescriptions over a period of 16 months, achieving a net profit off £289,000, justified a custodial sentence of 12 months (and a confiscation order)[17].

---

1. *R v Aramah* (1982) 147 JP 217 , 76 Cr App Rep 190; *R v Aranguren* (1994) 16 Cr App Rep (S) 211.

2. *R v Carter* (1986) 8 Cr App Rep (S) 410 (5 years' imprisonment on two counts of supplying heroin, one of possessing 3 grammes of heroin with intent to supply, involving retail dealing on a relatively small scale); *R v Ansari* (1985) 7 Cr App Rep (S) 312 (5 years' imprisonment for possession with intent to supply of 35 grammes of heroin found in offender's car, plus 4 ounces buried in his garden, where offender dealt only on a small scale, supplying to a small circle of friends); *R v Kelly* (1987) 9 Cr App Rep (S) 385, CA (2 years' imprisonment for social supply of one fold of heroin, not a sale, containing one-twenty fourth of a gram); *R v Doyle* (1988) 10 Cr App Rep (S) 5, CA (7 years' imprisonment upheld after contested trial for possessing 3.39 grammes of powder, of which 25% was diamorphine, with intent to supply, and supplying heroin on a small scale to friends, including teenagers); *R v Walker* [1998] 2 Cr App Rep (S) 245 (3 years, 11 months imprisonment for supplying crack cocaine in wraps containing 321, 253 and 197 milligrammes respectively; sentence consecutive to return to custody for 16 months under s 40 Criminal Justice Act 1991); *R v Iqbal* [2000] 2 Cr App Rep (S) 119 (4½ years' imprisonment upheld for possessing 2.59 grammes of crack cocaine with intent to supply).

3. *R v Hurley* [1998] 1 Cr App Rep (S) 299 (10 years' imprisonment for possession of LSD with intent to supply – in possession of 319 sheets of paper, each of which would contain about 900 6 mm squares, or a total of 287,000 marketable doses of LSD; the average content of each square being 31 microgrammes).

4. See para **3–229**, ante, with regard to Ecstasy and the normal form in which it is supplied.

5. *R v Allery* (1993) 14 Cr App Rep (S) 699 (5 years' imprisonment for possession of 19 Ecstasy tablets with intent to supply); *R v Broom* (1993) 14 Cr App Rep (S) 677 (3 years' imprisonment for possession of 190 Ecstasy tablets with intent to supply); *R v Burton* (1993) 14 Cr App Rep (S) 716 (5 years' imprisonment for possession of 1,470 Ecstasy tablets with intent to supply); *R v Catterall* (1993) 14 Cr App Rep (S) 724 (2 years' detention for supplying Ecstasy and possession with intent to supply Ecstasy and LSD – special mitigation: defendant's age – 20, small quantities involved, and fact the defendant's father called the police); *R v McLellan* (1993) 15 Cr App Rep (S) 351 (2 years' imprisonment for

supplying a single tablet of Ecstasy); *R v Jones* (1994) 15 Cr App Rep (S) 856 (4 years' imprisonment upheld for possessing 27 tablets of Ecstasy with intent to supply); *R v McLaughlin* (1994) 16 Cr App Rep (S) 357 (possession of 1,000 Ecstasy tablets as a courier with intent to supply – 5 years' imprisonment reduced to 4 years); *R v Kingham* (1994) 16 Cr App Rep (S) 399 (possession of 199 Ecstasy tablets and 79 LSD tablets – 4 years' imprisonment reduced to 3 years); *R v Asquith* (1994) 16 Cr App Rep (S) 453 (3 years' detention in a young offender institution upheld for possessing 48 Ecstasy tablets with intent to supply); *R v Spalding* (1995) 16 Cr App Rep (S) 803 (30 months' imprisonment for possessing 54 "Ecstasy" tablets with intent to supply as a "minder" reduced to 18 months) where it was accepted (applying *R v Arif* (1994) 15 Cr App Rep (S) 895) that a minder should not normally be dealt with as severely as a courier; *R v Byrne* (1995) 2 Cr App Rep (S) 34 (2 years' imprisonment reduced to 12 months for possessing 18 Ecstasy tablets to share with friends without financial gain); *R v Skidmore* (1996) 1 Cr App Rep (S) 15 (2 years' imprisonment upheld for offering to sell tablets believing they were Ecstasy, which were actually harmless, in a nightclub); *R v Harvey* [1997] 2 Cr App Rep (S) 306 (Sentence reduced to 3½ years' imprisonment for defendant who was acting as a warehouseman for possessing with intent to supply 900 ecstasy tablets – defendant worked at a cafe and was told to divide the consignment of 900 tablets into lots of 100 for collection by a dealer); *R v Wakeman* [1999] 1 Cr App Rep (S) 222 (2 years' imprisonment for offering to supply Ecstasy tablets reduced to 18 months on the basis that the defendant was willing to supply only to his friends); *R v Bull* [2000] 2 Cr App Rep (S) 195 (18 months' imprisonment imposed on a defendant aged 21,who supplied 2 Ecstasy tablets without payment to a friend who subsequently died from heart failure after apparently consuming one or more of the tablets, reduced to 9 months – held that the defendant should not receive a disproportionate sentence because of the tragic and appalling consequences).

6. *R v Thompson* [1997] 2 Cr App Rep (S) 223 (5 years' detention in a young offender institution reduced to 4 years for supplying Ecstasy tablets at a nightclub – defendant sold 4 tablets to 2 undercover police officers for £10 per tablet).

7. *R v Busby* [2000] 1 Cr App Rep (S) 279 (9 months' imprisonment for possessing 14 ecstasy tablets with the intention of sharing them with 2 friends reduced to 6 months). See also *A-G's Reference (No 71) of 2002* [2002] EWCA Crim 2217, [2003] 1 Cr App R (S) 99, where the Court stated that the appropriate level of sentence would have been about 18 months for the sale in a club of 17 ecstasy tablets and the offender had a further 32 tablets in his possession; and *R v Mapp* [2002] EWCA Crim 3182, [2003] 2 Cr App R (S), where 21 months' imprisonment was reduced to 8 for an offence involving the one-off supply of 2 tablets at cost price.

8. *R v Thomas* [2004] EWCA Crim 3092, [2005] 2 Cr App R (S) 10 (2 years' imprisonment upheld for possession of about 5,000 mushrooms with intent to supply).

9. *R v Prince* [1996] 1 Cr App Rep (S) 335 (5 years' imprisonment upheld for possessing heroin with intent to supply it to a serving prisoner – defendant was found in possession of 10 wraps of heroin at 27% purity weighing a total of 491 milligrammes and admitted supplying the heroin to his son who was serving a sentence of imprisonment).

10. *R v Chesterton* [1997] 2 Cr App Rep (S) 297 (3 years' detention under s 53(2) of the Children and Young Persons Act 1933 upheld on 2 youths, both aged 16 at the time of the offences, (one 17 at the time of hearing of appeal) for supplying LSD to schoolboys at school of which one defendant was an ex-pupil; 2 years' detention on 2 younger defendants aged 14 at time of offences reduced to 12 months' detention – all 4 defendants of previous good character and came from good homes).

11. *R v Aramah* (1982) 147 JP 217, 76 Cr App Rep 190. See also *R v Steventon* (1992) 13 Cr App Rep (S) 127 (2 years' imprisonment for a "medium level retailer" in possession of 730 grammes of cannabis resin, with unexplained financial transactions over 2½ years); *R v Nolan* (1992) 13 Cr App Rep (S) 144, (2½ years imprisonment for supplying half an ounce of cannabis to boys aged 15 and 16); *R v Netts* [1997] 2 Cr App Rep (S) 117 (5 years' imprisonment for possessing 94 kilograms of cannabis resin (most of which was contained in 24 packages – street value about £250,000) with intent to supply as a courier); *R v Fairburn* [1998] 2 Cr App Rep (S) 4 (two defendants pleaded guilty to possessing 92.8 kilogrammes of herbal cannabis – first defendant was a trusted and valued member of the distribution chain for whom a sentence of 5 years was appropriate; second defendant had been recruited merely as a driver on a single occasion – his sentence was reduced to 3½ years); *R v Kitching* [2000] 2 Cr App Rep (S) 194 (2 years' imprisonment on a school cleaner who supplied small quantities of cannabis to pupils aged between 15 and 17 at the school reduced to 18 months).

12. *R v Donovan* [2004] EWCA Crim 1327, [2005] 1 Cr App R(S) 16 (12 months' imprisonment reduced to 6 for conviction of possession of 409.9g cannabis with intent to supply, following a trial).

13. *R v Doyle* [1996] 1 Cr App Rep (S) 449 (12 months' imprisonment for possessing 380 grammes of cannabis with intent to supply reduced to six months on the ground that the defendant was in possession of the greater part of the cannabis on behalf of another person).

14. *R v Hole* (1991) 12 Cr App Rep (S) 766 (6 months' imprisonment on female offender aged 26 with 2 children, for possessing 6 ounces of amphetamine sulphate (street value £2,000) with intent to supply); *R v Lyth* (1994) 16 CR App Rep (S) 68 (possession of amphetamine worth about £7,500 with intent to supply where the drugs were held as a "minder" on behalf of the supplier and would have been returned to the supplier – 4 years' imprisonment reduced to 2 years).

15. *R v Savage* (1992) 14 Cr App Rep (S) 409 (6 months' imprisonment upheld for supplying a small quantity of cannabis to a prisoner during a visit – cannabis passed with £5 note rolled in a clenched fist); *R v Freeman* [1997] 2 Cr App Rep (S) 224 (21 months' imprisonment for possessing 5.5 grammes of cannabis with intent to supply a serving prisoner reduced to 15 months – defendant pleaded guilty – found to be in possession of cannabis having entered prison to visit an inmate – mitigation that defendant suffered from severe disability following car accident); *R v Doyle* [1998] 1 Cr App Rep (S) 79 (18 months' imprisonment for possessing cannabis with intent to supply a serving prisoner reduced to 12 months in view of the personal mitigation – defendant who pleaded guilty visited her boyfriend who was a serving prisoner; she took 8.7 grammes of cannabis resin and 10.4 grammes of herbal cannabis into the prison but was unable to pass the cannabis to her boyfriend and was detected as she left the prison); *R v Slater* [1998] 2 Cr App Rep (S) 415 (3 years' detention in a young offender institution upheld for attempting to smuggle 198 mg of heroin into a prison where the defendant's brother was serving a sentence); *R v Farooqi* [1999] 1 Cr App Rep (S) 379 (12 months' imprisonment upheld for taking 1.91 grammes of cannabis into a prison with the intention of supplying it to a prisoner); *R v Ellingham* [1999] 2 Cr App Rep (S) 243 (3 years' detention in a young offender institution upheld in the case of a woman aged 20, of previous good character, who attempted to take 0.1 grammes of heroin into prison to supply to her boyfriend who told her he was going to kill himself); *R v Cowap* [2000] 1 Cr App Rep (S) 284 (4 years' imprisonment upheld on a woman aged 31 who pleaded guilty to possessing a wrap containing half of one gramme of cocaine of 96% purity with intent to supply to her boyfriend who was a serving prisoner); *R v Hamilton* [2000] 1 Cr App Rep (S) 91 (2 years' imprisonment upheld on a woman who attempted to smuggle 6.02 grammes of heroin into a prison for use by a prisoner – defendant pleaded guilty to possession of heroin with intent to supply – defendant sole carer for 3 children aged between 9 and 15, one of whom had disabilities); *R v Young* [2000] 2 Cr App Rep (S) 248 (2½ years' imprisonment upheld in the case of a woman who pleaded guilty to possessing 10.7 grammes of heroin and 25.9 grammes of cannabis with intent to supply – defendant attempted to smuggle the drugs into a prison for her boyfriend who was serving a life sentence and the sentencer accepted the defendant believed she was attempting to smuggle only cannabis; had she known that she was taking heroin into prison she could have expected a sentence of 5 years).

16. *R v Appleton* [1999] 2 Cr App Rep (S) 289 (5 years' consecutive to an existing sentence of 7 years imposed on a serving prisoner for possession of small quantities of heroin, cannabis resin, herbal cannabis and amphetamine with intent to supply).

17. *R v Groombridge* [2003] EWCA Crim 1731, [2004] 1 Cr App R (S) 9.

3-288 Possession of controlled drugs.   *Class A drugs*: For offences of simple possession of controlled drugs the circumstances of the offender become of much greater importance. There are a variety of considerations to which the court may need to have regard, including often those of a medical nature, before determining sentence. Nevertheless, there will be many cases where for simple possession of class A drugs deprivation of liberty is both proper and expedient[1].

Possession of heroin in prison by a serving prisoner must attract a greater sentence than possession of a similar drug outside of prison, and there is a need to demonstrate to those inside and outside prison that the possession of Class A drugs is so serious that only a custodial sentence can be justified[2].

Save in exceptional circumstances, a court should not pass a sentence of imprisonment outside the range appropriate for the offence and for the particular offender on the grounds that the additional term of imprisonment will be of benefit to the offender in helping him to overcome some addiction to drugs or alcohol[3].

Class B drugs: For possessing cannabis when only small amounts are involved, being for personal use, the offence can often be met by a fine. If the history shows, however, a persistent flouting of the law, imprisonment may became necessary[4].

There is nothing in the guidance contained in *Aramah* to indicate that an offence of simple possession is not sufficiently serious to warrant a community sentence. Such an offence will usually cross that threshold, although there may well be circumstances which will render a fine more appropriate[5].

---

1. R v *Aramah* (1982) 147 JP 217, 76 Cr App Rep 190. See also R v *Diamond* (1985) 7 Cr App Rep (S) 152 (8 months' imprisonment – 2 months to serve, balance held in suspense – and a fine of £4,000, upheld on a man of 34 of previous good character for possessing 13.6 grams of powder containing 25% cocaine); R v *Layton* (1988) 10 Cr App Rep (S) 109, CA (3 months' imprisonment on a man of 30 with no previous convictions for drugs offences for possession of 5.6 grams of cocaine for personal use); R v *Gallagher* (1990) 12 Cr App Rep (S) 224 (6 months' imprisonment for possessing 3.3 grams of heroin for personal use); R v *Scarlett* (1994) 16 Cr App Rep (S) 745 (6 months' imprisonment upheld for possessing 1.69 grams of crack cocaine).
2. R v *Roberts* [1997] 2 Cr App Rep (S) 187 (15 months' imprisonment upheld for possession of 0.188 grams of heroin by a serving prisoner – defendant was serving a sentence of four years' imprisonment for possession of heroin with intent to supply when he was searched by prison officers and found to be in possession of the heroin – defendant admitted buying the heroin for personal consumption).
3. R v *Roote* (1980) 2 Cr App Rep (S) 368; R v *Bassett* (1985) 7 Cr App Rep (S) 75.
4. R v *Aramah* (1982) 147 JP 217, 76 Cr App Rep 190.
5. R v *Hughes* [1999] 2 Cr App Rep (S) 329 (a community service order for possessing 1.3 grams of cannabis approved in principle but reduced to 40 hours).

3-289 Permitting premises to be used for the supply of Class A drugs.   This offence covers a wide range of different degrees of involvement. In a case where there was no evidence of profit and the defendant was a vulnerable person who was used by people she tried to help, 18–24 months' imprisonment was too high a starting point[1].

---

1. R v *Doreen Jayne Setchall* [2002] EWCA Crim 1758, [2002] 1 Cr App Rep (S) 320 (12 months reduced to 4). See also R v *Melanie Jane Williams* [2002] EWCA Crim 2362, [2002] 1 Cr App Rep (S) 532 (18 months' imprisonment reduced to 8 where the defendant, who pleaded guilty, had failed to prevent her partner from supplying cocaine from her home),

3-300 Production of cannabis.   Production of *cannabis* on a commercial scale by means of a sophisticated operation will invariably attract a custodial sentence[1]. Where there is no element of commercial supply a substantially shorter term of imprisonment may be imposed[2]. Moreover, where the cannabis is cultivated for the offender's personal use to alleviate a medical condition from which he suffers, the medical condition may constitute a substantial mitigating factor[3].

The cultivation of cannabis is being increasingly adopted to overcome some of the problems involved in the importation of the drug. Accordingly, for offences of being concerned in the management of premises used for the production of cannabis deterrent sentences are required[4].

---

1. R v *Lyall* (1994) 16 Cr App Rep (S) 600 (3½ years' imprisonment upheld for producing cannabis on a commercial scale – defendant pleaded guilty to producing cannabis and was convicted of possessing cannabis with intent to supply; carefully planned and professional operation with intent of growing cannabis for sale and profit , with estimated output of up to 3 kilogrammes of cannabis in a year); R v *Booth* [1997] 2 Cr App Rep (S) 67 (4 years' imprisonment upheld for production of cannabis using the hydroponic method, whereby it could be expected between 8 and 12 kilogrammes of cannabis would be produced each year; R v *Blackham* [1997] 2 Cr App Rep (S) 275 (12 months' imprisonment for producing cannabis with 75 plants growing); R v *Green and Withers* [1998] 1 Cr App Rep (S) 437 (sentence of 4 years' imprisonment reduced to 3 years where sophisticated methods to produce cannabis were employed—47 cannabis plants growing – equipment installed to promote growth of the plants, but defendants had not begun to trade and it was accepted that they intended only to supply established cannabis users); R v *Knight* [1998] 2 Cr App Rep (S) 23 (3 years' imprisonment upheld for producing cannabis in a sophisticated manner with a view to financial gain – garage converted to grow cannabis by the hydroponic system – 11 growing plants found which would produce about 555 grammes of cannabis, at an estimated total value of £10,500 to just under £15,000); R v *Dibden* [2000] 1 Cr App Rep (S) 64 (21 months' imprisonment upheld for offender who grew sufficient cannabis plants to produce 400 grammes of cannabis with a view to supply to his friends for payment); R v *Evans* [2000] 1 Cr App Rep (S) 107 (12 months' imprisonment reduced to 9 months for cultivating 21 cannabis plants by the hydroponic system in a room set aside – defendant pleaded guilty on the basis that the cannabis was intended for his personal consumption only).
2. R v *Bennett* [1998] 1 Cr App Rep (S) 429 (sentence of 12 months' imprisonment for producing cannabis for personal use and for supply to friends without payment reduced to 6 months – 87 cannabis plants found, but no evidence of a sophisticated growing system). The re-classification of cannabis from Class B to Class C is relevant in cases where the cultivation was for own use, though such an offence still ordinarily crosses the custody threshold (see, for example R v

Donovan [2004] EWCA Crim 1237, [2005] 1 Cr App R (S) 16; *R v Herridge* [2005] EWCA Crim 1410, [2006] 1 Cr App R (S) 45, [2005] Crim LR 806; but the concurrent increase in maximum penalties for supply or intent to supply Class C drug means that no reduction is appropriate in cases involving an element of supply: *R v Herridge*, supra.

3. *R v Peters* [1999] 2 Cr App Rep (S) 334 (9 months' imprisonment for cultivating cannabis reduced to six months on the ground that the defendant cultivated cannabis for his own use to alleviate a medical condition).

4. *R v Chamberlain* [1998] 1 Cr App Rep (S) 49 (4½ years' imprisonment upheld for being concerned in the management of premises where cannabis was produced on a large scale – defendant was the owner of industrial premises which were licensed to others for the production of cannabis – premises found to contain 542 cannabis plants growing under the hydroponic method).

OFFENCES INVOLVING BAD DRIVING

3–301   Custodial sentences may be appropriate for *bad driving offences*, but there is no clear principle. Imprisonment has been held to be appropriate where blood-alcohol content exceeded by some three times the prescribed limit in an *excess alcohol* case[1], and where a defendant in a fairly advanced state of intoxication refused to supply a laboratory specimen[2] but inappropriate in a similar case, bad of its kind, where the defendant destroyed a laboratory specimen but where there was no suggestion of his being in an advanced state of intoxication[3]. The Magistrates' Association's *Suggestions for Assessing Penalties* indicate that where the offender has 100 microgrammes or more of alcohol per 100 millilitres of breath consideration should be given to imposing a custodial sentence. These guidelines have been approved by the Lord Chief Justice[4]. The propriety of custodial sentences for bad driving offences is not limited to offenders with bad records but is to be applied having regard to the seriousness of the offence charged[5]; short sentence resulting in one month served appropriate for recklessly ramming another car from behind on motorway at between 60 mph and 70 mph, then overtaking on the inside and braking in front of the other car[6]. Drivers who cause accidents resulting in injury or death when they have had too much to drink must expect to lose their liberty, in the absence of exceptional mitigating circumstances[7].

In *R v Cooksley, R v Stride, R v Cook, A-G's Reference (No 152 of 2002)*[8] the Court of Appeal, following consultation with the Sentencing Advisory Panel, established new sentencing guidelines for the offences of causing death by dangerous driving and causing death by careless driving when under the influence of drink or drugs. Aggravating factors include:

(*a*)   consumption of drugs (including legal medication known to cause drowsiness) or alcohol;

(*b*)   excessive speed, racing, competitive driving or 'showing off';

(*c*)   disregard of warnings from fellow passengers;

(*d*)   a prolonged, persistent, and deliberate course of very bad driving;

(*e*)   aggressive driving, eg driving much too close to the vehicle in front, persistent inappropriate attempts to overtake or cutting in after overtaking;

(*f*)   driving while avoidably distracted, eg by reading or by use of a mobile telephone (especially if hand-held);

(*g*)   driving when knowingly suffering from a medical condition that significantly impairs driving skills;

(*h*)   driving when knowingly deprived of adequate sleep or rest;

(*i*)   driving a poorly maintained or dangerously loaded vehicle, especially where that has been motivated by commercial concerns;

(*j*)   other offences committed at the same time, eg driving without ever holding a licence, driving while disqualified, driving without insurance, driving while a learner without supervision, taking a vehicle without consent, driving a stolen vehicle; (k) previous convictions for motoring offences, particularly offences involving bad driving or the consumption of excessive alcohol before driving;

(*l*)   more than one person killed as a result of the offence, especially if the offender knowingly puts more than one person at risk or the occurrence of multiple death is foreseeable;

(*m*)   injury to one or more victims in addition to any death(s);

(*n*)   behaviour at the time of the offence, eg failing to stop, falsely claiming that one of the victims was responsible for the crash or trying to throw the victim off the bonnet by swerving in order to escape;

(*o*)   causing death in the course of dangerous driving in an attempt to avoid detection or apprehension; and

(*p*)   committing the offence while on bail.

Mitigating factors include:

(*a*)   a good driving record;

(*b*)   the absence of previous convictions;

(*c*)   a timely plea of guilty;

(*d*)   genuine shock or remorse (which may be greater if the victim is either a close relation or a friend);

(*e*)   the offender's age (but only in cases where lack of driving experience has contributed to the commission of the offence); and

(*f*)   the fact that the offender has also been seriously injured as a result of the offence, but only very serious, or life-changing, injury should have a significant effect on the sentence.

In cases where there are no aggravating circumstances, the starting point for adult offenders, even when there is a plea of guilty, is a custodial sentence of perhaps 12 to 18 months, a custodial sentence only being avoidable if there are exceptional mitigating features. A starting point of two to three years is appropriate for an offence involving a momentary dangerous error of judgment or a short period of bad driving but which has been aggravated by an habitually unacceptable standard of driving on the part of the offender (aggravating factors (j) or (k)), by the death of more than one victim or serious injury to other victims (aggravating factors (l) and (m)) or by the offender's irresponsible behaviour at the time of the offence (aggravating factors (n) to (p)). In some cases, particularly where more than one of the above aggravating factors are present, five years may be appropriate. When the standard of the offender's driving is more highly dangerous (as indicated, for example, by the presence of one or two of aggravating factors (a) to (i)), a sentence of four to five years is the starting point in a contested case. For contested cases involving an extremely high level of culpability on the offender's part, the starting point is six years.

In "road rage" cases of dangerous driving, where no accident or injury resulted and there was no consumption of alcohol, but there was evidence to suggest furious driving in a temper with the intention of causing fear and possible injury, the appropriate sentencing bracket is 6–12 months[9].

In a case of dangerous driving, even where none of the (formerly "Boswell") aggravating features are present a custodial sentence may not be wrong in principle or manifestly excessive[10].

As a general rule, where driving on a single occasion gave rise to more than one offence (eg reckless driving and driving while disqualified) concurrent sentences are appropriate unless the circumstances were exceptional[11]. However, consecutive terms for dangerous driving and driving whilst disqualified were justified where the latter offence had been committed in full before the dangerous driving began and the reason for driving dangerously was to avoid arrest for driving whilst disqualified[12].

When judging the gravity of an offence of *aggravated vehicle taking*, the most important circumstances are that the vehicle was driven dangerously, for that concerns the culpability of the driver, whereas the incidence and severity of any injury or damage caused are to some extent a matter of chance[13]. Imprisonment in such cases may be justified even for those who are carried in a car which has been taken unlawfully and is driven dangerously[14]. However, it will be appropriate to make some distinction between the driver and the passenger, unless the passenger can be shown to have given some positive encouragement to the driver[15].

---

1. *R v Tupa* [1974] RTR 153. See also *R v Shoult* (1996) 2 Cr App Rep (S) 234, [1996] Crim LR 449.
2. *R v Horton* [1974] RTR 399.
3. *R v Welsh* [1974] RTR 478.
4. *R v Shoult* [1996] 2 Cr App Rep (S) 234, [1996] RTR 298, explaining and not following obiter dicta in *R v Cook* [1996] RTR 304n.
5. *R v Guilfoyle* [1973] 2 All ER 844, 137 JP 568; *R v Pashley* [1974] RTR 149; *R v Nokes* [1978] RTR 101.
6. *R v Till* [1982] Crim LR 540.
7. *R v Bilton* (1985) 7 Cr App Rep (S) 103, [1985] Crim LR 611.
8. [2003] EWCA Crim 996, [2003] 3 All ER 40, [2003] RTR 483, [2003] Crim LR 564.
9. *R v Howells* [2002] EWCA Crim 1608, [2003] 1 Cr App R (S) 61.
10. *R v Grant Anthony Smith* [2001] EWCA Crim 2822, [2002] 2 Cr App Rep (S) 103 (4 months' imprisonment upheld where a vocational driver aged 40 and of good character overtook a slow moving vehicle on a bend and collided with an oncoming car causing serious injuries to its driver).
11. *R v Skinner* (1986) 8 Cr App Rep (S) 166, CA.
12. *R v Philips* [2004] EWCA Crim 2651, [2005] 1 Cr App R (S) 113.
13. *R v Bird* [1993] RTR 1, [1993] Crim LR 85, 157 JP 488; applied in *R v Robinson and Scurry* (1993) 15 Cr App Rep (S) 452 (18 months and 21 months' detention for an appalling and dangerous piece of driving). See also *R v Carroll* (1994) 16 Cr App Rep (S) 488, [1995] Crim LR 92, CA (2 years' detention in a young offender institution for aggravated vehicle taking reduced to 18 months on the ground that it was wrong to impose the maximum sentence in a case where the defendant had pleaded guilty); *R v Timothy* (1995) 16 Cr App Rep (S) 1028 (15 months' imprisonment reduced to 9 months for aggravated vehicle taking involving driving at excessive speed while affected by alcohol on the basis that the sentence imposed should leave room for contested cases with more serious features).
14. *R v Sealey* (1993) 15 Cr App Rep (S) 189.
15. *R v Robinson and Scurry* (1993) 15 Cr App Rep (S) 452.

SEXUAL OFFENCES

3–302 For sentencing guidelines in respect of serious sexual offences, see *A-G's References (Nos 37, 38, 44, 54, 53, 35, 40, 43, 54, 421 and 42 of 2003)*[1]. For sentencing guidelines in respect of assault by penetration, contrary to s 2 of the Sexual Offences Act 2003, see *A-G's Reference (No 104 of 2004)*[2]. For sentencing guidelines in respect of battery with intent to commit a sexual offence, see para **3–305**, post.

In *R v Corran*[3] the Court of Appeal gave the following general guidance in relation to offences under the 2003 Act.

(1) The starting point for non-penile penetration should generally be lower than for penile penetration.

(2) So far as the offence of rape of a child under 13, contrary to s 5 of the Act, was concerned, no precise guidance could be given. The appropriate sentence was likely to lie within a very wide bracket, depending on all the circumstances of the particular offence. There would be very few cases in which immediate custody was not called for even in relation to a young offender, because the purpose of the legislation was to protect children under 13 from themselves as well as from others minded to prey on them. The offence was of such seriousness that custody was likely to be called for even when the new sentencing provisions of the Criminal Justice Act 2003 came into force. There would be some offences, for example, where there was no

question of consent, and where significant aggravating features were present, where a longer determinate sentence or a life sentence would be called for in accordance with existing authority on seriousness and dangerousness, as amplified by the Sentencing Guideline Council's guidelines on seriousness by reference to ss 142 and 143 of the Criminal Justice Act 2003. Although absence of consent was not an ingredient of the offence, presence of consent was material in relation to sentence, particularly with regard to younger defendants. The age of the defendant of itself and when compared with the age of the victim was also an important factor. A very short period of custody was likely to suffice for a teenager where the other party consented. In exceptional cases, a non-custodial sentence might be appropriate for a young defendant. If the offender was much older than the victim, a substantial term of imprisonment would usually be called for. Other factors included the nature of the relationship between the two and their respective characters and maturity, the number of occasions when penetration occurred, the circumstances of the penetration, including whether contraception was used, the consequences for the victim emotionally and physically, the degree of remorse shown by the defendant and the likelihood of repetition. A reasonable belief that the victim was 16 would also be a mitigating factor, particularly where the defendant was young. A plea of guilty would be pertinent. Pre-Act authorities such as *Bulmer*[4]; *Oakley*[5]; and *Brough*[6], which indicated a sentence of the order of 15 months for a defendant in his twenties, would continue to provide assistance, particularly bearing in mind that life imprisonment was the maximum sentence for the offence of having sexual intercourse with a girl under 13.

(3)   Before the coming into force of the Sexual Offences Act 2003, sexual intercourse by a man with the girl under the age of 16 was punishable by two years' imprisonment. Sexual activity other than intercourse with an under-16-year-old of either sex was now a criminal offence and the penalty had been increased substantially. Section 9 made it an offence punishable with up to 14 years' imprisonment to engage in penetrative sexual activity with a person under the age of 16 if the offender did not reasonably believe the other person to be 16 or over, or under the age of 13. If the offender was under 18, the maximum sentence by virtue of s 13, was five years. Section 10 contained similar provisions in relation to causing or inciting a child to engage in penetrative sexual activity. These increases in the maximum penalties must be appropriately reflected in sentences imposed by the courts in relation to offenders of whatever age.

(4)   The factors identified as relevant to sentence in relation to the rape of the child under 13 would also be relevant in relation to penetrative sexual activity under ss 9 and 10, subject to the difference that where the other party was 13 or over, reasonable belief that he or she was 16 or over would afford a defence rather than merely mitigation.

(5)   Sentencers should bear in mind that an offence contrary to s 5 would generally attract a heavier sentence than an offence, even where the victim was under 13, contrary to ss 9 or 10.

(6)   The sentence for ss 9 and 10 offences was likely to be less where the victim was under 16 rather than under 13[7].

(7)   Sections 7 and 8 provided for sexual offences against children under 13. The factors relevant to sentence would include the nature of the assault or penetrative activity and the period of time it lasted and other factors previously identified in relation to s 5 offences, appropriately adjusted.

(8)   Pre-Act authorities would continue to be of assistance, subject to their being viewed through the prism of the increased sentence for sexual assault from 10 to 14 years.

(9)   In relation to s 7 offences, the custody threshold would not always be passed. Generally speaking, s 7 offences would be less serious than offences contrary to ss 8, 9 or 10.

(10) Sections 11 and 12 created offences for persons over 18 engaging in sexual activity in the presence of children. The maximum penalty for these offences was 10 years on indictment. They would usually attract a lesser penalty than sexual activity with a child. The factors relevant to sentence would include the age and character of the defendant, the age of the child, the nature and situation of the sexual activity engaged in or depicted, the number of occasions when the activity was observed, the impact on the child, the degree of remorse shown by the defendant and the likelihood of repetition. A plea of guilty would call for the appropriate discount.

The offence of *voyeurism* may not cross the custody threshold[8].

In relation to the offence of sexual activity with a person with mental disorder impeding choice, there can similarly be cases where a non-custodial sentence is not unduly lenient[9].

Imprisonment is necessary for Intentional exposure where there is a relevant history of such behaviour[10].

---

1.   [2003] EWCA Crim 3045, (2003) 167 JPN 822
2.   (2004) 168 JPN, 886.
3.   [2005] EWCA Crim 192, [2005] 2 Cr App R (S) 73, [2005] Crim LR 404.
4.   (1989) 11 Cr App R (S.) 586.
5.   (1990) 12 Cr App R (S) 215.
6.   [1997] 1 Cr App R (S) 55.
7.   See, for example *R v Davies* [2005] EWCA Crim 1363, [2006] 1 Cr App R (S) 37 (sentence reduced to 9 months where 19 year-old had consensual intercourse with a drunken girl aged 13, when she had told him that she was 15)
8.   See *R v IP* [2004] EWCA Crim 2646, [2005] 1 Cr App R (S) 102, where the defendant secretly filmed his step-daughter in the shower, but there was no feature of showing the recording to others, or posting the pictures on the Internet

or selling them, the defendant had no previous convictions and his prompt admission had been followed by a timely guilty plea. See also, however, *R v Mark Turner* [2006] 2 EWCA Crim 63, [2006] 2 Cr App R (S) 51, where the manager of a health centre installed a video camera above female showers and filmed 3 women taking showers. It was held that the abuse of trust took the offences over the custody threshold (though the term was reduced from 14 to 9 months' imprisonment).

9. See, for example, *A-G's Reference (No 106 of 2005)* [2006] EWCA Crim 510, [2006] 2 Cr App R (S) 78, where the offender (45) had only one previous conviction, which was 20 years earlier for indecent assault, he knew the victim and her mother well, on each of the relevant 3 occasions the mother had asked the offender to take care of the victim, the sexual activity included intercourse and oral sex, the victim was 17 with an IQ of 65 and had a reasonable understanding of sexual matters: held, while a custodial sentence of at least 12–18 months might be expected, a sentence of a community rehabilitation order with a condition of residence at a probation hostel had not been unduly lenient in all the circumstances.

10. See *R v Stephen Paul Francis Mailer* [2006] EWCA Crim 665, [2006] 2 Cr App R (S) 84: the offender (26 at the time of the present offences) on 2 occasions sat next to the same young woman on a bus and exposed his penis and masturbated; his record included a number of offences of indecent exposure and he was subject to a CRO for similar offences: 6 months' imprisonment (with the CRO left to continue) upheld in view of the context of all that had gone before, though the offender was now making some positive progressive, was in a relationship and was in employment.

3–304   Supply or possession of indecent photographs of children.   In *R v Oliver*[1], the Court of Appeal, following consultation with the SAP, gave the following guidelines, which took into account the increased maximum penalties provided by the Criminal Justice and Courts Services Act 2000.

Two principle factors determined the seriousness of the offence: the nature of the material and the extent of the defendant's involvement with it. As to the former, it was desirable for sentencers to view the images for themselves, unless a description of what they depicted could be agreed. Descriptions of different levels of indecent activity were to be derived from the COPINE programme description of instruments. These were: level 1 indicated images depicting erotic posing with no sexual activity; level 2 indicated sexual activity between children or solo child masturbation; level 3 indicated non-penetrative sex between adults and children; level 4 indicated penetrative sexual activity between adults and children; and level 5 indicated sadism or bestiality.

With regard to the nature of the activity, the seriousness of offences increased in proportion to the defendant's proximity to, and responsibility for, the original abuse. Any element of commercial gain would place the offence at a high level of seriousness; and the swapping of images could properly be regarded as commercial activity, notwithstanding that it was not for commercial gain, because it was an activity that fuelled demand for the material. Widescale distribution, even without financial profit, was intrinsically more harmful than activity limited to 2 or 3 persons because it involved a risk that the material would be used by paedophiles, and a risk of shaming or degrading the original victims.

Taking the original film or photographs was more serious than downloading images, which, in turn, was more serious than merely locating images on the Internet. In such cases, it was difficult to make a choice between custody or a non-custodial sentence. On the one hand, there was social abhorrence of such offences and Parliament had increased the maximum penalties. On the other hand, there was evidence as to the effectiveness of sex offender treatment programmes. In any case that was close to the custody threshold, the defendant's suitability for treatment should be assessed with a view to the imposition of a CRO with a condition of attendance on a sex offender treatment programme. The appropriate sentence should not, however, be determined according to the availability of additional orders or to the availability of treatment programmes for offenders in custody.

The following factors were relevant to the level of sentence, but they should be treated as guidelines only. Prison overcrowding meant that custody should be imposed only when necessary. A fine would normally suffice for offences involving possession of material solely for the defendant's own use, including cases of downloading but non-distribution and cases involving material consisting entirely of pseudo-photographs, the making of which did not involve the exploitation of children and the activity depicted therein was of level 1 seriousness. In such cases, a conditional discharge might be appropriate if the defendant pleaded guilty and was of good character, but such an order should not be made for the purpose of avoiding registration under the SOA. Possession and downloading of artificially created pseudo photographs and the making of such images were less serious than cases involving the possession or making of photographic images of real children, unless the pseudo images were of a particularly grotesque nature. The indictment should, therefore, specify the type of images. A community sentence might be appropriate where the defendant was in possession of either large amounts of level 1 material or a small amount of level 2 material, provided there was no distribution. A CRO with a condition of attendance on a sex offender programme might also be appropriate if the defendant were sufficiently motivated.

The custody threshold was crossed where: the material was shown or distributed to others; or in cases of possession of either a large amount of level 2 material or a small amount of level 3 material or worse. Up to 6 months was appropriate where: the defendant was in possession of either a large amount of level 2 material or a small amount of level 3 material; or the defendant had shown, distributed, or exchanged material of level 1 or 2 seriousness on a limited scale without financial gain. Sentences of between 6 and 12 months were appropriate for: showing or distributing a large number of images of level 2 or 3 seriousness; or the possession of a small number of images of level 4 or 5 seriousness. More serious offences attracted a sentence in the range 1–3 years. Cases falling appropriately in this range were: possession of a large amount of material of level 4 or 5 seriousness, even without showing or distribution; showing or distributing a large number of level 3 images; and producing or trading in material of level 1–3 seriousness. Longer sentences should be reserved for: showing or distributing images at level 4 or 5; the active involvement in production of images at those levels, particularly if the offence involved a breach of trust, whether or not there was an element of commercial gain; and offences involving the commissioning or encouragement of such images.

Sentences approaching the 10-year maximum were appropriate in very serious cases where the defendant had previous convictions for dealing in child pornography or for abusing children sexually or violently. In less serious cases, previous convictions could cause the custody threshold to be crossed.

An extended sentence might also be appropriate, even if the custodial term was short[2].

The levels of sentences indicated above were for adult offenders, following a contested trial. The following factors were capable of aggravating the seriousness of an offence: showing or distributing to a child; numbers of images so large as to be unquantifiable; the organisation of the material in the collection might indicate sophistication, the defendant's part in trading and the level of personal interest involved; posting on public areas of the Internet or distribution in a way that increased likelihood of the images being found; responsibility for the original production of the material, particularly if the defendant had involved members of his own family or had drawn from vulnerable groups, or if he had abused a position of trust; and the age of the children, particularly if the effect on the child could not be quantified.

Cases involving babies or young children caused particular repugnance, particularly if the conduct depicted was such as to indicate a likelihood of injury to private parts. The level of fear or distress caused might also vary according to the age of the child.

A guilty plea was a mitigating factor, particularly if entered at an early stage.

Offences of this sort rarely resulted in the cautioning or prosecution of persons under 18. Where such a person fell to be sentenced, the appropriate sentence was likely to be a SO with a condition of attendance on a relevant programme. However, the Court wished to draw attention to the apparent shortage of adequate treatment programmes for young sex offenders[3].

The sentence must reflect the matters specifically identified in the charges[4]. Where, however, particularly aggravating features are present an extended sentence may be justified[5].

It was held that a restraining order under s 5A of the Sex Offenders Act 1997 could be made against an offender convicted of making indecent photographs by downloading pornographic images from the Internet as the knowledge on the part of the children concerned that they would be viewed by others can amount to serious psychological harm and thus meet the "serious harm" criterion in s 5A(2)[6]. Restraining orders have since been replaced by sexual offences prevention orders[7], and 'serious harm' has been changed to "serious sexual harm". It remains to be seen what effect these changes will have in this type of case.

---

1. [2002] EWCA Crim 2766, 2 Cr App R (S) 15.
2. Extended sentences have been superseded by imprisonment for public protection. If there is a significant risk of further specified offences of this type, it follows that there is a significant risk of serious harm and the sentencer is, accordingly, obliged to impose a sentence of imprisonment for public protection: *R v Duncan* [2005[EWCA Crim 3594, [2006] 2 Cr App R (S) 28, [2006] Crim LR 450.
3. For earlier authorities, see *R v Toomer* [2001] 2 Cr App Rep (S) 30. See also *R v Wild* and *R v Jefferson* [2001] EWCA Crim 1433, [2002] 1 Cr App Rep (S) 162; *R v Owens* [2001] EWCA Crim 1370, (2001) 165 JPN 495; *R v Makeham* [2001] 2 Cr App Rep (S) 198; *R v Malone* [2001] 2 Cr App Rep (S) 203; *R v Koeller* [2001] EWCA Crim 1854; *R v Allison* [2001] EWCA Crim 1971; *R v Knights* [2001] EWCA Crim 1694; and *R v Hopkinson* [2001] EWCA Crim 84, [2001] 2 Cr App Rep (S) 270.
4. *R v Pardue* [2003] EWCA Crim 1562, [2004] 1 Crim App R (S) 13 (defendant pleaded guilty to 17 charges encompassing a total of 28 indecent photographs should have been sentenced solely on the basis of that quantity, though he admitted in interview storing over 1,000 images on his computer hard drive).
5. *R v Grosvenor* [2003] EWCA Crim 1627, [2004] 1 Cr App R (S) 17 (case concerned offences of possession of over 8,000 images, many pornographic and some depicting sexual acts with young child committed by many on probation at the time for an offence of USI: a custodial term of 2 years and an extension period of 3 years upheld).
6. *R v Beaney* [2004] EWCA Crim 449, [2004] 2 Cr App R (S)82, followed in *R v Collard* [2004] EWCA Crim 1664, [2005] 1 Cr App R (S). It does not follow, however, that the court will be satisfied that it is necessary to make a restraining order in every downloading case; relevant factors are the number of offences, their duration, the nature of the material, the extent of publication, the use to which the material was put, the offender's antecedents, his personal characteristics and the risk of re-offending: *R v Collard*, supra.
7. See para **3–240**, post.

3–305   **Battery with intent to commit a sexual offence.**   In *R v Wisniewski*[1] the following guidance was given. Although the Sexual Offences Act 2003 had created new offences, the conduct giving rise to such offences was not new and the authorities relating to offences which had existed before the Act should continue to guide sentencers. In relation to battery with intent to commit a sexual offence, factors of particular relevance include: (i) the method and degree of force used by an offender; (ii) the nature and extent of the indecency intended; (iii) the degree of vulnerability of, and harm to, the victim; (iv) the circumstances of the attack, including the time of day and the place of the offence; and (v) the level of risk posed by the offender. Further, good character was only of limited mitigation. Furthermore, having regard to the maximum sentence of ten years' imprisonment for the offence as compared with the maximum sentence of life imprisonment for offences of rape and attempted rape, save where a great deal of violence was inflicted, the level of sentence for the instant offence was generally to be lower than was appropriate for offences of rape or attempted rape in similar circumstances.

---

1. [2004] EWCA Crim 3361, [2005] 2 Cr App R (S) 39

3–306

OTHER OFFENCES

Imprisonment for *harassment of a tenant* contrary to s 1 of the Protection from Eviction Act 1977 has been approved in principle[1]; as has imprisonment for having *obscene articles for publication for gain*

(28 days for participation in an offence of a minor and transient nature[2]); 12 months plus a fine of £5,000 for a second offence committed by a defendant concerned with a cinema club[3].

Persons engaged in *commercial exploitation of pornography*, on conviction of an offence under s 2(1) of the Obscene Publications Act 1959, should be sentenced to imprisonment. First offenders need only receive comparatively short sentences, but the full rigour of the law should come down on those who continued to offend. In addition the court should consider taking the profit out of such illegal trade by imposing substantial fines[4].

The importation of obscene videos as part of a commercial operation may justify a custodial sentence of significant length[5].

Possession of racially inflammatory material is viewed seriously because of the grave social damage done by offences and remarks of a racist nature. A sentence of 12 months' imprisonment for such an offence is not to be regarded as excessive[6].

For offences involving *false passports* sentencing levels must reflect the higher maximum penalties under ss 3 and 5(1) of the Forgery and Counterfeiting Act 1981 (using a false instrument/having a false instrument with intent that it shall be used), which is 10 years' imprisonment compared to 2 years' imprisonment for having a false instrument contrary to s 5(2), and increased public concern as a result of recent acts of international terrorism; where one false passport is being used or is being held with the intention of use, the appropriate sentence, even on a person of good character who pleads guilty, is 12–18 months' imprisonment[7].

The offence of *entering the UK without a passport*, contrary to s 2 of the Asylum and Immigration (Treatment of Claimants) Act 2004, has as its purpose the need to discourage people from destroying evidence of their identity, age or nationality in order to increase their chances of remaining in the UK; it was not intended to penalise those who never had an immigration document or those who used a forged passport to travel to the UK and who produced the document on arrival. Consequently, no assistance is to be found in the line of authority dealing with the use of false passports when asylum was not an issue. However, in normal circumstances a custodial sentence is inevitable, since such offences have the potential to undermine immigration control, they are prevalent and sentences need to have a deterrent effect[8].

Offences under s 24A of the Immigration Act 1971 (use of deception to obtain or to seek to leave to enter or to remain in the UK) are to an extent analogous with false passport offences and the tariff for the latter provides a helpful sentencing guide[9]. When dealing with an offence of *obtaining entry by deception*, it is not appropriate for the court routinely to assess the genuineness or strength of any claim to asylum[10].

Facilitating the illegal entry of an immigrant as part of a professional enterprise justifies a substantial prison sentence[11].

Passing a *forged banknote* is a serious offence which in the normal way demands a sentence of immediate imprisonment. For passing 3 counterfeit £50 notes in shops and possessing further counterfeit notes with intent to pass them as genuine, a sentence of 9 months' immediate imprisonment was upheld[12]; for 3 offences of passing £50 counterfeit notes and 32 similar offences to be taken into consideration, a sentence of 3 years' imprisonment was upheld[13]; for having custody of counterfeit currency (value about £3,000) and passing a counterfeit £20 note, a sentence of 2 years' imprisonment was upheld[14]; for possessing forged notes where there was no evidence of any intention to pass the notes as genuine, a sentence of 9 months' imprisonment was reduced to 4 months[15].

Offences of *counterfeiting* also usually attract at least a short sentence of imprisonment because they are difficult, time consuming and expensive to detect. The owners of copyright are entitled to be protected against their unlawful exploitation. They are entitled to have their commercial reputation protected against those who would seek unlawfully to damage it[16].

Sentences of immediate imprisonment of three months were upheld on persons, found to be in possession of 3 salmon and other fish, who were convicted of *unlawful fishing* for salmon and trout for commercial purposes; in such cases it is appropriate for the court to have regard to the incidence of unlicensed fishing in the area and experience of the state of the stock of fish in the area[17].

Offences of *making false statements as to the nature of services provided*, involving repairs to domestic appliances, contrary to s 20(1) of the Trade Descriptions Act 1968, are easy to commit and difficult to detect. It is important that dishonest tradesmen should be actively and sharply discouraged from taking advantage of the public who cannot check the work for themselves. A sentence of 3 months' imprisonment for 4 offences contrary to s 20(1) of the 1968 Act imposed on the director of a small company which was concerned with repairing washing machines was upheld[18]. The offence of "clocking" second-hand motor cars under the Trade Descriptions Act 1968, s 1(1)(*a*), is all too prevalent and it is one of which dishonest dealers make a great deal of money. Dishonest second-hand car dealers who "clock" vehicles should expect an immediate loss of liberty plus a substantial fine. Twelve months' imprisonment for "clocking" used cars, and related offences, varied by suspending 6 months of the sentence in view of the defendant's previous good character and plea of guilty[19]. Where, however, defendants are sentenced on the basis that they had not clocked the cars or connived at their clocking or had even turned a blind eye to clocking, but merely on the basis that they had failed to take the steps they should have taken to discover that the cars had been clocked by others, custody is wrong in principle[20].

Where a second-hand car dealer advertises and *sells a car with a false description* contrary to s 1(1)(*b*) of Trade Descriptions Act 1968 the offence is so serious that the imposition of a custodial sentence is required[21].

Making numerous false tachograph entries over a considerable period for a financial motive requires a sentence of significant length[22].

The owners of *trade marks* have a commercial asset which is entitled to legal protection. Deliberately suing someone else's trade mark is, in effect, stealing their commercial goodwill[23]. Where counterfeit pottery was manufactured for a period of 10 months and enabled the defendant to make a profit of £4,000 the sentence had to contain some element of deterrence[24]. Where, however, a defendant applied a false trade description by forging signatures on "celebrity" photographs that he sold from a stall at an exhibition centre, but only 27 photographs out of a stock of 1,000 examined by trading standards officers contained such forgeries, the defendant pleaded guilty and there was strong personal mitigation, the custody threshold was not crossed[25].

Imprisonment may be justified for an offence of *claiming to have contaminated goods* with intent to cause economic loss, contrary to the Public Order Act 1986, s 38(2), even though there was no disruption of trade, and there was no publicity[26].

Sentences for *fraud on the public purse* by dishonestly obtaining welfare benefits depend in the first instance on the scope of the fraud. A large scale carefully organised fraud involving considerable sums may merit an immediate sentence of two years imprisonment or more. Other considerations may be (i) a guilty plea, (ii) the amount involved and the length of time over which the defalcations persisted (bearing in mind that a large total may represent a very small amount weekly), (iii) the circumstances in which the offence began (eg there is a plain difference between a legitimate claim which becomes false owing to a change of situation and a claim which is false from the beginning), (iv) the use to which the money is put (the provision of household necessities is more excusable than spending the money on unnecessary luxury), (v) previous character, (vi) matters special to the offender, such as illness, disability, family difficulties, etc, (vii) any voluntary repayment. The court should ask itself, (*a*) is a custodial sentence really necessary? (*b*) if it is, can it make a community service order instead or suspend the whole sentence? (*c*) if not, what is the shortest sentence it can properly impose[27]?

Imprisonment will be justified for an offence of *communicating false information relating to a bomb* (Criminal Law Act 1977, s 51—bomb hoaxes) by making a telephone call to the emergency services stating that a bomb had been placed outside a Wimpy bar[28]. Telephone calls making *threats to kill* may also be treated seriously[29].

Intimidating a witness contrary to the Criminal Justice and Public Order Act 1994, s 51(2) must be viewed extremely seriously[30].

Possession of an offensive weapon, where the weapon has not been used and the person in possession has some ground to fear for his personal safety, may result in a custodial sentence[31].

Child abduction, where a parent takes a child away from the other parent in breach of a residence order, is always a serious matter. The offence, however, becomes much more serious if the child is taken out of the country[32].

Offences involving aircraft: Recklessly or negligently acting in a manner likely to endanger an aircraft or any person therein to such an extent that a defendant's violent behaviour caused distress and terror to other passengers and fear on the part of the air crew was held to merit a term of imprisonment near to the maximum sentence for the offence after giving credit for the defendant's plea and previous good character[33]. In the case of affray on board an aircraft an immediate custodial sentence is appropriate even though a non-custodial sentence might have met the gravity of the case if the offence had been committed in a public place on the ground[34]. It has been held that misconduct resulting from drunkenness by a passenger merits a custodial sentence even though no danger was involved[35]. However, in a case where the serious misconduct only started once the aircraft was on the ground it was held that a custodial sentence was not justified[36]. Passengers on an aircraft who assault members of the cabin crew can expect the sentence to be severe[37]. A personal flying log book is a record of critical importance and making false entries in such a record will merit a custodial sentence[38]. Custody is not wrong in principle for an offence having an article resembling a firearm at an aerodrome, even where the offence was a "criminal oversight"[39].

The offence of *facilitating the illegal entry of immigrants* into the United Kingdom contrary to s 25(1)(a) of the Immigration Act 1971 invariably attracts an immediate custodial sentence the severity of which is reflected by the presence or otherwise of a number of aggravating features which have been identified by the Court of Appeal[40]. Imprisonment is appropriate even where the defendant acted for humanitarian rather than commercial motives[41].

"*Escape from lawful custody* is always a serious offence. It is quite essential for the courts to mark out the seriousness of escapes from custody of this kind, whether in the magistrates' court or in the Crown Court, by immediate sentences of imprisonment. It is not only intended as a punishment. It is also intended to be a clear deterrent to others contemplating escapes from custody."[42] In the light of this guidance the court does not discriminate nicely between particular cases of escape from custody, particularly when they are escapes in the face of a court[43].

Money laundering is a serious matter and breaches of the legislation by professional people cannot be overlooked; custody (6 months) was, therefore, appropriate where a solicitor received £70,000 from a client later convicted of drug trafficking and failed to report his suspicions that the money came from that source[44].

The offence of *aggravated keeping of dogs dangerously out of control* requires courts to look at the consequences of the offence when determining the appropriate penalty, and it is entirely appropriate to pass a custodial sentence for such an offence[45].

Computer misuse by deliberately spreading 3 different viruses through e-mails, where the first was detected in 42 different countries and had stopped computer systems 2,700 times, and the second and third operated as "worms" and had affected the material on between 200 and 300 computers, justified a term of 2 years' imprisonment[46].

Criminal damage by spraying graffiti on to underground trains calls for a deterrent sentence[47].

---

1. *R v Spratt, Wood and Smylie* [1978] Crim LR 102.

2. *R v Sharman* [1981] Crim LR 347.

3. *R v Calleja* (1985) 7 Cr App Rep (S) 13, [1985] Crim LR 396.

4. *R v Holloway* (1982) 126 Sol Jo 359, 4 Cr App Rep (S) 128; followed in *R v Decozar* (1984) 6 Cr App Rep (S) 266. See also *R v Doorgashurn* (1988) 10 Cr App Rep (S) 195 (6 months' imprisonment for proprietor of small corner shop possessing obscene books and videotapes as part of general trade); *R v Knight* (1990) 12 Cr App Rep (S) 319 (6 months' imprisonment plus fine of £2,000 for offender who ran a secondhand book and video shop—pleaded guilty to 17 counts of possessing obscene articles for publication for gain, including videos depicting various sexual acts); *R v Holt* (1994) 16 Cr App Rep (S) 510 (2 months' imprisonment varied to fines totalling £500 where a schoolteacher imported by a post a number of magazines containing pictures of naked children); *R v Ibrahim* [1998] 1 Cr App Rep (S) 157 (total of 18 months' imprisonment upheld on offender who as a salesman working in a shop selling obscene video tapes pleaded guilty to 13 counts of having obscene articles for publication for gain; the fact that the offender persisted with the offences after an earlier warning by the police was held to be a seriously aggravating feature of the offences and a longer sentence was appropriate for the later offences).

5. *R v Hirst* [2001] 1 Cr App Rep (S) 152 (12 months upheld).

6. *R v Gray* [1999] 1 Cr App Rep (S) 50 (12 months' imprisonment upheld for defendant who was found to be in possession of a quantity of magazines which contained racist material and who was found to have been concerned in the distribution of the magazines); *R v Muca* (2001) 165 JPN 295 (12 months' imprisonment reduced to 8 in respect of an unsuccessful asylum seeker who attempted to leave the UK on a false Italian identity card).

7. *R v Kolawole* [2004] EWCA Crim 3047, [2005] Cr App R (S) 14. See also *R v Oliveira* [2005] EWCA Crim 3187, [2006] 2 Cr App R (S) 17 (15 months reduced 8 months on a guilty plea by offender of good character).

8. *R v Wang* [2005] EWCA Crim 293, [2005] 2 Cr App R (S) 79 (sentenced reduced from 10 months to 2 months' detention for 18 year-old who pleaded guilty and did not fall to be sentenced on the basis that she had destroyed her immigration documents). See also *R v Safari and Zanganeh* [2005] EWCA Crim 830, [2006] 1 Cr App R (S) 1 (sentence reduced from 9 to 3 months: the judge should not have sentenced the appellants on the basis that they had given their passports to their agent to conceal their identities and travel movements without a "Newton hearing"). In *R v Ai* [2005] EWCA Crim 936, [2006] 1 Cr App R (S) *Wang* was held not to be comparable where the appellant had left his country of origin (China) on his own passport, had lived in Russia for a year and then used a false passport and embarked on two further aeroplane journeys before arriving in the UK, he had returned the false passport to his agent, he was significantly older than Wang and would have been better placed to retain his documents: sentenced reduced to 5 months' imprisonment). It is not, however, for the criminal courts to determine whether or not the defendant is a genuine asylum seeker or an economic migrant, and a person should not be sentenced on the latter basis but simply for destruction of the documentation: *R v Da Hua Weng and Guo Xing Wang* [2005] EWCA Crim 2248, [2006] 1 Cr App R (S) 582.

9. *R v Nasir Ali* [2001] EWCA Crim 2874, [2002] 2 Cr App Rep (S) 115 (18 months' imprisonment reduced to 12 where asylum was sought using a false name, date of birth and nationality).

10. *R v Kishientine* [2004] EWCA Crim 3352, [2005] 2 Cr App R (S) 28 (9 months' imprisonment upheld where entry was gained by means of a false passport, correct details were given in an asylum claim made 2½ months later, but the appellant said she had arrived in the UK the previous day and had not been fingerprinted).

11. *R v Sackey* [2004] EWCA Crim 566, [2004] 2 Cr App R (S) 85 (2 years' imprisonment upheld on a guilty plea).

12. *R v Horrigan* (1985) 7 Cr App Rep (S) 112, [1985] Crim LR 604. See also *R v Pickard* (1985) 7 Cr App Rep (S) 279 (tendering and attempting to tender a counterfeit £20 note by a person who was not a prime mover in putting counterfeit notes into circulation: 9 months' imprisonment—6 months to serve, balance in suspense).

13. *R v Huntingdon* (1985) 7 Cr App Rep (S) 168.

14. *R v Howard* (1985) 82 Cr App Rep (S) 262, CA. See also *R v Dickens* (1992) 14 Cr App Rep (S) 76.

15. *R v Luxford* [1996] 1 Cr App Rep (S) 186.

16. *R v Lloyd* [1997] 2 Cr App Rep (S) 151 (12 months' imprisonment reduced to 6 months where a man of previous good character was convicted of making counterfeit copies of computer programmes). See also *R v Passley* [2003] EWCA Crim 2727, [2004] 1 Cr App R (S) 70 (21 months' imprisonment reduced to 12 where the appellant had antiquated and unsophisticated equipment for copying DVDs, etc, his turnover in the previous 2 years was £27,000, he was of positive good character and he pleaded guilty at the first opportunity).

17. *R v Jacobs and Gillespie* (1985) 7 Cr App Rep (S) 42.

18. *R v Burridge* (1985) 7 Cr App Rep (S) 125.

19. *R v Gupta* (1985) 7 Cr App Rep (S) 172, CA. See also *R v Canning* (1993) 15 Cr App Rep (S) 371 (6 months' imprisonment, plus compensation order for £990, for defendants who were dealers in used motor vehicles, for three counts of applying a false trade description and one of supplying goods to which a false trade description had been applied—each vehicle having been "clocked" from 20,000 to in excess of 50,000 miles).

20. *R v Richards, R v Evans* [2004] EWCA Crim 192, [2004] 2 Cr App R (S) 51.

21. *R v Gold* (1994) 16 Cr App Rep (S) 442 (9 months' imprisonment reduced to 4 months where a second-hand car dealer advertised and sold a car with serious defects which made it unroadworthy).

22. *R v Saunders, R v Hockings, R v Williams* [2001] EWCA Crim 93, [2001] 2 Cr App Rep (S) 301, (8 months' imprisonment upheld for numerous offences (respectively, 11, 10 and 6) of making false tachograph entries despite guilty pleas, the good character of 2 of the defendants and the adverse effect of custody upon them and their families).

23. *R v Bhad* [1999] 2 Cr App Rep (S) 139 (sentences of 4 months' imprisonment for possessing an article to which a trade mark had been applied without the consent of the prosecutor quashed).

24. *R v Bore* [2004] EWCA Crim 1452, (2005) 169 JP 245.

25. *R v Woolridge* [2005] EWCA Crim 1086, [2006] 1 Cr App R (S) 13 (9 months' imprisonment upheld following a guilty plea)

26. *R v Smith* (1993) 15 Cr App Rep (S) 106 (18 months' imprisonment for defendant who told a journalist that animal activists had contaminated bathroom products in a warehouse and that the goods would shortly go on sale).

27. *R v Stewart* [1987] 2 All ER 383, [1987] 1 WLR 559, CA. See also *R v Bolarin* (1990) 12 Cr App Rep (S) 543 (15 months' imprisonment for obtaining a total of £18,500 in income support and unemployment benefit over a period of 27 months by deception); *R v Tucker* (1993) 15 Cr App Rep (S) 349 (6 months' imprisonment upheld for benefit frauds involving £8,500 committed by a woman who began claiming lawfully but continued after her entitlement ceased); *R v Oyediran* [1997] 2 Cr App Rep (S) 277 (18 months' imprisonment upheld for obtaining over a period of 3 years a total of £18,000 from the DSS by false representations) and *R v Ellison* [1998] 2 Cr App Rep (S) 382 (10 months' imprisonment for 5 counts of obtaining about £11,000 in benefit by deception over a period of 4 years and 88 other offences taken into consideration).

In *R v Graham* [2004] EWCA Crim 2755, [2005] 1 Cr App (S) 115, [2005] Crim LR 247, the Court of Appeal considered the effect of inflation since the decision in *Stewart, supra,* and held that where imprisonment was necessary, short terms of up to about 9 to 12 months would usually be sufficient in contested cases where the overpayment was less than £20,000 (replacing the *Stewart* figure of £10,000).

28. *R v Rung-Ruangap* (1993) 15 Cr App Rep (S) 326 (12 months' imprisonment upheld notwithstanding that the defendant had suffered from psychiatric illness in the past and continued to suffer from stress and depression); *R v Harrison* [1997] 2 Cr App Rep (S) 174 (4 years' imprisonment upheld for making telephone calls giving false information relating to a bomb supposedly planted near a theatre by a man with previous convictions for similar offences); *R v Cann* [2004] EWCA Crim 1075, [2005] 1 Cr App R (S) (guilty plea to 3 offences of communicating a bomb hoax committed by man of previous good character: sentence reduced from 30 months to 21 months' imprisonment).

29. *R v Serzin* (1994) 16 Cr App Rep (S) 4 (3½ years' imprisonment upheld where a man of previous good character made telephone calls threatening to kill two police officers); *R v Parker* (1994) 16 Cr App Rep (S) 525 (3 years' imprisonment upheld for making threats by telephone to kill a former partner); *R v Walker* [1996] 1 Cr App Rep (S) 180 (4 years' imprisonment upheld for making threats to kill by telephone to two female former colleagues); *R v Winnington* [1996] 1 Cr App Rep (S) 210 (3 years' imprisonment reduced to 18 months for making a verbal threat after unsuccessful family proceedings for contact with a child).

30. *R v Williams* (1997) 2 Cr App Rep (S) 221 (2 years' imprisonment upheld for sending a threatening letter to a person who had given evidence). See also *R v Andrew John Chinery* [2002] EWCA Crim 32, [2002] 2 Cr App Rep (S) 244 (3 months' imprisonment plus 3 months consecutive upheld where the defendant, who was 43 and of good character, intimidated 2 different persons on different occasions who were witnesses to an alleged assault by the defendant's partner). See also *R v Atkin* [2002] EWCA Crim 3195, [2003] 2 Cr App R (S) (sentenced reduced to 15 months where a single mother with 4 children who was of previous good character carried out a vicious assault on the victim of a rape allegedly committed by her (the appellant's) brother); and *R v Lawrence* [2004] EWCA Crim 2219, [2005] 1 Cr App R (S) 83 (16 months varied to 8 months where the defendant threatened to kill his father in revenge after the latter had reported him to the police for stealing).

31. *R v Hopkins* [1996] 1 Cr App Rep (S) 18 (6 months' imprisonment reduced to 3 months for a taxi driver who carried a lemon juice bottle containing hydrochloric acid solution); *R v Buzzer* (1996) 2 Cr App Rep (S) 271 (6 months' imprisonment reduced to 3 months for possession of a flick knife by a man of previous good character); *R v Proctor* [2000] 1 Cr App Rep (S) 295 (9 months' imprisonment upheld for possessing a bottle containing a solution of ammonia for use as a weapon).

32. *R v Taylor* (1996) 1 Cr App Rep (S) 329 (4 months' imprisonment upheld for the abduction of a child by her mother, in breach of a residence order, where the child was taken out of the country).

33. *R v Mullaly* [1997] 2 Cr App Rep (S) 343 (sentences totalling 2 years' imprisonment for recklessly or negligently acting in a manner likely to endanger an aircraft or any person therein, and being drunk on an aircraft reduced to 18 months to give credit for the guilty plea and defendant's previous good conduct.

34. *R v Oliver* [1999] 1 Cr App Rep (S) 394 (sentence of 18 months reduced to 12 months: defendant lost his temper, became abusive towards cabin crew, struck his wife, used obscenities and had to be restrained by crew and returned to seat). See also *R v David James McCallum* [2001] EWCA Crim 2352, [2002] 1 Cr App Rep (S) 488 (12 months' imprisonment, following a guilty plea, upheld for an affray on an aircraft that involved the defendant fighting with and shouting threats at his female cousin and threatening to open the door of the plane).

35. *R v Hunter* (1998) Times, 26 February (sentence of 18 months reduced to 6 months for misconduct resulting from drunkenness which lasted for 3½ hours, although no danger to aircraft involved); *R v Abdulkarim* [2000] 2 Cr App Rep (S) 16 (9 months' imprisonment for being drunk on an international flight and refusing to refrain from smoking reduced to 6 months). See also *R v Ayodeji* [2001] 1 Cr App Rep (S) 370, (2000) Times, 20 October (8 months upheld where the defendant was drunk, urinated on the floor, persistently smoked on board when smoking was forbidden and was abusive on several occasions to a flight attendant).

36. *R v Cooper* [2003] EWCA Crim 3277, [2004] 2 Cr App R (S) 16.

37. *R v Beer* [1998] 2 Cr App Rep (S) 248.

38. *R v Grzybowski* [1998] 1 Cr App Rep (S) 4 (6 months' imprisonment upheld on a flying instructor who made false entries in the personal flying log of a pupil who was subsequently killed in an accident while flying).

39. *R v Burrows* [2004] EWCA Crim 677, [2004] 2 Cr App R (S) 89 (defendant had forgotten he had a ball bearing gun in his hand luggage – 4 months' imprisonment reduced to 28 days). See also *R v Charles* [2004] EWCA Crim 1977, [2005] 1 Cr App R (S) 56 in which the court upheld a sentence of 2 months' imprisonment, despite considerable mitigation, where the defendant had unintentionally included within his luggage a cosh, CS gas canister and lock knife.

40. *R v Van Binh Le and Stark* [1999] 1 Cr App Rep (S) 422. See also *R v Liddle* [2000] 2 Cr App Rep (S) 282 (4 years' imprisonment imposed on each of three men who were involved in arranging for 20 illegal immigrants to be brought into the UK concealed in a lorry reduced to 3 years).

41. *R v Angel* [1998] 1 Cr App Rep (S) 347 (15 months' imprisonment upheld on a man of previous good character who facilitated the illegal entry of a Sir Lankan citizen for humanitarian reasons; *R v Ahmetaj* [2000] 1 Cr App Rep (S) 66 (2 years' imprisonment for facilitating illegal entry by two men otherwise than for financial gain reduced to 18 months); *R v Toor & R v Toor* [2003] EWCA Crim 185, [2003] 2 Cr App R (S) 57 (2½ years upheld where 2 brothers attempted to facilitate the illegal entry of a further brother by providing a false passport).

42. *R v Sutcliffe* (1992) 13 Cr App Rep (S) 538, per Brooke LJ (six months' custody where there was an attempt to evade a police officer who was injured).

43. *R v Rumble* [2003] EWCA Crim 770, 167 JP 205 (six months' custody upheld where no security officers present and a great deal of unpleasant and aggressive abuse had been given to the chairman of the bench in the presence of the court clerk).

44. *R v Duff* [2002] EWCA Crim 2117, [2003] 1 Cr App R (S) 88.

45. *R v Cox* [2004] EWCA Crim 282, [2004] 2 Cr App R (S) 54 (9 months' imprisonment reduced to 3; 10 years' disqualification upheld).

46. *R v Vallor* [2003] EWCA Crim 2288, [2004] 1 Cr App R (S) 54.

47. *R v Verdi* [2004] EWCA Crim 1485, [2005] 1 Cr App R (S) 43 (2 years detention and a 10–year ABSO reduced to 18 months' detention (ASBO unchanged) for 9 offences of criminal damage to which the 18-year-old defendant pleaded guilty).

BREACH OF ANTI-SOCIAL BEHAVIOUR ORDERS

3–307   Breach of an ASBO, within days of completing a prison sentence following an earlier breach, justifies a substantial custodial term[1].

Breach of an ABSO made the previous day in respect of an offender with an appalling record of offences also justifies a custodial sentence[2].

Where the breach consists of conduct which itself constitutes a criminal offence the court is not restricted by the maximum punishment prescribed for that offence, though it is a factor to be borne in mind[3].

Where breaches do not involve harassment, alarm or distress, community penalties should be considered to help the offender learn to live within the terms of the ASBO to which he or is subject;

in those cases when there is no available community penalty (for example, because of the offender's unwillingness to co-operate), custodial sentences which are necessary to maintain the authority of the court should be kept as short as possible[4].

1. *R v Thomas* [2004] EWCA Crim 1173, [2005] 1 Cr App R (S) (order made in June 2003 prohibiting the defendant, who had previously been convicted of 451 offences including 263 for theft, from entering 4 stores in a particular town, breached within weeks for which the defendant received 5 months' imprisonment, then breached again 8 days after his release from that sentence: 18 months' imprisonment upheld). See also *R v Braxton* [2004] EWCA Crim 1374, [2005] 1 Cr App R (S) 36 (3½ years upheld for a breach committed by a young man with an appalling record of violence and public order offences who was "a menace . . . and a serious danger to the public").

2. *R v Dickinson* [2005] EWCA Crim 289, [2005] Cr App R (S) 78 (though the term was reduced from 18 to 8 months since the offender had not served a sentence of such length previously, it was his first breach and the breach was relatively minor). See also *R v Anthony* [2005] EWCA Crim 2055, [2006] 1 Cr App R (S) 74; and *R v Caiger* [2005] EWCA Crim 3114, [2006] 1 Cr App R (S) 7.

3. See *R v Tripp* [2005] EWCA Crim 2253, [2005] All ER (D) 71 (Aug) (12 months reduced to 8 for drunken disorderly behaviour committed shortly after community penalties had been imposed); followed in *R v L* [2005] EWCA Crim 2487 (22 months for 3 breaches reduced to 6: there was a history of offending and breaches, but none of the breaches resulted from anti-social behaviour as such) and *R v Stevens* [2006] EWCA Crim 255, [2006] 2 Cr App R (S) 68 (though the breach was conduct amounting to a non-imprisonable offence, after sentence was deferred the appellant again breached the order in a similar way: 8 months' imprisonment upheld). (Cf *R v Morrisson* [2005] EWCA Crim 2237.) See further *R v Bulmer* [2005] EWCA Crim 3516, [2006] 2 Cr App R (S) (21 months imposed on a severely chronic alcoholic of low intelligence reduced to 12 months on the ground of proportionality).

4. *R v L*, supra. See further *R v Lamb* [2005] EWCA Crim 3000, [2006] 2 Cr App R (S) 11 (persistent breaches of ABSO consisting of no more than using the Metro system in Newcastle, where no community penalty was available, merited no more than a short custodial sentence, and 22 months' imprisonment was reduced to 2 months).

BREACH OF PROTECTIVE ORDERS

3–308 *Restraining orders made for harassment offences*[1]. Factors relevant to the length of sentence include: the nature of the act giving rise to the breach; the use of actual violence and the threat of serious violence, which are aggravating features; the effect on the victim; whether or not this was a first breach; the offender's record and his response to previous community penalties; and the need to protect the person named in the order[2].

For a first offence, a short sentence may be appropriate; for a second offence a sentence of 15 months on a plea of guilty is appropriate[3]. A relevant consideration is whether the offence is a s 2 or s 4 offence[3]. However, even if it is the former, persistent breaches with associated criminal damage and a continuing high level of risk, merits a sentence in excess of 15 months[4].

The Sentencing Guidelines Council has published the following definitive guidelines for breach of restraining orders and non-molestation orders.

'A Statutory Provisions

1.1 For the purposes of this guideline, two protective orders are considered:

a(i) Restraining Order

1.2 It is an offence contrary to the Protection from Harassment Act 1997 to behave in a way which a person knows (or ought to know) causes someone else harassment (section 2) or fear of violence (section 4). When imposing sentence on an offender, a court may also impose a restraining order to prevent future conduct causing harassment or fear of violence.

1.3 An offence under these provisions may have occurred in a domestic context or may have occurred in other contexts. The Domestic Violence, Crime and Victims Act 2004 provides for such orders also to be made on conviction for any offence or following acquittal (when in force, s 12 of the 2004 Act amends s 5 of the 1997 Act and inserts a new s 5A to that Act).

1.4 It is an offence contrary to section 5(5) of the Act to fail to comply with the restraining order without reasonable excuse. That offence is punishable with a maximum of five years imprisonment.

(ii) Non-Molestation Order

1.5 Section 42 of the Family Law Act 1996 provides that, during family proceedings, a court may make a non-molestation order containing either or both of the following provisions:

(a) provision prohibiting a person ("the respondent") from molesting another person who is associated with the respondent;
(b) provision prohibiting the respondent from molesting a relevant child.

1.6 Section 1 of the Domestic Violence, Crime and Victims Act 2004 (when in force) inserts a new section 42A into the 1996 Act. Section 42A (1) will provide that it is an offence to fail to comply with the order without reasonable excuse. That offence is punishable with a maximum of five years imprisonment.

1.7 In addition, breach of a non-molestation order may be dealt with as a contempt of court.

B Sentencing for Breach

2.1 The facts that constitute a breach of a protective order may or may not also constitute a substantive offence. Where they do constitute a substantive offence, it is desirable that the substantive offence and the breach of the order should be charged as separate counts. Where necessary, consecutive sentences should be considered to reflect the seriousness of the counts and achieve the appropriate totality.

2.2 Sometimes, however, only the substantive offence or only the breach of the order will be charged. The basic principle is that the sentence should reflect all relevant aspects of the offence so that, provided the facts are not in issue, the result should be the same, regardless of whether one count or two has been charged. For example:

(i)   if the substantive offence only has been charged, the fact that it constitutes breach of a protective order should be treated as an aggravating factor;

(ii) if breach of the protective order only has been charged, the sentence should reflect the nature of the breach, namely, the conduct that amounts to the substantive offence, aggravated by the fact that it is also breach of an order.

2.3 If breach of a protective order has been charged where no substantive offence was involved, the sentence should reflect the circumstances of the breach, including whether it was an isolated breach, or part of a course of conduct in breach of the order; whether it was planned or unpremeditated; and any consequences of the breach, including psychiatric injury or distress to the person protected by the order.

C Factors Influencing Sentencing

3.1 In order to ensure that a protective order achieves the purpose it is intended for – protecting the victim from harm – it is important that the terms of the order are necessary and proportionate.

3.2 The circumstances leading to the making of one of the protective orders will vary widely. Whilst a restraining order will be made in criminal proceedings, it will almost certainly result from offences of markedly different levels of seriousness or even acquittal. A non molestation order will have been made in civil proceedings and, again, may follow a wide variety of conduct by the subject of the order.

3.3 **In all cases the order will have been made to protect an individual from harm and action in response to breach should have as its primary aim the importance of ensuring that the order is complied with and that it achieves the protection that it was intended to achieve.**

3.4 **When sentencing for a breach of an order, the main aim should be to achieve future compliance with that order where that is realist**ic.

The nature and context of the originating conduct or offence

3.5 The nature of the original conduct or offence is relevant in so far as it allows a judgement to be made on the level of harm caused to the victim by the breach and the extent to which that harm was intended by the offender.

3.6 If the original offence was serious, conduct which breaches the order might have a severe effect on the victim where in other contexts such conduct might appear minor. Even indirect contact, such as telephone calls, can cause significant harm or anxiety for a victim.

3.7 However, sentence following a breach is for the breach alone and must avoid punishing the offender again for the offence or conduct as a result of which the order was made.

The nature and context of the conduct that caused the breach

3.8 **The protective orders are designed to protect a victim. When dealing with a breach, a court will need to consider the extent to which the conduct amounting to breach put the victim at risk of harm.**

3.9 There may be exceptional cases where the nature of the breach is particularly serious but has not been dealt with by a separate offence being charged. In these cases, the risk posed by the offender and the nature of the breach will be particularly significant in determining the response. Where the order is breached by the use of physical violence, the starting point should normally be a custodial sentence.

3.10 Non-violent behaviour and/or indirect contact can also cause (or be intended to cause) a high degree of harm and anxiety. In such circumstances, it is likely that the custody threshold will have been crossed.

3.11 Where an order was made in civil proceedings, its purpose may have been to cause the subject of the order to modify behaviour rather than to imply that the conduct was especially serious. If so, it is likely to be disproportionate to impose a custodial sentence for a breach of the order if the breach did not involve threats or violence.

3.12 In some cases where a breach might result in a short custodial sentence but the court is satisfied that the offender genuinely intends to reform his or her behaviour and there is a real prospect of rehabilitation, the court may consider it appropriate to impose a sentence that will allow this. This may mean imposing a suspended sentence order or a community order (where appropriate with a requirement to attend an accredited domestic violence programme).

3.13 **Breach of a protective order will generally be more serious than breach of a conditional discharge.** Not only is a breach of a protective order an offence in its own right but it also undermines a specific prohibition imposed by the court. Breach of a conditional discharge amounts to an offender failing to take a chance that has been provided by the court.

D Aggravating and Mitigating Factors

4.1 Many of the aggravating factors which apply to an offence of violence in a domestic context will apply also to an offence arising from breach of a protective order.

Aggravating Factors

(i) Victim is particularly vulnerable

4.2 For cultural, religious, language, financial or any other reasons, some victims may be more vulnerable than others. This vulnerability means that the terms of a protective order are particularly important and a violation of those terms will warrant a higher penalty than usual.

4.3 Age, disability or the fact that the victim was pregnant or had recently given birth at the time of the offence may make a victim particularly vulnerable.

4.4 Any steps taken to prevent the victim reporting an incident or obtaining assistance will usually aggravate the offence.

(ii) Impact on children

4.5 If a protective order is imposed in order to protect children, either solely or in addition to another victim, then a breach of that order will generally be more serious (the definition of "harm" in s.31(9) of the Children Act 1989 as amended by s.120 of the Adoption and Children Act 2002 includes "impairment suffered from seeing or hearing the ill-treatment of another").

(iii) A proven history of violence or threats by the offender

4.6 Of necessity, a breach of a protective order will not be the first time an offender has caused fear or harassment towards a victim. However, the offence will be more serious if the breach is part of a series of prolonged violence or harassment towards the victim or the offender has a history of disobedience to court orders.

4.7 Where an offender has previously been convicted of an offence involving domestic violence, either against the same or a different person, or has been convicted for a breach of an order, this is likely to be a statutory aggravating factor (Criminal Justice Act 2003, s.143(2)).

(iv) Using contact arrangements with a child to instigate an offence

4.8 An offence will be aggravated where an offender exploits contact arrangements with a child in order to commit an offence.

(v) Victim is forced to leave home

4.9 A breach will be aggravated if, as a consequence, the victim is forced to leave home.

(vi) Additional aggravating factors

4.10 In addition to the factors listed above, the following will aggravate a breach of an order:
• the offence is a further breach, following earlier breach proceedings;
• the breach was committed immediately or shortly after the order was made.

Mitigating Factors

(i) Breach was committed after a long period of compliance

4.11 If the court is satisfied that the offender has complied with a protective order for a substantial period before a breach is committed, the court should take this into account when imposing sentence for the breach. The history of the relationship and the specific nature of the contact will be relevant in determining its significance as a mitigating factor.

(ii) Victim initiated contact

4.12 If the conditions of an order are breached following contact from the victim, this should be considered as mitigation. It is important to consider the history of the relationship and the specific nature of the contact in determining its significance as a mitigating factor.

4.13 Nonetheless it is important for the court to make clear that it is the responsibility of the offender and not the victim to ensure that the order is complied with.

E. Factors to take into Consideration

Aims of sentencing

(a) When sentencing for a breach of a protective order (which would have been imposed to protect a victim from further harm), the main aim should be to achieve future compliance with that order.

(b) A court will need to assess the level of risk posed by the offender. If the offender requires treatment or assistance for mental health or other issues, willingness to undergo treatment or accept help may influence sentence.

1. Key Factors

(a) The nature of the conduct that caused the breach of the order, in particular, whether the contact was direct or indirect, although it is important to recognise that indirect contact is capable of causing significant harm or anxiety.

(b) **There may be exceptional cases where the nature of the breach is particularly serious but has not been dealt with by a separate offence being charged. In these cases the risk posed by the offender and the nature of the breach will be particularly significant in determining the response**.

(c) The nature of the original conduct or offence is relevant to sentencing for the breach in so far as it allows a judgement to be made on the level of harm caused to the victim by the breach, and the extent to which that harm was intended by the offender.

(d) The sentence following a breach is for the breach alone and must avoid punishing the offender again for the offence or conduct as a result of which the order was made.

(e) Where violence is used to breach a restraining order or a molestation order, custody is the starting point for sentence.

(f) Non-violent conduct in breach may cross the custody threshold where a high degree of harm or anxiety has been caused to the victim.

(g) Where an order was made in civil proceedings, its purpose may have been to cause the subject of the order to modify behaviour rather than to imply that the conduct was especially serious. If so, it is likely to be disproportionate to impose a custodial sentence for a breach of the order if the breach did not involve threats or violence.

(h) In some cases where a breach might result in a short custodial sentence but the court is satisfied that the offender genuinely intends to reform his or her behaviour and there is a real prospect of rehabilitation, the court may consider it appropriate to impose a sentence that will allow this. This may mean imposing a suspended sentence order or a community order (where appropriate with a requirement to attend an accredited domestic violence programme).

(i) While, in principle, consecutive sentences may be imposed for each breach of which the offender is convicted, the overall sentence should reflect the totality principle.

2. General

(a) Breach of a protective order should be considered more serious than a breach of a conditional discharge.

(b) The principle of reduction in sentence for a guilty plea should be applied as set out in the Council guideline Reduction in Sentence for a Guilty Plea.

3. Non-custodial sentences

(a) It is likely that all breaches of protective orders will pass the threshold for a community sentence. The reference in the starting points to medium and low range community orders refers to the Council guideline New Sentences: Criminal Justice Act 2003 paragraphs 1.1.18–1.1.32.

(b) In accordance with general principle, the fact that the seriousness of an offence crosses a particular threshold does not preclude the court from imposing another type of sentence of a lower level where appropriate.

BREACH OF A PROTECTIVE ORDER

Breach of a Restraining Order

Section 5(5) Protection from Harassment Act 1997

Breach of a Non-Molestation Order

Section 42A Family Law Act 1996 (when in force)

Maximum Penalty: 5 years imprisonment

Where the conduct is particularly serious, it would normally be charged as a separate offence. These starting points are based on the premise that the activity has either been prosecuted separately as an offence or is not of a character sufficient to justify prosecution of it as an offence in its own right.

Nature of activity	Starting points Custodial Sentence
Breach (whether one or more) involving significant physical violence and significant physical or psychological harm to the victim	More than 12 months The length of the custodial sentence imposed will depend on the nature and seriousness of the breach(es).
More than one breach involving some violence and/or significant physical or psychological harm to the victim	26–39 weeks custody [Medium/High Custody Plus order]★★
Single breach involving some violence and/or significant physical or psychological harm to the victim	13–26 weeks custody [Low/Medium Custody Plus order]★★
	Non-Custodial Sentence
More than one breach involving no/minimal contact or some direct contact	MEDIUM range community order
Single breach involving no/minimal direct contact	LOW range community order

Additional aggravating factors	Additional mitigating factors
1. Victim is particularly vulnerable. 2. Impact on children. 3. A proven history of violence or threats by the offender. 4. Using contact arrangements with a child to instigate an offence. 5. Victim is forced to leave home. 6. Offence is a further breach, following earlier breach proceedings. 7. Offender has a history of disobedience to court orders. 8. Breach was committed immediately or shortly after the order was made.	1. Breach occurred after a long period of compliance. 2. Victim initiated contact.

Restraining orders made under the Sex Offenders Act 1997. Custody is inevitable where the breach is committed by an offender who presents a clear danger to children, and a substantial term is justified where the offender has demonstrated unwillingness or inability to address his sexual offending and has committed flagrant breach of court orders[5].

Breach of a notification requirement made under the Sexual Offences Act 2003. The notification provisions exist for the safety of the public and in some cases for the protection of the offender. Compliance is vital if those purposes are to be fulfilled, and a custodial sentence is therefore right in principle[6].

---

1. See also para **3–268**, ante.

2. *R v Pace* [2004] EWCA Crim 2019, [2005] 1 Cr App R (S) 74 (2 years reduced to 18 months for a first and unpremeditated breach arising from a chance encounter, though it lasted for 10 minutes, involved an implied threat of

serious violence ("I have got a blade, come here") and the offender's record showed a persistent disregard of community sentences).

　　3. *Liddle v Hayes* [2001] Cr App R (S) 131.

　　4. *R v Dadley* [2004] EWCA Crim 2216, [2005] 1 Cr App R (S) 87. See also *R v Bennett* [2005] EWCA Crim, [2005] Cr App R (S) 59 (18 months' imprisonment upheld for a third breach, even though there was no actual violence and it was not the most serious level of breaches of such orders. For an example of a persistent breach of an order made for a s 4 offence, see *R v Tetley* [2004] EWCA Crim 3228, [2005] 2 Cr App R (S) 35 (3 years 4 months' imprisonment upheld).

　　5. *R v Pylle* [2005] EWCA Crim 467, [2005] 2 Cr App R (S) 89 (order prohibiting offender from entering the vicinity of any grounds or recreational facility when occupied by one or more persons under 16 breached within weeks of the offender's release from prison: 3 years' imprisonment upheld where the offender's record included grave sexual offences, even though on this occasion he did not actually leave his parked vehicle or attempt to groom any child).

　　6. *R v B* [2005] EWCA Crim 158, [2005] 2 Cr App R (S) 65 (sentence reduced to 3 months on a guilty plea where the offender had an extensive record but only 1 previous sentence for a sexual offence).

Mentally disordered offenders

Orders in respect of mentally disordered offenders

3–320　It is implicit in passing sentence on a mentally disordered offender that the court considered that the offender was fit to plead and to stand trial[1]. However, in the case of a person suffering from mental illness or severe mental impairment, the court, if satisfied that the accused did the act or made the omission charged, may make a hospital or guardianship order (if all the usual requirements are met – see below) without convicting him[2].

　　The Crown Court has special powers to deal with an accused who is found not guilty by reason of insanity or where findings are recorded that the accused is under a disability and that he did the act or made the omission charged against him. In such cases, unless the sentence is fixed by law, the Crown Court shall: (*a*) make an order that the accused be admitted to such a hospital as may be specified by the Secretary of State; or (*b*) make in respect of the accused such one of the following orders as the court thinks most suitable in all the circumstances of the case—

　　(i)　a guardianship order;
　　(ii)　a supervision and treatment order;
　　(iii)　an order for his absolute discharge[3].

　　Although these powers under the Criminal Procedure (Insanity) Act 1964[5] are not available on summary trial, a magistrates' court has a limited jurisdiction with respect to the revocation or amendment of a supervision and treatment order made under the Criminal Procedure (Insanity and Unfitness to Plead) Act 1991[4].

---

　　1. See ante Part I: Magistrates' Courts, Procedure, para **1–308 Automatism, insanity, mental malfunction**, for procedures if the accused's mental state is too bad to allow the court to proceed to trial. See also para **3–55**, ante, **Medical reports** for provisions as to the reception of medical evidence.
　　2. Mental Health Act 1983, s 37(3) in Part VIII: Mental Health, post.
　　3. Criminal Procedure (Insanity) Act 1964, s 5, as substituted by the Criminal Procedure (Insanity and Unfitness to Plead) Act 1981, s 3.
　　4. See the Criminal Procedure (Insanity and Unfitness to Plead) Act 1991, s 5 and Sch 2, this Part, post.

Mental health treatment requirement in community order

3–321　*The following test applies only to offences committed on or after 4 April 2005. For offences committed before this date we refer readers to the paragraph* **3–490** *in the 2005 edition of this work.*

　　A community order or a suspended sentence order may include a mental health treatment requirement, ie a requirement that the offender must submit during a period or periods specified to treatment by or under the direction of a registered medical practitioner or a chartered psychologist (or both, for different periods) with a view to improving the offender's mental condition[1]. The order must specify the kind of treatment; this may be residential (but not in hospital premises where high security psychiatric services are provided), non-residential, or by or under the direction of a specified registered medical practitioner and/or chartered psychologist[2].

　　The prerequisites of a mental health treatment requirement are that: the court is satisfied on the evidence of a registered medical practitioner approved for the purposes of s 12 of the Mental Health Act 1983 that the mental condition of the offender is such that it requires and may be susceptible to treatment, but the case does not warrant making a hospital or guardianship order; arrangements have been made or can be made for the treatment that the court intends to specify; and the offender has expressed his willingness to comply with such a requirement[3].

　　Subject to certain conditions, mental health treatment may be carried out at a place other than that specified in the order[4].

---

　　1. Criminal Justice Act 207(1). See this Part, post.
　　2. CJA 2003, s 207(2). A "chartered psychologist" is a person for the time being listed in the British Psychological Society's Register of Chartered Psychologists: CJA 2003, s 207(6).
　　3. CJA 2003, s 207(3).
　　4. CJA 2003, s 208.

HOSPITAL AND GUARDIANSHIP ORDERS

3–322 Orders available on conviction: mental health hospital or guardianship orders.
(Important amendments were made to s 37 of the Mental Health Act 1983 by para 38 of Sch 32 to the Criminal Justice Act 2003, with this effect: in relation to offences committed on or after 4 April 2005[1], where a sentence would otherwise fall to be imposed under s 51A(2) of the Firearms Act 1968, ss 110(2) or 111(2) of the Powers of Criminal Courts (Sentencing) Act 2000, or under any of the provisions of ss 225–228 of the Criminal Justice Act 2003, nothing in those provisions shall prevent the court from making an order under s 37(1) for the admission of the offender to a hospital.)
A magistrates' court may place a person under the guardianship of a local social services authority or some other specified person approved by the authority, or authorise his admission to and detention in such hospital as may be specified in the order. The following requirements must first be fulfilled[2]—

   (1) the person must have been convicted of an offence punishable on summary conviction with imprisonment (but see below); and

   (2) the court must be satisfied, on the written or oral evidence[3] of two registered medical practitioners, that the offender is suffering from mental illness, psychopathic disorder, severe mental impairment or mental impairment and that either—

      (a) the mental disorder from which the offender is suffering is of a nature or degree which makes it appropriate for him to be detained in a hospital for medical treatment and, in the case of psychopathic disorder or mental impairment, that such treatment is likely to alleviate or prevent a deterioration of his condition; or

      (b) in the case of an offender who has attained the age of 16 years, the mental disorder is of a nature or degree which warrants his reception into guardianship under the Mental Health Act 1983,

      and,

   (3) the court must be of opinion, having regard to all the circumstances including the nature of the offence and the character and antecedents of the offender, and to the other available methods of dealing with him, that the most suitable method of disposing of the case is by means of a hospital or guardianship order; and

   (4) before making a hospital order, the court must be satisfied on the written or oral evidence of the registered medical practitioner who would be in charge of the offender's treatment or of some other person representing the managers of the hospital that arrangements have been made for his admission to that hospital in the event of such an order being made by the court, and for his admission to it within the period of 28 days beginning with the date of the making of the order; and the court may, pending his admission within that period, give such directions as it thinks fit for his conveyance to and detention in a place of safety; or

   (5) before making a guardianship order, the court must be satisfied that the local social services authority or other person who would be specified in the order would be willing to receive the offender into guardianship; a report may be requested[4].

As an alternative to (1) above, where a person is charged before a magistrates' court with any act or omission as an offence, and the court would have power, on convicting him of that offence, to make a hospital or guardianship order in his case as being a person suffering from mental illness or severe mental impairment, then, if the court is satisfied that the accused did the act or made the omission charged, the court may, if it thinks fit, make such an order without convicting him[5].

At least one of the medical practitioners must be approved for the purposes of s 12 of the Mental Health Act 1983 as having special experience in the diagnosis or treatment of mental disorders[6]. No order may be made unless the offender is described by each of the practitioners as suffering from the same one of those forms of mental disorder, whether or not he is also described as suffering from another of those forms[7].

When a hospital or guardianship order is made, the court shall not pass a sentence of imprisonment or detention or impose a fine or make a probation order in respect of the offence, or (in the case of a juvenile) make a supervision order or order the parent or guardian to enter into a recognizance to take proper care of him and exercise proper control over him[8], but may make any other order which it would have power to make.

The circumstances in which it will be appropriate to make a hospital order or guardianship order without convicting the accused will be very rare and will usually require the consent of those acting for him if he is under such a disability that he cannot be tried[9]. As there is no requirement for a trial in such a case, the provisions of section 20 of the Magistrates' Courts Act 1980 (procedure where summary trial appears more suitable for an offence triable either way) do not apply, and the court may proceed to make an order in the case of an offence triable either way, notwithstanding that the accused has not consented to summary trial[9]. However, a magistrates' court has no jurisdiction to adopt this procedure in respect of a defendant who is charged with an offence triable only on indictment[10].

The Court of Appeal has given guidance[11] to magistrates' courts as to the practical effects of a hospital order, contrasting it with a restriction order[12] for which the offender would have to be committed to the Crown Court, in the following terms.

It must be borne in mind that when only a hospital order is made—

   (1) It is only authority for the patient's detention for 6 months[13] in the first instance. This authority can be renewed if the medical practitioner in charge of the treatment of the patient . . . reports

to the hospital managers that it appears to him that the conditions set out in s 20(4) of the Mental Health Act 1983 are satisfied, and in particular that further detention is necessary in the interests of the patient's health or safety or for the protection of others. The hospital managers, however, are not bound to act on such a report and may refuse to extend the period and accordingly discharge the patient. Further, if the patient is sixteen or over he or his nearest relative can apply, at certain intervals to a mental health review tribunal who may in any case direct the patient's discharge and must do so if satisfied that he is no longer suffering from a mental disorder or that his further detention is not necessary.

(2) The patient can be discharged at any time by the hospital managers whose power is unlimited or by the responsible medical officer whose power is also unlimited or by a mental health review tribunal as already stated.

(3) Once discharged the patient is no longer liable to recall.

(4) A patient who is absent without leave cannot be re-taken into custody and indeed ceases to be liable to be detained (a) if he is over twenty-one and is classified as psychopathic or subnormal, after six months' absence, (b) in any other case, after twenty-eight days' absence.

If, however, a restriction order[14] is made in addition to a hospital order: (i) there is authority to detain the patient for at any rate the duration of that order, though the Secretary of State may terminate it at any time if satisfied that it is no longer required for the protection of the public; (ii) the patient can only be discharged with the consent of the Secretary of State or by the Secretary of State himself; (iii) the Secretary of State has power in discharging the patient himself to make the discharge conditional, in which case the patient remains liable to recall during the period up to the expiration of the restriction order. This power is particularly useful as a means of keeping a discharged patient under the supervision of a probation officer or mental welfare officer for a longer period than would be possible if there were no restriction order; lastly a patient who is absent without leave may be taken into custody again at any time.

Where an offender needs medical treatment but no hospital vacancy can be found, it is wrong to impose a custodial sentence; the courts must stand in the way of anyone who tries to sweep such an offender into the penal system and dispose of him by sending him to prison[15]. It is improper that hospital staff should be obstructive about the use of secure units, and once an order is made, to obstruct or counsel or procure any obstruction may amount to contempt of court[16].

In dealing with a minor, only a youth court may make a hospital or guardianship order[17]. It may commit to the Crown Court for a restriction order but only where the minor is aged 14 or over[18].

---

1. See para 5 of Sch 2 to the Criminal Justice Act 2003 (Commencement No 8 and Transitional and Saving Provisions) Order 2005, SI 2005/950. This does not apply, however, to an offender who qualifies for an automatic life sentence under s 109 of the Powers of Criminal Courts (Sentencing) Act 2000 for a pre-commencement offence; the deletion of the reference to s 109 from s 37(1) of the Mental Health Act 1983 does not does not affect such offences: para 6 of Sch 2, ibid.

2. Mental Health Act 1983, s 37, in PART VIII: MENTAL HEALTH, post.

3. As to presentation of the evidence, see para 3–55, ante.

4. Mental Health Act 1983, s 39A, in PART VIII: MENTAL HEALTH, post.

5. Mental Health Act 1983, s 37(3), in PART VIII: MENTAL HEALTH, post.

6. Mental Health Act 1983, s 54(1), in PART VIII: MENTAL HEALTH, post.

7. Mental Health Act 1983, s 37(7) in PART VIII: MENTAL HEALTH, post.

8. Mental Health Act 1983, s 37(8) in PART VIII: MENTAL HEALTH, post.

9. *R v Lincoln (Kesteven) Justices, ex p O'Connor* [1983] 1 All ER 901, [1983] 1 WLR 335, 147 JP 97.

10. *R v Chippenham Magistrates' Court, ex p Thompson* (1995) 160 JP 207.

11. In *R v Gardiner* [1967] 1 All ER 895, 131 JP 273.

12. Under Mental Health Act 1983, s 41 in PART VIII: MENTAL HEALTH, post. See also *R v Birch* (1989) 90 Cr App Rep 78, 11 Cr App Rep (S) 202, CA, for principles applicable to the imposition of a restriction order.

13. Mental Health Act 1983, s 20(2), which is applied to patients subject to a hospital or guardianship order by s 40(4) of and Sch 1 to the Act.

14. Under the Mental Health Act 1983, s 43 in PART VIII: MENTAL HEALTH, post.

15. *R v Clarke* (1975) 61 Cr App Rep 320; *R v Eaton* (1975) 119 Sol Jo 793.

16. See *R v Harding* (1984) 148 JP 595, CA.

17. Powers of Criminal Courts (Sentencing) Act 2000, s 8(6), this PART, post.

18. Mental Health Act 1983, s 43 in PART VIII: MENTAL HEALTH, post.

Restraining orders in proceedings brought by way of complaint

NOTIFICATION ORDERS

3–340   A chief officer of police may apply by complaint to a magistrates' court for a notification order in respect of a defendant dealt with for a relevant offence by a court in an overseas jurisdiction which has a similar effect to a notification requirement in respect of a domestic offence[1]. An interim order may be applied for where an application for such an order has not been determined[2]. An appeal from an order made by a magistrates' court is to the Crown Court[3]. Failure, without reasonable excuse, to comply with the notification requirements is an offence triable either way[4].

---

1. Sexual Offences Act 2003, s 97, in PART VIII: title SEXUAL OFFENCES, post

2. Sexual Offences Act 2003, s 100, in PART VIII: title SEXUAL OFFENCES, post.

3. Sexual Offences Act 2003, s 101, in PART VIII: title SEXUAL OFFENCES, post.
4. Sexual Offences Act 2003, ss 91 and 98, in Part VIII: title Sexual Offences, post.

RISK OF SEXUAL HARM ORDERS

3–341 A chief officer of police may by complaint to a magistrates' court apply for a risk of sexual harm order in respect of a person aged 18 or over if it appears to the chief officer that—

(*a*) the defendant has on at least two occasions, whether before or after the commencement of this Part has:

  – engaged in sexual activity involving a child or in the presence of a child;
  – caused or incited a child to watch a person engaging in sexual activity or to look at a moving or still image that is sexual;
  – given a child anything that relates to sexual activity or contains a reference to such activity;
  – communicated with a child, where any part of the communication is sexual; and

(*b*) as a result of those acts, there is reasonable cause to believe that it is necessary for such an order to be made[1].

The court may make a risk of sexual harm order if it is satisfied that:

  – the defendant has on at least two occasions, whether before or after the commencement of this section, done one of the above acts; and
  – it is necessary to make such an order, for the purpose of protecting children generally or any child from harm from the defendant[2].

A risk of sexual harm order prohibits the defendant from doing anything described in the order and has effect for a fixed period (not less than 2 years) specified in the order or until further order. Any prohibitions in the order may only be such as are necessary for protecting children generally or any child from harm from the defendant. On the making of an order any earlier such order ceases to have effect[3].

Provision is made for variations, renewals and discharges of such orders[4] and an interim order may be applied for where an application for such an order has not been determined[5]. Appeal is to the Crown Court[6].

If without reasonable excuse a person does anything which he is prohibited from doing by a foreign travel order, he shall be guilty of an offence which is triable either way[7].

---

1. Sexual Offences Act 2003, s 123(1)–(3), in PART VIII: title SEXUAL OFFENCES, post.
2. Sexual Offences Act 2003, s 123(4), in PART VIII: title SEXUAL OFFENCES, post.
3. Sexual Offences Act 2003, s 123(5)–(7), in PART VIII: title SEXUAL OFFENCES, post.
4. Sexual Offences Act 2003, s 125, in PART VIII: title SEXUAL OFFENCES, post.
5. Sexual Offences Act 2003, s 126, in PART VIII: title SEXUAL OFFENCES, post.
6. Sexual Offences Act 2003, s 127, in PART VIII: title SEXUAL OFFENCES, post.
7. Sexual Offences Act 2003, s 128, in PART VIII: title SEXUAL OFFENCES, post.

FOREIGN TRAVEL ORDERS

3–342 A chief officer of police may apply by way of complaint to a magistrates' court for a foreign travel order in respect of a person if it appears that the defendant is

  – a qualifying offender[1], and
  – he has since the appropriate date[2] acted in such a way as to give reasonable cause to believe that it is necessary for such an order to be made[3].

If the court is satisfied that he is a qualifying offender, and the defendant's behaviour since the appropriate date makes it necessary to make such an order for the purpose of protecting children generally or any child from serious sexual harm from the defendant outside the United Kingdom[4], the court may make an order for a fixed period not exceeding 6 months which prohibits the defendant from travelling outside the United Kingdom as specified[5]. Any prohibitions in the order may only be such as are necessary for protecting children generally or any child from serious sexual harm from the defendant outside the United Kingdom and the defendant will be subject to requirements to notify his travel arrangements[5]. Provision is made for variations, renewals and discharges of such orders[6] and for appeal to the Crown Court[7].

If without reasonable excuse a person does anything which he is prohibited from doing by a foreign travel order, he shall be guilty of an offence which is triable either way[8].

---

1. Sexual Offences Act 2003, s 116, in PART VIII: title SEXUAL OFFENCES, post.
2. Sexual Offences Act 2003, s 115(5), in PART VIII: title SEXUAL OFFENCES, post.
3. Sexual Offences Act 2003, s 114(1), in PART VIII: title SEXUAL OFFENCES, post.
4. Sexual Offences Act 2003, s 114(3), in PART VIII: title SEXUAL OFFENCES, post.
5. Sexual Offences Act 2003, s 117, in PART VIII: title SEXUAL OFFENCES, post.
6. Sexual Offences Act 2003, s 118, in PART VIII: title SEXUAL OFFENCES, post.
7. Sexual Offences Act 2003, s 119, in PART VIII: title SEXUAL OFFENCES, post.
8. Sexual Offences Act 2003, s 122, in PART VIII: title SEXUAL OFFENCES, post.

Binding over, recognizances[1]

3–360   The power to bind over derives from Statute and from the common law. Magistrates have power "to take of all them that be not of good fame, where they shall be found, sufficient surety and mainprise of their good behaviour towards the King and his people . . . to the intent that the peace be (not) blemished"[2], but this statutory provision is not exhaustive of the jurisdiction of magistrates in such circumstances[3]. A person may be bound over to keep the peace *and* be of good behaviour; or to keep the peace, or to be of good behaviour. A surety for good behaviour is more comprehensive than a surety of the peace, as good behaviour includes the peace[4]. Whereas a surety of the peace may only be required where there is evidence of fear of personal danger[5], a surety to be of good behaviour is not so restricted[3].

Binding over may be by way of order on complaint against the person named in the complaint[6]; or magistrates may bind over any person appearing before them whether as a party or witness[7] in the proceedings. Normally a person about to be bound over will be warned of the court's intention and given the opportunity of making representations[8]. The court will order the person being bound over to enter into a recognizance with or without other people acting as sureties, for a stipulated sum and for a stipulated time[9]. An acknowledgment by the person bound over of his indebtedness to the sovereign in the sum of the recognizance fixed by the court is of the essence, and the court cannot unilaterally impose a binding over order[10]. If the person refuses to acknowledge his indebtedness he may be committed to prison for a period not exceeding six months or until he sooner complies[11].

When justices have it in mind to order a binding over, before they do so: (1) there should be material before them justifying the conclusion that there is a risk of a breach of the peace unless action is taken to prevent it; (2) they have to indicate to the defendant their intention to bind him over and the reasons for it so that he or his lawyer may make representations; (3) before fixing the amount of the recognizance they should enquire as to the defendant's means; (4) the binding over should be for a finite period[12].

Although for some purposes binding over proceedings are treated as criminal proceedings, since the procedure is by way of complaint it is primarily a civil process[13]. The jurisdiction of the justices to deal with a complaint under s 115 of the Magistrates' Courts Act 1980 does not depend on a summons being issued, nor does the absence of a complaint in the form prescribed invalidate the procedure[14]. Where proceedings under s 115 are conducted by the CPS by virtue of s 3(2)(c) of the Prosecution of Offences Act 1985, and the complaint is dismissed, there is no power to order defence costs against the CPS but an order for costs may be made against the complainant[14].

---

1. The form of surety used to be "to keep the peace" and/or "be of good behaviour". However, in *Hashman and Harrup v United Kingdom* (1999) 8 BHRC 104, ECHR, the notion of "good behaviour" was found to breach the European Convention on Human Rights because it was too vague and uncertain and because the order did not comply with the requirement of art 10(2) of the Convention that it be "prescribed by law". But see also *Steel v United Kingdom* (1998) 28 EHRR 603.

2. Justices of the Peace Act 1361, this title, post.

3. *Lansbury v Riley* [1914] 3 KB 229, 77 JP 440.

4. See *R v Sandbach, ex p Williams* [1935] 2 KB 192, 99 JP 251.

5. *Vane's (Lord) Case* (1744) 73 East 172n; *R v Tregarthen* (1833) 5 B & Ad 678; *R v Dunn* (1840) 12 Ad & El 599, 4 JP 728; *Percy v DPP* (1994) 159 JP 337, [1995] 3 All ER 124.

6. Magistrates' Courts Act 1980, ss 115, 116.

7. See eg *R v Wilkins* [1907] 2 KB 330, 71 JP 327; *Sheldon v Bromfield Justices* [1964] 2 QB 573, [1964] 2 All ER 131.

8. *Sheldon v Bromfield Justices*, supra; *R v Keighley Justices, ex p Stoyles* [1976] Crim LR 573.

9. *R v Edgar* (1913) 77 JP 356.

10. *Veater v G* [1981] 2 All ER 304, [1981] 1 WLR 567, 145 JP 158.

11. Magistrates' Courts Act 1980, s 115(3); as to common law powers see 141 JP Jo 139 and *R v Trueman* (1913) 77 JP 428.

12. See *R v Crown Court at Lincoln, ex p Jude* [1997] 3 All ER 737, [1998] 1 WLR 24, [1998] 1 Cr App R 130.

13. However, under the European Convention on Human Rights binding over proceedings may be treated as criminal proceedings: see *Steel v United Kingdom* (1999) 28 EHRR 603.

14. *R v Coventry Magistrates' Court, ex p Crown Prosecution Service* (1996) 160 JP 741, [1996] Crim LR 723.

3–361   Binding over of parent or guardian.   Where a child or young person is found guilty of any offence, a court may, with the consent of his parent or guardian, order the parent or guardian to enter into a recognizance to take proper care of him and exercise proper control over him[1]. Where he has not attained 16, it is the court's duty to exercise these powers if it is satisfied, having regard to the circumstances of the case, that their exercise would be desirable in the interests of preventing the commission by him of further offences, and where it does not exercise them the court must state in open court that it is not so satisfied, and why[1]. The amount of the recognizance shall not exceed £1,000 and the period shall not exceed 3 years or until the minor attains the age of 18 years, whichever is shorter[2]. If the parent or guardian refuses consent and the court considers the refusal unreasonable, the court may order the parent or guardian to pay a fine not exceeding £1,000[3].

This power may be exercised by a magistrates' court that is not a youth court where, for example, a minor has been jointly charged and tried together with an adult[4]. It appears to be a sentence which should stand on its own and not in conjunction with some other sentence[5]. The recognizance will be fixed having regard to the means of the parent or guardian[1]. The parent or guardian may appeal against an order, or may seek to have it varied or revoked[1].

Proceedings to *forfeit a recognizance* proceed by way of order on complaint, and may result in estreatment of the whole or part of the recognizance, together with costs[4].

1. Powers of Criminal Courts (Sentencing) Act 2000, s 150(1), this PART, post.
2. Powers of Criminal Courts (Sentencing) Act 2000, s 150(3), (4), this PART, post.
3. Powers of Criminal Courts (Sentencing) Act 2000, s 150(2)(b), this PART, post.
4. Powers of Criminal Courts (Sentencing) Act 2000, s 8(6), (8), this PART, post.
5. Powers of Criminal Courts (Sentencing) Act 2000, s 150, this PART, post and Magistrates' Courts Act 1980, s 120 in PART I: MAGISTRATES' COURTS, PROCEDURE, ante.

Statutes on Sentencing

Justices of the Peace Act 1361
(34 Edw 3 c I)

3–580   First, that in every county of England shall be assigned for the keeping of the peace, one lord, and with him three or four of the most worthy in the county, with some learned in the law, and they shall have power to restrain the offenders, rioters, and all other barators and to pursue, arrest, take, and chastise them according their trespass or offence; and to cause them to be imprisoned and duly punished according to the law and customs of the realm, and according to that which to them shall seem best to do by their discretions and good advisement; . . . and to take and arrest all those that they may find by indictment, or by suspicion, and to put them in prison; and to take of all them that be [not][1] of good fame,[2] where they shall be found, sufficient surety[3] and mainprise of their good behaviour towards the King and his people, and the other duly to punish; to the intent that the people be not by such rioters or rebels troubled nor endamaged, nor the peace blemished, nor merchants nor other passing by the highways of the realm disturbed, nor [put in the peril which may happen[4]] of such offenders . . .[5]
[Justices of the Peace Act 1361.]

---

1. All translations read thus.
2. There is power for justices to bind over a man whether he is or is not of good fame; see *Lansbury v Riley* [1914] 3 KB 229, 77 JP 440. See also *R v County of London Quarter Sessions, ex p Metropolitan Police Comr* [1948] 1 KB 670, [1948] 1 All ER 72, 112 JP 118.
3. For a discussion of the origin and extent of this power in the exercise of preventive justice, see *Lansbury v Riley* [1914] 3 KB 229, 77 JP 440. Justices have power to bind over to keep the peace under this Act, and, by virtue of their commission, a person who is before them charged with any offence (*Wilson v Skeock* (1949) 113 JP 294).
4. Put in fear by peril which might happen.
5. Under the Human Rights Act 1998, this provision, so far as it is possible to do so, must be read and given effect in a way which is compatible with the Convention rights. For the position under the European Convention on Human Rights see *Steel v United Kingdom* (1998) 28 EHRR 603 and *Hashman and Harrup v United Kingdom* [2000] Crim LR 185.

Criminal Justice Act 1972
(1972 c 71)

PART I
POWERS FOR DEALING WITH OFFENDERS
Restitution orders

3–720   **6. Restitution orders.**   *Repealed.*

PART III
MISCELLANEOUS PROVISIONS

3–721   **34. Power of constable to take drunken offender to treatment centre.**   (1) On arresting an offender for an offence under—

    (*a*)   section 12 of the Licensing Act 1872; or
    (*b*)   section 91(1) of the Criminal Justice Act 1967,

a constable may, if he thinks fit, take him to any place approved for the purposes of this section by the Secretary of State as a treatment centre for alcoholics, and while a person is being so taken he shall be deemed to be in lawful custody.

(2) A person shall not by virtue of this section be liable to be detained in any such centre as aforesaid to which he has been taken, but the exercise in his case of the power conferred by this section shall not preclude his being charged with any offence.

(3) *Repealed.*
[Criminal Justice Act 1972, s 34, as amended by the Criminal Law Act 1977, Sch 12 and the Police and Criminal Evidence Act 1984 Schs 6 and 7.]

3–724   **46. Admissibility of written statements made outside England and Wales.**   (1) Section 9 of the Criminal Justice Act 1967 (written statements to be used as evidence in criminal proceedings) and section 89 of the said Act of 1967 (false statements which are tendered in evidence under the said section 9, shall apply to written statements made in Scotland or Northern Ireland as well as to written statements made in England and Wales.

(1A) The following provisions, namely—

(a) so much of section 5A of the Magistrates' Courts Act 1980 as relates to written statements and to documents or other exhibits referred to in them,

(b) section 5B of that Act, and

(c) section 106 of that Act,

shall apply where written statements are made in Scotland or Northern Ireland as well as where written statements are made in England and Wales.

(1B) The following provisions, namely—

(a) so much of section 5A of the Magistrates' Courts Act 1980 as relates to written statements and to documents or other exhibits referred to in them, and

(b) section 5B of that Act,

shall (subject to subsection (1C) below) apply where written statements are made outside the United Kingdom.

(1C) Where written statements are made outside the United Kingdom—

(a) section 5B of the Magistrates' Courts Act 1980 shall apply with the omission of subsections (2)(b) and (3A);

(b) paragraph 1 of Schedule 2 to the Criminal Procedure and Investigations Act 1996 (use of written statements at trial) shall not apply.

(2) *Repealed.*

[Criminal Justice Act, 1972, s 46 amended by the Magistrates' Courts Act 1980, Sch 7 and the Criminal Procedure and Investigations Act 1996, Schs 1 and 5.]

3–725   48. Proceedings under Indecency with Children Act 1960. *Repealed.*

3–727   51. Execution of process between England and Wales and Scotland. (1) *Repealed.*

(2) Where a warrant is issued for the apprehension of a child in pursuance of Part III of the Social Work (Scotland) Act 1968, that warrant may be executed in England and Wales in like manner as a warrant issued in Scotland for the apprehension of a person charged with an offence, and sections 17(1) and 325(1) of the Criminal Procedure (Scotland) Act 1975[1] shall apply accordingly.

(4) Section 4 of the said Act of 1881 shall have effect in relation to the service and execution in Scotland of process issued in England and Wales by a justices' clerk by virtue of section 28(1) of the Courts Act 2003, as it has as it has effect in relation to process issued in England and Wales by a court of summary jurisdiction as defined in the said Act of 1881.

[Criminal Justice Act 1972, s 51, as amended by the Powers of Criminal Courts Act 1973, Sch 6, the Criminal Procedure (Scotland) Act 1975, Sch 9, the Children Act 1989, Sch 15, the Criminal Justice Act 1991, Sch 11 and the Justices of the Peace Act 1997, Sch 5 and the Courts Act 2003, Sch 8.]

---

1. See now Pt X of the Criminal Justice and Public Order Act 1994, in PART I: MAGISTRATES' COURTS, PROCEDURE.

PART IV
ADMINISTRATIVE PROVISIONS

3–728   60. (1)–(5) *Power of entry in connection with acquisition of land for prisons.*

(6) Any person who wilfully obstructs a person acting in the exercise of his powers under this section shall be guilty of an offence and liable on summary conviction to a fine not exceeding **level 3** on the standard scale.

[Criminal Justice Act 1972, s 60 as amended by the Criminal Justice Act 1982, ss 38 and 46.]

PART V
SUPPLEMENTARY

3–729   66. Interpretation. (2) In this Act "court" does not include a court-martial; "sentence of imprisonment" does not include a committal in default of payment of any sum of money, or for want of sufficient distress to satisfy any sum of money, or for failure to do or abstain from doing anything required to be done or left undone or a committal or attachment for contempt of court, and "sentenced to imprisonment" shall be construed accordingly.

(5) Except where the context otherwise requires, any reference in this Act to any enactment shall be construed as a reference to that enactment as amended, and as including a reference thereto as extended or applied, by or under any other enactment, including this Act.

[Criminal Justice Act 1972, s 66, as amended by the Powers of Criminal Courts Act 1973, Sch 6.]

Rehabilitation of Offenders Act 1974
(1974 c 53)

3–940   1. Rehabilitated persons and spent convictions. (1) Subject to subsection (2) below, where an individual has been convicted, whether before or after the commencement of this Act, of any offence or offences, and the following conditions are satisfied, that is to say—

(a) he did not have imposed on him in respect of that conviction a sentence which is excluded from rehabilitation under this Act; and

(b) he has not had imposed on him in respect of a subsequent conviction during the rehabilitation period applicable to the first-mentioned conviction in accordance with section 6 below a sentence which is excluded from rehabilitation under this Act;

then, after the end of the rehabilitation period so applicable (including, where appropriate, any extension under section 6(4) below of the period originally applicable to the first-mentioned conviction) or, where that rehabilitation period ended before the commencement of this Act, after the commencement of this Act, that individual shall for the purposes of this Act be treated as a rehabilitated person in respect of the first-mentioned conviction and that conviction shall for those purposes be treated as spent[1].

(2) A person shall not become a rehabilitated person for the purposes of this Act in respect of a conviction unless he has served or otherwise undergone or complied with any sentence imposed on him in respect of that conviction; but the following shall not, by virtue of this subsection, prevent a person from becoming a rehabilitated person for those purposes—

(a) failure to pay a fine[2] or other sum adjudged to be paid by or imposed on a conviction, or breach of a condition of a recognizance or of a bond of caution to keep the peace or be of good behaviour;

(b) breach of any condition or requirement applicable in relation to a sentence which renders the person to whom it applies liable to be dealt with for the offence for which the sentence was imposed, or, where the sentence was a suspended sentence of imprisonment, liable to be dealt with in respect of that sentence whether or not, in any case, he is in fact so dealt with);

(c) failure to comply with any requirement of a suspended sentence supervision order;

(d) breach of any condition of a release supervision order made under section 16 of the Crime (Sentences) Act 1997.

(2A) Where in respect of a conviction a person has been sentenced to imprisonment with an order under section 47(1) of the Criminal Law Act 1977, he is to be treated for the purposes of subsection (2) above as having served the sentence as soon as he completes service of so much of the sentence as was by that order required to be served in prison.

(2B) In subsection (2)(a) above the reference to a fine or other sum adjudged to be paid by or imposed on a conviction does not include a reference to an amount payable under a confiscation order made under Part 2 or 3 of the Proceeds of Crime Act 2002.

(3) In this Act "sentence" includes any order made by a court in dealing with a person in respect of his conviction of any offence or offences, other than—

(a) an order for committal or any other order made in default of payment of any fine or other sum adjudged to be paid by or imposed on a conviction, or for want of sufficient distress to satisfy any such fine or other sum;

(b) an order dealing with a person in respect of a suspended sentence of imprisonment.

(4) In this Act, references to a conviction, however expressed, include references—

(a) to a conviction by or before a court outside Great Britain; and

(b) to any finding (other than a finding linked with a finding of insanity) in any criminal proceedings that a person has committed an offence or done the act or made the omission charged;

and notwithstanding anything in section 9 of the Criminal Justice (Scotland) Act 1949 or section 14 of the Powers of Criminal Courts (Sentencing) Act 2000 (conviction of a person discharged to be deemed not to be a conviction) a conviction in respect of which an order is made discharging the person concerned absolutely or conditionally shall be treated as a conviction for the purposes of this Act and the person in question may become a rehabilitated person in respect of that conviction and the conviction a spent conviction for those purposes accordingly[3].

[Rehabilitation of Offenders Act 1974, s 1, as amended by the Criminal Law Act 1977, Sch 9, the Children Act 1989, Sch 15, the Criminal Justice Act 1991, Sch 11, the Powers of Criminal Courts (Sentencing) Act 2000, Sch 9 and the Proceeds of Crime Act 2002, Sch 11 and the Crime (Sentences) Act 1997, Sch 4,.]

1. For effect of rehabilitation, see s 4(1), post; but see also s 7 which sets out circumstances where the Act will have no effect.

2. The reference here to "a fine or other sum adjudged to be paid by or imposed on a conviction" does not include a reference to an amount payable under a confiscation order within the meaning of s 2(9) of the Drug Trafficking Act 1994, in PART VIII: title MEDICINE AND PHARMACY, post (Drug Trafficking Act 1994, s 65(2)).

3. This provision is necessary because the effect of the Rehabilitation of Offenders Act 1974, once a person is rehabilitated and the conviction is spent, is wider than the provisions of s 14 of the 2000 Act taken alone. Whilst s 14 of the 2000 Act prevents the court appearance from ranking as a conviction, it does not enable any person to assert that they have never committed the offence or for that matter that they have never been found guilty of it. For the ability to contend that the offence has never been committed, the rehabilitated person has to look to the provisions of this Act, in particular s 4(2): *R v Patel* [2006] EWCA Crim 2689, [2007] 1 Cr App R 12.

3–941 2. Rehabilitation of persons dealt with in service disciplinary proceedings. (1) For the purposes of this Act any finding that a person is guilty of an offence in respect of any act or omission which was the subject of service disciplinary proceedings shall be treated as a conviction and any punishment awarded or order made by virtue of Schedule 5A to the Army Act 1955 or to the Air Force Act 1955 or Schedule 4A to the Naval Discipline Act 1957 in respect of any such findings shall be treated as a sentence.

(2)–(4) *Repealed.*

(5) In this Act, "service disciplinary proceedings" means any of the following—

(a) any proceedings under the Army Act 1955, the Air Force Act 1955, or the Naval Discipline Act 1957 (whether before a court-martial or before any other court or person authorised thereunder to award a punishment in respect of any offence);

(b) any proceedings under any Act previously in force corresponding to any of the Acts mentioned in paragraph (*a*) above;

(bb) any proceedings before a Standing Civilian Court established under the Armed Forces Act 1976;

(c) any proceedings under any corresponding enactment or law applying to a force, other than a home force, to which section 4 of the Visiting Forces (British Commonwealth) Act 1933 applies or applied at the time of the proceedings, being proceedings in respect of a member of a home force who is or was at that time attached to the first-mentioned force under that section;

whether in any event those proceedings take place in Great Britain or elsewhere.
[Rehabilitation of Offenders Act 1974, s 2, as amended by Armed Forces Act 1976, Sch 9, the Armed Forces Act 1981, Sch 4, and the Armed Forces Act 1996, s 13 and Sch 7.]

3–942 3. Special provision with respect to certain disposals by children's hearings under the Children (Scotland) Act 1995. Where a ground for the referral of a child's case to a children's hearing under the Children (Scotland) Act 1995 is that mentioned in section 52(2)(i) of that Act (commission by the child of an offence) and that ground has either been accepted by the child and, where necessary, by his parent or been established (or deemed established) to the satisfaction of the sheriff under section 68 or 85 of that Act, the acceptance, establishment (or deemed establishment) of that ground shall be treated for the purposes of this Act (but not otherwise) as a conviction, and any disposal of the case thereafter by a children's hearing shall be treated for those purposes as a sentence; and references in this Act to a person's being charged with or prosecuted for an offence shall be construed accordingly.
[Rehabilitation of Offenders Act 1974, s 3 as amended by the Children (Scotland) Act 1995, Sch 4.]

3–943 4. Effect of rehabilitation[1]. (1) Subject to sections 7[2] and 8 below, a person who has become a rehabilitated person for the purposes of this Act in respect of a conviction shall be treated for all purposes in law as a person who has not committed or been charged with or prosecuted for or convicted of or sentenced for the offence or offences which were the subject of that conviction; and, notwithstanding the provisions of any other enactment or rule of law to the contrary, but subject as aforesaid—

(a) no evidence shall be admissible in any proceedings before a judicial authority exercising its jurisdiction or functions in Great Britain to prove that any such person has committed or been charged with or prosecuted for or convicted of or sentenced for any offence which was the subject of a spent conviction; and

(b) a person shall not, in any such proceedings, be asked, and, if asked, shall not be required to answer, any question relating to his past which cannot be answered without acknowledging or referring to a spent conviction or spent convictions or any circumstances ancillary thereto.

(2) Subject to the provisions of any order made under subsection (4) below, where a question seeking information with respect to a person's previous convictions, offences, conduct or circumstances is put to him or to any other person otherwise than in proceedings before a judicial authority—

(a) the question shall be treated as not relating to spent convictions or to any circumstances ancillary to spent convictions, and the answer thereto may be framed accordingly; and

(b) the person questioned shall not be subjected to any liability or otherwise prejudiced in law by reason of any failure to acknowledge or disclose a spent conviction or any circumstances ancillary to a spent conviction to his answer to the question.

(3) Subject to the provisions of any order made under subsection (4) below—

(a) any obligation imposed on any person by any rule of law or by the provisions of any agreement or arrangement to disclose any matters to any other person shall not extend to requiring him to disclose a spent conviction or any circumstances ancillary to a spent conviction (whether the conviction is his own or another's); and

(b) a conviction which has become spent or any circumstances ancillary thereto, or any failure to disclose a spent conviction or any such circumstances, shall not be a proper ground for dismissing or excluding a person from any office, profession, occupation or employment, or for prejudicing him in any way in any occupation or employment.

(4) The Secretary of State may by order[3]—

(a) make such provision as seems to him appropriate for excluding or modifying the application of either or both of paragraphs (a) and (b) of subsection (2) above in relation to questions put in such circumstances as may be specified in the order;

(b) provide for such exceptions from the provisions of subsection (3) above as seem to him appropriate, in such cases or classes of case, and in relation to convictions of such a description, as may be specified in the order.

(5) For the purposes of this section and section 7 below any of the following are circumstances ancillary to a conviction, that is to say—

(a) the offence or offences which were the subject of that conviction;

(b) the conduct constituting that offence or those offences; and

(c) any process or proceedings preliminary to that conviction, any sentence imposed in respect of that conviction, any proceedings (whether by way of appeal or otherwise) for reviewing that conviction or any such sentence, and anything done in pursuance of or undergone in compliance with any such sentence.

(6) For the purposes of this section and section 7 below "proceedings before a judicial authority" includes, in addition to proceedings before any of the ordinary courts of law, proceedings before any tribunal, body or person having power—

(a) by virtue of any enactment, law, custom or practice;

(b) under the rules governing any association, institution, profession, occupation or employment; or

(c) under any provision of an agreement providing for arbitration with respect to questions arising thereunder;

to determine any question affecting the rights, privileges, obligations or liabilities of any person, or to receive evidence affecting the determination of any such question.
[Rehabilitation of Offenders Act 1974, s 4.]

---

1. For restrictions on the application of this section to a spent conviction for an offence involving fraud, dishonesty and other specified offences, see the Financial Services Act 1986, s 189 and Sch 14, in PART VIII, title COMPANIES, post.

2. Section 7 excludes the provisions of s 4(1) in specified circumstances: see that section and notes thereto, post. In particular, it may be noted that evidence relating to *any* previous convictions (whether "spent" or not) may be given in (1) any criminal proceedings: s 7(2)(a), but note terms of *Practice Direction (criminal: consolidated)* [2002] para I.6, in PART I: MAGISTRATES' COURTS, PROCEDURE, ante.and Home Office circulars 98/1975 and 130/1975 referred to in note to s 7(2)(a), post; (2) specified proceedings relating to children: s 7(2)(c) and (d); and (3) any other proceeding if the court is satisfied that justice cannot be done except by admitting evidence of "spent" convictions. See also *R v Evans* (1991) 156 JP 539, [1992] Crim LR 125, CA.

3. See the Rehabilitation of Offenders Act 1974 (Exceptions) Order 1975, SI 1975/1023, this PART: STATUTORY INSTRUMENTS ON SENTENCING, post.

3–944   **5. Rehabilitation periods for particular sentences.**   (1) The sentences excluded from rehabilitation under this Act are—

(a) a sentence of imprisonment for life;

(b) a sentence of imprisonment, youth custody, detention in a young offender institution or corrective training for a term exceeding thirty months;

(c) a sentence of preventive detention;

(d) a sentence of detention during Her Majesty's pleasure or for life or under section 90 or 91 or the Powers of Criminal Courts (Sentencing) Act 2000, 205(2) or (3) of the Criminal Procedure (Scotland) Act 1975, or a sentence of detention for a term exceeding thirty months passed under section 91 of the said Act of 2000, (young offenders convicted of grave crimes) or under section 206 of the said Act of 1975 (detention of children convicted on indictment) or a corresponding Court-martial punishment; and

(e) a sentence of custody for life; and

(f) a sentence of imprisonment for public protection under section 225 of the Criminal Justice Act 2003, a sentence of detention for public protection under section 226 of that Act or an extended sentence under section 227 or 228 of that Act

and any other sentence is a sentence subject to rehabilitation under this Act.

(1A) In subsection (1)(d) above "corresponding Court-martial punishment" means a punishment awarded under section 71A(3) or (4) of the Army Act 1955, section 71A(3) or (4) of the Air Force Act 1955 or section 43A(3) or (4) of the Naval Discipline Act 1957.

(2) For the purposes of this Act—

(a) the rehabilitation period applicable to a sentence specified in the first column of Table A below is the period specified in the second column of that Table in relation to that sentence, or, where the sentence was imposed on a person who was under eighteen years of age at the date of his conviction, half that period; and

(b) the rehabilitation period applicable to a sentence specified in the first column of Table B below is the period specified in the second column of that Table in relation to that sentence;

TABLE A
REHABILITATION PERIODS1 SUBJECT TO REDUCTION BY HALF FOR PERSONS UNDER 18*

Sentence	Rehabilitation period
A sentence of imprisonment detention in a young offender institution or youth custody or corrective training for a term exceeding six months but not exceeding thirty months.	Ten years.
A sentence of cashiering, discharge with ignominy or dismissal with disgrace from Her Majesty's service.	Ten years.
A sentence of imprisonment detention in a young offenders institution or youth custody for a term not exceeding six months.	Seven years.
A sentence of dismissal from Her Majesty's service.	Seven years.
Any sentence of detention in respect of a conviction in service disciplinary proceedings.	Five years.
A fine or any other sentence subject to rehabilitation under this Act, not being a sentence to which Table B below or any of subsections (3) to (8) below applies.	Five years.

TABLE B
REHABILITATION PERIODS FOR CERTAIN SENTENCES CONFINED TO YOUNG OFFENDERS

A sentence of Borstal training.	Seven years.
A custodial order under Schedule 5A to the Army Act 1955 or the Air Force Act 1955, or under Schedule 4A to the Naval Discipline Act 1957, where the maximum period of detention specified in the order is more than six months.	Seven years.
A custodial order under section 71AA of the Army Act 1955 or the Air Force Act 1955, or under section 43AA of the Naval Discipline Act 1957, where the maximum period of detention specified in the order is more than six months.	Seven years.
A sentence of detention for a term exceeding six months but not exceeding thirty months passed under section 91 of the said Powers of Criminal Courts (Sentencing) Act 2000 or under section 206 of the Criminal Procedure (Scotland) Act 1975.	Five years.
A sentence of detention for a term not exceeding six months passed under either of those provisions.	Three years.
An order for detention in a detention centre made under section 4 of the Criminal Justice Act 1982, section 4 of the Criminal Justice Act 1961.	Three years.
A custodial order under any of the Schedules to the said Acts of 1955 and 1957 mentioned above, where the maximum period of detention specified in the order is six months or less.	Three years.
A custodial order under section 71AA of the said Acts of 1955, or section 43AA of the said Act of 1957, where the maximum period of detention specified in the order is six months or less.	Three years.

reckoned in either case from the date of the conviction in respect of which the sentence was imposed.

(3) The rehabilitation period applicable—

(a) to an order discharging a person absolutely for an offence; and
(b) to the discharge by a children's hearing under section 69(1)(b) and (12) of the Children (Scotland) Act 1995 of the referral of a child's case;

shall be six months from the date of conviction.

(4) Where in respect of a conviction a person was conditionally discharged, bound over to keep the peace or be of good behaviour, the rehabilitation period applicable to the sentence shall be one year from the date of conviction or a period beginning with that date and ending when the order for conditional discharge or (as the case may be) the recognizance or bond of caution to keep the peace or be of good behaviour ceases or ceased to have effect, whichever is the longer.

(4A) Where in respect of a conviction a probation order or a community order under section 177 of the Criminal Justice Act 2003 was made, the rehabilitation period applicable to the sentence shall be—

(a) in the case of a person aged eighteen years or over at the date of his conviction, five years from the date of conviction;
(b) in the case of a person aged under the age of eighteen years at the date of his conviction, two and a half years from the date of conviction or a period beginning with the date of conviction and ending when the order in question ceases or ceased to have effect, whichever is the longer.

(4B) Where in respect of a conviction a referral order (within the meaning of the Powers of

Criminal Courts (Sentencing) Act 2000) is made in respect of the person convicted, the rehabilitation period applicable to the sentence shall be—

(a) if a youth offender contract takes effect under section 23 of that Act between him and a youth offender panel, the period beginning with the date of conviction and ending on the date when (in accordance with section 24 of that Act) the contract ceases to have effect;

(b) if no such contract so takes effect, the period beginning with the date of conviction and having the same length as the period for which such a contract would (ignoring any order under paragraph 11 or 12 of Schedule 1 to that Act) have had effect had one so taken effect.

(4C) Where in respect of a conviction an order is made in respect of the person convicted under paragraph 11 or 12 of Schedule 1 to the Powers of Criminal Courts (Sentencing) Act 2000 (extension of period for which youth offender contract has effect), the rehabilitation period applicable to the sentence shall be—

(a) if a youth offender contract takes effect under section 23 of that Act between the offender and a youth offender panel, the period beginning with the date of conviction and ending on the date when (in accordance with section 24 of that Act) the contract ceases to have effect;

(b) if no such contract so takes effect, the period beginning with the date of conviction and having the same length as the period for which, in accordance with the order, such a contract would have had effect had one so taken effect.

(5) Where in respect of a conviction any of the following sentences was imposed, that is to say—

(a) an order under section 57 of the Children and Young Persons Act 1933 or section 61 of the Children and Young Persons (Scotland) Act 1937 committing the person convicted to the care of a fit person;

(b) a supervision order under any provision of either of those Acts or of the Children and Young Persons Act 1963;

(c) an order under section 413 of the Criminal Procedure (Scotland) Act 1975 committing a child for the purpose of his undergoing residential training;

(d) an approved school order under section 61 of the said Act of 1937;

(e) a supervision order under section 63(1) of the Powers of Criminal Courts (Sentencing) Act 2000; or

(f) a supervision requirement under any provision of the Children (Scotland) Act 1995;

(g) a community supervision order under Schedule 5A to the Army Act 1955 or the Air Force Act 1955 or under Schedule 4A to the Naval Discipline Act 1957;

(h) *Repealed*;

the rehabilitation period applicable to the sentence shall be one year from the date of conviction or a period beginning with that date and ending when the order or requirement ceases or ceased to have effect, whichever is the longer.

(6) Where in respect of a conviction any of the following orders was made, that is to say—

(a) an order under section 54 of the said Act of 1933 committing the person convicted to custody in a remand home;

(b) an approved school order under section 57 of the said Act of 1933; or

(c) an attendance centre order under section 60 of the Powers of Criminal Courts (Sentencing) Act 2000; or

(d) a secure training order under section 1 of the Criminal Justice and Public Order Act 1994;

the rehabilitation period applicable to the sentence shall be a period beginning with the date of conviction and ending one year after the date on which the order ceases or ceased to have effect.

(6A) Where in respect of a conviction a detention and training order was made under section 100 of the Powers of Criminal Courts (Sentencing) Act 2000, the rehabilitation period applicable to the sentence shall be—

(a) in the case of a person aged fifteen years or over at the date of his conviction, five years if the order was, and three and a half years if the order was not, for a term exceeding six months;

(b) in the case of a person aged under fifteen years at the date of his conviction, a period beginning with that date and ending one year after the date on which the order ceases to have effect.

(7) Where in respect of a conviction a hospital order under Part III of the Mental Health Act 1983 or under Part VI of the Mental Health (Scotland) Act 1984 (with or without a restriction order) was made, the rehabilitation period applicable to the sentence shall be the period of five years from the date of conviction or a period beginning with that date and ending two years after the date on which the hospital order ceases or ceased to have effect, whichever is the longer.

(8) Where in respect of a conviction an order was made imposing on the person convicted any disqualification, disability, prohibition or other penalty[2], the rehabilitation period applicable to the sentence shall be a period beginning with the date of conviction and ending on the date on which the disqualification, disability, prohibition or penalty (as the case may be) ceases or ceased to have effect.

(9) For the purposes of this section—

(a) "sentence of imprisonment" includes a sentence of detention under section 207 or 415 of the Criminal Procedure (Scotland) Act 1975 and a sentence of penal servitude, and "term of imprisonment" shall be construed accordingly;

(b) consecutive terms of imprisonment or of detention under section 91 of the Powers of Criminal Courts (Sentencing) Act 2000 or section 206 of the said Act of 1975, and terms which are wholly or partly concurrent (being terms of imprisonment or detention imposed in respect of offences of which a person was convicted in the same proceedings) shall be treated as a single term;

(c) no account shall be taken of any subsequent variation, made by a court in dealing with a person in respect of a suspended sentence of imprisonment, of the term originally imposed; and

(d) a sentence imposed by a court outside Great Britain shall be treated as a sentence of that one of the descriptions mentioned in this section which most nearly corresponds to the sentence imposed.

(10) References in this section to the period during which a probation order, or a supervision order under the Powers of Criminal Courts (Sentencing) Act 2000, or a supervision requirement under the Children (Scotland) Act 1995, is or was in force include references to any period during which any order or requirement to which this subsection applies, being an order or requirement made or imposed directly or indirectly in substitution for the first-mentioned order or requirement, is or was in force.

This subsection applies—

(a) to any such order or requirement as is mentioned above in this subsection;

(b) to any order having effect under section 25(2) of the Children and Young Persons Act of 1969 as if it were a training school order in Northern Ireland; and

(c) to any supervision order made under section 72(2) of the said Act of 1968 and having effect as a supervision order under the Children and Young Persons Act (Northern Ireland) 1950.

(10A) *Scotland and Northern Ireland.*

(11) The Secretary of State may by order[3]—

(a) substitute different periods or terms for any of the periods or terms mentioned in subsections (1) to (8) above; and

(b) substitute a different age for the age mentioned in subsection (2)(a) above.

[Rehabilitation of Offenders Act 1974, s 5, as amended by the Armed Forces Act 1976, Sch 9, the Criminal Justice (Scotland) Act 1980, Schs 7 and 8, the Armed Forces Act 1981, Sch 4, the Criminal Justice Act 1982, Schs 14 and 16, the Mental Health (Amendment) Act 1982, Sch 3, the Mental Health Act 1983, Sch 4, the Mental Health (Scotland) Act 1984, Sch 3, the Criminal Justice Act 1988, Sch 8, the Children Act 1989, Sch 15, the Criminal Justice Act 1991, Sch 8, the Armed Forces Act 1991, Sch 3, the Criminal Justice and Public Order Act 1994, Schs 9, 10 and 11, the Children (Scotland) Act 1995, Sch 4, the Crime and Disorder Act 1998, Sch 8, the Youth Justice and Criminal Evidence Act 1999, Sch 4, the Powers of Criminal Courts (Sentencing) Act 2000, Sch 9, the Criminal Justice and Court Services Act 2000, Sch 7 and the Criminal Justice Act 2003, Sch 32.]

---

1. These periods may be extended by the period of a disqualification, etc; see sub-s (8), post.

2. An order for endorsement of a driving licence is a sentence for the purposes of s 1(3) of this Act and is therefore subject to the provisions for rehabilitation. However, an endorsement is simply a record which the sentencing court is obliged to make and is not in that sense a disqualification, disability, prohibition or other penalty within the terms of s 5(8). Accordingly the period of rehabilitation for an endorsement is calculated in accordance with Table A (five years) (and s 6(2) where appropriate) (*Power v Provincial Insurance* (1997) 161 JP 556, [1998] RTR 60, CA).

3. No order has yet been made.

3–945   6. The rehabilitation period applicable to a conviction.   (1) Where only one sentence is imposed in respect of a conviction (not being a sentence excluded from rehabilitation under this Act) the rehabilitation period applicable to the conviction is, subject to the following provisions of this section, the period applicable to the sentence in accordance with section 5 above.

(2) Where more than one sentence is imposed in respect of a conviction (whether or not in the same proceedings) and none of the sentences imposed is excluded from rehabilitation under this Act, then, subject to the following provisions of this section, if the periods applicable to those sentences in accordance with section 5 above differ, the rehabilitation period applicable to the conviction shall be the longer or the longest (as the case may be) of those periods.

(3) Without prejudice to subsection (2) above, where in respect of a conviction a person was conditionally discharged or a probation order was made and after the end of the rehabilitation period applicable to the conviction in accordance with subsection (1) or (2) above he is dealt with, in consequence of a breach of conditional discharge or a breach of the order, for the offence for which the order for conditional discharge or probation order was made, then, if the rehabilitation period applicable to the conviction in accordance with subsection (2) above (taking into account any sentence imposed when he is so dealt with) ends later than the rehabilitation period previously applicable to the conviction, he shall be treated for the purposes of this Act as not having become a rehabilitated person in respect of that conviction, and the conviction shall for those purposes be treated as not having become spent, in relation to any period falling before the end of the new rehabilitation period.

(4) Subject to subsection (5) below, where during the rehabilitation period applicable to a conviction—

(a) the person convicted is convicted of a further offence; and

(b) no sentence excluded from rehabilitation under this Act is imposed on him in respect of the later conviction;

if the rehabilitation period applicable in accordance with this section to either of the convictions would end earlier than the period so applicable in relation to the other, the rehabilitation period which would (apart from this subsection) end the earlier shall be extended so as to end at the same time as the other rehabilitation period.

(5) Where the rehabilitation period applicable to a conviction is the rehabilitation period applicable in accordance with section 5(8) above to an order imposing on a person any disqualification, disability, prohibition or other penalty, the rehabilitation period applicable to another conviction shall not by virtue of subsection (4) above be extended by reference to that period; but if any other sentence is imposed in respect of the first-mentioned conviction for which a rehabilitation period is prescribed by any other provision of section 5 above, the rehabilitation period applicable to another conviction shall, where appropriate, be extended under subsection (4) above by reference to the rehabilitation period applicable in accordance with that section to that sentence or, where more than one such sentence is imposed, by reference to the longer or longest of the periods so applicable to those sentences, as if the period in question were the rehabilitation period applicable to the first-mentioned conviction.

(6) For the purposes of subsection (4)(*a*) above there shall be disregarded—

(*a*) any conviction in England and Wales of [a summary offence or of a scheduled offence (within the meaning of section 22 of the Magistrates' Courts Act 1980 tried summarily in pursuance of subsection (2) of that section (summary trial where value involved is small), or of an offence under section 17 of the Crime (Sentences) Act 1997 (breach of conditions of release supervision order);

(*b*) any conviction in Scotland of an offence which is not excluded from the jurisdiction of inferior courts of summary jurisdiction by virtue of section 4 of the Summary Jurisdiction (Scotland) Act 1954 (certain crimes not to be tried in inferior courts of summary jurisdiction); and

(*bb*) any conviction in service disciplinary proceedings for an offence listed in the Schedule[1] to this Act;

(*c*) any conviction by or before a court outside Great Britain of an offence in respect of conduct which, if it had taken place in any part of Great Britain, would not have constituted an offence under the law in force in that part of Great Britain.

(7) *Repealed.*

[Rehabilitation of Offenders Act 1974, s 6, as amended by the Criminal Law Act 1977, Sch 12, the Magistrates' Courts Act 1980, Sch 7, the Armed Forces Act 1996, s 13 and Sch 7, the Crime (Sentences) Act 1997, Sch 4 and the Criminal Justice and Court Services Act 2000, Sch 7.]

---

1. The Schedule which was inserted by the Armed Forces Act 1996, Sch 4, is not reproduced in this Manual.

3–946   7. Limitations on rehabilitation under this Act, etc.   (1) Nothing in section 4(1) above shall affect[1]—

(*a*) any right of Her Majesty, by virtue of Her Royal prerogative or otherwise, to grant a free pardon, to quash any conviction or sentence, or to commute any sentence;

(*b*) the enforcement by any process or proceedings of any fine or other sum adjudged to be paid by or imposed on a spent conviction;

(*c*) the issue of any process for the purpose of proceedings in respect of any breach of a condition or requirement applicable to a sentence imposed in respect of a spent conviction; or

(*d*) the operation of any enactment by virtue of which, in consequence of any conviction, a person is subject, otherwise than by way of sentence, to any disqualification, disability, prohibition or other penalty the period of which extends beyond the rehabilitation period applicable in accordance with section 6 above to the conviction.

(2) Nothing in section 4(1) above shall affect the determination of any issue, or prevent the admission or requirement of any evidence, relating to a person's previous convictions or to circumstances ancillary thereto—

(*a*) in any criminal proceedings[2] before a court in Great Britain (including any appeal or reference in a criminal matter);

(*b*) in any service disciplinary proceedings or in any proceedings on appeal from any service disciplinary proceedings;

(*bb*) in any proceedings under Part 2 of the Sexual Offences Act 2993, or on appeal from any such proceedings;

(*c*) in any proceedings relating to adoption, the marriage of any minor, the exercise of the inherent jurisdiction of the High Court with respect to minors or the provision by any person of accommodation, care or schooling for minors;

(*cc*) in any proceedings brought under the Children Act 1989;

(*d*) in any proceedings relating to the variation or discharge of a supervision order under the Powers of Criminal Courts (Sentencing) Act 2000, or on appeal from any such proceedings;

(*e*) *Repealed;*

(*f*) in any proceedings in which he is a party or a witness, provided that, on the occasion when the issue or the admission or requirement of the evidence falls to be determined, he consents to the determination of the issue or, as the case may be, the admission or requirement of the evidence notwithstanding the provisions of section 4(1); or

(*g*) *Repealed.*

(3) If at any stage in any proceedings before a judicial authority[3] in Great Britain (not being

proceedings to which, by virtue of any of paragraphs (*a*) to (*e*) of subsection (2) above or of any order for the time being in force under subsection (6) below, section 4(1) above has no application, or proceedings to which section 8 below applies) the authority is satisfied, in the light of any considerations which appear to it to be relevant (including any evidence which has been or may thereafter be put before it), that justice cannot be done in the case except by admitting or requiring evidence relating to a person's spent convictions or to circumstances ancillary thereto, that authority may admit or, as the case may be, require the evidence in question notwithstanding the provisions of subsection (1) of section 4 above, and may determine any issue to which the evidence relates in disregard, so far as necessary, of those provisions.

(4) The Secretary of State may by order[4] exclude the application of section 4(1) above in relation to any proceedings specified in the order (other than proceedings to which section 8 below applies) to such extent and for such purposes as may be so specified.

(5) No order made by a court with respect to any person otherwise than on a conviction shall be included in any list or statement of that person's previous convictions given or made to any court which is considering how to deal with him in respect of any offence.

[Rehabilitation of Offenders Act 1974, s 7, as amended by the Banking Act 1979, s 43, the Banking Act 1987, Sch 7, the Children Act 1989, Sch 13, the Children (Scotland) Act 1995, Sch 4 and Sch 5, the Crime and Disorder Act 1998, Sch 8, the Powers of Criminal Courts (Sentencing) Act 2000, Sch 9, the Police Reform Act 2002, Sch 7 and the Sexual Offences Act 2003, Sch 6.]

---

1. The provisions of s 4 are also restricted for the purposes of determining whether to grant or revoke a licence under the National Lottery Act 1993 (s 19).

2. Previous convictions may be admissible during a trial (eg when the character of the accused or a witness is attacked, or to prove system); or after conviction as evidence of antecedents. In a *Practice Direction (criminal: consolidated)* [2002] para I.6, in PART I: MAGISTRATES' COURTS, PROCEDURE, *ante*, the Lord Chief Justice has stated that when previous "spent" convictions are admissible during a trial they should not be referred to if it can be reasonably avoided and, in any event, should not be referred to without the authority of the judge. However, a Practice Direction cannot determine the proper construction of a statute; on a true construction of ss 4 and 7 the latter is the prevailing provision and where a co-accused has "given evidence against" another within the meaning of s 1(*f*)(iii) of the Criminal Evidence Act 1898 then, provided the proposed question is relevant, the latter may cross-examine the former as to a spent conviction: *R v Corelli* [2001] EWCA Crim 974, [2001] Crim LR 913. Subject to that, we suggest that it would be proper to apply the principles stated in the Practice Direction in magistrates' courts. In Home Office circular 98/1975 the Secretary of State suggests (in para 2 of Part IV) that no *oral* reference should be made to any "spent" conviction unless it has influenced the court in determining sentence, and in Home Office circular 130/1975 it is intimated that magistrates' courts will no doubt wish to follow the guidance given by the Lord Chief Justice to the Crown Court. See also *R v Bailey* [1989] Crim LR 723.

3. The purpose of s 7(3) is not to confer a dispensing power to be exercised by way of discretion by adjudicating bodies but to ensure that spent convictions stay spent, unless in the classes of case where it is permissible to do so the party applying to put the spent conviction in can satisfy the judicial authority concerned that there is no other way of doing justice; see *R v Hastings Magistrates' Court, ex p McSpirit* (1994) 162 JP 44. For the procedure to be adopted when admitting spent convictions before a local authority or justices considering the grant of a licence to drive a hackney carriage, see *Adamson v Waveney District Council* [1997] 2 All ER 898, 161 JP 787, DC and the Local Government (Miscellaneous Provisions) Act 1976, s 59(1) and notes thereto in PART VIII title LOCAL GOVERNMENT, *post*. As to the admissibility of spent convictions on an application for forfeiture of cash under s 43(1) of the Drug Trafficking Act 1994, in PART III title MEDICINE AND PHARMACY, *post* see *R v Isleworth Crown Court, ex p Marland* (1997) 162 JP 251.

4. See the Rehabilitation of Offenders Act 1974 (Exceptions) Order 1975, this PART: STATUTORY INSTRUMENTS ON SENTENCING, *post*.

3–947 8. Defamation actions. (1) This section applies to any action for libel or slander begun after the commencement of this Act by a rehabilitated person and found upon the publication of any matter imputing that the plaintiff has committed or been charged with or prosecuted for or convicted of or sentenced for an offence which was the subject of a spent conviction.

(2) Nothing in section 4(1) above shall affect an action to which this section applies where the publication complained of took place before the conviction in question became spent, and the following provisions of this section shall not apply in any such case.

(3) Subject to subsections (5) and (6) below, nothing in section 4(1) above shall prevent the defendant in an action to which this section applies from relying on any defence of justification or fair comment or of absolute or qualified privilege which is available to him, or restrict the matters he may establish in support of any such defence.

(4) Without prejudice to the generality of subsection (3) above, where in any such action malice is alleged against a defendant who is relying on a defence of qualified privilege, nothing in section 4(1) above shall restrict the matters he may establish in rebuttal of the allegation.

(5) A defendant in any such action shall not by virtue of subsection (3) above be entitled to rely upon the defence of justification if the publication is proved to have been made with malice.

(6) Subject to subsection (7) below a defendant in any such action shall not, by virtue of subsection (3) above, be entitled to rely on any matter or adduce or require any evidence for the purpose of establishing (whether under section 14 of the Defamation Act 1996 or otherwise) the defence that the matter published constituted a fair and accurate report of judicial proceedings if it is proved that the publication contained a reference to evidence which was ruled to be inadmissible in the proceedings by virtue of section 4(1) above.

(7) Subsection (3) above shall apply without the qualifications imposed by subsection (6) above in relation to—

(*a*) any report of judicial proceedings contained in any bona fide series of law reports which does not form part of any other publication and consists solely of reports of proceedings in courts of law; and

(b) any report or account of judicial proceedings published for bona fide educational, scientific or professional purposes, or given in the course of any lecture, class or discussion given or held for any of those purposes.

(8) *(Applies to Scotland.)*

[Rehabilitation of Offenders Act 1974, s 8 as amended by the Defamation Act 1996, s 14.]

3–948   9. Unauthorised disclosure of spent convictions. (1) In this section—

"official record" means a record kept for the purposes of its functions by any court, police force, Government department, local or other public authority in Great Britain, or a record kept, in Great Britain or elsewhere, for the purposes of any of Her Majesty's forces; being in either case a record containing information about persons convicted of offences; and

"specified information" means information imputing that a named or otherwise identifiable rehabilitated living person has committed or been charged with or prosecuted for or convicted of or sentenced for any offence which is the subject of a spent conviction.

(2) Subject to the provisions of any order made under subsection (5) below, any person who, in the course of his official duties, has or at any time has had custody of or access to any official record[1] or the information contained therein, shall be guilty of an offence if, knowing or having reasonable cause to suspect that any specified information he has obtained in the course of those duties is specified information, he discloses it, otherwise than in the course of those duties, to another person[2].

(3) In any proceedings for an offence under subsection (2) above it shall be a defence for the defendant (or, in Scotland, the accused person) to show that the disclosure was made—

(a) to the rehabilitated person or to another person at the express request of the rehabilitated person; or

(b) to a person whom he reasonably believed to be the rehabilitated person or to another person at the express request of a person whom he reasonably believed to be the rehabilitated person.

(4) Any person who obtains any specified information from any official record by means of any fraud, dishonesty or bribe shall be guilty of an offence.

(5) The Secretary of State may by order[3] make such provision as appears to him to be appropriate for excepting the disclosure of specified information derived from an official record from the provisions of subsection (2) above in such cases or classes of case as may be specified in the order.

(6) Any person guilty of an offence under subsection (2) above shall be liable on summary conviction to a fine not exceeding **level 4** on the standard scale.

(7) Any person guilty of an offence under subsection (4) above shall be liable on summary conviction to a fine not exceeding **level 5** on the standard scale or to imprisonment for a term not exceeding **six months**, or both.

(8) Proceedings for an offence under subsection (2) above shall not, in England and Wales, be instituted except by or on behalf of the Director of Public Prosecutions.

[Rehabilitation of Offenders Act 1974, s 9, as amended by the Criminal Justice Act 1982, ss 38 and 46.]

---

1. This will include justices' clerks and their assistants.

2. We are of opinion that it would not be an offence under this subsection for a justices' clerk or his assistant to disclose information about a "spent" conviction if (a) he is under a statutory duty to do so (eg under r 66(12) of the Magistrates' Courts Rules 1981 or the Criminal Procedure Rules 2005, Part 6); (b) disclosure is made to a person who would have a lawful use for such information for the purposes of sub-s (1), (2) or (3) of s 7, supra; and (c) disclosure is made to a person who would have a lawful use for such information having regard to the exceptions set out in the Rehabilitation of Offenders Act 1974 (Exceptions) Order 1975 (this PART: STATUTORY INSTRUMENTS ON SENTENCING, post.) The Secretary of State has given guidance as to further circumstances in which, in his opinion, s 9(2) would not be contravened in para 8 of Part III of Home Office circular 98/1975 and, with regard to research projects, in Home Office letter, dated 17 May 1977.

3. No order has yet been made.

3–949   11. Citation, commencement and extent. (2) This Act shall come into force on 1st July 1975 or such earlier day as the Secretary of State may by order appoint.

3–949A   SCHEDULE
                                      SERVICE DISCIPLINARY CONVICTIONS
                                (Inserted by the Armed Forces Act 1996, Sch 4)

Licensed Premises (Exclusion of Certain Persons) Act 1980[1]
(1980 c 32)

3–960   1. Exclusion orders. (1) Where a court by or before which a person is convicted of an offence committed on licensed premises is satisfied that in committing that offence he resorted to violence or offered or threatened to resort to violence, the court may, subject to subsection (2) below, make an order[2] (in this Act referred to as an "exclusion order") prohibiting him from entering those premises or any other specified premises[3], without the express consent of the licensee of the premises or his servant or agent.

(2) An exclusion order may be made either—

(a) in addition to any sentence which is imposed in respect of the offence of which the person is convicted; or

(b) where the offence was committed in England or Wales, notwithstanding the provisions of sections 12 and 14 of the Powers of Criminal Courts (Sentencing) Act 2000 (cases in which absolute and conditional discharges may be made, and their effect), in addition to an order discharging him absolutely or conditionally; or

(c) where the offence was committed in Scotland, notwithstanding the provisions of sections 228, 246(2) and (3) and 247 of the Criminal Procedure (Scotland) Act 1995 (cases in which probation orders and absolute discharges may be made, and their effect), in addition to a probation order or an order discharging him absolutely;

but not otherwise.

(3) An exclusion order shall have effect for such period, not less than three months or more than two years, as is specified in the order, unless it is terminated under section 2(2) below.

[Licensed Premises (Exclusion of Certain Persons) Act 1980, s 1 as amended by the Criminal Justice Act 1991, Sch 11, the Criminal Procedure (Consequential Provisions) (Scotland) Act 1995, Sch 4, and the Powers of Criminal Courts (Sentencing) Act 2000, Sch 9.]

---

1. The Licensing Acts 1964 to 1976, the Licensing (Amendment) Act 1977, this Act, the Licensing (Amendment) Act 1980 and the Licensing (Alcohol Education and Research) Act 1981 may be cited as the Licensing Acts 1964 to 1981 (Licensing (Alcohol Education and Research) Act 1981, s 13(2)).

2. An exclusion order is designed for and justified in cases of those who might shortly be described as making a nuisance of themselves in public houses and as therefore qualifying to be debarred from going in to the annoyance of other customers and possible danger to the licensee (*R v Grady* (1990) 12 Cr App Rep (S) 152, CA). The court may make an order under this section on its own motion (*R v Penn* [1996] 2 Cr App Rep (S) 214, [1996] Crim LR 360). It is not wrong in principle for an exclusion order to specify a large number of public houses in an area where the offender might go to drink (*R v Arrowsmith* [2003] EWCA Crim 701, [2003] 2 Cr App R (S) 46).

3. A person who is a known troublemaker in public houses may be excluded from all the public houses that he might readily visit; "specified premises" means those specified in the order (in the instant case all the public house in the borough of Nantwich and Crewe) (*R v Arrowsmith* [2003] EWCA Crim 701, [2003] Crim LR 412).

3–961   2. Penalty for non-compliance with exclusion order.   (1) A person who enters any premises in breach of an exclusion order shall be guilty of an offence and shall be liable on summary conviction or, in Scotland, on conviction in a court of summary jurisdiction to a fine not exceeding **level 3** on the standard scale or to imprisonment for a term not exceeding **one month*** or **both**.

(2) The court by which a person is convicted of an offence under subsection (1) above shall consider whether or not the exclusion order should continue in force, and may, if it thinks fit, by order terminate the exclusion order or vary it by deleting the name of any specified premises, but an exclusion order shall not otherwise be affected by a person's conviction for such an offence.

[Licensed Premises (Exclusion of Certain Persons) Act 1980, s 2 as amended by the Criminal Justice Act 1982, s 46.]

---

*Words repealed and substituted with "51 weeks" by the Criminal Justice Act 2003, Sch 26, from a date to be appointed.

3–962   3. Power to expel person from licensed premises.   Without prejudice to any other right to expel a person from premises, the licensee of licensed premises or his servant or agent may expel from those premises any person who has entered or whom he reasonably suspects of having entered the premises in breach of an exclusion order; and a constable shall on the demand of the licensee or his servant or agent help to expel from licensed premises any person whom the constable reasonably suspects of having entered in breach of an exclusion order.

[Licensed Premises (Exclusion of Certain Persons) Act 1980, s 3.]

3–963   4. Supplemental.   (1) In this Act—

"licensed premises", in relation to England and Wales, means premises in respect of which there is in force a premises licence under the Licensing Act 2003 authorising the supply of alcohol (within the meaning of section 14 of that Act) for consumption on the premises and, in relation to Scotland, means premises in respect of which a licence under the Licensing (Scotland) Act 1976, other than an off-sales licence or a licence under Part III of that Act (licences for seamen's canteens), is in force; and

"licensee" in relation to any licensed premises means the holder of the licence granted in respect of those premises; and

"specified premises", in relation to an exclusion order, means any licensed premises which the court may specify by name and address in the order.

(2) *Scotland*.

(3) Where a court makes an exclusion order or an order terminating or varying an exclusion order, the proper officer of the court shall send a copy of the order to the licensee of the premises to which the order relates.

(4) For the purposes of subsection (3) above—

(a) the proper officer of a magistrates' court in England and Wales is the justices' chief executive for the court;

(b) the proper officer of the Crown Court is the appropriate officer; and

(*c*)   the proper officer of a court in Scotland is the clerk of the court.
[Licensed Premises (Exclusion of Certain Persons) Act 1980, s 4, as amended by the Access to Justice Act 1999, Sch 13 and the Licensing Act 2003, Sch 6.]

3–964   5. Short title, citation and extent.   (1)   This Act shall be cited as the Licensed Premises (Exclusion of Certain Persons) Act 1980 and this Act, in its application to Scotland, and the Licensing (Scotland) Act 1976 may be cited together as the Licensing (Scotland) Acts 1976 to 1980.
     (2)   This Act shall not extend to Northern Ireland.
[Licensed Premises (Exclusion of Certain Persons) Act 1980, s 5.]

Criminal Justice Act 1982
(1982 c 48)

PART I[1]
TREATMENT OF YOUNG OFFENDERS
Custody and detention of persons under 21

3–1090   1. General restriction on custodial sentences.   (1)   (5A) *Repealed.*
     (6)   For the purposes of any provision of this Act which requires the determination of the age of a person by the court or the Secretary of State his age shall be deemed to be that which it appears to the court or the Secretary of State (as the case may be) to be after considering any available evidence[2].
[Criminal Justice Act 1982, s 1 as amended by the Criminal Justice Act 1988, s 123, the Criminal Justice Act 1991, Schs 11 and 13, the Crime and Disorder Act 1998, Sch 8 and of the Powers of Criminal Courts (Sentencing) Act 2000, Sch 9.]

---

   1.   Part I contains ss 1–28.
   2.   If on the material before the court an offender is deemed to be 21, he shall be treated on that basis; the fact that he is subsequently found to be under 21 does not invalidate the sentence (*R v Brown* (1989) 11 Cr App Rep (S) 263).

3–1091   1A–19.   *Repealed.*

PART II[1]
PARTIAL SUSPENSION OF SENTENCES, EARLY RELEASE, RELEASE ON LICENCE OR BAIL ETC
Early release

3–1107   32. Early release of prisoners.   (1)   The Secretary of State may order that persons of any class specified in the order who are serving a sentence of imprisonment, other than—

(*a*)   imprisonment for life, imprisonment for public protection under section 225 of the Criminal Justice 2003 or an extended sentence under section 227 of that Act; or

(*b*)   imprisonment to which they were sentenced—

     (i)   for an excluded offence;

     (ii)   for attempting to commit such an offence;

     (iii)   for conspiracy to commit such an offence; or

     (iv)   for aiding or abetting, counselling, procuring or inciting the commission of such an offence,

shall be released from prison at such time earlier (but not more than six months earlier) than they would otherwise be so released as may be fixed by the order; but the Secretary of State shall not make an order under this section unless he is satisfied that it is necessary to do so in order to make the best use of the places available for detention.

     (2)   In this section "excluded offence" means—

(*a*)   an offence (whether at common law or under any enactment) specified in Part I of Schedule 1 to this Act; and

(*b*)   an offence under an enactment specified in Part II of that Schedule; and

(*c*)   an offence specified in Part III of that Schedule.

     (3)   No person may be released under this section if—

(*a*)   he is subject to more than one sentence of imprisonment; and

(*b*)   at least one of the terms that he has to serve is for an offence mentioned in subsection (1)(*b*)(i), (ii), (iii) or (iv) above.

     (4)   An order under this section—

(*a*)   may define a class of persons in any way;

(*b*)   may relate to one or more specified prisons, or to prisons of a specified class (however defined), or to prisons generally; and

(*c*)   may make the time at which a person of any specified class is to be released depend on any circumstances whatever.

     (5)   Where a person who is to be released from prison in pursuance of an order under this section is a person serving a sentence of imprisonment in respect of whom an extended sentence certificate (within the meaning of the Powers of Criminal Courts Act 1973) was issued when the sentence was

passed, his release shall be a release on licence under section 60 of the Criminal Justice Act 1967, irrespective of whether at the time of his release he could have been released on licence under that section by virtue of subsection (3) thereof.

(6) Where a person not within subsection (5) above is released from prison in pursuance of an order under this section, his sentence shall expire on his release.

(7) Subsections (1), (4) and (6) above shall apply in relation to any institution to which the Prison Act 1952 applies and to persons detained in any such institutions other than persons serving sentences of custody for life, as they apply in relation to prisons and persons serving such sentences of imprisonment as are mentioned in subsection (1) above.

(7A) Subsections (1) and (4) above shall apply in relation to secure training centres and persons detained in such centres as they apply, by virtue of section 43(5) of the Prison Act 1952, to young offenders institutions and to persons detained in such institutions.

(8) An order under this section shall be made by statutory instrument.

(9) No order under this section shall be made unless—

(a) a draft of the order has been laid before Parliament and approved by resolution of each House of Parliament; or

(b) the expedited procedure conditions are satisfied.

(10) The expedited procedure conditions are satisfied if—

(a) the order does not provide for the release of any persons before one month earlier than they would otherwise be released; and

(b) it is declared in the order that it appears to the Secretary of State that by reason of urgency it is necessary to make the order without a draft having been so approved.

(11) Every such order (except such an order of which a draft has been so approved)—

(a) shall be laid before Parliament; and

(b) shall cease to have effect at the expiry of a period of 40 days beginning with the date on which it was made unless, before the expiry of that period, the order has been approved by resolution of each House of Parliament, but without prejudice to anything previously done or to the making of a new order.

(12) In reckoning for the purposes of subsection (11) above any period of 40 days, no account shall be taken of any period during which Parliament is dissolved or prorogued or during which both Houses are adjourned for more than 4 days.

(13) An order under this section shall not remain in force after the expiration of 6 months beginning with the date on which it is made, but without prejudice to the power of the Secretary of State to revoke it or to make a further order under this section.

(14) Section 5 of the Imprisonment (Temporary Provisions) Act 1980 (which is superseded by this section) shall cease to have effect.

[Criminal Justice Act 1982, s 32 as amended by the Criminal Justice and Public Order Act 1994, Sch 10 and the Criminal Justice Act 2003, Sch 32.]

---

1. Part II contains ss 29–34.

PART III[1]

FINES ETC

Abolition of enhanced penalties

3–1108 35. Abolition of enhanced penalties on subsequent conviction of summary offences under Acts of Parliament. (1) Subject to subsection (3) below, this section applies where under an Act a person convicted of a summary offence—

(a) is liable to a fine or maximum fine of one amount in the case of a first conviction and of a different amount in the case of a second or subsequent conviction; or

(b) is liable to imprisonment for a longer term in the case of a second or subsequent conviction; or

(c) is only liable to imprisonment in the case of a second or subsequent conviction.

(2) Where this section applies, a person guilty of such an offence shall be liable on summary conviction—

(a) to a fine or, as the case may be, a maximum fine of an amount not exceeding the greatest amount;

(b) to imprisonment for a term not exceeding the longest or only term,

to which he would have been liable before this section came into force if his conviction had satisfied the conditions required for the imposition of a fine or maximum fine of that amount or imprisonment for that term.

(3) This section does not apply to offences under—

(a) sections 33 to 36 of the Sexual Offences Act 1956 (brothel-keeping and prostitution); or

(b) section 1(2) of the Street Offences Act 1959 (loitering and soliciting for the purpose of prostitution).

[Criminal Justice Act 1982, s 35.]

---

1. Part III contains ss 35–52.

3–1109   **36. Abolition of enhanced penalties under subordinate instruments.**   (1) This section applies where an Act (however framed or worded) confers power by subordinate instrument to make a person, as regards any summary offence (whether or not created by the instrument), liable on conviction—

(a)   to a fine or maximum fine of one amount in the case of a first conviction and of a different amount in the case of a second or subsequent conviction; or

(b)   to imprisonment for a longer term in the case of a second or subsequent conviction; or

(c)   to imprisonment only in the case of a second or subsequent conviction.

(2) Any such Act shall have effect as if it conferred power by subordinate instrument to make a person liable—

(a)   to a fine or, as the case may be, a maximum fine of an amount not exceeding the greatest amount;

(b)   to imprisonment for a term not exceeding the longest or only term,

to which he would have been liable before this section came into force if his conviction had satisfied the conditions required for the imposition of a fine or maximum fine of that amount or imprisonment for that term.

[Criminal Justice Act 1982, s 36.]

Introduction of standard scale of fines

3–1120   **37. The standard scale of fines for summary offences.**   (1) There shall be a standard scale of fines for summary offences, which shall be known as "the standard scale".

(2) The standard scale is shown below—

Level on the scale	Amount of fine
1	£200
2	£500
3	£1,000
4	£2,500
5	£5,000

(3) Where any enactment (whether contained in an Act passed before or after this Act) provides—

(a)   that a person convicted of a summary offence shall be liable on conviction to a fine or a maximum fine by reference to a specified level on the standard scale; or

(b)   confers power by subordinate instrument to make a person liable on conviction of a summary offence (whether or not created by the instrument) to a fine or maximum fine by reference to a specified level on the standard scale,

it is to be construed as referring to the standard scale for which this section provides as that standard scale has effect from time to time by virtue either of this section or of an order under section 143 of the Magistrates' Courts Act 1980.

[Criminal Justice Act 1982, s 37 as amended by the Criminal Justice Act 1991, s 17.]

Increase of fines

3–1121   **38. General increase of fines for summary offences under Acts of Parliament.**   (1) Subject to subsection (5) below and to section 39(1) below, this section applies to any enactment contained in an Act passed before this Act (however framed or worded) which, as regards any summary offence created not later than 29th July 1977 (the date of the passing of the Criminal Law Act 1977), makes a person liable on conviction to a fine or maximum fine which—

(a)   is less than £1,000; and

(b)   was not altered by section 30 or 31 of the Criminal Law Act 1977; and

(c)   has not been altered since 29th July 1977 or has only been altered since that date by section 35 above.

(2) Subject to subsection (7) below, where an enactment to which this section applies provides on conviction of a summary offence for a fine or maximum fine in respect of a specified quantity or a specified number of things, that fine or maximum fine shall be treated for the purposes of this section as being the fine or maximum fine for the offence.

(3) Where an enactment to which this section applies provides for different fines or maximum fines in relation to different circumstances or persons of different descriptions, they are to be treated separately for the purposes of this section.

(4) An enactment in which section 31(6) and (7) of the Criminal Law Act 1977 (pre-1949 enactments) produced the same fine or maximum fine for different convictions shall be treated for the purposes of this section as if there were omitted from it so much of it as before 29th July 1977 had the effect that a person guilty of an offence under it was liable on summary conviction to a fine or maximum fine less than the highest fine or maximum fine to which he would have been liable if his conviction had satisfied the conditions required for the imposition of the highest fine or maximum fine.

(5) This section shall not affect so much of any enactment as (in whatever words) makes a person

liable on summary conviction to a fine or maximum fine for each period of a specified length during which a continuing offence is continued.

(6) The fine or maximum fine for an offence under an enactment to which this section applies shall be increased to the amount at the appropriate level on the standard scale unless it is an enactment in relation to which section 39(2) below provides for some other increase.

(7) Where an enactment to which this section applies provides on conviction of a summary offence for a fine or maximum fine in respect of a specified quantity or a specified number of things but also specifies an alternative fine or maximum fine, subsection (6) above shall have effect to increase—

(*a*) the alternative fine; and

(*b*) any amount that the enactment specifies as the maximum which a fine under it may not exceed,

as well as the fine or maximum fine which it has effect to increase by virtue of subsection (2) above.

(8) Subject to subsection (9) below, the appropriate level on the standard scale for the purposes of subsections (6) and (7) above is the level on that scale next above the amount of the fine or maximum fine that falls to be increased.

(9) If the amount of the fine or maximum fine that falls to be increased is £400 or more but less than £500, the appropriate level is £1,000.

(10) Where section 35 above applies, the amount of the fine or maximum fine that falls to be increased is to be taken to be the fine or maximum fine to which a person is liable by virtue of that section.

[Criminal Justice Act 1982, s 38.]

3–1122   39. Special cases.   (1) Section 38 above does not apply—

(*a*) to any enactment specified in Schedule 2 to this Act; or

(*b*) to the following enactments—

(i) *Repealed*;

(ii) any enactment specified in the Schedule to the London Transport Act 1977 or in Schedule 1 to the British Railways Act 1977 to the extent that the enactment was amended by section 12(1)[1] of the former Act or section 13(1) of the latter;

(iii) any enactment specified in Part I of Schedule 2 to the City of London (Various Powers) Act 1977.

(2) The enactments specified in column 2 of Schedule 3 to this Act, which relate to the maximum fines for the offences mentioned (and broadly described) in column 1 of that Schedule, shall have effect as if the maximum fine that may be imposed on conviction of any offence so mentioned were a fine not exceeding the amount specified in column 4 of that Schedule instead of a fine not exceeding the amount specified in column 3.

(3) The enactments specified in column 2 of Schedule 4 to this Act, which relate to certain maximum fines that may be imposed on a person otherwise than on conviction of an offence, their broad effect being described in column 1 of that Schedule, shall have effect as if the maximum fine that may be imposed were a fine not exceeding the amount specified in column 4 of that Schedule instead of a fine not exceeding the amount specified in column 3.

[Criminal Justice Act 1982, s 39 as amended by the Road Traffic (Consequential Provisions) Act 1988 Sch 1.]

---

1. This shall be read as including s 12(1) as extended by Pt II of Sch 6 to the London Regional Transport Act 1984 (London Regional Transport Act 1984, Sch 6, Pt I, para 27).

3–1123   40. General increase of maximum fines under subordinate instruments.   (1) Subject to subsection (4) below, this section applies to any enactment contained in an Act passed before this Act (however framed or worded) which confers a power, created not later than 29th July 1977, by subordinate instrument to make a person, as regards any summary offence (whether or not created by the instrument), liable on conviction to a fine or maximum fine which—

(*a*) is less than £1,000; and

(*b*) was not altered by section 31 of the Criminal Law Act 1977,

if the fine or maximum fine to which a person may be made liable by virtue of the enactment has not been altered since 29th July 1977 or has only been altered since that date by section 36 above.

(2) Subject to subsection (7) below, where an enactment to which this section applies confers a power by subordinate instrument to make a person, as regards a summary offence, liable on conviction to a fine or maximum fine in respect of a specified quantity or a specified number of things, that fine or maximum fine shall be treated for the purposes of this section as being the fine or maximum fine to which a person may be made liable by virtue of the enactment.

(3) Where an enactment to which this section applies confers a power to provide for different fines or maximum fines in relation to different circumstances or persons of different descriptions, the amounts specified as those fines or maximum fines are to be treated separately for the purposes of this section.

(4) This section shall not affect so much of any enactment as (in whatever words) confers power by subordinate instrument to make a person liable on conviction to a fine or maximum fine for each period of a specified length during which a continuing offence is continued.

(5) Subject to subsection (6) below, the fine or maximum fine to which a person may be made liable by virtue of an enactment to which this section applies shall be increased to the amount at the appropriate level on the standard scale.

(6) Subsection (5) above does not apply—

(a) to section 67(3) of the Transport Act 1962 (byelaws for railways and railway shipping services);

(b) to section 25(2) of the London Transport Act 1969 (byelaws for road transport premises);

(c) to the enactments specified in Part II of Schedule 2 to the City of London (Various Powers) Act 1977; or

(d) to the enactments specified in Schedule 2 to the British Railways Act 1977.

(7) Where an enactment to which this section applies confers a power by subordinate instrument to make a person, as regards a summary offence, liable on conviction to a fine or maximum fine in respect of a specified quantity or a specified number of things but also confers a power by subordinate instrument to make a person, as regards such an offence, liable on conviction to an alternative fine or maximum fine, subsection (5) above shall have effect to increase—

(a) the alternative fine; and

(b) any amount that the enactment specifies as the maximum fine for which a subordinate instrument made in the exercise of the power conferred by it may provide,

as well as the fine or maximum fine which it has effect to increase by virtue of subsection (2) above.

(8) Subject to subsection (9) below, the appropriate level on the standard scale for the purposes of subsections (5) and (7) above is the level on that scale next above the amount that falls to be increased.

(9) If the amount that falls to be increased is £400 or more but less than £500, the appropriate level is £1,000.

(10) Where section 36 above applies, the amount that falls to be increased is the fine or maximum fine to which a person may be made liable by virtue of that section.
[Criminal Justice Act 1982, s 40.]

Application of standard scale to existing enactments

3–1125   46. Conversion of references to amounts to references to levels on scale.
(1) Where—

(a) either—

(i) a relevant enactment makes a person liable to a fine or maximum fine on conviction of a summary offence; or

(ii) a relevant enactment confers power by subordinate instrument to make a person liable to a fine or maximum fine on conviction of a summary offence (whether or not created by the instrument); and

(b) the amount of the fine or maximum fine for the offence is, whether by virtue of this Part of this Act or not, an amount shown in the second column of the standard scale,

a reference to the level in the first column of the standard scale corresponding to that amount shall be substituted for the reference in the enactment to the amount of the fine or maximum fine.

(2) Where a relevant enactment confers a power such as is mentioned in subsection (1)(a)(ii) above, the power shall be construed as a power to make a person liable to a fine or, as the case may be, a maximum fine not exceeding the amount corresponding to the level on the standard scale to which the enactment refers by virtue of subsection (1) above or not exceeding a lesser amount.

(3) If an order under section 143 of the Magistrates' Courts Act 1980 alters the sums specified in section 37(2) above, the second reference to the standard scale in subsection (1) above is to be construed as a reference to that scale as it has effect by virtue of the order.

(4) In this section "relevant enactment" means—

(a) any enactment contained in an Act passed before this Act;

(b) any enactment contained in this Act;

(c) any enactment contained in an Act passed on the same day as this Act; and

(d) any enactment contained in an Act passed after this Act but in the same Session as this Act.

(5) This section shall not affect so much of any enactment as (in whatever words) makes a person liable on summary conviction to a maximum fine not exceeding a specified amount for each period of a specified length during which a continuing offence is continued.
[Criminal Justice Act 1982, s 46 as amended by the Companies Consolidation (Consequential Provisions) Act 1985, Sch 1.]

3–1126   47. Provisions supplementary to sections 35 to 46.   (1) In sections 35 to 40 and 46 above "fine" includes a pecuniary penalty but does not include a pecuniary forfeiture or pecuniary compensation.

(2) Nothing in any provision contained in sections 35 to 46 above shall affect the punishment for an offence committed before that provision comes into force.
[Criminal Justice Act 1982, s 47.]

Shipping and oil pollution

3–1127   **49. Fines for certain offences under Merchant Shipping Acts and Prevention of Oil Pollution Act 1971.**   (1) Where a provision of the Merchant Shipping Acts 1894 to 1979 or the Prevention of Oil Pollution Act 1971—

     (*a*)   makes a person guilty of an offence triable either summarily or on indictment liable on summary conviction to a fine not exceeding £1,000; or

     (*b*)   confers power by subordinate instrument to make a person liable to a fine not exceeding £1,000 on summary conviction of an offence triable either summarily or on indictment,

the reference to £1,000 shall be construed as a reference to the statutory maximum.

     (2)–(4)   *Amendments to the Merchant Shipping Act 1979.*

[Criminal Justice Act 1982, s 49.]

3–1128   **50–52.** *Amendments to the Wireless Telegraphy Act 1949; the Magistrates' Courts Act 1980, and the Criminal Law Act 1977[1].*

---

    1. Appropriate amendments have been made in this work to the relevant enactments.

PART IV[1]

SCOTLAND

PART V[2]

MISCELLANEOUS

Persons remanded in custody

3–1129   **59. Remand in custody in absence of accused.**   (1) The Magistrates' Courts Act 1980 shall have effect subject to the amendments[3] specified in Schedule 9 to this Act, being amendments to modify the requirement that a person may not be remanded in custody without being brought before the court.

     (2) Nothing in this section shall affect the operation of section 2 of the Imprisonment (Temporary Provisions) Act 1980.

[Criminal Justice Act 1982, s 59.]

---

    1. Part IV contains ss 53–56.
    2. Part V contains ss 57–81.
    3. Appropriate amendments have been made in this work to the relevant enactments.

Community service

3–1130   **68. Community service orders.**   (1) Schedule 12[1] to this Act shall have effect with respect—

     (*a*)   to the powers of courts in England and Wales in relation to community service orders; and

     (*b*)   to arrangements for persons in England and Wales to perform work under such orders.

     (2) Schedule 13[2] to this Act shall have effect for the purpose of the enforcement in one part of the United Kingdom of community service orders made in another part.

[Criminal Justice Act 1982, s 68.]

---

    1. Schedule 12 amended the Powers of Criminal Courts Act 1973, s 14, *ante*, and the amendments have been incorporated into the text of that section.
    2. Part II of Sch 13 amended the Community Service by Offenders (Scotland) Act 1978, *ante*, with respect to the reciprocal arrangements governing community service orders, relating to persons residing in England or Wales, made by courts in Scotland. Part III of the Schedule, *post*, introduced reciprocal arrangements for community service orders, relating to persons residing in England and Wales, made by courts in Northern Ireland.

Unsworn statements

3–1131   **72. Abolition of right of accused to make unsworn statement.**   (1) Subject to subsections (2) and (3) below, in any criminal proceedings the accused shall not be entitled to make a statement without being sworn, and accordingly, if he gives evidence, he shall do so (subject to sections 55 and 56 of the Youth Justice and Criminal Evidence Act 1999) on oath and be liable to cross-examination; but this section shall not affect the right of the accused, if not represented by counsel or a solicitor, to address the court or jury otherwise than on oath on any matter on which, if he were so represented, counsel or a solicitor could address the court or jury on his behalf.

     (2) Nothing in subsection (1) above shall prevent the accused making a statement without being sworn—

     (*a*)   if it is one which he is required by law to make personally; or

     (*b*)   if he makes it by way of mitigation before the court passes sentence upon him.

     (3) Nothing in this section applies—

     (*a*)   to a trial; or

     (*b*)   to proceedings before a magistrates' court acting as examining justices,

which began before the commencement of this section.

[Criminal Justice Act 1982, s 72 as amended by the Youth Justice and Criminal Evidence Act 1999, Sch 4.]

Supplementary

3–1132 **77.** *Minor and consequential amendments.*

3–1133 **78.** *Repeals.*

3–1134 **79.** *Transitional.*

3–1135 **81.** *Citation and extent.*

SCHEDULES

Section 32   SCHEDULE 1
OFFENCES EXCLUDED FROM SECTION 32

(As amended by the Drug Trafficking Offences Act 1986, s 24, the Public Order Act 1986, Schs 2 and 3, the Criminal Justice Act 1988, Sch 15, the Road Traffic (Consequential Provisions) Act 1988 Sch 3, the Aviation and Maritime Security Act 1990, Sch 3, the Criminal Justice (International Co-operation) Act 1990, Sch 4, the Road Traffic Act 1991, Sch 4, the Criminal Justice Act 1993, s 74, the Drug Trafficking Act 1994, Sch 1, the Proceeds of Crime Act 2002, Sch 11, the Sexual Offences Act 2003, Schs 6 and 7 and the Domestic Violence, Crime and Victims Act 2004.)

PART I
OFFENCES MENTIONED IN SECTION 32(2)(A)

3–1136 **1.** Manslaughter.
2. *Repealed.*
3. Kidnapping.
4. Assault (of any description).

PART II
OFFENCES MENTIONED IN SECTION 32(2)(B)

MALICIOUS DAMAGE ACT 1861 (c 97)

3–1137 **1.** Sections 35, 47 and 48 (criminal damage).

OFFENCES AGAINST THE PERSON ACT 1861 (C 100)

2. Section 16 (making threats to kill).
3. Section 18 (wounding with intent to do grievous bodily harm or to resist apprehension).
4. Section 20 (wounding or inflicting grievous bodily harm).
5. Section 21 (garotting).
6. Section 23 (endangering life or causing harm by administering poison).
7. Section 28 (burning, maiming, etc by explosion).
8. Section 29 (causing explosions or casting corrosive fluids with intent to do grievous bodily harm).

EXPLOSIVE SUBSTANCES ACT 1883 (C 3)

9. Section 2 (causing explosion likely to endanger life or property).

INFANT LIFE (PRESERVATION) ACT 1929 (C 34)

10. Section 1 (child destruction).

INFANTICIDE ACT 1938 (C 36)

11. Section 1(1) (infanticide).
12. *Repealed.*
13. *Repealed.*
14. *Repealed.*

FIREARMS ACT 1968 (C 27)

15. Section 17(1) (use of firearms and imitation firearms to resist arrest).

THEFT ACT 1968 (C 60)

16. Section 8 (robbery).
17. Section 10 (aggravated burglary).

MISUSE OF DRUGS ACT 1971 (C 38)

18. Section 4 (production or supply of a controlled drug).
19. Section 5(3) (possession of a controlled drug with intent to supply it to another.
20. Section 20 (assisting in, or inducing the commission outside the United Kingdom of, an offence relating to drugs punishable under a corresponding law, as defined in section 36(1)).

CRIMINAL DAMAGE ACT 1971 (c 48)

21. Section 1(2)(*b*) (criminal damage, including arson, endangering life).

ROAD TRAFFIC ACT 1972 (c 20)

22. Section 1 (causing death by reckless driving).

CUSTOMS AND EXCISE MANAGEMENT ACT 1979 (c 2)

23. Section 85(2) (shooting at naval or revenue vessels).

AVIATION SECURITY ACT 1982 (c 36)

24. Section 1 (hijacking).
25. Sections 2, 3 and 6 (other offences relating to aircraft).

DRUG TRAFFICKING OFFENCES ACT 1986 (c 32)

25A. Section 23A (acquisition, possession or use of proceeds of drug trafficking).
26. Section 24 (assisting another to retain the benefit of drug trafficking).

PUBLIC ORDER ACT 1986 (c 64)

27. Section 1 (riot).
28. Section 2 (violent disorder).
29. Section 3 (affray).

CRIMINAL JUSTICE ACT 1988 (c 33)

29A. Section 93A (assisting another to retain the benefit of criminal conduct).
29B. Section 93B (acquisition, possession or use of proceeds of criminal conduct).
29C. Section 93C (concealing or transferring proceeds of criminal conduct).
30[1]. Section 134 (torture).

ROAD TRAFFIC ACT 1988 (c 52)

30. Section 1 (causing death by dangerous driving).
Section 3A (causing death by careless driving when under the influence of drink or drugs).

AVIATION AND MARITIME SECURITY ACT 1990 (c 31)

Section 1 (endangering safety at aerodromes).
Section 9 (hijacking of ships).
Section 10 (seizing or exercising control of fixed platforms).
Sections 11, 12, 13 and 14 (other offences relating to ships and fixed platforms.)

CRIMINAL JUSTICE (INTERNATIONAL CO-OPERATION) ACT 1990 (c 5)

Section 14 (concealing or transferring proceeds of drug trafficking).

DRUG TRAFFICKING ACT 1994 (c 37)

Section 49 (concealing or transferring the proceeds of drug trafficking).
Section 50 (assisting another person to retain the benefit of drug trafficking).
Section 51 (acquisition, possession or use of proceeds of drug trafficking).

PROCEEDS OF CRIME ACT 2002

Section 327 (concealing criminal property etc).
Section 328 (arrangements relating to criminal property).
Section 329 (acquisition, use and possession of criminal property).

SEXUAL OFFENCES ACT 2003

Sections 1 and 2 (rape, assault by penetration).
Section 4 (causing a person to engage in sexual activity without consent), where the activity caused involved penetration within subsection (4)(a) to (d) of that section.
Sections 5 and 6 (rape of a child under 13, assault of a child under 13 by penetration).
Section 8 (causing or inciting a child under 13 to engage in sexual activity), where an activity involving penetration within subsection (3)(a) to (d) of that section was caused.
Section 30 (sexual activity with a person with a mental disorder impeding choice), where the touching involved penetration within subsection (3)(a) to (d) of that section.
Section 31 (causing or inciting a person, with a mental disorder impeding choice, to engage in sexual activity), where an activity involving penetration within subsection (3)(a) to (d) of that section was caused.

DOMESTIC VIOLENCE, CRIME AND VICTIMS ACT 2004

Section 5 (causing or allowing the death of a child or vulnerable adult).

---

1. This paragraph which was inserted by the Criminal Justice Act 1988, Sch 15, was originally numbered "26" in the Queen's Printer's copy of the Criminal Justice Act 1988, but, notwithstanding the subsequent entry made by the Road Traffic (Consequential Provisions) Act 1988, has been amended to "30" in accordance with the Criminal Justice Act 1988, correction no 3 issued by HMSO.

PART III

OFFENCES MENTIONED IN SECTION 32(2)(C)

3–1138 Offences under sections 50(2) and (3), 68(2) and 170 of the Customs and Excise Management Act 1979 in connection with a prohibition or restriction on importation or exportation of a controlled drug which has effect by virtue of section 3 of the Misuse of Drugs Act 1971.

Section 39

SCHEDULE 2

FINES TO REMAIN AT THEIR PRESENT LEVEL

(Amended by the Road Traffic (Consequential Provisions) Act 1988, Sch 1)

Enactment Creating Offence 1	Penalty Enactment 2	Present Maximum Fine 3
TRANSPORT (LONDON) ACT 1969 (c 35)		
Offences under section 23(5) (providing a bus service without the agreement of the London Transport Executive)	Section 23(5)	£200
PATENTS ACT 1977 (c 37)		
Offences under section 110(1) (unauthorised claim of patent rights)	Section 110(1)	£200
Offences under section 111(1) (unauthorised claim that patent has been applied for)	Section 111(1)	£200
Offences under section 112 (misuse of title "Patent Office")	Section 112	£500
WEST MIDLANDS COUNTY COUNCIL ACT 1977 (c xiv)		
Offences under section 6(2) (contravention of bye-laws as to operation of aircraft at airports)	Section 6(2)	£500
CITY OF LONDON (VARIOUS POWERS) ACT 1977 (c xv)		
Offences under section 7(6) (contravention of notice prohibiting access to forest)	Section 7(6)	£50
Offences under section 24(6) (contravention of order under section 24)	Section 24(6)	£200
KENSINGTON AND CHELSEA CORPORATION ACT 1977 (c xix)		
Offences under section 5(2) (causing refuse to be deposited)	Section 5(3)	£50
NORTH WEST WATER AUTHORITY ACT 1977 (c xx)		
Offences under section 6(2) (failure to comply with notice and furnishing false information)	Section 6(2)	£200
PUBLIC PASSENGER VEHICLES ACT 1981 (c 14)		
Offences under section 26(2) (contravention of regulations relating to passengers)	Section 26(2)	£50
Offences under section 67 (contravention of regulations generally)	Section 67	£50

3–1150

SCHEDULE 3[1]

Special increases

----

1. Appropriate amendments have been made in this work to the penalties under the enactments to which this Schedule refers.

3–1151

SCHEDULE 4[1]

Fines imposed otherwise than on conviction

----

1. Appropriate amendments have been made in this work to the penalties under the enactments to which this Schedule refers.

3–1152

Section 68

SCHEDULE 13

COMMUNITY SERVICE ORDERS—RECIPROCAL ARRANGEMENTS

(As amended by the Criminal Justice Act 1991, Sch 13.)

PART I

Repealed.

3–1154

PART II[1]

RECIPROCAL ARRANGEMENTS (SCOTLAND)—PERSONS RESIDING IN ENGLAND AND WALES OR NORTHERN IRELAND

1. Amendments made by Pts I and II of Sch 13 have been incorporated in the text respectively of the Powers of Criminal Courts Act 1973 and the Community Service by Offenders (Scotland) Act 1978, *ante.*

3–1155

PART III

RECIPROCAL ARRANGEMENTS (NORTHERN IRELAND)—PERSONS RESIDING IN ENGLAND AND WALES OR SCOTLAND

Making and amendment of community service orders relating to persons residing in England and Wales

7. (1) Where a court in Northern Ireland considering the making of a community service order is satisfied that the offender resides, or will be residing when the order comes into force, in England or Wales, the Treatment of Offenders (Northern Ireland) Order 1976 shall have effect as if the following were substituted for Article 7(4)—

"(4) A court shall not make a community service order in respect of any offender unless the offender consents and—

    (*a*) it appears to the court that provision for the offender to perform work under such an order can be made under the arrangements for persons to perform work under such orders which exist in the petty sessions area in England or Wales in which he resides or will reside; and

    (*b*) the court is satisfied after considering a report by a probation officer about the offender and his circumstances and, if the court thinks it necessary, hearing a probation officer, that the offender is a suitable person to perform work under such an order.".

(2) Where a community service order has been made by a court in Northern Ireland and—

    (*a*) a court of summary jurisdiction acting for a petty sessions district in Northern Ireland for the time being specified in it is satisfied that the offender proposes to reside or is residing in England or Wales;

    (*b*) it appears to that court that provision can be made for him to perform work under the community service order under the arrangements for persons to perform work under such orders which exist in the petty sessions area in England or Wales in which he resides or will reside,

it may amend the order by specifying that the unpaid work required to be performed by the order be so performed.

(3) A community service order made or amended in accordance with this paragraph shall—

    (*a*) specify the petty sessions area in England or Wales in which the offender resides or will be residing when the order or the amendment comes into force; and

    (*b*) local probation board for that area (established under section 4 of the Criminal Justice and Court Services Act 2000) to appoint or assign an officer of the board who will discharge in respect of the order the functions in respect of community service orders conferred on responsible officers by the Powers of Criminal Courts (Sentencing) Act 2000.

Making and amendment of community service orders relating to persons residing in Scotland

3–1156   8. (1) Where a court in Northern Ireland considering the making of a community service order is satisfied that the offender resides, or will be residing when the order comes into force, in Scotland, the Treatment of Offenders (Northern Ireland) Order 1976 shall have effect as if the following were substituted for Article 7(4)—

"(4) A court shall not make a community service order in respect of any offender unless the offender consents and—

    (*a*) the court has been notified by the Secretary of State that arrangements exist for persons who reside in the locality in Scotland in which the offender resides or will be residing when the order comes into force, to perform work under community service orders made under section 1 of the Community Service by Offenders (Scotland) Act 1978; and

    (*b*) the court is satisfied after considering a report by a probation officer about the offender and his circumstances and, if the court thinks it necessary, hearing a probation officer, that the offender is a suitable person to perform work under such an order; and

    (*c*) it appears to the court that provision can be made for him to perform work under the arrangements mentioned in sub-paragraph (*a*) above.".

(2) Where a community service order has been made by a court in Northern Ireland and—

    (*a*) a court of summary jurisdiction acting for a petty sessions district in Northern Ireland for the time being specified in it is satisfied that the offender proposes to reside or is residing in Scotland;

    (*b*) that court has been notified by the Secretary of State that arrangements exist for persons who reside in the locality in Scotland in which the offender proposes to reside or is residing to perform work under community service orders made under section 1 of the Community Service by Offenders (Scotland) Act 1978;

    (*c*) it appears to that court that provision can be made for him to perform work under the community service order under those arrangements.

it may amend the order by specifying that the unpaid work required to be performed by the order be so performed.

(3) A community service order made or amended in accordance with this paragraph shall—

    (*a*) specify the locality in Scotland in which the offender resides or will be residing when the order or the amendment comes into force; and

    (*b*) require the regional or islands council in whose area the locality specified under paragraph (*a*) above is situated to appoint or assign an officer who will discharge in respect of the order the functions in respect of community service orders conferred on the local authority officer by the Community Service by Offenders (Scotland) Act 1978.

Community service orders relating to persons residing in England and Wales or Scotland—General

3–1157   9. (1) Where a community service order is made or amended in the circumstances specified in paragraph 7 or 8 above, the court which makes or amends the order shall send three copies of the order as made or amended to the home court, together with such documents and information relating to the case as it considers likely to be of assistance to that court.

(2) In this paragraph—

"home court" means—

    (a) if the offender resides in England or Wales, or will be residing in England or Wales at the relevant time, the magistrates' court acting for the petty sessions area in which he resides or proposes to reside; and

    (b) if he resides in Scotland, or will be residing in Scotland at the relevant time, the sheriff court having jurisdiction in the locality in which he resides or proposes to reside;

"the relevant time" means the time when the order or the amendment to it comes into force.

(3) A community service order made or amended in the circumstances specified in paragraph 7 or 8 above shall be treated, subject to the following provisions of this paragraph, as if it were a community service order made in the part of the United Kingdom in which the offender resides, or will be residing at the relevant time; and the legislation relating to community service orders which has effect in that part of the United Kingdom shall apply accordingly.

(4) Before making or amending a community service order in the circumstances specified in paragraph 7 or 8 above the court shall explain to the offender in ordinary language—

    (a) the requirements of the legislation relating to community service orders which has effect in the part of the United Kingdom in which he resides or will be residing at the relevant time;

    (b) the powers of the home court under that legislation, as modified by this Part of this Schedule; and

    (c) its own powers under this Part of this Schedule,

and an explanation given in accordance with this sub-paragraph shall be sufficient without the addition of an explanation under Article 7(7) of the Treatment of Offenders (Northern Ireland) Order 1976.

(5) The home court may exercise in relation to the community service order any power which it could exercise in relation to a community service order made by a court in the part of the United Kingdom in which the home court exercises jurisdiction, by virtue of the legislation relating to such orders which has effect in the part of the United Kingdom in which it has jurisdiction except—

    (a) a power to vary the order by substituting for the number of hours' work specified in it any greater number than the court which made the order could have specified;

    (b) a power to revoke the order; and

    (c) a power to revoke the order and deal with the offender for the offence in respect of which it was made in any manner in which he could have been dealt with for that offence by the court which made the order if the order had not been made.

(6) If at any time whilst legislation relating to community service orders which has effect in one part of the United Kingdom applies by virtue of sub-paragraph (3) above to a community service order made in another part—

    (a) it appears to the home court—

        (i) if that court is in England or Wales, on information to a justice of the peace acting for the petty sessions area for the time being specified in the order;

        (ii) if it is in Scotland, on evidence on oath from the local authority officer under the Community Service by Offenders (Scotland) Act 1978,

    that the offender has failed to comply with any of the requirements of the legislation applicable to the order; or

    (b) it appears to the home court on the application of the offender or—

        (i) if it is in England and Wales, of the relevant officer under the Powers of Criminal Courts Act 1973; and

        (ii) if it is in Scotland, of the local authority officer,

    that it would be in the interests of justice to exercise a power mentioned in sub-paragraph (5)(b) or (c) above.

the home court may require the offender to appear before the court by which the order was made.

(7) Where an offender is required to appear before a court by virtue of sub-paragraph (6) above, that court—

    (a) may issue a warrant for his arrest; and

    (b) may exercise any power which it could exercise in respect of the community service order if the offender resided in the part of the United Kingdom where the court has jurisdiction,

and any enactment relating to the exercise of such powers shall have effect accordingly.

Criminal Justice Act 1991

(1991 c 53)

PART I[1]
POWERS OF COURTS TO DEAL WITH OFFENDERS

3–1201   **1–15.** *Repealed.*

---

1. Part I contains ss 1–31.

3–1216   **16. Reciprocal enforcement of certain orders.**   Schedule 3 to this Act shall have effect for making provision for and in connection with—

    (a) *repealed*;

    (b) the making and amendment in Scotland or Northern Ireland of certain orders relating to persons residing in England and Wales.

[Criminal Justice Act 1991, s 16 as amended by the Powers of Criminal Courts (Sentencing) Act 2000, Sch 9.]

Financial penalties

3–1218   18. Fixing of fines.   *Repealed.*

3–1220   20. Statements as to offenders' means.   *Repealed.*

3–1221   20A. False statements as to financial circumstances.   (1) A person who is charged with an offence who, in furnishing a statement of his financial circumstances in response to an official request—

    (*a*)   makes a statement which he knows to be false in a material particular;

    (*b*)   recklessly furnishes a statement which is false in a material particular; or

    (*c*)   knowingly fails to disclose any material fact,

shall be liable on summary conviction to imprisonment for a term not exceeding **three months** or a fine not exceeding **level 4** on the standard scale or both.*

(1A) A person who is charged with an offence who fails to furnish a statement of his financial circumstances in response to an official request shall be liable on summary conviction to a fine not exceeding level 2 on the standard scale.

(2)   For the purposes of this section an official request is a request which—

    (*a*)   is made by the designated officer for the magistrates' court or the appropriate officer of the Crown Court, as the case may be; and

    (*b*)   is expressed to be made for informing the court, in the event of his being convicted, of his financial circumstances for the purpose of determining the amount of any fine the court may impose and how it should be paid.

(3)   Proceedings in respect of an offence under this section may, notwithstanding anything in section 127(1) of the 1980 Act (limitation of time), be commenced at any time within two years from the date of the commission of the offence or within six months from its first discovery by the prosecutor, whichever period expires the earlier.

[Criminal Justice Act 1991, s 20A, as inserted by the Criminal Justice and Public Order Act 1994, Sch 9 and amended by the Access to Justice Act 1999, Sch 13, the Courts Act 2003, s 95 and the Courts Act 2003, Sch 8.]

Financial penalties: supplemental

3–1222   21. Remission of fines.   *Repealed.*

3–1224   24. Recovery of fines etc by deductions from income support.   (1) The Secretary of State may by regulations¹ provide that where a fine has been imposed on an offender by a magistrates' court, or a sum is required to be paid by a compensation order which has been made against an offender by such a court, and (in either case) the offender is entitled to income support or a jobseeker's allowance or state pension credit—

    (*a*)   the court may apply to the Secretary of State asking him to deduct sums from any amounts payable to the offender by way of that benefit, in order to secure the payment of any sum which is or forms part of the fine or compensation; and

    (*b*)   the Secretary of State may deduct sums from any such amounts and pay them to the court towards satisfaction of any such sum.

(2)   The regulations may include—

    (*a*)   provision that, before making an application, the court shall make an enquiry as to the offender's means;*

   (*aa*)   provision that the court may require the offender to provide prescribed information in connection with an application;

    (*b*)   provision allowing or requiring adjudication as regards an application, and provision as to appeals to appeal tribunals constituted under Chapter I of Part I of the Social Security Act 1998 and decisions under section 9 or 10 of that Act;

    (*c*)   provision as to the circumstances and manner in which and the times at which sums are to be deducted and paid;

    (*d*)   provision as to the calculation of such sums (which may include provision to secure that amounts payable to the offender by way of income support, a jobseeker's allowance or state pension credit or a jobseeker's allowance* do not fall below prescribed figures);

    (*e*)   provision as to the circumstances in which the Secretary of State is to cease making deductions;

    (*f*)   provision requiring the Secretary of State to notify the offender, in a prescribed manner and at any prescribed time, of the total amount of sums deducted up to the time of notification; and

    (*g*)   provision that, where the whole amount to which the application relates has been paid, the court shall give notice of that fact to the Secretary of State.*

(2A)   An offender who fails to provide information required by the court by virtue of subsection (2)(*aa*) commits an offence.

(2B)   An offender commits an offence if, in providing information required by the court by virtue of that subsection, he—

    (*a*)   makes a statement which he knows to be false in a material particular,

    (*b*)   recklessly provides a statement which is false in a material particular, or

(c)   knowingly fails to disclose any material fact.

(2C)   A person guilty of an offence under subsection (2A) or (2B) is liable on summary conviction to a fine not exceeding level 2 on the standard scale.

(3)   In subsection (1) above—

(a)   the reference to a fine having been imposed by a magistrates' court includes a reference to a fine being treated, by virtue of section 140 of the Powers of Criminal Courts (Sentencing) Act 2000, as having been so imposed; and

(b)   the reference to a sum being required to be paid by a compensation order which has been made by a magistrates' court includes a reference to a sum which is required to be paid by such an order being treated, by virtue of section 41 of the Administration of Justice Act 1970, as having been adjudged to be paid on conviction by such a court;

(c)   the reference in paragraph (a) to "the court" includes a reference to a court to which the function in that paragraph has been transferred by virtue of a transfer of fine order under section 89(1) or (3) or 90(1)(a) of the 1980 Act (power of magistrates' court to make transfer of fine order) or under section 222(1)(a) or (b) of the Criminal Procedure (Scotland) Act 1995 (analogous provision as respects Scotland) and a reference to a court to which that function has been remitted by virtue of section 196(2) of the said Act of 1975 (enforcement of fine imposed by High Court of Justiciary).

(4)   In this section—

"fine" includes—

(a)   a penalty imposed under section 29 or 37 of the Vehicle Excise and Registration Act 1994 or section 102(3)(aa) of the Customs and Excise Management Act 1979 (penalties imposed for certain offences in relation to vehicle excise licences);

(b)   an amount ordered to be paid, in addition to any penalty so imposed, under section 30, 36 or 38 of the Vehicle Excise and Registration Act 1994 (liability to additional duty);

(c)   an amount ordered to be paid by way of costs which is, by virtue of section 41 of the Administration of Justice Act 1970, treated as having been adjudged to be paid on a conviction by a magistrates' court;

"income support" means income support within the meaning of the Social Security Act 1986, either alone or together with any incapacity benefit or retirement pension which is paid by means of the same instrument of payment;

"prescribed" means prescribed by regulations made by the Secretary of State.

(5)   *Scotland.*

[Criminal Justice Act 1991, s 24 as amended by the Vehicle Excise and Registration Act 1994, Sch 3, the Criminal Justice and Public Order Act 1994, s 47, the Jobseekers Act 1995, Schs 2 and 3, the Criminal Procedure (Consequential Provisions) (Scotland) Act 1995, Sch 4, the Powers of Criminal Courts (Sentencing) Act 2000, Sch 9, the Social Security Act 1998, Sch 7, the Welfare Reform and Pensions Act 1999, Sch 8, the State Pension Credit Act 2002, s 14 and the Courts Act 2003, s 96.]

---

1.   See the Fines (Deductions from Income Support) Regulations 1992, in this PART: STATUTORY INSTRUMENTS, post.

Miscellaneous

3–1226   26. Alteration of certain penalties.   (1) In section 7 of the Theft Act 1968 (theft), for the words "ten years" there shall be substituted the words "seven years".

(2)   For subsections (3) and (4) of section 9 of that Act (burglary) there shall be substituted the following subsections—

"(3)   A person guilty of burglary shall on conviction on indictment be liable to imprisonment for a term not exceeding—

(a)   where the offence was committed in respect of a building or part of a building which is a dwelling, fourteen years;

(b)   in any other case, ten years.

(4)   References in subsections (1) and (2) above to a building, and the reference in subsection (3) above to a building which is a dwelling, shall apply also to an inhabited vehicle or vessel, and shall apply to any such vehicle or vessel at times when the person having a habitation in it is not there as well as at times when he is."

(3)   In section 10(2) of the Badgers Act 1973 (enforcement, penalties etc), for the words preceding the proviso there shall be substituted the following—

"(2)   Any person guilty of an offence under this Act shall be liable on summary conviction—

(a)   in the case of an offence under section 1 or 2, to a fine not exceeding level 5 on the standard scale or to imprisonment for a term not exceeding six months or to both;

(b)   in the case of an offence under section 3 or 4, to a fine not exceeding that level; and

(c)   in the case of an offence under section 5, to a fine not exceeding level 3 on that scale;"

and in the proviso for the words "paragraph (b)" there shall be substituted the words "paragraph (a) or (b)".

(4)   In section 51(4) of the Criminal Law Act 1977 (penalties for bomb hoaxes)—

(*a*) in paragraph (*a*), for the words "three months" there shall be substituted the words "six months"; and

(*b*) in paragraph (*b*), for the words "five years" there shall be substituted the words "seven years".

(5) The power saved by subsection (1) of section 70 of the 1982 Act (vagrancy offences) shall not include, in the case of an offence mentioned in paragraph (*b*)(i) of that subsection (sleeping rough), power to impose a fine which exceeds level 1 on the standard scale.
[Criminal Justice Act 1991, s 26.]

Supplemental

3–1228   28. Savings for mitigation and mentally disordered offenders.   *Repealed.*

3–1229   29. Effect of previous convictions[1] and of offending while on bail.   *Repealed.*

3–1230   30. Rules, regulations and orders.   (1) Any power of the Secretary of State to make rules, regulations or orders under this Part—

(*a*) shall be exercisable by statutory instrument; and
(*b*) shall include power to make different provision for different cases or classes of case.

(2) A statutory instrument containing any rules, regulations or order under this Part shall be subject to annulment in pursuance of a resolution of either House of Parliament.
[Criminal Justice Act 1991, s 30, as amended by the Criminal Justice Act 1993, Sch 6 and the Powers of Criminal Courts (Sentencing) Act 2000, Sch 12.]

3–1231   31. Interpretation of Part I.   *Repealed.*

PART II[1]
EARLY RELEASE OF PRISONERS

3–1232   32–51.   *Repealed.*

---

1. Part II contains ss 32–51.

PART III[1]
CHILDREN AND YOUNG PERSONS

Children's evidence

3–1253   53. Notices of transfer in certain cases involving children[2].   (1) If a person has been charged with an offence to which section 32(2) of the 1988 Act applies (sexual offences and offences involving violence or cruelty) and the Director of Public Prosecutions is of the opinion—

(*a*) that the evidence of the offence would be sufficient for the person charged to be committed for trial;
(*b*) that a child who is alleged—
  (i) to be a person against whom the offence was committed; or
  (ii) to have witnessed the commission of the offence,
  will be called as a witness at the trial; and
(*c*) that, for the purpose of avoiding any prejudice to the welfare of the child, the case should be taken over and proceeded with without delay by the Crown Court,

a notice[3] ("notice of transfer") certifying that opinion may be given by or on behalf of the Director to the magistrates' court in whose jurisdiction the offence has been charged.

(2) A notice of transfer shall be given before the magistrates' court begins to inquire into the case as examining justices.

(3) On the giving of a notice of transfer the functions of the magistrates' court shall cease in relation to the case except as provided by paragraphs 2 and 3 of Schedule 6 to this Act or by paragraph 2 of Schedule 3 to the Access to Justice Act 1999.

(4) The decision to give a notice of transfer shall not be subject to appeal or liable to be questioned in any court.

(5) Schedule 6 to this Act (which makes further provision in relation to notices of transfer) shall have effect.

(6) In this section "child" means a person who—

(*a*) in the case of an offence falling within section 32(2)(*a*) or (*b*) of the 1988 Act, is under fourteen years of age or, if he was under that age when any such video recording as is mentioned in section 32A(2) of that Act was made in respect of him, is under fifteen years of age; or
(*b*) in the case of an offence falling within section 32(2)(*c*) of that Act, is under seventeen years of age or, if he was under that age when any such video recording was made in respect of him, is under eighteen years of age.

(7) Any reference in subsection (6) above to an offence falling within paragraph (*a*), (*b*) or (*c*) of section 32(2) of that Act includes a reference to an offence which consists of attempting or conspiring

to commit, or of aiding, abetting, counselling, procuring or inciting the commission of, an offence falling within that paragraph.

(8) This section shall not apply in any case in which section 51 of the Crime and Disorder Act 1998 (no committal proceedings for indictable-only offences) applies.

[Criminal Justice Act 1991, s 53 as amended by the Criminal Justice and Public Order Act 1994, Sch 9, the Crime and Disorder Act 1998, Sch 8 and the Access to Justice Act 1999, Sch 4.]

---

1. Part III contains ss 52–72.
2. See the Criminal Justice Act 1991 (Notice of Transfer) Regulations 1992 and the Criminal Procedure Rules 2005, Part 13 in PART I: MAGISTRATES' COURTS: PROCEDURE, ante. The *Practice Direction (criminal: consolidated)* [2002] para III.21, in PART I: MAGISTRATES' COURTS: PROCEDURE, ante, lists Crown Court centres which are equipped with live television link facilities. The decision to transfer for trial to the Crown Court a case involving child defendants should only be taken for very grave offences where if they were found guilty it ought to be possible to sentence them in pursuance of s 91(3) of the Powers of Criminal Courts (Sentencing) Act 2000 and a statement to that effect should be included in the transfer notice (*R v T and K* [2001] 1 Cr App Rep 446, 165 JP 306, [2001] Crim LR 398, CA).
3. Notice of transfer may be given with respect to a triable either way offence before a determination on mode of trial has been taken by the justices (*R v DPP, ex p Brewer* [1995] Crim LR 168). A notice of transfer may not reverse a determination as to mode of trial, and in the case of a person under the age of 18, where s 24(1) of the Magistrates' Court Act 1980, in PART I: MAGISTRATES' COURTS, PROCEDURE, ante, applies, it may only be given if the magistrates' court has decided in favour of trial on indictment (*R v Fareham Youth Court, ex p M* [1999] Crim LR 325).

Since the notice refers to the "case" rather than a charge, the notice may include offences not involving a child witness provided they may properly be joined on the indictment (*R v Wrench* [1996] Crim LR 265). Summary offences specified in s 40 of the Criminal Justice Act 1988 may not be committed for trial under those provisions which only apply where the principal offence is committed or sent for trial and not to cases where there is a transfer under these provisions (*R v T and K* [2001] 1 Cr App Rep 446, 165 JP 306, [2001] Crim LR 398, CA).

Responsibilities of parent or guardian

3–1258 **58. Binding over of parent or guardian.** *Repealed.*

Detention etc pending trial

3–1260 **60. Remands and committals to local authority accommodation.** (1) (*Amendment of s 23 of the Children and Young Persons Act 1969.*

(2) In section 37 of the 1980 Act (committal of young person to Crown Court for sentence)—

(a) in subsection (1), for the words "17 years old" there shall be substituted the words "18 years old".

(b) in subsection (2), for the words "A person committed in custody under subsection (1) above" there shall be substituted the words "Where a person committed in custody under subsection (1) above is not less than 17 years old, he"; and

(c) after that subsection there shall be inserted the following subsection—

"(3) Where a person committed in custody under subsection (1) above is less than 17 years old—

(a) he shall be committed to accommodation provided by or on behalf of a local authority (within the meaning of the Children Act 1989) and

(b) the court by which he is so committed shall impose a security requirement within the meaning of section 23 of the Children and Young Persons Act 1969."

(3) In the case of a child or young person who has been remanded or committed to local authority accommodation by a youth court or a magistrates' court other than a youth court, any application under section 25 of the Children Act 1989 (use of accommodation for restricting liberty) shall, notwithstanding anything in section 92(2) of that Act or section 65 of the 1980 Act, be made to that court[1].

[Criminal Justice Act 1991, s 60.]

---

1. The words "that court" are used in a generic sense meaning a youth court rather than a family proceedings court. Accordingly, an application for secure accommodation in these circumstances may be made to the appropriate youth court and jurisdiction is not confined to the remanding court (*Liverpool City Council v B* [1995] 1 WLR 505, [1995] 2 FCR 105, [1995] 2 FLR 84).

3–1261 **61. Provision by local authorities of secure accommodation.** (1) It shall be the duty of every local authority to secure that they are in a position to comply with any security requirement which may be imposed on them under—

(a) section 23(4) of the 1969 Act (remands and committals to local authority accommodation).

(b) *Repealed.*

(2) A local authority may discharge their duty under subsection (1) above either by providing secure accommodation themselves or by making arrangements with other local authorities for the provision by them of such accommodation or by making arrangements with persons carrying on an appropriate children's home for the provision or use by them of such accommodation.

(3) The Secretary of State may by regulations make provision as to the co-operation required of local authorities in the provision of secure accommodation.

(4) The power to make regulations under this section shall be exercisable by statutory instrument which shall be subject to annulment in pursuance of a resolution of either House of Parliament.

(5) In this section expressions used in section 23 of the 1969 Act have the same meanings as in

that section and expressions, other than "local authority", used in the Children Act 1989 have the same meanings as in that Act.
[Criminal Justice Act 1991, s 61 as amended by the Criminal Justice and Public Order Act 1994, s 19, the Crime and Disorder Act 1998, Sch 10 and the Care Standards Act 2000, Sch 4.]

3–1261A   61A. *Cost of secure accommodation.*

Young offenders

3–1265   65. Supervision of young offenders after release. (1) Where a person under the age of 22 years ("the offender") is released from★ a term of detention in a young offender institution or under section 91 of the Powers of Criminal Courts (Sentencing) Act 2000★★, he shall be under the supervision of—

(a) an officer of a local probation board;
(b) or a social worker of a local authority; or
(c) in the case of a person under the age of 18 years on his release, a member of a youth offending team.

(1A) Where the supervision is to be provided by an officer of a local probation board, the officer of a local probation board shall be an officer appointed for or assigned to the petty sessions area within which the offender resides for the time being.
(1B) Where the supervision is to be provided by—

(a) a social worker of a local authority; or
(b) a member of a youth offending team,

the social worker or member shall be a social worker of, or a member of a youth offending team established by, the local authority within whose area the offender resides for the time being.
(2) The supervision period ends on the offender's 22nd birthday if it has not ended before.
(3) Subject to subsection (2) above, where the offender is released otherwise than on licence under Part II of this Act, the supervision period begins on his release and ends three months from his release.
(4) Subject to subsection (2) above, where the offender is released on licence under Part II of this Act and the licence expires less than three months from his release, the supervision period begins on the expiry of the licence and ends three months from his release.
(5) Where a person is under supervision under this section, he shall comply with such requirements, if any, as may for the time being be specified in a notice from the Secretary of State.
(5A) The requirements that may be specified in a notice under subsection (5) above include—

(a) requirements for securing the electronic monitoring of the person's compliance with any other requirements specified in the notice;
(b) requirements for securing the electronic monitoring of his whereabouts (otherwise than for the purpose of securing his compliance with requirements specified in the notice);
(c) in the circumstances mentioned in subsection (5B) below, requirements to provide, when instructed to do so by an officer of a local probation board or a person authorised by the Secretary of State, any sample mentioned in the instruction for the purpose of ascertaining whether the person has any specified Class A drug in his body.

(5B) The circumstances referred to in subsection (5A)(c) above are that—

(a) the person has attained the age of 18 years;
(b) his term of detention was imposed for a trigger offence; and
(c) the requirements to provide samples are being imposed for the purpose of determining whether he is complying with any other requirements specified in the notice.

(5C) Requirements imposed by virtue of subsection (5A) above shall not have effect on or after the day on which the person would (but for his release) have served his term in full.
(5D) The function of giving such an instruction as is mentioned in subsection (5A)(c) above shall be exercised in accordance with guidance given from time to time by the Secretary of State; and the Secretary of State may make rules about the requirements that may be imposed by virtue of subsection (5A) above and the provision of samples in pursuance of such an instruction.]
(6) A person who without reasonable excuse fails to comply with a requirement imposed under subsection (5) above shall be liable on summary conviction-

(a) to a fine not exceeding level 3 on the standard scale; or
(b) to an appropriate custodial sentence for a period not exceeding 30 days,

but not liable to be dealt with in any other way.
(7) In subsection (6) above "appropriate custodial sentence" means—

(a) a sentence of imprisonment, if the offender has attained the age of 21★ years when he is sentenced; and
(b) a sentence of detention in a young offender institution★, if he has not attained that age.

(8) A person released from a custodial sentence passed under subsection (6) above shall not be liable to a period of supervision in consequence of his conviction under that subsection, but his conviction shall not prejudice any liability to supervision to which he was previously subject, and that liability shall accordingly continue until the end of the supervision period.

(9) The power to make rules under this section—

(a) shall be exercisable by statutory instrument which shall be subject to annulment in pursuance of a resolution of either House of Parliament;

(b) shall include power to make different provision for different cases or classes of case.

(10) In this section, "specified Class A drug" and "trigger offence" have the same meanings as in Part III of the Criminal Justice and Court Services Act 2000.★★★

[Criminal Justice Act 1991, s 65 as amended by the Crime and Disorder Act 1998, Sch 8, the Powers of Criminal Courts (Sentencing) Act 2000, Sch 9, the Criminal Justice and Court Services Act 2000, s 63, the Criminal Justice and Court Services Act 2000, s 63 and the Children Act 2004, Sch 5.]

★Amended by the Criminal Justice and Court Services Act 2000, Sch 7 from a date to be appointed.
★★Additional text to be inserted by virtue of the Criminal Justice and Court Services Act 2000, Sch 7 from a date to be appointed.
★★★Repealed by the Criminal Justice Act 2003, Sch 32 from a date to be appointed.

Miscellaneous

3–1268 68. Persons aged 17 to be treated as young persons for certain purposes. The following enactments, namely—

(a) the Children and Young Persons Acts 1933 to 1969;

(b) section 43(3) of the 1952 Act (remand centres, young offender institutions etc)★;

(c) section 5(2) of the Rehabilitation of Offenders Act 1974 (which provides for rehabilitation periods to be reduced by half for young offenders); and

(d) the 1980 Act,

shall have effect subject to the amendments specified in Schedule 8 to this Act, being amendments which, for certain purposes of those enactments, have the effect of substituting the age of 18 years for the age of 17 years.

[Criminal Justice Act 1991, s 68.]

★Repealed by the Criminal Justice and Court Services Act 2000, Sch 7 from a date to be appointed.

3–1270 70. Renaming of juvenile courts etc. (1) Juvenile courts shall be renamed youth courts and juvenile court panels shall be renamed youth court panels.

(2) Any reference to juvenile courts or juvenile court panels in any enactment passed or instrument made before the commencement of this section shall be construed in accordance with subsection (1) above.

[Criminal Justice Act 1991, s 70.]

3–1271

PART IV[1]
PROVISION OF SERVICES

1. Part IV contains ss 73–92.

Court security

3–1272 76–78. *Repealed.*

Prisoner escorts

3–1280 80. Arrangements for the provision of prisoner escorts. (1) The Secretary of State may make arrangements for any of the following functions, namely—

(a) the delivery of prisoners from one set of relevant premises to another;

(b) the custody of prisoners held on the premises of any court (whether or not they would otherwise be in the custody of the court) and their production before the court;

(c) the custody of prisoners temporarily held in a prison in the course of delivery from one prison to another; and

(e) the custody of prisoners while they are outside a prison for temporary purposes,

to be performed in such cases as may be determined by or under the arrangements by prisoner custody officers who are authorised to perform such functions.

(1A) In paragraph (a) of subsection (1) above "relevant premises" means a court, prison, police station or hospital; and either (but not both) of the sets of premises mentioned in that paragraph may be situated in a part of the British Islands outside England and Wales.

(2) Arrangements made by the Secretary of State under this section ("prisoner escort arrangements") may include entering into contracts with other persons for the provision by them of prisoner custody officers.

(3) Any person who, under a warrant or a hospital order or remand, is responsible for the performance of any such function as is mentioned in subsection (1) above shall be deemed to have complied with the warrant, order or remand if he does all that he reasonably can to secure that the function is performed by a prisoner custody officer acting in pursuance of prisoner escort arrangements.

(4) In this section—

"hospital" has the same meaning as in the Mental Health Act 1983;

"hospital order" means an order for a person's admission to hospital made under section 37, 38 or 44 of that Act, section 5 of the Criminal Procedure (Insanity) Act 1964 or section 6, 14 or 14A of the Criminal Appeal Act 1968;

"hospital remand" means a remand of a person to hospital under section 35 or 36 of the Mental Health Act 1983;

"warrant" means a warrant of commitment, a warrant of arrest or a warrant under section 46, 47, 48, 50 or 74 of that Act.

[Criminal Justice Act 1991, s 80 as amended by the Criminal Justice and Public Order Act 1994, s 93.]

3–1281   **81. Monitoring etc of prisoner escort arrangements.**   (1) Prisoner escort arrangements shall include the appointment of—

(a)   a prisoner escort monitor, that is to say, a Crown servant whose duty it shall be to keep the arrangements under review and to report on them to the Secretary of State; and

(b)   a panel of lay observers whose duty it shall be to inspect the conditions in which prisoners are transported or held in pursuance of the arrangements and to make recommendations to the Secretary of State.

(2) It shall also be the duty of a prisoner escort monitor to investigate and report to the Secretary of State on—

(a)   any allegations made against prisoner custody officers acting in pursuance of prisoner escort arrangements; and

(b)   any alleged breaches of discipline on the part of prisoners for whose delivery or custody such officers so acting are responsible.

(3) Any expenses incurred by members of lay panels may be defrayed by the Secretary of State to such extent as he may with the approval of the Treasury determine.

[Criminal Justice Act 1991, s 81.]

3–1282   **82. Powers and duties of prisoner custody officers acting in pursuance of such arrangements.**   (1) A prisoner custody officer acting in pursuance of prisoner escort arrangements shall have the following powers, namely—

(a)   to search in accordance with rules[1] made by the Secretary of State any prisoner for whose delivery or custody he is responsible in pursuance of the arrangements; and

(b)   to search any other person who is in or is seeking to enter any place where any such prisoner is or is to be held, and any article in the possession of such a person.

(2) The powers conferred by subsection (1)(b) above to search a person shall not be construed as authorising a prisoner custody officer to require a person to remove any of his clothing other than an outer coat, jacket or gloves.

(3) A prisoner custody officer shall have the following duties as respects prisoners for whose delivery or custody he is responsible in pursuance of prisoner escort arrangements, namely—

(a)   to prevent their escape from lawful custody;

(b)   to prevent, or detect and report on, the commission or attempted commission by them of other unlawful acts;

(c)   to ensure good order and discipline on their part;

(d)   to attend to their wellbeing; and

(e)   to give effect to any directions as to their treatment which are given by a court,

and the Secretary of State may make rules with respect to the performance by prisoner custody officers of their duty under paragraph (d) above.

(4) Where a prisoner custody officer acting in pursuance of prisoner escort arrangements is on any premises in which the Crown Court or a magistrates' court is sitting, it shall be his duty to give effect to any order of that court made—

(a)   in the case of the Crown Court, under section 142 of the Powers of Criminal Courts (Sentencing) Act 2000 (power of Court to order search of persons before it); or

(b)   in the case of a magistrates' court, under section 80 of the 1980 Act (application of money found on defaulter).

(5) The powers conferred by subsection (1) above, and the powers arising by virtue of subsections (3) and (4) above, shall include power to use reasonable force where necessary.

(6) The power to make rules under this section shall be exercisable by statutory instrument which shall be subject to annulment in pursuance of a resolution of either House of Parliament.

[Criminal Justice Act 1991, s 82 as amended by the Criminal Justice and Public Order Act 1994, s 94 and the Powers of Criminal Courts (Sentencing) Act 2000, Sch 9.]

---

1. The Prisoner Escorts Rules 1993, SI 1993/515 have been made.

3–1283   **83. Breaches of discipline by prisoners under escort.**   (1) This section applies where a prisoner for whose delivery or custody a prisoner custody officer has been responsible in pursuance of prisoner escort arrangements is delivered to a prison.

(2) For the purposes of such prison rules as relate to disciplinary offences, the prisoner shall be deemed to have been—

(a) in the custody of the governor of the prison; or

(b) in the case of a contracted out prison, in the custody of its director,

at all times during the period for which the prisoner custody officer was so responsible.

(3) In the case of any breach by the prisoner at any time during that period of such prison rules as so relate, a disciplinary charge may be laid against him by the prisoner custody officer.

(4) Nothing in this section shall enable a prisoner to be punished under prison rules for any act or omission of his for which he has already been punished by a court.

(5) In this section "prison rules", in relation to a prison situated in a part of the British Islands outside England and Wales, means rules made under any provision of the law of that part which corresponds to section 47 of the 1952 Act.

[Criminal Justice Act 1991, s 83, as substituted by the Criminal Justice and Public Order Act 1994, s 95.]

Contracted out prisons

3–1284 84. Contracting out prisons etc. (1) The Secretary of State may enter into a contract with another person for the provision or running (or the provision and running) by him, or (if the contract so provides) for the running by sub-contractors of his, of any prison or part of a prison.

(2) While a contract under this section for the running of a prison or part of a prison is in force—

(a) the prison or part shall be run subject to and in accordance with sections 85 and 86 below, the 1952 Act (as modified by section 87 below) and prison rules; and

(b) in the case of a part, that part and the remaining part shall each be treated for the purposes of sections 85 to 88A below as if they were separate prisons.

(3) Where the Secretary of State grants a lease or tenancy of land for the purposes of any contract under this section, none of the following enactments shall apply to it, namely—

(a) Part II of the Landlord and Tenant Act 1954 (security of tenure);

(b) section 146 of the Law of Property Act 1925 (restrictions on and relief against forfeiture);

(c) section 19(1), (2) and (3) of the Landlord and Tenant Act 1927 and the Landlord and Tenant Act 1988 (covenants not to assign etc); and

(d) the Agricultural Holdings Act 1986.

In this subsection "lease or tenancy" includes an underlease or sub-tenancy.

(4) In this Part—

"contracted out prison" means a prison or part of a prison for the running of which a contract under this section is for the time being in force;

"the contractor", in relation to a contracted out prison, means the person who has contracted with the Secretary of State for the running of it; and

"sub-contractor", in relation to a contracted out prison, means a person who has contracted with the contractor for the running of it or any part of it.

[Criminal Justice Act 1991, s 84 as substituted by the Criminal Justice and Public Order Act 1994, s 96.]

3–1285 85. Officers of contracted out prisons. (1) Instead of a governor, every contracted out prison shall have—

(a) a director, who shall be a prisoner custody officer appointed by the contractor and specially approved for the purposes of this section by the Secretary of State; and

(b) a controller, who shall be a Crown servant appointed by the Secretary of State;

and every officer of such a prison who performs custodial duties shall be a prisoner custody officer who is authorised to perform such duties or a prison officer who is temporarily attached to the prison.

(2) Subject to subsection (3) below, the director shall have such functions as are conferred on him by the 1952 Act (as modified by section 87 below) or as may be conferred on him by prison rules.

(3) The director shall not—

(a) inquire into a disciplinary charge laid against a prisoner, conduct the hearing of such a charge or make, remit or mitigate an award in respect of such a charge; or

(b) except in cases of urgency, order the removal of a prisoner from association with other prisoners, the temporary confinement of a prisoner in a special cell or the application to a prisoner of any other special control or restraint.

(4) The controller shall have such functions as may be conferred on him by prison rules and shall be under a duty—

(a) to keep under review, and report to the Secretary of State on, the running of the prison by or on behalf of the director; and

(b) to investigate, and report to the Secretary of State on, any allegations made against prisoner custody officers performing custodial duties at the prison or prison officers who are temporarily attached to the prison.

(5) The contractor and any sub-contractor of his shall each be under a duty to do all that he reasonably can (whether by giving directions to the officers of the prison or otherwise) to facilitate

the exercise by the controller of all such functions as are mentioned in or conferred by subsection (4) above.
[Criminal Justice Act 1991, s 85 as amended by the Criminal Justice and Public Order Act 1994, ss 97 and 101.]

3–1286   86. Powers and duties of prisoner custody officers employed at contracted out prisons.   (1) A prisoner custody officer performing custodial duties at a contracted out prison shall have the following powers, namely—

> (*a*)   to search in accordance with prison rules any prisoner who is confined in the prison; and
> (*b*)   to search any other person who is in or is seeking to enter the prison, and any article in the possession of such a person.

(2) The powers conferred by subsection (1)(*b*) above to search a person shall not be construed as authorising a prisoner custody officer to require a person to remove any of his clothing other than an outer coat, jacket or gloves.

(3) A prisoner custody officer performing custodial duties at a contracted out prison shall have the following duties as respects prisoners confined in the prison, namely—

> (*a*)   to prevent their escape from lawful custody;
> (*b*)   to prevent, or detect and report on, the commission or attempted commission by them of other unlawful acts;
> (*c*)   to ensure good order and discipline on their part; and
> (*d*)   to attend to their wellbeing.

(4) The powers conferred by subsection (1) above, and the powers arising by virtue of subsection (3) above, shall include power to use reasonable force where necessary.
[Criminal Justice Act 1991, s 86.]

3–1287   87. Consequential modifications of 1952 Act.   (1) In relation to a contracted out prison, the provisions of the 1952 Act specified in subsections (2) to (8) below shall have effect subject to the modifications so specified.

(2) In section 7(1) (prison officers), the reference to a governor shall be construed as a reference to a director and a controller.

(3) Section 8 (powers of prison officers) and section 8A (powers of search by authorised employees) shall not apply in relation to a prisoner custody officer performing custodial duties at the prison.

(4) In sections 10(5), 12(3), 13(1), 16A, 16B and 19(1) and (3) (various functions of the governor of a prison), references to the governor shall be construed as references to the director.

(4A) Section 11 (ejectment of prison officers and their families refusing to quit) shall not apply.

(5) In section 12(1) and (2) (place of confinement of prisoners), any reference to a prisoner or prisoners shall be construed as a reference to a remand prisoner or prisoners.

(6) In section 13(2) (legal custody of prisoner), the reference to an officer of the prison shall be construed as a reference to a prisoner custody officer performing custodial duties at the prison or a prison officer who is temporarily attached to the prison.

(7) In section 14(2) (cells), the reference to a prison officer shall be construed as a reference to a prisoner custody officer performing custodial duties at the prison or a prison officer who is temporarily attached to the prison.

(8) Section 35 (vesting of prison property in the Secretary of State) shall have effect subject to the provisions of the contract entered into under section 84(1) above.
[Criminal Justice Act 1991, s 87 as amended by the Criminal Justice and Public Order Act 1994, s 97 and Sch 10 and the Prisons (Alcohol Testing) Act 1997, s 2.]

3–1288   88. Intervention by the Secretary of State.   (1) This section applies where, in the case of a contracted out prison, it appears to the Secretary of State—

> (*a*)   that the director has lost, or is likely to lose, effective control of the prison or any part of it; and
> (*b*)   that the making of an appointment under subsection (2) below is necessary in the interests of preserving the safety of any person, or of preventing serious damage to any property.

(2) The Secretary of State may appoint a Crown servant to act as governor of the prison for the period—

> (*a*)   beginning with the time specified in the appointment; and
> (*b*)   ending with the time specified in the notice of termination under subsection (4) below.

(3) During that period—

> (*a*)   all the functions which would otherwise be exercisable by the director or the controller shall be exercisable by the governor;
> (*b*)   the contractor and any sub-contractor of his shall each do all that he reasonably can to facilitate the exercise by the governor of those functions; and
> (*c*)   the officers of the prison shall comply with any directions given by the governor in the exercise of those functions.

(4) Where the Secretary of State is satisfied—

(a) that the governor has secured effective control of the prison or, as the case may be, the relevant part of it; and

(b) that the governor's appointment is no longer necessary as mentioned in subsection (1)(b) above,

he shall, by a notice to the governor, terminate the appointment at a time specified in the notice.

(5) As soon as practicable after making or terminating an appointment under this section, the Secretary of State shall give a notice of the appointment, or a copy of the notice of termination, to the contractor, any sub-contractor of his, the director and the controller.

[Criminal Justice Act 1991, s 88 as amended by the Criminal Justice and Public Order Act 1994, s 101.]

Contracted out functions

3–1288A 88A. Contracted out functions at directly managed prisons. (1) The Secretary of State may enter into a contract with another person for any functions at a directly managed prison to be performed by prisoner custody officers who are provided by that person and are authorised to perform custodial duties.

(2) Section 86 above shall apply in relation to a prisoner custody officer performing contracted out functions at a directly managed prison as it applies in relation to such an officer performing custodial duties at a contracted out prison.

(3) In relation to a directly managed prison—

(a) the reference in section 13(2) of the 1952 Act (legal custody of prisoners) to an officer of the prison; and

(b) the reference in section 14(2) of that Act (cells) to a prison officer,

shall each be construed as including a reference to a prisoner custody officer performing custodial duties at the prison in pursuance of a contract under this section.

(4) Any reference in subsections (1) to (3) above to the performance of functions or custodial duties at a directly managed prison includes a reference to the performance of functions or such duties for the purposes of, or for purposes connected with, such a prison.

(5) In this Part—

"contracted out functions" means any functions which, by virtue of a contract under this section, fall to be performed by prisoner custody officers;

"directly managed prison" means a prison which is not a contracted out prison.

[Criminal Justice Act 1991, s 88A, as inserted by the Criminal Justice and Public Order Act 1994, s 99.]

Supplemental

3–1289 89. Certification of prisoner custody officers. (1) In this Part "prisoner custody officer" means a person in respect of whom a certificate is for the time being in force certifying—

(a) that he has been approved by the Secretary of State for the purpose of performing escort functions or custodial duties or both; and

(b) that he is accordingly authorised to perform them.

(2) The provisions of Schedule 10[1] to this Act shall have effect with respect to the certification of prisoner custody officers.

(3) In this section and Schedule 10 to this Act—

"custodial duties" means custodial duties at a contracted out or directly managed prison;

"escort functions" means the functions specified in section 80(1) above.

[Criminal Justice Act 1991, s 89 as amended by the Criminal Justice and Public Order Act 1994, s 101.]

---

1. See para **3–1352**, post.

3–1290 90. Protection of prisoner custody officers. (1) Any person who assaults a prisoner custody officer—

(a) acting in pursuance of prisoner escort arrangements;

(b) performing custodial duties at a contracted out prison; or

(c) performing contracted out functions at a directly managed prison,

shall be liable on summary conviction to a fine not exceeding **level 5** on the standard scale or to imprisonment for a term not exceeding **six months or to both**.

(2) Section 17(2) of the Firearms Act 1968 (additional penalty for possession of firearms when committing certain offences) shall apply to offences under subsection (1) above.

(3) Any person who resists or wilfully obstructs a prisoner custody officer—

(a) acting in pursuance of prisoner escort arrangements;

(b) performing custodial duties at a contracted out prison; or

(c) performing contracted out functions at a directly managed prison,

shall be liable on summary conviction to a fine not exceeding **level 3** on the standard scale.

(4) For the purposes of this section, a prisoner custody officer shall not be regarded as acting in pursuance of prisoner escort arrangements at any time when he is not readily identifiable as such an officer (whether by means of a uniform or badge which he is wearing or otherwise).

[Criminal Justice Act 1991, s 90 as amended by the Criminal Justice and Public Order Act 1994, s 101.]

3–1291　91. Wrongful disclosure of information. (1) A person who—

(a) is or has been employed (whether as a prisoner custody officer or otherwise) in pursuance of prisoner escort arrangements, or at a contracted out prison; or

(b) is or has been employed to perform contracted out functions at a directly managed prison,

shall be guilty of an offence if he discloses, otherwise than in the course of his duty or as authorised by the Secretary of State, any information which he acquired in the course of his employment and which relates to a particular prisoner.

(2) A person guilty of an offence under subsection (1) above shall be liable—

(a) on conviction on indictment, to imprisonment for a term not exceeding two years or a fine or both;

(b) on summary conviction, to imprisonment for a term not exceeding **six months** or a fine not exceeding **the statutory maximum or both**.

[Criminal Justice Act 1991, s 91 as amended by the Criminal Justice and Public Order Act 1994, s 101.]

3–1292　92. Interpretation of Part IV. (1) In this Part unless the context otherwise requires—

"contracted out prison" and "the contractor" have the meanings given by section 84(4) above;

"contracted out functions" and "directly managed prison" have the meanings given by section 88A(5) above;

"prison" includes a young offender institution or remand centre★;

"prisoner" means any person for the time being detained in legal custody as a result of a requirement imposed by a court or otherwise that he be so detained;

"prison officer" means an officer of a directly managed prison;

"prison rules" means rules made under section 47 of the 1952 Act;

"prisoner custody officer" has the meaning given by section 89(1) above;

"prisoner escort arrangements" has the meaning given by section 80(2) above.

"sub-contractor" has the meaning given by section 84(4) above.

(1A) Any reference in this Part to custodial duties at a contracted out prison includes a reference to custodial duties in relation to a prisoner who is outside such a prison for temporary purposes.

(2) *Repealed.*

(3) Sections 80, 81(1) and (2)(a), 82 and 89 to 91 above, subsection (1) above and Schedule 10 to this Act shall have effect as if—

(a) any reference in section 80(1), 81(1), 82 or 91 above to prisoners included a reference to persons remanded or committed to local authority accommodation under section 23 of the 1969 Act; and

(b) any reference in section 80(1)(c) or (e) or (1A) above to a prison included a reference to such accommodation.

(4) In sections 80, 82 and 83 above, "prison"—

(a) so far as relating to the delivery of prisoners to or from a prison situated in Scotland, includes a remand centre or young offenders institution within the meaning of section 19 of the Prisons (Scotland) Act 1989; and

(b) so far as relating to the delivery of prisoners to or from a prison situated in Northern Ireland, includes a remand centre or young offenders centre.

[Criminal Justice Act 1991, s 92 as amended by the Criminal Justice and Public Order Act 1994, ss 93, 98 and 101, the Justices of the Peace Act 1997, Sch 5 and the Courts Act 2003, Sch 8.]

★**Repealed by the Criminal Justice and Court Services Act 2000, Sch 7 from a date to be appointed.**

Part V[1]
Financial and Other Provisions
Miscellaneous

3–1293　95. Information for financial and other purposes. (1) The Secretary of State shall in each year publish such information as he considers expedient for the purpose of—

(a) enabling persons engaged in the administration of criminal justice to become aware of the financial implications of their decisions; or

(aa) enabling such persons to become aware of the relative effectiveness of different sentences—

(i) in preventing re-offending, and

(ii) in promoting public ocnfidence in the criminal justice system;

(b) facilitating the performance by such persons of their duty to avoid discriminating against any persons on the ground of race or sex or any other improper ground.

(2) Publication under subsection (1) above shall be effected in such manner as the Secretary of State considers appropriate for the purpose of bringing the information to the attention of the persons concerned.

[Criminal Justice Act 1991, s 95 and amended by the Criminal Justice Act 2003, 175.]

---

1. Part V contains ss 93–97. Whilst it contains matters relevant to the administration of the courts etc, we have kept all parts of this Act together until such time as appropriate amendments are made elsewhere in this work as various provisions come into force.

PART VI[1]
SUPPLEMENTAL

3–1294   **98.** *Expenses etc under Act.*

---

1. Part VI contains ss 98–102.

3–1295   **99. General interpretation.**   (1) In this Act—

"the 1933 Act" means the Children and Young Persons Act 1933;
"the 1952 Act" means the Prison Act 1952;
"the 1967 Act" means the Criminal Justice Act 1967;
"the 1969 Act" means the Children and Young Persons Act 1969;
"the 1973 Act" means the Powers of Criminal Courts Act 1973;
"the 1980 Act" means the Magistrates' Courts Act 1980;
"the 1982 Act" means the Criminal Justice Act 1982;
"the 1983 Act" means the Mental Health Act 1983;
"the 1988 Act" means the Criminal Justice Act 1988;
"child", unless the contrary intention appears, means a person under the age of fourteen years;
"local probation board" means a local probation board established under section 4 of the Criminal Justice and Court Services Act 2000;
"prison rules" means rules made under section 47 of the 1952 Act;
"young person" means a person who has attained the age of fourteen years and is under the age of eighteen years;
"youth offending team" means a team established under section 39 of the Crime and Disorder Act 1998.

(2) For the purposes of any provision of this Act which requires the determination of the age of a person by the court or the Secretary of State, his age shall be deemed to be that which it appears to the court or the Secretary of State to be after considering any available evidence.
[Criminal Justice Act 1991, s 99 as amended by the Justices of the Peace Act 1997, Sch 6, the Crime and Disorder Act 1998, Sch 8 and the Criminal Justice and Court Services Act 2000, Sch 7.]

3–1296   **100.** *Minor and consequential amendments*

3–1297   **101. Transitional provisions, savings and repeals.**   (1) The transitional provisions and savings contained in Schedule 12 to this Act shall have effect; but nothing in this subsection shall be taken as prejudicing the operation of sections 16 and 17 of the Interpretation Act 1978 (which relate to the effect of repeals).

(2) *(Repeals).*
[Criminal Justice Act 1991, s 101.]

3–1298   **102. Short title, commencement and extent.**   (1) This Act may be cited as the Criminal Justice Act 1991.

(2) This Act shall come into force on such day as the Secretary of State may by order[1] made by statutory instrument appoint, and different days may be appointed for different provisions or for different purposes.

(3) Without prejudice to the provisions of Schedule 12 to this Act, an order under subsection (2) above may make such transitional provisions and savings as appear to the Secretary of State necessary or expedient in connection with any provision brought into force by the order.

(4) Subject to subsections (5) to (8) below, this Act extends to England and Wales only.

(5) The following provisions of this Act, namely—

(a) this section;

(b) sections 16, 17(1) and (2), 24 and 26(3) and (4); and

(c) Schedule 3, paragraph 6 of Schedule 6, paragraph 5 of Schedule 8, and, so far as relating to the Social Work (Scotland) Act 1968, Schedule 13,

also extend to Scotland; and section 23(2) above and, in so far as relating to the Criminal Procedure (Scotland) Act 1975, Schedule 13 to this Act extend to Scotland only.

(6) This section, section 16 above, Schedule 3 to this Act, and, so far as relating to the Social Work (Scotland) Act 1968, Schedule 13 to this Act also extend to Northern Ireland.

(7) An Order in Council[2] under section 81(11) of the 1982 Act may direct that both or either of—

(a) section 37 of that Act as amended by section 17(1) above; and

(b) section 32 of the 1980 Act as amended by section 17(2) above,

shall extend, subject to such modifications as may be specified in the Order, to the Isle of Man or any of the Channel Islands.

(7A) Sections 80, 82 and 83 above, so far as relating to the delivery of prisoners to or from premises situated in a part of the British Islands outside England and Wales, extend to that part of those Islands.

(8) Nothing in subsection (4) above affects the extent of this Act in so far as it amends or repeals any provision of the Army Act 1955, the Air Force Act 1955, the Naval Discipline Act 1957 or the Armed Forces Act 1991.

[Criminal Justice Act 1991, s 102 as amended by the Criminal Justice and Public Order Act 1994, s 101 and the Powers of Criminal Courts (Sentencing) Act 2000, Sch 12.]

---

1. The following commencement orders have been made: Criminal Justice Act 1991 (Commencement No 1) Order 1991, SI 1991/2208; (Commencement No 2) Order 1991, SI 1991/2706 (Scotland); (Commencement No 3) Order 1992, SI 1992/333; (Commencement No 4) Order 1994, SI 1994/3191 and (Commencement No 3) (Amendment) Order, SI 1999/1280. See also note 1 to the short title of this Act, ante, for provisions not in force at the date of going to press.
2. The Criminal Justice Act 1982 (Guernsey) Order 1992, SI 1992/3202 has been made.

Section 16   SCHEDULE 3
RECIPROCAL ENFORCEMENT OF CERTAIN ORDERS

(As amended by SI 1995/756 and the Criminal Procedure (Consequential Provisions) (Scotland) Act 1995, Schs 4 and 5, SI 1996/3161, the Powers of Criminal Courts (Sentencing) Act 2000, Sch 9, the Criminal Justice and Court Services Act 2000, Sch 7, the Criminal Justice Act 2003, Sch 32 and SI 2005/886.)

PART II
TRANSFER OF CORRESPONDING ORDERS FROM SCOTLAND

Probation orders

3–1321   **7.** (1) The Criminal Procedure (Scotland) Act 1975 shall be amended as follows.

(2) In each of sections 183 and 384 (which provide, respectively, for probation orders in solemn and in summary proceedings) in subsection (1A) for the words "by the local authority in whose area he resides or is to reside" there shall be substituted the following paragraphs—

> "(*a*) in a case other than that mentioned in paragraph (*b*) below, by the local authority in whose area he resides or is to reside; or
>
> (*b*) in a case where, by virtue of section 188(1) of this Act, subsection (2) of this section would not apply, by the probation committee for the area which contains the petty sessions area which would be named in the order".

(3) In each of sections 188 and 389 (which provide, respectively, for probation orders relating to persons residing in England being made in solemn and in summary proceedings)—

(*a*) in subsection (1)—

> (i) for the words "that the offender shall perform unpaid work" there shall be substituted the words "which, while corresponding to a requirement mentioned in paragraph 2 or 3 of Schedule 1A to the Powers of Criminal Courts Act 1973, would if included in a probation order made under that Act fail to accord with a restriction as to days of presentation, participation or attendance mentioned in paragraph 2(4)(*a*) or (6)(*a*), or as the case may be 3(3)(*a*), of that Schedule;
>
> (ii) for the word "17" there shall be substituted the word "16";
>
> (iii) the word "and", where it secondly occurs, shall cease to have effect; and
>
> (iv) at the end there shall be added the words "; and where the order includes a requirement that the probationer perform unpaid work for a number of hours, the number specified shall not exceed one hundred.";

(*b*) in subsection (2)—

> (i) for the words "that the probationer has attained the age of 17 years and proposes to reside in or is residing in England" there shall be substituted the following paragraphs—
>
> "(*a*) that the probationer has attained the age of 16 years;
>
> (*b*) that he proposes to reside, or is residing, in England; and
>
> (*c*) that suitable arrangements for his supervision can be made by the probation committee for the area which contains the petty sessions area in which he resides or will reside"; and
>
> (ii) after the word "section", where it secondly occurs, there shall be inserted the words "or to vary any requirement for performance of unpaid work so that such hours as remain to be worked do not exceed one hundred";

(*c*) in subsection (3)—

> (i) in paragraph (*a*), for the words "section 3(2) of" and "section 3 of" there shall be substituted, respectively, the words "paragraph 5(3) of Schedule 1A to" and "paragraph 5 of Schedule 1A to"; and
>
> (ii) in paragraph (*b*), for the words "subsections (4) to (6) of section 3 of" there shall be substituted the words "sub-paragraphs (5) to (7) of paragraph 5 of Schedule 1A to";

(*d*) in subsection (4), for the words from "the Powers" to the end of the proviso there shall be substituted the words "Schedule 2 to the Criminal Justice Act 1991 shall apply to the order—

> (*a*) except in the case mentioned in paragraph (*b*) below, as if that order were a probation order made under section 2 of the Powers of Criminal Courts Act 1973; and
>
> (*b*) in the case of an order which contains a requirement such as is mentioned in subsection (5A) of section 183 or 384 of this Act, as if it were a combination order made under section 11 of the said Act of 1991:

Provided that Part III of that Schedule shall not so apply; and sub-paragraphs (3) and (4) of paragraph 2 of that Schedule shall so apply as if for the first reference in the said sub-paragraph (3) to the Crown Court there were substituted a reference to a court in Scotland and for the other references in those sub-paragraphs to the Crown Court there were substituted references to the court in Scotland."; and (*e*) in subsection (5), for the words from "for which" to "this section" there shall be substituted the words "named in a probation order made or amended under this section that the person to whom the order relates".

(4) Sections 189 and 390 (which make further provision as to probation orders in, respectively, solemn and summary proceedings) shall cease to have effect.

Community service orders

3–1322   **8.** *Repealed.*

Supervision requirements

3–1323   **9.** Section 72 of the Social Work (Scotland) Act 1968 (supervision of children moving to England and Wales or to Northern Ireland) shall be amended as follows—

(*a*) in subsection (1)(*b*), for the words "to a juvenile court acting for the petty sessions area" there shall be substituted the following sub-paragraphs—

"(i) in the case of residence in England and Wales, to a youth court acting for the petty sessions area (within the meaning of the Children and Young Persons Act 1969);

(ii) in the case of residence in Northern Ireland, to a juvenile court acting for the petty sessions district (within the meaning of Part III of the Magistrates' Courts (Northern Ireland) Order 1981).";

(*b*) in subsection (1A)—

(i) for the words "The juvenile court in England or Wales" there shall be substituted the words "A youth court";

(ii) after the word "12" there shall be inserted the words ", 12A, 12AA, 12B or 12C"; and

(iii) paragraph (*a*), and the word "and" immediately following that paragraph, shall cease to have effect;

(*c*) *Repealed*;

(*d*) in subsection (3), after the words "by a" there shall be inserted the words "youth court or, as the case may be"; and

(*e*) subsection (4) shall cease to have effect.

PART III
TRANSFER OF PROBATION ORDERS FROM NORTHERN IRELAND

3–1324   **10.** (1) Where a court in Northern Ireland considering the making of a probation order is satisfied that the offender resides in England and Wales, or will be residing there when the order comes into force, section 1 of the Probation Act (Northern Ireland) 1950 (probation orders) shall have effect as if after subsection (1) there were inserted the following subsection—

"(1A) A court shall not make a probation order in respect of any offender unless it is satisfied that suitable arrangements for his supervision can be made by the probation committee for the area which contains the local justice area in which he resides or will reside."

(2) Where a probation order has been made by a court in Northern Ireland and—

(*a*) a court of summary jurisdiction acting for the petty sessions district in Northern Ireland for the time being specified in the order is satisfied that the offender proposes to reside or is residing in England and Wales; and

(*b*) it appears to the court that suitable arrangements for his supervision can be made by the local probation board for the area which contains the local justice area in which he resides or will reside,

the power of the court to amend the order under Schedule 2 to the Probation Act (Northern Ireland) 1950 shall include power to amend it by requiring him to be supervised in accordance with arrangements so made.

(3) Where a court is considering the making or amendment of a probation order in accordance with this paragraph, schedule 1 to the Criminal Justice (Northern Ireland) Order 1996 shall have effect as if—

(*a*) any reference to a probation officer were a reference to an officer of a local probation board assigned to the local justice area in England and Wales in which the offender resides or will be residing when the order or amendment comes into force;

(*b*) the reference in paragraph 4(3) to treatment (whether as an in-patient or an out-patient) at such hospital as may be specified in the order, being a hospital within the meaning of the Health and Personal Social Services (Northern Ireland) Order 1972, approved by the Department of Health and Social Services for Northern Ireland for the purposes of that section were a reference to treatment as a resident patient in a hospital or mental nursing home within the meaning of the Mental Health Act 1983, not being hospital premises at which high security psychiatric services within the meaning of that Act are provided;

(*c*) the reference in section 2(5) to the Probation Board for Northern Ireland were a reference to the local probation board for the area in which the premises are situated; and

(*d*) references in paragraph 3to a day centre were references to a community rehabilitation centre within the meaning of section 201 of the Criminal Justice Act 2003.

(4) A probation order made or amended in accordance with this paragraph shall specify the local justice area in England and Wales in which the offender resides or will be residing when the order or amendment comes into force.

3–1325   **11.** (1) Where a probation order is made or amended in any of the circumstances specified in paragraph 10 above, the court which makes or amends the order shall send three copies of it as made or amended to the home court, together with such documents and information relating to the case as it considers likely to be of assistance to that court.

(2) Where a probation order is made or amended in any of the circumstances specified in paragraph 10 above, then, subject to the following provisions of this paragraph—

(*a*) the order shall be treated as if it were a community order made in England and Wales under section 177 of the Criminal Justice Act 2003; and

(b) the provisions of Part 12 of that Act (so far as relating to such orders) shall apply accordingly.

(3) Before making or amending a probation order in the circumstances specified in paragraph 10 above the court shall explain to the offender in ordinary language—

(a) the requirements of Part 12 of the Criminal Justice Act 2003 relating to community orders (within the meaning of that Part);

(b) the powers of the home court under Schedule 8 to that Act, as modified by this paragraph; and

(c) its own powers under this paragraph,

and an explanation given in accordance with this sub-paragraph shall be sufficient without the addition of an explanation under Article 10(3) of the Criminal Justice (Northern Ireland) Order 1996.

(4) The home court may exercise in relation to the probation order any power which it could exercise in relation to a community order made by a court in England and Wales under section 177 of the Criminal Justice Act 2003 except a power conferred by paragraph 9(1)(b) or (c) or 13(2)of Schedule 8 to that Act.

(5) If at any time while Part 12 of the Criminal Justice Act 2003 applies by virtue of sub-paragraph (2) above to a probation order made in Northern Ireland it appears to the home court—

(a) on information to a justice of the peace acting in the local justice area for the time being specified in the order, that the offender has failed to comply with any of the requirements of that Act applicable to the order; or

(b) on the application of the offender or the officer of a local probation board, that it would be in the interests of justice for the power conferred by paragraph 7 or 8 of Schedule 2 to the Criminal Justice (Northern Ireland) Order 1996 to be exercised,

the home court may require the offender to appear before the court which made the order.

(6) Where an offender is required by virtue of sub-paragraph (5) above to appear before the court which made the probation order, that court—

(a) may issue a warrant for his arrest; and

(b) may exercise any power which it could exercise in respect of the probation order if the offender resided in Northern Ireland,

and Schedule 2 to the Criminal Justice (Northern Ireland) Order 1996 shall have effect accordingly.

(7) Where an offender is required by virtue of paragraph (a) of sub-paragraph (5) above to appear before the court which made the probation order—

(a) the home court shall send to that court a certificate certifying that the offender has failed to comply with such of the requirements of the order as may be specified in the certificate, together with such other particulars of the case as may be desirable; and

(b) a certificate purporting to be signed by the clerk of the home court shall be admissible as evidence of the failure before the court which made the order.

(8) In this paragraph "home court" means, if the offender resides in England and Wales, or will be residing there at the time when the order or the amendment to it comes into force, the court of summary jurisdiction acting in the local justice area in which he resides or proposes to reside.

3–1327

Section 32(7)

SCHEDULE 5
THE PAROLE BOARD

Repealed.

3–1328

Section 53(5)

SCHEDULE 6
NOTICES OF TRANSFER: PROCEDURE IN LIEU OF COMMITTAL

(As amended by the Criminal Justice and Public Order Act 1994, Sch 10, the Criminal Procedure and Investigations Act 1996, s 45 and SI 2004/2035.)

Contents of notice of transfer

1. (1) A notice of transfer shall specify the proposed place of trial; and in selecting that place the Director of Public Prosecutions shall have regard to the considerations to which a magistrates' court committing a person for trial is required by section 7 of the 1980 Act to have regard when selecting the place at which he is to be tried.

(2) A notice of transfer shall specify the charge or charges to which it relates and include or be accompanied by such additional material as regulations under paragraph 4 below may require.

Remand

3–1329 2. (1) If a magistrates' court has remanded in custody a person to whom a notice of transfer relates, it shall have power, subject to section 4 of the Bail Act 1976, section 25 of the Criminal Justice and Public Order Act 1994 and regulations under section 22 of the Prosecution of Offences Act 1985—

(a) to order that he shall be safely kept in custody until delivered in due course of law; or

(b) to release him on bail in accordance with the Bail Act 1976, that is to say, by directing him to appear before the Crown Court for trial.

(2) Where—

(a) a person's release on bail under paragraph (b) of sub-paragraph (1) above is conditional on his providing one or more sureties; and

(b) in accordance with subsection (3) of section 8 of the Bail Act 1976, the court fixes the amount in which a surety is to be bound with a view to his entering into his recognisance subsequently in accordance with subsections (4) and (5) or (6) of that section, the court shall in the meantime make an order such as is mentioned in paragraph (*a*) of that sub-paragraph.

(3) If the conditions specified in sub-paragraph (4) below are satisfied, a court may exercise the powers conferred by sub-paragraph (1) above in relation to a person charged without his being brought before it in any case in which by virtue of subsection (3A) of section 128 of the 1980 Act it would have the power further to remand him on an adjournment such as is mentioned in that subsection.

(4) The conditions referred to in sub-paragraph (3) above are—

(*a*) that the person in question has given his written consent to the powers conferred by sub-paragraph (1) above being exercised without his being brought before the court; and

(*b*) that the court is satisfied that, when he gave his consent, he knew that the notice of transfer had been issued.

(5) Where a notice of transfer is given after a person to whom it relates has been remanded on bail to appear before a magistrates' court on an appointed day, the requirement that he shall so appear shall cease on the giving of the notice unless the notice states that it is to continue.

(6) Where that requirement ceases by virtue of sub-paragraph (5) above, it shall be the duty of the person in question to appear before the Crown Court at the place specified by the notice of transfer as the proposed place of trial or at any place substituted for it by a direction under section 76 of the Supreme Court Act 1981.

(7) If, in a case where the notice states that the requirement mentioned in sub-paragraph (5) above is to continue, a person to whom the notice relates appears before the magistrates' court, the court shall have—

(*a*) the powers and duties conferred on a magistrates' court by sub-paragraph (1) above but subject as there provided; and

(*b*) power to enlarge, in the surety's absence, a recognisance conditioned in accordance with section 128(4)(*a*) of the 1980 Act so that the surety is bound to secure that the person charged appears also before the Crown Court.

Witnesses

3–1330   **3.** For the purposes of the Criminal Procedure (Attendance of Witnesses) Act 1965—

(*a*) any magistrates' court for the petty sessions area for which the court from which a case was transferred sits shall be treated as examining magistrates; and

(*b*) a person indicated in the notice of transfer as a proposed witness shall be treated as a person who has been examined by the court.

Regulations

3–1331   **4.** (1) The Attorney General—

(*a*) shall by regulations[1] make provision requiring a copy of a notice of transfer, together with copies of the documents containing the evidence (including oral evidence) on which any charge to which it relates is based, to be given—

(i) to any person to whom the notice of transfer relates; and

(ii) to the Crown Court sitting at the place specified by the notice of transfer as the proposed place of trial; and

(*b*) may by regulations make such further provision in relation to notices of transfer, including provision as to the duties of the Director of Public Prosecutions in relation to such notices, as appears to him to be appropriate.

(1A) Regulations under sub-paragraph (1)(*a*) above may provide that there shall be no requirement for copies of documents to accompany the copy of the notice of transfer if they are referred to, in documents sent with the notice of transfer, as having already been supplied.

(2) The power to make regulations under this paragraph shall be exercisable by statutory instrument subject to annulment in pursuance of a resolution of either House of Parliament.

----

1. See the Criminal Justice Act 1991 (Notice of Transfer) Regulations 1992 and the Criminal Procedure Rules 2005, Part 13, in PART I: MAGISTRATES' COURTS, PROCEDURE, *ante.*

Applications for dismissal

3–1332   **5.** (1) Where a notice of transfer has been given, any person to whom the notice relates may, at any time before he is arraigned (and whether or not an indictment has been preferred against him), apply orally or in writing to the Crown Court sitting at the place specified by the notice of transfer as the proposed place of trial for the charge, or any of the charges, in the case to be dismissed.

(2) The judge shall dismiss a charge (and accordingly quash a count relating to it in any indictment preferred against the applicant) which is the subject of any such application if it appears to him that the evidence against the applicant would not be sufficient for a jury properly to convict him.

(3) No oral application may be made under sub-paragraph (1) above unless the applicant has given the Crown Court mentioned in that sub-paragraph written notice of his intention to make the application.

(4) Oral evidence may be given on such an application only with the leave of the judge or by his order; and the judge shall give leave or make an order only if it appears to him, having regard to any matters stated in the application for leave, that the interests of justice require him to do so.

(5) No leave or order under sub-paragraph (4) above shall be given or made in relation to oral evidence from a child (within the meaning of section 53 of this Act) who is alleged—

(a)　to be a person against whom an offence to which the notice of transfer relates was committed; or

(b)　to have witnessed the commission of such an offence.

(6)　If the judge gives leave permitting, or makes an order requiring, a person to give oral evidence, but that person does not do so, the judge may disregard any document indicating the evidence that he might have given.

(7)　Dismissal of the charge, or all the charges, against the applicant shall have the same effect as a refusal by examining magistrates to commit for trial, except that no further proceedings may be brought on a dismissed charge except by means of the preferment of a voluntary bill of indictment.

(8)　Criminal Procedure Rules may make provision for the purposes of this paragraph and, without prejudice to the generality of this sub-paragraph, may make provision—

(a)　as to the time or stage in the proceedings at which anything required to be done is to be done (unless the court grants leave to do it at some other time or stage);

(b)　as to the contents and form of notices or other documents;

(c)　as to the manner in which evidence is to be submitted; and

(d)　as to persons to be served with notices or other material.

Reporting restrictions

3–1333　6. (1)　Except as provided by this paragraph, it shall not be lawful—

(a)　to publish in Great Britain a written report of an application under paragraph 5(1) above; or

(b)　to include in a relevant programme for reception in Great Britain a report of such an application,

if (in either case) the report contains any matter other than that permitted by this paragraph.

(2)　An order that sub-paragraph (1) above shall not apply to reports of an application under paragraph 5(1) above may be made by the judge dealing with the application.

(3)　Where in the case of two or more accused one of them objects to the making of an order under sub-paragraph (2) above, the judge shall make the order if, and only if, he is satisfied, after hearing the representations of the accused, that it is in the interests of justice to do so.

(4)　An order under sub-paragraph (2) above shall not apply to reports of proceedings under sub-paragraph (3) above, but any decision of the court to make or not to make such an order may be contained in reports published or included in a relevant programme before the time authorised by sub-paragraph (5) below.

(5)　It shall not be unlawful under this paragraph to publish or include in a relevant programme a report of an application under paragraph 5(1) above containing any matter other than that permitted by sub-paragraph (8) below where the application is successful.

(6)　Where—

(a)　two or more persons were jointly charged; and

(b)　applications under paragraph 5(1) above are made by more than one of them,

sub-paragraph (5) above shall have effect as if for the words "the application is" there were substituted the words "all the applications are".

(7)　It shall not be unlawful under this paragraph to publish or include in a relevant programme a report of an unsuccessful application at the conclusion of the trial of the person charged, or of the last of the persons charged to be tried.

(8)　The following matters may be contained in a report published or included in a relevant programme without an order under sub-paragraph (2) above before the time authorised by sub-paragraphs (5) and (6)★ above, that is to say—

(a)　the identity of the court and the name of the judge;

(b)　the names, ages, home addresses and occupations of the accused and witnesses;

(c)　the offence or offences, or a summary of them, with which the accused is or are charged;

(d)　the names of counsel and solicitors engaged in the proceedings;

(e)　where the proceedings are adjourned, the date and place to which they are adjourned;

(f)　the arrangements as to bail;

(g)　whether legal aid was granted to the accused or any of the accused.

(9)　The addresses that may be published or included in a relevant programme under sub-paragraph (8) above are addresses—

(a)　at any relevant time; and

(b)　at the time of their publication or inclusion in a relevant programme.

(10)　If a report is published or included in a relevant programme in contravention of this paragraph, the following persons, that is to say—

(a)　in the case of a publication of a written report as part of a newspaper or periodical, any proprietor, editor or publisher of the newspaper or periodical;

(b)　in the case of a publication of a written report otherwise than as part of a newspaper or periodical, the person who publishes it;

(c)　in the case of the inclusion of a report in a relevant programme, any body corporate which is engaged in providing the service in which the programme is included and any person having functions in relation to the programme corresponding to those of the editor of a newspaper;

shall be liable on summary conviction to a fine not exceeding level 5 on the standard scale.

(11)　Proceedings for an offence under this paragraph shall not, in England and Wales, be instituted otherwise than by or with the consent of the Attorney General.

(12) Sub-paragraph (1) above shall be in addition to, and not in derogation from, the provisions of any other enactment with respect to the publication of reports of court proceedings.

(13) In this paragraph—

"publish", in relation to a report, means publish the report, either by itself or as part of a newspaper or periodical, for distribution to the public;

"relevant programme" means a programme included in a programme service (within the meaning of the Broadcasting Act 1990);

"relevant time" means a time when events giving rise to the charges to which the proceedings relate occurred.

---

*Amended in relation to a notice of transfer given under s 4 hereof, or served under the Criminal Justice Act 1991, s 53, by the Criminal Procedure and Investigations Act 1996, s 45(7), (8). In force in relation to notices of transfer served under the Criminal Justice Act, s 53, but has yet to be appointed for remaining purposes.

Avoidance of delay

3–1334   **7.** (1) Where a notice of transfer has been given in relation to any case—

(a) the Crown Court before which the case is to be tried; and

(b) any magistrates' court which exercises any functions under paragraph 2 or 3 above or section 20(4) of the Legal Aid Act 1988 in relation to the case,

shall, in exercising any of its powers in relation to the case, have regard to the desirability of avoiding prejudice to the welfare of any relevant child witness that may be occasioned by unnecessary delay in bringing the case to trial.

(2) In this paragraph "child" has the same meaning as in section 53 of this Act and "relevant child witness" means a child who will be called as a witness at the trial and who is alleged—

(a) to be a person against whom an offence to which the notice of transfer relates was committed; or

(b) to have witnessed the commission of such an offence.

Procedures for indictment of offenders

3–1335   **8.** (*Amends the Administration of Justice (Miscellaneous Provisions) Act 1933, s 2*)

Legal aid

3–1336   **9.** *Repealed*

Section 68

SCHEDULE 8[1]
AMENDMENTS FOR TREATING PERSONS AGED 17 AS YOUNG PERSONS

Children and Young Persons Act 1933 (c 12)

3–1338   **1.** (1) Section 31 of the 1933 Act shall be renumbered as subsection (1) of that section and after that provision as so renumbered there shall be inserted the following subsection—

"(2) In this section and section 34 of this Act, 'young person' means a person who has attained the age of fourteen and is under the age of seventeen years."

(2) In sections 46(1) and (1A), 48(2) and 99(1) of that Act, for the words "the age of seventeen" there shall be substituted the words "the age of eighteen".

(3) In section 107(1) of that Act, for the definition of "young person" there shall be substituted the following definition—

"'young person' means a person who has attained the age of fourteen and is under the age of eighteen years."

---

1. Only those provisions of Sch 8 which were not fully in force at the date of going to press are printed here.

Section 89

SCHEDULE 10
CERTIFICATION OF PRISONER CUSTODY OFFICERS

(*Amended by the Criminal Justice and Public Order Act 1994, s 101.*)

Preliminary

3–1352   **1.** In this Schedule—

"certificate" means a certificate under section 89 of this Act;

"the relevant functions", in relation to a certificate, means the escort functions or custodial duties authorised by the certificate.

3–1353

Issue of certificates

2. (1) Any person may apply to the Secretary of State for the issue of a certificate in respect of him.

(2) The Secretary of State shall not issue a certificate on any such application unless he is satisfied that the applicant—

(a) is a fit and proper person to perform the relevant functions; and

(b) has received training to such standard as he may consider appropriate for the performance of those functions.

(3) Where the Secretary of State issues a certificate, then, subject to any suspension under paragraph 3 or

revocation under paragraph 4 below, it shall continue in force until such date or the occurrence of such event as may be specified in the certificate.

(4) A certificate authorising the performance of both escort functions and custodial duties may specify different dates or events as respects those functions and duties respectively.

3–1353A **3–4.** *Suspension of certificate; revocation of certificate.*

False statements

3–1354 **5.** If any person, for the purpose of obtaining a certificate for himself or for any other person—

(a) makes a statement which he knows to be false in a material particular; or
(b) recklessly makes a statement which is false in a material particular,

he shall be liable on summary conviction to a fine not exceeding **level 4** on the standard scale.

Section 101(1)

SCHEDULE 12
TRANSITIONAL PROVISIONS AND SAVINGS

(As amended by the Criminal Justice and Public Order Act 1994, Sch 9, the Crime and Disorder Act 1998, Sch 10 and the Powers of Criminal Courts (Sentencing) Act 2000, Schs 9 and 12.)

Custodial and community sentences

3–1398 **1–4.** *Repealed.*

3–1399 **5.** *Repealed.*

3–1400 **6.** *Repealed.*

3–1400A **6A.** Section 17 of this Act shall not apply in relation to offences committed before the commencement of that section.

3–1401 **7.** Neither of subsections (3) and (4) of section 26 of this Act shall apply in relation to offences committed before the commencement of that subsection.

Early release: general

3–1402 **8.** (1) In this paragraph and paragraphs 9 to 11 below—

"existing licensee" means any person who, before the commencement of Part II of this Act, has been released on licence under section 60 of the 1967 Act and whose licence under that section is in force at that commencement;

"existing prisoner" means any person who, at that commencement, is serving a custodial sentence;

and sub-paragraphs (2) to (7) below shall have effect subject to those paragraphs.

(2) Subject to sub-paragraphs (3) to (7) below, Part II of this Act shall apply in relation to an existing licensee as it applies in relation to a person who is released on licence under that Part; and in its application to an existing prisoner, or to an existing licensee who is recalled under section 39 of this Act, that Part shall apply with the modifications made by those sub-paragraphs.

(3) *Repealed.*

(4) In relation to an existing prisoner whose sentence is for a term of twelve months, section 33(1) of this Act shall apply as if that sentence were for a term of less than twelve months.

(5) In relation to an existing prisoner or licensee whose sentence is for a term of—

(a) more than twelve months; and
(b) less than four years or, as the case may require, such other period as may for the time being be referred to in section 33(5) of this Act,

Part II of this Act shall apply as if he were or had been a long-term rather than a short-term prisoner.

(6) In relation to an existing prisoner or licensee whose sentence is for a term of more than twelve months—

(a) section 35(1) of this Act shall apply as if the reference to one half of his sentence were a reference to one-third of that sentence or six months, whichever is the longer; and
(b) sections 33(3) and 37(1) of this Act shall apply as if the reference to three-quarters of his sentence were a reference to two-thirds of that sentence.

(7) In relation to an existing prisoner or licensee—

(a) whose sentence is for a term of more than twelve months; and
(b) whose case falls within such class of cases as the Secretary of State may determine after consultation with the Parole Board,

section 35(1) of this Act shall apply as if the reference to a recommendation by the Board included in a reference to a recommendation by a local review committee established under section 59(6) of the 1967 Act.

(8) In this paragraph "custodial sentence" means—

(a) a sentence of imprisonment;
(b) a sentence of detention in a young offender institution;
(c) a sentence of detention (whether during Her Majesty's pleasure, for life or for a determinate term) under section 53 of the 1933 Act; or
(d) a sentence of custody for life under section 8 of the 1982 Act.

9. (1) This paragraph applies where, in the case of an existing life prisoner, the Secretary of State certifies his opinion that, if—

(*a*)   section 34 of this Act had been in force at the time when he was sentenced; and

(*b*)   the reference in subsection (1)(*a*) of that section to a violent or sexual offence the sentence for which is not fixed by law were a reference to any offence the sentence for which is not so fixed,

the court by which he was sentenced would have ordered that that section should apply to him as soon as he had served a part of his sentence specified in the certificate.

(2) In a case to which this paragraph applies, Part II of this Act except section 35(2) shall apply as if—

(*a*)   the existing life prisoner were a discretionary life prisoner for the purposes of that Part; and

(*b*)   the relevant part of his sentence within the meaning of section 34 of this Act were the part specified in the certificate, and

(*c*)   in section 34 of this Act, paragraph (*a*) of subsection (6) and subsection (6A) were omitted.

(3) In this paragraph "existing life prisoner" means a person who, at the commencement of Part II of this Act, is serving one or more of the following sentences, namely—

(*a*)   a sentence of life imprisonment;

(*b*)   a sentence of detention during Her Majesty's pleasure or for life under section 53 of the 1933 Act; or

(*c*)   a sentence of custody for life under section 8 of the 1982 Act.

(4) A person serving two or more such sentences shall not be treated as a discretionary life prisoner for the purposes of Part II of this Act unless the requirements of sub-paragraph (1) above are satisfied as respects each of those sentences; and subsections (3) and (5) of section 34 of this Act shall not apply in relation to such a person until after he has served the relevant part of each of those sentences.

10. Prison rules made by virtue of section 42 of this Act may include provision for applying any provisions of Part II of this Act, in relation to any existing prisoner or licensee who has forfeited any remission of his sentence, as if he had been awarded such number of additional days as may be determined by or under the rules.

Early release of young persons detained under 1933 Act

3–1403 11. In relation to an existing prisoner or licensee whose sentence is a determinate sentence of detention under section 53 of the 1933 Act—

(*a*)   Part II of this Act shall apply as if he were or had been a life rather than a long-term or short-term prisoner;

(*b*)   section 35(2) of this Act shall apply as if the requirement as to consultation were omitted; and

(*c*)   section 37(3) of this Act shall apply as if the reference to his death were a reference to the date on which he would (but for his release) have served the whole of his sentence.

Early release of prisoners serving extended sentences

3–1404 12. (1) In relation to an existing prisoner or licensee on the passing of whose sentence an extended sentence certificate was issued—

(*a*)   section 33(3) of this Act shall apply as if the duty to release him unconditionally were a duty to release him on licence; and

(*b*)   section 37(1) of this Act shall apply as if the reference to three-quarters of his sentence were a reference to the whole of that sentence.

(2) In this paragraph "extended sentence certificate" means a certificate issued under section 28 of the 1973 Act stating that an extended term of imprisonment was imposed on an offender under that section.

Early release of fine defaulters and contemnors

3–1405 13. Part II of this Act shall apply in relation to any person who, before the commencement of that Part, has been committed to prison or to be detained under section 9 of the 1982 Act—

(*a*)   in default of payment of a sum adjudged to be paid by a conviction; or

(*b*)   for contempt of court or any kindred offence,

as it applies in relation to any person who is so committed after that commencement.

3–1406 14. *Repealed.*

Remands and committals of children and young persons

3–1407 15. (1) In this paragraph—

"section 23" means section 23 of the 1969 Act as substituted by section 60(1) of this Act;

"the modifications" means the modifications of section 23 set out in section 62 of this Act;

"remand or committal" means a remand of a child or young person charged with or convicted of one or more offences, or a committal of a child or young person for trial or sentence.

(2) Section 23 as it has effect with the modifications shall not apply in relation to any remand or committal which is in force immediately before the commencement of sections 60 and 62 of this Act.

(3) Subject to sub-paragraphs (4) and (5) below, section 23 as it has effect without the modifications shall not apply in relation to any remand or committal which is in force immediately before the day appointed under section 62(1) of this Act.

(4) Any person who, in pursuance of any such remand or committal, is held in a remand centre or* prison shall be brought before the court which remanded or committed him before the end of the period of 8 days beginning with the day so appointed.

(5) Where any person is brought before a court under sub-paragraph (4) above, section 23 as it has effect without the modifications shall apply as if the court were just remanding or committing him as mentioned in subsection (1)(*a*) of that section.

---

*Repealed by the Criminal Justice and Court Services Act 2000, Sch 8 from a date to be appointed.

3–1407A   16. (1) Subsection (2)(*a*) of section 60 of this Act shall not apply in any case where proceedings for the offence in question have begun before the commencement of that section.

(2) Subject to sub-paragraphs (3) and (4) below, subsection (2)(*b*) and (*c*) of that section shall not apply in relation to any committal under section 37 of the 1980 Act which is in force immediately before that commencement.

(3) Any person less than 17 years old who, in pursuance of any such committal, is held in a remand centre or★ prison shall be brought before the court which committed him before the end of the period of 8 days beginning with that commencement.

(4) Where any person is brought before a court under sub-paragraph (3) above, section 37 of the 1980 Act shall apply as if the court were just committing him under that section.

★**Repealed by the Criminal Justice and Court Services Act 2000, Sch 8 from a date to be appointed.**

3–1408   17. *Repealed.*

3–1408A   18. Section 64 of this Act shall not apply in any case where the offence in question was committed before the commencement of that section and the offender is aged 16 at the date of his conviction.

Supervision of young offenders after release

3–1409   19. Section 65 of this Act shall not apply in relation to any person under the age of 22 years who, before the commencement of that section, is released from a term of detention in a young offender institution or under section 53 of the 1933 Act; and the repeal by this Act of section 15 of the 1982 Act shall not affect the operation of that section in relation to any such person who is so released.

3–1410   20. *Repealed.*

3–1411   21. *Repealed.*

Provisions for treating persons aged 17 as young persons

3–1412   22. (1) Paragraphs 1, 3, 4 and 6 of Schedule 8 shall not apply in any case where proceedings for the offence in question have begun before the commencement of that Schedule.

(2) Paragraph 5 of that Schedule shall apply in relation to any sentence imposed on any person who was convicted before that commencement and was aged 17 at the date of his conviction.

Renaming of juvenile courts etc

3–1413   23. In relation to any time before the commencement of section 70 of this Act, references in any other provision of this Act, or in any enactment amended by this Act, to youth courts shall be construed as references to juvenile courts.

Supplemental

3–1414   24. For the purposes of this Schedule proceedings for an offence shall be regarded as having begun as follows—

(*a*) in the case of an offence triable only summarily, when a plea is entered;

(*b*) in the case of an offence triable only on indictment, when the magistrates' court begins to inquire into the offence as examining magistrates;

(*c*) in the case of an offence triable either way, when the magistrates' court determines to proceed with the summary trial of the offence or, as the case may be, to proceed to inquire into the offence as examining justices.

Criminal Procedure (Insanity and Unfitness to Plead) Act 1991[1]

(1991 c 25)

3–1420   5. Orders under 1964 and 1968 Acts

1. This Act applies only to the higher courts except in so far as the magistrates' courts have power to revoke or amend supervision and treatment orders made in the higher courts. Only those provisions of the Act which relate to supervision and treatment orders are contained in this work.

3–1421   6. Interpretation etc.   (1) In this Act—

"the 1964 Act" means the Criminal Procedure (Insanity) Act 1964;

"the 1968 Act" means the Criminal Appeal Act 1968;

"the 1983 Act" means the Mental Health Act 1983;

"duly approved", in relation to a registered medical practitioner, means approved for the purposes of section 12 of the 1983 Act by the Secretary of State as having special experience in the diagnosis or treatment of mental disorder;

(2) *Repealed.*

[Criminal Procedure (Insanity and Unfitness to Plead) Act 1991, s 6, as amended by the Criminal Justice and Court Services Act 2000, Sch 7 and the Domestic Violence, Crime and Victims Act 2004, Sch 11.]

3–1422   8. *Transitional provisions, savings and repeals.*

3–1423   9. Short title, commencement and extent. (1) This Act may be cited as the Criminal Procedure (Insanity and Unfitness to Plead) Act 1991.

(2) This Act shall come into force on such day as the Secretary of State may by order made by statutory instrument appoint.

(3) This Act extends to England and Wales only.

[Criminal Procedure (Insanity and Unfitness to Plead) Act 1991, s 9.]

Section 5(3)   SCHEDULE 2
SUPERVISION AND TREATMENT ORDERS

3–1424 *Repealed.*

Prisoners and Criminal Proceedings (Scotland) Act 1993[1]
(1993 c 9)

PART I[2]

3–1425   12. Conditions in licence. (1) *Release on licence—Scotland.*

(2) Without prejudice to the generality of subsection (1) above and to the power of the Secretary of State under subsection (3) below to vary or cancel any condition, a licence granted under this Part of this Act shall include a condition requiring that the person subject to it—

(a) shall be under the supervision of a relevant officer of such local authority, or of an officer of a local probation board appointed for or assigned to such locla justice area, as may be specified in the licence; and

(b) shall comply with such requirements as that officer may specify for the purposes of the supervision.

(3), (4) *Variation etc of licence—Scotland.*

[Prisoners and Criminal Proceedings (Scotland) Act 1993, s 12 amended by the Criminal Justice and Public Order Act 1994, s 131, the Criminal Justice and Court Services Act 2000, s 74 and SI 2005/886.]

1. Only those provisions extended to England and Wales are reproduced.
2. Part I contains ss 1–27.

3–1425A   12A. Suspension of licence conditions. (1) Where a prisoner, who has been released on licence under this Part of this Act as respects a sentence of imprisonment—

(a) continues, by virtue of any enactment or rule of law, to be detained in prison notwithstanding such release; or

(b) is, by virtue of any enactment or rule of law, detained in prison subsequent to the date of such release but while the licence remains in force,

the conditions in the licence, other than those mentioned in subsection (3) below, shall by virtue of such detention be suspended.

(2) The suspension of the conditions shall have effect for so long as—

(a) the prisoner is so detained; and

(b) the licence remains in force.

(3) The conditions are any conditions, however expressed, requiring the prisoner—

(a) to be of good behaviour and to keep the peace; or

(b) not to contact a named person or class of persons (or not to do so unless with the approval of the person specified in the licence by virtue of section 12(2)(a) of this Act).

(4) The Scottish Ministers may by order amend subsection (3) above by—

(a) adding to the conditions mentioned in that subsection such other condition as they consider appropriate; or

(b) cancelling or varying a condition for the time being mentioned in that subsection.

[Prisoners and Criminal Proceedings (Scotland) Act 1993, s 12A as inserted by the Criminal Justice (Scotland) Act 2003, s 35.]

3–1425AA   12AA. Conditions for persons released on licence under section 3AA. (1) Without prejudice to the generality of section 12(1) of this Act, any licence granted under section 3AA of this Act must include—

(a) the standard conditions; and

(b) a curfew condition complying with section 12AB of this Act.

(2) Subsection (1) above is without prejudice to any power exercisable under section 12 of this Act.

(3) In this section, "the standard conditions" means such conditions as may be prescribed as such for the purposes of this section.

(4) In subsection (3) above, "prescribed" means prescribed by order by the Scottish Ministers.

(5) Different standard conditions may be so prescribed for different classes of prisoner.

(6) Subsection (4) of section 3AA of this Act applies in relation to—

(a) the exercise of the power of prescription conferred by subsection (3) above; and

(b) the specification, variation or cancellation of conditions, other than the standard conditions, in a licence granted under section 3AA of this Act,

as it applies in relation to the exercise of the power conferred by subsection (1) of that section.
[Prisoners and Criminal Proceedings (Scotland) Act 1993, s 12AA as inserted by the Management of Offenders etc (Scotland) Act 2005, s 15.]

3–1425AB 12AB. Curfew condition. (1) For the purposes of this Part, a curfew condition is a condition which—

(a) requires the released person to remain, for periods for the time being specified in the condition, at a place for the time being so specified; and

(b) may require him not to be in a place, or class of place, so specified at a time or during a period so specified.

(2) The curfew condition may specify different places, or different periods, for different days but a condition such as is mentioned in paragraph (a) of subsection (1) above may not specify periods which amount to less than nine hours in any one day (excluding for this purpose the first and last days of the period for which the condition is in force).

(3) Section 245C of the 1995 Act (contractual and other arrangements for, and devices which may be used for the purposes of, remote monitoring) applies in relation to the imposition of, and compliance with, a condition specified by virtue of subsection (1) above as that section applies in relation to the making of, and compliance with, a restriction of liberty order.

(4) A curfew condition is to be monitored remotely and the Scottish Ministers must designate in the licence a person who is to be responsible for the remote monitoring and must, as soon as practicable after they do so, send that person a copy of the condition together with such information as they consider requisite to the fulfilment of the responsibility.

(5) Subject to subsection (6) below, the designated person's responsibility—

(a) commences on that person's receipt of the copy so sent;

(b) is suspended during any period in which the curfew condition is suspended; and

(c) ends when the licence is revoked or otherwise ceases to be in force.

(6) The Scottish Ministers may from time to time designate a person who, in place of the person designated under subsection (4) above (or last designated under this subsection), is to be responsible for the remote monitoring; and on the Scottish Ministers amending the licence in respect of the new designation, that subsection and subsection (5) above apply in relation to the person designated under this subsection as they apply in relation to the person replaced.

(7) If a designation under subsection (6) above is made, the Scottish Ministers must, in so far as it is practicable to do so, notify the person replaced accordingly.
[Prisoners and Criminal Proceedings (Scotland) Act 1993, s 12AB as inserted by the Management of Offenders etc (Scotland) Act 2005, s 15.]

3–1425B 12B. Certain licences to be replaced by one. (1) Subsection (2) below applies where a prisoner—

(*a*) has been released on licence under this Part of this Act or under the 1989 Act as respects any sentence of imprisonment ("the original sentence"); and

(*b*) while so released, receives another sentence of imprisonment (whether for life or for a term) ("the subsequent sentence"),

and the licence as respects the original sentence has not been revoked.

(2) Where—

(*a*) this subsection applies; and

(*b*) the prisoner is to be released on licence under this Part of this Act as respects the subsequent sentence,

he shall instead be released on a single licence under this Part of this Act as respects both the original sentence and the subsequent sentence.

(3) The single licence—

(*a*) shall have effect in place of—

(i) the licence as respects the original sentence; and

(ii) any licence on which the prisoner would, apart from this section, be released as respects the subsequent sentence;

(*b*) shall be subject to such conditions as were in the licence as respects the original sentence immediately before that licence was replaced by the single licence; and

(*c*) shall (unless revoked) remain in force for so long as any licence as respects the original sentence or as respects the subsequent sentence would, apart from this section (and if not revoked), have remained in force.
[Prisoners and Criminal Proceedings (Scotland) Act 1993, s 12B as inserted by the Criminal Justice (Scotland) Act 2003, s 35.]

3–1426 14. Supervised release of short term prisoners. (1)–(3) *Repealed.*

(4) The Secretary of State shall, not later than thirty days before the date of release of a prisoner who is subject to a supervised release order, designate—

(a) the local authority for the area where the prisoner proposes to reside after release;
(b) the local authority for the area where the place from which he is to be released is situated; or
(c) the justices for the local justice area where he proposes to reside after release,

as the appropriate authority or, as the case may be, justices for the purposes of the order.

(5) As soon as practicable after designating a local authority or justices under subsection (4) above the Secretary of State shall—

(a) inform the prisoner in writing of the designation; and
(b) send to the authority or, as the case may be, to the designated officer for the justices a copy of the supervised release order and of the relevant documents and information received by the Secretary of State by virtue of section 209(6)(b) of the 1995 Act.

[Prisoners and Criminal Proceedings (Scotland) Act 1993, s 14 as amended by the Criminal Procedure (Consequential Provisions) (Scotland) Act 1995, Schs 4 and 5, the Crime and Disorder Act 1998, Schs 8 and 10, the Access to Justice Act 1999, s 90, the Crime and Punishment (Scotland) Act 1997, s 62 and SI 2005/886.]

3–1427   15. Variation of supervised release order etc.   (1) A person released subject to a supervised release order, or his supervising officer, may request the Secretary of State that a local authority or the justices for a local justice area (in this section referred to as the "second" designee) be designated under this subsection as the appropriate authority or justices for the purposes of the order in place of that or those for the time being designated under section 14(4) of this Act or this subsection (the "first" designee) if the person resides or proposes to reside in the area of the second designee.

(2) The Secretary of State shall, if he designates the second designee in accordance with the request, determine the date from which the designation shall have effect.

(3) As soon as practicable after a designation is made under subsection (1) above—

(a) the Secretary of State shall—

(i) inform the person subject to the supervised release order, the first designee and the second designee that the designation has been made and of the date determined under subsection (2) above; and
(ii) send a copy of the supervised release order to the second designee; and

(b) the first designee shall send to the second designee the relevant documents and information received by the first designee by virtue of section 14(5)(b) of this Act (or by virtue of this paragraph).

(4) The court which made a supervised release order may, on an application under this subsection by a person subject to the order (whether or not he has been released before the application is made) or by his supervising officer (or, if the person is not yet released, but a local authority stands or justices stand designated as the appropriate authority or justices in respect of the order, by a relevant officer of that authority or, as the case may be, an officer of a local probation board appointed for or assigned to the petty sessions area)—

(a) amend, vary or cancel any requirement specified in or by virtue of the order;
(b) insert in the order a requirement specified for the purpose mentioned in section 209(3)(b) of the 1995 Act,

whether or not such amendment, variation, cancellation or insertion accords with what is sought by the applicant; but the period during which the person is to be under supervision shall not thereby be increased beyond any period which could have been specified in making the order.

(5) If an application under subsection (4) above is by the supervising officer (or other relevant officer or an officer of a local probation board) alone, the court shall cite the person who is subject to the order to appear before the court and shall not proceed under that subsection until it has explained to the person, in as straightforward a way as is practicable, the effect of any proposed amendment, variation, cancellation or insertion.★

(5A) The unified citation provisions (as defined by section 307(1) of the Criminal Procedure (Scotland) Act 1995 (c 46)) apply in relation to a citation under subsection (5) above as they apply in relation to a citation under section 216(3)(a) of that Act.

(6) The clerk of the court by which an amendment, variation, cancellation or insertion is made under subsection (4) above shall forthwith send a copy of the resultant order to the person subject to it and to the supervising officer.

[Prisoners and Criminal Proceedings (Scotland) Act 1993, s 15 as amended by the Criminal Procedure (Consequential Provisions) (Scotland) Act 1995, Sch 4, the Criminal Justice and Court Services Act 2000, s 74, the Criminal Justice (Scotland) Act 2003, s 60 and SI 2005/886.]

3–1428   16. Commission of offence by released prisoner.   (1) This section applies to a short-term or long-term prisoner sentenced to a term of imprisonment (in this section referred to as "the original sentence") by a court in Scotland and released at any time under this Part of this Act or Part II of the Criminal Justice Act 1991 if—

(a) before the date on which he would (but for his release) have served his sentence in full, he commits an offence punishable with imprisonment (other than an offence in respect of which imprisonment for life is mandatory); and
(b) whether before or after that date, he pleads guilty to or is found guilty of that offence (in this section referred to as "the new offence") in a court in Scotland or England and Wales.

(2)　(*Powers of Scottish courts.*)

(3)　Where the court mentioned in subsection (1)(*b*) above is in England and Wales it may, instead of or in addition to making any other order in respect of the plea or finding, refer the case to the court which imposed the original sentence and shall, if it does so, send to that court such particulars of that case as may be relevant.

(4)–(8)　(*Scotland.*)

[Prisoners and Criminal Proceedings (Scotland) Act 1993, s 16 as amended by the Criminal Procedure (Consequential Provisions) (Scotland) Act 1995, Sch 4 and the Crime and Disorder Act 1998, s 111 and Sch 8.]

Criminal Procedure (Scotland) Act 1995[1]

(1995 c 46)

PART V[2]
CHILDREN AND YOUNG PERSONS

3–1440　**44. Detention of children.**　(1) Where a child appears before the sheriff in summary proceedings and pleads guilty to, or is found guilty of, an offence to which this section applies, the sheriff may order that he be detained in residential accommodation provided under Part II of the Children (Scotland) Act 1995 by the appropriate local authority for such period not exceeding one year as may be specified in the order in such place (in any part of the United Kingdom) as the local authority may, from time to time, consider appropriate.

(2)　This section applies to any offence (other than, if the child is under the age of 16 years, an offence under section 9(1) of the Antisocial Behaviour etc (Scotland) Act 2004 (asp 8) or that section as applied by section 234AA(11) of this Act) in respect of which it is competent to impose imprisonment on a person of the age of 21 years or more.

(3)　Where a child in respect of whom an order is made under this section is detained by the appropriate local authority, that authority shall have the same powers and duties in respect of the child as they would have if he were subject to a supervision requirement.

(4)　Where a child in respect of whom an order is made under this section is also subject to a supervision requirement, the supervision requirement shall be of no effect during any period for which he is required to be detained under the order.

(5)　The Secretary of State may, by regulations made by statutory instrument subject to annulment in pursuance of a resolution of either House of Parliament, make such provision as he considers necessary as regards the detention in secure accommodation of children in respect of whom orders have been made under this section.

(6)–(9)　*Repealed.*

(10)　Where a local authority consider it appropriate that a child in respect of whom an order has been made under subsection (1) or (8) above should be detained in a place in any part of the United Kingdom outside Scotland, the order shall be a like authority as in Scotland to the person in charge of the place to restrict the child's liberty to such an extent as that person may consider appropriate having regard to the terms of the order.

(11)　In this section—

"the appropriate local authority" means—

(*a*)　where the child usually resides in Scotland, the local authority for the area in which he usually resides;

(*b*)　in any other case, the local authority for the area in which the offence was committed; and

"secure accommodation" has the meaning assigned to it in Part II of the Children (Scotland) Act 1995.

[Criminal Procedure (Scotland) Act 1995, s 44 as amended by the Crime and Punishment (Scotland) Act 1997, Sch 1 and the Antisocial Behaviour etc (Scotland) Act 2004, s 10.]

1.　This Act consolidates certain enactments relating to criminal procedure in Scotland. Only those provisions which extend to England or Wales or are relevant to the work of magistrates' courts in England or Wales are printed here. The Act came into force on 1 April 1996 (s 309, post).

2.　Part V contains ss 41–51.

3–1441　**47. Restriction on report of proceedings involving children.**　(1) Subject to subsection (3) below, no newspaper report of any proceedings in a court shall reveal the name, address or school, or include any particulars calculated to lead to the identification, of any person under the age of 16 years concerned in the proceedings, either—

(*a*)　as being a person against or in respect of whom the proceedings are taken; or

(*b*)　as being a witness in the proceedings.

(2)　Subject to subsection (3) below, no picture which is, or includes, a picture of a person under the age of 16 years concerned in proceedings as mentioned in subsection (1) above shall be published in any newspaper in a context relevant to the proceedings.

(3)　The requirements of subsection (1) and (2) above shall be applied in any case mentioned in any of the following paragraphs to the extent specified in that paragraph—

(a) where a person under the age of 16 years is concerned in the proceedings as a witness only and no one against whom the proceedings are taken is under the age of 16 years, the requirements shall not apply unless the court so directs;

(b) where, at any stage of the proceedings, the court, if it is satisfied that it is in the public interest so to do, directs that the requirements (including the requirements as applied by a direction under paragraph (a) above) shall be dispensed with to such extent as the court may specify; and

(c) where the Secretary of State, after completion of the proceedings, if satisfied as mentioned in paragraph (b) above, by order dispenses with the requirements to such extent as may be specified in the order.

(4) This section shall, with the necessary modifications, apply in relation to sound and television programmes included in a programme service (within the meaning of the Broadcasting Act 1990) as it applies in relation to newspapers.

(5) A person who publishes matter in contravention of this section shall be guilty of an offence and liable on summary conviction to a fine not exceeding level 4 of the standard scale.

(6) In this section, references to a court shall not include a court in England, Wales or Northern Ireland.

[Criminal Procedure (Scotland) Act 1995, s 47.]

PART XI[1]
SENTENCING

3–1442 209. Supervised release orders. (1) Where a person is convicted on indictment of an offence, other than a sexual offence within the meaning of section 210A of this Act, and is sentenced to imprisonment for a term of less than four years, the court on passing sentence may, if it considers that it is necessary to do so to protect the public from serious harm from the offender on his release, make such order as is mentioned in subsection (3) below.★

(2) A court shall, before making an order under subsection (1) above, consider a report by a relevant officer of a local authority about the offender and his circumstances and, if the court thinks it necessary, hear that officer.

(3) The order referred to in subsection (1) above (to be known as a "supervised release order") is that the person, during a relevant period—

(a) be under the supervision either of a relevant officer of a local authority or of an officer of a local probation board appointed for or assigned to a petty sessions area (such local authority or the justices for such area to be designated under section 14(4) or 15(1) of the Prisoners and Criminal Proceedings (Scotland) Act 1993);

(b) comply with;

    (i) such requirements as may be imposed by the court in the order; and
    (ii) such requirements as that officer may reasonably specify,

for the purpose of securing the good conduct of the person or preventing, or lessening the possibility of, his committing a further offence (whether or not an offence of the kind for which he was sentenced); and

(c) comply with the standard requirements imposed by virtue of subsection (4)(a)(i) below.

(4) A supervised release order—

(a) shall—

    (i) without prejudice to subsection (3)(b) above, contain such requirements (in this section referred to as the "standard requirements"); and
    (ii) be as nearly as possible in such form,

as may be prescribed by Act of Adjournal;

(b) for the purposes of any appeal or review constitutes part of the sentence of the person in respect of whom the order is made; and

(c) shall have no effect during any period in which the person is subject to a licence under Part I of the said Act of 1993.

(5) Before making a supervised release order as respects a person the court shall explain to him, in as straightforward a way as is practicable, the effect of the order and the possible consequences for him of any breach of it.

(6) The clerk of the court by which a supervised release order is made in respect of a person shall—

(a) forthwith send a copy of the order to the person and to the Secretary of State; and

(b) within seven days after the date on which the order is made, send to the Secretary of State such documents and information relating to the case and to the person as are likely to be of assistance to a supervising officer.

(7) In this section —

"relevant officer" has the same meaning as in Part I of the Prisoners and Criminal Proceedings (Scotland) Act 1993;

"relevant period" means such period as may be specified in the supervised release order, being a period—

(a) not exceeding twelve months after the date of the person's release; and

(b) no part of which is later than the date by which the entire term of imprisonment specified in his sentence has elapsed; and★

"supervising officer" means, where an authority has or justices have been designated as is mentioned in subsection (3)(a) above for the purposes of the order, any relevant officer or, as the case may be, officer of a local probation board who is for the time being supervising for those purposes the person released.

(7A) Where a person—

(a) is serving a sentence of imprisonment and on his release from that sentence will be subject to a supervised release order; and

(b) is sentenced to a further term of imprisonment, whether that term is to run consecutively or concurrently with the sentenced mentioned in paragraph (a) above,

the relevant period for any supervised release order made in relation to him shall begin on the date when he is released from those terms of imprisonment; and where there is more than one such order he shall on his release be subject to whichever of them is for the longer, as the case may be, the longest period.

(8) This section applies to a person sentenced under section 207 of this Act as it applies to a person sentenced to a period of imprisonment.

(9) Subject to subsection (11) below, the periods referred to in the definition of "relevant period" in subsection (7) above are—

(a) a period, beginning on the day on which the person is released—

   (i) of not less than three months; and

   (ii) not exceeding whichever is the greater of two years or one quarter of the full sentence of imprisonment from which the person is being released; and

(b) a period, beginning on the day on which the person is released—

   (i) of not less than three months; and

   (ii) not exceeding ten years.

(10) For the purposes of this section "court" does not include a district court except where constituted by a stipendiary magistrate.

(11) No court may impose a supervised release order for a period longer than the maximum period of imprisonment which that court may impose for a common law offence.
[Criminal Procedure (Scotland) Act 1995, s 209 as amended by the Crime and Disorder Act 1998, s 86 and Sch 10, and the Crime and Punishment (Scotland) Act 1997, Sch 1 and the Criminal Justice and Court Services Act 2000, Sch 7.]

★**Section 209(1), (7) is amended by the Crime and Punishment (Scotland) Act 1997, s 4, when in force.**
1. Part XI contains ss 195–254.

3–1443 234. Probation orders: persons residing in England and Wales. (1) Where the court which made a probation order to which this subsection applies is satisfied that the offender has attained the age of 16 years and resides or will reside in England and Wales, subsections (3) and (4) of section 228 of this Act shall not apply to the order, but—

(a) the order shall contain a requirement that he be under the supervision of an officer of a local probation board appointed for or assigned to the local justice area in which the offender resides or will reside; and

(b) that area shall be named in the order

(2) Subsection (1) above applies to a probation order which is made under section 228 unless the order includes requirements which are more onerous than those which a court in England and Wales could impose on an offender under section 177 of the Criminal Justice Act 2003.

(3) Where a probation order has been made under the said section 228 and the court in Scotland which made the order or the appropriate court is satisfied—

(a) that the probationer has attained the age of 16 years;

(b) that he proposes to reside, or is residing, in England and Wales; and

(c) that suitable arrangements for his supervision can be made by the local probation board for the area which contains the local justice area in which he resides or will reside,

the power of that court to amend the order under Schedule 6 to this Act shall include power to insert the provisions required by subsection (1) above, and the court may so amend the order without summoning the probationer and without his consent.

(4) A probation order made or amended by virtue of this section may, notwithstanding section 230(9) of this Act, include a requirement that the probationer shall submit to treatment for his mental condition, and—

(a) subsection (1), (3) and (8) of the said section 230 and section 207(2) of the Criminal Justice Act 2003(all of which regulate the making of probation orders or, as the case may be, community orders under Part 12 of that Act which include any such requirement) shall apply to the making of an order which includes any such requirement by virtue of this subsection as they apply to the making of an order which includes any such requirement by virtue of the said section 230 and section 207 of the Criminal Justice Act 2003 respectively; and

(b)　sections 207(4) and 208(1) and (2) of the Criminal Justice Act 2003 (functions of supervising officer and registered medical practitioner where such a requirement has been imposed) shall apply in relation to a probationer who is undergoing treatment in England and Wales in pursuance of a requirement imposed by virtue of this subsection as they apply in relation to a probationer undergoing such treatment in pursuance of a requirement imposed by virtue of that section.

(4A)　A probation order made or amended under this section must specify as the corresponding requirements for the purposes of this section requirements which could be included in a community order made under section 177 of the Criminal Justice Act 2003.

(5)　Sections 231(1) and 232(1) of this Act shall not apply to any order made or amended under this section; but subject to subsection (6) below, Schedule 8 to the Criminal Justice Act 2003 shall apply as if it were a community order made by a magistrates' court under section 177 of that Act and imposing the requirements specified under subsection (4A) above.

(6)　In its application to a probation order made or amended under this section, Schedule 8 to the Criminal Justice Act 2003 has effect subject to the following modifications—

(a)　any reference to the responsible officer has effect as a reference to the person appointed or assigned under subsection (1)(a) above,

(b)　in paragraph 9—

(i)　paragraphs (b) and (c) of sub-paragraph (1) are omitted,

(ii)　in sub-paragraph (6), the first reference to the Crown Court has effect as a reference to a court in Scotland, and

(iii)　any other reference in sub-paragraphs (6) or (7) to the Crown Court has effect as a reference to the court in Scotland, and

(c)　Parts 3 and 5 are omitted.

(7)　If it appears on information to a justice acting in ther local justice area named in a probation order made or amended under this section that the person to whom the order relates has been convicted by a court in any part of Great Britain of an offence committed during the period specified in the order he may issue—

(a)　a summons requiring that person to appear, at the place and time specified in the summons, before the court in Scotland which made the probation order; or

(b)　if the information is in writing and on oath, a warrant for his arrest, directing that person to be brought before the last-mentioned court.

(8)　If a warrant for the arrest of a probationer issued under section 233 of this Act by a court is executed in England and Wales and the probationer cannot forthwith be brought before that court, the warrant shall have effect as if it directed him to be brought before a magistrates' court; and the magistrates' court shall commit him to custody or release him on bail (with or without sureties) until he can be brought or appear before the court in Scotland.

(9)　The court by which a probation order is made or amended in accordance with the provisions of this section shall send three copies of the order to the designated officer for the local justice area named in the order, together with such documents and information relating to the case as it considers likely to be of assistance to the court acting in that local justice area.

(10)　Where a probation order which is amended under subsection (3) above is an order to which the provisions of this Act apply by virtue of paragraph 8 of Schedule 9 (which relates to community orders under that Act relating to persons residing in Scotland) then, notwithstanding anything in that Schedule or this section, the order shall, as from the date of the amendment, have effect in all respects as if it were a community order made under Part 12 of that Act in the case of a person residing in England and Wales.

(11)　*Repealed.*.

[Criminal Procedure (Scotland) Act 1995, s 234 as amended by the Powers of Criminal Courts (Sentencing) Act 2000, Sch 9, the Access to Justice Act 1999, Sch 13, the Criminal Justice and Court Services Act 2000, Sch 7, the Criminal Justice Act 2003, Sch 32 and SI 2005/886.]

3–1443A　**234AA. Antisocial behaviour orders.**　(1) Where subsection (2) below applies, the court may, instead of or in addition to imposing any sentence which it could impose, make an antisocial behaviour order in respect of a person (the "offender").

(2)　This subsection applies where—

(a)　the offender is convicted of an offence;

(b)　at the time when he committed the offence, the offender was at least 12 years of age;

(c)　in committing the offence, he engaged in antisocial behaviour; and

(d)　the court is satisfied, on a balance of probabilities, that the making of an antisocial behaviour order is necessary for the purpose of protecting other persons from further antisocial behaviour by the offender.

(3)　For the purposes of subsection (2)(c) above, a person engages in antisocial behaviour if he—

(a)　acts in a manner that causes or is likely to cause alarm or distress; or

(b)　pursues a course of conduct that causes or is likely to cause alarm or distress, to at least one person who is not of the same household as him.

(4) Subject to subsection (5) below, an antisocial behaviour order is an order which prohibits, indefinitely or for such period as may be specified in the order, the offender from doing anything described in the order.

(5) The prohibitions that may be imposed by an antisocial behaviour order are those necessary for the purpose of protecting other persons from further antisocial behaviour by the offender.

(6) Before making an antisocial behaviour order, the court shall explain to the offender in ordinary language—

    (a) the effect of the order and the prohibitions proposed to be included in it;
    (b) the consequences of failing to comply with the order;
    (c) the powers the court has under subsection (8) below; and
    (d) the entitlement of the offender to appeal against the making of the order.

(7) Failure to comply with subsection (6) shall not affect the validity of the order.

(8) On the application of the offender in respect of whom an antisocial behaviour order is made under this section, the court which made the order may, if satisfied on a balance of probabilities that it is appropriate to do so—

    (a) revoke the order; or
    (b) subject to subsection (9) below, vary it in such manner as it thinks fit.

(9) Where an antisocial behaviour order specifies a period, the court may not, under subsection (8)(b) above, vary the order by extending the period.

(10) An antisocial behaviour order made under this section, and any revocation or variation of such an order under subsection (8) above, shall be taken to be a sentence for the purposes of an appeal.

(11) Sections 9 and 11 of the Antisocial Behaviour etc (Scotland) Act 2004 (asp 8) (which provide that breach of an antisocial behaviour order made under that Act is an offence for which a person is liable to be arrested without warrant) shall apply in relation to antisocial behaviour orders made under this section as those sections apply in relation to antisocial behaviour orders made under section 4 of that Act.

(12) In this section, "conduct" includes speech; and a course of conduct must involve conduct on at least two occasions.
[Criminal Procedure (Scotland) Act 1995, s 234AA as inserted by the Antisocial Behaviour etc (Scotland) Act 2004, s 118.]

3–1443B   234AB. Antisocial behaviour orders: notification. (1) Upon making an antisocial behaviour order under section 234AA of this Act, the court shall—

    (a) serve a copy of the order on the offender; and
    (b) give a copy of the order to the local authority it considers most appropriate.

(2) Upon revoking an antisocial behaviour order under subsection (8)(a) of that section, the court shall notify the local authority to whom a copy of the order was given under subsection (1)(b) above.

(3) Upon varying an antisocial behaviour order under subsection (8)(b) of that section, the court shall—

    (a) serve a copy of the order as varied on the offender; and
    (b) give a copy of the order as varied to the local authority to whom a copy of the order was given under subsection (1)(b) above.

(4) For the purposes of this section, a copy is served on an offender if—

    (a) given to him; or
    (b) sent to him by registered post or the recorded delivery service.

(5) A certificate of posting of a letter sent under subsection (4)(b) issued by the postal operator shall be sufficient evidence of the sending of the letter on the day specified in such certificate.

(6) In this section, "offender" means the person in respect of whom the antisocial behaviour order was made.
[Criminal Procedure (Scotland) Act 1995, s 234AB as inserted by the Antisocial Behaviour etc (Scotland) Act 2004, s 118.]

3–1444   242. Community service orders: persons residing in England and Wales. (1) Where a court is considering the making of a community service order and it is satisfied that the offender has attained the age of 16 years and resides, or will be residing when the order comes into force, in England or Wales, then—

    (a) section 238 of this Act shall have effect as if subsection (2) were amended as follows—

        (i) paragraph (b) shall be omitted;
        (ii) in paragraph (c) for the words "such an order" there shall be substituted the words "an unpaid work requirement imposed by a community order (within the meaning of Part 12 of the Criminal Justice Act 2003)"; and
        (iii) for paragraph (d) there shall be substituted the following paragraph—

        "(d) it appears to that court that provision can be made for the offender to perform work under the order made under subsection (1) above under the arrangements which exist in the petty sessions area in which he resides or will be residing for persons to perform work under unpaid work requirements imposed by community orders made under section 177 of the Criminal Justice Act 2003;"; and

(b) the order shall specify that the unpaid work required to be performed by the order shall be performed under the arrangements mentioned in section 238(2)(d) of this Act as substituted by paragraph (a) above.

(2) Where a community service order has been made and—

(a) the appropriate court is satisfied that the offender has attained the age of 16 years and proposes to reside or is residing in England or Wales; and

(b) it appears to that court that provision can be made for the offender to perform work under the order made under the arrangements which exist in the petty sessions area in which he proposes to reside or is residing for persons to perform work under unpaid work requirements imposed by community orders made under section 177 of the Criminal Justice Act 2003,

it may amend the order by specifying that the unpaid work required to be performed by the order shall be performed under the arrangements mentioned in paragraph (b) of this subsection.

(3) A community service order made under section 238(1) as amended by or in accordance with this section shall—

(a) specify the petty sessions area in England or Wales in which the offender resides or will be residing when the order or the amendment comes into force; and

(b) require the local probation board for that area to appoint or assign an officer of the board who will discharge in respect of the order the functions conferred on responsible officers by Part 12 of the Criminal Justice Act 2003 in respect of unpaid work requirements imposed by community orders (within the meaning of that Part).

[Criminal Procedure (Scotland) Act 1995, s 242 as amended by the Powers of Criminal Courts (Sentencing) Act 2000, Sch 9, the Criminal Justice and Court Services Act 2000, Sch 7 and the Criminal Justice Act 2003, Sch 32.]

3–1445   244. Community service orders: general provisions relating to persons living in England and Wales or Northern Ireland.   (1) Where a community service order is made or amended in the circumstances specified in section 242 or 243 of this Act, the court which makes or amends the order shall send three copies of it as made or amended to the home court, together with such documents and information relating to the case as it considers likely to be of assistance to that court.

(2) In this section—

"home court" means—

(a) if the offender resides in England or Wales, or will be residing in England or Wales at the relevant time, the magistrates' court acting for the petty sessions area in which he resides or proposes to reside; and

(b) if he resides in Northern Ireland, or will be residing in Northern Ireland, at the relevant time, the court of summary jurisdiction acting for the petty sessions district in which he resides or proposes to reside; and

"the relevant time" means the time when the order or the amendment to it comes into force.

(3) Subject to the following provisions of this section—

(a) a community service order made or amended in the circumstances specified in section 242 shall be treated as if it were a community order (within the meaning of Part 12 of the Criminal Justice Act 2003) made in England and Wales and the legislation relating to such community orders which has effect in England and Wales shall apply accordingly; and

(b) a community service order made or amended in the circumstances specified in section 243 shall be treated as if it were a community service order made in Northern Ireland and the legislation relating to community service orders which has effect in Northern Ireland shall apply accordingly.

(4) Before making or amending a community service order in those circumstances the court shall explain to the offender in ordinary language—

(a) the requirements of the legislation relating to community service orders or, as the case may be, community orders (within the meaning of Part 12 of the Criminal Justice Act 2003) which has effect in the part of the United Kingdom in which he resides or will be residing at the relevant time;

(b) the powers of the home court under that legislation, as modified by this section; and

(c) its own powers under this section,

and an explanation given in accordance with this section shall be sufficient without the addition of an explanation under section 238(4) of this Act.

(5) The home court may exercise in relation to the community service order any power which it could exercise in relation to a community service order, or, as the case may be, a community order (within the meaning of Part 12 of the Criminal Justice Act 2003) made by a court in the part of the United Kingdom in which the home court exercises jurisdiction, by virtue of the legislation relating to such orders which has effect in that part of the United Kingdom, except—

   (*a*) a power to vary the order by substituting for the number of hours' work specified in it any greater number than the court which made the order could have specified;

   (*b*) a power to revoke the order; and

   (*c*) a power to revoke the order and deal with the offender for the offence in respect of which it was made in any manner in which he could have been dealt with for that offence by the court which made the order if the order had not been made.

  (6) If at any time while legislation relating to community service orders or, as the case may be, community orders (within the meaning of Part 12 of the Criminal Justice Act 2003) which has effect in one part of the United Kingdom applies by virtue of subsection (3) above to a community service order made in another part—

   (*a*) it appears to the home court—

     (i) if that court is in England or Wales, on information to a justice of the peace acting for the petty sessions area for the time being specified in the order; or

     (ii) if it is in Northern Ireland, upon a complaint being made to a resident magistrate,

   that the offender has failed to comply with any of the requirements of the legislation applicable to the order; or

   (*b*) it appears to the home court on the application of—

     (i) the offender; or

     (ii) if that court is in England and Wales, the responsible officer under Part 12 of the Criminal Justice Act 2003; or

     (iii) if that court is in Northern Ireland, the relevant officer under the Treatment of Offenders (Northern Ireland) Order 1976,

   that it would be in the interests of justice to exercise a power mentioned in subsection (5)(*b*) or (*c*) above,

the home court may require the offender to appear before the court by which the order was made.

  (7) Where an offender is required by virtue of subsection (6) above to appear before the court which made a community service order, that court—

   (*a*) may issue a warrant for his arrest; and

   (*b*) may exercise any power which it could exercise in respect of the community service order if the offender resided in the part of the United Kingdom where the court has jurisdiction,

and any enactment relating to the exercise of such powers shall have effect accordingly.

[Criminal Procedure (Scotland) Act 1995, s 244, as amended by the Powers of Criminal Courts (Sentencing) Act 2000, Sch 9, the Criminal Justice and Court Services Act 2000, Sch 7, the Justice (Northern Ireland) Act 2002, Sch 4 and the Criminal Justice Act 2003, Sch 32.]

3–1446 252. Enforcement of compensation orders: application of provisions relating to fines. (1) The provisions of this Act specified in subsection (2) below shall, subject to any necessary modifications and to the qualifications mentioned in that subsection, apply in relation to compensation orders as they apply in relation to fines; and section 91 of the Magistrates' Courts Act 1980 and article 96 of the Magistrates' Courts (Northern Ireland) Order 1981 shall be construed accordingly.

  (2) The provisions mentioned in subsection (1) above are—

section 211(3), (4) and (7) to (9) (enforcement of fines);

section 212 (fines in summary proceedings);

section 213 (power to remit fines), with the omission of the words "or (4)" in subsection (2) of that section;

section 214 (time for payment) with the omission of—

   (*a*) the words from "unless" to "its decision" in subsection (4); and

   (*b*) subsection (5);

section 215 (further time for payment);

section 216 (reasons for default);

section 217 (supervision pending payment of fine);

section 218 (supplementary provisions), except that subsection (1) of that section shall not apply in relation to compensation orders made in solemn proceedings;

subject to subsection (3) below, section 219(1)(*b*), (2), (3), (5), (6) and (8) (maximum period of imprisonment for non-payment of fine);

section 220 (payment of fine in part by prisoner);

section 221 (recovery by civil diligence);

section 222 (transfer of fine orders);

section 223 (action of clerk of court on transfer of fine order); and

section 224 (discharge from imprisonment to be specified).

  (3) In the application of the provisions of section 219 of this Act mentioned in subsection (2) above for the purposes of subsection (1) above—

   (*a*) a court may impose imprisonment in respect of a fine and decline to impose imprisonment in respect of a compensation order but not vice versa; and (*b*) where a court imposes imprisonment both in respect of a fine and of a compensation order the amounts in respect of which imprisonment is imposed shall, for the purposes of subsection (2) of the said section 219, be aggregated.

[Criminal Procedure (Scotland) Act 1995, s 252.]

PART XIII[1]

MISCELLANEOUS

3–1447   303. Fixed penalty: enforcement.   (1) Subject to subsection (2) below, where an alleged offender accepts a conditional offer by paying the first instalment of the appropriate fixed penalty, any amount of the penalty which is outstanding at any time shall be treated as if the penalty were a fine imposed by the court, the clerk of which is specified in the conditional offer.

(2) In the enforcement of a penalty which is to be treated as a fine in pursuance of subsection (1) above—

(*a*) any reference, howsoever expressed, in any enactment whether passed or made before or after the coming into force of this section to—

(i) the imposition of imprisonment or detention in default of payment of a fine shall be construed as a reference to enforcement by means of civil diligence;

(ii) the finding or order of the court imposing the fine shall be construed as a reference to a certificate given in pursuance of subsection (3) below;

(iii) the offender shall be construed as a reference to the alleged offender;

(iv) the conviction of the offender shall be construed as a reference to the acceptance of the conditional offer by the alleged offender;

(*b*) the following sections of this Act shall not apply—

section 211(7);
section 213(2);
section 214(1) to (6);
section 216(7);
section 219, except subsection (1)(*b*);
section 220;
section 221(2) to (4);
section 222(8); and
section 224.

(3) For the purposes of any proceedings in connection with, or steps taken for, the enforcement of any amount of a fixed penalty which is outstanding, a document purporting to be a certificate signed by the clerk of court for the time being responsible for the collection or enforcement of the penalty as to any matter relating to the penalty shall be conclusive of the matter so certified.

(4) The Secretary of State may, by order made by statutory instrument subject to annulment in pursuance of a resolution of either House of Parliament, make such provision as he considers necessary for the enforcement in England and Wales or Northern Ireland of any penalty, treated in pursuance of subsection (1) above as a fine, which is transferred as a fine to a court in England and Wales or, as the case may be, Northern Ireland.

[Criminal Procedure (Scotland) Act 1995, s 303.]

---

1. Part XIII contains ss 287–303.

PART XIV[1]

GENERAL

3–1448   309. Short title, commencement and extent.   (1) This Act may be cited as the Criminal Procedure (Scotland) Act 1995.

(2) This Act shall come into force on 1 April 1996.

(3) Subject to subsections (4) and (5) below, this Act extends to Scotland only.

(4) The following provisions of this Act and this section extend to England and Wales—

section 44;
section 47;
section 209(3) and (7);
section 234(4) to (11);
section 244;
section 252 for the purposes of the construction mentioned in subsection (1) of that subsection;
section 303(4).

(5) The following provisions of this Act and this section extend to Northern Ireland—

section 44;
section 47;
section 244;
section 252 for the purposes of the construction mentioned in subsection (1) of that subsection;
section 303(4).

(6) Section 297(3) and (4) of this Act and this section also extend to the Isle of Man.

[Criminal Procedure (Scotland) Act 1995, s 309.]

---

1. Part XIV contains ss 304–309.

Crime (Sentences) Act 1997

(1997 c 43)

PART III[1]

MISCELLANEOUS AND SUPPLEMENTAL

Community sentences

3–1461   **35. Fine defaulters: general.**   (1) Subsection (2) below applies in any case where a magistrates' court—

(a)   has power under Part III of the Magistrates' Courts Act 1980 ("the 1980 Act") to issue a warrant of commitment for default in paying a sum adjudged to be paid by a conviction of a magistrates' court (other than a sum ordered to be paid under section 71 of the Criminal Justice Act 1988 or section 2 of the Drug Trafficking Act 1994 or section 6 of the Proceeds of Crime Act 2002); or

(b)   would, but for section 89 of the Powers of Criminal Courts (Sentencing) Act 2000 (restrictions on custodial sentences for persons under 21*), have power to issue such a warrant for such default.

(2)   The magistrates' court may—

(a)   subject to subsections (4) to (6) (10) and (11) below, make a community service order; or

(b)   subject to subsections (7) to (11) below, make a curfew order,

in respect of the person in default instead of issuing a warrant of commitment or, as the case may be, proceeding under section 81 of the 1980 Act (enforcement of fines imposed on young offenders).

(3)   Where a magistrates' court has power to make an order under subsection (2)(a) or (b) above, it may, if it thinks it expedient to do so, postpone the making of the order until such time and on such conditions, if any, as it thinks just.

(4)   In this section "community service order" has the same meaning as in the 1973 Act and—

(a)   section 14(2) of that Act; and

(b)   so far as applicable, the other provisions of that Act relating to community service orders and the provisions of Part I of the 1991 Act so relating,

shall have effect in relation to an order under subsection (2)(a) above as they have effect in relation to an order in respect of an offender, but subject to the exceptions in subsection (5) below.

(5)   The following are the exceptions, namely—

(a)   the reference in section 14(1A)(a) of the 1973 Act to 40 hours shall be construed as a reference to 20 hours;

(b)   section 14(3) of that Act shall not apply;

(c)   *repealed*

(d)   the power conferred by paragraph 3(1)(d) of Schedule 2 to the 1991 Act shall be construed as a power to revoke the order or deal with the person in respect of whom the order was made for his default in paying the sum in question or do both of those things;

(e)   sub-paragraphs (2)(a) and (2A) of paragraph 3 of that Schedule shall not apply.

(f)   the reference in paragraph 7(1)(b) of that Schedule to the offence in respect of which the order was made shall be construed as a reference to the default in respect of which the order was made;

(g)   the power conferred by paragraph 7(2)(b) of that Schedule to deal with an offender for the offence in respect of which the order was made shall be construed as a power to deal with the person in respect of whom the order was made for his default in paying the sum in question; and

(h)   paragraph 8(2)(b) of that Schedule shall not apply.

(6)   In the case of an amount in default which is described in the first column of the following Table, the period of community service specified in an order under subsection (2)(a) above shall not exceed the number of hours set out opposite that amount in the second column of that Table.

TABLE

Amount	*Number of hours*
An amount not exceeding £200	40 hours
An amount exceeding £200 but not exceeding £500	60 hours
An amount exceeding £500	100 hours

(7)   In this section "curfew order" has the same meaning as in Part I of the 1991 Act and—

(a)   section 12(6) of that Act; and

(b)   so far as applicable, the other provisions of that Part relating to curfew orders,

shall have effect in relation to an order under subsection (2)(b) above as they have effect in relation to an order in respect of an offender, but subject to the exceptions in subsection (8) below.

(8)   The following are the exceptions, namely—

(a) the power conferred by paragraph 3(1)(*d*) of Schedule 2 to the 1991 Act shall be construed as a power to revoke the order or deal with the person in respect of whom the order was made for his default in paying the sum in question or do both of those things;

(b) sub-paragraphs (2)(*a*) and (2A) of paragraph 3 of that Schedule shall not apply;

(c) the reference in paragraph 7(1)(*b*) of that Schedule to the offence in respect of which the order was made shall be construed as a reference to the default in respect of which the order was made;

(d) the power conferred by paragraph 7(2)(*b*) of that Schedule to deal with an offender for the offence in respect of which the order was made shall be construed as a power to deal with the person in respect of whom the order was made for his default in paying the sum in question; and

(e) paragraph 8(2)(*b*) of that Schedule shall not apply.

(9) In the case of an amount in default which is described in the first column of the following Table, the number of days to which an order under subsection (2)(*b*) above relates shall not exceed the number of days set out opposite that amount in the second column of that Table.

TABLE

Amount	Number of days
An amount not exceeding £200	20 days
An amount exceeding £200 but not exceeding £500	30 days
An amount exceeding £500 but not exceeding £1,000	60 days
An amount exceeding £1,000 but not exceeding £2,500	90 days
An amount exceeding £2,500	180 days

(10) A magistrates' court shall not make an order under subsection (2)(*a*) or (*b*) above in respect of a person who is under 16.

(11) A magistrates' court shall not make an order under subsection (2)(*a*) or (*b*) above unless the court has been notified by the Secretary of State that arrangements for implementing such orders are available in the relevant area and the notice has not been withdrawn.

(12) In subsection (11) above "the relevant area" means—

(a) in relation to an order under subsection (2)(*a*) above, the area proposed to be specified in the order;

(b) in relation to an order under subsection (2)(*b*) above, the area in which the place proposed to be specified in the order is situated.

(12A) Sections 35 and 36 of the Powers of Criminal Courts (Sentencing) Act 2000 (restrictions and procedural requirements for community sentences) do not apply in relation to an order under subsection (2)(*a*) or (*b*) above.

(13) Where an order has been made under subsection (2)(*a*) or (*b*) above for default in paying any sum—

(a) on payment of the whole sum to any person authorised to receive it, the order shall cease to have effect;

(b) on payment of a part of that sum to any such person, the total number of hours or days to which the order relates shall be reduced proportionately;

and the total number is so reduced if it is reduced by such number of complete hours or days as bears to the total number the proportion most nearly approximating to, without exceeding, the proportion which the part paid bears to the whole sum.

(14) The Secretary of State may by order direct that subsection (5)(*a*), (6) or (9) above shall be amended by substituting for any number of hours or days there specified such number of hours or days as may be specified in the order.

(15) The power to make an order under this section shall be exercisable by statutory instrument; but no such order shall be made unless a draft of the order has been laid before and approved by a resolution of each House of Parliament.**

[Crime (Sentences) Act 1997, s 35 as amended by the Crime and Disorder Act 1998, Schs 7,8 and 10, the Access to Justice Act 1999, Sch 9, the Powers of Criminal Courts (Sentencing) Act 2000, Sch 9 and the Proceeds of Crime Act 2002, Sch 11.]

---

*Amended by the Criminal Justice and Court Services Act 2000, Sch 7 from a date to be appointed.
**Repealed by the Criminal Justice Act 2003, Sch 37 from a date to be appointed.
1. Part III contains ss 35–57.

3–1462   37. Persistent petty offenders. *Repealed.*

Driving disqualifications

3–1463   39. Offenders. *Repealed.*

3–1464   40. Fine defaulters.   (1) This section applies in any case where a magistrates' court—

(a) has power under Part III of the 1980 Act to issue a warrant of commitment for default in paying a sum adjudged to be paid by a conviction of a magistrates' court (other than a sum ordered to be paid under section 71 of the Criminal Justice Act 1988 or section 2 of the Drug Trafficking Act 1994 or section 6 of the Proceeds of Crime Act 2002); or

(b) would, but for section 89 of the Powers of Criminal Courts (Sentencing) Act 2000 (restrictions on custodial sentences for persons under 21*), have power to issue such a warrant for such default.

(2) Subject to subsection (3) below, the magistrates' court may, instead of issuing a warrant of commitment or, as the case may be, proceeding under section 81 of the 1980 Act (enforcement of fines imposed on young offenders), order the person in default to be disqualified, for such period not exceeding twelve months as it thinks fit, for holding or obtaining a driving licence.

(3) A magistrates' court shall not make an order under subsection (2) above unless the court has been notified by the Secretary of State that the power to make such orders is exercisable by the court and the notice has not been withdrawn.

(4) Where an order has been made under subsection (2) above for default in paying any sum—

(a) on payment of the whole sum to any person authorised to receive it, the order shall cease to have effect;

(b) on payment of a part of that sum to any such person, the number of weeks or months to which the order relates shall be reduced proportionately;

and the total number is so reduced if it is reduced by such number of complete weeks or months as bears to the total number the proportion most nearly approximating to, without exceeding, the proportion which the part paid bears to the whole sum.

(5) The Secretary of State may by order made by statutory instrument vary the period specified in subsection (2) above; but no such order shall be made unless a draft of the order has been laid before and approved by a resolution of each House of Parliament.

(6) A court which makes an order under this section disqualifying a person for holding or obtaining a driving licence shall require him to produce any such licence held by him together with its counterpart.

(7) In this section—

"driving licence" means a licence to drive a motor vehicle granted under Part III of the Road Traffic Act 1988;

"counterpart", in relation to a driving licence, has the meaning given in relation to such a licence by section 108(1) of that Act.**

[Crime (Sentences) Act 1997, s 40 as amended by the Powers of Criminal Courts (Sentencing) Act 2000, Sch 9 and the Proceeds of Crime Act 2002, Sch 11.]

---

*Amended by the Criminal Justice and Court Services Act 2000, Sch 7 from a date to be appointed.
**Repealed by the Criminal Justice Act 2003, Sch 37 from a date to be appointed.

Transfer and repatriation of prisoners

3-1465   41. Transfer of prisoners within the British Islands.   Schedule 1 to this Act (which makes provision with respect to the transfer of prisoners within the British Islands) shall have effect.
[Crime (Sentences) Act 1997, s 41.]

3-1466   42. Repatriation of prisoners to the British Islands.   Schedule 2[1] to this Act (which makes provision, including retrospective provision, with respect to prisoners repatriated to the British Islands) shall have effect.
[Crime (Sentences) Act 1997, s 42.]

---

1. Schedule 2 is not reproduced in this work.

Mentally disordered offenders

3-1467   46. Power to make hospital and limitation directions.   *Amendment of the Mental Health Act 1983.*

3-1468   47. Power to specify hospital units.   (1) Subject to subsection (2) below, any power to specify a hospital which is conferred by—

(a) section 37 of the 1983 Act (hospital orders);

(b) section 45A of that Act (hospital and limitation directions);

(c) section 47 of that Act (transfer directions);

(d) *repealed*

includes power to specify a hospital unit; and where such a unit is specified in relation to any person in the exercise of such a power, any reference in any enactment (including one contained in this Act) to him being, or being liable to be, detained in a hospital shall be construed accordingly.

(2) In subsection (1) above—

(a) paragraph (a) shall not apply unless the court also makes an order under section 41 of the 1983 Act (restriction orders);

(*b*) paragraph (*c*) shall not apply unless the Secretary of State also gives a direction under section 49 of that Act (restriction directions);

(*c*) *repealed.*

(3) In this section—

"hospital", in relation to any exercise of a power, has the same meaning as in the enactment which confers the power;

"hospital unit" means any part of a hospital which is treated as a separate unit.

(4) A reference in this section to section 37 or 41 of the 1983 Act includes a reference to that section as it applies by virtue of—

(*a*) section 5 of the Criminal Procedure (Insanity) Act 1964'
(*b*) section 6 or 14 of the Criminal Appeal Act 1968,
(*c*) section 116A of the Army Act 1955 or the Air Force Act 1955 or section 63A of the Naval Discipline Act 1957, or
(*d*) section 16 or 23 of the Courts-Martial (Appeals) Act 1968.

[Crime (Sentences) Act 1997, s 47 as amended by the Domestic Violence, Crime and Victims Act 2004, Sch 12.]

Miscellaneous

3–1469   50. Disclosure of pre-sentence reports. *Repealed.*

3–1470   51. Committals for sentence. *Repealed.*

Supplemental

3–1471   53. *Financial provisions.*

3–1472   54. General interpretation. (1) In this Act—

"the 1933 Act" means the Children and Young Persons Act 1933;
"the 1969 Act" means the Children and Young Persons Act 1969;
"the 1973 Act" means the Powers of Criminal Courts Act 1973;
"the 1980 Act" means the Magistrates' Courts Act 1980;
"the 1982 Act" means the Criminal Justice Act 1982;
"the 1983 Act" means the Mental Health Act 1983;
"the 1991 Act" means the Criminal Justice Act 1991;
"local probation board" means a local probation board established under section 4 of the Criminal Justice and Court Services Act 2000.

(2) *Repealed.*

(3) Where an offence is found to have been committed over a period of two or more days, or at some time during a period of two or more days, it shall be taken for the purposes of this Act to have been committed on the last of those days.

(4) For the purposes of any provision of this Act which requires the determination of the age of a person by the court, his age shall be deemed to be that which it appears to the court to be after considering any available evidence.

[Crime (Sentences) Act 1997, s 54 as amended by Crime and Disorder Act 1998, Schs 7, 8 and 10 and the Criminal Justice and Court Services Act 2000, Sch 7.]

3–1473   55. Minor and consequential amendments. (1) The enactments mentioned in Schedule 4 to this Act shall have effect subject to the amendments there specified, being minor amendments and amendments consequential on the provisions of this Act.

(2) *Repealed.*

[Crime (Sentences) Act 1997, s 55 as amended by Crime and Disorder Act 1998, Sch 7, the Powers of Criminal Courts (Sentencing) Act 2000, Sch 12 and the Armed Services Act 2001, Sch 7.]

3–1474   56. Transitional provisions, savings and repeals. (1) The transitional provisions and savings contained in Schedule 5 to this Act shall have effect; but nothing in this subsection shall be taken as prejudicing the operation of sections 16 and 17 of the Interpretation Act 1978 (which relate to the effect of repeals).

(2) The enactments specified in Schedule 6 to this Act are hereby repealed to the extent specified in the third column of that Schedule.

[Crime (Sentences) Act 1997, s 56.]

3–1475   57. Short title, commencement and extent. (1) This Act may be cited as the Crime (Sentences) Act 1997.

(2) This Act shall come into force on such day as the Secretary of State may by order¹ made by statutory instrument appoint; and different days may be appointed for different purposes.

(3) Without prejudice to the provisions of Schedule 5 to this Act, an order under subsection (2) above may make such transitional provisions and savings as appear to the Secretary of State necessary or expedient in connection with any provision brought into force by the order.

(4) Subject to subsections (5) to (8) below, this Act extends to England and Wales only.

(5) The following provisions of this Act extend to Scotland, Northern Ireland and the Channel Islands, namely—

   (a) section 41 and Schedule 1; and
   (b) section 56(2) and Schedule 6 so far as relating to the repeal of Part III of the Criminal Justice Act 1961[2].

(6) The following provisions of this Act extend to Scotland, namely—

   (a) section 45;
   (b) paragraphs 1 and 5 to 8 of Schedule 2 and section 42 so far as relating to those paragraphs;
   (c) paragraphs 1 and 6 to 10 of Schedule 3 and section 48 so far as relating to those paragraphs;
   (d) paragraph 16 of Schedule 4 to this Act and section 55 so far as relating to that paragraph; and
   (e) paragraphs 9, 11 and 12 of Schedule 5 and section 56(1) so far as relating to those paragraphs.

(7) The following provisions of this Act extend to Northern Ireland, namely—

   (a) paragraphs 1, 9 and 10 of Schedule 2 and section 42 so far as relating to those paragraphs;
   (b) paragraphs 2, 3, 7 and 8 of Schedule 3 and section 48 so far as relating to those paragraphs; and
   (c) paragraphs 10 and 12 of Schedule 5 and section 56(1) so far as relating to those paragraphs.

(8) Nothing in subsection (4) above affects the extent of this Act in so far as it—

   (a) confers a power or imposes a duty on a court-martial or a Standing Civilian Court; or
   (b) amends any provision of the Army Act 1955, the Air Force Act 1955 or the Naval Discipline Act 1957,

or the extent of Chapter II of Part II so far as it relates to sentences passed by a court-martial.
[Crime (Sentences) Act 1997, s 57 as amended by the Criminal Justice and Court Services Act 2000, Sch 7.].]

1. At the date of going to press the following Commencement Orders had been made: Crime (Sentences) Act 1997 (Commencement) (No 1) Order 1997, SI 1997/1581; Crime (Sentences) Act 1997 (Commencement No 2 and Transitional Provisions) Order 1997, SI 1997/2200; Crime (Sentences) Act 1997 (Commencement No 3) Order 1999, SI 1999/3096).
2. Section 57(5)(b) shall have effect as if the reference to the Channel Islands included a reference to the Isle of Man (Crime and Disorder Act 1998, Sch 8, para 134).

SCHEDULES

Section 41

SCHEDULE 1
TRANSFER OF PRISONERS WITHIN THE BRITISH ISLANDS

(*As amended by the Crime and Disorder Act 1998, Schs 8 and 10, the Powers of Criminal Courts (Sentencing) Act 2000, Sch 9, the Criminal Justice, Court Services Act 2000, Sch 7 and the Justice (Northern Ireland) Act 2004, s 13, the Criminal Justice Act 2003, Sch 32 and the Management of Offenders etc (Scotland) Act 2005, s 21.*)

PART I
POWERS OF TRANSFER
Transfer of prisoners: general

3–1476 **1.** (1) The Secretary of State may, on the application of—

   (a) a person remanded in custody in any part of the United Kingdom in connection with an offence; or
   (b) a person serving a sentence of imprisonment in any part of the United Kingdom,

make an order for his transfer to another part of the United Kingdom or to any of the Channel Islands, there to be remanded in custody pending his trial for the offence or, as the case may be, to serve the whole or any part of the remainder of his sentence, and for his removal to an appropriate institution there.

(2) Where—

   (a) a person is remanded in custody in any of the Channel Islands in connection with an offence; or
   (b) a person has been sentenced to imprisonment in any of the Channel Islands,

the Secretary of State may, without application in that behalf, make an order for his transfer to any part of the United Kingdom, there to be remanded in custody pending his trial for the offence or, as the case may be, to serve the whole or any part of his sentence or the remainder of his sentence, and for his removal to an appropriate institution there.

(2A) If it appears to the Secretary of State that—

   (a) a person remanded in custody in Northern Ireland in connection with an offence, or
   (b) a person serving a sentence of imprisonment in Northern Ireland;

should be transferred to another part of the United Kingdom in the interests of maintaining security or good order in any prison in Northern Ireland, the Secretary of State may make an order for his transfer to that other part, there to be remanded in custody pending his trial or, as the case may be, to serve the whole or any part of the remainder of his sentence, and for his removal to an appropriate institution there.

(3) In this paragraph "appropriate institution"—

   (a) in relation to a person remanded in custody, means any prison or other institution;
   (b) in relation to a person sentenced to imprisonment, means, subject to sub-paragraph (4) below, any institution which would be appropriate for the detention of an offender of the same age serving an equivalent sentence passed by a court in the country or island to which he is transferred.

(4) Sub-paragraph (3)(b) above shall have effect in relation to a person serving a sentence of a length which could not have been passed on an offender of his age by a court in the place to which he has been transferred as if it defined "appropriate institution" as meaning such place as the Secretary of State may direct.

Transfer of prisoners for trial

3–1477   **2.** (1) If it appears to the Secretary of State that—

(*a*)   a person remanded in custody in any part of the United Kingdom in connection with an offence; or

(*b*)   a person serving a sentence of imprisonment in any part of the United Kingdom,

should be transferred to another part of the United Kingdom or to any of the Channel Islands for the purpose of attending criminal proceedings against him there, the Secretary of State may make an order for his transfer to that other part or that island and for his removal to a prison or other institution there.

(2) If it appears to the Secretary of State that—

(*a*)   a person remanded in custody in any of the Channel Islands in connection with an offence; or

(*b*)   a person serving a sentence of imprisonment in any of the Channel Islands,

should be transferred to a part of the United Kingdom for the purpose of attending criminal proceedings against him there, the Secretary of State may make an order for his transfer to that part and for his removal to a prison or other institution there.

(3) Where a person has been transferred under sub-paragraph (1)(*a*) or (2)(*a*) above for the purpose of any proceedings, the Secretary of State may, if that person is not sentenced to imprisonment in those proceedings, make an order for his return to the country or island from which he was transferred under that sub-paragraph.

(4) Where a person has been transferred under sub-paragraph (1)(*b*) or (2)(*b*) above for the purpose of any proceedings, the Secretary of State may—

(*a*)   if that person is sentenced to imprisonment in those proceedings, make an order under paragraph 1(1)(*b*) or (2)(*b*) above (but without application in that behalf) transferring him back to the country or island from which he was transferred under that sub-paragraph;

(*b*)   if he is not so sentenced, make an order for his return to the said country or island, there to serve the remainder of the sentence referred to in that sub-paragraph.

Transfer of prisoners for other judicial purposes

3–1478   **3.** (1) If the Secretary of State is satisfied, in the case of—

(*a*)   a person remanded in custody in any part of the United Kingdom in connection with an offence;

(*b*)   a person serving a sentence of imprisonment in any part of the United Kingdom; or

(*c*)   a person not falling within paragraph (*a*) or (*b*) above who is detained in a prison in any part of the United Kingdom,

that the attendance of that person at any place in that or any other part of the United Kingdom or in any of the Channel Islands is desirable in the interests of justice or for the purposes of any public inquiry, the Secretary of State may direct that person to be taken to that place.

(2) If the Secretary of State is satisfied, in the case of—

(*a*)   a person remanded in custody in any of the Channel Islands in connection with an offence;

(*b*)   a person serving a sentence of imprisonment in any of the Islands; or

(*c*)   a person not falling within paragraph (*a*) or (*b*) above who is detained in a prison in any of the Channel Islands,

that the attendance of that person at any place in the United Kingdom is desirable in the interests of justice or for the purposes of any public inquiry, the Secretary of State may direct that person to be taken to that place.

(3) Where any person is directed under this paragraph to be taken to any place he shall, unless the Secretary of State otherwise directs, be kept in custody while being so taken, while at that place, and while being taken back to the prison or other institution or place in which he is required in accordance with law to be detained.

Transfer of supervision of released prisoners

3–1479   **4.** (1) The Secretary of State may, on the application of a person undergoing or about to undergo supervision in any part of the United Kingdom, make an order for the transfer of his supervision to another part of the United Kingdom or to any of the Channel Islands, that is to say, an order—

(*a*)   for his supervision or, as the case may be, the remainder of his supervision to be undergone in that country or island; and

(*b*)   for responsibility for his supervision to be transferred to an appropriate person there.

(2) The Secretary of State may, on the application of a person undergoing or about to undergo supervision in any of the Channel Islands, make an order for the transfer of his supervision to any part of the United Kingdom, that is to say, an order—

(*a*)   for his supervision or, as the case may be, the remainder of his supervision to be undergone in that country; and

(*b*)   for responsibility for his supervision to be transferred to an appropriate person there.

Conditions of transfers

3–1480   **5.** (1) A transfer under this Part(other than a transfer under paragraph 1(2A)) shall have effect subject to such conditions (if any) as the Secretary of State may think fit to impose.

(2) Subject to sub-paragraph (3) below, a condition imposed under this paragraph may be varied or removed at any time.

(3) Such a condition as is mentioned in paragraph (6)(1)(*a*) below shall not be varied or removed except with the consent of the person to whom the transfer relates.

Conditions of transfer under paragraph 1(2A)

3–1480A   **5A.** (1) A transfer under paragraph 1(2A) shall have effect subject to—

(a)   such a condition as is mentioned in paragraph 6(1)(a); and
(b)   such other conditions (if any) as the Secretary of State may think fit to impose.

(2)   Such a condition as is mentioned in paragraph 6(1)(a) shall not be varied or removed.
(3)   A condition imposed under sub-paragraph (1)(b) may be varied or removed at any time.

PART II
EFFECT OF TRANSFERS

Preliminary

3–1481   **6.**—(1) For the purposes of this Part of this Schedule, a transfer under Part I of this Schedule—

(a)   is a restricted transfer if it is subject to a condition that the person to whom it relates is to be treated for the relevant purposes as if he were still subject to the provisions applicable for those purposes under the law of the place from which the transfer is made; and
(b)   is an unrestricted transfer if it is not so subject.

(2)   In this Part of this Schedule "the relevant purposes" means—

(a)   in relation to the transfer of a person under paragraph 1(1)(a) or (2)(a) or (2A)(a), 2(1)(a) or (2)(a) or 3(1)(a) or (2)(a) above, the purposes of his remand in custody and, where applicable, the purposes of his detention under and release from any sentence of imprisonment that may be imposed;
(b)   in relation to the transfer of a person under paragraph 1(1)(b) or (2)(b) or (2A)(b), 2(1)(b) or (2)(b) or 3(1)(b) or (2)(b) above, the purposes of his detention under and release from his sentence and, where applicable, the purposes of his supervision and possible recall following his release; and
(c)   in relation to the transfer of a person's supervision under paragraph 4(1) or (2) above, the purposes of his supervision and possible recall.

(3)   In this paragraph "recall" means—

(a)   in relation to a person who is supervised in pursuance of an order made for the purpose, being sentenced to imprisonment, or being recalled to prison, for a breach of any condition of the order;
(aa)   in relation to a person who is supervised in pursuance of a detention and training order, being ordered to be detained for any failure to comply with requirements under section 103(6)(b) of the Powers of Criminal Courts (Sentencing) Act 2000;
(b)   in relation to a person who is supervised in pursuance of a condition contained in a licence, being recalled or returned to prison, whether for a breach of any condition of the licence or otherwise.

(4)   In this Part of this Schedule—

"the 2003 Act" means the Criminal Justice Act 2003;
"custody plus order" has the meaning given by section 181(4) of that Act;
"intermittent custody order" has the meaning given by section 183(2) of that Act.

Restricted transfers: general

3–1482   **7.**—(1) Where—

(a)   a person's transfer under paragraph 1, 2 or 3 above; or
(b)   a transfer under paragraph 4 above of a person's supervision,

is a restricted transfer, that person or, as the case may be, his supervision may by order be transferred back to the country or island from which he or it was transferred.
(2)   Where a person's transfer under paragraph 1 or 2 above is a restricted transfer, that person shall while in the country or territory to which he is transferred be kept in custody except in so far as the Secretary of State may in any case or class of case otherwise direct.

Restricted transfers from England and Wales to Scotland

3–1483   **8.**—(1) Where a person's transfer under paragraph 1(1)(a), 2(1)(a) or 3(1)(a) above from England and Wales to Scotland is a restricted transfer—

(a)   regulations made under section 22 of the Prosecution of Offences Act 1985 (time limits in relation to preliminary stages of proceedings) shall apply to him in place of the corresponding provisions of the law of Scotland; but
(b)   subject to that and to any conditions to which the transfer is subject, he shall be treated for the relevant purposes as if he had been remanded for an offence committed in Scotland.

(2)   Where a person's transfer under paragraph 1(1)(b), 2(1)(b) or 3(1)(b) above from England and Wales to Scotland is a restricted transfer—

(a)   sections 241, 244, 247 to 252 and 254 to 264A of the 2003 Act (fixed-term prisoners) or, as the case may require, sections 102 to 104 of the Powers of Criminal Courts (Sentencing) Act 2000 (detention and training orders) or sections 28 to 34 of this Act (life sentences) shall apply to him in place of the corresponding provisions of the law of Scotland;
(aa)   sections 62 and 64 of the Criminal Justice and Court Services Act 2000 (which relate to licence conditions) shall apply to him in place of the corresponding provisions of the law of Scotland;
(ab)   where a custody plus order or intermittent custody order has effect in relation to him, the provisions of Chapters 3 and 4 of Part 12 of the 2003 Act relating to such orders shall also apply to him (subject to Schedule 11 to that Act); and (b) subject to that, sub-paragraph (3) below and to any conditions to which the transfer is subject, he shall be treated for the relevant purposes as if his sentence had been an equivalent sentence passed by a court in Scotland.

(3)   A person who has been sentenced to a sentence of a length which could not have been passed on an offender of his age in the place to which he has been transferred shall be treated for the purposes mentioned in sub-paragraph (2) above as the Secretary of State may direct.
(4)   Where a transfer under paragraph 4(1) above of a person's supervision from England and Wales to Scotland is a restricted transfer—

(a) sections 241, 249 264A of the 2003 Act (fixed-term prisoners) or, as the case may require, sections 103 and 104 of the Powers of Criminal Courts (Sentencing) Act 2000 (detention and training orders) or sections 31 to 34 of this Act (life sentences) shall apply to him in place of the corresponding provisions of the law of Scotland;

(aa) sections 62 and 64 of the Criminal Justice and Court Services Act 2000 (which relate to licence conditions) shall apply to him in place of the corresponding provisions of the law of Scotland;

(ab) where a custody plus order or intermittent custody order has effect in relation to him, the provisions of Chapters 3 and 4 of Part 12 of the 2003 Act relating to such orders shall also apply to him (subject to Schedule 11 to that Act); and

(b) subject to that and to any conditions to which the transfer is subject, he shall be treated for the relevant purposes as if his period of supervision had been an equivalent period of supervision directed to be undergone in Scotland.

(5) Section 31(2A) of this Act (conditions as to supervision after release), as applied by sub-paragraph (2) or (4) above, shall have effect as if for paragraphs (a) to (c) there were substituted the words "a relevant officer of such local authority as may be specified in the licence".

(6) Any provision of sections 102 to 104 of the Powers of Criminal Courts (Sentencing) Act 2000 which is applied by sub-paragraph (2) or (4) above shall have effect (as so applied) as if—

(a) any reference to secure accommodation were a reference to secure accommodation within the meaning of Part 2 of the Children (Scotland) Act 1995 or a young offenders institution provided under section 19(1)(b) of the Prisons (Scotland) Act 1989,

(b) except in section 103(2), any reference to the Secretary of State were a reference to the Scottish Ministers,

(c) any reference to an officer of a local probation board were a reference to a relevant officer as defined by section 27(1) of the Prisoners and Criminal Proceedings (Scotland) Act 1993,

(d) any reference to a youth court were a reference to a sheriff court,

(e) in section 103, any reference to a petty sessions area were a reference to a local government area within the meaning of the Local Government etc (Scotland) Act 1994,

(f) in section 103(3), for paragraphs (b) and (c) there were substituted a reference to an officer of a local authority constituted under that Act for the local government area in which the offender resides for the time being,

(g) section 103(5) were omitted,

(h) in section 104, for subsection (1) there were substituted—

"(1) Where a detention and training order is in force in respect of an offender and it appears on information to a sheriff court having jurisdiction in the locality in which the offender resides that the offender has failed to comply with requirements under section 103(6)(b), the court may—

(a) issue a citation requiring the offender to appear before it at the time specified in the citation, or

(b) issue a warrant for the offender's arrest.",

(i) section 104(2) were omitted, and

(j) in section 104(6), the reference to the Crown Court were a reference to the High Court of Justiciary.

TABLE

Expression	Substituted expression
Crown Court	High Court of Justiciary
Information on oath	Evidence on oath
Magistrates' court	Sheriff
Officer of a local probation board	Relevant officer within the meaning given by section 27(1) of the Prisoners and Criminal Proceedings (Scotland) Act 1993

Restricted transfers from England and Wales to Northern Ireland

3–1484 **9.** (1) Where a person's transfer under paragraph 1(1)(a), 2(1)(a) or 3(1)(a) above from England and Wales to Northern Ireland is a restricted transfer—

(a) Repealed.

(b) subject to any conditions to which the transfer is subject, he shall be treated for the relevant purposes as if he had been remanded for an offence committed in Northern Ireland.

(2) Where a person's transfer under paragraph 1(1)(b), 2(1)(b) or 3(1)(b) above from England and Wales to Northern Ireland is a restricted transfer—

(a) sections 241, 244, 247 to 252 and 254 to 264A of the 2003 Act (fixed-term prisoners) or, as the case may require, sections 102 to 104 of the Powers of Criminal Courts (Sentencing) Act 2000 (detention and training orders) or sections 28 to 34 of this Act (life sentences) shall apply to him in place of the corresponding provisions of the law of Northern Ireland;

(aa) sections 62 and 64 of the Criminal Justice and Court Services Act 2000 (which relate to licence conditions) shall apply to him in place of the corresponding provisions of the law of Northern Ireland;

(ab) where a custody plus order or intermittent custody order has effect in relation to him, the provisions of Chapters 3 and 4 of Part 12 of the 2003 Act relating to such orders shall apply to him (subject to Schedule 11 to that Act); and

(b) subject to that, to sub-paragraph (3) below and to any conditions to which the transfer is subject, he shall be treated for the relevant purposes as if that sentence had been an equivalent sentence passed by a court in Northern Ireland.

(3) A person who has been sentenced to a sentence of a length which could not have been passed on an offender of his age in the place to which he has been transferred shall be treated for the purposes mentioned in sub-paragraph (2) above as the Secretary of State may direct.

(4) Where a transfer under paragraph 4(1) above of a person's supervision from England and Wales to Northern Ireland is a restricted transfer—

(a) sections 241, 249 to 252 and 254 to 264 of the 2003 Act (fixed-term prisoners) or, as the case may require, sections 103 and 104 of the Powers of Criminal Courts (Sentencing) Act 2000 (detention and training orders) or sections 31 to 34 of this Act (life sentences) shall apply to him in place of the corresponding provisions of the law of Northern Ireland;

   (*aa*) sections 62 and 64 of the Criminal Justice and Court Services Act 2000 (which relate to licence conditions) shall apply to him in place of the corresponding provisions of the law of Northern Ireland;

   (*ab*) where a custody plus order or intermittent custody order has effect in relation to him, the provisions of Chapters 3 and 4 of Part 12 of the 2003 Act relating to such orders shall apply to him (subject to Schedule 11 to that Act); and

   (*b*) subject to that and to any conditions to which the transfer is subject, he shall be treated for the relevant purposes as if his period of supervision had been an equivalent period of supervision directed to be undergone in Northern Ireland.

(5) Section 31(2A) of this Act (conditions as to supervision after release), as applied by sub-paragraph (2) or (4) above, shall have effect as if for paragraphs (a) to (c) there were substituted the words "a probation appointed for or assigned to the petty sessions district within which the prisoner for the time being resides".

(8) Section 65(7)(*b*) of the 1991 Act, as applied by sub-paragraph (1), (2) or (4) above, shall have effect as if the reference to a young offender institution were a reference to a young offenders centre.

TABLE

Expression	Substituted expression
Community home	Training School
Information on oath	Complaint on oath
Prison rules	Rules made under section 13 of the Prison Act (Northern Ireland) 1953
Section 8 of the Police and Criminal Evidence Act 1984	Article 10 of the Police and Criminal Evidence (Northern Ireland) Order 1989
Social worker of a local authority social services department	Officer of a Board or an authorised Health and Social Services (HSS) Trust

Restricted transfers from Scotland to England and Wales

3–1485 **10.** (1) Where a person's transfer under paragraph 1(1)(*a*), 2(1)(*a*) or 3(1)(*a*) above from Scotland to England and Wales is a restricted transfer—

   (*a*) sections 65 and 147 of the Criminal Procedure (Scotland) Act 1995 (time limits for solemn and summary prosecutions where prisoner remanded in custody) shall apply to him in the place of the corresponding provisions of the law of England and Wales; but

   (*b*) subject to that and to any conditions to which the transfer is subject, he shall be treated for the relevant purposes as if he had been remanded for an offence committed in England and Wales.

(2) Where a person's transfer under paragraph 1(1)(*b*), 2(1)(*b*) or 3(1)(*b*) from Scotland to England and Wales is a restricted transfer—

   (*a*) sections 1, 1A, 3, 3AA, 3A, 5, 6(1)(*a*), 7, 9, 11 to 13, 15 to 21, 26A and 27 of, and Schedules 2 and 6 to, the Prisoners and Criminal Proceedings (Scotland) Act 1993 ("the 1993 Act") or, as the case may require, sections 1(4), 2, 3, 6(1)(*b*)(i) and (iii), 11 to 13 and 17 of the 1993 Act shall apply to him in place of the corresponding provisions of the law of England and Wales; but

   (*b*) subject to that, to sub-paragraph (3) below and to any conditions to which the transfer is subject, he shall be treated for the relevant purposes as if his sentence had been an equivalent sentence passed by a court in England and Wales.

(3) A person who has been sentenced to a sentence of a length which could not have been passed on an offender of his age in the place to which he is transferred shall be treated for the purposes mentioned in sub-paragraph (2) above as the Secretary of State may direct.

(4) *Repealed.*

(5) Where a transfer under paragraph 4(1) above of a person's supervision from Scotland to England and Wales is a restricted transfer—

   (*a*) sections 1AA, 1A, 2(4), 3A, 11 to 13, 15 to 21, 26A and 27 of, and Schedules 2 and 6 to, the 1993 Act or, as the case may require, sections 2(4), 11 to 13 and 17 of the 1993 Act shall apply to him in place of the corresponding provisions of the law of England and Wales; but

   (*b*) subject to that and to any conditions to which the transfer is subject, he shall be treated for the relevant purposes as if his period of supervision had been an equivalent period of supervision directed to be undergone in England and Wales.

(6) Any reference in—

   (*a*) sub-paragraphs (2) and (5) above to sections 15, 18 and 19 of the 1993 Act is a reference to those sections so far as relating to supervised release orders;

   (*b*) in the said sub-paragraph (2) the reference to section 6 (1)(*b*)(i) of the 1993 Act is a reference to that provision so far as it relates to a person sentenced under section 205(3) of the Criminal Procedure (Scotland) Act 1995.

(7) Any provision of Part I of the 1993 Act which is applied by sub-paragraph (2) or (5) above shall have effect (as so applied) as if any reference to a chief social work officer were a reference to a chief social worker of a local authority social services department.

TABLE

Expression	Substituted expression
Chief social work officer	Chief social worker of a local authority social services department
Young offenders institution	Young offender institution

Restricted transfers from Northern Ireland to England and Wales

3–1487   **12.** (1) Where a person's transfer under paragraph 1(1)(*a*) or (2A)(*a*), 2(1)(*a*) or 3(1)(*a*) above from Northern Ireland to England and Wales is a restricted transfer, subject to any conditions to which the transfer is subject, he shall be treated for the relevant purposes as if he had been remanded for an offence committed in England and Wales.

(2) Where a person's transfer under paragraph 1(1)(*b*) or (2A)(*b*), 2(1)(*b*) or 3(1)(*b*) above from Northern Ireland to England and Wales is a restricted transfer—

(*a*) sections 13(7), 23 and 24 of the Prison Act (Northern Ireland) 1953, Articles 3 to 6 of the Treatment of Offenders (Northern Ireland) Order 1976 and Articles 26 to 28 of the Criminal Justice (Northern Ireland) Order 1996 or, as the case may require, section 1 of the Northern Ireland (Remission of Sentences) Act 1995 shall apply to him in place of the corresponding provisions of the law of England and Wales; but**

(*b*) subject to that, to sub-paragraph (3) below and to any conditions to which the transfer is subject, he shall be treated for the relevant purposes as if that sentence had been an equivalent sentence passed by a court in England and Wales.

(3) A person who has been sentenced to a sentence of a length which could not have been passed on an offender of his age in the place to which he has been transferred shall be treated for the purposes mentioned in sub-paragraph (2) above as the Secretary of State may direct.

(4) Where a transfer under paragraph 4(1) of a person's supervision from Northern Ireland to England and Wales is a restricted transfer, subject to any conditions to which the transfer is subject, he shall be treated for the relevant purposes as if his period of supervision had been an equivalent period of supervision directed to be undergone in England and Wales.

(5) Any provision of the Prison Act (Northern Ireland) 1953, the Treatment of Offenders (Northern Ireland) Order 1976, the Criminal Justice (Northern Ireland) Order 1996 or the Northern Ireland (Remission of Sentences) Act 1995 which is applied by sub-paragraph (2) above shall have effect (as so applied) as if any reference to an expression specified in the first column of the following Table were a reference to the expression set out opposite it in the second column of that Table.

TABLE

Expression	Substituted expression
Complaint on oath	Information on oath
Court of summary jurisdiction	Magistrates' court

**Paragraph 12(2)(*a*) substituted by SI 2001/2565 from a date to be appointed.

3–1488   **13.** *Restricted transfers from Northern Ireland to Scotland.*

Restricted transfers between the United Kingdom and the Channel Islands

3–1489   **14.** (1) Her Majesty may by Order[1] in Council make, in relation to restricted transfers under Part I of this Schedule between any part of the United Kingdom and any of the Channel Islands, provision broadly corresponding to that made by any of paragraphs 8 to 13 above.

(2) An Order in Council under this paragraph may make such consequential, incidental, transitional and supplementary provision as Her Majesty considers appropriate.

(3) An order in Council under this paragraph shall be subject to annulment in pursuance of a resolution of either House of Parliament.

----

1. Paragraph 14 is applied to the Isle of Man, with the modification that in sub-para (1) for the words "any of the Channel Islands" there shall be substituted the words "the Isle of Man", by the Transfer of Prisoners (Isle of Man) Order 1997, SI 1997/1579. See also the Transfer of Prisoners (Restricted Transfers) (Channel Islands and Isle of Man) Order 1998, SI 1998/2798.

Unrestricted transfers: general

3–1490   **15.** (1) Where a person's transfer under paragraph 1(1)(*a*) or (2)(*a*), 2(1)*a*) or (2)(*a*) or 3(1)(*a*) or (2)(*a*) above to any part of the United Kingdom or to any of the Channel Islands is an unrestricted transfer, he shall be treated for the relevant purposes as if he had been remanded for an offence committed in the place to which he is transferred.

(2) Subject to sub-paragraph (3) below, where a person's transfer under paragraph 1(1)(*b*) or (2)(*b*), 2(1)(*b*) or (2)(*b*) or 3(1)(*b*) or (2)(*b*) above to any part of the United Kingdom or to any of the Channel Islands is an unrestricted transfer, he shall be treated for the relevant purposes as if his sentence had been an equivalent sentence passed by a court in the place to which he is transferred.

(3) A person who has been sentenced to a sentence of a length which could not have been passed on an offender of his age in the place to which he has been transferred shall be treated for the purposes mentioned in sub-paragraph (2) above as the Secretary of State may direct.

(4) Where a transfer under paragraph 4(1) or (2) above of a person's supervision to any part of the United Kingdom or to any of the Channel Islands is an unrestricted transfer—

(*a*) that person shall be treated for the relevant purposes as if his period of supervision had been an equivalent period of supervision directed to be undergone in the place to which he is transferred; and

(*b*) any functions of the Secretary of State under any provision of the law of that place which applies for those purposes shall be exercisable in relation to that person by any person appointed by the Secretary of State for the purpose.

(5) *Repealed.*

Transfers ceasing to be restricted

3–1491   **16.** (1) Where a transfer under Part I of this Schedule ceases to be a restricted transfer at any time by reason of the removal of such a condition as is mentioned in paragraph 6(1)(*a*) above, paragraph 15 above shall apply as if the transfer were an unrestricted transfer and had been effected at that time.

PART III

SUPPLEMENTAL

Prisoners unlawfully at large

3–1492 **17.** (1) The following enactments (relating to the arrest and return of prisoners and other persons unlawfully at large), namely—

    (*a*)   section 49(1) and (5) of the Prison Act 1952;

    (*b*)   section 40(1) of the Prisons (Scotland) Act 1989; and

    (*c*)   section 38(1) of the Prison Act (Northern Ireland) 1953,

shall extend throughout the United Kingdom and the Channel Islands.

    (2) Any reference in those enactments to a constable shall include a reference—

    (*a*)   to a person being a constable under the law of any part of the United Kingdom;

    (*b*)   to a police officer within the meaning of the Police Force (Jersey) Law 1974 or any corresponding law for the time being in force; and

    (*c*)   to an officer of police within the meaning of section 31(4) of the Theft (Bailiwick of Guernsey) Law 1983 or any corresponding law for the time being in force.

    (3) Those enactments shall also apply to persons who, being unlawfully at large under the law of any of the Channel Islands, are for the time being within the United Kingdom as they apply to persons unlawfully at large under the law of any part of the United Kingdom.

    (4) Any person arrested in the United Kingdom under those enactments as applied by sub-paragraph (3) above may be taken to the place in the Channel Islands in which he is required in accordance with the law in force there to be detained.

    (5) Where a person who, having been sentenced to imprisonment, is unlawfully at large during any period during which he is liable to be detained in a prison in any part of the United Kingdom is sentenced to imprisonment by a court in another part of the United Kingdom—

    (*a*)   the provisions of Part II of this Schedule relating to the treatment of persons transferred under sub-paragraph (1)(*b*) of paragraph 1 above shall apply to him, while he remains in that other part of the United Kingdom, as if he had been transferred there under that sub-paragraph immediately before he was so sentenced; and

    (*b*)   the Secretary of State may, if he thinks fit, make an order under that sub-paragraph (but without application in that behalf) transferring him back to the part of the United Kingdom from which he was unlawfully at large.

    (6) In the following provisions, namely—

    (*a*)   paragraph (*a*) of the proviso to section 49(2) of the Prison Act 1952 (which in effect enables a person who is unlawfully at large during the currency of his original sentence to count towards that sentence any period during which he is detained in pursuance of a sentence of any court);

    (*b*)   the proviso to section 40(2) of the Prisons (Scotland) Act 1989 (which contains corresponding provisions for Scotland); and

    (*c*)   section 38(3) of the Prisons Act (Northern Ireland) 1953 (which contains corresponding provisions for Northern Ireland),

references to a court shall include references to any court in the United Kingdom.

Subsequent sentence in case of transferred prisoners

3–1493 **18.** (1) The power of a court in any part of the United Kingdom to order that the term of any sentence of imprisonment passed by the court shall commence at or before the expiration of another term of imprisonment shall include power to make such an order where that other term was imposed by sentence of a court elsewhere in the United Kingdom or in any of the Channel Islands if the offender—

    (*a*)   is serving that other sentence in that part of the United Kingdom; or

    (*b*)   is for the time being present in that part of the United Kingdom,

by virtue of an order under this Schedule, or is unlawfully at large under the law of the country or island in which that other sentence was passed.

    (2) The provisions of this paragraph shall be without prejudice to the powers exercisable by any court apart from those provisions.

Application to the Isle of Man

3–1494 **19.** (1) Her Majesty may by Order[1] in Council direct that any of the foregoing provisions of this Schedule which extend to, or apply in relation to, the Channel Islands shall extend to, or apply in relation to, the Isle of Man with such modifications (if any) as Her Majesty considers appropriate.

    (2) An Order in Council under this paragraph may make such consequential, incidental, transitional and supplementary provision as Her Majesty considers appropriate.

    (3) An Order in Council under this paragraph shall be subject to annulment in pursuance of a resolution of either House of Parliament.

---

    1. See the Transfer of Prisoners (Isle of Man) (No 2) Order 1997, SI 1997/1775 amended by SI 1998/2797.

Interpretation

3–1495 **20.** (1) In this Schedule—

    "prison," unless the context otherwise requires, includes a young offender institution, a young offenders institution, a young offenders centre and a remand centre;

    "sentence of imprisonment" includes any sentence of detention and a sentence of custody for life under section 93 or 94 of the Powers of Criminal Courts (Sentencing) Act 2000, and cognate expressions shall be construed accordingly;

"supervision" means supervision in pursuance of an order made for the purpose or a detention or training order or, in the case of a person released from prison on licence, in pursuance of a condition contained in his licence.

(2) References in this Schedule to a person being remanded in custody are references to his being remanded in or committed to custody by an order of a court.

(3) In determining, in relation to any person serving a sentence of imprisonment, the time which is to be served in respect of an equivalent sentence treated as passed in another country or island, regard shall be had, not only to any time already served by him, but also to—

(a) any periods for which he has been remanded in custody, being either—

(i) periods by which his sentence falls to be reduced; or
(ii) periods which have been directed to count as time served as part of his sentence; and

(b) any early release or additional days awarded to him.

3–1495A

Section 42

SCHEDULE 2
REPATRIATION OF PRISONERS TO THE BRITISH ISLANDS

3–1496

Section 55

SCHEDULE 4
MINOR AND CONSEQUENTIAL AMENDMENTS

3–1497

Section 56(1)

SCHEDULE 5
TRANSITIONAL PROVISIONS AND SAVINGS

(As amended by Crime and Disorder Act 1998, Schs 8 and 10, the Powers of Criminal Courts (Sentencing) Act 2000, Sch 9 and the Criminal Justice and Court Services Act 2000, Sch 7.)

Sentences for offences committed before the commencement of Chapter I of Part II

3–1498 **1–4.** *Repealed.*

Duty to release certain life prisoners

3–1499 **5.** (1) *Repealed.*
(2) *Repealed.*
(3) Section 28(7) of this Act shall have effect as if—

(a) any reference of a prisoner's case made to the Parole Board under section 32(2) or 34(4) of the 1991 Act had been made under section 28(6) of this Act; and
(b) any such reference made under section 39(4) of that Act had been made under section 32(4) of this Act.

Life prisoners transferred to England and Wales

3–1500 **6.** *Repealed.*

Recall of life prisoners while on licence

3–1501 **7.** (1) Section 32(3) and (4) of this Act shall have effect as if any life prisoner recalled to prison under subsection (1) or (2) of section 39 of the 1991 Act had been recalled to prison under the corresponding subsection of section 32 of this Act.
(2) Section 32(4) of this Act shall have effect as if any representations made by a life prisoner under section 39(3) of the 1991 Act had been made under section 32(3) of this Act.

Transfers of prisoners: general

3–1502 **8.** *Repealed.*

Transfers of prisoners from England and Wales to Scotland

3–1503 **9.** (1) *Repealed.*
(2) In relation to any time before the commencement of Chapter II of Part II of this Act, paragraph 8 of Schedule 1 to this Act shall have effect if—

(a) references in sub-paragraph (2) to provisions of that Chapter were references to sections 34 to 37, 39, 43 and 46 of the 1991 Act and paragraphs 8 and 9 of Schedule 12 to that Act, so far as relating to life prisoners;
(b) references in sub-paragraph (4) to provisions of that Chapter were references to sections 37, 39, 43 and 46 of the 1991 Act and paragraphs 8 and 9 of Schedule 12 to that Act, so far as so relating; and
(c) the reference in sub-paragraph (5) to any provision of Part II of this Act were a reference to any provision of Part II of that Act.

Transfers of prisoners from England and Wales to Northern Ireland

3–1504 **10.** (1) *Repealed.*
(2) In relation to any time before the commencement of Chapter II of Part II of this Act, paragraph 9 of Schedule 1 to this Act shall have effect as if—

(a) references in sub-paragraph (2) to provisions of that Chapter were references to sections 34 to 37, 39, 43 and 46 of the 1991 Act and paragraphs 8 and 9 of Schedule 12 to that Act, so far as relating to life prisoners;
(b) references in sub-paragraph (4) to provisions of that Chapter were references to sections 37, 39, 43 and 46 of the 1991 Act and paragraphs 8 and 9 of Schedule 12 to that Act, so far as so relating; and
(c) the reference in sub-paragraph (5) to any provision of Part II of this Act were a reference to any provision of Part II of that Act.

Transfers of prisoners from Scotland to England and Wales

3–1505 11. (1) *Repealed.*

(2) In relation to any prisoner to whom the existing provisions apply, paragraph 10 of Schedule 1 to this Act shall have effect as if—

    (*a*)   references in sub-paragraph (2) to sections 1, 1A, 3, 3A, 5, 6(1)(*a*), 7, 9, 11 to 13, 15 to 21, 26A and 27 of, Schedules 2 and 6 to, the Prisoners and Criminal Proceedings (Scotland) Act 1993 ("the 1993 Act") were references to Schedule 6 to the 1993 Act and to the following existing provisions, namely, sections 18, 19(4), 22, 24, 26, 28 to 30, 32 and 43 of, and Schedule 1 to, the Prisons (Scotland) Act 1989 ("the 1989 Act") and any rules made under section 18 or 39 of that Act;

    (*b*)   references in sub-paragraph (5) to sections 1A, 2(4), 3A 11 to 13, 15 to 21, 26A and 27 of, and Schedules 2 and 6 to, the 1993 Act were references to the said Schedule 6 and to the following existing provisions, namely, sections 30, 32 and 43 of the 1989 Act; and

    (*c*)   the reference in sub-paragraph (7) to any provision of Part I of the 1993 Act were a reference to any provision of the said Schedule 6 or the 1989 Act.

(3) In sub-paragraph (2) above—

    (*a*)   the reference to section 19(4) of the 1989 Act is a reference to that provision so far as it applies section 24 of that Act in relation to persons detained in young offenders institutions; and

    (*b*)   any reference to the existing provisions is a reference to the existing provisions within the meaning of Schedule 6 to the 1993 Act.

3–1506 12. *Transfers of prisoners from Scotland to Northern Ireland.*

Interpretation

3–1507 13. In this Schedule—

"life prisoner" has the same meaning as in Chapter II of Part II of this Act;

"term of imprisonment" includes a sentence of detention in a young offender institution or under section 53 of the 1933 Act.

Crime and Disorder Act 1998[1]
(1998 c 37)

PART IV[2]
DEALING WITH OFFENDERS
CHAPTER I[3]
ENGLAND AND WALES

Sentencing: general

3–1545 80. Sentencing guidelines. (1) This section applies where the Court—

    (*a*)   is seised of an appeal against, or a reference under section 36 of the Criminal Justice Act 1988 with respect to, the sentence passed for an offence; or

    (*b*)   receives a proposal under section 81 below in respect of a particular category of offence;

and in this section "the relevant category" means any category within which the offence falls or, as the case may be, the category to which the proposal relates.

(2) The Court shall consider—

    (*a*)   whether to frame guidelines as to the sentencing of offenders for offences of the relevant category; or

    (*b*)   where such guidelines already exist, whether it would be appropriate to review them.

(3) Where the Court decides to frame or revise such guidelines, the Court shall have regard to—

    (*a*)   the need to promote consistency in sentencing;

    (*b*)   the sentences imposed by courts in England and Wales for offences of the relevant category;

    (*c*)   the cost of different sentences and their relative effectiveness in preventing re-offending;

    (*d*)   the need to promote public confidence in the criminal justice system; and

    (*e*)   the views communicated to the Court, in accordance with section 81(4)(*b*) below, by the Sentencing Advisory Panel.

(4) Guidelines framed or revised under this section shall include criteria for determining the seriousness of offences, including (where appropriate) criteria for determining the weight to be given to any previous convictions of offenders or any failures of theirs to respond to previous sentences.

(5) In a case falling within subsection (1)(*a*) above, guidelines framed or revised under this section shall, if practicable, be included in the Court's judgment in the appeal.

(6) Subject to subsection (5) above, guidelines framed or revised under this section shall be included in a judgment of the Court at the next appropriate opportunity (having regard to the relevant category of offence).

(7) For the purposes of this section, the Court is seised of an appeal against a sentence if—

    (*a*)   the Court or a single judge has granted leave to appeal against the sentence under section 9 or 10 of the Criminal Appeal Act 1968; or

    (*b*)   in a case where the judge who passed the sentence granted a certificate of fitness for appeal under section 9 or 10 of that Act, notice of appeal has been given,

and (in either case) the appeal has not been abandoned or disposed of.

(8)　For the purposes of this section, the Court is seised of a reference under section 36 of the Criminal Justice Act 1988 if it has given leave under subsection (1) of that section and the reference has not been disposed of.

(9)　In this section and section 81 below—

"the Court" means the criminal division of the Court of Appeal;

"offence" means an indictable offence.

[Crime and Disorder Act 1998, s 80.]

1.　The Crime and Disorder Act 1998 is printed partly in Part III and partly in Parts IV and V of this work. For commencement provisions see s 121 of the Act in PART I: MAGISTRATES' COURTS, PROCEDURE, ante.

2.　Part IV contains ss 58–96.

3.　Chapter 1 contains ss 58–85.

3–1546　81. The Sentencing Advisory Panel.　(1)　The Lord Chancellor, after consultation with the Secretary of State and the Lord Chief Justice, shall constitute a sentencing panel to be known as the Sentencing Advisory Panel ("the Panel") and appoint one of the members of the Panel to be its chairman.

(2)　Where, in a case falling within subsection (1)(a) of section 80 above, the Court decides to frame or revise guidelines under that section for a particular category of offence, the Court shall notify the Panel.

(3)　The Panel may at any time, and shall if directed to do so by the Secretary of State, propose to the Court that guidelines be framed or revised under section 80 above for a particular category of offence.

(4)　Where the Panel receives a notification under subsection (2) above or makes a proposal under subsection (3) above, the Panel shall—

(a)　obtain and consider the views on the matters in issue of such persons or bodies as may be determined, after consultation with the Secretary of State and the Lord Chief Justice, by the Lord Chancellor;

(b)　formulate its own views on those matters and communicate them to the Court; and

(c)　furnish information to the Court as to the matters mentioned in section 80(3)(b) and (c) above.

(5)　The Lord Chancellor may pay to any member of the Panel such remuneration as he may determine.

[Crime and Disorder Act 1998, s 81.]

3–1547　82. Increase in sentences for racial aggravation.　*Repealed.*

Miscellaneous and supplemental

3–1548　85. Interpretation etc of Chapter I.　*Repealed.*

Powers of Criminal Courts (Sentencing) Act 2000

(2000 c 6)

PART I[1]

POWERS EXERCISABLE BEFORE SENTENCE

Deferment of sentence

3–1553　1. Deferment of sentence[2].　(1)　The Crown Court or a magistrates' court may defer passing sentence on an offender for the purpose of enabling the court, or any other court to which it falls to deal with him, to have regard in dealing with him to—

(a)　his conduct after conviction (including, where appropriate, the making by him of reparation for his offence); or

(b)　any change in his circumstances;

but this is subject to subsections (2) and (3) below.

(2)　The power conferred by subsection (1) above shall be exercisable only if—

(a)　the offender consents; and

(b)　the court is satisfied, having regard to the nature of the offence and the character and circumstances of the offender, that it would be in the interests of justice to exercise the power.

(3)　Any deferment under this section shall be until such date as may be specified by the court, not being more than six months[3] after the date on which the deferment is announced by the court; and, subject to section 2(7) below, where the passing of sentence has been deferred under this section it shall not be further so deferred.

(4)　Notwithstanding any enactment, a court which under this section defers passing sentence on an offender shall not on the same occasion remand him.

(5)　Where the passing of sentence on an offender has been deferred by a court under this section, the court's power under this section to deal with the offender at the end of the period of deferment—

(a) is power to deal with him, in respect of the offence for which passing of sentence has been deferred, in any way in which it could have dealt with him if it had not deferred passing sentence; and

(b) without prejudice to the generality of paragraph (a) above, in the case of a magistrates' court includes the power conferred by section 3 below to commit him to the Crown Court for sentence.

(6) Nothing in this section or section 2 below shall affect—

(a) the power of the Crown Court to bind over an offender to come up for judgment when called upon; or

(b) the power of any court to defer passing sentence for any purpose for which it may lawfully do so apart from this section.

[Powers of Criminal Courts (Sentencing) Act 2000, s 1.]

1. Part I contains ss 1–11.
2. For full discussion of this power, see ante para **3–56**. Note Criminal Procedure Rules 2005, Part 45, in PART I: MAGISTRATES' COURTS, PROCEDURE, ante, which requires notification to be given if the offender is dealt with during the currency of a period of deferment ordered by another court.
3. But it would appear that the court can still sentence someone even if more than six months have elapsed since the deferment (*R v Ingle* [1974] 3 All ER 811, 59 Cr App Rep 306; see also *R v (James) Anderson* (1983) 5 Cr App Rep (S) 338, [1984] Crim LR 109).

3–1554 2. Further powers of courts where sentence deferred under section 1. (1) A court which under section 1 above has deferred passing sentence on an offender may deal with him before the end of the period of deferment if during that period he is convicted in Great Britain of any offence.

(2) Subsection (3) below applies where a court has under section 1 above deferred passing sentence on an offender in respect of one or more offences and during the period of deferment the offender is convicted in England or Wales of any offence ("the later offence").

(3) Where this subsection applies, then (without prejudice to subsection (1) above and whether or not the offender is sentenced for the later offence during the period of deferment), the court which passes sentence on him for the later offence may also, if this has not already been done, deal with him for the offence or offences for which passing of sentence has been deferred, except that—

(a) the power conferred by this subsection shall not be exercised by a magistrates' court if the court which deferred passing sentence was the Crown Court; and

(b) the Crown Court, in exercising that power in a case in which the court which deferred passing sentence was a magistrates' court, shall not pass any sentence which could not have been passed by a magistrates' court in exercising that power.

(4) Where—

(a) a court which under section 1 above has deferred passing sentence on an offender proposes to deal with him, whether on the date originally specified by the court or by virtue of subsection (1) above before that date, or

(b) the offender does not appear on the date so specified,

the court may issue a summons requiring him to appear before the court, or may issue a warrant for his arrest.

(5) In deferring the passing of sentence under section 1 above a magistrates' court shall be regarded as exercising the power of adjourning the trial conferred by section 10(1) of the Magistrates' Courts Act 1980, and accordingly sections 11(1) and 13(1) to (3A) and (5) of that Act (non-appearance of the accused) apply (without prejudice to subsection (4) above) if the offender does not appear on the date specified under section 1(3) above.

(6) Any power of a court under this section to deal with an offender in a case where the passing of sentence has been deferred under section 1 above—

(a) is power to deal with him, in respect of the offence for which passing of sentence has been deferred, in any way in which the court which deferred passing sentence could have dealt with him; and

(b) without prejudice to the generality of paragraph (a) above, in the case of a magistrates' court includes the power conferred by section 3 below to commit him to the Crown Court for sentence.

(7) Where—

(a) the passing of sentence on an offender in respect of one or more offences has been deferred under section 1 above, and

(b) a magistrates' court deals with him in respect of the offence or any of the offences by committing him to the Crown Court under section 3 below,

the power of the Crown Court to deal with him includes the same power to defer passing sentence on him as if he had just been convicted of the offence or offences on indictment before the court.

[Powers of Criminal Courts (Sentencing) Act 2000, s 2.]

Committal to Crown Court for sentence

3–1555 3. Committal for sentence on summary trial of offence triable either way[1].
(1) Subject to subsection (4) below, this section[1] applies where on the summary trial of an offence triable either way a person aged 18 or over is convicted of the offence.

(2) If the court is of the opinion—

(a) that the offence[2] or the combination of the offence and one or more offences associated with it[3] was so serious that greater punishment[4] should be inflicted for the offence than the court has power to impose, or

(b) in the case of a violent or sexual offence[3], that a custodial sentence for a term longer than the court has power to impose is necessary to protect the public from serious harm[3] from him,

the court may commit[5] the offender in custody or on bail[6] to the Crown Court for sentence[7] in accordance with section 5(1) below.

(3) Where the court commits a person under subsection (2) above, section 6 below (which enables a magistrates' court, where it commits a person under this section in respect of an offence, also to commit him to the Crown Court to be dealt with in respect of certain other offences) shall apply accordingly.

(4) This section does not apply in relation to an offence as regards which this section is excluded by section 33 of the Magistrates' Courts Act 1980 (certain offences where value involved is small).

(5) The preceding provisions of this section shall apply in relation to a corporation as if—

(a) the corporation were an individual aged 18 or over; and

(b) in subsection (2) above, paragraph (b) and the words "in custody or on bail" were omitted.

[Powers of Criminal Courts (Sentencing) Act 2000, s 3.]

1. For full discussion of this power, see ante para 3–560; and for the application of this section following the recording of an indication of plea before determination of venue, see *R v Warley Magistrates' Court, ex p DPP* (1998) 162 JP 559, [1998] Crim LR 684, CA, and PART I: MAGISTRATES' COURTS, PROCEDURE, para 1–508, **Guidance on whether to commit for sentence**, ante.

2. The context of this section does not enable the word "offence" to be construed plurally; s 6 of the Interpretation Act 1978 does not apply; justices would not therefore be empowered to aggregate sentences for three indictable offences and impose a suspended sentence supervision order themselves (see conditions in s 122(1), post); they should commit for sentence (*R v Rugby Justices, ex p Prince* [1974] 2 All ER 116, [1974] 1 WLR 736).

3. The terms "associated with it", "violent offence", "sexual offence", "serious harm" are all defined in s 161, post.

4. This is not restricted to imposing a custodial term outside the justices' powers but may include the situation where they consider the appropriate penalty is a fine but that their powers to impose a fine are restricted by the statutory limit at a figure which is too low in punishment for the particular offence. Before committing for sentence in these circumstances, the justices should intimate their intention to the defendant and, if the case is committed, should record their opinion for the benefit of the Crown Court judge although such opinion is not binding on the Crown Court (*R v North Essex Justices, ex p Lloyd* (2000) 165 JP 117, DC).

5. For rule relating to the documents to be sent to the appropriate officer of the Crown Court on a committal under this section, see Criminal Procedure Rules 2005, Part 43, in PART I MAGISTRATES' COURTS, PROCEDURE, ante. Where the justices determine a factual issue which is relevant to the sentence, and thereafter commit the defendant for sentence, the justices must ensure that the Crown Court is informed of the facts found; see *Munroe v Crown Prosecution Service* [1988] Crim LR 823. The method of challenging this committal is by application for judicial review, not by raising the matter in the Court of Appeal in an appeal under (what is now) the Criminal Appeal Act 1968, s 11 (*R v Warren* [1954] 1 All ER 597, [1954] 1 WLR 531, 118 JP 238; *R v Jones* [1969] 2 QB 33, [1969] 1 All ER 325, 133 JP 144).

6. For the decision as to whether the committal is on bail or in custody, see *R v Rafferty* [1999] 1 Cr App R 235, [1998] 2 Cr App Rep (S) 449, (1998) 162 JP 353, and PART I: MAGISTRATES' COURTS, PROCEDURE, para 1–502 **Procedures: plea before venue (and committal for sentence); committal for trial; sending for trial**, ante.

7. See s 7, post, as to the powers of the Crown Court, to which should be left endorsement and disqualification, although the magistrates' court may impose interim disqualification. Note the power to commit allied offences for sentence also (s 6).

It is unnecessary for justices to state their reasons for committing for sentence since the person so committed will have an opportunity to make full representations to the sentencing court: *R v Wirral Magistrates' Court, ex p Jermyn* [2001] 1 Cr App Rep (S) 485, [2001] Crim LR 45, DC. There is no right of appeal against a committal for sentence (*R v London Sessions, ex p Rogers* [1951] 2 KB 74, [1951] 1 All ER 343, 115 JP 108) but where a convicted person did not plead guilty he may appeal against his conviction under s 108 of the Magistrates' Courts Act 1980 in PART I: MAGISTRATES' COURTS, PROCEDURE, ante.

After committal for sentence following a plea of guilty, the Crown Court has jurisdiction to hear an application to change the plea, and if it accedes to the application will remit the case to the justices for a trial on the basis of a plea of not guilty (*R v Mutford and Lothingland Justices, ex p Harber* [1971] 2 QB 291, [1971] 1 All ER 81, 135 JP 107; *R v Fareham Justices, ex p Long* [1976] Crim LR 269).

Similarly, where a defendant who has been committed for sentence disagrees with the prosecution version of the facts, it is open to the Crown Court to remit the matter to the magistrates' court for it to find the correct version of the facts. Alternatively, the Crown Court has power to try the issue itself, and it should normally do so if the issue does not arise until the case is before the Crown Court (*Munroe v Crown Prosecution Service* [1988] Crim LR 823).

For procedure where committal for sentence is called on at the Crown Court before the time for lodging an appeal has expired, see *R v Faithful* [1950] 2 All ER 1251, 115 JP 20.

3–1556   4. Committal for sentence on indication of guilty plea to offence triable either way[1].

(1) This section applies where—

(a) a person aged 18 or over appears or is brought before a magistrates' court ("the court") on an information charging him with an offence triable either way ("the offence");

(b) he or his representative indicates that he would plead guilty if the offence were to proceed to trial; and

(c) proceeding as if section 9(1) of the Magistrates' Courts Act 1980 were complied with and he pleaded guilty under it, the court convicts him of the offence.

(2) If the court has committed the offender to the Crown Court for trial for one or more related offences, that is to say, one or more offences which, in its opinion, are related to the offence, it may commit him in custody or on bail to the Crown Court to be dealt with in respect of the offence in accordance with section 5(1) below.

(3) If the power conferred by subsection (2) above is not exercisable but the court is still to inquire, as examining justices, into one or more related offences—

(a) it shall adjourn the proceedings relating to the offence until after the conclusion of its inquiries; and

(b) if it commits the offender to the Crown Court for trial for one or more related offences, it may then exercise that power.

(4) Where the court—

(a) under subsection (2) above commits the offender to the Crown Court to be dealt with in respect of the offence, and

(b) does not state that, in its opinion, it also has power so to commit him under section 3(2) above,

section 5(1) below shall not apply unless he is convicted before the Crown Court of one or more of the related offences.

(5) Where section 5(1) below does not apply, the Crown Court may deal with the offender in respect of the offence in any way in which the magistrates' court could deal with him if it had just convicted him of the offence.

(6) Where the court commits a person under subsection (2) above, section 6 below (which enables a magistrates' court, where it commits a person under this section in respect of an offence, also to commit him to the Crown Court to be dealt with in respect of certain other offences) shall apply accordingly.

(7) For the purposes of this section one offence is related to another if, were they both to be prosecuted on indictment, the charges for them could be joined in the same indictment.

[Powers of Criminal Courts (Sentencing) Act 2000, s 4.]

---

1. For full discussion of this power, see ante para **3–560**.

3–1557 5. Power of Crown Court on committal for sentence under sections 3 and 4.
(1) Where an offender is committed by a magistrates' court for sentence under section 3 or 4 above, the Crown Court shall inquire into the circumstances of the case and may deal with the offender in any way in which it could deal with him if he had just been convicted of the offence on indictment before the court[1].

(2) In relation to committals under section 4 above, subsection (1) above has effect subject to section 4(4) and (5) above.

[Powers of Criminal Courts (Sentencing) Act 2000, s 5.]

---

1. Where the magistrates' court has make a mistake in the manner in which it has committed an offender to the Crown Court by committing under s 4(2) in circumstances where there are no related offences and with no statement under s 4(4)(b) instead of committing under s 3(2), the powers of the Crown Court are limited by s 5(2) to those of the magistrates' court (*R v Sallis* [2003] EWCA Crim 233, [2003] 2 Cr App Rep (S) 394.).

3–1558 6. Committal for sentence in certain cases where offender committed in respect of another offence. (1) This section applies where a magistrates' court ("the committing court") commits a person in custody or on bail to the Crown Court under any enactment mentioned in subsection (4) below to be sentenced or otherwise dealt with in respect of an offence ("the relevant offence")[1].

(2) Where this section applies and the relevant offence is an indictable offence, the committing court may also commit the offender, in custody or on bail as the case may require, to the Crown Court to be dealt with in respect of any other offence whatsoever in respect of which the committing court has power to deal with him (being an offence of which he has been convicted by that or any other court).

(3) Where this section applies and the relevant offence is a summary offence, the committing court may commit the offender, in custody or on bail as the case may require, to the Crown Court to be dealt with in respect of—

(a) any other offence of which the committing court has convicted him, being either—

   (i)   an offence punishable with imprisonment[2]; or

   (ii) an offence in respect of which the committing court has a power or duty to order him to be disqualified under section 34, 35 or 36 of the Road Traffic Offenders Act 1988[3] (disqualification for certain motoring offences); or

(b) any suspended sentence in respect of which the committing court has under section 120(1) below power to deal with him.

(4) The enactments referred to in subsection (1) above are—

(a) the Vagrancy Act 1824 (incorrigible rogues)[4];

(b) sections 3 and 4 above (committal for sentence for offences triable either way);

(c) section 13(5) below (conditionally discharged person convicted of further offence);

(d) section 116(3)(b) below (offender convicted of offence committed during currency of original sentence); and

(e) section 120(2) below (offender convicted during operational period of suspended sentence).

[Powers of Criminal Courts (Sentencing) Act 2000, s 6.]

1. The enactments to which this section applies are specified in sub-s (4). See Criminal Procedure Rules 2005, Part 43, in PART I MAGISTRATES' COURTS, PROCEDURE, ante, for provisions relating to this section.
2. This reference shall be construed without regard to any prohibition or restriction imposed in relation to a particular offender (s 164(2) post).
3. See PART VII: TRANSPORT, title ROAD TRAFFIC, post.
4. See PART VIII, title VAGRANTS, post.

3–1559 7. Power of Crown Court on committal for sentence under section 6. (1) Where under section 6 above a magistrates' court commits a person to be dealt with by the Crown Court in respect of an offence, the Crown Court may after inquiring into the circumstances of the case deal with him in any way in which the magistrates' court could deal with him if it had just convicted him of the offence[1].

(2) Subsection (1) above does not apply where under section 6 above a magistrates' court commits a person to be dealt with by the Crown Court in respect of a suspended sentence, but in such a case the powers under section 119 below (power of court to deal with suspended sentence) shall be exercisable by the Crown Court.

(3) Without prejudice to subsections (1) and (2) above, where under section 6 above or any enactment mentioned in subsection (4)[2] of that section a magistrates' court commits a person to be dealt with by the Crown Court, any duty or power[2] which, apart from this subsection, would fall to be discharged or exercised by the magistrates' court shall not be discharged[3] or exercised by that court but shall instead be discharged or may instead be exercised by the Crown Court.

(4) Where under section 6 above a magistrates' court commits a person to be dealt with by the Crown Court in respect of an offence triable only on indictment in the case of an adult (being an offence which was tried summarily because of the offender's being under 18 years of age), the Crown Court's powers under subsection (1) above in respect of the offender after he attains the age of 18 shall be powers to do either or both of the following—

(a) to impose a fine not exceeding £5,000;
(b) to deal with the offender in respect of the offence in any way in which the magistrates' court could deal with him if it had just convicted him of an offence punishable with imprisonment for a term not exceeding six months.

[Powers of Criminal Courts (Sentencing) Act 2000, s 7.]

1. See PART VIII, title VAGRANTS, post.
2. It should be noted that the transfer of duties and powers referred to in this sub-section operates, not only in respect of summary cases committed for sentence in accordance with s 6(2), (3), supra, but also (by the use of the words "any enactment mentioned in subsection (4) of that section") to any case committed for sentence under one of the enactments specified in s 6(4), supra. Consequently, whenever a person is committed for sentence, the duty or power to disqualify him from driving a motor vehicle or to order the endorsement of his driving licence will be exercised by the court to which he is committed for sentence.
Interim disqualification may be ordered; see s 26 of the Road Traffic Offenders Act 1988.
3. This provision does not operate to restrict the duty on a magistrates' court to order the disclosure of the date of birth of a defendant, when this is not previously known, in the event of an interim disqualification being imposed (ss 25(4) and 26(1) of the Road Traffic Act 1988).

Remission for sentence: young offenders etc

3–1560 8. Power and duty to remit young offenders to youth courts for sentence. (1) Subsection (2) below applies where a child or young person (that is to say, any person aged under 18) is convicted by or before any court of an offence other than homicide.

(2) The court may and, if it is not a youth court, shall[1] unless satisfied that it would be undesirable to do so, remit the case—

(a) if the offender was committed for trial or sent to the Crown Court for trial under section 51 of the Crime and Disorder Act 1998, to a youth court acting for the place where he was committed for trial or sent to the Crown Court for trial;
(b) in any other case, to a youth court acting either for the same place as the remitting court or for the place where the offender habitually resides;

but in relation to a magistrates' court other than a youth court this subsection has effect subject to subsection (6) below.

(3) Where a case is remitted under subsection (2) above, the offender shall be brought before a youth court accordingly, and that court may deal with him in any way in which it might have dealt with him if he had been tried and convicted by that court[2].

(4) A court by which an order remitting a case to a youth court is made under subsection (2) above—

(a) may, subject to section 25 of the Criminal Justice and Public Order Act 1994[3] (restrictions on granting bail), give such directions as appear to be necessary with respect to the custody of the offender or for his release on bail until he can be brought before the youth court; and
(b) shall cause to be transmitted to the justices' chief executive for the youth court a certificate setting out the nature of the offence and stating—

(i) that the offender has been convicted of the offence; and
(ii) that the case has been remitted for the purpose of being dealt with under the preceding provisions of this section.

(5) Where a case is remitted under subsection (2) above, the offender shall have no right of appeal against the order of remission, but shall have the same right of appeal against any order of the court to which the case is remitted as if he had been convicted by that court.

(6) Without prejudice to the power to remit any case to a youth court which is conferred on a magistrates' court other than a youth court by subsections (1) and (2) above, where such a magistrates' court convicts a child or young person of an offence it must exercise that power unless the case falls within subsection (7) or (8) below.

(7) The case falls within this subsection if the court would, were it not so to remit the case, be required by section 16(2) below to refer the offender to a youth offender panel (in which event the court may, but need not, so remit the case).

(8) The case falls within this subsection if it does not fall within subsection (7) above but the court is of the opinion that the case is one which can properly be dealt with by means of—

(a) an order discharging the offender absolutely or conditionally, or

(b) an order for the payment of a fine, or

(c) an order (under section 150 below) requiring the offender's parent or guardian to enter into a recognizance to take proper care of him and exercise proper control over him,

with or without any other order that the court has power to make when absolutely or conditionally discharging an offender.

(9) In subsection (8) above "care" and "control" shall be construed in accordance with section 150(11) below.

(10) A document purporting to be a copy of an order made by a court under this section shall, if it purports to be certified as a true copy by the justices' chief executive for the court, be evidence of the order.

[Powers of Criminal Courts (Sentencing) Act 2000, s 8.]

---

1. Since the powers of the Crown Court were aligned with those of the youth court by the Criminal Justice Act 1982, the former court will probably remit cases only very rarely; ss *R v Lewis* (1984) 148 JP 329.

2. The youth court receiving the case is not limited to passing sentence, but has jurisdiction to accept a change of plea to not guilty and then go on to try the information (*R v Stratford Youth Court, ex p Conde* [1997] 1 WLR 113, 161 JP 308, [1997] 2 Cr App Rep 1, DC. However, since the power of the youth court is to deal with the offender as if it had tried the offender and found him guilty, it does not extend to committing him to the Crown Court for trial (*R v Allen and Lambert* (1999) 163 JP 841).

3. See PART I: MAGISTRATES' COURTS, Procedure, *ante*.

3–1561   9. Power of youth court to remit offender who attains age of 18 to magistrates' court other than youth court for sentence[1]. (1) Where a person who appears or is brought before a youth court charged with an offence subsequently attains the age of 18, the youth court may, at any time after conviction and before sentence, remit him for sentence to a magistrates' court (other than a youth court) acting for the same petty sessions area as the youth court.

(2) Where an offender is remitted under subsection (1) above, the youth court shall adjourn proceedings in relation to the offence, and—

(a) section 128 of the Magistrates' Courts Act 1980 (remand in custody or on bail) and all other enactments, whenever passed, relating to remand or the granting of bail in criminal proceedings shall have effect, in relation to the youth court's power or duty to remand the offender on that adjournment, as if any reference to the court to or before which the person remanded is to be brought or appear after remand were a reference to the court to which he is being remitted; and

(b) subject to subsection (3) below, the court to which the offender is remitted ("the other court") may deal with the case in any way in which it would have power to deal with it if all proceedings relating to the offence which took place before the youth court had taken place before the other court.

(3) Where an offender is remitted under subsection (1) above, section 8(6) above (duty of adult magistrates' court to remit young offenders to youth court for sentence) shall not apply to the court to which he is remitted.

(4) Where an offender is remitted under subsection (1) above he shall have no right of appeal against the order of remission (but without prejudice to any right of appeal against an order made in respect of the offence by the court to which he is remitted).

(5) In this section—

(a) "enactment" includes an enactment contained in any order, regulation or other instrument having effect by virtue of an Act; and

(b) "bail in criminal proceedings" has the same meaning as in the Bail Act 1976.

[Powers of Criminal Courts (Sentencing) Act 2000, s 9.]

---

1. Remittal to the adult court is legally defective in the case of an offence triable only on indictment, and such an order can be rescinded under s 142 of the Magistrates' Courts Act 1980: *R (on the application of Denny) v Acton Youth Court Justices (DPP, interested party)* [2004] EWHC 948 (Admin), [2004] 2 All ER 961, (2004) 168 JP 388.

3–1562   10. Power of magistrates' court to remit case to another magistrates' court for sentence.   (1) Where a person aged 18 or over ("the offender") has been convicted by a magistrates' court ("the convicting court") of an offence to which this section applies ("the instant offence") and—

(a) it appears to the convicting court that some other magistrates' court ("the other court") has convicted him of another such offence in respect of which the other court has neither passed sentence on him nor committed him to the Crown Court for sentence nor dealt with him in any other way, and

(b) the other court consents to his being remitted under this section to the other court,

the convicting court may remit him to the other court to be dealt with in respect of the instant offence by the other court instead of by the convicting court.

(2) This section applies to—

(a) any offence punishable with imprisonment; and

(b) any offence in respect of which the convicting court has a power or duty to order the offender to be disqualified under section 34, 35 or 36 of the Road Traffic Offenders Act 1988 (disqualification for certain motoring offences).

(3) Where the convicting court remits the offender to the other court under this section, it shall adjourn the trial of the information charging him with the instant offence, and—

(a) section 128 of the Magistrates' Courts Act 1980 (remand in custody or on bail) and all other enactments, whenever passed, relating to remand or the granting of bail in criminal proceedings shall have effect, in relation to the convicting court's power or duty to remand the offender on that adjournment, as if any reference to the court to or before which the person remanded is to be brought or appear after remand were a reference to the court to which he is being remitted; and

(b) subject to subsection (7) below, the other court may deal with the case in any way in which it would have power to deal with it if all proceedings relating to the instant offence which took place before the convicting court had taken place before the other court.

(4) The power conferred on the other court by subsection (3)(b) above includes, where applicable, the power to remit the offender under this section to another magistrates' court in respect of the instant offence.

(5) Where the convicting court has remitted the offender under this section to the other court, the other court may remit him back to the convicting court; and the provisions of subsections (3) and (4) above (so far as applicable) shall apply with the necessary modifications in relation to any remission under this subsection.

(6) The offender, if remitted under this section, shall have no right of appeal against the order of remission (but without prejudice to any right of appeal against any other order made in respect of the instant offence by the court to which he is remitted).

(7) Nothing in this section shall preclude the convicting court from making any order which it has power to make under section 148 below (restitution orders) by virtue of the offender's conviction of the instant offence.

(8) In this section—

(a) "conviction" includes a finding under section 11(1) below (remand for medical examination) that the person in question did the act or made the omission charged, and "convicted" shall be construed accordingly;

(b) "enactment" includes an enactment contained in any order, regulation or other instrument having effect by virtue of an Act; and

(c) "bail in criminal proceedings" has the same meaning as in the Bail Act 1976.

[Powers of Criminal Courts (Sentencing) Act 2000, s 10.]

Remand by magistrates' court for medical examination

3–1563   11. Remand by magistrates' court for medical examination. (1) If, on the trial[1] by a magistrates' court of an offence punishable on summary conviction with imprisonment, the court—

(a) is satisfied that the accused did the act[2] or made the omission charged, but

(b) is of the opinion that an inquiry ought to be made into his physical or mental condition before the method of dealing with him is determined,

the court shall adjourn the case to enable a medical examination and report to be made, and shall remand him.

(2) An adjournment under subsection (1) above shall not be for more than three weeks at a time where the court remands the accused in custody, nor for more than four weeks at a time where it remands him on bail.

(3) Where on an adjournment under subsection (1) above the accused is remanded on bail, the court shall impose conditions under paragraph (d) of section 3(6) of the Bail Act 1976 and the requirements imposed as conditions under that paragraph shall be or shall include requirements that the accused—

(a) undergo medical examination by a registered medical practitioner or, where the inquiry is into his mental condition and the court so directs, two such practitioners; and

(b) for that purpose attend such an institution or place, or on such practitioner, as the court directs and, where the inquiry is into his mental condition, comply with any other directions which may be given to him for that purpose by any person specified by the court or by a person of any class so specified.

[Powers of Criminal Courts (Sentencing) Act 2000, s 11.]

---

1. This power is not available on inquiry by examining justices.
2. A hospital order may be made unusually without embarking on a trial, where those acting for the defendant consent; see *R v Lincolnshire (Kesteven) Justices, ex p O'Connor* [1983] 1 All ER 901, [1983] 1 WLR 335, 147 JP 97.

PART II[1]
ABSOLUTE AND CONDITIONAL DISCHARGE

3–1564   12. Absolute and conditional discharge[2]. (1) Where a court by or before which a person is convicted of an offence (not being an offence the sentence for which is fixed by law or falls to be imposed under section 109(2), 110(2) or 111(2) below) is of the opinion, having regard to the circumstances including the nature of the offence and the character of the offender, that it is inexpedient to inflict punishment, the court may make an order either—

(a) discharging him absolutely; or

(b) if the court thinks fit, discharging him subject to the condition that he commits no offence during such period, not exceeding three years from the date of the order, as may be specified in the order.

(2) Subsection (1)(b) above has effect subject to section 66(4) of the Crime and Disorder Act 1998 (effect of reprimands and warnings).

(3) An order discharging a person subject to such a condition as is mentioned in subsection (1)(b) above is in this Act referred to as an "order for conditional discharge"; and the period specified in any such order is in this Act referred to as "the period of conditional discharge".

(4) Before making an order for conditional discharge, the court shall explain to the offender in ordinary language that if he commits another offence during the period of conditional discharge he will be liable to be sentenced for the original offence.

(5) If (by virtue of section 13 below) a person conditionally discharged under this section is sentenced for the offence in respect of which the order for conditional discharge was made, that order shall cease to have effect.

(6) On making an order for conditional discharge, the court may, if it thinks it expedient for the purpose of the offender's reformation, allow any person who consents to do so to give security for the good behaviour of the offender[3].

(7) Nothing in this section shall be construed as preventing a court, on discharging an offender absolutely or conditionally in respect of any offence, from making an order for costs against the offender or imposing any disqualification on him or from making in respect of the offence an order under section 130, 143 or 148 below (compensation orders, deprivation orders and restitution orders).

[Powers of Criminal Courts (Sentencing) Act 2000, s 12.]

---

1. Part II contains ss 12–15.
2. For full discussion of these powers, see *ante*, para **3–200**.
3. This security will be by recognizance and the provisions of the Magistrates' Courts Act 1980, ss 117–120 will apply.

3–1565   13. Commission of further offence by person conditionally discharged[1]. (1) If it appears to the Crown Court, where that court has jurisdiction in accordance with subsection (2) below, or to a justice of the peace having jurisdiction in accordance with that subsection, that a person in whose case an order for conditional discharge has been made—

(a) has been convicted by a court in Great Britain of an offence committed during the period of conditional discharge, and

(b) has been dealt with in respect of that offence,

that court or justice may, subject to subsection (3) below, issue a summons requiring that person to appear at the place and time specified in it or a warrant for his arrest.

(2) Jurisdiction for the purposes of subsection (1) above may be exercised—

(a) if the order for conditional discharge was made by the Crown Court, by that court;

(b) if the order was made by a magistrates' court, by a justice acting for the petty sessions area for which that court acts.

(3) A justice of the peace shall not issue a summons under this section except on information and shall not issue a warrant under this section except on information in writing and on oath.

(4) A summons or warrant issued under this section shall direct the person to whom it relates to appear or to be brought before the court by which the order for conditional discharge was made.

(5) If a person in whose case an order for conditional discharge has been made by the Crown Court is convicted by a magistrates' court of an offence committed during the period of conditional discharge, the magistrates' court—

(a) may commit him to custody or release him on bail until he can be brought or appear before the Crown Court; and

(b) if it does so, shall send to the Crown Court a copy of the minute or memorandum of the conviction entered in the register, signed by the justices' chief executive by whom the register is kept.

(6) Where it is proved to the satisfaction of the court by which an order for conditional discharge was made that the person in whose case the order was made has been convicted of an offence committed during the period of conditional discharge, the court may deal with him, for the offence for which the order was made, in any way in which it could deal with him if he had just been convicted by or before that court of that offence.

(7) If a person in whose case an order for conditional discharge has been made by a magistrates' court—

(a) is convicted before the Crown Court of an offence committed during the period of conditional discharge, or

(b) is dealt with by the Crown Court for any such offence in respect of which he was committed for sentence to the Crown Court,

the Crown Court may deal with him, for the offence for which the order was made, in any way in which the magistrates' court could deal with him if it had just convicted him of that offence.

(8) If a person in whose case an order for conditional discharge has been made by a magistrates' court is convicted by another magistrates' court of any offence committed during the period of conditional discharge, that other court may, with the consent of the court which made the order, deal with him, for the offence for which the order was made, in any way in which the court could deal with him if it had just convicted him of that offence.

(9) Where an order for conditional discharge has been made by a magistrates' court in the case of an offender under 18 years of age in respect of an offence triable only on indictment in the case of an adult, any powers exercisable under subsection (6), (7) or (8) above by that or any other court in respect of the offender after he attains the age of 18 shall be powers to do either or both of the following—

(a) to impose a fine not exceeding £5,000 for the offence in respect of which the order was made;

(b) to deal with the offender for that offence in any way in which a magistrates' court could deal with him if it had just convicted him of an offence punishable with imprisonment for a term not exceeding six months.

(10) The reference in subsection (6) above to a person's having been convicted of an offence committed during the period of conditional discharge is a reference to his having been so convicted by a court in Great Britain.

[Powers of Criminal Courts (Sentencing) Act 2000, s 13.]

---

1. For full discussion of this power, see ante, para **3–201**.

3–1566   14. Effect of discharge[1]. (1) Subject to subsection (2) below, a conviction of an offence for which an order is made under section 12 above discharging the offender absolutely or conditionally shall be deemed not to be a conviction for any purpose other than the purposes of the proceedings[2] in which the order is made and of any subsequent proceedings which may be taken against the offender under section 13 above.

(2) Where the offender was aged 18 or over at the time of his conviction of the offence in question and is subsequently sentenced (under section 13 above) for that offence, subsection (1) above shall cease to apply to the conviction.

(3) Without prejudice to subsections (1) and (2) above, the conviction of an offender who is discharged absolutely or conditionally under section 12 above shall in any event be disregarded for the purposes of any enactment or instrument which—

(a) imposes any disqualification or disability[3] upon convicted persons; or

(b) authorises or requires the imposition of any such disqualification or disability.

(4) Subsections (1) to (3) above shall not affect—

(a) any right of an offender discharged absolutely or conditionally under section 12 above to rely on his conviction in bar of any subsequent proceedings for the same offence;

(b) the restoration of any property in consequence of the conviction of any such offender; or

(c) the operation, in relation to any such offender, of any enactment or instrument in force on 1st July 1974 which is expressed to extend to persons dealt with under section 1(1) of the Probation of Offenders Act 1907 as well as to convicted persons.

(5) In subsections (3) and (4) above—

"enactment" includes an enactment contained in a local Act; and

"instrument" means an instrument having effect by virtue of an Act.

(6) Subsection (1) above has effect subject to section 50(1A) of the Criminal Appeal Act 1968 and section 108(1A) of the Magistrates' Courts Act 1980 (rights of appeal); and this subsection shall not be taken to prejudice any other enactment that excludes the effect of subsection (1) or (3) above for particular purposes.

(7) Without prejudice to paragraph 1(3) of Schedule 11 to this Act (references to provisions of this Act to be construed as including references to corresponding old enactments), in this section—

(a) any reference to an order made under section 12 above discharging an offender absolutely or conditionally includes a reference to an order which was made under any provision of Part I of the Powers of Criminal Courts Act 1973 (whether or not reproduced in this Act) discharging the offender absolutely or conditionally;

(b) any reference to an offender who is discharged absolutely or conditionally under section 12 includes a reference to an offender who was discharged absolutely or conditionally under any such provision.

[Powers of Criminal Courts (Sentencing) Act 2000, s 14.]

---

1. The effect of sub-s (1) in former corresponding legislation was explained in *R v Harris* [1951] 1 KB 107, [1950] 2 All ER 816, 114 JP 535; *Cassidy v Cassidy* [1959] 3 All ER 187, 123 JP 454. See also *R v Stobbart* [1951] 2 All ER 753, 115 JP 561; and *R v Webb* [1953] 2 QB 390, [1953] 1 All ER 1156, 117 JP 319. Where an applicant for a post with a police force (which employment was exempt from the provisions of the Rehabilitation of Offenders Act 1974) had been asked "Have you ever been convicted?" and replied "no" whereas she had previously been made the subject of a conditional discharge, there was no offence of obtaining employment by deception. There was a distinction between this and "Have you ever been found guilty of an offence?" which would have been a false representation and capable of being a deception. However, it is perfectly open to such employers to ask a question such as "Have you ever been found guilty of a criminal offence?" or "Have you ever committed a criminal offence?" or, if necessary, "Have you ever appeared in court and been sentenced, including an absolute or conditional discharge, for an offence?": *R v Patel* [2006] EWCA Crim 2689, [2007] 1 Cr App R 12.

2. A conviction in respect of which a court has ordered that a person's driving licence shall be endorsed or that he be disqualified for holding or obtaining a licence shall be taken into account in determining his liability to punishment or disqualification for any offence specified in Sch 2 to the Road Traffic Offenders Act 1988, committed subsequently; see s 46 of the Road Traffic Offenders Act 1988 in PART VII: TRANSPORT title ROAD TRAFFIC, post. A conviction of an offence to which s 119(1) or (2)(a) of the Social Security Administration Act 1992 applies (failure to pay contributions), for which the offender is discharged absolutely or conditionally, shall apply as if it were a conviction for all purposes (Social Security Administration Act 1992, s 121(2), in PART VIII: SOCIAL SECURITY, post).

3. Nevertheless, a court convicting a person of an offence specified in Sch 2 to the Road Traffic Offenders Act 1988, and making an order discharging him absolutely or conditionally may order that his driving licence be endorsed or that he shall be disqualified for holding or obtaining a licence, and shall make such order of endorsement or disqualification as the court is required to make in accordance with ss 34, 36 or 44 of the said Act (Road Traffic Offenders Act 1988, s 46). See PART VII, TRANSPORT, title Road Traffic, post. A recommendation for deportation is not a disqualification or disability under this subsection (*R v Akan* [1973] QB 491, [1972] 3 All ER 285, 136 JP 766). The provisions of s 14 do not apply to disciplinary proceedings before a tribunal (*R v Statutory Committee of the Pharmaceutical Society of Great Britain, ex p Pharmaceutical Society of Great Britain* [1981] 2 All ER 805, [1981] 1 WLR 886), nor can they prevent a criminal conviction being taken into consideration in police disciplinary proceedings (*R v Secretary of State for the Home Department, ex p Thornton* [1987] QB 36, [1986] 2 All ER 641, CA).

3–1567   15. Discharge: supplementary.   (1) The Secretary of State may by order direct that subsection (1) of section 12 above shall be amended by substituting, for the maximum period specified in that subsection as originally enacted or as previously amended under this subsection, such period as may be specified in the order.

(2) Where an order for conditional discharge has been made on appeal, for the purposes of section 13 above it shall be deemed—

(a) if it was made on an appeal brought from a magistrates' court, to have been made by that magistrates' court;

(b) if it was made on an appeal brought from the Crown Court or from the criminal division of the Court of Appeal, to have been made by the Crown Court.

(3) In proceedings before the Crown Court under section 13 above, any question whether any person in whose case an order for conditional discharge has been made has been convicted of an offence committed during the period of conditional discharge shall be determined by the court and not by the verdict of a jury.

[Powers of Criminal Courts (Sentencing) Act 2000, s 15.]

PART III[1]
MANDATORY AND DISCRETIONARY REFERRAL OF YOUNG OFFENDERS

Referral orders

3–1568   16. Duty and power to refer certain young offenders to youth offender panels.
(1) This section applies where a youth court or other magistrates' court is dealing with a person aged under 18 for an offence and—

(a) neither the offence nor any connected offence is one for which the sentence is fixed by law;

(b) the court is not, in respect of the offence or any connected offence, proposing to impose a custodial sentence on the offender or make a hospital order (within the meaning of the Mental Health Act 1983) in his case; and

(c) the court is not proposing to discharge him absolutely in respect of the offence.

(2) If—

(a) the compulsory referral conditions are satisfied in accordance with section 17 below, and

(b) referral is available to the court,

the court shall sentence the offender for the offence by ordering him to be referred to a youth offender panel.

(3) If—

(a) the discretionary referral conditions are satisfied in accordance with section 17 below, and (*b*) referral is available to the court,

the court may sentence the offender for the offence by ordering him to be referred to a youth offender panel.

(4) For the purposes of this Part an offence is connected with another if the offender falls to be dealt with for it at the same time as he is dealt with for the other offence (whether or not he is convicted of the offences at the same time or by or before the same court).

(5) For the purposes of this section referral is available to a court if—

(*a*) the court has been notified by the Secretary of State that arrangements for the implementation of referral orders are available in the area in which it appears to the court that the offender resides or will reside; and

(*b*) the notice has not been withdrawn.

(6) An order under subsection (2) or (3) above is in this Act referred to as a "referral order".

(7) No referral order may be made in respect of any offence committed before the commencement of section 1 of the Youth Justice and Criminal Evidence Act 1999.

[Powers of Criminal Courts (Sentencing) Act 2000, s 16.]

---

1. Part III contains ss 16–32 and Sch 1. A referral order is only available to the court if the court has been notified by the Secretary of State that arrangements for the implementation of referral orders are available in the area in which it appears to the court that the offender resides or will reside; and the notice has not been withdrawn (s 16(5)).

For the interaction of parenting orders made under ss 8–10 of the Crime and Disorder Act 1998 and referral orders made under this Part of the Powers of Criminal Courts (Sentencing) Act 2000, see para **5–47AA** in PART V, YOUTH COURTS, post.

3–1569   17. The referral conditions.   (1) For the purposes of section 16(2) above the compulsory referral conditions are satisfied in relation to an offence if the offence is an offence punishable with imprisonment and the offender—

(*a*) pleaded guilty to the offence and to any connected offence;

(*b*) has never been convicted by or before a court in the United Kingdom of any offence other than the offence and any connected offence; and

(*c*) has never been bound over in criminal proceedings in England and Wales or Northern Ireland to keep the peace or to be of good behaviour.

(1A) For the purposes of section 16(3) above, the discretionary referral conditions are satisfied in relation to an offence if the offence is not an offence punishable with imprisonment but the offender meets the conditions in paragraphs (*a*) to (*c*) of subsection (1) above.

(2) For the purposes of section 16(3) above the discretionary referral conditions are also satisfied in relation to an offence if—

(*a*) the offender is being dealt with by the court for the offence and one or more connected offences (whether or not any of them is an offence punishable with imprisonment);

(*b*) although he pleaded guilty to at least one of the offences mentioned in paragraph (*a*) above, he also pleaded not guilty to at least one of them;

(*c*) he has never been convicted by or before a court in the United Kingdom of any offence other than the offences mentioned in paragraph (*a*) above; and

(*d*) he has never been bound over in criminal proceedings in England and Wales or Northern Ireland to keep the peace or to be of good behaviour.

(3) The Secretary of State may by regulations[1] make such amendments of this section as he considers appropriate for altering in any way the descriptions of offenders in the case of which the compulsory referral conditions or the discretionary referral conditions fall to be satisfied for the purposes of section 16(2) or (3) above (as the case may be).

(4) Any description of offender having effect for those purposes by virtue of such regulations may be framed by reference to such matters as the Secretary of State considers appropriate, including (in particular) one or more of the following—

(*a*) the offender's age;

(*b*) how the offender has pleaded;

(*c*) the offence (or offences) of which the offender has been convicted;

(*d*) the offender's previous convictions (if any);

(*e*) how (if at all) the offender has been previously punished or otherwise dealt with by any court; and

(*f*) any characteristics or behaviour of, or circumstances relating to, any person who has at any time been charged in the same proceedings as the offender (whether or not in respect of the same offence).

(5) For the purposes of this section an offender who has been convicted of an offence in respect of which he was conditionally discharged (whether by a court in England and Wales or in Northern Ireland) shall be treated, despite—

(*a*) section 14(1) above (conviction of offence for which offender so discharged deemed not a conviction), or

(*b*) Article 6(1) of the Criminal Justice (Northern Ireland) Order 1996 (corresponding provision for Northern Ireland), as having been convicted of that offence.

[Powers of Criminal Courts (Sentencing) Act 2000, s 17, as amended by SI 2003/1605.]

---

1. The Referral Orders (Amendment of Referral Conditions) Regulations 2003, SI 2003/1605 have been made, the effects of which have been noted in the text of section 17.

3–1570 18. Making of referral orders: general. (1) A referral order shall—

   (a)   specify the youth offending team responsible for implementing the order;

   (b)   require the offender to attend each of the meetings of a youth offender panel to be established by the team for the offender; and

   (c)   specify the period for which any youth offender contract taking effect between the offender and the panel under section 23 below is to have effect (which must not be less than three nor more than twelve months).

(2) The youth offending team specified under subsection (1)(a) above shall be the team having the function of implementing referral orders in the area in which it appears to the court that the offender resides or will reside.

(3) On making a referral order the court shall explain to the offender in ordinary language—

   (a)   the effect of the order; and

   (b)   the consequences which may follow—

      (i)   if no youth offender contract takes effect between the offender and the panel under section 23 below; or

      (ii)   if the offender breaches any of the terms of any such contract.

(4) Subsections (5) to (7) below apply where, in dealing with an offender for two or more connected offences, a court makes a referral order in respect of each, or each of two or more, of the offences.

(5) The orders shall have the effect of referring the offender to a single youth offender panel; and the provision made by them under subsection (1) above shall accordingly be the same in each case, except that the periods specified under subsection (1)(c) may be different.

(6) The court may direct that the period so specified in either or any of the orders is to run concurrently with or be additional to that specified in the other or any of the others; but in exercising its power under this subsection the court must ensure that the total period for which such a contract as is mentioned in subsection (1)(c) above is to have effect does not exceed twelve months.

(7) Each of the orders mentioned in subsection (4) above shall, for the purposes of this Part, be treated as associated with the other or each of the others.

[Powers of Criminal Courts (Sentencing) Act 2000, s 18.]

3–1571 19. Making of referral orders: effect on court's other sentencing powers. (1) Subsections (2) to (5) below apply where a court makes a referral order in respect of an offence.

(2) The court may not deal with the offender for the offence in any of the prohibited ways.

(3) The court—

   (a)   shall, in respect of any connected offence, either sentence the offender by making a referral order or make an order discharging him absolutely; and

   (b)   may not deal with the offender for any such offence in any of the prohibited ways.

(4) For the purposes of subsections (2) and (3) above the prohibited ways are—

   (a)   imposing a community sentence on the offender;

   (b)   ordering him to pay a fine;

   (c)   making a reparation order in respect of him; and

   (d)   making an order discharging him conditionally.

(5) The court may not make, in connection with the conviction of the offender for the offence or any connected offence—

   (a)   an order binding him over to keep the peace or to be of good behaviour; or

   (b)   an order under section 150 below (binding over of parent or guardian);

   (c)   *repealed.*

(6) Subsections (2), (3) and (5) above do not affect the exercise of any power to deal with the offender conferred by paragraph 5 (offender referred back to court by panel) or paragraph 14 (powers of a court where offender convicted while subject to referral) of Schedule 1 to this Act.

(7) Where section 16(2) above requires a court to make a referral order, the court may not under section 1 above defer passing sentence on him, but section 16(2) and subsection (3)(a) above do not affect any power or duty of a magistrates' court under—

   (a)   section 8 above (remission to youth court, or another such court, for sentence);

   (b)   section 10(3) of the Magistrates' Courts Act 1980 (adjournment for inquiries); or

   (c)   section 35, 38, 43 or 44 of the Mental Health Act 1983 (remand for reports, interim hospital orders and committal to Crown Court for restriction order).

[Powers of Criminal Courts (Sentencing) Act 2000, s 19 as amended by the Criminal Justice Act 2003, Sch 34.]

3–1572 20. Making of referral orders: attendance of parents etc. (1) A court making a referral order may make an order requiring—

(a) the appropriate person, or

(b) in a case where there are two or more appropriate persons, any one or more of them,

to attend the meetings of the youth offender panel.

(2) Where an offender is aged under 16 when a court makes a referral order in his case—

(a) the court shall exercise its power under subsection (1) above so as to require at least one appropriate person to attend meetings of the youth offender panel; and

(b) if the offender falls within subsection (6) below, the person or persons so required to attend those meetings shall be or include a representative of the local authority mentioned in that subsection.

(3) The court shall not under this section make an order requiring a person to attend meetings of the youth offender panel—

(a) if the court is satisfied that it would be unreasonable to do so; or

(b) to an extent which the court is satisfied would be unreasonable.

(4) Except where the offender falls within subsection (6) below, each person who is a parent or guardian of the offender is an "appropriate person" for the purposes of this section.

(5) Where the offender falls within subsection (6) below, each of the following is an "appropriate person" for the purposes of this section—

(a) a representative of the local authority mentioned in that subsection; and

(b) each person who is a parent or guardian of the offender with whom the offender is allowed to live.

(6) An offender falls within this subsection if he is (within the meaning of the Children Act 1989) a child who is looked after by a local authority.

(7) If, at the time when a court makes an order under this section—

(a) a person who is required by the order to attend meetings of a youth offender panel is not present in court, or

(b) a local authority whose representative is so required to attend such meetings is not represented in court,

the court must send him or (as the case may be) the authority a copy of the order forthwith.

[Powers of Criminal Courts (Sentencing) Act 2000, s 20.]

Youth offender panels

3–1573 21. Establishment of panels.   (1) Where a referral order has been made in respect of an offender (or two or more associated referral orders have been so made), it is the duty of the youth offending team specified in the order (or orders)—

(a) to establish a youth offender panel for the offender;

(b) to arrange for the first meeting of the panel to be held for the purposes of section 23 below; and

(c) subsequently to arrange for the holding of any further meetings of the panel required by virtue of section 25 below (in addition to those required by virtue of any other provision of this Part).

(2) A youth offender panel shall—

(a) be constituted,

(b) conduct its proceedings, and

(c) discharge its functions under this Part (and in particular those arising under section 23 below),

in accordance with guidance given from time to time by the Secretary of State.

(3) At each of its meetings a panel shall, however, consist of at least—

(a) one member appointed by the youth offending team from among its members; and

(b) two members so appointed who are not members of the team.

(4) The Secretary of State may by regulations make provision requiring persons appointed as members of a youth offender panel to have such qualifications, or satisfy such other criteria, as are specified in the regulations.

(5) Where it appears to the court which made a referral order that, by reason of either a change or a prospective change in the offender's place or intended place of residence, the youth offending team for the time being specified in the order ("the current team") either does not or will not have the function of implementing referral orders in the area in which the offender resides or will reside, the court may amend the order so that it instead specifies the team which has the function of implementing such orders in that area ("the new team").

(6) Where a court so amends a referral order—

(a) subsection (1)(a) above shall apply to the new team in any event;

(b) subsection (1)(b) above shall apply to the new team if no youth offender contract has (or has under paragraph (c) below been treated as having) taken effect under section 23 below between the offender and a youth offender panel established by the current team;

(c) if such a contract has (or has previously under this paragraph been treated as having) so taken effect, it shall (after the amendment) be treated as if it were a contract which had taken effect under section 23 below between the offender and the panel being established for the offender by the new team.

(7) References in this Part to the meetings of a youth offender panel (or any such meeting) are to the following meetings of the panel (or any of them)—

    (a)   the first meeting held in pursuance of subsection (1)(b) above;
    (b)   any further meetings held in pursuance of section 25 below;
    (c)   any progress meeting held under section 26 below; and
    (d)   the final meeting held under section 27 below.
[Powers of Criminal Courts (Sentencing) Act 2000, s 21.]

3–1574 22. Attendance at panel meetings.   (1) The specified team shall, in the case of each meeting of the panel established for the offender, notify—

    (a)   the offender, and
    (b)   any person to whom an order under section 20 above applies,

of the time and place at which he is required to attend that meeting.
    (2) If the offender fails to attend any part of such a meeting the panel may—

    (a)   adjourn the meeting to such time and place as it may specify; or
    (b)   end the meeting and refer the offender back to the appropriate court;

and subsection (1) above shall apply in relation to any such adjourned meeting.
    (2A) If—

    (a)   a parent or guardian of the offender fails to comply with an order under section 20 above (requirement to attend the meetings of the panel), and
    (b)   the offender is aged under 18 at the time of the failure,

the panel may refer that parent or guardian to a youth court acting for the petty sessions area in which it appears to the panel that the offender resides or will reside.
    (3) One person aged 18 or over chosen by the offender, with the agreement of the panel, shall be entitled to accompany the offender to any meeting of the panel (and it need not be the same person who accompanies him to every meeting).
    (4) The panel may allow to attend any such meeting—

    (a)   any person who appears to the panel to be a victim of, or otherwise affected by, the offence, or any of the offences, in respect of which the offender was referred to the panel;
    (b)   any person who appears to the panel to be someone capable of having a good influence on the offender.

    (5) Where the panel allows any such person as is mentioned in subsection (4)(a) above ("the victim") to attend a meeting of the panel, the panel may allow the victim to be accompanied to the meeting by one person chosen by the victim with the agreement of the panel.
[Powers of Criminal Courts (Sentencing) Act 2000, s 22 as amended by the Criminal Justice Act 2003, Sch 34.]

Youth offender contracts

3–1575 23. First meeting: agreement of contract with offender.   (1) At the first meeting of the youth offender panel established for an offender the panel shall seek to reach agreement with the offender on a programme of behaviour the aim (or principal aim) of which is the prevention of re-offending by the offender.
    (2) The terms of the programme may, in particular, include provision for any of the following—

    (a)   the offender to make financial or other reparation to any person who appears to the panel to be a victim of, or otherwise affected by, the offence, or any of the offences, for which the offender was referred to the panel;
    (b)   the offender to attend mediation sessions with any such victim or other person;
    (c)   the offender to carry out unpaid work or service in or for the community;
    (d)   the offender to be at home at times specified in or determined under the programme;
    (e)   attendance by the offender at a school or other educational establishment or at a place of work;
    (f)   the offender to participate in specified activities (such as those designed to address offending behaviour, those offering education or training or those assisting with the rehabilitation of persons dependent on, or having a propensity to misuse, alcohol or drugs);
    (g)   the offender to present himself to specified persons at times and places specified in or determined under the programme;
    (h)   the offender to stay away from specified places or persons (or both);
    (i)   enabling the offender's compliance with the programme to be supervised and recorded.

    (3) The programme may not, however, provide—

    (a)   for the electronic monitoring of the offender's whereabouts; or
    (b)   for the offender to have imposed on him any physical restriction on his movements.

    (4) No term which provides for anything to be done to or with any such victim or other affected person as is mentioned in subsection (2)(a) above may be included in the programme without the consent of that person.

(5) Where a programme is agreed between the offender and the panel, the panel shall cause a written record of the programme to be produced forthwith—

(*a*) in language capable of being readily understood by, or explained to, the offender; and
(*b*) for signature by him.

(6) Once the record has been signed—

(*a*) by the offender, and
(*b*) by a member of the panel on behalf of the panel,

the terms of the programme, as set out in the record, take effect as the terms of a "youth offender contract" between the offender and the panel; and the panel shall cause a copy of the record to be given or sent to the offender.
[Powers of Criminal Courts (Sentencing) Act 2000, s 23.]

3–1576   24. First meeting: duration of contract.   (1) This section applies where a youth offender contract has taken effect under section 23 above between an offender and a youth offender panel.

(2) The day on which the contract so takes effect shall be the first day of the period for which it has effect.

(3) Where the panel was established in pursuance of a single referral order, the length of the period for which the contract has effect shall be that of the period specified under section 18(1)(*c*) above in the referral order.

(4) Where the panel was established in pursuance of two or more associated referral orders, the length of the period for which the contract has effect shall be that resulting from the court's directions under section 18(6) above.

(5) Subsections (3) and (4) above have effect subject to—

(*a*) any order under paragraph 11 or 12 of Schedule 1 to this Act extending the length of the period for which the contract has effect; and
(*b*) subsection (6) below.

(6) If the referral order, or each of the associated referral orders, is revoked (whether under paragraph 5(2) of Schedule 1 to this Act or by virtue of paragraph 14(2) of that Schedule), the period for which the contract has effect expires at the time when the order or orders is or are revoked unless it has already expired.
[Powers of Criminal Courts (Sentencing) Act 2000, s 24.]

3–1577   25. First meeting: failure to agree contract.   (1) Where it appears to a youth offender panel to be appropriate to do so, the panel may—

(*a*) end the first meeting (or any further meeting held in pursuance of paragraph (*b*) below) without having reached agreement with the offender on a programme of behaviour of the kind mentioned in section 23(1) above; and
(*b*) resume consideration of the offender's case at a further meeting of the panel.

(2) If, however, it appears to the panel at the first meeting or any such further meeting that there is no prospect of agreement being reached with the offender within a reasonable period after the making of the referral order (or orders)—

(*a*) subsection (1)(*b*) above shall not apply; and
(*b*) instead the panel shall refer the offender back to the appropriate court.

(3) If at a meeting of the panel—

(*a*) agreement is reached with the offender but he does not sign the record produced in pursuance of section 23(5) above, and
(*b*) his failure to do so appears to the panel to be unreasonable,

the panel shall end the meeting and refer the offender back to the appropriate court.
[Powers of Criminal Courts (Sentencing) Act 2000, s 25.]

3–1578   26. Progress meetings.   (1) At any time—

(*a*) after a youth offender contract has taken effect under section 23 above, but
(*b*) before the end of the period for which the contract has effect,

the specified team shall, if so requested by the panel, arrange for the holding of a meeting of the panel under this section ("a progress meeting").

(2) The panel may make a request under subsection (1) above if it appears to the panel to be expedient to review—

(*a*) the offender's progress in implementing the programme of behaviour contained in the contract; or
(*b*) any other matter arising in connection with the contract.

(3) The panel shall make such a request if—

(*a*) the offender has notified the panel that—

(i) he wishes to seek the panel's agreement to a variation in the terms of the contract; or
(ii) he wishes the panel to refer him back to the appropriate court with a view to the referral order (or orders) being revoked on account of a significant change in his circumstances

(such as his being taken to live abroad) making compliance with any youth offender contract impractical; or

   (b) it appears to the panel that the offender is in breach of any of the terms of the contract.

(4) At a progress meeting the panel shall do such one or more of the following things as it considers appropriate in the circumstances, namely—

   (a) review the offender's progress or any such other matter as is mentioned in subsection (2) above;

   (b) discuss with the offender any breach of the terms of the contract which it appears to the panel that he has committed;

   (c) consider any variation in the terms of the contract sought by the offender or which it appears to the panel to be expedient to make in the light of any such review or discussion;

   (d) consider whether to accede to any request by the offender that he be referred back to the appropriate court.

(5) Where the panel has discussed with the offender such a breach as is mentioned in subsection (4)(b) above—

   (a) the panel and the offender may agree that the offender is to continue to be required to comply with the contract (either in its original form or with any agreed variation in its terms) without being referred back to the appropriate court; or

   (b) the panel may decide to end the meeting and refer the offender back to that court.

(6) Where a variation in the terms of the contract is agreed between the offender and the panel, the panel shall cause a written record of the variation to be produced forthwith—

   (a) in language capable of being readily understood by, or explained to, the offender; and

   (b) for signature by him.

(7) Any such variation shall take effect once the record has been signed—

   (a) by the offender; and

   (b) by a member of the panel on behalf of the panel;

and the panel shall cause a copy of the record to be given or sent to the offender.

(8) If at a progress meeting—

   (a) any such variation is agreed but the offender does not sign the record produced in pursuance of subsection (6) above, and

   (b) his failure to do so appears to the panel to be unreasonable,

the panel may end the meeting and refer the offender back to the appropriate court.

(9) Section 23(2) to (4) above shall apply in connection with what may be provided for by the terms of the contract as varied under this section as they apply in connection with what may be provided for by the terms of a programme of behaviour of the kind mentioned in section 23(1).

(10) Where the panel has discussed with the offender such a request as is mentioned in subsection (4)(d) above, the panel may, if it is satisfied that there is (or is soon to be) such a change in circumstances as is mentioned in subsection (3)(a)(ii) above, decide to end the meeting and refer the offender back to the appropriate court.
[Powers of Criminal Courts (Sentencing) Act 2000, s 26.]

3–1579 27. Final meeting. (1) Where the compliance period in the case of a youth offender contract is due to expire, the specified team shall arrange for the holding, before the end of that period, of a meeting of the panel under this section ("the final meeting").

(2) At the final meeting the panel shall—

   (a) review the extent of the offender's compliance to date with the terms of the contract; and

   (b) decide, in the light of that review, whether his compliance with those terms has been such as to justify the conclusion that, by the time the compliance period expires, he will have satisfactorily completed the contract;

and the panel shall give the offender written confirmation of its decision.

(3) Where the panel decides that the offender's compliance with the terms of the contract has been such as to justify that conclusion, the panel's decision shall have the effect of discharging the referral order (or orders) as from the end of the compliance period.

(4) Otherwise the panel shall refer the offender back to the appropriate court.

(5) Nothing in section 22(2) above prevents the panel from making the decision mentioned in subsection (3) above in the offender's absence if it appears to the panel to be appropriate to do that instead of exercising either of its powers under section 22(2).

(6) Section 22(2)(a) above does not permit the final meeting to be adjourned (or re-adjourned) to a time falling after the end of the compliance period.

(7) In this section "the compliance period", in relation to a youth offender contract, means the period for which the contract has effect in accordance with section 24 above.
[Powers of Criminal Courts (Sentencing) Act 2000, s 27.]

Further court proceedings

3–1580 28. Offender or parent referred back to court: offender convicted while subject to referral order. Schedule 1 to this Act, which—

(a) in Part I makes provision for what is to happen when a youth offender panel refers an offender back to the appropriate court, and

(aa) in Part 1A makes provision for what is to happen when a youth offender panel refers a parent or guardian to the court under section 22(2A) above, and

(b) in Part II makes provision for what is to happen when an offender is convicted of further offences while for the time being subject to a referral order,

shall have effect.

[Powers of Criminal Courts (Sentencing) Act 2000, s 28 as amended by the Criminal Justice Act 2003, Sch 34.]

Supplementary

3–1581   29. Functions of youth offending teams.   (1) The functions of a youth offending team responsible for implementing a referral order include, in particular, arranging for the provision of such administrative staff, accommodation or other facilities as are required by the youth offender panel established in pursuance of the order.

(2) During the period for which a youth offender contract between a youth offender panel and an offender has effect—

(a) the specified team shall make arrangements for supervising the offender's compliance with the terms of the contract; and

(b) the person who is the member of the panel referred to in section 21(3)(a) above shall ensure that records are kept of the offender's compliance (or non-compliance) with those terms.

(3) In implementing referral orders a youth offending team shall have regard to any guidance given from time to time by the Secretary of State.

[Powers of Criminal Courts (Sentencing) Act 2000, s 29.]

3–1582   30. Regulations under Part III.   (1) Any power of the Secretary of State to make regulations under section 17(3) or 21(4) above or paragraph 13(8) of Schedule 1 to this Act shall be exercisable by statutory instrument.

(2) A statutory instrument containing any regulations under section 21(4) shall be subject to annulment in pursuance of a resolution of either House of Parliament.

(3) No regulations shall be made under—

(a) section 17(3), or

(b) paragraph 13(8) of Schedule 1,

unless a draft of the regulations has been laid before, and approved by a resolution of, each House of Parliament.

(4) Any regulations made by the Secretary of State under section 17(3) or 21(4) or paragraph 13(8) of Schedule 1 may make different provision for different cases, circumstances or areas and may contain such incidental, supplemental, saving or transitional provisions as the Secretary of State thinks fit.

[Powers of Criminal Courts (Sentencing) Act 2000, s 30.]

3–1583   31. Rules of court.   (1) Criminal Procedure Rules may make such provision as appears to the Criminal Procedure Rule Committee to be necessary or expedient for the purposes of this Part (and nothing in this section shall be taken to affect the generality of any enactment conferring power to make such rules).

(2) *Repealed.*

[Powers of Criminal Courts (Sentencing) Act 2000, s 31 as amended by Si 2004/2035.]

3–1584   32. Definitions for purposes of Part III.   In this Part—

"the appropriate court" shall be construed in accordance with paragraph 1(2) of Schedule 1 to this Act;

"associated", in relation to referral orders, shall be construed in accordance with section 18(7) above;

"connected", in relation to offences, shall be construed in accordance with section 16(4) above;

"meeting", in relation to a youth offender panel, shall be construed in accordance with section 21(7) above;

"the specified team", in relation to an offender to whom a referral order applies (or two or more associated referral orders apply), means the youth offending team for the time being specified in the order (or orders).

[Powers of Criminal Courts (Sentencing) Act 2000, s 32.]

PART IV[1]
COMMUNITY ORDERS AND REPARATION ORDERS

CHAPTER I[2]
COMMUNITY ORDERS: GENERAL PROVISIONS

3–1585   33. Meaning of "youth community order" and "community sentence".   (1) In this Act "youth community order" means any of the following orders—

(a) a curfew order;

(b) an exclusion order;
(c) an attendance centre order;
(d) a supervision order;
(e) an action plan order.

(2) In this Act "community sentence" means a sentence which consists of or includes—

(a) a community order under section 177 of the Criminal Justice Act 2003, or
(b) one or more youth community orders.

[Powers of Criminal Courts (Sentencing) Act 2000, s 33 as substituted by the Criminal Justice Act 2003, Sch 32.]

---

1. Part IV contains ss 33–75 and Schs 2–8.
2. Chapter 1 contains ss 33–36.

3–1586   34. Community orders not available where sentence fixed by law etc.   None of the powers to make community orders which are conferred by this Part is exercisable in respect of an offence for which the sentence—

(a) is fixed by law; or
(b) falls to be imposed under section 109(2), 110(2) or 111(2) below (requirement to impose custodial sentences for certain repeated offences committed by offenders aged 18 or over).

[Powers of Criminal Courts (Sentencing) Act 2000, s 34.]

3–1587   35. Restrictions on imposing community sentences.   (1) A court shall not pass a community sentence on an offender unless it is of the opinion that the offence, or the combination of the offence and one or more offences associated with it, was serious enough to warrant such a sentence.

(2) In consequence of the provision made by section 51 below with respect to community punishment and rehabilitation orders, a community sentence shall not consist of or include both a community rehabilitation order and a community punishment order.[1]

(3) Subject to subsection (2) above and to section 69(5) below (which limits the community orders that may be combined with an action plan order), where a court passes a community sentence—

(a) the particular order or orders comprising or forming part of the sentence shall be such as in the opinion of the court is, or taken together are, the most suitable for the offender; and
(b) the restrictions on liberty imposed by the order or orders shall be such as in the opinion of the court are commensurate with the seriousness of the offence, or the combination of the offence and one or more offences associated with it.

(4) Subsections (1) and (3)(b) above have effect subject to section 59 below (curfew orders and community punishment orders for persistent petty offenders).

[Powers of Criminal Courts (Sentencing) Act 2000, s 35 as amended by the Criminal Justice and Court Services Act 2000, s 74.]

---

1. The effect of s 35(2) is to prevent a court from imposing a probation order and a community service order in relation to separate offences for which sentence is passed at the same hearing, except by way of a combination order under s 11, post; see *Gilding v DPP* (1998) Times, 20 May.

3–1588   36. Procedural requirements for community sentences: pre-sentence reports etc.
(1) In forming any such opinion as is mentioned in subsection (1) or (3)(b) of section 35 above, a court shall take into account all such information as is available to it about the circumstances of the offence or (as the case may be) of the offence and the offence or offences associated with it, including any aggravating or mitigating factors.

(2) In forming any such opinion as is mentioned in subsection (3)(a) of that section, a court may take into account any information about the offender which is before it.

(3) The following provisions of this section apply in relation to—

(a) a community rehabilitation order which includes additional requirements authorised by Schedule 2 to this Act;
(b) a community punishment order;
(c) a combination punishment and rehabilitation order;
(d) a drug treatment and testing order;
(e) a supervision order which includes requirements authorised by Schedule 6 to this Act.

(4) Subject to subsection (5) below, a court shall obtain and consider a pre-sentence report before forming an opinion as to the suitability for the offender of one or more of the orders mentioned in subsection (3) above[1].

(5) Subsection (4) above does not apply if, in the circumstances of the case, the court is of the opinion that it is unnecessary to obtain a pre-sentence report.

(6) In a case where the offender is aged under 18 and the offence is not triable only on indictment and there is no other offence associated with it that is triable only on indictment, the court shall not form such an opinion as is mentioned in subsection (5) above unless—

(a) there exists a previous pre-sentence report obtained in respect of the offender; and
(b) the court has had regard to the information contained in that report, or, if there is more than one such report, the most recent report.

(7) No community sentence which consists of or includes such an order as is mentioned in subsection (3) above shall be invalidated by the failure of a court to obtain and consider a pre-sentence report before forming an opinion as to the suitability of the order for the offender, but any court on an appeal against such a sentence—

(a) shall, subject to subsection (8) below, obtain a pre-sentence report if none was obtained by the court below; and

(b) shall consider any such report obtained by it or by that court.

(8) Subsection (7)(a) above does not apply if the court is of the opinion—

(a) that the court below was justified in forming an opinion that it was unnecessary to obtain a pre-sentence report; or

(b) that, although the court below was not justified in forming that opinion, in the circumstances of the case at the time it is before the court, it is unnecessary to obtain a pre-sentence report.

(9) In a case where the offender is aged under 18 and the offence is not triable only on indictment and there is no other offence associated with it that is triable only on indictment, the court shall not form such an opinion as is mentioned in subsection (8) above unless—

(a) there exists a previous pre-sentence report obtained in respect of the offender; and

(b) the court has had regard to the information contained in that report, or, if there is more than one such report, the most recent report.

(10) Section 156 below (disclosure of pre-sentence report to offender etc) applies to any pre-sentence report obtained in pursuance of this section.
[Powers of Criminal Courts (Sentencing) Act 2000, s 36 as amended by the Criminal Justice and Court Services Act 2000, s 74.]

---

1. The demands of a drug treatment and testing order and the need for the offender to be susceptible to treatment mean that a reasoned assessment should always be made, save in the most exceptional circumstances, of the offender's suitability for the order; and the court should be slow to act against the conclusions of a reasoned probation service assessment unless it has cogent reasons for doing so, see *R (on the application of Inner London Probation Service) v Tower Bridge Magistrates' Court* [2001] EWCH Admin 401, (2001) 165 JPN 394, [2001] 1 Cr App Rep (S) 179.

3–1589   36A. Pre-sentence drug testing.   (1) Where a person aged 18 or over is convicted of an offence and the court is considering passing a community sentence, it may make an order under subsection (2) below for the purpose of ascertaining whether the offender has any specified Class A drug in his body.

(2) The order shall require the offender to provide, in accordance with the order, samples of any description specified in the order.

(3) If it is proved to the satisfaction of the court that the offender has, without reasonable excuse, failed to comply with the order it may impose on him a fine of an amount not exceeding **level 4**.

In this subsection, "**level 4**" means the amount which, in relation to a fine for a summary offence, is level 4 on the standard scale.

(4) The court shall not make an order under subsection (2) above unless it has been notified by the Secretary of State that the power to make such orders is exercisable by the court and the notice has not been withdrawn.
[Powers of Criminal Courts (Sentencing) Act 2000, s 36A as inserted by the Criminal Justice and Court Services Act 2000, s 48.]

3–1590   36B. Electronic monitoring of requirement in community orders[1].   (1) Subject to subsections (2) to (4) below, a community order may include requirements for securing the electronic monitoring of the offender's compliance with any other requirements imposed by the order.

(2) A court shall not include in a community order a requirement under subsection (1) above unless the court—

(a) has been notified[2] by the Secretary of State that electronic monitoring arrangements are available in the relevant areas specified in subsections (7) to (10) below; and

(b) is satisfied that the necessary provision can be made under those arrangements.

(3) Where—

(a) it is proposed to include in an exclusion order a requirement for securing electronic monitoring in accordance with this section; but

(b) there is a person (other than the offender) without whose co-operation it will not be practicable to secure the monitoring,

the requirement shall not be included in the order without that person's consent.

(4) Where—

(a) it is proposed to include in a community rehabilitation order or a community punishment and rehabilitation order a requirement for securing the electronic monitoring of the offender's compliance with a requirement such as is mentioned in paragraph 8(1) of Schedule 2 to this Act; but

(b) there is a person (other than the offender) without whose co-operation it will not be practicable to secure the monitoring,

the requirement shall not be included in the order without that person's consent.

(5) An order which includes requirements under subsection (1) above shall include provision for making a person responsible for the monitoring; and a person who is made so responsible shall be of a description specified in an order³ made by the Secretary of State.

(6) The Secretary of State may make rules for regulating—

(a) the electronic monitoring of compliance with requirements included in a community order; and

(b) without prejudice to the generality of paragraph (a) above, the functions of persons made responsible for securing the electronic monitoring of compliance with requirements included in the order.

(7) In the case of a curfew order or an exclusion order, the relevant area is the area in which the place proposed to be specified in the order is situated.

In this subsection, "place", in relation to an exclusion order, has the same meaning as in section 40A below.

(8) In the case of a community rehabilitation order or a community punishment and rehabilitation order, the relevant areas are each of the following—

(a) where it is proposed to include in the order a requirement for securing compliance with a requirement such as is mentioned in sub-paragraph (1) of paragraph 7 of Schedule 2 to this Act, the area mentioned in sub-paragraph (5) of that paragraph;

(b) where it is proposed to include in the order a requirement for securing compliance with a requirement such as is mentioned in sub-paragraph (1) of paragraph 8 of that Schedule, the area mentioned in sub-paragraph (5) of that paragraph;

(c) where it is proposed to include in the order a requirement for securing compliance with any other requirement, the area proposed to be specified under section 41(3) below.

(9) In the case of a community punishment order, a drug treatment and testing order, a drug abstinence order, a supervision order or an action plan order, the relevant area is the petty sessions area proposed to be specified in the order.

(10) In the case of an attendance centre order, the relevant area is the petty sessions area in which the attendance centre proposed to be specified in the order is situated.★

[Powers of Criminal Courts (Sentencing) Act 2000, s 36B as inserted by the Criminal Justice and Court Services Act 2000, s 52.]

★Section amended by the Criminal Justice Act 2003, Sch 32 from a date to be appointed.

1. In relation to exclusion orders (but not exclusion requirements) this section was brought into force on 2 September 2004 by SI 2004/2171 but will apply only to those courts notified under sub-s (2).

2. For details of the piloting of electronic monitoring of a curfew as part of a community sentence and voice verification of the requirements of a community sentence, see Home Office Circular 34/2001. Courts in the police areas of West Midlands (Sandwell and Dudley only), Hampshire (Portsmouth and Southampton), Manchester (Salford and Bolton only) were notified by Home Office letter dated 24 August 2004 that arrangements for the electronic monitoring of exclusion orders under ss 36B and 40A by means of tracking were available as from 2 September 2004.

3. The Community Order (Electronic Monitoring of Requirements) (Responsible Officer) Order 2001, SI 2001/2233 amended by SI 2001/3346 and SI 2005/984 has been made.

CHAPTER II¹
COMMUNITY ORDERS AVAILABLE FOR OFFENDERS OF ANY AGE

Curfew orders

3–1591 37. Curfew orders. (1) Where a person aged under 16 is convicted of an offence, the court by or before which he is convicted may (subject to sections 148, 150 and 156 of the Criminal Justice Act 2003) make an order requiring him to remain, for periods specified in the order, at a place so specified.

(2) An order under subsection (1) above is in this Act referred to as a "curfew order".

(3) A curfew order may specify different places or different periods for different days, but shall not specify—

(a) periods which fall outside the period of six months beginning with the day on which it is made; or

(b) periods which amount to less than two hours or more than twelve hours in any one day.

(4) In relation to an offender aged under 16 on conviction, subsection (3)(a) above shall have effect as if the reference to six months were a reference to three months.★

(5) The requirements in a curfew order shall, as far as practicable, be such as to avoid—

(a) any conflict with the offender's religious beliefs or with the requirements of any other youth community order to which he may be subject; and

(b) any interference with the times, if any, at which he normally works or attends school or any other educational establishment.

(6) A curfew order shall include provision for making a person responsible for monitoring the offender's whereabouts during the curfew periods specified in the order; and a person who is made so responsible shall be of a description specified in an order² made by the Secretary of State.

(7) A court shall not make a curfew order unless the court has been notified³ by the Secretary of State that arrangements for monitoring the offender's whereabouts are available in the area in which the place proposed to be specified in the order is situated and the notice has not been withdrawn.

(8) Before making a curfew order, the court shall obtain and consider information about the place proposed to be specified in the order (including information as to the attitude of persons likely to be affected by the enforced presence there of the offender).

(9) Before making a curfew order in respect of an offender, the court shall obtain and consider information about his family circumstances and the likely effect of such an order on those circumstances.

(10) *Repealed.*

(11) The court by which a curfew order is made shall give a copy of the order to the offender and to the responsible officer.

(12) In this Act, "responsible officer", in relation to an offender subject to a curfew order, means—

(a) where the offender is also subject to a supervision order, the person who is the supervisor in relation to the supervision order, and

(b) in any other case, the person who is responsible for monitoring the offender's whereabouts during the curfew periods specified in the order.

[Powers of Criminal Courts (Sentencing) Act 2000, s 37 as amended by the Criminal Justice and Court Services Act 2000, s 74, the Anti-Social Behaviour Act 2003 and the Criminal Justice Act 2003, Sch 32.]

---

*Subsection (4) is omitted in relation to the following local authorities only: Birmingham City Council; Bolton Metropolitan Borough Council; Bridgend County Borough Council; Calderdale Metropolitan Borough Council; Cardiff County Council; City and County of Swansea Council; Coventry City Council; Kirklees Metropolitan Council; Leeds City Council; Liverpool City Council; London Borough of Barking and Dagenham; London Borough of Bexley; London Borough of Bromley; London Borough of Croydon; London Borough of Greenwich; London Borough of Havering; London Borough of Lewisham; London Borough of Merton; London Borough of Redbridge; London Borough of Richmond upon Thames; London Borough of Southwark; London Borough of Sutton; London Borough of Waltham Forest; Merthyr Tydfil County Borough Council; Neath Port Talbot County Borough Council; Nottingham City Council; Oldham Metropolitan Borough Council; Rhonda Cynon Taf County Borough Council; Royal Borough of Kingston upon Thames; Solihull Metropolitan Borough Council; Stockport Metropolitan Borough Council; Thameside Metropolitan Borough Council; and Vale of Glamorgan Council: see the Anti-social Behaviour Act 2003 (Commencement No 4) Order 2004, SI 2004/2168.

1. Chapter II contains ss 37–40.

2. The Curfew Order (Responsible Officer) Order 2001, SI 2001/2234 amended by SI 2001/3344 and SI 2005/984 has been made.

3. This section and section 38, post, re-enact ss 12 and 13 of the Criminal Justice Act 1991 which made provision for courts to impose curfew orders (with or without electronic monitoring) on those aged 16 or above and came into force on 9 January 1995. From this date curfew orders *without* electronic monitoring have been available throughout England and Wales for offenders aged 16 or over. Following pilot schemes in several areas, electronic monitoring of curfew orders has been available throughout England and Wales to support curfew orders on offenders aged 16 or over from 1 December 1999.

Curfew orders for offenders aged under 16 (with a maximum period of three months) have been available to all courts in England and Wales from 1 January 1998. Electronically-monitored curfew orders for offenders aged under 16 following pilot schemes in several areas have been made available to all courts in England and Wales from 1 February 2001.

3–1592 38. Electronic monitoring of curfew orders. *Repealed by the Criminal Justice and Court Services Act 2000, Sch 8.*

3–1593 39. Breach, revocation and amendment of curfew orders. Schedule 3 to this Act (which makes provision for dealing with failures to comply with the requirements of certain youth community orders, for revoking such orders with or without the substitution of other sentences and for amending such orders) shall have effect so far as relating to curfew orders.

[Powers of Criminal Courts (Sentencing) Act 2000, s 39 as amended by the Criminal Justice Act 2003, Sch 32.]

3–1594 40. Curfew orders: supplementary. (1) The Secretary of State may make rules for regulating—

(a) the monitoring of the whereabouts of persons who are subject to curfew orders; and

(b) without prejudice to the generality of paragraph (a) above, the functions of the responsible officers of persons who are subject to curfew orders.

(2) The Secretary of State may by order direct—

(a) that subsection (3) of section 37 above shall have effect with the substitution, for any period there specified, of such period as may be specified in the order; or

(b) that subsection (5) of that section shall have effect with such additional restrictions as may be so specified.

(3) An order under subsection (2)(a) above may make in paragraphs 2A(4) and (5) and 19(3)** of Schedule 3 to this Act any amendment which the Secretary of State thinks necessary in consequence of any substitution made by the order.*

[Powers of Criminal Courts (Sentencing) Act 2000, s 40 amended by the Criminal Justice and Court Services Act 2000, s 74.]

---

*In force except in so far as it relates to "2A(4) and (5) and 19(3)". Date in force for remaining purposes, to be appointed.

**Substituted by the Criminal Justice Act 2003, Sch 32 from a date to be appointed.

3–1595   40A. Exclusion orders[1].   (1) Where a person aged under 16 is convicted of an offence, the court by or before which he is convicted may (subject to sections 148, 150 and 156 of the Criminal Justice Act 2003) make an order prohibiting him from entering a place specified in the order for a period so specified of not more than three months.

(2) An order under subsection (1) above is in this Act referred to as an "exclusion order".

(3) An exclusion order—

(*a*) may provide for the prohibition to operate only during the periods specified in the order;

(*b*) may specify different places for different periods or days.

(4) *Repealed.*

(5) The requirements in an exclusion order shall, as far as practicable, be such as to avoid—

(*a*) any conflict with the offender's religious beliefs or with the requirements of any other youth community order to which he may be subject; and

(*b*) any interference with the times, if any, at which he normally works or attends school or any other educational establishment.

(6) An exclusion order shall include provision for making a person responsible for monitoring the offender's whereabouts during the periods when the prohibition operates; and a person who is made so responsible shall be of a description specified in an order[2] made by the Secretary of State.

(7) An exclusion order shall specify the petty sessions area in which the offender resides or will reside.

(8) A court shall not make an exclusion order unless the court has been notified[3] by the Secretary of State that arrangements for monitoring the offender's whereabouts are available in the area in which the place proposed to be specified in the order is situated and the notice has not been withdrawn.

(9) Before making an exclusion order in respect of an offender, the court shall obtain and consider information about his family circumstances and the likely effect of such an order on those circumstances.

(10) *Repealed.*

(11) The court by which an exclusion order is made shall—

(*a*) give a copy of the order to the offender and the responsible officer; and

(*b*) give to any affected person any information relating to the order which the court considers it appropriate for him to have.

(12) In this section, "place" includes an area.

(13) For the purposes of this Act, a person is an affected person in relation to an exclusion order if—

(*a*) a requirement under section 36B(1) above is included in the order by virtue of his consent; or

(*b*) a prohibition is included in the order for the purpose (or partly for the purpose) of protecting him from being approached by the offender.

(14) In this Act, "responsible officer", in relation to an offender subject to an exclusion order, means the person who is responsible for monitoring the offender's whereabouts during the periods when the prohibition operates.

[Powers of Criminal Courts (Sentencing) Act 2000, s 40A as inserted by the Criminal Justice and Courts Services Act 2000, s 46 and amended by the Criminal Justice Act 2003, Sch 32.]

---

1. This section was brought into force on 2 September 2004 by SI 2004/2171 but will apply only to those courts notified under sub-s (8).

2. The Exclusion Order (Monitoring of Offenders) Order 2005, SI 2005/979 has been made.

3. Courts in the police areas of West Midlands (Sandwell and Dudley only), Hampshire (Portsmouth and Southampton), Manchester (Salford and Bolton only) were notified by Home Office letter dated 24 August 2004 that arrangements for the electronic monitoring of exclusion orders under ss 36B and 40A by means of tracking were available as from 2 September 2004 (see HOC 61/2004).

3–1596   40B. Breach, revocation and amendment of exclusion orders.   Schedule 3 to this Act (which makes provision for dealing with failures to comply with the requirements of certain youth community orders, for revoking such orders with or without the substitution of other sentences and for amending such orders) shall have effect so far as relating to exclusion orders.

[Powers of Criminal Courts (Sentencing) Act 2000, s 40B as inserted by the Criminal Justice and Courts Services Act 2000, s 46 and amended by the Criminal Justice Act 2003, Sch 32.]

3–1597   40C. Exclusion orders: supplementary.   (1) The Secretary of State may make rules for regulating—

(*a*) the monitoring of the whereabouts of persons who are subject to exclusion orders; and

(*b*) without prejudice to the generality of paragraph (*a*) above, the functions of persons who are responsible officers in relation to offenders subject to exclusion orders.

(2) The Secretary of State may by order direct that section 40A(5) above shall have effect with such additional restrictions as may be specified in the order.

[Powers of Criminal Courts (Sentencing) Act 2000, s 40C as inserted by the Criminal Justice and Courts Services Act 2000, s 46.]

CHAPTER III

COMMUNITY ORDERS AVAILABLE ONLY WHERE OFFENDER AGED 16 OR OVER

Community rehabilitation orders²

3–1598　41–59. *Repealed.*

CHAPTER IV¹

ATTENDANCE CENTRE ORDERS: OFFENDERS UNDER 21 AND DEFAULTERS

3–1619　60. Attendance centre orders.　(1) Where—

(a) (subject to sections 148, 150 and 156 of the Criminal Justice Act 2003) a person aged under 16 is convicted by or before a court of an offence punishable with imprisonment, or

(b) a court* would have power, but for section 89 below (restrictions on imprisonment of young offenders and defaulters), to commit a person aged under 21 to prison in default of payment of any sum of money or for failing to do or abstain from doing anything required to be done or left undone, <u>or</u>

(c) a court has power to commit a person aged at least 21 but under 25 to prison in default of payment of any sum of money,*

the court may, if it has been notified² by the Secretary of State that an attendance centre is available for the reception of persons of his description, order him to attend at such a centre, to be specified in the order, for such number of hours as may be so specified.

(2) An order under subsection (1) above is in this Act referred to as an "attendance centre order".

(3) The aggregate number of hours for which an attendance centre order may require a person to attend at an attendance centre shall not be less than 12 except where—

(a) he is aged under 14; and

(b) the court is of the opinion that 12 hours would be excessive, having regard to his age or any other circumstances.

(4) The aggregate number of hours shall not exceed 12 except where the court is of the opinion, having regard to all the circumstances, that 12 hours would be inadequate, and in that case—

(a) shall not exceed 24 where the person is aged under 16; and

(b) shall not exceed 36 where the person is aged 16 or over but under 21 or (where subsection (1)(c) above applies) under 25.**

(5) A court may make an attendance centre order in respect of a person before a previous attendance centre order made in respect of him has ceased to have effect, and may determine the number of hours to be specified in the order without regard—

(a) to the number specified in the previous order; or

(b) to the fact that that order is still in effect.

(6) An attendance centre order shall not be made unless the court is satisfied that the attendance centre to be specified in it is reasonably accessible to the person concerned, having regard to his age, the means of access available to him and any other circumstances.

(7) The times at which a person is required to attend at an attendance centre shall, as far as practicable, be such as to avoid—

(a) any conflict with his religious beliefs or with the requirements of any other community order to which he may be subject; and

(b) any interference with the times, if any, at which he normally works or attends school or any other educational establishment.

(8) The first time at which the person is required to attend at an attendance centre shall be a time at which the centre is available for his attendance in accordance with the notification of the Secretary of State, and shall be specified in the order.

(9) The subsequent times shall be fixed by the officer in charge of the centre, having regard to the person's circumstances.

(10) A person shall not be required under this section to attend at an attendance centre on more than one occasion on any day, or for more than three hours on any occasion.

(11) Where a court makes an attendance centre order, the designated officer for the court shall—

(a) deliver or send a copy of the order to the officer in charge of the attendance centre specified in it; and

(b) deliver a copy of the order to the person in respect of whom it is made or send a copy by registered post or the recorded delivery service addressed to his last or usual place of abode.

(12) Where a person ("the defaulter") has been ordered to attend at an attendance centre in default of the payment of any sum of money—

(a) on payment of the whole sum to any person authorised to receive it, the attendance centre order shall cease to have effect;

(b) on payment of a part of the sum to any such person, the total number of hours for which the defaulter is required to attend at the centre shall be reduced proportionately, that is to say by such number of complete hours as bears to the total number the proportion most nearly approximating to, without exceeding, the proportion which the part bears to the whole sum.

[Powers of Criminal Courts (Sentencing) Act 2000, s 60, as amended by SI 2001/618 and the Criminal Justice Act 2003, Sch 32.]

---

*Additional text to be inserted by the Criminal Justice and Court Services Act 2000, Sch 7 from a date to be appointed.
**Amended by the Criminal Justice Act 2003, Sch 32 from a date to be appointed,
    1. Chapter IV contains ss 60–62 and Sch 5.
    2. See Home Office Circulars No 22/1986, dated 8 April 1986, No 58/1986, dated 19 August 1986, which list the attendance centres available to the Crown Court and all magistrates' courts and No 59/1987, dated 16 October 1987 and 72/1992, dated 28 July 1992. For further information about attendance centres, including their addresses, and the names, addresses and telephone numbers of the Officers-in-Charge, reference should be made to the Directory of Attendance Centres in England and Wales issued by the Home Office (25 August 1998).

3–1620 61. Breach, revocation and amendment of attendance centre orders. Schedule 5 to this Act (which makes provision for dealing with failures to comply with attendance centre orders, for revoking such orders with or without the substitution of other sentences and for amending such orders) shall have effect.
[Powers of Criminal Courts (Sentencing) Act 2000, s 61.]

3–1621 62. Provision, regulation and management of attendance centres. *Repealed.*

CHAPTER V[1]

COMMUNITY ORDERS AVAILABLE ONLY WHERE OFFENDER AGED UNDER 18

Supervision orders[2]

3–1622 63. Supervision orders. (1) Where a child or young person (that is to say, any person aged under 18) is convicted of an offence, the court by or before which he is convicted may (subject to s sections 148, 150 and 156 of the Criminal Justice Act 2003make an order placing him under the supervision of—

    (a) a local authority designated by the order;
    (b) an officer of a local probation board; or
    (c) a member of a youth offending team.

    (2) An order under subsection (1) above is in this Act referred to as a "supervision order".
    (3) In this Act "supervisor", in relation to a supervision order, means the person under whose supervision the offender is placed or to be placed by the order.
    (4) Schedule 6 to this Act (which specifies requirements that may be included in supervision orders) shall have effect.
    (5) A court shall not make a supervision order unless it is satisfied that the offender resides or will reside in the area of a local authority; and a court shall be entitled to be satisfied that the offender will so reside if he is to be required so to reside by a provision to be included in the order in pursuance of paragraph 1 of Schedule 6 to this Act.
    (6) A supervision order—

    (a) shall name the area of the local authority and the local justice area in which it appears to the court making the order (or to the court amending under Schedule 7 to this Act any provision included in the order in pursuance of this paragraph) that the offender resides or will reside; and
    (b) may contain such prescribed provisions as the court making the order (or amending it under that Schedule) considers appropriate for facilitating the performance by the supervisor of his functions under section 64(4) below, including any prescribed provisions for requiring visits to be made by the offender to the supervisor;

and in paragraph (b) above "prescribed" means prescribed by Criminal Procedure Rules.
    (7) A supervision order shall, unless it has previously been revoked, cease to have effect at the end of the period of three years, or such shorter period as may be specified in the order, beginning with the date on which the order was originally made.
    (8) A court which makes a supervision order shall forthwith send a copy of its order—

    (a) to the offender and, if the offender is aged under 14, to his parent or guardian;
    (b) to the supervisor;
    (c) to any local authority who are not entitled by virtue of paragraph (b) above to such a copy and whose area is named in the supervision order in pursuance of subsection (6) above;
    (d) where the offender is required by the order to reside with an individual or to undergo treatment by or under the direction of an individual or at any place, to the individual or the person in charge of that place; and
    (e) where a local justice area named in the order in pursuance of subsection (6) above is not that in which the court acts, to the designated officer for the local justice area so named;

and, in a case falling within paragraph (e) above, shall also send to the designated officer in question such documents and information relating to the case as the court considers likely to be of assistance to them.
    (9) If a court makes a supervision order while another such order made by any court is in force in respect of the offender, the court making the new order may revoke the earlier order (and paragraph 10 of Schedule 7 to this Act (supplementary provision) shall apply to the revocation).

[Powers of Criminal Courts (Sentencing) Act 2000, s 63, as amended by the Criminal Justice and Court Services Act 2000, s 74, the Criminal Justice Act 2003, Sch 32, SI 2004/2035 and SI 2005/886.]

---

1. Chapter V contains ss 63–72 and Sch 6–8.
2. For full discussion of this power see PART V: YOUTH COURTS, para **5–49**, post.

3–1623   64. Selection and duty of supervisor and certain expenditure of his.   (1) A court shall not designate a local authority as the supervisor by a provision of a supervision order unless—

(*a*) the authority agree; or

(*b*) it appears to the court that the offender resides or will reside in the area of the authority.

(2) Where a provision of a supervision order places the offender under the supervision of an officer of a local probation board, the supervisor shall be an officer of a local probation board appointed for or assigned to the local justice area named in the order in pursuance of section 63(6) above.

(3) Where a provision of a supervision order places the offender under the supervision of a member of a youth offending team, the supervisor shall be a member of a team established by the local authority within whose area it appears to the court that the offender resides or will reside.

(4) While a supervision order is in force, the supervisor shall advise, assist and befriend the offender.

(5) Where a supervision order—

(*a*) requires compliance with directions given by virtue of paragraph 2(1) of Schedule 6 to this Act, or

(*b*) includes by virtue of paragraph 3(2) of that Schedule a requirement which involves the use of facilities for the time being specified in a scheme in force under section 66 below for an area in which the offender resides or will reside,

any expenditure incurred by the supervisor for the purposes of the directions or requirements shall be defrayed by the local authority whose area is named in the order in pursuance of section 63(6) above.*

[Powers of Criminal Courts (Sentencing) Act 2000, s 64, as amended by the Criminal Justice and Court Services Act 2000, s 74 and SI 2005/886.]

3–1623A   64A. Supervision orders and curfew orders¹.   Nothing in this Chapter prevents a court which makes a supervision order in respect of an offender from also making a curfew order in respect of him.

[Powers of Criminal Courts (Sentencing) Act 2000, s 64A, as inserted by the Anti-social Behaviour Act 2003, Sch 2.]

---

1. Intensive Supervision and Surveillance Programmes (ISSP) are available under supervision orders and curfew orders. These allow intensive forms of supervision to run for up to 12 months. At the time of going to press, the following local authority areas were participating in ISSP pilot schemes: Birmingham City Council; Bolton Metropolitan Borough Council; Bridgend County Borough Council; Calderdale Metropolitan Borough Council; Cardiff County Council; City and County of Swansea Council; Coventry City Council; Kirklees Metropolitan Council; Leeds City Council; Liverpool City Council; London Borough of Barking and Dagenham; London Borough of Bexley; London Borough of Bromley; London Borough of Croydon; London Borough of Greenwich; London Borough of Havering; London Borough of Lewisham; London Borough of Merton; London Borough of Redbridge; London Borough of Richmond upon Thames; London Borough of Southwark; London Borough of Sutton; London Borough of Waltham Forest; Merthyr Tydfil County Borough Council; Neath Port Talbot County Borough Council; Nottingham City Council; Oldham Metropolitan Borough Council; Rhonda Cynon Taf County Borough Council; Royal Borough of Kingston upon Thames; Solihull Metropolitan Borough Council; Stockport Metropolitan Borough Council; Thameside Metropolitan Borough Council; and Vale of Glamorgan Council.

[Powers of Criminal Courts (Sentencing) Act 2000, s 64A inserted by the Anti-social Behaviour Act 2003, Sch 2.]

3–1624   65. Breach, revocation and amendment of supervision orders.   Schedule 7 to this Act (which makes provision for dealing with failures to comply with supervision orders and for revoking and amending such orders) shall have effect.

[Powers of Criminal Courts (Sentencing) Act 2000, s 65.]

3–1625   66. Facilities for implementing supervision orders.   (1) A local authority shall, acting either individually or in association with other local authorities, make arrangements with such persons as appear to them to be appropriate for the provision by those persons of facilities for enabling—

(*a*) directions given by virtue of paragraph 2(1) of Schedule 6 to this Act to persons resident in their area, and

(*b*) requirements that (because of paragraph 3(7) of that Schedule) may only be included in a supervision order by virtue of paragraph 3(2) of that Schedule if they are for the time being specified in a scheme,

to be carried out effectively.

(2) The authority or authorities making any arrangements in accordance with subsection (1) above shall consult each relevant local probation board as to the arrangements.

(3) Any such arrangements shall be specified in a scheme made by the authority or authorities making them.

(4) A scheme shall come into force on a date to be specified in it.

(5) The authority or authorities making a scheme shall send copies of it to the designated officer for each local justice area of which any part is included in the area to which the scheme relates.

(6) A copy of the scheme shall be kept available at the principal office of every authority who are a party to it for inspection by members of the public at all reasonable hours; and any such authority shall on demand by any person supply him with a copy of the scheme free of charge.

(7) The authority or authorities who made a scheme may at any time make a further scheme altering the arrangements or specifying arrangements to be substituted for those previously specified.

(8) A scheme which specifies arrangements to be substituted for those specified in a previous scheme shall revoke the previous scheme.

(9) The powers conferred by subsection (7) above shall not be exercisable by an authority or authorities unless they have first consulted each relevant local probation board.

(10) The authority or authorities who made a scheme shall send to the designated officer for each local justice area of which any part is included in the area for which arrangements under this section have been specified in the scheme notice of any exercise of a power conferred by subsection (7) above, specifying the date for the coming into force, and giving details of the effect, of the new or altered arrangements; and the new or altered arrangements shall come into force on that date.

(11) Arrangements shall not be made under this section for the provision of any facilities unless the facilities are approved or are of a kind approved by the Secretary of State for the purposes of this section.

(12) In this section "relevant local probation board" means a local probation board for an area of which any part is included in the area to which a scheme under this section relates.
[Powers of Criminal Courts (Sentencing) Act 2000, s 66 as amended by the Criminal Justice and Court Services Act 2000, s 74 and SI 2005/886.]

3–1626　67. Meaning of "local authority", "reside" and "parent".　(1) Unless the contrary intention appears, in sections 63 to 66 above and Schedules 6 and 7 to this Act—

"local authority" means the council of a county or of a county borough, metropolitan district or London borough or the Common Council of the City of London;
"reside" means habitually reside, and cognate expressions shall be construed accordingly except in paragraph 6(2) and (3) of Schedule 6.

(2) In the case of a child or young person—

(*a*)　whose father and mother were not married to each other at the time of his birth, and
(*b*)　with respect to whom a residence order is in force in favour of the father,

any reference in sections 63 to 66 and Schedules 6 and 7 to the parent of the child or young person includes a reference to the father.

(3) In subsection (2) above "residence order" has the meaning given by section 8(1) of the Children Act 1989, and subsection (2) above is without prejudice to the operation of section 1(1) of the Family Law Reform Act 1987 (construction of references to relationships) in relation to the provisions of this Act other than those mentioned in subsection (2).
[Powers of Criminal Courts (Sentencing) Act 2000, s 67.]

3–1627　68. Isles of Scilly.　(1) In their application to the Isles of Scilly, the following provisions of this Act, namely—

(*a*)　sections 63 to 67 and Schedules 6 and 7, and
(*b*)　section 163 (definitions) in its application to those sections and Schedules,

shall have effect with such modifications as the Secretary of State may by order specify.

(2) An order under this section may—

(*a*)　make different provision for different circumstances;
(*b*)　provide for exemptions from any provisions of the order; and
(*c*)　contain such incidental and supplemental provisions as the Secretary of State considers expedient for the purposes of the order.
[Powers of Criminal Courts (Sentencing) Act 2000, s 68.]

Action plan orders[1]

3–1628　69. Action plan orders.　(1) Where a child or young person (that is to say, any person aged under 18) is convicted of an offence and the court by or before which he is convicted is of the opinion mentioned in subsection (3) below, the court may (subject to sections 148, 150 and 156 of the Criminal Justice Act 2003) make an order which—

(*a*)　requires the offender, for a period of three months beginning with the date of the order, to comply with an action plan, that is to say, a series of requirements with respect to his actions and whereabouts during that period;
(*b*)　places the offender for that period under the supervision of the responsible officer; and
(*c*)　requires the offender to comply with any directions given by the responsible officer with a view to the implementation of that plan;

and the requirements included in the order, and any directions given by the responsible officer, may include requirements authorised by section 70 below.

(2) An order under subsection (1) above is in this Act referred to as an "action plan order".

(3) The opinion referred to in subsection (1) above is that the making of an action plan order is desirable in the interests of—

(a) securing the rehabilitation of the offender; or
(b) preventing the commission by him of further offences.

(4) In this Act "responsible officer", in relation to an offender subject to an action plan order, means one of the following who is specified in the order, namely—

(a) an officer of a local probation board;
(b) a social worker of a local authority;
(c) a member of a youth offending team.

(5) The court shall not make an action plan order in respect of the offender if—

(a) he is already the subject of such an order; or
(b) the court proposes to pass on him a custodial sentence or to make in respect of him a community order under section 177 of the Criminal Justice Act 2003, an attendance centre order, a supervision order or a referral order.

(6) Before making an action plan order, the court shall obtain and consider—

(a) a written report by an officer of a local probation board, a social worker of a local authority or a member of a youth offending team indicating—

(i) the requirements proposed by that person to be included in the order;
(ii) the benefits to the offender that the proposed requirements are designed to achieve; and
(iii) the attitude of a parent or guardian of the offender to the proposed requirements; and

(b) where the offender is aged under 16, information about the offender's family circumstances and the likely effect of the order on those circumstances.

(7) The court shall not make an action plan order unless it has been notified[2] by the Secretary of State that arrangements for implementing such orders are available in the area proposed to be named in the order under subsection (8) below and the notice has not been withdrawn.

(8) An action plan order shall name the local justice area in which it appears to the court making the order (or to the court amending under Schedule 8 to this Act any provision included in the order in pursuance of this subsection) that the offender resides or will reside.

(9) Where an action plan order specifies an officer of a local probation board under subsection (4) above, the officer specified must be an officer appointed for or assigned to the local justice area named in the order.

(10) Where an action plan order specifies under that subsection—

(a) a social worker of a local authority, or
(b) a member of a youth offending team,

the social worker or member specified must be a social worker of, or a member of a youth offending team established by, the local authority within whose area it appears to the court that the offender resides or will reside.

(11) *Repealed.*

[Powers of Criminal Courts (Sentencing) Act 2000, s 69, as amended by the Criminal Justice and Court Services Act 2000, s 74, the Children Act 2004, Sch 5 and SI 2005/886.]

---

1. For full discussion of this power see PART V: YOUTH COURTS, para **5–47D**, post.
2. All courts in England and Wales have been notified by Home Office letter dated 27 April 2000 that such orders were available from 1 June 2000.

3–1629　70. Requirements which may be included in action plan orders and directions.
(1) Requirements included in an action plan order, or directions given by a responsible officer, may require the offender to do all or any of the following things, namely—

(a) to participate in activities specified in the requirements or directions at a time or times so specified;
(b) to present himself to a person or persons specified in the requirements or directions at a place or places and at a time or times so specified;
(c) subject to subsection (2) below, to attend at an attendance centre specified in the requirements or directions for a number of hours so specified;
(d) to stay away from a place or places specified in the requirements or directions;
(e) to comply with any arrangements for his education specified in the requirements or directions;
(f) to make reparation specified in the requirements or directions to a person or persons so specified or to the community at large; and
(g) to attend any hearing fixed by the court under section 71 below.

(2) Subsection (1)(c) above applies only where the offence committed by the offender is an offence punishable with imprisonment.

(3) In subsection (1)(f) above "make reparation", in relation to an offender, means make reparation for the offence otherwise than by the payment of compensation.

(4) A person shall not be specified in requirements or directions under subsection (1)(f) above unless—

(*a*) he is identified by the court or (as the case may be) the responsible officer as a victim of the offence or a person otherwise affected by it; and

(*b*) he consents to the reparation being made.

(5) Requirements included in an action plan order and directions given by a responsible officer shall, as far as practicable, be such as to avoid—

(*a*) any conflict with the offender's religious beliefs or with the requirements of any other community order to which he may be subject; and

(*b*) any interference with the times, if any, at which he normally works or attends school or any other educational establishment.

[Powers of Criminal Courts (Sentencing) Act 2000, s 70.]

3–1630   71. Action plan orders: power to fix further hearings. (1) Immediately after making an action plan order, a court may—

(*a*) fix a further hearing for a date not more than 21 days after the making of the order; and

(*b*) direct the responsible officer to make, at that hearing, a report as to the effectiveness of the order and the extent to which it has been implemented.

(2) At a hearing fixed under subsection (1) above, the court—

(*a*) shall consider the responsible officer's report; and

(*b*) may, on the application of the responsible officer or the offender, amend the order—

(i) by cancelling any provision included in it; or

(ii) by inserting in it (either in addition to or in substitution for any of its provisions) any provision that the court could originally have included in it.

[Powers of Criminal Courts (Sentencing) Act 2000, s 71.]

3–1631   72. Breach, revocation and amendment of action plan orders. Schedule 8 to this Act (which makes provision for dealing with failures to comply with action plan orders and reparation orders and for revoking and amending such orders) shall have effect so far as relating to action plan orders.

[Powers of Criminal Courts (Sentencing) Act 2000, s 72.]

CHAPTER VI[1]
REPARATION ORDERS FOR YOUNG OFFENDERS[2]

3–1632   73. Reparation orders. (1) Where a child or young person (that is to say, any person aged under 18) is convicted of an offence other than one for which the sentence is fixed by law, the court by or before which he is convicted may make an order requiring him to make reparation specified in the order—

(*a*) to a person or persons so specified; or

(*b*) to the community at large;

and any person so specified must be a person identified by the court as a victim of the offence or a person otherwise affected by it.

(2) An order under subsection (1) above is in this Act referred to as a "reparation order".

(3) In this section and section 74 below "make reparation", in relation to an offender, means make reparation for the offence otherwise than by the payment of compensation; and the requirements that may be specified in a reparation order are subject to section 74(1) to (3).

(4) The court shall not make a reparation order in respect of the offender if it proposes—

(*a*) to pass on him a custodial sentence; or

(*b*) to make in respect of him a community order under section 177 of the Criminal Justice Act 2003, a supervision order which includes requirements authorised by Schedule 6 to this Act, an action plan order or a referral order.

(5) Before making a reparation order, a court shall obtain and consider a written report by an officer of a local probation board, a social worker of a local authority or a member of a youth offending team indicating—

(*a*) the type of work that is suitable for the offender; and

(*b*) the attitude of the victim or victims to the requirements proposed to be included in the order.

(6) The court shall not make a reparation order unless it has been notified[3] by the Secretary of State that arrangements for implementing such orders are available in the area proposed to be named in the order under section 74(4) below and the notice has not been withdrawn.

(7) *Repealed.*

(8) The court shall give reasons if it does not make a reparation order in a case where it has power to do so.

[Powers of Criminal Courts (Sentencing) Act 2000, s 73, as amended by the Criminal Justice and Court Services Act 2000, s 74, the Criminal Justice Act 2003, Sch 32 and the Children Act 2004, Sch 5.]

---

1. Chapter VI contains ss 73–75.

2. For full discussion of this power see PART V: YOUTH COURTS, para **5–47C**, post.

3. All courts in England and Wales have been notified by Home Office letter dated 27 April 2000 that such orders were available from 1 June 2000.

3–1633   74. Requirements and provisions of reparation order, and obligations of person subject to it. (1) A reparation order shall not require the offender—

(a)   to work for more than 24 hours in aggregate; or
(b)   to make reparation to any person without the consent of that person.

(2) Subject to subsection (1) above, requirements specified in a reparation order shall be such as in the opinion of the court are commensurate with the seriousness of the offence, or the combination of the offence and one or more offences associated with it.

(3) Requirements so specified shall, as far as practicable, be such as to avoid—

(a)   any conflict with the offender's religious beliefs or with the requirements of any community order or any youth community order to which he may be subject; and
(b)   any interference with the times, if any, at which he normally works or attends school or any other educational establishment.

(4) A reparation order shall name the local justice area in which it appears to the court making the order (or to the court amending under Schedule 8 to this Act any provision included in the order in pursuance of this subsection) that the offender resides or will reside.

(5) In this Act "responsible officer", in relation to an offender subject to a reparation order, means one of the following who is specified in the order, namely—

(a)   an officer of a local probation board;
(b)   a social worker of a local authority;
(c)   a member of a youth offending team.

(6) Where a reparation order specifies an officer of a local probation board under subsection (5) above, the officer specified must be an officer appointed for or assigned to the local justice area named in the order.

(7) Where a reparation order specifies under that subsection—

(a)   a social worker of a local authority, or
(b)   a member of a youth offending team,

the social worker or member specified must be a social worker of, or a member of a youth offending team established by, the local authority within whose area it appears to the court that the offender resides or will reside.

(8) Any reparation required by a reparation order—

(a)   shall be made under the supervision of the responsible officer; and
(b)   shall be made within a period of three months from the date of the making of the order.
[Powers of Criminal Courts (Sentencing) Act 2000, s 74, as amended by the Criminal Justice and Court Services Act 2000, s 74, the Criminal Justice Act 2003, Sch 32, SI 2005/886 and the Children Act 2004, Sch 5.]

3–1634   75. Breach, revocation and amendment of reparation orders. Schedule 8 to this Act (which makes provision for dealing with failures to comply with action plan orders and reparation orders and for revoking and amending such orders) shall have effect so far as relating to reparation orders.
[Powers of Criminal Courts (Sentencing) Act 2000, s 75.]

PART V[1]
CUSTODIAL SENTENCES ETC[2]

CHAPTER I[3]
GENERAL PROVISIONS
Meaning of "custodial sentence"

3–1635   76. Meaning of "custodial sentence". (1) In this Act "custodial sentence" means—

(a)   a sentence of imprisonment (as to which, see section 89(1)(a) below);
(b)   a sentence of detention under section 90 or 91 below;
(bb) a sentence of detention for public protection under section 226 of the Criminal Justice Act 2003;
(bc) a sentence of detention under section 228 of that Act;
(c)   a sentence of custody for life under section 93 or 94 below;★
(d)   a sentence of detention in a young offender institution (under section 96 below or otherwise); or★
(e)   a detention and training order (under section 100 below).

(2) In subsection (1) above "sentence of imprisonment" does not include a committal for contempt of court or any kindred offence.
[Powers of Criminal Courts (Sentencing) Act 2000, s 76 as amended by the Criminal Justice Act 2003, Sch 32.]

★Repealed by the Criminal Justice and Court Services Act 2000, Sch 7 from a date to be appointed.
1. Part V contains ss 76–125.
2. Chapter 1 contains ss 76–88.
3. For a discussion on custodial sentences see ante paras **3–218** to **3–241**.

Liability to imprisonment on conviction on indictment

3–1636   **77. Liability to imprisonment on conviction on indictment.**   Where a person is convicted on indictment of an offence against any enactment and is for that offence liable to be sentenced to imprisonment, but the sentence is not by any enactment either limited to a specified term or expressed to extend to imprisonment for life, the person so convicted shall be liable to imprisonment for not more than two years.
[Powers of Criminal Courts (Sentencing) Act 2000, s 77.]

General limit on magistrates' courts' powers

3–1637   **78. General limit on magistrates' court's power to impose imprisonment or detention in a young offender institution*.**   (1) A magistrates' court shall not have power to impose imprisonment, or detention in a young offender institution,* for more than six months in respect of any one offence.

(2) Unless expressly excluded, subsection (1) above shall apply even if the offence in question is one for which a person would otherwise be liable on summary conviction to imprisonment or detention in a young offender institution* for more than six months.

(3) Subsection (1) above is without prejudice to section 133 of the Magistrates' Courts Act 1980 (consecutive terms of imprisonment).

(4) Any power of a magistrates' court to impose a term of imprisonment for non-payment of a fine, or for want of sufficient distress to satisfy a fine, shall not be limited by virtue of subsection (1) above.

(5) In subsection (4) above "fine" includes a pecuniary penalty but does not include a pecuniary forfeiture or pecuniary compensation.

(6) In this section "impose imprisonment" means pass a sentence of imprisonment or fix a term of imprisonment for failure to pay any sum of money, or for want of sufficient distress to satisfy any sum of money, or for failure to do or abstain from doing anything required to be done or left undone.

(7) Section 132 of the Magistrates' Courts Act 1980 contains provision about the minimum term of imprisonment which may be imposed by a magistrates' court.**
[Powers of Criminal Courts (Sentencing) Act 2000, s 78.]

---

*Words 'or detention in a young offender institution' repealed by the Criminal Justice and Court Services Act 2000, Sch 7 from a date to be appointed.
**Section repealed the Criminal Justice Act 2003, Sch 32 from a date to be appointed.

General restrictions on discretionary custodial sentences

3–1638   **79–82.**   *Repealed.*

3–1642   **82A. Determination of tariffs.**   (1) This section applies if a court passes a life sentence in circumstances where the sentence is not fixed by law. (2) The court shall, unless it makes an order under subsection (4) below, order that the provisions of section 28(5) to (8) of the Crime (Sentences) Act 1997 (referred to in this section as the "early release provisions") shall apply to the offender as soon as he has served the part of his sentence which is specified in the order.

(3) The part of his sentence shall be such as the court considers appropriate taking into account—

(a) the seriousness of the offence, or of the combination of the offence and one or more offences associated with it;

(b) the effect of any direction which it would have given under section 240 of the Criminal Justice Act 2003 (crediting periods of remand in custody) if it had sentenced him to a term of imprisonment; and

(c) the early release provisions as compared with section 244(1) of the Criminal Justice Act 2003.

(4) If the offender was aged 21 or over when he committed the offence and the court is of the opinion that, because of the seriousness of the offence or of the combination of the offence and one or more offences associated with it, no order should be made under subsection (2) above, the court shall order that, subject to subsection (5) below, the early release provisions shall not apply to the offender.

(4A) No order under subsection (4) above may be made where the life sentence is—

(a) a sentence of imprisonment for public protection under section 225 of the Criminal Justice Act 2003, or

(b) a sentence of detention for public protection under section 226 of that Act.

(5) *Repealed.*
(6) *Repealed.*
(7) In this section—

"court" includes a court-martial;
"life sentence" has the same meaning as in Chapter II of Part II of the Crime (Sentences) Act 1997.

(8) So far as this section relates to sentences passed by a court-martial, section 167(1) below does not apply.*
[Powers of Criminal Courts (Sentencing) Act 2000, s 82A, as inserted by the Criminal Justice and Court Services Act 2000, s 60 and amended by the Criminal Justice Act 2003, Sch 32.].]

---

*In force in relation to sentences passed after 30 November 2000.

Other restrictions

3–1643　83. Restriction on imposing custodial sentences on persons not legally represented.
(1) A magistrates' court on summary conviction, or the Crown Court on committal for sentence or on conviction on indictment, shall not[1] pass a sentence of imprisonment on a person who—

(a) is not legally represented in that court, and
(b) has not been previously sentenced to that punishment by a court in any part of the United Kingdom,

unless he is a person to whom subsection (3) below applies.
(2) A magistrates' court on summary conviction, or the Crown Court on committal for sentence or on conviction on indictment, shall not—

(a) pass a sentence of detention under section 90 or 91 below,
(b) pass a sentence of custody for life under section 93 or 94 below*,
(c) pass a sentence of detention in a young offender institution, or*
(d) make a detention and training order,

on or in respect of a person who is not legally represented[2] in that court unless he is a person to whom subsection (3) below applies.
(3) This subsection applies to a person if either—

(a) he was granted a right to representation funded by the Legal Services Commission as part of the Criminal Defence Service but the right was withdrawn because of his conduct; or**
(b) having been informed of his right to apply for such representation and having had the opportunity to do so, he refused or failed to apply.

(4) For the purposes of this section a person is to be treated as legally represented in a court if, but only if, he has the assistance of counsel or a solicitor to represent him in the proceedings in that court at some time after he is found guilty and before he is sentenced.
(5) For the purposes of subsection (1)(b) above a previous sentence of imprisonment which has been suspended and which has not taken effect under section 119 below or under section 19 of the Treatment of Offenders Act (Northern Ireland) 1968 shall be disregarded.
(6) In this section "sentence of imprisonment" does not include a committal for contempt of court or any kindred offence.
[Powers of Criminal Courts (Sentencing) Act 2000, s 83.]

---

*Paragraphs 83(2)(b) and (c) are substituted by the Criminal Justice and Court Services Act 2000, Sch 7 from a date to be appointed.
**Subsection (3) para (a) amended and new para (aa) substituted by the Criminal Defence Service Act 2006, s 4(2)(c), (3) from a date to be appointed.
1. A sentence passed in breach of the provisions of this section is a sentence not authorised by law which will be quashed on appeal: see *R v Birmingham Justices, ex p Wyatt* [1975] 3 All ER 897, 140 JP 46; but we are of opinion that the justices could re-open the case under s 142 of the Magistrates' Courts Act 1980 and, possibly, also on the basis that the sentence was a nullity.
2. The requirements of this section will be satisfied if (unless paragraphs (a) or (b) of sub-s (3) apply) the defendant has legal representation after he has been found guilty. However, the court will often be able to anticipate the need for legal representation at an early stage of the proceedings and, if the defendant is not legally represented, advise him of his right to apply for representation. Where a right to representation is in force but an offender dismisses his advocate between conviction and sentence he is not legally represented within the meaning of 21 and it is therefore unlawful to impose a sentence of imprisonment without first withdrawing the right to representation (*R v Wilson* (1995) 16 Cr App Rep (S) 997, [1995] Crim LR 510).
See the Access to Justice Act 1999, s 14 and Sch 3 in PART I: MAGISTRATES' COURTS, PROCEDURE, ante, which set out the criteria for the grant of a right to representation.

3–1644　84. Restriction on consecutive sentences for released prisoners.　*Repealed.*

Sexual and violent offences: licences etc

3–1645　85. Sexual or violent offences: extension of certain custodial sentences for licence purposes.　*Repealed.*

3–1646　86. Sexual offences committed before 30th September 1998.　(1) Where, in the case of a long-term or short-term prisoner—

(a) the whole or any part of his sentence was imposed for a sexual offence committed before 30th September 1998, and
(b) the court by which he was sentenced for that offence, having had regard to the matters mentioned in section 32(6)(a) and (b) of the Criminal Justice Act 1991, ordered that this section should apply,

sections 33(3) and 37(1) of that Act shall each have effect as if for the reference to three-quarters of his sentence there were substituted a reference to the whole of that sentence.
(2) Expressions used in this section shall be construed as if they were contained in Part II of the Criminal Justice Act 1991.
(3) The reference in subsection (1) above to section 33(3) of the Criminal Justice Act 1991 is to

section 33(3) as it has effect without the amendment made by section 104(1) of the Crime and Disorder Act 1998 (which substituted the words "on licence" for the word "unconditionally" and does not apply in relation to a prisoner whose sentence or any part of whose sentence was imposed for an offence committed before 30th September 1998).
[Powers of Criminal Courts (Sentencing) Act 2000, s 86.]

Crediting of periods of remand in custody

3–1647 87. Crediting of periods of remand in custody: terms of imprisonment and detention[1]. *Repealed.*

3–1648 88. Meaning of "remand in custody"[1]. *Repealed.*

CHAPTER II[1]
DETENTION AND CUSTODY OF YOUNG OFFENDERS

Restriction on imposing imprisonment on persons under 21

3–1649 89. Restriction on imposing imprisonment on persons under 21[2]*.   (1) Subject to subsection (2) below, no court shall—

  (a)   pass a sentence of imprisonment on a person for an offence if he is aged under 21* when convicted of the offence; or
  (b)   commit a person aged under 21* to prison for any reason.

  (2) Nothing in subsection (1) above shall prevent the committal to prison of a person aged under 21* who is—

  (a)   remanded in custody;
  (b)   committed in custody for trial or sentence; or
  (c)   sent in custody for trial under section 51 of the Crime and Disorder Act 1998.
[Powers of Criminal Courts (Sentencing) Act 2000, s 89.]

> ***Amended by the Criminal Justice and Court Services Act 2000, Sch 7 from a date to be appointed.**
> 1. Chapter II contains ss 89–108.
> 2. If on the material before the court an offender is deemed to be 21, he shall be treated on that basis, the fact that he is subsequently found to be under 21 does not invalidate the sentence (*R v Brown* (1989) 11 Cr App Rep (S) 263).

Detention at Her Majesty's pleasure or for specified period

3–1650 90. Offenders who commit murder when under 18: duty to detain at Her Majesty's pleasure[1].   Where a person convicted of murder appears to the court to have been aged under 18 at the time the offence was committed, the court shall (notwithstanding anything in this or any other Act) sentence him to be detained[2] during Her Majesty's pleasure[3]*.
[Powers of Criminal Courts (Sentencing) Act 2000, s 90.]

> ***Amended by the Criminal Justice and Court Services Act 2000, s 60 from a date to be appointed.**
> 1. For further commentary on this section, see PART V: YOUTH COURTS, para **5–61**, post, and see Magistrates' Courts Act 1980 s 24 in PART I: MAGISTRATES' COURTS, PROCEDURE, ante, for provision as to committal to the Crown Court.
> 2. No child benefit is payable during detention (Social Security Contributions and Benefits Act 1992, Sch 9).
> 3. Young offenders sentenced under this provision are governed as to their release by s 35 of the Criminal Justice Act 1991 and for the principles applicable to children and young persons see *R v Secretary of State for the Home Department, ex p Venables* [1998] AC 407, [1997] 3 All ER 97, [1997] 2 FLR 471, HL. But see *T v United Kingdom; V v United Kingdom* [2000] Crim LR 187, ECtHR.

3–1651 91. Offenders under 18 convicted of certain serious offences: power to detain for specified period[1].   (1) Subsection (3) below applies where a person aged under 18 is convicted on indictment of—

  (a)   an offence punishable in the case of a person aged 21* or over with imprisonment for 14 years or more, not being an offence the sentence for which is fixed by law; or
  (b)   an offence under section 3 of the Sexual Offences Act 2003 (in this section, "the 2003 Act") (sexual assault); or
  (c)   an offence under section 13 of the 2003 Act (child sex offences committed by children or young persons); or
  (d)   an offence under section 25 of the 2003 Act (sexual activity with a child family member); or
  (e)   an offence under section 26 of the 2003 Act (inciting a child family member to engage in sexual activity).

  (1A) Subsection (3) below also applies where—

  (a)   a person aged under 18 is convicted on indictment of an offence—

     (i)   under subsection (1)(a), (ab), (aba), (ac), (ad), (ae), (af) or (c) of section 5 of the Firearms Act 1968 (prohibited weapons), or
     (ii) under subsection (1A)(a) of that section,

  (b)   the offence was committed after the commencement of section 51A of that Act and at a time when he was aged 16 or over, and (*c*)   the court is of the opinion mentioned in section 51A(2) of that Act (exceptional circumstances which justify its not imposing required custodial sentence).

(2) *Repealed.*

(3) If the court is of the opinion that none of the other methods in which the case may legally be dealt with** is suitable, the court may sentence[2] the offender to be detained for such period, not exceeding the maximum term of imprisonment with which the offence is punishable in the case of a person aged 21* or over, as may be specified in the sentence.

(4) Subsection (3) above is subject to (in particular) section 152 and 153 of the Criminal Justice Act 2003.

(5) Where subsection (2) of section 51A of the Firearms Act 1968 requires the imposition of a sentence of detention under this section for a term of at least the required minimum term (within the meaning of that section), the court shall sentence the offender to be detained for such period, of at least that term but not exceeding the maximum term of imprisonment with which the offence is punishable in the case of a person aged 18 or over, as may be specified in the sentence.

[Powers of Criminal Courts (Sentencing) Act 2000, s 91 as amended by the Sexual Offences Act 2003, Sch 6 and the Criminal Justice Act 2003, s 289 and Sch 32.]

---

*Amended by the Criminal Justice and Court Services Act 2000, Sch 7 from a date to be appointed.

1. For further commentary on this section, see PART V: YOUTH COURTS, para **5–61**, post, and see Magistrates' Courts Act 1980 s 24 in PART I: MAGISTRATES' COURTS, PROCEDURE, ante, for provision as to committal to the Crown Court.

2. For example see *R v Storey, Fuat, Duignam* [1973] 3 All ER 562, 137 JP 811. Where the minor was dangerous in the sense that he was likely to commit grave offences in future, the period selected should represent the maximum period within which the minor was thought likely to remain dangerous. The sentence can contain an element of deterrence. See commentary on *R v Woodbridge* [1978] Crim LR 376; also *R v Redmond* [1979] Crim LR 192 (a punitive or demonstrative sentence may be based on the length of imprisonment appropriate for an adult). Two years detention has been held appropriate in the case of two boys aged 14 who were guilty of arson, burglary and criminal damage value £70,000 at a school (*R v Padwick and New* (1985) 7 Cr App Rep (S) 452).

3–1652   92. Detention under sections 90 and 91: place of detention etc.   (1) A person sentenced to be detained under section 90 or 91 above shall be liable to be detained in such place and under such conditions—

(*a*)   as the Secretary of State may direct; or

(*b*)   as the Secretary of State may arrange with any person.

(2) A person detained pursuant to the directions or arrangements made by the Secretary of State under this section shall be deemed to be in legal custody.

(3) A direction of the Secretary of State under this section may be signified only—

(*a*)   under the hand of the Secretary of State or an Under-Secretary of State or an Assistant Under-Secretary; or

(*b*)   under the hand of an authorised officer;

and arrangements of the Secretary of State under this section may be signified only as mentioned in paragraph (*a*) above.

[Powers of Criminal Courts (Sentencing) Act 2000, s 92.]

Custody for life

3–1653   93. Duty to impose custody for life in certain cases where offender under 21.   Where a person aged under 21 is convicted of murder or any other offence the sentence for which is fixed by law as imprisonment for life, the court shall sentence him to custody for life unless he is liable to be detained under section 90 above.*

[Powers of Criminal Courts (Sentencing) Act 2000, s 93.]

---

*Repealed by the Criminal Justice and Court Services Act 2000, Sch 7 from a date to be appointed.

3–1654   94. Power to impose custody for life in certain other cases where offender at least 18 but under 21.   (1) Where a person aged at least 18 but under 21 is convicted of an offence—

(*a*)   for which the sentence is not fixed by law, but

(*b*)   for which a person aged 21 or over would be liable to imprisonment for life,

the court shall, if it considers that a sentence for life would be appropriate, sentence him to custody for life.

(2) Subsection (1) above is subject to (in particular) sections 79 and 80 above, but this subsection does not apply in relation to a sentence which falls to be imposed under section 109(2) below.*

[Powers of Criminal Courts (Sentencing) Act 2000, s 94.]

---

*Repealed by the Criminal Justice and Court Services Act 2000, Sch 7 from a date to be appointed.

3–1655   95. Custody for life: place of detention.   (1) Subject to section 22(2)(*b*) of the Prison Act 1952 (removal to hospital etc), an offender sentenced to custody for life shall be detained in a young offender institution unless a direction under subsection (2) below is in force in relation to him.

(2) The Secretary of State may from time to time direct that an offender sentenced to custody for life shall be detained in a prison or remand centre instead of a young offender institution.★

[Powers of Criminal Courts (Sentencing) Act 2000, s 95.]

★**Repealed by the Criminal Justice and Court Services Act 2000, Sch 7 from a date to be appointed.**

Detention in a young offender institution[1]

3–1656   96. Detention in a young offender institution for other cases where offender at least 18 but under 21.   Subject to sections 90, 93 and 94 above, where—

(a) a person aged at least 18 but under 21 is convicted of an offence[2] which is punishable with imprisonment in the case of a person aged 21 or over, and

(b) the court is of the opinion that either or both of paragraphs (a) and (b) of section 79(2) above apply or the case falls within section 79(3),

the sentence that the court is to pass is a sentence of detention in a young offender institution.★

[Powers of Criminal Courts (Sentencing) Act 2000, s 96.]

★**Repealed by the Criminal Justice and Court Services Act 2000, Sch 7 from a date to be appointed.**
1. For full discussion of this power see paras **3–243** ante and **5–24**, post. Where a defendant attains the age of 18 between the date of the commission of the offence and the date of conviction, the starting point for sentence is the sentence that the defendant would have been likely to receive at the former date; other factors might have to be considered, but there must be good reasons for departing from the starting point: *R v Ghafoor* [2002] EWCA Crim 1857, [2003] 1 Cr App R (S) 84, [2002] Crim LR 739 (offender charged with riot attained 18 before he was convicted; sentence reduced from 4½ years' detention to 18 months, the length of the DTO he would have received, taking his guilty plea into account, if he had been sentenced at the date of the commission of the offence. See also *R v M* [2002] All ER (D) 35 (Dec), [2002] 166 JPN 963 (DTO quashed where the defendant attained the age of 15 between the date of offence and the date of conviction).
2. A person guilty of contempt has not been "convicted of an offence" for the purposes of this section (*R v Byas*, (1995) 16 Cr App Rep (S) 869, 159 JP 458 [1995] Crim LR 439, CA) but for the detention of persons aged 18 to 20 for contempt, see s 108, post.

3–1657   97. Term of detention in a young offender institution, and consecutive sentences.
(1) The maximum term of detention in a young offender institution that a court may impose for an offence is the same as the maximum term of imprisonment that it may impose for that offence.

(2) Subject to subsection (3) below, a court shall not pass a sentence for an offender's detention in a young offender institution for less than 21 days[1].

(3) A court may pass a sentence of detention in a young offender institution for less than 21 days for an offence under section 65(6) of the Criminal Justice Act 1991 (breach of requirement imposed on young offender on his release from detention).

(4) Where—

(a) an offender is convicted of more than one offence for which he is liable to a sentence of detention in a young offender institution, or

(b) an offender who is serving a sentence of detention in a young offender institution is convicted of one or more further offences for which he is liable to such a sentence,

the court shall have the same power to pass consecutive sentences of detention in a young offender institution as if they were sentences of imprisonment.

(5) Subject to section 84 above (restriction on consecutive sentences for released prisoners), where an offender who—

(a) is serving a sentence of detention in a young offender institution, and

(b) is aged 21 or over,

is convicted of one or more further offences for which he is liable to imprisonment, the court shall have the power to pass one or more sentences of imprisonment to run consecutively upon the sentence of detention in a young offender institution[2].★

[Powers of Criminal Courts (Sentencing) Act 2000, s 97.]

★**Repealed by the Criminal Justice and Court Services Act 2000, Sch 7 from a date to be appointed.**
1. A court may not lawfully pass an individual term of detention for less than the minimum period applicable under s 97(2), and the requirement of s 97(2) is not satisfied by ordering consecutive terms which together exceed the minimum period (*R v Dover Youth Court, ex p K* [1998] 4 All ER 24, [1999] 1 WLR 27; sub nom *R v Kent Youth Centre, ex p Kingwell* [1999] Crim LR 168, [1999] 1 Cr App Rep (S) 263).
2. Section 97(5) has no bearing on the power of the court to pass a sentence of detention concurrently or consecutively in the normal way (*R v Williams (Robert Anthony)* (1994) Times, 19 August, CA).

3–1658   98. Detention in a young offender institution: place of detention.   (1) Subject to section 22(2)(b) of the Prison Act 1952 (removal to hospital etc), an offender sentenced to detention in a young offender institution shall be detained in such an institution unless a direction under subsection (2) below is in force in relation to him.

(2) The Secretary of State may from time to time direct that an offender sentenced to detention in a young offender institution shall be detained in a prison or remand centre instead of a young offender institution[1].★

[Powers of Criminal Courts (Sentencing) Act 2000, s 98.]

*Repealed by the Criminal Justice and Court Services Act 2000, Sch 7 from a date to be appointed.

1. Since detention in a prison or remand centre may be directed only for a temporary purpose, a warrant of commitment which directs the governor of a remand centre to hold the offender for the full period of the sentence will be invalid (*R v Accrington Youth Court, ex p Flood* [1998] 2 All ER 313, [1998] 1 WLR 156).

Conversion of sentence of detention or custody to sentence of imprisonment

3–1659 99. Conversion of sentence of detention or custody to sentence of imprisonment.
(1) Subject to the following provisions of this section, where an offender has been sentenced to a term of detention in a young offender institution and either—

(*a*) he has attained the age of 21, or

(*b*) he has attained the age of 18 and has been reported to the Secretary of State by the board of visitors of the institution in which he is detained as exercising a bad influence on the other inmates of the institution or as behaving in a disruptive manner to the detriment of those inmates,

the Secretary of State may direct that he shall be treated as if he had been sentenced to imprisonment for the same term.

(2) An offender who by virtue of this section falls to be treated as if he had been sentenced to imprisonment instead of detention in a young offender institution shall not be so treated for the purposes of section 65 of the Criminal Justice Act 1991 (supervision of young offenders after release).

(3) Where the Secretary of State gives a direction under subsection (1) above in relation to an offender, the portion of the term of detention in a young offender institution imposed by the sentence of detention in a young offender institution which he has already served shall be deemed to have been a portion of a term of imprisonment.

(4) Rules under section 47 of the Prison Act 1952 may provide that any award for an offence against discipline made in respect of an offender serving a sentence of detention in a young offender institution shall continue to have effect after a direction under subsection (1) above has been given in relation to him.

(5) This section applies to a person—

(*a*) who is detained under section 90 or 91 above, or

(*b*) who is serving a sentence of custody for life,

as it applies to a person serving a sentence of detention in a young offender institution.
[Powers of Criminal Courts (Sentencing) Act 2000, s 99.]

Detention and training orders[1]

3–1660 100. Offenders under 18: detention and training orders.   (1) Subject to sections 90 and 91 above, sections 226 and 228 of the Criminal Justice Act 2003, and subsection (2), where—

(*a*) a child or young person (that is to say, any person aged under 18[2]) is convicted of an offence which is punishable with imprisonment in the case of a person aged 21* or over, and

(*b*) the court is of the opinion that subsection (2) of section 152 of the Criminal Justice Act 2003 applies or the case falls within subsection (3) of that section,

the sentence that the court is to pass is a detention and training order.

(2) A court shall not make a detention and training order—

(*a*) in the case of an offender under the age of 15[3] at the time of the conviction, unless it is of the opinion that he is a persistent offender[4];

(*b*) in the case of an offender under the age of 12 at that time, unless—

(i) it is of the opinion that only a custodial sentence would be adequate to protect the public from further offending by him; and

(ii) the offence was committed on or after such date as the Secretary of State may by order appoint.

(3) A detention and training order is an order that the offender in respect of whom it is made shall be subject, for the term specified in the order, to a period of detention and training followed by a period of supervision.

(4) *Repealed.*
[Powers of Criminal Courts (Sentencing) Act 2000, s 100 as amended by the Criminal Justice Act 2003, Sch 32.]

*Amended by the Criminal Justice and Court Services Act 2000, Sch 7 from a date to be appointed.

1. For full discussion of this power see paras **5–60A** to **5–60D**, post.

2. In *Aldis v DPP* [2002] EWHC 403 (Admin), [2002] Crim LR 434 it was held, in relation to a defendant aged 17 at the time of mode of trial, at which hearing it must have been plain to all present that the possibility of a 2-year detention and training order was a factor in the court's decision to try the case summarily, that the attainment of 18 before the trial and conviction did not prevent the justices from imposing a detention and training order; Parliament's intention must have been that s 100 of the Powers of Criminal Courts (Sentencing) Act 2000 should be interpreted as subject to s 29 of the Children and Young Persons Act 1963.

3. Where a defendant crosses an important age threshold between the date of the commission of the offence and the date of conviction the starting point for sentencing is the sentence that the defendant would have been likely to receive at the former date; other facts might have to be considered, but there have to be good reasons for departing from the starting point: *R v Ghafoor* [2002] EWCA Crim 1857, [2003] 1 Cr App R (S) 84, [2002] Crim LR 739 (offender charged with riot attained 18 before he was convicted; sentenced reduced from 4½ years' detention to 18 months, the length of the DTO he would have received, taking his guilty plea into account, if he had been sentenced at the date of the commission of the

offence. See also *R v M* [2002] All ER (D) 35 (Dec), [2002] JPN 963 (DTO quashed where the defendant attained the age of 15 between the date of offence and the date of conviction); and *R v Jones* [2003] EWCA Crim 1609, [2003] Crim LR 639 (15 months' detention reduced to 12 because the defendant was 17 at the time of the offence and a DTO may not be made for such a period). See further *R v Jahmarl* [2004] EWCA Crim 2199, [2005] 1 Cr App R (S) 96, where, in "rather unusual circumstances", the Court substituted a sentence of one year's detention and training in respect of a youth aged 14 at the date of the offence, but 15 when convicted, who was of previous good character.

4. In the light of a series of robberies committed over a period of two days a defendant qualified as a persistent offender even though he had no previous convictions (*R v Smith* (2000) 164 JP 681, CA; followed in *R v Charlton* (2000) 164 JP 685, where it was said that the Home Office definition of "persistent young offender" for the purpose of fast tracking such cases was not appropriate to be adopted as definitive for the purpose of the statutory predecessor to s 100). The court is entitled to take into account offences for which the offender has been cautioned, and offences committed after the present offence, in determining whether an offender is "persistent": *R v B* [2001] Crim LR 50, CA.

3–1661   101. Term of order, consecutive terms and taking account of remands. (1) Subject to subsection (2) below, the term of a detention and training order made in respect of an offence (whether by a magistrates' court or otherwise) shall be 4, 6, 8, 10, 12, 18 or 24 months[1].

(2) The term of a detention and training order may not exceed the maximum term of imprisonment that the Crown Court could (in the case of an offender aged 21* or over) impose for the offence[2].

(3) Subject to subsections (4) and (6) below, a court making a detention and training order may order that its term shall commence on the expiry of the term of any other detention and training order made by that or any other court.

(4) A court shall not make in respect of an offender a detention and training order the effect of which would be that he would be subject to detention and training orders for a term which exceeds 24 months.

(5) Where the term of the detention and training orders to which an offender would otherwise be subject exceeds 24 months, the excess shall be treated as remitted.

(6) A court making a detention and training order shall not order that its term shall commence on the expiry of the term of a detention and training order under which the period of supervision has already begun (under section 103(1) below).

(7) Where a detention and training order ("the new order") is made in respect of an offender who is subject to a detention and training order under which the period of supervision has begun ("the old order"), the old order shall be disregarded in determining—

(a) for the purposes of subsection (4) above whether the effect of the new order would be that the offender would be subject to detention and training orders for a term which exceeds 24 months; and

(b) for the purposes of subsection (5) above whether the term of the detention and training orders to which the offender would (apart from that subsection) be subject exceeds 24 months.

(8) In determining the term of a detention and training order for an offence, the court shall take account of any period for which the offender has been remanded in custody in connection with the offence, or any other offence the charge for which was founded on the same facts or evidence.

(9) Where a court proposes to make detention and training orders in respect of an offender for two or more offences—

(a) subsection (8) above shall not apply; but

(b) in determining the total term of the detention and training orders it proposes to make in respect of the offender, the court shall take account of the total period (if any) for which he has been remanded in custody in connection with any of those offences, or any other offence the charge for which was founded on the same facts or evidence.

(10) Once a period of remand has, under subsection (8) or (9) above, been taken account of in relation to a detention and training order made in respect of an offender for any offence or offences, it shall not subsequently be taken account of (under either of those subsections) in relation to such an order made in respect of the offender for any other offence or offences.

(11) Any reference in subsection (8) or (9) above to an offender's being remanded in custody is a reference to his being—

(a) held in police detention;

(b) remanded in or committed to custody by an order of a court;

(c) remanded or committed to local authority accommodation under section 23 of the Children and Young Persons Act 1969 and placed and kept in secure accommodation or detained in a secure training centre pursuant to arrangements under subsection (7A) of that section; or

(d) remanded, admitted or removed to hospital under section 35, 36, 38 or 48 of the Mental Health Act 1983.

(12) A person is in police detention for the purposes of subsection (11) above—

(a) at any time when he is in police detention for the purposes of the Police and Criminal Evidence Act 1984; and

(b) at any time when he is detained under section 14 of the Terrorism Act 2000;

and in that subsection "secure accommodation" has the same meaning as in section 23 of the Children and Young Persons Act 1969.

(13) For the purpose of any reference in sections 102 to 105 below to the term of a detention and training order, consecutive terms of such orders and terms of such orders which are wholly or partly concurrent shall be treated as a single term if—

(a) the orders were made on the same occasion; or

(b) where they were made on different occasions, the offender has not been released (by virtue of subsection (2), (3), (4) or (5) of section 102 below) at any time during the period beginning with the first and ending with the last of those occasions.

[Powers of Criminal Courts (Sentencing) Act 2000, s 101, as amended by the Terrorism Act 2000, s 125 and the Criminal Justice and Police Act 2001, s 133.]

1. Where a new detention and training is made consecutive to one previously imposed the aggregate term does not need to correspond with one of the periods specified in (what is now) the Powers of Criminal Courts (Sentencing) Act 2000, s 101(1): *R v Norris* (2000) 164 JP 689, [2001] 1 Cr App Rep (S) 401, [2001] Crim LR 48, CA.

As the maximum custodial sentence for an adult is a term of imprisonment of three months' imprisonment, a youth convicted of criminal damage to the value of less than £5,000 is not liable to a custodial sentence in the youth court where the minimum sentence is a term of detention and training of four months: *Pye v Leeds Youth Court* [2006] EWHC 2527 (Admin).

Where a defendant aged 18 pleads guilty to an offence to which s 91, *supra*, is not available he should get credit for his plea; the fact that the prosecution did not pursue a charge that did attract s 91 is not a good reason for refusing a discount (*R v Wayne Robin March* [2002] EWCA Crim 551, [2002] 2 Cr App Rep (S) 448). (See also *R v Stuart Marley* [2001] EWCA Crim 2779, [2002] 2 Cr App Rep (S) 73; and *R v Gary Francis Kelly* [2001] EWCA Crim 1030. [2002] 1 Cr App Rep (S) 40 (in both cases s 91 detention was unavailable and the sentences for the offences (respectively, riot and s 20 wounding) were reduced from 24 to 18 months).

2. It is not possible to read the plural ("offences") for the singular ("offence") in s 101(2); therefore, while individual terms may not exceed the maximum term of imprisonment that the Crown Court can impose for the offence concerned, s 133 of the Magistrates' Court Act 1980, which places limitations on the maximum periods of imprisonment or detention in a young offender institution that magistrates may impose, does not apply to detention and training orders and the court may impose consecutive detention and training orders for summary offences to an aggregate that exceeds six months: *C v DPP* [2001] EWHC Admin 453, [2002] 1 Cr App Rep (S) 189, [2001] Crim LR 670, DC.

3–1662 **102. The period of detention and training.** (1) An offender shall serve the period of detention and training under a detention and training order in such secure accommodation as may be determined by the Secretary of State or by such other person as may be authorised by him for that purpose.

(2) Subject to subsections (3) to (5) below, the period of detention and training under a detention and training order shall be one-half of the term of the order.

(3) The Secretary of State may at any time release the offender if he is satisfied that exceptional circumstances exist which justify the offender's release on compassionate grounds.

(4) The Secretary of State may release the offender—

(a) in the case of an order for a term of 8 months or more but less than 18 months, one month before the half-way point of the term of the order; and

(b) in the case of an order for a term of 18 months or more, one month or two months before that point.

(5) If a youth court so orders on an application made by the Secretary of State for the purpose, the Secretary of State shall release the offender—

(a) in the case of an order for a term of 8 months or more but less than 18 months, one month after the half-way point of the term of the order; and

(b) in the case of an order for a term of 18 months or more, one month or two months after that point.

(6) An offender detained in pursuance of a detention and training order shall be deemed to be in legal custody.

[Powers of Criminal Courts (Sentencing) Act 2000, s 102.]

3–1663 **103. The period of supervision.** (1) The period of supervision of an offender who is subject to a detention and training order—

(a) shall begin with the offender's release, whether at the half-way point of the term of the order or otherwise; and

(b) subject to subsection (2) below, shall end when the term of the order ends.

(2) The Secretary of State may by order provide that the period of supervision shall end at such point during the term of a detention and training order as may be specified in the order under this subsection.

(3) During the period of supervision, the offender shall be under the supervision of—

(a) an officer of a local probation board;

(b) a social worker of a local authority; or

(c) a member of a youth offending team;

and the category of person to supervise the offender shall be determined from time to time by the Secretary of State.

(4) Where the supervision is to be provided by an officer of a local probation board, the officer of a local probation board shall be an officer appointed for or assigned to the local justicearea within which the offender resides for the time being.

(5) Where the supervision is to be provided by—

(a) a social worker of a local authority, or

(b) a member of a youth offending team,

the social worker or member shall be a social worker of, or a member of a youth offending team established by, the local authority within whose area the offender resides for the time being.

(6) The offender shall be given[1] a notice from the Secretary of State specifying—

(*a*) the category of person for the time being responsible for his supervision; and

(*b*) any requirements with which he must for the time being comply.

(7) A notice under subsection (6) above shall be given[1] to the offender—

(*a*) before the commencement of the period of supervision; and

(*b*) before any alteration in the matters specified in subsection (6)(*a*) or (*b*) above comes into effect.

[Powers of Criminal Courts (Sentencing) Act 2000, s 103, as amended by the Criminal Justice and Court Services Act 2000, s 74, SI 2005/886 and the Children Act 2004, Sch 5.]

---

1. Section 103(7) does not specify any particular formality, but it is desirable that when an offender is given such a notice he is asked to sign a copy so that there can be no dispute that he has received it: *S v Doncaster Youth Offending Team* [2003] EWHC 1128 (Admin), (2003) 167 JP 381.

3–1664 104. Breach of supervision requirements[1].

(1) Where a detention and training order is in force in respect of an offender and it appears on information to a justice of the peace that the offender has failed to comply with requirements under section 103(6)(*b*) above, the justice—

(*a*) may issue a summons requiring the offender to appear at the place and time specified in the summons; or

(*b*) if the information is in writing and on oath, may issue a warrant for the offender's arrest.

(2) Any summons or warrant issued under this section shall direct the offender to appear or be brought—

(*a*) before a youth court acting for the local justice area in which the offender resides; or

(*b*) if it is not known where the offender resides, before a youth court acting for same local justice area as the justice who issued the summons or warrant.

(3) If it is proved to the satisfaction of the youth court before which an offender appears or is brought under this section that he has failed to comply with requirements under section 103(6)(*b*) above, that court may—

(*a*) order the offender to be detained, in such secure accommodation as the Secretary of State may determine, for such period, not exceeding the shorter of three months or the remainder of the term of the detention and training order, as the court may specify; or

(*b*) impose on the offender a fine not exceeding level 3 on the standard scale.

(4) An offender detained in pursuance of an order under subsection (3)(*a*) above shall be deemed to be in legal custody.

(5) A fine imposed under subsection (3)(*b*) above shall be deemed, for the purposes of any enactment, to be a sum adjudged to be paid by a conviction.

(6) An offender may appeal to the Crown Court against any order made under subsection (3)(*a*) or (*b*) above.

[Powers of Criminal Courts (Sentencing) Act 2000, s 104 as amended by the Domestic Violence, Crime and Victims Act 2004, Sch 5 and SI 2005/886.]

---

1. Where a defendant is sentenced to detention and training orders in respect of a number of offences they constitute a single order for the purpose of breach proceedings and the court record should show a breach of only one order; where, however, there are two separate breaches of the licence – for example, failing to keep in touch with the supervising officer and failing to reside where directed – there is a need to lay separate informations in respect of each of the kinds of breach, though within each kind there is no need to allege each of the instances separately: *S v Doncaster Youth Offending Team* [2003] EWHC 1128 (Admin), (2003) 167 JP 381.

3–1665 105. Offences during currency of order.

(1) This section applies to a person subject to a detention and training order if—

(*a*) after his release and before the date on which the term of the order ends, he commits an offence punishable with imprisonment in the case of a person aged 21* or over ("the new offence"); and

(*b*) whether before or after that date, he is convicted of the new offence.

(2) Subject to section 8(6) above (duty of adult magistrates' court to remit young offenders to youth court for sentence), the court by or before which a person to whom this section applies is convicted of the new offence may, whether or not it passes any other sentence on him, order him to be detained in such secure accommodation as the Secretary of State may determine for the whole or any part of the period which—

(*a*) begins with the date of the court's order; and

(*b*) is equal in length to the period between the date on which the new offence was committed and the date mentioned in subsection (1) above.

(3) The period for which a person to whom this section applies is ordered under subsection (2) above to be detained in secure accommodation—

(*a*) shall, as the court may direct, either be served before and be followed by, or be served concurrently with, any sentence imposed for the new offence; and

(*b*) in either case, shall be disregarded in determining the appropriate length of that sentence.

(4) Where the new offence is found to have been committed over a period of two or more days, or at some time during a period of two or more days, it shall be taken for the purposes of this section to have been committed on the last of those days.

(5) A person detained in pursuance of an order under subsection (2) above shall be deemed to be in legal custody.

[Powers of Criminal Courts (Sentencing) Act 2000, s 105.]

---

*Amended by the Criminal Justice and Court Services Act 2000, Sch 7 from a date to be appointed.

3–1666 106. Interaction with sentences of detention in a young offender institution.
(1) Where a court passes a sentence of detention in a young offender institution in the case of an offender who is subject to a detention and training order, the sentence shall take effect as follows—

(*a*) if the offender has been released by virtue of subsection (2), (3), (4) or (5) of section 102 above, at the beginning of the day on which it is passed;

(*b*) if not, either as mentioned in paragraph (*a*) above or, if the court so orders, at the time when the offender would otherwise be released by virtue of subsection (2), (3), (4) or (5) of section 102.*

(2) *Repealed.*

(3) *Repealed.*

(4) Subject to subsection (5) below, where at any time an offender is subject concurrently—

(*a*) to a detention and training order, and

(*b*) to a sentence of detention in a young offender institution,

he shall be treated for the purposes of sections 102 to 105 above and of section 98 above** (place of detention), Chapter IV of this Part (return to detention) and Part II of the Criminal Justice Act 1991 (early release) as if he were subject only to the one of them that was imposed on the later occasion.

(5) Nothing in subsection (4) above shall require the offender to be released in respect of either the order or the sentence unless and until he is required to be released in respect of each of them.

(6) Where, by virtue of any enactment giving a court power to deal with a person in a way in which a court on a previous occasion could have dealt with him, a detention and training order for any term is made in the case of a person who has attained the age of 18, the person shall be treated as if he had been sentenced to detention in a young offender institution** for the same term.

[Powers of Criminal Courts (Sentencing) Act 2000, s 106 as amended by the Criminal Justice Act 2003, Sch 32.]

---

*Repealed by the Criminal Justice and Court Services Act 2000, Sch 7 from a date to be appointed.
**Amended by the Criminal Justice and Court Services Act 2000, Sch 7 from a date to be appointed.
1. The absence of an express power to make a detention and training order consecutive to detention under s 91, as opposed to detention in a young offender institution, implies that there is no power to make the former order: see *R v Hayward and Hayward* [2001] Crim LR 236, CA, and the commentary thereon.

3–1666A 106A. Interaction with sentences of detention. (1) In this section—

"the 2003 Act" means the Criminal Justice Act 2003;
"sentence of detention" means—

(a) a sentence of detention under section 91 above, or

(b) a sentence of detention under section 228 of the 2003 Act (extended sentence for certain violent or sexual offences: persons under 18).

(2) Where a court passes a sentence of detention in the case of an offender who is subject to a detention and training order, the sentence shall take effect as follows—

(a) if the offender has at any time been released by virtue of subsection (2), (3), (4) or (5) of section 102 above, at the beginning of the day on which the sentence is passed, and

(b) if not, either as mentioned in paragraph (a) above or, if the court so orders, at the time when the offender would otherwise be released by virtue of subsection (2), (3), (4) or (5) of section 102.

(3) Where a court makes a detention and training order in the case of an offender who is subject to a sentence of detention, the order shall take effect as follows—

(a) if the offender has at any time been released under Chapter 6 of Part 12 of the 2003 Act (release on licence of fixed-term prisoners), at the beginning of the day on which the order is made, and

(b) if not, either as mentioned in paragraph (a) above or, if the court so orders, at the time when the offender would otherwise be released under that Chapter.

(4) Where an order under section 102(5) above is made in the case of a person in respect of whom a sentence of detention is to take effect as mentioned in subsection (2)(b) above, the order is to be expressed as an order that the period of detention attributable to the detention and training order is to end at the time determined under section 102(5)(a) or (b) above.

(5) In determining for the purposes of subsection (3)(b) the time when an offender would

otherwise be released under Chapter 6 of Part 12 of the 2003 Act, section 246 of that Act (power of Secretary of State to release prisoners on licence before he is required to do so) is to be disregarded.

(6) Where by virtue of subsection (3)(b) above a detention and training order made in the case of a person who is subject to a sentence of detention under section 228 of the 2003 Act is to take effect at the time when he would otherwise be released under Chapter 6 of Part 12 of that Act, any direction by the Parole Board under subsection (2)(b) of section 247 of that Act in respect of him is to be expressed as a direction that the Board would, but for the detention and training order, have directed his release under that section.

(7) Subject to subsection (9) below, where at any time an offender is subject concurrently—

(a)   to a detention and training order, and
(b)   to a sentence of detention,

he shall be treated for the purposes of the provisions specified in subsection (8) below as if he were subject only to the sentence of detention.

(8) Those provisions are—

(a)   sections 102 to 105 above,
(b)   section 92 above and section 235 of the 2003 Act (place of detention, etc), and
(c)   Chapter 6 of Part 12 of the 2003 Act.

(9) Nothing in subsection (7) above shall require the offender to be released in respect of either the order or the sentence unless and until he is required to be released in respect of each of them.
[Powers of Criminal Courts (Sentencing) Act 2000, s 106A as inserted by the Criminal Justice Act 2003, Sch 32.]

3–1667   107. Meaning of "secure accommodation" and references to terms.   (1) In sections 102, 104 and 105 above "secure accommodation" means—

(*a*)   a secure training centre;
(*b*)   a young offender institution;
(*c*)   accommodation provided by a local authority for the purpose of restricting the liberty of children and young persons;
(*d*)   accommodation provided for that purpose under subsection (5) of section 82 of the Children Act 1989 (financial support by the Secretary of State); or
(*e*)   such other accommodation provided for the purpose of restricting liberty as the Secretary of State may direct.

(2) In sections 102 to 105 above references to the term of a detention and training order shall be construed in accordance with section 101(13) above.
[Powers of Criminal Courts (Sentencing) Act 2000, s 107.]

Detention of persons aged at least 18 but under 21 for default or contempt

3–1668   108. Detention of persons aged at least 18 but under 21 for default or contempt.
(1) In any case where, but for section 89(1) above, a court would have power—

(*a*)   to commit a person aged at least 18 but under 21 to prison for default in payment of a fine or any other sum of money, or
(*b*)   to make an order fixing a term of imprisonment in the event of such a default by such a person, or
(*c*)   to commit such a person[1] to prison for contempt of court or any kindred offence[2],

the court shall have power, subject to subsection (3) below, to commit him to be detained under this section or, as the case may be, to make an order fixing a term of detention under this section in the event of default, for a term not exceeding the term of imprisonment.

(2) For the purposes of subsection (1) above, the power of a court to order a person to be imprisoned under section 23 of the Attachment of Earnings Act 1971 shall be taken to be a power to commit him to prison.

(3) No court shall commit a person to be detained under this section unless it is of the opinion that no other method of dealing with him is appropriate; and in forming any such opinion, the court—

(*a*)   shall take into account all such information about the circumstances of the default or contempt (including any aggravating or mitigating factors) as is available to it; and
(*b*)   may take into account any information about that person which is before it.

(4) Where a magistrates' court commits a person to be detained under this section, it shall—

(*a*)   state in open court the reason for its opinion that no other method of dealing with him is appropriate; and
(*b*)   cause that reason to be specified in the warrant of commitment and to be entered in the register.

(5) Subject to section 22(2)(*b*) of the Prison Act 1952 (removal to hospital etc), a person in respect of whom an order has been made under this section is to be detained—

(*a*)   in a remand centre,

(b)   in a young offender institution, or
(c)   in any place in which a person aged 21 or over could be imprisoned or detained for default in payment of a fine or any other sum of money,

as the Secretary of State may from time to time direct.★
[Powers of Criminal Courts (Sentencing) Act 2000, s 108.]

★Repealed by the Criminal Justice and Court Services Act 2000, Sch 7 from a date to be appointed.
1. The powers of the court to deal with contempt where the offender is under 18 are very limited, see *R v Byas* (1995) 16 Cr App Rep (S) 869, 159 JP 458, [1995] Crim LR 439, CA and commentary.
2. In certain circumstances, a refusal to enter into a recognizance to keep the peace or be of good behaviour may amount to a "kindred offence" for the purposes of this paragraph; see *Howley v Oxford* (1985) 149 JP 363, 81 Cr App Rep 246.

CHAPTER III[1]
REQUIRED CUSTODIAL SENTENCES FOR CERTAIN OFFENCES

3–1669   109. Life sentence for second serious offence. *Repealed.*

---

1. Chapter III contains ss 109–115.

3–1670   110. Minimum of seven years for third class A drug trafficking offence[1]. (1) This section applies where—

(a)   a person is convicted of a class A drug trafficking offence committed after 30th September 1997;
(b)   at the time when that offence was committed, he was 18 or over and had been convicted in any part of the United Kingdom of two other class A drug trafficking offences; and
(c)   one of those other offences was committed after he had been convicted of the other.

(2)   The court shall impose an appropriate custodial sentence★ for a term of at least seven years except where the court is of the opinion that there are particular circumstances which—

(a)   relate to any of the offences or to the offender; and
(b)   would make it unjust to do so in all the circumstances.

(3)   *Repealed.*
(4)   Where—

(a)   a person is charged with a class A drug trafficking offence (which, apart from this subsection, would be triable either way), and
(b)   the circumstances are such that, if he were convicted of the offence, he could be sentenced for it under subsection (2) above,

the offence shall be triable only on indictment.
(5)   In this section "class A drug trafficking offence" means a drug trafficking offence committed in respect of a class A drug; and for this purpose—

"class A drug" has the same meaning as in the Misuse of Drugs Act 1971;
"drug trafficking offence" means an offence which is specified in—

(a)   paragraph 1 of Schedule 2 to the Proceeds of Crime Act 2002 (drug trafficking offences), or
(b)   so far as it relates to that paragraph, paragraph 10 of that Schedule.

(6)   In this section "an appropriate custodial sentence" means—

(a)   in relation to a person who is 21 or over when convicted of the offence mentioned in subsection (1)(a) above, a sentence of imprisonment;
(b)   in relation to a person who is under 21 at that time, a sentence of detention in a young offender institution.★★
[Powers of Criminal Courts (Sentencing) Act 2000, s 110, as amended by the Proceeds of Crime Act 2002, Sch 11and the Criminal Justice Act 2003, Sch 37.]

★Amended by the Criminal Justice and Court Services Act 2000, Sch 7 from a date to be appointed.
★★Repealed by the Criminal Justice and Court Services Act 2000, Sch 7 from a date to be appointed.
1. As to the approach to be adopted where s 110 applies, see *R v Jeffrey Hickson* [2001] EWCA 1595, [2002] 1 Cr App Rep (S) 298 ("particular circumstances" (see subsection (2), infra) are not the same as "exceptional circumstances", but the fact that the 2 previous convictions were in 1984 and 1987 and that the first was relatively minor did not, in the court's opinion, make it unjust to impose the minimum (as adjusted to reflect the guilty plea) of 5 years and 7 months),

---

3–1671   111. Minimum of three years for third domestic burglary. (1) This section applies where—

(a)   a person is convicted of a domestic burglary[1] committed after 30th November 1999;
(b)   at the time when that burglary was committed, he was 18 or over and had been convicted[2] in England and Wales of two other domestic burglaries; and
(c)   one of those other burglaries was committed after he had been convicted of the other, and both of them were committed after 30th November 1999.

(2) The court shall impose an appropriate custodial sentence* for a term of at least three years except where the court is of the opinion that there are particular circumstances which—

(a) relate to any of the offences or to the offender; and[3]

(b) would make it unjust to do so in all the circumstances.

(3) *Repealed.*

(4) Where—

(a) a person is charged with a domestic burglary which, apart from this subsection, would be triable either way, and

(b) the circumstances are such that, if he were convicted of the burglary, he could be sentenced for it under subsection (2) above,

the burglary shall be triable only on indictment.

(5) In this section "domestic burglary" means a burglary committed in respect of a building or part of a building which is a dwelling.

(6) In this section "an appropriate custodial sentence" means—

(a) in relation to a person who is 21 or over when convicted of the offence mentioned in subsection (1)(a) above, a sentence of imprisonment;

(b) in relation to a person who is under 21 at that time, a sentence of detention in a young offender institution.**

[Powers of Criminal Courts (Sentencing) Act 2000, s 111 as amended by the Criminal Justice Act 2003, Sch 37.]

---

*Amended by the Criminal Justice and Court Services Act 2000, Sch 7 from a date to be appointed.
**Repealed by the Criminal Justice and Court Services Act 2000, Sch 7 from a date to be appointed.
1. Attempted burglary is not a qualifying offence for the purposes of s 111 (*R v MaGuire* [2002] EWCA Crim 2689, [2003] 1 Cr App R (S) 10).
2. The sequence required by s 11 is: (a) the commission of a first offence; (b) the conviction for the first offence; (c) the commission of the second offence; d) the conviction for the second offence; (e) the commission of the third offence; and (f) the conviction for the third offence: *R v Hoare* [2004] EWCA Crim 191, [2004] 2 Cr App R (S) 50.
"Convicted" means a finding of guilt; thus, a conviction counts under this provision even though the defendant was awaiting sentence for that offence at the time of the commission of the instant offence: *R v Webster* [2003] EWCA Crim 3597, [2004] 2 Cr App R (S) 25. A burglary offence for which the offender was discharged absolutely or conditionally could not, however, qualify for the purposes of s 111: *R v Webster, supra.*
3. In arriving at its decision the Court is entitled to have regard not simply to the qualifying offences but to the whole of the offending history: *R v Smith* [2003] EWCA Crim 2531, [2003] 1 Cr App R (S) 120.

3–1672   **112. Appeals where previous convictions set aside.**   (1) This section applies where—

(a) a sentence has been imposed on any person under subsection (2) of section 110 or 111 above; and

(b) any previous conviction of his without which that section would not have applied has been subsequently set aside on appeal.

(2) Notwithstanding anything in section 18 of the Criminal Appeal Act 1968, notice of appeal against the sentence may be given at any time within 28 days from the date on which the previous conviction was set aside.

[Powers of Criminal Courts (Sentencing) Act 2000, s 112 as amended by the Criminal Justice Act 2003, Sch 37.]

3–1673   **113. Certificates of convictions for purposes of Chapter III.**   (1) Where—

(a) on any date after 30th September 1997 a person is convicted in England and Wales of a class A drug trafficking offence, or on any date after 30th November 1999 a person is convicted in England and Wales of a domestic burglary, and

(b) the court by or before which he is so convicted states in open court that he has been convicted of such an offence on that date, and

(c) that court subsequently certifies that fact,

the certificate shall be evidence, for the purposes of the relevant section of this Chapter, that he was convicted of such an offence on that date.

(2) Where—

(a) after 30th September 1997 a person is convicted in England and Wales of a class A drug trafficking offence or after 30th November 1999 a person is convicted in England and Wales of a domestic burglary, and

(b) the court by or before which he is so convicted states in open court that the offence was committed on a particular day or over, or at some time during, a particular period, and

(c) that court subsequently certifies that fact,

the certificate shall be evidence, for the purposes of the relevant section of this Chapter, that the offence was committed on that day or over, or at some time during, that period.

(3) In this section—

"class A drug trafficking offence" and "domestic burglary" have the same meanings as in sections 110 and 111 respectively; and

"the relevant section of this Chapter", in relation to any such offence, shall be construed accordingly.

[Powers of Criminal Courts (Sentencing) Act 2000, s 113 as amended by the Criminal Justice Act 2003, Sch 37.]

3–1674   114. Offences under service law.   (1) Where—

(a) a person has at any time been convicted of an offence under section 70 of the Army Act 1955, section 70 of the Air Force Act 1955 or section 42 of the Naval Discipline Act 1957, and

(b) the corresponding civil offence (within the meaning of that Act) was a class A drug trafficking offence or a domestic burglary,

the relevant section of this Chapter shall have effect as if he had at that time been convicted in England and Wales of the corresponding civil offence.

(2) Subsection (3) of section 113 above applies for the purposes of this section as it applies for the purposes of that section.

[Powers of Criminal Courts (Sentencing) Act 2000, s 114 as amended by the Criminal Justice Act 2003, Sch 37.]

3–1675   115. Determination of day when offence committed.   Where an offence is found to have been committed over a period of two or more days, or at some time during a period of two or more days, it shall be taken for the purposes of sections 110 and 111 above to have committed on the last of those days.

[Powers of Criminal Courts (Sentencing) Act 2000, s 115 as amended by the Criminal Justice Act 2003, Sch 37.]

CHAPTER IV[1]
RETURN TO PRISON ETC WHERE OFFENCE COMMITTED DURING ORIGINAL SENTENCE

3–1676   116–129.   *Repealed.*

Compensation orders

3–1690   130. Compensation orders against convicted persons.   (1) A court by or before which a person is convicted of an offence, instead of or in addition to dealing with him in any other way, may, on application or otherwise, make an order (in this Act referred to as a "compensation order"[1]) requiring him—

(a) to pay[2] compensation[3] for any personal injury, loss or damage resulting from[4] that offence or any other offence which is taken into consideration[5] by the court in determining sentence; or

(b) to make payments for funeral expenses or bereavement in respect of a death resulting from any such offence, other than a death due to an accident arising out of the presence of a motor vehicle on a road;

but this is subject to the following provisions of this section and to section 131 below.

(2) Where the person is convicted of an offence the sentence for which is fixed by law or falls to be imposed under section 110(2) or 111(2) above, section 51A(2) of the Firearms Act 1968 or section 225, 226, 227 or 228 of the Criminal Justice Act 2003, subsection (1) above shall have effect as if the words "instead of or" were omitted.

(3) A court shall give reasons, on passing sentence, if it does not make a compensation order in a case where this section empowers it to do so.

(4) Compensation under subsection (1) above shall be of such amount as the court considers appropriate, having regard to any evidence and to any representations that are made by or on behalf of the accused or the prosecutor[6].

(5) In the case of an offence under the Theft Act 1968, where the property in question is recovered, any damage to the property occurring while it was out of the owner's possession shall be treated for the purposes of subsection (1) above as having resulted from the offence, however and by whomever the damage was caused.

(6) A compensation order may only be made in respect of injury, loss or damage (other than loss suffered by a person's dependants in consequence of his death) which was due to an accident arising out of the presence of a motor vehicle on a road, if—

(a) it is in respect of damage which is treated by subsection (5) above as resulting from an offence under the Theft Act 1968; or

(b) it is in respect of injury, loss or damage as respects which—

(i) the offender is uninsured in relation to the use of the vehicle; and

(ii) compensation is not payable[7] under any arrangements to which the Secretary of State is a party[8].

(7) Where a compensation order is made in respect of injury, loss or damage due to an accident arising out of the presence of a motor vehicle on a road, the amount to be paid may include an amount representing the whole or part of any loss of or reduction in preferential rates of insurance attributable to the accident.

(8) A vehicle the use of which is exempted from insurance by section 144 of the Road Traffic Act 1988 is not uninsured for the purposes of subsection (6) above.

(9) A compensation order in respect of funeral expenses may be made for the benefit of anyone who incurred the expenses.

(10) A compensation order in respect of bereavement may be made only for the benefit of a person for whose benefit a claim for damages for bereavement could be made under section 1A of the Fatal Accidents Act 1976; and the amount of compensation in respect of bereavement shall not exceed the amount for the time being specified in section 1A(3) of that Act.

(11) In determining whether to make a compensation order against any person, and in determining

the amount to be paid by any person under such an order, the court shall have regard to his means so far as they appear or are known to the court.

(12) Where the court considers—

(a) that it would be appropriate both to impose a fine and to make a compensation order, but

(b) that the offender has insufficient means to pay both an appropriate fine and appropriate compensation,

the court shall give preference to compensation (though it may impose a fine as well).

[Powers of Criminal Courts (Sentencing) Act 2000, s 130 as amended by the Criminal Justice Act 2003, Sch 32.]

---

1. For full discussion of this power see para **3–202** et seq, ante.

2. Enforceable as a sum adjudged to be paid on conviction: Administration of Justice Act 1970, s 41 and Sch 9, in PART I, ante. In the case of a child or young person, his parent or guardian may be ordered to pay, s 137, post.

3. The amount of compensation payable is restricted by s 131(1), post. The machinery of a compensation order under this Act is intended for clear and simple cases. It must always be remembered that the civil rights of the victim remain, although the power to make a compensation order is not confined to cases where there is a civil liability (*R v Chappell* [1984] Crim LR 574). A compensation order made by the court of trial can be extremely beneficial as long as it is confined to simple, straightforward cases and generally cases where no great amount is at stake; see *R v Daly* [1974] 1 All ER 290, 138 JP 245; *R v Kneeshaw* [1974] 1 All ER 896; *R v Inwood* (1974) 60 Cr App Rep 70. For a summary of the principles to be followed when making a compensation order see *R v Miller* [1976] Crim LR 694. Where the issue of whether or not compensation is payble at all or by the defendant is raised, the court should normally refuse in its discretion to make a compensation order: see *R v Kneeshaw* [1975] QB 57, [1974] 1 All ER 896, 138 JP 291. Liabilities (eg costs and expenses) incurred in civil proceedings should not be regarded as a "loss" justifying a compensation order (*Hammerton Cars Ltd v London Borough of Redbridge* [1974] 2 All ER 216). Where stolen goods have been recovered, in the absence of evidence of damage to them, no compensation order ought to be made (*R v Sharkey* (1976) 120 Sol Jo 95). See also *R v Cadamarteris* [1977] Crim LR 236 and *R v Boardman* (1987) 9 Cr App Rep (S) 74 [1987] Crim LR 430, CA (compensation order for balance of purchase price of boat which was stolen inappropriate where owner was tricked into believing he had been paid in full, and boat was recovered intact). In special circumstances–for example where there had been the loss of use of a banknote, and the sum was large and the period long–the court may consider awarding interest on the compensation; see *R v Schofield* [1978] 2 All ER 705, [1978] 1 WLR 979.

4. "Personal injury" or "damage" includes terror and distress directly occasioned by the offence (*Bond v Chief Constable of Kent* [1983] 1 All ER 456, [1983] 1 WLR 40, 147 JP 107. Where the offender is convicted of *possession* of a controlled drug, any suffering caused to another person who partook of part of that drug could not be said to have resulted from the offence of simple possession (*Berkely v Orchard* (1975) 119 Sol Jo 353, [1975] Crim LR 225). It might be otherwise if the offender were convicted of supplying a drug to a person who suffered thereby. An offender convicted of handling a stolen oil painting was held to have been properly ordered to pay compensation for loss suffered by an innocent buyer to whom the painting had been subsequently sold (*R v Howell* (1978) 66 Cr App Rep 179).

5. Compensation orders can only be made in respect of loss resulting from offences actually charged or formally taken into consideration (*R v Crutchley and Tonks* (1994) 15 Cr App Rep (S) 627, [1994] Crim LR 309, CA applied in *R v Hose* (1994) 16 Cr App Rep (S) 682, [1995] Crim LR 259, CA).

6. Subsection (4) contemplates that the court can make assessments and approximations where the evidence is scanty or incomplete, and then make an order which is "appropriate". But where the basis for making any compensation order is challenged and issues are raised as to whether there has been loss, and if so what loss, the court must receive evidence to determine liability, and cannot act merely on the representations of the parties (*R v Horsham Justices, ex p Richards* [1985] 2 All ER 1114, [1985] 1 WLR 986).

7. A sum is "payable" not only where it is due for immediate payment but also where it will fall to be due to be paid at some future time. Since the Motor Insurer's Bureau will never pay out in respect of the first £300 of any claim, it will always be the case that compensation is not payable in respect of that amount. The power of the justices, however, to order compensation in such cases is limited to making an order of £300 (*DPP v Scott* [1995] RTR 40, 159 JP 261, [1995] Crim LR 91, 16 Cr App Rep (S) 292). See also *R v Austin* [1996] RTR 414, [1996] Crim LR 446.

8. This is a scheme arranged with the Motor Insurers' Bureau dated 13 August 1999.

3–1691   131. Limit on amount payable under compensation order of magistrates' court.

(1) The compensation to be paid under a compensation order made by a magistrates' court in respect of any offence of which the court has convicted the offender shall not exceed £5,000.

(2) The compensation or total compensation to be paid under a compensation order or compensation orders made by a magistrates' court in respect of any offence or offences taken into consideration in determining sentence shall not exceed the difference (if any) between—

(a) the amount or total amount which under subsection (1) above is the maximum for the offence or offences of which the offender has been convicted; and

(b) the amount or total amounts (if any) which are in fact ordered to be paid in respect of that offence or those offences.

[Powers of Criminal Courts (Sentencing) Act 2000, s 131.]

3–1692   132. Compensation orders: appeals etc.

(1) A person in whose favour a compensation order is made shall not be entitled to receive the amount due to him until (disregarding any power of a court to grant leave to appeal out of time) there is no further possibility of an appeal on which the order could be varied or set aside.

(2) Criminal Procedure Rules may make provision regarding the way in which the magistrates' court for the time being having functions (by virtue of section 41(1) of the Administration of Justice Act 1970[1] in relation to the enforcement of a compensation order is to deal with money paid in satisfaction of the order where the entitlement of the person in whose favour it was made is suspended.

(3) The Court of Appeal may by order annul or vary any compensation order made by the court of trial, although the conviction is not quashed; and the order, if annulled, shall not take effect and, if varied, shall take effect as varied.

(4) Where the House of Lords* restores a conviction, it may make any compensation order which the court of trial could have made.*

(5) Where a compensation order has been made against any person in respect of an offence taken into consideration in determining his sentence—

(a) the order shall cease to have effect if he successfully appeals against his conviction of the offence or, if more than one, all the offences, of which he was convicted in the proceedings in which the order was made;

(b) he may appeal against the order as if it were part of the sentence imposed in respect of the offence or, if more than one, any of the offences, of which he was so convicted.

[Powers of Criminal Courts (Sentencing) Act 2000, s 132 as amended by SI 2004/2035.]

---

*Words substituted by the Constitutional Reform Act 2005, Sch 9, and new subs (4A) inserted by the Domestic Violence, Crime and Victims Act 2004, Sch 10, from a date to be appointed.

1. See PART I : MAGISTRATES' COURTS, PROCEDURE, ante.

3–1693 133. Review of compensation orders[1]. (1) The magistrates' court for the time being having functions in relation to the enforcement of a compensation order (in this section referred to as "the appropriate court") may, on the application of the person against whom the compensation order was made, discharge the order or reduce the amount which remains to be paid; but this is subject to subsections (2) to (4) below.

(2) The appropriate court may exercise a power conferred by subsection (1) above only—

(a) at a time when (disregarding any power of a court to grant leave to appeal out of time) there is no further possibility of an appeal on which the compensation order could be varied or set aside; and

(b) at a time before the person against whom the compensation order was made has paid into court the whole of the compensation which the order requires him to pay.

(3) The appropriate court may exercise a power conferred by subsection (1) above only if it appears to the court—

(a) that the injury, loss or damage in respect of which the compensation order was made has been held in civil proceedings to be less than it was taken to be for the purposes of the order; or

(b) in the case of a compensation order in respect of the loss of any property, that the property has been recovered by the person in whose favour the order was made; or

(c) that the means of the person against whom the compensation order was made are insufficient to satisfy in full both the order and a confiscation order under Part VI of the Criminal Justice Act 1988, or Part 2 of the Proceeds of Crime Act 2002 made against him in the same proceedings; or

(d) that the person against whom the compensation order was made has suffered a substantial reduction in his means which was unexpected at the time when the order was made, and that his means seem unlikely to increase for a considerable period.[2]

(4) Where the compensation order was made by the Crown Court, the appropriate court shall not exercise any power conferred by subsection (1) above in a case where it is satisfied as mentioned in paragraph (c) or (d) of subsection (3) above unless it has first obtained the consent of the Crown Court.

(5) Where a compensation order has been made on appeal, for the purposes of subsection (4) above it shall be deemed—

(a) if it was made on an appeal brought from a magistrates' court, to have been made by that magistrates' court;

(b) if it was made on an appeal brought from the Crown Court or from the criminal division of the Court of Appeal, to have been made by the Crown Court.

[Powers of Criminal Courts (Sentencing) Act 2000, s 133, as amended by the Proceeds of Crime Act 2002, Sch 11.]

---

1. For procedure, see the Criminal Procedure Rules 2005, Part 53, in PART I: MAGISTRATES' COURTS, PROCEDURE, ante.

2. Any inability to comply with a compensation order caused by a change in financial circumstances should be the subject of an application under this section rather than by way of appeal (*R v Palmer* (1993) 15 Cr App Rep (S) 550).

3–1694 134. Effect of compensation order on subsequent award of damages in civil proceedings. (1) This section shall have effect where a compensation order, or a service compensation order or award, has been made in favour of any person in respect of any injury, loss or damage and a claim by him in civil proceedings for damages in respect of the injury, loss or damage subsequently falls to be determined.

(2) The damages in the civil proceedings shall be assessed without regard to the order or award, but the plaintiff may only recover an amount equal to the aggregate of the following—

(a) any amount by which they exceed the compensation; and

(b) a sum equal to any portion of the compensation which he fails to recover,

and may not enforce the judgment, so far as it relates to a sum such as is mentioned in paragraph (b) above, without the leave of the court.

(3) In this section a "service compensation order or award" means—

(a) an order requiring the payment of compensation under paragraph 11 of Schedule 5A to the Army Act 1955, of Schedule 5A to the Air Force Act 1955 or of Schedule 4A to the Naval Discipline Act 1957; or
(b) an award of stoppages payable by way of compensation under any of those Acts.
[Powers of Criminal Courts (Sentencing) Act 2000, s 134.]

Young offenders

3–1695   135. Limit on fines imposed by magistrates' courts in respect of young offenders.
(1) Where a person aged under 18 is found guilty by a magistrates' court of an offence for which, apart from this section, the court would have power to impose a fine of an amount exceeding £1,000, the amount of any fine imposed by the court shall not exceed £1,000.
(2) In relation to a person aged under 14, subsection (1) above shall have effect as if for "£1,000", in both places where it occurs, there were substituted "£250".
[Powers of Criminal Courts (Sentencing) Act 2000, s 135.]

3–1696   136. Power to order statement as to financial circumstances of parent or guardian.
(1) Before exercising its powers under section 137 below (power to order parent or guardian to pay fine, costs or compensation) against the parent or guardian of an individual who has been convicted of an offence, the court may make a financial circumstances order with respect to the parent or (as the case may be) guardian.
(2) In this section "financial circumstances order" has the meaning given by subsection (3) of section 162 of the Criminal Justice Act 2003, and subsections (4) to (6) of that section shall apply in relation to a financial circumstances order made under this section as they apply in relation to such an order made under that section.
[Powers of Criminal Courts (Sentencing) Act 2000, s 136 as amended by the Criminal Justice Act 2003, Sch 32.]

3–1697   137. Power to order parent or guardian to pay fine, costs or compensation[1*].
(1) Where—
(a) a child or young person (that is to say, any person aged under 18) is convicted of any offence for the commission of which a fine or costs may be imposed or a compensation order may be made, and
(b) the court is of the opinion that the case would best be met by the imposition of a fine[2] or costs or the making of such an order, whether with or without any other punishment,
the court shall order that the fine, compensation or costs awarded be paid by the parent or guardian[3] of the child or young person instead of by the child or young person himself, unless the court is satisfied—
(i) that the parent or guardian cannot be found; or
(ii) that it would be unreasonable[4] to make an order for payment, having regard to the circumstances of the case.*
(2) Where but for this subsection a court would impose a fine on a child or young person under—
(a) paragraph 4(1)(a) or 5(1)(a) of Schedule 3 to this Act (breach of curfew, probation, community service, combination or drug treatment and testing order),**
(b) paragraph 2(1)(a) of Schedule 5 to this Act (breach of attendance centre order or attendance centre rules),
(c) paragraph 2(2)(a) of Schedule 7 to this Act (breach of supervision order),
(d) paragraph 2(2)(a) of Schedule 8 to this Act (breach of action plan order or reparation order),
(e) section 104(3)(b) above (breach of requirements of supervision under a detention and training order), or
(f) section 4(3)(b) of the Criminal Justice and Public Order Act 1994 (breach of requirements of supervision under a secure training order),
the court shall order that the fine be paid by the parent or guardian of the child or young person instead of by the child or young person himself, unless the court is satisfied—
(i) that the parent or guardian cannot be found; or
(ii) that it would be unreasonable to make an order for payment, having regard to the circumstances of the case.
(3) In the case of a young person aged 16 or over, subsections (1) and (2) above shall have effect as if, instead of imposing a duty, they conferred a power to make such an order as is mentioned in those subsections.
(4) Subject to subsection (5) below, no order shall be made under this section without giving the parent or guardian an opportunity of being heard.
(5) An order under this section may be made against a parent or guardian who, having been required to attend, has failed to do so.
(6) A parent or guardian may appeal to the Crown Court[5] against an order under this section made by a magistrates' court.
(7) A parent or guardian may appeal to the Court of Appeal against an order under this section made by the Crown Court, as if he had been convicted on indictment and the order were a sentence passed on his conviction.

(8) In relation to a child or young person for whom a local authority have parental responsibility and who—

(a) is in their care, or

(b) is provided with accommodation by them in the exercise of any functions (in particular those under the Children Act 1989) which are social services functions within the meaning of the Local Authority Social Services Act 1970,

references in this section to his parent or guardian shall be construed as references to that authority[6].

(9) In subsection (8) above "local authority" and "parental responsibility" have the same meanings as in the Children Act 1989.

[Powers of Criminal Courts (Sentencing) Act 2000, s 137, as amended by SI 2001/2237 and SI 2002/808.]

---

*Section heading amended and new subs (1A) inserted by the Domestic Violence, Crime and Victims Act 2004, Sch 10, from a date to be appointed.
**Repealed by the Criminal Justice and Court Services Act 2000, Sch 7 from a date to be appointed.

1. For consideration of the powers of the court to order the parent or guardian, or the local authority, to pay a fine, costs or compensation, see paras **5–44** Compensation and **5–45** Fine, in PART V: YOUTH COURTS, post.

2. For enforcement of fines imposed on young offenders, see para **5–46, Fine: enforcement after finding of guilt**, in PART V: YOUTH COURTS, post.

3. For the purposes of an order under s 137 made against the parent or guardian of a child or young person see s 138, post. See also the Magistrates' Courts Act 1980, s 81, in PART I: MAGISTRATES' COURTS, PROCEDURE, ante, which enables the court to direct recovery from the parent or guardian where there is a default in payment. A means inquiry is necessary.

4. Where a court had decided it was unreasonable to require a local authority to pay compensation in respect of a young offender in its care, it was wrong to order the authority to pay the costs of the prosecution (*R v Leeds City Council* (1994) 16 Cr App Rep (S) 362). Furthermore, an order to pay compensation for offences committed by a young offender in the care of, or accommodated by, a local authority should not be made against the local authority if the authority has done everything it reasonably could to protect the public from the offender (*R v DPP* (1995) 16 Cr App Rep (S) 1040, [1995] Crim LR 748, [1995] 2 FLR 502.

5. For procedure, see the Criminal Procedure Rules 2005, Part 63, in PART I; MAGISTRATES' COURTS, PROCEDURE, ante.

6. For the purposes of an order under this section made against a local authority s 128(1) and s 130(11) shall not apply (s 138(2)). Where a juvenile is subject to a secure accommodation order and is placed by the local authority in accommodation provided by a company for "difficult to place" young people, there is no power to make a compensation order against the company for damage caused by the juvenile while in its care because the company is not a guardian for the purposes of s 137 (*Marlowe Child and Family Services Ltd v DPP* [1998] Crim LR 594, [1998] 2 Cr App Rep (S) 438).

3–1698   138. Fixing of fine or compensation to be paid by parent or guardian*. (1) For the purposes of any order under section 137 above made against the parent or guardian of a child or young person—*

(a) section 164 of the Criminal Justice Act 2003 (fixing of fines) shall have effect as if any reference in subsections (1) to (4) to the financial circumstances of the offender were a reference to the financial circumstances of the parent or guardian, and as if subsection (5) were omitted;

(b) section 130(11) above (determination of compensation order) shall have effect as if any reference to the means of the person against whom the compensation order is made were a reference to the financial circumstances of the parent or guardian; and

(c) section 130(12) above (preference to be given to compensation if insufficient means to pay both compensation and a fine) shall have effect as if the reference to the offender were a reference to the parent or guardian;

but in relation to an order under section 137 made against a local authority this subsection has effect subject to subsection (2) below.

(2) For the purposes of any order under section 137 above made against a local authority, section 164(1) of the Criminal Justice Act 2003 and section 130(11) above shall not apply.

(3) For the purposes of any order under section 137 above, where the parent or guardian of an offender who is a child or young person—

(a) has failed to comply with an order under section 136 above, or

(b) has otherwise failed to co-operate with the court in its inquiry into his financial circumstances,

and the court considers that it has insufficient information to make a proper determination of the parent's or guardian's financial circumstances, it may make such determination as it thinks fit.

(4) Where a court has, in fixing the amount of a fine, determined the financial circumstances of a parent or guardian under subsection (3) above, subsections (2) to (4) of section 165 of the Criminal Justice Act 2003 (remission of fines) shall (so far as applicable) have effect as they have effect in the case mentioned in section 165(1), but as if the reference in section 165(2) to the offender's financial circumstances were a reference to the financial circumstances of the parent or guardian.

(5) In this section "local authority" has the same meaning as in the Children Act 1989.

[Powers of Criminal Courts (Sentencing) Act 2000, s 138 as amended by the Criminal Justice Act 2003, Sch 32.]

---

*Section heading amended and new sub-para (1)(za) inserted by the Domestic Violence, Crime and Victims Act 2004, Sch 10, from a date to be appointed.

Miscellaneous powers and duties of Crown Court in relation to fines etc

3–1699   139. Powers and duties of Crown Court in relation to fines and forfeited recognizances. (1) Subject to the provisions of this section, if the Crown Court imposes a fine[1] on any person or forfeits his recognizance[2], the court may make an order—

   (a) allowing time for the payment of the amount of the fine or the amount due under the recognizance;

   (b) directing payment of that amount by instalments of such amounts and on such dates as may be specified in the order;

   (c) in the case of a recognizance, discharging the recognizance or reducing the amount due under it.

   (2) Subject to the provisions of this section, if the Crown Court imposes a fine on any person or forfeits his recognizance, the court shall make an order fixing a term of imprisonment[3] or of detention under section 108 above (detention of persons aged 18 to 20 for default)* which he is to undergo if any sum[4] which he is liable to pay is not duly paid or recovered.

   (3) No person shall on the occasion when a fine is imposed on him or his recognizance is forfeited by the Crown Court be committed to prison or detained* in pursuance of an order under subsection (2) above unless—

   (a) in the case of an offence punishable with imprisonment, he appears to the court to have sufficient means to pay the sum forthwith;

   (b) it appears to the court that he is unlikely to remain long enough at a place of abode in the United Kingdom to enable payment of the sum to be enforced by other methods; or

   (c) on the occasion when the order is made the court sentences him to immediate imprisonment, custody for life or detention in a young offender institution* for that or another offence, or so sentences him for an offence in addition to forfeiting his recognizance, or he is already serving a sentence of custody for life or a term—

      (i) of imprisonment;
      (ii) of detention in a young offender institution; or
      (iii) of detention under section 108 above.

   (4) The periods set out in the second column of the following Table shall be the maximum periods[5] of imprisonment or detention* under subsection (2) above applicable respectively to the amounts set out opposite them.

Table

An amount not exceeding £200	7 days
An amount exceeding £200 but not exceeding £500	14 days
An amount exceeding £500 but not exceeding £1,000	28 days
An amount exceeding £1,000 but not exceeding £2,500	45 days
An amount exceeding £2,500 but not exceeding £5,000	3 months
An amount exceeding £5,000 but not exceeding £10,000	6 months
An amount exceeding £10,000 but not exceeding £20,000	12 months
An amount exceeding £20,000 but not exceeding £50,000	18 months
An amount exceeding £50,000 but not exceeding £100,000	2 years
An amount exceeding £100,000 but not exceeding £250,000	3 years
An amount exceeding £250,000 but not exceeding £1 million	5 years
An amount exceeding £1 million	10 years

   (5) Where any person liable for the payment of a fine or a sum due under a recognizance to which this section applies is sentenced by the court to, or is serving or otherwise liable to serve, a term of imprisonment or detention in a young offender institution or a term of detention under section 108 above, the court may order that any term of imprisonment or detention* fixed under subsection (2) above shall not begin to run until after the end of the first-mentioned term.

   (6) The power conferred by this section to discharge a recognizance or reduce the amount due under it shall be in addition to the powers conferred by any other Act relating to the discharge, cancellation, mitigation or reduction of recognizances or sums forfeited under recognizances.

   (7) Subject to subsection (8) below, the powers conferred by this section shall not be taken as restricted by any enactment which authorises the Crown Court to deal with an offender in any way in which a magistrates' court might have dealt with him or could deal with him.

   (8) Any term fixed under subsection (2) above as respects a fine imposed in pursuance of such an enactment, that is to say a fine which the magistrates' court could have imposed, shall not exceed the period applicable to that fine (if imposed by the magistrates' court) under section 149(1) of the Customs and Excise Management Act 1979 (maximum periods of imprisonment in default of payment of certain fines).

   (9) This section shall not apply to a fine imposed by the Crown Court on appeal against a decision of a magistrates' court, but subsections (2) to (4) above shall apply in relation to a fine imposed or recognizance forfeited by the criminal division of the Court of Appeal, or by the House of Lords** on appeal from that division, as they apply in relation to a fine imposed or recognizance forfeited by

the Crown Court, and the references to the Crown Court in subsections (2) and (3) above shall be construed accordingly.

(10) For the purposes of any reference in this section, however expressed, to the term of imprisonment or other detention to which a person has been sentenced or which, or part of which, he has served, consecutive terms and terms which are wholly or partly concurrent shall, unless the context otherwise requires, be treated as a single term.

(11) Any reference in this section, however expressed, to a previous sentence shall be construed as a reference to a previous sentence passed by a court in Great Britain.

[Powers of Criminal Courts (Sentencing) Act 2000, s 139.]

---

*Repealed by the Criminal Justice and Court Services Act 2000, Sch 7 from a date to be appointed.
**Substituted by the Constitutional Reform Act 2005, Sch 9, from a date to be appointed.

1. This section does not apply to compensation and costs, thus imprisonment in default will be fixed by the magistrates' court; see *R v Komsta and Murphy* (1990) 154 JP 440 noted to s 41 of the Administration of Justice Act 1970, ante. However, s 139 does apply to a confiscation order under Pt VI of the Criminal Justice Act 1988; see Criminal Justice Act 1988 s 75(1) in PART I; MAGISTRATES' COURTS, PROCEDURE, ante, and to a confiscation order made under Pt I of the Drug Trafficking Act 1994; see Criminal Justice Act 1988 s 9 in PART VIII: MEDICINE AND PHARMACY, post.

2. Where a surety is unable to meet a recognizance the court should make such order as seems fair and just in the circumstances having regard to culpability and means (*R v Crown Court at Wood Green, ex p Howe* [1992] 3 All ER 366, 155 JP 652, DC.

3. The effect of ss 139(1) to (4) and 140(1) to (3) of this Act, when read with s 77(2) of the Magistrates' Courts Act 1980, is that the magistrates' court should approach enforcement of a Crown Court fine as if it had fixed a term of imprisonment in default, just as the Crown Court has done, and as if they had postponed the issue of the warrant for the period of time that the Crown Court has set for the fine to be paid. Accordingly, if in such circumstances the defendant defaults in payment of the sum ordered by the Crown Court, there is no requirement under s 82(3) of the 1980 Act to hold a means inquiry before issuing the warrant of commitment (*R v Hastings and Rother Justices, ex p Anscombe* (1998) 162 JP 340).

4. The term should be expressed to be in default of the fine and not in default of each individual instalment (*R v Power* (1986) 8 Cr App Rep (S) 8, CA).

5. Although the default term will normally fall in the band applicable to the amount of the order, the court has a discretion to fix a period below the maximum (*R v Szrajber* (1994) 15 Cr App Rep (S) 821, [1994] Crim LR 543, CA).

3–1700   140. Enforcement of fines imposed and recognizances forfeited by Crown Court.
(1) Subject to subsection (5) below, a fine imposed or a recognizance forfeited by the Crown Court shall be treated for the purposes of collection[1], enforcement and remission of the fine or other sum as having been imposed or forfeited—

(a) by a magistrates' court specified in an order made by the Crown Court, or

(b) if no such order is made, by the magistrates' court by which the offender was committed to the Crown Court to be tried or dealt with or by* which he was sent to the Crown Court for trial under section 51 or 51A of the Crime and Disorder Act 1998,

and, in the case of a fine, as having been so imposed on conviction by the magistrates' court in question.

(2) Subsection (3) below applies where a magistrates' court issues a warrant of commitment on a default in the payment of—

(a) a fine imposed by the Crown Court; or

(b) a sum due under a recognizance forfeited by the Crown Court.

(3) In such a case, the term of imprisonment or detention under section 108 above** specified in the warrant of commitment as the term which the offender is liable to serve shall be—

(a) the term fixed by the Crown Court under section 139(2) above, or

(b) if that term has been reduced under section 79(2) of the Magistrates' Courts Act 1980 (part payment) or section 85(2) of that Act (remission), that term as so reduced,

notwithstanding that that term exceeds the period applicable to the case under section 149(1) of the Customs and Excise Management Act 1979 (maximum periods of imprisonment in default of payment of certain fines).

(4) Subsections (1) to (3) above shall apply in relation to a fine imposed or recognizance forfeited by the criminal division of the Court of Appeal, or by the House of Lords*** on appeal from that division, as they apply in relation to a fine imposed or recognizance forfeited by the Crown Court; and references in those subsections to the Crown Court (except the references in subsection (1)(b)) shall be construed accordingly.

(5) A magistrates' court shall not, under section 85(1) or 120 of the Magistrates' Courts Act 1980 as applied by subsection (1) above, remit the whole or any part of a fine imposed by, or sum due under a recognizance forfeited by—

(a) the Crown Court,

(b) the criminal division of the Court of Appeal, or

(c) the House of Lords*** on appeal from that division,

without the consent of the Crown Court.

(6) Any fine or other sum the payment of which is enforceable by a magistrates' court by virtue of this section shall be treated for the purposes of the Justices of the Peace Act 1997 and, in particular, section 60 of that Act (application of fines and fees) as having been imposed by a magistrates' court, or as being due under a recognizance forfeited by such a court.

[Powers of Criminal Courts (Sentencing) Act 2000, s 140 as amended by the Criminal Justice Act 2003, Sch 3.]

*Repealed by the Criminal Justice Act 2003, Sch 3 from a date to be appointed.
**Repealed by the Criminal Justice and Court Services Act 2000, Sch 7 from a date to be appointed.
***Substituted by the Constitutional Reform Act 2005, Sch 9 from a date to be appointed.
  1. The Crown Court may allow time for payment by instalments, see ss 139 and 141.

3–1701   141. Power of Crown Court to allow time for payment, or payment by instalments, of costs and compensation. Where the Crown Court makes any such order as is mentioned in Part I of Schedule 9 to the Administration of Justice Act 1970 (orders against accused for the payment of costs or compensation), the court may—

  (*a*) allow time for the payment of the sum due under the order;
  (*b*) direct payment of that sum by instalments of such amounts and on such dates as the court may specify.

[Powers of Criminal Courts (Sentencing) Act 2000, s 141.]

3–1702   142. Power of Crown Court to order search of persons before it. (1) Where—

  (*a*) the Crown Court imposes a fine on a person or forfeits his recognizance,
  (*b*) the Crown Court makes against a person any such order as is mentioned in paragraph 3, 4 or 9 of Schedule 9 to the Administration of Justice Act 1970 (orders for the payment of costs),
  (*c*) the Crown Court makes a compensation order against a person,
  (*d*) the Crown Court makes against a person an order under section 137 above (order for parent or guardian to pay fine, costs or compensation), or
  (*e*) on the determination of an appeal brought by a person under section 108 of the Magistrates' Courts Act 1980 a sum is payable by him, whether by virtue of an order of the Crown Court or by virtue of a conviction or order of the magistrates' court against whose decision the appeal was brought,

then, if that person is before it, the Crown Court may order him to be searched.*

  (2) Any money found on a person in a search under this section may be applied, unless the court otherwise directs, towards payment of the fine or other sum payable by him; and the balance, if any, shall be returned to him.

[Powers of Criminal Courts (Sentencing) Act 2000, s 142.]

*Subsection (1) amended and new sub-para (*za*) inserted by the Domestic Violence, Crime and Victims Act 2004, Sch 10, from a date to be appointed.

PART VII[1]
FURTHER POWERS OF COURTS

Powers to deprive offender of property used etc for purposes of crime

3–1703   143. Powers to deprive offender of property used etc for purposes of crime[2].
  (1) Where a person is convicted of an offence and the court by or before which he is convicted[3] is satisfied that any property[4] which has been lawfully seized from him, or which was in his possession[5] or under his control at the time when he was apprehended for the offence or when a summons in respect of it was issued—

  (*a*) has been used for the purpose of committing, or facilitating the commission of, any offence[6], or
  (*b*) was intended by him to be used for that purpose,

the court may (subject to subsection (5) below) make an order under this section in respect of that property.

  (2) Where a person is convicted of an offence and the offence, or an offence which the court has taken into consideration in determining his sentence, consists of unlawful possession of property which—

  (*a*) has been lawfully seized from him, or
  (*b*) was in his possession or under his control at the time when he was apprehended for the offence of which he has been convicted or when a summons in respect of that offence was issued,

the court may (subject to subsection (5) below) make an order under this section in respect of that property.

  (3) An order under this section shall operate to deprive the offender of his rights, if any, in the property to which it relates, and the property shall (if not already in their possession) be taken into the possession of the police.

  (4) Any power conferred on a court by subsection (1) or (2) above may be exercised—

  (*a*) whether or not the court also deals with the offender in any other way in respect of the offence of which he has been convicted; and
  (*b*) without regard to any restrictions on forfeiture in any enactment contained in an Act passed before 29th July 1988.

  (5) In considering whether to make an order under this section in respect of any property, a court shall have regard—

  (*a*) to the value of the property; and

(b)   to the likely financial and other effects on the offender of the making of the order (taken together with any other order[7] that the court contemplates making).

(6)   Where a person commits an offence to which this subsection applies by—

(a)   driving, attempting to drive, or being in charge of a vehicle, or

(b)   failing to comply with a requirement made under section 7 or 7A of the Road Traffic Act 1988 (failure to provide specimen for analysis or laboratory test or to give permission for such a test) in the course of an investigation into whether the offender had committed an offence while driving, attempting to drive or being in charge of a vehicle, or

(c)   failing, as the driver of a vehicle, to comply with subsection (2) or (3) of section 170 of the Road Traffic Act 1988 (duty to stop and give information or report accident),

the vehicle shall be regarded for the purposes of subsection (1) above (and section 144(1)(b) below) as used for the purpose of committing the offence (and for the purpose of committing any offence of aiding, abetting, counselling or procuring the commission of the offence).

(7)   Subsection (6) above applies to—

(a)   an offence under the Road Traffic Act 1988 which is punishable with imprisonment;

(b)   an offence of manslaughter; and

(c)   an offence under section 35 of the Offences Against the Person Act 1861 (wanton and furious driving).

(8)   Facilitating the commission of an offence shall be taken for the purposes of subsection (1) above to include the taking of any steps after it has been committed for the purpose of disposing of any property to which it relates or of avoiding apprehension or detection.

[Powers of Criminal Courts (Sentencing) Act 2000, s 143 as amended by the Police Reform Act 2002, s 56.]

---

1. Part VII contains ss 143–150.

2. There is no power to make an order under this section to secure payment of fines and compensation (*R v Kingston-upon-Hull Justices, ex p Hartung* [1981] RTR 262, [1981] Crim LR 42), nor where the use of the vehicle was merely incidental to the commission of an offence (*R v Wilmott* (1985) 149 JP 428, CA). But it may be available when dealing with an offence such as driving whilst disqualified; see *R v Highbury Corner Stipendiary Magistrate, ex p Di Matteo* [1992] 1 All ER 102, [1991] 1 WLR 1374, 156 JP 61. An opportunity should be given of making representations before such an order is made: *R v Powell and Carvell* [1985] Crim LR 330. See also *R v Ball* [2002] EWCA Crim 2777, [2003] 2 Cr App R (S), [2003] Crim LR 122.

3. It is suggested that this subsection is qualified by s 6 ante, which thus enables the Crown Court on a committal from a magistrates' court to make an order of deprivation. A magistrates' court should not be misled into thinking that it alone has power to make an order in these circumstances.

4. "Property" does not include real property (*R v Khan* [1982] 3 All ER 969, [1982] 1 WLR 1405, [1982] Crim LR 752 and *R v Pearce* (1996) 2 Cr App Rep (S) 316, [1996] Crim LR 442, CA). It has been held that s 143 does not authorise the making of a deprivation order in respect of property which appears to be the proceeds of earlier offences (*R v Neville* (1987) 9 Cr App Rep (S) 222, [1987] Crim LR 585, CA; see, however, *R v O'Farrell* (1988) 10 Cr App Rep (S) 74 in which an offender's "working capital" for future drugs dealing was properly forfeited.

5. "Property" does not include real property (*R v Khan* [1982] 3 All ER 969, [1982] 1 WLR 1405, [1982] Crim LR 752 and *R v Pearce* (1996) 2 Cr App Rep (S) 316, [1996] Crim LR 442, CA). It has been held that s 143 does not authorise the making of a deprivation order in respect of property which appears to be the proceeds of earlier offences (*R v Neville* (1987) 9 Cr App Rep (S) 222, [1987] Crim LR 585, CA; see, however, *R v O'Farrell* (1988) 10 Cr App Rep (S) 74 in which an offender's "working capital" for future drugs dealing was properly forfeited.

6. There is no power to order forfeiture of an offender's right in property unless the property has been used for the purpose of committing or facilitating the commission of an offence by him, although it does not have to be the actual offence of which he has been convicted. However, there is nothing in s 143(1)(a) to require that the user and the offender have to be one and the same; see *R v Colville-Scott* [1990] 1 WLR 958 (defendant who was convicted of being concerned in the illegal importation of drugs found on arrest to have in his possession £125,000 which represented payment for arranging illegal drug deals–held that as the payments had been made to facilitate the commission of the defendant's offences of importation the court had power to make a deprivation order).

7. The deprivation order should be considered as part of the overall penalty for the offence and the other sentence should be adjusted accordingly (*R v Joyce* [1991] RTR 241, 11 Cr App Rep (S) 253, CA; *R v Priestly* (1996) 2 Cr App Rep (S) 144, [1996] Crim LR 356).

3–1704   **144. Property which is in possession of police by virtue of section 143.**   (1) The Police (Property) Act 1897 shall apply, with the following modifications, to property which is in the possession of the police by virtue of section 143 above—

(a)   no application shall be made under section 1(1) of that Act by any claimant of the property after the end of six months from the date on which the order in respect of the property was made under section 143 above; and

(b)   no such application shall succeed unless the claimant satisfies the court either—

(i)   that he had not consented to the offender having possession of the property; or

(ii)   where an order is made under subsection (1) of section 143 above, that he did not know, and had no reason to suspect, that the property was likely to be used for the purpose mentioned in that subsection.

(2)   In relation to property which is in the possession of the police by virtue of section 143 above, the power to make regulations under section 2 of the Police (Property) Act 1897 (disposal of property in cases where the owner of the property has not been ascertained and no order of a competent court has been made with respect to it) shall, subject to subsection (3) below, include power to make regulations for disposal (including disposal by vesting in the relevant authority) in cases where no application by a claimant of the property has been made within the period specified in subsection (1)(a) above or no such application has succeeded.

(3) The regulations may not provide for the vesting in the relevant authority of property in relation to which an order has been made under section 145 below (court order as to application of proceeds of forfeited property).

(4) Nothing in subsection (2A)(*a*) or (3) of section 2 of the Police (Property) Act 1897 limits the power to make regulations under that section by virtue of subsection (2) above.

(5) In this section "relevant authority" has the meaning given by section 2(2B) of the Police (Property) Act 1897.

[Powers of Criminal Courts (Sentencing) Act 2000, s 144.]

3–1705   145. Application of proceeds of forfeited property.   (1) Where a court makes an order under section 143 above in a case where—

(*a*)   the offender has been convicted of an offence which has resulted in a person suffering personal injury, loss or damage, or

(*b*)   any such offence is taken into consideration by the court in determining sentence,

the court may also make an order that any proceeds which arise from the disposal of the property and which do not exceed a sum specified by the court shall be paid to that person.

(2) The court may make an order under this section only if it is satisfied that but for the inadequacy of the offender's means it would have made a compensation order under which the offender would have been required to pay compensation of an amount not less than the specified amount.

(3) An order under this section has no effect—

(*a*)   before the end of the period specified in section 144(1)(*a*) above; or

(*b*)   if a successful application under section 1(1) of the Police (Property) Act 1897 has been made.

[Powers of Criminal Courts (Sentencing) Act 2000, s 145.]

Driving disqualifications

3–1706   146. Driving disqualification for any offence.   (1) The court by or before which a person is convicted of an offence committed after 31st December 1997 may[1], instead of or in addition to dealing with him in any other way, order him to be disqualified, for such period as it thinks fit, for holding or obtaining a driving licence.

(2) Where the person is convicted of an offence the sentence for which is fixed by law or falls to be imposed under section 110(2) or 111(2) above, section 51A(2) of the Firearms Act 1968 or section 225, 226, 227 or 228 of the Criminal Justice Act 2003, subsection (1) above shall have effect as if the words "instead of or" were omitted.*

(3) A court shall not make an order under subsection (1) above unless the court has been notified[2] by the Secretary of State that the power to make such orders is exercisable by the court and the notice has not been withdrawn.

(4) A court which makes an order under this section disqualifying a person for holding or obtaining a driving licence shall require him to produce—

(*a*)   any such licence held by him together with its counterpart;

(*aa*) in the case where he holds a Northern Ireland licence (within the meaning of Part 3 of the Road Traffic Act 1988), his Northern Ireland licence and its counterpart (if any) or;

(*b*)   in the case where he holds a Community licence (within the meaning of Part III of the Road Traffic Act 1988), his Community licence and its counterpart (if any).

(5) In this section—

"driving licence" means a licence to drive a motor vehicle granted under Part III of the Road Traffic Act 1988;

"counterpart"—

(*a*)   in relation to a driving licence, has the meaning given in relation to such a licence by section 108(1) of that Act;

(*aa*) in relation to a Northern Ireland licence, has the meaning given by section 109A of that Act; and

(*b*)   in relation to a Community licence, has the meaning given by section 99B of that Act.

[Powers of Criminal Courts (Sentencing) Act 2000, s 146 as amended by the Crime (International Co-operation) Act 2003, Sch 5 and the Criminal Justice Act 2003, Sch 32.]

---

*Amended by the Criminal Justice Act 2003, Sch 32 from a date to be appointed.

1. It is not necessary for the offence for which the defendant is being sentenced to be connected to the use of a motor car, though there must be sufficient reason for the disqualification: *R v Cliff* [2004] EWCA Crim 3139, [2005] RTR 11, [2005] Crim LR 250.

2. Notification of the power to exercise the power under this section was given to courts by HOC 59/2003 for implementation from 1 January 2004. See commentary at **3–522A**.

3–1707   147. Driving disqualification where vehicle used for purposes of crime.   (1) This section applies where a person—

(*a*)   is convicted before the Crown Court of an offence punishable on indictment with imprisonment for a term of two years or more; or (*b*) having been convicted by a magistrates' court of such an offence, is committed under section 3 above to the Crown Court for sentence.

(2) This section also applies where a person is convicted by or before any court of common assault or of any other offence involving an assault (including an offence of aiding, abetting, counselling or procuring, or inciting to the commission of, an offence)[1].

(3) If, in a case to which this section applies by virtue of subsection (1) above, the Crown Court is satisfied that a motor vehicle was used (by the person convicted or by anyone else) for the purpose of committing, or facilitating the commission of, the offence in question, the court may order the person convicted to be disqualified, for such period as the court thinks fit, for holding or obtaining a driving licence.

(4) If, in a case to which this section applies by virtue of subsection (2) above, the court is satisfied that the assault was committed by driving a motor vehicle, the court may order the person convicted to be disqualified, for such period as the court thinks fit, for holding or obtaining a driving licence.

(5) A court which makes an order under this section disqualifying a person for holding or obtaining a driving licence shall require him to produce—

(*a*) any such licence held by him together with its counterpart;

(*aa*) in the case where he holds a Northern Ireland licence (within the meaning of Part 3 of the Road Traffic Act 1988), his Northern Ireland licence and its counterpart (if any); or

(*b*) in the case where he holds a Community licence (within the meaning of Part III of the Road Traffic Act 1988), his Community licence and its counterpart (if any).

(6) Facilitating the commission of an offence shall be taken for the purposes of this section to include the taking of any steps after it has been committed for the purpose of disposing of any property to which it relates or of avoiding apprehension or detection.

(7) In this section "driving licence" and "counterpart" have the meanings given by section 146(5) above.

[Powers of Criminal Courts (Sentencing) Act 2000, s 147 as amended by the Crime (International Co-operation) Act 2003, Schs 5 and 6.]

---

1. Sub-ss (1) and (2) empower disqualification for offences other than those carrying endorsement and disqualification under the Road Traffic Act 1988; the disqualification will not be endorsed on the offender's licence, and s 35 of the Road Traffic Offenders Act 1988 (disqualification for repeated offences) will not apply. The power has been held not to apply to the offence of conspiracy (*R v Riley* [1984] Crim LR 40). For consideration of the principles to be applied in the use of this power, see *R v Arif* (1985) 7 Cr App Rep (S) 92, [1985] Crim LR 523, CA and *R v Rajesh Patel* (1995) 16 Cr App Rep (S) 827, [1995] Crim LR 440, CA and commentaries thereto. Where a vehicle is used for the fraudulent evasion of duty chargeable on cigarettes, disqualification under this section is appropriate and may be imposed whether or not any particular defendant was actually involved in the driving: *R v Skitt* [2004] EWCA Crim 3141, [2005] 2 Cr App R (S) 23.

Restitution orders[1]

3–1708 148. Restitution orders. (1) This section applies where goods have been stolen[2], and either—

(*a*) a person is convicted of any offence with reference to the theft (whether or not the stealing is the gist of his offence); or

(*b*) a person is convicted of any other offence, but such an offence as is mentioned in paragraph (*a*) above is taken into consideration in determining his sentence.

(2) Where this section applies, the court by or before which the offender is convicted may on the conviction (whether or not the passing of sentence is in other respects deferred) exercise any of the following powers—

(*a*) the court may order anyone having possession or control of the stolen goods to restore them to any person entitled to recover them from him; or

(*b*) on the application of a person entitled to recover from the person convicted any other goods directly or indirectly representing the stolen goods (as being the proceeds of any disposal or realisation of the whole or part of them or of goods so representing them), the court may order those other goods to be delivered or transferred to the applicant; or

(*c*) the court may order that a sum not exceeding the value of the stolen goods shall be paid, out of any money of the person convicted which was taken out of his possession on his apprehension, to any person who, if those goods were in the possession of the person convicted, would be entitled to recover them from him;

and in this subsection "the stolen goods" means the goods referred to in subsection (1) above.

(3) Where the court has power on a person's conviction to make an order against him both under paragraph (*b*) and under paragraph (*c*) of subsection (2) above with reference to the stealing of the same goods, the court may make orders under both paragraphs provided that the person in whose favour the orders are made does not thereby recover more than the value of those goods.

(4) Where the court on a person's conviction makes an order under subsection (2)(*a*) above for the restoration of any goods, and it appears to the court that the person convicted—

(*a*) has sold the goods to a person acting in good faith, or

(*b*) has borrowed money on the security of them from a person so acting,

the court may order that there shall be paid to the purchaser or lender, out of any money of the person convicted which was taken out of his possession on his apprehension, a sum not exceeding the amount paid for the purchase by the purchaser or, as the case may be, the amount owed to the lender in respect of the loan.

(5) The court shall not exercise the powers conferred by this section unless in the opinion of the court the relevant facts sufficiently appear from evidence given at the trial or the available documents, together with admissions made by or on behalf of any person in connection with any proposed exercise of the powers.

(6) In subsection (5) above "the available documents" means—

(a) any written statements or admissions which were made for use, and would have been admissible, as evidence at the trial; and

(b) such written statements, depositions and other documents as were tendered by or on behalf of the prosecutor at any committal proceedings.*

(7) Any order under this section shall be treated as an order for the restitution of property within the meaning of section 30 of the Criminal Appeal Act 1968 (which relates to the effect on such orders of appeals).

(8) Subject to subsection (9) below, references in this section to stealing shall be construed in accordance with section 1(1) of the Theft Act 1968 (read with the provisions of that Act relating to the construction of section 1(1)).

(9) Subsections (1) and (4) of section 24 of that Act (interpretation of certain provisions) shall also apply in relation to this section as they apply in relation to the provisions of that Act relating to goods which have been stolen.

(10) In this section and section 149 below, "goods", except in so far as the context otherwise requires, includes money and every other description of property (within the meaning of the Theft Act 1968) except land, and includes things severed from the land by stealing.

(11) An order may be made under this section in respect of money owed by the Crown.

[Powers of Criminal Courts (Sentencing) Act 2000, s 148.]

---

*Sub-para substituted by the Criminal Justice Act 2003, Sch 3, in force in relation to cases sent for trial under the Crime and Disorder Act 1998, ss 51 or 51A(3)(d) and for remaining purposes from a date to be appointed: '(b) such documents as were served on the offender in pursuance of regulations made under paragraph 1 of Schedule 3 to the Crime and Disorder Act 1998'.

1. For full discussion of this power see para **3–520**, ante.

2. Or obtained by deception or blackmail (sub-s (9), infra, and the Theft Act 1968, s 24(1) and (4), in PART VIII: THEFT, post).

3–1709   149. Restitution orders: supplementary.   (1) The following provisions of this section shall have effect with respect to section 148 above.

(2) The powers conferred by subsections (2)(c) and (4) of that section shall be exercisable without any application being made in that behalf or on the application of any person appearing to the court to be interested in the property concerned.

(3) Where an order is made under that section against any person in respect of an offence taken into consideration in determining his sentence—

(a) the order shall cease to have effect if he successfully appeals against his conviction of the offence or, if more than one, all the offences, of which he was convicted in the proceedings in which the order was made;

(b) he may appeal against the order as if it were part of the sentence imposed in respect of the offence or, if more than one, any of the offences, of which he was so convicted.

(4) Any order under that section made by a magistrates' court shall be suspended—

(a) in any case until the end of the period for the time being prescribed by law for the giving of notice of appeal against a decision of a magistrates' court;

(b) where notice of appeal is given within the period so prescribed, until the determination of the appeal;

but this subsection shall not apply where the order is made under section 148(2)(a) or (b) and the court so directs, being of the opinion that the title to the goods to be restored or, as the case may be, delivered or transferred under the order is not in dispute.

[Powers of Criminal Courts (Sentencing) Act 2000, s 149.]

Young offenders

3–1710   150. Binding over of parent or guardian.   (1) Where a child or young person (that is to say, any person aged under 18) is convicted of an offence, the powers conferred by this section shall be exercisable by the court by which he is sentenced for that offence, and where the offender is aged under 16 when sentenced it shall be the duty of that court—

(a) to exercise those powers if it is satisfied, having regard to the circumstances of the case, that their exercise would be desirable in the interests of preventing the commission by him of further offences; and

(b) if it does not exercise them, to state in open court that it is not satisfied as mentioned in paragraph (a) above and why it is not so satisfied;

but this subsection has effect subject to section 19(5) above and paragraph 13(5) of Schedule 1 to this Act (cases where referral orders made or extended).

(2) The powers conferred by this section are as follows—

   (a) with the consent of the offender's parent or guardian, to order the parent or guardian to enter into a recognizance to take proper care of him and exercise proper control over him; and

   (b) if the parent or guardian refuses consent and the court considers the refusal unreasonable, to order the parent or guardian to pay a fine not exceeding £1,000;

and where the court has passed a community sentence on the offender, it may include in the recognizance a provision that the offender's parent or guardian ensure that the offender complies with the requirements of that sentence.

(3) An order under this section shall not require the parent or guardian to enter into a recognizance for an amount exceeding £1,000.

(4) An order under this section shall not require the parent or guardian to enter into a recognizance—

   (a) for a period exceeding three years; or

   (b) where the offender will attain the age of 18 in a period shorter than three years, for a period exceeding that shorter period.

(5) Section 120 of the Magistrates' Courts Act 1980 (forfeiture of recognizances) shall apply in relation to a recognizance entered into in pursuance of an order under this section as it applies in relation to a recognizance to keep the peace.

(6) A fine imposed under subsection (2)(b) above shall be deemed, for the purposes of any enactment, to be a sum adjudged to be paid by a conviction.

(7) In fixing the amount of a recognizance under this section, the court shall take into account among other things the means of the parent or guardian so far as they appear or are known to the court; and this subsection applies whether taking into account the means of the parent or guardian has the effect of increasing or reducing the amount of the recognizance.

(8) A parent or guardian may appeal to the Crown Court against an order under this section made by a magistrates' court.

(9) A parent or guardian may appeal to the Court of Appeal against an order under this section made by the Crown Court, as if he had been convicted on indictment and the order were a sentence passed on his conviction.

(10) A court may vary or revoke an order made by it under this section if, on the application of the parent or guardian, it appears to the court, having regard to any change in the circumstances since the order was made, to be in the interests of justice to do so.

(11) For the purposes of this section, taking "care" of a person includes giving him protection and guidance and "control" includes discipline.

[Powers of Criminal Courts (Sentencing) Act 2000, s 150.]

PART VIII[1]
MISCELLANEOUS AND SUPPLEMENTARY

Factors to be taken into account in sentencing

3–1711   151–153.   *Repealed.*

---

1. Part VIII contains ss 151–168.

Commencement and alteration of Crown Court sentence

3–1714   154. Commencement of Crown Court sentence.   (1) A sentence imposed, or other order made, by the Crown Court when dealing with an offender shall take effect from the beginning of the day on which it is imposed, unless the court otherwise directs[1].

(2) The power to give a direction under subsection (1) above has effect subject to section 265 of the Criminal Justice Act 2003 (restriction on consecutive sentences for released prisoners).

(3) In this section "sentence" and "order" shall be construed in accordance with section 155(8) below.

[Powers of Criminal Courts (Sentencing) Act 2000, s 154 as amended by the Criminal Justice Act 2003, Sch 32.]

---

1. The court is not empowered to order a sentence to commence on a date earlier than the date that is pronounced (*R v Gilbert* [1975] 1 All ER 742, [1975] 1 WLR 1012, 139 JP 273).

3–1715   155. Alteration of Crown Court sentence.   (1) Subject to the following provisions of this section, a sentence imposed, or other order made, by the Crown Court when dealing with an offender may be varied[1] or rescinded by the Crown Court within the period of 28 days beginning with the day on which the sentence or other order was imposed or made or, where subsection (2) below applies, within the time allowed by that subsection.

(2) Where two or more persons are jointly tried on an indictment, then, subject to the following provisions of this section, a sentence imposed, or other order made, by the Crown Court on conviction of any of those persons on the indictment may be varied or rescinded by the Crown Court not later than the expiry of whichever is the shorter of the following periods, that is—

   (a) the period of 28 days beginning with the date of conclusion of the joint trial;

(b)   the period of 56 days beginning with the day on which the sentence or other order was imposed or made.

(3) For the purposes of subsection (2) above, the joint trial is concluded on the latest of the following dates, that is any date on which any of the persons jointly tried is sentenced or is acquitted or on which a special verdict is brought in.

(4) A sentence or other order shall not be varied or rescinded under this section except by the court constituted as it was when the sentence or other order was imposed or made, or, where that court comprised one or more justices of the peace, a court so constituted except for the omission of any one or more of those justices.

(5) Subject to subsection (6) below, where a sentence or other order is varied under this section the sentence or other order, as so varied, shall take effect from the beginning of the day on which it was originally imposed or made, unless the court otherwise directs.

(6) For the purposes of—

(a)   section 18(2) of the Criminal Appeal Act 1968 (time limit for notice of appeal or of application for leave to appeal), and

(b)   paragraph 1 of Schedule 3 to the Criminal Justice Act 1988 (time limit for notice of an application for leave to refer a case under section 36 of that Act),

the sentence or other order shall be regarded as imposed or made on the day on which it is varied under this section.

(7) Criminal Procedure Rules—

(a)   may, as respects cases where two or more persons are tried separately on the same or related facts alleged in one or more indictments, provide for extending the period fixed by subsection (1) above;

(b)   may, subject to the preceding provisions of this section, prescribe the cases and circumstances in which, and the time within which, any order or other decision made by the Crown Court may be varied or rescinded by that court.

(8) In this section—

"sentence" includes a recommendation for deportation made when dealing with an offender;
"order" does not include an order under section 17(2) of the Access to Justice Act 1999.
[Powers of Criminal Courts (Sentencing) Act 2000, s 155 as amended by SI 2004/2035.]

---

1. "Varied" has a wide meaning, including changing the nature of the sentence (*R v Sodhi* (1978) 66 Cr App Rep 260), and making a confiscation order under the Drug Trafficking Offences Act 1986, s 1, when originally no confiscation was ordered (*R v Miller* (1990) 155 JP 446, 92 Cr App Rep 191, CA). The court may not rescind a sentence within the 28 days and then impose a substitute sentence outside the period (*R v Stilwell and Jewell* (1991) 156 JP 335, CA). Apparently the Crown Court also possesses a wider inherent power, unlimited in time, to remedy mistakes in its record (*R v Saville* [1981] QB 12, [1980] 1 All ER 861).

Disclosure of pre-sentence reports etc

3–1716   156–158.   *Repealed.*

3–1719   159.   Execution of process between England and Wales and Scotland.   Section 4 of the Summary Jurisdiction (Process) Act 1881 (execution of process of English and Welsh courts in Scotland) shall apply to any process issued under—

section 1(7), 1B(3), 1C(4),] 13(1), 104(1)above,
paragraph 3(2) of Schedule 1* to this Act,
paragraph 3(1), 10(6) or 18(1) of Schedule 3 to this Act,
paragraph 1(1) of Schedule 5 to this Act,
paragraph 7(2) of Schedule 7 to this Act, or
paragraph 6(2) of Schedule 8 to this Act,

as it applies to process issued under the Magistrates' Courts Act 1980 by a magistrates' court.
[Powers of Criminal Courts (Sentencing) Act 2000, s 159 as amended by the Criminal Justice Act 2003, Schs 23, 36 and 37.]

---

*Substituted by the Criminal Justice Act 2003, Sch 36 from a date to be appointed.

3–1720   160.   *Rules and orders*

Interpretation

3–1721   161.   Meaning of "associated offence", "sexual offence", "violent offence" and "protecting the public from serious harm".   (1) For the purposes of this Act, an offence is associated with another if—

(a)   the offender is convicted of it in the proceedings in which he is convicted of the other offence, or (although convicted of it in earlier proceedings) is sentenced[1] for it at the same time as he is sentenced for that offence; or

(b) the offender admits the commission of it in the proceedings in which he is sentenced for the other offence and requests the court to take it into consideration in sentencing him for that offence.

(2)–(4) *Repealed.*

[Powers of Criminal Courts (Sentencing) Act 2000, s 161 as amended by the Sexual Offences Act 2003, Schs 6 and 7 and the Criminal Justice Act 2003, Sch 37.]

---

1. Activating a suspended sentence of imprisonment is not passing a new sentence and therefore the offence in respect of which it was imposed may not be an "associated offence" within the meaning of s 161(1) (*R v Crawford* (1993) 157 JP 667, 14 Cr App Rep (S) 782). The position is the same for an offence in respect of which a conditional discharge has been ordered (*R v Godfrey* [1993] Crim LR 540).

2. Whether the offence is a violent offence depends on the facts of the particular case; see *R v Cochrane* (1994) 15 Cr App Rep (S) 708 and *R v Bibby* [1994] 16 Cr App Rep (S) 127, Crim LR 611 (cases involving robbery at knife point); *R v Touriq Khan* (1994) 16 Cr App Rep (S) 180, [1994] Crim LR 862, CA (robbery with unloaded revolver). "Violent offence" does not extend to an offence leading to a reasonable apprehension of violence in the victim and so does not include a telephoned or mailed threat of violence (*R v Richart* (1995) 16 Cr App Rep (S) 977 [1995] Crim LR 574) except in the rare circumstances where the threat, in the circumstances of the victim, was intended to lead to death or injury (*R v Ragg* [1995] 4 All ER 155 [1995] Crim LR 664)

3. It should be noted that the section does not require the injury to be "serious"; see *R v Robinson* [1993] 2 All ER 1, [1993] 1 WLR 168).

4. It is not necessary for the offender to be a threat to the general public, an individual or small group of individuals will suffice (*R v Hashi* (1994) 16 Cr App Rep (S) 121 [1994] Crim LR 618). See also *R v S* [1994] Crim LR 868, CA (longer than normal sentence not justified for sexual offences committed against the children of the offender's own family where he was not a danger to children outside the family and was unlikely to form another family circle).

5. Where the relevant offence is a "violent offence" for the purposes of s 161(3), even though there is a record of previous violent offending which suggests the likelihood of violence in the future, there may be an issue as to whether the kind of violence likely to be committed in the future is likely to result in "serious physical injury" for the purposes of s 161(4). See *R v Gardiner* (1994) 15 Cr App Rep (S) 747, [1994] Crim LR 539, and *R v Ely* (1994) 15 Cr App Rep (S) 881, [1994] Crim LR 539.

3–1722 **162. Meaning of "pre-sentence report".** *Repealed.*

3–1723 **163. General definitions.** In this Act, except where the contrary intention appears—

"action plan order" means an order under section 69(1) above;

"affected person"—

(a) in relation to an exclusion order, has the meaning given by section 40A(13) above;

(b) *repealed*

(c) *repealed*

"associated", in relation to offences, shall be construed in accordance with section 161(1) above;

"attendance centre" has the meaning given by section 221(2) of the Criminal Justice Act 2003;★

"attendance centre order" means an order under section 60(1) above (and, except where the contrary intention is shown by paragraph 8 of Schedule 3 or paragraph 4 of Schedule 7 or 8 to this Act, includes orders made under section 60(1) by virtue of paragraph 4(1)(c) or 5(1)(c) of Schedule 3 or paragraph 2(2)(a) of Schedule 7 or 8);★

"child" means a person under the age of 14[1];

"community order" has the meaning given by section 177(1) of the Criminal Justice Act 2003;

"community sentence" has the meaning given by section 33(2) above;

"compensation order" has the meaning given by section 130(1) above;

"court" does not include a court-martial;

"curfew order" means an order under section 37(1) above (and, except where the contrary intention is shown by section 59 above or paragraph 3 of Schedule 7 or 8 to this Act or section 35 of the Crime (Sentences) Act 1997, includes orders made under section 37(1) by virtue of section 59 or paragraph 2(2)(a) of Schedule 7 or 8 or the said section 35);★

"custodial sentence" has the meaning given by section 76 above★;

"detention and training order" has the meaning given by section 100(3) above;

"exclusion order" means an order under section 40A(1) above;

"guardian" has the same meaning as in the Children and Young Persons Act 1933;

"local authority accommodation" means accommodation provided by or on behalf of a local authority, and "accommodation provided by or on behalf of a local authority" here has the same meaning as it has in the Children Act 1989 by virtue of section 105 of that Act;

"local probation board" means a local probation board established under section 4 of the Criminal Justice and Court Services Act 2000;

"offence punishable with imprisonment" shall be construed in accordance with section 164(2) below;

"operational period", in relation to a suspended sentence, has the meaning given by section 189(1)(b)(ii) of the Criminal Justice Act 2003;

"order for conditional discharge" has the meaning given by section 12(3) above;

"period of conditional discharge" has the meaning given by section 12(3) above;

"referral order" means an order under section 16(2) or (3) above;

"the register" means the register of proceedings before a magistrates' court required by Criminal Procedure Rules to be kept by the designated officer for the court;

"reparation order" means an order under section 73(1) above;

"responsible officer"—

(*a*) in relation to a curfew order, has the meaning given by section 37(12) above;
(*aa*) in relation to an exclusion order, has the meaning given by section 40A(14) above;
(*b*)–(*ee*) *repealed*
(*f*) in relation to an action plan order, has the meaning given by section 69(4) above; and
(*g*) in relation to a reparation order, has the meaning given by section 74(5) above;

"sentence of imprisonment" does not include a committal—

(*a*) in default of payment of any sum of money;
(*b*) for want of sufficient distress to satisfy any sum of money; or
(*c*) for failure to do or abstain from doing anything required to be done or left undone;

and references to sentencing an offender to imprisonment shall be construed accordingly;

"supervision order" means an order under section 63(1) above;
"supervisor", in relation to a supervision order, has the meaning given by section 63(3) above;
"suspended sentence" has the meaning given by section 189(7) of the Criminal Justice Act 2003;
"young person" means a person aged at least 14 but under 18[1];
"youth community order" has the meaning given by section 33(1) above;
"youth offending team" means a team established under section 39 of the Crime and Disorder Act 1998.

[Powers of Criminal Courts (Sentencing) Act 2000, s 163, as amended by the Criminal Justice and Court Services Act 2000, s 74, SI 2001/618 and the Criminal Justice and Court Services Act 2000, s 74 and the Criminal Justice Act 2003, Schs 32 and 37.]

---

*Amended by the Criminal Justice and Court Services Act 2000, Sch 7 from a date to be appointed.
1. A person attains a particular age at the commencement of the relevant anniversary of the date of his birth : s 9 of the Family Law Reform Act 1969.

3–1724   164. Further interpretive provisions. (1) For the purposes of any provision of this Act which requires the determination of the age of a person by the court or the Secretary of State, his age shall be deemed to be that which it appears to the court or (as the case may be) the Secretary of State to be after considering any available evidence[1].

(2) Any reference in this Act to an offence punishable with imprisonment shall be construed without regard to any prohibition or restriction imposed by or under this or any Act on the imprisonment of young offenders.

(3) References in this Act to a sentence falling to be imposed—

(*a*) under section 110(2) or 111(2) above,
(*b*) under section 51A(2) of the Firearms Act 1968, or
(*c*) under any of sections 225 to 228 of the Criminal Justice Act 2003,

are to be read in accordance with section 305(4) of the Criminal Justice Act 2003.
[Powers of Criminal Courts (Sentencing) Act 2000, s 164 as amended by the Criminal Justice Act 2003, Sch 32.]

---

1. Proof that a child was under a certain age was established by the evidence of a mistress of an elementary school attended by the child, corroborated by an officer of the Society for the Prevention of Cruelty to Children (*R v Cox* [1898] 1 QB 179). If on the material before the court an offender is deemed to be of a certain age, he shall be treated on that basis; the fact that he is subsequently found to be below that age does not invalidate a sentence not otherwise available to a person of his age (see *R v Brown* (1989) 11 Cr App Rep (S) 263 (imprisonment imposed on an offender subsequently found to be under 21 years).

Final provisions

3–1725   165. Consequential amendments, transitory modifications, transitional provisions and repeals. (1) Schedule 9 to this Act (which contains amendments consequential on this Act) shall have effect.

(2) Schedule 10 to this Act (which contains transitory modifications of this Act) shall have effect.
(3) Schedule 11 to this Act (which contains transitional provisions) shall have effect.
(4) The enactments mentioned in Part I of Schedule 12 to this Act and the instruments mentioned in Part II of that Schedule are hereby repealed or revoked to the extent specified in the third column of those Parts.
[Powers of Criminal Courts (Sentencing) Act 2000, s 165.]

3–1726   166. Short title. This Act may be cited as the Powers of Criminal Courts (Sentencing) Act 2000.
[Powers of Criminal Courts (Sentencing) Act 2000, s 166.]

3–1727   167. Extent. (1) Subject to subsections (2) to (4) below, this Act extends to England and Wales only.

(2) The following provisions also extend to Scotland, namely—

section 14;
sections 44, 49 and 51(6);
section 121(3);
section 159;
this section; and

Schedule 4.

(3) The following provisions also extend to Northern Ireland, namely—

sections 44, 49 and 51(6);
this section; and
Schedule 4.

(4) The extent of any amendment, repeal or revocation made by this Act is the same as that of the enactment amended, repealed or revoked.

(5) For the purposes of the Scotland Act 1998, any provision of this Act which extends to Scotland is to be taken to be a pre-commencement enactment within the meaning of that Act.
[Powers of Criminal Courts (Sentencing) Act 2000, s 167.]

3–1728 168. Commencement. (1) Subject to paragraph 11 of Schedule 11 (special provisions relating to referral orders), this Act shall come into force at the end of the period of three months beginning with the day on which it is passed (and references to the commencement of this Act are to its coming into force then).

(2) *Repealed.*

(3) *Repealed.*

[Powers of Criminal Courts (Sentencing) Act 2000, s 168 as amended by the Criminal Justice Act 2003, Sch 37.]

SCHEDULE 1

YOUTH OFFENDER PANELS: FURTHER COURT PROCEEDINGS

(*As amended by Criminal Justice Act 2003, Sch 34 and SI 2005/886*)

Section 28

PART I

REFERRAL BACK TO APPROPRIATE COURT

Introductory

3–1729 1. (1) This Part of this Schedule applies where a youth offender panel refers an offender back to the appropriate court under section 22(2), 25(2) or (3), 26(5), (8) or (10) or 27(4) of this Act.

(2) For the purposes of this Part of this Schedule and the provisions mentioned in sub-paragraph (1) above the appropriate court is—

(*a*) in the case of an offender aged under 18 at the time when (in pursuance of the referral back) he first appears before the court, a youth court acting in the local justice area in which it appears to the youth offender panel that the offender resides or will reside; and

(*b*) otherwise, a magistrates' court (other than a youth court) acting in that area.

Mode of referral back to court

2. The panel shall make the referral by sending a report to the appropriate court explaining why the offender is being referred back to it.

Bringing the offender before the court

3. (1) Where the appropriate court receives such a report, the court shall cause the offender to appear before it.

(2) For the purpose of securing the attendance of the offender before the court, a justice acting in the local justice area in which the court acts may—

(*a*) issue a summons requiring the offender to appear at the place and time specified in it; or

(*b*) if the report is substantiated on oath, issue a warrant for the offender's arrest.

(3) Any summons or warrant issued under sub-paragraph (2) above shall direct the offender to appear or be brought before the appropriate court.

Detention and remand of arrested offender

4. (1) Where the offender is arrested in pursuance of a warrant under paragraph 3(2) above and cannot be brought immediately before the appropriate court—

(*a*) the person in whose custody he is may make arrangements for his detention in a place of safety (within the meaning given by section 107(1) of the Children and Young Persons Act 1933) for a period of not more than 72 hours from the time of the arrest (and it shall be lawful for him to be detained in pursuance of the arrangements); and

(*b*) that person shall within that period bring him before a court which—

(i) if he is under the age of 18 when he is brought before the court, shall be a youth court; and

(ii) if he has then attained that age, shall be a magistrate's court other than a youth court.

(2) Sub-paragraphs (3) to (5) below apply where the court before which the offender is brought under sub-paragraph (1)(*b*) above ("the alternative court") is not the appropriate court.

(3) The alternative court may direct that he is to be released forthwith or remand him.

(4) Section 128 of the Magistrates' Courts Act 1980 (remand in custody or on bail) shall have effect where the alternative court has power under sub-paragraph (3) above to remand the offender as if the court referred to in subsections (1)(*a*), (3), (4)(*a*) and (5) were the appropriate court.

(5) That section shall have effect where the alternative court has power so to remand him, or the appropriate court has (by virtue of sub-paragraph (4) above) power to further remand him, as if in subsection (1) there were inserted after paragraph (*c*)

"or

(d) if he is aged under 18, remand him to accommodation provided by or on behalf of a local authority (within the meaning of the Children Act 1989) and, if it does so, shall designate as the authority who are to receive him the local authority for the area in which it appears to the court that he resides or will reside;".

Power of court where it upholds panel's decision

5. (1) If it is proved to the satisfaction of the appropriate court as regards any decision of the panel which resulted in the offender being referred back to the court—

(a) that, so far as the decision relied on any finding of fact by the panel, the panel was entitled to make that finding in the circumstances, and

(b) that, so far as the decision involved any exercise of discretion by the panel, the panel reasonably exercised that discretion in the circumstances,

the court may exercise the power conferred by sub-paragraph (2) below.

(2) That power is a power to revoke the referral order (or each of the referral orders).

(3) The revocation under sub-paragraph (2) above of a referral order has the effect of revoking any related order under paragraph 11 or 12 below.

(4) Where any order is revoked under sub-paragraph (2) above or by virtue of sub-paragraph (3) above, the appropriate court may deal with the offender in accordance with sub-paragraph (5) below for the offence in respect of which the revoked order was made.

(5) In so dealing with the offender for such an offence, the appropriate court—

(a) may deal with him in any way in which (assuming section 16 of this Act had not applied) he could have been dealt with for that offence by the court which made the order; and

(b) shall have regard to—

(i) the circumstances of his referral back to the court; and

(ii) where a contract has taken effect under section 23 of this Act between the offender and the panel, the extent of his compliance with the terms of the contract.

(6) The appropriate court may not exercise the powers conferred by sub-paragraph (2) or (4) above unless the offender is present before it; but those powers are exercisable even if, in a case where a contract has taken effect under section 23, the period for which the contract has effect has expired (whether before or after the referral of the offender back to the court).

Appeal

6. Where the court in exercise of the power conferred by paragraph 5(4) above deals with the offender for an offence, the offender may appeal to the Crown Court against the sentence.

Court not revoking referral order or orders

7. (1) This paragraph applies—

(a) where the appropriate court decides that the matters mentioned in paragraphs (a) and (b) of paragraph 5(1) above have not been proved to its satisfaction; or

(b) where, although by virtue of paragraph 5(1) above the appropriate court—

(i) is able to exercise the power conferred by paragraph 5(2) above, or

(ii) would be able to do so if the offender were present before it,

the court (for any reason) decides not to exercise that power.

(2) If either—

(a) no contract has taken effect under section 23 of this Act between the offender and the panel, or

(b) a contract has taken effect under that section but the period for which it has effect has not expired,

the offender shall continue to remain subject to the referral order (or orders) in all respects as if he had not been referred back to the court.

(3) If—

(a) a contract had taken effect under section 23 of this Act, but

(b) the period for which it has effect has expired (otherwise than by virtue of section 24(6)),

the court shall make an order declaring that the referral order (or each of the referral orders) is discharged.

Exception where court satisfied as to completion of contract

8. If, in a case where the offender is referred back to the court under section 27(4) of this Act, the court decides (contrary to the decision of the panel) that the offender's compliance with the terms of the contract has, or will have, been such as to justify the conclusion that he has satisfactorily completed the contract, the court shall make an order declaring that the referral order (or each of the referral orders) is discharged.

Discharge of extension orders

9. The discharge under paragraph 7(3) or 8 above of a referral order has the effect of discharging any related order under paragraph 11 or 12 below.

Part 1A

Referral of Parent or Guardian for Breach of Section 20 Order

Introductory

9A. (1) This Part of this Schedule applies where, under section 22(2A) of this Act, a youth offender panel refers an offender's parent or guardian to a youth court.

(2) In this Part of this Schedule—

(*a*) "the offender" means the offender whose parent or guardian is referred under section 22(2A);
(*b*) "the parent" means the parent or guardian so referred; and
(*c*) "the youth court" means a youth court as mentioned in section 22(2A).

Mode of referral to court

9B. The panel shall make the referral by sending a report to the youth court explaining why the parent is being referred to it.

Bringing the parent before the court

9C. (1) Where the youth court receives such a report it shall cause the parent to appear before it.

(2) For the purpose of securing the attendance of the parent before the court, a justice acting in the local justice area in which the court actsmay—

(*a*) issue a summons requiring the parent to appear at the place and time specified in it; or
(*b*) if the report is substantiated on oath, issue a warrant for the parent's arrest.

(3) Any summons or warrant issued under sub-paragraph (2) above shall direct the parent to appear or be brought before the youth court.

Power of court to make parenting order: application of supplemental provisions

9D. (1) Where the parent appears or is brought before the youth court under paragraph 9C above, the court may make a parenting order in respect of the parent if—

(*a*) it is proved to the satisfaction of the court that the parent has failed without reasonable excuse to comply with the order under section 20 of this Act; and
(*b*) the court is satisfied that the parenting order would be desirable in the interests of preventing the commission of any further offence by the offender.

(2) A parenting order is an order which requires the parent—

(*a*) to comply, for a period not exceeding twelve months, with such requirements as are specified in the order, and
(*b*) subject to sub-paragraph (4) below, to attend, for a concurrent period not exceeding three months, such counselling or guidance programme as may be specified in directions given by the responsible officer.

(3) The requirements that may be specified under sub-paragraph (2)(*a*) above are those which the court considers desirable in the interests of preventing the commission of any further offence by the offender.

(4) A parenting order under this paragraph may, but need not, include a requirement mentioned in subsection (2)(*b*) above in any case where a parenting order under this paragraph or any other enactment has been made in respect of the parent on a previous occasion.

(5) A counselling or guidance programme which a parent is required to attend by virtue of subsection (2)(*b*) above may be or include a residential course but only if the court is satisfied—

(*a*) that the attendance of the parent at a residential course is likely to be more effective than his attendance at a non-residential course in preventing the commission of any further offence by the offender, and
(*b*) that any interference with family life which is likely to result from the attendance of the parent at a residential course is proportionate in all the circumstances.

(6) Before making a parenting order under this paragraph where the offender is aged under 16, the court shall obtain and consider information about his family circumstances and the likely effect of the order on those circumstances.

(7) Sections 8(3) and (8), 9(3) to (7) and 18(3) and (4) of the Crime and Disorder Act 1998 apply in relation to a parenting order made under this paragraph as they apply in relation to any other parenting order.

Appeal

9E. (1) An appeal shall lie to the Crown Court against the making of a parenting order under paragraph 9D above.

(2) Subsections (2) and (3) of section 10 of the Crime and Disorder Act 1998 (appeals against parenting orders) apply in relation to an appeal under this paragraph as they apply in relation to an appeal under subsection (1)(*b*) of that section.

Effect on section 20 order

9F. (1) The making of a parenting order under paragraph 9D above is without prejudice to the continuance of the order under section 20 of this Act.

(2) Section 63(1) to (4) of the Magistrates' Courts Act 1980 (power of magistrates' court to deal with person for breach of order, etc) apply (as well as section 22(2A) of this Act and this Part of this Schedule) in relation to an order under section 20 of this Act.

PART II
FURTHER CONVICTIONS DURING REFERRAL

Extension of referral for further offences

3-1730 **10.** (1) Paragraphs 11 and 12 below apply where, at a time when an offender aged under 18 is subject to referral, a youth court or other magistrates' court ("the relevant court") is dealing with him for an offence in relation to which paragraphs (*a*) to (*c*) of section 16(1) of this Act are applicable.

(2) But paragraphs 11 and 12 do not apply unless the offender's compliance period is less than twelve months.

Extension where further offences committed pre-referral

11. If—

(a) the occasion on which the offender was referred to the panel is the only other occasion on which it has fallen to a court in the United Kingdom to deal with the offender for any offence or offences, and

(b) the offender committed the offence mentioned in paragraph 10 above, and any connected offence, before he was referred to the panel,

the relevant court may sentence the offender for the offence by making an order extending his compliance period.

Extension where further offence committed after referral

12. (1) If—

(a) paragraph 11(a) above applies, but

(b) the offender committed the offence mentioned in paragraph 10 above, or any connected offence, after he was referred to the panel,

the relevant court may sentence the offender for the offence by making an order extending his compliance period, but only if the requirements of sub-paragraph (2) below are complied with.

(2) Those requirements are that the court must—

(a) be satisfied, on the basis of a report made to it by the relevant body, that there are exceptional circumstances which indicate that, even though the offender has re-offended since being referred to the panel, extending his compliance period is likely to help prevent further re-offending by him; and

(b) state in open court that it is so satisfied and why it is.

(3) In sub-paragraph (2) above "the relevant body" means the panel to which the offender has been referred or, if no contract has yet taken effect between the offender and the panel under section 23 of this Act, the specified team.

Provisions supplementary to paragraphs 11 and 12

13. (1) An order under paragraph 11 or 12 above, or two or more orders under one or other of those paragraphs made in respect of connected offences, must not so extend the offender's compliance period as to cause it to exceed twelve months.

(2) Sub-paragraphs (3) to (5) below apply where the relevant court makes an order under paragraph 11 or 12 above in respect of the offence mentioned in paragraph 10 above; but sub-paragraphs (3) to (5) do not affect the exercise of any power to deal with the offender conferred by paragraph S or 14 of this Schedule.

(3) The relevant court may not deal with the offender for that offence in any of the prohibited ways specified in section 19(4) of this Act.

(4) The relevant court—

(a) shall, in respect of any connected offence, either—

(i) sentence the offender by making an order under the same paragraph; or

(ii) make an order discharging him absolutely; and

(b) may not deal with the offender for any connected offence in any of those prohibited ways.

(5) The relevant court may not, in connection with the conviction of the offender for the offence or any connected offence, make any such order as is mentioned in section 19(5) of this Act.

(6) For the purposes of paragraphs 11 and 12 above any occasion on which the offender was discharged absolutely in respect of the offence, or each of the offences, for which he was being dealt with shall be disregarded.

(7) Any occasion on which, in criminal proceedings in England and Wales or Northern Ireland, the offender was bound over to keep the peace or to be of good behaviour shall be regarded for those purposes as an occasion on which it fell to a court in the United Kingdom to deal with the offender for an offence.

(8) The Secretary of State may by regulations make such amendments of paragraphs 10 to 12 above and this paragraph as he considers appropriate for altering in any way the descriptions of offenders in the case of which an order extending the compliance period may be made; and subsection (4) of section 17 of this Act shall apply in relation to regulations under this sub-paragraph as it applies in relation to regulations under subsection (3) of that section.

Further convictions which lead to revocation of referral

14. (1) This paragraph applies where, at a time when an offender is subject to referral, a court in England and Wales deals with him for an offence (whether committed before or after he was referred to the panel) by making an order other than—

(a) an order under paragraph 11 or 12 above; or

(b) an order discharging him absolutely.

(2) In such a case the order of the court shall have the effect of revoking—

(a) the referral order (or orders); and

(b) any related order or orders under paragraph 11 or 12 above.

(3) Where any order is revoked by virtue of sub-paragraph (2) above, the court may, if appears to the court that it would be in the interests of justice to do so, deal with the offender for the offence in respect of which the revoked order was made in any way in which (assuming section 16 of this Act had not applied) he could have been dealt with for that offence by the court which made the order.

(4) When dealing with the offender under sub-paragraph (3) above the court shall, where a contract has taken effect between the offender and the panel under section 23 of this Act, have regard to the extent of his compliance with the terms of the contract.

Interpretation

15. (1) For the purposes of this Part of this Schedule an offender, is for the time being subject to referral if—

(a) a referral order has been made in respect of him and that order has not, or

(b) two or more referral orders have been made in respect of him and any of those orders has not, been discharged (whether by virtue of section 27(3) of this Act or under paragraph 7(3) or 8 above) or revoked (whether under paragraph 5(2) above or by virtue of paragraph 14(2) above).

(2) In this Part of this Schedule "compliance period", in relation to an offender who is for the time being subject to referral, means the period for which (in accordance with section 24 of this Act) any youth offender contract taking effect in his case under section 23 of this Act has (or would have) effect.

SCHEDULE 2
ADDITIONAL REQUIREMENTS WHICH MAY BE INCLUDED IN COMMUNITY REHABILITATION ORDERS

3–1731 *Repealed.*

Sections 39, 43, 48, 51, 56   SCHEDULE 3
BREACH, REVOCATION AND AMENDMENT OF CERTAIN COMMUNITY ORDERS

(Amended by the Criminal Justice and Court Services Act 2000, s 53 and Sch 7.)

PART I
PRELIMINARY

Definitions

3–1732   **1.** (1) In this Schedule "relevant order" means any of the following orders—

(a)   a curfew order;
(aa) an exclusion order;
(b)   a community rehabilitation order;
(c)   a community punishment order;
(d)   a community punishment and rehabilitation order;
(e)   a drug treatment and testing order;
(f)   a drug abstinence order.

(1A) The orders mentioned in paragraphs (a) to (d) and (f) of sub-paragraph (1) above and, if an order made by the Secretary of State so provides, any other order mentioned in that sub-paragraph are referred to in this Schedule as orders to which the warning provisions apply.

(2) In this Schedule "the petty sessions area concerned" means—

(a)   in relation to a curfew order, the petty sessions area in which the place for the time being specified in the order is situated; and
(b)   in relation to an exclusion, community rehabilitation, community punishment, community punishment and rehabilitation, drug treatment and testing or drug abstinence order, the petty sessions area for the time being specified in the order.

(3) In this Schedule, references to the court responsible for a drug treatment and testing order or drug abstinence order shall be construed in accordance with section 54(7) of this Act (or that subsection as applied by section 58B(2) of this Act).

(4) In this Schedule—

(a)   references to the community rehabilitation element of a community punishment and rehabilitation order are references to the order in so far as it imposes such a requirement as is mentioned in section 51(1)(a) of this Act (and in so far as it imposes any additional requirements included in the order by virtue of section 42); and
(b)   references to the community punishment element of such an order are references to the order in so far as it imposes such a requirement as is mentioned in section 51(1)(b).★

Orders made on appeal

2. (1) Where a curfew, exclusion, community rehabilitation, community punishment, community punishment and rehabilitation or drug abstinence order has been made on appeal, for the purposes of this Schedule it shall be deemed—

(a)   if it was made on an appeal brought from a magistrates' court, to have been made by a magistrates' court;
(b)   if it was made on an appeal brought from the Crown Court or from the criminal division of the Court of Appeal, to have been made by the Crown Court.

(2) Where a drug treatment and testing order has been made on an appeal brought from the Crown Court or from the criminal division of the Court of Appeal, for the purposes of this Schedule it shall be deemed to have been made by the Crown Court.★

★Substituted by the Criminal Justice Act 2003, Sch 32, from a date to be appointed.

PART II
BREACH OF REQUIREMENT OF ORDER

Functions of responsible officer★

2A. (1) Sub-paragraphs (2) and (3) below apply if the responsible officer is of the opinion that a person aged 18 or over ("the offender") has failed without reasonable excuse to comply with any of the requirements of an order to which the warning provisions apply other than a requirement to abstain from misusing specified Class A drugs.

(2) The officer shall give him a warning under this paragraph if—

(a) the offender has not within the specified period been given a warning under this paragraph in respect of a failure to comply with any of the requirements of the order; and

(b) the officer does not cause an information to be laid before a justice of the peace in respect of the failure in question.

(3) If the offender has within the specified period been given such a warning, the officer shall cause an information to be laid before a justice of the peace in respect of the failure in question.

(4) In sub-paragraphs (2) and (3) above, "specified period" means—

(a) in the case of a curfew order, the period of six months;

(b) in any other case, the period of twelve months;

ending with the failure in question.

(5) A warning under this paragraph must—

(a) describe the circumstances of the failure;

(b) state that the failure is unacceptable;

(c) inform the offender that if within the next six or (as the case may be) twelve months he again fails to comply with any requirement of the order, he will be liable to be brought before a court;

and the officer shall, as soon as is practicable after the warning has been given, record that fact.

(6) If a community sentence consists of or includes two or more orders to which the warning provisions apply, being orders in respect of the same offence—

(a) the preceding provisions of this paragraph shall have effect as if those orders were a single order to which the warning provisions apply; and

(b) where one of those orders is a curfew order that fact shall be disregarded for the purposes of sub-paragraph (4) above★.

★Paragraph 2A is printed as inserted by the Criminal Justice and Court Services Act 2000, s 53 from a date to be appointed.

Issue of summons or warrant

3. (1) If at any time while a relevant order is in force in respect of an offender it appears on information to a justice of the peace acting for the petty sessions area concerned that the offender has failed to comply with any of the requirements of the order, the justice may—

(a) issue a summons requiring the offender to appear at the place and time specified in it; or

(b) if the information is in writing and on oath, issue a warrant for his arrest.

(2) Any summons or warrant issued under this paragraph shall direct the offender to appear or be brought—

(a) in the case of a drug treatment and testing order or a drug abstinence order, before the court responsible for the order;

(b) in the case of any other relevant order which was made by the Crown Court and included a direction that any failure to comply with any of the requirements of the order be dealt with by the Crown Court, before the Crown Court; and

(c) in the case of a relevant order which is neither a drug treatment and testing order a drug abstinence order nor an order to which paragraph (b) above applies, before a magistrates' court acting for the petty sessions area concerned.

(3) Where a summons issued under sub-paragraph (1)(a) above requires an offender to appear before the Crown Court and the offender does not appear in answer to the summons, the Crown Court may issue a further summons requiring the offender to appear at the place and time specified in it.

(4) Where a summons issued under sub-paragraph (1)(a) above or a further summons issued under sub-paragraph (3) above requires an offender to appear before the Crown Court and the offender does not appear in answer to the summons, the Crown Court may issue a warrant for the arrest of the offender.

Powers of magistrates' court

4. (1) If it is proved[1] to the satisfaction of a magistrates' court before which an offender appears or is brought under paragraph 3 above that he has failed without reasonable excuse to comply with any of the requirements of the relevant order, the court may deal with him in respect of the failure in any one of the following ways—

(a) it may impose on him a fine not exceeding £1,000;

(b) where the offender is aged 16[2] or over it may, subject to paragraph 7 below, make a community service order in respect of him;

(c) where—

(i) the relevant order is a curfew order and the offender is aged under 16, or

(ii) the relevant order is a probation order or combination order and the offender is aged under 21,

it may, subject to paragraph 8 below, make an attendance centre order in respect of him; or

(d) where the relevant order was made by a magistrates' court, it may deal with him, for the offence in respect of which the order was made, in any way[3] in which it could deal with him if he had just been convicted by the court of the offence★.

(2) In dealing with an offender under sub-paragraph (1)(d)★ above, a magistrates' court—

(a) shall take into account the extent to which the offender has complied with the requirements of the relevant order; and

(b) in the case of an offender who has wilfully and persistently failed to comply with those requirements, may impose a custodial sentence (where the relevant order was made in respect of an offence punishable with such a sentence) notwithstanding anything in section 79(2) of this Act.

(3) Where a magistrates' court deals with an offender under sub-paragraph (1)(d)★★ above, it shall revoke the relevant order if it is still in force.

(4) Where a relevant order was made by the Crown Court and a magistrates' court has power to deal with the

offender under sub-paragraph (1)(a)**, (b) or (c) above, it may instead commit him to custody or release him on bail until he can be brought or appear before the Crown Court.

(5) A magistrate's court which deals with an offender's case under sub-paragraph (4) above shall send to the Crown Court—

(a)　a certificate signed by a justice of the peace certifying that the offender has failed to comply with the requirements of the relevant order in the respect specified in the certificate; and

(b)　such other particulars of the case as may be desirable;

and a certificate purporting to be so signed shall be admissible as evidence of the failure before the Crown Court.

(6) A person sentenced under sub-paragraph (1)(d)** above for an offence may appeal to the Crown Court against the sentence.

---

*Sub-paragraph 4(1) is to be substituted for new sub-paras (1), (1A), (1B) and (1C) by the Criminal Justice and Court Services Act 2000, s 53 from a date to be appointed.

**Amended by the Criminal Justice and Court Services Act 2000, Sch 7 from a date to be appointed.

1. The standard of proof is proof beyond reasonable doubt; where justices have before them evidence that the person summoned shares the same name, date of birth or address of the person who was convicted they may draw the inference that he is the same person, and they would be expected to draw that inference where all three of those personal details were the same: *West Yorkshire Probation Board v Boulter* [2005] EWHC 2342, [2006] 1 WLR 132, (2005) 169 JP 601.

2. Proof that a child was under a certain age was established by the evidence of a mistress of an elementary school attended by the child, corroborated by an officer of the Society for the Prevention of Cruelty to Children (*R v Cox* [1898] 1 QB 179). If on the material before the court an offender is deemed to be of a certain age, he shall be treated on that basis; the fact that he is subsequently found to be below that age does not invalidate a sentence not otherwise available to a person of his age (see *R v Brown* (1989) 11 Cr App Rep (S) 263 (imprisonment imposed on an offender subsequently found to be under 21 years).

3. In the case of an offence triable either way, this does not include committing the offender to the Crown Court for sentence pursuant to s 3 of this Act (*R v Jordan* [1998] Crim LR 353, but see reservations in the commentary). See also *R v Chute* [2003] EWCA Crim 177, [2003] Crim LR 295 (no power to commit breach of a DTTO made in the magistrates' court to the Crown Court for sentence).

Powers of Crown Court

5. (1) Where under paragraph 3 or by virtue of paragraph 4(4) above an offender is brought or appears before the Crown Court and it is proved to the satisfaction of that court that he has failed without reasonable excuse to comply with any of the requirements of the relevant order, the Crown Court may deal with him in respect of the failure in any one of the following ways—

(a)　it may impose on him a fine not exceeding £1,000;

(b)　where the offender is aged 16 or over it may, subject to paragraph 7 below, make a community service order in respect of him;

(c)　where—

(i)　the relevant order is a curfew order and the offender is aged under 16, or

(ii)　the relevant order is a probation order or combination order and the offender is aged under 21,

it may, subject to paragraph 8 below, make an attendance centre order in respect of him; or

(d)　it may deal with him, for the offence in respect of which the order was made, in any way in which it could deal with him if he had just been convicted before the Crown Court of the offence*.

(2) In dealing with an offender under sub-paragraph (1)(d) above, the Crown Court—

(a)　shall take into account the extent to which the offender has complied with the requirements of the relevant order; and

(b)　in the case of an offender who has wilfully and persistently failed to comply with those requirements, may impose a custodial sentence (where the relevant order was made in respect of an offence punishable with such a sentence) notwithstanding anything in section 79(2) of this Act.

(3) Where the Crown Court deals with an offender under sub-paragraph (1)(d) above, it shall revoke the relevant order if it is still in force.

(4) In proceedings before the Crown Court under this paragraph any question whether the offender has failed to comply with the requirements of the relevant order shall be determined by the court and not by the verdict of a jury.

---

*Sub-paragraph 5(1) is to be substituted for new sub-paras (1), (1A), (1B) and (1C) by the Criminal Justice and Court Services Act 2000, s 53 from a date to be appointed.

Exclusions from paragraphs 4 and 5

6. (1) Without prejudice to paragraphs 10 and 11 below, an offender who is convicted of a further offence while a relevant order is in force in respect of him shall not on that account be liable to be dealt with under paragraph 4 or 5 above in respect of a failure to comply with any requirement of the order.

(2) An offender who—

(a)　is required by a community rehabilitation order or community punishment and rehabilitation order to submit to treatment for his mental condition, or his dependency on or propensity to misuse drugs or alcohol, or

(b)　is required by a drug treatment and testing order to submit to treatment for his dependency on or propensity to misuse drugs;

shall not be treated for the purposes of paragraph 4 or 5 above as having failed to comply with that requirement on the ground only that he has refused to undergo any surgical, electrical or other treatment if, in the opinion of the court, his refusal was reasonable having regard to all the circumstances.

(3) Paragraphs 4(1A) and 5(1A) above do not apply in respect of a failure to comply with a requirement to abstain from misusing specified Class A drugs.

Curfew orders imposed for breach of relevant order*

6A. (1) Section 37(1) of this Act (curfew orders) shall apply for the purposes of paragraphs 4(1C)(*a*) and 5(1C)(*a*) above as if for the words from the beginning to "make" there were substituted "Where a court has power to deal with an offender under Part II of Schedule 3 to this Act for failure to comply with any of the requirements of a relevant order, the court may make in respect of the offender".

(2) In this paragraph—

"secondary order" means a curfew order made by virtue of paragraph 4(1C)(*a*) or 5(1C)(*a*) above;
"original order" means the relevant order the failure to comply with which led to the making of the secondary order.

(3) A secondary order—

(*a*) shall specify a period of not less than 14 nor more than 28 days for which the order is to be in force; and
(*b*) may specify different places, or different periods (within the period for which the order is in force), for different days, but shall not specify periods which amount to less than two hours or more than twelve hours in any one day.

(4) Part IV of this Act, except sections 35, 36, 37(3) and (4), 39 and 40(2)(*a*), has effect in relation to a secondary order as it has effect in relation to any other curfew order, but subject to the further modifications made below.

(5) Section 37(9) applies as if the reference to an offender who on conviction is under 16 were a reference to a person who on the date when his failure to comply with the original order is proved to the court is under 16.

(6) Paragraphs 2A, 4(1A) to (2) and 5(1A) to (2) above and 10 and 11 below apply as if, in respect of the period for which the secondary order is in force, the requirements of that order were requirements of the original order.

But in paragraphs 4 and 5 above, sub-paragraph (1C)(*c*) applies as if references to the relevant order were to the original order or the secondary order.

(7) In paragraphs 4 and 5 above, sub-paragraph (3) applies as if references to the relevant order were to the original order and the secondary order.

(8) Paragraph 19(3) below applies as if the reference to six months from the date of the original order were a reference to 28 days from the date of the secondary order.*

---

*Paragraph 6A printed as prospectively inserted by the Criminal Justice and Court Services Act 2000, Sch 7 from a date to be appointed.

Community punishment orders imposed for breach of relevant order

7. (1) Section 46(1) of this Act (community punishment orders) shall apply for the purposes of paragraphs 4(1)(*b*) and 5(1)(*b*)* above as if for the words from the beginning to "make" there were substituted "Where a court has power to deal with an offender aged 16 or over under Part II of Schedule 3 to this Act for failure to comply with any of the requirements of a relevant order, the court may make in respect of the offender".

(2) In this paragraph a "secondary order" means a community punishment order made by virtue of paragraph 4(1)(*b*) or 5(1)(*b*) above*.

(3) The number of hours which an offender may be required to work under a secondary order shall be specified in the order and shall not exceed 60 in the aggregate; and—

(*a*) where the relevant order is a community punishment order, the number of hours which the offender may be required to work under the secondary order shall not be such that the total number of hours under both orders exceeds the maximum specified in section 46(3) of this Act; and
(*b*) where the relevant order is a community punishment and rehabilitation order, the number of hours which the offender may be required to work under the secondary order shall not be such that the total number of hours under—

(i) the secondary order, and
(ii) the community punishment element of the community punishment and rehabilitation order,

exceeds the maximum specified in section 51(1)(*b*) of this Act.

(4) Section 46(4) of this Act and, so far as applicable—

(*a*) section 46(5) to (7) and (9) to (13), and
(*b*) section 47 and the provisions of this Schedule so far as relating to community service orders,

have effect in relation to a secondary order as they have effect in relation to any other community service order, subject to sub-paragraph (6) below**.

(5) Sections 35 and 36 of this Act (restrictions and procedural requirements for community sentences) do not apply in relation to a secondary order**.

(6) Where the provisions of this Schedule have effect as mentioned in sub-paragraph (4) above in relation to a secondary order—

(*a*) the power conferred on the court by each of paragraphs 4(1)(*d*) and 5(1)(*d*) above and paragraph 10(3)(*b*) below to deal with the offender for the offence in respect of which the order was made shall be construed as a power to deal with the offender, for his failure to comply with the original order, in any way in which the court could deal with him if that failure had just been proved to the satisfaction of the court;
(*b*) the references in paragraphs 10(1)(*b*) and 11(1)(*a*) below to the offence in respect of which the order was made shall be construed as references to the failure to comply in respect of which the order was made; and
(*c*) the power conferred on the Crown Court by paragraph 11(2)(*b*) below to deal with the offender for the offence in respect of which the order was made shall be construed as a power to deal with the offender, for his failure to comply with the original order, in any way in which a magistrate's court (if the original order was made by a magistrate's court) or the Crown Court (if the original order was made by the Crown Court) could deal with him if that failure had just been proved to its satisfaction;

and in this sub-paragraph "the original order" means the relevant order the failure to comply with which led to the making of the secondary order**.

*Amended by the Criminal Justice and Court Services Act 2000, Sch 7 from a date to be appointed.
**Sub-paragraphs (4) to (6) to be substituted by the Criminal Justice and Court Services Act 2000, Sch 7 from a date to be appointed.

Attendance centre orders imposed for breach of relevant order

8. (1) Section 60(1) of this Act (attendance centre orders) shall apply for the purposes of paragraphs 4(1)(*c*) and 5(1)(*c*)* above as if for the words from the beginning to "the court may," there were substituted

"Where a court—

    (*a*)   has power to deal with an offender aged under 16 under Part II of Schedule 3 to this Act for failure to comply with any of the requirements of a curfew order, or

    (*b*)   has power to deal with an offender aged under 21 under that Part of that Schedule for failure, to comply with any of the requirements of a probation or combination order,

the court may,".*

(2) The following provisions of this Act, namely—

    (*a*)   subsections (3) to (11) of section 60, and

    (*b*)   so far as applicable, section 36B and Schedule 5,

have effect in relation to an attendance centre order made by virtue of paragraph 4(1)(*c*) or 5(1)(*c**) above as they have effect in relation to any other attendance centre order, but as if there were omitted from each of paragraphs 2(1)(*b*), 3(1) and 4(3) of Schedule 5 the words ", for the offence in respect of which the order was made," and "for that offence".

(3) Sections 35 and 36 of this Act (restrictions and procedural requirements for community sentences) do not apply in relation to an attendance centre order made by virtue of paragraph 4(1)(*c*) or 5(1)(*c*)* above.

*Amended by the Criminal Justice and Court Services Act 2000, Sch 7 from a date to be appointed.

Supplementary

9. (1) Any exercise by a court of its powers under paragraph 4(1)(*a*), (*b*) or (*c*) or 5(1)(*a*), (*b*) or (*c*)* above shall be without prejudice to the continuance of the relevant order.

(2) A fine imposed under paragraph 4(1)(*a*) or 5(1)(*a*) above shall be deemed, for the purposes of any enactment, to be a sum adjudged to be paid by a conviction.**

(3) Where a relevant order was made by a magistrates' court in the case of an offender under 18 years of age in respect of an offence triable only on indictment in the case of an adult, any powers exercisable under paragraph 4(1)(*d*)* above in respect of the offender after he attains the age of 18 shall be powers to do either or both of the following—

    (*a*)   to impose a fine not exceeding £5,000 for the offence in respect of which the order was made;

    (*b*)   to deal with the offender for that offence in any way in which a magistrates' court could deal with him if it had just convicted him of an offence punishable with imprisonment for a term not exceeding six months.

*Amended by the Criminal Justice and Court Services Act 2000, Sch 7 from a date to be appointed.
**Repealed by the Criminal Justice and Court Services Act 2000, Sch 7 from a date to be appointed.

PART III
REVOCATION OF ORDER

Revocation of order with or without re-sentencing: powers of magistrates' court[1]

3–1733   **10.** (1) This paragraph applies where a relevant order made by a magistrates' court is in force in respect of any offender and on the application of the offender or the responsible officer it appears to the appropriate magistrates' court that, having regard to circumstances[2] which have arisen since the order was made, it would be in the interests of justice—

    (*a*)   for the order to be revoked; or

    (*b*)   for the offender to be dealt with in some other way for the offence in respect of which the order was made.

(2) In this paragraph "the appropriate magistrates court" means—

    (*a*)   in the case of a drug treatment and testing order or a drug abstinence order, the magistrates' court responsible for the order;

    (*b*)   in the case of any other relevant order, a magistrates' court acting for the petty sessions area concerned.

(3) The appropriate magistrates' court may—

    (*a*)   revoke the order; or

    (*b*)   both—

        (i)   revoke the order; and

        (ii)   deal with the offender, for the offence in respect of which the order was made, in any way in which it could deal with him if he had just been convicted by the court of the offence.

(4) The circumstances in which a probation, community rehabilitation, community punishment and rehabilitation or drug treatment and testing order may be revoked under sub-paragraph (3)(*a*) above shall include the offender's making good progress or his responding satisfactorily to supervision or, as the case may be, treatment.

(5) In dealing with an offender under sub-paragraph (3)(*b*) above, a magistrates' court shall take into account the extent to which the offender has complied with the requirements of the relevant order.

(6) A person sentenced under sub-paragraph (3)(*b*) above for an offence may appeal to the Crown Court against the sentence.

(7) Where a magistrates' court proposes to exercise its powers under this paragraph otherwise than on the application of the offender, it shall summon him to appear before the court and, if he does not appear in answer to the summons, may issue a warrant for his arrest.

(8) No application may be made by the offender under sub-paragraph (1) above while an appeal against the relevant order is pending.

---

1. For consideration of the application of this Schedule to re-sentencing, see *R v Oliver* [1993] 2 All ER 9, [1993] 1 WLR 177. See also commentary in para **3–217**, ante.
2. Disclosure after a community service order has been made that the offender suffers from a medical condition which existed before the order and which prevents him from performing community service is a "circumstance" for the purposes of para 10(1) (*R v Hammon* [1998] Crim LR 293, [1998] 2 Cr App Rep (S) 202).

Revocation of order with or without re-sentencing: powers of Crown Court on conviction etc

11. (1) This paragraph applies where—

(a) a relevant order made by the Crown Court is in force[1] in respect of an offender and the offender or the responsible officer applies to the Crown Court for the order to be revoked or for the offender to be dealt with in some other way for the offence in respect of which the order was made; or

(b) an offender in respect of whom a relevant order is in force is convicted of an offence before the Crown Court or, having been committed by a magistrates' court to the Crown Court for sentence, is brought or appears before the Crown Court.

(2) If it appears to the Crown Court to be in the interests of justice to do so, having regard to circumstances which have arisen since the order was made, the Crown Court[2] may—

(a) revoke the order; or

(b) both—

    (i) revoke the order; and

    (ii) deal with the offender, for the offence in respect of which the order was made, in any way in which the court which made the order could deal with him if he had just been convicted of that offence by or before the court which made the order[3].

(3) The circumstances in which a community rehabilitation order or community punishment and rehabilitation or drug treatment and testing order may be revoked under sub-paragraph (2)(a) above shall include the offender's making good progress or his responding satisfactorily to supervision or, as the case may be, treatment.

(4) In dealing with an offender under sub-paragraph (2)(b) above, the Crown Court shall take into account the extent to which the offender has complied with the requirements of the relevant order[4].

---

1. This power may only be exercised if the order is still in force when the offender is sentenced for the later offence or is otherwise brought before the Crown Court (*R v Bennett* (1993) 15 Cr App Rep (S) 213). Since para 11(1) focuses on the date of the offender's appearance before the Crown Court, courts need to be alive to the fact that, if the offender can delay his appearance until after the relevant order has expired, he can prevent the court from taking action under para 11; see *R v Cousin* (1993) 15 Cr App Rep (S) 516, [1994] Crim LR 300.
2. For consideration of the powers of the Crown Court under this provision see *R v Cawley* (1993) 15 Cr App Rep (S) 209, [1993] Crim LR 797, and commentary thereto. See also *R v Saphier and Pearsall* [1997] 1 Cr App Rep (S) 235 and *R v Day* [1997] Crim LR 529 and commentary.
3. For consideration of the application of this Schedule to re-sentencing, see *R v Oliver* [1993] 2 All ER 9, [1993] 1 WLR 177. The Crown Court may impose a condition in a probation order that the defendant should not commit any further offence during the currency of a probation order, breach of which may be dealt with under paragraph 11 (*R v Peacock* (1994) 159 JP 115, CA).
4. The allowance to be made for a partly completed period of community service is not to be calculated mathematically by the proportion of the hours served in relation to the total hours ordered to be served, because the offender has to perform the full period stipulated. Still less is such a period of a probation order as has been successfully completed to be approached mathematically (*R v Blight* [1999] Crim LR 426).

Substitution of conditional discharge for community rehabilitation or community punishment and rehabilitation order

12. (1) This paragraph applies where a probation order or community rehabilitation order or community punishment and rehabilitation order is in force in respect of any offender and on the application of the offender or the responsible officer to the appropriate court it appears to the court that, having regard to circumstances which have arisen since the order was made, it would be in the interests of justice—

(a) for the order to be revoked; and

(b) for an order to be made under section 12(1)(b) of this Act discharging the offender conditionally for the offence for which the community rehabilitation or community punishment and rehabilitation order was made.

(2) In this paragraph "the appropriate court" means—

(a) where the community rehabilitation or community punishment and rehabilitation order was made by a magistrates' court, a magistrates' court acting for the petty sessions area concerned;

(b) where the community rehabilitation or community punishment and rehabilitation order was made by the Crown Court, the Crown Court.

(3) No application may be made under paragraph 10 or 11 above for a community rehabilitation order or community punishment and rehabilitation order to be revoked and replaced with an order for conditional discharge under section 12(1)(b); but otherwise nothing in this paragraph shall affect the operation of paragraphs 10 and 11 above.

(4) Where this paragraph applies—

(a) the appropriate court may revoke the community rehabilitation or community punishment and rehabilitation order and make an order under section 12(1)(b) of this Act discharging the offender in respect of the offence for which the community punishment and rehabilitation order was made, subject to the condition that he commits no offence during the period specified in the order under section 12(1)(b); and

(b) the period specified in the order under section 12(1)(b) shall be the period beginning with the making of that order and ending with the date when the community rehabilitation period specified in the community punishment and rehabilitation order would have ended.

(5) For the purposes of sub-paragraph (4) above, subsection (1) of section 12 of this Act shall apply as if—

(a) for the words from the beginning to "may make an order either" there were substituted the words "Where paragraph 12 of Schedule 3 to this Act applies, the appropriate court may (subject to the provisions of sub-paragraph (4) of that paragraph) make an order in respect of the offender"; and

(b) paragraph (a) of that subsection were omitted.

(6) An application under this paragraph may be heard in the offender's absence if—

(a) the application is made by the responsible officer; and

(b) that officer produces to the court a statement by the offender that he understands the effect of an order for conditional discharge and consents to the making of the application;

and where the application is so heard section 12(4) of this Act shall not apply.

(7) No application may be made under this paragraph while an appeal against the community punishment and rehabilitation order is pending.

(8) Without prejudice to paragraph 15 below, on the making of an order under section 12(1)(b) of this Act by virtue of this paragraph the court shall forthwith give copies of the order to the responsible officer, and the responsible officer shall give a copy to the offender.

(9) Each of sections 1(11), 2(9) and 66(4) of the Crime and Disorder Act 1998 (which prevent a court from making an order for conditional discharge in certain cases) shall have effect as if the reference to the court by or before which a person is convicted of an offence there mentioned included a reference to a court dealing with an application under this paragraph in respect of the offence.

Revocation following custodial sentence by magistrates' court unconnected with order

13. (1) This paragraph applies where—

(a) an offender in respect of whom a relevant order is in force is convicted of an offence by a magistrates' court unconnected with the order;

(b) the court imposes a custodial sentence on the offender; and

(c) it appears to the court, on the application of the offender or the responsible officer, that it would be in the interests of justice to exercise its powers under this paragraph, having regard to circumstances which have arisen since the order was made.

(2) In sub-paragraph (1) above "a magistrates' court unconnected with the order" means—

(a) in the case of a drug treatment and testing order or a drug abstinence order, a magistrates' court which is not responsible for the order;

(b) in the case of any other relevant order, a magistrates' court not acting for the petty sessions area concerned.

(3) The court may—

(a) if the order was made by a magistrates' court, revoke it;

(b) if the order was made by the Crown Court, commit the offender in custody or release him on bail until he can be brought or appear before the Crown Court.

(4) Where the court deals with an offender's case under sub-paragraph (3)(b) above, it shall send to the Crown Court such particulars of the case as may be desirable.

14. Where by virtue of paragraph 13(3)(b) above an offender is brought or appears before the Crown Court and it appears to the Crown Court to be in the interests of justice to do so, having regard to circumstances which have arisen since the relevant order was made, the Crown Court may revoke the order.

Supplementary

15. (1) On the making under this Part of this Schedule of an order revoking a relevant order, the proper officer of the court shall forthwith give copies of the revoking order to the responsible officer.

(2) In sub-paragraph (1) above "proper officer" means—

(a) in relation to a magistrates' court, the justices' chief executive for the court; and

(b) in relation to the Crown Court, the appropriate officer.

(3) A responsible officer to whom in accordance with sub-paragraph (1) above copies of a revoking order are given shall give a copy to the offender and to the person in charge of any institution in which the offender was required by the order to reside.

16. Paragraph 9(3) above shall apply for the purposes of paragraphs 10 and 11 above as it applies for the purposes of paragraph 4 above, but as if for the words "paragraph 4(1)(d)* above" there were substituted "paragraph 10(3)(b)(ii) or 11 (2)(b)(ii) below".

17. Where under this Part of this Schedule a relevant order is revoked and replaced by an order for conditional discharge under section 12(1)(b) of this Act and—

(a) the order for conditional discharge is not made in the circumstances mentioned in section 13(9) of this Act (order made by magistrates' court in the case of an offender under 18 in respect of offence triable only on indictment in the case of an adult), but

(b) the relevant order was made in those circumstances,

section 13(9) shall have effect as if the order for conditional discharge had been made in those circumstances.

---

*Amended by the Criminal Justice and Court Services Act 2000, Sch 7 from a date to be appointed.

PART IV
AMENDMENT OF ORDER[1]

Amendment by reason of change of residence

3–1734   **18.** (1) This paragraph applies where, at any time while a relevant order (other than a drug treatment and testing order) is in force in respect of an offender, a magistrates' court acting for the petty sessions area concerned is satisfied that the offender proposes to change, or has changed, his residence from that petty sessions area to another petty sessions area.

(2) Subject to sub-paragraphs (3) to (5) below, the court may, and on the application of the responsible officer shall, amend the relevant order by substituting the other petty sessions area for the area specified in the order or, in the case of a curfew order, a place in that other area for the place so specified.

(3) The court shall not amend under this paragraph a community rehabilitation or curfew order which contains requirements which, in the opinion of the court, cannot be complied with unless the offender continues to reside in the petty sessions area concerned unless, in accordance with paragraph 19 below, it either—

(a) cancels those requirements; or
(b) substitutes for those requirements other requirements which can be complied with if the offender ceases to reside in that area.

(4) Sub-paragraph (3) above applies also in relation to a community punishment and rehabilitation order whose community rehabilitation element contains requirements such as are mentioned in that sub-paragraph.

(5) The court shall not amend a community punishment order or community punishment and rehabilitation order under this paragraph unless it appears to the court that provision can be made for the offender to perform work under the order under the arrangements which exist for persons who reside in the other petty sessions area to perform work under such orders.

(6) Where—

(a) the court amends a community rehabilitation, community punishment or community punishment and rehabilitation order under this paragraph,
(b) a local authority is specified in the order in accordance with section 41(5) or 46(9) of this Act, and
(c) the change, or proposed change, of residence also is or would be a change of residence from the area of that authority to the area of another such authority,

the court shall further amend the order by substituting the other authority for the authority specified in the order.

(7) In sub-paragraph (6) above "local authority" has the meaning given by section 42 of the Crime and Disorder Act 1998, and references to the area of a local authority shall be construed in accordance with that section.

---

*Part IV substituted by the Criminal Justice Act 2003, Sch 32 from a date to be appointed.

Amendment of requirements of community rehabilitation, community punishment and rehabilitation, curfew or exclusion order

19. (1) Without prejudice to the provisions of paragraph 18 above but subject to the following provisions of this paragraph, a magistrates' court acting for the petty sessions area concerned may, on the application of an eligible person, by order amend a community rehabilitation, curfew or exclusion order or the community rehabilitation element of a community punishment and rehabilitation order—

(a) by cancelling any of the requirements of the community rehabilitation, curfew or exclusion order or of the community rehabilitation element of the community punishment and rehabilitation order; or
(b) by inserting in the community rehabilitation, curfew or exclusion order or community rehabilitation element of the community punishment and rehabilitation order (either in addition to or in substitution for any of its requirements) any requirement which the court could include if it were then making the order.

(2) A magistrates' court shall not under sub-paragraph (1) above amend a community rehabilitation order or the probation element of a community punishment and rehabilitation order—

(a) by reducing the community rehabilitation period, or by extending that period beyond the end of three years from the date of the original order; or
(aa) by extending any curfew periods specified in a requirement order under the order beyond the end of six months from the date of the original order;
(ab) by extending the period during which the offender is prohibited from entering a place specified in a requirement under the order beyond the end of two years from the date of the original order;
(b) by inserting in it a requirement that the offender shall submit to treatment for his mental condition, or his dependency on or propensity to misuse drugs or alcohol, unless—

(i) the offender has expressed his willingness to comply with such a requirement; and
(ii) the amending order is made within three months after the date of the original order.

(3) A magistrates' court shall not under sub-paragraph (1) above amend a curfew order by extending the curfew periods beyond the end of six months (or for an offender aged under 16 on conviction, three months) from the date of the original order.

(4) A magistrates' court shall not under sub-paragraph (1) above amend an exclusion order by extending the period for which the offender is prohibited from entering the place in question beyond the end of two years (or, for an offender aged under 16 on conviction, three months) from the date of the original order.

(5) For the purposes of this paragraph the eligible persons are—

(a) the offender;
(b) the responsible officer; and
(c) in relation to an exclusion order, a community rehabilitation order or a community punishment and rehabilitation order, any affected person.

But an application under sub-paragraph (1) above by a person such as is mentioned in paragraph (c) above must be for the cancellation of a requirement which was included in the order by virtue of his consent or for the purpose (or partly for the purpose) of protecting him from being approached by the offender, or for the insertion of a requirement which will, if inserted, be such a requirement.

(6) Without prejudice to the provisions of paragraph 18 above, a magistrates' court acting for the petty sessions area concerned may, on the application of the offender or the responsible officer, by order amend a drug abstinence order by extending the period for which the order has effect (but not beyond the end of three years from the date of the original order).

Amendment of treatment requirements of community rehabilitation or community punishment and rehabilitation order on report of practitioner

20. (1) Where the medical practitioner or other person by whom or under whose direction an offender is, in pursuance of any requirement of a community rehabilitation or community punishment and rehabilitation order, being treated for his mental condition or his dependency on or propensity to misuse drugs or alcohol—

(a) is of the opinion mentioned in sub-paragraph (2) below, or
(b) is for any reason unwilling to continue to treat or direct the treatment of the offender,

he shall make a report in writing to that effect to the responsible officer and that officer shall apply under paragraph 19 above to a magistrates' court acting for the petty sessions area concerned for the variation or cancellation of the requirement.

(2) The opinion referred to in sub-paragraph (1) above is—

(a) that the treatment of the offender should be continued beyond the period specified in that behalf in the order;
(b) that the offender needs different treatment;
(c) that the offender is not susceptible to treatment; or
(d) that the offender does not require further treatment.

Amendment of drug treatment and testing order

21. (1) Without prejudice to the provisions of section 55(1), (6) and (8) of this Act, the court responsible for a drug treatment and testing order may by order—

(a) vary or cancel any of the requirements or provisions of the order on an application by the responsible officer under sub-paragraph (2) or (3)(a) or (b) below; or
(b) amend the order on an application by that officer under sub-paragraph (3)(c) below.

(2) Where the treatment provider is of the opinion that the treatment or testing requirement of the order should be varied or cancelled—

(a) he shall make a report in writing to that effect to the responsible officer; and
(b) that officer shall apply to the court for the variation or cancellation of the requirement.

(3) Where the responsible officer is of the opinion—

(a) that the treatment or testing requirement of the order should be so varied as to specify a different treatment provider,
(b) that any other requirement of the order, or a provision of the order, should be varied or cancelled, or
(c) that the order should be so amended as to provide for each subsequent periodic review (required by section 54(6)(a) of this Act) to be made without a hearing instead of at a review hearing, or vice versa,

he shall apply to the court for the variation or cancellation of the requirement or provision or the amendment of the order.

(4) The court—

(a) shall not amend the treatment or testing requirement unless the offender expresses his willingness to comply with the requirement as amended; and
(b) shall not amend any provision of the order so as to reduce the treatment and testing period below the minimum specified in section 52(1) of this Act, or to increase it above the maximum so specified.

(5) If the offender fails to express his willingness to comply with the treatment or testing requirement as proposed to be amended by the court, the court may—

(a) revoke the order; and
(b) deal with him, for the offence in respect of which the order was made, in any way in which it could deal with him if he had just been convicted by or before the court of the offence.

(6) In dealing with the offender under sub-paragraph (5)(b) above, the court—

(a) shall take into account the extent to which the offender has complied with the requirements of the order; and
(b) may impose a custodial sentence (where the order was made in respect of an offence punishable with such a sentence) notwithstanding anything in section 79(2) of this Act.

(7) Paragraph 9(3) above shall apply for the purposes of this paragraph as it applies for the purposes of paragraph 4 above, but as if for the words "paragraph 4(1)(*d*)* above" there were substituted "paragraph 21(5)(*b*) below".

---

*Amended by the Criminal Justice and Court Services Act 2000, Sch 7, from a date to be appointed.

Extension of community punishment or community punishment and rehabilitation order

22. Where—

(*a*) a community punishment order or community punishment and rehabilitation order is in force in respect of any offender, and

(*b*) on the application of the offender or the responsible officer, it appears to a magistrates' court acting for the petty sessions area concerned that it would be in the interests of justice to do so having regard to circumstances which have arisen since the order was made,

the court may, in relation to the order, extend the period of twelve months specified in section 47(3) of this Act.

Supplementary

23. No order may be made under paragraph 18 above, and no application may be made under paragraph 19 or 22 above or, except with the consent of the offender, under paragraph 21 above, while an appeal against the relevant order is pending.

24. (1) Subject to sub-paragraph (2) below, where a court proposes to exercise its powers under this Part of this Schedule, otherwise than on the application of the offender, the court—

(*a*) shall summon him to appear before the court; and

(*b*) if he does not appear in answer to the summons, may issue a warrant for his arrest.

(2) This paragraph shall not apply to an order cancelling a requirement of a relevant order or reducing the period of any requirement, or to an order under paragraph 18 above substituting a new petty sessions area or a new place for the one specified in a relevant order.

25. (1) On the making under this Part of this Schedule of an order amending a relevant order (other than a drug treatment and testing order), the justices' chief executive for the court shall forthwith—

(*a*) if the order amends the relevant order otherwise than by substituting by virtue of paragraph 18 above, a new petty sessions area or a new place for the one specified in the relevant order, give copies of the amending order to the responsible officer;

(*b*) if the order amends the relevant order in the manner excepted by paragraph (*a*) above, send to the chief executive to the justices for the new petty sessions area or, as the case may be, for the petty sessions area in which the new place is situated—

    (i) copies of the amending order; and

    (ii) such documents and information relating to the case as he considers likely to be of assistance to a court acting for that area in the exercise of its functions in relation to the order;

and in a case falling within paragraph (*b*) above the chief executive to the justices for that area shall give copies of the amending order to the responsible officer.

(2) On the making under this Part of this Schedule of an order amending a drug treatment and testing order, the justices' chief executive for the court shall forthwith give copies of the amending order to the responsible officer.*

(3) A responsible officer to whom in accordance with sub-paragraph (1) or (2)** above copies of an order are given shall give a copy to the offender and to the person in charge of any institution in which the offender is or was required by the order to reside.

26. (1) On the making under this Part of this Schedule of an order amending a drug treatment and testing order, the proper officer of the court shall (subject to sub-paragraph (3) below) forthwith give copies of the amending order to the responsible officer.

(2) In sub-paragraph (1) above, "proper officer" means—

(*a*) in relation to a magistrates' court, the justices' chief executive for the court; and

(*b*) in relation to the Crown Court, the appropriate officer.

(3) Where—

(*a*) a magistrates' court amends a drug treatment and testing order under this Part of this Schedule; and

(*b*) the amending order provides for a magistrates' court other than that mentioned in paragraph (*a*) above to be responsible for the order;

the court amending the order shall not give copies of the amending order as mentioned in sub-paragraph (1) above but shall send copies to the court responsible for the order and the justices' chief executive for that court shall forthwith give copies of the amending order to the responsible officer.

(4) A responsible officer to whom in accordance with sub-paragraph (1) or (3) above copies of an order are given shall give a copy to the offender and to the treatment provider.**

---

*Repealed by the Criminal Justice and Court Services Act 2000, Sch 7 from a date to be appointed.
**Paragraph 26 printed as inserted by the Criminal Justice and Court Services Act 2000, Sch 7 from a date to be appointed.

SCHEDULE 4
TRANSFER OF CERTAIN COMMUNITY ORDERS TO SCOTLAND OR NORTHERN IRELAND

3–1735   *Repealed.*

SCHEDULE 5
BREACH, REVOCATION AND AMENDMENT OF ATTENDANCE CENTRE ORDERS

(As amended by Criminal Justice Act 2003, Sch 32, the Domestic Violence, Crime and Victims Act 2004, Sch 5 and SI 2005/886)

Section 61

Breach of order or attendance centre rules

3–1736   **1.** (1) Where an attendance centre order is in force and it appears on information to a justice acting for a relevant petty sessions area that the offender—

    (a)   has failed to attend in accordance with the order, or

    (b)   while attending has committed a breach of rules made under section 222(1)(d) or (e) of the Criminal Justice Act 2003which cannot be adequately dealt with under those rules,

the justice may issue a summons requiring the offender to appear at the place and time specified in the summons or, if the information is in writing and on oath, may issue a warrant for the offender's arrest.

(2) Any summons or warrant issued under this paragraph shall direct the offender to appear or be brought—

    (a)   before a magistrates' court acting for the petty sessions area in which the offender resides; or

    (b)   if it is not known where the offender resides, before a magistrates' court acting for the petty sessions area in which is situated the attendance centre which the offender is required to attend by the order or by virtue of an order under paragraph 5(1)(b) below.

2. (1) If it is proved to the satisfaction of the magistrates' court before which an offender appears or is brought under paragraph 1 above that he has failed without reasonable excuse to attend as mentioned in sub-paragraph (1)(a) of that paragraph or has committed such a breach of rules as is mentioned in sub-paragraph (1)(b) of that paragraph, that court may deal with him in any one of the following ways—

    (a)   it may impose on him a fine not exceeding £1,000;

    (b)   where the attendance centre order was made by a magistrates' court, it may deal with him, for the offence in respect of which the order was made, in any way in which he could have been dealt with for that offence by the court which made the order if the order had not been made; or

    (c)   where the order was made by the Crown Court, it may commit him to custody or release him on bail until he can be brought or appear before the Crown Court.

(2) Any exercise by the court of its power under sub-paragraph (1)(a) above shall be without prejudice to the continuation of the order.

(3) A fine imposed under sub-paragraph (1)(a) above shall be deemed, for the purposes of any enactment, to be a sum adjudged to be paid by a conviction.

(4) Where a magistrates' court deals with an offender under sub-paragraph (1)(b) above, it shall revoke the attendance centre order if it is still in force.

(5) In dealing with an offender under sub-paragraph (1)(b) above, a magistrates' court—

    (a)   shall take into account the extent to which the offender has complied with the requirements of the attendance centre order; and

    (b)   in the case of an offender who has wilfully and persistently failed to comply with those requirements, may impose a custodial sentence notwithstanding anything in section 79(2) of this Act.

(5A) Where a magistrates' court dealing with an offender under sub-paragraph (1)(a) above would not otherwise have the power to amend the order under paragraph 5(1)(b) below (substitution of different attendance centre), that paragraph has effect as if references to an appropriate magistrates' court were references to the court dealing with the offender.

(6) A person sentenced under sub-paragraph (1)(b) above for an offence may appeal to the Crown Court against the sentence.

(7) A magistrates' court which deals with an offender's case under sub-paragraph (1)(c) above shall send to the Crown Court—

    (a)   a certificate signed by a justice of the peace giving particulars of the offender's failure to attend or, as the case may be, the breach of the rules which he has committed; and

    (b)   such other particulars of the case as may be desirable;

and a certificate purporting to be so signed shall be admissible as evidence of the failure or the breach before the Crown Court.

3. (1) Where by virtue of paragraph 2(1)(c) above the offender is brought or appears before the Crown Court and it is proved to the satisfaction of the court—

    (a)   that he has failed without reasonable excuse to attend as mentioned in paragraph 1(1)(a) above, or

    (b)   that he has committed such a breach of rules as is mentioned in paragraph 1(1)(b) above,

that court may deal with him, for the offence in respect of which the order was made, in any way in which it could have dealt with him for that offence if it had not made the order.

(2) Where the Crown Court deals with an offender under sub-paragraph (1) above, it shall revoke the attendance centre order if it is still in force.

(3) In dealing with an offender under sub-paragraph (1) above, the Crown Court—

    (a)   shall take into account the extent to which the offender has complied with the requirements of the attendance centre order; and

    (b)   in the case of an offender who has wilfully and persistently failed to comply with those requirements, may impose a custodial sentence notwithstanding anything in section 152(2) of the Criminal Justice Act 2003.

(4) In proceedings before the Crown Court under this paragraph any question whether there has been a failure to attend or a breach of the rules shall be determined by the court and not by the verdict of a jury.

Revocation of order with or without re-sentencing

4. (1) Where an attendance centre order is in force in respect of an offender, an appropriate court may, on an application made by the offender or by the officer in charge of the relevant attendance centre, revoke the order.

(2) In sub-paragraph (1) above "an appropriate court" means—

(*a*) where the court which made the order was the Crown Court and there is included in the order a direction that the power to revoke the order is reserved to that court, the Crown Court;

(*b*) in any other case, either of the following—

(i) a magistrates' court acting for the petty sessions area in which the relevant attendance centre is situated;

(ii) the court which made the order.

(3) Any power conferred by this paragraph—

(*a*) on a magistrates' court to revoke an attendance centre order made by such a court, or

(*b*) on the Crown Court to revoke an attendance centre order made by the Crown Court,

includes power to deal with the offender, for the offence in respect of which the order was made, in any way in which he could have been dealt with for that offence by the court which made the order if the order had not been made.

(4) A person sentenced by a magistrates' court under sub-paragraph (3) above for an offence may appeal to the Crown Court against the sentence.

(5) The proper officer of a court which makes an order under this paragraph revoking an attendance centre order shall—

(*a*) deliver a copy of the revoking order to the offender or send a copy by registered post or the recorded delivery service addressed to the offender's last or usual place of abode; and

(*b*) deliver or send a copy to the officer in charge of the relevant attendance centre.

(6) In this paragraph "the relevant attendance centre", in relation to an attendance centre order, means the attendance centre specified in the order or substituted for the attendance centre so specified by an order made by virtue of paragraph 5(1)(*b*) below.

(7) In this paragraph "proper officer" means—

(*a*) in relation to a magistrates' court, the designated officer for the court; and

(*b*) in relation to the Crown Court, the appropriate officer.

Amendment of order

5. (1) Where an attendance centre order is in force in respect of an offender, an appropriate magistrates' court may, on an application made by the offender or by the officer in charge of the relevant attendance centre, by order—

(*a*) vary the day or hour specified in the order for the offender's first attendance at the relevant attendance centre; or

(*b*) substitute for the relevant attendance centre an attendance centre which the court is satisfied is reasonably accessible to the offender, having regard to his age, the means of access available to him and any other circumstances.

(2) In sub-paragraph (1) above "an appropriate magistrates' court" means—

(*a*) a magistrates' court acting acting in the local justice area in which the relevant attendance centre is situated; or

(*b*) (except where the attendance centre order was made by the Crown Court) the magistrates' court which made the order.

(3) The designated officer for a court which makes an order under this paragraph shall—

(*a*) deliver a copy to the offender or send a copy by registered post or the recorded delivery service addressed to the offender's last or usual place of abode; and

(*b*) deliver or send a copy—

(i) if the order is made by virtue of sub-paragraph (1)(*a*) above, to the officer in charge of the relevant attendance centre; and

(ii) if it is made by virtue of sub-paragraph (1)(*b*) above, to the officer in charge of the attendance centre which the order as amended will require the offender to attend.

(4) In this paragraph "the relevant attendance centre" has the meaning given by paragraph 4(6) above.

Orders made on appeal

6. (1) Where an attendance centre order has been made on appeal, for the purposes of this Schedule it shall be deemed—

(*a*) if it was made on an appeal brought from a magistrates' court, to have been made by that magistrates' court;

(*b*) if it was made on an appeal brought from the Crown Court or from the criminal division of the Court of Appeal, to have been made by the Crown Court.

(2) In relation to an attendance centre order made on appeal, paragraphs 2(1)(*b*) and 4(3) above shall each have effect as if the words "if the order had not been made" were omitted and paragraph 3(1) above shall have effect as if the words "if it had not made the order" were omitted.

Orders for defaulters

7. (1) References in this Schedule to an "offender" include a person who has been ordered to attend at an attendance centre for such a default or failure as is mentioned in section 60(1)(*b*) or (*c*) of this Act.

(2) Where a person has been ordered to attend at an attendance centre for such a default or failure—

(a) paragraphs 2(1)(b), 3(1) and 4(3) above shall each have effect in relation to the order as if the words ", for the offence in respect of which the order was made," and "for that offence" were omitted; and

(b) paragraphs 2(5)(b) and 3(3)(b) above (which relate to custodial sentences for offences) do not apply.

Section 63   SCHEDULE 6
                    REQUIREMENTS WHICH MAY BE INCLUDED IN SUPERVISION ORDERS

(Amended by the Care Standards Act 2000, Sch 4, the Anti-social Behaviour Act 2003, Sch 2 and the Criminal Justice Act 2003, s 304, Sch 32 and the Criminal Defence Service Act 2006, s 4..)

Requirement to reside with named individual

3–1737 **1.** A supervision order may require the offender to reside with an individual named in the order who agrees to the requirement, but a requirement imposed by a supervision order in pursuance of this paragraph shall be subject to any such requirement of the order as is authorised by paragraph 2, 3, 6, 6A or 7 below.

Requirement to comply with directions of supervisor

2. (1) Subject to sub-paragraph (2) below, a supervision order may require the offender to comply with any directions given from time to time by the supervisor and requiring him to do all or any of the following things—

(a) to live at a place or places specified in the directions for a period or periods so specified;
(b) to present himself to a person or persons specified in the directions at a place or places and on a day or days so specified;
(c) to participate in activities specified in the directions on a day or days so specified.

(2) A supervision order shall not require compliance with directions given by virtue of sub-paragraph (1) above unless the court making it is satisfied that a scheme under section 66 of this Act (local authority schemes) is in force for the area where the offender resides or will reside; and no such directions may involve the use of facilities which are not for the time being specified in a scheme in force under that section for that area.

(3) A requirement imposed by a supervision order in pursuance of sub-paragraph (1) above shall be subject to any such requirement of the order as is authorised by paragraph 6 below (treatment for offender's mental condition).

(4) It shall be for the supervisor to decide—

(a) whether and to what extent he exercises any power to give directions conferred on him by virtue of sub-paragraph (1) above; and
(b) the form of any directions.

(5) The total number of days in respect of which an offender may be required to comply with directions given by virtue of paragraph (a), (b) or (c) of sub-paragraph (1) above shall not exceed 180 or such lesser number, if any, as the order may specify for the purposes of this sub-paragraph.

(6) For the purpose of calculating the total number of days in respect of which such directions may be given, the supervisor shall be entitled to disregard any day in respect of which directions were previously given in pursuance of the order and on which the directions were not complied with.

(7) Directions given by the supervisor by virtue of sub-paragraph (1)(b) or (c) above shall, as far as practicable, be such as to avoid—

(a) any conflict with the offender's religious beliefs or with the requirements of any other youth community order or any community order to which he may be subject; and
(b) any interference with the times, if any, at which he normally works or attends school or any other educational establishment.

Requirements as to activities, reparation, night restrictions etc

3. (1) This paragraph applies to a supervision order unless the order requires the offender to comply with directions given by the supervisor under paragraph 2(1) above.

(2) Subject to the following provisions of this paragraph, a supervision order to which this paragraph applies may require the offender—

(a) to live at a place or places specified in the order for a period or periods so specified;
(b) to present himself to a person or persons specified in the order at a place or places and on a day or days so specified;
(c) to participate in activities specified in the order on a day or days so specified;
(d) to make reparation specified in the order to a person or persons so specified or to the community at large;
(e) *repealed*
(f) to refrain from participating in activities specified in the order—

(i) on a specified day or days during the period for which the supervision order is in force; or
(ii) during the whole of that period or a specified portion of it;

and in this paragraph "make reparation" means make reparation for the offence otherwise than by the payment of compensation.

(3) The total number of days in respect of which an offender may be subject to requirements imposed by virtue of paragraph (a), (b), (c), or (d) or (e) of sub-paragraph (2) above shall not exceed 180.

(4) The court may not include requirements under sub-paragraph (2) above in a supervision order unless—

(a) it has first consulted the supervisor as to—

(i) the offender's circumstances, and
(ii) the feasibility of securing compliance with the requirements,

and is satisfied, having regard to the supervisor's report, that it is feasible to secure compliance with them;

(b) having regard to the circumstances of the case, it considers the requirements necessary for securing the good conduct of the offender or for preventing a repetition by him of the same offence or the commission of other offences; and

(c) if the offender is aged under 16, it has obtained and considered information about his family circumstances and the likely effect of the requirements on those circumstances.

(5) The court shall not by virtue of sub-paragraph (2) above include in a supervision order—

(a) any requirement that would involve the co-operation of a person other than the supervisor and the offender, unless that other person consents to its inclusion;

(b) any requirement to make reparation to any person unless that person—

(i) is identified by the court as a victim of the offence or a person otherwise affected by it; and
(ii) consents to the inclusion of the requirement;

(c) any requirement requiring the offender to reside with a specified individual; or
(d) any such requirement as is mentioned in paragraph 6(2) below (treatment for offender's mental condition).

(6) Requirements included in a supervision order by virtue of sub-paragraph (2)(b) or (c) above shall, as far as practicable, be such as to avoid—

(a) any conflict with the offender's religious beliefs or with the requirements of any other community order to which he may be subject; and

(b) any interference with the times, if any, at which he normally works or attends school or any other educational establishment;

and sub-paragraphs (7) and (8) below are without prejudice to this sub-paragraph.

(7) Subject to sub-paragraph (8) below, a supervision order may not by virtue of sub-paragraph (2) above include—

(a) any requirement that would involve the offender in absence from home—

(i) for more than two consecutive nights, or
(ii) for more than two nights in any one week, or

(b) if the offender is of compulsory school age, any requirement to participate in activities during normal school hours,

unless the court making the order is satisfied that the facilities whose use would be involved are for the time being specified in a scheme in force under section 66 of this Act for the area in which the offender resides or will reside.

(8) Sub-paragraph (7)(b) above does not apply to activities carried out in accordance with arrangements made or approved by the local education authority in whose area the offender resides or will reside.

(9) Expressions used in sub-paragraphs (7) and (8) above and in the Education Act 1996 have the same meaning in those sub-paragraphs as in that Act.

4. *Repealed.*

Requirement to live for specified period in local authority accommodation

5. (1) Where the conditions mentioned in sub-paragraph (2) below are satisfied, a supervision order may impose a requirement ("a local authority residence requirement") that the offender shall live for a specified period in local authority accommodation (as defined by section 163 of this Act).

(2) The conditions are that—

(a) a supervision order has previously been made in respect of the offender;

(b) that order imposed—

(i) a requirement under paragraph 1, 2, 3 or 7 of this Schedule; or
(ii) a local authority residence requirement;

(c) the offender fails to comply with that requirement, or is convicted of an offence committed while that order was in force; and

(d) the court is satisfied that—

(i) the failure to comply with the requirement, or the behaviour which constituted the offence, was due to a significant extent to the circumstances in which the offender was living; and
(ii) the imposition of a local authority residence requirement will assist in his rehabilitation;

except that sub-paragraph (i) of paragraph (d) above does not apply where the condition in paragraph (b)(ii) above is satisfied.

(3) A local authority residence requirement shall designate the local authority who are to receive the offender, and that authority shall be the authority in whose area the offender resides.

(4) The court shall not impose a local authority residence requirement without first consulting the designated authority.

(5) A local authority residence requirement may stipulate that the offender shall not live with a named person.

(6) The maximum period which may be specified in a local authority residence requirement is six months.

(7) A court shall not impose a local authority residence requirement in respect of an offender who is not legally represented at the relevant time in that court unless—

(a) he was granted a right to representation funded by the Legal Services Commission as part of the Criminal Defence Service for the purposes of the proceedings but the right was withdrawn because of his conduct or because it appeared that his financial resources were such that he was not eligible to be granted such a right;

(aa) he applied for such representation and the application was refused because it appeared that his financial resources were such that he was not eligible to be granted a right to it; or

(b) he has been informed of his right to apply for such representation for the purposes of the proceedings and has had the opportunity to do so, but nevertheless refused or failed to apply.

(8) In sub-paragraph (7) above—

(a) "the relevant time" means the time when the court is considering whether or not to impose the requirement; and

(b) "the proceedings" means—

    (i) the whole proceedings; or

    (ii) the part of the proceedings relating to the imposition of the requirement.

(9) A supervision order imposing a local authority residence requirement may also impose any of the requirements mentioned in paragraphs 2, 3, 6 and 7 of this Schedule.*

Requirement to live for specified period with local authority foster parent

5A. (1) Where the conditions mentioned in sub-paragraph (2) below are satisfied, a supervision order may impose a requirement ("a foster parent residence requirement") that the offender shall live for a specified period with a local authority foster parent.

(2) The conditions are that—

(a) the offence is punishable with imprisonment in the case of an offender aged 18 or over;

(b) the offence, or the combination of the offence and one or more offences associated with it, was so serious that a custodial sentence would normally be appropriate (or, where the offender is aged 10 or 11, would normally be appropriate if the offender were aged 12 or over); and

(c) the court is satisfied that—

    (i) the behaviour which constituted the offence was due to a significant extent to the circumstances in which the offender was living, and

    (ii) the imposition of a foster parent residence requirement will assist in his rehabilitation.

(3) A foster parent residence requirement shall designate the local authority who are to place the offender with a local authority foster parent under section 23(2)(a) of the Children Act 1989, and that authority shall be the authority in whose area the offender resides.

(4) A court shall not impose a foster parent residence requirement unless—

(a) the court has been notified by the Secretary of State that arrangements for implementing such a requirement are available in the area of the designated authority;

(b) the notice has not been withdrawn; and

(c) the court has consulted the designated authority.

(5) Subject to paragraph 5(2A) of Schedule 7 to this Act, the maximum period which may be specified in a foster parent residence requirement is twelve months.

(6) A court shall not impose a foster parent residence requirement in respect of an offender who is not legally represented at the relevant time in that court unless—

(a) he was granted a right to representation funded by the Legal Services Commission as part of the Criminal Defence Service for the purposes of the proceedings but the right was withdrawn because of his conduct or because it appeared that his financial resources were such that he was not eligible to be granted such a right;

(aa) he applied for such representation and the application was refused because it appeared that his financial resources were such that he was not eligible to be granted a right to it; or

(b) he has been informed of his right to apply for such representation for the purposes of the proceedings and has had opportunity to do so, but nevertheless refused or failed to apply.

(7) In sub-paragraph (6) above—

(a) "the relevant time" means the time when the court is considering whether or not to impose the requirement, and

(b) "the proceedings" means—

    (i) the whole proceedings, or

    (ii) the part of the proceedings relating to the imposition of the requirement.

(8) A supervision order imposing a foster parent residence requirement may also impose any of the requirements mentioned in paragraphs 2, 3, 6 and 7 of this Schedule.

(9) If at any time while a supervision order imposing a foster parent residence requirement is in force, the supervisor notifies the offender—

(a) that no suitable local authority foster parent is available, and

(b) that the supervisor has applied or proposes to apply under paragraph 5 of Schedule 7 for the variation or revocation of the order,

the foster parent residence requirement shall, until the determination of the application, be taken to require the offender to live in local authority accommodation (as defined by section 163 of this Act).

(10) This paragraph does not affect the power of a local authority to place with a local authority foster parent an offender to whom a local authority residence requirement under paragraph 5 above relates.

(11) In this paragraph "local authority foster parent" has the same meaning as in the Children Act 1989.

Requirements as to treatment for mental condition

6. (1) This paragraph applies where a court which proposes to make a supervision order is satisfied, on the evidence of a registered medical practitioner approved for the purposes of section 12 of the Mental Health Act 1983, that the mental condition of the offender—

(a) is such as requires and may be susceptible to treatment; but

(b) is not such as to warrant the making of a hospital order or guardianship order within the meaning of that Act.

(2) Where this paragraph applies, the court may include in the supervision order a requirement that the offender shall, for a period specified in the order, submit to treatment of one of the following descriptions so specified, that is to say—

(a) treatment as a resident patient in a an independent hospital or care home within the meaning of the Care Standards Act 2000 or a hospital within the meaning of the Mental Health Act 1983, but not a hospital at which high security psychiatric services within the meaning of that Act are provided;

(*b*) treatment as a non-resident patient at an institution or place specified in the order;

(*c*) treatment by or under the direction of a registered medical practitioner specified in the order; or

(*d*) treatment by or under the direction of a chartered psychologist specified in the order.★

(3) A requirement shall not be included in a supervision order by virtue of sub-paragraph (2) above—

(*a*) in any case, unless the court is satisfied that arrangements have been or can be made for the treatment in question and, in the case of treatment as a resident patient, for the reception of the patient;

(*b*) in the case of an order made or to be made in respect of a person aged 14 or over, unless he consents to its inclusion;

and a requirement so included shall not in any case continue in force after the offender attains the age of 18.

(4) Subsections (2) and (3) of section 54 of the Mental Health Act 1983 shall have effect with respect to proof for the purposes of sub-paragraph (1) above of an offender's mental condition as they have effect with respect to proof of an offender's mental condition for the purposes of section 37(2)(*a*) of that Act.

(5) In sub-paragraph (2) above "chartered psychologist" means a person for the time being listed in the British Psychological Society's Register of Chartered Psychologists.

Requirements as to drug treatment and testing

6A. (1) This paragraph applies where a court proposing to make a supervision order is satisfied—

(*a*) that the offender is dependent on, or has a propensity to misuse, drugs, and

(*b*) that his dependency or propensity is such as requires and may be susceptible to treatment.

(2) Where this paragraph applies, the court may include in the supervision order a requirement that the offender shall, for a period specified in the order ("the treatment period"), submit to treatment by or under the direction of a specified person having the necessary qualifications and experience ("the treatment provider") with a view to the reduction or elimination of the offender's dependency on or propensity to misuse drugs.

(3) The required treatment shall be—

(*a*) treatment as a resident in such institution or place as may be specified in the order, or

(*b*) treatment as a non-resident at such institution or place, and at such intervals, as may be so specified;

but the nature of the treatment shall not be specified in the order except as mentioned in paragraph (*a*) or (*b*) above.

(4) A requirement shall not be included in a supervision order by virtue of sub-paragraph (2) above—

(*a*) in any case, unless—

(i) the court is satisfied that arrangements have been or can be made for the treatment intended to be specified in the order (including arrangements for the reception of the offender where he is to be required to submit to treatment as a resident), and

(ii) the requirement has been recommended to the court as suitable for the offender by an officer of a local probation board or by a member of a youth offending team; and

(*b*) in the case of an order made or to be made in respect of a person aged 14 or over, unless he consents to its inclusion.

(5) Subject to sub-paragraph (6), a supervision order which includes a treatment requirement may also include a requirement ("a testing requirement") that, for the purpose of ascertaining whether he has any drug in his body during the treatment period, the offender shall during that period, at such times or in such circumstances as may (subject to the provisions of the order) be determined by the supervisor or the treatment provider, provide samples of such description as may be so determined.

(6) A testing requirement shall not be included in a supervision order by virtue of sub-paragraph (5) above unless—

(*a*) the offender is aged 14 or over and consents to its inclusion, and

(*b*) the court has been notified by the Secretary of State that arrangements for implementing such requirements are in force in the area proposed to be specified in the order.

(7) A testing requirement shall specify for each month the minimum number of occasions on which samples are to be provided.

(8) A supervision order including a testing requirement shall provide for the results of tests carried out on any samples provided by the offender in pursuance of the requirement to a person other than the supervisor to be communicated to the supervisor.★

***

★Para 6A inserted by the Criminal Justice Act 2003, s 279, Sch 24, and in force (for the purpose of sentencing persons resident in certain specified areas) 1 December 2004 (except in relation to the sentencing of a person convicted of an offence before that date): see SI 2004/3033, art 2.

Requirements as to education

7. (1) This paragraph applies to a supervision order unless the order requires the offender to comply with directions given by the supervisor under paragraph 2(1) above.

(2) Subject to the following provisions of this paragraph, a supervision order to which this paragraph applies may require the offender, if he is of compulsory school age, to comply, for as long as he is of that age and the order remains in force, with such arrangements for his education as may from time to time be made by his parent, being arrangements for the time being approved by the local education authority.

(3) The court shall not include such a requirement in a supervision order unless—

(*a*) it has consulted the local education authority with regard to its proposal to include the requirement; and

(*b*) it is satisfied that in the view of the local education authority arrangements exist for the offender to receive efficient full-time education suitable to his age, ability and aptitude and to any special educational need he may have.

(4) Expressions used in sub-paragraphs (2) and (3) above and in the Education Act 1996 have the same meaning in those sub-paragraphs as in that Act.

(5) The court may not include a requirement under sub-paragraph (2) above unless it has first consulted the

supervisor as to the offender's circumstances and, having regard to the circumstances of the case, it considers the requirement necessary for securing the good conduct of the offender or for preventing a repetition by him of the same offence or the commission of other offences.

Exercise of powers under paragraphs 3, 6 and 7

8. (1) Any power to include a requirement in a supervision order which is exercisable in relation to a person by virtue of paragraph 3, 6 or 7 above may be exercised in relation to him whether or not any other such power is exercised.

(2) Sub-paragraph (1) above is without prejudice to the power to include in a supervision order any other combination of requirements under different paragraphs of this Schedule that is authorised by this Schedule.

Section 65   SCHEDULE 7
                 BREACH, REVOCATION AND AMENDMENT OF SUPERVISION ORDERS

(Amended by the Anti-social Behaviour Act 2003, s 93 and Sch 2, Criminal Justice Act 2003, s 304, Sch 32 and SI 2005/886.)

Meaning of "relevant court", etc

3–1738 **1.** (1) In this Schedule, "relevant court", in relation to a supervision order, means—

(a) where the offender is under the age of 18, a youth court acting in the local justice area for the time being named in the order in pursuance of section 63(6) of this Act;

(b) where the offender has attained that age, a magistrates' court other than a youth court, being a magistrates' court acting in the local justice area for the time being so named.

(2) If an application to a youth court is made in pursuance of this Schedule and while it is pending the offender to whom it relates attains the age of 18, the youth court shall deal with the application as if he had not attained that age.

Breach of requirement of supervision order

2. (1) This paragraph applies if while a supervision order is in force in respect of an offender it is proved to the satisfaction of a relevant court, on the application of the supervisor, that the offender has failed to comply with any requirement included in the supervision order in pursuance of paragraph 1, 2, 3, 5, 5A, 6A or 7 of Schedule 6 to this Act or section 63(6)(b) of this Act.

(2) Where this paragraph applies, the court—

(a) whether or not it also makes an order under paragraph 5(1) below (revocation or amendment of supervision order)—

(i) may order the offender to pay a fine of an amount not exceeding £1,000; or

(ii) subject to sub-paragraph (2A) below and paragraph 3 below, may make a curfew order in respect of him; or

(iii) subject to paragraph 4 below, may make an attendance centre order in respect of him; or

(b) if the supervision order was made by a magistrates' court, may revoke the supervision order and deal with the offender, for the offence in respect of which the order was made, in any way in which he could have been dealt with for that offence by the court which made the order if the order had not been made; or

(c) if the supervision order was made by the Crown Court, may commit him in custody or release him on bail until he can be brought or appear before the Crown Court.⋆

(2A) The court may not make a curfew order under sub-paragraph (2)(a)(ii) above in respect of an offender who is already subject to a curfew order.

(3) Where a court deals with an offender under sub-paragraph (2)(c) above, it shall send to the Crown Court a certificate signed by a justice of the peace giving—

(a) particulars of the offender's failure to comply with the requirement in question; and

(b) such other particulars of the case as may be desirable;

and a certificate purporting to be so signed shall be admissible as evidence of the failure before the Crown Court.

(4) Where—

(a) by virtue of sub-paragraph (2)(c) above the offender is brought or appears before the Crown Court, and

(b) it is proved to the satisfaction of the court that he has failed to comply with the requirement in question,

that court may deal with him, for the offence in respect of which the supervision order was made, in any way in which it could have dealt with him for that offence if it had not made the order.

(5) Where the Crown Court deals with an offender under sub-paragraph (4) above, it shall revoke the supervision order if it is still in force.

(6) A fine imposed under this paragraph shall be deemed, for the purposes of any enactment, to be a sum adjudged to be paid by a conviction.

(7) In dealing with an offender under this paragraph, a court shall take into account the extent to which he has complied with the requirements of the supervision order.

(8) Where a supervision order has been made on appeal, for the purposes of this paragraph it shall be deemed—

(a) if it was made on an appeal brought from a magistrates' court, to have been made by that magistrates' court;

(b) if it was made on an appeal brought from the Crown Court or from the criminal division of the Court of Appeal, to have been made by the Crown Court;

and, in relation to a supervision order made on appeal, sub-paragraph (2)(b) above shall have effect as if the words "if the order had not been made" were omitted and sub-paragraph (4) above shall have effect as if the words "if it had not made the order" were omitted.

(9) This paragraph has effect subject to paragraph 7 below.

Curfew orders imposed for breach of supervision order

3.—(1) Section 37(1) of this Act (curfew orders) shall apply for the purposes of paragraph 2(2)(*a*)(ii) above as if for the words from the beginning to "make" there were substituted "Where a court considers it appropriate to make an order in respect of any person in pursuance of paragraph 2(2)(*a*)(ii) of Schedule 7 to this Act, it may make".

(2) The following provisions of this Act, namely—

(*a*)   section 37(3) to (12), and

(*b*)   so far as applicable, sections 36B and 40 and Schedule 3 so far as relating to curfew orders,

have effect in relation to a curfew order made by virtue of paragraph 2(2)(*a*)(ii) above as they have effect in relation to any other curfew order, subject to sub-paragraph (5) below.

(3) Sections 148 and 156 of the Criminal Justice Act 2003 (restrictions and procedural requirements for community sentences) do not apply in relation to a curfew order made by virtue of paragraph 2(2)(*a*)(ii) above.

(4) *Repealed.*

(5) Schedule 3 to this Act (breach, revocation and amendment of orders) shall have effect in relation to such a curfew order as if—

(*a*)   the power conferred on the court by each of paragraphs 4(2)(*c*) and and 10(3)(*b*) to deal with the offender for the offence in respect of which the order was made were a power to deal with the offender, for his failure to comply with the supervision order, in any way in which a relevant court could deal with him for that failure if it had just been proved to the satisfaction of that court;

(*b*)   the reference in paragraph 10(1)(*b*) to the offence in respect of which the order was made were a reference to the failure to comply in respect of which the curfew order was made; and

(*c*)   the power conferred on the Crown Court by paragraph 11(2)(*b*) to deal with the offender for the offence in respect of which the order was made were a power to deal with the offender, for his failure to comply with the supervision order, in any way in which a relevant court (if the supervision order was made by a magistrates' court) or the Crown Court (if the supervision order was made by the Crown Court) could deal with him for that failure if it had just been proved to its satisfaction.

(6) For the purposes of the provisions mentioned in paragraphs (*a*) and (*c*) of sub-paragraph (5) above, as applied by that sub-paragraph, if the supervision order is no longer in force the relevant court's powers shall be determined on the assumption that it is still in force.

Attendance centre orders imposed for breach of supervision order

4.—(1) Section 60(1) of this Act (attendance centre orders) shall apply for the purposes of paragraph 2(2)(*a*)(iii) above as if for the words from the beginning to "the court may," there were substituted "Where a court considers it appropriate to make an order in respect of any person in pursuance of paragraph 2(2)(*a*)(iii) of Schedule 7 to this Act, the court may,".

(2) The following provisions of this Act, namely—

(*a*)   subsections (3) to (11) of section 60, and

(*b*)   so far as applicable, Schedule 5,

have effect in relation to an attendance centre order made by virtue of paragraph 2(2)(*a*)(iii) above as they have effect in relation to any other attendance centre order, subject to sub-paragraph (4) below.

(3) Sections 148 and 156 of the Criminal Justice Act 2003 (restrictions and procedural requirements for community sentences) do not apply in relation to an attendance centre order made by virtue of paragraph 2(2)(*a*)(iii) above.

(4) Schedule 5 to this Act (breach, revocation and amendment of attendance centre orders) shall have effect in relation to such an attendance centre order as if there were omitted—

(*a*)   from each of paragraphs 2(1)(*b*) and 4(3) the words ", for the offence in respect of which the order was made," and "for that offence"; and

(*b*)   from paragraphs 2(6) and 4(4) the words "for an offence".

Revocation and amendment of supervision order

5.—(1) If while a supervision order is in force in respect of an offender it appears to a relevant court, on the application of the supervisor or the offender, that it is appropriate to make an order under this sub-paragraph, the court may—

(*a*)   make an order revoking the supervision order; or

(*b*)   make an order amending it—

(i)   by cancelling any requirement included in it in pursuance of Schedule 6 to, or section 63(6)(*b*) of, this Act; or

(ii)   by inserting in it (either in addition to or in substitution for any of its provisions) any provision which could have been included in the order if the court had then had power to make it and were exercising the power.

(2) Sub-paragraph (1) above has effect subject to paragraphs 7 to 9 below.★

(2A) In relation to a supervision order imposing a foster parent residence requirement under paragraph 5A of Schedule 6 to this Act, the power conferred by sub-paragraph (1)(*b*)(ii) above includes power to extend the period specified in the requirement to a period of not more than 18 months beginning with the day on which the requirement first had effect.

(3) The powers of amendment conferred by sub-paragraph (1) above do not include power—

(*a*)   to insert in the supervision order, after the end of three months beginning with the date when the order was originally made, a requirement in pursuance of paragraph 6 of Schedule 6 to this Act (treatment for mental condition), unless it is in substitution for such a requirement already included in the order;

(*b*)   *repealed.*

(4) Where an application under sub-paragraph (1) above for the revocation of a supervision order is dismissed, no further application for its revocation shall be made under that sub-paragraph by any person during the period of three months beginning with the date of the dismissal except with the consent of a court having jurisdiction to entertain such an application.

Amendment of order on report of medical practitioner

6. (1) If a medical practitioner by whom or under whose direction an offender is being treated for his mental condition in pursuance of a requirement included in a supervision order by virtue of paragraph 6 of Schedule 6 to this Act—

(a) is unwilling to continue to treat or direct the treatment of the offender, or
(b) is of the opinion mentioned in sub-paragraph (2) below,

the practitioner shall make a report in writing to that effect to the supervisor.
(2) The opinion referred to in sub-paragraph (1) above is—

(a) that the treatment of the offender should be continued beyond the period specified in that behalf in the order;
(b) that the offender needs different treatment;
(c) that the offender is not susceptible to treatment; or
(d) that the offender does not require further treatment.

(3) On receiving a report under sub-paragraph (1) above the supervisor shall refer it to a relevant court; and on such a reference the court may make an order cancelling or varying the requirement.
(4) Sub-paragraph (3) above has effect subject to paragraphs 7 to 9 below.

Presence of offender in court, remands etc

7. (1) Where the supervisor makes an application or reference under paragraph 2(1), 5(1) or 6(3) above to a court he may bring the offender before the court; and, subject to sub-paragraph (9) below, a court shall not make an order under paragraph 2, 5(1) or 6(3) above unless the offender is present before the court.
(2) Without prejudice to any power to issue a summons or warrant apart from this sub-paragraph, a justice may issue a summons or warrant for the purpose of securing the attendance of an offender before the court to which any application or reference in respect of him is made under paragraph 2(1), 5(1) or 6(3) above.
(3) Subsections (3) and (4) of section 55 of the Magistrates' Courts Act 1980 (which among other things restrict the circumstances in which a warrant may be issued) shall apply with the necessary modifications to a warrant under sub-paragraph (2) above as they apply to a warrant under that section, but as if in subsection (3) after the word "summons" there were inserted the words "cannot be served or".
(4) Where the offender is arrested in pursuance of a warrant issued by virtue of sub-paragraph (2) above and cannot be brought immediately before the court referred to in that sub-paragraph, the person in whose custody he is—

(a) may make arrangements for his detention in a place of safety for a period of not more than 72 hours from the time of the arrest (and it shall be lawful for him to be detained in pursuance of the arrangements); and
(b) shall within that period, unless within it the offender is brought before the court referred to in sub-paragraph (2) above, bring him before a justice;

and in paragraph (a) above "place of safety" has the same meaning as in the Children and Young Persons Act 1933.
(5) Where an offender is brought before a justice under sub-paragraph (4)(b) above, the justice may—

(a) direct that he be released forthwith; or
(b) subject to sub-paragraph (7) below, remand him to local authority accommodation.

(6) Subject to sub-paragraph (7) below, where an application is made to a youth court under paragraph 5(1) above, the court may remand (or further remand) the offender to local authority accommodation if—

(a) a warrant has been issued under sub-paragraph (2) above for the purpose of securing the attendance of the offender before the court; or
(b) the court considers that remanding (or further remanding) him will enable information to be obtained which is likely to assist the court in deciding whether and, if so, how to exercise its powers under paragraph 5(1) above.

(7) Where the offender is aged 18 or over at the time when he is brought before a justice under sub-paragraph (4)(b) above, or is aged 18 or over at a time when (apart from this sub-paragraph) a youth court could exercise its powers under sub-paragraph (6) above in respect of him, he shall not be remanded to local authority accommodation but may instead be remanded—

(a) to a remand centre, if the justice or youth court has been notified that such a centre is available for the reception of persons under this sub-paragraph; or*
(b) to a prison, if the justice or youth court has not been so notified.*

(8) A justice or court remanding a person to local authority accommodation under this paragraph shall designate, as the authority who are to receive him, the authority named in the supervision order.
(9) A court may make an order under paragraph 5(1) or 6(3) above in the absence of the offender if the effect of the order is confined to one or more of the following, that is to say—

(a) revoking the supervision order;
(b) cancelling a provision included in the supervision order in pursuance of Schedule 6 to, or section 63(6)(b) of, this Act;
(c) reducing the duration of the supervision order or any provision included in it in pursuance of that Schedule;
(d) altering in the supervision order the name of any area;
(e) changing the supervisor.

---

*Repealed by the Criminal Justice and Court Services Act 2000, Sch 7 from a date to be appointed.

Restrictions on court's powers to revoke or amend order

8. (1) A youth court shall not—

(a) exercise its powers under paragraph 5(1) above to make an order—

(i) revoking a supervision order, or

(ii) inserting in it a requirement authorised by Schedule 6 to this Act, or

(iii) varying or cancelling such a requirement,

except in a case where the court is satisfied that the offender either is unlikely to receive the care or control he needs unless the court makes the order or is likely to receive it notwithstanding the order;

(b) exercise its powers to make an order under paragraph 6(3) above except in such a case as is mentioned in paragraph (a) above;

(c) exercise its powers under paragraph 5(1) above to make an order inserting a requirement authorised by paragraph 6 of Schedule 6 to this Act in a supervision order which does not already contain such a requirement, unless the court is satisfied as mentioned in paragraph 6(1) of that Schedule on such evidence as is there mentioned.

(2) For the purposes of this paragraph "care" includes protection and guidance and "control" includes discipline.

9. Where the offender has attained the age of 14, then except with his consent a court shall not make an order under paragraph 5(1) or 6(3) above containing provisions—

(a) which insert in the supervision order a requirement authorised by paragraph 6 of Schedule 6 to this Act; or

(b) which alter such a requirement already included in the supervision order otherwise than by removing it or reducing its duration.

Copies of revoking or amending orders

10. A court which makes an order amending or revoking a supervision order shall forthwith send a copy of its order—

(a) to the offender and, if the offender is aged under 14, to his parent or guardian;

(b) to the supervisor and any person who has ceased to be the supervisor by virtue of the order;

(c) to any local authority who are not entitled by virtue of paragraph (b) above to such a copy and whose area is named in the supervision order in pursuance of section 63(6) of this Act or has ceased to be so named by virtue of the court's order;

(d) where the offender is required by the order, or was required by the supervision order before it was amended or revoked, to reside with an individual or to undergo treatment by or under the direction of an individual or at any place, to the individual or the person in charge of that place; and

(e) where a local justice area named in the order or revoked order in pursuance of section 63(6) of this Act is not that in which the court acts, to the designated officer for the local justice area so named;

and, in a case falling within paragraph (e) above, shall also send to the designated officer in question such documents and information relating to the case as the court considers likely to be of assistance to them.

Appeals

11. The offender may appeal to the Crown Court against—

(a) any order made under paragraph 2(2), 5(1) or 6(3) above by a relevant court, except—

(i) an order made or which could have been made in the absence of the offender (by virtue of paragraph 7(9) above); and

(ii) an order containing only provisions to which the offender consented in pursuance of paragraph 9 above;

(b) the dismissal of an application under paragraph 5(1) above to revoke a supervision order.

Power of parent or guardian to make application on behalf of young person

12. (1) Without prejudice to any power apart from this sub-paragraph to bring proceedings on behalf of another person, any power to make an application which is exercisable by a child or young person by virtue of paragraph 5(1) above shall also be exercisable on his behalf by his parent or guardian.

(2) In this paragraph "guardian" includes any person who was a guardian of the child or young person in question at the time when any supervision order to which the application relates was originally made.

SCHEDULE 8

BREACH, REVOCATION AND AMENDMENT OF ACTION PLAN ORDERS AND REPARATION ORDERS

(As amended by Criminal Justice and Court Services Act 2000, Sch 7, the Criminal Justice Act 2003, Sch 32 and SI 2005/886)

Sections 72 and 75

Meaning of "the appropriate court"

3–1739   1. In this Schedule, "the appropriate court", in relation to an action plan order or reparation order, means a youth court acting in the local justice area the time being named in the order in pursuance of section 69(8) or, as the case may be, 74(4) of this Act.

Breach of requirement of action plan order or reparation order

2. (1) This paragraph applies if while an action plan order or reparation order is in force in respect of an offender it is proved to the satisfaction of the appropriate court, on the application of the responsible officer, that the offender has failed to comply with any requirement included in the order.

(2) Where this paragraph applies, the court—

(*a*)   whether or not it also makes an order under paragraph 5(1) below (revocation or amendment of order)—

     (i)   may order the offender to pay a fine of an amount not exceeding £1,000; or

     (ii)   subject to paragraph 3 below, may make a curfew order in respect of him; or

     (iii)   subject to paragraph 4 below, may make an attendance centre order in respect of him; or

(*b*)   if the action plan order or reparation order was made by a magistrates' court, may revoke the order and deal with the offender, for the offence in respect of which the order was made, in any way in which he could have been dealt with for that offence by the court which made the order if the order had not been made; or

(*c*)   if the action plan order or reparation order was made by the Crown Court, may commit him in custody or release him on bail until he can be brought or appear before the Crown Court.

(3)   Where a court deals with an offender under sub-paragraph (2)(*c*) above, it shall send to the Crown Court a certificate signed by a justice of the peace giving—

(*a*)   particulars of the offender's failure to comply with the requirement in question; and

(*b*)   such other particulars of the case as may be desirable;

and a certificate purporting to be so signed shall be admissible as evidence of the failure before the Crown Court.

(4)   Where—

(*a*)   by virtue of sub-paragraph (2)(*c*) above the offender is brought or appears before the Crown Court, and

(*b*)   it is proved to the satisfaction of the court that he has failed to comply with the requirement in question,

that court may deal with him, for the offence in respect of which the order was made, in any way in which it could have dealt with him for that offence if it had not made the order.

(5)   Where the Crown Court deals with an offender under sub-paragraph (4) above, it shall revoke the action plan order or reparation order if it is still in force.

(6)   A fine imposed under this paragraph shall be deemed, for the purposes of any enactment, to be a sum adjudged to be paid by a conviction.

(7)   In dealing with an offender under this paragraph, a court shall take into account the extent to which he has complied with the requirements of the action plan order or reparation order.

(8)   Where a reparation order or action plan order has been made on appeal, for the purposes of this paragraph it shall be deemed—

(*a*)   if it was made on an appeal brought from a magistrates' court, to have been made by that magistrates' court;

(*b*)   if it was made on an appeal brought from the Crown Court or from the criminal division of the Court of Appeal, to have been made by the Crown Court;

and in relation to a reparation order or action plan order made on appeal, sub-paragraph (2)(*b*) above shall have effect as if the words "if the order had not been made" were omitted and sub-paragraph (4) above shall have effect as if the words "if it had not made the order" were omitted.

(9)   This paragraph has effect subject to paragraph 6 below.

Curfew orders imposed for breach of action plan order or reparation order

3.   (1)   Section 37(1) of this Act (curfew orders) shall apply for the purposes of paragraph 2(2)(*a*)(ii) above as if for the words from the beginning to "make" there were substituted "Where a court considers it appropriate to make an order in respect of any person in pursuance of paragraph 2(2)(*a*)(ii) of Schedule 8 to this Act, it may make".

(2)   The following provisions of this Act, namely—

(*a*)   section 37(3) to (12), and

(*b*)   so far as applicable, sections 36B and 40 and Schedule 3 so far as relating to curfew orders,

have effect in relation to a curfew order made by virtue of paragraph 2(2)(*a*)(ii) above as they have effect in relation to any other curfew order, subject to sub-paragraph (5) below.

(3)   Sections 148 and 156 of the Criminal Justice Act 2003 (restrictions and procedural requirements for community sentences) do not apply in relation to a curfew order made by virtue of paragraph 2(2)(*a*)(ii) above.

(4)   *Repealed.*

(5)   Schedule 3 to this Act (breach, revocation and amendment of orders) shall have effect in relation to such a curfew order as if—

(*a*)   the power conferred on the court by each of paragraphs 4(2)(*c*)* and 10(3)(*b*) to deal with the offender for the offence in respect of which the order was made were a power to deal with the offender, for his failure to comply with the action plan order or reparation order, in any way in which the appropriate court could deal with him for that failure if it had just been proved to the satisfaction of that court;

(*b*)   the reference in paragraph 10(1)(*b*) to the offence in respect of which the order was made were a reference to the failure to comply in respect of which the curfew order was made; and

(*c*)   the power conferred on the Crown Court by paragraph 11(2)(*b*) to deal with the offender for the offence in respect of which the order was made were a power to deal with the offender, for his failure to comply with the action plan order or reparation order, in any way in which the appropriate court (if the action plan order or reparation order was made by a magistrates' court) or the Crown Court (if that order was made by the Crown Court) could deal with him for that failure if it had just been proved to its satisfaction.

(6)   For the purposes of the provisions mentioned in paragraphs (*a*) and (*c*) of sub-paragraph (5) above, as applied by that sub-paragraph, if the action plan order or reparation order is no longer in force the appropriate court's powers shall be determined on the assumption that it is still in force.

---

*Amended by the Criminal Justice and Court Services Act 2000, Sch 7 from a date to be appointed.

Attendance centre orders imposed for breach of action plan or reparation order

4.   (1)   Section 60(1) of this Act (attendance centre orders) shall apply for the purposes of paragraph 2(2)(*a*)(iii) above as if for the words from the beginning to "the court may," there were substituted "Where a court considers it appropriate to make an order in respect of any person in pursuance of paragraph 2(2)(*a*)(iii) of Schedule 8 to this Act, the court may,".

(2) The following provisions of this Act, namely—

(a) subsections (3) to (11) of section 60, and

(b) so far as applicable, Schedule 5,

have effect in relation to an attendance centre order made by virtue of paragraph 2(2)(a)(iii) above as they have effect in relation to any other attendance centre order, subject to sub-paragraph (4) below.

(3) Sections 148 and 156 of the Criminal Justice Act 2003 (restrictions and procedural requirements for community sentences) do not apply in relation to an attendance centre order made by virtue of paragraph 2(2)(a)(iii) above.

(4) Schedule 5 to this Act (breach, revocation and amendment of attendance centre orders) shall have effect in relation to such an attendance centre order as if there were omitted—

(a) from each of paragraphs 2(1)(b) and 4(3) the words ", for the offence in respect of which the order was made," and "for that offence"; and

(b) from paragraphs 2(6) and 4(4) the words "for an offence".

Revocation and amendment of action plan order or reparation order

5. (1) If while an action plan order or reparation order is in force in respect of an offender it appears to the appropriate court, on the application of the responsible officer or the offender, that it is appropriate to make an order under this sub-paragraph, the court may—

(a) make an order revoking the action plan order or reparation order; or

(b) make an order amending it—

(i) by cancelling any provision included in it; or

(ii) by inserting in it (either in addition to or in substitution for any of its provisions) any provision which could have been included in the order if the court had then had power to make it and were exercising the power.

(2) Sub-paragraph (1) above has effect subject to paragraph 6 below.

(3) Where an application under sub-paragraph (1) above for the revocation of an action plan order or reparation order is dismissed, no further application for its revocation shall be made under that sub-paragraph by any person except with the consent of the appropriate court.*

---

*Repealed by the Criminal Justice and Court Services Act 2000, Sch 7 from a date to be appointed.

Presence of offender in court, remands etc

6. (1) Where the responsible officer makes an application under paragraph 2(1) or 5(1) above to the appropriate court he may bring the offender before the court; and, subject to sub-paragraph (9) below, a court shall not make an order under paragraph 2 or 5(1) above unless the offender is present before the court.

(2) Without prejudice to any power to issue a summons or warrant apart from this sub-paragraph, the court to which an application under paragraph 2(1) or 5(1) above is made may issue a summons or warrant for the purpose of securing the attendance of the offender before it.

(3) Subsections (3) and (4) of section 55 of the Magistrates' Courts Act 1980 (which among other things restrict the circumstances in which a warrant may be issued) shall apply with the necessary modifications to a warrant under sub-paragraph (2) above as they apply to a warrant under that section, but as if in subsection (3) after the word "summons" there were inserted the words "cannot be served or".

(4) Where the offender is arrested in pursuance of a warrant issued by virtue of sub-paragraph (2) above and cannot be brought immediately before the appropriate court, the person in whose custody he is—

(a) may make arrangements for his detention in a place of safety for a period of not more than 72 hours from the time of the arrest (and it shall be lawful for him to be detained in pursuance of the arrangements); and

(b) shall within that period bring him before a youth court;

and in paragraph (a) above "place of safety" has the same meaning as in the Children and Young Persons Act 1933.

(5) Where an offender is under sub-paragraph (4)(b) above brought before a youth court other than the appropriate court, the youth court may—

(a) direct that he be released forthwith; or

(b) subject to sub-paragraph (7) below, remand him to local authority accommodation.

(6) Subject to sub-paragraph (7) below, where an application is made to a court under paragraph 5(1) above, the court may remand (or further remand) the offender to local authority accommodation if—

(a) a warrant has been issued under sub-paragraph (2) above for the purpose of securing the attendance of the offender before the court; or

(b) the court considers that remanding (or further remanding) him will enable information to be obtained which is likely to assist the court in deciding whether and, if so, how to exercise its powers under paragraph 5(1) above.

(7) Where the offender is aged 18 or over at the time when he is brought before a youth court other than the appropriate court under sub-paragraph (4)(b) above, or is aged 18 or over at a time when (apart from this sub-paragraph) the appropriate court could exercise its powers under sub-paragraph (6) above in respect of him, he shall not be remanded to local authority accommodation but may instead be remanded—

(a) to a remand centre, if the court has been notified that such a centre is available for the reception of persons under this sub-paragraph; or*

(b) to a prison, if it has not been so notified.*

(8) A court remanding an offender to local authority accommodation under this paragraph shall designate, as the authority who are to receive him, the local authority for the area in which the offender resides or, where it appears to the court that he does not reside in the area of a local authority, the local authority—

(a) specified by the court; and

(b) in whose area the offence or an offence associated with it was committed.

(9) A court may make an order under paragraph 5(1) above in the absence of the offender if the effect of the order is confined to one or more of the following, that is to say—

(a) revoking the action plan order or reparation order;

(b) cancelling a requirement included in the action plan order or reparation order;

(c) altering in the action plan order or reparation order the name of any area;

(d) changing the responsible officer.

---

*Repealed by the Criminal Justice and Court Services Act 2000, Sch 7 from a date to be appointed.

Appeals

7. The offender may appeal to the Crown Court against—

(a) any order made under paragraph 2(2) or 5(1) above except an order made or which could have been made in his absence (by virtue of paragraph 6(9) above);

(b) the dismissal of an application under paragraph 5(1) above to revoke an action plan order or reparation order.

3–1740

Section 165   SCHEDULE 9
                   CONSEQUENTIAL AMENDMENTS

Section 165   SCHEDULE 10
                   TRANSITORY MODIFICATIONS

Section 8

3–1741   1. (1) This paragraph applies if paragraph 11 of Schedule 13 to the Access to Justice Act 1999 has not come into force before the commencement of this Act.

(2) If this paragraph applies, then until the relevant commencement date section 8(4) and (10) of this Act shall each have effect as if for the words "justices' chief executive for" there were substituted "clerk of".

2. (1) This paragraph applies if paragraph 5 of Schedule 4 to the Youth Justice and Criminal Evidence Act 1999 has not come into force before the commencement of this Act.

(2) If this paragraph applies, then until the appointed day section 8 of this Act shall have effect as if the words from "the case" in subsection (6) to "but" in subsection (8) were omitted.

(3) In this paragraph "the appointed day" means—

(a) if before the commencement of this Act an order has been made appointing a day for the coming into force of paragraph 5 of Schedule 4 to the Youth Justice and Criminal Evidence Act 1999, the day so appointed;

(b) otherwise, such day as the Secretary of State may by order appoint.

Section 13

3. (1) This paragraph applies if paragraph 84 of Schedule 13 to the Access to Justice Act 1999 has not come into force before the commencement of this Act.

(2) If this paragraph applies, then until the relevant commencement date section 13(5) of this Act shall have effect as if for the words "justices' chief executive" there were substituted "clerk of the court".

Sections 63 and 66 and Schedule 7

4. (1) This paragraph applies if paragraph 63 of Schedule 13 to the Access to Justice Act 1999 has not come into force before the commencement of this Act.

(2) If this paragraph applies, then until the relevant commencement date—

(a) sections 63(8) and 66(5) and (10) of this Act, and

(b) paragraph 10 of Schedule 7 to this Act,

shall each have effect as if for the words "justices' chief executive" (wherever occurring) there were substituted "clerk to the justices".

Section 67

5. (1) This paragraph applies if the repeal made by Part V(2) of Schedule 15 to the Access to Justice Act 1999 of the definition of "petty sessions area" in section 70(1) of the Children and Young Persons Act 1969 has not come into force before the commencement of this Act.

(2) If this paragraph applies, then until the relevant commencement date section 67(1) of this Act shall have effect as if after the definition of "local authority" there were inserted the following definition—

""petty sessions area", in relation to a youth court constituted for the metropolitan area within the meaning of Part II of Schedule 2 to the Children and Young Persons Act 1963, means such a division of that area as is mentioned in paragraph 14 of that Schedule;".

Section 69

6. (1) This paragraph applies if paragraph 30 of Schedule 4 to the Youth Justice and Criminal Evidence Act 1999 has not come into force before the commencement of this Act.

(2) If this paragraph applies, then until the appointed day section 69(5) of this Act shall have effect as if for the words ", a supervision order or a referral order" there were substituted "or a supervision order".

(3) In this paragraph "the appointed day" means—

(a) if before the commencement of this Act an order has been made appointing a day for the coming into force of paragraph 30 of Schedule 4 to the Youth Justice and Criminal Evidence Act 1999, the day so appointed;

(b) otherwise, such day as the Secretary of State may by order appoint.

Section 73

7. (1) This paragraph applies if paragraph 29 of Schedule 4 to the Youth Justice and Criminal Evidence Act 1999 has not come into force before the commencement of this Act.

(2) If this paragraph applies, then until the appointed day section 73(4) of this Act shall have effect as if for the words ", an action plan order or a referral order" there were substituted "or an action plan order".

(3) In this paragraph "the appointed day" means—

(a) if before the commencement of this Act an order has been made appointing a day for the coming into force of paragraph 29 of Schedule 4 to the Youth Justice and Criminal Evidence Act 1999, the day so appointed;

(b) otherwise, such day as the Secretary of State may by order appoint.

Section 83

8. (1) This paragraph applies if—

(a) paragraphs 9 and 25 of Schedule 4 to the Access to Justice Act 1999, and

(b) the repeals made by Part I of Schedule 15 to that Act in section 21 of the Powers of Criminal Courts Act 1973 and section 3 of the Criminal Justice Act 1982,

have not come into force before the commencement of this Act.

(2) If this paragraph applies, then until the relevant commencement date section 83 of this Act shall have effect as if—

(a) for paragraph (a) of subsection (3) there were substituted the following paragraph—

"(a) he applied for legal aid and had his application refused on the ground that it did not appear his resources were such that he required assistance; or"; and

(b) in paragraph (b) of that subsection, for the words "such representation" there were substituted "legal aid".

(3) If this paragraph applies, then until the relevant commencement date section 83 of this Act shall also have effect as if after subsection (4) there were inserted the following subsection—

"(4A) In this section "legal aid" means legal aid for the purposes of proceedings in that court, whether the whole proceedings or the proceedings on or in relation to sentence; but in the case of a person committed to the Crown Court for sentence or trial or sent to that court for trial under section 51 of the Crime and Disorder Act 1998 it is immaterial whether he applied for legal aid in the Crown Court to, or was informed of his right to apply by, that court or the court which committed or sent him."

Sections 122 and 124

9. (1) This paragraph applies if paragraph 85 of Schedule 13 to the Access to Justice Act 1999 has not come into force before the commencement of this Act.

(2) If this paragraph applies, then until the relevant commencement date sections 122(6) and 124(4) of this Act shall each have effect as if for the words "justices' chief executive" there were substituted "clerk to the justices".

Section 150

10. (1) This paragraph applies if paragraph 20 of Schedule 4 to the Youth Justice and Criminal Evidence Act 1999 has not come into force before the commencement of this Act.

(2) If this paragraph applies, then until the appointed day section 150(1) of this Act shall have effect as if the words from "but this subsection" onwards were omitted.

(3) In this paragraph "the appointed day" means—

(a) if before the commencement of this Act an order has been made appointing a day for the coming into force of paragraph 20 of Schedule 4 to the Youth Justice and Criminal Evidence Act 1999, the day so appointed;

(b) otherwise, such day as the Secretary of State may by order appoint.

Section 155

11. (1) This paragraph applies if paragraph 24 of Schedule 4 to the Access to Justice Act 1999 has not come into force before the commencement of this Act.

(2) If this paragraph applies, then until the relevant commencement date section 155(8) of this Act shall have effect as if for the words "an order under section 17(2) of the Access to Justice Act 1999" there were substituted "a contribution order made under section 23 of the Legal Aid Act 1988".

Schedule 3

12. (1) This paragraph applies if paragraph 166 of Schedule 13 to the Access to Justice Act 1999 has not come into force before the commencement of this Act.

(2) If this paragraph applies, then until the relevant commencement date Schedule 3 to this Act shall have effect as if—

(a) in paragraph 15(1), for the words "proper officer of" there were substituted "clerk to";

(b) paragraph 15(2) were omitted;

(c) in each of sub-paragraphs (1) and (2)* of paragraph 25, for the words 'justices' chief executive for the court" there were substituted "clerk to the court"; and**

(d) in sub-paragraph (1) of that paragraph, for the words "chief executive to the justices" (in both places where they occur) there were substituted "clerk to the justices";

(e) in sub-paragraph (2)(a) of paragraph 26, for the words "justices' chief executive for the court" there were substituted "clerk to the court"; and***

(f) in sub-paragraph (3) of that paragraph, for the words "justices' chief executive for that court" there were substituted "clerk to that court".***

---

*Amended by the Criminal Justice and Court Services Act 2000, Sch 7 from a date to be appointed.
**Repealed by the Criminal Justice and Court Services Act 2000, Sch 7 from a date to be appointed.

***Sub-paragraphs (*e*) and (*f*) printed as prospectively by the Criminal Justice and Court Services Act 2000, Sch 7 from a date to be appointed.**

Schedule 5

13. (1) This paragraph applies if paragraph 123 of Schedule 13 to the Access to Justice Act 1999 has not come into force before the commencement of this Act.

(2) If this paragraph applies, then until the relevant commencement date Schedule 5 to this Act shall have effect as if—

(*a*) in paragraph 4(5), for the words "proper officer of" there were substituted "clerk to";
(*b*) paragraph 4(7) were omitted; and
(*c*) in paragraph 5(3), for the words "justices' chief executive for" there were substituted "clerk to".

Schedule 6

14. (1) This paragraph applies if subsections (1) to (3) of section 71 of the Crime and Disorder Act 1998 have not come into force before the commencement of this Act.

(2) If this paragraph applies, then until the appointed day paragraph 3 of Schedule 6 to this Act shall have effect as if the following provisions were omitted—

(*a*) in sub-paragraph (2), paragraph (*d*);
(*b*) in sub-paragraph (3), the word ", (*d*)";
(*c*) in sub-paragraph (5), paragraph (*b*).

(3) In this paragraph "the appointed day" means—

(*a*) if before the commencement of this Act an order has been made appointing a day for the coming into force of section 71(1) to (3) of the Crime and Disorder Act 1998, the day so appointed;
(*b*) otherwise, such day as the Secretary of State may by order appoint.

15. (1) This paragraph applies if paragraph 5 of Schedule 4 to the Access to Justice Act 1999 has not come into force before the commencement of this Act.

(2) If this paragraph applies, then until the relevant commencement date paragraph 5(7) of Schedule 6 to this Act shall have effect as if—

(*a*) for paragraph (*a*) there were substituted the following paragraph—

"(*a*) he has applied for legal aid for the purposes of the proceedings and the application was refused on the ground that it did not appear that his resources were such that he required assistance; or"; and
(*b*) in paragraph (*b*), for the words "such representation" there were substituted the words "legal aid".

Meaning of "the relevant commencement date' etc

16. (1) Subject to sub-paragraph (2) below, in any of the preceding paragraphs "the relevant commencement date" means such day as the Lord Chancellor may by order made by statutory instrument appoint in relation to that paragraph; and different days may be appointed for different purposes.

(2) Where—

(*a*) a provision of the Access to Justice Act 1999 referred to in sub-paragraph (1) of paragraph 1, 3, 4, 5, 8, 9, 11, 12, 13 or 15 above has not come into force before the commencement of this Act, but
(*b*) before the commencement of this Act an order under the Access to Justice Act 1999 has been made appointing a day for the coming into force of that provision,

"the relevant commencement date", in relation to that provision, means the day so appointed.

17. An order under any of paragraphs 2, 6, 7, 10 and 14 above may appoint different days for different purposes or different areas.

Power to make transitional provision

18. Section 160(6) of this Act does not apply to an order made by the Secretary of State under any of the preceding provisions of this Schedule, but—

(*a*) an order under paragraph 14 or 16(1) above may make such transitional provisions and savings as appear to the Secretary of State or the Lord Chancellor necessary or expedient; and
(*b*) an order under any of paragraphs 2, 6, 7 and 10 above may make such provision as, by virtue of section 64(4) of the Youth Justice and Criminal Evidence Act 1999 (regulations and orders), is authorised to be made by an order under section 68(3) of that Act (commencement).

Saving for old transitional provisions

19. (1) This paragraph applies to any transitional provision or saving ("the transitional provision") made in connection with the coming into force of a provision of the Access to Justice Act 1999, the Youth Justice and Criminal Evidence Act 1999 or the Crime and Disorder Act 1998 mentioned in sub-paragraph (1) of any of paragraphs 1 to 15 above ("the old enactment").

(2) If the old enactment is in force before the commencement of the provision of this Act reproducing its effect ("the corresponding provision of this Act"), the transitional provision shall continue to have effect (so far as capable of doing so) in relation to the corresponding provision of this Act.

(3) If—

(*a*) sub-paragraph (2) above does not apply, but
(*b*) before the commencement of this Act an order has been made appointing a day for the coming into force of the old enactment,

the transitional provision shall, from the day so appointed, have effect in relation to the corresponding provision of this Act.

SCHEDULE 11
TRANSITIONAL PROVISIONS

PART I
GENERAL

Continuity of the law: general

3–1742 **1.** (1) The substitution of this Act for the provisions repealed by it shall not affect the continuity of the law.

(2) Any thing done (including subordinate legislation made), or having effect as if done, under or for the purposes of any provision repealed by this Act shall, if it could have been done under or for the purposes of the corresponding provision of this Act and if in force or effective immediately before the commencement of that corresponding provision, have effect thereafter as if done under or for the purposes of that corresponding provision.

(3) Any reference (express or implied) in this Act or any other enactment, instrument or document to a provision of this Act shall (so far as the context permits) be construed as including, as respects times, circumstances or purposes in relation to which the corresponding provision repealed by this Act had effect, a reference to that corresponding provision.

(4) Any reference (express or implied) in any enactment, instrument or document to a provision repealed by this Act shall (so far as the context permits) be construed, as respects times, circumstances and purposes in relation to which the corresponding provision of this Act has effect, as being or (according to the context) including a reference to the corresponding provision of this Act.

(5) Sub-paragraphs (1) to (4) above have effect instead of section 17(2) of the Interpretation Act 1978 (but are without prejudice to any other provision of that Act).

General saving for old transitional provisions and savings

2. (1) The repeal by this Act of a transitional provision or saving relating to the coming into force of a provision reproduced in this Act does not affect the operation of the transitional provision or saving, in so far as it is not specifically reproduced in this Act but remains capable of having effect in relation to the corresponding provision of this Act.

(2) The repeal by this Act of an enactment previously repealed subject to savings does not affect the continued operation of those savings.

(3) The repeal by this Act of a saving on the previous repeal of an enactment does not affect the operation of the saving in so far as it is not specifically reproduced in this Act but remains capable of having effect.

(4) Where the purpose of an enactment repealed by this Act was to secure that the substitution of the provisions of the Act containing that enactment for provisions repealed by that Act did not affect the continuity of the law, the enactment repealed by this Act continues to have effect in so far as it is capable of doing so.

Use of existing forms etc

3. Any reference to an enactment repealed by this Act which is contained in a document made, served or issued after the commencement of that repeal shall be construed, except so far as a contrary intention appears, as a reference or (as the context may require) as including a reference to the corresponding provision of this Act.

PART II
SPECIFIC PROVISIONS: REPLICATION OF OLD TRANSITIONAL PROVISIONS

Sections 37, 41. 46 and 79 and Schedules 2, 3 and 6: consent requirements

3–1743 **4.** (1) In relation to an offence committed before 1st October 1997—

(a) section 37 of this Act shall have effect as if at the end of subsection (10) (but not as part of paragraph (c)) there were added the words "and the court shall not make the order unless he expresses his willingness to comply with its requirements";

(b) section 41 of this Act shall have effect as if at the end of subsection (7) (but not as part of paragraph (c)) there were added the words "and the court shall not make the order unless he expresses his willingness to comply with its requirements";

(c) section 46(4) of this Act shall have effect as if after the word "unless" there were inserted "the offender consents and";

(d) section 79(3) of this Act shall have effect as if for the words from "he fails to" onwards there were substituted "he refuses to give his consent to a community sentence which is proposed by the court and requires that consent"; and

(e) Schedule 2 to this Act shall have effect as if there were omitted from each of paragraphs 5(4) and 6(5) paragraph (b) and the word "and" immediately preceding it.

(2) In relation to an offence committed before 1st October 1997, Schedule 3 to this Act shall have effect as if—

(a) for paragraph (b) of each of paragraphs 4(2) and 5(2) there were substituted the following paragraph—

"(b) may assume, in the case of an offender who has wilfully and persistently failed to comply with those requirements, that he has a refused to give his consent to a community sentence which has been proposed by the court and requires that consent.";

(b) paragraph 19(2)(b)(i) were omitted; and

(c) at the end of paragraph 20(2)(b) there were inserted ", being treatment of a kind to which he could be required to submit in pursuance of a probation or combination order".

(3) In relation to an offence committed before 1st October 1997, paragraph 3(4) of Schedule 6 to this Act shall have effect as if for paragraph (c) there were substituted the following paragraph—

"(c) the offender or, if he is a child, his parent or guardian, consents to their inclusion."

Section 37: minimum age for curfew order

5. In relation to an offence committed before 1st January 1998, section 37 of this Act shall have effect as if—

(a) in subsection (1), after the word "person" there were inserted "aged 16 or over"; and

(b) subsections (4) and (9) were omitted.

Custodial sentences for young offenders: section 98 and re-sentencing powers

6. In relation to an offender sentenced to detention in a young offender institution before 1st April 2000, section 98(2) of this Act shall have effect as if at the end there were inserted ", but if he is under 18 at the time of the direction, only for a temporary purpose".

7. A court to which it falls after the commencement of this Act to determine for the purposes of any enactment how a previous court could or might have dealt with an offender shall in the case of an offender aged under 18 make that determination—

(a) as if sections 100 to 107 of this Act (detention and training orders) and section 96 of this Act (detention in a young offender institution available only if offender is at least 18) had been in force; and

(b) as if sections 1 to 4 of the Criminal Justice and Public Order Act 1994 (secure training orders, repealed by the Crime and Disorder Act 1998) had not been in force.

Sections 143, 147, 148 and 150: miscellaneous transitional provisions

8. The following provisions of this Act, namely—

(a) subsections (6) and (7) of section 143, and

(b) subsections (2) and (4) of section 147,

do not apply in relation to an offence committed before 1st July 1992.

9. In relation to an offence into which a criminal investigation began before 1st April 1997, section 148 of this Act shall have effect as if for paragraph (b) of subsection (6) there were substituted the following paragraph—

"(b) the depositions taken at any committal proceedings and any written statements or admissions used as evidence in those proceedings."

10. In relation to an offence committed before 3rd February 1995, section 150 of this Act shall have effect as if there were omitted from subsection (2) the words from "and where the court" onwards.

PART III

SPECIFIC PROVISIONS: MISCELLANEOUS TRANSITIONAL PROVISIONS

Referral orders

3–1744   **11.**—(1) Any provision of Part III of this Act which re-enacts an enactment contained in the Youth Justice and Criminal Evidence Act 1999 which has not been brought into force before the commencement of this Act shall be of no effect until that enactment is brought into force.

(2) The repeal by this Act of any enactment contained in the Youth Justice and Criminal Evidence Act 1999 which has not been brought into force before the commencement of this Act shall not have effect until that enactment is brought into force.

(3) Sub-paragraph (2) above does not apply to the repeal by this Act of paragraph 5, 20, 29 or 30 of Schedule 4 to the Youth Justice and Criminal Evidence Act 1999.

(4) Any provision of Schedule 9 to this Act which amends an enactment as amended by Schedule 4 to the Youth Justice and Criminal Evidence Act 1999 shall, if the amendment in question made by Schedule 4 to that Act has not been brought into force before the commencement of this Act, be of no effect until that amendment is brought into force.

Modifications for Isles of Scilly

12. If immediately before the commencement of this Act an order made under section 71 of the Children and Young Persons Act 1969 (application to Isles of Scilly) is in force which modifies any provisions of that Act reproduced in this Act—

(a) the order shall have effect as if also made under section 68 of this Act; and

(b) the provisions modified by the order shall be deemed to include any provision of the sections and Schedules mentioned in section 68(1) which corresponds to a provision of the Children and Young Persons Act 1969 which, immediately before the commencement of this Act, was modified by the order.

Consequential amendments

13. The amendments made by Schedule 9 to this Act of subsections (5)(e) and (10) of section 5 of the Rehabilitation of Offenders Act 1974 shall not be taken to affect the operation of paragraph 36(7) of Schedule 14 to the Children Act 1989 (which saves the effect of section 5 in relation to certain care orders made under the Children and Young Persons Act 1969).

PART IV

INTERPRETATION

3–1745   **14.** In this Schedule, where the context permits, "repeal" includes revoke.

Section 165   **SCHEDULE 12**

REPEALS AND REVOCATIONS

3–1746

PART I

ACTS OF PARLIAMENT REPEALED

3–1747

PART II

SUBORDINATE LEGISLATION REVOKED

Proceeds of Crime Act 2002[1]
(2002 c 29)

PART 1
ASSETS RECOVERY AGENCY[2]

3–1748   The Director of the Assets Recovery Agency is appointed by the Secretary of State and must, acting through his staff (or other persons providing services under arrangements made by him if authorized generally or specifically for that purpose), exercise his functions in the way which he considers is best calculated to contribute to the reduction of crime having regard to any guidance issued by the Secretary of State (ss 1–2 and Sch 1). The Director must make provision for the training of financial investigators and provide a system for their accreditation (s 3). There is a mutual duty between the Director and persons who have functions relating to the investigation or prosecution of offences to co-operate in the exercise of their functions (s 4). The Director must also provide advice to the Secretary of State in relation to the Act and which is designed to help in the reduction of crime (s 5).

---

1. For commencement of this Act see s 458, post. The confiscation provisions of this Act apply to offences committed on or after 24 March 2003. For confiscation orders made in respect of offences committed before this date under Part VI of the Criminal Justice Act 1988 and Part I of the Drug Trafficking Offences Act 1994, see earlier editions of this work.
2. Part 1 comprises ss 1–5 and Sch 1.

PART 2
CONFISCATION: ENGLAND AND WALES[1]

Confiscation orders

3–1749   **6. Making of order.**   (1) The Crown Court must proceed under this section if the following two conditions are satisfied.

    (2) The first condition is that a defendant falls within any of the following paragraphs—

    (*a*)   he is convicted of an offence or offences in proceedings before the Crown Court;

    (*b*)   he is committed to the Crown Court for sentence in respect of an offence or offences under section 3, 4 or 6 of the Sentencing Act;

    (*c*)   he is committed to the Crown Court in respect of an offence or offences under section 70 below (committal with a view to a confiscation order being considered).

    (3) The second condition is that—

    (*a*)   the prosecutor or the Director asks the court to proceed under this section, or

    (*b*)   the court believes it is appropriate for it to do so.

    (4) The court must proceed as follows—

    (*a*)   it must decide whether the defendant has a criminal lifestyle;

    (*b*)   if it decides that he has a criminal lifestyle it must decide whether he has benefited from his general criminal conduct;

    (*c*)   if it decides that he does not have a criminal lifestyle it must decide whether he has benefited from his particular criminal conduct.

    (5) If the court decides under subsection (4)(*b*) or (*c*) that the defendant has benefited from the conduct referred to it must—

    (*a*)   decide the recoverable amount, and

    (*b*)   make an order (a confiscation order) requiring him to pay that amount.

    (6) But the court must treat the duty in subsection (5) as a power if it believes that any victim of the conduct has at any time started or intends to start proceedings against the defendant in respect of loss, injury or damage sustained in connection with the conduct.

    (7) The court must decide any question arising under subsection (4) or (5) on a balance of probabilities.

    (8) The first condition is not satisfied if the defendant absconds (but section 27 may apply).

    (9) References in this Part to the offence (or offences) concerned are to the offence (or offences) mentioned in subsection (2).

[Proceeds of Crime Act 2002, s 6.]

---

1. Part 2 comprises ss 6–91 and Sch 2.

3–1750   **7. Recoverable amount.**   (1) The recoverable amount for the purposes of section 6 is an amount equal to the defendant's benefit from the conduct concerned.

    (2) But if the defendant shows that the available amount is less than that benefit the recoverable amount is—

    (*a*)   the available amount, or

    (*b*)   a nominal amount, if the available amount is nil.

    (3) But if section 6(6) applies the recoverable amount is such amount as—

    (*a*)   the court believes is just, but

(b)   does not exceed the amount found under subsection (1) or (2) (as the case may be).

(4) In calculating the defendant's benefit from the conduct concerned for the purposes of subsection (1), any property in respect of which—

(a)   a recovery order is in force under section 266, or
(b)   a forfeiture order is in force under section 298(2),

must be ignored.

(5) If the court decides the available amount, it must include in the confiscation order a statement of its findings as to the matters relevant for deciding that amount.
[Proceeds of Crime Act 2002, s 7.]

3–1751   8. Defendant's benefit.   (1) If the court is proceeding under section 6 this section applies for the purpose of—

(a)   deciding whether the defendant has benefited from conduct, and
(b)   deciding his benefit from the conduct.

(2) The court must—

(a)   take account of conduct occurring up to the time it makes its decision;
(b)   take account of property obtained up to that time.

(3) Subsection (4) applies if—

(a)   the conduct concerned is general criminal conduct,
(b)   a confiscation order mentioned in subsection (5) has at an earlier time been made against the defendant, and
(c)   his benefit for the purposes of that order was benefit from his general criminal conduct.

(4) His benefit found at the time the last confiscation order mentioned in subsection (3)(c) was made against him must be taken for the purposes of this section to be his benefit from his general criminal conduct at that time.

(5) If the conduct concerned is general criminal conduct the court must deduct the aggregate of the following amounts—

(a)   the amount ordered to be paid under each confiscation order previously made against the defendant;
(b)   the amount ordered to be paid under each confiscation order previously made against him under any of the provisions listed in subsection (7).

(6) But subsection (5) does not apply to an amount which has been taken into account for the purposes of a deduction under that subsection on any earlier occasion.

(7) These are the provisions—

(a)   the Drug Trafficking Offences Act 1986 (c 32);
(b)   Part 1 of the Criminal Justice (Scotland) Act 1987 (c 41);
(c)   Part 6 of the Criminal Justice Act 1988 (c 33);
(d)   the Criminal Justice (Confiscation) (Northern Ireland) Order 1990 (SI 1990/2588 (NI 17));
(e)   Part 1 of the Drug Trafficking Act 1994 (c 37);
(f)   Part 1 of the Proceeds of Crime (Scotland) Act 1995 (c 43);
(g)   the Proceeds of Crime (Northern Ireland) Order 1996 (SI 1996/1299 (NI 9));
(h)   Part 3 or 4 of this Act.

(8) The reference to general criminal conduct in the case of a confiscation order made under any of the provisions listed in subsection (7) is a reference to conduct in respect of which a court is required or entitled to make one or more assumptions for the purpose of assessing a person's benefit from the conduct.
[Proceeds of Crime Act 2002, s 8.]

3–1752   9. Available amount.   (1) For the purposes of deciding the recoverable amount, the available amount is the aggregate of—

(a)   the total of the values (at the time the confiscation order is made) of all the free property then held by the defendant minus the total amount payable in pursuance of obligations which then have priority, and
(b)   the total of the values (at that time) of all tainted gifts.

(2) An obligation has priority if it is an obligation of the defendant—

(a)   to pay an amount due in respect of a fine or other order of a court which was imposed or made on conviction of an offence and at any time before the time the confiscation order is made, or
(b)   to pay a sum which would be included among the preferential debts if the defendant's bankruptcy had commenced on the date of the confiscation order or his winding up had been ordered on that date.

(3) "Preferential debts" has the meaning given by section 386 of the Insolvency Act 1986 (c 45).
[Proceeds of Crime Act 2002, s 9.]

3–1753   **10. Assumptions to be made in case of criminal lifestyle.**   (1) If the court decides under section 6 that the defendant has a criminal lifestyle it must make the following four assumptions for the purpose of—

    (a)   deciding whether he has benefited from his general criminal conduct, and
    (b)   deciding his benefit from the conduct.

   (2) The first assumption is that any property transferred to the defendant at any time after the relevant day was obtained by him—

    (a)   as a result of his general criminal conduct, and
    (b)   at the earliest time he appears to have held it.

   (3) The second assumption is that any property held by the defendant at any time after the date of conviction was obtained by him—

    (a)   as a result of his general criminal conduct, and
    (b)   at the earliest time he appears to have held it.

   (4) The third assumption is that any expenditure incurred by the defendant at any time after the relevant day was met from property obtained by him as a result of his general criminal conduct.

   (5) The fourth assumption is that, for the purpose of valuing any property obtained (or assumed to have been obtained) by the defendant, he obtained it free of any other interests in it.

   (6) But the court must not make a required assumption in relation to particular property or expenditure if—

    (a)   the assumption is shown to be incorrect, or
    (b)   there would be a serious risk of injustice if the assumption were made.

   (7) If the court does not make one or more of the required assumptions it must state its reasons.
   (8) The relevant day is the first day of the period of six years ending with—

    (a)   the day when proceedings for the offence concerned were started against the defendant, or
    (b)   if there are two or more offences and proceedings for them were started on different days, the earliest of those days.

   (9) But if a confiscation order mentioned in section 8(3)(c) has been made against the defendant at any time during the period mentioned in subsection (8)—

    (a)   the relevant day is the day when the defendant's benefit was calculated for the purposes of the last such confiscation order;
    (b)   the second assumption does not apply to any property which was held by him on or before the relevant day.

   (10) The date of conviction is—

    (a)   the date on which the defendant was convicted of the offence concerned, or
    (b)   if there are two or more offences and the convictions were on different dates, the date of the latest.
[Proceeds of Crime Act 2002, s 10.]

3–1754   **11. Time for payment.**   (1) The amount ordered to be paid under a confiscation order must be paid on the making of the order; but this is subject to the following provisions of this section.
   (2) If the defendant shows that he needs time to pay the amount ordered to be paid, the court making the confiscation order may make an order allowing payment to be made in a specified period.
   (3) The specified period—

    (a)   must start with the day on which the confiscation order is made, and
    (b)   must not exceed six months.

   (4) If within the specified period the defendant applies to the Crown Court for the period to be extended and the court believes there are exceptional circumstances, it may make an order extending the period.
   (5) The extended period—

    (a)   must start with the day on which the confiscation order is made, and
    (b)   must not exceed 12 months.

   (6) An order under subsection (4)—

    (a)   may be made after the end of the specified period, but
    (b)   must not be made after the end of the period of 12 months starting with the day on which the confiscation order is made.

   (7) The court must not make an order under subsection (2) or (4) unless it gives—

    (a)   the prosecutor, or
    (b)   if the Director was appointed as the enforcement authority for the order under section 34, the Director,

an opportunity to make representations.
[Proceeds of Crime Act 2002, s 11.]

3–1755   12. Interest on unpaid sums.   (1) If the amount required to be paid by a person under a confiscation order is not paid when it is required to be paid, he must pay interest on the amount for the period for which it remains unpaid.

(2)   The rate of interest is the same rate as that for the time being specified in section 17 of the Judgments Act 1838 (c 110) (interest on civil judgment debts).

(3)   For the purposes of this section no amount is required to be paid under a confiscation order if—

(a)   an application has been made under section 11(4),

(b)   the application has not been determined by the court, and

(c)   the period of 12 months starting with the day on which the confiscation order was made has not ended.

(4)   In applying this Part the amount of the interest must be treated as part of the amount to be paid under the confiscation order.
[Proceeds of Crime Act 2002, s 12.]

3–1756   13. Effect of order on court's other powers.   (1) If the court makes a confiscation order it must proceed as mentioned in subsections (2) and (4) in respect of the offence or offences concerned.

(2)   The court must take account of the confiscation order before—

(a)   it imposes a fine on the defendant, or

(b)   it makes an order falling within subsection (3).

(3)   These orders fall within this subsection—

(a)   an order involving payment by the defendant, other than an order under section 130 of the Sentencing Act (compensation orders);

(b)   an order under section 27 of the Misuse of Drugs Act 1971 (c 38) (forfeiture orders);

(c)   an order under section 143 of the Sentencing Act (deprivation orders);

(d)   an order under section 23 of the Terrorism Act 2000 (c 11) (forfeiture orders).

(4)   Subject to subsection (2), the court must leave the confiscation order out of account in deciding the appropriate sentence for the defendant.

(5)   Subsection (6) applies if—

(a)   the Crown Court makes both a confiscation order and an order for the payment of compensation under section 130 of the Sentencing Act against the same person in the same proceedings, and

(b)   the court believes he will not have sufficient means to satisfy both the orders in full.

(6)   In such a case the court must direct that so much of the compensation as it specifies is to be paid out of any sums recovered under the confiscation order; and the amount it specifies must be the amount it believes will not be recoverable because of the insufficiency of the person's means.
[Proceeds of Crime Act 2002, s 13.]

Procedural matters

3–1757   14. Postponement.   (1) The court may—

(a)   proceed under section 6 before it sentences the defendant for the offence (or any of the offences) concerned, or

(b)   postpone proceedings under section 6 for a specified period.

(2)   A period of postponement may be extended.

(3)   A period of postponement (including one as extended) must not end after the permitted period ends.

(4)   But subsection (3) does not apply if there are exceptional circumstances.

(5)   The permitted period is the period of two years starting with the date of conviction.

(6)   But if—

(a)   the defendant appeals against his conviction for the offence (or any of the offences) concerned, and

(b)   the period of three months (starting with the day when the appeal is determined or otherwise disposed of) ends after the period found under subsection (5),

the permitted period is that period of three months.

(7)   A postponement or extension may be made—

(a)   on application by the defendant;

(b)   on application by the prosecutor or the Director (as the case may be);

(c)   by the court of its own motion.

(8)   If—

(a)   proceedings are postponed for a period, and

(b)   an application to extend the period is made before it ends,

the application may be granted even after the period ends.

(9)   The date of conviction is—

(a)   the date on which the defendant was convicted of the offence concerned, or

(b) if there are two or more offences and the convictions were on different dates, the date of the latest.

(10) References to appealing include references to applying under section 111 of the Magistrates' Courts Act 1980 (c 43) (statement of case).

(11) A confiscation order must not be quashed only on the ground that there was a defect or omission in the procedure connected with the application for or the granting of a postponement.

(12) But subsection (11) does not apply if before it made the confiscation order the court—

(a) imposed a fine on the defendant;
(b) made an order falling within section 13(3);
(c) made an order under section 130 of the Sentencing Act (compensation orders).

[Proceeds of Crime Act 2002, s 14.]

3–1758 15. Effect of postponement.   (1) If the court postpones proceedings under section 6 it may proceed to sentence the defendant for the offence (or any of the offences) concerned.

(2) In sentencing the defendant for the offence (or any of the offences) concerned in the postponement period the court must not—

(a) impose a fine on him,
(b) make an order falling within section 13(3), or
(c) make an order for the payment of compensation under section 130 of the Sentencing Act.

(3) If the court sentences the defendant for the offence (or any of the offences) concerned in the postponement period, after that period ends it may vary the sentence by—

(a) imposing a fine on him,
(b) making an order falling within section 13(3), or
(c) making an order for the payment of compensation under section 130 of the Sentencing Act.

(4) But the court may proceed under subsection (3) only within the period of 28 days which starts with the last day of the postponement period.

(5) For the purposes of—

(a) section 18(2) of the Criminal Appeal Act 1968 (c 19) (time limit for notice of appeal or of application for leave to appeal), and
(b) paragraph 1 of Schedule 3 to the Criminal Justice Act 1988 (c 33) (time limit for notice of application for leave to refer a case under section 36 of that Act),

the sentence must be regarded as imposed or made on the day on which it is varied under subsection (3).

(6) If the court proceeds to sentence the defendant under subsection (1), section 6 has effect as if the defendant's particular criminal conduct included conduct which constitutes offences which the court has taken into consideration in deciding his sentence for the offence or offences concerned.

(7) The postponement period is the period for which proceedings under section 6 are postponed.

[Proceeds of Crime Act 2002, s 15.]

3–1759 16. Statement of information.   (1) If the court is proceeding under section 6 in a case where section 6(3)(a) applies, the prosecutor or the Director (as the case may be) must give the court a statement of information within the period the court orders.

(2) If the court is proceeding under section 6 in a case where section 6(3)(b) applies and it orders the prosecutor to give it a statement of information, the prosecutor must give it such a statement within the period the court orders.

(3) If the prosecutor or the Director (as the case may be) believes the defendant has a criminal lifestyle the statement of information is a statement of matters the prosecutor or the Director believes are relevant in connection with deciding these issues—

(a) whether the defendant has a criminal lifestyle;
(b) whether he has benefited from his general criminal conduct;
(c) his benefit from the conduct.

(4) A statement under subsection (3) must include information the prosecutor or Director believes is relevant—

(a) in connection with the making by the court of a required assumption under section 10;
(b) for the purpose of enabling the court to decide if the circumstances are such that it must not make such an assumption.

(5) If the prosecutor or the Director (as the case may be) does not believe the defendant has a criminal lifestyle the statement of information is a statement of matters the prosecutor or the Director believes are relevant in connection with deciding these issues—

(a) whether the defendant has benefited from his particular criminal conduct;
(b) his benefit from the conduct.

(6) If the prosecutor or the Director gives the court a statement of information—

(a) he may at any time give the court a further statement of information;
(b) he must give the court a further statement of information if it orders him to do so, and he must give it within the period the court orders.

(7) If the court makes an order under this section it may at any time vary it by making another one.
[Proceeds of Crime Act 2002, s 16.]

3–1760   **17. Defendant's response to statement of information.**   (1) If the prosecutor or the Director gives the court a statement of information and a copy is served on the defendant, the court may order the defendant—

(*a*)   to indicate (within the period it orders) the extent to which he accepts each allegation in the statement, and
(*b*)   so far as he does not accept such an allegation, to give particulars of any matters he proposes to rely on.

(2) If the defendant accepts to any extent an allegation in a statement of information the court may treat his acceptance as conclusive of the matters to which it relates for the purpose of deciding the issues referred to in section 16(3) or (5) (as the case may be).

(3) If the defendant fails in any respect to comply with an order under subsection (1) he may be treated for the purposes of subsection (2) as accepting every allegation in the statement of information apart from—

(*a*)   any allegation in respect of which he has complied with the requirement;
(*b*)   any allegation that he has benefited from his general or particular criminal conduct.

(4) For the purposes of this section an allegation may be accepted or particulars may be given in a manner ordered by the court.

(5) If the court makes an order under this section it may at any time vary it by making another one.

(6) No acceptance under this section that the defendant has benefited from conduct is admissible in evidence in proceedings for an offence.
[Proceeds of Crime Act 2002, s 17.]

3–1761   **18. Provision of information by defendant.**   (1) This section applies if—

(*a*)   the court is proceeding under section 6 in a case where section 6(3)(*a*) applies, or
(*b*)   it is proceeding under section 6 in a case where section 6(3)(*b*) applies or it is considering whether to proceed.

(2) For the purpose of obtaining information to help it in carrying out its functions the court may at any time order the defendant to give it information specified in the order.

(3) An order under this section may require all or a specified part of the information to be given in a specified manner and before a specified date.

(4) If the defendant fails without reasonable excuse to comply with an order under this section the court may draw such inference as it believes is appropriate.

(5) Subsection (4) does not affect any power of the court to deal with the defendant in respect of a failure to comply with an order under this section.

(6) If the prosecutor or the Director (as the case may be) accepts to any extent an allegation made by the defendant—

(*a*)   in giving information required by an order under this section, or
(*b*)   in any other statement given to the court in relation to any matter relevant to deciding the available amount under section 9,

the court may treat the acceptance as conclusive of the matters to which it relates.

(7) For the purposes of this section an allegation may be accepted in a manner ordered by the court.

(8) If the court makes an order under this section it may at any time vary it by making another one.

(9) No information given under this section which amounts to an admission by the defendant that he has benefited from criminal conduct is admissible in evidence in proceedings for an offence.
[Proceeds of Crime Act 2002, s 18.]

Reconsideration

3–1762   **19. No order made: reconsideration of case.**   (1) This section applies if—

(*a*)   the first condition in section 6 is satisfied but no court has proceeded under that section,
(*b*)   there is evidence which was not available to the prosecutor on the relevant date,
(*c*)   before the end of the period of six years starting with the date of conviction the prosecutor or the Director applies to the Crown Court to consider the evidence, and
(*d*)   after considering the evidence the court believes it is appropriate for it to proceed under section 6.

(2) If this section applies the court must proceed under section 6, and when it does so subsections (3) to (8) below apply.

(3) If the court has already sentenced the defendant for the offence (or any of the offences) concerned, section 6 has effect as if his particular criminal conduct included conduct which constitutes offences which the court has taken into consideration in deciding his sentence for the offence or offences concerned.

(4) Section 8(2) does not apply, and the rules applying instead are that the court must—

(a) take account of conduct occurring before the relevant date;
(b) take account of property obtained before that date;
(c) take account of property obtained on or after that date if it was obtained as a result of or in connection with conduct occurring before that date.

(5) In section 10—

(a) the first and second assumptions do not apply with regard to property first held by the defendant on or after the relevant date;
(b) the third assumption does not apply with regard to expenditure incurred by him on or after that date;
(c) the fourth assumption does not apply with regard to property obtained (or assumed to have been obtained) by him on or after that date.

(6) The recoverable amount for the purposes of section 6 is such amount as—

(a) the court believes is just, but
(b) does not exceed the amount found under section 7.

(7) In arriving at the just amount the court must have regard in particular to—

(a) the amount found under section 7;
(b) any fine imposed on the defendant in respect of the offence (or any of the offences) concerned;
(c) any order which falls within section 13(3) and has been made against him in respect of the offence (or any of the offences) concerned and has not already been taken into account by the court in deciding what is the free property held by him for the purposes of section 9;
(d) any order which has been made against him in respect of the offence (or any of the offences) concerned under section 130 of the Sentencing Act (compensation orders).

(8) If an order for the payment of compensation under section 130 of the Sentencing Act has been made against the defendant in respect of the offence or offences concerned, section 13(5) and (6) above do not apply.

(9) The relevant date is—

(a) if the court made a decision not to proceed under section 6, the date of the decision;
(b) if the court did not make such a decision, the date of conviction.

(10) The date of conviction is—

(a) the date on which the defendant was convicted of the offence concerned, or
(b) if there are two or more offences and the convictions were on different dates, the date of the latest.

[Proceeds of Crime Act 2002, s 19.]

3–1763　20. No order made: reconsideration of benefit. (1) This section applies if the following two conditions are satisfied.

(2) The first condition is that in proceeding under section 6 the court has decided that—

(a) the defendant has a criminal lifestyle but has not benefited from his general criminal conduct, or
(b) the defendant does not have a criminal lifestyle and has not benefited from his particular criminal conduct.

(3) If the court proceeded under section 6 because the Director asked it to, the second condition is that—

(a) the Director has evidence which was not available to him when the court decided that the defendant had not benefited from his general or particular criminal conduct,
(b) before the end of the period of six years starting with the date of conviction the Director applies to the Crown Court to consider the evidence, and
(c) after considering the evidence the court concludes that it would have decided that the defendant had benefited from his general or particular criminal conduct (as the case may be) if the evidence had been available to it.

(4) If the court proceeded under section 6 because the prosecutor asked it to or because it believed it was appropriate for it to do so, the second condition is that—

(a) there is evidence which was not available to the prosecutor when the court decided that the defendant had not benefited from his general or particular criminal conduct,
(b) before the end of the period of six years starting with the date of conviction the prosecutor or the Director applies to the Crown Court to consider the evidence, and
(c) after considering the evidence the court concludes that it would have decided that the defendant had benefited from his general or particular criminal conduct (as the case may be) if the evidence had been available to it.

(5) If this section applies the court—

(a) must make a fresh decision under section 6(4)(b) or (c) whether the defendant has benefited from his general or particular criminal conduct (as the case may be);
(b) may make a confiscation order under that section.

(6) Subsections (7) to (12) below apply if the court proceeds under section 6 in pursuance of this section.

(7) If the court has already sentenced the defendant for the offence (or any of the offences) concerned, section 6 has effect as if his particular criminal conduct included conduct which constitutes offences which the court has taken into consideration in deciding his sentence for the offence or offences concerned.

(8) Section 8(2) does not apply, and the rules applying instead are that the court must—

(a) take account of conduct occurring before the date of the original decision that the defendant had not benefited from his general or particular criminal conduct;

(b) take account of property obtained before that date;

(c) take account of property obtained on or after that date if it was obtained as a result of or in connection with conduct occurring before that date.

(9) In section 10—

(a) the first and second assumptions do not apply with regard to property first held by the defendant on or after the date of the original decision that the defendant had not benefited from his general or particular criminal conduct;

(b) the third assumption does not apply with regard to expenditure incurred by him on or after that date;

(c) the fourth assumption does not apply with regard to property obtained (or assumed to have been obtained) by him on or after that date.

(10) The recoverable amount for the purposes of section 6 is such amount as—

(a) the court believes is just, but

(b) does not exceed the amount found under section 7.

(11) In arriving at the just amount the court must have regard in particular to—

(a) the amount found under section 7;

(b) any fine imposed on the defendant in respect of the offence (or any of the offences) concerned;

(c) any order which falls within section 13(3) and has been made against him in respect of the offence (or any of the offences) concerned and has not already been taken into account by the court in deciding what is the free property held by him for the purposes of section 9;

(d) any order which has been made against him in respect of the offence (or any of the offences) concerned under section 130 of the Sentencing Act (compensation orders).

(12) If an order for the payment of compensation under section 130 of the Sentencing Act has been made against the defendant in respect of the offence or offences concerned, section 13(5) and (6) above do not apply.

(13) The date of conviction is the date found by applying section 19(10).

[Proceeds of Crime Act 2002, s 20.]

3–1764   21. Order made: reconsideration of benefit.   (1) This section applies if—

(a) a court has made a confiscation order,

(b) there is evidence which was not available to the prosecutor or the Director at the relevant time,

(c) the prosecutor or the Director believes that if the court were to find the amount of the defendant's benefit in pursuance of this section it would exceed the relevant amount,

(d) before the end of the period of six years starting with the date of conviction the prosecutor or the Director applies to the Crown Court to consider the evidence, and

(e) after considering the evidence the court believes it is appropriate for it to proceed under this section.

(2) The court must make a new calculation of the defendant's benefit from the conduct concerned, and when it does so subsections (3) to (6) below apply.

(3) If a court has already sentenced the defendant for the offence (or any of the offences) concerned section 6 has effect as if his particular criminal conduct included conduct which constitutes offences which the court has taken into consideration in deciding his sentence for the offence or offences concerned.

(4) Section 8(2) does not apply, and the rules applying instead are that the court must—

(a) take account of conduct occurring up to the time it decided the defendant's benefit for the purposes of the confiscation order;

(b) take account of property obtained up to that time;

(c) take account of property obtained after that time if it was obtained as a result of or in connection with conduct occurring before that time.

(5) In applying section 8(5) the confiscation order must be ignored.

(6) In section 10—

(a) the first and second assumptions do not apply with regard to property first held by the defendant after the time the court decided his benefit for the purposes of the confiscation order;

(b) the third assumption does not apply with regard to expenditure incurred by him after that time;

(c) the fourth assumption does not apply with regard to property obtained (or assumed to have been obtained) by him after that time.

(7) If the amount found under the new calculation of the defendant's benefit exceeds the relevant amount the court—

(a) must make a new calculation of the recoverable amount for the purposes of section 6, and
(b) if it exceeds the amount required to be paid under the confiscation order, may vary the order by substituting for the amount required to be paid such amount as it believes is just.

(8) In applying subsection (7)(a) the court must—

(a) take the new calculation of the defendant's benefit;
(b) apply section 9 as if references to the time the confiscation order is made were to the time of the new calculation of the recoverable amount and as if references to the date of the confiscation order were to the date of that new calculation.

(9) In applying subsection (7)(b) the court must have regard in particular to—

(a) any fine imposed on the defendant for the offence (or any of the offences) concerned;
(b) any order which falls within section 13(3) and has been made against him in respect of the offence (or any of the offences) concerned and has not already been taken into account by the court in deciding what is the free property held by him for the purposes of section 9;
(c) any order which has been made against him in respect of the offence (or any of the offences) concerned under section 130 of the Sentencing Act (compensation orders).

(10) But in applying subsection (7)(b) the court must not have regard to an order falling within subsection (9)(c) if a court has made a direction under section 13(6).

(11) In deciding under this section whether one amount exceeds another the court must take account of any change in the value of money.

(12) The relevant time is—

(a) when the court calculated the defendant's benefit for the purposes of the confiscation order, if this section has not applied previously;
(b) when the court last calculated the defendant's benefit in pursuance of this section, if this section has applied previously.

(13) The relevant amount is—

(a) the amount found as the defendant's benefit for the purposes of the confiscation order, if this section has not applied previously;
(b) the amount last found as the defendant's benefit in pursuance of this section, if this section has applied previously.

(14) The date of conviction is the date found by applying section 19(10).
[Proceeds of Crime Act 2002, s 21.]

3–1765   22. Order made: reconsideration of available amount.   (1) This section applies if—

(a) a court has made a confiscation order,
(b) the amount required to be paid was the amount found under section 7(2), and
(c) an applicant falling within subsection (2) applies to the Crown Court to make a new calculation of the available amount.

(2) These applicants fall within this subsection—

(a) the prosecutor;
(b) the Director;
(c) a receiver appointed under section 50 or 52.

(3) In a case where this section applies the court must make the new calculation, and in doing so it must apply section 9 as if references to the time the confiscation order is made were to the time of the new calculation and as if references to the date of the confiscation order were to the date of the new calculation.

(4) If the amount found under the new calculation exceeds the relevant amount the court may vary the order by substituting for the amount required to be paid such amount as—

(a) it believes is just, but
(b) does not exceed the amount found as the defendant's benefit from the conduct concerned.

(5) In deciding what is just the court must have regard in particular to—

(a) any fine imposed on the defendant for the offence (or any of the offences) concerned;
(b) any order which falls within section 13(3) and has been made against him in respect of the offence (or any of the offences) concerned and has not already been taken into account by the court in deciding what is the free property held by him for the purposes of section 9;
(c) any order which has been made against him in respect of the offence (or any of the offences) concerned under section 130 of the Sentencing Act (compensation orders).

(6) But in deciding what is just the court must not have regard to an order falling within subsection (5)(c) if a court has made a direction under section 13(6).

(7) In deciding under this section whether one amount exceeds another the court must take account of any change in the value of money.

(8) The relevant amount is—

(a) the amount found as the available amount for the purposes of the confiscation order, if this section has not applied previously;

(b) the amount last found as the available amount in pursuance of this section, if this section has applied previously.

(9) The amount found as the defendant's benefit from the conduct concerned is—

(a) the amount so found when the confiscation order was made, or

(b) if one or more new calculations of the defendant's benefit have been made under section 21 the amount found on the occasion of the last such calculation.

[Proceeds of Crime Act 2002, s 22.]

3–1766 23. Inadequacy of available amount: variation of order. (1) This section applies if—

(a) a court has made a confiscation order, and

(b) the defendant, or a receiver appointed under section 50 or 52, applies to the Crown Court to vary the order under this section.

(2) In such a case the court must calculate the available amount, and in doing so it must apply section 9 as if references to the time the confiscation order is made were to the time of the calculation and as if references to the date of the confiscation order were to the date of the calculation.

(3) If the court finds that the available amount (as so calculated) is inadequate for the payment of any amount remaining to be paid under the confiscation order it may vary the order by substituting for the amount required to be paid such smaller amount as the court believes is just.

(4) If a person has been adjudged bankrupt or his estate has been sequestrated, or if an order for the winding up of a company has been made, the court must take into account the extent to which realisable property held by that person or that company may be distributed among creditors.

(5) The court may disregard any inadequacy which it believes is attributable (wholly or partly) to anything done by the defendant for the purpose of preserving property held by the recipient of a tainted gift from any risk of realisation under this Part.

(6) In subsection (4) "company" means any company which may be wound up under the Insolvency Act 1986 (c 45) or the Insolvency (Northern Ireland) Order 1989 (SI 1989/2405 (NI 19)).

[Proceeds of Crime Act 2002, s 23.]

3–1767 24. Inadequacy of available amount: discharge of order. (1) This section applies if—

(a) a court has made a confiscation order,

(b) the designated officer for a magistrates' court applies to the Crown Court for the discharge of the order, and

(c) the amount remaining to be paid under the order is less than £1,000.

(2) In such a case the court must calculate the available amount, and in doing so it must apply section 9 as if references to the time the confiscation order is made were to the time of the calculation and as if references to the date of the confiscation order were to the date of the calculation.

(3) If the court—

(a) finds that the available amount (as so calculated) is inadequate to meet the amount remaining to be paid, and

(b) is satisfied that the inadequacy is due wholly to a specified reason or a combination of specified reasons,

it may discharge the confiscation order.

(4) The specified reasons are—

(a) in a case where any of the realisable property consists of money in a currency other than sterling, that fluctuations in currency exchange rates have occurred;

(b) any reason specified by the Secretary of State by order.

(5) The Secretary of State may by order vary the amount for the time being specified in subsection (1)(c).

[Proceeds of Crime Act 2002, s 24 as amended by the Courts Act 2003, Sch 8.]

3–1768 25. Small amount outstanding: discharge of order. (1) This section applies if—

(a) a court has made a confiscation order,

(b) the designated officer for a magistrates' court applies to the Crown Court for the discharge of the order, and

(c) the amount remaining to be paid under the order is £50 or less.

(2) In such a case the court may discharge the order.

(3) The Secretary of State may by order vary the amount for the time being specified in subsection (1)(c).

[Proceeds of Crime Act 2002, s 25 as amended by the Courts Act 2003, Sch 8.]

3–1769 26. Information. (1) This section applies if—

(a) the court proceeds under section 6 in pursuance of section 19 or 20, or

(b) the prosecutor or the Director applies under section 21.

(2) In such a case—

(a) the prosecutor or the Director (as the case may be) must give the court a statement of information within the period the court orders;

(b) section 16 applies accordingly (with appropriate modifications where the prosecutor or the Director applies under section 21);

(c) section 17 applies accordingly;

(d) section 18 applies as it applies in the circumstances mentioned in section 18(1).

[Proceeds of Crime Act 2002, s 26.]

Defendant absconds

3-1770 27. Defendant convicted or committed. (1) This section applies if the following two conditions are satisfied.

(2) The first condition is that a defendant absconds after—

(a) he is convicted of an offence or offences in proceedings before the Crown Court,

(b) he is committed to the Crown Court for sentence in respect of an offence or offences under section 3, 4 or 6 of the Sentencing Act, or

(c) he is committed to the Crown Court in respect of an offence or offences under section 70 below (committal with a view to a confiscation order being considered).

(3) The second condition is that—

(a) the prosecutor or the Director applies to the Crown Court to proceed under this section, and

(b) the court believes it is appropriate for it to do so.

(4) If this section applies the court must proceed under section 6 in the same way as it must proceed if the two conditions there mentioned are satisfied; but this is subject to subsection (5).

(5) If the court proceeds under section 6 as applied by this section, this Part has effect with these modifications—

(a) any person the court believes is likely to be affected by an order under section 6 is entitled to appear before the court and make representations;

(b) the court must not make an order under section 6 unless the prosecutor or the Director (as the case may be) has taken reasonable steps to contact the defendant;

(c) section 6(9) applies as if the reference to subsection (2) were to subsection (2) of this section;

(d) sections 10, 16(4), 17 and 18 must be ignored;

(e) sections 19, 20 and 21 must be ignored while the defendant is still an absconder.

(6) Once the defendant ceases to be an absconder section 19 has effect as if subsection (1)(a) read—

"(a) at a time when the first condition in section 27 was satisfied the court did not proceed under section 6,".

(7) If the court does not believe it is appropriate for it to proceed under this section, once the defendant ceases to be an absconder section 19 has effect as if subsection (1)(b) read—

"(b) there is evidence which was not available to the prosecutor or the Director on the relevant date,".

[Proceeds of Crime Act 2002, s 27.]

3-1771 28. Defendant neither convicted nor acquitted. (1) This section applies if the following two conditions are satisfied.

(2) The first condition is that—

(a) proceedings for an offence or offences are started against a defendant but are not concluded,

(b) he absconds, and

(c) the period of two years (starting with the day the court believes he absconded) has ended.

(3) The second condition is that—

(a) the prosecutor or the Director applies to the Crown Court to proceed under this section, and

(b) the court believes it is appropriate for it to do so.

(4) If this section applies the court must proceed under section 6 in the same way as it must proceed if the two conditions there mentioned are satisfied; but this is subject to subsection (5).

(5) If the court proceeds under section 6 as applied by this section, this Part has effect with these modifications—

(a) any person the court believes is likely to be affected by an order under section 6 is entitled to appear before the court and make representations;

(b) the court must not make an order under section 6 unless the prosecutor or the Director (as the case may be) has taken reasonable steps to contact the defendant;

(c) section 6(9) applies as if the reference to subsection (2) were to subsection (2) of this section;

(d) sections 10, 16(4) and 17 to 20 must be ignored;

(e) section 21 must be ignored while the defendant is still an absconder.

(6) Once the defendant has ceased to be an absconder section 21 has effect as if references to the date of conviction were to—

(a) the day when proceedings for the offence concerned were started against the defendant, or

(b) if there are two or more offences and proceedings for them were started on different days, the earliest of those days.

(7) If—

(a) the court makes an order under section 6 as applied by this section, and

(b) the defendant is later convicted in proceedings before the Crown Court of the offence (or any of the offences) concerned,

section 6 does not apply so far as that conviction is concerned.
[Proceeds of Crime Act 2002, s 28.]

3–1772 29. Variation of order. (1) This section applies if—

(a) the court makes a confiscation order under section 6 as applied by section 28,

(b) the defendant ceases to be an absconder,

(c) he is convicted of an offence (or any of the offences) mentioned in section 28(2)(a),

(d) he believes that the amount required to be paid was too large (taking the circumstances prevailing when the amount was found for the purposes of the order), and

(e) before the end of the relevant period he applies to the Crown Court to consider the evidence on which his belief is based.

(2) If (after considering the evidence) the court concludes that the defendant's belief is well founded—

(a) it must find the amount which should have been the amount required to be paid (taking the circumstances prevailing when the amount was found for the purposes of the order), and

(b) it may vary the order by substituting for the amount required to be paid such amount as it believes is just.

(3) The relevant period is the period of 28 days starting with—

(a) the date on which the defendant was convicted of the offence mentioned in section 28(2)(a), or

(b) if there are two or more offences and the convictions were on different dates, the date of the latest.

(4) But in a case where section 28(2)(a) applies to more than one offence the court must not make an order under this section unless it is satisfied that there is no possibility of any further proceedings being taken or continued in relation to any such offence in respect of which the defendant has not been convicted.
[Proceeds of Crime Act 2002, s 29.]

3–1773 30. Discharge of order. (1) Subsection (2) applies if—

(a) the court makes a confiscation order under section 6 as applied by section 28,

(b) the defendant is later tried for the offence or offences concerned and acquitted on all counts, and

(c) he applies to the Crown Court to discharge the order.

(2) In such a case the court must discharge the order.

(3) Subsection (4) applies if—

(a) the court makes a confiscation order under section 6 as applied by section 28,

(b) the defendant ceases to be an absconder,

(c) subsection (1)(b) does not apply, and

(d) he applies to the Crown Court to discharge the order.

(4) In such a case the court may discharge the order if it finds that—

(a) there has been undue delay in continuing the proceedings mentioned in section 28(2), or

(b) the prosecutor does not intend to proceed with the prosecution.

(5) If the court discharges a confiscation order under this section it may make such a consequential or incidental order as it believes is appropriate.
[Proceeds of Crime Act 2002, s 30.]

Appeals

3–1774 31. Appeal by prosecutor or Director. (1) If the Crown Court makes a confiscation order the prosecutor or the Director may appeal to the Court of Appeal in respect of the order.

(2) If the Crown Court decides not to make a confiscation order the prosecutor or the Director may appeal to the Court of Appeal against the decision.

(3) Subsections (1) and (2) do not apply to an order or decision made by virtue of section 19, 20, 27 or 28.
[Proceeds of Crime Act 2002, s 31.]

3–1775 *Powers of the Court of Appeal (s 32). Appeals to the House of Lords (s 33).*

Enforcement authority

3–1776   34. Enforcement authority.   (1) Subsection (2) applies if a court makes a confiscation order and any of the following paragraphs applies—

(a)   the court proceeded under section 6 after being asked to do so by the Director;

(b)   the court proceeded under section 6 by virtue of an application by the Director under section 19, 20, 27 or 28;

(c)   the court proceeded under section 6 as a result of an appeal by the Director under section 31(2) or 33;

(d)   before the court made the order the Director applied to the court to appoint him as the enforcement authority for the order.

(2) In any such case the court must appoint the Director as the enforcement authority for the order.

[Proceeds of Crime Act 2002, s 34.]

Enforcement as fines etc

3–1777   35. Director not appointed as enforcement authority.   (1) This section applies if a court—

(a)   makes a confiscation order, and

(b)   does not appoint the Director as the enforcement authority for the order.

(2) Sections 139(2) to (4) and (9) and 140(1) to (4) of the Sentencing Act (functions of court as to fines and enforcing fines) apply as if the amount ordered to be paid were a fine imposed on the defendant by the court making the confiscation order.

(3) In the application of Part 3 of the Magistrates' Courts Act 1980 (c 43) to an amount payable under a confiscation order—

(a)   ignore section 75 of that Act (power to dispense with immediate payment);

(b)   such an amount is not a sum adjudged to be paid by a conviction for the purposes of section 81 (enforcement of fines imposed on young offenders) or a fine for the purposes of section 85 (remission of fines) of that Act;

(c)   in section 87 of that Act ignore subsection (3) (inquiry into means).

[Proceeds of Crime Act 2002, s 35.]

3–1778   36. Director appointed as enforcement authority.   (1) This section applies if a court—

(a)   makes a confiscation order, and

(b)   appoints the Director as the enforcement authority for the order.

(2) Section 139(2) to (4) and (9) of the Sentencing Act (functions of court as to fines) applies as if the amount ordered to be paid were a fine imposed on the defendant by the court making the confiscation order.

[Proceeds of Crime Act 2002, s 36.]

3–1779   37. Director's application for enforcement.   (1) If the Director believes that the conditions set out in subsection (2) are satisfied he may make an ex parte application to the Crown Court for the issue of a summons against the defendant.

(2) The conditions are that—

(a)   a confiscation order has been made;

(b)   the Director has been appointed as the enforcement authority for the order;

(c)   because of the defendant's wilful refusal or culpable neglect the order is not satisfied;

(d)   the order is not subject to appeal;

(e)   the Director has done all that is practicable (apart from this section) to enforce the order.

(3) If it appears to the Crown Court that the conditions are satisfied it may issue a summons ordering the defendant to appear before the court at the time and place specified in the summons.

(4) If the defendant fails to appear before the Crown Court in pursuance of the summons the court may issue a warrant for his arrest.

(5) If—

(a)   the defendant appears before the Crown Court in pursuance of the summons or of a warrant issued under subsection (4), and

(b)   the court is satisfied that the conditions set out in subsection (2) are satisfied,

it may issue a warrant committing the defendant to prison or detention for default in payment of the amount ordered to be paid by the confiscation order.

(6) Subsection (7) applies if the amount remaining to be paid under the confiscation order when the warrant under subsection (5) is issued is less than the amount ordered to be paid.

(7) In such a case the court must substitute for the term of imprisonment or detention fixed in respect of the order under section 139(2) of the Sentencing Act such term as bears to the original term the same proportion as the amount remaining to be paid bears to the amount ordered to be paid.

(8) Subsections (9) and (10) apply if—

   (*a*) the defendant has been committed to prison or detention in pursuance of a warrant issued under subsection (5), and

   (*b*) a payment is made in respect of some or all of the amount remaining to be paid under the confiscation order.

  (9) If the payment is for the whole amount remaining to be paid the defendant must be released unless he is in custody for another reason.

  (10) If the payment is for less than that amount, the period of commitment is reduced so that it bears to the term fixed under section 139(2) of the Sentencing Act the same proportion as the amount remaining to be paid bears to the amount ordered to be paid.

[Proceeds of Crime Act 2002, s 37.]

3–1780 38. Provisions about imprisonment or detention.   (1) Subsection (2) applies if—

   (*a*) a warrant committing the defendant to prison or detention is issued for a default in payment of an amount ordered to be paid under a confiscation order in respect of an offence or offences, and

   (*b*) at the time the warrant is issued the defendant is liable to serve a term of custody in respect of the offence (or any of the offences).

  (2) In such a case the term of imprisonment or of detention under section 108 of the Sentencing Act (detention of persons aged 18 to 20 for default) to be served in default of payment of the amount does not begin to run until after the term mentioned in subsection (1)(*b*) above.

  (3) The reference in subsection (1)(*b*) to the term of custody the defendant is liable to serve in respect of the offence (or any of the offences) is a reference to the term of imprisonment, or detention in a young offender institution, which he is liable to serve in respect of the offence (or any of the offences).

  (4) For the purposes of subsection (3) consecutive terms and terms which are wholly or partly concurrent must be treated as a single term and the following must be ignored—

   (*a*) any sentence suspended under section 189(1) of the Criminal Justice Act 2003 which has not taken effect at the time the warrant is issued;

   (*b*) in the case of a sentence of imprisonment passed with an order under section 47(1) of the Criminal Law Act 1977 (c 45) (sentences of imprisonment partly served and partly suspended) any part of the sentence which the defendant has not at that time been required to serve in prison;

   (*c*) any term of imprisonment or detention fixed under section 139(2) of the Sentencing Act (term to be served in default of payment of fine etc) for which a warrant committing the defendant to prison or detention has not been issued at that time.

  (5) If the defendant serves a term of imprisonment or detention in default of paying any amount due under a confiscation order, his serving that term does not prevent the confiscation order from continuing to have effect so far as any other method of enforcement is concerned.

[Proceeds of Crime Act 2002, s 38 as amended by the Criminal Justice Act 2003.]

3–1781 39. Reconsideration etc: variation of prison term.   (1) Subsection (2) applies if—

   (*a*) a court varies a confiscation order under section 21, 22, 23, 29, 32 or 33,

   (*b*) the effect of the variation is to vary the maximum period applicable in relation to the order under section 139(4) of the Sentencing Act, and

   (*c*) the result is that that maximum period is less than the term of imprisonment or detention fixed in respect of the order under section 139(2) of the Sentencing Act.

  (2) In such a case the court must fix a reduced term of imprisonment or detention in respect of the confiscation order under section 139(2) of the Sentencing Act in place of the term previously fixed.

  (3) Subsection (4) applies if paragraphs (*a*) and (*b*) of subsection (1) apply but paragraph (*c*) does not.

  (4) In such a case the court may amend the term of imprisonment or detention fixed in respect of the confiscation order under section 139(2) of the Sentencing Act.

  (5) If the effect of section 12 is to increase the maximum period applicable in relation to a confiscation order under section 139(4) of the Sentencing Act, on the application of the appropriate person the Crown Court may amend the term of imprisonment or detention fixed in respect of the order under section 139(2) of that Act.

  (6) The appropriate person is—

   (*a*) the Director, if he was appointed as the enforcement authority for the order under section 34;

   (*b*) the prosecutor, in any other case.

[Proceeds of Crime Act 2002, s 39.]

Restraint orders

3–1782 40. Conditions for exercise of powers.   (1) The Crown Court may exercise the powers conferred by section 41 if any of the following conditions is satisfied.

  (2) The first condition is that—

   (*a*) a criminal investigation has been started in England and Wales with regard to an offence, and

(b) there is reasonable cause to believe that the alleged offender has benefited from his criminal conduct.

(3) The second condition is that—

(a) proceedings for an offence have been started in England and Wales and not concluded, and

(b) there is reasonable cause to believe that the defendant has benefited from his criminal conduct.

(4) The third condition is that—

(a) an application by the prosecutor or the Director has been made under section 19, 20, 27 or 28 and not concluded, or the court believes that such an application is to be made, and

(b) there is reasonable cause to believe that the defendant has benefited from his criminal conduct.

(5) The fourth condition is that—

(a) an application by the prosecutor or the Director has been made under section 21 and not concluded, or the court believes that such an application is to be made, and

(b) there is reasonable cause to believe that the court will decide under that section that the amount found under the new calculation of the defendant's benefit exceeds the relevant amount (as defined in that section).

(6) The fifth condition is that—

(a) an application by the prosecutor or the Director has been made under section 22 and not concluded, or the court believes that such an application is to be made, and

(b) there is reasonable cause to believe that the court will decide under that section that the amount found under the new calculation of the available amount exceeds the relevant amount (as defined in that section).

(7) The second condition is not satisfied if the court believes that—

(a) there has been undue delay in continuing the proceedings, or

(b) the prosecutor does not intend to proceed.

(8) If an application mentioned in the third, fourth or fifth condition has been made the condition is not satisfied if the court believes that—

(a) there has been undue delay in continuing the application, or

(b) the prosecutor or the Director (as the case may be) does not intend to proceed.

(9) If the first condition is satisfied—

(a) references in this Part to the defendant are to the alleged offender;

(b) references in this Part to the prosecutor are to the person the court believes is to have conduct of any proceedings for the offence;

(c) section 77(9) has effect as if proceedings for the offence had been started against the defendant when the investigation was started.

[Proceeds of Crime Act 2002, s 40.]

3–1783   41.   Restraint orders.   (1) If any condition set out in section 40 is satisfied the Crown Court may make an order (a restraint order) prohibiting any specified person from dealing with any realisable property held by him.

(2) A restraint order may provide that it applies—

(a) to all realisable property held by the specified person whether or not the property is described in the order;

(b) to realisable property transferred to the specified person after the order is made.

(3) A restraint order may be made subject to exceptions, and an exception may in particular—

(a) make provision for reasonable living expenses and reasonable legal expenses;

(b) make provision for the purpose of enabling any person to carry on any trade, business, profession or occupation;

(c) be made subject to conditions.

(4) But an exception to a restraint order must not make provision for any legal expenses which—

(a) relate to an offence[1] which falls within subsection (5), and

(b) are incurred by the defendant or by a recipient of a tainted gift.

(5) These offences fall within this subsection—

(a) the offence mentioned in section 40(2) or (3), if the first or second condition (as the case may be) is satisfied;

(b) the offence (or any of the offences) concerned, if the third, fourth or fifth condition is satisfied.

(6) Subsection (7) applies if—

(a) a court makes a restraint order, and

(b) the applicant for the order applies to the court to proceed under subsection (7) (whether as part of the application for the restraint order or at any time afterwards).

(7) The court may make such order as it believes is appropriate for the purpose of ensuring that the restraint order is effective.

(8) A restraint order does not affect property for the time being subject to a charge under any of these provisions—

(a) section 9 of the Drug Trafficking Offences Act 1986 (c 32);
(b) section 78 of the Criminal Justice Act 1988 (c 33);
(c) Article 14 of the Criminal Justice (Confiscation) (Northern Ireland) Order 1990 (SI 1990/2588 (NI 17));
(d) section 27 of the Drug Trafficking Act 1994 (c 37);
(e) Article 32 of the Proceeds of Crime (Northern Ireland) Order 1996 (SI 1996/1299 (NI 9)).

(9) Dealing with property includes removing it from England and Wales.
[Proceeds of Crime Act 2002, s 41.]

---

1. As Parliament intended to make public funding available to question restraint orders, this section prohibits the release of restrained funds for an application to vary or take advice upon a restraint order as these relate to the offence under investigation. Therefore a restraint order should state clearly on its face that public funding is available. Any application for public funding should be processed with the greatest expedition: *In re S (Restraint Order: Release of Assets)* [2004] EWCA Crim 3207, [2005] 1 WLR 1352, [2005] 1 Cr App R 17.

3–1784   42. Application, discharge and variation.   (1) A restraint order—

(a) may be made only on an application by an applicant falling within subsection (2);
(b) may be made on an ex parte application to a judge in chambers.

(2) These applicants fall within this subsection—

(a) the prosecutor;
(b) the Director;
(c) an accredited financial investigator.

(3) An application to discharge or vary a restraint order or an order under section 41(7) may be made to the Crown Court by—

(a) the person who applied for the order;
(b) any person affected by the order.

(4) Subsections (5) to (7) apply to an application under subsection (3).
(5) The court—

(a) may discharge the order;
(b) may vary the order.

(6) If the condition in section 40 which was satisfied was that proceedings were started or an application was made, the court must discharge the order on the conclusion of the proceedings or of the application (as the case may be).
(7) If the condition in section 40 which was satisfied was that an investigation was started or an application was to be made, the court must discharge the order if within a reasonable time proceedings for the offence are not started or the application is not made (as the case may be).
[Proceeds of Crime Act 2002, s 42.]

3–1785   *Appeal to the Court of Appeal and House of Lords* (ss 43–44).

3–1786   45. Seizure.   (1) If a restraint order is in force a constable or a customs officer may seize any realisable property to which it applies to prevent its removal from England and Wales.
(2) Property seized under subsection (1) must be dealt with in accordance with the directions of the court which made the order.
[Proceeds of Crime Act 2002, s 45.]

3–1787   46. Hearsay evidence.   (1) Evidence must not be excluded in restraint proceedings on the ground that it is hearsay (of whatever degree).
(2) Sections 2 to 4 of the Civil Evidence Act 1995[1] (c 38) apply in relation to restraint proceedings as those sections apply in relation to civil proceedings.
(3) Restraint proceedings are proceedings—

(a) for a restraint order;
(b) for the discharge or variation of a restraint order;
(c) on an appeal under section 43 or 44.

(4) Hearsay is a statement which is made otherwise than by a person while giving oral evidence in the proceedings and which is tendered as evidence of the matters stated.
(5) Nothing in this section affects the admissibility of evidence which is admissible apart from this section.
[Proceeds of Crime Act 2002, s 46.]

---

1. In PART II: EVIDENCE, ante.

3–1788   47. Supplementary.   (1) The registration Acts—

(a) apply in relation to restraint orders as they apply in relation to orders which affect land and are made by the court for the purpose of enforcing judgments or recognisances;

(b)   apply in relation to applications for restraint orders as they apply in relation to other pending land actions.

(2)   The registration Acts are—

(a)   the Land Registration Act 1925 (c 21);

(b)   the Land Charges Act 1972 (c 61);

(c)   the Land Registration Act 2002 (c 9).

(3)   But no notice may be entered in the register of title under the Land Registration Act 2002 in respect of a restraint order.

(4)   The person applying for a restraint order must be treated for the purposes of section 57 of the Land Registration Act 1925 (inhibitions) as a person interested in relation to any registered land to which—

(a)   the application relates, or

(b)   a restraint order made in pursuance of the application relates.

[Proceeds of Crime Act 2002, s 47.]

Management receivers

3–1789   48. Appointment.   (1) Subsection (2) applies if—

(a)   the Crown Court makes a restraint order, and

(b)   the applicant for the restraint order applies to the court to proceed under subsection (2) (whether as part of the application for the restraint order or at any time afterwards).

(2)   The Crown Court may by order appoint a receiver in respect of any realisable property to which the restraint order applies.

[Proceeds of Crime Act 2002, s 48.]

3–1790   49. Powers.   (1) If the court appoints a receiver under section 48 it may act under this section on the application of the person who applied for the restraint order.

(2)   The court may by order confer on the receiver the following powers in relation to any realisable property to which the restraint order applies—

(a)   power to take possession of the property;

(b)   power to manage or otherwise deal with the property;

(c)   power to start, carry on or defend any legal proceedings in respect of the property;

(d)   power to realise so much of the property as is necessary to meet the receiver's remuneration and expenses.

(3)   The court may by order confer on the receiver power to enter any premises in England and Wales and to do any of the following—

(a)   search for or inspect anything authorised by the court;

(b)   make or obtain a copy, photograph or other record of anything so authorised;

(c)   remove anything which the receiver is required or authorised to take possession of in pursuance of an order of the court.

(4)   The court may by order authorise the receiver to do any of the following for the purpose of the exercise of his functions—

(a)   hold property;

(b)   enter into contracts;

(c)   sue and be sued;

(d)   employ agents;

(e)   execute powers of attorney, deeds or other instruments;

(f)   take any other steps the court thinks appropriate.

(5)   The court may order any person who has possession of realisable property to which the restraint order applies to give possession of it to the receiver.

(6)   The court—

(a)   may order a person holding an interest in realisable property to which the restraint order applies to make to the receiver such payment as the court specifies in respect of a beneficial interest held by the defendant or the recipient of a tainted gift;

(b)   may (on the payment being made) by order transfer, grant or extinguish any interest in the property.

(7)   Subsections (2), (5) and (6) do not apply to property for the time being subject to a charge under any of these provisions—

(a)   section 9 of the Drug Trafficking Offences Act 1986 (c 32);

(b)   section 78 of the Criminal Justice Act 1988 (c 33);

(c)   Article 14 of the Criminal Justice (Confiscation) (Northern Ireland) Order 1990 (SI 1990/2588 (NI 17));

(d)   section 27 of the Drug Trafficking Act 1994 (c 37);

(e)   Article 32 of the Proceeds of Crime (Northern Ireland) Order 1996 (SI 1996/1299 (NI 9)).

(8)   The court must not—

(a)   confer the power mentioned in subsection (2)(b) or (d) in respect of property, or
(b)   exercise the power conferred on it by subsection (6) in respect of property,

unless it gives persons holding interests in the property a reasonable opportunity to make representations to it.

(9)   The court may order that a power conferred by an order under this section is subject to such conditions and exceptions as it specifies.

(10)   Managing or otherwise dealing with property includes—

(a)   selling the property or any part of it or interest in it;
(b)   carrying on or arranging for another person to carry on any trade or business the assets of which are or are part of the property;
(c)   incurring capital expenditure in respect of the property.

[Proceeds of Crime Act 2002, s 49.]

Enforcement receivers

3–1791   50. Appointment.   (1) This section applies if—

(a)   a confiscation order is made,
(b)   it is not satisfied, and
(c)   it is not subject to appeal.

(2)   On the application of the prosecutor the Crown Court may by order appoint a receiver in respect of realisable property.

[Proceeds of Crime Act 2002, s 50.]

3–1792   51. Powers.   (1) If the court appoints a receiver under section 50 it may act under this section on the application of the prosecutor.

(2)   The court may by order confer on the receiver the following powers in relation to the realisable property—

(a)   power to take possession of the property;
(b)   power to manage or otherwise deal with the property;
(c)   power to realise the property, in such manner as the court may specify;
(d)   power to start, carry on or defend any legal proceedings in respect of the property.

(3)   The court may by order confer on the receiver power to enter any premises in England and Wales and to do any of the following—

(a)   search for or inspect anything authorised by the court;
(b)   make or obtain a copy, photograph or other record of anything so authorised;
(c)   remove anything which the receiver is required or authorised to take possession of in pursuance of an order of the court.

(4)   The court may by order authorise the receiver to do any of the following for the purpose of the exercise of his functions—

(a)   hold property;
(b)   enter into contracts;
(c)   sue and be sued;
(d)   employ agents;
(e)   execute powers of attorney, deeds or other instruments;
(f)   take any other steps the court thinks appropriate.

(5)   The court may order any person who has possession of realisable property to give possession of it to the receiver.

(6)   The court—

(a)   may order a person holding an interest in realisable property to make to the receiver such payment as the court specifies in respect of a beneficial interest held by the defendant or the recipient of a tainted gift;
(b)   may (on the payment being made) by order transfer, grant or extinguish any interest in the property.

(7)   Subsections (2), (5) and (6) do not apply to property for the time being subject to a charge under any of these provisions—

(a)   section 9 of the Drug Trafficking Offences Act 1986 (c 32);
(b)   section 78 of the Criminal Justice Act 1988 (c 33);
(c)   Article 14 of the Criminal Justice (Confiscation) (Northern Ireland) Order 1990 (SI 1990/2588 (NI 17));
(d)   section 27 of the Drug Trafficking Act 1994 (c 37);
(e)   Article 32 of the Proceeds of Crime (Northern Ireland) Order 1996 (SI 1996/1299 (NI 9)).

(8)   The court must not—

(a)   confer the power mentioned in subsection (2)(b) or (c) in respect of property, or
(b)   exercise the power conferred on it by subsection (6) in respect of property,

unless it gives persons holding interests in the property a reasonable opportunity to make representations to it.

(9) The court may order that a power conferred by an order under this section is subject to such conditions and exceptions as it specifies.

(10) Managing or otherwise dealing with property includes—

(a) selling the property or any part of it or interest in it;

(b) carrying on or arranging for another person to carry on any trade or business the assets of which are or are part of the property;

(c) incurring capital expenditure in respect of the property.

[Proceeds of Crime Act 2002, s 51.]

Director's receivers

3–1793 52. Appointment. (1) This section applies if—

(a) a confiscation order is made, and

(b) the Director is appointed as the enforcement authority for the order under section 34.

(2) But this section does not apply if—

(a) the confiscation order was made by the Court of Appeal, and

(b) when the Crown Court comes to proceed under this section the confiscation order has been satisfied.

(3) If this section applies the Crown Court must make an order for the appointment of a receiver in respect of realisable property.

(4) An order under subsection (3)—

(a) must confer power on the Director to nominate the person who is to be the receiver, and

(b) takes effect when the Director nominates that person.

(5) The Director must not nominate a person under subsection (4) unless at the time he does so the confiscation order—

(a) is not satisfied, and

(b) is not subject to appeal.

(6) A person nominated to be the receiver under subsection (4) may be—

(a) a member of the staff of the Agency;

(b) a person providing services under arrangements made by the Director.

(7) If this section applies section 50 does not apply.

[Proceeds of Crime Act 2002, s 52.]

3–1794 53. Powers. (1) If the court makes an order for the appointment of a receiver under section 52 it may act under this section on the application of the Director.

(2) The court may by order confer on the receiver the following powers in relation to the realisable property—

(a) power to take possession of the property;

(b) power to manage or otherwise deal with the property;

(c) power to realise the property, in such manner as the court may specify;

(d) power to start, carry on or defend any legal proceedings in respect of the property.

(3) The court may by order confer on the receiver power to enter any premises in England and Wales and to do any of the following—

(a) search for or inspect anything authorised by the court;

(b) make or obtain a copy, photograph or other record of anything so authorised;

(c) remove anything which the receiver is required or authorised to take possession of in pursuance of an order of the court.

(4) The court may by order authorise the receiver to do any of the following for the purpose of the exercise of his functions—

(a) hold property;

(b) enter into contracts;

(c) sue and be sued;

(d) employ agents;

(e) execute powers of attorney, deeds or other instruments;

(f) take any other steps the court thinks appropriate.

(5) The court may order any person who has possession of realisable property to give possession of it to the receiver.

(6) The court—

(a) may order a person holding an interest in realisable property to make to the receiver such payment as the court specifies in respect of a beneficial interest held by the defendant or the recipient of a tainted gift;

(b) may (on the payment being made) by order transfer, grant or extinguish any interest in the property.

(7) Subsections (2), (5) and (6) do not apply to property for the time being subject to a charge under any of these provisions—

(a) section 9 of the Drug Trafficking Offences Act 1986 (c 32);
(b) section 78 of the Criminal Justice Act 1988 (c 33);
(c) Article 14 of the Criminal Justice (Confiscation) (Northern Ireland) Order 1990 (SI 1990/2588 (NI 17));
(d) section 27 of the Drug Trafficking Act 1994 (c 37);
(e) Article 32 of the Proceeds of Crime (Northern Ireland) Order 1996 (SI 1996/1299 (NI 9)).

(8) The court must not—
(a) confer the power mentioned in subsection (2)(b) or (c) in respect of property, or
(b) exercise the power conferred on it by subsection (6) in respect of property,

unless it gives persons holding interests in the property a reasonable opportunity to make representations to it.

(9) The court may order that a power conferred by an order under this section is subject to such conditions and exceptions as it specifies.

(10) Managing or otherwise dealing with property includes—
(a) selling the property or any part of it or interest in it;
(b) carrying on or arranging for another person to carry on any trade or business the assets of which are or are part of the property;
(c) incurring capital expenditure in respect of the property.

[Proceeds of Crime Act 2002, s 53.]

Application of sums

3–1795 54. Enforcement receivers. (1) This section applies to sums which are in the hands of a receiver appointed under section 50 if they are—
(a) the proceeds of the realisation of property under section 51;
(b) sums (other than those mentioned in paragraph (a)) in which the defendant holds an interest.

(2) The sums must be applied as follows—
(a) first, they must be applied in payment of such expenses incurred by a person acting as an insolvency practitioner as are payable under this subsection by virtue of section 432;
(b) second, they must be applied in making any payments directed by the Crown Court;
(c) third, they must be applied on the defendant's behalf towards satisfaction of the confiscation order.

(3) If the amount payable under the confiscation order has been fully paid and any sums remain in the receiver's hands he must distribute them—
(a) among such persons who held (or hold) interests in the property concerned as the Crown Court directs, and
(b) in such proportions as it directs.

(4) Before making a direction under subsection (3) the court must give persons who held (or hold) interests in the property concerned a reasonable opportunity to make representations to it.

(5) For the purposes of subsections (3) and (4) the property concerned is—
(a) the property represented by the proceeds mentioned in subsection (1)(a);
(b) the sums mentioned in subsection (1)(b).

(6) The receiver applies sums as mentioned in subsection (2)(c) by paying them to the appropriate designated officer on account of the amount payable under the order.

(7) The appropriate designated officer is the one for the magistrates' court responsible for enforcing the confiscation order as if the amount ordered to be paid were a fine.

[Proceeds of Crime Act 2002, s 54, as amended by the Courts Act 2003, Sch 8.]

3–1796 55. Sums received by designated officer. (1) This section applies if a designated officer receives sums on account of the amount payable under a confiscation order (whether the sums are received under section 54 or otherwise).

(2) The designated officer's receipt of the sums reduces the amount payable under the order, but he must apply the sums received as follows.

(3) First he must apply them in payment of such expenses incurred by a person acting as an insolvency practitioner as—
(a) are payable under this subsection by virtue of section 432, but
(b) are not already paid under section 54(2)(a).

(4) If the designated officer received the sums under section 54 he must next apply them—
(a) first, in payment of the remuneration and expenses of a receiver appointed under section 48, to the extent that they have not been met by virtue of the exercise by that receiver of a power conferred under section 49(2)(d);
(b) second, in payment of the remuneration and expenses of the receiver appointed under section 50.

(5) If a direction was made under section 13(6) for an amount of compensation to be paid out of sums recovered under the confiscation order, the designated officer must next apply the sums in payment of that amount.

(6) If any amount remains after the designated officermakes any payments required by the preceding provisions of this section, the amount must be treated for the purposes of section 38 of the Courts Act 2003 (application of fines etc) as if it were a fine imposed by a magistrates' court.

(7) Subsection (4) does not apply if the receiver is a member of the staff of the Crown Prosecution Service or of the Commissioners of Customs and Excise; and it is immaterial whether he is a permanent or temporary member or he is on secondment from elsewhere.

[Proceeds of Crime Act 2002, s 55 as amended by the Courts Act 2003, Sch 8.]

3–1797 56. Director's receivers. (1) This section applies to sums which are in the hands of a receiver appointed under section 52 if they are—

(a) the proceeds of the realisation of property under section 53;
(b) sums (other than those mentioned in paragraph (a)) in which the defendant holds an interest.

(2) The sums must be applied as follows—

(a) first, they must be applied in payment of such expenses incurred by a person acting as an insolvency practitioner as are payable under this subsection by virtue of section 432;
(b) second, they must be applied in making any payments directed by the Crown Court;
(c) third, they must be applied on the defendant's behalf towards satisfaction of the confiscation order by being paid to the Director on account of the amount payable under it.

(3) If the amount payable under the confiscation order has been fully paid and any sums remain in the receiver's hands he must distribute them—

(a) among such persons who held (or hold) interests in the property concerned as the Crown Court directs, and
(b) in such proportions as it directs.

(4) Before making a direction under subsection (3) the court must give persons who held (or hold) interests in the property concerned a reasonable opportunity to make representations to it.

(5) For the purposes of subsections (3) and (4) the property concerned is—

(a) the property represented by the proceeds mentioned in subsection (1)(a);
(b) the sums mentioned in subsection (1)(b).

[Proceeds of Crime Act 2002, s 56.]

3–1798 57. Sums received by Director. (1) This section applies if the Director receives sums on account of the amount payable under a confiscation order (whether the sums are received under section 56 or otherwise).

(2) The Director's receipt of the sums reduces the amount payable under the order, but he must apply the sums received as follows.

(3) First he must apply them in payment of such expenses incurred by a person acting as an insolvency practitioner as—

(a) are payable under this subsection by virtue of section 432, but
(b) are not already paid under section 56(2)(a).

(4) If the Director received the sums under section 56 he must next apply them—

(a) first, in payment of the remuneration and expenses of a receiver appointed under section 48, to the extent that they have not been met by virtue of the exercise by that receiver of a power conferred under section 49(2)(d);
(b) second, in payment of the remuneration and expenses of the receiver appointed under section 52.

(5) If a direction was made under section 13(6) for an amount of compensation to be paid out of sums recovered under the confiscation order, the Director must next apply the sums in payment of that amount.

(6) Subsection (4) does not apply if the receiver is a member of the staff of the Agency or a person providing services under arrangements made by the Director.

[Proceeds of Crime Act 2002, s 57.]

Restrictions

3–1799 58. Restraint orders. (1) Subsections (2) to (4) apply if a court makes a restraint order.

(2) No distress may be levied against any realisable property to which the order applies except with the leave of the Crown Court and subject to any terms the Crown Court may impose.

(3) If the order applies to a tenancy of any premises, no landlord or other person to whom rent is payable may exercise a right within subsection (4) except with the leave of the Crown Court and subject to any terms the Crown Court may impose.

(4) A right is within this subsection if it is a right of forfeiture by peaceable re-entry in relation to the premises in respect of any failure by the tenant to comply with any term or condition of the tenancy.

(5) If a court in which proceedings are pending in respect of any property is satisfied that a restraint order has been applied for or made in respect of the property, the court may either stay the proceedings or allow them to continue on any terms it thinks fit.

(6) Before exercising any power conferred by subsection (5), the court must give an opportunity to be heard to—

(a) the applicant for the restraint order, and
(b) any receiver appointed in respect of the property under section 48, 50 or 52.

[Proceeds of Crime Act 2002, s 58.]

3–1800   59. Enforcement receivers. (1) Subsections (2) to (4) apply if a court makes an order under section 50 appointing a receiver in respect of any realisable property.

(2) No distress may be levied against the property except with the leave of the Crown Court and subject to any terms the Crown Court may impose.

(3) If the receiver is appointed in respect of a tenancy of any premises, no landlord or other person to whom rent is payable may exercise a right within subsection (4) except with the leave of the Crown Court and subject to any terms the Crown Court may impose.

(4) A right is within this subsection if it is a right of forfeiture by peaceable re-entry in relation to the premises in respect of any failure by the tenant to comply with any term or condition of the tenancy.

(5) If a court in which proceedings are pending in respect of any property is satisfied that an order under section 50 appointing a receiver in respect of the property has been applied for or made, the court may either stay the proceedings or allow them to continue on any terms it thinks fit.

(6) Before exercising any power conferred by subsection (5), the court must give an opportunity to be heard to—

(a) the prosecutor, and
(b) the receiver (if the order under section 50 has been made).

[Proceeds of Crime Act 2002, s 59.]

3–1801   60. Director's receivers. (1) Subsections (2) to (4) apply if—

(a) the Crown Court has made an order under section 52 for the appointment of a receiver in respect of any realisable property, and
(b) the order has taken effect.

(2) No distress may be levied against the property except with the leave of the Crown Court and subject to any terms the Crown Court may impose.

(3) If the order is for the appointment of a receiver in respect of a tenancy of any premises, no landlord or other person to whom rent is payable may exercise a right within subsection (4) except with the leave of the Crown Court and subject to any terms the Crown Court may impose.

(4) A right is within this subsection if it is a right of forfeiture by peaceable re-entry in relation to the premises in respect of any failure by the tenant to comply with any term or condition of the tenancy.

(5) If a court (whether the Crown Court or any other court) in which proceedings are pending in respect of any property is satisfied that an order under section 52 for the appointment of a receiver in respect of the property has taken effect, the court may either stay the proceedings or allow them to continue on any terms it thinks fit.

(6) Before exercising any power conferred by subsection (5), the court must give an opportunity to be heard to—

(a) the Director, and
(b) the receiver.

[Proceeds of Crime Act 2002, s 60.]

Receivers: further provisions

3–1802   61. Protection. If a receiver appointed under section 48, 50 or 52—

(a) takes action in relation to property which is not realisable property,
(b) would be entitled to take the action if it were realisable property, and
(c) believes on reasonable grounds that he is entitled to take the action,

he is not liable to any person in respect of any loss or damage resulting from the action, except so far as the loss or damage is caused by his negligence.

[Proceeds of Crime Act 2002, s 61.]

3–1803   62. Further applications. (1) This section applies to a receiver appointed under section 48, 50 or 52.

(2) The receiver may apply to the Crown Court for an order giving directions as to the exercise of his powers.

(3) The following persons may apply to the Crown Court—

(a) any person affected by action taken by the receiver;
(b) any person who may be affected by action the receiver proposes to take.

(4) On an application under this section the court may make such order as it believes is appropriate.

[Proceeds of Crime Act 2002, s 62.]

3–1804   63. Discharge and variation.   (1) The following persons may apply to the Crown Court to vary or discharge an order made under any of sections 48 to 53—

   (a)   the receiver;

   (b)   the person who applied for the order or (if the order was made under section 52 or 53) the Director;

   (c)   any person affected by the order.

(2) On an application under this section the court—

   (a)   may discharge the order;

   (b)   may vary the order.

(3) But in the case of an order under section 48 or 49—

   (a)   if the condition in section 40 which was satisfied was that proceedings were started or an application was made, the court must discharge the order on the conclusion of the proceedings or of the application (as the case may be);

   (b)   if the condition which was satisfied was that an investigation was started or an application was to be made, the court must discharge the order if within a reasonable time proceedings for the offence are not started or the application is not made (as the case may be).

[Proceeds of Crime Act 2002, s 63.]

3–1805   64. Management receivers: discharge.   (1) This section applies if—

   (a)   a receiver stands appointed under section 48 in respect of realisable property (the management receiver), and

   (b)   the court appoints a receiver under section 50 or makes an order for the appointment of a receiver under section 52.

(2) The court must order the management receiver to transfer to the other receiver all property held by the management receiver by virtue of the powers conferred on him by section 49.

(3) But in a case where the court makes an order under section 52 its order under subsection (2) above does not take effect until the order under section 52 takes effect.

(4) Subsection (2) does not apply to property which the management receiver holds by virtue of the exercise by him of his power under section 49(2)(d).

(5) If the management receiver complies with an order under subsection (2) he is discharged—

   (a)   from his appointment under section 48;

   (b)   from any obligation under this Act arising from his appointment.

(6) If this section applies the court may make such a consequential or incidental order as it believes is appropriate.

[Proceeds of Crime Act 2002, s 64.]

3–1806   *Appeal to the Court of Appeal and House of Lords (ss 65–66).*

Seized money

3–1807   67. Seized money.   (1) This section applies to money which—

   (a)   is held by a person, and

   (b)   is held in an account maintained by him with a bank or a building society.

(2) This section also applies to money which is held by a person and which—

   (a)   has been seized by a constable under section 19 of the Police and Criminal Evidence Act 1984 (c 60) (general power of seizure etc), and

   (b)   is held in an account maintained by a police force with a bank or a building society.

(3) This section also applies to money which is held by a person and which—

   (a)   has been seized by a customs officer under section 19 of the 1984 Act as applied by order made under section 114(2) of that Act, and

   (b)   is held in an account maintained by the Commissioners of Customs and Excise with a bank or a building society.

(4) This section applies if the following conditions are satisfied—

   (a)   a restraint order has effect in relation to money to which this section applies;

   (b)   a confiscation order is made against the person by whom the money is held;

   (c)   the Director has not been appointed as the enforcement authority for the confiscation order;

   (d)   a receiver has not been appointed under section 50 in relation to the money;

   (e)   any period allowed under section 11 for payment of the amount ordered to be paid under the confiscation order has ended.

(5) In such a case a magistrates' court may order the bank or building society to pay the money to the designated officer for the court on account of the amount payable under the confiscation order.

(6) If a bank or building society fails to comply with an order under subsection (5)—

   (a)   the magistrates' court may order it to pay an amount not exceeding £5,000, and

   (b)   for the purposes of the Magistrates' Courts Act 1980 (c 43) the sum is to be treated as adjudged to be paid by a conviction of the court.

(7) In order to take account of changes in the value of money the Secretary of State may by order substitute another sum for the sum for the time being specified in subsection (6)(*a*).

(8) For the purposes of this section—

(*a*) a bank is a deposit-taking business within the meaning of the Banking Act 1987 (c 22);

(*b*) "building society" has the same meaning as in the Building Societies Act 1986 (c 53).

[Proceeds of Crime Act 2002, s 67 as amended by the Courts Act 2003, Sch 8.]

Financial investigators

3–1808   **68. Applications and appeals.**   (1) Subsections (2) and (3) apply to—

(*a*) an application under section 41, 42, 48, 49 or 63;

(*b*) an appeal under section 43, 44, 65 or 66.

(2) An accredited financial investigator must not make such an application or bring such an appeal unless he falls within subsection (3).

(3) An accredited financial investigator falls within this subsection if he is one of the following or is authorised for the purposes of this section by one of the following—

(*a*) a police officer who is not below the rank of superintendent,

(*b*) a customs officer who is not below such grade as is designated by the Commissioners of Customs and Excise as equivalent to that rank,

(*c*) an accredited financial investigator who falls within a description specified in an order made for the purposes of this paragraph by the Secretary of State under section 453.

(4) If such an application is made or appeal brought by an accredited financial investigator any subsequent step in the application or appeal or any further application or appeal relating to the same matter may be taken, made or brought by a different accredited financial investigator who falls within subsection (3).

(5) If—

(*a*) an application for a restraint order is made by an accredited financial investigator, and

(*b*) a court is required under section 58(6) to give the applicant for the order an opportunity to be heard,

the court may give the opportunity to a different accredited financial investigator who falls within subsection (3).

[Proceeds of Crime Act 2002, s 68.]

Exercise of powers

3–1809   **69. Powers of court and receiver.**   (1) This section applies to—

(*a*) the powers conferred on a court by sections 41 to 60 and sections 62 to 67;

(*b*) the powers of a receiver appointed under section 48, 50 or 52.

(2) The powers—

(*a*) must be exercised with a view to the value for the time being of realisable property being made available (by the property's realisation) for satisfying any confiscation order that has been or may be made against the defendant;

(*b*) must be exercised, in a case where a confiscation order has not been made, with a view to securing that there is no diminution in the value of realisable property;

(*c*) must be exercised without taking account of any obligation of the defendant or a recipient of a tainted gift if the obligation conflicts with the object of satisfying any confiscation order that has been or may be made against the defendant;

(*d*) may be exercised in respect of a debt owed by the Crown.

(3) Subsection (2) has effect subject to the following rules—

(*a*) the powers must be exercised with a view to allowing a person other than the defendant or a recipient of a tainted gift to retain or recover the value of any interest held by him;

(*b*) in the case of realisable property held by a recipient of a tainted gift, the powers must be exercised with a view to realising no more than the value for the time being of the gift;

(*c*) in a case where a confiscation order has not been made against the defendant, property must not be sold if the court so orders under subsection (4).

(4) If on an application by the defendant, or by the recipient of a tainted gift, the court decides that property cannot be replaced it may order that it must not be sold.

(5) An order under subsection (4) may be revoked or varied.

[Proceeds of Crime Act 2002, s 69.]

Committal

3–1810   **70. Committal by magistrates' court.**   (1) This section applies if—

(*a*) a defendant is convicted of an offence by a magistrates' court, and

(*b*) the prosecutor asks the court to commit the defendant to the Crown Court with a view to a confiscation order being considered under section 6.

(2) In such a case the magistrates' court—

(a) must commit the defendant to the Crown Court in respect of the offence, and
(b) may commit him to the Crown Court in respect of any other offence falling within subsection (3).

(3) An offence falls within this subsection if—

(a) the defendant has been convicted of it by the magistrates' court or any other court, and
(b) the magistrates' court has power to deal with him in respect of it.

(4) If a committal is made under this section in respect of an offence or offences—

(a) section 6 applies accordingly, and
(b) the committal operates as a committal of the defendant to be dealt with by the Crown Court in accordance with section 71.

(5) If a committal is made under this section in respect of an offence for which (apart from this section) the magistrates' court could have committed the defendant for sentence under section 3(2) of the Sentencing Act (offences triable either way) the court must state whether it would have done so.

(6) A committal under this section may be in custody or on bail.
[Proceeds of Crime Act 2002, s 70.]

3–1811 71. Sentencing by Crown Court. (1) If a defendant is committed to the Crown Court under section 70 in respect of an offence or offences, this section applies (whether or not the court proceeds under section 6).

(2) In the case of an offence in respect of which the magistrates' court has stated under section 70(5) that it would have committed the defendant for sentence, the Crown Court—

(a) must inquire into the circumstances of the case, and
(b) may deal with the defendant in any way in which it could deal with him if he had just been convicted of the offence on indictment before it.

(3) In the case of any other offence the Crown Court—

(a) must inquire into the circumstances of the case, and
(b) may deal with the defendant in any way in which the magistrates' court could deal with him if it had just convicted him of the offence.
[Proceeds of Crime Act 2002, s 71.]

Compensation

3–1812 72. Serious default. (1) If the following three conditions are satisfied the Crown Court may order the payment of such compensation as it believes is just.

(2) The first condition is satisfied if a criminal investigation has been started with regard to an offence and proceedings are not started for the offence.

(3) The first condition is also satisfied if proceedings for an offence are started against a person and—

(a) they do not result in his conviction for the offence, or
(b) he is convicted of the offence but the conviction is quashed or he is pardoned in respect of it.

(4) If subsection (2) applies the second condition is that—

(a) in the criminal investigation there has been a serious default by a person mentioned in subsection (9), and
(b) the investigation would not have continued if the default had not occurred.

(5) If subsection (3) applies the second condition is that—

(a) in the criminal investigation with regard to the offence or in its prosecution there has been a serious default by a person who is mentioned in subsection (9), and
(b) the proceedings would not have been started or continued if the default had not occurred.

(6) The third condition is that an application is made under this section by a person who held realisable property and has suffered loss in consequence of anything done in relation to it by or in pursuance of an order under this Part.

(7) The offence referred to in subsection (2) may be one of a number of offences with regard to which the investigation is started.

(8) The offence referred to in subsection (3) may be one of a number of offences for which the proceedings are started.

(9) Compensation under this section is payable to the applicant and—

(a) if the person in default was or was acting as a member of a police force, the compensation is payable out of the police fund from which the expenses of that force are met;
(b) if the person in default was a member of the Crown Prosecution Service or was acting on its behalf, the compensation is payable by the Director of Public Prosecutions;
(c) if the person in default was a member of the Serious Fraud Office, the compensation is payable by the Director of that Office;
(d) if the person in default was a member of or acting on behalf of the Revenue and Customs Prosecutions Office, the compensation is payable by the Director of Revenue and Customs Prosecutions;

(e) if the person in default was an officer of the Commissioners of Inland Revenue, the compensation is payable by those Commissioners.

[Proceeds of Crime Act 2002, s 72 as amended by the Commisssioners for Revenue and Customs Act 2005, Sch 4.]

3–1813 73. Order varied or discharged. (1) This section applies if—

(a) the court varies a confiscation order under section 29 or discharges one under section 30, and

(b) an application is made to the Crown Court by a person who held realisable property and has suffered loss as a result of the making of the order.

(2) The court may order the payment of such compensation as it believes is just.

(3) Compensation under this section is payable—

(a) to the applicant;

(b) by the Lord Chancellor.

[Proceeds of Crime Act 2002, s 73.]

Enforcement abroad

3–1814 74. Enforcement abroad. (1) This section applies if—

(a) any of the conditions in section 40 is satisfied,

(b) the prosecutor or the Director believes that realisable property is situated in a country or territory outside the United Kingdom (the receiving country), and

(c) the prosecutor or the Director (as the case may be) sends a request for assistance to the Secretary of State with a view to it being forwarded under this section.

(2) In a case where no confiscation order has been made, a request for assistance is a request to the government of the receiving country to secure that any person is prohibited from dealing with realisable property.

(3) In a case where a confiscation order has been made and has not been satisfied, discharged or quashed, a request for assistance is a request to the government of the receiving country to secure that—

(a) any person is prohibited from dealing with realisable property;

(b) realisable property is realised and the proceeds are applied in accordance with the law of the receiving country.

(4) No request for assistance may be made for the purposes of this section in a case where a confiscation order has been made and has been satisfied, discharged or quashed.

(5) If the Secretary of State believes it is appropriate to do so he may forward the request for assistance to the government of the receiving country.

(6) If property is realised in pursuance of a request under subsection (3) the amount ordered to be paid under the confiscation order must be taken to be reduced by an amount equal to the proceeds of realisation.

(7) A certificate purporting to be issued by or on behalf of the requested government is admissible as evidence of the facts it states if it states—

(a) that property has been realised in pursuance of a request under subsection (3),

(b) the date of realisation, and

(c) the proceeds of realisation.

(8) If the proceeds of realisation made in pursuance of a request under subsection (3) are expressed in a currency other than sterling, they must be taken to be the sterling equivalent calculated in accordance with the rate of exchange prevailing at the end of the day of realisation.

[Proceeds of Crime Act 2002, s 74.]

Interpretation

3–1815 75. Criminal lifestyle. (1) A defendant has a criminal lifestyle if (and only if) the following condition is satisfied.

(2) The condition is that the offence (or any of the offences) concerned satisfies any of these tests—

(a) it is specified in Schedule 2;

(b) it constitutes conduct forming part of a course of criminal activity;

(c) it is an offence committed over a period of at least six months and the defendant has benefited from the conduct which constitutes the offence.

(3) Conduct forms part of a course of criminal activity if the defendant has benefited from the conduct and—

(a) in the proceedings in which he was convicted he was convicted of three or more other offences, each of three or more of them constituting conduct from which he has benefited, or

(b) in the period of six years ending with the day when those proceedings were started (or, if there is more than one such day, the earliest day) he was convicted on at least two separate occasions of an offence constituting conduct from which he has benefited.

(4) But an offence does not satisfy the test in subsection (2)(b) or (c) unless the defendant obtains relevant benefit of not less than £5000.

(5) Relevant benefit for the purposes of subsection (2)(*b*) is—

(*a*) benefit from conduct which constitutes the offence;
(*b*) benefit from any other conduct which forms part of the course of criminal activity and which constitutes an offence of which the defendant has been convicted;
(*c*) benefit from conduct which constitutes an offence which has been or will be taken into consideration by the court in sentencing the defendant for an offence mentioned in paragraph (*a*) or (*b*).

(6) Relevant benefit for the purposes of subsection (2)(*c*) is—

(*a*) benefit from conduct which constitutes the offence;
(*b*) benefit from conduct which constitutes an offence which has been or will be taken into consideration by the court in sentencing the defendant for the offence mentioned in paragraph (*a*).

(7) The Secretary of State may by order amend Schedule 2.
(8) The Secretary of State may by order vary the amount for the time being specified in subsection (4).
[Proceeds of Crime Act 2002, s 75.]

3–1816   **76. Conduct and benefit.**   (1) Criminal conduct is conduct which—

(*a*) constitutes an offence in England and Wales, or
(*b*) would constitute such an offence if it occurred in England and Wales.

(2) General criminal conduct of the defendant is all his criminal conduct, and it is immaterial—

(*a*) whether conduct occurred before or after the passing of this Act;
(*b*) whether property constituting a benefit from conduct was obtained before or after the passing of this Act.

(3) Particular criminal conduct of the defendant is all his criminal conduct which falls within the following paragraphs—

(*a*) conduct which constitutes the offence or offences concerned;
(*b*) conduct which constitutes offences of which he was convicted in the same proceedings as those in which he was convicted of the offence or offences concerned;
(*c*) conduct which constitutes offences which the court will be taking into consideration in deciding his sentence for the offence or offences concerned.

(4) A person benefits from conduct if he obtains property as a result of or in connection with the conduct.
(5) If a person obtains a pecuniary advantage[1] as a result of or in connection with conduct, he is to be taken to obtain as a result of or in connection with the conduct a sum of money equal to the value of the pecuniary advantage.
(6) References to property or a pecuniary advantage obtained in connection with conduct include references to property or a pecuniary advantage obtained both in that connection and some other.
(7) If a person benefits from conduct his benefit is the value of the property obtained.
[Proceeds of Crime Act 2002, s 76.]

---

     1. The case of *R v Staines* [2006] EWCA Crim 15, [2006] Crim LR 453 established that the interpretation of "pecuniary advantage" that was adopted in respect of the Criminal Justice Act 1988, s 71(6) applies to the same use of the expression in s 76(5) of the 2002 Act, and that the earlier case law relating to the effect of an agreed basis of plea is equally applicable.

3–1817   **77. Tainted gifts.**   (1) Subsections (2) and (3) apply if—

(*a*) no court has made a decision as to whether the defendant has a criminal lifestyle, or
(*b*) a court has decided that the defendant has a criminal lifestyle.

(2) A gift is tainted if it was made by the defendant at any time after the relevant day.
(3) A gift is also tainted if it was made by the defendant at any time and was of property—

(*a*) which was obtained by the defendant as a result of or in connection with his general criminal conduct, or
(*b*) which (in whole or part and whether directly or indirectly) represented in the defendant's hands property obtained by him as a result of or in connection with his general criminal conduct.

(4) Subsection (5) applies if a court has decided that the defendant does not have a criminal lifestyle.
(5) A gift is tainted if it was made by the defendant at any time after—

(*a*) the date on which the offence concerned was committed, or
(*b*) if his particular criminal conduct consists of two or more offences and they were committed on different dates, the date of the earliest.

(6) For the purposes of subsection (5) an offence which is a continuing offence is committed on the first occasion when it is committed.
(7) For the purposes of subsection (5) the defendant's particular criminal conduct includes any

conduct which constitutes offences which the court has taken into consideration in deciding his sentence for the offence or offences concerned.

(8) A gift may be a tainted gift whether it was made before or after the passing of this Act.

(9) The relevant day is the first day of the period of six years ending with—

(a) the day when proceedings for the offence concerned were started against the defendant, or

(b) if there are two or more offences and proceedings for them were started on different days, the earliest of those days.

[Proceeds of Crime Act 2002, s 77.]

3–1818 78. Gifts and their recipients. (1) If the defendant transfers property to another person for a consideration whose value is significantly less than the value of the property at the time of the transfer, he is to be treated as making a gift.

(2) If subsection (1) applies the property given is to be treated as such share in the property transferred as is represented by the fraction—

(a) whose numerator is the difference between the two values mentioned in subsection (1), and

(b) whose denominator is the value of the property at the time of the transfer.

(3) References to a recipient of a tainted gift are to a person to whom the defendant has made the gift.

[Proceeds of Crime Act 2002, s 78.]

3–1819 79. Value: the basic rule. (1) This section applies for the purpose of deciding the value at any time of property then held by a person.

(2) Its value is the market value of the property at that time.

(3) But if at that time another person holds an interest in the property its value, in relation to the person mentioned in subsection (1), is the market value of his interest at that time, ignoring any charging order under a provision listed in subsection (4).

(4) The provisions are—

(a) section 9 of the Drug Trafficking Offences Act 1986 (c 32);

(b) section 78 of the Criminal Justice Act 1988 (c 33);

(c) Article 14 of the Criminal Justice (Confiscation) (Northern Ireland) Order 1990 (SI 1990/2588 (NI 17));

(d) section 27 of the Drug Trafficking Act 1994 (c 37);

(e) Article 32 of the Proceeds of Crime (Northern Ireland) Order 1996 (SI 1996/1299 (NI 9)).

(5) This section has effect subject to sections 80 and 81.

[Proceeds of Crime Act 2002, s 79.]

3–1820 80. Value of property obtained from conduct. (1) This section applies for the purpose of deciding the value of property obtained by a person as a result of or in connection with his criminal conduct; and the material time is the time the court makes its decision.

(2) The value of the property at the material time is the greater of the following—

(a) the value of the property (at the time the person obtained it) adjusted to take account of later changes in the value of money;

(b) the value (at the material time) of the property found under subsection (3).

(3) The property found under this subsection is as follows—

(a) if the person holds the property obtained, the property found under this subsection is that property;

(b) if he holds no part of the property obtained, the property found under this subsection is any property which directly or indirectly represents it in his hands;

(c) if he holds part of the property obtained, the property found under this subsection is that part and any property which directly or indirectly represents the other part in his hands.

(4) The references in subsection (2)(a) and (b) to the value are to the value found in accordance with section 79.

[Proceeds of Crime Act 2002, s 80.]

3–1821 81. Value of tainted gifts. (1) The value at any time (the material time) of a tainted gift is the greater of the following—

(a) the value (at the time of the gift) of the property given, adjusted to take account of later changes in the value of money;

(b) the value (at the material time) of the property found under subsection (2).

(2) The property found under this subsection is as follows—

(a) if the recipient holds the property given, the property found under this subsection is that property;

(b) if the recipient holds no part of the property given, the property found under this subsection is any property which directly or indirectly represents it in his hands;

(c) if the recipient holds part of the property given, the property found under this subsection is that part and any property which directly or indirectly represents the other part in his hands.

(3) The references in subsection (1)(*a*) and (*b*) to the value are to the value found in accordance with section 79.

[Proceeds of Crime Act 2002, s 81.]

3–1822   82. Free property.   Property is free unless an order is in force in respect of it under any of these provisions—

    (*a*)   section 27 of the Misuse of Drugs Act 1971 (c 38) (forfeiture orders);

    (*b*)   Article 11 of the Criminal Justice (Northern Ireland) Order 1994 (SI 1994/2795 (NI 15)) (deprivation orders);

    (*c*)   Part 2 of the Proceeds of Crime (Scotland) Act 1995 (c 43) (forfeiture of property used in crime);

    (*d*)   section 143 of the Sentencing Act (deprivation orders);

    (*e*)   section 23 or 111 of the Terrorism Act 2000 (c 11) (forfeiture orders);

    (*f*)   section 245A, 246, 255A, 256, 266, 295(2) or 298(2) of this Act.

[Proceeds of Crime Act 2002, s 82 as amended by the Serious Organised Crime and Police Act 2005, Sch 6.]

3–1823   83. Realisable property.   Realisable property is—

    (*a*)   any free property held by the defendant;

    (*b*)   any free property held by the recipient of a tainted gift.

[Proceeds of Crime Act 2002, s 83.]

3–1824   84. Property: general provisions.   (1) Property is all property wherever situated and includes—

    (*a*)   money;

    (*b*)   all forms of real or personal property;

    (*c*)   things in action and other intangible or incorporeal property.

(2) The following rules apply in relation to property—

    (*a*)   property is held by a person if he holds an interest in it;

    (*b*)   property is obtained by a person if he obtains an interest in it;

    (*c*)   property is transferred by one person to another if the first one transfers or grants an interest in it to the second;

    (*d*)   references to property held by a person include references to property vested in his trustee in bankruptcy, permanent or interim trustee (within the meaning of the Bankruptcy (Scotland) Act 1985 (c 66)) or liquidator;

    (*e*)   references to an interest held by a person beneficially in property include references to an interest which would be held by him beneficially if the property were not so vested;

    (*f*)   references to an interest, in relation to land in England and Wales or Northern Ireland, are to any legal estate or equitable interest or power;

    (*g*)   references to an interest, in relation to land in Scotland, are to any estate, interest, servitude or other heritable right in or over land, including a heritable security;

    (*h*)   references to an interest, in relation to property other than land, include references to a right (including a right to possession).

[Proceeds of Crime Act 2002, s 84.]

3–1825   85. Proceedings.   (1) Proceedings for an offence are started—

    (*a*)   when a justice of the peace issues a summons or warrant under section 1 of the Magistrates' Courts Act 1980 (c 43) in respect of the offence;

    (*b*)   when a person is charged with the offence after being taken into custody without a warrant;

    (*c*)   when a bill of indictment is preferred under section 2 of the Administration of Justice (Miscellaneous Provisions) Act 1933 (c 36) in a case falling within subsection (2)(*b*) of that section (preferment by Court of Appeal or High Court judge).

(2) If more than one time is found under subsection (1) in relation to proceedings they are started at the earliest of them.

(3) If the defendant is acquitted on all counts in proceedings for an offence, the proceedings are concluded when he is acquitted.

(4) If the defendant is convicted in proceedings for an offence and the conviction is quashed or the defendant is pardoned before a confiscation order is made, the proceedings are concluded when the conviction is quashed or the defendant is pardoned.

(5) If a confiscation order is made against the defendant in proceedings for an offence (whether the order is made by the Crown Court or the Court of Appeal) the proceedings are concluded—

    (*a*)   when the order is satisfied or discharged, or

    (*b*)   when the order is quashed and there is no further possibility of an appeal against the decision to quash the order.

(6) If the defendant is convicted in proceedings for an offence but the Crown Court decides not to make a confiscation order against him, the following rules apply—

    (*a*)   if an application for leave to appeal under section 31(2) is refused, the proceedings are concluded when the decision to refuse is made;

(b)   if the time for applying for leave to appeal under section 31(2) expires without an application being made, the proceedings are concluded when the time expires;

(c)   if on appeal under section 31(2) the Court of Appeal confirms the Crown Court's decision, and an application for leave to appeal under section 33 is refused, the proceedings are concluded when the decision to refuse is made;

(d)   if on appeal under section 31(2) the Court of Appeal confirms the Crown Court's decision, and the time for applying for leave to appeal under section 33 expires without an application being made, the proceedings are concluded when the time expires;

(e)   if on appeal under section 31(2) the Court of Appeal confirms the Crown Court's decision, and on appeal under section 33 the House of Lords confirms the Court of Appeal's decision, the proceedings are concluded when the House of Lords confirms the decision;

(f)   if on appeal under section 31(2) the Court of Appeal directs the Crown Court to reconsider the case, and on reconsideration the Crown Court decides not to make a confiscation order against the defendant, the proceedings are concluded when the Crown Court makes that decision;

(g)   if on appeal under section 33 the House of Lords directs the Crown Court to reconsider the case, and on reconsideration the Crown Court decides not to make a confiscation order against the defendant, the proceedings are concluded when the Crown Court makes that decision.

(7) In applying subsection (6) any power to extend the time for making an application for leave to appeal must be ignored.

(8) In applying subsection (6) the fact that a court may decide on a later occasion to make a confiscation order against the defendant must be ignored.

[Proceeds of Crime Act 2002, s 85.]

3–1826   86. Applications.   (1) An application under section 19, 20, 27 or 28 is concluded—

(a)   in a case where the court decides not to make a confiscation order against the defendant, when it makes the decision;

(b)   in a case where a confiscation order is made against him as a result of the application, when the order is satisfied or discharged, or when the order is quashed and there is no further possibility of an appeal against the decision to quash the order;

(c)   in a case where the application is withdrawn, when the person who made the application notifies the withdrawal to the court to which the application was made.

(2) An application under section 21 or 22 is concluded—

(a)   in a case where the court decides not to vary the confiscation order concerned, when it makes the decision;

(b)   in a case where the court varies the confiscation order as a result of the application, when the order is satisfied or discharged, or when the order is quashed and there is no further possibility of an appeal against the decision to quash the order;

(c)   in a case where the application is withdrawn, when the person who made the application notifies the withdrawal to the court to which the application was made.

[Proceeds of Crime Act 2002, s 86.]

3–1827   87. Confiscation orders.   (1) A confiscation order is satisfied when no amount is due under it.

(2) A confiscation order is subject to appeal until there is no further possibility of an appeal on which the order could be varied or quashed; and for this purpose any power to grant leave to appeal out of time must be ignored.

[Proceeds of Crime Act 2002, s 87.]

3–1828   88. Other interpretative provisions.   (1) A reference to the offence (or offences) concerned must be construed in accordance with section 6(9).

(2) A criminal investigation is an investigation which police officers or other persons have a duty to conduct with a view to it being ascertained whether a person should be charged with an offence.

(3) A defendant is a person against whom proceedings for an offence have been started (whether or not he has been convicted).

(4) A reference to sentencing the defendant for an offence includes a reference to dealing with him otherwise in respect of the offence.

(5) The Sentencing Act is the Powers of Criminal Courts (Sentencing) Act 2000 (c 6).

(6) The following paragraphs apply to references to orders—

(a)   a confiscation order is an order under section 6;

(b)   a restraint order is an order under section 41.

(7) Sections 75 to 87 and this section apply for the purposes of this Part.

[Proceeds of Crime Act 2002, s 88.]

General

3–1829   *Procedure on appeal to the Court of Appeal and to the House of Lords* (ss 89–90) *and Crown Court Rules* (s 91[1]).

PART 3
CONFISCATION: SCOTLAND[2]

PART 4
CONFISCATION: NORTHERN IRELAND[3]

PART 5
CIVIL RECOVERY OF THE PROCEEDS ETC OF UNLAWFUL CONDUCT[4]

CHAPTER 1
INTRODUCTORY[5]

3–1830 240. General purpose of this Part. (1) This Part has effect for the purposes of—

(a) enabling the enforcement authority to recover, in civil proceedings before the High Court or Court of Session, property which is, or represents, property obtained through unlawful conduct,

(b) enabling cash which is, or represents, property obtained through unlawful conduct, or which is intended to be used in unlawful conduct, to be forfeited in civil proceedings before a magistrates' court or (in Scotland) the sheriff.

(2) The powers conferred by this Part are exercisable in relation to any property (including cash) whether or not any proceedings have been brought for an offence in connection with the property.
[Proceeds of Crime Act 2002, s 240.]

---

1. See the Criminal Procedure Rules 2005, Parts 57–61, in PART I: MAGISTRATES' COURTS, PROCEDURE, ante..
2. Part 3 comprises ss 92–155 and Schs 3 and 4.
3. Part 4 comprises ss 156–239 and Sch 5.
4. Part 5 comprises ss 240–316 and Schs 6 and 7.
5. Chapter 1 comprises ss 240–242.

3–1831 241. "Unlawful conduct". (1) Conduct occurring in any part of the United Kingdom is unlawful conduct if it is unlawful under the criminal law of that part.

(2) Conduct which—

(a) occurs in a country or territory outside the United Kingdom and is unlawful under the criminal law applying in that country or territory, and

(b) if it occurred in a part of the United Kingdom, would be unlawful under the criminal law of that part,

is also unlawful conduct.

(3) The court or sheriff must decide on a balance of probabilities whether it is proved—

(a) that any matters alleged to constitute unlawful conduct have occurred, or

(b) that any person intended to use any cash in unlawful conduct.
[Proceeds of Crime Act 2002, s 241 as amended by the Serious Organised Crime and Police Act 2005, Sch 6.]

3–1832 242. "Property obtained through unlawful conduct". (1) A person obtains property through unlawful conduct (whether his own conduct or another's) if he obtains property by or in return for the conduct.

(2) In deciding whether any property was obtained through unlawful conduct—

(a) it is immaterial whether or not any money, goods or services were provided in order to put the person in question in a position to carry out the conduct,

(b) it is not necessary to show that the conduct was of a particular kind if it is shown that the property was obtained through conduct of one of a number of kinds, each of which would have been unlawful conduct.
[Proceeds of Crime Act 2002, s 242.]

CHAPTER 3
RECOVERY OF CASH IN SUMMARY PROCEEDINGS[1]

Searches

3–1833 289. Searches. (1) If a customs officer or constable who is lawfully on any premises has reasonable grounds for suspecting that there is on the premises cash—

(a) which is recoverable property or is intended by any person for use in unlawful conduct, and

(b) the amount of which is not less than the minimum amount,

he may search for the cash there.

(2) If a customs officer or constable has reasonable grounds for suspecting that a person (the suspect) is carrying cash—

(a) which is recoverable property or is intended by any person for use in unlawful conduct, and

(b) the amount of which is not less than the minimum amount,

he may exercise the following powers.

(3) The officer or constable may, so far as he thinks it necessary or expedient, require the suspect—

(a) to permit a search of any article he has with him,

(b) to permit a search of his person.

(4) An officer or constable exercising powers by virtue of subsection (3)(*b*) may detain the suspect for so long as is necessary for their exercise.

(5) The powers conferred by this section—

(*a*) are exercisable only so far as reasonably required for the purpose of finding cash,

(*b*) are exercisable by a customs officer only if he has reasonable grounds for suspecting that the unlawful conduct in question relates to an assigned matter (within the meaning of the Customs and Excise Management Act 1979 (c 2)).

(6) Cash means—

(*a*) notes and coins in any currency,

(*b*) postal orders,

(*c*) cheques of any kind, including travellers' cheques,

(*d*) bankers' drafts,

(*e*) bearer bonds and bearer shares,

found at any place in the United Kingdom.

(7) Cash also includes any kind of monetary instrument which is found at any place in the United Kingdom, if the instrument is specified by the Secretary of State by an order made after consultation with the Scottish Ministers.

(8) This section does not require a person to submit to an intimate search or strip search (within the meaning of section 164 of the Customs and Excise Management Act 1979 (c 2)).

[Proceeds of Crime Act 2002, s 289.]

---

1. Chapter 3 comprises ss 289–303.

3–1834 290. Prior approval. (1) The powers conferred by section 289 may be exercised only with the appropriate approval unless, in the circumstances, it is not practicable to obtain that approval before exercising the power.

(2) The appropriate approval means the approval of a judicial officer or (if that is not practicable in any case) the approval of a senior officer.

(3) A judicial officer means—

(*a*) in relation to England and Wales and Northern Ireland, a justice of the peace[1],

(*b*) in relation to Scotland, the sheriff.

(4) A senior officer means—

(*a*) in relation to the exercise of the power by a customs officer, a customs officer of a rank designated by the Commissioners of Customs and Excise as equivalent to that of a senior police officer,

(*b*) in relation to the exercise of the power by a constable, a senior police officer.

(5) A senior police officer means a police officer of at least the rank of inspector.

(6) If the powers are exercised without the approval of a judicial officer in a case where—

(*a*) no cash is seized by virtue of section 294, or

(*b*) any cash so seized is not detained for more than 48 hours (calculated in accordance with section 295(1B)),

the customs officer or constable who exercised the powers must give a written report to the appointed person.

(7) The report must give particulars of the circumstances which led him to believe that—

(*a*) the powers were exercisable, and

(*b*) it was not practicable to obtain the approval of a judicial officer.

(8) In this section and section 291, the appointed person means—

(*a*) in relation to England and Wales and Northern Ireland, a person appointed by the Secretary of State,

(*b*) in relation to Scotland, a person appointed by the Scottish Ministers.

(9) The appointed person must not be a person employed under or for the purposes of a government department or of the Scottish Administration; and the terms and conditions of his appointment, including any remuneration or expenses to be paid to him, are to be determined by the person appointing him.

[Proceeds of Crime Act 2002, s 290 as amended by the Serious Organised Crime and Police Act 2005, s 100.]

---

1. For procedure in respect of applications to a magistrates' court, see the Magistrates' Courts (Detention and Forfeiture of Cash) Rules 2002, in PART I: MAGISTRATES' COURTS, PROCEDURE, ante, see also for form of application and authority the Code of Practice for constables and customs officers under the Proceeds of Crime Act 2002, in this PART, post.

3–1835 291. Report on exercise of powers. (1) As soon as possible after the end of each financial year, the appointed person must prepare a report for that year.

"Financial year" means—

(*a*) the period beginning with the day on which this section comes into force and ending with the next 31 March (which is the first financial year), and

(*b*) each subsequent period of twelve months beginning with 1 April.

(2) The report must give his opinion as to the circumstances and manner in which the powers conferred by section 289 are being exercised in cases where the customs officer or constable who exercised them is required to give a report under section 290(6).

(3) In the report, he may make any recommendations he considers appropriate.

(4) He must send a copy of his report to the Secretary of State or, as the case may be, the Scottish Ministers, who must arrange for it to be published.

(5) The Secretary of State must lay a copy of any report he receives under this section before Parliament; and the Scottish Ministers must lay a copy of any report they receive under this section before the Scottish Parliament.
[Proceeds of Crime Act 2002, s 291.]

3–1836   292. Code of practice.   (1) The Secretary of State must make a code of practice[1] in connection with the exercise by customs officers and (in relation to England and Wales and Northern Ireland) constables of the powers conferred by virtue of section 289.

(2) Where he proposes to issue a code of practice he must—

(a) publish a draft,

(b) consider any representations made to him about the draft by the Scottish Ministers or any other person,

(c) if he thinks it appropriate, modify the draft in the light of any such representations.

(3) He must lay a draft of the code before Parliament.

(4) When he has laid a draft of the code before Parliament he may bring it into operation by order.

(5) He may revise the whole or any part of the code issued by him and issue the code as revised; and subsections (2) to (4) apply to such a revised code as they apply to the original code.

(6) A failure by a customs officer or constable to comply with a provision of the code does not of itself make him liable to criminal or civil proceedings.

(7) The code is admissible in evidence in criminal or civil proceedings and is to be taken into account by a court or tribunal in any case in which it appears to the court or tribunal to be relevant.
[Proceeds of Crime Act 2002, s 292.]

---

1. In this **PART**, post.

3–1837   293. Code of Practice.   *Scotland.*

Seizure and detention

3–1838   294. Seizure of cash.   (1) A customs officer or constable may seize any cash if he has reasonable grounds for suspecting that it is—

(a) recoverable property, or

(b) intended by any person for use in unlawful conduct.

(2) A customs officer or constable may also seize cash part of which he has reasonable grounds for suspecting to be—

(a) recoverable property, or

(b) intended by any person for use in unlawful conduct,

if it is not reasonably practicable to seize only that part.

(3) This section does not authorise the seizure of an amount of cash if it or, as the case may be, the part to which his suspicion relates, is less than the minimum amount.
[Proceeds of Crime Act 2002, s 294.]

3–1839   295. Detention of seized cash.   (1) While the customs officer or constable continues to have reasonable grounds for his suspicion, cash seized under section 294 may be detained initially for a period of 48 hours.

(1A) The period of 48 hours mentioned in subsection (1) is to be calculated in accordance with subsection (1B).

(1B) In calculating a period of 48 hours in accordance with this subsection, no account shall be taken of—

(a) any Saturday or Sunday,

(b) Christmas Day,

(c) Good Friday,

(d) any day that is a bank holiday under the Banking and Financial Dealings Act 1971 in the part of the United Kingdom within which the cash is seized, or

(e) any day prescribed under section 8(2) of the Criminal Procedure (Scotland) Act 1995 as a court holiday in a sheriff court in the sheriff court district within which the cash is seized.

(2) The period for which the cash or any part of it may be detained may be extended by an order made by a magistrates' court or (in Scotland) the sheriff; but the order may not authorise the detention of any of the cash—

(a) beyond the end of the period of three months beginning with the date of the order,

(b) in the case of any further order under this section, beyond the end of the period of two years beginning with the date of the first order.

(3) A justice of the peace may also exercise the power of a magistrates' court to make the first order under subsection (2) extending the period.

(4) An application[1] for an order under subsection (2)—

(a) in relation to England and Wales and Northern Ireland, may be made by the Commissioners of Customs and Excise or a constable,

(b) in relation to Scotland, may be made by the Scottish Ministers in connection with their functions under section 298 or by a procurator fiscal,

and the court, sheriff or justice may make the order if satisfied, in relation to any cash to be further detained, that either of the following conditions is met.

(5) The first condition is that there are reasonable grounds for suspecting that the cash is recoverable property and that either—

(a) its continued detention is justified while its derivation is further investigated or consideration is given to bringing (in the United Kingdom or elsewhere) proceedings against any person for an offence with which the cash is connected, or

(b) proceedings against any person for an offence with which the cash is connected have been started and have not been concluded.

(6) The second condition is that there are reasonable grounds for suspecting that the cash is intended to be used in unlawful conduct and that either—

(a) its continued detention is justified while its intended use is further investigated or consideration is given to bringing (in the United Kingdom or elsewhere) proceedings against any person for an offence with which the cash is connected, or

(b) proceedings against any person for an offence with which the cash is connected have been started and have not been concluded.

(7) An application for an order under subsection (2) may also be made in respect of any cash seized under section 294(2), and the court, sheriff or justice may make the order if satisfied that—

(a) the condition in subsection (5) or (6) is met in respect of part of the cash, and

(b) it is not reasonably practicable to detain only that part.

(8) An order under subsection (2) must provide for notice to be given to persons affected by it.
[Proceeds of Crime Act 2002, s 295 as amended by the Serious Organised Crime and Police Act 2005, s 100.]

---

1. For procedure in respect of applications to a magistrates' court, see the Magistrates' Courts (Detention and Forfeiture of Cash) Rules 2002, in PART I: MAGISTRATES' COURTS, PROCEDURE, ante.

3–1840   296. Interest.   (1) If cash is detained under section 295 for more than 48 hours (calculated in accordance with section 295(1B)), it is at the first opportunity to be paid into an interest-bearing account and held there; and the interest accruing on it is to be added to it on its forfeiture or release.

(2) In the case of cash detained under section 295 which was seized under section 294(2), the customs officer or constable must, on paying it into the account, release the part of the cash to which the suspicion does not relate.

(3) Subsection (1) does not apply if the cash or, as the case may be, the part to which the suspicion relates is required as evidence of an offence or evidence in proceedings under this Chapter.
[Proceeds of Crime Act 2002, s 296 as amended by the Serious Organised Crime and Police Act 2005, s 100.]

3–1841   297. Release of detained cash.   (1) This section applies while any cash is detained under section 295.

(2) A magistrates' court[1] or (in Scotland) the sheriff may direct the release of the whole or any part of the cash if the following condition is met.

(3) The condition is that the court or sheriff is satisfied, on an application by the person from whom the cash was seized, that the conditions in section 295 for the detention of the cash are no longer met in relation to the cash to be released.

(4) A customs officer, constable or (in Scotland) procurator fiscal may, after notifying the magistrates' court, sheriff or justice under whose order cash is being detained, release the whole or any part of it if satisfied that the detention of the cash to be released is no longer justified.
[Proceeds of Crime Act 2002, s 297.]

---

1. For procedure in respect of applications to a magistrates' court, see the Magistrates' Courts (Detention and Forfeiture of Cash) Rules 2002, in PART I: MAGISTRATES' COURTS, PROCEDURE, ante.

Forfeiture

3–1842   298. Forfeiture.   (1) While cash is detained under section 295, an application for the forfeiture of the whole or any part of it may be made—

(a) to a magistrates' court[1] by the Commissioners of Customs and Excise or a constable,

(b) (in Scotland) to the sheriff by the Scottish Ministers.

(2) The court or sheriff may order the forfeiture of the cash or any part of it if satisfied[2] that the cash or part—

(a) is recoverable property, or

(b) is intended by any person for use in unlawful conduct.

(3) But in the case of recoverable property which belongs to joint tenants, one of whom is an excepted joint owner, the order may not apply to so much of it as the court thinks is attributable to the excepted joint owner's share.

(4) Where an application for the forfeiture of any cash is made under this section, the cash is to be detained (and may not be released under any power conferred by this Chapter) until any proceedings in pursuance of the application (including any proceedings on appeal) are concluded.
[Proceeds of Crime Act 2002, s 298.]

1. For procedure in respect of applications to a magistrates' court, see the Magistrates' Courts (Detention and Forfeiture of Cash) Rules 2002, in PART I: MAGISTRATES' COURTS, PROCEDURE, ante.
2. The court need only be satisfied on a balance of probabilities that the cash is recoverable property or intended for use in unlawful conduct; there is no requirement for the applicant to identify a particular criminal activity and lies told by the person in possession of the cash can be used to support an inference that the cash was derived from crime and/or intended for use in crime: *Muneka v Customs and Excise Comrs* [2005] EWHC 495 (Admin), [2005] All ER (D) 21 (Feb), (2005) 169 JPN 145.

3–1843   299. Appeal against decision under section 298.   (1) Any party to proceedings for an order for the forfeiture of cash under section 298 who is aggrieved by an order under that section or by the decision of the court not to make such an order may appeal—

(a) in relation to England and Wales, to the Crown Court;
(b) in relation to Scotland, to the Sheriff Principal;
(c) in relation to Northern Ireland, to a county court.

(2) An appeal under subsection (1) must be made before the end of the period of 30 days starting with the day on which the court makes the order or decision.
(3) The court hearing the appeal may make any order it thinks appropriate.
(4) If the court upholds an appeal against an order forfeiting the cash, it may order the release of the cash.
[Proceeds of Crime Act 2002, s 299 as substituted by the Serious Organised Crime and Police Act 2005, s 101.]

3–1844   300. Application of forfeited cash.   (1) Cash forfeited under this Chapter, and any accrued interest on it—

(a) if forfeited by a magistrates' court in England and Wales or Northern Ireland, is to be paid into the Consolidated Fund,
(b) if forfeited by the sheriff, is to be paid into the Scottish Consolidated Fund.

(2) But it is not to be paid in—

(a) before the end of the period within which an appeal under section 299 may be made, or
(b) if a person appeals under that section, before the appeal is determined or otherwise disposed of.
[Proceeds of Crime Act 2002, s 300.]

Supplementary

3–1845   301. Victims and other owners.   (1) A person who claims that any cash detained under this Chapter, or any part of it, belongs to him may apply[1] to a magistrates' court or (in Scotland) the sheriff for the cash or part to be released to him.

(2) The application may be made in the course of proceedings under section 295 or 298 or at any other time.
(3) If it appears to the court or sheriff concerned that—

(a) the applicant was deprived of the cash to which the application relates, or of property which it represents, by unlawful conduct,
(b) the property he was deprived of was not, immediately before he was deprived of it, recoverable property, and
(c) that cash belongs to him,

the court or sheriff may order the cash to which the application relates to be released to the applicant.
(4) If—

(a) the applicant is not the person from whom the cash to which the application relates was seized,
(b) it appears to the court or sheriff that that cash belongs to the applicant,
(c) the court or sheriff is satisfied that the conditions in section 295 for the detention of that cash are no longer met or, if an application has been made under section 298, the court or sheriff decides not to make an order under that section in relation to that cash, and
(d) no objection to the making of an order under this subsection has been made by the person from whom that cash was seized,

the court or sheriff may order the cash to which the application relates to be released to the applicant or to the person from whom it was seized.
[Proceeds of Crime Act 2002, s 301.]

1. For procedure in respect of applications to a magistrates' court, see the Magistrates' Courts (Detention and Forfeiture of Cash) Rules 2002, in PART I: MAGISTRATES' COURTS, PROCEDURE, ante.

3–1846   302. Compensation.   (1) If no forfeiture order is made in respect of any cash detained under this Chapter, the person to whom the cash belongs or from whom it was seized may make an application to the magistrates' court[1] or (in Scotland) the sheriff for compensation.

(2) If, for any period beginning with the first opportunity to place the cash in an interest-bearing account after the initial detention of the cash for 48 hours (calculated in accordance with section 295(1B)), the cash was not held in an interest-bearing account while detained, the court or sheriff may order an amount of compensation to be paid to the applicant.

(3) The amount of compensation to be paid under subsection (2) is the amount the court or sheriff thinks would have been earned in interest in the period in question if the cash had been held in an interest-bearing account.

(4) If the court or sheriff is satisfied that, taking account of any interest to be paid under section 296 or any amount to be paid under subsection (2), the applicant has suffered loss as a result of the detention of the cash and that the circumstances are exceptional, the court or sheriff may order compensation (or additional compensation) to be paid to him.

(5) The amount of compensation to be paid under subsection (4) is the amount the court or sheriff thinks reasonable, having regard to the loss suffered and any other relevant circumstances.

(6) If the cash was seized by a customs officer, the compensation is to be paid by the Commissioners of Customs and Excise.

(7) If the cash was seized by a constable, the compensation is to be paid as follows—

(a)   in the case of a constable of a police force in England and Wales, it is to be paid out of the police fund from which the expenses of the police force are met,

(b)   in the case of a constable of a police force in Scotland, it is to be paid by the police authority or joint police board for the police area for which that force is maintained,

(c)   in the case of a police officer within the meaning of the Police (Northern Ireland) Act 2000 (c 32), it is to be paid out of money provided by the Chief Constable.

(8) If a forfeiture order is made in respect only of a part of any cash detained under this Chapter, this section has effect in relation to the other part.
[Proceeds of Crime Act 2002, s 302 as amended by the Serious Organised Crime and Police Act 2005, s 100.]

---

1. For procedure in respect of applications to a magistrates' court, see the Magistrates' Courts (Detention and Forfeiture of Cash) Rules 2002, in PART I: MAGISTRATES' COURTS, PROCEDURE, ante.

3–1847   303. "The minimum amount".   (1) In this Chapter, the minimum amount is the amount in sterling specified in an order[1] made by the Secretary of State after consultation with the Scottish Ministers.

(2) For that purpose the amount of any cash held in a currency other than sterling must be taken to be its sterling equivalent, calculated in accordance with the prevailing rate of exchange.
[Proceeds of Crime Act 2002, s 303.]

---

1. The Proceeds of Crime Act 2002 (Recovery of Cash in Summary Proceeding: Minimum Amount) Order 2006, SI 2006/1699 prescribes the minimum amount as £1,000.

CHAPTER 4
GENERAL

Recoverable property

3–1848   304. Property obtained through unlawful conduct.   (1) Property obtained through unlawful conduct is recoverable property.

(2) But if property obtained through unlawful conduct has been disposed of (since it was so obtained), it is recoverable property only if it is held by a person into whose hands it may be followed.

(3) Recoverable property obtained through unlawful conduct may be followed into the hands of a person obtaining it on a disposal by—

(a)   the person who through the conduct obtained the property, or

(b)   a person into whose hands it may (by virtue of this subsection) be followed.
[Proceeds of Crime Act 2002, s 304.]

3–1849   305. Tracing property, etc.   (1) Where property obtained through unlawful conduct ("the original property") is or has been recoverable, property which represents the original property is also recoverable property.

(2) If a person enters into a transaction by which—

(a)   he disposes of recoverable property, whether the original property or property which (by virtue of this Chapter) represents the original property, and

(b)   he obtains other property in place of it,

the other property represents the original property.

(3) If a person disposes of recoverable property which represents the original property, the property may be followed into the hands of the person who obtains it (and it continues to represent the original property).
[Proceeds of Crime Act 2002, s 305.]

3–1850   306. Mixing property.   (1) Subsection (2) applies if a person's recoverable property is mixed with other property (whether his property or another's).

(2) The portion of the mixed property which is attributable to the recoverable property represents the property obtained through unlawful conduct.

(3) Recoverable property is mixed with other property if (for example) it is used—

   (a)   to increase funds held in a bank account,
   (b)   in part payment for the acquisition of an asset,
   (c)   for the restoration or improvement of land,
   (d)   by a person holding a leasehold interest in the property to acquire the freehold.

[Proceeds of Crime Act 2002, s 306.]

3–1851   307. Recoverable property: accruing profits.   (1) This section applies where a person who has recoverable property obtains further property consisting of profits accruing in respect of the recoverable property.

(2) The further property is to be treated as representing the property obtained through unlawful conduct.

[Proceeds of Crime Act 2002, s 307.]

3–1852   308. General exceptions.   (1) If—

   (a)   a person disposes of recoverable property, and
   (b)   the person who obtains it on the disposal does so in good faith, for value and without notice that it was recoverable property,

the property may not be followed into that person's hands and, accordingly, it ceases to be recoverable.

(2) If recoverable property is vested, forfeited or otherwise disposed of in pursuance of powers conferred by virtue of this Part, it ceases to be recoverable.

(3) If—

   (a)   in pursuance of a judgment in civil proceedings (whether in the United Kingdom or elsewhere), the defendant makes a payment to the claimant or the claimant otherwise obtains property from the defendant,
   (b)   the claimant's claim is based on the defendant's unlawful conduct, and
   (c)   apart from this subsection, the sum received, or the property obtained, by the claimant would be recoverable property,

the property ceases to be recoverable.

In relation to Scotland, "claimant" and "defendant" are to be read as "pursuer" and "defender".

(4) If—

   (a)   a payment is made to a person in pursuance of a compensation order under Article 14 of the Criminal Justice (Northern Ireland) Order 1994 (SI 1994/2795 (NI 15)), section 249 of the Criminal Procedure (Scotland) Act 1995 (c 46) or section 130 of the Powers of Criminal Courts (Sentencing) Act 2000 (c 6), and
   (b)   apart from this subsection, the sum received would be recoverable property,

the property ceases to be recoverable.

(5) If—

   (a)   a payment is made to a person in pursuance of a restitution order under section 27 of the Theft Act (Northern Ireland) 1969 (c 16 (NI)) or section 148(2) of the Powers of Criminal Courts (Sentencing) Act 2000 or a person otherwise obtains any property in pursuance of such an order, and
   (b)   apart from this subsection, the sum received, or the property obtained, would be recoverable property,

the property ceases to be recoverable.

(6) If—

   (a)   in pursuance of an order made by the court under section 382(3) or 383(5) of the Financial Services and Markets Act 2000 (c 8) (restitution orders), an amount is paid to or distributed among any persons in accordance with the court's directions, and
   (b)   apart from this subsection, the sum received by them would be recoverable property,

the property ceases to be recoverable.

(7) If—

   (a)   in pursuance of a requirement of the Financial Services Authority under section 384(5) of the Financial Services and Markets Act 2000 (power of authority to require restitution), an amount is paid to or distributed among any persons, and
   (b)   apart from this subsection, the sum received by them would be recoverable property,

the property ceases to be recoverable.

(8) Property is not recoverable while a restraint order applies to it, that is—

   (a)   an order under section 41, 120 or 190, or
   (b)   an order under any corresponding provision of an enactment mentioned in section 8(7)(a) to (g).

(9) Property is not recoverable if it has been taken into account in deciding the amount of a person's benefit from criminal conduct for the purpose of making a confiscation order, that is—

(a)   an order under section 6, 92 or 156, or

(b)   an order under a corresponding provision[1] of an enactment mentioned in section 8(7)(a) to (g),

and, in relation to an order mentioned in paragraph (b), the reference to the amount of a person's benefit from criminal conduct is to be read as a reference to the corresponding amount under the enactment in question.

(10) Where—

(a)   a person enters into a transaction to which section 305(2) applies, and

(b)   the disposal is one to which subsection (1) or (2) applies,

this section does not affect the recoverability (by virtue of section 305(2)) of any property obtained on the transaction in place of the property disposed of.
[Proceeds of Crime Act 2002, s 308.]

---

1. Where a confiscation order made by the Crown Court under the Criminal Justice Act 1988 which was held on appeal to be invalid, it was not an order made under "a corresponding provision": *Satnam Singh v Assets Recovery Agency* [2005] EWCA Civ 580, [2005] Crim LR 665.

3–1853   309. Other exemptions.   (1) An order may provide that property is not recoverable or (as the case may be) associated property if—

(a)   it is prescribed property, or

(b)   it is disposed of in pursuance of a prescribed enactment or an enactment of a prescribed description.

(2) An order may provide that if property is disposed of in pursuance of a prescribed enactment or an enactment of a prescribed description, it is to be treated for the purposes of section 278 as if it had been disposed of in pursuance of a recovery order.

(3) An order under this section may be made so as to apply to property, or a disposal of property, only in prescribed circumstances; and the circumstances may relate to the property or disposal itself or to a person who holds or has held the property or to any other matter.

(4) In this section, an order[1] means an order made by the Secretary of State after consultation with the Scottish Ministers, and prescribed means prescribed by the order.
[Proceeds of Crime Act 2002, s 309.]

---

1. The Proceeds of Crime Act 2002 (Exemptions from Civil Recovery) Order 2003, SI 2003/336 has been made

3–1854   310. Granting interests.   (1) If a person grants an interest in his recoverable property, the question whether the interest is also recoverable is to be determined in the same manner as it is on any other disposal of recoverable property.

(2) Accordingly, on his granting an interest in the property ("the property in question")—

(a)   where the property in question is property obtained through unlawful conduct, the interest is also to be treated as obtained through that conduct,

(b)   where the property in question represents in his hands property obtained through unlawful conduct, the interest is also to be treated as representing in his hands the property so obtained.
[Proceeds of Crime Act 2002, s 310.]

Insolvency

3–1855   311. *Insolvency*

Delegation of enforcement functions

3–1856   312. *Performance of functions of Scottish Ministers by constables in Scotland*

3–1857   313. Restriction on performance of Director's functions by police.   (1) In spite of section 1(6), nothing which the Director is authorised or required to do for the purposes of this Part may be done by—

(a)   a member of a police force,

(b)   a member of the Police Service of Northern Ireland,

(c)   *repealed,*

(d)   *repealed.*

(2) In this section—

(a)   "member of a police force" has the same meaning as in the Police Act 1996 (c 16) and includes a person who would be a member of a police force but for section 97(3) of that Act (police officers engaged on service outside their force),

(b)   "member of the Police Service of Northern Ireland" includes a person who would be a member of the Police Service of Northern Ireland but for section 27(3) of the Police (Northern Ireland) Act 1998 (c 32) (members of that service engaged on other police service).
[Proceeds of Crime Act 2002, s 313 as amended by the Serious Organised Crime and Police Act 2005, Sch 4.]

disposing of a part of it, or

(b)   to his granting an interest in it,

(or to both); and references to the property disposed of are to any property obtained on the disposal.

(2) A person who makes a payment to another is to be treated as making a disposal of his property to the other, whatever form the payment takes.

(3) Where a person's property passes to another under a will or intestacy or by operation of law, it is to be treated as disposed of by him to the other.

(4) A person is only to be treated as having obtained his property for value in a case where he gave unexecuted consideration if the consideration has become executed consideration.

[Proceeds of Crime Act 2002, s 314.]

3-1859   315. *Northern Ireland courts*

3-1860   316. General interpretation.   (1) In this Part—

"associated property" has the meaning given by section 245,

"cash" has the meaning given by section 289(6) or (7),

"constable", in relation to Northern Ireland, means a police officer within the meaning of the Police (Northern Ireland) Act 2000 (c 32),

"country" includes territory,

"the court" (except in sections 253(2) and (3) and 262(2) and (3) and Chapter 3) means the High Court or (in relation to proceedings in Scotland) the Court of Session,

"dealing" with property includes disposing of it, taking possession of it or removing it from the United Kingdom,

"enforcement authority"—

(a)   in relation to England and Wales and Northern Ireland, means the Director,

(b)   in relation to Scotland, means the Scottish Ministers,

"excepted joint owner" has the meaning given by section 270(4),

"interest", in relation to land—

(a)   in the case of land in England and Wales or Northern Ireland, means any legal estate and any equitable interest or power,

(b)   in the case of land in Scotland, means any estate, interest, servitude or other heritable right in or over land, including a heritable security,

"interest", in relation to property other than land, includes any right (including a right to possession of the property),

"interim administration order" has the meaning given by section 256(2),

"interim receiving order" has the meaning given by section 246(2),

"the minimum amount" (in Chapter 3) has the meaning given by section 303,

"part", in relation to property, includes a portion,

"premises" has the same meaning as in the Police and Criminal Evidence Act 1984 (c 60),

"prohibitory property order" has the meaning given by section 255A(2);

"property freezing order" has the meaning given by section 245A(2);

"property obtained through unlawful conduct" has the meaning given by section 242,

"recoverable property" is to be read in accordance with sections 304 to 310,

"recovery order" means an order made under section 266,

"respondent" means—

(a)   where proceedings are brought by the enforcement authority by virtue of Chapter 2, the person against whom the proceedings are brought,

(b)   where no such proceedings have been brought but the enforcement authority has applied for a property freezing order, an interim receiving order, a prohibitory order or an interim administration order, the person against whom he intends to bring such proceedings,

"share", in relation to an excepted joint owner, has the meaning given by section 270(4),

"unlawful conduct" has the meaning given by section 241,

"value" means market value.

(2) The following provisions apply for the purposes of this Part.

(3) For the purpose of deciding whether or not property was recoverable at any time (including times before commencement), it is to be assumed that this Part was in force at that and any other relevant time.

(4) Property is all property wherever situated and includes—

(a)   money,

(b)   all forms of property, real or personal, heritable or moveable,

(c)   things in action and other intangible or incorporeal property.

(5) Any reference to a person's property (whether expressed as a reference to the property he holds or otherwise) is to be read as follows.

(6) In relation to land, it is a reference to any interest which he holds in the land.

(7) In relation to property other than land, it is a reference—

(a)   to the property (if it belongs to him), or

(b)   to any other interest which he holds in the property.

(8)   References to the satisfaction of the enforcement authority's right to recover property obtained through unlawful conduct are to be read in accordance with section 279.

(9)   Proceedings against any person for an offence are concluded when—

(a)   the person is convicted or acquitted,

(b)   the prosecution is discontinued or, in Scotland, the trial diet is deserted simpliciter, or

(c)   the jury is discharged without a finding otherwise than in circumstances where the proceedings are continued without a jury.*

[Proceeds of Crime Act 2002, s 316 as amended by the Serious Organised Crime and Police Act 2005, Sch 6 and the Criminal Justice Act 2003, Sch 36.]

---

*Reproduced as in force in England and Wales.

PART 6
REVENUE FUNCTIONS[1]

PART 7
MONEY LAUNDERING[2]

3–1861   327. Concealing etc.   (1)   A person commits an offence if he—

(a)   conceals criminal property[3];

(b)   disguises criminal property[3];

(c)   converts criminal property[3];

(d)   transfers criminal property[3];

(e)   removes criminal property[3] from England and Wales or from Scotland or from Northern Ireland.

(2)   But a person does not commit such an offence if—

(a)   he makes an authorised disclosure under section 338 and (if the disclosure is made before he does the act mentioned in subsection (1)) he has the appropriate consent;

(b)   he intended to make such a disclosure but had a reasonable excuse for not doing so;

(c)   the act he does is done in carrying out a function he has relating to the enforcement of any provision of this Act or of any other enactment relating to criminal conduct or benefit from criminal conduct.

(2A)   Nor does a person commit an offence under subsection (1) if—

(a)   he knows, or believes on reasonable grounds, that the relevant criminal conduct occurred in a particular country or territory outside the United Kingdom, and

(b)   the relevant criminal conduct—

(i)   was not, at the time it occurred, unlawful under the criminal law then applying in that country or territory, and

(ii)   is not of a description prescribed by an order[4] made by the Secretary of State.

(2B)   In subsection (2A) "the relevant criminal conduct" is the criminal conduct by reference to which the property concerned is criminal property.

(2C)   A deposit-taking body that does an act mentioned in paragraph (c) or (d) of subsection (1) does not commit an offence under that subsection if—

(a)   it does the act in operating an account maintained with it, and

(b)   the value of the criminal property concerned is less than the threshold amount determined under section 339A for the act.

(3)   Concealing or disguising criminal property includes concealing or disguising its nature, source, location, disposition, movement or ownership or any rights with respect to it.

[Proceeds of Crime Act 2002, s 327 as amended by the Serious Organised Crime and Police Act 2005, ss 102 and 103.]

---

1.   Part 6 comprises ss 317–326 and Sch 8.

2.   Part 7 comprises ss 327–340 and Sch 9.

3.   Offences under this section are only committed where the property is criminal when it is concealed etc and reliance cannot be placed on s 340, post, that the property was transferred for a criminal purpose (*R v Loizou* (2005) Times, 23 June, CA).

4.   The Proceeds of Crime Act 2002 (Money Laundering: Exceptions to Overseas Conduct Defence) Order 2006, SI 2006/1070 has been made.

3–1862   328. Arrangements.   (1)   A person commits an offence if he enters into or becomes concerned in an arrangement which he knows or suspects[1] facilitates (by whatever means) the acquisition, retention, use or control of criminal property by or on behalf of another person[2].

(2)   But a person does not commit such an offence if—

(a)   he makes an authorised disclosure under section 338 and (if the disclosure is made before he does the act mentioned in subsection (1)) he has the appropriate consent;

(b)   he intended to make such a disclosure but had a reasonable excuse for not doing so;

(*c*) the act he does is done in carrying out a function he has relating to the enforcement of any provision of this Act or of any other enactment relating to criminal conduct or benefit from criminal conduct.

(3) Nor does a person commit an offence under subsection (1) if—

(*a*) he knows, or believes on reasonable grounds, that the relevant criminal conduct occurred in a particular country or territory outside the United Kingdom, and

(*b*) the relevant criminal conduct—

(i) was not, at the time it occurred, unlawful under the criminal law then applying in that country or territory, and

(ii) is not of a description prescribed by an order[3] made by the Secretary of State.

(4) In subsection (3) "the relevant criminal conduct" is the criminal conduct by reference to which the property concerned is criminal property.

(5) A deposit-taking body that does an act mentioned in subsection (1) does not commit an offence under that subsection if—

(*a*) it does the act in operating an account maintained with it, and

(*b*) the arrangement facilitates the acquisition, retention, use or control of criminal property of a value that is less than the threshold amount determined under section 339A for the act.

[Proceeds of Crime Act 2002, s 328 as amended by the Serious Organised Crime and Police Act 2005, ss 102 and 103.]

---

1. For the working of this provision, see *Squirrell Ltd v National Westminster Bank plc* [2005] EWHC 664 (Ch), [2005] 2 All ER 784, [2006] 1 WLR 637. See also *K v National Westminster Bank plc* [2006] EWCA Civ 1039, [2006] 4 All ER 907, [2007] 1 WLR 311 where an injunction to compel the bank to carry out the customer's instructions was refused where the bank had acted in compliance with s 333 following an authorised disclosure.

2. Section 328 of the Proceeds of Crime Act 2002 was not intended to cover or affect the ordinary conduct of litigation by legal professionals, which included any step taken by them in litigation from the issue of proceedings up to its final disposal by judgment; Parliament could not have intended that proceedings or steps taken by lawyers to determine or secure legal rights and remedies for their clients should involve them in "becom(ing) concerned . . ." in the language of the section: *Bowman v Fels* [2005] EWCA Civ 226, [2005] 2 Cr App R 19, [2005] 2 FLR 247.

3. The Proceeds of Crime Act 2002 (Money Laundering: Exceptions to Overseas Conduct Defence) Order 2006, SI 2006/1070 has been made.

3–1863 **329. Acquisition, use and possession.** (1) A person commits an offence if he—

(*a*) acquires criminal property;

(*b*) uses criminal property;

(*c*) has possession of criminal property[1].

(2) But a person does not commit such an offence if—

(*a*) he makes an authorised disclosure under section 338 and (if the disclosure is made before he does the act mentioned in subsection (1)) he has the appropriate consent;

(*b*) he intended to make such a disclosure but had a reasonable excuse for not doing so;

(*c*) he acquired or used or had possession of the property for adequate consideration;

(*d*) the act he does is done in carrying out a function he has relating to the enforcement of any provision of this Act or of any other enactment relating to criminal conduct or benefit from criminal conduct.

(2A) Nor does a person commit an offence under subsection (1) if—

(*a*) he knows, or believes on reasonable grounds, that the relevant criminal conduct occurred in a particular country or territory outside the United Kingdom, and

(*b*) the relevant criminal conduct—

(i) was not, at the time it occurred, unlawful under the criminal law then applying in that country or territory, and

(ii) is not of a description prescribed by an order[2] made by the Secretary of State.

(2B) In subsection (2A) "the relevant criminal conduct" is the criminal conduct by reference to which the property concerned is criminal property.

(2C) A deposit-taking body that does an act mentioned in subsection (1) does not commit an offence under that subsection if—

(*a*) it does the act in operating an account maintained with it, and

(*b*) the value of the criminal property concerned is less than the threshold amount determined under section 339A for the act.

(3) For the purposes of this section—

(*a*) a person acquires property for inadequate consideration if the value of the consideration is significantly less than the value of the property;

(*b*) a person uses or has possession of property for inadequate consideration if the value of the consideration is significantly less than the value of the use or possession;

(*c*) the provision by a person of goods or services which he knows or suspects may help another to carry out criminal conduct is not consideration.

[Proceeds of Crime Act 2002, s 329 as amended by the Serious Organised Crime and Police Act 2005, ss 102 and 103.]

1. "Criminal property" is defined in s 340, post. Failure to declare profits made from trading in legitimate goods to the Inland Revenue or the Department for Work and Pensions cannot convert those profits into "criminal property"; failure to declare such profits or income tax purposes may give rise to an offence, but that does not make the legitimate trading an offence in itself; however, obtaining benefits obtained on the basis of a false declaration or a failure to disclose a change in circumstances may amount to obtaining a pecuniary advantage, namely the benefits: *R v Gabriel* [2006] EWCA Crim 229, [2006] Crim LR 852.

2. The Proceeds of Crime Act 2002 (Money Laundering: Exceptions to Overseas Conduct Defence) Order 2006, SI 2006/1070 has been made.

3–1864   **330. Failure to disclose: regulated sector.**   (1) A person commits an offence if the conditions in subsections (2) to (4) are satisfied.

(2) The first condition is that he—

(a) knows or suspects, or

(b) has reasonable grounds for knowing or suspecting,

that another person is engaged in money laundering.

(3) The second condition is that the information or other matter—

(a) on which his knowledge or suspicion is based, or

(b) which gives reasonable grounds for such knowledge or suspicion,

came to him in the course of a business in the regulated sector.

(3A) The third condition is—

(a) that he can identify the other person mentioned in subsection (2) or the whereabouts of any of the laundered property, or

(b) that he believes, or it is reasonable to expect him to believe, that the information or other matter mentioned in subsection (3) will or may assist in identifying that other person or the whereabouts of any of the laundered property.

(4) The fourth condition is that he does not make the required disclosure to—

(a) a nominated officer, or

(b) a person authorised for the purposes of this Part by the Director General of the Serious Organised Crime Agency,

as soon as is practicable after the information or other matter mentioned in subsection (3) comes to him.

(5) The required disclosure is a disclosure of—

(a) the identity of the other person mentioned in subsection (2), if he knows it,

(b) the whereabouts of the laundered property, so far as he knows it, and

(c) the information or other matter mentioned in subsection (3).

(5A) The laundered property is the property forming the subject-matter of the money laundering that he knows or suspects, or has reasonable grounds for knowing or suspecting, that other person to be engaged in.

(6) But he does not commit an offence under this section if—

(a) he has a reasonable excuse for not making the required disclosure,

(b) he is a professional legal adviser or other relevant professional adviser and—

(i) if he knows either of the things mentioned in subsection (5)(a) and (b), he knows the thing because of information or other matter that came to him in privileged circumstances, or

(ii) the information or other matter mentioned in subsection (3) came to him in privileged circumstances, or

(c) subsection (7) or (7B) applies to him.

(7) This subsection applies to a person if—

(a) he does not know or suspect that another person is engaged in money laundering, and

(b) he has not been provided by his employer with such training as is specified by the Secretary of State by order[1] for the purposes of this section.

(7A) Nor does a person commit an offence under this section if—

(a) he knows, or believes on reasonable grounds, that the money laundering is occurring in a particular country or territory outside the United Kingdom, and

(b) the money laundering—

(i) is not unlawful under the criminal law applying in that country or territory, and

(ii) is not of a description prescribed in an order made by the Secretary of State.

(7B) This subsection applies to a person if—

(a) he is employed by, or is in partnership with, a professional legal adviser or a relevant professional adviser to provide the adviser with assistance or support,

(b) the information or other matter mentioned in subsection (3) comes to the person in connection with the provision of such assistance or support, and

(c) the information or other matter came to the adviser in privileged circumstances.

(8) In deciding whether a person committed an offence under this section the court must consider whether he followed any relevant guidance which was at the time concerned—

(a) issued by a supervisory authority or any other appropriate body,
(b) approved by the Treasury, and
(c) published in a manner it approved as appropriate in its opinion to bring the guidance to the attention of persons likely to be affected by it.

(9) A disclosure to a nominated officer is a disclosure which—

(a) is made to a person nominated by the alleged offender's employer to receive disclosures under this section, and
(b) is made in the course of the alleged offender's employment.

(9A) But a disclosure which satisfies paragraphs (a) and (b) of subsection (9) is not to be taken as a disclosure to a nominated officer if the person making the disclosure—

(a) is a professional legal adviser or other relevant professional adviser,
(b) makes it for the purpose of obtaining advice about making a disclosure under this section, and
(c) does not intend it to be a disclosure under this section.

(10) Information or other matter comes to a professional legal adviser or other relevant professional adviser in privileged circumstances if it is communicated or given to him—

(a) by (or by a representative of) a client of his in connection with the giving by the adviser of legal advice to the client,
(b) by (or by a representative of) a person seeking legal advice from the adviser, or
(c) by a person in connection with legal proceedings or contemplated legal proceedings.

(11) But subsection (10) does not apply to information or other matter which is communicated or given with the intention of furthering a criminal purpose.

(12) Schedule 9 has effect for the purpose of determining what is—

(a) a business in the regulated sector;
(b) a supervisory authority.

(13) An appropriate body is any body which regulates or is representative of any trade, profession, business or employment carried on by the alleged offender.

(14) A relevant professional adviser is an accountant, auditor or tax adviser who is a member of a professional body which is established for accountants, auditors or tax advisers (as the case may be) and which makes provision for—

(a) testing the competence of those seeking admission to membership of such a body as a condition for such admission; and
(b) imposing and maintaining professional and ethical standards for its members, as well as imposing sanctions for non-compliance with those standards.

[Proceeds of Crime Act 2002, s 330 as amended by the Serious Organised Crime and Police Act 2005, ss 102, 104–106 and SI 2006/308.]

---

1. See the Proceeds of Crime Act 2002 (Failure to Disclose Money Laundering: Specified Training) Order 2003, SI 2003/171 amended by SI 2003/3075.

3–1865   331. Failure to disclose: nominated officers in the regulated sector. (1) A person nominated to receive disclosures under section 330 commits an offence if the conditions in subsections (2) to (4) are satisfied.

(2) The first condition is that he—

(a) knows or suspects, or
(b) has reasonable grounds for knowing or suspecting,

that another person is engaged in money laundering.

(3) The second condition is that the information or other matter—

(a) on which his knowledge or suspicion is based, or
(b) which gives reasonable grounds for such knowledge or suspicion,

came to him in consequence of a disclosure made under section 330.

(3A) The third condition is—

(a) that he knows the identity of the other person mentioned in subsection (2), or the whereabouts of any of the laundered property, in consequence of a disclosure made under section 330,
(b) that that other person, or the whereabouts of any of the laundered property, can be identified from the information or other matter mentioned in subsection (3), or
(c) that he believes, or it is reasonable to expect him to believe, that the information or other matter will or may assist in identifying that other person or the whereabouts of any of the laundered property.

(4) The fourth condition is that he does not make the required disclosure to a person authorised for the purposes of this Part by the Director General of the Serious Organised Crime Agency as soon as is practicable after the information or other matter mentioned in subsection (3) comes to him.

(5) The required disclosure is a disclosure of—

(a) the identity of the other person mentioned in subsection (2), if disclosed to him under section 330,

(b) the whereabouts of the laundered property, so far as disclosed to him under section 330, and

(c) the information or other matter mentioned in subsection (3).

(5A) The laundered property is the property forming the subject-matter of the money laundering that he knows or suspects, or has reasonable grounds for knowing or suspecting, that other person to be engaged in.

(6) But he does not commit an offence under this section if he has a reasonable excuse for not making the required disclosure.*

(6A) Nor does a person commit an offence under this section if—

(a) he knows, or believes on reasonable grounds, that the money laundering is occurring in a particular country or territory outside the United Kingdom, and

(b) the money laundering—

  (i) is not unlawful under the criminal law applying in that country or territory, and

  (ii) is not of a description prescribed in an order made by the Secretary of State.

(7) In deciding whether a person committed an offence under this section the court must consider whether he followed any relevant guidance which was at the time concerned—

(a) issued by a supervisory authority or any other appropriate body,

(b) approved by the Treasury, and

(c) published in a manner it approved as appropriate in its opinion to bring the guidance to the attention of persons likely to be affected by it.

(8) Schedule 9 has effect for the purpose of determining what is a supervisory authority.

(9) An appropriate body is a body which regulates or is representative of a trade, profession, business or employment.

[Proceeds of Crime Act 2002, s 331 as amended by the Serious Organised Crime and Police Act 2005, ss 102 and 104.]

---

*Subsection (6A) inserted by the Serious Organised Crime and Police Act 2005, s 102 from a date to be appointed.

3–1866 332. Failure to disclose: other nominated officers. (1) A person nominated to receive disclosures under section 337 or 338 commits an offence if the conditions in subsections (2) to (4) are satisfied.

(2) The first condition is that he knows or suspects that another person is engaged in money laundering.

(3) The second condition is that the information or other matter on which his knowledge or suspicion is based came to him in consequence of a disclosure made under the applicable section.

(3A) The third condition is—

(a) that he knows the identity of the other person mentioned in subsection (2), or the whereabouts of any of the laundered property, in consequence of a disclosure made under the applicable section,

(b) that that other person, or the whereabouts of any of the laundered property, can be identified from the information or other matter mentioned in subsection (3), or

(c) that he believes, or it is reasonable to expect him to believe, that the information or other matter will or may assist in identifying that other person or the whereabouts of any of the laundered property.

(4) The fourth condition is that he does not make the required disclosure to a person authorised for the purposes of this Part by the Director General of the Serious Organised Crime Agency as soon as is practicable after the information or other matter mentioned in subsection (3) comes to him.

(5) The required disclosure is a disclosure of—

(a) the identity of the other person mentioned in subsection (2), if disclosed to him under the applicable section,

(b) the whereabouts of the laundered property, so far as disclosed to him under the applicable section, and

(c) the information or other matter mentioned in subsection (3).

(5A) The laundered property is the property forming the subject-matter of the money laundering that he knows or suspects that other person to be engaged in.

(5B) The applicable section is section 337 or, as the case may be, section 338.

(6) But he does not commit an offence under this section if he has a reasonable excuse for not making the required disclosure.

(7) Nor does a person commit an offence under this section if—

(a) he knows, or believes on reasonable grounds, that the money laundering is occurring in a particular country or territory outside the United Kingdom, and

(b) the money laundering—

  (i) is not unlawful under the criminal law applying in that country or territory, and

  (ii) is not of a description prescribed in an order made by the Secretary of State.

[Proceeds of Crime Act 2002, s 332 as amended by the Serious Organised Crime and Police Act 2005, s 102.]

3–1867 **333. Tipping off.** (1) A person commits an offence if—

(a) he knows or suspects that a disclosure falling within section 337 or 338 has been made, and

(b) he makes a disclosure which is likely to prejudice any investigation which might be conducted following the disclosure referred to in paragraph (a).

(2) But a person does not commit an offence under subsection (1) if—

(a) he did not know or suspect that the disclosure was likely to be prejudicial as mentioned in subsection (1);

(b) the disclosure is made in carrying out a function he has relating to the enforcement of any provision of this Act or of any other enactment relating to criminal conduct or benefit from criminal conduct;

(c) he is a professional legal adviser and the disclosure falls within subsection (3).

(3) A disclosure falls within this subsection if it is a disclosure—

(a) to (or to a representative of) a client of the professional legal adviser in connection with the giving by the adviser of legal advice to the client, or

(b) to any person in connection with legal proceedings or contemplated legal proceedings.

(4) But a disclosure does not fall within subsection (3) if it is made with the intention of furthering a criminal purpose.
[Proceeds of Crime Act 2002, s 333.]

3–1868 **334. Penalties.** (1) A person guilty of an offence under section 327, 328 or 329 is liable—

(a) on summary conviction, to imprisonment for a term not exceeding six months or to a fine not exceeding the statutory maximum or to both, or

(b) on conviction on indictment, to imprisonment for a term not exceeding 14 years or to a fine or to both.

(2) A person guilty of an offence under section 330, 331, 332 or 333 is liable—

(a) on summary conviction, to imprisonment for a term not exceeding six months or to a fine not exceeding the statutory maximum or to both, or

(b) on conviction on indictment, to imprisonment for a term not exceeding five years or to a fine or to both.

(3) A person guilty of an offence under section 339(1A) is liable on summary conviction to a fine not exceeding level 5 on the standard scale.
[Proceeds of Crime Act 2002, s 334 as amended by the Serious Organised Crime and Police Act 2005, s 105.]

Consent

3–1869 **335. Appropriate consent.** (1) The appropriate consent is—

(a) the consent of a nominated officer to do a prohibited act if an authorised disclosure is made to the nominated officer;

(b) the consent of a constable to do a prohibited act if an authorised disclosure is made to a constable;

(c) the consent of a customs officer to do a prohibited act if an authorised disclosure is made to a customs officer.

(2) A person must be treated as having the appropriate consent if—

(a) he makes an authorised disclosure to a constable or a customs officer, and

(b) the condition in subsection (3) or the condition in subsection (4) is satisfied.

(3) The condition is that before the end of the notice period he does not receive notice from a constable or customs officer that consent to the doing of the act is refused.

(4) The condition is that—

(a) before the end of the notice period he receives notice from a constable or customs officer that consent to the doing of the act is refused, and

(b) the moratorium period has expired.

(5) The notice period is the period of seven working days starting with the first working day after the person makes the disclosure.

(6) The moratorium period is the period of 31 days starting with the day on which the person receives notice that consent to the doing of the act is refused.

(7) A working day is a day other than a Saturday, a Sunday, Christmas Day, Good Friday or a day which is a bank holiday under the Banking and Financial Dealings Act 1971 (c 80) in the part of the United Kingdom in which the person is when he makes the disclosure.

(8) References to a prohibited act are to an act mentioned in section 327(1), 328(1) or 329(1) (as the case may be).

(9) A nominated officer is a person nominated to receive disclosures under section 338.

(10) Subsections (1) to (4) apply for the purposes of this Part.
[Proceeds of Crime Act 2002, s 335.]

3–1870   336. Nominated officer: consent.   (1) A nominated officer must not give the appropriate consent to the doing of a prohibited act unless the condition in subsection (2), the condition in subsection (3) or the condition in subsection (4) is satisfied.

(2) The condition is that—

(a) he makes a disclosure that property is criminal property to a person authorised for the purposes of this Part by the Director General of the Serious Organised Crime Agency , and

(b) such a person gives consent to the doing of the act.*

(3) The condition is that—

(a) he makes a disclosure that property is criminal property to a person authorised for the purposes of this Part by the Director General of the Serious Organised Crime Agency, and

(b) before the end of the notice period he does not receive notice from such a person that consent to the doing of the act is refused.*

(4) The condition is that—

(a) he makes a disclosure that property is criminal property to a person authorised for the purposes of this Part by the Director General of the Serious Organised Crime Agency,

(b) before the end of the notice period he receives notice from such a person that consent to the doing of the act is refused, and

(c) the moratorium period has expired.

(5) A person who is a nominated officer commits an offence if—

(a) he gives consent to a prohibited act in circumstances where none of the conditions in subsections (2), (3) and (4) is satisfied, and

(b) he knows or suspects that the act is a prohibited act.

(6) A person guilty of such an offence is liable—

(a) on summary conviction, to imprisonment for a term not exceeding six months or to a fine not exceeding the statutory maximum or to both, or

(b) on conviction on indictment, to imprisonment for a term not exceeding five years or to a fine or to both.

(7) The notice period is the period of seven working days starting with the first working day after the nominated officer makes the disclosure.

(8) The moratorium period is the period of 31 days starting with the day on which the nominated officer is given notice that consent to the doing of the act is refused.

(9) A working day is a day other than a Saturday, a Sunday, Christmas Day, Good Friday or a day which is a bank holiday under the Banking and Financial Dealings Act 1971 (c 80) in the part of the United Kingdom in which the nominated officer is when he gives the appropriate consent.

(10) References to a prohibited act are to an act mentioned in section 327(1), 328(1) or 329(1) (as the case may be).

(11) A nominated officer is a person nominated to receive disclosures under section 338.

[Proceeds of Crime Act 2002, s 336 as amended by the Serious Organised Crime and Police Act 2005, Sch 4.]

Disclosures

3–1871   337. Protected disclosures.   (1) A disclosure which satisfies the following three conditions is not to be taken to breach any restriction on the disclosure of information (however imposed).

(2) The first condition is that the information or other matter disclosed came to the person making the disclosure (the discloser) in the course of his trade, profession, business or employment.

(3) The second condition is that the information or other matter—

(a) causes the discloser to know or suspect, or

(b) gives him reasonable grounds for knowing or suspecting,

that another person is engaged in money laundering.

(4) The third condition is that the disclosure is made to a constable, a customs officer or a nominated officer as soon as is practicable after the information or other matter comes to the discloser.

(4A) Where a disclosure consists of a disclosure protected under subsection (1) and a disclosure of either or both of—

(a) the identity of the other person mentioned in subsection (3), and

(b) the whereabouts of property forming the subject-matter of the money laundering that the discloser knows or suspects, or has reasonable grounds for knowing or suspecting, that other person to be engaged in,

the disclosure of the thing mentioned in paragraph (a) or (b) (as well as the disclosure protected under subsection (1)) is not to be taken to breach any restriction on the disclosure of information (however imposed).

(5) A disclosure to a nominated officer is a disclosure which—

(a) is made to a person nominated by the discloser's employer to receive disclosures under section 330 or this section, and

(b) is made in the course of the discloser's employment.

[Proceeds of Crime Act 2002, s 337 as amended by the Serious Organised Crime and Police Act 2005, ss 104 and 105.]

3–1872 338. Authorised disclosures. (1) For the purposes of this Part a disclosure is authorised if—

    (a) it is a disclosure to a constable, a customs officer or a nominated officer by the alleged offender that property is criminal property,

    (b) *repealed,* and

    (c) the first, second or third condition set out below is satisfied.

(2) The first condition is that the disclosure is made before the alleged offender does the prohibited act.

(2A) The second condition is that—

    (a) the disclosure is made while the alleged offender is doing the prohibited act,

    (b) he began to do the act at a time when, because he did not then know or suspect that the property constituted or represented a person's benefit from criminal conduct, the act was not a prohibited act, and

    (c) the disclosure is made on his own initiative and as soon as is practicable after he first knows or suspects that the property constitutes or represents a person's benefit from criminal conduct.

(3) The third condition is that—

    (a) the disclosure is made after the alleged offender does the prohibited act,

    (b) there is a good reason for his failure to make the disclosure before he did the act, and

    (c) the disclosure is made on his own initiative and as soon as it is practicable for him to make it.

(4) An authorised disclosure is not to be taken to breach any restriction on the disclosure of information (however imposed).

(5) A disclosure to a nominated officer is a disclosure which—

    (a) is made to a person nominated by the alleged offender's employer to receive authorised disclosures, and

    (b) is made in the course of the alleged offender's employment.

(6) References to the prohibited act are to an act mentioned in section 327(1), 328(1) or 329(1) (as the case may be).

[Proceeds of Crime Act 2002, s 338 as amended by the Serious Organised Crime and Police Act 2005, ss 105 and 106.]

3–1873 339. Form and manner of disclosures. (1) The Secretary of State may by order prescribe the form and manner in which a disclosure under section 330, 331, 332 or 338 must be made.

(1A) A person commits an offence if he makes a disclosure under section 330, 331, 332 or 338 otherwise than in the form prescribed under subsection (1) or otherwise than in the manner so prescribed.

(1B) But a person does not commit an offence under subsection (1A) if he has a reasonable excuse for making the disclosure otherwise than in the form prescribed under subsection (1) or (as the case may be) otherwise than in the manner so prescribed.

(2) The power under subsection (1) to prescribe the form in which a disclosure must be made includes power to provide for the form to include a request to a person making a disclosure that the person provide information specified or described in the form if he has not provided it in making the disclosure.

(3) Where under subsection (2) a request is included in a form prescribed under subsection (1), the form must—

    (a) state that there is no obligation to comply with the request, and

    (b) explain the protection conferred by subsection (4) on a person who complies with the request.

(4) A disclosure made in pursuance of a request under subsection (2) is not to be taken to breach any restriction on the disclosure of information (however imposed).

    (5) *Repealed.*

    (6) *Repealed.*

(7) Subsection (2) does not apply to a disclosure made to a nominated officer.

[Proceeds of Crime Act 2002, s 339 as amended by the Serious Organised Crime and Police Act 2005, s 105 and Sch 17.]

Threshold amounts

3–1873A 339A. Threshold amounts. (1) This section applies for the purposes of sections 327(2C), 328(5) and 329(2C).

(2) The threshold amount for acts done by a deposit-taking body in operating an account is £250 unless a higher amount is specified under the following provisions of this section (in which event it is that higher amount).

(3) An officer of Revenue and Customs, or a constable, may specify the threshold amount for acts done by a deposit-taking body in operating an account—

    (a) when he gives consent, or gives notice refusing consent, to the deposit-taking body's doing of an act mentioned in section 327(1), 328(1) or 329(1) in opening, or operating, the account or a related account, or

    (b) on a request from the deposit-taking body.

(4) Where the threshold amount for acts done in operating an account is specified under subsection (3) or this subsection, an officer of Revenue and Customs, or a constable, may vary the amount (whether on a request from the deposit-taking body or otherwise) by specifying a different amount.

(5) Different threshold amounts may be specified under subsections (3) and (4) for different acts done in operating the same account.

(6) The amount specified under subsection (3) or (4) as the threshold amount for acts done in operating an account must, when specified, not be less than the amount specified in subsection (2).

(7) The Secretary of State may by order vary the amount for the time being specified in subsection (2).

(8) For the purposes of this section, an account is related to another if each is maintained with the same deposit-taking body and there is a person who, in relation to each account, is the person or one of the persons entitled to instruct the body as respects the operation of the account.
[Proceeds of Crime Act 2002, s 339A as inserted by the Serious Organised Crime and Police Act 2005, s 103.]

Interpretation

3–1874　340. Interpretation.　(1) This section applies for the purposes of this Part.
(2) Criminal conduct is conduct which—

(a)　constitutes an offence in any part of the United Kingdom, or

(b)　would constitute an offence in any part of the United Kingdom if it occurred there.

(3) Property is criminal property[1] if—

(a)　it constitutes a person's benefit from criminal conduct or it represents such a benefit (in whole or part and whether directly or indirectly), and

(b)　the alleged offender knows or suspects that it constitutes or represents such a benefit.

(4) It is immaterial—

(a)　who carried out the conduct;

(b)　who benefited from it;

(c)　whether the conduct occurred before or after the passing of this Act.

(5) A person benefits from conduct if he obtains property as a result of or in connection with the conduct.

(6) If a person obtains a pecuniary advantage as a result of or in connection with conduct, he is to be taken to obtain as a result of or in connection with the conduct a sum of money equal to the value of the pecuniary advantage.

(7) References to property or a pecuniary advantage obtained in connection with conduct include references to property or a pecuniary advantage obtained in both that connection and some other.

(8) If a person benefits from conduct his benefit is the property obtained as a result of or in connection with the conduct.

(9) Property is all property wherever situated and includes—

(a)　money;

(b)　all forms of property, real or personal, heritable or moveable;

(c)　things in action and other intangible or incorporeal property.

(10) The following rules apply in relation to property—

(a)　property is obtained by a person if he obtains an interest in it;

(b)　references to an interest, in relation to land in England and Wales or Northern Ireland, are to any legal estate or equitable interest or power;

(c)　references to an interest, in relation to land in Scotland, are to any estate, interest, servitude or other heritable right in or over land, including a heritable security;

(d)　references to an interest, in relation to property other than land, include references to a right (including a right to possession).

(11) Money laundering is an act which—

(a)　constitutes an offence under section 327, 328 or 329,

(b)　constitutes an attempt, conspiracy or incitement to commit an offence specified in paragraph (a),

(c)　constitutes aiding, abetting, counselling or procuring the commission of an offence specified in paragraph (a), or

(d)　would constitute an offence specified in paragraph (a), (b) or (c) if done in the United Kingdom.

(12) For the purposes of a disclosure to a nominated officer—

(a)　references to a person's employer include any body, association or organisation (including a voluntary organisation) in connection with whose activities the person exercises a function (whether or not for gain or reward), and

(b)　references to employment must be construed accordingly.

(13) References to a constable include references to a person authorised for the purposes of this Part by the Director General of the Serious Organised Crime Agency.

(14) "Deposit-taking body" means—

(a)　a business which engages in the activity of accepting deposits, or

PART III.—*Sentencing* 1912

(*b*) the National Savings Bank.
[Proceeds of Crime Act 2002, s 340 as amended by the Serious Organised Crime and Police Act 2005, s 103 and Sch 4.]

---

1. Failure to declare profits made from trading in legitimate goods to the Inland Revenue or the Department for Work and Pensions cannot convert those profits into "criminal property"; failure to declare such profits or income tax purposes may give rise to an offence, but that does not make the legitimate trading an offence in itself; however, obtaining state benefits on the basis of a false declaration or a failure to disclose a change in circumstances may amount to obtaining a pecuniary advantage, namely the benefits: *R v Gabriel* [2006] EWCA Crim 229, [2006] Crim LR 852.

PART 8
INVESTIGATIONS[1]

CHAPTER 1
INTRODUCTION[2]

3–1875 341. Investigations. (1) For the purposes of this Part a confiscation investigation is an investigation into—

(*a*) whether a person has benefited from his criminal conduct, or
(*b*) the extent or whereabouts of his benefit from his criminal conduct.

(2) For the purposes of this Part a civil recovery investigation is an investigation into—

(*a*) whether property is recoverable property or associated property,
(*b*) who holds the property, or
(*c*) its extent or whereabouts.

(3) But an investigation is not a civil recovery investigation if—

(*a*) proceedings for a recovery order have been started in respect of the property in question,
(*b*) an interim receiving order applies to the property in question,
(*c*) an interim administration order applies to the property in question, or
(*d*) the property in question is detained under section 295.

(4) For the purposes of this Part a money laundering investigation is an investigation into whether a person has committed a money laundering offence.
[Proceeds of Crime Act 2002, s 341.]

---

1. Part 8 comprises ss 341–416.
2. Chapter 1 comprises ss 341–342.

3–1876 342. Offences of prejudicing investigation. (1) This section applies if a person knows or suspects that an appropriate officer or (in Scotland) a proper person is acting (or proposing to act) in connection with a confiscation investigation, a civil recovery investigation or a money laundering investigation which is being or is about to be conducted.

(2) The person commits an offence if—

(*a*) he makes a disclosure which is likely to prejudice the investigation, or
(*b*) he falsifies, conceals, destroys or otherwise disposes of, or causes or permits the falsification, concealment, destruction or disposal of, documents which are relevant to the investigation.

(3) A person does not commit an offence under subsection (2)(*a*) if—

(*a*) he does not know or suspect that the disclosure is likely to prejudice the investigation,
(*b*) the disclosure is made in the exercise of a function under this Act or any other enactment relating to criminal conduct or benefit from criminal conduct or in compliance with a requirement imposed under or by virtue of this Act, or
(*c*) he is a professional legal adviser and the disclosure falls within subsection (4).

(4) A disclosure falls within this subsection if it is a disclosure—

(*a*) to (or to a representative of) a client of the professional legal adviser in connection with the giving by the adviser of legal advice to the client, or
(*b*) to any person in connection with legal proceedings or contemplated legal proceedings.

(5) But a disclosure does not fall within subsection (4) if it is made with the intention of furthering a criminal purpose.

(6) A person does not commit an offence under subsection (2)(*b*) if—

(*a*) he does not know or suspect that the documents are relevant to the investigation, or
(*b*) he does not intend to conceal any facts disclosed by the documents from any appropriate officer or (in Scotland) proper person carrying out the investigation.

(7) A person guilty of an offence under subsection (2) is liable[1]—

(*a*) on summary conviction, to imprisonment for a term not exceeding six months or to a fine not exceeding the statutory maximum or to both, or
(*b*) on conviction on indictment, to imprisonment for a term not exceeding five years or to a fine or to both.

(8) For the purposes of this section—

(*a*) "appropriate officer" must be construed in accordance with section 378;

(*b*) "proper person" must be construed in accordance with section 412.
[Proceeds of Crime Act 2002, s 342.]

---

1. For procedure in respect of this offence, which is triable either way, see the Magistrates' Courts Act 1980, ss 17A–21, in PART I: MAGISTRATES' COURTS, PROCEDURE, ante.

CHAPTER 2
ENGLAND AND WALES AND NORTHERN IRELAND[1]
Disclosure orders

3–1877   343. Judges. (1) In this Chapter references to a judge in relation to an application must be construed in accordance with this section.

(2) In relation to an application for the purposes of a confiscation investigation or a money laundering investigation a judge is—

(*a*) in England and Wales, a judge entitled to exercise the jurisdiction of the Crown Court;
(*b*) in Northern Ireland, a Crown Court judge.

(3) In relation to an application for the purposes of a civil recovery investigation a judge is a judge of the High Court.
[Proceeds of Crime Act 2002, s 343.]

---

1. Chapter 2 comprises ss 343–379.

Judges and courts

3–1878   344. Courts. In this Chapter references to the court are to—

(*a*) the Crown Court, in relation to an order for the purposes of a confiscation investigation or a money laundering investigation;
(*b*) the High Court, in relation to an order for the purposes of a civil recovery investigation.
[Proceeds of Crime Act 2002, s 344.]

Production orders

3–1879   345. Production orders. (1) A judge may, on an application made to him by an appropriate officer, make a production order if he is satisfied that each of the requirements for the making of the order is fulfilled.

(2) The application for a production order must state that—

(*a*) a person specified in the application is subject to a confiscation investigation or a money laundering investigation, or
(*b*) property specified in the application is subject to a civil recovery investigation.

(3) The application must also state that—

(*a*) the order is sought for the purposes of the investigation;
(*b*) the order is sought in relation to material, or material of a description, specified in the application;
(*c*) a person specified in the application appears to be in possession or control of the material.

(4) A production order is an order either—

(*a*) requiring the person the application for the order specifies as appearing to be in possession or control of material to produce it to an appropriate officer for him to take away, or
(*b*) requiring that person to give an appropriate officer access to the material,

within the period stated in the order.

(5) The period stated in a production order must be a period of seven days beginning with the day on which the order is made, unless it appears to the judge by whom the order is made that a longer or shorter period would be appropriate in the particular circumstances.
[Proceeds of Crime Act 2002, s 345.]

3–1880   346. Requirements for making of production order. (1) These are the requirements for the making of a production order.

(2) There must be reasonable grounds for suspecting that—

(*a*) in the case of a confiscation investigation, the person the application for the order specifies as being subject to the investigation has benefited from his criminal conduct;
(*b*) in the case of a civil recovery investigation, the property the application for the order specifies as being subject to the investigation is recoverable property or associated property;
(*c*) in the case of a money laundering investigation, the person the application for the order specifies as being subject to the investigation has committed a money laundering offence.

(3) There must be reasonable grounds for believing that the person the application specifies as appearing to be in possession or control of the material so specified is in possession or control of it.

(4) There must be reasonable grounds for believing that the material is likely to be of substantial value (whether or not by itself) to the investigation for the purposes of which the order is sought.

(5) There must be reasonable grounds for believing that it is in the public interest for the material to be produced or for access to it to be given, having regard to—

(*a*) the benefit likely to accrue to the investigation if the material is obtained;

(*b*) the circumstances under which the person the application specifies as appearing to be in possession or control of the material holds it.

[Proceeds of Crime Act 2002, s 346.]

3–1881   347. Order to grant entry.   (1) This section applies if a judge makes a production order requiring a person to give an appropriate officer access to material on any premises.

(2) The judge may, on an application made to him by an appropriate officer and specifying the premises, make an order to grant entry in relation to the premises.

(3) An order to grant entry is an order requiring any person who appears to an appropriate officer to be entitled to grant entry to the premises to allow him to enter the premises to obtain access to the material.

[Proceeds of Crime Act 2002, s 347.]

3–1882   348. Further provisions.   (1) A production order does not require a person to produce, or give access to, privileged material.

(2) Privileged material is any material which the person would be entitled to refuse to produce on grounds of legal professional privilege in proceedings in the High Court.

(3) A production order does not require a person to produce, or give access to, excluded material.

(4) A production order has effect in spite of any restriction on the disclosure of information (however imposed).

(5) An appropriate officer may take copies of any material which is produced, or to which access is given, in compliance with a production order.

(6) Material produced in compliance with a production order may be retained for so long as it is necessary to retain it (as opposed to copies of it) in connection with the investigation for the purposes of which the order was made.

(7) But if an appropriate officer has reasonable grounds for believing that—

(*a*) the material may need to be produced for the purposes of any legal proceedings, and

(*b*) it might otherwise be unavailable for those purposes,

it may be retained until the proceedings are concluded.

[Proceeds of Crime Act 2002, s 348.]

3–1883   349. Computer information.   (1) This section applies if any of the material specified in an application for a production order consists of information contained in a computer.

(2) If the order is an order requiring a person to produce the material to an appropriate officer for him to take away, it has effect as an order to produce the material in a form in which it can be taken away by him and in which it is visible and legible.

(3) If the order is an order requiring a person to give an appropriate officer access to the material, it has effect as an order to give him access to the material in a form in which it is visible and legible.

[Proceeds of Crime Act 2002, s 349.]

3–1884   350. Government departments.   (1) A production order may be made in relation to material in the possession or control of an authorised government department.

(2) An order so made may require any officer of the department (whether named in the order or not) who may for the time being be in possession or control of the material to comply with it.

(3) An order containing such a requirement must be served as if the proceedings were civil proceedings against the department.

(4) If an order contains such a requirement—

(*a*) the person on whom it is served must take all reasonable steps to bring it to the attention of the officer concerned;

(*b*) any other officer of the department who is in receipt of the order must also take all reasonable steps to bring it to the attention of the officer concerned.

(5) If the order is not brought to the attention of the officer concerned within the period stated in the order (in pursuance of section 345(4)) the person on whom it is served must report the reasons for the failure to—

(*a*) a judge entitled to exercise the jurisdiction of the Crown Court or (in Northern Ireland) a Crown Court judge, in the case of an order made for the purposes of a confiscation investigation or a money laundering investigation;

(*b*) a High Court judge, in the case of an order made for the purposes of a civil recovery investigation.

(6) An authorised government department is a government department, or a Northern Ireland department, which is an authorised department for the purposes of the Crown Proceedings Act 1947 (c 44).

[Proceeds of Crime Act 2002, s 350.]

3–1885   351. Supplementary.   (1) An application for a production order or an order to grant entry may be made ex parte to a judge in chambers.

(2) Rules of court may make provision as to the practice and procedure to be followed in connection with proceedings relating to production orders and orders to grant entry.

(3) An application to discharge or vary a production order or an order to grant entry may be made to the court by—

(a)   the person who applied for the order;

(b)   any person affected by the order.

(4) The court—

(a)   may discharge the order;

(b)   may vary the order.

(5) If an accredited financial investigator, a constable or a customs officer applies for a production order or an order to grant entry, an application to discharge or vary the order need not be by the same accredited financial investigator, constable or customs officer.

(6) References to a person who applied for a production order or an order to grant entry must be construed accordingly.

(7) Production orders and orders to grant entry have effect as if they were orders of the court.

(8) Subsections (2) to (7) do not apply to orders made in England and Wales for the purposes of a civil recovery investigation.

[Proceeds of Crime Act 2002, s 351.]

Search and seizure warrants

3–1886   352. Search and seizure warrants.   (1) A judge may, on an application made to him by an appropriate officer, issue a search and seizure warrant if he is satisfied that either of the requirements for the issuing of the warrant is fulfilled.

(2) The application for a search and seizure warrant must state that—

(a)   a person specified in the application is subject to a confiscation investigation or a money laundering investigation, or

(b)   property specified in the application is subject to a civil recovery investigation.

(3) The application must also state—

(a)   that the warrant is sought for the purposes of the investigation;

(b)   that the warrant is sought in relation to the premises specified in the application;

(c)   that the warrant is sought in relation to material specified in the application, or that there are reasonable grounds for believing that there is material falling within section 353(6), (7) or (8) on the premises.

(4) A search and seizure warrant is a warrant authorising an appropriate person—

(a)   to enter and search the premises specified in the application for the warrant, and

(b)   to seize and retain any material found there which is likely to be of substantial value (whether or not by itself) to the investigation for the purposes of which the application is made.

(5) An appropriate person is—

(a)   a constable or a customs officer, if the warrant is sought for the purposes of a confiscation investigation or a money laundering investigation;

(b)   a named member of the staff of the Agency, if the warrant is sought for the purposes of a civil recovery investigation.

(6) The requirements for the issue of a search and seizure warrant are—

(a)   that a production order made in relation to material has not been complied with and there are reasonable grounds for believing that the material is on the premises specified in the application for the warrant, or

(b)   that section 353 is satisfied in relation to the warrant.

[Proceeds of Crime Act 2002, s 352.]

3–1887   353. Requirements where production order not available.   (1) This section is satisfied in relation to a search and seizure warrant if—

(a)   subsection (2) applies, and

(b)   either the first or the second set of conditions is complied with.

(2) This subsection applies if there are reasonable grounds for suspecting that—

(a)   in the case of a confiscation investigation, the person specified in the application for the warrant has benefited from his criminal conduct;

(b)   in the case of a civil recovery investigation, the property specified in the application for the warrant is recoverable property or associated property;

(c)   in the case of a money laundering investigation, the person specified in the application for the warrant has committed a money laundering offence.

(3) The first set of conditions is that there are reasonable grounds for believing that—

(*a*)   any material on the premises specified in the application for the warrant is likely to be of substantial value (whether or not by itself) to the investigation for the purposes of which the warrant is sought,

(*b*)   it is in the public interest for the material to be obtained, having regard to the benefit likely to accrue to the investigation if the material is obtained, and

(*c*)   it would not be appropriate to make a production order for any one or more of the reasons in subsection (4).

(4)   The reasons are—

(*a*)   that it is not practicable to communicate with any person against whom the production order could be made;

(*b*)   that it is not practicable to communicate with any person who would be required to comply with an order to grant entry to the premises;

(*c*)   that the investigation might be seriously prejudiced unless an appropriate person is able to secure immediate access to the material.

(5)   The second set of conditions is that—

(*a*)   there are reasonable grounds for believing that there is material on the premises specified in the application for the warrant and that the material falls within subsection (6), (7) or (8),

(*b*)   there are reasonable grounds for believing that it is in the public interest for the material to be obtained, having regard to the benefit likely to accrue to the investigation if the material is obtained, and

(*c*)   any one or more of the requirements in subsection (9) is met.

(6)   In the case of a confiscation investigation, material falls within this subsection if it cannot be identified at the time of the application but it—

(*a*)   relates to the person specified in the application, the question whether he has benefited from his criminal conduct or any question as to the extent or whereabouts of his benefit from his criminal conduct, and

(*b*)   is likely to be of substantial value (whether or not by itself) to the investigation for the purposes of which the warrant is sought.

(7)   In the case of a civil recovery investigation, material falls within this subsection if it cannot be identified at the time of the application but it—

(*a*)   relates to the property specified in the application, the question whether it is recoverable property or associated property, the question as to who holds any such property, any question as to whether the person who appears to hold any such property holds other property which is recoverable property, or any question as to the extent or whereabouts of any property mentioned in this paragraph, and

(*b*)   is likely to be of substantial value (whether or not by itself) to the investigation for the purposes of which the warrant is sought.

(8)   In the case of a money laundering investigation, material falls within this subsection if it cannot be identified at the time of the application but it—

(*a*)   relates to the person specified in the application or the question whether he has committed a money laundering offence, and

(*b*)   is likely to be of substantial value (whether or not by itself) to the investigation for the purposes of which the warrant is sought.

(9)   The requirements are—

(*a*)   that it is not practicable to communicate with any person entitled to grant entry to the premises;

(*b*)   that entry to the premises will not be granted unless a warrant is produced;

(*c*)   that the investigation might be seriously prejudiced unless an appropriate person arriving at the premises is able to secure immediate entry to them.

(10)   An appropriate person is—

(*a*)   a constable or a customs officer, if the warrant is sought for the purposes of a confiscation investigation or a money laundering investigation;

(*b*)   a member of the staff of the Agency, if the warrant is sought for the purposes of a civil recovery investigation.

[Proceeds of Crime Act 2002, s 353.]

3–1888   354. Further provisions: general.   (1) A search and seizure warrant does not confer the right to seize privileged material.

(2) Privileged material is any material which a person would be entitled to refuse to produce on grounds of legal professional privilege in proceedings in the High Court.

(3) A search and seizure warrant does not confer the right to seize excluded material.

[Proceeds of Crime Act 2002, s 354.]

3–1889   355. Further provisions: confiscation and money laundering.   (1) This section applies to—

(a) search and seizure warrants sought for the purposes of a confiscation investigation or a money laundering investigation, and

(b) powers of seizure under them.

(2) In relation to such warrants and powers, the Secretary of State may make an order[1] which applies the provisions to which subsections (3) and (4) apply subject to any specified modifications.

(3) This subsection applies to the following provisions of the Police and Criminal Evidence Act 1984 (c 60)—

(a) section 15 (search warrants – safeguards);

(b) section 16 (execution of warrants);

(c) section 21 (access and copying);

(d) section 22 (retention).

(4) This subsection applies to the following provisions of the Police and Criminal Evidence (Northern Ireland) Order 1989 (SI 1989/1341 (NI 12))—

(a) Article 17 (search warrants -safeguards);

(b) Article 18 (execution of warrants);

(c) Article 23 (access and copying);

(d) Article 24 (retention).

[Proceeds of Crime Act 2002, s 355.]

---

1. The Proceeds of Crime Act 2002 (Application of Police and Criminal Evidence Act 1984 and Police and Criminal Evidence (Northern Ireland) Order 1989) Order 2003, SI 2003/174 has been made.

3–1890   356. Further provisions: civil recovery.   (1) This section applies to search and seizure warrants sought for the purposes of civil recovery investigations.

(2) An application for a warrant may be made ex parte to a judge in chambers.

(3) A warrant may be issued subject to conditions.

(4) A warrant continues in force until the end of the period of one month starting with the day on which it is issued.

(5) A warrant authorises the person it names to require any information which is held in a computer and is accessible from the premises specified in the application for the warrant, and which the named person believes relates to any matter relevant to the investigation, to be produced in a form—

(a) in which it can be taken away, and

(b) in which it is visible and legible.

(6) If—

(a) the Director gives written authority for members of staff of the Agency to accompany the person a warrant names when executing it, and

(b) a warrant is issued,

the authorised members have the same powers under it as the person it names.

(7) A warrant may include provision authorising a person who is exercising powers under it to do other things which—

(a) are specified in the warrant, and

(b) need to be done in order to give effect to it.

(8) Copies may be taken of any material seized under a warrant.

(9) Material seized under a warrant may be retained for so long as it is necessary to retain it (as opposed to copies of it) in connection with the investigation for the purposes of which the warrant was issued.

(10) But if the Director has reasonable grounds for believing that—

(a) the material may need to be produced for the purposes of any legal proceedings, and

(b) it might otherwise be unavailable for those purposes,

it may be retained until the proceedings are concluded.

[Proceeds of Crime Act 2002, s 356.]

Disclosure orders

3–1891   357. Disclosure orders.   (1) A judge may, on an application made to him by the Director, make a disclosure order if he is satisfied that each of the requirements for the making of the order is fulfilled.

(2) No application for a disclosure order may be made in relation to a money laundering investigation.

(3) The application for a disclosure order must state that—

(a) a person specified in the application is subject to a confiscation investigation which is being carried out by the Director and the order is sought for the purposes of the investigation, or

(b) property specified in the application is subject to a civil recovery investigation and the order is sought for the purposes of the investigation.

(4) A disclosure order is an order authorising the Director to give to any person the Director

considers has relevant information notice in writing requiring him to do, with respect to any matter relevant to the investigation for the purposes of which the order is sought, any or all of the following—

(a)   answer questions, either at a time specified in the notice or at once, at a place so specified;
(b)   provide information specified in the notice, by a time and in a manner so specified;
(c)   produce documents, or documents of a description, specified in the notice, either at or by a time so specified or at once, and in a manner so specified.

(5) Relevant information is information (whether or not contained in a document) which the Director considers to be relevant to the investigation.
(6) A person is not bound to comply with a requirement imposed by a notice given under a disclosure order unless evidence of authority to give the notice is produced to him.
[Proceeds of Crime Act 2002, s 357.]

3–1892   358. Requirements for making of disclosure order.   (1) These are the requirements for the making of a disclosure order.
(2) There must be reasonable grounds for suspecting that—

(a)   in the case of a confiscation investigation, the person specified in the application for the order has benefited from his criminal conduct;
(b)   in the case of a civil recovery investigation, the property specified in the application for the order is recoverable property or associated property.

(3) There must be reasonable grounds for believing that information which may be provided in compliance with a requirement imposed under the order is likely to be of substantial value (whether or not by itself) to the investigation for the purposes of which the order is sought.
(4) There must be reasonable grounds for believing that it is in the public interest for the information to be provided, having regard to the benefit likely to accrue to the investigation if the information is obtained.
[Proceeds of Crime Act 2002, s 358.]

3–1893   359. Offences.   (1) A person commits an offence if without reasonable excuse he fails to comply with a requirement imposed on him under a disclosure order.
(2) A person guilty of an offence under subsection (1) is liable on summary conviction to—

(a)   imprisonment for a term not exceeding six months,
(b)   a fine not exceeding level 5 on the standard scale, or
(c)   both.

(3) A person commits an offence if, in purported compliance with a requirement imposed on him under a disclosure order, he—

(a)   makes a statement which he knows to be false or misleading in a material particular, or
(b)   recklessly makes a statement which is false or misleading in a material particular.

(4) A person guilty of an offence under subsection (3) is liable[1]—

(a)   on summary conviction, to imprisonment for a term not exceeding six months or to a fine not exceeding the statutory maximum or to both, or
(b)   on conviction on indictment, to imprisonment for a term not exceeding two years or to a fine or to both.
[Proceeds of Crime Act 2002, s 359.]

---

1. For procedure in respect of this offence, which is triable either way, see the Magistrates' Courts Act 1980, ss 17A–21, in PART I: MAGISTRATES' COURTS, PROCEDURE, ante.

3–1894   360. Statements.   (1) A statement made by a person in response to a requirement imposed on him under a disclosure order may not be used in evidence against him in criminal proceedings.
(2) But subsection (1) does not apply—

(a)   in the case of proceedings under Part 2 or 4,
(b)   on a prosecution for an offence under section 359(1) or (3),
(c)   on a prosecution for an offence under section 5 of the Perjury Act 1911 (c 6) or Article 10 of the Perjury (Northern Ireland) Order 1979 (SI 1979/1714 (NI 19)) (false statements), or
(d)   on a prosecution for some other offence where, in giving evidence, the person makes a statement inconsistent with the statement mentioned in subsection (1).

(3) A statement may not be used by virtue of subsection (2)(d) against a person unless—

(a)   evidence relating to it is adduced, or
(b)   a question relating to it is asked,

by him or on his behalf in the proceedings arising out of the prosecution.
[Proceeds of Crime Act 2002, s 360.]

3–1895   361. Further provisions.   (1) A disclosure order does not confer the right to require a person to answer any privileged question, provide any privileged information or produce any privileged document, except that a lawyer may be required to provide the name and address of a client of his.

(2) A privileged question is a question which the person would be entitled to refuse to answer on grounds of legal professional privilege in proceedings in the High Court.

(3) Privileged information is any information which the person would be entitled to refuse to provide on grounds of legal professional privilege in proceedings in the High Court.

(4) Privileged material is any material which the person would be entitled to refuse to produce on grounds of legal professional privilege in proceedings in the High Court.

(5) A disclosure order does not confer the right to require a person to produce excluded material.

(6) A disclosure order has effect in spite of any restriction on the disclosure of information (however imposed).

(7) The Director may take copies of any documents produced in compliance with a requirement to produce them which is imposed under a disclosure order.

(8) Documents so produced may be retained for so long as it is necessary to retain them (as opposed to a copy of them) in connection with the investigation for the purposes of which the order was made.

(9) But if the Director has reasonable grounds for believing that—

(a) the documents may need to be produced for the purposes of any legal proceedings, and
(b) they might otherwise be unavailable for those purposes,

they may be retained until the proceedings are concluded.
[Proceeds of Crime Act 2002, s 361.]

3–1896   362. Supplementary.   (1) An application for a disclosure order may be made ex parte to a judge in chambers.

(2) Rules of court may make provision as to the practice and procedure to be followed in connection with proceedings relating to disclosure orders.

(3) An application to discharge or vary a disclosure order may be made to the court by—

(a) the Director;
(b) any person affected by the order.

(4) The court—

(a) may discharge the order;
(b) may vary the order.

(5) Subsections (2) to (4) do not apply to orders made in England and Wales for the purposes of a civil recovery investigation.
[Proceeds of Crime Act 2002, s 362.]

Customer information orders

3–1897   363. Customer information orders.   (1) A judge may, on an application made to him by an appropriate officer, make a customer information order if he is satisfied that each of the requirements for the making of the order is fulfilled.

(2) The application for a customer information order must state that—

(a) a person specified in the application is subject to a confiscation investigation or a money laundering investigation, or
(b) property specified in the application is subject to a civil recovery investigation and a person specified in the application appears to hold the property.

(3) The application must also state that—

(a) the order is sought for the purposes of the investigation;
(b) the order is sought against the financial institution or financial institutions specified in the application.

(4) An application for a customer information order may specify—

(a) all financial institutions,
(b) a particular description, or particular descriptions, of financial institutions, or
(c) a particular financial institution or particular financial institutions.

(5) A customer information order is an order that a financial institution covered by the application for the order must, on being required to do so by notice in writing given by an appropriate officer, provide any such customer information as it has relating to the person specified in the application.

(6) A financial institution which is required to provide information under a customer information order must provide the information to an appropriate officer in such manner, and at or by such time, as an appropriate officer requires.

(7) If a financial institution on which a requirement is imposed by a notice given under a customer information order requires the production of evidence of authority to give the notice, it is not bound to comply with the requirement unless evidence of the authority has been produced to it.
[Proceeds of Crime Act 2002, s 363.]

3–1898   364. Meaning of customer information.   (1) "Customer information", in relation to a person and a financial institution, is information whether the person holds, or has held, an account or accounts or any safe deposit box at the financial institution (whether solely or jointly with another) and (if so) information as to—

(a) the matters specified in subsection (2) if the person is an individual;
(b) the matters specified in subsection (3) if the person is a company or limited liability partnership or a similar body incorporated or otherwise established outside the United Kingdom.

(2) The matters referred to in subsection (1)(a) are—

(a) the account number or numbers or the number of any safe deposit box;
(b) the person's full name;
(c) his date of birth;
(d) his most recent address and any previous addresses;
(e) in the case of an account or accounts, the date or dates on which he began to hold the account or accounts and, if he has ceased to hold the account or any of the accounts, the date or dates on which he did so;
(ee) in the case of any safe deposit box, the date on which the box was made available to him and if the box has ceased to be available to him the date on which it so ceased;
(f) such evidence of his identity as was obtained by the financial institution under or for the purposes of any legislation relating to money laundering;
(g) the full name, date of birth and most recent address, and any previous addresses, of any person who holds, or has held, an account at the financial institution jointly with him;
(h) the account number or numbers of any other account or accounts held at the financial institution to which he is a signatory and details of the person holding the other account or accounts.

(3) The matters referred to in subsection (1)(b) are—

(a) the account number or numbers or the number of any safe deposit box;
(b) the person's full name;
(c) a description of any business which the person carries on;
(d) the country or territory in which it is incorporated or otherwise established and any number allocated to it under the Companies Act 1985 (c 6) or the Companies (Northern Ireland) Order 1986 (SI 1986/ 1032 (NI 6)) or corresponding legislation of any country or territory outside the United Kingdom;
(e) any number assigned to it for the purposes of value added tax in the United Kingdom;
(f) its registered office, and any previous registered offices, under the Companies Act 1985 or the Companies (Northern Ireland) Order 1986 (SI 1986/1032 (NI 6)) or anything similar under corresponding legislation of any country or territory outside the United Kingdom;
(g) its registered office, and any previous registered offices, under the Limited Liability Partnerships Act 2000 (c 12) or anything similar under corresponding legislation of any country or territory outside Great Britain;
(h) in the case of an account or accounts, the date or dates on which it began to hold the account or accounts and, if it has ceased to hold the account or any of the accounts, the date or dates on which it did so;
(hh) in the case of any safe deposit box, the date on which the box was made available to him and if the box has ceased to be available to him the date on which it so ceased;
(i) such evidence of its identity as was obtained by the financial institution under or for the purposes of any legislation relating to money laundering;
(j) the full name, date of birth and most recent address and any previous addresses of any person who is a signatory to the account or any of the accounts.

(4) The Secretary of State may by order provide for information of a description specified in the order—

(a) to be customer information, or
(b) no longer to be customer information.

(5) Money laundering is an act which—

(a) constitutes an offence under section 327, 328 or 329 of this Act or section 18 of the Terrorism Act 2000 (c 11), or
(aa) constitutes an offence specified in section 415(1A) of this Act,
(b) would constitute an offence specified in paragraph (a) or (aa) if done in the United Kingdom.

(6) A "safe deposit box" includes and procedure under which a financial institution provides a facility to hold items for safe keeping on behalf of another person.
[Proceeds of Crime Act 2002, s 364 as amended by the Serious Organised Crime and Police Act 2005, ss 103 and SI 2005/1965.]

3–1899 365. Requirements for making of customer information order. (1) These are the requirements for the making of a customer information order.
(2) In the case of a confiscation investigation, there must be reasonable grounds for suspecting that the person specified in the application for the order has benefited from his criminal conduct.
(3) In the case of a civil recovery investigation, there must be reasonable grounds for suspecting that—

(a) the property specified in the application for the order is recoverable property or associated property;
(b) the person specified in the application holds all or some of the property.

(4) In the case of a money laundering investigation, there must be reasonable grounds for suspecting that the person specified in the application for the order has committed a money laundering offence.

(5) In the case of any investigation, there must be reasonable grounds for believing that customer information which may be provided in compliance with the order is likely to be of substantial value (whether or not by itself) to the investigation for the purposes of which the order is sought.

(6) In the case of any investigation, there must be reasonable grounds for believing that it is in the public interest for the customer information to be provided, having regard to the benefit likely to accrue to the investigation if the information is obtained.
[Proceeds of Crime Act 2002, s 365.]

3–1900 366. Offences. (1) A financial institution commits an offence if without reasonable excuse it fails to comply with a requirement imposed on it under a customer information order.

(2) A financial institution guilty of an offence under subsection (1) is liable[1] on summary conviction to a fine not exceeding level 5 on the standard scale.

(3) A financial institution commits an offence if, in purported compliance with a customer information order, it—

(*a*) makes a statement which it knows to be false or misleading in a material particular, or
(*b*) recklessly makes a statement which is false or misleading in a material particular.

(4) A financial institution guilty of an offence under subsection (3) is liable[1]—

(*a*) on summary conviction, to a fine not exceeding the statutory maximum, or
(*b*) on conviction on indictment, to a fine.
[Proceeds of Crime Act 2002, s 366.]

---

1. For procedure in respect of this offence, which is triable either way, see the Magistrates' Courts Act 1980, ss 17A–21, in PART I: MAGISTRATES' COURTS, PROCEDURE, ante.

3–1901 367. Statements. (1) A statement made by a financial institution in response to a customer information order may not be used in evidence against it in criminal proceedings.

(2) But subsection (1) does not apply—

(*a*) in the case of proceedings under Part 2 or 4,
(*b*) on a prosecution for an offence under section 366(1) or (3), or
(*c*) on a prosecution for some other offence where, in giving evidence, the financial institution makes a statement inconsistent with the statement mentioned in subsection (1).

(3) A statement may not be used by virtue of subsection (2)(*c*) against a financial institution unless—

(*a*) evidence relating to it is adduced, or
(*b*) a question relating to it is asked,

by or on behalf of the financial institution in the proceedings arising out of the prosecution.
[Proceeds of Crime Act 2002, s 367.]

3–1902 368. Disclosure of information. A customer information order has effect in spite of any restriction on the disclosure of information (however imposed).
[Proceeds of Crime Act 2002, s 368.]

3–1903 369. Supplementary. (1) An application for a customer information order may be made ex parte to a judge in chambers.

(2) Rules of court may make provision as to the practice and procedure to be followed in connection with proceedings relating to customer information orders.

(3) An application to discharge or vary a customer information order may be made to the court by—

(*a*) the person who applied for the order;
(*b*) any person affected by the order.

(4) The court—

(*a*) may discharge the order;
(*b*) may vary the order.

(5) If an accredited financial investigator, a constable or a customs officer applies for a customer information order, an application to discharge or vary the order need not be by the same accredited financial investigator, constable or customs officer.

(6) References to a person who applied for a customer information order must be construed accordingly.

(7) An accredited financial investigator, a constable or a customs officer may not make an application for a customer information order or an application to vary such an order unless he is a senior appropriate officer or he is authorised to do so by a senior appropriate officer.

(8) Subsections (2) to (6) do not apply to orders made in England and Wales for the purposes of a civil recovery investigation.
[Proceeds of Crime Act 2002, s 369.]

Account monitoring orders

3–1904   370. Account monitoring orders.   (1) A judge may, on an application made to him by an appropriate officer, make an account monitoring order if he is satisfied that each of the requirements for the making of the order is fulfilled.

(2) The application for an account monitoring order must state that—

(*a*) a person specified in the application is subject to a confiscation investigation or a money laundering investigation, or

(*b*) property specified in the application is subject to a civil recovery investigation and a person specified in the application appears to hold the property.

(3) The application must also state that—

(*a*) the order is sought for the purposes of the investigation;

(*b*) the order is sought against the financial institution specified in the application in relation to account information of the description so specified.

(4) Account information is information relating to an account or accounts held at the financial institution specified in the application by the person so specified (whether solely or jointly with another).

(5) The application for an account monitoring order may specify information relating to—

(*a*) all accounts held by the person specified in the application for the order at the financial institution so specified,

(*b*) a particular description, or particular descriptions, of accounts so held, or

(*c*) a particular account, or particular accounts, so held.

(6) An account monitoring order is an order that the financial institution specified in the application for the order must, for the period stated in the order, provide account information of the description specified in the order to an appropriate officer in the manner, and at or by the time or times, stated in the order.

(7) The period stated in an account monitoring order must not exceed the period of 90 days beginning with the day on which the order is made.
[Proceeds of Crime Act 2002, s 370.]

3–1905   371. Requirements for making of account monitoring order.   (1) These are the requirements for the making of an account monitoring order.

(2) In the case of a confiscation investigation, there must be reasonable grounds for suspecting that the person specified in the application for the order has benefited from his criminal conduct.

(3) In the case of a civil recovery investigation, there must be reasonable grounds for suspecting that—

(*a*) the property specified in the application for the order is recoverable property or associated property;

(*b*) the person specified in the application holds all or some of the property.

(4) In the case of a money laundering investigation, there must be reasonable grounds for suspecting that the person specified in the application for the order has committed a money laundering offence.

(5) In the case of any investigation, there must be reasonable grounds for believing that account information which may be provided in compliance with the order is likely to be of substantial value (whether or not by itself) to the investigation for the purposes of which the order is sought.

(6) In the case of any investigation, there must be reasonable grounds for believing that it is in the public interest for the account information to be provided, having regard to the benefit likely to accrue to the investigation if the information is obtained.
[Proceeds of Crime Act 2002, s 371.]

3–1906   372. Statements.   (1) A statement made by a financial institution in response to an account monitoring order may not be used in evidence against it in criminal proceedings.

(2) But subsection (1) does not apply—

(*a*) in the case of proceedings under Part 2 or 4,

(*b*) in the case of proceedings for contempt of court, or

(*c*) on a prosecution for an offence where, in giving evidence, the financial institution makes a statement inconsistent with the statement mentioned in subsection (1).

(3) A statement may not be used by virtue of subsection (2)(*c*) against a financial institution unless—

(*a*) evidence relating to it is adduced, or

(*b*) a question relating to it is asked,

by or on behalf of the financial institution in the proceedings arising out of the prosecution.
[Proceeds of Crime Act 2002, s 372.]

3–1907   373. Applications.   An application for an account monitoring order may be made ex parte to a judge in chambers.
[Proceeds of Crime Act 2002, s 373.]

3–1908   **374. Disclosure of information.**   An account monitoring order has effect in spite of any restriction on the disclosure of information (however imposed).
[Proceeds of Crime Act 2002, s 374.]

3–1909   **375. Supplementary.**   (1) Rules of court may make provision as to the practice and procedure to be followed in connection with proceedings relating to account monitoring orders.

(2) An application to discharge or vary an account monitoring order may be made to the court by—

    (a)   the person who applied for the order;
    (b)   any person affected by the order.

(3) The court—

    (a)   may discharge the order;
    (b)   may vary the order.

(4) If an accredited financial investigator, a constable or a customs officer applies for an account monitoring order, an application to discharge or vary the order need not be by the same accredited financial investigator, constable or customs officer.

(5) References to a person who applied for an account monitoring order must be construed accordingly.

(6) Account monitoring orders have effect as if they were orders of the court.

(7) This section does not apply to orders made in England and Wales for the purposes of a civil recovery investigation.
[Proceeds of Crime Act 2002, s 375.]

Evidence overseas

3–1910   **376. Evidence overseas.**   (1) This section applies if the Director is carrying out a confiscation investigation.

(2) A judge on the application of the Director or a person subject to the investigation may issue a letter of request if he thinks that there is evidence in a country or territory outside the United Kingdom—

    (a)   that such a person has benefited from his criminal conduct, or
    (b)   of the extent or whereabouts of that person's benefit from his criminal conduct.

(3) The Director may issue a letter of request if he thinks that there is evidence in a country or territory outside the United Kingdom—

    (a)   that a person subject to the investigation has benefited from his criminal conduct, or
    (b)   of the extent or whereabouts of that person's benefit from his criminal conduct.

(4) A letter of request is a letter requesting assistance in obtaining outside the United Kingdom such evidence as is specified in the letter for use in the investigation.

(5) The person issuing a letter of request must send it to the Secretary of State.

(6) If the Secretary of State believes it is appropriate to do so he may forward a letter received under subsection (5)*—

    (a)   to a court or tribunal which is specified in the letter and which exercises jurisdiction in the place where the evidence is to be obtained, or
    (b)   to an authority recognised by the government of the country or territory concerned as the appropriate authority for receiving letters of request.

(7) But in a case of urgency the person issuing the letter of request may send it directly to the court or tribunal mentioned in subsection (6)(a).

(8) Evidence obtained in pursuance of a letter of request must not be used—

    (a)   by any person other than the Director or a person subject to the investigation;
    (b)   for any purpose other than that for which it is obtained.

(9) Subsection (8) does not apply if the authority mentioned in subsection (6)(b) consents to the use.

(10) Evidence includes documents and other articles.

(11) Rules of court may make provision as to the practice and procedure to be followed in connection with proceedings relating to the issue of letters of request by a judge under this section.
[Proceeds of Crime Act 2002, s 376.]

***Subsection (5) repealed, sub–s (6) amended and sub–s (7) substituted by new sub–ss (7) and (7A) by the Crime (International Co-operation) Act 2003, Schs 5 and 6 from a date to be appointed.**

Code of practice

3–1911   **377.**   *Code of practice*[1]

---

1. The Proceeds of Crime Act 2002 (Investigations in England, Wales and Northern Ireland: Code of Practice) Order 2003, SI 2003/334 has been made.

Interpretation

3–1912 378. Officers. (1) In relation to a confiscation investigation these are appropriate officers—

(a) the Director;
(b) an accredited financial investigator;
(c) a constable;
(d) a customs officer.

(2) In relation to a confiscation investigation these are senior appropriate officers—

(a) the Director;
(b) a police officer who is not below the rank of superintendent;
(c) a customs officer who is not below such grade as is designated by the Commissioners of Customs and Excise as equivalent to that rank;
(d) an accredited financial investigator who falls within a description specified in an order made for the purposes of this paragraph by the Secretary of State under section 453.

(3) In relation to a civil recovery investigation the Director (and only the Director) is—

(a) an appropriate officer;
(b) a senior appropriate officer.

(4) In relation to a money laundering investigation these are appropriate officers—

(a) an accredited financial investigator;
(b) a constable;
(c) a customs officer.

(5) For the purposes of section 342, in relation to a money laundering investigation a person authorised for the purposes of money laundering investigations by the Director General of the Serious Organised Crime Agency is also an appropriate officer.

(6) In relation to a money laundering investigation these are senior appropriate officers—

(a) a police officer who is not below the rank of superintendent;
(b) a customs officer who is not below such grade as is designated by the Commissioners of Customs and Excise as equivalent to that rank;
(c) an accredited financial investigator who falls within a description specified in an order made for the purposes of this paragraph by the Secretary of State under section 453.

(7) But a person is not an appropriate officer or a senior appropriate officer in relation to a money laundering investigation if he is—

(a) a member of the staff of the Agency, or
(b) a person providing services under arrangements made by the Director.
[Proceeds of Crime Act 2002, s 378 as amended by the Serious Organised Crime and Police Act 2005, Sch 4.]

3–1913 379. Miscellaneous. "Document", "excluded material" and "premises" have the same meanings as in the Police and Criminal Evidence Act 1984 (c 60) or (in relation to Northern Ireland) the Police and Criminal Evidence (Northern Ireland) Order 1989 (SI 1989/1341 (NI 12)).
[Proceeds of Crime Act 2002, s 379.]

CHAPTER 4
INTERPRETATION[1]

3–1914 413. Criminal conduct. (1) Criminal conduct is conduct which—

(a) constitutes an offence in any part of the United Kingdom, or
(b) would constitute an offence in any part of the United Kingdom if it occurred there.

(2) A person benefits from conduct if he obtains property or a pecuniary advantage as a result of or in connection with the conduct.

(3) References to property or a pecuniary advantage obtained in connection with conduct include references to property or a pecuniary advantage obtained in both that connection and some other.

(4) If a person benefits from conduct his benefit is the property or pecuniary advantage obtained as a result of or in connection with the conduct.

(5) It is immaterial—

(a) whether conduct occurred before or after the passing of this Act, and
(b) whether property or a pecuniary advantage constituting a benefit from conduct was obtained before or after the passing of this Act.
[Proceeds of Crime Act 2002, s 413.]

---

1. Chapter 4 comprises ss 413–416.

PART 11
CO-OPERATION[1]

3–1915 443. *Enforcement in different parts of the United Kingdom*[2]

---

1. Part 11 comprises ss 443–447.
2. See the Proceeds of Crime Act 2002 (Enforcement in different parts of the United Kingdom) Order 2002,

SI 2002/3133 which makes provision for orders relating to restraint and receivership made in one part of the United Kingdom to be enforced in another part. Orders automatically have effect throughout the United Kingdom. However, proceedings for their enforcement may only be brought if the orders are registered in the Crown Court for England and Wales, the Court of Session for Scotland and the High Court for Northern Ireland. The court in which the order is registered then has the same powers to enforce the order as if it had made the order itself. See also the Proceeds of Crime Act 2002 (Investigations in different parts of the United Kingdom) Order 2003, SI 2003/425 which makes provision for orders and warrants made or issued under Part 8 of the Proceeds of Crime Act 2002 in one part of the United Kingdom to be enforced in another part of the United Kingdom. Part 8 of the Proceeds of Crime Act provides for various orders and warrants to be issued in relation to confiscation investigations, money laundering investigations and civil recovery investigations.

3–1916   444. *External requests and orders*

445. *External investigations*

446. *Rules of court*

447. *Interpretation*

PART 12
MISCELLANEOUS AND GENERAL[1]

Miscellaneous

3–1917   451. Revenue and Customs prosecutions.   (1) Proceedings for a specified offence may be started by the Director of Revenue and Customs Prosecutions or by order of the Commissioners for Her Majesty's Revenue and Customs (the Commissioners).

(2) Where proceedings under subsection (1) are instituted by the Commissioners, the proceedings must be brought in the name of an officer of Revenue and Customs.

(3) *Repealed.*

(4) If the Commissioners investigate, or propose to investigate, any matter to help them to decide—

(a) whether there are grounds for believing that a specified offence has been committed, or
(b) whether a person is to be prosecuted for such an offence,

the matter must be treated as an assigned matter within the meaning of the Customs and Excise Management Act 1979 (c 2).

(5) This section—

(a) does not prevent any person (including an officer of Revenue and Customs) who has power to arrest, detain or prosecute a person for a specified offence from doing so;
(b) does not prevent a court from dealing with a person brought before it following his arrest by an officer of Revenue and Customs for a specified offence, even if the proceedings were not started by an order under subsection (1).

(6) The following are specified offences—

(a) an offence under Part 7;
(b) an offence under section 342;
(c) an attempt, conspiracy or incitement to commit an offence specified in paragraph (a) or (b);
(d) aiding, abetting, counselling or procuring the commission of an offence specified in paragraph (a) or (b).

(7) This section does not apply to proceedings on indictment in Scotland.
[Proceeds of Crime Act 2002, s 451 as amended by the Commissioners for Revenue and Customs Act, Sch 4.]

---

1. Part 12 comprises ss 448–462 and Schs 10–12.

3–1918   452. Crown servants.   (1) The Secretary of State may by regulations[1] provide that any of the following provisions apply to persons in the public service of the Crown.

(2) The provisions are—

(a) the provisions of Part 7;
(b) section 342.
[Proceeds of Crime Act 2002, s 452.]

---

1. See the Proceeds of Crime Act 2002 (Crown Servants) Regulations 2003, SI 2003/173.

3–1919   453. References to financial investigators.   (1) The Secretary of State may by order[1] provide that a specified reference in this Act to an accredited financial investigator is a reference to such an investigator who falls within a specified description.

(2) A description may be framed by reference to a grade designated by a specified person.
[Proceeds of Crime Act 2002, s 453.]

---

1. The Proceeds of Crime Act 2002 (References to Financial Investigators) Order 2003, SI 2003/172 amended by SI 2004/8 and 3339, SI 2005/386 and SI 2006/57 has been made.

3–1920   454. Customs officers.   For the purposes of this Act a customs officer is a person commissioned by the Commissioners of Customs and Excise under section 6(3) of the Customs and Excise Management Act 1979 (c 2).
[*Proceeds of Crime Act 2002, s 454.*]

General

3–1921   458. Commencement.   (1) The preceding provisions of this Act (except the provisions specified in subsection (3)) come into force in accordance with provision made by the Secretary of State by order[1].

(2)–(3) *Scotland.*
[*Proceeds of Crime Act 2002, s 458.*]

---

1. At the date of going to press the following commencement orders had been made: (No 1 and Savings) Order 2002, SI 2002/3015; (No 2) Order 2002, SI 2002/3055; (No 3) Order, SI 2002/3145; (No 4, Transitional Provisions and Savings) Order 2003, SI 2003/120, amended by SI 2003/531; (No 5 Transitional, Savings and Amendment) SI 2003/333 amended by SI 2003/531. All the provisions reproduced here are in force.

3–1922   459. *Orders and regulations*

460. *Finance*

461. *Extent*

462. *Short title*

Section 75   SCHEDULE 2
                        LIFESTYLE OFFENCES: ENGLAND AND WALES

(*Amended by the Nationality, Immigration and Asylum Act 2002, s 114(3), the Sexual Offences Act 2003, Sch 6, the Asylum and Immigration (Treatment of Claimants, etc) Act 2004, s 5 and the Gangmasters (Licensing) Act 2004, s 29.*)

Drug trafficking

3–1923 1. (1) An offence under any of the following provisions of the Misuse of Drugs Act 1971 (c 38)—

(*a*)   section 4(2) or (3) (unlawful production or supply of controlled drugs);
(*b*)   section 5(3) (possession of controlled drug with intent to supply);
(*c*)   section 8 (permitting certain activities relating to controlled drugs);
(*d*)   section 20 (assisting in or inducing the commission outside the UK of an offence punishable under a corresponding law).

(2) An offence under any of the following provisions of the Customs and Excise Management Act 1979 (c 2) if it is committed in connection with a prohibition or restriction on importation or exportation which has effect by virtue of section 3 of the Misuse of Drugs Act 1971—

(*a*)   section 50(2) or (3) (improper importation of goods);
(*b*)   section 68(2) (exploration of prohibited or restricted goods);
(*c*)   section 170 (fraudulent evasion).

(3) An offence under either of the following provisions of the Criminal Justice (International Co-operation) Act 1990 (c 5)—

(*a*)   section 12 (manufacture or supply of a substance for the time being specified in Schedule 2 to that Act);
(*b*)   section 19 (using a ship for illicit traffic in controlled drugs).

Money laundering

2. An offence under either of the following provisions of this Act—

(*a*)   section 327 (concealing etc criminal property);
(*b*)   section 328 (assisting another to retain criminal property).

Directing terrorism

3. An offence under section 56 of the Terrorism Act 2000 (c 11) (directing the activities of a terrorist organisation).

People trafficking

4. (1) An offence under section 25, 25A or 25B of the Immigration Act 1971 (c 77) (assisting unlawful immigration etc).
(2) An offence under any of sections 57 to 59 of the Sexual Offences Act 2003 (trafficking for sexual exploitation).
(3) An offence under s 4 of the Asylum and Immigration (Treatment of Claimants, etc) Act 2004 (exploitation).

Arms trafficking

5. (1) An offence under either of the following provisions of the Customs and Excise Management Act 1979 if it is committed in connection with a firearm or ammunition—

(*a*) section 68(2) (exportation of prohibited goods);
(*b*) section 170 (fraudulent evasion).

(2) An offence under section 3(1) of the Firearms Act 1968 (c 27) (dealing in firearms or ammunition by way of trade or business).

(3) In this paragraph "firearm" and "ammunition" have the same meanings as in section 57 of the Firearms Act 1968 (c 27).

Counterfeiting

6. An offence under any of the following provisions of the Forgery and Counterfeiting Act 1981 (c 45)—

(*a*) section 14 (making counterfeit notes or coins);
(*b*) section 15 (passing etc counterfeit notes or coins);
(*c*) section 16 (having counterfeit notes or coins);
(*d*) section 17 (making or possessing materials or equipment for counterfeiting).

Intellectual property

7. (1) An offence under any of the following provisions of the Copyright, Designs and Patents Act 1988 (c 48)—

(*a*) section 107(1) (making or dealing in an article which infringes copyright);
(*b*) section 107(2) (making or possessing an article designed or adapted for making a copy of a copyright work);
(*c*) section 198(1) (making or dealing in an illicit recording);
(*d*) section 297A (making or dealing in unauthorised decoders).

(2) An offence under section 92(1), (2) or (3) of the Trade Marks Act 1994 (c 26) (unauthorised use etc of trade mark).

Prostitution and child sex

8. (1) An offence under section 33 or 34 of the Sexual Offences Act 1956 (keeping or letting premises for use as a brothel).

(2) An offence under any of the following provisions of the Sexual Offences Act 2003—

(*a*) section 14 (arranging or facilitating commission of a child sex offence);
(*b*) section 48 (causing or inciting child prostitution or pornography);
(*c*) section 49 (controlling a child prostitute or a child involved in pornography);
(*d*) section 50 (arranging or facilitating child prostitution or pornography);
(*e*) section 52 (causing or inciting prostitution for gain);
(*f*) section 53 (controlling prostitution for gain).Blackmail

9. An offence under section 21 of the Theft Act 1968 (c 60) (blackmail).

9A. An offence under section 12(1) or (2) of the Gangmasters (Licensing) Act 2004 (acting as a gangmaster other than under the authority of a licence, possession of false documents etc).

Inchoate offences

10. (1) An offence of attempting, conspiring or inciting the commission of an offence specified in this Schedule.
(2) An offence of aiding, abetting, counselling or procuring the commission of such an offence.

Section 330	SCHEDULE 9

REGULATED SECTOR AND SUPERVISORY AUTHORITIES

(*Amended by SI 2003/3074, the Enterprise Act 2002, s 2, the Gambling Act 2005, Sch 16 SI 2006/2385 and SI 2007/208.*)

PART 1
REGULATED SECTOR

Business in the regulated sector

3–1924 **1.** (1) A business is in the regulated sector to the extent that it engages in any of the following activities in the United Kingdom—

(*a*) a regulated activity specified in sub-paragraph (2);
(*b*) the activities of the National Savings Bank;
(*c*) any activity carried on for the purpose of raising money authorised to be raised under the National Loans Act 1968 (c 13) under the auspices of the Director of Savings;
(*d*) the business of operating a bureau de change, transmitting money (or any representation of monetary value) by any means or cashing cheques which are made payable to customers;
(*e*) any of the activities in points 1 to 12 or 14 of Annex 1 to the Banking Consolidation Directive when carried on by way of business, ignoring an activity falling within any of paragraphs (*a*) to (*d*);
(*f*) estate agency work;
(*g*) operating a casino by way of business;
(*h*) the activities of a person appointed to act as an insolvency practitioner within the meaning of section 388 of the Insolvency Act 1986 (c 45) or Article 3 of the Insolvency (Northern Ireland) Order 1989 (SI 1989/2405 (NI 19));
(*i*) the provision by way of business of advice about the tax affairs of another person by a body corporate or unincorporate or, in the case of a sole practitioner, by an individual;
(*j*) the provision by way of business of accountancy services by a body corporate or unincorporate or, in the case of a sole practitioner, by an individual;
(*k*) the provision by way of business of audit services by a person who is eligible for appointment as a company auditor under section 25 of the Companies Act 1989 (c 40) or Article 28 of the Companies (Northern Ireland) Order 1990 (SI 1990/593 (NI 5));

(*l*) the provision by way of business of legal services by a body corporate or unincorporate or, in the case of a sole practitioner, by an individual and which involves participation in a financial or real property transaction (whether by assisting in the planning or execution of any such transaction or otherwise by acting for, or on behalf of, a client in any such transaction);

(*m*) the provision by way of business of services in relation to the formation, operation or management of a company or a trust;

(*n*) the activity of dealing in goods of any description by way of business (including dealing as an auctioneer) whenever a transaction involves accepting a total cash payment of 15,000 euro or more.

(2) These are the regulated activities—

(*a*) accepting deposits;

(*b*) effecting or carrying out contracts of long-term insurance when carried on by a person who has received official authorisation pursuant to Article 4 or 51 of the Life Assurance Consolidation Directive;

(*c*) dealing in investments as principal or as agent;

(*d*) arranging deals in investments;

(*da*) operating a multilateral trading facility;

(*e*) managing investments;

(*f*) safeguarding and administering investments;

(*g*) sending dematerialised instructions;

(*h*) establishing (and taking other steps in relation to) collective investment schemes;

(*i*) advising on investments;

(*j*) issuing electronic money.

Excluded activities

2. A business is not in the regulated sector to the extent that it engages in any of the following activities—

(*a*) the issue of withdrawable share capital within the limit set by section 6 of the Industrial and Provident Societies Act 1965 (c 12) by a society registered under that Act;

(*b*) the acceptance of deposits from the public within the limit set by section 7(3) of that Act by such a society;

(*c*) the issue of withdrawable share capital within the limit set by section 6 of the Industrial and Provident Societies Act (Northern Ireland) 1969 (c 24 (NI)) by a society registered under that Act;

(*d*) the acceptance of deposits from the public within the limit set by section 7(3) of that Act by such a society;

(*e*) activities carried on by the Bank of England;

(*f*) any activity in respect of which an exemption order under section 38 of the Financial Services and Markets Act 2000 (c 8) has effect if it is carried on by a person who is for the time being specified in the order or falls within a class of persons so specified;

(*g*) the regulated activities of arranging deals in investments or advising on investments, in so far as the investment consists of rights under a regulated mortgage contract, rights under a regulated home reversion plan or rights under a regulated home purchase plan;

(*h*) the regulated activities of dealing in investments as agent, arranging deals in investments, managing investments or advising on investments, in so far as the investment consists of rights under, or any right to or interest in, a contract of insurance which is not a qualifying contract of insurance.

3. (1) This paragraph has effect for the purposes of paragraphs 1 and 2.

(2) Paragraphs 1(1)(*a*) and 2(*g*) and (*h*) must be read with section 22 of the Financial Services and Markets Act 2000, any relevant order under that section and Schedule 2 to that Act.

(3) The Banking Consolidation Directive is the Directive of the European Parliament and Council relating to the taking up and pursuit of the business of credit institutions (No 2000/12/EC), as amended.

(4) The Life Assurance Consolidation Directive is the Directive of the European Parliament and Council concerning life assurance (No 2002/83/EC).

(5) "Estate agency work" has the meaning given by section 1 of the Estate Agents Act 1979 (c 38) save for the omission of the words " (including a business in which he is employed)" in subsection (1) and includes a case where, in relation to a disposal or acquisition, the person acts as principal.

(6) References to amounts in euro include references to equivalent amounts in another currency.

(7) "Cash" means notes, coins or travellers' cheques in any currency.

(8) For the purpose of the application of this Part to Scotland, "real property" means "heritable property".

PART 2
SUPERVISORY AUTHORITIES

3–1925 **4.** (1) Each of the following is a supervisory authority—

(*a*) the Bank of England;

(*b*) the Financial Services Authority;

(*c*) the Council of Lloyd's;

(*d*) the Officel of Fair Trading;

(*e*) a body which is a designated professional body for the purposes of Part 20 of the Financial Services and Markets Act 2000 (c 8);

(*f*) Pensions Regulator;

(*g*) the Gambling Commission

(2) The Secretary of State is also a supervisory authority in the exercise, in relation to a person carrying on a business in the regulated sector, of his functions under the enactments relating to companies or insolvency or under the Financial Services and Markets Act 2000.

(3) The Treasury are also a supervisory authority in the exercise, in relation to a person carrying on a business in the regulated sector, of their functions under the enactments relating to companies or insolvency or under the Financial Services and Markets Act 2000.

PART 3
POWER TO AMEND

3–1926 **5.** The Treasury may by order amend Part 1 or 2 of this Schedule.

Criminal Justice Act 2003
2003 c 44

PART 12[1]
SENTENCING

CHAPTER 1[2]
General Provisions about Sentencing

Matters to be taken into account in sentencing

3–1930   142. Purposes of sentencing.   (1) Any court dealing with an offender in respect of his offence must have regard to the following purposes of sentencing—

    (a)   the punishment of offenders,
    (b)   the reduction of crime (including its reduction by deterrence),
    (c)   the reform and rehabilitation of offenders,
    (d)   the protection of the public, and
    (e)   the making of reparation by offenders to persons affected by their offences.

  (2) Subsection (1) does not apply—

    (a)   in relation to an offender who is aged under 18 at the time of conviction,
    (b)   to an offence the sentence for which is fixed by law,
    (c)   to an offence the sentence for which falls to be imposed under section 51A(2) of the Firearms Act 1968 (c 27) (minimum sentence for certain firearms offences), under subsection (2) of section 110 or 111 of the Sentencing Act (required custodial sentences) or under any of sections 225 to 228 of this Act (dangerous offenders), or
    (d)   in relation to the making under Part 3 of the Mental Health Act 1983 (c 20) of a hospital order (with or without a restriction order), an interim hospital order, a hospital direction or a limitation direction.

  (3) In this Chapter "sentence", in relation to an offence, includes any order made by a court when dealing with the offender in respect of his offence; and "sentencing" is to be construed accordingly.
[Criminal Justice Act 2003, s 142.]

---

  1. Part 12 contains ss 142–305. Individual section footnotes indicate the sections or parts of sections that had been brought into force at the date of going to press.
  2. Chapter 1 contains ss 142–176.

3–1931   143. Determining the seriousness of an offence.   (1) In considering the seriousness of any offence, the court must consider the offender's culpability in committing the offence and any harm which the offence caused, was intended to cause or might forseeably have caused.

  (2) In considering the seriousness of an offence ("the current offence") committed by an offender who has one or more previous convictions, the court must treat each previous conviction as an aggravating factor if (in the case of that conviction) the court considers that it can reasonably be so treated having regard, in particular, to—

    (a)   the nature of the offence to which the conviction relates and its relevance to the current offence, and
    (b)   the time that has elapsed since the conviction.

  (3) In considering the seriousness of any offence committed while the offender was on bail, the court must treat the fact that it was committed in those circumstances as an aggravating factor.

  (4) Any reference in subsection (2) to a previous conviction is to be read as a reference to—

    (a)   a previous conviction by a court in the United Kingdom, or
    (b)   a previous finding of guilt in service disciplinary proceedings.

  (5) Subsections (2) and (4) do not prevent the court from treating a previous conviction by a court outside the United Kingdom as an aggravating factor in any case where the court considers it appropriate to do so.
[Criminal Justice Act 2003, s 143.]

3–1932   144. Reduction in sentences for guilty pleas.   (1) In determining what sentence to pass on an offender who has pleaded guilty to an offence in proceedings before that or another court, a court must take into account—

    (a)   the stage in the proceedings for the offence at which the offender indicated his intention to plead guilty, and
    (b)   the circumstances in which this indication was given.

  (2) In the case of an offence the sentence for which falls to be imposed under subsection (2) of section 110 or 111 of the Sentencing Act, nothing in that subsection prevents the court, after taking into account any matter referred to in subsection (1) of this section, from imposing any sentence which is not less than 80 per cent of that specified in that subsection.
[Criminal Justice Act 2003, s 144.]

3–1933   145. Increase in sentences for racial or religious aggravation.   (1) This section applies where a court is considering the seriousness of an offence other than one under sections 29 to 32 of the Crime and Disorder Act 1998 (c 37) (racially or religiously aggravated assaults, criminal damage, public order offences and harassment etc).

(2)   If the offence was racially or religiously aggravated, the court—

(*a*)   must treat that fact as an aggravating factor, and

(*b*)   must state in open court that the offence was so aggravated.

(3)   Section 28 of the Crime and Disorder Act 1998 (meaning of "racially or religiously aggravated") applies for the purposes of this section as it applies for the purposes of sections 29 to 32 of that Act.
[Criminal Justice Act 2003, s 145.]

3–1934   146. Increase in sentences for aggravation related to disability or sexual orientation.   (1)   This section applies where the court is considering the seriousness of an offence committed in any of the circumstances mentioned in subsection (2).

(2)   Those circumstances are—

(*a*)   that, at the time of committing the offence, or immediately before or after doing so, the offender demonstrated towards the victim of the offence hostility based on—

(i)   the sexual orientation (or presumed sexual orientation) of the victim, or

(ii)   a disability (or presumed disability) of the victim, or

(*b*)   that the offence is motivated (wholly or partly)—

(i)   by hostility towards persons who are of a particular sexual orientation, or

(ii)   by hostility towards persons who have a disability or a particular disability.

(3)   The court—

(*a*)   must treat the fact that the offence was committed in any of those circumstances as an aggravating factor, and

(*b*)   must state in open court that the offence was committed in such circumstances.

(4)   It is immaterial for the purposes of paragraph (*a*) or (*b*) of subsection (2) whether or not the offender's hostility is also based, to any extent, on any other factor not mentioned in that paragraph.

(5)   In this section "disability" means any physical or mental impairment.
[Criminal Justice Act 2003, s 146.]

General restrictions on community sentences

3–1935   147. Meaning of "community sentence" etc.   (1)   In this Part "community sentence" means a sentence which consists of or includes—

(*a*)   a community order (as defined by section 177), or

(*b*)   one or more youth community orders.

(2)   In this Chapter "youth community order" means—

(*a*)   a curfew order as defined by section 163 of the Sentencing Act,

(*b*)   an exclusion order under section 40A(1) of that Act,

(*c*)   an attendance centre order as defined by section 163 of that Act,

(*d*)   a supervision order under section 63(1) of that Act, or

(*e*)   an action plan order under section 69(1) of that Act.
[Criminal Justice Act 2003, s 147.]

3–1936   148. Restrictions on imposing community sentences.   (1)   A court must not pass a community sentence on an offender unless it is of the opinion that the offence, or the combination of the offence and one or more offences associated with it, was serious enough to warrant such a sentence.

(2)   Where a court passes a community sentence which consists of or includes a community order—

(*a*)   the particular requirement or requirements forming part of the community order must be such as, in the opinion of the court, is, or taken together are, the most suitable for the offender, and

(*b*)   the restrictions on liberty imposed by the order must be such as in the opinion of the court are commensurate with the seriousness of the offence, or the combination of the offence and one or more offences associated with it.

(3)   Where a court passes a community sentence which consists of or includes one or more youth community orders—

(*a*)   the particular order or orders forming part of the sentence must be such as, in the opinion of the court, is, or taken together are, the most suitable for the offender, and

(*b*)   the restrictions on liberty imposed by the order or orders must be such as in the opinion of the court are commensurate with the seriousness of the offence, or the combination of the offence and one or more offences associated with it.

(4)   Subsections (1) and (2)(*b*) have effect subject to section 151(2).
[Criminal Justice Act 2003, s 148.]

3–1937 149. Passing of community sentence on offender remanded in custody. (1) In determining the restrictions on liberty to be imposed by a community order or youth community order in respect of an offence, the court may have regard to any period for which the offender has been remanded in custody in connection with the offence or any other offence the charge for which was founded on the same facts or evidence.

(2) In subsection (1) "remanded in custody" has the meaning given by section 242(2).

[Criminal Justice Act 2003, s 149.]

3–1938 150. Community sentence not available where sentence fixed by law etc. The power to make a community order or youth community order is not exercisable in respect of an offence for which the sentence—

(a) is fixed by law,

(b) falls to be imposed under section 51A(2) of the Firearms Act 1968 (c 27) (required custodial sentence for certain firearms offences),

(c) falls to be imposed under section 110(2) or 111(2) of the Sentencing Act (requirement to impose custodial sentences for certain repeated offences committed by offenders aged 18 or over), or

(d) falls to be imposed under any of sections 225 to 228 of this Act (requirement to impose custodial sentences for certain offences committed by offenders posing risk to public).

[Criminal Justice Act 2003, s 150.]

3–1939 151. Community order for persistent offender previously fined. (1) Subsection (2) applies where—

(a) a person aged 16 or over is convicted of an offence ("the current offence"),

(b) on three or more previous occasions he has, on conviction by a court in the United Kingdom of any offence committed by him after attaining the age of 16, had passed on him a sentence consisting only of a fine, and

(c) despite the effect of section 143(2), the court would not (apart from this section) regard the current offence, or the combination of the current offence and one or more offences associated with it, as being serious enough to warrant a community sentence.

(2) The court may make a community order in respect of the current offence instead of imposing a fine if it considers that, having regard to all the circumstances including the matters mentioned in subsection (3), it would be in the interests of justice to make such an order.

(3) The matters referred to in subsection (2) are—

(a) the nature of the offences to which the previous convictions mentioned in subsection (1)(b) relate and their relevance to the current offence, and

(b) the time that has elapsed since the offender's conviction of each of those offences.

(4) In subsection (1)(b), the reference to conviction by a court in the United Kingdom includes a reference to the finding of guilt in service disciplinary proceedings; and, in relation to any such finding of guilt, the reference to the sentence passed is a reference to the punishment awarded.

(5) For the purposes of subsection (1)(b), a compensation order does not form part of an offender's sentence.

(6) For the purposes of subsection (1)(b), it is immaterial whether on other previous occasions a court has passed on the offender a sentence not consisting only of a fine.

(7) This section does not limit the extent to which a court may, in accordance with section 143(2), treat any previous convictions of the offender as increasing the seriousness of an offence.

[Criminal Justice Act 2003, s 151.]

General restrictions on discretionary custodial sentences

3–1940 152. General restrictions on imposing discretionary custodial sentences. (1) This section applies where a person is convicted of an offence punishable with a custodial sentence other than one—

(a) fixed by law, or

(b) falling to be imposed under section 51A(2) of the Firearms Act 1968 (c 27), under 110(2) or 111(2) of the Sentencing Act or under any of sections 225 to 228 of this Act.

(2) The court must not pass a custodial sentence unless it is of the opinion that the offence, or the combination of the offence and one or more offences associated with it, was so serious that neither a fine alone nor a community sentence can be justified for the offence.

(3) Nothing in subsection (2) prevents the court from passing a custodial sentence on the offender if—

(a) he fails to express his willingness to comply with a requirement which is proposed by the court to be included in a community order and which requires an expression of such willingness, or

(b) he fails to comply with an order under section 161(2) (pre-sentence drug testing).

[Criminal Justice Act 2003, s 152.]

3–1941 153. Length of discretionary custodial sentences: general provision. (1) This section applies where a court passes a custodial sentence other than one fixed by law or falling to be imposed under section 225 or 226.

(2) Subject to section 51A(2) of the Firearms Act 1968 (c 27), sections 110(2) and 111(2) of the Sentencing Act and sections 227(2) and 228(2) of this Act, the custodial sentence must be for the shortest term (not exceeding the permitted maximum) that in the opinion of the court is commensurate with the seriousness of the offence, or the combination of the offence and one or more offences associated with it.
[Criminal Justice Act 2003, s 153.]

General limit on magistrates' court's power to impose imprisonment

3–1942   154. General limit on magistrates' court's power to impose imprisonment[1]. (1) A magistrates' court does not have power to impose imprisonment for more than 12 months in respect of any one offence.

(2) Unless expressly excluded, subsection (1) applies even if the offence in question is one for which a person would otherwise be liable on summary conviction to imprisonment for more than 12 months.

(3) Subsection (1) is without prejudice to section 133 of the Magistrates' Courts Act 1980 (c 43) (consecutive terms of imprisonment).

(4) Any power of a magistrates' court to impose a term of imprisonment for non-payment of a fine, or for want of sufficient distress to satisfy a fine, is not limited by virtue of subsection (1).

(5) In subsection (4) "fine" includes a pecuniary penalty but does not include a pecuniary forfeiture or pecuniary compensation.

(6) In this section "impose imprisonment" means pass a sentence of imprisonment or fix a term of imprisonment for failure to pay any sum of money, or for want of sufficient distress to satisfy any sum of money, or for failure to do or abstain from doing anything required to be done or left undone.

(7) Section 132 of the Magistrates' Courts Act 1980 contains provisions about the minimum term of imprisonment which may be imposed by a magistrates' court.
[Criminal Justice Act 2003, s 154.]

---

1. As to prison sentences of less than 12 months, or up to 65 weeks where consecutive prison sentences are imposed and none of the individual terms is 12 months or longer, see the provisions of Chapter 3, post. As to sentences of 12 months or longer, and to giving credit for periods of remand in custody, see the provisions of Chapter 6, post.

3–1943   155. Consecutive terms of imprisonment.   (1) Section 133 of the Magistrates' Courts Act 1980 (consecutive terms of imprisonment) is amended as follows.

(2) In subsection (1), for "6 months" there is substituted "65 weeks".

(3) Subsection (2) is omitted.

(4) In subsection (3) for "the preceding subsections" there is substituted "subsection (1) above".
[Criminal Justice Act 2003, s 155.]

Procedural requirements for imposing community sentences and discretionary custodial sentences

3–1944   156. Pre-sentence reports and other requirements.   (1) In forming any such opinion as is mentioned in section 148(1), (2)(b) or (3)(b), section 152(2) or section 153(2), a court must take into account all such information as is available to it about the circumstances of the offence or (as the case may be) of the offence and the offence or offences associated with it, including any aggravating or mitigating factors.

(2) In forming any such opinion as is mentioned in section 148(2)(a) or (3)(a), the court may take into account any information about the offender which is before it.

(3) Subject to subsection (4), a court must obtain and consider a pre-sentence report before—

(a) in the case of a custodial sentence, forming any such opinion as is mentioned in section 152(2), section 153(2), section 225(1)(b), section 226(1)(b), section 227(1)(b) or section 228(1)(b)(i), or

(b) in the case of a community sentence, forming any such opinion as is mentioned in section 148(1), (2)(b) or (3)(b) or any opinion as to the suitability for the offender of the particular requirement or requirements to be imposed by the community order.

(4) Subsection (3) does not apply if, in the circumstances of the case, the court is of the opinion that it is unnecessary to obtain a pre-sentence report.

(5) In a case where the offender is aged under 18, the court must not form the opinion mentioned in subsection (4) unless—

(a) there exists a previous pre-sentence report obtained in respect of the offender, and

(b) the court has had regard to the information contained in that report, or, if there is more than one such report, the most recent report.

(6) No custodial sentence or community sentence is invalidated by the failure of a court to obtain and consider a pre-sentence report before forming an opinion referred to in subsection (3), but any court on an appeal against such a sentence—

(a) must, subject to subsection (7), obtain a pre-sentence report if none was obtained by the court below, and

(b) must consider any such report obtained by it or by that court.

(7) Subsection (6)(a) does not apply if the court is of the opinion—

(a) that the court below was justified in forming an opinion that it was unnecessary to obtain a pre-sentence report, or

(b) that, although the court below was not justified in forming that opinion, in the circumstances of the case at the time it is before the court, it is unnecessary to obtain a pre-sentence report.

(8) In a case where the offender is aged under 18, the court must not form the opinion mentioned in subsection (7) unless—

(a) there exists a previous pre-sentence report obtained in respect of the offender, and

(b) the court has had regard to the information contained in that report, or, if there is more than one such report, the most recent report.

[Criminal Justice Act 2003, s 156.]

3–1945   157. Additional requirements in case of mentally disordered offender.   (1) Subject to subsection (2), in any case where the offender is or appears to be mentally disordered, the court must obtain and consider a medical report before passing a custodial sentence other than one fixed by law.

(2) Subsection (1) does not apply if, in the circumstances of the case, the court is of the opinion that it is unnecessary to obtain a medical report.

(3) Before passing a custodial sentence other than one fixed by law on an offender who is or appears to be mentally disordered, a court must consider—

(a) any information before it which relates to his mental condition (whether given in a medical report, a pre-sentence report or otherwise), and

(b) the likely effect of such a sentence on that condition and on any treatment which may be available for it.

(4) No custodial sentence which is passed in a case to which subsection (1) applies is invalidated by the failure of a court to comply with that subsection, but any court on an appeal against such a sentence—

(a) must obtain a medical report if none was obtained by the court below, and

(b) must consider any such report obtained by it or by that court.

(5) In this section "mentally disordered", in relation to any person, means suffering from a mental disorder within the meaning of the Mental Health Act 1983 (c 20).

(6) In this section "medical report" means a report as to an offender's mental condition made or submitted orally or in writing by a registered medical practitioner who is approved for the purposes of section 12 of the Mental Health Act 1983 by the Secretary of State as having special experience in the diagnosis or treatment of mental disorder.

(7) Nothing in this section is to be taken to limit the generality of section 156.

[Criminal Justice Act 2003, s 157.]

3–1946   158. Meaning of "pre-sentence report".   (1) In this Part "pre-sentence report" means a report which—

(a) with a view to assisting the court in determining the most suitable method of dealing with an offender, is made or submitted by an appropriate officer, and

(b) contains information as to such matters, presented in such manner, as may be prescribed by rules made by the Secretary of State[1].

(2) In subsection (1) "an appropriate officer" means—

(a) where the offender is aged 18 or over, an officer of a local probation board, and

(b) where the offender is aged under 18, an officer of a local probation board, a social worker of a local authority or a member of a youth offending team.

[Criminal Justice Act 2003, s 158 as amended by the Children Act 2004, Sch 5.]

---

1. Section 158(1)(a), (b) and (2) arein force: see Criminal Justice Act 2003 (Commencement No 7) Order 2005, SI 2005/373 and Criminal Justice Act 2003 (Commencement No 8 and Transitional and Saving Provisions) Order 2005.

Disclosure of pre-sentence reports etc

3–1947   159. Disclosure of pre-sentence reports.   (1) This section applies where the court obtains a pre-sentence report, other than a report given orally in open court.

(2) Subject to subsections (3) and (4), the court must give a copy of the report—

(a) to the offender or his counsel or solicitor,

(b) if the offender is aged under 18, to any parent or guardian of his who is present in court, and

(c) to the prosecutor, that is to say, the person having the conduct of the proceedings in respect of the offence.

(3) If the offender is aged under 18 and it appears to the court that the disclosure to the offender or to any parent or guardian of his of any information contained in the report would be likely to create a risk of significant harm to the offender, a complete copy of the report need not be given to the offender or, as the case may be, to that parent or guardian.

(4) If the prosecutor is not of a description prescribed by order made by the Secretary of State, a copy of the report need not be given to the prosecutor if the court considers that it would be inappropriate for him to be given it.[1]

(5) No information obtained by virtue of subsection (2)(c) may be used or disclosed otherwise than for the purpose of—

(a)   determining whether representations as to matters contained in the report need to be made to the court, or

(b)   making such representations to the court.

(6) In relation to an offender aged under 18 for whom a local authority have parental responsibility and who—

(a)   is in their care, or

(b)   is provided with accommodation by them in the exercise of any social services functions,

references in this section to his parent or guardian are to be read as references to that authority.

(7) In this section and section 160—

"harm" has the same meaning as in section 31 of the Children Act 1989 (c 41);

"local authority" and "parental responsibility" have the same meanings as in that Act;

"social services functions", in relation to a local authority, has the meaning given by section 1A of the Local Authority Social Services Act 1970 (c 42).

[Criminal Justice Act 2003, s 159.]

---

1. Section 159 is in force: see Criminal Justice Act 2003 (Commencement No 7) Order 2005, SI 2005/373.

3–1948   160. Other reports of local probation boards and members of youth offending teams.   (1) This section applies where—

(a)   a report by an officer of a local probation board or a member of a youth offending team is made to any court (other than a youth court) with a view to assisting the court in determining the most suitable method of dealing with any person in respect of an offence, and

(b)   the report is not a pre-sentence report.

(2) Subject to subsection (3), the court must give a copy of the report—

(a)   to the offender or his counsel or solicitor, and

(b)   if the offender is aged under 18, to any parent or guardian of his who is present in court.

(3) If the offender is aged under 18 and it appears to the court that the disclosure to the offender or to any parent or guardian of his of any information contained in the report would be likely to create a risk of significant harm to the offender, a complete copy of the report need not be given to the offender, or as the case may be, to that parent or guardian.

(4) In relation to an offender aged under 18 for whom a local authority have parental responsibility and who—

(a)   is in their care, or

(b)   is provided with accommodation by them in the exercise of any social services functions,

references in this section to his parent or guardian are to be read as references to that authority.

[Criminal Justice Act 2003, s 160.]

Pre-sentence drug testing

3–1949   161. Pre-sentence drug testing.   (1) Where a person aged 14 or over is convicted of an offence and the court is considering passing a community sentence or a suspended sentence, it may make an order under subsection (2) for the purpose of ascertaining whether the offender has any specified Class A drug in his body.

(2) The order requires the offender to provide, in accordance with the order, samples of any description specified in the order.

(3) Where the offender has not attained the age of 17, the order must provide for the samples to be provided in the presence of an appropriate adult.

(4) If it is proved to the satisfaction of the court that the offender has, without reasonable excuse, failed to comply with the order it may impose on him a fine of an amount not exceeding level 4.

(5) In subsection (4) "level 4" means the amount which, in relation to a fine for a summary offence, is level 4 on the standard scale.

(6) The court may not make an order under subsection (2) unless it has been notified by the Secretary of State that the power to make such orders is exercisable by the court and the notice has not been withdrawn.

(7) The Secretary of State may by order amend subsection (1) by substituting for the age for the time being specified there a different age specified in the order.

(8) In this section—

"appropriate adult", in relation to a person under the age of 17, means—

(a)   his parent or guardian or, if he is in the care of a local authority or voluntary organisation, a person representing that authority or organisation,

(b)   a social worker of a local authority, or

(c)   if no person falling within paragraph (a) or (b) is available, any responsible person aged 18 or over who is not a police officer or a person employed by the police;

"specified Class A drug" has the same meaning as in Part 3 of the Criminal Justice and Court Services Act 2000 (c 43).

[Criminal Justice Act 2003, s 161 as amended by the Children Act 2004, Sch 5.]

Fines

3–1950 162. Powers to order statement as to offender's financial circumstances. (1) Where an individual has been convicted of an offence, the court may, before sentencing him, make a financial circumstances order with respect to him.

(2) Where a magistrates' court has been notified in accordance with section 12(4) of the Magistrates' Courts Act 1980 (c 43) that an individual desires to plead guilty without appearing before the court, the court may make a financial circumstances order with respect to him.

(3) In this section "a financial circumstances order" means, in relation to any individual, an order requiring him to give to the court, within such period as may be specified in the order, such a statement of his financial circumstances as the court may require.

(4) An individual who without reasonable excuse fails to comply with a financial circumstances order is liable on summary conviction to a fine not exceeding level 3 on the standard scale.

(5) If an individual, in furnishing any statement in pursuance of a financial circumstances order—

(*a*) makes a statement which he knows to be false in a material particular,

(*b*) recklessly furnishes a statement which is false in a material particular, or

(*c*) knowingly fails to disclose any material fact,

he is liable on summary conviction to a fine not exceeding level 4 on the standard scale.

(6) Proceedings in respect of an offence under subsection (5) may, notwithstanding anything in section 127(1) of the Magistrates' Courts Act 1980 (c 43) (limitation of time), be commenced at any time within two years from the date of the commission of the offence or within six months from its first discovery by the prosecutor, whichever period expires the earlier.

[Criminal Justice Act 2003, s 162.]

3–1951 163. General power of Crown Court to fine offender convicted on indictment. Where a person is convicted on indictment of any offence, other than an offence for which the sentence is fixed by law or falls to be imposed under section 110(2) or 111(2) of the Sentencing Act or under any of sections 225 to 228 of this Act, the court, if not precluded from sentencing an offender by its exercise of some other power, may impose a fine instead of or in addition to dealing with him in any other way in which the court has power to deal with him, subject however to any enactment requiring the offender to be dealt with in a particular way.

[Criminal Justice Act 2003, s 163.]

3–1952 164. Fixing of fines. (1) Before fixing the amount of any fine to be imposed on an offender who is an individual, a court must inquire into his financial circumstances.

(2) The amount of any fine fixed by a court must be such as, in the opinion of the court, reflects the seriousness of the offence.

(3) In fixing the amount of any fine to be imposed on an offender (whether an individual or other person), a court must take into account the circumstances of the case including, among other things, the financial circumstances of the offender so far as they are known, or appear, to the court.

(4) Subsection (3) applies whether taking into account the financial circumstances of the offender has the effect of increasing or reducing the amount of the fine.

(5) Where—

(*a*) an offender has been convicted in his absence in pursuance of section 11 or 12 of the Magistrates' Courts Act 1980 (c 43) (non-appearance of accused), or

(*b*) an offender—

(i) has failed to furnish a statement of his financial circumstances in response to a request which is an official request for the purposes of section 20A of the Criminal Justice Act 1991 (c 53) (offence of making false statement as to financial circumstances),

(ii) has failed to comply with an order under section 162(1), or

(iii) has otherwise failed to co-operate with the court in its inquiry into his financial circumstances,

and the court considers that it has insufficient information to make a proper determination of the financial circumstances of the offender, it may make such determination as it thinks fit.

[Criminal Justice Act 2003, s 164.]

3–1953 165. Remission of fines. (1) This section applies where a court has, in fixing the amount of a fine, determined the offender's financial circumstances under section 164(5).

(2) If, on subsequently inquiring into the offender's financial circumstances, the court is satisfied that had it had the results of that inquiry when sentencing the offender it would—

(*a*) have fixed a smaller amount, or

(*b*) not have fined him,

it may remit the whole or part of the fine.

(3) Where under this section the court remits the whole or part of a fine after a term of imprisonment has been fixed under section 139 of the Sentencing Act (powers of Crown Court in

relation to fines) or section 82(5) of the Magistrates' Courts Act 1980 (magistrates' powers in relation to default) it must reduce the term by the corresponding proportion.

(4) In calculating any reduction required by subsection (3), any fraction of a day is to be ignored.
[Criminal Justice Act 2003, s 165.]

Savings for power to mitigate etc

3–1954 166. Savings for powers to mitigate sentences and deal appropriately with mentally disordered offenders. (1) Nothing in—

(*a*) section 148 (imposing community sentences),
(*b*) section 152, 153 or 157 (imposing custodial sentences),
(*c*) section 156 (pre-sentence reports and other requirements),
(*d*) section 164 (fixing of fines),

prevents a court from mitigating an offender's sentence by taking into account any such matters as, in the opinion of the court, are relevant in mitigation of sentence.

(2) Section 152(2) does not prevent a court, after taking into account such matters, from passing a community sentence even though it is of the opinion that the offence, or the combination of the offence and one or more offences associated with it, was so serious that a community sentence could not normally be justified for the offence.

(3) Nothing in the sections mentioned in subsection (1)(*a*) to (*d*) prevents a court—

(*a*) from mitigating any penalty included in an offender's sentence by taking into account any other penalty included in that sentence, and
(*b*) in the case of an offender who is convicted of one or more other offences, from mitigating his sentence by applying any rule of law as to the totality of sentences.

(4) Subsections (2) and (3) are without prejudice to the generality of subsection (1).
(5) Nothing in the sections mentioned in subsection (1)(*a*) to (*d*) is to be taken—

(*a*) as requiring a court to pass a custodial sentence, or any particular custodial sentence, on a mentally disordered offender, or
(*b*) as restricting any power (whether under the Mental Health Act 1983 (c 20) or otherwise) which enables a court to deal with such an offender in the manner it considers to be most appropriate in all the circumstances.

(6) In subsection (5) "mentally disordered", in relation to a person, means suffering from a mental disorder within the meaning of the Mental Health Act 1983.
[Criminal Justice Act 2003, s 166.]

Sentencing and allocation guidelines

3–1955 167. The Sentencing Guidelines Council. (1) There shall be a Sentencing Guidelines Council (in this Chapter referred to as the Council) consisting of—

(*a*) the Lord Chief Justice, who is to be chairman of the Council,
(*b*) seven members (in this section and section 168 referred to as "judicial members") appointed by the Lord Chief Justice after consultation with the Secretary of State and the Lord Chancellor, and
(*c*) four members (in this section and section 168 referred to as "non-judicial members") appointed by the Secretary of State after consultation with the Lord Chancellor and the Lord Chief Justice.

(2) A person is eligible to be appointed as a judicial member if he is—

(*a*) a Lord Justice of Appeal,
(*b*) a judge of the High Court,
(*c*) a Circuit judge,
(*d*) a District Judge (Magistrates' Courts), or
(*e*) a lay justice.

(3) The judicial members must include a Circuit judge, a District Judge (Magistrates' Courts) and a lay justice.

(4) A person is eligible for appointment as a non-judicial member if he appears to the Secretary of State to have experience in one or more of the following areas—

(*a*) policing,
(*b*) criminal prosecution,
(*c*) criminal defence, and
(*d*) the promotion of the welfare of victims of crime.

(5) The persons eligible for appointment as a non-judicial member by virtue of experience of criminal prosecution include the Director of Public Prosecutions.

(6) The non-judicial members must include at least one person appearing to the Secretary of State to have experience in each area.

(7) The Lord Chief Justice must appoint one of the judicial members or non-judicial members to be deputy chairman of the Council.

(8) In relation to any meeting of the Council from which the Lord Chief Justice is to be absent, he

may nominate any person eligible for appointment as a judicial member to act as a member on his behalf at the meeting.

(9) The Secretary of State may appoint a person appearing to him to have experience of sentencing policy and the administration of sentences to attend and speak at any meeting of the Council.

(10) In this section and section 168 "lay justice" means a justice of the peace who is not a District Judge (Magistrates' Courts).[1]

(10)[2] The Lord Chief Justice may nominate a judicial office holder (as defined in section 109(4) of the Constitutional Reform Act 2005) to exercise his functions under this section.

[Criminal Justice Act 2003, s 167 as amended by the Constitutional Reform Act 2005, Sch 4.]

1. This section came into force on 27 February 2004: see the Criminal Justice Act 2003 (Commencement No 2 and Saving Provisions) Order 2004, SI 2004/81.

2. It appears there was an error in the subsection numbering in the Constitutional Reform Act 2005.

3–1956 **168. Sentencing Guidelines Council: supplementary provisions[1].** (1) In relation to the Council, the Lord Chancellor may by order[2] make provision—

(a) as to the term of office, resignation and re-appointment of judicial members and non-judicial members,

(b) enabling the Lord Chancellor to remove a judicial member from office, with the concurrence of the Lord Chief Justice, on the grounds of incapacity or misbehaviour, and

(c) enabling the Secretary of State to remove a non-judicial member from office on the grounds of incapacity or misbehaviour

(1A) The following provisions apply to an order under subsection (1)—

(a) if the order includes provision falling within subsection (1)(a), the Lord Chancellor must consult the Lord Chief Justice about that provision before making the order;

(b) if the order includes provision falling within subsection (1)(b), the order may not be made unless the Lord Chief Justice agrees to the inclusion of that provision.

(1B) The Lord Chief Justice may, with the concurrence of the Lord Chancellor, by order make provision as to the proceedings of the Council.

(2) In subsection (1)(b) "the appropriate Minister" means—

(a) in relation to a judicial member, the Lord Chancellor, and

(b) in relation to a non-judicial member, the Secretary of State.

(3) The validity of anything done by the Council is not affected by any vacancy among its members, by any defect in the appointment of a member or by any failure to comply with section 167(3), (6) or (7).

(4) The Lord Chancellor may pay—

(a) to any judicial member who is appointed by virtue of being a lay justice, such remuneration or expenses as he may determine, and

(b) to any other judicial member or the Lord Chief Justice, such expenses as he may determine.

(5) The Secretary of State may pay to any non-judicial member such remuneration or expenses as he may determine.

(6) The Lord Chief Justice may nominate a judicial office holder (as defined in section 109(4) of the Constitutional Reform Act 2005) to exercise his functions under subsection (1B).

[Criminal Justice Act 2003, s 168 as amended by the Constitutional Reform Act 2005, s 15(1), Sch 4.]

1. Subsections (3)–(5) came into force on 27 February 2004: see the Criminal Justice Act 2003 (Commencement No 2 and Saving Provisions) Order 2004, SI 2004/81.

2. The Sentencing Guidelines Council (Supplementary Provisions) Order 2004, SI 2004/246 amended by SI 2006/680 has been made which makes provision for the term of office, resignation, re-appointment and removal of members of the Sentencing Guidelines Council.

3–1957 **169. The Sentencing Advisory Panel.** (1) There shall continue to be a Sentencing Advisory Panel (in this Chapter referred to as "the Panel") constituted by the Lord Chancellor after consultation with the Secretary of State and the Lord Chief Justice.

(2) The Lord Chancellor must, after consultation with the Secretary of State and the Lord Chief Justice, appoint one of the members of the Panel to be its chairman.

(3) The Lord Chancellor may pay to any member of the Panel such remuneration or expenses as he may determine.[1]

[Criminal Justice Act 2003, s 169.]

1. This section came into force on 27 February 2004: see the Criminal Justice Act 2003 (Commencement No 2 and Saving Provisions) Order 2004, SI 2004/81.

3–1958 **170. Guidelines relating to sentencing and allocation.** (1) In this Chapter—

(a) "sentencing guidelines" means guidelines relating to the sentencing of offenders, which may be general in nature or limited to a particular category of offence or offender, and

(b) "allocation guidelines" means guidelines relating to decisions by a magistrates' court under section 19 of the Magistrates' Courts Act 1980 (c 43) as to whether an offence is more suitable for summary trial or trial on indictment.

(2) The Secretary of State may at any time propose to the Council—

(a) that sentencing guidelines be framed or revised by the Council—

(i) in respect of offences or offenders of a particular category, or

(ii) in respect of a particular matter affecting sentencing, or

(b) that allocation guidelines be framed or revised by the Council.

(3) The Council may from time to time consider whether to frame sentencing guidelines or allocation guidelines and, if it receives—

(a) a proposal under section 171(2) from the Panel, or

(b) a proposal under subsection (2) from the Secretary of State,

must consider whether to do so.

(4) Where sentencing guidelines or allocation guidelines have been issued by the Council as definitive guidelines, the Council must from time to time (and, in particular, if it receives a proposal under section 171(2) from the Panel or under subsection (2) from the Secretary of State) consider whether to revise them.

(5) Where the Council decides to frame or revise sentencing guidelines, the matters to which the Council must have regard include—

(a) the need to promote consistency in sentencing,

(b) the sentences imposed by courts in England and Wales for offences to which the guidelines relate,

(c) the cost of different sentences and their relative effectiveness in preventing re-offending,

(d) the need to promote public confidence in the criminal justice system, and

(e) the views communicated to the Council, in accordance with section 171(3)(b), by the Panel.

(6) Where the Council decides to frame or revise allocation guidelines, the matters to which the Council must have regard include—

(a) the need to promote consistency in decisions under section 19 of the Magistrates' Courts Act 1980 (c 43), and

(b) the views communicated to the Council, in accordance with section 171(3)(b), by the Panel.

(7) Sentencing guidelines in respect of an offence or category of offences must include criteria for determining the seriousness of the offence or offences, including (where appropriate) criteria for determining the weight to be given to any previous convictions of offenders.

(8) Where the Council has prepared or revised any sentencing guidelines or allocation guidelines, it must—

(a) publish them as draft guidelines, and

(b) consult about the draft guidelines—

(i) the Secretary of State,

(ii) such persons as the Lord Chancellor, after consultation with the Secretary of State, may direct, and

(iii) such other persons as the Council considers appropriate.

(9) The Council may, after making any amendment of the draft guidelines which it considers appropriate, issue the guidelines as definitive guidelines.[1]

[Criminal Justice Act 2003, s 170.]

---

1. This section came into force on 27 February 2004: see the Criminal Justice Act 2003 (Commencement No 2 and Saving Provisions) Order 2004, SI 2004/81.

3–1959 171. Functions of Sentencing Advisory Panel in relation to guidelines. (1) Where the Council decides to frame or revise any sentencing guidelines or allocation guidelines, otherwise than in response to a proposal from the Panel under subsection (2), the Council must notify the Panel.

(2) The Panel may at any time propose to the Council—

(a) that sentencing guidelines be framed or revised by the Council—

(i) in respect of offences or offenders of a particular category, or

(ii) in respect of a particular matter affecting sentencing, or

(b) that allocation guidelines be framed or revised by the Council.

(3) Where the Panel receives a notification under subsection (1) or makes a proposal under subsection (2), the Panel must—

(a) obtain and consider the views on the matters in issue of such persons or bodies as may be determined, after consultation with the Secretary of State and the Lord Chancellor, by the Council, and

(b) formulate its own views on those matters and communicate them to the Council.

(4) Paragraph (a) of subsection (3) does not apply where the Council notifies the Panel of the

Council's view that the urgency of the case makes it impracticable for the Panel to comply with that paragraph.[1]
[Criminal Justice Act 2003, s 171.]

---

1. This section came into force on 27 February 2004: see the Criminal Justice Act 2003 (Commencement No 2 and Saving Provisions) Order 2004, SI 2004/81.

3–1960   172. Duty of court to have regard to sentencing guidelines.   (1) Every court must—

(a) in sentencing an offender, have regard to any guidelines which are relevant to the offender's case, and

(b) in exercising any other function relating to the sentencing of offenders, have regard to any guidelines which are relevant to the exercise of the function.

(2) In subsection (1) "guidelines" means sentencing guidelines issued by the Council under section 170(9) as definitive guidelines, as revised by subsequent guidelines so issued.[1]
[Criminal Justice Act 2003, s 172.]

---

1. This section came into force on 27 February 2004: see the Criminal Justice Act 2003 (Commencement No 2 and Saving Provisions) Order 2004, SI 2004/81.

3–1961   173. Annual report by Council.   (1) The Council must as soon as practicable after the end of each financial year make to the Ministers a report on the exercise of the Council's functions during the year.

(2) If section 167 comes into force after the beginning of a financial year, the first report may relate to a period beginning with the day on which that section comes into force and ending with the end of the next financial year.

(3) The Ministers must lay a copy of the report before each House of Parliament.

(4) The Council must publish the report once the copy has been so laid.

(5) In this section—

"financial year" means a period of 12 months ending with 31st March;

"the Ministers" means the Secretary of State and the Lord Chancellor.[1]
[Criminal Justice Act 2003, s 173.]

---

1. This section came into force on 27 February 2004: see the Criminal Justice Act 2003 (Commencement No 2 and Saving Provisions) Order 2004, SI 2004/81.

Duty of court to explain sentence

3–1962   174. Duty to give reasons for, and explain effect of, sentence.   (1) Subject to subsections (3) and (4), any court passing sentence on an offender—

(a) must state in open court, in ordinary language and in general terms, its reasons for deciding on the sentence passed, and

(b) must explain to the offender in ordinary language—

(i) the effect of the sentence,

(ii) where the offender is required to comply with any order of the court forming part of the sentence, the effects of non-compliance with the order,

(iii) any power of the court, on the application of the offender or any other person, to vary or review any order of the court forming part of the sentence, and

(iv) where the sentence consists of or includes a fine, the effects of failure to pay the fine.

(2) In complying with subsection (1)(a), the court must—

(a) where guidelines indicate that a sentence of a particular kind, or within a particular range, would normally be appropriate for the offence and the sentence is of a different kind, or is outside that range, state the court's reasons for deciding on a sentence of a different kind or outside that range,

(b) where the sentence is a custodial sentence and the duty in subsection (2) of section 152 is not excluded by subsection (1)(a) or (b) or (3) of that section, state that it is of the opinion referred to in section 152(2) and why it is of that opinion,

(c) where the sentence is a community sentence and the case does not fall within section 151(2), state that it is of the opinion that section 148(1) applies and why it is of that opinion,

(d) where as a result of taking into account any matter referred to in section 144(1), the court imposes a punishment on the offender which is less severe than the punishment it would otherwise have imposed, state that fact, and

(e) in any case, mention any aggravating or mitigating factors which the court has regarded as being of particular importance.

(3) Subsection (1)(a) does not apply—

(a) to an offence the sentence for which is fixed by law (provision relating to sentencing for such an offence being made by section 270), or

   (b)   to an offence the sentence for which falls to be imposed under section 51A(2) of the Firearms Act 1968 (c 27) or under subsection (2) of section 110 or 111 of the Sentencing Act (required custodial sentences).

  (4)   The Secretary of State may by order[1]—

   (a)   prescribe cases in which subsection (1)(a) or (b) does not apply, and
   (b)   prescribe cases in which the statement referred to in subsection (1)(a) or the explanation referred to in subsection (1)(b) may be made in the absence of the offender, or may be provided in written form.

  (5)   Where a magistrates' court passes a custodial sentence, it must cause any reason stated by virtue of subsection (2)(b) to be specified in the warrant of commitment and entered on the register.

  (6)   In this section—

"guidelines" has the same meaning as in section 172;
"the register" has the meaning given by section 163 of the Sentencing Act.
[Criminal Justice Act 2003, s 174.]

   1.   Section 174(4) came into force on 5 April 2004: see the Criminal Justice Act (Commencement No 3 and Transitional Provisions) Order 2004, SI 2004/929.

Publication of information by Secretary of State

3–1963   175. Duty to publish information about sentencing.   In section 95 of the Criminal Justice Act 1991 (c 53) (information for financial and other purposes) in subsection (1) before the "or" at the end of paragraph (a) there is inserted—

   "(aa) enabling such persons to become aware of the relative effectiveness of different sentences—

      (i)   in preventing re-offending, and
      (ii)   in promoting public confidence in the criminal justice system;".
[Criminal Justice Act 2003, s 175.]

Interpretation of Chapter

3–1964   176. Interpretation of Chapter 1[1].   In this Chapter—

"allocation guidelines" has the meaning given by section 170(1)(b);
"the Council" means the Sentencing Guidelines Council;
"the Panel" means the Sentencing Advisory Panel;
"sentence" and "sentencing" are to be read in accordance with section 142(3);
"sentencing guidelines" has the meaning given by section 170(1)(a);
"youth community order" has the meaning given by section 147(2).
[Criminal Justice Act 2003, s 176.]

   1.   Section 176 came into force on 5 April 2004: see the Criminal Justice Act (Commencement No 3 and Transitional Provisions) Order 2004, SI 2004/929.

CHAPTER 2[1]
Community Orders: Offenders Aged 16 or Over

3–1965   177. Community orders.   (1) Where a person aged 16 or over is convicted of an offence, the court by or before which he is convicted may make an order (in this Part referred to as a "community order") imposing on him any one or more of the following requirements—

   (a)   an unpaid work requirement (as defined by section 199),
   (b)   an activity requirement (as defined by section 201),
   (c)   a programme requirement (as defined by section 202),
   (d)   a prohibited activity requirement (as defined by section 203),
   (e)   a curfew requirement (as defined by section 204),
   (f)   an exclusion requirement (as defined by section 205),
   (g)   a residence requirement (as defined by section 206),
   (h)   a mental health treatment requirement (as defined by section 207),
   (i)   a drug rehabilitation requirement (as defined by section 209),
   (j)   an alcohol treatment requirement (as defined by section 212),
   (k)   a supervision requirement (as defined by section 213), and
   (l)   in a case where the offender is aged under 25, an attendance centre requirement (as defined by section 214).

  (2)   Subsection (1) has effect subject to sections 150 and 218 and to the following provisions of Chapter 4 relating to particular requirements—

   (a)   section 199(3) (unpaid work requirement),
   (b)   section 201(3) and (4) (activity requirement),
   (c)   section 202(4) and (5) (programme requirement),
   (d)   section 203(2) (prohibited activity requirement),
   (e)   section 207(3) (mental health treatment requirement),
   (f)   section 209(2) (drug rehabilitation requirement), and

(g)   section 212(2) and (3) (alcohol treatment requirement).

(3)   Where the court makes a community order imposing a curfew requirement or an exclusion requirement, the court must also impose an electronic monitoring requirement (as defined by section 215) unless—

(a)   it is prevented from doing so by section 215(2) or 218(4), or
(b)   in the particular circumstances of the case, it considers it inappropriate to do so.

(4)   Where the court makes a community order imposing an unpaid work requirement, an activity requirement, a programme requirement, a prohibited activity requirement, a residence requirement, a mental health treatment requirement, a drug rehabilitation requirement, an alcohol treatment requirement, a supervision requirement or an attendance centre requirement, the court may also impose an electronic monitoring requirement unless prevented from doing so by section 215(2) or 218(4).

(5)   A community order must specify a date, not more than three years after the date of the order, by which all the requirements in it must have been complied with; and a community order which imposes two or more different requirements falling within subsection (1) may also specify an earlier date or dates in relation to compliance with any one or more of them.

(6)   Before making a community order imposing two or more different requirements falling within subsection (1), the court must consider whether, in the circumstances of the case, the requirements are compatible with each other.
[Criminal Justice Act 2003, s 177.]

---

1.   Chapter 2 contains ss 177–180.

3-1966   178. Power to provide for court review of community orders.   (1)   The Secretary of State may by order[1]—

(a)   enable or require a court making a community order to provide for the community order to be reviewed periodically by that or another court,
(b)   enable a court to amend a community order so as to include or remove a provision for review by a court, and
(c)   make provision as to the timing and conduct of reviews and as to the powers of the court on a review.

(2)   An order under this section may, in particular, make provision in relation to community orders corresponding to any provision made by sections 191 and 192 in relation to suspended sentence orders.

(3)   An order under this section may repeal or amend any provision of this Part.[2]
[Criminal Justice Act 2003, s 178.]

---

1.   The Community Order (Review by Specified Courts in Liverpool and Salford) Order 2006, SI 2006/1006 has been made.
2.   Section 178 is in force: see Criminal Justice Act 2003 (Commencement No 7) Order 2005, SI 2005/373.

3-1967   179. Breach, revocation or amendment of community order.   Schedule 8 (which relates to failures to comply with the requirements of community orders and to the revocation or amendment of such orders) shall have effect.
[Criminal Justice Act 2003, s 179.]

3-1968   180. Transfer of community orders to Scotland or Northern Ireland.   Schedule 9 (transfer of community orders to Scotland or Northern Ireland) shall have effect.
[Criminal Justice Act 2003, s 180.]

CHAPTER 3[1]
Prison Sentences of Less than 12 Months
Prison sentences of less than twelve months

3-1969   181. Prison sentences of less than 12 months.   (1)   Any power of a court to impose a sentence of imprisonment for a term of less than 12 months on an offender may be exercised only in accordance with the following provisions of this section unless the court makes an intermittent custody order (as defined by section 183).

(2)   The term of the sentence—

(a)   must be expressed in weeks,
(b)   must be at least 28 weeks,
(c)   must not be more than 51 weeks in respect of any one offence, and
(d)   must not exceed the maximum term permitted for the offence.

(3)   The court, when passing sentence, must—

(a)   specify a period (in this Chapter referred to as "the custodial period") at the end of which the offender is to be released on a licence, and
(b)   by order require the licence to be granted subject to conditions requiring the offender's compliance during the remainder of the term (in this Chapter referred to as "the licence

period") or any part of it with one or more requirements falling within section 182(1) and specified in the order.

(4) In this Part "custody plus order" means an order under subsection (3)(b).

(5) The custodial period—

(a) must be at least 2 weeks, and

(b) in respect of any one offence, must not be more than 13 weeks.

(6) In determining the term of the sentence and the length of the custodial period, the court must ensure that the licence period is at least 26 weeks in length.

(7) Where a court imposes two or more terms of imprisonment in accordance with this section to be served consecutively—

(a) the aggregate length of the terms of imprisonment must not be more than 65 weeks, and

(b) the aggregate length of the custodial periods must not be more than 26 weeks.

(8) A custody plus order which specifies two or more requirements may, in relation to any requirement, refer to compliance within such part of the licence period as is specified in the order.

(9) Subsection (3)(b) does not apply where the sentence is a suspended sentence.
[Criminal Justice Act 2003, s 181.]

1. Chapter 3 contains ss 181–195.

3–1970 182. Licence conditions[1]. (1) The requirements falling within this subsection are—

(a) an unpaid work requirement (as defined by section 199),

(b) an activity requirement (as defined by section 201),

(c) a programme requirement (as defined by section 202),

(d) a prohibited activity requirement (as defined by section 203),

(e) a curfew requirement (as defined by section 204),

(f) an exclusion requirement (as defined by section 205),

(g) a supervision requirement (as defined by section 213), and

(h) in a case where the offender is aged under 25, an attendance centre requirement (as defined by section 214).

(2) The power under section 181(3)(b) to determine the conditions of the licence has effect subject to section 218 and to the following provisions of Chapter 4 relating to particular requirements—

(a) section 199(3) (unpaid work requirement),

(b) section 201(3) and (4) (activity requirement),

(c) section 202(4) and (5) (programme requirement), and

(d) section 203(2) (prohibited activity requirement).

(3) Where the court makes a custody plus order requiring a licence to contain a curfew requirement or an exclusion requirement, the court must also require the licence to contain an electronic monitoring requirement (as defined by section 215) unless—

(a) the court is prevented from doing so by section 215(2) or 218(4), or

(b) in the particular circumstances of the case, it considers it inappropriate to do so.

(4) Where the court makes a custody plus order requiring a licence to contain an unpaid work requirement, an activity requirement, a programme requirement, a prohibited activity requirement, a supervision requirement or an attendance centre requirement, the court may also require the licence to contain an electronic monitoring requirement unless the court is prevented from doing so by section 215(2) or 218(4).

(5) Before making a custody plus order requiring a licence to contain two or more different requirements falling within subsection (1), the court must consider whether, in the circumstances of the case, the requirements are compatible with each other.
[Criminal Justice Act 2003, s 182.]

1. Section 182(1) and (3)–(5) came into force on 26 January 2004. See the Criminal Justice Act 2003 (Commencement No 1) Order, SI 2003/3282.

Intermittent custody

3–1971 183. Intermittent custody[1]. (1) A court may, when passing a sentence of imprisonment for a term complying with subsection (4)—

(a) specify the number of days that the offender must serve in prison under the sentence before being released on licence for the remainder of the term, and

(b) by order—

(i) specify periods during which the offender is to be released temporarily on licence before he has served that number of days in prison, and

(ii) require any licence to be granted subject to conditions requiring the offender's compliance during the licence periods with one or more requirements falling within section 182(1) and specified in the order.

(2) In this Part "intermittent custody order" means an order under subsection (1)(*b*).

(3) In this Chapter—

"licence period", in relation to a term of imprisonment to which an intermittent custody order relates, means any period during which the offender is released on licence by virtue of subsection (1)(*a*) or (*b*)(i);

"the number of custodial days", in relation to a term of imprisonment to which an intermittent custody order relates, means the number of days specified under subsection (1)(*a*).

(4) The term of the sentence—

(*a*) must be expressed in weeks,
(*b*) must be at least 28 weeks,
(*c*) must not be more than 51 weeks in respect of any one offence, and
(*d*) must not exceed the maximum term permitted for the offence.

(5) The number of custodial days—

(*a*) must be at least 14, and
(*b*) in respect of any one offence, must not be more than 90.

(6) A court may not exercise its powers under subsection (1) unless the offender has expressed his willingness to serve the custodial part of the proposed sentence intermittently, during the parts of the sentence that are not to be licence periods.

(7) Where a court exercises its powers under subsection (1) in respect of two or more terms of imprisonment that are to be served consecutively—

(*a*) the aggregate length of the terms of imprisonment must not be more than 65 weeks, and
(*b*) the aggregate of the numbers of custodial days must not be more than 180.

(8) The Secretary of State may by order require a court, in specifying licence periods under subsection (1)(*b*)(i), to specify only—

(*a*) periods of a prescribed duration,
(*b*) periods beginning or ending at prescribed times, or
(*c*) periods including, or not including, specified parts of the week.

(9) An intermittent custody order which specifies two or more requirements may, in relation to any requirement, refer to compliance within such licence period or periods, or part of a licence period, as is specified in the order.
[Criminal Justice Act 2003, s 183.]

---

1. Section 183(1)–(7) and (9) came into force on January 26, 2004. See the Criminal Justice Act 2003 (Commencement No 1) Order, SI 2003/3282. By virtue of the Intermittent Custody (Transitory Provisions) Order, SI 2003/3283, in relation to any time before the commencement of the repeal of s 78 of the Powers of Criminal Courts (Sentencing) Act 2000 by the present Act, s 183 has effect with the following modifications:

    (*a*) in subs (4)(*b*) for "28" substitute "14";
    (*b*) in subs (4)(*c*) for "51" substitute "26";
    (*c*) in subs (5)(*b*) for "90" substitute "45";
    (*d*) in subs (7)(*a*) for "65" substitute "52"; and
    (*a*) in subs (7)(*b*) for "180" substitute "90".

3–1972   **184. Restrictions on power to make intermittent custody order[1].** (1) A court may not make an intermittent custody order unless it has been notified by the Secretary of State that arrangements for implementing such orders are available in the area proposed to be specified in the intermittent custody order and the notice has not been withdrawn.

(2) The court may not make an intermittent custody order in respect of any offender unless—

(*a*) it has consulted an officer of a local probation board,
(*b*) it has received from the Secretary of State notification that suitable prison accommodation is available for the offender during the custodial periods, and
(*c*) it appears to the court that the offender will have suitable accommodation available to him during the licence periods.

(3) In this section "custodial period", in relation to a sentence to which an intermittent custody order relates, means any part of the sentence that is not a licence period.
[Criminal Justice Act 2003, s 184.]

---

1. Sections 184–186 came into force on 26 January 2004. See the Criminal Justice Act 2003 (Commencement No 1) Order, SI 2003/3282.

3–1973   **185. Intermittent custody: licence conditions[1].** (1) Section 183(1)(*b*) has effect subject to section 218 and to the following provisions of Chapter 4 limiting the power to require the licence to contain particular requirements—

(*a*) section 199(3) (unpaid work requirement),
(*b*) section 201(3) and (4) (activity requirement),
(*c*) section 202(4) and (5) (programme requirement), and
(*d*) section 203(2) (prohibited activity requirement).

(2) Subsections (3) to (5) of section 182 have effect in relation to an intermittent custody order as they have effect in relation to a custody plus order.
[Criminal Justice Act 2003, s 185.]

---

1. Sections 184–186 came into force on 26 January 2004. See the Criminal Justice Act 2003 (Commencement No 1) Order, SI 2003/3282.

3–1974   186. Further provisions relating to intermittent custody[1]. (1) Section 21 of the 1952 Act (expenses of conveyance to prison) does not apply in relation to the conveyance to prison at the end of any licence period of an offender to whom an intermittent custody order relates.

(2) The Secretary of State may pay to any offender to whom an intermittent custody order relates the whole or part of any expenses incurred by the offender in travelling to and from prison during licence periods.

(3) In section 49 of the 1952 Act (persons unlawfully at large) after subsection (4) there is inserted—

"(4A) For the purposes of this section a person shall also be deemed to be unlawfully at large if, having been temporarily released in pursuance of an intermittent custody order made under section 183 of the Criminal Justice Act 2003, he remains at large at a time when, by reason of the expiry of the period for which he was temporarily released, he is liable to be detained in pursuance of his sentence."

(4) In section 23 of the Criminal Justice Act 1961 (c 39) (prison rules), in subsection (3) for "The days" there is substituted "Subject to subsection (3A), the days" and after subsection (3) there is inserted—

"(3A) In relation to a prisoner to whom an intermittent custody order under section 183 of the Criminal Justice Act 2003 relates, the only days to which subsection (3) applies are Christmas Day, Good Friday and any day which under the Banking and Financial Dealings Act 1971 is a bank holiday in England and Wales."

(5) In section 1 of the Prisoners (Return to Custody) Act 1995 (c 16) (remaining at large after temporary release) after subsection (1) there is inserted—

"(1A) A person who has been temporarily released in pursuance of an intermittent custody order made under section 183 of the Criminal Justice Act 2003 is guilty of an offence if, without reasonable excuse, he remains unlawfully at large at any time after becoming so at large by virtue of the expiry of the period for which he was temporarily released."

(6) In this section "the 1952 Act" means the Prison Act 1952 (c 52).
[Criminal Justice Act 2003, s 186.]

---

1. Sections 184–186 came into force on 26 January 2004. See the Criminal Justice Act 2003 (Commencement No 1) Order, SI 2003/3282.

Further provision about custody plus orders and intermittent custody orders

3–1975   187. Revocation or amendment of order[1]. Schedule 10 (which contains provisions relating to the revocation or amendment of custody plus orders and the amendment of intermittent custody orders) shall have effect.
[Criminal Justice Act 2003, s 187.]

---

1. Section 187 and Sch 10 came into force on 26 January 2004. See the Criminal Justice Act 2003 (Commencement No 1) Order, SI 2003/3282.

3–1976   188. Transfer of custody plus orders and intermittent custody orders to Scotland or Northern Ireland. Schedule 11 (transfer of custody plus orders and intermittent custody orders to Scotland or Northern Ireland) shall have effect.
[Criminal Justice Act 2003, s 188.]

Suspended sentences

3–1977   189. Suspended sentences of imprisonment[1]. (1) A court which passes a sentence of imprisonment for a term of at least 28 weeks but not more than 51 weeks in accordance with section 181 may—

(a) order the offender to comply during a period specified for the purposes of this paragraph in the order (in this Chapter referred to as "the supervision period") with one or more requirements falling within section 190(1) and specified in the order, and

(b) order that the sentence of imprisonment is not to take effect unless either—

  (i) during the supervision period the offender fails to comply with a requirement imposed under paragraph (a), or

  (ii) during a period specified in the order for the purposes of this sub-paragraph (in this Chapter referred to as "the operational period") the offender commits in the United Kingdom another offence (whether or not punishable with imprisonment),

and (in either case) a court having power to do so subsequently orders under paragraph 8 of Schedule 12 that the original sentence is to take effect.

(2) Where two or more sentences imposed on the same occasion are to be served consecutively, the power conferred by subsection (1) is not exercisable in relation to any of them unless the aggregate of the terms of the sentences does not exceed 65 weeks.

(3) The supervision period and the operational period must each be a period of not less than six months and not more than two years beginning with the date of the order.

(4) The supervision period must not end later than the operational period.

(5) A court which passes a suspended sentence on any person for an offence may not impose a community sentence in his case in respect of that offence or any other offence of which he is convicted by or before the court or for which he is dealt with by the court.

(6) Subject to any provision to the contrary contained in the Criminal Justice Act 1967 (c 80), the Sentencing Act or any other enactment passed or instrument made under any enactment after 31st December 1967, a suspended sentence which has not taken effect under paragraph 8 of Schedule 12 is to be treated as a sentence of imprisonment for the purposes of all enactments and instruments made under enactments.

(7) In this Part—

(a) "suspended sentence order" means an order under subsection (1),

(b) "suspended sentence" means a sentence to which a suspended sentence order relates, and

(c) "community requirement", in relation to a suspended sentence order, means a requirement imposed under subsection (1)(a).

[Criminal Justice Act 2003, s 189[1].]

---

1. Until s 78 of the Powers of Criminal Courts (Sentencing) Act (general limit on magistrates' courts' powers) is repealed by this Act and s 61 of this Act (abolition of sentences of detention in a young offender institution, custody for life etc) comes into force, this section is subject to the modifications in the Criminal Justice Act 2003 (Sentencing) (Transitory Provisions) Order 2005, in this PART, post.

3–1978 190. Imposition of requirements by suspended sentence order. (1) The requirements falling within this subsection are—

(a) an unpaid work requirement (as defined by section 199),

(b) an activity requirement (as defined by section 201),

(c) a programme requirement (as defined by section 202),

(d) a prohibited activity requirement (as defined by section 203),

(e) a curfew requirement (as defined by section 204),

(f) an exclusion requirement (as defined by section 205),

(g) a residence requirement (as defined by section 206),

(h) a mental health treatment requirement (as defined by section 207),

(i) a drug rehabilitation requirement (as defined by section 209),

(j) an alcohol treatment requirement (as defined by section 212),

(k) a supervision requirement (as defined by section 213), and

(l) in a case where the offender is aged under 25, an attendance centre requirement (as defined by section 214).

(2) Section 189(1)(a) has effect subject to section 218 and to the following provisions of Chapter 4 relating to particular requirements—

(a) section 199(3) (unpaid work requirement),

(b) section 201(3) and (4) (activity requirement),

(c) section 202(4) and (5) (programme requirement),

(d) section 203(2) (prohibited activity requirement),

(e) section 207(3) (mental health treatment requirement),

(f) section 209(2) (drug rehabilitation requirement), and

(g) section 212(2) and (3) (alcohol treatment requirement).

(3) Where the court makes a suspended sentence order imposing a curfew requirement or an exclusion requirement, it must also impose an electronic monitoring requirement (as defined by section 215) unless—

(a) the court is prevented from doing so by section 215(2) or 218(4), or

(b) in the particular circumstances of the case, it considers it inappropriate to do so.

(4) Where the court makes a suspended sentence order imposing an unpaid work requirement, an activity requirement, a programme requirement, a prohibited activity requirement, a residence requirement, a mental health treatment requirement, a drug rehabilitation requirement, an alcohol treatment requirement, a supervision requirement or an attendance centre requirement, the court may also impose an electronic monitoring requirement unless the court is prevented from doing so by section 215(2) or 218(4).

(5) Before making a suspended sentence order imposing two or more different requirements falling within subsection (1), the court must consider whether, in the circumstances of the case, the requirements are compatible with each other.

[Criminal Justice Act 2003, s 190.]

3–1979 191. Power to provide for review of suspended sentence order. (1) A suspended sentence order may—

(*a*) provide for the order to be reviewed periodically at specified intervals,

(*b*) provide for each review to be made, subject to section 192(4), at a hearing held for the purpose by the court responsible for the order (a "review hearing"),

(*c*) require the offender to attend each review hearing, and

(*d*) provide for the responsible officer to make to the court responsible for the order, before each review, a report on the offender's progress in complying with the community requirements of the order.

(2) Subsection (1) does not apply in the case of an order imposing a drug rehabilitation requirement (provision for such a requirement to be subject to review being made by section 210).

(3) In this section references to the court responsible for a suspended sentence order are references—

(*a*) where a court is specified in the order in accordance with subsection (4), to that court;

(*b*) in any other case, to the court by which the order is made.

(4) Where the area specified in a suspended sentence order made by a magistrates' court is not the area for which the court acts, the court may, if it thinks fit, include in the order provision specifying for the purpose of subsection (3) a magistrates' court which acts for the area specified in the order.

(5) Where a suspended sentence order has been made on an appeal brought from the Crown Court or from the criminal division of the Court of Appeal, it is to be taken for the purposes of subsection (3)(*b*) to have been made by the Crown Court.

[Criminal Justice Act 2003, s 191.]

3–1980 192. Periodic reviews of suspended sentence order. (1) At a review hearing (within the meaning of subsection (1) of section 191) the court may, after considering the responsible officer's report referred to in that subsection, amend the community requirements of the suspended sentence order, or any provision of the order which relates to those requirements.

(2) The court—

(*a*) may not amend the community requirements of the order so as to impose a requirement of a different kind unless the offender expresses his willingness to comply with that requirement,

(*b*) may not amend a mental health treatment requirement, a drug rehabilitation requirement or an alcohol treatment requirement unless the offender expresses his willingness to comply with the requirement as amended,

(*c*) may amend the supervision period only if the period as amended complies with section 189(3) and (4),

(*d*) may not amend the operational period of the suspended sentence, and

(*e*) except with the consent of the offender, may not amend the order while an appeal against the order is pending.

(3) For the purposes of subsection (2)(*a*)—

(*a*) a community requirement falling within any paragraph of section 190(1) is of the same kind as any other community requirement falling within that paragraph, and

(*b*) an electronic monitoring requirement is a community requirement of the same kind as any requirement falling within section 190(1) to which it relates.

(4) If before a review hearing is held at any review the court, after considering the responsible officer's report, is of the opinion that the offender's progress in complying with the community requirements of the order is satisfactory, it may order that no review hearing is to be held at that review; and if before a review hearing is held at any review, or at a review hearing, the court, after considering that report, is of that opinion, it may amend the suspended sentence order so as to provide for each subsequent review to be held without a hearing.

(5) If at a review held without a hearing the court, after considering the responsible officer's report, is of the opinion that the offender's progress under the order is no longer satisfactory, the court may require the offender to attend a hearing of the court at a specified time and place.

(6) If at a review hearing the court is of the opinion that the offender has without reasonable excuse failed to comply with any of the community requirements of the order, the court may adjourn the hearing for the purpose of dealing with the case under paragraph 8 of Schedule 12.

(7) At a review hearing the court may amend the suspended sentence order so as to vary the intervals specified under section 191(1).

(8) In this section any reference to the court, in relation to a review without a hearing, is to be read—

(*a*) in the case of the Crown Court, as a reference to a judge of the court, and

(*b*) in the case of a magistrates' court, as a reference to a justice of the peace acting for the commission area for which the court acts.

[Criminal Justice Act 2003, s 192.]

3–1981 193. Breach, revocation or amendment of suspended sentence order, and effect of further conviction. Schedule 12 (which relates to the breach, revocation or amendment of the community requirements of suspended sentence orders, and to the effect of any further conviction) shall have effect.

[Criminal Justice Act 2003, s 193.]

3–1982 194. Transfer of suspended sentence orders to Scotland or Northern Ireland. Schedule 13 (transfer of suspended sentence orders to Scotland or Northern Ireland) shall have effect.
[Criminal Justice Act 2003, s 194.]

Interpretation of Chapter

3–1983 195. Interpretation of Chapter 3[1]. In this Chapter—

"custodial period", in relation to a term of imprisonment imposed in accordance with section 181, has the meaning given by subsection (3)(*a*) of that section;
"licence period"—

    (*a*) in relation to a term of imprisonment imposed in accordance with section 181, has the meaning given by subsection (3)(*b*) of that section, and
    (*b*) in relation to a term of imprisonment to which an intermittent custody order relates, has the meaning given by section 183(3);

"the number of custodial days", in relation to a term of imprisonment to which an intermittent custody order relates, has the meaning given by section 183(3);
"operational period" and "supervision period", in relation to a suspended sentence, are to be read in accordance with section 189(1);
"sentence of imprisonment" does not include a committal for contempt of court or any kindred offence.
[Criminal Justice Act 2003, s 195.]

---

1. Section 195 came into force on 26 January 2004. See the Criminal Justice Act 2003 (Commencement No 1) Order, SI 2003/3282.

CHAPTER 4[1]
Further Provisions about Orders under Chapters 2 and 3

Introductory

3–1984 196. Meaning of "relevant order"[2]. (1) In this Chapter "relevant order" means—

    (*a*) a community order,
    (*b*) a custody plus order,
    (*c*) a suspended sentence order, or
    (*d*) an intermittent custody order.

(2) In this Chapter any reference to a requirement being imposed by, or included in, a relevant order is, in relation to a custody plus order or an intermittent custody order, a reference to compliance with the requirement being required by the order to be a condition of a licence.
[Criminal Justice Act 2003, s 196.]

---

1. Chapter 4 contains ss 196–223.
2. Section 196(1)(*d*) and (2) came into force on 26 January 2004. See the Criminal Justice Act 2003 (Commencement No 1) Order, SI 2003/3282.

3–1985 197. Meaning of "the responsible officer" [1]. (1) For the purposes of this Part, "the responsible officer", in relation to an offender to whom a relevant order relates, means—

    (*a*) in a case where the order—

        (i) imposes a curfew requirement or an exclusion requirement but no other requirement mentioned in section 177(1) or, as the case requires, section 182(1) or 190(1), and
        (ii) imposes an electronic monitoring requirement,

    the person who under section 215(3) is responsible for the electronic monitoring required by the order;

    (*b*) in a case where the offender is aged 18 or over and the only requirement imposed by the order is an attendance centre requirement, the officer in charge of the attendance centre in question;
    (*c*) in any other case, the qualifying officer who, as respects the offender, is for the time being responsible for discharging the functions conferred by this Part on the responsible officer.

(2) The following are qualifying officers for the purposes of subsection (1)(*c*)—

    (*a*) in a case where the offender is aged under 18 at the time when the relevant order is made, an officer of a local probation board appointed for or assigned to the petty sessions area for the time being specified in the order or a member of a youth offending team established by a local authority for the time being specified in the order;
    (*b*) in any other case, an officer of a local probation board appointed for or assigned to the petty sessions area for the time being specified in the order.

(3) The Secretary of State may by order—

    (*a*) amend subsections (1) and (2), and
    (*b*) make any other amendments of this Part that appear to him to be necessary or expedient in consequence of any amendment made by virtue of paragraph (*a*).[1]

(4) An order under subsection (3) may, in particular, provide for the court to determine which of two or more descriptions of "responsible officer" is to apply in relation to any relevant order.[1]
[Criminal Justice Act 2003, s 197.]

1. Sections 197–199 came into force (for the purposes of the passing of a sentence of imprisonment to which an intermittent custody order relates and the release on licence of a person serving such a sentence) on 26 January 2004. See the Criminal Justice Act 2003 (Commencement No 1) Order, SI 2003/3282. Sub-sections (3) and (4) now in force for remaining purposes: see Criminal Justice Act 2003 (Commencement No 7) Order 2005, SI 2005/373.

3–1986   198. Duties of responsible officer[1]. (1) Where a relevant order has effect, it is the duty of the responsible officer—

  (*a*)   to make any arrangements that are necessary in connection with the requirements imposed by the order,
  (*b*)   to promote the offender's compliance with those requirements, and
  (*c*)   where appropriate, to take steps to enforce those requirements.

(2) In this section "responsible officer" does not include a person falling within section 197(1)(*a*).
[Criminal Justice Act 2003, s 198.]

1. Sections 197–199 came into force on 26 January 2004. See the Criminal Justice Act 2003 (Commencement No 1) Order, SI 2003/3282.

Requirements available in case of all offenders

3–1986A   199. Unpaid work requirement[1]. (1) In this Part "unpaid work requirement", in relation to a relevant order, means a requirement that the offender must perform unpaid work in accordance with section 200.

(2) The number of hours which a person may be required to work under an unpaid work requirement must be specified in the relevant order and must be in the aggregate—

  (*a*)   not less than 40, and
  (*b*)   not more than 300.

(3) A court may not impose an unpaid work requirement in respect of an offender unless after hearing (if the courts thinks necessary) an appropriate officer, the court is satisfied that the offender is a suitable person to perform work under such a requirement.

(4) In subsection (3) "an appropriate officer" means—

  (*a*)   in the case of an offender aged 18 or over, an officer of a local probation board, and
  (*b*)   in the case of an offender aged under 18, an officer of a local probation board, a social worker of a local authority or a member of a youth offending team.

(5) Where the court makes relevant orders in respect of two or more offences of which the offender has been convicted on the same occasion and includes unpaid work requirements in each of them, the court may direct that the hours of work specified in any of those requirements is to be concurrent with or additional to those specified in any other of those orders, but so that the total number of hours which are not concurrent does not exceed the maximum specified in subsection (2)(*b*).
[Criminal Justice Act 2003, s 199 as amended by the Children Act 2004, Sch 5.]

1. Sections 197–199 came into force on 26 January 2004. See the Criminal Justice Act 2003 (Commencement No 1) Order, SI 2003/3282.

3–1987   200. Obligations of person subject to unpaid work requirement. (1) An offender in respect of whom an unpaid work requirement of a relevant order is in force must perform for the number of hours specified in the order such work at such times as he may be instructed by the responsible officer[1].

(2) Subject to paragraph 20 of Schedule 8 and paragraph 18 of Schedule 12 (power to extend order), the work required to be performed under an unpaid work requirement of a community order or a suspended sentence order must be performed during a period of twelve months.

(3) Unless revoked, a community order imposing an unpaid work requirement remains in force until the offender has worked under it for the number of hours specified in it.

(4) Where an unpaid work requirement is imposed by a suspended sentence order, the supervision period as defined by section 189(1)(*a*) continues until the offender has worked under the order for the number of hours specified in the order, but does not continue beyond the end of the operational period as defined by section 189(1)(*b*)(ii).
[Criminal Justice Act 2003, s 200.]

1. Section 200(1) came into force on 26 January 2004. See the Criminal Justice Act 2003 (Commencement No 1) Order, SI 2003/3282.

3–1988   201. Activity requirement[1]. (1) In this Part "activity requirement", in relation to a relevant order, means a requirement that the offender must do either or both of the following—

  (*a*)   present himself to a person or persons specified in the relevant order at a place or places so specified on such number of days as may be so specified;

(b)   participate in activities specified in the order on such number of days as may be so specified.

(2)   The specified activities may consist of or include activities whose purpose is that of reparation, such as activities involving contact between offenders and persons affected by their offences.

(3)   A court may not include an activity requirement in a relevant order unless—

(a)   it has consulted—

    (i)   in the case of an offender aged 18 or over, an officer of a local probation board,

    (ii)   in the case of an offender aged under 18, either an officer of a local probation board or a member of a youth offending team, and

(b)   it is satisfied that it is feasible to secure compliance with the requirement.

(4)   A court may not include an activity requirement in a relevant order if compliance with that requirement would involve the co-operation of a person other than the offender and the offender's responsible officer, unless that other person consents to its inclusion.

(5)   The aggregate of the number of days specified under subsection (1)(a) and (b) must not exceed 60.

(6)   A requirement such as is mentioned in subsection (1)(a) operates to require the offender—

(a)   in accordance with instructions given by his responsible officer, to present himself at a place or places on the number of days specified in the order, and

(b)   while at any place, to comply with instructions given by, or under the authority of, the person in charge of that place.

(7)   A place specified under subsection (1)(a) must be—

(a)   a community rehabilitation centre, or

(b)   a place that has been approved by the local probation board for the area in which the premises are situated as providing facilities suitable for persons subject to activity requirements.

(8)   Where the place specified under subsection (1)(a) is a community rehabilitation centre, the reference in subsection (6)(a) to the offender presenting himself at the specified place includes a reference to him presenting himself elsewhere than at the centre for the purpose of participating in activities in accordance with instructions given by, or under the authority of, the person in charge of the centre.

(9)   A requirement to participate in activities operates to require the offender—

(a)   in accordance with instructions given by his responsible officer, to participate in activities on the number of days specified in the order, and

(b)   while participating, to comply with instructions given by, or under the authority of, the person in charge of the activities.

(10)   In this section "community rehabilitation centre" means premises—

(a)   at which non-residential facilities are provided for use in connection with the rehabilitation of offenders, and

(b)   which are for the time being approved by the Secretary of State as providing facilities suitable for persons subject to relevant orders.

[Criminal Justice Act 2003, s 201.]

---

1. Sections 201–203 came into force on 26 January 2004. See the Criminal Justice Act 2003 (Commencement No 1) Order, SI 2003/3282.

3–1989   **202. Programme requirement[1].**   (1) In this Part "programme requirement", in relation to a relevant order, means a requirement that the offender must participate in an accredited programme specified in the order at a place so specified on such number of days as may be so specified.

(2)   In this Part "accredited programme" means a programme that is for the time being accredited by the accreditation body.

(3)   In this section—

(a)   "programme" means a systematic set of activities, and

(b)   "the accreditation body" means such body as the Secretary of State may designate for the purposes of this section by order[2].

(4)   A court may not include a programme requirement in a relevant order unless—

(a)   the accredited programme which the court proposes to specify in the order has been recommended to the court as being suitable for the offender—

    (i)   in the case of an offender aged 18 or over, by an officer of a local probation board, or

    (ii)   in the case of an offender aged under 18, either by an officer of a local probation board or by a member of a youth offending team, and

(b)   the court is satisfied that the programme is (or, where the relevant order is a custody plus order or an intermittent custody order, will be) available at the place proposed to be specified.

(5)   A court may not include a programme requirement in a relevant order if compliance with that requirement would involve the co-operation of a person other than the offender and the offender's responsible officer, unless that other person consents to its inclusion.

(6) A requirement to attend an accredited programme operates to require the offender—

(a) in accordance with instructions given by the responsible officer, to participate in the accredited programme at the place specified in the order on the number of days specified in the order, and

(b) while at that place, to comply with instructions given by, or under the authority of, the person in charge of the programme.

(7) A place specified in an order must be a place that has been approved by the local probation board for the area in which the premises are situated as providing facilities suitable for persons subject to programme requirements.
[Criminal Justice Act 2003, s 202.]

1. Sections 201–203 came into force (for the purposes of the passing of a sentence of imprisonment to which an intermittent custody order relates and the release on licence of a person serving such a sentence) on 26 January 2004. See the Criminal Justice Act 2003 (Commencement No 1) Order, SI 2003/3282. Section 202(3)(b) now in force for remaining purposes: Criminal Justice Act 2003 (Commencement No 7) Order 2005, SI 2005/373.
2. The Criminal Justice (Sentencing) (Programme and Electronic Monitoring Requirements) Order 2005, SI 2005/963 has been made which designates the Correctional Services Accreditation Panel.

3–1990 203. Prohibited activity requirement[1]. (1) In this Part "prohibited activity requirement", in relation to a relevant order, means a requirement that the offender must refrain from participating in activities specified in the order—

(a) on a day or days so specified, or
(b) during a period so specified.

(2) A court may not include a prohibited activity requirement in a relevant order unless it has consulted—

(a) in the case of an offender aged 18 or over, an officer of a local probation board;
(b) in the case of an offender aged under 18, either an officer of a local probation board or a member of a youth offending team.

(3) The requirements that may by virtue of this section be included in a relevant order include a requirement that the offender does not possess, use or carry a firearm within the meaning of the Firearms Act 1968 (c 27).
[Criminal Justice Act 2003, s 203.]

1. Sections 201–203 came into force on 26 January 2004. See the Criminal Justice Act 2003 (Commencement No 1) Order, SI 2003/3282.

3–1991 204. Curfew requirement[1]. (1) In this Part "curfew requirement", in relation to a relevant order, means a requirement that the offender must remain, for periods specified in the relevant order, at a place so specified.

(2) A relevant order imposing a curfew requirement may specify different places or different periods for different days, but may not specify periods which amount to less than two hours or more than twelve hours in any day.

(3) A community order or suspended sentence order which imposes a curfew requirement may not specify periods which fall outside the period of six months beginning with the day on which it is made.

(4) A custody plus order which imposes a curfew requirement may not specify a period which falls outside the period of six months beginning with the first day of the licence period as defined by section 181(3)(b).

(5) An intermittent custody order which imposes a curfew requirement must not specify a period if to do so would cause the aggregate number of days on which the offender is subject to the requirement for any part of the day to exceed 182.

(6) Before making a relevant order imposing a curfew requirement, the court must obtain and consider information about the place proposed to be specified in the order (including information as to the attitude of persons likely to be affected by the enforced presence there of the offender).
[Criminal Justice Act 2003, s 204.]

1. Section 204(1), (2), (5) and (6) came into force on 26 January 2004. See the Criminal Justice Act 2003 (Commencement No 1) Order, SI 2003/3282.

3–1992 205. Exclusion requirement[1]. (1) In this Part "exclusion requirement", in relation to a relevant order, means a provision prohibiting the offender from entering a place specified in the order for a period so specified.

(2) Where the relevant order is a community order, the period specified must not be more than two years.

(3) An exclusion requirement—

(a) may provide for the prohibition to operate only during the periods specified in the order, and
(b) may specify different places for different periods or days.

(4) In this section "place" includes an area.
[Criminal Justice Act 2003, s 205.]

1. Section 205(1), (3) and (4) came into force on 26 January 2004. See the Criminal Justice Act 2003 (Commencement No 1) Order, SI 2003/3282.

3–1993 206. Residence requirement. (1) In this Part, "residence requirement", in relation to a community order or a suspended sentence order, means a requirement that, during a period specified in the relevant order, the offender must reside at a place specified in the order.

(2) If the order so provides, a residence requirement does not prohibit the offender from residing, with the prior approval of the responsible officer, at a place other than that specified in the order.

(3) Before making a community order or suspended sentence order containing a residence requirement, the court must consider the home surroundings of the offender.

(4) A court may not specify a hostel or other institution as the place where an offender must reside, except on the recommendation of an officer of a local probation board.
[Criminal Justice Act 2003, s 206.]

3–1994 207. Mental health treatment requirement. (1) In this Part, "mental health treatment requirement", in relation to a community order or suspended sentence order, means a requirement that the offender must submit, during a period or periods specified in the order, to treatment by or under the direction of a registered medical practitioner or a chartered psychologist (or both, for different periods) with a view to the improvement of the offender's mental condition.

(2) The treatment required must be such one of the following kinds of treatment as may be specified in the relevant order—

(a) treatment as a resident patient in an independent hospital or care home within the meaning of the Care Standards Act 2000 (c 14) or a hospital within the meaning of the Mental Health Act 1983 (c 20), but not in hospital premises where high security psychiatric services within the meaning of that Act are provided;

(b) treatment as a non-resident patient at such institution or place as may be specified in the order;

(c) treatment by or under the direction of such registered medical practitioner or chartered psychologist (or both) as may be so specified;

but the nature of the treatment is not to be specified in the order except as mentioned in paragraph (a), (b) or (c).

(3) A court may not by virtue of this section include a mental health treatment requirement in a relevant order unless—

(a) the court is satisfied, on the evidence of a registered medical practitioner approved for the purposes of section 12 of the Mental Health Act 1983, that the mental condition of the offender—

(i) is such as requires and may be susceptible to treatment, but

(ii) is not such as to warrant the making of a hospital order or guardianship order within the meaning of that Act;

(b) the court is also satisfied that arrangements have been or can be made for the treatment intended to be specified in the order (including arrangements for the reception of the offender where he is to be required to submit to treatment as a resident patient); and

(c) the offender has expressed his willingness to comply with such a requirement.

(4) While the offender is under treatment as a resident patient in pursuance of a mental health requirement of a relevant order, his responsible officer shall carry out the supervision of the offender to such extent only as may be necessary for the purpose of the revocation or amendment of the order.

(5) Subsections (2) and (3) of section 54 of the Mental Health Act 1983 (c 20) have effect with respect to proof for the purposes of subsection (3)(a) of an offender's mental condition as they have effect with respect to proof of an offender's mental condition for the purposes of section 37(2)(a) of that Act.

(6) In this section and section 208, "chartered psychologist" means a person for the time being listed in the British Psychological Society's Register of Chartered Psychologists.
[Criminal Justice Act 2003, s 207.]

3–1995 208. Mental health treatment at place other than that specified in order. (1) Where the medical practitioner or chartered psychologist by whom or under whose direction an offender is being treated for his mental condition in pursuance of a mental health treatment requirement is of the opinion that part of the treatment can be better or more conveniently given in or at an institution or place which—

(a) is not specified in the relevant order, and

(b) is one in or at which the treatment of the offender will be given by or under the direction of a registered medical practitioner or chartered psychologist,

he may, with the consent of the offender, make arrangements for him to be treated accordingly.

(2) Such arrangements as are mentioned in subsection (1) may provide for the offender to receive part of his treatment as a resident patient in an institution or place notwithstanding that the institution or place is not one which could have been specified for that purpose in the relevant order.

(3) Where any such arrangements as are mentioned in subsection (1) are made for the treatment of an offender—

(a) the medical practitioner or chartered psychologist by whom the arrangements are made shall give notice in writing to the offender's responsible officer, specifying the institution or place in or at which the treatment is to be carried out; and

(b) the treatment provided for by the arrangements shall be deemed to be treatment to which he is required to submit in pursuance of the relevant order.

[Criminal Justice Act 2003, s 207.]

3–1996 209. Drug rehabilitation requirement. (1) In this Part "drug rehabilitation requirement", in relation to a community order or suspended sentence order, means a requirement that during a period specified in the order ("the treatment and testing period") the offender—

(a) must submit to treatment by or under the direction of a specified person having the necessary qualifications or experience with a view to the reduction or elimination of the offender's dependency on or propensity to misuse drugs, and

(b) for the purpose of ascertaining whether he has any drug in his body during that period, must provide samples of such description as may be so determined, at such times or in such circumstances as may (subject to the provisions of the order) be determined by the responsible officer or by the person specified as the person by or under whose direction the treatment is to be provided.

(2) A court may not impose a drug rehabilitation requirement unless—

(a) it is satisfied—

(i) that the offender is dependent on, or has a propensity to misuse, drugs, and

(ii) that his dependency or propensity is such as requires and may be susceptible to treatment,

(b) it is also satisfied that arrangements have been or can be made for the treatment intended to be specified in the order (including arrangements for the reception of the offender where he is to be required to submit to treatment as a resident),

(c) the requirement has been recommended to the court as being suitable for the offender—

(i) in the case of an offender aged 18 or over, by an officer of a local probation board, or

(ii) in the case of an offender aged under 18, either by an officer of a local probation board or by a member of a youth offending team, and

(d) the offender expresses his willingness to comply with the requirement.

(3) The treatment and testing period must be at least six months.

(4) The required treatment for any particular period must be—

(a) treatment as a resident in such institution or place as may be specified in the order, or

(b) treatment as a non-resident in or at such institution or place, and at such intervals, as may be so specified;

but the nature of the treatment is not to be specified in the order except as mentioned in paragraph (a) or (b) above.

(5) The function of making a determination as to the provision of samples under provision included in the community order or suspended sentence order by virtue of subsection (1)(b) is to be exercised in accordance with guidance given from time to time by the Secretary of State.

(6) A community order or suspended sentence order imposing a drug rehabilitation requirement must provide that the results of tests carried out on any samples provided by the offender in pursuance of the requirement to a person other than the responsible officer are to be communicated to the responsible officer.

(7) In this section "drug" means a controlled drug as defined by section 2 of the Misuse of Drugs Act 1971 (c 38).

[Criminal Justice Act 2003, s 209.]

3–1997 210. Drug rehabilitation requirement: provision for review by court. (1) A community order or suspended sentence order imposing a drug rehabilitation requirement may (and must if the treatment and testing period is more than 12 months)—

(a) provide for the requirement to be reviewed periodically at intervals of not less than one month,

(b) provide for each review of the requirement to be made, subject to section 211(6), at a hearing held for the purpose by the court responsible for the order (a "review hearing"),

(c) require the offender to attend each review hearing,

(d) provide for the responsible officer to make to the court responsible for the order, before each review, a report in writing on the offender's progress under the requirement, and

(e) provide for each such report to include the test results communicated to the responsible officer under section 209(6) or otherwise and the views of the treatment provider as to the treatment and testing of the offender.

(2) In this section references to the court responsible for a community order or suspended sentence order imposing a drug rehabilitation requirement are references—

(a) where a court is specified in the order in accordance with subsection (3), to that court;

(b) in any other case, to the court by which the order is made.

(3) Where the area specified in a community order or suspended sentence order which is made by a magistrates' court and imposes a drug rehabilitation requirement is not the area for which the court

acts, the court may, if it thinks fit, include in the order provision specifying for the purposes of subsection (2) a magistrates' court which acts for the area specified in the order.

(4) Where a community order or suspended sentence order imposing a drug rehabilitation requirement has been made on an appeal brought from the Crown Court or from the criminal division of the Court of Appeal, for the purposes of subsection (2)(*b*) it shall be taken to have been made by the Crown Court.

[Criminal Justice Act 2003, s 210.]

3–1998   211. Periodic review of drug rehabilitation requirement.   (1) At a review hearing (within the meaning given by subsection (1) of section 210) the court may, after considering the responsible officer's report referred to in that subsection, amend the community order or suspended sentence order, so far as it relates to the drug rehabilitation requirement.

(2) The court—

(*a*)   may not amend the drug rehabilitation requirement unless the offender expresses his willingness to comply with the requirement as amended,

(*b*)   may not amend any provision of the order so as to reduce the period for which the drug rehabilitation requirement has effect below the minimum specified in section 209(3), and

(*c*)   except with the consent of the offender, may not amend any requirement or provision of the order while an appeal against the order is pending.

(3) If the offender fails to express his willingness to comply with the drug rehabilitation requirement as proposed to be amended by the court, the court may—

(*a*)   revoke the community order, or the suspended sentence order and the suspended sentence to which it relates, and

(*b*)   deal with him, for the offence in respect of which the order was made, in any way in which he could have been dealt with for that offence by the court which made the order if the order had not been made.

(4) In dealing with the offender under subsection (3)(*b*), the court—

(*a*)   shall take into account the extent to which the offender has complied with the requirements of the order, and

(*b*)   may impose a custodial sentence (where the order was made in respect of an offence punishable with such a sentence) notwithstanding anything in section 152(2).

(5) Where the order is a community order made by a magistrates' court in the case of an offender under 18 years of age in respect of an offence triable only on indictment in the case of an adult, any powers exercisable under subsection (3)(*b*) in respect of the offender after he attains the age of 18 are powers to do either or both of the following—

(*a*)   to impose a fine not exceeding £5,000 for the offence in respect of which the order was made;

(*b*)   to deal with the offender for that offence in any way in which the court could deal with him if it had just convicted him of an offence punishable with imprisonment for a term not exceeding twelve months.

(6) If at a review hearing (as defined by section 210(1)(*b*)) the court, after considering the responsible officer's report, is of the opinion that the offender's progress under the requirement is satisfactory, the court may so amend the order as to provide for each subsequent review to be made by the court without a hearing.

(7) If at a review without a hearing the court, after considering the responsible officer's report, is of the opinion that the offender's progress under the requirement is no longer satisfactory, the court may require the offender to attend a hearing of the court at a specified time and place.

(8) At that hearing the court, after considering that report, may—

(*a*)   exercise the powers conferred by this section as if the hearing were a review hearing, and

(*b*)   so amend the order as to provide for each subsequent review to be made at a review hearing.

(9) In this section any reference to the court, in relation to a review without a hearing, is to be read—

(*a*)   in the case of the Crown Court, as a reference to a judge of the court;

(*b*)   in the case of a magistrates' court, as a reference to a justice of the peace acting for the commission area for which the court acts.

[Criminal Justice Act 2003, s 211.]

3–1999   212. Alcohol treatment requirement.   (1) In this Part "alcohol treatment requirement", in relation to a community order or suspended sentence order, means a requirement that the offender must submit during a period specified in the order to treatment by or under the direction of a specified person having the necessary qualifications or experience with a view to the reduction or elimination of the offender's dependency on alcohol.

(2) A court may not impose an alcohol treatment requirement in respect of an offender unless it is satisfied—

(*a*)   that he is dependent on alcohol,

(*b*)   that his dependency is such as requires and may be susceptible to treatment, and

(c) that arrangements have been or can be made for the treatment intended to be specified in the order (including arrangements for the reception of the offender where he is to be required to submit to treatment as a resident).

(3) A court may not impose an alcohol treatment requirement unless the offender expresses his willingness to comply with its requirements.

(4) The period for which the alcohol treatment requirement has effect must be not less than six months.

(5) The treatment required by an alcohol treatment requirement for any particular period must be—

(a) treatment as a resident in such institution or place as may be specified in the order,

(b) treatment as a non-resident in or at such institution or place, and at such intervals, as may be so specified, or

(c) treatment by or under the direction of such person having the necessary qualification or experience as may be so specified;

but the nature of the treatment shall not be specified in the order except as mentioned in paragraph (a), (b) or (c) above.
[Criminal Justice Act 2003, s 212.]

3–2000   213. Supervision requirement[1]. (1) In this Part "supervision requirement", in relation to a relevant order, means a requirement that, during the relevant period, the offender must attend appointments with the responsible officer or another person determined by the responsible officer, at such time and place as may be determined by the officer.

(2) The purpose for which a supervision requirement may be imposed is that of promoting the offender's rehabilitation.

(3) In subsection (1) "the relevant period" means—

(a) in relation to a community order, the period for which the community order remains in force,

(b) in relation to a custody plus order, the licence period as defined by section 181(3)(b),

(c) in relation to an intermittent custody order, the licence periods as defined by section 183(3), and

(d) in relation to a suspended sentence order, the supervision period as defined by section 189(1)(a).
[Criminal Justice Act 2003, s 213.]

---

1. Section 213(1), (2) and (3)(c) came into force on 26 January 2004. See the Criminal Justice Act 2003 (Commencement No 1) Order, SI 2003/3282.

Requirements available only in case of offenders aged under 25

3–2001   214. Attendance centre requirement[1]. (1) In this Part "attendance centre requirement", in relation to a relevant order, means a requirement that the offender must attend at an attendance centre specified in the relevant order for such number of hours as may be so specified.

(2) The aggregate number of hours for which the offender may be required to attend at an attendance centre must not be less than 12 or more than 36.

(3) The court may not impose an attendance centre requirement unless the court is satisfied that the attendance centre to be specified in it is reasonably accessible to the offender concerned, having regard to the means of access available to him and any other circumstances.

(4) The first time at which the offender is required to attend at the attendance centre is a time notified to the offender by the responsible officer.

(5) The subsequent hours are to be fixed by the officer in charge of the centre, having regard to the offender's circumstances.

(6) An offender may not be required under this section to attend at an attendance centre on more than one occasion on any day, or for more than three hours on any occasion.
[Criminal Justice Act 2003, s 214.]

---

1. Sections 214 and 215 came into force on 26 January 2004. See the Criminal Justice Act 2003 (Commencement No 1) Order, SI 2003/3282.

Electronic monitoring

3–2002   215. Electronic monitoring requirement[1]. (1) In this Part "electronic monitoring requirement", in relation to a relevant order, means a requirement for securing the electronic monitoring of the offender's compliance with other requirements imposed by the order during a period specified in the order, or determined by the responsible officer in accordance with the relevant order.

(2) Where—

(a) it is proposed to include in a relevant order a requirement for securing electronic monitoring in accordance with this section, but

(b) there is a person (other than the offender) without whose co-operation it will not be practicable to secure the monitoring,

the requirement may not be included in the order without that person's consent.

(3) A relevant order which includes an electronic monitoring requirement must include provision for making a person responsible for the monitoring; and a person who is made so responsible must be of a description specified in an order² made by the Secretary of State.

(4) Where an electronic monitoring requirement is required to take effect during a period determined by the responsible officer in accordance with the relevant order, the responsible officer must, before the beginning of that period, notify—

(a)   the offender,

(b)   the person responsible for the monitoring, and

(c)   any person falling within subsection (2)(b),

of the time when the period is to begin.

[Criminal Justice Act 2003, s 215.]

---

1. Sections 214 and 215 came into force (for the purposes of the passing of a sentence of imprisonment to which an intermittent custody order relates and the release on licence of a person serving such a sentence) on 26 January 2004. See the Criminal Justice Act 2003 (Commencement No 1) Order, SI 2003/3282. Section 215(3) now in force for remaining purposes: see Criminal Justice Act 2003 (Commencement No 7) Order 2005, SI 2005/373.

2. The Criminal Justice (Sentencing) (Programme and Electronic Monitoring Requirements) Order 2005, SI 2005/963 has been made.

Provisions applying to relevant orders generally

3–2003   216. Petty sessions area to be specified in relevant order¹. (1) A community order or suspended sentence order must specify the petty sessions area in which the offender resides or will reside.

(2) A custody plus order or an intermittent custody order must specify the petty sessions area in which the offender will reside—

(a)   in the case of a custody plus order, during the licence period as defined by section 181(3)(b), or

(b)   in the case of an intermittent custody order, during the licence periods as defined by section 183(3).

[Criminal Justice Act 2003, s 216.]

---

1. Section 216(2)(b) came into force on 26 January 2004. See the Criminal Justice Act 2003 (Commencement No 1) Order, SI 2003/3282.

3–2004   217. Requirement to avoid conflict with religious beliefs, etc¹. (1) The court must ensure, as far as practicable, that any requirement imposed by a relevant order is such as to avoid—

(a)   any conflict with the offender's religious beliefs or with the requirements of any other relevant order to which he may be subject; and

(b)   any interference with the times, if any, at which he normally works or attends school or any other educational establishment.

(2) The responsible officer in relation to an offender to whom a relevant order relates must ensure, as far as practicable, that any instruction given or requirement imposed by him in pursuance of the order is such as to avoid the conflict or interference mentioned in subsection (1).

(3) The Secretary of State may by order provide that subsection (1) or (2) is to have effect with such additional restrictions as may be specified in the order.¹

[Criminal Justice Act 2003, s 217.]

---

1. Sections 217 and 218 came into force (for the purposes of the passing of a sentence of imprisonment to which an intermittent custody order relates and the release on licence of a person serving such a sentence) on 26 January 2004. See the Criminal Justice Act 2003 (Commencement No 1) Order, SI 2003/3282. Section 217(3) now in force for remaining purposes: see Criminal Justice Act 2003 (Commencement No 7) Order 2005, SI 2005/373.

3–2005   218. Availability of arrangements in local area¹. (1) A court may not include an unpaid work requirement in a relevant order unless the court is satisfied that provision for the offender to work under such a requirement can be made under the arrangements for persons to perform work under such a requirement which exist in the petty sessions area in which he resides or will reside.

(2) A court may not include an activity requirement in a relevant order unless the court is satisfied that provision for the offender to participate in the activities proposed to be specified in the order can be made under the arrangements for persons to participate in such activities which exist in the petty sessions area in which he resides or will reside.

(3) A court may not include an attendance centre requirement in a relevant order in respect of an offender unless the court has been notified by the Secretary of State that an attendance centre is available for persons of his description.

(4) A court may not include an electronic monitoring requirement in a relevant order in respect of an offender unless the court—

(a)   has been notified by the Secretary of State that electronic monitoring arrangements are available in the relevant areas mentioned in subsections (5) to (7), and

(b)   is satisfied that the necessary provision can be made under those arrangements.

(5) In the case of a relevant order containing a curfew requirement or an exclusion requirement,

the relevant area for the purposes of subsection (4) is the area in which the place proposed to be specified in the order is situated.

(6) In the case of a relevant order containing an attendance centre requirement, the relevant area for the purposes of subsection (4) is the area in which the attendance centre proposed to be specified in the order is situated.

(7) In the case of any other relevant order, the relevant area for the purposes of subsection (4) is the petty sessions area proposed to be specified in the order.

(8) In subsection (5) "place", in relation to an exclusion requirement, has the same meaning as in section 205.
[Criminal Justice Act 2003, s 218.]

---

1. Sections 217 and 218 came into force on 26 January 2004. See the Criminal Justice Act 2003 (Commencement No 1) Order, SI 2003/3282.

3–2006   219. Provision of copies of relevant orders[1]. (1) The court by which any relevant order is made must forthwith provide copies of the order—

    (*a*) to the offender,
    (*b*) if the offender is aged 18 or over, to an officer of a local probation board assigned to the court,
    (*c*) if the offender is aged 16 or 17, to an officer of a local probation board assigned to the court or to a member of a youth offending team assigned to the court, and
    (*d*) where the order specifies a petty sessions area for which the court making the order does not act, to the local probation board acting for that area.

(2) Where a relevant order imposes any requirement specified in the first column of Schedule 14, the court by which the order is made must also forthwith provide the person specified in relation to that requirement in the second column of that Schedule with a copy of so much of the order as relates to that requirement.

(3) Where a relevant order specifies a petty sessions area for which the court making the order does not act, the court making the order must provide to the magistrates's court acting for that area—

    (*a*) a copy of the order, and
    (*b*) such documents and information relating to the case as it considers likely to be of assistance to a court acting for that area in the exercise of its functions in relation to the order.
[Criminal Justice Act 2003, s 219.]

---

1. Section 219(1)(*a*), (*b*) and (*d*), (2) and (3) and Sch 14 came into force on 26 January 2004. See the Criminal Justice Act 2003 (Commencement No 1) Order, SI 2003/3282.

3–2007   220. Duty of offender to keep in touch with responsible officer.   (1) An offender in respect of whom a community order or a suspended sentence order is in force—

    (*a*) must keep in touch with the responsible officer in accordance with such instructions as he may from time to time be given by that officer, and
    (*b*) must notify him of any change of address.

(2) The obligation imposed by subsection (1) is enforceable as if it were a requirement imposed by the order.
[Criminal Justice Act 2003, s 220.]

Powers of Secretary of State

3–2008   221. Provision of attendance centres[1].   (1) The Secretary of State may continue to provide attendance centres.

(2) In this Part "attendance centre" means a place at which offenders aged under 25 may be required to attend and be given under supervision appropriate occupation or instruction in pursuance of—

    (*a*) attendance centre requirements of relevant orders, or
    (*b*) attendance centre orders under section 60 of the Sentencing Act.

(3) For the purpose of providing attendance centres, the Secretary of State may make arrangements with any local authority or police authority for the use of premises of that authority.
[Criminal Justice Act 2003, s 221.]

---

1. Sections 221 and 222 came into force on 26 January 2004. See the Criminal Justice Act 2003 (Commencement No 1) Order, SI 2003/3282.

3–2009   222. Rules[1].   (1) The Secretary of State may make rules for regulating—

    (*a*) the supervision of persons who are subject to relevant orders,
    (*b*) without prejudice to the generality of paragraph (*a*), the functions of responsible officers in relation to offenders subject to relevant orders,
    (*c*) the arrangements to be made by local probation boards for persons subject to unpaid work requirements to perform work and the performance of such work,
    (*d*) the provision and carrying on of attendance centres and community rehabilitation centres,

(*e*) the attendance of persons subject to activity requirements or attendance centre requirements at the places at which they are required to attend, including hours of attendance, reckoning days of attendance and the keeping of attendance records,

(*f*) electronic monitoring in pursuance of an electronic monitoring requirement, and

(*g*) without prejudice to the generality of paragraph (*f*), the functions of persons made responsible for securing electronic monitoring in pursuance of such a requirement.

(2) Rules under subsection (1)(*c*) may, in particular, make provision—

(*a*) limiting the number of hours of work to be done by a person on any one day,

(*b*) as to the reckoning of hours worked and the keeping of work records, and

(*c*) for the payment of travelling and other expenses in connection with the performance of work.

[Criminal Justice Act 2003, s 222.]

---

1. Sections 221 and 222 came into force on 26 January 2004. See the Criminal Justice Act 2003 (Commencement No 1) Order, SI 2003/3282.

3–2010 223. Power to amend limits[1]. (1) The Secretary of State may by order amend—

(*a*) subsection (2) of section 199 (unpaid work requirement), or

(*b*) subsection (2) of section 204 (curfew requirement),

by substituting, for the maximum number of hours for the time being specified in that subsection, such other number of hours as may be specified in the order.

(2) The Secretary of State may by order amend any of the provisions mentioned in subsection (3) by substituting, for any period for the time being specified in the provision, such other period as may be specified in the order.

(3) Those provisions are—

(*a*) section 204(3) (curfew requirement);

(*b*) section 205(2) (exclusion requirement);

(*c*) section 209(3) (drug rehabilitation requirement);

(*d*) section 212(4) (alcohol treatment requirement).

[Criminal Justice Act 2003, s 223.]

---

1. Section 223 is in force: see Criminal Justice Act 2003 (Commencement No 1 Order SI 2003/3283, and Criminal Justice Act 2003 (Commencement No 7) Order 2005, SI 2005/373.

CHAPTER 5[1]
Dangerous Offenders

3–2011 224. Meaning of "specified offence" etc[2]. (1) An offence is a "specified offence" for the purposes of this Chapter if it is a specified violent offence or a specified sexual offence.

(2) An offence is a "serious offence" for the purposes of this Chapter if and only if—

(*a*) it is a specified offence, and

(*b*) it is, apart from section 225, punishable in the case of a person aged 18 or over by—

(i) imprisonment for life, or

(ii) imprisonment for a determinate period of ten years or more.

(3) In this Chapter—

"relevant offence" has the meaning given by section 229(4);

"serious harm" means death or serious personal injury, whether physical or psychological;

"specified violent offence" means an offence specified in Part 1 of Schedule 15;

"specified sexual offence" means an offence specified in Part 2 of that Schedule.

[Criminal Justice Act 2003, s 224.]

---

1. Chapter 5 contains ss 224–236.

2. Until s 61 of this Act (abolition of sentences of detention in a young offender institution, custody for life etc) comes into force, this section is subject to the modifications in the Criminal Justice Act 2003 (Sentencing) (Transitory Provisions) Order 2005, in this PART, post.

3–2012 225. Life sentence or imprisonment for public protection for serious offences[1]. (1) This section applies where—

(*a*) a person aged 18 or over is convicted of a serious offence committed after the commencement of this section, and

(*b*) the court is of the opinion that there is a significant risk to members of the public of serious harm occasioned by the commission by him of further specified offences.

(2) If—

(*a*) the offence is one in respect of which the offender would apart from this section be liable to imprisonment for life, and

(*b*) the court considers that the seriousness of the offence, or of the offence and one or more offences associated with it, is such as to justify the imposition of a sentence of imprisonment for life, the court must impose a sentence of imprisonment for life.

(3) In a case not falling within subsection (2), the court must impose a sentence of imprisonment for public protection.

(4) A sentence of imprisonment for public protection is a sentence of imprisonment for an indeterminate period, subject to the provisions of Chapter 2 of Part 2 of the Crime (Sentences) Act 1997 (c 43) as to the release of prisoners and duration of licences.

(5) An offence the sentence for which is imposed under this section is not to be regarded as an offence the sentence for which is fixed by law.

[Criminal Justice Act 2003, s 225.]

---

1. Until s 61 of this Act (abolition of sentences of detention in a young offender institution, custody for life etc) comes into force, this section is subject to the modifications in the Criminal Justice Act 2003 (Sentencing) (Transitory Provisions) Order 2005, in this PART, post.

3–2013　226. Detention for life or detention for public protection for serious offences committed by those under 18.　(1) This section applies where—

(a) a person aged under 18 is convicted of a serious offence committed after the commencement of this section, and

(b) the court is of the opinion that there is a significant risk to members of the public of serious harm occasioned by the commission by him of further specified offences.

(2) If—

(a) the offence is one in respect of which the offender would apart from this section be liable to a sentence of detention for life under section 91 of the Sentencing Act, and

(b) the court considers that the seriousness of the offence, or of the offence and one or more offences associated with it, is such as to justify the imposition of a sentence of detention for life,

the court must impose a sentence of detention for life under that section.

(3) If, in a case not falling within subsection (2), the court considers that an extended sentence under section 228 would not be adequate for the purpose of protecting the public from serious harm occasioned by the commission by the offender of further specified offences, the court must impose a sentence of detention for public protection.

(4) A sentence of detention for public protection is a sentence of detention for an indeterminate period, subject to the provisions of Chapter 2 of Part 2 of the Crime (Sentences) Act 1997 (c 43) as to the release of prisoners and duration of licences.

(5) An offence the sentence for which is imposed under this section is not to be regarded as an offence the sentence for which is fixed by law.

[Criminal Justice Act 2003, s 226.]

3–2014　227. Extended sentence for certain violent or sexual offences: persons 18 or over[1].
(1) This section applies where—

(a) a person aged 18 or over is convicted of a specified offence, other than a serious offence, committed after the commencement of this section, and

(b) the court considers that there is a significant risk to members of the public of serious harm occasioned by the commission by the offender of further specified offences.

(2) The court must impose on the offender an extended sentence of imprisonment, that is to say, a sentence of imprisonment the term of which is equal to the aggregate of—

(a) the appropriate custodial term, and

(b) a further period ("the extension period"[2]) for which the offender is to be subject to a licence and which is of such length as the court considers necessary for the purpose of protecting members of the public from serious harm occasioned by the commission by him of further specified offences.

(3) In subsection (2) "the appropriate custodial term" means a term of imprisonment (not exceeding the maximum term permitted for the offence) which—

(a) is the term that would (apart from this section) be imposed in compliance with section 153(2), or

(b) where the term that would be so imposed is a term of less than 12 months, is a term of 12 months.

(4) The extension period must not exceed—

(a) five years in the case of a specified violent offence, and

(b) eight years in the case of a specified sexual offence.

(5) The term of an extended sentence of imprisonment passed under this section in respect of an offence must not exceed the maximum term permitted for the offence.

[Criminal Justice Act 2003, s 227[1].]

---

1. Until s 61 of this Act (abolition of sentences of detention in a young offender institution, custody for life etc) comes into force, this section is subject to the modifications in the Criminal Justice Act 2003 (Sentencing) (Transitory Provisions) Order 2005, in this PART, post.

2. The extension period begins at the end of the custodial period determined by the court, whether or not part of that period is served on licence: *R v S, Burt* [2005] EWCA Crim 3616, [2006] 2 Cr App R (S) 35. Once a determination of dangerousness has been made, the court must impose an extended sentence in relation to any other specified offence; it is entitled to impose "no separate penalty" only for other offences which are not specified offences: *R v S, Burt*, supra.

3–2015 **228. Extended sentence for certain violent or sexual offences: persons under 18.**

(1) This section applies where—

    (*a*) a person aged under 18 is convicted of a specified offence committed after the commencement of this section, and

    (*b*) the court considers—

        (i) that there is a significant risk to members of the public of serious harm occasioned by the commission by the offender of further specified offences, and

        (ii) where the specified offence is a serious offence, that the case is not one in which the court is required by section 226(2) to impose a sentence of detention for life under section 91 of the Sentencing Act or by section 226(3) to impose a sentence of detention for public protection.

(2) The court must impose on the offender an extended sentence of detention, that is to say, a sentence of detention the term of which is equal to the aggregate of—

    (*a*) the appropriate custodial term, and

    (*b*) a further period ("the extension period"[1]) for which the offender is to be subject to a licence and which is of such length as the court considers necessary for the purpose of protecting members of the public from serious harm occasioned by the commission by him of further specified offences.

(3) In subsection (2) "the appropriate custodial term" means such term as the court considers appropriate, which—

    (*a*) must be at least 12 months, and

    (*b*) must not exceed the maximum term of imprisonment permitted for the offence.

(4) The extension period must not exceed—

    (*a*) five years in the case of a specified violent offence, and

    (*b*) eight years in the case of a specified sexual offence.

(5) The term of an extended sentence of detention passed under this section in respect of an offence must not exceed the maximum term of imprisonment permitted for the offence.

(6) Any reference in this section to the maximum term of imprisonment permitted for an offence is a reference to the maximum term of imprisonment that is, apart from section 225, permitted for the offence in the case of a person aged 18 or over.

[Criminal Justice Act 2003, s 228.]

_____

1. The extension period begins at the end of the custodial period determined by the court, whether or not part of that period is served on licence: *R v S, Burt* [2005] EWCA Crim 3616, [2006] 2 Cr App R (S) 35. Once a determination of dangerousness has been made, the court must impose an extended sentence in relation to any other specified offence; it is entitled to impose "no separate penalty" only for other offences which are not specified offences: *R v S, Burt*, supra.

3–2016 **229. The assessment of dangerousness.** (1) This section applies where—

    (*a*) a person has been convicted of a specified offence, and

    (*b*) it falls to a court to assess under any of sections 225 to 228 whether there is a significant risk to members of the public of serious harm occasioned by the commission by him of further such offences.

(2) If at the time when that offence was committed the offender had not been convicted in any part of the United Kingdom of any relevant offence or was aged under 18, the court in making the assessment referred to in subsection (1)(*b*)—

    (*a*) must take into account all such information as is available to it about the nature and circumstances of the offence,

    (*b*) may take into account any information which is before it about any pattern of behaviour of which the offence forms part, and

    (*c*) may take into account any information about the offender which is before it.

(3) If at the time when that offence was committed the offender was aged 18 or over and had been convicted in any part of the United Kingdom of one or more relevant offences, the court must assume that there is such a risk as is mentioned in subsection (1)(*b*) unless, after taking into account—

    (*a*) all such information as is available to it about the nature and circumstances of each of the offences,

    (*b*) where appropriate, any information which is before it about any pattern of behaviour of which any of the offences forms part, and

    (*c*) any information about the offender which is before it,

the court considers that it would be unreasonable to conclude that there is such a risk.

(4) In this Chapter "relevant offence" means—

    (*a*) a specified offence,

  (b) an offence specified in Schedule 16 (offences under the law of Scotland), or
  (c) an offence specified in Schedule 17 (offences under the law of Northern Ireland).
[Criminal Justice Act 2003, s 229.]

3–2017   230. Imprisonment or detention for public protection: release on licence.   Schedule 18 (release of prisoners serving sentences of imprisonment or detention for public protection) shall have effect.
[Criminal Justice Act 2003, s 230.]

3–2018   231. Appeals where previous convictions set aside.   (1) This section applies where—
  (a) a sentence has been imposed on any person under section 225 or 227, and
  (b) any previous conviction of his without which the court would not have been required to make the assumption mentioned in section 229(3) has been subsequently set aside on appeal.

(2) Notwithstanding anything in section 18 of the Criminal Appeal Act 1968 (c 19), notice of appeal against the sentence may be given at any time within 28 days from the date on which the previous conviction was set aside.
[Criminal Justice Act 2003, s 231.]

3–2019   232. Certificates of convictions for purposes of section 229.   Where—
  (a) on any date after the commencement of this section a person is convicted in England and Wales of a relevant offence, and
  (b) the court by or before which he is so convicted states in open court that he has been convicted of such an offence on that date, and
  (c) that court subsequently certifies that fact,

that certificate shall be evidence, for the purposes of section 229, that he was convicted of such an offence on that date.
[Criminal Justice Act 2003, s 232.]

3–2020   233. Offences under service law.   Where—
  (a) a person has at any time been convicted of an offence under section 70 of the Army Act 1955 (3 & 4 Eliz 2 c 18), section 70 of the Air Force Act 1955 (3 & 4 Eliz 2 c 19) or section 42 of the Naval Discipline Act 1957 (c 53), and
  (b) the corresponding civil offence (within the meaning of that Act) was a relevant offence,

section 229 shall have effect as if he had at that time been convicted in England and Wales of the corresponding civil offence.
[Criminal Justice Act 2003, s 233.]

3–2021   234. Determination of day when offence committed.   Where an offence is found to have been committed over a period of two or more days, or at some time during a period of two or more days, it shall be taken for the purposes of section 229 to have been committed on the last of those days.
[Criminal Justice Act 2003, s 234.]

3–2022   235. Detention under sections 226 and 228.   A person sentenced to be detained under section 226 or 228 is liable to be detained in such place, and under such conditions, as may be determined by the Secretary of State or by such other person as may be authorised by him for the purpose.
[Criminal Justice Act 2003, s 235.]

3–2023   236. Conversion of sentences of detention into sentences of imprisonment[1].   For section 99 of the Sentencing Act (conversion of sentence of detention and custody into sentence of imprisonment) there is substituted—

"Conversion of sentence of detention to sentence of imprisonment

99. Conversion of sentence of detention to sentence of imprisonment.   (1) Subject to the following provisions of this section, where an offender has been sentenced by a relevant sentence of detention to a term of detention and either—
  (a) he has attained the age of 21, or
  (b) he has attained the age of 18 and has been reported to the Secretary of State by the board of visitors of the institution in which he is detained as exercising a bad influence on the other inmates of the institution or as behaving in a disruptive manner to the detriment of those inmates,

the Secretary of State may direct that he shall be treated as if he had been sentenced to imprisonment for the same term.

(2) Where the Secretary of State gives a direction under subsection (1) above in relation to an offender, the portion of the term of detention imposed under the relevant sentence of detention which he has already served shall be deemed to have been a portion of a term of imprisonment.

(3) Where the Secretary of State gives a direction under subsection (1) above in relation to an

offender serving a sentence of detention for public protection under section 226 of the Criminal Justice Act 2003 the offender shall be treated as if he had been sentenced under section 225 of that Act; and where the Secretary of State gives such a direction in relation to an offender serving an extended sentence of detention under section 228 of that Act the offender shall be treated as if he had been sentenced under section 227 of that Act.

(4) Rules under section 47 of the Prison Act 1952 may provide that any award for an offence against discipline made in respect of an offender serving a relevant sentence of detention shall continue to have effect after a direction under subsection (1) has been given in relation to him.

(5) In this section "relevant sentence of detention" means—

(*a*) a sentence of detention under section 90, 91 or 96 above,

(*b*) a sentence of detention for public protection under section 226 or, in the case of a person aged at least 18 but under 21, a sentence of custody for life or detention in a young offender institution under section 225 of the Criminal Justice Act 2003, or

(*c*) an extended sentence of detention under section 228 or, in the case of a person aged at least 18 but under 21, an extended sentence of detention in a young offender institution under section 227 of that Act."

[Criminal Justice Act 2003, s 236[1].]

---

1. Until s 61 of this Act (abolition of sentences of detention in a young offender institution, custody for life etc) comes into force, this section is subject to the modifications in the Criminal Justice Act 2003 (Sentencing) (Transitory Provisions) Order 2005, in this PART, post.

CHAPTER 6[1]

Release on Licence

Preliminary

3–2024　237. Meaning of "fixed-term prisoner"[2]**.** (1) In this Chapter "fixed-term prisoner" means—

(*a*) a person serving a sentence of imprisonment for a determinate term, or

(*b*) a person serving a determinate sentence of detention under section 91 of the Sentencing Act or under section 228 of this Act.

(2) In this Chapter, unless the context otherwise requires, "prisoner" includes a person serving a sentence falling within subsection (1)(*b*); and "prison" includes any place where a person serving such a sentence is liable to be detained.

[Criminal Justice Act 2003, s 237.]

---

1. Chapter 6 contains ss 237–268.
2. Sections 237–239 and Sch 19 came into force on 26 January 2004. See the Criminal Justice Act 2003 (Commencement No 1) Order, SI 2003/3282. Until s 61 of this Act (abolition of sentences of detention in a young offender institution, custody for life etc) comes into force, this section is subject to the modifications in the Criminal Justice Act 2003 (Sentencing) (Transitory Provisions) Order 2005, in this PART, post.

Power of court to recommend licence conditions

3–2025　238. Power of court to recommend licence conditions for certain prisoners[1]**.** (1) A court which sentences an offender to a term of imprisonment of twelve months or more in respect of any offence may, when passing sentence, recommend to the Secretary of State particular conditions which in its view should be included in any licence granted to the offender under this Chapter on his release from prison.

(2) In exercising his powers under section 250(4)(*b*) in respect of an offender, the Secretary of State must have regard to any recommendation under subsection (1).

(3) A recommendation under subsection (1) is not to be treated for any purpose as part of the sentence passed on the offender.

(4) This section does not apply in relation to a sentence of detention under section 91 of the Sentencing Act or section 228 of this Act.

[Criminal Justice Act 2003, s 238.]

---

1. Sections 237–239 and Sch 19 came into force on 26 January 2004. See the Criminal Justice Act 2003 (Commencement No 1) Order, SI 2003/3282. Until s 61 of this Act (abolition of sentences of detention in a young offender institution, custody for life etc) comes into force, this section is subject to the modifications in the Criminal Justice Act 2003 (Sentencing) (Transitory Provisions) Order 2005, in this PART, post.

3–2026　239. The Parole Board[1]**.** (1) The Parole Board is to continue to be, by that name, a body corporate and as such is—

(*a*) to be constituted in accordance with this Chapter, and

(*b*) to have the functions conferred on it by this Chapter in respect of fixed-term prisoners and by Chapter 2 of Part 2 of the Crime (Sentences) Act 1997 (c 43) (in this Chapter referred to as "the 1997 Act") in respect of life prisoners within the meaning of that Chapter.

(2) It is the duty of the Board to advise the Secretary of State with respect to any matter referred to it by him which is to do with the early release or recall of prisoners.

(3) The Board must, in dealing with cases as respects which it makes recommendations under this Chapter or under Chapter 2 of Part 2 of the 1997 Act, consider—

(a) any documents given to it by the Secretary of State, and

(b) any other oral or written information obtained by it;

and if in any particular case the Board thinks it necessary to interview the person to whom the case relates before reaching a decision, the Board may authorise one of its members to interview him and must consider the report of the interview made by that member.

(4) The Board must deal with cases as respects which it gives directions under this Chapter or under Chapter 2 of Part 2 of the 1997 Act on consideration of all such evidence as may be adduced before it.

(5) Without prejudice to subsections (3) and (4), the Secretary of State may make rules with respect to the proceedings of the Board, including proceedings authorising cases to be dealt with by a prescribed number of its members or requiring cases to be dealt with at prescribed times.[1]

(6) The Secretary of State may also give to the Board directions as to the matters to be taken into account by it in discharging any functions under this Chapter or under Chapter 2 of Part 2 of the 1997 Act; and in giving any such directions the Secretary of State must have regard to—

(a) the need to protect the public from serious harm from offenders, and

(b) the desirability of preventing the commission by them of further offences and of securing their rehabilitation.[1]

(7) Schedule 19 shall have effect with respect to the Board.

[Criminal Justice Act 2003, s 239.]

---

1. Sections 237–239 and Sch 19 came into force (for the purposes of the passing of a sentence of imprisonment to which an intermittent custody order relates and the release on licence of a person serving such a sentence) on 26 January 2004. See the Criminal Justice Act 2003 (Commencement No 1) Order, SI 2003/3282. Section 239(5) and (6) now in force for remaining purposes: see Criminal Justice Act (Commencement No 7) Order 2005, SI 2005/373.

Effect of remand in custody

3–2027 **240. Crediting of periods of remand in custody: terms of imprisonment and detention[2].** (1) This section applies where—

(a) a court sentences an offender to imprisonment for a term in respect of an offence committed after the commencement of this section, and

(b) the offender has been remanded in custody (within the meaning given by section 242) in connection with the offence or a related offence, that is to say, any other offence the charge for which was founded on the same facts or evidence.

(2) It is immaterial for that purpose whether the offender—

(a) has also been remanded in custody in connection with other offences; or

(b) has also been detained in connection with other matters.

(3) Subject to subsection (4), the court must direct that the number of days for which the offender was remanded in custody in connection with the offence or a related offence is to count as time served by him as part of the sentence.

(4) Subsection (3) does not apply if and to the extent that—

(a) rules[3] made by the Secretary of State so provide in the case of—

(i) a remand in custody which is wholly or partly concurrent with a sentence of imprisonment, or

(ii) sentences of imprisonment for consecutive terms or for terms which are wholly or partly concurrent, or[1]

(b) it is in the opinion of the court just in all the circumstances not to give a direction under that subsection.

(5) Where the court gives a direction under subsection (3), it shall state in open court—

(a) the number of days for which the offender was remanded in custody, and

(b) the number of days in relation to which the direction is given.

(6) Where the court does not give a direction under subsection (3), or gives such a direction in relation to a number of days less than that for which the offender was remanded in custody, it shall state in open court—

(a) that its decision is in accordance with rules made under paragraph (a) of subsection (4), or

(b) that it is of the opinion mentioned in paragraph (b) of that subsection and what the circumstances are.

(7) For the purposes of this section a suspended sentence—

(a) is to be treated as a sentence of imprisonment when it takes effect under paragraph 8(2)(a) or (b) of Schedule 12, and

(b) is to be treated as being imposed by the order under which it takes effect.

(8) For the purposes of the reference in subsection (3) to the term of imprisonment to which a

person has been sentenced (that is to say, the reference to his "sentence"), consecutive terms and terms which are wholly or partly concurrent are to be treated as a single term if—

- (a) the sentences were passed on the same occasion, or
- (b) where they were passed on different occasions, the person has not been released under this Chapter at any time during the period beginning with the first and ending with the last of those occasions.

(9) Where an offence is found to have been committed over a period of two or more days, or at some time during a period of two or more days, it shall be taken for the purposes of subsection (1) to have been committed on the last of those days.

(10) This section applies to a determinate sentence of detention under section 91 of the Sentencing Act or section 228 of this Act as it applies to an equivalent sentence of imprisonment.
[Criminal Justice Act 2003, s 240.]

1. Section 240(4)(*a*) is in force: see Criminal Justice Act (Commencement No 7) Order 2005, SI 2005/373.
2. Until s 61 of this Act (abolition of sentences of detention in a young offender institution, custody for life etc) comes into force, this section is subject to the modifications in the Criminal Justice Act 2003 (Sentencing) (Transitory Provisions) Order 2005, in this PART, post.
3. The Remand in Custody (Effect of Concurrent and Consecutive Sentences of Imprisonment) Rules 2005 have been made, in this PART, STATUTORY INSTRUMENTS ON SENTENCING, post.

3–2028　241. Effect of direction under section 240 on release on licence[1]. (1) In determining for the purposes of this Chapter or Chapter 3 (prison sentences of less than twelve months) whether a person whose sentence falls to be reduced under section 67 of the Criminal Justice Act 1967 by any relevant period within the meaning of that section ("the relevant period")—

- (a) has served, or would (but for his release) have served, a particular proportion of his sentence, or
- (b) has served a particular period,

the relevant period is to be treated as having been served by him as part of that sentence or period.

(2) In determining for the purposes of section 183 (intermittent custody) whether any part of a sentence to which an intermittent custody order relates is a licence period, the number of custodial days, as defined by subsection (3) of that section, is to be taken to be reduced by the relevant period.
[Criminal Justice Act 2003, s 241 as amended by SI 2003/3283.]

1. Section 241 came into force on 26 January 2004. See the Criminal Justice Act 2003 (Commencement No 1) Order, SI 2003/3282.

3–2029　242. Interpretation of sections 240 and 241. (1) For the purposes of sections 240 and 241, the definition of "sentence of imprisonment" in section 305 applies as if for the words from the beginning of the definition to the end of paragraph (*a*) there were substituted—

""sentence of imprisonment" does not include a committal—

- (a) in default of payment of any sum of money, other than one adjudged to be paid on a conviction,";

and references in those sections to sentencing an offender to imprisonment, and to an offender's sentence, are to be read accordingly.

(2) References in sections 240 and 241 to an offender's being remanded in custody are references to his being—

- (a) remanded in or committed to custody by order of a court,
- (b) remanded or committed to local authority accommodation under section 23 of the Children and Young Persons Act 1969 (c 54) and kept in secure accommodation or detained in a secure training centre pursuant to arrangements under subsection (7A) of that section, or
- (c) remanded, admitted or removed to hospital under section 35, 36, 38 or 48 of the Mental Health Act 1983 (c 20).

(3) In subsection (2), "secure accommodation" has the same meaning as in section 23 of the Children and Young Persons Act 1969.
[Criminal Justice Act 2003, s 242.]

3–2030　243. Persons extradited to the United Kingdom. (1) A fixed-term prisoner is an extradited prisoner for the purposes of this section if—

- (a) he was tried for the offence in respect of which his sentence was imposed—
  - (i) after having been extradited to the United Kingdom, and
  - (ii) without having first been restored or had an opportunity of leaving the United Kingdom, and
- (b) he was for any period kept in custody while awaiting his extradition to the United Kingdom as mentioned in paragraph (*a*).

(2) In the case of an extradited prisoner, section 240 has effect as if the days for which he was kept in custody while awaiting extradition were days for which he was remanded in custody in connection

with the offence, or any other offence the charge for which was founded on the same facts or evidence.

(3) *Repealed.*

[Criminal Justice Act 2003, s 243 as amended by SI 2004/1897.]

Release on licence

3–2031   244. Duty to release prisoners[1, 2]. (1) As soon as a fixed-term prisoner, other than a prisoner to whom section 247 applies, has served the requisite custodial period, it is the duty of the Secretary of State to release him on licence under this section.

(2) Subsection (1) is subject to section 245.

(3) In this section "the requisite custodial period" means—

(a) in relation to a person serving a sentence of imprisonment for a term of twelve months or more or any determinate sentence of detention under section 91 of the Sentencing Act, one-half of his sentence,

(b) in relation to a person serving a sentence of imprisonment for a term of less than twelve months (other than one to which an intermittent custody order relates), the custodial period within the meaning of section 181,

(c) in relation to a person serving a sentence of imprisonment to which an intermittent custody order relates, any part of the term which is not a licence period as defined by section 183(3), and

(d) in relation to a person serving two or more concurrent or consecutive sentences, the period determined under sections 263(2) and 264(2).

[Criminal Justice Act 2003, s 244.]

---

1. Section 244(1), (2), (3)(c) and (d) came into force on 26 January 2004. See the Criminal Justice Act 2003 (Commencement No 1) Order, SI 2003/3282.

2. Until s 61 of this Act (abolition of sentences of detention in a young offender institution, custody for life etc) comes into force, this section is subject to the modifications in the Criminal Justice Act 2003 (Sentencing) (Transitory Provisions) Order 2005, in this PART, post.

3–2032   245. Restrictions on operation of section 244(1) in relation to intermittent custody prisoners[1]. (1) Where an intermittent custody prisoner returns to custody after being unlawfully at large within the meaning of section 49 of the Prison Act 1952 (c 52) at any time during the currency of his sentence, section 244(1) does not apply until—

(a) the relevant time (as defined in subsection (2)), or

(b) if earlier, the date on which he has served in prison the number of custodial days required by the intermittent custody order.

(2) In subsection (1)(a) "the relevant time" means—

(a) in a case where, within the period of 72 hours beginning with the return to custody of the intermittent custody prisoner, the Secretary of State or the responsible officer has applied to the court for the amendment of the intermittent custody order under paragraph 6(1)(b) of Schedule 10, the date on which the application is withdrawn or determined, and

(b) in any other case, the end of that 72-hour period.

(3) Section 244(1) does not apply in relation to an intermittent custody prisoner at any time after he has been recalled under section 254, unless after his recall the Board has directed his further release on licence.

[Criminal Justice Act 2003, s 245.]

---

1. Section 245 came into force on 26 January 2004. See the Criminal Justice Act 2003 (Commencement No 1) Order, SI 2003/3282.

3–2033   246. Power to release prisoners on licence before required to do so[1]. (1) Subject to subsections (2) to (4), the Secretary of State may—

(a) release on licence under this section a fixed-term prisoner, other than an intermittent custody prisoner, at any time during the period of 135 days ending with the day on which the prisoner will have served the requisite custodial period, and

(b) release on licence under this section an intermittent custody prisoner when 135 or less of the required custodial days remain to be served.

(2) Subsection (1)(a) does not apply in relation to a prisoner unless—

(a) the length of the requisite custodial period is at least 6 weeks,

(b) he has served—

(i) at least 4 weeks of his sentence, and

(ii) at least one-half of the requisite custodial period.

(3) Subsection (1)(b) does not apply in relation to a prisoner unless—

(a) the number of required custodial days is at least 42, and

(b) the prisoner has served—

(i) at least 28 of those days, and

(ii) at least one-half of the total number of those days.

(4) Subsection (1) does not apply where—

(a) the sentence is imposed under section 227 or 228,

(b) the sentence is for an offence under section 1 of the Prisoners (Return to Custody) Act 1995 (c 16),

(c) the prisoner is subject to a hospital order, hospital direction or transfer direction under section 37, 45A or 47 of the Mental Health Act 1983 (c 20),

(d) the sentence was imposed by virtue of paragraph 9(1)(b) or (c) or 10(1)(b) or (c) of Schedule 8 in a case where the prisoner has failed to comply with a curfew requirement of a community order,

(e) the prisoner is subject to the notification requirements of Part 2 of the Sexual Offences Act 2003 (c 42),

(f) the prisoner is liable to removal from the United Kingdom,

(g) the prisoner has been released on licence under this section during the currency of the sentence, and has been recalled to prison under section 255(1)(a),

(h) the prisoner has been released on licence under section 248 during the currency of the sentence, and has been recalled to prison under section 254, or

(i) in the case of a prisoner to whom a direction under section 240 relates, the interval between the date on which the sentence was passed and the date on which the prisoner will have served the requisite custodial period is less than 14 days or, where the sentence is one of intermittent custody, the number of the required custodial days remaining to be served is less than 14.

(5) The Secretary of State may by order—

(a) amend the number of days for the time being specified in subsection (1) (a) or (b), (3) or (4)(i),

(b) amend the number of weeks for the time being specified in subsection (2)(a) or (b)(i), and

(c) amend the fraction for the time being specified in subsection (2)(b)(ii) or (3)(b)(ii).[1]

(6) In this section—

"the required custodial days", in relation to an intermittent custody prisoner, means—

(a) the number of custodial days specified under section 183, or

(b) in the case of two or more sentences of intermittent custody, the aggregate of the numbers so specified;

"the requisite custodial period" in relation to a person serving any sentence other than a sentence of intermittent custody, has the meaning given by paragraph (a), (b) or (d) of section 244(3);

"sentence of intermittent custody" means a sentence to which an intermittent custody order relates.

[Criminal Justice Act 2003, s 246.]

---

1. Section 246(1)(b), (3), (4)(b)–(i), (5) and (6) came into force (for the purposes of the passing of a sentence of imprisonment to which an intermittent custody order relates and the release on licence of a person serving such a sentence) on 26 January 2004. See the Criminal Justice Act 2003 (Commencement No 1) Order, SI 2003/3282. Section 246(5) now in force for remaining purposes: see Criminal Justice Act (Commencement No 7) Order 2005, SI 2005/373.

3–2034 247. Release on licence of prisoner serving extended sentence under section 227 or 228. (1) This section applies to a prisoner who is serving an extended sentence imposed under section 227 or 228.

(2) As soon as—

(a) a prisoner to whom this section applies has served one-half of the appropriate custodial term, and

(b) the Parole Board has directed his release under this section,

it is the duty of the Secretary of State to release him on licence.

(3) The Parole Board may not give a direction under subsection (2) unless the Board is satisfied that it is no longer necessary for the protection of the public that the prisoner should be confined.

(4) As soon as a prisoner to whom this section applies has served the appropriate custodial term, it is the duty of the Secretary of State to release him on licence unless the prisoner has previously been recalled under section 254.

(5) Where a prisoner to whom this section applies is released on a licence, the Secretary of State may not by virtue of section 250(4)(b) include, or subsequently insert, a condition in the licence, or vary or cancel a condition in the licence, except after consultation with the Board.

(6) For the purposes of subsection (5), the Secretary of State is to be treated as having consulted the Board about a proposal to include, insert, vary or cancel a condition in any case if he has consulted the Board about the implementation of proposals of that description generally or in that class of case.

(7) In this section "the appropriate custodial term" means the period determined by the court as the appropriate custodial term under section 227 or 228.

[Criminal Justice Act 2003, s 247.]

3–2035 248. Power to release prisoners on compassionate grounds[1]. (1) The Secretary of State may at any time release a fixed-term prisoner on licence if he is satisfied that exceptional circumstances exist which justify the prisoner's release on compassionate grounds.

(2) Before releasing under this section a prisoner to whom section 247 applies, the Secretary of State must consult the Board, unless the circumstances are such as to render such consultation impracticable.
[Criminal Justice Act 2003, s 248.]

---

1. Section 248(1) came into force on 26 January 2004. See the Criminal Justice Act 2003 (Commencement No 1) Order, SI 2003/3282.

3–2036   249. Duration of licence[1]. (1) Subject to subsections (2) and (3), where a fixed-term prisoner is released on licence, the licence shall, subject to any revocation under section 254 or 255, remain in force for the remainder of his sentence.

(2) Where an intermittent custody prisoner is released on licence under section 244, the licence shall, subject to any revocation under section 254, remain in force—

(a)   until the time when he is required to return to prison at the beginning of the next custodial period of the sentence, or

(b)   where it is granted at the end of the last custodial period, for the remainder of his sentence.

(3) Subsection (1) has effect subject to sections 263(2) (concurrent terms) and 264(3) and (4) (consecutive terms).

(4) In subsection (2) "custodial period", in relation to a sentence to which an intermittent custody order relates, means any period which is not a licence period as defined by 183(3).
[Criminal Justice Act 2003, s 249.]

---

1. Section 249 came into force on 26 January 2004. See the Criminal Justice Act 2003 (Commencement No 1) Order, SI 2003/3282.

3–2037   250. Licence conditions[1]. (1) In this section—

(a)   "the standard conditions" means such conditions as may be prescribed for the purposes of this section as standard conditions, and

(b)   "prescribed" means prescribed by the Secretary of State by order[1,2].

(2) Subject to subsection (6) and section 251, any licence under this Chapter in respect of a prisoner serving one or more sentences of imprisonment of less than twelve months and no sentence of twelve months or more—

(a)   must include—

(i)   the conditions required by the relevant court order, and

(ii)   so far as not inconsistent with them, the standard conditions, and[1]

(b)   may also include—

(i)   any condition which is authorised by section 62 of the Criminal Justice and Court Services Act 2000 (c 43) (electronic monitoring) or section 64 of that Act (drug testing requirements) and which is compatible with the conditions required by the relevant court order, and

(ii)   such other conditions of a kind prescribed[2] for the purposes of this paragraph as the Secretary of State may for the time being consider to be necessary for the protection of the public and specify in the licence.

(3) For the purposes of subsection (2)(a)(i), any reference in the relevant court order to the licence period specified in the order is, in relation to a prohibited activity requirement, exclusion requirement, residence requirement or supervision requirement, to be taken to include a reference to any other period during which the prisoner is released on licence under section 246 or 248.

(4) Any licence under this Chapter in respect of a prisoner serving a sentence of imprisonment for a term of twelve months or more (including such a sentence imposed under section 227) or any sentence of detention under section 91 of the Sentencing Act or section 228 of this Act—

(a)   must include the standard conditions, and

(b)   may include—

(i)   any condition authorised by section 62 or 64 of the Criminal Justice and Court Services Act 2000, and

(ii)   such other conditions of a kind prescribed by the Secretary of State for the purposes of this paragraph as the Secretary of State may for the time being specify in the licence.[1]

(5) A licence under section 246 must also include a curfew condition complying with section 253.

(6) Where—

(a)   a licence under section 246 is granted to a prisoner serving one or more sentences of imprisonment of less than 12 months and no sentence of 12 months or more, and

(b)   the relevant court order requires the licence to be granted subject to a condition requiring his compliance with a curfew requirement (as defined by section 204),

that condition is not to be included in the licence at any time while a curfew condition required by section 253 is in force.

(7) The preceding provisions of this section have effect subject to section 263(3) (concurrent terms) and section 264(3) and (4) (consecutive terms).

(8) In exercising his powers to prescribe standard conditions or the other conditions referred to in subsection (4)(*b*)(ii), the Secretary of State must have regard to the following purposes of the supervision of offenders while on licence under this Chapter—

  (*a*) the protection of the public,

  (*b*) the prevention of re-offending, and

  (*c*) securing the successful re-integration of the prisoner into the community.[1]

[Criminal Justice Act 2003, s 250.]

---

1. Section 250(1)–(3) and (5)–(8) came into force (for the purposes of the passing of a sentence of imprisonment to which an intermittent custody order relates and the release on licence of a person serving such a sentence) on 26 January 2004. See the Criminal Justice Act 2003 (Commencement No 1) Order, SI 2003/3282. Section 250(1), (2)(*b*)(ii), (4)(*b*)(ii) and (8) now in force for remaining purposes: see Criminal Justice Act (Commencement No 7) Order 2005, SI 2005/373. Until s 61 of this Act (abolition of sentences of detention in a young offender institution, custody for life etc) comes into force, this section is subject to the modifications in the Criminal Justice Act 2003 (Sentencing) (Transitory Provisions) Order 2005, in this PART, post.

2. The Criminal Justice (Sentencing) (Licence Conditions) Order, SI 2005/648 has been made. See this PART, post.

3–2038 251. Licence conditions on re-release of prisoner serving sentence of less than 12 months[1]. (1) In relation to any licence under this Chapter which is granted to a prisoner serving one or more sentences of imprisonment of less than twelve months and no sentence of twelve months or more on his release in pursuance of a decision of the Board under section 254 or 256, subsections (2) and (3) apply instead of section 250(2).

(2) The licence—

  (*a*) must include the standard conditions, and

  (*b*) may include—

     (i) any condition authorised by section 62 or 64 of the Criminal Justice and Court Services Act 2000 (c 43), and

     (ii) such other conditions of a kind prescribed by the Secretary of State for the purposes of section 250(4)(*b*)(ii) as the Secretary of State may for the time being specify in the licence.

(3) In exercising his powers under subsection (2)(*b*)(ii), the Secretary of State must have regard to the terms of the relevant court order.

(4) In this section "the standard conditions" has the same meaning as in section 250.

[Criminal Justice Act 2003, s 251.]

---

1. Sections 251–257 came into force on 26 January 2004. See the Criminal Justice Act 2003 (Commencement No 1) Order, SI 2003/3282.

3–2039 252. Duty to comply with licence conditions[1]. A person subject to a licence under this Chapter must comply with such conditions as may for the time being be specified in the licence.

[Criminal Justice Act 2003, s 252.]

---

1. Sections 251–257 came into force on 26 January 2004. See the Criminal Justice Act 2003 (Commencement No 1) Order, SI 2003/3282.

3–2040 253. Curfew condition to be included in licence under section 246[1, 2]. (1) For the purposes of this Chapter, a curfew condition is a condition which—

  (*a*) requires the released person to remain, for periods for the time being specified in the condition, at a place for the time being so specified (which may be premises approved by the Secretary of State under section 9 of the Criminal Justice and Court Services Act 2000 (c 43)), and

  (*b*) includes requirements for securing the electronic monitoring of his whereabouts during the periods for the time being so specified.

(2) The curfew condition may specify different places or different periods for different days, but may not specify periods which amount to less than 9 hours in any one day (excluding for this purpose the first and last days of the period for which the condition is in force).

(3) The curfew condition is to remain in force until the date when the released person would (but for his release) fall to be released on licence under section 244.

(4) Subsection (3) does not apply in relation to a released person to whom an intermittent custody order relates; and in relation to such a person the curfew condition is to remain in force until the number of days during which it has been in force is equal to the number of the required custodial days, as defined in section 246(6), that remained to be served at the time when he was released under section 246.

(5) The curfew condition must include provision for making a person responsible for monitoring the released person's whereabouts during the periods for the time being specified in the condition; and a person who is made so responsible shall be of a description specified in an order[1] made by the Secretary of State.

(6) Nothing in this section is to be taken to require the Secretary of State to ensure that arrangements are made for the electronic monitoring of released persons' whereabouts in any particular part of England and Wales.

[Criminal Justice Act 2003, s 253.]

1. Sections 251–257 came into force (for the purposes of the passing of a sentence of imprisonment to which an intermittent custody order relates and the release on licence of a person serving such a sentence) on 26 January 2004. See the Criminal Justice Act 2003 (Commencement No 1) Order, SI 2003/3282. Section 253(5) now in force for remaining purposes: see Criminal Justice Act (Commencement No 7) Order 2005, SI 2005/373.

2. The Criminal Justice (Sentencing) (Curfew Conditions) Order 2005, SI 2005/986 has been made.

Recall after release

3–2041   254. Recall of prisoners while on licence[1]. (1) The Secretary of State may, in the case of any prisoner who has been released on licence under this Chapter, revoke his licence and recall him to prison.

(2) A person recalled to prison under subsection (1)—

(a) may make representations in writing with respect to his recall, and

(b) on his return to prison, must be informed of the reasons for his recall and of his right to make representations.

(3) The Secretary of State must refer to the Board the case of a person recalled under subsection (1).

(4) Where on a reference under subsection (3) relating to any person the Board recommends his immediate release on licence under this Chapter, the Secretary of State must give effect to the recommendation.

(5) In the case of an intermittent custody prisoner who has not yet served in prison the number of custodial days specified in the intermittent custody order, any recommendation by the Board as to immediate release on licence is to be a recommendation as to his release on licence until the end of one of the licence periods specified by virtue of section 183(1)(b) in the intermittent custody order.

(6) On the revocation of the licence of any person under this section, he shall be liable to be detained in pursuance of his sentence and, if at large, is to be treated as being unlawfully at large.

(7) Nothing in subsections (2) to (6) applies in relation to a person recalled under section 255.
[Criminal Justice Act 2003, s 254.]

1. Sections 251–257 came into force on 26 January 2004. See the Criminal Justice Act 2003 (Commencement No 1) Order, SI 2003/3282. Sections 254–256 supersede s 39 of the Criminal Justice Act 1991, and the Criminal Justice Act 2003 (Commencement No. 8 and Transitional and Savings Provisions) Order 2005 did not create a lacuna in relation to offenders sentenced to imprisonment for offences committed before 4 April 4 2005, who happened to be released on licence before that date; such offenders could be recalled by the Secretary of State under s 254: *R (on the application of Buddington) v Secretary of State for the Home Department* [2006] EWCA Civ 280, [2006] 2 Cr App R (S) 109.

Once a prisoner has been recalled under s 254, if he is subsequently released prior to the expiry of his sentence under s 254 or s 256 it is on licence in accordance with chapter 6 of Part 12 of the Act, ie his licence will continue until the expiry of his sentence, regardless of the date of the offence for which the sentence was imposed: *R (on the application of Stellato) v Secretary of State for the Home Department* [2006] EWHC 608, [2006] 2 Cr App R (S) 114.

3–2042   255. Recall of prisoners released early under section 246[1]. (1) If it appears to the Secretary of State, as regards a person released on licence under section 246—

(a) that he has failed to comply with any condition included in his licence, or

(b) that his whereabouts can no longer be electronically monitored at the place for the time being specified in the curfew condition included in his licence,

the Secretary of State may, if the curfew condition is still in force, revoke the licence and recall the person to prison under this section.

(2) A person whose licence under section 246 is revoked under this section—

(a) may make representations in writing with respect to the revocation, and

(b) on his return to prison, must be informed of the reasons for the revocation and of his right to make representations.

(3) The Secretary of State, after considering any representations under subsection (2)(b) or any other matters, may cancel a revocation under this section.

(4) Where the revocation of a person's licence is cancelled under subsection (3), the person is to be treated for the purposes of section 246 as if he had not been recalled to prison under this section.

(5) On the revocation of a person's licence under section 246, he is liable to be detained in pursuance of his sentence and, if at large, is to be treated as being unlawfully at large.
[Criminal Justice Act 2003, s 255.]

1. Sections 251–257 came into force on 26 January 2004. See the Criminal Justice Act 2003 (Commencement No 1) Order, SI 2003/3282.

3–2043   256. Further release after recall[1]. (1) Where on a reference under section 254(3) in relation to any person, the Board does not recommend his immediate release on licence under this Chapter, the Board must either—

(a) fix a date for the person's release on licence, or

(b) fix a date as the date for the next review of the person's case by the Board.

(2) Any date fixed under subsection (1)(a) or (b) must not be later than the first anniversary of the date on which the decision is taken.

(3) The Board need not fix a date under subsection (1)(*a*) or (*b*) if the prisoner will fall to be released unconditionally at any time within the next 12 months.

(4) Where the Board has fixed a date under subsection (1)(*a*), it is the duty of the Secretary of State to release him on licence on that date.

(5) On a review required by subsection (1)(*b*) in relation to any person, the Board may—

    (*a*)   recommend his immediate release on licence, or
    (*b*)   fix a date under subsection (1)(*a*) or (*b*).

[Criminal Justice Act 2003, s 256.]

---

   1. Sections 251–257 came into force on 26 January 2004. See the Criminal Justice Act 2003 (Commencement No 1) Order, SI 2003/3282.

Additional days

3–2044   **257. Additional days for disciplinary offences[1].**   (1) Prison rules, that is to say, rules made under section 47 of the Prison Act 1952 (c 52), may include provision for the award of additional days—

    (*a*)   to fixed-term prisoners, or
    (*b*)   conditionally on their subsequently becoming such prisoners, to persons on remand,

who (in either case) are guilty of disciplinary offences.

(2) Where additional days are awarded to a fixed-term prisoner, or to a person on remand who subsequently becomes such a prisoner, and are not remitted in accordance with prison rules—

    (*a*)   any period which he must serve before becoming entitled to or eligible for release under this Chapter,
    (*b*)   any period which he must serve before he can be removed from prison under section 260, and
    (*c*)   any period for which a licence granted to him under this Chapter remains in force,

is extended by the aggregate of those additional days.

[Criminal Justice Act 2003, s 257.]

---

   1. Sections 251–257 came into force on 26 January 2004. See the Criminal Justice Act 2003 (Commencement No 1) Order, SI 2003/3282.

Fine defaulters and contemnors

3–2045   **258. Early release of fine defaulters and contemnors[1].**   (1) This section applies in relation to a person committed to prison—

    (*a*)   in default of payment of a sum adjudged to be paid by a conviction, or
    (*b*)   for contempt of court or any kindred offence.

(2) As soon as a person to whom this section applies has served one-half of the term for which he was committed, it is the duty of the Secretary of State to release him unconditionally.

(3) Where a person to whom this section applies is also serving one or more sentences of imprisonment, nothing in this section requires the Secretary of State to release him until he is also required to release him in respect of that sentence or each of those sentences.

(4) The Secretary of State may at any time release unconditionally a person to whom this section applies if he is satisfied that exceptional circumstances exist which justify the person's release on compassionate grounds.

[Criminal Justice Act 2003, s 258.]

---

   1. Until s 61 of this Act (abolition of sentences of detention in a young offender institution, custody for life etc) comes into force, this section is subject to the modifications in the Criminal Justice Act 2003 (Sentencing) (Transitory Provisions) Order 2005, in this PART, post.

Persons liable to removal from the United Kingdom

3–2046   **259. Persons liable to removal from the United Kingdom[1].**   For the purposes of this Chapter a person is liable to removal from the United Kingdom if—

    (*a*)   he is liable to deportation under section 3(5) of the Immigration Act 1971 (c 77) and has been notified of a decision to make a deportation order against him,
    (*b*)   he is liable to deportation under section 3(6) of that Act,
    (*c*)   he has been notified of a decision to refuse him leave to enter the United Kingdom,
    (*d*)   he is an illegal entrant within the meaning of section 33(1) of that Act, or
    (*e*)   he is liable to removal under section 10 of the Immigration and Asylum Act 1999 (c 33).

[Criminal Justice Act 2003, s 259.]

---

   1. Section 259 came into force on 26 January 2004. See the Criminal Justice Act 2003 (Commencement No 1) Order, SI 2003/3282.

3–2047   **260. Early removal of prisoners liable to removal from United Kingdom.**   (1) Subject to subsections (2) and (3), where a fixed-term prisoner is liable to removal from the United Kingdom, the Secretary of State may remove him from prison under this section at any time during the period of 135 days ending with the day on which the prisoner will have served the requisite custodial period.

(2) Subsection (1) does not apply in relation to a prisoner unless—

(a) the length of the requisite custodial period is at least 6 weeks, and
(b) he has served—

(i) at least 4 weeks of his sentence, and
(ii) at least one-half of the requisite custodial period.

(3) Subsection (1) does not apply where—

(a) the sentence is imposed under section 227 or 228,
(b) the sentence is for an offence under section 1 of the Prisoners (Return to Custody) Act 1995 (c 16),
(c) the prisoner is subject to a hospital order, hospital direction or transfer direction under section 37, 45A or 47 of the Mental Health Act 1983 (c 20),
(d) the prisoner is subject to the notification requirements of Part 2 of the Sexual Offences Act 2003 (c 42), or
(e) in the case of a prisoner to whom a direction under section 240 relates, the interval between the date on which the sentence was passed and the date on which the prisoner will have served the requisite custodial period is less than 14 days.

(4) A prisoner removed from prison under this section—

(a) is so removed only for the purpose of enabling the Secretary of State to remove him from the United Kingdom under powers conferred by—

(i) Schedule 2 or 3 to the Immigration Act 1971, or
(ii) section 10 of the Immigration and Asylum Act 1999 (c 33), and

(b) so long as remaining in the United Kingdom, remains liable to be detained in pursuance of his sentence until he has served the requisite custodial period.

(5) So long as a prisoner removed from prison under this section remains in the United Kingdom but has not been returned to prison, any duty or power of the Secretary of State under section 244 or 248 is exercisable in relation to him as if he were in prison.

(6) The Secretary of State may by order—

(a) amend the number of days for the time being specified in subsection (1) or (3)(e),
(b) amend the number of weeks for the time being specified in subsection (2)(a) or (b)(i), and
(c) amend the fraction for the time being specified in subsection (2)(b)(ii).[1]

(7) In this section "the requisite custodial period" has the meaning given by paragraph (a), (b) or (d) of section 244(3).
[Criminal Justice Act 2003, s 260.]

---

1. Section 260(6) is in force: see Criminal Justice Act (Commencement No 7) Order 2005, SI 2005/373.

3–2048 261. Re-entry into United Kingdom of offender removed from prison early.
(1) This section applies in relation to a person who, after being removed from prison under section 260, has been removed from the United Kingdom before he has served the requisite custodial period.

(2) If a person to whom this section applies enters the United Kingdom at any time before his sentence expiry date, he is liable to be detained in pursuance of his sentence from the time of his entry into the United Kingdom until whichever is the earlier of the following—

(a) the end of a period ("the further custodial period") beginning with that time and equal in length to the outstanding custodial period, and
(b) his sentence expiry date.

(3) A person who is liable to be detained by virtue of subsection (2) is, if at large, to be taken for the purposes of section 49 of the Prison Act 1952 (c 52) (persons unlawfully at large) to be unlawfully at large.

(4) Subsection (2) does not prevent the further removal from the United Kingdom of a person falling within that subsection.

(5) Where, in the case of a person returned to prison by virtue of subsection (2), the further custodial period ends before the sentence expiry date, section 244 has effect in relation to him as if the reference to the requisite custodial period were a reference to the further custodial period.

(6) In this section—

"further custodial period" has the meaning given by subsection (2)(a);
"outstanding custodial period", in relation to a person to whom this section applies, means the period beginning with the date of his removal from the United Kingdom and ending with the date on which he would, but for his removal, have served the requisite custodial period;
"requisite custodial period" has the meaning given by paragraph (a), (b) or (d) of section 244(3);
"sentence expiry date", in relation to a person to whom this section applies, means the date on which, but for his removal from the United Kingdom, he would have ceased to be subject to a licence.
[Criminal Justice Act 2003, s 261.]

3–2049   262. Prisoners liable to removal from United Kingdom: modifications of Criminal Justice Act 1991[1].   Part 2 of the Criminal Justice Act 1991 (c 53) (early release of prisoners) shall (until the coming into force of its repeal by this Act) have effect subject to the modifications set out in Schedule 20 (which relate to persons liable to removal from the United Kingdom).
[Criminal Justice Act 2003, s 262.]

---

1. Section 262 came into force on 14 June 2004: see the Criminal Justice Act (Commencement No 3 and Transitional Provisions) Order 2004, SI 2004/929.

Consecutive or concurrent terms

3–2050   263. Concurrent terms[1].   (1) This section applies where—

  (a) a person ("the offender") has been sentenced by any court to two or more terms of imprisonment which are wholly or partly concurrent, and
  (b) the sentences were passed on the same occasion or, where they were passed on different occasions, the person has not been released under this Chapter at any time during the period beginning with the first and ending with the last of those occasions.

(2) Where this section applies—

  (a) nothing in this Chapter requires the Secretary of State to release the offender in respect of any of the terms unless and until he is required to release him in respect of each of the others,
  (b) section 244 does not authorise the Secretary of State to release him on licence under that section in respect of any of the terms unless and until that section authorises the Secretary of State to do so in respect of each of the others,
  (c) on and after his release under this Chapter the offender is to be on licence for so long, and subject to such conditions, as is required by this Chapter in respect of any of the sentences.

(3) Where the sentences include one or more sentences of twelve months or more and one or more sentences of less than twelve months, the terms of the licence may be determined by the Secretary of State in accordance with section 250(4)(b), without regard to the requirements of any custody plus order or intermittent custody order.

(4) In this section "term of imprisonment" includes a determinate sentence of detention under section 91 of the Sentencing Act or under section 228 of this Act.
[Criminal Justice Act 2003, s 263.]

---

1. Sections 263–265 came into force on 26 January 2004. See the Criminal Justice Act 2003 (Commencement No 1) Order, SI 2003/3282. Until s 61 of this Act (abolition of sentences of detention in a young offender institution, custody for life etc) comes into force, this section is subject to the modifications in the Criminal Justice Act 2003 (Sentencing) (Transitory Provisions) Order 2005, in this PART, post.

3–2051   264. Consecutive terms[1].   (1) This section applies where—

  (a) a person ("the offender") has been sentenced to two or more terms of imprisonment which are to be served consecutively on each other, and
  (b) the sentences were passed on the same occasion or, where they were passed on different occasions, the person has not been released under this Chapter at any time during the period beginning with the first and ending with the last of those occasions.

(2) Nothing in this Chapter requires the Secretary of State to release the offender on licence until he has served a period equal in length to the aggregate of the length of the custodial periods in relation to each of the terms of imprisonment.

(3) Where any of the terms of imprisonment is a term of twelve months or more, the offender is, on and after his release under this Chapter, to be on licence—

  (a) until he would, but for his release, have served a term equal in length to the aggregate length of the terms of imprisonment, and
  (b) subject to such conditions as are required by this Chapter in respect of each of those terms of imprisonment.

(4) Where each of the terms of imprisonment is a term of less than twelve months, the offender is, on and after his release under this Chapter, to be on licence until the relevant time, and subject to such conditions as are required by this Chapter in respect of any of the terms of imprisonment, and none of the terms is to be regarded for any purpose as continuing after the relevant time.

(5) In subsection (4) "the relevant time" means the time when the offender would, but for his release, have served a term equal in length to the aggregate of—

  (a) all the custodial periods in relation to the terms of imprisonment, and
  (b) the longest of the licence periods in relation to those terms.

(6) In this section—

  (a) "custodial period"—

    (i) in relation to an extended sentence imposed under section 227 or 228, means the appropriate custodial term determined under that section,
    (ii) in relation to a term of twelve months or more, means one-half of the term, and
    (iii) in relation to a term of less than twelve months complying with section 181, means the custodial period as defined by subsection (3)(a) of that section;

(b) "licence period", in relation to a term of less than twelve months complying with section 181, has the meaning given by subsection (3)(b) of that section.

(7) This section applies to a determinate sentence of detention under section 91 of the Sentencing Act or under section 228 of this Act as it applies to a term of imprisonment of 12 months or more.
[Criminal Justice Act 2003, s 264.]

---

1. Sections 263–265 came into force on 26 January 2004. See the Criminal Justice Act 2003 (Commencement No 1) Order, SI 2003/3282. Until s 61 of this Act (abolition of sentences of detention in a young offender institution, custody for life etc) comes into force, this section is subject to the modifications in the Criminal Justice Act 2003 (Sentencing) (Transitory Provisions) Order 2005, in this PART, post.

Restriction on consecutive sentences for released prisoners

3–2052   265. Restriction on consecutive sentences for released prisoners[1]. (1) A court sentencing a person to a term of imprisonment may not order or direct that the term is to commence on the expiry of any other sentence of imprisonment from which he has been released early under this Chapter.

(2) In this section "sentence of imprisonment" includes a sentence of detention under section 91 of the Sentencing Act or section 228 of this Act, and "term of imprisonment" is to be read accordingly.
[Criminal Justice Act 2003, s 265.]

---

1. Sections 263–265 came into force on 26 January 2004. See the Criminal Justice Act 2003 (Commencement No 1) Order, SI 2003/3282. Until s 61 of this Act (abolition of sentences of detention in a young offender institution, custody for life etc) comes into force, this section is subject to the modifications in the Criminal Justice Act 2003 (Sentencing) (Transitory Provisions) Order 2005, in this PART, post.

Drug testing requirements

3–2053   266. Release on licence etc: drug testing requirements. (1) Section 64 of the Criminal Justice and Court Services Act 2000 (c 43) (release on licence etc: drug testing requirements) is amended as follows.

(2) In subsection (1) for paragraph (a) there is substituted—

"(a) the Secretary of State releases from prison a person aged 14 or over on whom a sentence of imprisonment has been imposed,
(aa) a responsible officer is of the opinion—
  (i)   that the offender has a propensity to misuse specified Class A drugs, and
  (ii) that the misuse by the offender of any specified Class A drug caused or contributed to any offence of which he has been convicted, or is likely to cause or contribute to the commission of further offences, and".

(3) After subsection (4) there is inserted—

"(4A) A person under the age of 17 years may not be required by virtue of this section to provide a sample otherwise than in the presence of an appropriate adult."

(4) In subsection (5), after paragraph (e) there is inserted

"and
(f) a sentence of detention under section 226 or 228 of the Criminal Justice Act 2003,".

(5) After subsection (5) there is inserted—

"(6) In this section—

"appropriate adult", in relation to a person aged under 17, means—
  (a) his parent or guardian or, if he is in the care of a local authority or voluntary organisation, a person representing that authority or organisation,
  (b) a social worker of a local authority social services department, or
  (c) if no person falling within paragraph (a) or (b) is available, any responsible person aged 18 or over who is not a police officer or a person employed by the police;

"responsible officer" means—
  (a) in relation to an offender aged under 18, an officer of a local probation board or a member of a youth offending team;
  (b) in relation to an offender aged 18 or over, an officer of a local probation board."
[Criminal Justice Act 2003, s 266.]

Supplemental

3–2054   267. Alteration by order of relevant proportion of sentence. The Secretary of State may by order provide that any reference in section 244(3)(a), section 247(2) or section 264(6)(a)(ii) to a particular proportion of a prisoner's sentence is to be read as a reference to such other proportion of a prisoner's sentence as may be specified in the order.[1]
[Criminal Justice Act 2003, s 267.]

---

1. Section 267 is in force: see Criminal Justice Act (Commencement No 7) Order 2005, SI 2005/373.

3–2055 **268. Interpretation of Chapter 6[1].** In this Chapter—

"the 1997 Act" means the Crime (Sentences) Act 1997 (c 43);

"the Board" means the Parole Board;

"fixed-term prisoner" has the meaning given by section 237(1);

"intermittent custody prisoner" means a prisoner serving a sentence of imprisonment to which an intermittent custody order relates;

"prison" and "prisoner" are to be read in accordance with section 237(2);

"release", in relation to a prisoner serving a sentence of imprisonment to which an intermittent custody order relates, includes temporary release;

"relevant court order", in relation to a person serving a sentence of imprisonment to which a custody plus order or intermittent custody order relates, means that order.

[Criminal Justice Act 2003, s 268.]

1. Section 268 came into force on 26 January 2004. See the Criminal Justice Act 2003 (Commencement No 1) Order, SI 2003/3282.

CHAPTER 7[1]
Effect of Life Sentence

3–2056

1. Chapter 7 contains ss 269–277. These provisions relate to mandatory life sentences and are not reproduced in this work.

CHAPTER 8[1]
Other Provisions about Sentencing

Deferment of sentence

3–2057 **278. Deferment of sentence.** Schedule 23 (deferment of sentence) shall have effect.

[Criminal Justice Act 2003, s 278.]

1. Chapter 8 contains ss 278–301.

Power to include drug treatment and testing requirement in certain orders in respect of young offenders

3–2058 **279. Drug treatment and testing requirement in action plan order or supervision order.** Schedule 24 (which enables a requirement as to drug treatment and testing to be included in an action plan order or a supervision order) shall have effect.

[Criminal Justice Act 2003, s 279.]

Alteration of penalties for offences

3–2059 **280. Alteration of penalties for specified summary offences.** (1) The summary offences listed in Schedule 25 are no longer punishable with imprisonment.

(2) Schedule 26 (which contains amendments increasing the maximum term of imprisonment for certain summary offences from 4 months or less to 51 weeks) shall have effect.

(3) This section does not affect the penalty for any offence committed before the commencement of this section.

[Criminal Justice Act 2003, s 280.]

3–2060 **281. Alteration of penalties for other summary offences.** (1) Subsection (2) applies to any summary offence which—

(a) is an offence under a relevant enactment,

(b) is punishable with a maximum term of imprisonment of five months or less, and

(c) is not listed in Schedule 25 or Schedule 26.

(2) The Secretary of State may by order amend any relevant enactment so as to—

(a) provide that any summary offence to which this subsection applies is no longer punishable with imprisonment, or

(b) increase to 51 weeks the maximum term of imprisonment to which a person is liable on conviction of the offence.

(3) An order under subsection (2) may make such supplementary, incidental or consequential provision as the Secretary of State considers necessary or expedient, including provision amending any relevant enactment.

(4) Subsection (5) applies to any summary offence which—

(a) is an offence under a relevant enactment, and

(b) is punishable with a maximum term of imprisonment of six months.

(5) The maximum term of imprisonment to which a person is liable on conviction of an offence to which this subsection applies is, by virtue of this subsection, 51 weeks (and the relevant enactment in question is to be read as if it had been amended accordingly).

(6) Neither of the following—

(*a*) an order under subsection (2), or
(*b*) subsection (5),

affects the penalty for any offence committed before the commencement of that order or subsection (as the case may be).

(7) In this section and section 282 "relevant enactment" means any enactment contained in—

(*a*) an Act passed before or in the same Session as this Act, or
(*b*) any subordinate legislation made before the passing of this Act.

(8) In subsection (7) "subordinate legislation" has the same meaning as in the Interpretation Act 1978 (c 30).
[Criminal Justice Act 2003, s 281.]

3–2061   282.   Increase in maximum term that may be imposed on summary conviction of offence triable either way. (1) In section 32 of the Magistrates' Courts Act 1980 (c 43) (penalties on summary conviction for offences triable either way) in subsection (1) (offences listed in Schedule 1 to that Act) for "not exceeding 6 months" there is substituted "not exceeding 12 months".

(2) Subsection (3) applies to any offence triable either way which—

(*a*) is an offence under a relevant enactment,
(*b*) is punishable with imprisonment on summary conviction, and
(*c*) is not listed in Schedule 1 to the Magistrates' Courts Act 1980.

(3) The maximum term of imprisonment to which a person is liable on summary conviction of an offence to which this subsection applies is by virtue of this subsection 12 months (and the relevant enactment in question is to be read as if it had been amended accordingly).

(4) Nothing in this section affects the penalty for any offence committed before the commencement of this section.
[Criminal Justice Act 2003, s 282.]

3–2062   283.   Enabling powers: power to alter maximum penalties. (1) The Secretary of State may by order, in accordance with subsection (2) or (3), amend any relevant enactment which confers a power (however framed or worded) by subordinate legislation to make a person—

(*a*) as regards a summary offence, liable on conviction to a term of imprisonment;
(*b*) as regards an offence triable either way, liable on summary conviction to a term of imprisonment.

(2) An order made by virtue of paragraph (*a*) of subsection (1) may amend the relevant enactment in question so as to—

(*a*) restrict the power so that a person may no longer be made liable on conviction of a summary offence to a term of imprisonment, or
(*b*) increase to 51 weeks the maximum term of imprisonment to which a person may be made liable on conviction of a summary offence under the power.

(3) An order made by virtue of paragraph (*b*) of that subsection may amend the relevant enactment in question so as to increase the maximum term of imprisonment to which a person may be made liable on summary conviction of an offence under the power to 12 months.

(4) Schedule 27 (which amends the maximum penalties which may be imposed by virtue of certain enabling powers) shall have effect.

(5) The power conferred by subsection (1) shall not apply to the enactments amended under Schedule 27.

(6) An order under subsection (1) may make such supplementary, incidental or consequential provision as the Secretary of State considers necessary or expedient, including provision amending any relevant enactment.

(7) None of the following—

(*a*) an order under subsection (1), or
(*b*) Schedule 27,

affects the penalty for any offence committed before the commencement of that order or Schedule (as the case may be).

(8) In subsection (1) "subordinate legislation" has the same meaning as in the Interpretation Act 1978 (c 30).

(9) In this section "relevant enactment" means any enactment contained in an Act passed before or in the same Session as this Act.
[Criminal Justice Act 2003, s 283.]

3–2063   284.   Increase in penalties for drug-related offences. (*Introduces Sch 8, which increases the penalties for certain drug-related offences. Section 28 came into effect on 29 January 2004, but without affecting the penalties for offences committed before that date: see the Criminal Justice Act 2003 (Commencement No 2 and Saving Provisions) Order 2004, SI 2004/81.*)

3–2064   285.   Increase in penalties for certain driving-related offences. (*Increases the penalties for certain driver-related offences. Section 28 came into effect on 27 February 2004, but without affecting* *the penalties for offences committed before that date: see the Criminal Justice Act 2003 (Commencement No 2 and Saving Provisions) Order 2004, SI 2004/81.)*

3–2065   286. Increase in penalties for offences under section 174 of Road Traffic Act 1988. *(Increases the penalties for offences under s 174 of the Road Traffic Aft 1988. Section 286 came into effect on 29 January 2004, but without affecting the penalties for offences committed before that date: see the Criminal Justice Act 2003 (Commencement No 2 and Saving Provisions) Order 2004, SI 2004/81.)*

Firearms offences

3–2066   287. Minimum sentence for certain firearms offences. *(Imposes minimum sentences for certain firearms offences by inserting a new s 51A in the Firearms Act 1968. Section 287 came into effect on 22 January 2004, but without affecting the penalties for offences committed before that date: see the Criminal Justice Act 2003 (Commencement No 2 and Saving Provisions) Order 2004, SI 2004/81.)*

3–2067   288. Certain firearms offences to be triable only on indictment. *(Amends the Firearms Act 1968 to make certain offences, namely those for which minimum penalties are provided by s 287 above, triable only on indictment. Section 288 came into effect on 22 January 2004: see the Criminal Justice Act 2003 (Commencement No 2 and Saving Provisions) Order 2004, SI 2004/81.)*

3–2068   289. Power to sentence young offender to detention in respect of certain firearms offences: England and Wales. *(Amends s 91 of the Powers of Criminal Courts (Sentencing) Act 2000 to ensure that offenders age 16–17 can be sentenced to the minimum terms required by the new s 51A of the Firearms Act 1968. Section 288 came into effect on 22 January 2004: see the Criminal Justice Act 2003 (Commencement No 2 and Saving Provisions) Order 2004, SI 2004/81.)*

3–2069   290. Power to sentence young offender to detention in respect of certain firearms offences: Scotland

3–2070   291. Power by order to exclude application of minimum sentence to those under 18.
(1) The Secretary of State may by order—

   (*a*)   amend section 51A(1)(*b*) of the Firearms Act 1968 (c 27) by substituting for the word "16" the word "18",

   (*b*)   repeal section 91(1A)(*c*) and (5) of the Sentencing Act,

   (*c*)   amend subsection (3) of section 49 of the Criminal Procedure (Scotland) Act 1995 by repealing the exception to that subsection,

   (*d*)   repeal section 208(2) of that Act, and

   (*e*)   make such other provision as he considers necessary or expedient in consequence of, or in connection with, the provision made by virtue of paragraphs (*a*) to (*d*).

(2) The provision that may be made by virtue of subsection (1)(*e*) includes, in particular, provision amending or repealing any provision of an Act (whenever passed), including any provision of this Act[1].
[Criminal Justice Act 2003, s 291.]

---

1. Section 291 came into effect on 22 January 2004: see the Criminal Justice Act 2003 (Commencement No 2 and Saving Provisions) Order 2004, SI 2004/81.

3–2071   292. Sentencing for firearms offences in Northern Ireland

3–2072   293. Increase in penalty for offences relating to importation or exportation of certain firearms. *(Amends the Customs and Excise Management Act 1979 to increase the maximum penalty for smuggling prohibited weapons covered by the minimum sentence provisions. Section 293 came into effect on 22 January 2004, but without affecting the penalties for offences committed before that date: see the Criminal Justice Act 2003 (Commencement No 2 and Saving Provisions) Order 2004, SI 2004/81.)*

Offenders transferred to mental hospital

3–2073   294. Duration of directions under Mental Health Act 1983 in relation to offenders. *(Amends s 50 of the Mental Health Act 1983 in relation to arrangements for the release, or return to prison, of serving prisoners who have been transferred to hospital for medical treatment. Section 294 came into effect on 20 January 2004: see the Criminal Justice Act 2003 (Commencement No 2 and Saving Provisions) Order 2004, SI 2004/81.)*

3–2074   295. Access to Parole Board for certain patients serving prison sentences

3–2075   296. Duration of directions under Mental Health (Northern Ireland) Order 1986 in relation to offenders

3–2076   297. Access to Sentence Review Commissioners and Life Sentence Review Commissioners for certain Northern Ireland patients

Term of detention and training order

3–2077   298. Term of detention and training order.   (1) Section 101 of the Sentencing Act (which relates to detention and training orders) is amended as follows.

(2) In subsection (1), for "subsection (2)" there is substituted "subsections (2) and (2A)".

(3) After subsection (2) there is inserted—

"(2A) Where—

(*a*)   the offence is a summary offence,

(*b*)   the maximum term of imprisonment that a court could (in the case of an offender aged 18 or over) impose for the offence is 51 weeks,

the term of a detention and training order may not exceed 6 months."
[Criminal Justice Act 2003, s 298.]

Disqualification from working with children

3–2078   299. Disqualification from working with children[1].   Schedule 30 (which contains amendments of Part 2 of the Criminal Justice and Court Services Act 2000 (c 43) relating to disqualification orders under that Part) shall have effect.
[Criminal Justice Act 2003, s 299.]

---

1. Section 299 came into force on 1 May 2004: see the Criminal Justice Act (Commencement No 3 and Transitional Provisions) Order 2004, SI 2004/929.

Fine defaulters

3–2079   300. Power to impose unpaid work requirement or curfew requirement on fine defaulter.   (1) Subsection (2) applies in any case where, in respect of a person aged 16 or over, a magistrates' court—

(*a*)   has power under Part 3 of the Magistrates' Courts Act 1980 (c 43) to issue a warrant of commitment for default in paying a sum adjudged to be paid by a conviction (other than a sum ordered to be paid under section 6 of the Proceeds of Crime Act 2002 (c 29)), or

(*b*)   would, but for section 89 of the Sentencing Act (restrictions on custodial sentences for persons under 18), have power to issue such a warrant for such default.

(2) The magistrates' court may, instead of issuing a warrant of commitment or, as the case may be, proceeding under section 81 of the Magistrates' Courts Act 1980 (enforcement of fines imposed on young offender), order the person in default to comply with—

(*a*)   an unpaid work requirement (as defined by section 199), or

(*b*)   a curfew requirement (as defined by section 204).

(3) In this Part "default order" means an order under subsection (2).

(4) Subsections (3) and (4) of section 177 (which relate to electronic monitoring) have effect in relation to a default order as they have effect in relation to a community order.

(5) Where a magistrates' court has power to make a default order, it may, if it thinks it expedient to do so, postpone the making of the order until such time and on such conditions (if any) as it thinks just.

(6) Schedule 8 (breach, revocation or amendment of community order), Schedule 9 (transfer of community orders to Scotland or Northern Ireland) and Chapter 4 (further provisions about orders under Chapters 2 and 3) have effect in relation to default orders as they have effect in relation to community orders, but subject to the modifications contained in Schedule 31.[1]

(7) Where a default order has been made for default in paying any sum—

(*a*)   on payment of the whole sum to any person authorised to receive it, the order shall cease to have effect, and

(*b*)   on payment of a part of the sum to any such person, the total number of hours or days to which the order relates is to be taken to be reduced by a proportion corresponding to that which the part paid bears to the whole sum.

(8) In calculating any reduction required by subsection (7)(*b*), any fraction of a day or hour is to be disregarded.
[Criminal Justice Act 2003, s 300.]

---

1. Section 300(6) is in force for certain purposes: see Criminal Justice Act (Commencement No 7) Order 2005, SI 2005/373.

3–2080   301. Fine defaulters: driving disqualification.   (1) Subsection (2) applies in any case where a magistrates' court—

(*a*)   has power under Part 3 of the Magistrates' Courts Act 1980 (c 43) to issue a warrant of commitment for default in paying a sum adjudged to be paid by a conviction (other than a sum ordered to be paid under section 6 of the Proceeds of Crime Act 2002 (c 29)), or

(*b*)   would, but for section 89 of the Sentencing Act (restrictions on custodial sentences for persons under 18), have power to issue such a warrant for such default.

(2) The magistrates' court may, instead of issuing a warrant of commitment or, as the case may

be, proceeding under section 81 of the Magistrates' Courts Act 1980 (enforcement of fines imposed on young offenders), order the person in default to be disqualified, for such period not exceeding twelve months as it thinks fit, for holding or obtaining a driving licence.

(3) Where an order has been made under subsection (2) for default in paying any sum—

(a) on payment of the whole sum to any person authorised to receive it, the order shall cease to have effect, and

(b) on payment of part of the sum to any such person, the total number of weeks or months to which the order relates is to be taken to be reduced by a proportion corresponding to that which the part paid bears to the whole sum.

(4) In calculating any reduction required by subsection (3)(b) any fraction of a week or month is to be disregarded.

(5) The Secretary of State may by order amend subsection (2) by substituting, for the period there specified, such other period as may be specified in the order.[1]

(6) A court which makes an order under this section disqualifying a person for holding or obtaining a driving licence shall require him to produce—

(a) any such licence held by him together with its counterpart; or

(b) in the case where he holds a Community licence (within the meaning of Part 3 of the Road Traffic Act 1988 (c 52)), his Community licence and its counterpart (if any).

(7) In this section—

"driving licence" means a licence to drive a motor vehicle granted under Part 3 of the Road Traffic Act 1988;

"counterpart"—

(a) in relation to a driving licence, has the meaning given in relation to such a licence by section 108(1) of that Act; and

(b) in relation to a Community licence, has the meaning given by section 99B of that Act.

[Criminal Justice Act 2003, s 301.]

---

1. Section 301(5) is in force: see Criminal Justice Act (Commencement No 7) Order 2005, SI 2005/373.

CHAPTER 9[1]
Supplementary

3–2081   302. Execution of process between England and Wales and Scotland[2]. Section 4 of the Summary Jurisdiction (Process) Act 1881 (c 24) (execution of process of English and Welsh courts in Scotland) applies to any process issued by a magistrates' court under—

paragraph 7(2) or (4), 13(6) or 25(1) of Schedule 8,
paragraph 12 of Schedule 9,
paragraph 8(1) of Schedule 10, or
paragraph 6(2) or (4), 12(1) or 20(1) of Schedule 12,

as it applies to process issued under the Magistrates' Courts Act 1980 by a magistrates' court.
[Criminal Justice Act 2003, s 302.]

---

1. Chapter 9 contains ss 302–305.
2. Section 302 came into force on 26 January 2004. See the Criminal Justice Act 2003 (Commencement No 1) Order, SI 2003/3282.

3–2082   303. Sentencing: repeals. The following enactments (which are superseded by the provisions of this Part) shall cease to have effect—

(a) Part 2 of the Criminal Justice Act 1991 (c 53) (early release of prisoners),
(b) in the Crime (Sentences) Act 1997 (c 43)—

(i) section 29 (power of Secretary of State to release life prisoners to whom section 28 of that Act does not apply),
(ii) section 33 (transferred prisoners), and
(iii) sections 35 and 40 (fine defaulters),

(c) sections 80 and 81 of the Crime and Disorder Act 1998 (c 37) (sentencing guidelines), and
(d) in the Sentencing Act—

(i) Chapter 3 of Part 4 (community orders available only where offender 16 or over),
(ii) section 85 (sexual or violent offences: extension of custodial term for licence purposes),
(iii) sections 87 and 88 (remand in custody),
(iv) section 109 (life sentence for second serious offence), and
(v) Chapter 5 of Part 5 (suspended sentences).

[Criminal Justice Act 2003, s 303.]

3–2083   304. Amendments relating to sentencing[1]. Schedule 32 (which contains amendments related to the provisions of this Part) shall have effect.
[Criminal Justice Act 2003, s 304.]

1. Section 304 and paras 11, 12(1)–(3) and (6), 29, 57 and 58 of Sch 32 came into force on 26 January 2004. See the Criminal Justice Act 2003 (Commencement No 1) Order 2003, SI 2003/3282. Paras 48–50 of Sch 32 came into force on 26 January 2004: see the Criminal Justice Act 2003 (Commencement No 2 and Saving Provisions) Order 2004, SI 2004/81.

3–2084   305. Interpretation of Part 12[1].   (1) In this Part, except where the contrary intention appears—

"accredited programme" has the meaning given by section 202(2);

"activity requirement", in relation to a community order, custody plus order, intermittent custody order or suspended sentence order, has the meaning given by section 201;

"alcohol treatment requirement", in relation to a community order or suspended sentence order, has the meaning given by section 212;

"the appropriate officer of the court" means, in relation to a magistrates' court, the clerk of the court;

"associated", in relation to offences, is to be read in accordance with section 161(1) of the Sentencing Act;

"attendance centre" has the meaning given by section 221(2);

"attendance centre requirement", in relation to a community order, custody plus order, intermittent custody order or suspended sentence order, has the meaning given by section 214;

"community order" has the meaning given by section 177(1);

"community requirement", in relation to a suspended sentence order, has the meaning given by section 189(7);

"community sentence" has the meaning given by section 147(1);

"court" (without more), except in Chapter 7, does not include a service court;

"curfew requirement", in relation to a community order, custody plus order, intermittent custody order or suspended sentence order, has the meaning given by section 204;

"custodial sentence" has the meaning given by section 76 of the Sentencing Act;

"custody plus order" has the meaning given by section 181(4);

"default order" has the meaning given by section 300(3);

"drug rehabilitation requirement", in relation to a community order or suspended sentence order, has the meaning given by section 209;

"electronic monitoring requirement", in relation to a community order, custody plus order, intermittent custody order or suspended sentence order, has the meaning given by section 215;

"exclusion requirement", in relation to a community order, custody plus order, intermittent custody order or suspended sentence order, has the meaning given by section 205;

"guardian" has the same meaning as in the Children and Young Persons Act 1933 (c 12);

"intermittent custody order" has the meaning given by section 183(2);

"licence" means a licence under Chapter 6;

"local probation board" means a local probation board established under section 4 of the Criminal Justice and Court Services Act 2000 (c 43);

"mental health treatment requirement", in relation to a community order or suspended sentence order, has the meaning given by section 207;

"pre-sentence report" has the meaning given by section 158(1);

"programme requirement", in relation to a community order, custody plus order, intermittent custody order or suspended sentence order, has the meaning given by section 202;

"prohibited activity requirement", in relation to a community order, custody plus order, intermittent custody order or suspended sentence order, has the meaning given by section 203;

"residence requirement", in relation to a community order or suspended sentence order, has the meaning given by section 206;

"responsible officer", in relation to an offender to whom a community order, a custody plus order, an intermittent custody order or a suspended sentence order relates, has the meaning given by section 197;

"sentence of imprisonment" does not include a committal—

(a) in default of payment of any sum of money,

(b) for want of sufficient distress to satisfy any sum of money, or

(c) for failure to do or abstain from doing anything required to be done or left undone,

and references to sentencing an offender to imprisonment are to be read accordingly;

"the Sentencing Act" means the Powers of Criminal Courts (Sentencing) Act 2000 (c 6);

"service court" means—

(a) a court-martial constituted under the Army Act 1955 (3 & 4 Eliz 2 c 18), the Air Force Act 1955 (3 & 4 Eliz 2 c 19) or the Naval Discipline Act 1957 (c 53);

(b) a summary appeal court constituted under section 83ZA of the Army Act 1955, section 83ZA of the Air Force Act 1955 or section 52FF of the Naval Discipline Act 1957;

(c) the Courts-Martial Appeal Court; or

(d) a Standing Civilian Court;

"service disciplinary proceedings" means—

(a) any proceedings under the Army Act 1955, the Air Force Act 1955 or the Naval Discipline Act 1957 (whether before a court-martial or any other court or person authorised under any of those Acts to award a punishment in respect of any offence), and

(b) any proceedings before a Standing Civilian Court;

"supervision requirement", in relation to a community order, custody plus order, intermittent custody order or suspended sentence order, has the meaning given by section 213;
"suspended sentence" and "suspended sentence order" have the meaning given by section 189(7);
"unpaid work requirement", in relation to a community order, custody plus order, intermittent custody order or suspended sentence order, has the meaning given by section 199;
"youth offending team" means a team established under section 39 of the Crime and Disorder Act 1998 (c 37).

(2) For the purposes of any provision of this Part which requires the determination of the age of a person by the court or the Secretary of State, his age is to be taken to be that which it appears to the court or (as the case may be) the Secretary of State to be after considering any available evidence.

(3) Any reference in this Part to an offence punishable with imprisonment is to be read without regard to any prohibition or restriction imposed by or under any Act on the imprisonment of young offenders.

(4) For the purposes of this Part—

(a) a sentence falls to be imposed under subsection (2) of section 51A of the Firearms Act 1968 (c 27) if it is required by that subsection and the court is not of the opinion there mentioned,

(b) a sentence falls to be imposed under section 110(2) or 111(2) of the Sentencing Act if it is required by that provision and the court is not of the opinion there mentioned,

(c) a sentence falls to be imposed under section 225 or 227 if, because the court is of the opinion mentioned in subsection (1)(b) of that section, the court is obliged to pass a sentence complying with that section,

(d) a sentence falls to be imposed under section 226 if, because the court is of the opinion mentioned in subsection (1)(b) of that section and considers that the case falls within subsection (2) or (3) of that section, the court is obliged to pass a sentence complying with that section, and

(e) a sentence falls to be imposed under section 228 if, because the court is of the opinion mentioned in subsection (1)(b)(i) and (ii) of that section, the court is obliged to pass a sentence complying with that section.
[Criminal Justice Act 2003, s 305.]

1. Section 305(1)–(3) came into force on 26 January 2004. See the Criminal Justice Act 2003 (Commencement No 1) Order, SI 2003/3282.

3–2085
Section 179   SCHEDULE 8[1]
                    BREACH, REVOCATION OR AMENDMENT OF COMMUNITY ORDER

PART 1
PRELIMINARY
Interpretation

1. In this Schedule—
"the offender", in relation to a community order, means the person in respect of whom the order is made;
"the petty sessions area concerned", in relation to a community order, means the petty sessions area for the time being specified in the order;
"the responsible officer" has the meaning given by section 197.

2. In this Schedule—
(a) references to a drug rehabilitation requirement of a community order being subject to review are references to that requirement being subject to review in accordance with section 210(1)(b);
(b) references to the court responsible for a community order imposing a drug rehabilitation requirement which is subject to review are to be construed in accordance with section 210(2).

3. For the purposes of this Schedule—
(a) a requirement falling within any paragraph of section 177(1) is of the same kind as any other requirement falling within that paragraph, and
(b) an electronic monitoring requirement is a requirement of the same kind as any requirement falling within section 177(1) to which it relates.

1. Schedule 8 is of no effect in relation to offences committed before 4 April 2005: see the Criminal Justice Act 2003 (Commencement No 8 and Transitional and Saving Provisions) Order 2005, SI 2005/950.

Orders made on appeal
4. Where a community order has been made on appeal, it is to be taken for the purposes of this Schedule to have been made by the Crown Court.

PART 2
BREACH OF REQUIREMENT OF ORDER
Duty to give warning
5. (1) If the responsible officer is of the opinion that the offender has failed without reasonable excuse to comply with any of the requirements of a community order, the officer must give him a warning under this paragraph unless—

(a) the offender has within the previous twelve months been given a warning under this paragraph in relation to a failure to comply with any of the requirements of the order, or

(b) the officer causes an information to be laid before a justice of the peace in respect of the failure.

(2) A warning under this paragraph must—

(a) describe the circumstances of the failure,

(b) state that the failure is unacceptable, and

(c) inform the offender that, if within the next twelve months he again fails to comply with any requirement of the order, he will be liable to be brought before a court.

(3) The responsible officer must, as soon as practicable after the warning has been given, record that fact.

(4) In relation to any community order which was made by the Crown Court and does not include a direction that any failure to comply with the requirements of the order is to be dealt with by a magistrates' court, the reference in sub-paragraph (1)(b) to a justice of the peace is to be read as a reference to the Crown Court.

Breach of order after warning

6. (1) If—

(a) the responsible officer has given a warning under paragraph 5 to the offender in respect of a community order, and

(b) at any time within the twelve months beginning with the date on which the warning was given, the responsible officer is of the opinion that the offender has since that date failed without reasonable excuse to comply with any of the requirements of the order,

the officer must cause an information to be laid before a justice of the peace in respect of the failure in question.

(2) In relation to any community order which was made by the Crown Court and does not include a direction that any failure to comply with the requirements of the order is to be dealt with by a magistrates' court, the reference in sub-paragraph (1) to a justice of the peace is to be read as a reference to the Crown Court.

Issue of summons or warrant by justice of the peace

7. (1) This paragraph applies to—

(a) a community order made by a magistrates' court, or

(b) any community order which was made by the Crown Court and includes a direction that any failure to comply with the requirements of the order is to be dealt with by a magistrates' court.

(2) If at any time while a community order to which this paragraph applies is in force it appears on information to a justice of the peace acting for the petty sessions area concerned that the offender has failed to comply with any of the requirements of the order, the justice may—

(a) issue a summons requiring the offender to appear at the place and time specified in it, or

(b) if the information is in writing and on oath, issue a warrant for his arrest.

(3) Any summons or warrant issued under this paragraph must direct the offender to appear or be brought—

(a) in the case of a community order imposing a drug rehabilitation requirement which is subject to review, before the magistrates' court responsible for the order, or

(b) in any other case, before a magistrates' court acting for the petty sessions area concerned.

(4) Where a summons issued under sub-paragraph (2)(a) requires the offender to appear before a magistrates' court and the offender does not appear in answer to the summons, the magistrates' court may issue a warrant for the arrest of the offender.

Issue of summons or warrant by Crown Court

8. (1) This paragraph applies to a community order made by the Crown Court which does not include a direction that any failure to comply with the requirements of the order is to be dealt with by a magistrates' court.

(2) If at any time while a community order to which this paragraph applies is in force it appears on information to the Crown Court that the offender has failed to comply with any of the requirements of the order, the Crown Court may—

(a) issue a summons requiring the offender to appear at the place and time specified in it, or

(b) if the information is in writing and on oath, issue a warrant for his arrest.

(3) Any summons or warrant issued under this paragraph must direct the offender to appear or be brought before the Crown Court.

(4) Where a summons issued under sub-paragraph (2)(a) requires the offender to appear before the Crown Court and the offender does not appear in answer to the summons, the Crown Court may issue a warrant for the arrest of the offender.

Powers of magistrates' court

9. (1) If it is proved to the satisfaction of a magistrates' court before which an offender appears or is brought under paragraph 7 that he has failed without reasonable excuse to comply with any of the requirements of the community order, the court must deal with him in respect of the failure in any one of the following ways—

(a) by amending the terms of the community order so as to impose more onerous requirements which the court could include if it were then making the order;

(b) where the community order was made by a magistrates' court, by dealing with him, for the offence in respect of which the order was made, in any way in which the court could deal with him if he had just been convicted by it of the offence;

(c) where—

(i) the community order was made by a magistrates' court,

(ii) the offence in respect of which the order was made was not an offence punishable by imprisonment,

(iii) the offender is aged 18 or over, and

(iv) the offender has wilfully and persistently failed to comply with the requirements of the order,

by dealing with him, in respect of that offence, by imposing a sentence of imprisonment for a term not exceeding 51 weeks.

(2) In dealing with an offender under sub-paragraph (1), a magistrates' court must take into account the extent to which the offender has complied with the requirements of the community order.

(3) In dealing with an offender under sub-paragraph (1)(a), the court may extend the duration of particular requirements (subject to any limit imposed by Chapter 4 of Part 12 of this Act) but may not extend the period specified under section 177(5).

(4) In dealing with an offender under sub-paragraph (1)(b), the court may, in the case of an offender who has wilfully and persistently failed to comply with the requirements of the community order, impose a custodial sentence (where the order was made in respect of an offence punishable with such a sentence) notwithstanding anything in section 152(2).

(5) Where a magistrates' court deals with an offender under sub-paragraph (1)(b) or (c), it must revoke the community order if it is still in force.

(6) Where a community order was made by the Crown Court and a magistrates' court would (apart from this sub-paragraph) be required to deal with the offender under sub-paragraph (1)(a), (b) or (c), it may instead commit him to custody or release him on bail until he can be brought or appear before the Crown Court.

(7) A magistrates' court which deals with an offender's case under sub-paragraph (6) must send to the Crown Court—

(a) a certificate signed by a justice of the peace certifying that the offender has failed to comply with the requirements of the community order in the respect specified in the certificate, and

(b) such other particulars of the case as may be desirable;

and a certificate purporting to be so signed is admissible as evidence of the failure before the Crown Court.

(8) A person sentenced under sub-paragraph (1)(b) or (c) for an offence may appeal to the Crown Court against the sentence.

Powers of Crown Court

10. (1) Where under paragraph 8 or by virtue of paragraph 9(6) an offender appears or is brought before the Crown Court and it is proved to the satisfaction of that court that he has failed without reasonable excuse to comply with any of the requirements of the community order, the Crown Court must deal with him in respect of the failure in any one of the following ways—

(a) by amending the terms of the community order so as to impose more onerous requirements which the Crown Court could impose if it were then making the order;

(b) by dealing with him, for the offence in respect of which the order was made, in any way in which he could have been dealt with for that offence by the court which made the order if the order had not been made;

(c) where—

(i) the offence in respect of which the order was made was not an offence punishable by imprisonment,

(ii) the offender is aged 18 or over,

(iii) the offender has wilfully and persistently failed to comply with the requirements of the order,

by dealing with him, in respect of that offence, by imposing a sentence of imprisonment for a term not exceeding 51 weeks.

(2) In dealing with an offender under sub-paragraph (1), the Crown Court must take into account the extent to which the offender has complied with the requirements of the community order.

(3) In dealing with an offender under sub-paragraph (1)(a), the court may extend the duration of particular requirements (subject to any limit imposed by Chapter 4 of Part 12 of this Act) but may not extend the period specified under section 177(5).

(4) In dealing with an offender under sub-paragraph (1)(b), the Crown Court may, in the case of an offender who has wilfully and persistently failed to comply with the requirements of the community order, impose a custodial sentence (where the order was made in respect of an offence punishable with such a sentence) notwithstanding anything in section 152(2).

(5) Where the Crown Court deals with an offender under sub-paragraph (1)(b) or (c), it must revoke the community order if it is still in force.

(6) In proceedings before the Crown Court under this paragraph any question whether the offender has failed to comply with the requirements of the community order is to be determined by the court and not by the verdict of a jury.

Restriction of powers in paragraphs 9 and 10 where treatment required

11. (1) An offender who is required by any of the following requirements of a community order—

(a) a mental health treatment requirement,

(b) a drug rehabilitation requirement, or

(c) an alcohol treatment requirement,

to submit to treatment for his mental condition, or his dependency on or propensity to misuse drugs or alcohol, is not to be treated for the purposes of paragraph 9 or 10 as having failed to comply with that requirement on the ground only that he had refused to undergo any surgical, electrical or other treatment if, in the opinion of the court, his refusal was reasonable having regard to all the circumstances.

(2) A court may not under paragraph 9(1)(a) or 10(1)(a) amend a mental health treatment requirement, a drug rehabilitation requirement or an alcohol treatment requirement unless the offender expresses his willingness to comply with the requirement as amended.

Supplementary

12. Where a community order was made by a magistrates' court in the case of an offender under 18 years of age in respect of an offence triable only on indictment in the case of an adult, any powers exercisable under paragraph 9(1)(b) in respect of the offender after he attains the age of 18 are powers to do either or both of the following—

(a) to impose a fine not exceeding £5,000 for the offence in respect of which the order was made;

(b) to deal with the offender for that offence in any way in which a magistrates' court could deal with him if it had just convicted him of an offence punishable with imprisonment for a term not exceeding 51 weeks.

PART 3

REVOCATION OF ORDER

Revocation of order with or without re-sentencing: powers of magistrates' court

13. (1) This paragraph applies where a community order, other than an order made by the Crown Court and falling within paragraph 14(1)(*a*), is in force and on the application of the offender or the responsible officer it appears to the appropriate magistrates' court that, having regard to circumstances which have arisen since the order was made, it would be in the interests of justice—

(*a*) for the order to be revoked, or
(*b*) for the offender to be dealt with in some other way for the offence in respect of which the order was made.

(2) The appropriate magistrates' court may—

(*a*) revoke the order, or
(*b*) both—

    (i) revoke the order, and
    (ii) deal with the offender, for the offence in respect of which the order was made, in any way in which it could deal with him if he had just been convicted by the court of the offence.

(3) The circumstances in which a community order may be revoked under sub-paragraph (2) include the offender's making good progress or his responding satisfactorily to supervision or treatment (as the case requires).

(4) In dealing with an offender under sub-paragraph (2)(*b*), a magistrates' court must take into account the extent to which the offender has complied with the requirements of the community order.

(5) A person sentenced under sub-paragraph (2)(*b*) for an offence may appeal to the Crown Court against the sentence.

(6) Where a magistrates' court proposes to exercise its powers under this paragraph otherwise than on the application of the offender, it must summon him to appear before the court and, if he does not appear in answer to the summons, may issue a warrant for his arrest.

(7) In this paragraph "the appropriate magistrates' court" means—

(*a*) in the case of an order imposing a drug rehabilitation requirement which is subject to review, the magistrates' court responsible for the order, and
(*b*) in the case of any other community order, a magistrates' court acting for the petty sessions area concerned.

Revocation of order with or without re-sentencing: powers of Crown Court

14. (1) This paragraph applies where—

(*a*) there is in force a community order made by the Crown Court which does not include a direction that any failure to comply with the requirements of the order is to be dealt with by a magistrates' court, and
(*b*) the offender or the responsible officer applies to the Crown Court for the order to be revoked or for the offender to be dealt with in some other way for the offence in respect of which the order was made.

(2) If it appears to the Crown Court to be in the interests of justice to do so, having regard to circumstances which have arisen since the order was made, the Crown Court may—

(*a*) revoke the order, or
(*b*) both—

    (i) revoke the order, and
    (ii) deal with the offender, for the offence in respect of which the order was made, in any way in which he could have been dealt with for that offence by the court which made the order if the order had not been made.

(3) The circumstances in which a community order may be revoked under sub-paragraph (2) include the offender's making good progress or his responding satisfactorily to supervision or treatment (as the case requires).

(4) In dealing with an offender under sub-paragraph (2)(*b*), the Crown Court must take into account the extent to which the offender has complied with the requirements of the order.

(5) Where the Crown Court proposes to exercise its powers under this paragraph otherwise than on the application of the offender, it must summon him to appear before the court and, if he does not appear in answer to the summons, may issue a warrant for his arrest.

Supplementary

15. Paragraph 12 applies for the purposes of paragraphs 13 and 14 as it applies for the purposes of paragraph 9 above, but as if for the words "paragraph 9(1)(*b*)" there were substituted "paragraph 13(2)(*b*)(ii) or 14(2)(*b*)(ii)".

PART 4

AMENDMENT OF ORDER

Amendment by reason of change of residence

16. (1) This paragraph applies where, at any time while a community order is in force in respect of an offender, the appropriate court is satisfied that the offender proposes to change, or has changed, his residence from the petty sessions area concerned to another petty sessions area.

(2) Subject to sub-paragraphs (3) and (4), the appropriate court may, and on the application of the responsible officer must, amend the community order by substituting the other petty sessions area for the area specified in the order.

(3) The court may not under this paragraph amend a community order which contains requirements which, in the opinion of the court, cannot be complied with unless the offender continues to reside in the petty sessions area concerned unless, in accordance with paragraph 17, it either—

(*a*) cancels those requirements, or
(*b*) substitutes for those requirements other requirements which can be complied with if the offender ceases to reside in that area.

(4) The court may not amend under this paragraph a community order imposing a programme requirement unless it appears to the court that the accredited programme specified in the requirement is available in the other petty sessions area.

(5) In this paragraph "the appropriate court" means—

(a) in relation to any community order imposing a drug rehabilitation requirement which is subject to review, the court responsible for the order,

(b) in relation to any community order which was made by the Crown Court and does not include any direction that any failure to comply with the requirements of the order is to be dealt with by a magistrates' court, the Crown Court, and

(c) in relation to any other community order, a magistrates' court acting for the petty sessions area concerned.

Amendment of requirements of community order

17. (1) The appropriate court may, on the application of the offender or the responsible officer, by order amend a community order—

(a) by cancelling any of the requirements of the order, or

(b) by replacing any of those requirements with a requirement of the same kind, which the court could include if it were then making the order.

(2) The court may not under this paragraph amend a mental health treatment requirement, a drug rehabilitation requirement or an alcohol treatment requirement unless the offender expresses his willingness to comply with the requirement as amended.

(3) If the offender fails to express his willingness to comply with a mental health treatment requirement, drug rehabilitation requirement or alcohol treatment requirement as proposed to be amended by the court under this paragraph, the court may—

(a) revoke the community order, and

(b) deal with him, for the offence in respect of which the order was made, in any way in which he could have been dealt with for that offence by the court which made the order if the order had not been made.

(4) In dealing with the offender under sub-paragraph (3)(b), the court—

(a) must take into account the extent to which the offender has complied with the requirements of the order, and

(b) may impose a custodial sentence (where the order was made in respect of an offence punishable with such a sentence) notwithstanding anything in section 152(2).

(5) Paragraph 12 applies for the purposes of this paragraph as it applies for the purposes of paragraph 9, but as if for the words "paragraph 9(1)(b)" there were substituted "paragraph 17(3)(b)".

(6) In this paragraph "the appropriate court" has the same meaning as in paragraph 16.

Amendment of treatment requirements of community order on report of practitioner

18. (1) Where the medical practitioner or other person by whom or under whose direction an offender is, in pursuance of any requirement to which this sub-paragraph applies, being treated for his mental condition or his dependency on or propensity to misuse drugs or alcohol—

(a) is of the opinion mentioned in sub-paragraph (3), or

(b) is for any reason unwilling to continue to treat or direct the treatment of the offender,

he must make a report in writing to that effect to the responsible officer and that officer must apply under paragraph 17 to the appropriate court for the variation or cancellation of the requirement.

(2) The requirements to which sub-paragraph (1) applies are—

(a) a mental health treatment requirement,

(b) a drug rehabilitation requirement, and

(c) an alcohol treatment requirement.

(3) The opinion referred to in sub-paragraph (1) is—

(a) that the treatment of the offender should be continued beyond the period specified in that behalf in the order,

(b) that the offender needs different treatment,

(c) that the offender is not susceptible to treatment, or

(d) that the offender does not require further treatment.

(4) In this paragraph "the appropriate court" has the same meaning as in paragraph 16.

Amendment in relation to review of drug rehabilitation requirement

19. Where the responsible officer is of the opinion that a community order imposing a drug rehabilitation requirement which is subject to review should be so amended as to provide for each subsequent periodic review (required by section 211) to be made without a hearing instead of at a review hearing, or vice versa, he must apply under paragraph 17 to the court responsible for the order for the variation of the order.

Extension of unpaid work requirement

20. (1) Where—

(a) a community order imposing an unpaid work requirement is in force in respect of any offender, and

(b) on the application of the offender or the responsible officer, it appears to the appropriate court that it would be in the interests of justice to do so having regard to circumstances which have arisen since the order was made,

the court may, in relation to the order, extend the period of twelve months specified in section 200(2).

(2) In this paragraph "the appropriate court" has the same meaning as in paragraph 16.

PART 5
POWERS OF COURT IN RELATION TO ORDER FOLLOWING SUBSEQUENT CONVICTION

Powers of magistrates' court following subsequent conviction

21. (1) This paragraph applies where—

(a) an offender in respect of whom a community order made by a magistrates' court is in force is convicted of an offence by a magistrates' court, and

(b) it appears to the court that it would be in the interests of justice to exercise its powers under this paragraph, having regard to circumstances which have arisen since the community order was made.

(2) The magistrates' court may—

(a) revoke the order, or

(b) both—

    (i) revoke the order, and

    (ii) deal with the offender, for the offence in respect of which the order was made, in any way in which he could have been dealt with for that offence by the court which made the order if the order had not been made.

(3) In dealing with an offender under sub-paragraph (2)(b), a magistrates' court must take into account the extent to which the offender has complied with the requirements of the community order.

(4) A person sentenced under sub-paragraph (2)(b) for an offence may appeal to the Crown Court against the sentence.

22. (1) Where an offender in respect of whom a community order made by the Crown Court is in force is convicted of an offence by a magistrates' court, the magistrates' court may commit the offender in custody or release him on bail until he can be brought before the Crown Court.

(2) Where the magistrates' court deals with an offender's case under sub-paragraph (1), it must send to the Crown Court such particulars of the case as may be desirable.

Powers of Crown Court following subsequent conviction

23. (1) This paragraph applies where—

(a) an offender in respect of whom a community order is in force—

    (i) is convicted of an offence by the Crown Court, or

    (ii) is brought or appears before the Crown Court by virtue of paragraph 22 or having been committed by the magistrates' court to the Crown Court for sentence, and

(b) it appears to the Crown Court that it would be in the interests of justice to exercise its powers under this paragraph, having regard to circumstances which have arisen since the community order was made.

(2) The Crown Court may—

(a) revoke the order, or

(b) both—

    (i) revoke the order, and

    (ii) deal with the offender, for the offence in respect of which the order was made, in any way in which he could have been dealt with for that offence by the court which made the order if the order had not been made.

(3) In dealing with an offender under sub-paragraph (2)(b), the Crown Court must take into account the extent to which the offender has complied with the requirements of the community order.

PART 6
SUPPLEMENTARY

24. (1) No order may be made under paragraph 16, and no application may be made under paragraph 13, 17 or 20, while an appeal against the community order is pending.

(2) Sub-paragraph (1) does not apply to an application under paragraph 17 which—

(a) relates to a mental health treatment requirement, a drug rehabilitation requirement or an alcohol treatment requirement, and

(b) is made by the responsible officer with the consent of the offender.

25. (1) Subject to sub-paragraph (2), where a court proposes to exercise its powers under Part 4 or 5 of this Schedule, otherwise than on the application of the offender, the court—

(a) must summon him to appear before the court, and

(b) if he does not appear in answer to the summons, may issue a warrant for his arrest.

(2) This paragraph does not apply to an order cancelling a requirement of a community order or reducing the period of any requirement, or substituting a new petty sessions area or a new place for the one specified in the order.

26. Paragraphs 9(1)(a), 10(1)(a) and 17(1)(b) have effect subject to the provisions mentioned in subsection (2) of section 177, and to subsections (3) and (6) of that section.

27. (1) On the making under this Schedule of an order revoking or amending a community order, the proper officer of the court must—

(a) provide copies of the revoking or amending order to the offender and the responsible officer,

(b) in the case of an amending order which substitutes a new petty sessions area, provide a copy of the amending order to—

    (i) the local probation board acting for that area, and

    (ii) the magistrates' court acting for that area, and

(c) in the case of an amending order which imposes or amends a requirement specified in the first column of Schedule 14, provide a copy of so much of the amending order as relates to that requirement to the person specified in relation to that requirement in the second column of that Schedule.

(2) Where under sub-paragraph (1)(b) the proper officer of the court provides a copy of an amending order to a magistrates' court acting for a different area, the officer must also provide to that court such documents and information relating to the case as it considers likely to be of assistance to a court acting for that area in the exercise of its functions in relation to the order.

(3) In this paragraph "proper officer" means—

(a) in relation to a magistrates' court, the justices' chief executive for the court; and

(b) in relation to the Crown Court, the appropriate officer.

3–2086

Section 180

SCHEDULE 9[1]

TRANSFER OF COMMUNITY ORDERS TO SCOTLAND OR NORTHERN IRELAND

PART 1

SCOTLAND

1. (1) Where the court considering the making of a community order is satisfied that the offender resides in Scotland, or will reside there when the order comes into force, the court may not make a community order in respect of the offender unless it appears to the court—

(a) in the case of an order imposing a requirement mentioned in sub-paragraph (2), that arrangements exist for persons to comply with such a requirement in the locality in Scotland in which the offender resides, or will be residing when the order comes into force, and that provision can be made for him to comply with the requirement under those arrangements, and

(b) in any case, that suitable arrangements for his supervision can be made by the council constituted under section 2 of the Local Government etc (Scotland) Act 1994 (c 39) in whose area he resides, or will be residing when the order comes into force.

(2) The requirements referred to in sub-paragraph (1)(a) are—

(a) an unpaid work requirement,

(b) an activity requirement,

(c) a programme requirement,

(d) a mental health treatment requirement,

(e) a drug rehabilitation requirement,

(f) an alcohol treatment requirement, and

(g) an electronic monitoring requirement.

(3) Where—

(a) the appropriate court for the purposes of paragraph 16 of Schedule 8 (amendment by reason of change of residence) is satisfied that an offender in respect of whom a community order is in force proposes to reside or is residing in Scotland, and

(b) it appears to the court that the conditions in sub-paragraph (1)(a) and (b) are satisfied,

the power of the court to amend the order under Part 4 of Schedule 8 includes power to amend it by requiring it to be complied with in Scotland and the offender to be supervised in accordance with the arrangements referred to in sub-paragraph (1)(b).

(4) For the purposes of sub-paragraph (3), any reference in sub-paragraph (1)(a) and (b) to the time when the order comes into force is to be treated as a reference to the time when the amendment comes into force.

(5) The court may not by virtue of sub-paragraph (1) or (3) require an attendance centre requirement to be complied with in Scotland.

(6) A community order made or amended in accordance with this paragraph must—

(a) specify the locality in Scotland in which the offender resides or will be residing when the order or amendment comes into force;

(b) specify as the corresponding order for the purposes of this Schedule an order that may be made by a court in Scotland;

(c) specify as the appropriate court for the purposes of subsection (4) of section 228 of the Criminal Procedure (Scotland) Act 1995 (c 46) a court of summary jurisdiction (which, in the case of an offender convicted on indictment, must be the sheriff court) having jurisdiction in the locality specified under paragraph (a);

and section 216 (petty sessions area to be specified) does not apply in relation to an order so made or amended.

---

1. Schedule 9 is of no effect in relation to offences committed before 4 April 2005: see the Criminal Justice Act 2003 (Commencement No 8 and Transitional and Saving Provisions) Order 2005, SI 2005/950.

2. (1) Where a court is considering the making or amendment of a community order by virtue of paragraph 1, Chapter 4 of Part 12 of this Act has effect subject to the following modifications.

(2) Any reference to the responsible officer has effect as a reference to the officer of a council constituted under section 2 of the Local Government etc (Scotland) Act 1994 (c 39) responsible for the offender's supervision or, as the case may be, discharging in relation to him the functions in respect of community service orders assigned by sections 239 to 245 of the Criminal Procedure (Scotland) Act 1995.

(3) The following provisions are omitted—

(a) subsection (7) of section 201 (activity requirement),

(b) subsection (7) of section 202 (programme requirement),

(c) subsection (4) of section 206 (residence requirement), and

(d) subsection (4) of section 218 (availability of arrangements in local area).

(4) In section 207 (mental health treatment requirement), for subsection (2)(a) there is substituted—

"(a) treatment as a resident patient in a hospital within the meaning of the Mental Health (Care and Treatment) (Scotland) Act 2003, not being a State hospital within the meaning of that Act;".

(4) In section 215 (electronic monitoring requirement), in subsection (3), the words from "and" onwards are omitted.

PART 2

NORTHERN IRELAND

3. (1) Where the court considering the making of a community order is satisfied that the offender resides in Northern Ireland, or will reside there when the order comes into force, the court may not make a community order in respect of the offender unless it appears to the court—

(*a*) in the case of an order imposing a requirement mentioned in sub-paragraph (2), that arrangements exist for persons to comply with such a requirement in the petty sessions district in Northern Ireland in which the offender resides, or will be residing when the order comes into force, and that provision can be made for him to comply with the requirement under those arrangements, and

(*b*) in any case, that suitable arrangements for his supervision can be made by the Probation Board for Northern Ireland.

(2) The requirements referred to in sub-paragraph (1) are—

(*a*) an unpaid work requirement,

(*b*) an activity requirement,

(*c*) a programme requirement,

(*d*) a mental health treatment requirement,

(*e*) a drug rehabilitation requirement,

(*f*) an alcohol treatment requirement,

(*g*) an attendance centre requirement, and

(*h*) an electronic monitoring requirement.

(3) Where—

(*a*) the appropriate court for the purposes of paragraph 16 of Schedule 8 (amendment by reason of change of residence) is satisfied that the offender to whom a community order relates proposes to reside or is residing in Northern Ireland, and

(*b*) it appears to the court that the conditions in sub-paragraphs (1)(*a*) and (*b*) are satisfied,

the power of the court to amend the order under Part 4 of Schedule 8 includes power to amend it by requiring it to be complied with in Northern Ireland and the offender to be supervised in accordance with the arrangements referred to in sub-paragraph (1)(*b*).

(4) For the purposes of sub-paragraph (3), any reference in sub-paragraph (1)(*a*) and (*b*) to the time when the order comes into force is to be treated as a reference to the time when the amendment comes into force.

(5) A community order made or amended in accordance with this paragraph must specify the petty sessions district in Northern Ireland in which the offender resides or will be residing when the order or amendment comes into force; and section 216 (petty sessions area to be specified) does not apply in relation to an order so made or amended.

(6) A community order made or amended in accordance with this paragraph must also specify as the corresponding order for the purposes of this Schedule an order that may be made by a court in Northern Ireland.

4. (1) Where a court is considering the making or amendment of a community order by virtue of paragraph 3, Chapter 4 of Part 12 of this Act has effect subject to the following modifications.

(2) Any reference to the responsible officer has effect as a reference to the probation officer responsible for the offender's supervision or, as the case may be, discharging in relation to the offender the functions conferred by Part 2 of the Criminal Justice (Northern Ireland) Order 1996 (SI 1996/3160 (NI 24)).

(3) The following provisions are omitted—

(*a*) subsection (7) of section 201 (activity requirement),

(*b*) subsection (7) of section 202 (programme requirement),

(*c*) subsection (4) of section 206 (residence requirement), and

(*d*) subsection (4) of section 218 (availability of arrangements in local area).

(4) In section 207 (mental health treatment requirement), for subsection (2)(*a*) there is substituted—

"(*a*) treatment (whether as an in-patient or an out-patient) at such hospital as may be specified in the order, being a hospital within the meaning of the Health and Personal Social Services (Northern Ireland) Order 1972, approved by the Department of Health, Social Services and Public Safety for the purposes of paragraph 4(3) of Schedule 1 to the Criminal Justice (Northern Ireland) Order 1996 (SI 1996/3160 (NI 24));".

(5) In section 214 (attendance centre requirement), any reference to an attendance centre has effect as a reference to a day centre, as defined by paragraph 3(6) of Schedule 1 to the Criminal Justice (Northern Ireland) Order 1996 (SI 1996/3160 (NI 24)).

(5) In section 215 (electronic monitoring requirement), in subsection (3), the words from "and" onwards are omitted.

PART 3

GENERAL PROVISIONS

5. In this Part of this Schedule—

"corresponding order" means the order specified under paragraph 1(6)(*b*) or 3(6);

"home court" means—

(*a*) if the offender resides in Scotland, or will be residing there at the relevant time, the sheriff court having jurisdiction in the locality in which he resides or proposes to reside, and

(*b*) if he resides in Northern Ireland, or will be residing there at the relevant time, the court of summary jurisdiction acting for the petty sessions district in which he resides or proposes to reside;

"the local authority officer concerned", in relation to an offender, means the officer of a council constituted under section 2 of the Local Government etc (Scotland) Act 1994 (c 39) responsible for his supervision or, as the case may be, discharging in relation to him the functions in respect of community service orders assigned by sections 239 to 245 of the Criminal Procedure (Scotland) Act 1995 (c 46);

"the probation officer concerned", in relation to an offender, means the probation officer responsible for his supervision or, as the case may be, discharging in relation to him the functions conferred by Part 2 of the Criminal Justice (Northern Ireland) Order 1996;

"the relevant time" means the time when the order or the amendment to it comes into force.

6. Where a community order is made or amended in accordance with paragraph 1 or 3, the court which makes or amends the order must provide the home court with a copy of the order as made or amended, together with such other documents and information relating to the case as it considers likely to be of assistance to that court; and paragraphs (*b*) to (*d*) of subsection (1) of section 219 (provision of copies of relevant orders) do not apply.

7. In section 220 (duty of offender to keep in touch with responsible officer) the reference to the responsible officer is to be read in accordance with paragraph 2(2) or 4(2).

8. Where a community order is made or amended in accordance with paragraph 1 or 3, then, subject to the following provisions of this Part of this Schedule—

(*a*) the order is to be treated as if it were a corresponding order made in the part of the United Kingdom in which the offender resides, or will be residing at the relevant time, and

(*b*) the legislation relating to such orders which has effect in that part of the United Kingdom applies accordingly.

9. Before making or amending a community order in those circumstances the court must explain to the offender in ordinary language—

(*a*) the requirements of the legislation relating to corresponding orders which has effect in the part of the United Kingdom in which he resides or will be residing at the relevant time,

(*b*) the powers of the home court under that legislation, as modified by this Part of this Schedule, and

(*c*) its own powers under this Part of this Schedule.

10. The home court may exercise in relation to the community order any power which it could exercise in relation to the corresponding order made by a court in the part of the United Kingdom in which the home court exercises jurisdiction, by virtue of the legislation relating to such orders which has effect in that part, except the following—

(*a*) any power to discharge or revoke the order (other than a power to revoke the order where the offender has been convicted of a further offence and the court has imposed a custodial sentence),

(*b*) any power to deal with the offender for the offence in respect of which the order was made,

(*c*) in the case of a community order imposing an unpaid work requirement, any power to vary the order by substituting for the number of hours of work specified in it any greater number than the court which made the order could have specified, and

(*d*) in the case of a community order imposing a curfew requirement, any power to vary the order by substituting for the period specified in it any longer period than the court which made the order could have specified.

11. If at any time while legislation relating to corresponding orders which has effect in Scotland or Northern Ireland applies by virtue of paragraph 7 to a community order made in England and Wales—

(*a*) it appears to the home court—

(i) if that court is in Scotland, on information from the local authority officer concerned, or

(ii) if that court is in Northern Ireland, upon a complaint being made to a justice of the peace acting for the petty sessions district for the time being specified in the order,

that the offender has failed to comply with any of the requirements of the order, or

(*b*) it appears to the home court—

(i) if that court is in Scotland, on the application of the offender or of the local authority officer concerned, or

(ii) if it is in Northern Ireland, on the application of the offender or of the probation officer concerned,

that it would be in the interests of justice for a power conferred by paragraph 13 or 14 of Schedule 8 to be exercised,

the home court may require the offender to appear before the court which made the order or the court which last amended the order in England and Wales.

12. Where an offender is required by virtue of paragraph 11 to appear before a court in England and Wales that court—

(*a*) may issue a warrant for his arrest, and

(*b*) may exercise any power which it could exercise in respect of the community order if the offender resided in England and Wales,

and any enactment relating to the exercise of such powers has effect accordingly, and with any reference to the responsible officer being read as a reference to the local authority officer or probation officer concerned.

13. Paragraph 12(*b*) does not enable the court to amend the community order unless—

(*a*) where the offender resides in Scotland, it appears to the court that the conditions in paragraph 1(1)(*a*) and (*b*) are satisfied in relation to any requirement to be imposed, or

(*b*) where the offender resides in Northern Ireland, it appears to the court that the conditions in paragraph 3(1)(*a*) and (*b*) are satisfied in relation to any requirement to be imposed.

14. The preceding paragraphs of this Schedule have effect in relation to the amendment of a community order by virtue of paragraph 12(*b*) as they have effect in relation to the amendment of such an order by virtue of paragraph 1(3) or 3(3).

15. Where an offender is required by virtue of paragraph (*a*) of paragraph 11 to appear before a court in England and Wales—

(*a*) the home court must send to that court a certificate certifying that the offender has failed to comply with such of the requirements of the order as may be specified in the certificate, together with such other particulars of the case as may be desirable, and

(*b*) a certificate purporting to be signed by the clerk of the home court is admissible as evidence of the failure before the court which made the order.

3–2087

Section 187   SCHEDULE 10[1]
Revocation or Amendment of Custody Plus Orders and Amendment of Intermittent Custody
Orders

Interpretation

1. (1) In this Schedule—

"the appropriate court" means—

    (a) where the custody plus order or intermittent custody order was made by the Crown Court, the Crown
        Court, and

    (b) in any other case, a magistrates' court acting for the petty sessions area concerned;

"the offender", in relation to a custody plus order or intermittent custody order, means the person in respect of
      whom the order is made;

"the petty sessions area concerned", in relation to a custody plus order or intermittent custody order, means the
      petty sessions area for the time being specified in the order;

"the responsible officer" has the meaning given by section 197.

(2) In this Schedule any reference to a requirement being imposed by, or included in, a custody plus order or
intermittent custody order is to be read as a reference to compliance with the requirement being required by the
order to be a condition of a licence.

---

1. Schedule 10 is in force only for the purposes of the passing of a sentence of imprisonment to which an intermittent
custody order relates and the release on licence of a person serving such a sentence): 26 January 2004: see the Criminal
Justice Act 2003 (Commencement No 1) Order 2003, SI 2003/3282.

Orders made on appeal

2. Where a custody plus order or intermittent custody order has been made on appeal, it is to be taken for the
purposes of this Schedule to have been made by the Crown Court.

Revocation of custody plus order or removal from intermittent custody order of requirements as to licence conditions

3. (1) Where at any time while a custody plus order or intermittent custody order is in force, it appears to the
appropriate court on the application of the offender or the responsible officer that, having regard to circumstances
which have arisen since the order was made, it would be in the interests of justice to do so, the court may—

    (a) in the case of a custody plus order, revoke the order, and

    (b) in the case of an intermittent custody order, amend the order so that it contains only provision specifying
        periods for the purposes of section 183(1)(b)(i).

(2) The revocation under this paragraph of a custody plus order does not affect the sentence of imprisonment
to which the order relates, except in relation to the conditions of the licence.

Amendment by reason of change of residence

4. (1) This paragraph applies where, at any time during the term of imprisonment to which a custody plus
order or intermittent custody order relates, the appropriate court is satisfied that the offender proposes to change,
or has changed, his residence during the licence period from the petty sessions area concerned to another petty
sessions area.

(2) Subject to sub-paragraphs (3) and (4), the appropriate court may, and on the application of the Secretary
of State or the responsible officer must, amend the custody plus order or intermittent custody order by substituting
the other petty sessions area for the area specified in the order.

(3) The court may not amend under this paragraph a custody plus order or intermittent custody order which
contains requirements which, in the opinion of the court, cannot be complied with unless the offender resides in
the petty sessions area concerned unless, in accordance with paragraph 5, it either—

    (a) cancels those requirements, or
    (b) substitutes for those requirements other requirements which can be complied with if the offender does not
       reside in that area.

(4) The court may not amend under this paragraph any custody plus order or intermittent custody order
imposing a programme requirement unless it appears to the court that the accredited programme specified in the
requirement is available in the other petty sessions area.

Amendment of requirements of custody plus order or intermittent custody order

5. (1) At any time during the term of imprisonment to which a custody plus order or intermittent custody
order relates, the appropriate court may, on the application of the offender, the Secretary of State or the responsible
officer, by order amend any requirement of the custody plus order or intermittent custody order—

    (a) by cancelling the requirement, or
    (b) by replacing it with a requirement of the same kind imposing different obligations, which the court could
       include if it were then making the order.

(2) For the purposes of sub-paragraph (1)—

    (a) a requirement falling within any paragraph of section 182(1) is of the same kind as any other requirement
       falling within that paragraph, and
    (b) an electronic monitoring requirement is a requirement of the same kind as any requirement falling within
       section 182(1) to which it relates.

(3) Sub-paragraph (1)(b) has effect subject to the provisions mentioned in subsection (2) of section 182, and
to subsections (3) and (5) of that section.

Alteration of pattern of temporary release

6. (1) At any time during the term of imprisonment to which an intermittent custody order relates, the appropriate court may, on the application of the offender, the Secretary of State or the responsible officer, amend the order—

    (*a*) so as to specify different periods for the purposes of section 183(1)(*b*)(i), or

    (*b*) so as to provide that he is to remain in prison until the number of days served by him in prison is equal to the number of custodial days.

(2) The appropriate court may not by virtue of sub-paragraph (1) amend an intermittent custody order unless it has received from the Secretary of State notification that suitable prison accommodation is available for the offender during the periods which, under the order as amended, will be custodial periods.

(3) In this paragraph "custodial period" has the same meaning as in section 184(3).

Supplementary

7. No application may be made under paragraph 3(1), 5(1) or 6(1) while an appeal against the sentence of which the custody plus or intermittent custody order forms part is pending.

8. (1) Subject to sub-paragraph (2), where a court proposes to exercise its powers under paragraph 5 or 6, otherwise than on the application of the offender, the court—

    (*a*) must summon him to appear before the court, and

    (*b*) if he does not appear in answer to the summons, may issue a warrant for his arrest.

(2) This paragraph does not apply to an order cancelling any requirement of a custody plus or intermittent custody order.

9. (1) On the making under this Schedule of an order revoking or amending a custody plus order or amending an intermittent custody order, the proper officer of the court must—

    (*a*) provide copies of the revoking or amending order to the offender and the responsible officer,

    (*b*) in the case of an amending order which substitutes a new petty sessions area, provide a copy of the amending order to—

        (i) the local probation board acting for that area, and

        (ii) the magistrates' court acting for that area,

    (*c*) in the case of an order which cancels or amends a requirement specified in the first column of Schedule 14, provide a copy of so much of the amending order as relates to that requirement to the person specified in relation to that requirement in the second column of that Schedule.

(2) Where under sub-paragraph (1)(*b*) the proper officer of the court provides a copy of an amending order to a magistrates' court acting for a different area, the officer must also provide to that court such documents and information relating to the case as it considers likely to be of assistance to a court acting for that area in the exercise of its functions in relation to the order.

3–2088

Section 188   SCHEDULE 11[1]
TRANSFER OF CUSTODY PLUS ORDERS AND INTERMITTENT CUSTODY ORDERS TO SCOTLAND OR NORTHERN IRELAND

PART 1
INTRODUCTORY

1. In this Schedule—

    (*a*) "the 1997 Act" means the Crime (Sentences) Act 1997 (c 43), and

    (*b*) any reference to a requirement being imposed by, or included in a custody plus order or intermittent custody order is a reference to compliance with the requirement being required by the order to be a condition of a licence.

---

1. At the time of going to press Schedule 11 was not in force.

PART 2
SCOTLAND

2. (1) Where the court making a custody plus order is satisfied that the offender resides in Scotland, or will reside there during the licence period, the court may, subject to sub-paragraph (2), impose requirements that are to be complied with in Scotland and require the offender's compliance with the order to be supervised in accordance with arrangements made by the local authority in Scotland in whose area he resides or will reside.

(2) The court may not make an order by virtue of this paragraph unless it appears to the court—

    (*a*) in the case of an order imposing a requirement mentioned in sub-paragraph (3), that arrangements exist for persons to comply with such a requirement in the locality in Scotland in which the offender resides, or will be residing during the licence period, and that provision can be made for him to comply with the requirement under those arrangements, and

    (*b*) in any case, that suitable arrangements for supervising his compliance with the order can be made by the local authority in whose area he resides, or will be residing during the licence period.

(3) The requirements referred to in sub-paragraph (2)(*a*) are—

    (*a*) an unpaid work requirement,

    (*b*) an activity requirement,

    (*c*) a programme requirement, and

    (*d*) an electronic monitoring requirement.

(4) If an order has been made in accordance with this paragraph in relation to an offender but—

(*a*)   the Secretary of State decides not to make an order under paragraph 1 or 4 of Schedule 1 to the 1997 Act in relation to him, and

(*b*)   the offender has not applied under paragraph 22 of this Schedule for the amendment of the custody plus order or intermittent custody order,

the Secretary of State must apply to the court under paragraph 22 of this Schedule for the amendment of the order.

3. Where—

(*a*)   the appropriate court for the purposes of paragraph 4 of Schedule 10 (amendment by reason of change of residence) is satisfied that the offender in respect of whom a custody plus order or intermittent custody order is in force is residing in Scotland, or proposes to reside there during the licence period,

(*b*)   the Secretary of State has made, or has indicated his willingness to make, an order under paragraph 1 or 4 of Schedule 1 to the 1997 Act in relation to the offender, and

(*c*)   it appears to the court that the conditions in paragraph 2(2)(*a*) and (*b*) are satisfied,

the power of the court to amend the order under Schedule 10 includes power to amend it by requiring the requirements included in the order to be complied with in Scotland and the offender's compliance with them to be supervised in accordance with the arrangements referred to in paragraph 2(2)(*b*).

4. A court may not by virtue of paragraph 2 or 3 require an attendance centre requirement to be complied with in Scotland.

5. A custody plus order made in accordance with paragraph 2 or a custody plus order or intermittent order amended in accordance with paragraph 3 must—

(*a*)   specify the local authority area in which the offender resides or will reside during the licence period, and

(*b*)   require the local authority for that area to appoint or assign an officer who will be responsible for discharging in relation to him the functions conferred on responsible officers by Part 12 of this Act;

and section 216 (petty sessions area to be specified) does not apply in relation to an order so made or amended.

6. (1) Where a court makes a custody plus order in accordance with paragraph 2 or amends a custody plus order or intermittent custody order in accordance with paragraph 3, the court must provide the relevant documents to—

(*a*)   the local authority for the area specified in the order, and

(*b*)   the sheriff court having jurisdiction in the locality in which the offender resides or proposes to reside;

and paragraphs (*b*) to (*d*) of subsection (1) of section 219 (which relate to the provision of copies) do not apply in relation to an order so made or amended.

(2) In this paragraph, "the relevant documents" means—

(*a*)   a copy of the order as made or amended, and

(*b*)   such other documents and information relating to the case as the court making or amending the order considers likely to be of assistance.

7. (1) In relation to the making of a custody plus order by virtue of paragraph 2, in relation to the amendment of a custody plus order or intermittent custody order by virtue of paragraph 3, and (except for the purposes of paragraph 22) in relation to an order so made or amended, Chapter 4 of Part 12 of this Act has effect subject to the following modifications.

(2) Any reference to the responsible officer has effect as a reference to the officer appointed or assigned under paragraph 5(*b*).

(3) The following provisions are omitted—

(*a*)   subsection (7) of section 201 (activity requirement);

(*b*)   subsection (7) of section 202 (programme requirement);

(*c*)   subsection (4) of section 218 (availability of arrangements in local area).

(4) In section 215 (electronic monitoring requirement), in subsection (3), the words from "and" onwards are omitted.

8. In this Part of this Schedule "local authority" means a council constituted under section 2 of the Local Government etc (Scotland) Act 1994 (c 39); and any reference to the area of such an authority is a reference to the local government area within the meaning of that Act.

PART 3

NORTHERN IRELAND

9. (1) Where the court making a custody plus order is satisfied that the offender resides in Northern Ireland, or will reside there during the licence period, the court may, subject to sub-paragraph (2), impose requirements that are to be complied with in Northern Ireland and require the offender's compliance with the order to be supervised in accordance with arrangements made by the Probation Board for Northern Ireland.

(2) The court may not make an order by virtue of this paragraph unless it appears to the court—

(*a*)   in the case of an order imposing a requirement mentioned in sub-paragraph (3), that arrangements exist for persons to comply with such a requirement in the petty sessions district in Northern Ireland in which the offender resides, or will be residing during the licence period, and that provision can be made for him to comply with the requirement under those arrangements, and

(*b*)   in any case, that suitable arrangements for supervising his compliance with the order can be made by the Probation Board for Northern Ireland.

(3) The requirements referred to in sub-paragraph (1)(*a*) are—

(*a*)   an unpaid work requirement,

(*b*)   an activity requirement,

(*c*)   a programme requirement,

(*d*)   an attendance centre requirement, and

(*e*)   an electronic monitoring requirement.

(4) If an order has been made in accordance with this paragraph in relation to an offender but—

(a) the Secretary of State decides not to make an order under paragraph 1 or 4 of Schedule 1 to the 1997 Act in relation to him, and

(b) the offender has not applied under paragraph 22 of this Schedule for the amendment of the custody plus order or intermittent custody order,

the Secretary of State must apply to the court under paragraph 22 for the amendment of the order.

10. Where—

(a) the appropriate court for the purposes of paragraph 4 of Schedule 10 (amendment by reason of change of residence) is satisfied that the offender in respect of whom a custody plus order or intermittent custody order is in force is residing in Northern Ireland, or proposes to reside there during the licence period,

(b) the Secretary of State has made, or has indicated his willingness to make, an order under paragraph 1 or 4 of Schedule 1 to the 1997 Act in relation to the offender, and

(c) it appears to the court that the conditions in paragraph 9(2)(a) and (b) are satisfied,

the power of the court to amend the order under Schedule 10 includes power to amend it by requiring the requirements included in the order to be complied with in Northern Ireland and the offender's compliance with them to be supervised in accordance with the arrangements referred to in paragraph 9(2)(b).

11. A custody plus order made in accordance with paragraph 9 or a custody plus order or intermittent custody order amended in accordance with paragraph 10 must—

(a) specify the petty sessions district in Northern Ireland in which the offender resides or will reside during the licence period, and

(b) require the Probation Board for Northern Ireland to appoint or assign a probation officer who will be responsible for discharging in relation to him the functions conferred on responsible officers by Part 11 of this Act;

and section 216 (petty sessions area to be specified) does not apply in relation to an order so made or amended.

12. (1) Where a court makes a custody plus order in accordance with paragraph 9 or amends a custody plus order or intermittent custody order in accordance with paragraph 10, the court must provide the relevant documents to—

(a) the Probation Board for Northern Ireland, and

(b) the court of summary jurisdiction acting for the petty sessions district in which the offender resides or proposes to reside;

and paragraphs (b) to (d) of subsection (1) of section 219 (which relate to the provision of copies) do not apply in relation to an order so made or amended.

(2) In this paragraph, "the relevant documents" means—

(a) a copy of the order as made or amended, and

(b) such other documents and information relating to the case as the court making or amending the order considers likely to be of assistance.

13. (1) In relation to the making of a custody plus order by virtue of paragraph 9, in relation to the amendment of a custody plus order or intermittent custody order by virtue of paragraph 10, and (except for the purposes of paragraph 22) in relation to an order so made or amended, Chapter 4 of Part 12 of this Act has effect subject to the following modifications.

(2) Any reference to the responsible officer has effect as a reference to the probation officer appointed or assigned under paragraph 11(b).

(3) The following provisions are omitted—

(a) subsection (7) of section 201 (activity requirement);

(b) subsection (7) of section 202 (programme requirement);

(c) subsection (4) of section 218 (availability of arrangements in local area).

(4) In section 214 (attendance centre requirement), any reference to an attendance centre has effect as a reference to a day centre, as defined by paragraph 3(6) of Schedule 1 to the Criminal Justice (Northern Ireland) Order 1996 (SI 1996/3160 (NI 24).

(6) In section 215 (electronic monitoring requirement), in subsection (3), the words from "and" onwards are omitted.

PART 4
GENERAL PROVISIONS

14. This Part of this Schedule applies at any time while a custody plus order made in accordance with paragraph 2 or 9 or amended in accordance with paragraph 3 or 10, or an intermittent custody order amended in accordance with paragraph 3 or 10, is in force in respect of an offender.

15. In this Part of this Schedule—

"home court" means—

(a) if the offender resides in Scotland, or will be residing there during the licence period, the sheriff court having jurisdiction in the locality in which the offender resides or proposes to reside, and

(b) if he resides in Northern Ireland, or will be residing there during the licence period, the court of summary jurisdiction acting for the petty sessions district in which he resides or proposes to reside;

"local authority" and "local authority area" are to be read in accordance with paragraph 8;

"original court" means the court in England and Wales which made or last amended the custody plus order or intermittent custody order;

"the relevant officer" means—

(a) where the order specifies a local authority area in Scotland, the local authority officer appointed or assigned under paragraph 5(b), and

(b) where the order specifies a local authority district in Northern Ireland, the probation officer appointed or assigned under paragraph 11(b).

16. (1) Where this Part of this Schedule applies, Schedule 10 has effect subject to the following modifications.

(2) Any reference to the responsible officer has effect as a reference to the relevant officer.

(3) Any reference to the appropriate court has effect as a reference to the original court.

(4) Where the order specifies a local authority area in Scotland—

(a) any reference to the petty sessions area concerned has effect as a reference to that local authority area, and

(b) any other reference to a petty sessions area has effect as a reference to a local authority area.

(5) Where the order specifies a petty sessions district in Northern Ireland—

(a) any reference to the petty sessions area concerned has effect as a reference to that petty sessions district, and

(b) any other reference to a petty sessions area has effect as a reference to a petty sessions district.

(6) Paragraph 9 is omitted.

17. (1) The home court may exercise any power under paragraph 4 or 5 of Schedule 10 (amendment of custody plus order or intermittent custody order) as if it were the original court.

(2) Subject to sub-paragraph (3), where the home court proposes to exercise the power conferred by paragraph 5 of Schedule 10, otherwise than on the application of the offender, the court—

(a) if it is in Scotland—

(i) must issue a citation requiring the offender to appear before it, and

(ii) if he does not appear in answer to the citation, may issue a warrant for the offender's arrest;

(b) if it is in Northern Ireland—

(i) must issue a summons requiring the offender to appear before it, and

(ii) if he does not appear in answer to the summons, may issue a warrant for the offender's arrest;

and paragraph 8 of Schedule 10 does not apply to the home court.

(3) Sub-paragraph (2) does not apply to any order cancelling any requirement of a custody plus order or intermittent custody order.

(4) Where the home court is considering amending a custody plus or intermittent custody order, any reference in Chapter 4 of Part 12 of this Act to a local probation board has effect as a reference to a local authority in Scotland or, as the case may be, the Probation Board for Northern Ireland.

18. Where by virtue of paragraph 17 any application is made to the home court under paragraph 4 or 5 of Schedule 10, the home court may (instead of dealing with the application) require the offender to appear before the original court.

19. No court may amend or further amend a custody plus order or an intermittent custody order unless it appears to the court that the conditions in paragraph 2(2)(a) and (b) or, as the case may be, the conditions in paragraph 9(2)(a) and (b) are satisfied in relation to any requirement to be imposed; but this paragraph does not apply to any amendment made by virtue of paragraph 22(1).

20. The preceding paragraphs of this Schedule have effect in relation to any amendment of a custody plus or intermittent custody order by any court as they have effect in relation to the amendment of such an order by virtue of paragraph 3 or 10.

21. On the making of an order amending a custody plus order or intermittent custody order—

(a) the court must provide copies of the amending order to the offender and the relevant officer, and

(b) in the case of an amending order which substitutes a new local authority area or petty sessions district, paragraphs 5 and 6, or as the case may be paragraphs 11 and 12, have effect in relation to the order as they have effect in relation to an order made or amended in accordance with paragraph 2 or 3, or as the case may be, 9 or 10.

22. (1) Where—

(a) a custody plus order has been made in accordance with paragraph 2 or 9 or a custody plus or intermittent custody order has been amended in accordance with paragraph 3 or 10, but (in any of those cases) the Secretary of State has not made an order under paragraph 1 or 4 of Schedule 1 to the 1997 Act in relation to the offender, or

(b) the Secretary of State has made, or indicated his willingness to make, an order under paragraph 7(1) of Schedule 1 to the 1997 Act transferring the offender or his supervision back to England and Wales,

the court may, on the application of the offender or the Secretary of State, amend the custody plus order or intermittent custody order by requiring it to be complied with in England and Wales.

(2) In sub-paragraph (1) "the court", in a case falling within paragraph (a) of that sub-paragraph, means the original court.

(3) In a case where paragraph 2(4) or 9(4) requires the Secretary of State to apply under this paragraph, the court must make an amending order under this paragraph.

(4) Where under this paragraph the court amends a custody plus order or intermittent custody order which contains requirements which, in the opinion of the court, cannot be complied with in the petty sessions area in which the offender is residing or proposes to reside, the court must, in accordance with paragraph 5 of Schedule 10, either—

(a) cancel those requirements, or

(b) substitute for those requirements other requirements which can be complied with if the offender resides in that area.

(5) Where the court amends under this paragraph any custody plus order or intermittent custody order imposing a programme requirement, the court must ensure that the requirement as amended specifies a programme which is available in the petty sessions area in England and Wales in which the offender is residing or proposes to reside.

(6) The custody plus order or intermittent custody order as amended under this paragraph must specify the petty sessions area in which the offender resides or proposes to reside in the licence period.

(7) On the making under this paragraph of an order amending a custody plus order or intermittent custody order, the court must—

(a) provide copies of the amending order to the offender, the relevant officer and the local probation board acting for the new petty sessions area, and

(b) provide the magistrates' court acting for that area with a copy of the amending order and such other documents and information relating to the case as the home court considers likely to be of assistance to the court acting for that area in the exercise of its functions in relation to the order.

(7) Where an order has been amended under this paragraph, the preceding paragraphs of this Schedule shall cease to apply to the order as amended.

PART 5
SUPPLEMENTARY

23. Subsections (1) and (3) of section 245C of the Criminal Procedure (Scotland) Act 1995 (c 46) (provision of remote monitoring) have effect as if they included a reference to the electronic monitoring of the requirements of a custody plus order made in accordance with paragraph 2 or a custody plus order or intermittent custody order made in accordance with paragraph 3.

24. (1) Section 4 of the Summary Jurisdiction (Process) Act 1881 (c 24) (which provides, among other things, for service in England and Wales of Scottish citations or warrants) applies to any citation or warrant issued under paragraph 17(2)(a) as it applies to a citation or warrant granted under section 134 of the Criminal Procedure (Scotland) Act 1995.

(2) A summons issued by a court in Northern Ireland under paragraph 17(2)(b) may, in such circumstances as may be prescribed by rules of court, be served in England and Wales or Scotland.

3–2089

Section 193   SCHEDULE 12[1]
BREACH OR AMENDMENT OF SUSPENDED SENTENCE ORDER, AND EFFECT OF FURTHER CONVICTION

PART 1
PRELIMINARY

Interpretation

1. In this Schedule—

"the offender", in relation to a suspended sentence order, means the person in respect of whom the order is made;

"the petty sessions area concerned", in relation to a suspended sentence order, means the petty sessions area for the time being specified in the order;

"the responsible officer" has the meaning given by section 197.

---

1. Schedule 12 is of no effect in relation to offences committed before 4 April, 2005: see the Criminal Justice Act 2003 (Commencement No 8 and Transitional and Saving Provisions) Order 2005, SI 2005/950.

2. In this Schedule—

(a) any reference to a suspended sentence order being subject to review is a reference to such an order being subject to review in accordance with section 191(1)(b) or to a drug rehabilitation requirement of such an order being subject to review in accordance with section 210(1)(b);

(b) any reference to the court responsible for a suspended sentence order which is subject to review is to be construed in accordance with section 191(3) or, as the case may be, 210(2).

Orders made on appeal

3. Where a suspended sentence order is made on appeal it is to be taken for the purposes of this Schedule to have been made by the Crown Court.

PART 2
BREACH OF COMMUNITY REQUIREMENT OR CONVICTION OF FURTHER OFFENCE

Duty to give warning in relation to community requirement

4. (1) If the responsible officer is of the opinion that the offender has failed without reasonable excuse to comply with any of the community requirements of a suspended sentence order, the officer must give him a warning under this paragraph unless—

(a) the offender has within the previous twelve months been given a warning under this paragraph in relation to a failure to comply with any of the community requirements of the order, or

(b) the officer causes an information to be laid before a justice of the peace in respect of the failure.

(2) A warning under this paragraph must—

(a) describe the circumstances of the failure,

(b) state that the failure is unacceptable, and

(c) inform the offender that if within the next twelve months he again fails to comply with any requirement of the order, he will be liable to be brought before a court.

(3) The responsible officer must, as soon as practicable after the warning has been given, record that fact.

(4) In relation to any suspended sentence order which is made by the Crown Court and does not include a direction that any failure to comply with the community requirements of the order is to be dealt with by a magistrates' court, the reference in sub-paragraph (1)(b) to a justice of the peace is to be read as a reference to the Crown Court.

Breach of order after warning

5. (1) If—

(a) the responsible officer has given a warning under paragraph 4 to the offender in respect of a suspended sentence order, and

(b) at any time within the twelve months beginning with the date on which the warning was given, the responsible officer is of the opinion that the offender has since that date failed without reasonable excuse to comply with any of the community requirements of the order,

the officer must cause an information to be laid before a justice of the peace in respect of the failure in question.

(2) In relation to any suspended sentence order which is made by the Crown Court and does not include a direction that any failure to comply with the community requirements of the order is to be dealt with by a magistrates' court, the reference in sub-paragraph (1) to a justice of the peace is to be read as a reference to the Crown Court.

Issue of summons or warrant by justice of the peace

6. (1) This paragraph applies to—

(a) a suspended sentence order made by a magistrates' court, or
(b) any suspended sentence order which was made by the Crown Court and includes a direction that any failure to comply with the community requirements of the order is to be dealt with by a magistrates' court.

(2) If at any time while a suspended sentence order to which this paragraph applies is in force it appears on information to a justice of the peace acting for the petty sessions area concerned that the offender has failed to comply with any of the community requirements of the order, the justice may—

(a) issue a summons requiring the offender to appear at the place and time specified in it, or
(b) if the information is in writing and on oath, issue a warrant for his arrest.

(3) Any summons or warrant issued under this paragraph must direct the offender to appear or be brought—

(a) in the case of a suspended sentence order which is subject to review, before the court responsible for the order,
(b) in any other case, before a magistrates' court acting for the petty sessions area concerned.

(4) Where a summons issued under sub-paragraph (2)(a) requires the offender to appear before a magistrates' court and the offender does not appear in answer to the summons, the magistrates' court may issue a warrant for the arrest of the offender.

Issue of summons or warrant by Crown Court

7. (1) This paragraph applies to a suspended sentence order made by the Crown Court which does not include a direction that any failure to comply with the community requirements of the order is to be dealt with by a magistrates' court.

(2) If at any time while a suspended sentence order to which this paragraph applies is in force it appears on information to the Crown Court that the offender has failed to comply with any of the community requirements of the order, the Crown Court may—

(a) issue a summons requiring the offender to appear at the place and time specified in it, or
(b) if the information is in writing and on oath, issue a warrant for his arrest.

(3) Any summons or warrant issued under this paragraph must direct the offender to appear or be brought before the Crown Court.

(4) Where a summons issued under sub-paragraph (1)(a) requires the offender to appear before the Crown Court and the offender does not appear in answer to the summons, the Crown Court may issue a warrant for the arrest of the offender.

Powers of court on breach of community requirement or conviction of further offence

8. (1) This paragraph applies where—

(a) it is proved to the satisfaction of a court before which an offender appears or is brought under paragraph 6 or 7 or by virtue of section 192(6) that he has failed without reasonable excuse to comply with any of the community requirements of the suspended sentence order, or
(b) an offender is convicted of an offence committed during the operational period of a suspended sentence (other than one which has already taken effect) and either—

(i) he is so convicted by or before a court having power under paragraph 11 to deal with him in respect of the suspended sentence, or
(ii) he subsequently appears or is brought before such a court.

(2) The court must consider his case and deal with him in one of the following ways—

(a) the court may order that the suspended sentence is to take effect with its original term and custodial period unaltered,
(b) the court may order that the sentence is to take effect with either or both of the following modifications—

(i) the substitution for the original term of a lesser term complying with section 181(2), and
(ii) the substitution for the original custodial period of a lesser custodial period complying with section 181(5) and (6),

(c) the court may amend the order by doing any one or more of the following—

(i) imposing more onerous community requirements which the court could include if it were then making the order,
(ii) subject to subsections (3) and (4) of section 189, extending the supervision period, or
(iii) subject to subsection (3) of that section, extending the operational period.

(3) The court must make an order under sub-paragraph (2)(a) or (b) unless it is of the opinion that it would be unjust to do so in view of all the circumstances, including the matters mentioned in sub-paragraph (4); and where it is of that opinion the court must state its reasons.

(4) The matters referred to in sub-paragraph (3) are—

(a) the extent to which the offender has complied with the community requirements of the suspended sentence order, and

(b) in a case falling within sub-paragraph (1)(b), the facts of the subsequent offence.

(5) Where a court deals with an offender under sub-paragraph (2) in respect of a suspended sentence, the appropriate officer of the court must notify the appropriate officer of the court which passed the sentence of the method adopted.

(6) Where a suspended sentence order was made by the Crown Court and a magistrates' court would (apart from this sub-paragraph) be required to deal with the offender under sub-paragraph (2)(a), (b) or (c) it may instead commit him to custody or release him on bail until he can be brought or appear before the Crown Court.

(7) A magistrates' court which deals with an offender's case under sub-paragraph (6) must send to the Crown Court—

(a) a certificate signed by a justice of the peace certifying that the offender has failed to comply with the community requirements of the suspended sentence order in the respect specified in the certificate, and
(b) such other particulars of the case as may be desirable;

and a certificate purporting to be so signed is admissible as evidence of the failure before the Crown Court.

(8) In proceedings before the Crown Court under this paragraph any question whether the offender has failed to comply with the community requirements of the suspended sentence order and any question whether the offender has been convicted of an offence committed during the operational period of the suspended sentence is to be determined by the court and not by the verdict of a jury.

Further provisions as to order that suspended sentence is to take effect

9. (1) When making an order under paragraph 8(2)(a) or (b) that a sentence is to take effect (with or without any variation of the original term and custodial period), the court—

(a) must also make a custody plus order, and
(b) may order that the sentence is to take effect immediately or that the term of that sentence is to commence on the expiry of another term of imprisonment passed on the offender by that or another court.

(2) The power to make an order under sub-paragraph (1)(b) has effect subject to section 265 (restriction on consecutive sentences for released prisoners).

(3) For the purpose of any enactment conferring rights of appeal in criminal cases, any order made by the court under paragraph 8(2)(a) or (b) is to be treated as a sentence passed on the offender by that court for the offence for which the suspended sentence was passed.

Restriction of powers in paragraph 8 where treatment required

10. (1) An offender who is required by any of the following community requirements of a suspended sentence order—

(a) a mental health treatment requirement,
(b) a drug rehabilitation requirement, or
(c) an alcohol treatment requirement,

to submit to treatment for his mental condition, or his dependency on or propensity to misuse drugs or alcohol, is not to be treated for the purposes of paragraph 8(1)(a) as having failed to comply with that requirement on the ground only that he had refused to undergo any surgical, electrical or other treatment if, in the opinion of the court, his refusal was reasonable having regard to all the circumstances.

(2) A court may not under paragraph 8(2)(c)(i) amend a mental health treatment requirement, a drug rehabilitation requirement or an alcohol treatment requirement unless the offender expresses his willingness to comply with the requirement as amended.

Court by which suspended sentence may be dealt with under paragraph 8(1)(b)

11. (1) An offender may be dealt with under paragraph 8(1)(b) in respect of a suspended sentence by the Crown Court or, where the sentence was passed by a magistrates' court, by any magistrates' court before which he appears or is brought.

(2) Where an offender is convicted by a magistrates' court of any offence and the court is satisfied that the offence was committed during the operational period of a suspended sentence passed by the Crown Court—

(a) the court may, if it thinks fit, commit him in custody or on bail to the Crown Court, and
(b) if it does not, must give written notice of the conviction to the appropriate officer of the Crown Court.

Procedure where court convicting of further offence does not deal with suspended sentence

12. (1) If it appears to the Crown Court, where that court has jurisdiction in accordance with sub-paragraph (2), or to a justice of the peace having jurisdiction in accordance with that sub-paragraph—

(a) that an offender has been convicted in the United Kingdom of an offence committed during the operational period of a suspended sentence, and
(b) that he has not been dealt with in respect of the suspended sentence,

that court or justice may, subject to the following provisions of this paragraph, issue a summons requiring the offender to appear at the place and time specified in it, or a warrant for his arrest.

(2) Jurisdiction for the purposes of sub-paragraph (1) may be exercised—

(a) if the suspended sentence was passed by the Crown Court, by that court;
(b) if it was passed by a magistrates' court, by a justice acting for the petty sessions area for which that court acted.

(3) Where—

(a) an offender is convicted in Scotland or Northern Ireland of an offence, and
(b) the court is informed that the offence was committed during the operational period of a suspended sentence passed in England or Wales,

the court must give written notice of the conviction to the appropriate officer of the court by which the suspended sentence was passed.

(4) Unless he is acting in consequence of a notice under sub-paragraph (3), a justice of the peace may not issue a summons under this paragraph except on information and may not issue a warrant under this paragraph except on information in writing and on oath.

(5) A summons or warrant issued under this paragraph must direct the offender to appear or be brought before the court by which the suspended sentence was passed.

PART 3
AMENDMENT OF SUSPENDED SENTENCE ORDER
Cancellation of community requirements of suspended sentence order

13. (1) Where at any time while a suspended sentence order is in force, it appears to the appropriate court on the application of the offender or the responsible officer that, having regard to the circumstances which have arisen since the order was made, it would be in the interests of justice to do so, the court may cancel the community requirements of the suspended sentence order.

(2) The circumstances in which the appropriate court may exercise its power under sub-paragraph (1) include the offender's making good progress or his responding satisfactorily to supervision.

(3) In this paragraph "the appropriate court" means—

(a) in the case of a suspended sentence order which is subject to review, the court responsible for the order,

(b) in the case of a suspended sentence order which was made by the Crown Court and does not include any direction that any failure to comply with the community requirements of the order is to be dealt with by a magistrates' court, the Crown Court, and

(c) in any other case, a magistrates' court acting for the petty sessions area concerned.

Amendment by reason of change of residence

14. (1) This paragraph applies where, at any time while a suspended sentence order is in force, the appropriate court is satisfied that the offender proposes to change, or has changed, his residence from the petty sessions area concerned to another petty sessions area.

(2) Subject to sub-paragraphs (3) and (4), the appropriate court may, and on the application of the responsible officer must, amend the suspended sentence order by substituting the other petty sessions area for the area specified in the order.

(3) The court may not amend under this paragraph a suspended sentence order which contains requirements which, in the opinion of the court, cannot be complied with unless the offender resides in the petty sessions area concerned unless, in accordance with paragraph 15 it either—

(a) cancels those requirements, or

(b) substitutes for those requirements other requirements which can be complied with if the offender does not reside in that area.

(4) The court may not amend under this paragraph any suspended sentence order imposing a programme requirement unless it appears to the court that the accredited programme specified in the requirement is available in the other petty sessions area.

(5) In this paragraph "the appropriate court" has the same meaning as in paragraph 13.

Amendment of community requirements of suspended sentence order

15. (1) At any time during the supervision period, the appropriate court may, on the application of the offender or the responsible officer, by order amend any community requirement of a suspended sentence order—

(a) by cancelling the requirement, or

(b) by replacing it with a requirement of the same kind, which the court could include if it were then making the order.

(2) For the purposes of sub-paragraph (1)—

(a) a requirement falling within any paragraph of section 190(1) is of the same kind as any other requirement falling within that paragraph, and

(b) an electronic monitoring requirement is a requirement of the same kind as any requirement falling within section 190(1) to which it relates.

(3) The court may not under this paragraph amend a mental health treatment requirement, a drug rehabilitation requirement or an alcohol treatment requirement unless the offender expresses his willingness to comply with the requirement as amended.

(4) If the offender fails to express his willingness to comply with a mental health treatment requirement, drug rehabilitation requirement or alcohol treatment requirement as proposed to be amended by the court under this paragraph, the court may—

(a) revoke the suspended sentence order and the suspended sentence to which it relates, and

(b) deal with him, for the offence in respect of which the suspended sentence was imposed, in any way in which it could deal with him if he had just been convicted by or before the court of the offence.

(5) In dealing with the offender under sub-paragraph (4)(b), the court must take into account the extent to which the offender has complied with the requirements of the order.

(6) In this paragraph "the appropriate court" has the same meaning as in paragraph 13.

Amendment of treatment requirements on report of practitioner

16. (1) Where the medical practitioner or other person by whom or under whose direction an offender is, in pursuance of any requirement to which this sub-paragraph applies, being treated for his mental condition or his dependency on or propensity to misuse drugs or alcohol—

(a) is of the opinion mentioned in sub-paragraph (3), or

(b) is for any reason unwilling to continue to treat or direct the treatment of the offender,

he must make a report in writing to that effect to the responsible officer and that officer must apply under paragraph 15 to the appropriate court for the variation or cancellation of the requirement.

(2) The requirements to which sub-paragraph (1) applies are—

   (a) a mental health treatment requirement,
   (b) a drug rehabilitation requirement, and
   (c) an alcohol treatment requirement.

(3) The opinion referred to in sub-paragraph (1) is—

   (a) that the treatment of the offender should be continued beyond the period specified in that behalf in the order,
   (b) that the offender needs different treatment,
   (c) that the offender is not susceptible to treatment, or
   (d) that the offender does not require further treatment.

(4) In this paragraph "the appropriate court" has the same meaning as in paragraph 13.

Amendment in relation to review of drug rehabilitation requirement

17. Where the responsible officer is of the opinion that a suspended sentence order imposing a drug rehabilitation requirement which is subject to review should be so amended as to provide for each periodic review (required by section 211) to be made without a hearing instead of at a review hearing, or vice versa, he must apply under paragraph 15 to the court responsible for the order for the variation of the order.

Extension of unpaid work requirement

18. (1) Where—

   (a) a suspended sentence order imposing an unpaid work requirement is in force in respect of the offender, and
   (b) on the application of the offender or the responsible officer, it appears to the appropriate court that it would be in the interests of justice to do so having regard to circumstances which have arisen since the order was made,

the court may, in relation to the order, extend the period of twelve months specified in section 200(2).

(2) In this paragraph "the appropriate court" has the same meaning as in paragraph 13.

Supplementary

19. (1) No application may be made under paragraph 13, 15 or 18, and no order may be made under paragraph 14, while an appeal against the suspended sentence is pending.

(2) Sub-paragraph (1) does not apply to an application under paragraph 15 which—

   (a) relates to a mental health treatment requirement, a drug rehabilitation requirement or an alcohol treatment requirement, and
   (b) is made by the responsible officer with the consent of the offender.

20. (1) Subject to sub-paragraph (2), where a court proposes to exercise its powers under paragraph 15, otherwise than on the application of the offender, the court—

   (a) must summon him to appear before the court, and
   (b) if he does not appear in answer to the summons, may issue a warrant for his arrest.

(2) This paragraph does not apply to an order cancelling any community requirement of a suspended sentence order.

21. Paragraphs 8(2)(c) and 15(1)(b) have effect subject to the provisions mentioned in subsection (2) of section 190, and to subsections (3) and (5) of that section.

22. (1) On the making under this Schedule of an order amending a suspended sentence order, the proper officer of the court must—

   (a) provide copies of the amending order to the offender and the responsible officer,
   (b) in the case of an amending order which substitutes a new petty sessions area, provide a copy of the amending order to—

      (i) the local probation board acting for that area, and
      (ii) the magistrates' court acting for that area, and

   (c) in the case of an amending order which imposes or amends a requirement specified in the first column of Schedule 14, provide a copy of so much of the amending order as relates to that requirement to the person specified in relation to that requirement in the second column of that Schedule.

(2) Where under sub-paragraph (1)(b) the proper officer of the court provides a copy of an amending order to a magistrates' court acting for a different area, the officer must also provide to that court such documents and information relating to the case as it considers likely to be of assistance to a court acting for that area in the exercise of its functions in relation to the order.

(3) In this paragraph "proper officer" means—

   (a) in relation to a magistrates' court, the justices' chief executive for the court; and
   (b) in relation to the Crown Court, the appropriate officer.

3–2090

Section 194   SCHEDULE 13[1]
TRANSFER OF SUSPENDED SENTENCE ORDERS TO SCOTLAND OR NORTHERN IRELAND

PART 1
SCOTLAND

1. (1) Where the court considering the making of a suspended sentence order is satisfied that the offender resides in Scotland, or will reside there when the order comes into force, the court may not make a suspended sentence order in respect of the offender unless it appears to the court—

(a) in the case of an order imposing a requirement mentioned in sub-paragraph (2), that arrangements exist for persons to comply with such a requirement in the locality in Scotland in which the offender resides, or will be residing when the order comes into force, and that provision can be made for him to comply with the requirement under those arrangements, and

(b) in any case, that suitable arrangements for his supervision can be made by the local authority in whose area he resides, or will be residing when the order comes into force.

(2) The requirements referred to in sub-paragraph (1)(a) are—

(a) an unpaid work requirement,

(b) an activity requirement,

(c) a programme requirement,

(d) a mental health treatment requirement,

(e) a drug rehabilitation requirement,

(f) an alcohol treatment requirement, and

(g) an electronic monitoring requirement.

(3) Where—

(a) the appropriate court for the purposes of paragraph 14 of Schedule 12 (amendment by reason of change of residence) is satisfied that an offender in respect of whom a suspended sentence order is in force proposes to reside or is residing in Scotland, and

(b) it appears to the court that the conditions in sub-paragraph (1)(a) and (b) are satisfied,

the power of the court to amend the order under Part 3 of Schedule 12 includes power to amend it by requiring it to be complied with in Scotland and the offender to be supervised in accordance with the arrangements referred to in sub-paragraph (1)(b).

(4) For the purposes of sub-paragraph (3), any reference in sub-paragraph (1)(a) and (b) to the time when the order comes into force is to be treated as a reference to the time when the amendment comes into force.

(5) The court may not by virtue of sub-paragraph (1) or (3) require an attendance centre requirement to be complied with in Scotland.

(6) The court may not provide for an order made in accordance with this paragraph to be subject to review under section 191 or 210; and where an order which is subject to review under either of those sections is amended in accordance with this paragraph, the order shall cease to be so subject.

1. Schedule 13 is of no effect in relation to offences committed before 4 April, 2005: see the Criminal Justice Act 2003 (Commencement No 8 and Transitional and Saving Provisions) Order 2005, SI 2005/950.

2. A suspended sentence order made or amended in accordance with paragraph 1 must—

(a) specify the local authority area in which the offender resides or will be residing when the order or amendment comes into force, and

(b) require the local authority for that area to appoint or assign an officer who will be responsible for discharging in relation to him the functions conferred on responsible officers by Part 12 of this Act;

and section 216 (petty sessions area to be specified) does not apply in relation to an order so made or amended.

3. (1) Where a court makes or amends a suspended sentence order in accordance with paragraph 1, the court must provide the relevant documents to—

(a) the local authority for the area specified in the order, and

(b) the sheriff court having jurisdiction in the locality in which the offender resides or proposes to reside;

and paragraphs (b) to (d) of subsection (1) of section 219 (provision of copies of relevant orders) do not apply in relation to an order so made or amended.

(2) In this paragraph, "the relevant documents" means—

(a) a copy of the order as made or amended, and

(b) such other documents and information relating to the case as the court making or amending the order considers likely to be of assistance.

4. (1) In relation to the making or amendment of a suspended sentence order in accordance with paragraph 1, and (except for the purposes of paragraph 20) in relation to an order so made or amended, Chapter 4 of Part 12 of this Act has effect subject to the following modifications.

(2) Any reference to the responsible officer has effect as a reference to the officer appointed or assigned under paragraph 2(b).

(3) The following provisions are omitted—

(a) subsection (7) of section 201 (activity requirement),

(b) subsection (7) of section 202 (programme requirement),

(c) subsection (4) of section 206 (residence requirement),

(d) subsection (4) of section 218 (availability of arrangements in local area).

(4) In section 207 (mental health treatment requirement), for subsection (2)(a) there is substituted—

"(a) treatment as a resident patient in a hospital within the meaning of the Mental Health (Care and Treatment) (Scotland) Act 2003, not being a state hospital within the meaning of that Act;".

(5) In section 215 (electronic monitoring requirement), in subsection (3), the words from "and" onwards are omitted.

5. In this Part of this Schedule "local authority" means a council constituted under section 2 of the Local Government etc (Scotland) Act 1994 (c 39); and any reference to the area of such an authority is a reference to the local government area within the meaning of that Act.

PART 2
NORTHERN IRELAND

6. (1) Where the court considering the making of a suspended sentence order is satisfied that the offender resides in Northern Ireland, or will reside there when the order comes into force, the court may not make a suspended sentence order in respect of the offender unless it appears to the court—

(a) in the case of an order imposing a requirement mentioned in sub-paragraph (2), that arrangements exist for persons to comply with such a requirement in the petty sessions district in Northern Ireland in which the offender resides, or will be residing when the order comes into force, and that provision can be made for him to comply with the requirement under those arrangements, and

(b) in any case, that suitable arrangements for his supervision can be made by the Probation Board for Northern Ireland.

(2) The requirements referred to in sub-paragraph (1)(a) are—

(a) an unpaid work requirement,
(b) an activity requirement,
(c) a programme requirement,
(d) a mental health treatment requirement,
(e) a drug rehabilitation requirement,
(f) an alcohol treatment requirement,
(g) an attendance centre requirement, and
(h) an electronic monitoring requirement.

(3) Where—

(a) the appropriate court for the purposes of paragraph 14 of Schedule 12 (amendment by reason of change of residence) is satisfied that an offender in respect of whom a suspended sentence order is in force proposes to reside or is residing in Northern Ireland, and

(b) it appears to the court that the conditions in sub-paragraphs (1)(a) and (b) are satisfied,

the power of the court to amend the order under Part 3 of Schedule 12 includes power to amend it by requiring it to be complied with in Northern Ireland and the offender to be supervised in accordance with the arrangements referred to in sub-paragraph (1)(b).

(4) For the purposes of sub-paragraph (3), any reference in sub-paragraph (1)(a) and (b) to the time when the order comes into force is to be treated as a reference to the time when the amendment comes into force.

(5) The court may not provide for an order made in accordance with this paragraph to be subject to review under section 191 or 210; and where an order which is subject to review under either of those sections is amended in accordance with this paragraph, the order shall cease to be so subject.

7. A suspended sentence order made or amended in accordance with paragraph 6 must—

(a) specify the petty sessions district in Northern Ireland in which the offender resides or will be residing when the order or amendment comes into force, and

(b) require the Probation Board for Northern Ireland to appoint or assign a probation officer who will be responsible for discharging in relation to him the functions conferred on responsible officers by Part 12 of this Act;

and section 216 (petty sessions area to be specified) does not apply in relation to an order so made or amended.

8. (1) Where a court makes or amends a suspended sentence order in accordance with paragraph 6, the court must provide the relevant documents to—

(a) the Probation Board for Northern Ireland, and

(b) the court of summary jurisdiction acting for the petty sessions district in which the offender resides or proposes to reside;

and paragraphs (b) to (d) of subsection (1) of section 219 (provision of copies of relevant orders) do not apply in relation to an order so made or amended.

(2) In this paragraph, "the relevant documents" means—

(a) a copy of the order as made or amended, and

(b) such other documents and information relating to the case as the court making or amending the order considers likely to be of assistance.

9. (1) In relation to the making or amendment of a suspended sentence order in accordance with paragraph 6, and (except for the purposes of paragraph 20) in relation to an order so made or amended, Chapter 4 of Part 12 of this Act has effect subject to the following modifications.

(2) Any reference to the responsible officer has effect as a reference to the probation officer appointed or assigned under paragraph 7(b).

(3) The following provisions are omitted—

(a) subsection (7) of section 201 (activity requirement),
(b) subsection (7) of section 202 (programme requirement),
(c) subsection (4) of section 206 (residence requirement),
(d) subsection (4) of section 218 (availability of arrangements in local area).

(4) In section 207 (mental health treatment requirement), for subsection (2)(a) there is substituted—

"(a) treatment (whether as an in-patient or an out-patient) at such hospital as may be specified in the order, being a hospital within the meaning of the Health and Personal Social Services (Northern Ireland) Order 1972, approved by the Department of Health, Social Services and Public Safety for the purposes of paragraph 4(3) of Schedule 1 to the Criminal Justice (Northern Ireland) Order 1996 (SI 1996/3160 (NI 24));".

(5) In section 214 (attendance centre requirement), any reference to an attendance centre has effect as a reference to a day centre, as defined by paragraph 3(6) of Schedule 1 to the Criminal Justice (Northern Ireland) Order 1996 (SI 1996/3160 (NI 24).

(6) In section 215 (electronic monitoring requirement), in subsection (3), the words from "and" onwards are omitted.

PART 3
GENERAL PROVISIONS: BREACH OR AMENDMENT

10. This Part of this Schedule applies at any time while a suspended sentence order made or amended in accordance with paragraph 1 or 6 is in force in respect of an offender.

11. In this Part of this Schedule—

"home court" means—

    (*a*) if the offender resides in Scotland, or will be residing there at the relevant time, the sheriff court having jurisdiction in the locality in which the offender resides or proposes to reside, and

    (*b*) if he resides in Northern Ireland, or will be residing there at the relevant time, the court of summary jurisdiction acting for the petty sessions district in which he resides or proposes to reside;

"local authority" and "local authority area" are to be read in accordance with paragraph 5;

"original court" means the court in England and Wales which made or last amended the order;

"the relevant officer" means—

    (*a*) where the order specifies a local authority area in Scotland, the local authority officer appointed or assigned under paragraph 2(*b*), and

    (*b*) where the court specifies a petty sessions district in Northern Ireland, the probation officer appointed or assigned under paragraph 7(*b*);

"the relevant time" means the time when the order or the amendment to it comes into force.

12. (1) Where this Part of this Schedule applies, Schedule 12 has effect subject to the following modifications.

(2) Any reference to the responsible officer has effect as a reference to the relevant officer.

(3) Any reference to a magistrates' court acting for the petty sessions area concerned has effect as a reference to a magistrates' court acting for the same petty sessions area as the original court; and any reference to a justice of the peace acting for the petty sessions area concerned has effect as a reference to a justice of the peace acting for the same petty sessions area as that court.

(4) Any reference to the appropriate court has effect as a reference to the original court.

(5) In paragraphs 4 and 5, any reference to causing an information to be laid before a justice of the peace has effect—

    (*a*) if the home court is in Scotland, as a reference to providing information to the home court with a view to it issuing a citation, and

    (*b*) if the home court is in Northern Ireland, as a reference to making a complaint to a justice of the peace in Northern Ireland.

(6) In paragraph 14—

    (*a*) if the home court is in Scotland—

        (i) any reference to the petty sessions area concerned has effect as a reference to the local authority area specified in the order, and

        (ii) any other reference to a petty sessions area has effect as a reference to a local authority area, and

    (*b*) if the home court is in Northern Ireland—

        (i) any reference to the petty sessions area concerned has effect as a reference to the petty sessions district specified in the order, and

        (ii) any other reference to a petty sessions area has effect as a reference to a petty sessions district.

(7) Paragraph 22 is omitted.

(8) No court in England and Wales may—

    (*a*) exercise any power in relation to any failure by the offender to comply with any community requirement of the order unless the offender has been required in accordance with paragraph 14(1)(*b*) or (2)(*a*) of this Schedule to appear before that court;

    (*b*) exercise any power under Part 3 of Schedule 12 unless the offender has been required in accordance with paragraph 15(2) or 16 of this Schedule to appear before that court.

13. (1) Sub-paragraph (2) applies where it appears to the home court—

    (*a*) if that court is in Scotland, on information from the relevant officer, or

    (*b*) if that court is in Northern Ireland, upon a complaint being made by the relevant officer,

that the offender has failed without reasonable excuse to comply with any of the community requirements of the suspended sentence order.

(2) The home court may—

    (*a*) if it is in Scotland—

        (i) issue a citation requiring the offender to appear before it at the time specified in the citation, or

        (ii) issue a warrant for the offender's arrest;

    (*b*) if it is in Northern Ireland—

        (i) issue a summons requiring the offender to appear before it at the time specified in the summons, or

        (ii) issue a warrant for the offender's arrest.

14. (1) The court before which an offender appears or is brought by virtue of paragraph 13 must—

    (*a*) determine whether the offender has failed without reasonable excuse to comply with any of the community requirements of the suspended sentence order, or

    (*b*) require the offender to appear before the original court.

(2) If the home court determines that the offender has failed without reasonable excuse to comply with any of the community requirements of the order—

    (*a*) the home court must require the offender to appear before the original court, and

    (*b*) when the offender appears before the original court, paragraph 8 of Schedule 12 applies as if it had already been proved to the satisfaction of the original court that the offender failed without reasonable excuse to comply with such of the community requirements of the order as may have been determined.

(3) An offender who is required by any of the following community requirements of a suspended sentence order—

(*a*)   a mental health treatment requirement,
(*b*)   a drug rehabilitation requirement, or
(*c*)   an alcohol treatment requirement,

to submit to treatment for his mental condition, or his dependency on or propensity to misuse drugs or alcohol, is not to be treated for the purposes of sub-paragraph (2) as having failed to comply with that requirement on the ground only that he had refused to undergo any surgical, electrical or other treatment if, in the opinion of the court, his refusal was reasonable having regard to all the circumstances.

(4) The evidence of one witness shall, for the purposes of sub-paragraph (2), be sufficient.

(5) Where the home court is in Scotland and the order contains an electronic monitoring requirement, section 245H of the Criminal Procedure (Scotland) Act 1995 (c 46) (documentary evidence) applies to proceedings under this paragraph as it applies to proceedings under section 245F of that Act (breach of restriction of liberty order).

(6) Where an offender is required by virtue of sub-paragraph (2) to appear before the original court—

(*a*)   the home court must send to the original court a certificate certifying that the offender has failed without reasonable excuse to comply with the requirements of the order in the respect specified, and
(*b*)   such a certificate signed by the clerk of the home court is admissible before the original court as conclusive evidence of the matters specified in it.

15. (1) The home court may exercise any power under Part 3 of Schedule 12 (amendment of suspended sentence order) as if it were the original court, except that the home court may not exercise the power conferred by paragraph 15(4) of that Schedule.

(2) Where paragraph 15(4) of Schedule 12 applies the home court must require the offender to appear before the original court.

(3) Subject to sub-paragraph (4), where the home court proposes to exercise the power conferred by paragraph 15(1) of Schedule 12, otherwise than on the application of the offender, the court—

(*a*)   if it is in Scotland—

(i)   must issue a citation requiring the offender to appear before it, and
(ii)   if he does not appear in answer to the citation, may issue a warrant for the offender's arrest;

(*b*)   if it is in Northern Ireland—

(i)   must issue a summons requiring the offender to appear before it, and
(ii)   if he does not appear in answer to the summons, may issue a warrant for the offender's arrest;

and paragraph 20 of Schedule 12 does not apply to the home court.

(4) Sub-paragraph (3) does not apply to an order cancelling any community requirement of a suspended sentence order.

(5) Where the home court is considering amending a suspended sentence order, any reference in Chapter 4 of Part 12 of this Act to a local probation board has effect as a reference to a local authority in Scotland or, as the case may be, the Probation Board for Northern Ireland.

16. Where by virtue of paragraph 15 any application is made to the home court under Part 3 of Schedule 12, the home court may (instead of dealing with the application) require the offender to appear before the original court.

17. No court may amend or further amend a suspended sentence order unless it appears to the court that the conditions in paragraph 1(1)(*a*) and (*b*) or, as the case may be, paragraph 6(1)(*a*) and (*b*) are satisfied in relation to any requirement to be imposed; but this paragraph does not apply to any amendment by virtue of paragraph 20(2).

18. The preceding paragraphs of this Schedule have effect in relation to any amendment of a suspended order by any court as they have effect in relation to the amendment of such an order by virtue of paragraph 1(3) or 6(3).

19. On the making of an order amending a suspended sentence order—

(*a*)   the court must provide copies of the amending order to the offender and the relevant officer, and
(*b*)   in the case of an amending order which substitutes a new local authority area or petty sessions district, paragraphs 2 and 3 or, as the case may be, 7 and 8 have effect in relation to the order as they have effect in relation to an order made or amended in accordance with paragraph 1 or 6.

20. (1) This paragraph applies where the home court is satisfied that the offender is residing or proposes to reside in England and Wales.

(2) Subject to sub-paragraphs (3) and (4), the home court may, and on the application of the relevant officer must, amend the suspended sentence order by requiring it to be complied with in England and Wales.

(3) The court may not amend under this paragraph a suspended sentence order which contains requirements which, in the opinion of the court, cannot be complied with in the petty sessions area in which the offender is residing or proposes to reside unless, in accordance with paragraph 15 of Schedule 12 it either—

(*a*)   cancels those requirements, or
(*b*)   substitutes for those requirements other requirements which can be complied with if the offender resides in that area.

(4) The court may not amend under this paragraph any suspended sentence order imposing a programme requirement unless it appears to the court that the accredited programme specified in the requirement is available in the petty sessions area in England and Wales in which the offender is residing or proposes to reside.

(5) The suspended sentence order as amended must specify the petty sessions area in which the offender resides or proposes to reside.

(6) On the making under this paragraph of an order amending a suspended sentence order, the home court must—

(*a*)   provide copies of the amending order to the offender, the relevant officer and the local probation board acting for the new petty sessions area, and
(*b*)   provide the magistrates' court acting for that area with a copy of the amending order and such other documents and information relating to the case as the home court considers likely to be of assistance to a court acting for that area in the exercise of its functions in relation to the order.

(7) Where an order has been amended under this paragraph, the preceding paragraphs of this Schedule shall cease to apply to the order as amended.

PART 4
SUPPLEMENTARY

21. Subsections (1) and (3) of section 245C of the Criminal Procedure (Scotland) Act 1995 (c 46) (provision of remote monitoring) have effect as if they included a reference to the electronic monitoring of the community requirements of a suspended sentence order made or amended in accordance with paragraph 1 of this Schedule.

22.—(1) Section 4 of the Summary Jurisdiction (Process) Act 1881 (c 24) (which provides, among other things, for service in England and Wales of Scottish citations or warrants) applies to any citation or warrant issued under paragraph 13(2)(*a*) or 15(3)(*a*) as it applies to a citation or warrant granted under section 134 of the Criminal Procedure (Scotland) Act 1995.

(2) A summons issued by a court in Northern Ireland under paragraph 13(2)(*b*) or 15(3)(*b*) may, in such circumstances as may be prescribed by rules of court, be served in England and Wales or Scotland.

3–2091

Section 219

SCHEDULE 14
PERSONS TO WHOM COPIES OF REQUIREMENTS TO BE PROVIDED IN PARTICULAR CASES

Requirement	Person to whom copy of requirement is to be given
An activity requirement.	The person specified under section 201(1)(*a*).
An exclusion requirement imposed for the purpose (or partly for the purpose) of protecting a person from being approached by the offender.	The person intended to be protected.
A residence requirement relating to residence in an institution.	The person in charge of the institution.
A mental health treatment requirement.	The person specified under section 207(2)(*c*) or the person in charge of the institution or place specified under section 207(2)(*a*) or (*b*).
A drug rehabilitation requirement.	The person in charge of the institution or place specified under section 209(4)(*a*) or (*b*).
An alcohol treatment requirement.	The person specified under section 212(5)(*c*) or the person in charge of the institution or place specified under section 212(5)(*a*) or (*b*).
An attendance centre requirement.	The officer in charge of the attendance centre specified in the requirement.
An electronic monitoring requirement.	Any person who by virtue of section 215(3) will be responsible for the electronic monitoring. Any person by virtue of whose consent the requirement is included in the order.

3–2092

Section 224

SCHEDULE 15
SPECIFIED OFFENCES FOR PURPOSES OF CHAPTER 5 OF PART 12

PART 1
SPECIFIED VIOLENT OFFENCES

1. Manslaughter.

2. Kidnapping.

3. False imprisonment.

4. An offence under section 4 of the Offences against the Person Act 1861 (c 100) (soliciting murder).

5. An offence under section 16 of that Act (threats to kill).

6. An offence under section 18 of that Act (wounding with intent to cause grievous bodily harm).

7. An offence under section 20 of that Act (malicious wounding).

8. An offence under section 21 of that Act (attempting to choke, suffocate or strangle in order to commit or assist in committing an indictable offence).

9. An offence under section 22 of that Act (using chloroform etc to commit or assist in the committing of any indictable offence).

10. An offence under section 23 of that Act (maliciously administering poison etc so as to endanger life or inflict grievous bodily harm).

11. An offence under section 27 of that Act (abandoning children).

12. An offence under section 28 of that Act (causing bodily injury by explosives).

13. An offence under section 29 of that Act (using explosives etc with intent to do grievous bodily harm).

14. An offence under section 30 of that Act (placing explosives with intent to do bodily injury).

15. An offence under section 31 of that Act (setting spring guns etc with intent to do grievous bodily harm).

16. An offence under section 32 of that Act (endangering the safety of railway passengers).

17. An offence under section 35 of that Act (injuring persons by furious driving).

18. An offence under section 37 of that Act (assaulting officer preserving wreck).

19. An offence under section 38 of that Act (assault with intent to resist arrest).

20. An offence under section 47 of that Act (assault occasioning actual bodily harm).

21. An offence under section 2 of the Explosive Substances Act 1883 (c 3) (causing explosion likely to endanger life or property).

22. An offence under section 3 of that Act (attempt to cause explosion, or making or keeping explosive with intent to endanger life or property).

23. An offence under section 1 of the Infant Life (Preservation) Act 1929 (c 34) (child destruction).
24. An offence under section 1 of the Children and Young Persons Act 1933 (c 12) (cruelty to children).
25. An offence under section 1 of the Infanticide Act 1938 (c 36) (infanticide).
26. An offence under section 16 of the Firearms Act 1968 (c 27) (possession of firearm with intent to endanger life).
27. An offence under section 16A of that Act (possession of firearm with intent to cause fear of violence).
28. An offence under section 17(1) of that Act (use of firearm to resist arrest).
29. An offence under section 17(2) of that Act (possession of firearm at time of committing or being arrested for offence specified in Schedule 1 to that Act).
30. An offence under section 18 of that Act (carrying a firearm with criminal intent).
31. An offence under section 8 of the Theft Act 1968 (c 60) (robbery or assault with intent to rob).
32. An offence under section 9 of that Act of burglary with intent to—

(a) inflict grievous bodily harm on a person, or
(b) do unlawful damage to a building or anything in it.

33. An offence under section 10 of that Act (aggravated burglary).
34. An offence under section 12A of that Act (aggravated vehicle-taking) involving an accident which caused the death of any person.
35. An offence of arson under section 1 of the Criminal Damage Act 1971 (c 48).
36. An offence under section 1(2) of that Act (destroying or damaging property) other than an offence of arson.
37. An offence under section 1 of the Taking of Hostages Act 1982 (c 28) (hostage-taking).
38. An offence under section 1 of the Aviation Security Act 1982 (c 36) (hijacking).
39. An offence under section 2 of that Act (destroying, damaging or endangering safety of aircraft).
40. An offence under section 3 of that Act (other acts endangering or likely to endanger safety of aircraft).
41. An offence under section 4 of that Act (offences in relation to certain dangerous articles).
42. An offence under section 127 of the Mental Health Act 1983 (c 20) (ill-treatment of patients).
43. An offence under section 1 of the Prohibition of Female Circumcision Act 1985 (c 38) (prohibition of female circumcision).
44. An offence under section 1 of the Public Order Act 1986 (c 64) (riot).
45. An offence under section 2 of that Act (violent disorder).
46. An offence under section 3 of that Act (affray).
47. An offence under section 134 of the Criminal Justice Act 1988 (c 33) (torture).
48. An offence under section 1 of the Road Traffic Act 1988 (c 52) (causing death by dangerous driving).
49. An offence under section 3A of that Act (causing death by careless driving when under influence of drink or drugs).
50. An offence under section 1 of the Aviation and Maritime Security Act 1990 (c 31) (endangering safety at aerodromes).
51. An offence under section 9 of that Act (hijacking of ships).
52. An offence under section 10 of that Act (seizing or exercising control of fixed platforms).
53. An offence under section 11 of that Act (destroying fixed platforms or endangering their safety).
54. An offence under section 12 of that Act (other acts endangering or likely to endanger safe navigation).
55. An offence under section 13 of that Act (offences involving threats).
56. An offence under Part II of the Channel Tunnel (Security) Order 1994 (SI 1994/570) (offences relating to Channel Tunnel trains and the tunnel system).
57. An offence under section 4 of the Protection from Harassment Act 1997 (c 40) (putting people in fear of violence).
58. An offence under section 29 of the Crime and Disorder Act 1998 (c 37) (racially or religiously aggravated assaults).
59. An offence falling within section 31(1)(a) or (b) of that Act (racially or religiously aggravated offences under section 4 or 4A of the Public Order Act 1986 (c 64)).
60. An offence under section 51 or 52 of the International Criminal Court Act 2001 (c 17) (genocide, crimes against humanity, war crimes and related offences), other than one involving murder.
61. An offence under section 1 of the Female Genital Mutilation Act 2003 (c 31) (female genital mutilation).
62. An offence under section 2 of that Act (assisting a girl to mutilate her own genitalia).
63. An offence under section 3 of that Act (assisting a non-UK person to mutilate overseas a girl's genitalia).
64. An offence of—

(a) aiding, abetting, counselling, procuring or inciting the commission of an offence specified in this Part of this Schedule,
(b) conspiring to commit an offence so specified, or
(c) attempting to commit an offence so specified.

65. An attempt to commit murder or a conspiracy to commit murder.

PART 2
SPECIFIED SEXUAL OFFENCES

66. An offence under section 1 of the Sexual Offences Act 1956 (c 69) (rape).
67. An offence under section 2 of that Act (procurement of woman by threats).
68. An offence under section 3 of that Act (procurement of woman by false pretences).
69. An offence under section 4 of that Act (administering drugs to obtain or facilitate intercourse).
70. An offence under section 5 of that Act (intercourse with girl under thirteen).
71. An offence under section 6 of that Act (intercourse with girl under 16).
72. An offence under section 7 of that Act (intercourse with a defective).
73. An offence under section 9 of that Act (procurement of a defective).
74. An offence under section 10 of that Act (incest by a man).
75. An offence under section 11 of that Act (incest by a woman).
76. An offence under section 14 of that Act (indecent assault on a woman).
77. An offence under section 15 of that Act (indecent assault on a man).
78. An offence under section 16 of that Act (assault with intent to commit buggery).
79. An offence under section 17 of that Act (abduction of woman by force or for the sake of her property).

80. An offence under section 19 of that Act (abduction of unmarried girl under eighteen from parent or guardian).

81. An offence under section 20 of that Act (abduction of unmarried girl under sixteen from parent or guardian).

82. An offence under section 21 of that Act (abduction of defective from parent or guardian).

83. An offence under section 22 of that Act (causing prostitution of women).

84. An offence under section 23 of that Act (procuration of girl under twenty-one).

85. An offence under section 24 of that Act (detention of woman in brothel).

86. An offence under section 25 of that Act (permitting girl under thirteen to use premises for intercourse).

87. An offence under section 26 of that Act (permitting girl under sixteen to use premises for intercourse).

88. An offence under section 27 of that Act (permitting defective to use premises for intercourse).

89. An offence under section 28 of that Act (causing or encouraging the prostitution of, intercourse with or indecent assault on girl under sixteen).

90. An offence under section 29 of that Act (causing or encouraging prostitution of defective).

91. An offence under section 32 of that Act (soliciting by men).

92. An offence under section 33 of that Act (keeping a brothel).

93. An offence under section 128 of the Mental Health Act 1959 (c 72) (sexual intercourse with patients).

94. An offence under section 1 of the Indecency with Children Act 1960 (c 33) (indecent conduct towards young child).

95. An offence under section 4 of the Sexual Offences Act 1967 (c 60) (procuring others to commit homosexual acts).

96. An offence under section 5 of that Act (living on earnings of male prostitution).

97. An offence under section 9 of the Theft Act 1968 (c 60) of burglary with intent to commit rape.

98. An offence under section 54 of the Criminal Law Act 1977 (c 45) (inciting girl under sixteen to have incestuous sexual intercourse).

99. An offence under section 1 of the Protection of Children Act 1978 (c 37) (indecent photographs of children).

100. An offence under section 170 of the Customs and Excise Management Act 1979 (c 2) (penalty for fraudulent evasion of duty etc) in relation to goods prohibited to be imported under section 42 of the Customs Consolidation Act 1876 (c 36) (indecent or obscene articles).

101. An offence under section 160 of the Criminal Justice Act 1988 (c 33) (possession of indecent photograph of a child).

102. An offence under section 1 of the Sexual Offences Act 2003 (c 42) (rape).

103. An offence under section 2 of that Act (assault by penetration).

104. An offence under section 3 of that Act (sexual assault).

105. An offence under section 4 of that Act (causing a person to engage in sexual activity without consent).

106. An offence under section 5 of that Act (rape of a child under 13).

107. An offence under section 6 of that Act (assault of a child under 13 by penetration).

108. An offence under section 7 of that Act (sexual assault of a child under 13).

109. An offence under section 8 of that Act (causing or inciting a child under 13 to engage in sexual activity).

110. An offence under section 9 of that Act (sexual activity with a child).

111. An offence under section 10 of that Act (causing or inciting a child to engage in sexual activity).

112. An offence under section 11 of that Act (engaging in sexual activity in the presence of a child).

113. An offence under section 12 of that Act (causing a child to watch a sexual act).

114. An offence under section 13 of that Act (child sex offences committed by children or young persons).

115. An offence under section 14 of that Act (arranging or facilitating commission of a child sex offence).

116. An offence under section 15 of that Act (meeting a child following sexual grooming etc).

117. An offence under section 16 of that Act (abuse of position of trust: sexual activity with a child).

118. An offence under section 17 of that Act (abuse of position of trust: causing or inciting a child to engage in sexual activity).

119. An offence under section 18 of that Act (abuse of position of trust: sexual activity in the presence of a child).

120. An offence under section 19 of that Act (abuse of position of trust: causing a child to watch a sexual act).

121. An offence under section 25 of that Act (sexual activity with a child family member).

122. An offence under section 26 of that Act (inciting a child family member to engage in sexual activity).

123. An offence under section 30 of that Act (sexual activity with a person with a mental disorder impeding choice).

124. An offence under section 31 of that Act (causing or inciting a person with a mental disorder impeding choice to engage in sexual activity).

125. An offence under section 32 of that Act (engaging in sexual activity in the presence of a person with a mental disorder impeding choice).

126. An offence under section 33 of that Act (causing a person with a mental disorder impeding choice to watch a sexual act).

127. An offence under section 34 of that Act (inducement, threat or deception to procure sexual activity with a person with a mental disorder).

128. An offence under section 35 of that Act (causing a person with a mental disorder to engage in or agree to engage in sexual activity by inducement, threat or deception).

129. An offence under section 36 of that Act (engaging in sexual activity in the presence, procured by inducement, threat or deception, of a person with a mental disorder).

130. An offence under section 37 of that Act (causing a person with a mental disorder to watch a sexual act by inducement, threat or deception).

131. An offence under section 38 of that Act (care workers: sexual activity with a person with a mental disorder).

132. An offence under section 39 of that Act (care workers: causing or inciting sexual activity).

133. An offence under section 40 of that Act (care workers: sexual activity in the presence of a person with a mental disorder).

134. An offence under section 41 of that Act (care workers: causing a person with a mental disorder to watch a sexual act).

135. An offence under section 47 of that Act (paying for sexual services of a child).

136. An offence under section 48 of that Act (causing or inciting child prostitution or pornography).

137. An offence under section 49 of that Act (controlling a child prostitute or a child involved in pornography).
138. An offence under section 50 of that Act (arranging or facilitating child prostitution or pornography).
139. An offence under section 52 of that Act (causing or inciting prostitution for gain).
140. An offence under section 53 of that Act (controlling prostitution for gain).
141. An offence under section 57 of that Act (trafficking into the UK for sexual exploitation).
142. An offence under section 58 of that Act (trafficking within the UK for sexual exploitation).
143. An offence under section 59 of that Act (trafficking out of the UK for sexual exploitation).
144. An offence under section 61 of that Act (administering a substance with intent).
145. An offence under section 62 of that Act (committing an offence with intent to commit a sexual offence).
146. An offence under section 63 of that Act (trespass with intent to commit a sexual offence).
147. An offence under section 64 of that Act (sex with an adult relative: penetration).
148. An offence under section 65 of that Act (sex with an adult relative: consenting to penetration).
149. An offence under section 66 of that Act (exposure).
150. An offence under section 67 of that Act (voyeurism).
151. An offence under section 69 of that Act (intercourse with an animal).
152. An offence under section 70 of that Act (sexual penetration of a corpse).
153. An offence of—

   (a) aiding, abetting, counselling, procuring or inciting the commission of an offence specified in this Part of this Schedule,
   (b) conspiring to commit an offence so specified, or
   (c) attempting to commit an offence so specified.

SCHEDULE 23[1]
DEFERMENT OF SENTENCE

Substitutes new ss 1 and 2 of the Powers of Criminal Courts (Sentencing) Act 2000.

3–2093

Section 279   SCHEDULE 24[1]

DRUG TREATMENT AND TESTING REQUIREMENT IN ACTION PLAN ORDER OR SUPERVISION ORDER

1. (1) Section 70 of the Sentencing Act (requirements which may be included in action plan orders and directions) is amended as follows.
   (2) After subsection (4) there is inserted—

"(4A) Subsection (4B) below applies where a court proposing to make an action plan order is satisfied—

   (a) that the offender is dependent on, or has a propensity to misuse, drugs, and
   (b) that his dependency or propensity is such as requires and may be susceptible to treatment.

(4B) Where this subsection applies, requirements included in an action plan order may require the offender for a period specified in the order ("the treatment period") to submit to treatment by or under the direction of a specified person having the necessary qualifications and experience ("the treatment provider") with a view to the reduction or elimination of the offender's dependency on or propensity to misuse drugs.
(4C) The required treatment shall be—

   (a) treatment as a resident in such institution or place as may be specified in the order, or
   (b) treatment as a non-resident at such institution or place, and at such intervals, as may be so specified;

but the nature of the treatment shall not be specified in the order except as mentioned in paragraph (a) or (b) above.
(4D) A requirement shall not be included in an action plan order by virtue of subsection (4B) above—

   (a) in any case, unless—

      (i) the court is satisfied that arrangements have been or can be made for the treatment intended to be specified in the order (including arrangements for the reception of the offender where he is to be required to submit to treatment as a resident), and
      (ii) the requirement has been recommended to the court as suitable for the offender by an officer of a local probation board or by a member of a youth offending team; and

   (b) in the case of an order made or to be made in respect of a person aged 14 or over, unless he consents to its inclusion.

(4E) Subject to subsection (4F), an action plan order which includes a requirement by virtue of subsection (4B) above may, if the offender is aged 14 or over, also include a requirement ("a testing requirement") that, for the purpose of ascertaining whether he has any drug in his body during the treatment period, the offender shall during that period, at such times or in such circumstances as may (subject to the provisions of the order) be determined by the responsible officer or the treatment provider, provide samples of such description as may be so determined.
(4F) A testing requirement shall not be included in an action plan order by virtue of subsection (4E) above unless—

   (a) the offender is aged 14 or over and consents to its inclusion, and
   (b) the court has been notified by the Secretary of State that arrangements for implementing such requirements are in force in the area proposed to be specified in the order

(4G) A testing requirement shall specify for each month the minimum number of occasions on which samples are to be provided.
(4H) An action plan order including a testing requirement shall provide for the results of tests carried out on any samples provided by the offender in pursuance of the requirement to a person other than the responsible officer to be communicated to the responsible officer."

---

1. Schedule 24 is in for the purpose of sentencing persons resident in the petty sessions areas of Bradford, Calderdale, Keighley, Manchester and Newham, and that part of Teesside petty sessions area that is coterminous with the borough of

Middlesbrough, by courts in those areas: see the Criminal Justice Act 2003 (Commencement No 6 and Transitional Provisions) Order 2004, SI 2004/3033.

2. (1) Schedule 6 to the Sentencing Act (requirements which may be included in supervision orders) is amended as follows.

(2) In paragraph 1, after "6" there is inserted ",6A".

(3) After paragraph 6 there is inserted—

"*Requirements as to drug treatment and testing*

6A. (1) This paragraph applies where a court proposing to make a supervision order is satisfied—

(a)　that the offender is dependent on, or has a propensity to misuse, drugs, and

(b)　that his dependency or propensity is such as requires and may be susceptible to treatment.

(2) Where this paragraph applies, the court may include in the supervision order a requirement that the offender shall, for a period specified in the order ("the treatment period"), submit to treatment by or under the direction of a specified person having the necessary qualifications and experience ("the treatment provider") with a view to the reduction or elimination of the offender's dependency on or propensity to misuse drugs.

(3) The required treatment shall be—

(a)　treatment as a resident in such institution or place as may be specified in the order, or

(b)　treatment as a non-resident at such institution or place, and at such intervals, as may be so specified;

but the nature of the treatment shall not be specified in the order except as mentioned in paragraph (a) or (b) above.

(4) A requirement shall not be included in a supervision order by virtue of sub-paragraph (2) above—

(a)　in any case, unless—

(i)　the court is satisfied that arrangements have been or can be made for the treatment intended to be specified in the order (including arrangements for the reception of the offender where he is to be required to submit to treatment as a resident), and

(ii)　the requirement has been recommended to the court as suitable for the offender by an officer of a local probation board or by a member of a youth offending team; and

(b)　in the case of an order made or to be made in respect of a person aged 14 or over, unless he consents to its inclusion.

(5) Subject to sub-paragraph (6), a supervision order which includes a treatment requirement may also include a requirement ("a testing requirement") that, for the purpose of ascertaining whether he has any drug in his body during the treatment period, the offender shall during that period, at such times or in such circumstances as may (subject to the provisions of the order) be determined by the supervisor or the treatment provider, provide samples of such description as may be so determined.

(6) A testing requirement shall not be included in a supervision order by virtue of sub-paragraph (5) above unless—

(a)　the offender is aged 14 or over and consents to its inclusion, and

(b)　the court has been notified by the Secretary of State that arrangements for implementing such requirements are in force in the area proposed to be specified in the order.

(7) A testing requirement shall specify for each month the minimum number of occasions on which samples are to be provided.

(8) A supervision order including a testing requirement shall provide for the results of tests carried out on any samples provided by the offender in pursuance of the requirement to a person other than the supervisor to be communicated to the supervisor."

3. In Schedule 7 to the Sentencing Act (breach, revocation and amendment of supervision orders), in paragraph 2(1), before "or 7" there is inserted ",6A".

3–2094

Section 280(1)　　　　　　　　　　　SCHEDULE 25[1]
SUMMARY OFFENCES NO LONGER PUNISHABLE WITH IMPRISONMENT

Vagrancy Act 1824 (c 83)

1. The offence under section 3 of the Vagrancy Act 1824 (idle and disorderly persons) of causing or procuring or encouraging any child or children to wander abroad, or place himself or herself in any public place, street, highway, court, or passage, to beg or gather alms.

---

1. At the time of going to press the provisions of Schedule 25 were not in force.

2. The following offences under section 4 of that Act (rogues and vagabonds)—

(a)　the offence of going about as a gatherer or collector of alms, or endeavouring to procure charitable contributions of any nature or kind, under any false or fraudulent pretence,

(b)　the offence of being found in or upon any dwelling house, warehouse, coach-house, stable, or outhouse, or in any inclosed yard, garden, or area, for any unlawful purpose, and

(c)　the offence of being apprehended as an idle and disorderly person, and violently resisting any constable, or other peace officer so apprehending him or her, and being subsequently convicted of the offence for which he or she shall have been so apprehended.

Railway Regulation Act 1842 (c 55)

3. An offence under section 17 of the Railway Regulation Act 1842 (punishment of railway employees guilty of misconduct).

London Hackney Carriages Act 1843 (c 86)

4. An offence under section 28 of the London Hackney Carriages Act 1843 (punishment for furious driving etc).

Town Police Clauses Act 1847 (c 89)

5. An offence under section 26 of the Town Police Clauses Act 1847 (unlawful release of impounded stray cattle).
6. An offence under section 28 of that Act (offences relating to obstructions and nuisances).
7. An offence under section 29 of that Act (drunken persons, etc guilty of violent or indecent behaviour).
8. An offence under section 36 of that Act (keeping places for bear-baiting, cock-fighting etc).

Ecclesiastical Courts Jurisdiction Act 1860 (c 32)

9. An offence under section 2 of the Ecclesiastical Courts Jurisdiction Act 1860 (making a disturbance in churches, chapels, churchyards, etc).

Town Gardens Protection Act 1863 (c 13)

10. An offence under section 5 of the Town Gardens Protection Act 1863 (injuring gardens).

Public Stores Act 1875 (c 25)

11. An offence under section 8 of the Public Stores Act 1875 (sweeping, etc, near dockyards, artillery ranges, etc).

North Sea Fisheries Act 1893 (c 17)

12. An offence under section 2 of the North Sea Fisheries Act 1893 (penalty for supplying, exchanging, or otherwise selling spirits).
13. An offence under section 3 of that Act (penalty for purchasing spirits by exchange or otherwise).

Seamen's and Soldiers' False Characters Act 1906 (c 5)

14. An offence under section 1 of the Seamen's and Soldiers' False Characters Act 1906 (forgery of service or discharge certificate and personation).

Aliens Restriction (Amendment) Act 1919 (c 92)

15. An offence under section 3(2) of the Aliens Restriction (Amendment) Act 1919 (promoting industrial unrest).

Children and Young Persons Act 1933 (c 12)

16. An offence under section 4 of the Children and Young Persons Act 1933 (causing or allowing persons under sixteen to be used for begging).

Protection of Animals Act 1934 (c 21)

17. An offence under section 2 of the Protection of Animals Act 1934 (offences relating to the prohibition of certain public contests, performances, and exhibitions with animals).

Public Health Act 1936 (c 49)

18. An offence under section 287 of the Public Health Act 1936 (power to enter premises).

Essential Commodities Reserves Act 1938 (c 51)

19. An offence under section 4(2) of the Essential Commodities Reserves Act 1938 (enforcement).

London Building Acts (Amendment) Act 1939 (c xcvii)

20. An offence under section 142 of the London Building Acts (Amendment) Act 1939 (power of Council and others to enter buildings etc).

Cancer Act 1939 (c 13)

21. An offence under section 4 of the Cancer Act 1939 (prohibition of certain advertisements).

Civil Defence Act 1939 (c 31)

22. An offence under section 77 of the Civil Defence Act 1939 (penalty for false statements).

Hill Farming Act 1946 (c 73)

23. An offence under section 19(2) or (3) of the Hill Farming Act 1946 (offences in relation to the control of rams).

Polish Resettlement Act 1947 (c 19)

24. An offence under paragraph 7 of the Schedule to the Polish Resettlement Act 1947 (false representation or making a false statement).

Agriculture Act 1947 (c 48)

25. An offence under section 14(7) of the Agriculture Act 1947, as remaining in force for the purposes of section 95 of that Act, (directions to secure good estate management and good husbandry).

26. An offence under section 95 of that Act (failure to comply with a direction to secure production).

Civil Defence Act 1948 (c 5)

27. An offence under section 4 of the Civil Defence Act 1948 (powers as to land).

Agricultural Wages Act 1948 (c 47)

28. An offence under section 12 of the Agricultural Wages Act 1948 (hindering investigation of complaints etc).

Wireless Telegraphy Act 1949 (c 54)

29. An offence under section 11(7) of the Wireless Telegraphy Act 1949 (enforcement of regulations as to use of apparatus), other than one within section 14(1A)(c) of that Act.

Prevention of Damage by Pests Act 1949 (c 55)

30. An offence under section 22(5) of the Prevention of Damage by Pests Act 1949 (wrongful disclosure of information).

Coast Protection Act 1949 (c 74)

31. An offence under section 25(9) of the Coast Protection Act 1949 (powers of entry and inspection).

Pet Animals Act 1951 (c 35)

32. An offence under the Pet Animals Act 1951 (offences relating to licensing of pet shops and the sale of pets), other than one under section 4 of that Act.

Cockfighting Act 1952 (c 59)

33. An offence under section 1 of the Cockfighting Act 1952 (possession of appliances for use in fighting of domestic fowl).

Agricultural Land (Removal of Surface Soil) Act 1953 (c 10)

34. An offence under the Agricultural Land (Removal of Surface Soil) Act 1953 (removal of surface soil without planning permission).

Accommodation Agencies Act 1953 (c 23)

35. An offence under section 1 of the Accommodation Agencies Act 1953 (illegal commissions and advertisements).

Army Act 1955 (3 & 4 Eliz 2 c 18)

36. An offence under section 19 of the Army Act 1955 (false answers in attestation paper).

37. An offence under section 161 of that Act (refusal to receive persons billeted, etc).

38. An offence under section 171 of that Act (offences relating to the enforcement of provisions as to requisitioning).

39. An offence under section 191 of that Act (pretending to be a deserter).

40. An offence under section 193 of that Act (obstructing members of regular forces in execution of duty).

41. An offence under section 196 of that Act (illegal dealings in documents relating to pay, pensions, mobilisation etc).

42. An offence under section 197 of that Act (unauthorised use of and dealing in decorations etc).

Air Force Act 1955 (3 & 4 Eliz 2 c 19)

43. An offence under section 19 of the Air Force Act 1955 (false answers in attestation paper).

44. An offence under section 161 of that Act (refusal to receive persons billeted, etc).

45. An offence under section 171 of that Act (offences relating to the enforcement of provisions as to requisitioning).

46. An offence under section 191 of that Act (pretending to be a deserter).

47. An offence under section 193 of that Act (obstructing members of regular air force in execution of duty).

48. An offence under section 196 of that Act (illegal dealings in documents relating to pay, pensions, mobilisation etc).

49. An offence under section 197 of that Act (unauthorised use of and dealing in decorations etc).

Naval Discipline Act 1957 (c 53)

50. An offence under section 96 of the Naval Discipline Act 1957 (false pretence of desertion or absence without leave).

51. An offence under section 99 of that Act (illegal dealings in official documents).

Agricultural Marketing Act 1958 (c 47)

52. An offence under section 45 of the Agricultural Marketing Act 1958 (failure to comply with demand for information or knowingly making any false statement in reply thereto).

Rivers (Prevention of Pollution) Act 1961 (c 50)

53. An offence under section 12(1) of the Rivers (Prevention of Pollution) Act 1961 (restriction of disclosure of information).

Betting, Gaming and Lotteries Act 1963 (c 2)

54. An offence under section 8 of the Betting, Gaming and Lotteries Act 1963 (betting in streets and public places).

Children and Young Persons Act 1963 (c 37)

55. An offence under section 40 of the Children and Young Persons Act 1963 (offences relating to persons under 16 taking part in public performances etc).

Animal Boarding Establishments Act 1963 (c 43)

56. An offence under the Animal Boarding Establishments Act 1963 (offences in connection with the licensing and inspection of boarding establishments for animals), other than an offence under section 2 of that Act.

Agriculture and Horticulture Act 1964 (c 28)

57. An offence under Part 3 of the Agriculture and Horticulture Act 1964 (offences relating to the grading and transport of fresh horticultural produce), other than an offence under section 15(1) of that Act.

Emergency Laws (Re-enactments and Repeals) Act 1964 (c 60)

58. An offence under paragraph 1(3) or 2(4) of Schedule 1 to the Emergency Laws (Re-enactments and Repeals) Act 1964 (offences relating to the production of documents).

Riding Establishments Act 1964 (c 70)

59. An offence under the Riding Establishments Act 1964 (offences relating to the keeping of riding establishments), other than an offence under section 2(4) of that Act.

Industrial and Provident Societies Act 1965 (c 12)

60. An offence under section 16 of the Industrial and Provident Societies Act 1965 (cancellation of registration of society).
61. An offence under section 48 of that Act (production of documents and provision of information for certain purposes).

Cereals Marketing Act 1965 (c 14)

62. An offence under section 17(1) of the Cereals Marketing Act 1965 (failure to comply with a requirement of a scheme).

Gas Act 1965 (c 36)

63. An offence under paragraph 9 of Schedule 6 to the Gas Act 1965 (wrongful disclosure of information).

Armed Forces Act 1966 (c 45)

64. An offence under section 8 of the Armed Forces Act 1966 (false statements on entry into Royal Navy).

Agriculture Act 1967 (c 22)

65. An offence under section 6(9) of the Agriculture Act 1967 (compulsory use of systems of classification of carcases).
66. An offence under section 14(2) of that Act (levy schemes: requirements in relation to registration, returns and records).
67. An offence under section 69 of that Act (false statements to obtain grants etc).

Sea Fisheries (Shellfish) Act 1967 (c 83)

68. An offence under section 14(2) of the Sea Fisheries (Shellfish) Act 1967 (offences relating to the deposit and importation of shellfish).

Theatres Act 1968 (c 54)

69. An offence under section 13(1) or (2) of the Theatres Act 1968 (offences relating to licensing of premises for public performances of plays).

Theft Act 1968 (c 60)

70. An offence under paragraph 2(1) of Schedule 1 to the Theft Act 1968 (taking or destroying fish).

Agriculture Act 1970 (c 40)

71. An offence under section 106(8) of the Agriculture Act 1970 (eradication of brucellosis: obstructing or impeding an officer in the exercise of powers to obtain information).

Breeding of Dogs Act 1973 (c 60)

72. An offence under the Breeding of Dogs Act 1973 (offences connected with the licensing of breeding establishments for dogs), other than under section 2 of that Act.

Slaughterhouses Act 1974 (c 3)

73. An offence under section 4(5) of the Slaughterhouses Act 1974 (knacker's yard licences and applications for such licences).

National Health Service Act 1977 (c 49)

74. An offence under paragraph 8(3) or 9(4) of Schedule 11 to the National Health Service Act 1977 (offences relating to the production of documents etc).

Magistrates' Courts Act 1980 (c 43)

75. An offence under section 84(3) of the Magistrates' Courts Act 1980 (making of false statement as to means).

Animal Health Act 1981 (c 22)

76. An offence under paragraph 6 of Schedule 1 to the Animal Health Act 1981 (offences relating to the manufacture of veterinary therapeutic substances).

Fisheries Act 1981 (c 29)

77. An offence under section 5(4) of the Fisheries Act 1981 (alteration of records or furnishing false information).

Civil Aviation Act 1982 (c 16)

78. An offence under section 82 of the Civil Aviation Act 1982 (using an aircraft for advertising, etc).

Mental Health Act 1983 (c 20)

79. An offence under section 103 of the Mental Health Act 1983 (wrongful disclosure of a report made by a Visitor).
80. An offence under section 129 of that Act (obstruction).

Building Act 1984 (c 55)

81. An offence under section 96(3) of the Building Act 1984 (wrongful disclosure of information).

Surrogacy Arrangements Act 1985 (c 49)

82. An offence under section 2 of the Surrogacy Arrangements Act 1985 (negotiating surrogacy arrangements on a commercial basis, etc).

Animals (Scientific Procedures) Act 1986 (c 14)

83. An offence under section 22(3), 23 or 25(3) of the Animals (Scientific Procedures) Act 1986 (false statements and offences in relation to powers of entry).

Motor Cycle Noise Act 1987 (c 34)

84. An offence under paragraph 1 of Schedule 1 to the Motor Cycle Noise Act 1987 (supply of exhaust systems etc not complying with prescribed requirements).

Human Organ Transplants Act 1989 (c 31)

85. An offence under section 2 of the Human Organ Transplants Act 1989 (restrictions on organ transplants).

Town and Country Planning Act 1990 (c 8)

86. An offence under paragraph 14(4) of Schedule 15 to the Town and Country Planning Act 1990 (wrongful disclosure of information).

Environmental Protection Act 1990 (c 43)

87. An offence under section 118(1)(*g*), (*h*) or (*i*) of the Environmental Protection Act 1990 (offences relating to inspection of genetically modified organisms).

Criminal Justice Act 1991 (c 53)

88. An offence under section 20A of the Criminal Justice Act 1991 (false statements as to financial circumstances).

Deer Act 1991 (c 54)

89. An offence under section 10(3) of the Deer Act 1991 (offences relating to sale and purchase etc of venison).

Water Industry Act 1991 (c 56)

90. An offence under section 206(2) of the Water Industry Act 1991 (wrongful disclosure of information).
91. An offence that falls within paragraph 5(5) of Schedule 6 to that Act (wrongful disclosure of information).

Social Security Administration Act 1992 (c 5)

92. An offence under section 105 of the Social Security Administration Act 1992 (failure of person to maintain himself or another).
93. An offence under section 182 of that Act (illegal possession of documents).

Local Government Finance Act 1992 (c 14)

94. An offence under section 27(5) of the Local Government Finance Act 1992 (false statements in relation to properties).

Trade Union and Labour Relations (Consolidation) Act 1992 (c 52)

95. An offence under section 240 of the Trade Union and Labour Relations (Consolidation) Act 1992 (breach of contract involving injury to persons or property).

Merchant Shipping Act 1995 (c 21)

96. An offence under section 57 of the Merchant Shipping Act 1995 (offences relating to merchant navy uniforms).

Reserve Forces Act 1996 (c 14)

97. An offence under section 75(5) of the Reserve Forces Act 1996 (making false statements).
98. An offence under section 82(1) of that Act (offences in connection with regulations under sections 78 and 79 of that Act).
99. An offence under section 87(1) of that Act (offences in connection with claims for payment).
100. An offence under section 99 of that Act (false pretence of illegal absence).
101. An offence under paragraph 5(1) of Schedule 1 to that Act (false answers in attestation papers).

Housing Act 1996 (c 52)

102. An offence under paragraph 23 or 24 of Schedule 1 to the Housing Act 1996 (contravening order not to part with money etc held on behalf of a social landlord).

Broadcasting Act 1996 (c 55)

103. An offence under section 144 of the Broadcasting Act 1996 (providing false information in connection with licences).

Breeding and Sale of Dogs (Welfare) Act 1999 (c 11)

104. An offence under section 8 or 9(6) of the Breeding and Sale of Dogs (Welfare) Act 1999 (offences relating to the sale of dogs and connected matters).

Transport Act 2000 (c 38)

105. An offence under section 82(2) of the Transport Act 2000 (wrongful disclosure of information).

3–2095

Section 280(2)   **SCHEDULE 26**[1]
INCREASE IN MAXIMUM TERM FOR CERTAIN SUMMARY OFFENCES

Railway Regulation Act 1840 (c 97)

1. In section 16 of the Railway Regulation Act 1840 (obstructing officers or trespassing upon railway), for "one month", there is substituted "51 weeks".

---

1. At the time of going to press the provisions of Schedule 26 were not in force.

Licensing Act 1872 (c 94)

2. In section 12 of the Licensing Act 1872 (penalty for being found drunk), for "one month" there is substituted "51 weeks".

Regulation of Railways Act 1889 (c 57)

3. In section 5 of the Regulation of Railways Act 1889 (avoiding payment of fares, etc), in subsection (3), for "three months" there is substituted "51 weeks".

Witnesses (Public Inquiries) Protection Act 1892 (c 64)

4. In section 2 of the Witnesses (Public Inquiries) Protection Act 1892 (persons obstructing or intimidating witnesses), for "three months" there is substituted "51 weeks".

Licensing Act 1902 (c 28)

5. In section 2 of the Licensing Act 1902 (penalty for being drunk while in charge of a child), in subsection (1), for "one month" there is substituted "51 weeks".

Emergency Powers Act 1920 (c 55)

6. In section 2 of the Emergency Powers Act 1920 (emergency regulations), in subsection (3), for "three months" there is substituted "51 weeks".

Judicial Proceedings (Regulation of Reports) Act 1926 (c 61)

7. In section 1 of the Judicial Proceedings (Regulation of Reports) Act 1926 (restriction on publication of reports of judicial proceedings), in subsection (2), for "four months" there is substituted "51 weeks".

Public Order Act 1936 (1 Edw 8 & 1 Geo. 6 c 6)

8. In section 7 of the Public Order Act 1936 (enforcement), in subsection (2), for "three months" there is substituted "51 weeks".

Cinematograph Films (Animals) Act 1937 (c 59)

9. In section 1 of the Cinematograph Films (Animals) Act 1937 (prohibition of films involving cruelty to animals), in subsection (3), for "three months" there is substituted "51 weeks".

House to House Collections Act 1939 (c 44)

10. In section 8 of the House to House Collections Act 1939, in subsection (2), for "three months" there is substituted "51 weeks".

Fire Services Act 1947 (c 41)

11. In section 31 of the Fire Services Act 1947 (false alarms of fire), in subsection (1), for "three months" there is substituted "51 weeks".

National Assistance Act 1948 (c 29)

12. (1) The National Assistance Act 1948 is amended as follows.
(2) In section 51 (failure to maintain), in subsection (3)(*a*) and (*b*), for "three months" there is substituted "51 weeks".
(3) In section 52 (false statements), in subsection (1), for "three months" there is substituted "51 weeks".

Docking and Nicking of Horses Act 1949 (c 70)

13. (1) The Docking and Nicking of Horses Act 1949 is amended as follows.
(2) In section 1 (prohibition of docking and nicking except in certain cases), in subsection (3), for "three months" there is substituted "51 weeks".
(3) In section 2 (restriction on landing docked horses)—
(*a*) in subsection (3), and
(*b*) in subsection (4),
for "3 months" there is substituted "51 weeks".

Protection of Animals (Amendment) Act 1954 (c 40)

14. In section 2 of the Protection of Animals (Amendment) Act 1954 (breach of disqualification order), for "three months" there is substituted "51 weeks".

Children and Young Persons (Harmful Publications) Act 1955 (c 28)

15. In section 2 of the Children and Young Persons (Harmful Publications) Act 1955 (penalty for publishing certain works etc), in subsection (1), for "four months" there is substituted "51 weeks".

Agriculture Act 1957 (c 57)

16. In section 7 of the Agriculture Act 1957 (penalties)—
(*a*) in subsection (1), for "three months" there is substituted "51 weeks", and
(*b*) in subsection (2), for "one month" there is substituted "51 weeks".

Animals (Cruel Poisons) Act 1962 (c 26)

17. In section 1 of the Animals (Cruel Poisons) Act 1962 (offences and penalties under regulations), in paragraph (*b*), for "three months" there is substituted "51 weeks".

Plant Varieties and Seeds Act 1964 (c 14)

18. In section 27 of the Plant Varieties and Seeds Act 1964 (tampering with samples), in subsection (1), for "three months" there is substituted "51 weeks".

Agriculture Act 1967 (c 22)

19. (1) The Agriculture Act 1967 is amended as follows.
(2) In section 6 (penalties), in subsection (4), for "three months" there is substituted "51 weeks".
(3) In section 21 (inquiry by Meat and Livestock Commission), in subsection (11), for "three months" there is substituted "51 weeks".

Firearms Act 1968 (c 27)

20. (1) Part 1 of Schedule 6 to the Firearms Act 1968 (prosecution and punishment of offences) is amended as follows.
(2) In the entry relating to section 3(6) of that Act (business and other transactions with firearms and ammunition), in the fourth column, for "3 months" there is substituted "51 weeks".
(3) In the entry relating to section 6(3) of that Act (power to prohibit movement of arms and ammunition), in the fourth column, for "3 months" there is substituted "51 weeks".

(4) In the entry relating to section 20(2) of that Act (trespassing with firearm), in the fourth column, for "3 months" there is substituted "51 weeks".

(5) In the entry relating to section 22(1A) of that Act (acquisition and possession of firearms by minors), in the fourth column, for "3 months" there is substituted "51 weeks".

(6) In the entry relating to section 25 of that Act (supplying firearm to person drunk or insane), in the fourth column, for "3 months" there is substituted "51 weeks".

(7) In the entry relating to section 32C(6) of that Act (variation endorsement etc of European documents), in the fourth column, for "3 months" there is substituted "51 weeks".

(8) In the entry relating to section 42A of that Act (information as to transactions under visitors' permits), in the fourth column, for "3 months" there is substituted "51 weeks".

(9) In the entry relating to section 47(2) of that Act (powers of constables to stop and search), in the fourth column, for "3 months" there is substituted "51 weeks".

(10) In the entry relating to section 49(3) of that Act (police powers in relation to arms traffic), in the fourth column, for "3 months" there is substituted "51 weeks".

Agriculture (Miscellaneous Provisions) Act 1968 (c 34)

21. In section 7 of the Agriculture (Miscellaneous Provisions) Act 1968 (punishment of offences under Part 1), in subsection (1), for "three months" there is substituted "51 weeks".

Agriculture Act 1970 (c 40)

22. (1) The Agriculture Act 1970 is amended as follows.

(2) In section 68 (duty to give statutory statement), in subsection (4), for "three months" there is substituted "51 weeks".

(3) In section 69 (marking of material prepared for sale), in subsection (4), for "three months" there is substituted "51 weeks".

(4) In section 70 (use of names or expressions with prescribed meanings), in subsection (2), for "three months" there is substituted "51 weeks".

(5) In section 71 (particulars to be given of attributes if claimed to be present), in subsection (2), for "three months" there is substituted "51 weeks".

(6) In section 73 (deleterious ingredients in feeding stuff), in subsection (4), for "three months" there is substituted "51 weeks".

(7) In section 73A (unwholesome feeding stuff), in subsection (4), for "three months" there is substituted "51 weeks".

(8) In section 74A (regulations controlling the contents of feeding stuff), in subsection (3), for "three months" there is substituted "51 weeks".

(9) In section 79 (supplementary provision relating to samples and analysis), in subsection (10), for "three months" there is substituted "51 weeks".

(10) In section 83 (exercise of powers by inspectors), in subsection (3), for "three months" there is substituted "51 weeks".

(11) In section 106 (eradication of brucellosis), in subsection (7), for "three months" there is substituted "51 weeks".

Slaughterhouses Act 1974 (c 3)

23. (1) The Slaughterhouses Act 1974 is amended as follows.

(2) In section 20 (wrongful disclosure of information), in subsection (4), for "three months" there is substituted "51 weeks".

(3) In section 21 (obstruction), in subsection (1), for "one month" there is substituted "51 weeks".

(4) In section 23 (prosecution and punishment of offences), in subsection (2)(a), for "three months" there is substituted "51 weeks".

Criminal Law Act 1977 (c 45)

24. In section 8 of the Criminal Law Act 1977 (trespassing with a weapon of offence), in subsection (3), for "three months" there is substituted "51 weeks".

Refuse Disposal (Amenity) Act 1978 (c 3)

25. In section 2 of the Refuse Disposal (Amenity) Act 1978 (penalty for unauthorised dumping), in subsection (1), for "three months" there is substituted "51 weeks".

Customs and Excise Management Act 1979 (c 2)

26. (1) The Customs and Excise Management Act 1979 is amended as follows.

(2) In section 21 (control of movement of aircraft), in subsection (6), for "3 months" there is substituted "51 weeks".

(3) In section 33 (power to inspect aircraft etc), in subsection (4), for "3 months" there is substituted "51 weeks".

(4) In section 34 (power to prevent flight of aircraft)—

(a) in subsection (2), and
(b) in subsection (3),

for "3 months" there is substituted "51 weeks".

Licensed Premises (Exclusion of Certain Persons) Act 1980 (c 32)

27. In section 2 of the Licensed Premises (Exclusion of Certain Persons) Act 1980 (penalty for non-compliance with an exclusion order), in subsection (1), for "one month" there is substituted "51 weeks".

Criminal Attempts Act 1981 (c 47)

28. In section 9 of the Criminal Attempts Act 1981 (interference with vehicles), in subsection (3), for "three months" there is substituted "51 weeks".

British Nationality Act 1981 (c 61)

29. In section 46 of the British Nationality Act 1981 (offences and proceedings), in subsection (1) for "three months" there is substituted "51 weeks".

Civil Aviation Act 1982 (c 16)

30. (1) The Civil Aviation Act 1982 is amended as follows.
(2) In section 44 (offences relating to the power to obtain rights over land), in subsection (10), for "three months" there is substituted "51 weeks".
(3) In section 75 (investigation of accidents), in subsection (5), for "three months" there is substituted "51 weeks".

Anatomy Act 1984 (c 14)

31. In section 11 of the Anatomy Act 1984 (offences), in subsection (6), for "3 months" there is substituted "51 weeks".

Public Health (Control of Disease) Act 1984 (c 22)

32. (1) The Public Health (Control of Disease) Act 1984 is amended as follows.
(2) In section 29 (letting of house after recent case of notifiable disease), in subsection (1), for "one month" there is substituted "51 weeks".
(3) In section 30 (duty on ceasing to occupy house after recent case of notifiable disease), in subsection (1), for "one month" there is substituted "51 weeks".
(4) In section 62 (powers of entry), in subsection (3), for "3 months" there is substituted "51 weeks".

County Courts Act 1984 (c 28)

33. (1) The County Courts Act 1984 is amended as follows.
(2) In section 14 (penalty for assaulting officers), in subsection (1)(*a*), for "3 months" there is substituted "51 weeks".
(3) In section 92 (penalty for rescuing goods seized), in subsection (1)(*a*), for "one month" there is substituted "51 weeks."

Animal Health and Welfare Act 1984 (c 40)

34. In section 10 of the Animal Health and Welfare Act 1984 (artificial breeding of livestock), in subsection (6), for "three months" there is substituted "51 weeks".

Police and Criminal Evidence Act 1984 (c 60)

35. In section 63C of the Police and Criminal Evidence Act 1984 (testing for presence of drugs), in subsection (1), for "three months" there is substituted "51 weeks".

Sporting Events (Control of Alcohol etc) Act 1985 (c 57)

36. In section 8 of the Sporting Events (Control of Alcohol etc) Act 1985 (penalties for offences), in paragraph (*b*), for "three months" there is substituted "51 weeks".

Public Order Act 1986 (c 64)

37. (1) The Public Order Act 1986 is amended as follows.
(2) In section 12 (imposing conditions on public processions)—

(*a*) in subsection (8), and
(*b*) in subsection (10),

for "3 months" there is substituted "51 weeks".
(3) In section 13 (prohibiting public processions)—

(*a*) in subsection (11), and
(*b*) in subsection (13),

for "3 months" there is substituted "51 weeks".
(4) In section 14 (imposing conditions on public assemblies)—

(*a*) in subsection (8), and
(*b*) in subsection (10),

for "3 months" there is substituted "51 weeks".
(5) In section 14B (offences in connection with trespassory assemblies and arrest therefor)—

(*a*) in subsection (5), and
(*b*) in subsection (7),

for "3 months" there is substituted "51 weeks".

Road Traffic Offenders Act 1988 (c 53)

38. (1) Part 1 of Schedule 2 to the Road Traffic Offenders Act 1988 (prosecution and punishment of offenders) is amended as follows.

(2) In the entry relating to section 4(2) of the Road Traffic Act 1988 (driving, or being in charge, when under the influence of drink or drugs), in column 4, for "3 months" there is substituted "51 weeks".

(3) In the entry relating to section 5(1)(b) of that Act (driving or being in charge of a motor vehicle with alcohol concentration above prescribed limit), in column 4, for "3 months" there is substituted "51 weeks".

(4) In the entry relating to section 7 of that Act (provision of specimens for analysis), in column 4, for "3 months" there is substituted "51 weeks".

(5) In the entry relating to section 7A of that Act (failing to allow specimen to be subjected to analysis), in column 4, for "3 months" there is substituted "51 weeks".

Official Secrets Act 1989 (c 6)

39. In section 10 of the Official Secrets Act 1989 (penalties), in subsection (2), for "three months" there is substituted "51 weeks".

Human Organ Transplants Act 1989 (c 31)

40. In section 1 of the Human Organ Transplants Act 1989 (prohibition of commercial dealings in human organs), in subsection (5), for "three months" there is substituted "51 weeks".

Football Spectators Act 1989 (c 37)

41. In section 2 of the Football Spectators Act 1989 (unauthorised attendance at designated football matches), in subsection (3), for "one month" there is substituted "51 weeks".

Food Safety Act 1990 (c 16)

42. In section 35 of the Food Safety Act 1990 (punishment of offences), in subsection (1), for "three months" there is substituted "51 weeks".

Deer Act 1991 (c 54)

43. In section 9 of the Deer Act 1991 (penalties for offences relating to deer), in subsection (1), for "three months" there is substituted "51 weeks".

Social Security Administration Act 1992 (c 5)

44. In section 112 of the Social Security Administration Act 1992 (false representations for obtaining benefit etc), in subsection (2), for "3 months" there is substituted "51 weeks".

Criminal Justice and Public Order Act 1994 (c 33)

45. (1) The Criminal Justice and Public Order Act 1994 is amended as follows.

(2) In section 60 (failing to stop), in subsection (8), for "one month" there is substituted "51 weeks".

(3) In section 60AA (powers to require removal of disguises), in subsection (7), for "one month" there is substituted "51 weeks".

(4) In section 61 (power to remove trespasser on land), in subsection (4), for "three months" there is substituted "51 weeks".

(5) In section 62B (failure to comply with direction under section 62A: offences), in subsection (3), for "3 months" there is substituted "51 weeks".

(6) In section 63 (powers to remove persons attending or preparing for a rave), in subsections (6) and (7B), for "three months" there is substituted "51 weeks".

(7) In section 68 (offence of aggravated trespass), in subsection (3), for "three months" there is substituted "51 weeks".

(8) In section 69 (powers to remove persons committing or participating in aggravated trespass), in subsection (3), for "three months" there is substituted "51 weeks".

London Local Authorities Act 1995 (c x)

46. In section 24 of the London Local Authorities Act 1995 (enforcement), in subsection (1), for "three months" there is substituted "51 weeks".

Police Act 1996 (c 16)

47. In section 89 of the Police Act 1996 (assaults on constables etc), in subsection (2), for "one month" there is substituted "51 weeks".

Treasure Act 1996 (c 24)

48. In section 8 of the Treasure Act 1996 (duty of finder of treasure to notify coroner), in subsection (3)(a), for "three months" there is substituted "51 weeks".

Education Act 1996 (c 56)

49. (1) The Education Act 1996 is amended as follows.

(2) In section 444 (failure to secure regular attendance at school), in subsection (8A)(b), for "three months" there is substituted "51 weeks".

(3) In section 559 (prohibition or restriction on employment of children), in subsection (4)(b), for "one month" there is substituted "51 weeks".

Government of Wales Act 1998 (c 38)

50. In section 75 of the Government of Wales Act 1998 (witnesses and documents: supplementary), in subsection (3)(b), for "three months" there is substituted "51 weeks".*

Access to Justice Act 1999 (c 22)

51. In section 21 of the Access to Justice Act 1999 (misrepresentation etc), in subsection (2)(b), for "three months" there is substituted "51 weeks".

Greater London Authority Act 1999 (c 29)

52. In section 64 of the Greater London Authority Act 1999 (failure to attend proceedings etc), in subsection (2)(b), for "three months" there is substituted "51 weeks".

Immigration and Asylum Act 1999 (c 33)

53. (1) The Immigration and Asylum Act 1999 is amended as follows.
(2) In section 105 (false representation), in subsection (2), for "three months" there is substituted "51 weeks".
(3) In section 108 (failure of sponsor to maintain), in subsection (2), for "3 months" there is substituted "51 weeks".

Financial Services and Markets Act 2000 (c 8)

54. (1) The Financial Services and Markets Act 2000 is amended as follows.
(2) In section 177 (offences), in subsection (6), for "three months" there is substituted "51 weeks".
(3) In section 352 (offences), in subsection (5), for "three months" there is substituted "51 weeks".

Terrorism Act 2000 (c 11)

55. (1) The Terrorism Act 2000 is amended as follows.
(2) In section 36 (police powers), in subsection (4)(a), for "three months" there is substituted "51 weeks".
(3) In section 51 (offences in relation to parking), in subsection (6)(a), for "three months" there is substituted "51 weeks".
(4) In Schedule 5 (terrorist investigations: information)—

(a) in paragraph 3(8)(a), and
(b) in paragraph 15(5)(a),

for "three months" there is substituted "51 weeks".
(5) In Schedule 7 (ports and border controls), in paragraph 18(2)(a), for "three months" there is substituted "51 weeks".

Criminal Justice and Police Act 2001 (c 16)

56. (1) The Criminal Justice and Police Act 2001 is amended as follows.
(2) In section 25 (enforcement of closure orders)—

(a) in subsection (3)(a), for "one month" there is substituted "51 weeks", and
(b) in subsections (4) and (5), for "three months" there is substituted "51 weeks".

(3) In section 42 (prevention of intimidation), in subsection (7), for "three months" there is substituted "51 weeks".

Police Reform Act 2002 (c 30)

57. In section 46 of the Police Reform Act 2002 (offences against designated and accredited persons etc), in subsection (2), for "one month" there is substituted "51 weeks".

Nationality, Immigration and Asylum Act 2002 (c 41)

58. In section 137 of the Nationality, Immigration and Asylum Act 2002 (offences relating to the disclosure of information), in subsection (2)(a), for "three months" there is substituted "51 weeks".

Anti-social Behaviour Act 2003 (c 38)

59. In section 40 of the Anti-social Behaviour Act 2003 (closure of noisy premises), in subsection (5)(a), for "three months" there is substituted "51 weeks".

---

*Repealed by the Government of Wales Act 2006, s 163, Sch 12. This repeal comes into force immediately after the ordinary election (under the Government of Wales Act 1998, s 3) held in 2007.

3–2096

Section 283   SCHEDULE 27[1]
ENABLING POWERS: ALTERATION OF MAXIMUM PENALTIES ETC
(*Amended by the Legislative and Regulatory Reform Act 2006, Schedule.*)

Plant Health Act 1967 (c 8)

1. (1) Section 3 of the Plant Health Act 1967 (control of spread of pests in Great Britain) is amended as follows.
(2) In subsection (4A), for "three months" there is substituted "the prescribed term".
(3) After that subsection there is inserted—

"(4B) In subsection (4A) above, "the prescribed term" means—

(a) in relation to England and Wales, 51 weeks;
(b) in relation to Scotland, three months."

---

1. At the time of going to press the provisions of Schedule 27 were not in force.

Agriculture Act 1967 (c 22)

2. (1) Section 9 of the Agriculture Act 1967 (powers to meet future developments in livestock and livestock products industries) is amended as follows.

(2) In subsection (10), for "three months" there is substituted "the prescribed term".

(3) After that subsection there is inserted—

"(10A) In subsection (10), "the prescribed term" means—

   (*a*) in relation to England and Wales, 51 weeks;
   (*b*) in relation to Scotland, three months."

European Communities Act 1972 (c 68)

3. (1) Paragraph 1 of Schedule 2 to the European Communities Act 1972 (provisions as to powers conferred by section 2(2)) is amended as follows.

(2) In sub-paragraph (1)(*d*), for "three months" there is substituted "the prescribed term".

(3) After sub-paragraph (2) there is inserted—

"(3) In sub-paragraph (1)(*d*), "the prescribed term" means—

   (*a*) in relation to England and Wales, where the offence is a summary offence, 51 weeks;
   (*b*) in relation to England and Wales, where the offence is triable either way, twelve months;
   (*c*) in relation to Scotland and Northern Ireland, three months."

Slaughterhouses Act 1974 (c 3)

4. In section 38(5) of the Slaughterhouses Act 1974 (maximum penalties to be prescribed by regulations), the words "or imprisonment for a term of three months or both" are omitted.

Anatomy Act 1984 (c 14)

5. (1) Section 11 of the Anatomy Act 1984 (offences) is amended as follows.

(2) In subsection (7), for "3 months" there is substituted "the prescribed term".

(3) After that subsection there is inserted—

"(7A) In subsection (7), "the prescribed term" means—

   (*a*) in relation to England and Wales, 51 weeks;
   (*b*) in relation to Scotland, 3 months."

Environmental Protection Act 1990 (c 43)

6. (1) Section 141 of the Environmental Protection Act 1990 (power to prohibit or restrict the importation or exportation of waste) is amended as follows.

(2) In paragraph (*g*) of subsection (5), for "six months" there is substituted "the prescribed term".

(3) After that subsection there is inserted—

"(5A) In subsection (5)(*g*), "the prescribed term" means—

   (*a*) in relation to England and Wales, where the offence is a summary offence, 51 weeks;
   (*b*) in relation to England and Wales, where the offence is triable either way, twelve months;
   (*c*) in relation to Scotland and Northern Ireland, six months."

Scotland Act 1998 (c 46)

7. (1) Section 113 of the Scotland Act 1998 (subordinate legislation: scope of powers) is amended as follows.

(2) In paragraph (*a*) of subsection (10), for "three months" there is substituted "the prescribed term".

(3) After that subsection there is inserted—

"(10A) In subsection (10)(*a*), "the prescribed term" means—

   (*a*) in relation to England and Wales, where the offence is a summary offence, 51 weeks;
   (*b*) in relation to England and Wales, where the offence is triable either way, twelve months;
   (*c*) in relation to Scotland and Northern Ireland, three months."

8. *Repealed.*

3–2097

Section 300   SCHEDULE 31[1]
DEFAULT ORDERS: MODIFICATION OF PROVISIONS RELATING TO COMMUNITY ORDERS
General

1. Any reference to the offender is, in relation to a default order, to be read as a reference to the person in default.

---

1. At the time of going to press only para 5 of Schedule 31 was in force.

Unpaid work requirement

2. (1) In its application to a default order, section 199 (unpaid work requirement) is modified as follows.

(2) In subsection (2), for paragraphs (*a*) and (*b*) there is substituted—

"(*a*) not less than 20 hours, and
(*b*) in the case of an amount in default which is specified in the first column of the following Table, not more than the number of hours set out opposite that amount in the second column.

TABLE

Amount	Number of Hours
An amount not exceeding £200	40 hours
An amount exceeding £200 but not exceeding £500	60 hours
An amount exceeding £500	100 hours"

(3) Subsection (5) is omitted.

Curfew requirement

3. (1) In its application to a default order, section 204 (curfew requirement) is modified as follows.

(2) After subsection (2) there is inserted—

"(2A) In the case of an amount in default which is specified in the first column of the following Table, the number of days on which the person in default is subject to the curfew requirement must not exceed the number of days set out opposite that amount in the second column.

TABLE

Amount	Number of days
An amount not exceeding £200	20 days
An amount exceeding £200 but not exceeding £500	30 days
An amount exceeding £500 but not exceeding £1,000	60 days
An amount exceeding £1,000 but not exceeding £2,500	90 days
An amount exceeding £2,500	180 days"

Enforcement, revocation and amendment of default order

4. (1) In its application to a default order, Schedule 8 (breach, revocation or amendment of community orders) is modified as follows.

(2) Any reference to the offence in respect of which the community order was made is to be taken to be a reference to the default in respect of which the default order was made.

(3) Any power of the court to revoke the community order and deal with the offender for the offence is to be taken to be a power to revoke the default order and deal with him in any way in which the court which made the default order could deal with him for his default in paying the sum in question.

(4) In paragraph 4 the reference to the Crown Court is to be taken as a reference to a magistrates' court.

(5) The following provisions are omitted—

(a) paragraph 9(1)(c), (5) and (8),
(b) paragraph 12,
(c) paragraph 13(5),
(d) paragraph 15,
(e) paragraph 17(5),
(f) paragraph 21(4), and
(g) paragraph 23(2)(b).

Power to alter amount of money or number of hours or days

5. The Secretary of State may by order amend paragraph 2 or 3 by substituting for any reference to an amount of money or a number of hours or days there specified a reference to such other amount or number as may be specified in the order.

Transfer of default orders to Scotland or Northern Ireland

6. In its application to a default order, Schedule 9 (transfer of community orders to Scotland or Northern Ireland) is modified as follows.

7. After paragraph 8 there is inserted—

"**8A.** Nothing in paragraph 8 affects the application of section 300(7) to a default order made or amended in accordance with paragraph 1 or 3."

8. In paragraph 10, after paragraph (b) there is inserted—

"(bb) any power to impose a fine on the offender."

3–2097A

Section 304　　　　　　　　SCHEDULE 32[1]
　　　　　　AMENDMENTS RELATING TO SENTENCING

PART 1
GENERAL

Piracy Act 1837 (c 88)

1. Section 3 of the Piracy Act 1837 (punishment for offence under certain repealed Acts relating to piracy) shall cease to have effect.

1. A. Paras 1–10, 13–16, 18, 20–26, 30–32, 34–41, 44–47, 54–56, 59–61, 64, 65, 67, 68(1), (3), (4), 69–82, 84(4), 85–89, 91–98, 100, 101, 102(1), (2)(*a*), (4), 103–108, 109(3)(*a*), 110–121, 123(1), (2), (4), (5) (in part), (6)–(8), 124, 126–139, 141–144 came into effect on 4 April 2005: see the Criminal Justice Act 2003 (Commencement No 8 and Transitional and Saving Provisions) Order 2005, SI 2005/950, art 2(1), Sch 1, para 42; for transitional provisions see Sch 2, paras 5, 6(*a*), 9, 12, 13(*b*), 14, 18, 19(*b*), 25(*b*), 26–29, 31, 32 thereof.

B. Paras 11, 12(1)–(3), (6), 29, 57, 58 came into effect on 26 January 2004 for the purposes of the passing of a sentence of imprisonment to which an intermittent custody order relates and the release on licence of a person serving such a sentence): 26 January 2004: see the Criminal Justice Act 2003 (Commencement No 1) Order 2003, SI 2003/3282, art 2, Schedule.

C. Paras 12, 43(1), (2): Appointment (for remaining purposes) came into effect on 4 April 2005: see SI 2005/950, supra, art 2(1), Sch 1, paras 42(1), (7), (19); for transitional provisions see Sch 2, para 26 thereof.

D. Paras 48–50 came into effect on 22 January 2004: see Criminal Justice Act 2003 (Commencement No 2 and Saving Provisions) Order 2004, SI 2004/81, art 3(1), (2)(*d*).

Paras 52, 62, 90, 109(1): Appointment (for certain purposes) came into force on 4 April 2005: see SI 2005/950, supra, art 2(1), Sch 1, paras 42(1), (22), (25), (34).

E. Paras 99, 122, 123(3), (5) (remainder), 125 will come into force on 4 April 2007: see SI 2005/950, supra, art 4; for transitional provisions see Sch 2, paras 5, 11, thereof

Children and Young Persons Act 1933 (c 12)

2. (1) Section 49 of the Children and Young Persons Act 1933 (restrictions on reports of proceedings in which young persons are concerned) is amended as follows.

(2) In subsection (4A)(*d*), for "section 62(3) of the Powers of Criminal Courts (Sentencing) Act 2000" there is substituted "section 222(1)(*d*) or (*e*) of the Criminal Justice Act 2003".

(3) In subsection (11)—

(*a*) in the definition of "sexual offence", for "has the same meaning as in the Powers of Criminal Courts (Sentencing) Act 2000" there is substituted "means an offence listed in Part 2 of Schedule 15 to the Criminal Justice Act 2003", and

(*b*) in the definition of "violent offence", for "has the same meaning as in the Powers of Criminal Courts (Sentencing) Act 2000" there is substituted "means an offence listed in Part 1 of Schedule 15 to the Criminal Justice Act 2003".

Prison Act 1952 (c 52)

3. In section 53 of the Prison Act 1952 (interpretation), for "section 62 of the Powers of Criminal Courts (Sentencing) Act 2000" there is substituted "section 221 of the Criminal Justice Act 2003".

Criminal Justice Act 1967 (c 80)

4. The Criminal Justice Act 1967 is amended as follows.

5. In section 32 (amendments of Costs in Criminal Cases Act 1952), in subsection (3)(*a*), for "make an order under paragraph 5 of Schedule 2 to the Powers of Criminal Courts (Sentencing) Act 2000 (probation orders requiring treatment for mental condition) or" there is substituted "include in a community order (within the meaning of Part 12 of the Criminal Justice Act 2003) a mental health requirement under section 207 of that Act or make an order under".

6. In section 104 (general provisions as to interpretation)_

(*a*) in subsection (1), the definition of "suspended sentence" is omitted, and

(*b*) subsection (2) is omitted.

Criminal Appeal Act 1968 (c 19)

7. The Criminal Appeal Act 1968 is amended as follows.

8. (1) Section 10 (appeal against sentence in cases dealt with by Crown Court otherwise than on conviction on indictment) is amended as follows.

(2) In subsection (2)—

(*a*) in paragraph (*b*), for "or a community order within the meaning of the Powers of Criminal Courts (Sentencing) Act 2000" there is substituted "a youth community order within the meaning of the Powers of Criminal Courts (Sentencing) Act 2000 or a community order within the meaning of Part 12 of the Criminal Justice Act 2003", and

(*b*) paragraph (*c*) and the word "or" immediately preceding it are omitted.

9. In section 11 (supplementary provisions as to appeal against sentence), subsection (4) is omitted.

10. In Schedule 2 (procedural and other provisions applicable on order for retrial), in paragraph 2(4), for the words from the beginning to "apply" there is substituted "Section 240 of the Criminal Justice Act 2003 (crediting of periods of remand in custody: terms of imprisonment and detention) shall apply".

Firearms Act 1968 (c 27)

11. The Firearms Act 1968 is amended as follows.

12. (1) Section 21 (possession of firearms by persons previously convicted of crime) is amended as follows.

(2) In subsection (2A), after paragraph (*c*) there is inserted—

"(*d*) in the case of a person who has been subject to a sentence of imprisonment to which an intermittent custody order under section 183(1)(*b*) of the Criminal Justice Act 2003 relates, the date of his final release."

(3) After subsection (2A) there is inserted—

"(2B) A person who is serving a sentence of imprisonment to which an intermittent custody order under section 183 of the Criminal Justice Act 2003 relates shall not during any licence period specified for the purposes of subsection (1)(*b*)(i) of that section have a firearm or ammunition in his possession.".

(4) In subsection (3)(*b*), for "probation order" there is substituted "community order".

(5) After subsection (3) there is inserted—

"(3ZA) In subsection (3)(*b*) above, "community order" means—

   (*a*) a community order within the meaning of Part 12 of the Criminal Justice Act 2003 made in England and Wales, or

   (*b*) a probation order made in Scotland."

(6) In subsection (6), after " (2)" there is inserted ", (2B)".

13. (1) Section 52 (forfeiture and disposal of firearms; cancellation of certificate by convicting court) is amended as follows.

(2) In subsection (1)(*c*), for "probation order" there is substituted "community order".

(3) After subsection (1) there is inserted—

"(1A) In subsection (1)(*c*) "community order" means—

   (*a*) a community order within the meaning of Part 12 of the Criminal Justice Act 2003 made in England and Wales, or

   (*b*) a probation order made in Scotland."

Social Work (Scotland) Act 1968 (c 49)

14. In section 94 of the Social Work (Scotland) Act 1968 (interpretation), in the definition of "probation order" in subsection (1), for "community rehabilitation order" there is substituted "community order within the meaning of Part 12 of the Criminal Justice Act 2003".

Children and Young Persons Act 1969 (c 54)

15. In section 23 of the Children and Young Persons Act 1969 (remands and committals to local authority accommodation), for the definition of "sexual offence" and "violent offence" in subsection (12) there is substituted—

""sexual offence" means an offence specified in Part 2 of Schedule 15 to the Criminal Justice Act 2003; "violent offence" means murder or an offence specified in Part 1 of Schedule 15 to the Criminal Justice Act 2003;".

Immigration Act 1971 (c 77)

16. In section 7 of the Immigration Act 1971 (exemption from deportation for certain existing residents), in subsection (4), for "section 67 of the Criminal Justice Act 1967" there is substituted "section 240 of the Criminal Justice Act 2003".

Thames Barrier and Flood Prevention Act 1972 (c xiv)

17. In section 56 of the Thames Barrier and Flood Prevention Act 1972 (orders for carrying out certain defence works), in subsection (3)(*a*)(ii), for "six months" there is substituted "12 months".

Rehabilitation of Offenders Act 1974 (c 53)

18. (1) Section 5 of the Rehabilitation of Offenders Act 1974 (rehabilitation periods for particular offences) is amended as follows.

(2) In subsection (1)—

   (*a*) at the end of paragraph (*e*), there is inserted "and", and

   (*b*) after that paragraph, there is inserted the following paragraph—

      "(*f*) a sentence of imprisonment for public protection under section 225 of the Criminal Justice Act 2003, a sentence of detention for public protection under section 226 of that Act or an extended sentence under section 227 or 228 of that Act"

(3) In subsection (4A), after the words "probation order" there is inserted "or a community order under section 177 of the Criminal Justice Act 2003".

Armed Forces Act 1976 (c 52)

19. (1) Section 8 of the Armed Forces Act 1976 (powers of Standing Civilian Courts in relation to civilians) is amended as follows.

(2) In subsection (1)(*a*), for "six months" there is substituted "twelve months".

(3) In subsection (2), for "12 months" there is substituted "65 weeks".

Bail Act 1976 (c 63)

20. The Bail Act 1976 is amended as follows.

21. (1) Section 2 (other definitions) is amended as follows.

(2) In subsection (1)(*d*)—

   (*a*) the words "placing the offender on probation or" are omitted, and

   (*b*) for "him" there is substituted "the offender".

(3) In subsection (2), in the definition of "probation hostel", for the words from "by" onwards there is substituted "by a community order under section 177 of the Criminal Justice Act 2003".

22. In section 4 (general right to bail of accused persons and others), in subsection (3), for the words from "to be dealt with" onwards there is substituted

"or the Crown Court to be dealt with under—

   (*a*) Part 2 of Schedule 3 to the Powers of Criminal Courts (Sentencing) Act 2000 (breach of certain youth community orders), or (*b*) Part 2 of Schedule 8 to the Criminal Justice Act 2003 (breach of requirement of community order)."

23. In Part 3 of Schedule 1 (interpretation), in the definition of "default" in paragraph 4, for the words from "Part II" onwards there is substituted "Part 2 of Schedule 8 to the Criminal Justice Act 2003 (breach of requirement of order)".

Criminal Law Act 1977 (c 45)

24. In section 3 of the Criminal Law Act 1977 (penalties for conspiracy), in subsection (1), for "section 127 of the Powers of Criminal Courts (Sentencing) Act 2000" there is substituted "section 163 of the Criminal Justice Act 2003".

Magistrates' Courts Act 1980 (c 43)

25. The Magistrates' Courts Act 1980 is amended as follows.

26. In section 11 (non appearance of accused), in subsection (3), for "section 119 of the Powers of Criminal Courts (Sentencing) Act 2000" there is substituted "paragraph 8(2)(*a*) or (*b*) of Schedule 12 to the Criminal Justice Act 2003".

27. In section 33 (maximum penalties on summary conviction in pursuance of section 22), in subsection (1)(*a*), for "3 months" there is substituted "51 weeks".

28. In section 85 (power to remit fine), in subsection (2A), for "section 35(2)(*a*) or (*b*) of the Crime (Sentences) Act 1997" there is substituted "section 300(2) of the Criminal Justice Act 2003".

29. In section 131 (remand of accused already in custody), after subsection (2) there is inserted—

"(2A) Where the accused person is serving a sentence of imprisonment to which an intermittent custody order under section 183 of the Criminal Justice Act 2003 relates, the reference in subsection (2) to the expected date of his release is to be read as a reference to the expected date of his next release on licence.".

30. In section 133 (consecutive terms of imprisonment), in subsection (1), for "Subject to section 84 of the Powers of Criminal Courts (Sentencing) Act 2000," there is substituted "Subject to section 265 of the Criminal Justice Act 2003,".

Law Reform (Miscellaneous Provisions) (Scotland) Act 1980 (c 55)

31. In Schedule 1 to the Law Reform (Miscellaneous Provisions) (Scotland) Act 1980 (ineligibility for and disqualification and excusal from jury service), in Part 2, in paragraph (*bb*), for sub-paragraph (v) there is substituted—

"(v) a community order within the meaning of section 177 of the Criminal Justice Act 2003;
(va) a youth community order as defined by section 33 of the Powers of Criminal Courts (Sentencing) Act 2000;".

Public Passenger Vehicles Act 1981 (c 14)

32. (1) In Schedule 3 to the Public Passenger Vehicles Act 1981 (supplementary provisions as to qualifications for PSV operators licence), paragraph 1 is amended as follows.

(2) In sub-paragraph (4)(*a*), for "a community service order for more than sixty hours" there is substituted "a community order requiring the offender to perform unpaid work for more than sixty hours".

(3) In sub-paragraph (6), for the words from " "a community" onwards there is substituted ""a community order" means an order under section 177 of the Criminal Justice Act 2003, a community punishment order made before the commencement of that section or a community service order under the Community Service by Offenders (Scotland) Act 1978".

Criminal Attempts Act 1981 (c 47)

33. In section 4 of the Criminal Attempts Act 1981 (trials and penalties), in subsection (5)(*b*), for sub-paragraph (ii) there is substituted—

"(ii) in section 154(1) and (2) (general limit on magistrates' court's powers to impose imprisonment) of the Criminal Justice Act 2003.".

Criminal Justice Act 1982 (c 48)

34. The Criminal Justice Act 1982 is amended as follows.

35. In section 32 (early release of prisoners), in subsection (1)(*a*), after "life" there is inserted ", imprisonment for public protection under section 225 of the Criminal Justice Act 2003 or an extended sentence under section 227 of that Act".

36. (1) Part 3 of Schedule 13 (reciprocal arrangements (Northern Ireland): persons residing in England and Wales or Scotland) is amended as follows.

(2) In paragraph 7—

(*a*) in sub-paragraph (2)(*b*), for "such orders" there is substituted "an unpaid work requirement of a community order (within the meaning of Part 12 of the Criminal Justice Act 2003)", and

(*b*) in sub-paragraph (3)(*b*), for the words from "community service orders" onwards there is substituted "community orders within the meaning of Part 12 of the Criminal Justice Act 2003 conferred on responsible officers by that Part of that Act.".

(3) For paragraph 9(3) there is substituted—

"(3) Subject to the following provisions of this paragraph—

(*a*) a community service order made or amended in the circumstances specified in paragraph 7 above shall be treated as if it were a community order made in England and Wales under section 177 of the Criminal Justice Act 2003 and the provisions of Part 12 of that Act (so far as relating to such orders) shall apply accordingly; and

(b) a community service order made or amended in the circumstances specified in paragraph 8 above shall be treated as if it were a community service order made in Scotland and the legislation relating to community service orders in Scotland shall apply accordingly."

(4) In paragraph 9(4)(a), after "community service orders" there is inserted "or, as the case may be, community orders (within the meaning of Part 12 of the Criminal Justice Act 2003)".

(5) In paragraph 9(5), after "a community service order" there is inserted "or, as the case may be, a community order (within the meaning of Part 12 of the Criminal Justice Act 2003)".

(6) In paragraph 9(6)—

(a) after "community service orders", where first occurring, there is inserted "or, as the case may be, community orders (within the meaning of Part 12 of the Criminal Justice Act 2003)", and

(b) in paragraph (b)(i), for "the Powers of Criminal Courts (Sentencing) Act 2000" there is substituted "Part 12 of the Criminal Justice Act 2003".

Mental Health Act 1983 (c 20)

37. The Mental Health Act 1983 is amended as follows.

38. In section 37 (powers of courts to order hospital admission or guardianship)—

(a) in subsection (1), the words "or falls to be imposed under section 109(2) of the Powers of Criminal Courts (Sentencing) Act 2000" are omitted,

(b) for subsections (1A) and (1B) there is substituted—

"(1A) In the case of an offence the sentence for which would otherwise fall to be imposed—

(a) under section 51A(2) of the Firearms Act 1968,

(b) under section 110(2) or 111(2) of the Powers of Criminal Courts (Sentencing) Act 2000, or

(c) under any of sections 225 to 228 of the Criminal Justice Act 2003,

nothing in those provisions shall prevent a court from making an order under subsection (1) above for the admission of the offender to a hospital.

(1B) References in subsection (1A) above to a sentence falling to be imposed under any of the provisions mentioned in that subsection are to be read in accordance with section 305(4) of the Criminal Justice Act 2003."

(c) in subsection (8), for "probation order" there is substituted "community order (within the meaning of Part 12 of the Criminal Justice Act 2003)".

39. In section 45A (powers of higher courts to direct hospital admission), in subsection (1)(b), the words from "except" to "1997" are omitted.

Repatriation of Prisoners Act 1984 (c 47)

40. The Repatriation of Prisoners Act 1984 is amended as follows.

41. In section 2 (transfer out of the United Kingdom), in subsection (4)(b), for sub-paragraph (i) there is substituted—

"(i) released on licence under section 28(5) of the Crime (Sentences) Act 1997 or under section 244 or 246 of the Criminal Justice Act 2003; or".

42. In section 3 (transfer into the United Kingdom), subsection (9) is omitted.

43. (1) The Schedule (operation of certain enactments in relation to the prisoner) is amended as follows in relation to prisoners repatriated to England and Wales.

(2) In paragraph 2, for sub-paragraphs (1A) and (2) there is substituted—

"(2) If the warrant specifies a period to be taken into account for the purposes of this paragraph, the amount of time the prisoner has served shall, so far only as the question whether he has served a particular part of a life sentence is concerned, be deemed to be increased by that period.

(3) Where the prisoner's sentence is for a term of less than twelve months, Chapter 6 of Part 12 of the Criminal Justice Act 2003 shall apply as if the sentence were for a term of twelve months or more.

(4) In this paragraph—

"the enactments relating to release on licence" means section 28(5) and (7) of the Crime (Sentences) Act 1997 and Chapter 6 of Part 12 of the Criminal Justice Act 2003;

"sentence", means the provision included in the warrant which is equivalent to sentence.".

(3) Paragraph 3 is omitted.

Police and Criminal Evidence Act 1984 (c 60)

44. In section 38 of the Police and Criminal Evidence Act 1984 (duties of custody officer after charge), for the definitions of "sexual offence" and "violent offence" in subsection (6A) there is substituted—

""sexual offence" means an offence specified in Part 2 of Schedule 15 to the Criminal Justice Act 2003; "violent offence" means murder or an offence specified in Part 1 of that Schedule;".

Criminal Justice Act 1988 (c 33)

45. The Criminal Justice Act 1988 is amended as follows.

46. In section 36 (reviews of sentencing), in subsection (2), for the words from "erred in law" onwards there is substituted—

"(a) erred in law as to his powers of sentencing; or

(b) failed to impose a sentence required by—

(i) section 51A(2) of the Firearms Act 1968;

(ii) section 110(2) or 111(2) of the Powers of Criminal Courts (Sentencing) Act 2000; or

(iii) any of sections 225 to 228 of the Criminal Justice Act 2003."

47. In section 50 (suspended and partly suspended sentences on certain civilians in courts-martial and Standing

Civilian Courts), in subsection (3)(*b*)(i), for "Powers of Criminal Courts (Sentencing) Act 2000" there is substituted "Criminal Justice Act 2003".

Firearms (Amendment) Act 1988 (c 45)

48. The Firearms (Amendment) Act 1988 is amended as follows.
49. In section 1 (prohibited weapons and ammunition), in subsection (4A) after paragraph (*b*) there is inserted—

> "(*bb*)may amend subsection (1A)(*a*) of section 91 of the Powers of Criminal Courts (Sentencing) Act 2000 (offenders under 18 convicted of certain serious offences: power to detain for specified period) so as to include a reference to any provision added by the order to section 5(1) of the principal Act,
> (*bc*) may amend section 50(5A)(*a*), 68(4A)(*a*) or 170(4A)(*a*) of the Customs and Excise Management Act 1979 (offences relating to improper importation or exportation) so as to include a reference to anything added by the order to section 5(1) of the principal Act,".

50. In section 27(4) (which relates to Northern Ireland), after "Except for" there is inserted "section 1, so far as enabling provision to be made amending the Customs and Excise Management Act 1979, and".

Road Traffic Act 1988 (c 52)

51. In section 164 of the Road Traffic Act 1988 (power of constables to require production of driving licence and in certain cases statement of date of birth), in subsection (5), for "section 40 of the Crime (Sentences) Act 1997" there is substituted "section 301 of the Criminal Justice Act 2003".

Road Traffic Offenders Act 1988 (c 53)

52. The Road Traffic Offenders Act 1988 is amended as follows.
53. In section 27 (production of licence), in subsection (3), for "section 40 of the Crime (Sentences) Act 1997" there is substituted "section 301 of the Criminal Justice Act 2003".
54. In section 46 (combination of disqualification and endorsement with probation orders and orders for discharge), in subsection (1), paragraph (*a*) and the word "or" following it shall cease to have effect.

Football Spectators Act 1989 (c 37)

55. The Football Spectators Act 1989 is amended as follows.
56. In section 7 (disqualification for membership of scheme), subsection (9) is omitted.
57. In section 14E (banning orders: general), after subsection (6) there is inserted—

> "(7) A person serving a sentence of imprisonment to which an intermittent custody order under section 183 of the Criminal Justice Act 2003 relates is to be treated for the purposes of this section as having been detained in legal custody until his final release; and accordingly any reference in this section to release is, in relation to a person serving such a sentence, a reference to his final release."

58. In section 18 (information), after subsection (4) there is inserted—

> "(5) In relation to a person serving a sentence of imprisonment to which an intermittent custody order under section 183 of the Criminal Justice Act 2003 relates, any reference in this section to his detention or to his release shall be construed in accordance with section 14E(7)."

Children Act 1989 (c 41)

59. The Children Act 1989 is amended as follows.
60. (1) Section 68 (persons disqualified from being foster parents) is amended as follows.
(2) In subsection (2)(*d*), the words "a probation order has been made in respect of him or he has been" are omitted.
(3) After subsection (2) there is inserted—

> "(2A) A conviction in respect of which a probation order was made before 1st October 1992 (which would not otherwise be treated as a conviction) is to be treated as a conviction for the purposes of subsection (2)(*d*)."

61. (1) In Schedule 9A (child minding and day care for young children), paragraph 4 is amended as follows.
(2) In sub-paragraph (2)(*g*), the words "placed on probation or" are omitted.
(3) At the end there is inserted—

> "(7) A conviction in respect of which a probation order was made before 1st October 1992 (which would not otherwise be treated as a conviction) is to be treated as a conviction for the purposes of this paragraph.".

Criminal Justice Act 1991 (c 53)

62. The Criminal Justice Act 1991 is amended as follows.
63. Section 65 (supervision of young offenders after release) is omitted.
64. (1) Schedule 3 (reciprocal enforcement of certain orders) is amended as follows.
(2) In paragraph 10(3)(*d*), for the words from "paragraph 3 of Schedule 2" onwards there is substituted "section 201 of the Criminal Justice Act 2003".
(3) In paragraph 11(2)—

(*a*) in paragraph (*a*)—

(i) for "probation order" there is substituted "community order", and
(ii) after "England and Wales" there is inserted "under section 177 of the Criminal Justice Act 2003", and

(*b*) for paragraph (*b*) there is substituted—

> "(*b*) the provisions of Part 12 of that Act (so far as relating to such orders) shall apply accordingly.".

(4) In paragraph 11(3), for paragraphs (*a*) and (*b*) there is substituted—

> "(*a*) the requirements of Part 12 of the Criminal Justice Act 2003 relating to community orders (within the meaning of that Part);

(*b*) the powers of the home court under Schedule 8 to that Act, as modified by this paragraph; and".

(5) In paragraph 11(4), for the words from "probation order made by a court" onwards there is substituted "community order made by a court in England and Wales under section 177 of the Criminal Justice Act 2003, except a power conferred by paragraph 9(1)(*b*) or (*c*) or 13(2) of Schedule 8 to that Act".

(6) In paragraph 11(5), for "the Powers of Criminal Courts (Sentencing) Act 2000" there is substituted "Part 12 of the Criminal Justice Act 2003".

Aggravated Vehicle-Taking Act 1992 (c 11)

65. In section 1 of the Aggravated Vehicle-Taking Act 1992 (new offence of aggravated vehicle taking), in subsection (2)(*a*), for "section 127 of the Powers of Criminal Courts (Sentencing) Act 2000" there is substituted "section 163 of the Criminal Justice Act 2003".

Prisoners and Criminal Proceedings (Scotland) Act 1993 (c 9)

66. In section 10 of the Prisoners and Criminal Proceedings (Scotland) Act 1993 (life prisoners transferred to Scotland)—

(*a*) in subsection (1)—

    (i) in paragraph (*a*), sub-paragraph (i), and the succeeding "or", are omitted, and

    (ii) after paragraph (*a*)(ii) there is inserted

    "or

    (iii) subsections (5) to (8) of section 28 (early release of life prisoners to whom that section applies) of the Crime (Sentences) Act 1997 (c 43) (in this section, the "1997 Act") apply by virtue of an order made under section 28(2)(*b*) of that Act (while that provision was in force) or an order made under section 269(2) of, or paragraph 3(1)(*a*) of Schedule 22 to, the Criminal Justice Act 2003;", and

    (iii) for "28(2)(*b*) or 82A(2) or paragraph" there is substituted "82A(2), 28(2)(*b*) or 269(2) or paragraph 3(1)(*a*) or";

(*b*) after subsection (1) there is inserted—

"(1AA) This Part of this Act, except section 2(9), applies also to a transferred life prisoner—

(*a*) who is transferred from England and Wales on or after the date on which section 269 of the Criminal Justice Act 2003 comes into force,

(*b*) in relation to whom paragraph 3 of Schedule 22 to that Act applies by virtue of paragraph 2(*a*) of that Schedule, but

(*c*) in respect of whom, under the paragraph so applying, no order has been made,

as if the prisoner were a life prisoner within the meaning of section 2 of this Act and the punishment part of his sentence within the meaning of that section were the notified minimum term defined by paragraph 3(4) of that Schedule."; and

(*c*) in subsection (5)(*b*)—

    (i) for "the Crime (Sentences) Act 1997" there is substituted "the 1997 Act", and

    (ii) after the words "Powers of Criminal Courts (Sentencing) Act 2000 (c 6)" there is inserted "section 269(2) of, or paragraph 3(1)(*a*) of Schedule 22 to, the Criminal Justice Act 2003,".

Criminal Justice and Public Order Act 1994 (c 33)

67. In section 25 of the Criminal Justice and Public Order Act 1994 (no bail for defendants charged with or convicted of homicide or rape after previous conviction of such offences), in paragraph (*c*) of the definition of "conviction" in subsection (5)—

(*a*) the words "placing the offender on probation or" are omitted, and

(*b*) for "him" there is substituted "the offender".

Goods Vehicles (Licensing of Operators) Act 1995 (c 23)

68. (1) In Schedule 3 to the Goods Vehicles (Licensing of Operators) Act 1995 (qualifications for standard licence), paragraph 3 is amended as follows.

(2) In sub-paragraph (2)(*a*), for "exceeding three months" there is substituted "of 12 months or more or, before the commencement of section 181 of the Criminal Justice Act 2003, a term exceeding 3 months".

(3) In sub-paragraph (2)(*c*), for "community service order" there is substituted "community order".

(4) For sub-paragraph (3)(*b*), there is substituted—

"(*b*) "community order" means a community order under section 177 of the Criminal Justice Act 2003, a community punishment order made under section 46 of the Powers of Criminal Courts (Sentencing) Act 2000 or a community service order under the Community Service by Offenders (Scotland) Act 1978.".

Criminal Procedure (Scotland) Act 1995 (c 46)

69. The Criminal Procedure (Scotland) Act 1995 is amended as follows.

70. (1) Section 234 (probation orders: persons residing in England and Wales) is amended as follows.

(2) In subsection (1), the words after paragraph (*b*) are omitted.

(3) For subsection (2) there is substituted—

"(2) Subsection (1) above applies to any probation order made under section 228 unless the order includes requirements which are more onerous than those which a court in England and Wales could impose on an offender under section 177 of the Criminal Justice Act 2003."

(4) In subsection (3), the words from "or to vary" to "one hundred" are omitted.

(5) In subsection (4)—

(*a*) in paragraph (*a*)—

    (i) for "paragraph 5(3) of Schedule 2 to the 2000 Act" there is substituted "section 207(2) of the Criminal Justice Act 2003",

    (ii) for "or, as the case may be, community rehabilitation orders" there is substituted "or, as the case may be, community orders under Part 12 of that Act", and

    (iii) for "paragraph 5 of the said Schedule 2" there is substituted "section 207 of the Criminal Justice Act 2003", and

(*b*) in paragraph (*b*), for "sub-paragraphs (5) to (7) of the said paragraph 5" there is substituted "sections 207(4) and 208(1) and (2) of the Criminal Justice Act 2003".

(6) After subsection (4) there is inserted—

"(4A) A probation order made or amended under this section must specify as the corresponding requirements for the purposes of this section requirements which could be included in a community order made under section 177 of the Criminal Justice Act 2003."

(7) In subsection (5), for "Schedule 3" onwards there is substituted "Schedule 8 to the Criminal Justice Act 2003 shall apply as if it were a community order made by a magistrates' court under section 177 of that Act and imposing the requirements specified under subsection (4A) above".

(8) For subsection (6) there is substituted—

"(6) In its application to a probation order made or amended under this section, Schedule 8 to the Criminal Justice Act 2003 has effect subject to the following modifications—

(*a*) any reference to the responsible officer has effect as a reference to the person appointed or assigned under subsection (1)(*a*) above,

(*b*) in paragraph 9—

    (i) paragraphs (*b*) and (*c*) of sub-paragraph (1) are omitted,

    (ii) in sub-paragraph (6), the first reference to the Crown Court has effect as a reference to a court in Scotland, and

    (iii) any other reference in sub-paragraphs (6) or (7) to the Crown Court has effect as a reference to the court in Scotland, and

(*c*) Parts 3 and 5 are omitted."

(9) In subsection (10)—

(*a*) for the words from "paragraph 6" to "community rehabilitation orders" there is substituted "paragraph 8 of Schedule 9 (which relates to community orders)", and

(*b*) for "an order made under section 41" there is substituted "a community order made under Part 12".

71. In section 242 (community service orders: persons residing in England and Wales)—

(*a*) in subsection (1)—

    (i) in paragraph (*a*)(ii), for "a community punishment order" there is substituted "an unpaid work requirement imposed by a community order (within the meaning of Part 12 of the Criminal Justice Act 2003)", and

    (ii) in paragraph (*a*)(iii), for "community punishment orders made under section 46 of the Powers of Criminal Courts (Sentencing) Act 2000" there is substituted "unpaid work requirements imposed by community orders made under section 177 of the Criminal Justice Act 2003",

(*b*) in subsection (2)(*b*), for "community punishment orders made under section 46 of the Powers of Criminal Courts (Sentencing) Act 2000" there is substituted "unpaid work requirements imposed by community orders made under section 177 of the Criminal Justice Act 2003", and

(*c*) in subsection (3)(*b*), for "in respect of community punishment orders conferred on responsible officers by the Powers of Criminal Courts (Sentencing) Act 2000" there is substituted "conferred on responsible officers by Part 12 of the Criminal Justice Act 2003 in respect of unpaid work requirements imposed by community orders (within the meaning of that Part)".

72. In section 244 (community service orders: provisions relating to persons living in England and Wales or Northern Ireland)—

(*a*) in subsection (3)(*a*)—

    (i) for "community punishment order" there is substituted "community order (within the meaning of Part 12 of the Criminal Justice Act 2003)", and

    (ii) for "community punishment orders" there is substituted "such community orders",

(*b*) in subsection (4)(*a*), for "community punishment orders" there is substituted "community orders (within the meaning of Part 12 of the Criminal Justice Act 2003)",

(*c*) in subsection (5), for "community punishment order" there is substituted "a community order (within the meaning of Part 12 of the Criminal Justice Act 2003)", and

(*d*) in subsection (6)—

    (i) for "community punishment orders", where first occurring, there is substituted "community orders (within the meaning of Part 12 of the Criminal Justice Act 2003)", and

    (ii) in paragraph (*b*)(ii), for "the Powers of Criminal Courts (Sentencing) Act 2000" there is substituted "Part 12 of the Criminal Justice Act 2003".

Education Act 1996 (c 56)

73. In section 562 of the Education Act 1996 (Act not to apply to persons detained under order of a court), for "probation order" there is substituted "community order under section 177 the Criminal Justice Act 2003".

Criminal Justice (Northern Ireland) Order 1996 (SI 1996/3160 (NI 24))

74. The Criminal Justice (Northern Ireland) Order 1996 is amended as follows.

75. In Article 2 (interpretation) after paragraph (8) there is inserted—

"(9) For the purposes of this Order, a sentence falls to be imposed under paragraph (2) of Article 52A of the Firearms (Northern Ireland) Order 1981 if it is required by that paragraph and the court is not of the opinion there mentioned."

76. In Article 4 (absolute and conditional discharge), in paragraph (1), for " (not being an offence for which the sentence is fixed by law)" there is substituted " (not being an offence for which the sentence is fixed by law or falls to be imposed under Article 52A(2) of the Firearms (Northern Ireland) Order 1981)".

77. In Article 10 (probation orders), in paragraph (1) for " (not being an offence for which the sentence is fixed by law)" there is substituted " (not being an offence for which the sentence is fixed by law or falls to be imposed under Article 52A(2) of the Firearms (Northern Ireland) Order 1981)".

78. (1) Article 13 (community service orders) is amended as follows.

(2) In paragraph (1) for " (not being an offence for which the sentence is fixed by law)" there is substituted " (not being an offence for which the sentence is fixed by law or falls to be imposed under Article 52A(2) of the Firearms (Northern Ireland) Order 1981)".

(3) In paragraph (4)(b) as it has effect pursuant to paragraph 7(1) of Schedule 13 to the Criminal Justice Act 1982 (reciprocal arrangements), for "such orders" there is substituted "an unpaid work requirement of a community order (within the meaning of Part 12 of the Criminal Justice Act 2003)".

79. In Article 15 (orders combining probation and community service), in paragraph (1) for " (not being an offence for which the sentence is fixed by law)" there is substituted " (not being an offence for which the sentence is fixed by law or falls to be imposed under Article 52A(2) of the Firearms (Northern Ireland) Order 1981)".

80. In Article 19 (restrictions on imposing custodial sentences), at the end of paragraph (1) there is inserted "or falling to be imposed under Article 52A(2) of the Firearms (Northern Ireland) Order 1981".

81. (1) In Article 20 (length of custodial sentences), at the end of paragraph (1) there is inserted "or falling to be imposed under Article 52A(2) of the Firearms (Northern Ireland) Order 1981".

(2) In Article 24 (custody probation orders), in paragraph (1) for "other than one fixed by law" there is substituted ", other than an offence for which the sentence is fixed by law or falls to be imposed under Article 52A(2) of the Firearms (Northern Ireland) Order 1981,".

Crime (Sentences) Act 1997 (c 43)

82. The Crime (Sentences) Act 1997 is amended as follows.

83. (1) Section 31 (duration and conditions of licences) is amended as follows.

(2) In subsection (3), for the words from "except" onwards there is substituted "except in accordance with recommendations of the Parole Board".

(3) Subsection (4) is omitted.

(4) In subsection (6), for "section 46(3) of the 1991 Act" there is substituted "section 259 of the Criminal Justice Act 2003".

84. In section 32 (recall of life prisoners while on licence) for subsection (5) there is substituted—

"(5) Where on a reference under subsection (4) above the Parole Board directs the immediate release on licence under this section of the life prisoner, the Secretary of State shall give effect to the direction."

85. (1) Schedule 1 (transfers of prisoners within the British Islands) is amended as follows.

(2) In paragraph 6, after sub-paragraph (3) there is inserted—

"(4) In this Part of this Schedule—

"the 2003 Act" means the Criminal Justice Act 2003;
"custody plus order" has the meaning given by section 181(4) of that Act;
"intermittent custody order" has the meaning given by section 183(2) of that Act."

(3) In paragraph 8 (restricted transfers from England and Wales to Scotland)—

(a) for sub-paragraph (2)(a) there is substituted—

"(a) sections 241, 244, 247 to 252 and 254 to 264 of the 2003 Act (fixed-term prisoners) or, as the case may require, sections 102 to 104 of the Powers of Criminal Courts (Sentencing) Act 2000 (detention and training orders) or sections 28 to 34 of this Act (life sentences) shall apply to him in place of the corresponding provisions of the law of Scotland;

(aa) sections 62 and 64 of the Criminal Justice and Court Services Act 2000 (which relate to licence conditions) shall apply to him in place of the corresponding provisions of the law of Scotland;

(ab) where a custody plus order or intermittent custody order has effect in relation to him, the provisions of Chapters 3 and 4 of Part 12 of the 2003 Act relating to such orders shall also apply to him (subject to Schedule 11 to that Act); and",

(b) for sub-paragraph (4)(a) there is substituted—

"(a) sections 241, 249 to 252 and 254 to 264 of the 2003 Act (fixed-term prisoners) or, as the case may require, sections 103 and 104 of the Powers of Criminal Courts (Sentencing) Act 2000 (detention and training orders) or sections 31 to 34 of this Act (life sentences) shall apply to him in place of the corresponding provisions of the law of Scotland;

(aa) sections 62 and 64 of the Criminal Justice and Court Services Act 2000 (which relate to licence conditions) shall apply to him in place of the corresponding provisions of the law of Scotland;

(ab) where a custody plus order or intermittent custody order has effect in relation to him, the provisions of Chapters 3 and 4 of Part 12 of the 2003 Act relating to such orders shall also apply to him (subject to Schedule 11 to that Act); and", and

(c) for sub-paragraphs (5) to (7) there is substituted—

"(5) Section 31(2A) of this Act (conditions as to supervision after release), as applied by sub-paragraph (2) or (4) above, shall have effect as if for paragraphs (a) to (c) there were substituted the words "a relevant officer of such local authority as may be specified in the licence".

"(6) Any provision of sections 102 to 104 of the Powers of Criminal Courts (Sentencing) Act 2000 which is applied by sub-paragraph (2) or (4) above shall have effect (as so applied) as if—

(a) any reference to secure accommodation were a reference to secure accommodation within the meaning of Part 2 of the Children (Scotland) Act 1995 or a young offenders institution provided under section 19(1)(b) of the Prisons (Scotland) Act 1989,

(b) except in section 103(2), any reference to the Secretary of State were a reference to the Scottish Ministers,

(c) any reference to an officer of a local probation board were a reference to a relevant officer as defined by section 27(1) of the Prisoners and Criminal Proceedings (Scotland) Act 1993,

(d) any reference to a youth court were a reference to a sheriff court,

(e) in section 103, any reference to a petty sessions area were a reference to a local government area within the meaning of the Local Government etc (Scotland) Act 1994,

(f) in section 103(3), for paragraphs (b) and (c) there were substituted a reference to an officer of a local authority constituted under that Act for the local government area in which the offender resides for the time being,

(g) section 103(5) were omitted,

(h) in section 104, for subsection (1) there were substituted—

"(1) Where a detention and training order is in force in respect of an offender and it appears on information to a sheriff court having jurisdiction in the locality in which the offender resides that the offender has failed to comply with requirements under section 103(6)(b), the court may—

(a) issue a citation requiring the offender to appear before it at the time specified in the citation, or

(b) issue a warrant for the offender's arrest.",

(i) section 104(2) were omitted, and

(j) in section 104(6), the reference to the Crown Court were a reference to the High Court of Justiciary."

(4) In paragraph 9 (restricted transfers from England and Wales to Northern Ireland)—

(a) for sub-paragraph (2)(a) there is substituted—

"(a) sections 241, 244, 247 to 252 and 254 to 264 of the 2003 Act (fixed-term prisoners) or, as the case may require, sections 102 to 104 of the Powers of Criminal Courts (Sentencing) Act 2000 (detention and training orders) or sections 28 to 34 of this Act (life sentences) shall apply to him in place of the corresponding provisions of the law of Northern Ireland;

(aa) sections 62 and 64 of the Criminal Justice and Court Services Act 2000 (which relate to licence conditions) shall apply to him in place of the corresponding provisions of the law of Northern Ireland;

(ab) where a custody plus order or intermittent custody order has effect in relation to him, the provisions of Chapters 3 and 4 of Part 12 of the 2003 Act relating to such orders shall apply to him (subject to Schedule 11 to that Act); and",

(b) for sub-paragraph (4)(a) there is substituted—

"(a) sections 241, 249 to 252 and 254 to 264 of the 2003 Act (fixed-term prisoners) or, as the case may require, sections 103 and 104 of the Powers of Criminal Courts (Sentencing) Act 2000 (detention and training orders) or sections 31 to 34 of this Act (life sentences) shall apply to him in place of the corresponding provisions of the law of Northern Ireland;

(aa) sections 62 and 64 of the Criminal Justice and Court Services Act 2000 (which relate to licence conditions) shall apply to him in place of the corresponding provisions of the law of Northern Ireland;

(ab) where a custody plus order or intermittent custody order has effect in relation to him, the provisions of Chapters 3 and 4 of Part 12 of the 2003 Act relating to such orders shall apply to him (subject to Schedule 11 to that Act); and",

(c) for sub-paragraphs (5) to (7) there is substituted—

"(5) Section 31(2A) of this Act (conditions as to supervision after release), as applied by sub-paragraph (2) or (4) above, shall have effect as if for paragraphs (a) to (c) there were substituted the words "a probation appointed for or assigned to the petty sessions district within which the prisoner for the time being resides"."

(5) In paragraph 15 (unrestricted transfers: general provisions), sub-paragraph (5) is omitted.

86. In Schedule 2 (repatriation of prisoners to the British Islands) paragraphs 2 and 3 are omitted.

Crime and Disorder Act 1998 (c 37)

87. The Crime and Disorder Act 1998 is amended as follows.

88. In section 18 (interpretation etc of Chapter 1)—

(a) after the definition of "responsible officer" in subsection (1) there is inserted—

""serious harm" shall be construed in accordance with section 224 of the Criminal Justice Act 2003;"; and

(b) subsection (2) is omitted.

89. (1) Section 38 (local provision of youth justice services) is amended as follows.

(2) In subsection (4)(g), for "probation order, a community service order or a combination order" there is substituted "community order under section 177 of the Criminal Justice Act 2003".

(3) In subsection (4)(i), after "1997 Act")" there is inserted "or by virtue of conditions imposed under section 250 of the Criminal Justice Act 2003".

Powers of Criminal Courts (Sentencing) Act 2000 (c 6)

90. The Powers of Criminal Courts (Sentencing) Act 2000 is amended as follows.

91. (1) Section 6 (committal for sentence in certain cases where offender committed in respect of another offence) is amended as follows.

(2) In subsection (3)(b), for "section 120(1) below" there is substituted "paragraph 11(1) of Schedule 12 to the Criminal Justice Act 2003".

(3) For subsection (4)(e), there is substituted—

"(e) paragraph 11(2) of Schedule 12 to the Criminal Justice Act 2003 (committal to Crown Court where offender convicted during operational period of suspended sentence).".

92. In section 7 (power of Crown Court on committal for sentence under section 6), in subsection (2), for "section 119 below" there is substituted "paragraphs 8 and 9 of Schedule 12 to the Criminal Justice Act 2003".

93. In section 12 (absolute and conditional discharge)—

(a) in subsection (1) for "109(2), 110(2) or 111(2) below" there is substituted "section 110(2) or 111(2) below, section 51A(2) of the Firearms Act 1968 or section 225, 226, 227 or 228 of the Criminal Justice Act 2003)", and

(b) subsection (4) (duty to explain effect of order for conditional discharge) is omitted.

94. In the heading to Part 4, and the heading to Chapter 1 of that Part, for "COMMUNITY ORDERS" there is substituted "YOUTH COMMUNITY ORDERS".

95. For section 33 there is substituted—

"33. Meaning of "youth community order" and "community sentence". (1) In this Act "youth community order" means any of the following orders—

    (a) a curfew order;

    (b) an exclusion order;

    (c) an attendance centre order;

    (d) a supervision order;

    (e) an action plan order.

(2) In this Act "community sentence" means a sentence which consists of or includes—

    (a) a community order under section 177 of the Criminal Justice Act 2003, or

    (b) one or more youth community orders."

96. (1) Section 36B (electronic monitoring of requirements in community orders) is amended as follows.

(2) In the heading for "**community orders**" there is substituted "**youth community orders**", and

(3) In subsection (1)—

(a) for "to (4)" there is substituted "and (3)", and

(b) for "community order" there is substituted "youth community order".

(4) In subsection (2) and (6)(a), for "community order" there is substituted "youth community order".

97. (1) Section 37 (curfew orders) is amended as follows.

(2) In subsection (1)—

(a) after the word "person" there is inserted "aged under 16", and

(b) for "sections 34 to 36 above" there is substituted "sections 148, 150 and 156 of the Criminal Justice Act 2003".

(3) In subsection (5), for "community order" there is substituted "youth community order".

(4) Subsection (10) is omitted.

98. In section 39 (breach, revocation and amendment of curfew orders), for "community orders" there is substituted "youth community orders".

99. In section 40 (curfew orders: supplementary), in subsection (3), for "paragraphs 2A(4) and (5) and 19(3)" there is substituted "paragraph 16(2)".

100. (1) Section 40A (exclusion orders) is amended as follows.

(2) In subsection (1)—

(a) after "person" there is inserted "aged under 16",

(b) for "sections 34 to 36 above" there is substituted "sections 148, 150 and 156 of the Criminal Justice Act 2003", and

(c) for "two years" there is substituted "three months".

(3) In subsection (5), for "community order" there is substituted "youth community order".

(4) Subsection (10) is omitted.

101. In section 40B (breach, revocation and amendment of exclusion orders), for "community orders" there is substituted "youth community orders".

102. (1) Section 60 (attendance centre orders) is amended as follows.

(2) In subsection (1)—

(a) in paragraph (a), for "sections 34 to 36 above" there is substituted "sections 148, 150 and 156 of the Criminal Justice Act 2003" and for "21" there is substituted "16", and

(b) in paragraph (b), for "21" there is substituted "16", and

(c) paragraph (c) and the word "or" immediately preceding it are omitted.

(3) In subsection (4), for paragraphs (a) and (b) there is substituted "shall not exceed 24".

(4) In subsection (7), for "community order" there is substituted "youth community order".

103. In section 63 (supervision orders), in subsection (1), for "sections 34 to 36 above" there is substituted "sections 148, 150 and 156 of the Criminal Justice Act 2003".

104. (1) Section 69 (action plan orders) is amended as follows.

(2) In subsection (1), for "sections 34 to 36 above" there is substituted "sections 148, 150 and 156 of the Criminal Justice Act 2003", and

(3) In subsection (5)(b), for "a community rehabilitation order, a community punishment order, a community punishment and rehabilitation order," there is substituted "a community order under section 177 of the Criminal Justice Act 2003".

(4) Subsection (11) is omitted.

105. In section 70 (requirements which may be included in action plan orders and directions), in subsection (5)(a), after the word "other" there is inserted "youth community order or any".

106. (1) Section 73 (reparation orders) is amended as follows.

(2) In subsection (4)(b), for "a community punishment order, a community punishment and rehabilitation order," there is substituted "a community order under section 177 of the Criminal Justice Act 2003".

(3) Subsection (7) is omitted.

107. In section 74 (requirements and provisions of reparation order, and obligations of person subject to it), in subsection (3)(a), after "community order" there is inserted "or any youth community order".

108. In section 76 (meaning of custodial sentence), in subsection (1) after paragraph (b) there is inserted—

    "(bb) a sentence of detention for public protection under section 226 of the Criminal Justice Act 2003;

    (bc) a sentence of detention under section 228 of that Act;".

109. (1) Section 82A (determination of tariffs) is amended as follows.

(2) In subsection (1), for the words from "where" onwards there is substituted "where the sentence is not fixed by law".

(3) In subsection (3)—

(*a*) in paragraph (*b*), for "section 87" there is substituted "section 240 of the Criminal Justice Act 2003", and
(*b*) in paragraph (*c*), for "sections 33(2) and 35(1) of the Criminal Justice Act 1991" there is substituted "section 244(1) of the Criminal Justice Act 2003".

(4) In subsection (4)—

(*a*) after "If" there is inserted "the offender was aged 21 or over when he committed the offence and", and
(*b*) the words "subject to subsection (5) below" are omitted.

(5) Subsections (5) and (6) are omitted.

110. (1) Section 91 (offenders under 18 convicted of certain serious offences) is amended as follows.

(2) In subsection (3), for "none of the other methods in which the case may legally be dealt with" there is substituted "neither a community sentence nor a detention and training order".

(3) In subsection (4), for "section 79 and 80 above" there is substituted "section 152 and 153 of the Criminal Justice Act 2003".

111. (1) Section 100 (detention and training orders) is amended as follows.

(2) In subsection (1)—

(*a*) for the words from the beginning to "subsection (2)" there is substituted "Subject to sections 90 and 91 above, sections 226 and 228 of the Criminal Justice Act 2003, and subsection (2)", and
(*b*) for paragraph (*b*) there is substituted—

"(*b*) the court is of the opinion that subsection (2) of section 152 of the Criminal Justice Act 2003 applies or the case falls within subsection (3) of that section,".

(3) Subsection (4) is omitted.

112. In section 106 (interaction of detention and training orders with sentences of detention in a young offender institution), subsections (2) and (3) are omitted.

113. After section 106 there is inserted—

"106A. Interaction with sentences of detention. (1) In this section—

"the 2003 Act" means the Criminal Justice Act 2003;
"sentence of detention" means—

(*a*) a sentence of detention under section 91 above, or
(*b*) a sentence of detention under section 228 of the 2003 Act (extended sentence for certain violent or sexual offences: persons under 18).

(2) Where a court passes a sentence of detention in the case of an offender who is subject to a detention and training order, the sentence shall take effect as follows—

(*a*) if the offender has at any time been released by virtue of subsection (2), (3), (4) or (5) of section 102 above, at the beginning of the day on which the sentence is passed, and
(*b*) if not, either as mentioned in paragraph (*a*) above or, if the court so orders, at the time when the offender would otherwise be released by virtue of subsection (2), (3), (4) or (5) of section 102.

(3) Where a court makes a detention and training order in the case of an offender who is subject to a sentence of detention, the order shall take effect as follows—

(*a*) if the offender has at any time been released under Chapter 6 of Part 12 of the 2003 Act (release on licence of fixed-term prisoners), at the beginning of the day on which the order is made, and
(*b*) if not, either as mentioned in paragraph (*a*) above or, if the court so orders, at the time when the offender would otherwise be released under that Chapter.

(4) Where an order under section 102(5) above is made in the case of a person in respect of whom a sentence of detention is to take effect as mentioned in subsection (2)(*b*) above, the order is to be expressed as an order that the period of detention attributable to the detention and training order is to end at the time determined under section 102(5)(*a*) or (*b*) above.

(5) In determining for the purposes of subsection (3)(*b*) the time when an offender would otherwise be released under Chapter 6 of Part 12 of the 2003 Act, section 246 of that Act (power of Secretary of State to release prisoners on licence before he is required to do so) is to be disregarded.

(6) Where by virtue of subsection (3)(*b*) above a detention and training order made in the case of a person who is subject to a sentence of detention under section 228 of the 2003 Act is to take effect at the time when he would otherwise be released under Chapter 6 of Part 12 of that Act, any direction by the Parole Board under subsection (2)(*b*) of section 247 of that Act in respect of him is to be expressed as a direction that the Board would, but for the detention and training order, have directed his release under that section.

(7) Subject to subsection (9) below, where at any time an offender is subject concurrently—

(*a*) to a detention and training order, and
(*b*) to a sentence of detention,

he shall be treated for the purposes of the provisions specified in subsection (8) below as if he were subject only to the sentence of detention.

(8) Those provisions are—

(*a*) sections 102 to 105 above,
(*b*) section 92 above and section 235 of the 2003 Act (place of detention, etc), and
(*c*) Chapter 6 of Part 12 of the 2003 Act.

(9) Nothing in subsection (7) above shall require the offender to be released in respect of either the order or the sentence unless and until he is required to be released in respect of each of them."

114. In section 110 (required custodial sentence for third class A drug trafficking offence), subsection (3) is omitted.

115. In section 111 (minimum of three years for third domestic burglary) subsection (3) is omitted.

116. Sections 116 and 117 (return to prison etc where offence committed during original sentence) shall cease to have effect.

117. In section 130 (compensation orders against convicted persons), in subsection (2), for "109(2), 110(2) or 111(2) above," there is substituted "110(2) or 111(2) above, section 51A(2) of the Firearms Act 1968 or section 225, 226, 227 or 228 of the Criminal Justice Act 2003,".

118. In section 136 (power to order statement as to financial circumstances of parent or guardian) in subsection (2), for "section 126 above" there is substituted "section 162 of the Criminal Justice Act 2003".

119. (1) Section 138 (fixing of fine or compensation to be paid by parent or guardian) is amended as follows.

(2) In subsection (1)(*a*), for "section 128 above" there is substituted "section 164 of the Criminal Justice Act 2003".

(3) In subsection (2), for "sections 128(1) (duty to inquire into financial circumstances) and" there is substituted "section 164(1) of the Criminal Justice Act 2003 and section".

(4) In subsection (4)—

(*a*) for "section 129 above" there is substituted "section 165 of the Criminal Justice Act 2003",

(*b*) for "section 129(1)" there is substituted "section 165(1)", and

(*c*) for "section 129(2)" there is substituted "section 165(2)".

120. In section 146 (driving disqualification for any offence), in subsection (2), for "109(2), 110(2) or 111(2) above" there is substituted "110(2) or 111(2) above, section 51A(2) of the Firearms Act 1968 or section 225, 226, 227 or 228 of the Criminal Justice Act 2003".

121. In section 154 (commencement of Crown Court sentence), in subsection (2), for "section 84 above" there is substituted "section 265 of the Criminal Justice Act 2003".

122. In section 159 (execution of process between England and Wales and Scotland), for "10(7) or 24(1)" there is substituted "10(6) or 18(1)".

123. (1) Section 163 (interpretation) is amended as follows.

(2) In the definition of "attendance centre" for "section 62(2) above" there is substituted "section 221(2) of the Criminal Justice Act 2003".

(3) In the definition of "attendance centre order" for the words from "by virtue of" to "Schedule 3" there is substituted "by virtue of paragraph 4(2)(*b*) or 5(2)(*b*) of Schedule 3".

(4) In the definition of "community order", for "section 33(1) above" there is substituted "section 177(1) of the Criminal Justice Act 2003".

(5) For the definition of "curfew order" there is substituted—

"curfew order" means an order under section 37(1) above (and, except where the contrary intention is shown by paragraph 7 of Schedule 3 or paragraph 3 of Schedule 7 or 8, includes orders made under section 37(1) by virtue of paragraph 4(2)(*a*) or 5(2)(*a*) of Schedule 3 or paragraph 2(2)(*a*) of Schedule 7 or 8).".

(6) In the definition of "operational period", for "section 118(3) above" there is substituted "section 189(1)(*b*)(ii) of the Criminal Justice Act 2003".

(7) In the definition of "suspended sentence", for "section 118(3) above" there is substituted "section 189(7) of the Criminal Justice Act 2003".

(8) At the end there is inserted—

"youth community order" has the meaning given by section 33(1) above.".

124. In section 164 (further interpretative provision) for subsection (3) there is substituted—

"(3) References in this Act to a sentence falling to be imposed—

(*a*) under section 110(2) or 111(2) above,

(*b*) under section 51A(2) of the Firearms Act 1968, or

(*c*) under any of sections 225 to 228 of the Criminal Justice Act 2003,

are to be read in accordance with section 305(4) of the Criminal Justice Act 2003."

125. For Schedule 3 (breach revocation and amendment of certain community orders) there is substituted—

"SCHEDULE 3

BREACH, REVOCATION AND AMENDMENT OF CURFEW ORDERS AND EXCLUSION ORDERS

PART 1

PRELIMINARY

Definitions

1. In this Schedule—

"the petty sessions area concerned" means—

(*a*) in relation to a curfew order, the petty sessions area in which the place for the time being specified in the order is situated; and

(*b*) in relation to an exclusion order, the petty sessions area for the time being specified in the order;

"relevant order" means a curfew order or an exclusion order.

Orders made on appeal

2. Where a relevant order has been made on appeal, for the purposes of this Schedule it shall be deemed—

(*a*) if it was made on an appeal brought from a magistrates' court, to have been made by a magistrates' court;

(*b*) if it was made on an appeal brought from the Crown Court or from the criminal division of the Court of Appeal, to have been made by the Crown Court.

PART 2

BREACH OF REQUIREMENT OF ORDER

Issue of summons or warrant

3. (1) If at any time while a relevant order is in force in respect of an offender it appears on information to a justice of the peace acting for the petty sessions area concerned that the offender has failed to comply with any of the requirements of the order, the justice may—

(*a*) issue a summons requiring the offender to appear at the place and time specified in it; or

(*b*) if the information is in writing and on oath, issue a warrant for his arrest.

(2) Any summons or warrant issued under this paragraph shall direct the offender to appear or be brought—

(*a*) in the case of any relevant order which was made by the Crown Court and included a direction that any failure to comply with any of the requirements of the order be dealt with by the Crown Court, before the Crown Court; and

(*b*) in the case of a relevant order which is not an order to which paragraph (*a*) above applies, before a magistrates' court acting for the petty sessions area concerned.

(3) Where a summons issued under sub-paragraph (1)(*a*) above requires an offender to appear before the Crown Court and the offender does not appear in answer to the summons, the Crown Court may issue a further summons requiring the offender to appear at the place and time specified in it.

(4) Where a summons issued under sub-paragraph (1)(*a*) above or a further summons issued under sub-paragraph (3) above requires an offender to appear before the Crown Court and the offender does not appear in answer to the summons, the Crown Court may issue a warrant for the arrest of the offender.

Powers of magistrates' court

4. (1) This paragraph applies if it is proved to the satisfaction of a magistrates' court before which an offender appears or is brought under paragraph 3 above that he has failed without reasonable excuse to comply with any of the requirements of the relevant order.

(2) The magistrates' court may deal with the offender in respect of the failure in one of the following ways (and must deal with him in one of those ways if the relevant order is in force)—

(*a*) by making a curfew order in respect of him (subject to paragraph 7 below);

(*b*) by making an attendance centre order in respect of him (subject to paragraph 8 below); or

(*c*) where the relevant order was made by a magistrates' court, by dealing with him, for the offence in respect of which the order was made, in any way in which he could have been dealt with for that offence by the court which made the order if the order had not been made.

(3) In dealing with an offender under sub-paragraph (2)(*c*) above, a magistrates' court—

(*a*) shall take into account the extent to which the offender has complied with the requirements of the relevant order; and

(*b*) in the case of an offender who has wilfully and persistently failed to comply with those requirements, may impose a custodial sentence (where the relevant order was made in respect of an offence punishable with such a sentence) notwithstanding anything in section 152(2) of the Criminal Justice Act 2003.

(4) Where a magistrates' court deals with an offender under sub-paragraph (2)(*c*) above, it shall revoke the relevant order if it is still in force.

(5) Where a relevant order was made by the Crown Court and a magistrates' court has power to deal with the offender under sub-paragraph (2)(*a*) or (*b*) above, it may instead commit him to custody or release him on bail until he can be brought or appear before the Crown Court.

(6) A magistrates' court which deals with an offender's case under sub-paragraph (5) above shall send to the Crown Court—

(*a*) a certificate signed by a justice of the peace certifying that the offender has failed to comply with the requirements of the relevant order in the respect specified in the certificate; and

(*b*) such other particulars of the case as may be desirable;

and a certificate purporting to be so signed shall be admissible as evidence of the failure before the Crown Court.

(7) A person sentenced under sub-paragraph (2)(*c*) above for an offence may appeal to the Crown Court against the sentence.

Powers of Crown Court

5. (1) This paragraph applies where under paragraph 3 or by virtue of paragraph 4(5) above an offender is brought or appears before the Crown Court and it is proved to the satisfaction of that court that he has failed without reasonable excuse to comply with any of the requirements of the relevant order.

(2) The Crown Court may deal with the offender in respect of the failure in one of the following ways (and must deal with him in one of those ways if the relevant order is in force)—

(*a*) by making a curfew order in respect of him (subject to paragraph 7 below);

(*b*) by making an attendance centre order in respect of him (subject to paragraph 8 below); or

(*c*) by dealing with him, for the offence in respect of which the order was made, in any way in which he could have been dealt with for that offence by the court which made the order if the order had not been made.

(3) In dealing with an offender under sub-paragraph (2)(*c*) above, the Crown Court—

(*a*) shall take into account the extent to which the offender has complied with the requirements of the relevant order; and

(*b*) in the case of an offender who has wilfully and persistently failed to comply with those requirements, may impose a custodial sentence (where the relevant order was made in respect of an offence punishable with such a sentence) notwithstanding anything in section 152(2) of the Criminal Justice Act 2003.

(4) Where the Crown Court deals with an offender under sub-paragraph (2)(*c*) above, it shall revoke the relevant order if it is still in force.

(5) In proceedings before the Crown Court under this paragraph any question whether the offender has failed to comply with the requirements of the relevant order shall be determined by the court and not by the verdict of a jury.

Exclusions from paragraphs 4 and 5

6. Without prejudice to paragraphs 10 and 11 below, an offender who is convicted of a further offence while a relevant order is in force in respect of him shall not on that account be liable to be dealt with under paragraph 4 or 5 in respect of a failure to comply with any requirement of the order.

Curfew orders imposed for breach of relevant order

7. (1) Section 37 of this Act (curfew orders) shall apply for the purposes of paragraphs 4(2)(*a*) and 5(2)(*a*) above as if for the words from the beginning to "make" there were substituted "Where a court has power to deal with an offender under Part 2 of Schedule 3 to this Act for failure to comply with any of the requirements of a relevant order, the court may make in respect of the offender".

(2) The following provisions of this Act, namely—

(*a*) section 37(3) to (12), and

(*b*) so far as applicable, sections 36B and 40 and this Schedule so far as relating to curfew orders;

have effect in relation to a curfew order made by virtue of paragraphs 4(2)(*a*) and 5(2)(*a*) as they have effect in relation to any other curfew order, subject to sub-paragraph (3) below.

(3) This Schedule shall have effect in relation to such a curfew order as if—

(*a*) the power conferred on the court by each of paragraphs 4(2)(*c*), 5(2)(*c*) and 10(3)(*b*) to deal with the offender for the offence in respect of which the order was made were a power to deal with the offender, for his failure to comply with the relevant order, in any way in which the appropriate court could deal with him for that failure if it had just been proved to the satisfaction of the court;

(*b*) the reference in paragraph 10(1)(*b*) to the offence in respect of which the order was made were a reference to the failure to comply in respect of which the curfew order was made; and

(*c*) the power conferred on the Crown Court by paragraph 11(2)(*b*) to deal with the offender for the offence in respect of which the order was made were a power to deal with the offender, for his failure to comply with the relevant order, in any way in which the appropriate court (if the relevant order was made by the magistrates' court) or the Crown Court (if that order was made by the Crown Court) could deal with him for that failure if it had just been proved to its satisfaction.

(4) For the purposes of the provisions mentioned in paragraphs (*a*) and (*c*) of sub-paragraph (3) above, as applied by that sub-paragraph, if the relevant order is no longer in force the appropriate court's powers shall be determined on the assumption that it is still in force.

(5) Sections 148 and 156 of the Criminal Justice Act 2003 (restrictions and procedural requirements for community sentences) do not apply in relation to a curfew order made by virtue of paragraph 4(2)(*a*) or 5(2)(*a*) above.

Attendance centre orders imposed for breach of relevant order

8. (1) Section 60(1) of this Act (attendance centre orders) shall apply for the purposes of paragraphs 4(2)(*b*) and 5(2)(*b*) above as if for the words from the beginning to "the court may," there were substituted "Where a court has power to deal with an offender under Part 2 of Schedule 3 to this Act for failure to comply with any of the requirements of a relevant order, the court may,".

(2) The following provisions of this Act, namely—

(*a*) subsections (3) to (11) of section 60, and

(*b*) so far as applicable, section 36B and Schedule 5,

have effect in relation to an attendance centre order made by virtue of paragraph 4(2)(*b*) or 5(2)(*b*) above as they have effect in relation to any other attendance centre order, but as if there were omitted from each of paragraphs 2(1)(*b*), 3(1) and 4(3) of Schedule 5 the words ", for the offence in respect of which the order was made," and "for that offence".

(3) Sections 148 and 156 of the Criminal Justice Act 2003 (restrictions and procedural requirements for community sentences) do not apply in relation to an attendance centre order made by virtue of paragraph 4(2)(*b*) or 5(2)(*b*) above.

Supplementary

9. Any exercise by a court of its powers under paragraph 4(2)(*a*) or (*b*) or 5(2)(*a*) or (*b*) above shall be without prejudice to the continuance of the relevant order.

PART 3
REVOCATION OF ORDER

Revocation of order with or without re-sentencing: powers of magistrates' court

10. (1) This paragraph applies where a relevant order made by a magistrates' court is in force in respect of any offender and on the application of the offender or the responsible officer it appears to the appropriate magistrates' court that, having regard to circumstances which have arisen since the order was made, it would be in the interests of justice—

(*a*) for the order to be revoked; or

(*b*) for the offender to be dealt with in some other way for the offence in respect of which the order was made.

(2) In this paragraph "the appropriate magistrates' court" means a magistrates' court acting for the petty sessions area concerned.

(3) The appropriate magistrates' court may—

(*a*) revoke the order; or

(*b*) both—

(i) revoke the order; and

(ii) deal with the offender for the offence in respect of which the order was made, in any way in which he could have been dealt with for that offence by the court which made the order if the order had not been made.

(4) In dealing with an offender under sub-paragraph (3)(*b*) above, a magistrates' court shall take into account the extent to which the offender has complied with the requirements of the relevant order.

(5) A person sentenced under sub-paragraph (3)(*b*) above for an offence may appeal to the Crown Court against the sentence.

(6) Where a magistrates' court proposes to exercise its powers under this paragraph otherwise than on the application of the offender, it shall summon him to appear before the court and, if he does not appear in answer to the summons, may issue a warrant for his arrest.

(7) No application may be made by the offender under sub-paragraph (1) above while an appeal against the relevant order is pending.

Revocation of order with or without re-sentencing: powers of Crown Court on conviction etc

11. (1) This paragraph applies where—

(*a*) a relevant order made by the Crown Court is in force in respect of an offender and the offender or the responsible officer applies to the Crown Court for the order to be revoked or for the offender to be dealt with in some other way for the offence in respect of which the order was made; or

(*b*) an offender in respect of whom a relevant order is in force is convicted of an offence before the Crown Court or, having been committed by a magistrates' court to the Crown Court for sentence, is brought or appears before the Crown Court.

(2) If it appears to the Crown Court to be in the interests of justice to do so, having regard to circumstances which have arisen since the order was made, the Crown Court may—

(*a*) revoke the order; or

(*b*) both—

    (i) revoke the order; and

    (ii) deal with the offender for the offence in respect of which the order was made, in any way in which he could have been dealt with for that offence by the court which made the order if the order had not been made.

(3) In dealing with an offender under sub-paragraph (2)(*b*) above, the Crown Court shall take into account the extent to which the offender has complied with the requirements of the relevant order.

Revocation following custodial sentence by magistrates' court unconnected with order

12. (1) This paragraph applies where—

(*a*) an offender in respect of whom a relevant order is in force is convicted of an offence by a magistrates' court unconnected with the order;

(*b*) the court imposes a custodial sentence on the offender; and

(*c*) it appears to the court, on the application of the offender or the responsible officer, that it would be in the interests of justice to exercise its powers under this paragraph having regard to circumstances which have arisen since the order was made.

(2) In sub-paragraph (1) above "a magistrates' court unconnected with the order" means a magistrates' court not acting for the petty sessions area concerned.

(3) The court may—

(*a*) if the order was made by a magistrates' court, revoke it;

(*b*) if the order was made by the Crown Court, commit the offender in custody or release him on bail until he can be brought or appear before the Crown Court.

(4) Where the court deals with an offender's case under sub-paragraph (3)(*b*) above, it shall send to the Crown Court such particulars of the case as may be desirable.

13. Where by virtue of paragraph 12(3)(*b*) above an offender is brought or appears before the Crown Court and it appears to the Crown Court to be in the interests of justice to do so, having regard to circumstances which have arisen since the relevant order was made, the Crown Court may revoke the order.

Supplementary

14. (1) On the making under this Part of this Schedule of an order revoking a relevant order, the proper officer of the court shall forthwith give copies of the revoking order to the responsible officer.

(2) In sub-paragraph (1) above "proper officer" means—

(*a*) in relation to a magistrates' court, the justices' chief executive for the court; and

(*b*) in relation to the Crown Court, the appropriate officer.

(3) A responsible officer to whom in accordance with sub-paragraph (1) above copies of a revoking order are given shall give a copy to the offender and to the person in charge of any institution in which the offender was required by the order to reside.

PART 4
AMENDMENT OF ORDER

Amendment by reason of change of residence

15. (1) This paragraph applies where, at any time while a relevant order is in force in respect of an offender, a magistrates' court acting for the petty sessions area concerned is satisfied that the offender proposes to change, or has changed, his residence from that petty sessions area to another petty sessions area.

(2) Subject to sub-paragraph (3) below, the court may, and on the application of the responsible officer shall, amend the relevant order by substituting the other petty sessions area for the area specified in the order or, in the case of a curfew order, a place in that other area for the place so specified.

(3) The court shall not amend under this paragraph a curfew order which contains requirements which, in the opinion of the court, cannot be complied with unless the offender continues to reside in the petty sessions area concerned unless, in accordance with paragraph 16 below, it either—

(a) cancels those requirements; or

(b) substitutes for those requirements other requirements which can be complied with if the offender ceases to reside in that area.

Amendment of requirements of order

16.—(1) Without prejudice to the provisions of paragraph 15 above but subject to the following provisions of this paragraph, a magistrates' court acting for the petty sessions area concerned may, on the application of an eligible person, by order amend a relevant order—

(a) by cancelling any of the requirements of the order; or

(b) by inserting in the order (either in addition to or in substitution for any of its requirements) any requirement which the court could include if it were then making the order.

(2) A magistrates' court shall not under sub-paragraph (1) above amend a curfew order by extending the curfew periods beyond the end of six months from the date of the original order.

(3) A magistrates' court shall not under sub-paragraph (1) above amend an exclusion order by extending the period for which the offender is prohibited from entering the place in question beyond the end of three months from the date of the original order.

(4) For the purposes of this paragraph the eligible persons are—

(a) the offender;

(b) the responsible officer; and

(c) in relation to an exclusion order, any affected person.

But an application under sub-paragraph (1) by a person such as is mentioned in paragraph (c) above must be for the cancellation of a requirement which was included in the order by virtue of his consent or for the purpose (or partly for the purpose) of protecting him from being approached by the offender, or for the insertion of a requirement which will, if inserted, be such a requirement.

Supplementary

17. No order may be made under paragraph 15 above, and no application may be made under paragraph 16 above, while an appeal against the relevant order is pending.

18.—(1) Subject to sub-paragraph (2) below, where a court proposes to exercise its powers under this Part of this Schedule, otherwise than on the application of the offender, the court—

(a) shall summon him to appear before the court; and

(b) if he does not appear in answer to the summons, may issue a warrant for his arrest.

(2) This paragraph shall not apply to an order cancelling a requirement of a relevant order or reducing the period of any requirement, or to an order under paragraph 15 above substituting a new petty sessions area or a new place for the one specified in a relevant order.

19.—(1) On the making under this Part of this Schedule of an order amending a relevant order, the justices' chief executive for the court shall forthwith—

(a) if the order amends the relevant order otherwise than by substituting, by virtue of paragraph 15 above, a new petty session area or a new place for the one specified in the relevant order, give copies of the amending order to the responsible officer;

(b) if the order amends the relevant order in the manner excepted by paragraph (a) above, send to the chief executive to the justices for the new petty sessions area or, as the case may be, for the petty sessions area in which the new place is situated—

(i) copies of the amending order; and

(ii) such documents and information relating to the case as he considers likely to be of assistance to a court acting for that area in the exercise of its functions in relation to the order;

and in a case falling within paragraph (b) above the chief executive of the justices for that area shall give copies of the amending order to the responsible officer.

(2) A responsible officer to whom in accordance with sub-paragraph (1) above copies of an order are given shall give a copy to the offender and to the person in charge of any institution in which the offender is or was required by the order to reside."

126. In Schedule 5 (breach, revocation and amendment of attendance centre orders)—

(a) in paragraph 1(1)(b), for "section 62(3) of this Act" there is substituted "section 222(1)(d) or (e) of the Criminal Justice Act 2003",

(b) in paragraph 2(5)(b), for "section 79(2) of this Act" there is substituted "section 152(2) of the Criminal Justice Act 2003", and

(c) in paragraph 3(3)(b), for "section 79(2) of this Act" there is substituted "section 152(2) of the Criminal Justice Act 2003".

127. In Schedule 6 (requirements which may be included in supervision orders)—

(a) in paragraph 2(7)(a), after the word "other" there is inserted "youth community order or any", and

(b) in paragraph 3(6)(a), for "community order" there is substituted "youth community order".

128. In Schedule 7 (breach, revocation and amendment of supervision orders)—

(a) in paragraph 3—

(i) in sub-paragraph (2), for "sub-paragraphs (4) and (5)" there is substituted "sub-paragraph (5)",

(ii) in sub-paragraph (3), for "Sections 35 and 36 of this Act" there is substituted "Sections 148 and 156 of the Criminal Justice Act 2003",

(iii) sub-paragraph (4) is omitted, and

(iv) in sub-paragraph (5)(a), for the words from the beginning to "and" there is substituted "the power conferred on the court by each of paragraphs 4(2)(c) and", and

(b) in paragraph 4(3), for "Sections 35 and 36 of this Act" there is substituted "Sections 148 and 156 of the Criminal Justice Act 2003".

129. In Schedule 8 (breach, revocation and amendment of action plan orders and reparation orders)—

(*a*) in paragraph 3—

   (i) in sub-paragraph (2), for "sub-paragraphs (4) and (5)" there is substituted "sub-paragraph (5)",

   (ii) in sub-paragraph (3), for "Sections 35 and 36 of this Act" there is substituted "Sections 148 and 156 of the Criminal Justice Act 2003",

   (iii) sub-paragraph (4) is omitted, and

   (iv) in sub-paragraph (5)(*a*), for the words from the beginning to "and" there is substituted "The power conferred on the court by each of paragraphs 4(2)(*c*) and", and

(*b*) in paragraph 4(3), for "Sections 35 and 36 of this Act" there is substituted "Sections 148 and 156 of the Criminal Justice Act 2003".

Child Support, Pensions and Social Security Act 2000 (c 19)

130. The Child Support, Pensions and Social Security Act 2000 is amended as follows.

131. (1) Section 62 (loss of benefit for breach of community order) is amended as follows.

(2) In subsection (8), for the definition of "relevant community order" there is substituted—

""relevant community order" means—

   (*a*) a community order made under section 177 of the Criminal Justice Act 2003; or

   (*b*) any order falling in England or Wales to be treated as such an order."

(3) In subsection (11)(*c*)(ii), for "to (*e*)" there is substituted "and (*b*)".

132. In section 64 (information provision), in subsection (6)(*a*), after "community orders" there is inserted " (as defined by section 177 of the Criminal Justice Act 2003)".

Criminal Justice and Court Services Act 2000 (c 43)

133. The Criminal Justice and Court Services Act 2000 is amended as follows.

134. In section 1 (purposes of Chapter 1 of Part 1 of the Act), in subsection (2)—

(*a*) in paragraph (*a*), after "community orders" there is inserted " (as defined by section 177 of the Criminal Justice Act 2003)", and

(*b*) after paragraph (*c*) there is inserted—

"(*d*) giving effect to suspended sentence orders (as defined by section 189 of the Criminal Justice Act 2003)."

135. In section 42 (interpretation of Part 2), in subsection (2)(*a*), for "section 119 of the Powers of Criminal Court (Sentencing) Act 2000" there is substituted "paragraph 8(2)(*a*) or (*b*) of Schedule 11 of the Criminal Justice Act 2003".

136. (1) Section 62 (release on licence etc: conditions as to monitoring) is amended as follows.

(2) For subsection (3) there is substituted—

"(3) In relation to a prisoner released under section 246 of the Criminal Justice Act 2003 (power to release prisoners on licence before required to do so), the monitoring referred to in subsection (2)(*a*) does not include the monitoring of his compliance with conditions imposed under section 253 of that Act (curfew condition)."

(3) In subsection (5) after paragraph (*e*) there is inserted

", and

   (*f*) a sentence of detention under section 226 or 228 of the Criminal Justice Act 2003".

137. In section 69 (duties of local probation boards in connection with victims of certain offences), in subsection (8), for paragraph (*a*) there is substituted—

"(*a*) murder or an offence specified in Schedule 15 to the Criminal Justice Act 2003,".

138. In section 70 (general interpretation), in subsection (5), for the words "any community order" there is substituted "a curfew order, an exclusion order, a community rehabilitation order, a community punishment order, a community punishment and rehabilitation order, a drug treatment and testing order, a drug abstinence order, an attendance centre order, a supervision order or an action plan order".

International Criminal Court Act 2001 (c 17)

139. (1) Schedule 7 to the International Criminal Court Act 2001 (domestic provisions not applicable to ICC prisoners), is amended as follows.

(2) In paragraph 2(1), for paragraph (*d*) there is substituted—

"(*d*) section 240 of the Criminal Justice Act 2003 (crediting of periods of remand in custody)."

(3) In paragraph 3(1), for "Part 2 of the Criminal Justice Act 1991" there is substituted "sections 244 to 264 of the Criminal Justice Act 2003".

Armed Forces Act 2001 (c 19)

140. In section 30 of the Armed Forces Act 2001 (conditional release from custody), in subsection (6)(*a*) for "six months" there is substituted "the term specified in subsection (1)(*a*) of section 8 of the Armed Forces Act 1976 (powers of courts in relation to civilians)".

Proceeds of Crime Act 2002 (c 29)

141. In section 38 of the Proceeds of Crime Act 2002 (provisions about imprisonment or detention), in subsection (4)(*a*), for "section 118(1) of the Sentencing Act" there is substituted "section 189(1) of the Criminal Justice Act 2003".

Sexual Offences Act 2003 (c 42)

142. The Sexual Offences Act 2003 is amended as follows.
143. In section 131 (application of Part 2 to young offenders), after paragraph (*j*) there is inserted—

"(*k*) a sentence of detention for public protection under section 226 of the Criminal Justice Act 2003,
(*l*)   an extended sentence under section 228 of that Act,".

144. In section 133 (general interpretation), at the end of paragraph (*a*) of the definition of "community order" there is inserted " (as that Act had effect before the passing of the Criminal Justice Act 2003)".

PART 2
OFFENCES: ABOLITION OF IMPRISONMENT AND CONVERSION TO SUMMARY OFFENCE

Vagrancy Act 1824 (c 83)

145. In section 3 of the Vagrancy Act 1824 (idle and disorderly persons), for the words from "subject to" to the end there is substituted "it shall be lawful for any justice of the peace to impose on such person (being thereof convicted before him by his own view, or by the confession of such person, or by the evidence on oath of one or more credible witnesses) a fine not exceeding level 3 on the standard scale".
146. (1) Section 4 of that Act (rogues and vagabonds) is amended as follows.
(2) In that section, for the words from "shall be" to the end there is substituted "commits an offence under this section".
(3) At the end of that section (which becomes subsection (1)) there is inserted—

"(2) It shall be lawful for any justice of the peace to impose on any person who commits an offence under this section (being thereof convicted before him by the confession of such person, or by the evidence on oath of one or more credible witnesses)—

(*a*)   in the case of a person convicted of the offence of wandering abroad and lodging in any barn or outhouse, or in any deserted or unoccupied building, or in the open air, or under a tent, or in any cart or waggon, and not giving a good account of himself, a fine not exceeding level 1 on the standard scale, and
(*b*)   in the case of a person convicted of any other offence under this section, a fine not exceeding level 3 on the standard scale."

London Hackney Carriages Act 1843 (c 86)

147. In section 28 of the London Hackney Carriages Act 1843, after "for every such offence", there is inserted "of which he is convicted before the justice".

Town Police Clauses Act 1847 (c 89)

148. In section 26 of the Town Police Clauses Act 1847, for the words from "committed by them" to the end, there is substituted "liable to a fine not exceeding level 3 on the standard scale".
149. In section 28 of that Act, after "for each offence", there is inserted "of which he is convicted before the justice".
150. In section 29 of that Act, after "for every such offence", there is inserted "of which he is convicted before the justice".
151. In section 36 of that Act, after "liable", there is inserted "on conviction before the justices".

Seamen's and Soldiers' False Characters Act 1906 (c 5)

152. In section 1 of the Seamen's and Soldiers' False Characters Act 1906, for "imprisonment for a term not exceeding three months" there is substituted "a fine not exceeding level 2 on the standard scale".

Aliens Restriction (Amendment) Act 1919 (c 92)

153. In section 3(2) of the Aliens Restriction (Amendment) Act 1919, for "imprisonment for a term not exceeding three months" there is substituted "a fine not exceeding level 3 on the standard scale".

Polish Resettlement Act 1947 (c 19)

154. In the Schedule to the Polish Resettlement Act 1947, in paragraph 7, for "imprisonment for a term not exceeding three months" there is substituted "a fine not exceeding level 1 on the standard scale".

Army Act 1955 (3 & 4 Eliz 2 c 18)

155. In section 61 of the Army Act 1955, for the words from "the like" to "section nineteen of this Act" there is substituted "dismissal from Her Majesty's service with or without disgrace, to detention for a term not exceeding three months,".

Air Force Act 1955 (3 & 4 Eliz 2 c 19)

156. In section 61 of the Air Force Act 1955, for the words from "the like" to "section nineteen of this Act" there is substituted "dismissal from Her Majesty's service with or without disgrace, to detention for a term not exceeding three months,".

Naval Discipline Act 1957 (c 53)

157. In section 34A of the Naval Discipline Act 1957, for the words "imprisonment for a term not exceeding three months" there is substituted "dismissal from Her Majesty's service with or without disgrace, detention for a term not exceeding three months,".

Slaughterhouses Act 1974 (c 3)

158. In section 4 of the Slaughterhouses Act 1974, after subsection (5) there is inserted—

"(5A) A person guilty of an offence under subsection (5) above shall be liable to a fine not exceeding level 3 on the standard scale."

Water Industry Act 1991 (c 56)

159. In Schedule 6 to the Water Industry Act 1991, in paragraph 5(4), for paragraphs (*a*) and (*b*) there is substituted ", on summary conviction, to a fine not exceeding level 5 on the standard scale".

Water Resources Act 1991 (c 57)

160. In section 205(6) of the Water Resources Act 1991, for paragraphs (*a*) and (*b*) there is substituted "on summary conviction to a fine not exceeding level 5 on the standard scale".

Transport Act 2000 (c 38)

161. In section 82(4) of the Transport Act 2000, after "subsection (1)" there is inserted "or (2)".

Reserve Forces Act 1996 (c 14)

162. In paragraph 5(3) of Schedule 1 to the Reserve Forces Act 1996, for the words "imprisonment for a term not exceeding three months" there is substituted "dismissal from Her Majesty's service with or without disgrace, to detention for a term not exceeding 3 months,".

3–2098

SCHEDULE 34
PARENTING ORDERS AND REFERRAL ORDERS

(*Schedule 34, which was introduced by s 324 supra, makes provision in relation to the interaction between parenting orders made under ss 8–10 of the Crime and Disorder Act 1998 and referral orders made under Pt 3 of the Powers of Criminal Courts Act 2000. Section 324 came into force on 27 February 2004: see the Criminal Justice Act 2003 (Commencement No 2 and Saving Provisions) Order 2004, SI 2004/81.*)

3–2099

SCHEDULE 36
FURTHER MINOR AND CONSEQUENTIAL AMENDMENTS

(*This Schedule makes numerous, minor and consequential amendments. Those which effect statutory provisions reproduced in this work will be shown in the statutes concerned when they take effect.*)

3–2100

SCHEDULE 37
REPEALS

(*This Schedule makes repeals that are consequential on the changes made by the Act. Those which effect statutory provisions reproduced in this work will be shown in the statutes concerned when they take effect.*)

3–2101

Section 333(6)

SCHEDULE 38
TRANSITORY, TRANSITIONAL AND SAVING PROVISIONS

Sentencing of offenders aged 18 but under 21

1. If any provision of Part 12 ("the relevant provision") is to come into force before the day on which section 61 of the Criminal Justice and Court Services Act 2000 (abolition of sentences of detention in a young offender institution, custody for life, etc) comes into force (or fully into force) the provision that may be made by order under section 333(1) includes provision modifying the relevant provision with respect to sentences passed, or other things done, at any time before section 61 of that Act comes into force (or fully into force).

Sentencing guidelines

2. The repeal by this Act of sections 80 and 81 of the Crime and Disorder Act 1998 does not affect the authority of any guidelines with respect to sentencing which have been included in any judgment of the Court of Appeal given before the commencement of that repeal ("existing guidelines"), but any existing guidelines may be superseded by sentencing guidelines published by the Sentencing Guidelines Council under section 170 of this Act as definitive guidelines.

3. (1) Subject to sub-paragraph (2), the repeal by this Act of section 81 of the Crime and Disorder Act 1998 does not affect the operation of subsection (4) of that section in relation to any notification received by the Panel under subsection (2) of that section, or proposal made by the Panel under subsection (3) of that section, before the commencement of the repeal.

(2) In its application by virtue of sub-paragraph (1) after the commencement of that repeal, section 81(4) of that Act is to have effect as if any reference to "the Court" were a reference to the Sentencing Guidelines Council.

(3) In this paragraph "the Panel" means the Sentencing Advisory Panel.

Drug treatment and testing orders

4. A drug treatment and testing order made under section 52 of the Powers of Criminal Courts (Sentencing) Act 2000 before the repeal of that section by this Act is in force (or fully in force) need not include the provision referred to in subsection (6) of section 54 of that Act (periodic review by court) if the treatment and testing period (as defined by section 52(1) of that Act) is less than 12 months.

Drug testing as part of supervision of young offenders after release

5. (1) Until the coming into force of the repeal by this Act of section 65 of the Criminal Justice Act 1991 (c 53) (supervision of young offenders after release), that section has effect subject to the following modifications.

(2) In subsection (5B)—

(*a*) in paragraph (*a*), for "18 years" there is substituted "14 years",

(*b*) for paragraph (*b*) there is substituted—

"(*b*) a responsible officer is of the opinion—

(i) that the offender has a propensity to misuse specified Class A drugs, and

(ii) that the misuse by the offender of any specified Class A drug caused or contributed to any offence of which he has been convicted, or is likely to cause or contribute to the commission by him of further offences; and".

(3) After subsection (5D) there is inserted—

"(5E) A person under the age of 17 years may not be required by virtue of subsection (5A) to provide a sample otherwise than in the presence of an appropriate adult."

(4) For subsection (10) there is substituted—

"(10) In this section—

"appropriate adult", in relation to a person aged under 17, means—

(*a*) his parent or guardian or, if he is in the care of a local authority or voluntary organisation, a person representing that authority or organisation,

(*b*) a social worker of a local authority social services department, or

(*c*) if no person falling within paragraph (*a*) or (*b*) is available, any responsible person aged 18 or over who is not a police officer or a person employed by the police;

"responsible officer" means—

(*a*) in relation to an offender aged under 18, an officer of a local probation board or a member of a youth offending team;

(*b*) in relation to an offender aged 18 or over, an officer of a local probation board;

"specified Class A drug" has the same meaning as in Part 3 of the Criminal Justice and Court Services Act 2000 (c 43)."

Intermittent custody

6. If section 183 (intermittent custody) is to come into force for any purpose before the commencement of the repeal by this Act of section 78 of the Powers of Criminal Courts (Sentencing) Act 2000 (c 6) (which imposes a general limit on the power of a magistrates' court to impose imprisonment), the provision that may be made by order under section 333(1) includes provision modifying any period or number of days specified in section 183 with respect to sentences passed by magistrates' courts before the commencement of that repeal.

Transfer to Scotland of community orders and suspended sentence orders

7. (1) Until the coming into force of the repeal by the Mental Health (Care and Treatment) (Scotland) Act 2003 of the Mental Health (Scotland) Act 1984 (c 36), in the provisions mentioned in sub-paragraph (2) the reference to the Mental Health (Care and Treatment) (Scotland) Act 2003 has effect as a reference to the Mental Health (Scotland) Act 1984.

(2) Those provisions are—

(*a*) paragraph 2(4) of Schedule 9 (transfer of community orders to Scotland or Northern Ireland), and

(*b*) paragraph 4 of Schedule 13 (transfer of suspended sentence orders to Scotland or Northern Ireland).

Statutory Instruments on Sentencing

Rehabilitation of Offenders Act 1974 (Exceptions) Order 1975[1]

(SI 1975/1023 amended by 1986/1249 and 2268, the Osteopaths Act 1993, s 39, the Chiropractors Act 1994, s 40, SI 2001/1149, 1192 and 3816, SI 2002/441,SI 2003/965 and 1590,SI 2005/617, 848, 1082 and 2011 and SI 2006/594, 2143 and 3290)

3–3000 **1.** Citation and commencement.

1. Made under ss 4(4) and 7(4) of the Rehabilitation of Offenders Act 1974. Revoked in relation to Scotland by SSI 2003/231, as from 29 March 2003.

3–3001 **2.** (1) In this Order, except where the context otherwise requires—

"the 2000 Act" means the Financial Services and Markets Act 2000;

"the Act" means the Rehabilitation of Offenders Act 1974;

"administration of justice offence" means—

(*a*) the offence of perverting the course of justice,

(*b*) any offence under section 51 of the Criminal Justice and Public Order Act 1994 (intimidation etc of witnesses, jurors and others),

(*c*) an offence under section 1, 2, 6 or 7 of the Perjury Act 1911 (perjury),

or any offence committed under the law of any part of the United Kingdom (other than England or Wales) or of any other country where the conduct which constitutes the offence would, if it all took place in England or Wales, constitute one or more of the offences specified by paragraph (*a*) to (*c*);

"adoption agency" has the meaning given to it by section 1 of the Adoption Act 1976;

"associate", in relation to a person ("A"), means someone who is a controller, director or manager of A or, where A is a partnership, any partner of A;

"child minding" means—

(a) until section 79 of the Care Standards Act 2000 comes into force, acting as a child minder within the meaning of section 71 of the Children Act 1989; and

(b) when section 79 of the Care Standards Act 2000 is in force, child minding within the meaning of section 79A of the Children Act 1989;

"collective investment scheme" has the meaning given by section 235 of the 2000 Act;

"the competent authority for listing" means the competent authority for the purposes of Part VI of the 2000 Act (listing);

"contracting authority" means a contracting authority within the meaning of Article 1(9) of Directive 2004/18/EC;

"contracting entity" means a contracting entity within the meaning of Article 2(2) of Directive 2004/17/EC;

"controller" has the meaning given by section 422 of the 2000 Act;

"Council" has the meaning given to it by section 54 of the Care Standards Act 2000;

"Council of Lloyd's" means the council constituted by section 3 of Lloyd's Act 1982;

"day care" means—

(a) until section 79 of the Care Standards Act 2000 comes into force, day care for which registration is required by section 78(1) of the Children Act 1989; and

(b) when section 79 of the Care Standards Act 2000 is in force, day care for which registration is required by section 79D(5) of the Children Act 1989;

"day care premises" means any premises on which day care is provided, but does not include any part of the premises where children are not looked after;

"Directive 2004/17/EC" means Directive 2004/17/EC of the European Parliament and of the Council of 31 March 2004;

"Directive 2004/18/EC" means Directive 2004/18/EC of the European Parliament and of the Council of 31 March 2004;

"director" has the meaning given by section 417 of the 2000 Act;

"key worker", in relation to any body ("A"), means any individual who is likely, in the course of the duties of his office or employment—

(a) where A is the Authority, to play a significant role in the decision making process of the Authority in relation to the exercise of the Authority's public functions (within the meaning of section 349(5) of the 2000 Act) under any provision of the 2000 Act other than Part VI, or to support directly such a person;

(b) where A is the competent authority for listing, to play a significant role in the decision making process of the competent authority for listing in relation to the exercise of its functions under Part VI of the 2000 Act, or to support directly such a person;

"manager" has the meaning given by section 423 of the 2000 Act;

"open-ended investment company" has the meaning given by section 236 of the 2000 Act

"Part IV permission" has the meaning given by section 40(4) of the 2000 Act;

"relevant collective investment scheme" means a collective investment scheme which is recognised under section 264 (schemes constituted in other EEA States), 270 (schemes authorised in designated countries or territories) or 272 (individually recognised overseas schemes) of the 2000 Act;

"relevant offence" means—

(a) an offence involving fraud or other dishonesty; *or*

(b) an offence under legislation (whether or not of the United Kingdom) relating to building societies, companies (including insider dealing), industrial and provident societies, credit unions, friendly societies, insurance, banking or other financial services, money laundering, insolvency, consumer credit or consumer protection;

(c) an administration of justice offence; *or*

(d) an offence committed (whether or not under the law of, or of any part of, the United Kingdom) in connection with, or in relation to, taxation for which a person of 21 years of age or over may be sentenced to imprisonment for a term of 2 years or more;

"taxi driver licence" means a licence granted under—

(i) section 46 of the Town Police Clauses Act 1847;

(ii) section 8 of the Metropolitan Public Carriage Act 1869;

(iii) section 9 of the Plymouth City Council Act 1975;

(iv) section 51 of the Local Government (Miscellaneous Provisions) Act 1976; or

(v) section 13 of the Private Hire Vehicles (London) Act 1998;

"trustee", in relation to a unit trust scheme, has the meaning given by section 237 of the 2000 Act;

"UK recognised clearing house" means a clearing house in relation to which a recognition order under section 290 of the 2000 Act, otherwise than by virtue of section 292(2) of that Act (overseas clearing houses), is in force;

"UK recognised investment exchange" means an investment exchange in relation to which a recognition order under section 290 of the 2000 Act, otherwise than by virtue of section 292(2) of that Act (overseas investment exchanges), is in force;

"work" includes—

    (a) work of any kind, whether paid or unpaid, and whether under a contract of service or apprenticeship, under a contract for services, or otherwise than under a contract; and

    (b) an office established by or by virtue of an enactment;

"work with children" means work of the kind described in paragraph 14 of Schedule 1 to this Order.*

  (2) Where, by virtue of this Order, the operation of any of the provisions of the Act is excluded in relation to spent convictions the exclusion shall be taken to extend to spent convictions for offences of every description unless the said provisions are excluded only in relation to spent convictions for relevant offences.

  (3) Part IV of Schedule 1 to this Order shall have effect for the interpretation of expressions used in that Schedule.

  (4) In this Order a reference to any enactment shall be construed as a reference to that enactment as amended, extended or applied by or under any other enactment.

  (5) The Interpretation Act 1889 shall apply to the interpretation of this Order as it applies to the interpretation of an Act of Parliament.*

---

    *SI revoked in relation to Scotland by SSI 2003/231, as from 29 March 2003.

3–3002   **3.** None of the provisions of section 4(2) of the Act shall apply in relation to—

  (a) any question asked by or on behalf of any person, in the course of the duties of his office or employment, in order to assess the suitability—

    (i) of the person to whom the question relates for admission to any of the professions specified in Part I of Schedule 1 to this Order; or

    (ii) of the person to whom the question relates for any office or employment specified in Part II of the said Schedule 1 or for any other work specified in paragraph 12, 13, 20 or 21 of Part II of the said Schedule 1; or

    (iii) of the person to whom the question relates or of any other person to pursue any occupation specified in Part III of the said Schedule 1 or to pursue it subject to a particular condition or restriction; or

    (iv) of the person to whom the question relates or of any other person to hold a licence, certificate or permit of a kind specified in Schedule 2 to this Order or to hold it subject to a particular condition or restriction,

  where the person questioned is informed at the time the question is asked that, by virtue of this Order, spent convictions are to be disclosed;

  (aa) any question asked by or on behalf of any person, in the course of the duties of his work, in order to assess the suitability of a person to work with children, where—

    (i) the question relates to the person whose suitability is being assessed;

    (ii) the person whose suitability is being assessed lives on the premises where his work with children would normally take place and the question relates to a person living in the same household as him;

    (iii) the person whose suitability is being assessed lives on the premises where his work with children would normally take place and the question relates to a person who regularly works on those premises at a time when the work with children usually takes place; or

    (iv) the work for which the person's suitability is being assessed is child minding which would normally take place on premises other than premises where that person lives and the question relates to a person who lives on those other premises or to a person who regularly works on them at a time when the child minding takes place,

  and where the person to whom the question relates is informed at the time the question is asked that, by virtue of this Order, spent convictions are to be disclosed;

  (b) any question asked by or on behalf of any person, in the course of his duties as a person employed in the service of the Crown, the United Kingdom Atomic Energy Authority, or the Civil Aviation Authority, the Financial Services Authority in order to assess, for the purpose of safeguarding national security, the suitability of the person to whom the question relates or of any other person for any office or employment where the person questioned is informed at the time the question is asked that, by virtue of this Order, spent convictions are to be disclosed for the purpose of safeguarding national security;

  (bb) any question asked by or on behalf of

    (i) the Civil Aviation Authority,

    (ii) any other person authorised to provide air traffic services under section 4 or section 5 of the Transport Act 2000 (in any case where such person is a company, an "authorised company"),

    (iii) any company which is a subsidiary (within the meaning given by section 736(1) of the Companies Act 1985) of an authorised company, or

    (iv) any company of which an authorised company is a subsidiary,

  where, in the case of sub-paragraphs (iii) and (iv) of this paragraph the question is put in relation to the provision of air traffic services, and in all cases, where the question is put in order to assess, for the purpose of safeguarding national security, the suitability of the person to whom the question relates or of any other person for any office or employment where the person questioned is informed at the time the question is asked that, by virtue of this Order, spent convictions are to be disclosed for the purpose of safeguarding national security;*

(e)   any question asked by or on behalf of any person in the course of his duties as a person employed by an adoption agency for the purpose of assessing the suitability of any person to adopt children in general or a child in particular where—

   (i)   the question relates to the person whose suitability is being assessed; or
   (ii)   the question relates to a person over the age of 18 living in the same household as the person whose suitability is being assessed,

   and where the person to whom the question relates is informed at the time the question is asked that, by virtue of this Order, spent convictions are to be disclosed;

(f)   any question asked by or on behalf of any person, in the course of the duties of his work, in order to assess the suitability of a person to provide day care where—

   (i)   the question relates to the person whose suitability is being assessed; or
   (ii)   the question relates to a person who lives on the premises which are or are proposed to be day care premises,

   and where the person to whom the question relates is informed at the time the question is asked that, by virtue of this Order, spent convictions are to be disclosed;

(g)   any question asked by, or on behalf of, the person listed in the second column of any entry in the table below to the extent that it relates to a conviction for a relevant offence (or any circumstances ancillary to such a conviction) of any individual, but only if—

   (i)   the person questioned is informed at the time the question is asked that, by virtue of this Order, spent convictions for relevant offences are to be disclosed; and
   (ii)   the question is asked in order to assess the suitability of the individual to whom the question relates to have the status specified in the first column of that entry.

Status		Questioner
1	A person with Part IV permission.	The Financial Services Authority.
2	(a) An approved person (within the meaning of Part V of the 2000 Act (performance of regulated activities)).	The Financial Services Authority or the authorised person (within the meaning of section 31(2) of the 2000 Act) or the applicant for Part IV permission who made the application for the Authority's approval under section 59 of the 2000 Act in relation to the person mentioned in sub-paragraph (a) of the first column.
	(b) An associate of the person (whether or not an individual) mentioned in sub-paragraph (a).	
3	(a) The manager or trustee of an authorised unit trust scheme, within the meaning of section 237 of the 2000 Act.	The Financial Services Authority or the unit trust scheme mentioned in the first column.
	(b) An associate of the person (whether or not an individual) mentioned in sub-paragraph (a).	
4	(a) A director of an open-ended investment company.	The Financial Services Authority or the open-ended investment company mentioned in the first column.
	(b) An associate of the person (whether or not an individual) mentioned in sub-paragraph (a).	
5	An associate of the operator or trustee of a relevant collective investment scheme.	The Financial Services Authority or the collective investment scheme mentioned in the first column.
6	An associate of a UK recognised investment exchange or UK recognised clearing house.	The Financial Services Authority or the investment exchange or clearing house mentioned in the first column.
7	A controller of a person with Part IV permission.	The Financial Services Authority or the person with Part IV permission mentioned in the first column.
8	(a) A person who carries on a regulated activity (within the meaning of section 22 of the 2000 Act) but to whom the general prohibition does not apply by virtue of section 327 of the 2000 Act (exemption from the general prohibition for members of a designated professional body).	(a) The Financial Services Authority.

Status		Questioner
	(b) An associate of the person (whether or not an individual) mentioned in sub-paragraph (a).	(b) In the case of a person mentioned in sub-paragraph (b) of the first column, the person mentioned in sub-paragraph (a) of that column.
9	A key worker of the Financial Services Authority.	The Financial Services Authority.
10	An ombudsman (within the meaning of Schedule 17 to the 2000 Act) of the Financial Ombudsman Service.	The scheme operator (within the meaning of section 225 of the 2000 Act) of the Financial Ombudsman Service.
11	An associate of the issuer of securities which have been admitted to the official list maintained by the competent authority for listing under section 74 of the 2000 Act.	The competent authority for listing.
12	A sponsor (within the meaning of section 88(2) of the 2000 Act).	The competent authority for listing.
13	A key worker of the competent authority for listing.	The competent authority for listing.
14	An associate of a person who has Part IV permission and who is admitted to Lloyd's as an underwriting agent (within the meaning of section 2 of Lloyd's Act 1982).	(a) The Council of Lloyd's. (b) The person with Part IV permission specified in the first column (or a person applying for such permission).
15	An associate of the Council of Lloyd's.	The Council of Lloyd's.
16	(a) Any member of a UK recognised investment exchange or UK recognised clearing house.	(a) The UK recognised investment exchange or UK recognised clearing house specified in the first column.
	(b) Any associate of the person (whether or not an individual) mentioned in sub-paragraph (a).	(b) In the case of a person mentioned in sub-paragraph (b) of the first column, the person mentioned in sub-paragraph (a) of that column.

(*h*)   any question asked by or on behalf of the National Lottery Commission for the purpose of determining whether to grant or revoke a licence under Part I of the National Lottery etc Act 1993 where the question relates to an individual—

     (i)   who manages the business or any part of the business carried on under the licence (or who is likely to do so if the licence is granted), or

     (ii)   for whose benefit that business is carried on (or is likely to be carried on if the licence is granted),

and where the person to whom the question relates is informed at the time that the question is asked that, by virtue of this Order, spent convictions are to be disclosed.**

(*i*)   any question asked by or on behalf of the Council for the purpose of determining whether or not to grant an application for registration under Part IV of the Care Standards Act 2000, where the person questioned is informed at the time the question is asked that, by virtue of this Order, spent convictions are to be disclosed;

(*j*)   any question asked by or on behalf of a contracting authority or contracting entity in relation to a conviction within the meaning of Article 45(1) of Directive 2004/18/EC which is a spent conviction (or any circumstances ancillary to such a conviction) for the purpose of determining whether or not to treat a person as ineligible—

     (i)   for the purposes of regulation 23 of the Public Contracts Regulations 2006 or regulation 23 of the Utilities Contracts Regulations 2006; or

     (ii)   to participate in a design contest for the purposes of regulation 33 of the Public Contracts Regulations 2006 or regulation 34 of the Utilities Contracts Regulations 2006, where the person questioned is informed at the time the question is asked that, by virtue of this Order, convictions within the meaning of Article 45(1) of Directive 2004/18/EC which are spent convictions are to be disclosed;

(*k*)   any question asked, by or on behalf of the Football Association, Football League or Football Association Premier League in order to assess the suitability of the person to whom the question relates or of any other person to be approved as able to undertake, in the course of acting as a steward at a sports ground at which football matches are played or as a supervisor or manager of such a person, licensable conduct within the meaning of the Private Security Industry Act 2001 without a licence issued under that Act, in accordance with section 4 of that Act.

---

*Paragraph 3(*bb*) printed as prospectively inserted by SI 2002/441.
**SI revoked in relation to Scotland by SSI 2003/231, as from 29 March 2003.

3–3003   **4.** Paragraph (*b*) of section 4(3) of the Act shall not apply in relation to—

     (*a*)   the dismissal or exclusion of any person from any profession specified in Part I of Schedule 1 to this Order;

(b) any office, employment or occupation specified in Part II or Part III of the said Schedule 1 or any other work specified in paragraph 12, 13 20 or 21 of Part II of the said Schedule 1;

(c) any action taken for the purpose of safeguarding national security;

(d) any decision by the Financial Services Authority—

  (i) to refuse an application for Part IV permission under the 2000 Act,

  (ii) to vary or to cancel such permission (or to refuse to vary or cancel such permission) or to impose a requirement under section 43 of that Act or,

  (iii) to make, or to refuse to vary or revoke, an order under section 56 of that Act (prohibition orders),

  (iv) to refuse an application for the Authority's approval under section 59 of that Act or to withdraw such approval,

  (v) to refuse to make, or to revoke, an order declaring a unit trust scheme to be an authorised unit trust scheme under section 243 of the 2000 Act or to refuse to give its approval under section 251 of the 2000 Act to a proposal to replace the manager or trustee of such a scheme,

  (vi) to give a direction under section 257 of the 2000 Act (authorised unit trust schemes), or to vary (or to refuse to vary or revoke) such a direction,

  (vii) to refuse to make, or to revoke, an authorisation order under regulation 14 of the Open-Ended Investment Companies Regulations 2001 or to refuse to give its approval under regulation 21 of those Regulations to a proposal to replace a director or to appoint an additional director of an open-ended investment company,

  (viii) to give a direction to an open-ended investment company under regulation 25 of those Regulations or to vary (or refuse to vary or revoke) such a direction,

  (ix) to refuse to give its approval to a collective investment scheme being recognised under section 270 of the 2000 Act or to direct that such a scheme cease to be recognised by virtue of that section or to refuse to make, or to revoke, an order declaring a collective investment scheme to be a recognised scheme under section 272 of that Act,

  (x) to refuse to make, or to revoke, a recognition order under section 290 of the 2000 Act, otherwise than by virtue of section 292(2) of that Act, or to give a direction to a UK recognised investment exchange or UK recognised clearing house under section 296 of the 2000 Act,

  (xi) to make, or to refuse to vary or to revoke, an order under section 329 (orders in respect of members of a designated professional body in relation to the general prohibition), or

  (xii) to dismiss, fail to promote or exclude a person from being a key worker of the Authority,

by reason of, or partly by reason of, a spent conviction of an individual for a relevant offence, or of any circumstances ancillary to such a conviction or of a failure (whether or not by that individual) to disclose such a conviction or any such circumstances;

(e) any decision by the scheme operator (within the meaning of section 225 of the 2000 Act) of the Financial Ombudsman Service to dismiss, or not to appoint, an individual as, an ombudsman (within the meaning of Schedule 17 to the 2000 Act) of the Financial Ombudsman Service by reason of, or partly by reason of, his spent conviction for a relevant offence, or of any circumstances ancillary to such a conviction or of a failure (whether or not by that individual) to disclose such a conviction or any such circumstances;

(f) any decision of the competent authority for listing—

  (i) to refuse an application for listing under Part VI of the 2000 Act or to discontinue or suspend the listing of any securities under section 77 of that Act,

  (ii) to refuse to grant a person's application for approval as a sponsor under section 88 of the 2000 Act or to cancel such approval, or

  (iii) to dismiss, fail to promote or exclude a person from being a key worker of the competent authority for listing,

by reason of, or partly by reason of, a spent conviction of an individual for a relevant offence, or of any circumstances ancillary to such a conviction or of a failure (whether or not by that individual) to disclose such a conviction or any such circumstances;

(g) any decision of anyone who is specified in any of sub-paragraphs 2 to 4 or 5 to 7 of the second column of the table in article 3(g), other than the Authority, to dismiss an individual who has, or to fail to promote or exclude an individual who is seeking to obtain, the status specified in the corresponding entry in the first column of that table (but not, where applicable, the status of being an associate of another person), by reason of, or partly by reason of, a spent conviction of that individual or of his associate for a relevant offence, or of any circumstances ancillary to such a conviction or of a failure (whether or not by that individual) to disclose such a conviction or any such circumstances;

(h) any decision of anyone who is specified in sub-paragraph 8(a), 14(a) or 16(a) of the second column of the table in article 3(g) to dismiss an individual who has, or to fail to promote or exclude an individual who is seeking to obtain, the status specified in the corresponding entry in sub-paragraph (b) of the first column of that table (associate), by reason of, or partly by reason of, a spent conviction of that individual for a relevant offence, or of any circumstances ancillary to such a conviction or of a failure (whether or not by that individual) to disclose such a conviction or any such circumstances;

(i) any decision of the Council of Lloyd's—

  (i) to refuse to admit any person as, or to exclude, an underwriting agent (within the meaning of section 2 of Lloyd's Act 1982), where that person has, or who has applied for, Part IV permission, or

(ii) to dismiss, or to exclude a person from being, an associate of the Council of Lloyd's,

by reason of, or partly by reason of, a spent conviction of an individual for a relevant offence, or of any circumstances ancillary to such a conviction or of a failure (whether or not by that individual) to disclose such a conviction or any such circumstances;

(j) any decision of a UK recognised investment exchange or UK recognised clearing house to refuse to admit any person as, or to exclude, a member by reason of, or partly by reason of, a spent conviction of an individual for a relevant offence, or of any circumstances ancillary to such a conviction or of a failure (whether or not by that individual) to disclose such a conviction or any such circumstances.

(k) any decision by the Council to refuse to grant an application for registration under Part IV of the Care Standards Act 2000 or to suspend, remove or refuse to restore a person's registration under that Part;

(l) any decision to refuse to grant a taxi driver licence, to grant such a licence subject to conditions or to suspend, revoke or refuse to renew such a licence;

(m) any decision by the Security Industry Authority to refuse to grant a licence under section 8 of the Private Security Industry Act 2001, to grant such a licence subject to conditions, to modify such a licence (including any of the conditions of that licence) or to revoke such a licence;

(n) any decision by the Football Association, Football League or Football Association Premier League to refuse to approve a person as able to undertake, in the course of acting as a steward at a sports ground at which football matches are played or as a supervisor or manager of such a person, licensable conduct within the meaning of the Private Security Industry Act 2001 without a licence issued under that Act, in accordance with section 4 of that Act.*

*SI revoked in relation to Scotland by SSI 2003/231, as from 29 March 2003.

3–3004 5. (1) Section 4(1) of the Act shall not—

(a) apply in relation to any proceedings specified in Schedule 3 to this Order;

(b) apply in relation to any proceedings specified in paragraph (2) below to the extent that there falls to be determined therein any issue relating to a person's spent conviction for any relevant offence or to circumstances ancillary thereto;

(c) prevent, in any proceedings specified in paragraph (2) below, the admission or requirement of any evidence relating to a person's spent conviction for any relevant offence or to circumstances ancillary thereto.

(2) The proceedings referred to in paragraph (1) above are any proceedings with respect to a decision or proposed decision of the kind specified in article 4(d) to (j).*

*SI revoked in relation to Scotland by SSI 2003/231, as from 29 March 2003.

Articles 2(3), 3 and 4   SCHEDULE 1*
                    EXCEPTED PROFESSIONS, OFFICES, EMPLOYMENTS, WORK AND OCCUPATIONS

(Amended by SI 2001/1192 and SI 2005/848.)

*SI revoked in relation to Scotland by SSI 2003/231, as from 29 March 2003.

PART I

Professions

3–3005 1. Medical practitioner.
   2. Barrister (in England and Wales), advocate (in Scotland), solicitor.
   3. Chartered accountant, certified accountant.
   4. Dentist, dental hygienist, dental therapist.
   5. Veterinary surgeon.
   6. Nurse, midwife.
   7. Optometrist, dispensing optician.
   8. Pharmaceutical chemist.*
   9. Registered teacher (in Scotland).
   10. Any profession to which the Health Professions Order 2001 applies and which is undertaken following registration under that Act.
   11. Registered osteopath.
   12. Registered chiropractor.
   13. Chartered psychologist
   14. Actuary.
   15. Registered foreign lawyer.
   16. Legal executive.
   17. Receiver appointed by the Court of Protection.
   18. Home inspector.**

*Substituted by new terms "registered pharmacist" and "registered pharmacy technician" by SI 2007/289 from a date to be appointed.
**SI revoked in relation to Scotland by SSI 2003/231, as from 29 March 2003.

PART II

Offices, Employments and Work

3–3006   **1.** Judicial appointments.

   2. The Director of Public Prosecutions and any employment in his office.

   3. Revoked.

   4. Designated officers for magistrates' courts, for justices of the peace or for local justice areas, justices' clerks and assistants to justices' clerks.

   5. Clerks (including depute and assistant clerks) and officers of the High Court of Justiciary, the Court of Session and the district court, sheriff clerks (including sheriff clerks depute) and their clerks and assistants.

   6. Constables, persons appointed as police cadets to undergo training with a view to becoming constables and persons employed for the purposes of, or to assist the constables of, a police force established under any enactment; naval, military and air force police.

   7. Any employment which is concerned with the administration of, or is otherwise normally carried out wholly or partly within the precincts of, a prison, remand centre, removal centre, short-term holding facility, young offender institution or young offenders institution, and members of boards of visitors appointed under section 6 of the Prison Act 1952 or of visiting committees appointed under section 7 of the Prisons (Scotland) Act 1952.

   8. Traffic wardens appointed under section [95] of the Road Traffic Regulation Act [1984] or section 9 of the Police (Scotland) Act 1967.

   9. Probation officers appointed under Schedule 3 to the Powers of Criminal Courts Act 1973.

   10, 11. Revoked.

   12. Any office or employment which is concerned with:

    (*a*)   the provision of care services to vulnerable adults; or

    (*b*)   the representation of, or advocacy services for, vulnerable adults by a service that has been approved by the Secretary of State or created under any enactment;

and which is of such a kind as to enable a person, in the course of his normal duties, to have access to vulnerable adults in receipt of such services.

   13. Any employment or other work which is concerned with the provision of health services and which is of such a kind as to enable the holder of that employment or the person engaged in that work to have access to persons in receipt of such services in the course of his normal duties.

   14. Any work which is—

    (*a*)   work in a regulated position; or

    (*b*)   work in a further education institution where the normal duties of that work involve regular contact with persons aged under 18.

   15. Any employment in the Royal Society for the Prevention to Cruelty to Animals where the person employed or working, as part of his duties, may carry out the humane killing of animals.

   16. Any office or employment in the Serious Organised Crime Agency.

   17. Any office or employment in the Serious Organised Crime Agency.

   18. The Commissioners for Her Majesty's Revenue and Customs and any office or employment in their service.

   18A. The Director and any office or employment in the Revenue and Customs Prosecutions Office.

   19. Any employment which is concerned with the monitoring, for the purposes of child protection, of communications by means of the internet.

   20. Any employment or other work which is normally carried out in premises approved under section 9 of the Criminal Justice and Court Services Act 2000.

   21. Any employment or other work which is normally carried out in a hospital used only for the provision of high security psychiatric services.

   22. An individual designated under section 2 of the Traffic Management Act 2004.

   23. Judges' clerks, secretaries and legal secretaries within the meaning of section 98 of the Supreme Court Act 1981.

   24. Court officers and court contractors, who in the course of their work, have face to face contact with judges of the Supreme Court, or access to such judges' lodgings.

   25. Persons who in the course of their work have regular access to personal information relating to an identified or identifiable member of the judiciary.

   26. Court officers and court contractors, who, in the course of their work, attend either the Royal Courts of Justice or the Central Criminal Court.

   27. Court security officers, and tribunal security officers.

   28. Court contractors, who, in the course of their work, have unsupervised access to court-houses, offices and other accommodation used in relation to the courts.

   29. Contractors, sub-contractors, and any person acting under the authority of such a contractor or sub-contractor, who, in the course of their work, have unsupervised access to tribunal buildings, offices and other accommodation used in relation to tribunals.

   30. The following persons—

    (*a*)   Court officers who execute county court warrants;

    (*b*)   High Court enforcement officers;

    (*c*)   sheriffs and under-sheriffs;

    (*d*)   tipstaffs;

    (*e*)   any other persons who execute High Court writs or warrants who act under the authority of a person listed at (a) to (d);

    (*f*)   persons who execute writs of sequestration;

    (*g*)   civilian enforcement officers as defined in section 125A of the Magistrates' Courts Act 1980;

    (*h*)   persons who are authorised to execute warrants under section 125B(1) of the Magistrates' Courts Act 1980 , and any other person, (other than a constable), who is authorised to execute a warrant under section 125(2) of the 1980 Act;

    (*i*)   persons who execute clamping orders, as defined in paragraph 38(2) of Schedule 5 to the Courts Act 2003.

   31. The Official Solicitor and his deputy.

   32. Persons appointed to the office of Public Trustee or deputy Public Trustee, and officers of the Public Trustee.

   33. Court officers and court contractors who exercise functions in connection with the administration and management of funds in court including the deposit, payment, delivery and transfer in, into and out of any court of funds in court and regulating the evidence of such deposit, payment, delivery or transfer and court officers and court contractors, who receive payments in pursuance of a conviction or order of a magistrates' court.*

---

*SI revoked in relation to Scotland by SSI 2003/231, as from 29 March 2003.

PART III

Regulated occupations

3–3007 **1.** Firearms dealer.

2. Any occupation in respect of which an application to the Gaming Board for Great Britain for a licence, certificate or registration is required by or under any enactment.

3. Director, controller or manager of an insurer.

6. Any occupation which is concerned with—

(a) the management of a place in respect of which the approval of the Secretary of State is required by section 1 of the Abortion Act 1967; or

(b) in England and Wales, carrying on a nursing home in respect of which registration is required by section 187 of the Public Health Act 1936 or section 14 of the Mental Health Act 1959; or

(c) in Scotland, carrying on a nursing home in respect of which registration is required under section 1 of the Nursing Homes Registration (Scotland) Act 1938 or a private hospital in respect of which registration is required under section 15 of the Mental Health (Scotland) Act 1960.

7. Any occupation which is concerned with carrying on an establishment in respect of which registration is required by section 37 of the National Assistance Act 1948 or section 61 of the Social Work (Scotland) Act 1968.

8. Any occupation in respect of which the holder, as occupier of premises on which explosives are kept, is required pursuant to regulations 4 and 7 of the Control of Explosives Regulations 1991 to obtain from the chief officer of police a valid explosives certificate certifying him to be a fit person to acquire or acquire and keep explosives.

9. Revoked.*

---

*SI revoked in relation to Scotland by SSI 2003/231, as from 29 March 2003.

1. See now the Insurance Companies Act 1982.

PART IV

Interpretation

3–3008 In this Schedule—

"actuary" means a member of the Institute of Actuaries or a member or student of the Faculty of Actuaries;

"assistants to justices' clerks" has the meaning given by section 27(5) of the Courts Act 2003;

"care services" means

(i) accommodation and nursing or personal care in a care home (where "care home" has the same meaning as in the Care Standards Act 2000);

(ii) personal care or nursing or support for a person to live independently in his own home;

(iii) social care services; or

(iv) any services provided in an establishment catering for a person with learning difficulties;

"certified accountant" means a member of the Association of Certified Accountants;

"chartered accountant" means a member of the Institute of Chartered Accountants in England and Wales or of the Institute of Chartered Accountants of Scotland;

"chartered psychologist" means a psychologist included in the British Psychological Society's Register of Chartered Psychologists;

"court contractor" means a person who has entered into a contract with the Lord Chancellor under section 2(4) of the Courts Act 2003, such a person's sub-contractor, and persons acting under the authority of such a contractor or sub-contractor for the purpose of discharging the Lord Chancellor's general duty in relation to the courts;

"court officer" means a person appointed by the Lord Chancellor under section 2(1) of the Courts Act 2003;

"court security officers" has the meaning given by section 51 of the Courts Act 2003;

"firearms dealer" has the meaning assigned to that expression by section 57(4) of the Firearms Act 1968;

"funds in court" has the meaning given by section 47 of the Administration of Justice Act 1982;

"further education" has the meaning assigned to that expression by section 41 of the Education Act 1944 or, in Scotland, section 4 of the Education (Scotland) Act 1962;

"further education institution" has the meaning given to it by paragraph 3 of the Education (Restriction of Employment) Regulations 2000;

"health services" means services provided under the National Health Service Acts 1946 to 1973 or the National Health Service (Scotland) Acts 1947 to 1973 and similar services provided otherwise than under the National Health Service;

"high security psychiatric services" has the meaning given by section 4 of the National Health Service Act 1977;

"home inspector" means a person who is a member of a certification scheme approved by the Secretary of State in accordance with section 164(3) of the Housing Act 2004;

"judges of the Supreme Court" means the Lord Chief Justice, the Master of the Rolls, the President of the Queen's Bench Division, the President of the Family Division, the Chancellor of the High Court, the Lords Justices of Appeal and the puisne judges of the High Court;

"judicial appointment" means an appointment to any office by virtue of which the holder has power (whether alone or with others) under any enactment or rule of law to determine any question affecting the rights, privileges, obligations or liabilities of any person;

"legal executive" means a fellow of the Institute of Legal Executives;

"members of the judiciary" means persons appointed to any office by virtue of which the holder has power (whether alone or with others) under any enactment or rule of law to determine any question affecting the rights, privileges, obligations or liabilities of any person;

"personal information" means any information which is of a personal or confidential nature and is not in the public domain and it includes information in any form but excludes anything disclosed for the purposes of proceedings in a particular cause or matter;

"proprietor" and "independent school" have the meanings assigned to those expressions by section 114(1) of the Education Act 1944, or in Scotland, section 145 of the Education (Scotland) Act 1962;

"registered chiropractor" has the meaning given by section 43 of the Chiropractors Act 1994;

"registered foreign lawyer" has the meaning given by section 89 of the Courts and Legal Services Act 1990;

"registered osteopath" has the meaning given by section 41 of the Osteopaths Act 1993;*

"registered teacher" means a teacher registered under the Teaching Council (Scotland) Act 1965 and includes a provisionally registered teacher;

"regulated position" means a position which is a regulated position for the purposes of Part II of the Criminal Justice and Court Services Act 2000;

"removal centre" and "short-term holding facility" have the meaning given by section 147 of the Immigration and Asylum Act 1999;

"school" has the meaning assigned to that expression by section 114(1) of the Education Act 1944 or, in Scotland, section 145 of the Education (Scotland) Act 1962;

revoked;

"teacher" includes a warden of a community centre, leader of a youth club or similar institution, youth worker and, in Scotland, youth and community worker.

"tribunal security officers" means persons who, in the course of their work, guard tribunal buildings, offices and other accommodation used in relation to tribunals against unauthorised access or occupation, against outbreaks of disorder or against damage;

"tribunals" means any person exercising the judicial power of the State, that is not a court listed in section 1(1) of the Courts Act 2003;

"unit trust scheme" has the meaning assigned to that expression by section 26(1) of the Prevention of Fraud (Investments) Act 1958 and, in relation thereto, "manager" and "trustee" shall be construed in accordance with section 26(3) of that Act.**

"vulnerable adult" means a person aged 18 or over who has a condition of the following type:

(i)   a substantial learning or physical disability;

(ii)   a physical or mental illness or mental disorder, chronic or otherwise, including an addiction to alcohol or drugs; or

(iii) a significant reduction in physical or mental capacity.***

---

*New definitions "registered pharmacist" and "registered pharmacy technician" inserted by SI 2007/289 from a date to be appointed.

**Revoked by SI 1986/2268 from a date to be appointed.

***SI revoked in relation to Scotland by SSI 2003/231, as from 29 March 2003.

   1. Reference to s 7 shall include a reference to ss 96C and 96D of the Insurance Companies Act 1974 (Insurance Companies (Third Insurance Directives) Regulations 1994, SI 1994/1696).

3–3009

Article 3   SCHEDULE 2
                 EXCEPTED LICENCES, CERTIFICATES AND PERMITS

   1. Firearm certificates and shot gun certificates issued under the Firearms Act 1968, and permits issued under section 7(1), 9(2) or 13(1)(c) of that Act.

   2. Licences issued under section 25 of the Children and Young Persons Act 1933 (which relates to persons under the age of 18 going abroad for the purpose of performing or being exhibited for profit).

   3. Explosives certificates issued by a chief officer of police pursuant to regulations 4 and 7 of the Control of Explosives Regulations 1991 as to the fitness of a person to acquire or acquire and keep explosives.

   4. Taxi driver licences.

   5. Licences granted under section 8 of the Private Security Industry Act 2001.*

---

*SI revoked in relation to Scotland by SSI 2003/231, as from 29 March 2003.

3–3010

Article 5   SCHEDULE 3
                 EXCEPTED PROCEEDINGS

   1. Proceedings in respect of a person's admission to, or disciplinary proceedings against a member of, any profession specified in Part I of Schedule 1 to this Order.

   2. Proceedings before the Court of Appeal or the High Court in the exercise of their disciplinary jurisdiction in respect of solicitors.

   3. Disciplinary proceedings against a constable.

   4. Proceedings before the Gaming Board for Great Britain.

   5. Proceedings under the Mental Health Act [1983] before any Mental Health Review Tribunal, or under the Mental Health (Scotland) Act 1960 before the Sheriff or the Mental Welfare Commission for Scotland.

   6. Proceedings under the Firearms Act 1968 in respect of—

(a) the registration of a person as a firearms dealer, the removal of a person's name from a register of firearms dealers or the imposition, variation or revocation of conditions of any such registration; or

(b) the grant, renewal, variation or revocation of a firearm certificate; or

(c) the grant, renewal or revocation of a shot gun certificate; or

(d) the grant of a permit under section 7(1), 9(2) or 13(1)(c) of that Act.

   7. Proceedings in respect of the grant, renewal or variation of a licence under section 25 of the Children and Young Persons Act 1933 (which relates to persons under the age of 18 going abroad for the purpose of performing or being exhibited for profit).

   8. Proceedings—

(a) in respect of an application under the Financial Services and Markets Act 2000 for Part IV permission to effect or carry out contracts of insurance;

(b) in respect of a decision or proposed decision to impose a requirement under Part IV of that Act on an insurer on the ground that a director or a manager of that person is not, or may not be, a fit and proper person;

(c) in relation to a notice of control given under section 178 of that Act (acquiring or increasing control) in respect of an insurer.

   9. Proceedings in respect of a direction given under section 142 of the Education Act 2002 or of any

prohibition or restriction on a person's employment or work which has effect as if it were contained in such a direction.

10. Proceedings under the Prevention of Fraud (Investments) Act 1958 in respect of an application for, or revocation of,—

(a) a licence to deal in securities; or

(b) an order by the Secretary of State declaring a person to be an exempted dealer for the purposes of that Act; or

(c) an order by the Secretary of State declaring a unit trust scheme to be an authorised unit trust scheme for the purposes of that Act,

(including proceedings under section 6 of that Act before the tribunal of inquiry constituted under that section in respect of a licence to deal in securities).*

11. Proceedings in respect of an application for, or cancellation of,—

(a) the Secretary of State's approval of a place under section 1 of the Abortion Act 1967; or

(b) in England and Wales, registration in respect of a nursing home under section 187 of the Public Health Act 1936 or section 14 of the Mental Health Act 1959; or

(c) in Scotland, registration in respect of a nursing home under section 1 of the Nursing Homes Registration (Scotland) Act 1938 or of a private hospital under section 15 of the Mental Health (Scotland) Act 1960.

12. Proceedings in respect of an application for, or cancellation of, registration under section 37 of the National Assistance Act 1948 or section 61 of the Social Work (Scotland) Act 1968 in respect of any such establishment as is mentioned in those sections.

13. Proceedings on an application to the chief officer of police pursuant to regulations 4 and 7 of the Control of Explosives Regulations 1991 as to the fitness of the applicant to acquire or acquire and keep explosives.

14. Proceedings by way of appeal against, or review of, any decision taken, by virtue of any of the provisions of this Order, on consideration of a spent conviction.

15. Proceedings held for the receipt of evidence affecting the determination of any question arising in any proceedings specified in this Schedule.

16. Proceedings relating to a taxi driver licence.

17. Proceedings—

(a) before the National Lottery Commission in respect of the grant or revocation of a licence under Part I of the National Lottery etc Act 1993; or

(b) by way of appeal to the Secretary of State against the revocation of any such licence by the National Lottery Commission.**

18. Proceedings relating to registration under Part IV of the Care Standards Act 2000.

19. Proceedings under section 11 of the Private Security Industry Act 2001.

20. Proceedings before the Parole Board.

21. Proceedings under section 7D of the Criminal Injuries Compensation Act 1995.

22. The following proceedings under the Proceeds of Crime Act 2002—

(a) proceedings under Chapter 2 of Part 5;

(b) proceedings pursuant to a notice under section 317(2);

(c) proceedings pursuant to an application under Part 8 in connection with a civil recovery investigation (within the meaning of section 341).

23. Proceedings brought before the Football Association, Football League or Football Association Premier League against a decision taken by the body before which the proceedings are brought to refuse to approve a person as able to undertake, in the course of acting as a steward at a sports ground at which football matches are played or as a supervisor or manager of such a person, licensable conduct within the meaning of the Private Security Industry Act 2001 without a licence issued under that Act, in accordance with section 4 of that Act.***

---

*Paragraph 10 revoked by SI 1986/2268 from a date to be appointed.
**Reproduced as prospectively inserted when the Police Act 1997, s 133(d) comes into force, see SI 2002/441.
***SI revoked in relation to Scotland by SSI 2003/231, as from 29 March 2003.
1. See now the Insurance Companies Act 1982.

Magistrates' Courts (Attendance Centre) Rules 1992[1]
(SI 1992/2069 amended by SI 2001/615 and SI 2003/1236)

Citation, commencement and interpretation

3–3020 **1.** (1) Citation and commencement.

(2) In these Rules "relevant order" means an order under section 60 of the Powers of Criminal Courts (Sentencing) Act 2000 ordering a person who has attained the age of 18 to attend at an attendance centre.

---

1. Made by the Lord Chancellor, in exercise of the powers conferred on him by s 144 of the Magistrates' Courts Act 1980.

Forms

3–3021 **2.** Revoked.

Payment of money by person subject to relevant order

3–3022 **3.** (1) Where a relevant order has been made in default of payment of a sum of money—

(a) the whole of that sum may be paid to the justices' chief executive for the court which made the order ("the clerk"), or

(b) the whole or, subject to paragraph (2), a part of that sum may be paid to the officer in charge of the attendance centre specified in the order ("the officer in charge").

(2) The officer in charge may not accept a part payment that would not secure the reduction by one or more complete hours of the period of attendance specified in the order.

(3) On receiving a payment under paragraph (1) the justices' chief executive shall forthwith notify the officer in charge.

(4) The officer in charge shall pay any money received by him under paragraph (1) to the justices' chief executive and shall note the receipt of the money in the record maintained at the attendance centre.

3–3023   4. Revocations.

3–3024   SCHEDULE 1

(Revoked).

Fines (Deductions from Income Support) Regulations 1992[1]
(SI 1992/2182, amended by SI 1993/495, SI 1996/2344, SI 1998/563 and 865, SI 1999/3178, SI 2002/1397 and 3019, SI 2003/1360 and SI 2004/2889)

Citation, commencement and interpretation

3–3040   1. (1) Citation and commencement.

(2) In these Regulations, unless the context otherwise requires—

"the 1971 Act" means the Vehicles (Excise) Act 1971;

"the 1973 Act" means the Powers of Criminal Courts Act 1973;

"the 1998 Act" means the Social Security Act 1998;

"application" means an application made under regulation 2 containing the information specified in regulation 3(1);

"benefit week" has the meaning prescribed in regulation 2(1) of the Income Support Regulations or, as the case may be, regulation 1(2) of the State Pension Credit Regulations 2002 or regulation 1(3) of the Jobseeker's Allowance Regulations 1996;

"the Claims and Payments Regulations" means the Social Security (Claims and Payments) Regulations 1987;

"Commissioner" means the Chief or any other Social Security Commissioner appointed in accordance with section 52(1) or (2) of the 1992 Act and includes a Tribunal of Commissioners constituted in accordance with section 57(1) of that Act;

"contribution-based jobseeker's allowance", except in a case to which paragraph (*b*) of the definition of income-based jobseeker's allowance applies, means a contribution-based jobseeker's allowance under Part 1 of the Jobseekers Act 1995, but does not include any back to work bonus under section 26 of the Jobseekers Act which is paid as jobseeker's allowance;

"court" means in England and Wales a magistrates' court and in Scotland a court;

"5 per cent of the personal allowance for a single claimant aged not less than 25" means, where the percentage is not a multiple of 5 pence, the sum obtained by rounding that 5 per cent to the next higher such multiple;

"income-based jobseeker's allowance" means—

(*a*) an income-based jobseeker's allowance under Part 1 of the Jobseekers Act 1995; and

(*b*) in a case where, if there was no entitlement to contribution-based jobseeker's allowance, there would be entitlement to income-based jobseeker's allowance at the same rate, contribution-based jobseeker's allowance,

but does not include any back to work bonus under section 26 of the Jobseekers Act which is paid as jobseeker's allowance;

"income support" means income support under Part VII of the Social Security Contributions and Benefits Act 1992, but does not include any back to work bonus under section 26 of the Jobseekers Act which is paid as income support;

"Income Support Regulations" means the Income Support (General) Regulations 1987;

"Jobseekers Act" means the Jobseekers Act 1995;

"jobseeker's allowance" means an allowance under Part I of the Jobseekers Act but does not include any back to work bonus under section 26 of that Act which is paid as jobseeker's allowance;

"payments to third parties" means direct payments to third parties in accordance with Schedules 9 and 9A to the Claims and Payments Regulations, regulation 2(4) of the Community Charges (Deductions from Income Support) (No 2) Regulations 1990 and regulation 2(4) of the Community Charges (Deductions from Income Support) (Scotland) Regulations 1989 and regulation 2 of the Council Tax (Deductions from Income Support) Regulations 1993;

"personal allowance for a single claimant aged not less than 25" means—

(*a*) in the case of a person who is entitled to either income support or state pension credit, the amount for the time being specified in paragraph 1(1)(*e*) of column 2 of Schedule 2 to the Income Support Regulations; or,

(*b*) in the case of a person who is entitled to an income-based jobseeker's allowance, the amount specified in paragraph 1(1)(*e*) of Schedule 1 to the Jobseeker's Allowance Regulations 1996;

"social security office" means an office of the Department of Work and Pensions which is open to the public for the receipt of claims for income support or a jobseeker's allowance;

"state pension credit" means the benefit of that name payable under the State Pension Credit Act 2002;

"tribunal" means an appeal tribunal constituted in under Chapter I of Part I of the 1998 Act.

(3) Unless the context otherwise requires, any reference in these Regulations to a numbered regulation, Part or Schedule is a reference to the regulation, Part or Schedule bearing that number in these Regulations and any reference in a regulation or Schedule to a numbered paragraph is a reference to the paragraph of that regulation or Schedule having that number.

---

1. Made by the Secretary of State for Social Security, in exercise of powers conferred by sections 24 and 30 of the Criminal Justice Act 1991 and of all other powers enabling him in that behalf, after consultation with the Council on Tribunals in accordance with s 10 of the Tribunals and Inquiries Act 1971.

Application for deductions from income support, state pension credit or jobseeker's allowance

3–3041 **2.** (1) Where a fine has been imposed on an offender by a court or a sum is required to be paid by a compensation order which has been made against an offender by a court and (in either case) the offender is entitled to income support, state pension credit or jobseeker's allowance, the court may, subject to paragraph (2), apply to the Secretary of State asking him to deduct sums from any amounts payable to the offender by way of income support, state pension credit or jobseeker's allowance, in order to secure the payment of any sum which is or forms part of the fine or compensation.

(2) Before making an application the court shall make an enquiry as to the offender's means.

3–3041A **2A.** (1) Where an application is made the court may require the offender to provide his full name, full address, date of birth, national insurance number and the name of any benefits to which he is entitled.

(2) For the purposes of this regulation "benefits" means income support, state pension credit or a jobseeker's allowance.

Contents of application

3–3042 **3.** (1) An application shall contain the following information—

(a) the name and address of the offender, and, if it is known, his date of birth;

(b) the date when the fine was imposed or the compensation order made;

(c) the name and address of the court imposing the fine or making the compensation order;

(d) the amount of the fine or the amount payable by the compensation order as the case may be;

(e) the date on which the application is made;

(f) the date on which the court enquired into the offender's means;

(g) whether the offender has defaulted in paying the fine, compensation order or any instalment of either.

(2) A court making an application shall serve it on the Secretary of State by sending or delivering it to a social security office.

(3) Where it appears to the Secretary of State that an application from a court gives insufficient information to enable the offender to be identified, he may require the court to furnish such further information as he may reasonably require for that purpose.

Deductions from offender's income support, state pension credit or jobseeker's allowance

3–3043 **4.** (1) Subject to regulation 7, where—

(a) the Secretary of State receives an application from a court in respect of an offender who is entitled to income support[, state pension credit] or income-based jobseeker's allowance;

(b) the amount payable by way of that benefit, after any deduction under this paragraph, is 10 pence or more; and

(c) the aggregate amount payable under one or more of the following provisions, namely, paragraphs 3(2)(a), 5(6), 6(2)(a) and 7(3)(a) and (5)(a) of Schedule 9 to the Claims and Payments Regulations, and regulation 2 of the Council Tax (Deductions from Income Support) Regulations 1993, together with the amount to be deducted under this paragraph does not exceed an amount equal to 3 times 5 per cent of the personal allowance for a single claimant aged not less than 25 years,

the Secretary of State may deduct a sum from that benefit which is equal to 5 per cent of the personal allowance for a single claimant aged not less than 25 or £5, whichever is the greater amount allowed by sub-paragraphs (b) and (c) and pay that sum to the court towards satisfaction of the fine or the sum required to be paid by compensation order.

(2) Subject to paragraphs (3) and (4) and regulation 7, where—

(a) the Secretary of State receives an application from a court in respect of an offender who is entitled to contribution-based jobseeker's allowance; and

(b) the amount of contribution-based jobseeker's allowance payable before any deduction under this paragraph is equal to or more than one-third of the age-related amount applicable to the offender under section 4(1)(a) of the Jobseekers Act,

the Secretary of State may deduct a sum from that benefit which is equal to one-third of the age-related amount applicable to the offender under section 4(1)(a) of the Jobseekers Act and pay that sum to the court towards satisfaction of the fine or the sum required to be paid by compensation order.

(3) No deduction shall be made under paragraph (2) where a deduction is being made from the offender's contribution-based jobseeker's allowance under the Community Charges (Deductions from Income Support) (No 2) Regulations 1990, the Community Charges (Deductions from Income Support) (Scotland) Regulations 1989 or the Council Tax (Deductions from Income Support) Regulations 1993.

(4) Where the sum that would otherwise fall to be deducted under paragraph (2) includes a fraction of a penny, the sum to be deducted shall be rounded down to the next whole penny.

(5) The Secretary of State shall notify the offender and the court in writing of a decision to make a deduction under this regulation so far as is practicable within 14 days from the date on which he made the decision and at the same time shall notify the offender of his right of appeal.[1]

Circumstances, time of making and termination of deductions

3–3044 7. (1) The Secretary of State may make deductions from under regulation 4 only if—

(a) the offender is entitled to income support, state pension credit or jobseeker's allowance throughout any benefit week; and

(b) no deductions are being made in respect of the offender under any other application.

(2) The Secretary of State shall not make a deduction unless—

(a) the offender at the date of application by the court is aged not less than 18;

(b) the offender is entitled to income support, state pension credit or jobseeker's allowance; and

(c) the offender has defaulted in paying the fine, compensation order or any instalment of either.

(3) The Secretary of State shall make deductions from income support, state pension credit or jobseeker's allowance by reference to the times at which payment of income support, state pension credit or jobseeker's allowance is made to the offender.

(4) The Secretary of State shall cease making deductions from income support, state pension credit or jobseeker's allowance if—

(a) there is no longer sufficient entitlement to income support, state pension credit or jobseeker's allowance to enable him to make the deduction;

(b) entitlement to income support, state pension credit or jobseeker's allowance ceases;

(c) a court withdraws its application for deductions to be made; or

(d) the liability to make payment of the fine or under the compensation order as the case may be has ceased.

(5) The Secretary of State shall not determine any application under regulation 2 which relates to an offender in respect of whom—

(a) he is making deductions; or

(b) deductions fall to be made,

pursuant to an earlier application under that regulation until no deductions pursuant to that earlier application fall to be made.

(6) Payments of sums deducted from income support, state pension credit or jobseeker's allowance by the Secretary of State under these Regulations shall be made to the court at intervals of 13 weeks.

(7) Where the whole of the amount to which the application relates has been paid, the court shall so far as is practicable give notice of that fact within 21 days to the Secretary of State.

(8) The Secretary of State shall notify the offender in writing of the total of sums deducted by him under any application—

(a) on receipt of a written request for such information from the offender; or

(b) on the termination of deductions made under any such application.

Withdrawal of application

3–3045 8. A court may withdraw an application at any time by giving notice in writing to the social security office to which the application was sent or delivered.

Appeal

3–3046 9. (1) Where the adjudication officer has determined a question under regulation 4, the offender may appeal to a tribunal.

(2) Subject to paragraph (5), an appeal lies to a Commissioner from any decision of a tribunal on the grounds that the decision of that tribunal was erroneous in point of law and the persons who may appeal are the offender and the adjudication officer.

(3) If it appears to the Chief Commissioner or, in the case of his inability to act, to such other of the Commissioners, as he may have nominated to act for that purpose, that an appeal falling to be heard by one of the Commissioners involves a question of law of special difficulty, he may direct that the appeal be dealt with, not by that Commissioner alone but by a Tribunal consisting of any three of the Commissioners and if the decision is not unanimous, the decision of the majority shall be the decision of the Tribunal.

(4) Subject to paragraph (5), an appeal on a question of law lies to the appropriate appeal court from any decision of a Commissioner and the persons who may appeal are—

(a) the offender;
(b) the adjudication officer; and
(c) the Secretary of State.

(5) No appeal lies—

(a) to the Commissioner from a decision of a tribunal without the leave of the chairman of the tribunal which gave the decision or, if he refuses leave, without the leave of a Commissioner, or

(b) to the appropriate appeal court from a decision of a Commissioner, without the leave of the Commissioner who decided the case, or if he refuses, without the leave of the appropriate appeal court.

(6) Where in any case it is impracticable, or it would be likely to cause undue delay, for an application for leave to appeal against a decision of a tribunal to be determined by the person who was the chairman of that tribunal, that application shall be determined by any other person qualified under section 41(4) of the 1992 Act to act as a chairman of tribunals.

(7) In a case where the Chief Commissioner considers that it is impracticable, or would be likely to cause undue delay, for an application for leave to appeal to the appropriate appeal court to be determined by the Commissioner who decided the case, that application shall be determined—

(a) where the decision was a decision of an individual Commissioner, by the Chief Commissioner or a Commissioner selected by the Chief Commissioner, and

(b) where the decision was a decision of a Tribunal of Commissioners, by a differently constituted Tribunal of Commissioners selected by the Chief Commissioner.

(8) If the office of Chief Commissioner is vacant, or if the Chief Commissioner is unable to act, paragraph (7) shall have effect as if the expression "the Chief Commissioner" referred to such other of the Commissioners as may have been nominated to act for the purpose either by the Chief Commissioner or, if he has not made such a nomination, by the Lord Chancellor.

(9) On an application to a Commissioner for leave under this regulation it shall be the duty of the Commissioner to specify as the appropriate court—

(a) the Court of Appeal if it appears to him that the relevant place is in England and Wales; and
(b) the Court of Session if it appears to him that the relevant place is in Scotland;

except that if it appears to him, having regard to the circumstances of the case and in particular to the convenience of the persons who may be parties to the proposed appeal, that he should specify a different court mentioned in paragraphs (a) and (b) above as the appropriate court, it shall be his duty to specify that court as the appropriate court.

(10) In paragraph (9)—

"the relevant place", in relation to an application for leave to appeal from a decision of a Commissioner, means the premises where the tribunal whose decision was the subject of the Commissioner's decision usually exercises its functions.

Review

3–3047 **10.** (1) Any decision under these Regulations of an adjudication officer, a tribunal or a Commissioner may be reviewed at any time by an adjudication officer, if—

(a) the officer is satisfied that the decision was given in ignorance of, or was based on a mistake as to, some material fact; or

(b) there has been a relevant change of circumstances since the decision was given.

(2) Any decision of an adjudication officer may be reviewed by an adjudication officer on the grounds that the decision was erroneous in point of law.

(3) A question may be raised with a view to review under this regulation by means of an application in writing to an adjudication officer, stating the grounds of the application.

(4) On receipt of any such application, the adjudication officer shall take it into consideration and, so far as is practicable, dispose of it within 14 days of its receipt.

(5) A decision given by way of revision or a refusal to review under this regulation shall be subject to appeal in the same manner as an original decision and regulation 9(1) and Schedule 2 shall apply with the necessary modification in relation to a decision given on review as they apply to the original decision on a question.

Correction of accidental errors

3–3048 **11.** (1) Subject to regulation 13, accidental errors in any decision or record of a decision made under regulations 4, 9 and 10 and Schedule 2 may at any time be corrected by the person or tribunal by whom the decision was made or a person or tribunal of like status.

(2) A correction made to, or to the record of, a decision shall be deemed to be part of the decision, or of that record, and written notice of it shall be given as soon as is practicable to every party to the proceedings.

Setting aside decisions on certain grounds

3–3049 **12.** (1) Subject to regulation 13, on an application made by a party to the proceedings, a decision, made under regulation 4, 9, 10 and Schedule 2 by an adjudication officer, a tribunal or a Commissioner ("the adjudicating authority"), together with any determination given on an application for leave to appeal to a Commissioner or the appropriate appeal court against such a decision may be set aside by the adjudicating authority which gave the decision or an authority of like status, in a case where it appears just to set that decision aside on the grounds that—

(a) a document relating to the proceedings in which the decision was given was not sent to, or was not received at an appropriate time by a party to the proceedings or the party's representative or was not received at the appropriate time by the person or tribunal who gave the decision;

(b) in the case of an appeal to a tribunal or an oral hearing before a Commissioner a party to the proceedings in which the decision was given or the party's representative was not present at the hearing relating to the proceedings; or

(c) the interests of justice so require.

(2) An application under this regulation shall be made in accordance with regulation 14 and Schedule 1.

(3) Where an application to set aside is made under paragraph (1) every party to the proceedings shall be sent a copy of the application and shall be afforded a reasonable opportunity of making representations on it before the application is determined.

(4) Notice in writing of a determination on an application to set aside a decision shall be given to every party to the proceedings as soon as may be practicable and the notice shall contain a statement giving the reasons for the determination.

(5) For the purpose of determining under these Regulations an application to set aside a decision, there shall be disregarded, but subject to any contrary intention, any provision in any enactment or instrument to the effect that any notice or other document required or authorised to be given or sent to any person shall be deemed to have been given or sent if it was sent by post to that person's last known notified address.

Provisions common to regulations 11 and 12

3–3050   **13.** (1) In calculating any time specified in Schedule 1 there shall be disregarded any day falling before the day on which notice was given of a correction of a decision or the record thereof pursuant to regulation 11 or on which notice is given that a determination of a decision shall not be set aside following an application under regulation 12, as the case may be.

(2) There shall be no appeal against a correction made under regulation 11 or a refusal to make such a correction or against a determination under regulation 12.

(3) Nothing in regulation 11 or 12 shall be construed as derogating from any inherent or other power to correct or set aside decisions which is exercisable apart from these Regulations.

Manner of making applications or appeals and time limits

3–3051   **14.** (1) Any application or appeal set out in Column (1) of Schedule 1 shall be in writing and shall be made or given by sending or delivering it to the appropriate office within the specified time.

(2) In this regulation—

(a) "appropriate office" means the office specified in Column (2) of Schedule 1 opposite the description of the relevant application or appeal listed in Column (1); and

(b) "specified time" means the time specified in Column (3) of that Schedule opposite the description of the relevant application or appeal so listed.

(3) The time specified by this regulation and Schedule 1 for the making of any application or appeal (except an application to the chairman of a tribunal for leave to appeal to a Commissioner) may be extended for special reasons, even though the time so specified may already have expired, and any application for an extension of time under this paragraph shall be made to and determined by the person to whom the application or appeal is sought to be made or, in the case of a tribunal, its chairman.

(4) An application under paragraph (3) for an extension of time (except where it is made to a Commissioner) which has been refused may not be renewed.

(5) Any application of appeal set out in Column (1) of Schedule 1 shall be in writing and shall contain—

(a) the name and address of the appellant or applicant;

(b) the particulars of the grounds on which the appeal or application is to be made or given; and

(c) his address for service of documents if it is different from that in sub-paragraph (a);

and in the case of an appeal to the Commissioner, but subject to paragraph 21(2) of Schedule 2, the notice of appeal shall have annexed to it a copy of the determination granting leave to appeal and a copy of the decision against which leave to appeal has been granted.

(6) Where it appears to an adjudication officer, chairman of a tribunal or Commissioner that an application or appeal which is made to him, or to the tribunal, gives insufficient particulars to enable the question at issue to be determined, he may require, and in the case of a Commissioner, direct that the person making the application or appeal shall furnish such further particulars as may reasonably be required.

(7) The conduct and procedure in relation to any application or appeal shall be in accordance with Schedule 2.

Manner and time for the service of notices etc

3–3052   **15.** (1) Any notice or other document required or authorised to be given or sent to any person under these Regulations shall be deemed to have been given or sent if it was sent by post properly addressed and pre-paid to that person at his ordinary or last notified address.

(2) Any notice or other document required or authorised to be given or sent to an appropriate social security office or office of the clerk to a tribunal shall be treated as having been so given or sent on the day that it is received in the appropriate social security office or office of the clerk to the tribunal.

(3) Any notice or document required to be given, sent or submitted to, or served on, a Commissioner—

(a) shall be given, sent or submitted to an office of the Social Security Commissioners;
(b) shall be deemed to have been given, sent or submitted if it was sent by post properly addressed and pre-paid to an office of the Social Security Commissioners.

3–3053   SCHEDULE 1

(Time limits for making applications or appeals.)

3–3054   SCHEDULE 2

(Conduct and procedure in relation to appeals and applications.)

3–3055   SCHEDULE 3

(Repealed in relation to England and Wales).

Attendance Centre Rules 1995[1]
(SI 1995/3281)

3–3060 **1.** Citation and commencement.

1. Made by the Secretary of State in exercise of powers conferred on him by s 16(3) of the Criminal Justice Act 1982.

3–3061 **2.** Revocation.

Interpretation

3–3062 **3.** In these Rules, the expression—

"centre" means an attendance centre provided by the Secretary of State under section 16(1) of the Criminal Justice Act 1982;
"member of the staff" means any person for the time being carrying out any instructional or supervisory duties at a centre;
"officer in charge" means the member of the staff for the time being in charge of a centre;
"order" means an order made by a court under section 17 of the Criminal Justice Act 1982, section 15(3)(a) of the Children and Young Persons Act 1969 or Part II of Schedule 2 to the Criminal Justice Act 1991, requiring an offender to attend at a centre.

Occupation and instruction

3–3063 **4.** (1) The occupation and instruction given at a centre shall include a programme of group activities designed to assist offenders to acquire or develop personal responsibility, self-discipline, skills and interests.

(2) A female member of the staff shall, save in exceptional circumstances, always be in attendance at a centre which is available for the reception of female offenders; and female offenders attending at a centre shall, at any time when participating in physical training, so far as practicable be supervised by a female member of the staff.

Officer in charge

3–3064 **5.** (1) The officer in charge shall maintain a record in respect of each person required to attend showing—

(a) the number of hours specified in the order;
(b) every attendance or failure to attend;
(c) the duration of each attendance; and
(d) the commission by that person of any breach of these Rules and the manner in which it is dealt with.

(2) Subject to the provisions of rules 6(3)(b) and 11(2)(b) of these Rules, it shall be the duty of the officer in charge to ensure that any person attending at the centre who has not completed the period of attendance specified in the order is, before leaving the centre, informed (both orally and in writing) of the day and time when he is next required to attend at the centre, unless in any particular case it is impracticable to give this information.

Attendance

3–3065 **6.** (1) Persons required to attend at a centre shall so attend—

(a) on the first occasion, at the time specified in the order; and

(b) on any subsequent occasion, at such time as may be notified to them in accordance with rule 5(2) above, or, if no such notification has been given, at such time as may be notified to them in writing by or on behalf of the officer in charge;

and on attending shall report to, and place themselves under the direction of, the officer in charge.

(2) The occasions of a person's attendance at a centre and the duration of each attendance shall, so far as practicable and subject to the provisions of rules 11 and 12 of these Rules, be so arranged by the officer in charge that the duration of attendance on any occasion is not less than one hour.

(3) Where a person without reasonable excuse attends at the centre later than the time at which he was required to attend, the officer in charge may refuse to admit him; in such a case the person shall be regarded as having failed to attend on that occasion and shall either—

(a) be instructed in accordance with rule 5(2) above as to his further attendance at the centre; or

(b) be informed (both orally and in writing) that he is not required to attend at the centre again and that it is intended in respect of the failure to attend at the required time to take steps to bring him before a court under section 19(1) of the Criminal Justice Act 1982.

Admission to centre

3–3066 7. No person, other than a person on an occasion when he is required to attend in pursuance of an order, shall be admitted to, or remain in, a centre except with the permission of the Secretary of State or the officer in charge.

Unfitness for attendance

3–3067 8. (1) The officer in charge may at any time require a person attending at the centre to leave it if, in the opinion of that officer, that person is—

(a) so unwell as to be unfit to remain at the centre on that occasion; or

(b) suffering from any infectious disease or otherwise in a condition likely to be detrimental to other persons attending at the centre.

(2) Where a person is so required to leave, he shall be instructed in accordance with rule 5(2) above as to his further attendance at the centre.

Discipline

3–3068 9. The discipline of a centre shall be maintained by the personal influence of the officer in charge and other members of the staff.

3–3069 10. Persons shall while attending at a centre behave in an orderly manner and shall obey any instruction given by the officer in charge or any other member of the staff.

3–3070 11. (1) The officer in charge may at any time require any person committing a breach of these Rules to leave the centre.

(2) Where a person is so required to leave, he shall either—

(a) be instructed in accordance with rule 5(2) above as to his further attendance at the centre; or

(b) be informed (both orally and in writing) that he is not required to attend at the centre again and that it is intended in respect of the said breach to take steps to bring him before a court under section 19(1) of the Criminal Justice Act 1982.

3–3071 12. Without prejudice to rule 11 above, where a person is required to leave the centre in accordance with rule 8(1) or 11(1) above, the officer in charge shall not count towards the duration of his attendance on that occasion the period following the requirement to leave.

3–3072 13. Without prejudice to rules 6(3). 11 and 12 above, the officer in charge or any other member of the staff may deal with a person committing a breach of these Rules in either or both of the following ways, that is to say—

(a) by separating him from other persons attending at the centre;

(b) by giving him an alternative form of occupation;

during the whole or any part of the period of attendance specified in the order then remaining uncompleted.

Magistrates' Court Sentencing Guidelines[1]

Implementation Date: 1 January 2004

3–3080 These Guidelines have the support of the Lord Chancellor and the former Lord Chief Justice.

"They are of course only guidelines – they do not curtail your independent discretion to impose the sentences you think are right, case by case. But they exist to help you in that process. To give you a starting point. To give you more information in reaching your decisions.

And, importantly, they help to assist the magistracy to maintain an overall consistency of approach."

The Rt Hon Lord Irvine of Lairg

"I think it most important that, within discretionary limits, magistrates' courts up and down the country should endeavour to approach sentencing with a measure of consistency, and I have no doubt that these Guidelines will contribute powerfully to that end."

The Rt Hon Lord Bingham of Cornhill

Acknowledgements

1. These Sentencing Guidelines were issued by the Magistrates' Association in October 2003 and revised in December 2006. They are reproduced with the permission of the Magistrates' Association.

SECTION 1

USER GUIDE

IMPORTANT: THIS USER GUIDE IS AN INTEGRAL PART OF THE GUIDELINES – PLEASE READ IT

Introduction

These Sentencing Guidelines cover offences with which magistrates deal regularly and frequently in the adult criminal courts. They provide a sentencing structure which sets out how to:

— establish the seriousness of each case
— determine the most appropriate way of dealing with it.

The Sentencing Guidelines provide a method for considering individual cases and a guideline from which discussion should properly flow; but they are not a tariff and should never be used as such. **The guideline sentences are based on a first-time offender pleading not guilty.**

Using the sentencing structure

The sentencing structure used for these Guidelines was established by the Criminal Justice Act 1991. This reaffirms the principle of "just deserts" so that any penalty must reflect the seriousness of the offence for which it is imposed and the personal circumstances of the offender. Magistrates must always start the sentencing process by taking full account of all the circumstances of the offence and making a judicial assessment of the seriousness category into which it falls. It is important that the court makes clear the factual basis on which the sentence is based.

In every case, the Criminal Justice Act 1991 requires sentencers to consider:

— Is discharge or a fine appropriate?
— Is the offence serious enough for a community penalty?
— Is it so serious that only custody is appropriate?

If the last, in either way cases, justices will also need to consider if magistrates' courts' powers are sufficient.

Update December 2006

Criminal Justice Act 2003 (CJA 2003) now applies. See Sentencing Guidelines Council (SGC) guideline "Overarching principles: Seriousness", and page 1.39 of Adult Court Bench Book (ACBB).

The format of the Sentencing Guidelines

1. CONSIDER THE SERIOUSNESS OF THE OFFENCE

Magistrates must always make an assessment of seriousness following the structure of the Criminal Justice Act 1991. **The guideline sentences are based on a first-time offender pleading not guilty.**

Update December 2006: Following CJA 2003, in considering the seriousness of an offence, the court must consider the offender's culpability in committing the offence (whether the offence was intentional, reckless, likely outcome known, negligent etc). The court must also consider any harm which the offence caused, was intended to cause or might foreseeably have caused. The seriousness of an offence is determined by these two parameters of culpability and harm.

Where this guideline is discharge or fine, a suggested starting point guideline fine is also given. [There is also guidance where the starting point guideline is a community penalty.]

Where the starting point guideline is custody, think in terms of weeks and credit as appropriate for a timely guilty plea.

For some either way offences the guideline is "are your sentencing powers sufficient?". This indicates that magistrates should be considering whether the seriousness of the offence is such that six months (or 12 months in the case of two or more offences) is insufficient, so that the case must be committed to the Crown Court (consult the legal adviser with regard to Crown Court sentencing and guideline cases). If the case is retained in the magistrates' court a substantial custodial sentence is likely to be necessary.

It should be noted that if magistrates consider (say) nine months to be the appropriate sentence, to be reduced for a timely guilty plea to six months, then the case falls within their powers and must be retained. Subject to offender mitigation, six months would appear to be the appropriate sentence. However, if sentence is passed on this basis the court should specifically say so in its reasons.

2. CONSIDER AGGRAVATING AND MITIGATING FACTORS

Make sure that all aggravating and mitigating factors are considered. The lists in the Sentencing

Guidelines are neither exhaustive nor a substitute for the personal judgment of magistrates. **Factors which do not appear in the Guidelines may be important in individual cases.**

If the offence was racially or religiously aggravated, the court must treat that fact as an aggravating factor under statute (s 153 of the Powers of Criminal Courts (Sentencing) Act 2000).

If the offence was committed while the offender was on bail, the court must treat that as an aggravating factor under statute (s 151 Powers of Criminal Courts (Sentencing) Act 2000).

Consider previous convictions, or any failure to respond to previous sentences, in assessing seriousness. Courts should identify any convictions relevant for this purpose and then consider to what extent they affect the seriousness of the present offence.

3.　TAKE A PRELIMINARY VIEW OF SERIOUSNESS, THEN CONSIDER OFFENDER MITIGATION

When an initial assessment of the seriousness of the offence has been formed, consider the offender.The Guidelines set out some examples of offender mitigation but there are frequently others to be considered in individual cases. Any offender mitigation that the court accepts must lead to some downward revision of the provisional assessment of seriousness, although this revision may be minor. **Remember, however, that the guideline sentences are based on a first-time offender pleading not guilty.**

A previous criminal record may deprive the defendant of being able to say that he is a person of good character.

4.　CONSIDER YOUR SENTENCE

The law requires the court to consider reducing the sentence for a timely guilty plea. Credit for a timely guilty plea may result in a sentencing reduction of up to one-third but the precise amount of credit will depend upon the facts of each case and a last minute plea of guilty may attract only a minimal reduction.

Credit may be given in respect of the amount of a fine or periods of community service or custody. Periods of mandatory disqualification or mandatory penalty points cannot be reduced for a guilty plea.

5.　DECIDE YOUR SENTENCE

Remember that magistrates have a duty to consider the award of compensation in all appropriate cases, and to give reasons if compensation is not awarded. See Section Three.

Agree the form of words that the Chairman will use when announcing sentence.

SECTION 2

Affray

Public Order Act 1986 s.3 Triable either way – see Mode of Trial Guidelines Penalty: Level 5 and/or 6 months	**Affray**

CONSIDER THE SERIOUSNESS OF THE OFFENCE
(INCLUDING THE IMPACT ON THE VICTIM)

IS DISCHARGE OR FINE APPROPRIATE?

IS IT SERIOUS ENOUGH FOR A COMMUNITY PENALTY?

GUIDELINE: → IS IT SO SERIOUS THAT ONLY CUSTODY IS APPROPRIATE?

ARE YOUR SENTENCING POWERS SUFFICIENT?

THIS IS A GUIDELINE FOR A FIRST-TIME OFFENDER PLEADING NOT GUILTY

 ## CONSIDER AGGRAVATING AND MITIGATING FACTORS, CULPABILITY AND HARM

for example	**for example**
Busy public place	Provocation
Football related	Did not start the trouble
Group action	Stopped as soon as the police arrived
Injuries caused	*This list is not exhaustive*
People actually put in fear	
Vulnerable victim(s)	
This list is not exhaustive	

If racially or religiously aggravated, or offender is on bail, this offence is more serious
If offender has previous convictions, their relevance and any failure to respond to previous
sentences should be considered – they may increase the seriousness. The court should make
it clear, when passing sentence, that this was the approach adopted.

TAKE A PRELIMINARY VIEW OF SERIOUSNESS, THEN CONSIDER OFFENDER MITIGATION

for example
    Age, health (physical or mental)
    Co-operation with police
    Evidence of genuine remorse
    Voluntary compensation

CONSIDER YOUR SENTENCE

Compare it with the suggested guideline level of sentence and reconsider
your reasons carefully if you have chosen a sentence at a different level.
Consider a reduction for a timely guilty plea.

DECIDE YOUR SENTENCE
NB. COMPENSATION – Give reasons if not awarding compensation

Aggravated vehicle-taking	Theft Act 1968 s.12A as inserted by Aggravated Vehicle-Taking Act 1992 Triable either way – but in certain cases summarily only – consult legal adviser. Penalty: Level 5 and/or 6 months Must endorse and disqualify at least 12 months

CONSIDER THE SERIOUSNESS OF THE OFFENCE
(INCLUDING THE IMPACT ON THE VICTIM)

IS DISCHARGE OR FINE APPROPRIATE?
IS IT SERIOUS ENOUGH FOR A COMMUNITY PENALTY?
GUIDELINE: → IS IT SO SERIOUS THAT ONLY CUSTODY IS APPROPRIATE?
ARE YOUR SENTENCING POWERS SUFFICIENT?

THIS IS A GUIDELINE FOR A FIRST-TIME OFFENDER PLEADING NOT GUILTY

 ## CONSIDER AGGRAVATING AND MITIGATING FACTORS, CULPABILITY AND HARM

for example	for example
Competitive driving: racing, showing off	Passenger only
Disregard of warnings, eg from passengers or others in vicinity	Single incident of bad driving
Group action	Speed not excessive
Police pursuit	Very minor injury/damage
Pre-meditated	*This list is not exhaustive*
Serious injury/damage	
Serious risk	
Trying to avoid detection or arrest	
Vehicle destroyed	
This list is not exhaustive	

If racially or religiously aggravated, or offender is on bail, this offence is more serious
If offender has previous convictions, their relevance and any failure to respond to previous sentences should be considered – they may increase the seriousness. The court should make it clear, when passing sentence, that this was the approach adopted.

TAKE A PRELIMINARY VIEW OF SERIOUSNESS, THEN CONSIDER OFFENDER MITIGATION

for example
Health (physical or mental)
Co-operation with police
Evidence of genuine remorse
Voluntary compensation

CONSIDER YOUR SENTENCE

Compare it with the suggested guideline level of sentence and reconsider your reasons carefully if you have chosen a sentence at a different level. Consider a reduction for a timely guilty plea. Order a re-test unless good reason not to.

DECIDE YOUR SENTENCE

NB. COMPENSATION – Give reasons if not awarding compensation. In certain cases this offence is summary only – consult legal adviser.

Protection of Animals Act 1911 s.1 Triable only summarily Penalty: Level 5 and/or 6 months with powers to deprive ownership of the relevant animal and disqualify from keeping all or any animals	**Animal cruelty**

CONSIDER THE SERIOUSNESS OF THE OFFENCE

IS DISCHARGE OR FINE APPROPRIATE?

GUIDELINE: ➔   **IS IT SERIOUS ENOUGH FOR A COMMUNITY PENALTY?**

IS IT SO SERIOUS THAT ONLY CUSTODY IS APPROPRIATE?

THIS IS A GUIDELINE FOR A FIRST-TIME OFFENDER PLEADING NOT GUILTY

 ## CONSIDER AGGRAVATING AND MITIGATING FACTORS, CULPABILITY AND HARM

for example	for example
Adult involving children Animal(s) kept for livelihood Committed over a period or involving several animals Deriving pleasure from torturing or frightening Disregarded warnings of others Group action Offender in position of special responsibility towards the animal Premeditated/deliberate Prolonged neglect Serious injury or death Use of weapon *This list is not exhaustive*	Ignorance of appropriate care Impulsive Minor injury Offender induced by others Single incident *This list is not exhaustive*

If offender is on bail, this offence is more serious
If offender has previous convictions, their relevance and any failure to respond to previous sentences should be considered – they may increase the seriousness. The court should make it clear, when passing sentence, that this was the approach adopted.

TAKE A PRELIMINARY VIEW OF SERIOUSNESS, THEN CONSIDER OFFENDER MITIGATION

for example
     Age, health (physical or mental)
     Co-operation with police
     Evidence of genuine remorse

CONSIDER YOUR SENTENCE

*Compare it with the suggested guideline level of sentence and reconsider
your reasons carefully if you have chosen a sentence at a different level.
Consider a reduction for a timely guilty plea.*
***Always consider disqualifying the offender from having custody of animals,
or depriving him or her of owning the animal concerned.***

DECIDE YOUR SENTENCE

Assault – actual bodily harm	Offences Against the Person Act 1861 s.47 Triable either way – see Mode of Trial Guidelines Penalty: Level 5 and/or 6 months

CONSIDER THE SERIOUSNESS OF THE OFFENCE
(INCLUDING THE IMPACT ON THE VICTIM)

IS DISCHARGE OR FINE APPROPRIATE?

IS IT SERIOUS ENOUGH FOR A COMMUNITY PENALTY?

GUIDELINE: ➔ *IS IT SO SERIOUS THAT ONLY CUSTODY IS APPROPRIATE?*

ARE YOUR SENTENCING POWERS SUFFICIENT?

THIS IS A GUIDELINE FOR A FIRST-TIME OFFENDER PLEADING NOT GUILTY

 ## CONSIDER AGGRAVATING AND MITIGATING FACTORS, CULPABILITY AND HARM

for example	for example
Abuse of trust (domestic setting) Deliberate kicking or biting Extensive injuries (may be psychological) Headbutting Group action Offender in position of authority On hospital/medical or school premises Premeditated Victim particularly vulnerable Victim serving the public Weapon *This list is not exhaustive*	Minor injury Provocation Single blow *This list is not exhaustive*

If offender is on bail, this offence is more serious

If offender has previous convictions, their relevance and any failure to respond to previous sentences should be considered – they may increase the seriousness. The court should make it clear, when passing sentence, that this was the approach adopted.

TAKE A PRELIMINARY VIEW OF SERIOUSNESS, THEN CONSIDER OFFENDER MITIGATION

for example
Age, health (physical or mental)
Co-operation with police
Evidence of genuine remorse
Voluntary compensation

CONSIDER YOUR SENTENCE

Compare it with the suggested guideline level of sentence and reconsider your reasons carefully if you have chosen a sentence at a different level. Consider a reduction for a timely guilty plea.

DECIDE YOUR SENTENCE
NB. COMPENSATION – Give reasons if not awarding compensation

Assault on a police officer

Police Act 1996 s.89	
Police Act 1996 s.89 Triable only summarily Penalty: Level 5 and/or 6 months	**Assault on a police officer**

CONSIDER THE SERIOUSNESS OF THE OFFENCE
(INCLUDING THE IMPACT ON THE VICTIM)

IS DISCHARGE OR FINE APPROPRIATE?

IS IT SERIOUS ENOUGH FOR A COMMUNITY PENALTY?

GUIDELINE: → IS IT SO SERIOUS THAT ONLY CUSTODY IS APPROPRIATE?

THIS IS A GUIDELINE FOR A FIRST-TIME OFFENDER PLEADING NOT GUILTY

 ## CONSIDER AGGRAVATING AND MITIGATING FACTORS, CULPABILITY AND HARM

for example	for example
Any injuries caused Gross disregard for police authority Group action Premeditated Spitting *This list is not exhaustive*	Impulsive action Unaware that person was a police officer *This list is not exhaustive*

If racially or religiously aggravated, or offender is on bail, this offence is more serious
If offender has previous convictions, their relevance and any failure to respond to previous
sentences should be considered – they may increase the seriousness. The court should make
it clear, when passing sentence, that this was the approach adopted.

TAKE A PRELIMINARY VIEW OF SERIOUSNESS, THEN CONSIDER OFFENDER MITIGATION

for example
- Age, health (physical or mental)
- Co-operation with police
- Evidence of genuine remorse
- Voluntary compensation

CONSIDER YOUR SENTENCE

Compare it with the suggested guideline level of sentence and reconsider
your reasons carefully if you have chosen a sentence at a different level.
Consider a reduction for a timely guilty plea.

DECIDE YOUR SENTENCE
NB. COMPENSATION – Give reasons if not awarding compensation

<table>
<tr>
<td>

Breach of a community order

</td>
<td>

Update December 2006:
Pre April 2005 Criminal Justice Act 1991 sch.2. Post April 2005, CJA 2003 sch.8 – amendment to impose more onerous requirements or revocation of Order and re-sentence for original offence. If Order made by Crown Court, discretion to commit to the Crown Court. See new paragraph below.

</td>
</tr>
</table>

CONSIDER THE EXTENT OF THE BREACH

 ## CONSIDER AGGRAVATING AND MITIGATING FACTORS, CULPABILITY AND HARM

for example	for example
No attempt to start the sentence	Completed a significant part of the order
Unco-operative	*This list is not exhaustive*
This list is not exhaustive	

CONSIDER OFFENDER MITIGATION
(including timely admission)

DECIDE IF THE ORDER SHOULD CONTINUE

IF THE ORDER SHOULD CONTINUE

> *Is a fine appropriate? (Starting Point B)*

> *Is a community punishment order appropriate?*

> *Where the order is a community rehabilitation order, is an attendance centre order appropriate?*

> *Is a curfew order appropriate?*

IF THE ORDER SHOULD NOT CONTINUE AND IT IS A MAGISTRATES' COURT ORDER:

> *Revoke and re-sentence for original offence (see relevant guideline)*

NB. IF THE ORDER WAS MADE BY THE CROWN COURT, MAY FINE AND ALLOW ORDER TO CONTINUE, OR COMMIT TO CROWN COURT TO BE DEALT WITH (CONSULT LEGAL ADVISER)

Update December 2006
This page refers to pre April 2005 offences. For later matters, please refer to SGC guideline 'New Sentences CJA 2003' page 12 (iii). 'Breaches. In such proceedings the court must either increase the severity of the existing sentence (i.e. impose more onerous conditions including requirements aimed at enforcement, such as curfew or supervision requirement) or revoke the existing sentence and proceed as though sentencing for the original offence'. Consult your legal adviser.

Breach of anti-social behaviour order

Crime and Disorder Act 1998 s.1 Triable either way – see Mode of Trial Guidelines Penalty: Level 5 and/or 6 months	**Breach of anti-social behaviour order**

CONSIDER THE SERIOUSNESS OF THE OFFENCE
(INCLUDING THE IMPACT ON THE VICTIM)

IS FINE APPROPRIATE? (NB. A DISCHARGE IS NOT AVAILABLE FOR THIS OFFENCE)

IS IT SERIOUS ENOUGH FOR A COMMUNITY PENALTY?

GUIDELINE: →   IS IT SO SERIOUS THAT ONLY CUSTODY IS APPROPRIATE?

ARE YOUR SENTENCING POWERS SUFFICIENT?

THIS IS A GUIDELINE FOR A FIRST-TIME OFFENDER PLEADING NOT GUILTY

 ## CONSIDER AGGRAVATING AND MITIGATING FACTORS, CULPABILITY AND HARM

for example
- Breach of recently imposed order
- Breach amounted to commission of an offence
- Continues the pattern of behaviour the order sought to prohibit
- Group action
- Use of violence, threats, intimidation
- *This list is not exhaustive*

If racially or religiously aggravated, or offender is on bail, this offence is more serious
If offender has previous convictions, their relevance and any failure to respond to previous sentences should be considered – they may increase the seriousness. The court should make it clear, when passing sentence, that this was the approach adopted.

TAKE A PRELIMINARY VIEW OF SERIOUSNESS, THEN CONSIDER OFFENDER MITIGATION

for example
- Age, health (physical or mental)
- Co-operation with police
- Evidence of genuine remorse
- Voluntary compensation

CONSIDER YOUR SENTENCE

Compare it with the suggested guideline level of sentence and reconsider your reasons carefully if you have chosen a sentence at a different level. Consider a reduction for a timely guilty plea.

DECIDE YOUR SENTENCE
NB. COMPENSATION – Give reasons if not awarding compensation

Burglary (dwelling)	Theft Act 1968 s.9 Triable either way – see Mode of Trial Guidelines Penalty: Level 5 and/or 6 months

CONSIDER THE SERIOUSNESS OF THE OFFENCE
(INCLUDING THE IMPACT ON THE VICTIM)

IS DISCHARGE OR FINE APPROPRIATE?

IS IT SERIOUS ENOUGH FOR A COMMUNITY PENALTY?

IS IT SO SERIOUS THAT ONLY CUSTODY IS APPROPRIATE?

GUIDELINE: → **ARE YOUR SENTENCING POWERS SUFFICIENT?**

THIS IS A GUIDELINE FOR A FIRST-TIME OFFENDER PLEADING NOT GUILTY

 ## CONSIDER AGGRAVATING AND MITIGATING FACTORS, CULPABILITY AND HARM

for example	for example
Force used or threatened Group enterprise High value (in economic or sentimental terms) property stolen More than minor trauma caused Professional planning/organisation/ execution Significant damage or vandalism Victim injured Victim present at the time Vulnerable victim *IF ANY of the above factors are present you should commit for sentence.*	First offence of its type AND low value property stolen AND no significant damage or disturbance AND no injury or violence Minor part played Theft from attached garage Vacant property *ONLY if one or more of the above factors are present AND none of the aggravating factors listed are present should you consider NOT committing for sentence.*

If racially or religiously aggravated, or offender is on bail, this offence is more serious
If offender has previous convictions, their relevance and any failure to respond to previous sentences should be considered – they may increase the seriousness. The court should make it clear, when passing sentence, that this was the approach adopted.

TAKE A PRELIMINARY VIEW OF SERIOUSNESS, THEN CONSIDER WHETHER THE CASE SHOULD BE COMMITTED FOR SENTENCE, THEN CONSIDER OFFENDER MITIGATION

for example
Age, health (physical or mental)
Co-operation with police
Evidence of genuine remorse
Voluntary compensation

CONSIDER COMMITTAL OR YOUR SENTENCE

Compare it with the suggested guideline level of sentence and reconsider your reasons carefully if you have chosen a sentence at a different level.
Consider a reduction for a timely guilty plea.

DECIDE YOUR SENTENCE
NB. COMPENSATION – Give reasons if not awarding compensation

Burglary (non-dwelling)

Theft Act 1968 s.9 Triable either way – see Mode of Trial Guidelines Penalty: Level 5 and/or 6 months	Burglary (non-dwelling)

CONSIDER THE SERIOUSNESS OF THE OFFENCE
(INCLUDING THE IMPACT ON THE VICTIM)

IS DISCHARGE OR FINE APPROPRIATE?

GUIDELINE: →   *IS IT SERIOUS ENOUGH FOR A COMMUNITY PENALTY?*

IS IT SO SERIOUS THAT ONLY CUSTODY IS APPROPRIATE?

ARE YOUR SENTENCING POWERS SUFFICIENT?

THIS IS A GUIDELINE FOR A FIRST-TIME OFFENDER PLEADING NOT GUILTY

 ## CONSIDER AGGRAVATING AND MITIGATING FACTORS, CULPABILITY AND HARM

for example	for example
Forcible entry	Low value
Group offence	Nobody frightened
Harm to business	No damage or disturbance
Occupants frightened	*This list is not exhaustive*
Professional operation	
Repeat victimisation	
School or medical premises	
Soiling, ransacking, damage	
This list is not exhaustive	

If racially or religiously aggravated, or offender is on bail, this offence is more serious
If offender has previous convictions, their relevance and any failure to respond to previous sentences should be considered – they may increase the seriousness. The court should make it clear, when passing sentence, that this was the approach adopted.

TAKE A PRELIMINARY VIEW OF SERIOUSNESS, THEN CONSIDER OFFENDER MITIGATION

for example
     Age, health (physical or mental)
     Co-operation with police
     Evidence of genuine remorse
     Voluntary compensation

CONSIDER YOUR SENTENCE

Compare it with the suggested guideline level of sentence and reconsider your reasons carefully if you have chosen a sentence at a different level. Consider a reduction for a timely guilty plea.

DECIDE YOUR SENTENCE
NB. COMPENSATION – Give reasons if not awarding compensation

Common assault	Criminal Justice Act 1988 s.39 Triable only summarily Penalty: Level 5 and/or 6 months

CONSIDER THE SERIOUSNESS OF THE OFFENCE
(INCLUDING THE IMPACT ON THE VICTIM)

IS DISCHARGE OR FINE APPROPRIATE?

GUIDELINE: →   **IS IT SERIOUS ENOUGH FOR A COMMUNITY PENALTY?**

IS IT SO SERIOUS THAT ONLY CUSTODY IS APPROPRIATE?

THIS IS A GUIDELINE FOR A FIRST-TIME OFFENDER PLEADING NOT GUILTY

 ## CONSIDER AGGRAVATING AND MITIGATING FACTORS, CULPABILITY AND HARM

for example
- Abuse of trust (domestic setting)
- Group action
- Injury
- Offender in position of authority
- On hospital/medical or school premises
- Premeditated
- Spitting
- Victim particularly vulnerable
- Victim serving the public
- Weapon
- *This list is not exhaustive*

for example
- Impulsive
- Minor injury
- Provocation
- Single blow
- *This list is not exhaustive*

If offender is on bail, this offence is more serious
If offender has previous convictions, their relevance and any failure to respond to previous sentences should be considered – they may increase the seriousness. The court should make it clear, when passing sentence, that this was the approach adopted.

TAKE A PRELIMINARY VIEW OF SERIOUSNESS, THEN CONSIDER OFFENDER MITIGATION

for example
- Age, health (physical or mental)
- Co-operation with police
- Evidence of genuine remorse
- Voluntary compensation

CONSIDER YOUR SENTENCE

Compare it with the suggested guideline level of sentence and reconsider your reasons carefully if you have chosen a sentence at a different level. Consider a reduction for a timely guilty plea.

DECIDE YOUR SENTENCE
NB. COMPENSATION – Give reasons if not awarding compensation

Criminal damage

Criminal Damage Act 1971 s.1 Triable either way or summarily only. Consult legal adviser Penalty: Either way – Level 5 and/or 6 months Summarily – Level 4 and/or 3 months	Criminal damage

CONSIDER THE SERIOUSNESS OF THE OFFENCE
(INCLUDING THE IMPACT ON THE VICTIM)

GUIDELINE: →   ***IS DISCHARGE OR FINE APPROPRIATE?***

IS IT SERIOUS ENOUGH FOR A COMMUNITY PENALTY?

IS IT SO SERIOUS THAT ONLY CUSTODY IS APPROPRIATE?

ARE YOUR SENTENCING POWERS SUFFICIENT?

THIS IS A GUIDELINE FOR A FIRST-TIME OFFENDER PLEADING NOT GUILTY

GUIDELINE FINE – STARTING POINT C

 ## CONSIDER AGGRAVATING AND MITIGATING FACTORS, CULPABILITY AND HARM

for example	for example
Deliberate	Impulsive action
Group offence	Minor damage
Serious damage	Provocation
Targeting	*This list is not exhaustive*
Vulnerable victim	
This list is not exhaustive	

If offender is on bail, this offence is more serious
If offender has previous convictions, their relevance and any failure to respond to previous sentences should be considered – they may increase the seriousness. The court should make it clear, when passing sentence, that this was the approach adopted.

TAKE A PRELIMINARY VIEW OF SERIOUSNESS, THEN CONSIDER OFFENDER MITIGATION

for example
     Age, health (physical or mental)
     Co-operation with police
     Evidence of genuine remorse
     Voluntary compensation

CONSIDER YOUR SENTENCE

Compare it with the suggested guideline level of sentence and reconsider your reasons carefully if you have chosen a sentence at a different level. Consider a reduction for a timely guilty plea.

DECIDE YOUR SENTENCE
NB. COMPENSATION – Give reasons if not awarding compensation

Disorderly behaviour	Public Order Act 1986 s.5 Triable only summarily Penalty: Level 3

CONSIDER THE SERIOUSNESS OF THE OFFENCE
(INCLUDING THE IMPACT ON THE VICTIM)

GUIDELINE: →   ***IS DISCHARGE OR FINE APPROPRIATE?***

IS IT SERIOUS ENOUGH FOR A COMMUNITY PENALTY?

THIS IS A GUIDELINE FOR A FIRST-TIME OFFENDER PLEADING NOT GUILTY

GUIDELINE FINE – STARTING POINT B

 ## CONSIDER AGGRAVATING AND MITIGATING FACTORS, CULPABILITY AND HARM

for example	for example
Football related Group action Vulnerable victim *This list is not exhaustive*	Stopped as soon as police arrived Trivial incident *This list is not exhaustive*

If offender is on bail, this offence is more serious
If offender has previous convictions, their relevance and any failure to respond to previous sentences should be considered – they may increase the seriousness. The court should make it clear, when passing sentence, that this was the approach adopted.

TAKE A PRELIMINARY VIEW OF SERIOUSNESS, THEN CONSIDER OFFENDER MITIGATION

for example
    Age, health (physical or mental)
    Co-operation with police
    Evidence of genuine remorse
    Voluntary compensation

CONSIDER YOUR SENTENCE

Compare it with the suggested guideline level of sentence and reconsider your reasons carefully if you have chosen a sentence at a different level. Consider a reduction for a timely guilty plea.

DECIDE YOUR SENTENCE
NB. COMPENSATION – Give reasons if not awarding compensation

Disorderly behaviour with intent to cause harassment, alarm or distress

Public Order Act 1986 s.4A Triable only summarily Penalty: Level 5 and/or 6 months	**Disorderly behaviour with intent to cause harassment, alarm or distress**

CONSIDER THE SERIOUSNESS OF THE OFFENCE
(INCLUDING THE IMPACT ON THE VICTIM)

IS DISCHARGE OR FINE APPROPRIATE?
GUIDELINE: → IS IT SERIOUS ENOUGH FOR A COMMUNITY PENALTY?
IS IT SO SERIOUS THAT ONLY CUSTODY IS APPROPRIATE?

THIS IS A GUIDELINE FOR A FIRST-TIME OFFENDER PLEADING NOT GUILTY

 ## CONSIDER AGGRAVATING AND MITIGATING FACTORS, CULPABILITY AND HARM

for example	for example
Football related Group action High degree of planning Night time offence Victims specifically targeted Weapon *This list is not exhaustive*	Short duration *This list is not exhaustive*

If offender is on bail, this offence is more serious
If offender has previous convictions, their relevance and any failure to respond to previous sentences should be considered – they may increase the seriousness. The court should make it clear, when passing sentence, that this was the approach adopted.

TAKE A PRELIMINARY VIEW OF SERIOUSNESS, THEN CONSIDER OFFENDER MITIGATION

for example
  Age, health (physical or mental)
  Co-operation with police
  Evidence of genuine remorse
  Voluntary compensation

CONSIDER YOUR SENTENCE

Compare it with the suggested guideline level of sentence and reconsider your reasons carefully if you have chosen a sentence at a different level. Consider a reduction for a timely guilty plea.

DECIDE YOUR SENTENCE
NB. COMPENSATION – Give reasons if not awarding compensation

Drugs: Class A – possession	Misuse of Drugs Act 1971 s.5 Triable either way – see Mode of Trial Guidelines Penalty: Level 5 and/or 6 months

CONSIDER THE SERIOUSNESS OF THE OFFENCE

GUIDELINE: →

IS DISCHARGE OR FINE APPROPRIATE?
IS IT SERIOUS ENOUGH FOR A COMMUNITY PENALTY?
IS IT SO SERIOUS THAT ONLY CUSTODY IS APPROPRIATE?
ARE YOUR SENTENCING POWERS SUFFICIENT?

THIS IS A GUIDELINE FOR A FIRST-TIME OFFENDER PLEADING NOT GUILTY

 ## CONSIDER AGGRAVATING AND MITIGATING FACTORS, CULPABILITY AND HARM

for example An amount other than a very small quantity *This list is not exhaustive*	for example Very small quantity *This list is not exhaustive*

If offender is on bail, this offence is more serious
If offender has previous convictions, their relevance and any failure to respond to previous sentences should be considered – they may increase the seriousness. The court should make it clear, when passing sentence, that this was the approach adopted.

TAKE A PRELIMINARY VIEW OF SERIOUSNESS, THEN CONSIDER OFFENDER MITIGATION

for example
Age, health (physical or mental)
Co-operation with police
Evidence of genuine remorse

CONSIDER YOUR SENTENCE

Compare it with the suggested guideline level of sentence and reconsider
your reasons carefully if you have chosen a sentence at a different level.
Consider a reduction for a timely guilty plea. Consider forfeiture and destruction.

DECIDE YOUR SENTENCE

Drugs: Class A – production, supply

Misuse of Drugs Act 1971 s.4 Triable either way – see Mode of Trial Guidelines Penalty: Level 5 and/or 6 months	**Drugs: Class A – production, supply**

CONSIDER THE SERIOUSNESS OF THE OFFENCE
(INCLUDING THE IMPACT ON THE VICTIM)

IS DISCHARGE OR FINE APPROPRIATE?

IS IT SERIOUS ENOUGH FOR A COMMUNITY PENALTY?

IS IT SO SERIOUS THAT ONLY CUSTODY IS APPROPRIATE?

GUIDELINE: →   ***ARE YOUR SENTENCING POWERS SUFFICIENT?***

THIS IS A GUIDELINE FOR A FIRST-TIME OFFENDER PLEADING NOT GUILTY

CONSIDER AGGRAVATING AND MITIGATING FACTORS, CULPABILITY AND HARM

for example
- Commercial production
- Deliberate adulteration
- Quantity
- Sophisticated operation
- Supply to children
- Venue, eg prisons, educational establishments
- *This list is not exhaustive*

for example
- Small amount
- *This list is not exhaustive*

If offender is on bail, this offence is more serious

If offender has previous convictions, their relevance and any failure to respond to previous sentences should be considered – they may increase the seriousness. The court should make it clear, when passing sentence, that this was the approach adopted.

TAKE A PRELIMINARY VIEW OF SERIOUSNESS, THEN CONSIDER WHETHER THE CASE SHOULD BE COMMITTED FOR SENTENCE, THEN CONSIDER OFFENDER MITIGATION

for example
- Age, health (physical or mental)
- Co-operation with police
- Evidence of genuine remorse

CONSIDER COMMITTAL OR YOUR SENTENCE

Compare it with the suggested guideline level of sentence and reconsider your reasons carefully if you have chosen a sentence at a different level. Consider a reduction for a timely guilty plea. Consider forfeiture and destruction.

DECIDE YOUR SENTENCE

Drugs: Class B and C – possession	Misuse of Drugs Acts 1971 s.5 Triable either way – see Mode of Trial Guidelines Penalty: *Update December 2006*: Class B – level 4 and/or 3 months. Class C – level 3 and/or 3 months

CONSIDER THE SERIOUSNESS OF THE OFFENCE

GUIDELINE: →

IS DISCHARGE OR FINE APPROPRIATE?
IS IT SERIOUS ENOUGH FOR A COMMUNITY PENALTY?
IS IT SO SERIOUS THAT ONLY CUSTODY IS APPROPRIATE?
ARE YOUR SENTENCING POWERS SUFFICIENT?

THIS IS A GUIDELINE FOR A FIRST-TIME OFFENDER PLEADING NOT GUILTY

GUIDELINE FINE – STARTING POINT B

 ## CONSIDER AGGRAVATING AND MITIGATING FACTORS, CULPABILITY AND HARM

for example
    Large amount
    This list is not exhaustive
	for example
	    Small amount
	    This list is not exhaustive

If offender is on bail, this offence is more serious
If offender has previous convictions, their relevance and any failure to respond to previous sentences should be considered – they may increase the seriousness. The court should make it clear, when passing sentence, that this was the approach adopted.

TAKE A PRELIMINARY VIEW OF SERIOUSNESS, THEN CONSIDER OFFENDER MITIGATION

for example
    Age, health (physical or mental)
    Co-operation with police
    Evidence of genuine remorse

CONSIDER YOUR SENTENCE

Compare it with the suggested guideline level of sentence and reconsider
your reasons carefully if you have chosen a sentence at a different level.
Consider a reduction for a timely guilty plea. Consider forfeiture and destruction.

DECIDE YOUR SENTENCE

Drugs: Class B and C – supply, possession with intent to supply

Misuse of Drugs Acts 1971 s.5 Triable either way – see Mode of Trial Guidelines Penalty: *Update December 2006*: Class B – level 5 and/or 6 months. Class C – level 4 and/or 3 months	**Drugs: Class B and C – supply, possession with intent to supply**

CONSIDER THE SERIOUSNESS OF THE OFFENCE
(INCLUDING THE IMPACT ON THE VICTIM)

IS DISCHARGE OR FINE APPROPRIATE?

IS IT SERIOUS ENOUGH FOR A COMMUNITY PENALTY?

IS IT SO SERIOUS THAT ONLY CUSTODY IS APPROPRIATE?

GUIDELINE: →   **ARE YOUR SENTENCING POWERS SUFFICIENT?**

THIS IS A GUIDELINE FOR A FIRST-TIME OFFENDER PLEADING NOT GUILTY

 ## CONSIDER AGGRAVATING AND MITIGATING FACTORS, CULPABILITY AND HARM

for example	for example
Commercial supply	No commercial motive
Deliberate adulteration	Small amount
Large amount	*This list is not exhaustive*
Sophisticated operation	
Supply to children	
Venue, eg prisons, educational establishments	
This list is not exhaustive	

If offender is on bail, this offence is more serious
If offender has previous convictions, their relevance and any failure to respond to previous sentences should be considered – they may increase the seriousness. The court should make it clear, when passing sentence, that this was the approach adopted.

TAKE A PRELIMINARY VIEW OF SERIOUSNESS, THEN CONSIDER WHETHER THE CASE SHOULD BE COMMITTED FOR SENTENCE, THEN CONSIDER OFFENDER MITIGATION

for example
     Age, health (physical or mental)
     Co-operation with police
     Evidence of genuine remorse

CONSIDER COMMITTAL OR YOUR SENTENCE

Compare it with the suggested guideline level of sentence and reconsider your reasons carefully if you have chosen a sentence at a different level. Consider a reduction for a timely guilty plea. Consider forfeiture and destruction.

DECIDE YOUR SENTENCE

<table>
<tr><td>

Drugs:
Cultivation of cannabis

</td><td>

Misuse of Drugs Act 1971 s.6
Triable either way – see Mode of Trial Guidelines
Penalty: Level 5 and/or 6 months

</td></tr>
</table>

CONSIDER THE SERIOUSNESS OF THE OFFENCE
(INCLUDING THE IMPACT ON THE VICTIM)

IS DISCHARGE OR FINE APPROPRIATE?

GUIDELINE: →   IS IT SERIOUS ENOUGH FOR A COMMUNITY PENALTY?

IS IT SO SERIOUS THAT ONLY CUSTODY IS APPROPRIATE?

ARE YOUR SENTENCING POWERS SUFFICIENT?

THIS IS A GUIDELINE FOR A FIRST-TIME OFFENDER PLEADING NOT GUILTY

 ## CONSIDER AGGRAVATING AND MITIGATING FACTORS, CULPABILITY AND HARM

for example	for example
Commercial cultivation	For personal use
Large quantity	Not responsible for planting
Use of sophisticated system	Small scale cultivation
This list is not exhaustive	*This list is not exhaustive*

If offender is on bail, this offence is more serious
If offender has previous convictions, their relevance and any failure to respond to previous sentences should be considered – they may increase the seriousness. The court should make it clear, when passing sentence, that this was the approach adopted.

TAKE A PRELIMINARY VIEW OF SERIOUSNESS, THEN CONSIDER OFFENDER MITIGATION

for example
    Age, health (physical or mental)
    Co-operation with police
    Evidence of genuine remorse

CONSIDER YOUR SENTENCE

Compare it with the suggested guideline level of sentence and reconsider your reasons carefully if you have chosen a sentence at a different level. Consider a reduction for a timely guilty plea. Consider forfeiture and destruction.

DECIDE YOUR SENTENCE

Criminal Justice Act 1967 s.91 Triable only summarily Penalty: Level 3	**Drunk and disorderly**

CONSIDER THE SERIOUSNESS OF THE OFFENCE

GUIDELINE: → *IS DISCHARGE OR FINE APPROPRIATE?*
IS IT SERIOUS ENOUGH FOR A COMMUNITY PENALTY?

THIS IS A GUIDELINE FOR A FIRST-TIME OFFENDER PLEADING NOT GUILTY

GUIDELINE FINE – STARTING POINT A

 ## CONSIDER AGGRAVATING AND MITIGATING FACTORS, CULPABILITY AND HARM

for example Offensive language or behaviour On hospital/medical or school premises On public transport With group *This list is not exhaustive*	for example Induced by others No significant disturbance Not threatening *This list is not exhaustive*

If racially or religiously aggravated, or offender is on bail, this offence is more serious
If offender has previous convictions, their relevance and any failure to respond to previous
sentences should be considered – they may increase the seriousness. The court should make
it clear, when passing sentence, that this was the approach adopted.

TAKE A PRELIMINARY VIEW OF SERIOUSNESS, THEN CONSIDER OFFENDER MITIGATION

for example
Health (physical and mental)
Co-operation with police
Evidence of genuine remorse

CONSIDER YOUR SENTENCE

Compare it with the suggested guideline level of sentence and reconsider
your reasons carefully if you have chosen a sentence at a different level.
Consider a reduction for a timely guilty plea.

DECIDE YOUR SENTENCE

Evasion of duty	Customs and Excise Management Act 1979 s.170 Triable either way – see Mode of trial guidelines Penalty: 6 months and/or £5000/or 3 times the value of the goods (whichever is the greater)

CONSIDER THE SERIOUSNESS OF THE OFFENCE

IS DISCHARGE OR FINE APPROPRIATE?

GUIDELINE: →   *IS IT SERIOUS ENOUGH FOR A COMMUNITY PENALTY?*

IS IT SO SERIOUS THAT ONLY CUSTODY IS APPROPRIATE?

ARE YOUR SENTENCING POWERS SUFFICIENT?

THIS IS A GUIDELINE FOR A FIRST-TIME OFFENDER PLEADING NOT GUILTY

 ## CONSIDER AGGRAVATING AND MITIGATING FACTORS, CULPABILITY AND HARM

for example	for example

Abuse of power (eg use of children/
   vulnerable adults)
Offender is Customs/Police Officer
Playing an organisational role
Professional operation
Repeated imports over a period of time
Substantial amount of duty evaded
Threats of violence
Two or more types of goods
Warning previously given
This list is not exhaustive
	Co-operation with authorities
	No evidence of pre-planning
	Small amounts of duty evaded
	Under pressure from others to commit
	   offence
	This list is not exhaustive

If offender is on bail, this offence is more serious

If offender has previous convictions, their relevance and any failure to respond to previous sentences should be considered – they may increase the seriousness. The court should make it clear, when passing sentence, that this was the approach adopted.

TAKE A PRELIMINARY VIEW OF SERIOUSNESS, THEN CONSIDER OFFENDER MITIGATION

for example

Age, health (physical or mental)
Co-operation with authorities
Evidence of genuine remorse
Voluntary restitution

CONSIDER YOUR SENTENCE

Compare it with the suggested guideline level of sentence and reconsider your reasons carefully if you have chosen a sentence at a different level. Consider a reduction for a timely guilty plea. Consider forfeiture.

DECIDE YOUR SENTENCE

NB. The guideline above approximates to a low level offender with duty evaded in the region of £1000 to £10000. Restitution should be made. For offences above this level seek advice from legal adviser.

Bail Act 1976 s.6 Triable only summarily Penalty: level 5 and/or 3 months	**Failure to surrender to bail**

CONSIDER THE SERIOUSNESS OF THE OFFENCE

IS DISCHARGE OR FINE APPROPRIATE?

GUIDELINE: →   *IS IT SERIOUS ENOUGH FOR A COMMUNITY PENALTY?*

IS IT SO SERIOUS THAT ONLY CUSTODY IS APPROPRIATE?

THIS IS A GUIDELINE FOR A FIRST-TIME OFFENDER PLEADING NOT GUILTY

 ### CONSIDER AGGRAVATING AND MITIGATING FACTORS, CULPABILITY AND HARM

for example	for example
Leaves jurisdiction	Appears late on day of hearing
Long term evasion	Genuine misunderstanding
Results in ineffective trial date	Voluntary surrender
Wilful evasion	*This list is not exhaustive*
This list is not exhaustive	

A curfew order may be particularly suitable

Previous convictions for this offence increase the seriousness – consider custody

TAKE A PRELIMINARY VIEW OF SERIOUSNESS, THEN CONSIDER OFFENDER MITIGATION

for example
Age, health (physical or mental)
Co-operation with police
Evidence of genuine remorse

CONSIDER YOUR SENTENCE

Compare it with the suggested guideline level of sentence and reconsider your reasons carefully if you have chosen a sentence at a different level. Consider a reduction for a timely guilty plea.

DECIDE YOUR SENTENCE

Football-related offences: being drunk in, or whilst trying to enter ground

Football-related offences: being drunk in, or whilst trying to enter ground	Sporting Events (Control of Alcohol etc) Act 1985 s.2(2) Triable only summarily Penalty: Level 2

CONSIDER THE SERIOUSNESS OF THE OFFENCE

GUIDELINE: →   **IS DISCHARGE OR FINE APPROPRIATE?**
IS IT SERIOUS ENOUGH FOR A COMMUNITY PENALTY?

THIS IS A GUIDELINE FOR A FIRST-TIME OFFENDER PLEADING NOT GUILTY

GUIDELINE FINE – STARTING POINT A

 ## CONSIDER AGGRAVATING AND MITIGATING FACTORS, CULPABILITY AND HARM

for example	for example
Group action Offensive language/behaviour used *This list is not exhaustive*	No significant disturbance Not threatening *This list is not exhaustive*

If offender is on bail, this offence is more serious
If offender has previous convictions, their relevance and any failure to respond to previous sentences should be considered – they may increase the seriousness. The court should make it clear, when passing sentence, that this was the approach adopted.

TAKE A PRELIMINARY VIEW OF SERIOUSNESS, THEN CONSIDER OFFENDER MITIGATION

for example
    Age, health (physical or mental)
    Co-operation with police
    Evidence of genuine remorse

CONSIDER YOUR SENTENCE

Compare it with the suggested guideline level of sentence and reconsider your reasons carefully if you have chosen a sentence at a different level.
Consider a reduction for a timely guilty plea.

DECIDE YOUR SENTENCE
MUST CONSIDER IMPOSING A BANNING ORDER
IF NO BANNING ORDER IS MADE, COURT MUST GIVE REASONS
Seek advice from the legal adviser

Football-related offences: going onto playing area or adjacent area to which spectators are not admitted

Football (Offences) Act 1991 s.4 Triable only summarily Penalty: Level 3	**Football-related offences: going onto playing area or adjacent area to which spectators are not admitted**

CONSIDER THE SERIOUSNESS OF THE OFFENCE

GUIDELINE: →   ***IS DISCHARGE OR FINE APPROPRIATE?***
IS IT SERIOUS ENOUGH FOR A COMMUNITY PENALTY?

THIS IS A GUIDELINE FOR A FIRST-TIME OFFENDER PLEADING NOT GUILTY

GUIDELINE FINE – STARTING POINT A

 CONSIDER AGGRAVATING AND MITIGATING FACTORS, CULPABILITY AND HARM

for example
     Being drunk
     Deliberate provocative act
     Inciting others
     This list is not exhaustive

If offender is on bail, this offence is more serious
If offender has previous convictions, their relevance and any failure to respond to previous sentences should be considered – they may increase the seriousness. The court should make it clear, when passing sentence, that this was the approach adopted.

TAKE A PRELIMINARY VIEW OF SERIOUSNESS, THEN CONSIDER OFFENDER MITIGATION

for example
     Age, health (physical or mental)
     Co-operation with police
     Evidence of genuine remorse

CONSIDER YOUR SENTENCE

Compare it with the suggested guideline level of sentence and reconsider your reasons carefully if you have chosen a sentence at a different level.
Consider a reduction for a timely guilty plea.

DECIDE YOUR SENTENCE
MUST CONSIDER IMPOSING A BANNING ORDER
IF NO BANNING ORDER IS MADE, COURT MUST GIVE REASONS
Seek advice from the legal adviser

Football-related offences: possession of liquor whilst entering or trying to enter the ground	Sporting Events (Control of Alcohol etc) Act 1985 s.2(1) Triable only summarily Penalty: Level 3 and/or 3 months

CONSIDER THE SERIOUSNESS OF THE OFFENCE

GUIDELINE: →

IS DISCHARGE OR FINE APPROPRIATE?
IS IT SERIOUS ENOUGH FOR A COMMUNITY PENALTY?
IS IT SO SERIOUS THAT ONLY CUSTODY IS APPROPRIATE?

THIS IS A GUIDELINE FOR A FIRST-TIME OFFENDER PLEADING NOT GUILTY

GUIDELINE FINE – STARTING POINT B

 CONSIDER AGGRAVATING AND MITIGATING FACTORS, CULPABILITY AND HARM

for example	for example
Concealed	Low alcoholic-content liquor
Group action	Small amount of alcohol
High alcoholic-content liquor	*This list is not exhaustive*
Large amount of alcohol	
Offensive language/behaviour used	
This list is not exhaustive	

If offender is on bail, this offence is more serious
If offender has previous convictions, their relevance and any failure to respond to previous sentences should be considered – they may increase the seriousness. The court should make it clear, when passing sentence, that this was the approach adopted.

TAKE A PRELIMINARY VIEW OF SERIOUSNESS, THEN CONSIDER OFFENDER MITIGATION

for example
    Age, health (physical or mental)
    Co-operation with police
    Evidence of genuine remorse

CONSIDER YOUR SENTENCE

Compare it with the suggested guideline level of sentence and reconsider your reasons carefully if you have chosen a sentence at a different level.
Consider a reduction for a timely guilty plea.

DECIDE YOUR SENTENCE
MUST CONSIDER IMPOSING A BANNING ORDER
IF NO BANNING ORDER IS MADE, COURT MUST GIVE REASONS
Seek advice from the legal adviser

Football (Offences) Act 1991 s.2 Triable only summarily Penalty: Level 3	**Football-related offences: throwing missiles**

CONSIDER THE SERIOUSNESS OF THE OFFENCE

GUIDELINE: →   ***IS DISCHARGE OR FINE APPROPRIATE?***
IS IT SERIOUS ENOUGH FOR A COMMUNITY PENALTY?

THIS IS A GUIDELINE FOR A FIRST-TIME OFFENDER PLEADING NOT GUILTY

GUIDELINE FINE – STARTING POINT B

 ## CONSIDER AGGRAVATING AND MITIGATING FACTORS, CULPABILITY AND HARM

for example
     Object likely to cause injury (eg coin,
         glass bottle, stone)
     This list is not exhaustive

If racially or religiously aggravated, or offender is on bail, this offence is more serious
If offender has previous convictions, their relevance and any failure to respond to previous sentences should be considered – they may increase the seriousness. The court should make it clear, when passing sentence, that this was the approach adopted.

TAKE A PRELIMINARY VIEW OF SERIOUSNESS, THEN CONSIDER OFFENDER MITIGATION

for example
     Age, health (physical or mental)
     Co-operation with police
     Evidence of genuine remorse
     Voluntary compensation

CONSIDER YOUR SENTENCE

Compare it with the suggested guideline level of sentence and reconsider your reasons carefully if you have chosen a sentence at a different level. Consider a reduction for a timely guilty plea.

DECIDE YOUR SENTENCE
MUST CONSIDER IMPOSING A BANNING ORDER
IF NO BANNING ORDER IS MADE, COURT MUST GIVE REASONS
Seek advice from the legal adviser

Football-related offences: unauthorised sale or attempted sale of ticket	Criminal Justice and Public Order Act 1994 s.166 Triable only summarily Penalty: Level 5

CONSIDER THE SERIOUSNESS OF THE OFFENCE

GUIDELINE: →   ***IS DISCHARGE OR FINE APPROPRIATE?***
IS IT SERIOUS ENOUGH FOR A COMMUNITY PENALTY?

THIS IS A GUIDELINE FOR A FIRST-TIME OFFENDER PLEADING NOT GUILTY

GUIDELINE FINE – STARTING POINT B

CONSIDER AGGRAVATING AND MITIGATING FACTORS, CULPABILITY AND HARM

for example Commercial operation Counterfeit tickets In possession of a large number of tickets/ potential high value Sophisticated operation *This list is not exhaustive*	for example Single ticket *This list is not exhaustive*

If offender is on bail, this offence is more serious
If offender has previous convictions, their relevance and any failure to respond to previous sentences should be considered – they may increase the seriousness. The court should make it clear, when passing sentence, that this was the approach adopted.

TAKE A PRELIMINARY VIEW OF SERIOUSNESS, THEN CONSIDER OFFENDER MITIGATION

for example
Age, health (physical or mental)
Co-operation with police
Evidence of genuine remorse
Voluntary compensation

CONSIDER YOUR SENTENCE

Compare it with the suggested guideline level of sentence and reconsider your reasons carefully if you have chosen a sentence at a different level. Consider a reduction for a timely guilty plea.

DECIDE YOUR SENTENCE
MUST CONSIDER IMPOSING A BANNING ORDER
IF NO BANNING ORDER IS MADE, COURT MUST GIVE REASONS
Seek advice from the legal adviser

Going equipped for theft etc

Theft Act 1968 s.25 Triable either way – see Mode of Trial Guidelines Penalty: Level 5 and/or 6 months May disqualify where committed with reference to the theft or taking of a vehicle	Going equipped for theft etc.

CONSIDER THE SERIOUSNESS OF THE OFFENCE

GUIDELINE: →

IS DISCHARGE OR FINE APPROPRIATE?
IS IT SERIOUS ENOUGH FOR A COMMUNITY PENALTY?
IS IT SO SERIOUS THAT ONLY CUSTODY IS APPROPRIATE?
ARE YOUR SENTENCING POWERS SUFFICIENT?

THIS IS A GUIDELINE FOR A FIRST-TIME OFFENDER PLEADING NOT GUILTY

 ## CONSIDER AGGRAVATING AND MITIGATING FACTORS, CULPABILITY AND HARM

for example
> Group action
> Number of items
> People put in fear
> Sophisticated
> Specialised equipment
> *This list is not exhaustive*

If offender is on bail, this offence is more serious
If offender has previous convictions, their relevance and any failure to respond to previous sentences should be considered – they may increase the seriousness. The court should make it clear, when passing sentence, that this was the approach adopted.

TAKE A PRELIMINARY VIEW OF SERIOUSNESS, THEN CONSIDER OFFENDER MITIGATION

for example
> Age, health (physical or mental)
> Co-operation with police
> Evidence of genuine remorse

CONSIDER YOUR SENTENCE

Compare it with the suggested guideline level of sentence and reconsider your reasons carefully if you have chosen a sentence at a different level. Consider a reduction for a timely guilty plea. Consider forfeiture and destruction.

DECIDE YOUR SENTENCE

Handling stolen goods	Theft Act 1968 s.22 Triable either way – see Mode of Trial Guidelines Penalty: Level 5 and/or 6 months

CONSIDER THE SERIOUSNESS OF THE OFFENCE
(INCLUDING THE IMPACT ON THE VICTIM)

IS DISCHARGE OR FINE APPROPRIATE?

GUIDELINE: →   IS IT SERIOUS ENOUGH FOR A COMMUNITY PENALTY?

IS IT SO SERIOUS THAT ONLY CUSTODY IS APPROPRIATE?

ARE YOUR SENTENCING POWERS SUFFICIENT?

THIS IS A GUIDELINE FOR A FIRST-TIME OFFENDER PLEADING NOT GUILTY

CONSIDER AGGRAVATING AND MITIGATING FACTORS, CULPABILITY AND HARM

for example	for example
High level of profit accruing to handler High value (including sentimental) of goods Provision by handler of regular outlet for stolen goods Proximity of the handler to the primary offence Seriousness of the primary offence Sophistication The particular facts, eg the goods handled were the proceeds of a domestic burglary Threats of violence or abuse of power by handler in order to obtain goods *This list is not exhaustive*	Isolated offence Little or no benefit accruing to handler Low monetary value of goods *This list is not exhaustive*

If offender is on bail, this offence is more serious

If offender has previous convictions, their relevance and any failure to respond to previous sentences should be considered – they may increase the seriousness. The court should make it clear, when passing sentence, that this was the approach adopted.

TAKE A PRELIMINARY VIEW OF SERIOUSNESS, THEN CONSIDER OFFENDER MITIGATION

for example
Age, health (physical or mental)
Co-operation with police
Evidence of genuine remorse
Voluntary compensation

CONSIDER YOUR SENTENCE

Compare it with the suggested guideline level of sentence and reconsider your reasons carefully if you have chosen a sentence at a different level. Consider a reduction for a timely guilty plea.

DECIDE YOUR SENTENCE
NB. COMPENSATION – Give reasons if not awarding compensation

Harassment – Conduct causing fear of violence

Protection from Harassment Act 1997 s.4 Triable either way Penalty: Level 5 and/or 6 months Consider making a restraining order	**Harassment** Conduct causing fear of violence

CONSIDER THE SERIOUSNESS OF THE OFFENCE
(INCLUDING THE IMPACT ON THE VICTIM)

IS DISCHARGE OR FINE APPROPRIATE?

IS IT SERIOUS ENOUGH FOR A COMMUNITY PENALTY?

GUIDELINE: → *IS IT SO SERIOUS THAT ONLY CUSTODY IS APPROPRIATE?*

ARE YOUR SENTENCING POWERS SUFFICIENT?

THIS IS A GUIDELINE FOR A FIRST-TIME OFFENDER PLEADING NOT GUILTY

 ## CONSIDER AGGRAVATING AND MITIGATING FACTORS, CULPABILITY AND HARM

for example
- Disregard of warning
- Excessive persistence
- Interference with employment/business
- Invasion of victim's home
- Involvement of others
- Threat to use weapon or substance (including realistic imitations)
- Use of violence or grossly offensive material
- Where photographs or images of a personal nature are involved
- *This list is not exhaustive*

for example
- Initial provocation
- Short duration
- *This list is not exhaustive*

If offender is on bail, this offence is more serious
If offender has previous convictions, their relevance and any failure to respond to previous sentences should be considered – they may increase the seriousness. The court should make it clear, when passing sentence, that this was the approach adopted.

TAKE A PRELIMINARY VIEW OF SERIOUSNESS, THEN CONSIDER OFFENDER MITIGATION

for example
- Age, health (physical or mental)
- Co-operation with police
- Evidence of genuine remorse
- Voluntary compensation

CONSIDER YOUR SENTENCE

Compare it with the suggested guideline level of sentence and reconsider your reasons carefully if you have chosen a sentence at a different level.
Consider a reduction for a timely guilty plea.
Restraining order – consider making an order in addition to the sentence to protect the victim or any named person from further conduct which would amount to harassment, or which would cause the fear of violence.

DECIDE YOUR SENTENCE
NB. COMPENSATION – Give reasons if not awarding compensation

Harassment Conduct causing harassment	Protection from Harassment Act 1997 s.2 Triable only summarily Penalty: Level 5 and/or 6 months Consider making a restraining order

CONSIDER THE SERIOUSNESS OF THE OFFENCE
(INCLUDING THE IMPACT ON THE VICTIM)

IS DISCHARGE OR FINE APPROPRIATE?

GUIDELINE: →   *IS IT SERIOUS ENOUGH FOR A COMMUNITY PENALTY?*

IS IT SO SERIOUS THAT ONLY CUSTODY IS APPROPRIATE?

THIS IS A GUIDELINE FOR A FIRST-TIME OFFENDER PLEADING NOT GUILTY

 CONSIDER AGGRAVATING AND MITIGATING FACTORS, CULPABILITY AND HARM

for example	for example
Disregard of warning Excessive persistence Interference with employment/business Invasion of victim's home Involvement of others Use of violence or grossly offensive material Where photographs or images of a personal nature are involved *This list is not exhaustive*	Initial provocation Short duration *This list is not exhaustive*

If offender is on bail, this offence is more serious

If offender has previous convictions, their relevance and any failure to respond to previous sentences should be considered – they may increase the seriousness. The court should make it clear, when passing sentence, that this was the approach adopted.

TAKE A PRELIMINARY VIEW OF SERIOUSNESS, THEN CONSIDER OFFENDER MITIGATION

for example
> Age, health (physical or mental)
> Co-operation with police
> Evidence of genuine remorse
> Voluntary compensation

CONSIDER YOUR SENTENCE

Compare it with the suggested guideline level of sentence and reconsider your reasons carefully if you have chosen a sentence at a different level.
Consider a reduction for a timely guilty plea.
Restraining order – consider making an order in addition to the sentence to protect the victim or any named person from further conduct which would amount to harassment.

DECIDE YOUR SENTENCE
NB. COMPENSATION – Give reasons if not awarding compensation

Indecent assault

Sexual Offences Act 1956 ss.14&15 Triable either way – see Mode of Trial Guidelines Penalty: Level 5 and/or 6 months Entry in Sex Offender's Register (consult legal adviser)	**Indecent assault** Update December 2006: Offence now covered by Sexual Offences Act 2003. Consult your legal adviser

CONSIDER THE SERIOUSNESS OF THE OFFENCE
(INCLUDING THE IMPACT ON THE VICTIM)

IS DISCHARGE OR FINE APPROPRIATE?

IS IT SERIOUS ENOUGH FOR A COMMUNITY PENALTY?

GUIDELINE: → *IS IT SO SERIOUS THAT ONLY CUSTODY IS APPROPRIATE?*

ARE YOUR SENTENCING POWERS SUFFICIENT?

THIS IS A GUIDELINE FOR A FIRST-TIME OFFENDER PLEADING NOT GUILTY

 ## CONSIDER AGGRAVATING AND MITIGATING FACTORS, CULPABILITY AND HARM

for example 　Age differential 　Breach of trust 　Injury (may be psychological) 　Prolonged assault 　Very young victim 　Victim deliberately targeted 　Victim serving the public 　Vulnerable victim 　*This list is not exhaustive*	for example 　Slight contact 　*This list is not exhaustive*

If racially or religiously aggravated, or offender is on bail, this offence is more serious
If offender has previous convictions, their relevance and any failure to respond to previous
sentences should be considered – they may increase the seriousness. The court should make
it clear, when passing sentence, that this was the approach adopted.

TAKE A PRELIMINARY VIEW OF SERIOUSNESS, THEN CONSIDER OFFENDER MITIGATION

for example
　Age, health (physical or mental)
　Co-operation with police
　Evidence of genuine remorse
　Voluntary compensation

CONSIDER YOUR SENTENCE

Compare it with the suggested guideline level of sentence and reconsider
your reasons carefully if you have chosen a sentence at a different level.
Consider a reduction for a timely guilty plea.
Entry in Sex Offender's Register (consult legal adviser).

DECIDE YOUR SENTENCE
NB. COMPENSATION – Give reasons if not awarding compensation

Indecent photographs etc

Indecent photographs etc. Update December 2006: Offence now covered by Sexual Offences Act 2003. Consult your legal adviser	Protection of Children Act 1978 s.1(1) Criminal Justice Act 1988 s.160(1) Triable either way – see Mode of Trial Guidelines Penalty: Level 5 and/or 6 months Entry in Sex Offender's Register (consult legal adviser)

CONSIDER THE SERIOUSNESS OF THE OFFENCE
(INCLUDING THE IMPACT ON THE VICTIM)

IS DISCHARGE OR FINE APPROPRIATE?

IS IT SERIOUS ENOUGH FOR A COMMUNITY PENALTY?

IS IT SO SERIOUS THAT ONLY CUSTODY IS APPROPRIATE?

GUIDELINE: →   ***ARE YOUR SENTENCING POWERS SUFFICIENT?***

THIS IS A GUIDELINE FOR A FIRST-TIME OFFENDER PLEADING NOT GUILTY

 ## CONSIDER AGGRAVATING AND MITIGATING FACTORS, CULPABILITY AND HARM

for example	for example
Abuse of trust Commercial gain Involvement in production Large number of images Particularly young or vulnerable children *This list is not exhaustive*	Images at the lowest categories of COPINE* (seek advice from the legal adviser) One photograph only Possession for own use Pseudo images *This list is not exhaustive* **The COPINE (Combating Paedophile Information Networks in Europe) Project was founded in 1997, and is based in the Department of Applied Psychology, University College Cork, Ireland*

If racially or religiously aggravated, or offender is on bail, this offence is more serious
If offender has previous convictions, their relevance and any failure to respond to previous sentences should be considered – they may increase the seriousness. The court should make it clear, when passing sentence, that this was the approach adopted.

TAKE A PRELIMINARY VIEW OF SERIOUSNESS, THEN CONSIDER WHETHER THE CASE SHOULD BE COMMITTED FOR SENTENCE, THEN CONSIDER OFFENDER MITIGATION

for example
Age, health (physical or mental)
Co-operation with police
Evidence of genuine remorse
Voluntary compensation

CONSIDER COMMITTAL OR YOUR SENTENCE

Compare it with the suggested guideline level of sentence and reconsider your reasons carefully if you have chosen a sentence at a different level. Consider a reduction for a timely guilty plea. Consider forfeiture and destruction. Entry in Sex Offender's Register (consult legal adviser).

DECIDE YOUR SENTENCE

Making off without payment

Theft Act 1978 s.3 Triable either way – see Mode of Trial Guidelines Penalty: Level 5 and/or 6 months	**Making off without payment**

CONSIDER THE SERIOUSNESS OF THE OFFENCE
(INCLUDING THE IMPACT ON THE VICTIM)

GUIDELINE: →   *IS DISCHARGE OR FINE APPROPRIATE?*

IS IT SERIOUS ENOUGH FOR A COMMUNITY PENALTY?

IS IT SO SERIOUS THAT ONLY CUSTODY IS APPROPRIATE?

ARE YOUR SENTENCING POWERS SUFFICIENT?

THIS IS A GUIDELINE FOR A FIRST-TIME OFFENDER PLEADING NOT GUILTY

GUIDELINE FINE – STARTING POINT B

 ## CONSIDER AGGRAVATING AND MITIGATING FACTORS, CULPABILITY AND HARM

for example	for example
Deliberate plan	Impulsive action
High value	Low value
Two or more involved	*This list is not exhaustive*
Victim particularly vulnerable	
This list is not exhaustive	

If racially or religiously aggravated, or offender is on bail, this offence is more serious
If offender has previous convictions, their relevance and any failure to respond to previous sentences should be considered – they may increase the seriousness. The court should make it clear, when passing sentence, that this was the approach adopted.

TAKE A PRELIMINARY VIEW OF SERIOUSNESS, THEN CONSIDER OFFENDER MITIGATION

for example
     Age, health (physical or mental)
     Co-operation with police
     Evidence of genuine remorse
     Voluntary compensation

CONSIDER YOUR SENTENCE

Compare it with the suggested guideline level of sentence and reconsider your reasons carefully if you have chosen a sentence at a different level.
Consider a reduction for a timely guilty plea.

DECIDE YOUR SENTENCE
NB. COMPENSATION – Give reasons if not awarding compensation

Obstructing a police officer	Police Act 1996 s.89(2) Triable only summarily Penalty: Level 3 and/or 1 month

CONSIDER THE SERIOUSNESS OF THE OFFENCE
(INCLUDING THE IMPACT ON THE VICTIM)

GUIDELINE: →

IS DISCHARGE OR FINE APPROPRIATE?
IS IT SERIOUS ENOUGH FOR A COMMUNITY PENALTY?
IS IT SO SERIOUS THAT ONLY CUSTODY IS APPROPRIATE?

THIS IS A GUIDELINE FOR A FIRST-TIME OFFENDER PLEADING NOT GUILTY

GUIDELINE FINE – STARTING POINT B

 ## CONSIDER AGGRAVATING AND MITIGATING FACTORS, CULPABILITY AND HARM

for example	for example
Attempt to impede arrest	Genuine misjudgement
Group action	Impulsive action
Premeditated	Minor obstruction
This list is not exhaustive	*This list is not exhaustive*

If racially or religiously aggravated, or offender is on bail, this offence is more serious
If offender has previous convictions, their relevance and any failure to respond to previous sentences should be considered – they may increase the seriousness. The court should make it clear, when passing sentence, that this was the approach adopted.

TAKE A PRELIMINARY VIEW OF SERIOUSNESS, THEN CONSIDER OFFENDER MITIGATION

for example
Age, health (physical or mental)
Subsequent co-operation with police
Evidence of genuine remorse

CONSIDER YOUR SENTENCE

Compare it with the suggested guideline level of sentence and reconsider your reasons carefully if you have chosen a sentence at a different level. Consider a reduction for a timely guilty plea.

DECIDE YOUR SENTENCE

Obtaining by deception

Theft Act 1968 s.15 Triable either way – see Mode of Trial Guidelines Penalty: Level 5 and/or 6 months	**Obtaining by deception**

CONSIDER THE SERIOUSNESS OF THE OFFENCE
(INCLUDING THE IMPACT ON THE VICTIM)

IS DISCHARGE OR FINE APPROPRIATE?

GUIDELINE: →   IS IT SERIOUS ENOUGH FOR A COMMUNITY PENALTY?

IS IT SO SERIOUS THAT ONLY CUSTODY IS APPROPRIATE?

ARE YOUR SENTENCING POWERS SUFFICIENT?

THIS IS A GUIDELINE FOR A FIRST-TIME OFFENDER PLEADING NOT GUILTY

 ## CONSIDER AGGRAVATING AND MITIGATING FACTORS, CULPABILITY AND HARM

for example	for example
Committed over lengthy period Large sums or valuable goods Two or more involved Use of stolen credit/debit card, cheque books, or giros Victim particularly vulnerable *This list is not exhaustive*	Impulsive action Short period Small sum *This list is not exhaustive*

If offender is on bail, this offence is more serious
If offender has previous convictions, their relevance and any failure to respond to previous sentences should be considered – they may increase the seriousness. The court should make it clear, when passing sentence, that this was the approach adopted.

TAKE A PRELIMINARY VIEW OF SERIOUSNESS, THEN CONSIDER OFFENDER MITIGATION

for example
   Age, health (physical or mental)
   Co-operation with police
   Evidence of genuine remorse
   Voluntary compensation

CONSIDER YOUR SENTENCE

Compare it with the suggested guideline level of sentence and reconsider your reasons carefully if you have chosen a sentence at a different level. Consider a reduction for a timely guilty plea.

DECIDE YOUR SENTENCE
NB. COMPENSATION – Give reasons if not awarding compensation

Possession of a bladed instrument	Criminal Justice Act 1988 s.139 Triable either way – see Mode of Trial Guidelines Penalty: Level 5 and/or 6 months

CONSIDER THE SERIOUSNESS OF THE OFFENCE
(INCLUDING THE IMPACT ON THE VICTIM)

IS DISCHARGE OR FINE APPROPRIATE?

IS IT SERIOUS ENOUGH FOR A COMMUNITY PENALTY?

GUIDELINE: → *IS IT SO SERIOUS THAT ONLY CUSTODY IS APPROPRIATE?*

ARE YOUR SENTENCING POWERS SUFFICIENT?

THIS IS A GUIDELINE FOR A FIRST-TIME OFFENDER PLEADING NOT GUILTY

 ## CONSIDER AGGRAVATING AND MITIGATING FACTORS, CULPABILITY AND HARM

for example	for example
Group action or joint possession Location of offence Offender under influence of drink or drugs People put in fear/weapon brandished Planned use Very dangerous weapon *This list is not exhaustive*	Acting out of genuine fear Carried only on a temporary basis No attempt to use Not premeditated *This list is not exhaustive*

If racially or religiously aggravated, or offender is on bail, this offence is more serious
If offender has previous convictions, their relevance and any failure to respond to previous
sentences should be considered – they may increase the seriousness. The court should make
it clear, when passing sentence, that this was the approach adopted.

TAKE A PRELIMINARY VIEW OF SERIOUSNESS, THEN CONSIDER OFFENDER MITIGATION

for example
Age, health (physical or mental)
Co-operation with police
Evidence of genuine remorse

CONSIDER YOUR SENTENCE

Compare it with the suggested guideline level of sentence and reconsider
your reasons carefully if you have chosen a sentence at a different level.
Consider a reduction for a timely guilty plea. Consider forfeiture and destruction.

DECIDE YOUR SENTENCE

Possession of an offensive weapon

Prevention of Crime Act 1953 s.1 Triable either way – see Mode of Trial Guidelines Penalty: Level 5 and/or 6 months	Possession of an offensive weapon

CONSIDER THE SERIOUSNESS OF THE OFFENCE
(INCLUDING THE IMPACT ON THE VICTIM)

IS DISCHARGE OR FINE APPROPRIATE?

IS IT SERIOUS ENOUGH FOR A COMMUNITY PENALTY?

GUIDELINE: → *IS IT SO SERIOUS THAT ONLY CUSTODY IS APPROPRIATE?*

ARE YOUR SENTENCING POWERS SUFFICIENT?

THIS IS A GUIDELINE FOR A FIRST-TIME OFFENDER PLEADING NOT GUILTY

 ## CONSIDER AGGRAVATING AND MITIGATING FACTORS, CULPABILITY AND HARM

for example	**for example**
Group action or joint possession	Acting out of genuine fear
Location of offence	Carried only on a temporary basis
Offender under influence of drink or drugs	No attempt to use
People put in fear/weapon brandished	Not premeditated
Planned use	*This list is not exhaustive*
Very dangerous weapon	
This list is not exhaustive	

If racially or religiously aggravated, or offender is on bail, this offence is more serious
If offender has previous convictions, their relevance and any failure to respond to previous
sentences should be considered – they may increase the seriousness. The court should make
it clear, when passing sentence, that this was the approach adopted.

TAKE A PRELIMINARY VIEW OF SERIOUSNESS, THEN CONSIDER OFFENDER MITIGATION

for example
Age, health (physical or mental)
Co-operation with police
Evidence of genuine remorse
Voluntary compensation

CONSIDER YOUR SENTENCE

Compare it with the suggested guideline level of sentence and reconsider
your reasons carefully if you have chosen a sentence at a different level.
Consider a reduction for a timely guilty plea. Consider forfeiture and destruction.

DECIDE YOUR SENTENCE

Racially or religiously aggravated assault – actual bodily harm

Racially or religiously aggravated assault – actual bodily harm	Offences Against the Person Act 1861 s.47 Crime and Disorder Act 1998 s.29 Anti-Terrorism, Crime and Security Act 2001 Triable either way – see Mode of Trial Guidelines Penalty: Level 5 and/or 6 months

CONSIDER THE SERIOUSNESS OF THE OFFENCE
(INCLUDING THE IMPACT ON THE VICTIM)

IS DISCHARGE OR FINE APPROPRIATE?

IS IT SERIOUS ENOUGH FOR A COMMUNITY PENALTY?

IS IT SO SERIOUS THAT ONLY CUSTODY IS APPROPRIATE?

GUIDELINE: →   **ARE YOUR SENTENCING POWERS SUFFICIENT?**

THIS IS A GUIDELINE FOR A FIRST-TIME OFFENDER PLEADING NOT GUILTY

 ## CONSIDER AGGRAVATING AND MITIGATING FACTORS, CULPABILITY AND HARM

for example	for example
Deliberate kicking or biting Extensive injuries (may be psychological) Group action Headbutting **Motivation** for the offence was racial or religious Offender in position of authority On hospital/medical or school premises Premeditated Setting out to humiliate the victim Victim particularly vulnerable Victim serving the public Weapon *This list is not exhaustive*	Minor injury Provocation Single blow *This list is not exhaustive*

If offender is on bail, this offence is more serious
If offender has previous convictions, their relevance and any failure to respond to previous sentences should be considered – they may increase the seriousness. The court should make it clear, when passing sentence, that this was the approach adopted.

TAKE A PRELIMINARY VIEW OF SERIOUSNESS, THEN CONSIDER WHETHER THE CASE SHOULD BE COMMITTED FOR SENTENCE, THEN CONSIDER OFFENDER MITIGATION

for example
    Age, health (physical or mental)
    Co-operation with police
    Evidence of genuine remorse
    Voluntary compensation

CONSIDER COMMITTAL OR YOUR SENTENCE

Compare it with the suggested guideline level of sentence and reconsider your reasons carefully if you have chosen a sentence at a different level. Consider a reduction for a timely guilty plea.

DECIDE YOUR SENTENCE
NB. COMPENSATION – Give reasons if not awarding compensation

Racially or religiously aggravated common assault

Criminal Justice Act 1988 s.39 Crime and Disorder Act 1998 s.29 Anti-Terrorism, Crime and Security Act 2001 Triable either way – see Mode of Trial Guidelines Penalty: Level 5 and/or 6 months	**Racially or religiously aggravated common assault**

CONSIDER THE SERIOUSNESS OF THE OFFENCE
(INCLUDING THE IMPACT ON THE VICTIM)

IS DISCHARGE OR FINE APPROPRIATE?

IS IT SERIOUS ENOUGH FOR A COMMUNITY PENALTY?

GUIDELINE: → IS IT SO SERIOUS THAT ONLY CUSTODY IS APPROPRIATE?

ARE YOUR SENTENCING POWERS SUFFICIENT?

THIS IS A GUIDELINE FOR A FIRST-TIME OFFENDER PLEADING NOT GUILTY

 ## CONSIDER AGGRAVATING AND MITIGATING FACTORS, CULPABILITY AND HARM

for example
    Group action
    Injury
    Motivation for the offence was racial or religious
    Offender in position of authority
    On hospital/medical or school premises
    Premeditated
    Setting out to humiliate the victim
    Victim particularly vulnerable
    Victim serving the public
    Weapon
    This list is not exhaustive
	for example
	    Impulsive
	    Minor injury
	    Provocation
	    Single blow
	    This list is not exhaustive

If offender is on bail, this offence is more serious
If offender has previous convictions, their relevance and any failure to respond to previous sentences should be considered – they may increase the seriousness. The court should make it clear, when passing sentence, that this was the approach adopted.

TAKE A PRELIMINARY VIEW OF SERIOUSNESS, THEN CONSIDER OFFENDER MITIGATION

for example
    Age, health (physical or mental)
    Co-operation with police
    Evidence of genuine remorse
    Voluntary compensation

CONSIDER YOUR SENTENCE

Compare it with the suggested guideline level of sentence and reconsider your reasons carefully if you have chosen a sentence at a different level. Consider a reduction for a timely guilty plea.

DECIDE YOUR SENTENCE
NB. COMPENSATION – Give reasons if not awarding compensation

Racially or religiously aggravated criminal damage

Racially or religiously aggravated criminal damage	Criminal Damage Act 1971 s.1 Crime and Disorder Act 1998 s.30 Anti-Terrorism, Crime and Security Act 2001 Triable either way – see Mode of Trial Guidelines Penalty: Level 5 and/or 6 months

CONSIDER THE SERIOUSNESS OF THE OFFENCE
(INCLUDING THE IMPACT ON THE VICTIM)

IS DISCHARGE OR FINE APPROPRIATE?

GUIDELINE: ➜   *IS IT SERIOUS ENOUGH FOR A COMMUNITY PENALTY?*

IS IT SO SERIOUS THAT ONLY CUSTODY IS APPROPRIATE?

ARE YOUR SENTENCING POWERS SUFFICIENT?

THIS IS A GUIDELINE FOR A FIRST-TIME OFFENDER PLEADING NOT GUILTY

 ## CONSIDER AGGRAVATING AND MITIGATING FACTORS, CULPABILITY AND HARM

for example
- Deliberate
- Group offence
- **Motivation** for the offence was racial or religious
- Serious damage
- Setting out to humiliate the victim
- Vulnerable victim
- *This list is not exhaustive*

for example
- Impulsive action
- Minor damage
- Provocation
- *This list is not exhaustive*

If offender is on bail, this offence is more serious
If offender has previous convictions, their relevance and any failure to respond to previous sentences should be considered – they may increase the seriousness. The court should make it clear, when passing sentence, that this was the approach adopted.

TAKE A PRELIMINARY VIEW OF SERIOUSNESS, THEN CONSIDER OFFENDER MITIGATION

for example
- Age, health (physical or mental)
- Co-operation with police
- Evidence of genuine remorse
- Voluntary compensation

CONSIDER YOUR SENTENCE

Compare it with the suggested guideline level of sentence and reconsider your reasons carefully if you have chosen a sentence at a different level. Consider a reduction for a timely guilty plea.

DECIDE YOUR SENTENCE
NB. COMPENSATION – Give reasons if not awarding compensation

Racially or religiously aggravated disorderly behaviour

| Public Order Act 1986 s.5
Crime and Disorder Act 1998 s.31
Anti-Terrorism, Crime and Security Act 2001
Triable only summarily
Penalty: Level 4 | **Racially or religiously aggravated disorderly behaviour** |

CONSIDER THE SERIOUSNESS OF THE OFFENCE
(INCLUDING THE IMPACT ON THE VICTIM)

IS DISCHARGE OR FINE APPROPRIATE?

GUIDELINE: →   IS IT SERIOUS ENOUGH FOR A COMMUNITY PENALTY?

THIS IS A GUIDELINE FOR A FIRST-TIME OFFENDER PLEADING NOT GUILTY

 ## CONSIDER AGGRAVATING AND MITIGATING FACTORS, CULPABILITY AND HARM

for example	for example
Group action **Motivation** for the offence was racial or religious Setting out to humiliate the victim Vulnerable victim *This list is not exhaustive*	Stopped as soon as police arrived Trivial incident *This list is not exhaustive*

If offender is on bail, this offence is more serious
If offender has previous convictions, their relevance and any failure to respond to previous sentences should be considered – they may increase the seriousness. The court should make it clear, when passing sentence, that this was the approach adopted.

TAKE A PRELIMINARY VIEW OF SERIOUSNESS, THEN CONSIDER OFFENDER MITIGATION

for example
Age, health (physical or mental)
Co-operation with police
Evidence of genuine remorse
Voluntary compensation

CONSIDER YOUR SENTENCE

Compare it with the suggested guideline level of sentence and reconsider your reasons carefully if you have chosen a sentence at a different level. Consider a reduction for a timely guilty plea.

DECIDE YOUR SENTENCE
NB. COMPENSATION – Give reasons if not awarding compensation

Racially or religiously aggravated disorderly behaviour with intent to cause harassment, alarm or distress

Racially or religiously aggravated disorderly behaviour with intent to cause harassment, alarm or distress	Public Order Act 1986 s.4A Crime and Disorder Act 1998 s.31 Anti-Terrorism, Crime and Security Act 2001 Triable either way – see Mode of Trial Guidelines Penalty: Level 5 and/or 6 months

CONSIDER THE SERIOUSNESS OF THE OFFENCE
(INCLUDING THE IMPACT ON THE VICTIM)

IS DISCHARGE OR FINE APPROPRIATE?

IS IT SERIOUS ENOUGH FOR A COMMUNITY PENALTY?

GUIDELINE: → IS IT SO SERIOUS THAT ONLY CUSTODY IS APPROPRIATE?

ARE YOUR SENTENCING POWERS SUFFICIENT?

THIS IS A GUIDELINE FOR A FIRST-TIME OFFENDER PLEADING NOT GUILTY

 ## CONSIDER AGGRAVATING AND MITIGATING FACTORS, CULPABILITY AND HARM

for example
   Football related
   Group action
   High degree of planning
   Motivation for the offence was racial or religious
   Night time offence
   Setting out to humiliate the victim
   Victims specifically targeted
   Weapon
   This list is not exhaustive
	for example
	   Single incident
	   This list is not exhaustive

If offender is on bail, this offence is more serious

If offender has previous convictions, their relevance and any failure to respond to previous sentences should be considered – they may increase the seriousness. The court should make it clear, when passing sentence, that this was the approach adopted.

TAKE A PRELIMINARY VIEW OF SERIOUSNESS, THEN CONSIDER OFFENDER MITIGATION

for example
   Age, health (physical or mental)
   Co-operation with police
   Evidence of genuine remorse
   Voluntary compensation

CONSIDER YOUR SENTENCE

Compare it with the suggested guideline level of sentence and reconsider your reasons carefully if you have chosen a sentence at a different level. Consider a reduction for a timely guilty plea.

DECIDE YOUR SENTENCE

NB. COMPENSATION – Give reasons if not awarding compensation

Racially or religiously aggravated harassment – Conduct causing fear of violence

Protection from Harassment Act 1997 s.4 Crime and Disorder Act 1998 s.32 Anti-Terrorism, Crime and Security Act 2001 Triable either way – see Mode of Trial Guidelines Penalty: Level 5 and/or 6 months Consider making a restraining order	**Racially or religiously aggravated harassment** Conduct causing fear of violence

CONSIDER THE SERIOUSNESS OF THE OFFENCE
(INCLUDING THE IMPACT ON THE VICTIM)

IS DISCHARGE OR FINE APPROPRIATE?
IS IT SERIOUS ENOUGH FOR A COMMUNITY PENALTY?
IS IT SO SERIOUS THAT ONLY CUSTODY IS APPROPRIATE?
GUIDELINE: →   ARE YOUR SENTENCING POWERS SUFFICIENT?

THIS IS A GUIDELINE FOR A FIRST-TIME OFFENDER PLEADING NOT GUILTY

 ## CONSIDER AGGRAVATING AND MITIGATING FACTORS, CULPABILITY AND HARM

for example	for example

Disregard of warning
Excessive persistence
Interference with employment/business
Invasion of victim's home
Involvement of others
Motivation for the offence was racial or religious
Setting out to humiliate the victim
Threat to use weapon or substance (including
  realistic imitations)
Use of violence or grossly offensive material
Where photographs or images of a personal nature
  are involved
This list is not exhaustive
	Initial provocation
	Short duration
	This list is not exhaustive

If offender is on bail, this offence is more serious
If offender has previous convictions, their relevance and any failure to respond to previous
sentences should be considered – they may increase the seriousness. The court should make
it clear, when passing sentence, that this was the approach adopted.

TAKE A PRELIMINARY VIEW OF SERIOUSNESS, THEN CONSIDER WHETHER THE CASE SHOULD BE COMMITTED FOR SENTENCE, THEN CONSIDER OFFENDER MITIGATION

for example
  Age, health (physical or mental)
  Co-operation with police
  Evidence of genuine remorse
  Voluntary compensation

CONSIDER COMMITTAL OR YOUR SENTENCE

Compare it with the suggested guideline level of sentence and reconsider
your reasons carefully if you have chosen a sentence at a different level.
Consider a reduction for a timely guilty plea.
Restraining order – consider making an order in addition to the sentence to protect
the victim or any named person from further conduct which would amount to harassment,
or which would cause the fear of violence.

DECIDE YOUR SENTENCE
NB. COMPENSATION – Give reasons if not awarding compensation

Racially or religiously aggravated harassment Conduct causing harassment	Protection from Harassment Act 1997 s.2 Crime and Disorder Act 1998 s.32 Anti-Terrorism, Crime and Security Act 2001 Triable either way – see Mode of Trial Guidelines Penalty: Level 5 and/or 6 months Consider making a restraining order

CONSIDER THE SERIOUSNESS OF THE OFFENCE
(INCLUDING THE IMPACT ON THE VICTIM)

IS DISCHARGE OR FINE APPROPRIATE?
IS IT SERIOUS ENOUGH FOR A COMMUNITY PENALTY?
GUIDELINE: → IS IT SO SERIOUS THAT ONLY CUSTODY IS APPROPRIATE?
ARE YOUR SENTENCING POWERS SUFFICIENT?

THIS IS A GUIDELINE FOR A FIRST-TIME OFFENDER PLEADING NOT GUILTY

 ## CONSIDER AGGRAVATING AND MITIGATING FACTORS, CULPABILITY AND HARM

for example Disregard of warning Excessive persistence Interference with employment/business Invasion of victim's home Involvement of others **Motivation** for the offence was racial or religious Setting out to humiliate the victim Use of violence or grossly offensive material Where photographs or images of a personal nature are involved *This list is not exhaustive*	for example Initial provocation Short duration *This list is not exhaustive*

If offender is on bail, this offence is more serious
If offender has previous convictions, their relevance and any failure to respond to previous sentences should be considered – they may increase the seriousness. The court should make it clear, when passing sentence, that this was the approach adopted.

TAKE A PRELIMINARY VIEW OF SERIOUSNESS, THEN CONSIDER OFFENDER MITIGATION

for example
Age, health (physical or mental)
Co-operation with police
Evidence of genuine remorse
Voluntary compensation

CONSIDER YOUR SENTENCE

Compare it with the suggested guideline level of sentence and reconsider your reasons carefully if you have chosen a sentence at a different level.
Consider a reduction for a timely guilty plea.
Restraining order – consider making an order in addition to the sentence to protect the victim or any named person from further conduct which would amount to harassment.

DECIDE YOUR SENTENCE
NB. COMPENSATION – Give reasons if not awarding compensation

Racially or religiously aggravated threatening behaviour

Public Order Act 1986 s.4 Crime and Disorder Act 1998 s.32 Anti-Terrorism, Crime and Security Act 2001 Triable either way – see Mode of Trial Guidelines Penalty: Level 5 and/or 6 months	**Racially or religiously aggravated threatening behaviour**

CONSIDER THE SERIOUSNESS OF THE OFFENCE
(INCLUDING THE IMPACT ON THE VICTIM)

IS DISCHARGE OR FINE APPROPRIATE?

IS IT SERIOUS ENOUGH FOR A COMMUNITY PENALTY?

GUIDELINE: ➔ *IS IT SO SERIOUS THAT ONLY CUSTODY IS APPROPRIATE?*

ARE YOUR SENTENCING POWERS SUFFICIENT?

THIS IS A GUIDELINE FOR A FIRST-TIME OFFENDER PLEADING NOT GUILTY

 ## CONSIDER AGGRAVATING AND MITIGATING FACTORS, CULPABILITY AND HARM

for example 　Group action 　**Motivation** for the offence was racial or religious 　On hospital/medical or school premises 　People put in fear 　Setting out to humiliate the victim 　Victim serving the public 　Vulnerable victim 　*This list is not exhaustive*	for example 　Minor matter 　Short duration 　*This list is not exhaustive*

If offender is on bail, this offence is more serious
If offender has previous convictions, their relevance and any failure to respond to previous sentences should be considered – they may increase the seriousness. The court should make it clear, when passing sentence, that this was the approach adopted.

TAKE A PRELIMINARY VIEW OF SERIOUSNESS, THEN CONSIDER OFFENDER MITIGATION

for example
　Age, health (physical or mental)
　Co-operation with police
　Evidence of genuine remorse
　Voluntary compensation

CONSIDER YOUR SENTENCE

Compare it with the suggested guideline level of sentence and reconsider your reasons carefully if you have chosen a sentence at a different level. Consider a reduction for a timely guilty plea.

DECIDE YOUR SENTENCE
NB. COMPENSATION – Give reasons if not awarding compensation

Racially or religiously aggravated wounding – grievous bodily harm	Offences Against the Person Act 1861 s.20 Crime and Disorder Act 1998 s.29 Anti-Terrorism, Crime and Security Act 2001 Triable either way – see Mode of Trial Guidelines Penalty: Level 5 and/or 6 months

CONSIDER THE SERIOUSNESS OF THE OFFENCE
(INCLUDING THE IMPACT ON THE VICTIM)

IS DISCHARGE OR FINE APPROPRIATE?

IS IT SERIOUS ENOUGH FOR A COMMUNITY PENALTY?

IS IT SO SERIOUS THAT ONLY CUSTODY IS APPROPRIATE?

GUIDELINE: →   *ARE YOUR SENTENCING POWERS SUFFICIENT?*

THIS IS A GUIDELINE FOR A FIRST-TIME OFFENDER PLEADING NOT GUILTY

 ## CONSIDER AGGRAVATING AND MITIGATING FACTORS, CULPABILITY AND HARM

for example	for example
Deliberate kicking/biting Extensive injuries Group action **Motivation** for the offence was racial or religious Offender in position of authority On hospital/medical or school premises Premeditated Setting out to humiliate the victim Victim particularly vulnerable Victim serving the public Weapon *This list is not exhaustive*	Minor wound Provocation *This list is not exhaustive*

If offender is on bail, this offence is more serious
If offender has previous convictions, their relevance and any failure to respond to previous sentences should be considered – they may increase the seriousness. The court should make it clear, when passing sentence, that this was the approach adopted.

TAKE A PRELIMINARY VIEW OF SERIOUSNESS, THEN CONSIDER WHETHER THE CASE SHOULD BE COMMITTED FOR SENTENCE, THEN CONSIDER OFFENDER MITIGATION

for example
Age, health (physical or mental)
Co-operation with police
Evidence of genuine remorse
Voluntary compensation

CONSIDER COMMITTAL OR YOUR SENTENCE

Compare it with the suggested guideline level of sentence and reconsider your reasons carefully if you have chosen a sentence at a different level.
Consider a reduction for a timely guilty plea.

DECIDE YOUR SENTENCE
NB. COMPENSATION – Give reasons if not awarding compensation

Education Act 1996 s.444(1)A Penalty: Level 4 and/or 3 months Triable only summarily	**School non-attendance**

CONSIDER THE SERIOUSNESS OF THE OFFENCE

IS DISCHARGE OR FINE APPROPRIATE?

GUIDELINE: →   **IS IT SERIOUS ENOUGH FOR A COMMUNITY PENALTY?**

IS IT SO SERIOUS THAT ONLY CUSTODY IS APPROPRIATE?

THIS IS A GUIDELINE FOR A FIRST-TIME OFFENDER PLEADING NOT GUILTY

 ## CONSIDER AGGRAVATING AND MITIGATING FACTORS, CULPABILITY AND HARM

for example	for example
Harmful effect on other children in the family Lack of parental effort to ensure attendance Parental collusion Threats to teachers, pupils and/or officials *This list is not exhaustive*	Physical or mental health of child Substantiated history of bullying, drugs etc. *This list is not exhaustive*

If offender is on bail, this offence is more serious

If offender has previous convictions, their relevance and any failure to respond to previous sentences should be considered – they may increase the seriousness. The court should make it clear, when passing sentence, that this was the approach adopted.

TAKE A PRELIMINARY VIEW OF SERIOUSNESS, THEN CONSIDER OFFENDER MITIGATION

for example
Age, health (physical or mental)
Co-operation with the Education Authority
Evidence of genuine remorse

CONSIDER YOUR SENTENCE

Compare it with the suggested guideline level of sentence and reconsider your reasons carefully if you have chosen a sentence at a different level.
Consider a reduction for a timely guilty plea.
Consider a parenting order where appropriate.

DECIDE YOUR SENTENCE

Prosecutions under s.444(1) are penalty level 3 only – consult legal adviser.

Social Security – false representation to obtain benefit

Social Security – false representation to obtain benefit	Social Security Act 1992 s.112 Triable only summarily Penalty: Level 5 and/or 3 months

CONSIDER THE SERIOUSNESS OF THE OFFENCE

IS DISCHARGE OR FINE APPROPRIATE?
GUIDELINE: →   IS IT SERIOUS ENOUGH FOR A COMMUNITY PENALTY?
IS IT SO SERIOUS THAT ONLY CUSTODY IS APPROPRIATE?

THIS IS A GUIDELINE FOR A FIRST-TIME OFFENDER PLEADING NOT GUILTY

 CONSIDER AGGRAVATING AND MITIGATING FACTORS, CULPABILITY AND HARM

for example	for example
Claim fraudulent from the start Fraudulent claims over a long period Large amount Organised group offence Planned deception *This list is not exhaustive*	Misunderstanding of regulations Pressurised by others Small amount *This list is not exhaustive*

If offender is on bail, this offence is more serious
If offender has previous convictions, their relevance and any failure to respond to previous sentences should be considered – they may increase the seriousness. The court should make it clear, when passing sentence, that this was the approach adopted.

TAKE A PRELIMINARY VIEW OF SERIOUSNESS, THEN CONSIDER OFFENDER MITIGATION

for example
    Age, health (physical or mental)
    Co-operation with police
    Evidence of genuine remorse
    Voluntary compensation

CONSIDER YOUR SENTENCE

Compare it with the suggested guideline level of sentence and reconsider your reasons carefully if you have chosen a sentence at a different level. Consider a reduction for a timely guilty plea.

DECIDE YOUR SENTENCE
NB. COMPENSATION – Give reasons if not awarding compensation

Taking vehicle without consent

Theft Act 1968 s.12 Triable only summarily Penalty: Level 5 and/or 6 months May disqualify	**Taking vehicle without consent**

CONSIDER THE SERIOUSNESS OF THE OFFENCE
(INCLUDING THE IMPACT ON THE VICTIM)

IS DISCHARGE OR FINE APPROPRIATE?

GUIDELINE: →   **IS IT SERIOUS ENOUGH FOR A COMMUNITY PENALTY?**

IS IT SO SERIOUS THAT ONLY CUSTODY IS APPROPRIATE?

THIS IS A GUIDELINE FOR A FIRST-TIME OFFENDER PLEADING NOT GUILTY

 ## CONSIDER AGGRAVATING AND MITIGATING FACTORS, CULPABILITY AND HARM

for example	for example
Group action	Misunderstanding with owner
Premeditated	Soon returned
Related damage	Vehicle belonged to family or friend
Professional hallmarks	*This list is not exhaustive*
Vulnerable victim	
This list is not exhaustive	

If offender is on bail, this offence is more serious

If offender has previous convictions, their relevance and any failure to respond to previous sentences should be considered – they may increase the seriousness. The court should make it clear, when passing sentence, that this was the approach adopted.

TAKE A PRELIMINARY VIEW OF SERIOUSNESS, THEN CONSIDER OFFENDER MITIGATION

for example
- Health (physical or mental)
- Co-operation with police
- Evidence of genuine remorse
- Voluntary compensation

CONSIDER YOUR SENTENCE

Compare it with the suggested guideline level of sentence and reconsider your reasons carefully if you have chosen a sentence at a different level. Consider a reduction for a timely guilty plea.

DECIDE YOUR SENTENCE
NB. COMPENSATION – Give reasons if not awarding compensation

Theft	Theft Act 1968 s.1 Triable either way – see Mode of Trial Guidelines Penalty: Level 5 and/or 6 months May disqualify where committed with reference to the theft or taking of a vehicle

CONSIDER THE SERIOUSNESS OF THE OFFENCE
(INCLUDING THE IMPACT ON THE VICTIM)

IS DISCHARGE OR FINE APPROPRIATE?

GUIDELINE: →   *IS IT SERIOUS ENOUGH FOR A COMMUNITY PENALTY?*

IS IT SO SERIOUS THAT ONLY CUSTODY IS APPROPRIATE?

ARE YOUR SENTENCING POWERS SUFFICIENT?

THIS IS A GUIDELINE FOR A FIRST-TIME OFFENDER PLEADING NOT GUILTY

CONSIDER AGGRAVATING AND MITIGATING FACTORS, CULPABILITY AND HARM

for example	for example
High value	Impulsive action
Planned	Low value
Sophisticated	*This list is not exhaustive*
Adult involving children	
Organised team	
Related damage	
Vulnerable victim	
This list is not exhaustive	

If racially or religiously aggravated, or offender is on bail, this offence is more serious
If offender has previous convictions, their relevance and any failure to respond to previous sentences should be considered – they may increase the seriousness. The court should make it clear, when passing sentence, that this was the approach adopted.

TAKE A PRELIMINARY VIEW OF SERIOUSNESS, THEN CONSIDER OFFENDER MITIGATION

for example
Age, health (physical or mental)
Co-operation with police
Evidence of genuine remorse
Voluntary compensation

CONSIDER YOUR SENTENCE

Compare it with the suggested guideline level of sentence and reconsider your reasons carefully if you have chosen a sentence at a different level. Consider a reduction for a timely guilty plea.

DECIDE YOUR SENTENCE
NB. COMPENSATION – Give reasons if not awarding compensation

Theft in breach of trust

Theft Act 1968 s.1 Triable either way – see Mode of Trial Guidelines Penalty: Level 5 and/or 6 months	**Theft in breach of trust**

CONSIDER THE SERIOUSNESS OF THE OFFENCE
(INCLUDING THE IMPACT ON THE VICTIM)

IS DISCHARGE OR FINE APPROPRIATE?

IS IT SERIOUS ENOUGH FOR A COMMUNITY PENALTY?

GUIDELINE: ➜ *IS IT SO SERIOUS THAT ONLY CUSTODY IS APPROPRIATE?*

ARE YOUR SENTENCING POWERS SUFFICIENT?

THIS IS A GUIDELINE FOR A FIRST-TIME OFFENDER PLEADING NOT GUILTY

 ## CONSIDER AGGRAVATING AND MITIGATING FACTORS, CULPABILITY AND HARM

for example	for example
Casting suspicion on others	Impulsive action
Committed over a period	Low value
High value	Previous inconsistent attitude by employer
Organised team	Single item
Planned	Unsupported junior
Senior employee	*This list is not exhaustive*
Sophisticated	
Vulnerable victim	
This list is not exhaustive	

If racially or religiously aggravated, or offender is on bail, this offence is more serious
If offender has previous convictions, their relevance and any failure to respond to previous sentences should be considered – they may increase the seriousness. The court should make it clear, when passing sentence, that this was the approach adopted.

TAKE A PRELIMINARY VIEW OF SERIOUSNESS, THEN CONSIDER OFFENDER MITIGATION

for example
    Age, health (physical or mental)
    Co-operation with police
    Evidence of genuine remorse
    Voluntary compensation

CONSIDER YOUR SENTENCE

Compare it with the suggested guideline level of sentence and reconsider your reasons carefully if you have chosen a sentence at a different level. Consider a reduction for a timely guilty plea.

DECIDE YOUR SENTENCE
NB. COMPENSATION – Give reasons if not awarding compensation

Threatening behaviour	Public Order Act 1986 s.4 Triable only summarily Penalty: Level 5 and/or 6 months

CONSIDER THE SERIOUSNESS OF THE OFFENCE
(INCLUDING THE IMPACT ON THE VICTIM)

IS DISCHARGE OR FINE APPROPRIATE?

GUIDELINE: ➜   *IS IT SERIOUS ENOUGH FOR A COMMUNITY PENALTY?*

IS IT SO SERIOUS THAT ONLY CUSTODY IS APPROPRIATE?

THIS IS A GUIDELINE FOR A FIRST-TIME OFFENDER PLEADING NOT GUILTY

 ## CONSIDER AGGRAVATING AND MITIGATING FACTORS, CULPABILITY AND HARM

for example	for example
Football related	Minor matter
Group action	Short duration
On hospital/medical or school premises	*This list is not exhaustive*
People put in fear	
Victim serving the public	
Vulnerable victim	
This list is not exhaustive	

If offender is on bail, this offence is more serious
If offender has previous convictions, their relevance and any failure to respond to previous sentences should be considered – they may increase the seriousness. The court should make it clear, when passing sentence, that this was the approach adopted.

TAKE A PRELIMINARY VIEW OF SERIOUSNESS, THEN CONSIDER OFFENDER MITIGATION

for example
Age, health (physical or mental)
Co-operation with police
Evidence of genuine remorse
Voluntary compensation

CONSIDER YOUR SENTENCE

Compare it with the suggested guideline level of sentence and reconsider your reasons carefully if you have chosen a sentence at a different level. Consider a reduction for a timely guilty plea.

DECIDE YOUR SENTENCE
NB. COMPENSATION – Give reasons if not awarding compensation

TV licence payment evasion

Wireless Telegraphy Act 1949 s.1 Triable only summarily Penalty: Level 3	**TV licence payment evasion**

CONSIDER THE SERIOUSNESS OF THE OFFENCE

GUIDELINE: →   ***IS DISCHARGE OR FINE APPROPRIATE?***
              IS IT SERIOUS ENOUGH FOR A COMMUNITY PENALTY?

THIS IS A GUIDELINE FOR A FIRST-TIME OFFENDER PLEADING NOT GUILTY

GUIDELINE FINE – STARTING POINT A

 CONSIDER AGGRAVATING AND MITIGATING FACTORS, CULPABILITY AND HARM

for example	for example
Failure to respond to payment opportunities *This list is not exhaustive*	Accidental oversight Confusion of responsibility Licence immediately obtained Very short unlicensed use *This list is not exhaustive*

If offender is on bail, this offence is more serious
If offender has previous convictions, their relevance and any failure to respond to previous sentences should be considered – they may increase the seriousness. The court should make it clear, when passing sentence, that this was the approach adopted.

TAKE A PRELIMINARY VIEW OF SERIOUSNESS, THEN CONSIDER OFFENDER MITIGATION

for example
    Age, health (physical or mental)

CONSIDER YOUR SENTENCE

Compare it with the suggested guideline level of sentence and reconsider your reasons carefully if you have chosen a sentence at a different level.
Consider a reduction for a timely guilty plea.

DECIDE YOUR SENTENCE

Vehicle interference	Criminal Attempts Act 1981 s.9 Triable only summarily Penalty: Level 4 and/or 3 months

CONSIDER THE SERIOUSNESS OF THE OFFENCE
(INCLUDING THE IMPACT ON THE VICTIM)

IS DISCHARGE OR FINE APPROPRIATE?

GUIDELINE: → IS IT SERIOUS ENOUGH FOR A COMMUNITY PENALTY?

IS IT SO SERIOUS THAT ONLY CUSTODY IS APPROPRIATE?

THIS IS A GUIDELINE FOR A FIRST-TIME OFFENDER PLEADING NOT GUILTY

 ## CONSIDER AGGRAVATING AND MITIGATING FACTORS, CULPABILITY AND HARM

for example	for example
Disabled passenger vehicle	Impulsive action
Emergency service vehicle	*This list is not exhaustive*
Group action	
Planned	
Related damage	
This list is not exhaustive	

If racially or religiously aggravated, or offender is on bail, this offence is more serious
If offender has previous convictions, their relevance and any failure to respond to previous sentences should be considered – they may increase the seriousness. The court should make it clear, when passing sentence, that this was the approach adopted.

TAKE A PRELIMINARY VIEW OF SERIOUSNESS, THEN CONSIDER OFFENDER MITIGATION

for example
- Age, health (physical or mental)
- Co-operation with police
- Evidence of genuine remorse
- Voluntary compensation

CONSIDER YOUR SENTENCE

Compare it with the suggested guideline level of sentence and reconsider your reasons carefully if you have chosen a sentence at a different level. Consider a reduction for a timely guilty plea.

DECIDE YOUR SENTENCE
NB. COMPENSATION – Give reasons if not awarding compensation

Violent disorder

Public Order Act 1986 s.2 Triable either way – see Mode of Trial Guidelines Penalty: Level 5 and/or 6 months	**Violent disorder**

CONSIDER THE SERIOUSNESS OF THE OFFENCE
(INCLUDING THE IMPACT ON THE VICTIM)

IS DISCHARGE OR FINE APPROPRIATE?

IS IT SERIOUS ENOUGH FOR A COMMUNITY PENALTY?

IS IT SO SERIOUS THAT ONLY CUSTODY IS APPROPRIATE?

GUIDELINE: →   ***ARE YOUR SENTENCING POWERS SUFFICIENT?***

THIS IS A GUIDELINE FOR A FIRST-TIME OFFENDER PLEADING NOT GUILTY

 ## CONSIDER AGGRAVATING AND MITIGATING FACTORS, CULPABILITY AND HARM

for example	for example
Busy public place Fighting between rival groups Large group People in fear Planned Vulnerable victims Weapon *This list is not exhaustive*	Impulsive Provocation *This list is not exhaustive*

If racially or religiously aggravated, or offender is on bail, this offence is more serious
If offender has previous convictions, their relevance and any failure to respond to previous
sentences should be considered – they may increase the seriousness. The court should make
it clear, when passing sentence, that this was the approach adopted.

TAKE A PRELIMINARY VIEW OF SERIOUSNESS, THEN CONSIDER WHETHER THE CASE SHOULD BE COMMITTED FOR SENTENCE, THEN CONSIDER OFFENDER MITIGATION

for example
    Age, health (physical or mental)
    Co-operation with police
    Evidence of genuine remorse
    Voluntary compensation

CONSIDER COMMITTAL OR YOUR SENTENCE

Compare it with the suggested guideline level of sentence and reconsider
your reasons carefully if you have chosen a sentence at a different level.
Consider a reduction for a timely guilty plea.

DECIDE YOUR SENTENCE
NB. COMPENSATION – Give reasons if not awarding compensation

Wounding – grievous bodily harm	Offences Against the Person Act 1861 s.20 Triable either way – see Mode of Trial Guidelines Penalty: Level 5 and/or 6 months

CONSIDER THE SERIOUSNESS OF THE OFFENCE
(INCLUDING THE IMPACT ON THE VICTIM)

IS DISCHARGE OR FINE APPROPRIATE?

IS IT SERIOUS ENOUGH FOR A COMMUNITY PENALTY?

IS IT SO SERIOUS THAT ONLY CUSTODY IS APPROPRIATE?

GUIDELINE: →   ***ARE YOUR SENTENCING POWERS SUFFICIENT?***

THIS IS A GUIDELINE FOR A FIRST-TIME OFFENDER PLEADING NOT GUILTY

 ## CONSIDER AGGRAVATING AND MITIGATING FACTORS, CULPABILITY AND HARM

for example	for example
Abuse of trust (domestic setting) Deliberate kicking/biting Extensive injuries Group action Offender in position of authority On hospital/medical or school premises Premeditated Prolonged assault Victim particularly vulnerable Victim serving the public Weapon *This list is not exhaustive*	Minor wound Provocation *This list is not exhaustive*

If offender is on bail, this offence is more serious
If offender has previous convictions, their relevance and any failure to respond to previous sentences should be considered – they may increase the seriousness. The court should make it clear, when passing sentence, that this was the approach adopted.

TAKE A PRELIMINARY VIEW OF SERIOUSNESS, THEN CONSIDER WHETHER THE CASE SHOULD BE COMMITTED FOR SENTENCE, THEN CONSIDER OFFENDER MITIGATION

for example
- Age, health (physical or mental)
- Co-operation with police
- Evidence of genuine remorse
- Voluntary compensation

CONSIDER COMMITTAL OR YOUR SENTENCE

Compare it with the suggested guideline level of sentence and reconsider your reasons carefully if you have chosen a sentence at a different level. Consider a reduction for a timely guilty plea.

DECIDE YOUR SENTENCE
NB. COMPENSATION – Give reasons if not awarding compensation

Road Traffic Act 1988 s.3 Triable only summarily Penalty: Level 4 Must endorse (3-9 points OR may disqualify)	Careless driving

CONSIDER THE SERIOUSNESS OF THE OFFENCE

GUIDELINE: →   ***IS DISCHARGE OR FINE APPROPRIATE?***
           IS IT SERIOUS ENOUGH FOR A COMMUNITY PENALTY?

THIS IS A GUIDELINE FOR A FIRST-TIME OFFENDER PLEADING NOT GUILTY

GUIDELINE FINE – STARTING POINT B

 ## CONSIDER AGGRAVATING AND MITIGATING FACTORS, CULPABILITY AND HARM

for example	for example
Excessive speed	Minor risk
High degree of carelessness	Momentary lapse
Serious risk	Negligible/parking damage
Using a hand-held mobile telephone	Sudden change in weather conditions
This list is not exhaustive	*This list is not exhaustive*

Death, serious injury or damage is capable of being aggravation

If offender is on bail, this offence is more serious
If offender has previous convictions, their relevance and any failure to respond to previous sentences should be considered – they may increase the seriousness. The court should make it clear, when passing sentence, that this was the approach adopted.

TAKE A PRELIMINARY VIEW OF SERIOUSNESS, THEN CONSIDER OFFENDER MITIGATION

for example
     Co-operation with police
     Evidence of genuine remorse
     Voluntary compensation

CONSIDER YOUR SENTENCE

Endorse (3-9 points OR period of disqualification)
Consider other measures (including disqualification until test passed if appropriate –
for example, age, infirmity or medical condition)
Compare it with the suggested guideline level of sentence and reconsider
your reasons carefully if you have chosen a sentence at a different level.
Consider a reduction for a timely guilty plea.

DECIDE YOUR SENTENCE

Dangerous driving	Road Traffic Act 1988 s.2 Triable either way – see Mode of Trial Guidelines Penalty: Level 5 and/or 6 months Must endorse and disqualify at least 12 months Must endorse (3-11 points) if not disqualified **MUST ORDER EXTENDED RE-TEST**

CONSIDER THE SERIOUSNESS OF THE OFFENCE
(INCLUDING THE IMPACT ON THE VICTIM)

IS DISCHARGE OR FINE APPROPRIATE?
IS IT SERIOUS ENOUGH FOR A COMMUNITY PENALTY?
GUIDELINE: → IS IT SO SERIOUS THAT ONLY CUSTODY IS APPROPRIATE?
ARE YOUR SENTENCING POWERS SUFFICIENT?

THIS IS A GUIDELINE FOR A FIRST-TIME OFFENDER PLEADING NOT GUILTY

 ## CONSIDER AGGRAVATING AND MITIGATING FACTORS, CULPABILITY AND HARM

for example	for example
Avoiding detection or apprehension Competitive driving, racing, showing off Disregard of warnings, eg from passengers or others in vicinity Evidence of alcohol or drugs Excessive speed Police pursuit Prolonged, persistent, deliberate bad driving Serious risk Using a mobile telephone *This list is not exhaustive*	Emergency Speed not excessive *This list is not exhaustive*

Serious injury or damage is capable of being aggravation

If offender is on bail, this offence is more serious
If offender has previous convictions, their relevance and any failure to respond to previous sentences should be considered – they may increase the seriousness. The court should make it clear, when passing sentence, that this was the approach adopted.

TAKE A PRELIMINARY VIEW OF SERIOUSNESS, THEN CONSIDER OFFENDER MITIGATION

for example
   Co-operation with police
   Evidence of genuine remorse
   Voluntary compensation

CONSIDER YOUR SENTENCE

Endorse licence and disqualify at least 12 months unless special reasons apply.
MUST ORDER EXTENDED RE-TEST.
Compare it with the suggested guideline level of sentence and reconsider your reasons carefully if you have chosen a sentence at a different level.
Consider a reduction for a timely guilty plea.

DECIDE YOUR SENTENCE

| Road Traffic Act 1988 s.103
Triable only summarily
Penalty: Level 5 and/or 6 months
Must endorse: (6 points OR may disqualify again) | **Driving whilst disqualified** |

CONSIDER THE SERIOUSNESS OF THE OFFENCE

IS DISCHARGE OR FINE APPROPRIATE?

GUIDELINE: →   IS IT SERIOUS ENOUGH FOR A COMMUNITY PENALTY?

IS IT SO SERIOUS THAT ONLY CUSTODY IS APPROPRIATE?

THIS IS A GUIDELINE FOR A FIRST-TIME OFFENDER PLEADING NOT GUILTY

 ## CONSIDER AGGRAVATING AND MITIGATING FACTORS, CULPABILITY AND HARM

for example	for example
Driver has never passed a test Driving for remuneration Efforts to avoid detection Long distance driven Planned, long term evasion Recent disqualification *This list is not exhaustive*	Emergency established Full period expired but test not re-taken Short distance driven *This list is not exhaustive*

If offender is on bail, this offence is more serious
If offender has previous convictions, their relevance and any failure to respond to previous sentences should be considered – they may increase the seriousness. The court should make it clear, when passing sentence, that this was the approach adopted.

TAKE A PRELIMINARY VIEW OF SERIOUSNESS, THEN CONSIDER OFFENDER MITIGATION

for example
Co-operation with police
Evidence of genuine remorse

CONSIDER YOUR SENTENCE

Endorse (6 points OR period of disqualification)
Compare it with the suggested guideline level of sentence and reconsider your reasons carefully if you have chosen a sentence at a different level.
Consider a reduction for a timely guilty plea.

DECIDE YOUR SENTENCE

Excess alcohol (drive or attempt to drive)	Road Traffic Act 1988 s.5(1)(a) Penalty: Level 5 and/or 6 months Triable only summarily Must endorse and disqualify *at least* 12 months: disqualify at least 36 months for a further offence within 10 years

CONSIDER THE SERIOUSNESS OF THE OFFENCE

THE LEVEL OF SERIOUSNESS AND GUIDELINE SENTENCE ARE RELATED TO THE BREATH/BLOOD/URINE LEVEL

CONSIDER AGGRAVATING AND MITIGATING FACTORS, CULPABILITY AND HARM

for example	for example
Ability to drive seriously impaired Caused injury/fear/damage Police pursuit Evidence of nature of the driving Type of vehicle, eg carrying passengers for reward/large goods vehicle High reading (and in combination with above) *This list is not exhaustive*	Emergency Moving a vehicle a very short distance Spiked drinks *This list is not exhaustive*

If offender is on bail, this offence is more serious

If offender has previous convictions, their relevance and any failure to respond to previous sentences should be considered – they may increase the seriousness. The court should make it clear, when passing sentence, that this was the approach adopted.

TAKE A PRELIMINARY VIEW OF SERIOUSNESS, THEN CONSIDER OFFENDER MITIGATION

for example
    Co-operation with police

CONSIDER YOUR SENTENCE

Offer a rehabilitation course.
Compare your decision with the suggested guideline level of sentence and reconsider your reasons carefully if you have chosen a sentence at a different level.
Consider a reduction for a timely guilty plea.

DECIDE YOUR SENTENCE

BREATH	BLOOD	URINE	DISQUALIFY NOT LESS THAN	GUIDELINE
36-55	80-125	107-170	12 months	B
56-70	126-160	171-214	16 months	C
71-85	161-195	215-260	20 months	C
86-100	196-229	261-308	24 months	CONSIDER COMMUNITY PENALTY
101-115	230-264	309-354	28 months	
116-130	265-300	355-400	32 months	CONSIDER CUSTODY
131+	301+	401+	36 months	

Failing to stop, Failing to report

| Road Traffic Act 1988 s.170(4)
Triable only summarily
Penalty: Level 5 and/or 6 months
Must endorse: (5-10 points OR disqualify) | **Failing to stop
Failing to report** |

CONSIDER THE SERIOUSNESS OF THE OFFENCE

GUIDELINE: →   *IS DISCHARGE OR FINE APPROPRIATE?*
IS IT SERIOUS ENOUGH FOR A COMMUNITY PENALTY?
IS IT SO SERIOUS THAT ONLY CUSTODY IS APPROPRIATE?

THIS IS A GUIDELINE FOR A FIRST-TIME OFFENDER PLEADING NOT GUILTY

GUIDELINE FINE – STARTING POINT C

 CONSIDER AGGRAVATING AND MITIGATING FACTORS, CULPABILITY AND HARM

for example	for example
Evidence of drinking or drugs Serious injury Serious damage *This list is not exhaustive*	Believed identity to be known Failed to stop but reported Genuine fear of retaliation Negligible damage No one at scene but failed to report Stayed at scene but failed to give/left before giving full particulars *This list is not exhaustive*

If offender is on bail, this offence is more serious
If offender has previous convictions, their relevance and any failure to respond to previous sentences should be considered – they may increase the seriousness. The court should make it clear, when passing sentence, that this was the approach adopted.

TAKE A PRELIMINARY VIEW OF SERIOUSNESS, THEN CONSIDER OFFENDER MITIGATION

for example
    Co-operation with police
    Evidence of genuine remorse
    Voluntary compensation

CONSIDER YOUR SENTENCE

Endorse (5-10 points OR period of disqualification)
Compare it with the suggested guideline level of sentence and reconsider your reasons carefully if you have chosen a sentence at a different level.
Consider a reduction for a timely guilty plea.

DECIDE YOUR SENTENCE

<table>
<tr><td>

Fraudulent use etc.
Vehicle excise licence etc.

</td><td>

Vehicle Excise and Registration Act 1994 s.44
Triable either way – see Mode of Trial Guidelines
Penalty: Level 5

</td></tr>
</table>

CONSIDER THE SERIOUSNESS OF THE OFFENCE

GUIDELINE: →

IS DISCHARGE OR FINE APPROPRIATE?

IS IT SERIOUS ENOUGH FOR A COMMUNITY PENALTY?

ARE YOUR SENTENCING POWERS SUFFICIENT?

THIS IS A GUIDELINE FOR A FIRST-TIME OFFENDER PLEADING NOT GUILTY

GUIDELINE FINE – STARTING POINT B

 ## CONSIDER AGGRAVATING AND MITIGATING FACTORS, CULPABILITY AND HARM

for example
    Bought fraudulently
    Deliberately planned
    Disc forged or altered
    Long term defrauding
    LGV, HGV, PCV, PSV, taxi or private hire
      vehicle
    This list is not exhaustive

If offender is on bail, this offence is more serious
If offender has previous convictions, their relevance and any failure to respond to previous sentences should be considered – they may increase the seriousness. The court should make it clear, when passing sentence, that this was the approach adopted.

TAKE A PRELIMINARY VIEW OF SERIOUSNESS, THEN CONSIDER OFFENDER MITIGATION

for example
    Co-operation with police
    Evidence of genuine remorse

CONSIDER YOUR SENTENCE

Compare it with the suggested guideline level of sentence and reconsider your reasons carefully if you have chosen a sentence at a different level. Consider a reduction for a timely guilty plea.

DECIDE YOUR SENTENCE

No insurance

Road Traffic Act 1988 s.143 Triable only summarily Penalty: Level 5 Must endorse (6-8 points OR may disqualify)	No insurance

CONSIDER THE SERIOUSNESS OF THE OFFENCE

GUIDELINE: →   *IS DISCHARGE OR FINE APPROPRIATE?*
IS IT SERIOUS ENOUGH FOR A COMMUNITY PENALTY?

THIS IS A GUIDELINE FOR A FIRST-TIME OFFENDER PLEADING NOT GUILTY

GUIDELINE FINE – STARTING POINT B

 ## CONSIDER AGGRAVATING AND MITIGATING FACTORS, CULPABILITY AND HARM

for example	for example
Defective vehicle Deliberate driving without insurance Driver has never passed a test Gave false details LGV, HGV, PCV, PSV or taxi or private hire vehicle No reference to insurance ever having been held *This list is not exhaustive*	Accidental oversight Genuine mistake Responsibility for providing insurance resting with another – the parent/owner/lender/hirer Smaller vehicle, eg moped *This list is not exhaustive*

If offender is on bail, this offence is more serious
If offender has previous convictions, their relevance and any failure to respond to previous sentences should be considered – they may increase the seriousness. The court should make it clear, when passing sentence, that this was the approach adopted.

TAKE A PRELIMINARY VIEW OF SERIOUSNESS, THEN CONSIDER OFFENDER MITIGATION

for example
Difficult domestic circumstances
Evidence of genuine remorse

CONSIDER YOUR SENTENCE

Endorse licence.
Consider the option of a short period of disqualification where there are aggravating factors.
Compare your decision with the suggested guideline level of sentence and reconsider your reasons carefully if you have chosen a sentence at a different level.
Consider a reduction for a timely guilty plea.

DECIDE YOUR SENTENCE

Refuse evidential specimen (Drive or attempt to drive)

Refuse evidential specimen (Drive or attempt to drive)	Road Traffic Act 1988 s.7(6) Penalty: Level 5 and/or 6 months: Triable only summarily` Must endorse and disqualify at least 12 months: disqualify at least 36 months for a further offence within 10 years

CONSIDER THE SERIOUSNESS OF THE OFFENCE

IS DISCHARGE OR FINE APPROPRIATE?
GUIDELINE: →   *IS IT SERIOUS ENOUGH FOR A COMMUNITY PENALTY?*
IS IT SO SERIOUS THAT ONLY CUSTODY IS APPROPRIATE?

THIS IS A GUIDELINE FOR A FIRST-TIME OFFENDER PLEADING NOT GUILTY

 ## CONSIDER AGGRAVATING AND MITIGATING FACTORS, CULPABILITY AND HARM

for example	for example
Ability to drive seriously impaired Caused injury/fear/damage Evidence of nature of the driving Police pursuit Type of vehicle, eg carrying passengers for reward/large goods vehicle *This list is not exhaustive*	Not the driver

If offender is on bail, this offence is more serious
If offender has previous convictions, their relevance and any failure to respond to previous sentences should be considered – they may increase the seriousness. The court should make it clear, when passing sentence, that this was the approach adopted.

TAKE A PRELIMINARY VIEW OF SERIOUSNESS, THEN CONSIDER OFFENDER MITIGATION

for example
    Evidence of genuine remorse
    Voluntary completion of alcohol impaired driver course (if available)

CONSIDER YOUR SENTENCE

Offer a rehabilitation course.
Endorse licence. DISQUALIFY – a minimum period of 24 months is suggested.
Examine carefully aggravating/mitigating factors disclosed – do these justify any variation in period of disqualification suggested? If substantial aggravating factors, consider higher fine/community penalty/custody
Compare it with the suggested guideline level of sentence and reconsider your reasons carefully if you have chosen a sentence at a different level.
Consider a reduction for a timely guilty plea.

DECIDE YOUR SENTENCE

<table>
<tr><td>*Update December 2006:* Road Traffic Regulation Act 1984 s.89(1)
Triable only summarily
Penalty: Level 3 (Level 4 if motorway)
Must endorse (3-6 points OR may disqualify)</td><td>Speeding</td></tr>
</table>

CONSIDER THE SERIOUSNESS OF THE OFFENCE

GUIDELINE: →   *IS DISCHARGE OR FINE APPROPRIATE?*

THIS IS A GUIDELINE FOR A FIRST-TIME OFFENDER PLEADING NOT GUILTY

 ## CONSIDER AGGRAVATING AND MITIGATING FACTORS, CULPABILITY AND HARM

for example
   LGV, HGV, PCV or taxi or private-hire vehicles
   Location/time of day/visibility
   Serious risk
   Towing caravan/trailer
   This list is not exhaustive

for example
   Emergency established
   This list is not exhaustive

If offender is on bail, this offence is more serious
If offender has previous convictions, their relevance and any failure to respond to previous sentences should be considered – they may increase the seriousness. The court should make it clear, when passing sentence, that this was the approach adopted.

GUIDELINE PENALTY POINTS	LEGAL SPEED LIMITS	EXCESS SPEED – MPH	FINE
3	20-30 mph 40-50 mph 60-70 mph	Up to 10 mph Up to 15 mph Up to 20 mph	A
4 or 5 OR disqualify up to 42 days	20-30 mph 40-50 mph 60-70 mph	From 11-20 mph From 16-25 mph From 21-30 mph	B
6 OR disqualify up to 56 days	20-30 mph 40-50 mph 60-70 mph	From 21-30 mph From 26-35 mph From 31-40 mph	B

TAKE A PRELIMINARY VIEW OF SERIOUSNESS, THEN CONSIDER OFFENDER MITIGATION

for example
   Co-operation with police
   Fixed penalty not taken up for valid reason

CONSIDER YOUR SENTENCE

Endorse (3-6 points OR period of disqualification. If a new driver accumulates 6 points this will result in automatic revocation of the licence by the DVLA, see note on page 100.)
Consider other measures (including disqualification until test passed if appropriate).
Compare it with the suggested guideline level of sentence and reconsider your reasons carefully if you have chosen a sentence at a different level.
Consider a reduction for a timely guilty plea.

DECIDE YOUR SENTENCE

Vehicle Offences – Offences considered appropriate for guideline of discharge or fine, other than in exceptional circumstances

Offences considered appropriate for guideline of discharge or fine, other than in exceptional circumstances			
	PENALTY POINTS	MAXIMUM PENALTY	GUIDELINE FINE
ALCOHOL/DRUGS			
In charge over excess alcohol limit OR in charge whilst unfit through drink/drugs or refusing evidential specimen *Consider disqualification.*	10*	Level 4 and/or 3 months E	C
Refusing roadside breath test	4	Level 3 E	A
DRIVER			
Not supplying details *If company-owned, use higher fine when unable to apply endorsement as a minimum*	3*	Level 3 E	C
LICENCE OFFENCES			
† No driving licence, where could be covered, eg if licence not renewed, but would have covered class of vehicle driven, or holder of full licence has lost or misplaced it	–	Level 3	A
† Driving not in accordance with provisional licence (includes where no licence ever held)	3-6	Level 3 E	A
† No excise licence	–	Level 3 or 5 times annual duty (whichever greater)	Actual duty lost plus penalty of Guideline Fine – Starting Point A (1-3 months unpaid duty), B (4-6 months), C (7-12 months) consider a maximum of twice the annual duty
LIGHTS – Driving without	–	Level 3	A
OWNERSHIP – Not notifying DVLA of change etc.		Level 3	A
PARKING OFFENCES			
† Dangerous position	3	Level 3 E	A
† Pelican/zebra crossing	3	Level 3 E	A
TEST CERTIFICATE – Not held	–	Level 3	A
TRAFFIC DIRECTION OFFENCES			
† Fail to comply with height restriction	3	Level 3 E	A
† Fail to comply with red traffic light	3	Level 3 E	A
† Fail to comply with no entry sign	3	Level 3 E	A
† Fail to comply with stop sign/double white lines	3	Level 3 E	A
† Fail to give precedence – pelican/zebra crossing	3	Level 3 E	A
TRAFFIC OR POLICE SIGNS (non endorsable)			
† Fail to comply	–	3	A
† *These offences are eligible for fixed penalty offer. Where there is a valid reason why the case could not be dealt with by fixed penalty (eg holder of a non-uk driving licence, licence at DVLA for change of details etc), impose a fine equivalent to fixed penalty, endorse licence as appropriate and do not order costs.*			
In all cases, consider the safety factor, damage to roads, commercial gain and, if driver is not the owner, with whom prime responsibility should lie.			

E: Must ENDORSE (unless special reasons) and may disqualify

Vehicle Offences – Offences considered appropriate for guideline of discharge or fine, other than in exceptional circumstances – contd

Offences considered appropriate for guideline of discharge or fine, other than in exceptional circumstances – contd.			
	PENALTY POINTS	MAXIMUM PENALTY	GUIDELINE FINE
VEHICLE DEFECTS UP TO AND INCLUDING 3.5 TONNES GROSS VEHICLE WEIGHT			
DEFECTS			
† Brakes/Steering/Tyres (each)	3	Level 4 E	A
† Loss of wheel	3	Level 4 E	A
† Exhaust emission	–	Level 3	A
† Other offences	–	Level 3	A
LOADS			
† Condition of vehicle/accessories/equipment	3	Level 4 E	A
† Purpose of use/passenger numbers/how carried	3	Level 4 E	A
† Weight, position or distribution of load	3	Level 4 E	A
† Insecure load	3	Level 3	A
† Overloading or exceeding maximum axle weight	–	Level 5	A* Plus increase in proportion to percentage of overloading
* Examine carefully evidence of responsibility for overload and, if commercial gain relates to owner, increase the fine.			

† *These offences are eligible for fixed penalty offer. Where there is a valid reason why the case could not be dealt with by fixed penalty (eg holder of a non-UK driving licence, licence at DVLA for change of details etc), impose a fine equivalent to fixed penalty, endorse licence as appropriate and do not order costs.*

In all cases, **consider the safety factor, damage to roads, commercial gain** *and, if driver is not the owner, with whom prime responsibility should lie.*

E: Must ENDORSE (unless special reasons) and may disqualify

2125 Magistrates' Court Sentencing Guidelines 3–3080

Motorway offences

Motorway Offences

	PENALTY POINTS	MAXIMUM PENALTY	GUIDELINE FINE
DRIVING (Consider disqualification)			
† Driving in reverse on motorway	3	Level 4 E	B
† Driving in reverse on sliproad	3	Level 4 E	A
† Driving in wrong direction on motorway	3	Level 4 E	B
† Driving in wrong direction on sliproad	3	Level 4 E	A
† Driving off carriageway – central reservation	3	Level 4 E	A
† Driving off carriageway – hard shoulder	3	Level 4 E	A
† Driving on sliproad against no entry sign	3	Level 4 E	A
† Making U-Turn	3	Level 4 E	A
LEARNERS			
† Learner driver or excluded vehicle	3	Level 4 E	A
STOPPING			
† Stopping on hard shoulder of motorway	–	Level 4	A
† Stopping on hard shoulder of sliproad	–	Level 4	A
PROHIBITED LANE			
† Vehicle over 7.5 tonnes or drawing trailer, or prohibited PSV	3	Level 4 E	A
WALKING			
† Walking on motorway or sliproad	–	Level 4	A
† Walking on hard shoulder or verge	–	Level 4	A

† *These offences are eligible for fixed penalty offer. Where there is a valid reason why the case could not be dealt with by fixed penalty (eg holder of a non-UK driving licence, licence at DVLA for change of details etc), impose a fine equivalent to fixed penalty, endorse licence as appropriate and do not order costs.*

*In all cases, **consider the safety factor, damage to roads, commercial gain** and, if driver is not the owner, with whom prime responsibility should lie.*

Offences relating to buses and goods vehicles over 3.5 tonnes gross vehicle weight (GVW)

Offences relating to buses and goods vehicles over 3.5 tonnes gross vehicle weight (GVW)				
	PENALTY POINTS	MAXIMUM PENALTY	OWNER/ OPERATOR**	DRIVER
DEFECTS				
Brakes	3	Level 5 E	C	B
Steering	3	Level 5 E	C	B
Tyres (per tyre)	3	Level 5 E	C	B
Loss of wheel	3	Level 5 E	C	B
Exhaust emission	–	Level 4	C	B
Other offences	–	Level 4	C	B
LOADS				
Condition of vehicle/accessories/ equipment	3	Level 5 E	C	B
Purpose of use/number of passengers/ how carried	3	Level 5 E	C	B
Weight, position or distribution of load	3	Level 5 E	C	B
Insecure load	3	Level 4	C	B
Overloading or exceeding maximum axle weight	–	Level 5	C*	B*
			*Plus increase in proportion to percentage of overloading	
OPERATORS LICENCE				
Not held	–	Level 4	C	B
TACHOGRAPH				
Not properly used	–	Level 5	C	B
Falsification/fraudulent use	–	Level 5	C	B
SPEED LIMITERS – WHERE APPLICABLE				
Not being used or incorrectly calibrated	–	Level 5	C	B
** For an owner/operator, take net turnover into account as appropriate				

E: Must ENDORSE (unless special reasons) and may disqualify

SECTION 3

SERIOUSNESS

ESTABLISHING THE SERIOUSNESS OF THE OFFENCE

In establishing the seriousness of the case before them, courts should:

— make sure that all factors which aggravate or mitigate the offence are considered. The lists in the *Guidelines* are neither exhaustive nor a substitute for the personal judgment of magistrates. Factors which do not appear in the *Guidelines* may be important in individual cases;

— consider the various seriousness indicators, remembering that some will carry more weight than others **(see update below)**;

— take into account, as a seriousness factor, the impact of the offence upon the victim **(see update below)**;

— note that, by statute, racial and religious aggravation increases the seriousness of any offence – s 153 Powers of Criminal Courts (Sentences) Act 2000 – but see the note on specific racially aggravated offences created under ss 29–32 of the same Act on page 98;

— always bear in mind that, by statute, the commission of an offence on bail aggravates its seriousness;

— consider the effect of using previous convictions, or any failure to respond to previous sentences, in assessing seriousness. Courts should identify any convictions relevant for this purpose and then consider to what extent they affect the seriousness of the present offence;

— note that, when there are several offences to be sentenced, the court must have regard to the totality principle. This means that the overall effect of the sentence must be commensurate with the total criminality involved.

When the court has formed an initial assessment of the seriousness of the offence(s), consider any offender mitigation.

Update December 2006: CJA 2003 – "in considering the seriousness of any offence the court must consider the offender's culpability in committing the offence and any harm which the offence cause, was intended to cause or might foreseeably have caused".

VICTIM PERSONAL STATEMENTS

A victim personal statement gives victims a formal opportunity to say how a crime has affected them. Where the victim has chosen to make such a statement, a court should consider and take it into account prior to passing sentence. (LCJ Practice Direction made 16 October 2001.)

Evidence of the effects of an offence on the victim must be in the form of a s 9 witness statement or expert's report and served on the defence prior to sentence.

Except where inferences can properly be drawn from the nature or circumstances surrounding the offence, a sentencer must not make assumptions unsupported by evidence about the effects of an offence on the victim.

The court must pass what it judges to be the appropriate sentence having regard to the circumstances of the offence and of the offender, taking into account, so far as the court considers it appropriate, the consequences to the victim.

The opinions of the victim or the victim's close relatives as to what the sentence should be are not relevant.

REDUCTION IN SENTENCE FOR GUILTY PLEAS

(Section 152, Powers of Criminal Courts (Sentencing) Act 2000)

In deciding what sentence to pass on a person who has pleaded guilty the court has to take into account the stage in the proceedings at which that plea was indicated and the circumstances in which the indication was given. If the court imposes a less severe penalty than it would have given, it must state this in open court. It would be a matter of good practice for the court to say how much credit has been given, with a brief reason for the decision.

The principles of "discount" apply as much to magistrates' courts as they do to Crown Courts. A timely guilty plea may attract a sentencing reduction of up to a third but the precise amount will depend on the facts of each case. A change of plea on the day set down for trial may attract only a minimal reduction in sentence; the court must still consider whether credit should be given.

Reductions apply to fines, periods of community sentences and custody. An early guilty plea may also affect the length of a disqualification or the number of penalty points. However, minimum periods of disqualification and mandatory penalty points cannot be reduced for a guilty plea. Reasons should be given for decisions.

Update December 2006: Sentencers are referred to SGC guideline – "Reduction in Sentence for a Guilty Plea".

PRE-SENTENCE REPORTS

(See also the section on *community sentences*.)

The purpose of all reports is to provide information to help the court decide on the most suitable sentence. They are required in most cases where the threshold of "serious enough" (community penalties) or "so serious" (custody) is reached – and should only be sought in such cases. They can be in the form of a PSR (pre-sentence report) or SSR (specific sentence report).

PSRs are written reports to assist the courts in determining sentence. In accordance with National Standards 2002 they contain:
— a full risk assessment;
— a proposal for sentence commensurate with the risk of harm, likelihood of re-offending, the nature of the offence and the suitability of the offender.

A PSR must be provided within 15 working days or any agreed shorter period.

SSRs

An SSR is a PSR for legal purposes as it meets the definition of section 162 of the Powers of Criminal Courts (Sentencing) Act 2000. SSRs are designed to speed up the provision of information to courts to allow sentencing without delay in relatively straightforward cases. They are a specific limited enquiry undertaken at the request of the court into an offender's suitability for a particular community sentence.

They are designed to be available on the day requested (or next morning). If there is doubt about a defendant's suitability for a specific sentence report the probation officer may recommend an adjournment for a full PSR.

Update December 2006: A pre-sentence report under CJA 2003 may be oral or written. Current written formats are termed fast delivery and standard delivery. Which one will be appropriate will depend on the level of potential risk posed by the offender. When ordering a report, a court should first state its purpose(s) of sentence and decision on culpability and harm, normally using a sentencing form.

GIVING REASONS

Magistrates should normally give reasons for their findings and decisions; this is obligatory under the Human Rights Act.
— The offender should be told the reasons for the decision.
— The victim will want to know the reasons for the decision.
— The public are entitled to know what is going on in the criminal justice system, and to have confidence in it.
— If a sentence is unusual the importance of giving reasons is greater.
— Ill-informed criticism in the media may be reduced if reasons have been given in public and recorded.
— In preparing an SSR or a PSR, or in implementing a community sentence, the probation service must know what the magistrates had in mind and what findings of fact they made.
— If a case has to be adjourned, and a differently constituted bench sits next time, the later bench must know the reasons for the decisions and findings of the earlier bench.

And:
— The reasons will be necessary if there is an appeal by way of case stated.

There are now many instances where the giving of reasons is required by law.
— Why bail is refused.
— Why the offence is so serious as to justify prison.
— Why a defaulter is being sent to prison.
— If a compensation order is not awarded.
— If a sentence is reduced because of a guilty plea.
— If the court does not disqualify the driver or endorse his licence for 'special reasons'.
— If the court does not impose a 'totting up' disqualification.

Having reached their findings through a structured approach, it is perfectly proper for the magistrates to seek the advice and assistance of the legal adviser in how best to formulate and articulate their reasons for the purpose of the pronouncement.

It is the responsibility of the legal adviser to provide the justices with any advice they require properly to perform their functions, whether or not the justices have requested that advice. The Practice Direction on the functions and responsibilities of Justices' Clerks and authorised legal advisers, made by the Lord Chief Justice on 2 October 2000, makes it clear that this responsibility extends to giving advice on the appropriate decision-making structure to be applied in any given case, reminding the bench of the evidence, and assisting the court, where appropriate as to the formulation of reasons and the recording of those reasons.

FINANCIAL PENALTIES

FINING

Fines are suitable as punishment for cases which are not serious enough to merit a community penalty, nor so serious that a custodial sentence must be considered.

The aim should be for the fine to have equal impact on rich or poor and before fixing the amount of a fine, the court must enquire into the offender's financial circumstances, preferably using a standard means form.

A fine must not exceed the upper statutory limit. Where this is expressed in terms of a "level" the maxima are:

Level 1 £200
Level 2 £500
Level 3 £1,000
Level 4 £2,500
Level 5 £5,000

The fine must reflect the seriousness of the offence and must be proportionate to the offender's means.

A reduction must be considered for a guilty plea – up to a third if the plea was timely, and the appropriate announcement made.

Where compensation and costs are in issue then the order of priorities is compensation – fine – costs. The totality of the financial penalty must be considered in reaching a decision on the level of fine.

Where a defendant is to be fined for several offences and his means are limited it may be better to fix the relevant fine level for the most serious offence and order "no separate penalty" on the lesser matters.

The suggested fines in these *Guidelines* are given as either A, B or C. These represent 50%, 100% and 150% of the defendant's weekly take home pay/benefit. (Weekly take home pay or benefit means weekly income after all deductions made by an employer (take home pay) or the amount of weekly benefit payment.) These levels take into account ordinary living expenses. This guidance should not be used as a tariff and every offender's means must be individually considered.

The defendant should be given a document which sets out the total fines, rate of payment, date of first payment and place of payment before leaving the court.

Update December 2006: After the fine has been calculated and announced, a Collection Order should normally be made and explained to the offender, even when payment in full is to be made that day.

Assessing means

Before fixing the amount of any fine the Powers of Criminal Courts (Sentencing) Act 2000, section 128 requires the court to enquire into the financial circumstances of the offender so far as they are known. Defendants should be asked to complete a means form to provide this information.

The first figure needed is take home pay/benefit which is used to ensure the fairest approach to those in different financial circumstances – the guideline fines (which are only a starting point) are based on this income and reflect ordinary living expenses. The court should be aware of other information including:

– whether the offender has savings or other disposable or realisable capital assets;
– liability to pay outstanding fines;
– level of outgoings.

And should in every case consider individual circumstances, but outgoings will only be relevant if they are out of the ordinary and substantially reduce ability to pay, leading to undue hardship.

The financial circumstances of third parties, e.g. other members of the family, are irrelevant, save insofar as the offender derives income or benefit from such persons, or he is thereby relieved of a proportion of household expenses.

If for any reason the magistrates are not satisfied with the information they have received, and they feel they cannot sentence until they have such information, they may adjourn the case for further information to be supplied, and they may make a financial circumstances order requiring a statement of means to be provided, Powers of the Criminal Courts (Sentencing) Act 2000, section 126.

The fine is payable in full on the day and the defendant should always be asked for immediate payment. If periodic payments are allowed, the fine should normally be payable within a maximum of 12 months. It should be remembered however, that for those on very low incomes it is often unrealistic to expect them to maintain weekly payments for as long as a year.

The fine should be a hardship, depriving the offender of the capacity to spend the money on "luxuries", but care should be taken not to force him or her below a reasonable "subsistence" level.

Fining in the defendant's absence

If, having been given a reasonable opportunity to inform the court of his means, the offender refuses or fails to do so, the magistrates may draw such inference as to means as they think just in the circumstances, using all available information. It is inappropriate simply to fine the maximum level.

For further advice on the fines procedure, see the flowchart below and the guidance on **fine enforcement**.

FINES PROCEDURE FLOW CHART

1. DECIDE SENTENCING BAND ACCORDING TO SERIOUSNESS

Consider the aggravating and mitigating features of the offence, plus any personal mitigation relating to the offender – decide that a fine is appropriate

2. DECIDE LEVEL OF FINE ACCORDING TO SERIOUSNESS

Taking the above factors into account, decide on the level of fine
(A, B or C) that reflects those factors

3. OBTAIN FINANCIAL INFORMATION

The court is required by statute to enquire into financial circumstances and to take them into account so far as they are known. Full information (from means form/questioning in court) should cover income, savings (if any) and outgoings including other court fines.

4. SET FINE

A fine is meant to have an equal impact on rich and poor. To ensure a fair approach the starting point in all cases should be **weekly take home pay/weekly benefit payment**.

Select level A (50%), level B (100%) or level C (150%) of this weekly amount
according to decision on seriousness (see 2 above).
NB these levels already take into account ordinary living expenses.

5. CONSIDER FACTORS RELEVANT TO INDIVIDUAL CASE

OUTGOINGS: *These are only relevant if they are out of the ordinary and substantially reduce ability to pay, leading to undue hardship.*

TIMELY GUILTY PLEA: give credit where appropriate.

COMPENSATION/COSTS: If these are applicable then total financial penalty must be considered in relation to known means, including savings. If means insufficient for all three elements, apply usual priority of compensation – fine – costs.

CONFIRM ORIGINAL FIGURE OR JUSTIFY ANY CHANGE

6. ANNOUNCE AMOUNT OF FINE: SEEK IMMEDIATE PAYMENT

If payment in full not possible, seek immediate part payment
If time is asked for, consider all information above in setting
level of payments/time to clear total sum
Update December 2006: Courts Act 2003 applies: Normally a collection order
should be made and explained to the offender.

COSTS

The following guidance was given by the Court of Appeal in *R v Northallerton Magistrates' Court, ex p Dove*:

1. An order for costs to the prosecutor should never exceed the sum which, having regard to the defendant's means and any other financial order imposed upon him, he is able to pay and which it is reasonable to order him to pay.
2. Such an order should never exceed the sum which the prosecutor had actually and reasonably incurred.
3. The purpose of the order is to compensate the prosecutor and not to punish the defendant.
4. The costs ordered to be paid should not in the ordinary way be grossly disproportionate to the fine imposed for the offence. If the total of the proposed fine and the costs sought by the prosecutor exceeds the sum which the defendant could reasonably be ordered to pay, it was preferable to achieve an acceptable total by reducing the sum of costs ordered, rather than by reducing the fine.
5. It is for the defendant to provide the justices with such data relevant to his financial position as would enable them to assess what he could reasonably afford to pay, and if he fails to do so the justices are entitled to draw reasonable inferences as to his means from all the circumstances of the case.
6. It is incumbent on any court which proposed to make any financial order against a defendant to give him a fair opportunity to adduce any relevant financial information and to make any appropriate submissions.

COMPENSATION ORDERS

THE LEGAL FRAMEWORK

As well as assessing the seriousness of the offence, including the impact on the victim, and any mitigating factors affecting the offender, the court is under a duty to consider compensation in every case where loss, damage or injury has resulted from the offence, whether or not an application has been made (Powers of Criminal Courts (Sentencing) Act 2000, s 130).

PRIORITIES

If the sentence is to be financial, then the order of priorities is compensation, fine, costs. If the sentence is to be a community penalty, the court should consider carefully the overall burdens placed on the offender if a compensation order is to be made too. If the sentence is to be custody, then a compensation order will be unlikely unless the offender has financial resources available with which to pay immediately or on release.

GIVING REASONS

If, having considered making a compensation order, the court decides that it is not appropriate to make one, it has a statutory duty to give its reasons for not ordering compensation.

LIMITATIONS ON POWERS

Magistrates have the power to award compensation for personal injury, loss or damage up to a total of £5,000 for each offence. An exception is where the injury, loss or damage arises from a road accident: a compensation order may not be made in such a case unless there is conviction of an offence under the Theft Act or if the offender is uninsured and the Motor Insurers' Bureau will not cover the loss. If in doubt, seek advice from the legal adviser. Compensation should only be awarded in fairly clear, uncomplicated cases: if there are disputes and complications, the matter should be left to the civil courts.

NO DOUBLE COMPENSATION

Any victim may bring a civil action for damages against the offender: if that action is successful, the civil court will deduct the amount paid by the offender under a compensation order. In this way, there should be no double compensation. The same applies where the victim receives a payment under the Criminal Injuries Compensation Scheme. The magistrates' court should therefore take no account of these other possibilities.

CRIMINAL INJURIES COMPENSATION SCHEME

The Criminal Injuries Compensation Scheme provides state compensation for the victims of crimes of violence, particularly those who are seriously injured. The minimum award is currently £1,000. Courts are encouraged to make compensation orders, whether or not the case falls within the Criminal Injuries Compensation Scheme, in order to bring home to offenders themselves the consequences of their actions.

THE PURPOSE OF COMPENSATION ORDERS

The purpose of making a compensation order is to compensate the victim for his or her losses. The compensation may relate to offences taken into consideration, subject to a maximum of £5,000 per charge. Compensation for personal injury may include compensation for terror, shock or distress caused by the offence. The court must have regard to the means of the offender when calculating the amount of the order.

THE APPROACH TO COMPENSATION

In calculating the gross amount of compensation, courts should consider compensating the victim for two types of loss. The first, sometimes called "special damages", includes compensation for financial loss sustained as a result of the offence – e.g. the cost of repairing damage, or in cases of injury, any loss of earnings or dental expenses. If these costs are not agreed, the court should ask for evidence of them. The second type of loss, sometimes called "general damages", covers compensation for the pain and suffering of the injury itself and for any loss of facility.

CALCULATING THE COMPENSATION

The amount of compensation should be determined in the light of medical evidence, the victim's sex and age, and any other factors which appear to the court to be relevant in the particular case. If the court does not have sufficient information, then the matter should be adjourned to obtain more facts.

The Table below gives some general guidance on appropriate starting points for general damages for personal injuries.

Once the court has made a preliminary calculation of the appropriate compensation, it is required to have regard to the means of the offender before making an order. Where the offender has little money, the order may have to be scaled down significantly. However, even a compensation order for a fairly small sum may be important to the victim.

Type of injury	Description	Starting point
Graze	Depending on size	Up to £75
Bruise	Depending on size	Up to £100
Black eye		£125
Cut: no permanent scar	Depending on size and whether stitched	£100–£500
Sprain	Depending on loss of mobility	£100–£1,000
Finger	Fractured little finger, recovery within month	£1,000
Loss of non-front tooth	Depending on cosmetic effect	£500–1,000
Loss of front tooth		£1,500
Eye	Blurred or double vision	£1,000
Nose	Undisplaced fracture of nasal bone	£1,000
Nose	Displaced fracture of bone requiring manipulation	£1,500
Nose	Not causing fracture but displaced septum requiring sub-mucous resection	£2,000
Facial scar	However small, resulting in permanent disfigurement	£1,500
Wrist	Closed fracture, recovery within month	£3,000
Wrist	Displaced fracture, limb in plaster, recovery in 6 months	£3,500
Leg or arm	Closed fracture of tibia, fibula, ulna or radius, recovery within month	£3,500
Laparotomy	Stomach scar 6-8 inches (resulting from operation	£3,500

COMMUNITY SENTENCES

Update December 2006
[The material formerly covered here has] now been overtaken by CJA 2003 for offences from April 2005. Please refer instead to information including SGC guideline "New Sentences: CJA 3003", and to the adult court bench book pages 3–66 and 3–67, and pages 3–70 to 3–93.

BREACH OF COURT ORDERS

Update December 2006
[The material formerly covered here] has now been overtaken by CJA 2003 for offences from April 2005. Please refer instead to information including SGC guideline "New Sentences: CJA 2003", and to the adult court bench book pages 3–66 and 3–67, and pages 3–70 to 3–93.

ENVIRONMENTAL PROTECTION ACT 1990
HEALTH AND SAFETY AT WORK ACT 1974

LEGISLATION

The main environmental protection and drinking water offences are:
— Section 23 Environmental Protection Act 1990 – carrying on a prescribed process without, or in breach of, authorisation in integrated pollution control and local authority air pollution control.
— Section 33 Environmental Protection Act 1990 – depositing, recovering or disposing of waste without a site licence or in breach of its conditions.

- Sections 33 and 34 Environmental Protection Act 1990 – fly-tipping (offence is aggravated by dangerous or offensive material, tipping near housing etc., escape of waste, intention to avoid paying landfill tax.
- Section 85 Water Resources Act 1991 – polluting controlled waters.
- Section 70 Water Industry Act 1991 – supplying water unfit for human consumption.

The main health and safety offences are:

- Section 33 Health and Safety at Work Act 1974, sub-sections (1)(g) and (o) – failing to comply with an improvement or prohibition notice, or a court remedy order.
- Section 33(1)(a) – breaching general duties in sections 2 to 6 Health and Safety at Work Act.
- Section 33(1)(c) – breach of health and safety regulations or licensing conditions.

It is important to seek guidance from the legal adviser in all these serious cases. The Court of Appeal, in *R v Howe* [1999] 2 Cr App R (S) 37) gave guidance on health and safety sentencing.

SERIOUSNESS

Offences under these Acts are serious, especially where the maximum penalty in the magistrates' court is £20,000. Imprisonment is available for some offences. It is important to be careful when accepting jurisdiction as to whether the cases ought properly to be heard in the Crown Court. This is especially so when dealing with large companies. In *R v Howe*, the Court of Appeal said that a fine needs to be large enough to bring home to those who manage a company, and their shareholders, the need to protect the health and safety of workers and the public. A company is presumed to be able to pay any fine the court is minded to impose unless financial information to the contrary is available to the court before the hearing. A deliberate breach of the legislation by a company or an individual with a view to profit seriously aggravates the offence. If a guilty plea is made for an either way offence, again a committal for sentence under section 4 Powers of Criminal Courts (Sentencing) Act 2000 might be more appropriate. Simple cases can, of course, be dealt with by the magistrates' court.

In the case of *Friskies Petcare (UK) Ltd* [2000] 2 Cr App R (S) 401 it was recommended that the Health and Safety Executive should list in writing the aggravating features of the case, and the defence should do likewise with the mitigating features, so as to assist the court in coming to the proper basis for sentence after a guilty plea.

Matters to consider when assessing seriousness include:

- offence deliberate or reckless breach of the law rather than carelessness;
- action or lack of action prompted by financial motives – profit or cost-saving or neglecting to put in place preventative measures or avoiding payment for relevant licence;
- considerable potential for harm to workers or public;
- regular or continuing breach, not isolated lapse;
- failure to respond to advice, cautions or warning from regulatory authority;
- death or serious injury or ill-health has been a consequence of the offence;
- ignoring concerns raised by employees or others;
- an awareness of the specific risks likely to arise from action taken but ignoring them;
- previous offences of a similar nature;
- extent of damage and cost of rectifying it (expensive clean up operation required);
- attitude to the enforcing authorities;
- offending pattern;
- serious extent of damage resulting from offence (but lack of actual damage does not render the offence merely technical; it is still serious if there is risk);
- animal health or flora affected;
- defendant carrying out operations without an appropriate licence;
- other lawful activities interfered with.

Other factors may provide some mitigation:

- the offender's minor role with little personal responsibility;
- genuine lack of awareness or understanding of specific regulations;
- an isolated lapse.

There may be some offender mitigation:

- prompt reporting;
- ready co-operation with regulatory authority;
- good previous record;
- timely plea of guilt.

Sometimes in a case much more damage has occurred than could have been reasonably anticipated. Any sentence should give weight to the environmental impact but should primarily reflect the culpability of the offender.

THE LEVEL OF FINES – GENERAL APPROACH

A fine is considered by the Sentencing Advisory Panel to be the appropriate form of penalty for both companies and individuals for these offences. The normal principles of the Criminal Justice Act 1991 should apply and the seriousness of the offence and the financial circumstances of the defendant should be taken into account. The level of fine should reflect the extent to which the defendant's behaviour has fallen below the required standard. High culpability should be matched by a high fine even though actual damage turned out to be less than might reasonably have been anticipated.

In line with *R v Howe*, the level of the fine should reflect any economic gain from the offence by failure to take precautions. It has been said that a deliberate failure to take the necessary precautions can be a form of stealing commercial advantage from law-abiding competitors.

In all cases with corporate offenders the company's financial circumstances must be carefully considered. No single measure of ability to pay can apply in all cases. Turnover, profitability and liquidity should all be considered. It is not usual for an expert accountant to be available in summary cases.

If a company does not produce its accounts the court can assume that the company can pay whatever fine the court imposes. In most cases it is hard to imagine a company failing to provide such information, although with large known companies of national or international standing this may not be a necessary requirement. Where necessary the payment of fines can be spread over a longer period than the usual 12 months, if payment in full would be unduly burdensome on say, a smaller company.

FINING TOO LITTLE?

A fine suited to the circumstances of a small local company would make no impact at all on a multi-national corporation with a huge turnover. The fine to any company should be substantial enough to have a real economic impact, which together with attendant bad publicity would pressure both management and shareholders to tighten their regulatory compliance. Such fines on large companies might often be beyond the summary fines limit and in such circumstances the case should be transferred to the Crown Court for trial or sentence. Where the court does not transfer the case of a larger company to the higher court magistrates should look to a starting point near the maximum fine level then consider aggravating and mitigating factors.

FINING TOO MUCH?

Care should be taken to ensure that fines imposed on smaller companies are not beyond their capability to pay. The court might not wish the payment of the fine to result in the company not being able to pay for improved procedures or cause the company to go into liquidation or make its employees redundant.

OTHER SENTENCING OPTIONS

Whilst fines will be the usual outcome in proceedings of this sort, other sentencing options are available.
- A discharge will rarely be appropriate.
- Compensation should be considered if there is a specific victim who has suffered injury, loss or damage. You should give reasons if you decide not to make a compensation order. The current limit is £5,000 per offence, although substantial civil claims are often pending in such cases.
- The legislation provides for the possibility of directors and senior managers appearing before the courts, and custodial sentences are available in specific instances. The courts have power to disqualify directors under the Company Directors Disqualification Act 1986. This is important particularly in health and safety enforcement, and breach of an order is itself a criminal offence carrying a term of imprisonment for up to two years.

COSTS

The prosecution will normally claim the costs of investigation and presentation. These may be substantial, and can incorporate time and activity expended on containing and making the area safe. Remediation costs for pollution offences may also be significant. For water pollution offences enforcing authorities are able to recover them through the criminal courts (Water Resources Act 1991, as amended). In other cases there are powers for the courts to order offenders to remedy the cause of the offence, or for the Environment Agency to require them to undertake clean-up at their own expense, or for the agency to carry out remedial costs and seek to recover them through the civil courts.

The enforcing authorities' costs should be fully recouped from the offender.

The order for costs should not be disproportionate to the level of the fine imposed. The court should fix the level of the fine first, then consider awarding compensation, and then determine the costs. If the total sum exceeds the defendant's means, the order for costs should be reduced rather than the fine. Compensation should take priority over both the fine and costs.

As always, magistrates should seek the advice of the legal adviser on sentencing options and guidelines in all cases.

For more information, access the environmental offences training materials on the Magistrates' Association website. www.magistrates-association.org.uk

RACIALLY OR RELIGIOUSLY AGGRAVATED OFFENCES

There are special provisions on racial and religious aggravation, under the Crime and Disorder Act 1998 as amended. There are two forms of aggravation: an offence is racially or religiously aggravated EITHER if it is racially or religiously motivated, OR if in committing the offence the offender demonstrates racial or religious hostility (e.g. by making a racist remark). The guideline case for sentencing for these offences is *Kelly and Donnelly 2001*, and three situations should be treated separately:
(i) there are a few specific racially or religiously aggravated offences in the Crime and Disorder Act, which have higher maximum penalties than the non-aggravated versions of those offences (e.g. common assault, abh, criminal damage, etc). Where a defendant is convicted of one of these special offences, the court should determine its sentence for the basic offence (such as criminal damage or assault), and then decide how much to add for the

racial or religious aggravation. When the sentence is announced, the court should state how much it added to the basic offence in order to reflect the racial or religious aggravation.

(ii) most offences do not have a specific racially or religiously aggravated version, however. Here, the general principle applies, which is that racial or religious aggravation is a factor that should increase the severity of the sentence.

(iii) where an offender is convicted of an offence which has a racially or religiously aggravated version, but is convicted only of the basic offence, it is wrong in principle to pass a higher sentence on racial or religious grounds. If the racially or religiously aggravated version of the offence is not charged or not proved, that is the end of the matter.

ROAD TRAFFIC OFFENCES

DISQUALIFICATION

Some offences carry mandatory disqualification. This mandatory disqualification period may be automatically lengthened by the existence of certain previous convictions and disqualifications.

Sentencers should not disqualify defendants in their absence although there is provision in statute to do so provided that an offender is given adequate notice of the hearing at which the court will consider disqualification. This discretionary power should only be exercised in out of the ordinary circumstances. As with all decisions of this type, account should be taken of human rights legislation. The court must give cogent and explicit reasons for any decision to disqualify in absence.

PENALTY POINTS AND DISQUALIFICATION

All endorsable offences carry also as an alternative discretionary power to disqualify instead of imposing penalty points.

Dangerous driving carries an obligatory minimum disqualification of one year and a mandatory extended re-test.

For any offence which carries penalty points the courts have a discretion to order a re-test provided there is evidence of inexperience, incompetence or infirmity. It would be an ordinary test except where disqualification is obligatory when an extended test would be required.

The number of variable penalty points or the period of disqualification is targeted strictly at the seriousness of the offence and in either case must not be reduced below the statutory minimum, where applicable.

Offences committed on different occasions may carry points, even where they are dealt with on the same occasion.

DISQUALIFICATION UNTIL A TEST IS PASSED

A magistrates' court **must** disqualify an offender until he passes an *extended driving test* where he is convicted of an offence of dangerous driving.

The court has a **discretion** to disqualify until a test is passed where the offender has been convicted of an offence involving obligatory disqualification. In this case it is the ordinary driving test that must be undertaken.

An offender disqualified as a "totter" under the penalty points provisions **may** also be ordered to re-take a driving test, in which case it will be the *extended test.*

The discretion is likely to be exercised where there is evidence of inexperience, incompetence or infirmity; or the disqualification period imposed is lengthy (i.e. the offender is going to be "off the road" for a considerable time).

DISQUALIFICATIONS FOR LESS THAN 56 DAYS

A disqualification for less than 56 days is also more lenient in that it does not revoke the licence and cannot increase subsequent mandatory periods even if it is imposed under the points provisions.

REDUCTION FOR GUILTY PLEA

The precise amount of credit for a timely guilty plea will depend on the facts of each case. It should be given in respect of the fine or periods of community sentence or custody. An early guilty plea may also affect the length of a disqualification or the number of penalty points but cannot apply so as to reduce minimum mandatory periods of disqualification.

Update December 2006: Refer to SGC guideline – "Reduction in Sentence for a Guilty Plea". "A reduction in sentence should be applied to any of the elements of a penalty. The guilty plea reduction has no impact on sentencing decisions in relation to ancillary orders."

THE MULTIPLE OFFENDER

Where an offender is convicted of several offences committed on one occasion, it is suggested that the court should concentrate on the most serious offence, carrying the greatest number of penalty points or period of disqualification.

The application of the totality principle may then result in the court deciding to impose no separate penalty for the lesser offences, or to reduce fines for these offences below the level which might normally be imposed.

TOTTING

Repeat offenders who reach 12 points or more within a period of three years become liable to a minimum disqualification for 6 months, and in some instances 12 months or 2 years – but must be given an opportunity to address the court and/or bring evidence to show why such disqualification should not be ordered or should be reduced. Totting disqualifications, unlike other disqualifications, erase all penalty points.

Totting disqualifications can be reduced or avoided for exceptional hardship or other circumstances. No account is to be taken of non-exceptional hardship or circumstances alleged to make the offence(s) not serious. No such ground can be used again to mitigate totting, if previously taken into account in totting mitigation within the three years preceding the conviction.

NEW DRIVERS

Newly qualified drivers who incur 6 points or more during a two-year probationary period from the date of passing the driving test will automatically have their licence revoked by the Secretary of State and will have to apply for a provisional licence until they pass a repeat test. This total must include any points imposed prior to passing the test provided they are within three years.

FIXED PENALTIES

If a fixed penalty was offered, the court should consider any reasons for not taking it up and, if valid, fine the amount of the appropriate fixed penalty (provided the amount is within the means of the offender), endorse if required, waive costs and allow a maximum of 28 days to pay. If a fixed penalty was refused or not offered, the court should consider whether there are aggravating factors which merit increasing the fine or there should be any credit for a guilty plea.

FINE ENFORCEMENT

Unless an offender is appearing at the fine enforcement court because a review date was fixed when the fine was imposed, he will be either answering to a summons or on a warrant following a summons; in both instances he will probably have also had a reminder (court practices differ in this respect).

Update December 2006: Collection of fines – Courts Act 2003 now applies. Consult legal adviser for details. A court will normally make a collection order to enable a range of enforcement measures to be taken by a fines officer without the need for further referral to court. Courts enforcing unpaid sums are advised to make a collection order (and explain it to the defaulter) if this has not already been done. Collection orders may be made in the absence of defaulters.

The court should first receive information about the history of the case(s): the offence, the original means form, the date of the sentence, the order of the court regarding payment and the record of payment to date.

Then, an up-to-date means form should be considered, followed by questioning by the legal adviser and/or the magistrates to establish any change of circumstances since the fine was imposed and the reason given for the failure to pay as ordered.

The court can remit fines after a means enquiry and may order it if the court "thinks it just to do so having regard to a change of circumstances" which may reasonably be found where:
— the defaulter's means have changed;
— information available to the court on a means enquiry was not before the sentencing court;
— arrears have accumulated by the imposition of additional fines to a level which makes repayment of the total amount within a reasonable time unlikely;
— defaulters are serving a term of imprisonment, remission may be a more practical alternative than the lodging of concurrent warrants of imprisonment;
— compensation and costs cannot be remitted but in circumstances where payment is unlikely or impractical due to the defaulter's means or circumstances the sum may be discharged or reduced. Victims and claimants should be consulted and given an opportunity to attend a hearing.

NB: Excise penalties (which include fines and back duty for using an untaxed vehicle) cannot be remitted.

The Magistrates' Courts Act 1980 section 82 requires that before a court may issue a warrant of commitment for non-payment of fines it must have: "considered or tried all other methods of enforcing payment of the sum and it appears to the court that they are inappropriate or unsuccessful". The court must record the reasons for not trying each of the methods.

The options are:
— **Detention in the precincts of the court** (section 135 MCA 1980)
— **Money Payment Supervision Order**: for those under 21 years of age the court must place the defaulter under such an order (before making any decision to submit to detention) unless satisfied it is undesirable or impracticable so to do.
— **Attendance Centre Order**: for under 25 year olds only. It requires a defaulter to attend for two or three hours on a Saturday at a local attendance centre. The total number of hours must not exceed 24 if the defaulter is under 16, or 36 when he/she is 16 or over. NB. Not all sentencers have an Attendance Centre available to them.

— **Deduction from Benefit:** the court may request the Department for Work and Pensions to make payments direct from the offender's benefit, subject to any right of review or appeal he may have.

— **Attachment of Earnings Order:** the order requires an employer to make periodical payments from the defaulter's earnings to the court so this method is only suitable where the defaulter is in settled employment. A protected earnings rate (the rate below which his earnings will not be reduced as a result of the order) needs to be fixed together with a normal deduction rate, after enquiring into the defendant's means and needs and obligations.

— **Distress Warrant:** authorises the bailiffs to seize goods belonging to the defaulter and sell them in order to pay the fine, together with the bailiff's costs. Its issue may be postponed on terms.

— **Warrants of overnight detention:** the defaulter can be held overnight in the police station. He must be released at eight o'clock the following morning or the same morning if arrested after midnight.

— **Imprisonment:** the court must conduct a means enquiry before finding the defaulter guilty of culpable neglect or wilful refusal to pay. An opportunity must be provided for legal representation. The aim in fixing a period of commitment should be to identify the shortest period which is likely to succeed in obtaining payment and the periods prescribed in schedule 4 of the Magistrates' Courts Act 1980 (set out below) should be regarded as maxima rather than the norm. The period of imprisonment may be suspended pending regular payments. Where such payments are not made, the defaulter should be brought back before the court for consideration of whether the period of imprisonment should be implemented.

Maximum periods of imprisonment in default of payment

An amount not exceeding £200 7 days
An amount exceeding £200 but not exceeding £500 14 days
An amount exceeding £500 but not exceeding £1,000 28 days
An amount exceeding £1,000 but not exceeding £2,500 45 days
An amount exceeding £2,500 but not exceeding £5,000 3 months
An amount exceeding £5,000 but not exceeding £10,000 6 months
An amount exceeding £10,000 12 months

Notes

Search: magistrates can order the defaulter to be searched and any money found on him/her to be used to pay the fine.

STATING THE REASONS FOR SENTENCE

1. We are dealing with an offence of:
....
....

2. We have considered the impact on the victim which was
....

3. We have taken into account these features which make the offence more serious:
....
....

4. We have taken into account these features which make the offence less serious: ....
....

5. (*where relevant*) We have taken into account that the offence was:

	racially and/or religiously aggravated
	committed on bail

6. We have taken into account your previous record, specifically the offences of ....
and your failure to respond to the sentences imposed.

7. We have taken into account what we have heard in your favour about the offence and about you: ....
....

8. We have taken into account the fact that you pleaded guilty [at an earlier stage] [but not until ....] and we have reduced the sentence by [state how much].

9. And, as a result, we have decided that the most appropriate sentence for you is:
....
....

10. (*where relevant*) We have decided not to award compensation in this case because:
....

Update December 2006: Refer to the sentencing form and guidance notes at pages 1–48a to 1–48d of the adult court bench book.

Intermittent Custody (Transitory Provisions) Order 2003
(SI 2003/3283)

3–3090   1.   (1) This Order may be cited as the Intermittent Custody (Transitory Provisions) Order 2003 and shall come into force on 26th January 2004.

(2) In this Order, "the 2003 Act" means the Criminal Justice Act 2003.[1]

---

1. Made by the Secretary of State, in exercise of the powers conferred upon him by section 336(3) of the Criminal Justice Act 2003. A court may not make an intermittent custody order unless it has been notified by the Secretary of State that arrangements for implementing such orders are available in the area proposed to be specified in the intermittent custody order and the notice has not been withdrawn (Criminal Justice Act 2003, s 184(1)).

3–3091   2.   In relation to any time before the commencement of the repeal of section 78 of the Powers of Criminal Courts (Sentencing) Act 2000 by the 2003 Act, section 183 of the 2003 Act shall have effect with respect to sentences passed by magistrates' courts with the following modifications—

   (a)   in subsection (4)(b), for "28", substitute "14";
   (b)   in subsection (4)(c), for "51", substitute "26";
   (c)   in subsection (5)(b), for "90", substitute "45";
   (d)   in subsection (7)(a), for "65", substitute "52"; and
   (e)   in subsection (7)(b), for "180", substitute "90".

3–3092   3.   In relation to any time before the commencement of section 240 of the 2003 Act, section 241 of that Act shall have effect with the following modifications—

   (a)   in subsection (1)—
        (i)   for "to whom a direction under section 240 relates", substitute "whose sentence falls to be reduced under section 67 of the Criminal Justice Act 1967 by any relevant period within the meaning of that section ("the relevant period")"; and
        (ii)   for "number of days specified in the direction are", substitute "relevant period is"; and
   (b)   in subsection (2), for "number of days specified in a direction under section 240", substitute "relevant period".

Criminal Justice Act 2003 (Sentencing) (Transitory Provisions) Order 2005
(SI 2005/643)

3–3100   1. Citation, commencement and interpretation.   (1) This Order may be cited as the Criminal Justice Act 2003 (Sentencing) (Transitory Provisions) Order 2005 and shall come into force on 4th April 2005.

(2) In this Order "the 2003 Act" means the Criminal Justice Act 2003.

3–3101   2. Modifications for suspended sentence and community sentence.   (1) In relation to any time before the commencement of the repeal of section 78 of the Powers Criminal Courts (Sentencing) Act 2000 (general limit on magistrates' courts' powers) by the 2003 Act, the provisions of Part 12 of that Act shall have effect subject to the modifications set out in paragraphs (2) to (4).

(2) In section 189 (suspended sentences of imprisonment)—

   (a)   in subsection (1) for the words from "at least 28 weeks" to the words "section 181" substitute the words "at least 14 days but not more than twelve months, or in the case of a magistrates' court, at least 14 days but not more than six months";
   (b)   in subsection (2) for the words "65 weeks" substitute the words "twelve months, or in the case of a magistrates' court, six months".

(3) In Schedule 8 (breach, revocation or amendment of community order), in paragraphs 9(1)(c), 10(1)(c) and 12(b) for the words "51 weeks" substitute the words "6 months".

(4) In Schedule 12 (breach or amendment of suspended sentence order, and effect of further conviction)—

   (a)   in paragraph 8(2)—
        (i)   in sub-paragraph (a) omit the words "and custodial period"; and
        (ii)   in sub-paragraph (b) for the words for the words from "with either or both of" onwards substitute the words "subject to the substitution for the original term of a lesser term";
   (b)   in paragraph 9(1)—
        (i)   omit the words "and custodial period"; and
        (ii)   omit sub-paragraph (a).

3–3103   3. Modifications for sentencing of offenders aged 18 but under 21.   (1) In relation to any time before the coming into force of section 61 of the Criminal Justice and Court Services Act 2000 (abolition of sentences of detention in a young offender institution, custody for life etc), the provisions of Part 12 of the 2003 Act shall have effect subject to the modifications set out in paragraphs (2) to (17).

(2) In section 189 (suspended sentences of imprisonment)—

(a) in subsection (1)—

(i) after the words "sentence of imprisonment" where they first appear insert the words "or, in the case of a person aged at least 18 but under 21, detention in a young offender institution"; and

(ii) after those words the second time they appear insert the words "or detention in a young offender institution";

(b) in subsection (6), after the words "sentence of imprisonment" insert the words "or in the case of a person aged at least 18 but under 21, a sentence of detention in a young offender institution".

(3) In section 224(2) (meaning of "specified offence" etc)—

(a) in paragraph (b)(i), after the words "imprisonment for life" insert the words "or, in the case of a person aged at least 18 but under 21, custody for life";

(b) in paragraph (b)(ii), after the word "imprisonment" insert the words "or, in the case of a person aged at least 18 but under 21, detention in a young offender institution,".

(4) In section 225 (life sentence of imprisonment for public protection for serious offences)—

(a) in subsection (2), at the end, insert the words "or in the case of a person aged at least 18 but under 21, a sentence of custody for life";

(b) in subsection (3), at the end, insert the words "or in the case of a person aged at least 18 but under 21, a sentence of detention in a young offender institution for public protection";

(c) in subsection (4)—

(i) after the words "imprisonment for public protection" insert the words "or a sentence of detention in a young offender institution for public protection"; and

(ii) for the words "imprisonment for an indeterminate period" substitute the words "imprisonment or detention for an indeterminate period".

(5) In section 227 (extended sentence for certain violent or sexual offences: persons 18 or over)—

(a) in subsection (2)—

(i) after the words "extended sentence of imprisonment" insert the words "or, in the case of a person aged at least 18 but under 21, an extended sentence of detention in a young offender institution,"; and

(ii) after the words "a sentence of imprisonment" insert the words "or detention in a young offender institution";

(b) in subsection (3) after the words "a term of imprisonment" insert the words "or detention in a young offender institution";

(c) in subsection (5) after the words "sentence of imprisonment" insert the words "or detention in a young offender institution".

(6) In section 236 (conversion of sentences of detention into sentences of imprisonment), in section 99(5) of the Powers of Criminal Courts (Sentencing) Act 2000 ("the Sentencing Act") (as substituted by section 236)—

(a) in paragraph (a) for the words "section 90 or 91", substitute "section 90, 91 or 96";

(b) in paragraph (b) after the words "section 226" insert the words "or, in the case of a person aged at least 18 but under 21, a sentence of custody for life or detention in a young offender institution under section 225";

(c) in paragraph (c) after the words "section 228" insert the words "or, in the case of a person aged at least 18 but under 21, an extended sentence of detention in a young offender institution under section 227".

(7) In section 237 (meaning of "fixed-term prisoner") in subsection (1)(b) at the end insert the words "or a determinate sentence of detention in a young offender institution under section 96 of the Sentencing Act or section 227 of this Act".

(8) In section 238 (power of court to recommend licence conditions for certain prisoners) in subsection (1) after the words "a term of imprisonment" insert the words "or detention in a young offender institution".

(9) In section 240 (crediting periods of remand in custody: terms of imprisonment and detention), in subsection (10), after the words "of this Act" insert the words "or a sentence of detention in a young offender institution under section 96 of the Sentencing Act or section 227 of this Act".

(10) In section 244(3) (duty to release prisoners), in paragraph (a) after the words "section 91" insert the words "or 96".

(11) In section 250(4) (licence conditions), after the words "sentence of imprisonment" insert the words "or detention in a young offender institution".

(12) In section 258(3) (early release of fine defaulters and contemnors), after the words "sentences of imprisonment" insert the words "or detention in a young offender institution".

(13) In section 263(4) (concurrent terms) at the end insert the words "or a sentence of detention in a young offender institution under section 96 of the Sentencing Act or section 227 of this Act".

(14) In section 264(7) (consecutive terms) after the words "of this Act" insert the words "or a

sentence of detention in a young offender institution under section 96 of the Sentencing Act or section 227 of this Act".

(15) In section 265(2) (restriction on consecutive sentences for released prisoners) after the words "of this Act" insert the words "or a sentence of detention in a young offender institution under section 96 of the Sentencing Act or under section 227 of this Act".

(16) In Schedule 8 (breach, revocation or amendment of community order)—

(a) in paragraph 9(1)(c) after the words "sentence of imprisonment" insert the words "or, in the case of a person aged at least 18 but under 21, detention in a young offender institution,";

(b) in paragraph 10(1)(c) after the words "sentence of imprisonment" insert the words "or, in the case of a person aged at least 18 but under 21, detention in a young offender institution,".

(17) In Schedule 18 (release of prisoners serving sentences of imprisonment or detention for public protection)—

(a) in paragraph 2, in section 31A(5) of the Crime (Sentences) Act 1997 (as inserted by that paragraph), in the definition of "preventive sentence", after the words "a sentence of imprisonment" insert the words "or detention in a young offender institution";

(b) in paragraph 3, in section 34(2)(d) of the Crime (Sentences) Act 1997 (as inserted by that paragraph), after the words "a sentence of imprisonment" insert the words "or detention in a young offender institution";

(c) in paragraph 4, in section 82A(4A) of the Sentencing Act (as inserted by that paragraph), after the words "a sentence of imprisonment" insert the words "or detention in a young offender institution".

Criminal Justice (Sentencing) (Licence Conditions) Order 2005
(SI 2005/648)

3-3110   **1. Citation, commencement and interpretation.**   (1) This Order may be cited as the Criminal Justice (Sentencing) (Licence Conditions) Order 2005 and shall come into force on 4th April 2005.

(2) In this Order—

"the Act" means the Criminal Justice Act 2003;

"the 1991 Act" means the Criminal Justice Act 1991.

3-3111   **2. Standard conditions of licence.**   (1) The conditions set out in paragraph (2) are the standard conditions prescribed for the purposes of section 250 (1) of the Act.

(2) The prisoner must—

(a) keep in touch with the responsible officer as instructed by him;

(b) receive visits from the responsible officer as instructed by him;

(c) permanently reside at an address approved by the responsible officer and obtain the prior permission of the responsible officer for any stay of one or more nights at a different address;

(d) undertake work (including voluntary work) only with the approval of the responsible officer and obtain his prior approval in relation to any change in the nature of that work;

(e) not travel outside the United Kingdom, the Channel Islands or the Isle of Man without the prior permission of the responsible officer, except where he is deported or removed from the United Kingdom in accordance with the Immigration Act 1971 or the Immigration and Asylum Act 1999;

(f) be of good behaviour, and not behave in a way which undermines the purposes of the release on licence, which are to protect the public, prevent re-offending and promote successful re-integration into the community;

(g) not commit any offence.

3-3112   **3. Other conditions of licence.**   (1) Conditions of a kind set out in paragraph (2) are prescribed for the purposes of section 250(2)(b)(ii) and (4) (b) (ii) of the Act.

(2) The conditions are those which impose on a prisoner:

(a) a requirement that he reside at a certain place;

(b) a requirement relating to his making or maintaining contact with a person;

(c) a restriction relating to his making or maintaining contact with a person;

(d) a restriction on his participation in, or undertaking of, an activity;

(e) a requirement that he participate in, or co-operate with, a programme or set of activities designed to further one or more of the purposes referred to in section 250(8) of the Act;

(f) a requirement that he comply with a curfew arrangement;

(g) a restriction on his freedom of movement (which is not a requirement referred to in sub-paragraph (f));

(h) a requirement relating to his supervision in the community by a responsible officer.

(3) For the purpose of this article, "curfew arrangement" means an arrangement under which a prisoner is required to remain at a specified place for a specified period of time which is not an arrangement contained in a condition imposed by virtue of section 37A(1) of the 1991 Act or section 250(5) of the Act.

3–3113   4. Revocation and saving.   (1) The Criminal Justice (Sentencing) (Licence Conditions) Order 2003 is hereby revoked.

(2) The revocation of the instrument referred to in paragraph (1) does not affect the validity of conditions included in any licence granted under Chapter 6 of Part 12 of the Act before 4th April 2005 and in force on that date.

Remand in Custody (Effect of Concurrent and Consecutive Sentences of Imprisonment) Rules 2005
(SI 2005/2054)

3–3120   1.   (1) These Rules may be cited as the Remand in Custody (Effect of Concurrent and Consecutive Sentences of Imprisonment) Rules 2005 and shall come into force on the day after the day on which they are made.

(2) In these Rules "the 2003 Act" means the Criminal Justice Act 2003.

3–3121   2.   Section 240(3) of the 2003 Act does not apply in relation to a day for which an offender was remanded in custody—

(a) if on that day he was serving a sentence of imprisonment (and it was not a day on which he was on licence under Chapter 6 of Part 12 of the 2003 Act or Part 2 of the Criminal Justice Act 1991);or

(b) where the term of imprisonment referred to in subsection (1) of that section is ordered to be served consecutively on another term of imprisonment, if the length of that other term falls to be reduced by the same day by virtue of section 67 of the Criminal Justice Act 1967.

PART IV
ROAD TRAFFIC

Large Goods and Passenger Carrying Vehicles

Traffic Regulation

Construction and Use

Documentation (for Driver and Vehicle)

Drink Driving

The following references may be frequently required:

4–2 European Communities Act 1972: regulations. Within the scope of the title Road Traffic would logically fall the subject matter of a number of regulations made under the very wide enabling powers provided in s 2(2) of the European Communities Act 1972. Where such regulations create offences they are noted below in chronological order:

> Carriage of Goods (Prohibition of Discrimination) Regulations 1977, SI 1977/276;
> Motor Vehicles (Minimum Age for Driving) (Community Rules) Regulations 1975, in this Part, post;
> Passenger and Goods Vehicles (Recording Equipment) Regulations 1979, SI 1979/1746 amended by SI 1984/144, SI 1986/1457, SI 1986/2076, SI 1989/2016, SI 1991/381, SI 1994/1838, SI 1996/941 and SI 2006/3276;
> Motor Vehicles (Type Approval) (EEC Manufacturers) Regulations 1981, SI 1981/493;
> Road Transport (International Passenger Services) Regulations 1984, SI 1984/748 amended by SI 1987/1755, SI 1988/1809 and SI 2004/1882;
> Motor Vehicles (Type Approval) Regulations 1980, SI 1980/1182 amended by SI 1982/7, SI 1986/1501 and 1987, SI 1988/1103, SI 1989/2262 and SI 1991/2681 and 2830;
> Passenger and Goods Vehicles (Recording Equipment) Regulations 1989, SI 1989/2121;
> Motor Vehicles (EC Type Approval) Regulations 1992, SI 1992/3107 amended by SI 1998/2051 are revoked except in so far as they amend the Road Traffic Act 1988 and the Road Traffic Offenders Act 1988;
> Motor Vehicles (EC Type Approval) Regulations 1998, SI 1998/2051 amended by SI 1999/778 and 2324, SI 2000/869 and 2730, SI 2001/2908, SI 2002/1835 and 2743, SI 2003/1019 and 2428, SI 2004/73 and 2186, SI 2005/2454 and SI 2006/142, 1695, 2409 and 2816 make provision for the setting up of a system for granting EC Type-Approval for light passenger vehicles;
> Motor Cycles (EC Type Approval) Regulations 1999, SI 1999/2920 amended by SI 2001/368 and 1547, SI 2003/1099, SI 2004/1948 and 2539 and SI 2006/2935;
> Tractor etc (EC Type Approval) Regulations 2005, SI 2005/390 amended by SI 2006/2533.

Insurance claims between states within the EU or EEA. For the framework for satisfaction of claims and compensation, see the Motor Vehicles (Compulsory Insurance) (Information Centre and Compensation Body) Regulations 2003, SI 2003/37.

VEHICLES AND ROADS TO WHICH THE ACTS APPLY

4–3 Vehicles. The Road Traffic Act 1988 applies in the main to motor vehicles and trailers although specific sections relate to pedal cycles and pedestrians. A "motor vehicle" means a mechanically propelled vehicle intended or adapted for use on roads and "trailer" means a vehicle drawn by a "motor vehicle" (s 185(1)), but grass cutting machines controlled by a pedestrian and certain other pedestrian controlled vehicles to be specified by Regulations are excluded from the definition of "motor vehicle" (s 189(3)). The Vehicle Excise and Registration Act 1994 applies to mechanically propelled vehicles used or kept on any public road (ibid, s 1(1)).

A motor car does not necessarily cease to be a mechanically propelled vehicle by the mere temporary removal of its engine (*Newberry v Simmonds* [1961] 2 QB 345, [1961] 2 All ER 318, 125 JP 409). This case may be contrasted with *Smart v Allan* [1963] 1 QB 291, [1962] 3 All ER 893, 127 JP 35, where the contrary was held in respect of a vehicle that was a broken down wreck. See also *Binks v Department of the Environment* (1975) 119 Sol Jo 304 (car severely damaged but owner intending to repair it held to be a mechanically propelled vehicle). A pedal cycle fitted with an auxiliary motor, which was out of commission, was held not to be a mechanically propelled vehicle and therefore not a "motor vehicle" (*Lawrence v Howlett* [1952] 2 All ER 74, 116 JP 391). Contrast *Floyd v Bush* [1953] 1 All ER 265, 117 JP 88, where such a cycle was held to be a motor vehicle at a time when an efficient auxiliary motor, was not in use. See also *R v Tashin* [1970] RTR 88 (where it was held that the appropriate test in respect of cycles that can be propelled either by an engine or by the rider using the pedals was not "was the engine in working order" but "is the vehicle constructed so that it can be mechanically propelled") and *McEachran v Hurst* [1978] RTR 462. Generally, see (1966) 130 JP Jo 394.

"Intended or adapted for use on roads"—The test of whether a vehicle is "intended or adapted for use on roads" is whether a reasonable person, looking at the vehicle, and forming a view as to its general user, would say the vehicle might well be used on the road (*Chief Constable of Avon and Somerset v Fleming* [1987] 1 All ER 318, [1987] RTR 378). The burden of proving that a vehicle is intended or adapted for use on roads is on the prosecution (*Reader v Bunyard* [1987] RTR 406, [1987] Crim LR 274). In *Macdonald v Carmichael* 1941 JC 27, 106 JP Jo 53 (considered in *McCrone v J & L Rigby (Wigan) Ltd* [1951] 2 TLR 911), it was held that in the circumstances of the case a

diesel "dumper" was not intended or adapted for use on roads and was therefore not a "motor vehicle". It has been held in the absence of evidence supporting the contrary view, that a "dumper" used in the manner described in the case, was not "intended to be used on a road" (*Daley v Hargreaves* [1961] 1 All ER 552, 125 JP 193), but a 30-ton earth mover which because of its size was not transportable and had to move from site to site under its own power was held to be intended to be used on roads (*Childs v Coghlan* (1968) 112 Sol Jo 175, and see, related to the facts of the particular case, *Burns v Currell* [1963] 2 QB 433, [1963] 2 All ER 297, 127 JP 397, in which it was held that a Go-Kart was not "intended or adapted for use on roads"); also *Percy v Smith* [1986] RTR 252 in which a fork lift truck was in the circumstances of the case "intended . . . for use on roads", despite its licensing as a works truck. In *Chief Constable of North Yorkshire Police v Saddington* (2000) 165 JP 122, [2001] RTR 15, [2001] Crim LR 41. a motorised scooter known as a 'Go-ped' which did not comply with the Construction and Use Regulations, would not be accepted by DVLA for registration which the manufacturers stated did not comply with UK safety standards and was not intended for operation on public streets, roads or pathways and should not be used in traffic or on wet, frozen, oily or loose surfaces was held to be a motor vehicle intended for use on roads. The test was not whether a reasonable person would use the conveyance on a road but whether a reasonable person looking at the vehicle would say that one of its users would be a road user. Was some general use on the roads contemplated as one of its uses; the roadworthiness as a conveyance was not decisive. A reasonable person would say that one of its uses would be general use on the roads, not merely isolated use or use by a man losing his senses. Surrender to the temptation to use it on a road would not be an isolated occurrence. "Adapted" in this connotation means "fit" or "apt" (*Burns v Currell,* supra). It means "fit and apt for the purpose"—not "altered so as to be apt" (*Maddox v Storer* [1963] 1 QB 451, [1962] 1 All ER 831, 126 JP 263). When the word "adapted" is used disjunctively from "constructed", as in the definition of a "goods vehicle" (Road Traffic Act 1988, s 192(1)), it means not "suitable", but "altered so as to make the vehicle apt" (*French v Champkin* [1920] 1 KB 76, 83 JP 258; cf *Vincent v Whitehead* [1966] 1 All ER 917, 130 JP 214).

"*Trailer*"—This means anything on wheels (eg a poultry shed) drawn by a motor vehicle (*Garner v Burr* [1951] 1 KB 31, [1950] 2 All ER 683, 114 JP 484).

4–4 *Exemptions for invalid carriages*

(1) In the case of a vehicle which is an invalid carriage complying with the prescribed requirements[1] and which is being used in accordance with the prescribed conditions[1]—

    (a) no statutory provision prohibiting or restricting the use of footways shall prohibit or restrict the use of that vehicle on a footway;

    (b) if the vehicle is mechanically propelled, it shall be treated [for the purposes of the Road Traffic Regulation Act 1984 and the Road Traffic Act 1988 and the Road Traffic Offenders Act 1988, except section 22A of that Act (causing danger to road users by interfering with motor vehicles etc)] as not being a motor vehicle and sections 1 to 4, 163, 170 and 181 of the Road Traffic Act 1988 shall not apply to it; and

    (c) whether or not the vehicle is mechanically propelled, it shall be exempted from the requirements of [section 83 of the Road Traffic Act 1988].

(2) In this section—

"footway" means a way which is a footway, footpath or bridleway within the meaning of the Highways Act 1980;

"invalid carriage" means a vehicle, whether mechanically propelled or not, constructed or adapted for use for the carriage of one person, being a person suffering from some physical defect or disability;

"prescribed" means prescribed by regulations made by the Minister of Transport;

"statutory provision" means a provision contained in or having effect under, any enactment.

(3) Any regulations made under this section shall be made by statutory instrument, may make different provision for different circumstances and shall be subject to annulment in pursuance of a resolution of either House of Parliament.

[Chronically Sick and Disabled Persons Act 1970, s 20, as amended by the Highways Act 1980, Sch 24, the Road Traffic Act 1972, Sch 7, the Road Traffic Regulation Act 1984, Sch 13, the Road Traffic (Consequential Provisions) Act 1988, Sch 3 and the Road Traffic Act 1991, Sch 4.]

---

1. See the Use of Invalid Carriages on Highways Regulations 1988, in this PART, post. Disabled persons are able to use a badge on a motor vehicle allowing certain exemptions from parking restrictions; see the Road Traffic Regulation Act 1984, s 117, post as to wrongful use of such a badge.

SOME KEY TERMS AND CONCEPTS IN ROAD TRAFFIC LAW

4–5 **"Road".** "Road" means any highway and any other road to which the public has access and includes bridges over which a road passes (Road Traffic Act 1988, s 192(1)). In determining whether a place is a "road" for the purposes of the 1988 Act, the question to be asked, if the place is not a highway, is whether it is a road to which the general public have actual and legal access. A road has the physical character of a defined or definable route or way, with ascertained or ascertainable edges, leading from one point to another with the function of serving as a means of access enabling travellers to move conveniently from one point to another along a definable route and, accordingly, the question whether a place is a "road" is always one of fact. In the ordinary use of language a car park is not a "road" since they have separate and distinct characters and functions: the proper function of a road is to enable movement along it to a destination, whereas the proper function of a car park is to enable stationary vehicles to stand and wait (*Cutter v Eagle Star Insurance Co Ltd* [1998] 4 All ER 417, [1998] 1 WLR 1647, *sub nom Clarke v General Accident Fire and Life Assurance Corpn plc* [1999] RTR 153, HL).

It is irrelevant whether the way is a road within the ordinary meaning of the word; therefore, a footpath which is a highway is a road within the meaning of s 192(1) (*Lang v Hindhaugh* [1986] RTR 271). The expression "public road" in the Vehicle Excise and Registration Act 1994 means a road which is repairable at the public expense (ibid, s 62(1)). "Road" includes the footway as well as the carriageway (*Bryant v Marx* (1932) 96 JP 383, [1932] All ER Rep 518). A private occupation road leading to a farm, if at the time the public has access, is a road (*Harrison v Hill* 1932 SC 13). The mere fact that residents and their visitors used an access road to a council's housing estate does not mean that the public generally have access (see *Deacon v A T (a juvenile)* [1976] Crim LR 135). A road within the fenced boundaries of a factory (being a protected place), the factory being accessible only to those with a special pass, was held not to be within this definition (*O'Brien v Trafalgar Insurance Co Ltd* (1945) 109 JP 107; *Harrison v Hill* supra; *Bugge v Taylor* infra, distinguished). Inclusion of a lane as a footpath on a definitive map of a county drawn up under a National Parks and Access to the Countryside Act 1949 will not in itself extinguish ancient vehicular rights (*Suffolk County Council v Mason* (1977) Times, 16 March).

Similarly, in *Buchanan v Motor Insurers' Bureau* [1955] 1 All ER 607, 119 JP 227, it was held that a road in a dock area was not a road within this definition, the general public having no access thereto as a matter of legal right or by tolerance. For the purposes of s 78 of the Road Traffic Act 1988 (weighing of motor vehicles) harbour lands can be included in the definition of a road (s 178 (8)). By virtue of s 26 of the British Transport Commission Act 1961(9 & 10 Eliz 2 c xxxvi), as amended by the Transport Act 1962, 2nd Sch, the word "road" in ss 1, 2, 3, 4, 5, 17, 18, 19, 21, 22, 23, 24, 25, 29, 30, 84, 99, 143, 159, 161, 162 and 166 of the 1971 Act includes a dock road[1] of the Railways Board, the Docks Board, or the British Waterways Board.

Traffic regulation orders may be made in special areas of the countryside (see Road Traffic Regulation Act 1984, ss 1 and 22) and may include Crown roads[2] (see ibid, ss 131 and 132). A person who uses a road within the definition of the Road Traffic Act 1988, s 192(1) which is also a Crown Road will be bound by the road traffic enactments notwithstanding that the Minister has not made an order under s 131 of the 1984 Act[3].

By virtue of s 66 of the Airports Act 1986, the road traffic enactments[4] apply to roads which are within aerodromes owned or managed by the British Airports Authority, notwithstanding that the public does not have access to such roads. The Secretary of State may by order[5] direct that in their application to roads within these aerodromes the road traffic enactments shall have effect subject to such modifications as appear necessary. The Inward Freight Immigration lanes at Eastern Docks, Dover, have been held to be roads to which the public has access (*DPP v Coulman* [1993] RTR 230, [1993] Crim LR 399, explained in *DPP v Neville* (1995) 160 JP 758, DC).

In *Bugge v Taylor* [1941] 1 KB 198, 104 JP 467, it was held that the magistrates' court had rightly held to be a road the private forecourt of a hotel to which the public had access, but this decision was distinguished in *Thomas v Dando* [1951] 2 KB 620, [1951] 1 All ER 1010, 115 JP 344, when it was held that the magistrates' court was correct in deciding that an unpaved forecourt to a shop, unfenced from pavement and habitually crossed by customers was not a "road". Elements of tolerance and consent are irrelevant. The question is one of degree: a mere slight degree of access by the public is not enough to satisfy the definition of "road" in s 192 of the Road Traffic Act 1988 (*Cox v White* [1976] RTR 248, [1976] Crim LR 263).

A caravan park has been held to be a place to which the public have access; the questions to be asked are whether persons admitted formed a special class in that they passed through a screening process for a reason or on account of some characteristic personal to themselves, or whether they were members of the public being admitted as such and being processed simply so as to make them subject to payment and whatever other conditions the landowner chose to impose (*DPP v Vivier* [1991] 4 All ER 18, [1991] RTR 205, DC; see also *R v Spence* (1999) 163 JP 754, [1999] RTR 353, CA). A causeway, sometimes submerged, sometimes passable, linking a small island with only a few residents to the mainland, and with signs by the entrance to the approach road from the mainland to indicate that it was private, was not a "public place"[6].

The Road Traffic Act 1991 in substituting new ss 1, 2 and 3 to the 1988 Act made the offences of causing death by dangerous driving, dangerous driving, careless and inconsiderate driving apply to driving on a road or other public place, where previously such offences had applied only to driving on a road. Similarly the Motor Vehicles (Compulsory Insurance) Regulations 2000, SI 2000/726, made in the light of the decision in *Cutter v Eagle Star Insurance Co Ltd* supra that a car park is not a 'road', have extended the compulsory insurance requirements; the duty to provide name and address and produce documents to a constable: and the duty to stop and report an accident to a road 'or other public place'.

---

1. A dock road is defined as "any road, pier, wharf, quay, bridge, work or land which is situate within any dock or harbour premises of the Board (not being a road as defined by section 192 of the Road Traffic Act 1988)". Section 26 of the 1961 Act gives the protection of the 1988 Act to users of dock areas: see *Botwood v Phillips* [1976] RTR 260, [1976] Crim LR 68; followed in *R v Murray* [1984] RTR 203 (meaning of "dock road" under Mersey Docks and Harbour Board

Act 1971, s 11). The fact that staff drove their cars through a station car park on their way to a staff car park did not render the former capable of being a road (*Brewer v DPP* [2004] EWHC 355 (Admin), [2005] RTR 5).

    2. See the Crown Roads (Royal Parks) (Application of Road Traffic Enactments) Order 1987, SI 1987/363 and the Crown Roads (Industrial Estates) (Application of Road Traffic Enactments) Order 1978, SI 1978/749.

    3. See *Kellett v Daisy* [1977] RTR 396.

    4. For meaning of "the road traffic enactments" and "airports", see Airports Act 1986, s 63(3), post.

    5. See the Aerodrome Traffic (Gatwick) Order 1976, SI 1976/1494, the Aerodrome Traffic (Heathrow) Order 1976, SI 1976/1495, and the Aerodrome Traffic (Stansted) Order 1976, SI 1976/1496.

    6. *Planton v DPP* [2001] EWHC Admin 450, [2002] RTR 107, 166 JP 324.

4–6   "Using". A motor vehicle is "used on a road" where it has been placed on a road, with battery removed, and incapable of being driven[1]; or where the tyres were deflated, the handbrake was on, the rear brakes seized and the gearbox contained no oil because there was a leak in the transmission pipe[2]. The same principles apply to offences of using a vehicle without insurance (RTA 1988, s 143) and without a current test certificate (RTA 1988, s 47), namely that provided (i) a vehicle is a "motor vehicle" within the definition in s 185 of the Act, and (ii) the vehicle is on a road, the owner of the vehicle has the use of it on a road whether at the material time it can move on its wheels or not[2]. Even if the defendant had no intention of using the vehicle he may still be held to have "used" it, for "use" is to be interpreted to mean "to have the use of the motor vehicle on the road"[3].

    A passenger not driving or controlling a car but acting in concert with others as a joint enterprise[4], or being driven for his own purposes by another person[5] may still be using the vehicle. If the owner's employee in the strict sense of the master-servant relationship is driving the vehicle, the employer can be regarded as being vicariously responsible[6].

    Where an offence is not merely an offence of user, but can also be an offence of causing or permitting the user, a restricted meaning should be given to the word "use". This restricted meaning involves construing the word "use" as being limited to the driver of the vehicle and to the owner of the vehicle provided, first, that the driver is employed by the owner under a contract of service, that is, he is an employee; and secondly, that at the material time the driver was driving on his employer's business[7]. The same test of 'user' of a motor vehicle applies to prosecutions for use of a motor vehicle without third party insurance[8]. Nevertheless, it has been suggested that the principle stated above may not be appropriate with regard to the use of trailers[9], nor may it be applicable in certain circumstances to the use of a combination vehicle[10].

    1. *Elliott v Gray* [1960] 1 QB 367, [1959] 3 All ER 733, 124 JP 58; *B (a minor) v Knight* [1981] RTR 136.

    2. *Pumbien v Vines* [1996] RTR 37, [1996] Crim LR 124.

    3. *Eden v Mitchell* [1975] RTR 425, [1975] Crim LR 502, (1975) 119 Sol Jo 645. See also *Richmond upon Thames London Borough Council v Merton (West Yorkshire v Lex)* [2000] RTR 79 for the broader meaning of "use" in connection with the various Greater London (Restriction of Goods Vehicles) Traffic Orders.

    4. *Leathley v Tatton* [1980] RTR 21 and *Stinton v Stinton* [1995] RTR 167, CA.

    5. *Cobb v Williams* [1973] RTR 113.

    6. *Bennett v Richardson* [1980] RTR 358 (passenger, a business partner of the driver, not convicted).

    7. *West Yorkshire Trading Standards Service v Lex Vehicle Leasing Ltd* [1996] RTR 70 (self-employed contract or driving car transporter owned by the defendant company on company business—permitted laden weight exceeded by vehicle—held the company was not using the transporter).

    8. *Jones v DPP* (1998) 163 JP 121, [1999] RTR 1.

    9. See *NFC Forwarding Ltd v DPP* [1989] RTR 239.

    10. See *Hallett Silberman Ltd v Cheshire County Council* [1993] RTR 32 (wheeled trailer owned by defendant haulage company towed by vehicle owned by self-employed driver; defendant company responsible for loading, specifying and notifying highway authority of identity and route to be taken—held the defendant company had been properly convicted of using the heavy motor car drawing a wheeled trailer when the combined weight of the vehicle and trailer exceeded the maximum permitted laden weight).

4–7   "Causing" and "permitting". Many provisions of road traffic legislation in this title penalise one who causes or permits an offence. To *cause* the user involves some express mandate from the person 'causing' the other person, or some authority to the latter, arising in the circumstances of the case (*Redhead Freight Ltd v Shulman* [1989] RTR 1). The meaning of 'permits' depends on the context and on the provision contravened. It will include 'allowed' or 'authorised' and will usually import knowledge on the part of the person permitting of the activity being carried on or expected to be carried on. In some provisions however, for example, offences contrary to s 96(11A) of the Transport Act 1968 (breaches of community rules as to periods of driving) the meaning of 'permitted' is wider and embraces 'failed to take reasonable steps to prevent'. The prosecution may establish liability where it proves that the person permitting did so with actual knowledge of the activity and knowledge may be inferred from the nature of the act done; or that the defendant shut his eyes to an obvious means of knowledge (*Roper v Taylor's Central Garages (Exeter) Ltd* [1951] 2 TLR 284, DC). Thirdly, in those cases where there is a duty on the defendant to take reasonable steps to prevent the breach, the prosecution may prove that the defendant failed to take such reasonable steps (*Vehicle Inspectorate v Nuttall* [1999] 3 All ER 833, [1999] 1 WLR 629, [1999] RTR 264). The prosecution must nevertheless prove that the defendant must have perceived the possibility that the community rules on drivers hours might be contravened. This would be a matter for the court to draw such inferences as are appropriate from all the evidence in the case (*Vehicle Inspectorate v Nuttall* supra, *Yorkshire Traction v Vehicle Inspectorate* [2001] EWHC Admin 190, [2001] RTR 518).

    For a corporate body to be guilty of permitting an offence, it must be proved that some person, for whose criminal act the body was responsible permitted, and not merely committed, the offence (*James Smee & Son Ltd v Smee, Green v Burnett* [1955] 1 QB 78, [1954] 3 All ER 273, 118 JP 536).

The same principle applies to an allegation of causing an offence (*Ross Hillman Ltd v Bond* [1974] QB 435, [1974] 2 All ER 287, 138 JP 428). The court may infer from subsequent conduct that a person in effective control of a company had knowledge or means of knowledge of earlier irregularities (*Knowles Transport Ltd v Russell* [1975] RTR 87).

To make a person liable for permitting, he must be in a position to forbid another person to use the motor vehicle, eg the owner (*Goodbarne v Buck* [1940] 1 KB 771, [1940] 1 All ER 613), or the person otherwise in charge thereof (*Lloyd v Singleton* [1953] 1 QB 357, [1953] 1 All ER 291, 117 JP 97).

An express permission may be general or particular, as distinguished from a mandate. The other person is not told to use the vehicle in a particular way, but he is told that he may do so if he desires. However permission may also be inferred. If the other person is given the control of the vehicle, permission may be inferred if the vehicle is left at the other person's liberty to use it in the manner in which it was used (see *McLeod (Houston) v Buchanan* [1940] 2 All ER 179, per Lord Wright, approved in *Shave v Rosner* [1954] 2 QB 113, [1954] 2 All ER 280, 118 JP 364 and approved in *Sopp v Long* [1970] 1 QB 518, [1969] 1 All ER 855, 133 JP 261).

Permitting no insurance—A person who is ignorant of the fact that there is no insurance in force in relation to a vehicle, may, nevertheless, be guilty of the offence of permitting uninsured use if he permits the use of the vehicle (*Lyons v May* [1948] 2 All ER 1062, 113 JP 42; *Tapsell v Maslen* (1966) 110 Sol Jo 853). A mistaken belief that the use is covered by insurance would not be a defence to a charge of permitting, but a use contrary to the terms of the permission or authority to use the vehicle is capable of amounting to a good defence: see *Sheldon Deliveries Ltd v Willis* [1972] RTR 217; *Newbury v Davis* [1974] RTR 367; followed in *Baugh v Crago* [1975] RTR 453 (where the issue of insurance cover turned on whether the person permitted to drive held a driving licence). However, the decision in *Newbury v Davis*, supra, must be regarded with extreme caution, and its ratio is applicable only in exceptional circumstances (*Chief Constable of Norfolk v Fisher* (1991) 156 JP 93, [1991] Crim LR 787—a person who lends his car to another cannot avoid liability for permitting use of vehicle without insurance merely by asking the other to be insured before using it). This principle was applied also in *Ferrymasters Ltd v Adams* [1980] RTR 139, where an employer was convicted of an offence under s 84(2) of the Road Traffic Act 1972 (see now s 87 of the Road Traffic Act 1988) (employee failing to renew his driving licence and driving employer's vehicle in the course of his employment). The same construction of 'permits' in s 143 is applied to s 158:

> 'A permission which would arise only subject to and upon the fulfilment of a condition is not a permission until that condition is fulfilled. However, a permission is given for the purposes of the section when there is an honest, although mistaken, belief as to the circumstances of the person to whom permission is given. A permission does not cease to be a permission for the purposes of the statute because, in good faith, the person giving it believes that the person to whom it is given is covered by the policy when in fact that person is not.'

per Pill LJ in *Lloyd-Wolper v Moore* [2004] EWCA Civ 766, [2004] 3 All ER 741, [2004] 1 WLR 2350, [2004] RTR 30.

Hirers—A person hiring out a vehicle when he ought to know it may be used as a stage carriage, permits it to be used in the manner in which the hirer directs that person's servant to use it, because he has connived at what was going on (*Goldsmith v Deakin* (1933) 98 JP 4). But it would not be "permitting", if the person did not know that the vehicle was to be, or was being, used as a stage carriage, and did not deliberately refrain from making inquiries or shut his eyes to the obvious (*Evans v Dell* [1937] 1 All ER 349, 101 JP 149; *Goldsmith v Deakin*, supra, distinguished). Notwithstanding any agreement to the contrary, if warned that it will be so used, and he does not take adequate steps to prevent the user, he also permits it to be so used (*Webb v Maidstone and District Motor Services* (1934) 78 Sol Jo 336). But where there are no circumstances which ought either to have aroused his suspicion or put him on his guard, a dismissal was upheld on appeal (*Phillips v Autocars Services Ltd* (11 April 1936, unreported). Also where a driver did not know and had no reason to know that any part of a taxicab fare was or would be paid by other passengers—which by the Passenger Vehicles Act 1981, ss 1, 2 and Sch 1, does not now constitute an "express carriage"—a dismissal of a charge of permitting the vehicle to be used as an express carriage was upheld on appeal (*Newell v Cook*, *Newell v Chenery* [1936] 2 KB 632, [1936] 2 All ER 203, 100 JP 371).

4-8 "Driver" and "driving". The word "driver", except for the purposes of s 1 of the Road Traffic Act 1988 (causing death by dangerous driving), includes a separate person acting as steersman of a motor vehicle as well as any other person engaged in the driving of the vehicle and the word "drive" is to be construed accordingly (Road Traffic Act 1988, s 192 (1)). This section and the previous corresponding legislation contemplates that two persons, one acting as "steersman", can be classified as driving the same vehicle, eg on a traction engine, and this was so held in *Langman v Valentine* [1952] 2 All ER 803, 116 JP 576 and *R v Wilkins* (1951) 115 JP 443. The essence of driving is the use of the driver's controls in order to direct movement, however that movement is produced (*R v MacDonagh* [1974] QB 448, [1974] 2 All ER 257); accordingly a person who sits in the driver's seat of a vehicle and controls it while it is being towed is driving the vehicle (*McQuaid v Anderton* [1980] 3 All ER 540, [1981] 1 WLR 154, 144 JP 456), and so is a person sitting in the driver's seat and setting the car in motion, even though he had no keys, the engine was not running, and the steering was locked (*Burgoyne v Phillips* (1982) 147 JP 375, [1983] RTR 49). See also *Tyler v Whatmore* [1976] RTR 83 where the defendant was held to have been driving for the purposes of reg 104 of the Motor Vehicles (Construction and Use) Regulations 1986 (driver to be in position to have proper control) where she was in the passenger seat, leaning across and controlling the driving wheel, handbrake and ignition, whilst her companion in the driving seat operated the gears and foot controls. A limited company cannot "drive" a vehicle (*Richmond upon Thames London Borough Council v Pinn & Wheeler Ltd* (1989) 133 Sol Jo 389, [1989] Crim LR 510, DC).

A person can be said to be driving if the vehicle, when moving, is subject to his control and direction, and it has been held that he is not driving unless he is in the driving seat *or* in control of the steering wheel and has also something to do with the propulsion of the vehicle (*R v Roberts* [1965] 1 QB 85, [1964] 2 All ER 541, 128 JP 395; but see *Tyler v Whatmore*, supra). A front seat passenger who momentarily grabs the steering wheel cannot properly be said to be driving the car: in borderline cases it is important to consider the length of time the steering wheel or other control was handled (*Jones v Pratt* [1983] RTR 54; followed in *DPP v Hastings* (1993) 158 JP 118). The steersman of a towed vehicle is undoubtedly driving it for the purpose of the offence of driving while disqualified (*Caise v Wright, Fox v Wright* [1981] RTR 49). If the vehicle is being pushed, such a person at the wheel would be in the category of driver (*R v Spindley* [1961] Crim LR 486), if he is acting in common design with those pushing, and those pushing would be aiding and abetting him and could be properly charged (*Shimmell v Fisher* [1951] 2 All ER 672, 115 JP 526). A person walking beside a vehicle which is being pushed or moving under gravity will not be "driving" merely because he has his hand on the steering wheel (*R v MacDonagh* [1974] QB 448, [1974] 2 All ER 257, 138 JP 488). However, being in and using the brakes of a vehicle being towed to assist the towing vehicle is "driving" (and "using") (*R (on the application of Traves) v DPP* [2005] EWHC Admin 1482, (2005) 169 JP 421).

In the case of a motor cycle, it has been held that a person who sits astride it and propels it with his feet in a paddling movement, with hands on the handlebars so as to control direction, but without the engine running, was driving (*Gunnel v DPP* [1994] RTR 151 [1993] Crim LR 619). A defendant, wearing a crash helmet, who was astride a motorcycle, the exhaust of which was warm, and in substantial control of the movement and direction of the motorcycle was held to be driving although the engine was not actually running when he was apprehended (*McKoen v Ellis* (1986) 151 JP 60, [1987] RTR 26). In *Shaw v Knill* [1973] Crim LR 622, pushing a motor cycle on a car park which was not a public road, with the intent of riding it on a road, was held to be an attempt to drive while disqualified.

A person in the driving seat when a vehicle is in motion is deemed to be the driver and the onus is on him to show that he is not responsible, eg owing to a state of automatism induced by illness or accident (*Hill v Baxter* [1958] 1 QB 277, [1958] 1 All ER 193, 122 JP 134; *Watmore v Jenkins* [1962] 2 QB 572, [1962] 2 All ER 868, 126 JP 432).

In a case of alleged wheel spinning, it has been held that such an activity can constitute "driving" even though it is driving in such a way as to ensure that the vehicle does not move forwards while the drive wheels are turning (*DPP v Alderton* [2003] EWHC 2917 (Admin), [2004] RTR 23).

For the purposes of s 170 of the Road Traffic Act 1988 which imposes duties on drivers in the case of accidents, it has been held that the person who takes the vehicle on the road remains the driver while in the vehicle although both engine and vehicle have come to rest (*Jones v Prothero* [1952] 1 All ER 434, 116 JP 141).

Similarly, a defendant who had parked his car at the side of the road to post a letter and whilst he was not present, it had rolled down the road and struck a brick wall was the 'driver' for the purposes of s 170 of the 1988 Act (*Cawthorn v Newcastle upon Tyne Crown Court* (1999) 164 JP 527, DC).

4–9 "Dangerous" and "careless/inconsiderate driving". Causing death by dangerous driving is an indictable offence under s 1 of the Road Traffic Act 1988 and Sch 2 to the Road Traffic Offenders Act 1988; dangerous driving is a triable either way offence under s 2 and Sch 2; careless and inconsiderate driving is a summary offence under s 3 and Sch 2.

To summarise the position, in order to secure a conviction for driving without due care and attention, the prosecutor must prove beyond reasonable doubt that the defendant was not exercising that degree of care and attention that a reasonable and prudent driver would exercise in the circumstances. That standard is an objective one, impersonal and universal, fixed in relation to the safety of other users of the highway. If the facts are such that in the absence of an explanation put forward by the defendant, or that explanation is objectively inadequate, and the only possible conclusion is that he was careless, he should be convicted (*DPP v Cox* (1993) 157 JP 1044).

The meaning of "dangerous driving" is defined in s 2A of the 1988 Act as substituted by the Road Traffic Act 1991; the latter Act replaced the previous offence of reckless driving.

"Failure" to observe any provision of the Highway Code issued by the Minister (contained in this PART, post) may be relied upon by either party as tending to establish or negative liability in proceedings for an offence under the Road Traffic Act 1988 (see s 38 thereof, post). Evidence of the manner of driving three miles away may be given, the weight to be given to it being a matter for the justices (*R v Burdon* (1927) 20 Cr App Rep 80; *Hallett v Warren* (1929) 93 JP 225).

The same standard of care and attention is required from the learner as from the ordinary driver. The matter is governed by the essential needs of the public on the highway (*McCrone v Riding* [1938] 1 All ER 157, 102 JP 109). If someone was driving without due care and attention according to the objective and fixed standard required of all drivers, however inexperienced, it is immaterial to consider why he was so driving (*R v Preston Justices, ex p Lyons* [1982] RTR 173—learner driver failing to check that it was safe to perform a practice emergency stop where instructor directed that he need not check). In a civil case it has been held that good character evidence is of little, if indeed any, weight in determining fault for an accident; "Every driver is a careful driver until he makes a careless mistake": per Jonathan Parker LJ in *Hatton v Cooper* [2001] EWCA Civ 623, [2001] RTR 544. No motorist is called upon to achieve a standard of perfection when he is suddenly confronted with some kind of emergency (*Jones v Crown Court at Bristol* (1985) 150 JP 93, 83 Cr App Rep 109—driver of a laden articulated lorry on motorway in hours of darkness when lights failed). No special standards of due care and attention are applicable to police drivers summoned to an emergency: courts may however reflect the circumstances in the penalty, if any, imposed by them (*Wood v Richards* [1977] RTR 201). There is no rule of law that the driver of a vehicle must be able to pull up within the limits of his vision (see *Morris v Luton Corpn* [1946] KB 114, [1946] 1 All ER 1, 110 JP 102, in which was criticised a dictum of SCRUTTON LJ, in *Baker v E Longhurst & Sons Ltd* [1933] 2 KB 461). Each case must depend objectively on its own facts whether there was exercised that degree of care and attention which a reasonable and prudent driver would exercise in the circumstances; *Tidy v Battman* [1934] 1 KB 319, CA; *Stewart v Hancock* [1940] 2 All ER 427; *Simpson v Peat* [1952] 2 QB 24, [1952] 1 All ER 447, 116 JP 151; *Scott v M'Intosh* 1935 SLT 171; *Waring v Kenyon & Co (1927) Ltd* (1935) 79 Sol Jo 306; *Taylor v Rogers* (1960) 124 JP 217.

A following driver who collides with a vehicle making an emergency stop is not *prima facie* driving without due care and attention (*Scott v Warren* [1974] Crim LR 117); nor is a driver who emerges from a side road and collides with a vehicle on a main road; whether the driving is careless is a subjective matter (*Walker v Tolhurst* [1976] Crim LR 261). As to the effect of driving over crossings controlled by traffic lights, see *Joseph Eva Ltd v Reeves* [1938] 2 KB 393, [1938] 2 All ER 115, 102 JP 261, CA. As to the effect of failing to conform to a white line, see *Evans v Cross* [1938] 1 KB 694, [1938] 1 All ER 751, 102 JP 127. A skid may or may not be due to negligence (*Laurie v Raglan Building Co* [1942] 1 KB 152, [1941] 3 All ER 332; cf *Richley v Faull* [1965] 3 All ER 109, 129 JP 498). Where the rear of a lorry swung in an anti-clockwise direction, and then the other way, when there was no evidence of mechanical defect or other reason for those movements, and the justices found as fact that the driver had applied his brakes, something which he admitted in evidence would tend to "make matters worse" after such movements, the justices were entitled to convict of careless driving on the basis that the braking was not the action of a reasonable, prudent and competent driver (*R (on the application of Bingham) v DPP* [2003] EWHC 247 (Admin), (2003) 167 JP 422). Where a car left the road and rolled over, and no explanation was given, the inference that the defendant was not driving with due care and attention was not a matter of speculation but was an overwhelming inference which a court could properly draw (*Jarvis v Williams* [1979] RTR 497). In our view the concept of overwhelming inference should be applied with great care; see for example *Jarvis v Fuller* [1974] RTR 160 where it was held that the fact that the driver did not see a cyclist until he was 6 to 8 feet away did not justify a positive conclusion that he was driving at a speed which did not enable him to pull up within the limits of his vision; also *Webster v Wall* [1980] RTR 284 where the motorcyclist driving on dipped headlight in adverse weather conditions saw an unlighted parked car in sufficient time to start to pull out but not to avoid hitting it, and was acquitted of careless driving.

If a driver is adversely affected by drink, this fact is a circumstance relevant to the issue of whether he was driving dangerously. While evidence to this effect is of probative value and is admissible in law, the mere fact that the driver had had a drink is not of itself relevant. Moreover, in order to render evidence as to the drink taken by the driver admissible, such evidence must tend to show that the amount of drink taken was such as would adversely affect a driver or, alternatively, that the driver was in fact adversely affected (*R v McBride* [1962] 2 QB 167, [1961] 3 All ER 6; followed in *R v Woodward* [1995] 3 All ER 79, [1995] 1 WLR 375 [1995] 2 Cr App Rep 388). Where the prosecution can prove recent consumption of cocaine, that is per se relevant to the issue of driving dangerously in contrast to modest consumption of alcohol (*R v Pleydell* [2005] EWCA Crim 1447, [2006] 1 Cr App R 12, 169 JP 400, [2006] Crim LR 425).

That a driver allows himself to be overtaken by sleep is not a defence to a charge under s 3 (*Kay v Butterworth* (1945) 110 JP 75, followed by *Henderson v Jones* (1955) 119 JP 304, explaining the decision in *Edwards v Clarke* (1950) referred to in 115 JPJo 426). If a defendant raises the defence of automatism, he must introduce sufficient evidence to raise a doubt: this will usually be medical evidence (*Moses v Winder* [1980] Crim LR 232). Whether there is evidence of automatism is a question of law; the justices must decide on the evidence whether the defendant was not conscious of what he was doing and that his actions were automatic and involuntary throughout the period of the driving in question (*Broome v Perkins* [1987] RTR 321, 85 Cr App Rep 321). If the driving complained of is due to a mechanical defect in the vehicle, this will afford a defence to the charge, unless the defendant was aware of the defect or it could have been discovered by him by the exercise of reasonable prudence (*R v Spurge* [1961] 2 QB 205, [1961] 2 All ER 688, 125 JP 502). Evidence of regular servicing, which failed to cure a defect, will not necessarily provide a defence however; see *Haynes v Swain* [1974] Crim LR 483, [1974] RTR 40.

In s 3, the expression "other persons using the road" extends to passengers in the vehicle and is not confined to persons outside it (*Pawley v Wharldall* [1966] 1 QB 373, [1965] 2 All ER 757, 129 JP 444).

SUMMARY OF FIXED PENALTIES

4–10 Introduction. The law and procedure concerning these topics is complicated. The purpose of the ensuing paragraphs is to provide a simple guide. For more detailed study, users of this work should refer to the provisions to which reference is made in the footnotes[1].

1. The Road Safety Act 2006 makes a number of changes to the fixed penalty system. At the date at which this work states the law, those provisions had not been brought into force.

4–11   Fixed penalties: overview.   Many road traffic offences, including some that are endorsable, may be dealt with by way of a fixed penalty[1] rather than by way of prosecution.

Payment of the amount of the fixed penalty[2] discharges any liability to conviction of the offence to which the fixed penalty notice relates[3].

A fixed penalty may be given to a person or affixed to a vehicle.

It should be noted that the summaries that follow do not cover every procedural aspect of the fixed penalty system.

[1]   For the list of fixed penalty offences see Sch 3 to the Road Traffic Offenders Act 1988 (RTOA 1988), at para **4–1770**, post.
[2]   As to the amounts, see the Fixed Penalty Order 2000, SI 2000/2972, amended by SI 2003/1254, at para **4–4383**, post.
[3]   Fixed penalty notices are defined in RTOA 1988, s 52, at para **4–1706**, post.

4–12   *Fixed penalty given to a person on-the-spot or at a police station*
   (*a*)   Where a constable in uniform has reason to believe that a person he finds is committing or has on that occasion committed a fixed penalty offence the constable may give him a fixed penalty notice in respect of the offence.
   (*b*)   If the fixed penalty offence is an offence involving obligatory endorsement a fixed penalty notice may be given, provided the offender would not be liable to points disqualification if he were convicted of that offence[1] and he surrenders his licence and its counterpart to the constable.
   (*c*)   If the offender does not produce his licence and its counterpart to the constable for inspection, the constable may issue a "provisional" fixed penalty notice. If the licence and its counterpart are then surrendered at the police station specified in the notice within 7 days and the offender would not be liable to points' disqualification for the offence concerned, the offer of a fixed penalty must be confirmed.
   (*d*)   Where a fixed penalty notice is given to any person, this acts as a bar to any criminal proceedings against that person for the fixed penalty offence unless he requests a hearing in respect of the offence before the end of the suspended enforcement period[2].
   (*e*)   Failure to request a hearing or to pay the fixed penalty within the suspended enforcement period enables a sum equal to 150% of the value of the fixed penalty to be registered for enforcement against the recipient as a fine[3].

1. This operates to exclude the fixed penalty procedure by virtue of RTOA 1988, s 61, at para **4–1714**, post. Points disqualification is summarised in para **4–18**, post. The detailed provisions will be found in RTOA 1988, s 35, at para **4–1684**, post.
2. Defined in RTOA 1988, s 52, at para **4–1706**, post.
3. RTOA 1988, s 55(3), at para **4–1709**, post. The registration procedure is governed by RTOA 1988, ss 70 and 71, at paras **4–1730** and **4–1731**, post

4–13   *Conditional offer of fixed penalty.*   To enforce road traffic law, extensive use is made of automatic detection equipment, such as speed cameras. This inevitably means a delay between the commission and the discovery of the offence, and the need for investigation to establish the identity of the driver at the relevant time. To bring such cases within the fixed penalty scheme, provision is made for the issue of a conditional offer of fixed penalty, as described in detail below.
   (*a*)   Where a constable has reason to believe that a fixed penalty offence has been committed, and a fixed penalty notice has not already been given to a person or affixed to a vehicle in respect of that offence, a conditional offer may be sent to the alleged offender[1].
   (*b*)   The conditional offer must give sufficient particulars to amount to reasonable information about the alleged offence; it must state the amount of the fixed penalty; it must state that proceedings against the alleged offender cannot be commenced within 28 days (or such longer period as may be specified) of the issue of the offer[2]; it must also indicate that if the penalty is paid within the aforementioned period and, if the offence is endorsable, the licence and its counterpart are delivered to the fixed penalty clerk and he is satisfied there would be no liability to points disqualification if the alleged offender were convicted of the offence, any liability to conviction for the offence will be discharged[3].
   (*c*)   Following the issue of a conditional offer, proceedings for the alleged offence may not be brought against any person until the chief officer of police receives notice from the fixed penalty clerk that there has been a failure to fulfil the payment condition or, where applicable, the conditions concerning surrender of licence and counterpart and non liability to points disqualification[4].

In practice, a conditional offer will be issued at the same time as the notice requiring the registered keeper to give details of who was driving at the time of the alleged offence[5]. Indeed, the two are commonly included in the same document.

1. RTOA 1988, s 75(1), at para **4–1735**, post.
2. Failure to comply with this requirement does not preclude a subsequent prosecution or render such a prosecution an abuse of process: *DPP v Holden* [2006] EWHC 658 (Admin), [2007] RTR 5.

3. RTOA 1988, s 75(7), (8).
4. RTOA 1988, s 76(2)–(5), at para **4–1736**, post.
5. Ie a notice issued under RTA 1988, s 172, at para **4–1598**, post.

4–14 *Fixed penalty affixed to a vehicle*

(*a*) Provided that the offence does not involve obligatory endorsement, a fixed penalty may, instead of being given to a person, be affixed to the vehicle in respect of which the fixed penalty offence is being, or has on that occasion been, committed[1].

(*b*) During the subsequent suspended enforcement period only the driver of the vehicle on the occasion in question may request a court hearing[2]. If he does not do so, and the fixed penalty remains unpaid at the end of the suspended enforcement period, a notice to owner may be served on the person who appears to be the owner of the vehicle[3], and that person may then, within the period allowed for responding to the notice[4]:

    (i) pay the fixed penalty; or

    (ii) give notice requesting a hearing; or

    (iii) if somebody else was the driver on the relevant occasion and that person wishes to give notice requesting a hearing, furnish a statutory statement of ownership and a statutory statement of facts, and this renders ineffective any notice requesting a hearing that he purports to give on his own account[5]; or

    (iv) provide a statutory statement of ownership to the effect that he was not the owner of the vehicle at the time of the alleged offence.

(*c*) Subject to heads (*d*), (*e*) and (*f*) below, where the fixed penalty remains unpaid by the end of the period allowed for response to the notice to owner a sum equal to 150% of the value of the fixed penalty may be registered for enforcement against the person on whom the notice to owner was served[6].

(*d*) Where the recipient of the notice responds as in head (*b*)(ii) above (and in no other circumstances) he may be prosecuted for the offence and it shall conclusively be presumed that he was the driver of the vehicle on the occasion in question unless he proves that at that time the vehicle was in the possession of some other person without his consent[7].

(*e*) Where the recipient of the notice responds as in head (*b*)(iii) above the person identified as the driver of the vehicle may be prosecuted, but in no other circumstances may proceedings for the offence be brought against any person other than the person on whom the notice to owner was served[8] and, if no summons is served on that person within the period of two months immediately following the period allowed for response to the notice to owner, a sum equal to 150% of the value of the fixed penalty may be registered for enforcement against the person on whom the notice to owner was served[9].

(*f*) Where the recipient of the notice responds as in head (*b*)(iv) above he shall not be liable in respect of the alleged offence and a penalty may not be registered against him for enforcement as a fine[10].

There are separate provisions in relation to hired vehicles[11].

---

1. RTOA 1988, s 62, at para **4–1715**, post.
2. RTOA 1988, s 63(3), at para **4–1716**, post.
3. Under RTOA 1988, s 63(2).
4. This is 21 days from the date of service of the notice or such longer period as may be specified: RTOA 1988, s 63(5).
5. RTOA 1988, s 63(7)(*a*).
6. RTOA 1988, s 64(2), at para **4–1717**, post.
7. See RTOA 1988, 2 64(3), (5) and (6).
8. RTOA 1988, s 65(1), at para **4–1718**.
9. See RTOA 1988, s 63(7)(*b*).
10. RTOA 1988, s 64(4).
11. RTOA 1988, at para **4–1719**.

4–15 *Provisions concerning invalid registration and endorsement.*

There are provisions to deal with invalid registration and endorsement in the case of notices given on-the-spot or at a police station[1] and notices affixed to vehicles[2].

There are also provisions to deal with the case where the fixed penalty clerk is deceived into believing that the alleged offender is not liable to points disqualification[3].

---

1. RTOA 1988, s 72, at para **4–1732**, post.
2. RTOA 1988, s 73, at para **4–1733**, post.
3. RTOA 1988, s 83, at para **4–1743**, post.

CERTAIN PRELIMINARY MATTERS

4–16 **Duty to give information as to the identity of driver etc in certain circumstances: RTA 1988, s 172.**

It is often the case that a motor vehicle that has allegedly been involved in a road traffic offence is not stopped at the time. Accordingly, procedures are necessary for the identity of the person driving at the relevant time to be established so that that person can then be prosecuted (or offered a fixed penalty).

Where the driver of a vehicle is alleged to be guilty of any of certain specified offences[1] then:

(1) the person keeping the vehicle must give such information as to the identity of the driver as he may be required to give by or on behalf of a chief officer of police; and

(2) any other person must, if required as stated above, give any information which it is in his power to give and may lead to the identification of the driver[2].

A person who fails to comply with such a requirement is guilty of an offence[3]. A person is not, however, guilty of an offence by virtue of (1) above if he shows that he did not know, and could not with reasonable diligence have ascertained, who the driver of the vehicle was[4].

Where a body corporate is guilty of such an offence, officers of the company may additionally be found guilty of the offence in certain circumstances[5].

The requirement may be made in writing, in which case the information must be given within 28 days of service of the notice[6]. Where the requirement was so made, the person on whom it was served shall not be guilty of an offence if he shows either that he gave the information as reasonable practicable after the end of the 28-day period or it has not been reasonably practicable for him to give it[7].

It is often the case that a written notice will be served with, or will include, notice of intended prosecution where this must be given (see para **4-17**, infra) and, if appropriate, a conditional offer of a fixed penalty (see para **4-13**, supra).

---

1. For the specified offences, see RTA 1988, s 172(1), at para **4-1598**, post.
As to the duty to give such information in relation to certain offences under the Road Traffic Regulation Act 1984, see s 112 of that Act, at para **4-1212**, post. As to the duty to give such information in relation to offences under Part VI of the Transport Act 1968 and to the offence under the Goods Vehicle (Licensing of Operators) Act 1995, see Road Traffic Act 1960, s 232, at para **4-120**, post.
2. RTA 1988, s 172(2).
3. RTA 1988, 172(3).
4. RTA 1988, s 172(4).
5. RTA 1988, s 172(5).
6. RTA 1988, s 172(7).
7. RTA 1988, s 127(7)(b).

4-17 Requirement of warning of intended prosecution. A person cannot be convicted of certain specified offences[1] unless:

(1) he was warned at the time the offence was committed at the time that the question of prosecuting him for some one or other of the offences to which this applies would be taken into consideration, or

(2) within 14 days of the commission of the offence a summons for the offence was served on him, or

(3) within 14 days of the commission of the offence a notice of intended prosecution specifying the nature of the alleged offence and the time and place where it is alleged to have been committed was: (a) in the case of cycling offences, served on him, or (b) in the case of any other offence, served on him or on the person, if any, registered as the keeper of the vehicle at the time of the commission of the offence[2].

A notice of intended prosecution may be served by delivery to the person concerned, or by addressing it to him and leaving it at his last known address, or by posting it addressed to his last known address[3]. Where the latter method was used and postage was by recorded or registered delivery, the notice is deemed to have been served notwithstanding that it was returned as undelivered or was for any other reason not received by the addressee[4].

The requirement to give notice of intended prosecution is in every case deemed to have been complied with unless and until the contrary is proved[5].

The requirement to give notice of intended prosecution does not apply in relation to an offence if, at the time of the offence or immediately after it, an accident occurred owing to the presence on a road of the vehicle in respect of which the offence was committed[6]. Further, the requirement to give such notice does not apply in relation to an offence in respect of which a fixed penalty notice has been given or fixed, or a notice of an on the spot fine has been given[7].

Failure to comply with the requirement to give notice of intended prosecution is not a bar to the conviction of the accused in a case where the court is satisfied that neither the name and address of the accused nor the name and address of the registered keeper, if any, could with reasonable diligence have been ascertained in time for a summons or, as the case may be, complaint to be served or for a notice to be served or sent, or that the accused by his own conduct contributed to the failure[8].

Failure to comply with the requirement to give notice of intended prosecution is not a bar to a conviction in respect of an alternative offence[9].

---

1. For the offences to which this applies, see RTOA 1988, Sch 1, at para **4-1768**, post.
2. RTOA 1988, s 1(1), at para **4-1642**, post.
3. RTOA 1988, s 1(1A).
4. RTOA 1988, s 1(2).
5. RTOA 1988, s 1(3).
6. RTOA 1988, s 2(1), at para **4-1643**, post.
7. RTOA 1988, s 2(2).
8. RTOA 1988, s 2(3).
9. RTOA 1988, s 2(4).

SUMMARY OF PENALTY POINTS AND POINTS DISQUALIFICATION

4–18   Penalty points.   Where a person is convicted of an offence involving obligatory endorsement[1], and he is not ordered to be disqualified, the court must order there to be endorsed on the counterpart of any licence held by him particulars of the conviction and also the penalty points to be attributed to the offence[2] unless there are special reasons for not endorsing his licence[3].

Where there are 12 or more penalty points to be taken into account[4], the court must disqualify the offender for the minimum period[5] unless the court is satisfied, on the basis of non-excluded circumstances[6], that there are grounds for mitigating the normal consequences of the conviction.

There are three different three-year rules in relation to:

(1)   the aggregation of penalty points for different offences[7];
(2)   determining the minimum length of points' disqualification[8]; and
(3)   excluded circumstances for mitigating the normal consequences of the conviction[9].

Points' disqualification "wipes the slate clean" of any penalty points previously imposed[10].

The Road Safety Act 2006 prospectively provides for persons convicted of certain specified offences who would have 8–11 penalty points in the normal course to receive a reduction of 3 points (or, if lower, the number of points attributable to the instant offence) in return for completing an approved course[11].

---

1.   These are to be found in RTOA 1988, Sch 2, at para **4–1769**, post.
2.   As to the points to be attributed, see RTOA 1988, s 28, at para **4–1675**, post.
3.   RTOA 1988, s 44, at para **4–1693**, post. "Special reasons" are discussed in the notes to RTOA 1988, s 34, at para **4–1680**, post.
4.   RTOA 1988, s 29 governs the penalty points to be taken into account, at para **4–1676**, post.
5.   The minimum period is 6 months where there are no previous disqualifications to be taken into account; or 1 year or 2 years where there are, respectively, one or more than one previous disqualifications to be taken into account: see RTOA 1988, s 35(2), para **4–1684**, post.
6.   As to what is excluded, see RTOA 1988, s 35(4).
7.   See RTOA 1988, s 29(2). Penalty points are aggregated for offences committed within 3 years of each other unless an intervening points disqualification has been imposed.
8.   See RTOA 1988, s 35(2). A previous disqualification is relevant if it was for a period of 56 days or longer and was imposed within 3 years of the date of commission of the latest offence in respect of which penalty points are taken into account under s 29. Where one such disqualification is taken into account the minimum period of disqualification becomes 12 months; if more than one such disqualification is taken into account the minimum period becomes 24 months.
9.   See RTOA 1988, s 35(4)(*c*). A circumstance is excluded if, within the 3 years preceding the current conviction, it was taken into account in ordering the offender to be disqualified for less than the prescribed minimum period or not at all.
10.   See RTOA 1988, s 29(1)(*b*).
11.   See Road Safety Act 2006, s 34, at para **4–2015V**, post.

4–19   Disqualification.   The most serious road traffic offences carry obligatory disqualification[1] and the minimum period of such disqualification is increased where there are relevant, previous disqualifications[2]. Some of these offences further require the court to disqualify the offender until he has passed an extended driving test[3].

Where a person is convicted of an offence involving discretionary disqualification and the number of penalty points to be taken into account on that occasion is 12 or more the court must order the offender to be disqualified for the minimum period unless there are grounds for mitigating the normal consequences of the conviction[4].

Where a person is convicted of an offence involving discretionary disqualification, and the number of penalty points to be taken into account of that occasion is less than 12, the court may order the offender to be disqualified[5].

Where an offender is convicted of an offence involving obligatory endorsement the court may, whether or not it imposes any other form of disqualification, disqualify the offender until he passes a test of competence to drive[6].

There are other powers of disqualification from driving that are available either generally or in particular circumstances[7].

---

1.   These are to be found in RTOA 1988, Sch 2, at para **4–1769**, post.
2.   See RTOA 1988, s 34(3), at para **4–1680**, post.
3.   See RTOA 1988, s 36(2), at para **4–1685**, post.
4.   See para **4–18**, ante, for an introduction to points disqualification.
5.   See RTOA 1988, s 34(2).
6.   RTOA 1988, s 36(4). See further para **4–20**, post.
7.   See Powers of Criminal Courts (Sentencing) Act 2000, ss 146 and 147 in PART III: SENTENCING, ante.

4–20   Disqualification until test is passed.   Where a person is convicted of certain, serious road traffic offences and there are no special reasons not to impose the normal, obligatory disqualification the court must also order him to be disqualified until he passes the appropriate driving test[1].

Where a person is convicted of any other offence involving obligatory endorsement the court may order him to be disqualified until he passes the appropriate driving test[2].

The appropriate driving test is an extended driving test where the offender is convicted of an offence involving obligatory disqualification or is disqualified under the penalty points provisions; in any other case it is the normal test of competence to drive[3].

1. RTOA 1988, s 36(1) and (2), at para **4–1685**, post.
2. RTOA 1988, s 36(4). As to the relevant principles and factors, see Note 1 to s 36.
3. RTOA 1988, s 36(5).

4–21 **Effect of disqualification.** Where the holder of a driving licence is disqualified by an order of the court, the licence shall be treated as being revoked with effect from the beginning of the period of disqualification or, if the disqualification is suspended pending an appeal, from the date that the suspension ceases[1]. However, if the period of disqualification is less than 56 days, or is an order of interim disqualification, the licence has effect again at the end of the period of disqualification[2].

Where a person is subject to disqualification until passing a test, but is not otherwise disqualified, he is entitled to obtain a provisional driving licence and to drive a motor vehicle in accordance with its conditions[3].

There is mutual recognition of driving disqualifications between Northern Ireland and Great Britain, and this has been extended to the Isle of Man. Part 3 of the Crime (International Co-operation Act 2003[4] makes provision for EU wide recognition of disqualifications imposed in any Member State, but this has not yet taken effect.

It is an offence to obtain a licence, or to drive a motor vehicle on a road, while disqualified for holding or obtaining a licence, and this extends to disqualification imposed by a court in Northern Ireland, or in the Isle of Man or any of the Channel Islands, or in Gibratar[5].

Various provisions of the RTOA 1988 concerning endorsement and disqualification are applied to community licence holders[6].

1. RTOA 1988, s 37(1) and (3), at para **4–1686**, post. Accordingly, the disqualified person will need to apply for a new licence, but provided he has made such an application he may re-commence driving once the disqualification has expired: see RTA 1988, s 88(1)(*b*)(i), at para **4–1490**, post. In the case of persons convicted of certain alcohol-related offences, medical enquiries will be made by the DVLA before a new licence is issued.
2. RTOA 1988, s 37(2). In such a case it is unnecessary for the holder to apply for a new licence.
3. RTOA 1988, s 37(3).
4. In Part I: Magistrates' Courts, Procedure, ante.
5. RTA 1988, ss 102 and 103, at para **4–1512**, post. This offence does not apply to disqualification by reason of age: see s 103(4).
6. By RTOA 1988, s 91A, at para **4–1752**, post.

4–22 **Reduction/removal of disqualification.** In relation to persons convicted of certain alcohol-related driving offences who are disqualified for at least 12 months, the court may order that the period of disqualification shall be reduced by not less than 3 months and not more than one quarter of the unreduced period if the offender completes, no later than 2 months before the last day on which the reduced disqualification would expire, a course approved by the Secretary of State for this purpose[1].

A person ordered to be disqualified for more than 2 years may, after the expiration of the prescribed period or fraction of the original ban, apply to the court which imposed the disqualification for its removal, and on hearing such an application the court order the removal of the disqualification from such date as the court may specify or refuse the application[2].

1. RTOA 1988, s 34A, at para **4–1681**. Such an order requires the offender's consent: see s 34A(4)(*d*). The Road Safety Act 2006 prospectively provides an alternative, disqualification-reduction scheme of "alcohol ignition interlock programmes" for certain specified alcohol-related offences: see ss 15 and 16, at para **4–2015D** and **4–2015E**, post.
2. RTOA 1988, s 42, at para **4–1691**, post. The prescribed periods/fractions which must be served before the application can be made are: if the ban was less than 4 years, 2 years; if the ban was less than 10 years but not less than 4 years, one half of the period of disqualification; in any other case, 5 years.

4–23 **Requirement for drivers of motor vehicles to have driving licences.** A driving licence shows entitlement to drive vehicles of the category authorised. For this purpose vehicles are categorised as: motor cars; motorcycles; medium and large vehicles (3,500 kg or over); minibuses; and buses[1]. Each category must be applied for, and tested, separately.

It is an offence for a person to drive on a road a motor vehicle of any class otherwise than in accordance with a licence authorising him to drive a vehicle of that class[2]. It is also an offence for a person to cause or permit another person to drive on a road a motor vehicle of any class otherwise than in accordance with a licence authorising that other person to drive a vehicle of that class[3].

1. See Sch 2 to the Motor Vehicles (Driving Licences) Regulations 1999, at para **4–380C**, post.
2. RTA 1988, s 87(1), at para **4–1480**, post.
3. RTA 1988, s 87(2).

4–24 **Drivers visiting or newly resident in GB***European Economic Area licences.* The European Economic Area includes all EC countries and Liechtenstein, Iceland and Norway. A person who holds a valid licence as a result of a test passed in any EEA country may drive in the UK those vehicles which his licence authorises him to drive[1]. The licence will remain valid until whichever is the later of his 70th anniversary or the end of 3 years from the date he became normally resident here.

Exchangeable licences. EEA licences may be exchanged for UK licences to drive vehicles of corresponding classes[2].

Additionally, certain countries outside the EEA are legally designated in Great Britain for driver licensing exchange purposes. A new resident who holds a driving licence from one of these countries may, within 5 years, exchange it for a British licence to drive vehicles of corresponding classes without the need to pass a further driving test. For designated countries, "licences" do not include licences to drive vehicles over 3,500 kgs, or passenger carrying vehicles with more than 8 passenger seats.

Britain has also designated Gibraltar, the Channel Islands and the Isle of Man with additional entitlements. For these countries, "licences" include licences to drive larger vehicles, provided entitlement is shown on the driving licence.

The holder may drive on an exchangeable driving licence for up to one year, but cannot then drive unless the licence is exchanged for a GB licence.

Visitors and new residents from non-EEA or designated countries. By art 2 of the Motor Vehicles (International Circulation) Order 1975[3], persons resident outside the UK who hold either a Convention driving permit, a domestic driving permit issued in a country outside the UK or a British Forces driving licence may for up to one year drive such motor vehicles as their permits authorise without holding a licence under the RTA 1988. Article 3 of the Order makes similar provision in relation to members of visiting forces of civilian component parts thereof[4].

Provisions similar to art 3 are applied to persons who become resident in the UK[5].

---

1. RTA 1988, s 99A, at para **4–1504**, post. Vocational drivers can generally drive for up to 5 years on their EEA licences, but must then exchange them if they wish to continue driving.
2. RTA 1988, s 89(1)(*ea*), see para **4–1491**, post.
3. At para **4–4082**, post.
4. As to the application of the RTA 1988to such cases, see art 4 and Sch 3, at para **4–4087**, post.
5. By reg 80 of the Motor Vehicles (Driving Licences) Regulations, at para **4–4379Y**, post.

4–25 Endorsement of driving licences. Where a person is convicted of an offence involving obligatory endorsement, and the court does not find special reasons for not endorsing his licence, the conviction and certain particulars must be endorsed on the counterpart of any driving licence that he holds[1].

If the offender does not hold a current UK driving licence, the particulars will appear on any licence he subsequently obtains if the endorsement is still current[2]. There is separate provision dealing with the effect of endorsement on Community licence holders to whom a counterpart licence has been issued[3].

Most endorsements remain effective for 4 years or until an order is made imposing points disqualification on the offender, but if the offence was one of the principal drink driving offences the endorsement will remain effective for 11 years[4].

The Road Safety Act 2006 prospectively introduces a new system of endorsement[5]. This shifts the emphasis from licence counterparts to DVLA driver records. The principal aim is to bring non-UK licence holders to whom a counterpart has not been issued within the fixed penalty scheme for endorsable offences.

---

1. RTA 1988, s 44, at para **4–1693**, post.
2. RTA 1988, s 45.
3. RTOA 1988, s 91B, at para **4–1753**, post.
4. RTA 1988, s 45(5)–(7).
5. In ss 8–10, at paras **4–2014X** to **4–2014Z**, post.

4–26 Newly-qualified drivers. The Road Traffic (New Drivers) Act 1995[1] provides for the retesting of drivers who commit offences during the period of two years from the date of becoming qualified to drive. The Act applies to all GB licence holders regardless of whether the test was taken here or in a country with which we have reciprocal arrangements[2].

In summary, where, as a result of a conviction or a fixed penalty in respect of an endorsable offence committed during the probationary 2-year period, a driver has 6 or more penalty points, the court or fixed penalty clerk must notify the Secretary of State who must then issue a notice revoking the licence. The driver can then no longer drive as a full licence holder. He must apply for a new provisional licence and re-take the driving test.

---

1. From para **4–2008A**, post.
2. These are listed in s 1(2)(*b*).

Road and Rail Traffic Act 1933

(23 & 24 Geo 5 c 53)

Note.—The greater part of this Act has been repealed and replaced by the Road Traffic Act 1960, post. The unrepealed portions relevant to this work are printed below.

4–110   42. Non-compliance with Minister's direction that level crossing gates be kept closed across the railway at certain times. (1) The Minister[1] if upon an application made to him by the railway company[2] concerned he is satisfied that it is expedient so to do, may direct that the gates on any level crossing over a public road shall, instead of being kept closed across the road, be kept closed across the railway, either constantly, or on such days, or during such portions of any day, as he thinks fit, and, if he so directs, the gates shall, notwithstanding anything in any Act (whether a public general Act or not) to the contrary, be kept closed in accordance with his direction, except when engines or vehicles passing along the railway have occasion to cross the road, and, if the person entrusted with the care of the gates fails to comply with the direction of the Minister, he shall on summary conviction be liable to a penalty of **level 1** on the standard scale for each offence.

(2) The powers conferred upon the Minister by the preceding subsection shall be deemed to be in addition to, and not in derogation of, any powers conferred upon him by section 47 of the Railways Clauses Consolidation Act 1845, or section 40 of the Railways Clauses Consolidation (Scotland) Act 1845, or by any provision in a local and personal or private Act which relates to the closing of gates on level crossings.

[Road and Rail Traffic Act 1933, s 42, as amended by the Criminal Law Act 1977, s 31 and the Criminal Justice Act 1982, s 46.]

---

1. See now the Secretary of State for Transport Order 1976, SI 1976/1775.
2. "Railway company" includes any person or body of persons, whether incorporated or not, being the owner or owners, or lessee or lessees of, or working a railway. "Railway" includes a light railway, not being a light railway which is laid wholly or mainly along a public carriage-way, and is used wholly or mainly for the carriage of passengers (s 45).

Road Traffic Act 1960
(8 & 9 Eliz 2 c 16)

PART VII

4–120   232. Duty to give information as to identity of driver, etc, in certain cases. (1) This section applies—

(*a*) *Repealed*;
(*b*) to any offence under section 2 of the Goods Vehicles (Licensing of Operators) Act 1995;
(*c*)–(*e*) *Repealed*;
(*f*) to any offence under Part VI of the Transport Act 1968.

(2) Where the driver of a vehicle is alleged to be guilty of an offence to which this section applies[1]—

(*a*) the person keeping the vehicle shall give such information as to the identity of the driver as he may be required to give—

    (i) by or on behalf of a chief officer of police[2]; and
    (ii) *Repealed*

(*b*) any other person[3] shall if required as aforesaid give any information which it is in his power to give and may lead to the identification of the driver.

(3) A person who fails to comply with the requirements of paragraph (*a*) of the last foregoing subsection shall be guilty of an offence unless he shows to the satisfaction of the court that he did not know and could not with reasonable diligence have ascertained who the driver of the vehicle was, and a person who fails to comply with the requirement of paragraph (*b*) of that subsection shall be guilty of an offence; and a person guilty of an offence under this subsection shall be liable on summary conviction to a fine not exceeding **level 3** on the standard scale.

[Road Traffic Act 1960, s 232, amended by Road Traffic Act 1962, 1st Sch, Road Traffic Regulation Act 1967, Sch 7, Vehicle and Driving Licences Act 1969, Transport Act 1968, Schs 10 and 11, Road Traffic Act 1972, Sch 9, the Transport Act 1980, Sch 9, the Public Passenger Vehicles Act 1981, Sch 8, the Criminal Justice Act 1982, ss 38 and 46, the Goods Vehicles (Licensing of Operators) Act 1995, Sch 7 and the Statute Law (Repeals) Act 2004.]

---

1. The police are not bound to specify the nature of the alleged offence when they require information from an owner or other person (*Pulton v Leader* [1949] 2 All ER 747, 113 JP 537). For admissibility in evidence of a statement in writing, purporting to be signed by the accused, that the accused was the driver, etc of a particular vehicle on the particular occasion to which the information relates, see s 243, post.
2. A police officer properly acting in the course of his duty is not necessarily acting on behalf of the chief officer of police (*Record Tower Cranes Ltd v Gisbey* [1969] 1 All ER 418, 133 JP 167). A notice signed by an Inspector with the authority of his Superintendent who was held to have the implied delegated authority of the Commissioner of Police to further delegate to his Inspector was held to be a good and valid notice (*Nelms v Roe* [1969] 3 All ER 1379, 134 JP 88).
3. This expression includes the driver himself (*Bingham v Bruce* [1962] 1 All ER 186, 126 JP 81).

Forgery, false Statements, etc

4–123   242. Evidence by certificate. (1) In any proceedings in England or Wales for an offence to which s 232[1] of this Act applies a certificate in the prescribed form[2], purporting to be signed by a constable[3] and certifying that a person specified in the certificate stated to the constable—

(*a*) that a particular motor vehicle was being driven or used by, or belonged to, that person on a particular occasion[4]; or

(*b*) that a particular motor vehicle on a particular occasion was used by or belonged to a firm in which that person also stated that he was at the time of the statement a partner; or

(*c*) that a particular motor vehicle on a particular occasion was used by or belonged to a corporation of which that person also stated that he was at the time of the statement a director, officer or employee,

shall be admissible as evidence for the purpose of determining by whom the vehicle was being driven or used, or to whom it belonged, as the case may be, on that occasion.

(2) Nothing in the foregoing subsection shall be deemed to make a certificate admissible as evidence in proceedings for an offence except in a case where and to the like extent to which oral evidence to the like effect would have been admissible in those proceedings.

(3) Nothing in subsection (1) of this section shall be deemed to make a certificate admissible as evidence in proceedings for an offence—

(a) unless a copy thereof has, not less than seven days before the hearing or trial, been served in the prescribed manner[2] on the person charged with the offence; or

(b) if that person, not later than three days before the hearing or trial or within such further time as the court may in special circumstances allow, serves a notice in the prescribed form and manner[2] on the prosecutor requiring attendance at the trial of the person who signed the certificate.

(4) In this section "prescribed" means prescribed by rules made by the Secretary of State by statutory instrument.
[Road Traffic Act 1960, s 242, as amended by Road Traffic Act 1962, 4th Sch.]

---

1. Section 232, *ante*, relates to the duty of the owner of a vehicle to give information as to the driver.
2. Prescribed by the Evidence by Certificate Rules 1961, SI 1961/248 which require service to be in the following manner—

(a) where the person to be served is a corporation, by addressing it to the corporation and leaving it at, or sending it by registered post or by the recorded delivery service to, the registered office of the corporation or, if there is no such office, its principal office or place at which it conducts its business;

(b) in any other case, by delivering it personally to the person to be served or by addressing it to him and leaving it at, or sending it by registered post or by the recorded delivery service to, his last or usual place of abode or place of business.

3. Or a traffic warden acting in the discharge of functions authorised by the Functions of Traffic Wardens Order 1970, in this PART, *post*.
4. For admissibility in evidence of a statement in writing, purporting to be signed by the accused, that the accused was the driver, etc, of a particular vehicle on the particular occasion to which the information relates, see s 243, *post*.

4–124   243. Proof, in summary proceedings, of identity of driver of vehicle. Where on the summary trial in England or Wales of an information for an offence to which section 232[1] of this Act applies—

(a) it is proved to the satisfaction of the court, on oath or in manner prescribed by Criminal Procedure Rules[2], that a requirement under section 232(2)[1] to give information as to the identity of the driver of a particular vehicle on the particular occasion to which the information relates has been served on the accused by post; and

(b) a statement in writing is produced to the court purporting to be signed by the accused that the accused was the driver of that vehicle on that occasion,

the court may accept that statement as evidence that the accused was the driver of that vehicle on that occasion.
[Road Traffic Act 1960, s 243 as amended by the Courts Act 2003, Sch 8.]

---

1. Section 232, *ante*, relates to the duty of the owner of a vehicle to give information as to the driver.
2. See now s 69 of the Courts Act 2003. For the prescribed manner of proving service of a document by post, see Criminal Procedure Rules 2005, Part 4, in PART I: MAGISTRATES' COURTS, PROCEDURE, *ante*.

4–125   244. Time for commencing summary proceedings for certain offences. Summary proceedings for an offence under section 235 of this Act or an offence under section 99(5) of the Transport Act 1968 may be brought within a period of six months from the date on which evidence sufficient in the opinion of the prosecutor to warrant the proceedings came to his knowledge; but no such proceedings shall be brought by virtue of this section more than three years after the commission of the offence[1].

For the purposes of this section a certificate signed by or on behalf of the prosecutor and stating the date on which such evidence as aforesaid came to his knowledge shall be conclusive evidence of that fact; and a certificate stating that matter and purporting to be so signed shall be deemed to be so signed unless the contrary is proved.
[Road Traffic Act 1960, s 244, as amended by the Vehicle and Driving Licences Act 1969, Transport Act 1968, Sch 11, the Road Traffic Act 1972, Sch 9, the Road Traffic (Consequential Provisions) Act 1988, Sch 3 and the Goods Vehicles (Licensing of Operators) Act 1995, Schs 7 and 8.]

---

1. The application of this provision is noted against each of the relevant sections (*ante*). The extended limitation of time applies to aiding and abetting the specified offences (*Homolka v Osmond* [1939] 1 All ER 154).

Inquiries

4–126   248. General power to hold inquiries.   *Repealed.*

4–127   249. General provisions as to inquiries.   *Repealed.*

Interpretation

4–128   253. Interpretation of expressions relating to motor vehicles and classes or descriptions thereof.   (1) In this Act "motor vehicle" means a mechanically propelled vehicle intended or adapted[1] for use on roads[2], and "trailer" means a vehicle drawn by a motor vehicle[3].
Provided that a side-car attached to a motor cycle shall, if it complies with such conditions as may be

specified in regulations made by the Minister[4], be regarded as forming part of the vehicle to which it is attached and not as being a trailer.

(2) In this Act "motor car" means a mechanically propelled vehicle, not being a motor cycle or an invalid carriage, which is constructed itself to carry a load or passengers and the weight of which unladen—

(a) if it is constructed solely for the carriage of passengers and their effects, is adapted to carry not more than seven passengers exclusive of the driver, and is fitted with tyres of such type as may be specified in regulations made by the Minister[5], does not exceed 3050 kilograms[6];

(b) if it is constructed or adapted for use for the conveyance of goods or burden of any description, does not exceed 3050 kilograms, or 3500 kilograms if the vehicle carries a container or containers for holding for the purpose of its propulsion any fuel which is wholly gaseous at 17·5 degrees Celsius under a pressure of 1·013 bar or plant and materials for producing such fuel;

(c) does not exceed 2540 kilograms in a case falling within neither of the foregoing paragraphs.

(3) In this Act "heavy motor car" means a mechanically propelled vehicle, not being a motor car[7], which is constructed itself to carry a load or passengers and the weight of which unladen exceeds 2540 kilograms[6].

(4) In this Act (except for the purposes of the provisions thereof relating to the provisions by parish councils of parking places for bicycles and motor cycles[8]) "motor cycle" means a mechanically propelled vehicle, not being an invalid carriage, with less than four wheels and the weight of which unladen does not exceed 410 kilograms.

(5) In this Act "invalid carriage" means a mechanically propelled vehicle the weight of which unladen does not exceed 254 kilograms and which is specially designed and constructed, and not merely adapted, for the use of a person suffering from some physical defect or disability and is used solely by such a person.

(6) In this Act "motor tractor"[9] means a mechanically propelled vehicle which is not constructed itself to carry a load, other than the following articles, that is to say, water, fuel, accumulators and other equipment used for the purpose of propulsion, loose tools and loose equipment, and the weight of which unladen does not exceed 7370 kilograms.

(7) In this Act "light locomotive" means a mechanically propelled vehicle which is not constructed itself to carry a load, other than any of the articles aforesaid, and the weight of which unladen does not exceed 11690 kilograms but does exceed 7370 kilograms.

(8) In this Act "heavy locomotive" means a mechanically propelled vehicle which is not constructed itself to carry a load, other than any of the articles aforesaid, and the weight of which unladen exceeds 11690 kilograms.

(9) For the purposes of this section, in a case where a motor vehicle is so constructed that a trailer may by partial superimposition be attached to the vehicle in such manner as to cause a substantial part of the weight of the trailer to be borne by the vehicle, that vehicle shall be deemed to be a vehicle itself constructed to carry a load.

(10) For the purposes of this section, in the case of a motor vehicle fitted with a crane, dynamo, welding plant or other special appliance or apparatus which is a permanent or essentially permanent fixture, the appliance or apparatus[10] shall not be deemed to constitute a load or goods or burden of any description, but shall be deemed to form part of the vehicle.

(11) The Minister may by regulations vary any of the maximum or minimum weights specified in the foregoing provisions of this section, and such regulations may have effect either generally or in the case of vehicles of any class or description specified in the regulations and either for the purposes of this Act and of all regulations thereunder or for such of those purposes as may be so specified; and nothing in section 86 of the Road Traffic Regulation Act 1984[11], shall be construed as limiting the powers conferred by this subsection.

[Road Traffic Act 1960, s 253, as amended by SI 1981/1373 and 1374 and the Road Traffic Regulation Act 1984, Sch 13.]

---

1. For meaning of expression "intended or adapted for use on a road", see Headnote to this title, ante.

2. Therefore this is a definition for all Parts of the Act of "motor vehicles" and "trailers". A vehicle so constructed that it can be divided into two parts both of which are vehicles and one of which is a motor vehicle shall (when not so divided) be treated as a motor vehicle with a trailer attached (Road Traffic Act 1988, s 187, post).

3. This means anything on wheels (eg a poultry shed) drawn by a motor vehicle (*Garner v Burr* [1951] 1 KB 31, [1950] 2 All ER 683, 114 JP 484).

4. Power is given by the Road Traffic Act 1988, s 41, post, to the Minister to make regulations prescribing these conditions. If a sidecar attached to a motor cycle complies with reg 92 of the Road Vehicles (Construction and Use) Regulations 1986, in this PART, post, it is part of the cycle. If it does not comply, it is a trailer within sub-s (1), ante, and subject to the speed limit applicable to passenger and goods vehicles respectively, drawing a trailer, mentioned in Sch 6 to the Road Traffic Regulation Act 1984, post. See also the Motor Vehicles (Authorisation of Special Types) General Order, in this PART, post.

5. See reg 24 of the Road Vehicles (Construction and Use) Regulations, in this PART, post.

6. For method of calculating weight, see Road Traffic Act 1988, s 190, post.

7. As defined by sub-s (2), supra.

8. Now in s 57 of the Road Traffic Regulation Act 1984.

9. A chassis is not a tractor (*Millard v Turvey* [1968] 2 QB 390, [1968] 2 All ER 7, 132 JP 286).

10. As to a sound-recording van, although the apparatus is a permanent fixture, see *Burmingham v Lindsell* [1936] 2 All ER 159.

11. This section, post, prescribes speed limits for different classes of vehicles.

4–129   255. *Method of calculating weight of motor vehicles*[1]

---

1. This section has been replaced by s 190 of the Road Traffic Act 1988, post, in practically identical terms.

4–130   257. General interpretation provisions.   (1) In this Act, unless the context otherwise requires, the following expressions[1] have the meanings hereby assigned to them respectively, that is to say—

"driver", where a separate person acts as steersman[2] of a motor vehicle, includes that person as well as any other person engaged in the driving of the vehicle, and "drive" shall be construed accordingly;

"the Minister" means the Minister of Transport[3];

"road" means any highway and any other road to which the public has access[4], and includes bridges over which a road passes;

(2) References in this Act to any enactment shall be construed, except where the context otherwise requires, as references to that enactment as amended by or under any subsequent enactment.

[Road Traffic Act 1960, s 257, amended by London Government Act 1963, Sch 5, Police Act 1964, Sch 10, Road Traffic Regulation Act 1967, Schs 6, 7, the Road Traffic Act 1972, Sch 9, the Transport Act 1980, Schs 5 and 9, the Magistrates' Courts Act 1980, Sch 7, the Public Passenger Vehicles Act 1981, Sch 8 and the Statute Law (Repeals) Act 1993, Sch 1.]

---

1. The expressions "motor vehicle"; "trailer" and various classes or descriptions of motor vehicles are defined by s 253, ante.
2. "Steersman" in this definition would seem to refer to one of two people in charge of the same vehicle, as in a steam wagon. A person "drives" a vehicle in the act of steering it down an incline without the engine running (*Saycell v Bool* [1948] 2 All ER 83, 112 JP 341). Cf *R v Kitson* (1955) 39 Cr App Rep 66. For an instance of instructor and learner being joint drivers, see *Langman v Valentine* [1952] 2 All ER 803, 116 JP 576. Cf *Evans v Walkden* [1956] 3 All ER 64, 120 JP 495. See also the headnote to this title on "drivers" and "driving".
3. Functions of the Minister of Transport have been transferred to the Secretary of State by SI 1981/238.
4. For meaning of "Road", see Headnote to this title, ante.

Supplementary

4–133   266. Repeal of provisions as to use of bridges by locomotives.   *Repealed.*

4–135   269. Saving for law of nuisance.   Nothing in this Act shall authorise a person to use on a road a vehicle so constructed or used as to cause a public or private nuisance, or in Scotland a nuisance, or affect the liability, whether under statute or common law, of the driver or owner so using such a vehicle.

[Road Traffic Act 1960, s 269.]

Road Traffic (Amendment) Act 1967
(1967 c 70)

4–240   8. Extent of powers under Motor Vehicles (International Circulation) Act 1952.   It is hereby declared for the avoidance of doubt that—

(*a*) the power conferred on Her Majesty by section 1 of the Motor Vehicles (International Circulation) Act 1952 (Orders in Council for implementing international agreements about international road traffic) to make provision by Order in Council for modifying any enactment relating to vehicles or the drivers of vehicles includes power to make provision corresponding to any such enactment; and

(*b*) the reference in subsection (1)(*b*) of that section to any enactment is a reference to any enactment passed before or after that Act;

and that section 2 of that Act (Orders for implementing international agreements about international road traffic in Northern Ireland) has effect accordingly.

[Road Traffic (Amendment) Act 1967, s 8.]

4–241   10. Short title, citation, commencement and extent.   (1) This Act may be cited as the Road Traffic (Amendment) Act 1967.

(2), (3) *Repealed.*

(4) This Act, except section 8 thereof, does not extend to Northern Ireland.

[Road Traffic (Amendment) Act 1967, s 10 as amended by the Statute Law (Repeals) Act 1993, Sch 1.]

Transport Act 1968[1]
(1968 c 73)

4–260   Only the parts of this Act of relevance to magistrates' courts are included here. Amendments made by this Act to other enactments have been noted where appropriate.

---

1. The following section printed here has not yet been brought into force: s 99(10).

PART VI
DRIVERS' HOURS

4–279   95. Vehicles and drivers subject to control under Part VI.   (1) This Part of this Act shall have effect with a view to securing the observance of proper hours or periods of work by persons engaged in the carriage of passengers or goods by road and thereby protecting the public against the risks which arise in cases where the drivers of motor vehicles are suffering from fatigue, but the Secretary of State may by regulations[1] make such provision by way of substitution for or adaptation of the provisions of this Part, or supplemental or incidental to this Part, as he considers necessary or expedient to take account of the operation of any relevant Community provision[2].

(1A)   Regulations under subsection (1) above may in particular—

(a)   substitute different requirements for the requirements of the domestic drivers' hours code[2] or add to, make exceptions from or otherwise modify any of the requirements of that code;

(b)   apply to journeys and work to which no relevant Community provision[2] applies;

(c)   include provision as to the circumstances in which a period of driving or duty to which a relevant Community provision or the domestic drivers' hours code[2] applies is to be included or excluded in reckoning any period for purposes of the domestic drivers' hours code or any relevant Community provision respectively; and

(d)   may contain such transitional, supplemental or consequential provisions as the Secretary of State thinks necessary or expedient.

(2)   This Part of this Act applies to—

(a)   passenger vehicles, that is to say—

    (i)   public service vehicles; and

    (ii)   motor vehicles (other than public service vehicles) constructed or adapted to carry more than twelve passengers;

(b)   goods vehicles, that is to say—

    (i)   heavy locomotives, light locomotives, motor tractors and any motor vehicle so constructed that a trailer may by partial superimposition[3] be attached to the vehicle in such a manner as to cause a substantial part of the weight of the trailer to be borne by the vehicle; and

    (ii)   motor vehicles (except those mentioned in paragraph (a) of this subsection) constructed or adapted to carry goods other than the effects of passengers.

(c)   vehicles not falling within paragraph (a) or (b) of this subsection which

    (i)   are vehicles within the meaning given by Article 1 of Council Regulation (EEC) No 3820/85 of 29th December 1985 on the harmonization of certain social legislation relating to road transport; and

    (ii)   are not referred to in Article 4 of that Regulation.

(3)   This Part of this Act applies to any such person as follows (in this Part of this Act referred to as "a driver"), that is to say—

(a)   a person who drives a vehicle to which this Part of this Act applies in the course of his employment (in this Part of this Act referred to as "an employee-driver"); and

(b)   a person who drives such a vehicle for the purposes of a trade or business carried on by him (in this Part of this Act referred to as "an owner-driver");

and in this Part of this Act references to driving by any person are references to his driving as aforesaid[4].

[Transport Act 1968, s 95, as amended by the Road Traffic (Drivers' Ages and Hours of Work) Act 1976, s 2 and SI 1998/2006.]

---

1. See the Drivers' Hours (Harmonisation with Community Rules) Regulations 1986 in this PART, post.
2. See definition in s 103(1), post.
3. It would seem that the reference to a trailer being attached by partial superimposition is dealing with an articulated truck with a fifth wheel; see *National Trailer and Towing Association Ltd v DPP* [1999] RTR 89.
4. See *Lawson v Fox* [1974] AC 803, [1974] 1 All ER 783, 138 JP 368 as to driving abroad and see the Drivers' Hours (Harmonisation with Community Rules) Regulations 1986 in this PART, post.

4–280   96. Permitted driving time and periods of duty[1].   (1) Subject to the provisions of this section, a driver shall not on any working day drive a vehicle or vehicles to which this Part of this Act applies for periods amounting in the aggregate to more than ten hours[2].

(2)   Subject to the provisions of this section, if on any working day a driver has been on duty for a period of, or for periods amounting in the aggregate to, five and a half hours and—

(a)   there has not been during that period, or during or between any of those periods, an interval of not less than half an hour in which he was able to obtain rest and refreshment; and

(b)   the end of that period, or of the last of those periods, does not mark the end of the working day,

there shall at the end of that period, or of the last of those periods, be such an interval as aforesaid.

(3)   Subject to the provisions of this section, the working day of a driver—

(a)   except where paragraph (b) or (c) of this subsection applies, shall not exceed eleven hours[2];

(b) if during that day he is off duty for a period which is, or periods which taken together are, not less than the time by which his working day exceeds eleven hours[2], shall not exceed twelve and a half hours;

(c) if during that day—

    (i) all the time when he is driving vehicles to which this Part of the Act applies is spent in driving one or more express carriages or contract carriages; and

    (ii) he is able for a period of not less than four hours to obtain rest and refreshment,

shall not exceed fourteen hours.

(4) Subject to the provisions of this section, there shall be, between any two successive working days of a driver, an interval for rest which—

(a) subject to paragraph (b) of this subsection, shall not be of less than eleven hours;

(b) if during both those days all or the greater part of the time when he is driving vehicles to which the Part of this Act applies is spent in driving one or more passenger vehicles, may, on one occasion in each working week, be of less than eleven hours but not of less than nine and a half hours;

and for the purposes of this Part of this Act a period of time shall not be treated, in the case of an employee-driver, as not being an interval for rest by reason only that he may be called upon to report for duty if required.

(5) Subject to the provisions of this section a driver shall not be on duty in any working week for periods amounting in the aggregate to more than sixty hours.

(6) Subject to the provisions of this section, there shall be, in the case of each working week of a driver, a period of not less than twenty-four hours for which he is off duty, being a period either falling wholly in that week or beginning in that week and ending in the next week; but—

(a) where the requirements of the foregoing provisions of this subsection have been satisfied in the case of any week by reference to a period ending in the next week, no part of that period (except any part after the expiration of the first twenty-four hours of it) shall be taken into account for the purpose of satisfying those requirements in the case of the next week; and

(b) those requirements need not be satisfied in the case of any working week of a driver who on each working day falling wholly or partly in that week drives one or more stage carriages if that week is immediately preceded by a week in the case of which those requirements have been satisfied as respects that driver or during which he has not at any time been on duty.

(7) If in the case of the working week of any driver the following requirement is satisfied, that is to say, that, in each of the periods of twenty-four hours beginning at midnight which make up that week, the driver does not drive a vehicle to which this Part of this Act applies for a period of, or periods amounting in the aggregate to, more than four hours, the foregoing provisions of this section shall not apply to him in that week, except that the provisions of subsections (1), (2) and (3) shall nevertheless have effect in relation to the whole of any working day falling partly in that week and partly in a working week in the case of which that requirement is not satisfied.

(8) If on any working day a driver does not drive any vehicle to which this Part of this Act applies—

(a) subsections (2) and (3) of this section shall not apply to that day; and

(b) the period or periods of duty attributable to that day for the purposes of subsection (5) of this section shall, if amounting to more than eleven hours, be treated as amounting to eleven hours only.

(9) For the purposes of subsections (1) and (7) of this section no account shall be taken of any time spent driving a vehicle elsewhere than on a road if the vehicle is being so driven in the course of operations of agriculture or forestry.

(10) For the purpose of enabling drivers to deal with cases of emergency or otherwise to meet a special need, the Minister may by regulations[3]—

(a) create exemptions from all or any of the requirements of subsections (1) to (6) of this section in such cases and subject to such conditions as may be specified in the regulations;

(b) empower the traffic commissioner for any area, subject to the provisions of the regulations—

    (i) to dispense with the observance of all or any of those requirements (either generally or in such circumstances or to such extent as the commissioner thinks fit) in any particular case for which provision is not made under paragraph (a) of this subsection;

    (ii) to grant a certificate (which, for the purposes of any proceedings under this Part of this Act, shall be conclusive evidence of the facts therein stated) that any particular case falls or fell within any exemption created under the said paragraph (a);

and regulations under this subsection may enable any dispensation under paragraph (b)(i) of this subsection to be granted retrospectively and provide for a document purporting to be a certificate granted by virtue of paragraph (b)(ii) of this subsection to be accepted in evidence without further proof.

(11) If any of the requirements of the domestic drivers' code is contravened in the case of any driver—

(a) that driver; and

(b) any other person (being that driver's employer or a person to whose orders that driver was subject) who caused or permitted the contravention, shall be liable on summary conviction to a fine not exceeding **level 4** on the standard scale; but a person shall not be liable to be convicted under this subsection if he proves to the court—

    (i)   that the contravention was due to unavoidable delay[4] in the completion of a journey arising out of circumstances which he could not reasonably have foreseen; or

    (ii) in the case of a person charged under paragraph (*b*) of this subsection, that the contravention was due to the fact that the driver had for any particular period or periods driven or been on duty otherwise than in employment of that person or, as the case may be, otherwise than in the employment in which he is subject to the orders of that person, and that the person charged was not, and could not reasonably have become, aware of that fact.

(11A) Where, in the case of a driver of a motor vehicle, there is in Great Britain a contravention of any requirement of the applicable Community rules[5] as to periods of driving, or distance driven, or periods on or off duty, then the offender and any other person (being the offender's employer or a person to whose orders the offender was subject) who caused or permitted the contravention shall be liable on summary conviction to a fine not exceeding **level 4** on the standard scale;

(11B) But a person shall not be liable to be convicted under subsection (11A) if—

    (*a*) he proves the matters specified in paragraph (i) of subsection (11); or

    (*b*) being charged as the offender's employer a person to whose order the offender was subject, he proves the matters specified in paragraph (ii) of that subsection.

(12) The Minister may by order[6]—

    (*a*) direct that subsection (1) of this section shall have effect with the substitution for the reference to ten hours of a reference to nine hours, either generally or with such exceptions as may be specified in the order;

    (*b*) direct that paragraph (*a*) of subsection (3) of this section shall have effect with the substitution for the reference to eleven hours of a reference to any shorter period, or remove, modify or add to the provisions of that subsection containing exceptions to the said paragraph (*a*);

    (*c*) remove, modify or add to any of the requirements of subsections (2), (4), (5) or (6) of this section or any of the exemptions provided for by subsections (7), (8) and (9) thereof;

and any order under this subsection may contain such transitional and supplementary provisions as the Minister thinks necessary or expedient, including provisions amending any definition in section 103 of this Act which is relevant to any of the provisions affected by the order.

(13) In this Part of this Act "the domestic drivers' hours code" means the provisions of subsections (1) to (6) of this section as for the time being in force (and, in particular, as modified, added to or substituted by or under any instrument in force under section 95(1) of this Act or subsection (10) or (12) of this section).

[Transport Act 1968, s 96, as amended by the European Communities Act 1972, Sch 4, the Road Traffic (Drivers' Ages and Hours of Work) Act 1976, s 2, the Transport Act 1978, s 10, the Criminal Justice Act 1982, ss 38 and 46 and the Transport Act 1985, Sch 2 and SI 1986/1457.]

---

1. This section and regulations made thereunder will extend to foreign vehicles (Road Traffic (Foreign Vehicles) Act 1972, Sch 2, post. For modification of the effect of this section in respect of certain drivers of goods vehicles, see the Drivers' Hours (Goods Vehicles) (Modifications) Order 1986, SI 1986/1459; and for modifications in respect of drivers of passenger vehicles, see the Drivers' Hours (Passenger and Goods Vehicles) (Modifications) Order 1971, SI 1971/818 and SI 1986/1459. Further adjustments to the terms of s 96, as modified by the foregoing regulations, are made by the Drivers' Hours (Harmonisation with Community Rules) Regulations 1986, in this PART, post. A footnote to these Regulations explains their effect on s 96 and other Regulations, and reference should also be made to Regulation EEC 3820/85 as to drivers, hours and records, also in this PART, post. See as well *Paterson v Richardson* [1982] RTR 49.

The involved provisions of s 96 may be conveniently summarised as follows: they apply to an "employee-driver" or an "owner-driver"—s 95(3)—driving passenger and goods vehicles—ss 95(2) and 102A. He must not *drive* more than 10 hours on any "working-day"—ss 96(1) and 103(1)—ie during the time he is "on duty"—s 103(4)—which itself must not exceed 11 hours (with exceptions—s 93(3)) and must have at least ½ hour rest after 5½ hours at most—s 96(2).

There must be at least 11 hours rest between each working day—s 96(4)—and a minimum 24 hours period off duty each working week, with exceptions—s 96(6). The "working week"—s 103(1) and (5)—must not exceed 60 hours—s 96(5). Special exemptions are contained in s 96(7)–(10) and penalties and defences in s 96(11) and (11A).

2. It is irrelevant whether all or part of the ten hours of driving or eleven hours of work were whilst the driver was abroad provided that after more than ten hours' driving or after more than eleven hours on duty he drove or worked in England (*Lawson v Fox* [1974] AC 803, [1974] 1 All ER 783, 138 JP 368). If during this time he is not driving, the court must decide on the evidence why he was not driving and whether his employer would regard him as being on duty; whether he was on duty is a matter of fact to be determined from the circumstances of each case (*Carter v Walton* [1985] RTR 378).

3. See the Drivers' Hours (Passenger Vehicles) (Exemptions) Regulations 1970, SI 1970/145 amended by SI 1970/649 and 2003/2155 and the Drivers' Hours (Goods Vehicles) (Exemption) Regulations 1986, SI 1986/1492, in this PART, post.

4. This did not excuse a failure to have a minimum 11 hours' rest and led to convictions under ss 96(3) and 96(1) in *Whitby v Stead* [1975] Crim LR 240.

5. See definition in s 103(1), post.

6. See the Drivers' Hours (Goods Vehicles) (Modifications) Order 1970, SI 1970/257 amended by SI 1971/818 and SI 1986/1459, the Drivers' Hours (Passenger and Goods Vehicles) (Modifications) Order 1971, SI 1971/818 amended by SI 1986/1459, the Drivers' Hours (Goods Vehicles) Modifications) Order 1986, SI 1986/1459 and the Drivers' Hours (Passenger and Goods Vehicles) (Exemption) Regulations 1996, SI 1996/240.

4–281 97. Installation and use of recording equipment[1]. (1) No person shall use, or cause[2] or permit to be used, a vehicle to which this section applies

    (*a*) unless there is in the vehicle recording equipment which—

        (i) has been installed in accordance with the Community Recording Equipment Regulation;

(ii)   complies with the relevant Annexes to that Regulation; and
(iii)   is being used as provided by Articles 13 to 15 of that Regulation[3]; or

(b)   in which there is recording equipment which has been repaired (whether before or after installation) otherwise than in accordance with the Community Recording Equipment Regulation,

and any person who contravenes this subsection shall be liable on summary conviction to a fine not exceeding **level 5** on the standard scale.

(1A)   A person shall not be liable to be convicted under subsection (1) of this section if he proves to the court that he neither knew nor ought to have known that the recording equipment had not been installed or repaired, as the case may be, in accordance with the Community Recording Equipment Regulation.

(2)   A person shall not be liable to be convicted under subsection (1)(a) of this section if he proves to the court that the vehicle in question was proceeding to a place where recording equipment which would comply with the requirements of the relevant Annexes to the Community Recording Equipment Regulation was to be installed in the vehicle in accordance with that Regulation.

(3)   A person shall not be liable to be convicted under subsection (1)(a) of this section by reason of the recording equipment installed in the vehicle in question not being in working order if he proves to the court that—

(a)   it had not become reasonably practicable for the equipment to be repaired by an approved fitter or workshop; and
(b)   the requirements of Article 16(2) of the Community Recording Equipment Regulation were being complied with.

(4)   A person shall not be liable to be convicted under subsection (1)(a) of this section by reason of any seal on the recording equipment installed in the vehicle in question not being intact if he proves to the court that—

(a)   the breaking or removal of the seal could not have been avoided;
(b)   it had not become reasonably practicable for the seal to be replaced by an approved fitter or workshop; and
(c)   in all other respects the equipment was being used as provided by Articles 13 to 15 of the Community Recording Equipment Regulation.

(4A)   A person shall not be liable to be convicted under subsection (1)(a) of this section by reason of the driver card not being used with the recording equipment installed in the vehicle in question if he proves to the court that—

(a)   the driver card was damaged, malfunctioning, lost or stolen;
(b)   the requirements of Article 16(2) and, apart from the last paragraph thereof, Article 16(3) of the Community Recording Equipment Regulation were being complied with; and
(c)   in all other respects the recording equipment was being used as provided by Articles 13 to 15 of that Regulation.

(5)   For the purposes of this section recording equipment is used as provided by Articles 13 to 15 of the Community Recording Equipment Regulation if, and only if, the circumstances of its use are such that each requirement of those Articles is complied with.

(6)   This section applies at any time to any vehicle to which this Part of this Act applies if, at that time, Article 3 of the Community Recording Equipment Regulation requires recording equipment to be installed and used in that vehicle; and in this section and sections 97A and 97B of this Act any expression which is also used in that Regulation has the same meaning as in that Regulation.

(7)   In this Part of this Act—

"the Community Recording Equipment Regulation" means Council Regulation (EEC) No 3821/85[4] on recording equipment in road transport as it has effect in accordance with—

(a)   Commission Regulation (EEC) No 3314/90;
(b)   Commission Regulation (EEC) No 3688/92;
(c)   Commission Regulation (EC) No 2479/95;
(d)   Commission Regulation (EC) 1056/97;
(e)   Article 1 of Commission Regulation (EC) 2135/98;
(f)   Commission Regulation (EC) 1360/2002;
(g)   Commission Regulation (EC) 1882/2003;
(h)   Commission Regulation (EC) 432/2004; and
(i)   any regulations adopted in accordance with the procedure laid down in Article 18 to the Community Recording Equipment Regulation making amendments necessary to adapt the Annexes to that Regulation to technical progress;

and as read with the Community Drivers' Hours and Recording Equipment (Exemptions and Supplementary Provisions) Regulations 1986;
"recording equipment" means equipment for recording information as to the use of a vehicle;
"the relevant Annexes" to the Community Recording Equipment Regulation—

(a)   in the case of a vehicle put into service for the first time before 1st May 2006 means—

(i)   either Annex I or Annex IB to that Regulation; and
(ii)   Annex II to that Regulation; and

(b) in the case of a vehicle put into service for the first time on or after that date means—

    (i)   Annex IB to that Regulation; and

    (ii) Annex II to that Regulation.

[Transport Act 1968, s 97 as substituted by SI 1979/1746 and amended by the Criminal Justice Act 1982, ss 39 and 46 and Sch 3 and SI 1984/144, SI 1986/1457, SI 1989/2121, SI 1996/941,SI 2005/1904 and SI 2006/1117.]

---

1. This section and regulations made thereunder will extend to foreign vehicles (Road Traffic (Foreign Vehicles) Act 1972, Sch 2, post). This section was substituted by the Passenger and Goods Vehicles (Recording Equipment) Regulations 1979, SI 1979/1746 amended by SI 1984/144, SI 1986/1457, SI 1986/2076, SI 1989/2016, SI 1991/381, SI 1994/1838, SI 1996/941 and SI 2006/3276, made under s 2(2) of the European Communities Act 1972; the Regulations as amended also provide for the approval of fitters and workshops.

2. See introductory notes to this title, ante, "Causing permitting, etc".

3. Since this refers not just to the tachograph machinery itself, but also to record sheets which have emerged from the machine, failure to produce record sheets as provided by Article 15(7) of the Community Recording Equipment Regulation 3821/85 is an offence contrary to s 97(1)(a)(iii) (*Birkett and Naylor v Vehicle Inspectorate*) (1997) 161 JP 805, DC).

4. Council Regulation 3821/85/EEC is printed in this PART, post.

4–282   97A. Provisions supplementary to section 97.   (1) If an employed driver of a vehicle to which section 97 of this Act applies fails—

(a) without reasonable excuse to return any record sheet which relates to him to his employer within twenty-one days of completing it; or

(b) where he has two or more employers by whom he is employed as a driver of such a vehicle, to notify each of them of the name and address of the other or others of them,

he shall be liable on summary conviction to a fine not exceeding **level 4** on the standard scale.

(2) If the employer of drivers of a vehicle to which section 97 of this Act applies fails without reasonable excuse to secure that they comply with subsection (1)(a) of this section, he shall be liable on summary conviction to a fine not exceeding **level 4** on the standard scale.

(3) Where a driver of a vehicle to which section 97 of this Act applies has two or more employers by whom he is employed as a driver of such a vehicle, subsection (1)(a) and subsection (2) of this section shall apply as if any reference to his employer, or any reference which is to be construed as such a reference, were a reference to such of those employers as was the first to employ him in that capacity[1].

[Transport Act 1968, s 97A as added by SI 1979/1746 and amended by the Criminal Justice Act 1982, ss 39 and 46 and Sch 3 and SI 1986/1457.]

---

1. Transitional provisions provide for different commencement dates for s 97A in 1980 and 1981 depending on whether the vehicle is being used for international journeys or not; see SI 1979/1746.

4–283   97AA. Forgery, etc of seals on recording equipment.   (1) A person who, with intent to deceive, forges, alters or uses any seal on recording equipment installed in, or designed for installation in, a vehicle to which section 97 of this Act applies, shall be guilty of an offence.

(2) A person guilty of an offence under subsection (1) above shall be liable[1]—

(a) on conviction on indictment, to imprisonment for a term not exceeding two years, or

(b) on summary conviction, to a fine not exceeding the **statutory maximum**.

(3) In the application of this section to England and Wales a person "forges" a seal if he makes a false seal in order that it may be used as genuine.

[Transport Act 1968, s 97AA added by SI 1989/2121.]

---

1. For procedure in respect of an offence triable either way, see the Magistrates' Courts Act 1980, ss 17A–21 in PART I: MAGISTRATES' COURTS, PROCEDURE, ante.

4–284   97B. Records, etc produced by equipment may be used in evidence.   (1) Where recording equipment is installed in a vehicle to which this Part of this Act applies, any record produced by means of the equipment shall, in any proceedings under this Part of this Act, be evidence, and in Scotland sufficient evidence, of the matters appearing from the record.

(2) Any entry made on a record sheet or print out by a driver for the purposes of Article 15(2) or (5) or 16(2) of the Community Recording Equipment Regulation shall, in any proceedings under this Part of this Act, be evidence, and in Scotland sufficient evidence, of the matters appearing from that entry.

[Transport Act 1968, s 97B as added by SI 1979/1746 as amended by SI 1986/1457 and SI 2005/1904.]

4–285   98. Written records[1].   (1) The Minister may make regulations[2]—

(a) for requiring drivers to keep, and employers of employee-drivers to cause to be kept, in such books as may be specified in the regulations records with respect to such matters relevant to the enforcement of this Part of this Act as may be so specified; and

(b) for requiring owner-drivers and the employers of employee-drivers to maintain such registers as may be so specified with respect to any such books as aforesaid which are in their possession or in that of any employee-drivers in their employment.

(2) Regulations under this section may contain such supplementary and incidental provisions including provisions supplementary and incidental to the requirements of the applicable Community

rules[3] as to books, records or documents as the Minister thinks necessary or expedient, including in particular provisions—

(a) specifying the person or persons from whom books and registers required for the purposes of the regulations or of the international rules[3] are to be obtained and, if provision is made for them to be obtained from the Minister, charging a fee for their issue by him (which shall be payable into the Consolidated Fund);

(b) as to the form and manner of making of entries in such books and registers;

(c) as to the issue by and return to the employers of employee-drivers of books required to be kept by the latter for the purposes of the regulations;

(d) requiring any book in current use for the purposes of the regulation to be carried on, or by the driver of, any vehicle, as to the preservation of any books and registers used for those purposes, and otherwise as to the manner in which those books and registers are to be dealt with;

(e) for exemptions from all or any of the requirements of the regulations in respect of drivers of small goods vehicles as defined in section 103(6) of this Act and for other exemptions from all or any of those requirements.

(2A) The requirements of regulations made under this section shall not apply as respects the driving of a vehicle to which section 97 of this Act applies and which is installed with recording equipment complying with the relevant Annexes (within the meaning of that section).

(3) Subject to the provisions of any regulations made by the Minister, the traffic commissioner for any area may dispense with the observance by any employee-driver or his employer, or by any owner-driver, of any requirement imposed under this section, either generally or in such circumstances or to such extent as the commissioner thinks fit, but the traffic commissioner shall not grant such a dispensation unless satisfied that it is not reasonably practicable for the requirement dispensed with to be observed.

(4) Any person who contravenes any regulations made under this section or any requirements as to books, records or documents of the applicable Community rules[3] shall be liable on summary conviction to a fine not exceeding **level 4** on the standard scale; but the employer of an employee-driver shall not be liable to be convicted under this subsection by reason of contravening any such regulation whereby he is required to cause any records to be kept if he proves to the court that he has given proper instructions to his employees with respect to the keeping of the records and has from time to time taken reasonable steps to secure that those instructions are being carried out.

(4A) A person shall not be liable to be convicted under subsection (4) of this section by reason of contravening any regulation made under this section if he proves to the court that, if the vehicle in question had been such a vehicle as is mentioned in subsection (2A) of this section, there would have been no contravention of the provisions of this Part of this Act so far as they relate to the use of such vehicles.

(5) Any entry made by an employee-driver for the purposes of regulations under this section or of the applicable Community rules[4] shall, in any proceedings under this Part of this Act, be admissible in evidence against his employer.

[Transport Act 1968, s 98, as amended by the European Communities Act 1972, Sch 4, the Road Traffic (Drivers' Ages and Hours of Work) Act 1976, s 2, SI 1979/1746, the Criminal Justice Act 1982, ss 40 and 46, the Transport Act 1985, Sch 2 and SI 2005/1904.]

1. This section and regulations made thereunder will extend to foreign vehicles (Road Traffic (Foreign Vehicles) Act 1972, Sch 2, post).
2. See the Drivers' Hours (Keeping of Records) Regulations, in this PART, post, but note also Regulations EEC 3820/85 as to drivers' records, also in this PART.
3. See definition in s 103(1), post.
4. See definition in s 103(1), post.

4–286 99. Inspection of records and other documents[1]. (1) An officer may, on production if so required of his authority, require any person to produce[2] and permit him to inspect and copy—

(a) any book or register which that person is required by regulations under section 98 of this Act to carry or have in his possession for the purpose of making in it any entry required by those regulations or which is required under those regulations to be carried on any vehicle of which that person is the driver;

(b) any book or register which that person is required by regulations under section 98 of this Act to preserve;

(bb) *repealed*;

(c) if that person is the owner of a vehicle to which this Part of this Act applies, any other document of that person which the officer may reasonably require to inspect for the purpose of ascertaining whether the provisions of this Part of this Act or of regulations made thereunder have been complied with;

(d) *repealed*;

and that book, register or document shall, if the officer so requires by notice in writing served on that person, be produced at the office of the traffic commissioner specified in the notice within such time (not being less than ten days) from the service of the notice as may be so specified.

(2) An officer may, on production if so required of his authority—

(a) at any time, enter any vehicle to which this Part of this Act applies and inspect that vehicle and any recording equipment installed in it and inspect and copy any record sheet on the vehicle on which a record has been produced by means of the equipment or an entry has been made;

- (b) at any time which is reasonable having regard to the circumstances of the case, enter any premises on which he has reason to believe that such a vehicle is kept or that any such record sheets, books, registers or other documents as are mentioned in subsection (1) of this section are to be found, and inspect any such vehicle, and inspect and copy any such record sheet, book, register or document, which he finds there.

(3) For the purpose of exercising his powers under subsection (2)(*a*) and, in respect of a document carried on, or by the driver of, a vehicle under subsection (1)(*a*) of this section, an officer may detain the vehicle in question during such time as is required for the exercise of that power.

(4) Any person who—

- (a) fails to comply with any requirement[2] under subsection (1) of this section; or
- (b) obstructs an officer in the exercise of his powers under subsection (2) or (3) of this section,

shall be liable on summary conviction to a fine not exceeding **level 3** on the standard scale.

(4A) A person shall not be liable to be convicted under subsection (4) of this section by reason of failing to comply with any requirement under subsection (1)(*a*) or (*b*) of this section if he proves to the court that, if the vehicle in question had been such a vehicle as is mentioned in section 98(2A) of this Act, there would have been no contravention of the provisions of this Part of this Act so far as they relate to the use of such vehicles.

(5) Any person who makes, or causes to be made, any entry on a record sheet kept or carried for the purposes of the Community Recording Equipment Regulation or section 97 of this Act or any entry in a book, register or document kept or carried for the purposes of regulations under section 98 thereof which he knows to be false or, with intent to deceive, alters or causes to be altered any such record or entry shall be liable[3]—

- (a) on summary conviction, to a fine not exceeding **the prescribed sum**.
- (b) on conviction on indictment, to imprisonment for a term not exceeding two years.

(6) If an officer has reason to believe that an offence under subsection (5) of this section has been committed in respect of any record or document inspected by him under this section, he may seize that record or document; and where a record or document is seized as aforesaid and within six months of the date on which it was seized no person has been charged since that date with an offence in relation to that record or document under that subsection and the record or document has not been returned to the person from whom it was taken, a magistrate's court shall, on an application made for the purpose by that person or by an officer, make such order respecting the disposal of the record or document and award such costs as the justice of the case may require.

(7) *Scotland.*

(8) In this Part of this Act "officer" means an examiner appointed under section 66A of the Road Traffic Act 1988 and any person authorised for the purposes of this Part by the traffic commissioner for any area.

(9) The powers conferred by this Part of this Act on an officer shall be exercisable also by a police constable, who shall not, if wearing uniform, be required to produce any authority.

(10) In this section references to the inspection and copying of any record produced by means of recording equipment installed in a vehicle include references to the application to the record of any process for eliciting the information recorded thereby and to taking down the information elicited from it.

(11) Subsections (1) to (7) and (10) do not apply in respect of vehicles to which section 97 of this Act applies.

[Transport Act 1968, s 99, as amended by the Road Traffic Act 1972, Sch 7, the European Communities Act 1972, s 2, the Road Traffic (Drivers' Ages and Hours of Work) Act 1976, s 2, the Criminal Law Act 1977, s 28, SI 1979/1746, the Criminal Justice Act 1982, ss 38 and 46, the Transport Act 1985, Sch 2, SI 1986/1457, the Road Traffic (Consequential Provisions) Act 1988, Sch 3, the Road Traffic Act 1991, Sch 4 and SI 2005/1904.]

---

1. The functions of an examiner under this section extend to foreign vehicles (Road Traffic (Foreign Vehicles) Act 1972, Sch 1, post).
2. As an operator is required to retain tachograph records for a period of one year, more than one notice may be served to produce records for the same period. The practice of traffic examiners is to issue a preliminary request for the production of tachograph records in the form of a notice under s 9(1). If subsequent analysis reveals that there are missing records, the operator is given one or two further opportunities to produce the missing records by the service of further notices under s 9(1). Failure to comply with such notice is an offence, and the time limit for prosecution runs from the date of failure to produce records in accordance with the notice (*John Mann International Ltd v Vehicle Inspectorate* [2004] EWHC 1236 (Admin), [2004] 1 WLR 2731, 169 JP 171).
3. For procedure in respect of an offence triable either way, see the Magistrates' Courts Act 1980, ss 18–21, ante.

4–286ZA 99ZA. Inspection of records and other documents and data relating to recording equipment. (1) An officer may, on production if so required of his authority, require any person to produce, and permit him to inspect, remove, retain and copy—

- (a) if that person is the owner of a vehicle to which section 97 applies, any document of that person which the officer may reasonably require to inspect for the purpose of ascertaining whether the provisions of this Part of this Act have been complied with;
- (b) any record sheet or hard copy of electronically stored data which that person is required by the Community Recording Equipment Regulation to retain or to be able to produce;

(*c*)   any book, register or other document required by the applicable Community Rules or which the officer may reasonably require to inspect for the purpose of ascertaining whether the requirements of the applicable Community rules have been complied with.

(2)   An officer may, on production if so required of his authority, require any person—

(*a*)   to produce and permit him to inspect any driver card which that person is required by Article 15(7) of the Community Recording Equipment Regulation to be able to produce; and

(*b*)   to permit the officer to copy the data stored on the driver card (and to remove temporarily the driver card for the purpose of doing so) and to remove and retain the copy.

(3)   If the officer so requires by notice in writing, anything that a person is required to produce under subsection (1) or (2) of this section shall, instead of being produced when the requirement under those subsections is imposed, be produced at an address specified in the notice, within such time (not being less than ten days) from the service of the notice as is so specified.

(4)   Where a notice is served under subsection (3) of this section, the officer may exercise his powers under this section at the place specified in the notice.

(5)   In this Part of this Act any reference to copying data stored on a driver card or on digital recording equipment includes a reference to making a hard copy or an electronic copy of the data (and any reference to copies of data shall be construed accordingly).

(6)   In this Part of this Act—

"digital recording equipment" means recording equipment that complies with Annex IB to the Community Recording Equipment Regulation;

"driver card" has the meaning given in that Annex;

"electronic copy" of data means a copy of data stored electronically together with the data's digital signature (within the meaning of that Annex);

"hard copy" in relation to data stored electronically means a printed out version of the data.

[Transport Act 1968, s 99ZA as inserted by SI 2005/1904.]

4–286ZB   **99ZB. Power of entry.**   (1) An officer may, on production if so required of his authority, at any time enter any vehicle to which section 97 of this Act applies in order to inspect that vehicle and any recording equipment in or on it.

(2)   Where any officer enters any vehicle under subsection (1) of this section he may—

(*a*)   inspect, remove, retain and copy any record sheet that he finds there on which a record has been produced by means of analogue recording equipment or on which an entry has been made;

(*b*)   inspect, remove, retain and copy any hard copy of data that he finds there which was stored on any digital recording equipment or on a driver card;

(*c*)   inspect, remove, retain and copy any other document that he finds there which the officer may reasonably require to inspect for the purpose of ascertaining whether the requirements of the applicable Community rules have been complied with;

(*d*)   inspect any driver card that he finds there, copy the data stored on it (using any digital recording equipment in or on the vehicle or temporarily removing the driver card for the purpose of copying the data) and remove and retain the copy;

(*e*)   copy data stored on any digital recording equipment that is in or on the vehicle and remove and retain that copy;

(*f*)   inspect any recording equipment that is in or on the vehicle and, if necessary for the purposes of the inspection, remove it from the vehicle;

(*g*)   retain the recording equipment as evidence if he finds that it has been interfered with;

(*h*)   inspect the vehicle for the purpose of ascertaining whether there is in or on the vehicle any device which is capable of interfering with the proper operation of any recording equipment in or on the vehicle;

(*i*)   inspect anything in or on the vehicle which he believes is such a device and, if necessary for the purpose of the inspection, remove it from the vehicle;

(*j*)   retain the device as evidence if he finds that it is capable of interfering with the proper operation of the recording equipment.

(3)   Where any officer who is an examiner appointed under section 66A of the Road Traffic Act 1988, or any constable, enters any vehicle under subsection (1) of this section, he may, if he has reason to believe that—

(*a*)   any recording equipment in or on the vehicle has been interfered with so as to affect its proper operation, or

(*b*)   there is in or on the vehicle any device which is capable of interfering with the proper operation of any recording equipment in or on the vehicle,

require the driver or operator of the vehicle to take it to an address specified by the officer or constable for the purposes of enabling an inspection of the recording equipment, the vehicle or any device in or on it to be carried out.

(4)   An officer may, on production if so required of his authority, at any time which is reasonable having regard to the circumstances of the case, enter any premises on which he has reason to believe that—

(*a*)   a vehicle to which section 97 of this Act applies is kept;

(b) any such document as is mentioned in section 99ZA(1) of this Act is to be found;

(c) any driver card or copy of data previously stored on a driver card or on recording equipment is to be found; or

(d) any digital recording equipment is to be found.

(5) Where any officer enters any premises under subsection (4) of this section he may—

(a) inspect any vehicle which he finds there and to which section 97 of this Act applies;

(b) inspect, remove, retain and copy any such document as is mentioned in section 99ZA(1) of this Act that he finds there;

(c) make a copy of any such copy of data as is mentioned in subsection (4)(c) of this section that he finds there, and remove and retain the copies he makes;

(d) inspect any driver card that he finds there, copy the data stored on it (using any digital recording equipment on the premises or temporarily removing the driver card for the purpose of copying the data) and remove and retain the copy;

(e) copy data stored on any digital recording equipment that he finds there and remove and retain that copy;

(f) inspect any recording equipment that he finds there and, if necessary for the purposes of inspection, remove it from the premises;

(g) retain any such recording equipment as evidence if he finds that it has been interfered with;

(h) inspect anything that he finds there which he believes is a device capable of interfering with the proper operation of any recording equipment and, if necessary for the purpose of the inspection, remove it from the premises;

(i) retain any such device as evidence if he finds that it is capable of interfering with the proper operation of recording equipment.

(6) For the purposes of—

(a) exercising any of his powers under this section in relation to a vehicle or anything found in or on a vehicle, or

(b) exercising any of his powers under section 99ZA(1) or (2) of this Act in respect of a document or driver card carried by the driver of a vehicle,

an officer may detain the vehicle during such time as is required for the exercise of that power.

(7) If—

(a) at the time when a requirement is imposed under subsection (3) of this section the vehicle is more than five miles from the address specified by the officer or constable to which the vehicle is to be taken; and

(b) the Community Recording Equipment Regulation is found not to have been contravened in relation to the recording equipment, the vehicle or any device in or on it;

the relevant person must pay, in respect of loss occasioned, such amount as in default of agreement may be determined by a single arbitrator (in Scotland, arbiter) agreed upon by the parties or, in default of agreement, appointed by the Secretary of State.

(8) In subsection (7) of this section "relevant person" means—

(a) if the requirement was imposed by an examiner appointed under section 66A of the Road Traffic Act 1988, the Secretary of State, and

(b) if the requirement was imposed by a constable, the chief officer of police for the police area in which the requirement was imposed.

(9) In this Part of this Act "analogue recording equipment" means recording equipment that complies with Annex I to the Community Recording Equipment Regulation.
[Transport Act 1968, s 99ZB as inserted by SI 2005/1904.]

4–286ZC   99ZC. Sections 99ZA and 99ZB: supplementary.   (1) Where an officer makes any hard copy of data stored on a driver card or on recording equipment under section 99ZA or 99ZB of this Act he may require a person to sign the hard copy (if necessary with manual corrections) to confirm that it is a true and complete record of his activities during the period covered by it.

(2) Any record sheet, book, register, other document or any electronic copy of data that is retained by an officer under section 99ZA or 99ZB of this Act may only be retained—

(a) for six months; and

(b) if it is required as evidence in any proceedings, any further period during which it is so required.

(3) In sections 99ZA and 99ZB of this Act references to the inspection and copying of any record produced by means of equipment in or on a vehicle include references to the application to the record of any process for eliciting the information recorded by it and to taking down the information elicited from it.
[Transport Act 1968, s 99ZC as inserted by SI 2005/1904.]

4–286ZD   99ZD. Offence of failing to comply with requirements or obstructing an officer.
(1) A person commits an offence if he—

(a) fails without reasonable excuse to comply with any requirement imposed on him by an officer under any of sections 99ZA to 99ZC of this Act; or (*b*) obstructs an officer in the exercise of his powers under section 99ZB or 99ZF of this Act.

(2) A person guilty of an offence under subsection (1) of this section is liable on summary conviction to a fine not exceeding level 5 on the standard scale.
[Transport Act 1968, s 99ZD as inserted by SI 2005/1904.]

4–286ZE   99ZE. Offences: false records and data etc.   (1) A person commits an offence—

(*a*) if he makes, or causes or permits to be made, a relevant record or entry which he knows to be false;
(*b*) if, with intent to deceive, he alters, or causes or permits to be altered, a relevant record or entry;
(*c*) if he destroys or suppresses, or causes or permits to be destroyed or suppressed, a relevant record or entry; or
(*d*) if he fails without reasonable excuse to make a relevant record or entry, or causes or permits such a failure.

(2) For the purposes of subsection (1) of this section a "relevant record or entry" is—

(*a*) any record or entry required to be made by or for the purposes of the Community Recording Equipment Regulation or section 97 of this Act; or
(*b*) any entry in a book, register or document kept or carried for the purposes of the applicable Community rules.

(3) A person commits an offence—

(*a*) if he records or causes or permits to be recorded any data which he knows to be false on recording equipment or on a driver card;
(*b*) if he records or causes or permits to be recorded any data which he knows to be false on any hard copy of data previously stored on recording equipment or on a driver card;
(*c*) if, with intent to deceive, he alters, or causes or permits to be altered, any data stored on recording equipment or on a driver card or appearing on any copy of data previously so stored;
(*d*) if, with intent to deceive, he produces anything falsely purporting to be a hard copy of data stored on recording equipment or on a driver card;
(*e*) if he destroys or suppresses, or causes or permits to be destroyed or suppressed, any data stored in compliance with the requirements of the applicable Community rules on recording equipment or on a driver card; or
(*f*) if he fails without reasonable excuse to record any data on recording equipment or on a driver card, or causes or permits such a failure.

(4) A person guilty of an offence under subsection (1) or (3) of this section consisting otherwise than in permitting an act or omission is liable—

(*a*) on summary conviction, to a fine not exceeding the statutory maximum; or
(*b*) on conviction on indictment, to imprisonment for a term not exceeding two years or to a fine, or to both.

(5) A person guilty of an offence under subsection (1) or (3) of this section consisting in permitting an act or omission is liable on summary conviction to a fine not exceeding level 5 on the standard scale.

(6) A person commits an offence if he produces, supplies or installs any device—

(*a*) that is designed to interfere with the proper operation of any recording equipment, or
(*b*) that is designed to enable the falsification, alteration, destruction or suppression of data stored in compliance with requirements of the applicable Community Rules on any recording equipment or driver's card.

(7) A person commits an offence if without reasonable excuse he provides information which would assist other persons in producing any such device.

(8) A person shall not be liable to be convicted under subsection (6) or (7) of this section if he proves to the court that he produced, supplied or installed the device, or provided information to assist a person in producing a device, for use in connection with the enforcement of the provisions of this Part of this Act.

(9) A person guilty of an offence under subsection (6) or (7) of this section is liable on summary conviction to a fine not exceeding level 5 on the standard scale.

(10) For the purposes of this section, a person shall be taken to permit an act or omission if he is, or ought reasonably to be, aware of the act or omission, or of it being a likelihood, and takes no steps to prevent it.
[Transport Act 1968, s 99ZE as inserted by SI 2005/1904.]

4–286ZF   99ZF. Power to seize documents.   (1) If an officer has reason to believe that an offence under section 99ZE of this Act has been committed in respect of any document inspected by him under section 99ZA or 99ZB of this Act, he may seize that document.

(2) Where a document is so seized, a magistrates' court shall, on an application made for the purpose by that person or by an officer, make such order respecting the disposal of the document and award such costs as the justice of the case may require if—

(a) within six months of the date on which it was seized no person has been charged since that date with an offence under section 99ZE of this Act in relation to that document; and

(b) the document has not been returned to the person from whom it was taken.

(3) Any proceedings in Scotland under subsection (2) of this section shall be taken by way of summary application in the sheriff court.

In the application of that subsection to Scotland the reference to costs shall be construed as a reference to expenses.

[Transport Act 1968, s 99ZF as inserted by SI 2005/1904.]

4–286A 99A. Power to prohibit driving of vehicle. (1) If—

(a) the driver of a UK vehicle obstructs an authorised person in the exercise of his powers under subsection (2) or (3) of section 99 or under section 99ZB of this Act or fails to comply with any requirement made by an authorised person under subsection (1) section 99 or under any of sections 99ZA to 99ZC of this Act,

(b) it appears to an authorised person that, in relation to a UK vehicle or its driver, there has been a contravention of any of the provisions of—

(i) sections 96 to 98 of this Act and any orders or regulations under those sections, or

(ii) the applicable Community rules,

or that there will be such a contravention if the vehicle is driven on a road, or

(c) it appears to an authorised person that an offence under section 99(5) or section 99ZE of this Act has been committed in respect of a UK vehicle or its driver,

the authorised person may prohibit the driving of the vehicle on a road either for a specified period or without limitation of time.

(2) Where an authorised person prohibits the driving of a vehicle under this section, he may also direct the driver to remove the vehicle (and, if it is a motor vehicle drawing a trailer, also to remove the trailer) to such place and subject to such conditions as are specified in the direction; and the prohibition shall not apply to the removal of the vehicle in accordance with that direction.

(3) On imposing a prohibition under subsection (1) of this section, the authorised person shall give notice in writing of the prohibition to the driver of the vehicle, specifying the circumstances (as mentioned in paragraph (a), (b) or (c) of that subsection) in consequence of which the prohibition is imposed and stating whether it is imposed only for a specified period (and if so specifying the period) or without limitation of time.

(4) Any direction under subsection (2) of this section may be given—

(a) in the notice under subsection (3) of this section, or

(b) in a separate notice in writing given to the driver of the vehicle.

(5) In this section—

"authorised person" means—

(a) an examiner appointed by the Secretary of State under section 66A of the Road Traffic Act 1988, or

(b) a constable authorised to act for the purposes of this section by or on behalf of a chief officer of police;

"UK vehicle" means a vehicle registered under the Vehicle Excise and Registration Act 1994.

[Transport Act 1968, s 99A as inserted by the Transport Act 2000, s 266 and amended by SI 2005/1904.]

4–286B 99B. Duration and removal of prohibition. (1) Subject to any exemption granted under subsection (2) of this section, a prohibition under subsection (1) of section 99A of this Act shall come into force as soon as notice of it has been given in accordance with subsection (3) of that section and shall continue in force—

(a) until it is removed under subsection (3) of this section, or

(b) in the case of a prohibition imposed for a specified period, until it is removed under that subsection or that period expires, whichever first occurs.

(2) Where notice of a prohibition has been given under section 99A(3) of this Act in respect of a vehicle, an exemption in writing for the use of the vehicle in such manner, subject to such conditions and for such purposes as may be specified in the exemption may be granted by any authorised person.

(3) A prohibition under section 99A(1) of this Act may be removed by any authorised person, if he is satisfied that appropriate action has been taken to remove or remedy the circumstances (as mentioned in paragraph (a), (b) or (c) of section 99A(1) of this Act) in consequence of which the prohibition was imposed; and on doing so the authorised person shall give notice in writing of the removal of the prohibition to the driver of the vehicle.

(4) In this section, "authorised person" has the same meaning as in section 99A of this Act.

[Transport Act 1968, s 99B as inserted by the Transport Act 2000, s 266.]

4–286C 99C. Failure to comply with prohibition. Any person who—

(a) drives a vehicle on a road in contravention of a prohibition imposed under section 99A(1) of this Act,

(*b*) causes or permits a vehicle to be driven on a road in contravention of such a prohibition, or
(*c*) refuses or fails to comply within a reasonable time with a direction given under section 99A(2) of this Act,

shall be guilty of an offence and liable on summary conviction to a fine not exceeding level 5 on the standard scale."
[Transport Act 1968, s 99C as inserted by the Transport Act 2000, s 266.]

4–287 101. Orders and regulations under Part VI[1]**.** Power to make orders to give effect to international agreements[2] [s 100]; and power to make regulations under Part VI [s 101].
[Transport Act 1968, s 101 amended by the Transport Act 1982, s 64.]

1. Any orders made by virtue of s 100 will extend to foreign vehicles (Road Traffic (Foreign Vehicles) Act 1972, Sch 2, post).
2. Orders made under s 99 may provide for the punishment of contraventions (s 99(1)(*e*)).

4–288 102. Application to the Crown and exemption for police and fire brigade. (1) Subject to subsection (2) of this section, this Part of this Act shall apply to vehicles and persons in the public service of the Crown.
  (2) This Part of this Act shall not apply in the case of motor vehicles owned by the Secretary of State for Defence and used for naval, military or air force purposes or in the case of vehicles so used while being driven by persons for the time being subject to the orders of a member of the armed forces of the Crown.
  (3) Where an offence under this Part of this Act is alleged to have been committed in connection with a vehicle in the public service of the Crown, proceedings may be brought in respect of the offence against a person nominated for the purpose on behalf of the Crown; and subject to subsection (3A) below, where any such offence is committed any person so nominated shall also be guilty of the offence as well as any person actually responsible for the offence (but without prejudice to proceedings against any person so responsible)[1].
  (3A) Where a person is convicted of an offence by virtue of subsection (3) above—
(*a*) no order may be made on his conviction save an order imposing a fine;
(*b*) payment of any fine imposed on him in respect of that offence may not be enforced against him; and
(*c*) apart from the imposition of any such fine, the conviction shall be disregarded for all purposes other than any appeal (whether by way of case stated or otherwise)[1].
  (4) This Part of this Act shall not apply in the case of motor vehicles while being used for police or fire and rescue authority purposes.
[Transport Act 1968, s 102 amended by the Transport Act 1982, s 64 and the Fire and Rescue Services Act 2004, Sch 1.]

1. Section 102(3) and (3A) is printed as substituted by the Transport Act 1982, s 64 and repeated in Sch 3 to the Road Traffic (Consequential Provisions) Act 1988.

4–289 102A. Exclusion of application to tramcars and trolley vehicles. (1) This Part of this Act and section 255 of the Road Traffic Act 1960 in its application thereto shall not apply to tramcars or trolley vehicles operated under statutory powers.
  (2) In this section "operated under statutory powers" means, in relation to tramcars or trolley vehicles, that their use is authorised or regulated by special Act of Parliament or by an order having the force of an Act.
  (3) Subsection (1) above shall have effect subject to any such Act or order as is mentioned in subsection (2) above, and any such Act or order may apply to the tramcars or trolley vehicles to which it relates any of the provisions excluded by the said subsection (1).
[Transport Act 1968, s 102A inserted by Road Traffic Act 1972, Sch 7 and the Road Traffic (Consequential Provisions) Act 1988, Sch 3.]

4–290 103. Interpretation, supplementary provisions, etc, for Part VI[1]**.** (1) In this Part of this Act—
  "agriculture" has the meaning assigned by section 109(3) of the Agriculture Act 1947, or, in relation to Scotland, section 86(3) of the Agriculture (Scotland) Act 1948;
  "analogue recording equipment" has the meaning given by section 99ZB(9) of this Act;
  "the Community Recording Equipment Regulation" has the meaning given by section 97(7) of this Act;
  "driver", "employee-driver" and "owner-driver" have the meaning assigned by section 95(3) of this Act;
  "copying" and "copies", in relation to data stored on a driver card or digital recording equipment, is to be construed in accordance with section 99ZA(5) of this Act;
  "digital recording equipment" has the meaning given by section 99ZA(6) of this Act;
  "the domestic drivers' hours code" has the meaning given by section 96(13) of this Act;
  "driver", "employee-driver" and "owner-driver" have the meaning assigned by section 95(3) of this Act;
  "driver card" has the meaning given by section 99ZA(6) of this Act;

"electronic copy" of data has the meaning given by section 99ZA(6) of this Act;

"employer", in relation to an employee-driver, means the employer of that driver in the employment by virtue of which that driver is an employee-driver[2];

"the applicable Community rules" means any directly applicable Community provision for the time being in force about the driving of road vehicles;

"hard copy" in relation to data stored electronically has the meaning given by section 99ZA(6) of this Act;

repealed

"officer" has the meaning given by section 99(8) of this Act;

"prescribed" means prescribed by regulations made by the Minister;

"recording equipment" has the meaning given by section 97(7) of this Act;

"record sheet" includes a temporary sheet attached to a record sheet in accordance with Article 16(2) of the Community Recording Equipment Regulation;

"relevant Community provision" means any Community provision for the time being in force about the driving of road vehicles, whether directly applicable or not;

"working day", in relation to any driver, means—

    (a) any period during which he is on duty and which does not fall to be aggregated with any other such period by virtue of paragraph (b) of this definition; and

    (b) where a period during which he is on duty is not followed by an interval for rest of not less than eleven hours or (where permitted by virtue of section 96(4)(b) of this Act) of not less than nine and a half hours, the aggregate of that period an each successive such period until there is such an interval as aforesaid, together with any interval or intervals between periods so aggregated;

"working week" means, subject to subsection (5) of this section, a week beginning at midnight between Saturday and Sunday;

and any expression not defined above which is also used in the Act of 1960 has the same meaning as in that Act.

(2) For the purposes of this Part of this Act a director of a company shall be deemed to be employed by it.

(3) In this Part of this Act references to a person driving a vehicle are references to his being at the driving controls of the vehicle for the purpose of controlling its movement, whether it is in motion or is stationary with the engine running.

(4) In this Part of this Act references to a driver being on duty are references—

    (a) in the case of an employee-driver, to his being on duty (whether for the purpose of driving a vehicle to which this Part of this Act applies or for other purposes) in the employment by virtue of which he is an employee-driver, or in any other employment under the person who is his employer in the first-mentioned employment; and

    (b) in the case of an owner-driver, to his driving a vehicle to which this Part of this Act applies for the purposes of a trade or business carried on by him or being otherwise engaged in work for the purposes of that trade or business, being work in connection with such a vehicle or the load carried thereby.

(5) The traffic commissioner for any area may, on the application of an owner-driver or of the employer of an employee-driver, from time to time direct that a week beginning at midnight between two days other than Saturday and Sunday shall be, or be deemed to have been, a working week in relation to that owner-driver or employee-driver; but where by virtue of any such direction a new working week begins before the expiration of a previous working week, then without prejudice to the application of the provisions of this Part of this Act in relation to the new working week, those provisions shall continue to apply in relation to the previous working week until its expiration.

(6) In section 98(2)(e) of this Act "a small goods vehicle" means a goods vehicle which has a plated weight of the prescribed description not exceeding 3500 kilograms or (not having a plated weight) has an unladen weight not exceeding 1525 kilograms; but the Minister may by regulations direct that the foregoing provisions of this subsection shall have effect, in relation to either or both of those sections—

    (a) with the substitution for either of the weights there specified of such other weight as may be specified in the regulations;

    (b) with the substitution for either of those weights or for any other weight for the time being specified as aforesaid of a weight expressed in terms of the metric system, being a weight which is equivalent to that for which it is substituted or does not differ from it by more than five per cent thereof.

(7) An offence under this Part of this Act may be treated for the purpose of conferring jurisdiction on a court (but without prejudice to any jurisdiction it may have apart from this subsection) as having been committed in any of the following places, that is to say—

    (a) the place where the person charged with the offence was driving when evidence of the offence first came to the attention of a constable or vehicle examiner;

    (b) the place where that person resides or is or is believed to reside or be at the time when the proceedings are commenced; or

    (c) the place where at that time that person or, in the case of an employee-driver, that person's employer or, in the case of an owner-driver, the person for whom he was driving, has his place or principal place of business or his operating centre for the vehicle in question.

In this subsection "vehicle examiner" means an officer within the meaning of section 99 of this Act.

(8) The enactments specified in Schedule 11 to this Act shall have effect subject to the amendments there specified.

(9) Any order made under section 166(2) of this Act appointing a day for the purposes of any of the provisions of this Part of this Act may contain such transitional provision as the Minister thinks necessary or expedient as respects the application of any particular provision of this Part of this Act to a working week or working day falling partly before and partly after the date on which that provision comes into operation.

[Transport Act 1968, s 103, as amended by the European Communities Act 1972, Sch 4, the Road Traffic (Drivers' Ages and Hours of Work) Act 1976, s 3, SI 1979/1746, SI 1981/1373, the Transport Act 1985, Schs 2 and 8, SI 1986/1457 and SI 2005/1904.]

---

1. Functions of the Minister of Transport have been transferred to the Secretary of State by SI 1981/238.
2. This means that whilst he is driving, a driver is employed by the person who wants him to drive (*Alcock v G C Griston Ltd* [1981] RTR 34).

Road Traffic (Foreign Vehicles) Act 1972
(1972 c 27)

4–720   1. Power in certain cases to prohibit driving of foreign vehicle. (1) The provisions of this section shall have effect with respect to any foreign goods vehicle1 or foreign public service vehicle[1] where—

    (a) an examiner[1] or an authorised inspector exercises, in relation to the vehicle or its driver, any functions of the examiner or authorised inspector under an enactment or instrument specified in the first column of Schedule 1 to this Act, or any functions of the authorised inspecting officer under a Community instrument specified in that column, or

    (b) an authorised person exercises, in relation to the vehicle, any functions of that person under sections 78 and 79 of the Road Traffic Act 1988 (weighing of motor vehicles).

(2) If in any such case as is mentioned in subsection (1)(a) of this section—

    (a) the driver[1] obstructs the examiner or authorised inspector in the exercise of his functions under the enactment or instrument in question, or refuses, neglects or otherwise fails to comply with any requirement made by the examiner or authorised inspector under that enactment, or instrument or

    (b) it appears to the examiner or authorised inspector that, in relation to the vehicle or its driver, there has been a contravention of any of the enactments specified in the first column of Schedule 2 to this Act, or that there will be such a contravention if the vehicle is driven on a road,

the examiner or authorised inspector may prohibit the driving of the vehicle on a road, either absolutely or for a specified purpose, and either for a specified period or without any limitation of time.★

(3) If in any such case as is mentioned in subsection (1)(b) of this section—

    (a) the driver obstructs the authorised person in the exercise of his functions under the said sections 78 and 79, or refuses, neglects or otherwise fails to comply with any requirement made by the authorised person under those sections, or

    (b) it appears to the authorised person that any limit of weight applicable to the vehicle by virtue of regulations made under section 41 of the Road Traffic Act 1988 has been exceeded, or will be exceeded if the vehicle is driven on a road,

the authorised person may prohibit the driving of the vehicle on a road, either absolutely or for a specified purpose.

(4) Where an examiner or authorised inspector or an authorised person prohibits the driving of a vehicle under this section, he may also direct the driver to remove the vehicle (and, if it is a motor vehicle drawing a trailer, also to remove the trailer) to such place and subject to such conditions as are specified in the direction; and the prohibition shall not apply to the removal of the vehicle in accordance with that direction.

(5) Where a prohibition is imposed under subsection (2) or subsection (3) of this section, the examiner or authorised person shall forthwith give notice in writing of the prohibition to the driver of the vehicle, specifying the circumstances (as mentioned in paragraph (a) or paragraph (b) of either of those subsections) in consequence of which the prohibition is imposed, and—

    (a) stating whether the prohibition is on all driving of the vehicle or only on driving it for a specified purpose (and, if the latter, specifying the purpose), and★

    (b) where the prohibition is imposed under subsection (2) of this section, also stating whether it is imposed only for a specified period (and, if so, specifying the period) or without limitation of time;

and any direction under subsection (4) of this section may be given either in that notice or in a separate notice in writing given to the driver of the vehicle.

(6) In the case of a goods vehicle—

(a) a prohibition under subsection (2)(b) above, by reference to a supposed contravention of section 40A of the Road Traffic Act 1988 (using vehicle in dangerous condition etc) or regulations under section 41 of that Act (construction, weight, equipment etc of motor vehicles and trailers), may be imposed with a direction making it irremovable unless and until the vehicle has been inspected at an official testing station;

(b) a prohibition imposed under subsection (3) above may be against driving the vehicle on a road until the weight has been reduced and official notification has been given to whoever is for the time being in charge of the vehicle that it is permitted to proceed.

(7) Official notification for the purposes of subsection (6)(b) above must be in writing and be given by an authorised person and may be withheld until the vehicle has been weighed or re-weighed in order to satisfy the person giving the notification that the weight has been sufficiently reduced.
[Road Traffic (Foreign Vehicles) Act 1972, s 1, as amended by the Transport Act 1978, Sch 3, SI 1984/748, the Road Traffic (Consequential Provisions) Act 1988, Sch 3 and the Road Traffic Act 1991, Sch 4.]

*Amended by the Transport Act 1982, s 10, when in force.
1. For definition see s 7(1), post.

4–721 2. Provisions supplementary to s 1. (1) Subject to any exemption granted under subsection (2) of this section, a prohibition under section 1 of this Act shall come into force as soon as notice of it has been given in accordance with subsection (5) of that section, and shall continue in force until it is removed under the following provisions of this section (or, in the case of a prohibition imposed only for a specified period, shall continue in force until either it is removed under this section or that period expires, whichever first occurs).

(2) Where notice of a prohibition has been given under subsection (5) of section 1 of this Act in respect of a vehicle, an exemption in writing for the use of the vehicle in such manner, subject to such conditions and for such purpose as may be specified in the exemption may be granted—

(a) in the case of a prohibition under subsection (2) of that section, by any examiner, or
(b) in the case of a prohibition under subsection (3) of that section, by any authorised person.

(3) A prohibition under subsection (2) of section 1 of this Act may be removed by any examiner, and a prohibition under subsection (3) of that section may be removed by any authorised person, if he is satisfied that appropriate action has been taken to remove or remedy the circumstances (as mentioned in paragraph (a) or paragraph (b) of either of those subsections) in consequence of which the prohibition was imposed; and on doing so the examiner or authorised person shall forthwith give notice in writing of the removal of the prohibition to the driver of the vehicle.*

(3A) If the prohibition under section 1 of this Act has been imposed with a direction under subsection (6)(a) of that section, the prohibition shall not then be removed under subsection (3) above unless and until the vehicle has been inspected at an official testing station.

(3B) In the case of vehicles brought to an official testing station for inspection with a view to removal of a prohibition, section 72A of the Road Traffic Act 1988 (fees for inspection) applies.**

(4) In the exercise of his functions under section 1 of this Act or under this section an examiner shall act in accordance with any general directions given by the Secretary of State; and (without prejudice to the preceding provisions of this subsection) an examiner, in exercising his functions under subsection (2) of this section, shall act in accordance with any directions given by the Secretary of State with respect to the exercise of those functions in any particular case.
[Road Traffic (Foreign Vehicles) Act 1972, s 2, as amended by the Transport Act 1978, Sch 3, the Road Traffic (Consequential Provisions) Act 1988 Sch 3 and the Road Traffic Act 1991, Sch 4.]

*Amended by the Transport Act 1982, s 10, when in force.
**Amended by the Transport Act 1982, Sch 5, when in force.

4–722 3. Enforcement provisions. (1) Any person who—

(a) drives a vehicle on a road in contravention of a prohibition imposed under section 1 of this Act, or
(b) causes or permits a vehicle to be driven on a road in contravention of such a prohibition, or
(c) refuses, neglects or otherwise fails to comply within a reasonable time with a direction given under subsection (4) of that section,

shall be guilty of an offence and shall be liable on summary conviction to a fine not exceeding **level 5** on the standard scale.

(2) *Repealed.*

(3) Where a constable in uniform has reasonable cause to suspect the driver of a vehicle of having committed an offence under subsection (1) of this section, the constable may detain the vehicle, and for that purpose may give a direction, specifying an appropriate person and directing the vehicle to be removed by that person to such place and subject to such conditions as are specified in the direction; and the prohibition shall not apply to the removal of the vehicle in accordance with that direction.

(4) Where under subsection (3) of this section a constable—

(a) detains a motor vehicle drawing a trailer, or
(b) detains a trailer drawn by a motor vehicle,

then, for the purpose of securing the removal of the trailer, he may also (in a case falling within paragraph (*a*) of this subsection) detain the trailer or (in a case falling within paragraph (*b*) of this subsection) detain the motor vehicle; and a direction under subsection (3) of this section may require both the motor vehicle and the trailer to be removed to the place specified in the direction.

(5) A vehicle which, in accordance with a direction given under subsection (3) of this section, is removed to a place specified in the direction shall be detained in that place, or in any other place to which it is removed in accordance with a further direction given under that subsection, until a constable (or, if that place is in the occupation of the Secretary of State, the Secretary of State) authorises the vehicle to be released on being satisfied—

(*a*) that the prohibition (if any) imposed in respect of the vehicle under section 1 of this Act has been removed, or that no such prohibition was imposed, or

(*b*) that appropriate arrangements have been made for removing or remedying the circumstances in consequence of which any such prohibition was imposed, or

(*c*) that the vehicle will be taken forthwith to a place from which it will be taken out of Great Britain, or

(*d*) in the case of a vehicle detained under subsection (4) of this section, that (in the case of a motor vehicle) the purpose for which it was detained has been fulfilled or (in the case of a trailer) it is no longer necessary to obtain it for the purpose of safeguarding the trailer or its load.

(6) Any person who—

(*a*) drives a vehicle in accordance with a direction given under this section, or

(*b*) is in charge of a place at which a vehicle is detained under subsection (5) of this section,

shall not be liable for any damage to, or loss in respect of, the vehicle or its load unless it is shown that he did not take reasonable care of the vehicle while driving it or, as the case may be, did not, while the vehicle was detained in that place, take reasonable care of the vehicle or (if the vehicle was detained there with its load) did not take reasonable care of its load.

(7) In this section "appropriate person"—

(*a*) in relation to a direction to remove a motor vehicle, other than a motor vehicle drawing a trailer, means a person licensed to drive vehicles of the class to which the vehicle belongs, and

(*b*) in relation to a direction to remove a trailer, or to remove a motor vehicle drawing a trailer, means a person licensed to drive vehicles of a class which, when the direction is complied with, will include the motor vehicle drawing the trailer in accordance with that direction.

[Road Traffic (Foreign Vehicles) Act 1972, s 3 as amended by the Criminal Justice Act 1982, ss 39 and 46 and Sch 3 and the Police and Criminal Evidence Act 1984, Sch 7.]

4–723   4. Production of certain documents.   (1) Subsection (3) of this section shall have effect in relation to a vehicle where it appears to an examiner that the vehicle—

(*a*) is a foreign goods vehicle within the meaning of regulations for the time being in force under section 57(6) of the Goods Vehicles (Licensing of Operators) Act 1995 (which enables certain provisions of that Act to be modified in their application to vehicles brought temporarily into Great Britain), and

(*b*) is being used, or has been brought into Great Britain for the purposes of being used, in such circumstances as, by virtue of section 2(1) of that Act as modified by the regulations, to require a document of a description specified in the regulations to be carried on it.

(2) The next following subsection shall also have effect in relation to a vehicle where it appears to an examiner that the vehicle—

(*a*) is a foreign public service vehicle, and

(*b*) is being used, or has been brought into Great Britain for the purpose of being used, in such circumstances as, by virtue of section 12(1) of the Public Passenger Vehicles Act 1981 as modified by regulations for the time being in force under section 60(1)(*m*) of that Act (which enables certain provisions of that Act to be modified in their application to public service vehicles registered outside Great Britain), to require a document of a description specified in the regulations to be carried on it.

(3) In the circumstances mentioned in subsection (1) or subsection (2) of this section, the examiner, on production if so required of his authority—

(*a*) may require the driver of the vehicle to produce a document of the description in question and to permit the examiner to inspect and copy it, and

(*b*) may detain the vehicle for such time as is requisite for the purpose of inspecting and copying the document;

and, if the driver refuses or fails to comply with any such requirement (including any case where he does so by reason that no such document is carried on the vehicle), the examiner may prohibit the driving of the vehicle on a road, either absolutely or for a specified purpose, and either for a specified period or without limitation of time.

(4) In subsections (4) and (5) of section 1 and in sections 2 and 3 of this Act any reference to a prohibition imposed under section 1, or under subsection (2) of section 1, of this Act shall be construed as including a reference to a prohibition imposed under this section; and, in relation to a prohibition imposed under this section, so much of section 1(5) or of section 2(3) of this Act as

relates to the circumstances in consequence of which the prohibition was imposed shall be read subject to the appropriate modifications.

[Road Traffic (Foreign Vehicles) Act 1972, s 4, as amended by the Transport Act 1980, Sch 5, Part II, the Public Passenger Vehicles Act 1981, Sch 7 and the Goods Vehicles (Licensing of Operators) Act 1995, Sch 7.]

4–724 7. Interpretation and transitional provisions. (1) In this Act, except in so far as* the context otherwise requires, the following expressions have the meanings hereby assigned to them, respectively, that is to say—

"authorised person" means a person (whether an examiner or not) authorised to exercise the powers of section 78 of the Road Traffic Act 1988[1] with respect to the weighing of motor vehicles and trailers;
"driver"—

> (a) in relation to a motor vehicle, includes any person who is in charge of the vehicle and, if a separate person acts as steersman, includes that person as well as any other person in charge of the vehicle or engaged in the driving of it, and
>
> (b) in relation to a trailer, means any person who (in accordance with the preceding paragraph) is the driver of the motor vehicle by which the trailer is drawn;

"examiner" means an examiner appointed under section 66A of the Road Traffic Act 1988, or a constable authorised to act for the purposes of this Act by or on behalf of a chief officer of police;
"foreign goods vehicle" (except in section 4 of this Act) means a goods vehicle which has been brought into Great Britain and which, if a motor vehicle, is not registered in the United Kingdom or, if a trailer, is drawn by a motor vehicle not registered in the United Kingdom which has been brought into Great Britain;
"foreign public service vehicle" means a public service vehicle which has been brought into Great Britain and is not registered in the United Kingdom;
"goods vehicle" means a motor vehicle constructed or adapted for use for the carriage or haulage of goods or burden of any description, or a trailer so constructed or adapted;
"public service vehicle" shall be construed in accordance with the Public Passenger Vehicles Act 1981;
"road" means any highway and any other road to which the public has access, and includes bridges over which a road passes.**

(2) In this Act any reference to driving a vehicle shall, in relation to a trailer, be construed as a reference to driving the motor vehicle by which the trailer is drawn.

(3) In this Act any reference to a motor vehicle drawing a trailer, or to a motor vehicle by which a trailer is drawn, shall be construed as a reference to a motor vehicle to which a trailer is attached for the purpose of being drawn by it; and where, for the purpose of being drawn by a motor vehicle, two or more trailers (one of which is attached to the motor vehicle) are attached to each other, the motor vehicle shall for the purposes of this Act be treated as drawing each of those trailers.

(4) For the purposes of this Act a motor vehicle which does not for the time being have exhibited on it a licence or trade plates issued under the Vehicle Excise and Registration Act 1994 shall be presumed, unless the contrary is proved, not to be registered in the United Kingdom.

(5) Where, in accordance with subsection (4) of this section, a motor vehicle is presumed not to be registered in the United Kingdom, but is subsequently proved to have been so registered, anything which—

> (a) has been done in relation to the vehicle, or in relation to a trailer drawn by it, by a person relying in good faith on that presumption and purporting to act by virtue of any provision of this Act, and
>
> (b) would have been lawfully done by virtue of that provision if the vehicle had not been registered in the United Kingdom,

shall be treated as having been lawfully done by virtue of that provision.

(6) Any reference in any provision of this Act to regulations made under an enactment specified in that provision shall be construed as including a reference to any regulations which, by virtue of that or any other enactment, have effect, or are to be treated as if made under the enactment so specified.

[Road Traffic (Foreign Vehicles) Act 1972, s 7, as amended by the Road Traffic Act 1974, Sch 7, the Transport Act 1978, Sch 3, the Transport Act 1980, Sch 5, Part II, the Public Passenger Vehicles Act 1981, Sch 7, the Road Traffic (Consequential Provisions) Act 1988, Sch 3, the Road Traffic Act 1991, Sch 4 and the Vehicle Excise and Registration Act 1994, Sch 3.]

---

*Amended by the Transport Act 1982, Sch 5, when in force.
**Sub-section (1) is amended and a new sub-s (1A) added by the Transport Act 1982, Sch 5, when in force.
1. See sub-s (7), infra.

SCHEDULES[1]

SCHEDULE 1

PROVISIONS CONFERRING FUNCTIONS ON EXAMINERS

(Amended By SI 1979/1746, The Public Passenger Vehicles Act 1981, Sch 7, SI 1984/748, The Road Traffic (Consequential Provisions) Act 1988, Sch 3, The Road Traffic Act 1991, Sch 8, SI 1999/617 and 3413 and SI 2002/1415.)

Provisions	Function conferred
Section 99 of the Transport Act 1968.	To inspect and copy record sheets, books, registers and other documents required to be carried on goods vehicles and public service vehicles, to inspect recording equipment and to inspect and copy record sheets on which records have been produced by such equipment or entries have been made.
Section 67 of the Road Traffic Act 1988.	To test the condition of motor vehicles on roads.
Section 68 of the Road Traffic Act 1988.	To inspect vehicles to secure proper maintenance.
Regulation 16 of the Road Transport (International Passenger Services) Regulations 1984.	To require the production of, and to inspect, copy and mark, documents required to be kept or carried on certain passenger vehicles.
Article 3a(3) of Council Regulation (EEC) No 684/92 of 16 March 1992 on common rules for the international carriage of passengers by coach and bus, as amended by Council Regulation (EC) No 11/98 of 11 December 1997.	To require the production of a certain document which is required to be kept on board certain passenger vehicles.
Article 5(4) of Council Regulation (EEC) No 881/92 of 26th March 1992 on access to the market in the carriage of goods by road within the Community to or from the territory of a Member State or passing across the territory of one or more Member States.	To require the production of a certified copy of a Community authorisation which is required to be kept on board certain goods vehicles.
Regulation 7 of the Road Transport (Passenger Vehicles Cabotage) Regulations 1999.	To require the production of certain documents which are required to be kept on board certain passenger vehicles.

1. The provisions to which reference is made have been noted as to the effect of this Act.

SCHEDULE 2

PROVISIONS RELATING TO VEHICLES AND THEIR DRIVERS

(As amended by the European Communities Act 1972, Sch 4, the Road Traffic (Drivers' Ages and Hours of Work) Act 1976, s 2(3), SI 1977/777, reg 10(3), SI 1984/748, the Road Traffic (Consequential Provisions) Act 1988, Schs 1 and 3, the Road Traffic Act 1991, Sch 4, the Goods Vehicles (Licensing of Operators) Act 1995, SI 1999/3413 and SI 2002/1415.)

Provisions	Effect
Section 2 of the Goods Vehicles (Licensing of Operators) Act 1995.	To require users of certain goods vehicles to hold operators' licences unless exempted from doing so.
Regulations under section 57(2)(d) of the Goods Vehicles (Licensing of Operators) Act 1995.	To require goods vehicles to be identified by plates, marks etc
Sections 96 to 98 of the Transport Act 1968 and regulations and orders made under those sections and the applicable Community rules within the meaning of Part VI of that Act.	To limit driving time and periods of duty of drivers of goods and public service vehicles and to require the installation of recording equipment in, and the keeping of records on, such vehicles.
Any order under section 100 of the Transport Act 1968.	To give effect to international agreements relating to vehicles used on international journeys.
Section 40A of the Road Traffic Act 1988.	To create offence of using motor vehicle or trailer in dangerous condition etc.
Regulations under section 41 of the Road Traffic Act 1988.	To regulate the construction, weight, equipment and use of motor vehicles and trailers on roads.
Regulation 19 of the Road Transport (International Passenger Services) Regulations 1984.	To impose penalties for contravention of Community instruments relating to international passenger services.
Regulations 3 and 7 of the Goods Vehicles (Community Authorisations) Regulations 1992	To impose a penalty for contravention of certain requirements relating to the use of goods vehicles.
Regulations 3 and 7 of the Public Service Vehicles (Community Licenses) Regulations 1999.	To impose a penalty for contravention of certain requirements relating to international passenger services.
Regulation 3, 4 and 7 of the Road Transport (Passenger Vehicles Cabotage) Regulations 1999.	To impose penalties for contravention of certain requirements relating to national passenger services by a carrier registered in a foreign member State.

International Road Haulage Permits Act 1975
(1975 c 46)

4–830 1. Carriage on United Kingdom vehicles, and production, of international road haulage permits.   (1) The Secretary of State may by regulations[1] made by statutory instrument provide that—

(a) a goods vehicle registered in the United Kingdom, or

(b) a trailer drawn by a vehicle registered in the United Kingdom, or

(c) an unattached trailer which is for the time being in the United Kingdom

may not be used on a journey to which the regulations apply, being a journey—

(i)   for or in connection with the carriage or haulage of goods either for hire or reward or for or in connection with any trade or business carried on by the user of the vehicle, and

(ii) either between a place in the United Kingdom and a place outside the United Kingdom or, if the journey passes through any part of the United Kingdom, between places both of which are outside the United Kingdom,

unless a document of a description specified in the regulations is carried on the vehicle or, in the case of a trailer, is carried either on the vehicle drawing it or by a person in charge of it.

(2) If it appears to an examiner that a goods vehicle registered in the United Kingdom or a trailer is being used in such circumstances that, by virtue of regulations under subsection (1) above, a document of a description specified in the regulations is required to be carried as mentioned in that subsection he may, on production if so required of his authority—

(a) require the driver of the goods vehicle concerned or, in the case of a trailer, the driver of the vehicle drawing it or the person in charge of it to produce a document of the description in question and to permit the examiner to inspect and copy it,

(b) detain the goods vehicle or trailer concerned for such time as is requisite for the purpose of inspecting and copying the document,

(c) at any time which is reasonable having regard to the circumstances of the case enter any premises on which he has reason to believe that there is kept a vehicle (whether a goods vehicle or a trailer) which is being used on a journey to which regulations under subsection (1) above apply, and

(d) at any time which is reasonable having regard to the circumstances of the case enter any premises in which he has reason to believe that any document of a description specified in regulations under subsection (1) above is to be found and inspect and copy any such document which he finds there.

(3) If, without reasonable excuse, any person uses a goods vehicle or trailer in contravention of regulations under subsection (1) above he shall be liable on summary conviction to a fine not exceeding **level 4** on the standard scale.

(4) If the driver of a goods vehicle which is being used in such circumstances as are specified in subsection (2) above or the person in charge of, or the driver of a vehicle drawing, a trailer which is being so used—

(a) without reasonable excuse refuses or fails to comply with a requirement under subsection (2) above, or

(b) wilfully obstructs an examiner in the exercise of his powers under that subsection,

he shall be liable on summary conviction to a fine not exceeding **level 3** on the standard scale.

(5) If any person (other than a person specified in subsection (4) above) wilfully obstructs an examiner in the exercise of his powers under paragraph (d) of subsection (2) above, he shall be liable on summary conviction to a fine not exceeding **level 3** on the standard scale.

(6) For the purposes of this section a motor vehicle which for the time being has exhibited on it a licence or trade plates issued under the Vehicle Excise and Registration Act 1994 shall be presumed, unless the contrary is proved, to be registered in the United Kingdom.

(7) Before making any regulations under subsection (1) above the Secretary of State shall consult with such representative organisations as he thinks fit, and a statutory instrument containing any such regulations shall be subject to annulment in pursuance of a resolution of either House of Parliament.

(8) Any reference in this section to a person using a vehicle (whether a goods vehicle or a trailer) shall be construed as if this section were included in the Goods Vehicles (Licensing of Operators) Act 1995 or, as the case may require, Part III of the Transport Act (Northern Ireland) 1967 (operators' licences etc).

(9) In this section—

"examiner" means an examiner appointed under section 56(1) of the Road Traffic Act 1972 or section 66A of the Road Traffic Act 1988, an inspector appointed under section 37 of the Transport Act (Northern Ireland) 1967 or an inspector of vehicles, as defined in section 190(1) of the Road Traffic Act (Northern Ireland) 1970;

"goods vehicle" means a motor vehicle constructed or adapted for use for the carriage of goods or burden of any description;

"trailer" means a trailer so constructed or adapted;

and for the purposes of this subsection "motor vehicle" and "trailer" have the same meaning as in the Road Traffic Act 1988 or, in Northern Ireland, the Road Traffic Act (Northern Ireland) 1970.

[International Road Haulage Permits Act 1975, s 1 as amended by the Criminal Justice Act 1982, ss 38 and 46, the Road Traffic (Consequential Provisions) Act 1988, Sch 3, the Road Traffic Act 1991, Sch 4, the Vehicle Excise and the Goods Vehicles (Licensing of Operators) Act 1995, Sch 7.]

1. The Goods Vehicles (International Road Haulage Permits) Regulations 1975, SI 1975/2234, have been made.

4–831 **2. Power to prohibit vehicle or trailer being taken out of the United Kingdom.** (1) If it appears to an examiner—

(a) that a goods vehicle or a trailer is being used in such circumstances as are specified in subsection (2) of section 1 above, and

(b) that, without reasonable excuse, the driver of the goods vehicle or, as the case may require, the person in charge of, or the driver of a vehicle drawing, the trailer has refused or failed to comply with a requirement under that subsection,

the examiner may prohibit the removal of the goods vehicle or trailer out of the United Kingdom, either absolutely or for a specified purpose, and either for a specified period or without limitation of time.

(2) Where an examiner prohibits the removal of a goods vehicle or trailer out of the United Kingdom under subsection (1) above, he shall forthwith give notice in writing of the prohibition to the driver of the goods vehicle or, as the case may require, to the person in charge of, or the driver of the vehicle drawing, the trailer, specifying—

(a) the circumstances in consequence of which the prohibition is imposed,

(b) whether the prohibition applies absolutely or for a specified purpose, and

(c) whether the prohibition is for a specified period or without limit of time,

and the prohibition under subsection (1) above shall come into force as soon as notice thereof is given under this subsection.

(3) Where an examiner is satisfied, with respect to a goods vehicle or trailer to which a prohibition under subsection (1) above relates—

(a) that the goods vehicle or trailer is being used on a journey to which regulations under section 1(1) above do not apply, or

(b) that there is carried on the goods vehicle or, in the case of a trailer, on the vehicle drawing it or by a person in charge of it a document of a description specified in those regulations,

he may remove the prohibition and, where he does so, shall forthwith give notice in writing of the removal of the prohibition to the driver of the goods vehicle or, as the case may require, to the person in charge of, or the driver of the vehicle drawing, the trailer and the prohibition shall cease to have effect on the giving of that notice.

(4) Unless the person to whom a notice is given under subsection (2) or subsection (3) above is the person using the vehicle concerned, as soon as practicable after such a notice has been given, the examiner who gave it shall take steps to bring the contents of the notice to the attention of the person using the vehicle.

(5) In the exercise of his functions under this section, an examiner shall act in accordance with any general directions given by the Secretary of State.

(6) Any person who, without reasonable excuse—

(a) removes a goods vehicle or trailer out of the United Kingdom in contravention of a prohibition under subsection (1) above, or

(b) causes or permits a goods vehicle or trailer to be removed out of the United Kingdom in contravention of such a prohibition,

shall be guilty of an offence and liable on summary conviction to a fine not exceeding **level 4** on the standard scale.

(7) Subsections (8) and (9) of section 1 above shall apply in relation to this section as they apply in relation to that.

[International Road Haulage Permits Act 1975, s 2 as amended by the Criminal Justice Act 1982, ss 38 and 46.]

Transport Act 1980
(1980 c 34)

4–850 **42. Defences available to persons charged with certain offences.** (1) It shall be a defence for a person charged with an offence under any of the provisions mentioned in subsection (2) to prove that there was a reasonable excuse for the act or omission in respect of which he is charged.

(2) The provisions referred to in subsection (1) are—

(a) *Repealed*;

(b) in the 1960 Act—

(i)–(ii) *Repealed*;

(iii) so much of section 232(3) as relates to failure to comply with the requirement of section 232(2)(b); and

(iv) *Repealed*.

(3) It shall be a defence for a person charged with an offence under any of the provisions mentioned in subsection (4) to prove that he took all reasonable precautions and exercised all due diligence to avoid the commission of any offence under that provision.

(4) The provisions referred to in subsection (3) are

(a) sections 4(6) and (7), 17(3), 18(9)(b), 19(5), 22(7) and 24(4);

(b) in the 1960 Act—

    (i) so much of section 144(8) as relates to contravention of section 144(1)(b); and

    (ii) sections 148(2) and 157(2).

[Transport Act 1980, s 42, as amended by the Public Passenger Vehicles Act 1981, Sch 8.]

PART IV
MISCELLANEOUS AND GENERAL

4–851   64. Roof-signs on vehicles other than taxis.   (1) There shall not, in any part of England and Wales outside the metropolitan police district and the City of London, be displayed on or above the roof of any vehicle which is used for carrying passengers for hire or reward but which is not a taxi—

(a) any sign which consists of or includes the word "taxi" or "cab", whether in the singular or plural, or "hire", or any word of similar meaning or appearance to any of those words, whether alone or as part of another word; or

(b) any sign, notice, mark, illumination or other feature which may suggest[1] that the vehicle is a taxi.

(2) Any person who knowingly—

(a) drives a vehicle in respect of which subsection (1) is contravened; or

(b) causes or permits that subsection to be contravened in respect of any vehicle,

shall be liable on summary conviction to a fine not exceeding **level 3** on the standard scale.

(3) In this section "taxi" means a vehicle licensed under section 37 of the Town Police Clauses Act 1847, section 6 of the Metropolitan Carriage Act 1869, section 10 of the Civic Government (Scotland) Act 1982 or any similar local enactment.

[Transport Act 1980, s 64 as amended by the Criminal Justice Act 1982, s 46 and the Transport Act 1985, Sch 7.]

---

1. The correct test is to look at the vehicle of itself and in no particular context but with the sign on it and ask, as a matter of common sense, does this sign suggest that the vehicle is a taxi (as opposed, for example, to being available on hire on a telephone call or to identify a car a caller has ordered): *Yakhya v Tee* [1984] RTR 122.

Public Passenger Vehicles Act 1981
(1981 c 14)

PART I
PRELIMINARY

Definition and classification of public service vehicles

4–870   1. Definition of "public service vehicle".   (1) Subject to the provisions of this section, in this Act "public service vehicle" means a motor vehicle (other than a tramcar) which—

(a) being a vehicle adapted[1] to carry more than eight passengers, is used for carrying passengers for hire or reward[2]; or

(b) being a vehicle not so adapted, is used for carrying passengers for hire or reward at separate fares in the course of a business of carrying passengers.

(2) For the purposes of subsection (1) above a vehicle[3] "is used" as mentioned in paragraph (a) or (b) of that subsection if it is being so used or if it has been used as mentioned in that paragraph and that use has not been permanently discontinued.

(3) A vehicle carrying passengers at separate fares in the course of a business of carrying passengers, but doing so in circumstances in which the conditions set out in Part I, or III of Schedule 1 to this Act are fulfilled, shall be treated as not being a public service vehicle unless it is adapted to carry more than eight passengers.

(4) For the purposes of this section a journey made by a vehicle in the course of which one or more passengers are carried at separate fares shall not be treated as made in the course of a business of carrying passengers if—

(a) the fare or aggregate of the fares paid in respect of the journey does not exceed the amount of the running costs of the vehicle for the journey; and

(b) the arrangements for the payment of fares by the passenger or passengers so carried were made before the journey began;

and for the purposes of paragraph (a) above the running costs of a vehicle for a journey shall be taken to include an appropriate amount in respect of depreciation and general wear.

(5) For the purposes of this section, and Schedule 1 to this Act—

(*a*) a vehicle is to be treated as carrying passengers for hire or reward[4] if payment is made for, or for matters which include, the carrying of passengers, irrespective of the person to whom the payment is made and, in the case of a transaction effected by or on behalf of a member of any association of persons (whether incorporated or not) on the one hand and the association or another member thereof on the other hand, notwithstanding any rule of law as to such transactions;

(*b*) a payment made for the carrying of a passenger shall be treated as a fare notwithstanding that it is made in consideration of other matters in addition to the journey and irrespective of the person by or to whom it is made;

(*c*) a payment shall be treated as made for the carrying of a passenger if made in consideration of a person's being given a right to be carried[5], whether for one or more journeys and whether or not the right is exercised.

(6) Where a fare is paid for the carriage of a passenger on a journey by air, no part of that fare shall be treated for the purposes of subsection (5) above as paid in consideration of the carriage of the passenger by road by reason of the fact that, in case of mechanical failure, bad weather or other circumstances outside the operator's control, part of that journey may be made by road.
[Public Passenger Vehicles Act 1981, s 1 as amended by the Transport Act 1985, Sch 8.]

---

1. "Adapted" means "suitable"; see *Maddox v Storer* [1963] 1 QB 451, [1962] 1 All ER 831, 126 JP 263; *Wurzal v Addison* [1965] 2 QB 131, [1965] 1 All ER 20, 129 JP 86. Consideration of suitability should take place against the standard seat width per passenger provided by reg 28 of the Public Service (Conditions of Fitness, etc) Regulations 1981 (*Traffic Comrs for South Wales Traffic Area v Snape* [1977] RTR 367). In *Vehicle and Operator Services v Johnson* [2003] EWHC 2104 (Admin), (2003) 167 JP 497 it was held that justices had been entitled to conclude that a stretch limousine, though in fact carrying nine passengers at the relevant time, was not a public service vehicle; their decision was that in normal use it was not practicable for the vehicle to carry a ninth passenger and they were entitled, therefore, to find that the vehicle was not designed and laid out to carry more than eight passengers.
2. See *Evans v Dell* [1937] 1 All ER 349, 101 JP 149.
3. Section 1(2) does not apply to the use of a licensed taxi for the provision of a local service under a special licence (Transport Act 1985, s 12).
4. It is not necessary for the prosecution to establish a right to be carried or a legally enforceable agreement as this does not define the only circumstance in which a vehicle is used for carrying passengers for hire or reward (*Traffic Examiner of Metropolitan Traffic Area v Swallow Hotels Ltd* (1993) 157 JP 771, [1993] RTR 80, [1993] Crim LR 77).
5. The test in *Albert v Motor Insurers' Bureau* [1972] AC 301 was to be applied; was there a systematic carrying of passengers for reward not necessarily on a contractual basis going beyond the bounds of mere social kindness and amounting to a business activity (*DPP v Sikondar* (1992) 157 JP 659, [1993] RTR 90, [1993] Crim LR 76).

Traffic Areas and Traffic Commissioners

4–871   3. Traffic areas.   Great Britain is divided into eleven traffic areas; Secretary of State may alter these areas by order.
[Public Passenger Vehicles Act 1981, s 3 as amended by the Transport Act 1985, Sch 2—summarised.]

4–872   4–5. Traffic Commissioners.   Each traffic area to have a traffic commissioner appointed by Secretary of State, with terms of service stipulated.
[Public Passenger Vehicles Act 1981, ss 4, 5 as substituted by the Transport Act 1985, s 3—summarised.]

PART II[1]
GENERAL PROVISIONS RELATING TO PUBLIC SERVICE VEHICLES
Fitness of public service vehicles

4–873   6. Certificate of initial fitness (or equivalent) required for use as public service vehicles[2].   (1) A public service vehicle[3] adapted to carry more than eight passengers shall not be used on a road unless—

(*a*) an examiner appointed under section 66A of the Road Traffic Act 1988 has issued a certificate (in this Act referred to as a "certificate of initial fitness") that the prescribed conditions as to fitness[4] are fulfilled in respect of the vehicle; or*

(*b*) a certificate under section 10 of this Act has been issued in respect of the vehicle; or

(*c*) there has been issued in respect of the vehicle a certificate under section 47 of the Road Traffic Act 1972 or sections 55 to 58 of the Road Traffic Act 1988 (type approval) of a kind which by virtue of regulations is to be treated as the equivalent of a certificate of initial fitness.

(2) Subject to section 68(3) of this Act, if a vehicle is used in contravention of subsection (1) above, the operator of the vehicle shall be liable on summary conviction[5] to a fine not exceeding **level 4** on the standard scale.
[Public Passenger Vehicles Act 1981, s 6 as amended by the Criminal Justice Act 1982, s 46, the Road Traffic (Consequential Provisions) Act 1988, Sch 3 and the Road Traffic Act 1991, Sch 4.]

---

*Section 6(1) amended and a new s 6(1A) added by the Transport Act 1982, s 10, when in force.
1. Part II contains ss 6–29.
2. This Act shall have effect, in relation to a vehicle being used to carry out cabotage transport operations, as if this section was omitted, by virtue of the Road Transport (Passenger Vehicles Cabotage) Regulations 1999, SI 1999/3413.
3. Note exception for community bus service (s 45, post).
4. See the Public Service Vehicles (Conditions of Fitness, Use and Certification) Regulations 1981 in this PART, post.
5. See ss 68–74 post as to proceedings.

4–874   8. Powers of, and facilities for, inspection of public service vehicles.   (1)–(2) *Repealed.*

(3) The Secretary of State may—

(a)   provide and maintain stations where inspections of public service vehicles may be carried out;

(b)   designate premises as stations where such inspections may be carried out; and

(c)   provide and maintain apparatus for the carrying out of such inspections;

and in this Act "official PSV testing station" means a station provided, or any premises for the time being designated, under this subsection.

[Public Passenger Vehicles Act 1981, s 8 as amended by the Criminal Justice Act 1982, s 46, the Transport Act 1985, Sch 7 as amended by the Road Traffic Act 1991, s 11 and Sch 8.]

4–875   9A. Extension of sections 8 and 9 to certain passenger vehicles other than public service vehicles.   (1) Section 8 of this Act shall apply to any motor vehicle (other than a tramcar) which is adapted to carry more than eight passengers but was not a public service vehicle as it applies to a public service vehicle.

(2) *Repealed.*

[Public Passenger Vehicles Act 1981, s 9A added by the Transport Act 1985, s 33 and amended by the Road Traffic Act 1991, Sch 8.]

4–876   10. *Approval of type vehicle and effect thereof.*

4–877   11. *Modification of section 6 in relation to experimental vehicles.*

Public service vehicle operators' licences

4–880   12. PSV operators' licences[1].   (1) A public service vehicle shall not be used on a road for carrying passengers for hire or reward except under a PSV operator's licence[2] granted in accordance with the following provisions of this Part of this Act.

(2) The authority having power to grant a PSV operator's licence is the traffic commissioner for any traffic area in which, if the licence is granted, there will be one or more operating centres of vehicles used under the licence; and, subject to the provisions of this Part of this Act, a PSV operator's licence authorises the holder to use anywhere in Great Britain vehicles which have their operating centre in the area of the traffic commissioner by whom the licence was granted.

(3) A person may hold two or more PSV operator's licences each granted by the traffic commissioner for a different area, but shall not at the same time hold more than one such licence granted by the commissioner for the same area.

(4) An application for a PSV operator's licence shall be made in such form as the traffic commissioner may require, and an applicant shall give the commissioner such information as he may reasonably require for disposing of the application.

(5) Subject to section 68(3) of this Act, if a vehicle is used in contravention of subsection (1) above, the operator of the vehicle shall be liable on summary conviction to a fine not exceeding **level 4** on the standard scale.

[Public Passenger Vehicles Act 1981, s 12 as amended by the Criminal Justice Act 1982, s 46 and the Transport Act 1985, Schs 1 and 2.]

---

1. This Act shall have effect, in relation to a vehicle being used to carry out cabotage transport operations, as if this section was omitted, by virtue of the Road Transport (Passenger Vehicles Cabotage) Regulations 1999, SI 1999/3413.

2. Special licences granted under s 12 of the Transport Act 1985 (use of taxis) are to be disregarded for the purposes of this section. See also s 18 of the 1985 Act (use of buses by educational and other bodies).

4–881   13. Classification of licences.   (1) A PSV operator's licence may be either a standard licence or a restricted licence.

(2) A standard licence authorises the use of any description of public service and may authorise use either—

(a)   on both national and international operations; or

(b)   on national operations only.

(3) A restricted licence authorises the use (whether on national or international operations) of—

(a)   public service vehicles not adapted to carry more than eight passengers; and

(b)   public service vehicles not adapted to carry more than sixteen passengers when used—

(i)   otherwise than in the course of a business of carrying passengers; or

(ii)   by a person whose main occupation is not the operation of public service vehicles adapted to carry more than eight passengers.

(4) For the purposes of subsection (3)(b)(i) above, a vehicle used for carrying passengers by a local or public authority shall not be regarded as used in the course of a business of carrying passengers unless it is used by the public service vehicle undertaking of that authority.

[Public Passenger Vehicles Act 1981, s 13.]

4–882   14. *Grant of licences.*

4–883   14A. *Objections to application for PSV operator's licence.*

4–884 **15.** *Duration of licences.*

4–885 **16. Conditions attached to licences[1].** Power for commissioners to attach, add to, alter, remove conditions; subject to s 68(3) if a condition is contravened the licence holder shall be liable on summary conviction to a fine not exceeding **level 3** on the standard scale.
[Public Passenger Vehicles Act 1981, s 16 as amended by the Criminal Justice Act 1982, s 46 and the Transport Act 1985, s 24 and Schs 7 and 8—summarised.]

---

1. Several matters are prescribed by the Public Service Vehicles (Operators' Licences) Regulations 1995, in this PART, post. See also the Operation of Public Service Vehicles (Partnership) Regulations 1986, SI 1986/1628. Section 16(1A) and (2) do not apply to special licences under the Transport Act 1985, s 12. Conditions include those attached under s 26 of the 1985 Act.

4–885A **16A. Conditions as to matters required to be notified.** (1) On issuing a standard licence, a traffic commissioner shall attach to it the following conditions, namely—

  (a) a condition requiring the licence-holder to inform the commissioner of any event which could affect the fulfilment by the licence-holder of any of the requirements of section 14(1) of this Act, and to do so within 28 days of the event; and
  (b) a condition requiring the licence-holder to inform the commissioner of any event which could affect the fulfilment by a relevant transport manager of the requirements mentioned in section 14(1)(a) or (c) of this Act, and to do so within 28 days of the event coming to the licence-holder's knowledge.

  (2) In subsection (1)(b) above the reference to a "relevant transport manager" is a reference to any transport manager employed by the licence-holder who is relied on by the licence-holder to fulfil the requirements of section 14(1)(c) of this Act.
  (3) Any person who contravenes any condition attached under this section to a licence of which he is the holder is guilty of an offence and liable on summary conviction to a fine not exceeding **level 4** on the standard scale.
[Public Passenger Vehicles Act 1981, s 16A as inserted by SI 1999/2431.]

4–886 **17.** *Revocation, suspension etc of licences.*

4–887 **17A.** *Assessors to assist traffic commissioners.*

4–888 **18. Duty to exhibit operator's disc[1].** (1) Where a vehicle is being used in circumstances such that a PSV operator's licence is required, there shall be fixed and exhibited on the vehicle in the prescribed manner[2] an operator's disc issued under this section showing particulars of the operator of the vehicle and of the PSV operator's licence under which the vehicle is being used.
  (2) A traffic commissioner on granting a PSV operator's licence shall supply the person to whom the licence is granted—

  (a) with a number of operators' discs equal to the maximum number of vehicles that he may use under the licence in accordance with the condition or conditions attached to the licence under section 16(1) of this Act; or
  (b) with such lesser number of operators' discs as he may request.

  (2A) Where, in the case of any PSV operators' licence, the maximum number referred to in subsection (2)(a) above is increased on the variation of one or more of the conditions there referred to, the traffic commissioner on making the variation shall supply the holder of the licence—

  (a) with such number of additional operators' discs as will bring the total number of operators' discs held by him in respect of the licence to that maximum number, or
  (b) with such lesser number of additional operators' discs as he may request.

  (2B) Where the number of operators' discs currently held in respect of a PSV operators' licence is less than the maximum number referred to in subsection (2)(a) above, the traffic commissioner by whom the licence was granted shall on the application of the holder of the licence supply him with such number of additional operators' discs as is mentioned in subsection (2A)(a) or (b) above.
  (2C) Where, in accordance with regulations under subsection (3)(aa) below, all the operators' discs held in respect of a PSV operators' licence expire at the same time, the traffic commissioner by whom the licence was granted shall supply the holder of the licence with a number of new operators' discs equal to the number of discs that have expired.
  (3) Regulations may make provision—

  (a) as to the form of operator's discs and the particulars to be shown on them;
  (aa) as to the expiry of operators' discs;
  (b) with respect to the custody and production of operator's discs;
  (c) for the issue of new operators' discs in place of those lost, destroyed or defaced;
  (d) for the return of operators' discs on their expiry or otherwise ceasing to have effect, on the revocation or termination of a PSV operator's licence or in the event of a variation of one or more conditions attached to a licence under section 16(1) of this Act having the effect of reducing the maximum number of vehicles which may be used under the licence;
  (e) for the voluntary return of operators' discs by the holder of a PSV operators' licence.

(4) Subject to section 68(3) of this Act, if a vehicle is used in contravention of subsection (1) above, the operator of the vehicle shall be liable on summary conviction[3] to a fine not exceeding **level 3** on the standard scale.
[Public Passenger Vehicles Act 1981, s 18 as amended by the Criminal Justice Act 1982, s 46, the Transport Act 1985, s 24 and Sch 2 and the Deregulation and Contracting Out Act 1994, s 63 and Sch 14.]

1. This Act shall have effect, in relation to a vehicle being used to carry out cabotage transport operations, as if this section was omitted, by virtue of the Road Transport (Passenger Vehicles Cabotage) Regulations 1999, SI 1999/3413.
2. Several matters are prescribed by the Public Service Vehicles (Operators' Licences) Regulations 1995 in this PART, post. See also the Operation of Public Service Vehicles (Partnership) Regulations 1986, SI 1986/1628.
3. See ss 68–74 post as to proceedings. Section 18 does not apply to special licences under the Transport Act 1985, s 12.

4–889 19. Duty to inform traffic commissioner of relevant convictions etc. (1) A person who has applied for a PSV licence shall forthwith notify the traffic commissioner to whom the application was made if, in the interval between the making of the application and the date on which it is disposed of, a relevant conviction occurs of the applicant, or any employee or agent of his, or of any person proposed to be engaged as transport manager whose repute and competence are relied on in connection with the application.

(2) It shall be the duty of the holder of a PSV operator's licence to give notice in writing to the traffic commissioner by whom the licence was granted of—

(a) any relevant conviction of the holder; and
(b) any relevant conviction of any officer, employee or agent of the holder for an offence committed in the course of the holder's road passenger transport business,

and to do so within 28 days of the conviction in the case of a conviction of the holder or his transport manager and within 28 days of the conviction coming to the holder's knowledge in any other case.

(3) It shall be the duty of the holder of a PSV operator's licence within 28 days of the occurrence of—

(a) the bankruptcy or liquidation of the holder, or the sequestration of his estate or to the entry into administration of the holder or the appointment of a receiver, manager or trustee of his road passenger transport business, or
(b) any change in the identity of the transport manager of the holder's road passenger transport business,

to give notice in writing of that event to the traffic commissioner by whom the licence was granted.

(4) A traffic commissioner on granting or varying a PSV operator's licence, or at any time thereafter, may require the holder of the licence to inform him forthwith or within a time specified by him of any material change specified by him in any circumstances which were relevant to the grant or variation of the licence.

(5) Subject to the section 68(1) of this Act, a person who fails to comply with subsection (1), (2) or (3) above or any requirement under subsection (4) above shall be liable on summary conviction[1] to a fine not exceeding **level 3** on the standard scale.
[Public Passenger Vehicles Act 1981, s 19 as amended by the Criminal Justice Act 1982, s 46, the Transport Act 1985, Sch 2, the Insolvency Act 1985, Sch 8, the Insolvency Act 1986, Sch 14 and SI 2003/2096.]

1. See ss 68–74 post as to proceedings. Section 19 does not apply to special licences under the Transport Act 1985, s 12.

4–900 20. Duty to give traffic commissioners information about vehicles. (1) It shall be the duty of the holder of a PSV operator's licence, on the happening to any public service vehicle owned by him of any failure or damage of a nature calculated[1] to affect the safety of occupants of the public service vehicles or of persons using the road, to report the matter as soon as is practicable to the traffic commissioners who granted the licence.

(2) It shall be the duty of the holder of a PSV operator's licence, on any alteration otherwise than by replacement of parts being made in the structure or fixed equipment of any public service vehicle owned by him, to give notice of the alteration as soon as is practicable to the traffic commissioners who granted the licence.*

(3) The traffic commissioner by whom a PSV operator's licence was granted may—

(a) require the holder of the licence to supply him forthwith or within a specified time with such information as he may reasonably require about the public service vehicles owned by him and normally kept at an operating centre within the area of that commissioner, and to keep up to date information supplied by him under this paragraph; or
(b) require the holder or former holder of the licence to supply him forthwith or within a specified time with such information as he may reasonably require about the public service vehicles owned by him at any material time specified by him which were at that time normally kept at an operating centre within the area of that commissioner.

In this subsection "material time" means a time when the PSV operator's licence in question was in force.

(4) Subject to section 68(1) of this Act, a person who fails to comply with the provisions of subsection (1) or (2) above or with any requirement under subsection (3) above shall be liable on summary conviction[2] to a fine not exceeding **level 3** on the standard scale.

(5) A person who in purporting to comply with any requirement under subsection (3) above supplies any information which he knows to be false or does not believe to be true shall be liable on summary conviction[2] to a fine not exceeding **level 4** on the standard scale.

(6) *Repealed.*

[Public Passenger Vehicle Act 1981, s 20 as amended by the Criminal Justice Act 1982, s 46, the Transport Act 1985, Sch 2 and the Road Traffic Act 1991, Sch 8.]

---

*Amended by the Transport Act 1982, s 10, when in force.

  1. This appears to mean "likely to affect" and not "intended to affect"; see *Re London and Globe Finance Corpn Ltd* [1903] 1 Ch 728, 82 JP 447; *Collett v Co-operative Wholesale Society Ltd* [1970] 1 All ER 274; *Turner v Shearer* [1973] 1 All ER 397, [1972] 1 WLR 1387, 137 JP 191.

  2. See ss 68–74 post as to proceedings. Section 20 does not apply to special licences under the Transport Act 1985, s 12.

Regulation of conduct etc of drivers, inspectors, conductors and passengers

4–901   24. Regulation of conduct of drivers, inspectors and conductors. (1) Regulations[1] may make provision for regulating the conduct, when acting as such, of—

    (*a*)   drivers of public service vehicles, and

    (*b*)   inspectors and conductors of such vehicles, and

    (*c*)   drivers, inspectors and conductors of tramcars.

(2) Subject to section 68(1) of this Act, if a person to whom regulations having effect by virtue of this section apply contravenes, or fails to comply with, any of the provisions of the regulations, he shall be liable on summary conviction[2] to a fine not exceeding **level 2** on the standard scale and, in the case of an offence by a person acting as driver of a public service vehicle, the court by which he is convicted may, if it thinks fit, cause particulars of the conviction to be endorsed upon the counterpart of the licence granted to that person under Part III of the Road Traffic Act 1988 or, as the case may be, the counterpart (if any) of his Community licence (within the meaning of that Part).

(3) The person who has the custody of the licence and its counterpart shall, if so required by the convicting court, produce them within a reasonable time for the purpose of endorsement, and, subject to section 68(1) of this Act, if he fails to do so, shall be liable on summary conviction[2] to a fine not exceeding **level 3** on the standard scale.

(4) In this section and in section 25 of this Act "inspector", in relation to a public service vehicle, means a person authorised to act as an inspector by the holder of the PSV operator's licence under which the vehicle is being used.

(5) Notwithstanding section 1(1) of this Act, in this section and in sections 25 and 26 of this Act "public service vehicle" shall be construed as meaning a public service vehicle being used on a road for carrying passengers for hire or reward.

[Public Passenger Vehicles Act 1981, s 24 as amended by the Criminal Justice Act 1982, s 46, the Road Traffic (Driver Licensing and Information Systems) Act 1989, Sch 3 as amended by SI 1990/144, the Transport and Works Act 1992, s 61 and SI 1996/1974.]

---

  1. See the Public Service Vehicles (Conduct of Drivers, Conductors and Passengers) Regulations 1990 in this PART, post.

  2. See ss 68–74 post as to proceedings.

4–902   25. Regulation of conduct of passengers. (1) Regulations[1] may make provision generally as to the conduct of passengers on public service vehicles or tramcars and in particular (but without prejudice to the generality of the foregoing provision) for—

    (*a*)   authorising the removal from a public service vehicle or tramcar of a person infringing the regulations by the driver, inspector or conductor of the vehicle or on the request of the driver, inspector or conductor by a police constable;

    (*b*)   requiring a passenger in a public service vehicle or tramcar who is reasonably suspected by the driver, inspector or conductor thereof of contravening the regulations to give his name and address to the driver, inspector or conductor on demand;

    (*c*)   requiring a passenger to declare, if so requested by the driver, inspector or conductor, the journey he intends to take or has taken in the vehicle, and to pay the fare for the whole of that journey and to accept any ticket provided therefor;

    (*d*)   requiring, on demand being made for the purpose by the driver, inspector or conductor, production during the journey and surrender at the end of the journey by the holder thereof of any ticket issued to him;

    (*e*)   requiring a passenger, if so requested by the driver, inspector or conductor, to leave the vehicle on the completion of the journey the fare for which he has paid;

    (*f*)   requiring the surrender by the holder thereof on the expiry of the period for which it is issued of a ticket issued to him.

(2) *Repealed.*

(3) Subject to section 68(1) of this Act, if a person contravenes, or fails to comply with, a provision of regulations having effect by virtue of this section, he shall be liable on summary conviction[2] to a fine not exceeding **level 3** on the standard scale.

(4) *Applies to Scotland.*

[Public Passenger Vehicles Act 1981, s 25 as amended by the Criminal Justice Act 1982, s 46, the Police and Criminal Evidence Act 1984, Sch 7 and the Transport and Works Act 1992, s 61.]

1. See the Public Service Vehicles (Conduct of Drivers, Conductors and Passengers) Regulations 1990 in this PART, post.
2. See ss 68–74 post as to proceedings.

4–903   26. Control of number of passengers.   (1) Regulations may make provision with respect to public service vehicles for—

(a) the determination by or under the regulations of the number of the seated passengers and standing passengers respectively for whom a vehicle is constructed or adapted[1] and fit to carry;

(b) the determination by or under the regulations of the number of such passengers respectively who may be carried in a vehicle;

(c) the marks to be carried on a vehicle showing those numbers and the manner in which those marks are to be carried.

(2) Subject to section 68(1) and (3) of this Act, if a person contravenes, or fails to comply with, a provision of regulations[2] having effect by virtue of this section, he shall be liable on summary conviction[3] to a fine not exceeding **level 2** on the standard scale.
[Public Passenger Vehicles Act 1981, s 26 as amended by the Criminal Justice Act 1982, s 46.]

1. It would appear that this means originally constructed or subsequently altered to make it fit to carry; see eg *Flower Freight Co Ltd v Hammond* [1963] 1 QB 275, [1962] 3 All ER 950, 127 JP 42.
2. See the Public Service Vehicles (Carrying Capacity) Regulations 1984 in this PART, post.
3. See ss 68–74 post as to proceedings. Section 26 does not apply to special licences under the Transport Act 1985, s 12.

Supplementary provisions

4–904   27. *Repealed.*

PART IV[1]
MODIFICATION OF REQUIREMENTS OF PARTS II AND III IN RELATION TO CERTAIN VEHICLES
AND AREAS

Fare-paying passengers on school buses

4–905   46. Fare-paying passengers on school buses.   (1) Subject to subsection (2) below, a local education authority may—

(a) use a school bus, when it is being used to provide free school transport, to carry as fare-paying passengers persons other than those for whom the free school transport is provided;

(b) use a school bus belonging to the authority, when it is not being used to provide free school transport, to provide a local service;

and sections 6, 8, 9 and 12(1) of this Act shall not apply to a school bus belonging to a local education authority in the course of its use by the authority in accordance with this subsection.

(2) Subsection (1) above does not affect the duties of a local education authority in relation to the provision of free school transport or authorise a local education authority to make any charge for the carriage of a pupil on a journey which he is required to make in the course of his education in a school maintained by such an authority.

(3) In this section—

"free school transport" means transport provided by a local education authority free of charge—

(a) in pursuance of arrangements under section 509(1) or (1A) or section 509AA(7)(b) or (9)(a) of the Education Act 1996, or

(b) otherwise, in the exercise of any function of the authority, for the purpose of facilitating the attendance of persons receiving education or training at any premises;

"school bus", in relation to a local education authority, means a motor vehicle which is used by that authority to provide free school transport.

(4) *Applies to Scotland.*
[Public Passenger Vehicles Act 1981, s 46 as amended by the Transport Act 1985, Schs 1 and 8, the Road Traffic (Driver Licensing and Information Systems) Act 1989, Sch 3 and the Further and Higher Education Act 1992, Sch 8.]

1. Part IV comprises ss 42–49.

PART V[1]
MISCELLANEOUS AND SUPPLEMENTARY

Provisions relating to traffic commissioners etc

4–906   56. Records[2] of licences.   (1) The traffic commissioner for each traffic area shall keep a record in such form and containing such particulars as may be prescribed of all licences granted by him under this Act and shall allow the record to be inspected at all reasonable times by members of the public.

(2) *Repealed.*

(3) A record kept under this section shall be admissible in evidence of the matters required under this Act to be entered therein, and a copy of an entry made in such a record in pursuance of this section, purporting to be signed by or on behalf of the authority by whom the record is kept and to be certified to be a true copy shall be evidence of the matters stated in that entry without proof of the signature or authority of the person signing the same.
[Public Passenger Vehicles Act 1981, s 56 as amended by the Metropolitan Traffic Area (Transfer of Functions) Order 1984, SI 1984/31 and the Transport Act 1985, Schs 2, 7 and 8.]

1. Part V comprises ss 50–89.
2. Section 126 of the Transport Act 1985 applies s 56 of the 1981 Act to s 6 registrations, s 7 traffic regulation conditions and Part II London local service licences under that Act.

4–906A 56A. Correction of errors. Where it appears to the traffic commissioner for a traffic area that a document purporting to record, or issued in consequence of, a decision taken in the exercise of his functions contains a clerical error, he may issue a corrected document or a notice in writing that the document is to have effect with such corrections as are stated in the notice.
[Public Passenger Vehicles Act 1981, s 56A inserted by the Deregulation and Contracting Out Act 1994, s 65(3).]

Supplementary provisions as to licences etc

4–907 58. Partnerships and related matters[1].

1. The Operation of Public Service Vehicles (Partnership) Regulations, 1986, SI 1986/1628 have been made under this section. Section 58 is amended by the Transport Act 1985, Sch 1. Section 58(1) applies to the operation of vehicles and the provision of services under the Transport Act 1985 (ibid, s 132).

Regulations

4–908 59. Power to make regulations as to procedure on applications for licences[1].

1. The Public Service Vehicles (Operators' Licences) Regulations 1995, in this PART, post, have been made.

4–909 60. General power to make regulations for purposes of Act[1].

1. Relevant regulations are noted to individual sections of this Act. See also the Road Transport (Northern Ireland Passenger Services) Regulations 1980, SI 1980/1460 amended by SI 1981/462. Section 60 has effect as if Parts I and II of the Transport Act 1985 were contained in the 1981 Act (ibid, s 134). The 1985 Act has amended s 60, as has the Transport and Works Act 1992, s 61.

Provisions relating to Metropolitan Traffic Area

4–910 64. Exclusion of certain enactments as respects Metropolitan Traffic Area. (1) As respects the Metropolitan Traffic Area, the Metropolitan Public Carriage Act 1869 and the London Cab and Stage Carriage Act 1907 shall not apply to a public service vehicle or to the driver or conductor thereof.

(2) As respects the Metropolitan Traffic Area, no local authority shall exercise under the Town Police Clauses Act 1847 any powers with respect to public service vehicles or the licensing thereof or of their drivers or conductors.
[Public Passenger Vehicles Act 1981, s 64.]

Provisions relating to offences and legal proceedings

4–911 65. Forgery and misuse of documents etc. (1) This section applies to the following documents[1] and other things, namely—

(a) a licence under Part II of this Act;
(b) a certificate of initial fitness under section 6 of this Act;
(c) a certificate under section 10 of this Act that a vehicle conforms to a type vehicle;
(d) an operator's disc under section 18 of this Act;
(e) a certificate under section 21 of this Act as to the repute, financial standing or professional competence of any person;*
(e) a control document issued under Article 6 of Council Regulation (EC) No 12/98 of 11 December 1997;
(ea) a control document issued under Article 6 of Council Regulation (EC) No 12/98 of 11 December 1997;
(f) Repealed.

(2) A person who, with intent to deceive—

(a) forges or alters, or uses or lends to, or allows to be used by, any other person, a document or other thing to which this section applies[2], or
(b) makes or has in his possession[3] any document or other thing so closely resembling a document or other thing to which this section applies as to be calculated[4] to deceive,

shall be liable[5]—

  (i) on conviction on indictment, to imprisonment for a term not exceeding two years;
  (ii) on summary conviction, to a fine not exceeding the statutory maximum.

(3) In the application of this section to England and Wales—

"forges" means makes a false document or other thing in order that it may be used as genuine;

(4) *Repealed.*
[Public Passenger Vehicles Act 1981, s 65 as amended by the Forgery and Counterfeiting Act 1981, Sch and the Transport Act 1985, Sch 8 and the Road Traffic Act 1991, Sch 8, the Statute Law (Repeals) Act 1993, Sch 1 and SI 1999/3413.]

---

*Amended by the Transport Act 1982, s 23, when in force.
  1. The Transport Act 1985, s 127 applies this section to a permit under ss 19 and 22 of that Act and to a London local service licence under Part II of that Act.
  2. An offence would be committed by the use of a certificate which has ceased to be a valid certificate after the cancellation of a policy (*R v Cleghorn* [1938] 3 All ER 398).
  3. It may be sufficient to know that one has the document in one's control without knowledge of its qualities; see *Warner v Metropolitan Police Comr* [1969] 2 AC 256, [1968] 2 All ER 356, 132 JP 378. "Possession may be wider than mere physical possession; see *Towers & Co Ltd v Gray* [1961] 2 QB 351, [1961] 2 All ER 68, 125 JP 391.
  4. This appears to mean "likely to deceive" and not "intended to deceive"; see *Re London and Globe Finance Corpn Ltd* [1903 1 Ch 728, 82 JP 447; *Collett v Co-operative Wholesale Society Ltd* [1970] 1 All ER 274, 134 JP 227; *Turner v Shearer* [1973] 1 All ER 397, [1972] 1 WLR 1387, 137 JP 191.
  5. For procedure in respect of an offence triable either way, see the Magistrates' Courts Act 1980, ss 17A–21, in PART I: MAGISTRATES' COURTS, PROCEDURE, ante. See also ss 68–74 post as to proceedings.

4–912 66. False statements to obtain licence etc. A person who knowingly makes a false statement[1] for the purpose of—

  (a) obtaining the grant of a licence under Part II of this Act[2] to himself or any other person, obtaining the variation of any such licence, preventing the grant or variation of any such licence or procuring the imposition of a condition or limitation in relation to any such licence;
  (b) obtaining the issue of a certificate of initial fitness under section 6 of this Act;
  (c) obtaining the issue of a certificate under section 10 of this Act that a vehicle conforms to a type vehicle;
  (d) obtaining the issue of an operator's disc under section 18 of this Act;
  (e) obtaining the issue of a certificate under section 21 of this Act as to the repute, financial standing or professional competence of any person; or
  (f) obtaining the issue of a control document under article 6 of Council Regulation (EC) No 12/98 of 11 December 1997.

shall be liable on summary conviction[3] to a fine not exceeding **level 4** on the standard scale.*
[Public Passenger Vehicles Act 1981, s 66 as amended by the Criminal Justice Act 1982, s 46, the Transport Act 1985, Sch 8 and SI 1999/3413.]

---

*A new s 66A is added by the Transport Act 1982, s 24 and amended by the Road Traffic Act 1991, Sch 8, when in force.
  1. It is immaterial whether or not any gain or advantage would be derived as a result of the false statement (*Jones v Meatyard* [1939] 1 All ER 140).
  2. The Transport Act 1985, s 127 applies this section to a permit under ss 19 or 22 of that Act and to a London local service licence under Part II of that Act.
  3. See ss 68–74 post as to proceedings.

4–913 67. Penalty for breach of regulations. Subject to section 68(1) of this Act, if a person acts in contravention of, or fails to comply with, any regulations made by the Secretary of State under this Act[1] and contravention thereof, or failure to comply therewith, is not made an offence under any other provision of this Act, he shall for each offence be liable on summary conviction[2] to a fine not exceeding **level 2** on the standard scale.
[Public Passenger Vehicles Act 1981, s 67 as amended by the Criminal Justice Act 1982, s 46 and the Transport Act 1985, Sch 8.]

---

  1. Section 67 is to have effect as if Parts I and II of the Transport Act 1985 were contained in it, (ibid, s 127).
  2. See ss 68–74 post as to proceedings.

4–914 68. Defences available to persons charged with certain offences. (1) It shall be a defence for a person charged with an offence under any of the provisions of this Act mentioned in subsection (2) below to prove[1] that there was a reasonable excuse for the act or omission in respect of which he is charged.
  (2) The provisions referred to in subsection (1) above are—

  (a) sections 19(5), 20(4), 24(2) and (3), 25(3), 26(2), 67 and 70(3);
  (b) *Repealed.*

(3) It shall be a defence for a person charged with an offence under any of the provisions of this Act mentioned in subsection (4) below to prove that he took all reasonable precautions and exercised all due diligence to avoid the commission of any offence under that provision[2].
  (4) The provisions referred to in subsection (3) above are—

  (a) sections 6(2), 12(5), 16(7), 18(4), 26(2) and 27(2);

   (*b*) *Repealed.*
[Public Passenger Vehicles Act 1981, s 68 amended by the Transport Act 1985, Schs 1 and 8, the Road Traffic (Driver Licensing and Information Systems) Act 1989, Sch 6 and the Road Traffic Act 1991, Sch 8.]

---

   1. The burden of proof is on a preponderance of probabilities, less onerous than on the prosecution; *R v Carr-Briant* [1943] KB 607; *R v Dunbar* [1958] 1 QB 1, [1957] 2 All ER 737, 121 JP 506.
   2. The defence under s 68(3) applies in relation to offences under the Transport Act 1985, ss 23(5), 30(2), 35(6) and 38(7) (ibid, s 127).

4–915   69.   Restriction on institution in England and Wales of proceedings under Part II.
   (1) Subject to the provisions of this section proceedings for an offence under Part II of this Act[1] shall not, in England and Wales, be instituted except by or on behalf of the Director of Public Prosecutions or by a person authorised[2] in that behalf by a traffic commissioner, a chief officer of police, or the council of a county or district.
   (2) Subsection (1) above shall not apply to proceedings for the breach of regulations having effect by virtue of section 25 or 26 of this Act.
   (3) *Repealed.*
[Public Passenger Vehicles Act 1981, s 69 as amended by the Transport Act 1985, Schs 2 and 8 and the Statute Law (Repeals) Act 2004.]

---

   1. The provisions of s 69 apply to proceedings under Part I or II of the Transport Act 1985 (ibid, s 127).
   2. For example a police sergeant specially authorised by an Assistant Commissioner of Police acting under a general authorisation given by a Commissioner of Police (*Westminster Coaching Service Ltd v Piddlesden* (1933) 97 JP 185; cf *Tyler v Ferris* [1906] 1 KB 94, 70 JP 88. It is the duty of the justice or of the justices' clerk issuing process to satisfy himself that the authority has been given (*Price v Humphries* [1958] 2 QB 353, [1958] 2 All ER 725, 122 JP 423).

4–916   70.   Duty to give information as to identity of driver in certain cases.   (1) Where the driver of a vehicle is alleged to be guilty of an offence under Part II of this Act[1]—

   (*a*) the person keeping the vehicle shall give such information as to the identity of the driver as he may be required to give by or on behalf of a chief officer of police[2], and
   (*b*) any other person[3] shall if required as aforesaid give any information which it is in his power to give and may lead to the identification of the driver.

   (2) A person who fails to comply with the requirement of paragraph (*a*) of subsection (1) above shall, unless he shows to the satisfaction of the court that he did not know and could not with reasonable diligence ascertain who the driver of the vehicle was, be liable on summary conviction[4] to a fine not exceeding **level 2** on the standard scale.
   (3) Subject to section 68(1) of this Act, a person who fails to comply with the requirement of paragraph (*b*) of subsection (1) above shall be liable on summary conviction[4] to a fine not exceeding **level 2** on the standard scale.
[Public Passenger Vehicles Act 1981, s 70 as amended by the Criminal Justice Act 1982, s 46 and the Transport Act 1985, Sch 8.]

---

   1. The police are not bound to specify the nature of the alleged offence when they require information from an owner or other person (*Pulton v Leader* [1949] 2 All ER 747, 113 JP 537). The provisions of s 70 apply to proceedings under Part I or II of the Transport Act 1985 (ibid, s 127).
   2. A police officer properly acting in the course of his duty is not necessarily acting on behalf of the chief officer of police (*Record Tower Cranes Ltd v Gisbey* [1969] 1 All ER 418, 133 JP 167). A notice signed by a police inspector with the authority of his superintendent, who was held to have the implied delegated authority of a Commissioner of Police to further delegate to his inspector, was held to be a good and valid notice (*Nelms v Roe* [1969] 3 All ER 1379, 134 JP 88).
   3. This will include the driver himself (*Bingham v Bruce* [1962] 1 All ER 186, 126 JP 81).
   4. See ss 68–74, post, as to proceedings.

4–930   71.   Evidence by certificate.   (1) In any proceedings in England or Wales for an offence under Part II of this Act[1] a certificate in the prescribed form, purporting to be signed by a constable[2] and certifying that the person specified in the certificate stated to the constable—

   (*a*) that a particular motor vehicle was being driven or used by, or belonged to, that person on a particular occasion; or
   (*b*) that a particular motor vehicle on a particular occasion was used by or belonged to a firm in which that person also stated that he was at the time of the statement a partner; or
   (*c*) that a particular motor vehicle on a particular occasion was used by or belonged to a company of which that person also stated that he was at the time of the statement a director, officer or employee,

shall be admissible as evidence for the purpose of determining by whom the vehicle was being driven or used or to whom it belonged, as the case may be, on that occasion.
   (2) Nothing in subsection (1) above shall be deemed to make a certificate admissible as evidence in proceedings for an offence except in a case where and to the like extent to which oral evidence to the like effect would have been admissible in those proceedings.
   (3) Nothing in subsection (1) above shall be deemed to make a certificate admissible as evidence in proceedings for an offence—

   (*a*) unless a copy thereof has, not less than seven days before the hearing or trial, been served in the prescribed manner on the person charged with the offence; or

(b) if that person not later than three days before the hearing or trial or within such further time as the court may in special circumstances allow, serves a notice in the prescribed form and manner on the prosecutor requiring attendance at the trial of the person who signed the certificate.

(4) In this section "prescribed" means prescribed by rules made by the Secretary of State by statutory instrument.[3]
[Public Passenger Vehicles Act 1981, s 71 amended by the Transport Act 1985, Sch 8.]

----

1. The provisions of s 71 apply to proceedings under Part I or II of the Transport Act 1985 (ibid, s 127).
2. Probably including a traffic warden; cf Road Traffic Act 1960, s 242, ante.
3. No rules have been made, but comparison may be made with the Road Traffic Act 1960, s 242, ante.

4–931 72. Proof in summary proceedings of identity of driver of vehicle. Where on a summary trial in England or Wales of an information for an offence under Part II of this Act[1]—

(a) it is proved to the satisfaction of the court, on oath or in a manner prescribed by rules made under section 15 of the Justices of the Peace Act 1949[2], that a requirement under subsection (1) of section 70 of this Act to give information as to the identity of the driver of a particular vehicle on the particular occasions to which the information relates has been served on the accused by post; and
(b) a statement in writing is produced to the court purporting to be signed by the accused that the accused was the driver of that vehicle on that occasion,

the court may accept that statement as evidence that the accused was the driver of that vehicle on that occasion.
[Public Passenger Vehicles Act 1981, s 72 amended by the Transport Act 1985, Sch 8.]

----

1. The provisions of ss 72 and 74 apply to proceedings under Part I or II of the Transport Act 1985 (ibid, s 127).
2. Now replaced by the Courts Act 2003, s 69. For the prescribed manner of proving service of a document by post, see the Criminal Procedure Rules 2005, Part 4, in PART I: MAGISTRATES' COURTS, PROCEDURE, ante.

4–932 73. Time within which summary proceedings for certain offences may be commenced. Summary proceedings for an offence under section 65 or 66 of this Act may be brought within a period of six months from the date on which evidence sufficient in the opinion of the prosecutor to warrant the proceedings came to his knowledge; but no such proceedings shall be brought by virtue of this section more than three years after the commission of the offence[1].
For the purposes of this section a certificate signed by or on behalf of the prosecutor and stating the date on which such evidence as aforesaid came to his knowledge shall be conclusive evidence of that fact; and a certificate stating that matter and purporting to be so signed shall be deemed to be so signed unless the contrary is proved.
[Public Passenger Vehicles Act 1981, s 73.]

----

1. The extended limitation of time applies to aiding and abetting the specified offences (*Homolka v Osmond* [1939] 1 All ER 154).

4–933 74. Offences by companies. (1) Where an offence under Part II of this Act committed by a company is proved to have been committed with the consent or connivance of, or to be attributable to any neglect on the part of, any director, manager, secretary or other similar officer of the company, or any person who was purporting to act in any such capacity, he, as well as the company, shall be guilty of that offence and be liable to be proceeded against and punished accordingly.

(2) Where the affairs of a company are managed by its members, subsection (1) above shall apply in relation to the acts and defaults of a member in connection with his functions of management as if he were a director of the company.
[Public Passenger Vehicles Act 1981, s 74 amended by the Transport Act 1985, Sch 8.]

Inquiries

4–934 77. General provisions as to inquiries. *Repealed.*

Supplementary provisions

4–935 79. Vehicles excluded from regulation as private hire vehicles. At any time when a vehicle would apart from section 1(3) or (4)★ of this Act be a public service vehicle, it shall continue to be treated as such for the purposes only of provisions contained in a local Act, in sections 10 to 23 of the Civic Government (Scotland) Act 1982, in the Private Hire Vehicles (London) Act 1998 or in Part II of the Local Government (Miscellaneous Provisions) Act 1976, which regulate the use of private hire vehicles provided for hire with the services of a driver for the purpose of carrying passengers and exclude public service vehicles from the scope of that regulation.
[Public Passenger Vehicles Act 1981, s 79 as amended by the Civic Government (Scotland) Act 1982, Sch 3 and the Transport Act 1985, Sch 7 and the Private Hire Vehicles (London) Act 1998, Sch 1.]

★**Amended the Transport Act 2000, s 265(1) from a date to be appointed.**

4–935A 79A. Small PSVs subject to regulation as private hire vehicles.   (1) If a small bus is being provided for hire with the services of a driver for the purpose of carrying passengers otherwise than at separate fares, it is not to be regarded as a public service vehicle for the purpose of—

(*a*) Part II of the Local Government (Miscellaneous Provisions) Act 1976, or
(*b*) any local Act applying in any area in England and Wales which regulates the use of private hire vehicles provided for hire with the services of a driver for the purpose of carrying passengers and excludes public service vehicles from the scope of that regulation.

(2) If a small bus is being made available with a driver to the public for hire for the purpose of carrying passengers otherwise than at separate fares, it is not to be regarded as a public service vehicle for the purpose of the Private Hire Vehicles (London) Act 1998.

(3) But subsection (1) or (2) does not apply where the vehicle is being so provided or made available in the course of a business of carrying passengers by motor vehicles all but a small part of which involves the operation of large buses.

(4) In this section—

"small bus" means a public service vehicle within paragraph (b) of subsection (1) of section 1 of this Act; and
"large buses" means public service vehicles within paragraph (a) of that subsection."

(3) In section 167(4) of the Criminal Justice and Public Order Act 1994 (touting for hire car services: defence in case of public service vehicles), for "passengers for public service vehicles" substitute "passengers to be carried at separate fares by public service vehicles".
[Public Passenger Vehicles Act 1981, s 79A as inserted by the Transport Act 2000, s 265.]

4–936 81. Interpretation of references to the operator of a vehicle or service.   (1) For the purposes of this Act—

(*a*) regulations[1] may make provision as to the person who is to be regarded as the operator of a vehicle which is made available by one holder of a PSV operator's licence to another under a hiring arrangement; and
(*b*) where regulations under paragraph (*a*) above do not apply, the operator of a vehicle is—

(i) the driver, if he owns the vehicle; and
(ii) in any other case, the person for whom the driver works (whether under a contract of employment or any other description of contract personally to do work).

(2) *Repealed.*
[Public Passenger Vehicles Act 1981, s 81 as amended by the Transport Act 1985, Schs 1 and 8.]

---

1. See the Public Service Vehicles (Operators' Licences) Regulations 1995 in this PART, post.

4–937 82. General interpretation provisions.   (1) In this Act, unless the context otherwise requires—

"certificate of initial fitness" has the meaning given by section 6;
"company" means a body corporate;
"contravention", in relation to any condition or provision, includes a failure to comply with the condition or provision, and "contravene" shall be construed accordingly;
"director", in relation to a company, includes any person who occupies the position of a director, by whatever name called;
"driver"[1], where a separate person acts as steersman of a motor vehicle, includes that person as well as any other person engaged in the driving of the vehicle, and "drive" shall be construed accordingly;
"fares" includes sums payable in respect of a contract ticket or a season ticket;
"international operation" means a passenger transport operation starting or terminating in the United Kingdom and involving an international journey by the vehicle concerned, whether or not any driver leaves or enters the United Kingdom with that vehicle;
"local authority" means—

(*a*) in relation to England and Wales any local authority within the meaning of the Local Government Act 1972;
(*b*) *Applies to Scotland;*

"local service" has the same meaning as in the Transport Act 1985;
"magistrates' court" has the same meaning as in the Magistrates' Courts Act 1980[2];
"modification" includes addition, omission and alteration, and related expressions shall be construed accordingly;
"motor vehicle" means a mechanically propelled vehicle intended or adapted for use on roads;
"national operation" means a passenger transport operation wholly within the United Kingdom;
"official PSV testing station" has the meaning given by section 8(3);
"operating centre", in relation to a vehicle, means the base or centre at which the vehicle is normally kept;
"operator" has the meaning given by section 81;

"owner", in relation to a vehicle which is the subject of an agreement for hire, hire-purchase, conditional sale or loan, means the person in possession of the vehicle under that agreement, and references to owning a vehicle shall be construed accordingly;

"prescribed" has the meaning given by section 60(2);★

"PSV operator's licence" means a PSV operator's licence granted under the provisions of Part II of this Act;

"public service vehicle" has the meaning given by section 1;

"relevant conviction" means a conviction (other than a spent conviction) of any offence prescribed for the purposes of this Act, or an offence under the law of Northern Ireland, or of a country or territory outside the United Kingdom, corresponding to an offence so prescribed;

"restricted licence" means such a PSV operator's licence as is mentioned in section 13(3);

"road" means any highway and any other road to which the public has access, and includes bridges over which a road passes;

"standard licence" means a PSV operator's licence which is not a restricted licence;

"statutory provision" means a provision contained in an Act or in subordinate legislation within the meaning of the Interpretation Act 1978;

"traffic commissioner" means a person appointed to be the commissioner for a traffic area for the purposes of this Act;

"tramcar" includes any carriage used on any road by virtue of an order made under the Light Railways Act 1896;

"transport manager", in relation to a business, means an individual who, either alone or jointly with one or more other persons, has continuous and effective responsibility for the management of the road passenger transport operations of the business.

(2) Any reference in this Act to a Community instrument or to a particular provision of such an instrument—

(*a*) is a reference to that instrument or provision as amended from time to time, and

(*b*) if that instrument or provision is replaced, with or without modification, shall be construed as a reference to the instrument or provision replacing it.

(3) In this Act—

(*a*) any reference to a county shall be construed in relation to Wales as including a reference to a county borough;

(*b*) any reference to a county council shall be construed in relation to Wales as including a reference to a county borough council; and

(*c*) section 17(4) and (5) of the Local Government (Wales) Act 1994 (references to counties and districts to be construed generally in relation to Wales as references to counties and county boroughs) shall not apply.

[Public Passenger Vehicles Act 1981, s 82 as amended by the Transport Act 1985, Schs 1, 2 and 8, the Road Traffic Act 1991, Sch 8, the Local Government (Wales) Act 1994, Sch 7 and the Access to Justice Act 1999, Sch 10.]

★**A definition of "prescribed testing authority" and a new sub-s (1A) are added by the Transport Act 1982, Sch 5, when in force.**

1. See also Introductory Note to this PART under "Drivers and driving". "Steersman" in this definition would appear to refer to one of two people in charge of the same vehicle, for example, a steam wagon, or instructor and learner who are joint drivers (*Langman v Valentine* [1952] 2 All ER 803, 116 JP 576, and cf *Evans v Walkden* [1956] 3 All ER 64). A person "drives" a vehicle in the act of steering it down an incline without the engine running (*Saycell v Bool* [1948] 2 All ER 83, 112 JP 341) and cf *R v Kitson* (1955) 39 Cr App Rep 66.

2. See ss 148 and 150 thereof in PART I: MAGISTRATES' COURTS, PROCEDURE, ante.

4–938   83. Construction of references in other Acts etc to public service vehicles, licensing authorities etc. (1) A provision of an Act other than this Act or of an instrument having effect under an enactment not repealed by this Act which (however, expressed) defines "public service vehicle", by reference to the Road Traffic Act 1930 or the Road Traffic Act 1960 shall have effect as if it provided that that expression should be construed in like manner as if it were contained in this Act.

(2) *Repealed.*

[Public Passenger Vehicles Act 1981, s 83 as amended by the Transport Act 1985, Schs 1 and 8.]

4–939

SCHEDULES

Sections 1 and 2   SCHEDULE 1

PUBLIC SERVICE VEHICLES: CONDITIONS AFFECTING STATUS OR CLASSIFICATION

(*As amended by the Local Government Act 1985, Sch 5 and the Transport Act 1985, Schs 7 and 8.*)

PART I

SHARING OF TAXIS AND HIRE-CARS

1. The making of the agreement for the payment of separate fares must not have been initiated by the driver or by the owner of the vehicle, by any person who has made the vehicle available under any arrangement, or by any person who receives any remuneration in respect of the arrangements for the journey.

2. (1) The journey must be made without previous advertisement to the public of facilities for its being made

by passengers to be carried at separate fares, except where the local authorities concerned have approved the arrangements under which the journey is made as designed to meet the social and welfare needs of one or more communities, and their approvals remain in force.

(2) In relation to a journey the local authorities concerned for the purposes of this paragraph are those in whose area any part of the journey is to be made; and in this sub-paragraph "local authority" means—

(a) in relation to England and Wales, the council of a county, metropolitan district or London borough and the Common Council of the City of London;

(b) *(applies to Scotland).*

(3) *Repealed.*

PART III
ALTERNATIVE CONDITIONS AFFECTING STATUS OR CLASSIFICATION

5. Arrangements for the bringing together of all the passengers for the purpose of making the journey must have been made otherwise than by, or by a person acting on behalf of—

(a) the holder of the PSV operator's licence under which the vehicle is to be used, if such a licence is in force,

(b) the driver or the owner of the vehicle or any person who has made the vehicle available under any arrangement, if no such licence is in force.

and otherwise than by any person who receives any remuneration in respect of the arrangements.

6. The journey must be made without previous advertisement to the public of the arrangements therefor.

7. All passengers must, in the case of a journey to a particular destination, be carried to, or to the vicinity of, that destination, or, in the case of a tour, be carried for the greater part of the journey.

8. No differentiation of fares for the journey on the basis of distance or of time must be made.

PART IV
SUPPLEMENTARY

9. For the purposes of paragraphs 2 and 6 above no account shall be taken of any such advertisement as follows, that is to say—

(a) a notice displayed or announcement made—

(i) at or in any place of worship for the information of persons attending that place of worship;

(ii) at or in any place of work for the information of persons who work there; or

(iii) by any club or other voluntary association at or in any premises occupied or used by the club or association;

(b) a notice contained in any periodical published for the information of, and circulating wholly or mainly among—

(i) persons who attend or might reasonably be expected to attend a particular place of worship or a place of worship in a particular place; or

(ii) persons who work at a particular place of work or at any two or more particular places of work; or

(iii) the members of a club or other voluntary association.

Transport Act 1982[1]
(1982 c 49)

PART II[2]
TESTING, MARKING AND APPROVAL OF VEHICLES

Provision for private-sector plating and testing

4–1040   10. Provisions supplementary to section 8[3]. (1) To the extent that the terms of his authorisation so provide an authorised inspector shall have the duty to refuse any certificate or impose or remove any prohibition which he has power to refuse or (as the case may be) to impose or remove.

(2) In sections 45 and 46 of the 1988 Act (tests of satisfactory condition of vehicles other than goods vehicles to which section 49 applies)—

(a) in section 45(3) (persons who may carry out examinations under that section), after paragraph (a) there is inserted—

"(aa)any authorised inspector"

(b) in section 46(g) (keeping of registers of test certificates), after the words "authorised examiners" there shall be inserted the words "and, in the case of examinations carried out by authorised inspectors, by approved testing authorities"; and

(c) in section 46(h) (keeping of records), for the words "and authorised examiners" there shall be substituted the words "authorised examiners and approved testing authorities".

(3) The words "or an authorised inspector" shall be inserted—

(a) in sections 51(1)(b) and 61(2)(a) of the 1988 Act, after the words "a vehicle examiner", and

(b) in section 6(1)(a) and 10(2) of the 1981 Act, after the words "Act 1988";

and the words "or authorised inspector" shall be inserted after the word "examiner" wherever occurring in section 69 of the 1988 Act.

(4) In sections 1 and 2 of the Road Traffic (Foreign Vehicles) Act 1972—

(a) the words "or an authorised inspector" shall be inserted after the words "an examiner" (in each place where they appear); and

(b)   the words "or authorised inspector" shall be inserted after the words "the examiner" or "any examiner" (in each place where they appear).

(5) *Repealed.*

(6) In section 68(1) of the 1988 Act (powers of entry and inspection), the following words shall be inserted at the end—

"and an authorised inspector may exercise the powers given by paragraph (a) above in relation to any vehicle brought to the place of inspection in pursuance of a direction under subsection (3) below".

(7) The words "or the prescribed testing authority" shall be inserted after the words "the Secretary of State"—

(a)   in section 51(1)(a)(ii) and (d) of the 1988 Act (requirements with respect to the notification of alterations of goods vehicles to the Secretary of State and the specification of alterations required to be so notified in plating certificates);

(b)   in section 53(3) of that Act (offence to use vehicle where alteration not notified as required by regulations under section 49); and

(c)   in section 63(3) of that Act (offence to use vehicle where alteration not notified as required by regulations or directions under section 59);

and after those words (in the second place where they occur) in each of section 59(1), (2) and (3) of that Act (requirements and directions with respect to the notification of alterations relevant to type approval or plated weights).

(8) In section 6 of the 1981 Act (certificates of initial fitness required for use as public service vehicles), the following subsection shall be inserted after subsection (1)—

"(1A) Regulations may make provision with respect to the examination of vehicles for the purposes of subsection (1)(a) above by or under the direction of authorised inspectors and the issue or refusal of certificates of initial fitness by such inspectors on any such examinations.".

(9) In section 20 of that Act (duty of PSV operator to give information about his public service vehicles to traffic commissioners who granted his licence)—

(a)   for the words "to the traffic commissioners who granted the licence" in both subsections (1) and (2) (which relate respectively to failure or damage affecting safety and to structural alterations of vehicles) there shall be substituted the words "in accordance with regulations made by virtue of subsection (2A) below"; and

(b)   the following subsection shall be inserted after subsection (2)—

"(2A) Regulations may make provision—

(a)   for any report or notice required under subsection (1) or (2) above to be made or given to the Secretary of State or to the prescribed testing authority;

(b)   for requiring a public service vehicle to be submitted for examination in the event of any such failure or damage as is mentioned in subsection (1) above or any such alteration as is mentioned in subsection (2) above; and

(c)   for the examinations to be carried out under the regulations and, in particular, for authorising any such examination to be carried out by or under the direction of an examiner appointed under section 66A of the Road Traffic Act 1988 or an authorised inspector.".

(10) References in any regulations made under any enactment relating to any of the testing and surveillance functions before this section comes into operation to a vehicle examiner shall be read as including an authorised inspector authorised to exercise the function in question.

(11) Subject to the qualification mentioned below, regulations made under—

(a)   section 45, section 49 or section 61 of the 1988 Act;

(b)   section 6(1A), 10(4) or 20(2A) of the 1981 Act;

may include provision for the purpose of securing that private-sector examinations are properly carried out in accordance with the regulations, including (but without prejudice to the generality of the preceding provision) provision for the supervision or review of private-sector examinations by persons authorised for the purpose by or under the regulations.

No person other than an officer of the Secretary of State may be authorised by or under regulations so made to supervise or review an examination carried out in the course of a vehicle testing business carried on by a person other than his own employer.

In this subsection "private-sector examination" means, in relation to an examination under regulations so made, an examination carried out by or under the direction of an authorised inspector.

(12) Without prejudice to any existing power of the Secretary of State to determine the premises at which examinations under section 45 or 49 of the 1988 Act may be carried out—

(a)   the Secretary of State may designate premises as stations where examinations of vehicles of any description subject to examination under either of those sections may be carried out; and

(b)   regulations under either of those sections may require or authorise examinations of vehicles of any description specified in the regulations to be carried out at premises for the time being designated under this section as premises at which examinations of vehicles of that description may be carried out.

[Transport Act 1982, s 10 amended by the Road Traffic (Consequential Provisions) Act 1988, Sch 2 and the Road Traffic Act 1991, Schs 4 and 8.]

1. Only those parts of the Act of immediate concern to magistrates' courts are printed here. At the time of going to press, there had been the following Commencement Orders affecting the following relevant provisions: SI 1982/1561—ss 16, 58, 61, 72 (so far as it relates to ss 53 and 54), Sch 5 paras 25 and 26, and relating to s 72(2) and (4) of the Road Traffic Regulation Act 1967; SI 1982/1804—s 64; SI 1983/276—ss 57, 63 and 65; SI 1983/577—s 59 and para 13 of Sch 5; SI 1984/175—s 52, Sch 4, Sch 5, para 6 and Sch 6 so far as it relates to the Transport Act 1968; SI 1986/1326—ss 24–28 and 40–51, 73, 75, 76. Schs 1 and 3.
2. Part II includes ss 8–16.
3. At the date of going to press, this section had not been brought into force.

Miscellaneous and supplemental

4–1042　21. Amendments with respect to appeals. (1) Any examination of a vehicle on an appeal to the Secretary of State under section 45(4) of the 1988 Act (appeal against refusal of test certificate) shall be carried out by an officer of the Secretary of State; and accordingly, in section 45(5) of that Act, after the word "made" there shall be inserted the words "by an officer of the Secretary of State appointed by him for the purpose".

(2), (3) *Repealed.*

[Transport Act 1982, s 21(1)–(3) amended by the Road Traffic (Consequential Provisions) Act 1988, Sch 2 and the Road Traffic Act 1991, Sch 8.]

4–1043　22. Fees on notification of alterations notifiable under section 51 or 59 of the 1988 Act. (1) The following paragraph shall be inserted after paragraph (*a*) of section 51(1) of the 1988 Act (specific matters with which regulations under that section may deal)—

"(*aa*)require the payment of a fee on any notification of any alteration to a vehicle or its equipment which is required by the regulations to be notified to the Secretary of State or the prescribed testing authority;".

(2) For paragraph (*d*) of section 61(2) of that Act (power to make provision in relation to examinations, etc, following the notification of alterations notifiable under section 59 of that Act corresponding to provision authorised under certain paragraphs of section 51(1)) there shall be substituted the following paragraph—

"(*d*) may contain the like provisions with respect to any notification of any such alteration as is mentioned in paragraph (*a*) above, with respect to any examination of any vehicle in pursuance of regulations made by virtue of that paragraph and with respect to any appeal brought by virtue of paragraph (*c*) above as may be contained in regulations made by virtue of paragraphs (*aa*), (*b*), (*c*), (*g*) and (*h*) of section 51(1) of this Act in relation to the notifications, examinations and appeals there mentioned;".

[Transport Act 1982, s 22 amended by the Road Traffic (Consequential Provisions) Act 1988 Sch 2.]

4–1044　23. Forgery and misuse of documents etc. (1) A person who, with intent to deceive—

(*a*) uses or lends to, or allows to be used by, any other person, a document evidencing the authorisation of a person as an authorised inspector; or

(*b*) makes or has in his possession any document so closely resembling a document evidencing such an authorisation as to be calculated to deceive; or

(*c*) in Scotland, forges or alters a document evidencing such an authorisation;

shall be liable—

(i) on conviction on indictment, to imprisonment for a term not exceeding two years;

(ii) on summary conviction, to a fine not exceeding the statutory maximum.

(2) *Repealed.*

(3) In section 173 of the 1988 Act (forgery of documents etc), in subsection (2) the following paragraph shall be inserted after paragraph (*c*)—

"(*cc*)any notice removing a prohibition under section 69 or 70 of this Act;".

(4) *Repealed.*

[Transport Act 1982, s 23 amended by the Road Traffic (Consequential Provisions) Act 1988, Sch 2 and the Road Traffic Act 1991, Sch 8 and the Statute Law (Repeals) Act 1993, Sch 1.]

4–1045　24. Falsification of documents. (1) The following section shall be substituted for section 175 of the 1988 Act (issue of false documents)—

"**175. Falsification of documents.** (1) A person shall be guilty of an offence who issues—

(*a*) any such document as is referred to in paragraph (*a*) or (*b*) of section 174(5) of this Act;

(*b*) a test certificate, plating certificate, goods vehicle test certificate or certificate of conformity;

(*c*) a certificate of temporary exemption under regulations made under section 48(4) or 53(5)(*b*) of this Act; or

(*d*) a notice removing a prohibition under section 69 or 70 of this Act;

if the document or certificate so issued is to his knowledge false in a material particular.

(2) A person who amends a certificate of conformity shall be guilty of an offence if the certificate as amended is to his knowledge false in a material particular.

(3) Expressions used in subsections (1)(*b*) and (2) above have the same meanings as they respectively have for the purposes of Part II of this Act."*

(2) In section 176 of that Act (seizure of documents etc suspected of being false)—

(*a*)　in subsection (4) after the words "of this Act" there shall be inserted the words "or an authorised inspector appointed under section 8 of the Transport Act 1982";

(*b*)　in subsection (5) in paragraph (*b*), after the words "plating certificates" there shall be inserted the words "notices removing prohibitions under section 69 or 70 of this Act".

(3) In Part I of Schedule 2 to the Road Traffic Offenders Act 1988 (prosecution and punishment of offences)—

(*a*)　in column one of the entry relating to section 175, for "175" there shall be substituted "175(1)"; and

(*b*)　after that entry there shall be inserted the following entry—

"175 (2)	Falsely amending certificate of conformity	Summarily	Level 4 on the standard scale	—	—	".

and in Schedule 1 to the Road Traffic Offenders Act 1988, in the entry for section 175 of the Road Traffic Act 1988 there is added to the words in column 2 "falsely amending certificate of conformity".

(4) The following section shall be inserted after section 66 of the 1981 Act—

"66A. Issue of false documents.　(1) If a person issues—

(*a*)　a certificate of initial fitness under section 6 of this Act; or

(*b*)　a notice removing a prohibition under section 9(1) of this Act;

which he knows to be false in a material particular, he shall be liable on summary conviction to a fine not exceeding £500.

(2) If a constable, an examiner appointed under section 66A of the Road Traffic Act 1988 or an authorised inspector has reasonable cause to believe that a document produced to him or carried on a vehicle by its driver is a document in relation to which an offence has been committed under this section, he may seize the document.

(3) The power to seize a document under subsection (2) above includes power to detach a document carried on a vehicle from the vehicle.".

[Transport Act 1982, s 24 amended by the Road Traffic (Consequential Provisions) Act 1988, Schs 1 and 2 and the Road Traffic Act 1991, Sch 4.]

***As prospectively amended by the Transport Act 1982, s 24.**

4–1046　25. Impersonation of authorised inspector.　A person who, with intent to deceive, falsely represents himself to be an authorised inspector shall be liable on summary conviction to a fine not exceeding **level 3** on the standard scale.

[Transport Act 1982, s 25.]

4–1047　26. Interpretation of Part II.　In this Part of this Act—

"the 1981 Act" means the Public Passenger Vehicles Act 1981;

"the 1988 Act" means the Road Traffic Act 1988;

"approved testing authority" and "authorised inspector" have the meanings respectively given by section 8(3) and (4) of this Act;

"business" includes any activity carried on by a body of persons, whether corporate or unincorporate;

"goods vehicle" has the meaning given by section 192 of the 1988 Act; and

"vehicle testing business" has the meaning given by section 56(1) of and references to the testing and surveillance functions are references to the functions specified in section 9 of this Act.

[Transport Act 1982, s 26 amended by the Road Traffic (Consequential Provisions) Act 1988, Sch 2.]

Road Traffic Regulation Act 1984

(1984 c 27)

PART I[1]

GENERAL PROVISIONS FOR TRAFFIC REGULATION

Outside Greater London

4–1150　1. Traffic regulation orders[2] outside Greater London.　(1) The traffic authority for a road outside Greater London may make an order[3] under this section (referred to in this Act as a "traffic regulation order") in respect of the road where it appears to the authority making the order that it is expedient to make it—

   (*a*) for avoiding danger to persons or other traffic using the road or any other road or for preventing the likelihood of any such danger arising, or

   (*b*) for preventing damages to the road or to any building on or near the road, or

   (*c*) for facilitating the passage on the road or any other road of any class of traffic (including pedestrians), or

   (*d*) for preventing the use of the road by vehicular traffic of a kind which, or its use by vehicular traffic in a manner which, is unsuitable having regard to the existing character of the road or adjoining property, or

   (*e*) (without prejudice to the generality of paragraph (*d*) above) for preserving the character of the road in a case where it is specially suitable for use by persons on horseback or on foot, or

   (*f*) for preserving or improving the amenities of the area through which the road runs, or

   (*g*) for any of the purposes specified in paragraphs (*a*) to (*c*) of subsection (1) of section 87 of the Environment Act 1995 (air quality).

   (2) *Repealed.*

   (3) A traffic regulation order made by a local traffic authority may, with the consent of the Secretary of State or, as the case may be, the Scottish Ministers, extend to a road in relation to which he is or they are the traffic authority if the order forms part of a scheme of general traffic control relating to roads of which at least one has a junction with the length of road in question.

   (3A) A local traffic authority may make a traffic regulation order in respect of a road in relation to which the Secretary of State or the National Assembly for Wales is the traffic authority if—

   (*a*) the order is required for the provision of facilities pursuant to a quality partnership scheme under Part II of the Transport Act 2000, and

   (*b*) the Secretary of State, or the National Assembly for Wales, consents.

   (4), (5) *Repealed.*

[Road Traffic Regulation Act 1984, s 1 as amended by the Local Government Act 1985, Sch 5, the New Roads and Street Works Act 1991, Schs 8 and 9, the Environment Act 1995, Sch 22, the Transport Act 2000, s 161 and the Transport (Scotland) Act 2001, s 83.]

---

   1. Part I contains ss 1–13.

   2. As to exemptions in orders for vehicles displaying disabled persons' badges, see note 2 to ss 122–124, post.

   Tramcars are exempt from orders under this section; *trolley* vehicles are exempt from orders under this section other than prohibitions on waiting and loading: see SI 1992/1217, rr 3 and 5. *Transitional* provisions disapply any order made before 8 July 1992 in respect of tramcars and trolley vehicles except duo buses: see SI 1992/1217, rr 15 and 16.

   3. See, for example, the Various Trunk Roads (Prohibition on Waiting) (Clearways) Order 1963, SI 1963/1172.

4–1151   2. What a traffic regulation order may provide.   (1) A traffic regulation order may make any provision prohibiting, restricting or regulating the use of a road, or of any part of the width of a road, by vehicular traffic, or by vehicular traffic of any class specified in the order,—

   (*a*) either generally or subject to such exceptions[1] as may be specified in the order or determined in a manner provided for by it, and

   (*b*) subject to such exceptions as may be so specified or determined, either at all times or at times, on days or during periods so specified.

   (2) The provision that may be made by a traffic regulation order includes any provision—

   (*a*) requiring vehicular traffic, or vehicular traffic of any class specified in the order, to proceed in a specified direction or prohibiting its so proceeding;

   (*b*) specifying the part of the carriageway to be used by such traffic proceeding in a specified direction;

   (*c*) prohibiting or restricting the waiting of vehicles or the loading and unloading of vehicles;

   (*d*) prohibiting the use of roads by through traffic; or

   (*e*) prohibiting or restricting overtaking.

   (3) The provision that may be made by a traffic regulation order also includes provision prohibiting, restricting or regulating the use of a road, or of any part of the width of a road, by, or by any specified class of, pedestrians[2]—

   (*a*) either generally or subject to exceptions specified in the order, and

   (*b*) either at all times or at times, on days or during periods so specified.

   (4) A local traffic authority may include in a traffic regulation order any such provision—

   (*a*) specifying through routes for heavy commercial vehicles, or

   (*b*) prohibiting or restricting the use of heavy commercial vehicles (except in such cases, if any, as may be specified in the order) in such zones or on such roads as may be so specified,

as they consider expedient for preserving or improving the amenities of their area or of some part or parts of their area.

   (5) Nothing in subsection (4) above shall be construed as limiting the scope of any power or duty to control vehicles conferred or imposed on any local authority or the Secretary of State otherwise than by virtue of that subsection.

[Road Traffic Regulation Act 1984, s 2 as amended by the New Roads and Street Works Act 1991, Sch 8.]

1. Such exceptions will be strictly construed (*Clifford-Turner v Waterman* [1961] 3 All ER 974).
2. This includes persons driving, riding or leading a horse or other animal of draught or burden (s 127(1), post).

4–1152 3. Restrictions on traffic regulation orders. (1) A traffic regulation order shall not be made with respect to any road which would have the effect—

  (*a*) of preventing at any time access for pedestrians, or
  (*b*) of preventing for more than 8 hours in any period of 24 hours access for vehicles of any class,

to any premises situated on or adjacent to the road, or to any other premises accessible for pedestrians, or (as the case may be) for vehicles of that class, from, and only from, the road.

  (2) Subsection (1) above, so far as it relates to vehicles, shall not have effect in so far as the authority making the order are satisfied, and it is stated in the order that they are satisfied, that—

  (*a*) for avoiding danger to persons or other traffic using the road to which the order relates or any other road, or
  (*b*) for preventing the likelihood of any such danger arising, or
  (*c*) for preventing damage to the road or buildings on or near it, or
  (*d*) for facilitating the passage of vehicular traffic on the road, or
  (*e*) for preserving or improving the amenities of an area by prohibiting or restricting the use on a road or roads in that area of heavy commercial vehicles,

it is requisite that subsection (1) above should not apply to the order.

  (3) Provision for regulating the speed of vehicles on roads shall not be made by a traffic regulation order[1].

  (4) *Repealed.*
[Road Traffic Regulation Act 1984, s 3 as amended by the Transport Act 1985, Sch 8 and the New Roads and Street Works Act 1991, Schs 8 and 9.]

1. As to speed limits see Part VI (s 81 et seq).

4–1153 4. Provisions supplementary to ss 2 and 3. (1) A traffic regulation order may make provision for identifying any part of any road to which, or any time at which or period during which, any provision contained in the order is for the time being to apply by means of a traffic sign of a type or character specified in the order (being a type prescribed or character authorised under section 64 of this Act) and for the time being lawfully in place; and for the purposes of any such order so made any such traffic sign placed on and near a road shall be deemed to be lawfully in place unless the contrary is proved.

  (2) A traffic regulation order which imposes any restriction on the use by vehicles of a road, or the waiting of vehicles in a road, may include provision with respect to the issue and display of certificates or other means of identification of vehicles which are excepted from the restriction, whether generally or in particular circumstances or at particular times.

  (3) A traffic regulation order may also include provision with respect to the issue, display and operation of devices for indicating the time at which a vehicle arrived at, and the time at which it ought to leave, any place in a road in which waiting is restricted by the order, or one or other of those times, and for treating the indications given by any such device as evidence of such facts and for such purposes as may be prescribed by the order.
[Road Traffic Regulation Act 1984 s 4 as amended by SI 1996/1553.]

4–1154 5. Contravention of traffic regulation order. (1) A person who contravenes a traffic regulation order[1], or who uses a vehicle[2], or causes or permits a vehicle to be used[3] in contravention of a traffic regulation order, shall be guilty of an offence[4].

  (2) *Repealed.*
[Road Traffic Regulation Act 1984, s 5 as amended by the New Roads and Street Works Act 1991, Schs 8 and 9.]

1. Schedule 9 to this Act makes certain requirements in relation to the making of Orders: Failure to comply with these may mean that no offence was committed; see *James v Cavey* [1967] 2 QB 676, [1967] 1 All ER 1048, 131 JP 306. Where an order has been made under Sch 3 to the Road Traffic Act 1991, s 5 will to that extent cease to apply and any penalty charge will become payable under Sch 3.
2. This section does not apply to tramcars and trolley vehicles operated under statutory powers (s 141(1), post).
3. As to "use", "cause", "permit", see headnote to this title, ante. In *Cambridgeshire County Council v Associated Lead Mills Ltd* [2005] EWHC Admin 1627, (2005) 169 JP 489, [2006] RTR 8 their Lordships differed as to whether the words "cause or permit" gave rise to the need to prove a mental element where the defendant was the employer of the driver of the vehicle. Walker J was of the opinion that they did, and, so that "use" could not then be utilised in employer cases to circumvent the need to prove knowledge, construed s 5(1) as follows: (1) it is concerned to ensure that a person who contravenes a Traffic Regulation Order is guilty of an offence; (2) it identifies as an offender a person who uses a vehicle, or causes or permits a vehicle to be used, in contravention of a Traffic Regulation Order; (3) a Traffic Regulation Order does not have to identify the person who will contravene it, and it may be drafted in such a way that it is the vehicle, rather than a person, that contravenes the Order; (4) the words "uses a vehicle, or causes or permits a vehicle to be used" are there to cater for a case where the Regulation Order defines a vehicle, and not a person, as contravening it, and they are not engaged in cases where the Regulation Order identifies persons who contravene it.
4. For penalty see Sch 2 to the Road Traffic Offenders Act 1988, post.

In Greater London

4–1155 6. Orders similar to traffic regulation orders. (1) The traffic authority for a road in Greater London may make an order[1] under this section for controlling or regulating vehicular[2] and other traffic (including pedestrians).

Provision may, in particular, be made—

(a) for any of the purposes, or with respect to any of the matters, mentioned in Schedule 1 to this Act[3], and

(b) for any other purpose which is a purpose mentioned in any of paragraphs (a) to (g) to section 1(1) of this Act.

(2) In the case of a road for which the Secretary of State is the traffic authority, the power to make an order under this section is also exercisable, with his consent, by the local traffic authority.

(3) Any order under this section may be made so as to apply—

(a) to the whole area of a local authority, or to particular parts of that area, or to particular places or streets or parts of streets in that area;

(b) throughout the day, or during particular periods;

(c) on special occasions only, or at special times only;

(d) to traffic of any class;

(e) subject to such exceptions as may be specified in the order or determined in a manner provided for by it.

(4) *Repealed.*

(5) No order under this section shall contain any provision for regulating the speed of vehicles on roads[4].

(6) In this section, in section 7 of this Act and in Schedule 1 to this Act "street" includes any highway, any bridge carrying a highway and any lane, mews, footway, square, court, alley or passage whether a thoroughfare or not.

[Road Traffic Regulation Act 1984, s 6 as amended by the Local Government Act 1985, Sch 5, the New Roads and Street Works Act 1991, Schs 8 and 9 and the Environment Act 1995, Sch 22].

---

1. Where orders provide for a relevant traffic control to be subject to a relevant exception, the Secretary of State may replace or vary such exceptions pursuant to the Deregulation and Contracting Out Act 1994, s 34.

The Greater London (Restriction of Goods Vehicles) Traffic Order 1985 has been made. Within that Order for consideration of the term 'shortest practicable route': see *TNT Express (UK) Ltd v Richmond-upon-Thames London Borough* (1995) 160 JP 310. Breach of the conditions of a permit issued under art 4 (certain goods vehicles being driven in a restricted street during prescribed hours) incurs criminal liability under art 8 of the Order (*Post Office v London Borough of Richmond* (1994) 158 JP 919, [1995] RTR 28).

2. *Tramcars* are exempt from orders under this section; *trolley* vehicles are exempt from orders under this section other than matters referred to in para 15 of Sch 1: see SI 1992/1217, rr 3 and 5.

3. Sch 1 stipulates the following matters.

1. For prescribing the routes to be followed by all classes of traffic, or by any class or classes of traffic, from one specified point to another, either generally or between any specified times.

2. For prescribing streets which are not to be used for traffic by vehicles, or by vehicles of any specified class or classes, either generally or at specified times.

3. For regulating the relative position in the roadway of traffic of differing speeds or types.

4. For prescribing the places where vehicles, or vehicles of any class, may not turn so as to face in the opposite direction to that in which they were proceeding, or where they may only so turn under conditions prescribed by the order.

5. For prescribing the conditions subject to which, and the times at which, articles of exceptionally heavy weight or exceptionally large dimensions may be carried by road.

6. For prescribing the number and maximum size and weight of trailers which may be drawn on streets by vehicles, or by vehicles of any class, either generally or on streets of any class or description, and for prescribing that a man should be carried on the trailer or, where more than one trailer is drawn, on the rear trailer for signalling to the driver.

7. For prescribing the conditions subject to which, and the times at which, articles may be loaded on to or unloaded from vehicles, or vehicles of any class, on streets.

8. For prescribing the conditions subject to which, and the times at which, vehicles, or vehicles of any class, delivering or collecting goods or merchandise, or delivering goods or merchandise of any particular class, may stand in streets, or in streets of any class or description, or in specified streets.

9. For prescribing the conditions subject to which, and the times at which, vehicles, or vehicles of any class, may be used on streets for collecting refuse.

10. For prescribing rules as to precedence to be observed as between vehicles proceeding in the same direction, in opposite directions, or when crossing.

11. For prescribing the conditions subject to which, and the times at which, horses, cattle, sheep and other animals may be led or driven on streets within Greater London.

12. For requiring the erection, exhibition or removal of traffic notices, and as to the form, plan and character of such notices.

13. Broken down vehicles.

14. Vehicles, or vehicles of any class, when unattended.

15. Places in streets where vehicles, or vehicles of any class, may, or may not, wait, either generally or at particular times.

16. Cabs and hackney carriages not hired and being in a street elsewhere than on a cab rank.

17. for restricting the use of vehicles and animals, and sandwichmen and other persons, in streets for the purposes of advertisement of such a nature or in such a manner as is to be likely to be a source of danger or to cause obstruction to traffic.

18. The lighting and guarding of street works.

19. The erection or placing or the removal of any works or objects likely to hinder the free circulation of traffic in any street or likely to cause danger to passengers or vehicles.

20. Queues of persons waiting in streets.

21. Priority of entry to public vehicles.

22. For enabling any police, local or other public authority to do anything which under the order a person ought to have done and has failed to do, and to recover from the person so in default, summarily as a civil debt, the expenses of doing it.

4. As to speed limits see s 81 et seq of the Act, post.

4–1156   7. Supplementary provisions as to orders under s 6.   (1) Any order under section 6 of this Act may make provision for identifying any part of any road to which, or any time at which or period during which, any provision contained in the order is for the time being to apply by means of a traffic sign of a type or character specified in the order (being a type prescribed or character authorised under section 64 of this Act) and for the time being lawfully in place; and, for the purposes of any order so made, any such traffic sign placed on or near a street shall be deemed to be lawfully in place unless the contrary is proved.

(2) Any such order which imposes any restriction on the use by vehicles of streets in Greater London, or the waiting of vehicles in such streets, may include provision with respect to the issue and display of certificates or other means of identification of vehicles which are excepted from the restriction, whether generally or in particular circumstances or at particular times.

(3) Any such order may also include provision with respect to the issue, display and operation of devices for indicating the time at which a vehicle arrived at, and the time at which it ought to leave, any place in a street in which waiting is restricted by the order, or one or other of those times, and for treating the indications given by any such device as evidence of such facts and for such purposes as may be prescribed by the order.

(4) Any such order may provide for the suspension or modification, so long as the order remains in force, of any provisions of any Acts (whether public general or local or private, and including provisions contained in this Act), byelaws or regulations dealing with the same subject matter as the order, or of any Acts conferring power to make byelaws or regulations dealing with the same subject matter, so far as such provisions apply to any place or street to which the order applies.

(5)–(7) *Appeals, consultation.*

[Road Traffic Regulation Act 1984, s 7, amended by the Transport Act 1985, Sch 1 and SI 1996/1553.]

4–1157   8. Contravention of order under s 6.   (1) Any person who acts in contravention of, or fails to comply[1] with, an order[2] under section 6 of this Act shall be guilty of an offence[3].

(1A) Subsection (1) above does not apply in relation to any order under section 6 of this Act so far as it designates any parking places[4].*

(2) *Repealed.*

[Road Traffic Regulation Act 1984, s 8 as amended by the New Roads and Street Works Act 1991, Schs 8 and 9 and the Road Traffic Act 1991, s 65.]

---

*Repealed in relation to England and Wales by the Traffic Management Act 2005, Sch 12 from a date to be appointed.

1. Failing to comply with the conditions of a permit issued under art 4 of the Greater London (Restriction of Goods Vehicles) Traffic Order 1985 is an offence under art 3 (*Post Office v London Borough of Richmond* (1994) 158 JP 919, [1995] RTR 28).

Condition 5 of the Conditions Normally Considered for Attachment to a Permit under the London Boroughs Scheme for the Implementation and Enforcement of the Greater London (Restriction of Goods Vehicles) Traffic Order 1985 provides, *inter alia*, that the use of restricted roads be minimised and that the 'shortest practicable route' be taken; in this context 'practicable' means 'physically practicable', and the fact that a prolonged diversion would have the effect of increasing pollution in total is not a consideration open to justices when determining what was the 'shortest practicable route' for the purposes of condition 5: *Richmond-Upon-Thames London Borough Council v Express Ltd* [2003] EWHC 1181 (Admin), [2004] RTR 56.

2. Sch 9 to this Act makes certain requirements in relation to the making of Orders; failure to comply with these may mean that no offence was committed; see *James v Cavey* [1967] 2 QB 676, [1967] 1 All ER 1048, 131 JP 306.

3. The duty to give information as to the driver (s 112), applies here; this section applies to vehicles and persons in the public service of the Crown, except members of the armed forces on duty (s 130). For penalty for this offence see Sch 2 of the Road Traffic Offenders Act 1988, post.

4. For enforcement provisions for designated parking places in Greater London see the Road Traffic Act 1991, in PART VIII: title LONDON, post.

Experimental traffic schemes

4–1158   9–11.   *Experimental traffic orders[1,2] may be made by authorities in the same way as traffic regulation orders, and ss 1–4 will apply; a person acting in contravention or failing to comply will commit an offence under s 11[3].*

---

1. As to exemptions in orders under s 9 for vehicles displaying disabled persons' badges, see note 2 to ss 122–124, post. *Tramcars* are exempt from orders under this section; *trolley* vehicles are exempt from orders under this section other than prohibitions on waiting and loading: see SI 1992/1217, rr 3 and 5. Where an order has been made under Sch 3 to the Road Traffic Act 1991, s 11 will to that extent cease to apply and any penalty charge will become payable under Sch 3. It is unlawful to use the power under s 9 to make an order whose only purpose is to ban heavy goods vehicles from a road (*UK Waste Management Ltd v West Lancashire District Council* [1997] RTR 201, DC).

2. Where orders provide for a relevant traffic control to be subject to a relevant exception, the Secretary of State may replace or vary such exceptions pursuant to the Deregulation and Contracting Out Act 1994, s 34.

3. For penalty see Sch 2 to the Road Traffic Offenders Act 1988, post.

Experimental traffic schemes

4–1159   12, 13. *Repealed.*

PART II[1]
TRAFFIC REGULATION IN SPECIAL CASES

4–1160   14–16.   *Highway authority may make a temporary order[2] restricting or prohibiting traffic on a road by reason of works or danger or damage. Schedule 3 makes provision for notices. A person who contravenes* *or who uses or permits the use of a vehicle in contravention of a restriction or prohibition under s 14 commits an offence under s 16*[3].

1. Part II contains ss 14–22.

2. *Tramcars* are exempt from orders and notices under this section except in relation to speed restriction; *trolley* vehicles are exempt from orders or notices under this section except in relation to (i) waiting and loading, (ii) speed restriction, (iii) overtaking restriction, and (iv) vehicular prohibitions: see SI 1992/1217, rr 4 and 6. *Transitional* provisions disapply any order made before 8 July 1992 in respect of tramcars and trolley vehicles except duo buses: see SI 1992/1217, rr 15 and 16.

The powers of a local authority under these sections do not extend to the making of a prohibition or restriction order for the purpose of removing or reducing danger to the public from air pollution (*R v Greenwich London Borough, ex p W* (1995) 160 JP 270).

For procedure for making orders, see the Road Traffic (Temporary Restrictions) Procedure Regulations 1992, SI 1992/1215 amended by SI 2004/3168 (E) and SI 2006/1177.

3. For penalty see Sch 2 to the Road Traffic Offenders Act 1988 post. Sections 14 and 15 are substituted by the Road Traffic (Temporary Restrictions) Act 1991, s 1(1) and s 16(2) by s 1(2) thereof, when in force.

4–1160A　16A. Prohibition or restriction on roads in connection with certain events.

(1) In this section "relevant event" means any sporting event, social event or entertainment which is held on a road.

(2) If the traffic authority for a road are satisfied that traffic on the road should be restricted or prohibited for the purpose of—

(a)　facilitating the holding of a relevant event,

(b)　enabling members of the public to watch a relevant event, or

(c)　reducing the disruption to traffic likely to be caused by a relevant event.

the authority may by order restrict or prohibit temporarily the use of that road, or any part of it, by vehicles or vehicles of any class or by pedestrians, to such extent and subject to such conditions and exceptions as they may consider necessary or expedient.

(3) Before making an order under this section the authority shall satisfy themselves that it is not reasonably practicable for the event to be held otherwise than on a road.

(4) An order under this section—

(a)　may not be made in relation to any race or trial falling within subsection (1) of section 12 of the Road Traffic Act 1988 (motor racing on public ways);

(b)　may not be made in relation to any competition or trial falling within subsection (1) of section 13 of that Act (regulation of motoring events on public ways) unless the competition or trial is authorised by or under regulations under that section; and

(c)　may not be made in relation to any race or trial falling within subsection (1) of section 31 of that Act (regulation of cycle racing on public ways) unless the race or trial is authorised by or under regulations made under that section.

(5) An order under this section may relate to the road on which the relevant event is to be held or to any other road.

(6) In the case of a road for which the Secretary of State in the traffic authority, the power to make an order under this section is also exercisable, with his consent, by the local traffic authority or by any local traffic authority which is the traffic authority for any other road to which the order relates.

(7) In the case of a road for which a local traffic authority is the traffic authority, the power to make an order under this section is also exercisable, with the consent of that local traffic authority, by a local traffic authority which is the traffic authority for any other road to which the order relates.

(8) When considering the making of an order under this section, an authority shall have regard to the safety and convenience of alternative routes suitable for the traffic which will be affected by the order.

(9) The provision that may be made by an order under this section is—

(a)　any such provision as is mentioned in section 2(1), (2) or (3) or 4(1) of this Act;

(b)　any provision restricting the speed of vehicles; or

(c)　any provision restricting or prohibiting—

(i)　the riding of horses, or

(ii)　the leading or driving of horses, cattle, sheep or other animals,

but no such order shall be made with respect to any road which would have the effect of preventing at any time access for pedestrians to any premises situated on or adjacent to the road, or to any other premises accessible for pedestrians from, and only from, the road.

(10) An order under this section may—

(a)　suspend any statutory provision to which this subsection applies; or

(b)　for any of the purposes mentioned in subsection (2) above, suspend any such provision without imposing any such restriction or prohibition as is mentioned in that subsection.

(11) Subsection (10) above applies to—

(a)　any statutory provision of a description which could have been contained in an order under this section;

(b)　an order under section 32(1)(b), 35, 45, 46 or 49 of this Act or any such order as is mentioned in paragraph 11(1) of Schedule 10 to this Act; and (*c*) an order under section 6 of this Act so far as it designates any parking places in Greater London.

[Road Traffic Regulation Act 1984, s 16A, as inserted by the Road Traffic Regulation (Special Events) Act 1994, s 1.]

4–1160B 16B. Restrictions on orders under s 16A. (1) An order under section 16A of this Act shall not continue in force for a period of more than three days beginning with the day on which it comes into force unless—

(*a*) the order is made by the Secretary of State as the traffic authority for the road concerned; or
(*b*) before the order is made, he has agreed that it should continue in force for a longer period.

(2) Where an order under section 16A of this Act has not ceased to be in force and the relevant event to which it relates had not ended, the Secretary of State may, subject to subsections (4) and (5) below, from time to time direct that the order shall continue in force for a further period not exceeding three days beginning with the day on which it would otherwise cease to be in force.

(3) A direction under subsection (2) above may relate to all the roads to which the order under section 16A of this Act relates or only to specified roads.

(4) Where an order under section 16A of this Act relates only to roads for which the Secretary of State is not himself the traffic authority, he shall not give a direction under subsection (2) above except at the request of the traffic authority for any road to which the order relates.

(5) Where an order under section 16A of this Act relates to any road for which the Secretary of State is not himself the traffic authority, he shall not give a direction under subsection (2) above affecting that road except with the consent of the traffic authority for that road.

(6) Where an order had been made under section 16A of this Act in any calendar year, no further order may be made under that section in that year so as to affect any length of road affected by the previous order, unless the further order—

(*a*) is made by the Secretary of State as the traffic authority for the road concerned; or
(*b*) is made with his consent.

(7) For the purposes of subsection (6) above, a length of road is affected by an order under section 16A of this Act if the order contains provisions—

(*a*) prohibiting or restricting traffic on that length of road; or
(*b*) suspending any statutory provision applying to traffic on that length of road.

[Road Traffic Regulation Act 1984, s 16B, as inserted by the Road Traffic Regulation (Special Events) Act 1994, s 1.]

4–1160C 16C. Supplementary provisions as to orders under s 16A. (1) A person who contravenes, or who uses or permits the use of a vehicle in contravention of, a restriction or prohibition imposed by an order under section 16A of this Act shall be guilty of an offence.

(2) The Secretary of State may make regulations with respect to the procedure to be followed in connection with the making of orders under section 16A of this Act including provision for notifying the public of the exercise or proposed exercise of the powers conferred by that section and of the effect of orders made in the exercise of those powers.

(3) Without prejudice to the generality of subsection (2) above, the Secretary of State may by regulations under that subsection make, in relation to such orders as he thinks appropriate, provision—

(*a*) for the making and consideration of representations relating to a proposed order; and
(*b*) for any of the matters mentioned in paragraph 22(1)(*a*), (*c*), (*d*) or (*e*) of Schedule 9 to this Act;

and paragraph 25 of that Schedule shall apply to regulations under that subsection as it applies to regulations under Part III of that Schedule.

[Road Traffic Regulation Act 1984, s 16C, as inserted by the Road Traffic Regulation (Special Events) Act 1994, s 1.]

4–1161 17. Traffic regulation on special roads[1]. (1) A special road[2] shall not be used except by traffic of a class authorised to do so—

(*a*) in England and Wales, by a scheme made, or having effect as if made, under section 16 of the Highways Act 1980 or by virtue of paragraph 3 of Schedule 23 to that Act, or
(*b*) Scotland.

(2) The Secretary of State may make regulations[3] with respect to the use of special roads, and such regulations may in particular—

(*a*) regulate the manner in which and the conditions subject to which special roads may be used by traffic of the class authorised in that behalf by such a scheme as is mentioned in subsection (1)(*a*) above or, as the case may be, by virtue of the said paragraph 3;
(*b*) authorise, or enable such authority as may be specified in the regulations to authorise, the use of special roads on occasion or in an emergency or for the purpose of crossing, or for the purpose of securing access to premises abutting on or adjacent to the roads, by traffic other than that described in paragraph (*a*) above;
(*c*) relax, or enable any authority so specified to relax, any prohibition or restriction imposed by the regulations.

(3) Regulations made under subsection (2) above may make provision with respect to special roads generally, or may make different provision with respect to special roads provided for the use of different classes of traffic, or may make provision with respect to any particular special road.

(3A) *Scotland*

(4) If a person uses a special road in contravention of this section or of regulations under subsection (2) above, he shall be guilty of an offence[4].

(5) The provisions of this section and of any regulations under subsection (2) above do not apply in relation to a road, or part of a road, until the date declared by the traffic authority, by notice published in the prescribed[5] manner, to be the date on which the road or part is open for use as a special road.

This does not prevent the making of regulations under subsection (2) above before that date, so as to come into force in relation to that road or part on that date.

(6) In this section "use", in relation to a road, includes crossing.

[Road Traffic Regulation Act, 1984 s 17 as amended by the New Roads and Street Works Act 1991, Schs 8 and 9 and the National Parks (Scotland) Act 2000, Sch 5.]

1. This section does not apply to vehicles and persons in the public service of the Crown (s 130, post). For restrictions on the grant of a justices' licence for the sale of intoxicating liquor at premises on special roads, see the Licensing Act 1964, s 9(3) in PART VI, ante.
2. "Special road" is defined by s 142(1), post.
3. Regulations made under previous legislation and continued in force are Motorways Traffic (Speed Limit) Regulations 1974, SI 1974/502 specifying 70 mph generally with a few specified lower limits, and the Motorways Traffic (England and Wales) Regulations 1982, in this PART, post. There are other regulations of limited extent.
4. For penalty see Sch 2 to the Road Traffic Offenders Act 1988, post.
5. See the Special Roads (Notice of Opening) Regulations 1992, SI 1992/1371.

4–1162   17A. Further provisions as to special roads. (1) On the date declared by the traffic authority, by notice published in the prescribed manner, to be the date on which a special road, or a part of a special road, is open for use as a special road, any existing order under section 1, 6, 9 or 84 of this Act relating to that road or part shall cease to have effect.

(2) This is without prejudice to any power to make orders under those provisions in relation to the road or part as a special road; and any such power may be exercised before the date referred to above, so as to take effect on that date.

(3) The procedure for making an order applies in such a case with such modifications as may be prescribed.

[Road Traffic Regulation Act 1984, s 17A as inserted by the New Roads and Street Works Act 1991.]

4–1163   18. One-way traffic on trunk roads[1]. (1) Where the Secretary of State proposes to make an order[2] under section 10 of the Highways Act 1980, or (*Scotland*), directing that a road shall become a trunk road, and considers it expedient—

(a) that the road, when it becomes a trunk road, should be used only for traffic passing in one direction, and

(b) that any other road which is a trunk road, or is to become a trunk road by virtue of the order, should be used only for traffic passing in the other direction,

the order may make provision for restricting the use of those roads accordingly as from such date as may be specified in the order.

(2) Subsection (1) above shall have effect without prejudice to the powers of the Secretary of State under section 1 of this Act.

(3) A person who uses a vehicle, or causes or permits a vehicle to be used[3], in contravention of any provision made by virtue of subsection (1) above shall be guilty of an offence[4].

[Road Traffic Regulation Act 1984, s 18 as amended by the New Roads and Street Works Act 1991, Sch 8.]

1. This section does not apply to vehicles in the public service of the Crown (s 130, post) nor to tramcars or trolley vehicles operated under statutory powers (s 141, post).
2. *Tramcars* and *trolley* vehicles are exempt from orders under this section: see SI 1992/1217, rr 3 and 5. *Transitional* provisions disapply any order made before 8 July 1992 in respect of tramcars and trolley vehicles except duo buses: see SI 1992/1217, rr 15 and 16.
3. See headnote to this title, ante as to the meaning of "use", "cause", "permit".
4. For penalty see Sch 2 to the Road Traffic Offenders Act 1988, post.

4–1164   19. *Regulation of use of highways by public service vehicles.*

4–1165   20. *Prohibition or restriction of use of vehicles on roads of certain classes.*

4–1166   22–22BC. *Traffic regulation for special areas in the countryside.*
           22C, 22D. *Traffic regulation in relation to dangers connected with terrorism.*

PART III[1]
CROSSINGS AND PLAYGROUNDS

Pedestrian crossings

4–1167   23, 24. *Pedestrian crossings may be established on trunk roads by the Secretary of State and on other roads by a local authority.*

1. Part III contains ss 23–31.

4–1168 25. Pedestrian crossing regulations. (1) The Secretary of State may make regulations[1] with respect to the precedence of vehicles and pedestrians respectively, and generally with respect to the movement of traffic (including pedestrians), at and in the vicinity of crossings.

(2) Without prejudice to the generality of subsection (1) above, regulations under that subsection may be made—

(a) prohibiting pedestrian traffic on the carriageway within 100 yards of a crossing, and

(b) with respect to the indication of the limits of a crossing, or of any other matter whatsoever relating to the crossing, by marks or devices on or near the roadway or otherwise, and generally with respect to the erection of traffic signs in connection with a crossing.

(3) Different regulations may be made under this section in relation to different traffic conditions, and in particular (but without prejudice to the generality of the foregoing words) different regulations may be made in relation to crossings in the vicinity of, and at a distance from, a junction of roads, and in relation to traffic which is controlled by the police, and by traffic signals, and by different kinds of traffic signals, and traffic which is not controlled.

(4) Regulations may be made under this section applying only to a particular crossing or particular crossings specified in the regulations.

(5) A person who contravenes any regulations made under this section shall be guilty of an offence[2].

(6) In this section "crossing" means a crossing for pedestrians established—

(a) by a local authority under section 23 of this Act, or

(b) by the Secretary of State in the discharge of the duty imposed on him by section 24 of this Act,

and (in either case) indicated in accordance with the regulations having effect as respects that crossing; and, for the purposes of a prosecution for a contravention of the provisions of a regulation having effect as respects a crossing, the crossing shall be deemed to be established and indicated unless the contrary is proved[3].

[Road Traffic Regulation Act 1984 s 25.]

1. See the Zebra, Pelican and Puffin Pedestrian Crossings Regulations and General Directions 1997, this PART, post.
2. For penalty see Sch 2 to the Road Traffic Offenders Act 1988, post.
3. Schedule 10, para 9 provides savings for crossings established under the 1967 Act.

School crossings

4–1169 26. *Arrangements for patrolling school crossings.*

4–1170 28. Stopping of vehicles at school crossing. (1) When a vehicle is approaching a place in a road where a person is crossing or seeking to cross the road, a school crossing patrol wearing a uniform approved by the Secretary of State shall have power, by exhibiting a prescribed sign[1], to require the person driving or propelling the vehicle to stop it[2].

(2) When a person has been required under subsection (1) above to stop a vehicle—

(a) he shall cause the vehicle to stop before reaching the place where the person is crossing or seeking to cross and so as not to stop or impede his crossing[3], and

(b) the vehicle shall not be put in motion again so as to reach the place in question so long as the sign continues to be exhibited.

(3) A person who fails to comply with paragraph (a) of subsection (2) above, or who causes a vehicle to be put in motion in contravention of paragraph (b) of that subsection, shall be guilty of an offence[4].

(4) In this section—

(a) "prescribed sign" means a sign of a size, colour and type prescribed by regulations made by the Secretary of State or, if authorisation is given by the Secretary of State for the use of signs of a description not so prescribed, a sign of that description;

(b) "school crossing patrol" means a person authorised to patrol in accordance with arrangements under section 26 of this Act;

and regulations under paragraph (a) above may provide for the attachment of reflectors to signs or for the illumination of signs.

(5) For the purposes of this section—

(a) where it is proved that a sign was exhibited by a school crossing patrol, it shall be presumed, unless the contrary is proved, to be of a size, colour and type prescribed, or of a description authorised, under subsection (4)(b) above, and, if it was exhibited in circumstances in which it was required by the regulations to be illuminated, to have been illuminated in the prescribed manner; and

(b) where it is proved that a school crossing patrol was wearing a uniform, the uniform shall be presumed, unless the contrary is proved, to be a uniform approved by the Secretary of State;

(c) repealed.

[Road Traffic Regulation Act 1984, s 28, as amended by the Transport act 2000, Sch 31 and the Transport (Scotland) Act 2001, s 77.]

1. The School Crossing Patrol Sign (England and Wales) Regulations 2006, SI 2006/2215 prescribe the sign to be used.
2. The sign must be exhibited so that the driver can see the word "stop" (*Hoy v Smith* [1964] 3 All ER 670, 129 JP 33).
3. Once the sign has been properly exhibited the driver must stop unless by the time he reaches the crossing the sign has been removed (*Franklin v Langdown* [1971] 3 All ER 662, 135 JP 615). It is no defence to say that the driver did not stop or impeded any children in driving on (*Wall v Walwyn* [1973] Crim LR 376).
4. For penalty see Sch 2 to the Road Traffic Offenders Act 1988, post.

Street playgrounds

4–1171

A local traffic authority (s 29 as substituted by the New Roads and Street Works Act 1991, Sch 8) may make orders prohibiting traffic on roads to be used as playgrounds, and a person who uses a vehicle or causes or permits a vehicle to be used in contravention of such an order commits an offence: the local traffic authority having made an order may then make byelaws for the use of the road as a playground (s 31)1.

1. For penalty for offences under s 29 see Sch 2 to the Road Traffic Offenders Act 1988, post. Offences under byelaws under s 31 have a penalty as prescribed by the Local Government Act 1972, s 237, in PART VIII: title LOCAL GOVERNMENT, post.

PART IV[1]
PARKING PLACES
Provision of off-street parking, and parking on roads without payment

4–1172 32–34. *Powers of local authorities to provide off-street parking places and access to premises through them*[2].

1. Part IV contains ss 32–63.
2. See s 45 et seq for parking on highways for payment.

4–1173 35. Provisions as to use of parking places provided under s 32 or 33[1]. (1)–(3A) Local authority Orders[2].

(3B) In this section and in section 35A below "parking device" means either a card, disc, token, meter, permit, stamp or other similar device, whether used in a vehicle or not, which, being used either by itself, or in conjunction with any such apparatus as is referred to in subsection (3A)(*d*) above—

(*a*) indicates, or causes to be indicated, the payment of a charge, and—

   (i) the period in respect of which it has been paid and the time of the beginning or end of the period, or
   (ii) whether or not the period for which it has been paid or any further period has elapsed, or
   (iii) the period for which the vehicle in relation to which the parking device is used is permitted to park in the parking place, and the time of the beginning or end of the period, or
   (iv) whether or not the period for which the vehicle in relation to which the parking device is used is permitted to park in the parking place or any further period has elapsed; or

(*b*) operates apparatus controlling the entry of vehicles to or their exit from the parking place, or enables that apparatus to be operated;

or any other device of any such description as may from time to time be prescribed for the purposes of this section and section 35A below by order made by the Secretary of State.
(3C)–(3D) *Orders under subsection (3B).*
(4)–(9) *Repealed.*
[Road Traffic Regulation Act 1984, s 35 amended by the Road Traffic (Consequential Provisions) Act 1988, Sch 1, the Parking Act 1989, s 1, the Road Traffic Act 1991, s 44 and Sch 8 and SI 1996/1553.]

1. This section does not apply to vehicles and persons in the public service of the Crown (s 130, post).
2. As to exemptions to orders under s 35 for vehicles displaying disabled persons' badges, see note 2 to ss 122–124, post.

4–1174 35A. Offences and proceedings in connection with parking places provided under s 32 or 33. (1) In the event of any contravention of, or non-compliance with, a provision of an order under section 35(1) above, the person responsible shall be guilty of an offence[1].
(2) A person who, with intent to defraud—

(*a*) interferes with any such apparatus or device mentioned in section 35(3) above as is by an order under section 35(1) above to be used for the collection of charges at an off-street parking place, or operates or attempts to operate it by the insertion of objects other than current coins or bank notes of the appropriate denomination, or the appropriate credit or debit cards, or

(b) interferes with any such apparatus as is mentioned in section 35(3A)(d) above or with a parking device, or operates or attempts to operate any such apparatus or any parking device otherwise than in the manner prescribed, or

(c) displays a parking device otherwise than in the manner prescribed,

shall be guilty of an offence[2].

(3) *Orders under section 35(1).*

(4) *Repealed.*

(5) While a vehicle is within a parking place, it shall not be lawful for the driver or conductor of the vehicle, or for any person employed in connection with it, to ply for hire or accept passengers for hire; and if a person acts in contravention of this subsection he shall be guilty of an offence[2].

(6) In this section—

"credit card" means a card or similar thing issued by any person, use of which enables the holder to defer the payment by him of the charge for parking a vehicle; and

"debit card" means a card or similar thing issued by any person, use of which by the holder causes the charge for parking a vehicle to be paid by the electronic transfer of funds from any current account of his at a bank or other institution providing banking services.

[Road Traffic Regulation Act 1984, s 35A added by the Parking Act 1989, s 2 and amended by SI 1996/1553.]

---

1. As an alternative an order may be made by the Secretary of State under Sch 3 to the Road Traffic Act 1991 and where it has s 35A(1) will to that extent cease to apply and any penalty charge will become payable under Sch 3.
2. For penalties see the Road Traffic Offenders Act 1988, Sch 2, post.

4–1175   35B, 35C. *Display of information: regulations[1]: charges.*

---

1. For procedure for making regulations, see the Local Authorities' Traffic Orders (Procedure) (England and Wales) Regulations 1996, SI 1996 amended by SI 2004/3168 (E).

Control of off-street parking

4–1176   43. Control of off-street parking in Greater London[1]. (1)–(4) *In a controlled area only the local authority or the holder of a local authority licence is to operate a public off-street parking place; provision for licence.*

(5) *Offence[2] to disclose information or trade secret.*

(6)–(9) *Licensing procedures.*

(10) Subject to subsection (15) below and to the provisions of Part V of Schedule 4 to this Act[3], any holder of a licence who contravenes or fails to comply with any of the terms and conditions of the licence and who does not show that the contravention or failure was due to an act or omission of a person not connected with the operation of the licensed parking place which the persons so connected could not reasonably have been expected to prevent shall be guilty of an offence[2]; and on the conviction of the holder of a licence of an offence under this subsection the court before whom he is convicted may, if on an application made for the purpose by the local authority the court is satisfied that it is proper so to do by reason of the extent to which, or the period over which, or the frequency with which, the holder of the licence has contravened or failed to comply with the terms and conditions of the licence or by reason of the wilfulness of the offence, make an order for the revocation of the licence.

(11) *Revocation and appeal.*

(12) Subject to subsection (15) below and to the provisions of Part V of Schedule 4[3] to this Act, any person who, in contravention of subsection (2) above, operates a public off-street parking place without holding a licence for the purpose shall be guilty of an offence[2].

(13), (14) *Provision for regulations; definitions.*

(15) The Secretary of State, after consultation with a local authority, may at any time, if it appears to him expedient so to do by reason of any emergency which appears to him to have arisen or to be likely to arise, by order, which shall be laid before Parliament after being made, provide that this subsection shall apply either in relation to all areas for the time being designated by the local authority as controlled areas or in relation to such parts of any of those areas as may be specified in the order; and—

(a) during the period while any such order is in force in relation to any controlled area of part thereof, any public off-street parking place in that area or part may be operated as if that area or part were not, or, as the case may be, were not comprised in, a controlled area; and

(b) nothing in subsection (10) or (12) above shall apply to anything done at any such parking place during that period.

[Road Traffic Regulation Act 1984, s 43 as amended by the Local Government Act 1985, Sch 5 and the Airports Act 1986, Sch 6.]

---

1. This section and Sch 4 to the Act have also been applied to Metropolitan Districts in England and Wales by the Control of Off-Street Parking (England and Wales) (Metropolitan Districts) Order 1986, SI 1986/225.
2. For penalty for offences see Sch 7 of the Road Traffic Regulation Act 1984, post.
3. Schedule 4 is concerned with the making of regulations under s 43, and Part V thereof enables the unlicensed operation of a parking place between the time when an area first becomes a controlled area and the obtaining of a licence, and during periods allowed for appeals from licensing decisions.

Parking on highways for payment

4–1177 **45, 46, 46A.** *Designation[1] of paying parking places on highways, and charges at and regulation of such places.*

1. As to exemptions in orders under ss 45 and 46 for vehicles displaying persons' badges, see note 2 to ss 122–124, post.

4–1178 **47. Offences relating to designated parking places[1].** (1) A person who—

(a) being the driver of a vehicle, leaves the vehicle in a designated parking place[2] otherwise than as authorised by or under an order relating to the parking place, or leaves the vehicle in a designated parking place for longer after the excess charge[3] has been incurred than the time so authorised, or fails duly to pay any charge payable under section 45 of this Act, or contravenes or fails to comply with any provision of an order relating to the parking place as to the manner in which vehicles shall stand in, or be driven into or out of, the parking place, or

(b) whether being the driver of a vehicle or not, otherwise contravenes or fails to comply with any order relating to designated parking places,

shall, subject to section 48 of this Act, be guilty of an offence[4]; but this subsection does not apply in relation to any designated parking places in Greater London[5]*.

(2) In relation to an offence under paragraph (a) of subsection (1) above of leaving a vehicle for longer after the excess charge[3] has been incurred than the time authorised by an order relating to the parking place, or failing duly to pay any charge payable under section 45 of this Act, the reference in that paragraph to the driver of a vehicle shall be construed as a reference to the person driving the vehicle at the time when it was left in the parking place.

(3) A person who, with intent to defraud, interferes with a parking meter, or operates or attempts to operate a parking meter by the insertion of objects other than current coins or banknotes of the appropriate denomination, or the appropriate credit or debit cards[6] shall be guilty of an offence[4].

(4) Where, in any proceedings in England or Wales for an offence under this section of failing to pay any charge, it is proved that the amount which has become due, or any part of that amount, has not been duly paid, the court shall order the payment of the sum not paid; and any sum ordered to be paid by virtue of this subsection shall be recoverable as a penalty[7].

(5) *Repealed.*

(6) Where in any proceedings for an offence under this section of failing to pay an excess charge[3] it is not proved that the excess charge had become due, but it is proved that an initial charge has not been paid, the defendant may be convicted of an offence under this section of failing to pay an initial charge.

(7) *Repealed.*

[Road Traffic Regulation Act 1984, s 47 as amended by the Local Government Act 1985, Sch 17, the Road Traffic (Consequential Provisions) Act 1988 Sch 1, the Parking Act 1989, Sch, the Road Traffic Act 1991, s 65 and SI 1996/1553.]

*Words repealed by the Traffic Management Act 2004, Sch 12 from a date to be appointed.
1. This section shall not apply to contraventions of or failures to comply with designation orders under s 53(1), post.
2. In *Wilson v Arnott* [1977] 2 All ER 5, 141 JP 278 it was held that although the use of a parking bay had been suspended in accordance with the provisions of the local Order, the bay nevetheless remained a designated parking place. In *Strong v Dawtry* [1961] 1 All ER 926, 125 JP 378 the provisions of such an Order were strictly applied, it being held that a driver who left his vehicle for two minutes in order to obtain change to pay the initial charge had committed an offence against this section.
3. For enforcement of excess parking charges see ss 104–111, post.
4. For penalty see Sch 2 to the Road Traffic Offenders Act 1988, post. Where an order has been made under Sch 3 to the Road Traffic Act 1991, s 47(1) will to that extent cease to apply and any penalty charge will become payable under Sch 3.
5. For enforcement provisions for designated parking places in Greater London see the Road Traffic Act 1991, in PART VIII: title LONDON, post.
6. "Credit card" and "debit card" are defined by s 35A(6) above.
7. For procedure see Magistrates' Courts Act 1980, s 75 et seq in PART I: MAGISTRATES' COURTS, PROCEDURE, ante.

4–1179 **48. Acceptance of payment as bar to proceedings under s 47.** (1) Where a parking meter relating to the space in which a vehicle is left in a designated parking place indicates that the period for which payment was made for the vehicle by an initial charge has expired, but the authority by whom the parking place is controlled are satisfied that the initial charge was not paid, acceptance by the authority of payment of the excess charge shall be a bar to proceedings for an offence under section 47(1)(a) of this Act of failing to pay the initial charge.

(2) Where in the case of any vehicle—

(a) an authorisation by way of such a certificate, other means of identification or device as is referred to in section 4(2), 4(3), 7(2) or 7(3) of this Act, or such a permit or token as is referred to in section 46(2)(i) of this Act, has been issued with respect to the vehicle, and

(b) the authority by whom a designated parking place is controlled are satisfied that, in accordance with the terms on which the authorisation was issued, a charge has become payable and has not been paid in respect of any period for which the vehicle has been left in that parking place,

acceptance by that authority of payment of the amount of that charge shall be a bar to proceedings for an offence under section 47(1)(a) of this Act of failing duly to pay the charge.
[Road Traffic Regulation Act 1984, s 48.]

4–1180　50. *Repealed.*

4–1181　51. *Parking devices¹ for designated parking places in Greater London.*

---

1. "Parking device" is defined for the purposes of ss 51 and 52 by s 51(4) as amended by the Parking Act 1989, Schedule.

4–1182　52. Offences and proceedings in connection with parking devices and associated apparatus. (1) A person who, with intent to defraud—

(*a*)　interferes with any apparatus referred to in section 51(2)(*d*) of this Act or with a parking device, or operates or attempts to operate any such apparatus or any parking device otherwise than in the manner prescribed, or

(*b*)　displays a parking device otherwise than in the manner prescribed,

shall be guilty of an offence¹.

(2) *Repealed.*

(3) In section 48(1) of this Act the reference to a parking meter relating to the space in which a vehicle is left in a designated parking place shall include references to—

(*a*)　any such apparatus as is referred to in section 51(2)(*d*) of this Act which relates to the space in which a vehicle is so left, and

(*b*)　to a parking device used in respect of a vehicle left in a space in a designated parking place.

[Road Traffic Regulation Act 1984, s 52 as amended by the Parking Act 1989, Schedule and SI 1996/1553.]

---

1. For penalty for offences see Sch 2 to the Road Traffic Offenders Act 1988, post.

4–1183　53. Designation orders outside Greater London. (1) A designation order made in respect of highways or, in Scotland, roads in any area outside Greater London may include such provisions—

(*a*)　for any of the purposes specified in paragraphs (*a*) to (*c*) of section 2(2) of this Act, or

(*b*)　for authorising the use without charge (subject to such, if any, conditions as may be specified in the order) of any part of a road as a parking place for vehicles, or for vehicles of such classes as may be specified in the order,

as the authority making the order may consider appropriate in connection with the designation order.

(2) A designation order making provision for any of the purposes referred to in subsection (1)(*a*) above may vary or revoke any subsisting provision made for any of those purposes under section 1 of this Act.

(3) A designation order making such provision as is mentioned in subsection (1)(*b*) above may include provision for the removal, from any place authorised by virtue of that paragraph to be used as a parking place, of any vehicle left there in contravention of the order, and for the safe custody of the vehicle.

(4) Section 47 of this Act shall not apply to contraventions of, or failures to comply with, any provisions of a designation order having effect by virtue of subsection (1) above.

(5) A person who uses a vehicle, or causes or permits a vehicle to be used, in contravention of any provision of a designation order having effect by virtue of subsection (1)(*a*) above shall be guilty of an offence¹.

(6) In the event of a contravention of, or non-compliance with, a provision of a designation order having effect by virtue of subsection (1)(*b*) above, the person responsible (as determined in accordance with the order) shall be guilty of an offence.

(7) *Repealed.*

[Road Traffic Regulation Act 1984, s 53 as amended by the Local Government Act 1985, Sch 5, the Road Traffic (Consequential Provisions) Act 1988, Sch 1 and the New Roads and Street Works Act 1991, Sch 8.]

---

1. For penalty for offences see Sch 2 to the Road Traffic Offenders Act 1988, post.

4–1184　55–60. *Designation orders in Wales, financial provisions, grants, provision of parking places by parish or community councils.*

4–1185　61. *Land not part of a highway may be designated¹ a loading area; a person who without reasonable excuse causes a vehicle to be in any part of a loading area at a time when parking is prohibited shall be guilty of an offence².*

---

1. The Local Authorities' Traffic Orders (Procedures) (England and Wales) Regulations 1989, SI 1989/1120 in Part V, lay down the procedure to be followed by a local authority when making orders under this section controlling the parking of vehicles in areas used for loading or unloading goods vehicles.
2. For penalty for offences see Sch 2 to the Road Traffic Offenders Act 1988, post.

4–1186　62. Parking in Royal Parks. Regulations under section 2 of the Parks Regulation (Amendment) Act 1926 may make provision for imposing and recovering charges for the leaving of vehicles, or vehicles of any class, in any park to which that Act applies; and regulations made by virtue of this section may make, as respects charges and penalties recoverable under the regulations, provision corresponding to the provisions of section 47(4) of this Act.

[Road Traffic Regulation Act 1984, s 62.]

4–1187   63A. *Parking attendants.*

PART V[1]

TRAFFIC SIGNS

General provisions

4–1188   64–72. *Traffic signs may be prescribed by regulations[2] to give warnings, information, requirements, restrictions or prohibitions to traffic (s 64)[3]. Highway authority may cause or permit traffic signs to be placed in conformity with directions (s 65)[2]. A person acting under the instructions of the chief officer of police may place signs regulating traffic on public occasions (s 66), or in the event of emergencies (s 67). An authority having power to make certain orders under earlier provisions of this Act may place signs (s 68)[4]. The highway authority may require an owner or occupier of land to remove a sign and in default may itself remove the sign and recover the cost summarily as a civil debt (s 69)[5]. The Secretary of State has default powers and may recover the cost from the authority summarily as a civil debt (s 70)[5]. Power to enter land (s 71). Powers exercisable by parish or community councils (s 72).*

1. Part V contains ss 64–80.
2. The Zebra, Pelican and Puffin Pedestrian Crossings Regulations and General Directions 1997, in this TITLE, ,and the Traffic Signs and General Directions 2002, in this TITLE, post, have effect under ss 64 and 65; Welsh language versions are prescribed in the Traffic Signs (Welsh and English Language Provisions) Regulations and General Directions 1985, SI 1985/713. The Traffic Signs (Temporary Obstructions) Regulations 1997, SI 1997/3053 (red warning triangle which anyone may place to warn of a temporary obstruction on the carriageway, traffic cones, pyramids, warning lamps) also have effect under s 64. The signs must conform to the Directions contained in the Traffic Signs Regulations and General Directions before a motorist can be convicted of contravening them (*O'Halloran v DPP* (1989) 87 LGR 748, [1990] RTR 62—solid double white lines not preceded by arrow held not lawfully placed). See also the Temporary Traffic Signs (Prescribed Bodies) (England and Wales) Regulations 1998, SI 1998/111.
3. Under ss 64, 65 functions which are exerciseable jointly by the Secretaries of State charged with general responsibility under this Act in relation to England, Wales and Scotland, transferred to the Secretary of State, by SI 1999/3143.
4. Section 68(2) is amended by the Road Traffic (Temporary Restrictions) Act 1991, s 1(3).
5. See Magistrates' Courts Act 1980 s 58 ante in PART I: MAGISTRATES' COURTS, PROCEDURE, ante.

Provisions as to Greater London

4–1189   73–76. *Powers and duties of the Greater London Council[1] as a highway authority with regard to placing traffic signs[2] (s 73). Affixing of traffic signs to walls, where consent is unreasonably withheld from council, they may apply to a magistrates' court (or in the case of certain buildings specified in Sch 5 to the Secretary of State) who may allow the affixing subject to conditions thought fit, or disallow it (s 74), London borough councils and the London traffic control system (s 74A), transfer of traffic control systems between the Secretary of State and Transport for London (s 74B), the traffic authority for traffic signs (s 74C). Similar provisions in City of London (s 75).*

1. The functions conferred on the Greater London Council and the City of London have now been transferred to the Secretary of State (London Traffic Control System (Transfer) Order 1986, SI 1986/315).
2. Functions in respect of traffic signs which are traffic light signals controlling the movement of any class of road traffic (including pedestrians) which were transferred to the Secretary of State by orders under Local Government Act 1985, Sch 5, para 10 are, in so far as relating to GLA roads and roads in Greater London which are neither GLA roads nor trunk roads, transferred to Transport for London, by the Greater London Authority Act 1999, s 275.

PART VI[1]

SPEED LIMITS

4–1190   81. General speed limit for restricted roads.   (1) It shall not be lawful for a person to drive a motor vehicle on a restricted road at a speed exceeding 30 miles per hour[2].

(2)[3] The Ministers acting jointly[4] may by order made by statutory instrument and approved by a resolution of each House of Parliament increase or reduce the rate of speed fixed by subsection (1) above, either as originally enacted or as varied under this subsection.

[Road Traffic Regulation Act 1984, s 81.]

1. Part VI contains ss 81–91; ss 81–89 do not apply to tramcars and trolley vehicles (ibid, s 141).
2. The Traffic Signs Regulations and General Directions 2002, in this TITLE, post, prescribe the relevant signs and their method of display. It is no defence that the defendant did not see the speed limit signs (*Hood v Lewis* [1976] RTR 99). Savings for earlier legislation and orders are provided by Sch 10, paras 14–16.
3. Functions under sub-s (2) above which are exercisable jointly by the Secretaries of State charged with general responsibility under this Act in relation to England, Wales and Scotland, transferred to the Secretary of State, by SI 1999/3143, art 2(1).
4. Now the Secretary of State alone, see the Transfer of Functions (Road Traffic) Order 1999, SI 1999/3143.

4–1191   82. What roads are restricted roads.   (1) Subject to the provisions of this section and of section 84(3) of this Act, a road is a restricted road for the purposes of section 81 of this Act if—

(*a*) in England and Wales, there is provided on it a system of street lighting furnished by means of lamps placed not more than 200 yards apart[1];

(b) in Scotland, there is provided on it a system of carriageway lighting furnished by means of lamps placed not more than 185 metres apart and the road is of a classification or type specified for the purposes of this subsection in regulations made by the Secretary of State.

(2) The traffic authority for a road may direct—

(a) that the road[2] which is a restricted road for the purposes of section 81 of this Act shall cease to be a restricted road for those purposes, or

(b) that the road[2] which is not a restricted road for those purposes shall become a restricted road for those purposes[3].

(3) A special road is not a restricted road for the purposes of section 81 on or after the date declared by the traffic authority, by notice published in the prescribed manner, to be the date on which the special road, or the relevant part of the special road, is open for use as a special road.
[Road Traffic Regulation Act 1984, s 82 as amended by the New Roads and Street Works Act 1991, Sch 8.]

---

1. Subsections (1) and (2) must be read together. Prima facie, a road lighted as described in sub-s (1) is a restricted road. Any direction to the contrary must be given in accordance with s 72. On such a road, the absence of derestriction signs is evidence that the road is restricted (s 85(5), post). Conversely, a road not so lighted may, by direction, become a restricted road. This fact must then be indicated by restriction signs (s 85(4), post). The presence of signs (which must be deemed to have been lawfully erected) is prima facie proof that a direction has been given where there is no street lighting (*Gibbins v Skinner* [1951] 2 KB 379, [1951] 1 All ER 1049, 115 JP 360). A direction may be given with respect to the whole or any part of the width of any road (s 126, post). Where the distance between two lamps, in a system of 24 lamps, was 212 yards, it was held that the *de minimis* principle should apply; moreover, the fact that one street lamp in the system may be in a state of disrepair is irrelevant (*Spittle v Kent County Constabulary* [1986] RTR 142, [1985] Crim LR 744).
2. As to boundary roads, see s 125, post.
3. Section 82(2)(b) permits a local authority to direct that a road which is not a restricted road for the want of street lights should nonetheless become one; such an interpretation does not render s 84 otiose since the latter section allows the importation of speed limits other than 30 mph (*DPP v Evans* [2004] EWHC 2785, (2005) 169 JP 237).

4–1192   **83.** *Provisions as to directions under s 82(2).*

4–1193   **84. Speed limits on roads other than restricted roads.**   (1) An order made under this subsection as respects any road[1] may prohibit—

(a) the driving of motor vehicles on that road at a speed exceeding that specified in the order,

(b) the driving of motor vehicles on that road at a speed exceeding that specified in the order during periods specified in the order, or

(c) the driving of motor vehicles on that road at a speed exceeding the speed for the time being indicated by traffic signs in accordance with the order.

(1A) An order made by virtue of subsection (1)(c) above may—

(a) make provision restricting the speeds that may be indicated by traffic signs or the periods during which the indications may be given, and

(b) provide for the indications to be given only in such circumstances as may be determined by or under the order;

but any such order must comply with regulations made under subsection (1B) below, except where the Secretary of State authorises otherwise in a particular case.

(1B) The Secretary of State may make regulations governing the provision which may be made by orders of local authorities under subsection (1)(c) above, and any such regulations may in particular—

(a) prescribe the circumstances in which speed limits may have effect by virtue of an order,

(b) prescribe the speed limits which may be specified in an order, and

(c) make transitional provision and different provision for different cases.

(2) The power to make an order under subsection (1) is exercisable by the traffic authority, who shall before exercising it in any case give public notice of their intention to do so.

(3) While an order made by virtue of subsection (1)(a) above is in force as respects a road, that road shall not be a restricted road for the purposes of section 81 of this Act.

(4) This section does not apply to any part of a special road which is open for use as a special road.

(5) Section 68(1)(c) of this Act shall apply to any order made under subsection (1) above.

(6) Any reference in a local Act to roads subject to a speed limit shall, unless the contrary intention appears, be treated as not including a reference to roads subject to a speed limit imposed only by virtue of subsection (1)(b) or (c) above.
[Road Traffic Regulation Act 1984, s 84 as amended by the New Roads and Street Works Act 1991, Sch 8 and the Road Traffic Act 1991, s 45.]

---

1. As to boundary roads, see s 125, post. Where the distance between two lamps in a system of 24 lamps, was 212 yards it was held the de minimis principle should apply; moreover, the fact that one street lamp in the system may be in a state of disrepair is irrelevant (*Spittle v Kent County Constabulary* [1985] Crim LR 744).

4–1194   **85. Traffic signs for indicating speed restrictions.**   (1)–(3) *Duty of Secretary of State or local authority to erect and maintain signs.*

(4) Where no such system of street or carriageway lighting as is mentioned in section 82(1) is provided on a road, but a limit of speed is to be observed on the road, a person shall not be convicted

of driving a motor vehicle on the road at a speed exceeding the limit unless the limit is indicated by means of such traffic signs as are mentioned in subsection (1) or subsection (2) above.

(5) In any proceedings for a contravention of section 81 of this Act, where the proceedings relate to driving on a road provided with such a system of street or carriageway lighting, evidence of the absence of traffic signs displayed in pursuance of this section to indicate that the road is not a restricted road for the purposes of that section shall be evidence that the road is a restricted road for those purposes.

(5A) In any proceedings for a contravention of section 81 of this Act, a certificate of an officer of the Secretary of State or, where the function of specifying under section 82(1)(b) of this Act a classification or type of road is, by virtue of section 63 of the Scotland Act 1998, exercisable by the Scottish Ministers, a certificate of an officer of the Scottish Ministers that a road is of a specified classification or type shall be sufficient evidence of the facts certified; and a document purporting to be such a certificate and to be signed by such an officer shall be deemed to be such a certificate unless the contrary is shown.

(6) *This section not to apply to limit set by regulations made under s 17(2), ante (special roads).*

(7) *Directions under sub-s (2) by statutory instrument*[1].

[Road Traffic Regulation Act 1984, s 85 as amended by the New Roads and Street Works Act 1991, Sch 8 and SI 2000/2040, Schedule.]

---

1. The Traffic Signs Regulations and General Directions 2002, in this TITLE, post have been made.

4–1195   86. Speed limits for particular classes of vehicles.   (1) It shall not be lawful for a person to drive a motor vehicle of any class on a road at a speed greater than the speed specified in Schedule 6 to this Act as the maximum speed in relation to a vehicle of that class.

(2) Subject to subsections (4) and (5) below, the Secretary of State may by regulations vary, subject to such conditions as may be specified in the regulations, the provisions of that Schedule.

(3) Regulations under this section may make different provision as respects the same class of vehicles in different circumstances.

(4) *Repealed.*

(5) The Secretary of State shall not have power under this section to vary the speed limit imposed by section 81 of this Act.

(6) The Secretary of State shall not have power under this section to impose a speed limit, as respects driving on roads which are not restricted roads for the purposes of section 81 of this Act, on a vehicle[1] which—

(a)   is constructed solely for the carriage of passengers and their effects;
(b)   is not adapted to carry more than 8 passengers exclusive of the driver;
(c)   is neither a heavy motor car[1] nor an invalid carriage[1];
(d)   is not drawing a trailer[1]; and
(e)   is fitted with pneumatic tyres on all its wheels.

[Road Traffic Regulation Act 1984, s 86 as amended by the New Roads and Street Works Act 1991, Schs 8 and 9.]

---

1. See s 136, post for meaning of "motor vehicle", "heavy motor car", "invalid carriage", "trailer".

4–1196   87. Exemption of fire and rescue authority, ambulance and police vehicles from speed limits.   (1) No statutory provision imposing a speed limit on motor vehicles shall apply to any vehicle on an occasion when it is being used for fire and rescue authority, ambulance or police purposes[1], if the observance of that provision would be likely to hinder the use of the vehicle for the purpose for which it is being used on that occasion.

(2) Subsection (1) above applies in relation to a vehicle being used—

(a)   for Serious Organised Crime Agency purposes, or
(b)   for training persons to drive vehicles for use for Serious Organised Crime Agency purposes,

as it applies in relation to a vehicle being used for police purposes.

(3) But (except where it is being used for training the person by whom it is being driven) subsection (1) above does not apply in relation to a vehicle by virtue of subsection (2) above unless it is being driven by a person who has been trained in driving vehicles at high speeds.

[Road Traffic Regulation Act 1984, s 87 as amended by the Fire and Rescue Services Act 2004, Sch 1 and the Serious Organised Crime and Police Act 2005, Sch 4.]

---

1. The driving by a private person in order to obtain evidence of contravention of speed limit by a police car is not a police purpose (*Strathern v Gladstone* 1937 JC 11, 1937 SLT 62, 102 JP Jo 477). The exemption does not affect a driver's liability to prosecution for dangerous or careless driving: see *Gaynor v Allen* [1959] 2 QB 403, [1959] 2 All ER 644, 123 JP 413. The circumstances in which this exemption applies were considered in *Aitken v Yarwood* [1965] 1 QB 327, [1964] 2 All ER 537, 128 JP 470. It would appear that the section should be strictly construed.

4–1197   88. Temporary speed limits.   (1)–(6) *Secretary of State may by Order*[1] *impose temporary speed limits*[2] *on roads other than special roads; no traffic signs are required for this.*

(7) If a person drives a motor vehicle on a road in contravention of an order under subsection (1)(b) above, he shall be guilty of an offence; but a person shall not be liable to be convicted of so

driving solely on the evidence of one witness to the effect that, in the opinion of the witness, he was driving the vehicle at a speed less than that specified in the order[3].

(8) *Procedure for Order.*
[Road Traffic Regulation Act 1984, s 88.]

---

1. The 70 Miles Per Hour, 60 Miles Per Hour and 50 Miles Per Hour (Temporary Speed Limits) Order 1977 has been amended by an Order dated 16 August 1978 and is continued in force by SI 1978/1548.
2. Functions under sub-ss (1)(*a*), (4): certain functions under sub-ss (1)(*a*), (4) are transferred, in so far as they are exercisable in or as regards Scotland, to the Scottish Ministers, by SI 2000/1563, art 3, Schedule.
3. This relates to a minimum speed limit; an offence relating to a maximum speed limit is an offence under s 89 with penalty provided by Sch 2 to the Road Traffic Offenders Act 1988, post.

4–1198   89. Speeding offences generally.   (1) A person who drives[1] a motor vehicle[2] on a road at a speed exceeding a limit imposed by or under any enactment to which this section applies shall be guilty of an offence[3].

(2) A person prosecuted for such an offence shall not be liable to be convicted solely on the evidence of one witness to the effect that, in the opinion of the witness, the person prosecuted was driving the vehicle at a speed exceeding a specified limit[4].

(3) The enactments to which this section applies are—

(*a*) any enactment contained in this Act[5] except section 17(2);

(*b*) section 2 of the Parks Regulation (Amendment) Act 1926; and

(*c*) any enactment not contained in this Act, but passed after 1st September 1960, whether before or after the passing of this Act.

(4) If a person who employs other persons to drive motor vehicles on roads publishes or issues any time-table or schedule, or gives any directions, under which any journey, or any stage or part of any journey, is to be completed within some specified time, and it is not practicable in the circumstances of the case for that journey (or that stage or part of it) to be completed in the specified time without the commission of such an offence as is mentioned in subsection (1) above, the publication or issue of the time-table or schedule, or the giving of the directions, may be produced as prima facie evidence that the employer procured or (as the case may be) incited[6] the persons employed by him to drive the vehicles to commit such an offence.
[Road Traffic Regulation Act 1984, s 18.]

---

1. See headnote to this title for notes on "driver" and "driving". Where a defendant was found driving when the car was stopped, it was held, in the absence of any evidence to the contrary, to be some evidence that he was driving during the period the offence was committed (*Beresford v St Albans Justices* (1905) 22 TLR 1). A person who simply gave drivers of motor cars notice of a "police trap" was held not guilty of obstructing the constables in the execution of their duty (*Bastable v Little* [1907] 1 KB 59, 71 JP 52). The obstruction, however, is not limited to physical obstruction; so where cars, when warned of a "police trap", are being driven at an illegal speed, the person so warning and acting in concert with the drivers, may be convicted of obstructing (*Betts v Stevens* [1910] 1 KB 1, 73 JP 486; *Bastable v Little*, supra, distinguished). Cf *Hinchcliffe v Sheldon* [1955] 3 All ER 406, 120 JP 13.
  This section does not apply to tramcars or trolley vehicles operated under statutory powers (s 1(1), post).
2. For meaning of "motor vehicle" see s 136, post.
3. For penalty for offences under this section see Sch 2 to the Road Traffic Offenders Act 1988, post.
4. This does not imply that there must necessarily be more than one witness (*Russell v Beesley* [1937] 1 All ER 527). A single witness may be able to speak as to speed, not as a matter of opinion merely, but as a fact ascertained by measurement of distance and time (see *Plancq v Marks* (1906) 70 JP 216; *Scott v Jameson* 1914 SC (J) 187, and *Weatherhogg v Johns* (1931) 95 JP Jo 364). A person may be convicted on the evidence of one police officer supported by his own evidence of the reading of a speedometer or other mechanism where his evidence is of fact and not merely of opinion (*Nicholas v Penny* [1950] 2 KB 466, [1950] 2 All ER 89, 114 JP 335). As a matter of law, the reading on a police car's speedometer can be regarded as corroborative, whether or not that speedometer had been tested; the weight to be given to the corroborative evidence of a reading from an untested speedometer is a matter for the justices (*Swain v Gillet* [1974] RTR 446, [1974] Crim LR 433). The corroboration of the evidence of one witness must be as to the observations made at the same time (*Brighty v Pearson* [1938] 4 All ER 127, 102 JP 522).
  Where a police officer inspected the scene of an accident and from tests carried out calculated that the speed of the car had been not less than 41 mph at the start of the skid marks, it was held that the defendant had been properly convicted on the evidence of the single constable. Although the constable's evidence included a significant element of expert opinion, it did not amount solely to his opinion that the defendant had been driving at an excessive speed, since he also described in detail the objectively determined phenomena on which his expert opinion was based, namely the inspections and tests carried out at the scene of the accident (*Crossland v DPP* [1988] 3 All ER 712, 153 JP 63, [1988] RTR 417).
5. Speed limits for certain classes of vehicles are imposed by s 86, ante, and the 6th Sch, post. A general speed limit of 30 mph is imposed on restricted roads by s 1, and temporary speed limits may be imposed under s 88. For exemptions in respect of vehicles used for fire brigade, ambulance or police purposes, see s 87, ante. The Secretary of State may, by regulations, vary the statutory provisions in relation to naval, military or air force vehicles or for vehicles used for marine salvage; ss 130(3), 133, post (see note to 6th Sch, post). Other speed limits are imposed by orders made under the provisions of s 84, ante. Formerly, a direction could be given under s 19(2) of the Road Traffic Act 1960 (now repealed) imposing a limit of 40 mph in respect of a specified restricted road. Speed limits could also be imposed by traffic regulation orders made by virtue of s 26 of the 1960 Act (now repealed). Such directions and regulations as were in force prior to 1 November 1962 are deemed to have been made under s 84 of this Act (Sch 10, para 15, post).
6. A person aiding abetting counselling or procuring an offence is liable to the same penalties as a principal offender (Magistrates' Courts Act 1980, s 44 in PART I: MAGISTRATES' COURTS, PROCEDURE, ante.

PART VIII[1]
CONTROL AND ENFORCEMENT
Traffic wardens

4–1199   95. *Police authority may employ traffic wardens for the control and regulation of traffic or stationary vehicles, functions to be prescribed by Order of the Secretary of State*[2].

1. Part VIII contains ss 95–111.
2. The Functions of Traffic Wardens Order 1970 in this PART, post has effect under this section.

4–1200   **96. Additional powers of traffic wardens.**   (1) An order under section 95(5) of this Act may provide that, for the purposes of any functions which traffic wardens are authorised by the order to discharge, but subject to the provisions of subsection (3) below, references to a constable or police constable in all or any of the enactments specified in subsection (2) below shall include references to a traffic warden.

(2) The enactments referred to in subsection (1) above are—

(a) section 52 of the Metropolitan Police Act 1839, so far as it relates to the giving by the commissioner of directions to constables for preventing obstructions;

(b) section 22 of the local Act of the second and third year of the reign of Queen Victoria, chapter 94, so far as it makes similar provision with respect to the City of London;

(bb) in this Act—

(i) section 100(3) (which relates to the interim disposal of vehicles removed under section 99); and

(ii) sections 104 and 105 (which relate to the immobilisation of illegally parked vehicles);

(c) in the Road Traffic Act 1988—

(i) sections 35(1), 36 and 37 (which relate to compliance with traffic directions given by police constables);

(ia) section 67(3) (which relates to the power of a constable in uniform to stop vehicles);

(ii) section 163 (which relates to the power of a constable to stop vehicles);

(iii) section 164(1), (2) and (6) (which relate to the power of a constable to require the production of a driving licence in certain circumstances);

(iv) sections 165 and 169 (which relate to the powers of constables to obtain names and addresses of drivers and others and to require production of evidence of insurance or security and test certificates); and

(d) section 11 of the Road Traffic Offenders Act 1988.

(3) Any power of a constable for the purposes of the following provisions of the Road Traffic Act 1988, namely, sections 164(1), (2) and (6) and 165, shall be exercisable by a traffic warden under an order made by virtue of subsection (1) above only where—

(a) the traffic warden is assisting a constable, or

(b) the traffic warden has reasonable cause to believe that an offence has been committed of a description specified in relation to the section in question for the purposes of this paragraph by the order, and, in the case of a power for the purposes of section 165 of the Road Traffic Act 1988, the order authorises the use of that power in relation to that offence.

(4) Where an order has been made pursuant to subsection (2)(bb)(i) above, in section 100(3) of this Act the words "chief officer of the police force to which the constable belongs" shall be deemed to include a reference to a chief officer of police under whose direction a traffic warden acts.

(5) *Provision in order.*

[Road Traffic Regulation Act 1984, s 96 amended by the Road Traffic (Consequential Provisions) Act 1988, Sch 3, the Road Traffic Act 1991, Sch 4 and the Police Reform Act 2002, ss 44, 107 and 108.]

Removal or immobilisation of vehicles

4–1201   **99–103.**   *Removal of vehicles illegally, obstructively or dangerously parked, or abandoned or broken down; their disposal; charges for removal, storage and disposal; right of owner to recover vehicle or proceeds of sale*[1].

1. Charges are prescribed by SI 1989/744 amended by SI 1991/336 and SI 1993/550 and 1415. The Removal and Disposal of Vehicles Regulations SI 1986/183 amended by SI 1993/278 and 1708, SI 1994/1503, SI 1996/1003, SI 2002/746 and 2777 (England) and SI 2005/3252 (W) and the Removal and Disposal of Vehicles (Loading Areas) Regulations SI 1986/184 have been made. As to the functions of the National Assembly of Wales, see the National Assembly for Wales (Transfer of Functions) Order 2004, SI 2004/3044.

4–1202   **104. Immobilisation of vehicles illegally parked.**   (1) Subject to sections 105 and 106 of this Act, where a constable finds on a road a vehicle which has been permitted to remain at rest there in contravention of any prohibition or restriction imposed by or under any enactment, he may—

(a) fix an immobilisation device to the vehicle while it remains in the place in which he finds it; or

(b) move it from that place to another place on the same or another road and fix an immobilisation device to it in that other place;

or authorise another person to take under his direction any action he could himself take by virtue of paragraph (a) or (b) above.

(2) On any occasion when an immobilisation device is fixed to a vehicle in accordance with this section the constable or other person fixing the device shall also affix to the vehicle a notice—

(a) indicating that such a device has been fixed to the vehicle and warning that no attempt should be made to drive it or otherwise put it in motion until it has been released from that device;

(b) specifying the steps to be taken in order to secure its release; and
(c) giving such other information as may be prescribed.

(3) A vehicle to which an immobilisation device has been fixed in accordance with this section may only be released from that device by or under the direction of a person authorised to give such a direction by the chief officer of police within whose area the vehicle in question was found.

(4) Subject to subsection (3) above, a vehicle to which an immobilisation device has been fixed in accordance with this section shall be released from that device on payment in any manner specified in the notice affixed to the vehicle under subsection (2) above of such charge in respect of the release as may be prescribed[1].

(5) A notice affixed to a vehicle under this section shall not be removed or interfered with except by or under the authority of the person in charge of the vehicle or the person by whom it was put in the place where it was found by the constable; and any person contravening this subsection shall be guilty of an offence[2].

(6) Any person who, without being authorised to do so in accordance with this section, removes or attempts to remove an immobilisation device fixed to a vehicle in accordance with this section shall be guilty of an offence[2].

(7) Where a vehicle is moved in accordance with this section before an immobilisation device is fixed to it, any power of removal under regulations for the time being in force under section 99 of this Act which was exercisable in relation to that vehicle immediately before it was so moved shall continue to be exercisable in relation to that vehicle while it remains in the place to which it was so moved.

(8) In relation to any vehicle which is removed in pursuance of any such regulations or under section 3 of the Refuse Disposal (Amenity) Act 1978 (duty of local authority to remove abandoned vehicles) from a place to which it was moved in accordance with this section, references in the definition of "person responsible" in section 102(8) of this Act and section 5 of the said Act of 1978 mentioned above (recovery from person responsible of charges and expenses in respect of vehicles removed) to the place from which the vehicle was removed shall be read as references to the place in which it was immediately before it was moved in accordance with this section.

(9) In this section "immobilisation device" means any device or appliance designed or adapted to be fixed to a vehicle for the purpose of preventing it from being driven or otherwise put in motion, being a device or appliance of a type approved by the Secretary of State for use for that purpose in accordance with this section[3].

(10) *Repealed.*

(11) Any sum received by virtue of subsection (4) above shall be paid into the police fund.

(12) *Provision by regulations.*

(12A) For the purposes of this section, the suspension under section 13A or 49 of this Act of the use of a parking place is a restriction imposed under this Act.

[Road Traffic Regulation Act, 1984 s 104 as amended by the Road Traffic Act 1991, Schs 4 and 8.]

---

1. The Vehicles (Charges for Release from Immobilisation Devices) Regulations 1992, SI 1992/386 have been made and have effect under this section.
2. For penalty see Sch 2 to the Road Traffic Offenders Act 1988, post.
3. Section 106 provides for an initial experimental period for immobilisation of vehicles; a wheel-clamp device has been approved under s 104(9) for that.

4-1203 105. Exemptions from s 104. (1) Subject to the following provisions of this section, section 104(1) of this Act shall not apply in relation to a vehicle found by a constable in the circumstances mentioned in that subsection if*—

(a) a current disabled person's badge is displayed on the vehicle; or
(aa) a current recognised badge (within the meaning given by section 21A of the Chronically Sick and Disabled Persons Act 1970) is dispalyed on the vehicle; or
(b) the vehicle is in a meter bay within a parking place designated by a designation order.

(2) The exemption under subsection (1)(b) above shall not apply in the case of any vehicle found otherwise than in Greater London if—

(a) the meter bay in which it was found was not authorised for use as such at the time when it was left there (referred to below in this section as the time of parking); or
(b) an initial charge was not duly paid at the time of parking; or
(c) there has been since that time any contravention in relation to the relevant parking meter of any provision made by virtue of section 46(2)(c) of this Act; or
(d) more than two hours have elapsed since the end of any period for which an initial charge was duly paid at the time of parking or (as the case may be) since the end of any unexpired time in respect of another vehicle available on the relevant parking meter at the time of parking.

(2A) The exemption under subsection (1)(b) above shall not apply in the case of any vehicle found in Greater London if the meter bay in which it was found was not authorised for use as such at the time when it was left there.

(3) For the purposes of subsections (2)(a) and (2A) above, a meter bay in a parking place designated by a designation order is not authorised for use as such at any time when—

(a) by virtue of section 49(1)(a) of this Act the parking place is treated for the purposes of sections 46 and 47 of this Act as if it were not designated by that order; or

(b) the use of the parking place or of any part of it that consists of or includes that particular meter bay is suspended.

(4) In relation to any vehicle found in a meter bay within a parking place designated by a designation order, references in subsection (2) above to an initial charge are references to an initial charge payable in respect of that vehicle under section 45 or 50 of this Act.

(5) In any case where section 104(1) of this Act would apply in relation to a vehicle but for subsection (1)(a) above, the person guilty of contravening the prohibition or restriction mentioned in section 104(1) is also guilty of an offence under this subsection[1] if the conditions mentioned in subsection (6) below are met.

(6) Those conditions are that at the time when the contravention occurred—

(a) the vehicle was not being used in accordance with regulations under section 21 of the Chronically Sick and Disabled Persons Act 1970 (badges for display on motor vehicles used by disabled persons); and

(b) he was not using the vehicle in circumstances falling within section 117(2)(b) of this Act.

(6A) In any case where section 104(1) of this Act would apply in relation to a vehicle but for subsection (1)(aa) above, the person guilty of contravening the prohibition or restriction mentioned in section 104(1) is also guilty of an offence under this subsection if the conditions mentioned in subsection (6B) below are met.

(6B) Those conditions are that at the time when the contravention occurred—

(a) the vehicle was not being used in accordance with regulations under section 21A of the Chronically Sick and Disabled Persons Act 1970 (display of non-GB badges); and

(b) he was not using the vehicle in circumstances falling within section 117(1A)(b) of this Act.★

(7) In this section "meter bay" means a parking space equipped with a parking meter; and the references in subsection (2) above to the relevant parking meter are references to the parking meter relating to the meter bay in which the vehicle in question was found.★

[Road Traffic Regulation Act 1984, s 105 as amended by the Road Traffic Act 1991, Schs 4, 7 and 8 and the Disability Discrimination Act 2005, Sch 1.]

★Reproduced as in force in England.
1. For penalty see Sch 2 to the Road Traffic Offenders Act 1988, post.

Enforcement of excess parking charges

4–1204   107. Liability of vehicle owner in respect of excess parking charge.   (1) This section applies where—

(a) an excess charge has been incurred in pursuance of an order under sections 45 and 46 of this Act;

(b) notice of the incurring of the excess charge has been given or affixed as provided in the order; and

(c) the excess charge has not been duly paid in accordance with the order;

and in the following provisions of this Part of this Act "the excess charge offence" means the offence under section 47 of this Act of failing duly to pay the excess charge.

(2) Subject to the following provisions of this section—

(a) for the purposes of the institution of proceedings in respect of the excess charge offence against any person as being the owner of the vehicle at the relevant time, and

(b) in any proceedings in respect of the excess charge offence brought against any person as being the owner of the vehicle at the relevant time,

it shall be conclusively presumed (notwithstanding that that person may not be an individual) that he was the driver of the vehicle at that time and, accordingly, that acts or omissions of the driver of the vehicle at that time were his acts or omissions.

(3) Subsection (2) above shall not apply in relation to any person unless, within the period of 6 months beginning on the day on which the notice of the incurring of the excess charge was given or affixed as mentioned in subsection (1)(b) above, a notice under section 108 of this Act has been served on him—

(a) by or on behalf of the authority which is the local authority for the purposes of sections 45 and 46 of this Act in relation to the parking place concerned, or

(b) by or on behalf of the chief officer of police.

(4) If the person on whom a notice under section 108 of this Act is served in accordance with subsection (3) above was not the owner of the vehicle at the relevant time, subsection (2) above shall not apply in relation to him if he furnishes a statutory statement of ownership to that effect in compliance with the notice.

(5) The presumption in subsection (2) above shall not apply in any proceedings brought against any person as being the owner of the vehicle at the relevant time if, in those proceedings, it is proved—

(a) that at the relevant time the vehicle was in the possession of some other person without the consent of the accused, or

(b)   that the accused was not the owner of the vehicle at the relevant time and that he has a reasonable excuse for failing to comply with the notice under section 108 of this Act served on him in accordance with subsection (3) above.
[Road Traffic Regulation Act 1984, s 107.]

4–1205   108. Notice in respect of excess parking charge.   (1) A notice under this section shall be in the prescribed form, shall give particulars of the excess charge and shall provide that, unless the excess charge is paid before the expiry of the appropriate period, the person on whom the notice is served—

(a)   is required, before the expiry of that period, to furnish to the authority or chief officer of police by or on behalf of whom the notice was served a statutory statement of ownership (as defined in Part I of Schedule 8 to this Act), and

(b)   is invited, before the expiry of that period, to furnish to that authority or chief officer of police a statutory statement of facts (as defined in Part II of that Schedule).

(2)   If, in any case where—

(a)   a notice under this section has been served on any person, and

(b)   the excess charge specified in the notice is not paid within the appropriate period,

the person so served fails without reasonable excuse to comply with the notice by furnishing a statutory statement of ownership he shall be guilty of an offence[1].

(3)   If, in compliance with or in response to a notice under this section any person furnishes a statement which is false in a material particular, and does so recklessly or knowing it to be false in that particular, he shall be guilty of an offence[1].

(4)   Where a notice under this section has been served on any person in respect of any excess charge—

(a)   payment of the charge by any person before the date on which proceedings are begun for the excess charge offence, or, as the case may be, for an offence under subsection (2) above in respect of a failure to comply with the notice, shall discharge the liability of that or any other person (under this or any other enactment) for the excess charge offence or, as the case may be, for the offence under subsection (2) above;

(b)   conviction of any person of the excess charge offence shall discharge the liability of any other person (under this or any other enactment) for that offence and the liability of any person for an offence under subsection (2) above in respect of a failure to comply with the notice; and

(c)   conviction of the person so served of an offence under subsection (2) above in respect of a failure to comply with the notice shall discharge the liability of any person for the excess charge offence;

but, except as provided by this subsection, nothing in section 107 of this Act or this section shall affect the liability of any person for the excess charge offence.
[Road Traffic Regulation Act 1984, s 108.]

----

1. For penalty see Sch 2 to the Road Traffic Offenders Act 1988, post.

4–1206   109. Modifications of ss 107 and 108 in relation to hired vehicles.   (1) This section shall apply where—

(a)   a notice under section 108 of this Act has been served on a vehicle-hire firm, and

(b)   at the relevant time the vehicle in respect of which the notice was served was let to another person by the vehicle-hire firm under a hiring agreement to which this section applies.

(2)   Where this section applies, it shall be a sufficient compliance with the notice served on the vehicle-hire firm if the firm furnishes to the chief officer of police or local authority by or on behalf of whom the notice was served a statement in the prescribed form, signed by or on behalf of the vehicle-hire firm, stating that at the relevant time the vehicle concerned was hired under a hiring agreement to which this section applies, together with—

(a)   a copy of that hiring agreement, and

(b)   a copy of a statement of liability in the prescribed form, signed by the hirer under that hiring agreement;

and accordingly, in relation to the vehicle-hire firm on whom the notice was served, the reference in section 108(2) of this Act to a statutory statement of ownership shall be construed as a reference to a statement under this subsection together with the documents specified in paragraphs (a) and (b) above.

(3)   If, in a case where this section applies, the vehicle-hire firm has complied with the notice served on the firm by furnishing the statement and copies of the documents specified in subsection (2) above, then sections 107 and 108 of this Act shall have effect as if in those provisions—

(a)   any reference to the owner of the vehicle were a reference to the hirer under the hiring agreement, and

(b)   any reference to a statutory statement of ownership were a reference to a statutory statement of hiring.

(4)   Where, in compliance with a notice under section 108 of this Act, a vehicle-hire firm has

furnished copies of a hiring agreement and statement of liability as mentioned in subsection (2) above, a person authorised in that behalf by the chief officer of police or local authority to whom the documents are furnished may, at any reasonable time within 6 months after service of that notice, and on production of his authority, require the production by the firm of the originals of those documents; and if, without reasonable excuse, a vehicle-hire firm fails to produce the original of a document when required to do so under this subsection, the firm shall be treated as not having complied with the notice under section 108 of this Act.

(5) This section applies to a hiring agreement, under the terms of which the vehicle concerned is let to the hirer for a fixed period of less than 6 months (whether or not that period is capable of extension by agreement between the parties or otherwise); and any reference in this section to the currency of the hiring agreement includes a reference to any period during which, with the consent of the vehicle-hire firm, the hirer continues in possession of the vehicle as hirer, after the expiry of the fixed period specified in the agreement, but otherwise on terms and conditions specified in it.

(6) In this section "statement of liability" means a statement made by the hirer under a hiring agreement to which this section applies to the effect that the hirer acknowledges that he will be liable, as the owner of the vehicle, in respect of any excess charge which, during the currency of the hiring agreement, may be incurred with respect to the vehicle in pursuance of an order under sections 45 and 46 of this Act.

(7) In this section—

"hiring agreement" refers only to an agreement which contains such particulars as may be prescribed[1] and does not include a hire-purchase agreement within the meaning of the Consumer Credit Act 1974, and

"vehicle-hire firm" means any person engaged in hiring vehicles in the course of a business.

[Road Traffic Regulation Act 1984, s 109.]

---

1. Schedule 2 to the Road Traffic (Owner Liability) Regulations 1975 (SI 1975/324) requires the following particulars of the person signing the statement of liability—full name, date of birth, permanent address, address at time of hiring, serial number or drivers number and issuing authority and date of expiry of driving licence; it requires the following particulars of hiring arrangements—registration mark and make of hired vehicle and of any other vehicle substituted during the currency of the agreement, time and date of any change of vehicle, of commencement and expiry of original hiring period, and any authorised extension of hiring period.

4–1210 110. Time for bringing, and evidence in, proceedings for certain offences. (1) Proceedings in England or Wales for an offence under section 108(3) of this Act may be brought within a period of six months from the date on which evidence sufficient in the opinion of the prosecutor to warrant the proceedings came to his knowledge; but no such proceedings shall be brought by virtue of this section more than 3 years after the commission of the offence.

(2) (*Applies to Scotland.*)

(3) For the purposes of subsections (1) and (2) above a certificate signed by or on behalf of the prosecutor or, as the case may be, the Lord Advocate or the local authority, and stating the date on which evidence such as is mentioned in the subsection in question came to his or their knowledge, shall be conclusive evidence of that fact; and a certificate stating that matter and purporting to be so signed shall be deemed to be so signed unless the contrary is proved.

(4) Where any person is charged with the offence of failing to pay an excess charge, and the prosecutor produces to the court any of the statutory statements in Schedule 8 to this Act or a copy of a statement of liability (within the meaning of section 109 of this Act) purporting—

(*a*) to have been furnished in compliance with or in response to a notice under section 108 of this Act, and

(*b*) to have been signed by the accused,

the statement shall be presumed, unless the contrary is proved, to have been signed by the accused and shall be evidence (and, in Scotland, sufficient evidence) in the proceedings of any facts stated in it tending to show that the accused was the owner, the hirer or the driver of the vehicle concerned at a particular time.

[Road Traffic Regulation Act 1984, s 110.]

4–1211 111. Supplementary provisions as to excess charges. (1) The provisions of Schedule 8 to this Act shall have effect for the purposes of sections 107 to 109 of this Act (in this section referred to as "the specified sections").

(2) In the specified sections—

"appropriate period", in relation to a notice under section 108 of this Act, means the period of 14 days from the date on which the notice is served, or such longer period as may be specified in the notice or as may be allowed by the chief officer of police or authority by or on behalf of whom the notice is served;

"driver", in relation to an excess charge and in relation to an offence of failing duly to pay such a charge, means the person driving the vehicle at the time when it is alleged to have been left in the parking place concerned;

"relevant time", in relation to an excess charge, means the time when the vehicle was left in the parking place concerned, notwithstanding that the period in respect of which the excess charge was incurred did not begin at that time.

(3) For the purposes of the specified sections the owner of a vehicle shall be taken to be the person

by whom the vehicle is kept; and for the purpose of determining, in the course of any proceedings brought by virtue of the specified sections, who was the owner of the vehicle at any time, it shall be presumed that the owner was the person who was the registered keeper of the vehicle at that time.

(4) Notwithstanding the presumption in subsection (3) above, it shall be open to the defence in any proceedings to prove that the person who was the registered keeper of a vehicle at a particular time was not the person by whom the vehicle was kept at that time, and it shall be open to the prosecution to prove that the vehicle was kept by some other person at that time.

(5) A notice under section 108 of this Act may be served on any person—

(a) by delivering it to him or by leaving it at his proper address, or
(b) by sending it to him by post.

and, where the person on whom such a notice is to be served is a body corporate, it shall be duly served if it is served on the secretary or clerk of that body.

(6) For the purposes of subsection (5) above and of section 7 of the Interpretation Act 1978 (references to service by post) in its application to that subsection, the proper address of any person on whom such a notice is to be served—

(a) shall, in the case of the secretary or clerk of a body corporate, be that of the registered or principal office of that body or the registered address of the person who is the registered keeper of the vehicle concerned at the time of service, and
(b) shall in any other case be the last known address of the person to be served.

(7) References in this section to the person who was or is the registered keeper of a vehicle at any time are references to the person in whose name the vehicle was or is at that time registered under the Vehicle Excise and Registration Act 1994; and, in relation to any such person the reference in subsection (6)(a) above to that person's registered address is a reference to the address recorded in the record kept under that Act with respect to that vehicle as being that person's address.

(8) For the purposes of sections 1(2) and 2(1) of the Magistrates' Courts Act 1980 (power to issue summons or warrant and jurisdiction to try offences), any offence under subsection (2) of section 108 of this Act shall be treated as committed at any address which at the time of service of the notice under that section to which the offence relates was the accused's proper address (in accordance with subsection (6) above) for the service of any such notice as well as at the address to which any statutory statement furnished in response to that notice is required to be returned in accordance with the notice.
[Road Traffic Regulation Act 1984, s 111 amended by the Vehicle Excise and Registration Act 1994, Sch 3.]

PART IX[1]
FURTHER PROVISIONS AS TO ENFORCEMENT

General provisions

4–1212 112. Information as to identity of driver or rider. (1) This section applies to any offence under any of the foregoing provisions of this Act except—

(a) sections 43, 52, 88(7), 104, 105 and 108;
(b) the provisions of subsection (2) or (3) of section 108 as modified by subsections (2) and (3) of section 109; and
(c) section 35A(5) in its application to England and Wales.

(2) Where the driver of a vehicle is alleged to be guilty of an offence to which this section applies—

(a) the person keeping the vehicle shall give such information as to the identity of the driver as he may be required[2] to give—

(i) by or on behalf of a chief officer of police, or
(ii) in the case of an offence under section 35(a)(i) or against section 47 of this Act, by or on behalf of a chief officer of police or, in writing, by or on behalf of the local authority for the parking place in question; and

(b) any other person[3] shall, if required as mentioned in paragraph (a) above, give any information which it is in his power to give and which may lead to the identification of the driver.

(3) In subsection (2) above, references to the driver of a vehicle include references to the person riding a bicycle or tricycle (not being a motor vehicle); and—

(a) *Repealed*;
(b) in relation to an offence under section 61(5) of this Act, subsection (2)(a) above shall have effect as if, for subparagraphs (i) and (ii), there were substituted the words "by a notice in writing given to him by a local authority in whose area the loading area in question is situated",

and in subsection (2)(a) above, as modified by paragraph (b) of this subsection, "local authority" means any of the following, that is to say, a county council, a district council a London borough council and the Common Council of the City of London.

(4) Except as provided by subsection (5) below, a person who fails to comply with the requirements of subsection (2)(a) above shall be guilty of an offence unless he shows to the satisfaction of the court that he did not know, and could not with reasonable diligence have ascertained, who was the driver of the vehicle or, as the case may be, the rider of the bicycle or tricycle; and a person who fails to comply with the requirements of subsection (2)(b) above shall be guilty of an offence[4].

(5) (*Applies to Scotland.*)
[Road Traffic Regulation Act 1984, s 112 as amended by the Local Government Act 1985, Sch 17 and the Parking Act 1989.]

---

1. Part IX contains ss 112–118.
2. The information must be provided forthwith or within a reasonable time (*Lowe v Lester* [1987] RTR 30, [1986] Crim LR 339) and in accordance with any reasonable instructions, eg that it should be in writing (*Boss v Measures* [1990] RTR 26).
3. This expression includes the driver himself (*Bingham v Bruce* [1962] 1 All ER 136, 127 JP 81).
4. For penalty for this offence see Sch 2 to the Road Traffic Offenders Act 1988, post. Where an offence can be committed partly in one area and partly in another, it is sufficient that one lies within the jurisdictional area of the court trying it. The offence of failing to provide information as to the indentity of the driver of a vehicle allegedly involved in the commission of a traffic offence is committed at the point where the information was intended to be received, semble it can also be committed at the place where the defendant lives (*Kennet District Council v Young* [1999] RTR 235, 163 JP 622, DC).

4–1213 115. Mishandling of parking documents and related offences.   (1) A person shall be guilty of an offence[1] who, with intent to deceive,—

(*a*) uses, or lends to, or allows to be used by, any other person—

  (i)   any parking device or apparatus designed to be used in connection with parking devices;
  (ii) any ticket issued by a parking meter, parking device or apparatus designed to be used in connection with parking devices;
  (iii) any authorisation by way of such a certificate, other means of identification or device as is referred to in any of sections 4(2), 4(3), 7(2), and 7(3) of this Act; or
  (iv) any such permit or token as is referred to in section 46(2)(*i*) of this Act;

(*b*) makes or has in his possession anything so closely resembling any such thing as is mentioned in paragraph (*a*) above as to be calculated to deceive[2]; or
(*c*) Scotland.

(2) A person who knowingly makes a false statement for the purpose of procuring the grant or issue to himself or any other person of any such authorisation as is mentioned in subsection (1) above shall be guilty of an offence[1].
(2A) *Repealed.*
(3) *Scotland.*
[Road Traffic Regulation Act 1984, s 115 as substituted by the Road Traffic Regulation (Parking) Act 1986, s 2 and the Parking Act 1989 and amended by SI 1996/1553.]

---

1. For penalty see Sch 2 to the Road Traffic Offenders Act 1988, post.
2. "Calculated to deceive" means "likely to deceive"; see *R v Davison* [1972] 3 All ER 1121, [1972] 1 WLR 1540, CA; *Turner v Shearer* [1973] 1 All ER 397, 137 JP 191.

4–1214 116. Provisions supplementary to s 115.   (1) If any person authorised in that behalf by or under a designation order has reasonable cause to believe that a document or article carried on a vehicle, or by the driver or person in charge of a vehicle, is a document or article in relation to which an offence has been committed under subsection (1) of section 115 of this Act (so far as that subsection relates to such authorisations as are referred to in it) or under subsection (2) of that section, he may detain that document or article, and may for that purpose require the driver or person in charge of the vehicle to deliver up the document or article; and if the driver or person in charge of the vehicle fails to comply with that requirement, he shall be guilty of an offence[1].
(2) When a document or article has been detained under subsection (1) above and—

(*a*) at any time after the expiry of 6 months from the date when that detention began no person has been charged since that date with an offence in relation to the document or article under subsection (1) or (2) of section 115 of this Act, and
(*b*) the document or article has not been returned to the person to whom the authorisation in question was issued or to the person who at that date was the driver or person in charge of the vehicle,

then, on an application made for the purpose to a magistrates' court (or, in Scotland, on a summary application made for the purpose to the sheriff court), the court shall make such order respecting disposal of the document or article and award such costs (or, in Scotland, expenses) as the justice of the case may require.
(3) Any of the following, but no other, persons shall be entitled to make an application under subsection (2) above with respect to a document or article, that is to say—

(*a*) the person to whom the authorisation was issued;
(*b*) the person who, at the date when the detention of the document or article began, was the driver or person in charge of the vehicle; and
(*c*) the person for the time being having possession of the document or article.
[Road Traffic Regulation Act 1984, s 116.]

---

1. For penalty see Sch 2 to the Road Traffic Offenders Act 1988, post.

4–1215   117. Wrongful use of disabled person's badge. (1) A person who at any time acts in contravention of, or fails to comply with, any provision of an order under this Act relating to the parking of motor vehicles is also guilty of an offence under this subsection[1] if at that time—*

(*a*) there was displayed on the motor vehicle in question a badge purporting to be of a form prescribed under section 21 of the Chronically Sick and Disabled Persons Act 1970[2], and*

(*b*) he was using the vehicle in circumstances where a disabled person's concession would be available to a disabled person's vehicle,

but he shall not be guilty of an offence under this subsection if the badge was issued under that section and displayed in accordance with regulations made under it.*

(1A) A person who at any time acts in contravention of, or fails to comply with, any provision of an order under this Act relating to the parking of motor vehicles is also guilty of an offence under this subsection if at that time—

(*a*) there was displayed on the motor vehicle in question a badge purporting to be a recognised badge, and

(*b*) he was using the vehicle in circumstances where a concession would, by virtue of section 21B of the Chronically Sick and Disabled Persons Act 1970, be available to a vehicle lawfully displaying a recognised badge,

but he shall not be guilty of an offence under this subsection if the badge was a recognised badge and displayed in accordance with regulations made under section 21A of that Act.

(3) In this section—

"disabled person's concession" means—

(*a*) an exemption from an order under this Act given by reference to disabled persons' vehicles; or

(*b*) a provision made in any order under this Act for the use of a parking place by disabled persons' vehicles.

"recognised badge" has the meaning given in section 21A of the Chronically Sick and Disabled Persons Act 1970.*

[Road Traffic Regulation Act 1984, s 117 amended by the Road Traffic Act 1991, Sch 8 as amended by the Road Traffic Act 1991, s 35 and the Traffic Management Act 2004, s 94.]

---

*Reproduced as in force in England.
1. For penalty see Sch 2 to the Road Traffic Offenders Act 1988, post.
2. Section 21 of the Chronically Sick and Disabled Persons Act 1970 allows a badge to be displayed only in such circumstances and in such manner as may be prescribed; driving whilst displaying a badge otherwise is an offence under s 21(4B) punishable on summary conviction by a fine not exceeding level 3.

PART X[1]
GENERAL AND SUPPLEMENTARY PROVISIONS

4–1216 121A. Traffic authorities. (1) The Secretary of State is the traffic authority for every highway in England and Wales for which he is the highway authority within the meaning of the Highways Act 1980.

(1AA) The roads authority (as defined in section 151(1) of the Roads (Scotland) Act 1984) is the traffic authority for every road in Scotland.

(1A) Transport for London is the traffic authority for every GLA road.

(2) In Greater London, the council of the London borough or the Common Council of the City of London are the traffic authority for all roads in the borough or, as the case may be, in the City which are not GLA roads and for which the Secretary of State is not the traffic authority.

(3) In England and Wales outside Greater London, the council of the county or metropolitan district are the traffic authority for all roads in the county or, as the case may be, the district for which the Secretary of State is not the traffic authority.

(4) *Repealed.*

(5) In this Act "local traffic authority" means a traffic authority other than

(*a*) in relation to England and Wales, the Secretary of State; or

(*b*) in relation to Scotland, the Secretary of State or the Scottish Ministers.

[Road Traffic Regulation Act 1984, s 121A as inserted by the New Roads and Street Works Act 1991, Sch 7 and amended by the Greater London Authority Act 1999, s 271 and SI 2001/1400.]

4–1216A 121B. London borough council exercising powers so as to affect another traffic authority's roads. (1) No London borough council shall exercise any power under this Act in a way which will affect, or be likely to affect,—

(*a*) a GLA road, or

(*aa*) a strategic road, or

(*b*) a road in another London borough other than a GLA raod or strategic road,

unless the requirements of subsections (2) and (3) below have been satisfied.

(2) The first requirement is that the council has given notice of the proposal to exercise the power in the way in question—

(*a*) to Transport for London; and

(b) in a case where the road concerned is in another London borough, to the council for that borough.

(3) The second requirement is that—

(a) the proposal has been approved—

    (i) in the case of a GLA road, by Transport for London;

    (ii) in the case of a strategic road, by Transport for London and, where the road concerned is in another London borough, the council for that borough;

    (iii) in the case of a road with subsection (1)(b), or by the London borough council concerned; or;

(b) the period of one month beginning with the date on which Transport for London and, where applicable, the council received notice of the proposal has expired without Transport for London or the council having objected to the proposal; or

(c) any objection made by Transport for London or the council has been withdrawn; or

(d) where an objection has been made by Transport for London or a London borough council and not withdrawn, the Greater London Authority has given its consent to the proposal after consideration of the objection.

(3A) References in paragraphs (b) to (d) of subsection (3) to objections are to objections made by a person who, in the circumstances, has the power to give an approval under paragraph (a) of that subsection.

(4) Before deciding whether to give any consent for the purposes of subsection (3)(d) above, the Greater London Authority may cause a public inquiry to be held.

(5) If Transport for London has reason to believe—

(a) that a London borough council is proposing to exercise a power under this Act in a way which will affect, or be likely to affect,—

    (i) a GLA road,

    (ii) a strategic road, or

    (iii) a road in another London borough other than a GLA road or strategic road, and

(b) that notice of the proposal is required to be, but has not been, given in accordance with subsection (2) above,

Transport for London may give a direction to the council requiring it not to proceed with the proposal until the requirements of subsections (2) and (3) above have been satisfied.

(6) If a London borough council exercises any power in contravention of this section, Transport for London may take such steps as it considers appropriate to reverse or modify the effect of the exercise of that power.

(7) For the purposes of subsection (6) above, Transport for London shall have power to exercise any power of the London borough council on behalf of that council.

(8) Any reasonable expenses incurred by Transport for London in taking any steps under subsection (6) above shall be recoverable by Transport for London from the London borough council concerned as a civil debt.

(9) The Mayor of London may issue a direction dispensing with the requirements of subsections (2) and (3) above in such circumstances as may be specified in the direction.

(10) A direction under subsection (9) above may, in particular, dispense with those requirements as respects—

(a) all or any of the London borough councils;

(b) all or any of the GLA roads or strategic roads;

(c) all or any of the roads which are not GLA roads, strategic roads or trunk roads;

(d) the exercise of such powers as may be specified in the direction in such manner or circumstances as may be so specified.

(11) Any direction under subsection (9) above may be varied or revoked by a further direction under that subsection.

(12) For the purposes of this section—

(a) the City of London shall be treated as if it were a London borough;

(b) the Common Council shall be treated as if it were the council for a London borough; and

(c) the Inner Temple and the Middle Temple shall be treated as forming part of the City.

(13) In this section "strategic road" has the meaning given by section 60 of the Traffic Management Act 2004.

[Road Traffic Regulation Act 1984, s 121B as inserted by the Greater London Authority Act 1999, s 291 and amended by the Traffic Management Act 2004, s 63.]

4–1216B   **121C. Functions of GLA under this Act to be exercisable by the Mayor.**   (1) The functions of the Greater London Authority under this Act shall be functions of the Authority which are exercisable by the Mayor of London acting on behalf of the Authority.

(2) Subsection (1) above does not apply in relation to any function expressly conferred or imposed on, or made exercisable by, the London Assembly."

[Road Traffic Regulation Act 1984, s 121C as inserted by the Greater London Authority Act 1999, s 292.]

4-1217   122-124A. *Exercise of functions[2] by local authorities; delegation of functions by Greater London Council; Sch 9 to have effect as to the making, variation, revocation and validity of Orders[2]; GLA side roads.*

1. Part X contains ss 122–147.

2. For who may challenge the exercise of those functions, see Sch 9 and *R (LPC Group PLC) v Leicester City Council* [2002] EWHC Admin 2485, [2003] RTR 11.

3. The Secretary of State's Traffic Orders (Procedure) (England and Wales) Regulations 1990, SI 1990/1656 amended by SI 2004/3168 (E) lay down procedures for making Orders.

The Local Authorities' Traffic Orders (Procedures) (England and Wales) Regulations 1996, SI 1996/2489 amended by SI 2005/2929 (W) lay down the procedure to be followed by local authorities in England and Wales, including London, in connection with the making by them of the main types of traffic and parking place orders.

The Local Authorities' Traffic Orders (Exemptions for Disabled Persons) (England and Wales) Regulations 1986, SI 1986/178 amended by SI 1991/2709, apply to Orders, made under ss 1, 6, 9, 35, 45 and 46 of this Act, which, inter alia, prohibit vehicles from waiting at all times or during specified periods on roads marked by yellow lines, or prohibit beyond a certain period the waiting of vehicles in roads or in street parking places, whether a charge is made or not, and require such Orders to include an exemption from waiting prohibitions in certain circumstances, and from charges and time limits at places where vehicles may park or wait, in respect of vehicles displaying a disabled person's badge issued under s 21 of the Chronically Sick and Disabled Persons Act 1970 and the Disabled Persons (Badges for Motor Vehicles) Regulations 1982, SI 1982/1740. For the purpose of the Local Authorities' Traffic Orders (Exemptions for Disabled Persons) (England and Wales) Regulations 1986 and any Order referred to therein, a vehicle shall be regarded as displaying a disabled person's badge in the relevant position when—(a) in the case of a vehicle fitted with a front windscreen, the badge is exhibited thereon with the obverse side facing forwards on the near side of and immediately behind the windscreen; and (b) in the case of a vehicle not fitted with a front windscreen, the badge is exhibited in a conspicuous position on the vehicle (ibid, reg 4(7)).

4-1217A   124B. Orders of the Authority changing what are GLA side roads. (1) The Mayor of London shall keep under review the roads and proposed roads which have junctions with GLA roads or with other roads having such junctions and shall consider the extent to which such roads should be or cease to be GLA side roads.

(2) If the Mayor of London considers it expedient—

(*a*)   that any road or proposed road in Greater London, other than a trunk road or other road for which the Secretary of State is the highway authority, should become a GLA side road, or

(*b*)   that any GLA side road should cease to be such a road and should become a road for which the traffic authority is a London borough council or the Common Council of the City of London,

the Greater London Authority may by order direct that that road or proposed road shall become, or (as the case may be) that that GLA side road shall cease to be, a GLA side road as from such date as may be specified in that behalf in the order.

(3) Where an order under subsection (2) above directs that a road or proposed road shall become a GLA side road, it shall become such a road as from the date specified in that behalf in the order.

(4) Where an order under subsection (2) above directs that a GLA side road shall cease to be such a road, then, as from the date specified in that behalf in the order, the road shall cease to be a GLA side road and the following authority, that is to say—

(*a*)   where the road is situated in a London borough, the council for the London borough, and

(*b*)   where the road is situated in the City of London, the Common Council of the City of London,

shall become the traffic authority for the road.

(5) An order under subsection (2) above shall be of no effect unless—

(*a*)   it is made with the consent of the relevant traffic authority; or

(*b*)   if that consent is refused, it is confirmed (with or without modification) by the Secretary of State.

(6) For the purposes of subsection (5) above, the relevant traffic authority is—

(*a*)   in the case of an order directing that a road or proposed road shall become a GLA side road, the authority that is the traffic authority for the road or proposed road; and

(*b*)   in the case of an order directing that a GLA side road shall cease to be such a road, the authority that will become the traffic authority for the road in consequence of the order.

(7) An order under subsection (2) above may vary, revoke or re-enact with or without modifications—

(*a*)   any other order under that subsection (whether or not that other order was confirmed by the Secretary of State); or

(*b*)   an order of the Secretary of State under section 124A(1) of this Act.

(8) Where a GLA side road becomes a GLA road it shall cease to be a GLA side road.

(9) In this section, notwithstanding section 142(4) of this Act, a reference to a GLA road does not include a reference to a GLA side road.

[Road Traffic Regulation Act 1984, s 124B as inserted by SI 2000/2237, art 2(1), (4), Schedule.]

4-1217B   124C. Certification and records of GLA side roads. (1) A certificate by or on behalf of Transport for London that any road or proposed road is, or is not, for the time being a GLA side road shall be evidence of the facts stated in the certificate.

(2) A certificate under subsection (1) above may describe the road or proposed road in question by reference to a map.

(3) Transport for London shall prepare and maintain a record of the roads which are for the time being GLA side roads.

(4) The record required to be prepared and maintained under subsection (3) above may consist of—

(a) a list;
(b) a map; or
(c) a list and a map.

(5) Transport for London shall deposit a copy of that record with the Greater London Authority, each of the London borough councils and the Common Council of the City of London.

(6) Transport for London, and the Greater London Authority, each of the London borough councils and the Common Council of the City of London, shall make the record, or (as the case may be) the copies of the record deposited with them, available for inspection by the public at all reasonable hours.

(7) The record prepared and maintained by Transport for London under this section may be combined with the record which it is required to prepare and maintain under section 14C of the Highways Act 1980.

[Road Traffic Regulation Act 1984, s 124B as inserted by SI 2000/2237, art 2(1), (4), Schedule.]

4–1218 125. Boundary roads. (1) For the purposes of sections 6(1) and (2), 9, 73, 82(2) and 84(1) and (3) of this Act, where any part of the width of a road is in Greater London, the whole width of the road shall be deemed to be in Greater London.

(2) Subject to subsection (1) above, any powers which, under the provisions specified in subsection (3) below, are exercisable by a local authority as respects a road (including powers exercisable by such an authority as highway authority) shall, in the case of a road part of the width of which is in the area of one local authority and part in the area of another, be exercisable by either authority with the consent of the other.

(3) The provisions referred to in subsection (2) above are sections 1(2), 9, 14, 19(1), 23(1), 29(1), 32(1), 57(1) and (2), 68, 82(2) and 84.

(4) In this section "local authority" means the council of a county, metropolitan district, London borough, parish or community or the Common Council of the City of London.

(5) This section does not extend to Scotland.

[Road Traffic Regulation Act 1984, s 125 as amended by the Local Government Act 1985, Sch 5, the New Roads and Street Works Act 1991, Schs 8 and 9 and the Local Government (Wales) Act 1994, Sch 7.]

4–1219 126. Exercise of powers as respects part of width of road. (1) Any power which is exercisable in relation to any road under the provisions specified in subsection (2) below, otherwise than by virtue of section 125 of this Act, shall be exercisable with respect to the whole or any part of the width of the road.

(2) The provisions referred to in subsection (1) above are sections 9, 67(3), 82, 83, 84, 88 and 92 of this Act.

[Road Traffic Regulation Act 1984, s 126.]

4–1220 127. Footpaths, bridleways, restricted byways and byways open to all traffic. (1) In relation to any footpath, bridleway, restricted byway or byway open to all traffic—

(a) any reference in section 2(3) or 14 of this Act to pedestrians shall be construed as including a reference to persons to whom subsection (2) below applies, and
(b) any reference in any provision of this Act (except this section) to traffic shall be construed as including a reference to pedestrians and to persons to whom that subsection applies.

(2) This subsection applies to any person driving, riding or leading a horse or other animal of draught or burden.

(3) In this section—

(a) "footpath" does not include a highway over which the public have a right of way on foot only which is at the side of a public road; and
(b) "byway open to all traffic" means a highway over which the public have a right of way for vehicular and all other kinds of traffic, but which is used by the public mainly for the purpose for which footpaths and bridleways are so used.

(4) For the purposes of this section a highway at the side of a river, canal or inland navigation shall not be excluded from the definition of a footpath, bridleway, restricted byway or byway open to all traffic by reason only that the public have a right to use the highway for purposes of navigation, if the highway would fall within that definition if the public had no such right.

(5) This section does not extend to Scotland.

[Road Traffic Regulation Act 1984, s 127 as amended by SI 2006/1177.]

4–1221 128, 129. *Repealed.*

4–1222 130. Application of Act to Crown. (1) Subject to the provisions of this section and section 132 of this Act, the provisions of this Act specified in subsection (2) below shall apply to vehicles and persons in the public service of the Crown.

(2) The provisions referred to in subsection (1) above are

(a) sections 1 to 5, 9 to 16C, 21 to 26, 38, 42, 45 to 51, 52(3), 58 to 60, 62 to 67, 69 to 71, 76 to 90, 99, 100, 104, 105, 125 and 126;

(b) except in relation to vehicles and persons in the armed forces of the Crown when on duty, sections 6 to 8; and

(c) *Repealed.*

(3) In relation to vehicles used for naval, military or air force purposes, while being driven by persons for the time being subject to the orders of a member of the armed forces of the Crown, the Secretary of State may by regulations[1] vary the provisions of any statutory provision imposing a speed limit on motor vehicles; but regulations under this subsection may provide that any variation made by the regulations shall have effect subject to such conditions as may be specified in the regulations.

(4), (5) *Repealed.*

[Road Traffic Regulation Act 1984, s 130 amended by the Road Traffic (Consequential Provisions) Act 1988, Sch 1, the New Roads and Street Works Act 1991, Schs 8 and 9, the Road Traffic Regulation (Special Events) Act 1994, Schedule and SI 1996/1553.]

1. See the Motor Vehicles (Variation of Speed Limits) Regulations 1947, SI 1947/2192 amended by SI 1954/943 and SI 1964/489.

4–1223 131, 132, 132AA. *Secretary of State may with the consent of the appropriate Crown authority, make an Order applying road traffic enactments to Crown roads[1]; Royal Parks or highways in London affected by proposals relating to the other.*

1. "Crown road" means road, other than a highway, to which the public has access by permission granted by the appropriate Crown authority or otherwise granted by or on behalf of the Crown, and "road traffic enactments" means enactments relating to road traffic including the lighting and parking of vehicles and any order or other instruments having effect by virtue of any such enactment (s 131(7)). In the absence of an order under this section, a person who uses a Crown road which is a road within the definition of what is now s 192(1) of the Road Traffic Act 1988 is bound by the road traffic enactments; see *Kellett v Daisy* [1977] RTR 396.

The Crown Roads (Royal Parks) (Application of Road Traffic Enactments) Order 1987, SI 1987/363 has been made and the Crown Roads (Industrial Estates) (Application of Road Traffic Enactments) Order 1978, SI 1978/749 has effect under s 131.

4–1224 133. Vehicles used for marine salvage. (1) Subsection (3) of section 130 of this Act shall have effect in relation to motor vehicles used for salvage purposes pursuant to Part IX of the Merchant Shipping Act 1995 as it has effect in relation to vehicles used for naval, military or air force purposes while being driven as mentioned in that subsection.

(2) In this section "salvage" means the preservation of a vessel which is wrecked, stranded or in distress, or the lives of persons belonging to, or the cargo or apparel of, such a vessel.

[Road Traffic Regulation Act 1984, s 133 as amended by the Merchant Shipping Act 1995, Sch 13.]

4–1225 135. *Application of Act to Isles of Scilly[1].*

1. See the Isles of Scilly (Road Traffic Regulation) Order 1990, SI 1990/714.

4–1226 136. Meaning of "motor vehicle" and other expressions relating to vehicles[1]. (1) In this Act, subject to section 20 of the Chronically Sick and Disabled Persons Act 1970 (which makes special provision with respect to invalid carriages), "motor vehicle" means a mechanically propelled vehicle intended or adapted for use on roads, and "trailer" means a vehicle drawn by a motor vehicle.

(2) In this Act "motor car" means a mechanically propelled vehicle, not being a motor cycle or an invalid carriage, which is constructed itself to carry a load or passengers and of which the weight unladen—

(a) if it is constructed solely for the carriage of passengers and their effects, is adapted to carry not more than 7 passengers exclusive of the driver, and is fitted with tyres of such type as may be specified in regulations made by the Secretary of State, does not exceed 3050 kilograms;

(b) if it is constructed or adapted for use for the conveyance of goods or burden of any description, does not exceed 3050 kilograms (or 3500 kilograms if the vehicle carries a container or containers for holding, for the purposes of its propulsion, any fuel which is wholly gaseous at 17·5 degrees Celsius under a pressure of 1·013 bar or plant and materials for producing such fuel); or

(c) in a case falling within neither of the foregoing paragraphs, does not exceed 2540 kilograms.

(3) In this Act "heavy motor car" means a mechanically propelled vehicle, not being a motor car, which is constructed itself to carry a load or passengers and of which the weight unladen exceeds 2540 kilograms.

(4) In this Act (except for the purposes of sections 57 and 63) "motor cycle" means a mechanically propelled vehicle (not being an invalid carriage) with fewer than 4 wheels, of which the weight unladen does not exceed 410 kilograms.

(5) In this Act "invalid carriage" means a mechanically propelled vehicle of which the weight unladen does not exceed 254 kilograms and which is specially designed and constructed, and not

merely adapted, for the use of a person suffering from some physical defect or disability and is used solely by such a person.

(6) In this Act "motor tractor" means a mechanically propelled vehicle which is not constructed itself to carry a load, other than excepted articles, and of which the weight unladen does not exceed 7370 kilograms[2].

(7) In this Act "light locomotive" and "heavy locomotive" means a mechanically propelled vehicle which is not constructed itself to carry a load, other than excepted articles, and of which the weight unladen—

(a) in the case of a light locomotive, exceeds 7370 but does not exceed 11690 kilograms, and

(b) in the case of a heavy locomotive, exceeds 11690 kilograms[2].

(8) In subsections (6) and (7) above "excepted articles" means any of the following, that is to say, water, fuel, accumulators and other equipment used for the purpose of propulsion, loose tools and loose equipment.

[Road Traffic Regulation Act 1984, s 136 as amended by the Transport Act 2000, s 271 and the Transport (Scotland) Act 2001, s 78.]

---

1. See footnotes to similar provisions contained in the Road Traffic Act 1960, s 253, ante.
2. A recovery vehicle which was so constructed that a trailer might by partial superimposition be attached to the vehicle, so as to cause a substantial part of the weight of the trailer to be borne by the vehicle, was held not to be a motor tractor, a light locomotive or a heavy locomotive within s 136(6) and (7) (*DPP v Holtham* (1990) 154 JP 647, [1991] RTR 5, [1990] Crim LR 600).

4–1227 137. Supplementary provisions relating to s 136. (1) A sidecar attached to a motor vehicle shall, if it complies with such conditions as may be specified in regulations made by the Secretary of State, be regarded as forming part of the vehicle to which it is attached and not as being a trailer.

(2) For the purposes of section 136 of this Act, in a case where a motor vehicle is so constructed that a trailer may by partial superimposition be attached to the vehicle in such a manner as to cause a substantial part of the weight of the trailer to be borne by the vehicle, that vehicle shall be deemed to be a vehicle itself constructed to carry a load.

(3) For the purposes of that section, in the case of a motor vehicle fitted with a crane, dynamo, welding plant or other special appliance or apparatus which is a permanent or essentially permanent fixture, the appliance or apparatus shall not be deemed to constitute a load or goods or burden of any description, but shall be deemed to form part of the vehicle.

(4) The Secretary of State may by regulations vary any of the maximum or minimum weights specified in section 136 of this Act; and such regulations may have effect—

(a) either generally or in the case of vehicles of any class specified in the regulations, and

(b) either for the purposes of this Act and of all regulations made under it or for such of those purposes as may be so specified.

(5) Nothing in section 86 of this Act shall be construed as limiting the powers conferred by subsection (4) above.

[Road Traffic Regulation Act 1984, s 137.]

4–1228 138. Meaning of "heavy commercial vehicle". (1) Subject to subsections (4) to (7) below, in this Act "heavy commercial vehicle" means any goods vehicle which has an operating weight exceeding 7·5 tonnes[1].

(2) The operating weight of a goods vehicle for the purposes of this section is—

(a) in the case of a motor vehicle not drawing a trailer, or in the case of a trailer, its maximum laden weight;

(b) in the case of an articulated vehicle, its maximum laden weight (if it has one) and otherwise the aggregate maximum laden weight of all the individual vehicles forming part of that articulated vehicle; and

(c) in the case of motor vehicle (other than an articulated vehicle) drawing one or more trailers, the aggregate maximum laden weight of the motor vehicle and the trailer or trailers attached to it.

(3) In this section—

"articulated vehicle" means a motor vehicle with a trailer so attached to it as to be partially superimposed upon it;

"goods vehicle" means a motor vehicle constructed or adapted for use for the carriage of goods or burden of any description, or a trailer so constructed or adapted;

"trailer" means any vehicle other than a motor vehicle;

and references to the maximum laden weight of a vehicle are references to the total laden weight which must not be exceeded in the case of that vehicle if it is to be used in Great Britain without contravening any regulations for the time being in force under section 41 of the Road Traffic Act 1988 (construction and use regulations).

(4)–(6) *Limited power of Secretary of State to substitute different weights in sub-ss (1) and (2).*

(7), (8) *Repealed.*

[Road Traffic Regulation Act 1984, s 138 amended by the Road Traffic (Consequential Provisions) Act 1988, Sch 3 and the Statute Law (Repeals) Act 1993, Sch 1.]

1. Subsections (7) and (8) together with Sch 10, para 8, provide that for the purpose of determining whether or not any vehicle is a heavy commercial vehicle for the purposes of a traffic regulation order, or experimental traffic order (not including an order in Greater London), during the period from 28 October 1982 to 31 December 1989 "heavy commercial vehicle" means any vehicle whether mechanically propelled or not which is constructed or adapted for the carriage of goods and has an unladen weight exceeding 3 tons; the Secretary of State has power to substitute weights by regulations (but not below 3 tons). A vehicle drawing trailers shall be treated as one vehicle.

4–1229   139. Hovercraft. (1) For the purposes of this Act, a hovercraft—

  (*a*) shall be a motor vehicle, whether or not it is intended or adapted for use on roads; but

  (*b*) shall be treated, subject to subsection (2) below, as not being a vehicle of any of the classes defined in subsections (2) to (7) of section 136 of this Act.

  (2) The Secretary of State may by regulations provide—

  (*a*) that any provision of this Act, which would otherwise apply to hovercraft, shall not apply to them or shall apply to them subject to such modifications as may be specified in the regulations, or

  (*b*) that any such provision, which would not otherwise apply to hovercraft, shall apply to them subject to such modifications (if any) as may be so specified.

  (3) In this section "hovercraft" has the same meaning as in the Hovercraft Act 1968.
[Road Traffic Regulation Act 1984, s 139.]

4–1230   140. Certain vehicles not to be treated as motor vehicles. (1) For the purposes of this Act—

  (*a*) a mechanically propelled vehicle which is an implement for cutting grass, is controlled by a pedestrian and is not capable of being used or adapted for any other purpose;

  (*b*) any other mechanically propelled vehicle controlled by a pedestrian which may be specified by regulations made by the Secretary of State for the purposes of this section and of section 189 of the Road Traffic Act 1988; and

  (*c*) an electrically assisted pedal cycle of such class as may be prescribed by regulations[1] so made,

shall be treated as not being a motor vehicle.

  (2) In this section "controlled by a pedestrian" means that the vehicle either—

  (*a*) is constructed or adapted for use only under such control, or

  (*b*) is constructed or adapted for use either under such control or under the control of a person carried on it, but is not for the time being in use under, or proceeding under, the control of a person carried on it.
[Road Traffic Regulation Act 1984, s 140 amended by the Road Traffic (Consequential Provisions) Act 1988, Sch 3.]

1. The Electrically Assisted Pedal Cycle Regulations 1983, SI 1983/1168, have effect under this section; see also the Road Traffic Act 1988, ss 32 and 189, post.

4–1231   141A. *Tramcars and trolley vehicles: regulations.*

4–1240   142. General interpretation of Act. (1) In this Act, except where the context otherwise requires, the following expressions have the meanings hereby assigned to them respectively, that is to say—

   "bridge authority" means the authority or person responsible for the maintenance of a bridge;

   "bridleway" means a way over which the public[1] have the following, but no other, rights of way, that is to say, a right of way on foot and a right of way on horseback or leading a horse, with or without a right to drive animals of any description along the way;

   "credit card" and "debit card" have the meanings given by section 35A(6) of this Act;

   "designation order" means an order under section 45 of this Act (including any order so made by virtue of section 50(1) of this Act) and "designated parking place" means a parking place designated by a designation order;

   "disabled person's badge" means any badge issued, or having effect as if issued, under any regulations for the time being in force under section 21 of the Chronically Sick and Disabled Person's Act 1970;

   "disabled person's vehicle" means a vehicle lawfully displaying a disabled person's badge;

   "driver", where a separate person acts as steersman of a motor vehicle, includes that person as well as any other person engaged in the driving of the vehicle, and "drive" and "driving" shall be construed accordingly;

   "excess charge" has the meaning assigned to it by section 46(1) of this Act;

   "experimental traffic order" has the meaning assigned to it by section 9(1) of this Act;

   except in section 71(2) of this Act, "footpath" means a way over which the public has a right of way on foot only;

   "GLA road" (subject to subsection (4) below) has the same meaning as in the Highways Act 1980 (see sections 329(1) and 14D(1) of that Act);

   "GLA side road" shall be construed in accordance with section 124A(9) of this Act;

   "initial charge" has the meaning assigned to it by section 46(1) of this Act;

   "magistrates' court" has the same meaning as in the Magistrates' Courts Act 1980;

   "the Ministers" means the Secretaries of State charged with general responsibility under this Act in relation to England, Wales and Scotland respectively;

"off-street parking accommodation" means parking accommodation for motor vehicles off the highway or (*Scotland*);

subject to section 111(3) and (4) of, and paragraph 11(2) and (3) of Schedule 12 to, this Act, "owner", in relation to a vehicle which is subject to a hiring agreement or hire-purchase agreement, means the person in possession of the vehicle under that agreement;

"parking device" has the meaning assigned to it by section 35(3B) or, as the case may be section 51(4) of this Act;

"parking meter" has the meaning assigned to it by section 46(2)(*a*) of this Act;

"prescribed" means prescribed by regulations made by the Secretary of State;

"public road" has the same meaning as in the Roads (Scotland) Act 1984;

"public service vehicle" has the same meaning as in the Public Passenger Vehicles Act 1981;

"restricted byway" has the same meaning as in Part 2 of the Countryside and Rights of Way Act 2000;

"road"—

    (*a*) in England and Wales, means any length of highway or of any other road to which the public has access, and includes bridges over which a road passes, and

    (*b*) *Scotland*;

"special road", in England and Wales, has the same meaning as in the Highways Act 1980, and (*Scotland*).

"statutory", in relation to any prohibition, restriction, requirement or provision, means contained in, or having effect under, any enactment (including any enactment contained in this Act);

"street parking place" and "off-street parking place" refer respectively to parking places on land which does, and on land which does not, form part of a road;

"traffic authority" and "local traffic authority" has the meaning given by section 121A of this Act;

"traffic sign" has the meaning assigned to it by section 64(1) of this Act; and

"traffic regulation order" has the meaning assigned to it by section 1 of this Act;

"trunk road" has the same meaning as in the Highways Act 1980 (see section 329(1) of that Act).

(1A) In this Act—

    (*a*) any reference to a county shall be construed in relation to Wales as including a reference to a county borough;

    (*b*) any reference to a county council shall be construed in relation to Wales as including a reference to a county borough council; and

    (*c*) section 17(4) and (5) of the Local Government (Wales) Act 1994 (references to counties and districts to be construed generally in relation to Wales as references to counties and county boroughs) shall not apply.

(2) Any reference in this Act to a tricycle shall be construed as including a reference to a cycle which is not a motor vehicle and has 4 or more wheels.

(3) References in this Act to a class of vehicles or traffic (other than the references in section 17) shall be construed as references to a class defined or described by reference to any characteristics of the vehicles or traffic or to any other circumstances whatsoever.

(4) Any reference in this Act to a GLA road includes a reference to a GLA side road.

[Road Traffic Regulation Act 1984, s 142 as amended by the Local Government Act 1985, Schs 5 and 17, the Transport Act 1985, Sch 1, the Parking Act 1989, Sch, the New Roads and Street Works Act 1991, Sch 8, the Local Government (Wales) Act 1994, Sch 7, the Access to Justice Act 1999, Sch 10,the Greater London Authority Act 1999, s 292 and by SI 2006/1177.]

---

  1. See also s 27, ante as to any person driving, riding or leading a horse or other animal of draught or burden, and use of a highway at the side of a river, canal or inland navigation. Subject to any Orders made by a local authority and to any byelaws, the public have, as a right of way, the right to ride a pedal cycle on any bridleway, but must give way to pedestrians and persons on horseback; see the Countryside Act 1968, s 30.

4–1241 **143. Saving for law of nuisance.**   (1) Nothing in this Act shall authorise a person to use on a road a vehicle so constructed or used as to cause a nuisance, or affect the liability, whether under statute or common law, of the driver or owner so using such a vehicle.

(2) In this section, in its application to England and Wales, "nuisance" means a public or a private nuisance.

[Road Traffic Regulation Act 1984, s 143.]

SCHEDULES

4–1242 Schedule 1: *Matters as to which Orders can be made under s 6.*

4–1243 Schedule 2: *Matters as to which Regulations can be made under s 12.*

4–1244 Schedule 3: *Repealed*[1].

---

  1. Schedule 3 is repealed by the Road Traffic (Temporary Restrictions) Act 1991, Sch 2 when in force.

4–1245 Schedule 4: *Control of off-street parking (s 43).*

4–1246 Schedule 5: *Buildings in relation to which a Secretary of State is the appropriate authority for the purposes of s 74.*

Section 86

SCHEDULE 6
SPEED LIMITS FOR VEHICLES OF CERTAIN CLASSES[1]

(Amended by the Road Traffic (Consequential Provisions) Act 1988 Sch 3.)

PART I
VEHICLES FITTED WITH PNEUMATIC TYRES ON ALL WHEELS

(see application provisions below the following Table)

4–1247

TABLE

1	2	3		
Item No	Class of Vehicle	Maximum speed (in miles per hour) while vehicle is being driven on:		
		(a) Motorway	*(b)* Dual carriage-way road not being a motorway	*(c)* Other road
1	A passenger vehicle, motor caravan or dual-purpose vehicle not drawing a trailer being a vehicle with an unladen weight exceeding 3.05 tonnes or adapted to carry more than 8 passengers—			
	(i) if not exceeding 12 metres in overall length	70	60	50
	(ii) if exceeding 12 metres in overall length	60	60	50
2	An invalid carriage	not applicable	20	20
3	A passenger vehicle, motor caravan, car-derived van or dual-purpose vehicle drawing one trailer	60	60	50
4	A passenger vehicle, motor caravan, car-derived van or dual-purpose vehicle drawing more than one trailer	40	20	20
5	qc(1) A goods vehicle having a maximum laden weight not exceeding 7.5 tonnes and which is not—			
	(*a*) an articulated vehicle, or			
	(*b*) drawing a trailer, or			
	(*c*) a car-derived van	70	60	50
	(2) A goods vehicle which is—			
	(*a*)(i) an articulated vehicle having a maximum laden weight not exceeding 7.5 tonnes or			
	(ii) a motor vehicle, other than a car-derived van, which is drawing one trailer where the aggregate maximum laden weight of the motor vehicle and the trailer does not exceed 7.5 tonnes	60	60	50
	(*b*)(i) an articulated vehicle having a maximum laden weight exceeding 7.5 tonnes,			
	(ii) a motor vehicle having a maximum laden weight exceeding 7.5 tonnes and not drawing a trailer, or			
	(iii) a motor vehicle drawing one trailer where the aggregate maximum laden weight of the motor vehicle and the trailer exceeds 7.5 tonnes	60	50	40
	(*c*) a motor vehicle, other than a car-derived van, drawing more than one trailer	40	20	20
6	A motor tractor (other than an industrial tractor), a light locomotive or a heavy locomotive—			
	(*a*) if the provisions about springs and wings as specified in paragraph 3 of Part IV of this Schedule are complied with and the vehicle is not drawing a trailer, or if those provisions are complied with and the vehicle is drawing one trailer which also complies with those provisions	40	30	30
	(*b*) in any other case	20	20	20

1	2	3		
Item No	Class of Vehicle	Maximum speed (in miles per hour) while vehicle is being driven on:		
		(a) Motorway	(b) Dual carriage-way road not being a motorway	(c) Other road
7	A works truck	18	18	18
8	An industrial tractor	not applicable	18	18
9	An agricultural motor vehicle	40	40	40

Application

This Part applies only to motor vehicles, not being track-laying vehicles, every wheel of which is fitted with a pneumatic tyre and to such vehicles drawing one or more trailers, not being track-laying vehicles, every wheel of which is fitted with a pneumatic tyre.

PART II

VEHICLES (OTHER THAN TRACK-LAYING VEHICLES) NOT FITTED WITH PNEUMATIC TYRES ON ALL WHEELS

(see application provisions below the following Table)

4–1247A

1	2	3
Item No	Class of Vehicle	Maximum Speed (in miles per hour) while vehicle is being driven on a road
1	A motor vehicle, or in the case of a motor vehicle drawing one or more trailers, the combination, where— (a) every wheel is fitted with a resilient tyre, or (b) at least one wheel is fitted with a resilient tyre and every wheel which is not fitted with a resilient tyre is fitted with a pneumatic tyre	20
2	A motor vehicle, or in the case of a motor vehicle drawing one or more trailers, the combination, where any wheel is not fitted with either a pneumatic tyre or a resilient tyre	5

Application

This Part does not apply to—

(a) a motor vehicle which is a track-laying vehicle; or

(b) a motor vehicle which is not a track-laying vehicle but which is drawing one or more trailers any one of which is a track-laying vehicle.

PART III
TRACK-LAYING VEHICLES

(See application provisions below the following Table)

4–1247B   TABLE

1	2	3
Item No	Class of Vehicle	Maximum Speed (in miles per hour) while vehicle is being driven on a road
1	A motor vehicle being a track-laying vehicle which is fitted with— (*a*) springs between its frame and its weight-carrying rollers, and (*b*) resilient material between the rims of its weight-carrying rollers and the surface of the road, and which is not drawing a trailer	20
2	A vehicle specified in item 1 above drawing one or more trailers each one of which is either— (*a*) a track-laying vehicle fitted with springs and resilient material as mentioned in that item, or (*b*) not a track-laying vehicle and each wheel of which is fitted with either a pneumatic tyre or a resilient tyre	20
3	A vehicle specified in item 1 above drawing one or more trailers any one of which is either— (*a*) a track-laying vehicle not fitted with springs and resilient material as mentioned in that item, or (*b*) not a track-laying vehicle and at least one wheel of which is not fitted with either a pneumatic tyre or a resilient tyre	5
4	A motor vehicle being a track-laying vehicle which is not fitted with springs and resilient material as mentioned in item 1 above, whether drawing a trailer or not	5
5	A motor vehicle not being a track-laying vehicle, which is drawing one or more trailers any one or more of which is a track-laying vehicle— (*a*) if every wheel of the motor vehicle and of any non-track-laying trailer is fitted with a pneumatic tyre or with a resilient tyre, and every trailer which is a track-laying vehicle is fitted with springs and resilient material as mentioned in item 1 (*b*) in any other case	20 / 5

Application

This Part applies to—

(*a*) a motor vehicle which is a track-laying vehicle, and
(*b*) a motor vehicle of any description which is drawing one or more trailers any one or more of which is a track-laying vehicle.

PART IV
APPLICATION AND INTERPRETATION

4–1247C **1.** This Schedule does not apply to a vehicle which is being used for the purpose of experiments or trials under section 6 of the Road Improvements Act 1925 or section 283 of the Highways Act 1980.

    2. In this Schedule—

"agricultural motor vehicle", "articulated vehicle", "dual-purpose vehicle", "industrial tractor", "passenger vehicle", "pneumatic tyre", "track-laying", "wheel" and "works truck" have the same meanings as are respectively given to those expressions in Regulation 3(1) of the Motor Vehicles (Construction and Use) Regulations [1986];
"car-derived van" means a goods vehicle which is constructed or adapted as a derivative of a passenger vehicle and which has a maximum laden weight not exceeding 2 tonnes;
"construction and use requirements" has the same meaning as in section 41(7) of the Road Traffic Act 1988;

"dual-carriageway road" means a road part of which consists of a central reservation to separate a carriageway to be used by vehicles proceeding in one direction from a carriageway to be used by vehicles proceeding in the opposite direction;

"goods vehicle" has the same meaning as in section 192(1) of the Road Traffic Act 1988;

"maximum laden weight" in relation to a vehicle or a combination of vehicles means—

(a) in the case of a vehicle, or combination of vehicles, in respect of which a gross weight not to be exceeded in Great Britain is specified in construction and use requirements, that weight;

(b) in the case of any vehicle, or combination of vehicles, in respect of which no such weight is specified in construction and use requirements, the weight which the vehicle, or combination of vehicles, is designed or adapted not to exceed when in normal use and travelling on a road laden.

"motor caravan" has the same meaning as in Regulation 2(1) of the Motor Vehicles (Type Approval) (Great Britain) Regulations 1979;

"motorway" has the same meaning as in Regulation 3(1) of the Motorways Traffic (England and Wales) Regulations 1982, as regards England and Wales, and Regulation 2(2) of the Motorways Traffic (Scotland) Regulations 1964, as regards Scotland; and

"resilient tyre" means a tyre, not being a pneumatic tyre, which is soft or elastic.

3. The specification as regards springs and wings mentioned in item 6 of Part I of this Schedule is that the vehicle—

(i) is equipped with suitable and sufficient springs between each wheel and the frame of the vehicle, and

(ii) unless adequate protection is afforded by the body of the vehicle, is provided with wings or other similar fittings to catch, so far as practicable, mud or water thrown up by the rotation of the wheels.

4. A vehicle falling in two or more classes specified in Part I, II or III of this Schedule shall be treated as falling within the class for which the lower or lowest speed limit is specified.

---

1. The Secretary of State is empowered by s 86(2) to vary the provisions of Sch 6. The schedule is printed as amended by The Motor Vehicles (Variation of Speed Limits) Regulations 1986, SI 1986/1175. The Motor Vehicles (Variation of Speed Limit) Regulations 1947 SR & O 1947/2192 amended by SI 1954/943 and SI 1964/489 have effect under s 86 and provide that no speed limit is imposed in relation to motor vehicles of the types specified in the Schedule to the regulations which are owned by the Secretary of State for Defence and used for naval, military or air force purposes or which are so used whilst being driven by persons subject to the orders of any member of the armed forces of the Crown or which are vehicles in the service of a visiting force within the meaning of the Visiting Forces and International Headquarters (Application of Law) Order 1965, SI 1965/1536; or motor vehicles used for salvage purpose pursuant to the Merchant Shipping Act 1894, Part IX.

The type of vehicles specified in the Schedule are:—

1. motor vehicles constructed or adapted—
   (a) for actual combative purposes or for naval military or air force training in connection therewith, or
   (b) for the conveyance of personnel, or
   (c) for use with, or for the carriage or drawing of, guns or machine guns;
2. mobile cranes constructed or adapted for the raising of aircraft;
3. motor track laying vehicles constructed or adapted—
   (a) for actual combative purposes, or
   (b) for use with, or the carriage or drawing of guns, machine guns, ammunition, equipment or stores in connection therewith;
4. fire tenders;
5. ambulances.

For the exemption of fire brigade, ambulances and police vehicles from speed limits, see s 87, ante.

Section 111

SCHEDULE 8
STATUTORY STATEMENTS (EXCESS CHARGES)

PART I
STATUTORY STATEMENT OF OWNERSHIP OR HIRING

4–1248 **1.** For the purposes of the specified sections, a statutory statement of ownership is a statement in the prescribed form[1], signed by the person furnishing it and stating—

(a) whether he was the owner of the vehicle at the relevant time; and

(b) if he was not the owner of the vehicle at the relevant time, whether he ceased to be the owner before, or became the owner after, the relevant time, and, if the information is in his possession, the name and address of the person to whom, and the date on which, he disposed of the vehicle or, as the case may be, the name and address of the person from whom, and the date on which, he acquired it.

2. For the purposes of the specified sections, a statutory statement of hiring is a statement in the prescribed form[1], signed by the person furnishing it, being the person by whom a statement of liability was signed and stating—

(a) whether at the relevant time the vehicle was let to him under the hiring agreement to which the statement of liability refers; and

(b) if it was not, the date on which he returned the vehicle to the possession of the vehicle-hire firm concerned.

PART II
STATUTORY STATEMENT OF FACTS[2]

4–1248A **3.** For the purposes of the specified sections, a statutory statement of facts is a statement which is in the prescribed form[1] and which—

(a) states that the person furnishing it was not the driver of the vehicle at the relevant time;

(b) states the name and address at the time when the statement is furnished of the person who was the driver of the vehicle at the relevant time; and

(c) is signed both by the person furnishing it and by the person stated to be the driver of the vehicle at the relevant time.

1. The Road Traffic (Owner Liability) Regulations 1975, SI 1975/324, have effect under this Schedule and prescribe the appropriate forms.

2. At the time of going to press, para 3 of Sch 8 had not been brought into force. In its place Sch 10, para 20, defines a statutory statement of facts as follows:

"For the purposes of sections 107 to 109 of this Act, a statutory statement of facts is a statement which is in the prescribed form and which either—

(a) states that the person furnishing it was the driver of the vehicle at the relevant time and is signed by him; or

(b) states that the person was not the driver of the vehicle at the relevant time, states the name and address at the time the statement is furnished of the person who was the driver of the vehicle at the relevant time and is signed both by the person furnishing it and by the person stated to be the driver of the vehicle at the relevant time."

PART III

INTERPRETATION

4–1248B **4.** In this Schedule "the specified sections" has the meaning assigned to it by subsection (1) of section 111 of this Act.

5. Subsections (2) to (4) of that section shall have effect for the purposes of Parts I and II of this Schedule as they have effect for the purposes of the specified sections.

6. In paragraph 2 above "statement of liability", "hiring agreement" and "vehicle-hire firm" have the same meaning as in section 109 of this Act.

4–1249 Schedule 9: *Special provisions as to certain Orders (s 124). Schedule 9 has been amended to include an order made by the Secretary of State under s 34 of the Deregulation and Contracting Out Act 1994 and orders for which his consent would otherwise be required by paragraph 13 or 14 of this Schedule and any order made under section 84(1) which contains a provision applying to any road a speed limit of 20 miles an hour have been removed by SI 1999/1608.*

4–1250 Schedule 10: *Transitional provisions and savings (s 144).*

4–1251 Schedule 11: *Validation of provisions of Act taken from Instruments (s 144).*

Transport Act 1985[1]
(1985 c 67)

PART I[2]
GENERAL PROVISIONS RELATING TO ROAD PASSENGER TRANSPORT

Meaning of "local service"

4–1350 **2. Local services.** (1) In this Act "local service" means a service, using one or more public service vehicles, for the carriage of passengers by road at separate fares other than one—

(a) which is excluded by subsection (4) below; or

(b) in relation to which (except in an emergency) one or both of the conditions mentioned in subsection (2) below are met with respect to every passenger using the service.

(2) The conditions are that—

(a) the place where he is set down is fifteen miles or more, measured in a straight line, from the place where he was taken up;

(b) some point on the route between those places is fifteen miles or more, measured in a straight line, from either of those places.

(3) Where a service consists of one or more parts with respect to which one or both of the conditions are met, and one or more parts with respect to which neither of them is met, each of those parts shall be treated as a separate service for the purposes of subsection (1) above.

(4) A service shall not be regarded for the purposes of this Act as a local service if—

(a) the conditions set out in Part III of Schedule 1 to the 1981 Act (trips organised privately by persons acting independently of vehicle operators, etc) are met in respect of each journey made by the vehicles used in providing the service; or

(b) every vehicle used in providing the service is so used under a permit granted under section 19 of this Act.

(5) Subsections (5)(b), (c) and (6) of section 1 of the 1981 Act (meaning of "fares") shall apply for the purposes of this section.
[Transport Act 1985, s 2.]

1. A substantial amount of this Act has been brought into force by SI 1985/1887. Only those parts of the Act of relevance to magistrates' courts have been included here. The Commencement Order referred to above contains certain transitional provisions as well.

2. Part I contains ss 1–33.

4–1351 **6.** *Registration of local services[1].*

1. The Public Service Vehicles (Registration of Local Services) Regulations 1986, SI 1986/1671 amended by SI 1988/1879, SI 1989/1064, SI 1993/2752, SI 1994/3271, SI 2002/182 and SI 2004/10 have been made. Section 67 of

the Public Passenger Vehicles Act 1981, which deals with penalties for contravention of regulations, is applied to this Part of this Act; the maximum fine is **level 2** on the standard scale.

4–1352　　**7.** *Application of traffic regulation conditions to local services.*

4–1353　　**10–17.** *Taxis and hire cars; licensing and use.*

4–1354　　**18–23.** *Modifications of PSV requirements for vehicles used as buses by educational and other bodies, and as community buses*[1].

1. Contravention of a condition attaching to a community bus permit makes the holder liable on summary conviction to a fine not exceeding level 3 on the standard scale (s 23(5)). The Community Bus Regulations 1986 have been made under powers contained in s 23 and these are reproduced in this PART, post. The Minibus and Other Section 19 Permit Buses Regulations 1987, SI 1987/1230 amended by SI 1990/1708, SI 1995/1540, SI 1996/3088, SI 1997/535 and 2916 have been made under s 21. The maximum penalty not exceeding level 2 on the standard scale for contraventions of regulations is contained in s 67 of the Public Passenger Vehicles Act 1981 and is applied to these provisions as are the defences contained in s 68 of the 1981 Act.

4–1355　　**24–33.** *Further amendments with respect to PSV operators' licences: conditions, power to disqualify*[1].

1. An operator of a PSV adapted to carry more than eight passengers using the vehicle on a road in plying for hire as a whole is (subject to s 68(3) of the 1981 Act) liable on summary conviction to a fine not exceeding level 3 on the standard scale (s 30).

4–1356　　　　　　　　SCHEDULE 1
AMENDMENTS CONSEQUENTIAL ON THE ABOLITION OF ROAD SERVICE LICENSING

16. (1) Subject to any provision made by or under this Act, in any enactment or instrument passed or made before the commencement of section 1 of this Act—

(a) any reference to a stage carriage service shall be construed as a reference to a local service;
(b) any reference to an express carriage service shall be construed as a reference to any service for the carriage of passengers for hire or reward at separate fares which is neither a local service nor one provided by a vehicle to which subparagraph (2) below applies;
(c) any reference to a stage carriage shall be construed as a reference to a public service vehicle being used in the provision of a local service;
(d) any reference to an express carriage shall be construed as a reference to a public service vehicle being used to carry passengers for hire or reward at separate fares other than one being used in the provision of a local service; and
(e) any reference to a contract carriage shall be construed as a reference to a public service vehicle being used to carry passengers for hire or reward otherwise than at separate fares.

(2) When used in circumstances in which the conditions set out in Part III of Schedule 1 to the 1981 Act are fulfilled, a public service vehicle carrying passengers at separate fares shall be treated, for the purposes of any enactment or instrument to which paragraph (d) or (e) of sub-paragraph (1) above applies, as being used to carry passengers otherwise than at separate fares.

4–1357
Section 139(2)　　　　　　　　SCHEDULE 7
MINOR AND CONSEQUENTIAL AMENDMENTS
General

1. In England and Wales, the provisions made by or under any enactment which apply to motor vehicles used—

(a) to carry passengers under a contract express or implied for the use of the vehicle as a whole at or for a fixed or agreed rate or sum; and
(b) to ply for hire for such use;

shall apply to motor vehicles adapted to carry less than nine passengers as they apply to motor vehicles adapted to carry less than eight passengers.

Road Traffic Act 1988
(1988 c 52)

PART I[1]
PRINCIPAL ROAD SAFETY PROVISIONS
Driving offences

4–1370　　**1. Causing death by dangerous driving**[2]. A person who causes the death[3] of another person by driving[4] a mechanically propelled vehicle[5] dangerously on a road or other public place is guilty of an offence[6].
[Road Traffic Act 1988, s 1 as substituted by the Road Traffic Act 1991, s 1.]

---

1. Part I contains ss 1–40. Its provisions apply to vehicles and persons in the public service of the Crown (s 183, post).
2. See s 2A below for meaning of "dangerous driving".
3. The contribution of the driving to the death must be more than minute (*R v Hennigan* [1971] 3 All ER 133, 55 Cr

App Rep 262, 135 JP 504). The term "substantial cause" may imply a larger meaning whilst reference to more than a "slight or trifling" link is a useful way to avoid the term "de minimis" (*R v Kimsey* [1996] Crim LR 35).

4. See headnote to this title for notes on "driver" and "driving".

5. This section applies to tramcars and trolley vehicles operated under statutory powers (Sch 4, post). In this section, a separate person acting as steersman is not driving (s 192(1), post).

6. This offence is triable only on indictment (Road Traffic Offenders Act 1988, Sch 2). In our opinion, this offence is an offence of homicide so that by virtue of s 24 of the Magistrates' Courts Act 1980, ante, a juvenile charged with it may not be tried summarily but must be committed for trial at the Crown Court (in the same way as an adult). Note that the Coroners Act 1988, s 17 in title CORONERS, ante places the duty of notifying the coroner on the justices' clerk. Section 11 of the Road Traffic Offenders Act 1988 applies. The court must order a person convicted under s 1 to be disqualified until he passes an appropriate test.

4-1371   2. Dangerous driving[1]. A person who drives[2] a mechanically propelled vehicle dangerously[3] on a road or other public place is guilty of an offence[4].
[Road Traffic Act 1988, s 2 as substituted by the Road Traffic Act 1991, s 1.]

---

1. For defence of automatism, see PART I: MAGISTRATES' COURTS, PROCEDURE, ante and for general commentary including other defences see ante para **8–9 Dangerous and careless driving etc**. If the driver is alleged to be guilty of dangerous or careless driving, it is his duty to give his name and address to any person having reasonable ground for requiring it (s 168, post).

This section applies to trolley vehicles and tramcars; see Sch 4, post. The owner of the vehicle, though not actually driving, but allowing the vehicle to be driven in contravention of this section, is guilty of aiding and abetting, and, the offence being a misdemeanour, is liable to be convicted summarily as a principal (*Du Cros v Lambourne* [1907] 1 KB 40, 70 JP 525). The prosecution must prove that the defendant knew that the driver was, by virtue of the speed the vehicle was travelling, driving dangerously at a time when there was an opportunity to intervene. It is the defendant's failure to take that opportunity and exercise his right as owner of the vehicle, which would lead to the inference that he was associating himself with the dangerous driving (*R v Webster* [2006] EWCA Crim 415, [2006] 2 Cr App R 6).

The defendant must deliver his driving licence to the clerk of the court prior to the hearing or produce it on conviction (Road Traffic Offenders Act 1988, s 7, post). See Road Traffic Offenders Act 1988, ss 1 and 2, post, imposing restrictions on prosecutions under this section (notice of intended prosecution etc).

2. See Preliminary Note to this title for notes on "driver" and "driving".

3. See s 2A below for meaning of "dangerous driving".

4. For punishment see Road Traffic Offenders Act 1988, Sch 2, post, and notes thereto; and for power to "reduce" dangerous driving to careless driving, see s 24(3) of the Road Traffic Offenders Act 1988, post. Sections 1, 11 and 12(1) of the Road Traffic Offenders Act 1988 apply. The court must order a person convicted under s 2 to be disqualified until he passes an appropriate test. In relation to reckless driving it had been held that, unlike the offence of careless driving, a consequence such as personal injury can be taken into account for the purpose of sentence (*R v Steel* (1993) 14 Cr App Rep (S) 218) [1993] RTR 415, 96 Cr App Rep 121).

4-1372   2A. Meaning of dangerous driving.   (1) For the purposes of sections 1 and 2 above a person is to be regarded as driving dangerously if (and, subject to subsection (2) below, only if)—

(*a*) the way he drives[1] falls far below[2] what would be expected of a competent and careful driver, and

(*b*) it would be obvious to a competent and careful driver that driving in that way[3] would be dangerous.

(2) A person is also to be regarded as driving dangerously for the purposes of sections 1 and 2 above if it would be obvious[4] to a competent and careful driver that driving the vehicle in its current state[5] would be dangerous.

(3) In subsections (1) and (2) above "dangerous" refers to danger either of injury to any person or of serious damage to property; and in determining for the purposes of those subsections what would be expected of, or obvious to, a competent and careful driver in a particular case, regard shall be had not only to the circumstances[6] of which he could be expected to be aware but also to any circumstances shown to have been within the knowledge of the accused.

(4) In determining for the purposes of subsection (2) above the state of a vehicle, regard may be had to anything attached to or carried on or in it and to the manner in which it is attached or carried.
[Road Traffic Act 1988, s 2A added by the Road Traffic Act 1991, s 1.]

---

1. Where a defendant put his foot on the accelerator when he intended to put his foot on the brake, he was conscious of what he was doing (though not of the possible consequences), his movements were not involuntary, and a mistake of that nature was covered by the offence of dangerous driving: *A-G's Reference (No 4 of 2000) (R v GC)* [2001] EWCA Crim 780, [2001] RTR 415.

2. In a case of causing death by dangerous driving where the issue is whether the driving was dangerous it is very important to keep in mind, however tragic the outcome, the high threshold that s 2A establishes for the commission of the offence: *R v Conteh* [2003] EWCA Crim 962, [2004] RTR 1.

3. Speed alone is not sufficient to found a conviction for dangerous driving. It has to be a question of speed in the context of all the circumstances (*DPP v Milton* [2006] EWHC 242 (Admin), 170 JP 319).

4. The danger is obvious only if it can be seen or realised at first glance, or is evident to the competent or careful driver (*R v Strong* [1995] Crim LR 428, CA—driver acquitted where he was not aware of corrosion defect which would only have been revealed by going underneath the car). For where the defendant has particular knowledge see sub-s (3). More might be expected of a professional driver than an ordinary motorist. Where he is an employee it is important to consider the instructions he had concerning checks to be made on the vehicle. Provided they were apparently reasonable it would be wrong to expect him to do more than he was instructed to do (*R v Roberts and George* [1997] RTR 462, [1997] Crim LR 209, CA).

5. The immunity for vehicles specially authorised by the Secretary of State under s 44 post does not apply per se to offences under s 1 such as where the driver had manoeuvred dangerously. Where the vehicle had been authorised by the Secretary of State and the danger lay in the inherent design rather than lack of maintenance or positive alteration it might not be appropriate to prosecute the user (*R v Marchant* [2003] EWCA Crim 2099, [2004] 1 All ER 1187, [2004] 1 WLR 442, [2004] RTR 231, [2003] Crim LR 806).

6. Evidence of consumption of alcohol is admissible but only where it is to the effect that the defendant had consumed such a quantity of alcohol as might adversely affect a driver (*R v Woodward* [1995] 3 All ER 79, [1995] 1 WLR 375, [1995] 2 Cr App Rep 388, CA and see *R v Millington* [1996] 1 Cr App Rep (S) 45, 160 JP 39, [1996] RTR 80, CA). Evidence of recent consumption of cocaine however, is per se relevant to the issue of driving dangerously in contrast to modest consumption of alcohol (*R v Pleydell* [2005] EWCA Crim 1447, [2006] 1 Cr App R 12, 169 JP 400, [2006] Crim LR 425). The condition of the driver, eg where it is attributable to drink, is relevant and admissible. But it is not conclusive and it does not determine whether the way in which the defendant drove was dangerous (*R v Webster* [2006] EWCA Crim 415, [2006] 2 Cr App R 6). Where a diabetic driver, aware that there was a real risk that he would have a sudden hypoglycaemic attack, started to drive and suffered such an attack which resulted in a crash, that fell within the definition of dangerous driving (*R v Marison* [1997] RTR 457, [1996] Crim LR 909, CA).

While evidence of an additional hazard posed by the driver having consumed alcohol may be admissible (see *R v Woodward*, supra) Hallett LJ, without forming a concluded view, appeared inclined to accept that evidence of the defendant's particularly excellent driving skills were not a matter relevant to the independent bystander test. Her Ladyship could see considerable force in the argument that Parliament did not intend to open the floodgates to the admission of evidence as to an accused's driving skills (*DPP v Milton* [2006] EWHC 242 (Admin), 170 JP 319).

4–1372A   2B. Causing death by careless, or inconsiderate, driving. A person who causes the death of another person by driving a mechanically propelled vehicle on a road or other public place without due care and attention, or without reasonable consideration for other persons using the road or place, is guilty of an offence.*
[Road Traffic Act 1988, s 2B as inserted by the Road Safety Act 2006, s 20.]

---

*Inserted by the Road Safety Act 2006, s 20 from a date to be appointed.

4–1373   3. Careless, and inconsiderate, driving[1]. If a person drives[2] a mechanically propelled vehicle on a road or other public place without due care and attention[3], or without reasonable consideration for other persons using the road or place[4], he is guilty of an offence[5].
[Road Traffic Act 1988, s 3 as substituted by the Road Traffic Act 1991, s 2.]

---

1. This section applies to trolley vehicles operated under statutory powers but not to tramcars (Sch 4, post). See Road Traffic Offenders Act 1988, ss 1 and 2, post, imposing restrictions on prosecutions under this section (notice of intended prosecution etc). As to aiding and abetting, see *Thornton v Mitchell* [1940] 1 All ER 339, 104 JP 108. Where an accident involves a death, a charge of careless driving should not be preferred until after the coroner's inquest has been concluded (*R v Beresford* (1952) 116 JP Jo 194). The inquest will not be adjourned solely by reason of the institution of such proceedings (Coroners Rules 1984, SI 1984/552). Sections 11 and 12(1) of the Road Traffic Offenders Act 1988 (evidence by certificate etc) apply.
2. See Preliminary Note to this title for notes on "driver" and "driving".
3. See Preliminary Note to this title, ante, where the authorities relevant to this expression are considered.
4. This subsection creates two offences and a conviction using the word "or" is bad for duplicity (*R v Surrey Justices, ex p Witherick* [1932] 1 KB 450, 95 JP 219). "Other persons using the road" extends to passengers in the vehicle and is not confined to persons outside it (*Pawley v Wharldall* [1966] 1 QB 373, [1965] 2 All ER 757, 129 JP 444). As to the procedure when charges are taken separately against the drivers of vehicles involved in a collision, see *R v Chambers* (1939) 83 Sol Jo 439, ante.
5. For punishment see Road Traffic Offenders Act 1988, Sch 2, post, and notes thereto. In cases where death results from an offence of careless driving, the court must bear in mind the context of a statutory regime for road traffic offences that envisages the causing of death as a factor leading to an enhanced statutory sentencing bracket and where the courts regard additional deaths as an aggravating factor. Accordingly it would be anomalous in a case of careless driving for the court to disregard the fact that a death has occurred. Whilst culpability or criminality remains the primary consideration, the court is entitled to bear in mind that it is dealing with an offence that led to death. The relatively limited criminality of careless driving is balanced by the limited penalties that can be imposed for it. These include disqualification which is not limited to repeat offenders (*R v Simmonds* [1999] 2 Cr App Rep 18, [1999] Crim LR 241, CA (defendant in his sixties, previous good character and an excellent driving record, fined £1000 and disqualified for 1 year)). See also *R v King* [2001] EWCA Crim 709, [2001] 2 Cr App Rep (S) 503, [2002] RTR 1, (HGV driver with good driving record ploughed into slow-moving traffic on a straight road in good visibility killing 3 persons and causing a multiple pile-up, pleaded guilty and originally fined £2,250 and disqualified for 3 years, but reduced on appeal to £1,500 and 2 years, respectively).

4–1374   3A. Causing death by careless driving when under influence of drink or drugs.
(1) If a person causes the death of another person by driving a mechanically propelled vehicle on a road or other public place without due care and attention, or without reasonable consideration for other persons using the road or place, and—

(a) he is, at the time when he is driving, unfit to drive through drink or drugs, or
(b) he has consumed so much alcohol that the proportion of it in his breath, blood or urine at that time exceeds the prescribed limit, or
(c) he is, within 18 hours after that time, required to provide a specimen in pursuance of section 7 of this Act, but without reasonable excuse fails to provide it,

he is guilty of an offence[1].
(2) For the purposes of this section a person shall be taken to be unfit to drive at any time when his ability to drive properly is impaired.
(3) Subsection (1)(b) and (c) above shall not apply in relation to a person driving a mechanically propelled vehicle other than a motor vehicle.
[Road Traffic Act 1988, s 3A as added by the Road Traffic Act 1991, s 3.]

---

1. This offence is triable only on indictment (Road Traffic Offenders Act 1988, Sch 2). See comments on procedure and jurisdiction noted to s 1 ante which in our view apply also to this offence.

4–1374A   3ZA. Meaning of careless, or inconsiderate, driving. (1) This section has effect for the purposes of sections 2B and 3 above and section 3A below.

(2) A person is to be regarded as driving without due care and attention if (and only if) the way he drives falls below what would be expected of a competent and careful driver.

(3) In determining for the purposes of subsection (2) above what would be expected of a careful and competent driver in a particular case, regard shall be had not only to the circumstances of which he could be expected to be aware but also to any circumstances shown to have been within the knowledge of the accused.

(4) A person is to be regarded as driving without reasonable consideration for other persons only if those persons are inconvenienced by his driving.*

[Road Traffic Act 1988, s 3ZA as inserted by the Road Safety Act 2006, s 30.]

*Inserted by the Road Safety Act 2006, s 30 from a date to be appointed.

4-1374B 3ZB. Causing death by driving: unlicensed, disqualified or uninsured drivers. A person is guilty of an offence under this section if he causes the death of another person by driving a motor vehicle on a road and, at the time when he is driving, the circumstances are such that he is committing an offence under—

    (a) section 87(1) of this Act (driving otherwise than in accordance with a licence),

    (b) section 103(1)(b) of this Act (driving while disqualified), or

    (c) section 143 of this Act (using motor vehicle while uninsured or unsecured against third party risks).*

[Road Traffic Act 1988, s 2ZB as inserted by the Road Safety Act 2006, s 21.]

*Inserted by the Road Safety Act 2006, s 21 from a date to be appointed.

Motor vehicles: drink and drugs

4-1375 4. Driving, or being in charge, when under influence of drink or drugs. (1) A person who, when driving[1] or attempting to drive a mechanically propelled vehicle[2] on a road or other public place[3], is unfit to drive through drink or drugs[4] is guilty of an offence[7].

(2) Without prejudice to subsection (1) above, a person who, when in charge[5] of a mechanically propelled vehicle which is on a road or other public place, is unfit to drive through drink or drugs[6] is guilty of an offence[7].

(3) For the purposes of subsection (2) above, a person shall be deemed not to have been in charge of a mechanically propelled vehicle if he proves[8] that at the material time the circumstances were such that there was no likelihood of his driving it so long as he remained unfit to drive through drink or drugs.

(4) The court may, in determining whether there was such a likelihood as is mentioned in subsection (3) above, disregard any injury to him and any damage to the vehicle.

(5) For the purposes of this section, a person shall be taken to be unfit to drive if his ability to drive properly is for the time being impaired.

(6) *Repealed.*

(7) *Repealed.*

(8) Scotland.

[Road Traffic Act 1988, s 4 as amended by the Road Traffic Act 1991, s 4 and the Serious Organised Crime and Police Act 2005, Sch 7.]

1. See Headnote to this title for note on "driver" and "driving". Sections 11 and 12(1) of the Road Traffic Offenders Act 1988 (evidence by certificate etc) apply.

2. This subsection applies to trolley vehicles operated under statutory powers, but not to tramcars (Sch 4, post).

3. The other public place need not be a road. It must, however, be a place to which the public have access, eg a field to which the public are admitted on a certain day (*R v Collinson* (1931) 23 Cr App Rep 49); or a public house car park (*Elkins v Cartlidge* [1947] 1 All ER 829); or a multi-storey car park at a time when there was no barrier restricting entrance (*Bowman v DPP* [1991] RTR 263; but not such a car park at a time when the owner does not permit parking, eg out of licensing hours (*Sandy v Martin* (1974) 139 JP 241); nor land open only to the members and guests of a proprietary club (*Pugh v Knipe* [1972] RTR 286, nor to the car park of a private members' club (*Havell v DPP* (1993) 158 JP 680, [1993] Crim LR 621)). As to appropriate use of "road" in the charge where the vehicle left the road and collided with a stationary object, see *Redman v Taylor* [1975] Crim LR 348 and *Lewis v Ursell* (1983) Times, 23 April.

4. For admission of analytical evidence regarding the presence of alcohol or drug in the body of the accused, see the Road Traffic Offenders Act 1988, s 16, post, which, in its previous corresponding form, was considered in *R v Somers* [1963] 3 All ER 808, and in *R v Richards* [1974] QB 776, [1974] 3 All ER 696, 138 JP 789, where it was also stated to be in the interests of an accused person to be able to call evidence to show that the alcoholic level in his blood at the time the specimen was taken did not reflect the level at the time he was driving (s 4(1)), or in charge of (s 4(2)) the vehicle. The prosecution must prove not only the influence, but also that the defendant was thereby impaired in the proper control of this vehicle: see *R v Hawkes* (1931) 22 Cr App Rep 172. Intoximeter readings that are inadmissible on a charge of driving with excess alcohol, because the suspect failed to provide sufficient breath, may not be adduced in evidence to support a charge of driving whilst unfit through drink (*Willicott v DPP* [2001] EWHC Admin 415, (2002) 166 JP 385). The evidence of a medical man who has examined the defendant at the request of the police is admissible, even where he has used persuasion to overcome the defendant's refusal to be examined. "His evidence should be accepted as that of a professional man giving independent expert evidence with a desire to assist the court" (*per* Humphreys J, in *R v Nowell* [1948] 1 All ER 794, 112 JP 255, disagreeing with a Scottish case of *Reid v Nixon, Dumigan v Brown* 1948 SN 17), but the court should not be directed that his evidence ought therefore to be accepted in the absence of reasons for rejecting them. Such a direction would give a false impression of the weight to be attached to it (*per* Diplock J, in *R v Lanfear* [1968] 2 QB 77, [1968] 1 All ER 683, 132 JP 193). Evidence by a non-expert witness of the accused's condition may be given; but that witness's opinion that the accused was or was not fit to have control of a motor vehicle is inadmissible (*R v Davies* [1962] 3 All ER 97, 128 JP 455). A conviction for driving while under the influence of "drink or a drug . . ." is not bad for uncertainty (*Thomson v Knights* [1947] KB 336, [1947] 1 All ER 112, 111 JP 43). A driver who has wantonly caused

bodily harm can be prosecuted under the Offences against the Person Act 1861, s 35, in PART VII, PERSONS, OFFENCES AGAINST, ante (*R v Burdon* (1926) 20 Cr App Rep 80).

For the purposes of this section, a substance used as a medicine is a drug: an offence would be committed by, eg a person suffering from hypoglycæmic coma due to the over-action of a usual and prescribed insulin injection (*Armstrong v Clark* [1957] 2 QB 391, [1957] 1 All ER 433, 121 JP 193), a decision to be contrasted with that in *Watmore v Jenkins* [1962] 2 QB 572, [1962] 2 All ER 868, 126 JP 432, in which it was held, on special facts, that there was reasonable doubt whether the injected insulin was more than a predisposing or historical cause comprised in a situation or state of equilibrium on which the reduction of cortisone operated as an effective cause of the hypoglycæmic episode. See also *R v Ealing Magistrates' Court, ex p Woodman* [1994] RTR 189, 158 JP 997, [1994] Crim LR 372 (defendant a diabetic suffering hypoglycaemic attack—failure to follow medical advice not sufficient evidence to establish that the injection of insulin was the real effective cause of the defendant's unfitness to drive).

5. There is no hard and fast all-embracing test as to the meaning of "in charge". If the defendant is the owner or lawful possessor of the vehicle or has recently driven it he is prima facie in charge unless he has put the vehicle in someone else's charge; if he is not the owner, lawful possessor or recent driver, but is sitting in the vehicle or is otherwise involved with it, the question is whether he has assumed being in charge of it. The following circumstances will be relevant: (i) whether and where he is in the vehicle or how far he is from it; (ii) what he is doing at the relevant time; (iii) whether he is in possession of a key that fits the ignition; (iv) whether there is evidence of an intention to take or assert control of the car by driving or otherwise; (v) whether any other person is in, at, or near the vehicle and if so the like particulars in respect of that person. It will be for the court to consider all the above factors with any others which may be relevant and reach its decision as a question of fact and degree (*DPP v Watkins* [1989] QB 821, [1989] 1 All ER 1126).

6. The constituent chemicals of an adhesive, in particular toluene, are drugs for this purpose when deliberately inhaled by a "glue-sniffer" (*Bradford v Wilson* [1983] Crim LR 482).

7. For punishment see Road Traffic Offenders Act 1988, Sch 2 and notes thereto, post and see s 5 of that Act for restrictions on prosecutions under the Licensing Act 1872.

8. See note to s 5(2), post. Note also the assumption to be made by virtue of s 15(2) of the Road Traffic Offenders Act 1988, post. An arresting constable is not required to regard sub-s (3) in order to make the arrest valid or lawful (*R v Moore* [1975] RTR 285—removal of rotor arm). Case law earlier than the amendment of the Road Traffic Act 1972, s 5 by the Transport Act 1981 should be read subject to that amendment which enables courts to disregard injury to the defendant and damage to the vehicle in determining whether or not there was likelihood of his driving.

9. This power of arrest is preserved by the Police and Criminal Evidence Act 1984, s 26 and Sch 2. The power of arrest under this provision does not fall away where the police have embarked on administering a breath test in accordance with s 6. If the result of the test is negative, that would be a factor in whether there was reasonable cause to suspect the commission of an offence contrary to s 4 in order to effect an arrest under s 4(6) eg in the light of subsequent observations of the accused's conduct or demeanour (*DPP v Robertson* [2002] EWHC 542 (Admin), 166 JP 649, [2002] Crim LR 589, [2002] RTR 383).

4–1376   **5. Driving or being in charge of a motor vehicle with alcohol concentration above prescribed limit.**   (1) If a person—

(*a*)   drives[1] or attempts[2] to drive a motor vehicle on a road or other public place[3], or

(*b*)   is in charge of a motor vehicle on a road or other public place[3].

after consuming[4] so much alcohol that the proportion of it in his breath[5], blood or urine exceeds the prescribed limit[6] he is guilty of an offence[7].

(2) It is a defence for a person charged with an offence under subsection (1)(*b*) above to prove[8] that at the time he is alleged to have committed the offence the circumstances were such that there was no likelihood of his driving the vehicle whilst the proportion of alcohol in his breath, blood or urine remained likely to exceed the prescribed limit.

(3) The court may, in determining whether there was such a likelihood as is mentioned in subsection (2) above, disregard any injury to him and any damage[8] to the vehicle.
[Road Traffic Act 1988, s 5.]

---

1. Sections 11 and 12(1) of the Road Traffic Offenders Act 1988 (evidence by certificate etc) apply. It is not necessary for the prosecution to prove that the defendant drove *after* consuming excess alcohol; if it is proved or admitted that the defendant was driving, and that the specimen he gave was over the prescribed limit, the burden is then on the defendant, if he so chooses, to displace the assumption under s 15(2), post, that he was over the limit at the time when he drove (*Patterson v Charlton* (1985) 150 JP 29, [1986] RTR 18). Where both occupants of a vehicle are charged under s 5(1)(*a*) as principals, in accordance with s 44 of the Magistrates' Courts Act 1980, on the basis that one drove and the other aided and abetted the offence, it may not matter that the prosecutor is unable to prove who was the driver, provided there is evidence of a joint enterprise and, on the part of both, knowledge that each other had had too much to drink to be fit to drive or recklessness as to whether or not the driver had an excess amount of alcohol in his blood; see *Smith v Mellors* (1987) 84 Cr App Rep 279, [1987] RTR 210, [1987] Crim LR 421.

2. An attempt is a combination of an intention to do something and action directed towards accomplishing the event which failed to produce it, and it is not necessary to prove that the full offence is capable of achievement. See *R v Farrance* [1978] RTR 225, 67 Cr App Rep 136, and commentary thereon at Crim LR 496. There is no need for a constable's suspicion that the alcohol level might be above the prescribed limit to have arisen at a time when the defendant was driving (*Blake v Pope* [1986] 3 All ER 185, [1986] 1 WLR 1152).

3. See note to "road or other public place" in s 4 ante.

4. Alcohol may be consumed otherwise than by drinking; see *DPP v Johnson* [1994] Crim LR 601, [1995] RTR 9, [1995] 1 WLR 728. In this case an injection of the drug Kenalog, a month before the date of the alleged offence, amounted to consumption.

5. "Breath" means "air exhaled from anything", and that is the definition to adopt when construing "breath" in this provision; the term is not, therefore, limited to "deep lung air" so as to exclude "mouth alcohol": *Zafar v DPP* [2004] EWHC Div 2468, (2005) 169 JP 208, [2005] RTR 18, followed in *Woolfe v DPP* [2006] EWHC 1497 (Admin), [2007] RTR 16.

6. See s 11(1) post for the prescribed limits and see the Road Traffic Offenders Act 1988, ss 15 and 16 for provisions as to evidence; on a guilty plea, the court is not entitled to insist on the production of the original printout from a Lion Intoximeter (*R v Tower Bridge Magistrates' Court, ex p DPP* [1988] RTR 193).

Evidence which is material to the question of what was the proportion of alcohol at the moment of driving is admissible, and s 15 of the Road Traffic Offenders Act 1988, post, does not preclude evidence other than that revealed by a specimen. Accordingly, evidence may be admitted to show, by back-calculation, that the defendant's alcohol level was higher at the time of the offence than subsequently shown by a specimen of breath, blood or urine. However, the prosecution should not seek to rely on evidence of back-calculation unless that evidence is easily understood and clearly persuasive of the presence of excess alcohol at the time of the alleged offence (*Gumbley v Cunningham* [1989] AC 281, [1989] 1 All ER 5, [1989] RTR 49, HL).

In *Oswald v DPP* (1989) 153 JP 590, reference was made to the "common practice" of deducting six milligrams of alcohol from the results of blood-alcohol analysis "to allow for a margin of error"; the court is not bound to "round down" to the nearest whole milligram.

Where a sample of blood is split by a laboratory into a number of sub-samples for analysis it is lawful to use the average result and not necessary to use the lowest result (*DPP v Welsh* (1996) 161 JP 57, DC).

7. For punishment see the Road Traffic Offenders Act 1988, Sch 2 and notes thereto, post. The prosecution must specify in the information whether the excess of alcohol is in breath, blood or urine as appropriate; a charge in which the alternatives have not been deleted is duplicitous (*R v Bolton Justices, ex p Khan* [1999] Crim LR 912). Where the charge is aiding and abetting, it is sufficient if the defendant was aware that the principal offender had consumed excessive alcohol, even though the precise amount was not known (*Carter v Richardson* [1974] RTR 314, [1974] Crim LR 190). A person who surreptitiously laces a friend's drinks thus causing his later conviction can himself be convicted of aiding, abetting, counselling and procuring; the last of these elements does not require any shared intention (*Re A-G's Reference (No 1 of 1975)* [1975] QB 773, [1975] 2 All ER 684, 139 JP 569, and see also note to "special reasons" in s 34 of the Road Traffic Offenders Act 1988, post for other cases on "laced drinks").

8. In *Sheldrake v DPP* [2004] UKHL 43, [2005] 1 All ER 237, [2004] 3 WLR 976, [2005] RTR 13 the House of Lords held (reversing the decision of the Divisional Court) that s 5(2) imposed a legal burden on a defendant who was charged with an offence contrary to s 5(1)(*b*) and that the offence under s 5(1)(*b*) did not require proof that the defendant was likely to drive whilst unfit, but the defendant was given the opportunity by s 5(2) to exonerate himself if he could show that there was no such likelihood. The likelihood of the defendant driving was a matter so closely conditioned by his own knowledge and state of mind at the material time as to make it much more appropriate for him to prove on the balance of probabilities that he would not have been likely to drive than for the prosecution to prove, beyond reasonable doubt, that he would. The imposition of a legal burden upon the defendant did not go beyond what was necessary and reasonable, and was not in any way arbitrary.

Where the court is addressing the question of the rate of decline of alcohol in a person's blood over a given period, it will be unlikely to be able to reach a conclusion without the assistance of expert medical or scientific evidence; see *DPP v Frost* [1989] RTR 11, 153 JP 405.

Although there may be circumstances in which a person who was supervising a learner driver, and who was for the purposes of s 5(1)(*b*) in charge of the motor vehicle, may nevertheless establish that as a matter of fact there was no likelihood of driving, the supervisor will usually have a difficult task in proving that was so given that the very statutory purpose of having a person supervising the holder of a provisional driving licence is because they are a provisional driver and by statute not yet regarded as competent to drive on their own: *DPP v Janman* [2004] EWHC 101 (Admin), [2004] RTR 31, [2004] Crim LR 478. Where a person has assumed the role of supervisor of a learner driver it is unnecessary for the prosecution to adduce evidence that he met the legal criteria for supervising learning drivers: *DPP v Janman*, supra.

8. A wheel clamp cannot be disregarded as amounting to damage to the vehicle for the purposes of this subsection; see *Drake v DPP* [1994] RTR 411, [1994] Crim LR 855.

4–1377   **6. Power to administer preliminary tests[1].** (1) If any of subsections (2) to (5) applies a constable may require[2] a person to co-operate with any one or more preliminary tests[3] administered to the person by that constable or another constable.

(2) This subsection applies if a constable reasonably suspects[4] that the person—

(*a*) is driving, is attempting[5] to drive or is in charge of a motor vehicle on a road or other public place[6], and

(*b*) has alcohol or a drug[7] in his body or is under the influence of a drug.

(3) This subsection applies if a constable reasonably suspects[4] that the person—

(*a*) has been driving, attempting[5] to drive or in charge of a motor vehicle on a road or other public place[6] while having alcohol or a drug[7] in his body or while unfit to drive because of a drug, and

(*b*) still has alcohol or a drug[7] in his body or is still under the influence of a drug.

(4) This subsection applies if a constable reasonably suspects[4] that the person—

(*a*) is or has been driving, attempting[5] to drive or in charge of a motor vehicle on a road or other public place[6], and

(*b*) has committed a traffic offence[3] while the vehicle was in motion.

(5) This subsection applies if—

(*a*) an accident[8] occurs owing to the presence of a motor vehicle on a road or other public place[6], and

(*b*) a constable reasonably believes that the person was driving, attempting to drive or in charge of the vehicle at the time of the accident[8].

(6) A person commits an offence[9] if without reasonable excuse[10] he fails[11] to co-operate with a preliminary test in pursuance of a requirement imposed under this section.

(7) A constable may administer a preliminary test[3] by virtue of any of subsections (2) to (4) only if he is in uniform[12].

(8) In this section—

(*a*) a reference to a preliminary test is to any of the tests described in sections 6A to 6C, and

(*b*) "traffic offence" means an offence under—

(i)   a provision of Part II of the Public Passenger Vehicles Act 1981 (c 14),

(ii)   a provision of the Road Traffic Regulation Act 1984 (c 27),

(iii) a provision of the Road Traffic Offenders Act 1988 (c 53) other than a provision of Part III, or

(iv) a provision of this Act other than a provision of Part V.

[Road Traffic Act 1988, s 6 as substituted by the Railways and Transport Safety Act 2003, Sch 7.]

1. The provisions for preliminary breath tests under the substituted s 6 and ss 6A–6E came into force on 30 March 2004. The privilege against self-incrimination implied into art 6(2) of the European Convention on Human Rights does not extend to the provision of breath, blood, urine or other samples: *Saunders v United Kingdom* (1996) 23 EHRR 313, para 69.

2. The word "require" does not have to be used; all that is necessary is that the constable's language could fairly be said to amount to a requirement (*R v O'Boyle* [1973] RTR 445).

3. Defined in sub-s (8) post.

4. The following cases were decided under the former law based on a constable's having 'reasonable cause to suspect' that a driver had alcohol in his body. Evidence must be adduced to establish a reasonable cause to suspect alcohol (*Griffiths v Willett* [1979] RTR 195): a court may not infer reasonable grounds from the mere fact of asking for a breath test (*Siddiqui v Swain* [1979] RTR 454, [1979] Crim LR 318). There is no objection in law to a constable forming a reasonable suspicion from what another said, even from anonymous information, and it is admissible for him to say so: see *Moss v Jenkins* [1975] RTR 25 and *DPP v Wilson* [1991] RTR 284, [1991] Crim LR 441. Provided there is no malpractice, there is no restriction on the random stopping of motorists, but the subsequent requirement of a breath test can only be made if the constable has reasonable cause to suspect the ingestion of alcohol (*Chief Constable of Gwent v Dash* [1986] RTR 41, [1985] Crim LR 674) and see *DPP v McGladrigan* [1991] RTR 297, 155 JP 785. There is no obligation to warn the potential offender of the potential offence and failure to do so is not oppressive (*DPP v Wilson*, supra). There is no need for a constable's suspicion that the alcohol level might be above the prescribed limit to have arisen at a time when the defendant was driving (*Blake v Pope* [1986] 3 All ER 185, [1986] 1 WLR 1152). The fact that a person is seen to drive out of a public house car park does not in itself give rise to grounds to suspect a drink driving offence; accordingly, to question such a person about whether he has been drinking does not engage paras 10 and 11 of Code C and, therefore, a prior caution is unnecessary (*Sneyd v DPP* [2006] EWHC 560 (Admin), (2006) 170 JP 545, [2007] RTR 7).

5. An attempt is a combination of an intention to do something and action directed towards accomplishing the event which failed to produce it, and it is not necessary to prove that the full offence is capable of achievement. See *R v Farrance* (1978) 67 Cr App R 136, [1978] RTR 225, and commentary thereon at Crim LR 496 and see now the Criminal Attempts Act 1981, in PART I: MAGISTRATES' COURTS, PROCEDURE.

6. See note to "road or other public place" in s 4(1) ante. Sections 11 and 12(1) of the Road Traffic Offenders Act 1988 (evidence by certificate etc) apply.

7. Defined in s 11(2), post.

8. In *R v Morris* [1972] 1 All ER 384, [1972] 1 WLR 228, 136 JP 194, "accident", in relation to the particular facts of that case, was held to mean an unintended occurrence which has an adverse physical result. In *Chief Constable of West Midlands Police v Billingham* [1979] 2 All ER 182, [1979] RTR 446, it was held that the word "accident" should be given its ordinary popular meaning and not a technical one; accordingly an accident was held to have occurred in relation to a car which, having been left parked on a slope, was set in motion by a mischievous person and suffered damage; and also in a case where a car was deliberately driven into a gate (*Chief Constable of Staffordshire v Lees* [1981] RTR 506, (1981) 145 JP 208).

There must be a direct cause or connection between the motor vehicle and the occurrence of the accident; see *Quelch v Phipps* [1955] 2 QB 107, [1955] 2 All ER 302, 119 JP 430. The issue whether an accident has occurred is a question of fact (*R v Seward* [1970] 1 All ER 329, 134 JP 195); but if the primary facts are not in dispute the question of accident or no is a matter of law (*R v Morris*, supra).

9. For penalty see the Road Traffic Offenders Act 1988, Sch 2, post.

10. Such as a medical condition (*Hirst v Wilson* [1969] 3 All ER 1566; *R v Lennard* [1973] 2 All ER 831, 137 JP 585). A genuine but mistaken belief that a police officer is not acting bona fide is not a reasonable excuse (*McGrath v Vipas* [1984] RTR 58). The defendant must adduce sufficient evidence, including cross-examination where appropriate; once the defence is so raised, the onus is on the prosecution to negative it (*Parker v Smith* [1974] RTR 500, [1974] Crim LR 426) and see *Dawes v Taylor* [1986] RTR 81. For cases on what can constitute a reasonable excuse, see note to s 7(6) post, bearing in mind the fact that until 6 May 1983 the case law related to failure to provide a blood or urine specimen.

11. "Fail" includes "refuse" (s 11(2), post). See also s 11(3), post and notes thereto. A refusal to provide a specimen can be inferred from the defendant's conduct (see *R v Mackey* [1977] RTR 146); see also *R v Miles* [1979] RTR 509.

12. See *Wallwork v Giles* [1970] RTR 117 (policeman in uniform except for helmet nevertheless "in uniform") and *Taylor v Baldwin* [1976] RTR 265, [1976] Crim LR 137 (raincoat over uniform). In the absence of evidence to the contrary, a court is entitled to assume that the police officer was in uniform (*Richards v West* [1980] RTR 215—a special constable). See also *Gage v Jones* [1983] RTR 508.

4–1377A   6A. Preliminary breath test.   (1) A preliminary breath test is a procedure whereby the person to whom the test is administered provides a specimen of breath to be used for the purpose of obtaining, by means of a device of a type approved[1] by the Secretary of State, an indication whether the proportion of alcohol in the person's breath or blood is likely to exceed the prescribed limit[2].

(2) A preliminary breath test administered in reliance on section 6(2) to (4) may be administered only at or near the place where the requirement to co-operate with the test is imposed.

(3) A preliminary breath test administered in reliance on section 6(5) may be administered—

(a) at or near the place where the requirement to co-operate with the test is imposed, or

(b) if the constable who imposes the requirement thinks it expedient, at a police station specified by him.

[Road Traffic Act 1988, s 6A as inserted by the Railways and Transport Safety Act 2003, Sch 7.]

1. The following approval orders have been made under s 11(2) the relevant provision of which has been repealed.

Breath Test Device Approval 1999 as from 15 October 1999 the type of device known as the **Alcosensor IV UK** manufactured by Intoximeters UK Ltd.

Breath Test Device Approval 2000 as from 25 February 2000 the type of device known as the Lion Alcometer SL-400A (indicating display form), manufactured by Lion Laboratories plc. As to the instruction that the mouthpiece should not be reused, the relevant paragraph of the instructions does not clearly indicate that a mouthpiece must be disposed of after a suspect has failed tp provide sufficient breath for analysis (see *DPP v Kennedy* [2003] EWHC 2583 (Admin), 168 JP 185).

Breath Test Device Approval (No 2) 2000 as from 12 December 2002 the type of device known as the **Lion Alcolmeter SL 400B** manufactured by Lion Laboratories.

Authorities on earlier devices are set out below as they may be of assistance in interpreting requirements for the use of the modern machines. "**Alcotest 80**" and "**Alcotest 80A**" have been approved by Breath Test Device Approval Orders in 1968 and 1975 respectively The requirement of a breath test must start with a device fitted with a new and unsullied tube (*Price v Davies* [1979] RTR 204). The instructions on the device state that the bag must be filled by one single breath in not less than 10 and not more than 20 seconds. In *R v Chapman* [1969] 2 QB 436, [1969] 2 All ER 321, 133 JP 405, the Court of Appeal intimated that the Secretary of State's approval embraced the instructions of how the test was to be taken;

so that if a person took more than one blow he had failed to take the test in the manner prescribed. The manufacturer's instructions as to the use of the device should be followed, but provided the device is assembled correctly and the constable administering the test is acting bona fide and the test, on the information within his knowledge, is not likely to give a falsely high reading, then a departure from the instructions will not invalidate the test (*DPP v Carey* [1970] AC 1072, [1969] 3 All ER 1662, 133 JP 633; followed in *DPP v Kay* (1998) 163 JP 108, [1999] RTR 109, DC (SL400 breath testing device)). Breach of instructions about a single breath is to be regarded as not potentially prejudicial to the driver and does not vitiate the test (*A-G's Reference (No 1 of 1978)* [1978] RTR 377, 67 Cr App Rep 387). Although the manufacturer's instruction require the bag to be filled, by virtue of s 12(3) if the breath test is positive then, notwithstanding the bag was not filled, a specimen *has* been provided and an arrest for failing to provide a specimen under s 6(5) will probably be invalid (*R v Holah* [1973] 1 All ER 106, 137 JP 106; *Walker v Lovell* [1975] 3 All ER 107, 139 JP 708; followed in *Spicer v Holt* [1976] 3 All ER 71, 140 JP 545). These cases establish that if *some* breath goes into the bag the constable must inspect the crystals so that he can decide whether to make an arrest under s 6(5). But if *no* breath goes into the bag the constable is not required to inspect the crystals before making an arrest (*Stoddart v Balls* [1977] RTR 113, [1977] Crim LR 171; *Seneviratne v Bishop* [1978] RTR 92). The same principle would seem to apply where only a minimal amount of air goes into the bag (*R v Rey* [1978] RTR 413, 67 Cr App Rep 244). Where a bag was fully inflated by several short puffs, producing a negative result, it was held the defendant had failed to provide a specimen of breath for a breath test (*R v Littell* [1981] 3 All ER 1, [1981] 1 WLR 1146, 145 JP 451, CA). Where a defendant was arrested after failing fully to inflate a bag which showed a negative result, it was held that it was irrelevant to the validity of that arrest that 15 minutes later the crystals in the bag were found to have changed colour (*Kelly v Dolbey* [1984] RTR 67).

One of the instructions states that at least 20 minutes should elapse between the consumption of alcoholic liquor and using the device. In *DPP v Carey* (supra), it was stated that a police officer is under no obligation to enquire whether the suspect has been drinking within the previous 20 minutes; but if he knows that this is the case, or there are facts which make it probable, or the suspect so informs him, he must wait until 20 minutes have elapsed since the last drink before using the device; if the suspect refuses to wait he may be arrested for failing to supply a specimen of breath. But note *R v Aspden* [1975] RTR 456 where it was held that if the constable thinks it possible that no drink had been consumed within 20 minutes, notwithstanding that the defendant says he last drank "about fifteen minutes ago" an immediate breath test is valid; followed in *R v Moore* [1979] RTR 98.

For interpretation of instruction that the motorist is not to smoke "immediately" before the test, see *R v Gordon Wilson* (1973) 137 JP Jo 782. Smoking would be irrelevant unless it was so immediate as to raise a real possibility of contaminating the specimen (*Darnell v Portal* [1972] RTR 483, [1972] Crim LR 511; as explained in *Watkinson v Barley* [1975] 1 All ER 316, 139 JP 203, and *A-G's Reference (No 2 of 1974)* [1975] 1 All ER 658, 139 JP 267). Where the motorist has been smoking the police officer should examine the crystals in the breathalyser device and give evidence of what he observed, not merely that the test was "positive": see *R v Callum* [1975] RTR 415; *Butcher v Catterall* (1975) 119 Sol Jo 508.

There is a presumption that the constable acted in good faith and reasonably which may be rebutted (*Rendall v Hooper* [1970] 2 All ER 72, 134 JP 441). Approval need not be the personal approval of the Minister but may be given by the appropriate departmental official (*R v Skinner* [1968] 2 QB 700, [1968] 3 All ER 124, 132 JP 484). Production of a copy of the Order published and printed by HM Stationery Office is *prima facie* evidence of approval (*R v Clarke* [1969] 2 QB 91, [1969] 1 All ER 924, 133 JP 282). In *R v Jones* [1969] 3 All ER 1559, 134 JP 124, the Court of Appeal held that a court (including a jury) is entitled to take judicial notice that the Alcotest device is an approved type as the number of cases in which it had been proved was large and widely reported. To prove that the device used was the approved device it is not necessary to produce the device used; and evidence of a police officer that on the container of the device was the name of the approved device is some evidence of the nature of the device itself (*Miller v Howe* [1969] 3 All ER 451, 133 JP 665).

Further devices known as the "**Alcolyser**" and the "**Alcolmeter**" were approved in 1979. In *Horton v Twells* (1983) Times, 9 December, where the defendant has had his last drink ten minutes earlier and insisted on a breath test without waiting the further ten minutes required when using an Alcolmeter device, the court should have considered whether the police officer was acting bona fide in administering the test: the court suggested as well that where police officers were faced with a person who refused to wait 20 minutes before a test, they should arrest for failing to provide a specimen of breath.

Manufacturers' instructions for the Lion Alcometer S-L2 are not breached by the fact that the "READ" button is not kept depressed for the full 40 seconds where a red light indicating a positive reading comes on at once (*Woon v Maskell* [1985] RTR 289).

2. Defined in s 11(2), post.

4-1377B   6B. Preliminary impairment test.   (1) A preliminary impairment test is a procedure whereby the constable administering the test—

(a) observes the person to whom the test is administered in his performance of tasks specified by the constable, and

(b) makes such other observations of the person's physical state as the constable thinks expedient.

(2) The Secretary of State shall issue (and may from time to time revise) a code of practice about—

(a) the kind of task that may be specified for the purpose of a preliminary impairment test,

(b) the kind of observation of physical state that may be made in the course of a preliminary impairment test,

(c) the manner in which a preliminary impairment test should be administered, and

(d) the inferences that may be drawn from observations made in the course of a preliminary impairment test.

(3) In issuing or revising the code of practice the Secretary of State shall aim to ensure that a preliminary impairment test is designed to indicate—

(a) whether a person is unfit to drive, and

(b) if he is, whether or not his unfitness is likely to be due to drink or drugs[1].

(4) A preliminary impairment test may be administered—

(a) at or near the place where the requirement to co-operate with the test is imposed, or

(b) if the constable who imposes the requirement thinks it expedient, at a police station specified by him.

(5) A constable administering a preliminary impairment test shall have regard to the code of practice under this section.

(6) A constable may administer a preliminary impairment test only if he is approved for that purpose by the chief officer of the police force to which he belongs.

(7) A code of practice under this section may include provision about—

(a) the giving of approval under subsection (6), and

(b) in particular, the kind of training that a constable should have undergone, or the kind of qualification that a constable should possess, before being approved under that subsection.

[Road Traffic Act 1988, s 6B as inserted by the Railways and Transport Safety Act 2003, Sch 7.]

---

1. Defined in s 11(2), post.

4–1377C   6C. Preliminary drug test.   (1) A preliminary drug test is a procedure by which a specimen of sweat or saliva is—

(a) obtained, and

(b) used for the purpose of obtaining, by means of a device of a type approved[1] by the Secretary of State, an indication whether the person to whom the test is administered has a drug[2] in his body.

(2) A preliminary drug test may be administered—

(a) at or near the place where the requirement to co-operate with the test is imposed, or

(b) if the constable who imposes the requirement thinks it expedient, at a police station specified by him.

[Road Traffic Act 1988, s 6C as inserted by the Railways and Transport Safety Act 2003, Sch 7.]

---

1. At the date of going to press no approval orders had been made.
2. Defined in s 11(2), post.

4–1377D   6D. Arrest.   (1) A constable may arrest a person without warrant if as a result of a preliminary breath test[1] the constable reasonably suspects[2] that the proportion of alcohol in the person's breath or blood exceeds the prescribed limit[3].

(1A) The fact that specimens of breath have been provided under section 7 of this Act by the person concerned does not prevent subsection (1) above having effect if the constable who imposed on him the requirement to provide the specimens has reasonable cause to believe that the device used to analyse the specimens has not produced a reliable indication of the proportion of alcohol in the breath of the person.

(2) A constable may arrest a person without warrant if—

(a) the person fails to co-operate with a preliminary test in pursuance of a requirement imposed under section 6, and

(b) the constable reasonably suspects[2] that the person has alcohol or a drug in his body or is under the influence of a drug[3].

(2A) A person arrested under this section may, instead of being taken to a police station, be detained at or near the place where the preliminary test was, or would have been, administered, with a view to imposing on him there a requirement under section 7 of this Act.

(3) A person may not be arrested under this section while at a hospital as a patient[4].

[Road Traffic Act 1988, s 6D as inserted by the Railways and Transport Safety Act 2003, Sch 7 and amended by the Serious Organised Crime and Police Act 2005, s 154.]

---

1. See s 6A, ante.
2. See note to 'reasonably suspects' in s 6, ante.
3. Defined in s 11(2), post.
4. See post, s 9 for procedure at hospital.

4–1377E   6E. Power of entry.   (1) A constable may enter any place (using reasonable force if necessary) for the purpose of—

(a) imposing a requirement by virtue of section 6(5) following an accident in a case where the constable reasonably suspects that the accident involved injury of any person, or

(b) arresting a person under section 6D following an accident in a case where the constable reasonably suspects that the accident involved injury of any person.

(2) Scotland.

[Road Traffic Act 1988, s 6E as inserted by the Railways and Transport Safety Act 2003, Sch 7.]

4–1378   7. Provision of specimens for analysis.   (1) In the course of an investigation[1] into whether a person has committed an offence under section 3A, 4 or 5 of this Act a constable[2] may, subject to the following provisions of this section[3] and section 9 of this Act, require[4] him—

(a) to provide two[5] specimens of breath for analysis by means of a device of a type approved[6] by the Secretary of State, or

(b) to provide a specimen of blood[7] or urine for a laboratory test.

(2) A requirement under this section to provide specimens of breath can only be made—

(a) at a police station,

(b) at a hospital, or

(*c*)   at or near a place where a relevant breath test has been administered to the person concerned or would have been so administered but for his failure to co-operate with it.

(2A)   For the purposes of this section "a relevant breath test" is a procedure involving the provision by the person concerned of a specimen of breath to be used for the purpose of obtaining an indication whether the proportion of alcohol in his breath or blood is likely to exceed the prescribed limit.

(2B)   A requirement under this section to provide specimens of breath may not be made at or near a place mentioned in subsection (2)(c) above unless the constable making it—

(*a*)   is in uniform, or
(*b*)   has imposed a requirement on the person concerned to co-operate with a relevant breath test in circumstances in which section 6(5) of this Act applies.

(2C)   Where a constable has imposed a requirement on the person concerned to co-operate with a relevant breath test at any place, he is entitled to remain at or near that place in order to impose on him there a requirement under this section.

(2D)   If a requirement under subsection (1)(a) above has been made at a place other than at a police station, such a requirement may subsequently be made at a police station if (but only if)—

(*a*)   a device or a reliable device of the type mentioned in subsection (1)(a) above was not available at that place or it was for any other reason not practicable to use such a device there, or
(*b*)   the constable who made the previous requirement has reasonable cause to believe that the device used there has not produced a reliable indication of the proportion of alcohol in the breath of the person concerned.

(3)   A requirement[8] under this section to provide a specimen of blood or urine can only be made at a police station or at a hospital[9]; and it cannot be made at a police station unless[10]—

(*a*)   the constable making the requirement has reasonable cause to believe that for medical reasons[11] a specimen of breath cannot be provided or should not be required, or
(*b*)   specimens of breath have not been provided elsewhere and at the time the requirement is made a device or a reliable[12] device of the type mentioned in subsection (1)(a) above is not available[13] at the police station or it is then for any other reason not practicable[14] to use such a device there, or
(*bb*)   a device of the type mentioned in subsection (1)(a) above has been used (at the police station or elsewhere) but the constable who required the specimens of breath has reasonable cause to believe[15] that the device has not produced a reliable indication of the proportion of alcohol in the breath of the person concerned, or
(*bc*)   as a result of the administration of a preliminary drug test, the constable making the requirement has reasonable cause to believe that the person required to provide a specimen of blood or urine has a drug in his body, or
(*c*)   the suspected offence is one under section 3A or 4 of this Act and the constable making the requirement has been advised[16] by a medical practitioner that the condition of the person required to provide the specimen might be due to some drug;

but may then be made notwithstanding that the person required to provide the specimen has already provided or been required to provide two specimens of breath.

(4)   If the provision of a specimen other than a specimen of breath may be required in pursuance of this section the question whether it is to be a specimen of blood or a specimen of urine and, in the case of a specimen of blood, the question who is to be asked to take it shall be decided[17] (subject to subsection (4A)) by the constable making the requirement.

(4A)   Where a constable decides for the purposes of subsection (4) to require the provision of a specimen of blood, there shall be no requirement to provide such a specimen if—

(*a*)   the medical practitioner who is asked to take the specimen is of the opinion[18] that, for medical reasons, it cannot or should not be taken; or
(*b*)   the registered health care professional who is asked to take it is of that opinion[18] and there is no contrary opinion from a medical practitioner;

and, where by virtue of this subsection there can be no requirement to provide a specimen of blood, the constable may require a specimen of urine instead.

(5)   A specimen of urine[19] shall be provided within one hour[20] of the requirement for its provision being made and after the provision of a previous specimen of urine.

(6)   A person who, without reasonable excuse[21], fails[22] to provide a specimen when required to do so in pursuance of this section is guilty of an offence[23].

(7)   A constable must, on requiring any person to provide a specimen in pursuance of this section, warn him[24] that a failure to provide it may render him liable to prosecution.

[Road Traffic Act 1988, s 7 as amended by the Road Traffic Act 1991, Sch 4, the Criminal Procedure and Investigations Act 1996, s 63, the Police Reform Act 2002, s 55, the Railways and Transport Safety Act 2003, Sch 7 and the Serious Organised Crime and Police Act 2005, s 154.]

---

1.   "Investigation" is to be construed in accordance with the ordinary plain meaning of the word, namely "inquiring into" (*Graham v Albert* [1985] RTR 352). A constable with good reason to believe that one of several persons was driving a motor vehicle on a road and that they all had consumed alcohol may, in the course of the investigation, lawfully require each of those persons to provide specimens of breath (*Pearson v Metropolitan Police Comr* [1988] RTR 276). Where the question arises as to whether a constable had lawfully required a person to provide a specimen under s 7, the court trying the matter is simply concerned to know whether there was or was not a bona fide investigation of the question whether

the suspect had committed an offence under ss 4 or 5 of the Act (*Hawes v DPP* [1993] RTR 116). Accordingly, where a defendant had failed a roadside breath test administered bona fide by a constable in ignorance of the manufacturer's instructions that there should be a time interval of twenty minutes between the defendant's last drink and the administration of the test, the subsequent provision of specimens for analysis under s 7 was not vitiated. Although the court is not required to find mala fides on the part of the officer before exercising its discretion to exclude such evidence in accordance with s 78 of the Police and Criminal Evidence Act 1984, the failure of a police officer to allow twenty minutes to elapse from the defendant's last drink before administering a roadside breath test will not, in the absence of mala fides, justify the court in excluding under s 78 of the Police and Criminal Evidence Act 1984 the evidence of specimens provided under s 7. That is not to say that there cannot be circumstances where although the officer has not acted in bad faith, the court may still be justified in exercising the discretion under s 78 to exclude evidence. One such case might be where the breath test equipment had been wrongly assembled or where the officer had no ground for suspecting that the motorist had alcohol in his body (*DPP v Kay* (1998) 163 JP 108, [1999] RTR 109, DC). The discretion to exclude evidence in accordance with s 78 of the Police and Criminal Evidence Act 1984 must be exercised judicially and can only be exercised when the accused is able to point to something more than an improperly administered roadside test and a wrongful arrest. Although it may not be necessary to demonstrate bad faith or oppression by the police officers, a simple maladministration of the roadside test, will not do (*DPP v Kennedy* [2003] EWHC 2583 (Admin), 168 JP 185).

2. Where the constable did not know the machine's calibration limits it cast doubt on the weight to be given to her evidence that the machine was working properly, but that was a matter for the judge and it was for him to decide whether that undermined her evidence that she was a trained operator; merely because there were gaps in a trained person's knowledge did not mean that she could not be described as a trained operator (*Haggis v DPP* [2003] EWHC 2481 (Admin), [2004] Crim LR 583).

3. It is an open question whether a requirement to provide breath is lawful if the constable has reasonable to believe that for medical reasons a specimen of breath cannot or should not be required (see *Steadman v DPP*, infra, in which their lordships were divided on the point).

4. The word "require" does not have to be used; all that is necessary is that the constable's language could fairly be said to amount to a requirement (*R v O'Boyle* (1973) 137 JP 280). A lawful arrest is not an essential prerequisite to requiring a specimen for analysis. Accordingly, evidence of an offence which was obtained in accordance with the procedure laid down in the Act and without any inducement, threat or trick or other impropriety was held to be admissible notwithstanding that the accused had been wrongly arrested (*R v Fox* [1986] AC 281, [1985] 3 All ER 392, applied in *Hartland v Alden* [1987] RTR 253 and explained in *DPP v McGladrigan* (1991) 155 JP 785, [1991] RTR 297, DC). Where police officers act mala fides and oppressively, the court will consider exercising its discretion under s 78 of the Police and Criminal Evidence Act 1984 to exclude evidence (see *Matto v Crown Court at Wolverhampton* [1987] RTR 337, [1987] Crim LR 641), but the exercise of the discretion under s 78 is not confined to circumstances of mala fides (*Daniels v DPP* (1991) 156 JP 543). The contemporaneous recording of procedures under this section and s 8, post, do not constitute an interview for the purposes of the Code of Practice (C) for the Detention, Treatment and Questioning of persons by police officers (*DPP v D* [1992] RTR 246, 94 Cr App Rep 185).

5. A person arrested cannot be required to provide more than two specimens of breath for analysis (*Howard v Hallett* [1984] RTR 353, [1984] Crim LR 565; followed in *Chief Constable of Avon and Somerset Constabulary v Creech* [1986] RTR 87, [1986] Crim LR 62; followed in *Mercer v DPP* [2003] EWHC 225 (Admin), [2004] RTR 8 (where it was held that the fact that the Lion Intoxilyser does not recalibrate itself upon finding an interfering substance and aborting the test cycle did not make a material difference, so that the breath specimen supplied before the cycle was aborted could still be used in evidence). However, where a person fails to provide a specimen of breath for analysis in compliance with a requirement, nothing in the legislation precludes the making of a further request for such a breath specimen or renders inadmissible evidence of such a specimen (*Owen v Morgan* [1986] RTR 151). If a person provides two specimens of breath but the device fails to provide an accurate indication as to the level of alcohol in the specimens, there is nothing to prevent the officer from offering the option of a further breath test though he is not obliged to do so (*Stewart v DPP* [2003] EWHC 1323 (Admin), [2003] RTR 529). See also *Jubb v DPP* [2002] EWHC 2317 (Admin), (2003) 167 JP 50, [2003] RTR 272. (As to whether further breath specimens can be *required* in such circumstances, see the possibly conflicting observations at para 30 of *Stewart* and para 44 of *Judd*.)

The Intoximeter 6000, unlike its predecessor, is designed to cease a breath test cycle without re-calibrating when it detects an interfering substance in a breath specimen; when this occurs after the provision of a second specimen in a test cycle and the operator requires further specimens to be provided in a second cycle, the prosecution is entitled to proceed on the basis of the first specimen taken in the first cycle and the first specimen taken in the second (*Mercer v DPP* [2003] EWHC 225 (Admin), (2003) 167 JP 441).

There should not be a conviction under s 5(1) on the evidence of only one specimen of breath: offences under ss 5(1) and 7(6) are mutually exclusive and the court may therefore convict under the latter (*Cracknell v Willis* [1988] AC 450).

6. For "approved devices" see the Road Traffic Offenders Act 1988, s 15 and notes thereto.

7. A specimen of blood must be taken with a person's consent and by a medical practitioner; see s 11(4), post and the Road Traffic Offenders Act 1988, s 15(4), post. Where a person is incapable of giving consent because of his condition following an accident, a constable may request a medical practitioner to take a sample of blood without the patient's consent, see s 7A , post.

8. The effective and operative requirement is that first made in accordance with the statutory procedure; the provision of a specimen may take place at another police station, and neither the presence of a device at that other police station nor repetition of the requirement itself will affect the validity of the original requirement (*Chief Constable of Kent v Berry* [1986] RTR 321, [1986] Crim LR 748). The making of a requirement for a specimen of blood when the conditions under sub-s (3) are not satisfied, does not necessarily render inadmissible the evidence in relation to the specimen of breath required under s 7(1)(*a*) (*Sykes v DPP* [1988] RTR 129); similarly, evidence of the breath specimen may be admitted where the requirement for a blood sample was lawfully made but based on a mistaken belief in the unreliability of the device (*Hague v DPP* (1995) 160 JP 783, [1997] RTR 146). An invalid but unproductive request for a specimen of blood does not render inadmissible evidence of a subsequently correctly taken specimen of urine (*DPP v Garrett* [1995] RTR 302).

9. Where a constable requires the provision of a specimen of blood or urine from a patient in hospital, having regard to s 7(2), there is no obligation for the constable to inform the driver why a specimen of breath cannot be taken. However, at some stage during the process at the hospital the constable must ask the driver whether there is any reason why a specimen of blood should not be taken. There is no obligation for the constable to ask specifically whether there is any such reason based on medical grounds (*R v Burton-upon-Trent Justices, ex p Woolley* [1995] RTR 139, 159 JP 165).

10. There is a prohibition on requiring a specimen of blood or urine unless one of the exceptions in paras (*a*)–(*c*) applies; if a constable wrongly believes that one of the exceptions does apply, when it does not, his requirement for blood or urine will be invalid and the defendant will commit no offence by refusing; see *Woolman v Lenton* [1985] Crim LR 516 and commentary thereto; or where her emotional distress rendered her incapable of understanding what was required or the consequences of failure to comply (*Spalding v Paine* [1985] Crim LR 673).

11. All the constable can do is to determine, as a layman, whether or not he has reasonable cause to believe that for medical reasons a specimen of breath cannot be provided or should not be required; provided there is sufficient material to justify the constable's decision to give him cause to form such a belief, the decision is the constable's alone and he is not

required to summon a doctor to give an opinion *Dempsey v Catton* [1986] RTR 194. See also *Davis v DPP* [1988] RTR 156, [1988] Crim LR 249 and *Davies v DPP* (1989) 154 JP 336, [1989] RTR 391. See also *Steadman v DPP*, infra.

The question whether the constable had reasonable cause to believe that a specimen of breath could not be provided or should not be required is a question of fact to be objectively determined by the justices. Accordingly, a defendant's distressed condition, her being shaken up and upset, having obviously taken alcohol and being of slight build, were matters capable of amounting to a medical condition, and the justices were held to have come to a proper conclusion in finding that the constable had reasonable cause to believe that a breath specimen could not be provided (*Webb v DPP* [1992] RTR 299). Where because of her state of intoxication a defendant was rendered unable to provide a specimen of breath, it was held that the intoxication itself constituted a medical condition, and therefore a medical reason for the purpose of the subsection (*Young v DPP* (1992) 157 JP 606, [1992] RTR 328). A response that the defendant took tablets is capable of being a medical reason and should be considered by the constable before requiring a specimen of blood (*Wade v DPP* (1995) 159 JP 555). However, *Wade v DPP*, supra, was a case concerned with s 7(4); where a defendant was found to be in possession of a tablet, he was not asked what it was for, but he stated in response to questions that he took sleeping tablets, those facts could not have given the officer reasonable cause to believe that the defendant could not provide or should not be required to provide a specimen of breath (*Steadman v DPP* [2002] EWHC 810 (QB), [2003] RTR 10).

12. The words "reliable device" are to be construed subjectively, so as to mean "a device which the officer reasonably believed to be reliable" (*Thompson v Thyne* [1986] RTR 293); applied in *Haghigat-Khou v Chambers* [1988] RTR 954, [1987] Crim LR 340. A device which is not capable of producing an accurate date on the print-out cannot be said to be "reliable" (*Slender v Boothby* (1985) 149 JP 405, [1986] RTR 385n); but one which cannot produce a print-out may be "reliable" if the operator can establish from what was seen on the display panel that the device was functioning properly (*Morgan v Lee* (1985) 149 JP 583, [1985] RTR 409, [1985] Crim LR 515). The prosecution have to establish by evidence that the police officer did believe that the device was unreliable, and that there was some material or evidence on which at the time he could reasonably have formed that view (*Stokes v Sayers* [1988] RTR 89). The test to be applied in deciding whether or not the police officer reasonably believed that the device actually was at the material time unreliable is a subjective one (*Dixon v DPP* [1992] 158 JP 430). A police officer cannot reasonably believe that a reliable device is not available, if there is nothing wrong with the device, save that it has not been properly switched on, and he does not follow the routine procedures for operation of the device which would disclose the cause of the fault; see *Jones v DPP* (1990) 154 JP 1013, [1991] RTR 41. Once the constable forms the view that the device is unreliable and requests a blood sample, any prosecution must be based on the analysis of the blood and not the breath specimen (*Badkin v DPP* [1988] RTR 401, [1987] Crim LR 830 applied in *McLellan v DPP* [1993] RTR 401). As to whether a machine was in fact reliable, and for the admissibility in evidence of any sample, see the Road Traffic Offenders Act 1988, s 15 and notes thereto, in this PART, post.

13. A device which becomes unreliable before it has completed a full and proper analysis of the breath specimen is not "available" within the meaning of s 8(3)(b) (*Cotter v Kamil* [1984] RTR 371, [1984] Crim LR 569). The prosecution must prove that a device was not available (*Dye v Manns* [1986] Crim LR 337, [1987] RTR 90). If a device becomes unreliable, and thereby not available, before completion of its analysis of the two specimens of breath, this does not prevent the police officer requiring the motorist to provide two further specimens of breath for analysis by another device of the same type (*Denny v DPP* (1989) 154 JP 460, [1990] RTR 417, DC). Where the police officer genuinely believes there is something wrong with the device and requires a specimen of blood or urine, but later it is found the device was reliable evidence of the analysis of the breath specimen remains admissible (*Hague v DPP* (1995) 160 JP 783, [1997] RTR 146).

14. It may not be "practicable" to use the device because there is no trained police officer at the station to operate it; see *Chief Constable of Avon and Somerset Constabulary v Kelliher* [1987] RTR 305, [1986] Crim LR 635.

15. If a person provides two specimens of breath but the device fails to provide an accurate indication as to the level of alcohol in the specimens, the officer is not obliged to require blood or urine and he may, alternatively, offer the option of a further breath test (though he is not obliged to take the latter course) (*Stewart v DPP* [2003] EWHC 1323 (Admin), [2003] RTR 529, (2004) 168 JP 82).

Although an intoximeter machine may have self calibrated correctly, and was not itself unreliable a discrepancy of 30 per cent between two breath specimens taken within a space of a minute would lead any reasonable person to conclude that the indication given by the machine was unreliable. Further, an officer was able to rely on a police form of guidance to the same effect without the prosecution being required to call evidence as to the provenance of the form (*DPP v Smith (Robert James)* [2000] RTR 341, DC).

16. There should be a clear oral statement by the doctor to the police officer of his opinion as to the possible cause of the person's condition as found by him at the police station (*Cole v DPP* [1988] RTR 224).

17. In *DPP v Warren* [1992] 4 All ER 865, [1993] RTR 58 and *DPP v Jackson* [1999] 1 AC 406, [1998] 3 All ER 769, the House of Lords compared the requirements under s 7(3) (unavailable or unreliable breath specimens) and s 8(2) (marginal breath specimens). The guidance given in both these cases may be summarised as follows:

1   Requirements under s 7(3): The constable—

   (a)   must tell the driver the reason under s 7(3) why breath specimens cannot be taken or used;
   (b)   should tell the driver that in these circumstances he is required to give a specimen of blood or urine, but that it is for the constable to decide which;
   (c)   warn the driver that a failure to provide the specimen required may render him liable to prosecution; and then if the constable decides to require blood,
   (d)   ask the driver if there are any medical reasons why a specimen cannot or should not be taken from him by a doctor.

2   Requirements under s 8(2): The constable—

   (a)   should inform the driver of the nature of the option open to him and what will be involved if he exercises it;
   (b)   must inform the driver that the specimen of breath which he has given containing the lower proportion of alcohol exceeds the statutory limit, but does not exceed 50 microgrammes of alcohol in 100 millilitres of breath;
   (c)   should inform the driver that in these circumstances he is entitled to claim to have this specimen replaced by a specimen of blood or urine if he wishes; but that, if he does so, it will be for the constable to decide whether the replacement specimen is to be of blood or urine and that if the constable requires a specimen of blood it will be taken by a doctor unless the doctor considers that there are medical reasons for not taking blood, when urine may be given instead;
   (d)   ask the driver if there are any medical reasons why a specimen cannot or should not be taken from him by a doctor.

Requirements 1(a) and (c) in a s 7(3) case, and 2(b) in a s 8(2) case are mandatory and non-compliance should lead to an acquittal. The constable must seek to ensure that a driver is aware of the role of the doctor, but what is necessary is that the driver is aware (whether or not he is told by the constable) of the role of the doctor so that he does not suffer prejudice. Therefore, if the driver appreciates that a specimen of blood will be taken by a doctor and not by a police officer, the charge should not be dismissed by the justices because the police officer failed to tell the driver that the specimen would be taken by a doctor.

Accordingly, there are two issues for the justices to decide. The first issue is whether the matters set out in the requirements for a s 7(3) or 8(2) case have been brought to the attention of the driver by the constable. The second issue, if the answer to the first issue is "no", is whether in relation to the non-mandatory requirements the police officer's failure to give the full formula deprived the driver of the opportunity to exercise the option, or caused him to exercise it in a way which he would not have done had everything been said. If the answer to the second issue is "yes", then the driver should be acquitted, but if the answer is "no" the failure by the police officer to use the full formula should not be a reason for an acquittal. Since the second issue is directed to whether the driver has suffered prejudice, it will only be in exceptional cases that the justices should acquit on that ground without having heard evidence from the driver himself raising the issue that he has suffered prejudice. Both issues are issues of fact and, therefore, if the justices, having heard the evidence of the driver to raise the second issue, are left with a reasonable doubt as to whether or not he was prejudiced, they should acquit (*DPP v Jackson* [1999] 1 AC 406, [1998] 3 All ER 769, [1998] RTR 397, HL).

Where the driver makes a representation in answer to the question about whether a specimen of blood or a specimen of urine should be taken, the constable must consider whether the statement proffered is capable of being a medical reason. If he concludes that there is no medical reason, he may require a blood specimen, but otherwise if he is left in a state of doubt about the matter, he should seek the opinion of a medical practitioner (*Wade v DPP* (1995) 159 JP 555, [1996] RTR 177). But where a medical practitioner was present throughout, he did not express any medical opinion as to whether blood should or should not be taken, the defendant made no attempt to state any reason as why blood could or should be taken but merely stated "You are not going to examine me", those factors led irresistibly to the conclusion that no medical reason was being advanced to the officer as to why blood could or should not be taken: *DPP v Gibbons* [2001] EWHC Admin 385, 165 JP 812. It is not for the constable to substitute his opinion for that of the medical practitioner unless the driver's objection is obviously frivolous; accordingly, if the driver raises an objection based on his medical condition, even though unconvincing, the constable should delay requiring a blood specimen until after a medical practitioner has expressed an opinion (*DPP v Wythe* [1996] RTR 137).

Where the defendant claimed that his Rastafarian faith prevented him from giving blood, the officer should at least have considered whether blood or urine should be the choice, and to choose the specimen objected to without having any basis for doing so might be categorised as perverse and was accordingly a failure to comply with s 7(4): *Joseph v DPP* [2003] EWHC 3078 (Admin) , [2004] RTR 21, (2004) 168 JP 575.

The constable is entitled to change his mind as to the type of specimen to be required. That right continues up to the time at which the blood sample, if it be a blood specimen, is actually taken. An invalid but unproductive request for a specimen of blood does not render inadmissible evidence of the analysis of a subsequently correctly taken specimen of urine (*DPP v Garrett* (1995) 159 JP 561, [1995] RTR 302).

While it is essential from the terms of s 7(3) that the constable who requires the provision of a specimen of blood or urine must have cause to believe that there is no reliable device available to analyse the driver's breath at the police station, and the driver must be made aware of that fact, there is no requirement that the driver must be informed of that fact by the constable making the request (*Bobin v DPP* [1999] RTR 375). Section 7 applies to specimens required to be taken at a hospital as well as to those required to be taken at a police station; therefore, where, at a police station, a motorist gave a potential medical reason that might have led a medical practitioner to conclude that a specimen of blood could not or should not be given, and the motorist was then taken to hospital, that information given by the motorist should have been passed on to the doctor at the hospital who was in charge of the motorist's case: *Butler v DPP* [2001] RTR 430, [2001] Crim LR 580, DC.

18. Once the medical opinion is obtained, it is irrelevant to the constable's decision whether the medical practitioner's opinion is right or wrong. However, if as a result of an irrational medical opinion, a defendant has been deprived of his claim under s 8(2), post, to provide an alternative specimen, namely urine, it will be open to him to rely on s 78 of the Police and Criminal Evidence Act 1984. If he establishes that the doctor's opinion was seriously wrong, it will be difficult for the court to refuse to exercise discretion to exclude the breath analysis evidence; see *Andrews v DPP* [1992] RTR 1.

19. There is nothing in this subsection to prevent the specimen sent for analysis to be the third or subsequent one taken (*Nugent v Ridley* [1987] RTR 412, [1987] Crim LR 640, where the doctor took a prior specimen to satisfy himself of the subject's ability to provide one).

20. The significance of the period of one hour is to make finite the length of time available to the driver to provide the specimen required, so that, if he fails to provide the specimen within that time, he is liable to be charged with failing to provide a specimen. While the police officer conducting the procedure is not obliged to extend the time beyond the statutory limit of one hour, if he does permit the driver to provide a specimen after the hour has elapsed, that does not render the evidence of the analysis inadmissible (*DPP v Baldwin* [2000] RTR 314, DC).

21. **Reasonable excuse.** The defendant must adduce sufficient evidence, including cross-examination where appropriate: once the defence is so raised, the onus is on the prosecution to negative it (*Parker v Smith* [1974] Crim LR 426). The following case law must be read in the light of the fact that until 6 May 1983 the statutory provisions related to failure to provide a blood or urine specimen for a test, breath testing until then supplying only a preliminary screening and not a quantitative analysis. Nevertheless some of the principles may be adapted to the amended provisions. There is no obligation, statutory or otherwise, on the police to inform the defendant that he cannot see or consult a solicitor before providing a specimen (*DPP v Varley* (1998) 163 JP 443, [1999] Crim LR 753, DC). It is not a reasonable excuse that the defendant wishes to defer providing a specimen until his solicitor arrives (*Law v Stephens* [1971] RTR 358; *Pettigrew v Northumbria Police Authority* [1976] RTR 177); but it may be otherwise if the defendant merely requests to speak to his solicitor before deciding whether to give a specimen, see *Smith v Hand* [1986] RTR 265, applied in *DPP v Billington* [1988] 1 All ER 435, [1988] 1 WLR 535, 152 JP 1, where it was held that the refusal of the police to permit the defendant, under s 58 of the Police and Criminal Evidence Act 1984, to consult a solicitor before providing a specimen did not amount to a reasonable excuse, (and this remains the case following the Human Rights Act 1998; art 6(3) has not changed the position: see *Campbell v DPP* [2002] EWHC 1314 (Admin), (2002) 166 JP 742, [2004] RTR 5, [2003] Crim LR 118 (followed in *Kennedy v DPP* [2002] EWHC 2297 (Admin), [2004] RTR 6, [2003] Crim LR 120, and *Kirkup v DPP* [2003] EWHC Admin 2354, (2004) 168 JP 255, [2004] Crim LR 230. See also *Whitley v DPP* [2003] EWHC Admin 2512, (2004) 169 JP 350, [2004] Crim LR 585 and *Causey v DPP* [2004] EWHC Admin 3164, (2005) 169 JP 331) Nor was it a reasonable excuse that the defendant wished to consult a law book before providing a specimen (*DPP v Noe* [2000] RTR 351, DC). Where the defendant has been told positively that he could await his solicitor, there might be a reasonable excuse; otherwise the testing procedure is not to be unduly delayed by the right to consult a solicitor or to read Code C of the PACE Act 1984 codes of practice even where he believed he had been confused or misled by the police (*DPP v Skinner, DPP v Cornell* (1989) 153 JP 605, DC and see *DPP v Whalley* [1991] RTR 161, [1991] Crim LR 211). Where a defendant has been so confused or misled, depending on the circumstances, s 78 of the Police and Criminal Evidence Act 1984 may be applied to exclude evidence of the test procedure; see *Hudson v DPP* (1991) 156 JP 168, [1992] RTR 27. See also *Rush v DPP (DC)* [1994] RTR 268, noted in more detail at note 3 to s 8, post. Where a youth aged 16 was arrested after a positive roadside test and taken to a police station, he declined to have a solicitor notified or the custody officer, in breach of the PACE codes of practice, declined to notify an appropriate adult, justices were wrong to exclude the results of the substantive breath test; there was no difference between this situation and the cases concerning attempts to delay the procedure by awaiting the arrival of a solicitor or seeking to read the codes: *R (on the application of the DPP) v B* [2002] EWHC 2976 (Admin), (2003) 167 JP 144, [2003] Crim LR 338 (sub nom *DPP v E*).

The tests that have to be applied to establish reasonable excuse were identified in *DPP v Crofton* [1994] RTR 279 when it was held that the following matters had to be considered: (i) the need for evidence of physical or mental incapacity to provide the specimen; (ii) that medical evidence would normally be required to support such a claim and (iii) the necessary causative links between physical or mental conditions and the failure to provide the specimen. That causative link was held not to be present in the case of a man whose lung capacity was impaired to such an extent that he was incapable of providing a specimen, but who was unaware of that impairment; accordingly since he did not make a genuine attempt to provide the specimen he could not rely upon his impairment as a reasonable excuse (*DPP v Furby* [2000] RTR 181). While medical evidence will not be necessary in every case, in the vast majority of cases it will be necessary to have some medical or expert evidence (*Smith (Nicholas) v DPP* [1992] RTR 413). The finding of physical or mental inability is a finding which is achievable only upon the evidence, and in almost all cases this must be medical evidence; it is not open to justices to embark on an investigation of their own and reach a finding on an assumptive basis (*DPP v Ambrose* (1991) 156 JP 493, [1992] RTR 285 and see *DPP v Radford* [1995] RTR 86; nor are justices, however sympathetic they may be, entitled to use that sympathy to come to a conclusion which is not justified on the facts as they find them (*DPP v Brodzky* [1997] RTR 425n). The fact that the motorist has been detained by a police constable under s 136 of the Mental Health Act 1983 does not prevent him being requested to provide a specimen under s 7(6) if the police properly satisfy themselves that the motorist is capable of understanding the breath test procedure (*Francis v DPP* [1997] RTR 113)). The simple fact that the defendant has tried as hard as he could without success does not amount to a reasonable excuse (*Grady v Pollard* [1988] RTR 316). Where, however, the justices found that the defendant did her best to provide breath specimens and was prevented from doing so by shortness of breath brought on by a panic attack (even though a doctor called by the defence testified that during a panic attack there would be nothing to prevent the defendant providing breath specimens), and consequently found that the defendant had a reasonable excuse, those findings of fact disclosed a causative link between the physical/mental condition of the defendant and her failure to provide specimens and the Divisional Court could not go behind those findings (though the court expected that cases in which such a defence as this would succeed, where not fully supported by medical evidence, would be rare): *DPP v Falzarano* [2001] RTR 217. It is not a reasonable excuse for a person to claim he has not committed an offence (*Williams v Osborne* [1975] RTR 181, 61 Cr App Rep 1); nor that the sight of blood causing a person to become light-headed, and a fear of fainting, fear as well making him unable to give a specimen of urine (*Sykes v White* [1983] RTR 419); nor that in view of the danger of AIDS he would rather not give blood (*DPP v Fountain* [1988] RTR 385; *DPP v Eddowes* [1991] RTR 35; *DPP v Daley* [1992] RTR 155). In cases where the defendant claims an aversion to the sight of blood, it is important to distinguish between this and the taking of blood and that he might have avoided the sight of blood by closing his eyes or looking away (*DPP v Mukandiwa* [2005] EWHC 2977 (Admin), 170 JP 17. Failure to indicate to a motorist that there was a time limit for completion of the breathalyser test after which the machine stopped functioning does not necessarily amount to a reasonable excuse; in such cases the evidential burden is on the defendant to show he had good reason for being unable to comply with the test procedure (*DPP v Coyle* [1996] RTR 287). There is no principle of law that the defendant must necessarily be allowed the full three minutes, nor does he need to be told that he has three minutes at any stage of the procedure (*Cosgrove v DPP* [1997] RTR 153)). However, a defendant may have a reasonable excuse if the court accepts medical evidence as to the presence and genuineness of a phobia about contracting AIDS which prevented him from placing his lips on the mouthpiece of the breath-testing device (*De Freitas v DPP* (1992) 157 JP 413, [1993] RTR 98). It is not a reasonable excuse if the breath test procedure is explained to the defendant but he is too drunk, because of self-induced intoxication, to understand the procedure (*DPP v Beech* (1991) 156 JP 311, [1992] RTR 239). It is a reasonable excuse if the defendant was unable to understand the purpose of the requirement or the penalties (*Beck v Sager* [1979] Crim LR 257), or where her emotional distress rendered her incapable of understanding what was required or the consequences of failure to comply (*Spalding v Paine* [1985] Crim LR 673). Moreover, the fact that a solicitor has advised a defendant to refuse to provide a specimen, does not, if that advice is followed, amount to a reasonable excuse (*Dickinson v DPP* [1989] Crim LR 741).

If a man knows that he suffers from a medical condition which prevents him giving sufficient breath, his duty to provide a specimen includes, in those circumstances, a duty to inform the constable making the requirement of that medical condition; see *Teape v Godfrey* [1986] RTR 213. The fact that an arresting officer did not communicate to the custody sergeant, the defendant's contention at the roadside that he was suffering from bronchitis does not amount to a reasonable excuse (*DPP v Lonsdale* [2001] RTR 444, [2001] Crim LR 659, DC).

22. "Fail" includes "refuse" (s 11(1), post). A refusal to provide a specimen may be inferred from the defendant's conduct (see *R v Mackey* [1977] RTR 146; also *R v Miles* [1979] RTR 509). In assessing whether or not the defendant is refusing to provide a specimen, any relevant words and conduct should be taken into account; see *R v McAllister* [1974] RTR 408, 59 Cr App Rep 7. A statement by the defendant, "Can I change my mind?", and "I want to change my mind", following only five seconds after his answer "No" to the request for a specimen were held to be relevant words and conduct to be taken into account (*Smyth v DPP* [1996] RTR 59). There may be a failure where the defendant fails to reply to a request for a specimen; it is not necessary actually to show the device to the defendant in order to establish that the opportunity has been provided (*Campbell v DPP* [1989] RTR 256 [1989] Crim LR 380). A specimen of urine is *not* provided if the specimen is lost (eg by dropping the jar containing it) before a police officer has taken charge of it regardless of whether the loss is accidental or deliberate (*Ross v Hodges* [1975] RTR 55), but in *Beck v Watson* [1980] RTR 90, [1979] Crim LR 533, where the specimen of blood was accidentally spilled and a second specimen taken with the defendant's consent, the court declared the analyst's certificate as to the second sample inadmissible because there was no power to require a second sample. A defendant who steals a specimen is not to be convicted of failure to provide: *R v Rothery* [1976] RTR 550, [1976] Crim LR 691. In *Hier v Read* [1978] RTR 114, it was said the court had to establish whether or not there was an agreement to give a blood sample; it was wrong to treat a refusal to sign a form of consent to a blood sample being taken in all circumstances as being a refusal to give a blood sample. A defendant may comply with the section by agreeing to a specimen being taken by his own doctor but not by the police doctor (both doctors being present); *Bayliss v Thames Valley Police Chief Constable* [1978] RTR 328, [1978] Crim LR 363; however, *Bayliss* was a case determined on its own facts and there was no general right to insist on a particular medical practitioner (*DPP v Smith (Alan)* (1993) Times, 1 June). Before proceeding under this section, the police may allow the motorist to contact a solicitor, relative or doctor; they may withdraw the concession where for example the motorist is then trying to delay matters (*Brown v Ridge* [1979] RTR 136). There is no requirement for a person to give an immediate answer, however, but it is a matter for the reasonable exercise of discretion on the part of the police officer (*Edwards v Woods* [1981] Crim LR 414). A requirement to provide a specimen of blood involves a doctor exercising his medical skill and experience as to the site from which the blood is to be extracted. It is not open to a defendant to unreasonably refuse to allow a specimen to be taken from a site so selected (*Solesbury v Pugh* [1969] 2 All ER 1171, 133 JP 544). Once a person has complied with a request, he probably cannot be required to give a further specimen of blood or urine (*R v Hyams* [1972] 3 All ER 651, 136 JP 842; *Gabrielson v Richards* [1976] RTR 265, [1975] Crim LR 722). This does not prevent the police changing their minds as to the kind of specimen required, before there has been either a compliance or refusal (*R v Paduch* (1973) 57 Cr App Rep 676).

23. For penalty see the Road Traffic Offenders Act 1988, Sch 2, post. The offence under s 7(6) is one of failing without reasonable excuse to provide a specimen "when required to do so in pursuance of this section". The central test is whether the constable is carrying out an investigation into whether a person has committed any offence under s 4 or 5 of the Act. It does not have to be shown that the constable had in his mind a specific offence under one of these sections and that he was investigating that specific offence. It is not therefore necessary to specify in the charge which, if any, specific offence was being investigated by the constable. If the test is satisfied and the offence is proved, it will be necessary for the purposes of penalty for the court to conduct a separate and distinct inquiry in order to determine whether the defendant was driving or

in charge of the motor vehicle (*DPP v Butterworth* [1995] 1 AC 381, [1994] 3 All ER 289, [1994] RTR 330, [1995] Crim LR 71, HL, and see also *Worsley v DPP* [1995] Crim LR 572 and *Cawley v DPP* [2001] EWHC Admin 83). Justices should make it clear on which basis they are sentencing eg "We find you guilty of the offence and, furthermore, we are also satisfied that you were driving or attempting to drive"; or, alternatively, "We find you guilty of the offence but we are not satisfied that you were driving or attempting to drive but only that you were in charge" (*Crampsie v DPP* [1993] RTR 383).

On the trial of an information alleging an offence under s 7(6), the test record print-out of a breath-testing device is admissible as evidence since the print-out constitutes the product of a mechanical device which falls into the category of real evidence. Moreover, the constable operating the device may give evidence as to what he has observed and as to the result of what he observed, interpreting if necessary the print-out (*Castle v Cross* [1985] 1 All ER 87, [1984] 1 WLR 1372, [1985] RTR 62; applied in *Morgan v Lee* (1985) 149 JP 583, [1985] RTR 409, where the device was unable to produce a printout and it was held a police officer could give oral evidence of the result of a breath analysis which he had seen on the display panel of the device). The fact that the defendant provided a specimen of breath is admissible in a prosecution under s 7(6) since it shows an ability to provide a specimen and is, therefore, relevant evidence of a refusal to supply the second specimen; nevertheless, unless the defendant is charged under ss 4 and 5 of the Act, evidence of the value of the first specimen is irrelevant and may be highly prejudicial to the defendant (*Oldfield v Anderton* (1985) 150 JP 40, [1986] RTR 314, [1986] Crim LR 189 but may be relevant to sentence, see *Cracknell v Willis* [1988] AC 450, [1987] 3 All ER 801, [1987] 3 WR 1082, HL).

Where a suspect fails to provide breath in sufficient quantity to enable the readings obtained to be used in evidence to support a charge of driving with excess alcohol, those readings may not be taken into account when the court is determining the credibility of the suspect's evidence as to his reasons for failing to provide samples (*Willicott v DPP* [2001] EWHC Admin 415, (2001) 166 JP 385).

Sections 11 and 12(1) of the Road Traffic Offenders Act 1988 (evidence of identity by certificate etc) apply. There is nothing in the Act, in appropriate circumstances, to prevent a conviction for an offence under s 7(6) in addition to a conviction for the substantive offence under s 5(1), ante; see *Duddy v Gallagher* [1985] RTR 401.

24. This is a mandatory requirement, even where the subject is himself a police officer (*Simpson v Spalding* [1987] RTR 221). The warning must be understood as a warning by the person to whom it is applied, and if his lack of English prevents him understanding, the warning is not valid under s 7(7) (*Chief Constable of Avon and Somerset Constabulary v Singh* [1988] RTR 107). Failure to give the warning renders the results of the breath, blood or urine test inadmissible (*Murray v DPP* (1993) 158 JP 261 [1993] RTR 209, [1993] Crim LR 968). However, where the suspects is "invited" rather than "required" to provide further specimens of breath, the first specimens having failed to result in a reliable analysis (wide disparity in readings), it is unnecessary to repeat the warning under s 7(7): *Edmond v DPP* [2006] EWHC 463 (Admin), [2006] RTR 18.

4–1378A   7A. Specimens of blood taken from persons incapable of consenting.   (1) A constable may make a request to a medical practitioner for him to take a specimen of blood from a person ("the person concerned") irrespective of whether that person consents if—

(a) that person is a person from whom the constable would (in the absence of any incapacity of that person and of any objection under section 9) be entitled under section 7 to require the provision of a specimen of blood for a laboratory test;

(b) it appears to that constable that that person has been involved in an accident that constitutes or is comprised in the matter that is under investigation or the circumstances of that matter;

(c) it appears to that constable that that person is or may be incapable (whether or not he has purported to do so) of giving a valid consent to the taking of a specimen of blood; and

(d) it appears to that constable that that person's incapacity is attributable to medical reasons.

(2) A request under this section—

(a) shall not be made to a medical practitioner who for the time being has any responsibility (apart from the request) for the clinical care of the person concerned; and

(b) shall not be made to a medical practitioner other than a police medical practitioner unless—

(i)   it is not reasonably practicable for the request to made to a police medical practitioner; or

(ii) it is not reasonably practicable for such a medical practitioner (assuming him to be willing to do so) to take the specimen.

(3) It shall be lawful for a medical practitioner to whom a request is made under this section, if he thinks fit—

(a) to take a specimen of blood from the person concerned irrespective of whether that person consents; and

(b) to provide the sample to a constable.

(4) If a specimen is taken in pursuance of a request under this section, the specimen shall not be subjected to a laboratory test unless the person from whom it was taken—

(a) has been informed that it was taken; and

(b) has been required by a constable to give his permission for a laboratory test of the specimen; and

(c) has given his permission.

(5) A constable must, on requiring a person to give his permission for the purposes of this section for a laboratory test of a specimen, warn that person that a failure to give the permission may render him liable to prosecution.

(6) A person who, without reasonable excuse, fails to give his permission for a laboratory test of a specimen of blood taken from him under this section is guilty of an offence.

(7) In this section "police medical practitioner" means a medical practitioner who is engaged under any agreement to provide medical services for purposes connected with the activities of a police force.

[Road Traffic Act 1988, s 7A as inserted by the Police Reform Act 2002, s 56(1).]

4–1379   8. Choice of specimens of breath. (1) Subject to subsection (2) below, of any two[1] specimens of breath provided by any person in pursuance of section 7 of this Act that with the lower proportion of alcohol in the breath shall be used and the other shall be disregarded.

(2) If the specimen with the lower proportion of alcohol contains no more than 50 microgrammes of alcohol in 100 millilitres of breath, the person who provided it may claim[2] that it should be replaced by such specimen as may be required under section 7(4) of this Act[3] and, if he then provides such a specimen, neither specimen of breath shall be used[4].

(2A) If the person who makes a claim under subsection (2) above was required to provide specimens of breath under section 7 of this Act at or near a place mentioned in subsection (2)(c) of that section, a constable may arrest him without warrant.

(3) The Secretary of State may by regulations substitute another proportion of alcohol in the breath for that specified in subsection (2) above.

[Road Traffic Act 1988, s 8 as amended by the Serious Organised Crime and Police Act 2005, s 154.]

---

1. Evidence of both specimens of breath is admissible where each sample yields an identical reading on the print-out (*R v Brentford Magistrates' Court, ex p Clarke* (1986) 150 JP 495, [1986] Crim LR 633).

2. See *DPP v Warren* [1999] 1 AC 406, [1992] 4 All ER 865, [1993] RTR 58; *DPP v Jackson* [1998] 3 All ER 769, [1998] RTR 397, HL noted ante to s 7(4) as to the information to be given to the driver (who does not have a choice between blood or urine under either section; the choice is between the breath sample and its replacement under this section).

It has been held not to destroy the driver's choice where in reply to her question as to whether provision of blood would make any difference, the police officer replies "probably not" (*Sharp v Spencer* [1987] Crim LR 420). The onus is on a driver exercising this right to establish to the doctor that he is consenting to a blood sample being taken; if the doctor forms the impression that no such consent is being given so no specimen of blood is obtained, the prosecutor is then entitled to rely on the evidence provided by the specimen of breath with the lower proportion of alcohol (*Rawlins v Brown* [1987] RTR 238). The procedure provided by ss 7(4) and 8(1) and (2) is quite separate from that provided by ss 7(1) and (3) which means that the circumstances set out in s 7(3) do not have to apply before a requirement is made (*Sivyer v Parker* [1987] RTR 169, [1986] Crim LR 410).Where the defendant declines to give blood, then later changes his mind and a specimen of blood is taken, that does not prevent the evidence of the breath specimen being given; the defendant has a once-for-all option (*Smith v DPP* [1989] RTR 159, [1989] Crim LR 453). Similarly, where a defendant exercises his right under this subsection but later resiles from his agreement to provide a specimen of blood, he must take the consequences, namely that the prosecutor would be able to rely on the analysis of the breath specimen; see *Hope v DPP* [1992] RTR 305. In the procedure under s 8(2) there is no duty at any stage to warn the defendant under s 7(7), ante, that failure to provide either a urine or a blood sample will render him liable to prosecution because such failure does not render the defendant liable to prosecution (*Hayes v DPP* [1994] RTR 163). The defendant is not entitled to have legal advice before deciding whether to exercise this right (*R v DPP, ex p Ward* (1997) 162 JP 162, [1999] RTR 11, DC).

3. If by reason of his own actions the defendant frustrates the performance of the constable's duty to inform him of the options, he is not entitled to be acquitted (*DPP v Poole* [1992] RTR 177 but see also *Rush v DPP (DC)* [1994] RTR 268, in which it was held that where the prosecution had failed to prove beyond a reasonable doubt that the police officers had followed the correct statutory procedure and that as a result of unrecorded comments of the officers the defendant was waived her right to provide blood or urine, the defendant was entitled to be acquitted). If the defendant's consumption of alcohol contributed to his inability to comprehend the offer made to him to replace the breath specimen with a specimen under s 7(4), he cannot complain that he has been denied his rights and the evidence of the breath specimen is admissible (*DPP v Berry* (1995) 160 JP 707).

4. Section 8 is mandatory in precluding the use of the breath specimen; such specimen cannot be held in reserve to be used if a blood specimen is lost or is otherwise unusable (*Archbold v Jones* [1986] RTR 178, [1985] Crim LR 740), or if evidence of the analysis of the blood specimen is inadmissible because the procedure by which it was obtained was unlawful (*Wakeley v Hyams* [1987] RTR 49, [1987] Crim LR 342). Similarly, neither breath specimen may be relied upon even where the defendant is found to have falsified the analysis of his part of the blood specimen. Nevertheless, evidence of the readings from analysis of breath specimens by the Intoximeter may be admitted merely to allow the prosecution to establish that the proper procedure has been adhered to in order to establish their right to rely on the blood sample; see *Yhnell v DPP* (1988) 153 JP 364, [1989] RTR 250, DC.

However, if the court finds that the statutory procedure came to an end before a specimen of blood was provided, it may disregard that specimen, and the breath specimen may be used in evidence (*Smith v DPP* [1989] RTR 159, [1989] Crim LR 453, DC—motorist initially declining to provide optional blood specimen, but later changed his mind and did provide one). In *DPP v Winstanley* (1993) 158 JP 1062, [1993] RTR 222, it was held that a breath specimen could have been used where a defendant had requested a replacement specimen and a police officer had requested blood but had been unable to summon a doctor, the defendant then being unable to provide a urine sample. What a constable is obliged to say in accordance with the decision in *DPP v Warren*, noted ante to s 7(4), will depend on what stage he has reached in the decision-making process. Accordingly, if the constable first decides to require a urine sample he has no obligation at that stage to warn the defendant as to his right to object to giving a blood sample on medical grounds, but he would have to give such a warning if the procedure changed to a blood sample. What matters is that the defendant is warned of his rights before the option he is exercising under s 8(2) crystallises (*Hayes v DPP* [1994] RTR 163), and that the explanation is given fairly and properly so that he may make an informed decision (*Baldwin v DPP* [1996] RTR 238; *DPP v Hill-Brookes* [1996] RTR 279).

4–1379A   9. Protection for hospital patients. (1) While a person is at a hospital as a patient[1] he shall not be required to co-operate with a preliminary test or to provide a specimen under section 7 of this Act unless the medical practitioner in immediate charge of his case has been notified of the proposal to make the requirement; and—

    (*a*) if the requirement is then made, it shall be for the provision of a specimen at the hospital, but

    (*b*) if the medical practitioner objects on the ground specified in subsection (2) below, the requirement shall not be made.

(1A) While a person is at a hospital as a patient, no specimen of blood shall be taken from him under section 7A of this Act and he shall not be required to give his permission for a laboratory test of a specimen taken under that section unless the medical practitioner in immediate charge of his case—

    (*a*) has been notified of the proposal to take the specimen or to make the requirement; and

(b) has not objected on the ground specified in subsection (2).

(2) The ground on which the medical practitioner may object is—

(a) in a case falling within subsection (1), that the requirement or the provision of the specimen or (if one is required) the warning required by section 7(7) of this Act would be prejudicial to the proper care and treatment of the patient; and

(b) in a case falling within subsection (1A), that the taking of the specimen, the requirement or the warning required by section 7A(5) of this Act would be so prejudicial.

[Road Traffic Act 1988, s 9 as amended by the Police Reform Act 2002, s 56(2), the Railways and Transport Safety Act 2003, Sch 7 and the Serious Organised Crime and Police Act 2005, s 154.]

---

1. The words "at hospital" can be appropriate to anywhere within the precincts of a hospital. The phrase "as a patient" means someone who is at the hospital for the purpose of being treated, but that person ceases to be a patient as soon as the treatment contemplated for that visit is over (*A-G's Reference (No 1 of 1976)* [1977] 3 All ER 557, 64 Cr App Rep 222).

Once a person is at a hospital as a patient he must not be required to give a specimen unless a doctor has first been notified and has no objection (*R v Crowley* [1977] RTR 153, 64 Cr App Rep 225). It is not necessary to call the doctor to give evidence that he did not object, as evidence of non-objection is not hearsay and may, therefore, be given by the witness to whom the doctor indicated he had no objection (*R v Chapman* [1969] 2 QB 436, [1969] 2 All ER 321, 133 JP 405). A Divisional Court judgment that the doctor's right to object is a continuing one and is not restricted to the time at which he is first notified of the proposal to obtain a specimen (*Bosley v Long* [1970] 3 All ER 286, [1970] RTR 432) was disapproved by the House of Lords in *Bourlet v Porter* [1973] 2 All ER 800, 137 JP 649.

A requirement lawfully made of a patient at a hospital remains valid once that person is no longer a patient at the hospital and has been arrested under s 6(5)(b), ante, and taken to a police station at which an appropriate breath analysis machine is available; accordingly an analysis of the specimen of blood taken in these circumstances at the police station is admissible (*Webber v DPP* (Note) [1998] RTR 111).

Section 7(4) applies as well as s 9 where there is a proposal to require a specimen of blood or urine at a hospital; and, just as a constable is required by s 7(4) to consult a medical practitioner before he decides whether the specimen should be of blood or urine where he is aware of a potential medical reason affecting that decision, he is also required to tell the medical practitioner at the hospital of that potential medical reason when proceeding under s 9: *Butler v DPP* [2001] RTR 430, [2001] Crim LR 580, DC.

4–1380   10. Detention of persons affected by alcohol or a drug.   (1) Subject to subsections (2) and (3) below, a person required to provide a specimen of breath, blood or urine may afterwards be detained at a police station (or, if the specimen was provided otherwise than at a police station, arrested and taken to and detained at a police station) if a constable has reasonable grounds for believing that, were that person then driving or attempting to drive a mechanically propelled vehicle on a road, he would not commit an offence under section 4 or 5 of this Act.*

(2) Subsection (1) above does not apply to the person if it ought reasonably to appear to the constable that there is no likelihood of his driving or attempting to drive a mechanically propelled vehicle whilst his ability to drive properly is impaired or whilst the proportion of alcohol in his breath, blood or urine exceeds the prescribed limit.

(2A) A person who is at a hospital as a patient shall not be arrested and taken from there to a police station in pursuance of this section if it would be prejudicial to his proper care and treatment as a patient.

(3) A constable must consult a medical practitioner on any question arising under this section whether a person's ability to drive properly is or might be impaired through drugs and must act on the medical practitioner's advice.

[Road Traffic Act 1988, s 10 amended by the Road Traffic Act 1991, Sch 4 and the Serious Organised Crime and Police Act 2005, s 154.]

---

*Amended by the Railways and Transport Safety Act 2003, Sch 7 (in this PART, post), from a date to be appointed.

4–1381   11. Interpretation of sections 4 to 10.   (1) The following provisions apply for the interpretation of sections 3A to 10 of this Act.

(2) In those sections—

"drug" includes any intoxicant other than alcohol,

"fail" includes refuse,

"hospital" means an institution which provides medical or surgical treatment for in-patients or out-patients,

"the prescribed limit" means, as the case may require—

(a) 35 microgrammes of alcohol in 100 millilitres of breath,

(b) 80 milligrammes of alcohol in 100 millilitres of blood, or

(c) 107 milligrammes of alcohol in 100 millilitres of urine,

or such other proportion as may be prescribed by regulations made by the Secretary of State.

"registered health care professional" means a person (other than a medical practitioner) who is—

(a) a registered nurse; or

(b) a registered member of a health care profession which is designated for the purposes of this paragraph by an order[1] made by the Secretary of State.

(2A) A health care profession is any profession mentioned in section 60(2) of the Health Act 1999 (c 8) other than the profession of practising medicine and the profession of nursing.

(2B) An order under subsection (2) shall be made by statutory instrument; and any such statutory instrument shall be subject to annulment in pursuance of a resolution of either House of Parliament.

(3) A person does not co-operate with a preliminary test or provide[2] a specimen of breath for analysis unless his co-operation or the specimen—

(a) is sufficient to enable the test or the analysis to be carried out, and

(b) is provided in such a way as to enable the objective of the test or analysis to be satisfactorily achieved.

(4) A person provides a specimen of blood if and only if—

(a) he consents to the taking of such a specimen from him; and

(b) the specimen is taken from him by a medical practitioner or, if it is taken in a police station, either by a medical practitioner or by a registered health care professional.

[Road Traffic Act 1988, s 11 amended by the Road Traffic Act 1991, Sch 4, the Police Reform Act 2002, s 55 and the Railways and Transport Safety Act 2003, Sch 7.]

---

1. The Registered Health Care Profession (Designation No 2) Order 2003, SI 2003/2462 has been made which designates the profession of paramedics.

2. The objective of carrying out the test is to obtain a reliable positive or negative reading, not to obtain a reading which is reliable in some circumstances and not others. Therefore, a person fails to provide a specimen of breath for a roadside breath test if the person blows into the Alcolmeter testing device in such a way as to illuminate light "A" but not light "B", when the device so operates that, if in such circumstances, the "Read" button is pressed a positive result may be given which (if given) will be reliable, but a negative result may be given and (if given) may be false (*DPP v Heywood* [1998] RTR 1).

Motor racing and motoring events on public ways

4–1382   12. Motor racing on public ways.   (1) A person who promotes or takes part in a race or trial of speed between motor vehicles on a public way is guilty of an offence[1].

(2) In this section "public way" means, in England and Wales, a highway and, in Scotland, a public road.

[Road Traffic Act 1988, s 12 amended by the Road Traffic Act 1991, Sch 4.]

---

1. For punishment see the Road Traffic Offenders Act 1988, Sch 2, and notes thereto, post. Sections 11 and 12(1) of that Act (evidence by certificate etc) apply.

4–1383   13. Regulation of motoring events on public ways.   (1) A person who promotes or takes part in a competition or trial (other than a race or trial of speed) involving the use of motor vehicles on a public way is guilty of an offence[1] unless the competition or trial—

(a) is authorised, and

(b) is conducted in accordance with any conditions imposed,

by or under regulations[2] under this section.

(2) The Secretary of State may by regulations authorise, or provide for authorising, the holding of competitions or trials (other than races or trials of speed) involving the use of motor vehicles on public ways either—

(a) generally, or

(b) as regards any area, or as regards any class or description of competition or trial or any particular competition or trial,

subject to such conditions, including conditions requiring the payment of fees, as may be imposed by or under the regulations.

(3) Regulations under this section may—

(a) prescribe the procedure to be followed, and the particulars to be given, in connection with applications for authorisation under the regulations, and

(b) make different provision for different classes or descriptions of competition or trial.

(4) In this section "public way" means, in England and Wales, a highway[3] and, in Scotland, a public road.

[Road Traffic Act 1988, s 13 amended by the Road Traffic Act 1991, Sch 4.]

---

1. For punishment see the Road Traffic Offenders Act 1988, Sch 2, and notes thereto, post.

2. See Motor Vehicles (Competitions and Trials) Regulations 1969, SI 1969/414, as amended by SI 1974/1674, SI 1976/1657, SI 1982/1103 and SI 1993/2233.

3. There is no definition of a public highway.

4–1384   13A. Disapplication of sections 1 to 3 for authorised motoring events.   (1) A person shall not be guilty of an offence under sections 1, 2 or 3 of this Act by virtue of driving a vehicle in a public place other than a road if he shows that he was driving in accordance with an authorisation for a motoring event given under regulations[1] made by the Secretary of State.

(2) Regulations.

[Road Traffic Act 1988, s 13A as added by the Road Traffic Act 1991, s 5.]

---

1. See the Motor Vehicles (Off Road Events) Regulations 1995, SI 1995/1371.

Protective measures: seat belts, helmets, etc

4–1385   **14. Seat belts: adults.**   (1) The Secretary of State may make regulations[1] requiring, subject to such exceptions as may be prescribed, persons who are driving or riding in motor vehicles on a road to wear seat belts of such description as may be prescribed.

(2) Regulations under this section—

(*a*)   may make different provision in relation to different classes of vehicles, different descriptions of persons and different circumstances,

(*aa*) may, for the purpose of implementing the seat belt Directive, authorise the wearing of a seat belt approved under the law of a member State other than the United Kingdom,

(*b*)   shall include exceptions for—

    (i)   The driver of or a passenger in a motor vehicle constructed or adapted for carrying goods, while on a journey which does not exceed the prescribed distance and which is undertaken for the purpose of delivering or collecting any thing,

    (ii)   the drivers of vehicles while performing a manoeuvre which includes reversing,

    (iii)   any person holding a valid certificate signed by a medical practitioner to the effect that it is inadvisable on medical grounds for him to wear a seat belt,

(*bb*) shall, for the purpose of implementing the seat belt Directive, include an exception for any person holding a certificate to the like effect as that mentioned in paragraph (*b*)(iii) above which was issued in a member State other than the United Kingdom and which, under the law of that State, is valid for purposes corresponding to those of this section,

(*c*)   may make any prescribed exceptions subject to such conditions as may be prescribed, and

(*d*)   may prescribe cases in which a fee of a prescribed amount may be charged on an application for any certificate required as a condition of any prescribed exception.

(3) A person who drives or rides in a motor vehicle in contravention of regulations under this section is guilty of an offence[2]; but, notwithstanding any enactment or rule of law, no person other than the person actually committing the contravention is guilty of an offence by reason of the contravention.

(4) If the holder of any such certificate as is referred to in subsection (2)(*b*) or (*bb*) above is informed by a constable that he may be prosecuted for an offence under subsection (3) above, he is not in proceedings for that offence entitled to rely on the exception afforded to him by the certificate unless—

(*a*)   it is produced to the constable at the time he is so informed, or

(*b*)   it is produced—

    (i)   within seven days after the date on which he is so informed, or

    (ii)   as soon as is reasonably practicable,

    at such police station as he may have specified to the constable, or

(*c*)   where it is not produced at such police station, it is not reasonably practicable for it to be produced there before the day on which the proceedings are commenced.

(5) For the purposes of subsection (4) above, the laying of the information or, in Scotland, the service of the complaint on the accused shall be treated as the commencement of the proceedings.

(6) Regulations under this section requiring the wearing of seat belts by persons riding in motor vehicles shall not apply to children under the age of fourteen years.

(7) In this section, "the seat belt Directive" means the Directive of the Council of the European Communities, dated 16th December 1991 (No 91/671/EEC) on the approximation of the laws of the member States relating to compulsory use of safety belts in vehicles of less than 3·5 tonnes.
[Road Traffic Act 1988, s 14 amended by the Road Traffic Act 1991, Sch 4, SI 1992/3105 and the Railways and Transport Safety Act 2003, s 110.]

---

1. See the Motor Vehicles (Wearing of Seat Belts) Regulations 1993, in this PART, post.
2. For penalty see the Road Traffic Offenders Act 1988, Sch 2, post. Sections 11 and 12(1) of that Act (evidence by certificate etc) apply.

4–1386   **15. Restriction on carrying children not wearing seat belts in motor vehicles.**
(1) Except as provided by regulations[1], where a child under the age of fourteen years is in the front of a motor vehicle, a person must not without reasonable excuse drive the vehicle on a road unless the child is wearing a seat belt in conformity with regulations.

(1A) Where—

(*a*)   a child is in the front of a motor vehicle other than a bus,

(*b*)   the child is in a rear-facing child restraining device, and

(*c*)   the passenger seat where the child is placed is protected by a front air bag,

a person must not without reasonable excuse drive the vehicle on a road unless the air bag is deactivated.

(2) It is an offence[2] for a person to drive a motor vehicle in contravention of subsection (1) or (1A) above.

(3) Except as provided by regulations[3], where—

(*a*)   a child under the age of three years is in the rear of a motor vehicle, or

(b) a child of or over that age but under the age of fourteen years is in the rear of a motor vehicle and any seat belt is fitted in the rear of that vehicle,

a person must not without reasonable excuse drive the vehicle on a road unless the child is wearing a seat belt in conformity with regulations.

(3A) Except as provided by regulations, where—

(a) a child who is under the age of 12 years and less than 150 centimetres in height is in the rear of a passenger car,

(b) no seat belt is fitted in the rear of the passenger car, and

(c) a seat in the front of the passenger car is provided with a seat belt but is not occupied by any person,

a person must not without reasonable excuse drive the passenger car on a road.

(4) It is an offence for a person to drive a motor vehicle in contravention of subsection (3) or (3A) above.

(5) Provision may be made by regulations—

(a) excepting from the prohibition in subsection (1), (3) or (3A) above children of any prescribed description, vehicles of a prescribed class or the driving of vehicles in such circumstances as may be prescribed,

(b) defining in relation to any class of vehicle what part of the vehicle is to be regarded as the front of the vehicle for the purposes of subsection (1) or (3A) above or as the rear of the vehicle for the purposes of subsection (3) or (3A) above,

(c) prescribing for the purposes of subsection (1) or (3) above the descriptions of seat belt to be worn by children of any prescribed description and the manner in which such seat belt is to be fixed and used.

(5A) Without prejudice to the generality of subsection (5) above, regulations made by virtue of paragraph (c) of that subsection may, for the purpose of implementing the seat belt Directive—

(a) make different provision in relation to different vehicles and different circumstances,

(b) authorise the wearing of a seat belt approved under the law of any member State other than the United Kingdom.

(6) Regulations made for the purposes of subsection (3) or (3A) above—

(a) shall include an exemption for any child holding a valid certificate signed by a medical practitioner to the effect that it is inadvisable on medical grounds for him to wear a seat belt, and

(b) shall, for the purpose of implementing the seat belt Directive, include an exemption for any child holding a certificate to the like effect which was issued in any member State other than the United Kingdom and which, under the law of that State, is valid for purposes corresponding to those of this section,

but such regulations may, for the purpose of implementing that Directive, make either of those exemptions subject to such conditions as may be prescribed.

(7) If the driver of a motor vehicle is informed by a constable that he may be prosecuted for an offence under subsection (4) above, he is not in proceedings for that offence entitled to rely on an exception afforded to a child by a certificate referred to in subsection (6) above unless—

(a) it is produced to the constable at the time he is so informed, or

(b) it is produced—

(i) within seven days after the date on which he is so informed, or

(ii) as soon as is reasonably practicable,

at such police station as he may have specified to the constable, or

(c) where it is not produced at such police station, it is not reasonably practicable for it to be produced there before the day on which the proceedings are commenced.

(8) For the purposes of subsection (7) above, the laying of the information or, in Scotland, the service of the complaint on the accused shall be treated as the commencement of the proceedings.

(9) In this section—

"bus" means a motor vehicle that—

(a) has at least four wheels,

(b) is constructed or adapted for the carriage of passengers,

(c) has more than eight seats in addition to the driver's seat, and

(d) has a maximum design speed exceeding 25 kilometres per hour;

"maximum laden weight" has the meaning given by Part IV of Schedule 6 to the Road Traffic Regulation Act 1984;

"passenger car" means a motor vehicle which—

(a) is constructed or adapted for use for the carriage of passengers and is not a goods vehicle,

(b) has no more than eight seats in addition to the driver's seat,

(c) has four or more wheels,

(d) has a maximum design speed exceeding 25 kilometres per hour, and

(e) has a maximum laden weight not exceeding 3·5 tonnes,

"regulations" means regulations made by the Secretary of State under this section,

"seat belt" includes any description of restraining device for a child and any reference to wearing a seat belt is to be construed accordingly;

"the seat belt Directive" has the same meaning as in section 14.

(9A) The reference in subsection (1) above to the air bag being deactivated includes a reference to the case where the air bag is designed or adapted in such a way that it cannot inflate enough to pose a risk of injury to a child travelling in a rear-facing child restraining device in the seat in question.

(10) *Repealed.*

[Road Traffic Act 1988, s 15 amended by the Road Traffic Act 1991, Sch 8, SI 1992/3105 and SI 2006/1892.]

---

1. See the Motor Vehicles (Wearing of Seat Belts by Children in Front Seats) Regulations 1993, in this PART, post.
2. For penalty see the Road Traffic Offenders Act 1988, Sch 2; ss 11 and 12(1) of that Act (evidence by certificate etc) apply.
3. See the Motor Vehicles (Wearing of Seat Belts) Regulations 1993, in this PART, post.

4–1387 15A. Safety equipment for children in motor vehicles. (1) The Secretary of State may make regulations prescribing (by reference to shape, construction or any other quality) types of equipment of any description to which this section applies that are recommended as conducive to the safety in the event of accident of prescribed classes of children in prescribed classes of motor vehicles.

(2) Regulations under this section may make provision for securing that when equipment of a type prescribed by the regulations is sold or offered for sale as equipment which is so conducive—

(*a*) appropriate information is provided in relation to it in such manner as may be prescribed, and
(*b*) inappropriate information is not provided in relation to it.

(3) Except in such circumstances as may be prescribed, if a person sells, or offers for sale, equipment of any description for which a type is prescribed under this section as equipment which is so conducive and that equipment—

(*a*) is not of a type so prescribed, or
(*b*) is sold or offered for sale in contravention of regulations under this section,

he is, subject to subsection (5) below, guilty of an offence.

(4) Except in such circumstances as may be prescribed, if a person sells, or offers for sale, equipment of any description for which a type is prescribed under this section as equipment conducive to the safety in the event of accident—

(*a*) of children not of a class prescribed in relation to equipment of that type, or
(*b*) of children in motor vehicles not of a class prescribed in relation to equipment of that type,

he is, subject to subsection (5) below, guilty of an offence.

(5) A person shall not be convicted of an offence under this section in respect of the sale or offer for sale of equipment if he proves that it was sold or, as the case may be, offered for sale for export from Great Britain.

(6) The provisions of Schedule 1 to this Act shall have effect in relation to contraventions of this section.

(7) Regulations under this section may make different provision in relation to different circumstances.

(8) This section applies to equipment of any description for use in a motor vehicle consisting of—

(*a*) a restraining device for a child or for a carry-cot, or
(*b*) equipment designed for use by a child in conjunction with any description of restraining device.

(9) References in this section to selling or offering for sale include respectively references to letting on hire and offering to let on hire.

[Road Traffic Act 1988, s 15A added by the Motor Vehicles (Safety Equipment for Children) Act 1991, s 1.]

15B. Requirement to notify bus passengers to wear seat belts. (1) Subject to subsection (6) below, the operator of a bus in which any of the passenger seats are equipped with seat belts shall take all reasonable steps to ensure that every passenger is notified that he is required to wear a seat belt at all times when—

(*a*) he is in a seat equipped with a seat belt, and
(*b*) the bus is in motion.

(2) For the purposes of subsection (1) above, a passenger may be notified only by one or more of the following means—

(*a*) an official announcement, or an audio-visual presentation, made when the passenger joins the bus or within a reasonable time of his doing so;
(*b*) a sign prominently displayed at each passenger seat equipped with a seat belt.

In paragraph (a) above, "official announcement" means an announcement by the driver of the bus, by a conductor or courier or by a person who is a group leader in relation to any group of persons who are passengers on the bus.

(3) For the purposes of subsection (2)(*b*) above, a sign that takes the form of a pictorial symbol must be in the form shown in Schedule 2A, depicting a white figure on a blue background.

(4) An operator who fails to comply with subsection (1) above is guilty of an offence.

(5) Where an offence under subsection (4) above which has been committed by a body corporate is proved to have been committed with the consent or connivance of, or to be attributable to any neglect on the part of, a director, manager, secretary or other similar officer of the body corporate, or any person who was purporting to act in such a capacity, he as well as the body corporate shall be guilty of the offence and shall be liable to be proceeded against and punished accordingly.

(6) Subsection (1) above does not apply in relation to a bus—

(*a*) which is being used to provide a local service (within the meaning of the Transport Act 1985) in a built-up area, or

(*b*) which is constructed or adapted for the carriage of standing passengers and on which the operator permits standing.

For the purposes of paragraph (a) above, a local service is provided in a built-up area if the entire route used by that service consists of restricted roads.

(7) In this section—

"bus" has the same meaning as in section 15;
"operator", in relation to a bus, means—

(*a*) the owner of the bus, or

(*b*) if the bus is in the possession of any other person under an agreement for hire, hire-purchase, conditional sale, loan or otherwise, that person;

"passenger seat", in relation to a bus, means any seat other than the driver's seat;
"restricted road" means a road that is restricted for the purposes of section 81 of the Road Traffic Regulation Act 1984 (ignoring any direction under section 82(2)(b) of that Act) or would be so restricted but for a direction under section 82(2)(a) or an order under section 84(1) of that Act.

[Road Traffic Act 1988, s 15B as inserted by SI 2006/1892.]

4–1388　16. Wearing of protective headgear[1]. (1) The Secretary of State may make regulations[2] requiring, subject to such exceptions as may be specified in the regulations, persons driving or riding (otherwise than in side-cars) on motor cycles of any class specified in the regulations to wear protective headgear of such description as may be so specified.

(2) A requirement imposed by regulations under this section shall not apply to any follower of the Sikh religion while he is wearing a turban.

(3) Regulations under this section may make different provision in relation to different circumstances.

(4) A person who drives or rides on a motor cycle in contravention of regulations under this section is guilty of an offence[3]; but notwithstanding any enactment or rule of law no person other than the person actually committing the contravention is guilty of an offence by reason of the contravention unless the person actually committing the contravention is a child under the age of sixteen years.

[Road Traffic Act 1988, s 16.]

---

1. A requirement that protective headgear be worn will not necessarily breach art 9 (freedom of thought, conscience and religion) of the European Convention on Human Rights. See *X v United Kingdom* (1976) 5 DR 100, *X v United Kingdom* (1978) 14 DR 197 and *X v United Kingdom* (1982) 28 DR 5.
2. See the Motor Cycles (Protective Helmets) Regulations 1998, reg 4, this PART, POST.
3. For punishment see the Road Traffic Offenders Act 1988, Sch 2, post, and notes thereto. It is no defence to an offence alleged under s 17(2) of the Act to prove that the helmet was sold for off-road use; nor is it a defence to show that the helmet sold afforded a degree of protection similar to or greater than that provided by a type prescribed by the Motor Cycles (Protective Helmets) Regulations 1998, reg 5, this PART, post (*Losexis Ltd v Clarke* [1984] RTR 174).

4–1389　17. Protective helmets for motor cyclists. (1) The Secretary of State may make regulations[1] prescribing (by reference to shape, construction or any other quality) types of helmet recommended as affording protection to persons on or in motor cycles, or motor cycles of different classes, from injury in the event of accident.

(2) If a person sells, or offers for sale, a helmet as a helmet for affording such protection and the helmet is neither—

(*a*) of a type prescribed under this section, nor

(*b*) of a type authorised under regulations made under this section and sold or offered for sale subject to any conditions specified in the authorisation,

subject to subsection (3) below, he is guilty of an offence[2].

(3) A person shall not be convicted of an offence under this section in respect of the sale or offer for sale of a helmet if he proves that it was sold or, as the case may be, offered for sale for export from Great Britain.

(4) The provisions of Schedule 1[3] to this Act shall have effect in relation to contraventions of this section.

(5) In this section and that Schedule "helmet" includes any head-dress, and references in this section to selling or offering for sale include respectively references to letting on hire and offering to let on hire.

[Road Traffic Act 1988, s 17.]

1. The Motor Cycles (Protective Helmets) Regulations 1998, reg 5, this PART, post, prescribe the types of helmet by reference to British Standards.
2. For punishment see the Road Traffic Offenders Act 1988, Sch 2, post, and notes thereto. It is no defence to an offence alleged under sub-s (2) to prove that the helmet was sold for off-road use; nor is it a defence to show that the helmet sold afforded a degree of protection similar to or greater than that provided by a type prescribed by the Motor Cycles (Protective Helmets) Regulations 1998, reg 5, this PART, post (*Losexis Ltd v Clarke* [1984] RTR 174).
3. These provisions relate to the prosecution of the actual offender and to the pleading of a warranty.

4–1390 18. Authorisation of head-worn appliances for use on motor cycles. (1) The Secretary of State may make regulations[1] prescribing (by reference to shape, construction or any other quality) types of appliance of any description to which this section applies as authorised for use by persons driving or riding (otherwise than in sidecars) on motor cycles of any class specified in the regulations.
(2) Regulations under this section—

(*a*) may impose restrictions or requirements with respect to the circumstances in which appliances of any type prescribed by the regulations may be used, and
(*b*) may make different provision in relation to different circumstances.

(3) If a person driving or riding on a motor cycle on a road uses an appliance of any description for which a type is prescribed under this section and that appliance—

(*a*) is not of a type so prescribed, or
(*b*) is otherwise used in contravention of regulations under this section,

he is guilty of an offence[2].
(4) If a person sells, or offers for sale, an appliance of any such description as authorised for use by persons on or in motor cycles, or motor cycles of any class, and that appliance is not of a type prescribed under this section as authorised for such use, he is, subject to subsection (5) below, guilty of an offence[2].
(5) A person shall not convicted of an offence under this section in respect of the sale or offer for sale of an appliance if he proves that it was sold or, as the case may be, offered for sale for export from Great Britain.
(6) The provisions of Schedule 1[3] to this Act shall have effect in relation to contraventions of subsection (4) above.
(7) This section applies to appliances of any description designed or adapted for use—

(*a*) with any headgear, or
(*b*) by being attached to or placed upon the head,

(as, for example, eye protectors or earphones).
(8) References in this section to selling or offering for sale include respectively references to letting on hire and offering to let on hire.
[Road Traffic Act 1988, s 18.]

1. The Motor Cycles (Eye Protectors) Regulations 1999, in this PART, post, prescribe types of eye protectors by reference to conformity with a British Standard.
2. For punishment, see the Road Traffic Offenders Act 1988, Sch 2, post.
3. These provisions, post, relate to the prosecution of the actual offender and to the pleading of a warranty.

Stopping on verges, etc, or in dangerous positions, etc

4–1391 19. Prohibition of parking of HGVs on verges, central reservations and footways.
(1) Subject to subsection (2) below, a person who parks a heavy commercial vehicle (as defined in section 20 of this Act) wholly or partly—

(*a*) on the verge of a road, or
(*b*) on any land situated between two carriageways and which is not a footway, or
(*c*) on a footway,

is guilty of an offence[1].
(2) A person shall not be convicted of an offence under this section in respect of a vehicle if he proves to the satisfaction of the court—

(*a*) that it was parked in accordance with permission given by a constable in uniform, or
(*b*) that it was parked in contravention of this section for the purpose of saving life or extinguishing fire or meeting any other like emergency, or
(*c*) that it was parked in contravention of this section but the conditions specified in subsection (3) below were satisfied.

(3) The conditions mentioned in subsection (2)(*c*) above are—

(*a*) that the vehicle was parked on the verge of a road or on a footway for the purpose of loading or unloading, and
(*b*) that the loading or unloading of the vehicle could not have been satisfactorily performed if it had not been parked on the footway or verge, and
(*c*) that the vehicle was not left unattended at any time while it was so parked.

(4) In this section "carriageway" an "footway", in relation to England and Wales, have the same meanings as in the Highways Act 1980.

[Road Traffic Act 1988, s 19 amended by the Road Traffic (Consequential Provisions) Act 1988, Sch 2.]

---

1. For penalty see the Road Traffic Offenders Act 1988, Sch 2, post. Sections 11 and 12(1) of that Act (evidence by certificate etc) apply. Where an order has been made under Sch 3 to the Road Traffic Act 1991, s 19 will to that extent cease to apply and any penalty will become payable under Sch 3.

4–1400   20. Definition of "heavy commercial vehicle" for the purposes of section 19. (1) In section 19 of this Act, "heavy commercial vehicles" means any goods vehicle which has an operating weight exceeding 7.5 tonnes.

(2) The operating weight of a goods vehicle for the purposes of this section is—

(a) in the case of a motor vehicle not drawing a trailer or in the case of a trailer, its maximum laden weight;

(b) in the case of an articulated vehicle, its maximum laden weight (if it has one) and otherwise the aggregate maximum laden weight of all the individual vehicles forming part of that articulated vehicle, and

(c) in the case of a motor vehicle (other than an articulated vehicle) drawing one or more trailers, the aggregate maximum laden weight of the motor vehicle and the trailer or trailers attached to it.

(3) In this section "articulated vehicle" means a motor vehicle with a trailer so attached to it as to be partially superimposed upon it; and references to the maximum laden weight of a vehicle are references to the total laden weight which must not be exceeded in the case of that vehicle if it is to be used in Great Britain without contravening any regulations for the time being in force under section 41 of this Act.

(4) In this section, and in the definition of "goods vehicle" in section 192 of this Act as it applies for the purposes of this section, "trailer" means any vehicle other than a motor vehicle.

(5) The Secretary of State may by regulations amend subsections (1) and (2) above (whether as originally enacted or as previously amended under this subsection)—

(a) by substituting weights of a different description for any of the weights there mentioned, or

(b) in the case of subsection (1) above, by substituting a weight of a different description or amount, or a weight different both in description and amount, for the weight there mentioned.

(6) Different regulations may be made under subsection (5) above as respects different classes of vehicles or as respects the same class of vehicles in different circumstances and as respects different times of the day or night and as respects different localities.

(7) Regulations under subsection (5) above shall not so amend subsection (1) above that there is any case in which a goods vehicle whose operating weight (ascertained in accordance with subsection (2) above as originally enacted) does not exceed 7.5 tonnes is a heavy commercial vehicle for any of the purposes of section 19 of this Act.

[Road Traffic Act 1988, s 20.]

4–1401   21. Prohibition of driving or parking on cycle tracks. (1) Subject to the provisions of this section, any person who, without lawful authority, drives or parks a mechanically propelled vehicle wholly or partly on a cycle track is guilty of an offence[1].

(2) A person shall not be convicted of an offence under subsection (1) above with respect to a vehicle if he proves to the satisfaction of the court—

(a) that the vehicle was driven or (as the case may be) parked in contravention of that subsection for the purpose of saving life, or extinguishing fire or meeting any other like emergency, or

(b) that the vehicle was owned or operated by a highway authority or by a person discharging functions on behalf of a highway authority and was driven or (as the case may be) parked in contravention of that subsection in connection with the carrying out by or on behalf of that authority of any of the following, that is, the cleansing, maintenance or improvement of, or the maintenance or alteration of any structure or other work situated in, the cycle track or its verges, or the preventing or removing of obstructions to the cycle track or the preventing or abating in any other way of nuisances or other interferences with the cycle track, or

(c) that the vehicle was owned or operated by statutory undertakers and was driven or (as the case may be) parked in contravention of that subsection in connection with the carrying out by those undertakers of any works in relation to any apparatus belonging to or used by them for the purpose of their undertaking.

(3) In this section—

(a) "cycle track" and other expressions used in this section and in the Highways Act 1980 have the same meaning as in that Act,

(aa) in subsection (1) "mechanically propelled vehicle" does not include a vehicle falling within paragraph (a), (b) or (c) of section 189(1) of this Act.

(b) in subsection (2)(c) above "statutory undertakers" means any body who are statutory undertakers within the meaning of the Highways Act 1980, any sewerage authority within the meaning of that Act or the operator of an electronic communications code network and in relation to any such sewerage authority "apparatus" includes sewers or sewerage disposal works.

(4) This section does not extend to Scotland.

[Road Traffic Act 1988, s 21, as amended by the Countryside and Rights of Way Act 2000, Sch 7 and the Communications Act 2003, Sch 17.]

---

1. For penalty see the Road Traffic Offenders Act 1988, Sch 2, post. Where an order has been made under Sch 3 to the Road Traffic Act 1991, s 21 will to that extent cease to apply and any penalty will become payable under Sch 3.

4–1402   22. Leaving vehicles in dangerous positions.   If a person in charge of a vehicle[1] causes or permits the vehicle or a trailer[2] drawn by it to remain at rest on a road in such a position or in such condition or in such circumstances[3] as to involve a danger of injury to other persons using the road[4], he is guilty of an offence[5].

[Road Traffic Act 1988, s 22 amended by the Road Traffic Act 1991, Sch 4.]

---

1. This section applies to tramcars and trolley vehicles operated under statutory powers. It is not restricted to mechanically-propelled vehicles.
2. A "trailer" is defined as a vehicle drawn by a motor vehicle (s 186, post). If the object in question does not come within that definition, it will probably be a "vehicle".
3. This includes a vehicle which is likely to cause danger while moving after remaining at rest (*Maguire v Crouch* [1941] 1 KB 108, 104 JP 445).
4. For power to remove such vehicles, see ss 99 and 100 of the Road Traffic Regulation Act 1984, ante, and regulations made thereunder. See also Highway Code, paras 124, 125, in this PART, post.
5. For penalty see the Road Traffic Offenders Act 1988, Sch 2, post and notes thereto, post; ss 1 and 2 of that Act (notice of intended prosecution etc) imposes restrictions on prosecutions and ss 11 and 12(1) (evidence by certificate etc) also apply.

4–1403   22A. Causing danger to road-users.   (1) A person is guilty of an offence[1] if he intentionally and without lawful authority or reasonable cause—

  (*a*) causes anything to be on or over a road, or
  (*b*) interferes with a motor vehicle, trailer or cycle, or
  (*c*) interferes (directly or indirectly) with traffic equipment,

in such circumstances that it would be obvious to a reasonable person that to do so would be dangerous[2].

(2) In subsection (1) above "dangerous" refers to danger either of injury to any person while on or near a road, or of serious damage to property on or near a road; and in determining for the purposes of that subsection what would be obvious to a reasonable person in a particular case, regard shall be had not only to the circumstances of which he could be expected to be aware but also to any circumstances shown to have been within the knowledge of the accused.

(3) In subsection (1) above "traffic equipment" means—

  (*a*) anything lawfully placed on or near a road by a highway authority;
  (*b*) a traffic sign lawfully placed on or near a road by a person other than a highway authority;
  (*c*) any fence, barrier or light lawfully placed on or near a road—

    (i)   in pursuance of section 174 of the Highways Act 1980, section 8 of the Public Utilities Street Works Act 1950 or section 65 of the New Roads and Street Works Act 1991 (which provide for guarding, lighting and signing in streets where works are undertaken), or

    (ii) by a constable or a person acting under the instructions (whether general or specific) of a chief officer of police.

(4) For the purposes of subsection (3) above anything placed on or near a road shall unless the contrary is proved be deemed to have been lawfully placed there.

(5) In this section "road" does not include a footpath or bridleway.

(6) Scotland.

[Road Traffic Act 1988, s 22A as added by the Road Traffic Act 1991, s 6.]

---

1. For penalty see the Road Traffic Offenders Act 1988, Sch 2, post.
2. The reasonable man does not expect, and cannot be taken to expect, that motorists will drive well and carefully; the fact that a motorist driving carefully would have safely avoided the obstruction in question is not the correct approach, but rather whether a reasonable bystander, fully aware that not all drivers drive well, would consider it to represent an obvious danger: *DPP v D* [2006] EWHC 314 (Admin), (2006) 170 JP 421, [2006] RTR 38.

Other restrictions in interests of safety

4–1404   23. Restriction of carriage of persons on motor cycles.   (1) Not more than one person in addition to the driver may be carried on a motor bicycle.

(2) No person in addition to the driver may be carried on a motor bicycle otherwise than sitting astride the motor cycle and on a proper seat securely fixed to the motor cycle behind the driver's seat.

(3) If a person is carried on a motor cycle in contravention of this section, the driver of the motor cycle is guilty of an offence[1].

[Road Traffic Act 1988, s 23 as amended by the Road Traffic (Driver Licensing and Information Systems) Act 1989, Sch 3.]

1. For penalty see the Road Traffic Offenders Act 1988, Sch 2, post. Sections 11 and 12(1) of that Act (evidence by certificate etc) also apply.

4–1405　24. Restriction of carriage of persons on bicycles.　(1) Not more than one person may be carried on a road on a bicycle not propelled by mechanical power unless it is constructed or adapted for the carriage of more than one person.

(2) In this section—

(*a*) references to a person carried on a bicycle include references to a person riding the bicycle, and

(*b*) "road" includes bridleway.

(3) If a person is carried on a bicycle in contravention of subsection (1) above, each of the persons carried is guilty of an offence[1].
[Road Traffic Act 1988, s 24.]

1. For penalty, see the Road Traffic Offenders Act 1988, Sch 2, post. Sections 11 and 12(1) of that Act (evidence by certificate etc) apply.

4–1406　25. Tampering with motor vehicles.　If, while a motor vehicle is on a road or on a parking place provided by a local authority, a person—

(*a*) gets on to the vehicle, or

(*b*) tampers with the brake or other part of its mechanism,

without lawful authority or reasonable cause he is guilty of an offence[1].
[Road Traffic Act 1988, s 25.]

1. For penalty see the Road Traffic Offenders Act 1988, Sch 2, post. Section 11 of that Act (evidence by certificate) applies.

4–1407　26. Holding or getting on to vehicle in order to be towed or carried.　(1) If, for the purpose of being carried, a person without lawful authority or reasonable cause takes or retains hold of[1], or gets on to, a motor vehicle or trailer while in motion on a road he is guilty of an offence[2].

(2) If, for the purpose of being drawn, a person takes or retains hold of a motor vehicle or trailer while in motion on a road he is guilty of an offence[3].
[Road Traffic Act 1988, s 26.]

1. See also para 145 of the Highway Code in this PART, post.
2. For punishment see the Road Traffic Offenders Act 1988, Sch 2, post, and notes thereto. Section 11 of that Act (evidence by certificate) applies to s 26(1), and ss 11 and 12(1) apply to s 26(2).
3. This offence is committed even where the defendant obtains the consent of the driver of the drawing vehicle.

4–1408　27. Control of dogs on roads.　(1) A person who causes or permits a dog to be on a designated road without the dog being held on a lead is guilty of an offence[1].

(2) In this section "designated road" means a length of road specified by an order[2] in that behalf of the local authority in whose area the length of road is situated.

(3) The powers which under subsection (2) above are exercisable by a local authority in England and Wales are, in the case of a road part of the width of which is in the area of one local authority and part in the area of another, exercisable by either authority with the consent of the other.

(4) An order under this section may provide that subsection (1) above shall apply subject to such limitations or exceptions as may be specified in the order, and (without prejudice to the generality of this subsection) subsection (1) above does not apply to dogs proved—

(*a*) to be kept for driving or tending sheep or cattle in the course of a trade or business, or

(*b*) to have been at the material time in use under proper control for sporting purposes.

(5) An order under this section shall not be made except after consultation with the chief officer of police.

(6)–(8) Procedure for making regulations, meaning of "local authority", power to vary or revoke.
[Road Traffic Act 1988, s 27.]

1. For penalty see the Road Traffic Offenders Act 1988, Sch 2, post.
2. Made under the Control of Dogs on Roads Order (Procedure) (England and Wales) Regulations 1995, SI 1995/2767.

Cycling offences and cycle racing

4–1409　28. Dangerous cycling.　(1) A person who rides a cycle[1] on a road dangerously is guilty of an offence[2].

(2) For the purposes of subsection (1) above a person is to be regarded as riding dangerously if (and only if)—

(*a*) the way he rides falls far below what would be expected of a competent and careful cyclist, and

(*b*) it would be obvious to a competent and careful cyclist that riding in that way would be dangerous.

(3) In subsection (2) above "dangerous" refers to danger either of injury to any person or of serious damage to property; and in determining for the purposes of that subsection what would be obvious to a competent and careful cyclist in a particular case, regard shall be had not only to the circumstances of which he could be expected to be aware but also to any circumstances shown to have been within the knowledge of the accused.

[Road Traffic Act 1988 as substituted by the Road Traffic Act 1991, s 7.]

---

  1. Defined by s 192, post.
  2. For penalty see the the Road Traffic Offenders Act 1988, Sch 2, post and for restrictions on prosecution, see ss 1 and 2 thereof: ss 11 and 12(1) thereof (evidence by certificate etc) also apply.

4–1410   29. Careless, and inconsiderate, cycling.   If a person rides a cycle[1] on a road without due care and attention[2], or without reasonable consideration for other persons using the road, he is guilty of an offence.

[Road Traffic Act 1988, s 29 amended by the Road Traffic Act 1991, Sch 8.]

---

  1. Compare the offence under s 3 ante, and see preliminary note to this title.
  2. For penalty see the Road Traffic Offenders Act 1988, Sch 2, and for restrictions on prosecution see ss 1 and 2 thereof, post: ss 11 and 12(1) thereof (evidence by certificate etc) also apply.

4–1411   30. Cycling when under influence of drink or drugs.   (1) A person who, when riding a cycle on a road or other public place[1], is unfit to ride through drink or drugs (that is to say, is under the influence of drink or a drug to such an extent as to be incapable of having proper control of the cycle) is guilty of an offence[2].

  (2) Scotland.
  (3) Repealed.

[Road Traffic Act 1988, s 30 amended by the Road Traffic Act 1991, Sch 8.]

---

  1. See note to "road or other public place" in s 4, ante.
  2. For penalty see the Road Traffic Offenders Act 1988, Sch 2, post. Sections 11 and 12(1) thereof (evidence by certificate etc) also apply.

4–1412   31. Regulation of cycle racing on public ways.   (1) A person who promotes or takes part in a race or trial of speed on a public way between cycles is guilty of an offence[1], unless the race or trial—

  (a)   is authorised, and
  (b)   is conducted in accordance with any conditions imposed,

by or under regulations[2] under this section.

  (2), (3) Regulations.

  (4) Without prejudice to any other powers exercisable in that behalf, the chief officer of police may give directions with respect to the movement of, or the route to be followed by, vehicular traffic during any period, being directions which it is necessary or expedient to give in relation to that period to prevent or mitigate—

  (a)   congestion or obstruction of traffic, or
  (b)   danger to or from traffic,

in consequence of the holding of a race or trial of speed authorised by or under regulations under this section.

  (5) Directions under subsection (4) above may include a direction that any road or part of a road specified in the direction shall be closed during the period to vehicles or to vehicles of a class so specified.

  (6) In this section "public way" means, in England and Wales, a highway, and in Scotland, a public road but does not include a footpath.

[Road Traffic Act 1988, s 31 amended by the Road Traffic Act 1991, Sch 4.]

---

  1. For punishment see the Road Traffic Offenders Act 1988, Sch 2, post, and notes thereto,
  2. The Cycle Racing on Highways Regulations 1960, SI 1960/250 amended by SI 1963/929, SI 1980/1185, SI 1988/215 and SI 1995/3241 have been made. Sections 11 and 12(1) thereof (evidence by certificate etc) also apply.
  Periodically the Secretary of State authorises specified races and trials.

4–1413   32. Electrically assisted pedal cycles.   (1) An electrically assisted pedal cycle of a class specified in regulations[1] made for the purposes of section 189 of this Act and section 140 of the Road Traffic Regulation Act 1984 shall not be driven on a road by a person under the age of fourteen.

  (2) A person who—

  (a)   drives such a pedal cycle, or
  (b)   knowing or suspecting that another person is under the age of fourteen, causes or permits him to drive such a pedal cycle,

in contravention of subsection (1) above is guilty of an offence[2].

[Road Traffic Act 1988, s 32.]

1. The Electrically Assisted Pedal Cycles Regulations 1983, SI 1983/1168 have been made.
2. For penalty see the Road Traffic Offenders Act 1988, Sch 2, post.

Use of motor vehicles away from roads

4–1414   33. Control of use of footpaths, bridleways and restricted byways for motor vehicle trials.   (1) A person must not promote or take part in a trial of any description between motor vehicles on a footpath, bridleway or restricted bywaybyway[1] unless the holding of the trial has been authorised under this section by the local authority.

(2) A local authority shall not give an authorisation under this section unless satisfied that consent in writing to the use of any length of footpath, bridleway or restricted byway for the purposes of the trial has been given by the owner and by the occupier of the land over which that length of footpath, bridleway or restricted byway runs, and any such authorisation may be given subject to compliance with such conditions as the authority think fit.

(3) A person who—

   (a)   contravenes subsection (1) above, or

   (b)   fails to comply with any conditions subject to which an authorisation under this section has been granted,

is guilty of an offence[2].

(4) The holding of a trial authorised under this section is not affected by any statutory provision prohibiting or restricting the use of footpaths, bridleway or restricted byway a specified footpath, bridleway or restricted byway; but this section does not prejudice any right or remedy of a person as having any interest in land.

(5) In this section "local authority"—

   (a)   in relation to England and Wales, means the council of a county, metropolitan district or London borough, and

   (b)   Scotland.

(6) In this section "restricted byway" means a way over which the public have restricted byway rights within the meaning of Part 2 of the Countryside and Rights of Way Act 2000, with or without a right to drive animals of any description along the way, but no other rights of way.*
[Road Traffic Act 1988, s 33 as amended by SI 2006/1177.]

---

*Section reproduced as in force in England and Wales.
1. "Footpath" and "bridleway" are defined by s 192, post.
2. For penalty see the Road Traffic Offenders Act 1988, Sch 2, post. Sections 11 and 12(1) thereof (evidence by certificate etc) also apply.

4–1415   34. Prohibition of driving motor vehicles elsewhere than on roads.   (1) Subject to the provisions of this section, if without lawful authority a person drives a mechanically propelled vehicle—

   (a)   on to or upon any common land, moorland or land of any other description, not being land forming part of a road, or

   (b)   on any road being a footpath, bridleway or restricted byway,

he is guilty of an offence.

(2) For the purposes of subsection (1)(b) above, a way shown in a definitive map and statement as a footpath, bridleway or restricted byway is, without prejudice to section 56(1) of the Wildlife and Countryside Act 1981, to be taken to be a way of the kind shown, unless (subject to section 34A of this Act) the contrary is proved.

(2A) It is not an offence under this section for a person with an interest in land, or a visitor to any land, to drive a mechanically propelled vehicle on a road if, immediately before the commencement of section 47(2) of the Countryside and Rights of Way Act 2000, the road was—

   (a)   shown in a definitive map and statement as a road used as a public path, and

   (b)   in use for obtaining access to the land by the driving of mechanically propelled vehicles by a person with an interest in the land or by visitors to the land.

(3) It is not an offence under this section to drive a mechanically propelled vehicle on any land within fifteen yards of a road, being a road on which a motor vehicle may lawfully be driven, for the purpose only of parking the vehicle on that land.

(4) A person shall not be convicted of an offence under this section with respect to a vehicle if he proves to the satisfaction of the court that it was driven in contravention of this section for the purpose of saving life or extinguishing fire or meeting any other like emergency.

(5) It is hereby declared that nothing in this section prejudices the operation of—

   (a)   section 193 of the Law of Property Act 1925 (rights of the public over commons and waste lands), or

   (b)   any byelaws applying to any land,

or affects the law of trespass to land or any right or remedy to which a person may by law be entitled in respect of any such trespass or in particular confers a right to park a vehicle on any land.

(6) Subsection (2) above does not extend to Scotland.

(7) In this section—

"definitive map and statement" has the same meaning as in Part III of the Wildlife and Countryside Act 1981;

"interest", in relation to land, includes any estate in land and any right over land (whether exercisable by virtue of the ownership of an estate or interest in the land or by virtue of a licence or agreement) and, in particular, includes rights of common and sporting rights;

"mechanically propelled vehicle" does not include a vehicle falling within paragraph (*a*), (*b*) or (*c*) of section 189(1) of this Act; and

"restricted byway" means a way over which the public have restricted byway rights within the meaning of Part II of the Countryside and Rights of Way Act 2000, with or without a right to drive animals of any description along the way, but no other rights of way.

(8) A person—

(*a*) entering any land in exercise of rights conferred by virtue of section 2(1) of the Countryside and Rights of Way Act 2000, or

(*b*) entering any land which is treated by section 15(1) of that Act as being accessible to the public apart from that Act,

is not for the purposes of subsection (2A) a visitor to the land.]
[Road Traffic Act 1988, s 34 as substituted by the Countryside and Rights of Way Act 2000, Sch 7 and the Natural Environment And Rural Communities Act 2006, Sch 12.]

4–1415A 34A. Exceptions to presumption in section 34(2). (1) Where a person is charged with an offence under section 34 of this Act in respect of the driving of any vehicle, it is open to that person to prove under subsection (2) of that section that a way shown in a definitive map and statement as a footpath, bridleway or restricted byway is not a way of the kind shown only—

(*a*) if he proves to the satisfaction of the court—

  (i) that he was a person interested in any land and that the driving of the vehicle by him was reasonably necessary to obtain access to the land,

  (ii) that the driving of the vehicle by him was reasonably necessary to obtain access to any land, and was for the purpose of obtaining access to the land as a lawful visitor, or

  (iii) that the driving of the vehicle by him was reasonably necessary for the purposes of any business, trade or profession; or

(*b*) in such circumstances as may be prescribed by regulations made by the Secretary of State (and paragraph (*a*) above is without prejudice to this paragraph).

(2) In subsection (1) above—

"interest", in relation to land, includes any estate in land and any right over land, whether the right is exercisable by virtue of the ownership of an estate or interest in land or by virtue of a licence or agreement, and in particular includes rights of common and sporting rights, and the reference to a person interested in land shall be construed accordingly;

"lawful visitor", in relation to land, includes any person who enters the land for any purpose in the exercise of a right conferred by law.★
[Road Traffic Act 1988, s 34A as inserted by Countryside and Rights of Way Act 2000, s 67, Sch 7, para 6.]

★**Section 34A printed as prospectively inserted by the Countryside and Rights of Way Act 2000 from a date to be appointed.**

Directions to traffic and to pedestrians and traffic signs

4–1416 35. Drivers to comply with traffic directions. (1) Where a constable[1] or traffic officer★ is for the time being engaged in the regulation of traffic in a road, a person driving[2] or propelling a vehicle[3] who neglects[4] or refuses—

(*a*) to stop[5] the vehicle, or

(*b*) to make it proceed in, or keep to, a particular line of traffic,

when directed to do so by the constable in the execution of his duty[6] or traffic officer (as the case may be)★ is guilty of an offence[7].

(2) Where—

(*a*) a traffic survey of any description is being carried out on or in the vicinity of a road, and

(*b*) a constable or traffic officer★ gives to a person driving[2] or propelling a vehicle a direction—

  (i) to stop the vehicle,

  (ii) to make it proceed in, or keep to, a particular line of traffic, or

  (iii) to proceed to a particular point on or near the road on which the vehicle is being driven or propelled,

being a direction given for the purposes of the survey (but not a direction requiring any person to provide any information for the purposes of a traffic survey),

the person is guilty of an offence[7] if he neglects[4] or refuses to comply with the direction.

(3) The power to give such a direction as is referred to in subsection (2) above for the purposes

of a traffic survey shall be so exercised as not to cause any unreasonable delay to a person who indicates that he is unwilling to provide any information for the purposes of the survey.
[Road Traffic Act 1988, s 35 as amended by the Traffic Management Act 2004, s 6.]

---

*References to "traffic officer" in force in Wales from a date to be appointed.
1. Or a traffic warden if employed for the purposes of this section pursuant to the Functions of Traffic Wardens Order 1970, in this Part, post.
2. See Headnote to this title for notes on "driver" and "driving".
3. This is not limited to mechanically-propelled vehicles. This section applies to tramcars and trolley vehicles operated under statutory powers (Sch 4, post).
4. The use of the word "fail" in lieu of "neglect" in an information will not invalidate the conviction (*Pontin v Price* (1933) 97 JP 315).
5. "Stop" does not automatically mean the driver must remain at rest until signalled to proceed, unless the command was to remain stationary (*Kentesber v Waumsley* [1980] Crim LR 383).
6. He should be acting with a view to protecting life or property; see *Hoffman v Thomas* [1974] 2 All ER 233, 138 JP 414, and *Johnson v Philips* [1975] 3 All ER 682, widely interpreted in *R v Saunders* [1978] Crim LR 98.
7. For penalty, see Road Traffic Offenders Act 1988, Sch 2, post and for restrictions on prosecution, see s 1 thereof, ss 11 and 12(1) thereof (evidence by certificate etc) also apply.

4–1417   **36. Drivers to comply with traffic signs.**   (1) Where a traffic sign[1], being a sign—

(a) of the prescribed size, colour and type, or
(b) of another character authorised by the Secretary of State under the provisions in that behalf of the Road Traffic Regulation Act 1984,

has been lawfully placed on or near a road, a person driving or propelling a vehicle who fails to comply[2] with the indication given by the sign is guilty of an offence[3].

(2) A traffic sign shall not be treated for the purposes of this section as having been lawfully placed unless either—

(a) the indication given by the sign is an indication of a statutory prohibition, restriction or requirement, or
(b) it is expressly provided by or under any provision of the Traffic Acts that this section shall apply to the sign or to signs of a type of which the sign is one;

and, where the indication mentioned in paragraph (a) of this subsection is of the general nature only of the prohibition, restriction or requirement to which the sign relates, a person shall not be convicted of failure to comply with the indication unless he has failed to comply with the prohibition, restriction or requirement to which the sign relates.

(3) For the purposes of this section a traffic sign placed on or near a road shall be deemed—

(a) to be of the prescribed size, colour and type, or of another character authorised by the Secretary of State under the provisions in that behalf of the Road Traffic Regulation Act 1984, and
(b) (subject to subsection (2) above) to have been lawfully so placed,

unless the contrary is proved[4].

(4) Where a traffic survey of any description is being carried out on or in the vicinity of a road, this section applies to a traffic sign by which a direction is given—

(a) to stop a vehicle,
(b) to make it proceed in, or keep to, a particular line of traffic, or
(c) to proceed to a particular point on or near the road on which the vehicle is being driven or propelled,

being a direction given for the purposes of the survey (but not a direction requiring any person to provide any information for the purposes of the survey).

(5) Regulations made by the Secretary of State for Transport, the Secretary of State for Wales and the Secretary of State for Scotland acting jointly[5] may specify any traffic sign for the purposes of column 5 of the entry in Schedule 2 to the Road Traffic Offenders Act 1988 relating to offences under this section (offences committed by failing to comply with certain signs involve discretionary disqualification)[6].
[Road Traffic Act 1988, s 36.]

---

1. The Road Traffic Regulation Act 1984, s 64 defines "traffic sign". Section 36 of the 1988 Act is expressly applied to certain signs contained in the Traffic Signs Regulations and General Directions 2002: see reg 10 thereof in this Part, post. A single white line painted on the road way is not a traffic sign; see *Evans v Cross* [1938] 1 KB 694, [1938] 1 All ER 751, 102 JP 127 (decided upon the terminology of previous Regulations). See also the Highway Code in this Part, post. The section applies to emergency traffic signs erected by the police; Road Traffic Regulation Act 1984, s 67(2), ante.
2. The fact that the sign is not seen is no defence. Mens rea is not essential (*Rees v Taylor* (19 October 1939 unreported)). The significance of the "Stop" and "Give Way" signs is defined in reg 16 of the Traffic Sign Regulations and General Directions 2002, as amended which appear in this Part, post. See also *Brooks v Jefferies* [1936] 3 All ER 232, 717. Regulation 33(1)(b) makes special provision for vehicles used for fire brigade, ambulance or police purposes.
3. For punishment see the Road Traffic Offenders Act 1988, Sch 2, post, and notes thereto; s 1 thereof, post (notice of intended prosecution etc) imposes restrictions on prosecution. Sections 11 and 12(1) thereof (evidence by certificate etc) also apply.
4. In *Tingle Jacobs & Co v Kennedy* [1964] 1 All ER 888n, [1964] 1 WLR 638n, Lord Denning MR, expressed the view that the presumption should be that an automatic traffic light is in proper working order unless there is evidence to the contrary.
5. Now the Secretary of State alone, see Transfer of Functions (Road Traffic) Order, SI 1999/3143.

6. Functions under this section which are exercisable jointly by the Secretary of State for the Environment, Transport and the Regions, the Secretary of State for Scotland and the Secretary of State for Wales, transferred to the Secretary of State, by SI 1999/3143.

4–1418   37. Directions to pedestrians.   Where a constable in uniform[1] or traffic officer* is for the time being engaged in the regulation of vehicular traffic in a road, a person on foot[2] who proceeds across or along the carriageway in contravention of a direction to stop given by the constable in the execution of his duty or traffic officer (as the case may be)*, either to persons on foot or to persons on foot and other traffic, is guilty of an offence[3].
[Road Traffic Act 1988, s 37 as amended by the Traffic Management Act 2004, s 6.]

*References to "traffic officer" in force in Wales from a date to be appointed.
   1. Or a traffic warden if employed for the purposes of this section pursuant to the Functions of Traffic Wardens Order 1970, in this PART, post.
   2. A pedestrian offending against this section may be required by any constable to give his name and address (s 169, post).
   3. For punishment see the Road Traffic Offenders Act 1988, Sch 2, and notes thereto, post.

Promotion of road safety

4–1419   38. The Highway Code.   (1) The Highway Code[1] shall continue to have effect, subject however to revision in accordance with the following provisions of this section.
   (2)–(6) Revision, printing etc.
   (7) A failure[2] on the part of a person to observe a provision of the Highway Code shall not of itself render that person liable to criminal proceedings of any kind but any such failure may in any proceedings (whether civil or criminal, and including proceedings for an offence under the Traffic Acts, the Public Passenger Vehicles Act 1981 or sections 18 to 23 of the Transport Act 1985) be relied upon by any party to the proceedings as tending to establish or negative any liability which is in question in those proceedings.
   (8) In this section "the Highway Code" means the code comprising directions for the guidance of persons using roads issued under section 45 of the Road Traffic Act 1930, as from time to time revised under this section or under any previous enactment.
   (9) Definition.
[Road Traffic Act 1988, s 38.]

   1. The new edition published in on 24 May 2004 is contained in this PART, post.
   2. Observance is not mentioned. Seemingly a failure which negatives the defendant's liability is a failure by some one other than the defendant. See *Tart v G W Chitty & Co Ltd* (1931) 102 LJKB, 568, 149 LT 261, and *Baker v Longhurst & Sons Ltd* [1938] 2 KB 461, where failure to observe para 11 of the repealed Highway Code might have been pleaded as a defence. See also *Croston v Vaughan* [1938] 1 KB 540, [1937] 4 All ER 249, 102 JP 11; *Joseph Eva Ltd v Reeves* [1938] 2 KB 393, [1938] 2 All ER 115, 102 JP 261, CA.

PART II[1]
CONSTRUCTION AND USE OF VEHICLES AND EQUIPMENT
Using vehicle in dangerous condition

4–1420   40A. Using vehicle in dangerous condition etc[2].   A person is guilty of an offence[1] if he uses, or causes or permits another to use, a motor vehicle or trailer on a road when—
   (*a*)   the condition[3] of the motor vehicle or trailer, or of its accessories or equipment, or
   (*b*)   the purpose for which it is used, or
   (*c*)   the number of passengers carried[4] by it, or the manner in which they are carried, or
   (*d*)   the weight, position or distribution of its load, or the manner in which it is secured,

is such that the use of the motor vehicle or trailer involves a danger[3] of injury to any person.
[Road Traffic Act 1988, s 40A as added by the Road Traffic Act 1991, s 8(1).]

   1. For penalty see the Road Traffic Offenders Act 1988, Sch 2, post.
   2. This section does not apply to tramcars or trolley vehicles: SI 1992/1217, rr 7 and 9.
   3. The 'condition' may be that of a vehicle as manufactured. It is a matter for the justices, to determine each case as it arises having regard to all the circumstances. Accordingly where a car veered to the wrong side of the road and collided with a tractor which had its front link arms lowered and protruding more than in the raised position with the result that the driver of the car was killed, the justices were within their discretion in determining that the tractor was not in a dangerous condition (*DPP v Potts* [2000] RTR 1, DC).
See also authorities cited under reg 100 of the Construction and Use Regulations 1986, in this PART, post.
   4. The test to be applied under para (c) is an objective one and the court has to decide, looking at the evidence before it, whether it is satisfied that there was a danger of injury to any person, having regard to the way in which passengers were carried in the vehicle. The section is directed at the danger of injuries which might occur as a result of the ordinary problems of driving, such as sudden braking or having to swerve (*Gray v Crown Prosecution Service* (1999) 163 JP 710 [1999] RTR 339).

General regulation of construction, use etc

4–1421   41. Regulation of construction, weight, equipment and use of vehicles.   (1) The Secretary of State may make regulations[2] generally as to the use of motor vehicles[3] and trailers[4] on roads, their construction and equipment and the conditions under which they may be so used. Subsections (2) to (4) below do not affect the generality of this subsection.

(2)–(6)　Particulars matters to be contained in regulations.

(7)　In this Part of this Act—

"construction and use requirements" means requirements, whether applicable generally or at specified times or in specified circumstances, imposed under this section,

"plated particulars" means such particulars as are required to be marked on a goods vehicle in pursuance of regulations under this section by means of a plate,

"plated weights" means such weights as are required to be so marked.

[Road Traffic Act 1988, s 41 amended by the Road Traffic Act 1991, Schs 4 and 8.]

---

1. Part II contains ss 41–86. As to exceptions to the general rule that this Part applies to persons and vehicles in the public service of the Crown, see s 183, post.

2. The following regulations may be found in this Part, post; Public Service Vehicles (Conditions of Fitness, Equipment, Use and Certification) Regulations 1981, Road Transport (International Passenger Services) Regulations 1984, Road Vehicles (Construction and Use) Regulations 1986, Road Vehicles Lighting Regulations 1989, Road Vehicles (Authorised Weight) Regulations 1998. The following regulations have also been made; International Carriage of Dangerous Goods (Rear Marking of Motor Vehicles) Regulations 1975, SI 1975/2111 (by virtue of s 9(4) of the Road Traffic Act 1974), Minibus (Conditions of Fitness, Equipment and Use) Regulations 1977, SI 1977/2103 amended by SIs 1980/142, 1981/1599, 1982/1484, 1986/1813.

3. Regulations under this section will apply to foreign vehicles (Road Traffic (Foreign Vehicles) Act 1972, Sch 2, post). For the effect of regulations under this section made before 8 July 1992 on trolley vehicles see SI 1992/1217, r 17.

4. The Road Traffic Regulation Act 1984, s 21 enables local authorities to issue permits for a trailer to carry excess weight which would otherwise contravene regulations under this section.

4–1422　41A. Breach of requirement as to brakes, steering-gear or tyres.　A person who—

(a)　contravenes or fails to comply with a construction and use requirement as to brakes, steering-gear or tyres, or

(b)　uses on a road a motor vehicle or trailer which does not comply with such a requirement, or causes or permits a motor vehicle or trailer to be so used,

is guilty of an offence[1].

[Road Traffic Act 1988, s 41A as added by the Road Traffic Act 1991, s 8(2).]

---

1. For punishment see the Road Traffic Offenders Act 1988, Sch 2, post.

4–1423　41B. Breach of requirement as to weight, goods and passenger vehicles.　(1) A person who—

(a)　contravenes or fails to comply with a construction and use requirement as to any description of weight applicable to—

(i)　a goods vehicle, or

(ii)　a motor vehicle or trailer adapted to carry more than eight passengers, or

(b)　uses[1] on a road a vehicle which does not comply with such a requirement, or causes or permits[1] a vehicle to be so used,

is guilty of an offence[2].

(2)　In any proceedings for an offence under this section in which there is alleged a contravention of or failure to comply with a construction and use requirement as to any description of weight[3] applicable to a goods vehicle, it shall be a defence to prove[4] either—

(a)　that at the time when the vehicle was being used on the road—

(i)　it was proceeding to a weighbridge which was the nearest[5] available one to the place where the loading of the vehicle was completed for the purpose of being weighed, or

(ii)　it was proceeding from a weighbridge after being weighed to the nearest point at which it was reasonably practicable to reduce the weight to the relevant limit, without causing an obstruction on any road, or

(b)　in a case where the limit of that weight was not exceeded by more than 5 per cent—

(i)　that that limit was not exceeded at the time when the loading of the vehicle was originally completed, and

(ii)　that since that time no person has made any addition to the load.

[Road Traffic Act 1988, s 41B as added by the Road Traffic Act 1991, s 8(2).]

---

1. See Preliminary Note to this title for notes on "using", "causing", "permitting".

2. For penalty see Road Traffic Offenders Act 1988, Sch 2, post, ss 11 and 12(1) (evidence by certificate etc) also apply.

Where a weighbridge was used to measure the weight of the vehicle, it is not essential to adduce in evidence a certificate of accuracy; other evidence may suffice to prove that the weighbridge was accurate: *Kelly Communications v DPP* [2002] EWHC 2752 (Admin), (2003) 167 JP 73, [2003] Crim LR 479.

3. This subsection provides for a defence when it would be reasonable to assume that the person driving or the person in control of the vehicle or the owner could not reasonably know whether the vehicle was over its maximum weight in kilograms until he had taken the vehicle to the weighbridge in order to allow it to be weighed and had a reasonable opportunity of taking it back to get the excess of kilograms taken off the load; the expression "description of weight" is to be interpreted accordingly (*Hudson v Bushrod* [1982] RTR 87). See the Road Traffic Offenders Act 1988, s 17 for presumption about marked weight.

4. There is no onus on the prosecution to negative a possible defence. The defence bears the burden of proving their

case on the balance of probabilities, and it is not enough merely to raise a doubt (*Thurrock District Council v L A & A Pinch Ltd* [1974] RTR 269, [1974] Crim LR 425).

5. This means the nearest to which the lorry could go to be weighed: it is the road distance to which the Act refers. The "nearest available" weighbridge is the nearest one that is available and not the nearest available weighbridge of which the driver was aware (*Vehicle and Operator Services Agency v F & S Gibbs Transport Services Ltd* [2006] EWHC 1109 (Admin), (2006) 170 JP 586, [2007] RTR 17. The defence is not available to a driver going to a weighbridge solely to weigh the load in connection with delivering it (*Lovett v Payne* (1979) 143 JP 756, [1979] Crim LR 729). The fact that the nearest weighbridge is less convenient to use does not entitle the defendant to proceed to one further away; before it can be said the nearest weighbridge is not available, it must be established that it is not reasonably practicable to use it (*Halliday v Burl* [1983] RTR 21).

4–1423A   41C. Breach of requirement as to speed assessment equipment detection devices. A person who—

(*a*) contravenes or fails to comply with a construction or use requirement as to speed assessment equipment detection devices, or

(*b*) uses on a road a motor vehicle or trailer which does not comply with such a requirement, or causes or permits a motor vehicle or trailer to be so used,

is guilty of an offence.★
[Road Traffic Act 1988, s 41C as inserted by the Road Safety Act 2006, s 18.]

★**Inserted by the Road Safety Act 2006, s 18 from a date to be appointed.**

4–1423B   41D. Breach of requirements as to control of vehicle, mobile telephones etc. A person who contravenes or fails to comply with a construction and use requirement—

(*a*) as to not driving a motor vehicle in a position which does not give proper control or a full view of the road and traffic ahead, or not causing or permitting the driving of a motor vehicle by another person in such a position, or

(*b*) as to not driving or supervising the driving of a motor vehicle while using a hand-held mobile telephone or other hand-held interactive communication device, or not causing or permitting the driving of a motor vehicle by another person using such a telephone or other device,

is guilty of an offence.★
[Road Traffic Act 1988, s 41D as inserted by the Road Safety Act 2006, s 26.]

★**Inserted by the Road Safety Act 2006, s 26 from a date to be appointed.**

4–1424   42. Breach of other construction and use requirements. A person who—

(*a*) contravenes or fails to comply with any construction or use requirement other than one within section 41A(*a*) or 41B(1)(*a*) or 41D of this Act, or

(*b*) uses on a road a motor vehicle or trailer which does not comply with such a requirement, or causes or permits a motor vehicle or trailer to be so used,

is guilty of an offence[1].
[Road Traffic Act 1988, s 42 as substituted by the Road Traffic Act 1991, s 8(2) and amended by the Road Safety Act 2006.]

---

1. See Preliminary Note to this title for notes on "using", "causing", "permitting". This section does not apply to tramcars or trolley vehicles operated under statutory powers (Sch 4, post). Sections 11 and 12 of the Road Traffic Offenders Act (evidence by certificate etc) apply. For penalty see Road Traffic Offenders Act 1988, Sch 2, post.

4–1425   43. Temporary exemption from application of regulations under s 41.

4–1426   44. Authorisation of use on roads of special vehicles not complying with regulations under s 41[1].

---

1. See the Motor Vehicles (Authorisation of Special Types) General Order 1979, in this PART, post: Statutory Instruments, post.

4–1427   45. Tests of satisfactory condition of vehicles[1].

---

1. See the Motor Vehicles (Tests) Regulations 1981, SI 1981/1694 as amended, in this PART, post. Note exemption from duty for a vehicle proceeding to or from a compulsory test (Vehicle Excise and Registration Act 1994, s 5 and Sch 2, para 22, ante).

4–1428   46. Particular aspects of regulations under s 45.

4–1428A   46A. Use of records of vehicle examinations, etc. Use of such records by Secretary of State to maintain accuracy of test records and vehicle excise records.
[Road Traffic Act 1988, s 46A inserted by the Road Traffic (Vehicle Testing) Act 1999, s 3.]

4–1428B   46B. Evidence from records of vehicle registrations. (1) A statement to which this section applies is admissible in any proceedings as evidence (or, in Scotland, sufficient evidence) of any fact stated in it with respect to—

(*a*) the issue of a test certificate in respect of a vehicle, and

(*b*) the date of issue of such a certificate,

to the same extent as oral evidence of that fact is admissible in the proceedings.

(2) This section applies to a statement contained in a document purporting to be—

(*a*) a part of the records maintained under section 45(6B) of this Act,

(*b*) a copy of a document forming part of those records, or

(*c*) a note of any information contained in those records,

and to be authenticated by a person authorised to do so by the Secretary of State.

(3) In this section as it has effect in England and Wales—

"document" means anything in which information of any description is recorded;

"copy", in relation to a document, means anything onto which information recorded in the document has been copied, by whatever means and whether directly or indirectly; and

"statement" means any representation of fact, however made.

(4) In this section as it has effect in Scotland, "document" and "statement" have the same meanings as in section 17(3) of the Law Reform (Miscellaneous Provisions) (Scotland) Act 1968, and the reference to a copy of a document shall be construed in accordance with section 17(4) of that Act.

(5) Nothing in subsection (4) above limits to civil proceedings the reference to proceedings in subsection (1) above.

[Road Traffic Act 1988, s 46A inserted by the Road Traffic (Vehicle Testing) Act 1999, s 4.]

4–1429 47. Obligatory test certificates. (1) A person who uses[1] on a road at any time, or causes[1] or permits[1] to be so used, a motor vehicle to which this section applies, and as respects which no test certificate has been issued within the appropriate period before that time, is guilty of an offence[2].

In this section and section 48 of this Act, the "appropriate period" means a period of twelve months or such shorter period as may be prescribed.

(2) Subject to subsections (3) and (5) below, the motor vehicles to which this section applies at any time are—

(*a*) those first registered under the Vehicle Excise and Registration Act 1994 or any corresponding earlier legislation, not less than three years before that time, and

(*b*) those which, having a date of manufacture not less than three years before that time, have been used on roads (whether in Great Britain or elsewhere) before being so registered the Vehicles (Excise) Act 1971 or the Vehicles (Excise) Act 1962,

being, in either case, motor vehicles other than goods vehicles which are required by regulations under section 49 of this Act to be submitted for a goods vehicle test.

(3) As respects a vehicle being—

(*a*) a motor vehicle used for the carriage of passengers and with more than eight seats, excluding the driver's seat, or

(*b*) a taxi (as defined in section 64(3) of the Transport Act 1980), being a vehicle licensed to ply for hire, or

(*c*) an ambulance, that is to say, a motor vehicle which is constructed or adapted, and primarily used, for the carriage of persons to a place where they will receive, or from a place where they have received, medical or dental treatment, and which, by reason of design, marking or equipment is readily identifiable as a vehicle so constructed or adapted,

subsection (2)(*a*) above shall have effect as if for the period there mentioned there were substituted a period of one year.

(4) For the purposes of subsection (2)(*b*) above, there shall be disregarded—

(*a*) the use of a vehicle before it is sold or supplied by retail, and

(*b*) the use of a vehicle to which a motor dealer has assigned a mark under section 24 of the Vehicle Excise and Registration Act 1994 before it is registered by the Secretary of State under section 21(2) of that Act.

(5)–(7) Secretary of State may prescribe exemptions[3].

(8) For the purposes of this section the date of manufacture of a vehicle shall be taken to be the last day of the year during which its final assembly is completed, except where after that day modifications are made to the vehicle before it is sold or supplied by retail, and in that excepted case shall be taken to be the last day of the year during which the modifications are completed.

(9) Secretary of State may substitute periods in sub-s (2).

[Road Traffic Act 1988, s 47 amended by the Road Traffic (Consequential Provisions) Act 1988, Sch 2, the Finance Act 1994, Sch 2 and the Vehicle Excise and Registration Act 1994. Sch 3.]

---

1. See Preliminary Note to this title for "using", "causing", "permitting".

2. For penalty see the Road Traffic Offenders Act 1988, Sch 2, post. As to production of a test certificate, see s 165, post, and see also the Motor Vehicles (Production of Test Certificates) Regulations 1969, SI 1969/418. Once it has been established that the defendant was using a motor vehicle on a road the burden is on the defendant to prove on the balance of probabilities that he was covered by a current MOT certificate (if required for the vehicle) and current insurance and there is no requirement, although it is desirable, for there to have been a statutory demand to produce documents (*DPP v Kavaz* [1999] RTR 40, DC).

3. Exemptions are contained in the Motor Vehicles (Tests) Regulations 1981 in this PART, post.

4–1430   48. Supplementary provisions about test certificates.   (1) For the purpose of spreading the work of issuing certificates in contemplation of a change in—

(*a*)   the length of the appropriate period, or

(*b*)   the length of the period specified in section 47(2)(*a*) and (*b*) of this Act,

(and whether for the purposes of that section or section 66 of this Act), the order or, as the case may be, regulations changing the length of that period may be made so as to come into operation on different days as respects vehicles first registered under any of the enactments mentioned in section 47(2) of this Act at different times.

(1A)   A test certificate issued in respect of a vehicle within the period of one month ending immediately before the date on which section 47 of this Act first applies to the vehicle shall be treated for the purposes of that section as if issued at the end of that period.

(2)   Where—

(*a*)   within the appropriate period after a test certificate is issued or treated for the purposes of section 47 of this Act as issued, but

(*b*)   not earlier than one month before the end of that period,

a further test certificate is issued as respects the same vehicle, the further certificate shall be treated for the purposes of that section as if issued at the end of the appropriate period.

(3)   Where the particulars contained in a test certificate in accordance with regulations made under section 45 of this Act include a date of expiry falling later, but not more than one month later, than the end of the appropriate period after the date on which it is issued—

(*a*)   the certificate shall be deemed to have been issued in respect of the same vehicle as an earlier test certificate, and

(*b*)   the date on which it was issued shall be deemed to have been a date falling within the last month of the appropriate period after the date on which that earlier certificate was issued or treated for the purposes of section 47 of this Act as issued;

and any date of expiry contained in a test certificate shall be deemed to have been entered in accordance with regulations under section 45 of this Act unless the contrary is proved.

(4)   The Secretary of State may by regulations make provision for the issue, in such circumstances as may be prescribed, of a certificate of temporary exemption in respect of a public service vehicle adapted to carry more than eight passengers, exempting that vehicle from the provisions of section 47(1) of this Act for such period as may be specified in the certificate.

(5)   In relation to any public service vehicle so adapted—

(*a*)   subsections (1A), (2) and (3) above shall have effect as if for "one month" (in each place) there were substituted "two months", and

(*b*)   subsection (3) above shall have effect as if for "last month" there were substituted "last two months".

(6)   Repealed.

[Road Traffic Act 1988, s 48 amended by the Road Traffic Act 1991, Sch 8 and SI 1996/1700.]

Tests of certain classes of goods vehicles

4–1431   49. Tests of satisfactory condition of goods vehicles and determination of plated weights, etc[1].

---

1. The Goods Vehicles (Plating and Testing) Regulations 1988 have been made under this section, and are contained in this PART, post. Contravening or failing to comply with regulations is made an offence by s 51(2); for penalty see the Road Traffic Offenders Act 1988, Sch 2, post.

4–1432   50. Appeals against determinations.

4–1433   51. Particular aspects of regulations under s 49.

4–1434   52. Supplementary provisions about tests etc of goods vehicles.

4–1435   53. Obligatory goods vehicle test certificates.   (1) If any person at any time on or after the relevant date—

(*a*)   uses[1] on a road a goods vehicle of a class required by regulations under section 49 of this Act to have been submitted for examination for plating, or

(*b*)   causes or permits to be used[1] on a road a goods vehicle of such a class,

and at the time there is no plating certificate in force for the vehicle, he is guilty of an offence[2].
In this subsection "relevant date", in relation to any goods vehicle, means the date by which it is required by the regulations to be submitted for examination for plating.

(2)   If any person at any time on or after the relevant date—

(*a*)   uses[1] on a road a goods vehicle of a class required by regulations under section 49 of this Act to have been submitted for a goods vehicle test, or

(*b*)   causes or permits to be used[1] on a road a goods vehicle of such a class,

and at that time there is no goods vehicle test certificate in force for the vehicle, he is guilty of an offence[2].

In this subsection "relevant date", in relation to any goods vehicle, means the date by which it is required by the regulations to be submitted for its first goods vehicle test.

(3) Any person who—

(a) uses[1] a goods vehicle on a road, or

(b) causes or permits[1] a goods vehicle to be so used,

when an alteration has been made to the vehicle or its equipment which is required by regulations under section 49 of this Act to be, but has not been, notified to the Secretary of State is guilty of an offence[2].*

(4) In any proceedings for an offence under subsection (3) above, it shall be a defence to prove that the alteration was not specified in the relevant plating certificate in accordance with regulations under section 49 of this Act.

(5) Exemptions by regulations.

[Road Traffic Act 1988, s 53.]

---

*Amended by the Transport Act 1982, s 10 as amended by the Road Traffic (Consequential Provisions) Act 1988, Sch 2, when in force.

1. See Preliminary Note to this title for "using", "causing" and "permitting".

2. For penalty see the Road Traffic Offenders Act 1988, Sch 2, post. Sections 11 and 12(1) thereof (evidence by certificate etc) also apply. For application to a "tower wagon" see *Anderson & Heeley Ltd v Paterson* [1975] 1 All ER 523, [1975] 1 WLR 228, 139 JP 231.

Approval of design, construction, equipment and marking of vehicles

4–1436   54. Type approval requirements, certificates of conformity, Minister's approval certificates, appeals, regulations.

4–1437   63. Obligatory type approval certificates, certificates of conformity and Minister' approval certificates.   (1) If—

(a) any person at any time on or after the day appointed by regulations[1] made by the Secretary of State in relation to vehicles or vehicle parts of a prescribed class, being vehicles or vehicle parts to which type approval requirements prescribed by those regulations apply—

(i) uses[2] on a road, or

(ii) causes or permits to be so used[2],

a vehicle of that class or a vehicle to which is fitted a vehicle part of that class, and

(b) it does not appear from one or more certificates then in force under sections 54 to 58 of this Act that the vehicle or vehicle part complies with those requirements,

he is guilty of an offence[3].

Different days may be appointed under this subsection in relation to different classes of vehicles or vehicle parts.

(1A) For the purposes of subsection (1) above a vehicle shall be taken to comply with all relevant type approval requirements if an EC certificate of conformity has effect with respect to the vehicle.

(2) If a plating certificate—

(a) has been issued for a goods vehicle to which section 53(1) of this Act or subsection (1) above applies, but

(b) does not specify a maximum laden weight for the vehicle together with any trailer which may be drawn by it,

any person who on or after the relevant date within the meaning of section 53(1) of this Act or, as the case may be, the day appointed under subsection (1) above uses[2] the vehicle on a road for drawing a trailer, or causes or permits it to be so used[2], is guilty of an offence[3].

(3) Any person who—

(a) uses[2] a vehicle on a road, or

(b) causes or permits a vehicle to be so used[2],

when an alteration has been made to the vehicle or its equipment which is required by regulations or directions under section 59 of this Act to be, but has not been, notified to the Secretary of State is guilty of an offence[3].*

(4) In any proceedings for an offence under subsection (3) above, it shall be a defence to prove that the regulations were not or, as the case may be, the alteration was not, specified in the relevant certificate of conformity or Minister's approval certificate in accordance with regulations under section 59(3) of this Act.

(5) Exemptions by regulations.

[Road Traffic Act 1988, s 63 amended by SI 1992/3105.]

---

*Amended by the Transport Act 1982, s 10 as amended by the Road Traffic (Consequential Provisions) Act 1988, Sch 2 when in force.

1. The Motor Vehicles (Type Approval) (Great Britain) Regulations 1984, SI 1984/981, amended by SI 1984/1401 and 1761, SI 1985/1651, SI 1986/739, 1987/1509, 1988/1522, 1989/1580, SI 1990/94 and 1839, SI 1991/1022 and 1971, SI 1992/1341, 2161, 2908 and 3173, SI 1993/2201, SI 1994/2190, SI 1995/1322, SI 1996/2330 and 3015, SI 1997/1367, 1502 and 2933 and SI 1998/1005 and the Motor Vehicles (Type Approval for Goods Vehicles) (Great Britain) Regulations 1982, SI 1982/1271, amended by SI 1984/697 and 1402, SI 1985/46, SI 1986/427 and 1089, 1987/1508, 1990/94 and

1839, SI 1991/1021 and 1970, SI 1992/25, 1342 and 3084, SI 1993/2200, SI 1994/2191, SI 1995/1323, SI 1996/2331 and 3014, SI 1997/1365 and 2936, SI 1998/1006, SI 2003/582 and 1866, SI 2006/2565 and SI 2007/361 have been made. See also the Motor Vehicles (Type Approval of Reduced Pollution Adaptions) Regulations 1998, SI 1998/3093 amended by SI 2000/ 3275, the Motor Vehicles (Approval) Regulations 2001, SI 2001/25 amended by SI 2004/623 and the Motor Cycles Etc (Single Vehicle Approval) Regulations 2003, SI 2003/1959.

     2. See preliminary note to this title for "using", "causing" and "permitting".

     3. For penalty see the Road Traffic Offenders Act 1988, Sch 2, post. Sections 11 and 12 thereof (evidence by certificate etc) also apply.

4–1438   63A.   Alteration of plated weights for goods vehicles without examination.   (1) The Secretary of State may by regulations make provision—

     (a)   for the determination, in such circumstances as may be prescribed, of the plated weights (or any of the plated weights) for goods vehicles of any prescribed class otherwise than on an examination under regulations made under section 49 or 61 of this Act; and

     (b)   for the amendment of any approval certificate in force in respect of a vehicle of any such class so as to specify the weights determined for that vehicle under the regulations in place of any weights superseded by those weights or the cancellation of any such certificate and the issue in place of it of a different certificate specifying the weights so determined in place of any weights so superseded.

     (2)   Any person aggrieved by a determination of plated weights for a goods vehicle under regulations made under this section may appeal to the Secretary of State and on the appeal the Secretary of State shall cause the vehicle to be examined by an officer of the Secretary of State appointed by him for the purpose and shall make such determination on the basis of the examination as he thinks fit.

     (3)   Without prejudice to the generality of subsection (1) above, regulations under this section—

     (a)   may provide for the determination of any plated weights for a goods vehicle under the regulations to be made by the Secretary of State or by the prescribed testing authority;

     (b)   may contain the like provisions with respect to any appeal brought by virtue of subsection (2) above and any examination on any such appeal as may be contained in any regulations made by virtue of paragraphs (c), (g) and (h) of section 51(1) of this Act in relation to an appeal under section 50(1) and any examination on any such appeal;

     (c)   may specify the manner in which, and the time before or within which, applications may be made for the determination of plated weights of vehicles under the regulations, and the information to be supplied and documents to be produced on any such application;

     (d)   may make provision as to the fees to be paid on any such application;

     (e)   may provide for the issue of replacements for any plates fixed to a vehicle specifying weights superseded by weights specified in an approval certificate amended under the regulations or in any certificate issued under the regulations in place of an approval certificate, and for the payment of a fee for their issue; and

     (f)   may make different provision for different cases.

     (4)   In this section 'approval certificate' means a plating certificate and any certificate of conformity or Minister's approval certificate specifying any plated weights.

     (5)   Any certificate issued in respect of a goods vehicle under regulations made under this section in replacement of an approval certificate of any description mentioned in subsection (4) above—

     (a)   shall be in the form appropriate for an approval certificate of that description;

     (b)   shall be identical in content with the certificate it replaces, save for any alterations in the plated weights authorised by the regulations; and

     (c)   shall be treated for the purposes of this Part of this Act (including this section) and any regulations made under any provision of this Part of this Act as if it were the same certificate as the certificate it replaces;

and any plate so issued in replacement of a plate fixed to the vehicle under section 57 or 58 of this Act shall, when fixed to the vehicle, be treated as so fixed under that section.

[Road Traffic Act 1988, s 63A as inserted by the Transport Act 1982, s 18 as amended by the Road Traffic (Consequential Provisions) Act 1988 Sch 2.]

4–1439   64.   Using goods vehicle with unauthorised weights as well as authorised weights marked on it.   (1) If there is fixed to a goods vehicle a plate containing plated weights of any description—

     (a)   determined for that vehicle by virtue of sections 49 to 52 of this Act, or

     (b)   specified in a certificate for that vehicle under section 57(1) or (2) or 58(2) or (5) of this Act,

the vehicle shall not, while it is used on a road, be marked with any other weights, except other plated weights, other weights required or authorised to be marked on the vehicle by regulations under section 41 of this Act or weights so authorised for the purposes of this section by regulations[1] made by the Secretary of State and marked in the prescribed manner.

     (2)   In the event of a contravention of or failure to comply with this section the owner of the vehicle is guilty of an offence[2].

[Road Traffic Act 1988, s 64.]

---

     1. The Road Vehicles (Marking of Special Weights) Regulations 1983 in this PART, post, have been made.

     2. For punishment see the Road Traffic Offenders Act 1988, Sch 2, post, and notes thereto.

4–1440　64A. Failure to hold EC certificate of conformity for unregistered light passenger vehicle or motor cycle.　(1) Subject to subsections (2) to (5) below, if a person uses on a road a light passenger vehicle or a vehicle to which the motorcycle type approval Directive or tractor type approval Directive applies—

(*a*)　which has not been registered—

(i)　under section 21 of the Vehicle Excise and Registration Act 1994, or

(ii)　under the law of a member State other than the United Kingdom, and

(*b*)　in respect of which no EC certificate of conformity has effect,

he is guilty of an offence.

(2)　A person shall not be convicted of an offence under this section in respect of the use of a light passenger vehicle if he proves—

(*a*)　that the vehicle was one in respect of which the grant of a licence under the Vehicle Excise and Registration Act 1994 was not prohibited by regulation 10 of the Motor Vehicles (EC Type Approval) Regulations 1992, or

(*b*)　in the case of a vehicle in respect of which duty is not chargeable under that Act, that the vehicle was one whose registration under section 21 of that Act was not prohibited by that regulation.

(2A)　A person shall not be convicted of an offence under this section in respect of the use of a vehicle to which the motorcycle type approval Directive applies if he proves that the vehicle was one in respect of which the grant of a licence or nil licence under the Vehicle Excise and Registration Act 1994 was not prohibited by regulation 16 of the Motor Cycles Etc (EC Type Approval) Regulations 1999.

(3)　This section does not apply in relation to a vehicle in respect of which a Minister's approval certificate issued under section 58(1) of this Act or a Department's approval certificate issued under Article 31A(4) of the Road Traffic (Northern Ireland) Order 1981 has effect.

(4)　This section does not apply to the use of a vehicle under a trade licence (within the meaning of the Vehicle Excise and Registration Act 1994) in accordance with regulations made under section 12(2) of that Act.

(5)　This section does not apply in relation to a vehicle brought temporarily into Great Britain by a person resident outside the United Kingdom.

(6)　In the application of this section to a vehicle to which the motorcycle type approval Directive applies, any reference to a member State includes a reference to an EEA State.

[Road Traffic Act 1988, s 64A as inserted by SI 1992/3107 and amended by the Vehicle Excise and Registration Act 1994, Sch 3, SI 1999/2920 and SI 2005/390.]

4–1441　65. Vehicles and parts not to be sold without required certificate of conformity or Minister's approval certificate.　(1) If—

(*a*)　any person at any time on or after the day appointed by regulations under section 63(1) of this Act supplies a vehicle or vehicle part of a class to which those regulations apply, and

(*b*)　it does not appear from one or more certificates in force at that time under sections 54 to 58 of this Act that the vehicle or vehicle part complies with all the relevant type approval requirements prescribed by those regulations,

he is guilty of an offence[1].

(1A)　For the purposes of subsection (1) above a vehicle shall be taken to comply with all relevant type approval requirements if an EC certificate of conformity has effect with respect to the vehicle.

(2)　In this section references to supply include—

(*a*)　sell,

(*b*)　offer to sell or supply, and

(*c*)　expose for sale.

(3)　A person shall not be convicted of an offence under this section in respect of the supply of a vehicle or vehicle part if he proves—

(*a*)　that it was supplied for export from Great Britain,

(*b*)　that he had reasonable cause to believe that it would not be used on a road in Great Britain or, in the case of a vehicle part, that it would not be fitted to a vehicle used on a road in Great Britain or would not be so used or fitted until it had been certified under sections 54 to 58 of this Act, or

(*c*)　that he had reasonable cause to believe that it would only be used for purposes or in any area prescribed by the Secretary of State under section 63(5) of this Act or, in the case of a goods vehicle, under section 53(5) of this Act.

(4)　Nothing in subsection (1) above shall affect the validity of a contract or any rights arising under or in relation to a contract.

[Road Traffic Act 1988, s 65 amended by SI 1992/3105.]

1.　For penalty see the Road Traffic Offenders Act 1988, Sch 2, post.

4–1442　65A. Light passenger vehicles and motor cycles not to be sold without EC certificate of conformity.　(1) Subject to subsections (3) to (6) below, any person who supplies a light passenger vehicle or a vehicle to which the motorcycle type approval Directive applies—

(a) which has not been registered—

   (i) under section 21 of the Vehicle Excise and Registration Act 1994, or

   (ii) under the law of a member State other than the United Kingdom, and

(b) in respect of which no EC certificate of conformity has effect,

is guilty of an offence.

(2) In this section references to supply include—

(a) sell,

(b) offer to sell or supply, and

(c) expose for sale.

(3) A person shall not be convicted of an offence under this section in respect of the supply of a light passenger vehicle if he proves—

(a) that the vehicle was one in respect of which the grant of a licence under the Vehicle Excise and Registration Act 1994 was not prohibited by regulation 10 of the Motor Vehicles (EC Type Approval) Regulations 1992, or

(b) in the case of a vehicle in respect of which duty is not chargeable under that Act, that the vehicle was one whose registration under section 21 of that Act was not prohibited by that regulation.

(3A) A person shall not be convicted of an offence under this section in respect of the supply of a vehicle to which the motorcycle type approval Directive applies if he proves that the vehicle was one in respect of which the grant of a licence or nil licence under the Vehicle Excise and Registration Act 1994 was not prohibited by regulation 16 of the Motor Cycles Etc (EC Type Approval) Regulations 1999.

(4) A person shall not be convicted of an offence under this section in respect of the supply of a vehicle if he proves—

(a) that it was supplied for export from the United Kingdom to a country which is not a member State, or

(b) that he had reasonable cause to believe—

   (i) that it would not be used on a road in the United Kingdom or any other member State, or

   (ii) that it would not be so used until an EC certificate of conformity had been issued in respect of it.

(5) This section does not apply in relation to the supply of a vehicle—

(a) to the Crown for naval, military or air force purposes,

(b) for the purposes of the military forces of any country outside the United Kingdom,

(c) *repealed*

(d) to a police authority for police purposes, or

(e) to any public authority in a member State outside the United Kingdom which has responsibilities for maintaining public order.

(6) This section does not apply in relation to a vehicle in respect of which a Minister's approval certificate issued under section 58(1) of this Act or a Department's approval certificate issued under Article 31A(4) of the Road Traffic (Northern Ireland) Order 1981 has effect.

(7) Nothing in subsection (1) above shall affect the validity of a contract or any rights arising under or in relation to a contract.

(8) In the application of this section to a vehicle to which the motorcycle type approval Directive applies, any reference to a member State includes a reference to an EEA State.

[Road Traffic Act 1988, s 65A as inserted by SI 1992/3107 and amended by the Vehicle Excise and Registration Act 1994, Sch 3, SI 1999/2920 and the Civil Contigencies Act 2004, Sch 2.]

4–1443 66. Regulations prohibiting the grant of excise licences for certain vehicles except on compliance with certain conditions[1].

---

1. See the Motor Vehicles (Evidence of Test Certificates) Regulations 2004, SI 2004/1896 which provide for the producing of a test certificate in respect of a vehicle to which s 47 of this Act applies on an application for a vehicle excise licence, see also the Goods Vehicles (Evidence of Test Certificates) Regulations 2004, SI 2004/2577.

4–1444 66A. Appointment of examiners[1].

---

1. Section 66A as added by the Road Traffic Act 1991, s 9 empowers the Secretary of State to appoint vehicle examiners, replacing provisions under s 68(1) and (2) of this Act and s 7 of the Public Passenger Vehicles Act 1981.

Testing vehicles on roads

4–1450 67. Testing of condition of vehicles on roads. (1) An authorised examiner[1] may test a motor vehicle[2] on a road for the purpose of—

(a) ascertaining whether the following requirements, namely—

   (i) the construction and use requirements, and

    (ii) the requirement that the condition of the vehicle is not such that its use on a road would involve a danger of injury to any person,

are complied with as respects the vehicle;

    (b) bringing to the notice of the driver any failure to comply with those requirements.

(2) For the purpose of testing a vehicle under this section the examiner—

    (a) may require the driver to comply with his reasonable instructions, and
    (b) may drive the vehicle.

(3) A vehicle shall not be required to stop for a test except by a constable in uniform.

(4) The following persons may act as authorised examiners for the purposes of this section—

    (a) *repealed*,
    (b) a person appointed as an examiner under section 66A of this Act,
    (c) a person appointed to examine and inspect public carriage for the purposes of the Metropolitan Public Carriage Act 1869,
    (d) a person appointed to act for the purposes of this section by the Secretary of State,
    (e) a constable authorised so to act by or on behalf of a chief officer of police, and
    (f) a person appointed by the police authority for a police area to act, under the directions of the chief officer of police, for the purposes of this section.

(5) A person mentioned in subsection (4)(a) to (d) and (f) must produce his authority to act for the purposes of this section if required to do so.

(6) On the examiner proceeding to test a vehicle under this section, the driver may, unless the test is required under subsection (7) or (8) below to be carried out forthwith, elect that the test shall be deferred to a time, and carried out at a place, fixed in accordance with Schedule 2 to this Act, and the provisions of that Schedule shall apply accordingly.

(7) Where it appears to a constable that, by reason of an accident having occurred owing to the presence of the vehicle on a road, it is requisite that a test should be carried out forthwith, he may require it to be so carried out and, if he is not to carry it out himself, may require that the vehicle shall not be taken away until the test has been carried out.

(8) Where in the opinion of a constable the vehicle is apparently so defective that it ought not to be allowed to proceed without a test being carried out, he may require the test to be carried out forthwith.

(9) If a person obstructs an authorised examiner acting under this section, or fails to comply with a requirement of this section or Schedule 2 to this Act, he is guilty of an offence[3].

(10) In this section and in Schedule 2 to this Act—

    (a) "test" includes "inspect" or "inspection", as the case may require, and
    (b) references to a vehicle include references to a trailer drawn by it.

[Road Traffic Act 1988, s 67 amended by the Road Traffic Act 1991, s 10 and Sch 8.]

---

    1. A constable who is not an authorised examiner cannot rely on s 67 to authorise him to carry out the tests himself. Where however a defendant is co-operative and allows the constable to carry out tests, evidence of them would be admissible in later proceedings (*Stoneley v Richardson* [1973] Crim LR 310). See also *Phillips v Thomas* (1973) 137 JP Jo 469.
    2. This section will apply to foreign vehicles (Road Traffic (Foreign Vehicles) Act 1972, Sch 1, post).
    3. For punishment see the Road Traffic Offenders Act 1988, Sch 2 and notes thereto, post.

Inspection of public passenger vehicles and goods vehicles

4-1460   68. Inspection of public passenger vehicles[1] and goods vehicles[1]. (1) A vehicle examiner—

    (a) may at any time, on production if so required of his authority, inspect any vehicle to which this section applies and for that purpose detain the vehicle during such time as is required for the inspection, and
    (b) may at any time which is reasonable having regard to the circumstances of the case enter any premises on which he has reason to believe that such a vehicle is kept.

(2) The power conferred by subsection (1) above to inspect a vehicle includes power to test it and to drive it for the purpose of testing it.

(3) A person who intentionally obstructs an examiner in the exercise of his powers under subsection (1) above is guilty of an offence[2].

(4) A vehicle examiner or a constable in uniform may at any time require any person in charge of a vehicle to which this section applies and which is stationary on a road to proceed with the vehicle for the purpose of having it inspected under this section to any place where an inspection can be suitably carried out (not being more than five miles from the place where the requirement is made).

(5) A person in charge of a vehicle who refuses or neglects to comply with a requirement made under subsection (4) above is guilty of an offence[2].

(6) This section applies to—

    (a) goods vehicles,
    (b) public service vehicles, and
    (c) motor vehicles which are not public service vehicles but are adapted to carry more than eight passengers;

but subsection (1)(*b*) above shall not apply in relation to vehicles within paragraph (*c*) above or in relation to vehicles used to carry passengers for hire or reward only under permits granted under section 19 or 22 of the Transport Act 1985 (use of vehicles by educational and other bodies or in providing community bus services).
[Road Traffic Act 1988, s 68 as substituted by the Road Traffic Act 1991, s 11.]

---

1. This section does not apply to tramcars: SI 1992/1217, r 7. This section applies to trolley vehicles as if sub-s (4) were omitted: SI 1992/1217, r 10. This section applies fully to duo buses: SI 1992/1217, r 11.
2. For penalty see the Road Traffic Offenders Act 1988, Sch 2, post.

Prohibition of unfit vehicles[1]

4–1461   69. Power to prohibit driving of unfit vehicles.   (1) If on any inspection of a vehicle under section 41, 45, 49, 61, 67, 68 or 77 of this Act it appears to a vehicle examiner that owing to any defects in the vehicle it is, or is likely to become, unfit for service, he may prohibit the driving of the vehicle on a road—

(*a*) absolutely, or
(*b*) for one or more specified purposes, or
(*c*) except for one or more specified purposes.

(2) If on any inspection of a vehicle under any of the enactments mentioned in subsection (1) above it appears to an authorised constable that owing to any defects in the vehicle driving it (or driving it for any particular purpose or purposes or for any except one or more particular purposes) would involve a danger of injury to any person, he may prohibit the driving of the vehicle on a road—

(*a*) absolutely, or
(*b*) for one or more specified purposes, or
(*c*) except for one or more specified purposes.

(3) A prohibition under this section shall come into force as soon as the notice under subsection (6) below has been given if—

(*a*) it is imposed by an authorised constable, or
(*b*) in the opinion of the vehicle examiner imposing it the defects in the vehicle in question are such that driving it, or driving it for any purpose within the prohibition, would involve a danger of injury to any person.

(4) Except where subsection (3) applies, a prohibition under this section shall (unless previously removed under section 72 of this Act) come into force at such time not later than ten days from the date of the inspection as seems appropriate to the vehicle examiner imposing the prohibition, having regard to all the circumstances.

(5) A prohibition under this section shall continue in force until it is removed under section 72 of this Act.

(6) A person imposing a prohibition under this section shall forthwith give notice in writing of the prohibition to the person in charge of the vehicle at the time of the inspection—

(*a*) specifying the defects which occasioned the prohibition;
(*b*) stating whether the prohibition is on all driving of the vehicle or driving it for one or more specified purposes or driving it except for one or more specified purposes (and, where applicable, specifying the purpose or purposes in question); and
(*c*) stating whether the prohibition is to come into force immediately or at the end of a specified period.

(7) Where a notice has been given under subsection (6) above, any vehicle examiner or authorised constable may grant an exemption in writing for the use of the vehicle in such manner, subject to such conditions and for such purpose as may be specified in the exemption.

(8) Where such a notice has been given, any vehicle examiner or authorised constable may by endorsement on the notice vary its terms and, in particular, alter the time at which the prohibition is to come into force or suspend it if it has come into force.

(9) In this section "authorised constable" means a constable authorised to act for the purposes of this section by or on behalf of a chief officer of police.
[Road Traffic Act 1988, s 69 as substituted by the Road Traffic Act 1991, s 12.]

---

1. Sections 69 to 73 do not apply to tramcars: SI 1992/1217, r 7.

4–1462   69A. Prohibitions conditional on inspection etc.   (1) Where it appears to the person imposing a prohibition under section 69 of this Act that the vehicle is adapted to carry more than eight passengers, or is a public service vehicle not so adapted, the prohibition may be imposed with a direction making it irremovable unless and until the vehicle has been inspected at an official PSV testing station within the meaning of the Public Passenger Vehicles Act 1981.

(2) Where it appears to that person that the vehicle is of a class to which regulations under section 49 of this Act apply, the prohibition may be imposed with a direction making it irremovable unless and until the vehicle has been inspected at an official testing station.

(3) Where it appears to that person that the vehicle is one to which section 47 of this Act applies, or would apply if the vehicle had been registered under the Vehicle Excise and Registration Act 1994 more than three years earlier, the prohibition may be imposed with a direction making it irremovable

unless and until the vehicle has been inspected, and a test certificate issued, under section 45 of this Act.

(4) In any other case, the prohibition may be imposed with a direction making it irremovable unless and until the vehicle has been inspected in accordance with regulations under section 72 of this Act by a vehicle examiner or authorised constable (within the meaning of section 69 of this Act). [Road Traffic Act 1988, s 69A as added by the Road Traffic Act 1991, s 12 and amended by the Vehicle Excise and Registration Act 1994, Sch 3.]

4–1463   70. Power to prohibit driving of overloaded goods vehicles.   (1) Subsections (2) and (3) below apply where a goods vehicle or a motor vehicle adapted to carry more than eight passengers has been weighed in pursuance of a requirement imposed under section 78 of this Act and it appears to—

(*a*)   a vehicle examiner,

(*b*)   a person authorised with the consent of the Secretary of State to act for the purposes of this subsection by—

     (i)   a highway authority other than the Secretary of State, or

     (ii)   a local roads authority in Scotland, or

(*c*)   a constable authorised to act for those purposes by or on behalf of a chief officer of police,

that the limit imposed by construction and use requirements with respect to any description of weight which is applicable to that vehicle has been exceeded or would be exceeded if it were used on a road or that by reason of excessive overall weight or excessive axle weight on any axle driving the vehicle would involve a danger of injury to any person.

(2) The person to whom it so appears may, whether or not a notice is given under section 69(6) of this Act, give notice in writing to the person in charge of the vehicle prohibiting the driving of the vehicle on a road until—

(*a*)   that weight is reduced to that limit[1] or, as the case may be, so that it is no longer excessive, and

(*b*)   official notification has been given to whoever is for the time being in charge of the vehicle that it is permitted to proceed.

(3) The person to whom it so appears may also by direction in writing require the person in charge of the vehicle to remove it (and, if it is a motor vehicle drawing a trailer, also to remove the trailer) to such place and subject to such conditions as are specified in the direction; and the prohibition shall not apply to the removal of the vehicle or trailer in accordance with that direction.

(4) Official notification for the purposes of subsection (2) above—

(*a*)   must be in writing and be given by a vehicle examiner, a person authorised as mentioned in subsection (1) above or a constable authorised as so mentioned, and

(*b*)   may be withheld until the vehicle has been weighed or reweighed in order to satisfy the person giving the notification that the weight has been sufficiently reduced.

(5) Nothing in this section shall be construed as limiting the power of the Secretary of State to make regulations under section 71(2) of this Act. [Road Traffic Act 1988, s 70 as amended by the Road Traffic Act 1991, s 13.]

    1. In any subsequent proceedings under this section, if any question arises whether the weight has been so reduced, the burden of proof shall lie on the accused (Road Traffic Offenders Act 1988, s 17(3), post).

4–1464   71. Unfit and overloaded vehicles: offences.   (1) A person who—

(*a*)   drives[1] a vehicle in contravention of a prohibition under section 69 or 70 of this Act, or

(*b*)   causes or permits[1] a vehicle to be driven in contravention of such a prohibition, or

(*c*)   fails to comply within a reasonable time with a direction under section 70(3) of this Act,

is guilty of an offence[2].

(2) The Secretary of State may by regulations[3] provide for exceptions from subsection (1) above. [Road Traffic Act 1988, s 71 as substituted by the Road Traffic Act 1991, s 14.]

    1. See Preliminary Note to this title, ante, for "drive", "cause" and "permit". See also s 73(3) as to a trailer.
    2. For penalty see the the Road Traffic Offenders Act 1988, Sch 2, post. Sections 11 and 12(1) (evidence by certificate etc) also apply.
    3. See reg 3 of the Road Vehicles (Prohibition) Regulations 1992, in this Part post.

4–1465   72. Removal of prohibitions[1].

    1. See the Road Vehicles (Prohibition) Regulations 1992, in this Part post.

4–1466   73. Provisions supplementary to sections 69 to 72.   (1) Where it appears to a person giving a notice under section 69(6) or 70(2) of this Act that the vehicle concerned is, by virtue of section 5 of the Goods Vehicles (Licensing of Operators) Act 1995, authorised to be used under an operators' licence, he must as soon as practicable take steps to bring the contents of the notice to the attention of—

(*a*)   the traffic commissioner by whom the licence was issued and

(b) the holder of the licence if he is not in charge of the vehicle at the time when the notice is given.*

(1ZA) Where in a case within subsection (1) above it appears to the person giving the notice that the vehicle is authorised to be used under two or more operators' licences—

(a) if those licences were issued by different traffic commissioners, his duty under paragraph (a) of that subsection may be discharged by taking steps to bring the contents of the notice to the attention of any one of those commissioners,

(b) if those licences are held by different persons and none of those persons is in charge of the vehicle at the time when the notice is given, his duty under paragraph (b) of that subsection may be discharged by taking steps to bring the contents of the notice to the attention of any one of those persons, and

(c) if those licences are held by different persons and any of those persons is in charge of the vehicle at the time when the notice is given, no steps need be taken under that subsection to bring the contents of the notice to the attention of the others.

(d) the traffic commissioner by whom the licence was issued, and

(e) the holder of the licence if he is not in charge of the vehicle at the time when the notice is given.*

(1A) Where it appears to a person giving a notice under section 69(6) or 70(2) of this Act that the vehicle concerned is used under a PSV operator's licence, he must as soon as practicable take steps to bring the contents of the notice to the attention of—

(a) the traffic commissioner by whom the PSV operator's licence was granted for the vehicle, and

(b) the holder of the licence if he is not in charge of the vehicle at the time when the notice is given.

(1B) In a case not within subsection (1) or subsection (1A) above, a person giving a notice under section 69(6) or 70(2) of this Act must as soon as practicable take steps to bring the contents of the notice to the attention of the owner of the vehicle if he is not in charge of it at the time when the notice is given.

(1C) A person giving a notice to the owner of a vehicle under section 72(7) of this Act must as soon as practicable take steps to bring the contents of the notice to the attention of any other person—

(a) who was the person to whom the previous notice under section 69(6) or 70(2) was given and was then the owner of the vehicle, or

(b) to whose attention the contents of the previous notice were brought under this section.

(2) (Repealed).

(3) Any reference in sections 69 to 72 of this Act to the driving of a vehicle is, in relation to a trailer, a reference to the driving of the vehicle by which the trailer is drawn.**

(4) In this section "operator's licence" has the same meaning as in the Goods Vehicles (Licensing of Operators) Act 1995 and "PSV operator's licence" has the same meaning as in the Public Passenger Vehicles Act 1981.**

[Road Traffic Act 1988, s 73 amended by the Road Traffic Act 1991, Sch 4 and the Goods Vehicles (Licensing of Operators) Act 1995, Schs 7 and 8.]

---

*Amended by the Deregulation and Contracting Out Act 1994, s 57 and Sch 13, when in force.
**Amended by the Transport Act 1982, s 10 as amended by the Road Traffic (Consequential Provisions) Act 1988, Sch 2.

Miscellaneous provisions about vehicles and vehicle parts

4–1467 74. Operators' duty to inspect, and keep records of inspections of, goods vehicles.

(1) The Secretary of State may make regulations requiring the operator for the time being of a goods vehicle to which the regulations apply to secure—

(a) the carrying out by a suitably qualified person (including the operator if so qualified) of an inspection of the vehicle for the purpose of ascertaining whether the following requirements are complied with, namely—

(i) the construction and use requirements with respect to any prescribed matters, being requirements applicable to the vehicle, and

(ii) the requirement that the condition of the vehicle is not such that its use on a road would involve a danger of injury to any person, and

(b) the making and authentication of records of such matters relating to any such inspection as may be prescribed, including records of the action taken to remedy any defects discovered on the inspection,

and providing for the preservation of such records for a prescribed period not exceeding fifteen months and their custody and production during that period.

(2) Regulations under this section may—

(a) apply to all goods vehicles or to goods vehicles of such classes as may be prescribed,

(b) require the inspection of goods vehicles under the regulations to be carried out at such times, or before the happening of such events, as may be prescribed, and

(c) make different provision for different cases.

(3) Any person who contravenes or fails to comply with any provision of regulations under this section is guilty of an offence[1].

(4) In this section "the operator", in relation to a goods vehicle, means the person to whom it belongs or the hirer of it under a hire purchase agreement; but, if he has let it on hire (otherwise than by way of hire-purchase) or lent it to any other person, it means a person of a class prescribed by regulations under this section in relation to any particular class of goods vehicles or, subject to any such regulations, that other person.

[Road Traffic Act 1988, s 74 amended by the Road Traffic Act 1991, Sch 4.]

---

1. For penalty see the Road Traffic Offenders Act 1988, Sch 2, post.

4–1468   75. Vehicles not to be sold in unroadworthy condition or altered so as to be unroadworthy[1]. (1) Subject to the provisions of this section no person shall supply[2] a motor vehicle or trailer in an unroadworthy[3] condition.

(2) In this section references to supply include—

(a) sell,

(b) offer to sell[4] or supply, and

(c) expose for sale.

(3) For the purposes of subsection (1) above a motor vehicle or trailer is in an unroadworthy condition if—

(a) it is in such a condition that the use of it on a road in that condition would be unlawful by virtue of any provision made by regulations under section 41 of this Act as respects—

(i) brakes, steering gear or tyres, or

(ii) the construction, weight or equipment[4] of vehicles, or

(iii) *Repealed*, or

(b) it is in such a condition that its use on a road would involve a danger of injury to any person.

(4) Subject to the provisions of this section no person shall alter a motor vehicle or trailer so as to render its condition such that the use of it on a road in that condition—

(a) would be unlawful by virtue of any provision made as respects the construction, weight or equipment of vehicles by regulations under section 41[5],

(b) would involve a danger of injury to any person.

(5) A person who supplies or alters a motor vehicle or trailer in contravention of this section, or causes or permits[6] it to be so supplied or altered, is guilty of an offence[7].

(6) A person shall not be convicted of an offence under this section in respect of the supply or alteration of a motor vehicle or trailer if he proves—

(a) that it was supplied or altered, as the case may be, for export from Great Britain, or

(b) that he had reasonable cause to believe that the vehicle or trailer would not be used on a road in Great Britain, or would not be so used until it had been put into a condition in which it might lawfully be so used,

(c) *Repealed*.

(6A) Paragraph (b) of subsection (6) above shall not apply in relation to a person who, in the course of a trade or business—

(a) exposes a vehicle or trailer for sale, unless he also proves that he took all reasonable steps to ensure that any prospective purchaser would be aware that its use in its current condition on a road in Great Britain would be unlawful, or

(b) offers to sell a vehicle or trailer, unless he also proves that he took all reasonable steps to ensure that the person to whom the offer was made was aware of that fact.

(7) Nothing in the preceding provisions of this section shall affect the validity of a contract or any rights arising under a contract.

(8) Repealed.

[Road Traffic Act 1988, s 75 as amended by the Road Traffic Act 1991, s 16 and Sch 8.]

---

1. This section does not apply to tramcars: SI 1992/1217, r 7.

2. "Supply" involves no more than a transfer of physical control of a chattel from one person to another; thus, where a garage returned a vehicle to its owner having carried out repairs and having obtained an MOT test it supplied the vehicle to him: *Devon County Council v DB Cars Ltd* [2001] EWHC Admin 521, (2001) 166 JP 38, [2002] Crim LR 71.

3. No offence was committed where the defendant sold a trailer which was roadworthy in the circumstances in which it was driven away but which would be unroadworthy if used for the purpose for which it was designed and that he knew that the purchaser intended to use the vehicle for its designed purpose (*R (Newcastle upon Tyne City Council) v Le Quelelenec* (2005) Times 17 January, DC).

4. An auctioneer carrying out an auction in the ordinary way does not offer for sale but merely invites those present to make offers to buy (*British Car Auctions Ltd v Wright* [1972] 3 All ER 462).

5. See the Road Vehicles (Construction and Use) Regulations 1986 in this PART, post.

6. See headnote to this title, ante.

7. For punishment, see the Road Traffic Offenders Act 1988, Sch 2 and notes thereto, post. In a serious case the heavy sanctions of the Trade Descriptions Act 1968, including imprisonment, may be appropriate; see *R v Nash* [1990] RTR 343, CA.

4–1469   **76. Fitting and supply of defective or unsuitable vehicle parts[1].**   (1) If any person—

    (*a*)   fits a vehicle part[2] to a vehicle, or

    (*b*)   causes or permits[3] a vehicle part to be fitted to a vehicle,

in such circumstances that the use of the vehicle on a road would, by reason of that part being fitted to the vehicle involve a danger of injury to any person or, constitute a contravention of or failure to comply with any of the construction and use requirements, he is guilty of an offence[4].

    (2)   A person shall not be convicted of an offence under subsection (1) above if he proves—

    (*a*)   that the vehicle to which the part was fitted was to be exported from Great Britain, or

    (*b*)   that he had reasonable cause to believe that that vehicle—

        (i)   would not be used on a road in Great Britain, or

        (ii)   that it would not be so used until it had been put into a condition in which its use on a road would not constitute a contravention of or a failure to comply with any of the construction and use requirements and would not involve a danger of injury to any person.

    (3)   If a person—

    (*a*)   supplies a vehicle part or causes or permits a vehicle part to be supplied, and

    (*b*)   has reasonable cause to believe that the part is to be fitted to a motor vehicle, or to a vehicle of a particular class, or to a particular vehicle,

he is guilty of an offence[4] if that part could not be fitted to a motor vehicle or, as the case may require, to a vehicle of that class or of a class to which the particular vehicle belongs, except in such circumstances that the use of the vehicle on a road would, by reason of that part being fitted to the vehicle, constitute a contravention of or failure to comply with any of the construction and use requirements or involve a danger of injury to any person.

    (4)   In this section references to supply include—

    (*a*)   sell, and

    (*b*)   offer to sell or supply.

    (5)   A person shall not be convicted of an offence under subsection (3) above in respect of the supply of a vehicle part if he proves—

    (*a*)   that the part was supplied for export from Great Britain, or

    (*b*)   that he had reasonable cause to believe that—

        (i)   it would not be fitted to a vehicle used on a road in Great Britain, or

        (ii)   it would not be so fitted until it had been put into such a condition that it could be fitted otherwise than in such circumstances that the use of the vehicle on a road would, by reason of that part being fitted to the vehicle, constitute a contravention of or failure to comply with any of the construction and use requirements or involve a danger of injury to any person.

    (6)   An authorised examiner may at any reasonable hour enter premises where, in the course of a business, vehicle parts are fitted to vehicles or are supplied and test and inspect any vehicle or vehicle part found on those premises for the purpose of ascertaining whether—

    (*a*)   a vehicle part has been fitted to the vehicle in such circumstances that the use of the vehicle on a road would, by reason of that part being fitted to the vehicle, constitute a contravention of or failure to comply with any of the construction and use requirements or involve a danger of injury to any person, or

    (*b*)   the vehicle part could not be supplied for fitting to a vehicle used on roads in Great Britain without the commission of an offence under subsection (3) above.

    (7)   For the purpose of testing a motor vehicle and any trailer drawn by it the authorised examiner may drive it and for the purpose of testing a trailer may draw it with a motor vehicle.

    (8)   Any person who obstructs an authorised examiner acting under subsection (6) or (7) above is guilty of an offence[3].

    (9)   In subsections (6) to (8) above "authorised examiner" means a person who may act as an authorised examiner for the purposes of section 67 of this Act; and any such person, other than a constable in uniform, shall produce his authority to act for the purpose of subsections (6) and (7) above if required to do so.

    (10)   Nothing in this section shall affect the validity of a contract or of any rights arising under a contract.

[Road Traffic Act 1988, s 76 amended by the Road Traffic Act 1991, Sch 4.]

---

1. This section does not apply to tramcars: SI 1992/1217, r 7.
2. Defined by s 85, post.
3. See Headnote to this title, ante.
4. For punishment, see the Road Traffic Offenders Act 1988, Sch 2 and notes thereto, post.

4–1470   **77. Testing condition of used vehicles at sale rooms, etc[1].**   (1) An authorised examiner may at any reasonable hour enter premises where used motor vehicles or trailers are supplied in the course of a business and test and inspect any used motor vehicle or trailer found on the premises for the purpose of ascertaining whether it is in an unroadworthy condition for the purposes of section 75(1) of this Act.

(2) In this section (except paragraph (*d*) below) references to supply include—

(*a*) sell,
(*b*) offer for sale or supply,
(*c*) expose for sale, and
(*d*) otherwise keep for sale or supply.

(3) An authorised examiner may at any reasonable hour enter premises where vehicles or vehicle parts of a class prescribed for the purposes of section 63 of this Act are supplied in the course of a business and test and inspect any such vehicle or vehicle part for the purpose of ascertaining whether the vehicle or vehicle part complies with the type approval requirements applicable to a vehicle or vehicle part of that class.

(4) For the purpose of testing a motor vehicle and any trailer drawn by it the authorised examiner may drive it and for the purpose of testing a trailer may draw it with a motor vehicle.

(5) A person who obstructs an authorised examiner acting under this section is guilty of an offence[2].

(6) In this section "authorised examiner" means a person who may act as an authorised examiner for the purposes of section 67 of this Act; and any such person, other than a constable in uniform, shall produce his authority to act for the purposes of that section if required to do so.

(7) A motor vehicle or trailer shall be treated for the purposes of this section as used if, but only if, it has previously been sold or supplied by retail[3].
[Road Traffic Act 1988, s 77.]

_____

1. This section does not apply to tramcars or trolley vehicles: SI 1992/1217, rr 7 and 9.
2. For penalty see the Road Traffic Offenders Act 1988, Sch 2, post.
3. Defined by s 85, post.

4–1471   78. Weighing of motor vehicles[1]. (1) Subject to any regulations made by the Secretary of State, an authorised person[2] may, on production of his authority[3], require the person in charge of a motor vehicle—

(*a*) to allow the vehicle or any trailer drawn by it to be weighed, either laden or unladen, and the weight transmitted to the road by any parts of the vehicle or trailer in contact with the road to be tested[4], and
(*b*) for the purpose, to proceed to a weighbridge or other machine for weighing vehicles.

(2) For the purpose of enabling a vehicle or a trailer drawn by it to be weighed or a weight to be tested in accordance with regulations under subsection (1) above, an authorised person may require the person in charge of the vehicle to drive the vehicle or to do any other thing in relation to the vehicle or its load or the trailer or its load which is reasonably required to be done for that purpose.

(3) If a person in charge of a motor vehicle—

(*a*) refuses or neglects to comply with any requirement under subsection (1) or (2) above, or
(*b*) obstructs an authorised person in the exercise of his functions under this section,

he is guilty of an offence[5].

(4) An authorised person may not require the person in charge of the motor vehicle to unload the vehicle or trailer, or to cause or allow it to be unloaded, for the purpose of its being weighed unladen.

(5) Regulations under subsection (1) above may make provision with respect to—

(*a*) the manner in which a vehicle or trailer is to be weighed or a weight is to be tested as mentioned in subsection (1) above, and
(*b*) the limits within which, unless the contrary is proved, any weight determined by a weighbridge or other machine for weighing vehicles is to be presumed to be accurate for the purposes of any provision made by or under this Act or by or under any other enactment relating to motor vehicles or trailers,

and the regulations may make different provision in relation to vehicles of different classes, in relation to different types of weighbridges and other machines and in relation to different circumstances.

(6) If—

(*a*) at the time when the requirement is made the vehicle is more than five miles from the weighbridge or other machine, and
(*b*) the weight is found to be within the limits authorised by law,

the highway authority (in Scotland, roads authority) on whose behalf the requirement is made must pay, in respect of loss occasioned, such amount as in default of agreement may be determined by a single arbitrator (in Scotland, arbiter) agreed upon by the parties or, in default of agreement, appointed by the Secretary of State.

(7) The Secretary of State may by order designate areas in Great Britain where subsection (6) above is to have effect, in such cases as may be specified by the order, with the substitution for five miles of a greater distance so specified.

An order under this subsection shall be made by statutory instrument subject to annulment by a resolution of either House of Parliament.

(8) In this section—

(a) "road" includes any land which forms part of a harbour or which is adjacent to a harbour and is occupied wholly or partly for the purposes of harbour operations,

(b) "authorised person" means a person authorised by a highway authority (in Scotland, a roads authority) or a constable authorised on behalf of such an authority by a police authority or a chief officer of police,

and in this subsection "harbour" and "harbour operations" have the meanings given to them by section 57(1) of the Harbours Act 1964.

[Road Traffic Act 1988, s 78.]

---

1. This section does not apply to tramcars or trolley vehicles: SI 1992/1217, rr 7 and 9.
2. As to a duly authorised person by an authorised sign, "Stop, Road Traffic Officer—CC" requiring a motor vehicle to stop for the purpose of weighing it, see *Langley Cartage Co Ltd v Jenks, Adams v Jenks* [1937] 2 KB 382, [1937] 2 All ER 525, 101 JP 393. The appropriate sign is now prescribed by the Traffic Signs Regulations and General Directions 1981, in this PART, post.
3. Failure to produce an authority might prevent a successful prosecution under this section, but would not invalidate an ensuring conviction for exceeding weights shown in the plating certificate (*Wurzal v Reader Bros Ltd* [1974] RTR 383).
4. Regulations relating to the weights of vehicles are contained in the Road Vehicles (Construction and Use) Regulations 1986. The Weighing of Motor Vehicles (Use of Dynamic Axle Weighing Machines) Regulations 1978, SI 1978/1180, have been made.
5. For punishment see the Road Traffic Offenders Act 1988, Sch 2 and notes thereto, post. Sections 11 and 12(1) thereof (evidence by certificate etc) also apply.

4–1472 79. Further provisions relating to weighing of motor vehicles[1]. Certificate of weight must be given and will exempt from being further weighed while on same journey and carrying same load. Examiners etc may exercise powers under s 78. Certificate to be evidence.

[Road Traffic Act 1988, s 79 amended by the Road Traffic Act 1991, Schs 4 and 8—summarised.]

---

1. This section does not apply to tramcars or trolley vehicles: SI 1992/1217, rr 7 and 9.

4–1473 80. Approval marks[1].

---

1. See the Motor Vehicles (Designation of Approval Marks) Regulations 1979, SI 1979/1088, amended by SI 1980/582 and 2027, SI 1981/126 and 1732, SI 1982/1479, SI 1983/1602, SI 1985/113, SI 1986/369, SI 1989/1014, SI 1990/1838, SI 1991/1979, SI 1992/634 and 3086, SI 1993/1710, SI 1995/3342 and SI 1997/58. Unauthorised application of an approval mark is an offence under the Trade Descriptions Act 1968.

4–1474 81. Regulation of brakes, bells etc, on pedal cycles. (1)–(5) Matters to be covered by regulations.

(6) If a person sells, or supplies or offers to sell or supply a cycle in contravention of any prohibition imposed by regulations[1] made by virtue of subsection (5) above, he is guilty of an offence[2], unless he proves—

(a) that it was sold, supplied or offered for export from Great Britain, or

(b) that he had reasonable cause to believe that it would not be used on a road in Great Britain, or would not be so used until it had been put into a condition in which it might lawfully be so used.

[Road Traffic Act 1988, s 81.]

---

1. See the Pedal Cycle (Construction and Use) Regulations 1983 and the Road Vehicles Lighting Regulations 1989 in this PART, post.
2. For penalty see the Road Traffic Offenders Act 1988, Sch 2, post.

4–1475 82. Regulation of brakes on horse-drawn vehicles.

Miscellaneous

4–1476 83. Offences to do with reflectors and tail lamps[1]. A person who sells, or offers or exposes for sale, any appliance adapted for use as a reflector or tail lamp to be carried on a vehicle in accordance with the provisions of this Act or of any regulations made under it, not being an appliance which complies with the construction and use requirements[2] applicable to a class of vehicles for which the appliance is adapted, is guilty of an offence[3].

[Road Traffic Act 1988, s 83.]

---

1. This section does not apply to tramcars: SI 1992/1217, r 7.
2. See, for example, the Road Vehicles Lighting Regulations 1989 in this PART, post.
3. For penalty see the Road Traffic Offenders Act 1988, Sch 2.

4–1477 84. Appointment of officials and destination of fees.

4–1478   85. Interpretation of Part II.   In this Part of this Act—

"the Community Recording Equipment Regulation" means Council Regulation (EEC) No 3821/85 on recording equipment in road transport as it has effect in accordance with—

    (a)   Commission Regulation (EEC) No 3314/90;
    (b)   Commission Regulation (EEC) No 3688/92; and
    (c)   Commission Regulation (EC) No 2479/95;

and as read with the Community Drivers' Hours and Recording Equipment (Exemptions and Supplementary Provisions) Regulations 1986;

"EC certificate of conformity" means

    (a)   in the case of a light passenger vehicle, any certificate of conformity issued by a manufacturer—

        (a)   under regulation 4 of the Motor Vehicles (EC Type Approval) Regulations 1992, or
        (b)   under any provision of the law of a member State other than the United Kingdom giving effect to Article 6 of the light passenger vehicle type approval Directive,

      which is expressed to be a certificate for a complete or completed vehicle,

    (b)   in the case of a vehicle to which the motorcycle type approval Directive applies, any certificate of conformity—

        (i)   issued by a manufacturer under regulation 8(1) of the Motor Cycles Etc (EC Type Approval) Regulations 1999, whether before, on or after 9th November 2003, or
        (ii)   issued by a manufacturer under any provision of the law of an EEA State other than the United Kingdom giving effect to Article 7(1) of the motorcycle type approval directive or to Article 7(1) of Council Directive 92/61/EEC of 30th June 1992 relating to the type approval of two or three-wheeled motor vehicles,

"EEA Agreement" means the Agreement on the European Economic Area signed at Oporto on 2nd May 1992 as adjusted by the Protocol signed at Brussels on 17th March 1993;

"EEA State" means a State which is a contracting Party to the EEA Agreement;

"light passenger vehicle" means any motor vehicle which—

    (a)   has at least four wheels,
    (b)   is equipped with an internal combustion engine,
    (c)   is constructed or adapted for use for the carriage of passengers and is not a goods vehicle,
    (d)   has no more than eight seats in addition to the driver's seat, and
    (e)   has a maximum design speed exceeding 25 kilometres per hour,

but does not include a quadricycle within the meaning of Article 1(3) of the motorcycle type approval Directive or a vehicle used or intended for use for the purposes of any matter in relation to which a fire and rescue authority has functions (whoever uses it for those purposes),

"the light passenger vehicle type approval Directive" means Council Directive 70/156/EEC of 6th February 1970 on the approximation of the laws of the member States relating to the type-approval of motor vehicles and their trailers as amended by Council Directive 87/403/EEC of 25th June 1987 and Council Directive 92/53/EEC of 18th June 1992,

"the motorcycle type approval Directive" means Directive 2002/24/EC of the European Parliament and of the Council of 18th March 2002 relating to the type approval of two or three-wheel motor vehicles and repealing Council Directive 92/61/EEC, as corrected by a Corrigendum of 22nd February 2003,

"official testing station" means a testing station maintained by the Secretary of State under section 72A of this Act,*

"prescribed" means prescribed by regulations made by the Secretary of State,

"public service vehicle" has the same meaning as in the Public Passenger Vehicles Act 1981,

"sold or supplied by retail" means sold or supplied otherwise than to a person acquiring solely for the purpose of resale or of re-supply for a valuable consideration,

"tail lamp" means, in relation to a vehicle, any lamp carried attached to the vehicle for the purpose of showing a red light to the rear in accordance with regulations under section 41 of this Act,

"traffic area" has the same meaning as in the Public Passenger Vehicles Act 1981, and

"vehicle part" means any article which is a motor vehicle part, within the meaning of section 80 of this Act, and any other article which is made or adapted for use as part of, or as part of the equipment of, a vehicle which is intended or adapted to be used on roads but which is not a motor vehicle within the meaning of that section.

[Road Traffic Act 1988, s 85 amended by the Road Traffic Act 1991, Sch 4, SI 1992/3107, the Goods Vehicles (Licensing of Operators) Act 1995, Schs 7 and 8, SI 1996/941, SI 1999/2920, SI 2003/1099 and the Fire and Rescue Services Act 2004, Sch 1.]

---

*Section 85 is amended and added to by the Road Traffic (Consequential Provisions) Act 1988, Sch 2, para 17 when in force.

4–1479   86. Index to Part II.   The expressions listed in the left-hand column below are respectively defined or (as the case may be) fall to be construed in accordance with the provisions of this Part of this Act listed in the right-hand column in relation to those expressions.

Expression	Relevant Provision
Certificate of conformity	Section 57(1A)
Community Recording Equipment Regulation	Section 85
Construction and use requirements	Section 41(7)
Design weights	Section 54(3)
EC certificate of conformity	Section 85
Examination for plating	Section 49(4)
Goods vehicle test	Section 49(4)
Goods vehicle test certificate	Section 49(2)(*b*)
Light passenger vehicle	Section 85
Light passenger vehicle type approval Directive	Section 85
Minister's approval certificate	Section 58(1)
Motorcycle type approval Directive	Section 85
Official testing station	Section 85
Plating certificate	Section 49(2)(*a*)
Plated particulars	Section 41(7)
Plated weights	Section 41(7)
Prescribed	Section 85
Public service vehicle	Section 85
Relevant aspects of design, construction, equipment and marking	Section 54(6)
Sold or supplied by retail	Section 85
Tail lamp	Section 85
Test certificate	Section 45(2)
Traffic area	Section 85
Type approval certificate	Section 55(2)
Type approval requirements	Section 54(1)
Vehicle examiner	Section 66A
Vehicle part	Section 85

[Road Traffic Act 1988, s 86 amended by the Road Traffic Act 1991, Schs 4 and 8 and SI 1992/3107 and the Goods Vehicles (Licensing of Operators) Act 1995, Schs 7 and 8.]

PART III[1]
LICENSING OF DRIVERS OF VEHICLES

Requirement to hold licence

4–1480   **87. Drivers of motor vehicles to have driving licences.**   (1) It is an offence[2] for a person to drive[3] on a road a motor vehicle of any class otherwise than in accordance with a licence[4] authorising him to drive a motor vehicle of that class[5].

(2) It is an offence[2] for a person to cause or permit[3] another person to drive on a road a motor vehicle of any class otherwise than in accordance with a licence authorising that other person to drive a motor vehicle of that class.

(3) A licence authorising a person to drive a motor vehicle in category B within the meaning of the Motor Vehicles (Driving Licences) Regulations 1987, shall be regarded as authorising that person to drive a tramcar.

(3)[6] This section is subject to paragraph 11 of Schedule 1 to the Road Traffic (Driver Licensing and Information Systems) Act 1989[7].

(4) Notwithstanding subsection (1) above, a person may drive or cause or permit another person

to drive a tramcar if the driver was employed on duties which required the driving of tramcars on a road at any time during the one year period ending immediately before 1st July 1992.
[Road Traffic Act 1988, s 87 amended by the Road Traffic (Driver Licensing and Information Systems) Act 1989, Sch 3 and the Road Traffic Act 1991, s 17.]

---

1. Part III contains ss 87–109. As to exceptions to the general rule that this Part applies to persons and vehicles in the public service of the Crown, see s 183, post.
2. For penalty see the Road Traffic Offenders Act 1988, Sch 2, post.
3. For "drive", "cause", "permit", see Preliminary note to this title. The prosecution need only prove the granting of permission to drive and not that the owner was aware that the driver was unlicensed (*Ferrymasters Ltd v Adam* [1975] RTR 465, [1980] Crim LR 187). It was also held that the same principles apply to the interpretation of this subsection as apply to the interpretation of s 143(1) (use of motor vehicle without insurance), post.
Sections 11 and 12(1) of the Road Traffic Offenders Act 1988 (evidence by certificate etc) apply to s 87(1): s 11 applies to s 87(2).
4. The Motor Vehicles (Driving Licences) Regulations 1999 in this PART, post, make detailed provision. Part IV of this Act, post, deals with the licensing of LGV drivers.
The onus of proof that the driver had a licence lies upon him (*John v Humphreys* [1955] 1 All ER 793, 119 JP 309; *Tynan v Jones* [1975] RTR 465, [1975] Crim LR 458); and, once it has been proved that the defendant drove a vehicle on a road, it is irrelevant in this regard whether or not a police officer formally requested him to produce documents: *DPP v Hay* [2005] EWHC Admin 1395, (2005) 169 JP 429, [2006] RTR 3.
A licence taken out after detection, but on the same day, is not an answer to a charge (*Campbell v Strangeways* (1877) 3 CPD 105, 42 JP 39).
For special provisions regarding visitors see the Motor Vehicles (International Circulation) Order 1975, in this PART, post. It is not in principle incompatible with Community law for one Member State to require a national of another Member State who is permanently established in its territory to obtain a domestic driving licence, but there could be circumstances in which it could prejudice the right of freedom of movement, establishment, or to provide services; see Case 16/78 *Criminal Proceedings v Choquet* [1978] ECR 2293.
For provisions in respect of a probationary period after passing a test of competence to drive, see the Road Traffic (New Drivers) Act 1995, this PART, post.
5. See definition of "class of vehicles" in s 192(3), post. As to a disabled driver, see ss 92–94, 97(3)(*c*), 99(1)(*b*) and see *McKissock v Rees-Davies* [1976] RTR 419 (driver without right arm driving unadapted car).
6. In the course of amendment of this section, two subsections have been inadvertently numbered the same.
7. Sub-s (3) is added by the Road Traffic (Driver Licensing and Information Systems) Act 1989, Sch 3, para 7. Schedule 1, para 11 of that Act provides that:

"Notwithstanding section 87 of the 1988 Act, a person who is the holder of a licence to drive motor vehicles granted under Part III of that Act and coming into force on or after 1st June 1990 and is also the holder of—

(*a*) a licence under Part IV of that Act to drive heavy goods vehicles of any class, or
(*b*) a licence under section 22 of the 1981 Act to drive public service vehicles of any class,

may drive, or be caused or permitted to drive, a heavy goods vehicle or (as the case may be) a public service vehicle of that class notwithstanding that his licence under Part III of the 1988 Act does not authorise him to drive such a vehicle."

4–1490   88. Exceptions.   (1) Notwithstanding section 87 of this Act, a person may drive or cause or permit another person to drive a vehicle of any class if—

(*a*)   the driver has held—

   (i)   a licence under this Part of this Act to drive vehicles of that or a corresponding class, or
   (ia) a Community licence to drive vehicles of that or a corresponding class, or
   (ii) a Northern Ireland licence to drive vehicles of that or a corresponding class, or
   (iii) a British external licence or British Forces licence to drive vehicles of that or a corresponding class, or
   (iv) an exchangeable licence to drive vehicles of that or a corresponding class, and

(*b*)   either—

   (i)   a qualifying application by the driver for the grant of a licence to drive vehicles of that class for a period which includes that time has been received by the Secretary of State, or
   (ii) a licence to drive vehicles of that class granted to him has been revoked or surrendered in pursuance of section 99 (2A), (3) or (4) of this Act otherwise than by reason of a current disqualification or of its having been granted in error and he has complied with any requirements imposed on him under section 99 (7B) of this Act, and

(*c*)   any conditions which by virtue of section 97(3) or 98(2) of this Act apply to the driving under the authority of the licence of vehicles of that class are complied with.

(1A)   An application for the grant of a licence to drive vehicles of any class is a qualifying application for the purposes of subsection (1)(*b*)(i) above if—

(*a*)   the requirements of paragraphs (*a*), (*b*) so far as it relates to initial evidence and (*c*) of section 97(1) of this Act have been satisfied;
(*b*)   the applicant—

   (i)   is not subject to a current disqualification which is relevant to the licence he applies for, and
   (ii) is not prevented from obtaining it by section 89 of this Act or section 4 of or paragraph 6 or 9 of Schedule 1 to the Road Traffic (New Drivers) Act 1995; and

(*c*)   the declaration made in pursuance of section 92(1) of this Act indicates that he is not suffering from a relevant disability.

(1B)   A disqualification is relevant to a licence for which a person makes an application if—

(c) vehicles of all classes included in another such group, if a person passing the test is treated by virtue of regulations made for the purposes of this paragraph as competent also to drive vehicles of a class included in that other group.

(7) If vehicles of any classes are designated by regulations as a group (except where regulations otherwise provide) for the purposes of subsection (1)(b) above, a licence authorising the driving of vehicles of a class included in the group shall be deemed for the purposes of subsection (1)(b)(i) above or section 89A(4)(a) below to authorise the driving of—

(a) vehicles of all classes included in the group, and

(b) vehicles of all classes included in another such group, if a person holding the licence is treated by virtue of regulations as competent also to drive vehicles of a class included in that other group.

The reference in this subsection to a licence does not include a licence which has been revoked in pursuance of section 99(3) of this Act.

(8) For the purposes of this section and section 88(1) of this Act, an exchangeable licence issued in respect of a country or territory shall not be treated as authorising a person to drive a vehicle of any class if—

(a) the licence is not for the time being valid for that purpose, or

(b) it was issued in respect of that class for a purpose corresponding to that mentioned in section 97(2) of this Act.

(9) A test of competence falling within paragraphs (a)(ii), (c) or (e) of subsection (1) above shall be sufficient for the granting of a licence authorising the driving of—

(a) vehicles of all classes designated by regulations as a group for the purposes of subsection (1)(a) above, if (except where regulations otherwise provide) at the time the test was passed it authorised the granting of a licence to drive vehicles of any class included in the group, or of any class corresponding to a class included in the group, and

(b) vehicles of all classes included in another such group, if a person passing a test of competence authorising the granting of a licence to drive vehicles of a class included in the group mentioned in paragraph (a) above is treated by virtue of regulations as competent also to drive vehicles of a class included in that other group.

(10) A full Northern Ireland licence, a full British external licence, a full British Forces licence a Community licence or an exchangeable licence shall be treated for the purposes of paragraphs (b)(ii), (d), (ea) or (f) (as the case may be) of subsection (1) above as authorising the driving of—

(a) (except where regulations otherwise provide) vehicles of all classes designated by regulations as a group for the purposes of subsection (1)(b) above, if the licence authorises the driving of vehicles of any class included in the group, or any class corresponding to a class included in the group, and

(b) vehicles of all classes included in another such group, if by virtue of regulations a person holding a licence authorising him to drive vehicles of any class included in the group mentioned in paragraph (a) above is treated as competent also to drive vehicles of a class included in that other group.

(11) In this section and section 89A "the appointed day" means the day appointed for the coming into force of section 1 of the Road Traffic (Driver Licensing and Information Systems) Act 1989. [Road Traffic Act 1988, s 89 as amended by the Road Traffic (Driver Licensing and Information Systems) Act 1989, s 4 and 6 and Sch 3, the Road Traffic Act 1991, Sch 4 and SI 1996/1974.]

---

1. For further provisions about tests with respect to newly qualified drivers who have committed offences during the probationary period see the Road Traffic (New Drivers) Act 1995, this PART, post.

2. For appropriate offences in a case of impersonation, see *R v Potter* [1958] 2 All ER 51, [1958] 1 WLR 638, 122 JP 234.

3. The law of the following states or territories has been so designated by Driving Licences (Designation of Relevant External Law) Order: Jersey and the Isle of Man, SI 1996/3206; Guernsey, SI 2002/2590.

4. See the Motor Vehicles (Driving Licences) Regulations 1999 in this PART, post.

4–1492 89A. The alternative requirements to those in section 89. (1) The alternative requirements referred to in section 89(1) of this Act are the following.

(2) The requirement which is alternative to that specified in section 89(1)(a) on an application by a person for a licence authorising the driving of motor vehicles of any class other than any class of goods vehicle or passenger-carrying vehicle prescribed for the purposes of subsection (3) below—

(a) is available to that person if the application is made within the period of ten years beginning with the appointed day, and

(b) is that at some time before the appointed day and during the period of ten years ending with the date the application is made he has passed—

(i) the test of competence to drive prescribed by virtue of section 89(3) of this Act or a test of competence to drive which corresponds to such a test, or

(ii) a Northern Ireland test of competence to drive which corresponds to any test falling within (i) above, or

(iii) a test of competence which under section 89(6) of this Act is a sufficient test or a test of competence to drive which corresponds to such a test.

(3) The requirement which is alternative to that specified in section 89(1)(*a*) on an application by a person for a licence authorising the driving of any class of goods vehicle or passenger-carrying vehicle prescribed for the purposes of this subsection—

(*a*) is available to that person if the application is made within the period of five years beginning with the appointed day, and

(*b*) is that at some time before the appointed day and during the period of five years ending with the date the application is made he has passed—

(i) a test of competence to drive a heavy goods vehicle or public service vehicle of a class corresponding to the class of vehicle to which his application relates, or

(ii) a corresponding Northern Ireland test of competence to drive a heavy goods vehicle or public service vehicle of a class which corresponds to the class of goods vehicle or passenger-carrying vehicle to which his application relates.

(4) The requirement which is alternative to that specified in section 89(1)(*b*) on an application by a person for a licence authorising the driving of motor vehicles of any class other than any class of goods vehicle or passenger-carrying vehicle prescribed for the purposes of subsection (5) below is that at some time before the appointed day but not earlier than 1st January 1976 he has held—

(*a*) a full licence authorising the driving of vehicles of a class corresponding to the class of motor vehicle to which his application relates, or

(*b*) a full Northern Ireland licence authorising the driving of vehicles of a class corresponding to the class of motor vehicle to which his application relates.

(5) The requirement which is alternative to that specified in section 89(1)(*b*) on an application by a person for a licence authorising the driving of any class of goods vehicle or passenger-carrying vehicle prescribed for the purposes of this subsection is that at some time before the appointed day but not earlier than the beginning of the period of five years ending with the appointed day he has held—

(*a*) a full heavy goods vehicle or a public service vehicle driver's licence authorising the driving of vehicles of a class corresponding to the class of vehicle to which his application relates, or

(*b*) a full Northern Ireland licence to drive heavy goods vehicles of a class corresponding to the class of vehicle to which his application relates or a Northern Ireland licence to drive public service vehicles of a class corresponding to the class of vehicle to which his application relates.

(6) The requirement which is alternative to that specified in section 89(1)(*d*) on an application by a person for a licence authorising the driving of motor vehicles of any class—

(*a*) is available to that person if the application is made within the period of ten years beginning with the appointed day, and

(*b*) is that at some time before the appointed day and during the period of ten years ending with the date the application is made he has held a full British external licence or a full British Forces licence to drive vehicles of that or a corresponding class.

(7) In this section "heavy goods vehicle" and "public service vehicle" have the same meaning as they had for the purposes of Part IV of this Act or section 22 of the Public Passenger Vehicles Act 1981 before their repeal by section 1 of the Road Traffic (Driver Licensing and Information Systems) Act 1989.
[Road Traffic Act 1988, s 89A as added by the Road Traffic (Driver Licensing and Information Systems) Act 1989, s 4.]

4–1493 90. Review of conduct of test. (1) On the application of a person who has submitted himself for a test of competence to drive—

(*a*) a magistrates' court acting for the petty sessions area in which he resides, or

(*b*) in Scotland, the sheriff within whose jurisdiction he resides,

may determine whether the test was properly conducted in accordance with regulations[1].

(2) The court or, as the case may be, sheriff may, if it appears that the test was not so conducted—

(*a*) order that the applicant shall be eligible to submit himself for another test before the expiration of the period specified for the purposes of section 89(4)(*c*) of this Act, and

(*b*) order that any fee payable by the applicant in respect of the test shall not be paid or, if it has been paid, shall be repaid.

(3) If regulations make provision for a test of competence to drive to consist of separate parts, this section applies in relation to each part as well as in relation to the whole of the test.
[Road Traffic Act 1988, s 90.]

1. There is no general right of appeal. Jurisdiction is limited to an inquiry as to whether or not the test was conducted by an authorised person in conformity with the regulations; and, if so conducted there is no power to go behind or inquire into the findings of the examiner (*Geraghty v Morris* [1939] 2 All ER 269, 103 JP 175). Presumably Magistrates' Courts Rules 1981, r 34, in PART I, *ante*, will apply.

4–1494 91. Repayment of test fees.

Physical fitness

4–1495   92.   Requirements as to physical fitness of drivers.   (1) An application for the grant of a licence must include a declaration by the applicant, in such form as the Secretary of State may require, stating whether he is suffering or has at any time (or, if a period is prescribed for the purposes of this subsection, has during that period) suffered from any relevant disability or any prospective disability.

(2) In this Part of this Act—

"disability" includes disease and the persistent misuse of drugs or alcohol, whether or not such
    misuse amounts to dependency,
"relevant disability" in relation to any person means—

    (*a*)   any prescribed disability, and
    (*b*)   any other disability likely to cause the driving of a vehicle by him in pursuance of a licence
         to be a source of danger to the public, and

"prospective disability" in relation to any person means any other disability which—

    (*a*)   at the time of the application for the grant of a licence or, as the case may be, the material
         time for the purposes of the provision in which the expression is used, is not of such a
         kind that it is a relevant disability, but
    (*b*)   by virtue of the intermittent or progressive nature of the disability or otherwise, may
         become a relevant disability in course of time.

(3) If it appears from the applicant's declaration, or if on inquiry the Secretary of State is satisfied from other information, that the applicant is suffering from a relevant disability, the Secretary of State must, subject to the following provisions of this section, refuse[1] to grant the licence.

(4) The Secretary of State must not by virtue of subsection (3) above refuse to grant a licence—

    (*a*)   on account of any relevant disability which is prescribed for the purposes of this paragraph, if
         the applicant has at any time passed a relevant test and it does not appear to the Secretary of
         State that the disability has arisen or become more acute since that time or was, for whatever
         reason, not disclosed to the Secretary of State at that time,
    (*b*)   on account of any relevant disability which is prescribed for the purposes of this paragraph, if
         the applicant satisfies such conditions as may be prescribed with a view to authorising the
         grant of a licence to a person in whose case the disability is appropriately controlled,
    (*c*)   on account of any relevant disability which is prescribed for the purposes of this paragraph, if
         the application is for a provisional licence.

(5) Where as a result of a test of competence to drive or of information obtained under the relevant powers the Secretary of State is satisfied that the person who took the test or in relation to whom the information was obtained is suffering from a disability such that there is likely to be a danger to the public—

    (*a*)   if he drives any vehicle,
    (*b*)   if he drives a vehicle other than a vehicle of a particular class, or
    (*c*)   if he drives a vehicle except in accordance with particular conditions,

the Secretary of State must serve[2] notice in writing to that effect on that person and must include in the notice a description of the disability.

(6) Where a notice is served in pursuance of subsection (5)(*a*) above, then—

    (*a*)   if the disability is not prescribed under subsection (2) above, it shall be deemed to be so
         prescribed in relation to the person on whom the notice is served, and
    (*b*)   if the disability is prescribed for the purposes of subsection (4)(*c*) above it shall be deemed
         not to be so prescribed in relation to him.

(7) Where a notice is served in pursuance of subsection (5)(*b*) above, the Secretary of State may—

    (*a*)   if the person on whom the notice is served is an applicant for a licence, grant him a licence
         limited to vehicles of the particular class specified in the notice, or
    (*b*)   if he held a licence which is revoked by the Secretary of State and he complies with subsection
         (7ZB) below, grant him a licence limited to vehicles of that class,

and, if the Secretary of State so directs in the notice, his entitlement to drive other classes of vehicle by virtue of section 98(2) of this Act shall be limited as specified in the notice.

(7ZA) Where a notice is served in pursuance of subsection (5)(*c*) above, the Secretary of State may—

    (*a*)   if the person on whom the notice is served is an applicant for a licence, grant him a licence
         authorising him to drive vehicles subject to the particular conditions specified in the notice, or
    (*b*)   if he held a licence which is revoked by the Secretary of State and he complies with subsection
         (7ZB) below, grant him a licence authorising him to drive vehicles subject to those conditions,

and, if the Secretary of State so directs in the notice, any entitlement which the person has to drive vehicles by virtue of section 98(2) of this Act shall be subject to conditions as specified in the notice.

(7ZB) A person complies with this subsection if—

    (*a*)   he surrenders the existing licence and its counterpart, and

(b)   where the Secretary of State so requires, he provides evidence of his name, address, sex and date and place of birth and a photograph which is a current likeness of him.

(7A)   If he considers it appropriate to do so, the Secretary of State may, after serving a notice under any of the paragraphs of subsection (5) above, serve a further notice under that paragraph or a notice under another of those paragraphs; and on his serving the later notice the notice previously served shall cease to have effect and any licence previously granted in accordance with it shall be revoked by the later notice.

(7B)   In subsection (5) above the references to a test of competence to drive and to information obtained under the relevant powers are references respectively to a test of competence prescribed for the purposes of section 89 or so much of such a test as is required to be taken in pursuance of section 94(5)(c) of this Act and to information obtained in pursuance of section 94(5)(a) or (b) of this Act.

(7C)   A person whose licence is revoked by virtue of subsection (7A) above must deliver the licence or its counterpart to the Secretary of State forthwith after the revocation and a person who, without reasonable excuse, fails to do so is guilty of an offence.

(7D)   In subsection (7B) above the references to section 94 of this Act include references to that section as applied by section 99D or 109C of this Act.

(8)   In this section "relevant test", in relation to an application for a licence, means any such test of competence as is mentioned in section 89 of this Act or a test as to fitness or ability in pursuance of section 100 of the Road Traffic Act 1960 as originally enacted, being a test authorising the grant of a licence in respect of vehicles of the classes to which the application relates.

(9)   Without prejudice to subsection (8) above, for the purposes of subsection (4)(a) above—

(a)   an applicant shall be treated as having passed a relevant test if, and on the day on which, he passed a test of competence to drive which—

(i)   under a provision of the law of Northern Ireland or a relevant external law corresponding to subsections (3) and (4) or (6) of section 89 of this Act, either is prescribed in relation to vehicles of classes corresponding to the classes to which the application relates or is sufficient under that law for the granting of a licence authorising the driving of vehicles of those classes, or

(ii)   is sufficient for the granting of a British Forces licence authorising the driving of vehicles of those classes, and

(b)   in the case of an applicant who is treated as having passed a relevant test by virtue of paragraph (a) above, disclosure of a disability to his licensing authority shall be treated as disclosure to the Secretary of State.

(10)   A person who holds a licence authorising him to drive a motor vehicle of any class and who drives a motor vehicle of that class on a road is guilty of an offence if the declaration included in accordance with subsection (1) above in the application on which the licence was granted was one which he knew to be false.

[Road Traffic Act 1988, s 92 as amended by the Road Traffic (Driver Licensing and Information Systems) Act 1989, s 5 (amended by SI 1990/144), the Road Traffic Act 1991, s 18, SI 1996/1974, SI 1998/1420 and the Crime (International Co-operation) Act 2003, Sch 5.]

---

1.   A person aggrieved by this refusal may appeal to a magistrates' court (s 100, post). By reason of sub-s (3), there is no appeal if the applicant declares that he is suffering from a prescribed disease or disability (*R v Cumberland Justices, ex p Hepworth* [1931] WN 209, 95 JP 206, CA); but there is an appeal against the Secretary of State's refusal to grant a licence founded on information discovered by him on an inquiry made under this section (*R v Cardiff Justices, ex p Cardiff City Council* [1962] 2 QB 436, [1962] 1 All ER 751, 126 JP 175). A person suffering from a relevant disease that does not show itself when controlled by drugs is none the less suffering therefrom and must be refused a licence (*Devon County Council v Hawkins* [1967] 2 QB 26, [1967] 1 All ER 235, 131 JP 161).

The conditions subject to which an epileptic can be granted a licence are prescribed in the Motor Vehicles (Driving Licences) Regulations 1999, in this PART, post.

2.   Notice may be served by delivering it to him or by leaving it at his proper address or by sending it by post (s 107, post).

4–1496   93. Revocation of licence because of disability or prospective disability.   (1)   If the Secretary of State is at any time satisfied on inquiry—

(a)   that a licence holder is suffering from a relevant disability[1], and

(b)   that the Secretary of State would be required by virtue of section 92(3) of this Act to refuse an application for the licence made by him at that time,

the Secretary of State may serve notice[2] in writing on the licence holder revoking the licence[3] with effect from such date as may be specified in the notice, not being earlier than the date of service of the notice.

(2)   If the Secretary of State is at any time satisfied on inquiry that a licence holder is suffering from a prospective disability[1], the Secretary of State may—

(a)   serve notice[2] in writing on the licence holder revoking the licence[3] with effect from such date as may be specified in the notice, not being earlier than the date of service of the notice, and

(b)   on receipt of the licence so revoked and its counterpart and of an application made for the purposes of this subsection, grant to the licence holder, free of charge, a new licence for a period determined by the Secretary of State under section 99(1)(b) of this Act.

(2A)   The Secretary of State may require a person to provide—

(*a*)   evidence of his name, address, sex and date and place of birth, and

(*b*)   a photograph which is a current likeness of him,

before granting a licence to him on an application made for the purposes of subsection (2) above or subsection (6) below.

(3) A person whose licence and its counterpart is revoked under subsection (1) or (2) above must deliver up[4] the licence to the Secretary of State forthwith after the revocation and a person who, without reasonable excuse, fails to do so is guilty of an offence[5].

(4) Where a person whose licence is revoked under subsection (1) or (2) above—

(*a*)   is not in possession of his licence and its counterpart in consequence of the fact that he has surrendered them to a constable or authorised person (within the meaning of Part III of the Road Traffic Offenders Act 1988) on receiving a fixed penalty notice given to him under section 54 of that Act but

(*b*)   delivers them to the Secretary of State immediately on their return,

he is not in breach of the duty under subsection (3) above.

(5) Where the Secretary of State—

(*a*)   is at any time sent by the licensing authority in Northern Ireland a licence under a provision of Northern Ireland law corresponding to section 109B of this Act, and

(*b*)   by virtue of the reasons given by that authority for sending the licence is at that time satisfied as mentioned in subsection (1)(*a*) and (*b*) above or that the licence holder is suffering from a prospective disability,

the Secretary of State may serve notice in writing on the licence holder revoking the licence with effect from such date as may be specified in the notice, not being earlier than the date of service of the notice.

(6) Where the reasons given by the licensing authority in Northern Ireland for sending the licence relate to a prospective disability of the holder, the Secretary of State may, on an application made for the purposes of this subsection, grant to the holder, free of charge, a new licence for a period determined by the Secretary of State under section 99(1)(*b*) of this Act.

[Road Traffic Act 1988, s 93 as amended by the Road Traffic (Driver Licensing and Information Systems) Act 1989 s 5, SI 1990/144, SI 1996/1974, SI 1998/1420 and the Crime (International Co-operation) Act 2003, Sch 5,.]

---

    1. Defined in s 92, ante.
    2. See s 107 for service provisions.
    3. Appeal lies to the magistrates' court (s 100, post) and see notes to s 92(3), ante.
    4. In the event of default, s 164, post provides for enforcement.
    5. For penalty see the Road Traffic Offenders Act 1988, Sch 2, post.

4–1497   **94. Provision of information, etc relating to disabilities.**   (1) If at any time during the period for which his licence remains in force, a licence holder becomes aware—

(*a*)   that he is suffering from a relevant or prospective disability[1] which he has not previously disclosed to the Secretary of State, or

(*b*)   that a relevant or prospective disability[1] from which he has at any time suffered (and which has been previously so disclosed) has become more acute since the licence was granted,

the licence holder must forthwith notify the Secretary of State in writing of the nature and extent of his disability[1].

(2) The licence holder is not required to notify the Secretary of State under subsection (1) above if—

(*a*)   the disability is one from which he has not previously suffered, and

(*b*)   he has reasonable grounds for believing that the duration of the disability will not extend beyond the period of three months beginning with the date on which he first becomes aware that he suffers from it.

(3) A person who fails without reasonable excuse to notify the Secretary of State as required by subsection (1) above is guilty of an offence[2].

(3A) A person who holds a licence authorising him to drive a motor vehicle of any class and who drives a motor vehicle of that class on a road is guilty of an offence if at any earlier time while the licence was in force he was required by subsection (1) above to notify the Secretary of State but has failed without reasonable excuse to do so.

(4) If the prescribed circumstances obtain in relation to a person who is an applicant for, or the holder of, a licence or if the Secretary of State has reasonable grounds for believing that a person who is an applicant for, or the holder of, a licence may be suffering from a relevant or prospective disability, subsection (5) below applies for the purpose of enabling the Secretary of State to satisfy himself whether or not that person may be suffering from that or any other relevant or prospective disability.

(5) The Secretary of State may by notice in writing served[3] on the applicant or holder—

(*a*)   require him to provide the Secretary of State, within such reasonable time as may be specified in the notice, with such an authorisation as is mentioned in subsection (6) below, or

(*b*)   require him, as soon as practicable, to arrange to submit himself for examination—

(i)   by such registered medical practitioner or practitioners as may be nominated by the Secretary of State, or

(ii) with respect to a disability of a prescribed description, by such officer of the Secretary of State as may be so nominated,

for the purpose of determining whether or not he suffers or has at any time suffered from a relevant or prospective disability, or

(c)   except where the application is for, or the licence held is, a provisional licence, require him to submit himself for such a test of competence to drive as the Secretary of State directs in the notice,

as the case may be.

(6) The authorisation referred to in subsection (5)(a) above—

(a)   shall be in such form and contain such particulars as may be specified in the notice by which it is required to be provided, and

(b)   shall authorise any registered medical practitioner who may at any time have given medical advice or attention to the applicant or licence holder concerned to release to the Secretary of State any information which he may have, or which may be available to him, with respect to the question whether, and if so to what extent, the applicant or licence holder concerned may be suffering, or may at any time have suffered, from a relevant or prospective disability.

(7) If he considers it appropriate to do so in the case of any applicant or licence holder, the Secretary of State—

(a)   may include in a single notice under subsection (5) above requirements under more than one paragraph of that subsection, and

(b)   may at any time after the service of a notice under that subsection serve a further notice or notices under that subsection.

(8) If any person on whom a notice is served under subsection (5) above—

(a)   fails without reasonable excuse to comply with a requirement contained in the notice, or

(b)   fails any test of competence which he is required to take as mentioned in paragraph (c) of that subsection,

the Secretary of State may exercise his powers under sections 92 and 93 of this Act[4] as if he were satisfied that the applicant or licence holder concerned is suffering from a relevant disability which is not prescribed for the purposes of any paragraph of section 92(4) of this Act or, if the Secretary of State so determines, as if he were satisfied that the applicant or licence holder concerned is suffering from a prospective disability.

(9) Except where the requirement is made in the circumstances prescribed for the purpose of subsection (5) above, it shall be for the Secretary of State (and not for any other person) to defray any fees or other reasonable expenses of a registered medical practitioner in connection with—

(a)   the provision of information in pursuance of an authorisation required to be provided under subsection (5)(a) above, or

(b)   any examination which a person is required to undergo as mentioned in subsection (5)(b) above.

[Road Traffic Act 1988, s 94 as amended by the Road Traffic (Driver Licensing and Information Systems) Act 1989 s 5 and the Road Traffic Act 1991, s 18.]

---

1. Defined in s 92, ante.
2. For penalty see the Road Traffic Offenders Act 1988, Sch 2, post, and for restrictions on prosecution see s 3 thereof. Section 6 thereof (time limits) also applies.
3. See s 107, post, for service provisions.
4. Rights of appeal under s 100 will arise.

4–1498   94A. Driving after refusal or revocation of licence.   (1) A person who drives a motor vehicle of any class on a road otherwise than in accordance with a licence authorising him to drive a motor vehicle of that class is guilty of an offence if—

(a)   at any earlier time the Secretary of State—

(i)   has in accordance with section 92(3) of this Act refused to grant such a licence,

(ii) has under section 93 of this Act revoked such a licence, or

(iii) has served notice on that person in pursuance of section 99C(1) or (2) or 109B of this Act requiring him to deliver to the Secretary of State a Community licence or Northern Ireland licence authorising him to drive a motor vehicle of that or a corresponding class, and

(b)   since that earlier time he has not been granted—

(i)   a licence under this Part of this Act, or

(ii) a Community licence or Northern Ireland licence,

authorising him to drive a motor vehicle of that or a corresponding class.

(2) Section 88 of this Act shall apply in relation to subsection (1) above as it applies in relation to section 87.

[Road Traffic Act 1988, s 94A added by the Road Traffic Act 1991, s 18 and amended by SI 1996/1974 and the Crime (International Co-operation) Act 2003, Sch 5.]

4–1499   95. Notification of refusal of insurance on grounds of health.   Authorised insurer to notify Secretary of State.
[Road Traffic Act 1988, s 95—summarised.]

4–1500   96. Driving with uncorrected defective eyesight.   (1) If a person drives a motor vehicle on a road while his eyesight is such (whether through a defect which cannot be or one which is not for the time being sufficiently corrected) that he cannot comply[1] with any requirement as to eyesight prescribed under this Part of this Act for the purposes of tests of competence to drive, he is guilty of an offence[2].

(2) A constable having reason to suspect that a person driving a motor vehicle may be guilty of an offence under subsection (1) above may require him to submit to a test for the purpose of ascertaining whether, using no other means of correction than he used at the time of driving, he can comply[1] with the requirement concerned.

(3) If that person refuses to submit to the test he is guilty of an offence[2].
[Road Traffic Act 1988, s 96.]

---

1. The current standard is prescribed in the Motor Vehicles (Driving Licences) Regulations 1999 in this PART, post.
2. For penalty see the Road Traffic Offenders Act 1988, Sch 2, post.

Granting of licences, their form and duration

4–1501   97. Grant of licences.   (1) Secretary of State must grant on appropriate application.

(1A)   Secretary of State may require photograph.*

(1AA)   Northern Ireland.

(2)   Provisional licence with a view to passing a test.

(3)   A provisional licence—

(a)   shall be granted subject to prescribed conditions,

(b)   shall, in any cases prescribed for the purposes of this paragraph, be restricted so as to authorise only the driving of vehicles of the classes so prescribed,

(c)   may, in the case of a person appearing to the Secretary of State to be suffering from a relevant disability or a prospective disability, be restricted so as to authorise only the driving of vehicles of a particular construction or design specified in the licence,

(d)   shall not authorise a person under the age of 21 years, before he has passed a test of competence to drive a motor bicycle,—

   (i)   to drive a motor bicycle without a side-car unless it is a learner motor bicycle (as defined in subsection (5) below) or its first use (as defined in regulations) occurred before 1st January 1982 and the cylinder capacity of its engine does not exceed 125 cubic centimetres, or

   (ii)   to drive a motor bicycle with a side-car unless its power to weight ratio is less than or equal to 0.16 kilowatts per kilogram, and

(e)   except as provided under subsection (3B) below, shall not authorise a person, before he has passed a test of competence to drive, to drive on a road a motor bicycle or moped except where he has successfully completed an approved training course for motor cyclists or is undergoing training on such a course and is driving the motor bicycle or moped on the road as part of the training.*

(3A)   Regulations for training in driving of motor bicycles or mopeds.*

(3B)   Regulations prescribing exemptions from s 97(3)(e).*

(4)   Regulations.

(5)   A learner motor bicycle is a motor bicycle which either is propelled by electric power or has the following characteristics—

(a)   the cylinder capacity of its engine does not exceed 125 cubic centimetres,

(b)   the maximum net power output of the engine does not exceed eleven kilowatts.

(6)   In this section—

"maximum net power output", in relation to an engine, means the maximum net power output measured under full engine load, and

"power to weight ratio", in relation to a motor bicycle with a side-car, means the ratio of the maximum net power output of the engine of the motor bicycle to the weight of the combination with—

(a)   a full supply of fuel in the tank,

(b)   an adequate supply of other liquids needed for its propulsion, and

(c)   no load other than its normal equipment, including loose tools.

(7)   Repealed.

[Road Traffic Act 1988, s 97 as amended by the Road Traffic (Driver Licensing and Information Systems) Act 1989, Schs 3 and 6, the Road Traffic Act 1991, s 17 and Sch 8, SI 1996/1974, SI 1998/1420 and the Crime (International Co-operation) Act 2003, Sch 5.]

---

*Repealed by the Transport Act 2002, Sch 31, from a date to be appointed.

4-1502   98. Form of licence¹.

---

1. A full licence for certain classes only, shall authorise the driving of other classes subject to "provisional licence" conditions therefor; failure to comply with such conditions is an offence, for which a penalty is provided under Sch 2 of the Road Traffic Offenders Act 1988, post. Sections 11 and 12(1) thereof (evidence by certificate) apply. Section 98 is amended by the Road Traffic (Driver Licensing and Information Systems) Act 1989, s 5 (as amended by SI 1990/144) and Sch 3 and the Driving Licences (Community Driving Licence) Regulations 1998, 1998/1420, reg 7.

4-1502A   98A. Compulsory surrender of old-form licences.   (1) The Secretary of State may by order require the holders of licences of a specified description, or any specified description of the holders of such licences, to surrender the licences and their counterparts to the Secretary of State.

(2)–(4) *Further provisions as to orders*

(5) A replacement licence granted pursuant to provision made by virtue of subsection (4) above expires on the date on which the surrendered licence would have expired had it not been surrendered (but subject to subsection (6) below).

(6) Where the period for which the surrendered licence was granted was based on an error with respect to the licence holder's date of birth such that (if the error had not been made) that licence would have been expressed to expire on a different date, the replacement licence expires on that different date.

(7) A person who, without reasonable excuse, fails to comply with any requirement to surrender a licence and its counterpart imposed by an order under this section is guilty of an offence.

(8) – (11) *Orders**

[Road Traffic Act 1988, s 98A as inserted by the Road Safety Act 2006, 39.]

---

*Section in force from a date to be appointed.

4-1503   99. Duration of licences.   (1) In so far as a licence authorises its holder to drive motor vehicles of classes other than any prescribed class of goods vehicle or any prescribed class of goods vehicle or any prescribed class of passenger carrying vehicle, it shall, unless previously revoked or surrendered, remain in force, subject to subsection (2) below—

(a) except in a case falling within paragraph (b) or (c) of this subsection, for the period ending on the seventieth anniversary of the applicant's date of birth or for a period of three years, whichever is the longer,

(b) except in a case falling within paragraph (c) of this subsection, if the Secretary of State so determines in the case of a licence to be granted to a person appearing to him to be suffering from a relevant or prospective disability, for such period of not more than three years and not less than one year as the Secretary of State may determine¹, and

(c) in the case of a licence granted in exchange for a subsisting licence and in pursuance of an application requesting a licence for the period authorised by this paragraph, for a period equal to the remainder of that for which the subsisting licence was granted,

and any such period shall begin with the date on which the licence in question is expressed to come into force.

(1A) In so far as a licence authorises its holder to drive any prescribed class of goods vehicle or passenger-carrying vehicle, it shall, unless previously revoked, suspended or surrendered, remain in force—

(a) except in a case falling within paragraph (c) or (d) of this subsection—

  (i) for the period ending on the forty-fifth anniversary of the applicant's date of birth or for a period of five years, whichever is the longer, or

  (ii) where the applicant's age at the date on which the licence is to come into force will exceed forty-five but not sixty-five years, for the period ending on the sixty-sixth anniversary of the applicant's date of birth or for a period of five years, whichever is the shorter,

(b) except in a case falling within paragraph (d) of this subsection, where the applicant's age at that date will exceed sixty-five years, for a period of one year,

(c) except in a case falling within paragraph (b) or (d) of this subsection, if the Secretary of State so determines in the case of a licence to be granted to a person appearing to him to be suffering from a relevant or prospective disability, for such period of not more than three years and not less than one year as the Secretary of State may determine, and

(d) in the case of a licence granted in exchange for a subsisting licence and in pursuance of an application requesting a licence for the period authorised by this paragraph, for a period equal to the remainder of that for which the subsisting licence was granted,

and any such period shall begin with the date on which the licence in question is expressed to come into force.

(2) To the extent that a provisional licence authorises the driving of a motor bicycle or moped of a prescribed class it shall, unless previously surrendered or revoked, remain in force—

(a) for such period as may be prescribed, or

(b) if the licence is granted to the holder of a previous licence which was surrendered, revoked or treated as being revoked—

    (i) for the remainder of the period for which the previous licence would have authorised the driving of such a motor bicycle or moped, or

    (ii) in such circumstances as may be prescribed, for a period equal to that remainder at the time of surrender or revocation.

(2A) Where, in accordance with the preceding provisions of this section, a licence in the form of a photocard remains in force for a period of more than ten years, the holder of the licence must surrender it and its counterpart to the Secretary of State not later than the end of the period of ten years beginning with—

(a) the date shown on the licence as the date of its issue, or

(b) if the licence was granted by way of renewal or replacement of a licence bearing the same photograph, the date shown on the earliest licence bearing that photograph as the date of issue of that licence.

(3) Where it appears to the Secretary of State—

(a) that a licence granted by him to any person was granted in error or with an error or omission in the particulars specified in the licence, or

(aa) that the counterpart of a licence granted by him to any person is required to be endorsed in pursuance of any enactment or was issued with an error or omission in the particulars specified in the counterpart or required to be so endorsed on it, or

(b) that the particulars specified in a licence granted by him to any person or in its counterpart do not comply with any requirement imposed since the licence was granted by any provision made by or having effect under any enactment,

the Secretary of State may serve[2] notice in writing on that person revoking the licence and requiring him to surrender the licence and its counterpart forthwith to the Secretary of State and it shall be the duty of that person to comply with the requirement.

(3A) Where—

(a) the Secretary of State is sent under a provision of Northern Ireland law corresponding to section 97(1AA) of this Act a licence granted under this Part of this Act to a person to drive a motor vehicle of any class, and

(b) the Secretary of State is satisfied that a Northern Ireland licence to drive a motor vehicle of that or a corresponding class has been granted to that person,

the Secretary of State must serve notice in writing on that person revoking the licence granted under this Part of this Act.

(4) Where the name or address of the licence holder as specified in a licence ceases to be correct, its holder must forthwith surrender the licence and its counterpart to the Secretary of State.

(5) A person who without reasonable excuse fails to comply with the duty under subsection (2A), (3) or (4) above is guilty of an offence[3].

(6) Where a person who has a duty under this section to surrender his licence and its counterpart is not in possession of them in consequence of the fact that he has surrendered them to a constable or authorised person (within the meaning of Part III of the Road Traffic Offenders Act 1988) on receiving a fixed penalty notice given to him under section 54 of that Act, he does not fail to comply with the duty if he surrenders the licence and its counterpart to the Secretary of State immediately on and their return.

(7) On the surrender of a licence and its counterpart by a person in pursuance of subsection (2A), (3) or (4) above, the Secretary of State must (subject to the following provisions of this section) grant a new licence to that person.

(7ZA) The Secretary of State is not required by subsection (7) above to grant a new licence on the surrender of a licence and its counterpart by a person in pursuance of subsection (2A) above unless the person has paid the fee (if any) which is prescribed; but any other licence under that subsection is to be granted free of charge.

(7A) Where the surrendered licence was revoked because it was granted in error or in consequence of an error or omission appearing to the Secretary of State to be attributable to the fault of the licence holder or in consequence of a current disqualification, subsection (7) shall not apply but the Secretary of State may, if the person is not currently disqualified, grant a new licence to that person on payment of the fee (if any) which is prescribed.

(7B) The Secretary of State may require a person to provide—

(a) evidence of his name, address, sex and date and place of birth, and

(b) a photograph which is a current likeness of him,

before granting a new licence to him under subsection (7) or (7A) above.

(8) A replacement licence granted pursuant to subsection (7) or (7A) above shall expire on the date on which the surrendered licence would have expired had it not been surrendered except that, where the period for which the surrendered licence was granted was based on an error with respect to the licence holder's date of birth such that (if that error had not been made) that licence would have been expressed to expire on a different date, the replacement licence shall expire on that different date.

[Road Traffic Act 1988, s 99 as amended by the Road Traffic (Driver Licensing and Information Systems) Act 1989, s 2 and Sch 3, SI 1990/144, SI 1996/1974, SI 1998/1420, the Crime (International Co-operation) Act 2003, s 78 and the Road Safety Act 2006, s 40.]

1. Appeal from this determination lies to a magistrates' court; s 100, post.
2. See s 107, post for service provisions.
3. For penalty see the Road Traffic Offenders Act 1988, Sch 2, post. Section 6 thereof (time limits) also applies.

Driver training

4–1503A   99ZA. Compulsory driver training courses. Regulations may make provision about training in the driving of motor vehicles by means of courses provided in accordance with the regulations ("driver training courses").
[Road Traffic Act 1988, s 99ZA as inserted by the Transport Act 2000, s 257.]

4–1503B   99ZB. Requirements to complete training courses. (1) Regulations under section 99ZA of this Act may provide that persons who have not successfully completed a driver training course—

   (*a*) may not take a test of competence to drive motor vehicles of a prescribed class (or a prescribed part of such a test),

   (*b*) are not authorised to drive motor vehicles of a prescribed class (before having passed a test of competence to drive them) by a provisional licence (or by section 98(2) or 99A(5) of this Act),

   (*c*) are not granted a licence authorising the driving of motor vehicles of a prescribed class by virtue of regulations under section 89(6)(*b*) or (*c*) of this Act, or

   (*d*) are not authorised to drive motor vehicles of a prescribed class in prescribed circumstances (despite having passed a test of competence to drive them).

   (2) But a person is exempt from provision made by virtue of subsection (1)(*b*), (*c*) or (*d*) above if he is undergoing training on a driver training course and is driving a motor vehicle as part of the training.

   (3) And regulations under section 99ZA of this Act may include provision exempting persons from any provision made by virtue of subsection (1) above in other circumstances; and regulations including such provision may (in particular)—

   (*a*) limit an exemption to persons in prescribed circumstances,

   (*b*) limit an exemption to a prescribed period or in respect of driving in a prescribed area,

   (*c*) attach conditions to an exemption, and

   (*d*) regulate applications for an exemption.

   (4) Regulations under section 99ZA of this Act may include provision for the evidencing by a person of his being within—

   (*a*) the exemption specified in subsection (2) above, or

   (*b*) any exemption provided by virtue of subsection (3) above.

   (5) Regulations under section 99ZA of this Act may provide that a driver training course is not to be taken into account for the purposes of the regulations if it was completed before such time as is prescribed.
[Road Traffic Act 1988, s 99ZB as inserted by the Transport Act 2000, s 257.]

4–1503C   99ZC. Driver training courses: supplementary. (1) Regulations under section 99ZA of this Act may include—

   (*a*) provision about the nature of driver training courses,

   (*b*) provision for the approval by the Secretary of State of persons providing such courses and the withdrawal of approvals (including provision for appeals against refusal and withdrawal of approvals) and provision for exemptions from any requirement of approval,

   (*c*) provision for the training or assessment, or the supervision of the training or assessment, of persons providing driver training courses,

   (*d*) provision setting the maximum amount of any charges payable by persons undergoing such courses, and

   (*e*) provision for the evidencing of the successful completion of such courses.

   (2) Such regulations may include provision for the charging of reasonable fees in respect of the exercise of any function conferred or imposed on the Secretary of State by such regulations.

   (3) Such regulations may make different provision—

   (*a*) for different classes of motor vehicles,

   (*b*) for different descriptions of persons, or

   (*c*) otherwise for different circumstances.
[Road Traffic Act 1988, s 99ZC as inserted by the Transport Act 2000, s 257.]

Community licence holders

4–1504   99A. Authorisation to drive in Great Britain. (1) A Community licence holder may drive, and a person may cause or permit a Community licence holder to drive, in Great Britain, a motor vehicle of any class which—

   (*a*) he is authorised by his Community licence to drive, and

   (*b*) he is not disqualified for holding or obtaining a licence under this Part of this Act to drive, notwithstanding that he is not the holder of a licence under this Part of this Act.

(2) Subsections (3) and (4) below apply to a Community licence holder who is normally resident in Great Britain.

(3) In a case where the Community licence holder is authorised by his Community licence to drive motor vehicles of classes other than any prescribed class of goods vehicle or any prescribed class of passenger-carrying vehicle, he shall cease to be authorised by virtue of subsection (1) above to drive in Great Britain any such classes of motor vehicle from—

(a) the date on which he attains the age of seventy years, or

(b) the expiry of the period of three years beginning with the relevant date, whichever is the later.

(4) In a case where the Community licence holder is authorised by his Community licence to drive any prescribed class of goods vehicle or any prescribed class of passenger-carrying vehicle, he shall cease to be authorised by virtue of subsection (1) above to drive in Great Britain any such class of vehicle from—

(a) except in a case falling within paragraph (b) or (c) of this subsection—

(i) the date on which he attains the age of 45 years, or

(ii) the expiry of the period of five years beginning with the relevant date,

whichever is the later,

(b) where his age at the relevant date exceeds forty-five but not sixty-five years—

(i) the date on which he attains the age of sixty-six years, or

(ii) the expiry of the period of five years beginning with the relevant date, whichever is the earlier, and

(c) where his age at the relevant date exceeds sixty-five years, the expiry of the period of one year beginning with that date.

(5) A Community licence holder—

(a) to whom a counterpart of his Community licence is issued under section 99B of this Act, and

(b) who is authorised by virtue of subsection (1) above to drive in Great Britain motor vehicles of certain classes only,

may drive, in Great Britain, motor vehicles of all other classes subject to the same conditions as if he were authorised by a provisional licence to drive motor vehicles of those other classes.

(6) Subsections (3) and (4) of section 98 of this Act shall apply in relation to subsection (5) above as they apply in relation to subsection (2) of that section.

(7) For the purposes of this Part and Part IV of this Act a Community licence shall not be treated as authorising a person to drive a vehicle of any class if it is not for the time being valid for that purpose in the EEA State in respect of which it was issued.

(8) In this section "relevant date", in relation to a Community licence holder who is normally resident in Great Britain, means—

(a) in the case where he first became so resident on or before 1 January 1997, that date; and

(b) in any other case, the date on which he first became so resident.

[Road Traffic Act 1988, s 99A as inserted by SI 1996/1974 and amended by SI 1998/1420.]

4–1505 99B. Information about resident Community licence holders.   (1) A Community licence holder who—

(a) is normally resident in Great Britain, and

(b) is authorised by his Community licence to drive medium-sized or large goods vehicles or passenger-carrying vehicles of any class,

shall, on or before the expiry of the period of twelve months beginning with the relevant date, deliver his Community licence to the Secretary of State and provide him with the information specified in, or required under, subsection (4) below.

(2) Subsection (1) above shall not apply to a Community licence holder from whom the Secretary of State has received a qualifying application (within the meaning of section 88(1A) of this Act) for the grant of a licence under this Part of this Act.

(3) The Secretary of State may issue to any Community licence holder who—

(a) is normally resident in Great Britain, and

(b) has delivered his Community licence to the Secretary of State, and provided him with the information specified in, or required under, subsection (4) below, (whether or not in pursuance of this section),

a document (referred to in this Part of this Act in relation to a Community licence as a "counterpart") in such form and containing such information as the Secretary of State may determine but designed for the endorsement of particulars relating to the Community licence.

(4) The information referred to in subsections (1) and (3) above is—

(a) the name and address in Great Britain of the Community licence holder;

(b) his date of birth;

(c) the classes of vehicle which he is authorised by his Community licence to drive;

(d) the period of validity of the Community licence in the EEA State in respect of which it was issued;

(e) whether the licence was granted in exchange for a licence issued by a state other than an EEA State; and

(f) such other information as the Secretary of State may require for the purposes of the proper exercise of any of his functions under this Part or Part IV of this Act.

(5) The Secretary of State—

(a) may endorse a Community licence delivered to him (whether or not in pursuance of this section) in such manner as he may determine with any part of the information specified in, or required under, subsection (4) above or with information providing a means of ascertaining that information or any part of it; and

(b) must return the Community licence to the holder.

(6) Where it appears to the Secretary of State that a counterpart of a Community licence—

(a) is required to be endorsed in pursuance of any enactment or was issued with an error or omission in the information contained in it or in the particulars required to be endorsed on it, or

(b) does not comply with any requirement imposed since it was issued by any provision made by, or having effect under, any enactment,

the Secretary of State may serve notice in writing on the Community licence holder requiring him to surrender the counterpart immediately to the Secretary of State and it shall be the duty of the Community licence holder to comply with any such requirement.

(7) Where the name or address of a Community licence holder as specified in the counterpart of his Community licence issued to him under this section ceases to be correct, the Community licence holder must surrender the counterpart and, in the case of a change of name, deliver his Community licence, immediately to the Secretary of State and provide him with particulars of the alterations falling to be made in the name or address.

(8) On the surrender of a counterpart of a Community licence by any person in pursuance of subsection (6) or (7) above, the Secretary of State must issue to that person a new counterpart of the Community licence.

(9) On the delivery of a Community licence by any person in pursuance of subsection (7) above, the Secretary of State may endorse the Community licence with the correct name and must return the Community licence to that person.

(10) Where a Community licence holder has not complied with subsection (1) above, the Secretary of State may serve notice in writing on the holder requiring him to deliver his Community licence to the Secretary of State and to provide him with the information specified in, or required under, subsection (4) above within such period (not less than 28 days from the date of service of the notice) as is specified in the notice.

(11) A person who drives a motor vehicle on a road is guilty of an offence[1] if he fails without reasonable excuse—

(a) to comply with a requirement contained in a notice served on him in pursuance of subsection (10) above, or

(b) to comply with a requirement imposed under subsection (6) or (7) above.

(12) Where a Community licence holder who is required under subsection (6) or (7) above to surrender the counterpart of his Community licence or to deliver his Community licence is not in possession of it in consequence of the fact that he has surrendered it to a constable or authorised person (within the meaning of Part III of the Road Traffic Offenders Act 1988) on receiving a fixed penalty notice given to him under section 54 of that Act, he does not fail to comply with that requirement if he surrenders the counterpart or delivers the Community licence immediately on its return.

(13) In England and Wales, proceedings for an offence by virtue of subsection (11)(a) above shall not be instituted except by the Secretary of Sate or by a constable acting with the approval of the Secretary of State.

(14) In this section "relevant date" has the meaning given by section 99A(8) of this Act.
[Road Traffic Act 1988, s 99B as inserted by SI 1996/1974.]

---

1. For punishment see the Road Traffic Offenders Act 1988, Sch 2 and notes thereto, post.

4–1506 99C. Revocation of authorisation conferred by Community licence because of disability or prospective disability.   (1) If the Secretary of State is at any time satisfied on inquiry—

(a) that a Community licence holder who is normally resident in Great Britain at that time is suffering from a relevant disability, and

(b) that the Secretary of State would be required by virtue of section 92(3) of this Act to refuse an application made by him at that time for a licence authorising him to drive a vehicle of the class in respect of which his Community licence was issued or a class corresponding to that class,

the Secretary of State may serve notice in writing requiring the Community licence holder to deliver the Community licence and its counterpart (if any) immediately to the Secretary of State.

(2) If the Secretary of State is at any time satisfied on inquiry that a Community licence holder

who is normally resident in Great Britain at that time is suffering from a prospective disability, the Secretary of State may—

(a) serve notice in writing requiring the Community licence holder to deliver the Community licence and its counterpart (if any) immediately to the Secretary of State, and

(b) on receipt of the Community licence and its counterpart (if any) grant to the Community licence holder, free of charge, a licence for a period determined by the Secretary of State under section 99(1)(b) of this Act.

(3) Where, in relation to a Community licence holder who is normally resident in Great Britain, the Secretary of State is at any time under a duty to serve notice on him in pursuance of section 92(5) of this Act, the Secretary of State may include in that notice a requirement that the Community licence holder deliver the Community licence and its counterpart (if any) immediately to the Secretary of State.

(4) A person who—

(a) is required under, or by virtue of, any of subsections (1) to (3) above to deliver his Community licence and its counterpart (if any) to the Secretary of State, but

(b) without reasonable excuse, fails to do so,

is guilty of an offence[1].

(5) Where a Community licence holder to whom a counterpart of his Community licence is issued under section 99B of this Act—

(a) is required under, or by virtue of, any of subsections (1) to (3) above to deliver his Community licence and its counterpart to the Secretary of State, and

(b) is not in possession of them in consequence of the fact that he has surrendered them to a constable or authorised person (within the meaning of Part III of the Road Traffic Offenders Act 1988) on receiving a fixed penalty notice given to him under section 54 of that Act,

he does not fail to comply with any such requirement if he delivers the Community licence and its counterpart to the Secretary of State immediately on their return.

(6) Where a Community licence holder is served with a notice in pursuance of any of subsections (1) to (3) above, he shall cease to be authorised by virtue of section 99A(1) of this Act to drive in Great Britain a motor vehicle of any class from such date as may be specified in the notice, not being earlier than the date of service of the notice.

[Road Traffic Act 1988, s 99C as inserted by SI 1996/1974.]

1. For punishment see the Road Traffic Offenders Act 1988, Sch 2 and notes hereto, post.

4–1507 99D. Information relating to disabilities etc. Section 94 of this Act shall apply to a Community licence holder who is normally resident in Great Britain as if—

(a) in subsection (1), for the words from the beginning to "aware" there were substituted "If a Community licence holder who is authorised by virtue of section 99A(1) of this Act to drive in Great Britain a motor vehicle of any class, is aware immediately before the relevant date (as defined by section 99A(8) of this Act), or becomes aware on or after that date",

(b) for subsection (3A) there were substituted—

"(3A) A person who is authorised by virtue of section 99A(1) of this Act to drive in Great Britain a motor vehicle of any class and who drives on a road a motor vehicle of that class is guilty of an offence if at any earlier time while he was so authorised he was required by subsection (1) above to notify the Secretary of State but has failed without reasonable excuse to do so."

(c) in subsection (4), the words "an applicant for, or", in both places where they occur, were omitted,

(d) in subsection (5), the words "applicant or" and the words from the beginning of paragraph (c) to "provisional licence" were omitted,

(e) in subsection (6)(b), the words "applicant or", in both places where they occur, were omitted,

(f) in subsection (7), the words "applicant or" were omitted, and

(g) in subsection (8)—

(i) for "93" there were substituted "99C", and

(ii) the words "applicant or", in both places where they occur, were omitted.

[Road Traffic Act 1988, s 99D as inserted by SI 1996/1974.]

4–1508 99E. Return of Community licences delivered to Secretary of State. (1) This section applies where a Community licence is delivered to the Secretary of State in pursuance of section 99C or 115A of this Act.

(2) Subject to subsection (3) below, the Secretary of State must, on or after the expiry of the relevant period, forward the Community licence to the licensing authority in the EEA state in respect of which it was issued and explain to them his reasons for so doing.

(3) Where the Secretary of State is satisfied that the Community licence holder has ceased to be normally resident in Great Britain before the expiry of the relevant period, the Secretary of State must return the Community licence to the holder.

(4) In this section "relevant period" means—

(a) in a case where the Community licence holder appeals under section 100 or 119 of this Act against the requirement to surrender his Community licence, the period ending on the date on which the appeal is finally determined or abandoned, and

(b) in any other case, the period of seven months beginning with the date on which the Secretary of State received the Community licence.

[Road Traffic Act 1988, s 99E as inserted by SI 1996/1974.]

Appeals

4–1509   100. Appeals relating to licences.   (1) A person who is aggrieved by the Secretary of State's—

(a) refusal to grant or revocation of a licence in pursuance of section 92 or 93 of this Act, or

(b) determination under section 99(1)(b) of this Act to grant a licence for three years or less, or

(c) revocation of a licence in pursuance of section 99(3) or (3A of this Act,

or by a notice served on him in pursuance of section 92(5) or 99C or 109B of this Act may, after giving to the Secretary of State notice of his intention to do so, appeal[1] to a magistrate's court acting for the petty sessions area in which he resides or, in Scotland, to the sheriff within whose jurisdiction he resides.

(2) On any such appeal[1] the court or sheriff may make such order as it or he thinks fit and the order shall be binding on the Secretary of State.

(3) It is hereby declared that, without prejudice to section 90 of this Act, in any proceedings under this section the court or sheriff is not entitled to entertain any question as to whether the appellant passed a test of competence to drive if he was declared by the person who conducted it to have failed it.

[Road Traffic Act 1988, s 100 as amended by SI 1996/1974 and the Crime (International Co-operation) Act 2003, Sch 5.]

---

1. For procedure on this appeal, see rule 34 of the Magistrates' Courts Rules 1981, in PART I: MAGISTRATES' COURTS: PROCEDURE, ante, costs may be awarded (Magistrates' Courts Act 1980, s 64 in PART I: MAGISTRATES' COURTS, PROCEDURE, ante).

Disqualification (otherwise than on conviction)

4–1510   101. Disqualification of persons under age.   (1) A person is disqualified for holding or obtaining a licence to drive a motor vehicle of a class specified in the following Table if he is under the age specified in relation to it in the second column of the Table[1].

TABLE

Class of motor vehicle	Age (in years)
1. Invalid carriage	16
2. Moped	16
3. Motor bicycle	17
4. Agricultural or forestry tractor[2]	17
5. Small vehicle	17
6. Medium-sized goods vehicle	18
7. Other motor vehicles[3]	21

(2)–(5) Regulations[1].

[Road Traffic Act 1988, s 101 as amended by SI 1996/1974.]

---

1. Regulations have varied classes of vehicles and ages contained in the table; see the Motor Vehicles (Driving Licences) Regulations 1999 in this PART, post. A person attains a particular age at the commencement of the relevant anniversary of the date of his birth (Family Law Reform Act 1969, s 9 in PART VI: FAMILY LAW, ante. The onus of proving that the defendant is under age will be on the prosecution.

2. Defined by s 108(1), post.

3. Defined by s 185(1), post.

4. This subsection is modified by art 2(3) of the Motor Vehicles (International Circulation) Order 1975 in this PART, post. The restrictions on persons under 21 driving such vehicles do not apply to a military vehicle (s 183(5), post).

4–1511   102. Disqualification to prevent duplication of licences.   (1) A person is disqualified for obtaining a licence authorising him to drive a motor vehicle of any class so long as he is the holder of another licence authorising him to drive a motor vehicle of that class, whether the licence is suspended or not.

(2) A person is also disqualified for holding or obtaining a licence authorising him to drive a motor vehicle of any class so long as he is authorised by virtue of section 109(1) of this Act to drive a motor vehicle of that or a corresponding class.

[Road Traffic Act 1988, s 102 as amended by the Crime (International Co-operation) Act 2003, ss 76 and 78.]

Disqualification if disqualified in Northern Ireland etc

4–1511A   102A. Disqualification while disqualified in Northern Ireland, Isle of Man, Channel Islands or Gibraltar.   (1) A person is disqualified for holding or obtaining a licence to drive a motor vehicle of any class so long as he is subject to a relevant disqualification imposed outside Great Britain.

(2) For the purposes of this section a person is subject to a relevant disqualification imposed outside Great Britain if, in respect of any offence—

(a) a court in Northern Ireland disqualifies him for holding or obtaining a Northern Ireland licence,

(b) a court in the Isle of Man or any of the Channel Islands disqualifies him for holding or obtaining a British external licence, or

(c) a court in Gibraltar disqualifies him for holding or obtaining a licence to drive a motor vehicle granted under the law of Gibraltar.

(3) A certificate signed by the Secretary of State which states, in respect of a person, any matter relating to the question whether he is subject to a relevant disqualification imposed outside Great Britain shall be evidence (in Scotland, sufficient evidence) of the matter so stated.

(4) A certificate stating that matter and purporting to be so signed shall be deemed to be so signed unless the contrary is proved.

[Road Traffic Act 1988, s 102 as inserted by the Crime (International Co-operation) Act 2003, s 76.]

Effects of disqualification

4–1512 **103. Obtaining licence, or driving, while disqualified.** (1) A person is guilty of an offence[1] if, while disqualified[2] for holding or obtaining a licence, he—

(a) obtains a licence, or

(b) drives[3] a motor vehicle on a road.

(2) A licence obtained by a person who is disqualified is of no effect (or, where the disqualification relates only to vehicles of a particular class, is of no effect in relation to vehicles of that class).

(3) Repealed.

(4) Subsection (1) above does not apply in relation to disqualification by virtue of section 101 of this Act.

(5) Subsection (1)(b) does not apply in relation to disqualification by virtue of section 102 of this Act.

(6) In the application of subsection (1) above to a person whose disqualification is limited to the driving of motor vehicles of a particular class by virtue of—

(a) section 102, 117 or 117A of this Act, or

(b) subsection (9) of section 36 of the Road Traffic Offenders Act 1988 (disqualification until test is passed),

the references to disqualification for holding or obtaining a licence and driving motor vehicles are references to disqualification for holding or obtaining a licence to drive and driving motor vehicles of that class.

[Road Traffic Act 1988, s 103 as substituted by the Road Traffic Act 1991, s 19 and amended by SI 1996/1974 and the Police Reform Act 2002, ss107, 108.]

---

1. For punishment see the Road Traffic Offenders Act 1988, Sch 2 and notes thereto, post. Section 6 thereof (time limits) applies and ss 11 and 12(1) (evidence by certificate) to s 103(1)(b).

2. Including being disqualified by virtue of being under age (*R v Saddleworth Justices, ex p Staples* [1968] 1 All ER 1189, 132 JP 275). Knowledge of the disqualification need not be proved (*Taylor v Kenyon* [1952] 2 All ER 726, 116 JP 599); see also *R v Bowsher* [1973] Crim LR 373; nor is it a defence that the defendant thought that the place he was driving was not a road (*R v Miller* [1975] 2 All ER 974, 139 JP 613). Proof of a conviction pursuant to s 73 of the Police and Criminal Evidence Act 1984 requires strict proof of the identity of the person convicted which may be established by admission, by fingerprints or by evidence of a person in court at the time of the conviction to identify the defendant (*R v Derwentside Magistrates' Court, ex p Heaviside* (1995) 160 JP 317, [1996] RTR 384). It is not a breach of legal privilege to require the solicitor present at the original hearing to give evidence as to identity and to issue a witness summons to him to attend and produce his attendance note, although this is a method to be adopted by the prosecution where there is no reasonable alternative (*R (Howe) v South Durham Magistrates' Court* [2004] EWHC 362 (Admin), 168 JP 424). However, these methods of proof are not exhaustive and it is a matter for the justices in each case to determine on the evidence presented to them whether they are satisfied so they are sure that the defendant actually is the individual to whom the previous conviction refers (*R v Derwentside Magistrates' Court ex p Swift* (1995) 160 JP 468, [1997] RTR 89; *R v DPP, ex p Mansfield* (1995) 160 JP 472, [1997] RTR 96). See also *Bailey v DPP* (1998) 163 JP 518 in which it was held where a defendant contended that a memorandum of conviction bearing his name and address did not relate to him, evidence had to be adduced to disprove the suggestion that some other person had given the defendant's details to the police and the court in respect of an earlier offence. In that case evidence that the address given at the earlier hearing was that of the defendant's sister, and relatively few people knew he was living there, was held not be sufficient. See, however, *Pattison v DPP* [2005] EWHC Admin 2938, [2006] 2 All ER 317, (2006) 170 JP 51, [2006] RTR 13, in which Newman J reviewed the authorities and held that it would normally be possible to establish a prima facie case on the basis of consistency of details between the person's name in the memorandum and the accused and in this regard the personal details need not be uncommon, and if the accused failed to call evidence to contradict that prima facie case this would allow the court to be satisfied that identity has been proved. *Bailey* was explained on the basis that the accused had given evidence suggesting impersonation and no evidence had been adduced by the prosecution other than evidence of consistency of the details on the memorandum of conviction.

Evidence of disqualification will be a certified extract of the court register; see Criminal Procedure Rules 2005, Part 6 in PART I: MAGISTRATES' COURTS: PROCEDURE, ante. Even if the disqualification appears to be incorrectly expressed in the memorandum, the court is not allowed to go behind it in the absence of other evidence and purport to correct the error in law (*Holland v Phipp* [1982] 1 WLR 1150). The prosecution must, however, prove its case; if the prosecution fails to adduce evidence of the disqualification of the accused, the justices cannot consult their computerised records and, on finding the existence of a person with the same name, date of birth and address of the defendant before them, announce that the prosecution has proved the disqualification beyond reasonable doubt: *Kingsnorth v DPP, Debby v DPP* [2003] All ER (D) 235 (Mar), (2003) 167 JPN 202. The memorandum of an entry in the court register used for the purpose of proving the disqualification should show only the offence for which the disqualification was ordered; other matters being prejudicial to the defendant (*Stone v Bastick* [1967] 1 QB 74, [1965] 3 All ER 713, 130 JP 54). A person who is disqualified until he passes a driving test commits the offence of driving whilst disqualified if he drives a motor vehicle unless he has obtained a valid provisional licence and is driving in accordance with its conditions (ie accompanied by a qualified driver and displaying 'L' plates): *Scott v Jelf* [1974] RTR 256. Where a person is prosecuted on this basis, the burden is on him to show that he had a provisional licence and was complying with its convictions: *DPP v Barker* [2004] EWHC Admin 2502, (2004) 168 JP 617.

3. See headnote to this title for "drives" and "driving".

4. This power of arrest is preserved by the Police and Criminal Evidence Act 1984, s 26 and Sch 2. This power of arrest does not extend to any person "who has driven" a motor vehicle on a road (*James and Chorley v DPP* (1997) 163 JP 89, [1997] Crim LR 831), but the doctrine of fresh pursuit applies to an arrest under s 103(3) and an officer may, therefore, arrest a person whom he reasonably suspects of driving while disqualified where the arrest forms part of a continuous chain of events that included the person driving: *Shackleton v Chief Constable of Lancashire Constabulary* (2001) 165 JPN 875, CA. The power of arrest does not extend to someone who, although he had not actually been the driver of the vehicle in question, is reasonably suspected of being that driver: (*DPP v Swann* (1999) 163 JP 365, DC).

Miscellaneous

4–1513   104. Conduct of proceedings in certain courts by or against the Secretary of State.
(1) Any proceedings by or against the Secretary of State in a magistrates' court or before the registrar of a county court under this Part of this Act or Part II of the Road Traffic Offenders Act 1988 may be conducted on behalf of the Secretary of State by a person authorised by him for the purposes of this subsection.

(2) Scotland.

[Road Traffic Act 1988, s 104.]

4–1514   105. Regulations.   Secretary of State may make regulations for purposes of Part III and for the Road Traffic Offenders Act 1988 ss 2, 7, 8, 23–26, 27, 31 and 34–48[1].

[Road Traffic Act 1988, s 105 amended by the Road Traffic (Driver Licensing and Information Systems) Act 1989, Sch 3, SI 1996/1974, SI 1998/1420 and the Crime (International Co-operation) Act 2003, Sch 5—summarised.]

---

1. The Motor Vehicles (Driving Licences) Regulations 1999, in this PART, post have been made.

4–1515   106. Destination of fees for licences, etc.

4–1516   107. Service of notices.   A notice authorised to be served on any person under this Part or Part IV of this Act or a Community licence required to be returned to its holder by section 99B, 99E or 109A of this Act may be served on, or returned to him by delivering it to him or by leaving it at his proper address or by sending it to him by post; and for the purposes of this section and section 7 of the Interpretation Act 1978 in its application to this section the proper address of any person shall be his latest address as known to the person serving the notice.

[Road Traffic Act 1988, s 107, as amended by SI 1996/1974 and the Crime (International Co-operation) Act 2003, Sch 5.]

4–1520   108. Interpretation.   (1) In this Part of this Act—

"agricultural or forestry tractor" means a motor vehicle which—

    (*a*) has two or more axles,

    (*b*) is constructed for use as a tractor for work off the road in connection with agriculture or forestry, and

    (*c*) is primarily used as such[1],

"approved training course for motor cyclists" and, in relation to such a course, "prescribed certificate of completion" mean respectively any course of training approved under, and the certificate of completion prescribed in, regulations under section 97(3A) of this Act.*

"articulated goods vehicle" means a motor vehicle which is so constructed that a trailer designed to carry goods may by partial superimposition be attached to it in such manner as to cause a substantial part of the weight of the trailer to be borne by the motor vehicle, and "articulated goods vehicle combination" means an articulated goods vehicle with a trailer so attached,

"British external licence" and "British Forces licence" have the meanings given by section 88(8) of this Act,

"Community licence" means a document issued in respect of an EEA State other than the United Kingdom by an authority of that or another EEA State (including the United Kingdom) authorising the holder to drive a motor vehicle, not being—

    (*a*) a document containing a statement to the effect that that or a previous document was issued in exchange for a document issued in respect of a State other than an EEA State, or

    (*b*) a document in any of the forms for an international driving permit annexed to the Paris Convention on Motor Traffic of 1926, the Geneva Convention on Road Traffic of 1949 or the Vienna Convention on Road Traffic of 1968, or

    (*c*) a document issued for a purpose corresponding to that mentioned in section 97(2) of this Act,

"counterpart"—

(a) in relation to a licence under this Part of this Act, means a document in such form as the Secretary of State may determine, issued with the licence, containing such information as he determines and designed for the endorsement of particulars relating to the licence,

(aa) in relation to a Northern Ireland licence, has the meaning given by section 109A of this Act (except in the definition of "Northern Ireland counterpart" below), and

(b) in relation to a Community licence, has the meaning given by section 99B of this Act,

"disability" has the meaning given by section 92 of this Act,

"disqualified" means disqualified for holding or obtaining a licence (or, in cases where the disqualification is limited, a licence to drive motor vehicles of the class to which the disqualification relates), and "disqualification" is to be interpreted accordingly,

"EEA Agreement" means the Agreement on the European Economic Area signed at Oporto on 2nd May 1992 as adjusted by the Protocol signed at Brussels on 17th March 1993,

"EEA State" means a State which is a Contracting Party to the EEA Agreement,

"exchangeable licence" means a document authorising a person to drive a motor vehicle (not being a document mentioned in paragraph (b) of the definition of "Community licence")—

(a) issued in respect of Gibraltar by an authority of Gibraltar,

(b) issued in respect of a country or territory which is designed without restriction by an order under subsection (2)(a) below by an authority of that country or territory, or

(c) issued in respect of a country or territory which is designated by a restricted order under subsection (2)(b) below by an authority of that country or territory, being a document which is a licence of a description specified in that order,

and a licence of a description so specified as to which provision is made as mentioned in subsection (2B) below is only an exchangeable licence to the extent that it authorises its holder to drive vehicles of a class specified in the order.

"full licence" means a licence other than a provisional licence,

"large goods vehicle" has the meaning given by section 121(1) of this Act,

"licence" (except where the context otherwise requires) means a licence to drive a motor vehicle granted under this Part of this Act,

"maximum gross weight", in relation to a motor vehicle or trailer, means the weight of the vehicle laden with the heaviest load which it is constructed or adapted to carry,

"maximum train weight", in relation to an articulated goods vehicle combination, means the weight of the combination laden with the heaviest load which it is constructed or adapted to carry,

"medium-sized goods vehicle" means a motor vehicle—

(a) which is constructed or adapted to carry or to haul goods,

(b) which is not adapted to carry more than nine persons inclusive of the driver, and

(c) the permissible maximum weight of which exceeds 3.5 but not 7.5 tonnes,

and includes a combination of such a motor vehicle and a trailer where the relevant maximum weight of the trailer does not exceed 750 kilograms,

"moped" means a motor vehicle which has fewer than four wheels and—

(a) in the case of a vehicle the first use (as defined in regulations made for the purpose of section 97(3)(d) of this Act) of which occurred before 1st August 1977, has a cylinder capacity not exceeding 50 cubic centimetres and is equipped with pedals by means of which the vehicle is capable of being propelled, and

(b) in any other case, has a maximum design speed not exceeding 50 kilometres per hour and, if propelled by an internal combustion engine, has a cylinder capacity not exceeding 50 cubic centimetres,

"motor bicycle" means a motor vehicle which—

(a) has two wheels, and

(b) has a maximum design speed exceeding 45 kilometres per hour and, if powered by an internal combustion engine, has a cylinder capacity exceeding 50 cubic centimetres,

and includes a combination of such a motor vehicle and a side-car,

"Northern Ireland driving licence" or "Northern Ireland licence" means a licence to drive a motor vehicle granted under the law of Northern Ireland and "Northern Ireland counterpart" means the document issued with the Northern Ireland as a counterpart under the law of Norhern Ireland,

"passenger-carrying vehicle" has the meaning given by section 121(1) of this Act,

"permissible maximum weight", in relation to a goods vehicle (of whatever description), means

(a) in the case of a motor vehicle which neither is an articulated goods vehicle nor is drawing a trailer, the relevant maximum weight of the vehicle,

(b) in the case of an articulated goods vehicle—

(i) when drawing only a semi-trailer, the relevant maximum train weight of the articulated goods vehicle combination,

(ii) when drawing a trailer as well as a semi-trailer, the aggregate of the relevant maximum train weight of the articulated goods vehicle combination and the relevant maximum weight of the trailer,

(iii) when drawing a trailer but not a semi-trailer, the aggregate of the relevant maximum weight of the articulated goods vehicle and the relevant maximum weight of the trailer,

(iv) when drawing neither a semi-trailer nor a trailer, the relevant maximum weight of the vehicle,

(c) in the case of a motor vehicle (not being an articulated goods vehicle) which is drawing a trailer, the aggregate of the relevant maximum weight of the motor vehicle and the relevant maximum weight of the trailer,

"prescribed" means prescribed by regulations,
"prospective disability" has the meaning given by section 92 of this Act,
"provisional licence" means a licence granted by virtue of section 97(2) of this Act,
"regulations" means regulations made under section 105 of this Act,
"relevant disability" has the meaning given by section 92 of this Act,
"relevant external law" has the meaning given by section 88(8) of this Act,
"relevant maximum weight", in relation to a motor vehicle or trailer, means—

(a) in the case of a vehicle to which regulations under section 49 of this Act apply which is required by regulations under section 41 of this Act to have a maximum gross weight for the vehicle marked on a plate issued by the Secretary of State under regulations under section 41, the maximum gross weight so marked on the vehicle,

(b) in the case of a vehicle which is required by regulations under section 41 of this Act to have a maximum gross weight for the vehicle marked on the vehicle and does not also have a maximum gross weight marked on it as mentioned in paragraph (a) above, the maximum gross weight marked on the vehicle,

(c) in the case of a vehicle on which a maximum gross weight is marked by the same means as would be required by regulations under section 41 of this Act if those regulations applied to the vehicle, the maximum gross weight so marked on the vehicle,

(d) in the case of a vehicle on which a maximum gross weight is not marked as mentioned in paragraph (a), (b) or (c) above, the notional maximum gross weight of the vehicle, that is to say, such weight as is produced by multiplying the unladen weight of the vehicle by the number prescribed[1] by the Secretary of State for the class of vehicle into which that vehicle falls,

"relevant external law" has the meaning given by section 88(8) of this Act,
"relevant maximum train weight", in relation to an articulated goods vehicle combination, means—

(a) in the case of an articulated goods vehicle to which regulations under section 49 of this Act apply which is required by regulations under section 41 of this Act to have a maximum train weight for the combination marked on a plate issued by the Secretary of State under regulations under section 41, the maximum train weight so marked on the motor vehicle,

(b) in the case of an articulated goods vehicle which is required by regulations under section 41 of this Act to have a maximum train weight for the combination marked on the vehicle and does not also have a maximum train weight marked on it as mentioned in paragraph (a) above, the maximum train weight marked on the motor vehicle,

(c) in the case of an articulated goods vehicle on which a maximum train weight is marked by the same means as would be required by regulations under section 41 of this Act if those regulations applied to the vehicle, the maximum train weight so marked on the motor vehicle,

(d) in the case of an articulated goods vehicle on which a maximum train weight is not marked as mentioned in paragraph (a), (b) or (c) above, the notional maximum gross weight of the combination, that is to say, such weight as is produced by multiplying the sum of the unladen weights of the motor vehicle and the semi-trailer by the number prescribed[2] by the Secretary of State for the class of articulated goods vehicle combination into which that combination falls,

"semi-trailer", in relation to an articulated goods vehicle, means a trailer attached to it in the manner described in the definition of articulated goods vehicle,
"small vehicle" means a motor vehicle (other than an invalid carriage, moped or motor bicycle) which—

(a) is not constructed or adapted to carry more than nine persons inclusive of the driver, and
(b) has a maximum gross weight not exceeding 3.5 tonnes,

and includes a combination of such a motor vehicle and a trailer,

"test of competence to drive" means such a test conducted under section 89 of this Act.

(2) The Secretary of State may by order[3] made by statutory instrument designate a country or territory which neither is nor forms part of an EEA State for the purposes of the definition of "exchangeable licence" in subsection (1) above—

(a) as respects all licences authorising the driving of motor vehicles granted under the law of that country or territory, where the Secretary of State is satisfied that satisfactory provision is made by that law for the granting of licences to drive motor vehicles;

(*b*) as respects only licences authorising the driving of motor vehicles granted under the law of that country or territory of a description specified in the order, where the Secretary of State is satisfied that satisfactory provision is made by that law for the granting of licences of that description.

(2A) An order under subsection (2)(b) above may specify a description of licence by reference to any feature of the licences concerned (including in particular the circumstances in which they are granted, any conditions to which they are subject or the classes of vehicle which they authorise the holders to drive).

(2B) An order under subsection (2)(b) above may provide that a licence of a specified description shall only be an exchangeable licence in so far as it authorises its holder to drive vehicles of a class specified in the order.

(3) Consultation.

[Road Traffic Act 1988, s 108 as amended by the Road Traffic (Driver Licensing and Information Systems) Act 1989, Sch 3, SI 1990/144, SI 1996/1974,SI 1998/1420, SI 1998/1917 and the Crime (International Co-operation) Act 2003, Sch 5.]

---

*Definition repealed by the Transport Act 2002, Sch 31, from a date to be appointed.
1. A vehicle does not come within this definition if there is no evidence of its use, let alone primary use, as described in the definition: *Vehicle and Operator Services Agency v Greenfarms Ltd* [2005] EWHC 3156 (Admin), [2006] RTR 20.
2. See the Goods Vehicles (Ascertainment of Maximum Gross Weights) Regulations 1976, SI 1976/555.
3. The following countries have been designated for this purpose by Driving Licences (Exchangeable Licences) Orders: Australia, New Zealand, Norway, Singapore, Spain, Sweden and Switzerland, and the territory of Hong Kong (SI 1984/672 amended by SI 2002/1593); Barbados, the Republic of Cyprus, Finland, Malta and Zimbabwe, and the territory of the British Virgin Islands (SI 1985/65); Austria and Japan (SI 1985/1461), Korea and Monaco (SI 2002/2379), South Africa and Canada (SI 1999/1641 amended by SI 2007/96); Falkland Islands (SI 2004/301); Faroe Islands (SI 2007/95).

4–1521 109. Provisions as to Northern Ireland drivers' licences. (1) The holder of a Northern Ireland driving licence may drive, and a person may cause or permit the holder of such a licence to drive, in Great Britain, in accordance with that licence, a motor vehicle of any class which he is authorised by that licence to drive, and which he is not disqualified from driving under this or Part or Part IV of this Act, notwithstanding that he is not the holder of a licence under this Part of this Act.

(2) Any driver holding a Northern Ireland driving licence shall be under the like obligation to produce such a licence and its counterpart as if they had respectively been granted under this Part of this Act and the counterpart to such a licence, and the provisions—

(*a*) of this Act,
(*b*) Repealed

as to the production of licences and counterparts of licences granted under this Part of this Act shall apply accordingly.

(3) *Repealed.*
(4) *Repealed.*
(5) *Repealed.*

[Road Traffic Act 1988, s 109 as amended by the Road Traffic (Driver Licensing and Information Systems) Act 1989, Sch 3, SI 1990/144 and the Crime (International Co-operation) Act 2003, s 79 and Sch 5.]

4–1521A 109A. Counterparts issued to Northern Ireland licence holders. *Northern Ireland.*

4–1521B 109B. Revocation of authorisation conferred by Northern Ireland licence because of disability or prospective disability. *Northern Ireland.*

4–1521C 109C. Information relating to disabilities etc. *Northern Ireland.*

PART IV[1]
LICENSING OF DRIVERS OF LARGE GOODS VEHICLES AND PASSENGER-CARRYING VEHICLES

4–1522 110. Licensing of drivers of large goods vehicles and passenger-carrying vehicles.
(1) Licences under Part III of this Act to drive motor vehicles of classes which include large goods vehicles or passenger-carrying vehicles or large goods vehicles or passenger-carrying vehicles of any class shall be granted by the Secretary of State in accordance with this Part of this Act and shall, in so far as they authorise the driving of large goods vehicles or passenger-carrying vehicles, be otherwise subject to this Part of this Act in addition to Part III of this Act.

(2) In this Part of this Act—

"Community licence" has the same meaning as in Part III of this Act;
"LGV Community licence" means a Community licence in so far as it authorises a person to drive large goods vehicles of any class;
"large goods vehicle driver's licence" means a licence under Part III of this Act in so far as it authorises a person to drive large goods vehicles of any class;
"PVC Community licence" means a Community licence in so far as it authorises a person to drive passenger-carrying vehicles of any class; and
"passenger-carrying vehicle driver's licence" means a licence under Part III of this Act in so far as it authorises a person to drive passenger-carrying vehicles of any class.

[Road Traffic Act 1988, s 110 as substituted by the Road Traffic (Driver Licensing and Information Systems) Act 1989, Sch 2 and amended by SI 1996/1974.]

1. Part IV contains ss 110 to 122.

4–1522A Functions of traffic commissioners (s 111) Secretary of State not to grant licence unless satisfied having regard to applicant's conduct that he is a fit person (s 112); reference of matter for determination under s 112 to traffic commissioner, applicant may be required to furnish information, attend and answer questions, and failure may be notified to Secretary of State who may refuse licence (s 113).

4–1523   114. Conditions of certain licences.   (1) The following licences, that is to say—

(a) a large goods vehicle or passenger-carrying vehicle driver's licence issued as a provisional licence,

(b) a full large goods vehicle or passenger-carrying vehicle driver's licence granted to a person under the age of 21, and

(c) a LGV Community licence held by a person under the age of 21 who is normally resident in Great Britain,

shall be subject to the prescribed conditions, and if the holder of the licence fails, without reasonable excuse, to comply with any of the conditions he is guilty of an offence[1].

(2) It is an offence[1] for a person knowingly to cause or permit another person who is under the age of 21 to drive a large goods vehicle of any class or a passenger-carrying vehicle of any class in contravention of the prescribed conditions to which that other person's licence is subject.

[Road Traffic Act 1988, s 114 as substituted by the Road Traffic (Driver Licensing and Information Systems) Act 1989, Sch 2 and amended by SI 1996/1974.]

1. For penalty see the Road Traffic Offenders Act 1988, Sch 2, post.

4–1523A   115. Revocation or suspension of licences.   (1) A large goods vehicle or passenger-carrying vehicle driver's licence—

(a) must be revoked if there come into existence, in relation to its holder, such circumstances relating to his conduct as may be prescribed;

(b) must be revoked or suspended if his conduct is such as to make him unfit to hold such a licence;

and where the licence is suspended under paragraph (b) above it shall during the time of suspension be of no effect.

(2) Where it appears that the conduct of the holder of a licence falls within both paragraph (a) and paragraph (b) of subsection (1) above, proceedings shall be taken or continued under paragraph (a) and not under paragraph (b) and accordingly the power to suspend the licence, rather than revoke it, shall not be available.

(3) Regulations made for the purposes of this section or any of sections 115A, 117 or 117A of this Act—

(a) may make different provision for large goods vehicles and for passenger-carrying vehicles and for different descriptions of persons; and

(b) shall provide for the determination of the cases in which,—

(i) under section 117 of this Act, a person whose licence has been revoked, or

(ii) under section 117A of this Act, a person on whom a notice is served in pursuance of section 115A(1)(a) of this Act,

is to be disqualified indefinitely or for a period and, if for a period, for the determination of the period.

[Road Traffic Act 1988, s 115 as substituted by the Road Traffic (Driver Licensing and Information Systems, Act 1989, Sch 2 and amended by the Road Traffic Act 1991, Sch 4 and SI 1996/1974.]

4–1523B   115A. Community licence holders: cessation of authorisation, etc.   (1) Where, in relation to a holder of a LGV Community licence or PCV Community licence who is normally resident in Great Britain—

(a) there exist immediately before the relevant date, or there come into existence on or after that date, such circumstances relating to his conduct as may be prescribed; or

(b) his conduct is such as to make him unfit to be authorised by virtue of section 99A(1) of this Act to drive in Great Britain a large goods vehicle or passenger-carrying vehicle (as the case may be),

the Secretary of State must serve notice on the holder requiring him to deliver the Community licence and its counterpart (if any) immediately to the Secretary of State and it shall be the duty of the holder to comply with that requirement.

(2) Where a notice is served in pursuance of subsection (1)(a) or (b) above on the holder of a LGV Community licence or a PCV Community licence, he shall cease to be authorised by virtue of section 99A(1) of this Act to drive in Great Britain a large goods vehicle or passenger-carrying vehicle (as the case may be) from such date as is specified in the notice, not being earlier than the date of service of the notice.

(3) Where it appears to the Secretary of State that the conduct of a Community licence holder falls within both paragraph (a) and paragraph (b) of subsection (1) above, the Secretary of State must serve notice on the holder in pursuance of the former paragraph only.

(4) Any Community licence holder who fails without reasonable excuse to comply with his duty under subsection (1) above is guilty of an offence.[1]

(5) In this section "relevant date", in relation to a Community licence holder who is normally resident in Great Britain, has the same meaning as in section 99A(8) of this Act.

[Road Traffic Act 1988, s 115A as inserted by SI 1996/1974.]

---

1. For penalty see the Road Traffic Offenders Act 1988, Sch 2, post.

4–1523C   116. Revocation or suspension of licences: referral of matters of conduct to traffic commissioners.   (1) Any question arising—

   (*a*)   under section 115(1)(*b*) of this Act as to whether a person is or is not, by reason of his conduct, fit to hold a large goods vehicle or passenger-carrying vehicle driver's licence, as the case may be, or

   (*b*)   under section 115A(1)(*b*) of this Act as to whether the holder of a LGV Community licence or PCV Community licence is or is not, by reason of his conduct, fit to be authorised by virtue of section 99A(1) of this Act to drive in Great Britain a large goods vehicle or passenger-carrying vehicle (as the case may be),

may be referred by the Secretary of State to the traffic commissioner for the area in which the holder of the licence resides.

(2) Where, on any reference under subsection (1)(a) above, the traffic commissioner determines that the holder of the licence is not fit to hold a large goods vehicle or passenger-carrying vehicle driver's licence, as the case may be, he shall also determine whether the conduct of the holder of the licence is such as to require the revocation of his licence or only its suspension; and, if the former, whether the holder of the licence should be disqualified under section 117(2)(a) of this Act (and, if so, for what period) or under section 117(2)(b) of this Act.

(2A) Where, on any reference under subsection (1)(b) above, the traffic commissioner determines that a Community licence holder is not fit to be authorised by virtue of section 99A(1) of this Act to drive in Great Britain a large goods vehicle or passenger-carrying vehicle (as the case may be), he shall also determine whether the Community licence holder—

   (*a*)   should be disqualified under section 117A(2))(*a*) of this Act (and, if so, for what period) or under section 117A(2)(*b*) of this Act, or

   (*b*)   should be granted, free of charge, a large goods vehicle or passenger-carrying vehicle driver's licence (and, if so, from what date it shall take effect).

(3) A traffic commissioner to whom a reference has been made under subsection (1) above may require the holder of the licence to furnish the commissioner with such information as he may require and may, by notice to the holder, require him to attend before the commissioner at the time and place specified by the commissioner to furnish the information and to answer such questions (if any) relating to the subject matter of the reference as the commissioner may put to him.

(4) If the holder of the licence fails without reasonable excuse to furnish information to or to attend before or answer questions properly put by a commissioner when required to do so under subsection (3) above, the commissioner may notify the failure to the Secretary of State and, if the commissioner does so,

   (*a*)   in a case where the licence in question is a LGV Community licence or a PCV Community licence, the holder shall cease to be authorised by virtue of section 99A(1) of this Act to drive in Great Britain a large goods or passenger-carrying vehicle (as the case may be) from such date as is specified in a notice served on the holder by the Secretary of State; and—

   (*b*)   in any other case, revoke the licence or spend it for such period as he thinks fit.

(5) Except where he has given such a notification as is mentioned in subsection (4) above, the traffic commissioner to whom a reference has been made under subsection (1) above shall notify his determination in the matter to the Secretary of State and the holder of the licence and the decision of the commissioner shall be binding on the Secretary of State.

(6) Where the Secretary of State, without making such a reference, determines to revoke or suspend a person's licence under section 115(1) of this Act he shall notify his determination in the matter to the holder of the licence, and where he suspends it, to the traffic commissioner for the area in which the holder of the licence resides.

[Road Traffic Act 1988, s 116 as substituted by the Road Traffic (Driver Licensing and Information Systems) Act 1989, Sch 2 and amended by SI 1996/1974.]

4–1523D   117. Disqualification on revocation of licence.   (1) Where in pursuance of section 115(1)(a) of this Act the Secretary of State revokes a person's large goods vehicle or passenger-carrying vehicle driver's licence, the Secretary of State must, in accordance with the regulations made [in pursuance of section 115(3)], order that person to be disqualified indefinitely or for the period determined in accordance with the regulations.

(2) Where in pursuance of section 115(1)(b) of this Act the Secretary of State revokes a person's large goods vehicle or passenger-carrying vehicle driver's licence, the Secretary of State may—

(*a*) order the holder to be disqualified indefinitely or for such period as the Secretary of State thinks fit, or

(*b*) except where the licence is a provisional licence, if it appears to the Secretary of State that, owing to the conduct of the holder of the licence, it is expedient to require him to comply with the prescribed conditions applicable to provisional licences under Part III of this Act until he passes the prescribed test of competence to drive large goods vehicles or passenger-carrying vehicles of any class, order him to be disqualified for holding or obtaining a full licence until he passes such a test.

(2A) Regulations may make provision for the application of subsections (1) and (2) above, in such circumstances and with such modifications as may be prescribed, where a person's large goods vehicle or passenger-carrying vehicle driver's licence is treated as revoked by virtue of section 37(1) of the Road Traffic Offenders Act 1988 (effect of disqualification by order of a court).

(3) If, while the holder of a large goods vehicle or passenger-carrying vehicle driver's licence is disqualified under subsection (1) above, the circumstances prescribed for the purposes of section 115(1)(a) of this Act cease to exist in his case, the Secretary of State must, on an application made to him for the purpose, remove the disqualification.

(4) Where the holder of a large goods vehicle or passenger-carrying vehicle driver's licence is disqualified under subsection (2)(a) above, the Secretary of State may, in such circumstances as may be prescribed, remove the disqualification.

(5) Where the holder of a full licence is disqualified under subsection (2)(b) above, the Secretary of State must not afterwards grant him a full licence to drive a large goods vehicle or passenger-carrying vehicle of any class unless satisfied that he has since the disqualification passed the prescribed test of competence to drive vehicles of that class, and until he passes that test any full licence obtained by him shall be of no effect.

(6) So long as the disqualification under subsection (1) or (2)(a) above of the holder of a large goods vehicle or passenger-carrying vehicle driver's licence continues in force, a large goods vehicle or passenger-carrying vehicle driver's licence must not be granted to him and any such licence obtained by him shall be of no effect.

(7) In this section "disqualified"—

(*a*) in a case of revocation on the ground of the conduct of the holder of the licence as a driver, means disqualified for holding or obtaining a licence under Part III of this Act to drive large goods vehicles of the prescribed classes and passenger-carrying vehicles of the prescribed classes; and

(*b*) in a case of revocation of a passenger-carrying vehicle driver's licence on the ground of the conduct of the holder otherwise than as a driver, means disqualified for holding or obtaining a licence under Part III of this Act to drive passenger-carrying vehicles of the prescribed classes.

[Road Traffic Act 1988, s 117 as substituted by the Road Traffic (Driver Licensing and Information Systems) Act 1989, Sch 2 and amended by the Road Traffic Act 1991, Sch 4 and SI 1996/1974.]

4–1523E   117A. Community licences: disqualification etc.   (1) Where a notice is served on a Community licence holder in pursuance of section 115A(1)(a) of this Act, the Secretary of State must, in accordance with the regulations made in pursuance of section 115(3), order that person to be disqualified indefinitely or for the period determined in accordance with the regulations.

(2) Where a notice is served on a Community licence holder in pursuance of section 115A(1)(b) of this Act, the Secretary of State may—

(*a*) order that person to be disqualified indefinitely or for such period as the Secretary of State thinks fit,

(*b*) if it appears to the Secretary of State that, owing to the conduct of the Community licence holder, it is expedient to require him to comply with the prescribed conditions applicable to provisional licences under Part III of this Act until he passes the prescribed test of competence to drive large goods vehicles or passenger-carrying vehicles of any class, order him to be disqualified for holding or obtaining a full licence until he passes such a test, or

(*c*) on receipt of the Community licence and its counterpart (if any), grant to the Community licence holder, on payment of such fee (if any) as may be prescribed, a large goods vehicle or passenger-carrying vehicle driver's licence which shall take effect from such date as the Secretary of State may determine.

(3) Where, in pursuance of subsection (1) or (2) above, the Secretary of State orders a Community licence holder to be disqualified the Secretary of State must, on receipt of the Community licence and its counterpart (if any), grant to the Community licence holder, on payment of such fee (if any) as may be prescribed, a licence authorising the driving of the classes of vehicle which are unaffected by the disqualification.

(3A) The Secretary of State may require a person to provide—

(*a*) evidence of his name, address, sex and date and place of birth, and

(*b*) a photograph which is a current likeness of him,

before issuing a licence to him under subsection (3) above.

(4) If, while the holder of a LGV Community licence or a PCV Community licence is disqualified under subsection (1) above, the circumstances prescribed for the purposes of section 115A(1)(a) of

this Act cease to exist in his case, the Secretary of State must, on an application made to him for the purpose, remove the disqualification.

(5) Where the holder of a LGV Community licence or a PCV Community licence is disqualified under subsection (2)(a) above, the Secretary of State may, in such circumstances as may be prescribed, remove the disqualification.

(6) In this section "disqualified"—

(a) in a case where notice is served in pursuance of section 115A(1) of this Act on a Community licence holder on the ground of his conduct as a driver, means disqualified for holding or obtaining a licence under Part III of this Act to drive large goods vehicles of the prescribed classes and passenger-carrying vehicles of the prescribed classes; and

(b) in a case where notice is served in pursuance of section 115A(1) of this Act on a holder of a PCV Community licence on the ground of his conduct otherwise than as a driver, means disqualified for holding or obtaining a licence under Part III of this Act to drive passenger-carrying vehicles of the prescribed classes.

[Road Traffic Act 1988, s 117A as inserted by SI 1996/1974 and amended by SI 1998/1420 and the Road Safety Act 2006, s 40.]

4–1523F　118. Revoked or suspended licences: surrender, return and endorsement.
(1) Where, in pursuance of section 115 of this Act, the Secretary of State revokes a licence, he must serve notice on the holder of the licence requiring him to deliver the licence and its counterpart forthwith to the Secretary of State, and it shall be the duty of the holder of the licence to comply with the requirement.

(2) Where, in pursuance of section 115 of this Act, the Secretary of State suspends a licence, then—

(a) where he does so without making any reference under section 116 of this Act to a traffic commissioner, the Secretary of State must serve notice on the holder of the licence requiring him to deliver the licence and its counterpart forthwith to the traffic commissioner for the area in which the holder of the licence resides;

(b) where he does so in pursuance of a determination of a traffic commissioner on such a reference, the traffic commissioner must, if the licence and its counterpart have not previously been delivered to him serve notice on the holder of the licence requiring him to deliver them forthwith to the commissioner;

and it shall be the duty of the holder of the licence to comply with the requirement.

(3) Any holder of a licence who fails without reasonable excuse to comply with his duty under subsection (1) or (2) above is guilty of an offence[1].

(4) On the delivery of a licence and its counterpart by a person to the Secretary of State in pursuance of subsection (1) above, the Secretary of State must issue to him, on payment of such fee (if any) as may be prescribed, a licence authorising the driving of the classes of vehicles which are unaffected by the revocation.

(4A) The Secretary of State may require a person to provide—

(a) evidence of his name, address, sex and date and place of birth, and

(b) a photograph which is a current likeness of him,

before issuing a licence to him under subsection (4) above.

(5) On the delivery of a suspended licence and its counterpart to a traffic commissioner, the traffic commissioner must endorse the counterpart of the licence with particulars of the suspension and return the licence and its counterpart to the holder.

[Road Traffic Act 1988, s 118 as substituted by the Road Traffic (Driver Licensing and Information Systems) Act 1989, Sch 2 and amended by SI 1990/144, SI 1998/1420 and the Road Safety Act 2006, s 40.]

---

1. For penalty see the Road Traffic Offenders Act 1988, Sch 2, post.

4–1524　119. Appeals to magistrates' court or sheriff[1]. (1) A person who, being the holder of, or an applicant for, a large goods vehicle or passenger-carrying vehicle driver's licence or the holder of a LGV Community licence or PCV Community licence is aggrieved by the Secretary of State's—

(a) refusal or failure to grant such a licence in pursuance of section 112 or 113(4) of this Act,

(b) suspension or revocation of such a licence in pursuance of section 115 or 116(4) of this Act, or

(c) ordering of disqualification under section 117(2) or 117A(2) of this Act,

or by a notice served on him in pursuance of section 115A(1) or 116(4) of this Act may, after giving to the Secretary of State and any traffic commissioner to whom the matter was referred notice of his intention to do so, appeal to a magistrates' court acting for the petty sessions area in which the holder of or applicant for the licence resides or, in Scotland, to the sheriff within whose jurisdiction he resides.

(2) On any appeal under subsection (1) above (except under paragraph (c) of that subsection) the Secretary of State and, if the matter was referred to a traffic commissioner, the commissioner shall be respondent.

(3) On any appeal under subsection (1) above the court or sheriff may make such order as it or he thinks fit[2] and the order shall be binding on the Secretary of State.

[Road Traffic Act 1988, s 119 as substituted by the Road Traffic (Driver Licensing and Information Systems) Act 1989, Sch 2 and amended by SI 1996/1974.]

1. In deciding an appeal, the magistrates must exercise their own judgement. They may take account of any reasons given by the Traffic Commissioner for the decision appealed from, but they should not approach the appeal on the basis that it is to be dismissed unless there was something wrong in principle with the original decision (*R (Stace) v Milton Keynes Magistrates' Court* [2006] EWHC 1049 (Admin), 171 JP 1).

2. Where the Secretary of State has revoked a large goods vehicle driver's licence pursuant to s 115(1), ante, having acted under a mandatory duty in respect of which he had no discretion, on an appeal to a magistrates' court under s 119 against the revocation by the aggrieved licence holder, notwithstanding the words "make such order as it thinks fit", the magistrates' court does not have an absolute discretion that enables it to override the mandatory statutory duty of the Secretary of State (*Secretary of State for the Environment, Transport and the Regions v Elsy* [2000] RTR 29).

4–1525   120. Regulations.

4–1526   121. Interpretation.   (1) In this Part of this Act—

"conduct" means—

    (a) in relation to an applicant for or the holder of a large goods vehicle driver's licence, or the holder of a LGV Community licence, his conduct as a driver of a motor vehicle, and

    (b) in relation to an applicant for or the holder of a passenger-carrying vehicle driver's licence or the holder of a PCV Community licence, his conduct both as a driver of a motor vehicle and in any other respect[1] relevant to his holding a passenger-carrying vehicle driver's licence or (as the case may be) his authorisation by virtue of section 99A(1) of this Act to drive in Great Britain a passenger-carrying vehicle of any class,

    including, in either case, such conduct in Northern Ireland;

"counterpart", in relation to a licence to drive under Part III of this Act or a Community Licence, has the same meaning as in that Part;

"full licence" means a large goods vehicle or passenger-carrying vehicle driver's licence other than a provisional licence;

"large goods vehicle" means a motor vehicle (not being a medium-sized goods vehicle within the meaning of Part III of this Act) which is constructed or adapted to carry or to haul goods and the permissible maximum weight of which exceeds 7.5 tonnes;—

"passenger-carrying vehicle" means—

    (a) a large passenger-carrying vehicle, that is to say, a vehicle used for carrying passengers which is constructed or adapted to carry more than 16 passengers, or

    (b) a small passenger-carrying vehicle, that is to say, a vehicle used for carrying passengers for hire or reward which is constructed or adapted to carry more than 8 but not more than 16 passengers;

    and includes a combination of such a motor vehicle and a trailer

"notice" means notice in writing and "notify" shall be construed accordingly;

"prescribed" means, unless the context requires otherwise, prescribed by regulations under section 120 of this Act;

"provisional licence" means a licence granted by virtue of section 97(2) of this Act;

and "permissible maximum weight" has the same meaning as in Part III of this Act.

[Road Traffic Act 1988, s 121 as substituted by the Road Traffic (Driver Licensing and Information Systems) Act 1989, Sch 2 and amended by SI 1990/144 and SI 1996/1974.]

1. When considering fitness for a PCV licence and risk of re-offending, conviction of a sex offence and/or presence on the sex offender register does not automatically disqualify. All personal circumstances must be taken into account, both private and commercial including current employment status (*Secretary of State for Transport, Local Government and the Regions v Snowdon* [2002] EWHC 2394 (Admin), [2003] RTR 216). Accordingly, in relation to an appellant who had been convicted of three assaults on his wife, magistrates should have looked at the person's positive response to a community rehabilitation order, his failure to attend hearings before the traffic commissioner and his convictions in the context of whether conduct of that particular kind might affect his fitness to drive passenger-carrying vehicles. The magistrates should have asked the following questions: how serious was the conduct; what were the risks of any repetition of the violence; in what way did his propensity for violence impinge upon his abilities as a driver; and to what extent was he a risk to those passengers with whom he would come into contact? (*R (Stace) v Milton Keynes Magistrates' Court* [2006] EWHC 1049 (Admin), 171 JP 1).

4–1527   122. Provisions as to Northern Ireland licences.

Part V[1]

Driving Instruction

Instructors to be registered or licensed

4–1535   123. Driving instruction for payment to be given only by registered or licensed persons.   (1) No paid instruction in the driving of a motor car[2] shall be given unless—

    (a) the name of the person giving the instruction is in the register of approved instructors established in pursuance of section 23 of the Road Traffic Act 1962 (in this Part of this Act referred to as "the register"), or

(b) the person giving the instruction is the holder of a current licence granted under this Part of this Act authorising him to give such instruction.

(2) No paid instruction in the driving of a motor car[2] shall be given unless there is fixed to and exhibited on that motor car in such manner as may be prescribed by regulations either—

(a) a certificate[3] in such form as may be so prescribed that the name of the person giving the instruction is in the register, or

(b) a current licence granted under this Part of this Act authorising the person giving the instruction to give such instruction.

(3) For the purposes of subsections (1) and (2) above, instruction is paid instruction if payment of money or money's worth is, or is to be, made by or in respect of the person to whom the instruction is given for the giving of the instruction and for the purposes of this subsection instruction which is given—

(a) free of charge to a person who is not the holder of a current licence to drive a motor vehicle granted under Part III of this Act (other than a provisional licence),

(b) by, or in pursuance of arrangements made by, a person carrying on business in the supply of motor cars, and

(c) in connection with the supply of a motor car in the course of that business,

shall be deemed to be given for payment of money by the person to whom the instruction is given.

(4) Where instruction is given in contravention of subsection (1) above—

(a) the person by whom it is given, and

(b) if that person is employed by another to give that instruction, that other, as well as that person,

is guilty of an offence[4].

(5) In proceedings against a person for an offence under subsection (4) above it shall be a defence for him to prove that he did not know, and had no reasonable cause to believe, that his name or, as the case may be, that of the person employed by him, was not in the register at the material time.

(6) If instruction is given in contravention of subsection (2) above, the person by whom it is given is guilty of an offence[4].

(7) Any reference to this Part of this Act to a current licence or certificate is a reference to a licence or certificate which has not expired and has not been cancelled, revoked or suspended.

(8) In this Part[1] of this Act—

"paid instruction", in relation to instruction in the driving of a motor car, shall be construed in accordance with sub-section (3) above; and

"provisional licence" has the meaning as in Part III of this Act.

[Road Traffic Act 1988, s 123 as amended by the Road Traffic (Driving Instruction by Disabled Persons) Act 1993, Sch.]

1. Part V contains ss 123–142.
2. "Motor car" is defined in s 185, post. It will be observed that this section does not apply to other classes of motor vehicles.
3. In a prosecution for an offence contrary to s 123(4), a certificate, in a form prescribed by regulations under s 135 post, is a document on which the court may make prima facie findings of fact without the prosecution having to prove it was a valid certificate (*Toms v Hurst, Toms v Langton* [1996] RTR 226).
4. For punishment see the Road Traffic Offenders Act 1988, Sch 2 and notes thereto, post.

4–1536 **124.** Exemption of police instructors from prohibition imposed by s 123.

4–1537 **125.** The register of approved instructors.

4–1538 **125A.** Registration of disabled persons as driving instructors[1].

1. Failure, on application for registration as a disabled driving instructor, to notify Registrar of onset of, or deterioration in, relevant or prospective disability, is an offence contrary to sub-s (4) and punishable in accordance with Sch 2, post.

4–1539 **125B.** Provisions supplementary to section 125A.

4–1540 **126–131.** Registration, removal of names, licences for practical experience, revocation, appeals to Secretary of State.

4–1541 **132. Examinations and tests of ability to give driving instruction.** Regulations[1].

1. The Motor Cars (Driving Instruction) Regulations 2005, SI 2005/1902 amended by SI 2005/2716 and SI 2006/525 have been made.

4–1542 **133. Review of examinations.** (1) On the application of a person who has undergone a relevant examination, or a part of such an examination—

(a) the magistrates' court acting for the petty sessions area in which he resides, or

(b) in Scotland, the sheriff within whose jurisdiction he resides,

may determine whether that part of the examination was properly conducted[1].

(2) If it appears to the court or sheriff that the examination or part was not so conducted, the

court or sheriff may order that any fee payable by the application in respect of the examination or part shall not be paid or, if it has been paid, shall be repaid.

(3) No appeal shall lie under section 131 of this Act in respect of any matter in respect of which an application may be made to a magistrates' court or a sheriff under subsection (1) above.

(4) In this section "a relevant examination" means—

(*a*) an examination of ability to give instruction in the driving of motor cars,

(*b*) a test of continued ability and fitness to give instruction in the driving of motor cars (or appropriate motor cars), or

(*c*) an emergency control assessment.

[Road Traffic Act 1988, s 133, as amended by the Transport Act 2000, s 260 and SI 2002/658.]

---

1. See notes to the comparable s 90, ante.

4-1542A   133A–B. Assessment and further assessment of disabled person's ability to control a motor car in an emergency.

4-1543   133C. Duty to disclose further disability.   (1) This section applies to—

(*a*) registered disabled instructors[1], and

(*b*) persons who hold licences under section 129 of this Act granted by virtue of subsection (2)(*b*) of that section.

(2) If at any time a person to whom this section applies becomes aware—

(*a*) that he is suffering from a relevant or prospective disability[2] which he has not previously disclosed to the Secretary of State under section 125A(3) or 133A(3) or (4) of this Act, or

(*b*) that a relevant or prospective disability from which he has at any time suffered (and which has been previously so disclosed) has become more acute since his current emergency control certificate was granted,

he must forthwith notify the Registrar in writing of the nature and extent of his disability.

(3) Subsection (2) above does not require a person to notify the Registrar if—

(*a*) the disability is one from which he has not previously suffered, and

(*b*) he has reasonable grounds for believing that the duration of the disability will not extend beyond the period of three months beginning with the date on which he first becomes aware that he suffers from it.

(4) A person who fails without reasonable excuse to notify the Registrar as required by subsection (2) above is guilty of an offence[3].

[Road Traffic (Driving Instruction by Disabled Persons) Act 1993, s 133C.]

---

1. "Registered disabled instructor" means a person whose name is in the register with an indication that he is "disabled" (s 125A(8)).
2. "Disability" means a want of physical ability affecting the driving of motor cars; and

(i) "relevant disability", in relation to a person, means any disability which is prescribed in regulations or any other disability likely to cause the driving of a motor car by him to be a source of danger to the public; and

(ii) "prospective disabilty", in relation to a person, means any other disability which, at the material time, is not of such a kind that it is a relevant disability but, by virtue of the intermittent or progressive nature of the disability or otherwise, may become a relevant disability in course of time (s 125(8)).
3. For punishment, see Sch 2, post.

4-1544   133D. Offences relating to giving by disabled person of paid driving instruction.
(1) This section applies to—

(*a*) registered disabled instructors[1], and

(*b*) persons who hold licences under section 129 of this Act granted by virtue of subsection (2)(*b*) of that section.

(2) No person to whom this section applies shall give paid instruction in the driving of a motor car unless he is the holder of a current emergency control certificate[2].

(3) No person to whom this section applies shall give, in any unauthorised motor car, paid instruction in the driving of a motor car.

(4) Where instruction is given in contravention of this section—

(*a*) the person by whom it is given, and

(*b*) if that person is employed by another to give that instruction, that other, as well as that person,

is guilty of an offence[3].

(5) In subsection (3) above "unauthorised motor car", in relation to any person, means a motor car other than one which falls within the class of motor car specified in his current emergency control certificate and, where modifications are specified in that certificate, is modified in accordance with the specification.

[Road Traffic (Driving Instruction by Disabled Persons) Act 1993, s 133D.]

---

1. For "registered disabled instructor" see note 1 to s 133C, ante.
2. "Emergency control certificate" means a certificate under s 133A of this Act (s 125A(8)).
3. For punishment see Sch 2, post.

4–1545   134. Power to alter conditions for entry or retention in, and removal from, register and for grant or revocation of licences.

4–1546   135. Power to prescribe form of certificate of registration, etc.   (1) Regulations[1] may prescribe all or any of the following—

   (*a*)   a form of certificate for issue to persons whose names are in the register as evidence of their names' being in the register,

   (*b*)   a form of badge for use by such persons, and

   (*c*)   an official title for such use.

(2) If a person whose name is not in the register—

   (*a*)   take or uses a title prescribed under this section, or

   (*b*)   wears or displays a badge or certificate so prescribed, or

   (*c*)   take or uses any name, title, addition or description implying that his name is in the register,

he is guilty of an offence[2] unless he proves that he did not know, and had no reasonable cause to believe, that his name was not in the register at the material time.

(3) If a person carrying on business in the provision of instruction in the driving of motor vehicles—

   (*a*)   uses a title or description so prescribed in relation to any person employed by him whose name is not in the register, or

   (*b*)   issues any advertisement or invitation calculated to mislead with respect to the extent to which persons whose names are in the register are employed by him,

he is guilty of an offence[2] unless he proves that he did not know, and had no reasonable cause to believe, that the name or names in question were not in the register at the material time.
[Road Traffic Act 1988, s 135.]

---

1. The Motor Cars (Driving Instruction) Regulations 2005, SI 2005/1902 amended by SI 2005/2716 have been made.
2. For punishment see the Road Traffic Offenders Act 1988, Sch 2 and notes thereto, post.

4–1547   136. Surrender of certificates and licences.   Where—

   (*a*)   the name of a person to whom a certificate prescribed under section 135 of this Act has been issued is removed from the register in pursuance of this Part of this Act, or

   (*b*)   a licence granted under this Part of this Act to a person expires or is revoked,

that person must, if so required by the Registrar by notice in writing, surrender the certificate or licence, as the case may be, to the Registrar within the period of fourteen days beginning with that on which the notice is given and, if he fails to do so, he is guilty of an offence[1].
[Road Traffic Act 1988, s 136.]

---

1. For penalty see the Road Traffic Offenders Act 1988, Sch 2.

4–1548   137. Production of certificates and licences to constables and authorised persons.
(1) A person to whom a certificate prescribed under section 135 of this Act is issued, or to whom a licence under this Part of this Act is granted, must, on being so required by a constable or any person authorised in writing by the Secretary of State in that behalf, produce the certificate or licence for examination.

(2) Where—

   (*a*)   the name of a person is removed from the register, or

   (*b*)   a licence granted under this Part of this Act to a person expires or is revoked,

then, if that person fails to satisfy an obligation imposed on him by section 136 of this Act, a constable or a person authorised in writing by the Secretary of State in that behalf may require him to produce any such certificate issued to him or the licence, and upon its being produced may seize it and deliver it to the Registrar.

(3) A person who is required under subsection (1) or (2) above to produce a document and fails to do so is, subject to subsection (4) below, guilty of an offence[1].

(4) In proceedings against any person for an offence under subsection (3) above, it shall be a defence for him to show that—

   (*a*)   within seven days beginning with the day following that on which the production of the document was so required, it was produced—

      (i)   where the requirement was made by a constable, at a police station specified at the time the production was required by the person required to produce the document,

      (ii)   where the requirement was made by a person other than a constable, at a place specified at that time by that person, or

   (*b*)   the document was produced at that police station or, as the case may be, place as soon as was reasonably practicable, or

   (*c*)   it was not reasonably practicable for it to be produced at that police station or, as the case may be, place before the day on which the proceedings were commenced,

and for the purposes of this subsection the laying of the information or, in Scotland, the service of the complaint on the accused shall be treated as the commencement of the proceedings.
[Road Traffic Act 1988, s 137.]

---

1. For penalty see the Road Traffic Offenders Act 1988, Sch 2, post.

4-1549 138. Offences by corporations. Where a body corporate is guilty of an offence under this Part of this Act and the offence is proved to have been committed with the consent or connivance of, or to be attributable to neglect on the part of, a director, manager, secretary or other similar officer of the body corporate, or a person who was purporting to act in any such capacity, he, as well as the body corporate, is guilty of that offence and liable to be proceeded against and punished accordingly.
[Road Traffic Act 1988, s 128.]

4-1550 139. Service of notices. (1) A notice authorised or required to be given by this Part of this Act to a person may be given by delivering it to him, or by leaving it at his proper address, or by sending it to him by post.
(2) For the purposes of this section and of section 7 of the Interpretation Act 1978 in its application to this section, the proper address of a person shall be, in the case of a person whose name is included in the register, his address on the register, and in any other case, his usual or last known address.
[Road Traffic Act 1988, s 139.]

4-1551 140. Receipts.

4-1552 141. Regulations.

4-1553 141A. Meaning of "motor car". (1) Notwithstanding section 185(1) of this Act, in this Part of this Act "motor car" means a motor vehicle (other than an invalid carriage or motor cycle)—

(a) which is not constructed or adapted to carry more than nine persons inclusive of the driver, and

(b) which has a maximum gross weight not exceeding 3.5 tonnes

(2) In subsection (1) above "maximum gross weight" has the same meaning as in Part III of this Act.
[Road Traffic Act 1988 as inserted by SI 1996/1974.]

4-1554 142. Index to Part V. The expressions listed in the left-hand column below are respectively defined or (as the case may be) fall to be construed in accordance with the provisions of this Part of this Act listed in the right-hand column in relation to those expressions.

Expression	Relevant provision
Appropriate motor car	Section 125A(8)
Community licence and counterpart in relation thereto	Section 125(10)
Current licence	Section 123(7)
Disability, prospective disability and relevant disability	Section 125A(8)
Disabled person's limited driving licence	Section 125A(8)
Emergency control assessment and emergency control certificate	Section 125A(8)
Paid instruction	Section 123(8)
Provisional licence	Section 123(8)
The register	Section 123
Registered disabled instructor	Section 125A(8)
The Registrar	Section 125(2)
Regulations	Section 141

[Road Traffic Act 1988, s 142 as amended by the Road Traffic (Driving Instruction by Disabled Persons) Act 1993, Sch.]

PART VI[1]
THIRD-PARTY LIABILITIES

Compulsory insurance or security against third-party risks

4-1560 143. Users of motor vehicles to be insured or secured against third-party risks.
(1) Subject to the provisions of this Part[2] of this Act—

(a) a person must not use[3] motor vehicle on a road[4] or other public place unless there is in force in relation to the use of the vehicle[5] by that person such a policy of insurance or such a security in respect of third party risks as complies with the requirements of this Part of this Act, and

(b) a person must not cause or permit[3] any other person to use[6] a motor vehicle[7] on a road or other public place unless there is in force[8] in relation to the use of the vehicle by that other person such a policy of insurance[9] or such a security[10] in respect of third party risks[11] as complies[12] with the requirements of this Part of this Act.

(2) If a person acts in contravention of subsection (1) above he is guilty of an offence[13].

(3) A person charged with using a motor vehicle in contravention of this section shall not be convicted if he proves—

(a) that the vehicle did not belong to him and was not in his possession under a contract of hiring or of loan,

(b) that he was using the vehicle in the course of his employment, and

(c) that he neither knew nor had reason to believe that there was not in force in relation to the vehicle such a policy of insurance or security as is mentioned in subsection (1) above.

(4) This Part of this Act does not apply to invalid carriages[14].

[Road Traffic Act 1988, s 143 as amended by SI 2000/726.]

---

1. Part VI contains ss 143–162.

2. Exceptions are contained in s 144, post. By the Motor Vehicles (International Motor Insurance Card) Regulations 1971, SI 1971/792, as amended by SI 1977/895, visitors bringing motor vehicles temporarily into Great Britain and holding an international motor insurance card may register particulars thereof, whereby the card has effect as though it were a policy of insurance for the purposes of this Part of this Act.

3. See Preliminary Note to this title ante for "use", "cause", "permit".

4. See Preliminary Note to this title, ante, "Meaning of 'road'".

5. In determining whether a liability is covered by the terms of an insurance policy for the purposes of s 151 (infra) it is necessary to inquire as to the essential character or primary purpose of the journey in question: (*Keeley v Pashen* [2004] EWCA Civ 1491, [2005] RTR 10 (driving home after the vehicle had been used for hire or reward was covered, though the period of use for hire or reward had not been).

5. A breach of this statutory duty by the owner lending his motor vehicle when the required insurance as to the user by the borrower does not exist, renders the lender liable in damages to a third party for the injuries he has sustained (*Monk v Warbey* [1935] 1 KB 75, CA; *Corfield v Groves* [1950] 1 All ER 488), provided the damages are the result of such breach (*Daniels v Vaux* [1938] 2 KB 203, [1938] 2 All ER 271; but gives no right of action against the insurance company (*Richards v Port of Manchester Insurance Co and Brain* (1934) 152 LT 413). As to the use of a motor vehicle, after a sale by auction, where a policy is not in force, see *Watkins v O'Shaughnessy* [1939] 1 All ER 385.

A voidable policy of insurance, until avoided, is sufficient for the purposes of this section (*Goodbarne v Buck* [1940] 1 KB 107, [1939] 3 All ER 107; affd [1940] 1 KB 771, [1940] 1 All ER 613, CA). This is so even where the insurers are misled by the defendant's concealment of his disqualification from driving (*Adams v Dunn* [1978] Crim LR 365). An "exception clause" in a policy must be construed strictly: where such a clause avoids the policy in certain circumstances "to the knowledge of the insured", proof of actual, not constructive, knowledge of that circumstance is necessary in proof of guilt for "permitting" (*John T Ellis Ltd v Hinds* [1947] KB 475, [1947] 1 All ER 337; *Houghton v Trafalgar Insurance Co Ltd* [1954] 1 QB 247, [1953] 2 All ER 1409). For a case where permission to drive was held to continue after the death of the insured, see *Kelly v Cornhill Insurance Co Ltd* [1964] 1 All ER 321, HL.

If a policy is in force covering the user of the vehicle in respect of third-party risks, a policy covering the personal liability of the driver is not required. A vehicle, insured by an employer, was driven by a servant acting within the scope of his employment, although the driving was done in an unauthorised and improper way; if injury had been caused to a third party the employer would have been liable and it was this risk which was covered by the insurance policy and, therefore, no offence under this section was committed by the servant (*Marsh v Moores* [1949] 2 KB 208, [1949] 2 All ER 27, 113 JP 346). Where a policy excludes liability for the user who is disqualified for holding or obtaining a licence, these words must be construed as meaning a disqualification by a court under s 93 of the Act or, by virtue of non age (s 96 of the Act), and not disqualification on medical grounds (*Edwards v Griffiths* [1953] 2 All ER 874, 117 JP 514; *Mumford v Hardy* [1956] 1 All ER 337). Where the policy clearly excludes liability, the test of insurance is not whether an insurance company considers itself "on risk", but, where the interpretation of the conditions is doubtful, justices may have regard to the fact that the company accepts liability (*Carnill v Rowland* [1953] 1 All ER 486, 117 JP 127). For an instance of instructor and learner being joint drivers, see *Langman v Valentine* [1952] 2 All ER 803, 116 JP 576. The instructor must be in actual control of the vehicle, if his insurance policy is to be operative (*Evans v Walkden* [1956] 3 All ER 64, 120 JP 495).

The operation of this section was extensively reviewed in *Romford Ice and Cold Storage Co Ltd v Lister* [1956] 2 QB 180, [1955] 3 All ER 460; on appeal, *Lister v Romford Ice and Cold Storage Co Ltd* [1957] AC 555, [1957] 1 All ER 125, 121 JP 98.

6. A summons charging the use of a "motor car and trailer" without insurance is bad, but capable of amendment under the Magistrates' Courts Act 1980 s 123, ante: a motor car and a trailer are not a single entity (*Rogerson v Stephens* [1950] 2 All ER 144, 114 JP 372).

7. See the Magistrates' Courts Act 1980, s 101, ante (onus of proving exceptions etc).

It is not a sufficient defence for the accused to prove that he is contractually covered; he must also prove that he has *received* a certificate of insurance. See s 147, post. Once it has been established that the defendant was using a motor vehicle on a road the burden is on the defendant to prove on the balance of probabilities that he was covered by a current MOT certificate (if required for the vehicle) and current insurance and there is no requirement, although it is desirable, for there to have been a statutory demand to produce documents (*DPP v Kavaz* [1999] RTR 40, DC).

8. Described in s 145, post. It includes a covering note (s 161(1), post, and the Motor Vehicles (Third Party Risks) Regulations 1972, reg 4(1), in the PART, post), and an international motor insurance card issued in accordance with the Motor Vehicles (International Motor Insurance Card) Regulations 1971 (SI 1971/792 amended by SI 1977/895). Such a note is not a policy of insurance where the driver does not rely upon the offer of insurance contained therein (*Taylor v Allon* [1966] 1 QB 304, [1965] 1 All ER 557). See *Goodbarne v Buck* [1940] 1 KB 771, [1940] 1 All ER 613. A policy is not invalid because it covers a risk which is identified with an unlawful use of the vehicle (eg when drawing two laden trailers): the policy covers not unlawful user, but the consequences of negligent driving (*Leggate v Brown* [1950] 2 All ER 564, 114 JP 454).

9. See s 146, post.

10. As to requirements for cover for passengers see note 4 to s 145, post.

11. As by s 175, post, it is an offence for any person to issue a false certificate, the production of an apparently sufficient certificate will raise a rebuttable presumption that the required policy or security is in force (*R v Twyning* (1819) 2 B & Ald 386). The contents of the certificate can be proved by the constable to whom it was produced pursuant to s 165, post, without a notice to produce. *Semble*, the onus of proving that he holds a proper insurance policy is on the defendant (Magistrates' Courts Act 1980, s 101, ante; *Williams v Russell*, supra; cf *John v Humphreys* [1955] 1 All ER 93, 1179 JP 309), and *Davey v Towle* [1973] Crim LR 360. A letter from insurers is not admissible as evidence to prove terms of a policy (*Egan v Bower* (1939) 63 Ll L Rep 266). In *Edwards v Griffiths* [1953] 2 All ER 874, 117 JP 514, it was advised that

the prosecution should ensure that the policy is produced in court in cases where questions of its construction may arise. This may be done by means of a witness summons where the insured is not the defendant.

12. For punishment see the Road Traffic Offenders Act 1988 Sch 2 and notes thereto, post. Section 6 thereof (time limits) and ss 11 and 12(1) (evidence by certificate) apply.

13. Defined by s 185(1), post.

4–1561   144. Exceptions from requirement of third party insurance or security. (1) Section 143 of this Act does not apply[1] to a vehicle owned by a person[2] who has deposited and keeps deposited with the Accountant General of the Supreme Court* the sum of £500,000, at a time when the vehicle is being driven under the owner's control.

(1A) The Secretary of State may by order made by statutory instrument substitute a greater sum for the sum for the time being specified in subsection (1) above.

(1B) No order shall be made under subsection (1A) above unless a draft of it has been laid before and approved by resolution of each House of Parliament.

(2) Section 143 does not apply—

(a) to a vehicle owned—
   (i) by the council of a county or county district in England and Wales, the Broads Authority, the Common Council of the City of London, the council of a London borough, a National Park Authority, the Inner London Education Authority, the London Fire and Emergency Planning Authority, or a joint authority (other than a police authority), established by Part IV of the Local Government Act 1985,
   (ii) by a council constituted under section 2 of the Local Government etc (Scotland) Act 1994 in Scotland, or
   (iii) by a joint board or committee in England or Wales, or joint committee in Scotland, which is so constituted as to include among its members representatives of any such council,
   at a time when the vehicle is being driven under the owner's control,

(b) to a vehicle owned by a police authority, at a time when it is being driven under the owner's control, or to a vehicle at a time when it is being driven for police purposes[3] by or under the direction of a constable, or by a person employed by a police authority, or

(ba) repealedrepealed;

(c) to a vehicle at a time when it is being driven on a journey to or from any place undertaken for salvage purposes pursuant to Part IX of the Merchant Shipping Act 1995,

(d) to the use of a vehicle for the purpose of its being provided in pursuance of a direction under section 166(2)(b)[4] of the Army Act 1955 or under the corresponding provision of the Air Force Act 1955,

(da) to a vehicle owned by a health service body, as defined in section 60(7) of the National Health Service and Community Care Act 1990 by a Primary Care Trust established under section 16A of the National Health Service Act 1977 or by the Commission for Healthcare Audit and Inspection, at a time when the vehicle is being driven under the owner's control,

(db) to an ambulance owned by a National Health Service trust established under Part I of the National Health Service and Community Care Act 1990 or the National Health Service (Scotland) Act 1978, at a time when a vehicle is being driven under the owner's control,

(dc) to an ambulance owned by an NHS foundation trust, at a time when the vehicle is being driven under the owner's control,

(e) to a vehicle which is made available by the Secretary of State to any person, body or local authority in pursuance of section 23 or 26 of the National Health Service Act 1977 at a time when it is being used in accordance with the terms on which it is so made available,

(f) to a vehicle which is made available by the Secretary of State to any local authority, education authority or voluntary organisation in Scotland in pursuance of section 15 or 16 of the National Health Service (Scotland) Act 1978 at a time when it is being used in accordance with the terms on which it is so made available

(g) to a vehicle owned by the Commission for Social Care Inspection, at a time when the vehicle is being driven under the owner's control.

[Road Traffic Act 1988, s 144 as amended by the National Health Service and Community Care Act 1990, Sch 8, the Road Traffic Act 1991, s 20, the Merchant Shipping Act 1995, Sch 13, the Environment Act 1995, Sch 10, the Police Act 1997, Sch 9, SI 1999/2795, the Greater London Authority Act 1999, Schs 27 and 29, SI 2000/90, SI 2004/2987,the Health and Social Care (Community Health and Standards) Act 2003, Sch 4 and the Serious Organised Crime and Police Act 2005, Sch 4.]

*Words "Senior Courts" substituted by the Constitutional Reform Act 2005, Sch 11 from a date to be appointed.

1. But see reg 5 of the Motor Vehicles (Compulsory Insurance) (No 2) Regulations 1973, in this PART, post, whereby it is an offence (for which proceedings may be taken in Great Britain) to use a vehicle exempted under this section in a member state of the European Communities without insurance cover valid for those states.

2. This is designed to meet the case of important bodies who are their own insurers. The deposit will be liable to discharge the insurance liabilities first (s 152(1)). See the Motor Vehicles (Third Party Risks Deposits) Regulations 1992, SI 1992/1284.

3. This exception will apply to a constable's own car while it is being driven for police purposes (*Jones v Chief Constable of Bedfordshire* [1987] RTR 332, [1987] Crim LR 502).

4. This relates to a direction given under a requisitioning order.

4–1561A   144A. Offence of keeping vehicle which does not meet insurance requirements. (1) If a motor vehicle registered under the Vehicle Excise and Registration Act 1994 does not meet the insurance requirements, the person in whose name the vehicle is registered is guilty of an offence.

(2) For the purposes of this section a vehicle meets the insurance requirements if—

(a) it is covered by a such a policy of insurance or such a security in respect of third party risks as complies with the requirements of this Part of this Act, and

(b) either of the following conditions is satisfied.

(3) The first condition is that the policy or security, or the certificate of insurance or security which relates to it, identifies the vehicle by its registration mark as a vehicle which is covered by the policy or security.

(4) The second condition is that the vehicle is covered by the policy or security because—

(a) the policy or security covers any vehicle, or any vehicle of a particular description, the owner of which is a person named in the policy or security or in the certificate of insurance or security which relates to it, and

(b) the vehicle is owned by that person.

(5) For the purposes of this section a vehicle is covered by a policy of insurance or security if the policy of insurance or security is in force in relation to the use of the vehicle.★
[Road Traffic Act 1988, s 144A as inserted by the Road Safety Act 2006, s 22.]

★New ss 144A–144D inserted by the Road Safety Act 2006, s 22 from a date to be appointed.

4–1561B   144B. Exceptions to section 144A offence.   (1) A person ("the registered keeper") in whose name a vehicle which does not meet the insurance requirements is registered at any particular time ("the relevant time") does not commit an offence under section 144A of this Act at that time if any of the following conditions are satisfied.

(2) The first condition is that at the relevant time the vehicle is owned as described—

(a) in subsection (1) of section 144 of this Act, or

(b) in paragraph (a), (b), (da), (db), (dc) or (g) of subsection (2) of that section,

(whether or not at the relevant time it is being driven as described in that provision).

(3) The second condition is that at the relevant time the vehicle is owned with the intention that it should be used as described in paragraph (c), (d), (e) or (f) of section 144(2) of this Act.

(4) The third condition is that the registered keeper—

(a) is not at the relevant time the person keeping the vehicle, and

(b) if previously he was the person keeping the vehicle, he has by the relevant time complied with any requirements under subsection (7)(a) below that he is required to have complied with by the relevant or any earlier time.

(5) The fourth condition is that—

(a) the registered keeper is at the relevant time the person keeping the vehicle,

(b) at the relevant time the vehicle is not used on a road or other public place, and

(c) the registered keeper has by the relevant time complied with any requirements under subsection (7)(a) below that he is required to have complied with by the relevant or any earlier time.

(6) The fifth condition is that—

(a) the vehicle has been stolen before the relevant time,

(b) the vehicle has not been recovered by the relevant time, and

(c) any requirements under subsection (7)(b) below that, in connection with the theft, are required to have been complied with by the relevant or any earlier time have been complied with by the relevant time.

(7) Regulations may make provision—

(a) for the purposes of subsection (4)(b) and (5)(c) above, requiring a person in whose name a vehicle is registered to furnish such particulars and make such declarations as may be prescribed, and to do so at such times and in such manner as may be prescribed, and

(b) for the purposes of subsection (6)(c) above, as to the persons to whom, the times at which and the manner in which the theft of a vehicle is to be notified.

(8) Regulations may make provision amending this section for the purpose of providing for further exceptions to section 144A of this Act (or varying or revoking any such further exceptions).

(9) A person accused of an offence under section 144A of this Act is not entitled to the benefit of an exception conferred by or under this section unless evidence is adduced that is sufficient to raise an issue with respect to that exception; but where evidence is so adduced it is for the prosecution to prove beyond reasonable doubt that the exception does not apply.★
[Road Traffic Act 1988, s 144B as inserted by the Road Safety Act 2006, s 22.]

★New ss 144A–144D inserted by the Road Safety Act 2006, s 22 from a date to be appointed.

4–1561C   144C. Fixed penalty notices.   (1) Where on any occasion the Secretary of State has reason to believe that a person has committed an offence under section 144A of this Act, the Secretary of State may give the person a notice offering him the opportunity of discharging any liability to conviction for that offence by payment of a fixed penalty to the Secretary of State.

(2) Where a person is given a notice under this section in respect of an offence under section 144A of this Act—

(a) no proceedings may be instituted for that offence before the end of the period of 21 days following the date of the notice, and

(b) he may not be convicted of that offence if he pays the fixed penalty before the end of that period.

(3) A notice under this section must give such particulars of the circumstances alleged to constitute the offence as are necessary for giving reasonable information of the offence.

(4) A notice under this section must also state—

(a) the period during which, by virtue of subsection (2) above, proceedings will not be taken for the offence,

(b) the amount of the fixed penalty, and

(c) the person to whom and the address at which the fixed penalty may be paid.

(5) Without prejudice to payment by any other method, payment of the fixed penalty may be made by pre-paying and posting a letter containing the amount of the penalty (in cash or otherwise) to the person mentioned in subsection (4)(c) above at the address so mentioned.

(6) Where a letter is sent in accordance with subsection (5) above payment is to be regarded as having been made at the time at which that letter would be delivered in the ordinary course of post.

(7) Regulations may make provision as to any matter incidental to the operation of this section, and in particular—

(a) as to the form of a notice under this section,

(b) as to the information to be provided in such a notice by virtue of this section, and

(c) as to any further information to be provided in a such notice.

(8) The fixed penalty payable under this section is, subject to subsection (9) below, £100.

(9) Regulations may substitute a different amount for the amount for the time being specified in subsection (8) above.

(10) Regulations may make provision for treating a fixed penalty payable under this section as having been paid if a lesser amount is paid before the end of a prescribed period.

(11) In any proceedings a certificate which—

(a) purports to be signed by or on behalf of the Secretary of State, and

(b) states that payment of a fixed penalty was or was not received by a date specified in the certificate,

is evidence of the facts stated.*

[Road Traffic Act 1988, s 144C as inserted by the Road Safety Act 2006, s 22.]

---

*New ss 144A–144D inserted by the Road Safety Act 2006, s 22 from a date to be appointed.

4–1561D 144D. Section 144A offence: supplementary. (1) Schedule 2A makes provision about the immobilisation of vehicles as regards which it appears that an offence under section 144A of this Act is being committed and about their removal and disposal.

(2) A person authorised by the Secretary of State for the purposes of this subsection may on behalf of the Secretary of State conduct and appear in any proceedings by or against the Secretary of State in connection with the enforcement of an offence under section 144A of this Act or under regulations made under section 160 of this Act by virtue of Schedule 2A to this Act—

(a) in England and Wales, in a magistrates' court, and

(b) in Scotland, in any court other than the High Court of Justiciary or the Court of Session.*

[Road Traffic Act 1988, s 144D as inserted by the Road Safety Act 2006, s 22.]

---

*New ss 144A–144D inserted by the Road Safety Act 2006, s 22 from a date to be appointed.

4–1562 145. Requirements in respect of policies of insurance. (1) In order to comply with the requirements of this Part of this Act, a policy of insurance must satisfy the following conditions.

(2) The policy must be issued by an authorised insurer[1].

(3) Subject to subsection (4) below, the policy—

(a) must insure such person, persons or classes of persons[2] as may be specified in the policy in respect of any liability[3] which may be incurred by him or them in respect of the death of or bodily injury to any person[4] or damage to property caused by, or arising out of, the use of the vehicle on a road or other public place in Great Britain, and

(aa) must, in the case of a vehicle normally based in the territory of another member State, insure him or them in respect of any civil liability which may be incurred by him or them as a result of an event related to the use of the vehicle in Great Britain if—

(i) according to the law of that territory, he or they would be required to be insured in respect of a civil liability which would arise under that law as a result of that event if the place where the vehicle was used when the event occurred were in that territory, and

(ii) the cover required by that law would be higher than that required by paragraph (a) above, and

(b) must, in the case of a vehicle normally based in Great Britain, insure him or them in respect of any liability which may be incurred by him or them in respect of the use of the vehicle and of any trailer, whether or not coupled, in the territory other than Great Britain and Gibraltar of each of the member States of the Communities according to

(i) the law on compulsory insurance against civil liability in respect of the use of vehicles of the State in whose territory the event giving rise to the liability occurred; or

(ii) if it would give higher cover, the law which would be applicable under this Part of this Act if the place where the vehicle was used when that event occurred were in Great Britain; and

(c) must also insure him or them in respect of any liability which may be incurred by him or them under the provisions of this Part of this Act relating to payment for emergency treatment.

(4) The policy shall not, by virtue of subsection (3)(a) above, be required—

(a) to cover liability in respect of the death, arising out of and in the course of his employment, of a person in the employment of a person insured by the policy or of bodily injury sustained by such a person arising out of and in the course of his employment, or

(b) to provide insurance of more than £250,000 in respect of all such liabilities as may be incurred in respect of damage to property caused by, or arising out of, any one accident involving the vehicle, or

(c) to cover liability in respect of damage to the vehicle, or

(d) to cover liability in respect of damage to goods carried for hire or reward in or on the vehicle or in or on any trailer (whether or not coupled) drawn by the vehicle, or

(e) to cover any liability of a person in respect of damage to property in his custody or under his control, or

(f) to cover any contractual liability.

(4A) In the case of a person[4]—

(a) carried in or upon a vehicle, or

(b) entering or getting on to, or alighting from, a vehicle,

the provisions of paragraph (a) of subsection (4) above do not apply unless cover in respect of the liability referred to in that paragraph is in fact provided pursuant to a requirement of the Employers' Liability (Compulsory Insurance) Act 1969.

(5) "Authorised insurer" has the same meaning as in section 95.

(6) If any person or body of persons ceases to be a member of the Motor Insurers' Bureau, that person or body shall not by virtue of that cease to be treated as an authorised insurer for the purposes of this Part of this Act or the Road Traffic (NHS Charges) Act 1999*—

(a) in relation to any policy issued by the insurer before ceasing to be such a member, or

(b) in relation to any obligation (whether arising before or after the insurer ceased to be such a member) which the insurer may be called upon to meet under or in consequence of any such policy or under section 157 of this Act or section 1 of the Act 1999* by virtue of making a payment in pursuance of such an obligation.

[Road Traffic Act 1988, s 145 amended by the Motor Vehicles (Compulsory Insurance) Regulations 1992, SI 1992/3036, the Road Traffic (NHS Charges) Act 1999, s 18(1)(a) and (b), SI 2000/726, SI 2002/2640 and 3649.]

---

*Words repealed by the Health and Social Care (Community Health and Standards) Act 2003, Sch 14, from a date to be appointed.

1. But see reg 8 of the Motor Vehicles (Compulsory Insurance) (No 2) Regulations 1973 in this PART, post, as to insurance policies issued outside the UK for vehicles normally based in territory of member state of European Communities.

2. Although a policy may indemnify the insured against liability for his criminal act, it is not void as being against public policy (*Tinline v White Cross Insurance Co* [1921] 3 KB 327; *James v British General Insurance Co* [1927] 2 KB 311, doubted in *Haseldine v Hosken* [1933] 1 KB 822, CA). Cf *Davies v Hoskens* [1937] 3 All ER 192; *Leggate v Brown* [1950] 2 All ER 564, 114 JP 454, note 22, ante. Where a driver uses a vehicle in such a manner as to commit an offence against s 18 of the Offences against the Person Act 1861, the policy will cover a claim by an injured third party under s 151, even though the driver would have been debarred from recovering (*Hardy v Motor Insurer's Bureau* [1964] 2 All ER 742). A policy covering the policy holder and "his paid driver" covers a paid driver who is paid as a driver not necessarily by the policy holder or in the general employment of the policy holder (*Bryan v Forrow* [1950] 1 All ER 294, 114 JP 158). As to duty of insurers to satisfy judgments against persons insured, see s 151, and as to duty of insured to give particulars of his certificate of insurance, see s 154, post.

3. After delivery of a certificate, the conditions mentioned in s 148, post, shall be of no effect, so far as they restrict the insurance of the persons thereby insured. A contract of insurance is denominated a contract *uberrimae fidei* (*Glicksman v Lancashire and General Assurance Co Ltd* [1927] AC 139 at 143). A policy lapses on the sale by the assured of the insured car to another unless rights of insurance are specifically retained by the insured (*Boss v Kingston* [1963] 1 All ER 177). It is incapable of assignment without the consent of the insurers (*Peters v General Accident Fire and Life Assurance Corpn Ltd* [1938] 2 All ER 267). A policy obtained by misrepresentation of material facts insures no one (*Guardian Assurance Co Ltd v Sutherland* [1939] 2 All ER 246). A voidable policy is valid until avoided (*Goodbarne v Buck* [1940] 1 KB 771, [1940] 1 All ER 613).

4. See s 149, post as to the requirements for passenger liability. Where a policy provided for the indemnity of an authorised driver, in addition to the owner (policy owner), of a car, it was held that the driver was entitled to be indemnified against the damages awarded in favour of the policy-holder in the claim against him (*Digby v General Accident Fire and Life Assurance Corpn Ltd* [1943] AC 121, [1942] 2 All ER 319; *Richards v Cox* [1942] KB 139, [1942] 2 All ER 624).

The compulsory insurance scheme under the Road Traffic Act 1988 requires insurance to cover liability for personal injuries to all passengers other than the driver arising out of the use of a vehicle. Whilst the effect of sub-s (4A) read with sub-s 3(a) is that liability is required to be covered in respect of a person carried in or on a vehicle, this does not extend to the driver (*R v Secretary of State for Transport, ex p National Insurance Guarantee Corpn plc* (1996) Times, 3 June, DC).

For the Recovery from insurers and certain other persons of charges in connection with the treatment of road traffic casualties in national health service, and certain other, hospitals, see the Road Traffic (NHS charges) Act 1999.

4–1563   146. Requirements in respect of securities.   (1) In order to comply with the requirements of this Part of this Act, a security must satisfy the following conditions[1].

(2) The security must be given either by an authorised insurer or by some body of persons which carries on in the United Kingdom the business of giving securities of a like kind and has deposited and keeps deposited with the Accountant General of the Supreme Court the sum of £15,000 in respect of that business.

(3) Subject to subsection (4) below, the security must consist of an undertaking by the giver of the security to make good, subject to any conditions specified in it, any failure by the owner of the vehicle or such other persons or classes of persons as may be specified in the security duly to discharge any liability which may be incurred by him or them, being a liability required under section 145 of this Act to be covered by a policy of insurance.

(4) In the case of liabilities arising out of the use of a motor vehicle on a road or other public place in Great Britain the amount secured need not exceed—

(*a*) in the case of an undertaking relating to the use of public service vehicles (within the meaning of the Public Passenger Vehicles Act 1981), £25,000,

(*b*) in any other case, £5,000.

[Road Traffic Act 1988, s 146 as amended by SI 2000/726.]

---

1. For avoidance of certain exemptions, to securities, see s 148, post.

4–1564   147. Issue and surrender of certificates of insurance and of security.   (1) A policy of insurance shall be of no effect for the purposes of this Part of this Act unless and until there is delivered by the insurer to the person by whom the policy is effected a certificate (in this Part of this Act referred to as a "certificate of insurance"[1]) in the prescribed form[2] and containing such particulars of any conditions subject to which the policy is issued and of any other matters as may be prescribed.

(2) A security shall be of no effect for the purposes of this Part of this Act unless and until there is delivered by the person giving the security to the person to whom it is given a certificate (in this Part of this Act referred to as a "certificate of security") in the prescribed form and containing such particulars of any conditions subject to which the security is issued and of any other matters as may be prescribed.

(3) Different forms and different particulars may be prescribed for the purposes of subsection (1) or (2) above in relation to different cases or circumstances.

(4) Where a certificate has been delivered under this section and the policy or security to which it relates is cancelled by mutual consent or by virtue of any provision in the policy or security, the person to whom the certificate was delivered must, within seven days from the taking effect of the cancellation—

(*a*) surrender the certificate to the person by whom the policy was issued or the security was given, or

(*b*) if the certificate has been lost or destroyed, make a statutory declaration to that effect.

(5) A person who fails to comply with subsection (4) above is guilty of an offence[3].

[Road Traffic Act 1988, s 147.]

---

1. This certificate is not transferable to a new owner of the vehicle. But see reg 8 of the Motor Vehicles (Compulsory Insurance) (No 2) Regulations 1973, in this PART, post, as to insurance policies issued outside the UK for vehicles normally based in territory of member state of European Communities.

2. See the Motor Vehicles (Third Party Risks) Regulations 1972, reg 5(1), in this PART, post. A covering note must have printed on it or on the back thereof a certificate of insurance (reg 5(3)). The company must keep a record of certificates issued (reg 10).

3. For punishment see the Road Traffic Offenders Act 1988, Sch 2 and notes thereto, post.

4–1565   148. Avoidance of certain exceptions to policies or securities.   (1) Where a certificate of insurance or certificate of security has been delivered under section 147 of this Act to the person by whom a policy has been effected or to whom a security has been given, so much of the policy or security as purports to restrict—

(*a*) the insurance of the persons insured by the policy, or

(*b*) the operation of the security,

(as the case may be) by reference to any of the matters mentioned in subsection (2) below shall, as respects such liabilities as are required to be covered by a policy under section 145 of this Act, be of no effect.

(2) Those matters are—

(*a*) the age or physical or mental condition of persons driving the vehicle[1],

(*b*) the condition of the vehicle,

(*c*) the number of persons that the vehicle carries,

(*d*) the weight or physical characteristics of the goods that the vehicle carries,

(*e*) the time at which or the areas within which the vehicle is used,

(*f*) the horsepower or cylinder capacity or value of the vehicle,

(*g*) the carrying on the vehicle of any particular apparatus, or

(*h*) the carrying on the vehicle of any particular means of identification other than any means of identification required to be carried by or under the Vehicle Excise and Registration Act 1994.

(3) Nothing in subsection (1) above requires an insurer or the giver of a security to pay any sum in respect of the liability of any person otherwise than in or towards the discharge of that liability.

(4) Any sum paid by an insurer or the giver of a security in or towards the discharge of any liability of any person which is covered by the policy or security by virtue only of subsection (1) above is recoverable by the insurer or giver of the security from that person.

(5) A condition in a policy or security issued or given for the purposes of this Part of this Act providing—

(a) that no liability shall arise under the policy or security,[2] or

(b) that any liability so arising shall cease,

in the event of some specified thing being done or omitted to be done after the happening of the event giving rise to a claim under the policy or security, shall be of no effect in connection with such liabilities as are required to be covered by a policy under section 145 of this Act.

(6) Nothing in subsection (5) above shall be taken to render void any provision in a policy or security requiring the person insured or secured to pay to the insurer or the giver of the security any sums which the latter may have become liable to pay under the policy or security and which have been applied to the satisfaction of the claims of third parties.

(7) Notwithstanding anything in any enactment[3], a person issuing a policy of insurance under section 145[4] of this Act shall be liable to indemnify the persons[5] or classes of persons specified in the policy in respect of any liability which the policy purports to cover in the case of those persons or classes of persons[6].
[Road Traffic Act 1988, s 148 amended by the Vehicle Excise and Registration Act 1994, Sch 3.]

---

1. This does not apply to a condition to use all care and diligence to avoid accidents and to prevent loss (*National Farmers Union Mutual Insurance Society Ltd v Dawson* [1941] 2 KB 424).
2. The subsequent words "in the event", etc, govern "arise" as well as "cease". There is nothing in this Act to prevent an insurer and the insured effecting a policy which contains any conditions other than the cesser of liability after it has arisen. If the policy does not comply with the requirements of this Act, the insured is liable to a penalty (*Gray v Blackmore* [1943] 1 KB 95, 50 TLR 23). Therefore a condition in a policy that it did not cover the use of a motor cycle with a passenger, unless a sidecar is attached, may circumscribe the operation of the policy from the beginning (*Bright v Ashfold* [1932] KB 153, 96 JP 182).
3. By these words, Parliament intended to include the common law defence as well as the statutory defence contained in the Life Assurance Act 1774. Where a policy had been granted to A, providing that "the insurance shall extend to indemnify any person who is driving on the insured's order, or with his permission, in respect of any legal liability to third parties", it was held that notwithstanding he was not a party to the contract, B, who was driving with A's permission, might himself successfully sue on A's policy, and was therefore properly insured (*Vanderpitte v Preferred Accident Insurance Corpn of New York* [1933] AC 70, now followed (*Tattersal v Drysdale* [1935] 2 KB 174; *Austin v Zurich General Accident and Liability Insurance Co Ltd* [1945] KB 250, [1945] 1 All ER 316)).
4. The section does not apply to a policy obtained by fraud or misrepresentation or concealment (*McCormick v National Motor and Accident Insurance Union Ltd* (1934) 50 TLR 528; *Guardian Assurance Co Ltd v Sutherland* [1939] 2 All ER 246.)
5. See *Digby v General Accident Fire and Life Assurance Corpn Ltd* [1943] AC 121, [1942] 2 All ER 319.
6. By the Third Parties (Rights against Insurers) Act 1930, if an insured person, whether an individual or a company, becomes bankrupt, etc, but either before or after that event has insured a liability to a third person, the right of the bankrupt individual or company under their policy is transferred to and vests in the injured third party. The transfer is subject to all the rights of the insurance company against the assured (*Freshwater v Western Australian Assurance Co Ltd* [1933] 1 KB 515; *Stevens & Sons v Timber and General Mutual Accident Insurance Association Ltd* (1933) 102 LJKB 337, CA), but now subject to the provisions of s 7 of the Road Traffic (Consequential Provisions) Act 1988, post. As to bankruptcy, etc, of person insured, or, if dead, administration of his estate in bankruptcy, or, if a company, its winding up, etc, see s 153, post. As to cause of action surviving the death of the injured person, see the Law Reform (Miscellaneous Provisions) Act 1934, as amended by the Proceedings Against Estates Act 1970, and *Flint v Lovell* [1935] 1 KB 354, and *Slater v Spreag* [1936] 1 KB 83.

4-1566 149. Avoidance of certain agreements as to liability towards passengers. (1) This section applies where a person uses a motor vehicle in circumstances such that under section 143 of this Act there is required to be in force in relation to his use of it such a policy of insurance or such a security in respect of third-party risks as complies with the requirements of this Part of this Act.

(2) If any other person is carried in or upon the vehicle while the user is so using it, any antecedent agreement or understanding between them (whether intended to be legally binding or not) shall be of no effect so far as it purports or might be held—

(a) to negative or restrict any such liability of the user in respect of persons carried in or upon the vehicle as is required by section 145 of this Act to be covered by a policy of insurance, or

(b) to impose any conditions with respect to the enforcement of any such liability of the user.

(3) The fact that a person so carried has willingly accepted as his the risk of negligence on the part of the user shall not be treated as negativing any such liability of the user.

(4) For the purposes of this section—

(a) references to a person being carried in or upon a vehicle include references to a person entering or getting on to, or alighting from, the vehicle, and

(b) the reference to an antecedent agreement is to one made at any time before the liability arose.
[Road Traffic Act 1988, s 149.]

4-1567 150. Insurance or security in respect of private use of vehicle to cover use under car-sharing arrangements. (1) To the extent that a policy or security issued or given for the purposes of this Part of this Act—

(a) restricts the insurance of the persons insured by the policy or the operation of the security (as the case may be) to use of the vehicle for specified purpose (for example, social, domestic and pleasure purposes) of a non-commercial character, or

(b) excludes from that insurance or the operation of the security (as the case may be)—

(i) use of the vehicle for hire or reward, or

(ii) business or commercial use of the vehicle, or

(iii) use of the vehicle for specified purposes of a business or commercial character,

then, for the purposes of that policy or security so far as it relates to such liabilities as are required to be covered by a policy under section 145 of this Act, the use of a vehicle on a journey in the course of which one or more passengers are carried at separate fares shall, if the conditions specified in subsection (2) below are satisfied, be treated as falling within that restriction or as not falling within that exclusion (as the case may be).

(2) The conditions referred to in subsection (1) above are—

(a) the vehicle is not adapted to carry more than eight passengers and is not a motor cycle,

(b) the fare or aggregate of the fares paid in respect of the journey does not exceed the amount of the running costs of the vehicle for the journey (which for the purposes of this paragraph shall be taken to include an appropriate amount in respect of depreciation and general wear), and

(c) the arrangements for the payment of fares by the passenger or passengers carried at separate fares were made before the journey began.

(3) Subsections (1) and (2) above apply however the restrictions or exclusions described in subsection (1) are framed or worded.

(4) In subsections (1) and (2) above "fare" and "separate fares" have the same meaning as in section 1(4) of the Public Passenger Vehicles Act 1981.
[Road Traffic Act 1988, s 150.]

4–1568   151. Duty of insurers or persons giving security to satisfy judgment against persons insured or secured against third-party risks.

4–1569   152. Exceptions to s 151.

4–1580   153. Bankruptcy etc of insured or secured persons not to affect claims by third parties.

4–1581   154. Duty to give information as to insurance or security where claim made.   (1) A person against whom a claim is made in respect of any such liability as is required to be covered by a policy of insurance under section 145 of this Act must, on demand by or on behalf of the person making the claim—

(a) state whether or not, in respect of that liability—

(i) he was insured by a policy having effect for the purposes of this Part of this Act or had in force a security having effect for those purposes, or

(ii) he would have been so insured or would have had in force such a security if the insurer or, as the case may be, the giver of the security had not avoided or cancelled the policy or security, and

(b) if he was or would have been so insured, or had or would have had in force such a security—

(i) give such particulars with respect to that policy or security as were specified in any certificate of insurance or security delivered in respect of that policy or security, as the case may be, under section 147 of this Act, or

(ii) where no such certificate was delivered under that section, give the following particulars, that is to say, the registration mark or other identifying particulars of the vehicle concerned, the number or other identifying particulars of the insurance policy issued in respect of the vehicle, the name of the insurer and the period of the insurance cover.

(2) If without reasonable excuse, a person fails to comply with the provisions of subsection (1) above, or wilfully makes a false statement in reply to such demand as is referred to in that subsection, he is guilty of an offence[1].
[Road Traffic Act 1988, s 154.]

---

1. For penalty see the Road Traffic Offenders Act 1988, Sch 2, post.

4–1582   155. Deposits.

4–1583   156. Power to require evidence of insurance or security on application for vehicle excise licence[1].

---

1. See the Motor Vehicles (Third Party Risks) Regulations 1972, reg 9 in this PART, post.

4–1584   157. Payment for hospital treatment of traffic casualties.

4–1585   158. Payment for emergency treatment of traffic casualties.

4–1586   159.   Supplementary provisions as to payments for treatment.

4–1587   160.   Regulations[1].

---

1. See the Motor Vehicles (Third Party Risks) Regulations 1972, in this PART, post. The Motor Vehicles (International Motor Insurance Card) Regulations 1971, SI 1971/792, as amended by SI 1977/895 and the Motor Vehicles (Third Party Risks Deposits) Regulations 1992, SI 1992/1284, have also been made.

4–1588   **161. Interpretation.**   (1) In this Part of this Act—

"hospital" means any institution which provides medical or surgical treatment for in-patients, other than—

     (*a*)   a health service hospital within the meaning of the National Health Service Act 1977 or the National Health Service (Scotland) Act 1978,

     (*b*)   one which is a military hospital for the purposes of section 15 of the Road Traffic (NHS Charges) Act 1999,* or

     (*c*)   any institution carried on for profit,

"policy of insurers" includes a covering note,

"salvage" means the preservation of a vessel which is wrecked, stranded or in distress, or the lives of persons belonging to, or the cargo or apparel of, such a vessel, and

"under the owner's control" means, in relation to a vehicle, that it is being driven by the owner or by a servant of the owner in the course of his employment or is otherwise subject to the control of the owner.

(2) In any provisions of this Part of this Act relating to the surrender, or the loss or destruction, of a certificate of insurance or certificate of security, references to such a certificate—

     (*a*)   shall, in relation to policies or securities under which more than one certificate is issued, be construed as references to all certificates, and

     (*b*)   shall, where any copy has been issued of any certificate, be construed as including a reference to that copy.

(3) In this Part of this Act, any reference to an accident includes a reference to two or more causally related accidents.
[Road Traffic Act 1988, s 161 as amended by the National Health Service and Community Care Act 1990, Sch 9 and the Road Traffic (NHS Charges) Act 1999, s 18(3).]

---

*Repealed by the Health and Social Care (Community Health and Standards) Act 2003, Sch 14, from a date to be appointed.

4–1589   **162. Index to Part VI.**   The expressions listed in the left-hand column below are respectively defined or (as the case may be) fall to be construed in accordance with the provisions of this Part of his Act listed in the right-hand column in relation to those expressions.

Expression	*Relevant provision*
Accident	Section 161(3)
Authorised insurer	Section 145(2)
Certificate of insurance	Sections 147(1) and 161(2)
Certificate of security	Sections 147(2) and 161(2)
Hospital	Section 161(1)
Policy of insurance	Section 161(1)
Prescribed	Section 160(1)
Regulations	Section 160(1)
Salvage	Section 161(1)
Under the owner's control	Section 161(1)

[Road Traffic Act 1988, s 162, as amended by SI 2001/3649.]

PART VII[1]
MISCELLANEOUS AND GENERAL
Powers of constables and other authorised persons

4–1590   **162A. Approved test assistants.**   Secretary of State may make regulations permitting a person to be accompanied by an approved person to a specified test for the purpose, for example, in circumstances in which the person is likely to have difficulty in hearing, understanding or responding to instructions or the course of the relevant test without assistance.

163. Power of police to stop vehicles.   (1) A person driving[2] a mechanically propelled vehicle on a road must stop the vehicle on being required[3] to do so by a constable in uniform or a traffic officer*.

(2) A person driving a cycle on a road must stop the cycle on being required[3] to do so by a constable in uniform or a traffic officer*.

(3) If a person fails to comply with this section he is guilty of an offence[4].

Repealed(4) Repealed.
[Road Traffic Act 1988, s 163 amended by the Road Traffic Act 1991, Sch 4, the Police Reform Act 2002, s 49(1),the Traffic Management Act 2004, s 6 and the Serious Organised Crime and Police Act 2005, Sch 7.]

---

*References to "traffic officer" in force in Wales from a date to be appointed.
1. Part II contains ss 163–197.
2. See Preliminary Note to this title for "driving".
3. There is no power to detain a stationary vehicle (*R v Waterfield* [1964] 1 QB 164, [1963] 3 All ER 659, 128 JP 48; but the power to stop a vehicle is available provided the constable is acting *bona fide* and not capriciously (*Beard v Wood* [1980] RTR 454). A driver is under a duty to keep the vehicle at a standstill whilst a constable has a reasonable opportunity of exercising his powers, and this may include telling the driver his suspicions that a vehicle had been stolen and to arrest him and thus to detain the vehicle against the driver's will (*Lodwick v Sanders* [1985] 1 All ER 577, [1985] 1 WLR 382).
4. For punishment see the Road Traffic Offenders Act 1988 Sch 2 and notes thereto, post. Sections 11 and 12(1) thereof (evidence by certificate) apply.

4-1591   164. Power of constables to require production of driving licence and in certain cases statement of date of birth.   (1) Any of the following persons—

(*a*)   a person driving[1] a motor vehicle on a road,

(*b*)   a person whom a constable[2] or vehicle examiner has reasonable cause to believe to have been the driver of a motor vehicle at a time when an accident occurred owing to its presence on a road,

(*c*)   a person whom a constable[2] or vehicle examiner has reasonable cause to believe to have committed an offence in relation to the use of a motor vehicle on a road, or

(*d*)   a person—

   (i)   who supervises the holder of a provisional licence while the holder is driving a motor vehicle on a road, or

   (ii)   whom a constable[2] or vehicle examiner has reasonable cause to believe was supervising the holder of a provisional licence while driving, at a time when an accident occurred owing to the presence of the vehicle on a road or at a time when an offence is suspected of having been committed by the holder of the provisional licence in relation to the use of the vehicle on a road,

must, on being so required by a constable[2] or vehicle examiner, produce his licence and its counterpart for examination, so as to enable the constable or vehicle examiner to ascertain the name and address of the holder of the licence, the date of issue, and the authority by which they were issued.

(2)   A person required by a constable under subsection (1) above to produce his licence must in prescribed[3] circumstances, on being so required by the constable, state his date of birth.

(3)   If—

(*a*)   the Secretary of State has**

   (i)   revoked a licence under section 92, 93 or 99 of this Act, or

   (ii)   revoked or suspended a large goods vehicle driver's licence or a passenger carrying vehicle driver's licence under section 115 of this Act, or

   (iii)   served notice requiring the delivery of a licence to him in pursuance of section 99C, 109B or 115A of this Act, and

(*b*)   the holder of the licence fails to deliver it and its counterpart to the Secretary of State or the traffic commissioner as the case may be in pursuance of section 92, 93, 99, 99C, 109B, 115A or 118 or section 63 of the Crime (International Co-operation) Act 2003 (as the case may be),

a constable or vehicle examiner may require him to produce the licence and its counterpart, and upon their being produced may seize them and deliver them to the Secretary of State.*

(4)   Where a constable[4] has reasonable cause to believe that the holder of a licence, or any other person, has knowingly made a false statement for the purpose of obtaining the grant of the licence, the constable may require the holder of the licence to produce it and its counterpart to him.

(4A)   Where a constable to whom a provisional licence has been produced by a person driving a motor bicycle has reasonable cause to believe that the holder was not driving it as part of the training being provided on a training course for motor cyclists, the constable may require him to produce the prescribed certificate of completion of a training course for motor cyclists.***

(5)   Where a person has been required under section 26 or 27 of the Road Traffic Offenders Act 1988, section 40B of the Child Support Act 1991, section 40 of the Crime (Sentences) Act 1997****, section 146 or 147 of the Powers of Criminal Courts (Sentencing) Act 2000 or section 223A or 436A of the Criminal Procedure (Scotland) Act 1975 to produce a licence and its counterpart to the court and fails to do so, a constable may require him to produce them and, upon their being produced, may seize them and deliver them to the court.

(6)   If a person required under the preceding provisions of this section to produce a licence and its counterpart or state his date of birth or to produce his certificate of completion of a training course for motor cyclists*** fails to do so he is, subject to subsections (7) to (8A) below, guilty of an offence[5].

(7)   Subsection (6) above does not apply where a person required on any occasion under the preceding provisions of this section to produce a licence and its counterpart—

(a) produces on that occasion a current receipt for the licence and its counterpart issued under section 56 of the Road Traffic Offenders Act 1988 and, if required to do so, produces the licence and its counterpart in person immediately on their return at a police station that was specified on that occasion, or

(b) within seven days after that occasion produces such a receipt in person at a police station that was specified by him on that occasion and, if required to do so, produces the licence and its counterpart in person immediately on their return at that police station.

(8) In proceedings against any person for the offence of failing to produce a licence and its counterpart it shall be a defence for him show that—

(a) within seven days after the production of his licence and its counterpart was required he produced them in person at a police station that was specified by him at the time their production was required, or

(b) he produced them in person there as soon as was reasonably practicable, or

(c) it was not reasonably practicable for him to produce them there before the day on which the proceedings were commenced,

and for the purposes of this subsection the laying of the information or, in Scotland, the service of the complaint on the accused shall be treated as the commencement of the proceedings.

(8A) Subsection (8) above shall apply in relation to a certificate of completion of a training course for motor cyclists*** as it applies in relation to a licence.

(9) Where in accordance with this section a person has stated his date of birth to a constable, the Secretary of State may serve on that person a notice in writing requiring him to provide the Secretary of State—

(a) with such evidence in that person's possession or obtainable by him as the Secretary of State may specify for the purpose of verifying that date, and

(b) if his name differs from his name at the time of his birth, with a statement in writing specifying his name at that time,

and a person who knowingly fails to comply with a notice under this subsection is guilty of an offence[5].

(10) A notice authorised to be served on any person by subsection (9) above may be served on him by delivering it to him or by leaving it at his proper address or by sending it to him by post; and for the purposes of this subsection and section 7 of the Interpretation Act 1978 in its application to this subsection the proper address of any person shall be his latest address as known to the person giving the notice.

(11) In this section—

"licence" means a licence under Part III of this Act, a Northern Ireland licence or a Community licence,

"vehicle examiner" means an examiner appointed under section 66A of this Act:

and "Community licence", "counterpart", "a Northern Ireland licence", "provisional licence", "training course for motor cyclists" and, in relation to such a course, "the prescribed certificate of completion"** have the same meanings as in Part III of this Act.*

[Road Traffic Act 1988, s 164 amended by SI 1990/144, the Road Traffic (Driver Licensing and Information Systems) Act 1989, Sch 3, the Road Traffic Act 1991, Schs 4 and 8, SI 1996/1974, SI 1998/1420, the Powers of Criminal Courts (Sentencing) Act 2000, Sch 9 and the Crime (International Co-operation) Act 2003, Sch 5.]

---

*Section 164 is reproduced as prospectively amended by the Child Support, Pensions and Social Security Act 2000, s 16, when in force.
**Amended by the Crime (International Co-operation) Act 2003, Sch 5, from a date to be appointed.
***Substituted by the Transport Act 2000, Sch 29 from a date to be appointed.
****Words substituted by the Criminal Justice Act 2003, Sch 32 from a date to be appointed.
1. For notes on "driving" see Headnote to this title.
2. The reference to a constable in sub-ss (1) and (4) shall include references to a traffic warden in the limited circumstances specified in art 3(4) of the Functions of Traffic Wardens Order 1970, in this PART, post.
3. See the Motor Vehicles (Driving Licences) Regulations 1999 in this PART, post.
4. In this subsection "constable" does not appear to include a traffic warden.
5. For punishment see the Road Traffic Offenders Act 1988 Sch 2 and notes thereto, post. Sections 11 and 12(1) thereof (evidence by certificate) apply to s 164(6).

4–1592 **165. Power of constables to obtain names and addresses of drivers and others, and to require production of evidence of insurance or security and test certificates.** (1) Any of the following persons—

(a) a person driving a motor vehicle (other than an invalid carriage) on a road, or

(b) a person whom a constable[1] or vehicle examiner has reasonable cause to believe have been the driver of a motor vehicle (other than an invalid carriage) at a time when an accident occurred owing to its presence on a road or other public place, or

(c) a person whom a constable[1] or vehicle examiner has reasonable cause to believe to have committed an offence in relation to the use on a road of a motor vehicle (other than an invalid carriage),

must, on being so required by a constable[1] or vehicle examiner, give his name and address and the name and address of the owner of the vehicle and produce the following documents for examination.

(2) Those documents are—

(a) the relevant certificate of insurance[2] or certificate of security (within the meaning of Part VI of this Act), or such other evidence that the vehicle is not or was not being driven in contravention of section 143 of this Act as may be prescribed by regulations[3] made by the Secretary of State,

(b) in relation to a vehicle to which section 47 of this Act[4] applies, a test certificate issued in respect of the vehicle as mentioned in subsection (1) of that section, and

(c) in relation to a goods vehicle the use of which on a road without a plating certificate or goods vehicle test certificate is an offence under section 53(1) or (2) of this Act, any such certificate issued in respect of that vehicle or any trailer drawn by it.

(3) Subject to subsection (4) below, a person who fails to comply with a requirement under subsection (1) above is guilty of an offence[5].

(4) A person shall not be convicted of an offence under subsection (3) above by reason only of failure to produce any certificate or other evidence in proceedings against him for the offence he shows that—

(a) within seven days after the date on which the production of the certificate or other evidence was required it was produced[6] at a police station that was specified by him at the time when its production was required, or

(b) it was produced there as soon as was reasonably practicable, or

(c) it was not reasonably practicable for it to be produced there before the day on which the proceedings were commenced,

and for the purposes of this subsection the laying of the information or, in Scotland, the service of the complaint on the accused shall be treated as the commencement of the proceedings.

(5) A person—

(a) who supervises the holder of a provisional licence granted under Part III of this Act while the holder is driving on a road a motor vehicle (other than an invalid carriage), or

(b) whom a constable or vehicle examiner has reasonable cause to believe was supervising the holder of such a licence while driving, at a time when an accident occurred owing to the presence of the vehicle on a road or at a time when an offence is suspected of having been committed by the holder of the provisional licence in relation to the use of the vehicle on a road,

must, on being so required by a constable, give his name and address and the name and address of the owner of the vehicle.

(6) A person who fails to comply with a requirement under subsection (5) above is guilty of an offence[5].

(7) In this section "owner", in relation to a vehicle which is the subject of a hiring agreement, includes each party to the agreement and "vehicle examiner" means an examiner appointed under s 66A of this Act.

[Road Traffic Act 1988, s 165 as amended by the Road Traffic (Driver Licensing and Information Systems) Act 1989, Sch 3, the Road Traffic Act 1991, Schs 4 and 8 and SI 2000/726.]

---

1. These references to a police constable shall, so far as it applies to the furnishing of names and addresses, include references to a traffic warden if the warden has reasonable cause to believe that an offence specified in art 3(3) of the Functions of Traffic Wardens Order 1970, has been committed. The Order is set out in this PART, post.

2. An international motor insurance card issued in accordance with the Motor Vehicles (International Motor Insurance Card) Regulations 1971 (SI 1971/792), has effect as though it was a certificate of insurance issued for the purposes of this Act (reg 6(1)).

3. See the Motor Vehicles (Third Party Risks) Regulations 1972, reg 7, in this PART, post.

4. This provision of the section applies to a person in connection with a vehicle to which s 44 applies, notwithstanding that he or the driver is or was at any material time in the public service of the Crown (s 183(7), post).

5. For punishment see the Road Traffic Offenders Act 1988 Sch 2 and notes thereto, post. Sections 11 and 12(1) thereof (evidence by certificate) apply to s 165(3) and s 11 to s 165(6).

6. Not necessarily in person: contrast s 164(8), ante.

4–1592A 165A. Power to seize vehicles driven without licence or insurance. (1) Subsection (5) applies if any of the following conditions is satisfied.

(2) The first condition is that—

(a) a constable in uniform requires, under section 164, a person to produce his licence and its counterpart for examination,

(b) the person fails to produce them, and

(c) the constable has reasonable grounds for believing that a motor vehicle is or was being driven by the person in contravention of section 87(1).

(3) The second condition is that—

(a) a constable in uniform requires, under section 165, a person to produce evidence that a motor vehicle is not or was not being driven in contravention of section 143,

(b) the person fails to produce such evidence, and

(c) the constable has reasonable grounds for believing that the vehicle is or was being so driven.

(4) The third condition is that—

(a) a constable in uniform requires, under section 163, a person driving a motor vehicle to stop the vehicle,

(b) the person fails to stop the vehicle, or to stop the vehicle long enough, for the constable to make such lawful enquiries as he considers appropriate, and

(c) the constable has reasonable grounds for believing that the vehicle is or was being driven in contravention of section 87(1) or 143.

(5) Where this subsection applies, the constable may—

(a) seize the vehicle in accordance with subsections (6) and (7) and remove it;

(b) enter, for the purpose of exercising a power falling within paragraph (a), any premises (other than a private dwelling house) on which he has reasonable grounds for believing the vehicle to be;

(c) use reasonable force, if necessary, in the exercise of any power conferred by paragraph (a) or (b).

(6) Before seizing the motor vehicle, the constable must warn the person by whom it appears that the vehicle is or was being driven in contravention of section 87(1) or 143 that he will seize it—

(a) in a section 87(1) case, if the person does not produce his licence and its counterpart immediately;

(b) in a section 143 case, if the person does not provide him immediately with evidence that the vehicle is not or was not being driven in contravention of that section.

But the constable is not required to give such a warning if the circumstances make it impracticable for him to do so.

(7) If the constable is unable to seize the vehicle immediately because the person driving the vehicle has failed to stop as requested or has driven off, he may seize it at any time within the period of 24 hours beginning with the time at which the condition in question is first satisfied.

(8) The powers conferred on a constable by this section are exercisable only at a time when regulations under section 165B are in force.

(9) In this section—

(a) a reference to a motor vehicle does not include an invalid carriage;

(b) a reference to evidence that a motor vehicle is not or was not being driven in contravention of section 143 is a reference to a document or other evidence within section 165(2)(a);

(c) "counterpart" and "licence" have the same meanings as in section 164;

(d) "private dwelling house" does not include any garage or other structure occupied with the dwelling house, or any land appurtenant to the dwelling house.

[Road Traffic Act 1988, s 165A as inserted by the Serious Organised Crime and Police Act 2005, s 152.]

4–1592B   165B. Retention etc of vehicles seized under section 165A.   (1) The Secretary of State may by regulations[1] make provision as to—

(a) the removal and retention of motor vehicles seized under section 165A; and

(b) the release or disposal of such motor vehicles.

(2) Regulations under subsection (1) may, in particular, make provision—

(a) for the giving of notice of the seizure of a motor vehicle under section 165A to a person who is the registered keeper, the owner or the driver of that vehicle;

(b) for the procedure by which a person who claims to be the registered keeper or the owner of a motor vehicle seized under section 165A may seek to have it released;

(c) for requiring the payment, by the registered keeper, owner or driver of the vehicle, of fees, charges or costs in relation to the removal and retention of such a motor vehicle and to any application for its release;

(d) as to the circumstances in which a motor vehicle seized under section 165A may be disposed of;

(e) as to the destination—

(i) of any fees or charges payable in accordance with the regulations;

(ii) of the proceeds (if any) arising from the disposal of a motor vehicle seized under section 165A;

(f) for the delivery to a local authority, in circumstances prescribed by or determined in accordance with the regulations, of any motor vehicle seized under section 165A.

(3) Regulations under subsection (1) must provide that a person who would otherwise be liable to pay any fee or charge under the regulations is not liable to pay it if—

(a) he was not driving the motor vehicle at the time in question, and

(b) he did not know that the vehicle was being driven at that time, had not consented to its being driven and could not, by the taking of reasonable steps, have prevented it from being driven.

(4) Regulations under subsection (1) may make different provision for different cases.

(5) In this section—

"local authority"—

(a) in relation to England, means—

(i) a county council,

(ii) the council of a district comprised in an area for which there is no county council,

(iii) a London borough council,

(iv) the Common Council of the City of London, or

(v) Transport for London;

    (*b*) in relation to Wales, means the council of a county or county borough; and

    (*c*) in relation to Scotland, means a council constituted under section 2 of the Local Government etc (Scotland) Act 1994;

"registered keeper", in relation to a motor vehicle, means the person in whose name the vehicle is registered under the Vehicle Excise and Registration Act 1994.

[Road Traffic Act 1988, s 165B as inserted by the Serious Organised Crime and Police Act 2005, s 152.]

---

1. The Road Traffic Act 1988 (Retention and Disposal of Seized Motor Vehicles) Regulations 2005, SI 2005/1606 have been made.

4–1593 166. Powers of certain officers as respects goods vehicles and passenger-carrying vehicles. A person authorised for the purpose by a traffic commissioner appointed under the Public Passenger Vehicles Act 1981 may, on production if so required of his authority, exercise in the case of goods vehicles or passenger-carrying vehicles of any prescribed class all such powers as are, under section 164(1) or (3) or 165 of this Act, exercisable by a constable.

[Road Traffic Act 1988, s 166 as substituted by the Road Traffic (Driver Licensing and Information Systems) Act 1989, Sch 3 and amended by the Road Traffic Act 1991, Sch 4.]

Duty to give name and address

4–1594 168. Failure to give, or giving false, name and address in case of reckless or careless or inconsiderate driving or cycling. Any of the following persons—

    (*a*) the driver of a mechanically propelled vehicle who is alleged to have committed an offence under section 2 or 3 of this Act, or

    (*b*) the rider of a cycle who is alleged to have committed an offence under section 28 or 29 of this Act,

who refuses, on being so required by any person having reasonable ground for so requiring, to give his name or address, or gives a false name or address, is guilty of an offence[1].

[Road Traffic Act 1988, s 168 amended by the Road Traffic Act 1991, Sch 4.]

---

1. For penalty see the Road Traffic Offenders Act 1988 Sch 2. Sections 11 and 12(1) of the Road Traffic Offenders Act 1988 (evidence by certificate etc) apply.

4–1595 169. Pedestrian contravening constable's direction to stop to give name and address. A constable[1] may require a person committing an offence under section 37 of this Act to give his name and address, and if that person fails to do so he is guilty of an offence[2].

[Road Traffic Act 1988, s 169.]

---

1. Or a traffic warden (Functions of Traffic Wardens Order 1970 in this PART, post.
2. For penalty see the Road Traffic Offenders Act 1988 Sch 2.

Duties in case of accident

4–1596 170. Duty of driver to stop, report accident and give information or documents.

(1) This section applies in a case where, owing to the presence[1] of a mechanically propelled vehicle on a road, or other public place an accident occurs by which—

    (*a*) personal injury is caused to a person other than the driver[2] of that mechanically propelled vehicle, or

    (*b*) damage is caused—

        (i) to a vehicle[3] other than that mechanically propelled vehicle or a trailer drawn by that mechanically propelled vehicle, or

        (ii) to an animal other than an animal in or on that mechanically propelled vehicle or a trailer drawn by that mechanically propelled vehicle, or

        (iii) to any other property constructed on, fixed to, growing in or otherwise forming part of the land on which the road or place in question is situated or land adjacent to such land.

(2) The driver of the mechanically propelled vehicle must stop[4] and, if required to do so by any person having reasonable grounds[5] for so requiring, give his name and address[6] and also the name and address of the owner and the identification marks of the vehicle.

(3) If for any reason the driver of the mechanically propelled vehicle does not give his name and address[7] under subsection (2) above, he must report[8] the accident.

(4) A person who fails to comply with subsection (2) or (3) above is guilty of an offence[9].

(5) If, in a case where this section applies by virtue of subsection (1)(a) above, the driver of a motor vehicle does not at the time of the accident produce such a certificate of insurance or security, or other evidence, as is mentioned in section 165(2) of this Act—

    (*a*) to a constable, or

    (*b*) to some person who, having reasonable grounds for so doing, has required him to produce it,

the driver must report the accident and produce such a certificate or other evidence.

This subsection does not apply to the driver of an invalid carriage.

(6) To comply with a duty under this section to report an accident or to produce such a certificate of insurance or security, or other evidence, as is mentioned in section 165(2)(a) of this Act, the driver—

(a) must do so at a police station or to a constable, and

(b) must do so as soon as is reasonably practicable and, in any case, within twenty-four hours of the occurrence of the accident.

(7) A person who fails to comply with a duty under subsection (5) above is guilty of an offence[9], but he shall not be convicted by reason only of a failure to produce a certificate or other evidence if, within seven days after the occurrence of the accident, the certificate or other evidence is produced at a police station that was specified by him at the time when the accident was reported.

(8) In this section "animal" means horse, cattle, ass, mule, sheep, pig, goat or dog.

[Road Traffic Act 1988, s 170 amended by the Road Traffic Act 1991, Sch 4 and SI 2000/726.]

---

1. There must be a direct cause or connection between the motor vehicle and the occurrence of the accident (*Quelch v Phipps* [1955] 2 QB 107, [1955] 2 All ER 302, 119 JP 430).

2. See Preliminary Note to this title for "driver". For the purposes of s 170 the *driver* of a vehicle need not be *driving* the vehicle at the material time. Accordingly, a driver who stopped his vehicle, leaving it briefly with the hazard lights switched on to post a letter, did not cease to be the driver within the meaning of s 170(2) when before returning to the vehicle it rolled down a hill and collided with a brick wall (*Cawthorn v DPP* [2000] RTR 45, *sub nom Cawthorn v Newcastle upon Tyne Crown Court*, 164 JP 527, DC). Sections 11 and 12(1) of the Road Traffic Offenders Act 1988 (evidence by certificate) apply.

3. A bicycle is a vehicle (*Ellis v Nott-Bower* (1896) 60 JP 760).

4. The obligation to stop arises immediately the accident occurs. Accordingly, if the driver does not stop almost immediately as soon as he can safely and conveniently do so, he will fail to comply with the requirements of s 170(2) (*Hallinan v DPP* [1998] 163 JP 651, Crim LR 754). The obligation to stop applies where the only injury sustained as a result of the accident is to a passenger on board a bus (*Hallinan v DPP* [1998] 163 JP 651, Crim LR 754). After stopping the driver must personally remain where he has stopped for such a period of time as in the prevailing circumstances will enable him, if required, to give the information mentioned in what is now sub-s (2) (*Lee v Knapp* [1966] 3 All ER 961, 131 JP 110; *Ward v Rawson* [1978] RTR 498); but the driver is not obliged to go and seek out persons who may have a right to such information (*Mutton v Bates* (1983) 147 JP 459). The stopping and giving particulars (if required) is obligatory even if he subsequently complies with sub-s (3) (*Dawson v Winter* (1932) 149 LT 18; *North v Gerrish* (1959) 123 JP 313; *DPP v Bennett* [1993] 163 JP 175, [1993] Crim LR 71). Two offences are created by sub-ss (2) and (3) (*Roper v Sullivan* [1978] RTR 181, [1978] Crim LR 233), confirmed by *R v Sheffield City Justices, ex p Stubbs* (1987) unreported. For a consideration of circumstances whereby an offence of aiding and abetting a failure to stop after an accident may be committed by the supervisor of a learner driver, see *Bentley v Mullen* [1986] RTR 7.

5. A person does not cease to have reasonable grounds for the required particulars simply because he knows the driver involved (*R v Crown Court at Kingston upon Thames, ex p Scarll* (1989) Times, 28 April).

6. An address is where a person can be addressed and, so far as s 170 is concerned, to enable the purposes of the section to be satisfied and is not restricted to a person's residential address (*DPP v McCarthy* (1998) 163 JP 585, [1999] RTR 323, DC).

7. If he has given his name and address and other particulars to the other driver he need not report to the police under this subsection (*Green v Dunn* [1953] 1 All ER 550). The onus is on the prosecution to establish a *prima facie* case that the accident has occurred whereby a statutory duty was upon the defendant to stop and that he had failed to do so: if the defendant then satisfies the court (and the evidential burden is upon him) that he was unaware that an accident had occurred, he is entitled to be acquitted; *Harding v Price* [1948] 1 KB 695, [1948] 1 All ER 283, 112 JP 189, an appeal from a magistrates' court which had found as a fact that the driver of a "mechanical horse" to which a large trailer was attached was not aware that the trailer had collided with a stationary motor car. In this case Lord GODDARD CJ, commented, "It must not be thought that this decision provides an easy defence to motorists who fail to report an accident".

8. The obligation to report is not confined to where the driver has been required to give his name and address, and has not done so, but extends to every case where he has not, in fact, given his name and address, eg, where no one is present at the scene of the accident (*Peek v Towle* [1945] KB 458, [1945] 2 All ER 611, 109 JP 160). It makes no difference for this purpose that the accident was observed by a police officer but he made no request for information; the obligation to report still exists: *DPP v Hay* [2005] EWHC Admin 1395, (2005) 169 JP 429, [2006] RTR 3. If the driver satisfies the court that he was unaware that an accident had happened, he is entitled to be acquitted (*Harding v Price* [1948] 1 KB 695, [1948] 1 All ER 283, 112 JP 189); see note 7, supra. A driver who is not aware of an accident at the time it occurred, but subsequently becomes aware of it, has a duty to report the accident provided that he becomes so aware within 24 hours of the occurrence of the accident (*DPP v Drury* (1988) 153 JP 417, [1989] RTR 165, DC). It was decided in a Scottish case that the prosecution are not required to prove that the driver did not give his name and address to an interested person within twenty-four hours, if he has not done so at the time of the accident (*Wood v Maclean* 1947 SLT 22). In *Wisdom v Macdonald* [1983] RTR 186, [1982] Crim LR 758, on the facts of that case, it was held that reporting the accident by telephone did not avoid commission of an offence. When reporting an accident the driver is obliged to make clear to the police officer, whether at a police station or elsewhere, that the report is being made for the purposes of the obligation to report an accident, to identify the accident, giving the place, time, date, and to be prepared to give his name and address, and those of the owner of the vehicle and its identification marks; see *Wisdom v Macdonald* supra.

9. For punishment see the Road Traffic Offenders Act 1988 Sch 2, post, and notes thereto.

Other duties to give information or documents

4–1597 **171. Duty of owner of motor vehicle to give information for verifying compliance with requirement of compulsory insurance or security.** (1) For the purpose of determining whether a motor vehicle was or was not being driven in contravention of section 143 of this Act on any occasion when the driver was required under section 165(1) or 170 of this Act to produce such a certificate of insurance or security, or other evidence, as is mentioned in section 165(2)(a) of this Act, the owner of the vehicle must give such information as he may be required, by or on behalf of a chief officer of police, to give.

(2) A person who fails to comply with the requirement of subsection (1) above is guilty of an offence[1].

(3) In this section "owner", in relation to a vehicle which is the subject of a hiring agreement, includes each party to the agreement.
[Road Traffic Act 1988, s 171.]

---

1. For penalty see the Road Traffic Offenders Act 1988, Sch 2. Sections 11 and 12(1) of the Traffic Offenders Act 1988 (evidence by certificate) apply.

4–1598   172. Duty to give information as to identity of driver etc in certain circumstances.

(1) This section applies—

(a) to any offence under the preceding provisions of this Act except—

    (i) an offence under Part V, or

    (ii) an offence under section 13, 16, 51(2), 61(4), 67(9), 68(4), 96 or 120,

and to an offence under section 178 of this Act,

(b) to any offence under sections 25, 26 or 27 of the Road Traffic Offenders Act 1988,

(c) to any offence against any other enactment relating to the use of vehicles on roads, and

(d) to manslaughter, or in Scotland culpable homicide, by the driver of a motor vehicle.

(2) Where the driver of a vehicle is alleged[1] to be guilty of an offence to which this section applies[2]—

(a) the person keeping the vehicle shall give such information as to the identity of the driver as he may be required to give by or on behalf of a chief officer of police[3], and

(b) any other person[4] shall if required as stated above give any information which it is in his power to give and may lead to identification of the driver[5].

(3) Subject to the following provisions, a person who fails to comply with a requirement under subsection (2) above shall be guilty of an offence[6].

(4) A person shall not be guilty of an offence by virtue of paragraph (a) of subsection (2) above if he shows that he did not know and could not with reasonable diligence have ascertained who the driver of the vehicle was.

(5) Where a body corporate is guilty of an offence under this section and the offence is proved to have been committed with the consent or connivance of, or to be attributable to neglect on the part of, a director, manager, secretary or other similar officer of the body corporate, or a person who was purporting to act in any such capacity, he, as well as the body corporate, is guilty of that offence and liable to be proceeded against and punished accordingly.

(6) Where the alleged offender is a body corporate, or in Scotland a partnership or an unincorporated association, or the proceedings are brought against him by virtue of subsection (5) above or subsection (11) below, subsection (4) above shall not apply unless, in addition to the matters there mentioned, the alleged offender shows that no record was kept of the persons who drove the vehicle and that the failure to keep a record was reasonable.

(7) A requirement under subsection (2) may be made by written notice served by post; and where it is so made—

(a) it shall have effect as a requirement to give the information within the period of 28 days beginning with the day on which the notice is served, and

(b) the person on whom the notice is served shall not be guilty of an offence under this section if he shows either that he gave the information as soon as reasonably practicable after the end of that period or that it has not been reasonably practicable for him to give it.

(8) Where the person on whom a notice under subsection (7) above is to be served is a body corporate, the notice is duly served if it is served on the secretary or clerk of that body.

(9) For the purposes of section 7 of the Interpretation Act 1978 as it applies for the purposes of this section the proper address of any person in relation to the service on him of a notice under subsection (7) above is—

(a) in the case of the secretary or clerk of a body corporate, that of the registered or principal office of that body or (if the body corporate is the registered keeper of the vehicle concerned) the registered address, and

(b) in any other case, his last known address at the time of service.

(10) In this section—

"registered address", in relation to the registered keeper of a vehicle, means the address recorded in the record kept under the Vehicle Excise and Registration Act 1994 with respect to that vehicle as being that person's address, and

"registered keeper", in relation to a vehicle, means the person in whose name the vehicle is registered under that Act;

and references to the driver of a vehicle include references to the rider of a cycle.

(11) Scotland.
[Road Traffic Act 1988, s 172, as substituted by the Road Traffic Act 1991, s 21 amended by the Vehicle Excise and Registration Act 1994, Sch 3 and the Statute Law (Repeals) Act 2004.]

---

1. The leading of evidence by the prosecution of an admission obtained under s 172(2)(a) does not infringe a defendant's right to a fair trial under art 6 of the European Convention on Human Rights. While the *overall* fairness of a trial cannot be comprised otherwise article 6 of the European Convention on Human Rights is infringed, the constituent

rights comprised within art 6 are not themselves absolute and s 172 forms part of a regulatory regime imposed because driving cars has the potential to cause grave injury. Section 172 represents a proportionate legislative response to the problem of maintaining road safety. The answer to a question put under s 172 does not itself incriminate a suspect, since it is not without more an offence to drive a car and the section does not sanction prolonged questioning about the facts alleged to give rise to criminal offences. (*Brown v Stott (Procurator Fiscal, Dunfermline)* [2003] 1 AC 681,[2001] 2 All ER 97, sub nom *Brown v Procurator Fiscal, Dunfermline* [2001] RTR 121, PC).

2. The police are not bound to specify the nature of the alleged offence when they require information from an owner or other person (*Pulton v Leader* [1949] 2 All ER 747, 113 JP 637). For admissibility in evidence of a statement in writing, purporting to be signed by the accused, that the accused was the driver, etc, of a particular vehicle on the particular occasion to which the information relates, see the Road Traffic Offenders Act 1988 s 12, post. This section applies to tramcars and trolley vehicles operated under statutory powers (Sch 4, post).

3. Where there is a challenge to the validity of a request, provided justices exercise great care, test the notice and have regard to its authenticity, in the absence of any evidence to doubt that the document came into existence other than in an official way, they may rely on its appearance, its official nature and whether or not it could have other uses (*Pamplin v Gorman* [1980] RTR 54, [1980] Crim LR 52. Provided the justices are satisfied that the sender of the notice was acting 'on behalf of a chief officer of police', it is not necessary that the specially authorised person should sign every notice that is issued and justices were upheld in finding that there was a valid request where the computerised notice emanated from the central ticket office and was sent from a person 'for the Chief Constable' and was not signed (*Arnold v DPP* [1999] RTR 99).There should be annexed to s 9 statements a copy of the notice of intended prosecution to identify the alleged offence by the driver and a copy of the requirement to provide details so that it is clear that the latter has been made by or on behalf of the chief officer of police: *Mohindra v DPP* [2004] Admin 490, (2004) 168 JP 448, [2005] RTR 7.

4. This expression includes the driver himself (*Bingham v Bruce* [1962] 1 All ER 136, 126 JP 81); and a doctor who, under this section, may be required to give information about a patient which may lead to the identification of the driver (*Hunter v Mann* [1974] QB 767, [1974] 2 All ER 414, 138 JP 473).

5. It is implicit in the scheme that where the requirement is made by a written notice sent pursuant to s 172(7), and that notice specifies how the information is to be given and the manner that it specifies is reasonable, the information must be given in that way (*DPP v Broomfield* [2002] EWHC 1962 (Admin), (2002) 166 JP 736, [2003] RTR 108).

It was held in *Mawdesley v Chief Constable of Cheshire Constabulary, Yorke v DPP* [2003] EWHC 1586 (Admin), [2004] 1 All ER 58, [2004] 1 WLR 1035, [2004] RTR 13 that the insertion of a name in block capitals on the form, but with the space for the signature left blank, did not amount to a statement in writing purporting to be signed by the accused such as to be admissible under s 12 of the Road Traffic Offenders Act 1988 (but an unsigned form sent in response to a s 172 requirement to name the person driving at the time of the alleged offence [though not if completed and returned by a person acting as agent for the addressee] could amount to a confession under s 82 of PACE and could be proved under s 27 of the Criminal Justice Act 1988 and could give rise to a case to answer). In *Jones v DPP* [2004] Admin 236, (2004) 168 JP 393, the defendant responded to a s 172 by returning it almost blank but enclosing a signed letter stating that he was the owner of the vehicle (one of 6 in a medical practice fleet), but could not state who was driving on the relevant occasion. This was held to be so far as it went (there remained the question of whether this made out the defence under s 172(4), infra) a proper compliance with s 172(2). Similarly, in *R (Flegg) v Southampton and New Forest Justices* [2006] EWHC 396 (Admin), 170 JP 373 where the defendant had submitted a letter in response stating that he could not be sure which of two persons had been driving but gave no further details, it was held that in so doing he was in breach of s 172(2)(*a*) as he did not give the name of the driver or information in his power which would lead to the driver's identification and to avoid conviction he had to make good a defence under s 172(4). In considering such a defence, a request calls for an accurate response and statement of reasons. The provision of an inaccurate and misleading response does not constitute compliance with the requirements of the notice.

All the above cases were considered in *Francis v DPP* [2004] EWHC Admin 591, (2004) 168 JP 492, in which *Broomfield* (supra) was followed and it was held that the chief officer of police was entitled to require the addressee of the s 172 notice to sign it.

Section 172(2) specifies separate requirements in subparas (*a*) and (*b*), but s 172(3) creates only one offence and the information need allege no more than an offence under s 172(3): *Mohindra v DPP* [2004] Admin 490, (2004) 168 JP 448, [2004] Crim LR 667, [2005] RTR 7.

Where the police have already received information from an employer in response to a notice under s 172 (2)(*a*), although the defendant is a suspect, a caution is not required and in accordance with *Brown v Stott* supra, the defendant's response is admissible against him in subsequent proceedings. No distinction is to be drawn between the powers in s 172(2)(*a*) and (*b*) (*DPP v Wilson* [2001] EWHC Admin 198, 165 JP 715, [2002] RTR 37). See also *Francis v Director of Public Prosecutions* (supra).

6. For punishment see the Road Traffic Offenders Act 1988 Sch 2 and notes thereto, post. Where an offence can be committed partly in one area and partly in another, it is sufficient that one lies within the jurisdictional area of the court trying it. The offence of failing to provide information as to the identity of a driver of a vehicle allegedly involved in the commission of a traffic offence is committed at the point where the information was intended to be received, semble it can also be committed at the place where the defendant lives (*Kennet District Council v Young* [1999] RTR 235, (1998) 163 JP 622, DC (decided under the similarly worded provisions of s 112(4) of the Road Traffic Regulation Act 1984)).

Forgery, false statements, etc

4–1599   **173. Forgery of documents, etc.**   (1) A person who, within intent to deceive—

    (*a*)   forges, alters or uses[1] a document or other thing to which this section applies[2], or

    (*b*)   lends to, or allows to be used by, any other person a document or other thing to which this section applies, or

    (*c*)   makes or has in his possesion[3] any document or other thing so closely resembling a document or other thing to which this section applies as to be calculated to deceive[4],

is guilty of an offence[5].

    (2) This section applies to the following documents and other things—

    (*a*)   any licence under any Part of this Act or, in the case of a licence to drive, any counterpart of such a licence,

    (*aa*)   any counterpart of Northern Ireland licence or a Community licence,

    (*b*)   any test certificate, goods vehicle test certificate, plating certificate, certificate of conformity or Minister's approval certificate (within the meaning of Part II of this Act),*

    (*c*)   any certificate required as a condition of any exception prescribed under section 14 of this Act,

    (*cc*)   any seal required by regulations made under section 41 of this Act with respect to speed limiters,

(d) any plate containing particulars required to be marked on a vehicle by regulations under section 41 of this Act or containing other particulars required to be marked on a goods vehicle by sections 54 to 58 of this Act or regulations under those sections,*

(dd) any document evidencing the appointment of an examiner under section 66A of this Act,

(e) any records required to be kept by virtue of section 74 of this Act,*

(f) any document which, in pursuance of section 89(3) of this Act, is issued as evidence of the result of a test of competence to drive,

(ff) any certificate provided for by regulations under section 97(3A) of this Act relating to the completion of a training course for motor cyclists,

(g) any certificate under section 133A or any badge or certificate prescribed by regulations made by virtue of section 135 of this Act,

(h) any certificate of insurance or certificate of security under Part VI of this Act,

(j) any document produced as evidence of insurance in pursuance of Regulation 6 of the Motor Vehicles (Compulsory Insurance) (No 2) Regulations 1973,

(k) any document issued under regulations made by the Secretary of State in pursuance of his power under section 165(2)(a) of this Act to prescribe evidence which may be produced in lieu of a certificate of insurance or a certificate of security,

(l) any international road haulage permit, and

(m) a certificate of the kind referred to in section 34B(1) of the Road Traffic Offenders Act 1988.

(3) In the application of this section to England and Wales "forges" means makes a false document or other thing in order that it may be used as genuine.

(4) In this section "counterpart", "Community licence" and "Northern Ireland licence" have the same meanings as in Part III of this Act.

[Road Traffic Act 1988, s 173, amended by SI 1990/144 as amended by the Road Traffic (Driver Licensing and Information Systems) Act 1989, Sch 3, the Road Traffic Act 1991, Schs 4 and 8, the Road Traffic (Driving Instruction by Disabled Persons) Act 1993, Schedule, SI 1996/1974 and the Crime (International Co-operation) Act 2003, Sch 5.]

---

*Section 173(2)(b), (d) and (e) amended by the Transport Act 1982, s 23 as amended by the Road Traffic (Consequential Provisions) Act 1988, Sch 2, when in force.

1. A person may be convicted of "using" even if the document is a forgery and incomplete (*R v Pilditch* [1981] RTR 303, [1981] Crim LR 184). In *R v Howe* [1982] RTR 45, it was held that the production of a driving licence by the defendant and handing over of it to the police, which had nothing to do with driving a vehicle on the road, could not properly be said to be "use" for the purpose of s 173(1).

2. An offence would be committed by the use of a certificate which has ceased to be a valid certificate after the cancellation of the policy (*R v Cleghorn* [1938] 3 All ER 398).

3. See *R v Greenberg* [1942] 2 All ER 344.

4. This means "likely to deceive" and not "intended to deceive". (Cf *Re London and Globe Finance Corpn Ltd* [1903] 1 Ch 728). A pad of blank and bogus insurance certificates were held to constitute documents for the purposes of s 173(1)(c) because they so closely resembled any certificate of insurance as to be calculated, in the sense of likely to, deceive (*R v Aworinde* (1995) 159 JP 618, [1996] RTR 66, [1995] Crim LR 825).

5. For punishment see Sch 2 and notes thereto, post.

4–1610 174. False statements and withholding material information. (1) A person who knowingly makes a false statement[1] for the purpose—

(a) of obtaining the grant of a licence under any Part of this Act to himself or any other person, or

(b) of preventing the grant of any such licence, or

(c) of procuring the imposition of a condition or limitation in relation to any such licence, or

(d) of securing the entry or retention of the name of any person in the register of approved instructors maintained under Part V of this Act, or

(dd) of obtaining the grant to any person of a certificate under section 133A of this Act, or

(e) of obtaining the grant of an international road haulage permit to himself or any other person,

is guilty of an offence[3].

(2) A person who, in supplying information or producing documents for the purposes either of sections 53 to 60 and 63 of this Act or of regulations made under sections 49 to 51, 61, 62 and 66(3) of this Act—

(a) makes a statement which he knows to be false in a material particular or recklessly makes a statement which is false in a material particular, or

(b) produces, provides, sends or otherwise makes use of a document which he knows to be false in a material particular or recklessly produces, provides, sends or otherwise makes use of a document which is false in a material particular,

is guilty of an offence[3].

(3) A person who—

(a) knowingly produces false evidence for the purposes of regulations under section 66(1) of this Act, or

(b) knowingly makes a false statement in a declaration required to be made by the regulations,

is guilty of an offence[3].

(4) A person who—

(a) wilfully makes a false entry in any record required to be made or kept by regulations under section 74 of this Act, or

(b) with intent to deceive, makes use of any such entry which he knows to be false,

is guilty of an offence[3].

(5) A person who makes a false statement[2] or withholds any material information for the purpose of obtaining the issue—

(a) of a certificate of insurance or certificate of security under Part VI of this Act, or

(b) of any document issued under regulations made by the Secretary of State in pursuance of his power under section 165(2)(a) of this Act to prescribe evidence which may be produced in lieu of a certificate of insurance or a certificate of security,

is guilty of an offence[3].

[Road Traffic Act 1988, s 174 as amended by the Road Traffic (Driving Instruction by Disabled Persons) Act 1993, Sch.]

---

1. It is immaterial whether any gain or advantage would be derived as a result of the false statement (*Jones v Meatyard* [1939] 1 All ER 140).

2. The offence is absolute. A false statement need not have been made with conscious falsity, but it may be that the offence of withholding information predicates a conscious withholding by the defendant (*R v Cummerson* [1968] 2 QB 534, [1968] 2 All ER 863).

3. For punishment see the Road Traffic Offenders Act 1988, Sch 2 and notes thereto, post and s 6 thereof (time limits) also applies.

4–1611 175. Issue of false documents. If a person issues—

(a) any such document as is referred to in section 174(5)(a) or (b) of this Act, or

(b) a test certificate[1] or certificate of conformity (within the meaning of Part II of this Act),

and the document or certificate so issued is to his knowledge[2] false in a material particular, he is guilty of offence[3].★

[Road Traffic Act 1988, s 175.]

★**Section 175 is amended by the Transport Act 1982, s 24 as amended by the Road Traffic (Consequential Provisions) Act 1988, Sch 2, para 13 when in force.**

1. The prescribed form of certificate implies that the condition of a vehicle at the time of examination remains the same as at the date of issue of the certificate (*R v Evans* [1964] 3 All ER 666, 129 JP 29). See the Motor Vehicles (Tests) Regulations 1981 in this PART, post, which replace regulations clarifying questions raised in this case.

2. Knowledge in this subsection has no relation to any presumption or rules as to knowledge of law. It means that the defendant should know as a fact or have an honest opinion. It does not mean acting upon a mistaken view of the law (*Ocean Accident and Guarantee Corpn Ltd v Cole* [1932] 2 KB 100, 96 JP 191). An offence under this section is committed by a person who issues a "back-dated" test certificate (*Murphy v Griffiths* [1967] 1 All ER 424, 131 JP 204). In the case of a limited company, it is necessary to prove that the issue of the false document was committed by one who was the embodiment of the company, unless control of the company's operations in this respect has been delegated (*Essendon Engineering Co Ltd v Maile* [1982] RTR 260, [1982] Crim LR 510).

3. For penalty see the Road Traffic Offenders Act 1988, Sch 2, post. Section 6 thereof (time limits) also applies.

4–1612 176. Power to seize articles in respect of which offences under sections 173 to 175 may have been committed. (1) If a constable has reasonable cause to believe that a document produced to him—

(a) in pursuance of section 137 of this Act, or

(b) in pursuance of any of the preceding provisions of this Part of this Act,

is a document in relation to which an offence has been committed under section 173, 174 or 175 of this Act or under section 115 of the Road Traffic Regulation Act 1984, he may seize the document.

(1A) Where a licence to drive or a counterpart of any such licence or of any Northern Ireland licence or Community licence may be seized by a constable under subsection (1) above, he may also seize the counterpart, the licence to drive or the Northern Ireland licence or Community licence (as the case may be) produced with it.

(2) When a document is seized under subsection (1) above, the person from whom it was taken shall, unless—

(a) the document has been previously returned to him, or

(b) he has been previously charged with an offence under any of those sections,

be summoned before a magistrates' court or, in Scotland, the sheriff to account for his possession of the document.

(3) The court or sheriff must make such order respecting the disposal of the document and award such costs as the justice of the case may require.

(3A) An order under subsection (3) above respecting the disposal of any such licence or of a Northern Ireland licence or Community licence to drive or the counterpart of a licence may include an order respecting the disposal of any document seized under subsection (1A) above.

(4) If a constable, an examiner appointed under section 66A of this Act has reasonable cause to believe that a document or plate carried on a motor vehicle or by the driver of the vehicle is a document or plate to which this subsection applies, he may seize it.★

For the purposes of this subsection the power to seize includes power to detach from a vehicle.

(5) Subsection (4) above applies to a document or plate in relation to which an offence has been committed under sections 173, 174 or 175 of this Act in so far as they apply—

(a)   to documents evidencing the appointment of examiners under section 66A of this Act, or
(b)   to goods vehicle test certificates, plating certificates, certificates of conformity or Minister's approval certificates (within the meaning of Part II of this Act), or*
(c)   to plates containing plated particulars (within the meaning of that Part) or containing other particulars required to be marked on goods vehicles by sections 54 to 58 of this Act or regulations made under them, or
(d)   to records required to be kept by virtue of section 74 of this Act, or
(e)   to international road haulage permits.

(6) When a document or plate is seized under subsection (4) above, either driver or owner of the vehicle shall, if the document or plate is still detained and neither of them has previously been charged with an offence in relation to the document or plate under section 173, 174 or 175 of this Act, be summoned before a magistrates' court or, in Scotland, the sheriff to account for his possession of, or the presence on the vehicle of, the document or plate.

(7) The court or sheriff must make such order respecting the disposal of the document or plate and award such costs as the justice of the case may require.

(8) In this section "counterpart", "Community licence" and "Northern Ireland licence" have the same meanings as in Part III of this Act.
[Road Traffic Act 1988, s 176, amended by SI 1990/144, the Road Traffic Act 1991, Sch 4, SI 1996/1974 and the Crime (International Co-operation) Act 2003, Sch 5.]

---

*Amended by the Transport Act 1982, s 24, as amended by the Road Traffic (Consequential Provisions) Act 1988, Sch 2, para 13 when in force.

4–1613   177. Impersonation of authorised examiner, etc.   A person is guilty of an offence if, with intent to deceive, he falsely represents himself—

(a)   to be, or to be employed by, a person authorised in accordance with regulations made under section 41 of this Act with respect to the checking and sealing of speed limiters, or
(b)   to be a person entitled under section 45 of this Act to carry out examinations of vehicles under that section.1.
[Road Traffic Act 1988, s 177 amended by the Road Traffic Act 1991, Sch 4 and the Road Traffic (Vehicle Testing) Act 1999, Schedule.]

---

1. For penalty see the Road Traffic Offenders Act 1988, Sch 2, post.

Inquiries

4–1614   180. General provisions as to inquiries.   Secretary of State or person authorised by him may require attendance of witness to give evidence or produce documents; person who fails without reasonable excuse to comply with the order is guilty of an offence1.
[Road Traffic Act 1988, s 180—summarised.]

---

1. For penalty see the Road Traffic Offenders Act 1988, Sch 2, post.

4–1615   181. General provisions as to accident inquiries.   Secretary of State may authorise person to inspect vehicle; person obstructing is guilty of an offence1.
[Road Traffic Act 1988, s 181 amended by the Road Traffic Act 1991, Sch 4—summarised.]

---

1. For penalty see the Road Traffic Offenders Act 1988, Sch 2, post.

Application to the Crown

4–1616   183. Application to the Crown.   (1) Subject to the provisions of this section—

(a)   Part I of this Act,
(b)   Part II of this Act, except sections 68 to 74 and 77,
(c)   Part III of this Act,
(d)   Part IV of this Act, and
(e)   in this Part, sections 163, 164, 168, 169, 170(1) to (4), 177, 178, 181 and 182,

apply to vehicles and persons in the public service of the Crown1.

(2) Sections 49 to 63 and sections 64A, 65 and 65A2 of this Act apply—

(a)   to vehicles in the public service of the Crown only if they are registered or liable to be registered under the Vehicle Excise and Registration Act 1994, and
(b)   to trailers in the public service of the Crown only while drawn by vehicles (whether or not in the public service of the Crown) which are required to be so registered.*

(3) Where those sections so apply they do so subject to the following modifications—

(a)   examinations of such vehicles in pursuance of regulations under section 49 or 61(1)(a) of this Act may be made by or under the directions of examiners authorised by the Secretary of State for the purpose instead of by or under the directions of examiners appointed under section 66A of this Act,

(b) (*Repealed*).*

(4) Neither section 97(3) nor section 98(3) of this Act, in so far as they prevent such a licence as is there mentioned from authorising a person to drive certain motor bicycles and mopeds, applies—

(a) in the case of motor bicycles and mopeds owned by the Secretary of State for Defence and used for naval, military or air force purposes, or

(b) in the case of motor bicycles and mopeds so used while being ridden by persons for the time being subject to the orders of a member of the armed forces of the Crown.

(5) Subject to regulations made under subsection (2) of section 101 of this Act, that section (in so far as it prohibits persons under 21 from holding or obtaining a licence to drive motor vehicles or persons under 18 from holding or obtaining a licence to drive medium-sized goods vehicles) does not apply—

(a) in the case of motor vehicles owned by the Secretary of State for Defence and used for naval, military or air force purposes, or

(b) in the case of vehicles so used while being driven by persons for the time being subject to the orders of a member of the armed forces of the Crown.

(6) The functions under Part IV of this Act of traffic commissioners in relation to licences issued to persons subject to the Naval Discipline Act 1957, to military law or to air force law to drive large goods vehicles or passenger-carrying vehicles in the public service of the Crown shall be exercised by the prescribed authority.

(7) Section 165 of this Act, in so far as it provides for the production of test certificates and the giving of names and addresses, applies to a person in connection with a vehicle to which section 47 of this Act applies notwithstanding that he or the driver is or was at any material time in the public service of the Crown.

(8) Subsection (1) of section 165 of this Act, in so far as it provides for the production of any certificate mentioned in subsection (2)(c) of that section, applies to a person in connection with a goods vehicle so mentioned notwithstanding that he or the driver is or was at any material time in the public service of the Crown.

[Road Traffic Act 1988, s 183 as amended by the Road Traffic (Driver Licensing and Information Systems) Act 1989, Sch 3 and the Road Traffic Act 1991, Schs 4 and 8, SI 1992/3107, the Vehicle Excise and Registration Act 1994, Sch 3, SI 1996/1974, SI 1998/1420 and the Police Reform Act 2002, ss 107, 108.]

---

*Section 183(2) and (3) is amended by the Road Traffic (Consequential Provisions) Act 1988, Sch 2, para 18, when in force.

1. For the application of this subsection to vehicles in the service of a visiting force or international headquarters, see Visiting Forces and International Headquarters (Application of Law) Order 1965 (SI 1965/1536), art 9.

2. Sections 64A and 65A added by SI 1992/3107 with effect from 1 January 1996.

4–1617 **184.** Application of sections 5 to 10 to persons subject to service discipline.

Interpretation

4–1618 **185. Meaning of "motor vehicle" and other expressions relating to vehicles.** (1) In this Act—

"heavy locomotive" means a mechanically propelled vehicle which is not constructed itself to carry a load other than any of the excepted articles and the weight of which unladen exceeds 11690 kilograms[1],

"heavy motor car" means a mechanically propelled vehicle, not being a motor car, which is constructed itself to carry a load or passengers and the weight of which unladen exceeds 2540 kilograms[1],

"invalid carriage" means a mechanically propelled vehicle the weight of which unladen does not exceed 254 kilograms[1] and which is specially designed and constructed, and not merely adapted, for the use of a person suffering from some physical defect or disability and is used solely by such a person[2],

"light locomotive" means a mechanically propelled vehicle which is not constructed itself to carry a load other than any of the excepted articles and the weight of which unladen does not exceed 11690 kilograms but does exceed 7370 kilograms[1],

"motor car" means a mechanically propelled vehicle, not being a motor cycle or an invalid carriage, which is constructed itself to carry a load or passengers and the weight of which unladen—

(a) if it is constructed solely for the carriage of passengers and their effects, is adapted to carry not more than seven passengers exclusive of the driver and is fitted with tyres of such type as may be specified in regulations[3] made by the Secretary of State, does not exceed 3050 kilograms[1],

(b) if it is constructed or adapted for use for the conveyance of goods or burden of any description, does not exceed 3050 kilograms[1], or 3500 kilograms[1] if the vehicle carries a container or containers for holding for the purposes of its propulsion any fuel which is wholly gaseous at 17.5 degrees Celsius under a pressure of 1.013 bar or plant and materials for producing such fuel,

(c) does not exceed 2540 kilograms in a case not falling within sub-paragraph (a) or (b) above,

"motor cycle" means a mechanically propelled vehicle, not being an invalid carriage, with less than four wheels and the weight of which unladen does not exceed 410 kilograms[1],

"motor tractor" means a mechanically propelled vehicle which is not constructed itself to carry a load[4], other than the excepted articles, and the weight of which unladen does not exceed 7370 kilograms[1],

"motor vehicle" means[5], subject to section 20 of the Chronically Sick and Disabled Persons Act 1970 (which makes special provision about invalid carriages, within the meaning of that Act), a mechanically propelled vehicle intended or adapted for use on roads[6], and

"trailer" means a vehicle drawn by a motor vehicle[7].

(2) In subsection (1) above "excepted articles" means any of the following: water, fuel, accumulators and other equipment used for the purpose of propulsion, loose tools and loose equipment.
[Road Traffic Act 1988, s 185.]

---

1. For method of calculating weight see s 190 post.
2. See note 20, supra. For the purposes of Part II of this Act (relating to the licensing of drivers, etc) ante, the maximum weight of an invalid carriage is varied, from 254 kg to 510 kg) (Motor Vehicles (Driving Licences) Regulations 1999 in this PART, post.
3. See reg 24 of the Road Vehicles (Construction and Use) Regulations 1986, in this PART, post.
4. A chassis is not a tractor (*Millard v Turvey* [1968] 2 QB 390, [1968] 2 All ER 7, 132 JP 286).
5. See also s 189 post (certain vehicles not to be treated as motor vehicles). For application of this expression to a pedal cycle fitted with an auxiliary motor, see *Lawrence v Howlett* [1952] 2 All ER 74, 116 JP 391; *Floyd v Bush* [1953] 1 All ER 265, 117 JP 88.
6. For meaning of expression "intended or adapted for use on a road", see Preliminary Note to this title, para **4–3**, ante. See also s 189, post (certain vehicles not to be treated as motor vehicles).
7. This means anything on wheels (eg as poultry shed) drawn by a motor vehicle (*Garner v Burr* [1951] 1 KB 31, [1950] 2 All ER 688, 114 JP 484).

4–1619   186. Supplementary provisions about those expressions.   (1) For the purposes of section 185 of this Act, a side car attached to a motor vehicle, if it complies with such conditions[1] as may be specified in regulations made by the Secretary of State, is to be regarded as forming part of the vehicle to which it is attached and as not being a trailer[2].

(2) For the purposes of section 185 of this Act, in a case where a motor vehicle is so constructed that a trailer may by partial super-imposition be attached to the vehicle in such a manner as to cause a substantial part of the weight of the trailer to be borne by the vehicle, that vehicle is to be deemed to be a vehicle itself constructed to carry a load.

(3) For the purposes of section 185 of this Act, in the case of a motor vehicle fitted with a crane, dynamo, welding plant or other special appliance or apparatus[3] which is a permanent or essentially permanent fixture, the appliance or apparatus is not to be deemed to constitute a load or goods or burden of any description, but is to be deemed to form part of the vehicle.

(4)–(6) Regulations to vary s 185 weights.
[Road Traffic Act 1988, s 186.]

---

1. See the Road Vehicles (Construction and Use) Regulations 1986 reg 92 and the Motor Vehicles (Authorisation of Special Types) General Order 1979 in this PART, post.
2. A trailer must conform to the speed limit in Sch 6 to the Road Traffic Regulation Act 1984, ante, unless it complies with conditions in regulations.
3. As to a sound-recording van, although the apparatus is a permanent fixture, see *Burmingham v Lindsell* [1936] 2 All ER 159.

4–1620   187. Articulated vehicles.   (1) Unless it falls within subsection (2) below, a vehicle so constructed that it can be divided into two parts both of which are vehicles and one of which is a motor vehicle shall (when not so divided) be treated for the purposes of the enactments mentioned in subsection (3) below as that motor vehicle with the other part attached as a trailer.

(2) A passenger vehicle so constructed that—

(a) it can be divided into two parts, both of which are vehicles and one of which is a motor vehicle, but cannot be so divided without the use of facilities normally available only at a workshop, and

(b) passengers carried by it when not so divided can at all times pass from either part to the other,

shall (when not so divided) be treated for the purposes of the enactments mentioned in subsection (3) below as a single motor vehicle.

(3) The enactments referred to in subsections (1) and (2) above are the Road Traffic Act 1960, Parts I and II of the Public Passenger Vehicles Act 1981, and the Traffic Acts.

(4) In this section "passenger vehicle" means a vehicle constructed or adapted for use solely or principally for the carriage of passengers.
[Road Traffic Act 1988, s 187.]

4–1621   188. Hover vehicles.   (1) For the purposes of the Road Traffic Acts, a hovercraft within the meaning of the Hovercraft Act 1968 (in this section referred to as a hover vehicle)—

(a) is a motor vehicle, whether or not it is intended or adapted for use on roads, but

(b)   apart from that is to be treated, subject to subsection (2) below, as not being a vehicle of any of the classes defined in section 185 of this Act.

(2)   The Secretary of State may by regulations provide—

(a)   that any provisions of this Act which would otherwise apply to hover vehicles shall not apply to them or shall apply to them subject to such modifications as may be specified in the regulations, or

(b)   that any such provision which would not otherwise apply to hover vehicles shall apply to them subject to such modifications (if any) as may be specified in the regulations.

[Road Traffic Act 1988, s 188.]

4–1622   189.   Certain vehicles not to be treated as motor vehicles.   (1) For the purposes of the Road Traffic Acts—

(a)   a mechanically propelled vehicle being an implement for cutting grass which is controlled by a pedestrian and is not capable of being used or adapted for any other purpose,

(b)   any other mechanically propelled vehicle controlled by a pedestrian which may be specified by regulations made by the Secretary of State for the purposes of this section and section 140 of the Road Traffic Regulation Act 1984, and

(c)   an electrically assisted pedal cycle of such a class as may be prescribed by regulations[1] so made,

is to be treated as not being a motor vehicle.

(2)   In subsection (1) above "controlled by a pedestrian" means that the vehicle either—

(a)   is constructed or adapted for use only under such control, or

(b)   is constructed or adapted for use either under such control or under the control of a person carried on it, but is not for the time being in use under, or proceeding under, the control of a person carried on it.

[Road Traffic Act 1988, s 189.]

---

1.   The Electrically Assisted Pedal Cycles Regulations 1983 SI 1983/1168 have been made. Where is was impossible for anyone safely to use on the roads an electric scooter (called the "city bug") if reliance was placed on the pedals alone, condition (b) of the requirements of reg 4 of the aforementioned regulations was not satisfied and insurance, etc, was therefore required (*Winter v DPP* [2002] EWHC 2482 (Admin), [2003] RTR 14).

4–1623   190.   Method of calculating weight of motor vehicles and trailers[1].   (1) This section applies for the purposes of the Traffic Acts and of any other enactments relating to the use of motor vehicles or trailers on roads[2].

(2)   The weight unladen of a vehicle or trailer shall be taken to be the weight of the vehicle or trailer—

(a)   inclusive of the body and all parts (the heavier being taken where alternative bodies[3] or parts are used) which are necessary to or ordinarily used with the vehicle or trailer when working on a road, but

(b)   exclusive of the weight of water, fuel or accumulators used for the purpose of the supply of power for the propulsion of the vehicle or, as the case may be, of any vehicle by which the trailer is drawn, and of loose tools and loose equipment[4].

[Road Traffic Act 1988, s 190.]

---

1.   This section does not apply to tramcars: SI 1992/1217, r 7.

2.   Including the Vehicle Excise and Registration Act 1994. It is not permissible to change from one class to another without re-weighing and re-registration (*Scott v Dickson* (1939) 83 Sol Jo 317).

3.   A container, for carrying goods, fixed to the platform of a lorry is not an "alternative body" (*Cording v Halse* [1955] 1 QB 63, [1954] 3 All ER 287, 118 JP 558).

4.   The interpretation of this section was considered in *Lowe v Stone* [1948] 2 All ER 1076, 113 JP 59 and *LCC v Hay's Wharf Cartage Co Ltd* [1953] 2 All ER 34, 117 JP 304. Cf Vehicles (Excise) Act 1971, Sch 6, para 1, ante.

4–1624   191.   Interpretation of statutory references carriages[1].   A motor vehicle or trailer—

(a)   is to be deemed to be a carriage within the meaning of any Act of Parliament, whether a public general Act or a local Act, and of any rule, regulation or byelaw made under any Act of Parliament, and

(b)   if used as a carriage of any particular class shall for the purpose of any enactment relating to carriages of any particular class be deemed to be a carriage of that class.

[Road Traffic Act 1988, s 191.]

---

1.   This section does not apply to tramcars: SI 1992/1217, r 7.

4–1625   192.   General interpretation of Act[1].   (1) In this Act*—

"bridleway" means a way over which the public have the following, but no other, rights of way: a right of way on foot and a right of way on horseback or leading a horse, with or without a right to drive animals of any description along the way[2],

"carriage of goods" includes the haulage of goods,

"cycle" means a bicycle, a tricycle, or a cycle having four or more wheels, not being in any case a motor vehicle,

"driver", where a separate person acts as a steersman[3] of a motor vehicle, includes (except for the purposes of section 1[4] of this Act) that person as well as any other person engaged in the driving of the vehicle, and "drive" is to be interpreted accordingly,

"footpath", in relation to England and Wales, means a way over which the public have a right of way on foot only,

"goods" includes goods or burden of any description,

"goods vehicle" means a motor vehicle constructed or adapted for use for the carriage of goods, or a trailer so constructed or adapted,

"highway authority", in England and Wales, means—

(a) in relation to a road for which he is the highway authority within the meaning of the Highways Act 1980, the Secretary of State, and

(b) in relation to any other road, the council of the county, metropolitan district or London borough, or the Common Council of the City of London, as the case may be.

"international road haulage permit" means a licence, permit, authorisation or other document issued in pursuance of a Community instrument relating to the carriage of goods by road between member States or an international agreement to which the United Kingdom is a party and which relates to the international carriage of goods by road,

"owner", in relation to a vehicle which is the subject of a hiring agreement or hire-purchase agreement, means the person in possession of the vehicle under that agreement,

(Repealed)

"prescribed" means prescribed by regulations made by the Secretary of State,

"road"—

(a) in relation to England and Wales, means any highway and any other road to which the public has access, and includes bridges over which a road passes, and

(b) *Scotland.*

"the Road Traffic Acts" means the Road Traffic Offenders Act 1988, the Road Traffic (Consequential Provisions) Act 1988 (so far as it reproduces the effect of provisions repealed by that Act) and this Act,

"statutory", in relation to any prohibition, restriction, requirement or provision, means contained in, or having effect under, any enactment (including any enactment contained in this Act),

"the Traffic Acts" means the Road Traffic Acts and the Road Traffic Regulation Act 1984,

"traffic sign" has the meaning given by section 64(1) of the Road Traffic Regulations Act 1984,

"tramcar" includes any carriage used on any road by virtue of an order under the Light Railways Act 1896, and

"trolley vehicle" means a mechanically propelled vehicle adapted for use on roads without rails under power transmitted to it from some external source (whether or not there is in addition a source of power on board the vehicle).

(1A) In this Act—

(a) any reference to a county shall be construed in relation to Wales as including a reference to a county borough; and

(b) section 17(4) and (5) of the Local Government (Wales) Act 1994 (references to counties and districts to be construed generally in relation to Wales as references to counties and county boroughs) shall not apply.

(2) Scotland.

(3) References in this Act to a class of vehicles are to be interpreted as references to a class defined or described by reference to any characteristics of the vehicles or to any other circumstances whatsoever and accordingly as authorising the use of "category" to indicate a class of vehicles, however defined or described.

[Road Traffic Act 1988, s 192, as amended by the Road Traffic (Driver Licensing and Information Systems) Act 1989, Sch 3, the New Roads and Street Works Act 1991, Sch 8, the Road Traffic Act 1991, Sch 4, the Local Government (Wales) Act 1994, Sch 7 and the Access to Justice Act 1999 Sch 15.]

---

*A definition "approved testing authority" is added by the Road Traffic (Consequential Provisions) Act 1988, Sch 2 when in force.

1. The expression "motor vehicle", "trailer" and various classes or descriptions of motor vehicles are defined by s 185, ante.

2. Subject to any orders made by a local authority and to any byelaws, the public have a right of way, the right to ride a pedal cycle on any bridleway, but cyclists must give way to pedestrians and persons on horseback, see Countryside Act 1968, s 30.

3. "Steersman" in this definition would seem to refer to one of two people in charge of the same vehicle, as in a steam wagon. A person "drives" a vehicle in the act of steering it down an incline without the engine running (*Saycell v Bool* [1943] 2 All ER 83, 112 JP 341). Cf *R v Kitson* (1955) 39 Cr App Rep 66. For an instance of instructor and learner being joint drivers, see *Langman v Valentine* [1952] 2 All ER 803, 116 JP 576. Cf *Evans v Walkden* [1956] 3 All ER 64, 120 JP 495. See also the Headnote to this title on "drivers" and "driving".

4. This section, ante, relates to the offence of causing death by reckless driving.

4–1625A 192A. Tramcars and other guided vehicles: drink and drugs. (1) Sections 4 to 11 of this Act shall not apply (to the extent that apart from this subsection they would) to vehicles on any transport system to which Chapter I of Part II of the Transport and Works Act 1992 (offences involving drink or drugs on railways, tramways and certain other guided transport systems) applies.

    (2) Subject to subsection (1) above, the Secretary of State may by regulations provide that sections 4 to 11 of this Act shall apply to vehicles on a system of guided transport specified in the regulations with such modifications as he considers necessary or expedient.

    (3) Regulations under subsection (2) above may make different provision for different cases.

    (4) In this section—

"guided transport" means transport by vehicles guided by means external to the vehicles (whether or not the vehicles are also capable of being operated in some other way), and
"vehicle" includes mobile traction unit.
[Road Traffic Act 1988, s 192A added by the Transport and Works Act 1922, s 39.]

4–1626   193A. Tramcars and trolley vehicles.   Regulations may apply provisions of this Act and of the Road Traffic Offenders Act 1988 to tramcars and trolley vehicles.
[Road Traffic Act 1988, s 193A added by the Road Traffic Act 1991, s 46 and amended by SI 1996/1974 and the Crime (International Co-operation) Act 2003, Sch 5—summarised.]

4–1627   194. General index.   The expressions listed in the left-hand column below are respectively defined or (as the case may be) fall to be constructed in accordance with the provisions of this Act listed in the right-hand column in relation to those expressions.

Expression	Relevant provision
Bridleway	Section 192
Carriage of goods	Section 192
Carriageway	Section 192
Cycle	Section 192
Drive	Section 192
Driver	Section 192
Footpath	Section 192
Footway	Section 192
Goods	Section 192
Goods vehicle	Section 192
Goods vehicle test certificate	Section 49(2)(b)
Heavy locomotive	Section 185
Heavy motor car	Section 185
Highway authority	Section 192
International road haulage permit	Section 192
Invalid carriage	Section 185
Light locomotive	Section 185
Local roads authority	Section 192
Motor car	Section 185
Motor cycle	Section 185
Motor tractor	Section 185
Motor vehicle	Sections 185, 186(1), 187, 188, 189
Owner	Section 192
Plating certificate	Section 49(2)(a)
Prescribed	Section 192
Public road	Section 192
Road	Section 192
Roads authority	Section 192
Road Traffic Acts	Section 192
Special road	Section 192
Statutory	Section 192
Test certificate	Section 45(2)
Traffic Acts	Section 192
Traffic sign	Section 192
Trailer	Section 185
Tramcar	Section 192
Trolley vehicle	Section 192
Trunk road	Section 192
Unladen weight	Section 190

[Road Traffic Act 1988, s 194.]

Supplementary

4–1628   195. Provisions as to regulations.

4–1629   196. Provision, etc, of weighbridges.

SCHEDULES

SUPPLEMENTARY PROVISIONS IN CONNECTION WITH PROCEEDINGS FOR OFFENCES UNDER SECTIONS 15A, 17 AND 18(4)

(As amended by the Motor Vehicles (Safety Equipment for Children) Act 1991, s 2.)

Proceedings in England and Wales

4–1640   **1.** (1) A person against whom proceedings are brought in England and Wales for an offence under section 15A, 17 or 18(4) of this Act is, upon information duly laid by him and on giving the prosecution not less than three clear days' notice of his intention, entitled to have any person to whose act or default he alleges that the contravention of that section was due brought before the court in the proceedings.

(2) If, after the contravention has been proved, the original accused proves that the contravention was due to the act or default of that other person—

(*a*)   that other person may be convicted of the offence, and

(*b*)   if the original accused further proves that he has used all due diligence to secure that section 15A, 17 or, as the case may be, 18(4) was complied with, he shall be acquitted of the offence.

(3) Where an accused seeks to avail himself of the provisions of sub-paragraphs (1) and (2) above—

(*a*)   the prosecution, as well as the person whom the accused charges with the offence, has the right to cross-examine him, if he gives evidence, and any witness called by him in support of his pleas, and to call rebutting evidence, and

(*b*)   the court may make such order as it thinks fit for the payment of costs by any party to the proceedings to any other party to the proceedings.

2. (1) Where—

(*a*)   it appears that an offence under section 15A, 17 or 18(4) of this Act has been committed in respect of which proceedings might be taken in England and Wales against some person (referred to below in this paragraph as "the original offender"), and

(*b*)   a person proposing to take proceedings in respect of the offence is reasonably satisfied—

(i)   that the offence of which complaint is made was due to an act or default of some other person, being an act or default which took place in England and Wales, and

(ii)   that the original offender could establish a defence under paragraph 1 of this Schedule,

the proceedings may be taken against that other person without proceedings first being taken against the original offender.

(2) In any such proceedings the accused may be charged with, and on proof that the contravention was due to his act or default be convicted of, the offence with which the original offender might have been charged.

3. (1) Where proceedings are brought in England and Wales against a person (referred to below in this paragraph as "the accused") in respect of a contravention of section 15A, 17 or 18(4) of this Act and it is proved—

(*a*)   that the contravention was due to the act or default of some other person, being an act or default which took place in Scotland, and

(*b*)   that the accused used all due diligence to secure compliance with that section,

the accused shall, subject to the provisions of this paragraph, be acquitted of the offence.

(2) The accused is not entitled to be acquitted under this paragraph unless within seven days from the date of the service of the summons on him—

(*a*)   he has given notice in writing to the prosecution of his intention to rely upon the provisions of this paragraph, specifying the name and address of the person to whose act or default he alleges that the contravention was due, and

(*b*)   he has sent a like notice to that person.

(3) The person specified in a notice served under this paragraph is entitled to appear at the hearing and to give evidence and the court may, if it thinks fit, adjourn the hearing to enable him to do so.

(4) Where it is proved that the contravention of section 15A, 17 or 18(4) of this Act was due to the act or default of some person other than the accused, being an act or default which took place in Scotland, the court must (whether or not the accused in acquitted) cause notice of the proceedings to be sent to the Secretary of State.

4. Proceedings in Scotland.

Proceedings in Great Britain

5. (1) Subject to the provisions of this paragraph, in any proceedings (whether in England and Wales or Scotland) for an offence under section 17 or 18(4) of this Act it shall be a defence for the accused to prove—

(*a*)   that he purchased the helmet or appliance in question as being of a type which—

(i)   in the case of section 17, could be lawfully sold or offered for sale under that section, and

(ii)   in the case of section 18(4), could be lawfully sold or offered for sale under section 18 as authorised for use in the manner in question,

and with a written warranty to that effect, and

(*b*)   that he had no reason to believe at the time of the commission of the alleged offence that it was not of such a type, and

(*c*)   that it was then in the same state as when he purchased it.

(1A) Subject to the provisions of this paragraph, in any proceedings (whether in England and Wales or Scotland) for an offence under section 15A of this Act it shall be a defence for the accused to prove—

(*a*)   if the offence is under subsection (3)(*a*) of that section—

(i) that he purchased the equipment in question as being of a type which could be lawfully sold or offered for sale as conducive to the safety in the event of accident of prescribed classes of children in prescribed classes of motor vehicles and with a written warranty to that effect;
(ii) that he had no reason to believe at the time of the commission of the alleged offence that it was not of such a type; and
(iii) that it was then in the same state as when he purchased it;

(b) if the offence is under subsection (3)(b) of that section, he provided information in relation to the equipment and it is alleged that it did not include appropriate information or included or consisted of inappropriate information—

(i) that the information provided by him was information which had been provided to him with a written warranty to the effect that it was the information required to be provided by him under section 15A of this Act; and
(ii) that he had no reason to believe at the time of the commission of the alleged offence that the information provided by him was not the information required to be provided under that section; or

(c) if the offence is under subsection (3)(b) of that section, he provided information in relation to the equipment and it is alleged that it was not provided in the manner required under that section—

(i) that the information provided by him had been provided to him either with a written warranty to the effect that it was provided to him in the manner in which it was required to be provided by him under that section or with instructions as to the manner in which the information should be provided by him and with a written warranty to the effect that provision in that manner would comply with regulations under that section;
(ii) that he had no reason to believe at the time of the commission of the alleged offence that he was not providing the information in the manner required under that section; and
(iii) that the information was then in the same state as when it was provided to him or, as the case may be, that it was provided by him in accordance with the instructions given to him.

(2) A warranty is only a defence in any such proceedings if—
(a) the accused—

(i) has, not later than three clear days before the date of the hearing, sent to the prosecutor a copy of the warranty with a notice stating that he intends to rely on it and specifying the name and address of the person from whom he received it, and
(ii) has also sent a like notice of his intention to that person, and

(b) in the case of a warranty given by a person outside the United Kingdom, the accused proves that he had taken reasonable steps to ascertain, and did in fact believe in, the accuracy of the statement contained in the warranty.

(3) Where the accused is a servant of the person who purchased the equipment, helmet or appliance in question under a warranty, or to whom the information in question was provided in question under a warranty, he is entitled to rely on the provisions of this paragraph in the same way as his employer would have been entitled to do if he had been the accused.
(4) The person by whom the warranty is alleged to have been given is entitled to appear at the hearing and to give evidence and the court may, if it thinks fit, adjourn the hearing to enable him to do so.
6. (1) An accused who in any proceedings for an offence under section 15A, 17 or 18(4) of this Act wilfully applies to equipment, information, a helmet or, as the case may be, an appliance a warranty not given in relation to it is guilty of an offence[1].
(2) A person who, in respect of equipment, a helmet or an appliance sold by him, or information provided by him, being equipment, a helmet, an appliance or information in respect of which a warranty might be pleaded under paragraph 5 of this Schedule, gives to the purchaser a false warranty in writing, is guilty of an offence[1], unless he proves that when he gave the warranty he had reason to believe that the statements or description contained in it were accurate.
(3) Where the accused in a prosecution for an offence under section 15A, 17 or 18(4) of this Act relies successfully on a warranty given to him or his employer, any proceedings under sub-paragraph (2) above in respect of the warranty may, at the option of the prosecutor, be taken before a court having jurisdiction in the place—

(a) where the equipment, helmet or appliance, or any of the equipment, helmets or appliances, to which the warranty relates was procured;
(b) where the information, or any of it, to which the warranty relates was provided; or
(c) where the warranty was given.

7. In this Schedule, "equipment" means equipment to which section 15A of this Act applies and "appliance" means an appliance to which section 18 of this Act applies.

---

1. For penalty see the Road Traffic Offenders Act 1988, Sch 2, post.

4–1641
Section 67　　　　　　　　　　　SCHEDULE 2
DEFERRED TESTS OF CONDITIONS OF VEHICLES

SCHEDULE 2A★
FORM OF SEAT BELT SYMBOL FOR BUSES

SCHEDULE 2A★
OFFENCE OF KEEPING VEHICLE WHICH DOES NOT MEET INSURANCE REQUIREMENTS: IMMOBILISATION, REMOVAL AND DISPOSAL OF VEHICLES

Secretary of State may make regulations.

★**Two Schedules numbered "2A" have been inserted into the RTA 1988, the first by SI 2006/1892 and the second by the Road Safety Act 2006, Sch 5.**

4–1641A

Section 131

SCHEDULE 3
APPEALS UNDER SECTION 131 AGAINST DECISIONS OF THE REGISTRAR

Road Traffic Offenders Act 1988

(1988 c 53)

PART I[1]
TRIAL

Introductory

4–1642   1. Requirement of warning etc of prosecutions for certain offences. (1) Subject to section 2 of this Act, a person shall not be convicted of an offence to which this section applies[2] unless—

   (a) he was warned[3] at the time the offence was committed that the question of prosecuting him for some one or other of the offences to which this section applies would be taken into consideration, or

   (b) within fourteen days of the commission of the offence a summons (or, in Scotland, a complaint) for the offence was served[4] on him, or

   (c) within fourteen days of the commission of the offence a notice of the intended prosecution[5] specifying the nature of the alleged offence and the time and place[6] where it is alleged to have been committed, was—

      (i) in the case of an offence under section 28 or 29 of the Road Traffic Act 1988 (cycling offences), served[4] on him,

      (ii) in the case of any other offence, served[7] on him or on the person, if any, registered as the keeper of the vehicle at the time of the commission of the offence[8].

(1A) A notice required by this section to be served on any person may be served on that person—

   (a) by delivering it to him;

   (b) by addressing it to him and leaving it at his last known address; or

   (c) by sending it by registered post, recorded delivery service or first class post addressed to him at his last known address.

(2) A notice shall be deemed for the purposes of subsection (1)(c) above to have been served on a person if it was sent by registered post or recorded delivery service addressed to him at his last known address, notwithstanding that the notice was returned as undelivered or was for any other reason not received by him[9].

(3) The requirement of subsection (1) above shall in every case be deemed to have been complied with unless and until the contrary is proved[10].

(4) Schedule 1 to this Act shows the offences to which this section applies.

[Road Traffic Offenders Act 1988, s 1 amended by the Road Traffic Act 1991, Sch 4 and the Criminal Justice and Public Order Act 1994, Sch 9.]

---

  1. Part I contains ss 1–26.

  2. The effect of this section is noted against each of the provisions to which it applies, *ante*. Sections 1 and 2 do not apply to tramcars or trolley vehicles operated under statutory powers (Road Traffic Act 1988, Sch 4).

  3. The warning must be heard and understood by the person intended to take account of it (*Gibson v Dalton* [1980] RTR 410). The warning given "at the time the offence was committed" need not be in writing. A warning thirty-five minutes after the offence, but given at the earliest time reasonably possible after the arrival of the police, and while the parties were still at the scene of the offence, was held to be "at the time" (*Jeffs v Wells* (1936) 100 JP Jo 406). This case was applied in *Jollye v Dale* [1960] 2 QB 258, [1960] 2 All ER 369, 124 JP 333, and also in *R v Okike* [1978] RTR 489, where a warning given about 2½ hours after the offence was held not to have been unreasonable because during that time the police were actively involved in attempting to ascertain the identity of the driver. Whether a warning is given "at the time the offence was committed" may be a matter of degree depending upon the circumstances. It is a question of fact and degree for the magistrates' court and the High Court will not interfere if there is evidence supporting the finding. No exhaustive test exists to indicate clearly and beyond doubt whether or not the warning was so given (*R v Stacey* [1982] RTR 20). Where a constable stopped a car, and informed the driver thereof that he thought he was exceeding the speed limit, but that if, after he had compared the time taken by his watch with that of another constable, it appears that the driver had not exceeded the speed limit, he would hear nothing further about it, it was held that this was a sufficient warning under the repealed Motor Car Act 1903, s 9(2), of an intended prosecution (*Jessop v Clarke* (1908) 72 JP 358). But a warning that he was driving too fast, and would be *reported* for driving to the danger of the public, was held not to be sufficient under that subsection (*Parkes v Cole* (1922) 86 JP 122). This section only applies to prosecutions for the offences mentioned in it (cf *Staunton v Coates* (1924) 88 JP 193).

  4. It must be actually served. The laying of the information does not suffice. The Magistrates' Courts Act 1980, s 47, *ante* contains a saving provision to meet the case where a summons is sent by post within the prescribed period but is not served by reason of its non-acknowledgement by the defendant. A person may be convicted of careless or inconsiderate driving following a charge of reckless driving provided that the requirement of the section has been satisfied (or does not apply) as respects the major charge. This provision also relates to pedal cyclists.

  5. Paragraph (c) must be read in close connection with para (a). "Intended" means no more than "in contemplation". A warning or notice of an allegation of dangerous driving is a sufficient warning or notice when proceedings are later taken for driving without due care and attention: the section requires that "the nature" not "particulars" of the offence must be specified (*Milner v Allen* [1933] 1 KB 698, [1933] All ER Rep 734, 97 JP 111). The notice (if sent to the driver) must be addressed to the person summoned, so that a notice addressed and sent to a defendant's firm at the business address is not a sufficient notice to him (*Clarke v Mould* [1945] 2 All ER 551, 109 JP 175). As to a sufficient notice, see *Percival v Ball*

(1937) 107 JP Jo 614; *Venn v Morgan* [1949] 2 All ER 562, 113 JP 504; *Stewart v Chapman* [1951] 2 KB 792, [1951] 2 All ER 613, 115 JP 473; *Springate v Questier* [1952] 2 All ER 21, 116 JP 367; *Pope v Clarke* [1953] 2 All ER 704, 117 JP 429.

Each of these cases deals with a specific objection to a particular notice. It appears from the judgments that a notice should not be scrutinised with the formality accorded to a summons: it is adequate if it achieves its object of calling the attention of the driver to the time and circumstances in respect of which he may be charged. The requirement under s 1(1)(c) is satisfied where the defendant is charged within 14 days and is given a copy of the charge (*Sage v Townsend* (1986) Times, 27 May).

6. A court may have to consider whether the particulars given are sufficiently specific: see *Young v Day* (1959) 123 JP 317, discussed (1959) 109 LJ 519.

7. Service of the notice has been held to be good where it was served on the defendant's wife at his address, it being within the scope of her authority to accept letters on his behalf (*Burt v Kirkcaldy* [1965] 1 All ER 714, 129 JP 190, following *Hosier v Goodall* [1962] 1 All ER 30, 126 JP 52; although, per SACHS J, delivery to somebody who had not authority to take in letters, eg, a hall porter, might not have been good service).

8. Under the Road Vehicles (Registration and Licensing) Regulations 2002, in this PART, post, the registration is in the name of the 'keeper' of the vehicle, the term 'owner' is no longer used. A notice to the registered owner stating the nature, time and place of the offence, without particulars of the person to be prosecuted will suffice (*R v Bolkis* (1933) 97 JP 10).

9. The effect of this provision is that a notice under para (c) is deemed to have been served within 14 days provided it was posted, as required by the subsection, within 14 days of the commission of the offence even if, in fact, the notice was not received by him in 14 days (*Groome v Driscoll* [1969] 3 All ER 1638, 134 JP 83). If notice is given under para (c) by post, it will be deemed to be given at the time when the letter would be delivered in the ordinary course of post; this must be within 14 days (see *Nicholson v Tapp* [1972] 3 All ER 245, 136 JP 718); the words following para (c) prevent that presumption from being gainsaid by proof that the notice had not in fact been received within that period (*Nicholson v Tapp*, supra; *Groome v Driscoll* [1969] 3 All ER 1638, 134 JP 83).

10. The point may be raised by the defendant at any stage in the proceedings (*R v Edmonton Justices, ex p Brooks* [1960] 2 All ER 475, 124 JP 409). He will be required to establish non-compliance with each of the alternatives prescribed by sub-s 2(a)–(c) (*Sanders v Scott* [1961] 2 QB 326, [1961] 2 All ER 403, 125 JP 419). The onus is on the defendant to prove on a balance of probabilities that an effective warning was not given; merely to raise a doubt in the minds of the justices is not enough (*Offen v Ranson* [1980] RTR 484).

4-1643   2. Requirement of warning etc: supplementary.   (1) The requirement of section 1(1) of this Act does not apply in relation to an offence if, at the time of the offence or immediately after it, an accident[1] occurs owing to the presence on a road of the vehicle in respect of which the offence was committed.

(2) The requirement of section 1(1) of this Act does not apply in relation to an offence in respect of which—

    (a)   a fixed penalty notice (within the meaning of Part III of this Act) has been given or fixed under any provision of that Part, or

    (b)   a notice has been given under section 54(4) of this Act.

(3) Failure to comply with the requirement of section 1(1) of this Act is not a bar to the conviction of the accused in a case where the court is satisfied—

    (a)   that neither the name and address of the accused nor the name and address of the registered keeper, if any, could with reasonable diligence[2] have been ascertained in time for a summons or, as the case may be, a complaint to be served or for a notice to be served or sent in compliance with the requirement, or

    (b)   that the accused by his own conduct contributed to the failure.

(4) Failure to comply with the requirement of section 1(1) of this Act in relation to an offence is not a bar to the conviction of a person of that offence by virtue of the provisions of—

    (a)   section 24 of this Act, or

    (b)   any of the enactments mentioned in section 24(6);

but a person is not to be convicted of an offence by virtue of any of those provisions if section 1 applies to the offence with which he was charged and the requirement of section 1(1) was not satisfied in relation to the offence charged.

[Road Traffic Offenders Act 1988, s 2 amended by the Road Traffic Act 1991, Sch 4.]

---

1. As to evidence see *Metropolitan Police v Scarlett* [1978] Crim LR 234. The exemption provided by this subsection applies only to an accident of which at the time the defendant was aware (*Bentley v Dickinson* [1983] RTR 356, [1983] Crim LR 403 and see *DPP v Pidhajeckyj* (1990) 155 JP 318, [1991] RTR 136).

2. See *Clarke v Mould*, supra, and *R v Bolkis*, supra, for observations on "reasonable diligence". It frequently occurs that the name and address of the registered owner can be ascertained within the prescribed time as in *R v Bolkis*. If the prosecutor is able to rely on this subsection, there is no time within which he must give notice after he has ascertained the name and address of the defendant: see *Haughton v Harrison* [1976] RTR 208.

4-1644   3. Restriction on institution of proceedings for certain offences.   (1) Repealed.

(2) In England and Wales, proceedings[1] for an offence under section 94(3) of the Road Traffic Act 1988 (notice about relevant or prospective disability) shall not be instituted except by the Secretary of State or by a constable acting with the approval of the Secretary of State.

(2A) In subsection (2) above the reference to section 94(3) of the Road Traffic Act 1988 includes a reference to that section as applied by section 99D or 109C of that Act.

[Road Traffic Offenders Act 1988, s 3 as amended by the Road Traffic (Driver Licensing and Information Systems) Act 1989, Sch 6, SI 1996/1974 and the Crime (International Co-operation) Act 2003, Sch 5.]

---

1. There is a presumption that proceedings have been instituted in proper form, but where the defence request proof of compliance with the statutory formalities, it is for the prosecution to produce such evidence (*Anderton v Frost* [1984] RTR 106, [1983] Crim LR 553).

4–1645   4. Offences for which local authorities in England and Wales may institute proceedings[1].   (1) The council of a county, metropolitan district or London borough or the Common Council of the City of London may institute proceedings for an offence under section 15A of the Road Traffic Act 1988 (safety equipment for children in motor vehicles) or under section 17 or 18 of that Act (helmets and other head-worn appliances for motor cyclists).

(2) The council of a county, metropolitan district or London Borough or the Common Council of the City of London may institute proceedings for an offence under section 27 of that Act (dogs on roads) relating to a road in their area.

(3) The council of a county, district or London borough or the Common Council of the City of London may institute proceedings for offences under section 35A(1), (2) or (5) of the Road Traffic Regulation Act 1984 which are committed in connection with parking places provided by the council, or provided under any letting arrangements made by the council under section 33(4) of that Act.

(4) The council of a county, metropolitan district or London borough or the Common Council of the City of London may institute proceedings for an offence under section 47 or 52 of the Road Traffic Regulation Act 1984 in connection with a designated parking place controlled by the council.

(5) In England, the council of a county or metropolitan district and, in Wales, the council of a county or county borough may institute proceedings for an offence under section 53 of the Road Traffic Regulation Act 1984 in connection with a designated parking place in the council's area.

(6) In this section "parking place" means a place where vehicles, or vehicles of any class, may wait and "designated parking place" has the same meaning as in the Road Traffic Regulation Act 1984.

(7) This section extends to England and Wales only.

(8) In relation to Wales, any reference in subsections (1) to (4) above to a county shall be read as including a reference to a county borough.
[Road Traffic Offenders Act 1988, s 4 as amended by the Parking Act 1989, Sch, the Motor Vehicles (Safety Equipment for Children) Act 1991, s 3 and the Local Government (Wales) Act 1994, Sch 7.]

---

1. The express powers of prosecution provided by this section do not preclude the powers of a local authority to prosecute where the conditions in s 222 of the Local Government Act 1972 are satisfied (*Middlesborough Borough Council v Safeer* [2001] EWHC Admin 525, [2001] 4 All ER 630, [2002] 1 Cr App Rep 266, 166 JP 48).

4–1646   5. Exemption from Licensing Act offence.   A person liable to be charged with an offence under section 3A, 4, 5, 7 or 30 of the Road Traffic Act 1988 (drink and drugs) is not liable to be charged under section 12 of the Licensing Act 1872 with the offence of being drunk while in charge, on a highway or other public place, of a carriage.
[Road Traffic Offenders Act 1988, s 5 amended by the Road Traffic Act 1991, Sch 4.]

4–1647   6. Time within which summary proceedings for certain offences must be commenced.   (1) Subject to subsection (2) below, summary proceedings for an offence to which this section applies[1] may be brought within a period of six months from the date on which evidence sufficient in the opinion of the prosecutor[2] to warrant the proceedings came to his knowledge.

(2) No such proceedings shall be brought by virtue of this section more than three years after the commission of the offence.

(3) For the purposes of this section, a certificate signed by or on behalf of the prosecutor and stating the date on which evidence sufficient in his opinion to warrant the proceedings came to his knowledge shall be conclusive evidence of that fact.

(4) A certificate stating that matter and purporting to be so signed shall be deemed to be so signed unless the contrary is proved.

(5) Scotland.

(6) Schedule 1 to this Act shows the offences to which this section applies.
[Road Traffic Offenders Act 1988, s 6.]

---

1. The application of this provision is noted against each of the relevant sections. The extended limitation of time applies to aiding and abetting the specified offences (*Homolka v Osmond* [1939] 1 All ER 154).

2. A person authorised to investigate an offence but who has no authority to prosecute himself is not a prosecutor for the purposes of this subsection. Therefore although an investigating traffic examiner had interviewed a defendant and obtained a full confession, the prosecutor did not have knowledge of the evidence until a report was submitted to a senior traffic examiner who made the decision whether to prosecute (*Swan v Vehicle Inspectorate* (1996) 161 JP 293, [1997] RTR 187, DC).

4–1648   7. Duty of accused to provide licence[1].   (1) A person who is prosecuted for an offence involving obligatory or discretionary disqualification and who is the holder of a licence must—

(*a*)   cause it to be delivered to the proper officer of the court not later than the day before the date appointed for the hearing, or

(*b*)   post it, at such a time that in the ordinary course of post it would be delivered not later than that day, in a letter duly addressed to the clerk and either registered or sent by the recorded delivery service, or

(*c*)   have it with him at the hearing[2],

and the foregoing obligations imposed on him as respects the licence also apply as respects the counterpart to the licence.

(2) In subsection (1) above "proper officer" means—

(a) in relation to a magistrates' court in England and Wales, the justices' chief executive for the court, and

(b) in relation to any other court, the clerk of the court.

[Road Traffic Offenders Act 1988, s 7 amended by Road Traffic Act 1991, Sch 4 and the Access to Justice Act 1999, Sch 13.]

---

1. Also in the case of a newly qualified driver who holds a provisional licence, any certificate of passing a test of competence to drive (see the Road Traffic (New Drivers) Act 1995 Sch 2, this PART, post).

2. For consequences of failure to comply with s 7, see s 27, post.

4–1649 8. Duty to include date of birth and sex in written plea of guilty. A person who—

(a) gives a notification to a justices' chief executive in pursuance of section 12(4) of the Magistrates' Courts Act 1980 (written pleas of guilty), or

(b) gives a written intimation of a plea of guilty in pursuance of section 334(3) of the Criminal Procedure (Scotland) Act 1975,

in respect of an offence involving obligatory or discretionary disqualification or of such other offence as may be prescribed by regulations under section 105 of the Road Traffic Act 1988, must include in the notification or intimation a statement of the date of birth and sex of the accused[1].

[Road Traffic Offenders Act 1988, s 8 amended by SI 1990/144, the Magistrates' Courts (Procedure) Act 1998, s 4 and the Access to Justice Act 1999, Sch 13.]

---

1. See also s 25, post.

Trial

4–1650 9. Mode of trial. (1) An offence against a provision of the Traffic Acts specified in column 1 of Part I of Schedule 2 to this Act or regulations made under such a provision (the general nature of which offence is indicated in column 2) shall be punishable as shown against the offence in column 3 (that is, on summary conviction or on indictment or in either one way or the other).

(2) Column 3 of Part I of that Schedule is affected by Schedule 5 to the Road Traffic (Consequential Provisions) Act 1988 (transitory modifications).

[Road Traffic Offenders Act 1988, s 9.]

4–1651 11. Evidence by certificate as to driver, user or owner. (1) In any proceedings in England and Wales for an offence to which this section applies, a certificate in the prescribed form[1], purporting to be signed by a constable[2] and certifying that a person specified in the certificate stated to the constable—

(a) that a particular mechanically propelled vehicle was being driven or used by, or belonged to, that person on a particular occasion, or

(b) that a particular mechanically propelled vehicle on a particular occasion was used by, or belonged to, a firm and that he was, at the time of the statement, a partner in that firm, or

(c) that a particular mechanically propelled vehicle on a particular occasion was used by, or belonged to, a corporation and that he was, at the time of the statement, a director, officer or employee of that corporation,

shall be admissible as evidence for the purpose of determining by whom the vehicle was being driven or used, or to whom it belonged, as the case may be, on that occasion.

(2) Nothing in subsection (1) above makes a certificate admissible as evidence in proceedings for an offence except in a case where and to the like extent to which oral evidence to the like effect would have been admissible in those proceedings.

(3) Nothing in subsection (1) above makes a certificate admissible as evidence in proceedings for an offence—

(a) unless a copy of it has, not less than seven days before the hearing or trial, been served in the prescribed manner on the person charged with the offence, or

(b) if that person, not later than three days before the hearing or trial or within such further time as the court may in special circumstances allow, serves a notice in the prescribed form and manner on the prosecutor requiring attendance at the trial of the person who signed the certificate.

(3A) Where the proceedings mentioned in subsection (1) above are proceedings before a magistrates' court inquiring into an offence as examining justices this section shall have effect with the omission of—

(a) subsection (2), and

(b) in subsection (3), paragraph (b) and the word "or" immediately preceding it.

(4) In this section "prescribed" means prescribed by rules made by the Secretary of State by statutory instrument.

(5) Schedule 1 to this Act shows the offences to which this section applies.

[Road Traffic Offenders Act 1988, s 11 amended by the Road Traffic Act 1991, Sch 4 and the Criminal Procedure and Investigations Act 1996, Sch 1.]

---

1. Prescribed by the Evidence by Certificate Rules 1961 SI 1961/248 as follows—

(a) where the person to be served is a corporation, by addressing it to the corporation and leaving it at, or sending it by registered post or by the recorded delivery service to, the registered office of the corporation or, if there is no such office, its principal office or place at which it conducts its business;

(b) in any other case, by delivering it personally to the person to be served or by addressing it to him and leaving it at, or sending it by registered post or by the recorded delivery service to, his last or usual place of abode or place of business.

2. Or a traffic warden acting in the discharge of functions authorised by the Functions of Traffic Wardens Order 1970, in this PART, post.

4-1652   12. Proof, in summary proceedings, of identity of driver of vehicle. (1) Where on the summary trial in England and Wales of an information for an offence to which this subsection applies—

(a) it is proved to the satisfaction of the court, on oath or in manner prescribed[1] by Criminal Procedure Rules, that a requirement under section 172(2) of the Road Traffic Act 1988 to give information as to the identity of the driver of a particular vehicle on the particular occasion to which the information relates has been served on the accused by post, and

(b) a statement in writing is produced to the court purporting to be signed[2] by the accused that the accused was the driver of that vehicle on that occasion,

the court may accept that statement as evidence that the accused was the driver of that vehicle on that occasion.

(2) Schedule 1 to this Act shows the offences to which subsection (1) above applies.

(3) Where on the summary trial in England and Wales of an information for an offence to which section 112 of the Road Traffic Regulation Act 1984 applies—

(a) it is proved to the satisfaction of the court, on oath or in manner prescribed[1] by Criminal Procedure Rules,, that a requirement under section 112(2) of the Road Traffic Regulation Act 1984 to give information as to the identity of the driver of a particular vehicle on the particular occasion to which the information relates has been served on the accused by post, and

(b) a statement in writing is produced to the court purporting to be signed by the accused that the accused was the driver of that vehicle on that occasion,

the court may accept that statement as evidence that the accused was the driver of that vehicle on that occasion.

(4) Scotland.

[Road Traffic Offenders Act 1988, s 12 amended by the Road Traffic Act 1991, Sch 4 and SI 2004/2035.]

---

1. For the prescribed manner of proving service of a document by post, see Criminal Procedure Rules 2005, Part 4 in PART I: MAGISTRATES' COURTS: PROCEDURE, ante.

2. The insertion of a name in block capitals on the form, but with the space for the signature left blank, does not amount to a statement in writing purporting to be signed by the accused; but an unsigned form sent in response to a s 172 requirement to name the person driving at the time of the alleged offence (but not if completed and returned by a person acting as agent for the addressee) can amount to a confession under s 82 of PACE and can be proved under s 27 of the Criminal Justice Act 1988 and can give rise to a case to answer (*Mawdesley v Chief Constable of Cheshire Constabulary, Yorke v DPP* [2003] EWHC 1586 (Admin), [2004] 1 All ER 58, [2004] 1 WLR 1035, [2004] RTR 13.). Section 12 and s 172 of the Road Traffic Act 1988 were enacted at the same time and they both deal with the same subject matter; the chief officer of police is entitled, therefore, to require the addressee of a s 172 notice to sign it: *Francis v DPP* [2004] EWHC Admin 591, (2004) 168 JP 492.

4-1653   13. Admissibility of records as evidence. (1) This section applies to a statement contained in a document[1] purporting to be—

(a) a part of the records maintained by the Secretary of State in connection with any functions exercisable by him by virtue of Part III of the Road Traffic Act 1988 or a part of any other records maintained by the Secretary of State with respect to vehicles, or

(b) a copy of a document forming part of those records, or

(c) a note of any information contained in those records,

and to be authenticated by a person authorised in that behalf by the Secretary of State.*

(2) A statement to which this section applies shall be admissible in any proceedings as evidence (in Scotland, sufficient evidence) of any fact stated in it to the same extent as oral evidence of that fact is admissible in those proceedings.

(3) In the preceding subsections, except in Scotland—

"copy", in relation to a document, means anything onto which information recorded in the document has been copied, by whatever means and whether directly or indirectly;

"document" means anything in which information of any description is recorded; and

"statement" means any representation of fact, however made.

(3A) Scotland[2]

(3A) In any case where—

(a) a person is convicted by a magistrates' court of a summary offence under the Traffic Acts or the Road Traffic (Driver Licensing and Information Systems) Act 1989,

(b) a statement to which this section applies is produced to the court in the proceedings,

(c) the statement specifies an alleged previous conviction of the accused of an offence involving obligatory endorsement or an order made on the conviction, and (*d*)   the accused is not present in person before the court when the statement is so produced,

the court may take account of the previous conviction or order as if the accused had appeared and admitted it[2].

(3B)   Section 104 of the Magistrates' Courts Act 1980 (under which previous convictions may be adduced in the absence of the accused after giving him seven days' notice of them) does not limit the effect of subsection (3A) above.

(4)   In any case where—

(*a*)   a statement to which this section applies is produced to a magistrates' court in any proceedings for an offence involving obligatory or discretionary disqualification, other than a summary offence under any of the enactments mentioned in sub-section (3A)(*a*) above.

(*b*)   the statement specifies an alleged previous conviction of an accused person of any such offence or any order made on the conviction, and

(*c*)   it is proved to the satisfaction of the court, on oath or in such manner as may be prescribed[3] by Criminal Procedure Rules,, that not less than seven days before the statement is so produced a notice was served on the accused, in such form and manner as may be so prescribed, specifying the previous conviction or order and stating that it is proposed to bring it to the notice of the court in the event of or, as the case may be, in view of his conviction, and

(*d*)   the accused is not present in person before the court when the statement is so produced,

the court may take account of the previous conviction or order as if the accused had appeared and admitted it.

(5)   Nothing in the preceding provisions of this section enables evidence to be given in respect of any matter other than a matter of a description prescribed[4] by regulations made by the Secretary of State.

(6)   Regulations.

(7)   Where the proceedings mentioned in subsection (2) above are proceedings before a magistrates' court inquiring into an offence as examining justices this section shall have effect as if—

(*a*)   in subsection (2) the words "to the same extent as oral evidence of that fact is admissible in those proceedings" were omitted;

(*b*)   in subsection (4) the word "and" were inserted at the end of paragraph (*a*);

(*c*)   in subsection (4), paragraph (*c*) and (*d*) and the words "as if the accused had appeared and admitted it" were omitted.**

[Road Traffic Offenders Act 1988, s 13 as amended by the Civil Evidence Act 1995, Sch 1, the Criminal Procedure and Investigations Act 1996, Sch 1, the Magistrates' Courts (Procedure) Act 1998, s 2 and SI 2004/2035.]

---

*Amended by the Road Traffic (Consequential Provisions) Act 1988, Sch 2, para 20 when in force.
**Repealed by the Criminal Justice Act 2003, Sch 3 from a date to be appointed.
1.   This will usually be a computer print-out from the DVLC computer at Swansea, and a defendant present in court can admit or dispute the previous convictions. Where the defendant is not present, see sub-s (4).
2.   Two subsections (3A) have been inserted in s 13. The first subsection (3A), which is not reproduced here because it relates only to Scotland, was inserted by the Civil Evidence ACt 1995, Sch 1, para 15, and the second subsection (3A) was inserted by the Magistrates' Courts (Procedure) Act 1998, s 2.
3.   See Criminal Procedure Rules 2005, Part 37 in PART I, MAGISTRATES' COURTS, PROCEDURE, ante, and Form 30 in PART IX: PRECEDENTS AND FORMS, post.
4.   The Vehicle and Driving Licences Records (Evidence) Regulations 1970, SI 1970/1997, prescribe the following in reg 3 thereof—

"(1)   in connection with the licensing of drivers under Part II of the Road Traffic Act 1960—

(*a*)   a document being, forming part of, or submitted in connection with, an application for a driving licence;

(*b*)   a driving licence;

(*c*)   a certificate of competence to drive;

(*d*)   the conviction of an offence specified in Part I or Part II of Schedule 1 to the Road Traffic Act 1962 or of an offence treated as so specified by virtue of section 5 of the Road Safety Act 1967 of any person or any order made by the Court as a result of any such conviction;

(2)   in connection with the licensing and registration of mechanically propelled vehicles under the 1962 Act—

(*a*)   a document being, forming part of, or submitted in connection with, an application for—

(i)   a vehicle licence;

(ii)   a trade licence;

(iii)   a repayment of duty under section 9 of the 1962 Act or the recovery of underpayments or overpayments of duty under section 11 of that Act;

(*b*)   a vehicle licence, trade licence, registration book or registration mark;

(*c*)   a document containing a declaration and particulars such as are prescribed under the 1962 Act in relation to vehicles exempted from duty under that Act;

(*d*)   the conviction of an offence under the 1962 Act of any person;

(3)   in connection with the examination of a goods vehicle under regulations under section 9 of the Road Safety Act 1967—

(*a*)   an application for an examination of a vehicle under the said regulations;

(*b*)   a notifiable alteration made to a vehicle and required by the said regulations to be notified to the Secretary of State;

(*c*)   a plating certificate, goods vehicle test certificate, notification of the refusal of a goods vehicle test certificate, Ministry plate, Ministry test date disc or certificate of temporary exemption."

4–1654   14. Use of records kept by operators of goods vehicles.   In any proceedings for an offence under section 40A of the Road Traffic Act 1988 or for a contravention of or failure to comply with construction and use requirements (within the meaning of Part II of the Road Traffic Act 1988) or regulations under section 74 of that Act, any record purporting to be made and authenticated in accordance with regulations under that section shall be evidence (and in Scotland sufficient evidence) of the matters stated in the record and of its due authentication.

[Road Traffic Offenders Act 1988, s 14 amended by the Road Traffic Act 1991, Sch 4.]

4–1655 15. Use of specimens in proceedings for an offence under section 4 or 5 of the Road Traffic Act. (1) This section and section 16 of this Act apply in respect of proceedings for an offence under section 3A, 4 or 5 of the Road Traffic Act 1988 (driving offences connected with drink or drugs); and expressions used in this section and section 16 of this Act have the same meaning as in sections 3A to 10 of that Act.

(2) Evidence[1] of the proportion of alcohol or any drug in a specimen of breath, blood or urine provided by the accused shall, in all cases (including cases where the specimen was /not provided in connection with the alleged offence), be taken into account[2] and, subject to subsection (3) below, it shall be assumed[3] that the proportion of alcohol in the accused's breath, blood or urine at the time of the alleged offence was not less than in the specimen.

(3) That assumption shall not be made if the accused proves[4]—

(a) that he consumed[5] alcohol before he provided the specimen and—

   (i) in relation to an offence under section 3A, after the time of the alleged offence, and
   (ii) otherwise, after he had ceased to drive, attempt to drive or be in charge of a vehicle[6] on a road or other public place, and

(b) that had he not done so the proportion of alcohol in his breath, blood or urine would not have exceeded the prescribed limit and, if it is alleged that he was unfit to drive through drink, would not have been such as to impair his ability to drive properly.

(4) A specimen of blood shall be disregarded unless—

(a) it was taken from the accused with his consent and either—

   (i) in a police station by a medical practitioner or a registered health care professional; or
   (ii) elsewhere by a medical practitioner;

or

(b) it was taken from the accused by a medical practitioner under section 7A of the Road Traffic Act 1988 and the accused subsequently gave his permission for a laboratory test of the specimen.

(5) Where, at the time a specimen of blood or urine was provided by the accused, he asked to be provided with such a specimen, evidence of the proportion of alcohol or any drug found in the specimen is not admissible on behalf of the prosecution unless—

(a) the specimen in which the alcohol or drug was found is one of two parts into which the specimen provided by the accused was divided[6] at the time it was provided[8], and
(b) the other part was supplied[9] to the accused.

[Road Traffic Offenders Act 1988, s 15 amended by the Road Traffic Act 1991, Sch 4 and the Police Reform Act 2002, 57.]

---

1. Only evidence which has been obtained in accordance with the statutory procedure laid down in ss 7 *and 8 (and s 7A) of the Road Traffic Act 1988, ante, may be taken into account (Howard v Hallett* [1984] RTR 353, [1984] Crim LR 565). As to admissibility of evidence of an analysis when only a single specimen of breath is given, see notes to s 7(1) of the Road Traffic Act 1988, ante.

Approved devices The following approvals have been given under the Road Traffic Act 1988, s 7(1)(a):
Breath Analysis Devices Approval 1998 as from 1 March 1998 The device known as the **Camic Datamaster**, manufactured by Camic (Car and Medical Instrument Company) Ltd, composed of the Camic Datamaster, the Camic Gas System and software version 31-10-95; the device known as the **Lion Intoxilyzer 6000UK**, manufactured by Lion Laboratories plc, composed of the Lion Intoxilyzer 6000UK, the Lion Intoxilyzer 6000UK Gas Delivery System Type A or Type C and software version 2.33.
Breath Analysis Devices (No 2) Approval 1998 as from 1 March 1998 The device known as the **Intoximeter EC/IR**, manufactured by Intoximeters Inc. of Saint Louis Missouri, composed of the Intoximeter EC/IR, the Intoximeter EC/IR Gas Delivery System and software version EC/IR - UK 5.23.
Breath Analysis Devices Approval 1999 as from 2 November 1999 the device known as the **Lion Intoxilyzer 6000UK**, manufactured by Lion Laboratories plc, composed of the Lion Intoxilyzer 6000UK, the Lion Intoxilyzer 6000UK Gas Delivery System Type A, B and C software version 2.34.
Challenge to type approval of machine In 1998 the Secretary of State approved three devices to be used for breath analysis by Police Forces in England and Wales and by the Breath Analysis (No 2) Approval 1998 Intoximeter EC/IR was approved for use from 1 March 1998. The three breathalysers were approved on the basis that they complied with *A Guide to Type Approval Procedures for Evidential Breath Alcohol Testing Instruments used for Road Traffic Law Enforcement in Great Britain* (Home Office and Forensic Science Service October 1994). Individual machines are subject to quality control checks in accordance with the *Quality Framework Document of Evidential Breath Alcohol Testing Instruments*. It is not open to a defendant to challenge to grant of type approval to a particular type of machine and challenge its reliability in general in criminal proceedings: *R v Skegness Magistrates, ex p Cardy* [1985] RTR 49. Magistrates are only concerned with the particular intoximeter device used: *DPP v Browne* and *DPP v Teixeira* [2001] EWHC Admin 931, 166 JP 1 and a device would still be "of a type approved by the Secretary of State" even though it failed in one respect (detection of mouth alcohol) to comply with Home Office standards, and that any defect in the functioning of the device had to be relevant to the facts of the particular case to justify an acquittal on the ground of unreliability: *DPP v Browne* and *DPP v Teixeira*, supra. The fact that an EC/IR sometimes cannot detect mouth alcohol does not deprive it of type approval: *DPP v Memery* [2002] EWHC 1720 (Admin), 167 JP 238, [2003] RTR 249. See further *Fearnley v DPP* [2005] EWHC Admin 1393, (2005) 169 JP 450.

The inability to mount a challenge to the grant of an approval order is not inconsistent with the principle enunciated in *Boddington v British Transport Police* [1999] AC 143, [1998] 2 All ER 203, namely that "only the clear language of a statute can take away the right of a defendant in criminal proceedings to challenge the lawfulness of a by-law or administrative decision where the prosecution is premised on its validity" (per Lord Irvine at 162G). Having regard to the broad legislative context it cannot have been intended by Parliament that defendant should be able to challenge the approval of the device: *DPP v Memery*, supra; followed in *Grant v DPP* [2003] EWHC 130 (Admin), 167 JP 459.

However, alterations to an intoximeter can be so fundamental as to cause it to lose its status as an approved device or at least to lead to the conclusion that the device is no longer an example of the device as approved: *Young v Flint* [1987] RTR 300 (see also *Grant v DPP* supra, paras 42–44).

Where the court accepts evidence that, due to changes made to it, a device has become a different machine from the type the Secretary of State approved, that is fatal to the admissibility of the evidence produced by it and the court must acquit: *Kemsley v DPP* [2004] EWHC Admin 278, (2005) 169 JP 149.

Where the contention is that the device which was originally type approved has been altered without the Secretary of State's written consent in such a way as to take it out of type approval, and disclosure is sought to further that contention, the court will require more than the asserted fact of unapproved modification to justify disclosure. There will have to be some material which explains how the alteration could go to loss of type approval in the Schedule and how disclosure could advance that point. A change to a parameter in the software which was still described as UK5.23 would not be such a change. Where the edited printouts still showed that the software was UK5.23, the unedited ones would still show that the software was UK.5.23. Where there was nothing to suggest a change to the gas delivery system which took it out of type approval it would be difficult to see how allegedly defective maintenance practices could cause a device to lose its type approval, but they would have to be potentially of that gravity before becoming relevant to a loss of type approval argument. The material of which disclosure is sought must have some potential for bearing on the issue in respect of which is raised. The nature and degree of an alleged unreliability has to be such that it might be able to throw doubt on the excess in the reading to such an extent that the level of alcohol in the breath might have been below the level at which a prosecution would have been instituted. If on any view there would still be an excess leading to prosecution it is difficult to see how that could justify disclosure of the material sought to make an irrelevant point about reliability. The nature of the defence claims as to what alcohol had been consumed, and when, may matter. In considering disclosure applications based on a claim about a particular machine's unreliability, and its possible basis for a defence, the court needs explicitly to consider the effect of the safeguards provided by the taking of two specimens, the intervening clearances of the device and the evidential use of the lower specimen of the two, together with the opportunity to give specimens of blood or urine and the fact that there is leeway above the breath limit before prosecution takes place. They are relevant to whether the alleged unreliability could possibly advance the stated defence. Similarly the nature and extent of the possible changes to type had to be so fundamental that it could no longer be said that this was a type approved machine; that was the issue to which the disclosure material had to be addressed. (*DPP v Wood* [2006] EWHC 32 (Admin), 170 JP 177).

Reliability of an individual machine – burden of proof on prosecution Any challenge to admission of evidence which is based upon the reliability of the intoximeter machine needs to be considered in the light of *Cracknell v Willis* [1988] AC 450, [1987] 3 All ER 801, [1987] 3 WLR 1082, HL. The presumption is that the proportion of alcohol in the relevant specimen is no less that the proportion of alcohol in the breath at the time of the offence (Road Traffic Offenders Act 1988, s 15(2)). In the event of that assumption being challenged by the defendant, the justices have to be satisfied on relevant evidence that the reading provided by the machine is one on which they can rely, the burden being on the prosecution: *Cracknell v Willis*, supra.

Challenging reliability The functioning of the device may be challenged by relevant evidence.

It is not necessary in all cases in order to rebut the presumption of reliability of the intoximeter to adduce expert or technical evidence. It is the function of justices in each case to weigh the facts critically in each case and determine whether such evidence is necessary. In such cases, the justices should bear in mind the following factors:

— *discrepancy between claimed consumption and a reading*: consider the reliability of the defendant's evidence while having in mind the presumption of reliability of the device.
— *minimal claimed consumption, a high reading and little other evidence*: the discrepancy will be solely derived from the defendant's claimed consumption, which means it has to be weighed against the presumption that the machine is reliable. Rebutting the presumption in such circumstances is likely to be difficult.
— *no observable signs of alcohol save on the breath*: certain people can develop a high tolerance to alcohol and have high levels of alcohol without there being observable signs; expert evidence may be necessary.
— *claims of lower consumption*: signs of surprise by the defendant at the reading, or the very fact of a positive test, would be expected.
— *no notice given of claim the device was defective*: prosecution may apply for an adjournment:
— within the justices' discretion to order the defendant to pay the costs of the adjournment
— as a matter of general rule, there is no reason why a defendant should not be taken to be required to give notice in advance of trial that he intended to rely on the fact that the device was defective
— having regard to the presumption of reliability, the efficient administration of justice requires the prosecution to know that the defendant intended to rebut the presumption.

(*DPP v Spurrier* [2000] RTR 60, sub nom *R v Crown Prosecution Service, ex p Spurrier* 164 JP 369, DC).

It is essential for the prosecution to prove that the device was properly calibrated, either by production of the printout or by oral evidence of readings on the display panel; see *Mayon v DPP* [1988] RTR 281. Justices may not regard a device as reliable if it is operating in any way outside its area of tolerance, eg 0.1˚ above the maximum permissible temperature (*Waite v Smith* [1986] Crim LR 405). The mere fact that the device was defective does not however render evidence from it incapable of founding a conviction (*Wright v Taplin* [1986] RTR 388n, readings too low) applied in *Fawcett v Gasparics* [1986] RTR 375, [1987] Crim LR 53 (printout stating correct numerical date but wrong day) and see *DPP v McKeown* [1997] 1 All ER 737, [1997] 1 WLR 295, [1997] 2 Cr App Rep 155, HL, (the fact that the wrong time was displayed on the intoximeter was not relevant to the proper functioning of the computer (Lion Intoximeter) and the results of its analysis were thereby admissible under s 69 of Police and Criminal Evidence Act 1984 (now repealed); applied in *DPP v Barber* (1998) 163 JP 457 (printout with letters missing – held evidence of the printout and of a service engineer who remedied a fault on the printer was admissible).

Where the two readings produced a difference of 16 microgrammes, but nevertheless expert evidence showed that the defendant must have exceeded the permitted level and there was no other evidence to suggest that the machine was not working correctly, the court should convict: *Gordon v Thorpe* [1986] RTR 358. Where a device was found to be unreliable at the time breath specimens were provided, justices were entitled to conclude, in the absence of further evidence, that the device was not reliable 100 minutes later (*Oxford v Baxendale* [1987] RTR 247). Provided a Lion Intoximeter 3000 device is demonstrated to be calibrating properly, justices are entitled to infer that it was operating efficiently, despite evidence of substantial differences between readings (*Maharaj v Solomon* [1987] RTR 295 – 20.9% difference did not prevent conviction).

When an intoximeter device is all observable respects complying with its type approval and when supplied should have had the approved version of the operating software installed, and there is no evidence of any changes to the software, the court is entitled to assume that the device is functioning correctly: *Skinner v DPP* [2004] EWHC 2914 (Admin), [2005] RTR 17.

Blood specimens etc. If the evidence of the analyst called for the prosecution differs from that of an analyst called by the defence it is open to the justices, provided they are satisfied beyond a reasonable doubt, to prefer the analysis of the former analyst (*Froggatt v Allcock* [1975] RTR 372). What has to be proved is that the alcohol content exceeded the permitted maximum, not that any specific figure of alcohol content was correct; *R v Coomaraswamy* [1976] RTR 21, 62 Cr App Rep 80: distinguishing *R v Bowell* [1974] RTR 273 (where the charge had alleged a specific alcohol content). A defendant wishing to challenge prosecution evidence of analysis must do so with evidence of his part specimen. He may call evidence that he had nothing to drink or that a mistake has been made, but he may not call expert evidence to indulge in hypothetical calculations on uncertain and unproven facts (*R v Rutter* [1977] RTR 105).

2. If the evidence of the analyst called for the prosecution differs from that of an analyst called by the defence it is open to the justices, provided they are satisfied beyond a reasonable doubt, to prefer the analysis of the former analyst (*Froggatt v Allcock* [1975] RTR 372). What has to be proved is that the alcohol content exceeded the permitted maximum, not that any specific figure of alcohol content was correct; *R v Coomaraswamy* [1976] RTR 21, 62 Cr App Rep 80: distinguishing *R v Bowell* [1974] RTR 273 (where the charge had alleged a specific alcohol content). A defendant wishing to challenge prosecution evidence of analysis must do so with evidence of his part specimen. He may call evidence that he had nothing to drink or that a mistake has been made, but he may not call expert evidence to indulge in hypothetical calculations on uncertain and unproven facts (*R v Rutter* [1977] RTR 105).

3. The burden shifts so the defendant has to displace the assumption that he was over the limit at the time he had driven; see *DPP v Williams* [1989] Crim LR 382, DC. The assumption is irrebuttable (save as provided by s 15(3) and this does not infringe Convention rights viewed in the context of the legislation as a whole: *Parker v DPP* [2001] RTR 240, DC (where delay before testing had the effect of increasing the alcohol reading), followed in *Griffiths v DPP* [2002] EWHC 792 (Admin), (2002) 166 JP 629.

4. The imposition of a legal, rather than a persuasive, burden is not only justified but is also no greater than necessary; accordingly, it complies with art 6 of the ECHR (*R v Drummond* [2002] EWCA Crim 527, [2002] Cr App Rep 352, [2002] RTR 371). Unless the case is an obvious one where the justices can reliably and confidently say that the added liquor consumed after ceasing to drive must explain the excess alcohol, the only way in which the defendant can discharge the burden on him is by calling scientific evidence (*Dawson v Lunn* (1984) 149 JP 491, [1986] RTR 234n); *DPP v Singh* [1988] RTR 209.See also *Lonergan v DPP* [2002] EWHC 1263 (Admin), [2003] RTR 188. It is irrational for justices to accept scientific evidence based on a scenario as to pre and post driving consumption of alcohol unless a proper evidential basis has been laid for that scenario: *DPP v Chambers* [2003] EWHC Admin 2142, (2004) 168 JP 231. This provision does not allow a defendant to adduce evidence of retrospective calculation based on alcohol consumption by him both *before* and *after* driving so as to establish that the alcohol consumed before driving had not, when he drove, affected his blood; see *Millard v DPP* [1990] RTR 201, 91 Cr App Rep 108.

5. "Consumed" does not include regurgitating the contents of the stomach into the mouth or upper oesophagus and reabsorbing them: *Woolfe v DPP* [2006] EWHC 1497 (Admin), [2007] RTR 16.

6. If the defendant has been charged with driving contrary to s 5(1)(*a*), the defence is established if he can show he consumed alcohol after he ceased to drive; he should not be required to show he had ceased to be in charge unless he was proceeded against for being in charge (*Rynsard v Spalding* [1986] RTR 303). Whilst there is no specific reference here to the reliability of the device (unlike s 7(3)), if the evidence before the court is that a reading may be unreliable, the magistrates may not be sure that the offence is made out; but evidence of unreliability in general as opposed to evidence of a particular machine producing an unreliable reading should not prevent a conviction if the court does not form the view that the validity and accuracy of the printout has been attacked successfully (*Newton v Woods* (1986) 151 JP 436, [1987] RTR 41).

7. It is not essential for a proper division of the specimen that the totality of the blood in the syringe is divided into no more than two parts. (*Kidd v Kidd; Ley v Donegani* [1969] 1 QB 320, [1968] 3 All ER 226, 132 JP 536.) It is the product of one single specimen which has to be divided; evidence of an analysis of blood taken on two occasions and then divided is inadmissible (*Dear v DPP* [1988] RTR 148, 87 Cr App Rep 181).

8. It is a question of fact and degree whether the division occurred "at the time it was provided" (*DPP v Elstob* (1991) 157 JP 229, [1992] Crim LR 518—held that a period not exceeding two minutes between provision of the sample and its division into two parts was consistent with the two operations being closely linked and performed as part of the same event).

9. There must be a request by the accused to be provided with a specimen and without such a request the provisions of s 15(5) do not engage; if the accused does not take up the offer of a sample it cannot be said that it is not supplied to him: *Jones v Crown Prosecution Service* [2003] EWHC 1729 (Admin), (2003) 167 JP 481. Justices were entitled to find a specimen was "supplied" when the constable offered it to the defendant, a hospital patient, and then placed it in her handbag: *Jones v DPP* [2004] EWHC 3165, [2005] RTR 15. The accused should be supplied with his part within a reasonable time, not necessarily before he leaves the police station, but it is wise and proper practice to give it to him before he leaves (*R v Sharp* [1968] 2 QB 564, [1968] 3 All ER 182, 132 JP 491). The specimen provided must be one which is sufficient as to quantity to be capable of analysis by the use of ordinary equipment and skill (*Earl v Roy* [1969] 2 All ER 684, 133 JP 427; *R v Nixon* [1969] 2 All ER 688, 133 JP 520). Doubts thrown by experts on the *quality* of a specimen, and hence the accuracy of the results of its analysis, are relevant only in deciding whether an offence has been made out, and do not justify justices dismissing for non-compliance with this section (*Nicholson v Watts* [1973] RTR 208, [1973] Crim LR 246). The plain purpose of s 15(5) is to enable the defendant to obtain an independent analysis of the specimen provided by him; accordingly, where a defendant was misled by a prosecutor into thinking that she did not have a specimen which could be submitted to independent analysis, as a matter of justice the conviction was quashed (*Perry v McGovern* [1986] RTR 240). Where incompetent storage by the prosecution rendered a sample unfit for scientific testing by the defence, and such testing could well have established a line of defence, it was not enough for the judge to exclude the prosecution's evidence of analysis, the proceedings should have been stayed; although the scientific examination of samples is subject to the same principles as those enunciated in *R (on the application of Ebrahim) v Feltham Magistrates' Court* (see PART 1: MAGISTRATES' COURTS, Procedure, para **1–63**, ante), this situation is very different from the situation where a videotape is unavailable but witnesses may be able to testify as to the relevant events (*R v Boyd* [2002] EWCA Crim 2836, [2004] RTR 3). Where a part specimen was physically supplied to the defendant as required by s 15(5)(*b*), the fact that it was wrongly labelled did not mean that it was not supplied for the purposes of the section (*Butler v DPP* [1990] RTR 377); similarly the supply of the specimen in an envelope has been held to be a gloss on the procedure not part of the statutory requirement (*DPP v Snook* [1993] Crim LR 883). Subject to there being some relevant and clearly identified purpose for which it is to be adduced and subject to the exercise of the court's discretion, evidence of breath test results may properly be admissible in cases where the prosecution is based on the result of a blood alcohol analysis. Therefore, if the breath test result is compatible with, in the sense of being broadly equivalent to, the blood analysis result, it may provide evidence that is capable of tending to support the reliability of the blood analysis result (*Slasor v DPP* [1999] RTR 432).

4–1656   16. Documentary evidence as to specimens in such proceedings. (1) Evidence of the proportion of alcohol or a drug in a specimen of breath, blood or urine[1] may, subject to subsections (3) and (4) below and to section 15(5) of this Act, be given by the production[2] of a document[3] or documents purporting to be whichever of the following is appropriate, that is to say—

(a) a statement[4] automatically produced by the device by which the proportion of alcohol in a specimen of breath was measured and a certificate signed[5] by a constable (which may but need not be contained in the same document as the statement) that the statement relates to a specimen provided by the accused at the date and time[6] shown in the statement, and

(b) a certificate signed by an authorised analyst as to the proportion of alcohol or any drug found in a specimen of blood or urine identified in the certificate.

(2) Subject to subsections (3) and (4) below, evidence that a specimen of blood was taken from the accused with his consent by a medical practitioner or a registered health care professional may[7] be given by the production of a document purporting to certify that fact and to be signed by a medical practitioner or a registered health care professional.

(3) Subject to subsection (4) below—

(a) a document purporting to be such a statement or such a certificate (or both such a statement and such a certificate) as is mentioned in subsection (1)(a) above is admissible in evidence on behalf of the prosecution in pursuance of this section only if[8] a copy[9] of it either has been handed[10] to the accused when the document was produced or has been served[11] on him not later than seven days before the hearing[12], and

(b) any other document is so admissible only if a copy of it has been served on the accused not later than seven days before the hearing.

(4) A document purporting to be a certificate[13] (or so much of a document as purports to be a certificate) is not so admissible if the accused, not later than three days before the hearing or within such further time as the court may in special circumstances allow, has served notice on the prosecutor requiring the attendance at the hearing of the person by whom the document purports to be signed.

(5) Scotland.

(6) A copy of a certificate required by this section to be served on the accused or a notice required by this section to be served on the prosecutor may be served personally or sent by registered post or recorded delivery service[14].

(6A) Where the proceedings mentioned in section 15(1) of this Act are proceedings before a magistrates' court inquiring into an offence as examining justices this section shall have effect with the omission of subsection (4).

(7) In this section "authorised analyst" means—

(a) any person possessing the qualifications prescribed by regulations made under section 27 of the Food Safety Act 1990 as qualifying persons for appointment as public analyst under those Acts, and

(b) any other person authorised by the Secretary of State[15] to make analyses for the purposes of this section.

[Road Traffic Offenders Act 1988, s 16 as amended by the Food Safety Act 1990, Sch 3, the Criminal Procedure and Investigations Act 1996, Sch 1 and the Police Reform Act 2002, 57.]

---

1. A printout may, however, be adduced as evidence that the device had not produced a reliable indication of the proportion of alcohol, and that the police officer had reasonable cause so to believe, without satisfying the preconditions laid down in the subsequent provisions of this section; in such circumstances s 16(1) has no relevance: *Jubb v DPP* [2002] EWHC 2317 (Admin), (2003) 167 JP 50, [2003] RTR 272.

2. Once an exhibit is produced in evidence the court may examine it whenever it chooses (*R v Pydar Justices, ex p Foster* (1995) 160 JP 87—police officer produced print-out in evidence, handed to Crown Prosecutor but not passed to the bench. Court entitled to examine the print-out on submission of no case by the defence after the prosecution case had closed). See also *Leeson v DPP* [2000] RTR 385, DC.

3. Evidence of a printout is not rendered inadmissible merely because the breath testing device is shown to be unreliable; however, lack of reliability in a device may entitle the court to reject the evidence so given, except where the error in the printout is such that it can be explained or cured by expert evidence; see *Fawcett v Gasparics* [1986] RTR 375, [1987] Crim LR 53.

Evidence enabling the inference reasonably to be drawn that a breath-testing device was unreliable is admissible, for example the defendant's own evidence of the amount of alcohol he had drunk (*Cracknell v Willis* [1988] AC 450, [1987] 3 All ER 801, 86 Cr App Rep 196, HL), but the fact that it is possible as a matter of law to rebut the presumption in s 15(2), ante, by evidence does not mean that it is necessarily a comparatively easy thing to do; see *DPP v Hill* (1990) 156 JP 197, [1991] RTR 351.

4. The "test record" document produced by the Lion Intoximeter 3000 breath testing device may form part of the "statement" for the purposes of this section, and, therefore, is admissible in evidence. A police officer who is a trained operator of the breath testing device may give evidence to interpret the meaning of the contents of the document (*Gaimster v Marlow* [1984] QB 218, [1985] 1 All ER 82, 148 JP 624). It may be unwise for the printout to be altered in any way, for example substituting BST for GMT; where the court has to be informed of such a fact, it should be done by oral evidence at the hearing (*Beck v Scammell* [1986] RTR 162).

Where the first set of printouts were lost, shortly after being printed, it was held that provided there was evidence that the device was working properly and was accurately calibrated, a second printout might be admitted in evidence as an original document (*DPP v Hutchings* (1990) 156 JP 702, [1991] RTR 380).

Section 16(1) is merely an enabling section, which permits the printed statement of the device to be adduced in evidence. Nevertheless, in the absence of such a statement, the prosecution must establish not only the results of the analysis of the 2 breath specimens effected by the device, but also the results of the self calibration executed by the device before and after the breath specimens were provided (*Owen v Chesters* (1984) 149 JP 295, [1985] RTR 191, [1985] Crim LR 156). However, it is not necessary for the evidence to establish the actual calibration results (*Greenaway v DPP* (1993) 158 JP 27, [1994] RTR 17); provided the prosecution can establish that the machine was properly calibrated, oral evidence of the results of the analysis will be admissible (*Thom v DPP* [1994] RTR 11), (1993) 158 JP 414). An officer who gives such evidence must have been trained in the use and manner of performance of the device, understanding its calibration etc (*Denneny v Harding* [1986] RTR 350, [1986] Crim LR 254), but in the absence of any evidence that the officer lacked the requisite expertise the justices are entitled to decide for themselves what weight to place on his evidence and whether to accept it as establishing the reliability of the machine (*Sneyd v DPP* [2006] EWHC 560 (Admin), (2006) 170 JP 545,

[2007] RTR 7 . There is no difference in this regard between oral evidence as to the results displayed on the screen and oral evidence as to the results displayed on the printout; these are simply two different ways by which the machine displays its results (*Sneyd v DPP*, supra).

5. A failure by the constable to sign the certificate does not prevent oral evidence of the reading being given by the officer who operated the Intoximeter (*Garner v DPP* (1989) 154 JP 277, [1990] RTR 208, DC).

6. There is nothing wrong with a statement which shows the time recorded as Greenwich Mean Time instead of British Summer Time (*Parker v DPP* (1992) 157 JP 218).

7. Section 16(2) of the Road Traffic Offenders Act 1988 is not in mandatory terms and does not preclude evidence being given from another source as to consent or the qualifications of the medical practitioner (*Steward v DPP* [2003] EWHC 2251 (Admin), [2003] 4 All ER 1105).

8. This requirement is mandatory; no purported waiver can make the document or certificate admissible if it has not been served (*Tobi v Nicholas* (1987) 86 Cr App Rep 323, [1988] RTR 343). However, the defendant may waive the requirement of proof of service of the document or certificate (*Louis v DPP* (1997) 162 JP 287, [1998] RTR 354).

9. The omission of a signature on the copy given to the defendant does not affect its admissibility (*Chief Constable of Surrey v Wickens* (1984) 149 JP 333; nor does an incorrect forename on such copy where the error was purely formal and caused no prejudice to the defendant (*Toovey v Chief Constable of Northumbria* [1986] Crim LR 475).

10. It is insufficient compliance with this requirement for the document to be left on a counter and not offered to the defendant (*Walton v Rimmer* [1986] RTR 31). There is compliance with the "handed to" requirement of s 16(3)(a) where the defendant is offered a copy of the printout, but he refuses to accept it (*McCormack v DPP* [2002] EWHC 173 (Admin), [2002] RTR 20).

11. Notwithstanding sub-s (6), post, the requirement of service is satisfied by service upon an authorised agent, such as a solicitor, who has authority to receive and deal with documents (*Anderton v Kinnard* [1986] RTR 11). Service may be effected by handling to counsel, but he has a discretion to refuse to accept (*Penman v Parker* [1986] 2 All ER 862, [1986] 1 WLR 882, [1988] RTR 403).

12. If the defendant wishes to submit that a copy of the certificate has not been served on him as required by this provision he must object to the admission of the contents of the certificate before it is put in evidence; if he fails to do so his right to object is waived (*R v Banks* [1972] 1 All ER 1041, 136 JP 306). The "hearing" is that at which the document is to be adduced in evidence, not the hearing at which the defendant first appeared in answer to the summons (*Williams v DPP* [1991] 3 All ER 651; [1991] 1 WLR 1160).

13. Although in these circumstances the certificate is rendered inadmissible, the print-out remains admissible and can be put in by the operator (*Temple v Botha* [1985] Crim LR 517).

14. Unless the contrary is proved, justices may find that an acceptable method of delivery within the required time for the purposes of this subsection has been used on proof of service in accordance with the Criminal Procedure Rules 2005, Part 4, in PART I, ante (*Hawkins v Crown Prosecution Service* (1987) Times, 24th August).

15. See title, FOOD, post. Such authority has been given to named persons employed at the Home Office Forensic Science Laboratories and the Metropolitan Police Laboratory (Home Office Circular No 43/1963, dated 20 February, 1963).

4–1657　17. Provisions as to proceedings for certain offences in connection with the construction and use of vehicles and equipment. (1) If in any proceedings for an offence under section 40A, 41A, 41B or 42 of the Road Traffic Act 1988 (using a vehicle in dangerous condition or contravention of construction and use regulations)—

(*a*)　any question arises as to a weight of any description specified in the plating certificate for a goods vehicle, and

(*b*)　a weight of that description is marked on the vehicle,

it shall be assumed, unless the contrary is proved, that the weight marked on the vehicle is the weight so specified.

(2) If, in any proceedings for an offence—

(*a*)　under Part II of the Road Traffic Act 1988, except sections 47 and 75, or

(*b*)　under section 174(2) or (5) (false statements and deception) of that Act,

any question arises as to the date of manufacture of a vehicle, a date purporting to be such a date and marked on the vehicle in pursuance of regulations under that Part of that Act shall be evidence (and in Scotland sufficient evidence) that the vehicle was manufactured on the date so marked.

(3) If in any proceedings for the offence of driving a vehicle on a road, or causing or permitting a vehicle to be so driven, in contravention of a prohibition under section 70(2) of the Road Traffic Act 1988 any question arises whether a weight of any description has been reduced to a limit imposed by construction and use requirements, or so that it has ceased to be excessive, the burden of proof shall lie on the accused.

(4) Scotland.

[Road Traffic Offenders Act 1988, s 17 amended by the Road Traffic Act 1991, Schs 4 and 8.]

4–1658　18. Evidence by certificate as to registration of driving instructors and licences to give instruction. (1) A certificate signed by the Registrar and stating that, on any date—

(*a*)　a person's name was, or was not, in the register,

(*b*)　the entry of a person's name was made in the register or a person's name was removed from it,

(*c*)　a person was, or was not, the holder of a current licence under section 129 of the Road Traffic Act 1988, or

(*d*)　a licence under that section granted to a person came into force or ceased to be in force,

shall be evidence, and in Scotland sufficient evidence, of the facts stated in the certificate in pursuance of this section.

(2) A certificate so stating and purporting to be so signed by the Registrar shall be deemed to be so signed unless the contrary is proved.

(3) In this section "current licence", "Registrar" and "register" have the same meanings as in Part V of the Road Traffic Act 1988.

[Road Traffic Offenders Act 1988, s 18.]

4–1659   20. Speeding offences etc: admissibility of certain evidence.   (1) Evidence (which in Scotland shall be sufficient evidence) of a fact relevant to proceedings for an offence to which this section applies may be given by the production of—

(a) a record produced by a prescribed device, and

(b) (in the same or another document) a certificate as to the circumstances in which the record was produced signed by a constable or by a person authorised by or on behalf of the chief officer of police for the police area in which the offence is alleged to have been committed;

but subject to the following provisions of this section.

(2) This section applies to—

(a) an offence under section 16 of the Road Traffic Regulation Act 1984 consisting in the contravention of a restriction on the speed of vehicles imposed under section 14 of that Act;

(b) an offence under subsection (4) of section 17 of that Act consisting in the contravention of a restriction on the speed of vehicles imposed under that section;

(c) an offence under section 88(7) of that Act (temporary minimum speed limits);

(d) an offence under section 89(1) of that Act (speeding offences generally);

(e) an offence under section 36(1) of the Road Traffic Act 1988 consisting in the failure to comply with an indication given by a light signal that vehicular traffic is not to proceed.

(f) an offence under Part I or II of the Road Traffic Regulation Act 1984 of contravening or failing to comply with an order or regulations made under either of those Parts relating to the use of an area of road which is described as a bus lane or a route for use by buses only;

(g) an offence under section 29(1) of the Vehicle Excise and Registration Act 1994 (using or keeping an unlicensed vehicle on a public road).

(3) The Secretary of State may by order amend subsection (2) above by making additions to or deletions from the list of offences for the time being set out there; and an order under this subsection may make such transitional provision as appears to him to be necessary or expedient.

(4) A record produced or measurement made by a prescribed device shall not be admissible as evidence of a fact relevant to proceedings for an offence to which this section applies unless—

(a) the device is of a type approved[1] by the Secretary of State, and

(b) any conditions subject to which the approval was given are satisfied.

(5) Any approval given by the Secretary of State for the purposes of this section may be given subject to conditions as to the purposes for which, and the manner and other circumstances in which, any device of the type concerned is to be used.

(6) In proceedings for an offence to which this section applies, evidence (which in Scotland shall be sufficient evidence)—

(a) of a measurement made by a device, or of the circumstances in which it was made, or

(b) that a device was of a type approved for the purposes of this section, or that any conditions subject to which an approval was given were satisfied,

may be given by the production of a document which is signed as mentioned in subsection (1) above and which, as the case may be, gives particulars of the measurement or of the circumstances in which it was made, or states that the device was of such a type or that, to the best of the knowledge and belief of the person making the statement, all such conditions were satisfied.

(7) For the purposes of this section a document purporting to be a record of the kind mentioned in subsection (1) above, or to be a certificate or other document signed as mentioned in that subsection or in subsection (6) above, shall be deemed to be such a record, or to be so signed, unless the contrary is proved.

(8) Nothing in subsection (1) or (6) above makes a document admissible as evidence in proceedings for an offence unless a copy of it has, not less than seven days[2] before the hearing or trial, been served on the person charged with the offence; and nothing in those subsections makes a document admissible as evidence of anything other than the matters shown on a record produced by a prescribed device if that person, not less than three days before the hearing or trial or within such further time as the court may in special circumstances allow, serves a notice on the prosecutor requiring attendance at the hearing or trial of the person who signed the document.

(8A) *Scotland*[3].

(8A) Where the proceedings for an offence to which this section applies are proceedings before a magistrates' court inquiring into an offence as examining justices this section shall have effect as if in subsection (8) the words from "and nothing" to the end of the subsection were omitted[3].

(9) In this section "prescribed device" means device of a description specified in an order[4] made by the Secretary of State.

(10) The powers to make orders under subsections (3) and (9) above shall be exercisable by statutory instrument, which shall be subject to annulment in pursuance of a resolution of either House of Parliament.

[Road Traffic Offenders Act 1988, s 20 as substituted by the Road Traffic Act 1991, s 23 and amended by the Criminal Justice (Scotland) Act 1995, Sch 6, the Criminal Procedure and Investigations Act 1996, Sch 1, SI 1997/384 and SI 2001/1814.]

---

1. The prosecution is required to prove that the Secretary of State has approved the use of the device before the measurement of speed given by it can be admitted in evidence. Justices may not infer or assume that approval has been given, nor may they take judicial notice of the approval by reason of the fact that the device has been regularly used by the police. Normally, approval can be established by production of the approval order, or evidence of a police officer that the device he used was an approved device (*Roberts v DPP* [1994] RTR 31, a decision based on the original wording of s 20

of the Road Traffic Offenders Act 1988). A G R Speedman speed trap is a computer and evidence produced by it is admissible without a certificate under s 69 of the Police and Criminal Evidence Act 1984 where the burden of proving that there had been no improper use of the computer and that it had been operating properly is discharged by calling a non expert witness who is familiar with its operation (*Darby v DPP* (1994) 159 JP 533 following *R v Shepherd* [1993] AC 380, [1993] 1 All ER 225, 157 JP 145, HL).

2. The purpose of this section is to enable the record and certificate to be tendered in evidence at the hearing without the necessity of anybody being called to prove them. But it does not preclude such evidence being called in the conventional manner. Therefore, where the prosecution failed to comply with this section, it is not precluded from calling the police officer who may produce the record as real evidence. If the defendant is placed at a disadvantage thereby, the remedy is an adjournment and an application for costs thrown away, if appropriate (*DPP v Thornley* [2006] EWHC 312 (Admin), 170 JP 385).

3. Two subsections (8A) have been inserted in this section; the first by the Criminal Justice (Scotland) Act 1995, Sch 6, and the second which applies to England and Wales by the Criminal Procedure and Investigations Act 1996, Sch 1.

4. See the Road Traffic Offenders (Prescribed Devices) Order 1992, SI 1992/1209, the Road Traffic Offenders (Prescribed Devices) (No 2) Order 1992, SI 1992/2843, the Road Traffic Offenders (Prescribed Devices) Order 1993, SI 1993/1698, the Road Traffic Offenders (Prescribed Devices) Order 1999, SI 1999/162 and the Road Traffic Offenders (Additional Offences and Prescribed Devices) Order 2001, SI 2001/1814; a number of approval orders have been made.

4–1660 22. Notification of disability. (1) If in any proceedings for an offence committed in respect of a motor vehicle it appears to the court[1] that the accused may be suffering from any relevant disability or prospective disability (within the meaning of Part III of the Road Traffic Act 1988) the court must notify the Secretary of State.

(2) A notice sent by a court to the Secretary of State in pursuance of this section must be sent in such manner and to such address and contain such particulars as the Secretary of State may determine.

[Road Traffic Offenders Act 1988, s 22.]

1. There must be sufficient material before the court, even if only by way of something said in mitigation, suggesting that the defendant is suffering from a relevant disability or a prospective disability, before the court can properly refer the matter to the Secretary of State; see *R v Chichester Justices, ex p Crouch* (1982) 146 JP 26.

Verdict

4–1661 24. Alternative verdicts: general. (1) Where—

(a) a person charged with an offence under a provision of the Road Traffic Act 1988 specified in the first column of the Table below (where the general nature of the offences is also indicated) is found not guilty[1] of that offence, but

(b) the allegations in the indictment or information (or in Scotland complaint) amount to or include an allegation of an offence under one or more of the provisions specified in the corresponding entry in the second column,

he may be convicted of that offence or of one or more of those offences.

Offence charged	Alternative
Section 1 (causing death by dangerous driving)	Section 2 (dangerous driving) Section 3 (careless, and inconsiderate, driving)
Section 2 (dangerous driving)	Section 3 (careless, and inconsiderate, driving)
Section 3A (causing death by careless driving when under influence of drink or drugs)	Section 3 (careless, and inconsiderate, driving) Section 4(1) (driving when unfit to drive through drink or drugs) Section 5(1)(a) (driving with excess alcohol in breath, blood or urine) Section 7(6) (failing to provide specimen)
Section 4(1) (driving or attempting to drive when unfit to drive through drink or drugs)	Section 4(2) (being in charge of a vehicle when unfit to drive through drink or drugs)
Section 5(1)(a) (driving or attempting to drive with excess alcohol in breath, blood or urine)	Section 5(1)(b) (being in charge of a vehicle with excess alcohol in breath, blood or urine)
Section 28 (dangerous cycling)	Section 29 (careless, and inconsiderate, cycling)

(2) Where the offence with which a person is charged is an offence under section 3A of the Road Traffic Act 1988, subsection (1) above shall not authorise his conviction of any offence of attempting to drive.

(3) Where a person is charged with having committed an offence under section 4(1) or 5(1)(a) of the Road Traffic Act 1988 by driving a vehicle, he may be convicted of having committed an offence under the provision in question by attempting to drive.

(4) Where by virtue of this section a person is convicted before the Crown Court of an offence triable only summarily, the court shall have the same powers and duties as a magistrates' court would have had on convicting him of that offence.

(5) Scotland.

(6) This section has effect without prejudice to section 6(3) of the Criminal Law Act 1967 (alternative verdicts on trial on indictment), sections 295, 138(4), 256 and 293 of and Schedule 3 to the Criminal Procedure (Scotland) Act 1995 and section 23 of this Act.

[Road Traffic Offenders Act 1988, s 24 as substituted by the Road Traffic Act 1991, s 24 and amended by the Criminal Procedure (Consequential Provisions) (Scotland) Act 1995, Sch 4.]

1. A court which has dismissed a charge of dangerous driving on a submission of no case to answer has found the defendant not guilty and, depending on the circumstances, should go on to consider whether he is guilty of careless driving (*DPP v Smith* [2002] EWHC 1151 (Admin), [2002] Crim LR 970). However, a stay for abuse of process does not result in a conviction and s 24 is not available (*R v Khela* [2005] EWCA Crim 3446, [2006] 1 Cr App R 23).

After conviction

4–1672   25. Information as to date of birth and sex.   (1) If on convicting a person of an offence involving obligatory or discretionary disqualification or of such other offence as may be prescribed by regulations under section 105 of the Road Traffic Act 1988 the court does not know his date of birth, the court must order him to give that date to the court in writing.

(2) If a court convicting a person of such an offence in a case where—

(*a*) notification has been given to a justices' chief executive in pursuance of section 12(4) of the Magistrates' Courts Act 1980 (written pleas of guilty), or written intimation of a plea of guilty has been given in pursuance of section 334(3) of the Criminal Procedure (Scotland) Act 1975, and

(*b*) the notification or intimation did not include a statement of the person's sex,

does not know the person's sex, the court must order the person to give that information to the court in writing.

(3) A person who knowingly fails to comply with an order under subsection (1) or (2) above is guilty of an offence[1].

(4) Nothing in section 7 of the Powers of Criminal Courts (Sentencing) Act 2000 (where magistrates' court commits a person to the Crown Court to be dealt with, certain powers and duties transferred to that court) applies to any duty imposed upon a magistrates' court by subsection (1) or (2) above.

(5) Where a person has given his date of birth in accordance with this section or section 8 of this Act, the Secretary of State may serve on that person a notice in writing requiring him to provide the Secretary of State—

(*a*) with such evidence in that person's possession or obtainable by him as the Secretary of State may specify for the purpose of verifying that date, and

(*b*) if his name differs from his name at the time of his birth, with a statement in writing specifying his name at that time.

(6) A person who knowingly fails to comply with a notice under subsection (5) above is guilty of an offence[1].

(7) A notice to be served on any person under subsection (5) above may be served on him by delivering it to him or by leaving it at his proper address or by sending it to him by post; and for the purposes of this subsection and section 7 of the Interpretation Act 1978 in its application to this subsection the proper address of any person shall be his latest address as known to the person serving the notice.

[Road Traffic Offenders Act 1988, s 25 as amended by the Magistrates' Courts (Procedure) Act 1998, s 4, the Powers of Criminal Courts (Sentencing) Act 2000, Sch 9 and the Access to Justice Act 1999, Sch 13.]

1. For penalty see Sch 2, post. As to production of a driving licence, see s 27, post.

4–1673   26. Interim disqualification.   (1) Where a magistrates' court—

(*a*) commits an offender to the Crown Court under section 6 of the Powers of Criminal Courts (Sentencing) Act 2000 or any enactment mentioned in subsection (4) of that section, or any enactment to which that section applies, or

(*b*) remits an offender to another magistrates' court under section 10 of the Act,

to be dealt with for an offence involving obligatory or discretionary disqualification, it may order him to be disqualified until he has been dealt with in respect of the offence.

(2) Where a court in England and Wales—

(*a*) defers passing sentence on an offender under section 1 of that Act in respect of an offence involving obligatory or discretionary disqualification, or

(*b*) adjourns after convicting an offender of such an offence but before dealing with him for the offence,

it may order the offender to be disqualified until he has been dealt with in respect of the offence.

(3) Scotland.

(4) Subject to subsection (5) below, an order under this section shall cease to have effect at the end of the period of six months beginning with the day on which it is made, if it has not ceased to have effect before that time.

(5) Scotland.

(6) Where a court orders a person to be disqualified under this section ("the first order"), no court shall make a further order under this section in respect of the same offence or any offence in respect of which an order could have been made under this section at the time the first order was made.

(7) Where a court makes an order under this section in respect of any person it must—

(*a*)   require him to produce to the court any licence held by him and its counterpart, and
(*b*)   retain the licence and counterpart until it deals with him or (as the case may be) cause them to be sent to the proper officer of the court which is to deal with him.

(7A)   In subsection (7) above "proper officer" means—

(*a*)   in relation to a magistrates' court in England and Wales, the justices' chief executive for the court, and
(*b*)   in relation to any other court, the clerk of the court.

(8)   If the holder of the licence has not caused it and its counterpart to be delivered, or has not posted them, in accordance with section 7 of this Act and does not produce the licence and counterpart as required under subsection (7) above, then he is guilty of an offence.
(9)   Subsection (8) above does not apply to a person who—

(*a*)   satisfies the court that he has applied for a new licence and has not received it, or
(*b*)   surrenders to the court a current receipt for his licence and its counterpart issued under section 56 of this Act, and produces the licence and counterpart to the court immediately on their return.

(10)   Where a court makes an order under this section in respect of any person, sections 44(1), 47(2), 91ZA(7) and 91A(5) of this Act shall not apply in relation to the order, but—

(*a*)   the court must send notice of the order to the Secretary of State, and
(*b*)   if the court which deals with the offender determines not to order him to be disqualified under section 34 or 35 of this Act, it must send notice of the determination to the Secretary of State.

(11)   A notice sent by a court to the Secretary of State in pursuance of subsection (10) above must be sent in such manner and to such address and contain such particulars as the Secretary of State may determine.
(12)   Where on any occasion a court deals with an offender—

(*a*)   for an offence in respect of which an order was made under this section, or
(*b*)   for two or more offences in respect of any of which such an order was made,

any period of disqualification which is on that occasion imposed under section 34 or 35 of this Act shall be treated as reduced by any period during which he was disqualified by reason only of an order made under this section in respect of any of those offences.
(13)   Any reference in this or any other Act (including any Act passed after this Act) to the length of a period of disqualification shall, unless the context otherwise requires, be construed as a reference to its length before any reduction under this section.
(14)   In relation to licences which came into force before 1st June 1990, the references in this section to counterparts of licences shall be disregarded.
(15)   In subsection (7) above "proper officer" means—

(*a*)   in relation to a magistrates' court in England and Wales, the justices' chief executive for the court, and
(*b*)   in relation to any other court, the clerk of the court.
[Road Traffic Offenders Act 1988, s 26 as substituted by the Road Traffic Act 1991, s 25 and amended by SI 1996/1974, the Powers of Criminal Courts (Sentencing) Act 2000, Sch 9 and the Access to Justice Act 1999, Sch 13 and the Crime (International Co-operation) Act 2003, Sch 5.]

PART II[1]
SENTENCE[2]
Introductory

4–1674   27. Production of licence.   (1)   Where a person who is the holder of a licence is convicted of an offence involving obligatory or discretionary disqualification, and a court proposes to make an order disqualifying him or an order under section 44 of this Act, the court must, unless it has already received them, require the licence and its counterpart to be produced to it.
(2)   Repealed.
(3)   If the holder of the licence and its counterpart has not caused it and its counterpart to be delivered, or posted it, in accordance with section 7 of this Act and does not produce it and its counterpart as required under this section or section 40 of the Crime (Sentences) Act 1997*, section 146 or 147 of the Powers of Criminal Courts (Sentencing) Act 2000 or (Scotland), or if the holder of the licence does not produce it and its counterpart as required by section 40B of the Child Support Act 1991, then, unless he satisfies the court that he has applied for a new licence and has not received it—

(*a*)   he is guilty of an offence[3], and
(*b*)   the licence shall be suspended from the time when its production was required until it and its counterpart are produced[4] to the court and shall, while suspended, be of no effect.

(4)   Subsection (3) above does not apply where the holder of the licence—

(*a*)   has caused a current receipt for the licence and its counterpart issued under section 56 of this Act to be delivered to the proper officer of the court not later than the day before the date appointed for the hearing, or

(b)   has posted such a receipt, at such time that in the ordinary course of post it would be delivered not later than that day, in a letter duly addressed to the proper officer and either registered or sent by the recorded delivery service, or

(c)   surrenders such a receipt to the court at the hearing,

and produces the licence and its counterpart to the court immediately on their return.★★

(5)   In subsection (4) above "proper officer" means—

(a)   in relation to a magistrates' court in England and Wales, the justices' chief executive for the court, and

(b)   in relation to any other court, the clerk of the court.

[Road Traffic Offenders Act 1988, s 27 amended by SI 1990/144, the Road Traffic Act 1991, Sch 4, the Access to Justice ACt 1999, Sch 13, the Powers of Criminal Courts (Sentencing) Act 2000, Sch 9 and the Child SUpport, Pensions and Social Security Act 2000, s 16(5).]

★Substituted by the Criminal Justice Act 2003, Sch 32 from a date to be appointed.
★★Sub-section (4) repealed in relation to Scotland by the Statute Law (Repeals) Act 2004.

1.   Part II contains ss 24–50.

2.   This Part of the Act deals comprehensively with the sentencing of road traffic offenders, penalties for which are set out in Sch 2 to this Act, post. Numerous offences carry obligatory or discretionary disqualification and endorsement; it should be observed that disqualification may be ordered only for endorseable offences.

The following **sentencing procedure** is suggested; (1) announce conviction; (2) require production of licence (s 27); (3) examine any endorsement on the licence or, failing production of the licence, examine the document produced from records and admitted under s 13; (4) hear any necessary representations (see below); (5) order (at one and the same time) penalty (s 33), disqualification (ss 34, 35, 36), and endorsement (s 44).

Whenever dealing with **endorseable offences**, the court will need to consider the following matters: "present offence" means an offence for which the court is currently sentencing.

(1)   Is disqualification discretionary or obligatory for the present offence(s) (Sch 2); if the latter, are there special reasons (with reference to the offence *not* the offender) for not disqualifying or endorsing or should the period be increased for a serious or repeated offence under s 34(4) (ss 34, 44)?

(2)   Disregarding any offence for which obligatory disqualification is being ordered, if there is more than one present offence, was there more than one "occasion" and if not, should the offences count as if committed on more than one occasion (state reasons) (s 28)?

(3)   If the present offence carries a range of penalty points, select one (s 28, Sch 2).

(4)   If any 3 year period including at least one of the present offences, shows *commission* of offences for which penalty points total 12 or more (*occasions* and not individual offences count for this purpose), disqualify for minimum 6 months (s 35) (subject to (6) below).

(5)   Only points after previous disqualification for repeated offences count, but one previous disqualification for a fixed period of 56 days or more *imposed* in the three years previous to the date of the *commission* of the most recent offence increases today's minimum disqualification to one year, two previous increases it to 2 years (s 35) (subject to (6) below).

(6)   Mitigating circumstances may reduce or avoid disqualification for repeated offences, but excuse *cannot* be

—offence not serious
—hardship (unless exceptional)
—mitigation used in last 3 years (s 35(4)).

(7)   Disqualification(s) have effect from today and are concurrent only.

(8)   Should discretionary disqualification be ordered if none of the foregoing applied (s 34)?

Newly qualified drivers are subject to a probationary period of two years beginning on the day on which a test of competence to drive is passed. If a person is convicted of (or accepts a fixed penalty or conditional offer for) an enforcable offence committed during this period and the number of penalty points to be taken account of under section 29 of this Act is six or more the Secretary of State will revoke the licence and may not issue a full licence until a further test of competence to drive has been passed, see the Road Traffic (New Drivers) Act 1995, this PART, post.

3.   For penalty see Sch 2, post. The Road Traffic Act 1988, s 164(5) provides a "back-up" power where a licence has not been produced.

4.   If it is not produced, s 13, ante enables evidence of previous endorsements to be supplied to the court.

4–1675   28. Penalty points to be attributed to an offence.   (1) Where a person is convicted of an offence involving obligatory endorsement, then, subject to the following provisions of this section, the number of penalty points to be attributed to the offence is—

(a)   the number shown in relation to the offence in the last column of Part I or Part II of Schedule 2 to this Act, or

(b)   where a range of numbers is shown, a number within that range.

(2)   Where a person is convicted of an offence committed by aiding, abetting, counselling or procuring, or inciting to the commission of, an offence involving obligatory disqualification, then, subject to the following provisions of this section, the number of penalty points to be attributed to the offence is ten.

(3)   Where both a range of numbers and a number followed by the words "(fixed penalty)" is shown in the last column of Part I of Schedule 2 to this Act in relation to an offence, that number is the number of penalty points to be attributed to the offence for the purposes of sections 57(5) and 77(5) of this Act; and, where only a range of numbers is shown there, the lowest number in the range is the number of penalty points to be attributed to the offence for those purposes.

(4)   Where a person is convicted (whether on the same occasion or not) of two or more offences committed on the same occasion[1] and involving obligatory endorsement, the total number of penalty points to be attributed to them is the number or highest number that would be attributed on a conviction of one of them (so that if the convictions are on different occasions the number of penalty points to be attributed to the offences on the later occasion or occasions shall be restricted accordingly).

(5) In a case where (apart from this subsection) subsection (4) above would apply to two or more offences, the court may if it thinks fit determine that that subsection shall not apply to the offences (or, where three or more offences are concerned, to any one or more of them).

(6) Where a court makes such a determination it shall state its reasons in open court and, if it is a magistrates' court, or in Scotland a court of summary jurisdiction, shall cause them to be entered in the register (in Scotland, record) of its proceedings.

(7)–(9) The Secretary of State may by order alter penalty points.

[Road Traffic Offenders Act 1988, s 28 as substituted by the Road Traffic Act 1991, s 27.]

---

1. "Same occasion" is not defined in the Act, but it is suggested that there must be some close physical or temporal link before offences can be said to have been committed "on the same occasion". In *Johnson v Finbow* [1983] 1 WLR 879, [1983] RTR 363, [1983] Crim LR 480, where the defendant was convicted of failing to stop after an accident and failing to report the accident to the police, it was held that, although the second offence occurred some time after the first, the two offences should be attributed to the same occasion. In *Johnston v Over* (1984) 149 JP 286, [1985] RTR 240, it was stated that whether or not offences were committed on the same occasion was a question of fact; accordingly, where a defendant used two motor vehicles without insurance by leaving them parked in the road outside his house, it was held that common sense dictated that having regard to the use which was being made of the vehicles at the material times the offences were committed on the same occasion.

4-1676 29. Penalty points to be taken into account on conviction. (1) Where a person is convicted of an offence involving obligatory endorsement, the penalty points to be taken into account on that occasion[1] are (subject to subsection (2) below)—

(a) any that are to be attributed to the offence or offences of which he is convicted, disregarding any offence in respect of which an order under section 34 of this Act is made, and

(b) any that were on a previous occasion ordered to be endorsed on the counterpart of any licence held by him, unless the offender has since that occasion and before the conviction been disqualified under section 35 of this Act.

(2) If any of the offences was committed more than three years before another[2], the penalty points in respect of that offence shall not be added to those in respect of the other.

(3) In relation to licences which came into force before 1st June 1990, the reference in subsection (1) above to the counterpart of a licence shall be construed as a reference to the licence itself.

[Road Traffic Offenders Act 1988, s 29 as substituted by the Road Traffic Act 1991, s 28.]

---

1. The words "on that occasion" refer to the occasion of sentencing; therefore, the references in s 29 to "conviction" are to be given a wider interpretation and mean the date of sentence (*R v Brentwood Magistrates' Court, ex p Richardson* (1991) 156 JP 839, [1993] RTR 374).

2. This can be ascertained by looking three years before (and, if appropriate three years after) the dates of offences being dealt with today and adding together penalty points for these not more than three years apart from one another. It would seem that 1 November 1991 to 31 October 1994 would be three years, but to 1 November 1994 would be more than three years: but see PART II: EVIDENCE, para **2–744, Time,** ante.

4-1677 30. Penalty points: modification where fixed penalty also in question. (1) Sections 28 and 29 of this Act shall have effect subject to this section in any case where—

(a) a person is convicted of an offence involving obligatory endorsement, and

(b) the court is satisfied that the counterpart of his licence has been or is liable to be endorsed under section 57 or 77 of this Act in respect of an offence (referred to in this section as the "connected offence") committed on the same occasion as the offence of which he is convicted.

(2) The number of penalty points to be attributed to the offence of which he is convicted is—

(a) the number of penalty points to be attributed to that offence under section 28 of this Act apart from this section, less

(b) the number of penalty points required to be endorsed on the counterpart of his licence under section 57 or 77 of this Act in respect of the connected offence (except so far as they have already been deducted by virtue of this paragraph.

(3) *Repealed.**

[Road Traffic Offenders Act 1988, s 30 amended by SI 1990/144 and the Road Traffic Act 1991, Schs 4 and 8.]

---

*Section repealed in relation to Scotland by the Statute Law (Repeals) Act 2004.

4-1677A 30A. Reduced penalty points for attendance on course. (1) This section applies where—

(a) a person is convicted of a specified offence by or before a court,

(b) penalty points are to be attributed to the offence and the court does not order him to be disqualified, and

(c) at least seven but no more than eleven penalty points are to be taken into account on the occasion of the conviction.

(2) In this section "specified offence" means—

(a) an offence under section 3 of the Road Traffic Act 1988 (careless, and inconsiderate, driving),

(b) an offence under section 36 of that Act (failing to comply with traffic signs),

(c) an offence under section 17(4) of the Road Traffic Regulation Act 1984 (use of special road contrary to scheme or regulations), or (*d*)   an offence under section 89(1) of that Act (exceeding speed limit).

(3) But the Secretary of State may by regulations amend subsection (2) above by adding other offences or removing offences.

(4) Where this section applies, the court may make an order that three of the penalty points attributed to the offence (or all of them if three or fewer are so attributed) shall not be taken into account under section 29(1)(*b*) of this Act on the occasion of any conviction of an offence after the end of the period of twelve months beginning with the date of the order if, by the relevant date, the offender completes an approved course specified in the order.

(5) In subsection (4) above—

"an approved course" means a course approved by the appropriate national authority for the purposes of this section in relation to the description of offence of which the offender is convicted, and

"the relevant date" means such date, no later than ten months after the day on which the order is made, as is specified in the order.

(6) A court shall not make an order under this section in the case of an offender convicted of an offence if—

(*a*)   the offender has, during the period of three years ending with the date on which the offence was committed, committed a specified offence and successfully completed an approved course pursuant to an order made under this section or section 34A of this Act on conviction of that offence, or

(*b*)   the offence was committed during his probationary period.

(7) A court shall not make an order under this section in the case of an offender unless—

(*a*)   the court is satisfied that a place on the course specified in the order will be available for the offender,

(*b*)   the offender appears to the court to be of or over the age of 17,

(*c*)   the court has informed the offender (orally or in writing and in ordinary language) of the effect of the order and of the amount of the fees which he is required to pay for the course and when he must pay them, and

(*d*)   the offender has agreed that the order should be made.*

[Road Traffic Offenders Act 1988, s 30A as inserted by the Road Safety Act 2006, 34.]

---

*Section inserted by the Road Safety Act 2006, 34 from a date to be appointed.

4–1677B   30B. Certificates of completion of courses.   (1) An offender shall be regarded for the purposes of section 30A of this Act as having completed a course satisfactorily if (and only if) a certificate that he has done so is received by the proper officer of the supervising court.

(2) A course provider must give a certificate under subsection (1) above to the offender not later than fourteen days after the date specified in the order as the latest date for the completion of the course unless the offender—

(*a*)   fails to make due payment of fees for the course,

(*b*)   fails to attend the course in accordance with the course provider's reasonable instructions, or

(*c*)   fails to comply with any other reasonable requirement of the course provider.

(3) A certificate under subsection (1) above is to be given by the course provider and shall be in such form, and contain such particulars, as may be prescribed by, or determined in accordance with, regulations made by the appropriate national authority.

(4) Where a course provider decides not to give a certificate under subsection (1) above to the offender, he shall give written notice of the decision to the offender as soon as possible, and in any event not later than fourteen days after the date specified in the order as the latest date for completion of the course.

(5) An offender to whom a notice is given under subsection (4) above may, within such period as may be prescribed by rules of court, apply to the supervising court, or (if the supervising court is not the Crown Court, the High Court of Justiciary or the relevant local court) to either the supervising court or the relevant local court, for a declaration that the course provider's decision not to give a certificate under subsection (1) above was contrary to subsection (2) above.

(6) If the court grants the application, section 30A of this Act shall have effect as if the certificate had been duly received by the proper officer of the supervising court.

(7) If fourteen days after the date specified in the order as the latest date for completion of the course the course provider has given neither the certificate under subsection (1) above nor a notice under subsection (4) above, the offender may, within such period as may be prescribed by rules of court, apply to the supervising court, or (if the supervising court is not the Crown Court, the High Court of Justiciary or the relevant local court) to either the supervising court or the relevant local court, for a declaration that the course provider is in default.

(8) If the court grants the application, section 30A of this Act shall have effect as if the certificate had been duly received by the proper officer of the supervising court.

(9) A notice under subsection (4) above shall specify the ground on which it is given; and the appropriate national authority may by regulations make provision as to the form of notices under that subsection and as to the circumstances in which they are to be treated as given.

(10) Where the proper office of a court receives a certificate under subsection (1) above, or a

court grants an application under subsection (5) or (7) above, the proper officer or court must send notice of that fact to the Secretary of State; and the notice must be sent in such manner and to such address, and must contain such particulars, as the Secretary of State may determine.*
[Road Traffic Offenders Act 1988, s 30B as inserted by the Road Safety Act 2006, 34.]

*Section inserted by the Road Safety Act 2006, 34 from a date to be appointed.

4–1677C 30C. Approval of courses. (1) If an application is made to the appropriate national authority for the approval of a course for the purposes of section 30A of this Act, the appropriate national authority must decide whether to grant or refuse the application.

(2) In reaching that decision the appropriate national authority must have regard to—

(a) the nature of the course, and
(b) whether the course provider is an appropriate person to provide the course and administer its provision efficiently and effectively,

and may take into account any recommendations made by any persons appointed to consider the application.

(3) A course may be approved subject to conditions specified by the appropriate national authority.

(4) An approval of a course is for the period specified by the appropriate national authority (which must not exceed seven years), subject to withdrawal of approval.

(5) Regulations made by the appropriate national authority may make provision in relation to the approval of courses and may, in particular, include provision—

(a) in relation to the making of applications for approval,
(b) for the payment in respect of applications for approval, or of approvals, (or of both) of fees of such amounts as are prescribed by the regulations,
(c) specifying the maximum fees that a person may be required to pay for a course and by when they are to be paid,
(d) for the monitoring of courses and course providers,
(e) in relation to withdrawing approval,
(f) for an appeal to lie to the Transport Tribunal against a refusal of an application for approval, the imposition of conditions on the grant of such an application or the withdrawal of approval, and
(g) authorising the appropriate national authority to make available (with or without charge) information about courses and course providers.*
[Road Traffic Offenders Act 1988, s 30C as inserted by the Road Safety Act 2006, 34.]

*Section inserted by the Road Safety Act 2006, 34 from a date to be appointed.

4–1677D 30D. Provisions supplementary to sections 30A to 30C. (1) The appropriate national authority may issue guidance to course providers, or to any category of course provider, as to the conduct of courses approved for the purposes of section 30A of this Act; and—

(a) course providers shall have regard to any guidance given to them under this subsection, and
(b) in determining for the purposes of section 30B of this Act whether any instructions or requirements of a course provider were reasonable, a court shall have regard to any guidance given to him under this subsection.

(2) The Secretary of State may by regulations make provision—

(a) amending section 30A(1)(c) of this Act by substituting for the lower number of penalty points for the time being specified there a different number of penalty points, or
(b) amending section 30A(6)(a) of this Act by substituting for the period for the time being specified there a different period.

(3) In sections 30A to 30C of this Act and this section—

"appropriate national authority" means (as respects Wales) the National Assembly for Wales and (otherwise) the Secretary of State;
"course provider", in relation to a course, means the person by whom it is, or is to be, provided;
"probationary period" has the meaning given in section 1 of the Road Traffic (New Drivers) Act 1995;
"proper officer" means—

(a) in relation to a magistrates' court in England and Wales, the designated officer for the court, and
(b) otherwise, the clerk of the court;

"relevant local court", in relation to an order made under section 30A of this Act in the case of an offender, means—

(a) in England and Wales, a magistrates' court acting for the local justice area in which the offender resides, and
(b) in Scotland, the sheriff court for the district where the offender resides or, where the order is made by a stipendiary magistrate and the offender resides within his commission area, the district court for that area; and

"supervising court", in relation to an order under section 30A of this Act, means—

(a) in England and Wales, if the Crown Court made the order the Crown Court and otherwise a magistrates' court acting for the same local justice area as the court which made the order, and

(b) in Scotland, the court which made the order.

(4) Any power to make regulations under section 30A, 30B or 30C of this Act or this section includes power to make different provision for different cases, and to make such incidental or supplementary provision as appears to the appropriate national authority to be necessary or appropriate.

(5) Any power to make regulations under section 30A, 30B or 30C of this Act or this section shall be exercisable by statutory instrument.

(6) No regulations shall be made under section 30A of this Act or this section unless a draft of the regulations has been laid before, and approved by a resolution of, each House of Parliament.

(7) A statutory instrument containing regulations made under section 30B or 30C of this Act by the Secretary of State shall be subject to annulment in pursuance of a resolution of either House of Parliament.*

[Road Traffic Offenders Act 1988, s 30A as inserted by the Road Safety Act 2006, 34.]

---

*Section inserted by the Road Safety Act 2006, 34 from a date to be appointed.

4-1678   **31. Court may take particulars endorsed on licence into consideration.** (1) Where a person is convicted of an offence involving obligatory or discretionary disqualification and his licence and its counterpart are produced to the court—

(a) any existing endorsement on the counterpart of his licence is prima facie evidence[1] of the matters endorsed, and

(b) the court may, in determining what order to make in pursuance of the conviction, take those matters into consideration.

(2) Scotland.

[Road Traffic Offenders Act 1988, s 31 amended by SI 1990/144 and the Road Traffic Act 1991, Sch 4.]

---

1. As to proof of conviction, see the Police and Criminal Evidence Act 1984, ss 73–75, in PART II: EVIDENCE, ante, the Criminal Justice Act 1948, s 39 (fingerprints) and the Criminal Procedure Rules 2005, Part 6 (court register or extract) in PART I, MAGISTRATES' COURTS, PROCEDURE, ante.

Fine and imprisonment

4-1679   **33. Fine and imprisonment.** (1) Where a person is convicted of an offence against a provision of the Traffic Acts specified in column 1 of Part I of Schedule 2 to this Act or regulations made under any such provision, the maximum punishment by way of fine or imprisonment which may be imposed on him is that shown in column 4 against the offence and (where appropriate) the circumstances or the mode of trial there specified.

(2) Any reference in column 4 of that Part to a period of years or months is to be construed as a reference to a term of imprisonment of that duration.

[Road Traffic Offenders Act 1988, s 33.]

Disqualification

4-1680   **34. Disqualification for certain offences.** (1) Where a person is convicted of an offence involving obligatory disqualification[1], the court must order him to be disqualified[2] for such period not less than twelve months as the court thinks fit[3] unless the court for special reasons[4] thinks fit to order him to be disqualified for a shorter period or not to order him to be disqualified.

(1A) Where a person is convicted of an offence under section 12A of the Theft Act 1968 (aggravated vehicle-taking), the fact that he did not drive the vehicle in question at any particular time or at all shall not be regarded as a special reason for the purposes of subsection (1) above.

(2) Where a person is convicted of an offence involving discretionary disqualification[1], and either—

(a) the penalty points to be taken into account on that occasion number fewer than twelve, or

(b) the offence is not one involving obligatory endorsement[5],

the court may order him to be disqualified[2] for such period as the court thinks fit[3].

(3) Where a person convicted of an offence under any of the following provisions of the Road Traffic Act 1988, that is—

(a) section 4(1) (driving or attempting to drive while unfit),

(aa) section 3A (causing death by careless driving when under the influence of drink or drugs),

(b) section 5(1)(a) (driving or attempting to drive with excess alcohol), and

(c) section 7(6) (failing to provide a specimen) where that is an offence involving obligatory disqualification,

has within the ten years immediately preceding the commission of the offence been convicted of any such offence, subsection (1) above shall apply in relation to him as if the reference to twelve months were a reference to three years[6].

(4) Subject to subsection (3) above, subsection (1) above shall apply as if the reference to twelve months were a reference to two years—

(*a*) in relation to a person convicted of—

    (i) manslaughter, or in Scotland culpable homicide, or

    (ii) an offence under section 1 of the Road Traffic Act 1988 (causing death by dangerous driving), or

    (iii) an offence under section 3A of that Act (causing death by careless driving while under the influence of drink or drugs), and

(*b*) in relation to a person on whom more than one[7] disqualification for a fixed period of 56 days or more has been imposed within the three years immediately preceding the commission of the offence.

(4A) For the purposes of subsection (4)(*b*) above there shall be disregarded any disqualification imposed under section 26 of this Act or section 147 of the Powers of Criminal Courts (Sentencing) Act 2000 or section 223A or 436A of the Criminal Procedure (Scotland) Act 1975 (offences committed by using vehicles) and any disqualification imposed in respect of an offence of stealing a motor vehicle, an offence under section 12 or 25 of the Theft Act 1968, an offence under section 178 of the Road Traffic Act 1988, or an attempt to commit such an offence.

(5) The preceding provisions of this section shall apply in relation to a conviction of an offence committed by aiding, abetting, counselling or procuring, or inciting to the commission of, an offence involving obligatory disqualification as if the offence were an offence involving discretionary disqualification[8].

(6) This section is subject to section 48 of this Act.

[Road Traffic Offenders Act 1988, s 34 as amended by the Road Traffic Act 1991, s 29, the Aggravated Vehicle-Taking Act 1992, s 3 and the Powers of Criminal Courts (Sentencing) Act 2000, Sch 9.]

---

1. Schedule 2, *post* shows which offences carry obligatory or discretionary disqualification. A discretionary disqualification should not be imposed without a warning and an opportunity to address the court on the matter being given to the defendant or his legal representative; see *R v Ireland* [1989] Crim LR 458. Where the court is sentencing a defendant for an offence involving discretionary disqualification and a potential obligatory disqualification pursuant to s 35, *post*, the court is obliged to decide whether to impose a disqualification for the offence pursuant to s 34 of the Act before it can consider whether the provisions of s 35 of the Act apply. However, although the court should start with s 34 and consider whether to impose a disqualification for the offence, it is not limited in that consideration to the provisions and requirements of s 34 alone. It is open to the court in its discretion to decide not to impose such a disqualification, being conscious that the result will be the imposition of an obligatory disqualification under s 35 (*Jones v Chief Constable of West Mercia Police Authority* [2001] RTR 332, 165 JP 6, DC).

2. Disqualification shall not be ordered by a magistrates' court in a person's absence, except on resumption of the hearing after an adjournment following conviction but before sentence (Magistrates' Courts Act 1980, s 11(4), ante); magistrates considering a driving disqualification and adjourning under this section are under a duty to adjourn the whole question of sentence (*R v Talgarth Justices, ex p Bithell* [1973] 2 All ER 717, 137 JP 666). For combination of disqualification and endorsement with probation and discharge orders, see s 46, post. When committing to the Crown Court for sentence under s 56 of the Criminal Justice Act 1967, or remitting to another magistrates' court under s 39 of the Magistrates' Courts Act 1980, or deferring sentence under s 1 of the Powers of Criminal Courts Act 1973, or adjourning after conviction but before sentence, magistrates may order an interim disqualification (s 26, ante). Disqualification commences with the court's pronouncement. Disqualifications may not be ordered to be consecutive. Particulars endorsed on a licence are prima facie evidence of the matters endorsed (s 31, post).

3. **Use of disqualification.**—The imposition of a long period of disqualification may do more harm than good, particularly if the defendant does not have a bad *driving* record (*R v Dawtrey* [1975] RTR 101; *R v Rickeard* [1975] RTR 104); but would be justified if the defendant's record shows an irresponsible attitude to the use of motor vehicles or if the circumstances of the offence clearly warrant it; see *R v Davitt* [1974] Crim LR 719.

See also s 35, post for provisions as to disqualification for repeated offences. Disqualification, as a general rule, should be reserved for cases involving bad driving, for persistent motoring offences, or for cases involving the use of the vehicle for the purpose of crime (*R v Cooper* [1983] RTR 183). It is not to be ordered for an indefinite period (*R v Fowler* [1937] 2 All ER 380, 101 JP 244). A defendant should be allowed at least some hope that he may be able to drive again and, although disqualification for life is a valid order (*R v Tunde-Olarinde* [1967] 2 All ER 491, 131 JP 323); *R v Buckley* [1994] Crim LR 387) there are circumstances when such an order is not appropriate (*R v Bond* [1968] 2 All ER 1040, *R v King (Philip)* [1993] RTR 245; *R v Rivano* (1993) 14 Cr App Rep (S) 578 158 JP 288) and see *R v McCluskie* (1992) 13 Cr App Rep (S) 334. Long periods of disqualification may prove a severe handicap to a person desirous of rehabilitating himself. If the length of disqualification is overlong the penalty may well seem hopeless to the man and this sows the seeds of an incentive to disregard it. "However wrong such an attitude may be, it springs from a human factor which it is wise to take into account" (per SACHS LJ, in *R v Shirley* [1969] 3 All ER at 678, 133 JP 691).

It is accepted sentencing policy that with persons, who seem to be incapable of leaving motor vehicles alone, the imposition of a disqualification which will extend for a substantial period after their release from prison may well invite the offender to commit further offences, and so be counter productive and contrary to the public interest (*R v Thomas* [1983] 3 All ER 756, [1983] 1 WLR 1490, 5 Cr App Rep (S) 354, CA; followed in *R v Matthews* (1987) 9 Cr App Rep (S) 1, CA). However, different considerations will apply in the case of persons who because of their bad driving are shown to be a menace and for whom a sufficiently long period of disqualification is necessary to allow them to mature; see *R v Gibbons* (1987) 9 Cr App Rep (S) 21, CA.

In *R v McLaughlin* [1978] RTR 452, [1978] Crim LR 300, CA, a disqualification of 20 years was upheld on a driver with a drink problem convicted of four drink-driving offences. But in a case where the court held that circumstances where a defendant acted reasonably towards the police when stopped and who needed his car for his job could be regarded as mitigation notwithstanding that he had a bad driving record (*R v Aspden* [1975] RTR 456). In *R v Phelan* [1978] Crim LR 572 the defendant had deliberately driven recklessly in forcing a van off the road because its driving had annoyed him. His previous convictions were for criminal damage and minor road traffic offences; disqualified for 3 years. When the offence carries mandatory disqualification, the stated period is the minimum that must be imposed and is not the normal period (*R v Mills* [1974] RTR 215; *R v Sharman* [1974] RTR 213. Where a proposed disqualification would extend beyond the offender's release from a custodial sentence, the court should consider to what extent this might handicap him in trying to rehabilitate himself and lead an honest life (*R v West* (1986) 8 Cr App Rep (S) 266).

There is no tariff of 12 months' disqualification in the ordinary run of cases: the exact period is a matter for the court's wide discretion (*R v Sharman* [1974] RTR 213).

4. A **special reason** is one which is special to the facts of the particular case, that is, special to the facts which constitute the offence; and a circumstance peculiar to the offender (eg, that the licence is required for the purpose of carrying on his business) as distinguished from the offence is not a special reason (*R v Crossan* [1939] NI 106, KBD (Ir), Current Digest, col 159). The point was authoritatively decided in *Whittall v Kirby* [1947] KB 194, [1946] 2 All ER 552, 111 JP 1, in which the passage quoted supra, from *R v Crossan* was approved, and it was settled that considerations of financial hardship; previous good character; many years of driving without complaint, were not special reasons. See also the remarks of Lord GODDARD CJ, in *R v Recorder of Leicester, ex p Gabbitas* [1946] 1 All ER 615, 110 JP 228. As to combination of disqualification and endorsement with probation orders and orders for discharge, see s 46, post. Whether facts found by the Court amount to a "special reason" is a matter of law. If the court does find that there are special reasons, it must then exercise judicially its discretion whether or not to disqualify or endorse the licence and impose penalty points, as the case may be; see *Agnew v DPP* (1990) 155 JP 927, [1991] RTR 144 (police officer engaged in police driver training exercise convicted of driving without due care and attention—held that where there were two competing considerations, namely the need for realistic police driver training and the safety of lawful users of the highway, the second must always be paramount).

In *Holroyd v Berry* [1973] Crim LR 118 it was held not to be a special reason that the defendant was a **doctor** (who needed his car to answer calls) even though there was difficulty in obtaining doctors in the area where he practised and that it was in the public interest that medical services should be fully maintained. The fact that disqualification is considered a **severe penalty** in the circumstances is not a "special reason" (*Williamson v Wilson* [1947] 1 All ER 306, 111 JP 175). In *R v Jackson* [1970] 1 QB 647, [1969] 2 All ER 453, 133 JP 358, it was held that the fact that the offender is a **cripple** who required transport was peculiar to the offender and not the offence and therefore could not be a special reason. Followed in *Jarvis v DPP* (2000) 165 JP 15, DC, where it was held that an unexpected onset of hypoglycaemia suffered by a diabetic whilst driving did not constitute grounds for finding the existence of special reasons. Special reasons did not exist where it was claimed that the defendant would not have been over the limit if he had completed his journey as he had intended and that he had exceeded the limit only as a result of continued absorption of alcohol into his blood; this was a circumstance special to the offender and not to the offence (*Griffiths v DPP* [2002] EWHC 792 (Admin), (2002) 166 JP 629).The comparative **triviality** of the offence and marginal carelessness of the offender could not amount to special reasons, although they might justify a discharge or fine (*Hawkins v Roots*; *Hawkins v Smith* [1975] Crim LR 521) and see *Marks v West Midlands Police* [1981] RTR 471 where it was said that a special reason for not endorsing could never be constituted by the mere fact of the breach being small or the mere fact that the motorist did not notice that he was exceeding the speed limit, but that the unintentional commission of an offence could clearly be a special reason: the Divisional Court however said that account could properly be taken of a motorist's anxieties about his **passenger's health** which caused him to overlook excess speed which was in any event slight. See also *R v Lundt-Smith* [1964] 2 QB 167, [1964] 3 All ER 225, 128 JP 534, and *Brown v Dyerson* [1969] 1 QB 45, [1968] 3 All ER 39, 132 JP 495. A threat to cry rape which blackmailed the defendant into driving when over the alcohol limit can amount to an emergency which justices may consider when finding special reasons (*DPP v Enston* [1996] RTR 324). The fact that a person has been convicted of **theft** of a motor vehicle which did not involve bad driving, and had an unblemished record as a driver is not a special reason (*R v Preston* [1986] RTR 136). In *Walker v Rawlinson* [1957] Crim LR 523 it was held that a **motorist's ignorance** that a system of street lighting imposes a speed restriction is not a special reason for not disqualifying, but in *Burgess v West* [1982] RTR 269, [1982] Crim LR 235 the fact that the motorist thought he was still in a 40 mph area because nothing other than the street lighting system indicated a transition to a 30 mph area was accepted as a special reason for not endorsing. A claim that the motorist had consumed alcohol, gone to bed and slept for eight hours and was unaware that he had excess alcohol in his system the next day is not a special reason for not disqualifying (*DPP v O'Meara* [1989] RTR 24, 10 Cr App Rep (S) 56). It is not a special reason that he believed he was within the legal limit following an earlier negative breath test (*DPP v White* [1988] RTR 267, 10 Cr App Rep (S) 66).

The **amount** by which the blood-alcohol content exceeds the prescribed limit (*Delaroy-Hall v Tadman* [1969] 2 QB 208, [1969] 1 All ER 25, 133 JP 127), the fact that the accused's driving was not impaired and an accident was not his **fault** (*Taylor v Austin* [1969] 1 All ER 544, 133 JP 182), the fact that the accused had no idea that a combination of **sleeping tablets** and drink would produce a greater reaction in terms of her ability to drive than would drink alone (*R v Scott* [1970] 1 QB 661, [1969] 2 All ER 450, 133 JP 269) or the loss of the defendant's part of the specimen provided for a laboratory test (*Lodwick v Brow* [1984] RTR 394), cannot be special reasons for not imposing a disqualification for an offence under s 5 of the Road Traffic Act 1988, ante. The fact that a **motorist stopped** his car as soon as he felt incapacitated through drink is not a special reason (*Duck v Peacock* [1949] 1 All ER 318, 113 JP 135); but someone who realises on returning to his motor car that he is under the influence of drink and decides not to drive but to sleep in his car until a lift or taxi arrives can plead special reasons (*Jowett-Shooter v Franklin* [1949] 2 All ER 730, 113 JP 525; cf *Hopper v Stansfield* where the intoxicated driver was found sitting in his stationary car having earlier driven 6 miles. An injured motorist who took **drugs** not knowing that he would be more susceptible to the effect of alcohol (*Chapman v O'Hagan* [1949] 2 All ER 690, 113 JP 518, and a motorist ignorant of the fact that earlier prolonged exposure to trichloroethylene fumes would heighten the effect of later drinks (*Brewer v Metropolitan Police Comr* [1969] 1 All ER 513, 133 JP 185, could plead special reasons. Similarly, where a medical condition gave rise to a tendency to reflux, and the amount of alcohol consumed by the defendant would not have given a reading in excess of the limit, special reasons could be found: *Woolfe v DPP* [2006] EWHC 1497 (Admin), [2007] RTR 16. A first negative breath test followed some time later by a second, positive test could not excuse a motorist's **ignorance** of the delayed effect of alcohol and his consequent risk in driving (*DPP v White* [1988] RTR 267). Evidence that a defendant would, if he had not consumed a cough linctus, which unknown to him contained a small quantity of alcohol, have been in the range where the police would not have prosecuted, was held to be a special reason (*R v Cambridge Magistrates' Court and Crown Prosecution Service, ex p Wong* (1991) 156 JP 377, [1992] RTR 382).

Where a person has knowingly consumed alcoholic drink which is stronger than he believed because it is a "**laced drink**", it is open to the court to find special reasons (*R v Messom* (1973) 57 Cr App Rep 481). But for there to be special reasons in "laced drink" cases the defendant must show that there has been an intervention by a third party which misled him; it is not enough for the defendant to make no inquiry as to what he is drinking; a person who combines drinking with driving has a very heavy responsibility: see *R v Newton* [1974] RTR 451; *Alexander v Latter* [1972] RTR 441; *Adams v Bradley* [1975] Crim LR 168; *R v Krebs* [1977] RTR 406. When considering a submission of special reasons on the ground of a "laced drink", the prosecutor is entitled, provided this can be done by straightforward and relatively simple evidence, to show that, at the time of the offence, the defendant's blood-alcohol concentration was higher than that shown in his certified analysis tendered to the court (*Smith v Geraghty* [1986] RTR 222). Even if the court finds there is something which can be a special reason it may still find that the defendant merits disqualification: see *R v Newton*, supra; in this respect it is relevant to consider whether the defendant should have realised that he was not in a fit state to drive (*Pridige v Gant* [1985] RTR 196; *DPP v Barker* [1990] RTR 1; *Donahue v DPP* [1993] RTR 156). It is for the defendant to prove (on the balance of probabilities) that the added alcohol was responsible for the excess alcohol in his blood (*Weatherson v Connop* [1975] Crim LR 239), but it is unnecessary for medical evidence to be called in any case in which it must be obvious to the court that it is the alcohol which the defendant has unwittingly consumed which has been responsible for that excess (*Smith v DPP* [1990] RTR 17). See also *DPP Kinnersley* [1993] RTR 105, 14 Cr App Rep (S) 516.

Where a driver attends a function at which alcohol is being consumed and he is offered a drink that may contain alcohol he is under a duty to inquire what he is drinking; if he assumes without inquiry that the drink he is being offered is alcohol free he is taking a risk and if he turns out to be mistaken he must pay the price: *Robinson v DPP* [2003] EWHC Admin 2718, (2004) 168 JP 522, [2004] Crim LR 670. If a motorist not intending to drive consumes alcohol, and then an **emergency** requires him to take his car out, the situation is capable of amounting to special reasons; but discretion in his favour is to be exercised only in clear and compelling circumstances, for example an acute emergency, lack of alternative means of dealing with it, and the absence of traffic offences (*Taylor v Rajan* [1974] QB 424, [1974] 1 All ER 1087, 138 JP 328). See also *Evans v Bray* [1977] RTR 24, [1976] Crim LR 454; *Powell v Gliha* [1979] RTR 126; *Park v Hicks* [1979] RTR 259; *Vaughan v Dunn* [1984] RTR 376; *Williams v Tierney* [1988] RTR 118; *DPP v Waller* [1989] RTR 112; *DPP v Upchurch* [1994] RTR 336; *DPP v Knight* [1994] RTR 374; *DPP v Whittle* [1996] RTR 154 (illness of wife of defendant so she was no longer able to drive held not to be a medical emergency giving rise to the need for the defendant to drive); **DPP v Goddard** [1998] RTR 463 (defendant drove first to his sister's to escape from attackers but after being assaulted and then on to his own home—held that while there was an emergency for the first part of the journey to his sister's it was not an emergency to drive on to his own home. The question which justices should ask themselves in so-called emergency cases is this: What would a sober, reasonable and responsible friend of the defendant present at the time, but himself a non-driver and thus unable to help, have advised in the circumstances: drive or do not drive? Justices can only properly find special reasons and exercise discretion not to disqualify if they think it a real possibility rather than merely an off-chance that such a person would have advised the defendant to drive (*DPP v Bristow* (1996) 161 JP 35, [1998] RTR 100). Where a driver deliberately takes a decision to drink knowing that he will or probably will drive, even if he has a genuine fear for his safety, it is not open to the court to find special reasons existed (*DPP v Doyle* [1993] RTR 369). Where the suspicion of alcohol arose after the defendant moved his car at the **request** of the police officer, in considering whether this was a special reason, the court was entitled to take into account not only the driving which had taken place at the constable's request but also the defendant's previous driving which the constable had seen (*De Munthe v Stewart* [1982] RTR 27. In cases of **failure to provide a specimen of breath** for analysis, the fact that there is no reasonable excuse for such failure does not inevitably mean that there can be no special reasons for not disqualifying (*Daniels v DPP* (1991) 156 JP 543; see also *DPP v Daley (No 2)* [1994] RTR 107).

In *James v Hall* [1972] 2 All ER 59, 136 JP 385 it was held that the fact that the defendant was only trying to drive **a few yards** from the highway outside a house into the driveway of that house could amount to a special reason; but in *Coombs v Kehoe* [1972] 2 All ER 55, 136 JP 387, where the fact that the defendant had driven 200 yards to park his vehicle was held not to amount to a special reason, the Divisional Court held that *James v Hall* (supra) was a very special case and one which should not be extended, a view confirmed in *Haime v Walklett* (1983) 147 JP 570, but nevertheless contentions about short distance should be considered as they can amount to special reasons (*Redmond v Parry* [1986] RTR 146). Indeed, while recognising that the instances of special reasons being found in cases where a vehicle is moved only a short distance will be rare, the Divisional Court has suggested that the following matters should be taken into account by the court in determining whether special reasons exist—

   (*a*) how far the vehicle was in fact driven;
   (*b*) the manner in which it was driven;
   (*c*) the state of the vehicle;
   (*d*) whether the driver intended to drive any further;
   (*e*) the prevailing road and traffic conditions;
   (*f*) whether there was any possibility of danger by contact with other road users, and
   (*g*) the reason for the vehicle being driven at all,

      (*Chatters v Burke* [1986] 3 All ER 168, [1986] 1 WLR 1321, [1986] RTR 396); see however *DPP v Rose* (1992) 156 JP 733 where the fact of having driven only two feet, plus "justified resentment" at the manner and circumstances of a request to provide a specimen were held not to justify special reasons and *DPP v Humphries* [2000] RTR 52, [2000] 2 Cr App Rep (S) 1, 164 JP 502, where on a conviction for attempting to drive with excess alcohol it was held that it was not the fact that the car was only driven for six feet that mattered, it was the fact that the defendant had intended to drive it out on to the public highway in order to get home with all the attendant danger which that entailed; accordingly, there were no special reasons to justify non-disqualification.

For a no insurance case on shortness of distance driven see *DPP v Heritage* [2002] EWHC 2139 (Admin), (2002) 166 JP 772, where it was held that the justices had been entitled to find special reasons on this basis (the vehicle had been cleaned and moved onto the road, pending its sale, the owner wrongly, though reasonably, believing that it remained covered by insurance), though the prosecution case rested simply on the fact that the car had been left parked on a public road.

Where a child's motor cycle had been regarded by a defendant as a toy not requiring insurance or an "L" plate a finding of special reasons was upheld in the Divisional Court (*DPP v Powell* [1993] RTR 266).

Justices were held to be entitled to find special reasons for not endorsing the licences of motorists who performed U-turns across the central reservation of a motorway, which was not in normal use, and where, because of an apparent blockage, there was a long stationary traffic jam in the motorists' lane, with no on-coming traffic in the opposite carriageway for a considerable time: *DPP v Fruer, DPP v Siba, DPP v Ward* [1989] RTR 29.

Special reasons for expunging or reducing a term of disqualification below the minimum period cannot be widened so as to include and permit the granting of just satisfaction where that was required in response to an art 6 breach (here on the ground of delay): *Myles v DPP* [2004] EWHC 594 (Admin), [2004] 2 All ER 902, [2005] RTR 1.

Summary of rules as to special reasons: The rules emerging from the many cases cited above may be summarised as follows: (1) The duty to disqualify a convicted person for holding a licence to drive a motor vehicle, or to endorse such a licence with particulars of a conviction, falls not within the discretion of the convicting court, but is imposed by Act of Parliament: thus, it is not identified with the "maximum punishment" to be mitigated according to established principles. (2) The duty is mandatory, but the Act of Parliament has given a limited discretion to a conviction court, to be exercised judicially, to refrain from implementing the law's clearly expressed requirement for a reason which is special to the offence, but *not* for a reason special to the offender. (3) The High Court will interfere if the convicting court does not address its mind to the right considerations; but will not interfere if the convicting court properly and judicially directs itself, even though the High Court would have decided the matter differently if sitting as a court of original jurisdiction. It was further reviewed and summarised in *DPP v O'Connor* [1992] RTR 66, which also emphasised the two-stage process of first determining whether there are special reasons and then asking whether it is a case where in its discretion the court ought not to disqualify at all or for the full period.

In *R v Wickins* (1958) 42 Cr App Rep 236, the Court of Criminal Appeal prescribed four requirements that a "special reason" must fulfil—

   (*a*) It must be a mitigating or extenuating circumstance;
   (*b*) It must not amount in law to a defence to the charge;
   (*c*) It must be directly connected with the commission of the offence;
   (*d*) The matter must be one which the court ought properly to take into consideration when imposing punishment.

The law as to special reasons was comprehensively reviewed by the Court of Appeal in *R v Jackson* [1970] 1 QB 647, [1969] 2 All ER 453, 133 JP 358, and the principles stated above affirmed. It was stated that the special reasons which the court may take into account may well be different according to the offence committed; and the Court especially distinguished offences under s 6 of the Road Traffic Act 1960, from offences under the Road Safety Act 1967, now ss 4 and 5 of the Road Traffic Act 1988, ante. In *Jarvis v DPP* (2000) 165 JP 15 the Divisional Court affirmed that in breathalyser cases the appropriate authority to refer to was not *Wickins* but *Jackson* and that that the latter decision (liver complaint, of which the defendant was ignorant, that caused him to retain alcohol longer in his blood and thus be more susceptible to committing an excess alcohol offence not a special reason because it was a matter relating to the offender and not to the offence) applied to the offence of dangerous driving, which was concerned with the mode of driving and not the reasons for it. Therefore, the fact the bad driving was due to a hypoglycaemic episode brought on by diabetes did not afford special reasons.

Special reasons ought to be established by evidence, not merely by statements, per Lord GODDARD CJ, in *Jones v English* [1951] 2 All ER 853; the onus of proving the facts on which the plea of special reasons is based, lies on the defendant. It may be desirable for the defence to notify the prosecution in advance of such evidence; per Lord WIDGERY CJ, in *Pugsley v Hunter* [1973] 2 All ER 10, 137 JP 409 (a case on "laced drinks"). Inaccurate information given to a defendant by a constable which affected his decision not to provide a specimen for analysis is capable of amounting to a special reason (*Bobin v DPP* [1999] RTR 375).

If a court exercises its power not to order disqualification or endorsement, or to order disqualification for a shorter period than is prescribed, it shall state the grounds for doing so in open court, and, if it is a magistrates' court, such grounds shall be entered in the court register (s 47, post). Where the court does find special reasons exist, and where it is not suggested that the actual driving undertaken or contemplated could have posed any appreciable risk of danger to anyone, it will be hard to justify a period of disqualification in excess of the mandatory period (*R v Crown Court at St Albans, ex p O'Donovan* [2000] 1 Cr App Rep (S) 344).

5. See for example Powers of Criminal Courts Act 1973, s 44 in PART III SENTENCING ante, empowering the Crown Court to disqualify for offences other than those carrying endorsement.

6. Notwithstanding that for the previous offence the defendant escaped disqualification on the ground of special reasons, the court is bound to disqualify for at least 3 years for the subsequent offence and it cannot for the purposes of deciding whether there are special reasons for not disqualifying or reducing the period of disqualification on the second offence take into account the circumstances of the earlier offence (*Bolliston v Gibbons* [1985] RTR 176).

7. A double order of disqualification imposed for the *same offence* under the provisions of this Act as originally enacted does not count as "more than one disqualification" for this purpose (*Learmont v DPP* [1994] RTR 286).

8. This subsection applies only where the substantive offence committed by the aider and abettor carries a mandatory disqualification, and does not remove a requirement to disqualify under s 35 (*Ullah v Luckhurst* [1977] RTR 401, [1977] Crim LR 295); nor does it remove a requirement to disqualify under section 34(3) (*Makeham v Donaldson* [1981] RTR 511).

4–1681 34A. Reduced disqualification period for attendance on courses¹. (1) This section applies where—

(a) a person is convicted of an offence under section 3A (causing death by careless driving when under influence of drink or drugs), 4 (driving or being in charge when under influence of drink or drugs), 5 (driving or being in charge with excess alcohol) or 7 (failing to provide a specimen) of the Road Traffic Act 1988, and

(b) the court makes an order under section 34 of this Act disqualifying him for a period of not less than twelve months.

(2) Where this section applies, the court may make an order that the period of disqualification imposed under section 34 shall be reduced if, by a date specified in the order under this section, the offender satisfactorily completes a course approved by the Secretary of State for the purposes of this section and specified in the order.

(3) The reduction made by an order under this section in a period of disqualification imposed under section 34 shall be a period specified in the order of not less than three months and not more than one quarter of the unreduced period (and accordingly where the period imposed under section 34 is twelve months, the reduced period shall be nine months).

(4) The court shall not make an order under this section unless—

(a) it is satisfied that a place on the course specified in the order will be available for the offender,

(b) the offender appears to the court to be of or over the age of 17,

(c) the court has explained the effect of the order to the offender in ordinary language, and has informed him of the amount of the fees for the course and of the requirement that he must pay them before beginning the course, and

(d) the offender has agreed that the order should be made.

(5) The date specified in an order under this section as the latest date for completion of a course must be at least two months before the last day of the period of disqualification as reduced by the order.

(6) An order under this section shall name the petty sessions area (or in Scotland the sheriff court district or, where an order has been made under this section by a stipendiary magistrate, the commission area) in which the offender resides or will reside.
[Road Traffic Offenders Act 1988, s 34A added by the Road Traffic Act 1991, s 30.]

1. Following a six-year experimental period section 34A is now applied to all courts by the Courses for Drink-Drive Offenders (Experimental Period) (Termination of Restrictions) Order 1999, SI 1999/3130.

A Guide to the Operation of Approved Courses for Drink-Drive Offenders has been issued by the DETR to course organisers and the courts and is available on the DETR Website at http://www.detr.gov.uk/

The aim of the rehabilitation scheme is "to provide, for drink-drive offenders referred to an approved course, a period of guided reflection within a group enabling future non-offending behaviour to be developed and reduce incidences of reoffending" (DETR Guide).

Course providers have been approved by the Secretary of State for each Petty Sessional Area and these have been notified to courts.

The decision to refer an offender convicted of an offence specified in s 34(1)(a) and disqualified for a minimum period of 12 months to a course is a matter for the discretion of the court but the court may not make an order (a 'referral order') unless the criteria in s 34A(4) are met and the offender is willing to pay the course organiser's fee. Offenders who come within the criteria for High Risk Offenders (HRO) (see the Road Traffic Act s 94(4) and the Motor Vehicles (Driving Licences) Regulations 1999, reg 74 in this title, post (disqualified for being 2.5 times or more over the prescribed limit; disqualified for refusing to provide a specimen; or disqualified for a second drink-drive offence in ten years)) may be referred to a rehabilitation scheme but will still have to meet the requirements of the HRO scheme before their licence will be returned to them by the Secretary of State. Although referral to a rehabilitation scheme is not precluded, training courses for drink-drive offenders as a condition of a probation order may be more appropriate for offenders where the offences require a higher degree of intervention to match the seriousness of the offence (DETR Guide).

The making of a referral order is to be recorded in the court register and, where the court has determined the period of reduction, the period of reduction decided upon. The court must also specify the date for completion of the course being a date at least two months before the last day of the period of disqualification as reduced by the order.

Completion of the course Undertaking a course is voluntary and there is no penalty for refusing to accept a referral order or for failing to attend the course. On successfully completing a course, the course organiser will issue a *certificate of completion* which will be sent to the supervising court and a copy supplied to the offender. On receipt of the certificate of completion the court will notify the DVLA of the reduced period of disqualification. It will then be for the offender to apply for a new driving licence before the end of the reduced period of disqualification. If the offender fails to complete the course satisfactorily, the course supervisor will issue a *notice of non-completion*. The offender may apply within 28 days to the supervising court *against* the course organiser's decision not to give a certificate of completion.

4–1682 34B. Certificates of completion of courses. (1) An offender shall be regarded for the purposes of section 34A of this Act as having completed a course satisfactorily if (and only if) a certificate that he has done so is received by the proper officer of the supervising court before the end of the period of disqualification imposed under section 34.

(2) If the certificate referred to in subsection (1) above is received by the clerk of the supervising court before the end of the period of disqualification imposed under section 34 but after the end of the period as it would have been reduced by the order, the order shall have effect as if the reduced period ended with the day on which the certificate is received by the proper officer.

(3) The certificate referred to in subsection (1) above shall be a certificate in such form, containing such particulars, and given by such person, as may be prescribed by, or determined in accordance with, regulations[1] made by the Secretary of State.

(4) A course organiser shall give the certificate mentioned in subsection (1) above to the offender not later than fourteen days after the date specified in the order as the latest date for completion of the course, unless the offender fails to make due payment of the fees for the course, fails to attend the course in accordance with the organiser's reasonable instructions, or fails to comply with any other reasonable requirements of the organiser.

(5) Where a course organiser decides not to give the certificate mentioned in subsection (1) above, he shall give written notice of his decision to the offender as soon as possible, and in any event not later than fourteen days after the date specified in the order as the latest date for completion of the course.

(6) An offender to whom a notice is given under subsection (5) above may, within such period as may be prescribed by rules of court[2], apply to the supervising court for a declaration that the course organiser's decision not to give a certificate was contrary to subsection (4) above; and if the court grants the application section 34A of this Act shall have effect as if the certificate had been duly received by the proper officer of the court.

(7) If fourteen days after the date specified in the order as the latest date for completion of the course the course organiser has given neither the certificate mentioned in subsection (1) above nor a notice under subsection (5) above, the offender may, within such period as may be prescribed by rules of court[2], apply to the supervising court for a declaration that the course organiser is in default; and if the court grants the application section 34A of this Act shall have effect as if the certificate had been duly received by the proper officer of the court.

(8) A notice under subsection (5) above shall specify the ground on which it is given, and the Secretary of State may by regulations[1] make provision as to the form of notices under that subsection and as to the circumstances in which they are to be treated as given.

(9) Where the proper officer of a court receives a certificate of the kind referred to in subsection (1) above, or a court grants an application under subsection (6) or (7) above, the officer or court must send notice of that fact to the Secretary of State; and the notice must be sent in such manner and to such address, and must contain such particulars, as the Secretary of State may determine.
[Road Traffic Offenders Act 1988, s 34B as added by the Road Traffic Act 1991, s 30 and amended by the Access to Justice Act 1999, Sch 13.]

---

1. The Road Traffic (Courses for Drink-Drive Offenders) Regulations 1997 have been made, in this title, post.
2. The period of 28 days has been prescribed and for the procedure applicable see the Criminal Procedure Rules 2005, Part 55 in PART I: MAGISTRATES' COURTS, PROCEDURE, ante.

4–1683 34C. Provisions supplementary to sections 34A and 34B. (1) The Secretary of State may issue guidance to course organisers, or to any category of course organiser as to the conduct of courses approved for the purposes of section 34A of this Act; and—

(a) course organisers shall have regard to any guidance given to them under this subsection, and

(b) in determining for the purposes of section 34B(6) whether any instructions or requirements of an organiser were reasonable, a court shall have regard to any guidance given to him under this subsection.

(2) In sections 34A and 34B and this section—

"course organiser", in relation to a course, means the person who, in accordance with regulations made by the Secretary of State, is responsible for giving the certificates mentioned in section 34B(1) in respect of the completion of the course;

"proper officer" means—

(a) in relation to a magistrates' court in England and Wales, the justices' chief executive for the court, and

(b) in relation to a sheriff court in Scotland, the clerk of the court;

"supervising court", in relation to an order under section 34A, means—

(a) in England and Wales, a magistrates' court acting for the petty sessions area named in the order as the area where the offender resides or will reside;

(b) in Scotland, the sheriff court for the district where the offender resides or will reside or, where the order is made by a stipendiary magistrate and the offender resides or will reside within his commission area, the district court for that area.

(3) Any power to make regulations[1] under section 34B or this section—

(a) includes power to make different provision for different cases, and to make such incidental or supplemental provision as appears to the Secretary of State to be necessary or expedient;

(b) shall be exercisable by statutory instrument, which shall be subject to annulment in pursuance of a resolution of either House of Parliament.

[Road Traffic Offenders Act 1988, s 34C as added by the Road Traffic Act 1991, s 30 and as amended by the Access to Justice Act 1999, Schs 13 and 15.]

---

1. The Road Traffic (Courses for Drink-Drive Offenders) Regulations 1997 have been made, in this title, post.

4–1683A 34D. Reduced disqualification period: alcohol ignition interlock programme orders. (1) This section applies where—

(a) a person is convicted of a relevant drink offence by or before a court,

(b) he has committed another relevant drink offence at any time during the period of ten years ending with the date of the conviction,

(c) the court makes an order under section 34 of this Act but does not make an order under section 34A of this Act, and

(d) the period stated by the court as that for which, apart from this section, he would be disqualified ("the unreduced period") is not less than two years.

(2) In this section "relevant drink offence" means—

(a) an offence under paragraph (a) of subsection (1) of section 3A of the Road Traffic Act 1988 (causing death by careless driving when unfit to drive through drink) committed when unfit to drive through drink,

(b) an offence under paragraph (b) of that subsection (causing death by careless driving with excess alcohol),

(c) an offence under paragraph (c) of that subsection (failing to provide a specimen) where the specimen is required in connection with drink or consumption of alcohol,

(d) an offence under section 4 of that Act (driving or being in charge when under influence of drink) committed by reason of unfitness through drink,

(e) an offence under section 5(1) of that Act (driving or being in charge with excess alcohol),

(f) an offence under section 7(6) of that Act (failing to provide a specimen) committed in the course of an investigation into an offence within any of the preceding paragraphs, or

(g) an offence under section 7A(6) of that Act (failing to allow a specimen to be subjected to a laboratory test) in the course of an investigation into an offence within any of the preceding paragraphs.

(3) Where this section applies, the court may specify a lesser period of disqualification ("the reduced period") if it also makes an order (an "alcohol ignition interlock programme order") requiring the offender to comply with the alcohol ignition interlock conditions.

(4) The difference between the unreduced period and the reduced period shall be a period specified in the order of—

(a) not less than 12 months, and

(b) not more than one half of the unreduced period.

(5) If the offender contravenes the alcohol ignition interlock conditions, a further order under section 34 disqualifying him for the rest of the unreduced period is to be treated as having been made by the court immediately before the contravention.

(6) "The alcohol ignition interlock conditions" are that the offender—

(a) must participate fully in an approved alcohol ignition interlock programme specified in the order during such part of the unreduced period as is so specified, and

(b) during the part of that period following the reduced period, must not drive a motor vehicle unless it is fitted with an alcohol ignition interlock in good working order and must not drive a motor vehicle which is so fitted when not using the alcohol ignition interlock properly.

(7) A court shall not make an alcohol ignition interlock programme order in the case of an offender unless—

(a) the court is satisfied that a place on the approved alcohol ignition interlock programme specified in the order will be available for the offender,

(b) the offender appears to the court to be of or over the age of 17,

(c)   the court has informed the offender (orally or in writing and in ordinary language) of the effect of the order and the amount of the fees which he is required to pay for the programme and when he must pay them, and

(d)   the offender has agreed that the order should be made.

(8) For the purposes of this section an "approved alcohol ignition interlock programme" is a programme approved by the appropriate national authority and involving the provision of an alcohol ignition interlock for use by the offender, training in its use and other education and counselling relating to the consumption of alcohol and driving.

(9) For the purposes of this section "alcohol ignition interlock" means a device—

(a)   of a type approved by the Secretary of State, and

(b)   designed to be fitted to a motor vehicle with the purpose of preventing the driving of the vehicle by a person who does not, both before starting driving the vehicle and at regular intervals while driving it, provide specimens of breath in which the proportion of alcohol is likely not to exceed the limit specified in subsection (10) below.

(10) That limit is 9 microgrammes of alcohol in 100 millilitres of breath or such other proportion of alcohol to breath as the Secretary of State may by regulations prescribe.

(11) For the purposes of this section an offender uses an alcohol ignition interlock properly if (and only if) he is complying with all the instructions given to him about its use as part of the approved alcohol ignition interlock programme.

(12) Where an alcohol ignition interlock is fitted to a motor vehicle as part of an approved alcohol ignition interlock programme relating to an offender, a person commits an offence if—

(a)   he interferes with the alcohol ignition interlock with intent to cause it not to function or not to function properly, or

(b)   he is a person other than the offender and provides or attempts to provide a specimen of breath for the purposes of the alcohol ignition interlock with intent to enable the driving (or continued driving) of the vehicle by the offender.★

[Road Traffic Offenders Act 1988, s 34D as inserted by the Road Safety Act 2006, 15.]

★Section inserted by the Road Safety Act 2006, 15 from a date to be appointed.

4–1683B   34E. Certificates of failing fully to participate.   (1) An offender shall be regarded for the purposes of section 34D of this Act as not fully participating in an approved alcohol ignition interlock programme if (and only if) a certificate that that is so is received by the proper officer of the supervising court.

(2) A certificate under subsection (1) above may be given if (and only if) the offender has failed—

(a)   to make due payment of fees for the programme,

(b)   to attend for training, education or counselling forming part of the programme in accordance with the programme provider's reasonable instructions,

(c)   to attend at a place specified by the programme provider for the monitoring and maintenance of the alcohol ignition interlock, at a time specified by the programme provider or a person with whom the programme provider has made arrangements for its monitoring and maintenance, or

(d)   to comply with any other reasonable requirement of the programme provider.

(3) A certificate under subsection (1) above is to be given by the programme provider and shall be in such form, and contain such particulars, as may be prescribed by, or determined in accordance with, regulations made by the appropriate national authority.

(4) Where a programme provider decides to give a certificate under subsection (1) above, he shall give written notice of the decision to the offender as soon as possible.

(5) An offender to whom a notice is given under subsection (4) above may, within such period as may be prescribed by rules of court, apply to the supervising court, or (if the supervising court is not the Crown Court, the High Court of Justiciary or the relevant local court) to either the supervising court or the relevant local court, for a declaration that the programme provider has given the certificate under subsection (1) above in contravention of subsection (2) above.

(6) If the court grants the application, section 34D of this Act shall have effect as if the certificate had not been duly received by the proper officer of the supervising court.

(7) A notice under subsection (4) above shall specify the ground on which it is given; and the appropriate national authority may by regulations make provision as to the form of notices under that subsection and as to the circumstances in which they are to be treated as given.

(8) Where the proper office of a court receives a certificate under subsection (1) above, or a court grants an application under subsection (5) above, the proper officer or court must send notice of that fact to the Secretary of State; and the notice must be sent in such manner and to such address, and must contain such particulars, as the Secretary of State may determine.★

[Road Traffic Offenders Act 1988, s 34E as inserted by the Road Safety Act 2006, 15.]

★Section inserted by the Road Safety Act 2006, 15 from a date to be appointed.

4–1683C   34F. Approval of programmes.   (1) If an application is made to the appropriate national authority for the approval of a programme for the purposes of section 34D of this Act, the appropriate national authority must decide whether to grant or refuse the application.

(2) In reaching that decision the appropriate national authority must have regard to—

(a) the nature of the programme, and
(b) whether the programme provider is an appropriate person to provide the programme and administer its provision efficiently and effectively,

and may take into account any recommendations made by any persons appointed to consider the application.

(3) A programme may be approved subject to conditions specified by the appropriate national authority.

(4) An approval of a programme is for the period specified by the appropriate national authority (which must not exceed seven years), subject to withdrawal of approval.

(5) Regulations made by the appropriate national authority may make provision in relation to the approval of programmes and may, in particular, include provision—

(a) in relation to the making of applications for approval,
(b) for the payment in respect of applications for approval, or of approvals, (or of both) of fees of such amounts as are prescribed by the regulations,
(c) specifying the maximum fees that a person may be required to pay for a programme and by when they are to be paid,
(d) for the monitoring of programmes and programme providers,
(e) in relation to withdrawing approval,
(f) for an appeal to lie to the Transport Tribunal against a refusal of an application for approval, the imposition of conditions on the grant of such an application or the withdrawal of approval, and
(g) authorising the appropriate national authority to make available (with or without charge) information about programmes and programme providers.*

[Road Traffic Offenders Act 1988, s 34F as inserted by the Road Safety Act 2006, 15.]

Section inserted by the Road Safety Act 2006, 15 from a date to be appointed.

4–1683D 34G. Provisions supplementary to sections 34D to 34F. (1) The appropriate national authority may issue guidance to programme providers, or to any category of programme provider, as to the conduct of programmes approved for the purposes of section 34D of this Act; and—

(a) programme providers shall have regard to any guidance given to them under this subsection, and
(b) in determining for the purposes of section 34E of this Act whether any instructions or requirements of a programme provider were reasonable, a court shall have regard to any guidance given to him under this subsection.

(2) The Secretary of State may by regulations make provision—

(a) amending section 34D(1)(b) of this Act by substituting for the period for the time being specified there a different period,
(b) amending section 34D(1)(d) of this Act by substituting for the period for the time being specified there a different period, or
(c) amending section 34D(4) of this Act by substituting for the period for the time being specified there a different period, or by substituting for the fraction of the unreduced period for the time being specified there a different fraction of that period, (or by doing both).

(3) In sections 34D to 34F of this Act and this section—

"appropriate national authority" means (as respects Wales) the National Assembly for Wales and (otherwise) the Secretary of State;
"contravention" includes failure to comply;
"programme provider", in relation to an alcohol ignition interlock programme, means the person by whom it is, or is to be, provided;
"proper officer" means—

(a) in relation to a magistrates' court in England and Wales, the designated officer for the court, and
(b) otherwise, the clerk of the court;

"relevant local court", in relation to an alcohol ignition interlock programme order in the case of an offender, means—

(a) in England and Wales, a magistrates' court acting for the local justice area in which the offender resides, and
(b) in Scotland, the sheriff court for the district where the offender resides or, where the order is made by a stipendiary magistrate and the offender resides within his commission area, the district court for that area; and

"supervising court", in relation to an alcohol ignition interlock programme order, means—

(a) in England and Wales, if the Crown Court made the order the Crown Court and otherwise a magistrates' court acting for the same local justice area as the court which made the order, and (*b*) in Scotland, the court which made the order.

(4) Any power to make regulations under section 34D, 34E or 34F of this Act or this section includes power to make different provision for different cases, and to make such incidental or supplementary provision as appears to the appropriate national authority to be necessary or appropriate.

(5) Any power to make regulations under section 34D, 34E or 34F of this Act or this section shall be exercisable by statutory instrument.

(6) A statutory instrument containing regulations made under section 34D, 34E or 34F of this Act by the Secretary of State shall be subject to annulment in pursuance of a resolution of either House of Parliament.

(7) No regulations shall be made under this section unless a draft of the regulations has been laid before, and approved by a resolution of, each House of Parliament.*

[Road Traffic Offenders Act 1988, s 34G as inserted by the Road Safety Act 2006, 15.]

---

*Section inserted by the Road Safety Act 2006, 15 from a date to be appointed.

4-1684   35. Disqualification for repeated offences.   (1) Where—

(*a*) a person is convicted of an offence to which this subsection applies[1], and
(*b*) the penalty points to be taken into account on that occasion number twelve or more,

the court must order him to be disqualified[2] for not less than the minimum period unless the court is satisfied[3], having regard to all the circumstances[4], that there are grounds for mitigating[5] the normal consequences of the conviction and thinks fit to order him to be disqualified for a shorter period or not to order him to be disqualified.

(1A) Subsection (1) above applies to—

(*a*) an offence involving discretionary disqualification and obligatory endorsement, and
(*b*) an offence involving obligatory disqualification in respect of which no order is made under section 34 of this Act.

(2) The minimum period referred to in subsection (1) above is—

(*a*) six months if no previous disqualification imposed on the offender is to be taken into account, and
(*b*) one year if one, and two years if more than one, such disqualification is to be taken into account;

and a previous disqualification imposed on an offender is to be taken into account if it was for a fixed period of 56 days or more and was imposed within the three years immediately preceding the commission of the latest offence in respect of which penalty points are taken into account under section 29 of this Act.

(3) Where an offender is convicted[6] on the same occasion of more than one offence to which subsection (1) above applies—

(*a*) not more than one disqualification shall be imposed on him under subsection (1) above,
(*b*) in determining the period of the disqualification the court must take into account all[7] the offences, and
(*c*) for the purposes of any appeal any disqualification imposed under subsection (1) above shall be treated as an order made on the conviction of each of the offences.

(4) No account is to be taken under subsection (1) above of any of the following circumstances—

(*a*) any circumstances that are alleged to make the offence or any of the offences not a serious one,
(*b*) hardship, other than exceptional hardship, or
(*c*) any circumstances which, within the three years immediately preceding the conviction, have been taken into account[8] under that subsection in ordering the offender to be disqualified for a shorter period or not ordering him to be disqualified.

(5) References in this section to disqualification do not include a disqualification imposed under section 26 of this Act or section 147 of the Powers of Criminal Courts (Sentencing) Act 2000 or section 223A or 436A of the Criminal Procedure (Scotland) Act 1975 (offences committed by using vehicles) or a disqualification imposed in respect of an offence of stealing a motor vehicle, an offence under section 12 or 25 of the Theft Act 1968, an offence under section 178 of the Road Traffic Act 1988, or an attempt to commit such an offence.

(5A) The preceding provisions of this section shall apply in relation to a conviction of an offence committed by aiding, abetting, counselling, procuring, or inciting to the commission of, an offence involving obligatory disqualification as if the offence were an offence involving discretionary disqualification.

(6) Scotland.

(7) This section is subject to section 48 of this Act.

[Road Traffic Offenders Act 1988, s 35 amended by the Road Traffic Act 1991, Sch 4 and the Powers of Criminal Courts (Sentencing) Act 2000, Sch 9.]

---

1. See Sch 2, post, for list of such offences.
2. The operation of s 19 of the Transport Act 1981, which this section replaces, was considered in *R v Kent* [1983] 3

All ER 1, [1983] 1 WLR 794, 77 Cr App Rep 120 and *R v Yates* [1986] RTR 68, CA; note in particular that penalty points are not to be imposed at the same time as disqualification (see s 44(1), post) and that all periods of disqualification are to run concurrently. While multiple disqualification orders, under both ss 34 and 35, may theoretically be available in some exceptional circumstances, we are of the view that in practice such orders are best avoided since they add little to the sentencing process.

3. In the majority of cases justices will need evidence to satisfy themselves that there are grounds for mitigating the normal consequences of the conviction; but on rare occasions when considering the existence of exceptional hardship justices will be entitled to rely on their own knowledge, gathered from past events and experience, so as to be able to say that they can dispense with evidence and so be satisfied that exceptional hardship is established (*Owen v Jones* [1988] RTR 102, 9 Cr App Rep (S) 34).

4. It would seem that regard can be had to circumstances that relate to the offender or to his offence, or both. A sentencing policy, that the imposition on a young persistent offender of a long period of disqualification extending substantially beyond his release from prison, was counter-productive and contrary to the public interest by inviting him to commit further motoring offences, can constitute grounds for mitigation here (*R v Thomas* [1983] 3 All ER 756, [1983] 1 WLR 1490).

An excessive delay that breaches the defendant's rights under art 6 can be taken into account in deciding whether in all the circumstances there are grounds for mitigating the normal consequences of the defendant's conviction (*Miller v DPP* [2004] EWHC 595, [2005] RTR 3, where two and a half years elapsed between the defendant's guilty pleas and sentence, and a further year was wasted over the appeal).

5. Note the requirements of s 47, post, that the court should state the grounds in open court and cause them to be entered in the register. As to combination of disqualification and endorsement with probation orders and orders for discharge, see s 46, post. Mitigating circumstances may include good previous record where a driver has been convicted of theft of a motor vehicle but had an unblemished record as a driver and also evidence of the offender's rehabilitation (*R v Preston* [1986] RTR 136). See also *Owen v Jones* [1988] RTR 102, 9 Cr App Rep (S) 34 (evidence or justices' own knowledge).

6. We wonder whether "convicted" here should perhaps be read to mean "sentenced".

7. That is, when determining the disqualification under s 35. In respect of each offence, the court may also order disqualification under s 34. The periods of disqualification for the offence and for the repeated nature of the offence will be concurrent.

8. It is for the defendant to establish that the grounds are different from those put forward on an earlier occasion (*R v Sandbach Justices, ex p Pescud* (1983) 5 Cr App Rep (S) 177).

4–1685   36. Disqualification until test is passed.

(1) Where this subsection applies to a person the court must order him to be disqualified until he passes the appropriate driving test[1].

(2) Subsection (1) above applies to a person who is disqualified under section 34 of this Act on conviction of—

(*a*) manslaughter, or in Scotland culpable homicide, by the driver of a motor vehicle, or

(*b*) an offence under section 1 (causing death by dangerous driving) or section 2 (dangerous driving) of the Road Traffic Act 1988.

(3) Subsection (1) above also applies—

(*a*) to a person who is disqualified under section 34 or 35 of this Act in such circumstances or for such period as the Secretary of State may by order[2] prescribe, or

(*b*) to such other persons convicted of such offences involving obligatory endorsement as may be so prescribed.

(4) Where a person to whom subsection (1) above does not apply is convicted of an offence involving obligatory endorsement, the court may order him to be disqualified until he passes the appropriate driving test (whether or not he has previously passed any test).

(5) In this section—

"appropriate driving test" means—

(*a*) an extended driving test, where a person is convicted of an offence involving obligatory disqualification or is disqualified under section 35 of this Act,

(*b*) a test of competence to drive, other than an extended driving test, in any other case,

"extended driving test" means a test of competence to drive prescribed for the purposes of this section, and

"test of competence to drive" means a test prescribed by virtue of section 89(3) of the Road Traffic Act 1988.

(6) In determining whether to make an order under subsection (4) above, the court shall have regard to the safety of road users[3].

(7) Where a person is disqualified until he passes the extended driving test—

(*a*) any earlier order under this section shall cease to have effect, and

(*b*) a court shall not make a further order under this section while he is so disqualified.

(8) Subject to subsection (9) below, a disqualification by virtue of an order under this section shall be deemed to have expired on production to the Secretary of State of evidence, in such form as may be prescribed by regulations[4] under section 105 of the Road Traffic Act 1988, that the person disqualified has passed the test in question since the order was made.

(9) A disqualification shall be deemed to have expired only in relation to vehicles of such classes as may be prescribed in relation to the test passed by regulations under that section.

(10) Where there is issued to a person a licence on the counterpart of which are endorsed particulars of a disqualification under this section, there shall also be endorsed the particulars of any test of competence to drive that he has passed since the order of disqualification was made.

(11) For the purposes of an order under this section, a person shall be treated as having passed a

test of competence to drive other than an extended driving test if he passes a corresponding test conducted—

(a) under the law of Northern Ireland, the Isle of Man, any of the Channel Islands, another EEA State, Gibraltar or a designated country or territory, or

(b) for the purposes of obtaining a British Forces licence (as defined by section 88(8) of the Road Traffic Act 1988);

and accordingly subsections (8) to (10) above shall apply in relation to such a test as they apply in relation to a test prescribed by virtue of section 89(3) of that Act.

(11A) For the purposes of subsection (11) above "designated country or territory" means a country or territory designated by order under section 108(2) of the Road Traffic Act 1988 but a test conducted under the law of such a country or territory shall not be regarded as a corresponding test unless a person passing such a test would be entitled to an exchangeable licence as defined in section 108 (1) of that Act.

(12) This section is subject to section 48 of this Act.

(13) The power to make an order under subsection (3) above shall be exercisable by statutory instrument; and no such order shall be made unless a draft of it has been laid before and approved by resolution of each House of Parliament.

(14) The Secretary of State shall not make an order under subsection (3) above after the end of 2001 if he has not previously made such an order.

[Road Traffic Offenders Act 1988, s 36 as substituted by the Road Traffic Act 1991, s 32 and amended by SI 1996/1974.]

---

1. See s 89 of the Road Traffic Act 1988, ante. If no order of disqualification is made under s 34 or 35 or after any such order has expired, the person convicted may obtain a provisional licence under s 97, ante, to enable him to pass the prescribed test (s 37(3), post). It was said *obiter* in *Hunter v Coombs* [1962] 1 All ER 904, 126 JP 300, that a person disqualified under this section who contravenes the conditions under which a provisonal driving licence is held (eg by driving without "L" plates) is guilty of an offence of driving while disqualified under s 103 of the Road Traffic Act 1988.

Section 36 is not intended to be a punitive section but should be used in respect of people who are growing old or infirm, or show some incompetence in the offence, which requires looking into. See *R v Donnelly* [1975] 1 All ER 785, 139 JP 293, *R v Banks* [1978] RTR 535 and *R v Peat* [1985] Crim LR 110. Moreover, incompetence may take the form of not showing proper regard for other road users; see *R v Bannister* [1991] RTR 1, [1991] Crim LR 71, CA. Occasional incompetence to drive during an episode of hypomania arising from manic-depressive psychosis was held not to justify making an order under this section against a person who was found ordinarily to be a competent driver (*Hughes v Challes* (1983) 148 JP 170, [1984] RTR 283).

2. An offence under s 3A of the Road Traffic Act 1988 (causing death by dangerous driving when under the influence of drink or drugs) which is committed on or after 31 January 2002, and any person committing such an offence, are prescribed for the purposes of sub-s (1) by the Driving Licences (Disqualification until Test Passed) (Prescribed Offence) Order 2001, SI 2001/4051.

3. It is inappropriate to order the passenger convicted of an offence of aggravated vehicle taking to take an extended test (*R v Bradshaw, R v Waters* (Note-1994) [2001] RTR 41, CA).

4. See Motor Vehicles (Driving Licences) Regulations 1999 in this PART, post.

4–1686 37. Effect of order of disqualification.

(1) Where the holder of a licence is disqualified by an order of a court, the licence shall be treated as being revoked with effect from the beginning of the period of disqualification.

(1A) Where—

(a) the disqualification is for a fixed period shorter than 56 days in respect of an offence involving obligatory endorsement, or

(b) the order is made under section 26 of this Act,

subsection (1) above shall not prevent the licence from again having effect at the end of the period of disqualification.

(2) Where the holder of the licence appeals against the order and the disqualification is suspended under section 39 of this Act, the period of disqualification shall be treated for the purpose of subsection (1) above as beginning on the day on which the disqualification ceases to be suspended.

(3) Notwithstanding anything in Part III of the Road Traffic Act 1988, a person disqualified by an order of a court under section 36 of this Act is (unless he is also disqualified otherwise than by virtue of such an order) entitled to obtain and to hold a provisional licence and to drive a motor vehicle in accordance with the conditions subject to which the provisional licence is granted.

[Road Traffic Offenders Act 1988, s 37 as amended by the Road Traffic Act 1991, s 33 and Sch 4.]

4–1687 38. Appeal against disqualification.

(1) A person disqualified by an order of a magistrates' court under section 34 or 35 of this Act may appeal against the order in the same manner as against a conviction.

(2) Scotland.

[Road Traffic Offenders Act 1988, s 38.]

4–1688 39. Suspension of disqualification pending appeal.

(1) Any court in England and Wales (whether a magistrates' court or another) which makes an order disqualifying a person may, if it thinks fit, suspend the disqualification[1] pending an appeal against the order.

(2) Scotland.

(3) Where a court exercises its power under subsection (1) or (2) above, it must send notice of the suspension to the Secretary of State.

(4) The notice must be sent in such manner and to such address and must contain such particulars as the Secretary of State may determine.
[Road Traffic Offenders Act 1988, s 39.]

---

1. Disqualification runs from the date of the conviction or order, and (unless the operation of the order is suspended under this subsection) the service of a notice of appeal does not defer the operation of the suspension (*Kidner v Daniels* (1910) 74 JP 127). Although in practice an application will be made for suspension pending an appeal, it would seem that the court has power of its own volition to suspend the disqualification order; see *Taylor v Metropolitan Police Comr* [1987] RTR 118.

4–1689　40.　Power of appellate courts in England and Wales to suspend disqualification.

4–1690　41A.　Suspension of disqualification pending determination of applications under section 34B.　(1) Where a person makes an application to a court under section 34B of this Act, the court may suspend the disqualification to which the application relates pending the determination of the application.

(2) Where a court exercises its power under subsection (1) above it must send notice of the suspension to the Secretary of State.

(3) The notice must be sent in such manner and to such address, and must contain such particulars, as the Secretary of State may determine.
[Road Traffic Offenders Act 1988, s 41A as added by the Road Traffic Act 1991, Sch 4.]

4–1690A　41B.　Suspension of certificate pending determination of applications under section 34E.　(1) Where a person given a certificate under subsection (1) of section 34E of this Act makes an application to a court under subsection (5) of that section, the court may suspend the effect of the certificate pending the determination of the application.

(2) Where a court exercises its power under subsection (1) above it must send notice of the suspension to the Secretary of State.

(3) The notice must be sent in such manner and to such address and must contain such particulars, as the Secretary of State may determine.*
[Road Traffic Offenders Act 1988, s 41B as inserted by the Road Safety Act 2006, 15.]

---

*Section inserted by the Road Safety Act 2006, 15 from a date to be appointed.

4–1691　42.　Removal of disqualification.　(1) Subject to the provisions of this section, a person who by an order of a court is disqualified may apply[1] to the court by which the order was made[2] to remove the disqualification.

(2) On any such application the court may, as it thinks proper having regard to—

(*a*)　the character of the person disqualified and his conduct subsequent to the order,

(*b*)　the nature of the offence, and

(*c*)　any other circumstances of the case,

either by order[3] remove the disqualification as from such date as may be specified in the order or refuse the application.

(3) No application shall be made under subsection (1) above for the removal of a disqualification before the expiration of whichever is relevant of the following periods from the date of the order by which the disqualification was imposed, that is—

(*a*)　two years, if the disqualification is for less than four years,

(*b*)　one half of the period of disqualification, if it is for less than ten years but not less than four years,

(*c*)　five years in any other case;

and in determining the expiration of the period after which under this subsection a person may apply for the removal of a disqualification, any time after the conviction during which the disqualification was suspended or he was not disqualified shall be disregarded.

(4) Where an application under subsection (1) above is refused, a further application under that subsection shall not be entertained if made within three months after the date of the refusal.

(5) If under this section a court orders a disqualification to be removed, the court—

(*a*)　must cause particulars of the order to be endorsed on the counterpart of the licence, if any, previously held by the applicant, and

(*b*)　may in any case order the applicant to pay the whole or any part of the costs of the application.

(5A) Subsection (5)(a) above shall apply only where the disqualification was imposed in respect of an offence involving obligatory endorsement; and in any other case the court must send notice of the order made under this section to the Secretary of State.

(5B) A notice under subsection (5A) above must be sent in such manner and to such address, and must contain such particulars, as the Secretary of State may determine.

(6) The preceding provisions of this section shall not apply where the disqualification was imposed by order under section 36(1) of this Act.
[Road Traffic Offenders Act 1988, s 42 amended by SI 1990/144 and the Road Traffic Act 1991, Sch 4.]

1. This shall not apply to a person who has been disqualified until he has passed a driving test (see sub-s 6, infra). It is however, immaterial whether the disqualification was mandatory or discretionary and a person may apply under this section for the removal of a mandatory disqualification for more than 2 years (*Damer v Davison* [1976] RTR 44).

2. We understand this to mean not the individual persons who made the conviction or order, but any court of summary jurisdiction, sitting for the same petty sessional division, or the Crown Court (cf *McIntyre v Henderson* 1911 SC (J) 73, 48 Sc LR 588). An order of disqualification by the Crown Court on an appeal will have the same effect as if made by a court of summary jurisdiction (Magistrates' Courts Act 1980, s 110, ante). Where application is made to a magistrates' court, the Chief Constable should be summoned to show cause why the order applied for should not be made (Criminal Procedure Rules 2005, Part 55, in PART I: MAGISTRATES' COURTS, PROCEDURE, ante).

3. Notice of such order and copy of the endorsement are to be sent to the licensing authority to whom notice of the disqualification was sent (Criminal Procedure Rules 2005, Part 55, PART I, MAGISTRATES' COURTS, PROCEDURE, ante). The disqualification may not be removed in part (*R v Cottrell* [1955] 3 All ER 817). If a licence is restored as from a future date, eg six months hence, a further application for earlier restoration may be entertained, *semble* subject to sub-s (4), post (*R v Manchester Justices, ex p Gaynor* [1956] 1 All ER 610n).

4-1692   43. Rule for determining end of period of disqualification.   In determining the expiration of the period for which a person is disqualified by an order of a court made in consequence of a conviction, any time after the conviction during which the disqualification was suspended or he was not disqualified shall be disregarded.
[Road Traffic Offenders Act 1988, s 43.]

Endorsement

4-1693   44. Endorsement of licences.   (1) Where a person is convicted of an offence involving obligatory endorsement, the court must order[1] there to be endorsed on the counterpart of any licence held by him particulars of the conviction and also—

 (a) if the court orders[2] him to be disqualified, particulars of the disqualification, or
 (b) if the court does not order him to be disqualified—

  (i) particulars of the offence, including the date when it was committed, and
  (ii) the penalty points to be attributed to the offence.

(2) Where the court does not order the person convicted to be disqualified, it need not make an order under subsection (1) above if for special reasons[3] it thinks fit not to do so.
(3) Scotland.
(4) This section is subject to section 48 of this Act.
[Road Traffic Offenders Act 1988, s 44 amended by SI 1990/144.]

1. Cases in which conviction involves endorsement of a driving licence are not proper to be taken into consideration when passing sentence for another class of offence (*R v Collins* [1947] KB 560, [1947] 1 All ER 147, 111 JP 154), although they may be if the principal offence itself attracts endorsement: see *R v Jones* [1970] 3 All ER 815, 135 JP 36. Particulars of a disqualification or endorsement must not be entered on a visitor's driving licence; for position relating to such permits see the Motor Vehicles (International Circulation) Order 1975 in this PART, post. A list of the *endorsable offence codes* which appear on United Kingdom driving licences is printed immediately before statutory instruments in this PART, Also, if the court does not know the defendant's date of birth or sex, it will make an order under s 25, post.
2. This refers to any disqualification, whether obligatory or discretionary, which is ordered on the same occasion. Accordingly, a court, when dealing with offences committed on the same occasion, that orders an obligatory disqualification for one offence under s 34(1) has no power to impose penalty points for another offence that carries discretionary disqualification and obligatory endorsement (*Martin v DPP* [2000] RTR 188, [2000] 2 Cr App Rep (S) 18, 164 JP 405).See also the decision of the High Court of Justiciary in Scotland in *Ahmed v McLeod* [2000] RTR 201n, where it was held that when ordering an offender to be disqualified for driving until she passed a driving test for an offence of careless driving, the court had no power to impose penalty points for another offence committed on the same occasion of using a motor vehicle on a road without insurance.
3. For the meaning of "special reasons", see note to s 34(1), ante.

4-1693A   44A. Endorsement of driving record in accordance with order.   (1) Where the court orders the endorsement of a person's driving record with any particulars or penalty points it must send notice of the order to the Secretary of State.
(2) On receiving the notice, the Secretary of State must endorse those particulars or penalty points on the person's driving record.
(3) A notice sent by the court to the Secretary of State in pursuance of this section must be sent in such manner and to such address and contain such particulars as the Secretary of State may require.*
[Road Traffic Offenders Act 1988, s 44A as inserted by the Road Safety Act 2006, 9.]

*Section inserted by the Road Safety Act 2006, 9 from a date to be appointed.

4-1694   45. Effect of endorsement.   (1) An order that any particulars or penalty points are to be endorsed on the counterpart of any licence held by the person convicted shall, whether he is at the time the holder of a licence or not, operate as an order that the counterpart of any licence he may then hold or may subsequently obtain is to be so endorsed until he becomes entitled under subsection (4) below to have a licence issued to him with its counterpart free from the particulars or penalty points.
(2) On the issue of a new licence to a person, any particulars or penalty points ordered to be endorsed on the counterpart of any licence held by him shall be entered on the counterpart of the licence unless he has become entitled under subsection (4) below to have a licence issued to him with its counterpart free from those particulars or penalty points.

(3) (Repealed).

(4) A person the counterpart of whose licence has been ordered to be endorsed is entitled to have issued to him with effect from the end of the period for which the endorsement remains effective a new licence with a counterpart free from endorsement if he applies for a new licence in pursuance of section 97(1) of the Road Traffic Act 1988, surrenders any subsisting licence and its counterpart, pays the fee prescribed by regulations under Part III of that Act and satisfies the other requirements of section 97(1).

(5) An endorsement ordered on a person's conviction of an offence remains effective[1] (subject to subsections (6) and (7) below)—

    (a) if an order is made for the disqualification of the offender, until four years have elapsed since the conviction, and
    (b) if no such order is made, until either—

        (i) four years have elapsed since the commission of the offence, or
        (ii) an order is made for the disqualification of the offender under section 35 of this Act.

(6) Where the offence was one under section 1 or 2 of that Act (causing death by dangerous driving and dangerous driving), the endorsement remains in any case effective[1] until four years have elapsed since the conviction.

(7) Where the offence was one—

    (a) section 3A, 4(1) or 5(1)(a) of that Act (driving offences connected with drink or drugs), or
    (b) under section 7(6) of that Act (failing to provide specimen) involving obligatory disqualification,

the endorsement remains effective until eleven years have elapsed since the conviction[2].
[Road Traffic Offenders Act 1988, s 45 as amended by the Road Traffic (Driver Licensing a d Information Systems) Act 1989, Sch 3, SI 1990/144 and the Road Traffic Act 1991, Sch 4.]

---

    1. In determining sentence, courts are entitled to consider the record of previous convictions, whether or not evidenced by endorsements no longer effective within this subsection (*Chief Constable of West Mercia v Williams* [1987] RTR 188).
    2. The retention of an endorsement for an additional period after the conviction in question has become spent does not engage art 8 of the Convention; although the Rehabilitation of Offenders Act 1974 confers certain benefits on offenders, that is not to say that the continuation of an endorsement once a conviction has become spent interferes with a person's Convention rights (*R (Pearson) v Driver and Vehicle Licensing Authority* [2002] EWHC 2482 (Admin), [2003] RTR 292, [2003] Crim LR 199).

4–1694A 45A. Effect of endorsement of driving records. (1) An order that any particulars or penalty points are to be endorsed on a person's driving record shall operate as an order that his driving record is to be so endorsed until the end of the period for which the endorsement remains effective.

(2) At the end of the period for which the endorsement remains effective the Secretary of State must remove the endorsement from the person's driving record.

(3) On the issue of a new licence to a person, any particulars ordered to be endorsed on his driving record shall be entered on the counterpart of the licence unless he has become entitled under subsection (4) below to have a licence issued to him with its counterpart free from those particulars or penalty points.

(4) A person the counterpart of whose licence has been endorsed under subsection (3) above is entitled to have issued to him with effect from the end of the period for which the endorsement remains effective a new licence with a counterpart free from the endorsement if he applies for a new licence in pursuance of section 97(1) of the Road Traffic Act 1988, surrenders any subsisting licence and its counterpart, pays the fee prescribed by regulations under Part 3 of that Act and satisfies the other requirements of section 97(1).

(5) The period for which an endorsement remains effective is determined in accordance with section 45(5) to (7) of this Act.*
[Road Traffic Offenders Act 1988, s 45A as inserted by the Road Safety Act 2006, Sch 2.]

---

*Section inserted by the Road Safety Act 2006, Sch 2 from a date to be appointed.

General

4–1695 46. Combination of disqualification and endorsement with probation orders and orders for discharge. (1) Notwithstanding anything in section 14(3) of the Powers of Criminal Courts (Sentencing) Act 2000 (conviction of offender discharged to be disregarded for the purposes of enactments relating to disqualification), a court in England and Wales which on convicting a person of an offence involving obligatory or discretionary disqualification makes—

    (a) a probation order, or
    (b) an order discharging him absolutely or conditionally,

may on that occasion also exercise any power conferred, and must also discharge any duty imposed, on the court by sections 34, 35, 36 or 44 of this Act.

(2) A conviction—

    (a) in respect of which a court in England and Wales has ordered a person to be disqualified, or
    (b) of which particulars have been endorsed on the counterpart of any licence held by him,

is to be taken into account, notwithstanding anything in section 14(1) of the Powers of Criminal Courts (Sentencing) Act 2000 (conviction of offender discharged to be disregarded for the purpose of subsequent proceedings), in determining his liability to punishment or disqualification for any offence involving obligatory or discretionary disqualification committed subsequently.

(3) Scotland.

[Road Traffic Offenders Act 1988, s 46, amended by SI 1990/144 and the Criminal Justice Act 1991, Sch 11.]

4–1702 47. Supplementary provisions as to disqualifications and endorsements. (1) In any case where a court exercises its power under section 34, 35 or 44 of this Act not to order any disqualification or endorsement or to order disqualification for a shorter period than would otherwise be required, it must state[1] the grounds for doing so in open court and, if it is a magistrates' court or, in Scotland, a court of summary jurisdiction, must cause them to be entered in the register (in Scotland, record) of its proceedings.

(2) Where a court orders the endorsement of the counterpart of any licence held by a person it may, and where a court orders the holder of a licence to be disqualified for a period of 56 days or more it must send the licence and its counterpart, on their being produced to the court, to the Secretary of State; and if the court orders the endorsement but does not send the licence and its counterpart to the Secretary of State it must send him notice[2] of the endorsement.

(2A) Subsection (2) above is subject to section 2(2) of and paragraph 7(2) of Schedule 1 to the Road Traffic (New Drivers) Act 1995 (obligation of court to send licence and its counterpart to the Secretary of State).

(3) Where on an appeal against an order for the endorsement of a licence or the disqualification of a person the appeal is allowed, the court by which the appeal is allowed must send notice of that fact to the Secretary of State.

(4) A notice sent by a court to the Secretary of State in pursuance of this section must be sent in such manner and to such address and contain such particulars as the Secretary of State may determine, and a licence and the counterpart of a licence so sent in pursuance of this section must be sent to such address as the Secretary of State may determine.

[Road Traffic Offenders Act 1988, s 47, amended by SI 1990/144, the Road Traffic Act 1991, Sch 4 and the Road Traffic (New Drivers) Act 1995, Sch 2.]

---

1. The requirement to state the grounds is directory, not mandatory, so that failure to comply with this requirement does not provide a ground of appeal: see *Barnes v Gevaux* [1981] RTR 236.

2. The manner of notification is described in Home Office Circular No 145/1975. In the case of drivers from abroad, driving on their own country's driving permit, the court shall in no circumstances endorse such permit, but shall send particulars of the conviction to the Secretary of State. If disqualification is ordered, the permit should accompany these particulars (Motor Vehicles (International Circulation) Order 1975, SI 1975/1208). As to the application of this section to persons who become residents of Great Britain see Motor Vehicles (Driving Licences) Regulations 1996, in this PART, post, and as to Northern Ireland driving licences, see s 109 of the Road Traffic Act 1988.

4–1703 48. Exemption from disqualification and endorsement for certain construction and use offences. Where a person is convicted of an offence under section 40A of the Road Traffic Act 1988 (using vehicle in dangerous condition etc) the court must not—

(a) order him to be disqualified, or
(b) order any particulars or penalty points to be endorsed on the counterpart of any licence held by him,

if he proves that he did not know, and had no reasonable cause to suspect, that the use of the vehicle involved a danger of injury to any person.

(2) Where a person is convicted of an offence under section 41A of the Road Traffic Act 1988 (breach of requirement as to brakes, steering-gear or tyres) the court must not—

(a) order him to be disqualified, or
(b) order any particulars or penalty points to be endorsed on the counterpart of any licence held by him,

if he proves that he did not know, and had no reasonable cause to suspect, that the facts of the case were such that the offence would be committed.

(3) In relation to licences which came into force before 1st June 1990, the references in subsections (1) and (2) above to the counterpart of a licence shall be construed as references to the licence itself.

[Road Traffic Offenders Act 1988, s 48 as substituted by the Road Traffic Act 1991, Sch 4.]

4–1704 49. Offender escaping consequences of endorseable offence by deception. (1) This section applies where in dealing with a person convicted of an offence involving obligatory endorsement a court was deceived regarding any circumstances that were or might have been taken into account in deciding whether or for how long to disqualify him.

(2) If—

(a) the deception constituted or was due to an offence committed by that person, and
(b) he is convicted of that offence,

the court by or before which he is convicted shall have the same powers and duties regarding an order for disqualification as had the court which dealt with him for the offence involving obligatory

endorsement but must, in dealing with him, take into account any order made on his conviction of the offence involving obligatory endorsement.
[Road Traffic Offenders Act 1988, s 49.]

PART III[1]
FIXED PENALTIES

Introductory

4–1705　51. Fixed penalty offences.　(1) Any offence in respect of a vehicle under an enactment specified in column 1 of Schedule 3 to this Act is a fixed penalty offence for the purposes of this Part of this Act, but subject to subsection (2) below and to any limitation or exception shown against the enactment in column 2 (where the general nature of the offence is also indicated).

(2) An offence under an enactment so specified is not a fixed penalty offence for those purposes if it is committed by causing or permitting a vehicle to be used by another person in contravention of any provision made or restriction or prohibition imposed by or under any enactment.

(3) The Secretary of State may by order[2] provide for offences to become or (as the case may be) to cease to be fixed penalty offences for the purposes of this Part of this Act, and may make such modifications of the provisions of this Part of this Act as appear to him to be necessary for the purpose.
[Road Traffic Offenders Act 1988, s 51.]

───────────

1. Part III contains ss 51–90.
2. Orders have been noted to Sch 3, post.

4–1706　52. Fixed penalty notices.　(1) In this Part of this Act "fixed penalty notice" means a notice offering the opportunity of the discharge of any liability to conviction of the offence to which the notice relates by payment of a fixed penalty in accordance with this Part of this Act.

(2) A fixed penalty notice must give such particulars of the circumstances alleged to constitute the offence to which it relates as are necessary for giving reasonable information about the alleged offence.

(3) A fixed penalty notice must state—

(a) the period during which, by virtue of section 78(1) of this Act, proceedings cannot be brought against any person for the offence to which the notice relates, being the period of twenty-one days following the date of the notice or such longer period (if any) as may be specified in the notice (referred to in this Part of this Act as the "suspended enforcement period"),

(b) the amount of the fixed penalty, and

(c) the designated officer for a magistrates' court or in Scotland, the clerk of court to whom and the address at which the fixed penalty may be paid.

(4) Repealed.
[Road Traffic Offenders Act 1988, s 52, as amended by the Access to Justice Act 1999, Sch 13, the Statute Law (Repeals) Act 2004 and the Courts Act 2003, Sch 8.]

4–1707　53. Amount of fixed penalty.　(1) The fixed penalty for an offence is—

(a) such amount as the Secretary of State may by order[1] prescribe, or

(b) one-half of the maximum amount of the fine to which a person committing that offence would be liable on summary conviction,

whichever is the less.

(2) Any order made under subsection (1)(a) may make different provision for different cases or classes of case or in respect of different areas.★
[Road Traffic Offenders Act 1988, s 53 as substituted by the Road Traffic Act 1991, Sch 4.]

───────────

★Sub-section (3) inserted by the Domestic Violence, Crime and Victims Act 2004, s 16 from a date to be appointed.
1. See the Fixed Penalty Order 2000, this PART, post.

Giving notices to suspected offenders

4–1708　54. Notices on-the-spot or at a police station.　(1) This section applies where in England and Wales on any occasion a constable in uniform has reason to believe that a person he finds is committing or has on that occasion committed a fixed penalty offence.

(2) Subject to subsection (3) below, the constable may give him a fixed penalty notice in respect of the offence.

(3) Where the offence appears to the constable to involve obligatory endorsement, the constable may only give him a fixed penalty notice under subsection (2) above in respect of the offence if—

(a) he produces his licence and its counterpart for inspection by the constable,

(b) the constable is satisfied, on inspecting the licence and its counterpart, that he would not be liable to be disqualified under section 35 of this Act if he were convicted of that offence, and

(c) he surrenders his licence and its counterpart to the constable to be retained and dealt with in accordance with this Part of this Act.

(4) Where—

(a)   the offence appears to the constable to involve obligatory endorsement, and

(b)   the person concerned does not produce his licence and its counterpart for inspection by the constable,

the constable may give him a notice stating that if, within seven days after the notice is given, he produces the notice together with his licence and its counterpart in person to an authorised person at the police station specified in the notice (being a police station chosen by the person concerned) and the requirements of subsection (5)(a) and (b) below are met he will then be given a fixed penalty notice in respect of the offence.

(5)   If a person to whom a notice has been given under subsection (4) above produces the notice together with his licence and its counterpart in person to an authorised person at the police station specified in the notice within seven days after the notice was so given to him and the following requirements are met, that is—

(a)   the authorised person is satisfied, on inspecting the licence and its counterpart, that he would not be liable to be disqualified under section 35 of this Act if he were convicted of the offence, and

(b)   he surrenders his licence and its counterpart to the authorised person to be retained and dealt with in accordance with this Part of this Act,

the authorised person must give him a fixed penalty notice in respect of the offence to which the notice under subsection (4) above relates.

(6)   A notice under subsection (4) above shall give such particulars of the circumstances alleged to constitute the offence to which it relates as are necessary for giving reasonable information about the alleged offence.

(7)   A licence[1] and its counterpart surrendered in accordance with this section must be sent to the fixed penalty clerk.

(8)   Repealed.

(9)   In this Part of this Act "authorised person", in relation to a fixed penalty notice given at a police station, means a person authorised for the purposes of this section by or on behalf of the chief officer of police for the area in which the police station is situated.

This subsection is affected by Schedule 5 to the Road Traffic (Consequential Provisions) Act 1988 (transitory modifications).

(10)   In determining for the purposes of subsections (3)(b) and (5)(a) above whether a person convicted of an offence would be liable to disqualification under section 35, it shall be assumed, in the case of an offence in relation to which a range of numbers is shown in the last column of Part I of Schedule 2 to this Act, that the number of penalty points to be attributed to the offence would be the lowest in the range.

[Road Traffic Offenders Act 1988, s 54, amended by SI 1990/144 and the Road Traffic Act 1991, Sch 4.]

---

1. Also in the case of a newly qualified driver who holds a provisional licence, any certificate of passing a test of competence to drive (see the Road Traffic (New Drivers) Act 1995, Sch 1, Pt II, this PART, post).

4–1709 55. Effect of fixed penalty notice given under section 54.   (1) This section applies where a fixed penalty notice relating to an offence has been given to any person under section 54 of this Act, and references in this section to the recipient are to the person to whom the notice was given.

(2)   No proceedings shall be brought against the recipient for the offence to which the fixed penalty notice relates unless before the end of the suspended enforcement period he has given notice requesting a hearing in respect of that offence in the manner specified in the fixed penalty notice.

(3)   Where—

(a)   the recipient has not given notice requesting a hearing in respect of the offence to which the fixed penalty notice relates in the manner so specified, and

(b)   the fixed penalty has not been paid in accordance with this Part of this Act before the end of the suspended enforcement period,

a sum equal to the fixed penalty plus one-half of the amount of that penalty may be registered under section 71 of this Act for enforcement against the recipient as a fine.

[Road Traffic Offenders Act 1988, s 55.]

4–1710   56. Licence receipts.   (1) A constable or authorised person to whom a person surrenders his licence and its counterpart on receiving a fixed penalty notice given to him under section 54 of this Act must issue a receipt for the licence and its counterpart under this section.

(2)   The fixed penalty clerk may, on the application of a person who has surrendered his licence and its counterpart in those circumstances, issue a new receipt for them.

(3)   A receipt issued under this section ceases to a have effect—

(a)   if issued by a constable or authorised person, on the expiration of the period of one month beginning with the date of issue or such longer period as may be prescribed, and

(b)   if issued by the fixed penalty clerk, on such date as he may specify in the receipt,

or, if earlier, on the return of the licence and its counterpart to the licence holder.

[Road Traffic Offenders Act 1988, s 56, amended by SI 1990/144.]

4–1711 57. Endorsement of licences without hearings.   (1) Subject to subsection (2) below, where a person (referred to in this section as "the licence holder") has surrendered his licence and its counterpart to a constable or authorised person on the occasion when he was given a fixed penalty notice under section 54 of this Act, his licence and his counterpart may be endorsed in accordance with this section without any order of a court.

(2) The counterpart of a person's licence may not be endorsed under this section if at the end of the suspended enforcement period—

(a) he has given notice, in the manner specified in the fixed penalty notice, requesting a hearing in respect of the offence to which the fixed penalty notice relates, and
(b) the fixed penalty has not been paid in accordance with this Part of this Act.

(3) On the payment of the fixed penalty before the end of the suspended enforcement period, the fixed penalty clerk must endorse the relevant particulars on the counterpart of the licence and return it together with the licence to the licence holder.

(4) Where any sum determined by reference to the fixed penalty is registered under section 71 of this Act for enforcement against the licence holder as a fine, the fixed penalty clerk must endorse the relevant particulars on the counterpart of the licence and return it together with the licence to the licence holder—

(a) if he is himself the clerk who registers that sum, on the registration of that sum, and
(b) in any other case, on being notified of the registration by the clerk who registers that sum.

(5) References in this section to the relevant particulars are to—

(a) particulars of the offence, including the date when it was committed, and
(b) the number of penalty points to be attributed to the offence.

(6) On endorsing the counterpart of a person's licence under this section the fixed penalty clerk must send notice of the endorsement and of the particulars endorsed to the Secretary of State.

(7) Subsections (3) and (4) above are subject to section 2(4)(a) of and paragraph 7(4)(a) of Schedule 1 to the Road Traffic (New Drivers) Act 1995; and the fixed penalty clerk need not comply with subsection (6) above in a case where he sends a person's licence and its counterpart to the Secretary of State under section 2(4)(b) of or paragraph 7(4)(b) of Schedule 1 to that Act.
[Road Traffic Offenders Act 1988, s 57, amended by SI 1990/144 and the Road Traffic (New Drivers) Act 1995, Sch 2.]

4-1711A　57A. Endorsement of driving records without hearings. (1) Subject to subsection (2) below, where a person who is not the holder of a licence has been given a fixed penalty notice under section 54 of this Act in respect of an offence involving obligatory endorsement, his driving record may be endorsed in accordance with this section without any order of a court.

(2) A person's driving record may not be endorsed under this section if at the end of the suspended enforcement period—

(a) he has given notice, in the manner specified in the fixed penalty notice, requesting a hearing in respect of the offence to which the fixed penalty notice relates, and
(b) the fixed penalty has not been paid in accordance with this Part of this Act.

(3) If payment of the fixed penalty is made before the end of the suspended enforcement period and the person to whom the payment is made is the fixed penalty clerk, the fixed penalty clerk must send to the Secretary of State notice of the relevant particulars which are to be endorsed on the person's driving record.

(4) Where any sum determined by reference to the fixed penalty is registered under section 71 of this Act for enforcement against the person as a fine in a case where the fixed penalty is required to be paid to the fixed penalty clerk, the fixed penalty clerk must send to the Secretary of State notice of the relevant particulars which are to be endorsed on the person's driving record—

(a) if he is himself the person who registers the sum, on the registration of that sum, and
(b) in any other case, on being notified of the registration by the person who registers that sum.

(5) The Secretary of State must endorse the relevant particulars on the person's driving record if—

(a) he receives notice of them under subsection (3) or (4) above,
(b) the fixed penalty is paid to him before the end of the suspended enforcement period, or
(c) in a case where the fixed penalty is required to be paid to the Secretary of State, any sum determined by reference to the fixed penalty is registered under section 71 of this Act for enforcement against the person as a fine.

(6) References in this section to the relevant particulars are to—

(a) particulars of the offence, including the date when it was committed, and
(b) the number of penalty points to be attributed to the offence.*
[Road Traffic Offenders Act 1988, s 57A as inserted by the Road Safety Act 2006, 9.]

---

*Section inserted by the Road Safety Act 2006, 9 from a date to be appointed.

4-1712　58. Effect of endorsement without hearing. (1) Where the counterpart of a person's licence is endorsed under section 57 of this Act he shall be treated for the purposes of sections 13(4), 28, 29 and 45 of this Act and of the Rehabilitation of Offenders Act 1974 as if—

(a) he had been convicted of the offence,

(b)　the endorsement had been made in pursuance of an order made on his conviction by a court under section 44 of this Act, and

(c)　the particulars of the offence endorsed by virtue of section 57(5)(a) of this Act were particulars of his conviction of that offence.

(2)　In relation to any endorsement of the counterpart of a person's licence under section 57 of this Act—

(a)　the reference in section 45(4) of this Act to the order for endorsement, and

(b)　the references in section 13(4) of this Act to any order made on a person's conviction,

are to be read as references to the endorsement itself.
[Road Traffic Offenders Act 1988, s 58, amended by SI 1990/144.]

4–1712A　58A. Effect of endorsement of driving record without hearing.　(1) Where a person's driving record is endorsed under section 57A of this Act he shall be treated for the purposes of sections 13(4), 28, 29 and 45A of this Act and of the Rehabilitation of Offenders Act 1974 as if—

(a)　he had been convicted of the offence,

(b)　the endorsement had been made in pursuance of an order made on his conviction by a court under section 44 of this Act, and

(c)　the particulars of the offence endorsed by virtue of section 57A(6)(a) of this Act were particulars of his conviction of that offence.

(2)　In relation to any endorsement of a person's driving record under section 57A of this Act, the references in section 13(4) of this Act to any order made on a person's conviction are to be read as references to the endorsement itself.*
[Road Traffic Offenders Act 1988, s 58A as inserted by the Road Safety Act 2006, Sch 2.]

---

*Section inserted by the Road Safety Act 2006, Sch 2 from a date to be appointed.

4–1713　59. Notification of court and date of trial in England and Wales.　*Repealed by the Statute Law (Repeals) Act 2004.*

4–1714　61. Fixed penalty notice mistakenly given: exclusion of fixed penalty procedures.
(1)　This section applies where, on inspection of a licence and its counterpart sent to him under section 54(7) of this Act, it appears to the fixed penalty clerk that the person whose licence it is would be liable to be disqualified under section 35 of this Act if he were convicted of the offence in respect of which the fixed penalty notice was given.

(2)　The fixed penalty clerk must not endorse the counterpart of the licence under section 57 of this Act but must instead send it together with the licence to the chief officer of police.

(3)　Nothing in this Part of this Act prevents proceedings being brought in respect of the offence in respect of which the fixed penalty notice was given where those proceedings are commenced before the end of the period of six months beginning with the date on which that notice was given.

(4)　Where proceedings in respect of that offence are commenced before the end of that period, the case is from then on to be treated in all respects as if no fixed penalty notice had been given in respect of the offence.

(5)　Accordingly, where proceedings in respect of that offence are so commenced, any action taken in pursuance of any provision of this Part of this Act by reference to that fixed penalty notice shall be void (including, but without prejudice to the generality of the preceding provision—

(a)　the registration under section 71 of this Act of any sum, determined by reference to the fixed penalty for that offence, for enforcement against the person whose licence it is as a fine, and

(b)　any proceedings for enforcing payment of any such sum within the meaning of sections 73 and 74 of this Act (defined in section 74(5)).

(6)　In determining for the purposes of subsection (1) above whether a person convicted of an offence would be liable to disqualification under section 35, it shall be assumed, in the case of an offence in relation to which a range of numbers is shown in the last column of Part I of Schedule 2 to this Act, that the number of penalty points to be attributed to the offence would be the lowest in the range.
[Road Traffic Offenders Act 1988, s 61, amended by SI 1990/144 and the Road Traffic Act 1991, Sch 4.]

4–1714A　61A. Fixed penalty notice mistakenly given to unlicensed person: exclusion of fixed penalty procedures.　(1)　This section applies where, on accessing information held on the driving record of a person to whom a fixed penalty notice was given under section 54 of this Act, but who is not the holder of a licence, it appears to the fixed penalty clerk or the Secretary of State that the person would be liable to be disqualified under section 35 of this Act if he were convicted of the offence in respect of which the fixed penalty notice was given.

(2)　The person's driving record must not be endorsed under section 57A of this Act.

(3)　In a case where the fixed penalty is required to be paid to the fixed penalty clerk he must not send notice to the Secretary of State under section 57A of this Act but instead must notify the chief officer of police that the person to whom the fixed penalty notice was given would be liable to be disqualified under section 35 of this Act if he were convicted of the offence in respect of which the fixed penalty notice was given.

(4) Nothing in this Part of this Act prevents proceedings being brought in respect of the offence in respect of which the fixed penalty notice was given where those proceedings are commenced before the end of the period of six months beginning with the date on which that notice was given.

(5) Where proceedings in respect of that offence are commenced before the end of that period, the case is from then on to be treated in all respects as if no fixed penalty notice had been given in respect of the offence.

(6) Accordingly, where proceedings in respect of that offence are so commenced, any action taken in pursuance of this Part of this Act by reference to that fixed penalty notice shall be void (including, but without prejudice to the generality of the preceding provision—

(*a*) the registration under section 71 of this Act of any sum, determined by reference to the fixed penalty for that offence, for enforcement against the person to whom the fixed penalty notice was given, and

(*b*) any proceedings for enforcing payment of any such sum within the meaning of sections 73 and 74 of this Act (defined in section 74(5))).

(7) In determining for the purposes of subsection (1) above whether a person convicted of an offence would be liable to disqualification under section 35, it shall be assumed, in the case of an offence in relation to which a range of numbers is shown in the last column of Part 1 of Schedule 2 to this Act, that the number of penalty points to be attributed to the offence would be the lowest in the range.★

[Road Traffic Offenders Act 1988, s 61A as inserted by the Road Safety Act 2006, Sch 2.]

★Section inserted by the Road Safety Act 2006, Sch 2 from a date to be appointed.

Notices fixed to vehicles

4–1715 62. Fixing notices to vehicles. (1) Where on any occasion a constable has reason to believe in the case of any stationary vehicle that a fixed penalty offence is being or has on that occasion been committed in respect of it, he may fix a fixed penalty notice in respect of the offence to the vehicle unless the offence appears to him to involve obligatory endorsement.

(2) A person is guilty of an offence if he removes or interferes with any notice fixed to a vehicle under this section, unless he does so by or under the authority of the driver or person in charge of the vehicle or the person liable for the fixed penalty offence in question.

[Road Traffic Offenders Act 1988, s 62.]

4–1716 63. Service of notice to owner if penalty not paid. (1) This section applies where a fixed penalty notice relating to an offence has been fixed to a vehicle under section 62 of this Act.

(2) Subject to subsection (3) below, if at the end of the suspended enforcement period the fixed penalty has not been paid in accordance with this Part of this Act, a notice under this section may be served by or on behalf of the chief officer of police on any person who appears to him (or to any person authorised to act on his behalf for the purposes of this section) to be the owner of the vehicle. Such a notice is referred to in this Part of this Act as a "notice to owner".

(3) Subsection (2) above does not apply where before the end of the suspended enforcement period—

(*a*) any person has given notice requesting a hearing in respect of the offence in the manner specified in the fixed penalty notice, and

(*b*) the notice so given contains a statement by that person to the effect that he was the driver of the vehicle at the time when the offence is alleged to have been committed.

That time is referred to in this Part of this Act as the "time of the alleged offence".

(4) A notice to owner—

(*a*) must give particulars of the alleged offence and of the fixed penalty concerned,

(*b*) must state the period allowed for response to the notice, and

(*c*) must indicate that, if the fixed penalty is not paid before the end of that period, the person on whom the notice is served is asked to provide before the end of that period to the chief officer of police by or on whose behalf the notice was served a statutory statement of ownership (as defined in Part I of Schedule 4 to this Act).

(5) For the purposes of this Part of this Act, the period allowed for response to a notice to owner is the period of twenty-one days from the date on which the notice is served, or such longer period (if any) as may be specified in the notice.

(6) A notice to owner relating to any offence must indicate that the person on whom it is served may, before the end of the period allowed for response to the notice, either—

(*a*) give notice requesting a hearing in respect of the offence in the manner indicated by the notice, or

(*b*) if—

(i) he was not the driver of the vehicle at the time of the alleged offence, and

(ii) a person purporting to be the driver wishes to give notice requesting a hearing in respect of the offence,

provide, together with a statutory statement of ownership provided as requested in that notice, a statutory statement of facts (as defined by Part II of Schedule 4 to this Act) having the effect referred to in paragraph 3(2) of that Schedule (that is, as a notice requesting a hearing in respect of the offence given by the driver).

(7) In any case where a person on whom a notice to owner relating to any offence has been served provides a statutory statement of facts in pursuance of subsection (6)(b) above—

(a) any notice requesting a hearing in respect of the offence that he purports to give on his own account shall be of no effect, and

(b) no sum may be registered for enforcement against him as a fine in respect of the offence unless, within the period of two months immediately following the period allowed for response to the notice to owner, no summons or, in Scotland, complaint in respect of the offence in question is served on the person identified in the statement as the driver.

[Road Traffic Offenders Act 1988, s 63.]

4–1717   64. Enforcement or proceedings against owner.   (1) This section applies where—

(a) a fixed penalty notice relating to an offence has been fixed to a vehicle under section 62 of this Act,

(b) a notice to owner relating to the offence has been served on any person under section 63(2) of this Act before the end of the period of six months beginning with the day on which the fixed penalty notice was fixed to the vehicle, and

(c) the fixed penalty has not been paid in accordance with this Part of this Act before the end of the period allowed for response to the notice to owner.

(2) Subject to subsection (4) below and to section 63(7)(b) of this Act, a sum equal to the fixed penalty plus one-half of the amount of that penalty may be registered under section 71 of this Act for enforcement against the person on whom the notice to owner was served as a fine.

(3) Subject to subsection (4) below and to section 65 of this Act, proceedings may be brought in respect of the offence against the person on whom the notice to owner was served.

(4) If the person on whom the notice to owner was served—

(a) was not the owner of the vehicle at the time of the alleged offence, and

(b) provides a statutory statement of ownership to that effect in response to the notice before the end of the period allowed for response to the notice,

he shall not be liable in respect of the offence by virtue of this section nor shall any sum determined by reference to the fixed penalty for the offence be so registered by virtue of this section for enforcement against him as a fine.

(5) Subject to subsection (6) below—

(a) for the purposes of the institution of proceedings by virtue of subsection (3) above against any person on whom a notice to owner has been served, and

(b) in any proceedings brought by virtue of that subsection against any such person,

it shall be conclusively presumed (notwithstanding that that person may not be an individual) that he was the driver of the vehicle at the time of the alleged offence and, accordingly, that acts or omissions of the driver of the vehicle at that time were his acts or omissions.

(6) That presumption does not apply in any proceedings brought against any person by virtue of subsection (3) above if, in those proceedings, it is proved that at the time of the alleged offence the vehicle was in the possession of some other person without the consent of the accused.

(7) Where—

(a) by virtue of subsection (3) above proceedings may be brought in respect of an offence against a person on whom a notice to owner was served, and

(b) section 74(1) of this Act does not apply,

section 127(1) of the Magistrates' Courts Act 1980 (information must be laid within six months of time committed) and section 136(1) of the Criminal Procedure (Scotland) Act 1995 (proceedings must be commenced within six months of that time) shall have effect as if for the reference to six months there were substituted a reference to twelve months.

[Road Traffic Offenders Act 1988, s 64 as amended by the Criminal Procedure (Consequential Provisions) (Scotland) Act 1995, Sch 4.]

4–1718   65. Restrictions on proceedings against owner and others.   (1) In any case where a notice to owner relating to an offence may be served under section 63 of this Act, no proceedings shall be brought in respect of the offence against any person other than a person on whom such a notice has been served unless he is identified as the driver of the vehicle at the time of the alleged offence in a statutory statement of facts provided in pursuance of section 63(6)(b) of this Act by a person on whom such a notice has been served.

(2) Proceedings in respect of an offence to which a notice to owner relates shall not be brought against the person on whom the notice was served unless, before the end of the period allowed for response to the notice, he has given notice, in the manner indicated by the notice to owner, requesting a hearing in respect of the offence.

(3) Proceedings in respect of an offence to which a notice to owner relates may not be brought against any person identified as the driver of the vehicle in a statutory statement of facts provided in response to the notice if the fixed penalty is paid in accordance with this Part of this Act before the end of the period allowed for response to the notice.

(4) Once any sum determined by reference to the fixed penalty for an offence has been registered

by virtue of section 64 of this Act under section 71 for enforcement as a fine against a person on whom a notice to owner relating to that offence has been served, no proceedings shall be brought against any other person in respect of that offence.
[Road Traffic Offenders Act 1988, s 65.]

4–1719   66. Hired vehicles.   (1) This section applies where—

(a) a notice to owner has been served on a vehicle-hire firm,

(b) at the time of the alleged offence the vehicle in respect of which the notice was served was let to another person by the vehicle-hire firm under a hiring agreement to which this section applies, and

(c) within the period allowed for response to the notice the firm provides the chief officer of police by or on whose behalf the notice was served with the documents mentioned in subsection (2) below.

(2) Those documents are a statement on an official form, signed by or on behalf of the firm, stating that at the time of the alleged offence the vehicle concerned was hired under a hiring agreement to which this section applies, together with—

(a) a copy of that hiring agreement, and

(b) a copy of a statement of liability signed by the hirer under that hiring agreement.

(3) In this section a "statement of liability" means a statement made by the hirer under a hiring agreement to which this section applies to the effect that the hirer acknowledges that he will be liable, as the owner of the vehicle, in respect of any fixed penalty offence which may be committed with respect to the vehicle during the currency of the hiring agreement and giving such information as may be prescribed.

(4) In any case where this section applies, sections 63, 64 and 65 of this Act shall have effect as if—

(a) any reference to the owner of the vehicle were a reference to the hirer under the hiring agreement, and

(b) any reference to a statutory statement of ownership were a reference to a statutory statement of hiring,

and accordingly references in this Part of this Act (with the exceptions mentioned below) to a notice to owner include references to a notice served under section 63 of this Act as it applies by virtue of this section.
This subsection does not apply to references to a notice to owner in this section or in section 81(2)(b) of or Part I of Schedule 4 to this Act.

(5) In any case where this section applies, a person authorised in that behalf by the chief officer of police to whom the documents mentioned in subsection (2) above are provided may, at any reasonable time within six months after service of the notice to owner (and on the production of his authority) require the firm to produce the originals of the hiring agreement and statement of liability in question.

(6) If a vehicle-hire firm fails to produce the original of a document when required to do so under subsection (5) above, this section shall thereupon cease to apply (and section 64 of this Act shall apply accordingly in any such case after that time as it applies in a case where the person on whom the notice to owner was served has failed to provide a statutory statement of ownership in response to the notice within the period allowed).

(7) This section applies to a hiring agreement under the terms of which the vehicle concerned is let to the hirer for a fixed period of less than six months (whether or not that period is capable of extension by agreement between the parties or otherwise); and any reference in this section to the currency of the hiring agreement includes a reference to any period during which, with the consent of the vehicle-hire firm, the hirer continues in possession of the vehicle as hirer, after expiry of the fixed period specified in the agreement, but otherwise on the terms and conditions so specified.

(8) In this section—

"hiring agreement" refers only to an agreement which contains such particulars as may be prescribed and does not include a hire-purchase agreement within the meaning of the Consumer Credit Act 1974, and

"vehicle-hire firm" means any person engaged in hiring vehicles in the course of a business.
[Road Traffic Offenders Act 1988, s 66.]

4–1720   67. False statements in response to notices to owner.   A person who, in response to a notice to owner, provides a statement which is false in a material particular and does so recklessly or knowing it to be false in that particular is guilty of an offence[1].
[Road Traffic Offenders Act 1988, s 67.]

---

1. For penalty see Sch 2, post.

4–1721   68. "Owner", "statutory statement" and "official form".   (1) For the purposes of this Part of this Act, the owner of a vehicle shall be taken to be the person by whom the vehicle is kept; and for the purposes of determining, in the course of any proceedings brought by virtue of section 64(3) of this Act, who was the owner of a vehicle at any time, it shall be presumed that the owner was the person who was the registered keeper of the vehicle at that time.

(2) Notwithstanding the presumption in subsection (1) above, it is open to the defence in any proceedings to prove that the person who was the registered keeper of a vehicle at a particular time was not the person by whom the vehicle was kept at that time and to the prosecution to prove that the vehicle was kept by some other person at that time.

(3) References in this Part of this Act to statutory statements of any description are references to the statutory statement of that description defined in Schedule 4 to this Act; and that Schedule shall also have effect for the purpose of requiring certain information to be provided in official forms for the statutory statements so defined to assist persons in completing those forms and generally in determining what action to take in response to a notice to owner.

(4) In this Part of this Act "official form", in relation to a statutory statement mentioned in Schedule 4 to this Act or a statement under section 66(2) of this Act, means a document supplied by or on behalf of a chief officer of police for use in making that statement.

[Road Traffic Offenders Act 1988, s 68.]

The fixed penalty procedure

4–1729 69. Payment of penalty. (1) Payment of a fixed penalty under this Part of this Act must be made to such justices' chief executive or, in Scotland, clerk of court as may be specified in the fixed penalty notice relating to that penalty.

(2) Without prejudice to payment by any other method, payment of a fixed penalty under this Part of this Act may be made by properly addressing, pre-paying and posting a letter containing the amount of the penalty (in cash or otherwise) and, unless the contrary is proved, shall be regarded as having been made at the time at which that letter would be delivered in the ordinary course of post.

(3) A letter is properly addressed for the purposes of subsection (2) above if it is addressed to the fixed penalty clerk at the address specified in the fixed penalty notice relating to the fixed penalty as the address at which the fixed penalty may be paid.

(4) References in this Part of this Act (except in sections 75–77), in relation to any fixed penalty or fixed penalty notice, to the fixed penalty clerk are references to the justices chief executive or clerk specified in accordance with subsection (1) above in the fixed penalty notice relating to that penalty or (as the case may be) in that fixed penalty notice.

[Road Traffic Offenders Act 1988, s 69 amended by the Road Traffic Act 1991, Sch 4 and the Access to Justice Act 1999, Sch 13.]

4–1730 70. Registration certificates. (1) This section and section 71 of this Act apply where by virtue of section 55(3) or 64(2) of this Act a sum determined by reference to the fixed penalty for any offence may be registered under section 71 of this Act for enforcement against any person[1] as a fine.

In this section and section 71 of this Act—

(a) that sum is referred to as a "sum payable in default", and
(b) the person against whom that sum may be so registered is referred to as the "defaulter".

(2) Subject to subsection (3) below, the chief officer of police may in respect of any sum payable in default issue a certificate (referred to in this section and section 71 as a "registration certificate") stating that the sum is registered under section 71 for enforcement against the defaulter as a fine.

(3) Where the fixed penalty notice in question was given to the defaulter under section 54 in respect of an offence committed in Scotland—

(a) subsection (2) above does not apply, but
(b) the fixed penalty clerk must, unless the defaulter appears to him to reside within the jurisdiction of the court of summary jurisdiction of which he is himself the clerk, issue a registration certificate in respect of the sum payable in default.

(4) Where the chief officer of police or the fixed penalty clerk issues a registration certificate under this section, he must—

(a) if the defaulter appears to him to reside in England and Wales, cause it to be sent to the justices' chief executive for the petty sessions area in which the defaulter appears to him to reside, and
(b) if the defaulter appears to him to reside in Scotland, cause it to be sent to the clerk of a court of summary jurisdiction for the area in which the defaulter appears to him to reside.

(5) A registration certificate issued under this section in respect of any sum payable in default must—

(a) give particulars of the offence to which the fixed penalty notice relates,
(b) indicate whether registration is authorised under section 55(3) or 64(2) of this Act, and
(c) state the name and last known address of the defaulter and the amount of the sum payable in default.

[Road Traffic Offenders Act 1988, s 70. as amended by the Access to Justice Act 1999, Sch 13.]

---

1. "Person" includes an unincorporated body of persons, and the requirement in s 71(1) for the clerk to the justices to register a sum payable in default by such a defaulter is mandatory (*R v Clerk to the Croydon Justices, ex p Chief Constable of Kent* (1989) 154 JP 118, [1991] RTR 257, DC).

4–1731 71. Registration of sums payable in default. (1) Where, in England and Wales, a justices' chief executive receives a registration certificate issued under section 70 of this Act in respect of any sum payable in default—

(*a*) if it appears to him that the defaulter resides in a petty sessions area for which he is the justices' chief executive, he must register that sum for enforcement as a fine in that area by entering it in the register of a magistrates' court acting for that area,

(*b*) if it appears to him that the defaulter resides in any other petty sessions area in England and Wales, he must send the certificate to the justices' chief executive for that area, or

(*c*) if it appears to him that the defaulter resides in Scotland, he must send the certificate to the clerk of the court of summary jurisdiction for the area in which the defaulter appears to him to reside.

(2) Where, in Scotland, the clerk of a court receives a registration certificate issued under section 70 of this Act in respect of any sum payable in default—

(*a*) if it appears to him that the defaulter resides in the area of the court, he must register that sum for enforcement as a fine by that court,

(*b*) if it appears to him that the defaulter resides in the area of any other court of summary jurisdiction in Scotland, he must send the certificate to the clerk of that court, or

(*c*) if it appears to him that the defaulter resides in England and Wales, he must send the certificate to the justices' chief executive for the petty sessions area in which the defaulter appears to him to reside.

(2A) Subsections (1) and (2) apply to executives and clerks who receive certificates pursuant to the provision they contain as they apply to the original recipients.

(3) Where—

(*a*) the fixed penalty notice in question was given to the defaulter under section 54 of this Act in respect of an offence committed in Scotland, and

(*b*) the defaulter appears to the fixed penalty clerk to reside within the jurisdiction of the court of summary jurisdiction of which he is himself the clerk,

the fixed penalty clerk must register the sum payable in default for enforcement as a fine by that court.

(4) *Repealed.*

(5) Repealed.

(6) On registering any sum under this section for enforcement as a fine, the justices' chief executive for a petty sessions area or, as the case may be, the clerk of a court of summary jurisdiction must give to the defaulter notice of registration—

(*a*) specifying the amount of that sum, and

(*b*) giving the information with respect to the offence and the authority for registration included in the registration certificate by virtue of section 70(5)(*a*) and (*b*) of this Act or (in a case within subsection (3) above) the corresponding information.

(7) On the registration of any sum in a magistrates' court or a court of summary jurisdiction by virtue of this section any enactment referring (in whatever terms) to a fine imposed or other sum adjudged to be paid on the conviction of such a court shall have effect in the case in question as if the sum so registered were a fine imposed by that court on the conviction of the defaulter on the date of the registration.

(8) Accordingly, in the application by virtue of this section of the provisions of the Magistrates' Courts Act 1980 relating to the satisfaction and enforcement of sums adjudged to be paid on the conviction of a magistrates' court, section 85 of that Act (power to remit a fine in whole or in part) is not excluded by subsection (2) of that section (references in that section to a fine not to include any other sum adjudged to be paid on a conviction) from applying to a sum registered in a magistrates' court by virtue of this section.

(9) For the purposes of this section, where the defaulter is a body corporate, the place where that body resides and the address of that body are either of the following—

(*a*) the registered or principal office of that body, and

(*b*) the address which, with respect to the vehicle concerned, is the address recorded in the record kept under the Vehicle Excise and Registration Act 1994 as being that body's address.

[Road Traffic Offenders Act 1988, s 71, as amended by the Vehicle Excise and Registration Act 1994, Sch 3 and the Access to Justice Act 1999, Sch 13.]

---

1. He must do this even when the certificate names an unincorporated body of persons (*R v Clerk to Croydon Justices, ex p Chief Constable of Kent* (1989) 154 JP 118, [1991] RTR 257, [1989] Crim LR 910, DC).

4–1732 72. Notices on-the-spot or at a police station: when registration and endorsement invalid. (1) This section applies where—

(*a*) a person who has received notice of the registration, by virtue of section 55(3) of this Act, of a sum under section 71 of this Act for enforcement against him as a fine makes a statutory declaration to the effect mentioned in subsection (2) below, and

(*b*) that declaration is, within twenty-one days of the date on which the person making it received notice of the registration, served on the proper officer of the relevant court.

(2) The statutory declaration must state—

(*a*) that the person making the declaration was not the person to whom the relevant fixed penalty notice was given, or

(b) that he gave notice requesting a hearing in respect of the alleged offence as permitted by the fixed penalty notice before the end of the suspended enforcement period.

(3) In any case within subsection (2)(a) above, the relevant fixed penalty notice, the registration and any proceedings taken before the declaration was served for enforcing payment of the sum registered shall be void.

(4) Where in any case within subsection (2)(a) above the person to whom the relevant fixed penalty notice was given surrendered a licence and its counterpart held by the person making the declaration, any endorsement of that counterpart made under section 57 of this Act in respect of the offence in respect of which that notice was given shall be void.

(5) In any case within subsection (2)(b) above—

(a) the registration, any proceedings taken before the declaration was served for enforcing payment of the sum registered, and any endorsement, in respect of the offence in respect of which the relevant fixed penalty notice was given, made under section 57 of this Act before the declaration was served, shall be void, and

(b) the case shall be treated after the declaration is served as if the person making the declaration had given notice requesting a hearing in respect of the alleged offence as stated in the declaration.

(6) The proper officer of the relevant court must—

(a) cancel an endorsement of the counterpart of a licence under section 57 of this Act that is void by virtue of this section on production of the licence and its counterpart to him for that purpose, and

(b) send notice of the cancellation to the Secretary of State.

(7) References in this section to the relevant fixed penalty notice are to the fixed penalty notice relating to the fixed penalty concerned.

[Road Traffic Offenders Act 1988, s 72, amended by SI 1990/144 and the Access to Justice Act 1999, Sch 13.]

4–1733 73. Notices fixed to vehicles: when registration invalid. (1) This section applies where—

(a) a person who has received notice of the registration, by virtue of section 64(2) of this Act, of a sum under section 71 of this Act for enforcement against him as a fine makes a statutory declaration to the effect mentioned in subsection (2) below, and

(b) that declaration is, within twenty-one days of the date on which the person making it received notice of the registration, served on the proper officer of the relevant court.

(2) The statutory declaration must state either—

(a) that the person making the declaration did not know of the fixed penalty concerned or of any fixed penalty notice or notice to owner relating to that penalty until he received notice of the registration, or

(b) that he was not the owner of the vehicle at the time of the alleged offence of which particulars are given in the relevant notice to owner and that he has a reasonable excuse for failing to comply with that notice, or

(c) that he gave notice requesting a hearing in respect of that offence as permitted by the relevant notice to owner before the end of the period allowed for response to that notice.

(3) In any case within subsection (2)(a) or (b) above—

(a) the relevant notice to owner,

(b) the registration, and

(c) any proceedings taken before the declaration was served for enforcing payment of the sum registered,

shall be void but without prejudice, in a case within subsection (2)(a) above, to the service of a further notice to owner under section 63 of this Act on the person making the declaration.

This subsection applies whether or not the relevant notice to owner was duly served in accordance with that section on the person making the declaration.

(4) In any case within subsection (2)(c) above—

(a) no proceedings shall be taken, after the statutory declaration is served until the end of the period of twenty-one days following the date of that declaration, for enforcing payment of the sum registered, and

(b) where before the end of that period a notice is served by or on behalf of the chief officer of police on the person making the declaration asking him to provide a new statutory statement of ownership to that chief officer of police before the end of the period of twenty-one days from the date on which the notice is served, no such proceedings shall be taken until the end of the period allowed for response to that notice.

(5) Where in any case within subsection (2)(c) above—

(a) no notice is served by or on behalf of the chief officer of police in accordance with subsection (4) above, or

(b) such a notice is so served and the person making the declaration provides a new statutory statement of ownership in accordance with the notice, then—

(i)   the registration and any proceedings taken before the declaration was served for enforcing payment of the sum registered shall be void, and

(ii)   the case shall be treated after the time mentioned in subsection (6) below as if the person making the declaration had given notice requesting a hearing in respect of the alleged offence as stated in the declaration.

(6)   The time referred to in subsection (5) above is—

(a)   in a case within paragraph (a) of that subsection, the end of the period of twenty-one days following the date of the statutory declaration,

(b)   in a case within paragraph (b) of that subsection, the time when the statement is provided.

(7)   In any case where notice is served by or on behalf of the chief officer of police in accordance with subsection (4) above, he must cause the proper officer of the relevant court to be notified of that fact immediately on service of the notice.

(8)   References in this section to the relevant notice to owner are to the notice to owner relating to the fixed penalty concerned.

[Road Traffic Offenders Act 1988, s 73, as amended by the Access to Justice Act 1999, Sch 13.]

4–1734   74. Provisions supplementary to sections 72 and 73.   (1) In any case within section 72(2)(b) or 73(2) of this Act—

(a)   section 127(1) of the Magistrates' Courts Act 1980 (limitation of time), and

(b)   section 331(1) of the Criminal Procedure (Scotland) Act 1975 (statutory offences time limit),

shall have effect as if for the reference to the time when the offence was committed or (as the case may be) the time when the contravention occurred there were substituted a reference to the date of the statutory declaration made for the purposes of section 72(1) or, as the case may be, 73(1).

(2)   Where, on the application of a person who has received notice of the registration of a sum under section 71 of this Act for enforcement against him as a fine, it appears to the relevant court (which for this purpose may be composed of a single justice) that it was not reasonable to expect him to serve, within twenty-one days of the date on which he received the notice, a statutory declaration to the effect mentioned in section 72(2) or, as the case may be, 73(2) of this Act, the court may accept service of such a declaration by that person after that period has expired.

(3)   A statutory declaration accepted under subsection (2) above shall be taken to have been served as required by section 72(1) or, as the case may be, section 73(1) of this Act.

(4)   For the purposes of sections 72(1) and 73(1) of this Act, a statutory declaration shall be taken to be duly served on the proper officer of the relevant court if it is delivered to him, left at his office, or sent in a registered letter or by the recorded delivery service addressed to him at his office.

(5)   In sections 72, 73 and this section—

(a)   references to the relevant court are—

(i)   in the case of a sum registered under section 71 of this Act for enforcement as a fine in a petty sessions area in England and Wales, references to any magistrates' court acting for that area, and

(ii)   in the case of a sum registered under that section for enforcement as a fine by a court of summary jurisdiction in Scotland, references to that court,

(b)   references to the proper officer of the relevant court are—

(i)   in the case of a magistrates' court, references to the justices' chief executive for that court, and

(ii)   in the case of a court of summary jurisdiction in Scotland, references to the clerk of the court, and

(c)   references to proceedings for enforcing payment of the sum registered are references to any process issued or other proceedings taken for or in connection with enforcing payment of that sum.

(6)   For the purposes of sections 72, 73 and this section, a person shall be taken to receive notice of the registration of a sum under section 71 of this Act for enforcement against him as a fine when he receives notice either of the registration as such or of any proceedings for enforcing payment of the sum registered.

(7)   Nothing in the provisions of sections 72 or 73 or this section is to be read as prejudicing any rights a person may have apart from those provisions by virtue of the invalidity of any action purportedly taken in pursuance of this Part of this Act which is not in fact authorised by this Part of this Act in the circumstances of the case; and, accordingly, references in those provisions to the registration of any sum or to any other action taken under or by virtue of any provision of this Part of this Act are not to be read as implying that the registration or action was validly made or taken in accordance with that provision.

[Road Traffic Offenders Act 1988, s 74, as amended by the Access to Justice Act 1999, Sch 13.]

Conditional offer of fixed penalty

4–1735   75. Issue of conditional offer.   (1) Where in England and Wales—

(a)   a constable has reason to believe that a fixed penalty offence has been committed, and (*b*) no fixed penalty notice in respect of the offence has been given under section 54 of this Act or fixed to a vehicle under section 62 of this Act,

a notice under this section may be sent to the alleged offender by or on behalf of the chief officer of police.

(2), (3) Scotland.

(3) Where a constable is a constable of the British Transport Police Force subsection (3) shall have effect as if the reference to the chief constable were a references to the chief constable of that force.

(4) Scotland.

(5) A notice under this section is referred to in this section and sections 76 and 77 as a "conditional offer".

(6) Where a person issues a conditional offer, he must notify the designated officer, or in Scotland clerk of court, specified in it of its issue and its terms; and he is referred to in this section and sections 76 and 77 as "the fixed penalty clerk".

(7) A conditional offer must—

(*a*) give such particulars of the circumstances alleged to constitute the offence to which it relates as are necessary for giving reasonable information about the alleged offence,

(*b*) state the amount of the fixed penalty for that offence, and

(*c*) state that proceedings against the alleged offender cannot be commenced in respect of that offence until the end of the period of twenty-eight days following the date on which the conditional offer was issued or such longer period as may be specified in the conditional offer[1].

(8) A conditional offer must indicate that if the following conditions are fulfilled, that is—

(*a*) within the period of twenty-eight days following the date on which the offer was issued, or such longer period as may be specified in the offer, the alleged offender—

　(i) makes payment of the fixed penalty to the fixed penalty clerk, and

　(ii) where the offence to which the offer relates is an offence involving obligatory endorsement, at the same time delivers his licence[2] and its counterpart to that clerk, and

(*b*) where his licence and its counterpart are so delivered, that clerk is satisfied on inspecting them that, if the alleged offender were convicted of the offence, he would not be liable to be disqualified under section 35 of this Act,

any liability to conviction of the offence shall be discharged.

(9) For the purposes of the condition set out in subsection (8)(b) above, it shall be assumed, in the case of an offence in relation to which a range of numbers is shown in the last column of Part I of Schedule 2 to this Act, that the number of penalty points to be attributed to the offence would be the lowest in the range.

(10) The Secretary of State may by order provide for offences to become or (as the case may be) to cease to be offences in respect of which a conditional offer may be sent under subsection (2)(b) above, and may make such modifications of the provisions of this Part of this Act as appear to him to be necessary for the purpose.

(11) Scotland.

(12) In relation to licences which came into force before 1st June 1990, the references in subsection (8) above to the counterpart of a licence shall be disregarded.

[Road Traffic Offenders Act 1988, s 75 as substituted by the Road Traffic Act 1991, s 34, as amended by the Access to Justice Act 1999, Sch 13, the Railways and Transport Safety Act 2003, s 69 and the Courts Act 2003, s 109.]

---

1. Where a document incorporated both a requirement to provide information as to the identity of the driver, pursuant to s 172 of the Road Traffic Act 1988, and a conditional offer of fixed penalty, but the latter failed to comply with the s 75(7)(c) requirement to specify a period, that defect did not did not preclude the commencement of proceedings outside the period of 28 days from the date of the offer (the fixed penalty clerk having given notification under s 76(5), infra, of non payment of the fixed penalty following the expiry of that period), or render such a prosecution an abuse of process: *DPP v Holden* [2006] EWHC 658 (Admin), [2007] RTR 5.

2. Also in the case of a newly qualified driver who holds a provisional licence, any certificate of passing a test of competence to drive (see the Road Traffic (New Drivers) Act 1995 Sch 1 Pt II, this PART, post).

4–1736　76. Effect of offer and payment of penalty.　(1) This section applies where a conditional offer has been sent to a person under section 75 of this Act.

(2) No proceedings shall be brought against any person for the offence to which the conditional offer relates until—

(*a*) in England and Wales, the chief officer of police★, or

(*b*) *Scotland,*

receives notice in accordance with subsection (4) or (5) below.

(3) Where the alleged offender makes payment of the fixed penalty in accordance with the conditional offer, no proceedings shall be brought against him for the offence to which the offer relates.

(4) Where—

(*a*) the alleged offender tenders payment in accordance with the conditional offer and delivers his licence and its counterpart to the fixed penalty clerk, but (*b*) it appears to the clerk, on inspecting the licence and counterpart, that the alleged offender would be liable to be disqualified under section 35 of this Act if he were convicted of the offence to which the conditional offer relates,

then subsection (3) above shall not apply and the clerk must return the licence and its counterpart to the alleged offender together with the payment and give notice that he has done so to the person referred to in subsection (2)(*a*) or (*b*) above.

(5) Where, on the expiry of the period of twenty-eight days following the date on which the conditional offer was made or such longer period as may be specified in the offer, the conditions specified in the offer in accordance with section 75(8)(a) of this Act have not been fulfilled, the fixed penalty clerk must notify the person referred to in subsection (2)(a) or (b) above.

(6) In determining for the purposes of subsection (4)(b) above whether a person convicted of an offence would be liable to disqualification under section 35, it shall be assumed, in the case of an offence in relation to which a range of numbers is shown in the last column of Part I of Schedule 2 to this Act, that the number of penalty points to be attributed to the offence would be the lowest in the range.

(7) In any proceedings a certificate that by a date specified in the certificate payment of a fixed penalty was or was not received by the fixed penalty clerk shall, if the certificate purports to be signed by that clerk, be evidence, or in Scotland sufficient evidence, of the facts stated.

(8) In relation to licences which came into force before 1st June 1990, the references in subsection (4) above to the counterpart of a licence shall be disregarded.

(9) Scotland.

[Road Traffic Offenders Act 1988, s 76 as substituted by the Road Traffic Act 1991, s 34 and amended by the Railways and Transport Safety Act 2003, s 69.]

---

*Words repealed in relation to England and Wales by the Railways and Transport Safety Act 2003, s 69, from a date to be appointed.

4–1737 **77. Endorsement where penalty paid.** (1) Where—

(*a*) in pursuance of a conditional offer a person (referred to in this section as the "licence holder") makes payment of the fixed penalty to the fixed penalty clerk and delivers his licence and its counterpart to the clerk, and

(*b*) the clerk is not required by subsection (4) of section 76 of this Act to return the licence and its counterpart to him and did not, before the payment was tendered, notify the person referred to in section 76(2)(*a*) or (*b*) of this Act under subsection (5) of that section,

the clerk must forthwith endorse the relevant particulars on the counterpart of the licence and return it to the licence holder together with the licence.

(2) Scotland.

(3) Subject to subsection (4) below, where a cheque tendered in payment is subsequently dishonoured—

(*a*) any endorsement made by a clerk under subsection (1) above remains effective, notwithstanding that the licence holder is still liable to prosecution in respect of the alleged offence to which the endorsement relates, and

(*b*) the clerk must, upon the expiry of the period specified in the conditional offer or, if the period has expired, forthwith notify the person referred to in section 76(2)(*a*) or (*b*) of this Act that no payment has been made.

(4) When proceedings are brought against a licence holder after a notice has been given in pursuance of subsection (3)(b) above, the court—

(*a*) must order the removal of the fixed penalty endorsement from the counterpart of the licence, and

(*b*) may, on finding the licence holder guilty, make any competent order of endorsement or disqualification and pass any competent sentence.

(5) The reference in subsection (1) above to the relevant particulars is to—

(*a*) particulars of the offence, including the date when it was committed, and
(*b*) the number of penalty points to be attributed to the offence.

(6) The fixed penalty clerk must send notice to the Secretary of State—

(*a*) of any endorsement under subsection (1) above and of the particulars endorsed,
(*b*) of any amendment under subsection (2) above, and
(*c*) of any order under subsection (4)(*a*) above.

(7) Where the counterpart of a person's licence is endorsed under this section he shall be treated for the purposes of sections 13(4), 28, 29 and 45 of this Act and of the Rehabilitation of Offenders Act 1974 as if—

(*a*) he had been convicted of the offence,
(*b*) the endorsement had been made in pursuance of an order made on his conviction by a court under section 44 of this Act, and
(*c*) the particulars of the offence endorsed by virtue of subsection (5)(*a*) above were particulars of his conviction of that offence.

(8)	In relation to any endorsement of the counterpart of a person's licence under this section—

(a)	the reference in section 45(4) of this Act to the order for endorsement, and
(b)	the references in section 13(4) of this Act to any order made on a person's conviction,

are to be read as references to the endorsement itself.

(9)	In relation to licences which came into force before 1st June 1990, the references in this section to the counterpart of a licence shall be disregarded or, as the case may require, construed as references to the licence itself.

(10)	Subsection (1) above is subject to section 2(4)(a) of and paragraph 7(4)(a) of Schedule 1 to the Road Traffic (New Drivers) Act 1995; and the fixed penalty clerk need not send a notice falling within subsection (6)(a) above in a case where he sends a person's licence and its counterpart to the Secretary of State under section 2(4)(b) of or paragraph 7(4)(b) of Schedule 1 to that Act.

[Road Traffic Offenders Act 1988, s 77 as substituted by the Road Traffic Act 1991, s 34 and amended by the Road Traffic (New Drivers) Act 1995, Sch 2.]

**4–1737A	77A.	Endorsement of driving records where penalty paid.**	(1) Where—

(a)	in pursuance of a conditional offer issued under subsection (1), (2) or (3) of section 75 of this Act a person who is not the holder of a licence (referred to in this section as the "alleged offender") makes payment of the fixed penalty to the fixed penalty clerk, and
(b)	proceedings against the alleged offender for the offence to which the conditional offer relates are excluded by section 76 of this Act,

the fixed penalty clerk must forthwith send to the Secretary of State notice of the relevant particulars to be endorsed on the alleged offender's driving record.

(2)	The Secretary of State must endorse the relevant particulars on a person's driving record—

(a)	on receiving notice under subsection (1) above, or
(b)	if, in pursuance of a conditional offer issued under subsection (1A) or (3B) of section 75 of this Act, a person who is not the holder of a licence (also referred to in this section as the "alleged offender") makes payment of the fixed penalty to him and proceedings against the alleged offender are excluded by section 76 of this Act.

(3)	Where in Scotland the appropriate person is the fixed penalty clerk and it appears to him that there is an error in an endorsement made by virtue of this section on a person's driving record, he may send to the Secretary of State notice of the error.

(4)	Subject to subsection (5) below, where a cheque tendered in payment is subsequently dishonoured—

(a)	any endorsement made by the Secretary of State under subsection (2) above remains effective notwithstanding that the alleged offender is still liable to prosecution in respect of the alleged offence to which the endorsement relates, and
(b)	unless the appropriate person is the Secretary of State, the appropriate person must upon expiry of the period specified in the conditional offer or, if the period has expired, forthwith notify the person required to be notified that no payment has been made.

(5)	When proceedings are brought against an alleged offender where subsection (4) above applies, the court—

(a)	must order the removal of the fixed penalty endorsement from the driving record of the alleged offender,
(b)	may, on finding the alleged offender guilty, make any competent order of endorsement or disqualification and pass any competent sentence, and
(c)	must send to the Secretary of State notice of any order made under paragraph (a) or (b) above.

(6)	On receiving notice under subsection (3) above, the Secretary of State may correct the error in the endorsement on the driving record; and any endorsement corrected shall be treated for all purposes as if it had been correctly made on receipt of the fixed penalty.

(7)	On receiving a notice under subsection (5)(c) above, the Secretary of State must make any necessary adjustments to the endorsements on the alleged offender's driving record.

(8)	The references in subsection (1) and (2) above to the relevant particulars are to—

(a)	particulars of the offence, including the date when it was committed, and
(b)	the number of penalty points to be attributed to the offence.

(9)	Where a person's driving record is endorsed under this section he shall be treated for the purposes of sections 13(4), 28, 29 and 45A of this Act and of the Rehabilitation of Offenders Act 1974 as if—

(a)	he had been convicted of the offence,
(b)	the endorsement had been made in pursuance of an order made on his conviction by a court under section 44 of this Act, and
(c)	the particulars of the offence endorsed by virtue of subsection (8)(a) above were particulars of his conviction of that offence.

(10)	In relation to any endorsement of a person's driving record under this section, the references in section 13(4) of this Act to any order made on a person's conviction are to be read as references to the endorsement itself.★

[Road Traffic Offenders Act 1988, s 77A as inserted by the Road Safety Act 2006, Sch 2.]

*Section inserted by the Road Safety Act 2006, Sch 2 from a date to be appointed.

Proceedings in fixed penalty cases

4–1738   78. General restriction on proceedings.   (1) Proceedings shall not be brought against any person for the offence to which a fixed penalty notice relates until the end of the suspended enforcement period.

(2) Proceedings shall not be brought against any person for the offence to which a fixed penalty notice relates if the fixed penalty is paid in accordance with this Part of this Act before the end of the suspended enforcement period.

[Road Traffic Offenders Act 1988, s 78.]

4–1739   79. Statements by constables.   (1) In any proceedings a certificate that a copy of a statement by a constable with respect to the alleged offence (referred to in this section as a "constable's witness statement") was included in or given with a fixed penalty notice or a notice under section 54(3) of this Act given to the accused on a date specified in the certificate shall, if the certificate purports to be signed by the constable or authorised person who gave the accused the notice, be evidence of service of a copy of that statement by delivery to the accused on that date.

(2) In any proceedings a certificate that a copy of a constable's witness statement was included in or served with a notice to owner served on the accused in the manner and on a date specified in the certificate shall, if the certificate purports to be signed by any person employed by the police authority for the police area in which the offence to which the proceedings relate is alleged to have been committed, be evidence of service in the manner and on the date so specified both of a copy of that statement and of the notice to owner.

(3) Any address specified in any such certificate as is mentioned in subsection (2) above as being the address at which service of the notice to owner was effected shall be taken for the purposes of any proceedings in which the certificate is tendered in evidence to be the accused's proper address, unless the contrary is proved.

(4) Where a copy of a constable's witness statement is included in or served with a notice to owner served in any manner in which the notice is authorised to be served under this Part of this Act, the statement shall be treated as duly served for the purposes of section 9 of the Criminal Justice Act 1967 (proof by written statement) notwithstanding that the manner of service is not authorised by subsection (8) of that section.

(5) In relation to any proceedings in which service of a constable's witness statement is proved by certificate under this section—

  (*a*) that service shall be taken for the purposes of subsection (2)(*c*) of that section (copy of statement to be tendered in evidence to be served before hearing on other parties to the proceedings by or on behalf of the party proposing to tender it) to have been effected by or on behalf of the prosecutor, and

  (*b*) subsection (2)(*d*) of that section (time for objection) shall have effect with the substitution, for the reference to seven days from the service of the copy of the statement, of a reference to seven days from the relevant date.

(6) In subsection (5)(b) above "relevant date" means—

  (*a*) where the accused gives notice requesting a hearing in respect of the offence in accordance with any provision of this Part of this Act, the date on which he gives that notice, and

  (*b*) where a notice in respect of the offence was given to the accused under section 54(4) of this Act but no fixed penalty notice is given in respect of it, the last day for production of the notice under section 54(5) at a police station in accordance with that section.

(7) This section does not extend to Scotland.

[Road Traffic Offenders Act 1988, s 79.]

4–1740   80. Certificates about payment.   In any proceedings a certificate—

  (*a*) that payment of a fixed penalty was or was not received, by a date specified in the certificate, by the fixed penalty clerk, or

  (*b*) that a letter containing an amount sent by post in payment of a fixed penalty was marked as posted on a date so specified,

shall, if the certificate purports to be signed by the fixed penalty clerk, be evidence (and, in Scotland, sufficient evidence) of the facts stated.

[Road Traffic Offenders Act 1988, s 80.]

4–1741   81. Documents signed by the accused.   (1) Where—

  (*a*) any person is charged with a fixed penalty offence, and

  (*b*) the prosecutor produces to the court a document to which this subsection applies purporting to have been signed by the accused,

the document shall be presumed, unless the contrary is proved, to have been signed by the accused and shall be evidence (and, in Scotland, sufficient evidence) in the proceedings of any facts stated in it tending to show that the accused was the owner, the hirer or the driver of the vehicle concerned at a particular time.

(2) Subsection (1) above applies to any document purporting to be—

(a) a notice requesting a hearing in respect of the offence charged given in accordance with a fixed penalty notice relating to that offence, or
(b) a statutory statement of any description defined in Schedule 4 to this Act or a copy of a statement of liability within the meaning of section 66 of this Act provided in response to a notice to owner.
[Road Traffic Offenders Act 1988, s 81.]

Miscellaneous

4–1742   82. Accounting for fixed penalties: England and Wales.   (1) In England and Wales, sums paid by way of fixed penalty for an offence shall be treated for the purposes of section 60 of the Justices of the Peace Act 1997 (application of fines and fees) as if they were fines imposed on summary conviction for that offence.
(2) Where, in England and Wales, a justices' chief executive for a petty sessions area comprised in the area of one magistrates' courts committee ("the first committee") discharges functions in connection with a fixed penalty for an offence alleged to have been committed in a petty sessions area comprised in the area of another magistrates' courts committee ("the second committee")—

(a) the paying authority or authorities in relation to the second committee must make to the paying authority or authorities in relation to the first committee such payment in connection with the discharge of those functions as may be agreed between all the paying authorities concerned or, in default of such agreement, as may be determined by the Lord Chancellor, and
(b) any such payment between paying authorities shall be taken into account in determining for the purposes of section 57 of the Justices of the Peace Act 1997 the net cost to the responsible authorities of the functions referred to in subsection (1) of that section.

(2A) In subsection (2) above "paying authority" and "responsible authority" have the same meaning as in section 55 of the Justices of the Peace Act 1997, except that, in relation to the Greater London Magistrates' Courts Authority, the Authority is the paying authority and responsible authority.
(3) Subsection (2) above does not apply to functions discharged in connection with a fixed penalty on or after the registration of a sum determined by reference to the penalty under section 71 of this Act.
[Road Traffic Offenders Act 1988, s 82 amended by SI 1992/709, the Police and Magistrates' Courts Act 1994, Sch 8 and the Access to Justice Act 1999, Sch 12.]

4–1743   83. Powers of court where clerk deceived.   (1) This section applies where—

(a) in endorsing the counterpart of any person's licence under section 57 of this Act, the fixed penalty clerk is deceived as to whether endorsement under that section is excluded by section 61(2) of this Act by virtue of the fact that the licence holder would be liable to be disqualified under section 35 of this Act if he were convicted of the offence, or
(b) in endorsing the counterpart of any person's licence under section 77 of this Act the justices' chief executive or clerk of court specified in the conditional offer (within the meaning of that section) is deceived as to whether he is required by section 76(5) of this Act to return the licence and its counterpart without endorsing the counterpart by virtue of the fact that the licence holder would be liable to be disqualified under section 35 of this Act if he were convicted of the offence.

(2) If—
(a) the deception constituted or was due to an offence committed by the licence holder, and
(b) the licence holder is convicted of that offence,
the court by or before which he is convicted shall have the same powers and duties as it would have had if he had also been convicted by or before it of the offence of which particulars were endorsed under section 57 or, as the case may be, 77 of this Act.
[Road Traffic Offenders Act 1988, s 83, amended by SI 1990/144 and the Access to Justice Act 1999, Sch 13.]

4–1744   84. Regulations[1].

---

1. The Fixed Penalty (Procedure) Regulations 1986 have been made; see this PART, post. See also the Road Traffic (Owner Liability) Regulations 2000, SI 2000/2546 amended by SI 2001/1222 which prescribe forms for use in connection with ss 62–68 and Sch 4 (notices fixed to vehicles).

4–1744A   84A. Notices to Secretary of State.   Any notice sent to the Secretary of State under this Part must be sent in such manner and to such address and contain such particulars as the Secretary of State may determine.*
[Road Traffic Offenders Act 1988, s 84A as inserted by the Road Safety Act 2006, Sch 2.]

---

*Section inserted by the Road Safety Act 2006, Sch 2 from a date to be appointed.

4–1745   85. Service of documents.   (1) Subject to any requirement of this Part of this Act with respect to the manner in which a person may be provided with any such document, he may be provided with the following documents by post (but without prejudice to any other method of providing him with them), that is to say—

(a)   any of the statutory statements mentioned in Schedule 4 to this Act, and

(b)   any of the documents mentioned in section 66(2) of this Act.

(2)   Where a notice requesting a hearing in respect of an offence is permitted by a fixed penalty notice or notice to owner relating to that offence to be given by post, section 7 of the Interpretation Act 1978 (service of documents by post) shall apply as if that notice were permitted to be so given by this Act.

(3)   A notice to owner may be served on any person—

(a)   by delivering it to him or by leaving it at his proper address, or

(b)   by sending it to him by post,

and where the person on whom such a notice is to be served is a body corporate it is duly served if it is served on the secretary or clerk of that body.

(4)   For the purposes of this Part of this Act and of section 7 of the Interpretation Act 1978 as it applies for the purposes of subsection (3) above the proper address of any person in relation to the service on him of a notice to owner is—

(a)   in the case of the secretary or clerk of a body corporate, that of the registered or principal office of that body or the registered address of the person who is or was the registered keeper of the vehicle concerned at the time of service, and

(b)   in any other case, his last known address at the time of service.

(5)   In subsection (4) above, "registered address", in relation to the registered keeper of a vehicle, means the address recorded in the record kept under the Vehicle Excise and Registration Act 1994 with respect to that vehicle as being that person's address.

[Road Traffic Offenders Act 1988, s 85 amended by the Vehicle Excise and Registration Act 1994, Sch 3.]

4–1746   86. Functions of traffic wardens.   (1) An order under section 95(5) of the Road Traffic Regulation Act 1984 may not authorise the employment of a traffic warden to discharge any function under this Part of this Act in respect of an offence if the offence appears to the traffic warden to be an offence involving obligatory endorsement unless that offence was committed whilst the vehicle concerned was stationary.

(2)   In so far as an order under that section authorises the employment of traffic wardens for the purposes of this Part of this Act, references in this Part of this Act to a constable or, as the case may be, to a constable in uniform include a traffic warden.

[Road Traffic Offenders Act 1988, s 86 amended by the Road Traffic Act 1991, Sch 4.]

4–1747   87. Guidance on application of Part III.   The Secretary of State must issue guidance to chief officers of police for police areas in respect of the operation of this Part of this Act with the objective so far as possible of working towards uniformity.

[Road Traffic Offenders Act 1988, s 87.]

4–1748   88. Procedure for regulations and orders.

4–1749   89. Interpretation.   (1) In this Part of this Act—

"authorised person" has the meaning given by section 54(9) of this Act,

"chief constable" (*Scotland*)

"chief officer of police" (except in the definition of "authorised person") means, in relation to any fixed penalty notice, notice to owner or conditional offer, the chief officer of police for the police area in which the fixed penalty offence in question is alleged to have been committed,

"court of summary jurisdiction" has the same meaning as in section 307(1) of the Criminal Procedure (Scotland) Act 1995,

"driver" except in section 62 of this Act means, in relation to an alleged fixed penalty offence, the person by whom, assuming the offence to have been committed, it was committed,

and

"proceedings", except in relation to proceedings for enforcing payment of a sum registered under section 71 of this Act, means criminal proceedings.

(2)   In this Part of this Act—

(a)   references to a notice requesting a hearing in respect of an offence are references to a notice indicating that the person giving the notice wishes to contest liability for the offence or seeks a determination by a court with respect to the appropriate punishment for the offence,

(b)   references to an offence include an alleged offence, and

(c)   references to the person who is or was at any time the registered keeper of a vehicle are references to the person in whose name the vehicle is or was at that time registered under the Vehicle Excise and Registration Act 1994.

(3)   Subsection (1) of this section is affected by Schedule 5 to the Road Traffic (Consequential Provisions) Act 1988 (transitory modifications).

[Road Traffic Offenders Act 1988, s 89 amended by the Road Traffic Act 1991, Sch 4, the Vehicle Excise and Registration Act 1994, Sch 3, the Criminal Procedure (Consequential Provisions) (Scotland) Act 1995, Sch 4 and the Access to Justice Act 1999, Sch 15.]

4–1750 90. Index to Part III. The expressions listed in the left hand column below are respectively defined or (as the case may be) fall to be construed in accordance with the provisions of this Part of this Act listed in the right-hand column in relation to those expressions.

Expression	Relevant provision
Authorised person	Section 54(9)
Conditional offer	Section 75(3)
Fixed penalty	Section 53
Fixed penalty clerk	Section 69(4) and 75(4)
Fixed penalty notice	Section 52
Fixed penalty offence	Section 51
Notice to owner	Section 63(2) and 66(4)
Notice requesting a hearing in respect of an offence	Section 89(2)
Offence	Section 89(2)
Official form	Section 68(4)
Owner	Section 68(1)
Period allowed for response to a notice to owner	Section 63(5)
Proper address, in relation to the service of a notice to owner	Section 85(4)
Registered keeper	Section 89(2)
Statutory statement of facts	Part II of Schedule 4
Statutory statement of hiring	Part I of Schedule 4
Statutory statement of ownership	Part I of Schedule 4
Suspended enforcement period	Section 52(3)(a)
Time of the alleged offence	Section 63(3)

[Road Traffic Offenders Act 1988, s 90 amended by the Road Traffic Act 1991, Sch 4.]

PART 3A[1]
FINANCIAL PENALTY DEPOSITS

4–1750A 90A. Power to impose financial penalty deposit requirement. (1) A constable or vehicle examiner may impose a financial penalty deposit requirement on a person on any occasion if the conditions in this section are satisfied.

(2) The constable or vehicle examiner must have reason to believe—

(a) that the person is committing or has on that occasion committed an offence relating to a motor vehicle, and

(b) that the person, the offence and the circumstances in which the offence is committed are of a description specified in an order made by the Secretary of State.

(3) The person must be—

(a) given written notification that it appears likely that proceedings will be brought against him in respect of the offence, or

(b) (if the offence is a fixed penalty offence) either given such notification or given a fixed penalty notice (or, in Scotland, handed a conditional offer) in respect of the offence.

(4) The person must fail to provide a satisfactory address; and for this purpose "a satisfactory address" is an address in the United Kingdom at which the constable or vehicle examiner considers it likely that it would be possible to find the person whenever necessary to do so in connection with the proceedings, fixed penalty notice or conditional offer.

(5) The person who is to impose the financial penalty deposit requirement—

(a) if a constable, must be in uniform, and

(b) if a vehicle examiner, must produce his authority.★

[Road Traffic Offenders Act 1988, s 90A as inserted by the Road Safety Act 2006, 11.]

★**Section inserted by the Road Safety Act 2006, 11 from a date to be appointed.**
1. Part 3A comprises ss 90A–90F.

4–1750B 90B. Financial penalty deposit requirement. (1) For the purposes of this Part of this Act a financial penalty deposit requirement is a requirement to make a payment of the appropriate amount to the Secretary of State—

(a) in a manner specified in an order made by him, and

(b) either immediately or within the relevant period.

(2) In this Part of this Act "the appropriate amount", in relation to an offence and a person, is an amount specified in relation to the offence in an order made by the Secretary of State; and different amounts may be so specified—

(a) by reference to whether the person is given notification that it appears likely that proceedings will be brought against him or given a fixed penalty notice (or handed a conditional offer), and

(b) otherwise by reference to the circumstances of the offence.

(3) In this Part of this Act "the relevant period" means—

(a) if the person was given a fixed penalty notice and proceedings are not brought in respect of the offence by virtue of this Act before the end of the suspended enforcement period, the suspended enforcement period,

(b) if he was handed a conditional offer and proceedings are not brought in respect of the offence by virtue of this Act before the end of the period of 28 days following the date on which the conditional offer was given or any longer period specified in the conditional offer, that period, and

(c) otherwise, the period ending with the person being charged with the offence.*

[Road Traffic Offenders Act 1988, s 90B as inserted by the Road Safety Act 2006, 11.]

---

*Section inserted by the Road Safety Act 2006, 11 from a date to be appointed.

4–1750C   90C. Making of payment in compliance with requirement.   (1) This section applies where a person on whom a financial penalty deposit requirement is imposed in respect of an offence makes a payment of the appropriate amount in accordance with section 90B(1) of this Act (and any order made under it).

(2) On payment by the person of the appropriate amount the person by whom the payment is received must issue him with a written receipt for the payment specifying the effect of the following provisions of this section.

(3) If the person was handed a conditional offer—

(a) the person is entitled to give notice requesting a hearing in respect of the offence, and

(b) the written receipt must specify the manner in which such notice is to be given.

(4) In a case where—

(a) a fixed penalty notice relating to the offence has been given to the person or a conditional offer so relating has been handed to him,

(b) the person does not give notice requesting a hearing in respect of the offence before the end of the relevant period in the appropriate manner, and

(c) proceedings are not brought in respect of the offence by virtue of this Act,

subsection (6) below applies.

(5) In subsection (4)(b) above "the appropriate manner" means—

(a) if the person was given a fixed penalty notice, the manner specified in the fixed penalty notice, and

(b) if he was handed a conditional offer, the manner specified in the written receipt under subsection (2) above.

(6) Where this subsection applies, the Secretary of State must—

(a) apply so much of the payment as does not exceed the amount of the fixed penalty in or towards payment of the fixed penalty, and

(b) take the appropriate steps to make any appropriate refund to the person.

(7) In any other case—

(a) if the person is informed that he is not to be prosecuted for the offence, is acquitted of the offence or is convicted but not fined in respect of it, or the prosecution period comes to an end without a prosecution having been commenced against him in respect of it, subsection (9) below applies, and

(b) if a fine is imposed on the person in respect of the offence (otherwise than as a result of a conviction obtained on a prosecution commenced after the end of the prosecution period), subsection (10) below applies.

(8) In this Part of this Act "the prosecution period" means the period of twelve months beginning with the imposition of the financial penalty deposit requirement or, if shorter, any period after which no prosecution may be commenced in respect of the offence.

(9) Where this subsection applies, the Secretary of State must take the appropriate steps to make the appropriate refund to the person.

(10) Where this subsection applies, the Secretary of State must—

(a) apply so much of the payment as does not exceed the amount of the fine in or towards payment of the fine, and

(b) take the appropriate steps to make any appropriate refund to the person.

(11) Where the Secretary of State is required by this section to take the appropriate steps to make an appropriate refund, he must take such steps to trace the person and to make the refund to him, by such means, as are specified in an order made by the Secretary of State.

(12) In this Part of this Act "the appropriate refund", in any case, is a refund of—

(a)   where subsection (6) above applies, so much of the payment as exceeds the amount of the fixed penalty,
(b)   where subsection (9) above applies, the amount of the payment, and
(c)   where subsection (10) above applies, so much of the amount of the payment as exceeds the amount of the fine,

together with interest calculated in accordance with provision made by order made by the Treasury.*
[Road Traffic Offenders Act 1988, s 90C as inserted by the Road Safety Act 2006, 11.]

*Section inserted by the Road Safety Act 2006, 11 from a date to be appointed.

4–1750D   90D. Prohibition on driving on failure to make payment.   (1) This section applies where a person on whom a financial penalty deposit requirement is imposed does not make an immediate payment of the appropriate amount in accordance with section 90B(1) of this Act (and any order made under it).
(2) The constable or vehicle examiner by whom the requirement was imposed may prohibit the driving on a road of any vehicle of which the person was in charge at the time of the offence by giving to the person notice in writing of the prohibition.
(3) The prohibition—

(a)   shall come into force as soon as the notice is given, and
(b)   shall continue in force until the happening of whichever of the events in subsection (4) below occurs first.

(4) Those events are—

(a)   the person making a payment of the appropriate amount in accordance with section 90B(1) of this Act (and any order made under it) at any time during the relevant period,
(b)   (where a fixed penalty notice was given, or a conditional offer handed, to the person in respect of the offence) payment of the fixed penalty,
(c)   the person being convicted or acquitted of the offence,
(d)   the person being informed that he is not to be prosecuted for the offence, and
(e)   the coming to an end of the prosecution period.

(5) A constable or vehicle examiner may by direction in writing require the person to remove the vehicle to which the prohibition relates (and, if it is a motor vehicle drawing a trailer, also to remove the trailer) to such place and subject to such conditions as are specified in the direction; and the prohibition does not apply to the removal of the vehicle (or trailer) in accordance with the direction.
(6) A person who—

(a)   drives a vehicle in contravention of a prohibition under this section,
(b)   causes or permits a vehicle to be driven in contravention of such a prohibition, or
(c)   fails to comply within a reasonable time with a direction under subsection (5) above,

is guilty of an offence.
(7) The Secretary of State may by order provide for exceptions from subsection (6) above.
(8) Schedule 4 to the Road Safety Act 2006 makes provision about the immobilisation of vehicles the driving of which has been prohibited under this section and about their removal and disposal.*
[Road Traffic Offenders Act 1988, s 90D as inserted by the Road Safety Act 2006, 11.]

*Section inserted by the Road Safety Act 2006, 11 from a date to be appointed.

4–1750E   90E. Orders about financial penalty deposits.   (1) Any power conferred by section 90A, 90B, 90C or 90D of this Act on the Secretary of State or the Treasury to make an order shall be exercisable by statutory instrument.
(2) Before making an order under any of those sections the Secretary of State or the Treasury must consult with such representative organisations as appear appropriate.
(3) An order under any of those sections may make different provision for different cases.
(4) No order shall be made under section 90B(2) of this Act unless a draft of the instrument containing it has been laid before, and approved by a resolution of, each House of Parliament.
(5) A statutory instrument containing an order under section 90A, 90B(1), 90C or 90D of this Act shall be subject to annulment in pursuance of a resolution of either House of Parliament.*
[Road Traffic Offenders Act 1988, s 90E as inserted by the Road Safety Act 2006, 11.]

*Section inserted by the Road Safety Act 2006, 11 from a date to be appointed.

4–1750F   90F. Financial penalty deposits: interpretation.   In sections 90A to 90D of this Act—

"the appropriate amount" has the meaning given by section 90B(2) of this Act,
"the appropriate refund" has the meaning given by section 90C(12) of this Act,
"conditional offer" means a notice under section 75(3)(a) of this Act,
"financial penalty deposit requirement" has the meaning given by section 90B(1) of this Act,
"fixed penalty notice" has the meaning given by section 52 of this Act,
"fixed penalty offence" is to be construed in accordance with section 51 of this Act,
"the prosecution period" has the meaning given by section 90C(8) of this Act,
"the relevant period" has the meaning given by section 90B(3) of this Act,

"suspended enforcement period" is to be construed in accordance with section 52(3)(a) of this Act, and

"vehicle examiner" means an examiner appointed under section 66A of the Road Traffic Act 1988.*

[Road Traffic Offenders Act 1988, s 90F as inserted by the Road Safety Act 2006, 11.]

---

*Section inserted by the Road Safety Act 2006, 11 from a date to be appointed.

PART IV[1]
MISCELLANEOUS AND GENERAL

4–1751   91. Penalty for breach of regulations.   If a person acts in contravention of or fails to comply with—

(a) any regulations made by the Secretary of State under the Road Traffic Act 1988 other than regulations made under section 31, 45, or 132[2],

(b) any regulations made by the Secretary of State under the Road Traffic Regulation Act 1984, other than regulations made under section 28, Schedule 4, Part III of Schedule 9 or Schedule 12,

and the contravention or failure to comply is not made an offence under any other provision of the Traffic Acts[3], he shall for each offence be liable on summary conviction to a fine not exceeding **level 3** on the standard scale.

[Road Traffic Offenders Act 1988, s 91.]

---

1. Part IV contains ss 91–99.
2. In so far as regulations under these sections create offences, the penalties therefor are prescribed by the regulation itself.
3. Where an Act enables an authority to make regulations, the regulations become, for the purpose of obedience or disobedience, provisions of the Act (*Willingale v Norris* (1908) 72 JP 495). The regulations have the same force as if they were in the statute itself (*Bailey v Geddes* [1938] 1 KB 156, [1937] 3 All ER 671).

4–1751A   91ZA. Application to Northern Ireland licence holders.   (1) The references to a licence in the following provisions of this Act include references to a Northern Ireland licence—

(a) section 7,
(b) section 26(7) and (8) and (9)(b),
(c) section 27,
(d) section 29(1),
(e) section 30,
(f) section 31(1),
(g) section 32,
(h) section 42(5),
(i) section 44(1),
(j) section 46(2),
(k) section 47(2) and (3),
(l) section 48(1) and (2).

(2) Accordingly, the reference in section 27(3)(b) of this Act to the suspension of a licence is to be construed in relation to a Northern Ireland licence holder as a reference to his ceasing to be authorised by virtue of section 109(1) of the Road Traffic Act 1988 to drive in Great Britain a motor vehicle of any class.

(3) The references in sections 26(9)(a) and 27(3) of this Act to a new licence include references to a counterpart of a Northern Ireland licence.

(4) In relation to a Northern Ireland licence holder to whom a counterpart is issued under section 109A of the Road Traffic Act 1988, the references in Part 3 of this Act (except sections 75(12), 76(8) and 77(3)) to a licence include references to a Northern Ireland licence.

(5) Where a court orders the endorsement of the counterpart of any Northern Ireland licence held by a person, it must send notice of the endorsement to the Secretary of State.

(6) The notice must—

(a) be sent in such manner and to such address, and
(b) contain such particulars,

as the Secretary of State may determine.

(7) Where a court orders the holder of a Northern Ireland licence to be disqualified, it must send the Northern Ireland licence and its counterpart (if any), on their being produced to the court, to the Secretary of State.

(8) The licence and its counterpart must be sent to such address as the Secretary of State may determine.

(9) Where—

(a) a notice is sent to the Secretary of State under subsection (5) above, and
(b) the particulars contained in the notice include—

(i) particulars of an offence in respect of which the holder of a Northern Ireland licence is disqualified by an order of a court, and

(ii) particulars of the disqualification,

the Secretary of State must send a notice containing the particulars mentioned in paragraph (b)(i) and (ii) to the licensing authority in Northern Ireland.

[Road Traffic Offenders Act 1988, s 91ZA as inserted by the Crime (International Co-operation) Act 2003, s 77.]

4–1751B 91ZB. Effect of endorsement on Northern Ireland licence holders. Section 91B applies in relation to Northern Ireland licences as it applies in relation to Community licences.

[Road Traffic Offenders Act 1988, s 91ZB as inserted by the Crime (International Co-operation) Act 2003, s 77.]

4–1752 91A. Application to Community licence holders. (1) The references in sections 7, 26(7) and (8) and (9)(b), 27, 29(1), 30, 31(1), 32, 42(5), 44(1), 46(2), 47(3) and 48(1) and (2) of this Act to a licence includes references to a Community licence; and accordingly the reference in section 27(3)(b) of this Act to the suspension of a licence is to be construed in relation to a Community licence as a reference to the Community licence holder ceasing to be authorised by virtue of section 99(A)(1) of the Road Traffic Act 1988 to drive in Great Britain a motor vehicle of any class.

(2) The references in sections 26(9)(a) and 27(3) of this Act to a new licence include references to a counterpart of a Community licence.

(3) In relation to a Community licence holder to whom a counterpart is issued under section 99B of the Road Traffic Act 1988, the references in Part III of this Act (except sections 75(12), 76(8) and 77(9) of this Act) to a licence include references to a Community licence.

(4) Where a court orders the endorsement of the counterpart of any Community licence held by a person, it must send notice of the endorsement to the Secretary of State.

(5) Where a court orders the holder of a Community licence to be disqualified, it must send the Community licence and its counterpart (if any), on their being produced to the court, to the Secretary of State.

(6) A notice sent by a court to the Secretary of State in pursuance of subsection (4) above must be sent in such manner and to such address and contain such particulars as the Secretary of State may determine, and a Community licence and its counterpart (if any) so sent in pursuance of subsection (5) above must be sent to such address as the Secretary of State may determine.

(7) Where a Community licence held by a person who is ordered by the court to be disqualified is sent to the Secretary of State in pursuance of subsection (5) above, the Secretary of State—

(a) must send to the licensing authority in the EEA State in respect of which the Community licence was issued the holder's name and address and particulars of the disqualification, and

(b) must (subject to subsection (8) below) return the Community licence to the holder—

(i) on the expiry of the period of disqualification, or

(ii) if earlier, on being satisfied that the holder has left Great Britain and is not normally resident there.

(8) Where—

(a) the Secretary of State would, apart from this subsection, be under a duty on the expiry of the period of disqualification to return a Community licence to a person in pursuance of subsection (7)(b)(i) above, but

(b) at that time, the person would not be authorised by virtue of section 99A(1) of the Road Traffic Act 1988 to drive in Great Britain a motor vehicle of any class,

the Secretary of State must send the Community licence to the licensing authority in the EEA State in respect of which it was issued and explain to them his reasons for so doing.

(9) A Community licence to be returned to any person under subsection (7) above may be returned to him by delivering it to him or by leaving it at his proper address or by sending it to him by post; and for the purposes of this subsection and section 7 of the Interpretation Act 1978 in its application to this subsection the proper address of any person shall be his latest address as known to the person returning the Community licence.

(10) In this section "period of disqualification" means, in relation to a Community licence holder, the period for which he is ordered by the court to be disqualified (otherwise than under section 36 of this Act).

[Road Traffic Act 1988, s 91A as inserted by SI 1996/1974.]

4–1753 91B. Effect of endorsement on Community licence holders. (1) An order that any particulars or penalty points are to be endorsed on the counterpart of any Community licence held by the person convicted shall operate as an order that—

(a) the counterpart of any Community licence which he may then hold, or

(b) the counterpart of any licence or Community licence which he may subsequently obtain,

is to be so endorsed until he becomes entitled under subsection (3) below to have a counterpart of his Community licence, or a licence and its counterpart, issued to him free from the particulars or penalty points.

(2) On the issue of a new counterpart of a Community licence or a new licence to a person, any particulars or penalty points ordered to be endorsed on the counterpart of any Community licence held by him shall be entered on the new counterpart or the counterpart of the new licence (as the case

may be) unless he has become entitled under subsection (3) below to have a new counterpart of his Community licence or a new licence issued to him free from those particulars or penalty points.

(3) A person the counterpart of whose Community licence has been ordered to be endorsed is entitled to have issued to him with effect from the end of the period for which the endorsement remains effective (as determined in accordance with section 45(5) of this Act)—

(a) a new counterpart of any Community licence then held by him free from the endorsement if he makes an application to the Secretary of State for that purpose in such manner as the Secretary of State may determine, or

(b) a new licence with a counterpart free from the endorsement if he applies for a new licence in pursuance of section 97(1) of the Road Traffic Act 1988, surrenders any subsisting licence and its counterpart, pays the fee prescribed by regulations under Part III of that Act and satisfies the other requirements of section 97(1).

[Road Traffic Offenders Act 1988, s 91B as inserted by SI 1996/1974.]

4–1762   92. Application to Crown.   The following provisions of this Act apply to vehicles and persons in the public service of the Crown: sections 1, 2, 3, 15, 16, 20 and 49 and the provisions connected with the licensing of drivers.

[Road Traffic Offenders Act 1988, s 92 amended by the Road Traffic Act 1991, Sch 4.]

4–1763   93. Application of sections 15 and 16 to persons subject to service discipline.
(1) Sections 15 and 16, in their application to persons subject to service discipline, apply outside as well as within Great Britain and have effect as if—

(a) references to proceedings for an offence under any enactment included references to proceedings for the corresponding service offence,

(b) references to the court included a reference to any naval, military, or air force authority before whom the proceedings take place,

(c) references to a constable included references to a member of the provost staff, and

(d) in section 15, subsection (4) were omitted.

(2) Expressions used in this section have the same meaning as in sections 3A to 10 of the Road Traffic Act 1988.

[Road Traffic Offenders Act 1988, s 93 amended by the Road Traffic Act 1991, Sch 4.]

4–1764   94. Proceedings in respect of offences in connection with Crown vehicles.   (1) Where an offence under the Traffic Acts is alleged to have been committed in connection with a vehicle in the public service of the Crown, proceedings may be brought in respect of the offence against a person nominated[1] for the purpose on behalf of the Crown.

(2) Subject to subsection (3) below, where any such offence is committed any person so nominated shall also be guilty of the offence as well as any person actually responsible for the offence (but without prejudice to proceedings against any person so responsible).

(3) Where any person is convicted of an offence by virtue of this section—

(a) no order is to be made on his conviction save an order imposing a fine,

(b) payment of any fine imposed on him in respect of that offence is not to be enforced against him, and

(c) apart from the imposition of any such fine, the conviction is to be disregarded for all purposes other than any appeal (whether by way of case stated or otherwise).

[Road Traffic Offenders Act 1988, s 94.]

---

1. For consideration of the position of a person nominated, see *Barnett v French* [1981] 1 WLR 848, [1981] RTR 173, [1981] Crim LR 415. In *Secretary of State for the Environment v Hooper* [1981] RTR 169, it was held that it was wrong to convict the Secretary of State who did not as such own or use any vehicles.

4–1765   96. Meaning of "offence involving obligatory endorsement".   For the purposes of this Act, an offence involves obligatory endorsement if it is an offence under a provision of the Traffic Acts specified in column 1 of Part I of Schedule 2 to this Act or an offence specified in column 1 of Part II of that Schedule and either—

(a) the word "obligatory" (without qualification) appears in column 6 (in the case of Part I) or column 3 (in the case of Part II) against the offence, or

(b) that word appears there qualified by conditions relating to the offence which are satisfied.

[Road Traffic Offenders Act 1988, s 96.]

4–1766   97. Meaning of "offence involving obligatory disqualification" and "offence involving discretionary disqualification".   (1) For the purposes of this Act, an offence involves obligatory disqualification if it is an offence under a provision of the Traffic Acts specified in column 1 of Part I of Schedule 2 to this Act or an offence specified in column 1 of Part II of that Schedule and either—

(a) the word "obligatory" (without qualification) appears in column 5 (in the case of Part I) or column 2 (in the case of Part II) against the offence, or

(b) that word appears there qualified by conditions or circumstances relating to the offence which are satisfied or obtain.

(2) For the purposes of this Act, an offence involves discretionary disqualification if it is an offence under a provision of the Traffic Acts specified in column 1 of Part I of Schedule 2 to this Act or an offence specified in column 1 of Part II of that Schedule and either—

- (a) the word "discretionary" (without qualification) appears in column 5 (in the case of Part I) or column 2 (in the case of Part II) against the offence, or
- (b) that word appears there qualified by conditions or circumstances relating to the offence which are satisfied or obtain.

[Road Traffic Offenders Act 1988, s 97.]

4–1766A   97A. Meaning of "driving record".   (1) In this Act "driving record", in relation to a person, means a record in relation to the person maintained by the Secretary of State and designed to be endorsed with particulars relating to offences committed by the person under the Traffic Acts.

(2) The Secretary of State may make arrangements for the following persons to have access, by such means as the Secretary of State may determine, to information held on a person's driving record—

- (a) courts,
- (b) constables,
- (c) fixed penalty clerks,
- (d) the person in respect of whom the record is maintained and persons authorised by him, and
- (e) other persons prescribed in regulations made by the Secretary of State.

(3) The power to make regulations under subsection (2)(e) above shall be exercisable by statutory instrument.

(4) No regulations shall be made under subsection (2)(e) above unless a draft of the instrument containing them has been laid before, and approved by a resolution of, each House of Parliament.★

[Road Traffic Offenders Act 1988, s 97A as inserted by the Road Safety Act 2006, 8.]

★Section inserted by the Road Safety Act 2006, 8 from a date to be appointed.

4–1767   98. General interpretation.   (1) In this Act—

"disqualified" means disqualified for holding or obtaining a licence and "disqualification" is to be construed accordingly,

"driver" has the same meaning as in the Road Traffic Act 1988,

"licence" means a licence to drive a motor vehicle granted under Part III of that Act,

"provisional licence" means a licence granted by virtue of section 97(2) of that Act,

"the provisions connected with the licensing of drivers" means sections 7, 8, 22, 25 to 29, 31, 32, 34 to 48, 91ZA to 91B, 96 and 97 of this Act,

"road"—

- (a) in relation to England and Wales, means any highway and any other road to which the public has access, and includes bridges over which a road passes, and
- (b) (*Scotland*),

"the Road Traffic Acts" means the Road Traffic Act 1988, the Road Traffic (Consequential Provisions) Act 1988 (so far as it reproduces the effect of provisions repealed by that Act) and this Act, and

"the Traffic Acts" means the Road Traffic Acts and the Road Traffic Regulation Act 1984,

and "Community licence", "counterpart", "EEA State" and "Northern Ireland licence" have the same meanings as in Part III of the Road Traffic Act 1988.

(2) Sections 185 and 186 of the Road Traffic Act 1988 (meaning of "motor vehicle" and other expressions relating to vehicles) apply for the purposes of this Act as they apply for the purposes of that Act.

(3) In the Schedules to this Act—

"RTRA" is used as an abbreviation for the Road Traffic Regulation Act 1984, and

"RTA" is used as an abbreviation for the Road Traffic Act 1988 or, if followed by "1989", the Road Traffic (Driver Licensing and Information Systems) Act 1989.

(4) Subject to any express exception, references in this Act to any Part of this Act include a reference to any Schedule to this Act so far as relating to that Part.

[Road Traffic Offenders Act 1988, s 98, amended by SI 1990/144, the Road Traffic (Driver Licensing and Information Systems) Act 1989, Sch 3, the Road Traffic Act 1991, Sch 4, SI 1996/1974 and the Crime (International Co-operation) Act 2003, Sch 5.]

SCHEDULES

Sections 1 etc   SCHEDULE 1
OFFENCES TO WHICH SECTIONS 1, 6, 11 AND 12(1) APPLY

(Amended by the Road Traffic (Consequential Provisions) Act 1988 Sch 2, SI 1990/144, the Road Traffic (Driver Licensing and Information Systems) Act 1989, Schs 3 and 6, the Road Traffic Act 1991, Schs 1 and 8, the Road Traffic (New Drivers) Act 1995, Sch 2, SI 1996/1974, SI 1998/1420, Crime (International Co-operation) Act 2003, Sch 5, the Statute Law (Repeals) Act 2004 and the Road Safety Act 2006, s 26.)

4–1768   **1.** (1) Where section 1[1], 6, 11 or 12(1) of this Act[2] is shown in column 3 of this Schedule against a provision of the Road Traffic Act 1988 specified in column 1, the section in question applies to an offence under that provision.

(2) The general nature of the offence is indicated in column 2.

1A. Section 1 also applies to—

(a) an offence under section 16 of the Road Traffic Regulation Act 1984 consisting in the contravention of a restriction on the speed of vehicles imposed under section 14 of that Act,

(b) an offence under subsection (4) of section 17 of that Act consisting in the contravention of a restriction on the speed of vehicles imposed under that section, and

(c) an offence under section 88(7) or 89(1) of that Act (speeding offences).

2. Section 6 also applies—

(a) to an offence under section 67 of this Act,

(b) *Scotland*

(c) *(repealed)* and

(d) to an offence under paragraph 3(5) of Schedule 1 to the Road Traffic (New Drivers) Act 1995.

3. Section 11 also applies to—

(a) any offence to which section 112 of the Road Traffic Regulation Act 1984 (information as to identity of driver or rider) applies except an offence under section 61(5) of that Act,

(b) any offence which is punishable under section 91 of this Act,

(bb) *(repealed)* and

(c) any offence against any other enactment relating to the use of vehicles on roads.

4. Section 12(1) also applies to—

(a) any offence which is punishable under section 91 of this Act,

(aa) *(repealed)* and

(b) any offence against any other enactment relating to the use of vehicles on roads.

---

1. During consolidation, speeding offences under s 89 of the Road Traffic Regulation Act 1984 were omitted from Sch 1, and in the absence of amendment before commencement of this Act on 15 May 1989, s 1 will not therefore apply to those offences.

2. Section 1 precludes conviction unless there has been a warning at the time of the offence, or service of a summons or notice of intended prosecution within 14 days; s 6 enables summary proceedings within 6 months of sufficient evidence coming to the prosecutor's knowledge, his certificate is conclusive; s 11 enables evidence by certificate as to driver, user or owner; s 12(1) enables the identity of an accused driver to be established by his written statement.

(1) Provision creating offence	(2) General nature of offence	(3) Applicable provisions of this Act
RTA section 1	Causing death by dangerous driving.	Section 11 of this Act.
RTA section 2	Dangerous driving.	Sections 1, 11 and 12(1) of this Act.
RTA section 3	Careless, and inconsiderate, driving.	Sections 1, 11 and 12(1) of this Act.
RTA section 3A	Causing death by careless driving when under influence of drink or drugs.	Section 11 of this Act.
RTA section 4	Driving or attempting to drive, or being in charge of a mechanically propelled vehicle, when unfit to drive through drink or drugs.	Sections 11 and 12(1) of this Act.
RTA section 5	Driving or attempting to drive, or being in charge of a motor vehicle, with excess alcohol in breath, blood or urine.	Sections 11 and 12(1) of this Act.
RTA section 6	Failing to co-operate with a preliminary test.	Sections 11 and 12(1) of this Act.
RTA section 7	Failing to provide specimen for analysis or laboratory test.	Sections 11 and 12(1) of this Act.
RTA section 7A	Failing to allow specimen of blood to be subjected to laboratory test	Sections 11 and 12(1).
RTA section 12	Motor racing and speed trials.	Sections 11 and 12(1) of this Act.
RTA section 14	Driving or riding in a motor vehicle in contravention of regulations requiring wearing of seat belts.	Sections 11 and 12(1) of this Act.
RTA section 15	Driving motor vehicle with child not wearing seat belt.	Sections 11 and 12(1) of this Act.
RTA section 19	Prohibition of parking of heavy commercial vehicles on verges and footways.	Sections 11 and 12(1) of this Act.
RTA section 22	Leaving vehicles in dangerous positions.	Sections 1, 11 and 12(1) of this Act.
RTA section 23	Carrying passenger on motor-cycle contrary to section 23.	Sections 11 and 12(1) of this Act.
RTA section 24	Carrying passenger on bicycle contrary to section 24.	Sections 11 and 12(1) of this Act.
RTA section 25	Tampering with motor vehicles.	Section 11 of this Act.
RTA section 26(1)	Holding or getting into vehicle in order to be carried.	Section 11 of this Act.
RTA section 26(2)	Holding onto vehicle in order to be towed.	Sections 11 and 12(1) of this Act.
RTA section 28	Dangerous cycling.	Sections 1, 11 and 12(1) of this Act.
RTA section 29	Careless, and inconsiderate, cycling.	Sections 1, 11 and 12(1) of this Act.
RTA section 30	Cycling when unfit through drink or drugs.	Sections 11 and 12(1) of this Act.
RTA section 31	Unauthorised or irregular cycle racing, or trials of speed.	Sections 11 and 12(1) of this Act.
RTA section 33	Unauthorised motor vehicle trial on footpaths or bridleways.	Sections 11 and 12(1) of this Act.

(1) Provision creating offence	(2) General nature of offence	(3) Applicable provisions of this Act
RTA section 34	Driving motor vehicles elsewhere than on roads.	Sections 11 and 12(1) of this Act.
RTA section 35	Failing to comply with traffic directions.	Sections 1, 11 and 12(1) of this Act.
RTA section 36	Failing to comply with traffic signs.	Sections 1, 11 and 12(1) of this Act.
RTA section 40A	Using vehicle in dangerous condition etc.	Sections 11 and 12(1) of this Act.
RTA section 41A	Breach of requirement as to brakes, steering-gear or tyres.	Sections 11 and 12(1) of this Act.
RTA section 41B	Breach of requirement as to weight: goods and passenger vehicles.	Sections 11 and 12(1) of this Act.
RTA section 41D	Breach of requirements as to control of vehicle, mobile telephones etc.	Sections 11 and 12(1) of this Act.
RTA section 42	Breach of other construction and use requirements.	Sections 11 and 12(1) of this Act.
RTA section 47	Using, etc, vehicle without required test certificate being in force.	Sections 11 and 12(1) of this Act.
RTA section 53	Using, etc, vehicle without required plating certificate or goods vehicle test certificate being in force, or where Secretary State is required by regulations under section 49 to be notified of an alteration to the vehicle or its equipment but has not been notified.	Sections 11 and 12(1) of this Act.
RTA section 63	Using etc, vehicle without required certificate being in force showing that it, or a part fitted to it, complies with type approval requirements applicable to it, or using, etc, certain goods vehicles for drawing trailer when plating certificate does not specify maximum laden weight for vehicle and trailer, or using, etc, goods vehicle where Secretary of State has not been but is required to notified under section 48 of alteration to it or its equipment.	Sections 11 and 12(1) of this Act.
RTA section 71	Driving, etc, vehicle in contravention of prohibition on driving it as being unfit for service or overloaded, or refusing, neglecting or otherwise failing to comply with a direction to remove a vehicle found overloaded.	Sections 11 and 12(1) of this Act.
RTA section 78	Failing to comply with requirement about weighing motor vehicle or obstructing authorised person.	Sections 11 and 12(1) of this Act.
RTA section 87(1)	Driving otherwise than in accordance with a licence.	Sections 11 and 12(1) of this Act.
RTA section 87(2)	Causing or permitting a person to drive otherwise than in accordance with a licence.	Section 11 of this Act.
RTA section 92(10)	Driving after making false declaration as to physical fitness.	Sections 6, 11 and 12(1) of this Act.
RTA section 94(3) and that subsection as applied by RTA section 99D or 109C	Failure to notify the Secretary of State of onset of, or deterioration in, relevant or prospective disability.	Section 6 of this Act.
RTA section 94(3A) and that subsection as applied by RTA section 99D(b) or 109C(c)	Driving after such a failure.	Sections 6, 11 and 12(1) of this Act.
RTA section 94A	Driving after refusal of licence under section 92(3), revocation under section 93 or service of a notice under section 99C or 109B.	Sections 6, 11 and 12(1) of this Act.
RTA section 99B(11) and that subsection as applied by RTA section 109A(5)	Driving after failure to comply with a requirement under section 99B(6), (7) or (10) or a requirement under section 99B(6) or (7) as applied by section 109A(5)	Section 6 of this Act.
RTA section 103(1)(a)	Obtaining driving licence while disqualified.	Section 6 of this Act.
RTA section 103(1)(b)	Driving while disqualified.	Sections 6, 11 and 12(1) of this Act.
RTA section 114(1)	Failing to comply with conditions of LGV PCV licence or LGV Community licence.	Section 11 and 12(1) of this Act.
RTA section 114(2)	Causing or permitting a person under 21 to drive LGV or PCV in contravention of conditions of that person's licence.	Section 11 of this Act.
RTA section 143	Using motor vehicle, or causing or permitting it to be used, while uninsured or unsecured against third party risks.	Sections 6, 11 and 12(1) of this Act.
RTA section 163	Failing to stop vehicle when required by constable.	Sections 11 and 12(1) of this Act.
RTA section 164(6)	Failing to produce driving licence and counterpart etc or to state date of birth.	Sections 11 and 12(1) of this Act.

(1) Provision creating offence	(2) General nature of offence	(3) Applicable provisions of this Act
RTA section 165(3)	Failing to give constable certain names and addresses or to produce certificate of insurance or certain test and other like certificates.	Sections 11 and 12(1) of this Act.
RTA section 165(6)	Supervisor of learner driver failing to give constable certain names and addresses.	Section 11 of this Act.
RTA section 168	Refusing to give, or giving false, name and address in case of reckless, careless or inconsiderate driving or cycling.	Sections 11 and 12(1) of this Act.
RTA section 170	Failure by driver to stop, report accident or give information or documents.	Sections 11 and 12(1) of this Act.
RTA section 171	Failure by owner of motor vehicle to give police information for verifying compliance with requirement of compulsory insurance or security.	Sections 11 and 12(1) of this Act.
RTA section 174(1) or (5)	Making false statements in connection with licences under this Act and with registration as an approved driving instructor; or making false statement or withholding material information in order to obtain the issue of insurance certificates, etc.	Section 6 of this Act.
RTA section 175	Falsely amending certificate of conformity.*	Section 6 of this Act.

*As prospectively inserted by the Transport Act 1982, s 24(3) (as amended by the Road Traffic (Consequential Provisions) Act 1988, s 4, Sch 2, Part I), when in force.

4–1769

Section 9 etc

SCHEDULE 2

PROSECUTION AND PUNISHMENT OF OFFENCES

(Amended by the Road Traffic (Consequential Provisions) Act 1988 Sch 2, SI 1988/1906, the Parking Act 1989, Sch, the Road Traffic (Driver Licensing and Information Systems) Act 1989, Sch 3 as amended by SI 1990/144 and 6, the New Roads and Street Works Act 1991, Sch 9, the Motor Vehicles (Safety Equipment for Children) Act 1991, s 3, the Road Traffic Act 1991, Sch 2 and 8, the Aggravated Vehicle-Taking Act 1992, s 3, SI 1992/3207, the Road Traffic (Driving Instruction by Disabled Persons) Act 1993, Sch, the Criminal Justice Act 1993, s 67, the Road Traffic Regulation (Special Events) Act 1994, s 1, SI 1996/1974, SI 1998/1420, the Countryside and Rights of Way Act 2000, Sch 7, the Criminal Justice Act 2003, s 286 and Sch 26, the Railways and Transport Safety Act 2003, Sch 7, the Crime (International Co-operation) Act 2003, Sch 5, the Statute Law (Repeals) Act 2004, the Traffic Management Act 2004, Sch 12, the Disability Discrimination Act 2005, Sch 1 and the Road Safety Act 2006, s 26.)

PART I

OFFENCES UNDER THE TRAFFIC ACTS

(1) Provision creating offence	(2) General nature of offence	(3) Mode of prosecution	(4) Punishment
Offences under the Road Traffic Regulation Act 1984			
RTRA section 5	Contravention of traffic regulation order	Summarily	**Level 3** on the standard scale
RTRA section 8	Contravention of order regulating traffic in Greater London	Summarily	**Level 3** on the standard scale
RTRA section 11	Contravention of experimental traffic order	Summarily	**Level 3** on the standard scale
RTRA section 13	Contravention of experimental traffic scheme in Greater London	Summarily	**Level 3** on the standard scale
RTRA section 16(1)	Contravention of temporary prohibition or restriction	Summarily	**Level 3** on the standard scale
RTRA section 16C(1)	Contravention of prohibition or restriction relating to relevant event	Summarily	**Level 3** on the standard scale
RTRA section 17(4)	Use of special road contrary to scheme or regulations	Summarily	**Level 4** on the standard scale
RTRA section 18(3)	One-way traffic on trunk road	Summarily	**Level 3** on the standard scale
RTRA section 20(5)	Contravention of prohibition or restriction for roads of certain classes	Summarily	**Level 3** on the standard scale
RTRA section 25(5)	Contravention of pedestrian crossing regulations	Summarily	**Level 3** on the standard scale
RTRA section 28(3)	Not stopping at school crossing	Summarily	**Level 3** on the standard scale
RTRA section 29(3)	Contravention of order relating to street playground	Summarily	**Level 3** on the standard scale

(5) Disqualification	(6) Endorsement	(7) Penalty points
Discretionary[2] if committed in respect of a speed restriction	Obligatory[2] if committed in respect of a speed restriction	3–6 or 3 (fixed penalty)
Discretionary[2] if committed in respect of a motor vehicle otherwise than by unlawfully stopping or allowing the vehicle to remain at rest on a part of a special road on which vehicles are in certain circumstances permitted to remain at rest[3]	Obligatory[2] if committed as mentioned in the entry in column 5	3–6 or 3 (fixed penalty) if committed in respect of a speed restriction, 3 in any other case
Discretionary[2] if committed in respect of a motor vehicle	Obligatory[2] if committed in respect of a motor vehicle	3
Discretionary[2] if committed in respect of a motor vehicle	Obligatory[2] if committed in respect of a motor vehicle	3
Discretionary[2] if committed in respect of a motor vehicle	Obligatory[2] if committed in respect of a motor vehicle	2

SCHEDULE 2—*continued*

(1) Provision creating offence	(2) General nature of offence	(3) Mode of prosecution	(4) Punishment
Offences under the Road Traffic Regulation Act 1984—continued			
RTRA section 35A(1)	Contravention of order as to use of parking place	Summarily	(a) **Level 3** on the standard scale in the case of an offence committed by a person in a street parking place reserved for disabled persons' vehicles or in an off-street parking place reserved for such vehicles, where that person would not have been guilty of that offence if the motor vehicle in respect of which it was committed had been a disabled person's vehicle (b) **Level 2** on the standard scale in any other case
RTRA section 35A(2)	Misuse of apparatus for collecting charges or of parking device or connected apparatus	Summarily	**Level 3** on the standard scale
RTRA section 35A(5)	Plying for hire in parking place	Summarily	**Level 2** on the standard scale
RTRA section 43(5)	Unauthorised disclosure of information in respect of licensed parking place	Summarily	**Level 3** on the standard scale
RTRA section 43(10)	Failure to comply with term or conditions of licence to operate parking place	Summarily	**Level 3** on the standard scale
RTRA section 43(12)	Operation of public off-street parking place without licence	Summarily	**Level 5** on the standard scale
RTRA section 47(1)	Contraventions relating to designated parking places	Summarily	(a) **Level 3** on the standard scale in the case of an offence committed by a person in a street parking place reserved for disabled persons' vehicles where that person would not have been guilty of that offence if the motor vehicle in respect of which was committed had been a disabled person's vehicle (b) **Level 2** in any other case
RTRA section 47(3)	Tampering with parking meter	Summarily	**Level 3** on the standard scale
RTRA section 52(1)	Misuse of parking device	Summarily	**Level 2** on the standard scale
RTRA section 53(5)	Contravention of certain provisions of designation orders	Summarily	**Level 3** on the standard scale
RTRA section 53(6)	Other contraventions of designation orders	Summarily	**Level 2** on the standard scale
RTRA section 61(5)	Unauthorised use of loading area	Summarily	**Level 3** on the standard scale
RTRA section 88(7)	Contravention of minimum speed limit	Summarily	**Level 3** on the standard scale
RTRA section 89(1)	Exceeding speed limit	Summarily	**Level 3** on the standard scale
RTRA section 104(5)	Interference with notice as to immobilisation device	Summarily	**Level 2** on the standard scale
RTRA section 104(6)	Interference with immobilisation device	Summarily	**Level 3** on the standard scale
RTRA section 105(5)	Misuse of disabled person's badge (immobilisation devices)	Summarily	**Level 3** on the standard scale
RTRA section 105(6A)	Misuse of recognised badge (immobilisation devices)	Summarily	**Level 3** on the standard scale

(5) Disqualification	(4) Mode of prosecution	(6) Endorsement	(7) Penalty points
Discretionary[2]		Obligatory[2]	3–6 or 3 (fixed penalty)

SCHEDULE 2—*continued*

(1) Provision creating offence	(2) General nature of offence	(3) Mode of prosecution	(4) Punishment
Offences under the Road Traffic Regulation Act 1984—continued			
RTRA section 108(2) (or that subsection as modified by section 109(2) and (3))	Non-compliance with notice (excess charge)	Summarily	**Level 3** on the standard scale
RTRA section 108(3) (or that subsection as modified by section 109(2) and (3))	False response to notice (excess charge)	Summarily	**Level 5** on the standard scale
RTRA section 112(4)	Failure to give information as to identity of driver	Summarily	**Level 3** on the standard scale
RTRA 115(1)	Mishandling or faking parking documents	(*a*) Summarily[4] (*b*) On indictment	(*a*) The statutory maximum (*b*) 2 years
RTRA section 115(2)	False statement for procuring authorisation	Summarily	**Level 4** on the standard scale
RTRA section 116(1)	Non-delivery of suspect document or article	Summarily	**Level 3** on the standard scale
RTRA section 117(1)*	Wrongful use of disabled person's badge	Summarily	**Level 3** on the standard scale
RTRA section 117(1A)	Wrongful use of recognised badge	Summarily	**Level 3** on the standard scale
RTRA section 129(3)	Failure to give evidence at inquiry	Summarily	**Level 3** on the standard scale
Offences under the Road Traffic Act 1988			
RTA section 1	Causing death by dangerous driving[1]	On indictment	14 years
RTA section 2	Dangerous driving[1]	(*a*) Summarily[4] (*b*) On indictment	(*a*) **6 months** or the **statutory maximum** or both (*b*) 2 years or a fine or both
RTA section 3	Careless, and inconsiderate, driving[1]	Summarily	**Level 4** on the standard scale
RTA section 3A	Causing death by careless driving when under influence of drink or drugs[1]	On indictment	14 years or a fine or both
RTA section 4(1)	Driving or attempting to drive when unfit to drive through drink or drugs[1]	Summarily	**6 months** or **level 5** on the standard scale or both
RTA section 4(2)	Being in charge of a mechanically propelled vehicle when unfit to drive through drink or drugs[1]	Summarily	**3 months**** or **level 4** on the standard scale or both
RTA section 5(1)(a)	Driving or attempting to drive with excess alcohol in breath, blood or urine[1]	Summarily	**6 months** or **level 5** on the standard scale or both
RTA section 5(1)(b)	Being in charge of a motor vehicle with excess alcohol in breath, blood or urine[1]	Summarily	**3 months**** or **level 4** on the standard scale or both
RTA section 6	Failing to co-operate with a preliminary test[1]	Summarily	**Level 3** on the standard scale
RTA section 7	Failing to provide specimen for analysis or laboratory test[1]	Summarily	(*a*) Where the specimen was required to ascertain ability to drive or proportion of alcohol at the time offender was driving or attempting to drive, **6 months** or **level 5** on the standard scale or both (*b*) In any other case, **3 months**** or[6] **level 4** on the standard scale or both

(5) Disqualification	(6) Endorsement	(7) Penalty points
Obligatory[2]	Obligatory[2]	3–11[10]
Obligatory[2]	Obligatory[2]	3–11[10]
Discretionary[2]	Obligatory[2]	3–9
Obligatory	Obligatory	3–11[10]
Obligatory[2,5]	Obligatory[2]	3–11[10]
Discretionary[2]	Obligatory[2]	10
Obligatory[2,5]	Obligatory[2]	3–11[10]
Discretionary[2]	Obligatory[2]	10
Discretionary[2]	Obligatory[2]	4
(a) Obligatory[2,5] in case mentioned in column 4(a)	Obligatory[2]	(a) 3–11[10] in case mentioned in column 4(a)
(b) Discretionary[2] in any other case		(b) 10 in any other case

SCHEDULE 2—*continued*

(1) Provision creating offence	(2) General nature of offence	(3) Mode of prosecution	(4) Punishment
	Offences under the Road Traffic Act 1988—continued		
RTA section 7A	Failing to allow specimen to be subjected to laboratory test	Summarily	(a) Where the test would be for ascertaining ability to drive or proportion of alcohol at the time offender was driving or attempting to drive, **6 months** or **level 5** on the standard scale or both (b) In any other case, **3 months**** or level 4 on the standard scale or both
RTA section 12	Motor racing and speed trials on public ways[1]	Summarily	**Level 4** on the standard scale
RTA section 13	Other unauthorised or irregular competitions or trials on public ways	Summarily	**Level 3** on the standard scale
RTA section 14	Driving or riding in a motor vehicle in contravention of regulations requiring wearing of seat belts[1]	Summarily	**Level 2** on the standard scale
RTA section 15(2)	Driving motor vehicle with child not wearing seat belt[1]	Summarily	**Level 2** on the standard scale
RTA Section 15(4)	Driving motor vehicle with child in rear not wearing seatbelt	Summarily	**Level 1** on the standard scale
RTA section 15A(3) or (4)	Selling etc in certain circumstances equipment as conducive to the safety of children in motor vehicles	Summarily	**Level 3** on the standard scale
RTA section 16	Driving or riding motor cycles in contravention of regulations requiring wearing of protective headgear	Summarily	**Level 2** on the standard scale
RTA section 17	Selling, etc, helmet not of the prescribed type as helmet for affording protection for motor cyclists	Summarily	**Level 3** on the standard scale
RTA section 18(3)	Contravention of regulations with respect to use of head-worn appliances on motor cycles	Summarily	**Level 2** on the standard scale
RTA section 18(4)	Selling, etc, appliance not of prescribed type as approved for use on motor cycles	Summarily	**Level 3** on the standard scale
RTA section 19	Prohibition of parking of heavy commercial vehicles on verges, etc[1]	Summarily	**Level 3** on the standard scale
RTA section 21	Driving or parking on cycle track	Summarily	**Level 3** on the standard scale
RTA section 22	Leaving vehicles in dangerous positions[1]	Summarily	**Level 3** on the standard scale
RTA section 22A	Causing danger to road-users	(a) Summarily (b) On indictment	(a) **6 months** or the **statutory maximum** or both (b) **7 years** or a fine or both
RTA section 23	Carrying passenger on motor-cycle contrary to section 23[1]	Summarily	**Level 3** on the standard scale
RTA section 24	Carrying passenger on bicycle contrary to section 24[1]	Summarily	**Level 1** on the standard scale
RTA section 25	Tampering with motor vehicles[1]	Summarily	**Level 3** on the standard scale
RTA section 26	Holding or getting on to vehicle, etc, in order to be towed or carried[1]	Summarily	**Level 1** on the standard scale

(5) Disqualification	(6) Endorsement	(7) Penalty points
(a) Obligatory[2,5] in case mentioned in column 4(a)	Obligatory[2]	(a) 3–11[10] in cse mentioned in column 4(a)
(b) Discretionary[2] in any other case		(b) 10 in any other case
Obligatory[2]	Obligatory[2]	3–11[10]
Discretionary[2] if committed in respect of a motor vehicle	Obligatory[2] if committed in respect of a motor vehicle	3
Discretionary[2]	Obligatory[2]	3

SCHEDULE 2—*continued*

Offences under the Road Traffic Act 1988—continued

(1) Provision creating offence	(2) General nature of offence	(3) Mode of prosecution	(4) Punishment
RTA section 27	Dogs on designated roads without being held on lead[1]	Summarily	**Level 1** on the standard scale
RTA section 28	Dangerous cycling[1]	Summarily	**Level 4** on the standard scale
RTA section 29	Careless, and inconsiderate, cycling[1]	Summarily	**Level 3** on the standard scale
RTA section 30	Cycling when unfit through drink or drugs[1]	Summarily	**Level 3** on the standard scale
RTA section 31	Unauthorised or irregular cycle racing or trials of speed on public ways[1]	Summarily	**Level 1** on the standard scale
RTA section 32	Contravening prohibition on persons under 14 driving electrically assisted pedal cycles	Summarily	**Level 2** on the standard scale
RTA section 33	Unauthorised motor vehicle trial on footpaths or bridle-ways[1]	Summarily	**Level 3** on the standard scale
RTA section 34	Driving mechanically propelled vehicles elsewhere than on roads[1]	Summarily	**Level 3** on the standard scale
RTA section 35	Failing to comply with traffic directions[1]	Summarily	**Level 3** on the standard scale
RTA section 36	Failing to comply with traffic signs[1]	Summarily	**Level 3** on the standard scale
RTA section 37	Pedestrian failing to stop when directed by constable regulating traffic	Summarily	**Level 3** on the standard scale
RTA section 40A	Using vehicle in dangerous condition etc[1]	Summarily	(a) **Level 5** on the standard scale if committed in respect of a goods vehicle or a vehicle adapted to carry more than eight passengers (b) **Level 4** on the standard scale in any other case
RTA section 41A	Breach of requirement as to brakes[8], steering-gear or tyres[1]	Summarily	(a) **Level 5** on the standard scale if committed in respect of a goods vehicle or a vehicle adapted to carry more than eight passengers (b) **Level 4** on the standard scale in any other case
RTA section 41B	Breach of requirement as to weight: goods and passenger vehicles[1]	Summarily	**Level 5** on the standard scale
RTA section 41D	Breach of requirements as to control of vehicle, mobile telephones etc	Summarily	(a) **Level 4** on the standard scale if committed in respect of a goods vehicle or a vehicle adapted to carry more than eight passengers (b) **Level 3** on the standard scale in any other case
RTA section 42	Breach of other construction and use requirements[1]	Summarily	(a) **Level 4** on standard scale if committed in respect of a goods vehicle or a vehicle adapted to carry more than eight passengers (b) **Level 3** on the standard scale in any other case
RTA section 47	Using, etc, vehicle without required test certificate being in force[1]	Summarily	(a) **Level 4** on the standard scale in case of a vehicle adapted to carry more than eight passengers (b) **Level 3** on the standard scale in any other case

(5) Disqualification	(6) Endorsement	(7) Penalty points
Discretionary[2], if committed in respect of a motor vehicle by failure to comply with a direction of a constable or traffic warden	Obligatory[2] if committed as described in column 5	3
Discretionary[2], if committed in respect of a motor vehicle by failure to comply with an indication given by a sign specified for the purposes of this paragraph in regulations under RTA section 36[7]	Obligatory[2] if committed as described in column 5	3
Discretionary[2]	Obligatory[2]	3
Discretionary[2]	Obligatory[2]	3
Discretionary[2]	Obligatory[2]	3

SCHEDULE 2—*continued*

(1) Provision creating offence	(2) General nature of offence	(3) Mode of prosecution	(4) Punishment
	Offences under the Road Traffic Act 1988—continued		
Regulations under RTA section 49 made by virtue of section 51(2)	Contravention of requirement of regulations (which is declared by regulations to be an offence) that driver of goods vehicle being tested be present throughout test or drive, etc, vehicle as and when directed	Summarily	**Level 3** on the standard scale
RTA section 53(1)	Using, etc, goods vehicle without required plating certificate being in force[1]	Summarily	**Level 3** on the standard scale
RTA section 53(2)	Using, etc, goods vehicle without required goods vehicle test certificate being in force[1]	Summarily	**Level 4** on the standard scale
RTA section 53(3)	Using, etc, goods vehicle where Secretary of State is required by regulations under section 49 to be notified of an alteration to the vehicle or its equipment but has not been notified[1]	Summarily	**Level 3** on the standard scale
Regulations under RTA section 61 made by virtue of subsection (4).	Contravention of requirement of regulations (which is declared by regulations to be an offence) that driver of goods vehicle being tested after alteration be present throughout test and drive, etc, vehicle as when directed	Summarily	**Level 3** on the standard scale
RTA section 63(1)	Using, etc, goods vehicle without required certificate being in force showing that it complies with type approval requirements applicable to it[1]	Summarily	**Level 4** on the standard scale
RTA section 63(2)	Using, etc, certain goods vehicles for drawing trailer when plating certificate does not specify maximum laden weight for vehicle and trailer[1]	Summarily	**Level 3** on the standard scale
RTA section 63(3)	Using, etc, goods vehicle where Secretary of State is required to be notified under section 59 of alteration to it or its equipment but has not been notified[1]	Summarily	**Level 3** on the standard scale
RTA section 64	Using goods vehicle with unauthorised weights as well as authorised weights marked on it	Summarily	**Level 3** on the standard scale
RTA section 64A	Failure to hold EC certificate of conformity for unregistered light passenger vehicle or motor cycle	Summarily	**Level 3** on the standard scale
RTA section 65	Supplying vehicle or vehicle part without required certificate being in force showing that it complies with type approval requirements applicable to it	Summarily	**Level 5** on the standard scale
RTA section 65A	Light passenger vehicles and motor cycles not to be sold without EC certificate of conformity	Summarily	**Level 5** on the standard scale
RTA section 67	Obstructing testing of vehicle by examiner on road or failing to comply with requirements of RTA section 67 or Schedule 2	Summarily	**Level 3** on the standard scale

(5) Disqualification	(6) Endorsement	(7) Penalty points

SCHEDULE 2—*continued*

(1) Provision creating offence	(2) General nature of offence	(3) Mode of prosecution	(4) Punishment
Offences under the Road Traffic Act 198—continued			
RTA section 68	Obstructing inspection, etc, of vehicle by examiner or failing to comply with requirement to take vehicle for inspection	Summarily	**Level 3** on the standard scale
RTA section 71	Driving, etc, vehicle in contravention of prohibition on driving it as being unfit for service, or refusing, neglecting or otherwise failing to comply with direction to remove a vehicle found over-loaded[1]	Summarily	**Level 5** on the standard scale
RTA section 74	Contravention of regulations requiring goods vehicle operator to inspect, and keep records of inspection of, goods vehicles	Summarily	**Level 3** on the standard scale
RTA section 75	Selling, etc, unroad-worthy vehicle or trailer so as to make it unroad-worthy	Summarily	**Level 5** on the standard scale
RTA section 76(1)	Fitting of defective or unsuitable vehicle parts	Summarily	**Level 5** on the standard scale
RTA section 76(3)	Supplying defective or unsuitable vehicle parts	Summarily	**Level 4** on the standard scale
RTA section 76(8)	Obstructing examiner testing vehicles to ascertain whether defective or unsuitable part has been fitted, etc	Summarily	**Level 3** on the standard scale
RTA section 77	Obstructing examiner testing condition of used vehicles at sale rooms, etc	Summarily	**Level 3** on the standard scale
RTA section 78	Failing to comply with requirement about weighing motor vehicle or obstructing authorised person[1]	Summarily	**Level 5** on the standard scale
RTA section 81	Selling, etc, pedal cycle in contravention of regulations as to brakes, bells, etc	Summarily	**Level 3** on the standard scale
RTA section 83	Selling, etc, wrongly made tail lamps or reflectors	Summarily	**Level 5** on the standard scale
RTA section 87(1)	Driving otherwise than in accordance with a licence[1]	Summarily	**Level 3** on the standard scale
RTA section 87(2)	Causing or permitting a person to drive otherwise than in accordance with a licence[1]	Summarily	**Level 3** on the standard scale
RTA section 92(7C)	Failure to deliver licence revoked by virtue of section 92(7A) and counterpart to Secretary of State	Summarily	**Level 3** on the standard scale
RTA section 92(10)	Driving after making false declaration as to physical fitness[1]	Summarily	**Level 4** on the standard scale
RTA section 93(3)	Failure to deliver revoked licence and counterpart to Secretary of State	Summarily	**Level 3** on the standard scale
RTA section 94(3) and that subsection as applied by RTA section 99D or 109C	Failure to notify Secretary of State of onset of, or deterioration in, relevant or prospective disability[1]	Summarily	**Level 3** on the standard scale
RTA section 94(3A) and that subsection as applied by RTA section 99D(b) 109C(c)	Driving after such a failure[1]	Summarily	**Level 3** on the standard scale

(5) Disqualification	(6) Endorsement	(7) Penalty points
Discretionary² in a case where the offender's driving would not have been in accordance with any licence that could have been granted to him	Obligatory² in the case mentioned in column 5	3–6
Discretionary²	Obligatory²	3–6
Discretionary²	Obligatory²	3–6

SCHEDULE 2—*continued*

(1) Provision creating offence	(2) General nature of offence	(3) Mode of prosecution	(4) Punishment
Offences under the Road Traffic Act 1988—continued			
RTA section 94A	Driving after refusal of licence under section 92(3), revocation under section 93 or service of a notice under section 99C[1]	Summarily	**6 months** or **level 5** on the standard scale or both
RTA section 96	Driving with uncorrected defective eyesight sight, or refusing to submit to test of eyesight	Summarily	**Level 3** on the standard scale
RTA section 99(5)	Driving licence holder failing to surrender licence and counterpart[1]	Summarily	**Level 3** on the standard scale
RTA section 99B(11) and that subsection as applied by RTA section 109A(5)	Driving after failure to comply with a requirement under section 99B(6), (7) or (10)[1] or a requirement under section 99B(6) or (7) as applied by section 109A(5)	Summarily	**Level 3** on the standard scale
RTA section 99C(4)	Failure to deliver Community licence to Secretary of State when required by notice under section 99C	Summarily	**Level 3** on the standard scale
RTA section 103(1)(a)	Obtaining driving licence while disqualified[1]	Summarily	**Level 3** on the standard scale
RTA 103(1)(b)	Driving while disqualified[1]	(a) Summarily, in England and Wales (b) Summarily, in Scotland (c) On indictment, in Scotland	(a) **6 months** or **level 5** on the standard scale or both (b) **6 months** or the **statutory maximum** or both (c) **12 months** or a fine or both
Repealed RTA section 114	Failing to comply with conditions of LGV PCV licence or LGV Community licence, or causing or permitting person under 21 to drive LGV or PCV in contravention of such conditions[1]	Summarily	**Level 3** on the standard scale
RTA section 115A(4)	Failure to deliver LGV or PCV Community licence when required by notice under section 115A	Summarily	**Level 3** on the standard scale
RTA section 118	Failing to surrender revoked or suspended LGV or PCV licence and counterpart	Summarily	**Level 3** on the standard scale
Regulations made by virtue of RTA section 120(5)	Contravention of provision of regulations (which is declared by regulations to be an offence) about LGV or PCV driver's licences [or LGV or PCV Community licence	Summarily	**Level 3** on the standard scale
RTA section 123(4)	Giving of paid driving instruction by unregistered and unlicensed persons or their employers	Summarily	**Level 4** on the standard scale
RTA section 123(6)	Giving of paid instruction without there being exhibited on the motor car a certificate of registration or a licence under RTA Part V	Summarily	**Level 3** on the standard scale
RTA section 125A(4)	Failure, on application for registration as disabled driving instructor, to notify Registrar of onset of, or deterioration in, relevant or prospective disability	Summarily	**Level 3** on the standard scale

(5) Disqualification	(6) Endorsement	(7) Penalty points
Discretionary²	Obligatory²	3–6
Discretionary²	Obligatory²	3
Discretionary²	Obligatory²	6

SCHEDULE 2—*continued*

(1) Provision creating offence	(2) General nature of offence	(3) Mode of prosecution	(4) Punishment
*Offences under the Road Traffic Act 1988—continued*			
RTA section 133C(4)	Failure by registered or licensed disabled driving instructor to notify Registrar of onset of, or deterioration in, relevant or prospective disability	Summarily	**Level 3** on the standard scale
RTA section 133D	Giving of paid driving instruction by disabled persons or their employers without emergency control certificate or in unauthorised motor car	Summarily	**Level 3** on the standard scale
RTA section 135	Unregistered instructor using title or displaying badge, etc, prescribed for registered instructor, or employer using such title, etc, in relation to his unregistered instructor or issuing misleading advertisement, etc	Summarily	**Level 4** on the standard scale
RTA section 136	Failure of instructor to surrender to Registrar certificate or licence	Summarily	**Level 3** on the standard scale
RTA section 137	Failing to produce certificate of registration or licence as driving instructor	Summarily	**Level 3** on the standard scale
RTA section 143	Using motor vehicle while uninsured or unsecured or against third party risks[1]	Summarily	**Level 5** on the standard scale
RTA section 147	Failing to surrender certificate of insurance or security to insurer on cancellation or to make statutory declaration of loss or destruction	Summarily	**Level 3** on the standard scale
RTA section 154	Failing to give information, or wilfully making a false statement, as to insurance or security when claim made	Summarily	**Level 4** on the standard scale
RTA section 163	Failing to stop motor vehicle or cycle when required by constable[1]	Summarily	**Level 3** on the standard scale
RTA section 164	Failing to produce driving licence or counterpart etc or to state date of birth, or failing to provide the Secretary of State with evidence of date of birth, etc[1]	Summarily	**Level 3** on the standard scale
RTA section 165	Failing to give certain names and addresses or to produce certain documents[1]	Summarily	**Level 3** on the standard scale
RTA section 168	Refusing to give, or giving false, name and address in case of reckless, careless or inconsiderate driving or cycling[1]	Summarily	**Level 3** on the standard scale
RTA section 169	Pedestrian failing to give constable his name and address after failing to stop when directed by constable controlling traffic	Summarily	**Level 1** on the standard scale
RTA section 170(4)	Failing to stop after accident and give particulars or report accident[1]	Summarily	**Six months** or **level 5** on the standard scale or both

(5) Disqualification	(6) Endorsement	(7) Penalty points
Discretionary[2]	Obligatory	6–8
Discretionary[2]	Obligatory[2]	5–10

SCHEDULE 2—*continued*

(1) Provision creating offence	(2) General nature of offence	(3) Mode of prosecution	(4) Punishment
Offences under the Road Traffic Act 1988—continued			
RTA section 170(7)	Failure by driver, in case of accident involving injury to another, to produce evidence of insurance or security or to report accident[1]	Summarily	**Level 3** on the standard scale
RTA section 171	Failure by owner of motor vehicle to give police information for verifying compliance with requirement of compulsory insurance or security[1]	Summarily	**Level 4** on the standard scale
RTA section 172	Failure of person keeping vehicle and others to give police information as to identity of driver, etc, in the case of certain offences	Summarily	**Level 3** on the standard scale
RTA section 173	Forgery etc, of licences, counterparts of Community licences, test certificates, certificates of insurance and other documents and things	(*a*) Summarily[4]	(*a*) **The statutory maximum**
		(*b*) On indictment	(*b*) 2 years
RTA section 174	Making certain false statements, etc, and withholding certain material information[1]	(*a* Summarily***	(*a*) 6 months or the statutory maximum or both***
		(*b*) On indictment	(*b*) 2 years or a fine or both***
RTA section 175(1)***	Issuing false documents[1]	Summarily	**Level 4** on the standard scale
RTA section 175(2)	Falsely amending certificate of conformity	Summarily	**Level 4** on the standard scale***
RTA section 177	Impersonation of, or of person employed by, authorised examiner	Summarily	**Level 3** on the standard scale
RTA section 178	Taking, etc, in Scotland a motor vehicle without authority or, knowing that it has been so taken, driving it or allowing oneself to be carried in it without authority	(*a*) Summarily	(*a*) **3 months** or the **statutory maximum** or both
		(*b*) On indictment	(*b*) **12 months** or a fine or both
RTA section 180	Failing to attend, give evidence or produce documents to, inquiry held by Secretary of State, etc	Summarily	**Level 3** on the standard scale
RTA section 181	Obstructing inspection of vehicles after accident	Summarily	**Level 3** on the standard scale
RTA Schedule 1 paragraph 6	Applying warranty to equipment, protective helmet, appliance or information in defending proceedings under RTA section 15A, 17 or 18(4) where no warranty given, or applying false warranty	Summarily	**Level 3** on the standard scale
Offences under this Act			
Section 25 of this Act	Failing to give information as to date of birth or sex to court or to provide Secretary of State with evidence of date of birth, etc	Summarily	**Level 3** on the standard scale
Section 26 of this Act	Failing to produce driving licence and counterpart to court making order for interim disqualification.	Summarily	**Level 3** on the standard scale

(5) Disqualification	(6) Endorsement	(7) Penalty points
Discretionary, if committed otherwise than by virtue of subsection (5) or (11)	Obligatory, if committed otherwise than by virtue of subsection (5) or (11)	3
Discretionary		

SCHEDULE 2—*continued*

(1) Provision creating offence	(2) General nature of offence	(3) Mode of prosecution	(4) Punishment
Offences under the Road Traffic Act 1988			
Section 27 of this Act	Failing to produce licence and counterpart to court for endorsement on conviction of offence involving obligatory endorsement or on committal for sentence, etc, for offence involving obligatory or discretionary disqualification when no interim disqualification ordered	Summarily	**Level 3** on the standard scale
Section 62 of this Act	Removing fixed penalty notice fixed to vehicle	Summarily	**Level 2** on the standard scale
Section 67 of this Act	False statement in response to notice to owner	Summarily	**Level 5** on the standard scale

(5) Disqualification	(6) Endorsement	(7) Penalty points

SCHEDULE 2—*continued*

PART II
OTHER OFFENCES

(1) Offence
Manslaughter or, in Scotland, culpable homicide by the driver of a motor vehicle
An offence under section 12A of the Theft Act 1968 (aggravated vehicle-taking)
Stealing or attempting to steal a motor vehicle
An offence or attempt to commit an offence in respect of a motor vehicle under section 12 of the Theft Act 1968 (taking conveyance without consent of owner etc or, knowing it has been so taken, driving it or allowing oneself to be carried in it)
An offence under section 25 of the Theft Act 1968 (going equipped for stealing, etc) committed with reference to the theft or taking of motor vehicles

(2) Disqualification	(3) Endorsement	(4) Penalty points
Obligatory	Obligatory	3–11
Obligatory	Obligatory	3–11
Discretionary		
Discretionary		
Discretionary		

*Reproduced as in force in England.
**Amended by the Criminal Justice Act 2003, Sch 26, from a date to be appointed.
***Reproduced as amended and inserted respectively by the Transport Act 1982, s 24, from a date to be appointed.

1. Schedule 1, ante applies one or more provisions of the Act to offences under this section; reference should be made to see which apply. Section 1 precludes conviction unless there has been a warning at the time of the offence, or service of a summons or notice of intended prosecution within 14 days of it (but note the saving for alternative verdicts in ss 2 and 24, ante); s 6 enables summary proceedings within 6 months of sufficient evidence coming to the prosecutor's knowledge, his certificate is conclusive (but note overall limit of three years); s 11 enables evidence by certificate as to driver, user or owner; s 12(1) enables the identity of an accused driver to be established by his written statement.

2. See s 34 ante for provisions as to obligatory and discretionary disqualification, with notes thereon as to use of disqualification and special reasons for not disqualifying. Disqualification for repeated offences is provided by s 35, ante. See s 44, ante for provisions as to obligatory endorsement. A list of the endorseable offence codes which appear on United Kingdom driving licences is printed immediately before statutory instruments in this PART, post. A court not ordering disqualification or endorsement, or ordering it for a shorter period than would otherwise be required, must state its grounds in open court and have them entered in the register (s 47 ante). For disqualification pending a driving test see s 36, ante. For requirement to produce a driving licence to the court see ss 7 and 27, ante.

3. Regulation 7(2) of the Motorways Traffic (England and Wales) Regulations 1982 in this PART, post, creates a permission whereby in circumstances of necessity a vehicle may stop and remain at rest on a hard shoulder; therefore if a vehicle unlawfully stops on the hard shoulder contrary to reg 9, the exemption from discretionary disqualification would seem to apply whereas if the vehicle stops on the carriageway contrary to reg 7(1) the offence would appear to attract discretionary disqualification and obligatory endorsement; see *Mawson v Oxford* [1987] RTR 398, [1987] Crim LR 131.

4. For procedure in respect of an offence triable either way, see the Magistrates' Courts Act 1980, ss 17A–21 in PART I: MAGISTRATES' COURTS, COURTS, PROCEDURE, ante.

5. When a person convicted under ss 4(1), 5(1)(*a*) or 7(6) has within the 10 years immediately preceding the commission of the offence been convicted of any such offence, the minimum period of disqualification is 3 years (s 34(3), ante).

6. If the defendant is not prepared to accept that para (*a*) applies, the court must satisfy itself on hearing evidence from the prosecution that the heavier penalties apply, to which the defendant can call evidence in rebuttal: *R v Waltham Forest Justices, ex p Barton* [1990] RTR 49, DC.

7. Disqualification is limited to those signs specified by reg 10 of the Traffic Signs and General Directions 2002 in this PART, post.

8. "Load" can include a sheepdog sitting on a driver's lap (*Simpson v Vant* [1986] RTR 247).

9. In *Kenyon v Thorley* [1973] Crim LR 119 it was held that para 19(*b*) of Part II of Sch 1 to the Road Traffic Act 1962 referred to a breach in regard to the condition of brakes and *not* to a breach concerned with a failure to apply brakes under (what is now) reg 107 of the Construction and Use Regulations 1986. Although the wording in columns 4 and 5 of this Schedule relating to s 40(5) of the 1972 Act, which has been consolidated into s 42 of this Act, was not identical to that in para 19 of Sch 1 to the 1962 Act, it would appear that its effect is the same so that the offence of failing to set a brake effectually under reg 107 of the 1986 regulations does *not* carry endorsement or disqualification nor, in the case of goods vehicles, the higher penalty.

10. Offences under ss 1, 2, 4(1), 5(1)(*a*), 12 and (in stipulated circumstances) s 7(6) carry notional penalty points which are ordered only if special reasons are found for not imposing the obligatory disqualification which those offences carry, and which may thus be aggregated with other penalty points so as to result in disqualification for repeated offences. If the offence consists in aiding, abetting, counselling or procuring, or inciting to the commission of one of those offences, this does not carry obligatory disqualifications as such under Sch 2 but will attract 10 penalty points instead (see s 28(2) and s 34(5)).

4–1770

Section 51   SCHEDULE 3
              FIXED PENALTY OFFENCES

(*Amended by the Road Traffic (Consequential Provisions) Act 1988, Sch 2, the Parking Act 1989, Sch, SI 1990/335, the New Roads and Street Works Act 1991, Sch 9, the Road Traffic Act 1991, Schs 4 and 8, SI 1992/345, the Finance Act 1997, Sch 3, SI 1999/1851, the Countryside and Rights of Way Act 2000, Sch 7, SI 2003/1253, SI 2004/2922, the Traffic Management Act 2004, Sch 12, the Serious Organised Crime and Police Act 2005, s 150 and the Road Safety Act 2006, s 26.)*

(1) Provision creating offence	(2) General nature of offence
Offence under the Greater London Council (General Powers) Act 1974 (c xxiv)	
Section 15 of the Greater London Council (General Powers) Act 1974.	Parking vehicles on footways, verges, etc.
Offence under the Highways Act 1980 (c 60)	
Section 137 of the Highways Act 1980.	Obstructing a highway, but only where the offence is committed in respect of a vehicle.
Offences under the Road Traffic Regulation Act 1984 (c 27)	
RTRA section 5(1)	Using a vehicle in contravention of a traffic regulation order outside Greater London.
RTRA section 8(1)	Breach of traffic regulation order in Greater London.
RTRA section 11	Breach of experimental traffic order.
RTRA section 13	Breach of experimental traffic scheme regulations in Greater London.
RTRA section 16(1)	Using a vehicle in contravention of temporary prohibition or restriction of traffic in case of execution of works, etc.
RTRA section 17(4)	Wrongful use of special road.
RTRA section 18(3)	Using a vehicle in contravention of provision for one-way traffic on trunk road.
RTRA section 20(5)	Driving a vehicle in contravention of order prohibiting or restricting driving vehicles on certain classes of roads.

(1) Provision creating offence	(2) General nature of offence
RTRA section 25(5)	Breach of pedestrian crossing regulations, except an offence in respect of a moving motor vehicle [other than a contravention of regulations 23, 24, 25 and 26 of the Zebra, Pelican and Puffin Pedestrian Crossings Regulations and General Directions 1997.
RTRA section 29(3)	Using a vehicle in contravention of a street playground order.
RTRA section 35A(1)	Breach of an order regulating the use, etc, of a parking place provided by a local authority, but only where the offence is committed in relation to a parking place provided on a road.
RTRA section 47(1)	Breach of a provision of a parking place designation order and other offences committed in relation to a parking place designated by such an order, except any offence of failing to pay an excess charge within the meaning of section 46.
RTRA section 53(5)	Using vehicle in contravention of any provision of a parking place designation order having effect by virtue of section 53(1)(*a*) (inclusion of certain traffic regulation provisions).
RTRA section 53(6)	Breach of a provision of a parking place designation order having effect by virtue of section 53(1)(*b*) (use of any part of a road for parking without charge).
RTRA section 88(7)	Driving a motor vehicle in contravention of an order imposing a minimum speed limit under section 88(1)(*b*)
RTRA section 89(1)	Speeding offences under RTRA and other Acts.

Offences under the Road Traffic Act 1988 (c 52)

RTA section 14	Breach of regulations requiring wearing of seat belts.
RTA section 15(2)	Breach of restriction on carrying children in the front of vehicles.
RTA section 15(4)	Breach of restriction on carrying children in the rear of vehicles.
RTA section 16	Breach of regulations relating to protective headgear for motor cycle drivers and passengers.
RTA section 18(3)	Breach of regulations relating to head-worn appliances (eye protectors) for use on motor cycles
RTA section 19	Parking a heavy commercial vehicle on verge or footway.
RTA section 22	Leaving vehicle in dangerous position.
RTA section 23	Unlawful carrying of passengers on motor cycles.
RTA section 24	Carrying more than one person on a pedal cycle.
RTA section 34	Driving mechanically propelled vehicle elsewhere than on a road.
RTA section 35	Failure to comply with traffic directions.
RTA section 36	Failure to comply with traffic signs.
RTA section 40A	Using vehicle in dangerous condition etc.
RTA section 41A	Breach of requirement as to brakes, steering-gear or tyres.
RTA section 41B	Breach of requirement as to weight: goods and passenger vehicles.
RTA section 41D	Breach of requirement as to control of vehicle, mobile telephone etc.
RTA section 42	Breach of other construction and use requirements.
RTA section 47	Using, etc, vehicle without required test certificate being in force
RTA section 87(1)	Driving vehicle otherwise than in accordance with requisite licence.
RTA section 143	Using motor vehicle while uninsured or unsecured against third party risks
RTA section 163	Failure to stop vehicle on being so required*
RTA section 172	Failure of person keeping vehicle and others to give the police information as to identity of driver, etc, in the case of certain offences

Offences under the Vehicle Excise and Registration Act 1994 (c 22)

Section 33 of the Vehicle Excise and Registration Act 1994	Using or keeping a vehicle on a public road without vehicle licence, trade licence or nil licence being exhibited in manner prescribed by regulations.
Section 42 of that Act	Driving or keeping a vehicle without required registration mark.
Section 43 of that Act	Driving or keeping a vehicle with registration mark obscured etc.
Section 43C of that Act	Using an incorrectly registered vehicle.
Section 59 of that Act	Failure to fix prescribed registration mark to a vehicle in accordance with regulations made under section 23(4)(*a*) of that Act.

(1) Provision creating offence	(2) General nature of offence
Offences under the Highways Act 1835 and the Roads (Scotland) Act 1984	
Section 72 of the Highways Act 1835	Driving on the footway. Cycling on the footway.
Section 129(5) of the Roads (Scotland) Act 1984	Driving on the footway.

*Reproduced as in force in England.

Section 68

SCHEDULE 4
STATUTORY STATEMENTS

PART I
STATUTORY STATEMENT OF OWNERSHIP OR HIRING

4–1771 **1.** (1) For the purposes of Part III of this Act, a statutory statement of ownership is a statement on an official form signed by the person providing it and stating whether he was the owner of the vehicle at the time of the alleged offence and, if he was not the owner of the vehicle at that time, whether—

    (*a*) he was never the owner, or
    (*b*) he ceased to be the owner before, or became the owner after, that time,

and in a case within paragraph (*b*) above, stating, if the information is in his possession, the name and address of the person to whom, and the date on which, he disposed of the vehicle or (as the case may be) the name and address of the person from whom, and the date on which, he acquired it.

    (2) An official form for a statutory statement of ownership shall—

    (*a*) indicate that the person providing the statement in response to a notice to owner relating to an offence may give notice requesting a hearing in respect of the offence in the manner specified in the form, and
    (*b*) direct the attention of any person proposing to complete the form to the information provided in accordance with paragraph 3(3) below in any official form for a statutory statement of facts.

2. (1) For the purposes of Part III of this Act, a statutory statement of hiring is a statement on an official form, signed by the person providing it, being a person by whom a statement of liability was signed, and stating—

    (*a*) whether at the time of the alleged offence the vehicle was let to him under the hiring agreement to which the statement of liability refers, and
    (*b*) if it was not, the date on which he returned the vehicle to the possession of the vehicle-hire firm concerned.

    (2) An official form for a statutory statement of hiring shall—

    (*a*) indicate that the person providing the statement in pursuance of a notice relating to an offence served under section 63 of this Act by virtue of section 66 of this Act may give notice requesting a hearing in respect of the offence in the manner specified in the form, and
    (*b*) direct the attention of any person proposing to complete the form to the information provided in accordance with paragraph 3(3) below in any official form for a statutory statement of facts.

    (3) In sub-paragraph (1) above "statement of liability", "hiring agreement" and "vehicle-hire firm" have the same meaning as in section 66 of this Act.

PART II
STATUTORY STATEMENT OF FACTS

3. (1) For the purposes of Part III of this Act, a statutory statement of facts is a statement on an official form, signed by the person providing it, which—

    (*a*) states that the person providing it was not the driver of the vehicle at the time of the alleged offence, and
    (*b*) states the name and address at the time when the statement is provided of the person who was the driver of the vehicle at the time of the alleged offence.

    (2) A statutory statement of facts has effect as a notice given by the driver requesting a hearing in respect of the offence if it is signed by the person identified in the statement as the driver of the vehicle at the time of the alleged offence.

    (3) An official form for a statutory statement of facts shall indicate—

    (*a*) that if a person identified in the statement as the driver of the vehicle at the time of the alleged offence signs the statement he will be regarded as having given notice requesting a hearing in respect of the offence,
    (*b*) that the person on whom the notice to owner relating to the offence is served may not give notice requesting a hearing in respect of the offence on his own account if he provides a statutory statement of facts signed by a person so identified, and
    (*c*) that if the fixed penalty is not paid before the end of the period stated in the notice to owner as the period for response to the notice, a sum determined by reference to that fixed penalty may be registered without any court hearing for enforcement as a fine against the person on whom the notice to owner is served, unless he has given notice requesting a hearing in respect of the offence,

but that, in a case within paragraph (*c*) above, the sum in question may not be so registered if the person on whom the notice to owner is served provides a statutory statement of facts as mentioned in paragraph (*b*) above until two months have elapsed from the end of the period so stated without service of a summons or, in Scotland, complaint in respect of the offence on the person identified in that statement as the driver of the vehicle.

Road Traffic (Consequential Provisions) Act 1988
(1988 c 54)

4–1872   1. Meaning of "the Road Traffic Acts", "the repealed enactments", etc.   (1) In this Act—

"the Road Traffic Acts" means the Road Traffic Act 1988, the Road Traffic Offenders Act 1988 and, so far as it reproduces the effect of the repealed enactments, this Act, and

"the repealed enactments" means the enactments repealed or revoked by this Act.

(2) Expressions used in this Act and in the Road Traffic Act 1988 have the same meaning as in that Act.

[Road Traffic (Consequential Provisions) Act 1988, s 1.]

4–1873   2. Continuity, and construction of references to old and new law.   (1) The substitution of the Road Traffic Acts for the repealed enactments does not affect the continuity of the law.

(2) Anything done or having effect as if done under or for the purposes of a provision of the repealed enactments has effect, if it could have been done under or for the purposes of the corresponding provision of the Road Traffic Acts, as if done under or for the purposes of that corresponding provision.

(3) Any reference, whether express or implied, in the Road Traffic Acts or any other enactment, instrument or document to a provision of the Road Traffic Acts is to be read, in relation to the times, circumstances or purposes in relation to which the corresponding provision of the repealed enactments had effect and so far as the nature of the reference permits, as including a reference to that corresponding provision.

[Road Traffic (Consequential Provisions) Act 1988, s 2.]

4–1874   3, 4.   Repeals, prospective and consequential amendments (Schs 1–3 also).

4–1875   5.   Transitional provisions and savings, Sch 4.

4–1876   7. Saving for law of nuisance.   Nothing in the Road Traffic Acts authorises a person to use on a road a vehicle so constructed or used as to cause a public or private nuisance, or in Scotland a nuisance, or affects the liability, whether under statute or common law, of the driver or owner so using such a vehicle.

[Road Traffic (Consequential Provisions) Act 1988, s 7.]

4–1877   8. Short title, commencement and extent.   (1) Short title.

(2) This Act, except those provisions that may be brought into force in accordance with subsection (3) below, shall come into force at the end of the period of three months beginning with the day on which it is passed.

(3) Paragraphs 15 to 20 of Schedule 2 to this Act shall come into force on such day as the Secretary of State may by order made by statutory instrument appoint, and different days may be so appointed for different provisions and for different purposes.

(4) Transition.

(5) Extent.

[Road Traffic (Consequential Provisions) Act 1988, s 8 amended by the Road Traffic Act 1991, Sch 4.]

4–1878

Section 4   SCHEDULE 2
RE-ENACTMENT OR AMENDMENT OF CERTAIN ENACTMENTS NOT BROUGHT INTO FORCE

Repealed.

Section 5   SCHEDULE 4
TRANSITIONAL PROVISIONS AND SAVINGS
General rules for old savings and transitional provisions

4–1879   1.   (1) The repeal by this Act of an enactment previously repealed subject to savings does not affect the continued operation of those savings.

(2) The repeal by this Act of a saving made on the previous repeal of an enactment does not affect the operation of the saving in so far as it is not specially reproduced in the Road Traffic Acts but remains capable of having effect.

(3) Where the purpose of a repealed enactment was to secure that the substitution of the provisions of the Act containing that enactment for provisions repealed by that Act did not affect the continuity of the law, the repealed enactment, so far as it is not specifically reproduced in the Road Traffic Acts, shall continue to have effect, so far as it is capable of doing so, for the purposes of the Road Traffic Acts.

Old Offences

2. The Road Traffic Acts (including this Act so far as not included in that expression) do not affect the operation of the repealed enactments in relation to offences committed before the commencement of those Acts or to appeals against or suspension of disqualification by virtue of convictions for offences so committed or against orders made in consequence of such convictions.

Road Traffic Act 1974 (c 3)

3. (1) Any provision contained in an enactment passed or instrument made before 31 July 1974 which was not repealed by the Road Traffic Act 1974 and in which any expression was given the same meaning as in, or was otherwise to be construed by reference to, any provision of sections 68 to 82 of the Road Traffic Act 1972 which was repealed by that Act shall continue to be construed as if that provision had not been so repealed.

(2) The Secretary of State may by regulations made by statutory instrument make such amendments as he considers appropriate to take account of section 9 of the Road Traffic Act 1974—

(a) in any enactment passed or instrument made before 31 July 1974 which refers (whether directly or by virtue of the Interpretation Act 1978 or otherwise) to any provision of sections 68 to 82 of the Road Traffic Act 1972 which was repealed by the Road Traffic Act 1974,

(b) in the reference in paragraph 4 of Schedule 4 to the Road Traffic Act 1988 to section 83 of that Act, and

(c) in the definition of "hours of darkness" in paragraph 2(2)(a) of Schedule 12 to the Road Traffic Regulation Act 1984.

(3) A statutory instrument containing regulations under sub-paragraph (2) above shall be subject to annulment in pursuance of a resolution of either House of Parliament.

Road Traffic (Drivers' Ages and Hours of Work) Act 1976 (c 3)

4. (1) Subject to sub-paragraph (2) below, a person who, immediately before 1st January 1976, fulfilled any of the conditions in paragraph 2(1) of Schedule 2 to the Road Traffic (Drivers' Ages and Hours of Work) Act 1976 shall not, by reason only of the provisions of section 101 of the Road Traffic Act 1988, be disqualified for holding or obtaining a licence authorising him to drive motor vehicles falling within the class described in paragraph 5 or 6 of the Table set out in section 101(1) of that Act.

(2) A person shall not be treated, by virtue of sub-paragraph (1) above, as entitled to the grant of a licence authorising him to drive a goods vehicle the permissible maximum weight of which exceeds 10 tonnes or a motor vehicle constructed solely for the carriage of passengers and their effects which is adapted to carry more than fifteen passengers inclusive of the driver.

Road Traffic Regulation Act 1984 (c 27)

5. (1) Notwithstanding the repeal by this Act of the provisions of section 98 of and Schedule 7 to the Road Traffic Regulation Act 1984 (prosecution of offences), those provisions shall, in relation to the interim period (within the meaning of Schedule 12 to that Act), continue to have effect in relation to offences under Schedule 12 to that Act.

(2) To the extent that section 135 of that Act (application to Isles of Scilly) applied to the repealed enactments, it shall continue to apply to the corresponding provisions of the Road Traffic Acts.

Payments for traffic casualties

6. Where an accident giving rise to death or bodily injury in respect of which a payment is made under section 157 of the Road Traffic Act 1988, or claimed under section 158 of that Act, occurred before 1st April 1987, the amount payable shall not exceed the amount that would have been payable under the corresponding repealed enactment.

Licences, disqualification and endorsement

7. (1) For the purposes of section 92(4)(a) of the Road Traffic Act 1988, a person to whom a licence was granted after the making of a declaration under paragraph (c) of the proviso to section 5(2) of the Road Traffic Act 1930 (which contained transitional provisions with respect to certain disabilities) shall be treated as having passed, at the time of the declaration, a relevant test in respect of vehicles of the classes to which the licence related.

(2) The references in sections 125(3)(d), 127(3)(d), 128(2)(b) and 130(2)(b) of the Road Traffic Act 1988 to section 34 or 36 of the Road Traffic Offenders Act 1988 and to Part III of the Road Traffic Act 1988 include a reference—

(a) to section 93 of the Road Traffic Act 1972 and to Part III of that Act, and

(b) to section 5 of the Road Traffic Act 1962 and Part II of the Road Traffic Act 1960 (but not to section 104 of the 1960 Act).

(3) For the purposes of section 29 of the Road Traffic Offenders Act 1988, an order for endorsement which was made before the commencement of section 19 of the Transport Act 1981 counts as an order made in pursuance of section 44 of the Road Traffic Offenders Act 1988 for the endorsement of three penalty points, unless a disqualification was imposed on the offender on that or any subsequent occasion.

(4) For the purposes of section 2 of this Act as it has effect for the purposes of section 34(3) of the Road Traffic Offenders Act 1988—

(a) a previous conviction of an offence under section 6(1) of the Road Traffic Act 1972, as it had effect immediately before the substitution of a new section 6(1) by the Transport Act 1981, shall be treated as a conviction of an offence under section 5(1)(a) of the Road Traffic Act 1988, and

(b) a previous conviction of an offence under section 9(3) of the 1972 Act, as it had effect immediately before the substitution of a new section 8(7) by the 1981 Act, shall be treated as a conviction of an offence under section 7(6) of the Road Traffic Act 1988.

(5) The references in sections 36(4), 37(3) and 42(6) of the Road Traffic Offenders Act 1988 to an order under subsection (1) of section 36 include a reference to an order under section 93(7) of the Road Traffic Act 1972, section 5(7) of the Road Traffic Act 1962 or section 104(3) of the Road Traffic Act 1960.

(6) Where, in pursuance of section 93(5) of the Road Traffic Act 1972, a period of disqualification was imposed on an offender in addition to any other period or periods then, for the purpose of determining whether an application may be made under section 42 of the Road Traffic Offenders Act 1988 for the removal of either or any of the disqualifications the periods shall be treated as one continuous period of disqualification.

Hovercraft

8. For the purposes of the Hovercraft Act 1968 (under which enactments and instruments relating, amongst other things, to motor vehicles may, if passed before the commencement of that Act, be applied to hovercraft) any enactment contained in the Road Traffic Acts, being an enactment or instrument derived from an enactment so passed, and any instrument made or having effect as if made under such an enactment, shall be treated as included among the enactments and instruments which can be so applied.

Road Traffic (Driver Licensing and Information Systems) Act 1989[1]
(1989 c 22)

PART I
DRIVING LICENCES

PART II
DRIVER INFORMATION SYSTEMS
Preliminary

4–1891   8. Definitions of driver information systems etc.   (1) The following provisions shall have effect for the interpretation of this Part of this Act.

(2) Subject to subsection (7) below, "driver information" is information (including guidance and warnings) of use to the drivers of motor vehicles relating to routes for or the position of their vehicles or traffic conditions and "route guidance" is to be construed accordingly.

(3) A "driver information system" is—

(a) a system for the collection, storage and processing of data from which driver information is derived, or

(b) a system for the transmission of data from which driver information is derived, by means of apparatus situated otherwise than in motor vehicles to motor vehicles equipped to receive the transmissions, or

(c) a system for both of the above;

but data is not "collected" unless it is collected from motor vehicles whether or not also from other sources.

(4) A person "operates" a driver information system if (otherwise than as an employee)—

(a) he collects, stores and processes data from which driver information is derived, or

(b) he transmits such data to motor vehicles;

and he operates a driver information system "in relation to" public roads if he collects data from or, as the case may be, transmits data to, motor vehicles on public roads; and related expressions shall be construed accordingly.

(5) "Data" means information recorded in a form in which it can be processed by equipment operating automatically in response to instructions given for that purpose.

(6) The "system apparatus", in relation to a driver information system, is the apparatus by means of which the system is operated.

(7) The Secretary of State may by order prescribe descriptions of information which is not to be driver information for the purposes of any provision of this Part of this Act.

(8) In this Part of this Act—

(a) "highway authority" is used with reference to England and Wales and has the same meaning as in the Highways Act 1980;

(b) "roads authority" is used with reference to Scotland and has the same meaning as in the Roads (Scotland) Act 1984; and

(c) "public road" means, with reference to England and Wales, a highway maintainable at the public expense within the meaning of the Highways Act 1980, and, (*Scotland*).

[Road Traffic (Driver Licensing and Information Systems) Act 1989, s 8.]

Licensing for driver information systems

4–1892   9. Requirement for licence to operate driver information system.   (1) Except as provided under subsection (2) below, no person shall operate a driver information system in relation to public roads in England or Wales or Scotland unless he is authorised to do so by a licence granted to him by the Secretary of State.

(2) The Secretary of State may, by order[1], direct that this Part of this Act shall not apply to any description of driver information system specified in the order; and the description of a system may be framed by reference to any of its characteristics, its effects or any other circumstances.

(3) The holding by a person of a licence under this section shall not relieve him of—

(a) any liability in respect of a failure to hold a licence under section 1 of the Wireless Telegraphy Act 1949; or

(b) any obligation to comply with requirements imposed by or under Chapter 1 of Part 2 of the Communications Act 2003 (electronic communications networks and electronic communications services).

(4) Any person who operates a driver information system in contravention of this section commits an offence.

(5) A person guilty of an offence under this section shall be liable[2]—

(a) on summary conviction, to a fine not exceeding the **statutory maximum**; and

(b) on conviction on indictment, to a fine.

[Road Traffic (Driver Licensing and Information Systems) Act 1989, s 9 as amended by the Communications Act 2003, Sch 17.]

1. See the Driver Information Systems (Exemption) Order 1990, SI 1990/865.
2. For procedure in respect of an offence triable either way, see the Magistrates' Courts Act 1980, ss 17A–21 in PART I: MAGISTRATES' COURTS, PROCEDURE, ante.

4–1893   11. Sanctions for operating outside licence area or for breach of licence conditions.
(1)–(4) *Secretary of State may revoke or suspend licence for operating outside area or for breach of conditions.*

(5) Subject to subsection (6) below, if a condition attached to an operator's licence is broken, the holder of the licence commits an offence.

(6) It shall be a defence for a person charged with an offence under subsection (5) above to prove that he took all reasonable precautions and exercised all due diligence to avoid a breach of that condition.

(7) A person guilty of an offence under subsection (5) above shall be liable on summary conviction to a fine not exceeding **level 5** on the standard scale.
[Road Traffic (Driver Licensing and Information Systems) Act 1989, s 11.]

4–1894   14. Offences by officers of bodies corporate.   (1) Where a body corporate is guilty of an offence under any provision of this Part of this Act and that offence is proved to have been committed with the consent or connivance of, or to be attributable to any neglect on the part of, a director, manager, secretary or other similar officer of the body corporate or any person who was purporting to act in any such capacity, he as well as the body corporate shall be guilty of that offence and shall be liable to be proceeded against and punished accordingly.

(2) Where the affairs of a body corporate are managed by its members, subsection (1) shall apply in relation to the acts and defaults of a member in connection with his functions of management as if he were a director of the body corporate.
[Road Traffic (Driver Licensing and Information Systems) Act 1989, s 14.]

Section 13(2)   SCHEDULE 5
DRIVER INFORMATION SYSTEMS: UNDERTAKERS' WORKS

4–1896   This Schedule provides for relevant undertakers such as persons authorised to carry on transport undertakings, telecommunications, gas supply etc to give notice to a licensed operator of a driver information system of proposed works. "Relevant undertaker" and "undertaker's works" are defined by para 8 of the Schedule.

Penalty

4–1897   7. (1) If the relevant undertaker or any of his agents—

(a) executes any works without the notice required by paragraph 2 above having been given, or
(b) fails without reasonable excuse to comply with any reasonable requirement of the operator under this Schedule,

he shall be guilty of an offence.

(2) A person guilty of an offence under this paragraph shall be liable on summary conviction to a fine which—

(a) if the service provided by the operator's system is interrupted by the works or failure, shall not exceed **level 4** on the standard scale; and
(b) if that service is not so interrupted, shall not exceed **level 3** on the standard scale.

Vehicle Excise and Registration Act 1994
(1994 c 22)

PART I
VEHICLE EXCISE DUTY AND LICENCES

Main provisions

4–1910   1. Duty and licences.   (1) A duty of excise ("vehicle excise duty") shall be charged in respect of every mechanically propelled vehicle[1] that—

(a) is registered under this Act (see section 21), or
(b) is not so registered but is used, or kept, on a public road[2] in the United Kingdom.

(1A) Vehicle excise duty shall also be charged in respect of every thing (whether or not it is a vehicle) that has been, but has ceased to be, a mechanically propelled vehicle and—

(a) is registered under this Act, or
(b) is not so registered but is used, or kept, on a public road in the United Kingdom.

(1B) In the following provisions of this Act "vehicle" means—

(a) a mechanically propelled vehicle, or
(b) any thing (whether or not it is a vehicle) that has been, but has ceased to be, a mechanically propelled vehicle.

(1C) Vehicle excise duty charged in respect of a vehicle by subsection (1)(a) or (1A)(a) shall be paid on a licence to be taken out—

(a) by the person in whose name the vehicle is registered under this Act, or
(b) if that person is not the person keeping the vehicle, by either of those persons.

(1D) Vehicle excise duty charged in respect of a vehicle by subsection (1)(*b*) or (1A)(*b*) shall be paid on a licence to be taken out by the person keeping the vehicle.

(2) A licence taken out for a vehicle is in this Act referred to as a "vehicle licence"[1].

[Vehicle Excise and Registration Act 1994, s 1, as amended by the Finance Act 2002, s 19.]

---

1. Prima facie this expression should be given the same meaning as in the Road Traffic Act 1960, see s 253(1) thereof and headnote to this title. For vehicles exempt from duty see s 5 and Sch 2, post.

2. "Public road" means a road repairable at public expense (s 62, post).

4–1911   2. Annual rates of duty.   (1) Vehicle excise duty in respect of a vehicle of any description is chargeable by reference to the annual rate currently applicable to it in accordance with the provisions of Schedule 1 which relate to vehicles of that description.

(2) Subsection (1) applies subject to the following provisions of this section.

(3) Where vehicle excise duty is charged by section 1(1)(*b*) or (1A)(*b*) in respect of the keeping of a vehicle on a road (and not in respect of its use), duty in respect of such keeping is chargeable by reference to the general rate currently specified in paragraph 1(2) of Schedule 1.

(4) Subsections (5) and (6) apply where—

(*a*) vehicle excise duty is charged by section 1(1)(*a*) or (1A)(*a*) in respect of a vehicle, and

(*b*) were the vehicle not registered under this Act, duty would not be charged by section 1(1)(*b*) or (1A)(*b*) in respect of the use of the vehicle on a road.

(5) Where one or more use licences have previously been issued for the vehicle, the duty charged by section 1(1)(*a*) or (1A)(*a*) is chargeable by reference to the annual rate currently applicable to a vehicle of the same description as that of the vehicle on the occasion of the issue of that licence (or the last of those licences).

(6) In any other case, the duty charged by section 1(1)(*a*) or (1A)(*a*) is chargeable by reference to the general rate currently specified in paragraph 1(2) of Schedule 1.

(7) In subsection (5) "use licence" means—

(*a*) a vehicle licence issued for the use of a vehicle, or

(*b*) a vehicle licence that is issued by reason of a vehicle being registered under this Act but which would have been issued for the use of the vehicle if the vehicle had not been registered under this Act.

[Vehicle Excise and Registration Act 1994, s 2 as amended by the Finance Act 1996, s 18 and the Finance Act 2002, s 19.]

4–1912   3. Duration of licences.   (1) A vehicle licence may be taken out for any vehicle for any period of twelve months running from the beginning of the month in which the licence first has effect[1].

(2) Where the annual rate of vehicle excise duty in respect of vehicles of any description exceeds £50, a vehicle licence may be taken out for a vehicle of that description for a period of six months running from the beginning of the month in which the licence first has effect.

(3) The Secretary of State may by order[2] provide that a vehicle licence may be taken out for a vehicle for such period as may be specified in the order.

(4) An order under subsection (3) may specify—

(*a*) a period of a fixed number of months (not exceeding fifteen) running from the beginning of the month in which the licence first has effect,

(*b*) in the case of a licence taken out on the first registration under this Act of a vehicle of such description as may be specified in the order, a period exceeding by such number of days (not exceeding thirty) as may be determined by or under the order the period for which the licence would otherwise have effect by virtue of subsection (1) or (2) or of an order under paragraph (*a*), or

(*c*) in the case of a vehicle of such description (or of such description and used in such circumstances) as may be specified in the order, a period of less than one month.

(5) An order under subsection (3)—

(*a*) may be made so as to apply only to vehicles of specified descriptions, and

(*b*) may make different provision for vehicles of different descriptions or for different circumstances.

(6) The power to make an order under subsection (3) includes power to make transitional provisions and to amend or repeal subsection (1) or (2).

[Vehicle Excise and Registration Act 1994, s 3.]

---

1. There are no "days of grace", but in practice, except for trade licences, 14 days are allowed for payment. As to the production of a certificate of insurance on application for a licence, see the Motor Vehicles (Third Party Risks) Regulations 1972, reg 9, in this PART, post. Where applicable, there must be produced a test certificate issued under s 47 of the Road Traffic Act 1988 or a declaration that the vehicle will not be used except for a purpose or in an area in respect of which it may be used without a certificate (Motor Vehicles (Production of Test Certificates) Regulations 1969, SI 1969/418).

2. See the Vehicle Licences (Duration of First Licences and Rate of Duty) Order 1986, SI 1986/1428, amended by SI 1994/3095.

4–1913   4. Amount of duty.   (1) Where a vehicle licence for a vehicle of any description is taken out for any period of twelve months, vehicle excise duty shall be paid on the licence at the annual rate of duty applicable to vehicles of that description.

(2) Where a vehicle licence for a vehicle of any description is taken out for period of six months, vehicle excise duty shall be paid on the licence at a rate equal to fifty-five per cent of that annual rate.

(3) In determining a rate of duty under subsection (2) any fraction of five pence—

(*a*) if it exceeds two and a half pence, shall be treated as five pence, and

(*b*) otherwise, shall be disregarded.

(4) Where a vehicle licence for a vehicle of any description is taken out for a period specified in an order under section 3(3), vehicle excise duty shall be paid on the licence at such rate as may be specified in the order.

(5) A rate of vehicle excise duty specified in an order under section 3(3) in relation to a licence taken out for a vehicle for a period of—

(*a*) a fixed number of months other than twelve, or

(*b*) less than one month,

shall be such as to bear to the annual rate of duty applicable to the vehicle no less proportion than the period for which the licence is taken out bears to a year.

(6) A rate of vehicle excise duty specified in an order under section 3(3) in relation to a licence taken out for a vehicle for a period of three months or a period of four months shall not exceed for each month of the period ten per cent. of the annual rate of duty applicable to the vehicle.

(7) The power to make an order under section 3(3) includes power to amend or repeal subsection (2) or (3) of this section.

[Vehicle Excise and Registration Act 1994, s 4.]

4–1914   5. Exempt vehicles.   (1) No vehicle excise duty shall be charged in respect of a vehicle if it is an exempt vehicle.

(2) Schedule 2 specifies descriptions of vehicles which are exempt vehicles.

[Vehicle Excise and Registration Act 1994, s 5.]

4–1915   6. Collection etc of duty.   (1) Vehicle excise duty shall be levied by the Secretary of State.

(2) For the purpose of levying vehicle excise duty the Secretary of State and his officers (including any body or person authorised by the Secretary of State to act as his agent for the purposes of this Act) have the same powers, duties and liabilities as the Commissioners of Customs and Excise and their officers have with respect to—

(*a*) duties of excise (other than duties on imported goods),

(*b*) the issue and cancellation of licences on which duties of excise are imposed, and

(*c*) other matters (not being matters relating only to duties on imported goods),

under the enactments relating to duties of excise and excise licences.

(3) The enactments relating to duties of excise, or punishments and penalties in connection with those duties, (other than enactments relating only to duties on imported goods) apply accordingly.

(4) Subsections (2) and (3) have effect subject to the provisions of this Act (including in particular, in the case of subsection (3), subsection (6) of this section and sections 47[1], 48 and 56).

(5) The Secretary of State has with respect to vehicle excise duty and licences under this Act the powers given to the Commissioners of Customs and Excise by the enactments relating to duties of excise and excise licences for the mitigation or remission of any penalty or part of a penalty.

(6) Vehicle excise duty, and any sums received by the Secretary of State by virtue of this Act by way of fees, shall be paid into the Consolidated Fund.

[Vehicle Excise and Registration Act 1994, s 6.]

---

1. Section 47, post, makes provision regarding the time within which summary proceedings may be instituted in respect of offences against ss 29, 34 or 37 of this Act or regulations made thereunder, and regarding the person by whom such proceedings may be taken. Section 48 applies to Scotland and s 56 relates to the application of fines, etc.

Vehicle licences

4–1916   7. Issue of vehicle licences.   (1) Every person applying for a vehicle licence shall—

(*a*) make any such declaration, and

(*b*) furnish any such particulars and any such documentary or other evidence,

(whether or not with respect to the vehicle for which the licence is to be taken out) as may be specified by the Secretary of State.

(2) The declarations, particulars and evidence which may be so specified include, in relation to a person applying for a licence for a goods vehicle or a special vehicle, a declaration as to, particulars of and evidence in relation to, any of the matters specified in subsection (3) as to which the Secretary of State may require information with a view to an alteration in the basis on which vehicle excise duty is chargeable in respect of goods vehicles or, as the case may be, special vehicles.

(3) The matters referred to in subsection (2) are—

(*a*) the construction of the vehicle,

(*b*) the vehicle's revenue weight;

(*ba*) the place where the vehicle has been or is normally kept, and

(*c*) the use to which the vehicle has been or is likely to be put.

(3A) A person applying for a licence shall not be required to make a declaration specified for the purposes of subsection (1) (*a*) if he agrees to comply with such conditions as may be specified in relation to him by the Secretary of State.

(3B) The conditions which may be specified under subsection (3A) include

(*a*) a condition that particulars for the time being specified for the purposes of subsection (1)(*b*) are furnished by being transmitted to the Secretary of State by such electronic means as he may specify; and

(*b*) a condition requiring such payments as may be specified by the Secretary of State to be made to him in respect of—

    (i) steps taken by him for facilitating compliance by any person with any condition falling within paragraph (*a*); and

    (ii) in such circumstances as may be so specified, the processing of applications for vehicle licences where particulars are transmitted in accordance with that paragraph.

(4) A vehicle licence is issued for the vehicle specified in the application for the licence (and for no other)

(5) The Secretary of State is not required to issue a vehicle licence for which an application is made unless he is satisfied—

(*a*) that the licence applied for is the appropriate licence for the vehicle specified in the application, and

(*b*) in the case of an application for a licence for a vehicle purporting to be the first application for a licence for the vehicle, that a licence has not previously been issued for the vehicle.

(6) Regulations[1] made by the Secretary of State may provide for—

(*aa*) the return of any vehicle licence which is damaged or contains any particulars which have become illegible or inaccurate,

(*a*) the issue of a new vehicle licence in the place of a licence which is or may be lost, stolen, destroyed or damaged, or which contains any particulars which have become illegal or inaccurate and

(*b*) the fee to be paid on the issue of a new licence in any of those circumstances.

(7) Where, following an application made in accordance with regulations under paragraph 13 of Schedule 1, a licence is issued for a goods vehicle at the rate of duty applicable to a weight specified in the application which is lower than its actual weight, that lower weight is to be shown on the licence.

(8) In this section 'special vehicle' has the same meaning as in paragraph 4 of Schedule 1.

[Vehicle Excise and Registration Act 1994, s 7 as amended by the Finance Act 1995, Sch 4, the Finance Act 1996, s 17 and Sch 2, the Finance (No 2) Act 1997, s 14, SI 2002/2377 and the Finance Act 2002, s 19.]

---

1. See the Road Vehicles (Registration and Licensing) Regulations 2002, reg 8, in this PART, post.

4–1916A   **7A. Supplement payable on vehicle ceasing to be appropriately covered.** (1) Regulations may make provision for a supplement of a prescribed amount to be payable where—

(*a*) a vehicle has ceased to be appropriately covered,

(*b*) the vehicle is not, before the end of the relevant prescribed period, appropriately covered as mentioned in paragraph (*a*) or (*b*) of subsection (1A) below with effect from the time immediately after it so ceased or appropriately covered as mentioned in paragraph (*d*) of that subsection, and

(*c*) the circumstances are not such as may be prescribed.

(1A) For the purposes of this section and section 7B a vehicle is appropriately covered if (and only if)—

(*a*) a vehicle licence or trade licence is in force for or in respect of the vehicle,

(*b*) the vehicle is an exempt vehicle in respect of which regulations under this Act require a nil licence to be in force and a nil licence is in force in respect of it,

(*c*) the vehicle is an exempt vehicle that is not one in respect of which regulations under this Act require a nil licence to be in force, or

(*d*) the vehicle is neither kept nor used on a public road and the declarations and particulars required to be delivered by regulations under section 22(1D) have been delivered in relation to it in accordance with the regulations within the immediately preceding period of 12 months.

(1B) Where a vehicle for or in respect of which a vehicle licence is in force is transferred by the holder of the vehicle licence to another person, the vehicle licence is to be treated for the purposes of subsection (1A) as no longer in force unless it is delivered to the other person with the vehicle.

(1C) Where—

(*a*) an application is made for a vehicle licence for any period, and

(*b*) a temporary licence is issued pursuant to the application,

subsection (1B) does not apply to the licence applied for if, on a transfer of the vehicle during the currency of the temporary licence, the temporary licence is delivered with the vehicle to the transferee.

(1D) In subsection (1)(*b*) "the relevant prescribed period" means such period beginning with the date on which the vehicle ceased to be appropriately covered as is prescribed.

(2) A supplement under this section—

(a) shall be payable by such person, or jointly and severally by such persons, as may be prescribed;

(b) shall become payable at such time as may be prescribed;

(c) may be of an amount that varies according to the length of the period between—

(i) the time of a notification (in accordance with regulations under section 7B(1)) to, or in relation to, a person by whom it is payable, and

(ii) the time at which it is paid.

(3) A supplement under this section that has become payable—

(a) is in addition to any vehicle excise duty charged in respect of the vehicle concerned;

(b) does not cease to be payable by reason of a vehicle licence being taken out for the vehicle after the supplement has become payable;

(c) may, without prejudice to section 6 or 7B(2) or (3) or any other provision of this Act, be recovered as a debt due to the Crown.

(4) In this section—

(a) references to the expiry of a vehicle licence include a reference to—

(i) its surrender, and—

(ii) its being treated as no longer in force for the purposes of subsection (2) of section 31A by subsection (4) of that section;

(b) "prescribed" means prescribed by, or determined in accordance with, regulations;

(c) "regulations" means regulations made by the Secretary of State with the consent of the Treasury.

(5) No regulations to which subsection (6) applies shall be made under this section unless a draft of the regulations has been laid before, and approved by a resolution of, each House of Parliament.

(6) This subsection applies to regulations under this section that—

(a) provide for a supplement to be payable in a case where one would not otherwise be payable,

(b) increase the amount of a supplement,

(c) provide for a supplement to become payable earlier than it would otherwise be payable, or

(d) provide for a supplement to be payable by a person by whom the supplement would not otherwise be payable.

[Vehicle Excise and Registration Act 1994, s 7A as inserted by the Finance Act 2002, Sch 5 and amended by the Finance (No 2) 2005, s 66.]

4–1916A 7B. Section 7A supplements: further provisions. (1) The Secretary of State may by regulations make provision for notifying the person in whose name a vehicle is registered under this Act about—

(a) any supplement under section 7A that may or has become payable in relation to the vehicle;

(b) when the vehicle ceasing to be appropriately covered may result in the person being guilty of an offence under section 31A.

(2) The Secretary of State may by regulations make provision—

(a) for assessing an amount of supplement due under section 7A from any person and for notifying that amount to that person or any person acting in a representative capacity in relation to that person;

(b) for an amount assessed and notified under such regulations to be deemed to be an amount of vehicle excise duty due from the person assessed and recoverable accordingly;

(c) for review of decisions under such regulations and for appeals with respect to such decisions or decisions on such reviews.

(3) Regulations under subsection (2) may, in particular, make provision that, subject to any modifications that the Secretary of State considers appropriate, corresponds or is similar to—

(a) any provision made by sections 12A and 12B of the Finance Act 1994 (assessments related to excise duty matters), or

(b) any provision made by sections 14 to 16 of that Act (customs and excise reviews and appeals).

(4) Sums received by way of supplements under section 7A shall be paid into the Consolidated Fund.

[Vehicle Excise and Registration Act 1994, s 7B as inserted by the Finance Act 2002, Sch 5 and amended by the Finance (No 2) Act 2005, s 66.]

7C. Recovery of section 7A supplements: Scotland

4–1917 8. Vehicles removed into UK. Where an application is made for a vehicle licence for a vehicle which—

(a) appears to the Secretary of State to have been removed into the United Kingdom from a place outside the United Kingdom, and

(b) is not already registered under this Act,

the Secretary of State may refuse to issue the licence unless subsection (2) applies to the vehicle.

(2) This subsection applies to a vehicle if the Secretary of State is satisfied in relation to the removal of the vehicle into the United Kingdom—

(*a*) that any value added tax charged on the acquisition of the vehicle from another member State, or on any supply involving its removal into the United Kingdom, has been or will be paid or remitted,

(*b*) that any value added tax or customs duty charged on the importation of the vehicle from a place outside the member States has been or will be paid or remitted, or

(*c*) that no such tax or duty has been charged on the acquisition or importation of the vehicle or on any supply involving its removal into the United Kingdom.

[Vehicle Excise and Registration Act 1994, s 8.]

4–1918   9. Temporary vehicle licences.   (1) Where an application is made for a vehicle licence for a vehicle for any period, the Secretary of State may, if he thinks fit, instead of issuing immediately a vehicle licence for that period—

(*a*) issue a vehicle licence (a "temporary licence") for fourteen days, or such other period as may be prescribed by regulations made by the Secretary of State, having effect from such day as may be so prescribed, and

(*b*) from time to time issue a further temporary licence for the vehicle.

(2) Nothing in this section affects the amount of any duty payable on a vehicle licence.

(3) Where an application for a vehicle licence is made to a body authorised by the Secretary of State to act as his agent for the purpose of issuing licences, the body may, before issuing a licence under subsection (1)(*a*), require the applicant to pay to it in connection with the issue a fee of £2.

(4) The Secretary of State may by regulations substitute for the sum for the time being specified in subsection (3) such other sum as may be prescribed[1] by the regulations.

[Vehicle Excise and Registration Act 1994, s 9.]

4–1919   10. Transfer and surrender of vehicle licences.   (1) Any vehicle licence may be transferred in the manner prescribed by regulations[1] made by the Secretary of State.

(2) The holder of a vehicle licence may at any time surrender the licence to the Secretary of State.

(3) Where—

(*a*) a person surrenders under subsection (2) a temporary licence issued pursuant to an application for a vehicle licence, and

(*b*) a further vehicle licence issued pursuant to the application is either held by him at the time of the surrender of the temporary licence or received by him after that time,

the further licence ceases to be in force and the person shall immediately return it to the Secretary of State.

[Vehicle Excise and Registration Act 1994, s 10.]

---

1. See the Road Vehicles (Registration and Licensing) Regulations 2002, regs 18–25, in this PART, post.

Trade licences

4–1920   11. Issue of trade licences.   (1) Where—

(*a*) a motor trader or vehicle tester, or

(*b*) a person who satisfies the Secretary of State that he intends to commence business as a motor trader or vehicle tester,

applies to the Secretary of State (in the manner specified made by the Secretary of State) to take out a licence under this section (a "trade licence"), the Secretary of State may, subject to the conditions prescribed by regulations[1] made by the Secretary of State, issue such a licence to him on payment of vehicle excise duty at the rate applicable to the licence.

(1A) The power to prescribe conditions under subsection (1) includes, in particular, the power to prescribe conditions which are to be complied with after the licence is issued.

(2) In the case of a motor trader who is a manufacturer of vehicles, a trade licence is a licence for—

(*a*) all vehicles which are from time to time temporarily in his possession in the course of his business as a motor trader,

(*b*) all vehicles kept and used by him solely for purposes of conducting research and development in the course of his business as such a manufacturer, and

(*c*) all vehicles which are from time to time submitted to him by other manufacturers for testing on roads in the course of that business.

(3) In the case of any other motor trader, a trade licence is a licence for all vehicles which are from time to time temporarily in his possession in the course of his business as a motor trader.

(4) In the case of a vehicle tester, a trade licence is a licence for all vehicles which are from time to time submitted to him for testing in the course of his business as a vehicle tester.

[Vehicle Excise and Registration Act 1994, s 11 as amended by the Finance Act 1995, Sch 4 and the Finance Act 1996, Sch 2.]

---

1. See the Road Vehicles (Registration and Licensing) Regulations 2002, reg 37 and Sch 6 Pt I, in this PART, post.

4–1921   12. Use of vehicles by holders of trade licences.   (1) The holder of a trade licence is not entitled by virtue of the licence—

(a) to use more than one vehicle at any one time,

(b) to use a vehicle for any purpose other than a purpose prescribed by regulations[1] made by the Secretary of State, or

(c) except in such circumstances as may be so prescribed[1], to keep any vehicle on a road if it is not being used on the road.

(2) The Secretary of State shall by regulations[1] prescribe—

(a) the conditions subject to which trade licences are to be issued, and

(b) the purposes for which the holder of a trade licence may use a vehicle by virtue of the licence.

(3) The purposes which may be prescribed as those for which the holder of a trade licence may use a vehicle under the licence shall not include the conveyance of goods or burden of any description other than—

(a) a load which is carried solely for the purpose of testing or demonstrating the vehicle or any of its accessories or equipment and which is returned to the place of loading without having been removed from the vehicle except for that purpose or in the case of accident,

(b) in the case of a vehicle which is being delivered or collected, a load consisting of another vehicle used or to be used for travel from or to the place of delivery or collection,

(c) a load built in as part of the vehicle or permanently attached to it,

(d) a load consisting of parts, accessories or equipment designed to be fitted to the vehicle and of tools for fitting them to the vehicle, or

(e) a load consisting of a trailer other than trailer which is for the time being disabled vehicle.

(4) For the purposes of subsection (3), where a vehicle is so constructed that a trailer may by partial superimposition be attached to the vehicle in such a manner as to cause a substantial part of the weight of the trailer to be borne by the vehicle, the vehicle and the trailer are deemed to constitute a single vehicle.

(5) In subsection (3)(e) "disabled vehicle" includes a vehicle which has been abandoned or is scrap.

[Vehicle Excise and Registration Act 1994, s 12.]

---

1. See the Road Vehicles (Registration and Licensing) Regulations 2002, reg 38 and Sch 6 Pt II, in this PART, post.

4–1922 13. Trade licences: duration and amount of duty. (1) A trade licence may be taken out—

(a) for one calendar year,

(b) for a period of six months beginning with the first day of January or of July, or

(c) where subsection (2) applies, for a period of seven, eight, nine, ten or eleven months beginning with the first day of any month other than January or July and ending no later than the relevant date.

(1A) In subsection (1)(c) "the relevant date" means—

(a) in relation to a licence taken out for a period beginning with the first day of any of the months February to June in any year, 31st December of that year;

(b) in relation to a licence taken out for a period beginning with the first day of any of the months August to December in any year, 30th June of the following year.

(2) This subsection applies where the person taking out the licence—

(a) is not a motor trader or vehicle tester (having satisfied the Secretary of State as mentioned in section 11(1)(b)), or

(b) does not hold any existing trade licence.

(3) The rate of duty applicable to a trade licence taken out for a calendar year is—

(a) the annual rate currently applicable to a vehicle under sub-paragraph (1)(c) of paragraph 2 of Schedule 1 if the licence is to be used only for vehicles to which that paragraph applies, and

(b) otherwise, the annual rate currently applicable to a vehicle under paragraph 1(2) of Schedule 1.

(4) The rate of duty applicable to a trade licence taken out for a period of six months is fifty-five per cent of the rate applicable to the corresponding trade licence taken out for a calendar year.

(5) The rate of duty applicable to a trade licence taken out for a period of seven, eight, nine, ten or eleven months is the aggregate of—

(a) fifty-five per cent of the rate applicable to the corresponding trade licence taken out for a calendar year, and

(b) one-sixth of the amount arrived at under paragraph[1] in respect of each month in the period in excess of six.

(6) In determining a rate of duty under subsection (4) or (5) any fraction of five pence—

(a) if it exceeds two and a half pence, shall be treated as five pence, and

(b) otherwise, shall be disregarded.★

[Vehicle Excise and Registration Act 1994, s 13 as amended by the Finance Act 1995, Sch 4, the Finance Act 1996, s 18 and the finance act 1999, s 8.]

*A new s 13 is substituted by Sch 4, para 8 to this Act from a date to be appointed.

4–1923   14. Trade licences: supplementary.   (1) Nothing in sections 11 to 13 prevents a person entitled to take out a trade licence from holding two or more trade licences.

(2) The holder of a trade licence may at any time surrender the licence to the Secretary of State.

(3) Where—

(a) the Secretary of State refuses an application for a trade licence by a person entitled to make such an application, and

(b) the applicant, within the period prescribed by regulations made by the Secretary of State, requests him to review his decision,

the Secretary of State shall comply with the request and (in doing so) consider any representations made to him in writing during that period by the applicant.

(4) Regulations[1] made by the Secretary of State may provide for—

(a) the issue of a new trade licence in the place of a licence which is or may be lost, stolen, destroyed or damaged, and

(b) the fee to be paid on the issue of a new licence.

[Vehicle Excise and Registration Act 1994, s 14.]

---

1. See the Road Vehicles (Registration and Licensing) Regulations 2002, reg 41, in this PART, post.

Additional duty, rebates etc

4–1924   15. Vehicles becoming chargeable to duty at higher rate.   (1) Where—

(a) a vehicle licence has been taken out for a vehicle at any rate of vehicle excise duty, and

(b) at any time while the licence is in force the vehicle is used so as to subject it to a higher rate,

duty at the higher rate become chargeable in respect of the licence for the vehicle.

(2) For the purposes of subsection (1) a vehicle is used so as to subject it to a higher rate if it is used in an altered condition[1], in a manner or for a purpose which—

(a) brings it within, or

(b) if it was used solely in that condition, in that manner or for that purpose, would bring it within,

a description of vehicle to which a higher rate of duty is applicable.

(2A) For the purposes of subsection (1) a vehicle is also used so as to subject it to a higher rate if—

(a) the rate of vehicle excise duty paid on a vehicle licence taken out for the vehicle was the rate applicable to a vehicle of the same description with respect to which the reduced pollution requirements are satisfied, and

(b) while the licence is in force, the vehicle is used at a time when those requirements are not satisfied with respect to it.

(3) For the purposes of subsection (1) a vehicle in respect of which a lower rate of duty is chargeable by virtue of regulations under paragraph 13 of Schedule 1 is also used so as to subject it to a higher rate if it is used in contravention of a condition imposed under or by virtue of sub-paragraph (2) of that paragraph.

(4) Subject to section 7(5), where duty at a higher rate becomes chargeable under subsection (1) in respect of a vehicle licence, the licence may be exchanged for a new vehicle licence for the period—

(a) beginning with the date on which the higher rate of duty becomes chargeable, and

(b) ending with the period for which the original licence was issued.

(5) A new vehicle licence may be obtained under subsection (4) only on payment of the appropriate proportion of the difference between—

(a) the amount of duty payable on the original licence, and

(b) the amount of duty payable on a vehicle licence taken out for the period for which the original licence was issued but at the higher rate of duty.

(6) For the purposes of subsection (5) "the appropriate proportion" means the proportion which the number of months in the period—

(a) beginning with the date on which the higher rate of duty becomes chargeable, and

(b) ending with the period for which the original licence was issued,

bears to the number of months in the whole of the period for which the original licence was issued (any incomplete month being treated as a whole month).

(7) If the higher rate has been changed since the issue of the original licence, the amount under subsection (5)(b) is calculated as if that rate had been in force at all material times at the level at which it is in force when it becomes chargeable.

[Vehicle Excise and Registration Act 1994, s 15 as amended by the Finance Act 1995, Sch 4 and the Finance Act 1998, Sch 1.]

---

1. The fixing of loose boards in slots set in the sides of a vehicle so as to enable a greater load to be carried has been held to be an alteration within the meaning of similar provisions of the repealed Finance Act 1922 (*Lowe v Stone* [1948] 2 All ER 1076, 113 JP 59).

4–1925   16. Exceptions from charge at higher rate in case of tractive units. (1) Subject to subsection (9) duty at a higher rate does not become chargeable under section 15—

(a)   where subsection (2) applies in relation to a tractive unit, by reason of the tractive unit being used in accordance with subsection (3),

(b)   where subsection (4) applies in relation to a tractive unit, by reason of the tractive unit being used in accordance with subsection (5), or

(c)   where subsection (6) applies in relation to a tractive unit, by reason of the tractive unit being used in accordance with subsection (7).

(2) This subsection applies in relation to a tractive unit where—

(a)   a vehicle licence for—

     (i)   a tractive unit having two axles which is to be used only with semi-trailers with not fewer than two axles, or

     (ii)   a tractive unit having two axles which is to be used only with semi-trailers with not fewer than three axles,

     has been taken out for the tractive unit, and

(b)   the rate of duty paid on taking out the licence is equal to or exceeds the rate of duty applicable to a tractive unit having two axles which—

     (i)   has a revenue weight equal to the maximum laden weight at which a tractive unit having two axles may lawfully be used in Great Britain with a semi-trailer with a single axle, and

     (ii)   is to be used with semi-trailers with any number of axles.

(3) The tractive unit is being used in accordance with this subsection where—

(a)   it is used with a semi-trailer with a single axle, and

(b)   when so used, the laden weight of the tractive unit and semi-trailer taken together does not exceed the maximum laden weight mentioned in subsection (2)(b)(i).

(4) This subsection applies in relation to a tractive unit where—

(a)   a vehicle licence for a tractive unit having two axles which is to be used only with semi-trailers with not fewer than three axles has been taken out for the tractive unit, and

(b)   the rate of duty paid on taking out the licence is equal to or exceeds the rate of duty applicable to a tractive unit having two axles which—

     (i)   has a revenue weight of 33,000 kilograms, and

     (ii)   is to be used with semi-trailers with not fewer than two axles.

(5) The tractive unit is being used in accordance with this subsection where—

(a)   it is used with a semi-trailer with two axles, and

(b)   when so used, the laden weight of the tractive unit and semi-trailer taken together does not exceed 33,000 kilograms.

(6) This subsection applies in relation to a tractive unit where—

(a)   a vehicle licence for a tractive unit having three or more axles which is to be used only with semi-trailers with not fewer than two axles has been taken out for the tractive unit, and

(b)   the rate of duty paid on taking out the licence is equal to or exceeds the rate of duty applicable to a tractive unit having three or more axles which—

     (i)   has a revenue weight equal to the maximum laden weight at which a tractive unit having three or more axles may lawfully be used in Great Britain with a semi-trailer with a single axle, and

     (ii)   is to be used with semi-trailers with any number of axles.

(7) The tractive unit is being used in accordance with this subsection where—

(a)   it is used with a semi-trailer with a single axle, and

(b)   when so used, the laden weight of the tractive unit and semi-trailer taken together does not exceed the maximum laden weight mentioned in subsection (6)(b)(i).

(8) This subsection applies to a tractive unit ("the relevant tractive unit") in relation to which subsection (2), (4) or (6) applies if—

(a)   the rate of duty paid on taking out the licence for the relevant tractive unit is the rate applicable to a tractive unit of the appropriate description with respect to which the reduced pollution requirements are satisfied; and

(b)   while the licence is in force, the relevant tractive unit is used at a time when the reduced pollution requirements are not satisfied with respect to it.

(9) Where subsection (8) applies, subsection (1) does not prevent duty becoming payable under section 15 at the rate applicable to a tractive unit of the appropriate description with respect to which the reduced pollution requirements are not satisfied.

(10) In this section "the appropriate description" means the description mentioned in paragraph (b) of whichever of subsections (2), (4) and (6) applies in relation to the relevant tractive unit.

[Vehicle Excise and Registration Act 1994, s 16 as amended by the Finance Act 1995, Sch 4 and the Finance Act 1998, Sch 1.]

4–1926 **17. Other exceptions from charge at higher rate.** (1) Where a vehicle licence has been taken out for a vehicle of any description, duty at a higher rate applicable to a vehicle of another description does not[1] become chargeable under section 15 unless the vehicle as used while the licence is in force satisfies all the conditions which must be satisfied in order to bring the vehicle into the other description of vehicle for the purposes of vehicle excise duty.

(2) Where—

(a) duty has been paid in respect of a vehicle at a rate applicable under Part VIII of Schedule 1, and

(b) the vehicle is to a substantial extent being used for the conveyance of goods or burden belonging to a particular person (whether the person keeping the vehicle or not),

duty at a higher rate does not become chargeable under section 15 by reason only that the vehicle is used for the conveyance without charge in the course of their employment of employees of the person to whom the goods or burden belong.

(3)–(7) *Repealed.*

(8) This section does not have effect where section 15 applies by reason of the use of a vehicle in contravention of a condition imposed under or by virtue of paragraph 13(2) of Schedule 1.

[Vehicle Excise and Registration Act 1994, s 17 as amended by the Finance Act 1995, Schs 4 and 29.]

---

1. Previous legislation, replaced by this section, reversed the decision in *Payne v Allcock* [1932] 2 KB 413, 96 JP 283, that mere user of the vehicle for the carriage of goods in a private motor car, not adapted or constructed for the carriage of goods, attracted a higher rate of duty.

4–1927 **18. Vehicles for export becoming liable to VAT.** (1) Where, by virtue of sub-paragraph (2) of paragraph 23 of Schedule 2, a vehicle which is an exempt vehicle under sub-paragraph (1) of that paragraph is deemed never to have been an exempt vehicle under that sub-paragraph, vehicle excise duty is payable—

(a) by the person by whom the vehicle was acquired from its manufacturer, in relation to the whole period since the registration of the vehicle, or

(b) by any other person who is for the time being the keeper of the vehicle, in relation to the period since the vehicle was first kept by him,

unless, or except to the extent that, the Secretary of State waives payment of the duty.

(2) Subsection (1) is without prejudice to section 30; but duty with respect to a vehicle is not payable by a person under that subsection in relation to any part of a period if an amount with respect to it has been ordered to be paid by him under that section in relation to the part of the period.

[Vehicle Excise and Registration Act 1994, s 18.]

4–1928 **19. Surrender of licences.** (1) Where a licence is surrendered to the Secretary of State under section 10(2) or 14(2), the holder is entitled to receive from the Secretary of State (by way of rebate of the duty paid on the licence) an amount equal to one-twelfth of the annual rate of duty chargeable on the licence in respect of each complete month of the period of the currency of the licence which is unexpired at the date of the surrender.

(1A) Subsection (1B) applies where the holder of a licence—

(a) has notified the Secretary of State that he wishes to surrender the licence under section 10(2),

(b) has agreed to comply with such conditions as may be specified in relation to him by the Secretary of State, and

(c) if the conditions so specified in relation to him include a condition such as is mentioned in subsection (1C)(a), has complied with that condition.

(1B) If the holder has not surrendered the licence before the time when paragraphs (a) to (c) of subsection (1A) are first all satisfied, then at that time—

(a) the holder becomes entitled to rebate under subsection (1) as if he had surrendered the licence at that time,

(b) the licence ceases to be in force, and

(c) the provisions of section 10(2) and subsection (1) cease to apply to the licence.

(1C) The conditions which may be specified under subsection (1A)(b) include—

(a) a condition that particulars for the time being prescribed under section 22(1D)(a) are furnished by being transmitted to the Secretary of State by such electronic means as he may specify; and

(b) a condition that the licence be returned to the Secretary of State within such period as may be specified by the Secretary of State.

(2) If during the currency of a temporary licence issued in pursuance of an application for a vehicle licence for any period the temporary licence is surrendered under section 10(2), it is treated for the purposes of subsection (1) as issued for that period.

(3) *Repealed.*

[Vehicle Excise and Registration Act 1994, s 19 as amended by the Finance Act 1996, Sch 2 and the Finance Act 2001, s 14.]

4–1928A **19A. Payment for licences by cheque.** (1) The Secretary of State may, if he thinks fit, issue a vehicle or a trade licence on receipt of a cheque for the amount of the duty payable on it.

(2) In a case where—

(a) a vehicle licence or an trade licence is issued to a person on receipt of a cheque which is subsequently dishonoured, and

(b) the Secretary of State sends a notice by post to the person informing him that the licence is void as from the time when it was granted,

the licence shall be void as from the time when it was granted.

(3) In a case where—

(a) a vehicle licence or a trade licence is issued to a person on receipt of a cheque which is subsequently dishonoured,

(b) the Secretary of State sends a notice by post to the person requiring him to secure that the duty payable on the licence is paid within such reasonable period as is specified in the notice,

(c) the requirement in the notice is not complied with, and

(d) the Secretary of State sends a further notice by post to the person informing him that the licence is void as from the time when it was granted,

the licence shall be void as from the time when it was granted.

(4) Section 102 of the Customs and Excise Management Act 1979 (payment for excise licences by cheque) shall not apply in relation to a vehicle licence or a trade licence.

[Vehicle Excise and Registration Act 1994, s 19A, as inserted by the Finance Act 1995, Sch 4.]

4-1928B 19B. Issue of licences before payment of duty.

(1) The Secretary of State may, if he thinks fit, issue a vehicle licence or a trade licence to a person who has agreed with the Secretary of State to pay the duty payable on the licence in a manner provided for in the agreement.

(2) In a case where—

(a) a vehicle licence or a trade licence is issued to a person in accordance with subsection (1),

(b) the duty payable on the licence is not received by the Secretary of State in accordance with the agreement, and

(c) the Secretary of State sends a notice by post to the person informing him that the licence is void as from the time when it was granted,

the licence shall be void as from the time when it was granted.

(3) In a case where—

(a) paragraphs (a) and (b) of subsection (2) apply,

(b) the Secretary of State sends a notice by post to the person requiring him to secure that the duty payable on the licence is paid within such reasonable period as is specified in the notice,

(c) the requirement in the notice is not complied with, and

(d) the Secretary of State sends a further notice by post to the person informing him that the licence is void as from the time when it was granted,

the licence shall be void as from the time when it was granted.

[Vehicle Excise and Registration Act 1994, s 19B, as inserted by the Finance Act 1997, s 19.]

4-1928C 19C. Fee for payment of duty by credit card.

(1) This section applies where—

(a) a person applies for a vehicle licence or a trade licence, and

(b) the Secretary of State, or an authorised body, accepts a credit card payment in respect of the duty payable on the licence.

(2) Before issuing the licence, the Secretary of State, or the authorised body, shall require—

(a) the applicant, or

(b) a person acting on behalf of the applicant,

to pay to him, or it, such fee (if any) in respect of the acceptance of the credit card payment as may be prescribed by, or determined in accordance with, regulations.

(3) In cases of such descriptions as the Secretary of State may, with the consent of the Treasury, determine, the whole or a part of a fee paid under this section may be refunded.

(4) In this section—

"authorised body" means a body (other than a Northern Ireland department) which is authorised by the Secretary of State[1] to act as his agent for the purpose of issuing licences;

"credit card" has such meaning as may be prescribed by regulations;

"regulations" means regulations made by the Secretary of State.*

[Vehicle Excise and Registration Act 1994, s 19C, as inserted by the Finance Act 2004, s 18.]

---

*This amendment has effect in relation to licences issued on or after 14 October 2005: see the Finance Act 2004, s 18(4) and SI 2005/2356, art 2.

1. The Road Vehicles (Payment of Duty) by Credit Card) (Prescribed Fee) Regulations 2005, SI 2005/2460 have been made.

4-1929 20. Combined road-rail transport of goods[1].

(1) This section applies where—

(a) goods are loaded on a relevant goods vehicle for transport between member States,

(b) the vehicle is transported by rail between the nearest suitable rail loading station to the point of loading and the nearest suitable rail unloading station to the point of unloading, and (*c*)   part of the rail transport of the vehicle takes place in the United Kingdom at a time when a vehicle licence for it is in force.

(2)   Where this section applies, the holder of the licence is, on making a claim, entitled to receive from the Secretary of State (by way of rebate of the duty paid on the licence) an amount calculated by the method prescribed by regulations made by the Secretary of State.

(3)   In this section "relevant goods vehicle" means any vehicle the rate of duty applicable to which is provided for in Part VIII of Schedule 1 or which would be such a vehicle if Part VI of that Schedule did not apply to the vehicle.

(4)   The Secretary of State may by regulations prescribe—

  (*a*)   when and how a claim for a rebate under this section is to be made, and

  (*b*)   the evidence to be provided in support of such a claim.

[Vehicle Excise and Registration Act 1994, s 20 as amended by the Finance Act 1995, Sch 4.]

---

1. Section 20 is to be brought into force by an order under Sch 4, para 9. At the time of going to press no order had been made.

PART II
REGISTRATION OF VEHICLES

Registration

4–1930   21. Registration of vehicles.   (1) Subject to subsection (3), on the issue by the Secretary of State for a vehicle which is not registered under this section of either—

  (*a*)   a vehicle licence, or

  (*b*)   a nil licence,

the Secretary of State shall register the vehicle in such manner as he thinks fit without any further application by the person to whom the licence is issued.

(2)   Subject to subsection (3) where particulars in respect of a vehicle are furnished to the Secretary of State in accordance with regulations under section 24 before he first issues a vehicle licence for the vehicle, he shall so register the vehicle on receiving the particulars.

(3)   The Secretary of State may by regulations provide that in such circumstances as may be prescribed[1] by the regulations a vehicle shall not be registered under this section until a fee of such amount as may be so prescribed is paid.

(4)   The Secretary of State may by regulations make provision about repayment of any sum paid by way of a fee mentioned in subsection (3), and the regulations may in particular include provision—

  (*a*)   that repayment shall be made only if a specified person is satisfied that specified conditions are met or in other specified circumstances;

  (*b*)   that repayment shall be made in part only;

  (*c*)   that, in the case of partial repayment, the amount repaid shall be a specified sum or determined in a specified manner;

  (*d*)   for repayment of different amounts in different circumstances;

and "specified" here means specified in the regulations.

---

1. See the Road Vehicles (Registration and Licensing) Regulations 2002, reg 10(1), in this PART, post which provides that, subject to exceptions, a vehicle must not be registered unless a fee of £25 is paid.

[Vehicle Excise and Registration Act 1994, s 21 as amended by the Finance Act 1995, Sch 4 and the Finance Act 1997, Sch 3.]

4–1931   22. Registration regulations.   (1) The Secretary of State may by regulations[1]—

  (*a*)   make provision with respect to the registration of vehicles (including, in particular, the form of and the particulars to be included in the register of trade licences),

  (*b*)   require the Secretary of State to make with respect to registered vehicles the returns prescribed by the regulations,

  (*c*)   provide for making any particulars contained in the register available for use by the persons prescribed by the regulations on payment, in cases so prescribed, of a fee of such amount as appears to the Secretary of State reasonable in the circumstances of the case,

  (*d*)   require a person by, through or to whom any vehicle is sold or disposed of to furnish the particulars prescribed by the regulations in the manner so prescribed,

 (*dd*)   require a person by, or through whom any vehicle is sold or disposed of to furnish the person to whom it is sold or disposed of with such document relating to the vehicle's registration as may be prescribed by the regulations, and to do so at such time as may be so prescribed.

  (*e*)   provide for the issue of registration documents in respect of the registration of a vehicle,

  (*f*)   provide for the transfer, surrender and production of registration documents,

  (*g*)   provide for the inspection of registration documents by the persons prescribed by the regulations,

  (*h*)   provide for the issue of new registration documents in place of registration documents which are or may be lost, stolen, surrendered, destroyed or damaged. or which contain any particulars which have become illegible or inaccurate.

(*i*)   provide for a fee of such amount as appears to the Secretary of State to be reasonable to be paid on the issue of new registration documents in any of the circumstances mentioned in paragraph (*h*).

(1A) The Secretary of State may make regulations providing for the sale of information derived from particulars contained in the register—

(*a*)   to such persons as the Secretary of State thinks fit, and

(*b*)   for such price and on such other terms, and subject to such restrictions, as he thinks fit,

if the information does not identify any person or contain anything enabling any person to be identified.

(1B) Without prejudice to the generality of paragraph (*d*) of subsection (1), regulations under that paragraph may require—

(*a*)   any person there mentioned to furnish particulars to another person there mentioned or to the Secretary of State or to another such person and to the Secretary of State;

(*b*)   any person there mentioned who is furnished with particulars in pursuance of the regulations to furnish them to the Secretary of State.

(1C) Regulations under subsection (1)(*e*) may, in particular, provide that registration documents need not be issued in respect of the registration of a vehicle until the vehicle has been inspected by a person specified by the Secretary of State.

(1D) The Secretary of State may by regulations require a person—

(*a*)   who surrenders a vehicle licence under section 10(2);

(*aa*) who does not renew a licence for a vehicle registered under this Act in his name,

(*b*)   who does not renew a vehicle licence for a vehicle kept by him, or

(*c*)   who keeps an unlicensed vehicle at any place in the United Kingdom

to furnish such particulars and make such declarations as may be prescribed by the regulations, and to do so at such times and in such manner as may be so prescribed.

(1DA) For the purposes of subsection (1D)(*aa*) a person shall be regarded as not renewing a vehicle licence for a vehicle registered in his name if—

(*a*)   a vehicle for which a vehicle licence is in force is registered in his name, and

(*b*)   he does not, at such time as may be prescribed by the regulations or within such period as may be so prescribed, take out a vehicle licence to have effect from the expiry of the vehicle licence mentioned in paragraph (*a*).

(1E) For the purposes of subsection (1D)(*b*) a person shall be regarded as not renewing a vehicle licence for a vehicle kept by him if—

(*a*)   he keeps a vehicle for which a vehicle licence is in force, and

(*b*)   he does not, at such times as may be prescribed by the regulations or within such period as may be so prescribed, take out a vehicle licence to have effect from the expiry of the vehicle licence mentioned in paragraph (*a*).

(1F) For the purposes of subsection (1D)(*c*) a vehicle is unlicensed if no vehicle licence is in force for the vehicle.

(1G) Regulations under subsection (1D) may make such transitional provision as appears to the Secretary of State to be appropriate.

(2) Regulations made by the Secretary of State may—

(*a*)   extend any of the provisions as to registration (and provisions incidental to any of those provisions) to,

(*b*)   provide for the identification of,

any exempt vehicles, any vehicles belonging to the Crown or any trailers (within the meaning of Part VIII of Schedule 1).

(2A) Regulations under subsection (2) may, in particular—

(*a*)   require a person applying for a nil licence—

(i)   to make any such declaration, and

(ii) to furnish any such particulars and any such documentary or other evidence

(whether or not with respect to the vehicle for which the licence is to be taken out) as may be prescribed by the regulations,

(*b*)   provide for any requirement to make such a declaration not to apply in such circumstances as may be so prescribed,

(*c*)   make provision (including provision requiring the payment of a fee) for cases where a nil licence is or may be lost, stolen, destroyed or damaged or contains particulars which have become illegible or inaccurate,

(*d*)   require a person issue with a nil licence which ceases to be in force in circumstances prescribed by the regulations to furnish to the Secretary of State any such particulars and any such documentary or other evidence and make any such declarations as may be so prescribed, and to do so at such times and in such manner as may be so prescribed.*

(2B) The circumstances which may be prescribed by the regulations by virtue of subsection

(2A) (b) include where a person applying for a nil licence agrees to comply with such conditions as may be specified in relation to him by the Secretary of State.

(2C) The conditions which may be specified by virtue of subsection (2B) include—

(a) a condition that particulars for the time being prescribed by the regulations by virtue of subsection (2A)(a) are furnished by being transmitted to the Secretary of State by such electronic means as he may specify; and

(b) a condition such as is mentioned in section 7(3B)(b) (treating the references to paragraph (a) of subsection (3B) as references to paragraph (a) of this subsection).

(3) *Repealed.*

(4) Regulations made by the Secretary of State may make provision for the return of any nil licence to the Secretary of State in such circumstances as may be prescribed by the regulations.

[Vehicle Excise and Registration Act 1994, s 22 as amended by the Finance Act 1995, Sch 4, the Finance Act 1996, Schs 2 and 41, the Finance (No 2) Act 1997, s 14 and Sch 8, the Finance Act 1997, Sch 3, the Finance Act 1998, s 18 and Sch 27, the Vehicles (Crime) Act 2001, s 32, the Finance Act 2002, Sch 5 and SI 2002/2377.]

---

1. See the Road Vehicles (Registration and Licensing) Regulations 2002, in this PART, post.

4–1931A   22ZA.   Nil licences for vehicles for disabled persons: information.   (1) This section applies to information that—

(a) is held for the purposes of functions relating to social security or war pensions—

(i) by the Secretary of State or a Northern Ireland department, or

(ii) by a person providing services to the Secretary of State or a Northern Ireland department, in connection with the provision of those services, and

(b) is of a description prescribed by regulations made by the Secretary of State.

(2) Information to which this section applies may, if the consent condition is satisfied, be supplied—

(a) to the Secretary of State, or

(b) to a person providing services to the Secretary of State, for use for the purposes of relevant nil licence functions.

(3) The "consent condition", in relation to any information, is that—

(a) if the information was provided by a person other than the person to whom the information relates, the person who provided the information, or

(b) in any other case, the person to whom the information relates,

has consented to the supply of the information and has not withdrawn that consent.

(4) Information supplied under subsection (2) shall not—

(a) be supplied by the recipient to any other person unless—

(i) it could be supplied to that person under subsection (2), or

(ii) it is supplied for the purposes of any civil or criminal proceedings relating to this Act;

(b) be used otherwise than for the purposes of relevant nil licence functions or any such proceedings.

(5) In this section "relevant nil licence functions" means functions relating to applications for, and the issue of, nil licences in respect of vehicles that are exempt vehicles under—

(a) paragraph 19 of Schedule 2, or

(b) paragraph 7 of Schedule 4.

[Vehicle Excise and Registration Act 1994, s 22ZA as inserted by the Finance Act 2002, s 17, and amended by the Finance Act 2003, s 15.]

4–1931B   22A.   Vehicle identity checks.   (1) This section applies to regulations under section 22(1)(h) which confer a power on the Secretary of State to refuse to issue a new registration document in respect of a registered vehicle if he is not satisfied that the vehicle for which the document is being sought is the registered vehicle.

(2) Such regulations may, in particular, provide for—

(a) the examination (whether by the Secretary of State or by persons authorised by him) of all vehicles for which new registration documents are being sought, or such vehicles of a particular description, for the purpose of ascertaining whether they are the registered vehicles concerned,

(b) the provision of other evidence in relation to all vehicles for which new registration documents are being sought, or such vehicles of a particular description, for the purpose of ascertaining whether they are the registered vehicles concerned.

(3) Regulations made by virtue of subsection (2) may, in particular, provide for—

(a) notification of examinations (including their purpose), the issue of certificates as to the outcome of examinations and the keeping of records in relation to examinations and certificates,

(b) the issue of duplicates or copies of certificates and the fees to be paid on applications for such duplicates or copies,

(c) the correction of errors in certificates,

(d) the payment of fees for examinations, and for re-examinations resulting from appeals and the repayment of the whole or part of the fee paid for such a re-examination where it appears to the Secretary of State that there were substantial grounds for contesting the whole or part of the decision appealed against,

(e) the making of appeals against the outcome of examinations,

(f) the carrying out of examinations in the absence of the keepers or owners of the vehicles concerned,

(g) courses of instruction in connection with the carrying out of examinations and the charging of fees in respect of attendance on such courses,

(h) the authorisation of examiners, the imposition of conditions to be complied with by authorised examiners (including the payment of fees to the Secretary of State) and the withdrawal of authorisations,

(i) the manner in which, conditions under which and apparatus with which examinations are carried out by authorised examiners, and the inspection of premises at which and apparatus with which such examinations are being, or are to be, carried out,

(j) the charges to be paid by authorised examiners to the Secretary of State in connection with—

(i) the issue of certificates,
(ii) the issue of duplicates or copies of certificates, and
(iii) the correction of errors in certificates.

(4) The Secretary of State may use information contained in relevant records—

(a) to check the accuracy of information which has been obtained under regulations made by virtue of subsection (2), and

(b) where appropriate, to amend or supplement any such information.

(5) The Secretary of State may use information which has been obtained under regulations made by virtue of subsection (2)—

(a) to check the accuracy of relevant records, and
(b) where appropriate, to amend or supplement information contained in those records.

(6) In subsections (4) and (5) "relevant records" means records—

(a) maintained by the Secretary of State in connection with any functions exercisable by him under or by virtue of this Act,

(b) records maintained by the Secretary of State (or caused by him to be maintained) under section 45(6B) of the Road Traffic Act 1988 (c 52).

(7) Subsections (4) to (6) do not limit any powers of the Secretary of State apart from those subsections.

(8) This section is without prejudice to the generality of the powers conferred by section 22.
[Vehicle Excise and Registration Act 1994, s 22A as inserted by the Vehicles (Crime) Act 2001, Sch.]

Registration marks

4–1932 23. Registration marks. (1) Where the Secretary of State registers a vehicle under section 21(1) he shall assign to the vehicle a mark (a "registration mark") indicating the registered number of the vehicle.

(2) The Secretary of State may, in such circumstances as he may determine—

(a) assign a registration mark to a vehicle to which another registration mark has previously been assigned,

(b) assign to a vehicle (whether on its first registration or later) a registration mark previously assigned to another vehicle,

(c) (whether or not in connection with an assignment within paragraph (a) or (b)) withdraw any registration mark for the time being assigned to a vehicle, and

(d) re-assign to a vehicle a registration mark previously assigned to it but subsequently withdrawn.

(3) The Secretary of State may by regulations[1] provide that the registration mark for the time being assigned to a vehicle shall be fixed, in the manner prescribed by the regulations, on the vehicle, on any other vehicle drawn by the vehicle or on both.

(4) The Secretary of State may be regulations[1] prescribe—

(a) the size, shape and character of registration marks to be fixed on any vehicle, and

(b) the manner in which registration marks are to be displayed and rendered easily distinguishable (whether by day or by night).

(5) The Secretary of State may by regulations[2]—

(a) make provision for assigning general registration marks to persons holding trade licences and (in particular) prescribe the registration marks to be carried by vehicles the use of which is authorised by a trade licence, and

(b) make provisions for the issue of trade plates to holders of trade licences and for the charging of a fee for the replacement of trade plates which are or may be lost, stolen, destroyed or damaged.
[Vehicle Excise and Registration Act 1994, s 23.]

1. See the Road Vehicles (Display of Registration Marks) Regulations 2001, in this PART, post, regs 12–15.
2. See the Road Vehicles (Registration and Licensing) Regulations 2002, reg 39, in this PART, post.

4–1933   **24. Assignment of registration marks by motor dealers.**   (1) The Secretary of State may by regulations make such provisions and he considers appropriate with respect to the allocation of registration marks for vehicles to motor dealers who—

(a) apply for such allocations, and
(b) appear to the Secretary of State suitable to receive them,

and with respect to the assigning of the marks to vehicles by motor dealers.

(2) Regulations under this section may, in particular, include provision—

(a) as to the mode of application for the allocation of registration marks,
(b) as to the transfer of registration marks allocated to a motor dealer in cases where the motor dealer dies or becomes incapacitated or bankrupt and in such other cases as may be prescribed by the regulations, and
(c) as to the cancellation of allocations of registration marks.

(3) The provision which may be made by regulations under this section also includes provision for—

(a) restricting the circumstances in which a motor dealer may assign a registration mark to a vehicle,
(b) securing that registration marks allocated to a motor dealer are assigned by him in such sequence as the Secretary of State considers appropriate and that no registration mark is assigned to a vehicle to which a registration mark has already been assigned, and
(c) requiring a motor dealer to furnish to the Secretary of State within the period prescribed by the regulations such particulars in respect of each vehicle to which the motor dealer assigns a registration mark as are so prescribed.

(4) Where—

(a) the Secretary of State—

   (i) rejects an application by a motor dealer for an allocation of registration marks, or
   (ii) cancels an allocation of registration marks made to a motor dealer, and

(b) the motor dealer, within the period prescribed by regulations made by the Secretary of State, requests him to review his decision,

the Secretary of State shall comply with the request and (in doing so) consider any representations made to him in writing during that period by the motor dealer.

(5) Where the Secretary of State cancels an allocation of registration marks made to a motor dealer—

(a) the cancellation does not take effect before the end of the period prescribed by regulations made by the Secretary of State, and
(b) where during that period the motor dealer requests the Secretary of State to review his decision, the cancellation does not take effect before the Secretary of State gives notice in writing of the result of the review to the motor dealer.

(6) For the purposes of subsection (5)(b) notice may be given to a person by—

(a) delivering it to him,
(b) leaving it at his proper address, or
(c) sending it to him by post;

and for the purposes of this subsection, and of section 7 of the Interpretation Act 1978 in its application to this subsection, the proper address of a person is his latest address as known to the Secretary of State.

[Vehicle Excise and Registration Act 1994, s 24.]

4–1934   **25.** *Charge on request for registration mark.*

4–1935   **26.** *Retention of registration mark pending transfer.*

4–1936   **27.** *Sale of rights to particular registration marks*[1].

1. The Sale of Registration Marks Regulations 1995, SI 1995/2880, make a new scheme providing for registration marks to be assigned to vehicles registered in the names of persons who have acquired rights under the scheme to have the marks so assigned.

4–1936A   **27A. Registration plates.**   (1) The Secretary of State may by regulations—

(a) prescribe specifications for registration plates (whether relating to their size, shape, material of manufacture or otherwise),
(b) provide for registration plates to contain or display such information other than registration marks or (as the case may be) special registration marks as may be specified or described in the regulations.

(2) Regulations under subsection (1)(*b*) may, in particular, prescribe the form and manner in which any such information is to be contained or displayed.

(3) In this section "registration plates" means—

(*a*) plates or other devices for displaying registration marks and for fixing them on vehicles or trailers in accordance with regulations under section 23(3), or

(*b*) plates or other devices for displaying special registration marks and for fixing them on vehicles or trailers in accordance with regulations under section 22(2),

and includes plates or other devices which are also for containing or displaying information other than registration marks or (as the case may be) special registration marks (whether or not such information is to be contained or displayed by virtue of regulations under this section).

(4) In this section—

"special registration mark" means a mark indicating the registered number of a vehicle or trailer and assigned to the vehicle or trailer by virtue of regulations under section 22(2), and

"trailer" has the same meaning as in Part 8 of Schedule 1.*

[Vehicle Excise and Registration Act 1994, s 27A as inserted by the Vehicles (Crime) Act 2001, s 34.]

---

*Section 27A is printed as inserted by the Vehicles (Crime) Act 2001, s 34, from a date to be appointed.

Marking

4–1937   28. Marking of engines and bodies.   (1) The Secretary of State may by regulations make such provision as he thinks appropriate with respect to the marking of the engines and bodies of vehicles.

(2) Regulations under this section may, in particular, include provision—

(*a*) as to the persons by whom and the times at which engines and bodies of vehicles are to be marked,

(*b*) as to the form of any mark and the manner and position in which it is to be made, and

(*c*) for requiring particulars of marks made under the regulations to be furnished to the Secretary of State.

[Vehicle Excise and Registration Act 1994, s 28.]

Power of constables etc to require production of documents

4–1937A   28A. Power of constables etc to require production of registration documents.
(1) A person using a vehicle in respect of which a registration document has been issued must produce the document for inspection on being so required by—

(*a*) a constable, or

(*b*) a person authorised by the Secretary of State for the purposes of this section (an "authorised person").

(2) An authorised person exercising the power conferred by subsection (1) must, if so requested, produce evidence of his authority to exercise the power.

(3) A person is guilty of an offence if he fails to comply with subsection (1).

(4) Subsection (3) does not apply if any of the following conditions is satisfied.

(5) The first condition is that—

(*a*) the person produces the registration document, in person, at a police station specified by him at the time of the request, and

(*b*) he does so within 7 days after the date on which the request was made or as soon as is reasonably practicable.

(6) The second condition is that—

(*a*) the vehicle is subject to a lease or hire agreement,

(*b*) the vehicle is not registered in the name of the lessee or hirer under that agreement and is not required to be so registered,

(*c*) the person produces appropriate evidence of the agreement to the constable or authorised person at the time of the request or he produces such evidence in person, at a police station specified by him at the time of the request—

(i) within 7 days after the date of the request, or

(ii) as soon as is reasonably practicable, and

(*d*) the person has reasonable grounds for believing, or it is reasonable for him to expect, that the person from whom the vehicle has been leased or hired is able to produce, or require the production of, the registration document.

(7) In subsection (6)(*c*) "appropriate evidence" means—

(*a*) a copy of the agreement, or

(*b*) such other documentary evidence of the agreement as is prescribed in regulations under this section.

(8) The third condition is that any exception prescribed in regulations under this section is met.

(9) Where a requirement is imposed under subsection (1) by an authorised person, a testing

station provided under section 52(2) of the Road Traffic Act 1988 may be specified under subsection (5)(*a*) or (6)(*c*) instead of a police station.

(10) A person accused of an offence under this section is not entitled to the benefit of an exception conferred by or under this section unless evidence is adduced that is sufficient to raise an issue with respect to that exception, but where evidence is so adduced it is for the prosecution to prove beyond reasonable doubt that the exception does not apply.

(11) A person guilty of an offence under this section is liable on summary conviction to a fine not exceeding level 2 on the standard scale.

(12) The Secretary of State may make regulations—

(*a*) prescribing descriptions of evidence for the purposes of subsection (7);

(*b*) prescribing, varying or revoking exceptions for the purposes of subsection (8).

(13) In this section "registration document" means a registration document issued in accordance with regulations under section 22(1)(*e*).

[Vehicle Excise and Registration Act 1994, s 28A as inserted by the Serious Organised Crime and Police Act 2005, s 151.]

PART III
OFFENCES

Offence of using or keeping unlicensed vehicle

4–1938 29. Penalty for using or keeping unlicensed vehicle. (1) If a person uses[1], or keeps, on a public road[2] a vehicle (not being an exempt vehicle) which is unlicensed he is guilty of an offence[3].

(2) For the purposes of subsection (1) a vehicle is unlicensed if no vehicle licence or trade licence is in force[4] for or in respect of the vehicle.

(3) Subject to subsection (3A) person guilty of an offence under subsection (1) is liable on summary conviction to an excise penalty[5] of—

(*a*) **level 3** on the standard scale, or

(*b*) **five times the amount of the vehicle excise duty**[6] chargeable in respect of the vehicle,

whichever is the greater.

(3A) In the case of a person who—

(*a*) has provided the Secretary of State with a declaration or statement (in pursuance of regulations under section 22) that the vehicle will not during a period specified in the declaration or statement be used or kept on a public road, and,

(*b*) commits an offence under subsection (1) within a period prescribed by regulations,

subsection (3) applies as if the reference in paragraph (*a*) to level 3 were a reference to level 4.

(4) Where a vehicle for which a vehicle licence is in force is transferred by the holder of the licence to another person, the licence is to be treated for the purposes of subsection (2) as no longer in force unless it is delivered to the other person with the vehicle.

(5) Where—

(*a*) an application is made for a vehicle licence for any period, and

(*b*) a temporary licence is issued pursuant to the application,

subsection (4) does not apply to the licence applied for if, on a transfer of the vehicle during the currency of the temporary licence, the temporary licence is delivered with the vehicle to the transferee.

(6) The amount of the vehicle excise duty chargeable in respect of a vehicle is to be taken for the purposes of subsection (3)(*b*) to be an amount equal to the annual rate of duty applicable to the vehicle at the date on which the offence was committed[7].

(7) Where in the case of a vehicle kept (but not used) on a public road that annual rate differs from the annual rate by reference to which the vehicle was at that date chargeable under section 2(3) to (6) the amount of the vehicle excise duty chargeable in respect of the vehicle is to be taken for those purposes to be an amount equal to the latter rate.

(8) In the case of a conviction for a continuing offence, the offence is to be taken for the purposes of subsections (6) and (7) to have been committed on the date or latest date to which the conviction relates.

[Vehicle Excise and Registration Act 1994, s 29 as amended by the Finance Act 1996, Sch 2 and the Finance Act 2002, Sch 5.]

---

1. The user, not within the scope of any authority from the owner, is not the user of the owner (*Abercromby v Morris* (1932) 96 JP 392, [1932] All ER Rep 676). It may be an oppressive course to prosecute the driver of an unlicensed vehicle who is an employee and not responsible for licensing the vehicle (*Carpenter v Campbell* [1953] 1 All ER 280, 117 JP 90). For exempt vehicles, see Sch 2, post.

2. Ie a road which is repairable at the public expense (s 62, post).

3. The burden of proof is on the prosecutor throughout to show that it was the defendant who was the keeper of the vehicle on the road on the relevant day. If there is proof that the defendant was the registered keeper of the vehicle and no more, the burden of proof may not be discharged. However, a failure to respond to a notice under s 46, post, requesting the keeper of the vehicle to give information as to the identity of the person who kept the vehicle on the road gives rise to an adverse inference which discharges the burden of proof and entitles justices to convict (*Secretary of State for the Environment, Transport and the Regions v Holt* [2000] RTR 309, DC).

4. The onus is on the defendant to prove that a vehicle excise licence was in force in respect of the vehicle (*Guyll v Bright* [1987] RTR 104, 84 Cr App Rep 260). Where a licence is granted upon receipt of a cheque, subsequently dihonoured, the licence is void as from the time it was granted (Customs and Excise Management Act 1979, s 102 in

PART VIII: title CUSTOMS AND EXCISE, post). The burden shall be on the defendant as to certain questions of fact mentioned in s 53, post, touching the vehicle and the purpose for which it was used.

5. Recoverable on summary conviction (Customs and Excise Management Act 1979, s 156(2), in PART VIII: title CUSTOMS AND EXCISE, post; applied by virtue of s 6(2)(3), ante). For powers of the Secretary of State to mitigate or remit penalties see s 6(5), ante. Proceedings may be instituted by the Secretary of State or a constable with the approval of the Secretary of State at any time within six months from which evidence of the offence came to his knowledge but not more than three years from the commission of the offence (s 47, post). A person charged with an offence should be informed in the information or in an accompanying notice under which part of Sch 1 to the Act penalties and back duty will be recoverable; see *Halls Construction Services Ltd v DPP* [1989] RTR 399, DC.

Where a person convicted is a person by whom the vehicle in respect of which the offence was committed was kept at the time of the commission of the offence, there should be an additional payment of an amount calculated in accordance with s 30(2)–(5), post.

6. See sub-s (6), post.

7. In proceeding under this section the burden of proof regarding specified matters lies upon the defendant (s 53, post).

4–1939   **30. Additional liability for keeper of unlicensed vehicle.**   (1) Where the person convicted of an offence under section 29 is the person by whom the vehicle in respect of which the offence was committed was kept at the time at which it was committed, the court shall (in addition to any penalty which it may impose under that section) order[1] him to pay the amount specified in subsection (2)[2].

(2) The amount referred to in subsection (1) is an amount equal to one-twelfth of the annual rate of vehicle excise duty appropriate to the vehicle for each month, or part of a month, in the relevant period (within the meaning of section 31).

(3) In relation to any month or part of a month in the relevant period, the reference in subsection (2) to the annual rate of vehicle excise duty appropriate to the vehicle is a reference to the annual rate applicable to it at the beginning of that month or part.

(4) A vehicle is to be taken for the purposes of this section to have belonged throughout the relevant period to the description of vehicle to which it belonged for the purposes of vehicle excise duty at—

(*a*)   the date on which the offence was committed, or

(*b*)   if the prosecution so elect, the date when a vehicle licence for it was last issued,

except so far as it is proved to have fallen within some other description for the whole of any month or part of a month in that period.

(5) In the case of a conviction for a continuing offence, the offence is to be taken for the purposes of this section to have been committed on the date or latest date to which the conviction relates.

[Vehicle Excise and Registration Act 1994, s 30.]

---

1. Section 35 of the Magistrates' Courts Act 1980 (fixing amount of fine) has no application to the recovery of back duty and justices have no discretion to reduce the sums payable under this section (*Chief Constable of Kent v Mather* [1986] RTR 36).

2. Home Office Circular 158/1967 contains detailed recommendations to enable the necessary information to be provided for the court. In the case of a person convicted in his absence in pursuance of the Magistrates' Courts Act 1980, s 12(2) the court is required to proceed as if the amount of the additional duty had been calculated in accordance with this section unless the defendant states in his notice that the specified amount is inappropriate (s 55(4), post).

4–1940   **31. Relevant period for purposes of section 30.**   (1) For the purposes of section 30 the relevant period is the period—

(*a*)   ending with the date on which the offence was committed, and

(*b*)   beginning as provided by subsections (2) to (4).

(2) Subject to subsection (4), if the person convicted has before the date of the offence notified the Secretary of State of his acquisition of the vehicle in accordance with regulations[1] made by the Secretary of State, the relevant period begins with—

(*a*)   the date on which the notification was received by the Secretary of State, or

(*b*)   the expiry of the vehicle licence last in force for the vehicle,

whichever is the later.

(3) Subject to subsection (4), in any other case the relevant period begins with—

(*a*)   the expiry of the vehicle licence last in force for the vehicle before the date on which the offence was committed, or

(*b*)   if there has not at any time before that date been a vehicle licence in force for the vehicle, the date on which the vehicle was first kept by the person convicted.

(4) Where—

(*a*)   the person convicted has been ordered to pay an amount under section 30 on the occasion of a previous conviction for an offence in respect of the same vehicle, and

(*b*)   that offence was committed after the date specified in subsection (2) or (3) as the date with which the relevant period begins,

the relevant period instead begins with the month immediately following that in which the earlier offence was committed.

(5) Where the person convicted proves—

(*a*)   that throughout any month or part of a month in the relevant period the vehicle was not kept by him, or

(b) that he has paid the duty due in respect of the vehicle for any such month or part of a month,

any amount which the person is ordered to pay under section 30 is to be calculated as if that month or part of a month were not in the relevant period.

(6) Where a person has previously been ordered under section 36 to pay an amount for a month or part of a month in the case of a vehicle, any amount which he is ordered to pay under section 30 in the case of the vehicle is to be calculated as if no part of that month were in the relevant period.

(7) In this section references to the expiry of a vehicle licence include a reference to—

(a) its surrender, and

(b) its being treated as no longer in force for the purposes of subsection (2) of section 29 by subsection (4) of that section.

(8) In the case of a conviction for a continuing offence, the offence is to be taken for the purposes of this section to have been committed on the date or latest date to which the conviction relates.
[Vehicle Excise and Registration Act 1994, s 31 as amended by the Finance Act 1995, Schs 4 and 29.]

---

1. See the Road Vehicles (Registration and Licensing) Regulations 2002, reg 12, in this PART, post where however, the regulation applies in terms to a change of keeper rather than acquisition of ownership as in the predecessor regulations.

4–1940A 31A. Offence by registered keeper where vehicle unlicensed. (1) If a vehicle registered under this Act is unlicensed, the person in whose name the vehicle is registered is guilty of an offence.

(2) For the purposes of this section a vehicle is unlicensed if no vehicle licence or trade licence is in force for or in respect of the vehicle.

(3) Subsection (1) does not apply to a vehicle if—

(a) it is an exempt vehicle in respect of which regulations under this Act require a nil licence to be in force and a nil licence is in force in respect of the vehicle, or

(b) it is an exempt vehicle that is not one in respect of which regulations under this Act require a nil licence to be in force.

(4) Where a vehicle for which a vehicle licence is in force is transferred by the holder of the licence to another person, the licence is to be treated for the purposes of subsection (2) as no longer in force unless it is delivered to the other person with the vehicle.

(5) Where—

(a) an application is made for a vehicle licence for any period, and

(b) a temporary licence is issued pursuant to the application,

subsection (4) does not apply to the licence applied for if, on a transfer of the vehicle during the currency of the temporary licence, the temporary licence is delivered with the vehicle to the transferee.
[Vehicle Excise and Registration Act 1994, s 31A as inserted by the Finance Act 2002, Sch 5.]

4–1940B 31B. Exceptions to section 31A. (1) A person ("the registered keeper") in whose name an unlicensed vehicle is registered at any particular time ("the relevant time") does not commit an offence under section 31A at that time if any of the following conditions are satisfied.

(2) The first condition is that the registered keeper—

(a) is not at the relevant time the person keeping the vehicle, and

(b) if previously he was the person keeping the vehicle, he has by the relevant time complied with any requirements under section 22(1)(d)—

(i) that are prescribed for the purposes of this condition, and

(ii) that he is required to have complied with by the relevant or any earlier time.

(3) The second condition is that—

(a) the registered keeper is at the relevant time the person keeping the vehicle,

(b) at the relevant time the vehicle is neither kept nor used on a public road, and

(c) the registered keeper has by the relevant time complied with any requirements under section 22(1D)—

(i) that are prescribed for the purposes of this condition, and

(ii) that he is required to have complied with by the relevant or any earlier time.

(4) The third condition is that—

(a) the vehicle has been stolen before the relevant time,

(b) the vehicle has not been recovered by the relevant time, and

(c) any requirements under subsection (6) that, in connection with the theft, are required to have been complied with by the relevant or any earlier time have been complied with by the relevant time.

(5) The fourth condition is that the relevant time falls within a period ("the grace days")—

(a) beginning with the expiry of the last vehicle licence to be in force for the vehicle, and

(b) of a prescribed length,

and a vehicle licence for the vehicle is taken out within the grace days for a period beginning with the grace days.

(6) The Secretary of State may by regulations make provision for the purposes of subsection

(4)(c) as to the persons to whom, the times at which and the manner in which the theft of a vehicle is to be notified.

(7) The Secretary of State may by regulations make provision amending this section for the purpose of providing for further exceptions to section 31A(1) (or varying or revoking any such further exceptions).

(8) A person accused of an offence under section 31A(1) is not entitled to the benefit of an exception conferred by or under this section unless evidence is adduced that is sufficient to raise an issue with respect to that exception, but where evidence is so adduced it is for the prosecution to prove beyond reasonable doubt that the exception does not apply.

(9) In this section—

(a) references to the expiry of a vehicle licence include a reference to—

(i) its surrender, and
(ii) its being treated as no longer in force for the purposes of subsection (2) of section 31A by subsection (4) of that section;

(b) "prescribed" means prescribed by regulations made by the Secretary of State.

[Vehicle Excise and Registration Act 1994, s 31B as inserted by the Finance Act 2002, Sch 5.]

4–1940C   31C. Penalties for offences under section 31A.   (1) A person guilty of an offence under section 31A(1) is liable on summary conviction to—

(a) an excise penalty of—

(i) level 3 on the standard scale, or
(ii) five times the amount of vehicle excise duty chargeable in respect of the vehicle concerned,

whichever is the greater; and

(b) if subsection (3) applies to him, an excise penalty (in addition to any under paragraph (a)) of an amount that complies with subsection (2).

(2) An amount complies with this subsection if it—

(a) is not less than the greater of—

(i) the maximum of the penalty to which the person is liable under subsection (1)(a), and
(ii) the amount of the supplement (if any) that became payable by him by reason of non-renewal of the vehicle licence for the vehicle that last expired before the commission of the offence; and

(b) is not more than the greatest of—

(i) the maximum of the penalty to which the person is liable under subsection (1)(a),
(ii) the amount mentioned in paragraph (a)(ii), and
(iii) ten times the amount of vehicle excise duty chargeable in respect of the vehicle.

(3) This subsection applies to the person if—

(a) he was, at the time proceedings for the offence were commenced, the person in whose name the vehicle concerned was registered under this Act, and
(b) that vehicle was unlicensed throughout the period beginning with the commission of the offence and ending with the commencement of those proceedings.

(4) The amount of vehicle excise duty chargeable in respect of a vehicle is to be taken for the purposes of subsections (1) and (2) to be an amount equal to the annual rate of duty applicable to the vehicle at the date on which the offence was committed.

(5) Where in the case of a vehicle kept (but not used) on a public road that annual rate differs from the annual rate by reference to which the vehicle was at that date chargeable under section 2(3) to (6), the amount of the vehicle excise duty chargeable in respect of the vehicle is to be taken for those purposes to be an amount equal to the latter rate.

(6) In the case of a conviction for a continuing offence, the offence is to be taken for the purposes of subsections (4) and (5) to have been committed on the date or latest date to which the conviction relates.

(7) In this section, references to the expiry of a vehicle licence include a reference to—

(a) its surrender, and
(b) its being treated as no longer in force for the purposes of subsection (2) of section 31A by subsection (4) of that section.]

[Vehicle Excise and Registration Act 1994, s 31C as inserted by the Finance Act 2002, Sch 5.]

4–1941   32. Sections 29 to 31C: supplementary.   (1) Where in the case of an offence under section 29 or 31A there is made against a person—

(a) an order under section 12 of the Powers of Criminal Courts (Sentencing) Act 2000 discharging him absolutely or conditionally,
(b) Scotland,
(c) Northern Ireland.

he is to be treated for the purposes of sections 29 to 31or (as the case may be) sections 31A to 31C as having been convicted.

(2) Section 30 has effect subject to the provisions (applying with the necessary modifications) of any enactment relating to the imposition of fines by magistrates' courts and courts of summary jurisdiction, other than any conferring a discretion as to their amount.

(3) Where a sum is payable by virtue of an order under section 30—

(*a*) in England and Wales, the sum is to be treated as a fine, and the order as a conviction, for the purposes of Part III of the Magistrates' Courts Act 1980 (including any enactment having effect as if contained in that Part) and of any other enactment relating to the recovery or application of sums ordered to be paid by magistrates' courts,

(*b*) Scotland.

(*c*) *Northern Ireland.*

[Vehicle Excise and Registration Act 1994, s 32 as amended by the Powers of Criminal Courts (Sentencing) Act 2000, Sch 9 and the Finance Act 2002, Sch 5.]

Other offences relating to licences

4–1941A 32A. Immobilisation, removal and disposal of vehicles. Schedule 2A (which relates to the immobilisation of vehicles as regards which it appears that an offence under section 29(1) is being committed and to their removal and disposal) shall have effect.

[Vehicle Excise and Registration Act 1994, s 32A, as inserted by the Finance Act 1995, Sch 4.]

4–1942 33. Not exhibiting licence. (1) A person is guilty of an offence if—

(*a*) he uses, or keeps, on a public road[1] a vehicle in respect of which vehicle excise duty is chargeable, and

(*b*) there is not fixed to and exhibited on the vehicle in the manner prescribed by regulations[2] made by the Secretary of State a licence for, or in respect of, the vehicle which is for the time being in force.

(1A) A person is guilty of an offence if—

(*a*) he uses, or keeps, on a public road an exempt vehicle,

(*b*) that vehicle is one in respect of which regulations[2] under this Act require a nil licence to be in force, and

(*c*) there is not fixed to and exhibited on the vehicle in the manner prescribed by regulations made by the Secretary of State a nil licence for that vehicle which is for the time being in force.

(2) A person guilty of an offence under subsection (1) or (1A) is liable on summary conviction to a fine not exceeding **level 1** on the standard scale.

(3) Subsections (1) and (1A)—

(*a*) have effect subject to the provisions of regulations[2] made by the Secretary of State, and

(*b*) are without prejudice to sections 29, 31A and 43A[3].

(4) The Secretary of State may make regulations[2] prohibiting a person from exhibiting on a vehicle which is kept or used on a public road anything—

(*a*) which is intended to be, or

(*b*) which could reasonably be,

mistaken for a licence which is for, or in respect of, the vehicle and which is for the time being in force.

(5) The reference to a licence in subsection (4) includes a reference to a nil licence.

[Vehicle Excise and Registration Act 1994, s 33 as amended by the Finance Act 1996, Sch 2 and the Finance Act 1997, Sch 3 and the Finance Act 2002, Sch 5.]

---

1. "Public road" means a road repairable at public expense (s 62, post).
2. See the Road Vehicles (Registration and Licensing) Regulations 2002, regs 6 and 7, in this PART, post
3. It is not defence to a charge for this offence that the defendant has been convicted of an offence under (s 29) of using or keeping the vehicle without a licence at the same time or place (*Pilgrim v Dean* [1974] 2 All ER 751, 138 JP 502).

4–1943 34. Trade licences: penalties. (1) A person holding a trade licence or trade licences is guilty of an offence if he—

(*a*) uses at any one time on a public road[1] a greater number of vehicles[2] (not being vehicles for which vehicle licences are for the time being in force) than he is authorised to use by virtue of the trade licence or licences,

(*b*) uses a vehicle (not being a vehicle for which a vehicle licence is for the time being in force) on a public road[1] for any purpose other than a purpose which has been prescribed under section 12(2)(*b*), or

(*c*) uses the trade licence, or any of the trade licences, for the purposes of keeping on a public road in any circumstances other than circumstances which have been prescribed under section 12(1)(*c*) a vehicle which is not being used on that road

(2) A person guilty of an offence under subsection (1) is liable on summary conviction to an **excise penalty**[3] of—

(*a*) **level 3** on the standard scale, or

(*b*) **five times the amount of the vehicle excise duty** chargeable in respect of (in the case of an offence under subsection (1)(*a*)) the vehicles which he is not authorised to use or (in the case of an offence under subsection (1)(*b*) or (*c*)) the vehicle concerned,

whichever is the greater.

(3) The amount of the vehicle excise duty chargeable in respect of a vehicle is to be taken for the purposes of subsection (2) to be an amount equal to the annual rate of duty applicable to the vehicle at the date on which the offence was committed[4].

(4) Where in the case of a vehicle kept (but not used) on a public road[1] that annual rate differs from the annual rate by reference to which the vehicle was at that date chargeable under section 2(3) to (6), the amount of the vehicle excise duty chargeable in respect of the vehicle is to be taken for those purposes to be an amount equal to the latter rate.

(5) In the case of a conviction for a continuing offence, the offence is to be taken for the purposes of subsections (3) and (4) to have been committed on the date or latest date to which the conviction relates.

[Vehicle Excise and Registration Act 1994, s 34, as amended by the Finance Act 2002, Sch 5.]

---

1. "Public road" means a road repairable at public expense (s 62, post).
2. If any question arises as to the number of vehicles used, the burden of proof in respect thereof lies upon the defendant (s 53, post).
3. See note 4 to s 29, ante.
4. In proceedings under this section the burden of proof regarding specified matters lies upon the defendant (s 53, post).

4–1944   **35. Failure to return licence.**   (1) A person who knowingly fails to comply with section 10(3) is guilty of an offence.

(2) A person guilty of an offence under subsection (1) is liable on summary conviction to a fine not exceeding **level 3** on the standard scale.

[Vehicle Excise and Registration Act 1994, s 35.]

4–1944A   **35A. Dishonoured cheques.**   (1) In a case where—

(*a*) a notice sent as mentioned in section 19A(2)(*b*) or 19B(2)(*c*) or a further notice sent as mentioned in section 19A(3)(*d*) or 19B(3)(*d*) contains a relevant requirement, and
(*b*) the person fails to comply with the requirement contained in the notice,

he shall be liable on summary conviction to a penalty of an amount found under subsection (2).

(2) The amount is whichever is the greater of—

(*a*) level 3 on the standard scale;
(*b*) an amount equal to five times the annual rate of duty that was payable on the grant of the licence or would have been so payable if it had been taken out for a period of twelve months.

(3) For the purposes of subsection (1)(*a*), a relevant requirement is—

(*a*) a requirement to deliver up the licence within such reasonable period as is specified in the notice; or
(*b*) a requirement to deliver up the licence within such reasonable period as is so specified and, on doing so, to pay the amount specified in subsection (4).

(4) The amount referred to in subsection (3)(*b*) is an amount equal to one-twelfth of the appropriate annual rate of vehicle excise duty for each month, or part of a month, in the relevant period.

(5) The reference in subsection (4) to the appropriate annual rate of vehicle excise duty is a reference to the annual rate which at the beginning of the relevant period—

(*a*) in the case of a vehicle licence, was applicable to a vehicle of the description specified in the application, or
(*b*) in the case of a trade licence, was applicable to a vehicle falling within paragraph 1(2) of Schedule 1 (or to a vehicle falling within sub-paragraph (1)(*c*) of paragraph 2 of that Schedule if the licence was to be used only for vehicles to which that paragraph applies).

(6) For the purposes of subsection (4) the relevant period is the period—

(*a*) beginning with the first day of the period for which the licence was applied for or, if later, the day on which the licence first was to have effect, and
(*b*) ending with whichever is the earliest of the times specified in subsection (7).

(7) In a case where the requirement is a requirement to deliver up a vehicle licence, those times are—

(*a*) the end of the month during which the licence was required to be delivered up,
(*b*) the end of the month during which the licence was actually delivered up,
(*c*) the date on which the licence was due to expire, and
(*d*) the end of the month preceding that in which there first had effect a new vehicle licence for the vehicle in question;

and, in a case where the requirement is a requirement to deliver up a trade licence, those times are the times specified in paragraphs (*a*) to (*c*).

[Vehicle Excise and Registration Act 1994, s 35A, as inserted by the Finance Act 1995, Sch 4 and amended by the Finance Act 1997, s 19, the Finance Act 1998, s 19 and the finance act 1999, s 8.]

4–1945   36. Dishonoured cheques: additional liability.   (1) Where a person has been convicted of an offence under section 35A in relation to a vehicle licence or a trade licence, the court shall (in addition to any penalty which it may impose under that section) order him to pay the amount specified in subsection (2).

(2) The amount referred to in subsection (1) is an amount equal to one-twelfth of the appropriate annual rate of vehicle excise duty for each month, or part of a month, in the relevant period.

(3) The reference in subsection (2) to the appropriate annual rate of vehicle excise duty is a reference to the annual rate which at the beginning of the relevant period—

(*a*) in the case of a vehicle licence, was applicable to a vehicle of the description specified in the application, or

(*b*) in the case of a trade licence, was applicable to a vehicle falling within paragraph 1(2) of Schedule 1 (or to a vehicle falling within sub-paragraph (1)(*c*) of paragraph 2 of that Schedule if the licence was to be used only for vehicles to which that paragraph applies).

(4) For the purposes of this section the relevant period is the period—

(*a*) beginning with the first day of the period for which the licence was applied for or, if later, the day on which the licence first was to have effect, and

(*b*) ending with whichever is the earliest of the times specified in subsection (4A).

(4A) In the case of a vehicle licence those times are—

(*a*) the end of the month in which the order is made,

(*b*) the date on which the licence was due to expire,

(*c*) the end of the month during which the licence was delivered up, and

(*d*) the end of the month preceding that in which there first had effect a new licence for the vehicle in question;

and, in the case of a trade licence, those times are the times specified in paragraphs (*a*) to (*c*).

(5) Where a person has previously been ordered under section 30 to pay an amount for a month or part of a month in the case of a vehicle, any amount which he is ordered to pay under this section in the case of a vehicle licence for the vehicle is to be calculated as if no part of that month were in the relevant period.

(6) Where—

(*a*) a person has been convicted of an offence under section 35A in relation to a vehicle licence or a trade licence, and

(*b*) a requirement to pay an amount with respect to that licence has been imposed on that person by virtue of section 35A(3)(*b*),

the order to pay an amount under this section shall have effect instead of that requirement and the amount to be paid under the order shall be reduced by any amount actually paid in pursuance of the requirement.

[Vehicle Excise and Registration Act 1994, s 36 as amended by the Finance Act 1995, Sch 4, the Finance Act 1996, s 18, the Finance Act 1998, s 19 and the finance act 1999, s 8.]

Offence of not paying duty chargeable at higher rate

4–1946   37. Penalty for not paying duty chargeable at higher rate.   (1) Where—

(*a*) a vehicle licence has been taken out for a vehicle at any rate of vehicle excise duty,

(*b*) at any time while the licence is in force the vehicle is so used that duty at a higher rate becomes chargeable in respect of the licence for the vehicle under section 15, and

(*c*) duty at that higher rate was not paid before the vehicle was so used,

the person so using the vehicle is guilty of an offence[1].

(2) A person guilty of an offence under subsection (1) is liable on summary conviction to an excise penalty[2] of—

(*a*) level 3 on the standard scale, or

(*b*) five times the difference between the duty actually paid on the licence and the amount of the duty at the higher rate[3].

whichever is the greater.

[Vehicle Excise and Registration Act 1994, s 37 as amended by the Finance Act 1995, Schs 4 and 29.]

---

1. In proceedings under this section the burden of proof regarding specified matters lies upon the defendant (s 53, post).

2. See note 4 to s 29, ante.

3. A person charged with using an undertaxed vehicle should be informed in the information or in an accompanying notice under which Part of Sch 1 to the Act penalties and back duty will be recoverable (*Halls Construction Services Ltd v DPP* [1989] RTR 399, DC).

4–1947   38. Additional liability for keeper of vehicle chargeable at higher rate.   (1) Where the person convicted of an offence under section 37 is the person by whom the vehicle in respect of which the offence was committed was kept at the time at which it was committed, the court shall (in addition to any penalty which it may impose under that section) order him to pay the amount specified in subsection (2).

(2) The amount referred to in subsection (1) is an amount equal to one-twelfth of the difference between—

(a) the rate of duty at which the licence in relation to which the offence was committed was taken out, and

(b) the relevant higher rate of duty (within the meaning of section 39) in relation to the vehicle,

for each month, or part of a month, in the relevant period (within the meaning of section 40).

(3) A vehicle is to be taken for the purposes of subsection (2) to have belonged throughout the relevant period to the description of vehicle to which it belonged for the purposes of vehicle excise duty at the date on which the offence was committed, except so far as it is proved to have fallen within some other description for the whole of any month or part of a month in that period.

(4) Where a person is convicted of more than one offence under section 37 in respect of the same vehicle (whether or not in the same proceedings), the court shall (in calculating the amount payable under this section in respect of any of the offences) reduce the amount in relation to any period by any amount ordered to be paid under this section in relation to the period in respect of any other such offence.

[Vehicle Excise and Registration Act 1994, s 38.]

4–1948   39. Relevant higher rate of duty for purposes of section 38.   (1) For the purposes of section 38 the relevant higher rate of duty in relation to a vehicle is the rate provided by this section.

(2) Where—

(a) at the time of the offence the vehicle had a revenue weight which exceeded that which it had when the licence in relation to which the offence was committed was taken out, and

(b) the licence was taken out at the rate applicable to the previous weight,

the relevant higher rate of duty is the rate which would have been applicable had the licence been taken out by reference to the higher weight.

(3) Where—

(a) the vehicle is a tractive unit,

(b) the licence in relation to which the offence was committed was taken out at a rate applicable to the use of the vehicle—

(i)   only with semi-trailers having not fewer than two axles, or

(ii) only with semi-trailers having not fewer than three axles, and

(c) the offence consisted in using the vehicle with a semi-trailer with a smaller number of axles,

the relevant higher rate of duty is the rate which would have been applicable had the licence been taken out by reference to the use of the vehicle which constituted the offence.

(4) Where—

(a) the licence in relation to which the offence was committed was taken out at a rate applicable, by virtue of paragraph 13 of Schedule 1, to a weight lower than the revenue weight of the vehicle, and

(b) the offence consisted of using the vehicle in contravention of a condition imposed under or by virtue of sub-paragraph (2) of that paragraph,

the relevant higher rate of duty is the rate which would have been applicable had the licence been taken out by reference to the revenue weight of the vehicle.

(5) Where—

(a) the licence in relation to which the offence was committed was taken out at a rate lower than that applicable to it by reference to its revenue weight, and

(b) none of subsections (2) to (4) apply,

the relevant higher rate of duty is the rate which would have been applicable had the licence been taken out by reference to the revenue weight of the vehicle.

(6) Where—

(a) the licence in relation to which the offence was committed was taken out at a rate lower than that at which duty was chargeable in respect of the condition, manner or purpose of use of the vehicle which constituted the offence, and

(b) none of subsections (2) to (5) apply,

the relevant higher rate of duty is the rate which would have been applicable had the licence been taken out by reference to the condition, manner or purpose of use of the vehicle which constituted the offence.

[Vehicle Excise and Registration Act 1994, s 39 as amended by the Finance Act 1995, Sch 4.]

4–1949   40. Relevant period for purposes of section 38.   (1) For the purposes of section 38 the relevant period is the period—

(a) ending on the date on which the offence was committed, and

(b) beginning as provided by subsection (2) or (3).

(2) If the offence consists in the vehicle having a revenue weight which exceeds that which it had

when the licence in relation to which the offence was committed was taken out, the relevant period begins with the date on which the vehicle became a vehicle with a higher revenue weight.

(3) In any other case, the relevant period begins with the date on which the licence in relation to which the offence was committed first took effect.

(4) Where the person convicted proves—

(a) that throughout any month or part of a month in the relevant period the vehicle was not kept by him, or

(b) that he has paid the duty due (or an amount equal to the duty due) at the relevant higher rate in respect of the vehicle for any such month or part of a month,

any amount which the person is ordered to pay under section 38 is to be calculated as if that month or part of a month were not in the relevant period.

[Vehicle Excise and Registration Act 1994, s 40, as amended by the Finance Act 1995, Sch 4.]

4–1950　41. Sections 37 to 40; supplementary. (1) Where in the case of an offence under section 37 there is made against a person—

(a) an order under section 12 of the Powers of Criminal Courts (Sentencing) Act 2000 discharging him absolutely or conditionally,

(b) Scotland,

(c) Northern Ireland.

he is to be treated for the purposes of sections 38 to 40 as having been convicted.

(2) Section 38 has effect subject to the provisions (applying with the necessary modifications) of any enactment relating to the imposition of fines by magistrates' courts and courts of summary jurisdiction, other than any conferring a discretion as to their amount.

(3) Where a sum is payable by virtue of an order under section 38—

(a) in England and Wales, the sum is to be treated as a fine, and the order as a conviction, for the purposes of Part III of the Magistrates' Courts Act 1980 (including any enactment having effect as if contained in that Part) and of any other enactment relating to the recovery or application of sums ordered to be paid by magistrates' courts,

(b) Scotland,

(c) Northern Ireland.

[Vehicle Excise and Registration Act 1994, s 41 as amended by the Finance Act 1995, Schs 4 and 29 and the Powers of Criminal Courts (Sentencing) Act 2000, Sch 9.]

Offences relating to registration marks

4–1951　42. Not fixing registration mark. (1) If a registration mark is not fixed on a vehicle as required by virtue of section 23, the relevant person is guilty of an offence.

(2) A person guilty of an offence under subsection (1) is liable on summary conviction to a fine not exceeding **level 3** on the standard scale.

(3) In subsection (1) "the relevant person" means the person driving the vehicle or, where it is not being driven, the person keeping it.

(4) It is a defence for a person charged with an offence under subsection (1) to prove that—

(a) he had no reasonable opportunity to register the vehicle under this Act, and

(b) the vehicle was being driven for the purpose of being so registered.

(5) It is a defence for a person charged with an offence under subsection (1) in relation to a vehicle—

(a) to which section 47 of the Road Traffic Act 1988 applies by virtue of subsection (2)(b) of that section, or

(b) Northern Ireland,

(vehicles manufactured before the prescribed period and used before registration) to prove that he had no reasonable opportunity to register the vehicle under this Act and that the vehicle was being driven in accordance with subsection (6).

(6) A vehicle is being driven in accordance with this subsection if—

(a) it is being driven for the purposes of, or in connection with, its examination under section 45 of the Road Traffic Act 1988 in circumstances in which its use is exempted from subsection (1) of section 47 of that Act by regulations under subsection (6) of that section, or

(b) Northern Ireland.

[Vehicle Excise and Registration Act 1994, s 42.]

4–1952　43. Obscured registration mark. (1) If a registration mark fixed on a vehicle as required by virtue of section 23 is in any way—

(a) obscured, or

(b) rendered, or allowed to become, not easily distinguishable,

the relevant person is guilty of an offence.

(2) A person guilty of an offence under subsection (1) is liable on summary conviction to a fine not exceeding **level 3** on the standard scale.

(3) In subsection (1) "the relevant person" means the person driving the vehicle or, where it is not being driven, the person keeping it.

(4) It is a defence for a person charged with an offence under this section to prove that he took all steps which it was reasonably practicable to take to prevent the mark being obscured or rendered not easily distinguishable.

[Vehicle Excise and Registration Act 1994, s 43.]

Other offences

4–1952A 43A. Failure to have nil licence for exempt vehicle. (1) A person is guilty of an offence if—

(*a*) he uses, or keeps on a public road an exempt vehicle,

(*b*) that vehicle is one in respect of which regulations under this Act require a nil licence to be in force, and

(*c*) a nil licence is not for the time being in force in respect of the vehicle.

(2) A person guilty of an offence under subsection (1) is liable on summary conviction to a fine not exceeding **level 2** on the standard scale.

(3) Subsection (1) has effect subject to the provisions of regulations made by the Secretary of State.

(4) The Secretary of State may, if he thinks fit, compound any proceedings for an offence under this section.

[Vehicle Excise and Registration Act 1994, s 43A, as inserted by the Finance Act 1997, Sch 3.]

4–1952B 43B. Vehicle identity checks: impersonation of authorised examiners. (1) A person is guilty of an offence if, with intent to deceive, he falsely represents himself to be a person entitled under regulations made by virtue of section 22A(2) to carry out examinations of vehicles in accordance with regulations so made.

(2) A person guilty of an offence under subsection (1) is liable on summary conviction to a fine not exceeding level 3 on the standard scale.

[Vehicle Excise and Registration Act 1994, s 43B, as inserted by the Vehicles (Crime) Act 2001, Sch.]

4–1952C 43C. Offence of using an incorrectly registered vehicle. (1) A person is guilty of an offence if, on a public road or in a public place, he uses a vehicle to which subsection (2) applies and in respect of which—

(*a*) the name and address of the keeper are not recorded in the register, or

(*b*) any of the particulars recorded in the register are incorrect.

(2) This subsection applies to a vehicle if—

(*a*) vehicle excise duty is chargeable in respect of it, or

(*b*) it is an exempt vehicle in respect of which regulations under this Act require a nil licence to be in force.

(3) It is a defence for a person charged with an offence under subsection (1) to show (as the case may be)—

(*a*) that there was no reasonable opportunity, before the material time, to furnish the name and address of the keeper of the vehicle, or

(*b*) that there was no reasonable opportunity, before the material time, to furnish particulars correcting the incorrect particulars.

(4) It is also a defence for a person charged with an offence under subsection (1) to show—

(*a*) that he had reasonable grounds for believing, or that it was reasonable for him to expect, that the name and address of the keeper or the other particulars of registration (as the case may be) were correctly recorded in the register, or

(*b*) that any exception prescribed in regulations under this section is met.

(5) A person guilty of an offence under this section is liable on summary conviction to a fine not exceeding level 3 on the standard scale.

(6) The Secretary of State may make regulations prescribing, varying or revoking exceptions for the purposes of subsection (4)(*b*).

(7) In this section—

"keeper", in relation to a vehicle, means the person by whom it is kept at the material time;

"the register" means the register kept by the Secretary of State under Part 2.

[Vehicle Excise and Registration Act 1994, s 43C, as inserted by the Serious Organised Crime and Police Act 2005, s 150.]

4–1953 44. Forgery and fraud. (1) A person is guilty of an offence if he forges[1], fraudulently[2] alters, fraudulently uses[3], fraudulently lends or fraudulently allows to be used by another person anything to which subsection (2) applies.

(2) This subsection applies to—

(*a*) a vehicle licence,

(*b*) a trade licence,

(c) a nil licence,
(d) a registration mark,
(e) a registration document, and
(f) a trade plate (including a replacement trade plate).

(3) A person guilty of an offence under this section is liable—

(a) on summary conviction, to a fine not exceeding the **statutory maximum**, and
(b) on conviction on indictment, to imprisonment for a term not exceeding **two years or to a fine** or (except in Scotland) to **both**[4].

[Vehicle Excise and Registration Act 1994, s 44, as amended by the Finance Act 1997, Sch 3.]

---

1. The definition of forgery in the Forgery and Counterfeiting Act 1981, s 1, should be applied. Accordingly a person charged under s 44 with forgery of a licence will be guilty of an offence if (i) he made a false licence; (ii) with the intent that he or another should use it to include another to accept it as genuine; and (iii) by reason of so accepting it to do or not to do some act, to his own or another's prejudice as a result of such acceptance of the false licence as genuine in connection with the performance of any duty (*R v Macrae* (1993) 159 JP 359, [1994] Crim LR 363). In *Clifford v Bloom* [1977] RTR 351, where the terminal letter on registration plates was altered, "forges" was defined as the making of a false registration mark upon a number plate with the intention that it should be regarded as genuine.

2. In *R v Terry* [1984] AC 374, [1984] 1 All ER 65, 78 Cr App Rep 101 "fraudulently" was given a wide meaning, following *Welham v DPP* [1961] AC 103, [1960] 1 All ER 805, 124 JP 280, not confined to economic loss but including the purpose of deceiving a police officer into thinking a motor car was properly licensed.

3. The offence of fraudulently using a vehicle licence is only committed where there is evidence that the vehicle was being or had been used on a public road while displaying the offending licence. Accordingly, exhibiting an altered licence on private land, with an intention to use the vehicle with the licence in future, is insufficient to constitute an offence (*R v Johnson (Tony)* (1994) 158 JP 788, [1995] RTR 15, [1995] Crim LR 250, CA).

4. For procedure in respect of an offence triable either way, see the Magistrates' Courts Act 1980, ss 17A–21, PART I, MAGISTRATES' COURTS, PROCEDURE, *ante.*

4–1954   45. False or misleading declarations and information.   (1) A person who in connection with—

(a) an application for a vehicle licence or a trade licence,
(b) a claim for a rebate under section 20, or
(c) an application for an allocation of registration marks,

makes a declaration which to his knowledge is either false or in any material respect misleading[1] is guilty of an offence.

(2) A person who makes a declaration which—

(a) is required by regulations under this Act to be made in respect of a vehicle which is an exempt vehicle under paragraph 19 of Schedule 2, and
(b) to his knowledge is either false or in any material respect misleading[1],

is guilty of an offence.

(2A) A person who makes a declaration or statement which—

(a) is required to be made in respect of a vehicle by regulations under section 22, and
(b) to his knowledge is either false or in any material respect misleading,

is guilty of an offence.

(3) A person who—

(a) is required by virtue of this Act to furnish particulars relating to, or to the keeper of, a vehicle, and
(b) furnishes particulars which to his knowledge are either false or in any material respect misleading[1],

is guilty of an offence.

(3A) A person who, in supplying information or producing documents for the purposes of any regulations made under section 61A or 61B—

(a) makes a statement which to his knowledge is false or in any material respect misleading or recklessly makes a statement which is false or in any material respect misleading, or
(b) produces or otherwise makes use of a document which to his knowledge is false or in any material respect misleading,

is guilty of an offence.

(3B) A person who—

(a) with intent to deceive, forges, alters or uses a certificate issued by virtue of section 61A or 61B;
(b) knowing or believing that it will be used for deception lends such a certificate to another or allows another to alter or use it; or
(c) without reasonable excuse makes or has in his possession any document so closely resembling such a certificate as to be calculated to deceive,

is guilty of an offence.

(4) A person guilty of an offence under this section is liable—

(a) on summary conviction, to a fine not exceeding the **statutory maximum**, and
(b) on conviction on indictment, to imprisonment for a term not exceeding **two years** or to a fine or (except in Scotland) to **both**[2].

[Vehicle Excise and Registration Act 1994, s 45 as amanded by the Finance Act 1995, Sch 4, the Finance Act 1996, Sch 2 and the Finance Act 1998, Sch 1.]

---

1. In proceedings under this section the burden of proof regarding specified matters lies upon the defendant (s 53, post).
2. For procedure in respect of an offence triable either way, see the Magistrates' Courts Act 1980, ss 17A–21, PART I, MAGISTRATES' COURTS, PROCEDURE, ante.

4–1955   46. Duty to give information[1]. (1) Where it is alleged that a vehicle has been used on a road in contravention of section 29[2], 34[3], 37[4] or 43A—

(a) the person keeping the vehicle shall give such information as he may be required to give in accordance with subsection (7) as to the identity of the driver of the vehicle or any person who used the vehicle, and

(b) any other person shall give such information as it is in his power to give and which may lead to the identification of the driver of the vehicle or any person who used the vehicle if he is required to do so in accordance with subsection (7).

(2) Where it is alleged that a vehicle has been kept on a road in contravention of section 29 or 43A—

(a) the person keeping the vehicle shall give such information as he may be required to give in accordance with subsection (7) as to the identity of the person who kept the vehicle on the road, and

(b) any other person shall give such information as it is in his power to give and which may lead to the identification of the person who kept the vehicle on the road if he is required to do so in accordance with subsection (7).

(3) Where it is alleged that a vehicle has at any time been used on a road in contravention of section 29 or 43A, the person who is alleged to have so used the vehicle shall give such information as it is in his power to give as to the identity of the person who was keeping the vehicle at that time if he is required to do so in accordance with subsection (7).

(4) A person who fails to comply with subsection (1), (2) or (3) is guilty of an offence.

(5) A person guilty of an offence under subsection (4) is liable on summary conviction to a fine not exceeding **level 3** on the standard scale.

(6) If a person is charged with an offence under subsection (4) consisting of failing to comply with subsection (1)(a) or (2)(a), it is a defence for him to show to the satisfaction of the court that he did not know, and could not with reasonable diligence have ascertained, the identity of the person or persons concerned.

(7) A person is required to give information in accordance with this subsection if he is required to give the information by or on behalf of—

(a) a chief officer of police or, in Northern Ireland, the Chief Constable of the Royal Ulster Constabulary, or

(b) the Secretary of State.

[Vehicle Excise and Registration Act 1994, s 46, as amended by the Finance Act 1997, Sch 3.]

---

1. This section corresponds to s 172 of the Road Traffic Act 1988, post, and s 70 of the Public Passenger Vehicles Act 1981, post. The notes to that section are relevant hereto. For evidence by written admission of the identity of the driver, see s 32, post.
2. Using or keeping a vehicle without a licence, ante.
3. Using excessive number of vehicles under a trade licence, ante.
4. Failure to pay a higher rate of duty, ante.

4–1955A   46A. Duty to give information: offences under regulations. (1) Subsection (2) applies where it appears to the Secretary of State—

(a) that a person is a person by, through or to whom a vehicle has been sold or disposed of and that he has failed to comply with regulations made by virtue of section 22(1)(d) requiring him to furnish particulars prescribed by the regulations;

(b) that a person is a person by or through whom a vehicle has been sold or disposed of an that he has failed to comply with regulations made by virtue of section 22(1)(dd) requiring him to furnish a document prescribed by the regulations; or

(c) that a person is a person who is surrendering a vehicle licence, or who is not renewing a vehicle licence for a vehicle kept by him or who is keeping an unlicensed vehicle and that he has failed to comply with regulations made by virtue of section 22(1D) requiring him to furnish particulars or make a declaration prescribed by the regulations.

(2) The Secretary of State may serve a notice on the person in question requiring him to give the Secretary of State such information as it in his power to give—

(a) as to the identity of any person who is keeping a specified vehicle or who has kept it at a specified time or during a specified period;

(b) as to the identity of any person by, through or to whom a specified vehicle has been sold or disposed of at a specified time or during a specified period; or

(c) which may lead to the identification of a person falling within paragraph (a) or (b).

(3) A person who fails to comply with a notice under subsection (2) is guilty of an offence.

(4) A person guilty of an offence under subsection (3) is liable on summary conviction to a fine not exceeding **level 3** on the standard scale.

(5) In this section 'specified' means specified in a notice under subsection (2).

[Vehicle Excise and Registration Act 1994, s 46A, as inserted by the Finance Act 1996, Sch 2.]

PART IV
LEGAL PROCEEDINGS

Institution and conduct of proceedings

4–1956 47. Proceedings in England and Wales or Northern Ireland. (1) No proceedings for an offence under section 29[1], 31A, 34[2], 35A or 37[3] shall be instituted in England and Wales or Northern Ireland except by the Secretary of State or a constable; and no such proceedings shall be instituted there by a constable except with the approval of the Secretary of State.

(2) Proceedings for an offence under—

(a) section 29, 31A, 34, 35A or 37, or

(b) regulations under this Act,

may be commenced in England or Wales or Northern Ireland by the Secretary of State or a constable at any time within six months from the date on which evidence sufficient in his opinion to justify the proceedings came to his knowledge[4].

(3) No proceedings for any offence may be commenced by virtue of subsection (2) more than three years after the commission of the offence.

(4) A certificate—

(a) stating that the Secretary of State's approval is given for the institution by a constable of any proceedings specified in the certificate, and

(b) signed by or on behalf of the Secretary of State,

is conclusive evidence of that approval.

(5) A certificate—

(a) stating the date on which evidence such as is mentioned in subsection (2) came to the knowledge of the Secretary of State or a constable, and

(b) signed by or on behalf of the Secretary of State or constable,

is conclusive evidence of that date.

(6) A certificate—

(a) including a statement such as is mentioned in paragraph[1] of subsection (4) or (5), and

(b) purporting to be signed as mentioned in paragraph[2] of the subsection concerned,

is to be deemed to be so signed unless the contrary is proved.

(7) The following provisions of the Customs and Excise Management Act 1979 do not apply to proceedings in England and Wales or Northern Ireland for any offence under this Act—

(a) section 145 (which would require such proceedings to be instituted by order of the Secretary of State and certain such proceedings to be commenced in the name of an officer of his), and

(b) section 146A (which would impose time-limits for bringing such proceedings).

[Vehicle Excise and Registration Act 1994, s 47 as amended by the Finance Act 1996, Sch 2 and the Finance Act 2002, Sch 5.]

---

1. Using or keeping a vehicle without a licence, ante.
2. Using excessive number of vehicles under a trade licence, ante.
3. Failure to pay a higher rate of duty, ante.
4. Where a police officer notifies facts to the Secretary of State, the six months' period runs from the date on which evidence sufficient in the opinion of the Secretary of State to warrant proceedings came to his knowledge, and not from the date on which the police officer became aware of the facts (_Algar v Shaw_ [1987] RTR 229).

4–1957 48. _Proceedings in Scotland._

4–1958 49. Authorised persons. A person authorised by the Secretary of State for the purposes of this section may on behalf of the Secretary of State conduct and appear in any proceedings by or against the Secretary of State under this Act—

(a) in England and Wales, in a magistrates' court or before a district judge of a county court,

(b) Scotland,

(c) Northern Ireland.

[Vehicle Excise and Registration Act 1994, s 49.]

4–1959 50. Time-limit for recovery of underpayments and overpayments. No proceedings shall be brought—

(a) by the Secretary of State for the recovery of any under-payment of duty on a vehicle licence, or

(b) by any person for the recovery of any overpayment of duty on a vehicle licence taken out by him,

after the end of the period of twelve months beginning with the end of the period in respect of which the licence was taken out.
[Vehicle Excise and Registration Act 1994, s 50.]

Evidence

4–1960   51. Admissions[1]**.**   (1) This section applies where in any proceedings in England and Wales or Northern Ireland for an offence under section 29[2], 34[3] or 43A—

(a) it is appropriately proved that there has been served on the accused by post a requirement under section 46(1) or (2) to give information as to the identity of—

   (i)   the driver of, or a person who used, a particular vehicle, or
   (ii) the person who kept a particular vehicle on a road,

on the particular occasion on which the offence is alleged to have been committed, and

(b) a statement in writing is produced to the court purporting to be signed by the accused that he was—

   (i)   the driver of, or a person who used, that vehicle, or
   (ii) the person who kept that vehicle on a road, on that occasion.

(2) Where this section applies, the court may accept the statement as evidence that the accused was—

(a) the driver of, or a person who used, that vehicle, or
(b) the person who kept that vehicle on a road, on that occasion.

(3) In subsection (1) "appropriately proved" means proved to the satisfaction of the court—

(a) on oath, or
(b) in the manner prescribed—

   (i)   in England and Wales, by Criminal Procedure Rules, or
   (ii) *Northern Ireland.*

[Vehicle Excise and Registration Act 1994, s 51, as amended by the Finance Act 1997, Sch 3 and the Courts Act 2003, Sch 8.]

---

1. This section corresponds to s 243 of the Road Traffic Act 1960, *ante*, and s 12 of the Road Traffic Offenders Act 1988, *post*.
2. Using or keeping a vehicle without a licence.
3. Using an excessive number of vehicles under a trade licence.

4–1960A   51A. Admissions: offences under regulations.   (1) Subsection (2) applies in relation to any proceedings in England, Wales or Northern Ireland against a person for an offence on the grounds that—

(a) a vehicle has been sold or disposed of by, through or to him and he has failed to furnish particulars prescribed by regulations made by virtue of section 22(1)(*d*);
(b) a vehicle has been sold or disposed of by or through him and he has failed to furnish a document prescribed by regulations made by virtue of section 22(1)(*dd*); or
(c) he has surrendered, or not renewed, a vehicle licence, or is keeping an unlicensed vehicle, and has failed to furnish any particulars or make a declaration prescribed by regulations made by virtue of section 22(1D).

(2) If—

(a) it is appropriately proved that there has been served on the accused by post a requirement under section 46A to give information as to the identity of the person keeping the vehicle at a particular time, and
(b) a statement in writing is produced to the court purporting to be signed by the accused that he was keeping the vehicle at that time,

the court may accept the statement as evidence that the accused was keeping the vehicle at that time.

(3) In subsection (2) 'appropriately proved' has the same meaning as in section 51.

[Vehicle Excise and Registration Act 1994, s 51A, as inserted by the Finance Act 1996, Sch 2.]

4–1961   52. Records.   (1) A statement to which this section applies is admissible in any proceedings as evidence (or, in Scotland, sufficient evidence) of any fact[1] stated in it with respect to matters prescribed by regulations[2] made by the Secretary of State to the same extent as oral evidence of that fact is admissible in the proceedings.

(2) This section applies to a statement contained in a document purporting to be—

(a) a part of the records maintained by the Secretary of State in connection with any functions exercisable by him under or by virtue of this Act,
(b) a copy of a document forming part of those records, or
(c) a note of any information contained in those records,

and to be authenticated by a person authorised to do so by the Secretary of State.

(3) In this section as it has effect in England and Wales—

"document" means anything in which information of any description is recorded;

"copy", in relation to a document, means anything onto which information recorded in the document has been copied, by whatever means and whether directly or indirectly; and "statement" means any representation of fact, however made.

(4)–(6) *Scotland; Northern Ireland.*
[Vehicle Excise and Registration Act 1994, s 52 as amended by the Finance Act 1995, Sch 4 and the Civil Evidence Act 1995, Sch 1.]

---

1. Such facts are not limited to those which prove the history of the registration and/or licensing of a vehicle but may, for example, prove that in the process of manufacture a given vehicle was marked with one or more unique serial numbers without recourse to section 24 of the Criminal Justice Act 1988 (*R v McCarthy* [1998] RTR 374, CA).
2. These matters are prescribed by the Vehicle and Driving Licences Records (Evidence) Regulations 1970, SI 1970/1997 amended by SI 2002/2742.

4–1962 53. Burden of proof. (1) Where in any proceedings for an offence under section 29[1], 31A, 34[2], 37[3] or 45 any question arises as to—

(*a*) the number of vehicles used,
(*b*) the character, weight or cylinder capacity of a vehicle,
(*c*) the seating capacity of a vehicle, or
(*d*) the purpose for which a vehicle has been used,

the burden of proof in respect of the matter lies on the accused.
[Vehicle Excise and Registration Act 1994, s 55 as amended by the Finance Act 2002, Sch 5.]

---

1. Using or keeping a vehicle without a licence, ante.
2. Using excessive number of vehicles under a trade licence, ante.
3. Failure to pay a higher rate of duty, ante.

4–1963 54. *Scotland.*

4–1964 55. Guilty plea by absent accused. (1) This section applies where, under section 12(5) of the Magistrates' Courts Act 1980, a person is convicted in his absence of an offence under section 29 or 35A and it is appropriately proved that a relevant notice was served on the accused with the summons.

(2) In subsection (1) "appropriately proved" means—

(*a*) in England and Wales, proved to the satisfaction of the court—

(i) on oath, or
(ii) in the manner prescribed by Criminal Procedure Rules, and

(*b*) *Northern Ireland.*

(3) In this section "relevant notice", in relation to an accused, means a notice stating that, in the event of his being convicted of the offence, it will be alleged that an order requiring him to pay an amount specified in the notice falls to be made by the court—

(*a*) in a case within subsection (1)[1], under section 30, or
(*b*) in a case within subsection (1)[2], under section 36.

(4) Where this section applies, the court shall proceed under section 30, or section 36, as if the amount specified in the relevant notice were the amount calculated in accordance with that section.

(5) The court shall not so proceed if it is stated in the notification purporting to be given by or on behalf of the accused under—

(*a*) section 12(4) of the Magistrates' Courts Act 1980, or
(*b*) *Northern Ireland,*

that the amount specified in the relevant notice is inappropriate.
[Vehicle Excise and Registration Act 1994, s 55 as amended by the Finance Act 1996, Sch 2 and the Magistrates' Courts (Procedure) Act 1998, s 4 and the Courts Act 2003, Sch 8.]

Penalties etc

4–1965 56. Penalties and fines. (1) Any penalty recovered under or by virtue of this Act shall be paid into the Consolidated Fund.

(2) Section 151 of the Customs and Excise Management Act 1979 (application of penalties) does not apply to penalties recovered under or by virtue of this Act.

(3) Any fine imposed under or by virtue of this Act which (apart from this subsection) would not be paid into the Consolidated Fund shall be so paid.
[Vehicle Excise and Registration Act 1994, s 56.]

PART V
SUPPLEMENTARY
Regulations and orders

4–1966 57. Regulations. (1) The Secretary of State may make regulations[1] generally for the purpose of carrying into effect the provisions of this Act.

(2) Regulations under this Act—

(a)　may make different provision for different cases or circumstances, and

(b)　may contain such incidental, consequential and supplemental provisions as the Secretary of State considers expedient for the purposes of the regulations.

(3)　Regulations under this Act (other than regulations under section 26 or 27)—

(a)　may make different provision for different parts of the United Kingdom, and

(b)　may provide for exemptions from any provision of the regulations.

(4)　Nothing in any other provision of this Act limits subsections (1) to (3).

(5)　Regulations under sections 20(4), 22, 23(4) and (5), 24(1) to (3) and 28 may provide that any document for which provision is made by the regulations—

(a)　is to be in such form, and

(b)　is to contain such particulars,

as may be specified by a person prescribed by the regulations.

(6)　Any power to make regulations under this Act is exercisable by statutory instrument.

(7)　A statutory instrument containing regulations under this Act is subject to annulment in pursuance of a resolution of either House of Parliament.

(7A)　Subsection (7) does not apply to a statutory instrument containing regulations under section 7A to which subsection (6) of that section applies.

[Vehicle Excise and Registration Act 1994, s 57 as amended by the Finance Act 1996, Schs 2 and 41 and the Finance Act 2002, Schs 5 and 40.]

1.　Regulations made under enactments repealed by this Act are to have effect as if made under this Act (Sch 4, para 2(1), post). The Motor Vehicles (International Circulation) Regulations 1985, have been made, in this PART, post

Regulations made under the provisions of this Act include: Vehicle Excise Duty (Immobilisation, Removal and Disposal of Vehicles) Regulations 1997, SI 1997/2439 amended by SI 1997/3063, SI 1998/1217, SI 1999/35, SI 2001/936 and SI 2002/745; and the Road Vehicles (Registration and Licensing) Regulations 2002, in this **PART**, post.

4–1966A　**58.**　*Fees prescribed by Regulations.*

4–1967　**59. Regulations: offences.**　(1) A person who contravenes or fails to comply with any regulations under this Act (other than any regulations under section 24, 26, 27 or 28) is guilty of an offence.

(2)　A person guilty of an offence under subsection (1) is liable on summary conviction to a fine not exceeding—

(a)　in the case of regulations prescribed by regulations[1] made by the Secretary of State as regulations to which this paragraph applies, **level 3** on the standard scale, and

(b)　in any other case, **level 2** on the standard scale.

(3)　The prescribing of regulations as regulations to which subsection (2)[1] applies does not affect the punishment for a contravention of, or failure to comply with, the regulations before they were so prescribed.

(4)　Regulations under section 24 or 28 may provide that a person who contravenes or fails to comply with any specified provision of the regulations is guilty of an offence.

(5)　A person guilty of such an offence is liable on summary conviction to a fine not exceeding—

(a)　in the case of regulations under section 24, **level 1** on the standard scale, and

(b)　in the case of regulations under section 28, **level 3** on the standard scale.

(6)　The Secretary of State may, if he sees fit, compound any proceedings for an offence—

(a)　under subsection (1), or

(b)　under regulations under section 24 or 28.

[Vehicle Excise and Registration Act 1994, s 59 as amended by the Finance Act 1996, Sch 2.]

1.　See the Road Vehicles (Registration and Licensing) Regulations 2002, reg 47, in this PART, post, which prescribes offences under the following of the 2002 regulations: 16(1), 17, 18(1), 19(1), 21, 22, 23, 24, 25, 26 (including Sch 4), 40(5) and 42..

4–1968　**60.**　*Orders.*

4–1968A　**60A. Meaning of "revenue weight".**　(1) Any reference in this Act to the revenue weight of a vehicle is a reference—

(a)　where it has a confirmed maximum weight, to that weight; and

(b)　in any other case, to the weight determined in accordance with the following provisions of this section.

(2)　For the purposes of this Act a vehicle which does not have a confirmed maximum weight shall have a revenue weight which, subject to the following provisions of this section, is equal to its design weight.

(3)　Subject to subsection (4), the design weight of a vehicle is, for the purposes of this section—

(a)　in the case of a tractive unit, the weight which is required, by the design and any subsequent adaptations of that vehicle, not to be exceeded by an articulated vehicle which—

(i)　consists of the vehicle and any semi-trailer capable of being drawn by it, and

(ii)   is in normal use and travelling on a road laden; and

(b)   in the case of any other vehicle, the weight which the vehicle itself is designed or adapted not to exceed when in normal use and travelling on a road laden.

(4)   Where, at any time, a vehicle—

(a)   does not have a confirmed maximum weight,

(b)   has previously had such a weight, and

(c)   has not acquired a different design weight by reason of any adaptation made since the most recent occasion on which it had a confirmed maximum weight,

the vehicle's design weight at that time shall be equal to its confirmed maximum weight on that occasion.

(5)   An adaptation reducing the design weight of a vehicle shall be disregarded for the purposes of this section unless it is a permanent adaptation.

(6)   For the purposes of this Act where—

(a)   a vehicle which does not have a confirmed maximum weight is used on a public road in the United Kingdom, and

(b)   at the time when it is so used—

(i)   the weight of the vehicle, or

(ii)   in the case of a tractive unit used as part of an articulated vehicle consisting of the vehicle and a semi-trailer, the weight of the articulated vehicle,

exceeds what, apart from this subsection, would be the vehicle's design weight,

it shall be conclusively presumed, as against the person using the vehicle, that the vehicle has been temporarily adapted so as to have a design weight while being so used equal to the actual weight of the vehicle or articulated vehicle at that time.

(7)   For the purposes of this Act limitations on the space available on a vehicle for carrying a load shall be disregarded in determining the weight which the vehicle is designed or adapted not to exceed when in normal use and travelling on a road laden.

(8)   A vehicle which does not have a confirmed maximum weight shall not at any time be taken to have a revenue weight which is greater than the maximum laden weight at which that vehicle or, as the case may be, an articulated vehicle consisting of that vehicle and a semi-trailer may lawfully be used in Great Britain.

(9)   A vehicle has a confirmed maximum weight at any time if at that time—

(a)   it has a plated gross weight or a plated train weight; and

(b)   that weight is the maximum laden weight at which that vehicle or, as the case may be, an articulated vehicle consisting of that vehicle and a semi-trailer may lawfully be used in Great Britain;

and the confirmed maximum weight of a vehicle with such a weight shall be taken to be the weight referred to in paragraph (a).

(10)–(11)   *Northern Ireland.*

[Vehicle Excise and Registration Act 1994, s 60A as inserted by the Finance Act 1995, Sch 4.]

Interpretation

4–1970   61. Vehicle weights.   (1) In this Act a reference to the plated gross weight of a goods vehicle or trailer is a reference—

(a)   in the case of a trailer which may lawfully be used in Great Britain without a Ministry plate (within the meaning of regulations under section 41 or 49 of the Road Traffic Act 1988), to the maximum laden weight at which the trailer may lawfully be used in Great Britain, and

(b)   otherwise, to the weight which is the maximum gross weight which may not be exceeded in Great Britain for the vehicle or trailer as indicated on the appropriate plate.

(2)   In this Act a reference to the plated train weight of a vehicle is a reference to the weight which is the maximum gross weight which may not be exceeded in Great Britain for an articulated vehicle consisting of the vehicle and any semi-trailer which may be drawn by it as indicated on the appropriate plate.

(3)   In subsections (1) and (2) "appropriate plate", in relation to a vehicle or trailer, means—

(a)   where a Ministry plate (within the meaning of regulations under section 41 or 49 of the Road Traffic Act 1988) has been issued, or has effect as if issued, for the vehicle or trailer following the issue or amendment of a plating certificate (within the meaning of Part II of that Act), that plate, and

(b)   where paragraph (a) does not apply but such a certificate is in force for the vehicle or trailer, that certificate.

(c)   *Repealed.*

(3A)   Where it appears to the Secretary of State that there is a description of document which—

(a)   falls to be treated for some or all of the purposes of the Road Traffic Act 1988 as if it were a plating certificate, or

(b)   is issued under the law of any state in the European Economic Area for purposes which are or include purposes corresponding to those for which such a certificate is issued, he may by regulations provide for references in this section to a plating certificate to have effect as if they included references to a document of that description.

(4)–(5) *Repealed.*

(6) In this Act "weight unladen"—

(*a*) In England and Wales, has the same meaning as it has for the purposes of the Road Traffic Act 1988 by virtue of section 190 of that Act, and

(*b*) *Northern Ireland.*

(7) *Repealed.*

(8) In this section "trailer" has the same meaning as in Part VIII of Schedule 1.

[Vehicles Excise and Registration Act 1994, s 61 as amended by the Finance Act 1995, Schs 4 and 29.]

4–1970A   61A. Certificates etc as to vehicle weight.   *Power of Secretary of State to make regulation*[1].

---

1. The Vehicles Excise (Design Weight Certificate) Regulations 1995, SI 1995/1455 have been made.

4–1970B   61B. Certificates as to reduced pollution.   (1) The Secretary of State may by regulations[1] make provision—

(*a*) for the making of an application to the Secretary of State for the issue in respect of an eligible vehicle of a reduced pollution certificate;

(*b*) for the manner in which any determination of whether to issue such a certificate on such an application is to be made;

(*c*) for the examination of an eligible vehicle, for the purposes of the determination mentioned in paragraph (*b*), by such persons, and in such manner, as may be prescribed;

(*d*) for a fee to be paid for such an examination;

(*e*) for a reduced pollution certificate to be issued in respect of an eligible vehicle if, and only if, it is found, on a prescribed examination, that the reduced pollution requirements are satisfied with respect to it;

(*f*) for the form and content of such a certificate;

(*g*) for such a certificate to be valid for such period as the Secretary of State may determine;

(*h*) for the revocation, cancellation or surrender of such a certificate before the end of any such period;

(*i*) for the Secretary of State to be entitled to require the return to him of such a certificate that has been revoked;

(*j*) for the fact that such a certificate is, or is not, in force in respect of a vehicle to be treated as having conclusive effect for the purposes of this Act as to such matters as may be prescribed;

(*k*) for the Secretary of State to be entitled, in prescribed cases, to require the production of such a certificate before making a determination for the purposes of section 7(5); and

(*l*) for appeals against any determination not to issue such a certificate.

(2) For the purposes of this Act, the reduced pollution requirements are satisfied with respect to a vehicle at any time if, at that time, prescribed requirements relating to the vehicle's emissions are satisfied as a result of—

(*a*) the design, construction or equipment of the vehicle as manufactured; or

(*b*) adaptations of a prescribed description having been made to the vehicle after a prescribed date.

(2A) Different requirements may be prescribed under subsection (2) for vehicles first registered at different times.

(3) Without prejudice to the generality of subsection (1), for the purpose of enabling the Secretary of State to determine whether the reduced pollution requirements are satisfied at any time with respect to a vehicle in respect of which a reduced pollution certificate is in force, regulations under this section—

(*a*) may authorise such person as may be prescribed to require the vehicle to be re-examined in accordance with the regulations;

(*b*) may provide for a fee to be paid for such a re-examination;

(*c*) may provide for the refund of such a fee if it is found, on the prescribed re-examination, that the reduced pollution requirements are satisfied with respect to the vehicle.

(4) In this section "eligible vehicle" means—

(*a*) a bus, as defined in paragraph 3(2) of Schedule 1;

(*b*) a vehicle to which paragraph 6 of Schedule 1 applies;

(*c*) a haulage vehicle, as defined in paragraph 7(2) of Schedule 1, other than a showman's vehicle; or

(*d*) a goods vehicle, other than one falling within paragraph 9(2) or 11(2) of Schedule 1.

(5) In this section "prescribed" means prescribed by regulations made by the Secretary of State.

[Vehicle Excise and Registration Act 1994, s 61B as inserted by the Finance Act 1998, Sch 1 and amended by the Finance Act 2006, s 14.]

---

1. See the Road Vehicles (Registration and Licensing) Regulations 2002, reg 5 and Sch 2, in this PART, post.

4–1971 62. Other definitions. (1) In this Act, unless the context otherwise requires—

"axle", in relation to the vehicle, includes—

(a) two or more stub axles which are fitted on opposite sides of the longitudinal axis of the vehicle so as to form a pair in the case of two stub axles or pairs in the case of more than two stub axles,

(b) a single stub axle which is not one of a pair, and

(c) a retractable axle,

("stub axle" meaning an axle on which only one wheel is mounted),

"business" includes the performance by a local or public authority of its functions,

"disabled person" means a person suffering from a physical or mental defect or disability,

"exempt vehicle" means a vehicle in respect of which vehicle excise duty is not chargeable,

"goods vehicle"[1] means a vehicle constructed or adapted[2] for use and used for the conveyance of goods or burden of any description, whether in the course of trade or not,

"motor dealer" means a person carrying on the business of selling or supplying vehicles,

"motor trader" means—

(a) a manufacturer or repairer of, or dealer in, vehicles, or

(b) any other description of person who carries on a business of such description as may be prescribed by regulations made by the Secretary of State,

and a person is treated as a dealer in vehicles if he carries on a business consisting wholly or mainly of collecting and delivering vehicles, and not including any other activities except activities[3] as a manufacturer or repairer of, or dealer in, vehicles,

"nil licence" means a document which is in the form of a vehicle licence and is issued by the Secretary of State in pursuance of regulations under this Act in respect of a vehicle which is an exempt vehicle,

"public road"—

(a) in England and Wales and Northern Ireland, means a road which is repairable at the public expense, and

(b) in Scotland, has the same meaning as in the Roads (Scotland) Act 1984,

"registration mark" is to be construed in accordance with section 23(1),

"relevant right" is to be construed in accordance with section 27(3)(a) and (b),

"right of retention" is to be construed in accordance with section 26(1) and (2)(a),

"rigid goods vehicle" means a goods vehicle which is not a tractive unit,

"showman's goods vehicle" means a showman's vehicle which—

(a) is a goods vehicle, and

(b) is permanently fitted with a living van or some other special type of body or superstructure forming part of the equipment of the show of the person in whose name the vehicle is registered under this Act,

"showman's vehicle" means a vehicle—

(a) registered under this Act in the name of a person following the business of a travelling showman, and

(b) used solely by him for the purposes of his business and for no other purpose,

"temporary licence" is to be construed in accordance with section 9(1),

"tractive unit" means a goods vehicle to which a semi-trailer may be so attached that—

(a) part of the semi-trailer is superimposed on part of the goods vehicle, and

(b) when the semi-trailer is uniformly loaded, not less than twenty per cent. of the weight of its load is borne by the goods vehicle,

"trade licence" is to be construed in accordance with section 11,

"vehicle" shall be construed in accordance with section 1(1B),

"vehicle excise duty" is to be construed in accordance with section 1(1),

"vehicle licence" is to be construed in accordance with section 1(2), and

"vehicle tester" means a person, other than a motor trader, who regularly in the course of his business engages in the testing on roads of vehicles belonging to other persons.

(1A) For the purposes of this Act, a vehicle is not an electrically propelled vehicle unless the electrical motive power is derived from—

(a) a source external to the vehicle, or

(b) an electrical storage battery which is not connected to any source of power when the vehicle is in motion.

(2) For the purposes of this Act and any other enactment relating to the keeping of vehicles on public roads, a person keeps a vehicle on a public road if he causes it to be on such a road for any period, however short, when it is not in use there.

[Vehicle Excise and Registration Act 1994, s 62 as amended by the Finance Act 1995, Sch 29, the Finance Act 1996, s 15 and the Finance Act 1997, Sch 3 and the Finance Act 2002, Sch 5.]

---

1. This definition of "goods vehicle" and the reference to a vehicle for conveying machines in para 14 of Sch 1, post, are not mutually exclusive and are intended to be read together, so that "burden" is intended to have the same meaning in both places (*Department of Transport v Caird Environmental Services Ltd* [1999] RTR 137).

2. "Adapted" means not "suitable" but "altered so as to make the vehicle apt for the conveyance of goods" (*French v Champkin* [1920] 1 KB 76, 83 JP 258). "Constructed or adapted" means "originally or where the structure is subsequently altered" (*Taylor v Mead* [1961] 1 All ER 626, 125 JP 286). The test to be applied to an altered vehicle is whether it would have been a goods vehicle if it had been constructed in its altered state (*Flowers Freight Co Ltd v Hammond* [1963] 1 QB 275, [1962] 3 All ER 950, 127 JP 42).

3. This modifies the decision in *Carey v Heath* [1952] 1 KB 62, [1951] 2 All ER 774, 115 JP 577.

SCHEDULES

Section 2

SCHEDULE 1
Annual Rates of Duty

(*As amended by the Finance Act 1995, Schs 4 and 29, the Finance Act 1996, ss 14, 15, 16, 17, 18 and 22, and Sch 41, the Finance Act 1997, s 16, the Finance (No 2) Act 1997, s 13, the Finance Act 1998, Schs 1 and 27, the Finance Act 1999, s 8, the Finance Act 2000, Schs 3, 5 and ss 20, 21, the Finance Act 2001, Sch 2 and the Finance Act 2002, s 20.*)

Part I
General

4–1972   **1.** (1) The annual rate of vehicle excise duty applicable to a vehicle in respect of which no other annual rate is specified by this Schedule is the general rate.

(2) Except in the case of a vehicle having an engine with a cylinder capacity not exceeding 1,549 cubic centimetres, the general rate is £160.

(2A) In the case of a vehicle having an engine with a cylinder capacity not exceeding 1,549 cubic centimetres, the general rate is £105.

(2B) For the purposes of this Schedule the cylinder capacity of an engine shall be calculated in accordance with regulations made by the Secretary of State.

(3)–(5) *Repealed.*

Part IA[1]
Light Passenger Vehicles: Graduated Rates of Duty

4–1972A

Vehicles to which this Part applies

1A. (1) This Part of this Schedule applies to a vehicle which—

(a) is first registered on or after 1st March 2001, and

(b) is so registered on the basis of an EC certificate of conformity or UK approval certificate that—

(i) identifies the vehicle as having been approved as a light passenger vehicle, and

(ii) specifies a CO2 emissions figure in terms of grams per kilometre driven

(2) In sub-paragraph (1)(b)(i) a "light passenger vehicle" means a vehicle within Category M1 of Annex II to Council Directive 70/156/EEC (vehicle with at least four wheels used for carriage of passengers and comprising no more than 8 seats in addition to the driver's seat).

(3) For the purposes of this Part of this Schedule "the applicable CO2 emissions figure" is—

(a) where the EC certificate of conformity or UK approval certificate specifies only one CO2 emissions figure, that figure, and

(b) where it specifies more than one, the figure specified as the CO2 emissions (combined) figure.

(4) Where the car is registered on the basis of an EC certificate of conformity, or UK approval certificate, that specifies separate CO2 emissions figures in terms of grams per kilometre driven for different fuels, "the applicable CO2 emissions figure" is the lowest figure specified or, in a case within sub-paragraph (3)(b), the lowest CO2 emissions (combined) figure specified.

(5) If a vehicle is on first registration a vehicle to which this Part of this Schedule applies—

(a) its status as such a vehicle, and

(b) the applicable CO2 emissions figure,

are not affected by any subsequent modification of the vehicle.

Graduated rates of duty

1B. The annual rate of vehicle excise duty applicable to a vehicle to which this Part of this Schedule applies shall be determined in accordance with the following table by reference to—

(a) the applicable CO2 emissions figure, and

(b) whether the vehicle qualifies for the reduced rate of duty, or is liable to the standard rate or the premium rate of duty.

CO2 emissions figure		Rate		
(1) Exceeding	(2) Not Exceeding	(3) Reduced rate	(4) Standard rate	(5) Premium rate
g/km	g/km	£	£	£
—	150	90	100	110
150	165	110	120	130
165	185	130	140	150
185	—	150	155	160

The reduced rate

1C. (1) A vehicle qualifies for the reduced rate of duty if condition A, B or C below is met.

(2) Condition A is that the vehicle is constructed or modified—

(*a*) so as to be propelled by a prescribed type of fuel, or

(*b*) so as to be capable of being propelled by any of a number of prescribed types of fuel,

and complies with any other requirements prescribed for the purposes of this condition.

(3) Condition B is that the vehicle—

(*a*) incorporates before its first registration equipment enabling it to meet such vehicle emission standards as may be prescribed for the purposes of this condition, and

(*b*) has incorporated such equipment since its first registration.

(4) Condition C is that the vehicle is of a description certified by the Secretary of State, before the vehicle's first registration, as meeting such vehicle emission standards as may be prescribed for the purposes of this condition.

(5) The Secretary of State may make provision by regulations—

(*a*) for the making of an application to the Secretary of State for the issue of a certificate under sub-paragraph (4);

(*b*) for the manner in which any determination of whether to issue such a certificate on such an application is to be made;

(*c*) for the examination of one or more vehicles of the description to which the application relates, for the purposes of the determination mentioned in paragraph (b), by such persons, and in such manner, as may be prescribed;

(*d*) for a fee to be paid for such an examination;

(*e*) for the form and content of such a certificate;

(*f*) for the revocation, cancellation or surrender of such a certificate;

(*g*) for the fact that such a certificate is, or is not, in force in respect of a description of vehicle to be treated as having conclusive effect for the purposes of this Act as to such matters as may be prescribed; and

(*h*) for appeals against any determination not to issue such a certificate.

The standard rate

1D. A vehicle is liable to the standard rate of duty if it does not qualify for the reduced rate and is not liable to the premium rate.

The premium rate

1E. (1) A vehicle is liable to the premium rate of duty if—

(*a*) it is constructed or modified so as to be propelled solely by diesel, and

(*b*) it is not of a prescribed description.

(2) In sub-paragraph (1)(*a*) "diesel" means any diesel fuel within the definition in Article 2 of Directive 98/70/EC of the European Parliament and of the Council.

Meaning of "prescribed"

1F. In this Part of this Schedule "prescribed" means prescribed by regulations[2] made by the Secretary of State with the consent of the Treasury.

Meaning of "EC certificate of conformity" and "UK approval certificate"

1G. (1) References in this Part of this Schedule to an "EC certificate of conformity" are to a certificate of conformity issued by a manufacturer under any provision of the law of a Member State implementing Article 6 of Council Directive 70/156/EEC, as amended.

(2) References in this Part of this Schedule to a "UK approval certificate" are to a certificate issued under—

(*a*) section 58(1) or (4) of the Road Traffic Act 1988, or

(*b*) Article 31A(4) or (5) of the Road Traffic (Northern Ireland) Order 1981.★

★**Part IA is printed as inserted by the Finance Act 2000, Sch 3. This amendment has effect with respect to vehicle excise duty on light passenger vehicles and light goods vehicles first registered on or after 1 March 2001: see the Finance Act 2000, s 22.**

1. For the enforcement provisions with respect to vehicles for which there are different rates of vehicle excise duty, see the Finance Act 2000, s 23 and Sch 4, in PART VIII: title CUSTOMS AND EXCISE, post.

2. The Graduated Vehicle Excise Duty (Prescribed Types of Fuel) Regulations 2001, SI 2001/93 have been made.

PART IB
LIGHT GOODS VEHICLES

Vehicles to which this Part applies

1H. (1) This Part of this Schedule applies to a vehicle which—

(*a*) is first registered on or after 1st March 2001, and

(*b*) is so registered on the basis of an EC certificate of conformity or UK approval certificate that identifies the vehicle as having been approved as a light goods vehicle.

(2) In sub-paragraph (1)(*b*) a "light goods vehicle" means a vehicle within Category N1 of Annex II to Council Directive 70/156/EEC (vehicle with four or more wheels used for carriage of goods and having a maximum mass not exceeding 3.5 tonnes).

(3) If a vehicle is on first registration a vehicle to which this Part of this Schedule applies its status as such a vehicle is not affected by a subsequent modification of the vehicle.

(4) In this paragraph "EC certificate of conformity" and "UK approval certificate" have the same meaning as in Part IA of this Schedule.

Annual rate of duty

1J. The annual rate of vehicle excise duty applicable to a vehicle to which this Part of this Schedule applies is—

(a) if the vehicle is not a lower-emission van, £160;

(b) if the vehicle is a lower-emission van, £105.

1K. For the purposes of paragraph 1J, a vehicle to which this Part of this Schedule applies is a "lower-emission van" if—

(a) the vehicle is first registered on or after 1st March 2003, and

(b) the limit values given for the vehicle by the Table (which is extracted from the new table inserted in section 5.3.1.4 of Annex I of Council Directive 70/220/EEC by Directive 98/69/EC of the European Parliament and of the Council) are not exceeded during a Type I test.]

Reference mass of vehicle		Limit values for types of emissions by reference to vehicle type						
		CO		HC	NOx		HC+ NOx	PM
Exceeding	Not exceeding	Petrol	Diesel	Petrol	Petrol	Diesel	Diesel	Diesel
kg	kg	g/km	g/km	g/km	g/km	g/km	g/km	g/km
—	1,305	1.0	0.5	0.1	0.08	0.25	0.3	0.025
1,305	1760	1.81	0.63	0.13	0.1	0.33	0.39	0.04
1,760	3,500	2.27	0.74	0.16	0.11	0.39	0.46	0.06

1L. In paragraph 1K—

"Type I test" means a test as described in section 5.3 of Annex I to Council Directive 70/220/EEC as amended (test for simulating/verifying the average tailpipe emissions after a cold start and carried out using the procedure described in Annex III of that Directive as amended);

"the reference mass" of a vehicle means the mass of the vehicle with bodywork and, in the case of a towing vehicle, with coupling device, if fitted by the manufacturer, in running order, or mass of the chassis or chassis with cab, without bodywork and/or coupling device if the manufacturer does not fit the bodywork and/or coupling device (including liquids and tools, and spare wheel if fitted, and with the fuel tank filled to 90% and the other liquid containing systems, except those for used water, to 100% of the capacity specified by the manufacturer), increased by a uniform mass of 100 kilograms;

"CO" means mass of carbon monoxide;

"HC" means mass of hydrocarbons;

"NOx" means mass of oxides of nitrogen;

"PM" means mass of particulates (for compression ignition engines).

PART II
MOTORCYCLES

4–1973   2. (1)

(a) if the cylinder capacity of the engine does not exceed 150 cubic centimetres, 10 per cent of the general rate specified in paragraph 1(2);

(b) if the vehicle is a motorbicycle and the cylinder capacity of the engine exceeds 150 cubic centimetres but does not exceed 250 cubic centimetres, 25 per cent of the general rate specified in paragraph 1(2);

(c) in any other case, 40 per cent of the general rate specified in paragraph 1(2).

(1A) Where an amount arrived at in accordance with sub-paragraph (1)(a), (b) or (c) is an amount—

(a) which is not a multiple of £5, and

(b) which on division by five does not produce a remainder of £2.50,

the rate is the amount arrived at rounded (either up or down) to the nearest amount which is a multiple of £5.

(1B) Where an amount arrived at in accordance with sub-paragraph (1)(a), (b) or (c) is an amount which on division by five produces a remainder of £2.50, the rate is the amount arrived at increased by £2.50.

(2) *Repealed.*

(3) In this paragraph—

"motorcycle" means a motorbicycle or a motortricycle but does not include an electrically propelled vehicle,

"motorbicycle" includes a two-wheeled motor scooter, a bicycle with an attachment for propelling it by mechanical power and a motorbicycle to which a side-car is attached, and

"motortricycle" includes a three-wheeled motor scooter and a tricycle with an attachment for propelling it by mechanical power.

(4) *Repealed.*

---

1. Cylinder capacity of vehicles is calculated in accordance with the Road Vehicles (Registration and Licensing) Regulations 2002, reg 43, in this PART, post.

PART III
BUSES

4–1974   3. (1) The annual rate of vehicle excise duty applicable to a bus with respect to which the reduced pollution requirements are not satisfied is—

(a) if its seating capacity is nine to sixteen, the same as the basic goods vehicle rate;
(b) if its seating capacity is seventeen to thirty-five, 133 per cent of the basic goods vehicle rate;
(c) if its seating capacity is thirty-six to sixty 200 per cent of the basic goods vehicle rate;
(d) if its seating capacity is over sixty, 300 per cent of the basic goods vehicle rate.

(1A) The annual rate of vehicle excise duty applicable to a bus with respect to which the reduced pollution requirements are satisfied is the general rate specified in paragraph 1(2).
(2) In this paragraph "bus" means a vehicle which—

(a) is a public service vehicle (within the meaning given by section 1 of the Public Passenger Vehicles Act 1981), and
(b) is not an excepted vehicle or a special concessionary vehicle.

(3) For the purposes of this paragraph an excepted vehicle is—

(a) a vehicle which has a seating capacity under nine,
(b) a vehicle which is a community bus,
(c) a vehicle used under a permit granted under section 19 of the Transport Act 1985 (educational and other bodies) and used in circumstances where the requirements mentioned in subsection (2) of that section are met, or
(d) (*Northern Ireland*).

(4) In sub-paragraph (3)(b) "community bus" means a vehicle—

(a) used on public roads solely in accordance with a community bus permit (within the meaning given by section 22 of the Transport Act 1985), and
(b) not used for providing a service under an agreement providing for service subsidies (within the meaning given by section 63(10)(b) of that Act).

(5) For the purposes of this paragraph the seating capacity of a vehicle shall be determined in accordance with regulations made by the Secretary of State.
(6) In sub-paragraph (1) references to the basic goods vehicle rate are to the rate applicable, by virtue of sub-paragraph (1) of paragraph 9, to a rigid goods vehicle which—

(a) is not a vehicle with respect to which the reduced pollution requirements are satisfied; and
(b) falls within column (3) of the table in that sub-paragraph and has a revenue weight exceeding 3,500 kilograms and not exceeding 7,500 kilograms.

(7) Where an amount arrived at in accordance with sub-paragraph (1)(b), (c) or (d) is an amount—

(a) which is not a multiple of £10, and
(b) which on division by ten does not produce a remainder of £5,

the rate is the amount arrived at rounded (either up or down) to the nearest amount which is a multiple of £10.
(8) Where an amount arrived at in accordance with sub-paragraph (1)(b), (c) or (d) is an amount which on division by ten produces a remainder of £5, the rate is the amount arrived at increased by £5.

PART IV
SPECIAL VEHICLES

4–1975 **4.** (1) The annual rate of vehicle excise duty applicable to a special vehicle is the same as the basic goods vehicle rate.
(2) In sub-paragraph (1) "special vehicle" means a vehicle which has a revenue weight exceeding 3,500 kilograms which is not a special concessionary vehicle and which is—

(a)–(b) *Repealed,*
(bb) a vehicle falling within sub-paragraph (2A) or (2B),
(c) a digging machine,
(d) a mobile crane,
(dd) mobile pumping vehicle,
(e) a works truck, or
(ee) a road roller,
(f) *Repealed.*

(2A) A vehicle falls within this sub-paragraph if—

(a) it is designed or adapted for use for the conveyance of goods or burden of any description; but
(b) it is not so used or is not so used for hire or reward or for or in connection with a trade or business

(2B) A vehicle falls within this sub-paragraph if—

(a) it is designed or adapted for use with a semi-trailer attached; but
(b) it is not so used or, if it is so used, the semi-trailer is not used for the conveyance of goods or burden of any description.

(3) *Repealed.*
(4) In sub-paragraph (2)(c) "digging machine" means a vehicle which is designed, constructed and used for the purpose of trench digging, or any kind of excavating or shovelling work, and which—

(a) is used on public roads only for that purpose or for the purpose of proceeding to and from the place where it is to be or has been used for that purpose, and
(b) when so proceeding does not carry any load except such as is necessary for its propulsion or equipment.

(5) In sub-paragraph (2)(d) "mobile crane" means a vehicle which is designed and constructed as a mobile crane and which—

(a) is used on public roads only as a crane in connection with work carried on on a site in the immediate vicinity or for the purpose of proceeding to and from a place where it is to be or has been used as a crane, and
(b) when so proceeding does not carry any load except such as is necessary for its propulsion or equipment.

(5A) In sub-paragraph (2)(dd) "mobile pumping vehicle" means a vehicle—

(a) which is constructed or adapted for use and used for the conveyance of a pump and a jib satisfying the requirements specified in sub-paragraph (5B),

(b) which is used on public roads only—

(i) when the vehicle is stationary and the pump is being used to pump material from a point in the immediate vicinity to another such point, or

(ii) for the purpose of proceeding to and from a place where the pump is to be or has been used, and

(c) which, when so proceeding, does not carry—

(i) the material that is to be or has been pumped, or

(ii) any other load except such as is necessary for the propulsion or equipment of the vehicle or for the operation of the pump.

(5B) The requirements are that each of the pump and the jib is—

(a) built in as part of the vehicle, and

(b) designed so that material pumped by the pump is delivered to a desired height or depth through piping that—

(i) is attached to the pump and the jib, and

(ii) is raised or lowered to that height or depth by operation of the jib.

(6) In sub-paragraph (2)(e) "works truck" means a goods vehicle which is—

(a) designed for use in private premises, and

(b) used on public roads only—

(i) for carrying goods between private premises and a vehicle on a road in the immediate vicinity,

(ii) in passing from one part of private premises to another or between private premises and other private premises in the immediate vicinity, or

(iii) in connection with road works at or in the immediate vicinity of the site of the works.

(7) In sub-paragraph (1) the reference to the basic goods vehicle rate is to the rate applicable, by virtue of sub-paragraph (1) of paragraph 9, to a rigid goods vehicle which—

(a) is not a vehicle with respect to which the reduced pollution requirements are satisfied; and

(b) falls within column (3) of the table in that sub-paragraph and has a revenue weight exceeding 3,500 kilograms and not exceeding 7,500 kilograms.

PART IVA
SPECIAL CONCESSIONARY VEHICLES

4–1975A *Repealed.*

PART V
RECOVERY VEHICLES

4–1976 5. (1) The annual rate of vehicle excise duty applicable to a recovery vehicle[1] is—

(a) if it has a revenue weight exceeding 3,500 kilograms and not exceeding 25,000 kilograms, the same as the basic goods vehicle rate;

(c) if it has a revenue weight exceeding 25,000 kilograms, 250 per cent of the basic goods vehicle rate.

(2) In sub-paragraph (1) "recovery vehicle" means a vehicle which is constructed or permanently adapted primarily for any one or more of the purposes of lifting, towing and transporting a disabled vehicle[2].

(3) A vehicle is not a recovery vehicle if at any time it is used for a purpose other than—

(a) the recovery of a disabled vehicle,

(b) the removal of a disabled vehicle from the place where it became disabled to premises at which it is to be repaired or scrapped,

(c) the removal of a disabled vehicle from premises to which it was taken for repair to other premises at which it is to be repaired or scrapped,

(d) carrying fuel and other liquids required for its propulsion and tools and other articles required for the operation of, or in connection with, apparatus designed to lift, tow or transport a disabled vehicle, and

(e) any purpose prescribed for the purposes of this sub-paragraph by regulations[3] made by the Secretary of State.

(4) At any time when a vehicle is being used for either of the purposes specified in paragraphs (a) and (b) of sub-paragraph (3), use for—

(a) the carriage of a person who, immediately before the vehicle became disabled, was the driver of or a passenger in the vehicle,

(b) the carriage of any goods which, immediately before the vehicle became disabled, were being carried in the vehicle, or

(c) any purpose prescribed for the purposes of this sub-paragraph by regulations[3] made by the Secretary of State,

shall be disregarded in determining whether the vehicle is a recovery vehicle.

(5) A vehicle is not a recovery vehicle if at any time the number of vehicles which it is used to recover exceeds a number specified for the purposes of this sub-paragraph by an order[4] made by the Secretary of State.

(5A) *Repealed.*

(6) In sub-paragraph (1) references to the basic goods vehicle rate are to the rate applicable, by virtue of sub-paragraph (1) of paragraph 9, to a rigid goods vehicle which—

(a) is not a vehicle with respect to which the reduced pollution requirements are satisfied; and

(b) falls within column (3) of the table in that sub-paragraph and has a revenue weight exceeding 3,500 kilograms and not exceeding 7,500 kilograms.

(7) Where an amount arrived at in accordance with sub-paragraph (1)(b) or (c) is an amount—

(*a*) which is not a multiple of £10, and
(*b*) which on division by ten does not produce a remainder of £5,

the rate is the amount arrived at rounded (either up or down) to the nearest amount which is a multiple of £10.
(8) Where an amount arrived at in accordance with sub-paragraph (1)(b) or (c) is an amount which on division by ten produces a remainder of £5, the rate is the amount arrived at increased by £5.

---

1. For vehicle to be a "recovery" vehicle any equipment or apparatus by which disabled vehicles are lifted, towed or transported, has to be permanently mounted on to or has to form an integral part of the vehicle and it is not sufficient that the vehicle simply carries such equipment as part of its tools or accessories as otherwise its status will change according to the equipment carried at any particular time. Nor is it sufficient to come within the definition that the vehicle is part of a team to assist other vehicles which have the capacity to lift or tow (*Vehicle Inspectorate v Richard Read Transport Ltd* [1998] RTR 288n, DC).
2. A disabled vehicle is one which has suffered some disability other than simply having the rotor arm removed (*Robertson v Crew* [1977] RTR 141). Moreover, it is not only a vehicle that suffers from a significant disability, but it is a vehicle which has broken down because of that disability (*Squires v Mitchell* [1983] RTR 400). A "disabled vehicle" is to be construed to mean one vehicle only, and it does not include a scrap vehicle (*Gibson v Nutter* [1984] RTR 8).
3. See the Road Vehicles (Registration and Licensing) Regulations 2002, reg 45 and Sch 7, in this PART, post
4. The number is two; see the Recovery Vehicles (Number of Vehicles Recovered) Order 1989, SI 1989/1226.

PART VI
VEHICLES USED FOR EXCEPTIONAL LOADS

4–1977 **6.** (1) This paragraph applies to a vehicle which is—

(*a*) a heavy motor car used for the carriage of exceptional loads, or
(*b*) a heavy locomotive, light locomotive or motor tractor used to draw trailers carrying exceptional loads.

and which is not a special concessionary vehicle.
(2) The annual rate of vehicle excise duty applicable to a vehicle to which this paragraph applies in respect of use for the carriage of exceptional loads, or to draw trailers carrying exceptional loads, which is authorised by virtue of an order under—

(*a*) section 44 of the Road Traffic Act 1988, or
(*b*) *Northern Ireland,*

is the rate specified in sub-paragraph (2A).
(2A) The rate referred to in sub-paragraph (2) is—

(*a*) in the case of a vehicle with respect to which the reduced pollution requirements are not satisfied, £2,585; and
(*b*) in the case of a vehicle with respect to which those requirements are satisfied, £2,085.

(3) For the purposes of this paragraph an exceptional load is a load which—

(*a*) by reason of its dimensions cannot be carried by a heavy motor car or trailer, or a combination of a heavy motor car and trailer, which complies in all respects with requirements of regulations under section 41 of the Road Traffic Act 1988 or (in Northern Ireland) Article 55 of the Road Traffic (Northern Ireland) Order 1995, or
(*b*) by reason of its weight cannot be carried by a heavy motor car or trailer, or a combination of a heavy motor car and trailer, which has a total laden weight of not more than 41,000 kilograms and which complies in all respects with such requirements.

(3A) *Repealed.*
(4) Expressions used in this paragraph and in the Road Traffic Act 1988 or the Road Traffic (Northern Ireland) Order 1995 have the same meanings in this paragraph as in that Act.

PART VII
HAULAGE VEHICLES

4–1978 **7.** (1) The annual rate of vehicle excise duty applicable to a haulage vehicle is—

(*a*) if it is a showman's vehicle, the same as the basic goods vehicle rate;
(*b*) in any other case, the rate specified in sub-paragraph (3A).

(2) In sub-paragraph (1) "haulage vehicle" means a vehicle (other than a vehicle to which Part IV, V or VI applies) which is constructed and used on public roads solely for haulage and not for the purpose of carrying or having superimposed on it any load except such as is necessary for its propulsion or equipment[1].
(3) In sub-paragraph (1) the reference to the basic goods vehicle rate is to the rate applicable, by virtue of sub-paragraph (1) of paragraph 9, to a rigid goods vehicle which—

(*a*) is not a vehicle with respect to which the reduced pollution requirements are satisfied; and
(*b*) falls within column (3) of the table in that sub-paragraph and has a revenue weight exceeding 3,500 kilograms and not exceeding 7,500 kilograms.

(3A) The rate referred to in sub-paragraph (1)(b) is—

(*a*) in the case of a vehicle with respect to which the reduced pollution requirements are not satisfied, £350; and
(*b*) in the case of a vehicle with respect to which those requirements are satisfied, the general rate specified in paragraph 1(2).

(4)–(6) *Repealed.*

---

1. The carriage of tools, ballast or other articles to assist in propulsion or haulage does not prevent a vehicle being a "haulage vehicle" as distinct from a "goods vehicle" (*LCC v Hay's Wharf Cartage Co Ltd* [1953] 2 All ER 34, 117 JP 304).

PART VIII
GOODS VEHICLES
Basic rate

4–1979 8. Repealed.

Rigid goods vehicles exceeding 7,500 kilograms plated gross weight or relevant maximum weight

4–1980 9. (1) Subject to sub-paragraphs (2) and (3), the annual rate of vehicle excise duty applicable to a rigid goods vehicle which is not a vehicle with respect to which the reduced pollution requirements are satisfied and which has a revenue weight exceeding 3,500 kilograms shall be determined in accordance with the following table by reference to—

  (a) the revenue weight of the vehicle, and
  (b) the number of axles on the vehicle.

Revenue weight of vehicle		Rate		
(1) Exceeding	(2) Not Exceeding	(3) Two axle vehicle	(4) Three axle vehicle	(5) Four or more axle vehicle
kgs	Kgs	£	£	£
3,500	7,500	165	165	165
7,500	12,000	200	200	200
12,000	13,000	200	200	200
13,000	14,000	200	200	200
14,000	15,000	200	200	200
15,000	17,000	650	200	200
17,000	19,000	650	200	200
19,000	21,000	650	200	200
21,000	23,000	650	450	200
23,000	25,000	650	650	450
25,000	27,000	650	650	650
27,000	29,000	650	650	1,200
29,000	31,000	650	650	1,200
31,000	44,000	650	650	1,200

(2) The annual rate of vehicle excise duty applicable—

  (a) to any rigid goods vehicle which is a showman's goods vehicle with a revenue weight exceeding 3,500 kilograms but not exceeding 44,000 kilograms,
  (b) to any rigid goods vehicle which is an island goods vehicle with a revenue weight exceeding 3,500 kilograms, and
  (c) to any rigid goods vehicle which is used loaded only in connection with a person learning to drive the vehicle or taking a driving test,

shall be the basic goods vehicle rate.
  (3) The annual rate of vehicle excise duty applicable to a rigid goods vehicle which—

  (a) is not a vehicle with respect to which the reduced pollution requirements are satisfied,
  (b) has a revenue weight exceeding 44,000 kilograms, and
  (c) is not an island goods vehicle,

shall be £2,585.
  (4) In sub-paragraph (2) the reference to the basic goods vehicle rate is to the rate applicable, by virtue of sub-paragraph (1), to a rigid goods vehicle which—

  (a) is not a vehicle with respect to which the reduced pollution requirements are satisfied; and
  (b) falls within column (3) of the table in that sub-paragraph and has a revenue weight exceeding 3,500 kilograms and not exceeding 7,500 kilograms.

  (5) *Repealed.*

4–1980A 9A. (1) This paragraph applies to a rigid goods vehicle which—

  (a) is a vehicle with respect to which the reduced pollution requirements are satisfied;
  (b) is not a vehicle for which the annual rate of vehicle excise duty is determined under paragraph 9(2); and
  (c) has a revenue weight exceeding 3,500 kilograms.

  (2) Subject to sub-paragraph (3), the annual rate of vehicle excise duty applicable to a rigid goods vehicle to which this paragraph applies shall be determined in accordance with the table set out in paragraph 9B by reference to—

  (a) the revenue weight of the vehicle, and
  (b) the number of axles on the vehicle.

  (3) The annual rate of vehicle excise duty applicable to a rigid goods vehicle to which this paragraph applies which has a revenue weight exceeding 44,000 kilograms shall be £2,085.

4–1980B   **9B.** That table is as follows—

Revenue weight of vehicle		Rate		
(1) Exceeding	(2) Not Exceeding	(3) Two axle vehicle	(4) Three axle vehicle	(5) Four or more axle vehicle
kgs	Kgs	£	£	£
3,500	7,500	160	160	160
7,500	12,000	160	160	160
12,000	13,000	160	160	160
13,000	14,000	160	160	160
14,000	15,000	160	160	160
15,000	17,000	280	160	160
17,000	19,000	280	160	160
19,000	21,000	280	160	160
21,000	23,000	280	210	160
23,000	25,000	280	280	210
25,000	27,000	280	280	280
27,000	29,000	280	280	700
29,000	31,000	280	280	700
31,000	44,000	280	280	700

4–1980C   **10.** (1) The annual rate of vehicle excise duty application, in accordance with paragraphs 9 and 9A, to a rigid goods vehicle which has a revenue weight exceeding 12,000 kilograms, which does not fall within paragraph 9(2)(b) or (c) and which is used for drawing a trailer which—

(a) has a plated gross weight exceeding 4,000 kilograms, and

(b) when so drawn, is used for the conveyance of goods or burden,

shall be increased by the amount of the supplement (the "trailer supplement") which is appropriate to the plated gross weight of the trailer being drawn.

(2) Where the plated gross weight of the trailer—

(a) exceeds 4,000 kilograms, but

(b) does not exceed 12,000 kilograms,

the amount of the trailer supplement is an amount equal to the amount of the general rate specified in paragraph 1(2).

(3) Where the plated gross weight of the trailer exceeds 12,000 kilograms, the amount of the trailer supplement is an amount equal to 140 per cent of the amount of the general rate specified in paragraph 1(2).

(3A) Where an amount arrived at in accordance with sub-paragraph (3) is an amount—

(a) which is not a multiple of £10, and

(b) which on division by ten does not produce a remainder of £5,

the amount of the trailer supplement is the amount arrived at rounded (either up or down) to the nearest amount which is a multiple of £10.

(3B) Where an amount arrived at in accordance with sub-paragraph (3) is an amount which on division by ten produces a remainder of £5, the amount of the trailer supplement is the amount arrived at increased by £5.

(4) *Repealed.*

Tractive units exceeding 7,500 kilograms train weight

4–1981   **11.** (1) Subject to sub-paragraphs (2) and (3) and paragraph 11C, the annual rate of vehicle excise duty applicable to a tractive unit which is not a vehicle with respect to which the reduced pollution requirements are satisfied and which has a revenue weight exceeding 3,500 kilograms shall be determined in accordance with the following table by reference to—

(a) the revenue weight of the tractive unit,

(b) the number of axles on the tractive unit, and

(c) the types of semi-trailers, distinguished according to the number of their axles, which are to be drawn by it.

Revenue weight of tractive unit		Rate for tractive unit with two axles			Rate for tractive unit with three or more axles		
(1) Exceeding	(2) Not ex- ceeding	(3) Any no of semi- trailer ax- les	(4) 2 or more semi- trailer ax- les	(5) 3 or more semi- trailer ax- les	(6) Any no of semi- trailer ax- les	(7) 2 or more semi- trailer ax- les	(8) 3 or more semi- trailer axles
kgs	kgs	£	£	£	£	£	£
3,500	7,500	165	165	165	165	165	165
7,500	12,000	165	165	165	165	165	165
12,000	16,000	165	165	165	165	165	165
16,000	20,000	165	165	165	165	165	165
20,000	23,000	165	165	165	165	165	165
23,000	25,000	165	165	165	165	165	165
25,000	26,000	450	165	165	165	165	165
26,000	28,000	450	165	165	165	165	165

Revenue weight of tractive unit		Rate for tractive unit with two axles			Rate for tractive unit with three or more axles		
(1) Exceeding	(2) Not exceeding	(3) Any no of semi-trailer axles	(4) 2 or more semi-trailer axles	(5) 3 or more semi-trailer axles	(6) Any no of semi-trailer axles	(7) 2 or more semi-trailer axles	(8) 3 or more semi-trailer axles
kgs	kgs	£	£	£	£	£	£
28,000	31,000	650	650	165	450	165	165
31,000	33,000	1,200	1,200	450	1,200	450	165
33,000	34,000	1,200	1,200	450	1,200	650	165
34,000	35,000	1,500	1,500	1,200	1,200	650	450
35,000	36,000	1,500	1,500	1,200	1,200	650	450
36,000	38,000	1,500	1,500	1,200	1,500	1,200	650
38,000	41,000	1,850	1,850	1,850	1,850	1,850	1,200
41,000	44,000	1,850	1,850	1,850	1,850	1,850	1,200

(2) The annual rate of vehicle excise duty applicable—

    (a) to any tractive unit which is a showman's goods vehicle with a revenue weight exceeding 3,500 kilograms but not exceeding 44,000 kilograms,

    (b) to any tractive unit which is an island goods vehicle with a revenue weight exceeding 3,500 kilograms, and

    (c) to any tractive unit to which a semi-trailer is attached which is used loaded only in connection with a person learning to drive the tractive unit or taking a driving test,

shall be the basic goods vehicle rate.

(3) The annual rate of vehicle excise duty applicable to a tractive unit which—

    (a) is not a vehicle with respect to which the reduced pollution requirements are satisfied,

    (b) has a revenue weight exceeding 44,000 kilograms, and

    (c) is not an island goods vehicle,

shall be £2,585.

(4) In sub-paragraph (2) the reference to the basic goods vehicle rate is to the rate applicable, by virtue of sub-paragraph (1) of paragraph 9, to a rigid goods vehicle which—

    (a) is not a vehicle with respect to which the reduced pollution requirements are satisfied; and

    (b) falls within column (3) of the table in that sub-paragraph and has a revenue weight exceeding 3,500 kilograms and not exceeding 7,500 kilograms.

    (5) *Repealed.*

4–1981A　**11A.** (1) This paragraph applies to a tractive unit which—

    (a) is a vehicle with respect to which the reduced pollution requirements are satisfied;

    (b) is not a vehicle for which the annual rate of vehicle excise duty is determined under paragraph 11(2); and

    (c) has a revenue weight exceeding 3,500 kilograms.

(2) Subject to sub-paragraph (3) and paragraph 11C, the annual rate of vehicle excise duty applicable to a tractive unit to which this paragraph applies shall be determined, in accordance with the table set out in paragraph 11B, by reference to—

    (a) the revenue weight of the tractive unit,

    (b) the number of axles on the tractive unit, and

    (c) the types of semi-trailers, distinguished according to the number of their axles, which are to be drawn by it.

(3) The annual rate of vehicle excise duty applicable to a tractive unit to which this paragraph applies which has a revenue weight exceeding 44,000 kilograms shall be £2,085.

4–1981B　**11B.** That table is as follows—

Revenue weight of tractive unit		Rate for tractive unit with two axles			Rate for tractive unit with three or more axles		
(1) Exceeding	(2) Not exceeding	(3) Any no of semi-trailer axles	(4) 2 or more semi-trailer axles	(5) 3 or more semi-trailer axles	(6) Any no of semi-trailer axles	(7) 2 or more semi-trailer axles	(8) 3 or more semi-trailer axles
kgs	kgs	£	£	£	£	£	£
3,500	7,500	160	160	160	160	160	160
7,500	12,000	160	160	160	160	160	160
12,000	16,000	160	160	160	160	160	160
16,000	20,000	160	160	160	160	160	160
20,000	23,000	160	160	160	160	160	160
23,000	25,000	160	160	160	160	160	160
25,000	26,000	210	160	160	160	160	160
26,000	28,000	210	160	160	160	160	160

Revenue weight of tractive unit		Rate for tractive unit with two axles			Rate for tractive unit with three or more axles		
(1) Exceeding	(2) Not exceeding	(3) Any no of semi-trailer axles	(4) 2 or more semi-trailer axles	(5) 3 or more semi-trailer axles	(6) Any no of semi-trailer axles	(7) 2 or more semi-trailer axles	(8) 3 or more semi-trailer axles
kgs	kgs	£	£	£	£	£	£
28,000	31,000	280	280	160	210	160	160
31,000	33,000	700	700	210	700	210	160
33,000	34,000	700	700	210	700	280	160
34,000	35,000	1,000	1,000	700	700	280	210

4–1981C **11C.** (1) This paragraph applies to a tractive unit that—

(a) has a revenue weight exceeding 41,000 kilograms but not exceeding 44,000 kilograms,
(b) has 3 or more axles and is used exclusively for the conveyance of semi-trailers with 3 or more axles,
(c) is of a type that could lawfully be used on a public road immediately before 21st March 2000, and
(d) complies with the requirements in force immediately before that date for use on a public road.

(2) The annual rate of vehicle excise duty applicable to a vehicle to which this paragraph applies is—

(a) in the case of a vehicle with respect to which the reduced pollution requirements are not satisfied, £650;
(b) in the case of a vehicle with respect to which those requirements are satisfied, £280.

4–1982 **12.** *Repealed.*

Vehicles with reduced plated weights

4–1983 **13.** (1) The Secretary of State may by regulations provide that, on an application relating to a goods vehicle which is made in accordance with the regulations, the vehicle is treated for the purposes of this Part as if its revenue weight were such lower weight as may be specified in the application.
(2) The regulations may provide that the treatment of the vehicle as being of a lower weight is subject to—

(a) conditions prescribed by the regulations, or
(b) such further conditions as the Secretary of State may think fit to impose in any particular case.

Vehicles for conveying machines

4–1984 **14.** A vehicle which—

(a) is constructed or adapted for use and used for the conveyance of a machine or device and no other load except articles used in connection with the machine or device,
(b)–(c) *Repealed,*

is chargeable with vehicle excise duty at the rate which would be applicable to it if the machine or device were burden even if it is built in as part of the vehicle[1].

1. The definition of "goods vehicle" in s 62(1), ante, and the reference in para 14 to a vehicle for carrying machines are not mutually exclusive, and are intended to be read together so that "burden" is intended to have the same meaning in both places (*Department of Transport v Caird Environmental Services Ltd* [1999] RTR 137). By virtue of s 60A, ante, in the absence of any other evidence as to weight, the plated weight of a vehicle is the revenue weight for the purposes of paras 9 and 14 of this Schedule (*Department of Transport v Caird Environmental Services Ltd*, supra).

Goods vehicles used partly for private purposes

4–1985 **15.** *Repealed.*

Exceptions

4–1986 **16.** (1) This Part does not apply to

(a) a vehicle to which Part II, IV, V or VII applies,
(b) *repealed.*

(2) This Part applies to a goods vehicle which is a vehicle to which paragraph 6 applies only if it is used on a public road and the use is not such as is mentioned in sub-paragraph (2) of that paragraph.

Meaning of "trailer"

4–1987 **17.** (1) In this Part "trailer" does not include—

(a) an appliance constructed and used solely for the purpose of distributing on the road loose gritting material, or
(b) a snow plough,
(c)–(e) *Repealed.*

(2) *Repealed.*

Meaning of "island goods vehicle"

4–1987A   18. (1) In this Part "island goods vehicle" means any goods vehicle which—

(a) is kept for use wholly or partly on the roads of one or more small islands; and

(b) is not kept or used on any mainland road, except in a manner authorised by sub-paragraph (2) or (3).

(2) The keeping or use of a goods vehicle on a mainland road is authorised by this sub-paragraph if—

(a) the road is one used for travel between a landing place and premises where vehicles disembarked at that place are loaded or unloaded, or both;

(b) the length of the journey, using that road, from that landing place to those premises is not more than five kilometres;

(c) the vehicle in question is one which was disembarked at that landing place after a journey by sea which began on a small island; and

(d) the loading or unloading of that vehicle is to take place, or has taken place, at those premises.

(3) The keeping or use of a goods vehicle on a mainland road is authorised by this sub-paragraph if—

(a) that vehicle has a revenue weight not exceeding 17,000 kilograms;

(b) that vehicle is normally kept at a base or centre on a small island; and

(c) the only journeys for which that vehicle is used are ones that begin or end at that base or centre.

(4) References in this paragraph to a small island are references to any such island falling within sub-paragraph (5) as may be designated as a small island by an order[1] made by the Secretary of State.

(5) An island falls within this sub-paragraph if—

(a) it has an area of 230,000 hectares or less; and

(b) the absence of a bridge, causeway, tunnel, ford or other way makes it at all times impracticable for road vehicles to be driven under their own power from that island as far as the mainland.

(6) The reference in sub-paragraph (5) to driving a road vehicle as far as the mainland is a reference to driving it as far as any public road in the United Kingdom which is not on an island with an area of 230,000 hectares or less and is not a road connecting two such islands.

(7) In this paragraph—

"island" includes anything that is an island only when the tide reaches a certain height;

"landing place" means any place at which vehicles are disembarked after sea journeys;

"mainland road" means any public road in the United Kingdom, other than one which is on a small island or which connects two such islands; and

"road vehicles" means vehicles which are designed or adapted primarily for being driven on roads and which do not have any special features for facilitating their being driven elsewhere;

and references in this paragraph to the loading or unloading of a vehicle include references to the loading or unloading of its trailer or semi-trailer.

---

1. The Vehicle Excise Duty (Designation of Small Islands) Order 1995, SI 1995/1397 amended by SI 2002/1072, designates the islands referred to in this Schedule as small islands.

Other expressions

4–1987B   19. (1) In this Part "driving test" means any test of competence to drive mentioned in section 89(1) of the Road Traffic Act 1988.

(2) For the purposes of this Part a vehicle or a semi-trailer is used loaded if the vehicle or, as the case may be, the semi-trailer is used for the conveyance of goods or burden of any description.

Section 5   SCHEDULE 2
                        Exempt vehicles[1]

(Amended by the Value Added Tax Act 1994, Sch 14, the Finance Act 1995, Schs 4 and 29, the Finance Act 1996, ss 15, 18, 19, 20 and 21, and Sch 41, the Finance Act 1997, s 17, Schs 3 and 18, the Finance Act 1998, s 17 and Sch 1, the Finance Act 2001, s 13, SI 1999/2795, SI 2000/90, the Vehicles (Crime) Act 2002, Sch, the Fire and Rescue Services Act 2004, Sch 1, SI 2004/2987 and the Health and Social Care (Community Health and Standards) Act 2003, Sch 4.)

Electrically propelled vehicles

4–1988   1. *Repealed.*

---

1. The burden of proving exemption lies upon the defendant (s 53, ante). In some of the cases, the court is required to look at the use of the vehicle. Otherwise, where for example a fire engine has been modified (see *Coote v Winfield* [1980] RTR 42) to serve some other purpose, it may no longer be capable of reasonably being regarded as fitting its original description.

For special reliefs where a vehicle licence was taken out on or after 1 July 1995 and before 1 July 1996 and an exemption under this Schedule was abolished by the Finance Act 1995, Sch 4, para 41.

Old vehicles

4–1988A   1A. (1) Subject to sub-paragraph (2), a vehicle is an exempt vehicle at any time if it was constructed before 1st January 1973.

(2) A vehicle is not an exempt vehicle by virtue of sub-paragraph (1) if—

(a) an annual rate is specified in respect of it by any provision of Part III, V, VI, VII or VIII of Schedule 1; or

(b) it is a special vehicle, within the meaning of Part IV of Schedule 1, which—

(i) falls within sub-paragraph (3) or (4); and

(ii) is not a digging machine, mobile crane, mobile pumping vehicle, works truck or road roller.

(3) A vehicle falls within this sub-paragraph if—

(a)   it is designed or adapted for use for the conveyance of goods or burden of any description;
(b)   it is put to a commercial use on a public road; and
(c)   that use is not a use for the conveyance of goods or burden of any description.

(4)   A vehicle falls within this sub-paragraph if—

(a)   it is designed or adapted for use with a semi-trailer attached;
(b)   it is put to a commercial use on a public road; and
(c)   in a case where that use is a use with a semi-trailer is not used for the conveyance of goods or burden of any description.

(5)   In sub-paragraph (2) "digging machine", "mobile crane", "mobile pumping vehicle", and "works truck" have the same meanings as in paragraph 4 of Schedule 1.
(6)   In sub-paragraph (3) and (4) "commercial use" means use for hire or reward or for or in connection with a trade or business.

Trams

4–1989   **2.** A vehicle used on tram lines is an exempt vehicle.

Electrically assisted pedal cycles

4–1989A   **2A.** (1) An electrically assisted pedal cycle is an exempt vehicle.
(2) For the purposes of sub-paragraph (1) an electrically assisted pedal cycle is a vehicle of a class complying with such requirements as may be prescribed by regulations made by the Secretary of State for the purposes of this paragraph.

Vehicles not for carriage

4–1990   **3.** A vehicle which is not constructed or adapted for use, or used, for the carriage of a driver or passenger is an exempt vehicle.

Police vehicles

4–1990A   **3A.** A vehicle is an exempt vehicle when it is being used for police purposes.

Fire engines etc

4–1991   **4.** (1) A fire engine is an exempt vehicle.
(2) In sub-paragraph (1) "fire engine" means a vehicle which—

(a)   is constructed or adapted for use for the purpose of fire fighting or salvage (or both), and
(b)   is used solely for purposes in relation to which a fire and rescue authority under the Fire and Rescue Services Act 2004 has functions (whoever uses it for those purposes)

5. A vehicle which is kept by a fire and rescue authority is an exempt vehicle when it is being used or kept on a road for the purposes of the authority's functions.

Ambulances and health service vehicles

4–1992   **6.** (1) An ambulance is an exempt vehicle.
(2) In sub-paragraph (1) "ambulance" means a vehicle which—

(a)   is constructed or adapted for, and used for no purpose other than, the carriage of sick, injured or disabled people to or from welfare centres or places where medical or dental treatment is given, and
(b)   is readily identifiable as a vehicle used for the carriage of such people by being marked "Ambulance" on both sides.

7. A vehicle is an exempt vehicle when it is being used or kept on a road by—

(a)   a health service body (as defined in section 60(7) of the National Health Service and Community Care Act 1990) or a health and social services body (as defined in Article 7(6) of the Health and Personal Social Services (Northern Ireland) Order 1991), or
(b)   a National Health Service trust established under Part I of the National Health Service and Community Care Act 1990 or the National Health Service (Scotland) Act 1978 or a Health and Social Services Trust established under the Health and Personal Social Services (Northern Ireland) Order 1991 or★
(ba) an NHS foundation trust, or
(c)   the Commission for Healthcare Audit and Inspection or
(d)   a Primary Care Trust established under section 16A of the National Health Service Act 1977 or
(e)   a Local Health Board established under section 16BA of that Act or
(f)   the Commission for Social Care Inspection.

8. A vehicle which is made available by the Secretary of State—

(a)   to a person, body or local authority under section 23 or 26 of the National Health Service Act 1977, or
(b)   to a local authority, education authority or voluntary organisation in Scotland under section 15 or 16 of the National Health Service (Scotland) Act 1978,

and which is used in accordance with the terms on which it is so made available is an exempt vehicle.
9. (1) A veterinary ambulance is an exempt vehicle.
(2) In sub-paragraph (1) "veterinary ambulance" means a vehicle which—

(a)   is used for no purpose other than the carriage of sick or injured animals to or from places where veterinary treatment is given, and
(b)   is readily identifiable as a vehicle used for the carriage of such animals by being marked "Veterinary Ambulance" on both sides.

Mine rescue vehicles etc

4–1993   **10.** A vehicle used solely—

(a) as a mine rescue vehicle, or
(b) for the purpose of conveying or drawing emergency winding-gear at a mine,

is an exempt vehicle.

Lifeboat vehicles

4–1994   **11.** A vehicle used or kept on a road for no purpose other than the haulage of a lifeboat and the conveyance of the necessary gear of the lifeboat which is being hauled is an exempt vehicle.

Road construction and maintenance vehicles

4–1995   **12–17.** *Repealed.*

Vehicles for disabled people

4–1996   **18.** A vehicle (including a cycle with an attachment for propulsion by mechanical power) which—

(a) is adapted, and used or kept on a road, for an invalid, and
(b) does not exceed 508 kilograms in weight unladen,

is an exempt vehicle.

19. (1) A vehicle is an exempt vehicle when it is being used, or kept for use, by or for the purposes of a disabled person who satisfies sub-paragraph (2) if—

(a) the vehicle is registered under this Act in the name of the disabled person, and
(b) no other vehicle is registered in his name under this Act is an exempt vehicle under this paragraph or paragraph 7 of Schedule 4.

(2) A disabled person satisfies this sub-paragraph if—

(a) he is in receipt of a disability living allowance by virtue of entitlement to the mobility component at the higher rate,
(b) he is in receipt of a mobility supplement, or
(c) he has obtained, or is eligible for, a grant under—

(i) paragraph 2 of Schedule 2 to the National Health Service Act 1977,
(ii) *Scotland,*
(iii) *Northern Ireland.*

in relation to the vehicle.

(2A) This paragraph shall have effect as if a person were in receipt of a disability living allowance by virtue of entitlement to the mobility component at the higher rate in any case where—

(a) he has ceased to be in receipt of it as a result of having ceased to satisfy a condition of receiving the allowance or of receiving the mobility component at that rate;
(b) that condition is either—

(i) a condition relating to circumstances in which he is undergoing medical or other treatment as an in-patient in a hospital or similar institution; or
(ii) a condition specified in regulations made by the Secretary of State;

and

(c) he would continue to be entitled to receive the mobility component of the allowance at the higher rate but for his failure to satisfy that condition.

(3) For the purposes of sub-paragraph (1) a vehicle is deemed to be registered under this Act in the name of a person in receipt of a disability living allowance by virtue of entitlement to the mobility component at the higher rate, or of a mobility supplement, if it is so registered in the name of—

(a) an appointee, or
(b) a person nominated for the purposes of this paragraph by the person or an appointee.

(4) In sub-paragraph (3) "appointee" means—

(a) a person appointed pursuant to regulations made under (or having effect as if made under) the Social Security Administration Act 1992 to exercise any of the rights and powers of a person in receipt of a disability living allowance, or
(b) a person to whom a mobility supplement is paid for application for the benefit of another person in receipt of the supplement.

(5) In this paragraph "mobility supplement" means a mobility supplement under—

(a) a scheme under the Personal Injuries (Emergency Provisions) Act 1939, or
(b) an Order in Council under section 12 of the Social Security (Miscellaneous Provisions) Act 1977,

or a payment appearing to the Secretary of State to be of a similar kind and specified for the purposes of this paragraph by an order[1] made by him.

---

1. See the Motor Vehicles (Exemption from Vehicles Excise Duty) Order 1985, SI 1985/722.

4–1996A   **20.** (1) A vehicle (other than an ambulance within the meaning of paragraph 6) used for the carriage of disabled people by a body for the time being recognised by the Secretary of State for the purposes of this paragraph is an exempt vehicle.

(2) The Secretary of State shall recognise a body for the purposes of this paragraph if, on an application made to him in such manner as he may specify, it appears to him that the body is concerned with the care of disabled people.

(3) The issue by the Secretary of State of a nil licence in respect of a vehicle under this paragraph is to be

treated as recognition by him for the purposes of this paragraph of the body by reference to whose use of the vehicle the document is issued.

(4) *Repealed.*

(5) The Secretary of State may withdraw recognition of a body for the purposes of this paragraph if it appears to him that the body is no longer concerned with the care of disabled people.

Vehicles used between different parts of land

4–1996B　20A. A vehicle is an exempt vehicle if—

(a)　it is used only for purposes relating to agriculture, horticulture or forestry,

(b)　it is used on public roads only in passing between different areas of land occupied by the same person, and

(c)　the distance it travels on public roads in passing between any two such areas does not exceed 1·5 kilometres.

Tractors

4–1996C　20B. (1) A vehicle is an exempt vehicle if it is—

(a)　an agricultural tractor, or

(b)　an off-road tractor.

(2) In sub-paragraph (1) "agricultural tractor" means a tractor used on public roads solely for purposes relating to agriculture, horticulture, forestry or activities falling within sub-paragraph (3).

(3) The activities falling within this sub-paragraph are—

(a)　cutting verges bordering public roads;

(b)　cutting hedges or trees bordering public roads or bordering verges which border public roads.

(4) In sub-paragraph (1) "off-road tractor" means a tractor which is not an agricultural tractor (within the meaning given by sub-paragraph (2)) and which is—

(a)　designed and constructed primarily for use otherwise than on roads, and

(b)　incapable by reason of its construction of exceeding a speed of twenty-five miles per hour on the level under its own power.

Light agricultural vehicles

4–1996D　20C. (1) A vehicle is an exempt vehicle if it is a light agricultural vehicle.

(2) In sub-paragraph (1) "light agricultural vehicle" means a vehicle which—

(a)　has a revenue weight not exceeding 1,000 kilograms,

(b)　is designed and constructed so as to seat only the driver,

(c)　is designed and constructed primarily for use otherwise than on roads, and

(d)　is used solely for purposes relating to agriculture, horticulture or forestry.

Agricultural engines

4–1996E　20D. An agricultural engine is an exempt vehicle.[1]

---

1. The Act does not impose a condition that when such a vehicle is being used as a vehicle for the carriage or haulage of goods it ceases to be exempt: *Vehicle Operators Services Agency v Law Fertilisers Ltd* [2004] EWHC 3000, [2005] RTR 21.

Mowing machines

4–1996F　20E. A mowing machine is an exempt vehicle.

Steam powered vehicles

4–1996G　20F. A steam powered vehicle is an exempt vehicle.

Electrically propelled vehicles

4–1996H　20G. An electrically propelled vehicle is an exempt vehicle.

Snow ploughs

4–1996I　20H. A vehicle is an exempt vehicle when it is—

(a)　being used,

(b)　going to or from the place where it is to be or has been used, or

(c)　being kept for use,

for the purpose of clearing snow from public roads by means of a snow plough or similar device (whether or not forming part of the vehicle).

Gritters

4–1996J　20J. A vehicle is an exempt vehicle if it is constructed or adapted, and used, solely for the conveyance of machinery for spreading material on roads to deal with frost, ice or snow (with or without articles or material used for the purposes of the machinery).

4–1997　21. *Repealed.*

Vehicle testing etc

4–1998　22. (1) A vehicle is an exempt vehicle when it is being used solely for the purpose of—

(a) submitting it (by previous arrangement for a specified time on a specified date) for a compulsory test, a vehicle identity check, a vehicle weight test or a reduced pollution test, or

(b) bringing it away from any such test or check[1].

(1A) A vehicle is an exempt vehicle when it is being used solely for the purpose of—

(a) taking it (by previous arrangement for a specified time on a specified date) for a relevant re-examination, or

(b) bringing it away from such a re-examination.

(2) A vehicle is an exempt vehicle when it is being used by an authorised person in the course of a compulsory test, a vehicle weight test, or a vehicle identity check or a reduced pollution test or a relevant re-examination and is being so used solely for the purpose of—

(a) taking it to, or bringing it away from, a place where a part of the test, check or re-examination is to be, or has been, carried out, or

(b) carrying out a part of the check, test or re-examination.

(2A) A vehicle is an exempt vehicle when it is being used by an authorised person solely for the purpose of warming up its engine in preparation for the carrying out of—

(a) a compulsory test or a reduced pollution test, or

(b) relevant re-examination that is to be carried out for the purposes of an appeal relating to a determination made on a compulsory test or a reduced pollution test.

(3) Where the relevant certificate is refused on a compulsory test or a reduced pollution test of a vehicle or as a result of a relevant re-examination, the vehicle is an exempt vehicle when it is being used solely for the purpose of—

(a) delivering it (by previous arrangement for a specified time on a specified date) at a place where relevant work is to be done on it, or

(b) bringing it away from a place where relevant work has been done on it.

(4) In this paragraph "compulsory test" means, as respects England and Wales and Scotland—

(a) in the case of a vehicle for which by virtue of section 66(3) of the Road Traffic Act 1988 a vehicle licence cannot be granted unless certain requirements are satisfied, an examination such as is specified in sub-paragraph (5), and

(b) otherwise, an examination under section 45 of the Road Traffic Act 1988 with a view to obtaining a test certificate without which a vehicle licence cannot be granted for the vehicle.

(5) The examinations referred to in sub-paragraph (4)(a) are—

(a) an examination under regulations under section 49(1)(b) or (c) of the Road Traffic Act 1988 (examination as to compliance with construction and use or safety requirements),

(b) an examination for the purposes of sections 54 to 58 of that Act (examination as to a vehicle's compliance with type approval requirements), and

(c) *Repealed*;

(d) an examination under regulations under section 61(2)(a) of that Act (examinations in connection with alterations to vehicles subject to type approval requirements).

(6) *Northern Ireland*.

(6ZA) In this paragraph "a vehicle identity check" means any examination of a vehicle for which provision is made by regulations made by virtue of section 22A(2) of this Act.

(6A) In this paragraph "a vehicle weight test" means any examination of a vehicle for which provision is made by regulations under—

(a) section 61A of this Act

(b) section 49(1)(a) of the Road Traffic Act 1988 (tests for selecting plated weights and other plated particulars), or

(c) Article 65(1)(a) of the Road Traffic (Northern Ireland) Order 1995.

(6AA) In this paragraph "a reduced pollution test" means any examination of a vehicle for which provision is made by regulations under section 61B of this Act.

(6B) In this paragraph "a relevant re-examination" means any examination or re-examination which is carried out in accordance with any provision or requirement made or imposed for the purposes of an appeal relating to a determination made on a compulsory test, a vehicle identity check, a vehicle weight test or a reduced pollution test.

(7) In this paragraph "authorised person" means—

(a) in the case of an examination within sub-paragraph (4)(b), a person who is, or is acting on behalf of, an examiner or inspector entitled to carry out such an examination or a person acting under the personal direction of such a person,

(b) in the case of an examination within sub-paragraph (5), an examiner appointed under section 66A of the Road Traffic Act 1988, a person carrying out the examination under the direction of such an examiner or a person driving the vehicle in accordance with a requirement to do so under the regulations under which the examination is carried out,

(c) *Northern Ireland*, and

(ca) in the case of an examination of a vehicle for which provision is made by regulations made by virtue of section 22A(2) of this Act, the Secretary of State or a person authorised by him to carry out the examination; and

(d) in the case of a relevant re-examination—

(i) the person to whom the appeal in question is made, or

(ii) any person who, by virtue of an appointment made by that person, is authorised by or under any enactment to carry out that re-examination

(8) In this paragraph "the relevant certificate" means, as respects England and Wales and Scotland—

(a) a test certificate (as defined in section 45(2) of the Road Traffic Act 1988), or

(b) a goods vehicle test certificate (as defined in section 49 of that Act), or

(c) a type approval certificate or Minister's approval certificate (as defined in sections 54 to 58 of that Act), or

(d) a certificate issued by virtue of section 61B of this Act.

(9) *Northern Ireland*.

(10) In this paragraph "relevant work" means—

(a) where the relevant certificate which is refused is a test certificate, work done or to be done to remedy for a further compulsory test the defects on the ground of which the relevant certificate was refused, and

(b) in any other case, work done or to be done to remedy the defects on the ground of which the relevant certificate was refused (including work to alter the vehicle in some aspect of design, construction, equipment or marking on account of which the relevant certificate was refused).

---

1. Whether a vehicle is being used solely for this purpose is a matter of fact and degree and it would be ridiculous to hold that a driver could not buy petrol or make a short stop provided that he is on his way to the test (*Secretary of State for Transport v Richards* (1997) 162 JP 682, [1998] RTR 456, DC).

Vehicles for export

4–1999 23. (1) A vehicle is an exempt vehicle if—

(a) it has been supplied to the person keeping it by a taxable person within the meaning of section 3 of the Value Added Tax Act 1994, and

(b) the supply has been zero-rated under subsection (8) of section 30 of that Act.

(2) If at any time the value added tax that would have been chargeable on the supply but for the zero-rating becomes payable under subsection (10) of that section (or would have become payable but for any authorisation or waiver under that subsection), the vehicle is deemed never to have been an exempt vehicle under sub-paragraph (1).

Vehicles imported by members of foreign armed forces etc

4–2000 24. The Secretary of State may by regulations[1] provide that, in such cases, subject to such conditions and for such period as may be prescribed by the regulations, a vehicle is an exempt vehicle if it has been imported by—

(a) a person for the time being appointed to serve with any body, contingent or detachment of the forces of any country prescribed by the regulations which is for the time being present in the United Kingdom on the invitation of Her Majesty's Government in the United Kingdom,

(b) a member of any country's military forces, except Her Majesty's United Kingdom forces, who is for the time being appointed to serve in the United Kingdom under the orders of any organisation so prescribed,

(c) a person for the time being recognised by the Secretary of State as a member of a civilian component of a force within sub-paragraph (a) or as a civilian member of an organisation within sub-paragraph (b), or

(d) any dependant of a description so prescribed of a person within sub-paragraph (a), (b), (c).

---

1. See the Road Vehicles (Registration and Licensing) Regulations 2002, reg 34 and Sch 5, in this PART, post.

SCHEDULE 2A
IMMOBILISATION, REMOVAL AND DISPOSAL OF VEHICLES

(As inserted by the Finance Act 1995, Sch 4.)

Immobilisation

4–2000A 1. (1) The Secretary of State may make regulations[1] under this Schedule with respect to any case where an authorised person has reason to believe that, on or after such date as may be prescribed, an offence under section 29(1) is being committed as regards a vehicle which is stationary on a public road.

(2) The regulations may provide that the authorised person or a person acting under his direction may—

(a) fix an immobilisation device to the vehicle while it remains in the place where it is stationary, or

(b) move it from that place to another place on the same or another public road and fix an immobilisation device to it in that other place.

(3) The regulations may provide that on any occasion when an immobilisation device is fixed to a vehicle in accordance with the regulations the person fixing the device shall also fix to the vehicle a notice—

(a) indicating that the device has been fixed to the vehicle and warning that no attempt should be made to drive it or otherwise put it in motion until it has been released from the device;

(b) specifying the steps to be taken to secure its release;

(c) giving such other information as may be prescribed.

(4) The regulations may provide that—

(a) a vehicle to which an immobilisation device has been fixed in accordance with the regulations may only be released from the device by or under the direction of an authorised person;

(b) subject to that, such a vehicle shall be released from the device if the first and second requirements specified below are met.

(5) The first requirement is that such charge in respect of the release as may be prescribed is paid in any manner specified in the immobilisation notice.

(6) The second requirement is that—

(a) a vehicle licence is produced in accordance with instructions specified in the immobilisation notice, and the licence is one which is in force for the vehicle concerned at the time the licence is produced, or

(b) where such a licence is not produced, such sum as may be prescribed is paid in any manner specified in the immobilisation notice.

(7) The regulations may provide that they shall not apply in relation to a vehicle if—

(a) a current disabled person's badge is displayed on the vehicle, or

(b) such other conditions as may be prescribed are fulfilled;

and "disabled person's badge" here means a badge issued, or having effect as if issued, under any regulations for the time being in force under section 21 of the Chronically Sick and Disabled Persons Act 1970 or any regulations for the time being in force under section 14 of the Chronically Sick and Disabled Persons (Northern Ireland) Act 1978.

(8) The regulations may provide that an immobilisation notice shall not be removed or interfered with except by or on the authority of a person falling within a prescribed description.

---

1. The Vehicle Excise Duty (Immobilisation, Removal and Disposal of Vehicles) Regulations 1997, SI 1997/2439 amended by SI 1997/3063, SI 1998/1217, SI 1999/35 and SI 2001/936 have been made.

Offences connected with immobilisation

4–2000B **2.** (1) The regulations may provide that a person contravening provision made under paragraph 1(8) is guilty of an offence and liable on summary conviction to a fine not exceeding level 2 on the standard scale.

(2) The regulations may provide that a person who, without being authorised to do so in accordance with provision made under paragraph 1, removes or attempts to remove an immobilisation device fixed to a vehicle in accordance with the regulations is guilty of an offence and liable on summary conviction to a fine not exceeding level 3 on the standard scale.

(3) The regulations may provide that where they would apply in relation to a vehicle but for provision made under paragraph 1(7)(a) and the vehicle was not, at the time it was stationary, being used—

    (a) in accordance with regulations under section 21 of the Chronically Sick and Disabled Persons Act 1970 or regulations under section 14 of the Chronically Sick and Disabled Persons (Northern Ireland) Act 1978, and

    (b) in circumstances falling within section 117(1)(b) of the Road Traffic Regulation Act 1984 or Article 174A(2)(b) of the Road Traffic (Northern Ireland) Order 1981 (use where a disabled person's concession would be available),

the person in charge of the vehicle at that time is guilty of an offence and liable on summary conviction to a fine not exceeding level 3 on the standard scale.

(4) The regulations may provide that where—

    (a) a person makes a declaration with a view to securing the release of a vehicle from an immobilisation device purported to have been fixed in accordance with the regulations,

    (b) the declaration is that the vehicle is or was an exempt vehicle, and

    (c) the declaration is to the person's knowledge either false or in any material respect misleading,

he is guilty of an offence.

(5) The regulations may provide that a person guilty of an offence by virtue of provision made under sub-paragraph (4) is liable—

    (a) on summary conviction, to a fine not exceeding the statutory maximum, and

    (b) on conviction on indictment, to imprisonment for a term not exceeding two years or to a fine or (except in Scotland) to both.

Removal and disposal of vehicles

4–2000C **3.** (1) The regulations may make provision as regards a case where—

    (a) an immobilisation device is fixed to a vehicle in accordance with the regulations, and

    (b) such conditions as may be prescribed are fulfilled.

(2) The regulations may provide that an authorised person, or a person acting under the direction of an authorised person, may remove the vehicle and deliver it into the custody of a person—

    (a) who is identified in accordance with prescribed rules, and

    (b) who agrees to accept delivery in accordance with arrangements agreed between that person and the Secretary of State;

and the arrangements may include provision as to the payment of a sum to the person into whose custody the vehicle is delivered.

(3) The regulations may provide that the person into whose custody the vehicle is delivered may dispose of it, and in particular provision may be made as to—

    (a) the time at which the vehicle may be disposed of;

    (b) the manner in which it may be disposed of.

(4) The regulations may make provision allowing a person to take possession of the vehicle if—

    (a) he claims it before it is disposed of, and

    (b) any prescribed conditions are fulfilled.

(5) The regulations may provide for a sum of an amount arrived at under prescribed rules to be paid to a person if—

    (a) he claims after the vehicle's disposal to be or to have been its owner,

    (b) the claim is made within a prescribed time of the disposal, and

    (c) any other prescribed conditions are fulfilled.

(6) The regulations may provide that—

    (a) the Secretary of State, or

    (b) a person into whose custody the vehicle is delivered under the regulations,

may recover from the vehicle's owner (whether or not a claim is made under provision made under sub-paragraph (4) or (5)) such charges as may be prescribed in respect of all or any of the following, namely, its release, removal, custody and disposal; and "owner" here means the person who was the owner when the immobilisation device was fixed.

(7) The conditions prescribed under sub-paragraph (4) may include conditions as to—

    (a)   satisfying the person with custody that the claimant is the vehicle's owner;
    (b)   the payment of prescribed charges in respect of the vehicle's release, removal and custody;
    (c)   the production of a vehicle licence;
    (d)   payment of a prescribed sum where a vehicle licence is not produced.

    (8) Without prejudice to anything in the preceding provisions of this paragraph, the regulations may include provision for purposes corresponding to those of sections 101 and 102 of the Road Traffic Regulation Act 1984 (disposal and charges) subject to such additions, omissions or other modifications as the Secretary of State thinks fit.

Offences as to securing possession of vehicles

4–2000D   **4.**—(1) The regulations may provide that where—

    (a)   a person makes a declaration with a view to securing possession of a vehicle purported to have been delivered into the custody of a person in accordance with provision made under paragraph 3,
    (b)   the declaration is that the vehicle is or was an exempt vehicle, and
    (c)   the declaration is to the person's knowledge either false or in any material respect misleading,

he is guilty of an offence.

    (2) The regulations may provide that a person guilty of such an offence is liable—

    (a)   on summary conviction, to a fine not exceeding the statutory maximum, and
    (b)   on conviction on indictment, to imprisonment for a term not exceeding two years or to a fine or (except in Scotland) to both.

Payment of sum where licence not produced

4–2000E   **5.**—(1) The regulations may make provision as regards a case where a person pays a prescribed sum in pursuance of provision made under—

    (a)   paragraph 1(6)(*b*), or
    (b)   paragraph 3(7)(*d*).

    (2) The regulations may—

    (a)   provide for a voucher to be issued in respect of the sum;
    (b)   provide for setting the sum against the amount of any vehicle excise duty payable in respect of the vehicle concerned;
    (c)   provide for the refund of any sum;
    (d)   provide that where a voucher has been issued section 29(1) and any other prescribed provision of this Act shall not apply, as regards the vehicle concerned, in relation to events occurring in a prescribed period.

    (3) The regulations may make provision—

    (a)   as to the information to be provided before a voucher is issued;
    (b)   as to the contents of vouchers;
    (c)   specifying conditions subject to which any provision under sub-paragraph (2)(*b*) to (*d*) is to have effect.

    (4) The regulations may make provision as to any case where a voucher is issued on receipt of a cheque which is subsequently dishonoured, and in particular the regulations may—

    (a)   provide for a voucher to be void;
    (b)   provide that, where the sum concerned is set against the amount of any vehicle excise duty, the licence concerned shall be void;
    (c)   make provision under which a person is required to deliver up a void voucher or void licence.

Offences relating to vouchers

4–2000F   **6.**—(1) The regulations may provide that—

    (a)   a person is guilty of an offence if within such reasonable period as is found in accordance with prescribed rules he fails to deliver up a voucher that is void by virtue of provision made under paragraph 5(4);
    (b)   a person guilty of such an offence shall be liable on summary conviction to a fine not exceeding level 3 on the standard scale.

    (2) The regulations may provide that a person is guilty of an offence if within such reasonable period as is found in accordance with prescribed rules he fails to deliver up a licence that is void by virtue of provision made under paragraph 5(4), and that a person guilty of such an offence shall be liable on summary conviction to a penalty of whichever is the greater of—

    (a)   level 3 on the standard scale;
    (b)   an amount equal to five times the annual rate of duty that was payable on the grant of the licence or would have been so payable if it had been taken out for a period of twelve months.

    (3) The regulations may provide that where a person is convicted of an offence under provision made by virtue of sub-paragraph (2) he must pay, in addition to any penalty, an amount found in accordance with prescribed rules.

    (4) The regulations may provide that if—

    (a)   a voucher is void by virtue of provision made under paragraph 5(4),
    (b)   a person seeks to set the sum concerned against the amount of any vehicle excise duty, and
    (c)   he knows the voucher is void,

he is guilty of an offence and liable on summary conviction to a fine not exceeding level 5 on the standard scale.

    (5) The regulations may provide that a person who in connection with—

    (a)   obtaining a voucher for which provision is made under paragraph 5, or
    (b)   obtaining a refund of any sum in respect of which such a voucher is issued,

makes a declaration which to his knowledge is either false or in any material respect misleading is guilty of an offence.

(6) The regulations may provide that a person is guilty of an offence if he forges, fraudulently alters, fraudulently uses, fraudulently lends or fraudulently allows to be used by another person a voucher for which provision is made under paragraph 5.

(7) The regulations may provide that a person guilty of an offence under provision made under sub-paragraph (5) or (6) is liable—

(*a*) on summary conviction, to a fine not exceeding the statutory maximum, and

(*b*) on conviction on indictment, to imprisonment for a term not exceeding two years or to a fine or (except in Scotland) to both.

Vouchers: general

4–2000G 7. Without prejudice to anything in paragraphs 5(4) and 6 the regulations may include provision for purposes corresponding to those of sections 19A and 36 subject to such additions, omissions or other modifications as the Secretary of State thinks fit.

Disputes

4–2000H 8. The regulations may make provision about the proceedings to be followed where a dispute occurs as a result of the regulations, and in particular provision may be made—

(*a*) for an application to be made to a magistrates' court or (in Northern Ireland) a court of summary jurisdiction;

(*b*) for a court to order a sum to be paid by the Secretary of State.

Authorised persons

4–2000I 9. As regards anything falling to be done under the regulations (such as receiving payment of a charge or other sum or issuing a voucher) the regulations may provide that it may be done—

(*a*) by an authorised person, or

(*b*) by an authorised person or a person acting under his direction.

Application of provisions

4–2000J 10. (1) The regulations may provide that they shall only apply where the authorised person has reason to believe that the offence mentioned in paragraph 1(1) is being committed before such date as may be prescribed.

(2) The regulations may provide that they shall only apply where the vehicle mentioned in paragraph 1(1) is in a prescribed area.

(3) Different dates may be prescribed under paragraph 1(1) or sub-paragraph (1) above in relation to different areas prescribed under sub-paragraph (2) above.

Interpretation

4–2000K 11. (1) The regulations may make provision as to the meaning for the purposes of the regulations of "owner" as regards a vehicle.

(2) In particular, the regulations may provide that for the purposes of the regulations—

(*a*) the owner of a vehicle at a particular time shall be taken to be the person by whom it is then kept;

(*b*) the person by whom a vehicle is kept at a particular time shall be taken to be the person in whose name it is then registered by virtue of this Act.

12. (1) The regulations may make provision as to the meaning in the regulations of "authorised person".

(2) In particular, the regulations may provide that—

(*a*) references to an authorised person are to a person authorised by the Secretary of State for the purposes of the regulations;

(*b*) an authorised person may be a local authority or an employee of a local authority or a member of a police force or some other person;

(*c*) different persons may be authorised for the purposes of different provisions of the regulations.

13. In this Schedule—

(*a*) references to an immobilisation device are to a device or appliance which is an immobilisation device for the purposes of section 104 of the Road Traffic Regulation Act 1984 (immobilisation of vehicles illegally parked);

(*b*) references to an immobilisation notice are to a notice fixed to a vehicle in accordance with the regulations;

(*c*) "prescribed" means prescribed by regulations made under this Schedule.

SCHEDULE 4
TRANSITIONALS ETC

(*As amended by the Finance Act 1995, Sch 4, the Finance Act 1996, s 18 and the Finance Act 1999, s 8.*)

General transitionals and savings

4–2001 1. The substitution of this Act for the provisions repealed or revoked by this Act does not affect the continuity of the law.

2. (1) Anything done, or having effect as done, (including the making of subordinate legislation and the issuing of licences) under or for the purposes of any provision repealed or revoked by this Act has effect as if done under or for the purposes of any corresponding provision of this Act.

(2) Sub-paragraph (1) does not apply to the Vehicle Licences (Duration and Rate of Duty) Order 1980.

3. Any reference (express or implied) in this Act or any other enactment, or in any instrument or document, to a provision of this Act is (so far as the context permits) to be read as (according to the context) being or including in relation to times, circumstances and purposes before the commencement of this Act a reference to the corresponding provision repealed or revoked by this Act.

4. Any reference (express or implied) in any enactment, or in any instrument or document, to a provision repealed or revoked by this Act is (so far as the context permits) to be read as (according to the context) being or including in relation to times, circumstances and purposes after the commencement of this Act a reference to the corresponding provision of this Act.

5. Paragraphs 1 to 4 have effect in place of section 17(2) of the Interpretation Act 1978 (but are without prejudice to any other provision of that Act).

Preservation of old transitionals and savings

4–2002 6. (1) The repeal by this Act of an enactment previously repealed subject to savings (whether or not in the repealing enactment) does not affect the continued operation of those savings.

(2) The repeal by this Act of a saving made on the previous repeal of an enactment does not affect the operation of the saving in so far as it remains capable of having effect.

(3) Where the purpose of an enactment repealed by this Act was to secure that the substitution of the provisions of the Act containing that enactment for provisions repealed by that Act did not affect the continuity of the law, the enactment repealed by this Act continues to have effect in so far as it is capable of doing so.

Exemption for disabled passengers

4–2003 7. (1) Where—

(a) a vehicle is suitable for use by persons having a particular disability that so incapacitates them in the use of their limbs that they have to be driven and cared for by a full-time constant attendant,

(b) the vehicle is registered under this Act in the name of a person who has such a disability and is a person to whom this paragraph applies,

(c) that person is sufficiently disabled to be eligible for an invalid tricycle under the National Health Service Act 1977, the National Health Service (Scotland) Act 1978 or the Health and Personal Social Services (Northern Ireland) Order 1972 but too disabled to drive it, and

(d) no other vehicle registered in that person's name under this Act, or deemed to be so registered under sub-paragraph (3) of paragraph 19 of Schedule 2, is an exempt vehicle under that paragraph,

the vehicle is an exempt vehicle if used or kept for use by or for the purposes of that person.

(2) This paragraph applies to a person if—

(a) there remains valid a relevant certificate issued in respect of him before 13th October 1993 (the day on which the repeal of the provisions specified in section 12(1) of the Finance (No. 2) Act 1992 came into force), or

(b) an application for a relevant certificate in respect of him had been received by the Secretary of State or the Department of Health and Social Services for Northern Ireland before that date and a relevant certificate issued pursuant to that application remains valid.

(3) In this paragraph a "relevant certificate" means—

(a) a certificate issued by the Secretary of State (or the Minister of Transport) containing a statement as described in Regulation 26(2)(b)(i) and (ii) of the Road Vehicles (Registration and Licensing) Regulations 1971 (as in force on 29th December 1972) or a statement to similar effect, or

(b) a certificate issued by the Department of Health and Social Services for Northern Ireland (or the Ministry of Health and Social Services for Northern Ireland) containing a statement as described in Regulation 27(2)(b)(i) and (ii) of the Road Vehicles (Registration and Licensing) Regulations (Northern Ireland) 1973 (as originally in force) or a statement to similar effect,

including (in either case) any renewal or continuation of such a certificate.

(4) For the purposes of sub-paragraph (2) a relevant certificate issued in respect of a person remains valid for as long as the matters stated in the certificate in relation to the person's disability remain unaltered.

(5) Where immediately before 13th October 1993 a person to whom this paragraph applies was under the age of five, the person ceases to be a person to whom this paragraph applies—

(a) if a relevant licence document is in force on the day on which he attains the age of five in respect of a vehicle used or kept for use for his purposes, when that licence document expires, and

(b) otherwise, on attaining the age five.

(6) In sub-paragraph (5) "relevant licence document" means a document in the form of a licence issued under—

(a) Regulation 26(3A)(b) of the Road Vehicles (Registration and Licensing) Regulations 1971,

(b) Regulation 27(4)(b) of the Road Vehicles (Registration and Licensing) Regulations (Northern Ireland) 1973, or

(c) paragraph 4 or 6 of the Schedule to the Finance (No. 2) Act 1992 (Commencement No. 6 and Transitional Provisions and Savings) Order 1993,

or any re-enactment (with or without modifications) of any of those provisions.

(7) Regulations under section 22(2) of this Act which require a person to furnish information relating to a vehicle which is an exempt vehicle under this paragraph may require him to furnish (in addition) such evidence of the facts giving rise to the exemption as is prescribed by the regulations.

(8) In spite of the repeal by this Act of section 12(2) of the Finance (No. 2) Act 1992, paragraphs 4 to 8 of the Schedule to the Finance (No. 2) At 1992 (Commencement No. 6 and Transitional Provisions and Savings) Order 1993 shall, until the coming into force of the first regulations made by virtue of sub-paragraph (7) (unless revoked and subject to any amendments), continue to have effect but subject to the modifications specified in sub-paragraph (9).

(9) The modifications referred to in sub-paragraph (8) are—

(a) the substitution of a reference to this paragraph for any reference to paragraph 2 of that Schedule,

(b) the addition of a reference to this Act after the first reference to the Vehicles (Excise) Act 1971 in paragraphs 4(4)(a) and 6(4)(a),

(c) the substitution of a reference to this Act for each other reference to the Vehicles (Excise) Act 1971, and

(d) the substitution of a reference to section 23 of this Act for any reference to section 19 of that Act and of a reference to subsection (3) of section 23 of this Act for any reference to subsection (2) of section 19 of that Act.

(10) Sections 44 and 45 of this Act have effect in relation to a vehicle which is an exempt vehicle under this paragraph as they have effect in relation to a vehicle which is an exempt vehicle under paragraph 19 of Schedule 2 to this Act.

(11) If and to the extent that, immediately before the coming into force of this Act, the Secretary of State had power to amend or revoke by order any provision of the Finance (No. 2) Act 1992 (Commencement No. 6 and Transitional provisions and Savings) Order 1993, he has the same power in relation to so much of this paragraph as reproduces that provision.

Trade licences

4–2004 8. (1) On and after such day as the Secretary of State may by order appoint this Act shall have effect as if for section 13 there were substituted—

13. "Trade licences: duration and amount of duty.   (1) A trade licence may be taken out—

> (*a*) for a period of twelve months, or
> (*b*) for a period of six months.

(2) A trade licence taken out by a person who is not a motor trader or vehicle tester (having satisfied the Secretary of State as mentioned in section 11(1)(*b*)) may be taken out only for a period of six months.

(3) The Secretary of State may require that a trade licence taken out by a motor trader or vehicle tester who does not hold an existing trade licence may be taken out only for a period of six months.

(4) The rate of duty applicable to a trade licence taken out for a period of twelve months is—

> (*a*) the annual rate currently applicable to a vehicle under sub-paragraph (1)(*c*) of paragraph 2 of Schedule 1 if the licence is to be used only for vehicles to which that paragraph applies, and
> (*b*) otherwise, the annual rate currently applicable to a vehicle under paragraph 1(2) of Schedule 1.

(5) The rate of duty applicable to a trade licence taken out for a period of six months is fifty-five per cent of the rate applicable to the corresponding trade licence taken out for a period of twelve months.

(6) In determining a rate of duty under subsection (5) any fraction of five pence—

> (*a*) if it exceeds two and a half pence, shall be treated as five pence, and
> (*b*) otherwise, shall be disregarded."

(2) An order under sub-paragraph (1) may appoint different days for different cases.

(3) A licence in force when such an order substitutes for section 13 the provisions set out in sub-paragraph (1) is not affected by that substitution.

Combined road-rail transport of goods

4–2005 9. Section 20 (and the references to it in sections 45(1)(*b*) and 57(5)) shall not come into force until such day as the Secretary of State may by order appoint.

Regulations about registration and licensing

4–2006 10. Regulation 12(1) of the Road Vehicles (Registration and Licensing) Regulations 1971 continues to have effect (until revoked) as if the amendments of section 23 of the Vehicles (Excise) Act 1971, as set out in paragraph 20 of Schedule 7 to that Act, which were made by paragraph 16(3) of Part III of Schedule 1 to the Finance Act 1987 had been in force when those Regulations were made.

Assignment of registration marks

4–2007 11. The inclusion in this Act of subsection (2), and the words "for the time being" in subsection (3), of section 23 (which reproduce the amendments of the Vehicles (Excise) Act 1971 made by section 10(2) and (3) of the Finance Act 1989) shall not be construed as affecting the operation of—

> (*a*) the Vehicles (Excise) Act 1971 or the Vehicles (Excise) Act (Northern Ireland) 1972, or
> (*b*) any regulations made under either of those Acts,

in relation to any time before 27th July 1989 (the day on which the Finance Act 1989 was passed).

Road Traffic (New Drivers) Act 1995[1]

(1995 c 13)

Introductory

4–2008A 1. Probationary period for newly qualified drivers.   (1) For the purposes of this Act, a person's probationary period is, subject to section 7, the period of two years beginning with the day[2] on which he becomes a qualified driver.

(2) For the purposes of this Act, a person becomes a qualified driver on the first occasion on which he passes—

> (*a*) any test of competence to drive mentioned in paragraph (*a*) or (*c*) of section 89(1) of the Road Traffic Act 1988;
> (*b*) any test of competence to drive conducted under the law of
>
> > (i)   another EEA State,
> > (ii) the Isle of Man,
> > (iii) any of the Channel Islands, or
> > (iv) Gibraltar.

(3) In subsection (2) "EEA State" means a State which is a contracting party to the EEA

Agreement but until the EEA Agreement comes into force in relation to Liechtenstein does not include the State of Liechtenstein.

(4) In subsection (3) "EEA Agreement" means the Agreement on the European Economic Area signed at Oporto on 2nd May 1992 as adjusted by the Protocol signed at Brussels on 17th March 1993.

[Road Traffic (New Drivers) Act 1995, s 1 as amended by SI 1996/1974.]

---

1. For applicability of this Act to Crown servants, see s 8, post. Expressions used in this Act are to be construed in the same way as those in Part III of the Road Traffic Act 1988 and in the Road Traffic Offenders Act 1988 (s 91(2)). The Act was brought into force by orders made under s 10(2), post.

2. These provisions apply to a driver who first passes a test of competence to drive on or after 1 June 1997, see sub-s (2) and the commencement provisions in s 10(3), post.

Revocation of licences and re-testing

4–2008B   2. Surrender of licences.   (1) Subsection (2) applies where—

(a) a person is the holder of a licence[1];

(b) he is convicted of an offence involving obligatory[2] endorsement;

(c) the penalty points to be taken into account under section 29 of the Road Traffic Offenders Act 1988[3] on that occasion number six or more;

(d) the court makes an order falling within section 44(1)(b)[4] of that Act in respect of the offence;

(e) the person's licence shows the date on which he became a qualified driver, or that date has been shown by other evidence in the proceedings; and

(f) it appears to the court, in the light of the order and the date so shown, that the offence was committed during the person's probationary period.

(2) Where this subsection applies, the court must send to the Secretary of State—

(a) a notice containing the particulars required to be endorsed on the counterpart of the person's licence in accordance with the order referred to in subsection (1)(d); and

(b) on their production[5] to the court, the person's licence and its counterpart.

(3) Subsection (4) applies where—

(a) a person's licence and its counterpart[6] have been sent to the fixed penalty clerk under section 54(7) of the Road Traffic Offenders Act 1988 or delivered to the fixed penalty clerk in response to a conditional offer issued under section 75 of that Act;

(b) the offence to which the fixed penalty notice or the conditional offer relates is one involving obligatory endorsement;

(c) the fixed penalty clerk endorses the number of penalty points to be attributed to the offence on the counterpart of the licence;

(d) the penalty points to be taken into account by the fixed penalty clerk in respect of the offence number six or more;

(e) the licence shows the date on which the person became a qualified driver; and

(f) it appears to the fixed penalty clerk, in the light of the particulars of the offence endorsed on the counterpart of the licence and the date so shown, that the offence was committed during the person's probationary period.

(4) Where this subsection applies, the fixed penalty clerk—

(a) may not return the licence and its counterpart under section 57(3) or (4) or 77(1) of the Road Traffic Offenders Act 1988; but

(b) must send them[6] to the Secretary of State.

(5) For the purposes of subsection (3)(d) the penalty points to be taken into account by the fixed penalty clerk in respect of the offence are the penalty points which would have been taken into account under section 29 of the Road Traffic Offenders Act 1988 if—

(a) the person in question had been convicted of the offence; and

(b) the number of penalty points to be attributed to the offence on that occasion had been determined in accordance with section 28(3)[7] of that Act.

(6) In this section and section 3 "licence" includes a Northern Ireland licence.

[Road Traffic (New Drivers) Act 1995, s 2 as amended by the Crime (International Co-operation) Act 2003, Sch 5.]

---

1. Where the person holds a licence and certificate of passing a test of competence to drive (a "test certificate"), see Sch 1, post.

2. For exemption from endorsement for certain construction and use offences, see s 48 of the Road Traffic Offenders Act 1988 and for special reasons for not endorsing the licence see s 44(2) and the note to s 34(1) respectively of the Road Traffic Offenders Act 1988, in this PART, ante.

3. In this PART, ante.

4. Endorsement on the counterpart of any licence of the particulars of the conviction and the particulars of the offence and any penalty points to be attributed to it.

5. For production of licence see ss 7 and 27 of the Road Traffic Offenders Act 1988, in this PART, ante, and for production of a certificate of competence to drive where relevant, and for the requirement for the court to send it to the Secretary of State, see Sch 1, post.

6. For circumstances where a certificate of passing a test of competence to drive must be included, see Sch 1, post.

7. The number of points indicated in Sch 2 to the Road Traffic Offenders Act 1988 attributable to an offence dealt with by means of a fixed penalty, or where a range of points is shown, the lowest number in the range.

4–2008C 3. Revocation of licences. (1) Where the Secretary of State receives—

(*a*) a notice sent to him under section 2(2)(*a*) of particulars required to be endorsed on the counterpart of a person's licence, or

(*b*) a person's licence and its counterpart sent to him in accordance with section 2(2)(*b*) or (4),

the Secretary of State must by notice[1] served[2] on that person revoke the licence.★

(1A) Where the Secretary of State serves on the holder of a Northern Ireland licence a notice under subsection (1), the Secretary of State must send to the licensing authority in Northern Ireland—

(*a*) particulars of the notice; and

(*b*) the Northern Ireland licence.

(1B) Where the Secretary of State is sent by that licensing authority particulars of a notice served on the holder of a licence under a provision of Northern Ireland law corresponding to subsection (1), he must by notice served on the holder revoke the licence.

(2) A revocation under subsection (1) shall have effect from a date specified in the notice of revocation which may not be earlier than the date of service of that notice.

(3) In this section references to the revocation of a person's Northern Ireland licence are references to its revocation as respects Great Britain; and, accordingly, the person ceases to be authorised by virtue of section 109(1) of the Road Traffic Act 1988 to drive in Great Britain a motor vehicle of any class.

[Road Traffic (New Drivers) Act 1995, s 3 as amended by the Crime (International Co-operation) Act 2003, Sch 5.]

1. Notice must be in writing (s 9(3), post).
2. For service see s 9(4), post.

4–2008D 4. Re-testing. (1) Subject to subsection (5) and section 5, the Secretary of State may not under Part III of the Road Traffic Act 1988 grant a person whose licence has been revoked under section 3 a full licence to drive any class of vehicles in relation to which the revoked licence was issued as a full licence or (as the case may be) full Northern Ireland licence unless he satisfies the Secretary of State that within the relevant period he has passed a relevant driving test.

(1A) Subject to subsection (5), the Secretary of State may not under that Part grant a person whose Northern Ireland licence has been revoked under a provision of Northern Ireland law corresponding to section 3(1) a full licence to drive any class of vehicles in relation to which the revoked licence was issued as a full Northern Ireland licence unless he satisfies the Secretary of State as mentioned in subsection (1).

(2) In this section "relevant driving test" means, in relation to a person whose licence has been revoked, any test which—

(*a*) falls within paragraph (*a*) or (*b*) of section 1(2); and

(*b*) is a test of competence to drive any vehicle included in any class of vehicles in relation to which the revoked licence was issued as a full licence or (as the case may be) full Northern Ireland licence.

(3) If the Secretary of State grants a full licence to a person who is required to pass a relevant driving test in order to be granted that licence, the licence granted must (subject to section 92[1] and Part IV[2] of the Road Traffic Act 1988) be one authorising that person to drive all the classes of vehicles in relation to which the revoked licence was issued as a full licence or (as the case may be) full Northern Ireland licence.

(4) In subsection (1) "the relevant period" means the period beginning—

(*a*) after the date of the revocation of the licence; and

(*b*) not more than two years before the date on which the application for the full licence is made.

(5) Subsections (1) and (1A) do not apply to a person whose licence has been revoked under section 3 or whose Northern Ireland licence has been revoked under a provision of Northern Ireland law corresponding to section 3(1) if, before he passes a relevant driving test, an order is made in relation to him under section 36 of the Road Traffic Offenders Act 1988 (disqualification until test is passed).

[Road Traffic (New Drivers) Act 1995, s 4 as amended by the Crime (International Co-operation) Act 2003, Sch 5.]

1. Requirements as to physical fitness of drivers.
2. Licensing of drivers of large goods vehicles and passenger carrying vehicles.

4–2008E 5. Restoration of licence without re-testing in certain cases. (1) If the Secretary of State receives notice that a person whose licence has been revoked under section 3 is appealing against a conviction or endorsement which was the basis or formed part of the basis for the revocation, he must grant that person free of charge a full licence for a period prescribed by regulations[1].

(2) Regulations under subsection (1) may in particular prescribe—

(*a*) a period expiring when the appeal is finally determined or abandoned; or

2551 Road Traffic (New Drivers) Act 1995 4–2008H

(b)   a period expiring on the date on which the revoked licence would have expired if it had not been revoked.

(3) If the regulations prescribe a period other than that mentioned in subsection (2)(a), a licence granted under subsection (1) shall be treated as revoked if—

(a)   following the appeal, the penalty points taken into account for the purposes of section 2 or (as the case may be) the provision of Northern Ireland law corresponding to that section are not reduced to a number smaller than six; or

(b)   the appeal is abandoned.

(4) If, in the case of a person whose licence has been revoked under section 3, the Secretary of State receives notice that a court—

(a)   has quashed a conviction which was the basis or formed part of the basis for the revocation of the licence,

(b)   has quashed an endorsement which was the basis or formed part of the basis for the revocation of the licence and has not on doing so ordered him to be disqualified, or

(c)   has made an order which has the effect of reducing the penalty points taken into account for the purposes of section 2 or (as the case may be) the provision of Northern Ireland law corresponding to that section to a number smaller than six,

then, subject to subsection (5), the Secretary of State must grant that person free of charge a full licence for a period expiring on the date on which the revoked licence would have expired if it had not been revoked.

(5) Subsection (4) does not require the Secretary of State to grant a licence to a person who has been granted a previous licence which has not been surrendered unless that person provides the Secretary of State with an explanation for not surrendering the previous licence that the Secretary of State considers adequate.

(6) If, in accordance with subsection (1) or (4), the Secretary of State grants a full licence to a person whose licence has been revoked under section 3, the licence granted must be one authorising that person to drive all the classes of vehicles in relation to which the revoked licence was issued as a full licence.

(7) Any licence granted in accordance with subsection (1) or (4) shall have effect for the purposes of the Road Traffic Acts as if it were a licence granted under Part III of the Road Traffic Act 1988.

(8) Regulations may make provision for requiring such courts as may be prescribed to give notice to the Secretary of State—

(a)   that a person whose licence has been or is due to be revoked under section 3(1) is appealing against a conviction or endorsement which is the basis or forms part of the basis for the revocation;

(b)   that such an appeal has been abandoned.

(9)–(10) *Regulations.*

(11) Nothing in this section applies in relation to a person whose Northern Ireland licence has been revoked under section 3(1).

[Road Traffic (New Drivers) Act 1995, s 5 as amended by the Crime (International Co-operation) Act 2003, Sch 5,.]

---

1.   The New Drivers (Appeals Procedure) Regulations 1997, have been made, in this PART, post.

Miscellaneous and general

4–2008F   6. Newly qualified drivers holding test certificates.   Schedule 1 (which makes provision about newly qualified drivers who hold test certificates) shall have effect.
[Road Traffic (New Drivers) Act 1995, s 6.]

4–2008G   7. Early termination of probationary period.   For the purposes of this Act a person's probationary period comes to an end[1] if—

(a)   an order is made in relation to him under section 36 of the Road Traffic Offenders Act 1988 (order that a person be disqualified until he passes the appropriate driving test);

(b)   after his licence is revoked under section 3, he is granted a full licence following the passing of a test which is a relevant driving test for the purposes of section 4; or

(c)   after his test certificate is revoked under paragraph 5 of Schedule 1, or his licence and test certificate are revoked under paragraph 8(1) of that Schedule, he is granted a full licence following the passing of a test which is a relevant driving test for the purposes of paragraph 8 of that Schedule.

[Road Traffic (New Drivers) Act 1995, s 7 as amended by the Crime (International Co-operation) Act 2003, Sch 5.]

---

1.   Accordingly, where a new licence is subsequently granted, there will not be a further probationary period.

4–2008H   8. The Crown.   This Act applies to persons in the public service of the Crown.
[Road Traffic (New Drivers) Act 1995, s 8.]

4–2008I   9. Interpretation etc.   (1) Expressions used in this Act which are also used in Part III of the Road Traffic Act 1988 shall be construed in the same way as in that Act.

(2) Expressions used in this Act which are also used in the Road Traffic Offenders Act 1988 shall be construed in the same way as in that Act.

(2A) In this Act—

"full Northern Ireland licence" means a Northern Ireland licence other than a Northern Ireland provisional licence,

"Northern Ireland provisional licence" means a Northern Ireland licence which corresponds to a provisional licence.

(3) In this Act "notice" means notice in writing.

(4) Section 107 of the Road Traffic Act 1988 (service of notices) applies to a notice served under section 3 or paragraph 5 or 8 of Schedule 1 as it applies to a notice served under Part III or IV of that Act.

(5) Any requirement under any provision of this Act that a licence and its counterpart, a test certificate or a notice must be sent to the Secretary of State is a requirement that the licence and its counterpart, the test certificate or the notice must be sent to the Secretary of State at such address as the Secretary of State may determine.

[Road Traffic (New Drivers) Act 1995, s 9 as amended by SI 1996/1974 and the Crime (International Co-operation) Act 2003, Sch 5.]

4–2008J   10. Short title, commencement, extent etc.   (1) *Short title.*

(2) The provisions of this Act shall come into force on such day as the Secretary of State may by order[1] made by statutory instrument appoint and different days may be so appointed for different provisions.

(3) Nothing in any provision of this Act applies to a person who becomes a qualified driver before the day on which the provision comes into force.

(4) *Consequential amendments effect.*

(5) *Extent.*

[Road Traffic (New Drivers) Act 1995, s 10.]

---

1. The Road Traffic (New Drivers) Act 1995 (Commencement) Order 1997, SI 1997/267 has been made which brought the Act into force on the following dates:

1 March 1997: ss 5(1), (2), (8)–(10), 6 (see Sch 1), 10(1), (5), Sch 1
1 June 1997: ss 1–4, 5(3)–(7), 6 (Sch 1), 4–9, 10(2)–(4), Sch 1 paras 1–10, Sch 2.

Section 6   SCHEDULE 1
NEWLY QUALIFIED DRIVERS HOLDING TEST CERTIFICATES
(Amended by the Crime (International Co-operation) Act 2003, Sch 5.)

PART I
GENERAL

Interpretation

4–2008K   1. (1) In this Schedule "test certificate" means a certificate or other document which by virtue of regulations under section 89 of the Road Traffic Act 1988 is evidence that a person has not more than two years previously passed a test of competence to drive prescribed by virtue of such regulations.

(2) In this Schedule "prescribed conditions" means the prescribed conditions referred to in section 97(3) of the 1988 Act (subject to which provisional licences are granted).

(3) In this Schedule "licence" includes a Northern Ireland licence, "full licence" includes a full Northern Ireland licence and "provisional licence" includes a Northern Ireland provisional licence.

(4) In relation to the holder of a Northern Ireland licence, the following sub-paragraphs have effect for the purposes of this Schedule.

(5) References to a test certificate are references to a certificate or other document (in this Schedule referred to as a "Northern Ireland test certificate") which is evidence that he has not more than two years previously passed a Northern Ireland test of competence to drive corresponding to the test mentioned in sub-paragraph (1).

(6) References to prescribed conditions are references to conditions subject to which the Northern Ireland provisional licence was granted.

Application of Schedule

4–2008L   2. (1) Part II of this Schedule applies to any person to whom Part III or IV of this Schedule applies.

(2) Part III of this Schedule applies to a person who holds—

(a) a licence issued as a provisional licence; and
(b) a test certificate.

(3) Part IV of this Schedule applies to a person who falls within sub-paragraph (4) or (5).
(4) A person falls within this sub-paragraph if—

(a) he holds a licence issued as a full licence in relation to a class or certain classes of vehicles;
(b) he is treated under section 98(2) of the Road Traffic Act 1988 as authorised by a provisional licence to drive another class or other classes of vehicles; and
(c) he holds a test certificate which relates to that other class of vehicles or any of those other classes of vehicles.*

(4A) In relation to the holder of a Northern Ireland licence, the reference in sub-paragraph (4)(b) to section

98(2) of the Road Traffic Act 1988 is a reference to the corresponding provision under the law of Northern Ireland.

(5) A person falls within this sub-paragraph if he holds—

(a) a licence issued as a full licence in relation to a class or certain classes of vehicles and as a provisional licence in relation to another class or other classes of vehicles; and

(b) a test certificate which relates to that other class of vehicles or any of those other classes of vehicles.

PART II
DUTY TO PROVIDE TEST CERTIFICATE

4–2008M   **3.** (1) Sub-paragraph (2) applies where—

(a) a person to whom this Part of this Schedule applies is prosecuted for an offence involving obligatory endorsement; and

(b) the time at which the offence for which he is prosecuted is alleged to have occurred is a time during his probationary period.

(2) Any obligations imposed on the person under section 7 of the Road Traffic Offenders Act 1988 as respects his licence and its counterpart shall also apply as respects his test certificate.

(3) If, in a case where sub-paragraph (2) applies—

(a) the person is convicted in the proceedings in question of an offence involving obligatory endorsement, and

(b) he has not previously caused his test certificate to be delivered or posted it to the proper officer of the court,

he must produce his test certificate to the court.

(3A) In sub-paragraph (3) "proper officer" means—

(a) in relation to a magistrates' court in England and Wales, the justices' chief executive for the court, and

(b) in relation to any other court, the clerk of the court.

(4) In a case where—

(a) the licence of a person to whom this Part of this Schedule applies has (with its counterpart) been sent to the fixed penalty clerk under section 54(7) of the Road Traffic Offenders Act 1988 or delivered to the fixed penalty clerk in response to a conditional offer issued under section 75 of that Act,

(b) the offence to which the fixed penalty notice or the conditional offer relates is one involving obligatory endorsement and occurring during his probationary period, and

(c) the person proposes to pay the fixed penalty to the fixed penalty clerk,

the person must ensure that when the fixed penalty is paid his test certificate is sent to the fixed penalty clerk to whom the payment is made.

(5) A person who without reasonable excuse fails to comply with sub-paragraph (3) or (4) is guilty of an offence and shall be liable on **summary conviction** to a **fine** not exceeding **level 3** on the standard scale.

PART III
NEWLY QUALIFIED DRIVER WITH PROVISIONAL LICENCE AND TEST CERTIFICATE

Surrender of test certificate

4–2008N   **4.** (1) Where the circumstances mentioned in section 2(1) exist with respect to a person to whom this Part of this Schedule applies, sub-paragraph (2) applies instead of section 2(2).

(2) The court must send to the Secretary of State—

(a) a notice containing the particulars required to be endorsed on the counterpart of the person's licence in accordance with the order referred to in section 2(1)(d); and

(b) on its production to the court, the person's test certificate.

(3) Where—

(a) the circumstances mentioned in section 2(3)(a) to (d) and (f) exist with respect to a person to whom this Part of this Schedule applies,

(b) the fixed penalty clerk has received the person's test certificate in accordance with paragraph 3(4), and

(c) the test certificate shows the date on which the person became a qualified driver,

sub-paragraph (4) applies instead of section 2(4).

(4) The fixed penalty clerk must send to the Secretary of State—

(a) a notice containing the particulars endorsed on the counterpart of the person's licence; and

(b) the person's test certificate.

Revocation of test certificate

4–2008P   **5.** (1) Where the Secretary of State—

(a) has received a notice sent to him under paragraph 4 of particulars required to be endorsed or endorsed on the counterpart of a person's licence, and

(b) has received the person's test certificate sent to him under paragraph 4(2)(b) or (4)(b) or is satisfied that the person has been issued with a test certificate,

the Secretary of State must by notice served on that person revoke the test certificate.

(1A) Where the Secretary of State serves on the holder of a Northern Ireland licence a notice under sub-paragraph (1), the Secretary of State must send to the licensing authority in Northern Ireland particulars of the notice together with the Northern Ireland test certificate.

(1B) Where the Secretary of State is sent by that licensing authority particulars of a notice served on the holder of a licence under a provision of Northern Ireland law corresponding to sub-paragraph (1), he must by notice served on that person revoke his test certificate.

(2) A revocation under sub-paragraph (1) or (1B) shall have effect from a date specified in the notice of revocation which may not be earlier than the date of service of that notice.

(3) The effect of the revocation of a person's test certificate is that any prescribed conditions to which his provisional licence ceased to be subject when he became a qualified driver shall again apply.

(4) In this paragraph and paragraph 8 references to the revocation of a person's Northern Ireland test certificate are references to its revocation as respects Great Britain.

(5) The effect of the revocation of a person's Northern Ireland test certificate as respects Great Britain is that any prescribed conditions to which his Northern Ireland provisional licence ceased to be subject when he became a qualified driver shall again apply for the purposes of section 109(1) of the Road Traffic Act 1988.

Re-testing

4–2008Q 6. (1) Subject to Part V of this Schedule, the Secretary of State may not under Part III of the Road Traffic Act 1988 grant a person whose test certificate has been revoked under paragraph 5, or whose Northern Ireland test certificate has been revoked under a provision of Northern Ireland law corresponding to paragraph 5(1), a full licence to drive any class of vehicles that, immediately before his test certificate was revoked, he was permitted to drive without observing prescribed conditions, unless he satisfies the Secretary of State that within the relevant period he has passed a relevant driving test.*

(2) In this paragraph "relevant driving test" means, in relation to a person whose test certificate has been revoked, any test which—

(a) falls within paragraph (a) or (b) of section 1(2); and
(b) is a test of competence to drive any vehicle included in any class of vehicles that, immediately before his test certificate was revoked, he was permitted to drive without observing prescribed conditions.

(3) If the Secretary of State grants a full licence to a person who is required to pass a relevant driving test in order to be granted that licence, the licence granted must (subject to section 92 and Part IV of the Road Traffic Act 1988) be one authorising that person to drive all the classes of vehicles that, immediately before his test certificate was revoked, he was permitted to drive without observing prescribed conditions.

(4) In sub-paragraph (1) "the relevant period" means the period beginning—

(a) after the date of the revocation of the test certificate; and
(b) not more than two years before the date on which the application for the full licence is made.

PART IV
NEWLY QUALIFIED DRIVER WITH FULL AND PROVISIONAL ENTITLEMENTS AND TEST CERTIFICATE

Surrender of licence and test certificate

4–2008R 7. (1) Where the circumstances mentioned in section 2(1) exist with respect to a person to whom this Part of this Schedule applies, sub-paragraph (2) applies instead of section 2(2).

(2) The court must send to the Secretary of State—

(a) a notice containing the particulars required to endorsed on the counterpart of the person's licence in accordance with the order referred to in section 2(1)(d);
(b) on their production to the court, the person's licence and its counterpart; and
(c) on its production to the court, the person's test certificate.

(3) Where—

(a) the circumstances mentioned in section 2(3) exist with respect to a person to whom this Part of this Schedule applies, and
(b) the fixed penalty clerk has received the person's test certificate in accordance with paragraph 3(4),

sub-paragraph (4) applies instead of section 2(4).

(4) The fixed penalty clerk—

(a) may not return the person's licence and its counterpart under section 57(3) or (4) or 77(1) of the Road Traffic Offenders Act 1988; but
(b) must send them and the person's test certificate to the Secretary of State.

Revocation of licence and test certificate

4–2008S 8. (1) Where the Secretary of State—

(a) has received a notice sent to him under paragraph 7(2)(a) of particulars required to be endorsed on the counterpart of a person's licence or has received the licence and its counterpart under paragraph 7(2)(b) or (4)(b), and
(b) has received the person's test certificate sent to him under paragraph 7(2)(b) or (4)(b) or is satisfied that the person has been issued with a test certificate,

the Secretary of State must by notice served on that person revoke the licence and the test certificate.

(1A) Where the Secretary of State serves on the holder of a Northern Ireland licence a notice under sub-paragraph (1), the Secretary of State must send to the licensing authority in Northern Ireland particulars of the notice together with the Northern Ireland licence and the Northern Ireland test certificate.

(1B) Where the Secretary of State is sent by that licensing authority particulars of a notice served on the holder of a licence under a provision of Northern Ireland law corresponding to sub-paragraph (1), he must by notice served on that person revoke his licence and test certificate.

(2) A revocation under sub-paragraph (1) or (1B) shall have effect from a date specified in the notice of revocation which may not be earlier than the date of service of that notice.

(3) In this paragraph references to the revocation of a person's Northern Ireland licence are references to its revocation as respects Great Britain; and, accordingly, the person ceases to be authorised by virtue of section 109(1) of the Road Traffic Act 1988 to drive in Great Britain a motor vehicle of any class.

Re-testing

4–2008T 9. (1) Subject to Part V of this Schedule, the Secretary of State may not under Part III of the Road Traffic Act 1988 grant a person whose licence and test certificate have been revoked under paragraph 8, or whose Northern Ireland licence and Northern Ireland test certificate have been revoked under a provision of Northern

Ireland law corresponding to paragraph 8(1), a full licence to drive any class of vehicles mentioned in sub-paragraph (4), unless he satisfies the Secretary of State that within the relevant period he has passed a relevant driving test.*

(2) In this paragraph "relevant driving test" means any test which—

(a) falls within paragraph (a) or (b) of section 1(2); and

(b) is a test of competence to drive any vehicle included in any class of vehicles mentioned in sub-paragraph (4).

(3) If the Secretary of State grants a full licence to a person who is required to pass a relevant driving test in order to be granted that licence, the licence granted must (subject to section 92 and Part IV of the Road Traffic Act 1988) be one authorising that person to drive all the classes of vehicles mentioned in sub-paragraph (4).

(4) The classes of vehicles are—

(a) any class of vehicles in relation to which the revoked licence was issued as a full licence; and

(b) any class of vehicles—

   (i) that he was treated under section 98(2) of the Road Traffic Act , or under a provision of Northern Ireland law corresponding to that section as authorised to drive under a provisional licence, or

   (ii) in relation to which the revoked licence was issued as a provisional licence,

and that, immediately before the test certificate was revoked, he was permitted to drive without observing prescribed conditions.*

(5) In sub-paragraph (1) "the relevant period" means the period beginning—

(a) after the date of the revocation of the licence and the test certificate; and

(b) not more than two years before the date on which the application for the full licence is made.

PART V
SUPPLEMENTARY

Effect of disqualification until test is passed on re-testing rule

4–2008U   **10.** Where—

(a) a person's test certificate has been revoked under paragraph 5 (or a person's Northern Ireland test certificate has been revoked under a provision of Northern Ireland law corresponding to paragraph 5(1)) or his licence and test certificate have been revoked under paragraph 8 (or a person's Northern Ireland licence and Northern Ireland test certificate have been revoked under a provision of Northern Ireland law corresponding to paragraph 8(1)), but

(b) before he passes a relevant driving test, an order is made in relation to him under section 36 of the Road Traffic Offenders Act 1988 (disqualification until test is passed)

paragraph 6(1) or, as the case may be, paragraph 9(1) shall not apply to him.*

Regulations

4–2009   **11.** (1) The Secretary of State may by regulations make provision for cases where, after the Secretary of State has revoked a person's test certificate under paragraph 5, or a person's licence and test certificate under paragraph 8, he receives notice—

(a) that the person is appealing against a conviction or endorsement which was the basis or formed part of the basis for the revocation;

(b) that a court has quashed a conviction which was the basis or formed part of the basis for the revocation;

(c) that a court has quashed an endorsement which was the basis or formed part of the basis for the revocation and has not on doing so ordered that person to be disqualified;

(d) that a court has made an order which has the effect of reducing the penalty points taken into account for the purposes of section 2 or (as the case may be) the provision of Northern Ireland law corresponding to that section to a number smaller than six.

(2) Regulations under sub-paragraph (1) may in particular make provision for—

(a) issuing licences for such period as may be prescribed;

(b) licences issued under the regulations to be treated as revoked in such circumstances as may be prescribed;

(c) re-issuing a test certificate which has been revoked under paragraph 5 or 8;

(d) suspending or terminating any prescribed conditions applied by virtue of paragraph 5(3);

(e) requiring such courts as may be prescribed to give notice to the Secretary of State of the matters mentioned in sub-paragraph (3).

(3) The matters referred to are—

(a) that a person whose certificate has been or is due to be revoked under paragraph 5(1) or whose licence and certificate have been or are due to be revoked under paragraph 8(1) is appealing against a conviction or endorsement which is the basis or forms part of the basis for the revocation;

(b) that such an appeal has been abandoned.

(4) Any regulations under this paragraph may—

(a) include such incidental or supplementary provision as appears to the Secretary of State to be expedient;

(b) make different provision for different cases.

(5) Any regulations under this paragraph shall be made by statutory instrument which shall be subject to annulment in pursuance of a resolution of either House of Parliament.

---

1. The New Drivers (Appeals Procedure) Regulations 1997, have been made, in this PART, post.

Goods Vehicles (Licensing of Operators) Act 1995[1]

(1995 c 23)

Functions of traffic commissioners

4–2009A   **1. Functions of traffic commissioners.** (1) The traffic commissioner for any traffic area constituted for the purposes of the Public Passenger Vehicles Act 1981[2] shall exercise the functions conferred on him by this Act.

(2) In the exercise of his functions under this Act a traffic commissioner shall act under the general directions of the Secretary of State.
[Goods Vehicles (Licensing of Operators) Act 1995, s 1.]

---

1. This Act consolidates Part V of the Transport Act 1968 and related provisions concerning the licensing of operators of certain goods vehicles.
The Goods Vehicles (Licensing of Operators) Act 1995 is to be brought into force in accordance with s 61, post.
2. See this title, ante.

Operators' licences

4–2009B   2. Obligation to hold operator's licence[1]. (1) Subject to subsection (2)[2] and section 4, no person shall use[3] a goods vehicle on a road for the carriage of goods[4]—

(a) for hire or reward, or

(b) for or in connection with any trade or business[5] carried on by him,

except under a licence issued under this Act; and in this Act such a licence is referred to as an "operator's licence".

(2) Subsection (1) does not apply to—

(a) the use of a small goods vehicle within the meaning given in Schedule 1;

(b) the use of a goods vehicle for international carriage by a haulier established in a member State other than the United Kingdom and not established in the United Kingdom[2];

(c) the use of a goods vehicle for international carriage by a haulier established in Northern Ireland and not established in Great Britain; or

(d) the use of a vehicle of any class specified in regulations[6].

(3) In subsection (2)(b) and (c) "established", "haulier" and "international carriage" have the same meaning as in Community Council Regulation (EEC) No 881/92 dated 26 March 1992 concerning access to the market in the carriage of goods by road within the Community to or from the territory of a member State or passing across the territory of one or more member States.

(4) It is hereby declared that, for the purposes of this Act, the performance by a local or public authority of their functions constitutes the carrying on of a business.

(5) A person who uses a vehicle in contravention of this section is guilty of an offence and liable on summary conviction to a fine not exceeding **level 5** on the standard scale.
[Goods Vehicles (Licensing of Operators) Act 1995, s 2, as amended by the Transport Act 2000, s 261.]

---

1. This section is extended to foreign vehicles by the Road Traffic (Foreign Vehicles) Act 1972, Sch 2, post. For application to a "tower wagon" see *Anderson & Healey Ltd v Paterson* [1975] 1 All ER 523, 139 JP 231.
2. For exemption of certain foreign goods vehicles used in Great Britain see the Goods Vehicles (Operators Licences) (Temporary Use in Great Britain) Regulations 1996, SI 1996/2186.
3. For provisions as to the user of a vehicle, see s 58(2), post.
4. For the meaning of "carriage of goods" and "goods", see s 58(1), post.
5. In *Stirk v McKenna* [1984] RTR 330 it was held that a defendant who drove a converted motor coach to transport a vehicle in which he carried on stock car racing for pleasure and a hobby, and for which he competed for prize money and received sponsorship, was not using the motor coach for or in connection with any trade or business.
6. See the Goods Vehicles (Licensing of Operators) Regulations 1995, in this PART, POST.

4–2009BB   2A. Detention of vehicle used without operator's licence. Schedule 1A (which relates to the detention, removal and disposal of goods vehicles in respect of which it appears that section 2 is contravened) shall have effect.
[Goods Vehicles (Licensing of Operators) Act 1995, s 2A inserted by the Transport Act 2000, s 262.]

4–2009C   3. "Standard" and "restricted" licences. (1) An operator's licence may be either a standard licence or a restricted licence.

(2) A standard licence is an operator's licence under which a goods vehicle may be used on a road for the carriage of goods—

(a) for hire or reward, or

(b) for or in connection with any trade or business carried on by the holder of the licence.

(3) A restricted licence is an operator's licence under which a goods vehicle may be used on a road for the carriage of goods for or in connection with any trade or business carried on by the holder of the licence, other than that of carrying goods for hire or reward.

(4) Notwithstanding subsections (2) and (3), a company may use a goods vehicle on a road for the carriage of goods for hire or reward under a restricted licence instead of a standard licence if (but only if) the goods concerned are the property of a company which is—

(a) a subsidiary of the first company.

(b) a holding company for the first company, or

(c) a subsidiary of a company which is a holding company both for that subsidiary and for the first company.

(5) A standard licence may authorise a goods vehicle to be used for the carriage of goods—

(a) on both national and international transport operations; or

(b) on national transport operations only.

(6) Except as provided in subsection (4) and subject to section 4, a person who uses a goods

vehicle under a restricted licence for carrying goods for hire or reward is guilty of an offence and liable on summary conviction to a fine not exceeding £500.

(7) A person who uses a goods vehicle for carrying goods for hire or reward on international transport operations under a standard licence which covers the carriage of goods on national transport operations only is guilty of an offence and liable on summary conviction to a fine not exceeding £500.
[Goods Vehicles (Licensing of Operators) Act 1995, s 3.]

4–2009D   4. Temporary exemptions.   (1) A traffic commissioner may, for the purpose of—

    (a) enabling an emergency to be dealt with, or
    (b) enabling some other special need to be met,

by notice in writing grant to any person falling within subsection (2) a temporary exemption from any requirement to hold a standard licence which would otherwise be imposed on him by sections 2 and 3 in respect of any vehicle specified in the notice or any vehicle of a class so specified.

(2) A person falls within this subsection if he is engaged exclusively in national transport operations which have only a minor impact on the transport market because of the nature of the goods carried or the short distances over which goods are carried.

(3) A temporary exemption granted under subsection (1) permits the person to whom it is granted to use the specified vehicle or (as the case may be) any vehicle of the specified class for the carriage of goods for hire or reward for the purposes of transport operations of his such as are referred to in subsection (2) (and, accordingly, sections 2(1) and 3(6) shall not to that extent apply to that person's use of goods vehicles).

(4) A temporary exemption has effect until consultations with the European Commission for the purposes of Article 2(2) of the 1974 Council Directive are completed.
[Goods Vehicles (Licensing of Operators) Act 1995, s 4.]

Vehicles authorised to be used under a licence

4–2009E   5. Vehicles authorised to be used under operator's licence.   (1) Subject to the following provisions of this section, the vehicles authorised to be used under an operator's licence are—

    (a) any motor vehicle in the lawful possession of the licence-holder (whether that motor vehicle is specified in the licence or not); and
    (b) any trailer in the lawful possession of the licence-holder.

(2) An operator's licence may provide—

    (a) that no motor vehicle, or no trailer, whose relevant weight exceeds a weight specified in the licence is authorised to be used under it;
    (b) that no trailers are authorised to be used under the licence; or
    (c) that no motor vehicle that is not specified in the licence is authorised to be used under it.

(3) In subsection (2) "relevant weight", in relation to a motor vehicle or trailer of any prescribed class, means a weight of the description specified in relation to motor vehicles or trailers of that class by regulations.

(4) An operator's licence shall not authorise the use of any vehicle unless the place which is for the time being its operating centre—

    (a) is in the area of the traffic commissioner by whom the licence was issued; or
    (b) is outside that area but has not been the operating centre of that vehicle for a period of more than three months.

(5) For the purposes of subsection (4)(b), two or more successive periods which are not separated from each other by an interval of at least three months shall be treated as a single period having a duration equal to the total duration of those periods.

(6) A motor vehicle which is not specified in an operator's licence is not authorised to be used under that licence by virtue of subsection (1) after the period of one month beginning with—

    (a) the day on which the vehicle was first in the lawful possession of the licence-holder, or
    (b) (if later) the day on which the licence came into force,

unless, during that period, the licence-holder has given to the traffic commissioner by whom the licence was issued a notice in such form and containing such information about the vehicle as the commissioner may require, and has paid to him a prescribed fee.

(7) Where notice of a vehicle has been duly given and the prescribed fee has been duly paid under subsection (6), the traffic commissioner shall vary the licence by directing that the vehicle be specified in it.

(8) A motor vehicle specified in an operator's licence shall not, while it remains so specified, be capable of being effectively specified in any other operator's licence.

(9) Where it comes to the knowledge of the traffic commissioner by whom an operator's licence ("the first licence") was issued that a vehicle specified in that licence—

    (a) has ceased to be used under the licence (otherwise than because of a fluctuation in business or because it is undergoing repair or maintenance), or
    (b) is specified in another operator's licence,

he may vary the first licence by directing that the vehicle be removed from it.
[Goods Vehicles (Licensing of Operators) Act 1995, s 5.]

4–2009F **6. Maximum numbers of vehicles.** (1) An operator's licence—

(a) shall specify a maximum number for motor vehicles, and
(b) may specify a maximum number for motor vehicles whose relevant weight exceeds a weight specified in the licence.

(2) An operator's licence that does not contain a provision such as is mentioned in section 5(2)(b)—

(a) shall specify a maximum number for trailers, and
(b) may specify a maximum number for trailers whose relevant weight exceeds a weight specified in the licence.

(3) The number of motor vehicles which at any one time are being used under an operator's licence while not specified in that licence may not exceed the maximum number specified in the licence under subsection (1)(a) less however many motor vehicles are specified in the licence.

(4) Where, under subsection (1)(b), an operator's licence specifies a maximum number for motor vehicles whose relevant weight exceeds a specified weight—

(a) the number of such motor vehicles which at any one time are being used under the licence while not specified in it may not exceed that maximum number less however many motor vehicles whose relevant weight exceeds the specified weight are specified in the licence, and
(b) the number of such motor vehicles that are specified in the licence and are being used under it at any one time may not exceed that maximum number.

(5) The number of trailers being used under an operator's licence at any one time may not exceed the maximum number specified in the licence under subsection (2)(a).

(6) Where, under subsection (2)(b), an operator's licence specifies a maximum number for trailers whose relevant weight exceeds a specified weight, the number of such trailers being used under the licence at any one time may not exceed that maximum number.

(7) The definition of "relevant weight" in section 5(3) applies for the purposes of this section as it applies for the purposes of section 5(2).

(8) If subsection (3), (4)(a) or (b), (5) or (6) is contravened, the licence-holder is guilty of an offence and liable on summary conviction to a fine not exceeding **level 4** on the standard scale.
[Goods Vehicles (Licensing of Operators) Act 1995, s 6.]

Operating centres

4–2009G **7. Operating centres to be specified in operators' licences.** (1) A person may not use a place in the area of any traffic commissioner as an operating centre for vehicles authorised to be used under any operator's licence issued to him by that commissioner unless that place is specified as an operating centre of his in that licence.

(2) Any person who contravenes subsection (1) is guilty of an offence and liable on summary conviction to a fine not exceeding **level 4** on the standard scale.

(3) In this Act "operating centre", in relation to any vehicle, means the base or centre at which the vehicle is normally kept, and references to an operating centre of the holder of an operator's licence are references to any place which is an operating centre for vehicles used under that licence.
[Goods Vehicles (Licensing of Operators) Act 1995, s 7.]

Applications for licences

4–2009H **8. Applications for operators' licences.** (1) An application for an operator's licence shall be made to the traffic commissioner for each area in which, if the licence is issued, the applicant will have an operating centre or operating centres.

(2) Accordingly, a person may hold separate operators' licences in respect of different areas; but he shall not at any time hold more than one such licence in respect of the same area.

(3) A person applying for an operator's licence shall give to the traffic commissioner a statement—

(a) containing such particulars as the commissioner may require of the motor vehicles proposed to be used under the licence and stating the number and type of any trailers proposed to be used under the licence; and
(b) containing such particulars as the commissioner may require of each place in the area of the commissioner which will be an operating centre of the applicant if the licence is issued.

(4) A person applying for an operator's licence shall also give to the traffic commissioner any further information which the commissioner may reasonably require for the discharge of his duties in relation to the application, and in particular shall, if required by the commissioner to do so, give to him any of the information specified in paragraph 1 of Schedule 2.

(5) Without prejudice to subsection (4), a person applying for an operator's licence shall also, if required by the traffic commissioner to do so, give to him such particulars as he may require with respect to the use which the applicant proposes to make, for vehicles used under the licence, of any place referred to in the statement under subsection (3)(b).

(6) Any statement, information or particulars to be given to a traffic commissioner under this section shall be given in such form as the commissioner may require.
[Goods Vehicles (Licensing of Operators) Act 1995, s 8.]

4–2009I   9. Convictions etc subsequent to the making of an application.   (1) A person who has made an application for an operator's licence shall forthwith notify the traffic commissioner to whom it was made if, in the interval between the making of the application and the date on which it is disposed of, there occurs a notifiable conviction within the meaning given in paragraph 4 of Schedule 2.

(2) A person who—

(*a*)   has made an application for a standard licence, and
(*b*)   has included in that application particulars of a transport manager,

shall forthwith notify the traffic commissioner to whom the application was made if, in the interval between the making of the application and the date on which it is disposed of, there occurs any event affecting any information about the transport manager given to the commissioner under section 8.

(3) A person is guilty of an offence[1] if he—

(*a*)   knowingly fails to comply with subsection (1), or
(*b*)   knowingly fails to comply with subsection (2) in a case where the event which occurs as mentioned in that subsection is the conviction of the transport manager of an offence such as is mentioned in paragraph 5 of Schedule 2;

and a person who is guilty of an offence under paragraph (*a*) or (*b*) is liable on summary conviction to a fine not exceeding **level 4** on the standard scale.

(4) For the purposes of this section an application shall be taken to be disposed of—

(*a*)   in a case where the traffic commissioner is required, by virtue of regulations under section 57(2)(*a*), to cause a statement containing his decision on the application to be issued, on the date on which that statement is issued, and
(*b*)   in any other case, on the date on which the applicant receives notice from the traffic commissioner of his decision on the application.

[Goods Vehicles (Licensing of Operators) Act 1995, s 9.]

---

1. As to the time limit for bringing proceedings under this section, see s 51, post.

Determination of applications

4–2009J   15. Issue of operators' licences.   (1) Subject to subsection (2) and to sections 14(6), 21, 22, 23 and 45(2), on granting an application for an operator's licence a traffic commissioner shall issue that licence in the terms applied for.

(2) If a traffic commissioner has determined that any of the requirements of subsection (5) or (6) of section 13 that he has taken into consideration in accordance with subsection (1) or (as the case may be) (2) of that section would not be satisfied unless he were to exercise any of his powers under subsection (3) below, he shall exercise those powers accordingly.

(3) A traffic commissioner may issue the licence in terms that differ from the terms applied for in any of the following respects—

(*a*)   more or fewer motor vehicles are specified in the licence;
(*b*)   different motor vehicles are specified in it;
(*c*)   it includes a provision such as is mentioned in section 5(2);
(*d*)   it includes a provision such as is mentioned in section 6(1)(*b*) or (2)(*b*);
(*e*)   higher or lower maximum numbers are specified in it under section 6;
(*f*)   fewer places are specified in it as operating centres of the licence-holder.

(4) Any undertakings taken into account by the traffic commissioner under section 13(8) that he considers to be material to the granting of the application shall be recorded in the licence issued.

(5) A statement shall appear on the face of every operator's licence indicating whether it is a standard licence or a restricted licence.

(6) A statement shall appear on the face of every standard licence indicating whether it covers both national and international transport operations or national transport operations only.
[Goods Vehicles (Licensing of Operators) Act 1995, s 15.]

4–2009K   16. Duration of operators' licences.   (1) The date on which an operator's licence is to come into force shall be specified in the licence.

(2) Subject to its revocation or other termination under any provision of this Act or any other statutory provision, an operator's licence (other than an interim licence issued under section 24) shall continue in force indefinitely.

(3) If the holder of an operator's licence requests the traffic commissioner by whom it was issued to terminate it at any time, the commissioner shall, subject to subsection (4), comply with the request.

(4) The traffic commissioner may refuse to comply with the request if he is considering giving a direction in respect of the licence under section 26 or 27.

(5) An operator's licence held by an individual terminates if he dies, if he becomes a patient within the meaning of Part VII of the Mental Health Act 1983, or if (in Scotland) a curator bonis[1] is

appointed in respect of him on the ground that he is incapable, by reason of mental disorder, of adequately managing and administering his property and affairs.
[Goods Vehicles (Licensing of Operators) Act 1995, s 16.]

---

1. By virtue of the Adults With Incapacity (Scotland) Act 2000, Sch 5, The Reference In sub-s (5) to a curator bonis shall be construed as a reference to a guardian with similar powers appointed under that Act.

4–2009L   14–20. *Variation of licences.*

Conditions attached to licences

4–2009M   21. Conditions for securing road safety. (1) On issuing an operator's licence, or on varying such a licence under section 17, a traffic commissioner may attach to the licence such conditions as he thinks fit for preventing vehicles that are authorised to be used under it from causing danger to the public—

(a) at any point where vehicles first join a public road on their way from an operating centre of the licence-holder (or last leave a public road on their way to such an operating centre); and

(b) on any road (other than a public road) along which vehicles are driven between such a point and the operating centre.

(2) On varying an operator's licence under section 17 a traffic commissioner may vary or remove any condition attached to the licence under this section.

(3) The traffic commissioner shall not—

(a) attach to an operator's licence any condition such as is mentioned in this section, or

(b) vary in such manner as imposes new or further restrictions or requirements any condition attached to an operator's licence under this section,

without first giving the applicant for the licence or (as the case may be) the licence-holder an opportunity to make representations to the commissioner with respect to the effect on his business of the proposed condition or variation.

(4) The traffic commissioner shall give special consideration to any representations made under subsection (3) in determining whether to attach the proposed condition or make the proposed variation.

(5) In this section "public road"—

(a) in relation to England and Wales, means a highway maintainable at the public expense for the purposes of the Highways Act 1980; and

(b) in relation to Scotland, has the same meaning as in the Roads (Scotland) Act 1984.

(6) Any person who contravenes any condition attached under this section to a licence of which he is the holder is guilty of an offence and liable on summary conviction to a fine not exceeding **level 4** on the standard scale.
[Goods Vehicles (Licensing of Operators) Act 1995, s 21.]

4–2009N   22. Conditions as to matters required to be notified to traffic commissioner.
(1) On issuing an operator's licence, a traffic commissioner may attach to the licence such conditions as he thinks fit for requiring the holder to inform him—

(a) of any change of a kind specified in the conditions in the organisation, management or ownership of the trade or business in the course of which vehicles are used under the licence or, if the licence is at any time suspended under section 26 or 28, were used under the licence immediately before its suspension;

(b) where the licence-holder is a company, of any change, or of any change of a kind specified in the conditions, in the persons holding shares in the company; or

(c) of any other event of a kind specified in the conditions which affects the licence-holder and which is relevant to the exercise of any powers of the traffic commissioner in relation to the licence.

(2) On issuing a standard licence, a traffic commissioner shall attach to it the following conditions, namely—

(a) a condition requiring the licence-holder to inform the commissioner of any event which could affect the fulfilment by the licence-holder of any of the requirements of section 13(3), and to do so within 28 days of the event; and

(b) a condition requiring the licence-holder to inform the commissioner of any event which could affect the fulfilment by a relevant transport manager of the requirements mentioned in section 13(3)(a) or (c), and to do so within 28 days of the event coming to the licence-holder's knowledge.

(3) In subsection (2)(b) the reference to a "relevant transport manager" is a reference to any transport manager employed by the licence-holder who is relied on by the licence-holder to fulfil the requirements of section 13(3)(c).

(4) In a case where the licence-holder is a company, no condition attached under subsection (2) shall be taken to require the company to inform the traffic commissioner of any change in the identity of the persons holding shares in the company unless the change is such as to cause a change in the control of the company.

(5) for the purposes of subsection (4), a change in the control of a company occurs when the beneficial ownership of more than half its equity share capital (as defined in section 744 of the Companies Act 1985) passes from one person to another person or from one group of persons to a wholly or substantially different group of persons.

(6) Any person who contravenes any condition attached under this section to a licence of which he is the holder is guilty of an offence and liable on summary conviction to a fine not exceeding **level 4** on the standard scale.

[Goods Vehicles (Licensing of Operators) Act 1995, s 22.]

4–2009P 23. Conditions as to use of operating centres.　(1) On issuing an operator's licence, or on varying such a licence on an application of which notice has been published under section 17(3), a traffic commissioner may attach to the licence such conditions as he thinks fit for preventing or minimising any adverse effects on environmental conditions arising from the use of a place in his area as an operating centre of the licence-holder.

(2) The conditions which may be attached to a licence under this section shall be of such description as may be prescribed; and, without prejudice to the generality of the preceding provision, the descriptions which may be prescribed include conditions regulating—

(a) the number, type and size of motor vehicles or trailers which may at any one time be at any operating centre of the licence-holder in the area of the traffic commissioner for any prescribed purpose;

(b) the parking arrangements to be provided at or in the vicinity of any such centre; and

(c) the hours at which operations of any prescribed description may be carried on at any such centre.

(3) On varying an operator's licence on an application of which notice has been published under section 17(3), a traffic commissioner may vary or remove any condition attached to the licence under this section.

(4) The traffic commissioner shall not—

(a) attach any condition such as is mentioned in this section to an operator's licence, or

(b) vary in such manner as imposes new or further restrictions or requirements any condition attached to an operator's licence under this section,

without first giving the applicant for the licence or (as the case may be) the licence-holder an opportunity to make representations to the commissioner with respect to the effect on his business of the proposed condition or variation.

(5) The traffic commissioner shall give special consideration to any representations made under subsection (4) in determining whether to attach the proposed condition or make the proposed variation.

(6) Any person who contravenes any condition attached under this section to a licence of which he is the holder is guilty of an offence and liable on summary conviction to a fine not exceeding **level 4** on the standard scale.

[Goods Vehicles (Licensing of Operators) Act 1995, s 23.]

Interim licences and interim variations

4–2009Q 24. Interim operators' licences.　(1) On an application for an operator's licence (a "full" licence), a traffic commissioner may, if the applicant so requests, issue to him an interim licence.

(2) An interim licence is an operator's licence that (subject to its revocation or other termination under any provision of this Act or any other statutory provision) will continue in force until it terminates under subsection (4), (5) or (6).

(3) The traffic commissioner may issue an interim licence in the same terms as those applied for in relation to the full licence or in terms that differ from those terms in any of the respects mentioned in section 15(3).

(4) If the traffic commissioner grants the application and issues to the applicant a full licence that—

(a) is in the terms applied for, or

(b) is in those terms subject only to the attachment under section 21, 22 or 23 of any conditions that are also attached to the interim licence,

the interim licence shall terminate on the date on which the full licence comes into force.

(5) If, on an appeal under section 37 arising out of the application, the Transport Tribunal orders the traffic commissioner to issue a full licence to the applicant, the interim licence shall terminate—

(a) on the date on which the full licence issued in pursuance of the order comes into force, or

(b) at the time at which the application is withdrawn or treated as withdrawn by virtue of section 45(3).

(6) If neither subsection (4) nor subsection (5) applies, the interim licence shall terminate on the date on which the application is finally disposed of or such earlier date as the applicant may specify in a written request to the traffic commissioner.

(7) Where, in a case within subsection (6), the application is granted, the full licence issued to the applicant shall be of no effect before the interim licence terminates (notwithstanding any statement in it to the contrary).

(8) A request for the issuing of an interim licence—

(*a*)   shall not be treated as an application for an operator's licence for the purposes of section 10, 11, 12, 13, 14, 15(1) to (4), 36 or 37 or Schedule 4, but

(*b*)   shall be treated as such an application for the purposes of any other provision of this Act.

(9) In this section and section 25 references to the date on which an application is finally disposed of are references

(*a*)   subject to paragraph (*b*), to the earliest date by which the application and any appeal to the Transport Tribunal arising out of the application have been determined and any time for bringing such an appeal has expired, or

(*b*)   if the application is withdrawn or any such appeal is abandoned, to the date of the withdrawal or abandonment.

[Goods Vehicles (Licensing of Operators) Act 1995, s 24.]

Revocation etc of operators' licences

4–2009R   26. Revocation, suspension and curtailment of operators' licences. (1) *Grounds on which the traffic commissioner by whom an operator's licence was issued may direct that it be revoked, suspended or curtailed.*

(2) Where the traffic commissioner has power to give a direction in respect of a licence under subsection (1), the commissioner also has power to direct that a condition, or additional condition, such as is mentioned in section 22(1) be attached to the licence.

(3) In this Act any reference, in relation to an operator's licence, to a condition attached to the licence under section 22(1) includes any condition attached to the licence under subsection (2) above.

(4) Where the existence of any of the grounds mentioned in subsection (1) is brought to the notice of the traffic commissioner in the case of the holder of any licence issued by him, the commissioner shall consider whether or not to give a direction under this section in respect of that licence.

(5) Where, in a case falling within subsection (1)(*c*)(i)—

(*a*)   the conviction in question is a conviction of the licence-holder of an offence under section 3(6) or of the corresponding offence under regulation 33(2) of the Goods Vehicles (Operators' Licences, Qualifications and Fees) Regulations 1984, and

(*b*)   there has been, within the 5 years preceding that conviction, a previous conviction of the licence-holder of an offence under either of those provisions,

the traffic commissioner shall give a direction under subsection (1) to revoke the licence.

(6) Where the traffic commissioner directs that an operator's licence be suspended or curtailed, the commissioner may order—

(*a*)   in the case of a suspension, that any motor vehicle specified in the licence may not be used under any other operator's licence (notwithstanding anything in section 5(1)(*a*)), or

(*b*)   in the case of a curtailment having the effect of removing any motor vehicle from the licence, that the motor vehicle may not be used as mentioned in paragraph (*a*) and shall not be capable of being effectively specified in any other operator's licence.

(7) An order made under subsection (6) shall cease to have effect—

(*a*)   on such date, not being more than 6 months after the order is made, as may be specified in the order, or

(*b*)   if, before that date, the licence which is directed to be suspended or curtailed ceases to be in force, on the date on which it ceases to be in force.

(8) The traffic commissioner by whom any direction suspending or curtailing a licence under subsection (1) was given may at any time—

(*a*)   cancel the direction together with any order under subsection (6) that was made when the direction was given;

(*b*)   cancel any such order; or

(*c*)   with the consent of the licence-holder, vary the direction or any such order (or both the direction and any such order).

(9) Where an operator's licence is suspended under this section, the licence remains in force during the time of its suspension subject to the limitation that no vehicles are authorised to be used under it.

(10) In subsection (1)(*g*) the reference to an individual having been adjudged bankrupt shall, as respects Scotland, be construed as a reference to an award of sequestration having been made of his estate.

(11) In this Act references to directing that an operator's licence be curtailed are references to directing (with effect for the remainder of the duration of the licence or for any shorter period) all or any of the following, that is to say—

(*a*)   that one or more of the vehicles specified in the licence be removed from it;

(*b*)   that a provision such as is mentioned in section 5(2) or 6(1)(*b*) or (2)(*b*) be included in the licence;

(*c*)   that any maximum number specified in the licence under section 6 be reduced;

    (*d*)   that any one or more of the places specified in the licence as operating centres be removed from it.

[Goods Vehicles (Licensing of Operators) Act 1995, s 26.]

4–2009S   27. Revocation of standard licences.   (1) The traffic commissioner by whom a standard licence was issued shall direct that it be revoked if at any time it appears to him that the licence-holder is no longer—

    (*a*)   of good repute,

    (*b*)   of the appropriate financial standing, or

    (*c*)   professionally competent;

and the traffic commissioner shall determine whether or not that is the case in accordance with Schedule 3.

    (2) Before giving a direction under subsection (1) in respect of a licence, the traffic commissioner shall give to its holder notice in writing that he is considering giving such a direction.

    (3) A notice under subsection (2) shall state the grounds on which the traffic commissioner is considering giving a direction under subsection (1) and shall also state—

    (*a*)   that written representations with respect to those grounds may be made to the commissioner by the licence-holder, and

    (*b*)   that any such representations must be received by the commissioner within 21 days of the date of the notice;

and the traffic commissioner shall consider any representations duly made under this subsection.

    (4) This section has effect subject to section 29 (and, in particular, nothing in subsection (3) above shall be taken to affect a person's right under section 29(1) to require the holding of an inquiry).

[Goods Vehicles (Licensing of Operators) Act 1995, s 27.]

4–2009T   28. Disqualification.   (1) Where, under section 26(1) or 27(1), a traffic commissioner directs that an operator's licence be revoked, the commissioner may order the person who was the holder of the licence to be disqualified (either indefinitely or for such period as the commissioner thinks fit) from holding or obtaining an operator's licence; and so long as the disqualification is in force—

    (*a*)   any operator's licence held by him at the date of the making of the order (other than the licence revoked) shall be suspended, and

    (*b*)   notwithstanding anything in section 13 or 24, no operator's licence may be issued to him.

    (2) If a person applies for or obtains an operator's licence while he is disqualified under subsection (1)—

    (*a*)   he is guilty of an offence and liable on summary conviction to a fine not exceeding **level 4** on the standard scale, and

    (*b*)   any operator's licence issued to him on the application, or (as the case may be) the operator's licence obtained by him, shall be void.

    (3) An order under subsection (1) may be limited so as to apply only to the holding or obtaining of an operator's licence in respect of one or more specified traffic areas and, if the order is so limited—

    (*a*)   paragraphs (*a*) and (*b*) of that subsection and subsection (2) shall apply only to any operator's licence to which the order applies, but

    (*b*)   notwithstanding section 5(4)(*b*), no other operator's licence held by the person in question shall authorise the use by him of any vehicle at a time when its operating centre is in a traffic area in respect of which he is disqualified by virtue of the order.

    (4) Where the traffic commissioner makes an order under subsection (1) in respect of any person, the commissioner may direct that if that person, at any time or during such period as the commissioner may specify—

    (*a*)   is a director of, or holds a controlling interest in—

        (i)   a company which holds a licence of the kind to which the order in question applies, or

        (ii) a company of which such a company is a subsidiary, or

    (*b*)   operates any goods vehicles in partnership with a person who holds such a licence,

that licence of that company or, as the case may be, of that person, shall be liable to revocation, suspension or curtailment under section 26.

    (5) The powers conferred by subsections (1) and (4) in relation to the person who was the holder of a licence shall be exercisable also—

    (*a*)   where that person was a company, in relation to any director of that company, and

    (*b*)   where that person operated vehicles under the licence in partnership with other persons, in relation to any of those other persons;

and any reference in this section or in section 26 or 29 to subsection (1) or (4) above includes a reference to that subsection as it applies by virtue of this subsection.

    (6) The traffic commissioner by whom any order disqualifying a person was made under subsection (1) may at any time—

(a) cancel that order together with any direction that was given under subsection (4) when the order was made;

(b) cancel any such direction; or

(c) with the consent of the person disqualified, vary the order or any such direction (or both the order and any such direction).

(7) Where an operator's licence is suspended under this section, the licence remains in force during the time of its suspension subject to the limitation that no vehicles are authorised to be used under it.

(8) For the purposes of this section a person holds a controlling interest in a company if he is the beneficial owner of more than half its equity share capital (as defined in section 744 of the Companies Act 1985).

[Goods Vehicles (Licensing of Operators) Act 1995, s 28.]

4–2009U   29. Revocation and disqualification etc: supplementary provisions. (1) A traffic commissioner shall not—

(a) give a direction under section 26(1) or (2) or 27(1) in respect of any licence,

(b) make an order under section 26(6) in respect of any vehicle, or

(c) make an order or give a direction under section 28(1) or (4) in respect of any person,

without first holding an inquiry if the holder of the licence or (as the case may be) the person concerned requests him to do so.

(2) The traffic commissioner may direct that any direction or order given or made by him under—

(a) section 26(1), (2) or (6),

(b) section 27(1), or

(c) section 28(1) or (4),

shall not take effect until the expiry of the time within which an appeal may be made to the Transport Tribunal against the direction or order and, if such an appeal is made, until the appeal has been disposed of.

(3) If the traffic commissioner refuses to give a direction under subsection (2) the holder of the licence or, as the case may be, the person in respect of whom the direction or order was given or made may apply to the Tribunal for such a direction.

(4) The Tribunal shall give its decision on any application under subsection (3) within 14 days.

[Goods Vehicles (Licensing of Operators) Act 1995, s 29.]

Inquiries

4–2009V   35. Power of traffic commissioners to hold inquiries. (1) A traffic commissioner may hold such inquiries as he thinks necessary for the proper exercise of his functions under this Act.

(2)–(3) *Supplementary provision as to inquiries.*

(4) Information with respect to any particular trade or business which is given at any such inquiry while admission to the inquiry is restricted in accordance with regulations shall not, so long as that trade or business continues to be carried on, be disclosed except—

(a) with the consent of the person for the time being carrying on that trade or business;

(b) for the purpose of the discharge by any person of his functions under this Act; or

(c) with a view to the institution of, or otherwise for the purposes of, any legal proceedings pursuant to or arising out of this Act, including proceedings before the Transport Tribunal.

(5) Any person who discloses any information in contravention of subsection (4) is guilty of an offence and liable on summary conviction to a fine not exceeding **level 4** on the standard scale.

[Goods Vehicles (Licensing of Operators) Act 1995, s 35.]

4–2009VA   36–37. *Review of decisions and appeals.*

Forgery, false statements, etc

4–2009W   38. Forgery of documents, etc. (1) A person is guilty of an offence if, with intent to deceive, he—

(a) forges, alters or uses a document or other thing to which this section applies[1];

(b) lends to, or allows to be used by, any other person a document or other thing to which this section applies; or

(c) makes or has in his possession[2] any document or other thing so closely resembling a document or other thing to which this section applies as to be calculated to deceive[3].

(2) This section applies to the following documents and other things, namely—

(a) any operator's licence;

(b) any document, plate, mark or other thing by which, in pursuance of regulations, a vehicle is to be identified as being authorised to be used, or as being used, under an operator's licence;

(c) any document evidencing the authorisation of any person for the purposes of sections 40 and 41;

(d) any certificate of qualification under section 49; and

(e) any certificate or diploma such as is mentioned in paragraph 13(1) of Schedule 3.

(3) A person guilty of an offence under subsection (1) is liable[4]—

(*a*) on summary conviction[5], to a fine not exceeding **the statutory maximum**;

(*b*) on conviction on indictment, to imprisonment for a term not exceeding **two years** or to a **fine** or to **both**.

(4) In the application of subsection (1) to England and Wales, "forges" means makes a false document or other thing in order that it may be used as genuine.

[Goods Vehicles (Licensing of Operators) Act 1995, s 38.]

---

1. An offence would be committed by the use of a certificate which has ceased to be a valid certificate after the cancellation of the policy (*R v Cleghorn* [1938] 3 All ER 398).

2. See *R v Greenberg* [1942] 2 All ER 344.

3. This means "likely to deceive" and not "intended to deceive" (cf *Re London and Globe Finance Corpn Ltd* [1903] 1 Ch 728, 82 JP 447).

4. For procedure in respect of an offence triable either way, see the Magistrates' Courts Act 1980, ss 18–21, ante.

5. As to the time limit for bringing the proceedings under this section, see s 51, post.

4–2009X   **39. False statements.**   (1) A person is guilty of an offence if he knowingly makes a false statement[1] for the purpose of

(*a*) obtaining the issue to himself or any other person of an operator's licence;

(*b*) obtaining the variation of any such licence;

(*c*) preventing the issue or variation of any such licence;

(*d*) procuring the imposition of a condition or limitation in relation to any such licence; or

(*e*) obtaining the issue to himself or any other person of a certificate of qualification under section 49 or a certificate or diploma such as is mentioned in paragraph 13(1) of Schedule 3.

(2) A person guilty of an offence[2] under subsection (1) is liable on summary conviction to a fine not exceeding **level 4** on the standard scale.

[Goods Vehicles (Licensing of Operators) Act 1995, s 39.]

---

1. It is immaterial that any gain or advantage would be derived as a result of the false statement (*Jones v Meatyard* [1939] 1 All ER 140).

2. As to the time limit for bringing proceedings under this section, see s 51, post.

Enforcement etc

4–2009Y   **40. Inspection of maintenance facilities.**   (1) An officer may, at any time which is reasonable having regard to the circumstances of the case, enter any premises of an applicant for an operator's licence or of the holder of such a licence and inspect any facilities on those premises for maintaining the vehicles used under the licence in a fit and serviceable condition.

(2) Any person who obstructs an officer in the exercise of his powers under subsection (1) is guilty of an offence and liable on summary conviction to a fine not exceeding **level 3** on the standard scale.

[Goods Vehicles (Licensing of Operators) Act 1995, s 40.]

4–2009Z   **41. Power to seize documents etc.**   (1) If an officer has reason to believe that—

(*a*) a document or article carried on or by the driver of a vehicle, or

(*b*) a document produced to him in pursuance of this Act,

is a document or article in relation to which an offence has been committed under section 38 or 39, he may seize that document or article.

(2) Where—

(*a*) a document or article is seized under subsection (1),

(*b*) no person has, within six months of the date on which the document or article was seized, been charged since that date with an offence in relation to it under section 38 or 39, and

(*c*) the document or article is still detained,

then any of the persons mentioned in subsection (3) may make an application to a magistrates' court or (in the case of an application made in Scotland) the sheriff.

(3) The persons who may make an application under subsection (2) are—

(*a*) an officer;

(*b*) the driver or owner of the vehicle;

(*c*) the person from whom the document was seized.

(4) On an application under subsection (2), the magistrates' court or the sheriff shall—

(*a*) make such order respecting the disposal of the document or article, and

(*b*) award such costs or (in Scotland) expenses,

as the justice of the case may require.

(5) Any application made under subsection (2) to the sheriff shall be made by way of summary application.

[Goods Vehicles (Licensing of Operators) Act 1995, s 41.]

4–2009ZA 42. Meaning of "officer" and powers of police constables. (1) In sections 40 and 41 "officer" means—

- (a) an examiner appointed under section 66A of the Road Traffic Act 1988, or
- (b) any person authorised for the purposes of sections 40 and 41 by the traffic commissioner for any area.

(2) The powers conferred by sections 40 and 41 on an officer shall be exercisable also by a police constable.
[Goods Vehicles (Licensing of Operators) Act 1995, s 42.]

4–2009ZB 43. Evidence by certificate. (1) In any proceedings for an offence under this Act a certificate such as is mentioned in subsection (2) shall be evidence, and in Scotland sufficient evidence, of the facts stated in it.

(2) The certificate referred to in subsection (1) is a certificate signed by or on behalf of a traffic commissioner which states—

- (a) that, on any date, a person was or was not the holder of an operator's licence issued by the commissioner;
- (b) that, by virtue of a direction given by the commissioner under regulations made under section 48(2)(b) or (3), a person is to be treated as having been the holder of an operator's licence on any date;
- (c) the date of the coming into force of any operator's licence issued by the commissioner;
- (d) the date on which any operator's licence issued by the commissioner ceased to be in force;
- (e) the terms and conditions of any operator's licence issued by the commissioner;
- (f) that a person is by virtue of an order of the commissioner disqualified from holding or obtaining an operator's licence, either indefinitely or for a specified period;
- (g) that a direction, having effect indefinitely or for a specified period, has been given by the commissioner under section 28(4) in relation to any person;
- (h) that an operator's licence was on any date or during any specified period suspended by virtue of a direction given by the commissioner under section 26(1); or
- (i) that, by virtue of a direction given by the commissioner under regulations made under section 48(2)(a), an operator's licence is to be treated as having been suspended on any date or during any specified period.

(3) Any such certificate which purports to be signed by or on behalf of a traffic commissioner shall be taken to be so signed unless the contrary is proved.
[Goods Vehicles (Licensing of Operators) Act 1995, s 43.]

Miscellaneous

4–2009ZC 46. Holding companies and subsidiaries. (1) The Secretary of State may by regulations[1] make provision for the purpose of enabling any company or other body corporate which has one or more subsidiaries to hold an operator's licence under which the vehicles authorised to be used consist of or include vehicles belonging to or in the possession of any of its subsidiaries.

(2) Regulations under this section may—

- (a) modify or supplement any of the provisions of this Act, other than the excepted provisions, so far as appears to the Secretary of State to be necessary or expedient for or in connection with the purpose mentioned in subsection (1), and
- (b) may contain such other supplementary and incidental provisions as appear to the Secretary of State to be requisite.

(3) In this Act "the excepted provisions" means the following provisions (which are provisions that reproduce the effect of provisions of the Goods Vehicles (Operators' Licences, Qualifications and Fees) Regulations 1984), namely—

- (a) sections 3, 4, 9(2) and (3)(b), 13(3), 15(5) and (6), 20, 22(2) to (5), 27 and 49;
- (b) in section 58, in subsection (1), the definitions of "international transport operations", "national transport operations", "road transport undertaking" and "transport manager", and subsection (4); and
- (c) Schedule 3.
[Goods Vehicles (Licensing of Operators) Act 1995, s 46.]

---

1. See the Goods Vehicles (Licensing of Operators) Regulations 1996, reg 30, in this PART, post.

4–2009ZD 47. Partnerships. Regulations may provide for this Act to apply in relation to partnerships with such modifications as may be specified in the regulations; but nothing in any such regulations may make modifications in any of the excepted provisions (within the meaning given in section 46(3)).
[Goods Vehicles (Licensing of Operators) Act 1995, s 47.]

4–2009ZE 48. Operators' licences not to be transferable etc. (1) Subject to any regulations under section 46, an operator's licence is neither transferable nor assignable.

(2) Regulations may make provision enabling a traffic commissioner, where the holder of an

operator's licence issued by him has died or become a patient within the meaning of Part VII of the Mental Health Act 1983, to direct that the licence be treated—

(a) as not having terminated at the time when the licence-holder died or became a patient but as having been suspended (that is, as having remained in force but subject to the limitation that no vehicles were authorised to be used under it) from that time until the time when the direction comes into force; and

(b) as having effect from the time when the direction comes into force for a specified period and as being held during that period (for such purposes and to such extent as may be specified) not by the person to whom it was issued but by such other person carrying on that person's business, or part of that person's business, as may be specified.

(3) Regulations may make provision enabling a traffic commissioner in prescribed circumstances to direct that any operator's licence issued by him is to be treated (for such purposes, for such period and to such extent as may be specified) as held not by the person to whom it was issued but by such other person carrying on that person's business, or part of that person's business, as may be specified.

(4) Regulations may make provision enabling a traffic commissioner to direct, for the purpose of giving effect to or supplementing a direction given by him by virtue of subsection (2) or (3), that this Act is to apply with specified modifications in relation to the person who is to be treated under the direction as the holder of an operator's licence; but nothing in any such regulations shall permit the commissioner to modify the operation of any of the excepted provisions (within the meaning given in section 46(3)).

(5) In subsection (2) references to a person becoming a patient within the meaning of Part VII of the Mental Health Act 1983 include references to a curator bonis[1] being appointed in respect of him in Scotland on the ground that he is incapable, by reason of mental disorder, of adequately managing and administering his property and affairs.

(6) In this section "specified", in relation to a direction, means specified—

(a) in the regulations under which the direction was given; or

(b) in the direction in accordance with those regulations.

[Goods Vehicles (Licensing of Operators) Act 1995, s 48.]

---

1. By virtue of the Adults with Incapacity (Scotland) Act 2000, Sch 5, the reference in sub-s (5) to a curator bonis shall be construed as a reference to a guardian with similar powers appointed under that act.

4–2009ZF   49.   *Certificates of qualification.*

Large goods vehicles

4–2009ZG   50. Large goods vehicles.   (1) Schedule 5 (which requires certain documents to be carried by the drivers of large goods vehicles and makes other provision in connection with such vehicles) shall have effect.

(2) This section and Schedule 5 shall come into force[1] on such day as the Secretary of State may by order appoint; and different days may be appointed for different purposes and different provisions.

[Goods Vehicles (Licensing of Operators) Act 1995, s 50.]

---

1. At the date of going to press, s 50 and Sch 5 had not been brought into force; see s 61, post.

General provisions

4–2009ZH   51. Time for bringing proceedings.   Section 6 of the Road Traffic Offenders Act 1988[1] (time for bringing summary proceedings for certain offences) shall apply to an offence under section 9(3)[1] or, 38 or 39.

[Goods Vehicles (Licensing of Operators) Act 1995, s 51.]

---

1. See this PART, post.

4–2009ZI   53. Method of calculating weight of motor vehicles.   For the purposes of this Act the weight unladen of a vehicle shall be taken to be the weight of the vehicle inclusive of the body and all parts (the heavier being taken where alternative bodies or parts are used) which are necessary to or ordinarily used with the vehicle when working on a road, but exclusive of the weight of water, fuel or accumulators used for the purpose of the supply of power for the propulsion of the vehicle, and of loose tools and loose equipment.

[Goods Vehicles (Licensing of Operators) Act 1995, s 53.]

4–2009ZJ   54. Saving for law of nuisance.   Nothing in this Act shall authorise a person to use on a road a vehicle so constructed or used as to cause a public or private nuisance, or in Scotland a nuisance, or affect the liability, whether under statute or common law, of the driver or owner so using such a vehicle.

[Goods Vehicles (Licensing of Operators) Act 1995, s 54.]

4–2009ZK   55. Protection of public interests.   It is hereby declared that nothing in this Act is to be treated as conferring on the holder of an operator's licence any right to the continuance of any benefits arising from this Act or from any such licence or from any conditions attached to any such licence.

[Goods Vehicles (Licensing of Operators) Act 1995, s 55.]

Regulations and orders

4–2009ZL   57. Regulations and orders. (1) The Secretary of State may make regulations[1] for any purpose for which regulations may be made under this Act, and for prescribing anything which may be prescribed under this Act, and generally for carrying this Act into effect.

(2) In particular, but without prejudice to the generality of subsection (1), the Secretary of State may make regulations with respect to the following matters—

(a) the procedure on applications for, and the determination of questions in connection with, the issuing and variation of operators' licences and the procedure under, and the determination of questions for the purposes of, sections 26 to 32 and 36;

(b) the issue of operators' licences and the issue on payment of the prescribed fee of copies of such licences in the case of licences lost or defaced;

(c) the forms which operators' licences are to take in order to show a distinction—

(i) between a standard licence and a restricted licence; and

(ii) between a licence covering both international and national transport operations and a licence covering national transport operations only;

(d) the means by which vehicles may be identified, whether by plates, marks or otherwise, as being used or authorised to be used under an operator's licence;

(e) the custody, production, return and cancellation of operators' licences and of documents, plates and any other means of identification prescribed under paragraph (d);

(f) the payment of a prescribed fee in respect of any document, plate or other means of identification so prescribed that has been lost, defaced or broken;

(g) the notification to a traffic commissioner of vehicles which have ceased to be used under an operator's licence;

(h) the repayment (or partial repayment) in the prescribed circumstances of fees paid under this Act;

(i) the circumstances in which goods are to be treated for the purposes of this Act as carried for hire or reward and the circumstances in which goods are to be treated for those purposes as carried by any person for or in connection with a trade or business carried on by him.

(3) The power under subsection (2)(a) shall include power to require a person applying for an operator's licence to state in his application—

(a) whether his application is for a standard licence or a restricted licence, and

(b) (if his application is for a standard licence) whether his application is for a licence to cover both international and national transport operations or for one to cover national transport operations only.

(4) The power under subsection (2)(d) shall include power to require that any means of identification prescribed for a vehicle shall be carried notwithstanding that for the time being the vehicle is not being used for a purpose for which an operator's licence is required.

(5) The power under subsection (2)(d) shall also include power to make provision with respect to the means by which—

(a) any vehicle may be identified as being used under a standard licence or, as the case may be, a restricted licence; and

(b) any vehicle which is being used under a standard licence may be identified as being used under a licence that permits it to be used—

(i) for both international and national transport operations, or

(ii) for national transport operations only.

(6) The Secretary of State may make regulations for providing that any provision of this Act shall, in relation to vehicles brought temporarily into Great Britain, have effect subject to such modifications as may be prescribed.

(7) Any regulations under this Act may make—

(a) different provision for different cases or classes of case and different circumstances, and

(b) transitional provision,

and regulations made by virtue of subsection (2)(d) may make different provision for different traffic areas.

(8) A definition or description of a class of vehicles for the purposes of any regulation under this Act may be framed by reference to any characteristic of the vehicles or to any other circumstances whatever.

(9) Any person who contravenes a provision of regulations under this section, a contravention of which is declared by the regulations to be an offence, is guilty of an offence and liable on summary conviction to a fine not exceeding **level 1** on the standard scale.

(10) No regulations shall be made under section 30(3) unless a draft of them has been laid before, and approved by a resolution of, each House of Parliament.

(11) Any regulations made by the Secretary of State under this Act, other than regulations under

section 30(3), shall be subject to annulment in pursuance of a resolution of either House of Parliament.

(12) Before making any regulations under this Act the Secretary of State shall consult with such representative organisations as he thinks fit.

(13) Any power to make orders or regulations conferred on the Secretary of State by any provision of this Act shall be exercisable by statutory instrument.

[Goods Vehicles (Licensing of Operators) Act 1995, s 57.]

---

1. See the Goods Vehicles (Licensing of Operators) Regulations 1995, in this PART, post. See also the Goods Vehicles (Licensing of Operators) (Temporary Use in Great Britain) Regulations 1996, SI 1996/2186 amended by SI 2004/462.

Interpretation

4–2009ZM   58.   General interpretation.   (1) In this Act, unless the context otherwise requires—

"area", in relation to a traffic commissioner, means the traffic area for which he is the traffic commissioner;

"articulated combination" means a combination made up of—

     (*a*)   a motor vehicle which is so constructed that a trailer may by partial superimposition be attached to the vehicle in such a manner as to cause a substantial part of the weight of the trailer to be borne by the vehicle, and

     (*b*)   a trailer attached to it as described in paragraph (*a*);

"carriage of goods" includes haulage of goods;

"contravention", in relation to any condition or provision, includes a failure to comply with the condition or provision, and "contravenes" shall be construed accordingly;

"the 1974 Council Directive" means Community Council Directive No 74/561/EEC dated 12 November 1974 on admission to the occupation of road haulage operator in national and international transport operations, as amended by Community Council Directive No 89/438/EEC dated 21 June 1989;

"the 1977 Council Directive" means Community Council Directive No 77/796/EEC dated 12 December 1977 concerning the mutual recognition of diplomas, certificates and other evidence of formal qualifications for goods haulage operators and road passenger transport operators, including measures to encourage such operators effectively to exercise their right of freedom of establishment, as amended by Community Council Directive No 89/438/EEC dated 21 June 1989;

"driver"—

     (*a*)   where a separate person acts as steersman of a motor vehicle, includes that person as well as any other person engaged in the driving of the vehicle; and

     (*b*)   in relation to a trailer, means the driver of the vehicle by which the trailer is drawn;

     and "drive" shall be construed accordingly;

"functions" includes powers, duties and obligations;

"goods" includes goods or burden of any description[1];

"goods vehicle" means a motor vehicle constructed or adapted for use for the carriage of goods, or a trailer so constructed or adapted, but does not include a tramcar or trolley vehicle within the meaning of the Road Traffic Act 1988;

"holding company" and "subsidiary" have the meaning given by section 736 of the Companies Act 1985;

"international transport operations" and "national transport operations" have the same meaning as in the 1974 Council Directive;

"modification" includes addition, omission and alteration, and related expressions shall be construed accordingly;

"motor vehicle" and "trailer" have the same meaning as in section 253 of the Road Traffic Act 1960;

"operating centre" has the meaning given in section 7(3);

"operator's licence" has the meaning given in section 2(1);

"owner", in relation to any land in England and Wales, means a person, other than a mortgagee not in possession, who, whether in his own right or as trustee for any other person, is entitled to receive the rack rent of the land or, where the land is not let at a rack rent, would be so entitled if it were so let;

"plated weight", in relation to a vehicle, means a weight required to be marked on it by means of a plate in pursuance of regulations made by virtue of section 41 of the Road Traffic Act 1988 or required to be so marked by section 57 or 58 of that Act;

"prescribed" means prescribed by regulations;

"regulations" means regulations made by the Secretary of State under this Act;

"restricted licence" has the meaning given in section 3(3);

"road"—

     (*a*)   in relation to England and Wales, means any highway and any other road to which the public has access, and includes bridges over which a road passes; and

     (*b*)   in relation to Scotland, has the same meaning as in the Roads (Scotland) Act 1984;

"road transport undertaking" means an undertaking which involves the use of goods vehicles—

    (*a*)   under an operator's licence, or

    (*b*)   in accordance with the law of Northern Ireland or the law of any member State other than the United Kingdom;

"standard licence" has the meaning given in section 3(2);

"statutory provision" means a provision contained in an Act or in subordinate legislation within the meaning of the Interpretation Act 1978;

"traffic area" means a traffic area constituted for the purposes of the Public Passenger Vehicles Act 1981;

"transport manager", in relation to a business, means an individual who is in, or who is engaged to enter into, the employment of the holder of a standard licence and who, either alone or jointly with one or more other persons, has continuous and effective responsibility for the management of the transport operations of the business in so far as they relate to the carriage of goods;

"vehicle combination" means a combination of goods vehicles made up of one or more motor vehicles and one or more trailers all of which are linked together when travelling.

(2)   For the purposes of this Act, the driver of a vehicle, if it belongs to him or is in his possession under an agreement for hire, hire-purchase or loan, and in any other case the person whose servant[2] or agent the driver is, shall be deemed to be the person using the vehicle; and references to using a vehicle shall be construed accordingly.

(3)   In this Act references to vehicles being authorised to be used under an operator's licence are to be read in accordance with section 5.

(4)   For the purposes of this Act, a person who is an applicant for, or a holder of, a standard licence, or who is a transport manager, shall be regarded as being engaged in a road transport undertaking if—

    (*a*)   in a case where that person is an individual, he is either—

        (i)   the holder, or one of the joint holders, of an operator's licence, or

        (ii)   in the employment of a person who carries on a road transport undertaking and that undertaking gives him responsibility for the operation of goods vehicles used under an operator's licence; or

    (*b*)   in a case where that person is a company, either—

        (i)   the company is the holder of an operator's licence, or

        (ii)   the company is a subsidiary of the holder of an operator's licence and goods vehicles used under that licence belong to the company or are in its possession.

(5)   Anything required or authorised by this Act to be done by or to a traffic commissioner by whom a licence was issued may be done by or to any person for the time being acting as traffic commissioner for the area for which the first-mentioned commissioner was acting at the time of the issuing of the licence

[Goods Vehicles (Licensing of Operators) Act 1995, s 58.]

---

    1. A trailer being transported for testing or repair and towed by a tractor unit has been held to be goods for the purposes of s 2 of this Act (*Booth v DPP* [1993] RTR 379).

    2. This is a question of fact, see *Alderton v Richard Burgon Associates Ltd* [1974] RTR 422 (where the defendants, an employment agency, were held not to be the employers of a driver). The word "servant" in sub-s (2) includes a person for whom the putative employer is vicariously liable and includes deemed temporary employees. The paramount test is control over the relevant activity. Therefore where a parcels delivery company which had an operators licence used a contractor who did not have an operators licence to provide some of the drivers for the company's vehicles and the company gave instructions to the contractor as to the delivery of the vehicles for servicing, the completion of daily defect reports, the cleaning of the cab and the completion of time sheets, specified the driver qualifications necessary, required and provided any necessary training at its expense and was able to institute disciplinary proceedings the necessary element of control was present to regard the drivers as temporary deemed servants of the company (*Interlink Express Parcels Ltd v Night Trunkers Ltd* [2001] EWCA Civ 360, [2001] RTR 338).

Supplementary provisions

4–2009ZN 59. Transitional provision etc.   (1) The transitional provisions and transitory modifications of this Act contained in Schedule 6[1] shall have effect.

(2)   Without prejudice to the generality of paragraphs 2 to 4 of that Schedule, an existing licence shall continue in force as if it had been issued under this Act, and in this Act or any other enactment, instrument or document, any reference to, or including a reference to, an operator's licence issued under this Act shall, so far as the nature of the reference permits, be construed as including a reference to an existing licence.

(3)   In subsection (2) "existing licence" means any operator's licence within the meaning of Part V of the Transport Act 1968 which was in force immediately before the commencement of this Act.

[Goods Vehicles (Licensing of Operators) Act 1995, s 59.]

---

    1. See, post.

4–2009ZP   **60.**   *Consequential amendments and repeals.*

4–2009ZQ   61. Commencement.   (1) Subject to section 50(2) (which makes provision in relation to the commencement of section 50 and Schedule 5) this Act shall come into force on such day as the Secretary of State may by order[1] appoint.

(2) An order under subsection (1) may contain such transitional provisions and savings as appear to the Secretary of State to be necessary or expedient in connection with the coming into force of any provision of this Act which reproduces the effect of any provision of the Deregulation and Contracting Out Act 1994 which was not brought into force before the appointed day.

(3) Where any provision of the Deregulation and Contracting Out Act 1994 was brought into force before the appointed day by an order containing transitional provisions or savings in connection with the coming into force of that provision, an order under subsection (1) may contain corresponding transitional provisions or savings in connection with the coming into force of any provision of this Act which reproduces the effect of that provision of that Act.

(4) In subsections (2) and (3) "the appointed day" means the day appointed under subsection (1).

[Goods Vehicles (Licensing of Operators) Act 1995, s 61.]

---

1. The Goods Vehicles (Licensing of Operators) Act 1995 (Commencement and Transitional Provisions) Order 1995, SI 1995/2181, has been made and provides that the whole of the Act, save for s 50 and Sch 5, shall come into force on 1 January 1996. At the date of going to press, no date had been appointed for the commencement of s 50 and Sch 5.

4–2009ZR   62. Short title and extent.   (1) This Act may be cited as the Goods Vehicles (Licensing of Operators) Act 1995.

(2) The amendments specified in Schedule 7 and the repeals and revocations specified in Schedule 8 have the same extent as the enactments and instruments to which they relate.

(3) Subject to subsection (2), this Act does not extend to Northern Ireland.

[Goods Vehicles (Licensing of Operators) Act 1995, s 62.]

SCHEDULES

Section 2   SCHEDULE 1

MEANING OF "SMALL GOODS VEHICLE"

4–2009ZS   1. For the purposes of section 2 a small goods vehicle is a goods vehicle falling within any of paragraphs 2 to 4.

2. A goods vehicle falls within this paragraph if it does not form part of a vehicle combination and—

(a) has a relevant plated weight not exceeding 3.5 tonnes, or
(b) if it does not have a relevant plated weight, has an unladen weight not exceeding 1525 kilograms.

3. (1) A goods vehicle falls within this paragraph if it forms part of a vehicle combination, other than an articulated combination, and the combination is such that—

(a) in a case where all the vehicles comprised in it, or all of those vehicles except any small trailer, have relevant plated weights, the aggregate of the relevant plated weights of those vehicles, exclusive of any such trailer, does not exceed 3.5 tonnes, or
(b) in any other case, the aggregate of the unladen weights of the vehicles comprised in the combination, exclusive of any small trailer, does not exceed 1525 kilograms.

(2) In this paragraph "small trailer" means a trailer having an unladen weight not exceeding 1020 kilograms.

4. A goods vehicle falls within this paragraph if it forms part of an articulated combination which is such that—

(a) in a case where the trailer comprised in the combination has a relevant plated weight, the aggregate of—

(i) the unladen weight of the motor vehicle comprised in the combination, and
(ii) the relevant plated weight of that trailer, does not exceed 3.5 tonnes, or

(b) in any other case, the aggregate of the unladen weights of the motor vehicle and the trailer comprised in the combination does not exceed 1525 kilograms.

5. In any provision of paragraphs 2 to 4 "relevant plated weight" means a plated weight of the description specified in relation to that provision by regulations.

4–2009ZSA

Section 2   SCHEDULE 1A

DETENTION OF VEHICLES USED WITHOUT OPERATOR'S LICENCE[1]

---

1. The Goods Vehicles (Enforcement Powers Regulations 2001 this title post have been made under this Schedule which permit an authorised person to detain a heavy goods vehicle and its contents where the person using the vehicle did not hold an operator's licence for that or any other vehicle.

Sections 8, 9 and 26.   SCHEDULE 2

INFORMATION ABOUT, AND CONVICTIONS OF, APPLICANTS FOR AND HOLDERS OF OPERATORS' LICENCES

Information to be given under section 8

4–2009ZT   1. The information referred to in section 8(4) is the following—

(a) such particulars as the traffic commissioner may require with respect to the purposes for which the vehicles referred to in the statement under section 8(3) are proposed to be used;

(b) particulars of the arrangements for securing that—

   (i) Part VI of the Transport Act 1968 (drivers' hours), and
   (ii) the applicable Community rules, within the meaning of that Part,

will be complied with in the case of those vehicles;

(c) particulars of the arrangements for securing that those vehicles will not be overloaded;
(d) particulars of the facilities and arrangements for securing that those vehicles will be maintained in a fit and serviceable condition;
(e) particulars of any relevant activities carried on, at any time before the making of the application, by any relevant person;
(f) particulars of any notifiable convictions which have occurred during the five years preceding the making of the application;
(g) particulars of the financial resources which are or are likely to be available to the applicant;
(h) where the applicant is a company, the names of the directors and officers of—

   (i) the company, and
   (ii) any company of which that company is a subsidiary;

where the vehicles referred to in the statement under section 8(3) are proposed to be operated

(i) by the applicant in partnership with other persons, the names of those other persons.

"Relevant person"

4–2009ZU 2. In this Schedule "relevant person" means any of the following persons, namely—

(a) the applicant;
(b) any company of which the applicant is or has been a director;
(c) where the applicant is a company, any person who is a director of the company;
(d) where the applicant proposes to operate the vehicles referred to in the statement under section 8(3) in partnership with other persons, any of those other persons;
(e) any company of which any such person as is mentioned in sub-paragraph (c) or (d) is or has been a director; or
(f) where the applicant is a company, any company of which the applicant is a subsidiary.

"Relevant activities"

4–2009ZV 3. In paragraph 1(e) "relevant activities" means any of the following—

(a) activities in carrying on any trade or business in the course of which vehicles of any description are operated;
(b) activities as a person employed for the purposes of any such trade or business; or
(c) activities as a director of a company carrying on any such trade or business.

"Notifiable convictions"

4–2009ZW 4. The following are "notifiable convictions", namely—

(a) any conviction of a relevant person of an offence such as is mentioned in paragraph 5, and
(b) any conviction of a servant or agent of a relevant person of an offence such as is mentioned in sub-paragraph (a), (b), (d), (f), (g), (i) or (j) of that paragraph.

Offences

4–2009ZX 5. The offences are—

(a) an offence under section 53 of the Road Traffic Act 1988 (plating certificates and goods vehicle test certificates);
(b) an offence committed in relation to a goods vehicle consisting in the contravention of any provision (however expressed) contained in or having effect under any enactment (including any enactment passed after this Act) relating to—

   (i) the maintenance of vehicles in a fit and serviceable condition;
   (ii) limits of speed and weight laden and unladen, and the loading of goods vehicles; or
   (iii) the licensing of drivers;

(c) an offence under—

   (i) this Act;
   (ii) Part V of the Transport Act 1968 or section 233 or 235 of the Road Traffic Act 1960 so far as applicable (by virtue of Schedule 10 to the 1968 Act) to licences or means of identification under that Part;
   (iii) regulation 33(2) or (3) of the Goods Vehicles (Operators' Licences, Qualifications and Fees) Regulations 1984; or
   (iv) any regulation made under this Act or the Transport Act 1968 which is prescribed for the purposes of this paragraph;

(d) an offence under, or of conspiracy to contravene, Part VI of the Transport Act 1968 (drivers' hours) committed in relation to a goods vehicle;
(e) an offence under, or of conspiracy to contravene, section 13 of the Hydrocarbon Oil Duties Act 1979 (unlawful use of rebated fuel oil) committed in relation to a goods vehicle;
(f) an offence under section 173 or 174 of the Road Traffic Act 1988 (forgery, false statements and withholding of information) committed in relation to an international road haulage permit within the meaning of that Act;
(g) an offence under section 2 of the International Road Haulage Permits Act 1975 (removing, or causing or permitting the removal of, a goods vehicle or trailer from the United Kingdom in contravention of a prohibition imposed under that section);

(*h*) an offence under section 74 of the Road Traffic Act 1988 (operator's duty to inspect, and keep records of inspection of, goods vehicles);

(*i*) an offence under—

    (i) section 3 of the Control of Pollution Act 1974

    (ii) section 2 of the Refuse Disposal (Amenity) Act 1978;

    (iii) section 1 of the Control of Pollution (Amendment) Act 1989; or

    (iv) section 33 of the Environmental Protection Act 1990;

(*j*) an offence committed in relation to a goods vehicle consisting in the contravention of—

    (i) any provision (however expressed) prohibiting or restricting the waiting of vehicles which is contained in an order made under section 1, 6, 9 or 12 of the Road Traffic Regulation Act 1984, including any such order made by virtue of paragraph 3 of Schedule 9 to that Act (local authority powers to be exercisable also by Secretary of State); or

    (ii) any provision which is contained in a traffic regulation order, within the meaning of section 1 of that Act, by virtue of section 2(4) of that Act (lorry routes).

Repealed enactments

4–2009ZY   **6.** (1) In paragraph 5 any reference to an offence under a provision of the Road Traffic Act 1988 includes a reference to an offence under any corresponding provision of the Road Traffic Act 1972 repealed by the Road Traffic (Consequential Provisions) Act 1988.

(2) In paragraph 5(*j*)

(*a*) the reference to a provision contained in an order made under section 1, 6, 9 or 12 of the Road Traffic Regulation Act 1984 includes a reference to a provision contained in an order made under any enactment repealed by the 1984 Act and re-enacted by any of those sections, including any such order made by virtue of section 84A(2) of the Road Traffic Regulation Act 1967; and

(*b*) the reference to a provision contained in a traffic regulation order by virtue of section 2(4) of the 1984 Act includes a reference to a provision included in such an order by virtue of section 1(3AA) of the 1967 Act.

4–2010

Sections 13 and 27

SCHEDULE 3

QUALIFICATIONS FOR STANDARD LICENCE

(*Amended by SI 2004/3222.*)

4–2010A

Section 33

SCHEDULE 4

TRANSFER OF OPERATING CENTRES

Section 50

SCHEDULE 5[1]

LARGE GOODS VEHICLES

Meaning of "large goods vehicle"

4–2010B   **1.** (1) For the purposes of this Schedule, a large goods vehicle is a goods vehicle, other than a hauling vehicle, falling within any of sub-paragraphs (2) to (4).

(2) A goods vehicle falls within this sub-paragraph if—

(*a*) it has a relevant plated weight exceeding 16260 kilograms, or

(*b*) in the case of a vehicle which does not have a relevant plated weight, it has an unladen weight exceeding 5080 kilograms.

(3) A goods vehicle falls within this sub-paragraph if it forms part of a vehicle combination, other than an articulated combination, and the combination is such that—

(*a*) in a case where all the vehicles comprised in the combination, or all of those vehicles except any small trailer, have relevant plated weights, the aggregate of the relevant plated weights of the vehicles comprised in the combination, exclusive of any such trailer, exceeds 16260 kilograms, or

(*b*) in any other case, the aggregate of the unladen weights of the vehicles comprised in it, exclusive of any small trailer, exceeds 5080 kilograms;

and in this sub-paragraph "small trailer" means a trailer having an unladen weight not exceeding 1020 kilograms.

(4) A goods vehicle falls within this sub-paragraph if it forms part of an articulated combination which is such that—

(*a*) in a case where the trailer comprised in the combination has a relevant plated weight, the aggregate of—

    (i) the unladen weight of the motor vehicle comprised in the combination, and

    (ii) the relevant plated weight of that trailer,

exceeds 16260 kilograms, or

(*b*) in any other case, the aggregate of the unladen weights of the motor vehicle and the trailer comprised in the combination exceeds 5080 kilograms.

(5) In any provision of sub-paragraphs (2) to (4) "relevant plated weight" means a plated weight of the description specified in relation to that provision by regulations.

(6) In sub-paragraph (1) "hauling vehicle" means a motor tractor, a light locomotive, a heavy locomotive or the motor vehicle comprised in an articulated combination; and in this sub-paragraph "motor tractor", "light locomotive" and "heavy locomotive" have the same meaning as in the Road Traffic Act 1960.

---

1. At the date of going to press Sch 5 had not been brought into force; see s 50 and s 61, ante.

Consignment notes

4–2010C   **2.** (1) Subject to sub-paragraph (2), no goods shall be carried on a large goods vehicle unless a document (a "consignment note") in the prescribed form and containing the prescribed particulars has been completed and signed in the prescribed manner and is carried by the driver of the vehicle.

(2) Sub-paragraph (1) shall not apply—

     (*a*) to the carriage of goods on any journey or on a vehicle of any class exempted from that sub-paragraph by regulations; or

     (*b*) to any carriage of goods which is lawful without the authority of an operator's licence.

(3) Subject to the provisions of regulations, a traffic commissioner may dispense with the observance, as respects the carriage of goods under an operator's licence issued by him, of any requirement of sub-paragraph (1), where he is satisfied that it is not reasonably practicable for that requirement to be observed.

(4) Such a dispensation may be granted—

     (*a*) generally;

     (*b*) as respects a particular vehicle; or

     (*c*) as respects the use of vehicles for a particular purpose.

(5) The consignment note relating to the goods carried on a vehicle on any journey shall, at the conclusion of that journey, be preserved for the prescribed period by the person who used the vehicle for carrying the goods on that journey.

(6) Any person who—

     (*a*) uses or drives a vehicle in contravention of sub-paragraph (1), or

     (*b*) fails to comply with sub-paragraph (5),

is guilty of an offence and liable on summary conviction to a fine not exceeding **level 4** on the standard scale.

Powers of entry and inspection

4–2010D   **3.** (1) An officer may require any person to produce and permit him to inspect and copy—

     (*a*) any document which is required by or under paragraph 2 to be carried by that person as driver of a vehicle; or

     (*b*) any document which that person is required by or under that paragraph to preserve;

and that document shall, if the officer so requires by notice in writing served on that person, be produced at the office of the traffic commissioner specified in the notice within such time (not being less than 10 days) from the service of the notice as may be so specified.

(2) An officer may at any time enter any large goods vehicle and inspect that vehicle and any goods carried on it

(3) Where an officer has reason to believe—

     (*a*) that a large goods vehicle is being kept on any premises, or

     (*b*) that any such documents as are mentioned in sub-paragraph (1) are to be found on any premises,

he may, at any time which is reasonable having regard to the circumstances of the case, enter those premises and inspect any such vehicle, and inspect and copy any such document, which he finds there.

(4) For the purpose of exercising his powers under sub-paragraph (1)(*a*) or (2), an officer may detain the vehicle in question during such time as is required for the exercise of that power.

(5) The powers conferred by sub-paragraphs (1) to (4) are exercisable on production by the officer, if so required, of his authority.

(6) Any person who—

     (*a*) fails to comply with any requirement under sub-paragraph (1), or

     (*b*) obstructs any officer in the exercise of his powers under sub-paragraph (2), (3) or (4),

is guilty of an offence and liable on summary conviction to a fine not exceeding **level 3** on the standard scale.

(7) In this paragraph "officer" has meaning given in section 42(1) (as amended by paragraph 5 below).

(8) The powers conferred by this paragraph on an officer shall be exercisable also by a police constable who shall not, if wearing uniform, be required to produce any authority.

Falsification of consignment notes and records

4–2010E   **4.** (1) Any person who—

     (*a*) makes, or causes to be made, any document required to be made under paragraph 2 which he knows to be false, or

     (*b*) with intent to deceive, alters or causes to be altered any document required to be made under that paragraph,

is guilty of an offence.

(2) A person guilty of an offence under sub-paragraph (1) is liable[1]—

     (*a*) on summary conviction, to a fine not exceeding **the statutory maximum**;

     (*b*) on conviction on indictment, to imprisonment for a term not exceeding **two years** or to a **fine** or to **both**.

---

1. For procedure in respect of this offence which is triable either way, see the Magistrates' Courts Act 1980, ss 17A–21, in PART I: MAGISTRATES' COURTS, PROCEDURE, *ante*.

Amendment of section 38, 41 and 42 of this Act

4–2010F   **5.** (1) The following amendments shall take effect on the day appointed for the coming into force of paragraph 3, namely, in sections 38(2)(*c*) and 42(1)(*b*), after the words "sections 40 and 41" there shall be inserted the words "and paragraph 3 of Schedule 5".

(2) The following amendments shall take effect on the day appointed for the coming into force of paragraph 4, namely, in section 41(1) and (2)(*b*), after the words "section 38 or 39" there shall be inserted the words "or paragraph 4(1) of Schedule 5".

SCHEDULE 6
TRANSITIONAL PROVISIONS, TRANSITORY MODIFICATIONS AND SAVINGS
(*As amended by the Statute Law (Repeals) Act 2004.*)

General transitional provisions

4–2010G   1. The substitution of this Act for the provisions repealed and revoked by it shall not affect the continuity of the law.

2. In so far as any thing done (including any subordinate legislation made or other instrument issued) under a provision repealed or revoked by this Act could have been done under the corresponding provision of this Act, it shall have effect as if done under that corresponding provision.

3. Any reference (express or implied) in this Act or any other enactment, instrument or document to—

(*a*)   any provision of this Act, or

(*b*)   things done or falling to be done under or for the purposes of any provision of this Act,

shall, so far as the nature of the reference permits, be construed as including, in relation to the times, circumstances or purposes in relation to which the corresponding provision repealed or revoked by this Act had effect, a reference to that corresponding provision or (as the case may be) to things done or failing to be done under or for the purposes of that corresponding provision.

(4)   Any reference (express or implied) in any enactment, instrument or document to—

(*a*)   a provision repealed or revoked by this Act, or

(*b*)   things done or falling to be done under or for the purposes of such a provision,

shall, so far as the nature of the reference permits, be construed as including, in relation to the times, circumstances or purposes in relation to which the corresponding provision of this Act has effect, a reference to that corresponding provision or (as the case may be) to things done or falling to be done under or for the purposes of that corresponding provision.

5. Paragraphs 1 to 4 have effect, in relation to the substitution of this Act for the provisions repealed and revoked by it, in place of section 17(2) of the Interpretation Act 1978 (but without prejudice to any other provision of that Act).

4–2010H   6. *Repealed.*

Meaning of "holding company" and "subsidiary"

4–2010I   7. For the purposes of this Act as it applies in relation to licences granted before 11 November 1990 (the date on which section 144(1) of the Companies Act 1989 came into force) the expressions "holding company" and "subsidiary" have the meaning given by section 736 of the Companies Act 1985 as originally enacted.

Transport Act 2000
(2000 c 38)

4–2011   Part II of the Act (ss 108–162 and Schs 10 and 11) makes provision for local transport including local transport plans and strategies and in particular the provision of bus services[1]. Sections 145–150 provide for mandatory travel concessions outside Greater London for pensioners and specified disabled persons and an operator commits an offence under s 148(2) punishable by a fine not exceeding **level 3** if he systematically fails to comply with the obligations imposed by section 145(1) during any period. Proceedings may not be instituted except by a travel concession authority or by or with the consent of the Director of Public Prosecutions (s 148(3)). Similar provisions are made for the Greater London Area by amendments to the Greater London Authority Act 1999. Provision is made for road charging (s 168)[2].

---

1. See the Bus Lane Contraventions (Approved Local Authorities) (England) Order 2005, SI 2005/2755 amended by SI 2005/3406 and SI 2006/593, 1447, 1516, 2632, 2820, 3212, 3419 and 3425, the Bus Lanes (Approved Devices) Order 2005, SI 2005/2756 and the Bus Lane Contravention (Penalty Charges, Adjudication and Enforcement) (England) Regulations 2005, SI 2005/2757, made under s 144.

2. See the Trunk Road Charging Schemes (Bridges and Tunnels) (England) Procedure Regulations 2001, SI 2001/2303 amended by SI 2004/3168 (E).

Traffic Management Act 2004[1]
(2004 c 18)

PART 1[2]
TRAFFIC OFFICERS

Traffic officers for England and for Wales

4–2012   1. Traffic officers: introduction.   (1)   This Part makes provision for the designation of individuals as traffic officers by, or under an authorisation given by, the Secretary of State or the Assembly.

(2)   The duties assigned to traffic officers must be connected with, or intended to facilitate or to be conducive or incidental to—

(*a*)   the management of traffic on the relevant road network; or (*b*)   the performance of any other functions of the appropriate national authority (in its capacity as a traffic authority or highway authority).

(3) In subsection (2) "the relevant road network" means—

(*a*)   the network of relevant roads in England (in the case of traffic officers designated by, or under an authorisation given by, the Secretary of State); or

(*b*)   the network of relevant roads in Wales (in the case of traffic officers designated by, or under an authorisation given by, the Assembly).

(4) Traffic officers shall have such special powers (for use in connection with the performance of their duties) as are referred to in section 5(1).

(5) In this Part "relevant road" means a road in England for which the Secretary of State is the traffic authority or a road in Wales for which the Assembly is the traffic authority.

[Traffic Management Act 2004, s 1.]

---

1. This Act is to be brought into force in accordance with orders made under s 99. At the date of going to press the following commencement order had been made: (No 1 and Transitional Provision) (England) SI 2004/2380 (ss 1–12, 13 (part), 14–15, 40 (part), 60–63, 95, 97, 98 (part) on 4 October 2004; (No 2) (England) SI 2004/3110 (Part 2, s 43(1), (2) and (4) on 4 January 2005); (No 1) (England) SI 2006/1736 (s 94 on 29 January 2006); (No 1) (Wales) SI 2006/2826 (ss 5(4), 5(5) and 10, 16 to 31, 72 to 93, 94, 95 and 96 98, insofar as it relates to Part 2 of Sch 12 on 26 October 2006; (No 3) (England) SI 2006/1736 (s 94 as from 29 September 2006).

The legislation has the overall aim of improving management of traffic on the roads. In particular, Part 1 of the Act provides for an enhanced role for the Highways Agency as 'strategic road network operator' and provides for the establishing of a uniformed traffic officer service which may undertake some traffic management functions of the police on motorways and trunk roads. These responsibilities in essence relate to keeping traffic moving, preventing congestion and avoiding danger to persons or other traffic and preventing damage e.g. dealing with the knock-on effects of accidents and breakdowns by directing traffic and implementing other traffic management measures. Part 2 makes provision for network management of their road networks by local authorities. Part 3 provides for 'permit schemes' to regulate of street works and Part 4 strengthens enforcement of existing legislation regulating street works and introduces a fixed penalty scheme for offences under the New Roads and Street Works Act 1991. Part 5 makes specific provision for the designation of strategic roads in London and introduces a fixed penalty scheme for certain offences under the Highways Act 1980. Part 6 makes provision for a single scheme for civil enforcement for road traffic contraventions.

2. Part 1 comprises ss 1–15.

4–2012A   2. Designation of traffic officers

Jurisdiction and powers of traffic officers

4–2012B   3. Jurisdiction of traffic officers.   (1) A traffic officer has jurisdiction—

(*a*)   over any relevant road in England (if he was designated by, or under an authorisation given by, the Secretary of State); or

(*b*)   over any relevant road in Wales (if he was designated by, or under an authorisation given by, the Assembly),

unless his designation provides that this subsection does not apply to him.

(2) If subsection (1) does not apply to a traffic officer, he has jurisdiction only over such relevant roads, or relevant roads of such descriptions, as may be specified in his designation.

[Traffic Management Act 2004, s 3.]

4–2012C   4. Powers to direct traffic officers.   (1) A traffic officer shall, when carrying out his duties, comply with any direction of a constable.

(2) Subject to that, a traffic officer designated by an authorised person shall, when carrying out his duties, comply with any direction of the appropriate national authority.

[Traffic Management Act 2004, s 4.]

4–2012D   5. The special powers of a traffic officer.   (1) For the purposes of this Part the special powers of a traffic officer are the following—

(*a*)   powers conferred by sections 6 and 7;

(*b*)   powers conferred by orders under section 8; and

(*c*)   powers conferred by or under any other Act which are expressed to be special powers for the purposes of this section.

(2) The exercise of those powers is subject to the following restrictions.

(3) Those powers may only be exercised for one or more of the following purposes—

(*a*)   maintaining or improving the movement of traffic on a relevant road over which the traffic officer has jurisdiction by virtue of section 3;

(*b*)   preventing or reducing the effect of anything causing (or which has the potential to cause) congestion or other disruption to the movement of traffic on such a road;

(*c*)   avoiding danger to persons or other traffic using such a road (or preventing risks of any such danger arising);

(*d*)   preventing damage to, or to anything on or near, such a road;

or for a purpose incidental to any of those purposes.

(4) Subject to that, those powers may be exercised—

(a)   on or in relation to any relevant road over which the traffic officer has jurisdiction to act by virtue of section 3; or

(b)   if the condition specified in subsection (5) is met, on or in relation to any other road in England and Wales.

(5)   The condition is that the traffic officer is acting—

(a)   at the direction of the chief officer of police for the area in which the road is situated; or

(b)   with the consent of the traffic authority for the road.

(6)   A traffic officer may not exercise his special powers on a road unless he is in uniform.

[Traffic Management Act 2004, s 5.]

4–2012E   6. Powers to stop or direct traffic.   (1) This section confers the following powers on a traffic officer—

(a)   a power, when the traffic officer is engaged in the regulation of traffic in a road, to direct a person driving or propelling a vehicle—

    (i)   to stop the vehicle, or

    (ii)   to make it proceed in, or keep to, a particular line of traffic;

(b)   a power, for the purposes of a traffic survey of any description which is being carried out on or in the vicinity of a road, to direct a person driving or propelling a vehicle—

    (i)   to stop the vehicle, or

    (ii)   to make it proceed in, or keep to, a particular line of traffic, or

    (iii)   to proceed to a particular point on or near the road on which the vehicle is being driven or propelled;

    (subject to the restriction in section 35(3) of the Road Traffic Act 1988 (c 52));

(c)   a power, when the traffic officer is engaged in the regulation of vehicular traffic in a road, to direct persons on foot (or such persons and other traffic) to stop;

(d)   a power to direct a person driving a mechanically propelled vehicle, or riding a cycle, on a road to stop the vehicle or cycle.

(2)   In section 35 of the Road Traffic Act 1988 (drivers to comply with traffic directions)—

(a)   in subsection (1)—

    (i)   after "a constable" there is inserted "or traffic officer";

    (ii)   after "duty" there is inserted "or the traffic officer (as the case may be)";

(b)   in subsection (2)(b) after "constable" there is inserted "or traffic officer".

(3)   In section 37 of that Act (directions to pedestrians)—

(a)   after "uniform" there is inserted "or traffic officer";

(b)   after "duty" there is inserted "or the traffic officer (as the case may be)".

(4)   In section 163 of that Act (power of police to stop vehicles), in subsections (1) and (2) after "uniform" there is inserted "or a traffic officer".

(5)   In Part 1 of Schedule 2 to the Road Traffic Offenders Act 1988 (c 53) (prosecution and punishment of offences under the Traffic Acts), in column 5 of the entry relating to section 35 of the Road Traffic Act 1988 after "constable" there is inserted ", traffic officer".

[Traffic Management Act 2004, s 6.]

4–2012F   7. Powers to place temporary traffic signs.   (1) A traffic officer has the powers of a constable under section 67(1) of the Road Traffic Regulation Act 1984 (c 27) (power in the case of emergencies and temporary obstructions etc to place and temporarily maintain traffic signs on a road or on any structure on a road).

(2)   The references in section 67(1) and (2) to powers conferred by subsection (1) of that section include a reference to the corresponding powers of a traffic officer by virtue of this section.

[Traffic Management Act 2004, s 7.]

4–2012G   8. Power to confer further special powers on traffic officers

4–2012H   9. Removal of certain vehicles by traffic officers.   *Regulations made under the Road Traffic Regulation Act 1984 may make consequential provision for removal by traffic officers.*

Miscellaneous and supplementary

4–2012I   10. Offences.   (1) A person who assaults a traffic officer in the execution of his duties is guilty of an offence and liable, on summary conviction, to imprisonment for a term not exceeding 51 weeks or to a fine not exceeding level 5 on the standard scale (or both).

(2)   A person who resists or wilfully obstructs a traffic officer in the execution of his duties is guilty of an offence and liable, on summary conviction, to imprisonment for a term not exceeding 51 weeks or to a fine not exceeding level 3 on the standard scale (or both).

(3)   A person who, with intent to deceive—

    (*a*)   impersonates a traffic officer,

    (*b*)   makes any statement or does any act calculated falsely to suggest that he is a traffic officer, or

    (*c*)   makes any statement or does any act calculated falsely to suggest that he has powers as a traffic officer that exceed the powers he actually has,

is guilty of an offence and liable, on summary conviction, to imprisonment for a term not exceeding 51 weeks or to a fine not exceeding level 5 on the standard scale (or both).

    (4) A person to whom this subsection applies who fails to give his name and address to a traffic officer in uniform on being required to do so by that officer is guilty of an offence and liable on summary conviction to a fine not exceeding level 3 on the standard scale.

    (5) Subsection (4) applies to a person whom the traffic officer reasonably believes to have been the driver of a vehicle at a time of a failure to comply with—

    (*a*)   a direction given in relation to that vehicle under a power conferred by section 6, or

    (*b*)   the indication given by a traffic sign placed under a power conferred by section 7.

    (6) In the case of offences committed before the commencement of section 281(5) of the Criminal Justice Act 2003—

    (*a*)   subsections (1) and (3) apply as if for "51 weeks" there were substituted "six months"; and

    (*b*)   subsection (2) applies as if for "51 weeks" there were substituted "one month".

[Traffic Management Act 2004, s 10.]

4–2012J   11.   Uniform

4–2012K   12.   Power to charge for traffic officer services provided on request

4–2012L   13.   Power to acquire land. *Acquisition of land for use by, or in connection with the activities of traffic officers*

4–2012M   14.   Financial assistance to authorised persons

4–2012N   15.   Interpretation of Part 1.   In this Part—

"the appropriate national authority" means—

    (*a*)   the Secretary of State, as respects England; and

    (*b*)   the Assembly, as respects Wales;

"the Assembly" means the National Assembly for Wales;

"authorised person" means a person who is authorised under section 2;

"designation" means designation as a traffic officer under section 2;

"relevant road" has the meaning given by section 1(5);

"road" means any length of highway or of any other road to which the public has access, and includes bridges over which a road passes;

"traffic authority" has same meaning as in the Road Traffic Regulation Act 1984 (c 27);

"traffic officer" means an individual designated under section 2.

[Traffic Management Act 2004, s 15.]

4–2012O

PART 2[1]

NETWORK MANAGEMENT BY LOCAL TRAFFIC AUTHORITIES

---

    1. Part 2 comprises ss 16–31 and imposes a duty on every local traffic authority manage its road network to secure, so far as is reasonably practicable, the expeditious movement of traffic on its road network, and on the road networks of other authorities.

4–2012P

PART 3[1]

PERMIT SCHEMES

---

    1. Part 3 comprises ss 32–39 and makes provision for permit schemes prepared by local highway authorities, the Secretary of State (or the National Assembly for Wales) to regulate street works and other prescribed works or activities which are, or correspond to activities regulated or controlled by the Highways Act 1980.

4–2012Q

PART 4[1]

STREET WORKS

Enforcement

4–2012R   40.   Increase in penalties for summary offences under 1991 Act. (1) The maximum fine for each offence under a provision of the New Roads and Street Works Act 1991 (c 22) (in this Part referred to as "the 1991 Act") listed in column 1 of the table in Schedule 1 is increased from level 3 on the standard scale to the level specified for that provision in column 3 of the table.

(2) Accordingly, in each provision so listed, for "level 3" there is substituted "level 4" or "level 5" (as specified in column 3 of the table).

(3) In section 70(6) of the 1991 Act, for the words from "to a" to the end there is substituted—

"(a) in the case of an offence consisting of a failure to comply with subsection (3) or (4A), to a fine not exceeding level 4 on the standard scale; and
  (b) in any other case, to a fine not exceeding level 5 on that scale."

(4) In section 74(7B) and 74A(11) of the 1991 Act (maximum fine for offences in regulations in respect of failure to comply with notice requirement) for "level 3" there is substituted "level 4".

(5) In section 88(6) of the 1991 Act (failure to comply with duties relating to street works affecting the structure of a bridge) for the words from "to a" to the end there is substituted—

"(a) in the case of an offence consisting of a failure to take all reasonably practicable steps to comply with subsection (5)(a), to a fine not exceeding level 4 on the standard scale; and
  (b) in any other case, to a fine not exceeding level 5 on that scale."

[Traffic Management Act 2004, s 40.]

---

1. Part 4 comprises ss 40–59 and Schs 1–4 and makes amendments to the New Roads and Street Works Act 1991. There is an increase in penalties for a number of summary offences and the 1991 Act is also amended to introduce a new fixed penalty notice system for offences. Further provisions in Part 4 amend the 1991 Act in order to strengthen the powers of authorities to impose restrictions on and make directions to, those undertaking streetworks in order to minimise disruption to traffic.

4–2012S 41. Fixed penalty offences. (1) After section 95 of the 1991 Act (offences) there is inserted—

"95A. Fixed penalties for certain offences under this Part. (1) Any offence under this Part relating to any street works which is listed in the first column of Schedule 4A (and described in general terms in the second column) is a fixed penalty offence for the purposes of this Part.

(2) Offences listed in that Schedule which are committed by virtue of section 166 (offences by bodies corporate and Scottish partnerships) are not fixed penalty offences.

(3) The Secretary of State may by order modify that Schedule so as to provide for offences under this Part relating to any street works to become (or cease to be) fixed penalty offences.

(4) Such an order may not be made unless a draft of the order has been laid before and approved by resolution of each House of Parliament.

(5) Schedule 4B (which makes provision about fixed penalties for fixed penalty offences) has effect."

(2) In section 106 of that Act (index for Part 3), the following entry is inserted in the appropriate place—

"fixed penalty offence   section 95A(1)".

(3) After Schedule 4 to that Act there is inserted Schedules 4A and 4B as set out in Schedules 2 and 3 to this Act.

[Traffic Management Act 2004, s 41.]

Direction-making powers

4–2012T 43. Directions relating to timing of street works. (1) Section 56 of the 1991 Act (power to give directions as to timing of street works) is amended as follows.

(2) In subsection (1)—

(a) in paragraph (b), after "at certain times" there is inserted "or on certain days (or at certain times on certain days)";
(b) after "the times" there is inserted "or days (or both)".

(3) After subsection (1) there is inserted—

"(1A) Where it appears to a street authority—

(a) that subsisting street works are causing or are likely to cause serious disruption to traffic, and
(b) that the disruption would be avoided or reduced if the works were to continue to be carried out only at certain times or on certain days (or at certain times on certain days),

the authority may give the undertaker such directions as may be appropriate as to the times or days (or both) when the works may or may not continue to be carried out."

(4) After subsection (3) there is inserted—

"(3A) An undertaker shall be taken not to have failed to fulfil any statutory duty to afford a supply or service if, or to the extent that, his failure is attributable to a direction under this section."

[Traffic Management Act 2004, s 43.]

4–2012U 44. Directions as to placing of apparatus. In the 1991 Act, after section 56 there is inserted—

"56A. Power to give directions as to placing of apparatus. (1) Where—

    (*a*) an undertaker is proposing to execute street works consisting of the placing of apparatus in a street ("street A"),

    (*b*) placing the apparatus in street A is likely to cause disruption to traffic, and

    (*c*) it appears to the street authority that—

        (i) there is another street ("street B") in which the apparatus could be placed, and

        (ii) the conditions in subsection (2) are satisfied,

the authority may by direction require the undertaker not to place the apparatus in street A (but may not require him to place the apparatus in street B).

    (2) The conditions referred to in subsection (1)(*c*) are that—

    (*a*) disruption to traffic would be avoided or reduced if the apparatus were to be placed in street B;

    (*b*) placing the apparatus in street B would be a reasonable way of achieving the purpose for which the apparatus is to be placed; and

    (*c*) it is reasonable to require the undertaker not to place the apparatus in street A.

    (3) A direction under this section may be varied or revoked by a further such direction.

    (4) The procedure for giving a direction under this section shall be prescribed by the Secretary of State.

    (5) The Secretary of State may by regulations make provision for appeals against directions under this section, including provision as to the persons who may determine appeals and the procedure to be followed on an appeal.

    (6) An undertaker who executes works in contravention of a direction under this section commits an offence and is liable on summary conviction to a fine not exceeding level 5 on the standard scale.

    (7) An undertaker shall be taken not to have failed to fulfil any statutory duty to afford a supply or service if, or to the extent that, his failure is attributable to a direction under this section.

    (8) The Secretary of State may issue or approve for the purposes of this section a code of practice giving practical guidance as to the exercise by street authorities of the power conferred by this section; and in exercising that power a street authority shall have regard to the code of practice."

[Traffic Management Act 2004, s 44.]

4–2012V 46. Records of location of apparatus. (1) Section 79 of the 1991 Act (records of location of apparatus) is amended as follows.

    (2) After subsection (1) there is inserted—

    "(1A) An undertaker may, except in such cases as may be prescribed, include in his records under subsection (1) a record of the location of any item of apparatus belonging to him which is not required to be so included, stating the nature of the apparatus and (if known) whether it is for the time being in use."

    (3) After subsection (2) there is inserted—

    "(2A) Regulations under subsection (2) which alter the form or manner in which the records are to be kept may apply to records made before (as well as records made after) the alterations take effect."

    (4) After subsection (3) there is inserted—

    "(3A) In subsections (2) to (3) the references to an undertaker's records are to the records kept by him under subsection (1) (including anything included in those records by virtue of any provision of this Act or any other enactment)."

[Traffic Management Act 2004, s 46.]

4–2012W 47. Duties relating to the location of unexpected apparatus. (1) Section 80 of the 1991 Act (duties where person finds unidentified apparatus) is amended as follows.

    (2) In subsection (1) for "made available by the undertaker" there is substituted "kept by the undertaker under section 79(1) and made available by him".

    (3) After subsection (1) there is inserted—

    "(1A) Subsection (1) has effect subject to such exceptions as may be prescribed."

    (4) For subsections (2) and (3) there is substituted—

    "(2) Where a person executing works of any description in the street finds apparatus which does not belong to him and is unable, after taking such steps as are reasonably practicable, to ascertain to whom the apparatus belongs, he shall comply with such requirements (if any) as may be prescribed for the purpose of securing that he—

    (*a*) makes and keeps a record of the location of the apparatus and (so far as appears from external inspection) its nature and whether it is in use; and

    (*b*) informs the street authority or any other person of those matters.

    (2A) Regulations under subsection (2) may make provision—

    (*a*) as to the form and manner in which records are to be kept;

    (*b*)   as to the form and manner in which, or the time at or by which, information is to be given; and

    (*c*)   for records which are to be kept by undertakers to be included in the records kept by them under section 79(1)."

(5) In subsection (4) for " (2)" there is substituted "any requirement imposed on him by regulations under subsection (2)".

(6) After subsection (4) there is added—

"(5) The Secretary of State may by regulations make provision for and in connection with the keeping (whether by the Secretary of State or a person with whom he has made appropriate arrangements) of a register of information recorded by undertakers in pursuance of a requirement imposed under subsection (2).

(6) Regulations under subsection (5) may make provision about the inspection of the register by any person having authority to execute works of any description in the street or otherwise appearing to the person responsible for keeping the register to have a sufficient interest."

[Traffic Management Act 2004, s 47.]

Miscellaneous

4–2012X   **49. Notices of street works.**   (1) In section 54 of the 1991 Act (advance notice of certain works)—

    (*a*)   in subsection (3) for "contain such" there is substituted "state the date on which it is proposed to begin the works and shall contain such other";

    (*b*)   after subsection (4) there is inserted—

"(4A) If an undertaker who has given advance notice under this section has not, before the starting date specified in the notice, given to the street authority a notice under section 55 in respect of the works, he shall within such period as may be prescribed give to that authority a notice containing such information as may be prescribed.

(4B) An advance notice under this section shall cease to have effect in relation to the proposed works (so that subsection (1) applies again in relation to the works) if those works are not substantially begun before the end of such period beginning with the starting date specified in the notice as may be prescribed, or such further period as the street authority may allow.

(4C) Different periods may be prescribed under subsection (4B) for different descriptions of works."

(2) In section 55 of that Act (notice of starting date of works) after subsection (7) there is inserted—

"(8) If a notice under this section ceases to have effect the undertaker shall, within such period as may be prescribed, give a notice containing such information as may be prescribed to those to whom the notice under this section was required to be given.

(9) An undertaker who fails to give notice in accordance with subsection (8) commits an offence and is liable on summary conviction to a fine not exceeding level 4 on the standard scale."

(3) In section 93 of that Act (works affecting level crossings or tramways) in subsection (2) for "(7)" there is substituted "(9)".

[Traffic Management Act 2004, s 49.]

4–2012Y   **50. Qualifications of supervisors and operatives.**   (1) Section 67 of the 1991 Act (qualifications of supervisors and operatives) is amended as follows.

(2) After subsection (1) there is inserted—

"(1A) A street authority may (unless the case is one excepted from subsection (1)) by notice require an undertaker executing street works—

    (*a*)   to notify them of the name of—

        (i)   the person who is currently the qualified supervisor required by subsection (1); and

        (ii)   each person who has previously been the qualified supervisor so required; and

    (*b*)   to provide them with such evidence of the requisite qualification of each person named as may be prescribed."

(3) After subsection (2) there is inserted—

"(2A) A street authority may (unless the case is one excepted from subsection (2)) by notice require an undertaker executing street works—

    (*a*)   to notify them of the name of—

        (i)   a person whose presence on site at any time specified in the notice (being a time when the works were in progress) enabled the undertaker to comply with his duty under subsection (2); or

        (ii)   each person whose presence on site during the progress of the works enabled the undertaker to comply with his duty in subsection (2); and

    (*b*)   to provide them with such evidence of the requisite qualification of each person named as may be prescribed.

(2B) A notice under subsection (1A) or (2A) may be given at any time while the works are being executed or within such period after their completion as may be prescribed.

(2C) The undertaker shall comply with a notice under subsection (1A) or (2A) within such period as may be prescribed."

(4) In subsection (3) for "or (2)" there is substituted ", (2) or (2C)".

(5) In subsection (4), after paragraph (*b*) there is inserted

"and

(*c*) the form of any document to be issued by an approved body to certify or otherwise show that a qualification has been conferred on any person."

[Traffic Management Act 2004, s 50.]

4–2012Z 51. Restriction on works following substantial road works. (1) Section 58 of the 1991 Act (restriction on works following substantial road works) is amended as specified in subsections (2) to (8).

(2) In subsection (1), for the words "twelve months" there is substituted "prescribed period".

(3) In subsection (2), after "prescribed" there is inserted "form and" and for "three months" there is substituted "such period as may be prescribed".

(4) In subsection (3) after paragraph (*e*) there is inserted

"and

(*f*) any other person of a prescribed description;"

(and the word "and" after paragraph (*d*) is omitted).

(5) In subsection (4), for paragraphs (*a*) and (*b*) there is substituted "within such period as may be prescribed".

(6) In subsection (6), at the beginning of paragraph (*b*) there is inserted "if he is convicted of an offence under this subsection".

(7) In subsection (7), for "by arbitration" there is substituted "in the prescribed manner".

(8) After that subsection there is inserted—

"(7A) Regulations under subsection (7) may in particular make provision for the question referred to in that subsection to be settled—

(*a*) by arbitration;

(*b*) by a person designated by the Secretary of State on appeal by the undertaker."

(9) In section 55 of the 1991 Act (notice of starting date of works), in subsection (2), after "works," there is inserted "or in cases where the undertaker has been given notice under section 58(1),".

[Traffic Management Act 2004, s 51.]

4–2013 52. Restriction on works following substantial street works. (1) After section 58 of the 1991 Act there is inserted—

"58A. Restriction on works following substantial street works. Schedule 3A shall have effect."

(2) After Schedule 3 to that Act there is inserted Schedule 3A as set out in Schedule 4 to this Act.

(3) In section 57 of that Act (notice of emergency works)—

(*a*) in subsection (1) after "works)" there is inserted "or paragraph 2(1)(*d*) or 3(1) of Schedule 3A (notification of proposed works or directions as to timings of works)";

(*b*) in subsection (2) after "is" there is inserted "(or would, but for paragraph 2(6) of Schedule 3A, be)".

(4) In section 64 of that Act (traffic-sensitive streets) in subsection (1) after "works)" there is inserted "or paragraph 2 of Schedule 3A".

(5) In section 74 of that Act (charge for occupation of highway where works unreasonably prolonged)in subsection (3)(*b*) after "date)" there is inserted "or notification under paragraph 2(1)(*d*) of Schedule 3A (notification of proposed works)".

(6) In section 88 of that Act (provisions relating to bridges)in subsection (4) after "date)" there is inserted ", or making a notification under paragraph 2(1)(*d*) of Schedule 3A (notification of proposed works),".

(7) In section 89 of that Act (provisions relating to sewers)in subsection (2) after "date)" there is inserted ", or making a notification under paragraph 2(1)(*d*) of Schedule 3A (notification of proposed works),".

[Traffic Management Act 2004, s 52.]

4–2013A 54. Duty to notify street authority of reinstatement. (1) Section 70 of the 1991 Act (duty of undertaker to reinstate) is amended as follows.

(2) After subsection (1) there is inserted—

"(1A) The reinstatement required by subsection (1) may be permanent or interim."

(3) For subsections (3) and (4) there is substituted—

"(3) He shall within 7 working days from the date on which the reinstatement is completed give notice to the street authority of that completion—

(*a*) stating whether the reinstatement is permanent or interim; and

(*b*) giving such other information about the reinstatement as may be prescribed.

(4) If the reinstatement is interim, he shall complete the permanent reinstatement of the street as soon as reasonably practicable, and in any event within 6 months from the date on which the interim reinstatement was completed.

(4A) He shall, within 7 working days from the date on which the permanent reinstatement required by subsection (4) is completed, give notice to the street authority of that completion, giving such other information about the reinstatement as may be prescribed.

(4B) The Secretary of State may by regulations modify the period specified in subsection (3), (4) or (4A)."

[Traffic Management Act 2004, s 54.]

PART 5[1]
HIGHWAYS AND ROADS

4–2013B 60–63. *Strategic roads in London.*

---

1. Part 5 comprises ss 60–71 and Schs 5 and 6 and makes amendments to the provisions as to the designation of certain roads in London as strategic roads. Also, amendments are made to the Highways Act 1980 to enable the creation of a fixed penalty notice scheme for certain offences under Part 9 of the 1980 Act, and to the provisions in that Act which regulate charges for builder's skips, scaffolding etc, in the highway.

4–2013C 64. Fixed penalty offences under the Highways Act 1980. (1) After section 314 of the 1980 Act (offences by body corporate) there is inserted—

"**314A. Fixed penalties for certain offences under Part 9.** (1) A fixed penalty offence is any offence under Part 9 which—

(*a*) is listed in the first column in Schedule 22A (and described in general terms in the second column), and

(*b*) is prescribed in regulations made by the Secretary of State.

(2) Offences listed in that Schedule which are committed by virtue of section 314 (offences committed by bodies corporate, etc) are not fixed penalty offences.

(3) Schedule 22B (which makes provision about fixed penalties for fixed penalty offences) has effect.

(4) Regulations under subsection (1)(*b*) may—

(*a*) make provision for Greater London different from that made for the rest of England;

(*b*) make consequential provision (including provision disapplying sections 8 to 11 of, and Schedule 2 to, the London Local Authorities and Transport for London Act 2003 in relation to any offence prescribed in such regulations);

(*c*) make transitional provision."

(2) In section 322(5) of that Act (service of notices etc), after paragraph (*a*) there is inserted—

"(*ab*) a notice under Schedule 22B to this Act;".

(3) After Schedule 22 to that Act there is inserted Schedules 22A and 22B as set out in Schedules 5 and 6 to this Act.

(4) In the New Roads and Street Works Act 1991 (c 22), in section 97 (service of notices etc) after subsection (2) there is inserted—

"(3) References in this section to notices authorised to be given or served for the purposes of this Part include a reference to notices under Schedule 22B to the Highways Act 1980 (fixed penalties for certain offences under that Act)."

(5) In the London Local Authorities and Transport for London Act 2003 (c iii), in section 11 (fixed penalties: reserve powers of Secretary of State) after subsection (6) there is inserted—

"(7) The Secretary of State may make regulations increasing the level of fixed penalty under this Act in respect of an offence listed in Schedule 22A to the Highways Act 1980 (as well as Schedule 4 to this Act).

(8) While regulations under subsection (7) are in force in respect of an offence, the borough councils and Transport for London may not set the level of fixed penalty in respect of that offence below that set by the regulations."

[Traffic Management Act 2004, s 64.]

4–2013D 66. Builders' skips: charge for occupation of highway for unreasonable period.
For section 140A of the 1980 Act there is substituted—

"**140A. Builders' skips: charge for occupation of highway for unreasonable period.**
(1) The Secretary of State may make provision by regulations requiring the owner of a builder's

skip deposited on a highway maintainable at the public expense to pay a charge to the highway authority where the period for which the skip remains in the highway exceeds—

    (a)   such period as may be prescribed, and

    (b)   a reasonable period.

(2) For this purpose "a reasonable period" means such period as is agreed by the authority and the owner of the skip to be reasonable or, in default of such agreement, is determined by arbitration to be reasonable in the circumstances.

(3) In default of agreement, the authority's view as to what is a reasonable period shall be acted upon pending the decision of the arbitrator.

(4) The regulations may prescribe exemptions from the requirement to pay charges.

(5) The regulations may provide—

    (a)   that in prescribed circumstances (including in particular where any person makes an application for permission under section 139) the owner of the skip shall give to the authority, in such manner and within such period as may be prescribed, notice containing an estimate of the likely duration of the occupation of the highway, and

    (b)   that the period stated in the notice shall be taken to be agreed by the authority to be reasonable unless the authority give notice, in such manner and within such period as may be prescribed, objecting to the estimate.

(6) The regulations may also provide—

    (a)   that in prescribed circumstances the owner of the skip shall give to the authority, in such manner and within such period as may be prescribed, notice containing a revised estimate of the likely duration of the occupation of the highway, and

    (b)   that upon the notice being given any previous agreement to or determination of a reasonable period ceases to have effect, and the period stated in the notice shall be taken to be agreed by the authority to be reasonable unless the authority give notice, in such manner and within such period as may be prescribed, objecting to the revised estimate.

(7) The amount of the charge shall be determined in such manner as may be prescribed by reference to the period for which the highway is occupied by the skip.

(8) The regulations may prescribe different rates of charge according to—

    (a)   the extent to which the skip occupies the highway;

    (b)   the place and time of the occupation;

    (c)   such other factors as appear to the Secretary of State to be relevant.

(9) The regulations may provide—

    (a)   that the authority are to set the rate of charge, up to a prescribed maximum, and

    (b)   that different rates of charge may be set according to such factors as the authority consider relevant.

(10) The regulations may make provision for the determination of the duration of the occupation of the highway for the purposes of the regulations.

(11) And they may, in particular, make provision for an occupation to be treated as beginning or ending on the giving of, or as stated in, a notice given by the owner of the skip to the authority, in the prescribed manner, in accordance with a requirement imposed by the regulations.

(12) The regulations may make provision requiring the owner of the skip to provide the authority, in such manner and within such period as may be prescribed, with such information as the authority may specify in a notice to that person, being information required for the purposes of—

    (a)   determining whether a charge is payable by him;

    (b)   calculating the amount of any charge payable by him.

(13) The regulations may make provision as to the time and manner of making payment of charges.

(14) The regulations shall provide that a highway authority may reduce the amount, or waive payment, of a charge—

    (a)   in any particular case,

    (b)   in such classes of case as they may decide or as may be prescribed, or

    (c)   in all cases or in all cases other than a particular case or such class of case as they may decide or as may be prescribed.

(15) The regulations may make provision as to—

    (a)   the application by local highway authorities of sums paid by way of charges, and

    (b)   the keeping of accounts, and the preparation and publication of statements of account, relating to sums paid by way of charges.

(16) The regulations may create in respect of any failure to give a notice, or to provide information, required by the regulations a criminal offence triable summarily and punishable with a fine not exceeding level 4 on the standard scale.

(17) The regulations may provide that where a skip is the subject of a prescribed description of hiring agreement or hire purchase agreement, the person in possession of the skip under the agreement is for the purposes of the regulations to be treated as the owner of the skip.

(18) The regulations may make provision about their application to a series of deposits of skips.

(19) And they may, in particular, provide that a series of deposits of skips is to be treated as a single deposit of a skip—

(a) beginning at the time the first in the series was deposited, and
(b) ending at the time the last in the series was removed.

(20) In this section—

"builder's skip" has the meaning given by section 139(11);
"prescribed" means prescribed by the Secretary of State by regulations, which may make different provision for different cases."

[Traffic Management Act 2004, s 66.]

Guidance as to safety precautions

4–2013E   71. Guidance to local highway authorities as to safety precautions.   In section 174 of the 1980 Act (precautions to be taken by persons executing works in streets), after subsection (1) there is inserted—

"(1A) The Secretary of State may give guidance to local highway authorities as to the discharge by them of their obligations under subsection (1)(a) and (b) where they are executing works for road purposes.
(1B) A local highway authority must in executing any works for road purposes have regard to any guidance given under subsection (1A).
(1C) In subsections (1A) and (1B) "works for road purposes" has the same meaning as in Part 3 of the New Roads and Street Works Act 1991.""

[Traffic Management Act 2004, s 71.]

PART 6[1]
CIVIL ENFORCEMENT OF TRAFFIC CONTRAVENTIONS
Civil penalties for road traffic contraventions

4–2013F   72. Civil penalties for road traffic contraventions.   (1) The appropriate national authority may make provision by regulations for or in connection with—

(a) the imposition of penalty charges in respect of road traffic contraventions that—
    (i)   are subject to civil enforcement (see section 73), and
    (ii) are committed in an area that is a civil enforcement area for contraventions of that description (see section 74), and
(b) the payment of such penalty charges.

(2) The regulations shall include provision specifying the person or persons by whom a penalty charge in respect of a contravention is to be paid (who may be the owner of the vehicle involved in the contravention, its driver at the time of the contravention or any other appropriate person).

(3) The regulations shall include provision in respect of any description of conduct for which a penalty charge may be imposed—

(a) prohibiting criminal proceedings or the issuing of a fixed penalty notice in respect of conduct of that description, or
(b) securing that a penalty charge is not required to be paid, or is refunded, where the conduct is the subject of criminal proceedings or of a fixed penalty notice.

(4) The regulations may include provision prohibiting the imposition of a penalty charge except on the basis of—

(a) a record produced by an approved device, or
(b) information given by a civil enforcement officer as to conduct observed by him.

(5) The regulations may—

(a) specify exemptions from penalty charges, and
(b) make provision for discounts or surcharges, or both.

[Traffic Management Act 2004, s 72.]

---

1. Part 6 comprises ss 72–93 and Schs 4–11 and provides for a single framework for the civil enforcement by local authorities of parking and waiting restrictions, bus lane restrictions and some moving traffic offences.

4–2013G   73. Contraventions subject to civil enforcement.   (1) Schedule 7 specifies the road traffic contraventions that are subject to civil enforcement.

(2) These are—

(a) parking contraventions (see Part 1 of the Schedule);
(b) bus lane contraventions (see Part 2 of the Schedule);
(c) London lorry ban contraventions (see Part 3 of the Schedule);
(d) moving traffic contraventions (see Part 4 of the Schedule).

(3) Regulations under this Part of this Act may make different provision in relation to different descriptions of contravention.

(4) The appropriate national authority may by regulations make such consequential amendment of Schedule 7 as appears to the authority to be required in consequence of the amendment, replacement or revocation of any provision of subordinate legislation referred to in that Schedule.

[Traffic Management Act 2004, s 73.]

4–2013H   **74. Civil enforcement areas.**   (1) Schedule 8 makes provision—

(*a*) as to the areas that are civil enforcement areas for the purposes of different descriptions of road traffic contravention, and

(*b*) as to the meaning of "enforcement authority" in relation to road traffic contraventions committed in a civil enforcement area.

(2) In that Schedule—

Part 1 makes provision for Greater London, and
Part 2 makes provision for the rest of England and Wales.

[Traffic Management Act 2004, s 74.]

4–2013I   **75. Power to require authority to apply for civil enforcement powers**

4–2013J   **76. Civil enforcement officers.**   (1) A local authority may provide for the enforcement of road traffic contraventions for which it is the enforcement authority by individuals to be known as civil enforcement officers.

(2) A civil enforcement officer must be—

(*a*) an individual employed by the authority, or

(*b*) where the authority have made arrangements with any person for the purposes of this section, an individual employed by that person to act as a civil enforcement officer.

(3) Civil enforcement officers—

(*a*) when exercising specified functions must wear such uniform as may be determined by the enforcement authority in accordance with guidelines issued by the appropriate national authority, and

(*b*) must not exercise any of those functions when not in uniform.

(4) In subsection (3)(*a*) "specified" means specified by regulations made by the appropriate national authority.

(5) A parking attendant appointed under section 63A of the Road Traffic Regulation Act 1984 (c 27) by a local authority that is an enforcement authority—

(*a*) is a civil enforcement officer in relation to parking contraventions for which that authority is the enforcement authority, and

(*b*) may be appointed a civil enforcement officer in relation to other road traffic contraventions for which they are the enforcement authority.

[Traffic Management Act 2004, s 76.]

4–2013K   **77. Setting the level of penalty charges.**   (1) Schedule 9 provides for the setting of the levels of penalty charges and certain other charges.

(2) In that Schedule—

Part 1 specifies the charges to which the Schedule applies,
Part 2 provides for charges applicable in Greater London, and
Part 3 provides for charges applicable outside Greater London.

[Traffic Management Act 2004, s 77.]

Notification, adjudication and enforcement

4–2013L   **78. Notification of penalty charge.**   (1) The Lord Chancellor may make regulations for and in connection with the notification of penalty charges.

(2) The regulations may provide for notification of a penalty charge to be given in respect of a stationary vehicle—

(*a*) by a notice affixed to the vehicle,

(*b*) by a notice given to a person appearing to be in charge of the vehicle, or

(*c*) in such other manner as may be specified by the regulations.

(3) The regulations may provide for notification of a penalty charge otherwise than in respect of a stationary vehicle to be given in such manner as may be specified by the regulations.

(4) The regulations may not confer power to stop vehicles.

(5) The regulations may provide that, if it appears to the enforcement authority that both the operator of a vehicle and the person in control of the vehicle are liable to a penalty charge, they may give notice to the operator requiring him to provide them with the name and address of the person who was in control of the vehicle at the time of the alleged contravention.

(6) The regulations may include provision creating criminal offences to be triable summarily and

punishable with a fine not exceeding level 5 on the standard scale or such lower amount as may be specified.

[Traffic Management Act 2004, s 78.]

4–2013M   **79. Immobilisation of vehicle where penalty charge payable.**   (1) The appropriate national authority may make provision by regulations for or in connection with—

   (*a*)   the fixing of an immobilisation device to a stationary vehicle found in any place where there is reason to believe the vehicle has been permitted to remain at rest there in circumstances in which a penalty charge has become payable, and

   (*b*)   the release of the vehicle from the device only on payment of—

     (i)   the penalty charge mentioned in paragraph (*a*),

     (ii)   such unpaid earlier penalty charges relating to the vehicle as may be specified in the regulations, and

     (iii)   the charge payable in respect of the release.

   (2) The regulations may make provision authorising—

   (*a*)   the fixing of an immobilisation device to the vehicle while it remains in the place where it was found, or

   (*b*)   the moving of the vehicle to another place and the fixing of an immobilisation device to it in that other place,

and providing for any power of removal that was exercisable in relation to the vehicle before it was so moved to continue to be exercisable in relation to the vehicle while it remains in the place to which it was so moved.

   (3) The regulations may provide—

   (*a*)   that on any occasion when an immobilisation device is fixed to a vehicle in accordance with the regulations, the person fixing the device shall also fix to the vehicle a notice—

     (i)   indicating that such a device has been fixed to the vehicle and warning that no attempt should be made to drive it or otherwise put it in motion unless it has been released from the device;

     (ii)   specifying the steps to be taken in order to secure its release; and

     (iii)   giving such other information as may be specified by the regulations; and

   (*b*)   that a notice fixed to a vehicle in accordance with the regulations shall not be removed or interfered with except by or under the authority of—

     (i)   the owner or person in charge of the vehicle, or

     (ii)   the enforcement authority,

and that a person contravening that prohibition commits an offence and is liable on summary conviction to a fine not exceeding level 2 on the standard scale.

   (4) The regulations may also provide—

   (*a*)   that a vehicle to which an immobilisation device has been fixed in accordance with the regulations may only be released from the device by or under the direction of a person authorised by the enforcement authority; and

   (*b*)   that a person who, without being authorised to do so in accordance with the regulations, removes or attempts to remove an immobilisation device fixed to a vehicle in accordance with the regulations commits an offence and is liable on summary conviction to a fine not exceeding level 3 on the standard scale.

   (5) The regulations shall provide—

   (*a*)   that an immobilisation device must not be fixed to a vehicle if a current disabled person's badge is displayed on the vehicle; and

   (*b*)   that if, in a case in which an immobilisation device would have been fixed to a vehicle but for paragraph (*a*), the vehicle was not being used—

     (i)   in accordance with regulations under section 21 of the Chronically Sick and Disabled Persons Act 1970 (c 44), and

     (ii)   in circumstances falling within section 117(1)(*b*) of the Road Traffic Regulation Act 1984 (c 27) (use where a disabled person's concession would be available),

the person in charge of the vehicle commits an offence and is liable on summary conviction to a fine not exceeding level 3 on the standard scale.

   (5A) The regulations shall provide—

   (*a*)   that an immobilisation device must not be fixed to a vehicle if a current recognised badge is displayed on the vehicle; and

   (*b*)   that if, in a case in which an immobilisation device would have been fixed to a vehicle but for paragraph (*a*), the vehicle was not being used—

     (i)   in accordance with regulations under section 21A of the Chronically Sick and Disabled Persons Act 1970, and

(ii) in circumstances falling within section 117(1A)(b) of the Road Traffic Regulation Act 1984 (use where a disabled person's concession would be available by virtue of displaying a non-GB badge),

the person in charge of the vehicle commits an offence and is liable on summary conviction to a fine not exceeding level 3 on the standard scale.★

(6) The regulations shall also provide that an immobilisation device must not be fixed to a vehicle in a parking place in respect of a contravention consisting of, or arising out of, a failure—

(a) to pay a parking charge with respect to the vehicle,
(b) properly to display a ticket or parking device, or
(c) to remove the vehicle from the parking space by the end of a period for which the appropriate charge was paid,

until 15 minutes have elapsed since the giving of a notification of a penalty charge in respect of the contravention.

(7) In this section—

"disabled person's badge" has the same meaning as in section 142(1) of the Road Traffic Regulation Act 1984;

"parking device" means a parking device within the meaning of section 35(3B) or 51(4) of that Act;

"parking place" means—

(a) a parking place designated by an order under section 45 of that Act, or
(b) an off-street parking place provided under section 32(1)(a) or 57(1)(b), or under a letting or arrangement made under section 33(4), of that Act;

"recognised badge" has the meaning given by section 21A of the Chronically Sick and Disabled Persons Act 1970.★

[Traffic Management Act 2004, s 79 as amended by the Disability Discrimination Act 2005, Sch 1.]

★. Reproduced as in force in England. In force in Wales from a date to be appointed.

4–2013N   80. Representations and appeals.   (1) The Lord Chancellor may make provision by regulations entitling a person—

(a) who is or may be liable to pay a penalty charge, or
(b) who secures the release of a vehicle from an immobilisation device on payment of an amount in accordance with regulations under section 79,

to make representations to the enforcement authority and to appeal to an adjudicator if his representations are not accepted.

(2) The regulations may make such provision in connection with the rights conferred as appears to the Lord Chancellor to be appropriate, and may in particular make provision—

(a) requiring the authority to give a person notice of the rights conferred by the regulations,
(b) as to the grounds on which, and time within which, representations may be made,
(c) requiring supporting evidence in such circumstances as may be specified,
(d) as to the duties of the authority when representations are received,
(e) as to the circumstances in which there is a right of appeal to an adjudicator,
(f) generally as to the making, determination and effect of, and procedure in connection with, appeals, and
(g) enabling an adjudicator to review any decision made on, or in the course of, an appeal.

(3) The regulations may provide that, as respects a ground on which representations may be made, the adjudicator's function on an appeal is to decide whether to direct the enforcement authority to consider or re-consider (as the case may be) any representations relating to that ground.

(4) The regulations may include provision—

(a) authorising an adjudicator to require a person—

(i) to attend to give evidence at the hearing of an appeal, and
(ii) to produce any documents in his custody or under his control relating to any matter relevant for the purposes of the appeal, and

(b) making it a criminal offence triable summarily and punishable with a fine not exceeding level 2 on the standard scale to fail to comply with such a requirement.

(5) The regulations may provide that a person who makes a representation that is false in a material particular, and does so recklessly or knowing it to be false, commits an offence triable summarily and punishable with a fine not exceeding level 5 on the standard scale.

(6) The regulations may include provision authorising an adjudicator to make an order for the payment of costs and expenses by a party to an appeal in such circumstances as may be specified.

[Traffic Management Act 2004, s 80.]

4–2013O   81. Adjudicators.   (1) The Lord Chancellor may make provision by regulations for and in connection with the appointment of adjudicators for the purposes of this Part.

(2) The following provisions apply in relation to the office of adjudicator—

(a) to be qualified for appointment as an adjudicator, a person must have a 5-year general qualification (within the meaning of section 71 of the Courts and Legal Services Act 1990 (c 41));

(b) an adjudicator is appointed for a term, not exceeding five years, specified in his instrument of appointment;

(c) on the expiry of a term of appointment an adjudicator is eligible for re-appointment;

(d) an adjudicator may be removed from office only for misconduct or on the ground that he is unable or unfit to discharge his functions, but otherwise holds and vacates office in accordance with the terms of his appointment.

(3) The regulations shall provide—

(a) for adjudicators to be appointed by the relevant enforcement authorities on such terms as those authorities may decide, and

(b) for the consent of the Lord Chancellor to be required for any decision by those authorities to appoint a person as an adjudicator;

(c) for the consent of the Lord Chancellor and the Lord Chief Justice to be required for any decision by those authorities—

    (i) not to re-appoint a person as an adjudicator, or

    (ii) to remove a person from his office as an adjudicator.

(3A) The regulations may provide for the Lord Chief Justice to nominate a judicial office holder (as defined in section 109(4) of the Constitutional Reform Act 2005) to exercise any of his functions under the regulations.

(a)(b)(4) The relevant enforcement authorities shall—

(a) provide, or make arrangements for the provision of, accommodation and administrative staff and facilities for adjudicators, and

(b) determine the places where adjudicators are to sit,

and shall defray all the expenses of the adjudication process and, in particular, expenses in relation to the remuneration of adjudicators.

(5) The regulations shall provide—

(a) for each adjudicator to make an annual report to the relevant enforcement authorities in accordance with such requirements as may be imposed by those authorities, and

(b) for those authorities to make and publish an annual report to the appropriate national authority on the discharge by the adjudicators of their functions.

(6) In this section "the relevant enforcement authorities" means the authorities who are enforcement authorities for the purposes of this Part in relation to road traffic contraventions (of any description).

(7) The regulations may provide for the functions of the relevant enforcement authorities under this section—

(a) to be discharged separately for Greater London, England (outside Greater London) and Wales;

(b) to be discharged by means of arrangements under section 101 of the Local Government Act 1972 (c 70) (arrangements for discharge of functions by local authorities) or in such other way as the regulations may provide.

(8) The regulations may make provision—

(a) for treating adjudicators appointed before the commencement of this Part under section 73 of the Road Traffic Act 1991 (c 40), or under regulations made under section 144 of the Transport Act 2000 (c 38), as if they had been appointed under this section;

(b) for continuing in force for the purposes of this section any arrangements in force immediately before the commencement of this Part for the discharge of functions corresponding to the functions of relevant enforcement authorities under this section.

(9) The expenses of the relevant enforcement authorities under this section shall be defrayed by them in such proportions—

(a) as they may decide, or

(b) in default of a decision by them, as may be determined in accordance with regulations made—

    (i) by the Secretary of State, or

    (ii) if the functions of those authorities are discharged separately for Wales, by the appropriate national authority.

(10) Regulations under subsection (9)(b) may, in particular, provide—

(a) for the matter to be determined by an arbitrator appointed by a body specified in the regulations, and

(b) for the giving of directions by the Secretary of State or, as the case may be, the appropriate national authority in order to secure that the matter is referred to arbitration.

[Traffic Management Act 2004, s 81 as amended by SI 2006/1016.]

4–2013P 82. Enforcement of penalty charges. (1) The Lord Chancellor may make regulations for or in connection with the enforcement of penalty charges.

(2) The regulations may include provision—

(a) creating criminal offences to be triable summarily and punishable with a fine not exceeding level 5 on the standard scale or such lower amount as may be specified;

(b) for amounts payable under or by virtue of any provision of this Part to be recoverable, if a county court so orders, as if they were payable under a county court order.

An amount to which paragraph (b) applies that is so recoverable is referred to below as a "traffic contravention debt".

(3) The Lord Chancellor may by order make provision—

(a) for warrants of execution in respect of traffic contravention debts, or such class or classes of traffic contravention debts as may be specified in the order, to be executed by certificated bailiffs;

(b) as to the requirements that must be satisfied before a person takes any other step of a kind specified in the order, with a view to enforcing the payment of—

(i) a traffic contravention debt, or

(ii) such class or classes of traffic contravention debts as may be so specified.

(4) Any such order may make such incidental and supplementary provision (including modifications of any enactment other than this Act) as the Lord Chancellor considers appropriate in consequence of the provision made by the order.

(5) Any order in force immediately before the commencement of this Part under section 78(2) of the Road Traffic Act 1991 (c 40) shall have effect after that commencement as if made under the corresponding provisions of this section and shall apply in relation to the enforcement of any traffic contravention debt.

[Traffic Management Act 2004, s 82.]

4–2013Q 83. Certificated bailiffs. (1) For the purposes of section 82 (enforcement of penalty charges) a person is a certificated bailiff if he is authorised to act as such by a certificate signed—

(a) by a judge assigned to a county court district, or

(b) in such circumstances as may be specified in regulations made by the Lord Chancellor, by a district judge.

(2) The Lord Chancellor may by regulations make provision in connection with the certification of bailiffs under this section and the execution of warrants of execution by such bailiffs.

(3) The regulations may, in particular, make provision—

(a) as to the security (if any) to be required from certificated bailiffs,

(b) as to the fees and expenses payable with respect to execution by certificated bailiffs, and

(c) for the suspension or cancellation of certificates issued under this section and with respect to the effect of any such suspension or cancellation.

(4) Any regulations in force immediately before the commencement of this Part under section 78(4) to (6) of the Road Traffic Act 1991 shall have effect after that commencement as if made under the corresponding provisions of this section and anything done by or in relation to any person under such regulations shall be treated, so far as may be necessary for continuing their effect, as if done under regulations made under this section.

(5) A person who is not a certificated bailiff but who purports to levy a distress as such a bailiff, and any person authorising him to levy it, shall be deemed to have committed a trespass.

[Traffic Management Act 2004, s 83.]

Additional contraventions in special enforcement areas

4–2013R 84. Designation of special enforcement areas. Schedule 10 provides for the designation of areas ("special enforcement areas") where the following sections apply—

section 85 (prohibition of double parking etc);
section 86 (prohibition of parking at dropped footways etc).

[Traffic Management Act 2004, s 84.]

4–2013S 85. Prohibition of double parking etc. (1) In a special enforcement area a vehicle must not be parked on the carriageway in such a way that no part of the vehicle is within 50 centimetres of the edge of the carriageway.

This is subject to the following exceptions.

(2) The first exception is where the vehicle is parked wholly within a designated parking place or any other part of the carriageway where parking is specifically authorised.

A "designated parking place" means a parking place designated by order under section 6, 9, 32(1)(b) or 45 of the Road Traffic Regulation Act 1984 (c 27).

(3) The second exception is where the vehicle is being used for fire brigade, ambulance or police purposes.

(4) The third exception is where—

(a) the vehicle is being used for the purposes of delivering goods to, or collecting goods from, any premises, or is being loaded from or unloaded to any premises,

(b) the delivery, collection, loading or unloading cannot reasonably be carried out in relation to those premises without the vehicle being parked as mentioned in subsection (1), and

(c) the vehicle is so parked for no longer than is necessary and for no more than 20 minutes.

(5) The fourth exception is where—

(a) the vehicle is being used in connection with any of the following—

(i) undertaking any building operation, demolition or excavation,

(ii) the collection of waste by a local authority,

(iii) removing an obstruction to traffic,

(iv) undertaking works in relation to a road, a traffic sign or road lighting, or

(v) undertaking works in relation to a sewer or water main or in relation to the supply of gas, electricity, water or communications services,

(b) it cannot be so used without being parked as mentioned in subsection (1), and

(c) it is so parked for no longer than is necessary.

(6) In this section "carriageway" has the meaning given by section 329(1) of the Highways Act 1980 (c 66).

(7) References in this section to parking include waiting, but do not include stopping where—

(a) the driver is prevented from proceeding by circumstances beyond his control or it is necessary for him to stop to avoid an accident, or

(b) the vehicle is stopped, for no longer than is necessary, for the purpose of allowing people to board or alight from it.

(8) The prohibition in this section is enforceable as if imposed—

(a) in Greater London, by an order under section 6 of the Road Traffic Regulation Act 1984;

(b) elsewhere in England and Wales, by an order under section 1 of that Act.

[Traffic Management Act 2004, s 85.]

4–2013T 86. Prohibition of parking at dropped footways etc. (1) In a special enforcement area a vehicle must not be parked on the carriageway adjacent to a footway, cycle track or verge where—

(a) the footway, cycle track or verge has been lowered to meet the level of the carriageway for the purpose of—

(i) assisting pedestrians crossing the carriageway,

(ii) assisting cyclists entering or leaving the carriageway, or

(iii) assisting vehicles entering or leaving the carriageway across the footway, cycle track or verge; or

(b) the carriageway has, for a purpose within paragraph (a)(i) to (iii), been raised to meet the level of the footway, cycle track or verge.

This is subject to the following exceptions.

(2) The first exception is where the vehicle is parked wholly within a designated parking place or any other part of the carriageway where parking is specifically authorised.

A "designated parking place" means a parking place designated by order under section 6, 9, 32(1)(b) or 45 of the Road Traffic Regulation Act 1984 (c 27).

(3) The second exception is where the vehicle is parked outside residential premises by or with the consent (but not consent given for reward) of the occupier of the premises.

This exception does not apply in the case of a shared driveway.

(4) The third exception is where the vehicle is being used for fire brigade, ambulance or police purposes.

(5) The fourth exception is where—

(a) the vehicle is being used for the purposes of delivering goods to, or collecting goods from, any premises, or is being loaded from or unloaded to any premises,

(b) the delivery, collection, loading or unloading cannot reasonably be carried out in relation to those premises without the vehicle being parked as mentioned in subsection (1), and

(c) the vehicle is so parked for no longer than is necessary and for no more than 20 minutes.

(6) The fifth exception is where—

(a) the vehicle is being used in connection with any of the following—

(i) undertaking any building operation, demolition or excavation,

(ii) the collection of waste by a local authority,

(iii) removing an obstruction to traffic,

(iv) undertaking works in relation to a road, a traffic sign or road lighting, or

(v) undertaking works in relation to a sewer or water main or in relation to the supply of gas, electricity, water or communications services,

(b) it cannot be so used without being parked as mentioned in subsection (1), and

(c) it is so parked for no longer than is necessary.

(7) In this section "carriageway", "cycle track" and "footway" have the meanings given by section 329(1) of the Highways Act 1980 (c 66).

(8) References in this section to parking include waiting, but do not include stopping where—

(a) the driver is prevented from proceeding by circumstances beyond his control or it is necessary for him to stop to avoid an accident, or

(b) the vehicle is stopped, for no longer than is necessary, for the purpose of allowing people to board or alight from it.

(9) The prohibition in this section is enforceable as if imposed—

(a) in Greater London, by an order under section 6 of the Road Traffic Regulation Act 1984 (c 27),

(b) elsewhere in England and Wales, by an order under section 1 of that Act.

[Traffic Management Act 2004, s 86.]

4–2013U   87. Guidance to local authorities

4–2013V   88. Financial provisions

4–2013W   89. Regulations and orders

4–2013X   90. Application to Crown and visiting forces.   (1) This Part does not apply in relation to a vehicle that—

(a) at the relevant time is used or appropriated for use for naval, military or airforce purposes, or

(b) belongs to any visiting forces (within the meaning of the Visiting Forces Act 1952 (c 67)) or is at the relevant time used or appropriated for use by any such forces.

(2) The provisions of this Part apply to—

(a) vehicles in the public service of the Crown that are required to be registered under the Vehicle Excise and Registration Act 1994 (c 22) (other than those exempted by subsection (1)(a) above), and

(b) persons in the public service of the Crown.

(3) This Part does not apply in relation to Crown roads within the meaning of section 131 of the Road Traffic Regulation Act 1984 (c 27) (application of road traffic enactments to Crown roads) unless applied by order under that section.

[Traffic Management Act 2004, s 90.]

4–2013Y   91. Consequential amendments

4–2013Z   92. Minor definitions.   (1) In this Part—

"appropriate national authority" means—

(a) as regards England, the Secretary of State, and

(b) as regards Wales, the National Assembly for Wales;

"approved device" means a device of a description specified in an order made by the appropriate national authority;

"fixed penalty notice" has the meaning given by section 52(1) of the Road Traffic Offenders Act 1988 (c 53);

"GLA road" means—

(a) a GLA road within the meaning of the Highways Act 1980 (c 66) (see sections 329(1) and 14D(1) of that Act), or

(b) a GLA side road within the meaning of the Road Traffic Regulation Act 1984 (c 27) (see sections 124A(9) and 142(1) of that Act);

"immobilisation device" has the same meaning as in section 104(9) of the Road Traffic Regulation Act 1984;

"local authority" means—

(a) as regards England, a county council, a London authority, a metropolitan district council or the Council of the Isles of Scilly,

(b) as regards Wales, a county or county borough council;

"London authority" means a London local authority or Transport for London;

"London local authority" means a London borough council or the Common Council of the City of London;

"operator", in relation to a vehicle, means a person who holds an operator's licence in respect of the vehicle under section 2 of the Goods Vehicles (Licensing of Operators) Act 1995 (c 23);

"owner", in relation to a vehicle, means the person by whom the vehicle is kept, which in the case of a vehicle registered under the Vehicle Excise and Registration Act 1994 (c 22) is presumed (unless the contrary is proved) to be the person in whose name the vehicle is registered;

"penalty charge" means a penalty charge imposed under this Part;

"road" has the same meaning as in the Road Traffic Regulation Act 1984;

"subordinate legislation" has the same meaning as in the Interpretation Act 1978 (c 30) (see section 21(1) of that Act);

"traffic sign" has the meaning given by section 64 of the Road Traffic Regulation Act 1984.

(2) Any reference in this Part to contravention of an order, or of provision made by or under an order, includes a failure to comply with the order or provision.

[Traffic Management Act 2004, s 92.]

4–2014 93. Index of defined expressions. In this Part the expressions listed below are defined or otherwise explained by the provisions indicated—

appropriate national authority	section 92
approved device	section 92
bus lane contravention	Part 2 of Schedule 7
civil enforcement area	Schedule 8
civil enforcement officer	Section 76
enforcement authority	Schedule 8
fixed penalty notice	section 92
GLA road	section 92
immobilisation device	section 92
local authority	section 92
London local authority	section 92
London lorry ban contravention	Part 3 of Schedule 7
moving traffic contravention	Part 4 of Schedule 7
operator	section 92
owner	section 92
parking contravention	Part 1 of Schedule 7
penalty charge	section 92
road	section 92
road traffic contravention	Schedule 7
special enforcement area	Schedule 10
subordinate legislation	section 92
traffic sign	section 92

[Traffic Management Act 2004, s 93.]

PART 7[1]

MISCELLANEOUS AND GENERAL

4–2014A 96. Wales. References in Schedule 1 to the National Assembly for Wales (Transfer of Functions) Order 1999 (SI 1999/672) to—

(*a*) the Highways Act 1980 (c 66),

(*b*) the Road Traffic Regulation Act 1984 (c 27), and

(*c*) the New Roads and Street Works Act 1991 (c 22),

are to be treated as references to those Acts as amended by this Act.

[Traffic Management Act 2004, s 96.]

---

1. Part 7 comprises ss 94–100 and Sch 12.

4–2014B 98. Repeals

4–2014C 99. Commencement, transitionals and savings. (1) The preceding provisions of this Act shall come into force on such day as the Secretary of State (as respects England) or the National Assembly for Wales (as respects Wales) may appoint by order made by statutory instrument.

(2) Different days may be appointed for different purposes.

(3) For the purposes of Part 6 (civil enforcement of road traffic contraventions), and related repeals, different days may be appointed for different areas.

(4) The Secretary of State (as respects England) or the National Assembly for Wales (as respects Wales) may by order made by statutory instrument make transitional provision or savings in connection with the coming into force of any provision of this Act.

[Traffic Management Act 2004, s 99.]

4–2014D 100. Short title and extent

Section 40

SCHEDULE 1
INCREASE IN MAXIMUM FINES FOR CERTAIN SUMMARY OFFENCES UNDER THE 1991 ACT

Provision specifying fine	Brief description of offence or offences to which the fine relates	New maximum fine
Section 51(2)	Offences under s 51(1) (prohibition of authorised street works)	level 5
Section 54(5)	Failure to comply with duties under s 54 (advance notice of certain works, etc)	level 4
Section 55(5)	Beginning to execute works in contravention of s 55 (notice of starting date of works)	level 4
Section 56(3)	Execution of works in contravention of direction under s 56 (directions as to timing of street works)	level 5
Section 57(4)	Failure to give notice in accordance with s 57 (notice of emergency works)	level 4
Section 58(6)(a)	Carrying out works in contravention of a restriction imposed under s 58 (restriction on works following substantial road works)	level 5
Section 60(3)	Failure to comply with duty under s 60(1) (general duty of undertakers to co-operate)	level 5
Section 65(4)	Failure to comply with s 65(1) or (2) (safety measures)	level 5
Section 65(6)	Interference with safety measures taken by undertaker	level 5
Section 66(2)	Failure to comply with s 66(1) (duty to carry on and complete certain street works with all reasonably practicable dispatch)	level 5
Section 67(3)	Failure to comply with s 67(1), (2) or (2C) (duties relating to the use of qualified supervisors and operatives)	level 5
Section 68(2)	Failure by undertaker to afford street authority with reasonable facilities for ascertaining whether he is complying with his duties under Part 3	level 4
Section 69(2)	Failure to comply with s 69(1) (requirements relating to street works likely to affect another person's apparatus in the street)	level 4
Section 71(5)	Failure to comply with duties under s 71 (prescribed requirements as to materials and workmanship and performance standards for reinstatements)	level 5
Section 79(4)	Failure to comply with duties under s 79(1) to (3) (records of location of apparatus)	level 5
Section 80(4)	Failure to comply with s 80(1) (duty to inform other undertaker of location of certain apparatus) or requirements imposed under s 80(2) (duties applicable where ownership of certain apparatus cannot be ascertained)	level 4
Section 83(3)	Failure by authority to comply with s 83(2) (requirements relating to certain road works likely to affect apparatus in the street)	level 4
Section 92(2)	Failure to comply with a special requirement as to the displaying of lights imposed by a transport authority under s 92(1)	level 5
Schedule 3, paragraph 5(3)	Failure to comply with obligation under paragraph 5 (obligations to give notice to street authority)	level 4
Schedule 4, paragraph 6	Execution of works in street with special engineering difficulties in contravention of paragraph 2 (requirement for agreed plan and section before executing works) or paragraph 3 (requirement to furnish plan and section after emergency works)	level 5

Provision specifying fine	Brief description of offence or offences to which the fine relates	New maximum fine
Schedule 4, paragraph 12(5)	Failure to execute works in such a street in accordance with a direction under paragraph 12	level 5
Schedule 4, paragraph 13(2)	Failure to comply with paragraph 13(1) (requirement to execute works in such a street in accordance with plan or agreed modification)	level 5

4–2014F

Section 41

SCHEDULE 2
SCHEDULE 4A TO THE NEW ROADS AND STREET WORKS ACT 1991

Section 95A

"SCHEDULE 4A
FIXED PENALTY OFFENCES UNDER PART 3

Offence	Brief description
An offence under section 54(5)	Failure to comply with duties under s 54 (advance notice of certain works, etc)
An offence under section 55(5)	Beginning to execute works in contravention of s 55 (notice of starting date)
An offence under section 55(9)	Failure to give notice in accordance with s 55(8) (notice to be given on s 55 notice ceasing to have effect)
An offence under section 57(4)	Failure to give notice in accordance with s 57 (notice of emergency works)
An offence under section 70(6) consisting of a failure to comply with subsection (3) or (4A)	Failure to comply with requirements to give notice of completion of reinstatement
An offence created by regulations made under section 74(7B)	Failure to give a notice required by regulations under s 74 (charge for occupation of the highway where works unreasonably delayed)
An offence created by regulations made under section 74A(11)	Failure to give a notice required by regulations under s 74A (charge determined by reference to duration of works)"

4–2014G

Section 41

SCHEDULE 3
SCHEDULE 4B TO THE NEW ROADS AND STREET WORKS ACT 1991

Section 95A

"SCHEDULE 4B
FIXED PENALTIES FOR CERTAIN OFFENCES UNDER PART 3

Power to give fixed penalty notices

1. (1) An authorised officer of a street authority may, if he has reason to believe that a person is committing or has committed a fixed penalty offence, give him a fixed penalty notice in relation to that offence.

(2) In this Schedule "fixed penalty notice" means a notice offering a person the opportunity of discharging any liability to conviction for a fixed penalty offence by payment of a penalty.

2. A fixed penalty notice for an offence may not be given after such time relating to the offence as the Secretary of State may by regulations prescribe.

Contents of fixed penalty notice

3. (1) A fixed penalty notice must identify the offence to which it relates and give reasonable particulars of the circumstances alleged to constitute that offence.

(2) A fixed penalty notice must also state—

(a) the amount of the penalty and the period within which it may be paid;
(b) the discounted amount and the period within which it may be paid;
(c) the person to whom and the address at which payment may be made;
(d) the method or methods by which payment may be made;
(e) the person to whom and the address at which any representations relating to the notice may be addressed;
(f) the consequences of not making a payment within the period for payment.

(3) The person specified under sub-paragraph (2)(c) must be the street authority or a person acting on their behalf.

The amount of the penalty and the period for payment

4. (1) The penalty for a fixed penalty offence is (subject to paragraph 5) such amount, not exceeding 30 per cent of the maximum fine for that offence, as may be prescribed.

(2) The period for payment of the penalty is the period of 29 days beginning with the day on which the notice is given.

(3) The street authority may extend the period for paying the penalty in any particular case if they consider it appropriate to do so.

The discounted amount

5. (1) A discounted amount is payable instead of the amount prescribed under paragraph 4(1) if payment is made before the end of the period of 15 days beginning with the day on which the notice is given.

(2) The discounted amount for a fixed penalty offence is such amount, not exceeding 25 per cent of the maximum fine for the offence, as may be prescribed.

(3) If the last day of the period specified in sub-paragraph (1) does not fall on a working day, the period for payment of the discounted amount is extended until the end of the next working day.

Effect of notice and payment of penalty

6. (1) This paragraph applies where a person is given a fixed penalty notice in respect of a fixed penalty offence.

(2) No proceedings for the offence may be commenced before the end of the period for payment of the penalty.

(3) No such proceedings may be commenced or continued if payment of the penalty is made before the end of that period or is accepted by the street authority after that time.

(4) Payment of the discounted amount only counts for the purposes of sub-paragraph (3) if it is made before the end of the period for payment of the discounted amount.

(5) In proceedings for the offence a certificate which—

(*a*) purports to be signed by or on behalf of the person having responsibility for the financial affairs of the street authority; and

(*b*) states that payment of an amount specified in the certificate was or was not received by a date so specified,

is evidence of the facts stated.

Power to withdraw notices

7. (1) If the street authority consider that a fixed penalty notice which has been given ought not to have been given, they may give to the person to whom it was given a notice withdrawing the fixed penalty notice.

(2) Where a notice under sub-paragraph (1) is given—

(*a*) the authority shall repay any amount which has been paid by way of penalty in pursuance of the fixed penalty notice; and

(*b*) no proceedings shall be commenced or continued against that person for the offence in question.

(3) The street authority shall consider any representations made by or on behalf of the recipient of a fixed penalty notice and decide in all the circumstances whether to withdraw the notice.

General and supplementary

8. The Secretary of State may, with the consent of the Treasury, make regulations about—

(*a*) the application by street authorities of fixed penalties paid under this Schedule;

(*b*) the keeping of accounts, and the preparation and publication of statements of account, relating to fixed penalties paid under this Schedule.

9. The Secretary of State may by regulations—

(*a*) prescribe circumstances in which fixed penalty notices may not be given;

(*b*) modify paragraph 4(2) or 5(1) so as to substitute a different period for the period for the time being specified there;

(*c*) prescribe the method or methods by which penalties may be paid."

4–2014H

Section 52   SCHEDULE 4
SCHEDULE 3A TO THE NEW ROADS AND STREET WORKS ACT 1991

"SCHEDULE 3A
RESTRICTION ON WORKS FOLLOWING SUBSTANTIAL STREET WORKS

Introductory

1. (1) This Schedule applies where a street authority receive a notice under section 54 or 55 that an undertaker is proposing to execute substantial street works in a highway.

(2) For the purposes of this Schedule, "substantial street works" means street works of such description as may be prescribed.

Notice by authority of proposed restriction

2. (1) The street authority may publish a notice—

(*a*) specifying the nature and location of the proposed works and the date on which it is proposed to begin them;

(*b*) stating that the authority propose to issue a direction under paragraph 4 imposing a restriction on street works;

(*c*) stating the duration of the proposed restriction and the part of the highway to which it relates;

(*d*) requiring any other undertakers who propose to execute street works in that part of the highway, and who have not already done so, to notify the authority of their proposed works within the period specified in the notice ("the notice period").

(2) The notice period shall not be less than such period as may be prescribed.

(3) A notice under this paragraph shall—

(*a*) be published in the prescribed form and manner; and

(*b*) comply with such requirements as to its form and content as may be prescribed.

(4) A copy of a notice under this paragraph shall be given to each of the following—

(*a*) where there is a public sewer in the part of the highway specified under sub-paragraph (1)(*c*), to the sewer authority;

(b) where that part of the highway is carried or crossed by a bridge vested in a transport authority, or crosses or is crossed by any other property held by or used for the purposes of a transport authority, to that authority;

(c) where in any other case that part of the highway is carried or crossed by a bridge, to the bridge authority;

(d) any person who has given notice under section 54 of his intention to execute street works in that part of the highway;

(e) any person who has apparatus in that part of the highway;

(f) any other person of a prescribed description.

(5) Notification under sub-paragraph (1)(d) shall be in such form, contain such information, and be made in such manner as may be prescribed.

(6) Section 55 does not apply in relation to works in the part of the highway specified under sub-paragraph (1)(c) that are begun between the end of the notice period and completion of the works referred to in paragraph 3(1)(a) to (c).

This sub-paragraph does not apply to cases prescribed under paragraph 3(5)(b).

Completion of notified works

3. (1) After the expiry of the notice period the street authority may issue directions to—

(a) the undertaker proposing to execute the substantial street works,

(b) any undertakers who have given notice under paragraph 2 in respect of works they propose to execute, and

(c) any undertakers who have previously given notice of works they propose to execute in the part of the highway specified under paragraph 2(1)(c).

(2) A direction to an undertaker under this paragraph is a direction as to the date on which he may begin to execute the works proposed by him.

(3) Where—

(a) a direction is given to an undertaker under this paragraph as respects the date on which he may begin to execute the works proposed by him, and

(b) he begins to execute those works before that date,

he is guilty of an offence.

(4) After the expiry of the notice period, any undertaker who, before completion of the works referred to in sub-paragraph (1)(a) to (c), executes any other street works in the part of the highway specified under paragraph 2(1)(c), commits an offence.

(5) Sub-paragraph (4) does not apply—

(a) where an undertaker executes emergency works; or

(b) in such other cases as may be prescribed.

(6) A person guilty of an offence under this paragraph is liable on summary conviction to a fine not exceeding level 5 on the standard scale.

Direction restricting further works

4. (1) After the expiry of the notice period and before completion of the works referred to in paragraph 3(1)(a) to (c) the authority may give a direction under this paragraph.

(2) A direction under this paragraph is a direction restricting the execution of street works in the part of the highway specified under paragraph 2(1)(c) for such period following completion of the works referred to in paragraph 3(1)(a) to (c) as may be specified in the direction.

(3) The duration of the period specified under sub-paragraph (2) may not exceed the duration of the restriction proposed by the authority under paragraph 2(1)(c).

(4) The period specified in a direction under this paragraph may not in any case exceed such period as may be prescribed.

(5) A direction under this paragraph shall—

(a) be given in the prescribed manner;

(b) comply with such requirements as to its form and content as may be prescribed.

(6) The street authority must send a copy of any direction under this paragraph to the persons specified in paragraph 2(4).

(7) A direction under this paragraph shall cease to have effect if the works referred to in paragraph 3(1)(a) to (c) to which it relates are not completed within such period as may be prescribed.

(8) A direction under this paragraph may be revoked at any time by the authority which gave it.

(9) Where a direction under this paragraph ceases to have effect by virtue of sub-paragraph (7), or is revoked by virtue of sub-paragraph (8), the street authority must notify the persons specified in paragraph 2(4).

(10) If the street authority decides not to give a direction under this paragraph, it must notify the persons specified in paragraph 2(4) accordingly.

Effect of direction imposing restriction

5. (1) Where a direction under paragraph 4 is in force, an undertaker may not during the period specified in the direction execute street works in the part of the highway to which the restriction relates.

(2) Sub-paragraph (1) does not apply—

(a) where an undertaker executes emergency works;

(b) where an undertaker executes works with the consent of the street authority; or

(c) in such other cases as may be prescribed.

(3) The consent of the street authority under sub-paragraph (2)(b) shall not be unreasonably withheld; and any question whether the withholding of consent is unreasonable shall be settled in such manner as may be prescribed.

(4) Regulations under sub-paragraph (3) may in particular make provision for the question referred to in that sub-paragraph to be settled—

(*a*) by arbitration;

(*b*) by a person specified by the Secretary of State on appeal by the undertaker.

(5) An undertaker who contravenes sub-paragraph (1) commits an offence and is liable on summary conviction to a fine not exceeding level 5 on the standard scale.

(6) An undertaker convicted of an offence under sub-paragraph (5) is liable to reimburse the street authority any costs reasonably incurred by them in reinstating the highway.

Supplementary

6. An undertaker shall be taken not to have failed to fulfil any statutory duty to afford a supply or service if, or to the extent that, his failure is attributable to a restriction imposed under this Schedule."

4–2014I

Section 64

SCHEDULE 5
SCHEDULE 22A TO THE HIGHWAYS ACT 1980

Section 314A

"SCHEDULE 22A
FIXED PENALTY OFFENCES UNDER PART 9

Offence	Brief description
An offence under section 139(3)	Deposit of builder's skip on highway without permission of highway authority.
An offence under section 139(4)	Failure of owner of skip to ensure skip properly lit and marked and removed as soon as practicable once filled or to ensure conditions of permission complied with.
An offence created by regulations made under section 140A, consisting of a failure to give a notice	Failure to give a notice required by regulations under s 140A (charge for occupation of the highway by builder's skip for unreasonable period).
An offence created by regulations made under section 140B, consisting of a failure to give a notice	Failure to give a notice required by regulations under s 140B (charge determined by reference to duration of occupation of the highway by builder's skip).
An offence under section 169(5)	Offences relating to the erection or retention of scaffolding etc which obstructs the highway.
An offence under section 170(1)	Mixing or depositing mortar etc on highway.
An offence under section 171(6)	Offences relating to the deposit of materials on highway or the making of temporary excavations in it.
An offence created by regulations made under section 171A, consisting of a failure to give a notice	Failure to give a notice required by regulations under s 171A (charge for occupation of the highway by scaffolding etc for unreasonable period).
An offence created by regulations made under section 171B, consisting of a failure to give a notice	Failure to give a notice required by regulations under s 171B (charge determined by reference to duration of occupation of the highway by scaffolding etc)."

4–2014J

Section 64

SCHEDULE 6
SCHEDULE 22B TO THE HIGHWAYS ACT 1980

Section 314A

"SCHEDULE 22B
FIXED PENALTIES FOR CERTAIN OFFENCES UNDER PART 9

Power to give fixed penalty notices

1. (1) An authorised officer of a highway authority may, if he has reason to believe that a person is committing or has committed a fixed penalty offence, give him a fixed penalty notice in relation to that offence.

(2) In this Schedule "fixed penalty notice" means a notice offering a person the opportunity of discharging any liability to conviction for a fixed penalty offence by payment of a penalty.

2. A fixed penalty notice for an offence may not be given after such time relating to the offence as the Secretary of State may by regulations prescribe.

Contents of fixed penalty notice

3. (1) A fixed penalty notice must identify the offence to which it relates and give reasonable particulars of the circumstances alleged to constitute that offence.

(2) A fixed penalty notice must also state—

(*a*) the amount of the penalty and the period within which it may be paid;

(*b*) the discounted amount and the period within which it may be paid;

(*c*) the person to whom and the address at which payment may be made;

(*d*) the method or methods by which payment may be made;

(*e*) the person to whom and the address at which any representations relating to the notice may be addressed;

(*f*) the consequences of not making any payment within the period for payment.

(3) The person specified under sub-paragraph (2)(*c*) must be the highway authority or a person acting on their behalf.

The amount of the penalty and the period for payment

4. (1) The penalty for a fixed penalty offence is (subject to paragraph 5) such amount, not exceeding 30 per cent of the maximum fine for that offence, as may be prescribed.

(2) The period for payment of the penalty is the period of 29 days beginning with the day on which the notice is given.

(3) The highway authority may extend the period for paying the penalty in any particular case if they consider it appropriate to do so.

The discounted amount

5. (1) A discounted amount is payable instead of the amount prescribed under paragraph 4(1) if payment is made before the end of the period of 15 days beginning with the day on which the notice is given.

(2) The discounted amount for a fixed penalty offence is such amount, not exceeding 25 per cent of the maximum fine for the offence, as may be prescribed.

(3) If the last day of the period specified in sub-paragraph (1) does not fall on a working day, the period for payment of the discounted amount is extended until the end of the next working day.

(4) In sub-paragraph (3) "working day" means a day other than a Saturday, a Sunday, Christmas Day, Good Friday or a bank holiday in the locality in which the highway in question is situated.

Effect of notice and payment of penalty

6. (1) This paragraph applies where a person is given a fixed penalty notice in respect of a fixed penalty offence.

(2) No proceedings for the offence may be commenced before the end of the period for payment of the penalty.

(3) No such proceedings may be commenced or continued if payment of the penalty is made before the end of that period or is accepted by the highway authority after that time.

(4) Payment of the discounted amount only counts for the purposes of sub-paragraph (3) if it is made before the end of the period for payment of the discounted amount.

(5) In proceedings for the offence a certificate which—

(a) purports to be signed by or on behalf of the person having responsibility for the financial affairs of the highway authority; and

(b) states that payment of an amount specified in the certificate was or was not received by a date so specified,

is evidence of the facts stated.

Power to withdraw notices

7. (1) If the highway authority consider that a fixed penalty notice which has been given ought not to have been given, they may give to the person on whom it was given a notice withdrawing the fixed penalty notice.

(2) Where a notice under sub-paragraph (1) is given—

(a) the authority shall repay any amount which has been paid by way of penalty in pursuance of the fixed penalty notice; and

(b) no proceedings may be commenced or continued against that person for the offence in question.

(3) The highway authority shall consider any representations made by or on behalf of the recipient of a fixed penalty notice and decide in all the circumstances whether to withdraw the notice.

General and supplementary

8. (1) In this Schedule "prescribed" means prescribed in regulations made by the Secretary of State.

(2) The Secretary of State may, with the consent of the Treasury, make regulations about—

(a) the application by highway authorities of fixed penalties paid under this Schedule;

(b) the keeping of accounts, and the preparation and publication of statements of account, relating to penalties paid under this Schedule.

(3) The Secretary of State may by regulations—

(a) prescribe circumstances in which fixed penalty notices may not be given;

(b) modify paragraph 4(2) or 5(1) so as to substitute a different period for the period for the time being specified there;

(c) prescribe the method or methods by which penalties may be paid.

(4) Regulations under this Schedule may—

(a) make different provision (including provision prescribing the amount of the penalty or the discounted amount) for different purposes or areas;

(b) make consequential or transitional provision.

9. Section 323(1)(b) (reckoning of periods of 8 days or less) does not apply for the purposes of this Schedule."

4–2014K

Section 73

SCHEDULE 7
ROAD TRAFFIC CONTRAVENTIONS SUBJECT TO CIVIL ENFORCEMENT

PART 1
PARKING CONTRAVENTIONS

Parking contraventions

1. References in this Part of this Act to a parking contravention shall be construed as follows.

2. (1) In Greater London there is a parking contravention in relation to a vehicle if the vehicle is stationary in a parking place and—

(a) the vehicle has been left—

(i) otherwise than as authorised by or under any order relating to the parking place, or

(ii) beyond the period of parking that has been paid for,

(b) no parking charge payable with respect to the vehicle has been paid, or

(c) there has been, with respect to the vehicle, a contravention of any provision made by or under any order relating to the parking place.

(2) In sub-paragraph (1) "parking place" means—

(a) a parking place designated by an order made under section 6, 9 or 45 of the Road Traffic Regulation Act 1984 (c 27), or

(b) an off-street parking place provided under section 32(1)(a) of that Act.

Other parking contraventions in Greater London

3. (1) In Greater London there is a parking contravention in relation to a vehicle if it is stationary in circumstances in which any of the offences listed below is committed.

(2) The offences are—

(a) an offence under section 15 of the Greater London Council (General Powers) Act 1974 (c xxiv) (parking on footways, verges, etc);

(b) an offence under section 8, 11, 16(1) or 16C of the Road Traffic Regulation Act 1984 (contravention of certain traffic orders) of contravening—

(i) a prohibition or restriction on waiting of vehicles, or

(ii) provision relating to any of the matters mentioned in paragraph 7 or 8 of Schedule 1 to that Act (conditions for loading or unloading, or delivering or collecting);

(c) an offence under section 25(5) of the Road Traffic Regulation Act 1984 of contravening regulation 18 or 20 of the Zebra, Pelican and Puffin Pedestrian Crossings Regulations and General Directions 1997 (SI 1997/2400) (prohibition on stopping vehicles on or near pedestrian crossings);

(d) an offence under section 35A(1) of the Road Traffic Regulation Act 1984 (contravention of orders relating to parking places provided under section 32 or 33 of that Act);

(e) an offence under section 61(5) of the Road Traffic Regulation Act 1984 (parking in loading areas);

(f) an offence under section 19 of the Road Traffic Act 1988 (c 52) (parking of HGVs on verges, central reservations or footways);

(g) an offence under section 21 of the Road Traffic Act 1988 (offences relating to cycle tracks) of parking a vehicle wholly or partly on a cycle track;

(h) an offence under section 36(1) of the Road Traffic Act 1988 (failure to comply with traffic sign) of failing to comply with a sign of a type referred to in—

(i) regulation 10(1)(b) of the Traffic Signs Regulations and General Directions 2002 (SI 2002/3113) (zig-zag lines relating to certain crossings), or

(ii) regulation 29(1) of those regulations (bus stop or bus stand markings).

(3) This paragraph does not apply to a contravention within paragraph 2 above (contraventions relating to parking places).

Parking contraventions outside Greater London

4. (1) Outside Greater London there is a parking contravention in relation to a vehicle if it is stationary in circumstances in which any of the offences listed below is committed.

(2) The offences are—

(a) an offence under section 64(3) of the Local Government (Miscellaneous Provisions) Act 1976 (c 57) of causing a vehicle to stop on part of a road appointed, or deemed to have been appointed, as a hackney carriage stand;

(b) an offence under section 5, 11, 16(1) or 16C of the Road Traffic Regulation Act 1984 (c 27) (contravention of certain traffic orders) of contravening a prohibition or restriction on waiting, or loading or unloading, of vehicles;

(c) an offence under section 25(5) of the Road Traffic Regulation Act 1984 of contravening regulation 18 or 20 of the Zebra, Pelican and Puffin Pedestrian Crossings Regulations and General Directions 1997 (SI 1997/2400) (prohibition on stopping vehicles on or near pedestrian crossings);

(d) an offence under section 35A(1), 47(1) or 53(5) or (6) of the Road Traffic Regulation Act 1984 (offences in connection with parking places);

(e) an offence under section 61(5) of the Road Traffic Regulation Act 1984 (parking in loading areas);

(f) an offence under section 6(6) of the Essex Act 1987 (c xx) of leaving a vehicle on any land in contravention of a prohibition under that section (prohibitions relating to verges and certain other land adjoining or accessible from highway);

(g) an offence under section 19 of the Road Traffic Act 1988 (c 52) (parking of HGVs on verges, central reservations or footways);

(h) an offence under section 21 of the Road Traffic Act 1988 (offences relating to cycle tracks) of parking a vehicle wholly or partly on a cycle track;

(i) an offence under section 36(1) of the Road Traffic Act 1988 (failure to comply with traffic sign) of failing to comply with a sign of a type referred to in—

(i) regulation 10(1)(b) of the Traffic Signs Regulations and General Directions 2002 (SI 2002/3113) (zig-zag lines relating to certain crossings), or

(ii)   regulation 29(1) of those regulations (bus stop or bus stand markings).

Power to add further offences

5. (1)   The appropriate national authority may by regulations amend paragraph 3 or 4 so as to add further offences (but only in so far as they relate to stationary vehicles).

(2)   Before making regulations amending paragraph 3 the Secretary of State shall consult—

(a)   the Commissioner of Police of the Metropolis and the Commissioner of Police for the City of London, and

(b)   such associations of London authorities (if any) as he thinks appropriate.

(3)   Before making regulations amending paragraph 4 the appropriate national authority shall consult—

(a)   such representatives of chief officers of police, and

(b)   such associations of local authorities (if any),

as the authority considers appropriate.

PART 2
BUS LANE CONTRAVENTIONS

Bus lane contraventions

6. (1)   A bus lane contravention is a contravention of any provision of a traffic order relating to the use of an area of road that is or forms part of a bus lane.

(2)   An area of road is or forms part of a bus lane if the order provides that it may be used—

(a)   only by buses (or a particular description of bus), or

(b)   only by buses (or a particular description of bus) and some other class or classes of vehicular traffic.

(3)   In this paragraph—

"bus" includes a tramcar (within the meaning of section 141A of the Road Traffic Regulation Act 1984 (c 27)) and a trolley vehicle (within the meaning of that section); and

"traffic order" means an order under section 1, 6, 9 or 14 of that Act.

PART 3
LONDON LORRY BAN CONTRAVENTIONS

London lorry ban contraventions

7. A London lorry ban contravention is a contravention of the Greater London (Restriction of Goods Vehicles) Traffic Order 1985 made by the Greater London Council under section 6 of the Road Traffic Regulation Act 1984, or any order replacing that order, as amended from time to time.

PART 4
MOVING TRAFFIC CONTRAVENTIONS

Moving traffic contraventions

8. (1)   A moving traffic contravention is—

(a)   an offence under section 36 of the Road Traffic Act 1988 (c 52) of failing to comply with the indication given by a traffic sign that is subject to civil enforcement (see paragraph 9), or

(b)   an offence of failing to comply with a traffic order in so far as it makes provision for a requirement, restriction or prohibition that is conveyed by a traffic sign subject to civil enforcement.

(2)   In sub-paragraph (1)(b) "traffic order" means an order under section 1, 6, 9, 14 or 16A of the Road Traffic Regulation Act 1984 (c 27).

(3)   If conduct is both a moving traffic contravention and a London lorry ban contravention (see Part 3 above), a penalty charge may only be imposed on the latter basis.

(4)   If in any other case the same conduct is a moving traffic contravention under sub-paragraph (1)(a) and (b), a penalty charge may be imposed on either basis but not both.

Traffic signs subject to civil enforcement

9. (1)   The table below specifies the traffic signs that are subject to civil enforcement.

(2)   In the table—

(a)   column 1 sets out the description, corresponding to the description in the Traffic Signs Regulations and General Directions 2002 (SI 2002/3113), of the requirement, restriction or prohibition conveyed by the sign, and

(b)   column 2 sets out the number given to the diagram illustrating the sign in that instrument.

(3)   References in the table to any sign include any permitted variant of that sign.

(4)   The table is as follows:

Description	Diagram number
Vehicular traffic must turn ahead in the direction indicated by the arrow	609
Vehicular traffic must comply with the requirements in regulation 15	610
No right turn for vehicular traffic	612
No left turn for vehicular traffic	613
No U-turns for vehicular traffic	614
Priority must be given to vehicles from the opposite direction	615, 615.1
No entry for vehicular traffic (when the restriction or prohibition is one that may be indicated by another traffic sign subject to civil enforcement)	616
All vehicles prohibited except non-mechanically propelled vehicles being pushed by pedestrians	617

Description	Diagram number
Entry to pedestrian zone restricted (alternative types)	618.2
Entry to and waiting in pedestrian zone restricted (alternative types)	618.3
Entry to and waiting in pedestrian zone restricted (variable message sign)	618.3A
Motor vehicles prohibited	619
Motor vehicles except solo motor cycles prohibited	619.1
Solo motor cycles prohibited	619.2
Goods vehicles exceeding the maximum gross weight indicated on the goods vehicle symbol prohibited	622.1A
One way traffic	652
Buses prohibited	952
Route for use by buses and pedal cycles only	953
Route for use by tramcars only	953.1
Route for use by pedal cycles only	955
Route for use by pedal cycles and pedestrians only	956
Route comprising two ways, for use by pedal cycles only and by pedestrians only	957
With-flow cycle lane	959.1
Contra-flow cycle lane	960.1
Box junction markings	1043, 1044

Power to amend table

10.—(1) The appropriate national authority may by regulations amend the table in paragraph 9(4) so as to add further traffic signs.

(2) A traffic sign may only be added to the table if it is of a type—

(a) regulating the movement of vehicles (and not stationary vehicles),

(b) to which section 36 of the Road Traffic Act 1988 (c 52) applies (offence of failure to comply with traffic sign), and

(c) failure to comply with which is not an offence involving obligatory endorsement.

In paragraph (c) "offence involving obligatory endorsement" has the meaning given by section 96 of the Road Traffic Offenders Act 1988 (c 53).

(3) Before making regulations under this paragraph the appropriate national authority shall consult—

(a) such representatives of chief officers of police, and

(b) such associations of local authorities (if any),

as the authority considers appropriate.

4–2014L   SCHEDULE 8
CIVIL ENFORCEMENT AREAS AND ENFORCEMENT AUTHORITIES

4–2014M   SCHEDULE 9
CIVIL ENFORCEMENT: SETTING THE LEVEL OF CHARGES

4–2014N   SCHEDULE 10
CIVIL ENFORCEMENT: SPECIAL ENFORCEMENT AREAS

4–2014O
Section 91   SCHEDULE 11
CIVIL ENFORCEMENT: CONSEQUENTIAL AMENDMENTS

Road Traffic Regulation Act 1984

1.—(1) Section 46 of the Road Traffic Regulation Act 1984 (c 27) (charges at, and regulation of, designated parking places) is amended as follows.

(2) In subsection (1) after "outside Greater London" insert ", and not in a civil enforcement area for parking contraventions,".

(3) In subsection (1A) after "in Greater London" insert ", or outside Greater London in a civil enforcement area for parking contraventions,".

(4) After subsection (5) add—

"(6) In this section "civil enforcement area for parking contraventions" has the same meaning as in Part 6 of the Traffic Management Act 2004.".

2. In section 63A of the Road Traffic Regulation Act 1984 (parking attendants), for subsection (4) (requirement to wear uniform) substitute—

"(4) Parking attendants in an area that is a civil enforcement area for parking contraventions—

(a) when exercising prescribed functions must wear such uniform as may be determined by the enforcement authority in accordance with guidance issued by the appropriate national authority, and

(b) must not exercise any of those functions when not in uniform.

Expressions used in this subsection that are defined for the purposes of Part 6 of the Traffic Management Act 2004 have the same meaning as in that Part.".

3.—(1) In section 101 of the Road Traffic Regulation Act 1984 (disposal of vehicles removed under that Act)—

(a) in subsection (1) (power of competent authority to dispose of vehicle) for "Subject to subsections (3) to (5A) below" substitute "Subject to subsection (3) and section 101A below";

(b) omit subsections (4) to (6) (right of owner to recover vehicle or proceeds of sale).

(2) After that section insert—

"**101A. Right of owner to recover vehicle or proceeds of sale.**—(1) If before a vehicle is disposed of by an authority under section 101 above it is claimed by a person who—

(*a*) satisfies the authority that he is its owner, and
(*b*) pays the relevant charges,

the authority shall permit him to remove the vehicle from their custody within such period as they may specify or, in the case of an authority other than a local authority, as may be prescribed.

(2) If before the end of the period of one year beginning with the date on which a vehicle is sold by an authority under section 101 above a person satisfies the authority that at the time of the sale he was the owner of the vehicle, the authority shall pay him any sum by which the proceeds of sale exceed the amount of the relevant charges.

(3) In the case of a vehicle found in an area that is a civil enforcement area for parking contraventions, the relevant charges are—

(*a*) any penalty charge payable in respect of the parking of the vehicle in the place from which it was removed,
(*b*) such unpaid earlier penalty charges relating to the vehicle as may be prescribed, and
(*c*) such sums in respect of the removal and storage of the vehicle—

(i) as the authority may require in accordance with Schedule 9 of the Traffic Management Act 2004, or
(ii) in the case of an authority other than a local authority, as may be prescribed.

(4) In any other case the relevant charges are such sums in respect of the removal and storage of the vehicle as may be prescribed.

(5) If in the case of any vehicle it appears to the authority in question that more than one person is or was its owner at the relevant time, such one of them as the authority think fit shall be treated as its owner for the purposes of this section.

(6) In this section—

"civil enforcement area for parking contraventions" and "penalty charge" have the same meaning as in Part 6 of the Traffic Management Act 2004; and

"owner" has the same meaning as in section 101 above.

101B. Representations and appeals. (1) The Lord Chancellor may make regulations entitling a person who in the case of a vehicle found in an area that is a civil enforcement area for parking contraventions—

(*a*) is required to pay an amount on recovering the vehicle under section 101A(1), or
(*b*) receives a sum in respect of the vehicle under section 101A(2) or is informed that the proceeds of sale did not exceed the aggregate amount mentioned in that provision,

to make representations to the authority concerned and to appeal to an adjudicator if his representations are not accepted.

(2) The regulations may make such provision in connection with the rights conferred as appears to the Lord Chancellor to be appropriate, and may in particular make provision—

(*a*) requiring the authority to give a person notice of the rights conferred by the regulations,
(*b*) as to the grounds on which, and time within which, representations may be made;
(*c*) requiring supporting evidence in such circumstances as may be specified;
(*d*) as to the duties of the authority when representations are received;
(*e*) as to the circumstances in which there is a right of appeal to an adjudicator,
(*f*) generally as to the making, determination and effect of, and procedure in connection with, such appeals, and
(*g*) enabling an adjudicator to review any decision made on, or in the course of, an appeal.

(3) The regulations may include provision authorising an adjudicator to require a person—

(*a*) to attend to give evidence at the hearing of an appeal, and
(*b*) to produce any documents in his custody or under his control relating to any matter relevant for the purposes of the appeal,

and making it a criminal offence triable summarily and punishable with a fine not exceeding level 2 on the standard scale to fail to comply with such a requirement.

(4) The regulations may include provision authorising an adjudicator to make an order for the payment of costs and expenses by a party to an appeal in such circumstances as may be specified.

(5) The functions of adjudicators under this section shall be discharged by the persons appointed as adjudicators for the purposes of Part 6 of the Traffic Management Act 2004 (civil enforcement of road traffic contraventions) and any arrangements made for the discharge of their functions under that Part also have effect for the purposes of this section.".

4. (1) Section 102 of the Road Traffic Regulation Act 1984 (c 27) (charges for removal, storage and disposal of vehicles) is amended as follows.

(2) For subsection (2) (recovery of charges) substitute—

"(2) If the place from which the vehicle is removed is in an area that is not a civil enforcement area for parking contraventions—

(*a*) the appropriate authority is entitled to recover from any person responsible such charges as may be prescribed in respect of the removal of the vehicle;
(*b*) the chief officer of a police force or a local authority in whose custody the vehicle is during any period is entitled to recover from any person responsible charges ascertained by reference to a prescribed scale in respect of that period; and
(*c*) the chief officer of a police force or a local authority who dispose of the vehicle in pursuance of section 101 of this Act is entitled to recover from any person responsible charges determined in the prescribed manner in respect of its disposal.

(2A) If the place from which the vehicle is removed is in an area that is a civil enforcement area for parking contraventions, the enforcement authority is entitled to recover from any person responsible such charges in respect of the removal, storage and disposal of the vehicle as they may require in accordance with Schedule 9 of the Traffic Management Act 2004.".

(3) In subsection (8) (interpretation) at the appropriate place insert—

""civil enforcement area for parking contraventions" and "enforcement authority" have the same meaning as in Part 6 of the Traffic Management Act 2004;";

(4) In subsection (9) (application of provisions to parking places provided under letting or other arrangements), for "subsection (2)(*d*)" substitute "subsection (2A)".

Tribunals and Inquiries Act 1992

5. In Part 1 of Schedule 1 to the Tribunals and Inquiries Act 1992 (c 53) (tribunals under direct supervision of Council on Tribunals), in paragraph 40 (road traffic) for sub-paragraph (*b*) substitute—

"(*b*) an adjudicator appointed for the purposes of Part 6 of the Traffic Management Act 2004 (civil enforcement of road traffic contraventions).".

London Local Authorities Act 1995

6. In the London Local Authorities Act 1995 (c x)—

(*a*) in section 2 (interpretation), for the definition of "special parking area" substitute—

""special enforcement area" means a special enforcement area designated by order of the Secretary of State under Schedule 10 of the Traffic Management Act 2004;";

(*b*) in section 9(1) (special temporary prohibitions) for "special parking area" substitute "special enforcement area".

London Local Authorities and Transport for London Act 2003

7. In section 20 of the London Local Authorities and Transport for London Act 2003 (c iii) (disclosure of information about identity of owner of vehicle), in subsection (2) (enactments for purposes of which disclosure may be made) for paragraphs (*b*) to (*d*) substitute—

"(*b*) Part 6 of the Traffic Management Act 2004 (civil enforcement of road traffic contraventions).".

4–2014P

Section 98

SCHEDULE 12
REPEALS
PART 1
CIVIL ENFORCEMENT

Short title and chapter	Extent of repeal
Road Traffic Regulation Act 1984 (c 27)	Section 8(1A) and (1B). Section 11(2) and (2A). In section 47(1), the words "; but this subsection does not apply in relation to any designated parking place in Greater London". Section 101(4) to (6). In section 102(8), the definition of "London authority" and the word "and" preceding it.
Road Traffic Act 1988 (c 52)	Section 36(1A).
Road Traffic Act 1991 (c 40)	Section 43. Sections 65 to 67. Section 68(2) and (3)(*c*). Sections 69 to 74A. Sections 76 to 79. Schedule 3. Schedule 6.
Local Government Wales Act 1994 (c 19)	In Schedule 7, paragraph 43(*b*).
London Local Authorities Act 1995 (c x)	Sections 4, 5, 7 and 8.
Greater London Authority Act 1999 (c 29)	Section 283(2) and (4). Section 284. Section 286.
Transport Act 2000 (c 38)	Section 144.
London Local Authorities Act 2000 (c vii)	In section 3(1), the definition of "special parking area". Sections 4 to 14.
London Local Authorities and Transport for London Act 2003 (c iii)	Sections 4 to 7. Sections 14 and 15. Schedule 1. In Schedule 2— (*a*) in the heading, the words from "4" to "and"; (*b*) paragraph 1(*a*); (*c*) paragraphs 5 and 6. Schedule 3.

Road Safety Act 2006[1]
(2006 c 49)

Payments for road safety

4–2014Q 1. Road safety grants. *Substitutes s 40 of the Road Traffic Act 1988.*

[Road Safety Act 2006, s 1.]

---

1. This Act is to be brought into force in accordance with the provisions of s 61 and commencement orders made thereunder. Sections 51, 58 and 60 and Sch 7 came into force on 8 November 2006 and ss 1 and 49 came into force on 8 February 2007. At the date of going to press, the following commencement orders had been made: (No 1) Order 2007, SI 2007/237, (No 1) (England and Wales) Order 2007, SI 2007/466.

4–2014R 2. Application of surplus income from safety camera enforcement. (1) Section 38 of the Vehicles (Crime) Act 2001 (c 3) (unified power for Secretary of State to fund speed cameras etc) is amended as follows.

(2) In subsections (3) and (4), for "this section" substitute "subsection (1)".

(3) After subsection (4) insert—

"(4A) The Secretary of State may by regulations make provision for making to public authorities for road safety purposes payments calculated by reference to any amount by which—

(*a*) the amount of the sums paid into the Consolidated Fund in consequence of the commission of offences to which subsection (2) applies and which are detected by cameras, exceeds

(*b*) the amount of any payments made under subsection (1)."

[Road Safety Act 2006, s 2.]

Fixed penalties

4–2014S 3. Graduated fixed penalties. (1) The Road Traffic Offenders Act 1988 (c 53) is amended as follows.

(2) In section 53 (amount of fixed penalty), for subsections (2) and (3) substitute—

"(2) Any order made under subsection (1)(*a*) above in relation to an offence may make provision for the fixed penalty for the offence to be different depending on the circumstances, including (in particular)—

(*a*) the nature of the contravention or failure constituting the offence,

(*b*) how serious it is,

(*c*) the area, or sort of place, where it takes place, and

(*d*) whether the offender appears to have committed any offence or offences of a description specified in the order during a period so specified."

(3) In section 84(2) (regulations about surcharge notices), for paragraphs (*b*) and (*c*) substitute

"and

(*b*) the amount of the penalty stated in the offer is less than the fixed penalty applicable in the circumstances,".

[Road Safety Act 2006, s 3.]

4–2014T 4. Graduated fixed penalty points. (1) Section 28 of the Road Traffic Offenders Act 1988 (penalty points to be attributed to an offence) is amended as follows.

(2) For subsection (3) substitute—

"(3) For the purposes of sections 57(5) and 77(5) of this Act, the number of penalty points to be attributed to an offence is—

(*a*) where both a range of numbers and a number followed by the words " (fixed penalty)" is shown in the last column of Part 1 of Schedule 2 to this Act in relation to the offence, that number,

(*b*) where a range of numbers followed by the words "or appropriate penalty points (fixed penalty)" is shown there in relation to the offence, the appropriate number of penalty points for the offence, and

(*c*) where only a range of numbers is shown there in relation to the offence, the lowest number in the range.

(3A) For the purposes of subsection (3)(*b*) above the appropriate number of penalty points for an offence is such number of penalty points as the Secretary of State may by order made by statutory instrument prescribe.

(3B) An order made under subsection (3A) above in relation to an offence may make provision for the appropriate number of penalty points for the offence to be different depending on the circumstances, including (in particular)—

(*a*) the nature of the contravention or failure constituting the offence,

(*b*) how serious it is,

(*c*) the area, or sort of place, where it takes place, and (*d*) whether the offender appears to have committed any offence or offences of a description specified in the order during a period so specified."

(3) In subsection (7), in paragraph (*b*), after "penalty)" insert "or the words "or appropriate penalty points (fixed penalty)" ".

(4) Before the word "and" at the end of that paragraph insert—

"(ba)substitute the words "or appropriate penalty points (fixed penalty)" for a number together with the words " (fixed penalty)", or substitute a number together with the words " (fixed penalty)" for the words "or appropriate penalty points (fixed penalty)", in relation to an offence in the last column of Part 1 or 2,".

(5) After subsection (8) insert—

"(8A) Before making any order under subsection (3A) above the Secretary of State must consult with such representative organisations as he thinks fit."

(6) In subsection (9), for "subsection (7) above" substitute "this section".

[Road Safety Act 2006, s 4.]

4–2014U   5. Giving of fixed penalty notices by vehicle examiners.   Schedule 1 contains provision about the giving of fixed penalty notices by vehicle examiners and connected matters.

[Road Safety Act 2006, s 5.]

4–2014V   6. Goods vehicles operator licensing.   (1) The Goods Vehicles (Licensing of Operators) Act 1995 (c 23) is amended as follows.

(2) In subsection (1) of section 9 (duty of applicant for operator's licence to notify traffic commissioner of notifiable conviction subsequent to making of application), insert at the end "or there is issued a notifiable fixed penalty notice within the meaning given in paragraph 7 of that Schedule."

(3) In subsection (3)(*b*) of that section (offence of failing to notify conviction of transport manager), insert at the end "or the issue to the transport manager of a fixed penalty notice or conditional offer under Part 3 of the Road Traffic Offenders Act 1988 in respect of such an offence."

(4) In subsection (1) of section 26 (revocation, suspension and curtailment of operators' licences), after paragraph (*c*) insert—

"(ca)that during those five years a fixed penalty notice or conditional offer has been issued under Part 3 of the Road Traffic Offenders Act 1988 to the licence-holder in respect of an offence within sub-paragraph (i) of paragraph (*c*) or to a servant or agent of the licence-holder in respect of an offence within sub-paragraph (ii) of that paragraph;".

(5) In paragraph (*d*) of that subsection, insert at the end "or an issue of a fixed penalty notice or conditional offer under Part 3 of the Road Traffic Offenders Act 1988 to the licence-holder or a servant or agent of his in respect of such an offence;".

(6) In paragraph 1 of Schedule 2 (information about, and convictions of, applicants for and holders of operators' licences), after paragraph (*f*) insert—

"(fa)particulars of any notifiable fixed penalty notices which have been issued during those five years;".

(7) After paragraph 6 of that Schedule insert—

7. ""Notifiable fixed penalty notices".   In paragraph 1(fa) "notifiable fixed penalty notice" means any fixed penalty notice or conditional offer under Part 3 of the Road Traffic Offenders Act 1988—

(*a*) issued to a relevant person in respect of an offence such as is mentioned in paragraph 5, or

(*b*) issued to a servant or agent of a relevant person in respect of an offence within paragraph 4(*b*)."

[Road Safety Act 2006, s 6.]

4–2014W   7. Public passenger vehicle licensing.   (1) The Public Passenger Vehicles Act 1981 (c 14) is amended as follows.

(2) In section 19 (duty of applicant for PSV operator's licence to inform traffic commissioners of relevant convictions etc), after subsection (2) insert—

"(2A) For the purposes of subsections (1) and (2) above the issue to a person of a fixed penalty notice or conditional offer under Part 3 of the Road Traffic Offenders Act 1988 in respect of an offence prescribed for the purposes of this Act is to be treated as if it were a relevant conviction of him."

(3) In sub-paragraph (1) of paragraph 1 of Schedule 3 (supplementary provisions as to qualifications for PSV operator's licence), before the word "and" at the end of paragraph (*a*) insert—

"(aa)relevant fixed penalty notices issued to him and to his employees and agents;".

(4) In sub-paragraph (2) of that paragraph, before the word "and" at the end of paragraph (*a*) insert—

"(aa)relevant fixed penalty notices issued to the company's officers, employees and agents;".

(5) After that sub-paragraph insert—

"(2A) In sub-paragraphs (1)(aa) and (2)(aa) above "relevant fixed penalty notice" means a fixed penalty notice or conditional offer issued under Part 3 of the Road Traffic Offenders Act 1988 in respect of an offence prescribed for the purposes of this Act."

[Road Safety Act 2006, s 7.]

New system of endorsement

4–2014X   8.   Driving record.   *Inserts s 97A into the Road Traffic Offenders Act 1988.*

4–2014Y   9.   Unlicensed and foreign drivers.   (1) The Road Traffic Offenders Act 1988 is amended as follows.

(2) In section 44 (endorsement of licences)—

(*a*) after subsection (3) insert—

"(3A) Where a person who is not the holder of a licence is convicted of an offence involving obligatory endorsement, subsection (1) above applies as if the reference to the counterpart of any licence held by him were a reference to his driving record.", and

(*b*) for the heading substitute **"Orders for endorsement"**.

(3) *Inserts s 44A into the Road Traffic Offenders Act 1988.*

(4) In section 54 (notices on-the-spot etc), after subsection (5) insert—

"(5A) Where the offence appears to the constable or vehicle examiner to involve obligatory endorsement, and the person is not the holder of a licence, the constable or vehicle examiner may only give him a fixed penalty notice under subsection (2) above in respect of the offence if the constable or vehicle examiner is satisfied, on accessing information held on his driving record, that he would not be liable to be disqualified under section 35 of this Act if he were convicted of that offence.

(5B) Subsection (5C) below applies where—

(*a*) the offence appears to the constable or vehicle examiner to involve obligatory endorsement,
(*b*) the person concerned is not the holder of a licence, and
(*c*) the constable or vehicle examiner is unable to satisfy himself, by accessing information held on his driving record, that he would not be liable to be disqualified under section 35 of this Act if he were convicted of that offence.

(5C) Where this subsection applies, the constable or vehicle examiner may give the person a notice stating that if—

(*a*) he delivers the notice in accordance with subsection (5D) below, and
(*b*) the person to whom it is delivered is satisfied, on accessing information held on his driving record, that he would not be liable to be disqualified under section 35 of this Act if he were convicted of the offence,

he will then be given a fixed penalty notice in respect of the offence.

(5D) Delivery must—

(*a*) if the notice is given by a constable, be made in person, within seven days after the notice is given, to a constable or authorised person at the police station specified in the notice (being a police station chosen by the person concerned), or
(*b*) if the notice is given by a vehicle examiner, be made (either by post or in person), within fourteen days after the notice is given, to the Secretary of State at the place specified in the notice.

(5E) If a person to whom a notice has been given under subsection (5C) above delivers the notice in accordance with subsection (5D) above, and the person to whom it is delivered is satisfied, on accessing information held on his driving record, that he would not be liable to be disqualified under section 35 of this Act if he were convicted of the offence, that person must give him a fixed penalty notice in respect of the offence to which the notice under subsection (5C) relates."

(5) *Inserts s 57A into the Road Traffic Offenders Act 1988.*

(6) Schedule 2 contains further amendments about the endorsement of driving records in the case of unlicensed and certain foreign drivers.

[Road Safety Act 2006, s 9.]

4–2014Z   10.   All drivers.   (1) The Road Traffic Offenders Act 1988 (c 53) (as amended by section 9 and Schedule 2) is amended as follows.

(2) In section 44 (orders for endorsement)—

(*a*) in subsection (1), for "the counterpart of any licence held by him" substitute "his driving record", and
(*b*) omit subsection (3A).

(3) Section 54 (notices on-the-spot etc) is amended as follows.

(4) For subsections (3) to (5E) substitute—

"(3) Where the offence appears to the constable or vehicle examiner to involve obligatory endorsement, the constable or vehicle examiner may only give him a fixed penalty notice under subsection (2) above in respect of the offence if—

(a) the constable or vehicle examiner is satisfied, on accessing information held on his driving record, that he would not be liable to be disqualified under section 35 of this Act if he were convicted of that offence, and

(b) in the case of a person who is the holder of a licence, he produces it for inspection by the constable or vehicle examiner and surrenders it to him to be retained and dealt with in accordance with this Part of this Act.

(4) Where the offence appears to the constable or vehicle examiner to involve obligatory endorsement, subsection (5) below applies if—

(a) the constable or vehicle examiner is unable to satisfy himself, by accessing information held on his driving record, that he would not be liable to be disqualified under section 35 of this Act if he were convicted of that offence, or

(b) in the case of a person who is the holder of a licence, he does not produce it for inspection by the constable or vehicle examiner.

(5) Where this subsection applies, the constable or vehicle examiner may give the person a notice stating that if—

(a) he delivers the notice and (if he is the holder of a licence) his licence in accordance with subsection (5A) below, and

(b) the requirements of subsection (5B) below are met,

he will then be given a fixed penalty notice in respect of the offence.

(5A) Delivery must—

(a) if the notice is given by a constable, be made in person, within seven days after the notice is given, to a constable or authorised person at the police station specified in the notice (being a police station chosen by the person concerned), or

(b) if the notice is given by a vehicle examiner, be made (either by post or in person), within fourteen days after the notice is given, to the Secretary of State at the place specified in the notice.

(5B) If a person to whom a notice has been given under subsection (5) above delivers the notice and (if he is the holder of a licence) his licence in accordance with subsection (5A) above, and the following requirements are met, that is—

(a) the person to whom the notice is delivered is satisfied, on accessing information held on his driving record, that he would not be liable to be disqualified under section 35 of this Act if he were convicted of the offence, and

(b) if he is the holder of a licence, it is delivered to be retained and dealt with in accordance with this Part of this Act,

the person to whom the notice is delivered must give him a fixed penalty notice in respect of the offence to which the notice under subsection (5) above relates."

(5) In subsection (6), for " (4) or (5C)" substitute " (5)".

(6) In subsection (7), omit "and a counterpart of a licence".

(7) Omit section 57 (endorsement of counterparts without hearings).

(8) Section 57A (endorsement of driving records without hearings) is amended as follows.

(9) In subsection (1), omit "who is not the holder of a licence".

(10) In subsection (3), at the end insert "and return to that person any licence surrendered by him under section 54 of this Act."

(11) In subsection (4), after "record" insert "and return to that person any licence surrendered by him under section 54 of this Act".

(12) Schedule 3 contains further amendments about the endorsement of driving records in the case of all drivers.

[Road Safety Act 2006, s 10.]

Deposits and prohibition on driving

4–2015 11. Financial penalty deposits. (1) *Inserts Part 3A into the Road Traffic Offenders Act 1988.*

(2) In Part 1 of Schedule 2 to the Road Traffic Offenders Act 1988 (c 53) (prosecution and punishment of offences: offences under the Traffic Acts), after the entry relating to section 67 of that Act insert—

| "Section 90D(6) of this Act | Driving, etc, vehicle in contravention of prohibition for failure to pay financial penalty deposit, etc | Summarily. | Level 5 on the standard scale. | | " |

(3) Schedule 4 makes provision about the immobilisation of vehicles the driving of which has been prohibited and about their removal and disposal.

[Road Safety Act 2006, s 11.]

4–2015A 12. Prohibition on driving: immobilisation, removal and disposal of vehicles. (1) In section 99A of the Transport Act 1968 (c 73) (powers to prohibit driving of vehicles in connection with contravention of provisions about drivers' hours), after subsection (5) insert—

"(6) Schedule 4 to the Road Safety Act 2006 makes provision about the immobilisation of vehicles the driving of which has been prohibited under subsection (1) of this section and about their removal and disposal."

(2) In section 3 of the Road Traffic (Foreign Vehicles) Act 1972 (c 27) (prohibition on driving of foreign vehicles: enforcement provisions), after subsection (7) insert—

"(8) Schedule 4 to the Road Safety Act 2006 makes provision about the immobilisation of vehicles the driving of which has been prohibited under section 1 of this Act and about their removal and disposal."

(3) In section 73 of the Road Traffic Act 1988 (c 52) (prohibition on driving of unfit or overloaded vehicles: supplementary provisions), after subsection (4) insert—

"(5) Schedule 4 to the Road Safety Act 2006 makes provision about the immobilisation of vehicles the driving of which has been prohibited under section 69 or 70 of this Act and about their removal and disposal."

[Road Safety Act 2006, s 12.]

Drink-driving etc

4–2015B 13. High risk offenders: medical enquiries following disqualification. (1) In section 88 of the Road Traffic Act 1988 (exceptions to requirement to hold driving licence), after subsection (2) insert—

"(2A) Subsection (1) above does not apply by virtue of an application mentioned in paragraph (*b*) of that subsection having been received by the Secretary of State if—

(*a*) the application was made as a result of, or in anticipation of, the expiry of a disqualification relevant to the licence applied for,

(*b*) either the nature of the disqualification or its imposition within a particular period after an earlier disqualification amounted to circumstances prescribed under subsection (4) of section 94 of this Act (disqualification: high risk offenders), and

(*c*) the Secretary of State has notified the applicant that, because of that, he will be subject to a requirement under paragraph (*a*) or (*b*) of subsection (5) of that section."

(2) The amendment made by subsection (1) does not apply where the conviction in respect of which the disqualification was ordered was imposed before the coming into force of that subsection.

[Road Safety Act 2006, s 13.]

4–2015C 14. Period of endorsement for failure to allow specimen to be tested. In section 45(7) of the Road Traffic Offenders Act 1988 (c 53) (effect of endorsement: period for which effective), after paragraph (*b*) insert

"or

(*c*) under section 7A(6) of that Act (failing to allow a specimen to be subjected to laboratory test),".

[Road Safety Act 2006, s 14.]

4–2015D 15. Alcohol ignition interlocks. (1), (2) *Insert ss 34D–34G and 41B into the Road Traffic Offenders Act 1988.*

(3) In Schedule 1 to that Act (offences to which certain sections apply)—

(*a*) in paragraph 3, after paragraph (*a*) insert—

"(aa) an offence under section 34D(12) of this Act,", and

(*b*) in paragraph 4, before paragraph (*a*) insert—

"(za) an offence under section 34D(12) of this Act,".

(4) In Part 1 of Schedule 2 to that Act (prosecution and punishment of offences: offences under the Traffic Acts), after the entry relating to section 27 of that Act insert—

"Section 34D(12) of this Act	Interference etc with alcohol ignition interlock.	Summarily.	Level 4 on the standard scale if the motor vehicle to which the alcohol ignition interlock is fitted is a oods vehicle or a vehicle adapted to carry more than eight passengers. Level 3 on the standard scale in any other case."		

[Road Safety Act 2006, s 15.]

4–2015E   16. Experimental period for section 15.   (1) Subject as follows, no order shall be made under section 34D of the Road Traffic Offenders Act 1988 (c 53) (inserted by section 15) after—

(a) the end of 2010, or
(b) such later time as may be specified in an order made by the Secretary of State.

(2) But at any time before the restriction imposed by subsection (1) has taken effect, the Secretary of State may by order provide that it shall not do so.
(3)–(9) *Further provisions as to orders.*

[Road Safety Act 2006, s 16.]

Speeding

4–2015F   17. Penalty points.   In Part 1 of Schedule 2 to the Road Traffic Offenders Act 1988 (c 53) (prosecution and punishment of offences: offences under the Traffic Acts), in column (7) (penalty points)—

(a) for the entry relating to section 17(4) of the Road Traffic Regulation Act 1984 (c 27) (traffic regulation on special roads), substitute "2–6 or appropriate penalty points (fixed penalty) if committed in respect of a speed limit, 3 in any other case", and
(b) for the entry relating to section 89(1) of that Act (speeding offences other than those on special roads), substitute "2–6 or appropriate penalty points (fixed penalty)".

[Road Safety Act 2006, s 17.]

4–2015G   18. Speed assessment equipment detection devices.   (1) In section 41 of the Road Traffic Act 1988 (c 52) (regulation of construction, weight, equipment and use of vehicles)—

(a) in subsection (2), at the end insert—

"(m)speed assessment equipment detection devices.", and
(b) in subsection (7), at the end insert—

""speed assessment equipment detection device" means a device the purpose, or one of the purposes, of which is to detect, or interfere with the operation of, equipment used to assess the speed of motor vehicles."

(2) *Inserts s 41C into the Road Traffic Offenders Act 1988.*
(3) In section 42(a) of that Act (breach of other construction and use requirements), for "or 41B(1)(a)" substitute ", 41B(1)(a), 41C(a)".
(4) In section 98(1) of the Road Traffic Offenders Act 1988 (c 53) (interpretation), at the appropriate place insert—

""special road" in England and Wales has the same meaning as in the Highways Act 1980 and in Scotland has the same meaning as in the Roads (Scotland) Act 1984,".

(5) In Schedule 1 to that Act (offences to which certain sections apply), after the entry relating to section 41B of the Road Traffic Act 1988 (c 52) insert—

"RTA section 41C	Breach of requirement as to speed assessment equipment detection device.	Sections 11 and 12(1) of t Act."

(6) In Part 1 of Schedule 2 to that Act (prosecution and punishment of offences: offences under the Traffic Acts), after the entry relating to section 41B of the Road Traffic Act 1988 insert—

"RTA section 41C	Breach of requirement as to speed assessment equipment detection devices.	Summarily.	(*a*) Level 4 on the standard scale if committed on a special road. (*b*) Level 3 on the standard scale in any other case.	Discretionary.	Obligatory.	3–6 or 3 (fixed penalty)."

(7) In Schedule 3 to that Act (fixed penalty offences), after the entry relating to section 41B of the Road Traffic Act 1988 insert—

[Road Safety Act 2006, s 18.]

4–2015H **19. Exemptions from speed limits.** For section 87 of the Road Traffic Regulation Act 1984 (c 27) (exemption of fire, ambulance and police vehicles from speed limits) substitute—

87. "Exemptions from speed limits. (1) No statutory provision imposing a speed limit on motor vehicles shall apply to any vehicle on an occasion when—

(*a*) it is being used for fire and rescue authority purposes or for or in connection with the exercise of any function of a relevant authority as defined in section 6 of the Fire (Scotland) Act 2005, for ambulance purposes or for police or Serious Organised Crime Agency purposes,

(*b*) it is being used for other prescribed purposes in such circumstances as may be prescribed, or

(*c*) it is being used for training persons to drive vehicles for use for any of the purposes mentioned in paragraph (*a*) or (*b*) above,

if the observance of that provision would be likely to hinder the use of the vehicle for the purpose for which it is being used on that occasion.

(2) Subsection (1) above does not apply unless the vehicle is being driven by a person who—

(*a*) has satisfactorily completed a course of training in the driving of vehicles at high speed provided in accordance with regulations under this section, or

(*b*) is driving the vehicle as part of such a course.

(3) The Secretary of State may by regulations make provision about courses of training in the driving of vehicles at high speed.

(4) The regulations may include—

(*a*) provision about the nature of courses,

(*b*) provision for the approval by the Secretary of State of persons providing courses or giving instruction on courses and the withdrawal of approvals (including provision for appeals against refusal and withdrawal of approvals),

(*c*) provision specifying the maximum fees that a person may be required to pay for a course,

(*d*) provision for the training or assessment, or the supervision of the training or assessment, of persons providing courses or giving instruction on courses,

(*e*) provision for the evidencing of the successful completion of courses,

(*f*) provision authorising the Secretary of State to make available information about persons providing courses or giving instruction on courses, and

(*g*) provision treating courses of training in the driving of vehicles at high speed which have been completed before the coming into force of the regulations as if they had been provided in accordance with the regulations.

(5) The regulations may include provision for the charging of reasonable fees in respect of any function conferred or imposed on the Secretary of State by the regulations.

(6) The regulations may make different provision—

(*a*) for different classes of vehicle,

(*b*) for different descriptions of persons, or

(*c*) otherwise for different circumstances."

[Road Safety Act 2006, s 19.]

New offences

4–2015I **20. Causing death by careless, or inconsiderate, driving.** (1) *Inserts s 2B into the Road Traffic Act 1988.*

(2) In section 24(1) of the Road Traffic Offenders Act 1988 (c 53) (alternative verdicts), in the Table—

(a) in the entry relating to section 1 of the Road Traffic Act 1988 (c 52) (causing death by dangerous driving), in the second column, after "Section 2 (dangerous driving)" insert "Section 2B (causing death by careless, or inconsiderate, driving)",

(b) after the entry relating to section 2 of that Act insert—

"Section 2B (causing death by careless, or inconsiderate, driving)	Section 3 (careless, and inconsiderate, driving),"

(c) in the entry relating to section 3A of that Act (causing death by careless driving when under influence of drink or drugs), in the second column, before "Section 3 (careless, and inconsiderate, driving)" insert "Section 2B (causing death by careless, or inconsiderate, driving)".

(3) In Schedule 1 to the Road Traffic Offenders Act 1988 (offences to which certain sections apply), after the entry relating to section 2 of the Road Traffic Act 1988 insert—

"RTA section 2B	Causing death by careless, or inconsiderate, driving.	Sections 11 and 12(1) of this Act."

(4) In Part 1 of Schedule 2 to that Act (prosecution and punishment of offences: offences under the Traffic Acts), after the entry relating to section 2 of the Road Traffic Act 1988 insert—

"RTA section 2B	Causing death by careless, or inconsiderate, driving.	(a) Summarily. (b) On indictment	(a) 12 months (in England and Wales) or 6 months (in Scotland) or the statutory maximum or both. (b) 5 years or a fine or both.	Obligatory.	Obligatory.	3–11"

(5) In sections 16(1)(a)(ii) and 17(1)(b) and (2)(b) of the Coroners Act 1988 (c 13) (informing coroners)—

(a) after "1" insert ", 2B", and

(b) after "dangerous driving" insert ", careless driving".

(6) In paragraph 3 of Schedule 3 to the Crime (International Co-operation) Act 2003 (c 32) (offences where notice must be given to authority of State in which offender is normally resident), after paragraph (b) insert—

"(ba)section 2B (causing death by careless, or inconsiderate, driving),".

[Road Safety Act 2006, s 20.]

4–2015J   21. Causing death by driving: unlicensed, disqualified or uninsured drivers.

(1) *Inserts s 3ZB into the Road Traffic Act 1988.*

(2) In Schedule 1 to the Road Traffic Offenders Act 1988 (c 53) (offences to which certain sections apply), after the entry relating to section 3 of the Road Traffic Act 1988 insert—

"RTA section 3ZB	Causing death by driving: unlicensed, disqualified or uninsured drivers.	Sections 11 and 12(1) of this Act."

(3) In Part 1 of Schedule 2 to that Act (prosecution and punishment of offences: offences under the Traffic Acts), after the entry relating to section 3 of the Road Traffic Act 1988 insert—

"RTA section 3ZB	Causing death by driving: unlicensed, disqualified or uninsured drivers.	(a) Summarily. (b) On indictment.	(a) 12 months (in England and Wales) or 6 months (in Scotland) or the statutory maximum or both. (b) 2 years or a fine or both.	Obligatory.	Obligatory.	3–11"

(4) In sections 16(1)(a)(ii) and 17(1)(b) and (2)(b) of the Coroners Act 1988 (c 13) (informing coroners)—

(a) before "or 3A" insert ", 3ZB", and

(b) before "or careless" insert ", unlicensed, disqualified or uninsured drivers".

(5) In paragraph 3 of Schedule 3 to the Crime (International Co-operation) Act 2003 (c 32)

(offences where notice must be given to authority of State in which offender is normally resident), after paragraph (*c*) insert—

"(ca)section 3ZB (causing death by driving: unlicensed, disqualified or uninsured drivers),".

[Road Safety Act 2006, s 21.]

4–2015K   22. Offence of keeping vehicle which does not meet insurance requirements.   (1),
(2) *Insert ss 144A–144D and 159A into the Road Traffic Act 1988.*
(3) After Schedule 2 to that Act insert the Schedule 2A set out in Schedule 5 to this Act.
(4) In section 91(*a*) of the Road Traffic Offenders Act 1988 (c 53) (penalty for breach of regulations: application to regulations under Road Traffic Act 1988), after "132" insert "or under section 160 by virtue of Schedule 2A".
(5) In Schedule 1 to that Act (offences to which certain sections apply), after the entry relating to section 143 of the Road Traffic Act 1988 insert—

"RTA section 144A	Keeping vehicle which does not meet insurance requirements.	Sections 6, 11 and 12(1) of this Act."

(6) Part 1 of Schedule 2 to that Act (prosecution and punishment of offences: offences under the Traffic Acts) is amended as follows.
(7) After the entry relating to section 143 of the Road Traffic Act 1988 insert—

"RTA section 144A	Keeping vehicle which does not meet insurance requirements.	Summarily.	Level 3 on the standard scale.			"

(8) After the entry relating to section 154 of the Road Traffic Act 1988 insert—

"Regulations under RTA section 160 made by virtue of paragraph 2(1) of Schedule 2A	Contravention of provision of regulations (which is declared by regulations to be an offence) prohibiting removal of or interference with immobilisation notice.	Summarily.	Level 2 on the standard scale.			
Regulations under RTA section 160 made by virtue of paragraph 2(2) of Schedule 2A	Contravention of provision of regulations (which is declared by regulations to be an offence) prohibiting removal or attempted removal of immobilisation device.	Summarily.	Level 3 on the standard scale.			
Regulations under RTA section 160 made by virtue of paragraph 2(3) of Schedule 2A	Contravention of provision of regulations (which is declared by regulations to be an offence) about display of disabled person's badge.	Summarily.	Level 3 on the standard scale.			
Regulations under RTA section 160 made by virtue of paragraph 2(4) of Schedule 2A	Contravention of provision of regulations (which is declared by regulations to be an offence) prohibiting making of false or misleading declaration to secure release of vehicle from immobilisation device.	(*a*) Summarily. (*b*) On indictment.	(*a*) The statutory maximum. (*b*) 2 years or a fine or both.			

Regulations under RTA section 160 made by virtue of paragraph 4 of Schedule 2A	Contravention of provision of regulations (which is declared by regulations to be an offence) prohibiting making of false or misleading declaration to secure possession of vehicle in person's custody.	(*a*) Summarily. (*b*) On indictment.	(*a*) The statutory maximum. (*b*) 2 years or a fine or both.	``

[Road Safety Act 2006, s 22.]

Increases in penalties

4–2015L 23. Careless, and inconsiderate, driving. In Part 1 of Schedule 2 to the Road Traffic Offenders Act 1988 (c 53) (prosecution and punishment of offences: offences under the Traffic Acts), in the entry relating to section 3 of the Road Traffic Act 1988 (c 52) (careless, and inconsiderate, driving), in column (4) (punishment), for "Level 4" substitute "Level 5".

[Road Safety Act 2006, s 23.]

4–2015M 24. Breach of requirements relating to children and seat belts. In Part 1 of Schedule 2 to the Road Traffic Offenders Act 1988 (prosecution and punishment of offences: offences under the Traffic Acts), in the entry relating to section 15(4) of the Road Traffic Act 1988 (driving a motor vehicle in contravention of requirements relating to seat belts where children in rear seat), in column (4) (punishment), for "Level 1" substitute "Level 2".

[Road Safety Act 2006, s 24.]

4–2015N 25. Using vehicle in dangerous condition etc. (1) In Part 1 of Schedule 2 to the Road Traffic Offenders Act 1988 (c 53) (prosecution and punishment of offences: offences under the Traffic Acts), in the entry relating to section 40A of the Road Traffic Act 1988 (c 52) (using vehicle in dangerous condition etc), in column (5) (disqualification), for "Discretionary." substitute—

"(*a*) Obligatory if committed within three years of a previous conviction of the offender under section 40A.

(*b*) Discretionary in any other case."

(2) In section 34 of that Act (disqualification for certain offences), after subsection (4A) insert—

"(4B) Where a person convicted of an offence under section 40A of the Road Traffic Act 1988 (using vehicle in dangerous condition etc) has within the three years immediately preceding the commission of the offence been convicted of any such offence, subsection (1) above shall apply in relation to him as if the reference to twelve months were a reference to six months."

[Road Safety Act 2006, s 25.]

4–2015O 26. Breach of requirements as to control of vehicle, mobile telephones etc.
(1) *Inserts s 41D into the Road Traffic Act 1988.*

(2) In section 42(*a*) of that Act (breach of other construction and use requirements), before "of" insert "or 41D".

(3) In Schedule 1 to the Road Traffic Offenders Act 1988 (offences ... apply), before the entry relating to section 42 of the Road Traffic Act 1988 insert—

"RTA section 41D. | Breach of requirements as to control of vehicle, mobile telephones etc | Sections 11 and 12(1) of the Act."

(4) In Part 1 of Schedule 2 to that Act (prosecution and punishment of offences: offences under the Traffic Acts), before the entry relating to section 42 of the Road Traffic Act 1988 (c 52) insert—

| "RTA section 41D | Breach of requirements as to control of vehicle, mobile telephones etc | Summarily. | (*a*) Level 4 on the standard scale if committed in respect of a goods vehicle or a vehicle adapted to carry more than eight passengers. (*b*) Level 3 on the standard scale in any other case. | Discretionary. | Obligatory. | 3." |

(5) In Schedule 3 to that Act (fixed penalty offences), before the entry relating to section 42 of the Road Traffic Act 1988 insert—

| "RTA section 41D | Breach of requirement as to control of vehicle, mobile telephone etc" |

[Road Safety Act 2006, s 26.]

4–2015P   27. Power of police to stop vehicle.   In Part 1 of Schedule 2 to the Road Traffic Offenders Act 1988 (c 53) (prosecution and punishment of offences: offences under the Traffic Acts), in the entry relating to section 163 of the Road Traffic Act 1988 (failing to stop mechanically propelled vehicle or cycle when required to do so), in column (4) (punishment), for "Level 3 on the standard scale." substitute—

"(*a*) Level 5 on the standard scale if committed by a person driving a mechanically propelled vehicle.
(*b*) Level 3 on the standard scale if committed by a person riding a cycle."
and, in column (2) (general nature of offence), for "motor" substitute "mechanically propelled".

[Road Safety Act 2006, s 27.]

4–2015Q   28. Furious driving.   In Part 2 of Schedule 2 to the Road Traffic Offenders Act 1988 (prosecution and punishment of offences: offences otherwise than under the Traffic Acts), after the entry relating to manslaughter and culpable homicide insert—

| "An offence under section 35 of the Offences against the Person Act 1861 (furious driving). | Discretionary. | Obligatory if committed in respect of a mechanically propelled vehicle. | 3–9" |

[Road Safety Act 2006, s 28.]

4–2015R   29. Breach of duty to give information as to identity of driver etc.   In Part 1 of Schedule 2 to the Road Traffic Offenders Act 1988 (c 53) (prosecution and punishment of offences: offences under the Traffic Acts), in the entry relating to section 172 of the Road Traffic Act 1988 (c 52) (duty to give information as to identity of driver etc in certain circumstances), in column (7) (penalty points), for "3" substitute "6".

[Road Safety Act 2006, s 29.]

Other provisions about offences

4–2015S   30. Meaning of driving without due care and attention.   *Inserts s 3ZA into the Road Traffic Act 1988.*

4–2015T   31. Extension of offence in section 3A of Road Traffic Act 1988.   (1) Section 3A of the Road Traffic Act 1988 (causing death by careless driving when under influence of drink or drugs etc) is amended as follows.
(2) In subsection (1), after paragraph (*c*) insert

"or
(*d*) he is required by a constable to give his permission for a laboratory test of a specimen of blood taken from him under section 7A of this Act, but without reasonable excuse fails to do so,".

(3) In subsection (3), for "and (*c*)" substitute ", (*c*) and (*d*)".
(4) In section 24(1) of the Road Traffic Offenders Act 1988 (alternative verdicts), in the Table, in the entry relating to section 3A of the Road Traffic Act 1988, in the second column, after "Section 7(6) (failing to provide specimen)" insert "Section 7A(6) (failing to give permission for laboratory test)".

[Road Safety Act 2006, s 31.]

32. Alternative verdict on unsuccessful culpable homicide prosecution.   *Scotland.*

4–2015U   33. Alternative verdict on unsuccessful manslaughter prosecution.   In section 24 of the Road Traffic Offenders Act 1988 (alternative verdicts), before subsection (1) insert—

"(A1) Where—
(*a*) a person charged with manslaughter in connection with the driving of a mechanically propelled vehicle by him is found not guilty of that offence, but
(*b*) the allegations in the indictment amount to or include an allegation of any of the relevant offences,

he may be convicted of that offence.
(A2) For the purposes of subsection (A1) above the following are the relevant offences—

(a) an offence under section 1 of the Road Traffic Act 1988 (causing death by dangerous driving),

(b) an offence under section 2 of that Act (dangerous driving),

(c) an offence under section 3A of that Act (causing death by careless driving when under influence of drink or drugs), and

(d) an offence under section 35 of the Offences against the Person Act 1861 (furious driving)."

[Road Safety Act 2006, s 33.]

Attendance on courses

4–2015V   34. Penalty points.   (1) The Road Traffic Offenders Act 1988 is amended as follows.

(2) In section 29 (penalty points to be taken into account on conviction), after subsection (2) insert—

"(2A) Subsection (1)(b) above has effect subject to section 30A(4) of this Act."

(3) *Inserts ss 30A–30D into the Road Traffic Offenders Act 1988,*

[Road Safety Act 2006, s 34.]

4–2015W   35. Reduced disqualification period for attendance on course.   For sections 34A to 34C of the Road Traffic Offenders Act 1988 (c 53) substitute—

34A. "Reduced disqualification for attendance on courses.   (1) This section applies where—

(a) a person is convicted of a relevant drink offence or a specified offence by or before a court, and

(b) the court makes an order under section 34 of this Act disqualifying him for a period of not less than twelve months.

(2) In this section "relevant drink offence" means—

(a) an offence under paragraph (a) of subsection (1) of section 3A of the Road Traffic Act 1988 (causing death by careless driving when unfit to drive through drink) committed when unfit to drive through drink,

(b) an offence under paragraph (b) of that subsection (causing death by careless driving with excess alcohol),

(c) an offence under paragraph (c) of that subsection (failing to provide a specimen) where the specimen is required in connection with drink or consumption of alcohol,

(d) an offence under section 4 of that Act (driving or being in charge when under influence of drink) committed by reason of unfitness through drink,

(e) an offence under section 5(1) of that Act (driving or being in charge with excess alcohol),

(f) an offence under section 7(6) of that Act (failing to provide a specimen) committed in the course of an investigation into an offence within any of the preceding paragraphs, or

(g) an offence under section 7A(6) of that Act (failing to allow a specimen to be subjected to a laboratory test) in the course of an investigation into an offence within any of the preceding paragraphs.

(3) In this section "specified offence" means—

(a) an offence under section 3 of the Road Traffic Act 1988 (careless, and inconsiderate, driving),

(b) an offence under section 36 of that Act (failing to comply with traffic signs),

(c) an offence under section 17(4) of the Road Traffic Regulation Act 1984 (use of special road contrary to scheme or regulations), or

(d) an offence under section 89(1) of that Act (exceeding speed limit).

(4) But the Secretary of State may by regulations amend subsection (3) above by adding other offences or removing offences.

(5) Where this section applies, the court may make an order that the period of disqualification imposed under section 34 of this Act ("the unreduced period") shall be reduced if, by the relevant date, the offender satisfactorily completes an approved course specified in the order.

(6) In subsection (5) above—

"an approved course" means a course approved by the appropriate national authority for the purposes of this section in relation to the description of offence of which the offender is convicted, and

"the relevant date" means such date, at least two months before the last day of the period of disqualification as reduced by the order, as is specified in the order.

(7) The reduction made in a period of disqualification by an order under this section is a period specified in the order of—

(a) not less than three months, and

(b) not more than one quarter of the unreduced period,

(and, accordingly, where the unreduced period is twelve months, the reduced period is nine months).

(8) A court shall not make an order under this section in the case of an offender convicted of a specified offence if—

(a) the offender has, during the period of three years ending with the date on which the offence was committed, committed a specified offence and successfully completed an approved course pursuant to an order made under this section or section 30A of this Act on conviction of that offence, or

(b) the specified offence was committed during his probationary period.

(9) A court shall not make an order under this section in the case of an offender unless—

(a) the court is satisfied that a place on the course specified in the order will be available for the offender,

(b) the offender appears to the court to be of or over the age of 17,

(c) the court has informed the offender (orally or in writing and in ordinary language) of the effect of the order and of the amount of the fees which he is required to pay for the course and when he must pay them, and

(d) the offender has agreed that the order should be made.

34B. Certificates of completion of courses. (1) An offender shall be regarded for the purposes of section 34A of this Act as having completed a course satisfactorily if (and only if) a certificate that he has done so is received by the proper officer of the supervising court before the end of the unreduced period.

(2) If a certificate under subsection (1) above is so received before the end of the unreduced period but after the end of the period which would (apart from this subsection) be the reduced period, the reduced period is to be taken to end with the day on which the certificate is so received.

(3) A certificate under subsection (1) above is to be given by the course provider and shall be in such form, and contain such particulars, as may be prescribed by, or determined in accordance with, regulations made by the appropriate national authority.

(4) A course provider must give a certificate under subsection (1) above to the offender not later than fourteen days after the date specified in the order as the latest date for the completion of the course unless the offender—

(a) fails to make due payment of fees for the course,

(b) fails to attend the course in accordance with the course provider's reasonable instructions, or

(c) fails to comply with any other reasonable requirement of the course provider.

(5) Where a course provider decides not to give a certificate under subsection (1) above to the offender, he shall give written notice of the decision to the offender as soon as possible, and in any event not later than fourteen days after the date specified in the order as the latest date for completion of the course.

(6) An offender to whom a notice is given under subsection (5) above may, within such period as may be prescribed by rules of court, apply to the supervising court, or (if the supervising court is not the Crown Court, the High Court of Justiciary or the relevant local court) to either the supervising court or the relevant local court, for a declaration that the course provider's decision not to give a certificate under subsection (1) above was contrary to subsection (4) above.

(7) If the court grants the application, section 34A of this Act shall have effect as if the certificate had been duly received by the proper officer of the supervising court.

(8) If fourteen days after the date specified in the order as the latest date for completion of the course the course provider has given neither a certificate under subsection (1) above nor a notice under subsection (5) above, the offender may, within such period as may be prescribed by rules of court, apply to the supervising court, or (if the supervising court is not the Crown Court, the High Court of Justiciary or the relevant local court) to either the supervising court or the relevant local court, for a declaration that the course provider is in default.

(9) If the court grants the application, section 34A of this Act shall have effect as if the certificate had been duly received by the proper officer of the supervising court.

(10) A notice under subsection (5) above shall specify the ground on which it is given; and the appropriate national authority may by regulations make provision as to the form of notices under that subsection and as to the circumstances in which they are to be treated as given.

(11) Where the proper officer of a court receives a certificate under subsection (1) above, or a court grants an application under subsection (6) or (8) above, the proper officer or court must send notice of that fact to the Secretary of State; and the notice must be sent in such manner and to such address, and must contain such particulars, as the Secretary of State may determine.

34BA. Approval of courses. (1) If an application is made to the appropriate national authority for the approval of a course for the purposes of section 34A of this Act, the appropriate national authority must decide whether to grant or refuse the application.

(2) In reaching that decision the appropriate national authority must have regard to—

(a) the nature of the course, and

(b) whether the course provider is an appropriate person to provide the course and administer its provision efficiently and effectively,

and may take into account any recommendations made by any persons appointed to consider the application.

(3) A course may be approved subject to conditions specified by the appropriate national authority.

(4) An approval of a course is for the period specified by the appropriate national authority (which must not exceed seven years), subject to withdrawal of approval.

(5) Regulations made by the appropriate national authority may make provision in relation to the approval of courses and may, in particular, include provision—

    (a) in relation to the making of applications for approval,

    (b) for the payment in respect of applications for approval, or of approvals, (or of both) of fees of such amounts as are prescribed by the regulations,

    (c) specifying the maximum fees that a person may be required to pay for a course and by when they are to be paid,

    (d) for the monitoring of courses and course providers,

    (e) in relation to withdrawing approval,

    (f) for an appeal to lie to the Transport Tribunal against a refusal of an application for approval, the imposition of conditions on the grant of such an application or the withdrawal of approval, and

    (g) authorising the appropriate national authority to make available (with or without charge) information about courses and course providers.

34C. Provisions supplementary to sections 34A to 34BA. (1) The appropriate national authority may issue guidance to course providers, or to any category of course provider, as to the conduct of courses approved for the purposes of section 34A of this Act; and—

    (a) course providers shall have regard to any guidance given to them under this subsection, and

    (b) in determining for the purposes of section 34B of this Act whether any instructions or requirements of a course provider were reasonable, a court shall have regard to any guidance given to him under this subsection.

(2) The Secretary of State may by regulations make provision—

    (a) amending section 34A(1)(b) of this Act by substituting for the period for the time being specified there a different period,

    (b) amending section 34A(7) of this Act by substituting for the period for the time being specified there a different period, or by substituting for the fraction of the unreduced period for the time being specified there a different fraction of that period, (or by doing both), or

    (c) amending section 34A(8)(a) of this Act by substituting for the period for the time being specified there a different period.

(3) In sections 34A to 34BA of this Act and this section—

"appropriate national authority" means (as respects Wales) the National Assembly for Wales and (otherwise) the Secretary of State;

"course provider", in relation to a course, means the person by whom it is, or is to be, provided;

"probationary period" has the meaning given in section 1 of the Road Traffic (New Drivers) Act 1995;

"proper officer" means—

    (a) in relation to a magistrates' court in England and Wales, the designated officer for the court, and

    (b) otherwise, the clerk of the court;

"relevant local court", in relation to an order under section 34A of this Act in the case of an offender, means—

    (a) in England and Wales, a magistrates' court acting for the local justice area in which the offender resides, and

    (b) in Scotland, the sheriff court for the district where the offender resides or, where the order is made by a stipendiary magistrate and the offender resides within his commission area, the district court for that area; and

"supervising court", in relation to an order under section 34A of this Act, means—

    (a) in England and Wales, if the Crown Court made the order the Crown Court and otherwise a magistrates' court acting for the same local justice area as the court which made the order, and

    (b) in Scotland, the court which made the order.

(4) Any power to make regulations under section 34A, 34B or 34BA of this Act or this section includes power to make different provision for different cases, and to make such incidental or supplementary provision as appears necessary or appropriate.

(5) Any power to make regulations under section 34A, 34B or 34BA of this Act or this section shall be exercisable by statutory instrument.

(6) No regulations shall be made under section 34A of this Act or this section unless a draft of the regulations has been laid before, and approved by a resolution of, each House of Parliament.

(7) A statutory instrument containing regulations made under section 34B or 34BA of this Act

by the Secretary of State shall be subject to annulment in pursuance of a resolution of either House of Parliament."

[Road Safety Act 2006, s 35.]

Driving standards

4–2015X **36. Driving tests.** (1) Section 89 of the Road Traffic Act 1988 (c 52) (driving tests) is amended as follows.

(2) In subsection (3) (regulations about nature of tests)—

(*a*) in paragraph (*a*), insert at the end "and the administrative arrangements for submitting for such tests",

(*b*) in paragraph (*b*), after "conducted" insert ", conditions which must be satisfied during the currency of an appointment, the charging of reasonable fees in respect of applications for appointment or appointments or in connection with any examination or assessment which may be required before appointment or during the currency of any appointment", and

(*c*) after that paragraph insert—

"(ba)the duty of a person submitting himself for a test to produce, and in prescribed circumstances surrender, any licence previously granted to him,".

(3) In subsection (4) (provision that may be included in regulations under subsection (3))—

(*a*) for "In particular, regulations may, without prejudice to the generality of subsection (3) above," substitute "Regulations under subsection (3)(*a*) above may in particular",

(*b*) in paragraph (*a*) (provision by person submitting himself for driving test of vehicle which, if loading requirements are prescribed, is loaded in accordance with prescribed requirements), for "a vehicle" substitute "a safe and suitable vehicle",

(*c*) in that paragraph, for the words after "the test" substitute "and for requiring that, if the vehicle is a vehicle of a prescribed description, it has been certified in the prescribed manner after a prescribed inspection as satisfying such requirements as may be prescribed,", and

(*d*) for paragraph (*b*) substitute—

"(*b*) for the charging (whether on the making of an appointment for a test or otherwise) of reasonable fees for or in connection with the test and any inspection of a vehicle required by regulations under paragraph (*a*) above in relation to the test,".

(4) In subsection (5) (driving tests in parts), omit paragraph (*b*) and the word "and" before it.

(5) After that subsection insert—

"(5ZA) Regulations under subsection (3)(*b*) above may in particular provide—

(*a*) for the supply by the Secretary of State to persons by whom tests of competence to drive, or parts of such tests, may be conducted of forms for certificates evidencing the results of such tests or parts of such tests, and

(*b*) for the charging of reasonable fees in respect of the exercise of any function conferred or imposed on the Secretary of State by the regulations."

(6) In section 91 of that Act (repayment of test fees), for "A fee" substitute "The whole or any part of a fee".

[Road Safety Act 2006, s 36.]

4–2015Y **37. Disqualification until test is passed.** (1) Section 36 of the Road Traffic Offenders Act 1988 (c 53) (duty of court to order disqualification until test is passed) is amended as follows.

(2) In subsection (3) (order to be made in case of person disqualified in circumstances, or for period, prescribed by order)—

(*a*) for "in such circumstances or for such period" substitute "for such period, in such circumstances or for such period and in such circumstances",

(*b*) for "prescribe" substitute "specify", and

(*c*) for "may be so prescribed" substitute "the Secretary of State may by order specify".

(3) In subsection (5) (interpretation), for the definition of "appropriate driving test" substitute—

""appropriate driving test" means—

(*a*) in such circumstances as the Secretary of State may prescribe, an extended driving test, and

(*b*) otherwise, a test of competence to drive which is not an extended driving test,";

and, in the definition of "extended driving test", after "section" insert "by regulations made by the Secretary of State".

(4) In subsection (8) (disqualification to expire on production in accordance with regulations under section 105 of Road Traffic Act 1988 of evidence of having passed test), for "under section 105 of the Road Traffic Act 1988" substitute "made by the Secretary of State".

(5) In subsection (9) (disqualification to expire by reason of passing of test only in relation to vehicles of such classes as are prescribed by such regulations), for "under that section" substitute "made by the Secretary of State".

(6) After subsection (13) insert—

"(13A) Before making an order under subsection (3) above the Secretary of State must consult with such representative organisations as he thinks fit."

(7) Omit subsection (14) (no order to be made under subsection (3) after end of 2001 unless one previously made).

(8) In section 173(2) of the Road Traffic Act 1988 (c 52) (forgery of documents etc), insert at the end

"and
(*n*) any document produced as evidence of the passing of an appropriate driving test within the meaning of section 36 of that Act."

[Road Safety Act 2006, s 37.]

4-2015Z   38. Granting of full licence.   (1) In section 89(1) of the Road Traffic Act 1988 (c 52) (licence not to be granted unless conditions satisfied), for—

(*a*) the words in paragraph (*a*) before sub-paragraph (i), and
(*b*) the words from "that" to "passed" in paragraphs (*c*) and (*e*),

substitute "that he has, at such time or within such period as is prescribed, passed".

(2) In section 97 of that Act (grant of licences), after subsection (1) insert—

"(1ZA) Regulations may provide that in prescribed circumstances a licence granted by the Secretary of State may be granted subject to prescribed conditions having effect—

(*a*) for a prescribed period, or
(*b*) until the happening of a prescribed event."

(3) In section 98(1)(*c*) of that Act (provisional licence to specify conditions subject to which it is granted)—

(*a*) omit "in the case of a provisional licence", and
(*b*) for "the conditions" substitute "any conditions".

(4) In section 195 of that Act (provisions as to regulations)—

(*a*) in subsection (3), omit "is exercised" and after "189)" insert "is exercised (otherwise than for the purposes of section 97(1ZA) of this Act)", and
(*b*) in subsection (4), after "Act" insert ", or for the purposes of section 97(1ZA) of this Act,".

[Road Safety Act 2006, s 38.]

4-2016   39. Compulsory surrender of old-form licences.   (1) *Inserts s 98A into the Road Traffic Act 1988.*

(2) In Schedule 1 to the Road Traffic Offenders Act 1988 (c 53) (offences to which certain sections apply), after the entry relating to section 94A of the Road Traffic Act 1988 (c 52) insert—

"RTA section 98A(7)	Driving licence holder failing to surrender licence and counterpart	Section 6 of this Act."

(3) In Part 1 of Schedule 2 to that Act (prosecution and punishment of offences: offences under the Traffic Acts), after the entry relating to section 96 of the Road Traffic Act 1988 insert—

"RTA section 98A(7).	Driving licence holder failing to surrender licence and counterpart.	Summarily.	Level 3 on the standard scale.".

[Road Safety Act 2006, s 39.]

4-2016A   40. Fee for renewal of photocard licence and issue of certain alternative licences.
(1) In section 99 of the Road Traffic Act 1988 (duration of licence)—

(*a*) in subsection (7) (grant of new licence free of charge on surrender of photocard licence after ten years, in cases of error and on change of name or address), omit "and any licence granted under this subsection shall be granted free of charge", and
(*b*) After that subsection insert—

"(7ZA) The Secretary of State is not required by subsection (7) above to grant a new licence on the surrender of a licence and its counterpart by a person in pursuance of subsection (2A) above unless the person has paid the fee (if any) which is prescribed; but any other licence under that subsection is to be granted free of charge."

(2) In section 117A(2)(*c*) and (3) of that Act (disqualification etc of holders of Community licences: issue of alternative licences), for ", free of charge," substitute ", on payment of such fee (if any) as may be prescribed,".

[Road Safety Act 2006, s 40.]

4-2016B   41. Driver training.   (1) Section 99ZC(1) of the Road Traffic Act 1988 (c 52) (driver training courses: supplementary) is amended as follows.

(2) In paragraphs (*b*) and (*c*), after "courses" insert "or giving instruction on such courses".

(3) After paragraph (*e*) insert

"and

(*f*) provision authorising the Secretary of State to make available information about persons providing driver training courses or giving instruction on such courses."

(4) In section 173(2) of that Act (forgery of documents etc), for paragraph (ff) substitute—

"(ff) any document evidencing the successful completion of a driver training course provided in accordance with regulations under section 99ZA of this Act,".

(5) In section 174(1) of that Act (false statements), after paragraph (*c*) insert—

"(ca) of obtaining a document evidencing the successful completion of a driver training course provided in accordance with regulations under section 99ZA of this Act, or".

[Road Safety Act 2006, s 41.]

4–2016C 42. Driving instruction. Schedule 6 contains amendments about driving instruction.

[Road Safety Act 2006, s 42.]

43. Tests: approved assistants. *Inserts s 162A into the Road Traffic Act 1988.*

Regulation of registration plate suppliers

44. Enforcement authorities. *Amends Part 2 of the Vehicles (Crime) Act 2001.*

4–2016D 45. Registration plates. (1) Part 2 of the Vehicles (Crime) Act 2001 (c 3) (regulation of registration plate suppliers) is amended as follows.

(2) In section 31(1) (interpretation of Part 2), in paragraph (*a*) of the definition of "registration plate", for "a registration mark" substitute "in accordance with regulations under paragraph (*b*) of subsection (4) of section 23 of the 1994 Act a registration mark which complies with regulations under paragraph (*a*) of that subsection".

(3) Section 28 (offences) is amended as follows.

(4) After subsection (1) insert—

"(1A) A person who sells a plate or other device which is not a registration plate only because the registration mark displayed by it—

(*a*) does not comply with regulations under paragraph (*a*) of subsection (4) of section 23 of the 1994 Act, or

(*b*) is displayed otherwise than in accordance with regulations under paragraph (*b*) of that subsection,

(or both) shall be guilty of an offence.

(1B) The Secretary of State may by regulations provide that the offence under subsection (1A) is not committed in circumstances prescribed by the regulations."

(5) In subsection (2), after " (1)" insert "or (1A)".

(6) In subsection (3), for "subsection (1) or (2)" substitute "this section".

(7) In the heading, for **"counterfeit registration plates"** substitute **"plates etc"**.

[Road Safety Act 2006, s 45.]

46. Extension to Scotland and Northern Ireland

Information

4–2016E 47. Particulars to be included in vehicles register. (1) Section 7 of the Vehicle Excise and Registration Act 1994 (c 22) (issue of vehicle licences) is amended as follows.

(2) After subsection (1) insert—

"(1A) The particulars which may be so specified include any particulars which are required by regulations under section 22(1)(aa) to be recorded on the register in the case of the vehicle for which the licence is to be taken out; and the declarations and evidence which may be so specified include declarations and evidence relating to any such particulars."

(3) In subsection (5), before paragraph (*a*) insert—

"(za) that the requirements imposed by this section in the case of the vehicle specified in the application have been complied with,".

(4) Section 22 of that Act (registration regulations) is amended as follows.

(5) In paragraph (*a*) of subsection (1) (provision with respect to registration), for " (including, in particular, the form of and the particulars to be included in the register of trade licences)" substitute "and trade licences".

(6) After that paragraph insert—

"(aa) prescribe the form of, and the particulars to be included in, the register of vehicles and the register of trade licences,".

(7) In paragraph (*d*) of that subsection (requirement on person by, through or to whom vehicle is sold or disposed of to furnish particulars)—

(*a*) after "person" insert "by whom any vehicle is kept or",

(*b*) for "furnish the particulars" substitute "make any such declarations and furnish any such particulars and any such documentary or other evidence as may be", and

(*c*) for "in the manner" substitute "and to do so at such times and in such manner as may be".

(8) In paragraph (*h*) of that subsection (new registration documents), for "or inaccurate" substitute "or which have become inaccurate for any reason (in particular by reason of a change in the person by whom the vehicle to which they relate is being kept)".

(9) After subsection (1A) insert—

"(1AA) The particulars which may be required to be included in the register by regulations under subsection (1)(aa), or to be furnished by regulations under subsection (1)(*d*), in the case of a vehicle include—

(*a*) particulars relating to the vehicle, and

(*b*) particulars relating to the person by whom the vehicle is kept;

and the declarations and evidence which may be required to be furnished by regulations under subsection (1)(*d*) in the case of a vehicle include declarations and evidence relating to such particulars."

(10) After subsection (1B) insert—

"(1BA) Regulations under subsection (1)(*e*) and (*h*) may, in particular, provide that registration documents, or new registration documents, need not be issued in respect of a vehicle if particulars required in the case of the vehicle by regulations under paragraph (*d*) have not been furnished."

(11) Section 45 of that Act (false or misleading declarations and information) is amended as follows.

(12) In subsection (1), after "misleading" insert ", or produces a document which to his knowledge is false or in any material respect misleading,".

(13) In subsection (2A)—

(*a*) after "statement" insert "or produces a document", and

(*b*) for "made in respect of a vehicle" substitute "made or produced".

[Road Safety Act 2006, s 47.]

4–2016F   48. Records of goods vehicle examinations.   (1) In section 49 of the Road Traffic Act 1988 (c 52) (tests of satisfactory condition of goods vehicles and determination of plated weights etc), after subsection (3) insert—

"(3A) The Secretary of State must maintain, or cause to be maintained, records containing such particulars as he thinks fit of—

(*a*) goods vehicles submitted for examination under this section, and

(*b*) the carrying out of and the results of the examinations."

(2) After that section insert—

"49A. Use of records of goods vehicle examinations, etc.   (1) This section applies to—

(*a*) the records maintained by the Secretary of State (or caused by him to be maintained) under section 49(3A) of this Act, and

(*b*) the records maintained by the Secretary of State in connection with any functions exercisable by him under or by virtue of the Vehicle Excise and Registration Act 1994.

(2) The Secretary of State may use the information contained in records falling within either paragraph of subsection (1) above—

(*a*) to check the accuracy of the records falling within the other paragraph of that subsection, and

(*b*) where appropriate, to amend or supplement information contained in those records.

(3) The Secretary of State may also use the information contained in records falling within paragraph (*b*) of that subsection for the purpose of promoting compliance with section 53 of this Act.

(4) This section does not limit any powers of the Secretary of State apart from this section."

(3) In section 22A(6) of the Vehicle Excise and Registration Act 1994 (c 22) (vehicle identity checks), after "45(6B)" insert "or 49(3A)".

[Road Safety Act 2006, s 48.]

49. Disclosure to foreign authorities of licensing and registration information

Level crossings

50–51.   *Safety arrangements at level crossings and delegation of power to make level crossing orders.*

Hackney carriages and private hire vehicles

4–2016G   52. Immediate suspension and revocation of drivers' licences. *Amends Part 2 of the Local Government (Miscellaneous Provisions) Act 1976.*

4–2016H   53. Abolition of "contract exemption".   In section 75(1) of the Local Government (Miscellaneous Provisions) Act 1976 (hackney carriages and private hire vehicles in England and Wales outside London: savings), omit paragraph (*b*) (vehicles used only for carrying passengers for hire or reward under contract for hire for not less than 7 day period).

[Road Safety Act 2006, s 53.]

4–2016I   54. Private hire vehicles in London.   In the definition of "private hire vehicle" in section 1(1)(*a*) of the Private Hire Vehicles (London) Act 1998 (c 34) (vehicle, other than a taxi or public service vehicle, seating fewer than nine passengers made available with a driver to the public for hire to carry passengers), omit "to the public".

[Road Safety Act 2006, s 54.]

Miscellaneous

55. Trunk road picnic areas

4–2016J   56. Vehicles modified to run on fuel stored under pressure.   (1) The Road Traffic Act 1988 (c 52) is amended as follows.

(2) Section 41 (regulation of construction, weight, equipment and use of vehicles) is amended as follows.

(3) In subsection (2), after paragraph (*b*) insert—

"(ba)the modification of motor vehicles to enable them to be propelled using fuel stored under pressure,".

(4) After that subsection insert—

"(2A) Regulations under this section with respect to the modification of motor vehicles to enable them to be propelled using fuel stored under pressure may include provision—

(*a*) as to the examination, by persons authorised in accordance with regulations, of motor vehicles that have been so modified, the issuing of certificates by them in respect of such vehicles and the making of charges by them,

(*b*) requiring authorised persons to notify the Secretary of State of any such examinations carried out by them,

(*c*) as to appeals against any decision by an authorised person not to issue a certificate,

(*d*) as to applications to the Secretary of State for authorisation and charges in connection with them,

(*e*) imposing or providing for the imposition of conditions to be complied with by authorised persons,

(*f*) as to the withdrawal of authorisations."

(5) In section 66 (regulations prohibiting the grant of excise licences for certain vehicles except on compliance with certain conditions), after subsection (7) insert—

"(7A) The Secretary of State may by regulations provide, in relation to vehicles required to be examined and certified by regulations under section 41(2A)(*a*) of this Act, that the first licence for such a vehicle under the Vehicle Excise and Registration Act 1994 for a period after the requirement applies to the vehicle is to be granted only if evidence is provided that a certificate has been issued in accordance with those regulations."

[Road Safety Act 2006, s 56.]

4–2016K   57. Powers to regulate transport of radioactive material.   (1) Section 2 of the Radioactive Material (Road Transport) Act 1991 (c 27) (regulations for preventing injury or damage from transport by road of radioactive material) is amended as follows.

(2) In subsection (2), for paragraph (*d*) and the word "and" before it substitute—

"(*d*) the keeping of records and the production, inspection, removal, retention and copying of records and other documents;

(*e*) the provision of information and the answering of questions (including the making of declarations as to the truth of answers and their admissibility in evidence); and

(*f*) the provision of facilities and assistance in connection with the carrying out of functions conferred by the regulations."

(3) In subsection (3), before paragraph (*a*) insert—

"(za)make provision for the imposition of requirements by inspectors and examiners;".

(4) In subsection (4), after "with any" insert "requirement imposed by or by virtue of".

[Road Safety Act 2006, s 57.]

58. Minor corrections

Supplementary

59. Repeals and revocations

60. Power to make amendments

4–2016L 61. Commencement.   (1) The preceding provisions of this Act come into force on such day as the Secretary of State may by order made by statutory instrument appoint (but subject to subsections (7) to (10)).

(2) Different days may be appointed for different purposes.

(3) Any provision of this Act which alters any penalty for an offence has effect only in relation to offences committed after the coming into force of the provision.

(4) Section 2B of the Road Traffic Act 1988 (c 52) (inserted by section 20) has effect only in relation to driving occurring after the coming into force of that section; and section 3ZB of that Act (inserted by section 21) has effect only in relation to driving occurring after the coming into force of that section.

(5) In relation to an offence under section 2B or 3ZB of the Road Traffic Act 1988 committed before the commencement of section 154(1) of the Criminal Justice Act 2003 (c 44), the references in column 4 of Part 1 of Schedule 2 to the Road Traffic Offenders Act 1988 (c 53) relating to offences under those sections have effect with the omission of the words "12 months (in England and Wales) or" and "(in Scotland)".

(6) The Secretary of State may by order made by statutory instrument make such transitional provisions and savings as he considers appropriate in connection with the coming into force of any provision of this Act.

(7) The following provisions come into force at the end of the period of two months beginning with the day on which this Act is passed—

    (*a*) section 1, and

    (*b*) section 49.

(8) The day on which sections 8 and 9 and Schedule 2 (and the repeals contained in Schedule 7 under the heading "Endorsement: unlicensed and foreign drivers") come into force must be—

    (*a*) later than the day on which section 5 and Schedule 1 (and the repeals contained in Schedule 7 under the heading "Giving of fixed penalty notices by vehicle examiners") come into force, but

    (*b*) earlier than the day on which section 10 and Schedule 3 (and the repeals contained in Schedule 7 under the heading "Endorsement: all drivers") come into force.

(9) Sections 51, 58 and 60, and the repeals contained in Schedule 7 under the heading "Spent enactments" (and section 59 so far as relating to them), come into force on the day on which this Act is passed; but—

    (*a*) section 51(2) does not affect anything done or omitted to be done before that day, and

    (*b*) section 58(6) has effect only in relation to offences committed on or after that day.

(10) Any power to make an order or regulations which is conferred by any provision of this Act may be exercised at any time after the passing of this Act.

[Road Safety Act 2006, s 61.]

62. Extent

63. Short title

SCHEDULE 1

GIVING OF FIXED PENALTY NOTICES BY VEHICLE EXAMINERS ETC

Section 9

SCHEDULE 2

ENDORSEMENT: UNLICENSED AND FOREIGN DRIVERS

Public Passenger Vehicles Act 1981 (c 14)

1. (1) Section 24 of the Public Passenger Vehicles Act 1981 (regulation of conduct of drivers, inspectors and conductors) is amended as follows.

(2) In subsection (2), insert at the end "or, if he is not the holder of a licence (within the meaning of Part 3 of the Road Traffic Act 1988), on his driving record (within the meaning of section 97A of the Road Traffic Offenders Act 1988)".

(3) In subsection (3)—

    (*a*) for "the licence and its counterpart" substitute "any counterpart of a licence which is to be endorsed under subsection (2) above", and

    (*b*) for "them" substitute "it and the licence".

Road Traffic Offenders Act 1988 (c 53)

2. The Road Traffic Offenders Act 1988 is amended as follows.

3. In section 28(3) (penalty points to be attributed to an offence), for "and 77(5)" substitute ", 57A(6), 77(5) and 77A(8)".

4. In section 29(1)(*b*) (penalty points to be taken into account on conviction), after "him" insert "or on his driving record".

5. (1) Section 30 (modification of sections 28 and 29 in case where fixed penalty also in question) is amended as follows.

(2) In subsection (1)(*b*)—

(*a*) after "licence" insert "or his driving record", and

(*b*) for "or 77" substitute ", 57A, 77 or 77A".

(3) In subsection (2)(*b*)—

(*a*) after "licence" insert "or on his driving record", and

(*b*) for "or 77" substitute ", 57A, 77 or 77A".

6. (1) Section 31 (court may take particulars endorsed on licence into consideration) is amended as follows.

(2) For subsection (1) substitute—

"(1) Where a person is convicted of an offence involving obligatory or discretionary disqualification—

(*a*) any existing endorsement on the counterpart of his licence or on his driving record is prima facie evidence of the matters endorsed, and

(*b*) the court may, in determining what order to make in pursuance of the conviction, take those matters into consideration."

(3) In the heading, omit **"on licence"**.

7. In section 36 (disqualification until test passed), after subsection (10) insert—

"(10A) Where a person's driving record is endorsed with particulars of a disqualification under this section, it shall also be endorsed with the particulars of any test of competence to drive that he has passed since the order of disqualification was made."

8. (1) Section 42 (removal of disqualification) is amended as follows.

(2) In subsection (5), for paragraph (*a*) substitute—

"(*a*) must—

(i) if particulars of the disqualification were previously endorsed on the counterpart of any licence previously held by the applicant, cause particulars of the order to be endorsed on that counterpart, and

(ii) if particulars of the disqualification were previously endorsed on the driving record of the applicant, send notice of the order to the Secretary of State,".

(3) In subsection (5A), for " (5)(*a*)" substitute " (5)(*a*)(i)".

(4) After that subsection insert—

"(5AA) If the disqualification was imposed in respect of an offence involving obligatory endorsement, the Secretary of State must, on receiving notice of an order under subsection (5)(*a*)(ii) above, make any necessary adjustments to the endorsements on the person's driving record to reflect the order."

(5) In subsection (5B), after "subsection" insert " (5)(*a*)(ii) or".

9. (1) Section 45 (effect of endorsement) is amended as follows.

(2) In subsection (1), omit ", whether he is at the time the holder of a licence or not,".

(3) In the heading, insert at the end **"of counterparts"**.

10. *Inserts s 45A into the Road Traffic Offenders Act 1988.*

11. (1) Section 46 (combination of disqualification and endorsement with certain other orders) is amended as follows.

(2) In subsection (1), for "or 44" substitute ", 44 or 44A".

(3) In subsection (2)(*b*), insert at the end "or on his driving record".

(4) In subsection (3), for "and 45" substitute ", 45 and 45A".

12. (1) Section 47 (supplementary provisions as to disqualification and endorsements) is amended as follows.

(2) In subsection (3), after "licence" insert "or a driving record".

(3) After that subsection insert—

"(3A) On receiving such a notice in relation to a person who is not the holder of a licence, the Secretary of State must make any necessary adjustments to the endorsements on the person's driving record to reflect the outcome of the appeal."

13. In section 48(1)(*b*) and (2)(*b*) (exemption from disqualification and endorsement for certain construction and use offences), after "him" insert "or on his driving record".

14. (1) Section 54 (notices on-the-spot etc) is amended as follows.

(2) In subsection (2), for "subsection (3) below" substitute "the following provisions of this section".

(3) In subsection (3), after "endorsement" insert ", and the person is the holder of a licence,".

(4) In subsection (4)—

(*a*) for the word "and" at the end of paragraph (*a*) substitute—

"(aa) the person concerned is the holder of a licence, and",

(*b*) in paragraph (*b*), for "the person concerned" substitute "he".

(5) In subsection (6), after "subsection (4)" insert "or (5C)".

(6) In subsection (10), for "subsections (3)(*b*) and (5)(*a*) above" substitute "this section".

15. (1) Section 57 (endorsement without hearings) is amended as follows.

(2) In subsection (1), after "a person" insert "who is the holder of a licence".

(3) In the heading, for **"licences"** substitute **"counterparts"**.

16. In section 58 (effect of endorsement without hearing), in the heading, after **"endorsement"** insert **"of counterpart"**.

17. *Inserts s 58A into the Road Traffic Offenders Act 1988.*

18. In section 61 (fixed penalty notice mistakenly given: exclusion of fixed penalty procedures), in the heading, after **"given"** insert **"to licence holder"**.

19. *Inserts s 61A into the Road Traffic Offenders Act 1988.*

20. In section 69(4) (payment of penalty), for "77" substitute "77A".

21. (1) In section 70(4) (registration certificates), after paragraph (*b*) insert "and

(c) otherwise—

(i) if the offence to which the fixed penalty notice or conditional offer relates was committed in England or Wales, cause it to be sent to the designated officer for the local justice area in which the offence was committed, or

(ii) if the offence was committed in Scotland, cause it to be sent to the clerk of a court of summary jurisdiction for the area in which the offence was committed."

(2) An order under section 61 may provide that sub-paragraph (1) is to come into force only in relation to an area specified in the order.

(3) If such an order provides that sub-paragraph (1) is to come into force only in relation to an area specified in the order, it may also provide that (unless continued in force by a subsequent order) sub-paragraph (1) is to remain in force there only for a period specified in the order.

22. (1) Section 71 (registration of sums payable in default) is amended as follows.

(2) In subsection (1), after paragraph (a) insert "or" and after paragraph (c) insert

"or

(d) if it appears to him that the defaulter does not reside in England, Wales or Scotland—

(i) in a case where the offence to which the fixed penalty notice or conditional offer relates was committed in the local justice area for which he is the designated officer, he must register that sum for enforcement as a fine in that area by entering it in the register of a magistrates' court acting in that area,

(ii) in a case where it was committed in another local justice area in England and Wales, he must send the certificate to the designated officer for that area, and

(iii) in a case where it was committed in Scotland, he must send the certificate to the clerk of a court of summary jurisdiction for the area in which the offence was committed."

(3) In subsection (2), after paragraph (a) insert "or" and after paragraph (c) insert

"or

(d) if it appears to him that the defaulter does not reside in England, Wales or Scotland—

(i) in a case where the offence to which the fixed penalty notice or conditional offer relates was committed in the area of the court, he must register that sum for enforcement as a fine by that court,

(ii) in a case where it was committed in an area of any other court of summary jurisdiction in Scotland, he must send the certificate to the clerk of that court, and

(iii) in a case where it was committed in England or Wales, he must send the certificate to the designated officer for the local justice area in which the offence was committed."

(4) An order under section 61 may provide that sub-paragraphs (1) to (3) are to come into force only in relation to an area specified in the order.

(5) If such an order provides that sub-paragraphs (1) to (3) are to come into force only in relation to an area specified in the order, it may also provide that (unless continued in force by a subsequent order) sub-paragraphs (1) to (3) are to remain in force there only for a period specified in the order.

23. (1) Section 72 (notices on-the-spot etc: when registration and endorsement invalid) is amended as follows.

(2) After subsection (4) insert—

"(4A) Where in any case within subsection (2)(a) above the driving record of the person to whom the relevant fixed penalty notice was given was endorsed under section 57A of this Act in respect of the offence in respect of which the notice was given, the endorsement shall be void."

(3) In subsection (5)(a), after "57" insert "or 57A".

(4) After subsection (6) insert—

"(6A) The proper officer of the relevant court must send notice to the Secretary of State of any endorsement of a person's driving record that is void by virtue of this section and the Secretary of State must adjust the endorsements on that record accordingly."

24. (1) Section 75 (issue of conditional offer) is amended as follows.

(2) In subsection (5), for "and 77" substitute ", 77 and 77A".

(3) In subsection (6), for "and 77" substitute ", 77 and 77A".

(4) In subsection (8), after "conditional offer" insert "sent to an alleged offender who is the holder of a licence".

(5) After subsection (8) insert—

"(8A) A conditional offer sent to an alleged offender who is not the holder of a licence must indicate that if the following conditions are fulfilled, that is—

(a) within the period of twenty-eight days following the date on which the offer was issued, or such longer period as may be specified in the offer, the alleged offender makes payment of the fixed penalty to the appropriate person, and

(b) the appropriate person is satisfied, on accessing information held on the driving record of the alleged offender, that if he were convicted of the offence, he would not be liable to be disqualified under section 35 of this Act,

any liability to conviction of the offence shall be discharged."

(6) In subsection (9)—

(a) for "condition" substitute "conditions", and

(b) after " (8)(b)" insert "and (8A)(b)".

(7) In subsection (11A), for "and 77" substitute ", 77 and 77A".

25. (1) Section 76 (effect of offer and payment of penalty) is amended as follows.

(2) In subsection (3)—

(a) in paragraph (a), after "counterpart" insert "or (where the alleged offender is not the holder of a licence) accessing information held on his driving record", and

(b) in paragraph (b), after "with" insert " (where he is the holder of a licence)".

(3) In subsection (4), after "75(8)(a)" insert "or (8A)(a)".

26. (1) Section 77 (endorsement where penalty paid) is amended as follows.

(2) In subsection (1)(a), after "a person" insert "who is the holder of a licence".

(3) In the heading, after **"endorsement"** insert **"of counterparts"**.

27. Inserts s 77A into the Road Traffic Offenders Act 1988.

28. (1) Section 83 (powers of court in cases of deception) is amended as follows.

(2) After subsection (1) insert—

"(1A) This section also applies where—

(a) particulars are endorsed on a person's driving record under section 57A of this Act because the fixed penalty clerk or the Secretary of State is deceived as to whether endorsement under that section is excluded by section 61A(2) of this Act by virtue of the fact that the person to whom the fixed penalty notice was given would be liable to be disqualified under section 35 of this Act if he were convicted of the offence, or

(b) particulars are endorsed on a person's driving record under section 77A of this Act because the appropriate person or court is deceived as to whether proceedings against the person are excluded by section 76 of this Act by virtue of the fact that the person to whom the conditional offer is issued would be liable to be disqualified under section 35 of this Act if he were convicted of the offence."

(3) In subsection (2)—

(a) in paragraph (a), for "licence holder" substitute "person to whom the fixed penalty notice was given or conditional offer was issued",

(b) in paragraph (b), for "the licence holder" substitute "he",

(c) after "57" insert "or 57A", and

(d) after "77" insert "or 77A".

29. In section 84(1) (regulations), after "54(4)" insert "or (5C)".

30. Inserts s 84A into the Road Traffic Offenders Act 1988.

31. In section 91ZA(1) (application to Northern Ireland licence holders)—

(a) in paragraph (i), after "44(1)" insert "and (3A)", and

(b) in paragraph (k), for "and (3)" substitute ", (3) and (3A)".

32. In section 91A(1) (application to Community licence holders)—

(a) after "44(1)" insert "and (3A)", and

(b) after "47(3)" insert "and (3A)".

Child Support Act 1991 (c 48)

33. In section 40B(9) of the Child Support Act 1991 (disqualification from driving: further provision), for "the driving" substitute "any driving".

Section 10

SCHEDULE 3
ENDORSEMENT: ALL DRIVERS

Public Passenger Vehicles Act 1981 (c 14)

1. (1) Section 24 of the Public Passenger Vehicles Act 1981 (regulation of conduct of drivers, inspectors and conductors) (as amended by Schedule 2) is amended as follows.

(2) In subsection (2), for the words from "cause particulars" to the end substitute "send notice of the particulars of the conviction to the Secretary of State requiring the Secretary of State to endorse them on the person's driving record (within the meaning of section 97A of the Road Traffic Offenders Act 1988)".

(3) Omit subsection (3).

Road Traffic Act 1988 (c 52)

2. The Road Traffic Act 1988 is amended as follows.

3. In section 88(6) (requirement for driving licence: exceptions), omit ", counterparts of licences".

4. In section 92(7ZB)(a) and (7C) (requirements as to physical fitness of drivers), omit "and its counterpart".

5. (1) Section 93 (revocation of licence because of disability or prospective disability) is amended as follows.

(2) In subsections (2)(b) and (3), omit "and its counterpart".

(3) In subsection (4)(a)—

(a) omit "or its counterpart", and

(b) for "them" substitute "it".

(4) In subsection (4)(b)—

(a) for "them" substitute "it", and

(b) for "their" substitute "its".

6. (1) Section 97 (grant of licences) is amended as follows.

(2) In subsection (1)(c)—

(a) in sub-paragraph (i), omit "and its counterpart",

(b) in sub-paragraph (ia), omit the words from "together" to the end, and

(c) in sub-paragraph (ii), omit "and its counterpart (if any) issued to him".

(3) In subsection (1AA), omit—

(a) "together with the counterparts mentioned in that sub-paragraph", and

(b) "and its Northern Ireland counterpart".

7. In section 98(1)(c) (form of licence), omit "or its counterpart".

8. (1) Section 98A (compulsory surrender of old-form licences) (inserted by section 29) is amended as follows.

(2) In subsection (1), omit "and their counterparts".

(3) In subsection (3), omit " (and their counterparts)".

(4) In subsection (4), omit " (with its counterpart)".

(5) In subsection (7), omit "and its counterpart".

9. (1) Section 99 (duration of licences) is amended as follows.

(2) In subsection (2A), omit "and its counterpart".

(3) In subsection (3)—

(a) omit paragraph (aa),

(b) in paragraph (b), omit "or in its counterpart", and

(c) omit "and its counterpart".

(4) In subsection (4), omit "and its counterpart".

(5) In subsection (6)—

(a) omit "and its counterpart", in both places,

(b) for "them", in both places, substitute "it", and

(c) for "their" substitute "its".

(6) In subsection (7), omit "and its counterpart".

(7) In subsection (7ZA) (inserted by section 30), omit "and its counterpart".

10. In section 99A (authorisation to drive in Great Britain), omit subsections (5) and (6).

11. (1) Section 99B (information about resident Community licence holders) is amended as follows.

(2) Omit subsection (3).

(3) In subsection (4), for "subsections (1) and (3)" substitute "subsection (1)".

(4) In subsection (5), for "a Community licence delivered to him (whether or not in pursuance of this section) in such manner as he may determine" substitute "the driving record of a person who delivers to him a Community licence (whether or not in pursuance of this section)".

(5) Omit subsection (6).

(6) For subsection (7) substitute—

"(7) Where the name of a Community licence holder as specified in his Community licence ceases to be correct, he must deliver his Community licence immediately to the Secretary of State and provide him with particulars of the alterations falling to be made in the name on it."

(7) Omit subsection (8).

(8) In subsection (9), after "endorse the Community licence" insert "and that person's driving record".

(9) In subsection (11)(b), omit " (6) or".

(10) Omit subsection (12).

12. (1) Section 99C (revocation of authorisation conferred by Community licence because of disability or prospective disability) is amended as follows.

(2) In subsections (1) to (4), omit "and its counterpart (if any)" in each place.

(3) Omit subsection (5).

13. (1) Section 105 (regulations) is amended as follows.

(2) In subsection (2)—

(a) in paragraph (a), for "Community licences and counterparts of such licences" substitute "and Community licences",

(b) in paragraph (b), after sub-paragraph (i) insert "or" and omit sub-paragraph (iii) and the word "or" before it,

(c) in paragraph (e), omit "and counterparts of licences" and "or counterparts of licences", and

(d) omit paragraph (ea).

(3) In subsection (5), for "and 91ZA to 91B" substitute ", 91ZA and 91A".

14. In section 108 (interpretation), omit the definition of "counterpart".

15. In section 109 (provisions as to Northern Ireland drivers' licences), for subsection (2) substitute—

"(2) For the purposes of this Act, any driver holding a Northern Ireland licence shall be under the same obligation to produce such a licence as if it had been a licence granted under this Part of this Act, and the provisions of this Act as to the production of licences granted under this Part of this Act shall apply accordingly."

16. (1) Section 109A (counterparts issued to Northern Ireland licence holders) is amended as follows.

(2) For subsections (1) and (2) substitute—

"(1) The Secretary of State may endorse the driving record of a Northern Ireland licence holder who delivers to him a Northern Ireland licence together with the information specified in, or required under, subsection (3) below with any part of that information."

(3) For subsections (4) and (5) substitute—

"(4) Where the name of a Northern Ireland licence holder as specified in his Northern Ireland licence ceases to be correct, he may deliver his Northern Ireland licence immediately to the Secretary of State and provide him with particulars of the alterations falling to be made in the name on it.

(5) On the delivery of a Northern Ireland licence by any person in pursuance of subsection (4) above, the Secretary of State may endorse the Northern Ireland licence and that person's driving record with the correct name and must return the Northern Ireland licence to that person."

(4) In the heading, for **"Counterparts issued to"** substitute **"Information about"**.

17. (1) Section 109B (revocation of authorisation conferred by Northern Ireland licence because of disability or prospective disability) is amended as follows.

(2) In subsection (1), omit the words from "together" to the end.

(3) In subsection (2)—

(a) in paragraph (a), omit "together with the relevant counterparts", and

(b) in paragraph (b), omit "and those counterparts".

(4) In subsection (4), omit "and the relevant counterparts".

(5) Omit subsection (5).

18. In section 115A(1) (community licence holders: cessation of authorisation), omit "and its counterpart (if any)".

19. In section 117A (community licences: disqualification, etc), omit "and its counterpart (if any)" in both places.

20. (1) Section 118 (revoked or suspended licences: surrender, return and endorsement) is amended as follows.

(2) In subsection (1), omit "and its counterpart".

(3) For subsection (2) substitute—

"(2) Where, in pursuance of section 115 of this Act, the Secretary of State suspends a licence, he must (unless the holder of the licence has already delivered his licence to a traffic commissioner on a reference under section 116 of this Act) serve notice on the holder of the licence requiring him to deliver the licence forthwith to the Secretary of State at the address specified in the notice, and it shall be the duty of the holder of the licence to comply with the requirement.

(2A) On the delivery of the licence or, where the licence has already been delivered to a traffic commissioner, on suspending the licence, the Secretary of State must endorse the particulars of the suspension on the licence holder's driving record.

(2B) The Secretary of State or, as the case may be, the traffic commissioner, must then return the licence to the holder."

(4) In subsection (4), omit "and its counterpart".

(5) Omit subsection (5).

21. In section 121 (interpretation), omit the definition of "counterpart".

22. In section 122(3) (provisions as to Northern Ireland licences)—

(*a*) for "and its counterpart are" substitute "is", and

(*b*) for "them" substitute "it".

23. In section 125A(8) (registration of disabled persons), in paragraph (*c*) of the definition of "disabled person's limited driving licence", omit "and a counterpart of that licence".

24. In section 141A(5) (interpretation of Part 5) (as substituted by Schedule 6), omit "and "counterpart", in relation to a Community licence".

25. In section 142 (index to Part 5) (as substituted by Schedule 6), omit "and counterpart".

26. (1) Section 164 (power of constables to require production of driving licence and in certain cases statement of date of birth) is amended as follows.

(2) Omit "and its counterpart" in each place.

(3) In subsection (1), for "they were" substitute "it was".

(4) In subsection (3)—

(*a*) for "their" substitute "its", and

(*b*) for "them", in both places, substitute "it".

(5) In subsection (5)—

(*a*) for "them", in each place, substitute "it", and

(*b*) for "their" substitute "its".

(6) In subsection (7), for "their", in both places, substitute "its".

(7) In subsection (8)—

(*a*) for "them", in each place, substitute "it", and

(*b*) for "their" substitute "its".

(8) In subsection (11), omit the reference to "counterpart".

27. In section 167(*a*) (power of arrest in Scotland for reckless or careless driving or cycling), for the words from "and the counterpart" to the end substitute "or, as the case may be, his Northern Ireland licence or Community licence within the meaning of that Part."

28. (1) Section 173 (forgery of documents etc) is amended as follows.

(2) In subsection (2)—

(*a*) in paragraph (*a*), omit the words from "or" to the end, and

(*b*) omit paragraph (aa).

(3) In subsection (4), omit ""counterpart",".

29. In section 176 (power to seize articles), omit subsections (1A), (3A) and (8).

Road Traffic Offenders Act 1988 (c 53)

30. The Road Traffic Offenders Act 1988 (as amended by Schedule 2) is amended as follows.

31. In section 7(1) (duty of accused to provide licence), omit the words from "and the foregoing" to the end.

32. (1) Section 26 (interim disqualification) is amended as follows.

(2) In subsection (7)—

(*a*) in paragraph (*a*), omit "and its counterpart", and

(*b*) in paragraph (*b*), omit "and counterpart" and for "them" substitute "it".

(3) In subsection (8)—

(*a*) omit "and its counterpart",

(*b*) for "them" substitute "it", and

(*c*) omit "and counterpart".

(4) In subsection (9)(*b*)—

(*a*) omit "and its counterpart",

(*b*) omit "and counterpart", and

(*c*) for "their" substitute "its".

(5) Omit subsection (14).

33. (1) Section 27 (production of licence) is amended as follows.

(2) Omit "and its counterpart" in each place.

(3) In subsection (1), for "them" substitute "it".

(4) In subsection (3)(*b*), for "are produced" substitute "is produced".

(5) In subsection (4), for "their" substitute "its".

34. In section 28(3) (penalty points to be attributed to an offence), for "57(5), 57A(6), 77(5)" substitute "57A(6)".

35. (1) Section 29 (penalty points to be taken into account on conviction) is amended as follows.

(2) In subsection (1)(*b*), omit "the counterpart of any licence held by him or on".

(3) Omit subsection (3).

36. (1) Section 30 (modification of sections 28 and 29 in case where fixed penalty also in question) is amended as follows.

(2) In subsection (1)(*b*)—

(*a*) omit "the counterpart of his licence or", and

(*b*) for "57, 57A, 77" substitute "57A".

(3) In subsection (2)(*b*)—

(*a*) omit "on the counterpart of his licence or", and

(*b*) for "57, 57A, 77" substitute "57A".

37. In section 31(1) (court may take particulars endorsed into consideration), omit "the counterpart of his licence or on".

38. Omit section 32 (in Scotland court may take extract from licensing records into account).

39. In section 36 (disqualification until test passed), omit subsection (10).

40. (1) Section 42 (removal of disqualification) is amended as follows.

(2) In subsection (5), for paragraph (*a*) substitute—

"(*a*) must send notice of the order to the Secretary of State,".

(3) Omit subsection (5A).

(4) In subsection (5AA), for " (5)(*a*)(ii)" substitute " (5)(*a*)".

(5) In subsection (5B), for " (5)(*a*)(ii) or (5A)" substitute " (5)(*a*)".

41. Omit section 45 (effect of endorsement of counterparts).

42. In section 45A (effect of endorsement of driving records), for subsections (3) to (5) substitute—

"(3) An endorsement ordered on a person's conviction of an offence remains effective (subject to subsections (4) and (5) below)—

(*a*) if an order is made for the disqualification of the offender, until four years have elapsed since the conviction, and

(*b*) if no such order is made, until either—

(i) four years have elapsed since the commission of the offence, or

(ii) an order is made for the disqualification of the offender under section 35 of this Act.

(4) Where the offence was one under section 1 or 2 of the Road Traffic Act 1988 (causing death by dangerous driving and dangerous driving), the endorsement remains in any case effective until four years have elapsed since the conviction.

(5) Where the offence was one—

(*a*) under section 3A, 4(1) or 5(1)(*a*) of that Act (driving offences connected with drink or drugs),

(*b*) under section 7(6) of that Act (failing to provide specimen) involving obligatory disqualification, or

(*c*) under section 7A(6) of that Act (failing to allow a specimen to be subjected to laboratory test),

the endorsement remains effective until eleven years have elapsed since the conviction."

43. In section 46(2)(*b*) (combination of disqualification and endorsement with probation orders and orders for discharge), omit "the counterpart of any licence held by him or on".

44. (1) Section 47 (supplementary provisions as to disqualifications and endorsements) is amended as follows.

(2) For subsection (2) substitute—

"(2) Where a court orders the endorsement of a person's driving record it may, and where a court orders a person to be disqualified for a period of 56 days or more it must, send any licence of the person that is produced to the court, to the Secretary of State."

(3) In subsection (2A), omit "and its counterpart".

(4) In subsection (3), omit "a licence or".

(5) In subsection (3A), omit "in relation to a person who is not the holder of a licence,".

(6) In subsection (4), omit "and the counterpart of a licence".

45. (1) Section 48 (exemption from disqualification and endorsement for certain construction and use offences) is amended as follows.

(2) In subsections (1) and (2), omit "the counterpart of any licence held by him or on".

(3) Omit subsection (3).

46. (1) Section 56 (licence receipts) is amended as follows.

(2) Omit "and its counterpart" in each place.

(3) In subsection (2), for "them" substitute "it".

47. Omit section 58 (effect of endorsement of counterpart without hearing).

48. Omit section 61 (fixed penalty notice mistakenly given to licence holder: exclusion of fixed penalty procedures).

49. (1) Section 61A (fixed penalty notice mistakenly given to unlicensed person: exclusion of fixed penalty procedures) is amended as follows.

(2) In subsection (1), omit "but who is not the holder of a licence,".

(3) In subsection (3), insert at the end "and send the chief officer of police any licence sent to him under section 54(7) of this Act."

(4) In the heading, omit **"to unlicensed person"**.

50. (1) Section 72 (notices on-the-spot etc: when registration and endorsement invalid) is amended as follows.

(2) Omit subsection (4).

(3) In subsection (5), omit "57 or".

(4) Omit subsection (6).

51. (1) Section 75 (issue of conditional offer) is amended as follows.

(2) In subsections (5) and (6), for ", 77 and 77A", substitute "and 77A".

(3) Omit subsection (8).

(4) In subsection (8A)—

(a) omit "who is not the holder of a licence", and
(b) in paragraph (a), for the words after "offender" substitute—

> "(i) makes payment of the fixed penalty to the appropriate person, and
> (ii) where he is the holder of a licence and the offence to which the offer relates is an offence involving obligatory endorsement, at the same time delivers his licence to the appropriate person, and".

(5) In subsection (11A), for ", 77 and 77A", substitute "and 77A".
(6) Omit subsection (12).
52. (1) Section 76 (effect of offer and payment of penalty) is amended as follows.
(2) In subsection (3)—

(a) in paragraph (a), omit "inspecting the licence and its counterpart or (where the alleged offender is not the holder of a licence)" and for "his" substitute "the alleged offender's", and
(b) in paragraph (b), omit "and its counterpart".

(3) In subsection (4), for "75(8)(a) or (8A)(a)" substitute "75(8A)(a)".
(4) Omit subsection (8).
53. Omit section 77 (endorsement of counterparts where penalty paid).
54. (1) Section 77A (endorsement of driving records where penalty paid) is amended as follows.
(2) In subsection (1)—

(a) omit "who is not the holder of a licence",
(b) after "to the fixed penalty clerk" insert "and (if he is the holder of a licence) delivers his licence to the fixed penalty clerk", and
(c) insert at the end "together with any licence delivered under paragraph (a) above".

(3) In subsection (2)—

(a) after "record" insert "and return any licence delivered to him under this section to the alleged offender",
(b) omit "who is not the holder of a licence", and
(c) after "to him" insert "and (if he is the holder of a licence) delivers his licence to him,".

55. (1) Section 83 (powers of court in cases of deception) is amended as follows.
(2) Omit subsection (1).
(3) In subsection (1A), omit "also".
(4) In subsection (2), omit—

(a) "57 or", and
(b) "77 or".

56. In section 84(1)(a) (regulations), for "54(4) or (5C)" substitute "54(5)".
57. (1) Section 91ZA (application to Northern Ireland licence holders) is amended as follows.
(2) In subsection (1)—

(a) in paragraph (b), omit "and (9)(b)",
(b) omit paragraphs (d) to (f),
(c) omit paragraphs (h) to (j),
(d) in paragraph (k), omit ", (3) and (3A)", and
(e) omit paragraph (l).

(3) Omit subsections (3) to (6).
(4) In subsection (7)—

(a) omit "and its counterpart (if any)", and
(b) for "their" substitute "its".

(5) In subsection (8), omit "and its counterpart".
(6) In subsection (9)—

(a) in paragraph (a), for "subsection (5) above" substitute "section 44A above of an order for the endorsement of a person's driving record", and
(b) in paragraph (b)(i), after "licence" insert ", or a person normally resident in Northern Ireland who does not hold a licence,".

58. Omit section 91ZB (effect of endorsement on Northern Ireland licence holders).
59. (1) Section 91A (application to Community licence holders) is amended as follows.
(2) In subsection (1), for the words from "27" to "48(1) and (2)" substitute "and 32".
(3) Omit subsections (2) to (4).
(4) In subsection (5)—

(a) omit "and its counterpart (if any)", and
(b) for "their" substitute "its".

(5) Omit subsection (6).
(6) For subsection (7) substitute—

"(7) Where—

> (a) a notice is sent to the Secretary of State under section 44A above for the endorsement of a person's driving record with any particulars or penalty points, and
> (b) the particulars contained in the notice include—
>
>> (i) particulars of an offence in respect of which the holder of a Community licence, or a person normally resident in another EEA state who does not hold a licence, is disqualified by an order of a court, and
>> (ii) particulars of the disqualification,

the Secretary of State must send a notice containing the particulars mentioned in paragraph (b)(i) and (ii) to the licensing authority in the EEA state in respect of which the Community licence was issued or, where the person disqualified is not the holder of a licence, the licensing authority in the EEA state where the person is normally resident.

(7A) Where a Community licence has been sent to the Secretary of State in pursuance of subsection (5) above, he must return the Community licence to the holder—

(*a*) on the expiry of the period of disqualification, or

(*b*) if earlier, on being satisfied that the holder has left Great Britain and is not normally resident there."

(7) Omit subsections (8) to (10).

60. Omit section 91B (effect of endorsement on Community licence holders).

61. In section 98(1) (interpretation)—

(*a*) in the definition of "the provisions connected with the licensing of drivers", for "91ZA to 91B" substitute "91ZA, 91A", and

(*b*) in the words following the definition of "the Traffic Acts", omit " "counterpart",".

62. (1) Schedule 1 (offences to which sections 1, 6, 11 and 12(1) apply) is amended as follows.

(2) In the entries relating to sections 98A(7) and 99(5) of the Road Traffic Act 1988 (c 52), omit "and counterpart".

(3) In the entry relating to section 164(6) of that Act, omit "and counterpart etc".

63. (1) Part 1 of Schedule 2 (prosecution and punishment of offences: offences under the Traffic Acts) is amended as follows.

(2) In the entries relating to the following provisions, omit "and counterpart"—

(*a*) section 92(7C) of the Road Traffic Act 1988,

(*b*) section 93(3) of that Act,

(*c*) section 98A(7) of that Act,

(*d*) section 99(5) of that Act,

(*e*) section 118 of that Act,

(*f*) section 26 of the Road Traffic Offenders Act 1988 (c 53), and

(*g*) section 27 of that Act.

(3) In the entry relating to section 164 of the Road Traffic Act 1988, omit "or counterpart etc".

(4) In the entry relating to section 173 of that Act, omit "counterparts of Community licences,".

64. In Schedule 5 (Scotland: additional offences open to conditional offer), in the entry relating to section 99(5) of the Road Traffic Act 1988, omit—

(*a*) "and its counterpart", and

(*b*) "and counterpart".

Child Support Act 1991 (c 48)

65. (1) Section 40B of the Child Support Act 1991 (disqualification from driving: further provision) is amended as follows.

(2) In subsection (4), omit the words from "and" to the end.

(3) In subsection (9)—

(*a*) omit "and its counterpart", and

(*b*) for "their" substitute "its".

Road Traffic (New Drivers) Act 1995 (c 13)

66. The Road Traffic (New Drivers) Act 1995 is amended as follows.

67. (1) Section 2 (surrender of licences) is amended as follows.

(2) For subsection (2) substitute—

"(2) Where this subsection applies, the court must, together with the notice of the order referred to in subsection (1)(*d*) required to be sent to the Secretary of State under section 44A of the Road Traffic Offenders Act 1988, send the person's licence on its production to the court."

(3) In subsection (3)—

(*a*) in paragraph (*a*), for "and its counterpart have" substitute "has",

(*b*) in paragraph (*c*)—

(i) omit "appropriate person endorses the number of", and

(ii) for "on the counterpart of the licence" substitute "are to be endorsed on the person's driving record", and

(*c*) in paragraph (*f*)—

(i) before "endorsed" insert "to be", and

(ii) for "counterpart of the licence" substitute "person's driving record".

(4) In subsection (4)—

(*a*) in paragraph (*a*)—

(i) omit "and its counterpart", and

(ii) for "57(3) or (4) or 77(1)" substitute "57A(3) or (4) or 77A(2)", and

(*b*) in paragraph (*b*), insert at the end "together with the notice he is required to send under section 57A or 77A of that Act of the particulars to be endorsed on the person's driving record".

68. In section 3 (revocation of licences), for subsection (1) substitute—

"(1) Where the Secretary of State receives—

(*a*) a notice sent to him under section 44A, 57A or 77A of the Road Traffic Offenders Act 1988 of particulars required to be endorsed on a person's driving record, and

(*b*) a person's licence sent to him in accordance with section 2(2) or (4)(*b*),

the Secretary of State must by notice served on that person revoke the licence."

69. In section 9(5) (interpretation etc), omit "and its counterpart" in both places.

70. (1) Schedule 1 (newly qualified drivers holding test certificates) is amended as follows.
(2) In paragraph 3—

(*a*) in sub-paragraph (2), omit "and its counterpart", and
(*b*) in sub-paragraph (4)(*a*), omit " (with its counterpart)".

(3) In paragraph 4—

(*a*) for sub-paragraph (2) substitute—

"(2) The court must send to the Secretary of State, on its production to the court, the person's test certificate, together with the notice of the order referred to in section 2(1)(*d*).", and

(*b*) in sub-paragraph (4), for the words following "State" substitute "the person's test certificate together with the notice he is required to send under section 57A or 77A of the particulars to be endorsed on the person's driving record."

(4) In paragraph 5(1)—

(*a*) for "paragraph 4" substitute "section 44A, 57A or 77A of the Road Traffic Offenders Act 1988",
(*b*) for "or endorsed on the counterpart of a person's licence" substitute "on a person's driving record", and
(*c*) for " (4)(*b*)" substitute " (4)".

(5) In paragraph 7—

(*a*) for sub-paragraph (2) substitute—

"(2) The court must, together with the notice of the order referred to in section 2(1)(*d*), send to the Secretary of State—

    (*a*) on its production to the court, the person's licence, and
    (*b*) on its production to the court, the person's test certificate.", and

(*b*) in sub-paragraph (4)—

    (i) in paragraph (*a*), omit "and its counterpart",
    (ii) in that paragraph, for "57(3) or (4) or 77(1)" substitute "57A(3) or (4) or 77A(2)", and
    (iii) in paragraph (*b*), for "them" substitute "it" and insert at the end "together with the notice he is required to send under section 57A or 77A of that Act of the particulars to be endorsed on the person's driving record."

(6) In paragraph 8(1)(*a*),—

(*a*) for "paragraph 7(2)(*a*)" substitute "section 44A, 57A or 77A of the Road Traffic Offenders Act 1988",
(*b*) for "the counterpart of a person's licence" substitute "a person's driving record,
(*c*) omit "and its counterpart", and
(*d*) for "7(2)(*b*)" substitute "7(2)(*a*)".

Powers of Criminal Courts (Sentencing) Act 2000 (c 6)

71. The Powers of Criminal Courts (Sentencing) Act 2000 is amended as follows.
72. (1) Section 146 (driving disqualification for any offence) is amended as follows.
(2) In subsection (4)—

(*a*) in paragraph (*a*), omit "together with its counterpart", and
(*b*) in paragraphs (aa) and (*b*), omit "and its counterpart (if any)".

(3) In subsection (5), omit the definition of "counterpart".
73. (1) Section 147 (driving disqualification where vehicle used for purposes of crime) is amended as follows.
(2) In subsection (5)—

(*a*) in paragraph (*a*), omit "together with its counterpart", and
(*b*) in paragraphs (aa) and (*b*), omit "and its counterpart (if any)".

(3) In subsection (7), for "and "counterpart" have the meanings" substitute "has the meaning".

Crime (International Co-operation) Act 2003 (c 32)

74. The Crime (International Co-operation) Act 2003 is amended as follows.
75. (1) Section 63 (production of licence: Great Britain) is amended as follows.
(2) Omit "and its counterpart" in each place.
(3) In subsections (3)(*b*) and (4)(*b*), for "them" substitute "it".
(4) In subsection (7), omit the second sentence.
76. (1) Section 64 (production of licence: Northern Ireland) is amended as follows.
(2) Omit "and its counterpart" in each place.
(3) In subsections (3)(*b*) and (4)(*b*), for "them" substitute "it".
(4) In subsection (7), omit the second sentence.
77. (1) Section 68 (endorsement of licence: Great Britain) is amended as follows.
(2) For subsections (2) to (5) substitute—

"(2) The Secretary of State must secure that the particulars of the disqualification are endorsed on the person's driving record until the end of the period for which the endorsement remains effective.
   (3) At the end of the period for which the endorsement remains effective the Secretary of State must remove the endorsement from the person's driving record."

(3) For subsection (7) substitute—

"(7) Where the person ceases to be disqualified by virtue of section 57(6), the Secretary of State must endorse the relevant particulars on his driving record.
   In this section and section 69 "driving record" has the meaning given by section 97A of the Road Traffic Offenders Act 1988."

78. (1) Section 69 (endorsement of licence: Northern Ireland) is amended as follows.
(2) For subsections (2) to (5) substitute—

"(2) The Department must secure that the particulars of the disqualification are endorsed on the person's driving record until the end of the period for which the endorsement remains effective.

(3) At the end of the period for which the endorsement remains effective the Department must secure that the endorsement is removed from the person's driving record."

(3) For subsection (7) substitute—

"(7) Where the person ceases to be disqualified by virtue of section 57(6), the Department must secure that the relevant particulars are endorsed on his driving record."

79. In section 74(1) (interpretation), omit the definition of "counterpart".

Criminal Justice Act 2003 (c 44)

80. (1) Section 301 of the Criminal Justice Act 2003 (fine defaulters: driving disqualification) is amended as follows.

(2) In subsection (6)—

(*a*) in paragraph (*a*), omit "together with its counterpart", and
(*b*) in paragraph (*b*), omit "and its counterpart (if any)".

(3) In subsection (7), omit the definition of "counterpart".

SCHEDULE 4
PROHIBITION ON DRIVING: IMMOBILISATION, REMOVAL AND DISPOSAL OF VEHICLES
Secretary of State may make regulations.

SCHEDULE 5
NEW SCHEDULE 2A TO THE ROAD TRAFFIC ACT 1988

4–2016O

Section 42   SCHEDULE 6
                                   DRIVING INSTRUCTION

Road Traffic Act 1988 (c 52)

1. The Road Traffic Act 1988 is amended as follows.

2. For section 123 (instruction in the driving of motor cars to be given only by registered or licensed person) and the heading before it substitute—

"Instructors and instruction businesses to be registered

123. Requirement of registration.   (1) A person—

(*a*) must not give paid driving instruction of any prescribed description unless he is registered in respect of the giving of that description of driving instruction, and
(*b*) must not carry on business in the provision of paid driving instruction of any prescribed description unless he is registered in respect of the carrying on of business in the provision of that description of driving instruction.

(2) A person—

(*a*) must not give paid driving instruction of any prescribed description unless prescribed requirements as to the displaying of evidence that he is registered in respect of the giving of that description of driving instruction are complied with, and
(*b*) must not carry on business in the provision of paid driving instruction of any prescribed description unless prescribed requirements as to the displaying of evidence that he is registered in respect of the carrying on of business in the provision of that description of driving instruction are complied with.

(3) In this Part of this Act "driving instruction" means instruction in relation to the driving of a motor vehicle.

(4) Regulations under this Part which prescribe a description of driving instruction may do so by reference to—

(*a*) the class of motor vehicle to which the instruction relates,
(*b*) the description of persons to whom the instruction is given or provided, or
(*c*) the nature of the instruction or where or how it is given or provided.

(5) For the purposes of this Part of this Act instruction is paid instruction if payment of money or money's worth is, or is to be, made for the instruction by or in respect of the person to whom the instruction is given or provided.

(6) Regulations may prescribe circumstances in which instruction provided free of charge shall be deemed to be given for payment of money by or in respect of the person to whom the instruction is given or provided.

(7) For the purposes of this Part of this Act a person is "registered" if his name is in the register together with—

(*a*) an indication as to whether he is registered in respect of the giving of driving instruction or the carrying on of business in the provision of driving instruction (or both),
(*b*) an indication as to the description of driving instruction in respect of which he is registered, and
(*c*) such other particulars as may be prescribed,

and "registration" shall be construed accordingly.

(8) In this Part of this Act "the register" means the register established for the purposes of this Part of this Act under section 125 of this Act.

123A. Paid driving instruction: offences.   (1) If driving instruction is given in contravention of section 123(1)(*a*) of this Act—

(a) the person by whom it is given,

(b) if that person is employed by another to give that instruction, that other (as well as that person), and

(c) if that person is a franchisee under a driving instruction franchise, the franchisor under the driving instruction franchise (as well as that person),

is guilty of an offence.

(2) If a person contravenes section 123(1)(*b*) of this Act he is guilty of an offence.

(3) In proceedings against a person for an offence under subsection (1) or (2) above it shall be a defence for him to prove that he did not know, and had no reasonable cause to believe, that—

(a) in a case within paragraph (*a*) of subsection (1) above, or within subsection (2) above, he,

(b) in a case within paragraph (*b*) of subsection (1) above, the person employed by him, or

(c) in a case within paragraph (*c*) of that subsection, the person who was the franchisee under the driving instruction franchise,

was not at the material time registered in respect of the description of driving instruction in question.

(4) If a person contravenes section 123(2) of this Act he is guilty of an offence."

3. For section 124 (exemption of police instructors) substitute—

"124. Exemption from prohibitions imposed by section 123. (1) Regulations may prescribe circumstances in which section 123 of this Act shall not apply in relation to driving instruction, or driving instruction of a prescribed description.

(2) The regulations may, in particular, make provision for section 123(1)(*a*) and (2)(*a*) of this Act not to apply in prescribed circumstances for the purpose of enabling persons to acquire experience in giving driving instruction."

4. For section 125 (register of approved instructors) substitute—

"125. Register. (1) Regulations shall make provision for the establishment and maintenance of a register for the purposes of this Part of this Act.

(2) An application to be registered in respect of any description of driving instruction must be made to the officer of the Secretary of State (in this Part of this Act referred to as "the Registrar") by whom the register is, on behalf of the Secretary of State, compiled and maintained.

(3) An application under subsection (2) above shall be made in such manner, and shall be accompanied by such particulars, as the Secretary of State may determine.

(4) The Registrar must, on making a decision on an application under subsection (2) above, give notice in writing of the decision to the applicant which, in the case of a decision to refuse the application, must state the grounds for the refusal.

(5) Regulations may make provision authorising the Secretary of State to make available information about persons registered under this section.

(6) Subsections (2) to (5) above and section 125ZA of this Act do not apply in relation to an application by a person to be registered, or to a person's registration, as a disabled instructor in respect of the giving of instruction in the driving of a motor vehicle in the motor vehicle."

5. After that section insert—

"125ZA. Conditions of registration. (1) Where a person duly applies to be registered in respect of a description of driving instruction, the Registrar must register him in respect of that description of driving instruction if he satisfies the Registrar that the conditions prescribed under this subsection are fulfilled.

(2) In the case of applications by persons to be registered in relation to the giving of a description of driving instruction, those conditions may (in particular) include—

(a) conditions requiring the persons to have passed such examinations of ability and fitness to give driving instruction of that description as may be prescribed under section 132 of this Act,

(b) conditions requiring the persons to hold, or to have held for a prescribed period, such licences to drive motor vehicles of a prescribed description as may be prescribed, and

(c) conditions requiring the persons not to have been disqualified during a prescribed period under prescribed provisions for holding or obtaining a licence to drive motor vehicles.

(3) A person may be registered in respect of a description of driving instruction subject to fulfilling the conditions prescribed under this subsection for so long as he continues to be so registered.

(4) In the case of the registration of persons in relation to the giving of a description of driving instruction, those conditions may (in particular) include—

(a) conditions requiring the persons, if at any time required to do so by the Registrar, to submit themselves for such examinations of continued ability and fitness to give driving instruction of that description as may be prescribed under section 132 of this Act,

(b) conditions requiring the persons to have passed those examinations,

(c) conditions within subsection (2)(*b*) and (*c*) above, and

(d) conditions requiring the persons to follow guidance issued by the Registrar as to the giving of driving instruction of that description.

(5) In the case of the registration of persons in relation to the carrying on of business in the provision of a description of driving instruction, those conditions may (in particular) include—

(a) conditions requiring the persons to secure that motor vehicles and premises used by them in the carrying on of the business meet prescribed standards throughout the period of registration,

(b) conditions requiring the persons, if at any time required to do so by the Registrar, to allow those motor vehicles and premises to be inspected, and

(c) conditions requiring the persons to follow guidance issued by the Registrar as to the carrying on of business in the provision of driving instruction of that description.

(6) The conditions prescribed under subsection (1) or (3) above may (in particular) include a condition that persons are fit and proper persons to be, or to continue to be, registered.

(7) Regulations may include provision for persons of a prescribed description to be exempt from any condition, to such extent as is prescribed, in prescribed circumstances."

6. (1) Section 125A (registration of disabled persons) is amended as follows.

(2) For subsection (1) substitute—

"(1) A person may apply to the Registrar to be registered as a disabled instructor in respect of the giving of instruction in the driving of a motor vehicle of a prescribed description in such a motor vehicle if he—

(a) suffers from a disability or prospective disability affecting the driving of motor vehicles of that description,

(b) holds a current disabled person's limited driving licence relating to motor vehicles of that description, and

(c) holds a current emergency control certificate specifying motor vehicles of that description."

(3) For subsections (5) to (7) substitute—

"(5) Where a person duly applies to be registered as a disabled instructor in respect of the giving of instruction in the driving of a motor vehicle of a prescribed description in such a motor vehicle, the Registrar must (subject to section 125B(4) of this Act) so register him if he satisfies the Registrar that the conditions prescribed under this subsection are fulfilled.

(6) Those conditions may (in particular) include—

(a) conditions requiring the person to have passed such examinations of ability and fitness to give driving instruction of that description as may be prescribed under section 132 of this Act,

(b) conditions requiring the person to hold, or to have held for a prescribed period, such licences to drive motor vehicles of a prescribed description as may be prescribed, and

(c) conditions requiring the person not to have been disqualified during a prescribed period under prescribed provisions for holding or obtaining a licence to drive motor vehicles.

(7) A person may be so registered subject to fulfilling the conditions prescribed under this subsection for so long as he continues to be so registered.

(7A) Those conditions may (in particular) include—

(a) conditions requiring the person, if at any time required to do so by the Registrar, to submit himself for such examinations of continued ability and fitness to give driving instruction of that description as may be prescribed under section 132 of this Act,

(b) conditions requiring the person to have passed those examinations,

(c) conditions requiring the person, if at any time required to do so by the Registrar, to submit himself for a further emergency control assessment on the day (within such period as may be prescribed) and at the place specified by the Registrar,

(d) conditions within subsection (6)(b) and (c) above, and

(e) conditions requiring the person to follow guidance issued by the Registrar as to the giving of instruction in the driving of a motor vehicle of a prescribed description in such a motor vehicle.

(7B) The conditions prescribed under subsection (5) or (7) above may (in particular) include a condition that persons are fit and proper persons to be, or to continue to be, registered.

(7C) In considering whether to exercise, in respect of any person, his power under subsection (7A)(c) above, the Registrar must have regard to any recommendation included in the person's current emergency control certificate as to the period after which he should undergo a further emergency control assessment.

(7D) Regulations may include provision for prescribed persons to be exempt from any prescribed condition, to such extent as is prescribed, in prescribed circumstances.

(7E) Regulations may make provision authorising the Secretary of State to make available information about persons registered under this section."

(4) In subsection (8)—

(a) for the definition of "appropriate motor car" substitute—

""appropriate motor vehicle" means, subject to section 125B(2) of this Act, a motor vehicle equipped with automatic transmission;",

(b) in the definition of "disability", for "means a want of physical ability affecting the driving of motor cars" substitute ", in respect of motor vehicles of any description, means a want of physical ability affecting the driving of motor vehicles of that description",

(c) in the definition of "relevant disability", for "car" substitute "vehicle of the description in question",

(d) in the definition of "disabled person's limited driving licence", for "car", in each place, substitute "vehicle",

(e) in the definition of "modifications", for "car" substitute "vehicle",

(f) in the definition of "registered disabled instructor", for "whose name is in the register with an indication that he is disabled" substitute "registered as a disabled instructor in respect of instruction in the driving of a motor vehicles of a prescribed description given in a motor vehicle of that description", and

(g) in the words following that definition, for "car", in both places, substitute "vehicle".

7. (1) Section 125B (provisions supplementary to section 125A) is amended as follows.

(2) In subsection (2), for "car", in each place, substitute "vehicle".

(3) For subsection (3) substitute—

"(3) Regulations may make provision for prescribed persons to be exempt from section 125A(1)(c) of this Act in prescribed circumstances."

(4) In subsection (4), for "enter the name of a person in the register under section 125A of this Act as that of a disabled instructor" substitute "register a person under section 125A of this Act".

(5) Omit subsections (6) and (7).

8. For section 126 (duration of registration) substitute—

"**126. Duration of registration.** (1) Unless previously terminated under the following provisions of this Part of this Act, a person's registration in respect of any description of driving instruction shall (subject to subsection (3) below) be terminated at the end of the period of four years beginning with the day specified in subsection (2) below.

(2) That day is—

(a) the first day of the month next after that in which the person became registered in respect of that description of driving instruction, or

(b) where his registration in respect of that description of driving instruction has been extended under section 127 of this Act, the day on which the last further period for which the registration was last extended began.

(3) If an application for the extension of a person's registration in respect of any description of driving instruction is made under section 127 of this Act, the registration is not terminated under subsection (1) above.

(4) Where a person whose registration in respect of any description of driving instruction has been terminated under subsection (1) above applies under section 125 of this Act to be registered again in respect of that description of driving instruction, he shall be required again to fulfil such of the conditions prescribed under section 125ZA(1) of this Act as may be prescribed.

(5) But if the person was a registered disabled instructor he shall instead be required again to fulfil such of the conditions prescribed under section 125A(5) of this Act as may be prescribed."

9. (1) Section 127 (extension of duration of registration) is amended as follows.

(2) For subsections (1) to (4) substitute—

"(1) A person may, no later than such time before his registration in respect of any description of driving instruction is terminated under section 126(1) of this Act as is prescribed, apply to the Registrar for the extension of that registration for a further period of four years.

(2) An application under subsection (1) above shall be made in such manner, and shall be accompanied by such particulars, as the Secretary of State may determine.

(3) On an application under subsection (1) above, the applicant shall be entitled to have the registration extended for the further period of four years if he satisfies the Registrar that the prescribed requirements are fulfilled.

(4) The continued registration of a person by virtue of an extension under this section may be made subject to—

(a) in the case of a registered disabled instructor, the conditions prescribed under section 125A(7) of this Act, and

(b) in any other case, the conditions prescribed under section 125ZA(3) of this Act."

(3) In subsection (7), after "application" insert "under subsection (1) above".

(4) In subsection (7A), for "A decision to refuse" substitute "The termination of a person's registration on a decision to refuse such".

(5) In subsection (8), for "decision shall" substitute "termination of registration shall".

10. For section 128 (removal of names from register) substitute—

"128. Termination of registration by Registrar. (1) The Registrar may terminate a person's registration in respect of any description of driving instruction if he is satisfied that any relevant prescribed condition has not been complied with in the case of the person—

(a) in a case where his registration has not been extended under section 127 of this Act, at any time since he became registered, or

(b) in a case where his registration has been so extended, at any time since it was last extended.

(2) For the purposes of subsection (1) above "relevant prescribed condition" means—

(a) in the case of a registered disabled instructor, a condition prescribed under section 125A(7) of this Act, and

(b) in any other case, a condition prescribed under section 125ZA(3) of this Act.

(3) The Registrar may also terminate a person's registration in respect of a description of driving instruction if the person's registration, or (if the person's registration has been extended) the last extension of his registration, was made by mistake or procured by fraud.

(4) Before terminating a person's registration in respect of any description of driving instruction, the Registrar must give him written notice stating that he is considering terminating the registration and giving particulars of the grounds on which he is considering it.

(5) Where the Registrar gives notice to a person under subsection (4) above—

(a) that person may, within the period of 28 days beginning with the day on which the notice is given, make representations with respect to the proposed termination,

(b) the Registrar must not decide to terminate the registration until after the end of that period, and

(c) before deciding whether or not to terminate the registration, the Registrar must take into consideration any such representations made by him within that period.

(6) The Registrar must, on making a decision to terminate a person's registration in respect of any description of driving instruction, give notice in writing of the decision to the person.

(7) A decision to terminate a person's registration in respect of any description of driving instruction shall take effect at the end of the period of 14 days beginning with the day on which notice of the decision is given (or, if any appeal brought against the decision under the following provisions of this Part of this Act is previously withdrawn or dismissed, when the appeal is withdrawn or dismissed).

(8) But the Registrar may, when giving notice of his decision to terminate a person's registration in respect of any description of driving instruction, direct that the decision shall instead take effect—

(a) where no appeal under the following provisions of this Part of this Act is brought against the decision within the time limited for the appeal, at the end of that time,

(b) where such an appeal is brought and is withdrawn or struck out for want of prosecution, on the withdrawal or striking out of the appeal, or

(c) where such an appeal is brought and not withdrawn or struck out for want of prosecution, if and when the appeal is dismissed, and not otherwise."

11. After that section insert—

"128A. Power to give direction as to further applications. (1) This section applies when the Registrar decides—

    (*a*) to refuse to register a person,
    (*b*) to refuse an application for the extension of a person's registration, or
    (*c*) to terminate a person's registration,

in respect of any description of driving instruction.

    (2) The Registrar may direct that any application by that person to be registered in respect of that description of driving instruction shall not be entertained before the end of such period, not exceeding four years beginning with the day on which the decision takes effect, as may be specified in the direction.

    (3) Notice of any such direction must be included in the notice of the decision in connection with which it is given."

12. Omit sections 129 and 130 (licences for giving instruction so as to obtain practical experience) and the heading before them.

13. (1) Section 131 (appeals) is amended as follows.

    (2) In subsection (1), for paragraphs (*a*) to (*c*) substitute—

    "(*a*) to refuse an application for his registration or for the extension of his registration,
    (*b*) to terminate his registration,
    (*c*) to give a direction under section 128A of this Act,".

    (3) Omit subsection (2).

    (4) In subsection (3), for paragraph (*b*) and the word "or" before it substitute—

    "(*b*) for the continuation or termination of the registration, or
    (*c*) for the revocation or confirmation of the direction or the alteration of the period specified in the direction,".

    (5) In subsection (4), for the words from the beginning to the end of paragraph (*b*) substitute "An order for refusal or termination under subsection (3)(*a*) or (*b*) above may direct that an application by the appellant to be registered".

    (6) In subsection (4B), for ", 128(7) or 130(6)" substitute "or 128(8)".

    (7) In subsection (4D)—

    (*a*) for "retention of a name in the register, to remove a name from the register or to revoke a licence granted under section 129 of this Act" substitute "extension of a person's registration or to terminate a person's registration", and
    (*b*) for ", 128(7) or 130(6)" substitute "or 128(8)".

    (8) In subsection (4F), for "instruction in the driving of a motor car" substitute "driving instruction".

14. For sections 132 and 133 and the heading before them substitute—

"Examinations and training

132. Examinations. (1) Regulations may make provision with respect to—

    (*a*) the nature of examinations of the ability and fitness (or continued ability and fitness) to give driving instruction (which may consist of practical tests and other tests and means of assessment) and the administrative arrangements for submitting for such examinations,
    (*b*) the qualification, selection and appointment of persons by whom they may be conducted, conditions which must be satisfied during the currency of an appointment, the charging of reasonable fees in respect of applications for appointment or appointments or in connection with any examination or assessment which may be required before appointment or during the currency of any appointment and the revocation of any appointment,
    (*c*) evidence of the results of such examinations, and
    (*d*) the making available of information about the results of such examinations,

and generally with respect to such examinations.

    (2) In particular, the regulations may make provision—

    (*a*) for requiring a person submitting himself for any part of an examination which consists of practical tests, to provide a safe and suitable vehicle for the purposes of the practical tests and for requiring that, if the vehicle is a vehicle of a prescribed description, the vehicle has been certified in the prescribed manner after a prescribed inspection as satisfying such requirements as may be prescribed,
    (*b*) for the charging (whether on the making by a person of arrangements to submit himself for any part of an examination or otherwise) of reasonable fees for or in connection with the examination, or any part of it, and any inspection and certification of a vehicle required by regulations under paragraph (*a*) above in relation to any part of the examination,
    (*c*) for requiring a person who desires to submit himself, or is required to submit himself, for an examination, or any part of it, to supply the Registrar with such particulars as the Secretary of State may determine, and
    (*d*) for ensuring that a person submitting himself for an examination, or any part of it, and failing to pass it shall not be eligible to submit himself for another examination, or any part of it, by the same or any other person before the end of a prescribed period, except under an order made by a court or sheriff under the power conferred by section 133 of this Act.

133. Review of examinations etc. (1) On the application of a person who has undergone a relevant instructor examination, or a part of a relevant instructor examination—

    (*a*) a magistrates' court, or
    (*b*) in Scotland, the sheriff within whose jurisdiction he resides,

may determine whether the examination, or the part of the examination, was properly conducted.

    (2) In this Part of this Act "relevant instructor examination" means—

    (*a*) an examination of ability and fitness referred to in section 125ZA(2)(*a*) or 125A(6)(*a*) of this Act,
    (*b*) an examination of continued ability and fitness referred to in section 125ZA(4)(*a*) or 125A(7A)(*a*) of this Act, or

(c) an emergency control assessment under section 133A of this Act.

(3) If it appears to the court or sheriff that it was not properly conducted, the court or sheriff may—

(a) (except in the case of an emergency control assessment) order that the applicant shall be eligible to submit himself for another examination before the end of the period prescribed under section 132(2)(d) of this Act, and

(b) (in any case) order that any fee payable by the applicant in respect of the examination shall not be paid or, if it has been paid, shall be repaid.

(4) No appeal shall lie under section 131 of this Act in respect of any matter in respect of which an application may be made to a magistrates' court or a sheriff under subsection (1) above.

133ZA. Training. (1) Regulations may provide that a person—

(a) shall not be permitted to take any part of a relevant instructor examination,
(b) shall not be registered, or
(c) shall not have his registration extended,

unless he has successfully completed training in accordance with the regulations.

(2) Regulations may make provision in relation to training—

(a) by means of courses provided in accordance with the regulations,
(b) by means of study conducted in accordance with the regulations, and
(c) by any other prescribed means.

(3) Regulations under this section may include provision exempting persons from any requirement imposed by virtue of subsection (1) above; and regulations including such provision may (in particular)—

(a) limit an exemption to persons in prescribed circumstances,
(b) attach conditions to an exemption,
(c) regulate applications for an exemption, and
(d) include provision for the evidencing by a person of his being within an exemption.

(4) Regulations under this section may provide that training is not to be taken into account for the purposes of the regulations if it was completed before such time as is prescribed.

(5) Regulations under this section may, in particular, include—

(a) provision about the nature of training,
(b) provision for the approval by the Secretary of State of persons providing training or giving instruction as part of training and the withdrawal of approval (including provision for appeals to the Transport Tribunal against refusal and withdrawal of approval) and provision for exemptions from any requirement of approval,
(c) provision for the training or assessment, or the supervision of training or assessment, of persons providing training or giving instruction as part of training,
(d) provision setting the maximum amount of any charges payable by persons undergoing training,
(e) provision for the evidencing of the successful completion of training, and
(f) provision authorising the Secretary of State to make available information about persons providing training or giving instruction as part of training.

(6) Regulations under this section may include provision for the charging of reasonable fees in respect of the exercise of any function conferred or imposed on the Secretary of State by the regulations."

15. In section 133A (assessment of disabled person's ability to control a motor car in an emergency), for "car" in each place (including in the heading) substitute "vehicle".

16. (1) Section 133B (further assessments) is amended as follows.

(2) In subsection (1), for "125B(6)(a)" substitute "125A(7A)(c)".

(3) In subsection (2), for "whose name is not on the register" substitute "who is not registered".

(4) In subsection (4)(b), for "car" substitute "vehicle".

17. (1) Section 133C (duty to disclose further disability) is amended as follows.

(2) Omit subsection (1).

(3) In subsection (2), for "person to whom this section applies" substitute "registered disabled instructor".

18. (1) Section 133D (offences relating to giving by disabled person of paid driving instruction) is amended as follows.

(2) Omit subsection (1).

(3) For "car" in each place substitute "vehicle".

(4) In subsections (2) and (3), for "person to whom this section applies" substitute "registered disabled instructor".

(5) For subsection (4) substitute—

"(4) Where a registered disabled instructor gives instruction in contravention of this section—

(a) the instructor,
(b) if the instructor is employed by another person to give that instruction, that other person (as well as the instructor), and
(c) if the instructor is a franchisee under a driving instruction franchise, the franchisor (as well as the instructor),

is guilty of an offence."

19. For section 134 (power to alter conditions for entry or retention in, and removal from, register etc) substitute—

"134. Power to alter registration period. (1) Regulations may alter—

(a) the period at the end of which a person's registration is terminated (unless extended or further extended),
(b) the period for which a person's registration may be extended or further extended, and
(c) the period before the end of which it may be directed that any application by a person to be registered shall not be entertained.

(2) Regulations under this section may contain amendments of this Part of this Act."
20. For section 135 substitute—

"135. Evidence of registration. (1) Regulations may prescribe—

(*a*) certificates or other items that may be issued to registered persons to be displayed as evidence of their registration, and

(*b*) a title or other description which may be used as such evidence.

(2) If at any time a person who is not registered—

(*a*) displays a certificate or other item prescribed under subsection (1)(*a*) above,

(*b*) uses a title or other description prescribed under subsection (1)(*b*) above, or

(*c*) uses a title or other description implying that he is registered,

he is guilty of an offence unless he proves that he did not know, and did not have reasonable cause to believe, that he was not registered at that time.

(3) If a person carrying on business in the provision of driving instruction at any time—

(*a*) uses a title or other description prescribed under subsection (1)(*b*) above in relation to any relevant person who is not appropriately registered, or

(*b*) issues any advertisement or invitation calculated to mislead with respect to the extent to which relevant persons are appropriately registered,

he is guilty of an offence unless he proves that he did not know, and did not have reasonable cause to believe, that the relevant person was, or relevant persons were, not appropriately registered at that time.

(4) For the purposes of subsection (3) above—

(*a*) a relevant person is a person who is employed by the person carrying on business to give driving instruction, or is a franchisee giving driving instruction under a driving instruction franchise under which that person is the franchisor, and

(*b*) a relevant person is appropriately registered if he is registered in respect of the giving of the description of driving instruction which he is employed to give or which is given by him under the driving instruction franchise."

21. In section 136 (surrender of certificates)—

(*a*) for paragraphs (*a*) and (*b*) substitute "the registration of a person to whom a certificate or other item prescribed under section 135(1)(*a*) of this Act has been issued is terminated,",

(*b*) for "licence, as the case may be," substitute "other item", and

(*c*) in the heading for **"and licences"** substitute **"etc"**.

22. (1) Section 137 (production of certificates to constables and authorised persons) is amended as follows.
(2) In subsection (1)—

(*a*) after "a certificate" insert "or other item",

(*b*) omit ", or to whom a licence under this Part of this Act is granted,", and

(*c*) for "or licence" substitute "or other item".

(3) In subsection (2), for the words before "constable" substitute

"Where—

(*a*) a person's registration is terminated, and

(*b*) he fails to satisfy an obligation imposed on him by section 136 of this Act,

a".

(4) In that subsection, for "issued to him or the licence" substitute "or other item issued to him".
(5) In subsection (3), for "document" substitute "certificate or other item".
(6) In subsection (4), for "document", in each place, substitute "certificate or other item".
(7) In the heading for **"and licences"** substitute **"etc"**.
23. (1) Section 140 (receipts) is to be renumbered as subsection (3) of that section.
(2) Before that subsection insert—

"(1) Regulations may make provision for the payment of such fees (if any) as may be prescribed in connection with registration or extension of registration.
(2) Regulations may make provision for the repayment (in whole or in part) of any fee payable by virtue of any provision of this Part of this Act in such circumstances as may be prescribed."
(3) For the heading substitute **"Fees"**.
24. (1) Section 141 (regulations) is to be renumbered as subsection (1) of that section.
(2) In that subsection, after "by regulations" insert "and for prescribing anything which may be prescribed under this Part of this Act".
(3) After that subsection insert—

"(2) Regulations under this section—

(*a*) may be expressed to apply generally or only in particular circumstances,

(*b*) may make different provision in relation to different cases or other circumstances or otherwise for different purposes, and

(*c*) may make incidental, supplementary, consequential or transitional provision or savings."

25. For section 141A (meaning of "motor car") substitute—

"141A. Interpretation of Part 5. (1) For the purposes of this Part of this Act persons may carry on business in the provision of driving instruction in any way, including in particular—

(*a*) by giving instruction themselves,

(*b*) by arranging for the giving of driving instruction by their employees, or

(*c*) by arranging for the giving of driving instruction by persons who are franchisees under driving instruction franchises under which they are the franchisor.

(2) In this Part of this Act "driving instruction franchise" means an agreement under which one party (the "franchisor") grants to another party (a "franchisee") rights consisting of or including the right to use a particular trading name, style or design in the carrying on of business in the giving of driving instruction.

(3) In this Part of this Act references to "the franchisor" and "a franchisee", in relation to a driving instruction franchise, shall be construed accordingly.

(4) In this Part of this Act "current", in relation to a licence or certificate, means one which has not expired and has not been cancelled, revoked or suspended.

(5) In this Part of this Act—

(a) "Community licence" and "counterpart", in relation to a Community licence, and

(b) "provisional licence",

have the same meanings as in Part 3 of this Act."

26. For section 142 substitute—

"142. Index to Part 5.   The expressions listed in the left-hand column below are respectively defined or (as the case may be) fall to be construed in accordance with the provisions of this Part of this Act listed in the right-hand column in relation to those expressions.

Expression	Relevant provision
Appropriate motor vehicle	Section 125A(8)
Carry on business in the provision of driving instruction	Section 141A(1)
Community licence and counterpart	Section 141A(5)
Current (in relation to a licence or certificate)	Section 141A(4)
Disability, prospective disability and relevant disability	Section 125A(8)
Disabled person's limited driving licence	Section 125A(8)
Driving instruction	Section 123(3)
Driving instruction franchise (and franchisor and franchisee)	Section 141A(2) and (3)
Emergency control assessment and emergency control certificate	Section 125A(8)
Modifications, in relation to a motor vehicle	Section 125A(8)
Paid instruction	Section 123(5) and (6)
Provisional licence	Section 141A(5)
Registered and registration	Section 123(7)
The register	Section 123(8)
Registered disabled instructor	Section 125A(8)
The Registrar	Section 125(2)
Regulations	Section 141
Relevant instructor examination	Section 133(2)"

27. In section 173(2) (forgery of documents etc), for paragraph (g) substitute—

"(g) any document evidencing the passing of an examination (or part of an examination) required by regulations under section 132 of this Act or the successful completion of training provided in accordance with regulations under section 133ZA of this Act,

(ga) any certificate under section 133A of this Act,

(gb) any certificate or other item prescribed under section 135(1)(a) of this Act,".

28. In section 174(1) (false statements), after paragraph (d) insert—

"(da)f obtaining a document evidencing the passing of an examination (or part of an examination) required by regulations under section 132 of this Act or the successful completion of training provided in accordance with regulations under section 133ZA of this Act, or".

29. In section 183 (application to Crown), after subsection (6) insert—

"(6A) The Secretary of State may by regulations provide that Part 5 of this Act is to apply in relation to persons in the public service of the Crown but subject to any prescribed omissions, additions or other modifications."

30. In section 195(2) (duty to consult before making regulations under any provision other than section 8(3) and Part 5), omit "or Part 5".

Road Traffic Offenders Act 1988 (c 53)

31. The Road Traffic Offenders Act 1988 is amended as follows.

32. (1) Section 18 (evidence by certificate as to registration of driving instructors and licences to give instruction) is amended as follows.

(2) In subsection (1), for paragraphs (a) to (d) substitute—

"(a) a person was, or was not, registered,

(b) a person became registered or a person's registration was terminated, or

(c) a person was, or was not, exempt from the prohibitions imposed by section 123 of the Road Traffic Act 1988 (requirement of registration) by virtue of provision made by regulations under section 124 of that Act,".

(3) In subsection (3), for the words from ""current" to ""register"" substitute ""Registrar", "registered" and "registration"".

(4) In the heading, for **"of driving instructors and licences to give instruction"** substitute **"etc of driving instructors etc"**.

33. (1) Part 1 of Schedule 2 (prosecution and punishment of offences: offences under the Traffic Acts) is amended as follows.

(2) In the entry relating to section 123(4) of the Road Traffic Act 1988 (c 52)—

(*a*) in column 1, for "123(4)" substitute "123A(1) and (2)", and
(*b*) in column 2, for "by unregistered and unlicensed persons or their employers" substitute ", and carrying on of business in provision of driving instruction, by unregistered persons".

(3) In the entry relating to section 123(6) of that Act—

(*a*) in column 1, for "123(6)" substitute "123A(4)", and
(*b*) in column 2, for "without there being exhibited on the motor car a certificate of registration or a licence under RTA Part 5" substitute ", and carrying on of business in provision of driving instruction, without prescribed requirements relating to displaying of evidence of registration under RTA Part 5 being complied with".

(4) In the entry relating to section 133C(4) of that Act, in column 2, omit "or licensed".
(5) In the entry relating to section 133D of that Act, in column 2, omit "or their employers".
(6) In the entry relating to section 135 of that Act, for the words in column 2 substitute "Misuse of evidence of registration etc".
(7) In the entries relating to sections 136 and 137 of that Act, in column 2, for "or licence" substitute "etc".

4–2016P

Section 59   SCHEDULE 7
                                     REPEALS AND REVOCATIONS

(1) Graduated fixed penalties

Short title and chapter	Extent of repeal
Domestic Violence, Crime and Victims Act 2004 (c 28)	Section 16(2).

(2) Giving of fixed penalty notices by vehicle examiners

Short title and chapter	Extent of repeal
Road Traffic Offenders Act 1988 (c 53)	In section 54(5), the words "he surrenders". In section 61(2), the words "fixed penalty clerk must not endorse the". In section 66(8), the word "and" after the definition of "hiring agreement". In section 73, in subsection (5), the words "by or on behalf of the chief officer of police" and the word "such" and, in subsection (7), the words "by or on behalf of the chief officer of police". In section 79(1), the words "constable or authorised". In section 89(1), the word "and" before the definition of "proceedings".
Road Traffic (New Drivers) Act 1995 (c 13)	In section 2, in subsection (4), the words ", the fixed penalty clerk" and, in subsection (5), the words "by the fixed penalty clerk".
Police Reform Act 2002 (c 30)	Section 76(4).
Railways and Transport Safety Act 2003 (c 20)	Section 69(3). Section 109.
Crime (International Co-operation) Act 2003 (c 32)	In Schedule 5, paragraphs 47(*b*), 55(*b*) and 57(*b*).
Courts Act 2003 (c 39)	In Schedule 8, paragraphs 314 and 321.

(3) Endorsement: unlicensed and foreign drivers

Short title or title and reference	Extent of repeal or revocation
Road Traffic Offenders Act 1988 (c 53)	In the heading of section 31, the words "on licence". In section 45(1), the words ", whether he is at the time the holder of a licence or not,". In section 70(4), the word "and" at the end of paragraph (*a*).
Road Traffic (Driver Licensing and Information Systems) Act 1989 (c 22)	In Schedule 3, paragraph 2(bb).
The Driving Licences (Community Driving Licence) Regulations 1990 (SI 1990/144)	In Schedule 2, paragraphs 6 and 9. In Schedule 3, paragraph 3(2)(*b*).
Road Traffic Act 1991 (c 40)	In Schedule 4, paragraph 93.

(4) Endorsement: all drivers

Short title or title and reference	Extent of repeal or revocation
Public Passenger Vehicles Act 1981 (c 14) Road Traffic Act 1988 (c 52)	Section 24(3). In section 88(6), the words ", counterparts of licences". In section 92(7ZB)(*a*) and (7C), the words "and its counterpart". In section 93— (*a*) in subsections (2)(*b*) and (3), the words "and its counterpart", and (*b*) in subsection (4)(*a*), the words "or its counterpart". In section 97— (*a*) in sub-paragraph (i) of paragraph (*c*) of subsection (1), the words "and its counterpart", (*b*) in sub-paragraph (ia) of that paragraph, the words from "together" to the end, (*c*) in sub-paragraph (ii) of that paragraph, the words "and its counterpart (if any) issued to him", and (*d*) in subsection (1AA), the words "together with the counterparts mentioned in that sub-paragraph" and the words "and its Northern Ireland counterpart". In section 98(1)(*c*), the words "or its counterpart". In section 98A— (*a*) in subsection (1), the words "and their counterparts", (*b*) in subsection (3), the words " (and their counterparts)", (*c*) in subsection (4), the words " (with its counterpart)", and (*d*) in subsection (7), the words "and its counterpart". In section 99— (*a*) in subsection (2A), the words "and its counterpart", (*b*) in subsection (3), paragraph (aa), in paragraph (*b*), the words "or in its counterpart" and the words "and its counterpart", (*c*) in subsection (4), the words "and its counterpart", (*d*) in subsection (6), the words "and its counterpart" in both places, and (*e*) in subsections (7) and (7ZA), the words "and its counterpart". Section 99A(5) and (6). Section 99B— (*a*) subsections (3), (6) and (8), (*b*) in subsection (11)(*b*), the words " (6) or", and (*c*) subsection (12). In section 99C— (*a*) in subsections (1) to (4), the words "and its counterpart (if any)" in each place, and (*b*) subsection (5). In section 105(2)— (*a*) sub-paragraph (iii) of paragraph (*b*) and the word "or" before it, (*b*) in paragraph (*e*), the words "and counterparts of licences" and the words "or counterparts of licences", and (*c*) paragraph (ea). In section 108, the definition of "counterpart". In section 109B— (*a*) in subsection (1), the words from "together" to the end, (*b*) in subsection (2), in paragraph (*a*), the words "together with the relevant counterparts" and, in paragraph (*b*), the words "and those counterparts", (*c*) in subsection (4), the words "and the relevant counterparts", and (*d*) subsection (5). In section 115A(1), the words "and its counterpart (if any)". In section 117A, the words "and its counterpart (if any)" in both places. In section 118—

Short title or title and reference	Extent of repeal or revocation
	(a) in subsection (1), the words "and its counterpart",
	(b) in subsection (4), the words "and its counterpart", and
	(c) subsection (5).
	In section 121, the definition of "counterpart".
	In section 125A(8), in paragraph (c) of the definition of "disabled person's limited driving licence", the words "and a counterpart of that licence".
	In section 141A(5), the words "and "counterpart", in relation to a Community licence".
	In section 142, the words "and counterpart".
	In section 164—
	(a) the words "and its counterpart" in each place, and
	(b) in subsection (11), the reference to "counterpart".
	In section 173—
	(a) in paragraph (a) of subsection (2), the words from "or" to the end,
	(b) paragraph (aa) of that subsection, and
	(c) in subsection (4), the word ""counterpart",".
	Section 176(1A), (3A) and (8).
Road Traffic Offenders Act 1988 (c 53)	In section 7(1), the words from "and the foregoing" to the end.
	In section 26—
	(a) in subsections (7), (8) and (9)(b), the words "and its counterpart" and the words "and counterpart", and
	(b) subsection (14).
	In section 27, the words "and its counterpart" in each place.
	In section 29—
	(a) in subsection (1)(b), the words "the counterpart of any licence held by him or on", and
	(b) subsection (3).
	In section 30—
	(a) in subsection (1)(b), the words "the counterpart of his licence or", and
	(b) in subsection (2)(b), the words "on the counterpart of his licence or".
	In section 31(1), the words "the counterpart of his licence or on".
	Section 32.
	Section 36(10).
	Section 42(5A).
	Section 44(3A).
	Section 45.
	In section 46(2), the words "the counterpart of any licence held by him or on".
	In section 47—
	(a) in subsection (2A), the words "and its counterpart",
	(b) in subsection (3), the words "a licence or",
	(c) in subsection (3A), the words "in relation to a person who is not the holder of a licence,", and
	(d) in subsection (4), the words "and the counterpart of a licence".
	In section 48—
	(a) in subsections (1) and (2), the words "the counterpart of any licence held by him or on", and
	(b) subsection (3).
	In section 54(7), the words "and a counterpart of a licence".
	In section 56, the words "and its counterpart" in each place.
	Section 57.
	In section 57A(1), the words "who is not the holder of a licence".
	Section 58.
	Section 61.
	In section 61A—
	(a) in subsection (1), the words "but who is not the holder of a licence,", and
	(b) in the heading, the words "to unlicensed person".
	In section 72—

Short title or title and reference	Extent of repeal or revocation
	(a) subsection (4), (b) in subsection (5), the words "57 or", and (c) subsection (6). In section 75— (a) subsection (8), (b) in subsection (8A), the words "who is not the holder of a licence", and (c) subsection (12). In section 76— (a) in paragraph (a) of subsection (3), the words "inspecting the licence and its counterpart or (where the alleged offender is not the holder of a licence)", (b) in paragraph (b) of that subsection, the words "and its counterpart", and (c) subsection (8). Section 77. In section 77A(1) and (2), the words "who is not the holder of a licence". In section 83— (a) subsection (1), (b) in subsection (1A), the word "also", and (c) in subsection (2), the words "57 or" and the words "77 or". In section 91ZA— (a) in paragraph (b) of subsection (1), the words "and (9)(b)", (b) paragraphs (d) to (f) and (h) to (j) of that subsection, (c) in paragraph (k) of that subsection, the words ", (3) and (3A)", (d) paragraph (l) of that subsection, (e) subsections (3) to (6), (f) in subsection (7), the words "and its counterpart (if any)", and (g) in subsection (8), the words "and its counterpart". Section 91ZB. In section 91A— (a) subsections (2) to (4), (b) in subsection (5), the words "and its counterpart (if any)", and (c) subsections (6) and (8) to (10). Section 91B. In section 98(1), the word ""counterpart",". In Schedule 1— (a) in the entries relating to sections 98A(7) and 99(5) of the Road Traffic Act 1988, the words "and counterpart", and (b) in the entry relating to section 164(6) of that Act, the words "and counterpart etc". In Part 1 of Schedule 2, in the entries relating to the following provisions, the words "and counterpart"— (a) section 92(7C) of the Road Traffic Act 1988 (c 52), (b) section 93(3) of that Act, (c) section 98A(7) of that Act, (d) section 99(5) of that Act, (e) section 118 of that Act, (f) section 26 of the Road Traffic Offenders Act 1988, and (g) section 27 of that Act. In Part 1 of Schedule 2— (a) in the entry relating to section 164 of the Road Traffic Act 1988 (c 52), the words "or counterpart etc", and (b) in the entry relating to section 173 of that Act, the words "counterparts of Community licence,". In Schedule 5, in the entry relating to section 99(5) of the Road Traffic Act 1988— (a) the words "and its counterpart", and (b) the words "and counterpart".
Road Traffic (Driver Licensing and Information Systems) Act 1989 (c 22)	In Schedule 3— (a) paragraph 2(b), (b) paragraph 16(b), and

Short title or title and reference	Extent of repeal or revocation
	(c) paragraph 25.
The Driving Licences (Community Driving Licence) Regulations 1990 (SI 1990/144)	In Schedule 1—
	(a) paragraphs 1 to 3,
	(b) paragraph 5(a)(ii) and (iii),
	(c) paragraph 5(b) to (d),
	(d) paragraph 8,
	(e) paragraph 9(a), (b)(i), (iii) and (iv) and (c) to (h), and
	(f) paragraphs 10 to 12.
	In Schedule 2—
	(a) paragraphs 1 and 2,
	(b) paragraph 3(a) and (c),
	(c) paragraph 5,
	(d) paragraph 8, and
	(f) paragraphs 10 to 28.
	In Schedule 3—
	(a) paragraph 1(a),
	(b) paragraph 2, and
	(c) paragraph 3(2)(a).
Road Traffic Act 1991 (c 40)	In Schedule 4—
	(a) paragraph 99,
	(b) paragraph 100(2), and
	(c) paragraph 104.
Child Support Act 1991 (c 48)	In section 40B—
	(a) in subsection (4), the words from "and" to the end, and
	(b) in subsection (9), the words "and its counterpart".
Road Traffic (New Drivers) Act 1995 (c 13)	In section 2—
	(a) in subsection (3)(c), the words "appropriate person endorses the number of", and
	(b) in subsection (4)(a), the words "and its counterpart".
	In section 9(5), the words "and its counterpart" in both places.
	In Schedule 1—
	(a) in paragraph 3(2), the words "and its counterpart",
	(b) in paragraph 3(4)(a), the words " (with its counterpart)",
	(c) in paragraph 7(4)(a), the words "and its counterpart", and
	(d) in paragraph 8(1)(a), the words "and its counterpart".
	In Schedule 2, paragraph 6.
The Driving Licences (Community Driving Licence) Regulations 1996 (SI 1996/1974)	In Schedule 1—
	(a) paragraph 17(b),
	(b) paragraph 19(2)(c),
	(c) paragraph 28(2)(b),
	(d) paragraph 31, and
	(e) paragraph 32(2).
	In Schedule 2—
	(a) paragraph 5, and
	(b) paragraph 6(a).
	In Schedule 4, paragraph 4.
Powers of Criminal Courts (Sentencing) Act 2000 (c 6)	In section 146—
	(a) in paragraph (a) of subsection (4), the words "together with its counterpart",
	(b) in paragraphs (aa) and (b) of that subsection, the words "and its counterpart (if any)", and
	(c) in subsection (5), the definition of "counterpart".
	In section 147(5)—
	(a) in paragraph (a), the words "together with its counterpart", and
	(b) in paragraphs (aa) and (b), the words "and its counterpart (if any)".
Crime (International Co-operation) Act 2003 (c 32)	In section 63—
	(a) the words "and its counterpart" in each place, and
	(b) in subsection (7), the second sentence.
	In section 64—
	(a) the words "and its counterpart" in each place, and
	(b) in subsection (7), the second sentence.

Short title or title and reference	Extent of repeal or revocation
Criminal Justice Act 2003 (c 44)	In section 74(1), the definition of "counterpart". In Schedule 5— (*a*) paragraph 23(*a*)(ii) and (iii) and (*b*), (*b*) paragraph 25(*a*), (*c*) paragraph 26(*b*), (*d*) paragraph 28, (*e*) paragraph 29(*a*), (*f*) paragraph 35(*a*), and (*g*) paragraph 73(*b*). In section 301— (*a*) in paragraph (*a*) of subsection (6), the words "together with its counterpart", (*b*) in paragraph (*b*) of that subsection, the words "and its counterpart (if any)", and (*c*) in subsection (7), the definition of "counterpart".
Road Safety Act 2006 (c 49)	Section 9(2)(*a*) and (4). Section 14. Section 58(3). In Schedule 1— (*a*) paragraph 3(4) to (7), (*b*) paragraph 5, (*c*) paragraph 6, (*d*) paragraph 13(2), (*e*) paragraph 15(6), (*f*) paragraph 16(6), (*g*) paragraph 17, (*h*) paragraph 21(2), (*i*) in paragraph 25(2)(*b*), the word " (*c*),", and (*j*) paragraph 26(2). In Schedule 2— (*a*) paragraph 1, (*b*) paragraph 8(2), (3) and (5), (*c*) paragraph 9, (*d*) paragraph 14(3), (4) and (5), (*e*) paragraph 15, (*f*) paragraph 16, (*g*) paragraph 18, (*h*) paragraph 24(2) to (4) and (7), (*i*) paragraph 25(3), (*j*) paragraph 26, (*k*) paragraph 29, (*l*) paragraph 31, and (*m*) paragraph 32.

(5) Period of endorsement for failure to allow specimen to be tested

Short title and chapter	Extent of repeal
Road Traffic Offenders Act 1988 (c 53)	In section 45(7), the word "or" at the end of paragraph (*a*).

(6) Speeding: penalty points

Short title and chapter	Extent of repeal
Road Traffic Act 1991 (c 40)	In Schedule 2, paragraphs 3 and 4.

(7) Exemption from speed limits

Short title and chapter	Extent of repeal
Fire and Rescue Services Act 2004 (c 21)	In Schedule 1, paragraph 55.
Serious Organised Crime and Police Act 2005 (c 15)	In Schedule 4, paragraph 42.
Fire (Scotland) Act 2005 (asp 5)	In Schedule 3, paragraph 12.

(8) Reduced disqualification period for attendance on course

Short title and chapter	Extent of repeal
Road Traffic Act 1991 (c 40)	Section 30.
Access to Justice Act 1999 (c 22)	In Schedule 13, paragraphs 145 and 146.

(9) Driving tests

Short title and chapter	Extent of repeal
Road Traffic Act 1988 (c 52)	In section 89(5), paragraph (*b*) and the word "and" before it.
Road Traffic (Driver Licensing and Information Systems) Act 1989 (c 22)	In Schedule 3, paragraph 8(*a*).

(10) Disqualification until test is passed

Short title and chapter	Extent of repeal
Road Traffic Act 1988 (c 52)	In section 173(2), the word "and" after paragraph (*l*).
Road Traffic Offenders Act 1988 (c 53)	Section 36(14).

(11) Granting of full licence

Short title and chapter	Extent of repeal
Road Traffic Act 1988 (c 52)	In section 98(1)(*c*), the words "in the case of a provisional licence". In section 195(3), the words "is exercised".

(12) Fee for renewal of photocard licence and issue of certain alternative licences

Short title and chapter	Extent of repeal
Road Traffic Act 1988 (c 52)	In section 99(7), the words "and any licence granted under this subsection shall be granted free of charge".

(13) Driver training

Short title and chapter	Extent of repeal
Road Traffic Act 1988 (c 52)	In section 99ZC(1), the word "and" at the end of paragraph (*d*).
Road Traffic Act 1991 (c 40)	In Schedule 4, paragraph 73(5).

(14) Driving instruction

Short title or title and reference	Extent of repeal or revocation
Road Traffic Act 1988 (c 52)	Section 125B(6) and (7). Sections 129 and 130. Section 131(2). Section 133C(1). Section 133D(1). In section 137(1), the words ", or to whom a licence under this Part of this Act is granted,". In section 195(2), the words "or Part 5".
Road Traffic Offenders Act 1988 (c 53)	In Schedule 2, in column 2— (*a*) in the entry relating to section 133C(4) of the Road Traffic Act 1988, the words "or licensed", and (*b*) in the entry relating to section 133D of that Act, the words "or their employers".
Road Traffic (Driving Instruction by Disabled Persons) Act 1993 (c 31)	Section 2. In the Schedule, paragraphs 2 to 9.
Driving Licences (Community Driving Licence) Regulations 1996 (SI 1996/1974)	In Schedule 1, paragraph 29.
Police Act 1997 (c 50)	In Schedule 9, paragraph 58.
Motor Cars (Driving Instruction) (Admission of Community Licence Holders) Regulations 1999 (SI 1999/357)	Regulation 2(2), (4) and (5).
Transport Act 2000 (c 38)	In section 258(2), the words "and (2)". Section 259(2) and (3). In Schedule 29, paragraphs 7, 8, 9 and 11.
Courts Act 2003 (c 39)	In Schedule 8, paragraph 309.
Serious Organised Crime and Police Act 2005 (c 15)	In Schedule 4, paragraph 53.

(15) Registration plate suppliers: extension to Scotland and Northern Ireland

Short title and chapter	Extent of repeal
Vehicles (Crime) Act 2001 (c 3)	In section 17(1), the words "in England or Wales".

(16) Safety arrangements at level crossings

Short title and chapter	Extent of repeal
Level Crossings Act 1983 (c 16)	In section 1— (a) in subsection (3)(b), the words "barriers or other", and (b) in subsection (11), the definition of "local authority".

(17) Hackney carriages and private hire vehicles

Short title and chapter	Extent of repeal
Local Government (Miscellaneous Provisions) Act 1976 (c 57)	Section 75(1)(b).
Private Hire Vehicles (London) Act 1998 (c 34)	In section 1(1)(a), in the definition of "private hire vehicle", the words "to the public".

(18) Trunk road picnic areas

Short title and chapter	Extent of repeal
Highways Act 1980 (c 66)	In section 112— (a) in subsection (1), the words "that is not a special road", (b) in subsection (4), the words ", other than a council,", and (c) in subsection (5), the words "that is not a special road".

(19) Spent enactments

Short title and chapter	Extent of repeal
Criminal Justice Act 1972 (c 71)	Section 24(3).
Road Traffic Act 1988 (c 52)	In section 89— (a) in subsection (1)(a) and (d), the words "or that, if it is available to him, he satisfies the alternative requirement of section 89A of this Act", and (b) in subsection (6), the words "or section 89A(2)(b)(iii) below". Section 89A(2), (3) and (6).
Road Traffic Offenders Act 1988 (c 53)	In section 84(1), the words "60(1),".

Road Traffic

Endorseable Offence Codes and Penalty Points[1]

4–2019 *The following codes are extracted from instructions issued by the Driver and Vehicle Licensing Agency and are of value in interpreting United Kingdom driving licences. A few codes are used primarily by Scottish courts. Crown copyright material is reproduced with the permission of the Controller of HMSO and the Queen's Printer for Scotland.*

Code	Offences	Penalty points
Offences in relation to accidents		
AC10	Failing to stop after an accident	5–10
AC20	Failing to give particulars or to report an accident within 24 hours	5–10
AC30	Undefined accident offence	4–9
Offences of driving while disqualified		
BA10	Driving while disqualified by order of court	6
BA20	Driving while disqualified as under age	(*obsolete*)
BA30	Attempting to drive while disqualified by order of court (England/Wales only)	6
Careless driving offences		
CD10	Driving without due care and attention	3–9
CD20	Driving without reasonable consideration for other road users	3–9
CD30	Driving without due care and attention or without reasonable consideration for other road users	3–9
CD40	Causing death by careless driving when unfit through drink	(2)
CD50	Causing death by careless driving when unfit through drugs	(2)
CD60	Causing death by careless driving with alcohol level above the limit	(2)
CD70	Causing death by careless driving then failing to supply specimen for analysis	3–11
Construction and use offences (vehicles or parts dangerous)		
CU10	Using a vehicle with defective brakes	3
CU20	Causing or likely to cause danger by reason of use of unsuitable vehicle or using a vehicle with parts or accessories (excluding brakes, steering or tyres) in dangerous condition	3
CU30	Using a vehicle with defective tyres	3
CU40	Using a vehicle with defective steering	3
CU50	Causing or likely to cause danger by reason of load or passengers	3
CU60	Undefined failure to comply with constructions and use regulations	3
Reckless driving offences		
DD30	Reckless driving	(*obsolete*)
DD40	Dangerous driving	(2)
DD60	Manslaughter or, in Scotland, culpable homicide while driving a motor vehicle	(2)
DD70	Causing death by reckless driving	(*obsolete*)
DD80	Causing death by dangerous driving	(2)
Drink or drugs offences		
DR10	Driving or attempting to drive with alcohol concentration above limit	(2)
DR20	Driving or attempting to drive when unfit through drink	(2)
DR30	Driving or attempting to drive, then refusing to provide a specimen for analysis	(2)
DR40	In charge of a vehicle with alcohol concentration above limit	10
DR50	In charge of a vehicle when unfit through drink	10
DR60	Failure to provide a specimen for analysis in circumstances other than driving or attempting to drive	10
DR70	Failing to provide a specimen for breath test	4
DR80	Driving or attempting to drive when unfit through drugs	[2]
DR90	In charge of vehicle when unfit through drugs	10
Insurance offences		
IN10	Using a vehicle uninsured against third-party risks	6–8
Licence offences		
LC10	Driving without a licence	(*obsolete*)
LC20	Driving otherwise than in accordance with a licence	3–6
LC30	Driving after making a false declaration about fitness when applying for a licence	3–6
LC40	Driving vehicle having failed to notify a disability	3–6
LC50	Driving after a licence has been revoked or refused on medical grounds	3–6
Miscellaneous offences		
MS10	Leaving vehicle in a dangerous position	3
MS20	Unlawful pillion riding	1
MS30	Playstreet offence	2
MS40	Driving with uncorrected defective eyesight or refusing to submit to a test of eyesight	(*obsolete*)2
MS50	Motor racing on the highway	(2)
MS60	Offences not covered by other codes	as appropriate
MS70	Driving with uncorrected defective eyesight	3
MS80	Refusing to submit to eyesight test	3
MS90	Failing to give information as to identity of driver in certain cases	3

Code	Offences	Penalty points
Motorway offence		
MW10	Contravention of special roads regulations (excluding speed limits)	3
Non-endorsable offences		
NE 98	A disqualification under section 146 of the Powers of Criminal Courts (Sentencing) Act 2000	
NE99	A disqualification under section 24 of the Criminal Justice Act 1972 and section 44 of the Powers of Criminal Courts Act (and for offences of unauthorised taking formerly designated by codes UT10–UT40)	
Pedestrian crossing offences		
PC10	Undefined contravention of pedestrian crossing regulations	3
PC20	Contravention of pedestrian crossing regulations with moving vehicle	3
PC30	Contravention of pedestrian crossing regulations with stationary vehicle	3
Provisional licence offences		
PL10	Driving without L-plates	(obsolete)
PL20	Not accompanied by a qualified person	(obsolete)
PL30	Carrying a person not qualified	(obsolete)
PL40	Drawing an unauthorised trailer	(obsolete)
PL50	Undefined failure to comply with the conditions of a provisional licence	(obsolete)
Speed limits offences		
SP10	Exceeding goods vehicle speed limit	3–6
SP20	Exceeding speed limit for type of vehicle (excluding goods/passenger vehicles)	3–6
SP30	Exceeding statutory speed limit on a public road	3–6
SP40	Exceeding passenger vehicle speed limit	3–6
SP50	Exceeding speed limit on a motorway	3–6
SP60	Undefined speed limit offence	3–6
Traffic directions and signs offences		
TS10	Failing to comply with traffic light signals	3
TS20	Failing to comply with double white lines	3
TS30	Failing to comply with a "stop" sign	3
TS40	Failing to comply with a direction of a constable or traffic warden	3
TS50	Failing to comply with a traffic sign (excluding stop signs, traffic lights or double white lines)	3
TS60	Failure to comply with a school crossing patrol sign	3
TS70	Undefined failure to comply with a traffic direction or sign	3
Offences of theft or unauthorised taking		
UT10	Taking and driving away a vehicle without consent or an attempt threat (in England and Wales prior to Theft Act 1968 only). Driving a vehicle knowing it to have been taken without consent. Allowing oneself to be carried in or on a vehicle knowing it to have been taken without consent. (Primarily for use by Scottish Courts.)	(obsolete)
UT20	Stealing or attempting to steal a vehicle	(obsolete)
UT30	Going equipped for stealing or taking a motor vehicle	(obsolete)
UT40	Taking or attempting to take a vehicle without consent. Driving or attempting to drive a vehicle knowing it to have been taken without consent. Allowing oneself to be carried in or on a vehicle knowing it to have been taken without consent.	(obsolete)
UT50	Aggravated taking of a vehicle	(2)
Special code		
TT99	ONLY to be used to indicate a disqualification under the penalty points procedures i.e. where the number of penalty points totals 12 or more—including any penalty points "taken into account", but not endorsed because a driver has been disqualified. *NB* When using this code, a date of conviction must always be shown on the licence.	

Aiding and/or abetting and/or counselling and/or procuring
Offences as coded above but with zero changed to "2", eg UT10 becomes UT12.

Causing or permitting
Offences coded as above but with zero changed to "4", eg PL10 becomes PL14.

Inciting
Offences as coded above but with zero changed to "6", eg DD30 becomes DD36.

Obsolete special code
XX99   To signify a disqualification under the old "totting-up" procedure
Following the introduction of the penalty points scheme XX99 can no longer be used, but will continue to appear on existing licences for some time.

1. Appended to Home Office Circular No 85/1982, amended by Home Office Circulars Nos 16 and 46 of 1983 and HOC 59/2003.
2. This offence carries obligatory disqualification except for special reasons when 3–11 points are imposed.

Sentence Codes[1]

A — Imprisonment

B — Detention in a place specified by the Secretary of State

C — Suspended Prison Sentence

D — Suspended Sentence Supervision Order

E — Conditional Discharge (maximum 3 years)

F — Bound Over

G — Probation (minimum 6 months maximum 3 years)

H — Supervision Order

J — Absolute discharge

K — Attendance Centre (minimum 12 hours, maximum 24 hours)

L — detention Centre (minimum 3 months, maximum 6 months)

X — Total period of partially suspended sentence, ie period sentence served and period sentence suspended

M — Community Service Order (minimum 40 hours, maximum 240)

N — Cumulative Sentence (Scottish Courts only)

P — Youth Custody Sentence

Q — Parent or Guardian Order

R — Borstal (minimum 6 months, maximum 2 years)

S — Compensation Orders (Scottish Courts)

T — Hospital Guardianship Order

U — Admonition (Scottish Courts only)

V — Young Offenders Institution (Scottish Courts only)

W — Care order

---

1. See footnote and italic headnote to the Endorseable Offence Codes, *ante.*

Highway Code[1]

4–2031 *Issued by the Secretary of State for Transport with the authority of Parliament (Resolutions passed November 1977) in pursuance of the Road Traffic Act 1972, s 37 and continued in effect by the Road Traffic Act 1988, s 38, in this* PART, *ante. Crown copyright material is reproduced with the permission of the Controller of HMSO and the Queen's Printer for Scotland.*

---

1. A print purporting to be printed under the superintendence or authority of Her Majesty's Stationery Office is admissible in evidence (Documentary Evidence Act 1882, PART II, EVIDENCE, *ante*). As to the legal effect of this code, see the Road Traffic Act 1988, s 38, in this PART, *ante.* Reproduced as published 24 May 2004.

RULES FOR PEDESTRIANS

GENERAL GUIDANCE

4–2032   1. Pavements or footpaths should be used if provided. Where possible, avoid walking next to the kerb with your back to the traffic. If you have to step into the road, look both ways first.

2. If there is no pavement or footpath, walk on the right-hand side of the road so that you can see oncoming traffic. You should take extra care and

- be prepared to walk in single file, especially on narrow roads or in poor light
- keep close to the side of the road.
- It may be safer to cross the road well before a sharp right-hand bend (so that oncoming traffic has a better chance of seeing you). Cross back after the bend.

3. Help other road users to see you. Wear or carry something light coloured, bright or fluorescent in poor daylight conditions. When it is dark, use reflective materials (e.g. armbands, sashes, waistcoats and jackets), which can be seen by drivers using headlights, up to three times as far away as non-reflective materials.

4. Young children should not be out alone on the pavement or road (see Rule 7). When taking children out, walk between them and the traffic and hold their hands firmly. Strap very young children into push-chairs or use reins

5. Organised walks. Groups of people should use a path if available; if one is not, they should keep to the left. Look-outs should be positioned at the front and back of the group, and they should wear fluorescent clothes in daylight and reflective clothes in the dark. At night, the look-out in front should carry a white light and the one at the back a red light. People on the outside of large groups should also carry lights and wear reflective clothing.

6. Motorways. You MUST NOT walk on motorways or their slip roads except in an emergency (see Rule 249).

[Laws RTRA s 17, MT(E&W)R 1982 as amended & MT(S)R regs 2 & 13.]

CROSSING THE ROAD

4–2033   7. The Green Cross Code. The advice given below on crossing the road is for all pedestrians. Children should be taught the Code and should not be allowed out alone until they can understand and use it properly. The age when they can do this is different for each child. Many children cannot judge how fast vehicles are going or how far away they are. Children learn by example, so parents and carers should always use the Code in full when out with their children. They are responsible for deciding at what age children can use it safely by themselves.

a. First find a safe place to cross.

It is safer to cross using a subway, a footbridge, an island, a zebra, pelican, toucan or puffin crossing, or where there is a crossing point controlled by a police officer, a school crossing patrol or a traffic warden. Where there is a crossing nearby, use it. Otherwise choose a place where you can see clearly in all directions. Try to avoid crossing between parked cars (see Rule 14) and on blind bends and brows of hills. Move to a space where drivers can see you clearly.

b. Stop just before you get to the kerb

Stop just before you get to the kerb, where you can see if anything is coming. Do not get too close to the traffic. If there is no pavement, keep back from the edge of the road but make sure you can still see approaching traffic.

c. Look all around for traffic and listen.

Traffic could come from any direction. Listen as well because you can sometimes hear traffic before you see it.

d. If traffic is coming, let it pass

Look all round again and listen. Do not cross until there is a safe gap in the traffic and you are certain that there is plenty of time. Remember, even if traffic is a long way off, it may be approaching very quickly.

e. When it is safe, walk straight across the road—do not run.

Keep looking and listening for traffic while you cross, in case there is any traffic you did not see, or in case other traffic appears suddenly.

8. At a junction. When crossing the road, look out for traffic turning into the road, especially from behind you.

9. Pedestrian Safety Barriers. Where there are barriers, cross the road only at the gaps provided for pedestrians. Do not climb over the barriers or walk between them and the road.

10. Tactile paving. Small raised studs which can be felt underfoot may be used to advise blind or partially sighted people that they are approaching a crossing point with a dropped kerb.

11. One-way streets. Check which way the traffic is moving. Do not cross until it is safe to do so without stopping. Bus and cycle lanes may operate in the opposite direction to the rest of the traffic.

12. Bus and cycle lanes. Take care when crossing these lanes as traffic may be moving faster than in the other lanes, or against the flow of traffic.

13. Routes shared with cyclists. Cycle tracks may run alongside footpaths, with a dividing line segregating the two. Keep to the section for pedestrians. Take extra care where cyclists and pedestrians share the same path without separation (see Rule 48).

14. Parked vehicles. If you have to cross between parked vehicles, use the outside edges of the vehicles as if they were the kerb. Stop there and make sure you can see all around and that the traffic can see you. Never cross the road in front of, or behind, any vehicle with its engine running, especially a large vehicle, as the driver may not be able to see you.

15. Reversing vehicles. Never cross behind a vehicle which is reversing, showing white reverse lights or sounding a warning.

16. Moving vehicles. You MUST NOT get on to or hold on to a moving vehicle.
[Law RTA 1988 s 26.]

17. At night. Wear something reflective to make it easier for others to see you (see Rule 3). If there is no pedestrian crossing nearby, cross the road near a street light so that traffic can see you more easily.

CROSSINGS

4–2034   **18. At all crossings.** When using any type of crossing you should

- always check that the traffic has stopped before you start to cross or push a pram onto a crossing
- always cross between the studs or over the zebra markings. Do not cross at the side of the crossing or on the zig-zag lines, as it can be dangerous.

You MUST NOT loiter on zebra, pelican or puffin crossings.
[Laws ZPPPCRGD reg 19 & RTRA s 25(5).]

19. Zebra crossings. Give traffic plenty of time to see you and to stop before you start to cross. Vehicles will need more time when the road is slippery. Remember that traffic does not have to stop until someone has moved onto the crossing. Wait until traffic has stopped from both directions or the road is clear before crossing. Keep looking both ways, and listening, in case a driver or rider has not seen you and attempts to overtake a vehicle that has stopped.

20. Where there is an island in the middle of a zebra crossing, wait on the island and follow Rule 19 before you cross the second half of the road – it is a separate crossing.

21. At traffic lights. There may be special signals for pedestrians. You should only start to cross the road when the green figure shows. If you have started to cross the road and the green figure goes out, you should still have time to reach the other side, but do not delay. If no pedestrian signals have been provided, watch carefully and do not cross until the traffic lights are red and the traffic has stopped. Keep looking and check for traffic that may be turning the corner. Remember that traffic lights may let traffic move in some lanes while traffic in other lanes has stopped.

22. Pelican crossings. These are signal-controlled crossings operated by pedestrians. Push the control button to activate the traffic signals. When the red figure shows, do not cross. When a steady green figure shows, check the traffic has stopped then cross with care. When the green figure begins to flash you should not start to cross. If you have already started you should have time to finish crossing safely.

23. At some pelican crossings there is a bleeping sound to indicate to blind or partially-sighted people when the steady green figure is showing, and there may be a tactile signal to help deafblind people.

24. When the road is congested, traffic on your side of the road may be forced to stop even though their lights are green. Traffic may still be moving on the other side of the road, so press the button and wait for the signal to cross.

25. Puffin and toucan crossings. These differ from pelican crossings as there is no flashing green figure phase. On puffin crossings the red and green figures are above the control box on your side of the road. Press the button and wait for the green figure to show. On toucan crossings cyclists are permitted to ride across the road (see Rule 65).

26. 'Staggered' pelican or puffin crossings. When the crossings on each side of the central refuge are not in line they are two separate crossings. On reaching the central island press the button again and wait for a steady green figure.

27. Crossings controlled by an authorised person. Do not cross the road unless you are signalled to do so by a police officer, traffic warden or school crossing patrol. Always cross in front of them.

28. Where there are no controlled crossing points available it is advisable to cross where there is an island in the middle of the road. Use the Green Cross Code to cross to the island and then stop and use it again to cross the second half of the road.

SITUATIONS NEEDING EXTRA CARE

4–2035   29. Emergency vehicles. If an ambulance, fire engine, police or other emergency vehicle approaches using flashing blue lights, headlights and/or sirens, keep off the road.

30. Buses. Get on or off a bus only when it has stopped to allow you to do so. Watch out for cyclists when you are getting off. Never cross the road directly behind or in front of a bus; wait until it has moved off and you can see clearly in both directions.

31. Tramways. These may run through pedestrian areas. Their path will be marked out by shallow kerbs, changes in the paving or other road surface, while lines or yellow dots. Cross at designated crossings where provided. Flashing amber lights may warn you that a tram is approaching. Elsewhere look both ways along the track before crossing. Do not walk along the track. Trams move quickly and silently and cannot steer to avoid you.

32. Railway level crossings. Do not cross if the red lights show, an alarm is sounding or the barriers are being lowered. The tone of the alarm will change if another train is approaching. If there are no lights, alarms or barriers, stop, look both ways and listen before crossing.

33. Street and pavement repairs. A pavement may be closed temporarily because it is not safe to use. Take extra care if you are directed to walk in or to cross the road.

RULES ABOUT ANIMALS

HORSERIDERS

4–2036   34. Safety equipment. Children under the age of 14 MUST wear a helmet which complies with the Regulations. It MUST be fastened securely. Other riders should also follow this advice. [Law H(PHYR)R.]

35. Other clothing. You should wear

- boots or shoes with hard soles and heels
- light-coloured or fluorescent clothing in daylight
- reflective clothing if you have to ride at night or in poor visibility.

36. At night. It is safer not to ride on the road at night or in poor visibility, but if you do, make sure your horse has reflective bands above the fetlock joints. Carry a light which shows white to the front and red to the rear.

Riding

37. Before you take a horse on to a road, you should

- Ensure all tack fits well and is in good condition
- Make sure you can control the horse.

Always ride with other, less nervous horses if you think that your horse will be nervous of traffic. Never ride a horse without a saddle or bridle.

38. Before riding off or turning, look behind you to make sure it is safe, then give a clear arm signal.

39. When riding on the road you should

- keep to the left
- keep both hands on the reins unless you are signalling
- keep both feet in the stirrups
- not carry another person
- not carry anything which might affect your balance or get tangled up with the reins
- keep a horse you are leading to your left
- move in the direction of the traffic flow in a one-way street
- never ride more than two abreast, and ride in single file where the road narrows or on the approach to a bend.

40. You MUST NOT take a horse on to a footpath, pavement or cycle track. Use a bridleway where possible.
[Laws HA 1835 s 72 & R(S)A s 129(5)]

41. Avoid roundabouts wherever possible. If you use them you should

- keep to the left and watch out for vehicles crossing you path to leave or join the roundabout
- signal right when riding across exits to show you are not leaving
- signal left just before you leave the roundabout.

OTHER ANIMALS

4–2037 **42. Dogs.** Do not let a dog out on the road on its own. Keep it on a short lead when walking on the pavement, road or path shared with cyclists.

43. When in a vehicle make sure dogs or other animals are suitably restrained so they cannot distract you while you are driving or injure you if you stop quickly.

44. Animals being herded. These should be kept under control at all times. You should, if possible, send another person along the road in front to warn other road users, especially at a bend or the brow of a hill. It is safer not to move animals after dark, but if you do, then wear reflective clothing and ensure that lights are carried (white at the front and red at the rear of the herd).

RULES FOR CYCLISTS

4–2038 These rules are in addition to those in the following sections, which apply to all vehicles (except the motorway section). See also choosing and maintaining your bicycle.

45. Clothing. You should wear

- a cycle helmet which conforms to current regulations
- appropriate clothes for cycling. Avoid clothes which may get tangled in the chain, or in a wheel or may obscure your lights
- light-coloured or fluorescent clothing which helps other road users to see you in daylight and poor light
- reflective clothing and/or accessories (belt, arm or ankle bands) in the dark.

46. At night your cycle MUST have front and rear lights lit. It MUST also be fitted with a red rear reflector (and amber pedal reflectors, if manufactured after 1/10/85). Flashing lights and other reflectors may help you to be seen but MUST NOT be used alone.
[Law RVLR regs 18 and 24.]

WHEN CYCLING

4–2039 **47.** Use cycle routes when practicable. They can make your journey safer.

48. Cycle Tracks. These are normally located away from the road, but may occasionally be found alongside footpaths or pavements. Cyclists and pedestrians may be segregated or they may share the same space (unsegregated). When using segregated tracks you MUST keep to the side intended for cyclists. Take care when passing pedestrians, especially children, elderly or disabled people, and allow them plenty of room. Always be prepared to slow down and stop if necessary.
[Law HA 1835 s 72.]

49. Cycle Lanes. These are marked by a white line (which may be broken) along the carriageway (see Rule 119). Keep within the lane wherever possible.

50. You MUST obey all traffic signs and traffic light signals.
[Laws RTA 1988 s 36, TSRGD reg 10(1).]

51. You should

- keep both hands on the handlebars except when signalling or changing gear
- keep both feet on the pedals
- not ride more than two abreast
- ride in single file on narrow or busy roads
- not ride close behind another vehicle
- not carry anything which will affect your balance or may get tangled up with your wheels or chain
- be considerate of other road users, particularly blind and partially sighted pedestrians. Let them know you are there when necessary, for example by ringing your bell.

52. You should

- look all around before moving away from the kerb, turning or manoeuvring, to make sure it is safe to do so. Give a clear signal to show other road users what you intend to do
- look well ahead for obstructions in the road, such as drains, pot-holes and parked vehicles so that you do not have to swerve suddenly to avoid them. Leave plenty of room when passing parked vehicles and watch out for doors being opened into your path
- take extra care near road humps, narrowing and other traffic calming features.

53. You MUST NOT

- carry a passenger unless your cycle has been built or adapted to carry one
- hold on to a moving vehicle or trailer
- ride in a dangerous, careless or inconsiderate manner
- ride when under the influence of drink or drugs.

[Law RTA 1988 sects 24, 26, 28, 29 & 30 as amended by RTA 1991.]

54. You MUST NOT cycle on a pavement. Do not leave your cycle where it would endanger or obstruct other road users or pedestrians, for example, lying on the pavement. Use cycle parking facilities where provided.
[Laws HA 1835 s 72 & R(S)A s 129.]

55. You MUST NOT cross the stop line when the traffic lights are red. Some junctions have an advanced stop line to enable you to position yourself ahead of other traffic (see Rule 154).
[Laws RTA 1988 s 36, TSRGD regs 10 and 36(1).]

56. Bus Lanes. These may be used by cyclist only if the signs include a cycle symbol. Watch out for people getting on or off a bus. Be very careful when overtaking a bus or leaving a bus lane as you will be entering a busier traffic flow.

Road junctions

57. On the left. When approaching a junction on the left, watch out for vehicles turning in front of you, out of or into the side road. Do not ride on the inside of vehicles signalling of slowing down to turn left.

58. Pay particular attention to long vehicles which need a lot of room to manoeuvre at corners. They may have to move over to the right before turning left. Wait until they have completed the manoeuvre because the rear wheels come very close to the kerb while turning. Do not be tempted to ride in the space between them and the kerb.

59. On the right. If you are turning right, check the traffic to ensure it is safe, then signal and move to the centre of the road. Wait until there is a safe gap in the oncoming traffic before completing the turn. It may be safer to wait on the left if there is a safe gap or to dismount and push your cycle across the road.

60. Dual carriageways. Remember that traffic on most dual carriageways moves quickly. When crossing wait for a safe gap and cross each carriageway in turn. Take extra care when crossing slip roads.

Roundabouts

61. Full details about the correct procedure at roundabouts are contained in Rules 160-166. Roundabouts can be hazardous and should be approached with care.

62. You may feel safer either keeping to the left on the roundabout or dismounting and walking your cycle round on the pavement or verge. If you decide to keep to the left you should

- be aware that drivers may not easily see you
- take extra care when cycling across exits and you may need to signal right to show you are not leaving the roundabout
- watch out for vehicles crossing your path to leave or join the roundabout.

63. Give plenty of room to long vehicles on the roundabout as they need more space to manoeuvre. Do not ride in the space they need to get round the roundabout. It may be safer to wait until they have cleared the roundabout.

Crossing the road

64. Do not ride across a pelican, puffin or zebra crossing. Dismount and wheel your cycle across.

65. Toucan crossings. These are light-controlled crossings which allow cyclists and pedestrians to cross at the same time. They are push button operated. Pedestrians and cyclists will see the green signal together. Cyclists are permitted to ride across.

66. Cycle-only crossings. Cycle tacks opposite sides of the road may be linked by signalled crossings. You may ride across but you MUST NOT cross until the green cycle symbol is showing.
[Law TSRGD reg 36(1).]

RULES FOR MOTORCYCLISTS

These Rules are in addition to those in the following sections which apply to all vehicles. For motorcycle licence requirements see Annex 2.

General

4–2040　67. On all journeys, the rider and pillion passenger on a motorcycle, scooter or moped MUST wear a protective helmet. Helmets MUST comply with the Regulations and they MUST be fastened securely. It is also advisable to wear eye protectors, which MUST comply with the Regulations. Consider wearing ear protection. Strong boots, gloves and suitable clothing may help to protect you if you fall off.
[Laws RTA 1988 ss 16 & 17 & MC(PH)R as amended reg 4, & RTA s 18 & MC(EP)R as amended reg 4.]

68. You MUST NOT carry more than one pillion passenger and he/she MUST sit astride the machine on a proper seat and should keep both feet on the footrests.
[Law RTA 1988 s 23.]

69. Daylight riding. Make yourself as visible as possible from the side as well as the front and rear. Wear a white helmet and fluorescent clothing or strips. Dipped headlights, even in good daylight, may also make you more conspicuous.

70. Riding in the dark. Wear reflective clothing or strips to improve your chances of being seen in the dark. These reflect light from the headlamps of other vehicles making you more visible from a long distance. See Rules 93–96 for lighting requirements.

71. Manoeuvring. You should be aware of what is behind and to the sides before manoeuvring. Look behind you; use mirrors if they are fitted. When overtaking traffic queues look out for pedestrians crossing between vehicles and vehicles emerging from junctions.
Remember: Observation – Signal – Manoeuvre.

RULES FOR DRIVERS AND MOTORCYCLISTS

4–2041 **72. Vehicle condition.** You MUST ensure your vehicle and trailer complies with the full requirements of the Road Vehicles (Construction and Use) Regulations and Road Vehicles Lighting Regulations. (See *Annex 6.*)

73. Before setting off. You should ensure that

- you have planned your route and allowed sufficient time
- clothing and footwear do not prevent you using the controls in the correct manner
- you know where all the controls are and how to use them before you need them. All vehicles are different; do not wait until it is too late to find out
- your mirrors and seat are adjusted correctly to ensure comfort, full control and maximum vision
- head restraints are properly adjusted to reduce the risk of neck injuries in the event of an accident
- you have sufficient fuel before commencing your journey, especially if it includes motorway driving. It can be dangerous to lose power when driving in traffic.

74. Vehicle towing and loading. As a driver

- you MUST NOT tow more than your licence permits you to
- you MUST NOT overload your vehicle or trailer. You should not tow a weight greater than that recommended by the manufacturer of your vehicle
- you MUST secure your load and it MUST NOT stick out dangerously
- you should properly distribute the weight in your caravan or trailer with heavy items mainly over the axle(s) and ensure a downward load on the tow ball. Manufacturer's recommended weight and tow ball load should not be exceeded. This should avoid the possibility of swerving or snaking and going out of control. If this does happen, ease off the accelerator and reduce speed gently to regain control.

[Law CUR reg 100, MVDL reg 43.]

75. Seat belts. You MUST wear a seat belt if one is available, unless you are exempt. Those exempt from the requirement include the holders of medical exemption certificates and people making local deliveries in a vehicle designed for the purpose.

[Laws RTA 1988 ss 14 & 15, MV(WSB)R & MV(WSBCFS)R.]

Seat belt requirements. This table summarises the main legal requirements for wearing seat belts.

	Front seat (all vehicles)	Rear seat (cars and small minibuses*)	Whose responsibility
Driver	**Must** be worn if fitted	—	**Driver**
CHILD under 3 years of age	Appropriate child restraint **must** be worn	Appropriate child restraint **must** be worn *if available*	**Driver**
CHILD aged 3 to 11 and under 1.5 metres (about 5 feet) in height	Appropriate child restraint **must** be worn *if available*. If not, an adult seat belt **must** be worn	Appropriate child restraint **must** be worn if available. If not, an adult seat belt **must** be worn *if available*	**Driver**
CHILD aged 12 or 13 or younger child 1.5 metres or more in height	Adult seat belt **must** be worn *if available*	Adult seat belt **must** be worn *if available*	**Driver**
PASSENGER over the age of 14	**Must** be worn *if available*	**Must** be worn *if available*	*Passenger*

*Minibuses with an unladen weight of 2540kg or less

76. The driver MUST ensure that all children under 14 years of age wear seat belts or sit in an approved child restraint, This should be a baby seat, child seat, booster seat or booster cushion appropriate to the child's weight and size, fitted to the manufacture's instructions.

[Laws RTA 1988 ss 14 & 15, MV(WSB)R & MV(WSBCFS)R.]

77. You MUST wear seatbelts in minibuses with an unladen weight of 2540 kgs or less. You should wear them in large min-buses and coaches where available.

[Laws RTA 1988 ss 14 & 15, MV(WSB)R & MV(WSBCFS)R.]

78. Children in cars. Drivers who are carrying children in cars should ensure that

- children do not sit behind the rear seats in an estate car or hatchback, unless a special child seat has been fitted
- the child safety door locks, where fitted, are used when children are in the car
- children are kept under control
- a rear-facing baby seat is NEVER fitted into a seat protected by an airbag.

FITNESS TO DRIVE

4–2042 **79. Make sure that you are fit to drive.** You MUST report to the Driver and Vehicle Licensing Agency (DVLA) any health condition likely to affect your driving.

[Law RTA 1988 s 94.]

80. Driving when you are tired greatly increases your accident risk. To minimise this risk

- make sure you are fit to drive. Do not undertake a long journey (longer than an hour) if you feel tired
- avoid undertaking long journeys between midnight and 6am, when natural alertness is at a minimum
- plan your journey to take sufficient breaks. A minimum break of at least 15 minutes after two hours of driving is recommended
- if you feel at all sleepy, stop in a safe place. Do not stop on the hard shoulder of a motorway
- the most effective ways to counter sleepiness are to take a short nap (up to 15 minutes) or drink, for example, two cups of strong coffee. Fresh air, exercise or turning up the radio may help for a short time, but are *not* as effective.

81. **Vision.** You MUST be able to read a vehicle number plate from a distance of 20.5 metres (67 feet – about five car lengths) in good daylight. From September 2001, you MUST be able to read a new style number plate from a distance of 20 metres (66 feet). If you need to wear glasses (or contact lenses) to do this, you MUST wear them at all times whilst driving. The police have the power to require a driver, at any time, to undertake an eyesight test in good daylight.
[Laws RTA 1988 s 96 & MV(DL)R reg 40 & Sch 8.]

82. At night or in poor visibility, do not use tinted glasses, lenses or visors or anything that restricts vision.

Alcohol and drugs

83. **Do not drink and drive** as it will seriously affect your judgement and abilities. You MUST NOT drive with a breath alcohol level higher than 35μg/100ml or a blood alcohol level of more than 80 mg/100 ml. Alcohol will

- give a false sense of confidence
- reduce co-ordination and slow down reactions
- affect judgement of speed, distance and risk
- reduce your driving ability, even if you are below the legal limit
- take time to leave your body; you may be unfit to drive in the evening after drinking at lunchtime, or in the morning after drinking the previous evening. If you are going to drink, arrange another means of transport.

[Law RTA 1988 ss 4, 5 and 11(2).]

84. You MUST NOT drive under the influence of drugs or medicine. Check the instructions or ask your doctor or pharmacist. Using illegal drugs is highly dangerous. Never take them before driving; the effects are unpredictable, but can be even more severe than alcohol and may result in fatal or serious road accidents.
[Law RTA 1988 s 4.]

GENERAL RULES, TECHNIQUES AND ADVICE FOR ALL DRIVERS AND RIDERS
SIGNALS

4–2043 85. Signals warn and inform other road users, including pedestrians, of your intended actions. You should

- give clear signals in plenty of time, having checked it is not misleading to signal at that time
- use them, if necessary, before changing course or direction, stopping or moving off
- cancel them after use
- make sure your signals will not confuse others. If, for instance you want to stop after a side road, do not signal until you are passing the road. If you signal earlier it may give the impression that you intend to turn into the road. Your brake lights will warn traffic behind you that you are slowing down.
- use an arm signal to emphasise or reinforce your signal if necessary. Remember that signalling does not give you priority.

86. You should also

- watch out for signals given by other road users and proceed only when you are satisfied that it is safe
- be aware that an indicator on another vehicle may not have been cancelled.

87. You MUST obey signals given by police officers and traffic wardens (see *Signals by authorised persons* section) and signs used by school crossing patrols.
[Laws RTRA s 28, RTA 1988 s 35 and FTWO art 3.]

TRAFFIC LIGHT SIGNALS AND TRAFFIC SIGNS

4–2044 88. You MUST obey all traffic light signals (see *Light signals controlling traffic* section) and traffic signs giving orders, including temporary signals & signs (see *Traffic signs and Road works signs* sections). Make sure you know, understand and act on all other traffic and information signs and road markings (see sections on *Warning signs, Direction signs, Information signs, Road works signs* and *Road markings*).
[Laws RTA 1988 s 36, TSRGD regs 10, 15, 16, 25, 26 and 33.]

89. **Police stopping procedures.** If the police want to stop your vehicle they will, where possible, attract your attention by

- Flashing blue lights or headlights or sounding their siren or horn
- Directing you to pull over to the side by pointing and/or using the left indicator.

You MUST then pull over and stop as soon as it is safe to do so. Then switch off your engine.
[Law RTA 1988 s 163.]

90. Flashing headlights. Only flash your headlights to let other road users know that you are there. Do not flash your headlights in an attempt to intimidate other road users.

91. If another driver flashes his headlights never assume that it is a signal to go. Use your own judgement and proceed carefully.

92. The horn. Use only while your vehicle is moving and you need to warn other road users of your presence. Never sound your horn aggressively. You MUST NOT use your horn

- while stationary on the road
- when driving in a built up area between the hours of 11.30pm and 7.00am

except when another vehicle poses a danger.
[Law CUR reg 99.]

Lighting requirements

93. You MUST

- use headlights at night, except on restricted roads (those with street lights not more than 185 metres (600 feet) apart and which are generally subject to a speed limit of 30 mph)
- use headlights when visibility is seriously reduced (see Rule 201).
- Ensure all sidelights and rear registration plate lights are lit at night.
[Laws RVLR regs 24 & 25 RV(R&L)R reg 19.]

94. You MUST NOT

- use any lights in a way which would dazzle or cause discomfort to other road users
- use front or rear fog lights unless visibility is seriously reduced. You MUST switch them off when visibility improves to avoid dazzling other road users.
[Law RVLR reg 27.]

95. You should also

- use dipped headlights, or dim-dip if fitted, at night in built-up areas and in dull daytime weather, to ensure that you can be seen
- keep your headlights dipped when overtaking until you are level with the other vehicle and then change to main beam if necessary, unless this would dazzle oncoming traffic
- slow down, and if necessary stop, if you are dazzled by oncoming headlights.

96. Hazard warning lights. These may be used when your vehicle is stationary, to warn that it is temporarily obstructing traffic. Never use them as an excuse for dangerous or illegal parking. You MUST NOT use hazard warning lights whilst driving unless you are on a motorway or unrestricted dual carriageway and you need to warn drivers behind you of a hazard or obstructing ahead. Only use them for long enough to ensure that your warning has been observed.
[Law RVLR reg 27.]

Control of the vehicle

Braking

4–2045 **97. In normal circumstances.** The safest way to brake is to do so early and lightly. Brake more firmly as you begin to stop. Ease the pressure off just before the vehicle comes to rest to avoid a jerky stop.

98. In an emergency. Brake immediately. Try to avoid braking so harshly that you lock your wheels. Locked wheels can lead to skidding.

99. Skids. Skidding is caused by the driver braking, accelerating or steering too harshly or driving too fast for the road conditions. If skidding occurs, ease off the brake or accelerator and try to steer smoothly in the direction of the skid. For example, if the rear of the vehicle skids to the right, steer quickly and smoothly to the right to recover.

100. ABS. The presence of an anti-lock braking system should not cause you to alter the way you brake from that indicated in Rule 97. However in the case of an emergency, apply the footbrake rapidly and firmly; do not release the pressure until the vehicle has slowed to the desired speed. The ABS should ensure that steering control will be retained.

101. Brakes affected by water. If you have driven through deep water your brake may be less effective. Test them at the first safe opportunity by pushing gently on the brake pedal to make sure that they work. If they are not fully effective, gently apply light pressure while driving slowly. This will help to dry them out.

102. Coasting. This term describes a vehicle travelling in neutral or with the clutch pressed down. Do not coast, whatever the driving conditions. It reduces driver control because

- engine braking is eliminated
- vehicle speed downhill will increase quickly
- increased use of the footbrake can reduce its effectiveness
- steering response will be effected particularly on bends and corners
- it may be more difficult to select the appropriate gear when needed.

Speed limits

103. You MUST NOT exceed the maximum speed limits for the road and for your vehicle (see the table below). Street lights usually mean that there is a 30 mph speed limit unless there are signs showing another limit.
[Law RTRA ss 81, 86, 89 & Sch 6.]

Speed limits

| Type of vehicle | Built-up areas* | Elsewhere | | Motorways |
		Single carriage-ways	Dual carriage-ways	
	Mph	Mph	Mph	Mph
Cars & motorcycles (including car derived vans up to 2 tonnes maximum laden weight)	30	60	70	70
Cars towing caravans or trailers (including car derived vans and motorcycles)	30	50	60	60
Buses & coaches (not exceeding 12 metres in overall length)	30	50	60	70
Goods vehicles (not exceeding 7.5 tonnes maximum laden weight)	30	50	60	70¹
Goods vehicles (exceeding 7.5 tonnes maximum laden weight)	30	40	50	60

These are the national speed limits and apply to all roads unless signs show otherwise.

The 30mph limit applies to all traffic on all roads in England and Wales (only Class C and unclassified roads in Scotland) with street lighting unless signs show otherwise.

1. 60 if articulated or towing a trailer.

104. The speed limit is the absolute maximum and does not mean it is safe to drive at that speed irrespective of conditions. Driving at speeds too fast for the road and traffic conditions can be dangerous. You should always reduce your speed when

- the road layout or condition presents hazards, such as bends
- sharing the road with pedestrians and cyclists, particularly children, and motorcyclists
- weather conditions make it safer to do so
- driving at night as it is harder to see other road users.

Stopping distances

105. Drive at a speed that will allow you to stop well within the distance you can see to be clear. You should

- leave enough space between you and the vehicle in front so that you can pull up safely if it suddenly slows down or stops. The safe rule is never to get closer than the overall stopping distance (see Typical Stopping Distances diagram, below).
- Allow at least a two-second gap between and the vehicle in front on roads carrying fast traffic. The gap should be at least doubled on wet roads and increased still further on icy roads
- Remember, large vehicles and motorcycles need a greater distance to stop.

Use a fixed point to help measure a two second gap.

TYPICAL STOPPING DISTANCES

	Thinking Distance	Stopping Distance	Average car length = 4 metres
20 mph	6 metres	6 metres	= 12 metres (40 feet) or 3 car lengths
30 mph	9 metres	14 metres	= 23 metres (75 feet) or 6 car lengths
40 mph	12 metres	24 metres	= 36 metres (120 feet) or 9 car lengths
50 mph	15 metres	38 metres	= 53 metres (175 feet) or 13 car lengths
60 mph	18 metres	55 metres	= 73 metres (240 feet) or 18 car lengths
70 mph	21 metres	75 metres	= 96 metres (315 feet) or 24 car lengths

LINES AND LANE MARKINGS ON THE ROAD

4–2046 106. A broken white line. This marks the centre of the road. When this line lengthens and the gaps shorten, it means that there is a hazard ahead. Do not cross it unless you can see the road is clear well ahead and wish to overtake or turn off.

107. Double white lines where the line nearest to you is broken. This means you may cross the lines to overtake if it is safe, provided you can complete the manoeuvre before reaching a solid white line on your side. White arrows on the road indicate when you need to get back onto your side of the road.

108. Double white lines where the line nearest you is solid. This means you MUST NOT cross or straddle it unless it is safe and you need to enter adjoining premises or a side road. You may cross the line if necessary to pass a stationary vehicle, or overtake a pedal cycle, horse or road maintenance vehicle if they are travelling at 10mph or less.
[Laws RTA s 36 & TSRGD regs 10 & 26.]

109. Areas of white diagonal stripes or chevrons painted on the road. These are to separate traffic lanes or to protect traffic turning right.

- If the area is bordered by a broken white line, you should not enter the area unless it is necessary and you can see that it is safe to do so.
- If the area is marked with diagonal stripes and bordered by solid white lines, you should not enter it except in an emergency.
- If the area is marked with chevrons and bordered by solid white lines you MUST NOT enter it except in an emergency.

[Laws MT(E&W)R regs 5, 9, 10 & 16, MT(S)R regs 4, 8, 9 & 14, RTA s 36 & TSRGD 10(1).]

110. Lane dividers. These are short broken white lines which are used on wide carriageways to divide them into lanes. You should keep between them.

111. Reflective road studs may be used with white lines.

- White studs mark the lanes or the middle of the road.
- Red studs mark the left edge of the road.
- Amber studs mark the central reservation of a dual carriageway or motorway.
- Green studs mark the edge of the main carriageway at lay-bys, side roads and slip roads.

MULTI-LANE CARRIAGEWAYS

4–2047

Lane discipline

112. If you need to change lane, first use your mirrors and check your blind spots (the areas you are unable to see in the mirrors) to make sure you will not force another driver or rider to swerve or slow down. When it is safe to do so, signal to indicate your intentions to other road users and when clear move over.

113. You should follow the signs and road markings and get into lane as directed. In congested road conditions do not change lanes unnecessarily.

Single carriageway

114. Where a single carriageway has three lanes and the road markings or signs do not give priority to traffic in either direction

- use the middle lane only for overtaking or turning right. Remember, you have no more right to use the middle lane than a driver coming from the opposite direction
- do not use the right-hand lane.

115. Where a single carriageway has four or more lanes, use only the lanes that signs or markings indicate.

Dual carriageways

116. On a two-lane dual carriageway you should stay in the left-hand lane. Use the right-hand lane for overtaking or turning right. If you use it for overtaking move back to the left-hand lane when it is safe to do so.

117. On a three-lane dual carriageway, you may use the middle lane or the right-hand lane to overtake but return to the middle and then the left-hand lane when it is safe.

Climbing and crawler lanes

118. These are provided on some hills. Use this lane if you are driving a slow moving vehicle or if there are vehicles behind you wishing to overtake.

Cycle lanes

119. These are shown by road markings and signs. You MUST NOT drive or park in a cycle lane marked by a solid white line during its times of operation. Do not drive or park in a cycle lane marked by a broken white line unless it is unavoidable. You MUST NOT park in any cycle lane whilst waiting restrictions apply.
[Law RTRA ss 5 & 8.]

120. Bus and tram lanes. These are shown by road markings and signs. You MUST NOT drive or stop in a tram lane or in a bus lane during its period of operation unless the signs indicate you may do so.
[Law RTRA ss 5 & 8.]

121. One-way streets. Traffic MUST travel in the direction indicated by signs. Buses and/or cycles may have a contraflow lane. Choose the correct lane for your exit soon as you can. Do not change lanes suddenly. Unless road signs or markings indicate otherwise, you should use

- the left-hand lane when going left
- the right-hand lane when going right
- the most appropriate lane when going straight ahead.

- Remember – traffic could be passing on both sides.
[Laws RTA 1988 s 36 & RTRA ss 5 & 8.]

4–2048 122. You MUST NOT

- drive dangerously
- drive without due care and attention
- drive without reasonable consideration for other road users.

[Law RTA 1988 ss 2 & 3 as amended by RTA 1991.]

123. You MUST NOT drive on or over a pavement, footpath or bridleway except to gain lawful access to property.
[Laws HA 1835 s 72 & RTA s 34.]

124. Adapt your driving to the appropriate type and condition of road you are on. In particular

- do not treat speed limits as a target. It is often not appropriate or safe to drive at the maximum speed limit
- take the road and traffic conditions into account. Be prepared for unexpected or difficult situations, for example, the road being blocked beyond a blind bend. Be prepared to adjust your speed as a precaution
- where there are junctions, be prepared for vehicles emerging
- in side roads and country lanes look out for unmarked junctions where nobody has priority
- try to anticipate what pedestrians and cyclists might do. If pedestrians, particularly children, are looking the other way, they may step out into the road without seeing you.

125. Be considerate. Be careful of and considerate towards other road users. You should

- try to be understanding if other drivers cause problems; they may be inexperienced or not know the area well
- be patient; remember that anyone can make a mistake
- not allow yourself to become agitated or involved if someone is behaving badly on the road. This will only make the situation worse. Pull over, calm down and, when you feel relaxed, continue your journey
- slow down and hold back if a vehicle pulls out into your path at a junction. Allow it to get clear. Do not over-react by driving too close behind it.

126. Safe driving needs concentration. Avoid distractions when driving such as

- loud music (this may mask other sounds)
- trying to read maps
- inserting a cassette or CD or tuning a radio
- arguing with your passengers or other road users
- eating and drinking.

Mobile phones and in-car technology

127. You MUST exercise proper control of your vehicle at all times. You MUST NOT use a hand-held mobile phone, or similar device, when driving or when supervising a learner driver, except to call 999 or 112 in a genuine emergency when it is unsafe or impractical to stop. Never use a hand-held microphone when driving. Using hands free equipment is also likely to distract your attention from the road. It is far safer not to use any telephone while you are driving - find a safe place to stop first.
[Law RTA 1988 ss 2 & 3 & CUR regs 104 & 110.]

128. There is a danger of driver distraction being caused by in-vehicle systems such as route guidance and navigation systems, congestion warning systems, PCs, multi-media, etc. Do not operate, adjust or view any such system if it will distract your attention while you are driving; you MUST exercise proper control of your vehicle at all times. If necessary find a safe place to stop first.
[Law RTA 1988 ss 2 & 3 & CUR reg 104.]

In slow moving traffic

129. You should

- reduce the distance between you and the vehicle ahead to maintain traffic flow
- never get so close to the vehicle in front that you cannot stop safely
- leave enough space to be able to manoeuvre if the vehicle in front breaks down or an emergency vehicle needs to get past
- not change lanes to the left to overtake
- allow access into and from side roads, as blocking these will add to congestion.

Driving in built up areas

130. Narrow residential streets. You should drive slowly and carefully on streets where there are likely to be pedestrians, cyclists and parked cars. In some areas a 20 mph maximum speed limit may be in force. Look out for

- vehicles emerging from junctions
- vehicles moving off
- car doors opening
- pedestrians
- children running out from between parked cars
- cyclists and motorcyclists.

131. Traffic calming measures. On some roads there are features such as road humps, chicanes and narrowings which are intended to slow you down. When you approach these features reduce your speed. Allow cyclists and motorcyclists room to pass through them. Maintain a reduced speed along the whole of the stretch of road within the calming measures. Give way to contouring traffic if directed to do so by signs. You should not overtake other moving vehicles whilst in these areas.

Country roads

132. Take extra care on country roads and reduce your speed at approaches to bends, which can be sharper than they appear, and at minor junctions and turnings, which may be partially hidden. Be prepared for pedestrians, horse riders and cyclists walking or riding in the road. You should also reduce your speed where country roads enter villages.

133. Single-track roads. These are only wide enough for one vehicle. They may have special passing places. If you see a vehicle coming towards you, or the driver behind wants to overtake, pull into a passing place on your left, or wait opposite a passing place on your right. Give way to vehicles coming uphill whenever you can. If necessary, reverse until you reach a passing place to let the other vehicle pass.

134. Do not park in passing places.

USING THE ROAD
GENERAL RULES

4–2049   **135. Before moving off** you should

- use all mirrors to check the road is clear
- look round to check the blind spots (the areas you are unable to see in the mirrors)
- signal if necessary before moving out
- look round for a final check.

Move off only when it is safe to do so.

136. Once moving you should

- keep to the left, unless road signs or markings indicate otherwise. The exceptions are when you want to overtake, turn right to pass parked vehicles or pedestrians in the road
- keep well to the left on right-hand bends. This will improve your view of the road and help avoid the risk of colliding with traffic approaching from the opposite direction
- keep both hands on the wheel, where possible. This will help you to remain in full control of the vehicle at all times
- be aware of other vehicles especially cycles and motorcycles. These are more difficult to see than larger vehicles and their riders are particularly vulnerable. Give them plenty of room, especially if you are driving a long vehicle or towing a trailer
- select a lower gear before you reach a long downhill slope. This will help to control your speed
- when towing, remember the extra length will affect overtaking and manoeuvring. The extra weight will also affect the braking and acceleration.

Mirrors

137. All mirrors should be used effectively throughout you journey. You should

- use your mirrors frequently so that you always know what is behind and to each side of you
- use them in good time before you signal or change direction or speed
- be aware that mirrors do not cover all areas and there will be blind spots. You will need to look round and check.

Remember: Mirrors – Signal – Manoeuvre

OVERTAKING

138. Before overtaking you should make sure

- the road is sufficiently clear ahead
- the vehicle behind is not beginning to overtake you
- there is a suitable gap in front of the vehicle you plan to overtake.

139. Overtake only when it is safe to do so. You should

- not get too close to the vehicle you intend to overtake
- use your mirrors, signal when it is safe to do so, take a quick sideways glance into the blind spot area and then start to move out
- not assume that you can simply follow a vehicle ahead which is overtaking; there may only be enough room for one vehicle
- move quickly past the vehicle you are overtaking, once you have started to overtake. Allow plenty of room. Move back to the left as soon as you can but do not cut in
- take extra care at night and in poor visibility when it is harder to judge speed and distance
- give way to oncoming vehicles before passing parked vehicles or other obstructions on your side of the road
- only overtake on the left if the vehicle in front is signalling to turn right, and there is room to do so

- stay in your lane if traffic is moving slowly in queues. If the queue on your right is moving more slowly than you are, you may pass on the left
- give motorcyclists, cyclists and horse riders at least as much room as you would a car when overtaking (see Rules 188, 189 and 191).

Remember: Mirrors – Signal – Manoeuvre

140. Large vehicles. Overtaking these is more difficult. You should

- drop back to increase your ability to see ahead. Getting too close to large vehicles will obscure your view of the road ahead and there may be another slow moving vehicle in front
- make sure that you have enough room to complete your overtaking manoeuvre before committing yourself. It takes longer to pass a large vehicle. If in doubt do not overtake
- not assume you can follow a vehicle ahead which is overtaking a long vehicle. If a problem develops, they may abort overtaking and pull back in.

141. You MUST NOT overtake

- if you would have to cross or straddle double white lines with a solid line nearest to you (but see Rule 108)
- if you would have to enter an area designed to divide traffic, if it is surrounded by a solid white line
- the nearest vehicle to a pedestrian crossing, especially when it has stopped to let pedestrians cross
- if you would have to enter a lane reserved for buses, trams or cycles during its hours of operation
- after a 'No Overtaking' sign and until you pass a sign cancelling the restriction.

[Laws RTA 1988 s 36, TSRGD regs 10, 22 23 & 24, ZPPPCR reg 24.]

142. DO NOT overtake if there is any doubt, or where you cannot see far enough ahead to be sure it is safe. For example, when you are approaching

- a corner or bend
- a hump bridge
- the brow of a hill.

143. DO NOT overtake where you might come into conflict with other road users. For example

- approaching or at a road junction on either side of the road
- where the road narrows
- when approaching a school crossing patrol
- between the kerb and a bus or tram when it is at a stop
- where traffic is queuing at junctions or road works
- when you would force another vehicle to swerve or slow down
- at a level crossing
- when a vehicle is indicating right, even if you believe the signal should have been cancelled. Do not take a risk; wait for the signal to be cancelled.

144. Being overtaken. If a driver is trying to overtake you, maintain a steady course and speed, slowing down if necessary to let the vehicle pass. Never obstruct drivers who wish to pass. Speeding up or driving unpredictably while someone is overtaking you is dangerous. Drop back to maintain a two-second gap if someone overtakes and pulls into the gap in front of you.

145. Do not hold up a long queue of traffic, especially if you are driving a large or slow moving vehicle. Check your mirrors frequently, and if necessary, pull in where it is safe and let traffic pass.

ROAD JUNCTIONS

4–2050 **146.** Take extra care at junctions. You should

- watch out for cyclists, motorcyclists and pedestrians as they are not always easy to see
- watch out for pedestrians crossing a road into which you are turning. If they have started to cross they have priority, so give way
- watch out for long vehicles which may be turning at a junction ahead; they may have to use the whole width of the road to make the turn (see Rule 196)
- not assume, when waiting at a junction, that a vehicle coming from the right and signalling left will actually turn. Wait and make sure
- not cross or join a road until there is a gap large enough for you to do so safely.

147. You MUST stop behind the line at a junction with a 'Stop' sign and a solid white line across the road. Wait for a safe gap in the traffic before you move off.

[Laws RTA 1988 s 36 & TSRGD regs 10 & 16.]

148. The approach to a junction may have a 'Give Way' sign or a triangle marked on the road. You MUST give way to traffic on the main road when emerging from a junction with broken white lines across the road.

[Laws RTA 1988 s 36 & TSRGD regs 10(1), 16(1) & 25.]

149. Dual carriageways. When crossing or turning right, first assess whether the central reservation is deep enough to protect the full length of your vehicle.

- if it is, then you should treat each half of the carriageway as a separate road. Wait in the central reservation until there is a safe gap in the traffic on the second half of the road.

- If the central reservation is too shallow for the length of your vehicle, wait until you can cross both carriageways in one go.

150. Box junctions. These have criss-cross yellow lines painted on the road (see *Other road markings* section). You MUST NOT enter the box until your exit road or lane is clear. However, you may enter the box and wait when you want to turn right, and are only stopped from doing so by oncoming traffic, or by other vehicles waiting to turn right. At signalled roundabouts you MUST NOT enter the box unless you can cross over it completely without stopping.
[Law TSRGD reg 10(1) & 29(2).]

Junctions controlled by traffic lights

151. You MUST stop behind the white 'Stop' line across your side of the road unless the light is green. If the amber light appears you may go on only if you have already crossed the stop line or are so close to it that to stop might cause an accident.
[Laws RTA 1988 s 36 & TSRGD regs 10 & 36.]

152. You MUST NOT move forward over the white line when the red light is showing. Only go forward when the traffic lights are green if there is room for you to clear the junction safely or you are taking up a position to turn right. If the traffic lights are not working, proceed with caution. Allow cyclists and buses time and space to move off when the green signal shows.
[Laws RTA 1988 s 36 & TSRGD regs 10 & 36.]

153. Green filter arrow. This indicates a filter lane only. Do not enter that lane unless you want to go in the direction of the arrow. You may proceed in the direction of the green arrow when it, or the full green light shows. Give other traffic, especially cyclists, time and room to move into the correct lane.

154. Advanced stop lines. Some junctions have advanced stop lines or bus advance areas to allow cycles and buses to be positioned ahead of other traffic. Motorists, including motorcyclists, MUST wait behind the first white line reached, and not encroach on the marked area. Allow cyclists and buses time and space to move off when the green signal shows. If your vehicle has proceeded over the first white line at the time the signal goes red, you MUST stop at the second white line, even if your vehicle is in the marked area.
[Laws RTA 1988 s 36 & TSRGD regs 10 & 43(2).]

Turning right

155. Well before you turn right you should

- use your mirrors to make sure you know the position and movement of traffic behind you
- give a right-turn signal
- take up a position just left of the middle of the road or in the space marked for traffic turning right
- leave room for other vehicles to pass on the left, if possible.

156. Wait until there is a safe gap between you and any oncoming vehicle. Watch out for cyclists, motorcyclists and pedestrians. Check your mirrors and blind spot again to make sure you are not being overtaken, then make the turn. Do not cut the corner. Take great care when turning into a main road; you will need to watch for traffic in both directions and wait for a safe gap.
Remember: Mirrors – Signal – Manoeuvre

157. When turning at a cross roads where an oncoming vehicle is also turning right, there is a choice of two methods

- turn right side to right side; keep the other vehicle on your right and turn behind it. This is generally the safest method as you have a clear view of any approaching traffic when completing your turn
- left side to left side, turning in front of each other. This can block your view of oncoming vehicles, so take extra care. Road layout, markings or how the other vehicle is positioned can determine which course should be taken.

Road layout, markings or how the other vehicle is positioned can determine which course should be taken.

Turning left

158. Use your mirrors and give a left-turn signal well before you turn left. Do not overtake just before you turn left and watch out for traffic coming up on your left before you make the turn, especially if driving a large vehicle. Cyclists and motorcyclists in particular may be hidden from your view.

159. When turning

- keep as close to the left as is safe and practical
- give way to any vehicles using a bus lane, cycle lane or tramway from either direction.

ROUNDABOUTS

4–2051 160. On approaching a roundabout take notice and act on all the information available to you, including traffic signs, traffic lights and lane markings which direct you into the correct lane. You should

- use **Mirrors – Signal – Manoeuvre** at all stages

- decide as early as possible which exit you need to take
- give an appropriate signal (see Rule 162). Time your signals so as not to confuse other road users
- get into the correct lane
- adjust your speed and position to fit in with traffic conditions
- be aware of the speed and position of all the traffic around you.

161. When reaching the roundabout you should

- give priority to traffic approaching from your right, unless directed otherwise by signs, road markings or traffic lights
- check whether road markings allow you to enter the roundabout without giving way. If so, proceed, but still look to the right before joining
- watch out for vehicles already on the roundabout; be aware they may not be signalling correctly or at all
- look forward before moving off to make sure traffic in front has moved off.

162. Signals and position, unless signs or markings indicate otherwise.
When taking the first exit

- signal left and approach in the left-hand lane
- keep to the left on the roundabout and continue signalling left to leave.

When taking any intermediate exit

- select the appropriate lane on approach to and on the roundabout, signalling as necessary
- stay in this lane until you need to alter course to exit the roundabout
- signal left after you have passed the exit before the one you want.

When taking the last exit or going full circle

- signal right and approach in the right-hand lane
- keep to the right on the roundabout until you need to change lanes to exit the roundabout
- signal left after you have passed the exit before the one you want.

When there are more than three lanes at the entrance to a roundabout, use the most appropriate lane on approach and through it.

163. In all cases watch out for and give plenty of room to

- pedestrians who may be crossing the approach and exit roads
- traffic crossing in front of you on the roundabout, especially vehicles intending to leave by the next exit
- traffic which may be straddling lanes or positioned incorrectly
- motorcyclists
- cyclists and horse riders who may stay in the left-hand lane and signal right if they intend to continue round the roundabout
- long vehicles (including those towing trailers) which might have to take a different course approaching or on the roundabout because of their length. Watch out for their signals.

164. Mini-roundabouts. Approach these in the same way as normal roundabouts. All vehicles MUST pass round the central markings except large vehicles which are physically incapable or doing so. Remember, there is less space to manoeuvre and less time to signal. Beware of vehicles making U-turns.
[Laws RTA 1988 s 36 & TSRGD 10(1), 16(1).]

165. At double mini-roundabouts treat each roundabout separately and give way to traffic from the right.

166. Multiple roundabouts. At some complex junctions, there may be a series of mini-roundabouts at the intersections. Treat each mini-roundabout separately and follow the normal rules.

PEDESTRIAN CROSSINGS

4–2052 **167.** You MUST NOT park on a crossing or in the area covered by the zig-zag lines. You MUST NOT overtake the moving vehicle nearest the crossing or the vehicle nearest the crossing which has stopped to give way to pedestrians.
[Laws ZPPPCRGD regs 18, 20 & 24, RTRA s 25(5) & TSRGD regs 10, 27 & 28.]

168. In queuing traffic, you should keep the crossing clear.

169. You should take extra care where the view of either side of the crossing is blocked by queuing traffic or incorrectly parked vehicles. Pedestrians may be crossing between stationary vehicles.

170. Allow pedestrians plenty of time to cross and do not harass them by revving you engine or edging forward.

171. Zebra crossings. As you approach a zebra crossing

- look out for people waiting to cross and be ready to slow down or stop to let them cross
- you MUST give way when someone has moved onto a crossing
- allow more time for stopping on wet or icy roads
- do not wave people across; this could be dangerous if another vehicle is approaching
- be aware of pedestrians approaching from the side of the crossing

[Law ZPPPCR reg 25.]

Signal-controlled crossings

172. Pelican crossings. These are signal-controlled crossings where flashing amber follows the red 'Stop' light. You MUST stop when the red light shows. When the amber light is flashing,

you MUST give way to any pedestrians on the crossing. If the amber light is flashing and there are no pedestrians on the crossing, you may proceed with caution.
[Laws ZPPPCRGD regs 23 & 26 & RTRA s 25(5).]

173. Pelican crossings which go straight across the road are one crossing, even when there is a central island. You MUST wait for pedestrians who are crossing from the other side of the island.
[Law ZPPPCRGD reg 26 & RTRA s 25(5).]

174. Give way to pedestrians who are still crossing after the signal for vehicles has changed to green.

175. Toucan and puffin crossings. These are similar to pelican crossings, but there is no flashing amber phase.

REVERSING

4–2053 176. Choose an appropriate place to manoeuvre. If you need to turn your car around, wait until you find a safe place. Try not to reverse or turn in a busy road; find a quiet side road or drive round a block of side streets.

177. Do not reverse from a side road into a main road. When using a driveway, reverse in and drive out if you can.

178. Look carefully before you start reversing. You should

- use all you mirrors
- check the 'blind spot' behind you (the part of the road you cannot see easily in the mirrors)
- check there are no pedestrians, particularly children, cyclists, or obstructions in the road behind you
- look mainly through the rear window
- check all around just before you start to turn and be aware that the front of your vehicle will swing out as you turn
- get someone to guide you if you cannot see clearly.

179. You MUST NOT reverse your vehicle further than necessary.
[Law CUR reg 106.]

ROAD USERS REQUIRING EXTRA CARE

180. The most vulnerable road users are pedestrians, cyclists, motorcyclists and horse riders. It is particularly important to be aware of children, elderly and disabled people, and learner and inexperienced drivers and riders.

PEDESTRIANS

4–2054 181. In urban areas there is a risk of pedestrians, especially children, stepping unexpectedly into the road. You should drive with the safety of children in mind at a speed suitable for the conditions.

182. Drive carefully and slowly when

- in crowded shopping streets or residential areas
- driving past bus and tram stops; pedestrians may emerge suddenly into the road
- passing parked vehicles, especially ice cream vans; children are more interested in ice cream than traffic and may run into the road unexpectedly
- needing to cross a pavement; for example, to reach a driveway
- reversing into a side road; look all around the vehicle and give way to any pedestrians who may be crossing the road
- turning at road junctions; give way to pedestrians who are already crossing the road into which you are turning
- the pavement is closed due to street repairs and pedestrians are directed to use the road.

183. Particularly vulnerable pedestrians. These include

- children and elderly pedestrians who may not be able to judge your speed and could step into the road in front of you. At 40 mph your vehicle will probably kill any pedestrians it his. At 20 mph there is only a 1 in 20 chance of the pedestrian being killed. So kill your speed
- elderly pedestrians who may need more time to cross the road. Be patient and allow them to cross in their own time. Do not hurry them by revving your engine or edging forward
- blind and partially sighted people who may be carrying a white cane (white with a red band for deaf and blind people) or using a guide dog
- people with disabilities. Those with hearing problems may not be aware of your vehicle approaching. Those with walking difficulties require more time.

184. Near schools. Drive slowly and be particularly aware of young cyclists and pedestrians. In some places, there may be a flashing amber signal below the 'School' warning sign which tells you that there may be children crossing the road ahead. Drive very slowly until you are clear of the area.

185. Drive carefully when passing a stationary bus showing a 'School Bus' sign (see *Vehicle markings* section) as children may be getting on or off.

186. You MUST stop when a school crossing patrol shows a 'Stop' for children sign (see *Traffic signs* section).
[Law RTRA s 28.]

Motorcyclists and cyclists

187. It is often difficult to see motorcyclists and cyclists especially when they are coming up from behind, coming out of junctions and at roundabouts. Always look out for them when you are emerging from a junction.

188. When passing motorcyclists and cyclists, give them plenty of room (see Rule 139). If they look over their shoulder whilst you are following them it could mean that they may soon attempt to turn right. Give them time and space to do so.

189. Motorcyclists and cyclists may suddenly need to avoid uneven road surfaces and obstacles such as draincovers or oily, wet or icy patches on the road. Give them plenty of room.

Other road users

190. Animals. When passing animals, drive slowly. Give them plenty of room and be ready to stop. Do not scare animals by sounding your horn or revving your engine. Look out for animals being led or ridden on the road and take extra care and keep your speed down at left-hand bends and on narrow country roads. If a road is blocked by a herd of animals, stop and switch off your engine until they have left the road. Watch out for animals on unfenced roads.

191. Horse riders. Be particularly careful of horses and riders, especially when overtaking. Always pass wide and slow. Horse riders are often children, so take extra care and remember riders may ride in double file when escorting a young or inexperienced horse rider. Look out for horse riders' signals and heed a request to slow down or stop. Treat all horses as a potential hazard and take great care.

192. Elderly drivers. Their reactions may be slower than other drivers. Make allowance for this.

193. Learners and inexperienced drivers. They may not be so skilful at reacting to events. Be particularly patient with learner drivers and young drivers. Drivers who have recently passed their test may display a 'new driver' plate or sticker.

Other vehicles

4–2055 194. Emergency vehicles. You should look and listen for ambulances, fire engines, police or other emergency vehicles using flashing blue, red or green lights, headlights or sirens. When one approaches do not panic. Consider the route of the emergency vehicle and take appropriate action to let it pass. If necessary, pull to the side of the road and stop, but do not endanger other road users.

195. Powered vehicles used by disabled people. These small vehicles travel at a maximum speed of 8 mph. On a dual carriageway they MUST have a flashing amber light, but on other roads you may not have that advance warning.
[Law RVLR reg 17(1).]

196. Large vehicles. These may need extra road space to turn or to deal with a hazard that you are not able to see. If you are following a large vehicle, such as a bus or articulated lorry, be prepared to stop and wait if it needs room or time to turn.

197. Large vehicles can block your view. Your ability to see and to plan ahead will be improved if you pull back to increase your separation distance.

198. Buses, coaches and trams. Give priority to these vehicles when you can do so safely, especially when they signal to pull away from stops. Look out for people getting off a bus or tram and crossing the road.

199. Electric vehicles. Be careful of electric vehicles such as milk floats and trams. Trams move quickly but silently and cannot steer to avoid you.

200. Vehicles with flashing amber lights. These warn of a slow-moving vehicle (such as a road gritter or recovery vehicle) or a vehicle which has broken down, so approach with caution.

DRIVING IN ADVERSE WEATHER CONDITIONS

4–2056 201. You MUST use headlights when visibility is seriously reduced, generally when you cannot see for more than 100 metres (328 feet). You may also use front or rear fog lights (in addition to headlights) but you MUST switch them off when visibility improves (see Rule 211).
[Law RVLR regs 25 & 27.]

Wet weather

202. In wet weather, stopping distances will be at least double those required for stopping on dry roads (see *Stopping Distances*). This is because your tyres have less grip on the road. In wet weather

- you should keep well back from the vehicle in front. This will increase your ability to see and plan ahead
- if the steering becomes unresponsive, it probably means that water is preventing the tyres from gripping the road. Ease off the accelerator and slow down gradually
- the rain and spray from vehicles may make it difficult to see and be seen.

Icy and snowy weather

203. In winter check the local weather forecast for warnings of icy or snowy weather. DO NOT drive in these conditions unless your journey is essential. If it is, take great care. Carry a spade, warm clothing, a warm drink and emergency food in case your vehicle breaks down.

204. Before you set off

- you MUST be able to see, so clear all snow and ice from all your windows
- you MUST ensure that lights and number plates are clean

- make sure the mirrors are clear and the windows are de-misted thoroughly.
[Laws CUR reg 30 & RVLR reg 23.]

205. When driving in icy or snowy weather

- drive with care, even if the roads have been gritted
- keep well back from the vehicle in front as stopping distances can be ten times greater than on dry roads
- take care when overtaking gritting vehicles, particularly if you are riding a motorcycle
- watch out for snowploughs which may throw out snow on either side. Do not overtake them unless the lane you intend to use has been cleared
- be prepared for the road conditions changing over relatively short distances.

206. Drive extremely carefully when the roads are icy. Avoid sudden actions as these could cause a skid. You should

- drive at a l sow speed in as high a gear as possible; accelerate and brake very gently
- drive particularly slowly on bends where skids are more likely. Brake progressively on the straight before you reach a bend. Having slowed down, steer smoothly round the bend, avoiding sudden actions
- check your grip on the road surface when there is snow or ice by choosing a safe place to brake gently. If the steering feels unresponsive this may indicate ice and your vehicle losing its grip on the road. When travelling on ice, tyres make virtually no noise.

Windy weather

207. High sided vehicles are most affected by windy weather, but strong gusts can also blow a car, cyclist or motorcyclist off course. This can happen at open stretches of the road exposed to strong cross winds, or when passing bridges or gaps in hedges.

208. In very windy weather your vehicle may be affected by turbulence created by large vehicles. Motorcyclists are particularly affected, so keep well back from them when they are overtaking a high-sided vehicle.

Fog

209. Before entering fog check you mirrors then slow down. If the word 'Fog' is shown on a roadside signal but the road is clear, be prepared for a bank of fog or drifting patchy fog ahead. Even if it seems to be clearing, you can suddenly find yourself in thick fog.

210. When driving in fog you should

- use your lights as required in Rule 201
- keep a safe distance behind the vehicle in front. Rear lights can give a false sense of security
- be able to pull up within the distance you can see clearly. This is particularly important on motorways and dual carriageways, as vehicles are travelling faster
- use your windscreen wipers and demisters
- beware of other drivers not using headlights
- not accelerate to get away from a vehicle which is too close behind you
- check your mirrors before you slow down. Then use your brakes so that your brake lights warn drivers behind you that you are slowing down
- stop in the correct position at a junction with limited visibility and listen for traffic. When you are sure it is safe to emerge, do so positively and do not hesitate in a position that puts you directly in the path of approaching vehicles.

211. You MUST NOT use front or rear fog lights unless visibility is seriously reduced (see Rule 201) as they dazzle other road users and can obscure your brake lights. You MUST switch them off when visibility improves.
[Law RVLR regs 25 & 27.]

Hot weather

212. Keep your vehicle well ventilated to avoid drowsiness. Be aware that the road surface may become soft or if it rains after a dry spell it may become slippery. These conditions could affect your steering and braking.

WAITING AND PARKING

4–2057 213. You MUST NOT wait or park where there are restrictions shown by

- yellow lines along the edge of the carriageway
- school entrance markings on the carriageway (see *Along the edge of the carriageway* section)

The periods when restrictions apply are shown on upright signs, usually at intervals along the road, parallel to the kerb.
[Law RTRA ss 5 & 8.]

PARKING

4–2058 214. Use off-street parking areas, or bays marked out with white lines on the road as parking places, wherever possible. If you have to stop on the road side

- stop as close as you can to the side

- do not stop too close to a vehicle displaying s Blue Badge, remember, they may need more room to get in or out
- you MUST switch off the engine, headlights and fog lights
- you MUST apply the handbrake before leaving the vehicle
- you MUST ensure you do not hit anyone when you open your door
- it is safer for your passengers (especially children) to get out of the vehicle on the side next to the kerb
- lock your vehicle.

[Laws CSDPA s 21, CUR regs 98, 105 & 107, RVLR reg 27 & RTA 1988 s 42.]

215. You MUST NOT stop or park on

- the carriageway or the hard shoulder of a motorway except in an emergency (see Rule 244)
- a pedestrian crossing, including the area marked by the zig-zag lines (see Rule 167)
- a Clearway (see *Traffic signs* section)
- a Bus Stop Clearway within its hours of operation
- taxi bays as indicated by upright signs and markings
- an Urban Clearway within its hours of operation, except to pick up or set down passengers (see *Traffic signs* section)
- a road marked with double white lines, except to pick up or set down passengers
- a bus, tram or cycle lane during its period of operation
- a cycle track
- red lines, in the case of specially designated 'red routes', unless otherwise indicated by signs.

[Laws MT(E&W)R regs 7 & 9, MT(S)R regs 6 & 8, ZPPPCRGD regs 18 & 20, RTRA ss 5 & 8, TSRGD regs 10, 26, 27 & 29(1), RTA 1988 ss 36 & 21(1).]

216. You MUST NOT park in parking spaces reserved for specific users, such as Blue Badge holders or residents, unless entitled to do so.
[Law CSDPA s 21 & RTRA ss 5 & 8.]

217. **DO NOT** park your vehicle or trailer on the road where it would endanger, inconvenience or obstruct pedestrians or other road users. For example, do not stop

- near a school entrance
- anywhere you would prevent access for Emergency Services
- at or near a bus stop or taxi rank
- on the approach to a level crossing
- opposite or within 10 metres (32 feet) of a junction, except in an authorised parking space
- near the brow of a hill or hump bridge
- opposite a traffic island or (if this would cause an obstruction) another parked vehicle
- where you would force other traffic to enter a tram lane
- where the kerb has been lowered to help wheelchair users
- in front of an entrance to a property
- on a bend.

218. **DO NOT** park partially or wholly on the pavement unless signs permit it. Parking on the pavement can obstruct and seriously inconvenience pedestrians, people in wheelchairs, the visually impaired and people with prams or pushchairs.

219. Controlled Parking Zones. The zone entry signs indicate the times when the waiting restrictions within the zone are in force. Parking may be allowed in some places at other times. Otherwise parking will be within separately signed and marked bays.

220. Goods vehicles. Vehicles with a maximum laden weight of over 7.5 tonnes (including any trailer) MUST NOT be parked on a verge, pavement or any land situated between carriageways, without police permission. The only exception is when parking is essential for loading and unloading, in which case the vehicle MUST NOT be left unattended.
[Law RTA 1988 s 19.]

221. Loading and unloading. Do not load or unload where there are yellow markings on the kerb and upright signs advise restrictions are in place. This may be permitted where parking is otherwise restricted. On red routes, specially marked and signed bays indicate where and when loading and unloading is permitted.
[Law RTRA ss 5 & 8.]

Parking at night

222. You MUST NOT park on a road at night facing against the direction of the traffic flow unless in a recognised parking space.
[Laws CUR reg 101 & RVLR reg 24.]

223. All vehicles MUST display parking lights when parked on a road or a lay-by on a road with a speed limit greater than 30 mph.
[Law RVLR reg 24.]

224. Cars, goods vehicles not exceeding 1525kg unladen, invalid carriages and motorcycles may be parked without lights on a road (or lay-by) with a speed limit of 30 mph or less if they are

- at least 10 metres (32 feet) away from any junction, close to the kerb and facing in the direction of the traffic flow
- in a recognised parking place or lay-by.

Otherwise vehicles and trailers, and all vehicles with projecting loads, MUST NOT be left on a road at night without lights.

[Law RVLR reg 24.]

225. Parking in fog. It is especially dangerous to park on the road in fog. If it is unavoidable, leave your parking lights or sidelights on.

226. Parking on hills. If you park on a hill you should

- park close to the kerb and apply the handbrake firmly
- select a forward gear and turn your steering wheel away from the kerb when facing uphill
- select reverse gear and turn your steering wheel towards the kerb when facing downhill
- use 'park' if your car has an automatic gearbox.

MOTORWAYS

Many other Rules apply to motorway driving, either wholly or in part: Rules 43,67–105, 109–113, 118, 122, 126–128, 135, 137, 194, 196, 200, 201–212, 248–252, 254–264.

GENERAL

4–2059 **227. Prohibited vehicles.** Motorways MUST NOT be used by pedestrians, holders of provisional car or motorcycles driving licences unless exempt, riders of motorcycles under 50cc, cyclists and horse riders. Certain slow-moving vehicles and those carrying oversized loads (except by special permission), agricultural vehicles and most invalid carriages are also prohibited.
[Laws HA 1980 ss 16, 17 & Sch 4, MT(E&W)R reg 4, MT(E&W)(A)R, R(S)A ss 7, 8 & Sch 3 & MT(S)R reg 10.]

228. Traffic on motorways (see *Motorway signals* section) usually travels faster than on other roads, so you have less time to react. It is especially important to use your mirrors earlier and look much further ahead than you would on other roads.

Motorway signals

229. Motorway signals are used to warn you of a danger ahead. For example, there may be an accident, fog, or a spillage, which you may not immediately be able to see.

230. Signals situated on the central reservation apply to all lanes. On very busy stretches, signal may be overhead with a separate signal for each lane.

231. Amber flashing lights. These warn of a hazard ahead. The signal may show a temporary maximum speed limit, lanes that are closed or a message such as 'Fog'. Adjust your speed and look out for the danger until you pass a signal which is not flashing or one that gives the 'All clear' sign and you are sure it is safe to increase your speed.

232. Red flashing lights. If red lights on the overhead signals flash above your lane (there may also be a red 'X') you MUST NOT go beyond the signal in that lane. If red lights flash on a signal in the central reservation or at the side of the road, you MUST NOT go beyond the signal in any lane.
[Laws RTA 1988 s 36 & TSRGD reg 10.]

DRIVING ON THE MOTORWAY

Joining the motorway

4–2060 **233.** When you join the motorway you will normally approach it from a road on the left (a slip road) or from an adjoining motorway. You should

- give priority to traffic already on the motorway
- check the traffic on the motorway and adjust your speed to fit safely into the traffic flow in the left-hand lane
- not cross solid white lines that separate lanes
- stay on the slip road if it continues as an extra lane on the motorway
- remain in the left-hand lane long enough to adjust to the speed of traffic before considering overtaking.

On the motorway

234. When you can see well ahead and the road conditions are good, you should

- drive at a steady cruising speed which you and your vehicle can handle safely and is within the speed limit (see table)
- keep a safe distance from the vehicle in front and increase the gap on wet or icy roads, or in fog (see Rules 105 & 210).

235. You MUST NOT exceed 70 mph, or the maximum speed limit permitted for your vehicle (see table). If a lower speed limit is in force, either permanently or temporarily, at roadworks for example, you MUST NOT exceed the lower limit. On some motorways, mandatory motorways signals (which display the speed within a red ring) are used to vary the maximum speed limit to improve traffic flow. You MUST NOT exceed this speed limit.
[Law RTRA ss 17, 86, 89 & Sch 6.]

236. The monotony of driving on a motorway can make you feel sleepy. To minimise the risk, follow the advice in Rule 80.

237. You MUST NOT reverse, cross the central reservation, or drive against the traffic flow. If you have missed your exit, or have taken the wrong route, carry on to the next exit.
[Laws MT(E&W)R regs 6, 7 & 10 & MT(S)R regs 4, 5, 7 & 9.]

Lane discipline

238. You should drive in the left-hand lane if the road ahead is clear. If you are overtaking a number of slower moving vehicles it may be safer to remain in the centre or outer lanes until the manoeuvre is completed rather than continually changing lanes. Return to the left-hand lane once you have overtaken all the vehicles or if you are delaying traffic behind you. Slow moving or speed restricted vehicles should always remain in the left-hand lane of the carriageway unless overtaking. You MUST NOT drive on the hard shoulder except in an emergency or if directed to do so by signs.
[Laws MT(E&W)R regs 5, 9 & 16(1)(a) & MT(S)R regs 4, 8 & 14(1)(a).]

239. The right-hand lane of a motorway with three or more lanes MUST NOT be used (except in prescribed circumstances) if you are driving

- any vehicle drawing a trailer
- a goods vehicle with a maximum laden weight over 7.5 tonnes
- a passenger vehicle with a maximum laden weight exceeding 7.5 tonnes constructed or adapted to carry more than eight seated passengers in addition to the driver.
[Laws MT(E&W)R reg 12 & MT(S)R reg 11.]

240. Approaching a junction. Look well ahead for signals or signs. Direction signs may be placed over the road. If you need to change lanes, do so in good time. At some junctions a lane may lead directly off the motorway. Only get in that lane if you wish to go in the direction indicated on the overhead signs.

Overtaking

241. Do not overtake unless you are sure it is safe to do so. Overtake only on the right. You should

- check your mirrors
- take time to judge the speeds correctly
- make sure that the lane you will be joining is sufficiently clear ahead and behind
- take a quick sideways glance into the blind spot area to verify the position of a vehicle that may have disappeared from your view in the mirror
- remember that traffic may be coming up behind you very quickly. Check you mirrors carefully. When it is safe to do so, signal in plenty of time, then move out
- ensure you do not cut in on the vehicle you have overtaken
- be especially careful at night and in poor visibility when it is harder to judge speed and distance.

242. Do not overtake on the left or move to a lane on your left to overtake. In congested conditions, where adjacent lanes of traffic are moving at similar speeds. Traffic in left-hand lanes may sometimes be moving faster than traffic to the right. In these conditions you may keep up with the traffic in your lane even if this means passing traffic in the lane to your right. Do not weave in and out of lanes to overtake.

243. You MUST NOT use the hard shoulder for overtaking.
[Laws MT(E&W)R regs 5 & 9 & MT(S)R regs 4 & 8.]

Stopping

244. You MUST NOT stop on the carriageway, hard shoulder, slip road, central reservation or verge except in an emergency, or when told to do so by the police, an emergency sign or by flashing red light signals.
[Laws MT(E&W)R regs 7(1), 9, 10 & 16 & MT(S)R regs 6(1), 8, 9 & 14.]

245. You MUST NOT pick up or set down anyone, or walk on a motorway, except in an emergency.
[Laws RTRA s 17 & MT(E&W)R reg 15.]

Leaving the motorway

246. Unless signs indicate that a lane leads directly off the motorway, you will normally leave the motorway by a slip road on your left. You should

- watch for the signs letting you know you are getting near your exit
- move into the left-hand lane well before reaching your exit
- signal left in good time and reduce your speed on the slip road as necessary.

247. On leaving the motorway or using a link road between motorways, your speed may be higher than you realise – 50 mph may feel like 30 mph. Check your speedometer and adjust your speed accordingly. Some slip-roads and link roads have sharp bends, so you will need to slow down.

BREAKDOWNS AND ACCIDENTS
BREAKDOWNS

4–2061   **248.** If your vehicle breaks down, think first of other road users and

- get your vehicle off the road if possible
- warn other traffic by using your hazard warning lights if your vehicle is causing an obstruction

- put a warning triangle on the road at least 45 metres (147 feet) behind your broken down vehicle on the same side of the road, or use other permitted warning devices if you have them. Always take great care when placing them, but never use them on motorways
- keep your sidelights on if it is dark or visibility is poor
- do not stand (or let anybody else stand), between your vehicle and oncoming traffic
- at night or in poor visibility do not stand where you will prevent other road users seeing your lights.

Additional rules for the motorway

249. If your vehicle develops a problem, leave the motorway at the next exit or pull into a service area. If you cannot do so, you should

- pull on to the hard shoulder and stop as far to the left as possible, with your wheels turned to the left
- try to stop near an emergency telephone (situated at approximately one mile intervals along the hard shoulder)
- leave the vehicle by the left-hand door and ensure you passengers do the same. You MUST leave any animals in the vehicle or, in an emergency, keep them under proper control on the verge
- do not attempt even simple repairs
- ensure that passengers keep away from the carriageway and hard shoulder, and that children are kept under control
- walk to an emergency telephone on your side of the carriageway (follow the arrows on the posts at the back of the hard shoulder) – the telephone is free of charge and connects directly to the police. Use these in preference to a mobile phone (see Rule 257)
- give full details to the police; also inform them if you are a vulnerable motorist such as a woman travelling alone
- return and wait near your vehicle (well away from the carriageway and hard shoulder)
- if you feel at risk from another person, return to your vehicle by a left-hand door and lock all doors. Leave your vehicle again as soon as you feel this danger has passed.

[Laws MT(E&W)R reg 14 & MT(S)R reg 12.]

250. Before you rejoin the carriageway after a breakdown, build up speed on the hard shoulder and watch for a safe gap in the traffic. Be aware that other vehicles may be stationary on the hard shoulder.

251. If you cannot get your vehicle on to the hard shoulder

- do not attempt to place any warning device on the carriageway
- switch on your hazard warning lights
- leave your vehicle only when you can safely get clear of the carriageway.

Disabled drivers

252. If you have a disability which prevents you from following the above advice you should

- stay in your vehicle
- switch on your hazard warning lights
- display a 'Help' pennant or, if you have a car or mobile telephone, contact the emergency services and be prepared to advise them of your location.

Obstructions

4–2062 **253.** If anything falls from your vehicle (or any other vehicle) on to the road, stop and retrieve it only if it is safe to do so.

254. Motorways. On a motorway so not try to remove the obstruction yourself. Stop at the next emergency telephone and call the police.

Accidents

4–2063 **255. Warning signs or flashing lights.** If you see or hear emergency vehicles in the distance be aware there may be an accident ahead.

256. When passing the scene of an accident do not be distracted or slow down unnecessarily (for example if an accident is on the other side of a dual carriageway). This may cause another accident or traffic congestion, but see Rule 257 below.

257. If you are involved in an accident or stop to give assistance

- use your hazard warning lights to warn other traffic
- ask drivers to switch off their engines and stop smoking
- arrange for the emergency services to be called immediately with full details of the accident location and any casualties (on a motorway, use the emergency telephone which allows easy location by the emergency services. If you use a mobile phone, first make sure you have identified your location from the marker posts on the side of the hard shoulder)
- move uninjured people away from the vehicles to safety; on a motorway this should, if possible, be well away from the traffic, the hard shoulder and the central reservation

- do not move injured people from their vehicles unless they are in immediate danger from fire or explosion
- do not remove a motorcyclist's helmet unless it is essential to do so
- be prepared to give first aid as shown in *Annex 7*
- stay at the scene until emergency services arrive.

If you are involved in any other medical emergency on the motorway you should contact the emergency services in the same way.

Accidents involving dangerous goods

258. Vehicles carrying dangerous goods in packages will be marked with plain orange reflective plates. Road tankers and vehicles carrying tank containers or dangerous goods will have hazard warning plates (see *Vehicle markings* section).

259. If and accident involves a vehicle containing dangerous goods, follow the advice in Rule 257 above and, in particular

- switch off engines and DO NOT SMOKE
- keep well away from the vehicle and do not be tempted to try to rescue casualties as you yourself could become one
- call the emergency services and give as much information as possible about the labels and markings on the vehicle.

DO NOT use a mobile phone close to a vehicle carrying flammable loads.

Documentation

260. If you are involved in an accident which causes damage or injury to any other person, vehicle, animal or property, you MUST

- stop
- give your own and the vehicle owner's name and address, and the registration number of the vehicle, to anyone having reasonable grounds for requiring them
- if you do not give your name and address at the time of the accident, report the accident to the police as soon as reasonably practicable, and in any case within 24 hours.

[Law RTA 1988 s 170.]

261. If another person is inured and you do not produce your insurance certificate at the time of the accident to a police officer or to anyone having reasonable grounds to request it you MUST

- report the accident to the police as soon as possible and in any case within 24 hours
- produce your insurance certificate for the police within seven days.

[Law RTA 1988 s 170.]

ROAD WORKS

4–2064   **262.** When the 'Road Works Ahead' sign is displayed, you will need to be more watchful and look for additional signs providing more specific instructions.

- You MUST NOT exceed any temporary maximum speed limit.
- Use you mirrors and get into the correct land for your vehicle in good time and as signs direct.
- Do not switch lanes to overtake queuing traffic.
- Do not drive through an area marked off by traffic cones.
- Watch out for traffic entering or leaving the works area, but do not be distracted by what is going on there.
- Bear in mind that the road ahead may be obstructed by the works or by slow moving or stationary traffic.

[Law RTRA s 16.]

Additional rules for high speed roads

263. Take special care on motorways and other high speed dual carriageways.

- One or more lanes may be closed to traffic and a lower speed limit may apply.
- Works vehicles that are slow moving or stationary with a large 'Keep Left' or 'Keep Right' sign on the back are sometimes used to close lanes for repairs.
- Check mirrors, slow down and change lanes if necessary.
- Keep a safe distance from the vehicle in front (see Rule 105).

264. Contraflow systems means that you may be travelling in a narrower lane than normal and with no permanent barrier between you and oncoming traffic. The hard shoulder may be used for traffic, but be aware that there may be broken down vehicles ahead of you. Keep a good distance from the vehicle ahead and observe any temporary speed limits.

RAILWAY LEVEL CROSSINGS

4–2065   **265.** A level crossing is where a road crosses a railway line. Approach and cross it with care. Never drive on to a crossing until the road is clear on the other side and do not get too close to the car in front. Never stop or park on, or near, a crossing.

266. Most crossings have traffic lights signals with a steady amber light, twin flashing red stop lights (see *Lights controlling traffic* section and *Warning signs* section) and an audible alarm for pedestrians. They may have full, half or no barriers.

- You MUST always obey the flashing red stop lights.
- You MUST stop behind the white line across the road.
- Keep going if you have already crossed the white line when the amber light comes on.
- You MUST wait if a train goes by and the red light continues to flash. This means another train will be passing soon.
- Only cross when the lights go off and barriers open.
- Never zig-zag around half-barriers, they lower automatically because a train is approaching.
- At crossings where there are no barriers, a train is approaching when the lights show.

[Laws RTA 1988 s 36 & TSRGD regs 10 & 40.]

267. Railway telephones. If you are driving a large or slow-moving vehicle, or herding animals, a train could arrive before you are clear of the crossing. You MUST obey any sign instructing you to use the railway telephone to obtain permission to cross. You MUST also telephone when clear of the crossing.

[Laws RTA 1988 s 36 & TSRGD regs 10 & 16(1).]

268. Crossing without traffic lights. Vehicles should stop and wait at the barrier or gate when it begins to close and not cross until the barrier or gate opens.

User-operated gates or barriers

269. Some crossings have 'Stop' signs and small red and green lights. You MUST NOT cross when the red light is showing, only cross if the green light is on. If crossing with a vehicle, you should

- open the gates or barriers on both sides of the crossing
- check that the green light is still on and cross quickly
- close the gates or barriers when you are clear of the crossing.

[Laws RTA 1988 s 36 & TSRGD regs 10 & 52(2).]

270. If there are no lights, follow the procedure in Rule 269 above. Stop, look both ways and listen before you cross. If there is a railway telephone, always use it to contact the signal operator to make sure it is safe to cross. Inform the signal operator again when you are clear of the crossing.

Open crossings

269. These have no gates, barriers, attendant or traffic lights but will have a 'Give Way' sign. You should look both ways, listen and make sure there is no train coming before you cross.

Accidents and breakdowns

271. If your vehicle breaks down, or if you have an accident on a crossing you should

- get everyone out of the vehicle and clear of the crossing immediately
- use a railway telephone if available to tell the signal operator. Follow the instructions you are given
- move the vehicle clear of the crossing if there is time before a train arrives. If the alarm sounds, or the amber light comes on, leave the vehicle and get clear of the crossing immediately.

TRAMWAYS

4–2066 273. You MUST NOT enter a road, lane or other route reserved for trams. Take extra care where trams run along the road. The width taken up by trams is often shown by tram lanes marked by white lines, yellow dots or by a different type of road surface. Diamond-shaped signs give instructions to tram drivers only.
[Law RTRA ss 5 & 8.]

274. Take extra care where the track crosses from one side of the road to the other and where the road narrows and the tracks come close to the kerb. Tram drivers usually have their own traffic signals and may be permitted to move when you are not. Always give way to trams. Do not try to race or overtake them.

275. You MUST NOT park your vehicle where it would get in the way of trams or where it would force other drivers to do so.
[Law RTRA ss 5 & 8.]

276. Tram stops. Where the tram stops at a platform, either in the middle or at the side of the road, you MUST follow the route shown by the road signs and markings. At stops without platforms you MUST NOT drive between a tram and the left-hand kerb when a tram has stopped to pick up passengers.
[Law RTRA ss 5 & 8.]

277. Look out for pedestrians, especially children, running to catch a tram approaching a stop.

278. Cyclists and motorcyclists should take extra care when riding close to or crossing the tracks, especially if the rails are wet. It is safest to cross the tracks directly at right angles.
Annexes not reproduced in this work.

LARGE GOODS AND PASSENGER CARRYING VEHICLES

Public Service Vehicles (Lost Property) Regulations 1978[1]
(SI 1978/1684 amended by SI 1981/1623 and SI 2003/1615)

4–2111   1, 2. *Commencement, citation, revocation and saving.*

---

1. Made under s 160 of the Road Traffic Act 1960 now the Public Passenger Vehicles Act 1981, s 60; penalty for contravention or failure to comply is a fine not exceeding **level 2** on the standard scale (Public Passenger Vehicles Act 1981, s 67, and see the Criminal Justice Act 1982, s 40).

Interpretation

4–2112   3. (1) In these Regulations, unless the context otherwise requires, the following expressions have the meanings hereby respectively assigned to them, that is to say—

"operator" means, in relation to a vehicle, or to any property accidentally left in a vehicle, the person providing the service upon which the vehicle is being used as a public service vehicle;

"owner" means in relation to any property which is the subject of an agreement for hire, hire-purchase or loan, the person entitled to possession of the property under that agreement and the expressions "owned" and "ownership" shall be construed accordingly;

"vehicle" means a public service vehicle;

"the 1934 Regulations" means the Public Service Vehicles (Lost Property) Regulations 1934.

(2) Any reference in these Regulations to the conductor of a vehicle shall, as respects a vehicle which has no conductor, be construed as a reference to the driver of the vehicle.

(3) Any reference in these Regulations to any enactment or instrument shall be construed, unless the context otherwise requires, as a reference to that enactment or instrument as amended, re-enacted or replaced by any subsequent enactment or instrument.

(4) Any reference in these Regulations to a numbered Regulation or Schedule is a reference to the Regulation or Schedule bearing that number in these Regulations except where otherwise expressly provided.

(5) The Interpretation Act [1978] shall apply for the interpretation of these Regulations as it applies for the interpretation of an Act of Parliament and as if, for the purposes of [sections 16(1) and 17(2)] of that Act, these Regulations were an Act of Parliament and the Regulations revoked by Regulation 2 were Acts of Parliament thereby repealed.

Application of Regulations

4–2113   4. (1) Subject to paragraph (2) below, these Regulations apply in relation to the safe custody and redelivery or disposal of property accidentally left in any vehicle whether before or after these Regulations come into operation.

(2) These Regulations do not apply in relation to the safe custody and redelivery or disposal of any property accidentally left in a vehicle belonging to and under the control of Transport for London or any of its subsidiaries (within the meaning of the Greater London Authority Act 1999).

Lost property to be handed to conductor

4–2114   5. Any person who finds property accidentally left in a vehicle shall immediately hand it in the state in which he finds it to the conductor of the vehicle or, where this is not practicable, deliver it to the operator's lost property office.

Search of vehicles for lost property and delivery to operator or his representative

4–2115   6. (1) Immediately before, or on, the termination of any journey of a vehicle the conductor of the vehicle shall search the vehicle so far as practicable for any property accidentally left in the vehicle.

(2) The conductor of a vehicle to whom any property is handed, in accordance with Regulation 4 of the 1934 Regulations or Regulation 5 above, or who himself finds any property in a vehicle shall, as soon as possible and in any case within 24 hours (unless the property has been returned to its owner under paragraph (3) below), deliver the property for safe custody in the state in which it came into his possession to the operator of the vehicle or his representative.

(3) If any such property as is referred to in paragraph (2) above is claimed by a person who satisfies the conductor that he is the owner of the property, it shall be returned to that person forthwith, without charge, on that person giving his name and address to the conductor who shall, as soon as may be, report the facts and give the claimant's name and address and a description of the property to the operator or his representative.

Safe custody and recording of property

4–2116   7. (1) An operator's representative to whom any property is delivered in pursuance of the 1934 Regulations or these Regulations, shall either (a) within 48 hours deliver it to the operator in the state in which he received it, together with particulars of the property the circumstances in which it was found and the name of the conductor into whose possession it first came, or (b) forward to the operator such particulars as aforesaid and the address of the place at which he has custody of the property.

(2) Any operator or any operator's representative to whom any property is delivered under these Regulations or the 1934 Regulations shall keep it in safe custody until it is returned to its owner or otherwise disposed of in pursuance of these Regulations:

Provided that—

(a) official documents, including licences passports and alien's identity books, shall wherever practicable be returned forthwith to the appropriate government department, local authority or other public body or person responsible for issuing or for controlling or dealing with them;

(b) where the name and address of a person who may be the owner of any property other than the documents referred to in the preceding proviso are readily ascertainable, the operator or his representative shall forthwith notify him that the property is in his possession and may be claimed in accordance with these Regulations.

(3) An operator to whom particulars of any property are given under paragraph (1) of this Regulation or Regulation 6 of the 1934 Regulations shall, whether or not the property is delivered to him, keep for a period of not less than twelve months a record of such particulars and the ultimate disposal of each item of property under these Regulations or the 1934 Regulations, and such record shall at all reasonable times during the said period be available for inspection by a constable or any person authorised in that behalf by the traffic commissioners for the area in which the record is kept.

Return of lost property to owner on payment of charges

4–2117 **8.** If any property accidentally left in a vehicle is claimed while it is in the custody of an operator or his representative, and the claimant gives his name and address and satisfies such operator or representative that he is the owner thereof, it shall thereupon be returned to him on payment to such operator or representative of a charge of the amount specified, or at the rate specified, in column (2) of Schedule 2 for property of that kind.

Disposal of property by operator or his representative

4–2118 **9.** (1) If any property which is in the custody of an operator in accordance with these Regulations is not claimed within a period of—

(a) one month in the case of property (other than a document mentioned in sub-paragraph (b) below) the value of which in the opinion of the operator or his representative is 50p or less,

(b) three months in the case of any document mentioned in sub-paragraph (a) of the proviso to Regulation 7(2) above, whatever may be its value, or

(c) three months in the case of any property not mentioned in sub-paragraph (a) or (b) above,

from the date on which it was delivered to the operator or his representative and proved to the satisfaction of the operator or his representative to be owned by the claimant or if the claimant shall refuse or neglect to pay the charge mentioned in Regulation 8 above within the said period of one month or, as the case may be, three months, such property shall thereupon vest in the operator.

(2) In the event of an operator becoming entitled to—

(a) a charge paid in accordance with Regulation 8, or

(b) property in accordance with paragraph (1) above,

the operator is entitled to dispose of the charge or, as the case may be, the property as he, in his discretion, thinks fit including returning the charge or the property to the claimant.

Perishable property

4–2119 **10.** Notwithstanding the foregoing provisions of these Regulations, if any property held by an operator or his representative under these Regulations appears to such operator or representative to be of a perishable nature, and if, within 48 hours from the time when it was found, it has not been claimed and proved to the satisfaction of such operator or representative to be owned by a person who has paid the charge payable under Regulation 8 and taken delivery of the property, then the property shall thereupon vest in the operator who may destroy or otherwise dispose of it as he thinks fit.

Provided that any property which is, or which becomes, objectionable may be destroyed or disposed of at any time in the discretion of the operator or his representative having custody of it.

Cost of packing and carriage

4–2120 **11.** Where any property is to be forwarded to a claimant by the operator or his representative all costs of packing and carriage reasonably incurred shall be paid in advance by the claimant to the operator or his representative.

Examination of property

4–2121 **12.** Where any property is contained in a package, bag or other receptacle the operator or his representative may cause such receptacle to be opened and the contents examined, or require any claimant to open it and submit it and its contents for examination, if the operator or his representative deems it necessary for the purpose—

(*a*) of identifying and tracing the owner of the property, or

(*b*) of ascertaining the nature of the contents or valuing the property.

4–2122   SCHEDULE 1
                                     REGULATIONS REVOKED BY REGULATION 2

4–2123   SCHEDULE 2
                  CHARGES PAYABLE UNDER REGULATION 8 BEFORE DELIVERY OF PROPERTY TO OWNER

                                               Revoked.

Public Service Vehicles (Conditions of Fitness, Equipment, Use and Certification) Regulations 1981[1]

(SI 1981/257 amended by SI 1982/20, 1058 and 1482, SI 1984/1763, 1986/370 and 1812, SI 1988/340, SI 1989/322 and 2359, SI 1990/450, SI 1991/456, SI 1992/565 and SI 1993/3012, SI 1995/305, SI 1997/84, SI 1998/1670, SI 2000/1431, SI 2001/1649, SI 2002/335 and 489, SI 2003/1817, SI 2004/1880 and SI 2005/1403, 2342, 2986 and 3128)

PART I
PRELIMINARY

4–2131 1, 2. *Commencement, citation and revocation.*

1. Made by the Minister of Transport under ss 130, 159 and 160(1) of the Road Traffic Act 1960, s 40(1) and (3) of the Road Traffic Act 1972 and ss 17(1) and 28(9) of the Transport Act 1980; see now the Public Passenger Vehicles Act 1981, ss 6, 10, 50, 52, 60. The Regulations have been annotated to accord with the 1981 Act.

Interpretation

4–2132 3. (1) In these Regulations, unless the context otherwise requires, the following expressions have the meanings hereby respectively assigned to them—

"the Act" means the Public Passenger Vehicles Act 1981;

"the 1995 Act" means the Disability Discrimination Act 1995;

"the 2000 Regulations" means the Public Service Vehicles Accessibility Regulations 2000;

"articulated bus" means a passenger vehicle so constructed that—

(*a*) it can be divided into two parts, both of which are vehicles and one of which is a motor vehicle, but cannot be so divided without the use of facilities normally available only at a workshop; and

(*b*) passengers carried by it when not so divided can at all times pass from either part to the other;

"certificate of conformity" means a certificate issued by the Minister in pursuance of section [11(3)] of the Act;

"certificate of initial fitness" has the same meaning as in section 6 of the Act;

"the Commissioners" means the traffic commissioners for any traffic area constituted for the purposes of the Act . . .;

"crew seat" means a seat fitted to a vehicle and intended for use by crew (other than the driver), including any arm rests and foot rest with which the vehicle is fitted in relation to the seat, and which complies with the requirements specified in Regulation 28A;

"deck" means a floor or platform upon which seats are provided for the accommodation of passengers;

"double-decked vehicle" means a vehicle having two decks one of which is wholly or partly above the other and each deck of which is provided with a gangway serving seats on that deck only;

"ECE Regulation 36" means Regulation No 36 (uniform provisions concerning the construction of public service vehicles) which entered into force on 1st March 1976, annexed to the Agreement concerning the adoption of uniform conditions of approval and reciprocal recognition of approval for motor vehicle equipment and parts concluded at Geneva on 20th March 1958 as amended, to which the United Kingdom is a party;

"emergency exit" means an exit which is provided for use only in case of emergency;

"entrance" means any aperture or space provided to enable passengers to board the vehicle;

"exit" means any aperture or space provided to enable passengers to leave the vehicle;

"gangway" means the space provided for obtaining access from any entrance to the passengers' seats or from any such seat to an exit other than an emergency exit but does not include a staircase or any space in front of a seat or row of seats which is required only for the use of passengers occupying that seat or that row of seats;

"half-decked vehicle" means any vehicle not being a single-decked vehicle or a double-decked vehicle;

"minibus" means a motor vehicle which is constructed or adapted to carry more than 8 but not more than 16 seated passengers in addition to the driver;

"permanent top" means any covering of a vehicle other than a hood made of canvas or other flexible material which is capable of being readily folded back so that no portion of such hood or any fixed structure of the roof remains vertically above any part of any seat of the vehicle, or, in the case of a double-decked vehicle, of any seat on the upper deck of the vehicle;

"priority seat" means a seat which is designated as such in accordance with paragraph 3 of Schedule 2 to the 2000 Regulations (priority seats);

"registered" in relation to a vehicle, means registered under the Roads Act 1920 or, as the case may be, the Vehicles (Excise) Act 1949, the Vehicles (Excise) Act 1962 or the Vehicles (Excise) Act 1971 and references to a vehicle being registered are references to the date on which it was first so registered;

"regulated public service vehicle" means a public service vehicle to which the 2000 Regulations apply;

"safety glass', "safety glazing" and "specified safety glass" have the same meanings as are respectively assigned to them in Regulation 32(13) of the Motor Vehicles (Construction and Use) Regulations 1986;

"single-decked vehicle" means a vehicle on which no part of a deck or gangway is placed vertically above another deck or gangway;

"type approval certificate" means a certificate issued by the Minister in pursuance of section 10 of the Act;

"vehicle" means a public service vehicle within section [1 of the Act]; and

"vehicle in the service of a visiting force or headquarters" has the same meaning as in Article 8(6) of the Visiting Forces and International Headquarters (Application of Law) Order 1965;

"wheelchair user" has the same meaning as in paragraph 1 of Schedule 1 to the 2000 Regulations.

(2) For the purposes of these Regulations, the date when a motor vehicle is first used shall be taken to be such date as is the earlier of the undermentioned relevant dates applicable to that vehicle, that is to say—

(a) in the case of a vehicle registered under the Roads Act 1920, the Vehicles (Excise) Act 1949, the Vehicles (Excise) Act 1962 or the Vehicles (Excise) Act 1971 the relevant date is the date on which it was first so registered; and

(b) in each of the following cases, that is to say—

(i) in the case of a vehicle which is being or has been used under a trade licence within the meaning of section 16(1) of the Vehicles (Excise) Act 1971 (otherwise than for the purposes of demonstration or testing or of being delivered from premises of the manufacturer by whom it was made, or of a distributor of vehicles or dealer in vehicles to premises of a distributor of vehicles, dealer in vehicles or purchaser thereof, or to premises of a person obtaining possession thereof under a hiring agreement or hire purchase agreement);

(ii) in the case of a vehicle belonging, or which has belonged, to the Crown which is or was used or appropriated for use for naval, military or air force purposes;

(iii) in the case of a vehicle belonging, or which has belonged, to a visiting force or a headquarters within the meaning of Article 3 of the Visiting Forces and International Headquarters (Application of Law) Order 1965;

(iv) in the case of a vehicle which has been used on roads outside Great Britain and which has been imported into Great Britain; and

(v) in the case of a vehicle which has been used otherwise than on roads after being sold or supplied by retail and before being registered,

the relevant date is the date of manufacture of the vehicle.

In case (v) above "sold or supplied by retail" means sold or supplied otherwise than to a person acquiring the vehicle solely for the purpose of resale or re-supply for valuable consideration.

(3) Unless the context otherwise requires, any reference in these Regulations—

(a) to a numbered Regulation or Schedule is a reference to the Regulation or Schedule bearing that number in these Regulations, and

(b) to a numbered paragraph is to the paragraph bearing that number in the Regulation in which the reference occurs.

(4) The provisions of the Regulations in Part IV of these Regulations are in addition to, and not in derogation of, the provisions of any other Regulations made or having effect as if made under section [41] of the Road Traffic Act 1988.

Exemptions

4–2133 **4.** (1) Part IV of these Regulations does not apply to any vehicle in the public service of the Crown or in the service of a visiting force or headquarters.

(2) Parts III and IV of these Regulations do not apply to a motor vehicle belonging to a local education authority and which is from time to time used by that authority to provide free school transport whether the vehicle is being used wholly or partly to provide such transport or to provide a local bus service.

(2A) Notwithstanding regulation 5, regulations 6 to 33, 35 to 44 and 45A shall not apply to a minibus which either complies with, or is required to comply with, or is exempted from the requirements specified in regulations 41 to 43 of the Road Vehicles (Construction and Use) Regulations 1986 for a minibus first used within the meaning of those Regulations on or after 1st April 1988.

(3) Regulation 43 does not apply to a motor vehicle not belonging to a local education authority at any time when that vehicle is being used by that authority to provide free school transport, and

to carry as the only fare-paying passengers pupils other than those for whom free school transport is provided.

(4) In this Regulation—

(a) "free school transport" has the meaning given by section 46(3) of the Public Passenger Vehicles Act 1981 as regards England and Wales and by section 46(4) of that Act as regards Scotland;

(b) "pupil" has the meaning given by section 114(1) of the Education Act 1944 as regards England and Wales and by section 135(1) of the Education (Scotland) Act 1980 as regards Scotland; and

(c) references to a local education authority relate, as regards Scotland, to an education authority.

PART II

REGULATIONS RELATING TO THE CONDITIONS AS TO FITNESS OF PUBLIC SERVICE VEHICLES

Conditions of fitness

4–2133A   4A. Alternative prescribed conditions. The prescribed conditions as to the fitness of a vehicle contained in Part II may alternatively be met by a vehicle satisfying the requirements in such of the Annexes to Directive 2001/85/EC of the European Parliament and of the Council of 20 November 2001, relating to special provisions for vehicles used for the carriage of passengers comprising more than eight seats in addition to the drivers seat, and amending Directives 70/156/EEC and 97/27/EC, as apply to it.

4–2134   5. (1) Except as provided in paragraph (2), the prescribed conditions as to the fitness of a vehicle are for the purpose of the issue of a certificate of initial fitness in accordance with section 6 of the Act compliance with the provisions specified in the Regulations in this Part of these Regulations.

(2) Paragraph (1) shall not apply to—

(a) an articulated bus, or

(b) a vehicle to which there is applied a marking designated as an approval mark in relation to ECE Regulation 36 by Regulation 4 of, and Schedule 2 (at item 36) to, the Motor Vehicles (Designation of Approval Marks) Regulations 1979 as read with paragraphs 1 and 7 of Schedule 3 to those Regulations and which satisfies the requirements of paragraph 5 (Specifications) of ECE Regulation 36.

(3) The prescribed conditions as to the fitness of a vehicle mentioned in sub-paragraph (a) or (b) above are compliance with the provisions specified in—

(i) paragraph 5 of ECE Regulation 36, and

(ii) those of the Regulations contained in this Part of these Regulations, or the paragraphs thereof, which are specified in Schedule 3.

Stability

4–2135   6. (1) The stability of a vehicle shall be such that—

(a) in the case of a double-decked vehicle, the point at which overturning occurs would not be passed if, when the vehicle is complete, fully equipped for service and loaded with weights placed in the correct relative positions to represent the driver, a full complement of passengers on the upper deck only and a conductor (if carried), the surface on which the vehicle stands were tilted to either side to an angle of 28 degrees from the horizontal; and

(b) in the case of a single-decked vehicle and of a half-decked vehicle, the point at which overturning occurs would not be passed if, when the vehicle is complete, fully equipped for service and loaded with weights placed in the correct relative positions to represent a full complement of passengers (including any passengers who are wheelchair users), a driver, any crew for whom a crew seat is provided, and any conductor intended to be carried on the vehicle otherwise than in a crew seat, the surface on which the vehicle stands were tilted to either side to an angle of 35 degrees from the horizontal.

(2) For the purpose of ascertaining whether the requirements of paragraph (1) have been complied with, the height of any stop used to prevent a wheel of the vehicle from slipping sideways shall not be greater than two-thirds of the distance between the surface upon which the vehicle stands before it is tilted and that part of the rim of that wheel which is nearest to that surface when the vehicle is loaded in accordance with the said requirements.

(3) For the purpose of this regulation—

(a) 63.5 kilograms shall be deemed to represent the weight of one person other than a wheelchair user, and

(b) 180 kilograms shall be deemed to represent the weight of one wheelchair and wheelchair user.

Suspension

4–2136   7. (1) Subject to paragraph 1 of Schedule 2, every vehicle shall—

(a) be fitted with an efficient suspension system so designed and constructed that there is no excessive body sway, and (*b*) be so constructed or adapted that a failure of a spring, torsion bar or other resilient component of the suspension system is not likely to cause the driver to lose directional control of the vehicle.

(2) For the purpose of this Regulation a tyre shall not be regarded as forming part of the suspension system.

Guard rails

4–2137   **8.** If any two wheels on either side of a vehicle have a clear space of more than 610 millimetres between the nearest points that space shall be effectively guarded to within—

(i)   230 millimetres of the front wheel,
(ii)   155 millimetres of the rear wheel, and
(iii)   310 millimetres of the ground when the vehicle is carrying no passengers and is otherwise unladen and is standing on level ground.

Brakes

4–2138   **9.** Revoked.

Brake and steering connections

4–2139   **10.** Revoked.

Locking of nuts

4–2140   **11.** Revoked.

Steering

4–2141   **12.** Revoked.

Fuel tanks, carburettors, etc

4–2142   **13.** (1) Subject to paragraph 3 of Schedule 2—

(*a*) in the case of a single-decked vehicle which has a seating capacity exceeding 12 passengers, a half-decked vehicle or the lower deck of a double-decked vehicle, no fuel tank shall be placed under any part of any gangway or under any part of any passage leading to a primary emergency exit as defined in Regulation 21(1) if that part of the gangway or passage is within 600 millimetres of any entrance or exit not being an emergency exit other than a primary emergency exit;

(*b*) in the case of a single-decked vehicle which has a seating capacity not exceeding 12 passengers, no fuel tank shall be placed immediately under any entrance or exit or within 300 millimetres of any entrance or exit and no filling point for such a tank shall be situated at the rear of the vehicle;

(*c*) no part of any fuel tank or apparatus for the supply of fuel shall be placed in the compartments or other spaces provided for the accommodation of the driver or passengers; and

(*d*) a device shall be provided by means of which the supply of fuel to any carburettor or, in the case of a fuel injection pump, to the injection nozzles, can be readily cut off and the following requirements shall be complied with—

(i)   the means of operation shall at all times be readily accessible from outside the vehicle and, except in the case of a vehicle fitted with an engine having a fuel injection system, shall be readily visible from the outside of the vehicle; and

(ii)   in a case where the device is so visible, the "off" position of the means of operation thereof shall be clearly marked also on the outside of the vehicle, and in a case where the said device is not so visible, its position shall be clearly marked on the outside of the vehicle and the means of operation shall also be clearly indicated.

(2) All fuel tanks and all apparatus supplying fuel to the engine shall be so placed or shielded that no fuel overflowing or leaking therefrom can fall or accumulate upon any woodwork forming part of the vehicle or upon any other part of the vehicle or fitting thereto such that it might readily be ignited or that it can fall into any receptacle where it might accumulate.

(3) The filling points for all fuel tanks shall be accessible only from the outside of the vehicle and filler caps shall be so designed and constructed that they cannot be dislodged by accidental operation and any vent hole shall be protected from danger of penetration by fire and shall be so designed as to prevent fuel from being ejected by splashing.

Exhaust pipe

4–2143   **14.** Subject to paragraph 3A of Schedule 2, the exhaust pipe shall be so fitted or shielded that no inflammable material can fall or be thrown upon the pipe from any other part of the vehicle and so that it is not likely to cause a fire through proximity to any inflammable material on the vehicle, and the outlet of the pipe shall be either at the rear or on the offside and far enough to the rear, to prevent so far as practicable fumes from entering the vehicle.

Luggage racks

4-2144   15. All baggage racks fitted in a vehicle shall be so designed and constructed that any article placed thereon, if it becomes dislodged whilst the vehicle is in motion, is not likely to fall on the driver or interfere with his control of the vehicle.

Artificial lighting

4-2145   16. Subject to paragraph 4 of Schedule 2, adequate internal lighting shall be provided in every vehicle for the illumination—

(a)   of each deck having a permanent top; and

(b)   of any step or platform forming part of any entrance or exit other than an emergency exit;

and all lighting circuits shall be so arranged that an electrical failure of any lighting sub-circuit shall not be capable of extinguishing all the lights on any deck and at least one lamp shall be provided as near as practicable to the top of every staircase leading to an upper deck not having a permanent top.

Electrical equipment

4-2146   17. (1) All electrical apparatus and circuits in a vehicle shall be so constructed and installed as to guard adequately against the risk of electric shock or the outbreak of fire.

(2) Subject to paragraph 5 of Schedule 2, where the voltage exceeds 100 volts in one or more electrical circuits in a vehicle, a manually operated isolating switch which is capable of disconnecting all such circuits from the main electrical supply shall be connected in each pole of that supply which is not electrically connected to earth, and shall be located inside the vehicle in a position readily accessible to the driver or conductor:

Provided that no such isolating switch shall be capable of disconnecting any electrical circuit supplying the lamps carried for the purposes of section 68 of the Road Traffic Act 1972 (which provides for lights to be carried by vehicles during the hours of darkness).

(3) In this Regulation any reference to an electrical circuit is a reference to an electrical circuit not being a high tension ignition circuit or a circuit within a unit of equipment.

Body

4-2147   18. The body of a vehicle shall be securely fixed to the chassis, every trap door in the floor of a vehicle shall be so fitted or fastened that it cannot become dislodged by vibration, and no lifting device fitted to a trap door shall project above the level of the floor.

Height of sides of body

4-2148   19. (1) Subject to paragraph 6 of Schedule 2, the top of the side rails or panels of a vehicle not having a permanent top shall be at least 910 millimetres above the deck and at least 455 millimetres above the highest part of any passenger seat, and the top of the front and back rails or panels shall be at least 1·21 metres above any part of the deck.

(2) For the purposes of this Regulation a back rest shall not be deemed to be part of a seat, and the expression "deck", in relation to a vehicle with more than one deck, means the upper deck.

Steps, platforms and stairs

4-2149   20. (1) Subject to paragraph 7 of Schedule 2—

(a)   a platform from which passengers can step directly to the ground through an exit without any step intervening, or the top of the tread of the lowest step provided at any entrance or exit, other than an emergency exit, shall not be more than 435 millimetres above the ground when the vehicle is empty; all steps and the outer edge of any platform shall be fitted with non-slip treads; and fixed steps shall be not less than 225 millimetres wide and shall in no case project laterally beyond the body of the vehicle unless they are so protected by the front wings of the vehicle or otherwise are such that they are not liable to injure pedestrians; and

(b)   in the case of a double-decked vehicle—

(i)   the risers of all steps leading from the lower to the upper deck shall be closed and no unguarded aperture shall be left at the top landing board;

(ii)   all steps leading from the lower to the upper deck shall be fitted with non-slip treads;

(iii) the horizontal distance from the nearest point of the riser of the top step to the vertical line passing through the nearest point of the seat opposite to the top tread of the staircase, excluding any grab rail which does not project more than 105 millimetres from the back of the seat, shall be not less than 660 millimetres; and

(iv) the outer stringer of an outside staircase shall be constructed, or a band shall be placed, to act as a sufficient screen to persons ascending or descending, and the height of the outer guard rail shall not be less than 1·21 metres above the front of the tread of each step.

(2) Paragraph (1)(a) shall not apply to an entrance provided with a lifting platform or a ramp for the benefit of disabled passengers if—

(a)   another entrance is provided in the vehicle and in relation to such other entrance the requirements specified in paragraph (1)(a) are met, and

(b)   that other entrance is placed—

(i)   in the case of any vehicle, on the near side, or

(ii) in the case of such a vehicle as is mentioned in the proviso to Regulation 21(4), on the rear face of the vehicle.

(3) Paragraph (1)(*a*) shall not apply to an exit provided with a lifting platform or a ramp for the benefit of disabled passengers if—

(*a*) another exit is provided in the vehicle and in relation to such other exit the requirements specified in paragraph (1)(*a*) are met, and

(*b*) that other exit is placed—

(i)   in the case of any vehicle, on the near side, or

(ii) in the case of such a vehicle as is mentioned in the proviso to Regulation 21(4), on the rear face of the vehicle.

(4) Paragraph (1)(*a*) shall not apply to any steps on a regulated public service vehicle which are steps at an entrance or an exit of the vehicle for which requirements are imposed by paragraph 4 of Schedule 2 or paragraph 4 of Schedule 3 to the 2000 Regulations and which meet those requirements.

Number, position and size of entrances and exits

4–2150 21. (1) For the purposes of this Regulation and Regulations 13, 22, 23, 24, 25 and 26—

(*a*) "primary emergency exit" means an emergency exit being an exit provided in a single-decked vehicle or in the lower deck of a double-decked vehicle which, subject to paragraph 8 of Schedule 2—

(i)   is situated so that passengers can step directly from the passage referred to in Regulation 26(1)(*g*) to the outside of the vehicle,

(ii) has a clear height—

(A) in the case of a vehicle which has a seating capacity not exceeding 14 passengers, of not less than 1·21 metres, and

(B) in the case of any other vehicle, of not less than 1·37 metres,

(iii) has a width of not less than 530 millimetres;

(*b*) "secondary emergency exit" means an emergency exit of which the dimensions are not less than 910 millimetres by 530 millimetres and which does not satisfy all the requirements of a primary emergency exit and which is not in the roof of a vehicle;

(*c*) neither of the foregoing definitions shall apply in relation to an emergency exit as required by paragraphs (7) and (8) but the exit so required shall be of dimensions not less than 1·52 metres by 455 millimetres;

(*d*) references to the seating capacity of a vehicle shall, in the case of a double-decked vehicle, be treated as references to the seating capacity of its lower deck;

(*e*) references to the distance between the centres or between the nearest points of the openings of two exits in a vehicle are references to the distance between lines drawn at right-angles to the longitudinal axis of the vehicle and passing respectively through the centres or, as the case may be, the nearest points of the openings of the exits at gangway level; and

(*f*) the reference to the distance between the centre of an exit placed at the front end of a vehicle and the foremost part of the vehicle is a reference to the distance between lines drawn at right-angles to the longitudinal axis of the vehicle and passing through the centre of that exit and the said foremost part and the reference to the distance between the centre of an exit placed at the rear end of a vehicle and the rearmost part of the vehicle is a reference to the distance between lines drawn as aforesaid and passing through the centre of that exit and the said rearmost part.

(2) In this Regulation—

(*a*) "pre-October 1981 vehicle" means a vehicle manufactured before 1st October 1981 or first used before 1st April 1982; and

(*b*) "post-October 1981 vehicle" means a vehicle manufactured on or after 1st October 1981 and first used on or after 1st April 1982.

(3) Subject to paragraph 8 of Schedule 2, the following provisions of this Regulation shall apply with respect to the number and position of entrances and exits which shall be provided in a vehicle but a vehicle shall not be treated as failing to comply with any of those provisions by reason only that a number of exits is provided in a vehicle in excess of the number specified in relation to it by any provision of this Regulation.

(4) Subject to paragraphs (5) and (11), a vehicle which has a seating capacity for not more than 45 passengers shall be provided with two exits so placed as not to be on the same side of the vehicle, and

(*a*) in the case of a pre-October 1981 vehicle, one of which may be a primary emergency exit but neither of which shall be a secondary emergency exit;

(*b*) in the case of a post-October 1981 vehicle, one of which shall be a primary emergency exit and the other of which shall have dimensions which are not less than those specified in paragraph (1)(*a*) above in relation to a primary emergency exit:

Provided that this paragraph shall not apply in the case of a vehicle which has a seating capacity—

    (i) exceeding 23 passengers and which is provided with an exit by virtue of its having a platform of a type described in Regulation 20(1)(*a*) which communicates with a deck (being in the case of a double-decked vehicle, the lower deck) by means of a doorless opening and has a doorless opening on the nearside of the vehicle continuous with another such opening at the rear of the vehicle, these openings serving together as a means of entrance to or exit from the vehicle, and

    (ii) not exceeding 12 passengers and of which the fuel tank is not placed behind the rear wheels if one exit of which, in the case of a post-October 1981 vehicle, the dimensions are not less than 1·21 metres in height by 530 millimetres in width is provided and is placed at the rear of the vehicle.

(5) Where the exits provided in accordance with paragraph (4) are so placed that the distance between their centres is—

    (*a*) in the case of a vehicle first used before 1st January 1974 which has a seating capacity exceeding 30 passengers, less than 3·05 metres;

    (*b*) in the case of a vehicle first used on or after 1st January 1974 which has a seating capacity exceeding 23 passengers, less than 3·05 metres;

    (*c*) in the case of a vehicle first used on or after 1st January 1974 which has a seating capacity exceeding 14 but not exceeding 23 passengers, less than 2·44 metres,

a primary or secondary emergency exit shall be provided and placed so that there is a distance between the nearest points of the openings of that exit and one of the two exits mentioned in paragraph (4) of—

    (i) in the cases mentioned in sub-paragraphs (*a*) and (*b*) above, not less than 3·05 metres, and

    (ii) in the case mentioned in sub-paragraph (*c*) above, not less than 2·44 metres.

(6) Subject to paragraph (11), a vehicle which has a seating capacity exceeding 45 passengers shall be provided with three exits in respect of which the following provisions shall apply:—

    (*a*) in the case of a pre-October 1981 vehicle one of the exits, but not more than one, may be a secondary emergency exit, and in the case of a post-October 1981 vehicle one of the exits shall be a primary emergency exit and any other exit (not being a secondary emergency exit) shall have dimensions not less than those specified in paragraph (1)(*a*) above in relation to primary emergency exits;

    (*b*) two of the exits (neither being a secondary emergency exit) shall be so placed as not to be on the same side of the vehicle;

    (*c*) where two exits are placed on the same side of the vehicle, the distance between their centres shall not be less than 3·05 metres; and

    (*d*) one of the exits (not being a secondary emergency exit) shall be placed at the front end of the vehicle so that the distance between its centre and the foremost part of the vehicle is not more than 3·05 metres and another of the exits (not being a secondary emergency exit) shall be placed at the rear end of the vehicle so that the distance between its centre and the rearmost part of the vehicle is not more than 3·05 metres:

Provided that—

    (i) in the case of a vehicle registered on or after 28th October 1964 and before 19th June 1968 the reference in sub-paragraph (*c*) above to 3·05 metres shall be replaced by a reference to 4·75 metres and sub-paragraph (*d*) shall not apply, and

    (ii) in the case of any other vehicle first used before 1st January 1974 sub-paragraph (*d*) above shall apply with the omission of the words "(not being a secondary emergency exit)" in both places where they occur.

(7) In the case of a half-decked vehicle an emergency exit shall be provided in the roof of the vehicle so placed that the transverse centre line of that exit lies within 610 millimetres of the mid-point between the front edges of the foremost and of the rearmost passenger seats in the vehicle.

(8) Where, in the case of a double-decked vehicle which has a permanent top, access to the upper-deck is obtained by means of an enclosed staircase, an emergency exit shall be provided on that deck and placed otherwise than on the nearside of the vehicle.

(9) Every entrance provided in a vehicle shall be placed on the nearside of the vehicle, but one or more entrances may be provided on the offside of the vehicle if—

    (*a*) as respects any entrance so provided it is not also an exit provided in accordance with any of the foregoing provisions in this Regulation;

    (*b*) every such entrance is fitted with a door which can be controlled only by the driver while sitting in his seat; and

    (*c*) the device available to the driver for opening or closing that door is a separate and readily distinguishable device from that available to the driver for opening or closing any door fitted to the nearside of the vehicle:

and one or more entrances may be provided on the rear face of the vehicle if each of those entrances is provided with a lifting platform or ramp for the benefit of disabled passengers.

Provided that this paragraph shall not apply in the case of any such vehicle as is mentioned in the proviso to paragraph (4).

(10) A grab handle shall be fitted to every entrance and exit (other than an emergency exit) to assist passengers to board or alight from the vehicle.

(11) In the case of a vehicle—

    (*a*) being a post-October 1981 vehicle,

    (*b*) having a seating capacity for more than 16 passengers, and (*c*) being a single-decked vehicle or a half-decked vehicle,

there shall be at least one emergency exit which complies with the requirements specified in paragraph (12) and which is either—

(i)   in the front face of the vehicle, or
(ii) in the rear face of the vehicle, or
(iii) in the roof of the vehicle.

(12) The requirements referred to in paragraph (11) are, in respect of each exit therein referred to, as follows:—

(*a*) the dimensions of the aperture shall be such that it has a total area of not less than 4,000 square centimetres and shall include a rectangular area the dimensions of which are not less than 70 centimetres by 50 centimetres;

(*b*) the exit shall be so constructed that it can be opened by means available to persons inside the vehicle, and it may be so constructed that it can be opened also by persons outside the vehicle; and

(*c*) the exit shall be—

(i)   ejectable, or
(ii) constructed of specified safety glass which can be readily broken by the application of reasonable force so as to afford a clear aperture having the dimensions referred to in sub-paragraph (*a*) above, and provided in a position adjacent to the exit with a suitable means, readily available to persons inside the vehicle, for breaking the glass, or
(iii) except where the exit is an exit in the roof, hinged.

(13) The width requirements of paragraphs (4)(*b*) and (6)(*a*) shall not apply to those parts of an exit which have a clear unobstructed width of not less than 800 millimetres for wheelchair access.

Width of entrances and exits

4–2151 **22.** (1) The width of every entrance and exit (other than a secondary emergency exit, an emergency exit provided in accordance with Regulation 21(7), (8) and (11) or an exit referred to in paragraph (2), shall—

(*a*) (save as provided in paragraph (3)) in the case of an entrance or an exit which serves both decks of a double-decked vehicle (disregarding any stanchion), being an entrance or an exit which is either—

(i)   the only such entrance or exit in the vehicle, or
(ii) the entrance or exit most readily and directly associated with a staircase serving the upper deck,

be not less than 910 millimetres; and

(*b*) in any other case, be not less than 530 millimetres.

(2) The requirements specified in paragraph (1) shall not apply in the case of an exit referred to in paragraph (i) of the proviso to Regulation 21(4) if the width of that exit measured along the side of the vehicle is not less than 530 millimetres and its width measured along the rear of the vehicle is not less than 455 millimetres.

(3) A vehicle shall not be regarded as failing to fulfil condition (*a*) of paragraph (1) by reason only of the fact that, in a case where the entrance or exit is fitted with a pair of power operated doors, one door may be opened independently of the other, if the width of the aperture thereby provided is not less than 530 millimetres and if the doors are capable of being opened together by means of the devices required by Regulation 23(1)(*b*).

(4) The width requirements of paragraph (1)(*b*) and paragraph (2) shall not apply to those parts of an entrance or exit which have a clear unobstructed width of not less than 800 millimetres for wheelchair access.

Doors

4–2152 **23.** (1) Subject to paragraph 9 of Schedule 2 and paragraph (4) the following conditions shall be complied with in the case of every vehicle—

(*a*) means shall be provided for holding every entrance and exit door securely in the closed position and, where any such door is capable of remaining open when the vehicle is in motion or of being accidentally closed by the movement of the vehicle, means shall also be provided for holding that door securely in the open position;

(*b*) subject to paragraph (2) and paragrpah (5), every entrance and exit door shall be provided with at least two devices (of which one may be a device provided for use in circumstances of normal operation only by a person authorised by the owner of the vehicle, and one, but not more than one, shall be provided on the outside of the vehicle) being in each case a device for operating the means for holding the door securely in the closed position, and every such device shall be so designed that a single movement of it will allow that door to be readily opened;

(*c*) the method of operation of any device mentioned in condition (*b*) above, the position of such a device where it is not placed on the door and the direction and points of application of any manual effort required to open any door, shall be clearly indicated; and there shall, in the case of a power-operated door, also be an indication that the said device may not be used by passengers except in an emergency;

(d) where any device mentioned in condition (b) above is not placed on the door, it shall be placed so as to be readily associated with that door and so that a person of normal height may conveniently operate the device without risk of being injured by movement of the door;

(e) in the case of every entrance and exit, any device mentioned in condition (b) above, other than such a device provided on the outside of an emergency exit on the upper deck of a double-decked vehicle or in the roof of a vehicle, shall be easily accessible to persons of normal height;

(f) the means and devices mentioned in conditions (a) and (b) above shall be so designed and fitted that they are unlikely to become dislodged or be operated accidentally but (subject to paragraph (5)) there shall be in the vehicle no means of a mechanical nature the operation of which would prevent the devices mentioned in the said condition (b) (devices for allowing entrance and exit doors to be opened in an emergency) when deliberately used, from allowing the entrance or exit doors for which they are provided to be readily opened;

(g) every door shall operate so as not to obstruct clear access to any entrance or exit from inside or outside the vehicle;

(h) being a vehicle having power-operated door which, when open or being operated, projects laterally beyond the body of the vehicle at its widest point by more than 80 millimetres, shall be so constructed or adapted that it cannot move from rest under its own power when the door is open, and the door shall not be capable of being operated while the vehicle is in motion, except by the operation of such a device as is mentioned in condition (b) above;

(i) the storage and transmission system of the power for operating any power-operated door shall be such that operation of the doors does not adversely affect the efficient operation of the braking system of the vehicle and the apparatus shall be so designed and constructed that in the event of the system becoming inoperative the door shall be capable of being operated manually from inside and outside the vehicle; and

(j) the design of power-operated doors and their associated equipment at entrances and exits shall be such that, when opening or closing, the doors are unlikely to injure any passengers, and the vertical edges of any power-operated door which, when open or being operated, projects laterally beyond the body of the vehicle at its widest point by not more than 80 millimetres and which is installed in a vehicle not constructed or adapted as mentioned in condition (h) above, shall be fitted with soft rubber.

(1A) Schedule 3A shall have effect for the purpose of supplementing paragraph (1) in relation to power-operated doors fitted to certain vehicles.

(2) A vehicle shall not be deemed to fail to comply with condition (b) or (f) of paragraph (1) by reason only of the fact that, for the purposes of securing the vehicle when unattended, any entrance or exit door has been fitted with a supplementary lock with or without an actuating mechanism if the lock is so designed and constructed that a single movement of any device mentioned in condition (b) above, being a device provided on the inside of the vehicle, will at all times allow that door to be readily opened.

(3) In determining for the purposes of conditions (h) and (j) of paragraph (1) whether, or the distance by which, a power-operated door, when open or being operated, projects laterally beyond the body of the vehicle at its widest point any moulding on the outside of the vehicle shall be disregarded.

(4) The references to exits in paragraph (1) do not include an emergency exit provided in accordance with the provisions of Regulation 21(11) unless such exit is a primary emergency exit or a secondary emergency exit.

(5) In relation to securing the closed position of an entrance or exit door of a vehicle whilst that vehicle is in motion, any such door may be fitted with a device so designed that the motion of the vehicle will operate to prevent that door from being readily opened.

Marking, positioning and operation of emergency exits

4–2153   **24.** (1) Subject to the provisions of paragraph 10 of Schedule 2, every emergency exit, other than an emergency exit with which a vehicle is required to be fitted under Regulation 21(11) shall comply with the following conditions—

(a) the emergency exit shall—

(i) be clearly marked as such inside and outside the vehicle;

(ii) be fitted with doors which open outwards or, in the case of a secondary emergency exit, be constructed of specified safety glass which can be readily broken by the application of reasonable force so as to afford a clear aperture of dimensions not less than those referred to in Regulation 21(1)(b);

(iii) except in the case of an emergency exit provided in the roof of a vehicle, be readily accessible to passengers;

(iv) in the case of a single-decked or half-decked vehicle or the lower deck of a double-decked vehicle, be so situated that passengers can step directly from the passage referred to in Regulation 26(1)(g) to the outside of the vehicle:

Provided that this requirement shall not apply in the case of an emergency exit provided in the roof of the vehicle or in the case of a secondary emergency exit;

(b) the means of operation of doors fitted to the emergency exit shall be clearly indicated;

(c) the doors of the emergency exit shall not be fitted with any system of power operation and (*d*) the means of operation of the doors of the emergency exit, other than those provided in the upper deck of a double-decked vehicle or in the roof of a vehicle, shall be readily accessible to persons of normal height standing at ground level outside the vehicle.

(2) Every emergency exit with which a vehicle is required to be fitted under Regulation 21(11) shall—

(*a*) be clearly marked as an emergency exit—

(i) on the inside of the vehicle, and
(ii) in a case where the emergency exit can be opened from the outside, on the outside of the vehicle;

(*b*) be accessible to persons inside the vehicle when the vehicle is tilted to either side through an angle of 90 degrees, measured from the normal vertical plane of the vehicle;
(*c*) be clearly marked with its means of operation;
(*d*) if hinged, open outwards; and
(*e*) if ejectable, be fitted with a restraint which will prevent the part of the emergency exit which is ejected from becoming completely detached from the vehicle but which will not prevent egress from the vehicle by persons within it.

Access to exits

4–2154 **25.** (1) Subject to paragraphs (2) and (3) the following conditions shall be complied with in the case of every vehicle—

(*a*) there shall be unobstructed access from every seat in the vehicle—

(i) in a case where the vehicle is, in accordance with the provisions of these Regulations, provided with only one exit, to that exit, and
(ii) in a case where the vehicle is, in accordance with those provisions, provided with two or more exits, to both or, as the case may be to at least two, of those exits;

(*b*) no seat in a vehicle shall be fitted to any door of the vehicle; and
(*c*) being a half-decked vehicle, there shall be no obstruction in the space between the floor in front of any passenger seat and the roof of the vehicle.

(2) Condition (*a*) of paragraph (1) shall not apply in relation to—

(*a*) any seat in a vehicle which is placed—

(i) beside the driver's seat if there is unobstructed access to that seat by means of an entrance other than the driver's entrance, or
(ii) on a deck which does not have a permanent top if there is unobstructed access from every seat on that deck to an exit; or

(*aa*) a crew seat occupied by crew; or
(*b*) an exit provided in accordance with the provisions of Regulation 21(11) unless such exit be a primary emergency exit or a secondary emergency exit.

(3) In the case of a double-decked vehicle as respects which provision is made for the placing of a barrier at the foot of the staircase leading to the upper deck, the vehicle shall not be treated as failing to comply with the requirements of the condition (*a*) of paragraph (1) by reason only that when that barrier is in position it would effectively prevent passengers from gaining access to the upper deck.

Width of gangways

4–2155 **26.** (1) Subject to paragraphs (2), (3) and (5) and to paragraph 11 of Schedule 2, the following conditions shall be complied with in the case of every vehicle:—

(*a*) the width of every gangway shall be not less than—

(i) 305 millimetres up to a height of 765 millimetres above the level of the deck of the vehicle,
(ii) 355 millimetres at heights exceeding 765 millimetres but not exceeding 1·22 metres above the level of the deck of the vehicle, and
(iii) 455 millimetres at heights exceeding 1·22 metres above the level of the deck of the vehicle;

(*b*) a vertical line projected upwards from the centre line of any gangway at deck level shall, to the height prescribed in Regulation 27 as the height of that gangway, be laterally not less than 150 millimetres from any part of the vehicle other than the roof above the gangway;
(*c*) being a vehicle which has a seating capacity exceeding 12 passengers, no part of any gangway which is within 910 millimetres of an entrance or exit (other than an emergency exit) to which it provides access shall be less than 530 millimetres in width;

(*d*) (*repealed*)

(*e*) where a part of a gangway which adjoins an entrance or exit is divided by a handrail, the width of that part of the gangway at any point on each side of the handrail shall not be less than 455 millimetres;
(*f*) where two seats (being either two seats each for one passenger only or two portions of a continuous seat, each of such portions being for one passenger only measured in accordance with condition (*b*) of Regulation 28(1)) are placed parallel to the longitudinal axis of a vehicle and face each other and the space between those seats is not required for

the purpose of obtaining access from an entrance to any other seat or from any other seat to an exit (not being an emergency exit), that space shall not for the purposes of this Regulation and Regulation 27 be treated as forming part of the gangway;

(g) between every exit, not being either—

   (i) an emergency exit provided in the roof of a vehicle, or

   (ii) an exit provided in accordance with the provisions of Regulation 21(11) unless it be a primary or secondary emergency exit,

and a gangway there shall be a passage—

   A   of dimensions not less than those prescribed for a gangway in condition (a) of paragraph (1);

   B   so designed that a vertical line projected upwards from the centre line of the passage at floor level to a height of 760 millimetres from the level of the deck is laterally not less than 150 millimetres from any part of the vehicle (excluding any cowling or cover which projects not more than 230 millimetres from the bulkhead of the vehicle into the passage at floor level and not more than 230 millimetres above the deck level and the provision of which is required by the projection of part of the chassis or mechanism of the vehicle into the body);

   C   which has a clear height at every point along the centre line of the passage of 1·52 metres from the deck level:

Provided that—

   (i) for the purposes of sub-paragraphs A and B of this paragraph a seat placed below or in front of an emergency exit, being such an exit provided on the upper deck of a double-decked vehicle or in the roof of a vehicle or which is a secondary emergency exit within the meaning of Regulation 21 shall be deemed to form part of such a passage, and

   (ii) sub-paragraph C of this paragraph shall not apply in the case of a passage leading to an emergency exit, being such an exit provided on the upper deck of a double-decked vehicle or in the roof of a vehicle or which is a secondary emergency exit within the meaning of Regulation 21, nor shall it apply in the case of a passage in a single-decked vehicle having a permanent top if the vehicle has a seating capacity not exceeding 14 passengers.

(2) Subject to paragraph 11 of Schedule 2, where any space in front of a seat in a vehicle adapted to carry more than 12 passengers is required for the accommodation of seated passengers, the space within 225 millimetres of the seat shall not be taken into account in measuring the width of a gangway:

(3) The provisions of paragraph (1)(c) and (g) do not apply as regards a crew seat occupied by crew.

(4) The provisions of paragraph (1)(a) shall not apply to a gangway of a vehicle if the width of that gangway is not less than—

   (i) 450 millimetres up to a height of 1400 millimetres measured vertically from the floor of the vehicle, and

   (ii) 550 millimetres at heights exceeding 1400 millimetres measured vertically from the floor of the vehicle.

Height of gangways

4–2156   **27.** (1) Subject to paragraph 12 of Schedule 2, the following conditions shall be complied with in the case of every vehicle adapted to carry more than 12 passengers—

   (a) the clear height at every point along the centre line of any gangway between the limits specified in paragraph (2) shall be—

     (i) in the case of a single-decked vehicle being a vehicle having a permanent top, and in the case of a half-decked vehicle and the lower deck of a double-decked vehicle, not less than 1·77 metres if the seating capacity of the vehicle exceeds 14 passengers and not less than 1·6 metres in any other case, and

     (ii) in the case of the top deck of a double-decked vehicle having a permanent top, not less than 1·72 metres;

   (b) except as respects any part of any gangway placed on the offside of the vehicle which is required only to provide access to the foremost passenger seat in the vehicle, the said clear height shall, outside the limits specified in paragraph (2), be not less than the clear height as prescribed in relation to the vehicle in condition (a) above reduced by 105 millimetres;

   (c) in the case of a single-decked vehicle not having a permanent top, when the hood of the vehicle is extended or raised, the said clear height from the level of the deck shall in no place (except over the driver's seat) be less than 1·52 metres;

   (d) in the case of the top deck of a double-decked vehicle, no part of any gangway shall project into the compartment or other space provided for the accommodation of the driver in such a manner as to incommode the driver or cause his view of the road to the front of the vehicle or to the sides thereof to be restricted.

(2) The clear height prescribed in condition (a) of paragraph (1) shall, in the case of the lower deck of a double-decked vehicle, extend throughout the gangway and in any other case shall

extend from the front edge of the foremost passenger seat adjacent to the gangway to the front edge of the rearmost passenger seat adjacent to the gangway:

Provided that where the gangway is on the offside of the vehicle it shall be a sufficient compliance with the requirements of sub-paragraph (ii) of the said condition (a) if the clear height of 1·72 metres extends from a point 460 millimetres behind the front edge of the foremost passenger seat adjacent to that gangway to the front edge of the rearmost passenger seat adjacent thereto.

(3) In the case of a vehicle which has a seating capacity not exceeding 12 passengers, the clear height at every point along the centre line of any gangway in the vehicle, except for a distance of 305 millimetres along the line measured from each entrance and exit, shall be not less than 1·42 metres and, in the case of the said distance, shall be not less than 1·21 metres.

Seats

4–2157 **28.** (1) Subject to paragraph (5) of this regulation and to paragraph 13 of Schedule 2, the following conditions shall, as regards every passenger seat, be complied with in the case of every vehicle—

(a) the supports of all seats shall be securely fixed in position;

(b) a length of at least 400 millimetres measured horizontally along the front of each seat shall be allowed for the accommodation of a seated passenger:

Provided that in the case of a continuous seat fitted with arms for the purpose of separating the seating spaces, being arms so constructed that they can be folded back or otherwise put out of use, the seat shall be measured for the purposes of this paragraph as though it were not fitted with arms;

(c) every seat shall have a back rest so closed or otherwise constructed as to prevent, as far as practicable, the pockets of passengers from being picked;

(d) all passenger seats shall be so fitted—

(i) that the distance between any part of the back rest of any seat placed lengthwise and the corresponding part of the back rest of the seat facing it shall be, in the case of a vehicle which has a seating capacity not exceeding 12 passengers, not less than 1·37 metres, and in any other case, not less than 1·60 metres, and

(ii) that there is a clear space of at least 610 millimetres in front of the back rest of any seat measured from the centre of each complete length of the seat allowed for the accommodation of a seated passenger in accordance with condition (b) above and a clear space of 200 millimetres in front of any part of that seat:

Provided that in the case of a seat for more than three passengers—

(a) in the case of a vehicle being used as a stage carriage, and

(b) in the case of any vehicle to which this regulation applies and which is first used on or after 1st April 1982

where access to that seat can be obtained only from one end of the seat, the said clear spaces shall respectively be at least 685 millimetres and 300 millimetres;

(e) there shall be a clear space of at least 480 millimetres between any part of the front edge of any transverse seat and any part of any other seat which faces it:

Provided that any support provided for a table shall be disregarded if there is a clear space of at least 225 millimetres between that support and the front edge of the nearest seat and the support is not in such a position as to cause discomfort to passengers occupying the seats;

(f) (repealed);

(g) there shall, as respects every seat, be a clear space measured vertically from the centre of each complete length of the seat allowed for the accommodation of a seated passenger in accordance with condition (b) above which shall be, in the case of a vehicle which has a seating capacity not exceeding 12 passengers, not less than 910 millimetres, and, in any other case, not less than 965 millimetres;

(h) where any seat is so placed that a passenger seated upon it is liable to be thrown through any entrance to or exit from the vehicle or down a stairway in the vehicle, an effective screen or guard shall be placed so as to afford adequate protection against that occurrence to a passenger occupying that seat; and

(i) the shortest distances between the edge of the well of any step in the vehicle and a vertical plane passing through the front edge of any seat shall be not less than 225 millimetres:

Provided that this condition shall not apply in the case of the well of a step provided as a means of obtaining access only to any forward-facing front passenger seat placed alongside the driver in a vehicle which has a seating capacity not exceeding 1.

(2) In this Regulations and in paragraph 13 of Schedule 2 the expression "back rest" includes any part of the vehicle which is available for seated passengers to lean against.

(3) Paragraph (1)(b) above shall not apply to a wheelchair carried in a vehicle.

(4) Where a table is fitted to the rear of a seat and is so constructed that it can be folded back or otherwise put out of use, distances shall be measured for the purposes of paragraph (1)(d) with the table so folded or put out of use.

(5) In the case of a regulated public service vehicle, the provisions of this regulation shall apply with the following modifications—

(a) where, in accordance with paragraph 3(1) of Schedule 2 to the 2000 Regulations, such a vehicle is fitted with priority seats that comply with the requirements set out in paragraph 3(2) of that Schedule, paragraph (1)(d)(ii) and paragraph (1)(g) shall not apply to such seats; and (*b*) where seats fitted to such a vehicle comply with the requirements set out in paragraph 3(1) of Schedule 3 to the 2000 Regulations, paragraph (1)(*d*)(ii) shall not apply to such seats:

Provided that in the case of a seat for more than three passengers, or one or more priority seats in a seat for more than three passengers, and where access to that seat can be obtained only from one end of the seat, there shall be a clear space of—

(i) at least 685 millimetres in front of the back rest of any of those seats (measured from the centre of each complete length of the seat allowed for the accommodation of a seated passenger in accordance with paragraph (1) (*b*)), and

(ii) 300 millimetres in front of any part of those seats.

Crew seats

4–2158   **28A.** (1) Every crew seat shall be so constructed and located that when it is in use—

(*a*) the person by whom it is occupied—

(i) is adequately protected by means of arm rests from falling sideways either to the left or to the right,

(ii) may conveniently place his feet either on a deck of the vehicle or on a foot rest, and

(iii) does not impede the driving of the vehicle either by obstructing the driver's field of vision or otherwise; and

(*b*) a space of at least 300 millimetres exists, along the whole width of the seat, between the foremost edge of the seat and any other part of the vehicle.

(2) Every crew seat shall be so constructed and located that when it is not in use—

(*a*) no part of it impedes the driving of the vehicle either by obstructing the driver's field of vision or otherwise; and

(*b*) every part of it which, when the seat is ready for or in use, protrudes into a gangway so that the provisions of Regulation 26(1)(*c*) and (*g*) are not complied with, is, as a result of automatic mechanism, retracted so that those provisions are complied with.

(3) The words "FOR CREW USE ONLY" shall be marked either on or near and in relation to every crew seat in letters not less than 10 millimetres tall and in a colour which contrasts with their background.

(4) The provisions of paragraph (1)(*a*) to (*e*) of Regulation 28 apply as respects a crew seat in the same manner as they apply as respects a seat to which that Regulation applies.

Passenger protection

4–2159   **29.** (1) Subject to paragraph 14 of Schedule 2, all transverse glass windows or panels not made of safety glass or specified safety glass shall be adequately protected against the likelihood of breakage in the event of passengers being thrown against them.

(2) No emergency exit or ventilating panel (not being a window) shall be fitted to the roof of any vehicle manufactured on or after 1st October 1981 unless such exit or panel is constructed of metal, specified safety glass or safety glazing.

Ventilation

4–2160   **30.** Adequate ventilation shall be provided for passengers and the driver without the necessity for opening any main window or windscreen.

Driver's accommodation

4–2161   **31.** Subject to paragraph 15 of Schedule 2, the following conditions shall be complied with in the case of every vehicle—

(*a*) the vehicle shall be so designed that the driver, when sitting in his seat, has adequate room and can readily reach and operate the controls;

(*b*) the controls shall be so placed as to allow reasonable access to the driver's seat;

(*c*) the accommodation for the driver shall be so arranged as to afford adequate protection from the weather;

(*d*) means shall be provided to prevent light from the interior of the vehicle from incommoding the driver and, in respect of any window placed on that side of the centre line of the vehicle occupied by the driver, the means so provided shall be capable of being operated by the driver when in his seat;

(*e*) except in the case of a vehicle which has a seating capacity not exceeding 12 passengers, the driver's seat shall be capable of being adjusted in a vertical direction and in a horizontal direction parallel to the longitudinal axis of the vehicle and of being firmly secured in any desired position within the limits of such adjustments: the range of such adjustments shall permit the seat to be fixed in a position such that the horizontal distance between the nearest part of the steering wheel and the backrest of the seat is 355 millimetres and the vertical distance between the lowest part of the steering wheel and the horizontal plane level with the top of the seat cushion is 200 millimetres and also as to permit the seat to be adjusted at least 50 millimetres forwards, backwards, upwards and downwards from that position;

(*f*) except in the case of a vehicle which has a seating capacity not exceeding 12 passengers, where direct and reasonable access is provided to the driver's seat, such access shall be provided to that seat either from the offside of the vehicle or by means of a passage which shall be not less than 300 millimetres in width up to a height of 765 millimetres above the floor of the vehicle and not less than 355 millimetres above that height and shall comply with the requirement prescribed in relation to the gangway of the vehicle by condition (*b*) of Regulation 26(1);

(*g*) where access to the driver's seat is obtained from the offside of the vehicle—

(i) an opening in the side of the vehicle shall be provided which shall have a clear width of not less than 455 millimetres except where this dimension cannot be provided by reason only of the presence of a portion of the wheel arch in that opening,

(ii) except in the case of a vehicle which has a seating capacity not exceeding 12 passengers where direct and reasonable access is provided to the driver's seat, a grab handle shall be fitted to assist the driver in boarding and alighting from the vehicle, and

(iii) a step shall be provided on the vehicle at a convenient position and height adjacent to the opening if the lowest point of the sill of that opening is more than 690 millimetres from ground level when the vehicle is unladen;

(*h*) where a separate and enclosed compartment is provided for the driver and access to the driver's seat is obtained from the offside of the vehicle, an emergency escape window shall be provided (otherwise than on the offside of that compartment) which shall be readily accessible to the driver and shall have a clear opening with the dimensions of not less than 530 millimetres by 455 millimetres;

(*i*) where any seat for passengers is placed to the side of the driver's seat (whether to one side or to both sides of that seat and whether or not that seat is continuous with the driver's seat) then—

(i) whether the seat is a separate seat or is continuous with the driver's seat, a space of at least 455 millimetres measured from the centre of the steering column on the side on which the seat is placed shall be reserved for use solely by the driver, and

(ii) if the seat is continuous with the driver's seat or if it is a separate seat so placed that any part of it is nearer to the centre of the steering column then 455 millimetres the said space shall be divided off by means of a solid partition having a height of at least 225 millimetres measured from the seat level of the driver's seat and extending for the whole depth of the seat.

Windscreens

4–2162   32. Where a vehicle is fitted with a front windscreen for the driver the windscreen shall, except where an adequate demisting and defrosting device is fitted, be capable of being opened so as to give the driver a clear view of the road ahead.

Passengers' communication with driver

4–2163   33. Except in the case of a vehicle which has a seating capacity not exceeding 12 passengers, adequate means shall be provided in every vehicle to enable passengers on any deck to signal to the driver.

General construction

4–2164   34. (1) The requirements as to the construction, weight and equipment of motor vehicles contained in any regulations for the time being in force under section [41] of the Road Traffic Act [1988] shall be complied with in the case of every vehicle; and all bodywork, upholstery and fittings, shall be soundly and properly constructed of suitable materials, well finished and in good and serviceable condition, and of such design as to be capable of withstanding the loads and stresses likely to be met with in normal operation of the vehicle.

(2) No vehicle shall be constructed or adapted as to be incapable of being fitted with a lighting system which complies in all respects with the requirements of the Road Traffic Act 1972 and any regulations for the time being in force under that Act.

PART III
REGULATIONS RELATING TO THE EQUIPMENT OF PUBLIC SERVICE VEHICLES
Fire extinguishing apparatus

4–2165   35. (1) There shall be carried by every vehicle suitable and efficient apparatus for extinguishing fire which is of one or more of the types specified in Schedule 4.

(2) The apparatus referred to in paragraph (1) shall be—

(a) readily available for use,

(b) clearly marked with the appropriate British Standards Institution specification number, and

(c) maintained in good and efficient working order.

(3) Paragraph (1) shall not apply to a vehicle if it carries apparatus for extinguishing fire which would meet the requirements of that paragraph were there substituted—

(a) for a reference in Schedule 4 to any British Standard, a reference to a corresponding standard;

(b) for the reference in Schedule 4 to a test fire rating of 8A or the reference in that Schedule to a test fire rating of 21B, a reference to an equivalent level of performance specified in the corresponding standard; and

(c) for the reference in paragraph (2)(*b*) to the appropriate British Standards Institution specification number, a reference to a marking indicating compliance with the corresponding standard.

(4) For the purposes of this regulation, "corresponding standard", in relation to a British Standard, means—

(*a*) a standard or code of practice of a national standards body or equivalent body of any EEA State;

(*b*) any international standard recognised for use as a standard by any EEA State; or

(*c*) a technical specification or code of practice which, whether mandatory or not, is recognised for use as a standard by a public authority of any EEA State,

where the standard, code of practice, international standard or technical specification provides, in relation to fire extinguishers, a level of safety equivalent to that provided by the British Standard and contains a requirement as respects the markings of fire extinguishers equivalent to that provided by the British Standard.

(5) For the purposes of this regulation—

"EEA State" means a state which is a contracting party to the EEA Agreement but, until the EEA Agreement comes into force as regards Liechtenstein, does not include the State of Liechtenstein; and

"EEA Agreement" means the Agreement on the European Economic Area signed at Oporto on 2 May 1992 as adjusted by the Protocol signed at Brussels on 17 March 1993.

First aid equipment

4–2166   36. (1) There shall be carried by every vehicle being used as an express carriage or as a contract carriage a receptacle which contains the items specified in Schedule 5.

(2) The receptacle referred to in paragraph (1) shall be—

(*a*) maintained in a good condition,

(*b*) suitable for the purpose of keeping the items referred to in the said paragraph in good condition,

(*c*) readily available for use, and

(*d*) prominently marked as a first aid receptacle.

(3) The items referred to in paragraph (1) shall be maintained in good condition and shall be of a good and reliable quality and of a suitable design.

PART IV
REGULATIONS RELATING TO THE USE OF PUBLIC SERVICE VEHICLES

Obstruction of entrances, exits and gangways

4–2167   37. No person shall, while passengers are being carried by a vehicle, cause or permit any unnecessary obstruction to any entrance or exit or gangway of the vehicle.

Obstruction of driver

4–2168   38. No person shall cause or permit any unnecessary obstruction of the driver of a vehicle.

Body maintenance

4–2169   39. No person shall use a vehicle while it is carrying passengers or cause or permit it to be so used unless the inside and the outside of the body of the vehicle and all windows and fittings and all passengers' seats are maintained in clean and good condition.

Lamps

4–2170   40. (1) No person shall use a vehicle during the hours of darkness while it is carrying passengers or cause or permit it to be so used unless every lamp provided in compliance with Regulation 16 for the internal illumination of the vehicle is at all times during such use kept lighted to such extent as is necessary to provide adequate illumination of every access from any seat in the vehicle to every exit in the vehicle and of every such marking as is required by Regulation 24 to be provided in relation to every emergency exit in the vehicle:

Provided that it shall not be necessary to keep lighted any lamp provided on the upper deck of a double-decked vehicle if a barrier is secured across the bottom of all staircases leading to that deck so as effectively to prevent passengers using any such staircase.

(2) In this Regulation, "hours of darkness" means the time between half-an-hour after sunset and half-an-hour before sunrise.

Use of device for operating power-operated doors

4–2171   41. (1) Except as provided by paragraph (2), no person shall use or cause or permit to be used any device for operating the doors of a vehicle having power-operated doors, being a device such as is mentioned in condition (*b*) of Regulation 23(1) or, as the case may be, in paragraph 9(*b*)(ii) of Schedule 2.

(2) Paragraph (1) shall not apply—

(*a*) in an emergency, as to the use of a device by any person;

(*b*) otherwise than in an emergency, as to the use of a device by a person in accordance with an authorisation by the operator of the vehicle, save that no such use shall occur if—

(i) the vehicle is in motion, and
(ii) the doors, when fully opened, project more than 80 millimetres from the side of the vehicle.

Filling of petrol tank

4–2172   42. While the engine of a vehicle is running no person shall cause or permit the filler cap fitted to the petrol tank of the vehicle to be removed or petrol to be put into its petrol tank.

Carriage of conductor

4–2173   43. No person shall use or cause or permit to be used as a stage carriage any vehicle which has a seating capacity exceeding 20 passengers unless a person authorised to act as conductor of the vehicle is carried thereby:
Provided that this Regulation shall not apply—

(i) in the case of a single-decked vehicle which has a seating capacity not exceeding 32 passengers and which is provided with only one emergency exit, if that exit and the entrance to the vehicle are both placed at the front of the vehicle and are readily visible to the driver from his seat and means are provided for the driver to be aware if any person outside the vehicle has been trapped by the closure of any door provided at that entrance, or
(ii) in the case of any other vehicle, if a certifying officer has stated in writing that the construction and design of the vehicle is such that a conductor is not required for the purpose of the safety of the passengers.

Carriage of inflammable or dangerous substances

4–2174   44. (1) No person shall use or cause or permit to be used any vehicle by which any highly inflammable or otherwise dangerous substance is carried unless that substance is carried in containers so designed and constructed, or unless the substance is so packed, that, notwithstanding an accident to the vehicle, it is unlikely that damage to the vehicle or injury to passengers carried by the vehicle will be caused by reason of the presence on it of that substance.
(2) The requirements of this Regulation are in addition to and not in derogation of the requirements of regulations made under the Petroleum (Consolidation) Act 1928 or under any other Act.

Markings

4–2175   45. No vehicle in respect of which, by virtue of section [6 of the Act], a certificate of initial fitness, or a certificate under section 130 of the Road Traffic Act 1960, or a certificate under section [55] of the Road Traffic Act [1988] is required shall be used on a road unless the vehicle is marked with clearly legible characters—

(i) not less than 25 millimetres tall,
(ii) in a conspicuous position on the nearside of the vehicle,
(iii) in colours which contrast with their background, and
(iv) indicating the name of the owner (as defined in section 44(1) of the said Act[1] of 1980 in relation to a vehicle to which that definition applies) of the vehicle and the owner's principal place of business.

---

1. See now s 82(1) of the Public Passenger Vehicles Act 1981.

Use of seats

4–2176   45A. (1) No passenger shall be permitted to use a seat provided for a passenger unless it complies with the requirements specified in Regulation 28.
(2) No crew shall be permitted to use a crew seat unless it complies with the requirements specified in Regulation 28A.

4–2176A   45B. Route and destination displays.   (1) No person shall use or cause or permit to be used on a road any regulated public service vehicle unless any route number or any destination fitted in the positions provided for such displays with respect to the vehicle in accordance (as the case may be) with either paragraph 8 of Schedule 2 or paragraph 7 of Schedule 3 to the 2000 Regulations is displayed in characters which—

(*a*) in the case of a route number, are not less than 200 millimetres in height on the front and rear of the vehicle and not less than 70 millimetres in height on the side of the vehicle,
(*b*) in the case of a destination, are not less than 125 millimetres in height on the front of the vehicle and not less than 70 millimetres in height on the side of the vehicle,
(*c*) contrast with the display background, and
(*d*) in the case of destination information, is not written in capital letters only.

(2) In this regulation—

"character" means capital letters or numbers of a height (as specified in paragraph (1)(*a*) and (*b*) above) and lower case letters of a size relative to the text of a capital letter for a given typeface;

"destination" means a word or words to describe the route or final destination; and

"route number" means any combination of numbers or letters which designate a route.

PART V

REGULATIONS RELATING TO CERTIFICATES OF INITIAL FITNESS, APPROVAL AS A TYPE VEHICLE AND CONFORMITY TO AN APPROVED TYPE VEHICLE

[Regulations 46–57]

4–2177   SCHEDULE 1

Regulations revoked by regulation 2

SCHEDULE 2

EXCEPTIONS FROM THE CONDITIONS PRESCRIBED IN PART II AS APPLICABLE TO VEHICLES REGISTERED BEFORE CERTAIN DATES

4–2178 **1.** Regulation 7(2) (Suspension) shall not apply in the case of a vehicle registered before 1st April 1959.

2. Regulation 9(1) and (2) (Brakes) shall not apply in the case of a vehicle registered before 1st January 1955.

3. Regulation 13(1) (Fuel tanks, carburettors, etc) shall not apply—

(*a*) in the case of a vehicle registered before 1st April 1959 if, in the case of a single-decked vehicle or a half-decked vehicle, no fuel tank is placed under any part of any gangway which is within 600 millimetres of any entrance or exit and, in the case of a double-decked vehicle, no such tank is placed under any part of any gangway on the lower deck of that vehicle which is within 600 millimetres of any entrance or exit on that deck;

(*b*) in the case of a single-decked vehicle registered before 28th October 1964 which has a seating capacity not exceeding 12 passengers, if no fuel tank is placed immediately under any entrance or exit and no filling point for such a tank is situated under or immediately adjacent to any entrance or exit;

(*c*) in so far as it consists of sub-paragraph (*c*), in the case of a vehicle registered before 1st April 1959;

(*d*) in so far as it consists of sub-paragraph (*d*), in the case of a vehicle registered before 1st April 1959 if—

   (i)   the vehicle is fitted with an engine having a fuel injection system; or

   (ii) the vehicle is not so fitted, but a cock is fitted by means of which the supply of fuel to any carburettor can be immediately cut off and the "off" position of the means of operation is clearly marked on the outside of the vehicle.

3A. Regulation 14 (exhaust pipe) shall not apply in the case of a steam-powered vehicle which was manufactured before 1st January 1955, whether or not it has subsequently been used as a public service vehicle.

4. Regulation 16 (Artificial lighting) in so far as it consists of sub-paragraph (*b*), shall not apply in the case of a vehicle registered before 1st April 1959 and the requirements as to lighting circuits in that Regulation shall not apply in the case of a vehicle registered before 28th October 1964.

5. Regulation 17(2) (Electrical equipment) shall not apply in the case of a vehicle registered before 19th June 1968 if one or more electrical circuits in which the voltage exceeds 100 volts has been installed in the vehicle on or after that date.

6. Regulation 19 (Height of sides of body) shall not apply in the case of a vehicle registered before 1st April 1959—

(*a*) in the case of a vehicle not being a single-decked vehicle, if it otherwise complies with the requirements of that Regulation with the substitution of a reference to 990 millimetres for the reference therein to 1·21 metres; and

(*b*) in the case of a single-decked vehicle, if the height of the body sides from the deck measured at the sides of the vehicle is not less than 710 millimetres.

7. Regulation 20 (Steps, platforms and stairs) shall not apply—

(*a*) in so far as it consists of paragraph (*a*), in the case of a vehicle registered before 1st April 1982 in respect of any platform except a rear platform, and

(*b*) in so far as it consists of paragraph (*b*)(iv) in the case of a vehicle registered before 1st April 1959 if it otherwise complies with the requirements of the said condition (*b*) with the substitution of a reference to 990 millimetres for the reference therein to 1.21 metres.

8. Regulation 21 (Number, position and size of entrances and exits) shall not apply—

(*a*) in so far as it consists of paragraphs (4) and (6) in the case of a vehicle registered before 1st April 1959 if it is provided with two exits so placed as not to be on the same side of the vehicle;

(*b*) in so far as it consists of paragraph (6) in the case of a vehicle registered on or after 1st April 1959 and before 28th October 1964 which has a seating capacity exceeding 45 passengers if—

   (i)   the vehicle is provided with two exits (of which neither is a secondary emergency exit) and those exits are not on the same side of the vehicle, and

   (ii) in a case where those exits are so placed that the distance between their centres is less than 3·05 metres, a secondary emergency exit is provided in such a position that there is a distance of not less than 3·05 metres between the nearest points of the openings of that exit and of whichever of the exits mentioned in sub-paragraph paragraph (i) above is the nearer to that exit. For the purpose of this paragraph the reference to the distance between the centres and between the nearest points of the openings of the two exits there mentioned shall be construed in accordance with Regulation 21(1)(*e*);

(*c*) in so far as it consists of paragraph (9)—

   (i)   in the case of a vehicle registered before 1st April 1959 (not being a single-decked vehicle having a permanent top) if it is provided with two exits so placed as not to be on the same side of the vehicle; or

   (ii) in the case of a vehicle which—

      A   is provided with a platform such as is mentioned in proviso (i) to Regulation 21(4); or

      B   has a seating capacity not exceeding 14 passengers, if one means of exit and entrance is provided and is placed behind the rear wheels.

9. Regulation 23(1) (Doors) shall not apply—

  (*a*) in so far as it consists of sub-paragraph (*j*) in the case of a vehicle registered before 1st August 1968;

  (*b*) save in so far as it consists of sub-paragraph (*j*) in the case of a vehicle registered before 19th June 1968 if—

    (i) every entrance door and every exit door can be readily opened from inside and outside the vehicle by one operation of the locking mechanism:

    Provided that a vehicle shall not be deemed to fail to comply with this sub-paragraph by reason only of the fact that, for the purpose of securing the vehicle when unattended, any entrance or exit door has been fitted with a supplementary lock with or without an actuating mechanism if the lock is so designed and constructed that the door can at all times be opened by a person inside the vehicle by one operation of the ordinary locking mechanism;

    (ii) except in the case of a vehicle registered before 1st April 1959, the device provided outside the vehicle for operating the locking mechanism of the door (not being a device provided in relation to an emergency exit on the upper deck of a double-decked vehicle or in the roof of a half-decked vehicle) is readily accessible to persons of normal height standing at ground level outside the vehicle;

    (iii) except in the case of a vehicle registered before 1st April 1959, means are provided for holding every entrance and exit door securely in the closed position;

    (iv) except in the case of a vehicle registered before 1st April 1959, all locks and fastenings fitted to entrance and exit doors are so designed and fitted that they are not likely to become dislodged or be operated accidentally, and, in the said excepted case, door handles or levers to door catches are so designed and fitted that they are not likely to become dislodged or be operated accidentally;

    (v) where any entrances are provided with doors which are designed to remain open when the vehicle is in motion, suitable fastenings are provided to hold such doors securely in the opened position;

    (vi) except in the case of a vehicle registered before 1st April 1959, every sliding door and every folding door fitted to an entrance or exit is provided with suitable fastenings to prevent it from being closed by any movement of the vehicle;

    (vii) all doors can open so as not to obstruct clear access to any entrance or exit from inside or outside the vehicle; and

    (viii) except in the case of a vehicle registered before 1st April 1959, the means by which a power-operated door may be opened are provided inside the vehicle on or adjacent to the door and their position is clearly indicated and there is also an indication that the said means may be used by passengers only in an emergency; and the storage and transmission system of the power for operating the door is such that operation of the doors does not adversely affect the efficient operation of the braking system of the vehicle and the apparatus is so designed and constructed that in the event of the system becoming inoperative the door can be operated manually from inside and outside the vehicle.

10. Regulation 24(1)(*b*)(iv) (Marking, positioning and operation of emergency exits) shall not apply in the case of a vehicle registered before 1st April 1959, being a vehicle which is provided with a rear platform, if an emergency exit (of which the clear height at the centre line is not less than 1·52 metres and of which the width is not less than 455 millimetres) is provided from that platform to the rear of the vehicle and is enclosed by means of a door placed on the near side of that platform.

11. The provisions of Regulation 26 (Width of gangways) specified in column 1 of the Table below shall not apply in the case of a vehicle specified, in relation to those provisions, in column 2 of that Table.

TABLE

1	2
Paragraph (1)(*e*) Paragraph (1)(*a*), (*c*) and (*g*)C.	A vehicle registered before 19th June 1968. A vehicle registered before 1st April 1959 if the width of every gangway is not less than 305 millimetres up to a height of 765 millimetres above the level of the deck and not less than 355 millimetres above that height.
Paragraph 1(*c*)	A vehicle registered after 1st April 1959 and before 19th June 1968 if no part of any gangway which is within 915 millimetres of an exit (other than an emergency exit) to which it leads is less than 530 millimetres in width.

12. Regulation 27 (Height of gangways) shall not apply in the case of a half-decked vehicle registered before 8th August 1950, and Regulation 27(1)(*d*) shall not apply in the case of a vehicle registered before 1st January 1947.

13. Regulation 28 (Seats) shall not apply—

  (*a*) in so far as it consists of paragraph (1)(*d*) in the case of a vehicle registered before 1st April 1959 if all the passengers' seats in the vehicle are so fitted—

    (i) that no part of the back rest of any seat placed lengthwise is less than 1·37 metres from the corresponding part of the back rest of the seat facing it; and

    (ii) there is in relation to every transverse seat in the vehicle a clear space of at least 660 millimetres in front of the whole length of the top of the back rest of that seat measured from the centre of each complete length of the seat allowed for the accommodation of a seated passenger in accordance with condition (*b*) of the said paragraph (1) but disregarding any handles or grips which do not project more than 105 millimetres from the back rest;

  (*b*) in so far as it consists of paragraph (1)(*g*) in the case of a vehicle registered before 1st April 1959 if no seat placed over the arch of a wheel of the vehicle is in such a position as to cause discomfort to passengers;

  (*c*) in so far as it consists of paragraph (1)(*h*) in the case of a vehicle registered before 1st April 1959 if, as respects any transverse seat in the vehicle which is so placed that a passenger seated upon it is liable to be thrown through any entrance to or exit from the vehicle or down a stairway in the vehicle, an effective screen or guard is placed so as to afford adequate protection against that occurrence to a passenger occupying that seat.

14. Regulation 29 (Passenger protection) shall not apply in the case of a vehicle registered before 1st April 1959 if all glass windows or panels which face any transverse seat in the vehicle are adequately protected against the likelihood of breakage in the event of passengers being thrown against them.

15. Regulation 31 (Driver's accommodation) shall not apply—

(a) in so far as it consists of sub-paragraphs (b) and (e) in the case of a vehicle registered before 1st April 1959;

(b) in so far as it consists of sub-paragraph (d) in the case of a vehicle registered before 1st April 1959 if means are provided (where necessary) to prevent light from the interior of the vehicle from incommoding the driver; and

(c) in so far as it consists of sub-paragraphs (g) and (h) in the case of a vehicle registered before 1st April 1959.

4–2179

(see Regulation 5)   SCHEDULE 3

CONDITIONS PRESCRIBED IN REGULATIONS IN PART II, OR PROVISIONS THEREOF, APPLICABLE TO CERTAIN VEHICLES BEARING A DESIGNATED APPROVAL MARK

Regulation 6 (Stability);
Regulation 7 (Suspension);
Regulation 8 (Guard rails);
Regulation 9 (Brakes);
Regulation 10 (Brake and Steering Connections);
Regulation 11 (Locking of nuts);
Regulation 12 (Steering);
Regulation 14 (Exhaust pipe);
Regulation 15 (Luggage racks);
Regulation 16 (Artificial lighting);
Regulation 17 (Electrical equipment);
Regulation 18 (Body);
Regulation 23 (Doors);
Regulation 24 (Positioning and operation of emergency exits);
Paragraph (1)(a) and (h) of Regulation 28 (Seats);
Regulation 29 (Passenger protection);
Regulation 30 (Ventilation);
Regulation 31 (Driver's accommodation);
Regulation 32 (Windscreens);
Regulation 33 (Passengers' communication);
Regulation 34 (General construction).

4–2180

(See Regulation 23(1A))   SCHEDULE 3A

Application

1. This schedule applies to every vehicle registered on or after the 1st April 1980.

Conditions

2. Save as provided below, the following conditions shall be complied with in relation to every power-operated door which is—

(a) fitted to a vehicle to which this Schedule applies, and

(b) so situated in the vehicle that the whole of the door opening is more than 500 millimetres behind the transverse vertical plane that touches the back of the driver's seat when the seat is in its rearmost position.

3. (1) The first condition is that when the door is prevented from closing by the presence of a fixed vertical surface that is 60 millimetres high placed at right angles to the direction of movement of the closing edge—

(a) the force exerted on the surface does not exceed 150 newtons and

(b) the door re-opens automatically and remains open until a closing control is operated manually.

(2) This condition shall not have to be met when a door is within 30 millimetres of its fully closed position, but shall otherwise apply wherever the surface is placed within the door opening (regardless of the stage of closure when the door first strikes the surface or of the part of the closing edge that strikes the surface).

4. (1) The second condition is that whenever the door is closed on to the fingers or the palm of the hand—

(a) the door re-opens automatically and remains open until a closing control is operated manually, or

(b) the fingers or hand can be readily extracted from the doors without injury.

(2) this condition shall not apply to a door fitted to a coach manufactured before the 1st of October 1992 or registered before the 1st of April 1992.

(3) In this paragraph "coach" has the same meaning as in the Road Vehicles (Construction and Use) Regulations 1986.

5. The third condition is that a visual warning device, clearly visible to the driver at all times, is activated whenever the door is not fully closed.

Transitional and Savings

6. (1) This schedule shall not have effect until 1st April 1993 in relation to a vehicle manufactured before the 14th May 1990 or first used before the 1st October 1990.

(2) Nothing in this Schedule shall be construed as derogating from the requirements of regulation 23(1).

4–2181

(See Regulation 35)   SCHEDULE 4

FIRE EXTINGUISHING APPARATUS

A fire extinguisher which complies in all respects with the specification for portable fire extinguishers issued by the British Standards Institution numbered BS 5423: 1977 or BS 5423: 1980 or BS 5423: 1987 and which—

(a) has a minimum test fire rating of 8A or 21B, and
(b) contains water or foam or contains, and is marked to indicate that it contains, halon 1211 or halon 1301.

4–2182

(See Regulation 36)   SCHEDULE 5
                                  FIRST AID EQUIPMENT

(i) Ten antiseptic wipes, foil packed.
(ii) One conforming disposable bandage (not less than 7·5 centimetres wide).
(iii) Two triangular bandages.
(iv) One packet of 24 assorted adhesive dressings.
(v) Three large sterile unmedicated ambulance dressings (not less than 15·0 centimetres I 20·0 centimetres).
(vi) Two sterile eye pads, with attachments.
(vii) Twelve assorted safety pins.
(viii) One pair of rustless blunt-ended scissors.

Road Vehicles (Marking of Special Weights) Regulations 1983[1]
(SI 1983/910 amended by SI 1987/1326)

4–2191 **1.** *Commencement and citation.*

1. Made by the Secretary of State for Transport under s 172 of the Road Traffic Act 1972 and now having effect under s 64 of the Road Traffic Act 1988.

4–2192 **2.** (1) The weights specified in Regulation 3 below are authorised for the purposes of section [64] of the Road Traffic Act [1988].
(2) The prescribed manner in which the weights mentioned in paragraph (1) above shall be marked is that they shall be clearly and indelibly marked on a plate securely affixed to the vehicle in a conspicuous and readily accessible position and all letters and figures shown on the plate shall be not less than 4 millimetres in height.

4–2193 **3.** (1) The weights mentioned in Regulation 2(1) above are the weights mentioned in paragraph (2) below at which the vehicle on which they are marked can, in the opinion of the manufacturer of the vehicle, be used at a speed not exceeding each of the following—

(i) 12 miles per hour;
(ii) 20 miles per hour;
(iii) 25 miles per hour;
(iv) 30 miles per hour;
(v) 35 miles per hour;
(vi) 40 miles per hour,

on a road by virtue of any order for the time being in force under section [44] of the Road Traffic Act [1988], provided any conditions (whether or not relating to limits of weight) imposed by or under any such order are complied with.
(2) the weights referred to in paragraph (1) above are—
(i) in the case of a motor vehicle

  —its maximum gross weight,
  —the maximum axle weight for each axle, and
  —the maximum train weight; and

(ii) in the case of a trailer (whether forming part of an articulated vehicle or not)

  —its maximum gross weight, and
  —the maximum axle weight for each axle.

(3) In this Regulation "maximum gross weight", maximum axle weight for each axle" and "maximum train weight" have the meanings respectively given to those expressions in Schedule 2 to the Motor Vehicles (Construction and Use) Regulations 1978[1].

1. See now the Road Vehicles (Construction and Use) Regulations 1986, Part I of Sch 8.

Road Transport (International Passenger Services) Regulations 1984[1]
(SI 1984/748, amended by SI 1987/1755, SI 1988/1809, SI 1990/1103, SI 2003/1118 and SI 2004/1882)

PART I—GENERAL

4–2241 **1.** *Citation, commencement and revocation.*

1. These regulations are made under s 2(2) of the European Communities Act 1972, s 40(1) and (3) of the Road Traffic Act 1972 and s 60(1) of the Public Passenger Vehicles Act 1981.

Interpretation

4–2242   **2.**—(1) In these Regulations—

(a) the references to the following provisions, that is to say—

Council Regulation No 117/66
Council Regulation No 516/72
Council Regulation No 517/72 and
Commission Regulation No 1016/68

are references, respectively, to the Community provisions more particularly described in Schedule 1 and references to "the Council Regulations" or "the Commission Regulation" shall be construed accordingly;

(b) "ASOR" means the Agreement on the International Carriage of Passengers by Road by means of Occasional Coach and Bus Services (ASOR)[1], approved on behalf of the Economic Community pursuant to Council Decision (EEC) of 20th July 1982 concluding the Agreement[2], entering into force for the Economic Community on 1st December 1983, as read with Council Regulation (EEC) No 56/83 on measures implementing the Agreement[3];

(c) "ASOR State" means—

   (i) a state, not being a member State, which is a Contracting Party to ASOR and to which the provisions of Sections II and III of ASOR apply in accordance with Article 18 thereof, or

   (ii) the Economic Community;

(d) "ASOR regulated" means, in relation to the carriage of passengers, the international carriage of passengers by road to which ASOR applies, namely in the circumstances specified in Article 1 thereof, that is to say, by means of occasional services (within the meaning of that Agreement) effected—

   (i) between the territories of two ASOR States, or starting and finishing in the territory of the same ASOR State; and

   (ii) should the need arise during such services, in transit through the territory of another ASOR State or through the territory of a state which is not an ASOR State; and

   (iii) using vehicles registered in the territory of an ASOR State which by virtue of their construction and their equipment, are suitable for carrying more than nine persons, including the driver, and are intended for that purpose,

and references to the carriage of passengers which is ASOR regulated include unladen journeys of the vehicles concerned with such carriage;

(e) "Community regulated" means, in relation to the carriage of passengers, the international carriage of passengers by road to which Council Regulation No 117/66 applies, namely in the circumstances mentioned in Article 4(1) thereof, that is to say—

   (i) where the place of departure is in the territory of a member State and the destination is in the territory of the same or another member State; and

   (ii) the vehicle is registered in a member State and in construction and equipment is suitable for carrying more than nine persons, including the driver, and is intended for that purpose,

and references to the carriage of passengers which is Community regulated include unladen journeys of the vehicles concerned with such carriage;

(f) "ECMT State" means a State which is a member of the European Conference of Ministers of Transport of the 17th November 1953 but not a member State or an ASOR State;

(g) "the Secretary of State" means the Secretary of State for Transport;

(h) "examiner" has the same meaning as in section 7(1) of the Road Traffic (Foreign Vehicles) Act 1972[4];

(i) "public service vehicle" shall be construed in accordance with section 1 of the Act of 1981;

(j) "the Act of 1981" means the Public Passenger Vehicles Act 1981.

(2) Any reference in these Regulations to a numbered Regulation or Schedule is a reference to the Regulation or Schedule bearing that number in these Regulations.

---

1. OJ No L230, 5.8.82, p 39.
2. OJ No L230, 5.8.82, p 38.
3. OJ No L10, 13.1.83, p 1.
4. 1972 c 27; s 7(1) has been amended by s 88 of, and para 17 of Sch 7 to, the Public Passenger Vehicles Act 1981.

Extent

4–2243   **3.** These Regulations do not extend to Northern Ireland.

PART II—MODIFICATIONS OF THE ACT OF 1981 IN RELATION TO VEHICLES REGISTERED IN THE UNITED KINGDOM WHEN USED FOR THE INTERNATIONAL CARRIAGE OF PASSENGERS

Community regulated regular, shuttle and works services by vehicles registered in the United Kingdom

4–2244   **4.**—(1) This Regulation applies to a vehicle registered in the United Kingdom which is being used for Community regulated carriage of passengers in so far as the vehicle—

(a) is used to provide any service for the carriage of passengers such as is mentioned in Article 1, 2 or 6 of Council Regulation No 117/66; and

(b) is so used in accordance with such of the requirements of the Council Regulations as apply in relation to the service in question.

(2) The provisions of the Act of 1981 shall have effect as if—

(a) in relation to a vehicle to which this Regulation applies registered in Great Britain, section 30 (Road service licences required for operation of stage carriage services) of the Act of 1981 were omitted; and

(b) in relation to a vehicle to which this Regulation applies registered in Northern Ireland, sections 6, 12, 18, 22 and 30 of the Act of 1981 were omitted.

Non-Community regulated regular and shuttle services by public service vehicles registered in the United Kingdom

4–2245 **5.** (1) This Regulation applies to a public service vehicle registered in the United Kingdom which is being used for the international carriage of passengers by road which is not Community regulated but where the vehicle is being used to provide a service for the carriage of passengers of a description such as is mentioned in Article 1 or 2 of Council Regulation 117/66 (that is to say, a regular service, a special regular service or a shuttle service as defined in those Articles).

(2) The provisions of the Act of 1981 and Parts I and II of the Transport Act 1985 shall have effect as if—

(a) in relation to a vehicle to which this Regulation applies registered in Northern Ireland, sections 6, 12, 18 and 22 of the Act of 1981 were omitted; and

(b) in relation to a vehicle to which this Regulation applies registered in Great Britain or in Northern Ireland, for section 6 of the Transport Act 1985 there were substituted the following section and section 35 of that Act shall be omitted—

"**6.** (1) No person shall cause or permit a public service vehicle to be used on a road for the international carriage of passengers unless there is in force in relation to the use of the vehicle, and is carried on the vehicle, an international passenger transport authorisation.

(2) A certifying officer or a public service vehicle examiner may at any time, on production if so required of his authority, require the operator or the driver of any such vehicle as is referred to in subsection (1) above, to produce and to permit him to inspect and copy an international passenger transport authorisation relating to the use of the vehicle, and for that purpose may require the vehicle to be stopped and may detain the vehicle for such time as is requisite for the purpose of inspecting and copying the authorisation.

(3) A person who—

(a) without reasonable excuse contravenes subsection (1) of this section, or

(b) without reasonable excuse fails to comply with a requirement of a certifying officer or public service vehicle examiner, or wilfully obstructs such officer or examiner, in the exercise of his powers under subsection (2) of this section,

shall be guilty of an offence and shall be liable on summary conviction to a fine not exceeding **level 3** on the standard scale (within the meaning of section 75 of the Criminal Justice Act 1982),

(4) In this section "international passenger transport authorisation" means licence, permit, authorisation or other document issued by the Secretary of State in pursuance of an international agreement or arrangement to which the United Kingdom is for the time being a party.".

Occasional services by vehicles registered in the United Kingdom (whether ASOR or Community regulated or not)

4–2246 **6.** (1) This Regulation applies to a vehicle registered in the United Kingdom which is being used for the international carriage of passengers by road—

(a) in so far as the vehicle is used to provide a service for the carriage of passengers which is Community regulated and is such as is mentioned—

(i) in paragraph 1(a) of Article 3 of Council Regulation No 117/66 (that is to say, an occasional service described in that paragraph as a closed-door tour), or

(ii) in paragraph 1(b) of the said Article 3 (that is to say, an occasional service described in that paragraph where the passengers are carried on the outward journey and the return journey is made unladen), or

(iii) in paragraph 1(c) of the said Article 3 (that is to say, an occasional service, as mentioned in that paragraph, of any other description); or

(b) in so far as the vehicle is used to provide a service for the carriage of passengers which is ASOR regulated; or

(c) in so far as the vehicle is used as a public service vehicle for the carriage of passengers which is not ASOR regulated or Community regulated but is a service of a description such as is mentioned in any of the paragraphs of Article 3 of Council Regulation No 117/66.

(2) The provision of the Act of 1981 and Parts I and II of the Transport Act 1985 shall have effect as if—

(a) in relation to a vehicle to which this Regulation applies registered in Northern Ireland, sections 6, 12, 18 and 22 of the Act of 1981 were omitted; and (*b*) in relation to a vehicle to which this Regulation applies registered in Great Britain or in Northern Ireland, for section 6 of the Transport Act 1985 there were substituted the following section and section 35 of that Act shall be omitted—

"**6.** (1) No person shall cause or permit a vehicle to be used on a road for the international carriage or passengers unless—

(*a*) in relation to the use of the vehicle, in the case of such carriage which is ASOR regulated, the requirements of Articles 7, 8 and 9 of, and the Annex to, ASOR (which provide for the completion by the person by whom, or on whose behalf, a vehicle is used to provide an occasional service of a passenger way-bill in respect of the service in question and for the carrying of the top copy of such waybill on the vehicle at all times while it is used on that service) are complied with and, in the case of any other such carriage, the requirements of Articles 2, 3 and 4 of, and of Annex 2 to, Commission Regulation No 1016/68 (which provide as aforesaid) are complied with, or would be complied with if those provisions applied to the service; and

(*b*) the vehicle is used on the service in question in circumstances which accord in all respects with the particulars which have been specified in the said passenger waybill as applicable to that service.

(2) A certifying officer or a public service vehicle examiner may, at any time which is reasonable having regard to the circumstances of the case, enter any premises from which he has reason to believe that a vehicle is or is to be operated on a service for the international carriage of passengers and may, on production if so required of his authority, require the operator of the vehicle to produce and to permit him to inspect and copy a control document duly completed for the service, in the case of ASOR regulated carriage, in accordance with Articles 7, 8 and 9 of, and the Annex to, ASOR and, in the case of any other such carriage, in accordance with Articles 2, 3, and 4 of, and Annex 2 to, Commission Regulations No 1016/68.

(3) A certifying officer or a public service vehicle examiner may, on production if so required of his authority—

(*a*) require the driver of a vehicle used for the international carriage of passengers to produce and to permit him to inspect and copy and to mark with an official stamp, in the case of a vehicle used for ASOR regulated carriage, the document required by Article 8(2) of ASOR and, in the case of any other such carriage, the document required by Article 3(2) of Commission Regulations No 1016/68, to be kept on a vehicle to which that Article applies; and

(*b*) detain the vehicle for such time as is required for the purpose of inspecting, copying and marking the document.

(4) A person who—

(*a*) without reasonable excuse contravenes subsection (1) above, or

(*b*) without reasonable excuse fails to comply with a requirement of an officer or examiner, under subsection (2) or (3) above, or

(*c*) wilfully obstructs an officer or examiner in the exercise of his powers under either of those subsections,

shall be guilty of an offence and shall be liable on summary conviction to a fine not exceeding **level 3** on the standard scale (within the meaning of section 75 of the Criminal Justice Act 1982).

(5) In this section—

"ASOR" means the Agreement on the International Carriage of Passengers by Road by means of Occasional Coach and Bus Services (ASOR) approved on behalf of the Economic Community pursuant to Council Decision (EEC) of July 20th 1982 concluding the Agreement entering into force for the Economic Community on December 1st 1983, as read with Council Regulation (EEC) No 56/83 on measures implementing the Agreement;

"ASOR" State means—

(*a*) a state, not being a member State, which is a Contracting Party to ASOR and to which the provisions of Sections II and III of ASOR apply in accordance with Article 18 thereof; or

(*b*) the Economic Community;

"ASOR regulated" means, in relation to the carriage of passengers, the international carriage of passengers by road to which ASOR applies namely in the circumstances specified in Article 1 thereof, that is to say, by means of occasional services (within the meaning of that Agreement) effected—

(*a*) between the territories of two ASOR States, or starting and finishing in the territory of the same ASOR State; and

(*b*) should the need arise during such services, in transit through the territory of another ASOR State or through the territory of a state which is not an ASOR State; and

(*c*) using vehicles registered in the territory of an ASOR State which, by virtue of their construction and their equipment, are suitable for carrying more than nine persons, including the driver, and are intended for that purpose,

and references to the carriage of passengers which is ASOR regulated include unladen journeys of the vehicles concerned with such carriage;

"Commission Regulation No 1016/68" means Regulation (EEC) No 1016/68 of the Commission of 9th July 1968 prescribing the model control documents referred to in Articles 6 and 9 of Council Regulation No 117/66/EEC as amended by and as read with Regulation (EEC) No 2485/82 of the Commission of 13th September 1982; and

"Council Regulation No 117/66" means Regulation No 117/66/EEC of the Council of 28th July 1966 on the introduction of common rules for the international carriage of passengers by coach and bus.".

PART III—MODIFICATIONS OF THE ACT OF 1981 IN RELATION TO VEHICLES REGISTERED OUTSIDE THE UNITED KINGDOM

Small vehicles registered outside the United Kingdom visiting Great Britain temporarily

4–2247 **7.** (1) This Regulation applies to a public service vehicle registered outside the United Kingdom which—

(a) in construction and equipment is suitable for carrying not more than nine persons, including the driver, and is intended for that purpose;

(b) is brought into Great Britain for the purpose of carrying passengers who are travelling to Great Britain from a place outside the United Kingdom, or who are travelling from the United Kingdom to any such place; and

(c) remains in Great Britain for a period not exceeding three months from the date of its entry therein.

(2) The provisions of the Act of 1981 shall, in relation to a vehicle to which this Regulation applies, have effect as if sections 6, 12, 18, 22 and 30 of the Act of 1981 were omitted.

Community regulated regular, shuttle and works services by vehicles registered outside the United Kingdom

4–2248 **8.** (1) This Regulation applies to a vehicle registered outside the United Kingdom which is being used for Community regulated carriage of passengers in so far as the vehicle—

(a) is being used to provide any service for the carriage of passengers such as is mentioned in Article 1, 2 or 6 of Council Regulation 117/66; and

(b) is being so used in accordance with such of the requirements of the Council Regulations or, as the case may be, the Commission Regulation as apply to the service in question.

(2) The provisions of the Act of 1981 shall, in relation to a vehicle to which this Regulation applies, have effect as if sections 6, 12, 18, 22 and 30 of the Act of 1981 were omitted.

Non-Community regulated regular and shuttle services by vehicles registered outside the United Kingdom

4–2249 **9.** (1) This Regulation applies to a public service vehicle registered outside the United Kingdom which is being used for the international carriage of passengers which is not Community regulated in so far as the vehicle—

(a) is being used to provide a service for the carriage of passengers of a description such as is mentioned in Article 1 or 2 of Council Regulation 117/66 (that is to say, a regular service, a special regular service or a shuttle service as defined in those Articles), and

(b) is so used by or on behalf of a person who is authorised, under the law of the country in which the vehicle is registered, to use the vehicle for the carriage of passengers on the journey in question or such parts thereof as are situated within that country.

(2) The provisions of the Act of 1981 shall in relation to a vehicle to which this Regulation applies, have effect as if sections 6, 18, 22 and 30 of the Act of 1981 were omitted, and as if for section 12 of the Act of 1981 there were substituted the section set out in Schedule 2.

ASOR or Community regulated occasional services by vehicles registered outside the United Kingdom

4–2250 **10.** (1) This Regulation applies to a vehicle registered outside the United Kingdom which is being used for ASOR or Community regulated carriage of passengers—

(a) in so far as the vehicle is used to provide a service for the carriage of passengers such as is mentioned—

(i) in paragraph 1(a) of Article 2 of ASOR or paragraph 1(a) of Article 3 of Council Regulation No 117/66 (that is to say, an occasional service described in that paragraph as a closed-door tour), or

(ii) in paragraph 1(b) of each of those Articles (that is to say an occasional service as described in that paragraph where passengers are carried on the outward journey and the return journey is made unladen), or

(iii) in paragraph 1(c) of each of those Articles (that is to say, an occasional service as mentioned in that paragraph of any other description); and

(b) in so far as, in relation to the use of the vehicle—

(i) in the case of a vehicle being used for ASOR regulated carriage, the requirements of Articles 7, 8 and 9 of, and the Annex to, ASOR (which provides for the completion, by the person by whom or on whose behalf a vehicle is used to provide such an occasional service as aforesaid, of a passenger waybill in respect of the service in question and for the carrying of the top copy of such waybill on the vehicle at all times while it is used on that service) and in the case of a vehicle being used for Community regulated carriage, the requirements of Articles 2, 3 and 4 of, and Annex 2 to, Commission Regulation No 1016/68 (which provides as aforesaid), have been complied with, and

(ii) the vehicle is used on the service in question in circumstances which accord in all respects with the particulars which, in pursuance of the said requirements, have been specified in the said passenger waybill as applicable to that service.

(2) In relation to a vehicle to which this Regulation applies, the provisions of the Act of 1981 shall have effect as if sections 6, 18, 22 and 30 of the Act of 1981 were omitted and—

(a) in so far as the vehicle is used to provide a service for the carriage of passengers such as is mentioned—

(i) in Article 2(1)(a) or (b) of ASOR or Article 3(1)(a) or (b) of Council Regulation No 117/66, or

(ii) in a case where the service is ASOR regulated and all the conditions mentioned in Article 5(2) of ASOR are fulfilled, in Article 2(1)(c) of ASOR, or

(iii) in a case where the service is Community regulated and all the conditions mentioned in Article 5(2) of the said Council Regulation are fulfilled, in Article 2(1)(c) of that Regulation,

as if section 12 of the Act of 1981 were omitted; and

(b) in so far as the vehicle is used as a public service vehicle to provide a service for the carriage of passengers such as is mentioned in Article 2(1)(c) of ASOR or Article 2(1)(c) of the said Council Regulation and—

(i) in a case where the service is ASOR regulated any of the conditions mentioned in Article 5(2) of ASOR are not fulfilled, or

(ii) in a case where the service is Community regulated, any of the conditions mentioned in Article 5(2) of the said Council Regulation are not fulfilled,

as if for the said section 12 there were substituted the section set out in Schedule 2.

Certain occasional services by vehicles registered in ECMT States

4–2251   **11.** (1) This Regulation applies to a public service vehicle—

(a) which is registered in the territory of a State which is an ECMT State;

(b) which is brought into Great Britain for the purpose of carrying passengers who are making only a temporary stay therein or are in transit; and

(c) which remains in Great Britain for a period not exceeding three months from the date of its entry therein,

in so far as the vehicle

(i) is used to provide a service for the carriage of passengers which is not ASOR or Community regulated but which is of a description such as is mentioned in Article 3(1)(a), (b) or (c) of Council Regulation No 117/66, where the journey made by the vehicle in providing that service starts from a place situated in the territory of an ECMT State and ends at a place situated in the territory of such a State or in Great Britain, and

(ii) is so used by or on behalf of a person who is authorised, under the law in force in the State, in the territory of which it is registered to use the vehicle for the carriage of passengers on the journey in question or such part thereof as lies within the territory of that State.

(2) In relation to a vehicle to which this Regulation applies, the provisions of the Act of 1981 shall have effect as if sections 6, 18, 22 and 30 of the Act of 1981 were omitted and as if—

(a) in so far as the vehicle is used to provide a service for the carriage of passengers such as is mentioned in paragraph 1(a) and 1(b) of Article 3 of Council Regulation No 117/66, for section 12 of the Act of 1981 there were substituted the following sections—

"**12.** No person shall cause or permit a public service vehicle to be used on a road for the international carriage of passengers unless there is in force in relation to the use of the vehicle, and is carried on the vehicle, a document which is issued by the competent authority of the country in which the vehicle is registered in the form set out in Schedule 3 to the Road Transport (International Passenger Service) Regulations 1984 and which is duly completed."; and

(b) in so far as the vehicle is used for the carriage of passengers such as is mentioned in paragraph 1(c) of the said Article 3, for section 12 of the Act of 1981 there were substituted the section set out in Schedule 2.

Certain occasional services by vehicles not registered in a member State, an ASOR State or an ECMT State

4–2252   **12.** (1) This Regulation applies to a public service vehicle—

(a) which is registered in the territory of a State which is not a member State, an ASOR State or an ECMT State;

(b) which is brought into Great Britain for the purpose of carrying passengers who are making only a temporary stay therein or are in transit, being passengers who commenced their journey from the state in the territory of which the vehicle is registered or, as the case may be, from Northern Ireland; and (*c*) which remains in Great Britain for a period not exceeding three months from the date of its entry therein,

in so far as the vehicle—

(i) is used to provide a service for the carriage of passengers which is not Community regulated but which is of a description such as is mentioned in Article 3(1)(*a*), (*b*) or (*c*) of Regulation No 117/66, and

(ii) is so used by or on behalf of a person who is authorised, under the law in force in the state in the territory of which it is registered to use the vehicle for the carriage of passengers on the journey in question or such parts thereof as lies within the territory of that state.

(2) The provisions of the Act of 1981 shall, in relation to a vehicle to which this Regulation applies, have effect as if sections 6, 18, 22 and 30 of the Act of 1981 were omitted and as if for section 12 of the Act of 1981 there were substituted—

(*a*) in the case of a public service vehicle registered in the Union of Soviet Socialist Republics used to provide a service of a description such as is mentioned in article 3(1)(*a*) or (*b*) of regulation No. 117/66, the following section—

"**12.** No person shall cause or permit a public service vehicle to be used on a road for the international carriage of passengers unless there is carried on the vehicle a list of the passengers carried by the vehicle"; and

(*b*) in any other case, the section set out in Schedule 2.

PART IV—APPLICATIONS FOR ISSUE OF AUTHORISATIONS AND OTHER DOCUMENTS AND FEES IN RESPECT THEREOF

Competent authority for the purposes of ASOR, the Council Regulations and the Commission Regulation

4–2253   **13.** (1) The Secretary of State shall be the competent authority of the United Kingdom for all purposes of ASOR, the Council Regulations and the commission Regulation, in relation to the international carriage of passengers to, from or through Great Britain.

(2) The Bus and Coach Council is hereby designated as a duly authorised agency for the purposes of Article 6 of ASOR and of Article 9 of Council Regulation No 117/66.

Applications for, issue of, and fees payable in respect of, authorisations for international passenger services

4–2254   **14.** (1) An application for, or for the variation of the conditions of, a regular service authorisation, a special regular service authorisation or a shuttle service authorisation shall be made to the Secretary of State on the form prescribed by Regulation (EEC) No 1172/72 of the Commission of 26th May 1972[1].

(2) An application for any other authorisation required by these Regulations or by the Act of 1981 as modified by these Regulations, for the use of a vehicle for the international carriage of passengers by road shall be made to the Secretary of State.

(2A) An application for a certified copy of any such authorisation as is referred to in paragraph (1) or (2) above shall be made to the Secretary of State and the applicant shall pay a free of £11 in respect of each such copy.

(3) An applicant for a special regular service authorisation, or an international passenger transport authorisation required by section 6 of the Transport Act 1985, as modified by Regulation 5 shall pay, when the application is made, a fee of £160 in respect of the application.

(3A) An applicant for a shuttle service authorisation or a regular service authorisation shall pay, when the application is made, a fee of £163 in respect of the application.

(4) An applicant for a regular, or special regular, service authorisation shall pay, before the authorisation is issued, in addition to the fee required by paragraph (3) above, a fee of £34 in respect of each year of validity of the authorisation.

(5) An applicant for a control document referred to in paragraph (1) of Regulation 15 shall pay to the Bus and Coach council, when the application is made, a fee of such amount as may, with approval of the Secretary of State, be required by the council.

(5A) An applicant for an own account certificate shall pay, when the application is made, a fee of £5 in respect of each year of validity of the certificate.

(6) In this Regulation "shuttle service authorisation" means such an authorisation under Council Regulation No 516/72 and "regular service authorisation" and "special regular service authorisation" means such an authorisation under Council Regulation No 517/72 and "own-account certificate" means a certificate issued in respect of an own-account road transport operation under Regulation (EEC) No 684/92 of the Commission of 16th March 1992 on common rules for the international carriage of passengers by coach and bus as amended by Regulation (EC) No 11/98 of the Council of 11th December 1997.

---

1. OJ No L 134; 12.6.72, p 527.

Applications for, and issue of, certificates and control documents for works and occasional services

4–2255   **15.** (1) The following provisions of this Regulation shall have effect with respect to the issue of a certificate (specified in Article 1 of Commission Regulation No 1016/68 being the certificate which by virtue of Article 6 of Council Regulation No 117/66 is required to be in force in respect of the provision of a service such as is mentioned in that Article) or of a control document (specified in Article 7 of ASOR or in Article 2 of Commission Regulation No 1016/68 being the document applicable in respect of the provision of a service such as is mentioned in Article 2 of ASOR or Article 3 of council Regulation No 117/66).

(2) An application for the issue of a certificate referred to in paragraph (1) above shall be made to the Secretary of State and an application for the issue of a control document referred to in that paragraph shall be made to the Bus and Coach Council.

(3) The period of validity of a control document shall be five years.

(4) The top copy of every passenger waybill (being the document which, as mentioned in Article 7 of ASOR or Article 2 of the Commission Regulation is the document applicable in respect of the provision of a service for the carriage of passengers such as is mentioned in Article 2 of ASOR or Article 3 of Council Regulation No 117/66), shall be retained, after the service in question has been provided, by the person by whom or on whose behalf it was provided and shall be sent to the Secretary of State so as to reach him not later than 31st March next following the end of the calendar year in which the service to which the waybill relates was provided.

(5) The duplicate of every such passenger waybill (being the duplicate which by virtue of Article 7(1) of ASOR or Article 2(1) of Commission Regulation No 1016/68 is required to be contained in a control document such as is mentioned in those Articles shall not be detached from that document at any time during its period of validity.

PART V—PENALTIES, ENFORCEMENT, SUPPLEMENTARY AND CONSEQUENTIAL

Production, inspection and copying of documents in relation to ASOR or Community regulated services

4–2256   16. (1) Paragraph (2) below shall have effect in relation to a vehicle where it appears to an examiner that the vehicle—

(a) is being used for the provision of an ASOR regulated or Community regulated service; and
(b) is being used, or has been brought into Great Britain for the purpose of being used, in such circumstances as, by virtue of any of the provisions specified in paragraph (3) below, to require a document of a description referred to in that provision to be kept or carried on the vehicle.

(2) An examiner may, on production if so required of his authority—

(a) require the driver of a vehicle referred to in paragraph (1) above to produce the document and to permit him to inspect and copy it and (in the case of a document of a description referred to in any of the provisions specified in paragraph (3)(c) or (e) below) to mark it with an official stamp; and
(b) may detain the vehicle for such time as is required for the purpose of inspecting, copying and marking the document.

(3) The provisions referred to in paragraph (1) above as being specified in this paragraph are—

(a) Article 17 of Council Regulation No 517/72 (which provides, inter alia, that the authorisation required by that Regulation for the use of a vehicle to provide a service for the carriage of passengers such as is mentioned in Article 1 thereof shall be carried on the vehicle);
(b) Articles 17 and 18 of Council Regulation No 516/72 (which respectively provide, inter alia, that the authorisation required by that Regulation for the use of a vehicle to provide a service for the carriage of passengers such as is mentioned in Article 1 thereof shall be carried on the vehicle and that passengers using that service shall be provided with a ticket throughout the journey in question);
(c) Article 8(2) of ASOR and Article 3(2) of Commission Regulation No 1016/68 (which provide that the top copy of the passenger waybill being the document which, by virtue of Article 7 of ASOR or Article 2 of Commission Regulation No 1016/68, has been detached from the control document such as is mentioned in those Articles, and is the document applicable in respect of the provision of a service for the carriage of passengers such as is mentioned in Article 2 of ASOR or Article 3 of Council Regulation No 117/66, shall be kept on the vehicle);
(d) Article 11(3) of ASOR and Article 5a(3) of Commission Regulation No 1018/68 (which provide that the model document with stiff green covers referred to in Article 11 of ASOR must be carried on the vehicle); and
(e) Regulation 17.

Carriage on the vehicle of certificate issued under Article 6 of Council Regulation No 117/66

4–2257   17. (1) In relation to a vehicle being used to provide a Community regulated service for the carriage of passengers such as is mentioned in Article 6 of Council Regulation No 117/66 there shall be carried on the vehicle, at all times while it is being used, the certificate specified in Article 1 of Commission Regulation No 1016/68, being the certificate which, by virtue of the said Article 6, is required to be in force in respect of the provision of that service.

(2) An examiner may, on production if so required of his authority—

(a) require the driver of a vehicle referred to in paragraph (1) above to produce the document and to permit him to inspect and copy it and to mark it with an official stamp; and
(b) may detain the vehicle for such time as is required for the purpose of inspecting, copying and marking the document.

Withdrawal of regular, special regular and shuttle service authorisations

4–2258   **18.** (1) If the Secretary of State is at any time satisfied that a holder of a regular, special regular or shuttle service authorisation issued by him—

    (a)   has failed to comply with the relevant Council Regulation, with the authorisation or any conditions specified therein; or

    (b)   has failed to operate, or is no longer operating, a service under the authorisation,

he may, by notice in writing to the holder, withdraw the authorisation.

    (2) Where the Secretary of State decides to withdraw an authorisation in exercise of his powers under Council Regulation No 516/72 or Council Regulation No 517/72 he may do so by notice in writing to the holder of the authorisation.

    (3) The withdrawal of an authorisation in accordance with this Regulation shall take effect on the date specified in the notice which shall be not earlier than 28 days after the date of the notice.

    (4) Where an authorisation is withdrawn in accordance with this Regulation it shall be of no effect and the holder shall forthwith surrender the authorisation to the Secretary of State.

    (5) At any time that is reasonable having regard to the circumstances of the case, an examiner may, on production if so required of his authority, enter any premises of the holder of an authorisation which has been withdrawn in accordance with this Regulation and may require the holder to produce the authorisation and, on its being produced, may seize it and deliver it to the Secretary of State.

    (6) Where it appears to an examiner that a document produced to him in pursuance of Regulation 16 is an authorisation which has been withdrawn in accordance with this Regulation he may seize it and deliver it to the Secretary of State.

    (7) In paragraph (1) of this Regulation "relevant Council Regulation" means in the case of a regular or special regular service authorisation Council Regulation No 517/72 and in the case of a shuttle service authorisation Council Regulation No 516/72.

Penalty for contravention of ASOR, the Council Regulations or the Commission Regulation

4–2259   **19.** (1) A person is guilty of an offence under this Regulation if without reasonable excuse, he uses a vehicle for Community regulated carriage of passengers by road or causes or permits such a vehicle to be used—

    (a)   to provide a service for the carriage of passengers such as is mentioned in Article 1 of Council Regulation No 117/66 (that is to say, a regular service or a special regular service as defined in that Article), not being, in either such case, a service such as is mentioned in Article 6 of that Regulation, otherwise than under and in accordance with the terms of an authorisation issued under Article 2 of Council Regulation No 517/72; or

    (b)   to provide a service for the carriage of passengers such as is mentioned in Article 2 of Council Regulation No 117/66 (that is to say, a shuttle service as defined in that Article), not being a service such as is mentioned in Article 6 of that Regulation, otherwise than under and in accordance with the terms of an authorisation issued under Article 2 of Council Regulation No 516/72; or

    (c)   to provide a service for the carriage of passengers such as is mentioned in Article 6 of Council Regulation No 117/66 (that is to say, a service provided by an undertaking for its own workers in relation to which the conditions mentioned in paragraph 1(a) and (b) of that Article are fulfilled) without there being in force in relation to the service a certificate issued under Article 1 of Commission Regulation No 1016/68.

    (2) A person shall be guilty of an offence under this Regulation if, without reasonable excuse, he uses a vehicle for ASOR regulated or Community regulated carriage by road, or causes or permits a vehicle to be so used, to provide a service for the carriage of passengers such as is mentioned in paragraph 1 of, Article 2 of ASOR or Article 3 of Council Regulation No 117/66 when there is not duly and correctly completed for the vehicle a passenger waybill, or when the top copy of the passenger waybill is not kept on the vehicle throughout the journey to which it refers, as required, in the case of a vehicle being used for ASOR regulated carriage, by Articles 7 and 8 of ASOR and, in the case of a vehicle being used for Community regulated carriage, by Articles 2 and 3 of Council Regulation No 1016/68.

    (3) A person guilty of an offence under this Regulation shall be liable on summary conviction to a fine not exceeding **£400**.

Penalty relating to documents required in respect of ASOR and Community regulated services

4–2260   **20.** A person who—

    (a)   without reasonable excuse contravenes, or fails to comply with a requirement imposed by or under Regulation 15(4) or (5), 16(2)(a), 17(1) or (2), or 18(4) or (5), or by or under any provision of ASOR, the Council Regulations or the Commission Regulation referred to in any of those provisions; or

    (b)   wilfully obstructs an examiner in the exercise of his powers under Regulation 16(2), 17(1) or (2), or 18(5) or (6), or under any provision of ASOR, the Council Regulations or Commission Regulation referred to in any of those provisions

shall be liable on summary conviction to a fine not exceeding **£400**.

Forgery and false statements, etc

4–2261   **21.** In sections 65(1)(a) (forgery) and 66(a) (false statements) of the Act of 1981 the references to a licence under any Part of that Act shall include references to an authorisation, certificate or other document required by ASOR, any of the Council Regulations or the Commission Regulation, or by these Regulations, or by the Act of 1981 as modified by these Regulations, to be in force in relation to a vehicle, or to be kept or carried on a vehicle, used for the international carriage of passengers.

Disapplication of requirements as to fitness, equipment type approval and certification of public service vehicles

4–2262   23. None of the provisions of Parts II, III, IV and V of the Public Service Vehicles (Conditions of Fitness, Equipment Use and Certification) Regulations 1981 shall have effect in relation to a vehicle to which any provision of Part III of these Regulations applies or to a vehicle registered in Northern Ireland to which any provision of Part II of these Regulations applies.

Public Service Vehicles (Carrying Capacity) Regulations 1984[1]
(SI 1984/1406 amended by SI 1996/167)

4–2271   1, 2. *Commencement, citation, revocation.*

1. These regulations are made under ss 26(1) and 60(1) of the Public Passenger Vehicles Act 1981 by the Secretary of State for Transport.

Interpretation

4–2272   3. (1) In these Regulations—

"the Act" means the Public Passenger Vehicles Act 1981;
"certificate of conformity" means a certificate issued in pursuance of section 10(2) of the Act;
"certificate of initial fitness" has the same meaning as in section 6(1) of the Act;
"certifying officer" has the same meaning as in section 7(1) of the Act;
"crew seat", "deck", "double-decked vehicle", "gangway" and "half-decked vehicle" have the meanings given to those expressions in Regulation 3(1) of the Public Service Vehicles (Conditions of Fitness, Equipment, Use and Certification) Regulations 1981; and
"vehicle" means a public service vehicle to which section 1(1)(a) of the Act applies.

(2) Unless the context otherwise requires, any reference in these Regulations to—

(a) a numbered Regulation is a reference to the Regulation of these Regulations bearing that number;
(b) a numbered paragraph is a reference to the paragraph bearing that number in the Regulation in which the reference appears.

Maximum seating capacity

4–2273   4. (1) Save as provided in paragraph (2), the maximum seating capacity of a vehicle is—

(a) in a case where on or after 1st April 1981 there is issued in respect of the vehicle a certificate of initial fitness or a certificate of conformity either—
(i) the seating capacity specified in such certificate, or
(ii) such greater or lesser capacity than that so specified as is authorised by a certifying officer either pursuant to a notification under Regulation 9 or otherwise;
(b) in a case where no certificate of a kind mentioned in sub-paragraph (a) is issued on or after 1st April 1981, either—
(i) the seating capacity calculated in accordance with Regulation 42 of the Road Vehicles (Registration and Licensing) Regulations 1971[1], whether or not the vehicle is one to which that Regulation applies; or
(ii) such greater or lesser capacity than that so calculated as is authorised by a certifying officer either pursuant to a notification under Regulation 9 or otherwise.

(2) The maximum seating capacity of a vehicle as mentioned in paragraph (1) does not include a driver's seat or a crew seat.

1. See now the Road Vehicles (Registration and Licensing) Regulations 2002, reg 44, in this PART, post.

Carriage of seated passengers

4–2274   5. (1) Save as provided in paragraph (2), no person shall drive, or cause or permit to be driven, on a road a vehicle if the number of seated passengers exceeds the number of seats available for passengers.
(2) For the purposes of paragraph (1)—
(a) a child under 5 years of age who is not occupying a seat does not count as a passenger; and
(b) subject to sub-paragraph (a) above, three seated children each of whom is under 14 years of age and none of whom are occupying a seat provided with a seat belt shall count as two passengers.

(3) In this Regulation "seat belt" has the meaning given in regulation 47 of the Road Vehicles (Construction and Use) Regulations 1986.

(4) For the purposes of this Regulation, in relation to a continuous seat which is designed for the accommodation of more than one adult, each part of the seat which is designed to accommodate one adult shall be regarded as a separate seat.

(5) For the purposes of this Regulation, a child shall be deemed to be under 14 years of age until the last day of August following his fourteenth birthday.

Maximum standing capacity

4–2275 **6.** (1) Save as provided in paragraph (2), the maximum standing capacity of a vehicle is—

(a) in a case where on or after 1st April 1981 there is issued in respect of the vehicle a certificate of initial fitness or a certificate of conformity, either—

    (i) the number of standing passengers specified in such certificate, or

    (ii) such greater or lesser number than that so specified as is authorised by a certifying officer either pursuant to a notification under Regulation 9 or otherwise;

(b) in a case where no certificate of a kind mentioned in sub-paragraph (a) is issued on or after 1st April 1981, either—

    (i) one third of the number of passengers for which the vehicle, or, in the case of a double-deck vehicle, the lower deck, has seating capacity, or 8, whichever is the less; or

    (ii) such greater or lesser number than that mentioned in sub-paragraph (i) as is authorised by a certifying officer either pursuant to a notification under Regulation 9 or otherwise.

(2) The maximum standing capacity of—

(a) a vehicle with a seating capacity for less than 13 passengers,

(b) a vehicle with a gangway any part of the height of which is less than 1·77 metres, and

(c) a half-decked vehicle

is nil.

Carriage of standing passengers

4–2276 **7.** (1) No person shall drive, or cause or permit to be driven, on a road a vehicle if the number of standing passengers exceeds the maximum specified in relation to that vehicle in Regulation 6.

(2) No person shall stand on—

(a) the upper deck or on any step leading to the upper deck of any double-decked vehicle,

(b) any part of a gangway of a vehicle forward of the rearmost part of the driver's seat; or

(c) any part of a vehicle in which the operator has indicated by a notice, the letters on which are at least 10 millimetres tall and in a colour contrasting with the colour of their background, that no standing shall occur.

Markings on vehicles

4–2277 **8.** The operator of a vehicle shall mark on the inside of the vehicle with letters not less than 25 millimetres in height, in a colour contrasting with the colour of their background, and which may be read from inside or outside the vehicle—

(a)

    (i) the maximum seating capacity of the vehicle as specified in Regulation 4, or, if it be less and the operator so wishes,

    (ii) the number of passenger seats with which the vehicle is fitted; and

(b)

    (i) the standing capacity (be it nil or otherwise) of the vehicle as specified in Regulation 6, or, if it be less,

    (ii) the number of standing passengers which the operator of the vehicle is willing to have on the vehicle.

Notification of increase of seating or standing capacity

4–2278 **9.** Any person who increases the seating or standing capacity of a vehicle which is being used by virtue of a PSV operator's licence shall, when the increase occurs, in writing notify the traffic commissioners who granted that licence of the increase, and the vehicle shall not be used on a road as a public service vehicle after such increase has been made until such notification has been made and a certificate has been issued in pursuance of such notice.

Forms of certificate

4–2279 **10.** Any authorisation of a kind mentioned in Regulation 4(1)(a)(ii) or (b)(ii) issued on or after 4th October 1984 and any authorisation of a kind mentioned in Regulation 6(1)(a)(ii) or (b)(ii) issued on or after 4th October 1984 shall be in writing and signed and dated by the person giving the authorisation.

Exemptions

4–2280 **11.** Nothing in these Regulations applies to a vehicle to which Part III of the Road Transport (International Passenger Services) Regulations 1980 or the Road Transport (Northern Ireland Passenger Services) Regulations 1980 applies.

4–2281 **12.** *Appeals from refusal or grant of certificate under regs 4 and 6.*

Community Drivers' Hours Regulations
Harmonisation of Certain Social Legislation Relating to Road Transport[1]
(Regulation (EEC) 3820/85)

SECTION I
DEFINITIONS

4–2291   Article 1. In this Regulation:

1. "carriage by road" means any journey made on roads open to the public[2] of a vehicle, whether laden or not, used for the carriage of passengers or goods;

2. "vehicles" means motor vehicles, tractors, trailers and semi-trailers, defined as follows:

   (a) "motor vehicle": any mechanically self-propelled vehicle circulating on the road, other than a vehicle running on rails, and normally used for carrying passengers or goods;

   (b) "tractor": any mechanically self-propelled vehicle circulating on the road, other than a vehicle running on rails, and specially designed to pull, push or move trailers, semi-trailers, implements or machines;

   (c) "trailer": any vehicle designed to be coupled to a motor vehicle or a tractor;

   (d) "semi-trailer": a trailer without a front axle coupled in such a way that a substantial part of its weight and of the weight of its load is borne by the tractor or motor vehicle;

3. "driver" means any person who drives the vehicle even for a short period, or who is carried in the vehicle in order to be available for driving if necessary[3];

4. "week" means the period between 00.00 hours on Monday and 24.00 hours on Sunday;

5. "rest" means any uninterrupted period of at least one hour during which the driver may freely dispose of his time;

6. "permissible maximum weight"[4] means the maximum authorized operating weight of the vehicle fully laden;

7. "regular passenger services" means national and international services as defined in Article 1 of Council Regulation No 117/66/EEC of 28 July 1966 on the introduction of common rules for the international carriage of passengers by coach and bus[5].

---

1. This is a Regulation of the Council of the European Communities and contravention of its provisions is punishable under s 96(11A) of the Transport Act 1968 by a fine not exceeding **level 4** on the standard scale. In so far as any contravention relates to books, records or documents it will be punishable by the same maximum fine under s 98(4) of the Act. Exemptions and modifications are given in the Community Drivers' Hours and Recording Equipment (Exemptions and Supplementary Provisions) Regulations 1986, SI 1986/1456 amended by SI 1986/1669, SI 1987/805, SI 1988/760 and SI 2006/3276.

2. The expression "roads open to the public" means roads to which the public has access (*DPP v Cargo Handling Ltd* [1992] RTR 318).

3. Employees of a coach company who travelled as passengers with the purpose of taking over the driving at an appropriate point later in the journey where they were due to take over the driving but were drivers within the meaning of art 1(3) and were obliged to record the time they were carried on the coach but not driving (*Vehicle Inspectorate v Southern Coaches Ltd* (1999) 164 JP 492, [2000] RTR 165, [2000] Crim LR 595, DC).

4. The expression "permissible maximum weight" in the case of a motor vehicle which is not itself an articulated goods vehicle but is drawing a trailer, relates to the aggregate of the relevant maximum weight of the vehicle and the relevant maximum weight of the trailer. The relevant maximum weight of the vehicle and of the trailer relates to the maximum gross weight which is marked upon the vehicle that is towing and marked, in cases where it is required to be marked, on the trailer which is being towed, and it does not relate to the maximum train weight (*Small v DPP* [1995] RTR 95, [1995] Crim LR 165). See also *Laverick v DPP* [1999] RTR 417.

5. The definition provides that "regular services are services which provide for the carriage of passengers at specified intervals along specified routes, passengers being taken up and set down at predetermined stopping points".

SECTION II
SCOPE

4–2292   Article 2. 1. This Regulation applies to carriage by road, as defined in Article 1(1), within the Community.

2. The European Agreement concerning the Work of Crews of Vehicles engaged in International Road Transport (AETR) shall apply instead of the present rules to international road transport operations:

   —to and/or from third countries which are Contracting Parties to the Agreement, or in transit through such countries, for the whole of the journey where such operations are carried out by vehicles registered in a Member State or in one of the said third countries;

   —to and/or from a third country which is not a Contracting Party to the Agreement in the case of any journey made within the Community where such operations are carried out by vehicles registered in one of those countries.

Article 3. The Community shall enter into any negotiations with third countries which may prove necessary for the purpose of implementing this Regulation.

Article 4. This Regulation shall not apply to carriage by[1]:

1. vehicles used for the carriage of goods where the maximum permissible weight of the vehicle, including any trailer or semi-trailer, does not exceed 3·5 tonnes[2];

2. vehicles used for the carriage of passengers which, by virtue of their construction and

equipment, are suitable for carrying not more than nine persons, including the driver, and are intended for that purpose;

3. vehicles used for the carriage of passengers on regular services[3] where the route covered by the service in question does not exceed 50 kilometres;

4. vehicles with a maximum authorized speed not exceeding 30 kilometres per hour;

5. vehicles used by or under the control of the armed services, civil defence, fire services, and forces responsible for maintaining public order;

6. vehicles used in connection with the sewerage, flood protection, water[4], gas[5] and electricity services, highway maintenance[6] and control, refuse collection and disposal[7], telegraph and telephone services, carriage of postal articles, radio and television broadcasting and the detection of radio or television transmitters or receivers;

7. vehicles used in emergencies or rescue operations;

8. specialized vehicles used for medical purposes;

9. vehicles transporting circus and fun-fair equipment[8];

10. specialized breakdown vehicles[9];

11. vehicles undergoing road tests for technical development, repair or maintenance purposes, and new or rebuilt vehicles which have not yet been put into service;

12. vehicles used for non-commercial carriage of goods for personal use;

13. vehicles used for milk collections from farms and the return to farms of milk containers or milk products.

---

1. It should be noted that the vehicles which are exempted under art 4 are types of vehicle rather than individual vehicles according to their use on a particular occasion (*DPP v Guy* (1997) 161 JP 727, [1998] RTR 82).

2. This exemption did not cover a pick up vehicle with a plated weight of 3.4 tonnes which was towing a single axle hoist with an unladen weight of 950K; a purposive approach required that the aggregate weight be taken: *Pritchard v DPP* [2003] EWHC 1851 (Admin), [2004] RTR 355.

3. A passenger transport service, supplied on a number of occasions pursuant to a block reservation made by a tour operator and providing for a single journey from an airport to an hotel with a stop, on occasions, at a tourist attraction where the precise route to be taken was not predetermined, was held not to constitute a regular service within the meaning of art 4(3) (*Clarke (E) and Son (Coaches) Ltd and D J Ferne* (Case No C–47/97) [1998] ECR I-2147, [1998] RTR 333).

4. This applies to a vehicle used for winch and lifting work in connection with drilling water wells (*DPP v Ryan* (1991) 155 JP 456).

5. All the services, envisaged by art 4(6), are general services performed in the public interest. Accordingly, it has been held that the provision applies solely to vehicles used, at the relevant time, for carriage wholly and exclusively in connection with the production, transport or distribution of gas, or the maintenance of the necessary installations for that purpose. It does not apply to vehicles wholly or partly used at the relevant time in connection with the carriage of domestic gas appliances (*Licensing Authority South Eastern Traffic Area v British Gas plc—Case C-116/91—*[1992] ECR I-4071, 158 JP 606).

6. A transporter lorry which carried a line marking machine 35 miles to the site of road marking operations was not being used in connection with "highway maintenance and control" even though when it arrived at the site it would be used in conjunction with the line marking machine to mark the road as a guide to indicate the position of the line to be painted: *Lewis v Moss* (1998) Times, 23 March, DC; see also *Vehicle Inspectorate v Bruce Cook Road Planing Ltd* [1999] 4 All ER 761, HL, [2000] RTR 90, 164 JP 415 (a tipper lorry and trailer which were being used to transport a road planting machine, which could not be driven independently, to a site so that it could be operated, was held not to be within the exemption for vehicles used in connection with highway maintenance).

7. The concept of 'vehicles used in connection with . . . refuse collection and disposal' is to be interpreted as covering vehicles used for the collection of waste of all kinds which is not subject to more specific rules and for the transportation of such waste over short distances, within the context of a general service in the public interest provided directly by public authorities or by private undertakings under their control (*Re Mrozek and Jager* C-335/94; *Re Goupil* C-39/95 [1997] RTR 238, EC). A lorry equipped with tachograph recording equipment which was used in the course of a commercial business solely for the delivery and collection of builders' skips is not within art 4(6) (*Swain v McCaul* [1997] RTR 102, DC).

8. This exemption is restricted to vehicles used to transport equipment currently employed in a circus or funfair; accordingly, a tent used for a music festival was held not to constitute "circus equipment" (*Creek v Fossett, Eccles and Supertents Ltd* [1986] Crim LR 256).

9. A specialised breakdown vehicle should be regarded as a vehicle which is specially built or adapted, and kept, for the purpose of going to the assistance of a broken down vehicle and which generally, has the capability, for this purpose, of raising a broken down vehicle (wholly or partially) with a view to its recovery either by conveyance on, or by towing behind, the breakdown vehicle. This description should not be regarded as a precise definition but rather as a working description which can, if necessary, be refined in the light of experience (*Universal Salvage Ltd v Boothby* [1984] RTR 289). It means a vehicle whose construction, fitments or other permanent characteristics were such that it would be used mainly for removing vehicles that had recently been involved in an accident or had broken down for another reason; such a vehicle is exempt whatever use is made of it by its owner (*Hamilton v Whitelock*: 79/86 [1987] 3 CMLR 190, [1988] RTR 23, ECJ).

SECTION III
CREW

4–2293   **Article 5. 1.** The minimum ages[1] for drivers engaged in the carriage of goods shall be as follows:

    (a)   for vehicles, including, where appropriate, trailers or semi-trailers, having a permissible maximum weight of not more than 7·5 tonnes, 18 years;

    (b)   for other vehicles:

         —21 years, or

         —18 years provided that the person concerned holds a certificate of professional competence recognized by one of the Member States confirming that he has completed a training course for drivers of vehicles intended for the carriage of goods by road, in conformity with Community rules on the minimum level of training for road transport drivers.

2. Any driver engaged in the carriage of passengers shall have reached the age[1] of 21 years.

Any driver engaged in the carriage of passengers on journeys beyond a 50 kilometre radius from the place where the vehicle is normally based must also fulfil one of the following conditions:

(a) he must have worked for at least one year in the carriage of goods as a driver of vehicles with a permissible maximum weight exceeding 3·5 tonnes;

(b) he must have worked for at least one year as a driver of vehicles used to provide passenger services on journeys within a 50 kilometre radius from the place where the vehicle is normally based, or other types of passenger services not subject to this Regulation, provided the competent authority considers that he has by so doing acquired the necessary experience;

(c) he must hold a certificate of professional competence recognized by one of the Member States confirming that he has completed a training course for drivers of vehicles intended for the carriage of passengers by road, in conformity with Community rules on the minimum level of training for road transport drivers.

3. The minimum age for drivers' mates and conductors shall be 18 years.

4. A driver engaged in the carriage of passengers shall not be subject to the conditions laid down in paragraph 2, second subparagraph, (a), (b) and (c) if he has carried on that occupation for at least one year prior to 1 October 1970.

5. In the case of internal transport operations carried out within a 50 kilometre radius of the place where the vehicle is based, including local administrative areas the centres of which are situated within that radius, Member States may reduce the minimum age for drivers' mates to 16 years, on condition that this is for purposes of vocational training and subject to the limits imposed by their national law on employment matters.

---

1. See modification of paras 1 and 2 of art 5 in the Motor Vehicles (Minimum Age for Driving) (Community Rules) Regulations 1975, post.

SECTION IV
DRIVING PERIODS

4–2294   Article 6. 1. The driving period between any two daily rest periods or between a daily rest period and a weekly rest period, hereinafter called "daily driving period", shall not exceed nine hours. It may be extended twice in any one week to 10 hours.

A driver must, after[1] no more than six daily[2] driving periods, take a weekly rest period as defined in Article 8(3).

The weekly rest period may be postponed until the end of the sixth day[2] if the total driving time over the six days does not exceed the maximum corresponding to six daily driving periods.

In the case of the international carriage of passengers, other than on regular services, the terms "six" and "sixth" in the second and third subparagraphs shall be replaced by "twelve" and "twelfth" respectively.

Member States may extend the application of the previous subparagraph to national passenger services within their territory, other than regular services.

2. The total period of driving in any one fortnight shall not exceed 90 hours.

---

1. A "day" is any period of 24 hours beginning with a driver's resumption of driving after his last weekly rest period, not a fixed 24-hour period beginning at midnight (*Kelly v Shulman* [1989] 1 All ER 106, [1988] 1 WLR 1134, [1989] RTR 84, DC).

2. The weekly rest obligation arises after the period of driving. Where, in the case of international carriage of passengers other than on regular services, the weekly rest period is postponed for twelve days, and a rest period has straddled the beginning of the initial week, art 8.4 does not operate so as to permit a rest period of 36 hours taken before driving began to relieve the operator of any longer period at the end of the second week than 36 hours (*Vehicle Inspectorate v York Pullman Ltd* [2001] RTR 273).

SECTION V
BREAKS AND REST PERIODS

4–2295   Article 7. 1[1]. After four-and-a-half hours' driving, the driver shall observe a break of at least 45 minutes, unless he begins a rest period.

2[1]. This break may be replaced by breaks of at least 15 minutes each distributed over the driving period or immediately after this period in such a way as to comply with the provisions of paragraph 1.

3. By way of exception from paragraph 1, in the case of national carriage of passengers on regular services Member States may fix the minimum break at not less than 30 minutes after a driving period not exceeding four hours. Such exceptions may be granted only in cases where breaks in driving of over 30 minutes could hamper the flow of urban traffic and where it is not possible for drivers to take a 15-minute break within four-and-a-half hours of driving prior to a 30-minute break.

4. During these breaks, the driver may not carry out any other work. For the purposes of this Article, the waiting time and time not devoted to driving spent in a vehicle in motion, a ferry, or a train shall not be regarded as "other work".

5. The breaks observed under this article may not be regarded as daily rest periods.

1. Article 7(1) and (2) is to be interpreted as prohibiting drivers to which it applies from driving continuously for more than $4^1/_2$ hours. But where a driver has taken 45 minutes break either as a single break or as several breaks of at least 15 minutes during or at the end of a $4^1/_2$-hour period, the calculation provided for by art 7(1) of the regulation should begin afresh, without taking into account the driving time and breaks previously completed by the driver. The calculation under art 7(1) begins at the moment when the driver sets in motion the recording equipment provided for by Council Regulation (EEC) No 3821/85 of 20 December 1985 on recording equipment in road transport and begins driving (Case C-116/92 *Charlton v DPP* (1993) 158 JP 766 [1994] RTR 133, ECJ).

4-2295A   Article 8. 1. In each period of 24 hours, the driver shall have a daily rest period of at least 11 consecutive hours, which may be reduced to a minimum of nine consecutive hours not more than three times in any one week, on condition that an equivalent period of rest be granted as compensation before the end of the following week.

On days when the rest is not reduced in accordance with the first subparagraph, it may be taken in two or three separate periods during the 24-hour period, one of which must be of at least eight consecutive hours. In this case the minimum length of the rest shall be increased to 12 hours.

2. During each period of 30 hours when a vehicle is manned[1] by at least two drivers, each driver shall have a rest period of not less than eight consecutive hours.

3. In the course of each week, one of the rest periods referred to in paragraphs 1 and 2 shall be extended, by way of weekly rest, to a total of 45 consecutive hours. This rest period may be reduced to a minimum of 36 consecutive hours if taken at the place where the vehicle is normally based or where the driver is based, or to a minimum of 24 consecutive hours if taken elsewhere. Each reduction shall be compensated by an equivalent rest taken *en bloc* before the end of the third week following the week in question.

4. A weekly rest period which begins in one week and continues into the following week may be attached to either of these weeks.

5. In the case of the carriage of passengers to which Article 6(1), fourth or fifth subparagraph, applies, the weekly rest period may be postponed until the week following that in respect of which the rest is due and added on to that second week's weekly rest.

6. Any rest taken as compensation for the reduction of the daily and/or weekly rest periods must be attached to another rest of at least eight hours and shall be granted, at the request of the person concerned, at the vehicle's parking place or driver's base.

7. The daily rest period may be taken in a vehicle, as long as it is fitted with a bunk and is stationary[2].

1. This demands the presence of two drivers on the vehicle while it is in motion (*Williams v Boyd* [1986] RTR 185).
2. Accordingly the period spent by an employee of a coach firm as a passenger on a coach he was due to drive from a stage later in the journey, was not a rest period for the purposes of this article (*Vehicle Inspectorate v Southern Coaches Ltd* (1999) 164 JP 492, [2000] RTR 165, [2000] Crim LR 595, DC).

4-2295B   Article 9. Notwithstanding Article 8(1) where a driver engaged in the carriage of goods or passengers accompanies a vehicle which is transported by ferryboat or train, the daily rest period may be interrupted not more than once, provided the following conditions are fulfilled:

— that part of the daily rest period spent on land must be able to be taken before or after the portion of the daily rest period taken on board the ferryboat or the train,
— the period between the two portions of the daily rest period must be as short as possible and may on no account exceed one hour before embarkation or after disembarkation, customs formalities being included in the embarkation or disembarkation operations,
— during both portions of the rest period the driver must be able to have access to a bunk or couchette.

The daily rest period, interrupted in this way, shall be increased by two hours.

SECTION VI
PROHIBITION OF CERTAIN TYPES OF PAYMENT

4-2296   Article 10. Payments to wage-earning drivers, even in the form of bonuses or wage supplements, related to distances travelled and/or the amount of goods carried shall be prohibited, unless these payments are of such a kind as not to endanger road safety.

SECTION VII
EXCEPTIONS

4-2297   Article 11. Each Member may apply higher minima or lower maxima than those laid down in Articles 5 to 8 inclusive. Nevertheless, the provisions of this Regulation shall remain applicable to drivers engaged in international transport operations on vehicles registered in another Member State.

Article 12. Provided that road safety is not thereby jeopardized and to enable him to reach a suitable stopping place, the driver may depart from the provisions of this Regulation to the extent necessary to ensure the safety of persons, of the vehicle or of its load. The driver shall indicate the nature of and reason for his departure from those provisions on the record sheet of the recording equipment or in his duty roster[1].

1. Article 12 does not authorise a driver to derogate from the provisions of arts 6, 7 or 8 of the Regulations for reasons known before the journey was commenced (*R v Bird* [1996] RTR 49, ECJ).

4–2297A   Article 13. 1. *Member States may grant exemptions for specified operations*[1].

2. Member States may, after authorization by the Commission, grant exceptions from the application of the provisions of this Regulation to transport operations carried out in exceptional circumstances, if such exceptions do not seriously jeopardize the objectives of the Regulation.

In urgent cases they may grant a temporary exception[2] for a period not exceeding 30 days, which shall be notified immediately to the Commission.

The Commission shall notify the other Member State of any exception granted pursuant to this Regulation.

1. See the Community Drivers' Hours and Recording Equipment (Exemptions and Supplementary Provisions) Regulations in this PART, post.
2. Various Community Drivers' Hours (Temporary Exception) Regulations have been made.

SECTION VIII
CONTROL PROCEDURES AND PENALTIES

4–2298   Article 14. 1. In the case of:

— regular national passenger services, and
— regular international passenger services whose route terminals are located within a distance of 50 kilometres as the crow flies from a frontier between two Member States and whose route length does not exceed 100 kilometres,

which are subject to this Regulation, a service timetable and a duty roster shall be drawn up by the undertaking.

2. The duty roster shall show, in respect of each driver, the name, place where based and the schedule laid down in advance for various periods of driving, other work and availability.

3. The duty roster shall include all the particulars specified in paragraph 2 for a minimum period covering both the current week and the weeks immediately preceding and following that week.

4. The duty roster shall be signed by the head of the undertaking or by a person authorized to represent him.

5. Each driver assigned to a service referred to in paragraph 1 shall carry an extract from the duty roster and a copy of the service timetable.

6. The duty roster shall be kept by the undertaking for one year after expiry of the period covered. The undertaking shall give an extract from the roster to the drivers concerned who request it.

7. This Article shall not apply to the drivers of vehicles fitted with recording equipment used in accordance with the provisions of Council Regulation (EEC) No 3821/85 of 20 December 1985 on recording equipment in road transport.

Article 15. 1. The transport undertaking shall organize drivers' work in such a way that drivers are able to comply with the relevant provisions of this Regulation and of Regulation (EEC) No 3821/85.

2. The undertaking shall make periodic checks[1] to ensure that the provisions of these two Regulations have been complied with. If breaches are found to have occurred, the undertaking shall take appropriate steps to prevent their repetition.

1. This necessarily imposes a duty on the owner to take reasonable steps (although it is not clear whether the prosecution must also prove that the defendant must have perceived the possibility that the rules might be contravened) (*Vehicle Inspectorate v Nuttall* [1999] 3 All ER 833, [1999] 1 WLR 629, [1999] RTR 264, HL).

Community Recording Equipment Regulations Recording Equipment in Road Transport[1]

(Regulation (EEC) 3821/85)

CHAPTER I
PRINCIPLES AND SCOPE

4–2311   Article 1. Recording equipment within the meaning of this Regulation shall, as regards construction, installation, use and testing, comply with the requirements of this Regulation and of Annexes I and II thereto, which shall form an integral part of this Regulation.

Article 2. For the purposes of this Regulation the definitions set out in Article 1 of Regulation (EEC) No 3820/85 shall apply.

Article 3. 1. Recording equipment shall be installed and used in vehicles registered in a Member State which are used[2] for the carriage of passengers or goods by road, except the vehicles referred to in Articles 4 and 14(1) of Regulation (EEC) No 3820/85.

2. Member States may exempt[3] vehicles mentioned in Article 13(1) of Regulation (EEC) No 3820/85 from application of this Regulation. Member States shall inform the Commission of any exemption granted under this paragraph.

3. Member States may, after authorization by the Commission, exempt from application of this Regulation vehicles used for the transport operations referred to in Article 13(2) of Regulation

(EEC) No 3820/85. In urgent cases they may grant a temporary exemption for a period not exceeding 30 days, which shall be notified immediately to the Commission. The Commission shall notify the other Member States of any exemption granted pursuant to this paragraph.

4. In the case of national transport operations, Member States may require the installation and use of recording equipment in accordance with this Regulation in any of the vehicles for which its installation and use are not required by paragraph 1.

---

1. This is a Regulation of the Council of the European Communities and contravention of its provisions is punishable under s 97 of the Transport Act 1968 by a fine not exceeding **level 5** on the standard scale. Under art 3 of the Regulation, Member States may grant certain exemptions from the application of the Regulation; for such exemptions see the Community Drivers' Hours and Recording Equipment (Exemptions and Supplementary Provisions) Regulations 1986, post.

2. Subject to the exceptions in EEC 3820/85, liability is attached to vehicles 'constructed or adapted for use for the carriage of passengers or goods by road' not, 'actually used' for that purpose. Therefore a tractor unit being driven to docks for the purpose of export was required to be fitted with a tachograph (*Vehicle Services Operations Agency v North Leicester Vehicle Movements Ltd* [2003] EWHC 2638 (Admin), 168 JP 285, [2004] RTR 449).

3. See the Community Drivers' Hours and Recording Equipment (Exemptions and Supplementary Provisions) Regulations 1986, post.

CHAPTER II
TYPE APPROVAL

4–2312   Article 4. Applications for EEC approval of a type of recording equipment or of a model record sheet shall be submitted, accompanied by the appropriate specifications, by the manufacturer or his agent to a Member State. No application in respect of any one type of recording equipment or of any one model record sheet may be submitted to more than one Member State.

Article 5. A Member State shall grant EEC approval to any type of recording equipment or to any model record sheet which conforms to the requirements laid down in Annex I to this Regulation, provided the Member State is in a position to check that production models conform to the approved prototype.

Any modifications or additions to an approved model must receive additional EEC type approval from the Member State which granted the original EEC type approval.

Article 6. Member States shall issue to the applicant an EEC approval mark, which shall conform to the model shown in Annex II, for each type of recording equipment or model record sheet which they approve pursuant to Article 5.

Article 7. The competent authorities of the Member State to which the application for type approval has been submitted shall, in respect of each type of recording equipment or model record sheet which they approve or refuse, either send within one month to the authorities of the other Member States a copy of the approval certificate accompanied by copies of the relevant specifications, or, if such is the case, notify those authorities that approval has been refused; in cases of refusal they shall communicate the reasons for their decision.

Article 8. 1. If a Member State which has granted EEC type approval as provided for in Article 5 finds that certain recording equipment or record sheets bearing the EEC type approval mark which it has issued do not conform to the prototype which it has approved, it shall take the necessary measures to ensure that production models conform to the approved prototype. The measures taken may, if necessary, extend to withdrawal of EEC type approval.

2. A Member State which has granted EEC type approval shall withdraw such approval if the recording equipment or record sheet which has been approved is not in conformity with this Regulation or its Annexes or displays in use any general defect which makes it unsuitable for the purpose for which it is intended.

3. If a Member State which has granted EEC type approval is notified by another Member State of one of the cases referred to in paragraphs 1 and 2, it shall also, after consulting the latter Member State, take the steps laid down in those paragraphs, subject to paragraph 5.

4. A Member State which ascertains that one of the cases referred to in paragraph 2 has arisen may forbid until further notice the placing on the market and putting into service of the recording equipment or record sheets. The same applies in the cases mentioned in paragraph 1 with respect to recording equipment or record sheets which have been exempted from EEC initial verification, if the manufacturer, after due warning, does not bring the equipment into line with the approved model or with the requirements of this Regulation.

In any event, the competent authorities of the Member States shall notify one another and the Commission, within one month, of any withdrawal of EEC type approval or of any other measures taken pursuant to paragraphs 1, 2 and 3 and shall specify the reasons for such action.

5. If a Member State which has granted an EEC type approval disputes the existence of any of the cases specified in paragraphs 1 or 2 notified to it, the Member States concerned shall endeavour to settle the dispute and the Commission shall be kept informed.

If talks between the Member States have not resulted in agreement within four months of the date of the notification referred to in paragraph 3 above, the Commission, after consulting experts from all Member States and having considered all the relevant factors, eg economic and technical factors, shall within six months adopt a decision which shall be communicated to the Member States concerned and at the same time to the other Member States. The Commission shall lay down in each instance the time limit for implementation of its decision.

Article 9. 1. An applicant for EEC type approval of a model record sheet shall state on his application the type or types of recording equipment on which the sheet in question is designed to be used and shall provide suitable equipment of such type or types for the purpose of testing the sheet.

2. The competent authorities of each Member State shall indicate on the approval certificate for the model record sheet the type or types of recording equipment on which that model sheet may be used.

Article 10. No Member State may refuse to register any vehicle fitted with recording equipment, or prohibit the entry into service or use of such vehicle for any reason connected with the fact that the vehicle is fitted with such equipment, if the equipment bears the EEC approval mark referred to in Article 6 and the installation plaque referred to in Article 12.

Article 11. All decisions pursuant to this Regulation refusing or withdrawing approval of a type of recording equipment or model record sheet shall specify in detail the reasons on which they are based. A decision shall be communicated to the party concerned, who shall at the same time be informed of the remedies available to him under the laws of the Member States and of the time-limits for the exercise of such remedies.

CHAPTER III
INSTALLATION AND INSPECTION

4–2313 Article 12. 1. Recording equipment may be installed or repaired only by fitters or workshops approved by the competent authorities of Member States for that purpose after the latter, should they so desire, have heard the views of the manufacturers concerned.

2. The approved fitter or workshop shall place a special mark on the seals which it affixes. The competent authorities of each Member State shall maintain a register of the marks used.

3. The competent authorities of the Member States shall send each other their lists of approved fitters or workshops and also copies of the marks used.

4. For the purpose of certifying that installation of recording equipment took place in accordance with the requirements of this Regulation an installation plaque affixed as provided in Annex I shall be used.

CHAPTER IV
USE OF EQUIPMENT

4–2314 Article 13. The employer and drivers shall be responsible for seeing that the equipment functions correctly.

Article 14. 1. The employer[1] shall issue a sufficient number of record sheets to drivers, bearing in mind the fact that these sheets are personal in character, the length of the period of service and the possible obligation to replace sheets which are damaged, or have been taken by an authorized inspecting officer. The employer shall issue to drivers only sheets of an approved model suitable for use in the equipment installed in the vehicle.

2. The undertaking shall keep the record sheets in good order for at least a year after their use and shall give copies to the drivers concerned who request them. The sheets shall be produced or handed over at the request of any authorized inspecting officer.

Article 15. 1. Drivers shall not use dirty or damaged record sheets. The sheets shall be adequately protected on this account.

In case of damage to a sheet bearing recordings, drivers shall attach the damaged sheet to the spare sheet used to replace it.

2. Drivers shall use the record sheets every day on which they are driving, starting from the moment they take over the vehicle[2]. The record sheet shall not be withdrawn[3] before the end of the daily working period[4] unless its withdrawal is otherwise authorized. No record sheet may be used to cover a period longer than that for which it is intended.

When, as a result of being away from the vehicle, a driver is unable to use the equipment fitted to the vehicle, the periods of time indicated in paragraph 3, second indent (b), (c) and (d) below shall be entered on the sheet, either manually, by automatic recording or other means, legibly and without dirtying the sheet.

Drivers shall amend the record sheets as necessary should there be more than one driver on board the vehicle, so that the information referred to in Chapter II(1) to (3) of Annex I is recorded on the record sheet of the driver who is actually driving.

3. Drivers shall:

—ensure that the time recorded on the sheet agrees with the official time in the country of registration of the vehicle,

—operate the switch mechanisms enabling the following periods of time to be recorded separately and distinctly:

    (a) under the sign:

    driving time:

    (b) under the sign:

    all other periods of work[5];

    (c) under the sign:

other periods of availability, namely:

—waiting time, ie the period during which drivers need remain at posts only for the
     purpose of answering any calls to start or resume driving or to carry out other work,
—time spent beside the driver while the vehicle is in motion,
—time spent on a bunk while the vehicle is in motion;

(*d*) under the sign:

breaks in work and daily rest periods.

4. Each Member State may permit all the periods referred to in paragraph 3, second indent (*b*)
and (*c*) to be recorded under the sign

on the record sheets used on vehicles registered in its territory.

5. Each crew member shall enter the following information on his record sheet:

(*a*) on beginning to use the sheet—his surname and first name;
(*b*) the date and place where use of the sheet begins and the date and place where such use
     ends;
(*c*) the registration number of each vehicle to which he is assigned, both at the start of the first
     journey recorded on the sheet and then, in the event of a change of vehicle during use of
     the sheet;
(*d*) the odometer reading:

—at the start of the first journey recorded on the sheet,
—at the end of the last journey recorded on the sheet,
—in the event of a change of vehicle during a working day (reading on the vehicle to which
     he was assigned and reading on the vehicle to which he is to be assigned);

(*e*) the time of any change of vehicle.

6. The equipment shall be so designed that it is possible for an authorised inspecting officer, if
necessary after opening the equipment, to read the recordings relating to the nine hours
preceding the time of the check without permanently deforming, damaging or soiling the sheet.

The equipment shall, furthermore, be so designed that it is possible, without opening the case,
to verify that recordings are being made.

7. Whenever requested by an authorised inspecting officer to do so, the driver must be able to
produce record sheets for the current week, and in any case for the last day of the previous week
on which he drove.

---

1. As the duty falls on the employer (the carrier), a haulage company governed by French law which hired
out vehicles without drivers for the carriage of goods by road to a company of another Member State might
not continue to manage the tachograph discs of the hired vehicles (*Bourasse v Ministère Public* ECJ Case C-
228/01, [2003] RTR 335).
2. The regulations are intended to cover not only the person driving at the material time but any other drivers
present upon the vehicle who are drivers for the purposes of the journey which the vehicle is making.
Accordingly, a relief driver takes over a vehicle when he boards the vehicle notwithstanding that he does not
actually drive the vehicle for the first part of the journey (*Vehicle Inspectorate v Anelay* [1998] RTR 279).
3. A broad purposive approach to the construction of "withdrawn" is required; thus, any action which lifts
the record sheet from the styli before the end of the working period can be regarded as falling within that word:
Vehicle and Operator Services Agency v Jones [2005] EWHC Admin 2278, (2005) 169 JP 611, [2006] RTR 6.
4. For the purposes of art 15(2) the driver's "daily working period" does not end until, at the earliest, he
ceases to drive the tachograph vehicle (*DPP v Guy* (1997) 161 JP 727, [1998] RTR 82—period taken for driving a
tachograph vehicle home cannot count as part of the driver's rest period).
5. "Other periods of work" include all other periods of work forming part of the driver's daily working period.
Accordingly, working overtime on general labouring in the employer's yard should be recorded even though
the driver may have no intention of resuming driving until the following day (*Prime v Hosking* [1995] RTR 189).
And the obligation extends to time which a driver necessarily spends travelling to take over a vehicle subject to
the obligation to install and use a tachograph, and which is not at the driver's home or the employer's
operational centre, regardless of whether the employer gave instructions as to when and how to travel or
whether that choice was left to the driver, and to periods of driving spent by him whilst performing a transport
service falling outside the scope of these regulations before taking over a vehicle to which these Regulations
apply (*Skills Motor Coaches Ltd* (Case C – 297/99) [2001] RTR 305, ECJ).

Article 16. 1. In the event of breakdown or faulty operation of the equipment, the employer
shall have it repaired by an approved fitter or workshop, as soon as circumstances permit.

If the vehicle is unable to return to the premises within a period of one week calculated from
the day of the breakdown or of the discovery of defective operation, the repair shall be carried
out *en route*.

Measures taken by Member States pursuant to Article 19 may give the competent authorities
power to prohibit the use of the vehicle in cases where breakdown or faulty operation has not
been put right as provided in the foregoing sub-paragraphs.

2. While the equipment is unserviceable or operating defectively, drivers shall mark on the
record sheet or sheets, or on a temporary sheet to be attached to the record sheet, all information
for the various periods of time which is not recorded correctly by the equipment.

Community Bus Regulations 1986[1]
(SI 1986/1245, amended by SI 1990/1020, SI 1996/3087, SI 1997/2917, SI 2002/2537, SI 2004/2252 and SI 2005/2353)

4-2321 1. *Citation and commencement.*

1. Made by the Secretary of State in exercise of powers under sections 52(1) and 60(1) of the Public Passenger Vehicles Act 1981 and section 23(2)(*b*) and (8) of the Transport Act 1985. Contravention of the regulations carries a maximum fine not exceeding **level 2** on the standard scale as s 67 of the Public Passenger Vehicles Act 1981 has been applied to these regulations by s 127 of the Transport Act 1985; the defences contained in s 68 of the 1981 Act are similarly applied.

Interpretation

4-2322 2. In these Regulations—

"the 1985 Act" means the Transport Act 1985;
"the 1988 Act" means the Road Traffic Act 1988;
"holder" means a body to which a permit has been granted;
"permit" means a community bus permit as defined in section 22(1) of the 1985 Act; and
"traffic regulation conditions" has the meaning given in section 7(1) of the 1985 Act.

Conditions to be fulfilled by driver

4-2323 3. (1) The driver of a vehicle used under a permit, if he is not the holder of—

(*a*) a passenger-carrying vehicle driver's licence,
(*b*) a PCV Community licence, or
(*c*) a Northern Ireland licence corresponding to a passenger-carrying vehicle driver's licence,

which authorises the driving of that vehicle must fulfil the conduct condition specified in paragraph (2) and, if he does not also fulfil the licence conditions specified in paragraph (3), must fulfil the alternative licence conditions specified in paragraph (4).

(2) The conduct condition is that he shall, while he is for the time being responsible for driving the vehicle, comply with regulations 4 and 5(1) and sub-paragraph (*a*), in so far as it relates to giving particulars of his licence and name, and (*b*) of regulation 5(3) of the Public Service Vehicles (Conduct of Drivers, Inspectors, Conductors and Passengers) Regulations 1990.

(3) The licence conditions are that he—

(*a*) is the holder of—

(i) a valid full licence granted under Part III of the 1988 Act,
(ii) a valid Northern Ireland licence corresponding to such a licence, or
(iii) a valid Community licence,

authorising the driver of motor vehicles included in category B other than vehicles included in sub-category B1;

(*b*) has held such a licence for a period of, or periods amounting in aggregate to, not less than two years,
(*c*) is 21 years of age or over, and
(*d*) if he is 70 years of age or over, is not suffering from a relevant disability in respect of which the Secretary of State would be bound to refuse to grant him a licence authorising the driving of a class of vehicle in sub-category D1.

(4) The alternative licence conditions are that he—

(*a*) was first granted a full licence under Part III of the 1988 Act before 1st January 1997,
(*b*) is the holder of a valid full licence granted under that Part of that Act authorising the driving of motor vehicles included in Category B, other than vehicles included in sub-category B1, and sub-category D1 (not for hire or reward), and
(*c*) is 21 years of age or over.

(5) For the purposes of this regulation—

(*a*) any expression which is also used in Parts III and IV of the 1988 Act has the same meaning as in those Parts of that Act;
(*b*) expressions relating to vehicle categories shall be construed in accordance with regulation 4(2)(*a*) and (*b*) of the Motor Vehicles (Driving Licences) Regulations 1996;
(*c*) a person holds a valid full licence granted under Part III of the 1988 Act authorising the driving of motor vehicles included in any category or sub-category if he is authorised to drive such vehicles by virtue of section 88(1) of that Act.

Permits, discs and fees

4-2324 4. (1) *Fees.*

(2) There shall be issued by the traffic commissioner with each permit a disc which shall contain the name of the holder of the permit to which the disc relates, the number of that permit and the words "Community Bus Disc".

(3) The holder shall during such time as the vehicle is being used under the permit cause the disc related to that permit to be affixed to the inside of the vehicle in such a position that the disc—

(*a*) does not interfere unduly with the driver's view, and (*b*) can easily be read in daylight from the outside of the vehicle.

(4) If a permit or disc has been lost, destroyed or defaced, the holder shall forthwith give notice in writing of the fact to the traffic commissioner who granted or issued it.

(5) If upon receipt of the notice referred to in paragraph (4) of this regulation and, in the case where a permit or disc has been defaced, upon surrender of that document, the traffic commissioner is satisfied that the permit or disc has been lost, destroyed or defaced, he shall issue to the holder a duplicate of the document in question (marked as such), and the provisions of these Regulations shall apply to the duplicate as they applied to the original.

(6) If, at any time after notice has been given under paragraph (4) of this regulation, the permit or disc notified as having been lost or destroyed comes into the possession of the holder, that holder shall forthwith return that permit or disc to the traffic commissioner who granted or issued it.

(7) In the event of revocation of a permit or the holder ceasing to operate local services, the holder shall forthwith surrender the permit and disc to the traffic commissioner who granted and issued them.

Attaching traffic regulation conditions to permits

4–2325 5. (1) The holder of a permit shall, upon being required to do so in writing by the traffic commissioner who granted the permit, produce it to a person authorised by that traffic commissioner in order that traffic regulation conditions may be attached to it.

(2) A notice by a traffic commissioner requiring production of a permit may be left at, or sent by the recorded delivery service to, the address last notified to the traffic commissioner by the holder.

(3) The permit shall be produced within 14 days (excluding any day which is a bank holiday under the Banking and Financial Dealings Act 1971 of the date on which the notice is received at the address mentioned in paragraph (2) of this regulation.

(4) The permit shall be produced at the address in the traffic area of the traffic commissioner, and within the business hours, specified in the notice, and if sent by post shall not be treated as having been produced until actually received by the traffic commissioner.

Conditions of fitness for use

4–2326 6. (1) The date on which a vehicle is first used for the purposes of this regulation shall be determined in accordance with regulation 3(3) of the Road Vehicles (Construction and Use) Regulations 1986.

(2) The prescribed conditions of fitness for use for the purpose of section 23(2)(*c*) of the 1985 Act shall be that the vehicle either—

(*a*) complies with the requirements specified in regulations 41 to 43 of the Road Vehicles (Construction and Use) Regulations 1986 for a minibus first used on or after 1st April 1988; or

(*b*) in respect of a vehicle first used before 1st April 1988, complies with the requirements specified in regulations 5 to 28 of the Community Bus Regulations 1978.

Community Drivers' Hours and Recording Equipment (Exemptions and Supplementary Provisions) Regulations 1986[1]

(SI 1986/1456 as amended by SI 1986/1669, SI 1987/805, SI 1988/760, SI 1994/857, SI 1998/2006, SI 2001/1149, SI 2002/2469, SI 2003/1615 and SI 2006/3276)

Citation, commencement, interpretation and revocation

4–2371 1. (1) *Citation and commencement*

(2) In these Regulations—

"the Community Drivers' Hours Regulations" means Council Regulation (EEC) No 3820/85 of 20th December 1985 on the harmonisation of certain social legislation relating to road transport;

"the Community Recording Equipment Regulation" means Council Regulation (EEC) No 3821/85 on recording equipment in road transport as it has effect in accordance with—

(*a*) Commission Regulation (EEC) No 3314/90;

(*b*) Commission Regulation (EEC) No 3688/92;

(*c*) Commission Regulation (EC) No 2479/95;

(*d*) Commission Regulation (EC) No 1056/97;

(*e*) Article 1 of Council Regulation (EC) No 2135/98;

(*f*) Commission Regulation (EC) No 1360/2002;

(*g*) Act concerning the conditions of accession of the Czech Republic, the Republic of Estonia, the Republic of Cyprus, the Republic of Latvia, the Republic of Lithuania, the Republic of Hungary, the Republic of Malta, the Republic of Poland, the Republic of Slovenia and the Slovak Republic and the adjustments to the Treaties on which the European Union is founded;

(*h*) Regulation (EC) No 1882/2003 of the European Parliament and of the Council;

(*i*) Commission Regulation (EC) No 432/2004; and

(*j*) Regulation (EC) No 561/2006 of the European Parliament and of the Council.

"permissible maximum weight" has the same meaning as in section [108] of the Road Traffic Act [1988].

(3) Subject to paragraph (2) above, any expression used in these Regulations which is used in the Community Drivers' Hours Regulation has the same meaning as in that Regulation.

(4) *Revocation.*

1. Made by the Secretary of State in exercise of powers under section 2(2) of the European Communities Act 1972.

Exemption from the Community Drivers' Hours Regulation

4–2372   2. (1) Pursuant to Article 13(1) of the Community Drivers' Hours Regulation, exemption is granted from all the provisions of that Regulation, except Article 5 (minimum ages for drivers) in respect of any vehicle falling within a description specified in Part I of the Schedule to these Regulations.

(2) Pursuant to Article 13(2) of the Community Drivers' Hours Regulation, exemption is granted from all the provision of that Regulation, except Article 5, in respect of any vehicle falling within a description specified in Part II of the Schedule to these Regulations.

Supplementary provisions relating to the Community Drivers' Hours Regulation

4–2373   3. (1) Pursuant to Article 6(1) of the Community Drivers' Hours Regulation, the application to the fourth sub-paragraph of that Article shall be extended to national passenger services other than regular passenger services.

(2) Pursuant to Article 7(3) of the Community Drivers' Hours Regulation, if—

(a) the driver of a vehicle which is engaged in the national carriage of passengers on a regular service observes in a relevant area, immediately after any period of driving not exceeding four hours, a break of at least 30 minutes; and
(b) it was not possible for him to observe at any time during that period of driving, a break of at least 15 minutes.

that period of driving shall be disregarded for the purposes of Article 7(1) of that Regulation.

(3) In paragraph (2) above "relevant area", in relation to the driver of a vehicle which is engaged in the national carriage of passengers on a regular service, means any of the following areas, namely—

(a) The London Borough of Camden;
(b) the Royal Borough of Kensington and Chelsea;
(c) the London Borough of Islington;
(d) the City of Westminster;
(e) in the City of Birmingham, an area comprising Digbeth Coach Station, Rea Street, Bradford Street, Barford Street, Cheapside and Birchall Street;
(f) in the City of Bristol an area comprising Marlborough Street Coach Station, Marlborough Street, Maudlin Street, Lower Maudlin Street, Earl Street and Whitson Street;
(g) in the City of Leeds an area comprising Wellington Street Coach Station, Wellington Street, York Place, Queen Street, Little Queen Street and King Street;
(h) in the City of Leicester, an area comprising St Margaret's Bus Station, Abbey Street, Gravel Street, Church Gate, Mansfield Street, Sandacre Street, New Road, Burleys Way and St Margaret's Way;
(i) in the City of Nottingham, an area comprising Victoria Bus Station, Glasshouse Street, Huntingdon Street, York Street, Cairns Street, Woodborough Road, Mansfield Road, Milton Street, Lower Parliament Street and Union Road; and
(j) in the City of Oxford an area comprising Oxpens Coach Park, Oxpens Road, Thames Street and Holybush Hill,

in which passengers are taken up or set down in the course of the service.

Exemption from the Community Recording Equipment Regulation

4–2374   4. (1) Pursuant to Article 3(2) of the Community Recording Equipment Regulation, exemption is granted from the provisions of that Regulation in respect of any vehicle falling within a description specified in Part I of the Schedule to these Regulations.

(2) Pursuant to Article 3(3) of the Community Recording Equipment Regulation, exemption is granted from the provisions of that Regulation in respect of:

(a) any vehicle falling within a description specified in Part II of the Schedule to these Regulations; and
(b) any vehicle which is being used for collecting sea coal.

Application of the Community Recording Equipment Regulation

4–2375   5. (1) Pursuant to Article 3(4) of the Community Recording Equipment Regulation, that Regulation shall apply (notwithstanding the exception in Article 3(1) to vehicles used for the carriage of postal articles on national transport operations except—

(a) vehicles which have a permissible maximum weight which does not exceed 3·5 tonnes;
(b) revoked.

(2) Revoked.

(3) This Regulation shall not have effect—

(a) before 1st April 1988 in relation to vehicles which have a permissible maximum weight of 7·5 tonnes or more; or

(b) before 1st January 1990 in relation to vehicles which have a permissible maximum weight which exceeds 3·5 tonnes but which is less than 7·5 tonnes.

4–2376

SCHEDULE
EXEMPTED VEHICLES

PART I
VEHICLES EXEMPTED BY REGULATIONS 2(1) AND 4(1)

1. Any vehicle used for the carriage of passengers which is by virtue of its construction and equipment suitable for carrying not more than 17 persons including the driver and is intended for that purpose.

2. (1) Any vehicle which, on or after 1st January 1990, is being used by a public authority to provide public services otherwise than in competition with professional road hauliers.

(2) A vehicle does not fall within the description specified in this paragraph unless the vehicle—

(a) is being used by a health service body—

(i) to provide ambulance services in pursuance of its duty under the National Health Service Act 1977, the National Health Service and Community Care Act 1990 or the National Health Service (Scotland) Act 1978; or

(ii) to carry staff, patients, medical supplies or equipment in pursuance of its general duties under that Act;.

(b) is being used by a local authority for the purposes of the Local Authority Social Services Act 1970 or the Social Work (Scotland) Act 1968 to provide, in the exercise of social services functions—

(i) services for old persons; or

(ii) services for persons to whom section 29 of the National Assistance Act 1948 (welfare arrangements for physically and mentally handicapped persons) applies;

(c) is being used by Her Majesty's Coastguard, a general lighthouse authority or a local lighthouse authority;

(d) is being used by a harbour authority within the limits of a harbour for the improvement, maintenance or management of which the authority is responsible;

(e) is being used for an airports authority within the perimeter of an airport owned or managed by the authority;

(f) is being used by the British Railways Board or any holder of a network licence (within the meaning of Part I of the Railways Act 1993) which is a company wholly owned by the Crown (within the meaning of that Act), Transport for London, any wholly-owned subsidiary of Transport for London, a Passenger Transport Executive or a local authority for the purpose of maintaining railways; or

(g) is being used by the British Waterways Board for the purpose of maintaining navigable waterways.

(3) In this paragraph—

"airport" means an aerodrome within the meaning given by section 105(1) of the Civil Aviation Act 1982;

"airports authority" means the British Airports Authority or a local authority which owns or manages an airport;

"general lighthouse authority" and "local lighthouse authority" have the meanings given by section 634 of the Merchant Shipping Act 1894;

"harbour" and "harbour authority" have the meanings given by section 57(1) of the Harbours Act 1964;

"health service body"—

(a) in relation to England, means a Strategic Health Authority, a Special Health Authority, an NHS trust or a Primary Care Trust (each within the meaning of the National Health Service Act 1977);

(aa) in relation to Wales, means a Health Authority, a Special Health Authority or an NHS trust (each within the meaning of the National Health Service Act 1977);

(b) in relation to Scotland, means the Agency, a Health Board, a Special Health Board or an NHS trust (each within the meaning of the National Health Service (Scotland) Act 1978).

"local authority", unless the contrary intention appears, means—

(a) in relation to England and Wales, a county or district council, a London borough council or the Common Council of the City of London; and

(b) in relation to Scotland, a regional, islands or district council;

"social services functions"—

(a) in relation to England and Wales, has the meaning given by section 3(1) of the Local Authority Social Services Act 1970; and

(b) in relation to Scotland, means functions under the enactments referred to in section 2(2) of the Social Work (Scotland) Act 1968;

"wholly owned subsidiary", in relation to Transport for London, has the meaning given by section 736(2) of the Companies Act 1985.

3. (1) Any vehicle which is being used by an agricultural, horticultural, forestry or fishery undertaking to carry goods within a 50 kilometre radius of the place where the vehicle is normally based, including local administrative areas the centres of which are situated within that radius.

(2) A vehicle which is being used by a fishery undertaking does not fall within the description specified in this paragraph unless the vehicle is being used—

(a) to carry live fish; or

(b) to carry a catch of fish from the place of landing to a place where it is to be processed.

4. Any vehicle which is being used to carry animal waste or carcases which are not intended for human consumption.

5. Any vehicle which is being used to carry live animals between a farm and a local market or from a market to a local slaughterhouse.

6. Any vehicle which is being used—

(a)　as a shop at a local market;
(b)　for door-to-door selling²;
(c)　for mobile banking, exchange or saving transactions;
(d)　for worship;
(e)　for the lending of books, records or cassettes; or
(f)　for cultural events or exhibitions,

and is specially fitted for that use.

7. (1) Any vehicle used for the carriage of goods which has a permissible maximum weight not exceeding 7·5 tonnes and is carrying material¹ or equipment for the driver's use in the course of his work within a 50 kilometre radius of the place where the vehicle is normally based.

(2) A vehicle does not fall within the description specified in this paragraph if driving the vehicle constitutes the driver's main activity.

8. Any vehicle which operates exclusively on an island which does not exceed 2300 square kilometres in area and is not linked to the rest of Great Britain by a bridge, ford or tunnel open for use by motor vehicles.

9. Any vehicle used for the carriage of goods which has a permissible maximum weight not exceeding 7·5 tonnes and is propelled by means of gas produced on the vehicle or by means of electricity.

10. (1) Any vehicle which is being used for driving instruction with a view to obtaining a driving licence.

(2) A vehicle does not fall within the description specified in this paragraph if the vehicle or any trailer or semi-trailer drawn by it is being used for the carriage of goods—

(a)　for hire or reward; or
(b)　for or in connection with any trade or business.

11. Any tractor which, on or after 1st January 1990, is used exclusively for agricultural and forestry work.

---

1. The word "material" does not apply to a retailer's or any vendor's stock in trade; accordingly the exemption was held not to apply to a vehicle used by a greengrocer for transporting fruit and vegetables from a wholesale market to his own retail market stall (*DPP v Aston* [1989] RTR 196, DC). Where a goods vehicle was being driven by a driver for whom driving the vehicle was not his main activity to an auction for sale, and no goods were being carried, the registration document in his possession did not constitute 'material or equipment' which the vehicle was carrying for the driver's use in the course of his work. 'Material' means goods which are in the possession of the person who has them, for the purpose of either being worked on so as to produce some other article, or particularly, as in the case of building materials, where they are proposed to be incorporated into some other article or structure (*Vehicle Inspectorate v Norman* [1999] RTR 366, DC).

2. The delivery of concessionary coal to miners or retired miners by an autobagger vehicle, while a door-to-door activity, was held not to be "door-to-door selling" since the acquisition of the coal was not by way of sale (*DPP v Digby* (1992) 156 JP 420).

PART II
VEHICLES EXEMPTED BY REGULATIONS 2(2) AND 4(2)

4–2377　12. Any vehicle which is being used by the Royal National Lifeboat Institution for the purpose of hauling lifeboats.

13. Any vehicle which was manufactured before 1st January 1947.

14. Any vehicle which is propelled by steam.

15. (1) Any vehicle which is by virtue of its construction and equipment suitable for carrying passengers and which on the occasion on which it is being driven—

(a)　is a vintage vehicle;
(b)　is not carrying more than 9 persons including the driver;
(c)　is not used for carrying passengers with a view to profit; and
(d)　is being driven—

　(i)　in a vintage vehicle rally or to or from such a rally, or
　(ii)　to or from a museum, or other place where the vehicle is to be or has been displayed to members of the public, or
　(iii)　to or from a place where the vehicle is to be or has been repaired, maintained or tested.

(2) For the purposes of this paragraph:—

(a)　a vehicle is a vintage vehicle on any occasion on which it is being driven if it was manufactured more than 25 years before that occasion; and
(b)　"vintage vehicle rally" means an event in which a collection of historic vehicles are driven on a road open to the public along a pre-determined route.

Drivers' Hours (Harmonisation with Community Rules) Regulations 1986¹
(SI 1986/1458)

4–2391　1. (1) *Citation and commencement.*
(2) In these Regulations "the 1968 Act" means the Transport Act 1968.
(3) *Revocation.*

---

1. Made by the Secretary of State in exercise of powers conferred by sections 95(1) and (1A) of the Transport Act 1968.

Domestic drivers' hours code etc

4–2392　2. (1) Subject to the provisions of this Regulation, the domestic drivers' hours code shall not apply in relation to any Community driving or work of a driver of a vehicle to which Part VI of the 1968 Act applies.

(2) Paragraphs (3) and (4) below apply where during any working day a driver of a vehicle to

which Part VI of the 1968 Act applies spends time both on Community driving or work and on domestic driving or work.

(3) Any time spent on Community driving or work shall be regarded for the purpose of—

(a) applying the limits in the domestic drivers' hours code on periods of driving or length of working day; or

(b) calculating periods of driving for the purposes of section 96(7) of the 1968 Act,

as time spent on domestic driving or, as the case may be, domestic work.

(4) Without prejudice to paragraph (3) above, any time spent on Community driving or work shall not be regarded for the purposes of any of the provisions of the domestic drivers' hours code as constituting or forming part of an interval for rest or an interval for rest and refreshment.

(5) In this Regulation "the domestic drivers' hours code" has the meaning given by section 96(13) of the 1968 Act.

(6) In this Regulation—

(a) any reference to Community driving or work is a reference to driving or, as the case may be, work to which the applicable Community Rules apply; and

(b) any reference to domestic driving or work is a reference to driving or, as the case may be, work to which Part VI of the 1968 Act applies and those Rules do not apply.

Meaning of "working week"

4–2393   3. (1) In subsection (1) of section 103 of the 1968 Act, for the definition of "working week" there shall be substituted the following definition—

" 'working week' means, subject to subsection (5) of this section, a week beginning at midnight between Sunday and Monday;".

(2) In subsection (5) of that section, for the words "Saturday and Sunday" there shall be substituted the words "Sunday and Monday".

Drivers' Hours (Goods Vehicles) (Modifications) Order 1986[1]
(SI 1986/1459)

4–2411   1. (1) *Citation and commencement.*

(2) In this Order "the 1968 Act" means the Transport Act 1968.

(3) *Revocation.*

---

1. Made by the Secretary of State in exercise of powers conferred by sections 96(12), 101(2) and 157 of the Transport Act 1968.

Goods vehicles generally

4–2412   2. Where during any working day a driver spends all or the greater part of the time when he is driving vehicles to which Part VI of the 1968 Act applies in driving goods vehicles, that Part of that Act shall have effect, as respects that driver and that working day, as if—

(a) subsections (2), (3)(b), (4) to (6) and (8)(b) of section 96 were omitted;

(b) for the words "subsections (1), (2) and (3)" in subsection (7) of that section there were substituted the words "subsections (1) and 3(a)";

(c) for the words "'subsections (2) and (3)" in subsection (8)(a) of that section there were substituted the words "subsection (3)(a)"; and

(d) for the definition of "working day", in section 103(1) there were substituted the following definition—

"working day", in relation to any driver, means—

(a) any working period (that is to say, any period during which he is on duty) which does not fall to be aggregated with the whole or part of any other such period or periods by virtue of paragraph (b) of this definition; and

(b) where a working period is followed by one or more other such periods beginning within the 24 hours next after the beginning of that working period, the aggregate of that working period and so much of the other such period or periods as fall within those 24 hours;

Light goods vehicles

4–2413   3. (1) Where during any working week a driver spends all of the time when he is driving vehicles to which Part VI of the 1968 Act applies in driving light goods vehicles and, in so far as he drives such a vehicle during that week otherwise than for social, domestic or pleasure purposes, he does so—

(a) solely in connection with the carrying on by him or by his employer of the profession of medical practitioner, nurse, midwife, dentist or veterinary surgeon;

(b) wholly or mainly in connection with the carrying out of any service of inspection, cleaning, maintenance, repair, installation or fitting;

(c) solely while he is acting as a commercial traveller and is carrying in the vehicle (apart from the effects of any person carried in it) no goods other than goods carried for the purpose of soliciting orders;

(d) solely while he is acting in the course of his employment by the Automobile Association, the Royal Automobile Club or Royal Scottish Automobile Club; or

(e) solely in connection with the carrying on by him or by his employer of the business of cinematography or of radio or television broadcasting,

that Part of that Act shall have effect, as respects that driver and any working day falling wholly within that working week, not only with the modifications made by article 2 above but also as if subsections (3)(a) and (8)(a) of section 96 were omitted.

(2) In this article "light goods vehicle" means a vehicle which—

(a) is a goods vehicle which has a permissible maximum weight within the meaning of section [108] of the Road Traffic Act [1988] not exceeding 3·5 tonnes; or

(b) is a dual purpose vehicle within the meaning of Regulation 3(1) of the Motor Vehicles (Construction and Use) Regulations 1978[1], and (in either case) is a vehicle to which Part VI of the 1968 Act applies.

---

1. See now reg 3 of the Road Vehicles (Construction and Use) Regulations 1986 in this PART, ante.

Drivers' Hours (Goods Vehicles) (Exemptions) Regulations 1986[1]
(SI 1986/1492 amended by SI 2003/2155)

4-2421   1. *Citation, commencement and revocation.*

---

1. Made by the Secretary of State in exercise of powers conferred by section 96(10) of the Transport Act 1968.

Exemptions from requirements as to drivers hours

4-2422   2. (1) A driver who during any working day spends all or the greater part of the time when he is driving vehicles to which Part VI of the Transport Act 1968 applies in driving goods vehicles and who spends time on duty during that working day to deal with any of the cases of emergency specified in paragraph (2) below is exempted from the requirements of sections 96(1) and (3)(a) of that Act in respect of that working day subject to the condition that he does not spend time on such duty (otherwise than to deal with the emergency) for a period of or periods amounting in the aggregate to more than 11 hours.

(2) The cases of emergency referred to in paragraph (1) above are—

(a) events which cause or are likely to cause such—

  (i) danger to life or health of one or more individuals or animals or

  (ii) a serious interruption in the maintenance of public services for the supply of water, gas, electricity or drainage or of electronic communications or postal services, or

  (iii) a serious interruption in the use of roads, railways, ports or airports,

  as to necessitate the taking of immediate action to prevent the occurrence or continuance of such danger or interruption and

(b) events which are likely to cause such serious damage to property as to necessitate the taking of immediate action to prevent the occurrence of such damage.

Drivers' Hours (Goods Vehicles) (Keeping of Records) Regulations 1987[1]
(SI 1987/1421)

4-2471   1. *Commencement and citation.*

---

1. Made by the Secretary of State for Transport in exercise of powers conferred by ss 98 and 101(2) of the Transport Act 1968. The penalty for contravention is a fine not exceeding level 4 on the standard scale: s 98(4) of the Transport Act 1968.

4-2472   2. *Revocation.*

Interpretation

4-2473   3. In these Regulations, unless the context otherwise requires—

"the Act" means the Transport Act 1968;

"driver's record book" means a book which complies with regulation 5, and any reference in relation to a driver's record book to a front sheet, instructions to drivers for completion of sheets, and weekly record sheets is a reference to those components of a driver's record book referred to in regulation 5.

"operator's licence" has the same meaning as in section 60(1) of the Act; and

"passenger vehicles" and "goods vehicles" have the same meaning as in section 95(2) of the Act.

Application of Regulations

4–2474 **4.** Subject to the provisions of regulations 12 and 13 these Regulations apply to drivers[1] of goods vehicles and to employers of employee-drivers of such vehicles but they do not so apply in relation to a journey made or work done by a driver in a case where the journey or, as the case may be, the work is a journey or work to which the applicable Community rules apply.

---

1. "Driver" is defined in s 95(3) of the Act.

4–2475 **5.** *Form of driver's record book.*

Issue of Driver's Record Books

4–2476 **6.** (1) Where an employee-driver[1] is required by these Regulations to enter information in a driver's record book the employer[2] shall issue to him and from time to time as may be necessary while the employee-driver remains in the employment of that employer supply him with a new driver's record book.

(2) If on the date of the coming into operation of these Regulations or at any time thereafter an employee-driver has more than one employer in relation to whom he is an employee-driver of a vehicle, the employer who is to issue a new driver's record book to him shall be the employer for whom the employee-driver first acts in the course of his employment on or after the said date or time.

(3) Where during the currency of a driver's record book an employee-driver ceases to be employed by an employer who has issued that book to him he shall return that book, (including all unused weekly record sheets), to that employer and, if he is at that time employed by some other person or persons in relation to whom he is an employee-driver of a vehicle, that other person, or if there is more than one such other person, that one of them for whom he first acts in the course of his employment after ceasing to be so employed as aforesaid, shall issue a new driver's record book to him in accordance with the provisions of paragraph (1) above.

---

1. "Employee-driver" is defined in s 95(3) of the Act.
2. "Employer" is defined in s 103(1) of the Act.

Entries in driver's record books

4–2477 **7.** (1) An employer of an employee-driver or an owner-driver[1] shall enter or secure that there is entered on the front sheet the information specified in items 4 and 6 of that sheet.

(2) The entries referred to in paragraph (1) shall be made—

(a) in the case of an employer, before the driver's record book is issued to the driver pursuant to regulation 6, and

(b) in the case of an owner-driver before the book is used.

(3)

(a) For the purpose of entering the information specified in item 4, the address shall, in the case of an owner-driver, be the address of the driver's place of business.

(b) For the purpose of entering the information specified in item 6 the Operator's Licence No shall be the serial number of the operator's licence granted under Part V of the Act by virtue of which each goods vehicle used by the driver during the currency of the record book is an authorised vehicle for the purposes of the said Part V.

(4) A driver shall enter, and where he is an employee-driver, his employer shall cause him to enter, in accordance with the instructions to drivers for the completion of sheets—

(a) on the front sheet the information specified in relation to the front sheet in those instructions; and

(b) in the appropriate boxes in the weekly record sheet the information specified in relation to weekly record sheets in those instructions.

(5) A driver when making an entry in a weekly record sheet (including signing such a sheet) shall ensure by the use of carbon paper or otherwise, that the entry is simultaneously reproduced on the duplicate of that sheet.

---

1. "Owner-driver" is defined in s 95(3) of the Act.

Manner of keeping driver's record books—supplementary

4–2478 **8.** (1) Where a weekly record sheet has been completed by an employee-driver he shall deliver the driver's record book (including the duplicate of the weekly record sheet which has been completed) to the employer who issued or should have issued the record book to him within a period of seven days from the date when the weekly record sheet was completed or earlier if so required by the employer.

(2) An employer to whom a driver's record book has been delivered pursuant to paragraph 1 above shall—

(a) examine the weekly record sheet which has been completed and sign it and its duplicate;

(b) detach the duplicate sheet; and

(c) return the book to the driver before he is next on duty.

(3) When all the weekly record sheets in a driver's record book have been used, the driver shall

retain the book for a period of fourteen days from the date on which the book was last returned to him pursuant to paragraph (2)(c) above and shall then return the book to the employer as soon as is reasonably practicable.

(4) When a weekly record sheet has been completed by an owner-driver he shall, within a period of seven days from the date of its being completed, detach the duplicate sheet and deliver it to the address which is required to be entered in item 4 on the front sheet.

(5) An employee-driver or an owner-driver shall not be treated as having failed to comply with any of the requirements of paragraphs (1) and (4) above with respect to the period within which the duplicate of a weekly record sheet shall be delivered if he can show that it was not reasonably practicable to comply with that requirement and that the duplicate of the weekly record sheet was delivered as soon as it was reasonably practicable to do so.

(6) A driver who is in possession of a driver's record book in which he has made any entry pursuant to regulation 7 shall not, until all the weekly record sheets in that book have been completed, make any entry in any other record book.

(7) An employee-driver shall not make any entry in a driver's record book pursuant to regulation 7 if the book was not supplied to him by his employer unless a driver's record book so supplied was not available to him.

(8) No person shall erase or obliterate any entry once made in a driver's record book, and if a correction is required it shall be made by striking the original entry through in such a way that it may still be read and by writing the appropriate correction near to the entry so struck through, and any person making such a correction shall initial it.

Production of driver's record books by employee-drivers

4-2479   9. (1) Where an employee-driver has or has had during any period more than one employer in relation to whom he is an employee-driver each employer, who is not the employer who is required by these Regulations to issue a driver's record book to that employee-driver, shall require that driver to produce his current driver's record book and shall enter on the front sheet the information contained in item 5.

(2) An employee-driver shall produce his current driver's record book for inspection by the employer who issued it to him, or by any other person in relation to whom he is at any time during the period of the currency of that book an employee-driver, whenever required to do so by that employer or that other person.

Driver's record books to be carried by drivers

4-2480   10. A driver shall have his current driver's record book (including all unused record sheets) in his possession at all times when he is on duty.

Preservation of driver's record books

4-2481   11. (1) An owner-driver shall preserve his driver's record book intact when it has been completed or he has ceased to use it, and the employer of an employee-driver to whom any driver's record book relating to that employee-driver has been returned shall preserve that book intact[1], for the period specified in paragraph (3) below.

(2) An employer of an employee-driver or an owner-driver who has detached duplicates of weekly sheets pursuant to regulation 8(2)(b) or as the case may be regulation 8(4) shall preserve those sheets for the period specified in paragraph (3) below.

(3) The period for which driver's record books and duplicates of weekly record sheets must be preserved as required by this regulation shall be one year reckoned, in the case of an owner-driver, from the day on which that book was completed or ceased to be used by him, or in the case of an employee-driver, from the day on which that book was returned to his employer pursuant to regulation 8(3).

---

1. An employer will not preserve a record book intact if he re-issues it to a second driver and permits it to be used by him (*Blakey Transport Ltd v Casebourne* [1975] RTR 221).

Exemptions

4-2482   12. (1) Where a driver does not during any working day drive any goods vehicle other than a vehicle the use of which is exempted from any requirement to have an operator's licence or, in the case of a vehicle in the public service of the Crown, would be so exempted by virtue of section 60(2) of the Act, were it not such a vehicle, that driver and, if he is an employee-driver, his employer, shall be exempted for that period from the specified requirements.

(2)

(a) Where in any working day a driver does not drive a goods vehicle for more than four hours and does not drive any such vehicle outside a radius of 50 kilometres from the operating centre of the vehicle, then he and, if he is an employee-driver, his employer shall be exempted for that period from the specified requirements.

(b) For the purposes of computing the period of four hours mentioned in sub-paragraph (a) above no account shall be taken of any time spent in driving a vehicle elsewhere than on a road if the vehicle is being so driven in the course of operations of agriculture, forestry or quarrying or in the course of carrying out work in the construction, reconstruction, alteration or extension or maintenance of, or of a part of, a building, or of any other fixed works of construction of civil engineering (including works for the construction, improvement or maintenance of a road) and, for the purposes of this sub-paragraph, where the vehicle is being driven on, or on a part of, a road in the course of carrying out of any work for the improvement or maintenance of, or of that part of, that road, it shall be treated as being driven elsewhere than on a road.

(3) Where during any working day a driver does not spend all or the greater part of the time when he is driving vehicles to which Part VI of the Act applies in driving goods vehicles, then he and, if he is an employee-driver, his employer shall be exempted for that working day from the specified requirements.

(4) Where a vehicle is used in such circumstances that by virtue of regulation 5 of the Community Drivers' Hours and Recording Equipment (Exemptions and Supplementary Provisions) Regulations 1986 Council Regulation (EEC) No 3821/85 of 20th December 1985 on recording equipment in road transport[1] applies to the vehicle, the driver of the vehicle and, if he is an employee-driver, his employer shall be exempted from the specified requirements in relation to the use of the vehicle in those circumstances.

(5)

(a) In this regulation "the specified requirements" means the provisions of regulations 7 and 10.

(b) In paragraph (2)(a) above "operating centre" has the same meaning as in section 92 of the Act.

---

1. OJ L370, 31.12.85, p 8.

Drivers of goods vehicles and passenger vehicles

4–2483 **13.** (1) Subject to the provisions of regulation 12(3), regulations 7 and 10 apply to a driver who in any working week drives goods and passenger vehicles as they apply to a driver who only drives a goods vehicle and the information to be entered in the driver's record book pursuant to regulation 7 shall be information in relation to his employments in connection with both goods and passenger vehicles.

(2) If a driver of both goods vehicles and passenger vehicles has a different employer in relation to his employment in connection with goods vehicles from his employer in relation to his employment in connection with passenger vehicles his employer for the purpose of regulation 6 shall be his employer in relation to his employment in connection with goods vehicles notwithstanding the provisions of regulation 6(2).

4–2484   SCHEDULE
                     Model for Driver's Record Book

Goods Vehicles (Plating and Testing) Regulations 1988[1]

(SI 1988/1478 amended by SI 1989/320 and 1693, SI 1990/448, SI 1991/252 and 454, SI 1992/564 and 2447, SI 1993/2048 and 3013, SI 1994/328, SI 1995/1456, SI 1997/82 and 263 and SI 1998/1671, 1998/3113, SI 2000/1433, SI 2001/307 and 1650, SI 2002/487, SI 2003/1816, SI 2004/1873[2])

4–2491 **1, 2.** *Citation and commencement and revocation.*

---

1. Made by the Secretary of State under ss 45, 46(5) and 51 of the Road Traffic Act 1972 and now having effect under ss 49 to 53, 63 and 68 of the Road Traffic Act 1988.
2. Those instruments which amend scales of fees are not listed.

Interpretation

4–2492 **3.** (1) In these Regulations, except where the context otherwise requires, the following expressions have the meanings hereby respectively assigned to them:—

"the 1971 Act" means the Vehicles (Excise) Act 1971;

"the 1988 Act" means the Road Traffic Act 1988;

"the Construction and Use Regulations" means the Road Vehicles (Construction and Use) Regulations 1986;

"the National Type Approval for Goods Vehicles Regulations" means the Motor Vehicles (Type Approval for Goods Vehicles) (Great Britain) Regulations 1982;

"agricultural motor vehicle", "agricultural trailer", "agricultural trailed appliance", "agricultural trailed appliance conveyor", "articulated vehicle", "converter dolly", "dual-purpose vehicle", "engineering plant", "exhaust system," "Ministry plate", "registered", "semi-trailer", "straddle carrier", "track laying", "works trailer", and "works truck" have the same meanings respectively as in the Construction and Use Regulations;

"appeal officer" means the person appointed by the Secretary of State for the purposes of appeals to the Secretary of State;

"appropriate day", means—

(a) in relation to a vehicle which is a motor vehicle, the last day of the calendar month in which falls the first anniversary of the date on which it was registered; and

(b) in relation to a vehicle which is a trailer, the last day of the calendar month in which falls the first anniversary of the date on which it was first sold or supplied by retail;

"auxiliary station" means a vehicle testing station which is regularly not open for the carrying out of re-tests on certain normal working days;

"break-down vehicle" means a motor vehicle—

(a) on which is permanently mounted apparatus designed for raising one disabled[1] vehicle partly from the ground and for drawing that vehicle when so raised; and

(b) which is not equipped to carry any load other than articles required for the operation of, or in connection with, that apparatus or for repairing disabled vehicles;

"design gross weight" means—

(a) in the case of a vehicle equipped with a Ministry plate, the weight shown thereon as the design weight or, if no weight is so shown thereon, the weight shown thereon as the weight not to be exceeded in Great Britain;

(b) in the case of a vehicle which is not equipped with a Ministry plate, but which is equipped with a plate in accordance with regulation 66 of the Construction and Use Regulations, the maximum gross weight shown on the plate in respect of item 7 of Part I of Schedule 8 to those Regulations; and

(c) in any other case, the weight which the vehicle is designed or adapted not to exceed when in normal use and travelling on a road laden;

"examination" means any operation being—

(a) a first examination;

(b) a re-test;

(c) a periodical test;

(d) a re-examination under Regulation 33; or

(e) an examination or re-examination for the purposes of an appeal against a determination made under these Regulations;

"first examination" means an examination or, as the case may be, examinations for which a vehicle is submitted under regulation 9;

"Goods Vehicle Centre" means the Goods Vehicle Centre at Welcombe House, 91–92 The Strand, Swansea, SA1 2DH;

"living van" means a vehicle whether mechanically propelled or not which is used as living accommodation by one or more persons, and which is also used for the carriage of goods or burden which are not needed by such one or more persons for the purpose of their residence in the vehicle;

"Ministry test date disc" means a plate issued by the Secretary of State for a goods vehicle being a trailer, following the issue of a goods vehicle test certificate for that trailer under these Regulations and containing—

(a) the identification mark allotted to that trailer and shown in that certificate;

(b) the date until which that certificate is valid; and

(c) the number of the vehicle testing station shown in the said certificate;

"notifiable alteration", in relation to a vehicle, means—

(a) an alteration made in the structure or fixed equipment of the vehicle which varies the carrying capacity or towing capacity of the vehicle;

(b) an alteration, affecting any part of a braking system or the steering system with which the vehicle is equipped or of the means of operation of either of those systems; or

(c) any other alteration made in the structure or fixed equipment of the vehicle which renders or is likely to render the vehicle unsafe to travel on roads at any weight equal to any plated weight shown in the plating certificate for that vehicle.

"out of hours" means at any time either—

(a) on any day which is a Saturday, Sunday, Good Friday, Christmas Day or a Bank holiday (as defined in the Banking and Financial Dealings Act 1971); or

(b) on any other day, other than between—

(i) 8.00 am and 5.00 pm on a Monday to Thursday inclusive, or

(ii) 8.00 am and 4.30 pm on a Friday;

"periodical test", in relation to a vehicle, means a goods vehicle test carried out under Part IV of these Regulations on a vehicle in respect of which a goods vehicle test certificate has been issued on a first examination of it or as a result of a re-test following that examination or as a result of an appeal under any provision in these Regulations;

"plated particulars" means those particulars which are required to be shown in a Ministry plate under Schedule 10B to the Construction and Use Regulations;

"plated weights" means such of the plated particulars related to gross weight, axle weight for each axle and train weight as are required to be shown in column (2) on the Ministry plate;

"play bus" means a motor vehicle which was originally constructed to carry more than 12 passengers but which has been adapted primarily for the carriage of play things for children (including articles required in connection with the use of those things);

"the prescribed construction and use requirements", in relation to a vehicle, means those of the requirements specified in Part I of Schedule 3 which apply to the vehicle and the requirements of Part II of that Schedule;

"re-test", in relation to a vehicle, means an examination which is—

(a) an examination for plating and a goods vehicle test carried out on a vehicle under Part III of these Regulations subsequent to a first examination of that vehicle as a result of which a notice of refusal was issued; or (*b*) a goods vehicle test carried out on a vehicle under Part IV of these Regulations subsequent to a periodical test of that vehicle as a result of which a notice of refusal was issued;

"Secretary of State" means the Secretary of State for Transport;

"sender" means a person who informs the Secretary of State of a notifiable alteration under regulation 30;

"sold or supplied by retail", in relation to a trailer, means sold or supplied otherwise than to a person acquiring solely for the purpose of resale or of resupply for a valuable consideration;

"the standard lists" means lists—

(*a*) prepared by the Secretary of State after consultation with representative organisations of the motor manufacturing and road transport industries and other connected organisations and published by the Goods Vehicle Centre; and

(*b*) showing, as respects goods vehicles of a make, model and type specified in the lists and complying in the case of motor vehicles with certain particulars relating to the engine, transmission, brakes and dimensions so specified and in the case of trailers with certain particulars relating to type of coupling, dimensions, brakes and tyres so specified (hereinafter referred to as "the constructional particulars") the gross weight for, and the axle weight for each axle of, vehicles of that make, model and type and, in the case of motor vehicles, the train weight for vehicles of that make, model and type, the said weights being weights at or below which the Secretary of State considers vehicles of that make, model and type could safely be driven on roads having regard to—

  (i) the weights at which vehicles of that make, model and type were originally designed to operate;

  (ii) in the case of motor vehicles, the requirements as to brakes of Regulations 15, 16 and 18 of the Construction and Use Regulations;

  (iii) in the case of trailers, the requirements of Regulations 15 and 16 of the Construction and Use Regulations and the provisions of Schedule 1 as respects braking force; and

"vehicle testing station" means a station provided by the Secretary of State under section 52(2) of the 1988 Act or such other place as he may consider appropriate for the purposes of carrying out an examination.

(2) Any reference in these Regulations to—

(*a*) an examination for plating includes, in relation to a vehicle to which regulation 18 applies, an examination provided for in that regulation; and

(*b*) a vehicle of a make, model and type shall in relation to a trailer, include a reference to a vehicle of a make and bearing a serial number.

(3) For the purpose of these Regulations, in counting the number of axles of a vehicle, where the centres of the areas of contact between all the wheels and the road surface can be included between any two vertical planes at right angles to the longitudinal axis of the vehicle less than 0·5 metres apart, those wheels shall be treated as constituting one axle.

(4) For the purpose of these Regulations, in determining when a trailer is first sold or supplied by retail the date of such first sale or supply by retail shall in the case of a trailer which is constructed with a chassis be taken to be the date on which that chassis (with or without a body mounted on it) is first sold or supplied by retail and in the case of any other trailer be taken to be the date the trailer is first sold or supplied by retail.

(5) Unless the context otherwise requires, any reference in these Regulations to—

(*a*) a numbered Regulation or Schedule is a reference to the Regulation or Schedule bearing that number in these Regulations;

(*b*) a numbered paragraph is a reference to the paragraph bearing that number in the Regulation or Schedule in which the reference appears;

(*c*) a vehicle is a reference to a vehicle to which these Regulations apply.

---

1. A scrap vehicle is not a disabled vehicle (*Gibson v Nutter* [1984] RTR 8).

Application

4–2493   **4.** (1) Subject to paragraph (2), these Regulations apply to goods vehicles being—

(*a*) heavy motor cars and motor cars constructed or adapted for the purpose of forming part of an articulated vehicle;

(*b*) other heavy motor cars;

(*c*) other motor cars, the design gross weight of which exceeds 3,500 kilograms;

(*d*) semi-trailers;

(*e*) converter dollies of any unladen weight manufactured on or after 1st January 1979; or

(*f*) trailers, not being converter dollies or semi-trailers, the unladen weight of which exceeds 1020 kilograms.

(2) Nothing in these Regulations applies to goods vehicles of any of the classes of vehicle specified in Schedule 2.

4–2493A   **4A.** Without prejudice to section 17 of the Interpretation Act 1978 and subject to the context, a reference in these Regulations to any enactment comprised in subordinate legislation (within the meaning of that Act) is a reference to that enactment as from time to time amended or as from time to time re-enacted with or without modification.

Prescribed requirements for tests

4–2494 5. (1) Subject to these Regulations, every vehicle submitted for a goods vehicle test in accordance with these Regulations shall be examined for the purpose of ascertaining whether the prescribed construction and use requirements are complied with.

(2) For the purposes of these Regulations the applicability of any of the prescribed construction and use requirements to a vehicle is not affected by Item 5 in the Table in regulation 4(4) of the Construction and Use Regulations (which exempts vehicles being used in the course of a goods vehicle test from certain construction and use requirements).

Supervision of tests

4–2495 6. Subject to these Regulations, every examination for plating and every goods vehicle test shall be carried out by or under the direction of a goods vehicle examiner.

Authority to drive and duties of driver

4–2496 7. (1) The person who drove the vehicle to an examination shall, except so far as he is permitted to be absent by the person who is carrying out the examination, be present throughout the whole of the examination, and shall drive the vehicle and operate its controls when and in such a manner as he may be directed by the person who is carrying out the examination to do so.

(2) The person who is carrying out an examination is authorised to drive the vehicle on a road or elsewhere.

(3) A contravention of this regulation is hereby declared to be an offence.

Conditions of acceptance of vehicle

4–2497 8. (1) In this Regulation, "examiner" means—

(a)   in relation to an examination not being an examination for the purposes of an appeal against a determination under these Regulations, a vehicle examiner; or

(b)   in relation to an examination for the purposes of an appeal against a determination under these Regulations, the appeal officer.

(2) An examiner shall not be under an obligation to accept a vehicle for examination or to proceed with an examination in any case where—

(a)   the vehicle is not submitted for examination at the time fixed under these Regulations for the examination;

(b)   the applicant for the examination does not, after being requested to do so, produce the notice of appointment (if any) relating to the examination and—

(i)   in the case of a motor vehicle, either the registration document relating to the vehicle or other evidence of the date of its first registration or, in the case of a motor vehicle not registered before the date of the examination, evidence of the date of its manufacture; or

(ii)   in the case of a trailer, evidence of the date of its manufacture;

(c)   the fee in respect of that examination has not been paid and is not tendered in cash;

(d)   the particulars relating to the vehicle and shown in any application form relevant to that examination are found to be substantially incorrect;

(e)   the vehicle is one as respects which it has been stated in the application form that it is to be used on roads to draw a trailer and in the last notice of appointment preceding the examination it was required that the vehicle should be accompanied by a trailer which is to be so drawn, and the vehicle is not accompanied by such a trailer;

(f)   the vehicle is a trailer and is not accompanied by a motor vehicle suitable for drawing that trailer and capable of operating any braking system with which the trailer is equipped;

(g)   there is not permanently affixed to the chassis or main structure of the vehicle in a conspicuous and easily accessible position so as to be readily legible either—

(i)   the chassis or serial number shown in the registration document relating to the vehicle; or

(ii)   if no such number is shown or exists, the identification mark allotted to the vehicle by the Secretary of State;

(h)   the vehicle, or any motor vehicle by which it is accompanied, or any part of or any equipment of the vehicle is so dirty or dangerous as to make it unreasonable for the examination to be carried out in accordance with these Regulations or with any directions given under section 52(1) of the 1988 Act, or the applicant for the examination does not produce any certificate required in the last notice of appointment preceding the examination, that a vehicle used for carrying toxic, corrosive or inflammable loads has been properly cleaned or otherwise made safe;

(i)   an examiner is not able to complete the examination without the vehicle or, in the case of a trailer the motor vehicle by which it is accompanied being driven and such vehicle or, as the case may be, accompanying vehicle is not provided with fuel and oil to enable it to be driven to such extent as may be necessary for the purpose of the examination;

(*j*) an examiner is not able to complete the examination of a trailer unless the motor vehicle by which it is accompanied is driven on a road, and that motor vehicle cannot be so driven in compliance with section 8 of the 1971 Act because no licence under that Act is in force for such vehicle;

(*k*) the vehicle or any trailer by which it is accompanied is not loaded or unloaded in the manner (if any) specified for the purpose of the examination in the last notice of appointment preceding the examination or as otherwise notified in writing by the Secretary of State;

(*l*) an examiner is not able to complete the examination due to the failure of a part of the vehicle, or of any vehicle by which it is drawn or intended to be drawn, which renders the vehicle, or any such accompanying vehicle incapable of being moved in safety under the power of the vehicle or, as the case may be, the accompanying vehicle;

(*m*) on the submission of a vehicle for a periodical test, or a re-test following a periodical test the driver of the vehicle or, in the case of a trailer, the driver of the vehicle which accompanies it, does not produce to an examiner the last plating certificate (or a photocopy of it) and the last goods vehicle test certificate (or a photocopy of it) which have been issued in respect of the vehicle submitted;

(*n*) *revoked;*

(*o*) on the submission of the vehicle for a periodical test or a re-test following a periodical test, the Ministry plate issued in respect of the vehicle—

  (i) is not affixed in accordance with regulation 70(1) of the Construction and Use Regulations; or

  (ii) contains particulars which do not correspond to the vehicle to which it is affixed;

(*p*) the vehicle or any motor vehicle by which it is accompanied emits substantial quantities of avoidable smoke;

(*q*) the vehicle is a vehicle propelled by a compression ignition system to which regualtion 61(10BA) of the Construction and Use Regulations applies and the exhaust system has been so altered that the examiner is not able, with the facilities and apparatus available to him at the place at which the examination would otherwise be carried out, to determine whether Part II of Schedule 7B to those Regulations applies to the vehicle; or

(*r*) an examiner is not able to open and examine recording equipment fitted to the vehicle in accordance with the Community Recording Equipment Regulation.

Part II
Timing and Method of Application for Examinations
Dates by which vehicles are to be submitted for first examinations

4–2498 **9.** (1) Every motor vehicle to which paragraph (3) applies shall be submitted for a goods vehicle test on or before the appropriate day.

(2) Every motor vehicle to which paragraph (3) does not apply and every trailer shall be submitted for both a plating examination and a goods vehicle test on or before the appropriate day.

(3) This paragraph applies to a motor vehicle if the following requirements are met, namely—

(*a*) a plating certificate is in force for the vehicle; and

(*b*) that plating certificate is a certificate of conformity or a Minister's approval certificate that is treated as a plating certificate by virtue of section 59(4) of the 1988 Act.

(4) Paragraphs (1) and (2) shall not prevent the Secretary of State authorising the submission of a vehicle for a first examination after the date by which the vehicle is required by those paragraphs to be submitted for first examination.

Dates by which vehicles are to be submitted for periodical tests

4–2499 **10.** (1) Where a goods vehicle test certificate for a vehicle is issued on an examination, the vehicle shall be submitted for a further examination before the certificate expires.

(2) Where a goods vehicle test certificate for a vehicle is refused on an examination, the vehicle shall be submitted for a further examination—

(*a*) if one goods vehicle certificate is in force for the vehicle at the time of the refusal, before the expiration of the certificate;

(*b*) if more than one goods vehicle is in force for the vehicle at the time of the refusal, before the expiration of the last of those certificates to have been issued; or

(*c*) in any other case, on or before the appropriate day or before the vehicle is used on a road (whichever is the later).

(3) Paragraphs (1) and (2) and regulation 11 shall not prevent the Secretary of State authorising the submission of a vehicle for a periodical test after the date by which the vehicle is required by those provisions to be submitted for a periodical test.

Period of validity of goods vehicle test certificate

4–2500 **11.** (1) A goods vehicle test certificate issued in the circumstances described in column (2) of an item in the Table below shall be valid for the period described in column (3) of that item.

(1) Item	(2) Circumstances	(3) Period of validity
1	Vehicle submitted for a first examination during the two month period ending with the appropriate day.	The period beginning with the date of issue of the certificate and ending with the first anniversary of the appropriate day.
2	Vehicle submitted for a periodical test during the two month period ending with the expiry date of a current goods vehicle test certificate.	The period beginning with the date of issue of the certificate and ending with the first anniversary of the expiry date of that certificate.
3	Vehicle submitted for a periodical test in circumstances other than those described in items 1 and 2 of this Table.	The period beginning with the date of issue of the certificate and ending with the last day of the same calendar month in the following year.

(2) In this regulation, a reference to the end of a period is a reference to the end of the final day of that period.

Manner of making application for first examinations or periodical tests, and fees

4–2501 **12.**—(1) Any person wishing to have a first examination or periodical test carried out on a vehicle shall make an application for that purpose either to the Secretary of State
  (2) *Revoked.*
  (3) *Forms and fees.*
  (4), (4A), (5) *Fees.*

Time of application for first examinations and periodical tests

4–2502 **13.**—(1) Except as provided in paragraph (2), every application for a first examination or periodical test of a vehicle shall be made—
  (a) at least one calendar month before the date on which the applicant desires to submit the vehicle for the examination or test, and
  (b) not more than three calendar months before the last day by which the vehicle is required by these Regulations to be submitted for the examination or test.

  (2) If the Secretary of State is satisfied that there are reasonable grounds for an application for a first examination or periodical test of a vehicle not being made within the period specified in paragraph (1) he may permit the application to be accepted and dealt with as if it had been made within that period.

Notice of place and time of first examinations or periodical tests

4–2503 **14.**—(1) As soon as reasonably practicable after the date of the receipt of an application for a first examination or periodical test of a vehicle under Regulation 12(1) the Secretary of State shall send to the applicant notice of the vehicle testing station at which the examination or test is to take place, and the date and time reserved by the Secretary of State for that examination or test.
  (2) *Revoked.*

Application for re-tests following first examinations or periodical tests

4–2504 **15.**—(1) Where, under Regulation 23(1) or 26, a notification of the refusal of a goods vehicle test certificate in respect of a vehicle is issued the vehicle may be submitted, if need be on more than one occasion, at a vehicle testing station for a re-test.
  (2) Where an applicant desires to submit a vehicle for a re-test he shall make arrangements with the Secretary of State as to the vehicle testing station at which the vehicle is to be submitted for a re-test and as to the date and time at which the vehicle is to be submitted to that vehicle testing station.

4–2505 **16.** *Fees for re-tests.*

PART III
EXAMINATION FOR PLATING ON A FIRST EXAMINATION
Examination for plating

4–2506 **14–19.** *Revoked.*

4–2509 **20.**—(1) Where a vehicle is submitted for an examination for plating on a first examination, a vehicle examiner shall determine the plated weights of the vehicle having regard—
  (a) to any information which may have been supplied by the Secretary of State as to the plated weights which have been determined for similar vehicles under these Regulations;
  (b) to the design, construction and equipment of the vehicle, and the stresses to which it is likely to be subject when in use on roads;
  (c) to any information which may be available about the weights at which the vehicle was originally designed to be driven on roads;

(*d*) if the vehicle or its equipment has, or appears to have, been altered since the date of its manufacture, to the likely effect of any such alteration in making the vehicle fit to be driven safely on roads at weights different from those at which it appears to the examiner the vehicle was originally designed to be so driven;

(*e*) if the vehicle is a motor vehicle, the requirements of regulations 15, 16 and 18 of the Construction and Use Regulations;

(*f*) if the vehicle is a trailer, to—

(i) the requirements of Regulations 15 and 16 of the Construction and Use Regulations; and

(ii) the provisions of Schedule 1; and

(*g*) to the need to comply with Regulations 25, 75, 78 and 79 of the Construction and Use Regulations or of the Road Vehicles (Authorised Weight) Regulations 1998[1], and with the requirement that—

(i) no plated weight relating to train weight, other than a plated train weight applicable only to combined transport operations, shall exceed the maximum train weight at which the vehicle can lawfully be driven on a road in Great Britain by virtue of the Construction and Use Regulations, ignoring Schedule 11A to those Regulations; and

(ii) no plated weight relating to train weight applicable only to combined transport operations can exceed the maximum train weight at which the vehicle can lawfully be driven on a road in Great Britain by virtue of the Construction and Use Regulations (having regard to Schedule 11A to those Regulations);

(2) In this regulation, a reference to use on a road is a reference to use on a road other than for international transport.

(3) For the purposes of this regulation, the Construction and Use Regulations shall have effect as if regulation 80 were omitted.

1. In this title, post.

Issue of plating certificates, and particulars to be contained therein

4–2510 21. (1) After the determination of the plated weights of a vehicle submitted for an examination for plating on a first examination there shall, unless there is a refusal to issue a goods vehicle test certificate in respect of that vehicle, be issued a plating certificate in respect of that vehicle.

(2) *Revoked.*

(3) Every plating certificate issued in relation to a vehicle shall—

(*a*) be signed either by the goods vehicle examiner who carried out, or under whose direction the examination for plating was carried out, or by a person authorised in that behalf by the Secretary of State; and

(*b*) contain—

(i) the date on which it was issued;

(ii) the number allotted by the Secretary of State to the vehicle testing station at which it was issued or the letters GVC if it was issued at the Goods Vehicle Centre;

(iii) the plated weights determined for that vehicle under Regulation 20 or 24;

(iv) *revoked,*

(v) where any such plated weight determined under Regulation 20 is less than the weight which would have been determined but for paragraph (*g*) of that Regulation the weight which would have been determined but for that paragraph shall be shown as a design weight;

(vi) the other plated particulars ascertained from the application mentioned in regulation 12 and an inspection of the vehicle;

(vii) any alteration in the vehicle or its equipment which is required by these Regulations to be notified to the Secretary of State; and

(viii) the sizes of the tyres fitted to the wheels of the vehicle at the time of the issue of the certificate, and the particular conditions, if any, in which a vehicle should be used on roads at or below its plated weights when fitted with those types properly maintained.

(4) A plating certificate issued in relation to a vehicle under the provisions of these Regulations may contain (in addition to the particulars mentioned in paragraph (3))—

(*a*) the DOE (Department of the Environment) or DTp (Department of Transport) reference number for the particular type of vehicle, and

(*b*) the maximum authorised weights and dimensions in accordance with article 2 of Council Directive 85/3/EEC[1].

1. OJ No L2, 3.1.1985, p 14.

Goods vehicle test

4–2511 22. After an examination for plating has been carried out on a vehicle, a goods vehicle examiner shall arrange for the vehicle to undergo a goods vehicle test.

Issue of goods vehicle test certificates (or of notices of refusal) and particulars to be contained therein

4–2512 23. (1) Where as a result of a goods vehicle test a vehicle is found not to comply with the prescribed construction and use requirements there shall be issued a notice of the refusal of a goods vehicle test certificate, and such notice shall state the grounds of such refusal.

(2) Where as a result of a goods vehicle test a vehicle is found to comply with the prescribed construction and use requirements a goods vehicle test certificate shall be issued as respects that vehicle and such certificate shall state the period of the validity of the certificate and that the vehicle was found to comply with the prescribed construction and use requirements.

(3) Every notice issued under paragraph (1) and every certificate issued under paragraph (2) shall—

(a) be signed by either the goods vehicle examiner who carried out, or under whose direction the goods vehicle test was carried out, or by a person authorised in that behalf by the Secretary of State; and

(b) contain—

(i) the date on which it was issued;

(ii) the number allotted by the Secretary of State to the vehicle testing station at which it was issued;

(iii) in the case of a certificate or notice issued for a motor vehicle, the registration mark (if any) exhibited on the vehicle or, if no such mark is so exhibited, the chassis or serial number marked on the vehicle or, if no such number is so marked, the identification mark which shall have been allotted to the vehicle by the Secretary of State in the notice of appointment relating to the first examination of the vehicle; and

(iv) in the case of a certificate or notice issued for a trailer, the identification mark which shall have been allotted to the trailer by the Secretary of State in the notice of appointment (if any) relating to the first examination of the trailer or shall have otherwise been allotted to the trailer by the Secretary of State under these Regulations.

Re-test procedure, and issue of plating and test certificates (or notices of refusal)

4–2513   24. (1) Where on a first examination of a vehicle no plating certificate has been issued in respect of that vehicle and it is submitted for a re-test under regulation 15 a goods vehicle examiner shall determine as the plated weights of the vehicle—

(a) if after examination of the vehicle he is satisfied that no alteration has been made to the vehicle or its equipment which would render inapplicable the plated weights determined for the vehicle on its first examination, the weights so determined; or,

(b) if he is not so satisfied, weights consistent with Regulation 19 or, as the case may be, Regulation 20.

(2) A goods vehicle examiner in carrying out an examination pursuant to Regulation 15(2) and (3) shall be under an obligation only to examine the vehicle for the purpose of ascertaining whether it complies with the particular items of the prescribed construction and use requirements with which it was shown in the last notice of a refusal of a test certificate not to comply.

(3) Where a goods vehicle examiner finds that the vehicle complies with the particular items of the prescribed construction and use requirements mentioned in paragraph (2) and has no reason to believe that the other prescribed construction and use requirements are not complied with in relation to the vehicle, there shall be issued a goods vehicle test certificate and also a plating certificate for the vehicle.

(4) Where a goods vehicle examiner finds that the vehicle does not comply with the particular items of the prescribed construction and use requirements mentioned in paragraph (2) or that the other prescribed construction and use requirements is not complied with in relation to the vehicle, there shall be issued a notice of the refusal of a goods vehicle test certificate and in that event no plating certificate shall be issued for the vehicle.

(5) On completion of an examination of a vehicle pursuant to Regulation 15(4) a goods vehicle examiner shall arrange for the vehicle to undergo a goods vehicle test, and when that test has been completed there shall be issued—

(a) where the vehicle is found to comply with the prescribed construction and use requirements, a goods vehicle test certificate and also a plating certificate for that vehicle; or

(b) where the vehicle is found not to comply with the prescribed construction and use requirements, a notice of the refusal of a goods vehicle test certificate, and in that event no plating certificate shall be issued for the vehicle.

4–2514   25. *Appeals.*

Interpretation of this Part

4–2514A   25A. In this Part, a reference to a periodical test includes a goods vehicle test carried out pursuant to regulation 22.

PART IV
REGULATIONS GOVERNING PERIODICAL TESTS

Periodical tests, and issue of test certificates (or notices of refusal)

4–2515   26. On the submission of a vehicle for a periodical test a goods vehicle examiner shall arrange for the vehicle to undergo that test, and when that test has been completed there shall be issued—

(a) where the vehicle is found to comply with the prescribed construction and use requirements, a goods vehicle test certificate; or (*b*) where the vehicle is found not to comply with the prescribed construction and use requirements, a notice of the refusal of a goods vehicle test certificate.

Re-test procedure, and issue of test certificates (or notices of refusal)

4–2516   27. (1) Where a vehicle is submitted for a re-test at a vehicle testing station in circumstances where the fee for the retest is payable under paragraph (1) or (3) of regulation 16 or would have been so payable but for paragraph (6) of that regulation, a goods vehicle examiner shall in carrying out the test be under an obligation only to examine the vehicle for the purpose of ascertaining whether it complies with the particular items of the prescribed construction and use requirements with which it was shown in the last notice of a refusal of a test certificate not to comply.

(2) Where a goods vehicle examiner finds that the vehicle complies with the particular items of the prescribed construction and use requirements mentioned in paragraph (1) and has no reason to believe that the other prescribed construction and use requirements are not complied with in relation to the vehicle, there shall be issued a goods vehicle test certificate.

(3) Where a goods vehicle examiner does not find that the vehicle complies with the particular items of the prescribed construction and use requirements mentioned in paragraph (1) or finds that any other prescribed construction and use requirement is not complied with in relation to the vehicle, there shall be issued a notice of the refusal of a test certificate.

(4) Where a vehicle is submitted for a re-test at a vehicle testing station in circumstances where a fee for the retest is payable under regulation 16(2), a goods vehicle examiner shall arrange for the vehicle to undergo a goods vehicle test, and when that test has been completed there shall be issued—

(*a*) where the vehicle is found to comply with the prescribed construction and use requirements, a goods vehicle test certificate;

(*b*) where the vehicle is found not to comply with the prescribed construction and use requirements, a notice of the refusal of a goods vehicle test certificate.

Form of test certificates and notices of refusal

4–2517   28. Goods vehicle test certificates and notices of the refusal of a goods vehicle test certificate issued under Regulation 24, 26 or 27 shall contain the same particulars as are appropriate in the case of goods vehicle test certificates and notices of the refusal of a goods vehicle test certificate mentioned in regulation 23 and shall be signed in the same manner as is provided in Regulation 23.

4–2518   29. *Appeals.*

Part V
Regulations Governing Notifiable Alterations, Amendments of Plating Certificates and Re-examinations in Connection Therewith
Secretary of State to be informed of notifiable alterations

4–2519   30. In the event of a notifiable alteration being made to a vehicle in respect of which a plating certificate has been issued, and before the vehicle to which the alteration has been made is used on roads, particulars of that alteration on a form approved by the Secretary of State shall be sent to him at the Goods Vehicle Centre, and any such form may contain a request by the sender for an amendment to be made as respects a plated weight shown on the plating certificate for the vehicle.

4–2520   31. In the following provisions of this Part, a reference to a re-examination shall where appropriate be read as a reference to an examination that is not a re-examination.

Other amendments to the plating certificate

4–2521   32. Where, otherwise than by reason of a notifiable alteration, any particular (with reference to a plated weight or any other matter) contained in a plating certificate for a vehicle becomes or may have become no longer applicable to that vehicle, an application on a form approved by the Secretary of State may be sent to him, for the purpose of having the vehicle re-examined with a view to that particular being amended.

Provision as to re-examination

4–2522   33. (1) Where, under Regulation 30, particulars of a notifiable alteration are sent to the Secretary of State and the form contains a request as provided in that regulation the Secretary of State shall by notice to the sender require him to submit the vehicle for re-examination.

(2) Where, under Regulation 30, particulars of a notifiable alteration are sent to the Secretary of State and the form does not contain a request as provided in that regulation the Secretary of State shall determine whether to require a re-examination of the vehicle. If the Secretary of State determines that no re-examination is required he shall by notice inform the sender accordingly, and if the Secretary of State determines that a re-examination is required he shall by notice require the sender to submit the vehicle for re-examination.

(3) Where, under Regulation 32, an application to have a vehicle re-examined is received by the Secretary of State he shall by notice require the sender to submit the vehicle for re-examination.

(4) Any notice by which the Secretary of State requires a vehicle to be submitted for re-examination under paragraph (1), (2) or (3) shall specify the vehicle testing station, date and time appointed by the Secretary of State for that re-examination.

4–2523   34. *Fee for re-examination.*

Condition of acceptance of vehicle

4–2524   35. A goods vehicle examiner shall not be under an obligation to proceed with a re-examination of a vehicle under this Part of the Regulations where on the submission of a vehicle for the re-examination the sender does not, after being required to do so, produce to the examiner the plating certificate relating to the vehicle, and nothing in this paragraph shall be taken to derogate from Regulation 8.

Re-examination procedure, and issue or amendment of plating certificates (or notices of refusal)

4–2525   36. (1) Where a vehicle is submitted for a re-examination under this Part of these Regulations a goods vehicle examiner shall—

(a) in a case where the re-examination is carried out by reason of a notifiable alteration examine the vehicle for the purpose of determining to what extent that notifiable alteration has rendered the plated weights shown in the plating certificate relating to that vehicle no longer appropriate; or

(b) in any other case examine the vehicle for the purpose of determining to what extent any particular contained in the said plating certificate is no longer applicable.

(2) On completion of the re-examination the goods vehicle examiner shall either—

(a) by notice inform the sender that—

(i) the notifiable alteration has not rendered any of the plated weights shown in the plating certificate no longer appropriate;

(ii) the particular is still applicable; or

(b) amend the plating certificate to show any new plated weights or any new particulars which the examiner has determined for the vehicle; or

(c) issue a new plating certificate in place of the certificate required to be produced under Regulation 35 and mark as cancelled the certificate so produced.

(3) Any goods vehicle examiner amending or cancelling a plating certificate shall authenticate the amendment or cancellation by showing on the certificate or on a document securely attached to it his name, the address of the place at which the examination as a result of which the amendment or cancellation occurs, and the date on which the amendment or cancellation takes effect.

(4) Where a new plating certificate is issued for a vehicle it shall contain—

(a) particulars of any plated weights determined for the vehicle under this Regulation;

(b) *revoked;*

(c) where any such plated weight so determined is less than the weight that would have been otherwise determined under Regulation 20 but for paragraph (g) of that regulation, particulars of the last mentioned weight which shall be shown as a design weight;

(d) any other new particular determined for the vehicle under this Regulation; and

(e) subject to sub-paragraphs (a) to (d) above, the same particulars as are appropriate in the case of the plating certificate mentioned in Regulation 21.

(5) A new plating certificate shall be signed by the goods vehicle examiner who carried out, or under whose direction the re-examination was carried out, or shall be signed on behalf of that examiner by a person authorised in that behalf by the Secretary of State.

4–2526   37. *Appeals.*

PART Va
ALTERATION OF PLATED WEIGHTS WITHOUT EXAMINATION
Introduction

4–2526A   37A. (1) This Part of these Regulations has effect by virtue of section 63A of the 1988 Act.

(2) The plated weights (or any of the plated weights) for a vehicle may be determined in accordance with the provisions of this Part, without an examination under these Regulations or under regulations made under section 61 of the 1988 Act.

(3) The plated weights for a vehicle may only be determined under this regulation if—

(a) a plating certificate is in force for the vehicle, and

(b) the alteration applied for would not affect the safety of the vehicle on the road.

4–2526B   37B. *Application for alteration of plated weights without examination.*

4–2526C   37C. *Disposal of applications.*

4–2526D   37D. *Appeals.*

PART VI
MISCELLANEOUS MATTERS

4–2527 38. *Revoked.*

4–2528 39. *General provisions as to fees.*

4–2529 40. *Provisions as to fees on appeal.*

Replacements of plates and certificates

4–2530 41. (1) If a Ministry plate, a plating certificate (whether issued under these Regulations or being treated as a plating certificate by virtue of section 59(4) of the 1988 Act), a goods vehicle test certificate or a Ministry test date disc has been lost or defaced, an application for the issue of a replacement for the plate, certificate or disc lost or defaced may be made in writing to the Secretary of State and every such application shall be accompanied by the payment of a fee of £11.

(2) On the receipt of an application and fee mentioned in paragraph (1) the Secretary of State shall determine whether the vehicle shall be re-examined, and if he determines—

(*a*) that no re-examination of the vehicle is required he shall issue to the applicant a replacement for the plate, certificate or disc to which the application relates and any such replacement shall have the same effect as the plate, certificate or disc which it replaces and shall be marked "replacement";

(*b*) that a re-examination of the vehicle is required, he shall by notice to the sender require the vehicle to be submitted for re-examination at a vehicle testing station specified in the notice and appoint a date and time for the examination.

(3) A re-examination under paragraph 2(*b*) shall be carried out as if it were a first examination under Regulations 20 to 23, the appropriate fee shall be paid as if the examination were a first examination, and the appropriate documents shall be issued in accordance with Regulations 21 and 23.

Provisions as to notices

4–2531 42. (1) Except as otherwise provided in these Regulations, every notice under these Regulations shall be in writing and may be given by post.

(2) For the purposes of calculating the period of any notice given in accordance with the provisions of these Regulations a Saturday, Sunday, Good Friday, Christmas Day or a bank holiday (as defined in the Banking and Financial Dealings Act 1971) shall be excluded from the period.

(3) When giving any notice referred to in Regulation 14(1), 15(4) or 33 the Secretary of State shall have regard, so far as is reasonably practicable, to any preference expressed by the person to whom the notice is addressed as to the vehicle testing station and the date and time at which the examination shall take place.

4–2531A 42A. Any plating certificate, goods vehicle test certificate, notice of the refusal of a goods vehicle test certificate or certificate of temporary exemption which has been issued under the provisions of these Regulations and which bears a facsimile, by whatever process reproduced, of the signature of, as the case may be, the relevant goods vehicle examiner, authorised or appointed person or appeal officer, shall be deemed to have been duly signed.

PART VII
CROWN VEHICLES

Provision as to Crown Vehicles

4–2532 43. (1) Except as provided in paragraphs (2) and (3), these Regulations apply to goods vehicles which are of a class specified in Regulation 4 and which are—

(*a*) goods vehicles in the public service of the Crown which are registered or liable to be registered under the 1971 Act; or

(*b*) trailers in the public service of the Crown while drawn by goods vehicles (whether or not in the public service of the Crown) which are registered or liable to be registered under the 1971 Act.

(2) A first examination of a vehicle, a periodical test or a re-examination of a vehicle under Part V of these Regulations may be made by or under the direction of an examiner (in this Regulation referred to as an "authorised examiner") authorised for the purpose by the Secretary of State instead of by or under the direction of a goods vehicle examiner, and in relation to any such examination made by an authorised examiner these Regulations shall apply as if—

(*a*) Regulations 6, 8, 12, 13, 14, 15, 25, 29 and 37 were omitted;

(*b*) any reference to a goods vehicle examiner included a reference to an authorised examiner, and any reference to a vehicle testing station included a reference to premises approved by the Secretary of State for the carrying out of examinations under these Regulations by an authorised examiner;

(*c*) in Regulation 21(3)(*b*)(vi) the reference to the application included a reference to a form approved by the Secretary of State for the purpose of an application for an examination under these Regulations by an authorised examiner; and

(d) in Regulation 23(3)(b)(iii) and (iv) the reference to the identification mark included a reference to an identification mark allotted by the Secretary of State for the purpose of an examination under these Regulations by an authorised examiner.

(3) Any person aggrieved by a determination of an authorised examiner on a first examination of a vehicle, a periodical test or a re-examination of a vehicle under Part V of these Regulations may appeal to the Secretary of State and on the appeal the Secretary of State shall cause the vehicle to be re-examined by an officer appointed by him for the purpose and may make such determination on the basis of the re-examination as he thinks fit and, where appropriate, may issue a plating certificate, a goods vehicle test certificate or a notice of the refusal of a goods vehicle test certificate.

PART VIII
EXEMPTIONS
Exemptions from section 53(1) and (2) of the 1988 Act

4–2533 44. (1) The provisions of section 53(1) and (2) of the 1988 Act do not apply to the use of a vehicle for any of the following purposes—

   (a) the purpose of submitting it by previous arrangement for, or of bringing it away from, or being used in the course of or in connection with any examination;
   (b) where a goods vehicle test certificate is refused on an examination—

      (i) the purpose of delivering it by previous arrangement at, or bringing it away from, a place where work is to be or has been done on it to remedy the defects on the grounds of which the certificate was refused; or
      (ii) the purpose of delivering it, by towing it, to a place where it is to be broken up.

   (c) when unladen, the purpose of being driven or drawn unladen by a vehicle driven under a trade licence issued under section 16 of the 1971 Act;
   (d) the purpose of being driven or drawn where it has been imported into Great Britain after arrival in Great Britain on the journey from the place where it has arrived in Great Britain to a place where it is to be kept by the person importing the vehicle or by any other person on whose behalf the vehicle has been imported, and in this sub-paragraph the reference to a vehicle being imported into Great Britain is a reference, in the case of a vehicle which has been so imported more than once, to the first such importation, and in determining for the purposes of this sub-paragraph when a vehicle was first so imported any such importation as is referred to in paragraph 24 of Schedule 2 shall be disregarded;
   (e) any purpose for which it is authorised to be used on roads by an order under section 44 of the 1988 Act;
   (f) any purpose connected with its seizure or detention by a constable;
   (g) any purpose connected with its removal, detention, seizure, condemnation or forfeiture under any provision in the Customs and Excise Management Act 1979; and
   (h) the purpose of removing it under section 3 of the Refuse Disposal (Amenity) Act 1978, or under section 99 of the Road Traffic Regulation Act 1984, or of removing it from a parking place in pursuance of an order under section 35(1) of the Road Traffic Regulation Act 1984, an order relating to a parking place designated under section 45 thereof, or a provision of a designation order having effect by virtue of section 53(3) thereof.

(2) The provisions of section 53(1) and (2) of the 1988 Act shall not apply to the use of a vehicle in so far as such use occurs in any place (excluding the Isle of Wight, the islands of Lewis, Mainland (Orkney), Mainland (Shetland) and Skye) being any island and to any area mainly surrounded by water, being an island or area from which motor vehicles not constructed for special purposes can at no time be conveniently driven to a road in any other part of Great Britain by reason of the absence of any bridge, tunnel, ford or other way suitable for the passage of such motor vehicles.

Exemption from section 63(2) of the 1988 Act

4–2534 45. Motor vehicles, other than those manufactured on or after 1st October 1982 and first used on or after 1st April 1983, not constructed or adapted to form part of an articulated vehicle are hereby exempted from the provisions of section 63(2) of the 1988 Act.

Certificates of temporary exemption

4–2535 46. (1) The Secretary of State may issue in respect of a vehicle a certificate of temporary exemption, by virtue of which that vehicle shall not, during the period specified in paragraph (2)(d), be subject to the provisions of section 53(1) or (2) of the 1988 Act, where—

   (a) he is satisfied that by reason of exceptional circumstances, as defined in Regulation 39(1) affecting either a vehicle testing station or the vehicle, an examination cannot be completed by a date fixed under these Regulations for carrying out the examination; and
   (b) the use of the vehicle on or after that date would be unlawful by virtue of the said provisions.

(2) Every certificate of temporary exemption shall be on a form approved by the Secretary of State and shall be signed by a person duly authorised on his behalf and shall contain—

   (a) in the case of a certificate issued for a motor vehicle, the registration mark (if any) exhibited on the vehicle or, if no such mark is so exhibited, the chassis or serial number marked on the vehicle or, if no such number is so marked, the identification mark which shall have been allotted to the vehicle by the Secretary of State in the notice of appointment relating to the first examination of the vehicle;

(b) in the case of a certificate issued for a trailer, the identification mark which shall have been allotted to the trailer by the Secretary of State in the notice of appointment (if any) relating to the first examination of the trailer or shall have otherwise been allotted to the trailer by the Secretary of State under these Regulations;

(c) the date on which the certificate is issued; and

(d) the period during which the vehicle is exempted from the provisions of section 53(1) or (2) of the 1988 Act so, however, that no such period shall exceed three months in duration.

(Regulations 3 (1) and 20)   **SCHEDULE 1**
PROVISIONS AS TO BRAKING FORCE OF TRAILERS

4–2541   **1.** In this Schedule—
the letter "W" represents—

(a) in the case of a trailer so designed that part of the weight of the trailer is imposed on the drawing vehicle, the axle weight, or, as the case may be, the sum of the axle weights which is or are to be determined for the trailer on an examination for plating;

(b) in any other case the gross weight of the trailer which is to be so determined.

2. The minimum braking force capable of being developed by the brakes of a trailer manufactured before 1st January 1968 should in the case of—

(a) a trailer, not being a semi-trailer, be 0·4W;

(b) a semi-trailer for which a gross weight of 6100 kilogrammes or more is to be determined for the vehicle on an examination for plating, be 0·35W;

(c) a semi-trailer for which a gross weight of less than 6100 kilogrammes is to be so determined, be 0·32W.

3. The minimum braking force capable of being developed by the brakes of a trailer manufactured on or after 1st January 1968 but before 1st October 1982 should in the case of—

(a) a trailer, not being a semi-trailer, be 0·5W;

(b) a semi-trailer, be 0·4W.

4. The minimum braking force capable of being developed by the brakes of a trailer manufactured on or after 1st October 1982 should be 0·45W.

(Regulation 4)   **SCHEDULE 2**
CLASSES OF VEHICLE TO WHICH THESE REGULATIONS DO NOT APPLY

(*Amended by SI 2002/487.*)

4–2542   **1.** Dual-purpose vehicles not constructed or adapted to form part of an articulated vehicle.

2. Mobile cranes as defined in Schedule 3 to the 1971 Act.

3. Break-down vehicles.

4. Engineering plant and plant, not being engineering plant, which is movable plant or equipment being a motor vehicle or trailer (not constructed primarily to carry a load) especially designed and constructed for the special purpose of engineering operations.

5. Trailers being drying or mixing plant designed for the production of asphalt or of bituminous or tar macadam.

6. Tower wagons as defined in—

(a) paragraph 8 of Schedule 1 to the Vehicle Excise and Registration Act 1994 as originally enacted; or

(b) paragraph 17 of Schedule 2 to that Act as originally enacted.

7. Road construction vehicles as defined in section 61 of the Vehicle Excise and Registration Act 1994 as originally enacted and road rollers.

8. Vehicles designed and used solely for fire fighting or fire salvage purposes.

9. Works trucks, straddle carriers used solely as works trucks, and works trailers.

10. Electrically-propelled motor vehicles.

11. Vehicles used solely for one or both of the following purposes—

(a) clearing frost, ice or snow from roads by means of a snow plough or similar contrivance, whether forming part of the vehicle or not, and

(b) spreading material on roads to deal with frost, ice or snow.

12. Motor vehicles used for no other purpose than the haulage of lifeboats and the conveyance of the necessary gear of the lifeboats which are being hauled.

13. Living vans the design gross weight of which does not exceed 3,500 kilograms.

14. Vehicles constructed or adapted for, and used primarily for the purpose of, carrying equipment permanently fixed to the vehicle¹ which equipment is used for medical, dental, veterinary, health, educational, display, clerical or experimental laboratory purposes, such use—

(a) not directly involving the sale, hire or loan of goods from the vehicle; and

(b) not directly or indirectly involving drain cleaning or sewage or refuse collection.

15. Trailers which have no other brakes than a parking brake and brakes which automatically come into operation on the over-run of the trailer.

16. A motor vehicle at a time when it is being used on a public road during any calendar week if—

(a) it is being used only in passing from land in the occupation of the person keeping the vehicle to other land in his occupation, and

(b) it has not been used on public roads for distances exceeding an aggregate of six miles in that calendar week, and to a trailer drawn by a motor vehicle that is being used on a public road in such circumstances.

For the purposes of this paragraph "public road" has the meaning given in section 62(1) the Vehicle Excise and Registration Act 1994.

17. Agricultural motor vehicles and agricultural trailed appliances.

18. Agricultural trailers and agricultural trailed appliance conveyors drawn on roads only by an agricultural motor vehicle.

18A. Converter dollies used solely for the purposes of agriculture, horticulture and forestry, or for any one or two of those purposes.

19. Public service vehicles (as defined in section 1 of the Public Passenger Vehicles Act 1981).

20. Licensed taxis (as defined in section 13(3) of the Transport Act 1985).

21. Vehicles used solely for the purposes of funerals.

22. Goods vehicles to which any of the prescribed construction and use requirements do not apply by virtue of either of the following items in the Table in Regulation 4(4) of the Construction and Use Regulations namely—

(a) item 1 (which relates to vehicles proceeding to a port for export);

(b) item 4 (which relates to vehicles in the service of a visiting force or of a headquarters).

23. Vehicles equipped with new or improved equipment or types of equipment and used, solely by a manufacturer of vehicles or their equipment or by an importer of vehicles, for or in connection with the test or trial of any such equipment.

24. Motor vehicles brought into Great Britain and displaying a registration mark mentioned in Regulation 5 of the Motor Vehicles (International Circulation) Regulations 1971, a period of twelve months not having elapsed since the vehicle in question was last brought into Great Britain.

25. Motor vehicles in respect of which a test certificate issued in accordance with Article 34 of the Road Traffic (Northern Ireland) Order 1981 is in force or which are for the time being licensed under the Vehicles (Excise) Act (Northern Ireland) 1972.

26. Vehicles having a base or centre in any of the following islands, namely, Arran, Bute, Great Cumbrae, Islay, Mull, Tiree or North Uist from which the use of the vehicle on a journey is normally commenced.

27. Trailers brought into Great Britain and having a base or centre in a country outside Great Britain from which the use of the vehicle on a journey is normally commenced, a period of twelve months not having elapsed since the vehicle in question was last brought into Great Britain.

28. Track laying vehicles.

29. Steam propelled vehicles.

30. Motor vehicles first used before 1st January 1960, used unladen and not drawing a laden trailer, and trailers manufactured before 1st January 1960 and used unladen.

For the purposes of this paragraph any determination as to when a motor vehicle is first used shall be made as provided in Regulation 3(3) of the Construction and Use Regulations.

31. Motor vehicles constructed, and not merely adapted, for the purpose of street cleansing, or the collection or disposal of refuse or the collection or disposal of the contents of gullies and which are either—

(a) three-wheeled vehicles, or

(b) vehicles which—

(i) are incapable by reason of their construction of exceeding a speed of 20 miles per hour on the level under their own power, or

(ii) have an inside track width of not more than 1100mm.

32. Vehicles designed and used for the purpose of servicing or controlling or loading or unloading air craft while so used—

(a) on an aerodrome as defined in section 105(1) of the Civil Aviation Act 1982;

(b) on roads outside such an aerodrome if, except when proceeding directly from one part of such an aerodrome to another part thereof, the vehicles are unladen and are not drawing a laden trailer.

33. Vehicles designed for use, and used on an aerodrome mentioned in paragraph 32 solely for the purpose of road cleansing, the collection or disposal of refuse or the collection or disposal of the contents of gullies or cesspools.

34. Vehicles provided for police purposes and maintained in workshops approved by the Secretary of State as suitable for such maintenance, being vehicles provided in England and Wales by a police authority or the Receiver for the metropolitan police district, or, in Scotland by a police authority or a joint police committee.

35. Heavy motor cars or motor cars constructed or adapted for the purpose of forming part of an articulated vehicle and which are used for drawing only a trailer falling within a class of vehicle specified in paragraph 13, 14 or 15 of this Schedule or a trailer being used for or in connection with any purpose for which it is authorised to be used on roads by an order under section 44(1) of the 1988 Act, being an order authorising that trailer or any class or description of trailers comprising that trailer to be used on roads.

36. Play buses.

---

1. In a case decided under the predecessor regulation it was held that equipment that is permanently fixed to the vehicle must be used for some activity to be carried on, in part at least in the vehicle (*Creek v Fossett, Eccles and Supertents Ltd* [1986] Crim LR 256).

37. A vehicle—

(a) which complies with the requirements specified in regulation 4(2) of the Motor Vehicles (Approval) Regulations 2001;

(b) in respect of which a Minister's approval certificate has been issued under section 58 of the 1988 Act for the purposes of the type approval requirements prescribed by those Regulations; and

(c) in respect of which a Minister's approval certificate has not subsequently been issued under that section for the purposes of the type approval requirements prescribed by the National Type Approval for Goods Vehicles Regulations.

(Regulations 3 and 16)   SCHEDULE 3
                 The Prescribed Construction and Use Requirements

                            Part I

4–2543   **1.** The requirements contained in the provisions of the Construction and Use Regulations set out in column (2) of Table I below.

                            Table I

(1) Item No	(2) Regulation	(3) Subject Matter
1	15 to 18	Braking systems
2	24 to 27	Tyres
3	29	Maintenance of steering gear
4	30	View to the front
5	33	Mirrors
6	34	Windscreen wipers and washers
7	35 and 36	Speedometer
8	36B	Speed limiters
9	37	Audible warning
10	46, 47 and 48	Seat Belts
11	49 and 50	Rear under-run protection
12	51 and 52	Side guards
13	54	Maintenance of silencer
14	61	Smoke emission, oil etc
15	64 and 65	Spray suppression equipment
16	70A	Speed limiter plates

2. The requirements contained in the provisions of the Road Vehicles Lighting Regulations 1989 set out in column (2) of Table II below to the extent shown in column (4) of that Table (expressions used in that Table having the same meanings as they have in those Regulations).

                            Table II

(1) Item No	(2) Regulation	(3) Subject matter	(4) Extent
17	18	Obligatory lamps, reflectors, rear markings and devices	Except in so far as the regulation relates to dim-dip devices, running lamps, front fog lamps, reversing lamps and warning beacons.
18	20	Optional lamps, reflectors, rear markings and devices	In so far as the regulation relates to— headlamps fitted to motor vehicles; direction indicators; rear fog lamps; stop lamps; and rear markings.
19	23	Maintenance of lamps, reflectors, rear markings and devices	Except in so far as the regulation relates to dim-dip devices, running lamps, front fog lamps, reversing lamps and warning beacons.

3. The requirements, in so far as they relate to the installation of recording equipment in Article 3, and the seals to be affixed to such equipment in Article 12 and paragraph 4 of Section V of Annex 1 of the Community Recording Equipment Regulation (as defined in section 85 of the 1988 Act).

                            Part II

4. The requirements of this Part of this Schedule, in relation to a vehicle, are that the condition of the vehicle is such that its use on a road would not involve a danger of injury to any person having regard in particular to items of the following descriptions—

    spare wheel carrier;
    trailer coupling on a motor vehicle;
    coupling on a trailer;
    the chassis;
    electrical wiring and equipment;
    landing legs;
    engine mountings;
    fuel tanks and system;
    transmission shafts and associated equipment;
    exhaust system;
    battery;
    wheels and hubs;
    suspension system;
    axles and steering gear;
    shock absorbers;
    bumpers;
    wings;
    the cab;
    driving seat;
    the body;
    driver's controls;
    cab step or step rings;
    glass, or other transparent material in windscreen or windows;
    loading devices;
    load securing devices.

Public Service Vehicles (Conduct of Drivers, Inspectors, Conductors and Passengers) Regulations 1990[1]

(SI 1990/1020, amended by SI 1995/186 and SI 2002/1724)

4-2561   1. *Citation and commencement.*

---

1. Made by the Secretary of State for Transport in exercise of powers conferred by ss 24(2), 25(1) and (4) and 60 of the Public Passenger Vehicles Act 1981 and ss 23(2)(*b*), 134(1) and 137(1) of the Transport Act 1985. Breaches of the regulations which would be offences under s 24(2) of the 1981 Act punishable with a fine not exceeding **level 2** on the standard scale and breaches of the regulations which would be offences under s 25(3) of the 1981 Act punishable with a fine not exceeding **level 3** on the standard scale.

4-2562   2. *Revocation.*

Interpretation

4-2563   3. (1) In this Part of the Regulations unless the context otherwise requires—

"the 1981 Act" means the Public Passenger Vehicles Act 1981;
"the 1985 Act" means the Transport Act 1985;
"the 1995 Act" means the Disability Discrimination Act 1995;*
"the 1984 Regulations" means the Public Service Vehicles (Carrying Capacity) Regulations 1984;
"the 2000 Regulations" means the Public Service Vehicles Accessibility Regulations 2000;
"assistance dog" means a dog which—

(a) is trained by a specified charity to assist a disabled person with a physical impairment for the purpose of section 1 of the 1995 Act which—

   (i) consists of epilepsy; or
   (ii) otherwise affects his mobility, manual dexterity, physical coordination or ability to lift, carry or otherwise move everyday objects; and

(b) at the time it is providing assistance to a disabled person, is wearing a jacket inscribed with the name of one of the following charities, that is to say—

   (i) "Dogs for the Disabled" registered with the Charity Commission under registration number 700454;
   (ii) "Support Dogs" registered with the Charity Commission under registration number 1017237; or
   (iii) "Canine Partners for Independence" registered with the Charity Commission under registration number 803680;

"boarding lift" means a lift fitted to a regulated public service vehicle for the purpose of allowing wheelchair users to board and alight from the vehicle;
"boarding ramp" means a ramp fitted to a regulated public service vehicle for the purpose of allowing wheelchair users to board and alight from the vehicle;
"disabled person" has the same meaning as in section 1 of the 1995 Act;
"guide dog" has the same meaning as in section 37(11) of the 1995 Act;
"hearing dog" has the same meaning as in section 37(11) of the 1995 Act;
"licence" means a licence to drive a vehicle granted under section 22 of the 1981 Act;
"local service" has the same meaning as in section 2 of the 1985 Act;
"maximum seating capacity" has the same meaning as in regulation 4 of the 1984 Regulations;
"maximum standing capacity" has the same meaning as in regulation 6 of the 1984 Regulations;
"portable ramp" means a ramp which is carried on a regulated public service vehicle for the purpose of allowing wheelchair users to board or alight from the vehicle;
"regulated public service vehicle" means a public service vehicle to which the 2000 Regulations apply;
"scheduled service" means a service, using one or more public service vehicles, for the carriage of passengers at separate fares—

(a) along specified routes,
(b) at specified times, and
(c) with passengers being taken up and set down at pre-determined stopping points,

but does not include a tour service (being a service where a public service vehicle is used for or in conjunction with the carriage of passengers to a particular location, or particular locations, and back to their point of departure);

"ticket" means a document which, in accordance with the terms and conditions under which it has been issued, constitutes a valid authority to travel on a vehicle;
"vehicle" means any vehicle used as a public service vehicle as defined in the 1981 Act but excluding any vehicle used under a permit granted by virtue of section 19 of the 1985 Act;
"wheelchair restraint system" means a system which is designed to keep a wheelchair restrained within the wheelchair space;
"wheelchair space" means a space for a wheelchair with which a regulated public service vehicle is fitted in accordance with paragraph 2 of Schedule 1 to the 2000 Regulations;
"wheelchair user" means a disabled person using a wheelchair; and
"wheelchair user restraint" means a system which is designed to keep a wheelchair user restrained in the wheelchair.*

(2) For the purposes of this Part of the Regulations, a sum payable by a passenger on the vehicle shall not be regarded as a fare unless—

(a) it is computed in accordance with a fare table available on the vehicle; and
(b) the fare table contains sufficient information to enable the passenger to ascertain the fare for his journey or the manner in which it is computed.

(3) In this Part of the Regulations, in relation to a vehicle—

"conductor" means a person, not being the driver, who is authorised by the operator to act as a conductor on the vehicle, but does not include an inspector; and
"driver" means a person who is the holder of a licence and who is for the time being responsible for driving the vehicle.

(4) In this Part of the Regulations, any reference to a numbered regulation is a reference to the regulation bearing that number in this Part of the Regulations.

(5) In this Part of the Regulations, any reference to a numbered or lettered paragraph or sub-paragraph is a reference to the paragraph or sub-paragraph bearing that number or letter in the regulation or (in the case of a sub-paragraph) paragraph in which the reference appears.

The conduct of drivers, inspectors and conductors

4–2564   **4.** (1) A driver shall not, when a vehicle is in motion, hold a microphone or any attachment thereto unless it is necessary for him, either in an emergency or on the grounds of safety, to speak into the microphone.

(2) Subject to paragraph (3), a driver shall not, when a vehicle is in motion, speak to any person either directly or by means of a microphone.

(3) Nothing in paragraph (2) shall prevent—

(a) the driver of a vehicle from—

(i) speaking in circumstances when he is obliged to do so by reason of an emergency or on grounds of safety; or
(ii) speaking to a relevant person in relation to the operation of the vehicle provided that he can do so without being distracted from his driving of the vehicle; and

(b) the driver of a vehicle which is being used to provide a relevant service from making short statements from time to time limited to indicating the location of the vehicle or operational matters provided that he can do so without being distracted from his driving of the vehicle.

(4) In this regulation—

(a) "relevant person" is a person fulfilling one of the following descriptions—

(i) an employee of the operator;
(ii) when the operator is a firm, a partner of the firm;
(iii) if the operator is an individual, that individual; or
(iv) if the operator is a company, a director; and

(b) "relevant service" is a service for the carriage of passengers for hire or reward at separate fares which is neither—

(i) an excursion or tour within the meaning of section 137(1) of the 1985 Act; nor
(ii) a service the primary purpose of which is sightseeing, not falling within sub-paragraph (i).

4–2565   **5.** (1) A driver and a conductor shall take all reasonable precautions[1] to ensure the safety of passengers who are on, or who are entering or leaving, the vehicle.

(2) A driver, inspector and conductor shall take all reasonable steps to ensure that the provisions of these Regulations relating to the conduct of passengers are complied with.

(3) A driver, inspector or conductor—

(a) shall, if so requested by a constable or other person having reasonable cause, give his name, the person by whom he is employed and, in the case of a driver, particulars of the licence by virtue of which he drives the vehicle; and
(b) shall not smoke in or on a vehicle except in one of the circumstances specified in paragraph (4).

(4) The circumstances referred to in paragraph (3)(b) are that—

(a) the vehicle is not available for the carriage of passengers and the person concerned is in or on any part of the vehicle where smoking by passengers is not prohibited by regulation 6(1)(d); or
(b) the vehicle is hired as a whole and the person concerned has the permission of the operator and the hirer.

(5) A driver shall, when picking up or setting down passengers, stop the vehicle as close as is reasonably practicable to the left or near side of the road.

(6) A conductor shall not, while the vehicle is in motion and without reasonable cause, distract the driver's attention or obstruct his vision.

(7) A driver, inspector and a conductor shall not, subject to there being a suitable space available, prevent a disabled person accompanied by an assistance dog, a guide dog or a hearing dog, being allowed to board and travel in the vehicle with his dog.

1. In *Edwards v Rigby* [1980] RTR 353, where the information was dismissed, the lack of visibility behind a door panel was balanced against the difficult and risky manoeuvre if the driver were to leave his seat.

The conduct of passengers

4–2566   6. (1) No passenger on a vehicle shall—

(a) where the vehicle has a door which passengers are by a notice informed is for a particular purpose, use that door for any other purpose, unless otherwise directed or authorised by a driver, inspector or conductor;

(b) put at risk or unreasonably impede or cause discomfort to any person travelling on or entering or leaving the vehicle, or a driver, inspector, conductor or employee of the operator when doing his work on the vehicle;

(c) throw or trail any article from the vehicle;

(d) smoke or carry lighted tobacco or light a match or a cigarette lighter in or on any part of the vehicle where passengers are by a notice informed that smoking is prohibited, unless the vehicle has been hired as a whole and both the operator and the hirer have given their permission to the contrary;

(e) except with the permission of the operator, distribute any paper or other article for the purpose of giving or seeking information about or comment upon any matter;

(f) except with the permission of the operator, sell or offer for sale any article;

(g) speak to the driver whilst the vehicle is in motion except—

   (i) in an emergency;

   (ii) for reasons of safety; or

   (iii) to give directions as to the stopping of the vehicle;

(h) without reasonable cause distract the driver's attention, obstruct his vision or give any signal which might reasonably be interpreted by the driver as a signal—

   (i) to stop the vehicle in an emergency; or

   (ii) to start the vehicle;

(j) travel on any part of the vehicle which is not provided for the carriage of passengers;

(k) remain on the vehicle, when directed to leave by the driver, inspector or conductor on the following grounds—

   (i) that his remaining would result in the number of passengers exceeding the maximum seating capacity or the maximum standing capacity marked on the vehicle in accordance with the Public Service Vehicles (Carrying Capacity) Regulations 1984;

   (ii) that he has been causing a nuisance; or

   (iii) that his condition is such as would be likely to cause offence to a reasonable passenger or that the condition of his clothing is such that his remaining would be reasonably expected to soil the fittings of the vehicle or the clothing of other passengers;

(l) play or operate any musical instrument or sound reproducing equipment to the annoyance of any person on the vehicle or in a manner which is likely to cause annoyance to any person on the vehicle; or

(m) intentionally interfere with any equipment with which the vehicle is fitted.

(1A) Paragraph (1)(k)(ii) and (iii) shall not apply to a direction given by a driver, inspector or conductor solely on the grounds that a person is a disabled person.

(2) Subject to paragraph (3), a passenger on a vehicle who has with him any article or substance mentioned in paragraph (4) or any animal—

(a) if directed by the driver, inspector or conductor to put it in a particular place on the vehicle, shall put it where directed; and

(b) if requested to move it from the vehicle by the driver, inspector or conductor, shall remove it.

(3) Paragraph (2)(b) does not require the removal of an animal where the passenger is a disabled person and the animal is an assistance dog, a guide dog or a hearing dog.

(3A) Without prejudice to regulation 5(7), a disabled person shall comply with any direction given by a driver, inspector or conductor to remove his assistance dog, guide dog or hearing dog from the gangway.

(4) The article or substance referred to in paragraph (2) is—

(a) any bulky or cumbersome article;

(b) any article or substance which causes or is likely to cause annoyance to any person on the vehicle; or

(c) any article or substance which would be reasonably expected to constitute—

   (i) a risk of injury to any person on the vehicle; or

   (ii) a risk of damage to the property of any person on the vehicle or to the vehicle.

(5) In this regulation, "double-decked vehicle", "single-decked vehicle" and "overall length" have the meanings given by the Road Vehicles (Construction and Use) Regulations 1986.

4–2567   7. (1) No passenger on a vehicle being used for the carriage of passengers at separate fares shall use any ticket which has—

(a) been altered or defaced;

(b) been issued for use by another person on terms that it is not transferable; or

(c) expired.

(2) Save as provided in paragraph (3), every passenger on a vehicle being used for the carriage of passengers at separate fares shall—

(a) declare, if so requested by the driver, inspector or conductor, the journey which he intends to take, is taking or has taken in the vehicle;

(b) where the vehicle is being operated by the driver without a conductor—

(i) save as provided in (ii) below, immediately on boarding the vehicle, pay the fare for the journey he intends to take to the driver or, where appropriate, by inserting in any fare-collection equipment provided on the vehicle the money or token required to pay that fare; or

(ii) if otherwise directed by the driver, an inspector or a notice displayed on the vehicle, shall pay the fare for his journey in accordance with the direction;

(c) where the vehicle is being operated by the driver with a conductor, pay the fare for the journey which he intends to take, is taking, or has taken in the vehicle to the conductor immediately on being requested to do so by the conductor or an inspector;

(d) accept and retain for the rest of his journey any ticket which is provided on payment of a fare in accordance with sub-paragraph (b) or (c);

(e) produce during his journey any ticket which has been issued to him either under sub-paragraph (d) or before he started his journey for inspection by the driver, inspector or conductor on being requested to do so by the driver, inspector or conductor; and

(f) as soon as he has completed the journey for which he has a ticket, either—

(i) leave the vehicle; or

(ii) pay the fare for any further journey which he intends to take on the vehicle.

(3) Paragraph (2)(b) and (c) do not apply to a passenger who has with him a ticket which was issued to him before his journey in respect of that journey, provided he complies with all such directions in relation to the ticket as may be—

(a) printed on the ticket;

(b) displayed on the vehicle; or

(c) given by the driver, inspector or conductor.

(4) Any passenger who—

(a) fails to comply with paragraph 2(b) or (c); or

(b) does not have with him a ticket which was issued to him before his journey in respect of that journey;

shall pay the fare for his journey to the driver, inspector or conductor on request and in any case before he leaves the vehicle unless otherwise agreed by the driver, inspector or conductor.

(5) Any passenger on a vehicle being used for the carriage of passengers at separate fares who has with him a ticket which he is not entitled to retain for any reason including—

(a) the alteration or defacement of the ticket;

(b) the fact that the ticket, having been issued for use by another person, was not transferable to him;

(c) the expiry of the ticket; or

(d) a mistake in consequence of which the ticket was issued;

shall surrender the ticket to a driver, inspector or conductor on being required to do so.

4–2568 8. (1) Any passenger on a vehicle who is reasonably suspected by the driver, inspector or conductor of the vehicle of contravening any provision of these Regulations shall give his name and address to the driver, inspector or conductor on demand.

(2) Any passenger on a vehicle who contravenes any provision of these Regulations may be removed from the vehicle by the driver, inspector or conductor of the vehicle or, on the request of the driver, inspector or conductor, by a police constable.

4–2569 9. In its application to Scotland, regulation 8(1) shall have effect as if after the word "address" there were inserted the words "to a police constable or".

4–2569A 10. (Repealed).

The Conduct of Drivers and Conductors of Regulated Public Service Vehicles with Respect to Wheelchair Users and Other Disabled Persons

4–2569B 11. In this Part—

"Schedule 1" means Schedule 1 (wheelchair accessibility requirements) to the 2000 Regulations;

"Schedule 2" means Schedule 2 (general accessibility requirements for single-deck and double-deck buses) to the 2000 Regulations;

"Schedule 3" means Schedule 3 (general accessibility requirements for single-deck and double-deck coaches) to the 2000 Regulations;

a "Schedule 1 vehicle" means a regulated public service vehicle which is required to comply with the provisions of Schedule 1; and

a "Schedule 2 or 3 vehicle" means a regulated public service vehicle which is required to comply (as the case may be) with the provisions of either Schedule 2 or Schedule 3.

4–2569C   12. (1) This regulation applies (subject to regulation 15(1) (duties requiring the proper functioning of equipment)) in relation to a driver and a conductor of a Schedule 1 vehicle.

(2) If there is an unoccupied wheelchair space on the vehicle, a driver and a conductor shall allow a wheelchair user to board if—

(a) the wheelchair is of a type or size that can be correctly and safely located in that wheelchair space, and

(b) in so doing, neither the maximum seating nor standing capacity of the vehicle would be exceeded.

(3) For the purpose of paragraph (2), a wheelchair space is occupied if—

(a) there is a wheelchair user in that space; or

(b) passengers or their effects are in that space and they or their effects cannot readily and reasonably vacate it by moving to another part of the vehicle.

(4) A driver and a conductor shall ensure—

(a) where the carriage of a portable ramp is required by Schedule 1, that a portable ramp is carried on the vehicle where the vehicle is operating on a local service or on a scheduled service;

(b) that any boarding lift, boarding ramp or portable ramp is in its normal position for vehicle travel and is securely stowed before the vehicle is driven;

(c) where the vehicle is operating on a local or a scheduled service and it is fitted with a boarding lift or a boarding ramp which, in order to comply with Schedule 1, requires a means of control for it to be capable of being operated manually in the event of a power failure, that such a separate means of control is carried on the vehicle;

(d) that wheelchair users can gain access into and can get out of a wheelchair space;

(e) before the vehicle is driven, that any wheelchair user is correctly and safely positioned in a wheelchair space and that any retractable rail (being a rail fitted in accordance with the requirements of paragraph 4(3)(b) of Schedule 1) or any similar device is in a position to restrict the lateral movement of the wheelchair; and

(f) where a wheelchair user using a wheelchair space faces the front of the vehicle, that the wheelchair restraint system is attached in accordance with the relevant instructions pursuant to paragraph 8(3) of Schedule 1.

(5) If the vehicle has a seat in a wheelchair space which is capable of being quickly dismantled or removed, a driver and a conductor shall ensure that any such seat—

(a) when it is not in use and is stowed on the vehicle, is safely stowed; and

(b) whenever it is in position for use within the wheelchair space, is secured.

4–2569D   13. (1) This regulation (subject to regulations 15 (effects of faulty or malfunctioning equipment) and 17 (extent of driver's and conductor's duty)) applies in relation to a driver and to a conductor of a Schedule 2 and 3 vehicle where that vehicle is equipped with—

(a) a kneeling system, or

(b) a folding or retractable step.

(2) A driver and a conductor shall operate the kneeling system or the folding or retractable step—

(a) whenever they consider that a disabled person will need the system to be operated or the step to be deployed, or

(b) if requested to do so,

for the purpose of enabling that person to board or to alight from the vehicle, and in such a manner that the distance between the vehicle and the ground or the vehicle and the kerb is the minimum that is reasonably practicable.

(3) "Kneeling system" means any system which enables the bodywork of the vehicle to be lowered relative to its normal height of travel and a "folding or retractable step" means a step which can either fold or retract and which meets the requirements applicable to external steps pursuant to paragraph 4 of Schedule 2 or Schedule 3 (as the case may be).

(4) A driver and a conductor shall ensure that disabled persons who are not wheelchair users may, when boarding or alighting from the vehicle, use an entrance or an exit which is provided in compliance with (as the case may be) the provisions of either Schedule 2 or Schedule 3.

4–2569E   14. (1) Where a wheelchair user wishes to board or to alight from a Schedule 1 vehicle, a driver and a conductor shall first safely deploy (subject to regulation 15(1) (duties requiring the proper functioning of equipment)) any boarding lift, boarding ramp or portable ramp in its correct operating position.

(2) Where a wheelchair user wishes to board or to alight from a Schedule 1 vehicle and requests assistance to do so, a driver and a conductor shall provide assistance to him.

(3) Where a disabled person who is not a wheelchair user wishes to board or to alight from a Schedule 2 or 3 vehicle and requests assistance to do so, a driver and a conductor shall provide assistance to him.

(4) Where a wheelchair user wishes to occupy a wheelchair space in a Schedule 1 vehicle which is fitted with a wheelchair user restraint, a driver and a conductor shall—

(a) offer to provide such assistance as may be required so as to enable the wheelchair user to wear that restraint, and

(b) in providing that assistance, apply (subject to regulation 15(1) (duties requiring the proper functioning of equipment)) the wheelchair user restraint only in accordance with the user instructions which are displayed pursuant to paragraph 8(3) of Schedule 1.

4–2569F   15. (1) Where the fulfilment of a duty owed by a driver or a conductor under—

(a) regulation 12 (duties towards wheelchair users of Schedule 1 vehicles),
(b) regulation 13 (duties concerning kneeling systems etc towards disabled persons using Schedule 2 or 3 vehicles) or
(c) regulation 14 (general duties towards wheelchair users and other disabled persons),

requires the use or operation of any equipment, kneeling system or folding or retractable step and there is a fault in, or a failure in the operation of, that equipment, system or step, the person owing the duty shall not permit a wheelchair user, or other disabled person or any other passenger to board or alight from the vehicle or (if already on board) to travel on the vehicle unless he is satisfied that such persons can do so in safety.

(2) A driver or a conductor shall not be considered to have failed to ensure fulfilment of the duty under either regulation 13(2) (duties concerning kneeling systems etc) or regulation 16 (display of route numbers etc) if, and to the extent that, the performance of that duty involves the proper functioning of equipment on the vehicle but there is a fault in, or a failure in the operation of, that equipment which prevents it being used.

(3) In this regulation—

"equipment" means any equipment fitted to a regulated public service vehicle in order to comply with Schedule 1, Schedule 2 or Schedule 3 and which a driver and a conductor must operate for the safe fulfilment of the relevant duty; and

"kneeling system or folding or retractable step" has the same meaning as in regulation 13(3).

4–2569G   16. (1) Subject to regulation 15(2) (equipment failure preventing use), a driver and a conductor of a regulated public service vehicle shall ensure that—

(a) a route number (if any) and a destination is displayed in the positions provided for such displays with respect to the vehicle in accordance (as the case may be) with either paragraph 8 of Schedule 2 or paragraph 7 of Schedule 3;
(b) a route number and a destination displayed in accordance with sub-paragraph (a) which is required to be provided with a means of illumination shall have characters that are kept illuminated between sunset and sunrise; and
(c) the vehicle shall at all times display the correct route number and destination.

(2) Sub-paragraphs (a) and (b) of paragraph (1) shall not apply to an emergency replacement vehicle or to a temporary service vehicle until 21 days has elapsed from the day when the vehicle is first used as an emergency replacement vehicle or as a temporary service vehicle, provided that—

(a) the route number (if any) and a destination shall be displayed either on the front or on the nearside of the vehicle as close as practical to the foremost passenger entrance; and
(b) the requirement of sub-paragraph (c) of paragraph (1) is complied with.

(3) In this regulation, "destination" and "route number" have the same meanings as in paragraph 7(6) of Schedule 3 to the 2000 Regulations and—

"emergency replacement vehicle" means a public service vehicle which has been brought into service on the route in question to provide emergency cover; and

"temporary service vehicle" means a public service vehicle which is in service on a temporary route or service.

4–2569H   17. (1) Where, in any of the preceding provisions of this Part, a duty is expressed to be owed by the driver and the conductor of a vehicle, but a function to be performed to fulfil that duty is, according to arrangements made by the operator of the vehicle, the responsibility of one only of them, then that one only, and not the other, owes that duty in relation to that function.

(2) The duties which a driver or a conductor owes under regulation 13 (duties concerning kneeling systems etc) and 14 (general duties towards wheelchair users and other disabled persons) are duties—

(a) to take such care as in all the circumstances of the case is reasonable to see that the wheelchair user or other disabled person will be reasonably safe in boarding or in alighting from the vehicle, and
(b) shall not oblige the person owing the duty to take any steps if, on reasonable grounds, he considers that—

(i) there will be a risk to his health, safety or security or to that of the wheelchair user or other disabled person or to that of any other passenger or member of the public; or
(ii) there will be a risk to the safety and security of the vehicle.

(3) The duties which a driver or a conductor owes under regulations 13 (duties concerning kneeling systems etc) and 14 (general duties towards wheelchair users and other disabled persons) are duties to operate the kneeling system or the folding or retractable step, or to deploy the boarding lift, boarding ramp or portable ramp to the extent that it is practicable having regard to the construction of the vehicle and the condition of the road.

Road Vehicles (Prohibition) Regulations 1992[1]
(SI 1992/1285 amended by SI 1997/83)

4–2600 **1.** *Citation and commencement.*

---

1. Made by the Secretary of State for Transport, in exercise of the powers conferred by section 71(2), and 72 of the Road Traffic Act 1988.

Interpretation

4–2601 **2.** (1) In these Regulations—

"the 1981 Regulations" means the Motor Vehicles (Tests) Regulations 1981 as from time to time amended;

"the 1988 Regulations" means the Goods Vehicles (Plating and Testing) Regulations 1988 as from time to time amended;

"the 1988 Act" means the Road Traffic Act 1988;

"authorised constable" means a constable authorised to act for the purpose of section 72 of the 1988 Act by or on behalf of a chief officer of police;

"vehicle examiner" has the meaning given by section 66A of the 1988 Act;

"prohibition" means a prohibition under section 69 of the 1988 Act; and

"relevant test certificate", in relation to a prohibition, means a test certificate issued in respect of the vehicle after the prohibition had been imposed.

(2) A reference to an inspection by a vehicle examiner shall be read as including a reference to an inspection under the direction of a vehicle examiner.

Exemptions from section 71(1) of the 1988 Act

4–2602 **3.** (1) The driving of a vehicle on a road—

(a) solely for the purpose of submitting it by previous arrangement for a specified time on a specified date for an inspection by a vehicle examiner or authorised constable with a view to the removal of the prohibition;

(b) solely for the purpose of submitting it by previous arrangement for a specified time on a specified date for an inspection by a vehicle examiner with a view to the removal of the prohibition and the issue of either a test certificate or a goods vehicle test certificate;

(c) in the course of an inspection with a view to the removal of a prohibition; or

(d) within 3 miles from where it is being, or has been, repaired solely for the purpose of its test or trial with a view to the removal of a prohibition,

is exempted from section 71(1)(a) and (b) of the 1988 Act.

(2) Where a prohibition has been imposed with a direction under section 69A(3) of the 1988 Act, the driving of the vehicle on a road solely for the purpose of submitting it by previous arrangement at a specified time for an examination under section 45(3) of the 1988 Act with a view to obtaining a test certificate or bringing it away from such an examination is exempted from section 71(1)(a) and (b) of that Act.

(3) Where—

(a) a prohibition has been imposed with a direction under section 69A(3) of the 1988 Act, and

(b) a relevant test certificate has been issued,

the driving of the vehicle on a road to a police station with a view to the prohibition being removed under regulation 4(3) of these Regulations is exempted from section 71(1)(a) and (b) of that Act.

Removal of prohibitions imposed with a direction under section 69A(3) of the 1988 Act

4–2603 **4.** (1) This regulation applies where a prohibition has been imposed with a direction under section 69A(3) of the 1988 Act.

(2) Where a vehicle examiner has issued a relevant test certificate, the prohibition may be removed by—

(a) the vehicle examiner who issued the certificate, or

(b) a person who has been authorised for the purpose by or on behalf of the Secretary of State and to whom the certificate has been produced.

3. The prohibition may also be removed by a person who has been authorised for the purpose by or on behalf of a chief officer of police and to whom a relevant test certificate has been produced at a police station.

Removal of prohibitions imposed with a direction under section 69A(4)

4–2604 **5.** (1) This regulation applies where a prohibition has been imposed under section 69A(4) of the 1988 Act.

(2) The requirements relating to the inspection of the vehicle which have to be complied with before the prohibition can be removed are that the vehicle must have been inspected by a vehicle examiner or an authorised constable.

Appeals relating to prohibitions

4–2605 6. (1) This regulation applies to appeals to the Secretary of State under section 72(5) of the 1988 Act (appeals against the refusal of a vehicle examiner or authorised constable to remove a prohibition).

(2) Every appeal to which the section applies shall be made within 14 days of the date on which the vehicle examiner or authorised constable refused to remove the prohibition in question.

(3) Every such appeal shall—

(a) be in writing; and

(b) contain a statement of the grounds on which it is made,

and shall be delivered to the Secretary of State.

(4) Every such appeal relating to a goods vehicle shall be accompanied by such fee as is payable in respect of the vehicle under regulation 25 of the 1988 Regulations on an appeal to the Secretary of State under those Regulations.

(5) Every such appeal relating to a vehicle other than a goods vehicle shall be accompanied by such a fee as is payable in respect of the vehicle under regulation 21 of the 1981 Regulations on an appeal under those Regulations.

4–2606 7. *Fees relating to inspection of goods vehicles*

4–2607 8. *Fees relating to the inspection of vehicles other than goods vehicles*

4–2608 9. *Revocations*

Goods Vehicles (Licensing of Operators) Regulations 1995

(SI 1995/2869 amended by the Adults with Incapacity (Scotland) Act 2000, Sch 5, SI 2003/2096, SI 2004/3168 (E), SI 2005/2929 (W) and SI 2006/594)

PART I
GENERAL

4–2609 1. *Commencement and citation.*

4–2610 2. *Revocation.*

Interpretation

4–2611 3. (1) In these Regulations, unless the context otherwise requires, any reference to—

(a) a numbered section is a reference to the section bearing that number in the Goods Vehicles (Licensing of Operators) Act 1995;

(b) a numbered regulation or Schedule is a reference to the regulation or, as the case may be, the Schedule bearing that number in these Regulations; and

(c) a numbered paragraph is a reference to the paragraph bearing that number in the regulation in which the reference appears.

(2) In these Regulations, unless the context otherwise requires—

"the 1995 Act" means the Goods Vehicles (Licensing of Operators) Act 1995;

"application for a licence" means an application for an operator's licence for which publication is required by section 10(1);

"application for the variation of a licence" means an application for the variation of an operator's licence for which publication is required by section 17(3) and,

"application" when used otherwise than as part of those expressions means—

(a) an application for a licence, or

(b) an application for the variation of a licence;

"Applications and Decisions" means a statement issued by a traffic commissioner under regulation 21;

"company" shall be construed as provided in section 735 of the Companies Act 1985;

"disc" means a disc issued in accordance with regulation 23(1) and (2) or 27(2);

"dual purpose vehicle" has the meaning given in column 2 of the Table in regulation 3(2) of the Road Vehicles (Construction and Use) Regulations 1986;

"farm" includes a market garden;

"firm" has the same meaning as in section 4 of the Partnership Act 1890;

"goods vehicle" has the same meaning as in section 58(1) but excludes a small goods vehicle as described in Schedule 1 to the 1995 Act;

"keeper", in relation to a goods vehicle, is the person in whose name the vehicle is registered under the Vehicle Excise and Registration Act 1994;

"licence" means an operator's licence (whether standard or restricted) as defined in section 2(1) and, where the context so requires, includes the documentation which evidences the grant of an application;

"licence-holder", and "holder' in relation to a licence, mean the person to whom the licence was issued;

"motor vehicle" means a mechanically propelled vehicle intended or adapted for use on roads;

"maintenance" in relation to a goods vehicle includes inspection, repair and fuelling;

"officer" has the meaning given in section 42;

"recovery vehicle" has the same meaning as in Part V of Schedule 1 to the Vehicle Excise and Registration Act 1994;

"relevant conviction" means any conviction mentioned in paragraph 5 of Schedule 2 to the 1995 Act or any conviction of contravening any provision of the law of Northern Ireland or of a country or territory outside the United Kingdom corresponding to any such conviction, not being in either case a spent conviction within the meaning of section 1(1) of the Rehabilitation of Offending Act 1974;

"showman's goods vehicle" has the same meaning as in section 62 of the Vehicle Excise and Registration Act 1994;

"tower wagon" has the same meaning as in paragraph 17(2) of Schedule 2 to the Vehicle Excise and Registration act 1994 (as originally enacted);

"trade licence" is a licence granted under section 11 of the Vehicle Excise and Registration Act 1994;

"visiting force", "headquarters" and "vehicle in the service of a visiting force or a headquarters" have the same meanings as in the Visiting Forces and International Headquarters (Application of Law) Order 1965.

PART III

Consideration of objections and representations

4–2612　13. (1) The traffic commissioner shall consider every objection duly made in considering whether or not to hold an inquiry as provided in section 35.

(2) The traffic commissioner shall consider every representation duly made in considering whether or not to hold an inquiry as provided in section 35.

PART IV
OPERATING CENTRES

Conditions which may be attached to a licence

4–2613　14. The condition which may be attached under section 23 to a licence are conditions regulating—

(a) the number, type and size of authorised motor vehicles or trailers which may at any one time be at any operating centre of the licence-holder in the area of the traffic commissioner for the purposes of maintenance and parking;

(b) the parking arrangements to be provided for authorised motor vehicles or trailers at or in the vicinity of every such operating centre;

(c) the times between which there may be carried out at every such operating centre any maintenance or movement of any authorised motor vehicle or trailer and the times at which any equipment may be used for any such maintenance or movement; and

(d) the means of ingress to and egress from every such operating centre for any authorised motor vehicle or trailer.

Considerations relevant to determinations

4–2614　15. (1) The considerations prescribed as relevant to any determination of a kind specified in section 34(2) are—

(a) the nature and the use of any other land in the vicinity of the land used or proposed to be used as an operating centre, and any effect which the use of the land as an operating centre has, or would be likely to have, on the environment of that vicinity;

(b) in a case where the land proposed to be used as an operating centre is, or has previously been, used as an operating centre, the extent to which the grant of the application would result in any material change as regards that operating centre, or its use, which would adversely affect the environment of the vicinity of that land;

(c) in the case of an application which, if granted, would result in land which has not previously been used as an operating centre being used as one, any information known to the traffic commissioner to whom the application is made about any planning permission or application for planning permission relating to the land or any other land in the vicinity of that land;

(d) the number, type and size of motor vehicles or trailers;

(e) the arrangements for the parking of motor vehicles or trailers or the proposed or likely arrangements for such parking;

(f) the nature and the times of the use of the land for the purpose of an operating centre or the proposed nature and times of the use of the land proposed to be used for that purpose;

(g) the nature and the times of the use of any equipment installed on the land used as an operating centre for the purpose of the use of that land as an operating centre or of any equipment proposed or likely to be installed on the land proposed to be used as an operating centre for that purpose; and

(h) the means and frequency of vehicular ingress to, and egress from, the land used as an operating centre or the proposed means and frequency of such ingress to, and egress from, the land proposed to be used as an operating centre.

(2) In this regulation—

"operating centre" includes part of an operating centre and the place which would be the operating centre if the application were granted; and

"planning permission" has the same meaning, as regards England and Wales, as in section 336(1) of the Town and Country Planning Act 1990, and, as regards Scotland, as in section 274(1) of the Town and Country Planning (Scotland) Act 1972.

Conditions to be satisfied in relation to specified operating centres

4–2615   16. The prescribed condition under sections 14(5)(c) and paragraphs 1(7)(b) and 3(7)b) of Schedule 4 to the 1995 Act is that either—

(a) proceedings on any appeal (including any proceedings on or in consequence of an appeal) have been determined and any time for appealing or further appealing has expired; or

(b) any review under section 36 has been determined or the time for giving notice of intention to review under section 36(2) has expired and no such notice of review has been served,

and if appeal or notice of intention is withdrawn or abandoned the date of such withdrawal or abandonment shall be taken to be the time of expiry.

Period for service of notice on review of an operating centre

4–2616   17. The period prescribed for the purpose of section 30(1) is two months.

Manner of service of notice on review of an operating centre

4–2616A   18. Paragraph 6 of Schedule 4 shall have effect in relation to serving of notices by the traffic commissioner on a licence-holder for the purposes of section 30(1), as if "section 30" were substituted for "the Schedule" in sub-paragraph (1) of that paragraph.

Manner of making representations in relation to a review

4–2617   19. Without prejudice to section 31(5), the prescribed manner of making representations in relation to a review is by delivering a document to the traffic commissioner at the office of his traffic area—

(a) setting out the representations;

(b) clearly identifying

(i) the person making the representations,

(ii) the place specified in the operator's licence to which the representations relate,

(iii) land or property in the vicinity which is owned or occupied by the person making the representations; and

(c) signed—

(i) if made by an individual, by that person,

(ii) if made by a firm, by all of the partners of that firm or by one of them with the authority of the others,

(iii) if made by any other body or group of persons, by one or more individual persons authorised for that purpose by the body or group,

or, in any of the above cases, by a solicitor acting on behalf of (as the case may be) the person, firm, body or group.

PART V
INQUIRIES
Provisions about inquiries

4–2618   20. Schedule 4 shall effect in relation to any inquiry held by a traffic commissioner.

PART VI
APPLICATIONS AND DECISIONS
Statement to be issued by the traffic commissioner

4–2619   21. (1) The traffic commissioner shall publish as occasion may require a statement known as "Applications and Decisions" which shall contain (unless previously notified)—

(a) as regards applications

(i) notices of the applications,

(ii) the dates on which and the places at which he proposes to hold inquiries and the applications which he proposes to consider at those inquiries, and

(iii) the traffic commissioners' decisions on applications, other than his decisions to issue an interim licence under section 24, or to make an interim direction under section 25;

(b) any direction to revoke, suspend or curtail a licence given under section 26 or section 27;

(c) the dates on which and the places at which he proposes to hold any inquiries other than those mentioned in sub-paragraph (a)(ii) above; and

(d) any decision of his following a review under section 30.

(2) The publication of the date of any inquiry in Applications and Decisions shall not prevent the traffic commissioner from adjourning, cancelling or postponing the consideration of any

application and in particular any inquiry held or proposed to be held in connection with the application.

(3) Copies of Applications and Decisions may be inspected at the office of the traffic area of the traffic commissioner by whom it was issued and at such other places (if any) as he may determine and copies of the whole or the relevant parts thereof shall be supplied to any person requiring them on payment of such sum as the traffic commissioner may require to cover the cost of supplying the copy.

Notification of decisions

4-2620 22. (1) Subject to paragraph (2), where a traffic commissioner grants or refuses an application, he shall send a written statement of his reasons to—

(a) the applicant;
(b) every objector; and
(c) every person who has made a representation in accordance with sections 12(4), 19(2) or 19(4) and asked the traffic commissioner for such a statement.

(2) Paragraph (1) does not apply where—

(a) the traffic commissioner grants an application in the terms applied for; and
(b) no objection or representations has been made in accordance with sections 12(1), 12(4), 19(2) or 19(4).

(3) Where a traffic commissioner makes a direction under section 31 or 32, he shall send a written statement of his seasons to the licence-holder.

PART VII
OTHER MATTERS

Identifications of motor vehicles

4-2621 23. (1) The traffic commissioner shall, when any motor vehicle to be used under a licence is specified in the licence, issue to the licence-holder a disc in respect of the vehicle.—

(2) The disc shall clearly indicate (by colour or other means)—

(a) whether a vehicle is being used under a standard licence or under a restricted licence; and
(b) in the case of a vehicle being used under a standard licence, whether the vehicle covers both international and national transport operations or national transport operations only.

(3) The licence-holder shall, during such time as any motor vehicle is specified in the licence and whether or not for the time being the vehicle is being used for the purpose for which a licence is required, cause a disc appropriate to the vehicle to be fixed to, and exhibited in a legible condition on, that vehicle in a waterproof container—

(a) in the case of a vehicle fitted with a front windscreen, on the near side and near the lower edge of the windscreen with the obverse side facing forwards;
(b) in the case of a vehicle not fitted with a front windscreen, in a conspicuous position on the front or nearside of the vehicle

(4) At no time shall any person except the traffic commissioner, or a person authorised to do so on his behalf, write on or make any other alteration to a disc.

Temporary addition of a motor vehicle

4-2622 24. Where—

(a) a motor vehicle specified in an operator's licence ("the specified vehicle") has been rendered unfit for service, or withdrawn from service for overhaul or repair, and the licence-holder informs the traffic commissioner of his desire to have a variation of the licence specifying another motor vehicle in its place ("the additional vehicle"); or
(b) the specified vehicle has been rendered fit for service again, and the licence-holder informs the traffic commissioner of his desire to have a variation of the licence whereby the additional vehicle will cease to be specified on the licence,

the provisions of regulations 4 and 5 shall not apply.

Notification of change of address

4-2623 25. If during the currency of a licence the address for correspondence as notified in the licence-holder's application or as subsequently notified under this regulation cases to be an effective address for correspondence the licence-holder shall within 28 days from the date of such event notify the traffic commissioner by whom the licence was granted of an effective address for correspondence.

Production of licence for examination

4-2624 26. (1) The licence-holder shall produce the licence for inspection by an officer or a police constable on being required by such a person to do so, and the licence-holder may do so at any operating centre covered by the licence or at his head or principal place of business within the traffic area in which any such operating centre lies or, if the requirement is made by a police constable, at a police station chosen by the licence-holder.

(2) The licence-holder shall comply with any requirement mentioned in paragraph (1) within 14 days of the day on which the requirement is made.

Issue of copies of licences and discs

4–2625   27. (1) If a licence or disc has been lost, destroyed or defaced, the person to whom it was issued shall forthwith notify in writing the traffic commissioner by whom the licence or disc was issued.

(2) If—

(a) the traffic commissioner is satisfied that a licence or disc has been lost, destroyed or defaced; and

(b) in the case of a licence or disc which has been defaced, it is surrendered to the traffic commissioner,

the traffic commissioner shall issue a copy (so marked) which shall have effect as the original licence or disc.

(3) Where a licence or disc has been lost and after a copy has been issued the lost licence or disc is found by or comes into the possession of the licence-holder he shall forthwith return the original licence or disc to the traffic commissioner.

Return of licences and discs

4–2626   28. (1) If a licence-holder ceases to use under the licence any motor vehicle specified in the licence he shall within 21 days beginning with the date of ceasing to use the vehicle or vehicles notify the traffic commissioner by whom the licence was issued and return to that traffic commissioner the licence for variation and the disc relating to the vehicle.

(2) If a licence is varied under section 17, 31, 32 or 36 its holder shall, when required by the traffic commissioner so to do, return to the traffic commissioner

(a) the licence; and

(b) if the number of motor vehicles specified in the licence has been reduced, the disc relating to any vehicle no longer specified in the licence.

(3) If a licence is revoked, surrendered, suspended, curtailed or terminated for any other reason, or if a traffic commissioner has given a direction in respect of a licence under section 26(2), the licence-holder shall on or before the date specified in a notice to that effect, send or deliver to the office of the traffic area of the traffic commissioner by whom the licence was issued—

(a) the licence; and

(b) the disc relating to any motor vehicle which the traffic commissioner may specify, for cancellation, retention during the time of suspension, or alteration as the case may be.

(4) The notice referred to in paragraph (3) shall be delivered personally to the licence-holder or sent to him by recorded delivery service at the address shown in his application or last notified in accordance with regulation 25.

(5) In the event of the traffic commissioner deciding to make a variation under paragraph 9 of the Schedule to the Goods Vehicles (Licensing of Operators) Act 1995 (Commencement and Transitional Provisions) Order 1995 the licence-holder shall return the licence to the traffic commissioner for him to amend the licence so that it conforms to the variation before returning it to the holder.

Partnerships

4–2627   29. (1) The provision in section 8(2) that a person shall not at the same time hold more than one operator's licence in respect of the same area shall apply so that a firm shall be treated as a person separate from any partner of that firm or an individual in any other partnership.

(2) For the purposes of authorising goods vehicles to be used under section 5(1) when the licence-holder is a firm, any vehicle in the lawful possession of any partner of a firm shall be regarded as in the lawful possession of the firm.

(3) The provisions of section 13(3) shall apply in any case where an applicant for a standard licence is a firm so that the traffic commissioner is required to satisfy himself that—

(a) every one of the partners of that firm is of good repute;

(b) the firm satisfies the requirement of appropriate financial standing; and

(c) either—

(i) if one of the firm's partners manage the road transport business carried on by the firm, he, or if more than one each of them, is professionally competent, or

(ii) the firm employs a transport manager or transport managers who, or if more than one each of whom, is of good repute and professionally competent.

(4) The provisions of section 13(4) shall apply in any case where an applicant for a restricted licence is a firm so that the traffic commissioner is required to satisfy himself that every one of the partners of that firm is not unfit to hold an operator's licence by reason of any activities or convictions covered by section 34(a) of (b).

(5) The provisions of section 13(6) shall apply in any case where an applicant is a firm and in such case the financial resources referred to in the subsection shall be those of the firm.

(6) The provisions of section 26 shall apply in any case where the licence-holder is a firm and in such a case any act, omission or conviction of a partner of that firm shall be regarded as the act, omission or conviction of the firm.

(7) The provisions of section 27(1) shall apply in any case where the licence-holder is a firm if—

- (a) any one or more of the partners of that firm cease to satisfy the requirement to be of good repute; or
- (b) the firm ceases to satisfy the requirement to be of appropriate financial standing; or
- (c) when the requirement as to professional competence is satisfied by one or more of the firm's partners who manage the road transport business carried on by the firm, he, or if more than one each of them, ceases to do so, or when the firm employs a transport manager or transport managers such manager, or if more than one any of them, ceases to be of good repute, or when the firm relies upon the employment of a single transport manager to satisfy the requirement as to professional competence, that transport manager ceases to be employed by the firm.

(8) The provisions of section 28 shall apply to the revocation of an operator's licence held by a firm and in such a case the powers conferred by subsections (1) and (4) shall be exercisable in respect of each and every partner of that firm.

(9) Except in a case falling within paragraph (9) any requirement, obligation or prohibition (however expressed) placed on a person making an application or on the licence-holder by, or in pursuance of, a provision in the 1995 Act or these Regulations, shall apply where the licence-holder is a firm and the duty to meet the requirement or obligation or to comply with the prohibition, shall apply to the partners of that firm severally as well as jointly.

(10) Where an application is made by, or the licence-holder is a firm a requirement or obligation placed on the applicant or licence-holder by virtue of section 8(4), 9(1) or 17(2) of the 1995 Act to inform the traffic commissioner of a notifiable conviction within the meaning given in paragraph 4 of Schedule 2 to the 1995 Act shall apply in relation to the notifiable conviction of each partner of that firm, and the duty to meet the requirement shall apply to the person convicted.

(11) The provisions in section 16(5) as to the events on which an operator's licence held by an individual terminates apply in a case where such a licence is held by a firm, if—

- (a) the partnership is dissolved; or
- (b) one or more of the persons dies or becomes a patient within the meaning of Part VII of the Mental Health Act 1983, or if (in Scotland) a curator bonis[1] is appointed in respect of him, with the result that only one other of such persons who is not such a patient or so incapable remains in the partnership

(12) In the Schedule 3 to the 1995 Act—

- (a) the provisions in paragraph 1 as regards determining whether an individual is of good repute apply, in a case of a firm in respect of each of the partners of that firm as they apply to an individual;
- (b) the provision in paragraph 6 as regards determining whether the applicant for, or the holder of, a licence is of appropriate financial standing shall apply, in the case of a firm, to the financial standing of the firm;
- (c) the provision in paragraph 8(2) that a company satisfies the requirement as to professional competence if, and so long as, if has a transport manager or transport managers of its road transport business who, or if more than one each of whom, is of good repute and professionally competent shall apply in the case of a firm so that the firm satisfies the said requirement if, and so long as, each of its partners is of good repute, and either,—
  - (i) if one or more of the firm's partners manage the road transport business carried on by the firm, he, or if more than one each of them, is professionally competent, or
  - (ii) the firm employs a transport manager or transport managers of its road transport business who, or if more than one each of whom, if (if on QP copy) of good repute and professionally competent; and
- (d) in a case where one or more partners of a firm manage the road transport business carried on by that firm or the firm employs a transport manager or transport managers the provision in paragraph 10 and 11 shall apply—
  - (i) as regards one such person or a single transport manager employed by the firm as it applies as regards a single transport manager employed by a company, and
  - (ii) as regards two or more such persons or two or more transport managers employed by the firm as it applies as regards two or more transport managers employed by a company.

---

1. By virtue of the Adults with Incapacity (Scotland) Act 2000, Sch 5, the reference in para (11)(b) to a curator bonis shall be construed as a reference to a guardian with similar powers appointed under that Act.

Holding companies and subsidies

4–2628 30. (1) A holding company may apply to the traffic commissioner for any traffic area—

- (a) if it does not already hold a licence in respect of that area, for the issue of a licence; or
- (b) if it already holds a licence in respect of that area, for a variation of its licence by a direction under 17(1)(a).

which would have the effect, if the application were granted, of including in the licence to be issued to, or already held by, the holding company, goods vehicles in the lawful possession of a subsidiary of that company specified in the application.

(2) An application by holding company under paragraph (1) shall, unless

- (a) the subsidiary is not the licence-holder; or

(b) the licence or variation applied for by the holding company will not take effect until any licence held by the subsidiary has been surrendered or has otherwise terminated,

be accompanied by an application by the subsidiary for the variation of the licence held by the subsidiary by a direction under section 17(1)(b) for the removal therefrom of all or some of the goods vehicles authorised to be used thereunder, being the vehicles to which the application of the holding company relates.

(3) Where a holding company, on an application under paragraph (1) signifies to the traffic commissioner its desire that the provisions of this regulation should have effect as respects a subsidiary of that company, then, in relation to the application and to any licence granted to the holding company, or held by the holding company and varied, on that application, and to the use of any goods vehicles authorised to be used under any such licence, the 1995 Act and these Regulations shall have effect subject to the modification specified Schedule 2[1].

(4) The provisions of this regulation shall cease to have effect as respects a holding company and its subsidiary—

    (a) if the holding company gives notice to the traffic commissioner who issued or varied its licence that it desires that this regulation should, as from any date, cease to apply to the holding company and that subsidiary, as from that date; or

    (b) as from the date on which that subsidiary ceases to be a subsidiary of that holding company.

(5) Where by virtue of the provisions of paragraphs (1) to (3) a holding company holds a licence which includes goods vehicles in the lawful possessions of a subsidiary of that company, and the holding company gives notice under paragraph (4)(a), then, in relation to any application by the subsidiary for the issue of a licence in respect of all or any of those vehicles, section 10 shall have effect as if for sub-section (1) there were substituted the following sub-section—

    "(1) The traffic commissioner may publish in the prescribed manner notice of any application to him for an operator's licence made by a company or other body corporate in pursuance of Regulations made under section 46 of this Act."

(6) Where the provisions of this regulation cease to have effect as respects a holding company and its subsidiary by virtue of paragraph (4)(b) the company which was the holding company shall within 21 days of the event which caused the subsidiary to cease to be a subsidiary of that company—

    (a) notify the traffic commissioner by whom the licence was issued, and

    (b) supply all material details of the event and

    (c) return to the traffic commissioner the licence and the discs relating to the motor vehicles authorised to be used thereunder,

and in so far as the holding company fails to satisfy those requirements the company which was the subsidiary company shall, on being so directed by the traffic commissioner, within 7 days of that direction supply the details, or return the licence and the discs, as the case may require.

(7) In a case where the applicant for, or the holder of, standard licence is a holding company and the goods vehicles used, or to be used, under the licence belong to, or are in the possession of, a subsidiary of that holding company, the provisions of these Regulations apply as if—

    (a) the road transport undertaking and any operating centre of the subsidiary were the road transport undertaking and an operating centre of the holding company;

    (b) for purposes of, or relating to, the reputation and financial standing of the holding company, the activities, relevant convictions and financial resources of the subsidiary were activities, convictions and resources of the holding company; and

    (c) in relation to a transport manager, his employment by the subsidiary were employment by the holding company.

---

1. Schedule 2 is not reproduced in this work.

Continuance of licence on death, bankruptcy etc

4–2629   **31.** (1) In this regulation, "actual holder" in relation to a licence means the person to whom the licence was issued.

(2) This regulation applies in the event—

    (a) of the death of the actual holder of a licence;

    (b) of the actual holder of a licence becoming a patient under Part VII of the Mental Health Act 1983, or in Scotland a curator bonis[1] being appointed in respect of him on the ground that he is incapable, by reason of mental disorder, of adequately managing his property and affairs;

    (c) of the bankruptcy of the actual holder of a licence;

    (d) in the case of a company, of the actual holder of a licence going into liquidation or entering administration; or

    (e) of the appointment of a receiver or manager of the trade or business of the actual holder of a licence.

(3) After the happening of either of the events mentioned in paragraph (2)(a) or (b) the traffic commissioner may direct that the licence shall not be treated as terminated when the actual holder died or became a patient but suspended until the date when a direction under paragraph (4) comes into force.

(4) After the happening of any of the events mentioned in paragraph (2) the traffic commissioner

may direct that a person carrying on the trade or business of the actual holder of the licence is to be treated for the purposes of the 1995 Act as if he were the holder thereof for such purpose and to such extent as is specified in the direction for a period not exceeding—

(a) if it appears to the traffic commissioner that there are special circumstances, 18 months;
(b) in any other case, 12 months,

from the date of the coming into force of that direction.

(5) The powers under paragraph (4) shall be exercisable in relation to a standard licence whether or not the person carrying on the trade or business of the actual holder of the licence satisfies the requirement of professional competence.

(6) Where a person is treated as if he were the licence-holder by virtue of a direction under this regulation—

(a) any goods vehicle which had been in the lawful possession of the actual holder of the licence shall for the purposes of the 1995 Act be treated as if it was in the lawful possession of that person; and
(b) if the licence is a standard licence, nothing in section 27 shall oblige the traffic commissioner to revoke the licence by reason only of that person not satisfying the requirement of professional competence.

---

1. By virtue of the Adults with Incapacity (Scotland) Act 2000, Sch 5, the reference in para (2)(*b*) to a curator bonis shall be construed as a reference to a guardian with similar powers appointed under that Act.

Offences

4–2630   32. (1) Any contravention of, or failure to comply with, a provision in regulation 23(3), 23(4), 25, 26, 27(1), 27(3), 28(1), 28(2), 28(3), 28(4) or 30(6), is hereby declared to be an offence and for the purposes of section 57(9) any provision mentioned above shall be regarded as made under the 1995 Act.

Classes of vehicle for which a licence is not required

4–2631   33. (1) The classes of vehicle specified under section 2(2)(*d*) as those to which section 2(1) does not apply are the classes mentioned in Part I of Schedule 3.

(2) The relevant plated weight of a goods vehicle, for the purposes of Schedule 1 to the 1995 Act (meaning of "small goods vehicle") is the gross weight not to be exceeded in Great Britain of the vehicle as shown on a Ministry plate as defined in column 2 of the Table in regulation 3(2) of the Road Vehicles (Construction and Use) Regulations 1986 or, if no such plate has been issued in respect of that vehicle, the maximum gross weight of the vehicle as shown on a plate affixed to the vehicle by virtue of regulation 66 of those Regulations.

Period for service of notice of review on ground of procedural irregularity

4–2632   34. The period prescribed for the purposes of section 36(2) is two months.

Manner of service of notice of review on ground of procedural irregularity

4–2633   35. Paragraph 6 of Schedule 4 shall have effect in relation to the serving of notices by the traffic commissioner on the applicant or (as the case may be) the licence-holder which state his intention to review a decision referred to in section 36(1), and in such a case "section 36(2)(*a*)" shall be substituted for "this Schedule" in sub-paragraph (1) of that paragraph.

Meaning of "relevant weight"

4–2634   36. (1) A motor vehicle or trailer of any prescribed class referred to in section 5(3) means any vehicle described in section 2(1) as needing an operator's licence, and the relevant weight of such a vehicle is its revenue weight.

(2) For the purposes of this regulation "revenue weight" shall have the meaning given in section 60A of the Vehicle Excise and Registration Act 1994.

(3) In its application to this regulation, section 60A of that Act shall have effect as if—

(a) subsection (6) of that section were omitted; and
(b) no provision had been made under section 61A(2) of that Act.

Regulation 33   SCHEDULE 3
          CLASSES OF VEHICLE FOR WHICH A LICENCE IS NOT REQUIRED
                              PART I

4–2635   1. Any tractor as defined in paragraph 4(3) of Part IV of Schedule 1 to the Vehicle Excise and Registration Act 1994 (as originally enacted) while being used for one or more of the purposes specified in Part II of this Schedule.

2. A dual-purpose vehicle and any trailer drawn by it.

3. A vehicle used on a road only in passing from private premises to other private premises in the immediate neighbourhood belonging (except in the case of a vehicle so used only in connection with excavation or demolition) to the same person, provided that the distance travelled on a road by any such vehicle does not exceed in the aggregate 9.654 kilometres, (6 miles), in any one week.

4. A motor vehicle constructed or adapted primarily for the carriage of passengers and their effects, and any trailer drawn by it, while being so used.

5. A vehicle which is being used for funerals.

6. A vehicle which is being used for police, relevant authority (as defined in section 6 of the Fire (Scotland)

Act 2005 (asp 5)) or, in England or Wales, fire and rescue authority or ambulance or Serious Organised Crime Agency purposes.

7. A vehicle which is being used for fire-fighting or rescue operations at mines.

8. A vehicle on which no permanent body has been constructed, which is being used only for carrying burden which either is carried solely for the purpose of test or trial, or consists of articles and equipment which will form part of the completed vehicle when the body is constructed.

9. A vehicle which is being used under a trade licence.

10. A vehicle in the service of a visiting force or of a headquarters.

11. A vehicle used by or under the control of Her Majesty's United Kingdom forces.

12. A trailer not constructed primarily for the carriage of goods but which is being used incidentally for that purpose in connection with the construction, maintenance or repair of roads.

13. A road roller and any trailer drawn by it.

14. A vehicle while being used under the direction of HM Coastguard or of the Royal National Lifeboat Institution for the carriage of life-boats, live-saving appliances or crew.

15. A vehicle fitted with a machine, appliance, apparatus or other contrivance which is a permanent or essentially permanent fixture, provided that the only goods carried[1] on the vehicle are—

(a) required for use in connection with the machine, appliance, apparatus or contrivance or the running of the vehicle;

(b) to be mixed by the machine, appliance, apparatus or contrivance with other goods not carried on the vehicle on a road in order to thrash, grade, clean or chemically treat grain;

(c) to be mixed by the machine, appliance, apparatus or contrivance with other goods not carried on the vehicle in order to make fodder for animals; or

(d) mud or other matter swept up from the surface of a road by the use of the machine, appliance, apparatus or other contrivance.

16. A vehicle while being used by a local authority for the purposes of the enactments relating to weights and measures or the sale of food and drugs.

17. A vehicle while being used by a local authority in the discharge of any function conferred on or exercisable by that authority under Regulations made under the Civil Defence Act 1948.

18. A steam-propelled vehicle.

19. A tower wagon or trailer drawn thereby, provided that the only goods carried on the trailer are goods required for use in connection with the work on which the tower wagon is ordinarily used as such.

20. A vehicle while being used for the carriage of goods within an aerodrome within the meaning of section 105(1) of the Civil Aviation Act 1982.

21. An electrically propelled vehicle.

22. A showman's goods vehicle and any trailer drawn thereby.

23. A vehicle permitted to carry out cabotage in the United Kingdom under Community Council Regulation (EEC) No. 3118/93 dated 25 October 1993, laying down conditions under which non-resident carriers may operate national road haulage services within a Member State.

24. A goods vehicle first used before 1 January 1977 which has an unladen weight not exceeding 1525 kilograms and for which the maximum gross weight, as shown on a plate affixed to the vehicle by virtue of regulation 66 of the Motor Vehicles (Construction and Use) Regulation 1986 or any provision which that regulation replaced, exceeds 3500 kilograms but does not exceed 3556.21 kilograms (3½ tons).

25. A vehicle while being used by a highway authority for the purposes of section 196 of the Road Traffic Act 1988.

26. A vehicle being held ready for use in an emergency by an undertaking for the supply of water, electricity, gas or telephone services[2].

27. A recovery vehicle[3].

28. A vehicle which is being used for snow clearing, or for the distribution of grit, salt or other materials on frosted, icebound or snow-covered roads or for going to or from the place where it is to be used for the said purposes or for any other purpose directly connected with those purposes.

29. A vehicle proceeding to or from a station provided by the Secretary of State under section 45 of the Road Traffic Act 1988 for the purposes of an examination of that vehicle under that section provided that—

(a) the only load being carried is a load required for the purposes of the examination; and

(b) it is being carried at the request of the Secretary of State.

---

1. The exemption is for a vehicle on which goods are being "carried", not for a vehicle hauling: further, the "goods" being carried must be required for use in connection with the machine, etc, rather than for use in connection with the operation in which the machine was going to be used: *Vehicle Operators Services Agency v Law Fertilisers Ltd* [2004] EWHC 3000, [2005] RTR 21 (see also *North West Traffic Area Licensing Authority v Post Office* [2982] RTR 304).

2. The vehicle is required to be held by its owners for the purpose of use in an emergency and must not be doing any other task which will impinge on its responding to an emergency. A vehicle carrying materials and equipment used to excavate a site, lay telephone cables supplied by another and make good the surface back to the depot at the end of the working day for safekeeping was not "held ready for use in an emergency" even though the owners were under contract to provide a 24 hour call-out service. Nor could the owners be properly described as a "supplier" of telephone services (*Vehicle Inspectorate v TD & C Kelly* [1998] RTR 297, DC).

3. For the definition of a "recovery" vehicle see paragraph 5(2) (3) in Part V of Sch 1 to the Vehicle Excise and Registration Act 1994, in this title, ante (*Vehicle Inspectorate v Richard Read Transport Ltd* [1998] RTR 288n, DC).

PART II
PURPOSES REFERRED TO IN PARAGRAPH 1 OF PART I OF THIS SCHEDULE

4–2636 **1.** Hauling—

(a) threshing appliances;

(b) farming implements;

(c) a living van for the accommodation of persons employed to drive the tractor; or

(d) supplies of water or fuel required for the tractor

2. Hauling articles for a farm required by the keeper, being either the occupier of the farm or a contractor employed to do agricultural work on the farm by the occupier of the farm.

3. Hauling articles for a forestry estate required by the keeper where the keeper is the occupier of that estate or employed to do forestry work on the estate by the occupier or a contractor employed to do forestry work on the estate by the occupier.

4. Hauling within 24.135 kilometres, (15 miles), of a farm or a forestry estate occupied by the keeper, agricultural or woodland produce of that farm or estate.

5. Hauling within 24.135 kilometres, (15 miles), of a farm or a forestry estate occupied by the keeper, material to be spread on roads to deal with frost, ice or snow.

6. Hauling a snow plough or as a similar contrivance for the purpose of clearing snow; and

7. Hauling—

(a) soil for landscaping or similar works; or

(b) a mowing machine.

where the keeper is a local authority.

Public Service Vehicles (Operators' Licences) Regulations 1995
(SI 1995/2908 amended by SI 2001/1149)

4-2637   **1.** *Citation and commencement.*

4-2638   **2.** *Revocation.*

Interpretation

4-2639   **3.** (1) In these Regulations, unless the context otherwise requires—

"the 1981 Act" means the Public Passenger Vehicles Act 1981;

"the 1985 Act" means the Transport Act 1985;

"designated sporting event" has the same meaning as in the Sporting Events (Control of Alcohol) Act 1985;

"disc" means an operator's disc issued under section 18;

"fax" means the making of a facsimile copy of a documentary by the transmission of electronic signals;

"holder" in relation to a licence means the person to whom that licence was granted;

"licence" means a PSV operator's licence and "special licence" has the same meaning as in section 12(12) of the 1985 Act;

"local authority" has the meaning given by section 14A(4);

"Notices and Proceedings" has the same meaning as in regulation 3 of the Public Service Vehicles (Traffic Commissioners: Publications and Inquiries) Regulations 1986;

"traffic regulation conditions" has the meaning given by section 7(1) of the 1985 Act; and

"vehicle examiner" means an examiner appointed under section 66A of the Road Traffic Act 1988.

(2) Unless the context otherwise requires, any reference in these Regulations to:

(a) a numbered section is a reference to the section bearing that number in the 1981 Act;

(b) a numbered regulation is a reference to the regulation bearing that number in these Regulations

(c) a numbered paragraph is a reference to the paragraph bearing that number in the regulation in which the reference appears.

Inspection of applications

4-2640   **4.** (1) The traffic commissioner who receives an application for a licence shall, until that application is determined, make it (or any part of it) available for inspection by any person who is authorised in that behalf by any chief officer of police or local authority and who so requests in writing.

(2) The traffic commissioner may satisfy his obligation under paragraph (1) by either:

(a) making the application, or, as the case may be, part of it, available for inspection at the office of his Traffic area; or

(b) on prior receipt of his expenses, posting a copy of the application, or, as the case may be, part of it, to the person making the request.

Objections to applications for licences

4-2641   **5.** (1) The prescribed time within which an objection under section 14A must be made is the period of 21 days beginning with the day after the date when the notice of the application is published in Notices and Proceedings.

(2) The prescribed manner for making an objection for the purposes of section 14A is by serving on the traffic commissioner a document—

(a) setting out the objection; and

(b) signed by or on behalf of the person making the objection.

(3) Service of a document on the traffic commissioner shall, for the purposes of this regulation be effected by—

(a) delivering it; or

(b) sending it by post; or

(c) transmitting it by fax,

to the traffic commissioner at the office of his traffic area.

(4) A copy of every document setting out an objection shall be sent by the objector to the applicant on the day or the next working day after it is made.

Determination of applications

4–2642 **6.** A traffic commissioner shall not refuse an application for a licence, or grant it other than as requested without giving to the applicant an opportunity to state his case at an inquiry save where the application or the applicant's conduct in relation to it is frivolous or unreasonable.

Description of conditions attached to licences

4–2643 **7.** (1) For the purpose of section 16(3), the prescribed description of conditions is any condition regulating any of the matters specified in paragraph (2) in relation to a journey, or part of a journey, the purpose or the main purpose of which is to carry passengers to or from a designated sporting event.

(2) The matters referred to in paragraph (1) are—

(a) the times of departure and arrival of the outward journey and of the homeward journey; and

(b) the length of any break in the outward journey or the homeward journey and the places at which any such break may occur.

Requirements of notice and consideration of representations

4–2644 **8.** Before—

(a) attaching to a licence, except on granting the licence, any condition or additional condition in exercise of his powers under section 16(3), or

(b) altering, in exercise of his powers under section 16(5)(a) other than at the holder's request, any condition attached to a licence under section 16(3) (except a condition treated as so attached by virtue of section 27(4) of the 1985 Act),

the traffic commissioner who granted the licence shall give the holder notice of his proposal to attach or alter any such condition, and that commissioner shall consider any written representations from the holder about that proposal which he receives within 14 days of such notice.

4–2645 **9.** (1) Before—

(a) exercising any of his powers under section 17(1) or (2), or

(b) attaching to a licence, except on granting the licence and except if section 27(2) of the 1985 Act applies, any condition under section 26 of the 1985 Act or varying any such condition, or

(c) making an order under section 28(1) of the 1985 Act,

the traffic commissioner who granted the licence shall give notice to the holder or former holder.

(2) The notice shall state—

(a) that he is considering one or more of such actions

(b) the grounds on which that consideration is based

(c) that within 14 days of such notice the holder or former holder may make representations to him with respect to the action or actions being considered;

(d) that those representations shall be written; and

(e) either

  (i) that he proposes to hold an inquiry in relation to the action or actions being considered and the data (being a date not less than 14 days from the notice) on which that inquiry will be held, or,

  (ii) that he does not propose to hold an inquiry in relation to that action or those actions unless the holder or former holder, within 14 days of the notice, in writing requests him to do so

(3) The traffic commissioner shall take into account any representations which he receives by virtue of and in accordance with any notice which he gives under paragraph (1) before he decides whether or not to take any action which the notice stated he was considering.

(4) The provisions of paragraph (3) shall not prevent the traffic commissioner at his discretion from hearing and considering any representations other than those made in accordance with paragraph (1) including any which are advanced (whether orally or in writing) at the inquiry, of any, which he holds.

(5) The prescribed period for the purpose of section 27(3) of the 1985 Act shall be 14 days beginning with the date that a notice is given to the holder that the condition has been attached to the licence.

Forms of and particulars to be contained on discs

4–2646 **10.** (1) There shall be specified on every disc the date on which it comes into force and the date on which it expires.

(2) The disc shall clearly indicate (by colour or other means)—

(a) whether a vehicle is being used under a standard licence or under a restricted licence; and

(b) in the case of a vehicle being used under a standard licence, whether the licence covers both international and national transport operations or national transport operations only.

The coming into force and expiry of discs

4–2647   11. (1) A disc shall not come into force more than a month after it is used.—

(2) A disc shall expire—

(a) if paragraph (3) applies to the disc, at the end of the 1 year period of the relevant licence in which the disc comes into force;

(b) in any other case, at the end of the 5 year period of the relevant licence in which the disc comes into force.

(3) This paragraph applies—

(a) to a disc which comes into force during the first 5 year period of the relevant licence if and only if a notice of election is in force immediately before the licence is granted; and

(b) to a disc which comes into force during any other 5 year period of the relevant licence if and only if a notice of election is in force immediately before the beginning of the period.

(4) For the purposes of this regulation a notice of election, in relation to a licence, is a notice in which the holder states (or stated when he was applying for the licence) that he wishes to pay the fee for the issue of any disc connected with the licence on an annual basis.

(5) A notice of election shall come into force on the day on which the holder serves it on the traffic commissioner and shall remain in force until revoked in accordance with paragraph (6).

(6) The holder of a licence may not earlier than 42 days before the end of a 5 year period of the relevant licence serve a notice on the traffic commissioner revoking a notice of election.

(7) Paragraph (3) of regulation 5 shall apply to the service of a notice under this regulation as it applies to service of a notice under that paragraph.

(8) For the purposes of this regulation, "relevant licence", in relation to a disc, means the licence in respect of which the disc is issued.

(9) For the purposes of this regulation, the 1 year periods of a licence, are—

(a) the period of 1 year beginning with the first day of the month in which the relevant licence comes into force; and

(b) each consecutive period of 1 year.

(10) For the purposes of this regulation, the 5 year periods of licence, are—

(a) the period of 5 years beginning with the first day of the month in which the relevant licence comes into force; and

(b) each consecutive period of 5 years.

(11) Notwithstanding anything in the foregoing provisions of this regulation, paragraph (2)(a) shall not apply to a disc unless at the time the disc is issued a provision in regulations under the 1981 Act is in force which prescribes different fees for the issue of a disc according to whether paragraph (3) does or does not apply.

Manner in which discs are to be fixed and exhibited

4–2648   12. The prescribed manner in which a disc is to be fixed and exhibited for the purposes of section 8 is by so fixing it to the vehicle that it—

(a) is adjacent to the licence issued under the Vehicles Excise and Registration Act 1994;

(b) does not interfere unduly with the driver's view; and

(c) can easily be read in daylight from the outside of the vehicle.

Issue of a duplicate licence or disc and prohibition on unauthorised alteration of a disc

4–2649   13. (1) If a licence or disc has been lost or destroyed, the holder shall forthwith notify the traffic commissioner who granted the licence or disc so that he may provide a duplicate, marked as such.

(2) If a licence or disc has been notified as lost or destroyed in accordance with paragraph (1) and is subsequently recovered by the holder, then the holder, then the holder shall use the duplicate licence or disc and return the original to the traffic commissioner.

(3) At no time shall any person except the traffic commissioner, or a person authorised to do so on his behalf, write on or otherwise alter a disc, but in the event that a disc becomes illegible by ordinary wear and tear the holder shall forthwith return the illegible disc so that the traffic commissioner may provide a duplicate, marked as such

Compulsory return of licences and discs

4–2650   14. (1) In the event of the suspension, surrender or other termination—

(a) at any time of a continuous licence; or

(b) prior to the date of expiry specified in a term licence,

the holder shall return that licence to the traffic commissioner by whom it was granted for retention during the time of the suspension, or for cancellation, as the case may be, and shall at the same time return to that commissioner any discs which have been issued in relation to the licence .

(2) On the removal of a suspension referred to in paragraph (1) the commissioner shall return the licence together with any discs which were issued in relation to the licence.

(3) In the event of the traffic commissioner deciding—

(a) to attach an additional condition or any traffic regulation conditions to a licence;

(b) to alter or remove a condition or any traffic regulation conditions attached to a licence; or (*c*) to vary or remove any undertaking in a licence,

the holder shall return that licence to the traffic commissioner for him to make the appropriate addition, alteration, variation or removal before returning it to the holder.

(4) In the event of the traffic commissioner deciding to vary one or more conditions attached to a licence under section 16(1), so reducing the maximum number of vehicles which may be used under the licence below the number of discs which have been issued to the holder, the holder shall return to that commissioner such number of discs as will leave the holder with only the same number of discs as is equal to the reduced maximum number of vehicles.

(5) In the event of a disc ceasing to have effect prior to the date of expiry, the holder shall return the disc to the traffic commissioner who issued it.

(6) For the purposes of this regulation, a requirement to return a licence or disc to a traffic commissioner is a requirement for it to be—

(*a*) delivered to the office of his traffic area; or
(*b*) sent to the traffic commissioner at the office of his traffic area by recorded delivery service,

within the period of 14 days beginning with the date on which the holder receives the notice from the traffic commissioner requiring it to be returned.

(7) For the purposes of this regulation, if a licence or disc is sent by recorded delivery service in accordance with paragraph (6), it shall be regarded as having been returned at the date that it is delivered at the appropriate office in the traffic area.

(8) In this regulation—

"term licence" means a licence which by virtue of the Deregulation and Contracting Out (Commencement) (No 4) Order 1995, has an expiry date; and

"continuous licence" means a licence that is not a term licence.

Voluntary return of discs

4–2651   15. (1) The holder of the licence may, if he so wishes, at any time return a disc to the traffic commissioner by whom the licence was issued by delivering it to him at the office of his traffic area or sending it to him at that address by recorded delivery service.

(2) For the purposes of these Regulations, if a disc is sent by recorded delivery service in accordance with paragraph (1), it shall be regarded as having been returned on the date that it is delivered at the appropriate office in the traffic area.

Production of licences and discs for examination

4–2652   16. (1) Unless its loss or destruction has been previously notified to the traffic commissioner in accordance with regulation 13(1) or (2), a licence or a disc shall be produced by the holder for examination if he is so required by any police constable, vehicle examiner or by any person authorised by the traffic commissioner for any traffic area to examine the licence or disc, and any such requirement shall be complied within not more than 14 days.

(2) Any such requirement in paragraph (1) may be complied with by the holder producing the licence or disc within the traffic area of the traffic commissioner by whom the licence was granted at the operating centre or principal place of business of the holder.

Notification of decisions

4–2653   17. The traffic commissioner shall, as regards any application made to him with respect to a licence, inform the applicant of his decision upon the application, and the traffic commissioner shall inform any applicant and any objector of the reasons for his decision when he refuses an application, grants an application other than as requested, or grants an application despite objection to it.

Review of decisions

4–2654   18. The period after taking a decision that is prescribed for the purposes of section 49A of the 1981 Act is 2 months.

Notices generally

4–2655   19. (1) A notice required or authorised to be given to a person (other than a traffic commissioner) under the 1981 Act and these Regulations may be effected by—

(*a*) delivering to him at his proper address; or
(*b*) sending it to him by post to his proper address; or
(*c*) transmitting it to him by fax if he has indicated expressly in writing or by providing a fax number on his letter heading that he will accept transmission by fax

(2) Any such document may—

(*a*) in the case of a body corporate, be sent to the secretary or clerk of that body;
(*b*) in the case of a partnership, be sent to any partner.

(3) For the purposes of this paragraph and section 7 of the Interpretation Act 1978, the proper address of any person is his last known address (whether or his residence or a place where he carries on business or is employed) and in the case of a body corporate, its secretary or its clerk, the address of its registered or principal office in the United Kingdom.

(4) If a notice under section 49A is sent by registered post or the recorded delivery service addressed to the applicant or (as the case may be) the licence holder at his proper address, the

notice shall, for the purposes of that section, be deemed to have been given when it would have been delivered in the ordinary course of post, notwithstanding that—

   (a) the notice was returned as undelivered or was for any reason not received by him; or
   (b) was in fact delivered or received by him at some other time.

and notwithstanding anything in section 7 of the Interpretation Act 1978.

(5) Where a person has notified the traffic commissioner of an address or a new address at which documents may be given to him for the purposes of the 1981 Act and these Regulations, that address shall also be his proper address for service for the purposes mentioned in paragraph (3) or (4) or, as the case may be, his proper address for those purposes in substitution for that previously notified.

Notification of change of address

4–2656   20. If during the currency of a licence the address for correspondence as notified in the licence holder's application or as subsequently notified under this regulation ceases to be an effective address for correspondence the holder shall within 28 days from the date of such event notify the traffic commissioner by whom the licence was granted of an effective address for correspondence.

Relevant convictions

4–2657   21. The convictions specified in the Schedule hereto are hereby prescribed as relevant convictions for the purposes of the 1981 Act.

Operations under hiring arrangements

4–2658   22. The person who is to be regarded as the operator of a vehicle which is made available by one holder of a licence to another under a hiring arrangement is the holder from whom the vehicle is hired in a case where—

   (a) the holder to whom the vehicle is hired is not, under the hiring arrangement, entitled to keep the vehicle in his possession for a total period of more than 14 days);
   (b) not less than 14 days have elapsed between the finish of any previous period (of whatever duration) in which the hirer to whom the vehicle is hired was entitled to the use of the vehicle under a hiring arrangement with the holder from whom the vehicle is hired and the start of the period mentioned in sub-paragraph (a) above.;
   (c) at all times when the vehicle is being used for carrying passengers for hire or reward during the period mentioned in sub-paragraph (a) above there is affixed to the vehicle a disc which has been issued to the holder from whom the vehicle is hired;
   (d) the vehicle, is made available to the holder of a restricted licence, is not adapted to carry more than sixteen passengers; and
   (e) the vehicle is not a licensed taxi made available to or by the holder of a special licence.

Terminating of licences held by companies

4–2659   23. In a case where a licence is held by a company the events relating to the holder on the occurrence of which the licence is to terminate are as follows—

   (a) the making of a winding up order; and
   (b) the passing of a resolution for voluntary winding up.

Computation of time

4–2660   24. Any day which is a bank holiday under the Banking and Financial Dealings Act 1971 shall be excluded from the computation of any period of a specified number of days prescribed in these Regulations.

Post Office

4–2661   25. Section 16(1A) (limit on number of vehicles to be used under a restricted licence) shall not apply in respect of a licence held at any time by a universal service provider (within the meaning of the Postal Services Act 2000) for any purposes in connection with the provision of a universal postal service (within the meaning of that Act).

Savings

4–2662   26. Notwithstanding the revocation of the Public Service Vehicles (Operators' Licences) Regulations 1986 by these Regulations, regulation 12(3) of those Regulations (which require a licence to be returned if its period of validity is curtailed) shall continue to have effect in relation to a licence if its period of validity is curtailed before 1st January 1996.

SCHEDULE
RELEVANT CONVICTIONS PRESCRIBED BY REGULATION 21

4–2663   1. A conviction of any of the offences specified in paragraph 2 below—

   (a) of the holder of a licence, or the applicant for a licence;
   (b) where the holder of a licence, or the applicant for a licence, is a partnership, of a partner in that partnership;

(c)   of any transport manager whom the holder of a licence employs or proposes to employ, and
(d)   of any person appointed or otherwise engaged as an officer, employee or agent of the holder of, or of an applicant for, a licence in relation to any business which such holder or applicant carries on, or proposes to carry on.

(2) The offences referred to in paragraph 1 above are offences in relation to a public service vehicle or the operation thereof—

(a)   under or by virtue of the 1981 Act;
(b)   under sections 5(1), 8(1), 11, 13, 16(1), 17(4) and 18(3) of the Road Traffic Regulation Act 1984;
(c)   under section 1(2) of the Sporting Events (Control of Alcohol etc) Act 1985;
(d)   under or by virtue of Parts I and II and Section 101 of the 1985 Act;
(e)   under or by virtue of Parts I, II, III, IV and VI are sections 164(6) and (9), 165(3) and (6), 168, 170(7), 171(2), 172(3) and (4), 173(1), 174(1) and (2) and (5) in Part VII of the Road Traffic Act 1988;
(f)   under section 91 of the Road Traffic Offenders Act 1988;
(g)   relating to—
   (i)   the speed at which vehicles may be driven,
   (ii)   drivers' hours or the keeping of drivers' records under or by virtue of Part VI of the Transport Act 1968,
   (iii) new bus grants under section 32 of, and Schedule 8 to, the Transport Act 1968, grants towards bus fuel duty under section 92 of the Finance Act 1965,
   (iv)   a duty of exercise imposed by or under the Vehicles (Excise) Act 1971 or the Vehicle Excise and Registration Act 1994, and
(h)   under section 92 of the Licensing (Scotland) Act 1976 and section 70 of the Criminal Justice (Scotland) Act 1980;

or other offences under the law in force in any part of Great Britain which are serious offences as defined in paragraph 1(4) of Schedule 3 or road transport offences as defined in paragraph 1(5) of that Schedule.

Council Regulation (EC) No 12/98 of 11 December 1997

LAYING DOWN THE CONDITIONS UNDER WHICH NON-RESIDENT CARRIERS MAY OPERATE NATIONAL ROAD PASSENGER TRANSPORT SERVICES WITHIN A MEMBER STATE[1]

4–2664   Article 1. Any carrier who operates road passenger transport services for hire or reward, and who holds the Community licence provided for in Article 3a of Council Regulation (EEC) No 684/92 of 16 March 1992 on common rules for the international carriage of passengers by coach and bus, shall be permitted, under the conditions laid down in this Regulation and without discrimination on grounds of the carrier's nationality or place of establishment, temporarily to operate national road passenger services for hire or reward in another Member State, hereinafter referred to as the 'host Member State', without being required to have a registered office or other establishment in that State.

Such national transport services are hereinafter referred to as 'cabotage transport operations'.

Article 2. For the purposes of this Regulation:

(1) 'Regular services' means services which provide for the carriage of passengers at specified intervals along specified routes, passengers being taken up and set down at predetermined stopping points. Regular services shall be open to all - subject, where appropriate, to compulsory reservation.
The fact that the operating conditions of the service may be adjusted shall not affect its classification as a regular service.

(2) 'Special regular services' means regular services which provide for the carriage of specified categories of passengers, to the exclusion of other passengers, at specified intervals along specified routes, passengers being taken up and set down at predetermined stopping points.
Special regular services shall include:
   (a)   the carriage of workers between home and work;
   (b)   carriage to and from the educational institution for school pupils and students;
   (c)   the carriage of soldiers and their families between their homes and the area of their barracks.
The fact that a special service may be varied according to the needs of users shall not affect its classification as a regular service.

(3) 'Occasional services' means services which do not fall within the definition of regular services, including special regular services, and whose main characteristic is that they carry groups constituted on the initiative of a customer or of the carrier himself. These services shall not cease to be occasional services solely because they are provided at certain intervals.

(4) 'Vehicles' means motor vehicles which, by virtue of their type of construction and equipment, are suitable for carrying more than nine persons - including the driver - and are intended for that purpose.

Article 3. Cabotage transport operations shall be authorized for the following services:

(1) special regular services provided that they are covered by a contract concluded between the organizer and the carrier;
(2) occasional services;
(3) regular services, provided they are performed by a carrier not resident in the host Member State in the course of a regular international service in accordance with Regulation (EEC) No 684/92.

Cabotage transport cannot be performed independently of such international service.
Urban and suburban services shall be excluded from the scope of this point.
'Urban and suburban services' means transport services meeting the needs of an urban centre or conurbation, and transport needs between it and the surrounding areas.

Article 4. 1 The performance of the cabotage transport operations referred to in Article 3 shall be subject, save as otherwise provided in Community legislation, to the laws, regulations and administrative provisions in force in the host Member State in relation to the following areas:

(*a*) rates and conditions governing the transport contract;

(*b*) weights and dimensi0ons of road vehicles; such weights and dimensions may, where appropriate, exceed those applicable in the carrier's Member State of establishment, but they may under no circumstances exceed the technical standards set out in the certificate of conformity;

(*c*) requirements relating to the carriage of certain categories of passengers, viz. schoolchildren, children and persons with reduced mobility;

(*d*) driving and rest time;

(*e*) VAT (value added tax) on transport services; in this area Article 21 (1) (*a*) of Council Directive 77/388/EEC of 17 May 1977 on the harmonization of the laws of the Member States relating to turnover taxes - common system of value added tax: uniform basis of assessment shall apply to the services referred to in Article 1 of this Regulation.

2 Save as otherwise provided in Community legislation, cabotage transport operations which form part of the transport services provided for in Article 3 (3) shall be subject to the existing laws, regulations and administrative provisions in force in the host Member State regarding authorizations, tendering procedures, the routes to be operated and the regularity, continuity and frequency of services as well as itineraries.

3 The technical standards of construction and equipment which must be met by vehicles used to carry out cabotage transport operations shall be those laid down for vehicles put into circulation in international transport.

4 The national provisions referred to in paragraphs 1 and 2 shall be applied by the Member States to non-resident carriers on the same conditions as those imposed on their own nationals, so as effectively to prevent any open or hidden discrimination on grounds of nationality or place of establishment.

5 If it is established that, in the light of experience, the list of areas covered by the host Member State's provisions, as referred to in paragraph 1, needs to be amended, the Council shall do so by a qualified majority, on a proposal from the Commission.

Article 5. The Community licence or a certified true copy thereof shall be kept on board the vehicle and be produced when requested by an authorized inspecting officer.

Article 6. 1 Cabotage transport operations in the form of occasional services shall be carried out under cover of a control document - the journey form - which must be kept on board the vehicle and be produced when requested by an authorized inspecting officer.

2 The journey form, the model for which shall be adopted by the Commission in accordance with the procedure laid down in Article 8, shall comprise the following information:

(*a*) the points of departure and destination of the service;

(*b*) the date of departure and the date on which the service ends.

3 The journey forms shall be supplied in books certified by the competent authority or agency in the Member State of establishment. The model for the book of journey forms shall be adopted by the Commission in accordance with the procedure laid down in Article 8.

4 In the case of special regular services, the contract concluded between the carrier and the transport organizer, or a certified true copy of the contract, shall serve as the control document.
However, the journey form shall be completed in the form of a monthly statement.

5 The journey forms used shall be returned to the competent authority or agency in the Member State of establishment in accordance with procedures to be laid down by that authority or agency.

Articles 4–15. *Commission procedures and obligations of Member States.*

---

1. Given effect in respect of the United Kingdom by the Road Transport (Passenger Services Cabotage) Regulations 1999, in this title, post.

Road Transport (Passenger Vehicles Cabotage) Regulations 1999[1]
(SI 1999/3413 amended by SI 2000/3114)

4–2665 **1. Commencement, citation and interpretation.** (1) These Regulations may be cited as the Road Transport (Passenger Vehicles Cabotage) Regulations 1999 and shall come into force on 28th January 2000.

(2) In these Regulations—

"the Council Regulation" means Council Regulation (EC) No 12/98 of 11 December 1997[2] laying down the conditions under which non-resident carriers may operate national road passenger transport services within a member State;

"the 1981 Act" means the Public Passenger Vehicles Act 1981;

"Community carrier" means a road passenger transport carrier established in a member state of the European Community other than the United Kingdom;

"road" has the meaning given in section 192(1) of the Road Traffic Act 1988;
"traffic commissioner" has the meaning given in section 4 of the 1981 Act;
"UK cabotage operations" means cabotage transport operations in Great Britain or between Great Britain and Northern Ireland[3].

1. Made by the Secretary of State for the Environment, Transport and the Regions being a Minister designated for the purposes of section 2(2) of the European Communities Act 1972 in relation to the carriage of passengers by road, in exercise of the powers conferred by that section.
2. In this title, ante.
3. For definition of 'cabotage' see EC Council Regulation 12/98, art 1, in this title, ante.

4–2666　2. Extent.　These Regulations apply in Great Britain.

4–2667　3. Cabotage without a Community licence.　(1) A person commits an offence if he uses a vehicle on a road, or causes or permits a vehicle to be so used, for the purpose of UK cabotage operations which are carried out by a Community carrier without a valid Community licence.
(2) A person who is guilty of an offence under paragraph (1) above shall be liable on summary conviction to a fine not exceeding *level 4* on the standard scale.

4–2668　4. Use of a vehicle in Great Britain without a control document.　(1) A person commits an offence if he uses a vehicle on a road, or causes or permits a vehicle to be so used, for the purposes of UK cabotage operations which—
(a) take the form of occasional services in Great Britain or between Great Britain and Northern Ireland, and
(b) are carried out in contravention of Article 6(1) of the Council Regulation.
(2) A person who is guilty of an offence under paragraph (1) above shall be liable on summary conviction to a fine not exceeding level 4 on the standard scale.

4–2669　5. Competent Authorities in Great Britain.　*Repealed.*

4–2670　6. Appeals.　(1) A carrier who is aggrieved by an administrative penalty imposed on him by the Secretary of State under Article 11(2) of the Council Regulation may request the Secretary of State to review that decision.
(2) A carrier who is aggrieved by an administrative penalty imposed on him by the appropriate traffic commissioner under Article 11(4) of the Council Regulation may appeal to the Transport Tribunal.

4–2671　7. Production of documents.　(1) The driver of a vehicle which is required, under Article 5 of the Council Regulation, to have on board a Community licence commits an offence if he fails, without reasonable cause, to produce the licence when requested to do so by an authorised inspecting officer.
(2) References in paragraph (1) above to a Community licence include references to a certified true copy of a licence.
(3) The driver of a vehicle which is required, under Article 6(1) of the Council Regulation, to have on board a control document commits an offence if he fails, without reasonable cause, to produce the control document when requested to do so by an authorised inspecting officer.
(4) A person who is guilty of an offence under paragraph (1) or (3) above is liable on summary conviction to a fine not exceeding level 3 on the standard scale.

4–2672　8. Authorised inspecting officers.　Authorised inspecting officers for the purposes of the Council Regulation shall in Great Britain be constables in uniform, and examiners appointed under section 66A of the Road Traffic Act 1988.

4–2673　9. Bodies corporate.　(1) Where an offence under these Regulations has been committed by a body corporate and it is proved to have been committed with the consent or connivance of, or to be attributable to any neglect on the part of, any director, manager, secretary or other similar officer of the body corporate or any person who was purporting to act in any such capacity, he as well as the body corporate shall be guilty of the offence and shall be liable to be proceeded against and punished accordingly.
(2) Where the affairs of a body corporate are managed by its members, paragraph (1) above shall apply in relation to the acts and defaults of a member in connection with his functions of management as if he were a director of the body corporate.
(3) Where an offence under these Regulations has been committed by a Scottish partnership and is proved to have been committed with the consent or connivance of, or to be attributable to any neglect on the part of a partner, he as well as the partnership shall be guilty of the offence and shall be liable to be proceeded against and punished accordingly.

4–2674　10. Modification of certain enactments and of the Public Service Vehicles (Conditions of Fitness, Equipment Use and Certification) Regulations 1981.　(1) *Amendment of the Road Traffic (Foreign Vehicles) Act 1972*
(2) The provisions of the 1981 Act shall have effect, in relation to a vehicle being used to carry out cabotage transport operations, as if sections 6, 12 and 18 were omitted.
(3) *Amendment of section 65(1) of the 1981*

(4) In section 66 of the 1981 Act, the word "or" at the end of paragraph (*d*) shall be omitted and after paragraph (*e*) there shall be inserted

(5) *Amendment of paragraph 9 of Schedule 4 to the Transport Act 1985.*

(6) None of the provisions of Parts II, III, IV and V of the Public Service Vehicles (Conditions of Fitness, Equipment, Use and Certification) Regulations 1981 shall have effect in relation to a vehicle which is carrying out a cabotage transport operation in Great Britain in accordance with the Council Regulation.

Goods Vehicles (Enforcement Powers) Regulations 2001[1]
(SI 2001/3981)

4–2680 1. *Citation and commencement*

---

1. Made by the Secretary of State in exercise of powers unders Sch 1A to the Goods Vehicles (Licensing of Operators) Act 1995.

4–2681 2. Interpretation. In these Regulations—

"the 1995 Act" means the Goods Vehicles (Licensing of Operators) Act 1995;

"hiring agreement" has the same meaning as in section 66 of the Road Traffic Offenders Act 1988;

"immobilisation notice" has the meaning given in regulation 5(3);

"licence" means an operator's licence (whether standard or restricted) as defined in section 2(1) of the 1995 Act;

"owner" means, in relation to a vehicle or trailer which has been detained in accordance with regulation 3—

    (*a*) in the case of a vehicle which at the time of its detention was not hired from a vehicle-hire firm under a hiring agreement but was registered under the Vehicle Excise and Registration Act 1994, the person who can show to the satisfaction of an authorised person that he was at the time of its detention the lawful owner (whether or not he was the person in whose name it was so registered);

    (*b*) in the case of a vehicle or trailer which at the time of its detention was hired from a vehicle-hire firm under a hiring agreement, the vehicle-hire firm; or

    (*c*) in the case of any other vehicle or trailer, the person who can show to the satisfaction of an authorised person that he was at the time of its detention the lawful owner.

"release" in relation to a vehicle means release from an immobilisation device;

"vehicle" has the same meaning as "goods vehicle" in section 58(1) of the 1995 Act but excludes a small goods vehicle as described in Schedule 1 to that Act; and

"vehicle-hire firm" has the same meaning as in section 66 of the Road Traffic Offenders Act 1988.

4–2682 3. *Detention of property*

4–2683 4. *Release of detained vehicles*

4–2684 5. *Power to immobilise vehicles*

4–2685 6. Removal of, or interference with, an immobilisation notice or device. (1) An immobilisation notice shall not be removed or interfered with except by or on the authority of an authorised person.

(2) A person contravening paragraph (1) shall be guilty of an offence and liable on summary conviction to a fine not exceeding level 2 on the standard scale.

(3) Any person who, without being authorised to do so in accordance with regulation 7, removes or attempts to remove an immobilisation device fixed to a vehicle in accordance with these Regulations shall be guilty of an offence and shall be liable on summary conviction to a fine not exceeding level 3 on the standard scale.

4–2686 7. *Release of immobilised vehicles*

4–2687 8. Removal and delivery of property detained. (1) An authorised person may direct in writing that any property detained in accordance with regulation 3 be removed and delivered into the custody of a person specified in the direction.

(2) A vehicle may be driven, towed or removed by such means as are reasonable in the circumstances and any necessary steps may be taken in relation to the vehicle in order to facilitate its removal.

(3) The contents of a vehicle may be removed separately in cases where—

    (*a*) it is reasonable to do so to facilitate removal of the vehicle;

    (*b*) there is good reason for storing them at a different place from the vehicle; or

    (*c*) their condition requires them to be disposed of without delay.

(4) A person may be specified in a direction only if—

(a) he is a person appointed by an authorised person; and

(b) he has made arrangements with the Secretary of State and agreed to accept delivery of the property in accordance with those arrangements; and

(c) he has agreed with the Secretary of State to take such steps as are necessary for the safe custody of such property.

(5) The arrangements made by virtue of paragraph (4) may include the payment of a sum to a person into whose custody any property is delivered.

(6) Where an authorised person has given a direction by virtue of paragraph (1) in respect of a vehicle, he may allow the driver of the vehicle to deliver its contents to their destination or some other suitable place before delivering the vehicle into the custody of the person specified in the direction.

(7) Subject to the powers of a person specified in a direction by virtue of paragraph (1) to sell or destroy any property, it shall be the duty of that person while any property is in his custody to take such steps as are necessary for the safe custody of that property.

4–2688   **9. Notification of detention of a vehicle and its contents.**   (1) Where a vehicle has been detained in accordance with regulation 3, an authorised person shall—

(a) publish a notice in the London Gazette if the vehicle was detained in England or Wales or in the Edinburgh Gazette if the vehicle was detained in Scotland—

  (i) giving a brief description of the property detained and the vehicle's registration mark (if any);

  (ii) indicating the time and place at which, and the powers under which, it was detained by the authorised person;

  (iii) stating that it may be claimed at the place and at the times specified in the notice and that, if no-one establishes within the period specified in the notice that he is entitled to the return of the vehicle, the authorised person intends to dispose of it after the expiry of that period in accordance with regulation 15;

  (iv) stating that any contents which are not disposed of in accordance with regulation 17(1) may be claimed at the place and at the times specified in the notice and that, if no-one establishes within the period specified in the notice that he is entitled to the return of the contents, the authorised person intends to dispose of them after the expiry of that period in accordance with regulation 17(2); and

(b) not less than 21 days before the expiry of the period given in the notice serve a copy of the notice on—

  (i) the owner of the vehicle;

  (ii) the traffic commissioner in whose area the vehicle was detained;

  (iii) the chief officer of the police force in whose area the property was detained;

  (iv) the Association of British Insurers; and

  (v) the British Vehicle Rental and Leasing Association.

(2) The period specified in a notice under paragraph (1)(a)(iii) and (iv) shall be 21 days, beginning with the date on which the notice is published under regulation 9(1)(a) or, if later, a copy of the notice is served under regulation 9(1)(b).

4–2689   **10. Applications to a traffic commissioner.**   (1) The owner of a vehicle detained in accordance with regulation 3 may, within the period specified in regulation 9(2), apply to the traffic commissioner for the area in which the vehicle was detained for the return of the vehicle.

(2) An application under paragraph (1) shall be given in writing and shall be accompanied by—

(a) a statement of one or more of the grounds specified in paragraph (4) on which the application is declared to be based; and

(b) a statement indicating whether the applicant wishes the traffic commissioner to hold a hearing.

(3) An application under paragraph (1) shall be served before the expiry of the period specified in regulation 9(2).

(4) An application under paragraph (1) may be made on any of the following grounds -

(a) that at the time the vehicle was detained the person using the vehicle held a licence (whether or not authorising the use of the vehicle);

(b) that at the time the vehicle was detained the vehicle was not being, and had not been, used in contravention of section 2 of the 1995 Act; or

(c) that, although at the time the vehicle was detained it was being, or had been, used in contravention of section 2 of the 1995 Act, the owner did not know that it was being, or had been, so used.

4–2690   **11.** *Hearings*

4–2691   **12.** *Notification of determinations*

4–2692   **13.** *Appeals from a determination of a traffic commissioner to the Transport Tribunal*

4–2693   **14.** *Return of a vehicle detained*

4–2694   **15.** *Disposal of vehicles*

4–2695 16. Return of contents. (1) The person specified in a direction by virtue of regulation 8 may retain custody of the contents of a vehicle until they are disposed of in accordance with regulation 17, or returned to a person who establishes that he is entitled to them in accordance with the provisions of this regulation.

(2) Unless the contents of a vehicle have already been disposed of in accordance with regulation 17, an authorised person shall return any contents detained under regulation 3 to a person who has given notice in writing of his claim to an authorised person within the period specified in the notice given under regulation 9(1)(*a*)(iv) and who—

(*a*) produces satisfactory evidence of his entitlement to them and of his identity and address; or

(*b*) where he seeks to recover the contents as the agent of another person, produces satisfactory evidence of his status as agent and of his principal's identity, address and entitlement to the contents.

(3) Where the person claiming to be entitled to a vehicle establishes his entitlement, he shall be treated for the purposes of this regulation as also entitled to its contents unless and to the extent that another person has claimed them.

(4) Where there is more than one claim to the contents, an authorised person shall determine which person is entitled to them on the basis of the evidence provided to him.

4–2696 17. Disposal of contents. (1) Where the condition of the contents of a vehicle requires them to be disposed of without delay they may be disposed of without the authorised person complying with the requirements of regulation 9.

(2) Where the contents of a vehicle are not disposed of in accordance with paragraph (1) and either—

(*a*) one or more persons has given notice of a claim in respect of them in accordance with regulation 16(2) but no person establishes his entitlement to them in accordance with regulation 16; or

(*b*) no notice of a claim has been given in respect of them in accordance with regulation 16(2),

the authorised person may sell or destroy those contents as he thinks fit.

4–2697 18. Application of proceeds of sale. (1) The proceeds of sale of any property sold by an authorised person under regulation 15 or 17 shall be applied towards meeting expenses incurred by the authorised person in exercising his functions under these Regulations and, in so far as they are not so applied, in meeting any claim to the proceeds of sale made and established in accordance with paragraph (2).

(2) A claim to the proceeds of sale of any property shall be established if the claimant provides the authorised person with satisfactory evidence that he would have been entitled to the return of the property under regulation 14 or 16 if the property had not been sold.

(3) Where the conditions specified in paragraph (4) are fulfilled, there shall be payable to him by the authorised person a sum calculated in accordance with paragraph (5).

(4) The conditions are that—

(*a*) the person claiming satisfies the authorised person that he was the owner of the property at the time it was disposed of; and

(*b*) the claim is made before the end of the period of one year beginning with the date on which the property was disposed of.

(5) The sum payable under paragraph (2) shall be calculated by deducting from the proceeds of sale the expenses incurred by the authorised person in exercising his functions under these Regulations, including the detention, removal, storage and disposal of the property.

4–2698 19. Disputes. (1) This regulation applies to a dispute which has arisen in relation to the return or disposal of the contents of a vehicle, or the application of the proceeds of sale of a vehicle or its contents.

(2) The claimant under a dispute to which this regulation applies may apply in writing to the Secretary of State on the grounds that the authorised person did not comply with the requirements of regulation 9, 16, 17 or 18.

(3) The Secretary of State shall consider any representations duly made and any evidence provided in support of them and notify the claimant in writing whether or not he accepts that the grounds of the application have been established and—

(*a*) if the Secretary of State notifies the claimant that the grounds have been established, the authorised person shall pay the claimant any amount due to him;

(*b*) if the Secretary of State rejects the application he shall so inform the claimant in writing and at the same time notify him of his right to make an appeal under paragraph (4).

(4) An appeal may be made from the Secretary of State's determination to the appropriate court by a claimant whose—

(*a*) application under paragraph (2) has been rejected under paragraph (3) and the subsequent appeal is made within 21 days of the claimant being served with notification to that effect under paragraph (3)(*b*); or

(*b*) the Secretary of State has not notified the claimant of the outcome of the application in accordance with paragraph (3) and 56 days have elapsed since the application was made,

and, if the appropriate court finds that the grounds of the appeal have been established, the authorised person shall be ordered to pay the claimant the amount due to him.

(5) In paragraph (4), "appropriate court" means—

  (a) the magistrates' court for the petty sessions area, or in Scotland, the sheriff court in the sheriffdom—

    (i) in which the claimant resides (in the case of an individual);

    (ii) where the principal or last known place of business of the claimant is situated (in the case of a partnership); or

    (iii) where the registered or principal office of the claimant is situated (in the case of an incorporated or unincorporated body).

4–2699   20. Offences as to obstruction of an authorised person.   Where a person intentionally obstructs an authorised person in the exercise of his powers under regulation 3 or 8, he is guilty of an offence and shall be liable on summary conviction to a fine not exceeding level 3 on the standard scale.

4–2700   21. Offences as to securing possession of property.   (1) Where a person makes a declaration with a view to securing the return of a vehicle and the declaration is that the vehicle was not being, or had not been, used in contravention of section 2 of the 1995 Act, and the declaration is to the person's knowledge either false or in any material respect misleading, he is guilty of an offence.

(2) A person guilty of an offence under paragraph (1) shall be liable—

  (a) on summary conviction, to a fine not exceeding the statutory maximum, and

  (b) on conviction on indictment, to imprisonment for a term not exceeding two years or to a fine or to both.

4–2701   22. Giving of notice.   (1) Any notice or application under these Regulations may be served by post (or in such other form as is agreed between the person to be served and the person serving the notice).

(2) Subject to paragraph (1), any such document shall be regarded as having been served on that party if it is—

  (a) delivered to him;

  (b) left at his proper address;

  (c) sent by post to him at that address; or

  (d) transmitted to him by FAX or other means of electronic data transmission in accordance with paragraph (3).

(3) A document may be transmitted by FAX or other means of electronic data transmission where the receiving party has indicated in writing to the sending party that he is willing to regard a document as having been duly sent to him if it is transmitted to him in a specified manner and the document is accordingly transmitted to him.

(4) Where the proper address includes a numbered box number at a document exchange, delivery of a document may be effected by leaving the document addressed to that numbered box at that document exchange or at a document exchange which transmits documents on every business day to that exchange.

(5) Any document which is left at a document exchange in accordance with paragraph (4) shall, unless the contrary is proved, be deemed to have been delivered on the second business day after the day on which it is left.

(6) If no address for service has been specified, the proper address for the purposes of these Regulations and of section 7 of the Interpretation Act 1978 shall be—

  (a) in the case of an individual, his usual or last known address;

  (b) in the case of a partnership, the principal or last known place of business of the partnership within the United Kingdom; or

  (c) in the case of an incorporated or unincorporated body, the registered or principal office of the body.

(7) A party may at any time by notice to another party change his proper address for service for the purposes of these Regulations and of section 7 of the Interpretation Act 1978.

(8) A party may by notice in writing delivered to another party vary or revoke any indication given by him under paragraph (3).

Road Transport (Working Time) Regulations 2005[1]
(SI 2005/639)

4–2701A   1. Citation, commencement and extent.   (1) These Regulations may be cited as the Road Transport (Working Time) Regulations 2005 and shall come into force on 4th April 2005.

(2) These Regulations extend to Great Britain only.

---

1. Made by the Secretary of State, being a Minister designated for the purposes of s 2(2) of the European Communities Act.

4–2701B   2.   In these Regulations—

"AETR" means the European agreement concerning the work of crews of vehicles engaged in international road transport of 1st July 1970;

"collective agreement" means a collective agreement within the meaning of section 178 of the Trade Union and Labour Relations (Consolidation) Act 1992, the trade union parties to which are independent trade unions within the meaning of section 5 of that Act;

"the Community Drivers' Hours Regulation" means Council Regulation (EEC) No3820/85 of 20th December 1985 on the harmonisation of certain social legislation relating to road transport;

"employer" in relation to a worker, means the person by whom the worker is (or, where the employment has ceased, was) employed;

"employment" in relation to a worker, means employment under his contract, and "employed" shall be construed accordingly;

"goods" includes goods or burden of any description;

"goods vehicle" means a motor vehicle constructed or adapted for use for the carriage of goods, or a trailer so constructed or adapted;

"inspector" means a person appointed under paragraph 1 of Schedule 2;

"mobile worker" means any worker forming part of the travelling staff, including trainees and apprentices, who is in the service of an undertaking which operates transport services for passengers or goods by road for hire or reward or on its own account;

"night time" means in respect of goods vehicles the period between midnight and 4 a.m. and in respect of passenger vehicles the period between 1am and 5am;

"motor vehicle" means a mechanically propelled vehicle intended or adapted for use on roads;

"night work" means any work performed during night time;

"passenger vehicle" means a motor vehicle which is constructed or adapted to carry more than eight seated passengers in addition to the driver;

"period of availability" means a period during which the mobile worker is not required to remain at his workstation, but is required to be available to answer any calls to start or resume driving or to carry out other work , including periods during which the mobile worker is accompanying a vehicle being transported by a ferry or by a train as well as periods of waiting at frontiers and those due to traffic prohibitions;

"reference period" means the period for calculation of the average maximum weekly working time;

"relevant requirements" means regulations 4(8), 7(5), 8(2), 9(4), 10, 11 and 12;

"self-employed driver" means anyone whose main occupation is to transport passengers or goods by road for hire or reward within the meaning of Community legislation under cover of a Community licence or any other professional authorisation to carry out such transport, who is entitled to work for himself and who is not tied to an employer by an employment contract or by any other type of working hierarchical relationship, who is free to organise the relevant working activities, whose income depends directly on the profits made and who has the freedom, individually or through a co-operation between self-employed drivers, to have commercial relations with several customers;

"vehicle" means a goods vehicle or a passenger vehicle;

"week" means a period of seven days beginning at midnight between Sunday and Monday;

"worker" means an individual who has entered into or works under (or, where employment has ceased, worked under)—

(a) a contract of employment; or

(b) any other contract, whether express or implied and (if it is express) whether oral or in writing, whereby the individual undertakes to do or perform personally any work or services for another party to the contract;

and any reference to a worker's contract shall be construed accordingly;

"workforce agreement" means an agreement between an employer and mobile workers employed by him or their representatives in respect of which the conditions set out in Schedule 1 to these Regulations are satisfied;

"working time" means the time from the beginning to the end of work during which the mobile worker is at his workstation, at the disposal of his employer and exercising his functions or activities, being

(a) time devoted to all road transport activities, including, in particular—

(i) driving;
(ii) loading and unloading;
(iii) assisting passengers boarding and disembarking from the vehicle;
(iv) cleaning and technical maintenance;
(v) all other work intended to ensure the safety of the vehicle, its cargo and passengers or to fulfil the legal or regulatory obligations directly linked to the specific transport operation under way, including monitoring of loading and unloading and dealing with administrative formalities with police, customs, immigration officers and others; or

(b) time during which the mobile worker cannot dispose freely of his time and is required to be at his workstation, ready to take up normal work, with certain tasks associated with being on duty, in particular during periods awaiting loading or unloading where their foreseeable duration is not known in advance, that is to say either before departure or just before the actual start of the period in question, or under collective agreements or workforce agreements;

"workstation" means

(a) the location of the main place of business of the undertaking for which the person performing mobile transport activities carries out duties, together with its various subsidiary places of business, regardless of whether they are located in the same place as its head office or its main place of business;

(b) the vehicle which the person performing mobile road transport activities uses when he carries out duties; or

(c) any other place in which activities connected with transport are carried out.

4–2701C 3. Application. (1) These Regulations apply to mobile workers who are employed by, or who do work for, undertakings established in a Member State of the European Union, and to whom paragraph (2) or paragraph (3) applies.

(2) This paragraph applies to mobile workers who in the course of that employment or work drive, or travel in, vehicles

(a) which fall within the meaning of 'vehicles' in Article 1 of the Community Drivers' Hours Regulation;

(b) which are not referred to in Article 4 of that Regulation; and

(c) in respect of which exemption from provisions of the Community Drivers' Hours Regulation has not been granted by regulation 2 of the Community Drivers' Hours and Recording Equipment (Exemptions and Supplementary Provisions) Regulations 1986.

(3) This paragraph applies to mobile workers, to whom paragraph (2) does not apply, who in the course of that employment or work drive, or travel in, vehicles

(a) which fall within the meaning of a "vehicle" in Article 1 of the AETR;

(b) which are not referred to in Article 2(2)(b) of the AETR; and

(c) which are performing international transport.

(4) These Regulations do not apply to—

(a) self-employed drivers, or

(b) any worker who does work which is included in the calculation of working time—

(i) where the reference period is shorter than 26 weeks, on fewer than 11 days in a reference period applicable to that worker, or

(ii) in any other case on fewer than 16 days in a reference period applicable to that worker.

4–2701D 4. Working time. (1) Subject to paragraph (2) below, the working time, including overtime, of a mobile worker shall not exceed 60 hours in a week.

(2) In any reference period which is applicable to his case, a mobile worker's working time shall not exceed an average of 48 hours for each week.

(3) The reference periods which apply in the case of a mobile worker shall be—

(a) where a collective agreement or a workforce agreement provides for the application of this regulation in relation to successive periods of 17 weeks, each such period,

(b) in a case where—

(i) there is no such provision, and

(ii) the employer gives written notice to the mobile worker in writing that he intends to apply this subparagraph,

any period of 17 weeks in the course of the worker's employment, or

(c) in any other case, the period ending at midnight between Sunday 31st July 2005 and Monday 1st August 2005 and thereafter, in each year, the successive periods beginning at midnight at the beginning of the Monday which falls on, or is the first Monday after, a date in column 1 below and ending at midnight at the beginning of the Monday which falls on, or is the first Monday after, the date on the same line in column 2 below.

Column 1 (beginning)	Column 2 (end)
1st December	1st April
1st April	1st August
1st August	1st December

(4) The reference period may be extended in relation to particular mobile workers or groups of mobile workers for objective or technical reasons or reasons concerning the organisation of work, by a collective agreement or a workforce agreement, by the substitution for 17 weeks of a period not exceeding 26 weeks in the application of paragraphs (2) and (3)(a) above.

(5) A mobile worker's average weekly working time during a reference period shall be determined according to the formula—

(A + B) / C

where—

A is the aggregate number of hours comprised in the mobile worker's working time during the course of the reference period;

B is the number of excluded hours during the reference period; and

C is the number of weeks in the reference period.

(6) In paragraph (5), "excluded hours" means hours comprised in—

(a) any period of annual leave taken by the mobile worker in exercise of entitlement under regulation 13 of the Working Time Regulations 1998;

(b) any period of sick leave taken by the mobile worker;

(c) any period of maternity, paternity, adoption or parental leave taken by the mobile worker;

(7) For the purposes of paragraph (5), the number of hours in a whole day shall be eight and the number of hours in a whole week shall be forty-eight.

(8) An employer shall take all reasonable steps, in keeping with the need to protect the health and safety of the mobile worker, to ensure that the limits specified above are complied with in the case of each mobile worker employed by him.

4–2701E 5.   The times of breaks, rests and periods of availability shall not be included in the calculation of working time.

4–2701F 6. Periods of availability.   (1) A period shall not be treated as a period of availability unless the mobile worker knows before the start of the relevant period about that period of availability and its reasonably foreseeable duration.

(2) The time spent by a mobile worker, who is working as part of a team, travelling in, but not driving, a moving vehicle as part of that team shall be a period of availability for that mobile worker.

(3) Subject to paragraph (4) a period of availability shall not include a period of rest or a break.

(4) A period of availability may include a break taken by a mobile worker during waiting time or time which is not devoted to driving by the mobile worker and is spent in a moving vehicle, a ferry or a train.

4–2701G 7. Breaks.   (1) No mobile worker shall work for more than six hours without a break.

(2) Where a mobile worker's working time exceeds six hours but does not exceed nine hours, the worker shall be entitled to a break lasting at least 30 minutes and interrupting that time.

(3) Where a mobile worker's working time exceeds nine hours, the worker shall be entitled to a break lasting at least 45 minutes and interrupting that period.

(4) Each break may be made up of separate periods of not less than 15 minutes each.

(5) An employer shall take all reasonable steps, in keeping with the need to protect the health and safety of the mobile worker, to ensure that the limits specified above are complied with in the case of each mobile worker employed by him.

4–2701H 8. Rest periods.   (1) In the application of these Regulations, the provisions of the Community Drivers' Hours Regulation relating to daily and weekly rest shall apply to all mobile workers to whom they do not apply under that Regulation as they apply to other mobile workers under that Regulation.

(2) An employer shall take all reasonable steps, in keeping with the need to protect the health and safety of the mobile worker, to ensure that those provisions are complied with in the case of each mobile worker employed by him, to whom they are applied by paragraph (1).

4–2701I 9. Night work.   (1) The working time of a mobile worker, who performs night work in any period of 24 hours, shall not exceed 10 hours during that period.

(2) The period of 10 hours may be extended in relation to particular mobile workers or groups of mobile workers for objective or technical reasons or reasons concerning the organisation of work, by a collective agreement or a workforce agreement.

(3) Compensation for night work shall not be given to a mobile worker in any manner which is liable to endanger road safety.

(4) An employer shall take all reasonable steps in keeping with the need to protect the health and safety of mobile workers to ensure that the limit specified in paragraph (1), or extended in accordance with paragraph (2), is complied with in the case of each mobile worker employed by him.

4–2701J 10. Information and records.   An employer of mobile workers shall notify each worker of the provisions of these Regulations and the provisions of any collective or workforce agreement which is capable of application to that worker.

4–2701K 11.   An employer of a mobile worker shall

(a) request from each mobile worker details of any time worked by that worker for another employer;

(b) include time worked for another employer in the calculation of the mobile worker's working time;

(c) keep records which are adequate to show whether the requirements of these Regulations are being complied with in the case of each mobile worker employed by him to whom they apply;

(d) retain such records for at least two years after the end of the period covered by those records;

(e) provide, at the request of a mobile worker, a copy of the record of hours worked by that worker;

(f) provide to an enforcement officer copies of such records relating to mobile workers as the officer may require;

(g) provide to a mobile worker or enforcement officer copies of such documentary evidence in the employer's possession as may be requested by the worker or officer in relation to records provided to him in accordance with paragraph (e) or (f) above.

4–2701L 12. A mobile worker shall, at the request of his employer under regulation 11(*a*), notify his employer in writing of time worked by the worker for another employer for inclusion in the calculation of the mobile worker's working time.

4–2701M 13. (1) The Secretary of State shall arrange for the publication, in such form and manner as he considers appropriate, of information and advice concerning the operation of these Regulations.
(2) The information and advice shall be such as appear to him best calculated to enable employers and workers affected by these Regulations to understand their respective rights and obligations.

4–2701N 14. Agency workers not otherwise mobile workers. (1) This regulation applies in any case where an individual ("the agency worker")—

   (*a*) is supplied by a person ("the agent") to do the work of a mobile worker for another ("the principal") under a contract or other arrangements made between the agent and the principal; but
   (*b*) is not, as respects that work, a worker, because of the absence of a worker's contract between the individual and the agent or the principal; and
   (*c*) is not a party to a contract under which he undertakes to do the work for another party to the contract whose status is, by virtue of the contract, that of a client or customer or any profession or business undertaking carried on by the individual.

(2) In a case where this regulation applies, the other provisions of these Regulations shall have effect as if there were a contract for the doing of the work by the agency worker made between the agency worker and—

   (*a*) whichever of the agent and the principal is responsible for paying the agency worker in respect of the work; or
   (*b*) if neither the agent nor the principal is so responsible, whichever of them pays the agency worker in respect of the work,
   (*c*) and as if that person were the agency worker's employer.

4–2701O 15. Individual carrying on trade or business. (1) This regulation applies in any case where an individual, who is not a self-employed driver, drives a vehicle described in regulation 3(1)(*b*) for the purpose of a trade or business carried on by him.
(2) Where this regulation applies—

   (*a*) subject to paragraph (*b*), the other provisions of these Regulations shall have effect as if—

      (i) the individual were a mobile worker, and
      (ii) the individual were the employer of that mobile worker;

   (*b*) regulations 10, 11(*a*) and (*e*) and 12 shall not have effect.

(3) This regulation shall not apply in any case where regulation 14 applies.

4–2701P 16. Enforcement. (1) It shall be the duty of the Secretary of State to enforce the requirements of these Regulations.
(2) Schedule 2 shall apply in relation to the enforcement of the relevant requirements.

4–2701Q 17. (1) Any person who fails to comply with any of the relevant requirements shall be guilty of an offence.
(2) The provisions of paragraph (3) shall apply where an inspector is exercising or has exercised any power conferred by Schedule 2.
(3) It is an offence for a person—

   (*a*) to contravene any requirement imposed by an inspector under paragraph 2 of Schedule 2;
   (*b*) to prevent or attempt to prevent any other person from appearing before an inspector or from answering any question to which an inspector may by virtue of paragraph 2(2)(*e*) of Schedule 2 require an answer;
   (*c*) to contravene any requirement or prohibition imposed by an improvement notice or a prohibition notice referred to in paragraphs 3 and 4 of Schedule 2 (including any such notice as is modified on appeal);
   (*d*) intentionally to obstruct an inspector in the exercise or performance of his powers;
   (*e*) to use or disclose any information in contravention of paragraph 7 of Schedule 2;
   (*f*) to make a statement which he knows to be false or recklessly to make a statement which is false where the statement is made in purported compliance with a requirement to furnish any information imposed by or under these Regulations.

(4) Any person guilty of an offence under paragraph (1) shall be liable—

   (*a*) on summary conviction, to a fine not exceeding the statutory maximum;
   (*b*) on conviction on indictment, to a fine.

(5) A person guilty of an offence under paragraph (3)(*b*) or (*d*) shall be liable on summary conviction to a fine not exceeding level 5 on the standard scale.
(6) A person guilty of an offence under paragraph (3)(*c*) shall be liable—

   (*a*) on summary conviction, to imprisonment for a term not exceeding three months, or a fine not exceeding the statutory maximum;

   (b) on conviction on indictment, to imprisonment for a term not exceeding two years, or a fine or both.

   (7) A person guilty of an offence under paragraph (3)(*a*), (*e*) or (*f*) shall be liable—

   (a) on summary conviction, to a fine not exceeding the statutory maximum;
   (b) on conviction on indictment—

      (i) if the offence is under paragraph (3)(*e*), to imprisonment for a term not exceeding two years or a fine or both,
      (ii) if the offence is under paragraph (3)(*a*) or (*f*), to a fine.

   (8) The provisions set out in regulations 18 to 22 shall apply in relation to the offences provided for in paragraphs (1) and (3).

4–2701R   18. Offences due to fault of other person. Where the commission by any person of an offence is due to the act or default of some other person, that other person shall be guilty of the offence, and a person may be charged with the conviction of the offence by virtue of this regulation whether or not proceedings are taken against the first-mentioned person.

4–2701S   19. Offences by bodies corporate. (1) Where an offence committed by a body corporate is proved to have been committed with the consent or connivance of, or to have been attributable to any neglect on the part of, any director, manager, secretary or other similar officer of the body corporate or a person who was purporting to act in any such capacity, he as well as the body corporate shall be guilty of that offence and shall be liable to be proceeded against and punished accordingly.

   (2) Where the affairs of a body corporate are managed by its members, the preceding paragraph shall apply in relation to the acts and defaults of a member in connection with his functions of management as if he were a director of the body corporate.

4–2701T   20. Restriction on institution of proceedings in England and Wales. Proceedings for an offence shall not be instituted in England or Wales except by an inspector or by, or with the consent of, the Director of Public Prosecutions.

4–2701U   21. (1) If authorised in that behalf by the Secretary of State an inspector may prosecute proceedings for an offence before a magistrates court even though the inspector is not of counsel or a solicitor.

   (2) This regulation shall not apply in Scotland.

4–2701V   22. Power of court to order cause of offence to be remedied. (1) This regulation applies where a person is convicted of an offence in respect of any matter which appears to the court to be a matter which it is in his power to remedy.

   (2) In addition to or instead of imposing any punishment, the court may order the person in question to take such steps as may be specified in the order for remedying the said matters within such time as may be fixed by the order.

   (3) The time fixed by an order under paragraph (2) may be extended or further extended by order of the court on an application made before the end of that time as originally fixed or as extended under this paragraph, as the case may be.

   (4) Where a person is ordered under paragraph (2) to remedy any matters, that person shall not be liable under these Regulations in respect of that matter in so far as it continues during the time fixed by the order or any further time allowed under paragraph (3).

4–2701W

Regulation 2   SCHEDULE 1
                              WORKFORCE AGREEMENTS

   1. An agreement is a workforce agreement for the purposes of these Regulations if the following conditions are satisfied—

   (a) the agreement is in writing;
   (b) it has effect for a specified period not exceeding five years;
   (c) it applies either—

      (i) to all of the relevant members of the workforce, or
      (ii) to all of the relevant members of the workforce who belong to a particular group;

   (d) the agreement is signed—

      (i) in the case of an agreement of the kind referred to in sub-paragraph (*c*)(i), by the representatives of the workforce, and in the case of an agreement of the kind referred to in sub-paragraph (*c*)(ii), by the representatives of the group to which the agreement applies (excluding, in either case, any representative not a relevant member of the workforce on the date on which the agreement was first made available for signature), or
      (ii) if the employer employed 20 or fewer workers on the date referred to in sub-paragraph (*d*)(i), either by the appropriate representatives in accordance with that sub-paragraph or by the majority of the workers employed by him; and

   (e) before the agreement was made available for signature, the employer provided all the workers to whom it was intended to apply on the date on which it came into effect with copies of the text of the agreement and such guidance as those employees might reasonably require in order to understand it in full.

   2. For the purposes of this Schedule—

"a particular group" is a group of the relevant members of a workforce who undertake a particular function, work at a particular workplace or belong to a particular department or unit within their employer's business;

"relevant members of the workforce" are all of the workers employed by a particular employer, excluding any worker whose terms and conditions of employment are provided for, wholly or in part, in a collective agreement;

"representatives of the group" are workers duly elected to represent the members of a particular group;

"representatives of the workforce" are workers duly elected to represent the relevant members of the workforce;

and representatives are "duly elected" if the election at which they were elected satisfied the requirements of paragraph 3.

3. The requirements concerning elections referred to in paragraph 2 are that—

(a) the number of representatives to be elected is determined by the employer;

(b) the candidates for election as representatives of the workforce are relevant members of the workforce, and candidates for election as representatives of the group are members of the group;

(c) no worker who is eligible to be a candidate is unreasonably excluded from standing for election;

(d) all the relevant members of the workforce are entitled to vote for representatives of the workforce, and all the members of a particular group are entitled to vote for representatives of the group;

(e) the workers entitled to vote may vote for as many candidates as there are representatives to be elected; and

(f) the election is conducted so as to secure that—

(i) so far as is reasonably practicable, those voting do so in secret, and

(ii) the votes given at the election are fairly and accurately counted.

4–2701X

Regulation 16(2)

SCHEDULE 2
ENFORCEMENT

Appointment of inspectors

1. (1) The Secretary of State may appoint as inspectors (under whatever title he may from time to time determine) such persons having suitable qualifications as he thinks necessary for carrying into effect these Regulations, and may terminate any appointment made under this paragraph.

(2) Every appointment of a person as an inspector under this paragraph shall be made by an instrument in writing specifying which of the powers conferred on inspectors by these Regulations are to be exercisable by the person appointed; and an inspector shall in right of his appointment under this paragraph be entitled to exercise only such of those powers as are so specified.

(3) So much of an inspector's instrument of appointment as specifies the powers which he is entitled to exercise may be varied by the Secretary of State.

(4) An inspector shall, if so required when exercising or seeking to exercise any power conferred on him by these Regulations, produce his instrument of appointment or a duly authenticated copy thereof.

Powers of inspectors

2. (1) Subject to the provisions of paragraph 1 and this paragraph, an inspector may for the purpose of carrying into effect these Regulations exercise the powers set out in sub-paragraph (2).

(2) The powers of an inspector are the following, namely—

(a) at any reasonable time (or in a situation which in his opinion may be dangerous, at any time) to enter any premises which he has reason to believe it is necessary for him to enter for the purposes mentioned in sub-paragraph (1);

(b) to take with him a constable if he has reasonable cause to apprehend any serious obstruction in the execution of his duty;

(c) without prejudice to paragraph (b), on entering any premises by virtue of paragraph (a) to take with him—

(i) any other person duly authorised by the Secretary of State; and

(ii) any equipment or material required for any purpose for which the power of entry is being exercised;

(d) to make such examination and investigation as may in any circumstances be necessary for the purpose mentioned in sub-paragraph (1);

(e) to require any person whom he has reasonable cause to believe to be able to give any information relevant to any examination or investigation under paragraph (d) to answer (in the absence of persons other than a person nominated by him to be present and any persons whom the inspector may allow to be present) such questions as the inspector thinks fit to ask and to sign a declaration of the truth of his answers;

(f) to require the production of, inspect, and take copies of, or of any entry in—

(i) any records which by virtue of these Regulations are required to be kept, and

(ii) any other books, records or documents which it is necessary for him to see for the purposes of any examination or investigation under paragraph (d);

(g) to require any person to afford him such facilities and assistance with respect to any matters or things within that person's control or in relation to which that person has responsibilities as are necessary to enable the inspector to exercise any of the powers conferred on him by this sub-paragraph;

(h) any other power which is necessary for the purpose mentioned in sub-paragraph (1).

(3) No answer given by a person in pursuance of a requirement imposed under sub-paragraph (2)(e) shall be admissible in evidence against that person or the husband or wife of that person in any proceedings.

(4) Nothing in this paragraph shall be taken to compel the production by any person of a document of which he would on grounds of legal professional privilege be entitled to withhold production on an order for discovery in an action in the High Court or, as the case may be, an order for the production of documents in an action in the Court of Session.

Improvement notices

3. If an inspector is of the opinion that a person—

(a) is contravening one or more of these Regulations; or

(b) has contravened one or more of these Regulations in circumstances that make it likely that the contravention will continue or be repeated,

he may serve on him a notice (in this Schedule referred to as "an improvement notice") stating that he is of that opinion, specifying the provision or provisions as to which he is of that opinion, giving particulars of the reasons why he is of that opinion, and requiring that person to remedy the contravention or, as the case may be, the matter occasioning it within such period (ending not earlier than the period within which an appeal against the notice can be brought under paragraph (6)) as may be specified in the notice.

Prohibition notices

4. (1) This paragraph applies to any activities which are being, or are likely to be, carried on by or under the control of any person, being activities to or in relation to which any of these Regulations apply or will, if the activities are so carried on, apply.

(2) If as regards any activities to which this paragraph applies an inspector is of the opinion that, as carried on by or under the control of the person in question, the activities involve or, as the case may be, will involve a risk of serious personal injury, the inspector may serve on that person a notice (in this Schedule referred to as "a prohibition notice").

(3) A prohibition notice shall—

(a) state that the inspector is of the said opinion;
(b) specify the matters which in his opinion give or, as the case may be, will give rise to the said risk;
(c) where in his opinion any of those matters involves or, as the case may be, will involve a contravention of any of these Regulations, state that he is of that opinion, specify the regulation or regulations as to which he is of that opinion, and give particulars of the reasons why he is of that opinion; and
(d) direct that the activities to which the notice relates shall not be carried on by or under the control of the person on whom the notice is served unless the matters specified in the notice in pursuance of paragraph (b) and any associated contraventions of provisions so specified in pursuance of paragraph (c) have been remedied.

(4) A direction contained in a prohibition notice in pursuance of sub-paragraph (3)(d) shall take effect—

(a) at the end of the period specified in the notice; or
(b) if the notice so declares, immediately.

Provisions supplementary to paragraphs 3 and 4

5. (1) In this paragraph "a notice" means an improvement notice or a prohibition notice.

(2) A notice may (but need not) include directions as to the measures to be taken to remedy any contravention or matter to which the notice relates; and any such directions—

(a) may be framed to any extent by reference to any approved code of practice; and
(b) may be framed so as to afford the person on whom the notice is served a choice between different ways of remedying the contravention or matter.

(3) Where an improvement notice or prohibition notice which is not to take immediate effect has been served—

(a) the notice may be withdrawn by an inspector at any time before the end of the period specified therein in pursuance of paragraph 3 or paragraph 4(4) as the case may be; and
(b) the period so specified may be extended or further extended by an inspector at any time when an appeal against the notice is not pending.

Appeal against improvement or prohibition notice

6. (1) In this paragraph "a notice" means an improvement or prohibition notice.

(2) A person on whom a notice is served may within 21 days from the date of its service appeal to an employment tribunal; and on such an appeal the tribunal may either cancel or affirm the notice and, if it affirms it, may do so either in its original form or with such modifications as the tribunal may in the circumstances think fit.

(3) Where an appeal under this paragraph is brought against a notice within the period allowed under the preceding sub-paragraph, then—

(a) in the case of an improvement notice, the bringing of the appeal shall have the effect of suspending the operation of the notice until the appeal is finally disposed of or, if the appeal is withdrawn, until the withdrawal of the appeal;
(b) in the case of a prohibition notice, the bringing of the appeal shall have the like effect if, but only if, on the application of the appellant the tribunal so directs (and then only from the giving of the direction).

(4) One or more assessors may be appointed for the purposes of any proceedings brought before an employment tribunal under this paragraph.

Restrictions on disclosure of information

7. (1) In this paragraph—

"relevant information" means information obtained by an inspector in pursuance of a requirement imposed under paragraph 2;
"relevant statutory provisions" means the provisions of Part 6 of the Transport Act 1968 and of any orders or regulations made under powers contained in that Part; and
"the recipient", in relation to any relevant information, means the person by whom that information was so obtained or to whom that information was so furnished, as the case may be.

(2) Subject to the following sub-paragraph, no relevant information shall be disclosed without the consent of the person by whom it was furnished.

(3) The preceding sub-paragraph shall not apply to—

(a) disclosure of information to a government department;
(b) without prejudice to paragraph (a), disclosure by the recipient of information to any person for the purpose of any function conferred on the recipient by or under any of the relevant statutory provisions or under these Regulations;
(c) without prejudice to paragraph (a), disclosure by the recipient of information to—

(i) an officer of a local authority who is authorised by that authority to receive it: or
(ii) a constable authorised by a chief officer of police to receive it; or

(d) disclosure by the recipient of information in a form calculated to prevent it from being identified as relating to a particular person or case.

(4) A person to whom information is disclosed in pursuance of sub-paragraph (3) shall not use the information for a purpose other than—

(a) in a case falling within sub-paragraph (3)(a), a purpose of a government department or local authority in connection with these Regulations or with the relevant statutory provisions, or any enactment whatsoever relating to working time;

(*b*) in the case of information given to a constable, the purposes of the police in connection with these Regulations, the relevant statutory provisions or any enactment relating to working time.

(5) A person shall not disclose any information obtained by him as a result of the exercise of any power conferred by paragraph 2 (including in particular any information with respect to any trade secret obtained by him in any premises entered by him by virtue of any such power) except—

(*a*) for the purposes of his functions; or
(*b*) for the purposes of any legal proceedings; or
(*c*) with the relevant consent.

In this sub-paragraph "the relevant consent" means, in the case of information furnished in pursuance of a requirement imposed under paragraph 2, the consent of the person who furnished it, and, in any other case, the consent of a person having responsibilities in relation to the premises where the information was obtained.

(6) Notwithstanding anything in sub-paragraph (5) an inspector shall, in circumstances in which it is necessary to do so for the purpose of assisting in keeping persons (or the representatives of persons) adequately informed about matters affecting their health, safety and welfare or working time, give to such persons or their representatives the following descriptions of information, that is to say—

(*a*) factual information obtained by him as mentioned in that sub-paragraph which relates to their working environment; and
(*b*) information with respect to any action which he has taken or proposes to take in or in connection with the performance of his functions in relation to their working environment;

and, where an inspector does as aforesaid, he shall give the like information to the employer of the first-mentioned persons.

Passenger and Goods Vehicles (Recording Equipment) (Tachograph Card) Regulations 2006[1]

(SI 2006/1937 amended by SI 2006/3276)

4–2701Y 1.   These Regulations may be cited as the Passenger and Goods Vehicles (Recording Equipment) (Tachograph Card) Regulations 2006 and shall come into force on 21st August 2006.

---

1. Made by the Secretary of State, in exercise of the powers conferred by s 2(2) of the European Communities Act 1972.

4–2701Z 2.   In these Regulations—

"the Community Recording Equipment Regulation" means Council Regulation (EEC) No 3821/85 on recording equipment in road transport as it has effect in accordance with—

(*a*) Commission Regulation (EEC) No 3314/90;
(*b*) Commission Regulation (EEC) No 3688/92;
(*c*) Commission Regulation (EC) No 2479/95;
(*d*) Commission Regulation (EC) No 1056/97;
(*e*) Article 1 of Council Regulation (EC) No 2135/98;
(*f*) Commission Regulation (EC) No 1360/2002;
(*g*) Act concerning the conditions of accession of the Czech Republic, the Republic of Estonia, the Republic of Cyprus, the Republic of Latvia, the Republic of Lithuania, the Republic of Hungary, the Republic of Malta, the Republic of Poland, the Republic of Slovenia and the Slovak Republic and the adjustments to the Treaties on which the European Union is founded;
(*h*) Regulation (EC) No 1882/2003 of the European Parliament and of the Council;
(*i*) Commission Regulation (EC) No 432/2004; and
(*j*) Regulation (EC) No 561/2006 of the European Parliament and of the Council;

and as read with the Community Drivers' Hours and Recording Equipment (Exemptions and Supplementary Provisions) Regulations 1986;

"company card", "control card", "driver card" and "workshop card" have the meanings given by Annex IB to the Community Recording Equipment Regulation;

"PIN" means personal identification number for use in connection with a workshop card;

"relevant vehicle" means a vehicle in which there is recording equipment

(i) which has been installed in accordance with the Community Recording Equipment Regulation; and
(ii) complies with Annexes IB and II to that regulation; and

"tachograph card" means a company card, control card, driver card or workshop card.

4–2702 3. Driver cards.   (1) A person commits an offence—

(*a*) if, subject to paragraph (3), he uses, attempts to use or is in possession of, more than one driver card on which he is identified as the holder;
(*b*) if he uses or attempts to use a driver card on which he is not identified as the holder;
(*c*) if, with intent to deceive, he makes a false statement, or forges or alters a document, for the purpose of obtaining a driver card;
(*d*) if he uses, or is in possession of, a driver card issued in consequence of an application which included, with intent to deceive, a false statement or forged or altered document; or
(*e*) if he uses, or is in possession of, a driver card which has been forged or altered.

(2) A person commits an offence if he causes or permits—

(a) any use or possession of a driver card; or
(b) the making of any false statement or forgery or alteration of a document
specified in paragraph (1).
(3) It shall not be an offence—

(a) to hold a card which will become time-expired within one month and the card which has been issued by the Secretary of State in renewal of the former card; or
(b) to hold a card, which has become time-expired, in combination with another card.

(4) A person guilty of an offence under paragraph (1)(a) or (b) is liable on summary conviction to a fine not exceeding level 5 on the standard scale.
(5) A person guilty of an offence under paragraph (1)(c) is liable—

(a) on summary conviction, to imprisonment for a term not exceeding 3 months or to a fine not exceeding the statutory maximum, or to both; or
(b) on conviction on indictment, to imprisonment for a term not exceeding two years, or to a fine, or to both.

(6) A person guilty of an offence under paragraph (1)(d) or (e) or paragraph (2) is liable—

(a) on summary conviction, to a fine not exceeding the statutory maximum; or

(b) on conviction on indictment, to imprisonment for a term not exceeding two years or to a fine, or to both.

4–2702A   4. Workshop cards.   (1) A person commits an offence—

(a) if, subject to paragraph (3) he uses, attempts to use or is in possession of more than one workshop card, on which he is identified as the holder, or more than one PIN, in respect of the same place of work;
(b) if he uses or attempts to use a workshop card, or PIN, of which he is not the identified holder;
(c) if he uses or attempts to use a workshop card, or PIN, in circumstances unconnected with the place of work for which that card, or PIN, was issued;
(d) if, with intent to deceive, he makes a false statement, or forges or alters a document, for the purpose of obtaining a workshop card or PIN;
(e) if he uses, or is in possession of, a workshop card, or PIN, issued in consequence of an application which included, with intent to deceive, a false statement or forged or altered document;
(f) if he uses, or is in possession of, a workshop card, which has been forged or altered; or
(g) if he divulges to another person, or permits another person to use, the PIN used in connection with a workshop card of which he is identified as the holder.

(2) A person commits an offence if he causes or permits—

(a) any use, alteration or possession of a workshop card or PIN, or
(b) the making of any false statement or forgery or alteration of a document,
specified in paragraph (1).
(3) It shall not be an offence—

(a) to hold a workshop card which will become time-expired within one month and the workshop card which has been issued by the Secretary of State in renewal of the former workshop card; or
(b) to hold a workshop card, which has become time-expired, in combination with another workshop card.

(4) A person guilty of an offence under paragraph (1)(a), (b), (c) or (g) is liable on summary conviction to a fine not exceeding level 5 on the standard scale.
(5) A person guilty of an offence under paragraph (1)(d) is liable—

(a) on summary conviction, to imprisonment for a term not exceeding 3 months or to a fine not exceeding the statutory maximum, or to both; or
(b) on conviction on indictment, to imprisonment for a term not exceeding two years, or to a fine, or to both.

(6) A person guilty of an offence under paragraph (1)(e) or (f) or paragraph (2) is liable—

(a) on summary conviction, to a fine not exceeding the statutory maximum; or
(b) on conviction on indictment, to imprisonment for a term not exceeding two years or to a fine, or both.

4–2702B   5. Lost, stolen, damaged or malfunctioning cards.   (1) If a tachograph card is lost or stolen, the person to whom that card was issued shall notify the Secretary of State in writing and shall provide such information or documents concerning the loss or theft as the Secretary of State may require.
(2) If a tachograph card is found at any time after the Secretary of State has been notified in accordance with paragraph (1) of the loss or theft of it, the person to whom that card was issued, if it is in his possession, shall return it to the Secretary of State, or if it is not in his possession, but he becomes aware that it is found, shall take all reasonable steps to take possession of it and if successful shall return it as soon as may be to the Secretary of State.
(3) If a tachograph card is damaged or malfunctions, the person to whom that card was issued shall return it to the Secretary of State and shall provide such information or documents concerning the damage or malfunction as the Secretary of State may require.

(4) A person who fails to comply with the requirements of paragraph (1), (2) or (3) commits an offence.

(5) A person guilty of an offence under paragraph (4) is liable on summary conviction to a fine not exceeding level 5 on the standard scale.

4–2702C 6. Card particulars. (1) Where the details of the holder of a tachograph card specified on the card cease to be correct, the holder—

(a) must forthwith notify the Secretary of State of the details which require correction, and
(b) must surrender the card when required to do so, to such address as may be specified, by the Secretary of State.

(2) Where it appears to the Secretary of State that a tachograph card issued by him to any person was issued in error or with an error or omission in the particulars specified in the card, he may serve notice in writing on that person requiring him to surrender that card and it shall be the duty of that person to comply with the requirement.

(3) Subject to paragraph (4), on surrender of a card by a person in accordance with paragraph (1) or (2) the Secretary of State shall, if so requested by that person, issue a replacement card to him.

(4) The Secretary of State may require the person surrendering the card to provide such information and documents as the Secretary of State may require to enable him to correct the details, error or omission before issuing a new card under paragraph (3).

(5) A person who fails to comply with the requirements of paragraph (1) or (2) commits an offence.

(6) A person guilty of an offence under paragraph (5) is liable on summary conviction to a fine not exceeding level 5 on the standard scale.

4–2702D 7. Unauthorised cards. (1) A person in possession of a tachograph card described in paragraph (3) shall surrender that card to the Secretary of State, by such means and to such address as may be specified by the Secretary of State.

(2) A constable or a vehicle examiner appointed under section 66A of the Road Traffic Act 1988 may remove and retain a tachograph card described in paragraph (3) which has not been surrendered to the Secretary of State.

(3) A tachograph card to which paragraphs (1) and (2) refer is a card—

(a) on which the person using the card is not identified as the holder;
(b) which has been falsified; or
(c) which has been issued in consequence of an application which included a false statement or forged or altered document.

(4) A person who does not surrender a card in accordance with paragraph (1) commits an offence.

(5) A person guilty of an offence under paragraph (3) is liable on summary conviction to a fine not exceeding level 5 on the standard scale.

TRAFFIC REGULATION

Functions of Traffic Wardens Order 1970[1]
(SI 1970/1958 amended by SI 1986/1328, SI 1993/1334 and SI 2002/2975)

4–2731 1. *Citation, commencement, revocation and extent.*

---

1. Made by the Home Secretary under s 81(3), (4A) and (4B) of the Road Traffic Regulation Act 1967 and now having effect under s 95 of the Road Traffic Regulations Act 1984.

4–2732 2. In this Order—

"the Act of 1960" and "the Act of 1967" mean respectively the Road Traffic Act, 1960[1] and the Road Traffic Regulation Act, 1967[1];
"street parking place order" means an order made under the Act of 1967 relating to a street parking place;
"traffic order" means an order made under section 1, 5, 6, 9, 11 or 84A of the Act of 1967[2].

---

1. The Road Traffic Act 1972 and the Road Traffic (Consequential Provisions) Act 1988 have successively repealed and replaced the relevant provisions of the 1960 Act and the Road Traffic Regulation Act 1984 has repealed and replaced the provisions of the 1967 Act. The text of these regulations has been amended accordingly. References to the "Act of 1988" are to the Road Traffic Act 1988.
2. Traffic orders are now made under the Road Traffic Regulation Act 1984, ss 1, 6, 9, 10, 12, 37, Sch 9.

4–2733 3. (1) The functions set out in the Schedule to this Order are hereby prescribed as appropriate for discharge by traffic wardens.

(2) For the purposes of the discharge by traffic wardens of such functions, references to a constable or police constable in the following enactments shall include references to a traffic warden—

(a) section 52 of the Metropolitan Police Act, 1839 so far as it relates to the giving by the commissioner of directions to constables for preventing obstruction;

(b) section 22 of the local Act of the second and third year of the reign of Queen Victoria, chapter 94, so far as it makes similar provision with respect to the City of London;

(c) sections 35 and 37 of the Act of 1988 (drivers and pedestrians to comply with traffic directions given by police constables);

(d) section 169 of the Act of 1988 (the power of constables to obtain the names and addresses of pedestrians failing to comply with traffic directions);

(e) section 11 of the Road Traffic Offenders Act 1988 and section 113 of the Act of 1984 (the giving of evidence of an admission by certificate);

(f) section 100(3) of the Road Traffic Regulation Act 1984 (the interim disposal of vehicles removed under section 99 of that Act);

(g) sections 104 and 105 of the Road Traffic Regulation Act 1984 (the immobilisation of illegally parked vehicles).

(h) section 67(3) of the Road Traffic Act 1988 (power to stop vehicles for testing);

(i) section 163 of the Road Traffic Act 1988 (power to stop vehicles).

(3) For the purposes of the discharge by traffic wardens of the functions set out in the Schedule to this Order, references in section 165(1) of the Act of 1988 to a police constable shall, in so far as it applies to the furnishing of names and addresses, include references to a traffic warden if the traffic warden has reasonable cause to believe that there has been committed an offence—

(a) in respect of a vehicle by its being left or parked on a road during the hours of darkness (as defined by the Road Traffic Act, 1972[1]) without the lights or reflectors required by law;

(b) in respect of a vehicle by its obstructing a road, or waiting, or being left or parked, or being loaded or unloaded, in a road;

(c) in contravention of section 35 of the Act of 1988;

(d) in contravention of a provision of the Vehicle Excise and Registration Act 1994;

(e) created by section 47 of the Act of 1984 (offences relating to parking places on highways where charges made).

(4) References in section 164(1), (2) and (6) of the Road Traffic Act 1988 to a constable or police constable shall include references to a traffic warden only where—

(a) the traffic warden has reasonable cause to believe that there has been committed an offence by causing a vehicle, or any part of it, to stop in contravention of regulations made under section 25 of the Road Traffic Regulation Act 1984 or an offence in contravention of section 22 of the Road Traffic Act 1988 (leaving vehicles in dangerous positions); or

(b) the traffic warden is employed to perform functions in connection with the custody of vehicles removed from a road or land in the open air in pursuance of regulations made under section 99 of the Road Traffic Regulation Act 1984 or from a parking place in pursuance of a street parking place order, and he has reasonable cause to believe that there has been committed an offence in respect of a vehicle by its obstructing a road, or waiting, or being left or parked, or being loaded or unloaded, in a road.

---

1. The definition of "hours or darkness" is to be found now in the Road Vehicles Lighting Regulations in this PART.

Article 3   SCHEDULE
                              FUNCTIONS OF TRAFFIC WARDENS

4–2734 1. (1) Traffic wardens may be employed to enforce the law with respect to an offence—

(a) committed in respect of a vehicle by its being left or parked on a road during the hours of darkness (as defined by the Road Traffic Act, 1972[1]) without the lights or reflectors required by law; or

(b) committed in respect of a vehicle by its obstructing a road, or waiting, or being left or parked, or being loaded or unloaded, in a road or other public place; or

(c) committed in contravention of a provision of the Vehicle Excise and Registration Act 1994;

(d) created by section 47 of the Act of 1984 (offences relating to parking places on highways where charges made);

(e) committed by causing a vehicle, or any part of it, to stop in contravention of regulations made under section 25 of the Road Traffic Regulation Act 1984.

(2) For the purposes of the enforcement of the law with respect to such of the offences described in sub-paragraph (1) of this paragraph as are fixed penalty offences within the meaning of section 51 of the Road Traffic Offenders Act 1988, traffic wardens may exercise the functions conferred on constables by Part III of the said Act of 1988.

2. (1) Traffic wardens may, under arrangements made with the Secretary of State or a local authority, be employed to act as parking attendants at street parking places provided or controlled by the Secretary of State or local authority.

(2) A traffic warden may exercise functions conferred on a traffic warden by a traffic order or a street parking place order.

3. Without prejudice to the generality of paragraph 1 above, traffic wardens may be employed in connection with obtaining information under section 172 of the Act of 1988 or section 112 of the Act of 1984 (duty to give information as to identity of driver, etc in certain cases).

4. Traffic wardens may be employed to perform functions in connection with the custody of vehicles removed from a road or land in the open air in pursuance of regulation under section 99 of the Act of 1984 or from a parking place in pursuance of a street parking place order.

5. Where a police authority provides school crossing patrols under section 26 of the Act of 1984, whether as the appropriate authority or by agreement with the appropriate authority, traffic wardens appointed by that police authority may be employed to act as school crossing patrols.

5A. Traffic wardens may be employed to stop vehicles for the purposes of a test under subsection (1) of section 67 of the Road Traffic Act 1988 (testing of conditions of vehicles on roads).

5B. Traffic wardens may be employed to escort vehicles or trailers carrying loads of exceptional dimensions the use of which is authorised by an order made by the Secretary of State under section 44(1)(*d*) of the Road Traffic Act 1988.

6. (1) Subject to the foregoing paragraphs, traffic wardens may be employed in the control and regulation of traffic (including foot passengers) or vehicles whether on a highway or not and to discharge any other functions normally undertaken by the police in connection with the control and regulation of traffic (including foot passengers) or vehicles.

---

1. The definition of "hours of darkness" is to be found now in the Road Vehicles Lighting Regulations in this PART, ante.

Motorways Traffic (England and Wales) Regulations 1982[1]

(SI 1982/1163 amended by SI 1983/374, SI 1984/1479, SI 1992/1364, SI 1995/158, SI 1996/3053, SI 2004/3168 (E) and 3258, SI 2005/2929 (W) and SI 2006/594)

4–2811 1. *Citation and commencement.*

---

1. Made by the Secretary of State for Transport in exercise of powers conferred by s 13(2) and (3) of the Road Traffic Regulation Act 1967. Contravention of the Regulations is an offence punishable in accordance with ss 17(4), of the Road Traffic Regulation Act 1984 with penalty provided by Sch 2 to the Road Traffic Offenders Act 1988, in this PART, ante.

4–2812 2. *Revocation.*

Interpretation

4–2813 3. (1) In these Regulations, the following expressions have the meanings hereby respectively assigned to them—

- (*a*) "the 1984 Act" means the Road Traffic Regulation Act 1984;
- (*b*) "carriageway" means that part of a motorway which—

  - (i) is provided for the regular passage of vehicular motor traffic along the motorway; and
  - (ii) where a hard shoulder is provided, has the approximate position of its left-hand or near-side edge marked with a traffic sign of the type shown in diagram 1012·1 in Schedule 2 to the Traffic Signs Regulations and General Directions 1981[1].

- (*c*) "central reservation" means that part of a motorway which separates the carriageway to be used by vehicles travelling in one direction from the carriageway to be used by vehicles travelling in the opposite direction;
- (*d*) "excluded traffic" means traffic which is not traffic of Classes I or II;
- (*e*) "hard shoulder" means a part of the motorway which is adjacent to and situated on the left hand or near side of the carriageway when facing in the direction in which vehicles may be driven in accordance with Regulation 6, and which is designed to take the weight of a vehicle;
- (*f*) "motorway" means any road or part of a road to which these Regulations apply by virtue of Regulation 4;
- (*ff*) "traffic officer" means an individual designated as such by, or under an authority given by, the Secretary of State or the National Assembly for Wales in accordance with section 2 of the Traffic Management Act 2004;
- (*g*) "verge" means any part of a motorway which is not a carriageway, a hard shoulder, or a central reservation.

(2) A vehicle shall be treated for the purposes of any provision of these Regulations as being on any part of a motorway specified in that provision if any part of the vehicle (whether it is at rest or not) is on the part of the motorway so specified.

(3) Any provision of these Regulations containing any prohibition or restriction relating to the driving, moving or stopping of a vehicle, or to its remaining at rest, shall be construed as a provision that no person shall use a motorway by driving, moving or stopping the vehicle or by causing or permitting it to be driven or moved, or to stop or remain at rest, in contravention of that prohibition or restriction.

(4) In these Regulations references to numbered classes of traffic are references to the classes of traffic set out in Schedule 4 to the Highways Act 1980.

---

1. These Regulations have been repealed and replaced by the Traffic Signs Regulations and General Directions 1994, SI 1994/1519, post, save in so far as they relate to the Traffic Signs (Welsh and English Language Provisions) Regulations 1985.

Application

4–2814   **4.** Subject to section 17(5) of the 1984 Act, these Regulations apply to every special road or part of a special road which can be used only by traffic of Class I or II.

Vehicles to be driven on the carriageway only

4–2815   **5.** Subject to the following provisions of these Regulations, no vehicle shall be driven on any part of a motorway which is not a carriageway.

Direction of driving

4–2816   **6.** (1) Where there is a traffic sign indicating that there is no entry to a carriageway at a particular place, no vehicle shall be driven or moved onto that carriageway at that place.

(2) Where there is a traffic sign indicating that there is no left or right turn into a carriageway at a particular place, no vehicle shall be so driven or moved as to cause it to turn to the left or (as the case may be) to the right into that carriageway at that place.

(3) Every vehicle on a length of carriageway which is contiguous to a central reservation, shall be driven in such a direction that the central reservation is at all times on the right hand or off side of the vehicle.

(4) Where traffic signs are so placed that there is a length of carriageway (being a length which is not contiguous to a central reservation) which can be entered at one end only by vehicles driven in conformity with paragraph (1) of this Regulation, every vehicle on that length of carriageway shall be driven in such a direction only as to cause it to proceed away from that end of that length of carriageway towards the other end thereof.

(5) Without prejudice to the foregoing provisions of this Regulation, no vehicle which—

(*a*) is on a length of carriageway on which vehicles are required by any of the foregoing provisions of this Regulation to be driven in one direction only and is proceeding in or facing that direction, or

(*b*) is on any other length of carriageway and is proceeding in or facing one direction,

shall be driven or moved so as to cause it to turn and proceed in or face the opposite direction.

Restriction on stopping

4–2817   **7.** (1) Subject to the following provisions of this Regulation, no vehicle shall stop or remain at rest on a carriageway[1].

(2) Where it is necessary for a vehicle which is being driven on a carriageway to be stopped while it is on a motorway—

(*a*) by reason of a breakdown or mechanical defect or lack of fuel, oil or water, required for the vehicle; or

(*b*) by reason of any accident, illness or other emergency; or

(*c*) to permit any person carried in or on the vehicle to recover or move any object which has fallen onto a motorway; or

(*d*) to permit any person carried in or on the vehicle to give help which is required by any other person in any of the circumstances specified in the foregoing provisions of this paragraph,

the vehicle shall, as soon and in so far as is reasonably practicable, be driven or moved off the carriageway on to, and may stop and remain at rest on, any hard shoulder which is contiguous to that carriageway.

(3) (*a*) A vehicle which is at rest on a hard shoulder shall so far as is reasonably practicable be allowed to remain at rest on that hard shoulder in such a position only that no part of it or of the load carried thereby shall obstruct or be a cause of danger to vehicles using the carriageway.

(*b*) A vehicle shall not remain at rest on a hard shoulder for longer than is necessary in the circumstances or for the purposes specified in paragraph (2) of this Regulation.

(4) Nothing in the foregoing provisions of this Regulation shall preclude a vehicle from stopping or remaining at rest on a carriageway while it is prevented from proceeding along the carriageway by the presence of any other vehicle or any person or object[1].

---

1. Regulation 7(4) does not contemplate vehicles being permitted to stop on the carriageway or to remain at rest on the carriageway in any circumstances at all, but simply excludes from the ambit of the Regulation vehicles stopped because of the presence of other vehicles, persons or objects on the carriageway. Therefore, as reg 7(4) is not permissive for the purposes of applying Sch 7 to the Road Traffic Regulation Act 1984 (maximum penalties on conviction), an offence, contrary to s 17(4) of that Act and reg 7(1), attracts discretionary disqualification and carries an obligatory endorsement; see *Mawson v Oxford* [1987] RTR 398.

Restriction on reversing

4–2818   **8.** No vehicle on a motorway shall be driven or moved backwards except in so far as it is necessary to back the vehicle to enable it to proceed forwards or to be connected to any other vehicle.

Restriction on the use of hard shoulders

4–2819 **9.** No vehicle shall be driven or stop or remain at rest on any hard shoulder except in accordance with paragraphs (2) and (3) of Regulation 7.

Vehicles not to use the central reservation or verge

4–2820 **10.** No vehicle shall be driven or moved or stop or remain at rest on a central reservation or verge.

Vehicles not to be driven by learner drivers

4–2821 **11.** (1) Subject to paragraph (3), a person shall not drive on a motorway a motor vehicle to which this regulation applies if he is authorised to drive that vehicle only by virtue of his being the holder of a provisional licence.

(2) This regulation applies to—

(a) a motor vehicle in category A or B or sub-category C1+E (8.25 tonnes), D1 (not for hire or reward), D1+E (not for hire or reward) or P, and

(b) a motor vehicle in category B+E or sub-category C1 if the provisional licence authorising the driving of such a motor vehicle was in force at a time before 1st January 1997.

(3) Paragraph (1) shall not apply in relation to a vehicle if the holder of the provisional licence has passed a test of competence prescribed under section 89 of the Road Traffic Act 1988 for the grant of a licence to drive that vehicle.

(4) In this regulation—

(a) the expression "in force" and expressions relating to vehicle categories shall be construed in accordance with regulations 3(2) and 4(2) respectively of the Motor Vehicles (Driving Licences) Regulations 1996;

(b) "provisional licence", in relation to any vehicle, means a licence—

(i) granted under section 97(2) of the Road Traffic Act 1988, or

(ii) treated, by virtue of section 98 of that Act and regulations made thereunder, as authorising its holder to drive that vehicle as if he were authorised by a provisional licence to do so.

Restriction on use of right-hand or off side lane

4–2822 **12.** (1) This Regulation applies to—

(a) a goods vehicle having a maximum laden weight exceeding 7·5 tonnes;

(aa) a goods vehicle—

(i) having a maximum laden weight exceeding 3.5 tonnes but not exceeding 7.5 tonnes, and

(ii) to which regulation 36B of the Road Vehicles (Construction and Use) Regulations 1986 applies or would apply but for paragraph (14)(a) or (b) of that regulation;

(b) a passenger vehicle which is constructed or adapted to carry more than eight seated passengers in addition to the driver the maximum laden weight of which exceeds 7.5 tonnes;

(bb) a passenger vehicle—

(i) which is constructed or adapted to carry more than eight seated passengers in addition to the driver the maximum laden weight of which does not exceed 7.5 tonnes, and

(ii) to which regulation 36A of the Road Vehicles (Construction and Use) Regulations 1986 (Speed limiters) applies or would apply but for paragraph (13)(a) or (b) of that regulation;

(c) a motor vehicle drawing a trailer, and

(d) a vehicle which is a motor tractor, a light locomotive or a heavy locomotive.

(2) Subject to the provisions of paragraph (3) below, no vehicle to which this Regulation applies shall be driven, or moved, or stop or remain at rest on the right hand or off side lane of a length of carriageway which has three or more traffic lanes at any place where all the lanes are open for use by traffic proceeding in the same direction.

(3) The prohibition contained in paragraph (2) above shall not apply to a vehicle while it is being driven on any right hand or off side lane such as is mentioned in that paragraph in so far as it is necessary for the vehicle to be driven to enable it to pass another vehicle which is carrying or drawing a load of exceptional width.

(4) Nothing in this regulation shall have effect so as to require a vehicle to change lane during a period when it would not be reasonably practicable for it to do so without involving danger of injury to any person or inconvenience to other traffic.

(5) In this Regulation "goods vehicle", "passenger vehicle" and "maximum laden weight" have the same meanings as in Schedule 6 to the 1984 Act.

4–2823 **13.** *Revoked.*

Restrictions affecting animals carried in vehicles

4–2824   14. The person in charge of any animal which is carried by a vehicle using a motorway shall, so far as is practicable, secure that—

(a) the animal shall not be removed from or permitted to leave the vehicle while the vehicle is on a motorway, and

(b) if it escapes from, or it is necessary for it to be removed from, or permitted to leave, the vehicle—

(i) it shall not go or remain on any part of the motorway other than a hard shoulder, and

(ii) it shall whilst it is not on or in the vehicle be held on a lead or otherwise kept under proper control.

Use of motorway by excluded traffic

4–2825   15. (1) Excluded traffic is hereby authorised to use a motorway on the occasions or in the emergencies and to the extent specified in the following provisions of this paragraph, that is to say—

(a) traffic of Classes III or IV may use a motorway for the maintenance, repair, cleaning or clearance of any part of a motorway or for the erection, laying, placing, maintenance, testing, alteration, repair or removal of any structure, works or apparatus in, on, under or over any part of a motorway;

(b) pedestrians may use a motorway—

(i) when it is necessary for them to do so as a result of an accident or emergency or of a vehicle being at rest on a motorway in any of the circumstances specified in paragraph (2) of Regulation 7, or

(ii) in any of the circumstances specified in sub-paragraphs (b), (d), (e) or (f) of paragraph (1) of Regulation 16.

(2) The Secretary of State may authorise the use of a motorway by any excluded traffic on occasion or in emergency or for the purpose of enabling such traffic to cross a motorway or to secure access to premises abutting on or adjacent to a motorway.

(3) Where by reason of any emergency the use of any road (not being a motorway) by any excluded traffic is rendered impossible or unsuitable the Chief Officer of Police of the police area in which a motorway or any part of a motorway is situated, or any officer of or above the rank of superintendent authorised in that behalf by that Chief Officer, may—

(a) authorise any excluded traffic to use that motorway or that part of a motorway as an alternative road for the period during which the use of the other road by such traffic continues to be impossible or unsuitable, and

(b) relax any prohibition or restriction imposed by these Regulations in so far as he considers it necessary to do so in connection with the use of that motorway or that part of a motorway by excluded traffic in pursuance of any such authorisation as aforesaid.

Exceptions and relaxations

4–2826   16. (1) Nothing in the foregoing provisions of these Regulations shall preclude any person from using a motorway otherwise than in accordance with the provisions in any of the following circumstances, that is to say—

(a) where he does so in accordance with any direction or permission given by a constable in uniform, a traffic officer in uniform or with the indication given by a traffic sign;

(b) where, in accordance with any permission given by, a traffic officer in uniform or a constable, he does so for the purpose of investigating any accident which has occurred on or near a motorway;

(c) where it is necessary for him to do so to avoid or prevent an accident or to obtain or give help required as the result of an accident or emergency, and he does so in such manner as to cause as little danger or inconvenience as possible to other traffic on a motorway;

(d) where he does so in the exercise of his duty as a constable, a traffic officer, when in uniform as a member of the Serious Organised Crime Agency for the purposes of that Agency, or as a member of an ambulance service or as an employee of a fire and rescue authority employed for the purposes of that authority;

(e) where it is necessary for him to do so to carry out in an efficient manner—

(i) the maintenance, repair, cleaning, clearance, alteration or improvement of any part of a motorway, or

(ii) the removal of any vehicle from any part of a motorway, or

(iii) the erection, laying, placing, maintenance, testing, alteration, repair or removal of any structure, works or apparatus in, on, under or over any part of a motorway; or

(f) where it is necessary for him to do so in connection with any inspection, survey, investigation or census which is carried out in accordance with any general or special authority granted by the Secretary of State.

(2) Without prejudice to the foregoing provisions of these Regulations, the Secretary of State may relax any prohibition or restriction imposed by these Regulations.

Zebra, Pelican and Puffin Pedestrian Crossings Regulations and General Directions 1997[1]

(SI 1997/2400 amended by SI 2003/2155, SI 2004/3168 (E),SI 2005/2929 (W) and SI 2006/594)

PART I

THE ZEBRA, PELICAN AND PUFFIN PEDESTRIAN CROSSINGS REGULATIONS 1997

SECTION I

PRELIMINARY

4-2909   1. *Citation and commencement*

1. These Regulations and Directions have been made by the Secretary of State for Transport, the Secretary of State for Scotland and the Secretary of State for Wales in exercise of the powers specified in the Appendix to this Instrument.

Revocation

4-2910   2. (1) The "Zebra" Pedestrian Crossings Regulations 1971, the "Zebra" Pedestrian Crossings (Amendment) Regulations 1990 and, so far as they consist of or comprise regulations, the "Pelican" Pedestrian Crossings Regulations and General Directions 1987 are hereby revoked.

(2) Any crossing which, immediately before the coming into force of these Regulations, was constituted a Pelican or a Zebra crossing in accordance with the regulations revoked by paragraph (1) which were applicable to it ("the applicable regulations") shall, notwithstanding the revocation of the applicable regulations, be treated as constituted in accordance with these Regulations for so long as the traffic signs situated at or near it and the manner in which its presence and limits are indicated comply with the applicable regulations.

(3) Paragraph (2) shall cease to have effect on 15th December 2002.

Interpretation

4-2911   3. (1) In these Regulations unless the context otherwise requires—

"the 1984 Act" means the Road Traffic Regulation Act 1984;

"the 1994 Regulations" means the Traffic Signs Regulations 1994;

"carriageway" means—

(a) in relation to a crossing on a highway in England or Wales or on a road in Scotland, a way constituting or comprised in the highway or road being a way over which the public has a right of way for the passage of vehicles; and

(b) in relation to a crossing on any other road in England or Wales to which the public has access, that part of the road to which vehicles have access,

but does not include in either case any central reservation (whether within the limits of the crossing or not);

"central reservation" means—

(a) in relation to a road comprising a single carriageway, any provision (including a refuge for pedestrians) which separates one part of the carriageway from another part;

(b) in relation to a road which comprises two or more carriageways any land or permanent work which separates those carriageways from one another;

"controlled area" means a Pelican controlled area, a Puffin controlled area or a Zebra controlled area;

"crossing" means a crossing for pedestrians established—

(a) in the case of a trunk road, by the Secretary of State pursuant to section 24 of the 1984 Act; and

(b) in the case of any other road, by a local traffic authority pursuant to section 23 of that Act;

"driver" in relation to a vehicle which is a motor cycle or pedal cycle means the person riding the vehicle who is in control of it;

"give-way line" means a road marking placed adjacent to a Zebra crossing in accordance with regulation 6(1) and Schedule 1;

"indicator for pedestrians" means the traffic sign of that description prescribed for the purposes of a Pelican crossing by regulation 5(2)(a) and paragraphs 2(c) and 5 of Part I and Part II of Schedule 2;

"layout or character" in relation to a road means the layout or character of the road itself and does not include the layout or character of any land or premises adjacent to the road;

"mm" means millimetres;

"one-way street" means a road on which the driving of vehicles otherwise than in one particular direction is prohibited;

"pedestrian demand unit" means the traffic sign of that description prescribed for the purposes of a Puffin crossing by regulation 5(3)(a) and paragraphs 1(b) and 3 of Part I and Part II of Schedule 3;

"pedestrian light signals" means the traffic sign of that description prescribed for the purposes of a Pelican crossing by regulation 5(2)(a) and paragraphs 2(b) and 4 of Part I of Schedule 2;

"Pelican controlled area" means an area of carriageway in the vicinity of a Pelican crossing the limits of which are indicated in accordance with regulation 6(2) and Schedule 4;

"Pelican crossing" means a crossing—

    (a)   at which there are traffic signs of the size, colour and type prescribed by regulation 5(2)(a) and Schedule 2;

    (b)   the limits of which are indicated in accordance with regulation 5(2)(b) and Schedule 4;

"primary signal" means vehicular light signals so placed as to face vehicular traffic approaching a Pelican or a Puffin crossing and placed beyond the stop line and in front of the line of studs nearest the stop line indicating the limits of the crossing in accordance with regulation 6(3) and Schedule 4;

"Puffin controlled area" means an area of the carriageway in the vicinity of a Puffin crossing the limits of which are indicated in accordance with regulation 6(2) and Schedule 4;

"Puffin crossing" means a crossing—

    (a)   at which there are traffic signs of the size, colour and type prescribed by regulation 5(3)(a) and Schedule 3;

    (b)   the limits of which are indicated in accordance with regulation 5(3)(b) and Schedule 4;

"refuge for pedestrians" means a part of a road to which vehicles do not have access and on which pedestrians may wait after crossing one part of the carriageway and before crossing the other;

"retroreflecting material" means material which reflects a ray of light back towards the source of that light;

"road marking" means a traffic sign consisting of a line or mark or legend on a road and includes a stud;

"secondary signal" means vehicular light signals so placed as to face vehicular traffic approaching a Pelican or Puffin crossing but sited beyond the furthest limit of the crossing as viewed from the direction of travel of the traffic;

"stop line" means, in relation to a vehicle approaching a Pelican or Puffin crossing, the transverse continuous white line (indicated in accordance with regulation 6(3) and Schedule 4 and parallel to the limits of the crossing) which is on the same side of the crossing as the vehicle;

"stud" means a mark or device on the carriageway, whether or not projecting above the surface of the carriageway;

"system of staggered crossings" means two or more Pelican crossings or two or more Puffin crossings provided on a road on which there is a central reservation and where—

    (a)   there is one crossing on each side of the central reservation; and

    (b)   taken together the two crossings do not lie along a straight line;

"two-way street" means a road which is not a one-way street;

"vehicular light signals" means, in relation to a Pelican or Puffin crossing, the traffic sign of that description prescribed (in the case of a Pelican crossing) by regulation 5(2)(a) and paragraphs 2(a) and 3 of Part I of Schedule 2 or (in the case of a Puffin crossing) by regulation 5(3)(a) and paragraphs 1(a) and 2 of Part I of Schedule 3;

"Zebra controlled area" means an area of carriageway in the vicinity of a Zebra crossing the limits of which are indicated in accordance with regulation 6(1) and Part II of Schedule 1; and

"Zebra crossing" means a crossing—

    (a)   at which there are traffic signs of the size, colour and type prescribed by regulation 5(1)(a) and Part I of Schedule 1; and

    (b)   the limits of which are indicated in accordance with regulation 5(1)(b) and Part II of Schedule 1.

(2) In these Regulations, unless it is expressly provided otherwise or the context otherwise requires—

    (a)   a reference to a numbered regulation or Schedule is a reference to the regulation or, as the case may be, the Schedule so numbered in these Regulations;

    (b)   a reference in a regulation or Schedule to a numbered paragraph is a reference to the paragraph so numbered in the regulation or, as the case may be, in the Schedule in which the reference occurs; and

    (c)   a reference to a sub-paragraph followed by a number or letter is a reference to the sub-paragraph bearing that number or letter in the paragraph in which the reference occurs.

Application of Regulations

4–2912   **4.** These Regulations apply to a crossing which is a Zebra, Pelican or Puffin crossing.

SECTION II
FORM OF CROSSINGS

Traffic signs and road markings for indicating crossings

4–2913   **5.** (1) A Zebra crossing shall be indicated by—

(a) the placing at or near the crossing of traffic signs of the size, colour and type specified in Part I of Schedule 1;

(b) the placing on the carriageway to indicate the limits of the crossing of road markings of the size, colour and type specified in Part II of Schedule 1.

(2) A Pelican crossing shall be indicated by—

(a) the placing at or near the crossing of traffic signs of the size, colour and type specified in Schedule 2;

(b) the placing on the carriageway to indicate the limits of the crossing of road markings of the size, colour and type specified in Schedule 4.

(3) A Puffin crossing shall be indicated by—

(a) the placing at or near the crossing of traffic signs of the size, colour and type specified in Schedule 3;

(b) the placing on the carriageway to indicate the limits of the crossing of road markings of the size, colour and type specified in Schedule 4.

Give-way and stop lines and controlled areas

4–2914   **6.** (1) On each side of a Zebra crossing, there shall be laid out a Zebra controlled area (including a give-way line) indicated by road markings of the size, colour and type, and generally in the manner, specified in Part II of Schedule 1.

(2) On each side of a Pelican or Puffin crossing, there shall be laid out a Pelican controlled area or a Puffin controlled area indicated by road markings of the size, colour and type, and generally in the manner, specified in Schedule 4.

(3) A stop line or stop lines of the size, colour and type specified in Schedule 4 shall be placed next to a Pelican or Puffin crossing in the manner specified in that Schedule.

Dimensions

4–2915   **7.** (1) Dimensions indicated on any diagram shown in the Schedules to these Regulations are expressed in millimetres.

(2) A dimension (other than one specified as a maximum or minimum dimension) specified in a diagram in Schedule 2 or 3 may be varied if, in the case of a dimension of the length specified in column (2) of an item in the table below, the variation does not exceed the extent specified in column (3) of the item.

TABLE

(1) Item	(2) Length of dimension	(3) Extent of variation
(1)	less than 10 mm	1 mm
(2)	10 mm or more but less than 50 mm	10% of the dimension
(3)	50 mm or more but less than 300 mm	7.5% of the dimension
(4)	300 mm or more	5% of the dimension

(3) A dimension (other than one specified as a maximum or minimum dimension) specified in any diagram in Schedule 1 or in Schedule 4 may be varied if, in the case of a dimension of the length specified in column (2) of an item in the table below, the variation does not exceed the extent specified in column (3) of the item.

TABLE

(1) Item	(2) Length of dimension	(3) Extent of variation
(1)	300 mm or more	(i) 20% of the dimension where the varied dimension is greater than the specified dimension; or
		(ii) 10% of the dimension where the varied dimension is less than the specified dimension
(2)	Less than 300 mm	(i) 30% of the dimension where the varied dimension is greater than the specified dimension; or
		(ii) 10% of the dimension where the varied dimension is less than the specified dimension.

(4) Where maximum and minimum dimensions are specified for any element of a traffic sign or road marking, the dimension chosen for that element must not be less than the minimum and must not exceed the maximum.

(5) Where any diagram in a Schedule to these Regulations specifies a dimension for an element of a traffic sign or road marking together with a dimension for that element in brackets, the dimensions so specified shall be alternatives.

(6) A dimension specified in the 1994 Regulations in relation to a traffic sign prescribed by those Regulations and referred to in these Regulations may be varied to the extent permitted by the 1994 Regulations.

Additional equipment

4–2916   8. A traffic authority may provide at, or fix to any traffic sign or post placed for the purposes of, a crossing in accordance with these Regulations any object, device, apparatus or equipment—

    (*a*)   in connection with the proper operation of the crossing; or

    (*b*)   which they consider appropriate for giving information or assistance to disabled persons wishing to use the crossing.

Additional traffic signs

4–2917   9. In addition to the traffic signs prescribed in regulation 5 a traffic sign shown in diagram 610, 611, 612, 613 or 616 in Schedule 2 or diagram 810 in Schedule 4, or a road marking shown in diagram 1029 or the white triangular markings included in the road marking shown in diagram 1061 of Schedule 6, to the 1994 Regulations may, if the traffic authority think fit, be placed at or near a crossing.

Non-compliance with requirements of this Section

4–2918   10. (1) Where, as respects a crossing or controlled area, the requirements of this Section of these Regulations as to the placing of traffic signs and road markings to indicate the crossing or controlled area have not been complied with in every respect, the crossing or, as the case may be, the controlled area shall nevertheless be treated as complying with these Regulations if the non-compliance—

    (*a*)   is not such as materially to affect the general appearance of the crossing or the controlled area;

    (*b*)   does not, in the case of a Pelican or Puffin crossing, affect the proper operation of the vehicular and pedestrian signals at the crossing; and

    (*c*)   does not relate to the size of the controlled area.

(2) Nothing in any other provision of these Regulations shall be taken to restrict the generality of paragraph (1).

SECTION III

SIGNIFICANCE OF TRAFFIC SIGNS AT CROSSINGS

Scope of Section III

4–2919   11. The provisions of this Section of these Regulations (except regulation 16) are made under section 64(1) of the Road Traffic Regulation Act 1984 for the purpose of prescribing the warnings, information, requirements, restrictions and prohibitions which are to be conveyed to traffic by traffic signs and road markings of the size, colour and type prescribed by Section II.

Significance of vehicular light signals at Pelican crossings

4–2920   12. (1) The significance of the vehicular light signals prescribed by regulation 5(2)(*a*) and paragraph 3 of Schedule 2 for the purpose of indicating a Pelican crossing shall be as follows—

    (*a*)   the green signal shall indicate that vehicular traffic may proceed beyond the stop line and across the crossing;

    (*b*)   the green arrow signal shall indicate that vehicular traffic may proceed beyond the stop line and through the crossing only for the purpose of proceeding in the direction indicated by the arrow;

    (*c*)   except as provided by sub-paragraph (*e*) and sub-paragraph (*ea*) and sub-paragraph (*eb*) the steady amber signal shall convey the same prohibition as the red signal except that, as respects a vehicle which is so close to the stop line that it cannot safely be stopped without proceeding beyond the stop line, it shall convey the same indication as the green signal or, if the amber signal was immediately preceded by a green arrow signal, as that green arrow signal;

    (*d*)   except as provided in sub-paragraph (*e*) and sub-paragraph (*ea*) and sub-paragraph (*eb*), the red signal shall convey the prohibition that vehicular traffic shall not proceed beyond the stop line;

    (*e*)   when a vehicle is being used for <u>fire brigade</u>* or, in England, fire and rescue authority, ambulance, national blood service or police purposes and the observance of the prohibition conveyed by the steady amber or the red signal in accordance with sub-paragraph (*c*) or (*d*) would be likely to hinder the use of that vehicle for the purpose for which it is being used, then those sub-paragraphs shall not apply to the vehicle, and the steady amber and the red signal shall each convey the information that the vehicle may proceed beyond the stop line if the driver—

        (i)   accords precedence to any pedestrian who is on that part of the carriageway which lies within the limits of the crossing or on a central reservation which lies between two crossings which do not form part of a system of staggered crossings; and

(ii) does not proceed in a manner or at a time likely to endanger any person or any vehicle approaching or waiting at the crossing, or to cause the driver of any such vehicle to change its speed or course in order to avoid an accident; and

(*ea*) as regards England and Wales, and so far as relating to the functions of the Serious Organised Crime Agency which are exercisable in or as regards Scotland and which relate to reserved matters (within the meaning of the Scotland Act 1998), when a vehicle is being used for Serious Organised Crime Agency purposes and the observance of the prohibition conveyed by the steady amber or the red signal in accordance with sub-paragraph (*c*) or (*d*) would be likely to hinder the use of that vehicle for those purposes, then those sub-paragraphs shall not apply to the vehicle, and the steady amber and the red signal shall each convey the information that the vehicle may proceed beyond the stop line if the driver—

(i) accords precedence to any pedestrian who is on that part of the carriageway which lies within the limits of the crossing or on a central reservation which lies between two crossings which do not form part of a system of staggered crossings; and

(ii) does not proceed in a manner or at a time likely to endanger any person or any vehicle approaching or waiting at the crossing, or to cause the driver of any such vehicle to change its speed or course in order to avoid an accident; and

(*eb*) *Scotland*;

(*f*) the flashing amber signal shall convey the information that traffic may proceed across the crossing but that every pedestrian who is on the carriageway or a central reservation within the limits of the crossing (but not if he is on a central reservation which lies between two crossings forming part of a system of staggered crossings) before any part of a vehicle has entered those limits, has the right of precedence within those limits over that vehicle, and the requirement that the driver of a vehicle shall accord such precedence to any such pedestrian.

(2) Vehicular traffic proceeding beyond a stop line in accordance with paragraph (1) shall proceed with due regard to the safety of other road users and subject to any direction given by a constable in uniform or a traffic warden or to any other applicable prohibition or restriction.

(3) In this regulation, references to the "stop line" in relation to a Pelican crossing where the stop line is not visible are to be treated as references to the post or other structure on which the primary signal is mounted.

---

*In relation to Scotland 'relevant authority (as defined in section 6 of the Fire (Scotland) Act 2005 (asp 5)' substituted by SSI 2005/344.

Significance of vehicular light signals at Puffin crossings

4–2921 **13.** (1) The significance of the vehicular light signals at a Puffin crossing prescribed by regulation 5(3)(*a*) and paragraph 2 of Schedule 3 shall be as follows—

(*a*) the green signal shall indicate that vehicular traffic may proceed beyond the stop line and across the crossing;

(*b*) the green arrow signal shall indicate that vehicular traffic may proceed beyond the stop line and through the crossing only for the purpose of proceeding in the direction indicated by the arrow;

(*c*) except as provided by sub-paragraph (*f*) and sub-paragraph (*g*) and sub-paragraph (*h*), the amber signal shall, when shown alone, convey the same prohibition as the red signal, except that, as respects any vehicle which is so close to the stop line that it cannot safely be stopped without proceeding beyond the stop line, it shall convey the same indication as the green signal or, if the amber signal was immediately preceded by a green arrow signal, as that green arrow signal;

(*d*) except as provided in sub-paragraph (*f*) and sub-paragraph (*g*) and sub-paragraph (*h*),, the red signal shall convey the prohibition that vehicular traffic shall not proceed beyond the stop line;

(*e*) except as provided by sub-paragraph (*f*) and sub-paragraph (*g*) and sub-paragraph (*h*),, the red-with-amber signal shall denote an impending change to green in the indication given by the signals but shall convey the same prohibition as the red signal;

(*f*) when a vehicle is being used for fire brigade* or, in England, fire and rescue authority, ambulance, national blood service or police purposes and the observance of the prohibition conveyed by the amber, red or red-with-amber signal in accordance with sub-paragraph (*c*), (*d*) or (*e*) would be likely to hinder the use of that vehicle for the purpose for which it is being used, then those sub-paragraphs shall not apply to the vehicle, and the red signal, red-with-amber and amber signals shall each convey the information that the vehicle may proceed beyond the stop line if the driver—

(i) accords precedence to any pedestrian who is on that part of the carriageway which lies within the limits of the crossing or on a central reservation which lies between two crossings which do not form part of a system of staggered crossings; and

(ii) does not proceed in a manner or at a time likely to endanger any person or any vehicle approaching or waiting at the crossing, or to cause the driver of any such vehicle to change its speed or course in order to avoid an accident;

(*g*) as regards England and Wales, and so far as relating to the functions of the Serious Organised Crime Agency which are exercisable in or as regards Scotland and which relate to reserved matters (within the meaning of the Scotland Act 1998), when a vehicle is being used for Serious Organised Crime Agency purposes and the observance of the prohibition conveyed by the amber, red or red-with-amber signal in accordance with sub-paragraph (c), (d) or (e) would be likely to hinder the use of that vehicle for those purposes, then those sub-paragraphs shall not apply to the vehicle, and the red signal, red-with-amber and amber signals shall each convey the information that the vehicle may proceed beyond the stop line if the driver—

(i) accords precedence to any pedestrian who is on that part of the carriageway which lies within the limits of the crossing or on a central reservation which lies between two crossings which do not form part of a system of staggered crossings; and

(ii) does not proceed in a manner or at a time likely to endanger any person or any vehicle approaching or waiting at the crossing, or to cause the driver of any such vehicle to change its speed or course in order to avoid an accident;

(h) *Scotland.*

(2) Vehicular traffic proceeding beyond a stop line in accordance with paragraph (1) shall proceed with due regard to the safety of other road users and subject to any direction given by a constable in uniform or a traffic warden or to any other applicable prohibition or restriction.

(3) In this regulation, references to the "stop line" in relation to a Puffin crossing where the stop line is not visible are to be treated as references to the post or other structure on which the primary signal is mounted.

*In relation to Scotland 'relevant authority (as defined in section 6 of the Fire (Scotland) Act 2005 (asp 5)' substituted by SSI 2005/344.

Significance of give-way lines at Zebra crossings

4-2922 **14.** A give-way line included in the markings placed pursuant to regulation 5(1)(b) and Part II of Schedule 1 shall convey to vehicular traffic proceeding towards a Zebra crossing the position at or before which a vehicle should be stopped for the purpose of complying with regulation 25 (precedence of pedestrians over vehicles at Zebra crossings).

Significance of pedestrian light signals and figures on pedestrian demand units

4-2923 **15.** (1) The significance of the red and steady green pedestrian light signals whilst they are illuminated at a Pelican crossing and of the red and green figures on a pedestrian demand unit whilst they are illuminated at a Puffin crossing shall be as follows—

(a) the red pedestrian light signal and the red figure shall both convey to a pedestrian the warning that, in the interests of safety, he should not cross the carriageway; and

(b) the steady green pedestrian light signal and the steady green figure shall both indicate to a pedestrian that he may cross the carriageway and that drivers may not cause vehicles to enter the crossing.

(2) The flashing green pedestrian light signal at a Pelican crossing shall convey—

(a) to a pedestrian who is already on the crossing when the flashing green signal is first shown the information that he may continue to use the crossing and that, if he is on the carriageway or a central reservation within the limits of that crossing (but not if he is on a central reservation which lies between two crossings which form part of a system of staggered crossings) before any part of a vehicle has entered those limits, he has precedence over that vehicle within those limits; and

(b) to a pedestrian who is not already on the crossing when the flashing green light is first shown the warning that he should not, in the interests of safety, start to cross the carriageway.

(3) Any audible signal emitted by any device for emitting audible signals provided in conjunction with the steady green pedestrian light signal or the green figure, and any tactile signal given by any device for making tactile signals similarly provided, shall convey to a pedestrian the same indication as the steady green pedestrian light signal or as the green figure as the case may be.

Significance of additional traffic signs

4-2924 **16.** A traffic sign placed in accordance with regulation 9 shall convey the information, prohibition or requirement specified in relation to it by the 1994 Regulations.

SECTION IV
MOVEMENT OF TRAFFIC AT CROSSINGS
Scope of Section IV

4-2925 **17.** This Section of these Regulations is made under section 25 of the 1984 Act with respect to the movement of traffic at and in the vicinity of crossings[1].

1. For penalty for contravention and provisions regarding disqualification and endorsement, see s 25(5) and PART 1 of Sch 2 to the Road Traffic Offenders Act 1988 in this PART, ante.

Prohibition against the stopping of vehicles on crossings

4–2926   **18.** The driver of a vehicle shall not cause the vehicle or any part of it to stop within the limits of a crossing unless he is prevented from proceeding by circumstances beyond his control[1] or it is necessary for him to stop to avoid injury or damage to persons or property.

---

1. A driver who parked within the limits of a crossing believing he had run out of petrol but not knowing that he had a reserve petrol tank was not allowed to avail himself of this defence under the predecessor regulations: *Oakley-Moore v Robinson* [1982] RTR 74.

Pedestrians not to delay on crossings

4–2927   **19.** No pedestrian shall remain on the carriageway within the limits of a crossing longer than is necessary for that pedestrian to pass over the crossing with reasonable despatch.

Prohibition against the stopping of vehicles in controlled areas

4–2928   **20.** (1) For the purposes of this regulation and regulations 21 and 22 the word "vehicle" shall not include a pedal bicycle not having a sidecar attached to it, whether or not additional means of propulsion by mechanical power are attached to the bicycle.

(2) Except as provided in regulations 21 and 22 the driver of a vehicle shall not cause it or any part of it to stop in a controlled area.

Exceptions to regulation 20

4–2929   **21.** Regulation 20 does not prohibit the driver of a vehicle from stopping it in a controlled area—

(a) if the driver has stopped it for the purpose of complying with regulation 25 or 26;

(b) if the driver is prevented from proceeding by circumstances beyond his control[1] or it is necessary for him to stop to avoid injury or damage to persons or property; or

(c) when the vehicle is being used for police, fire brigade* or, in England, fire and rescue authority or ambulance purposes; or

(d) as regards England and Wales, and so far as relating to the functions of the Serious Organised Crime Agency which are exercisable in or as regards Scotland and which relate to reserved matters (within the meaning of the Scotland Act 1998), when the vehicle is being used for Serious Organised Crime Agency purposes; or

(e) *Scotland.*

---

*In relation to Scotland 'relevant authority (as defined in section 6 of the Fire (Scotland) Act 2005 (asp 5)' substituted by SSI 2005/344.
1. See note to reg 18, ante.

Further exceptions to regulation 20

4–2930   **22.** (1) Regulation 20 does not prohibit the driver of a vehicle from stopping it in a controlled area—

(a) for so long as may be necessary to enable the vehicle to be used for the purposes of—

(i) any building operation, demolition or excavation;

(ii) the removal of any obstruction to traffic;

(iii) the maintenance, improvement or reconstruction of a road; or

(iv) the laying, erection, alteration, repair or cleaning in or near the crossing of any sewer or of any main, pipe or apparatus for the supply of gas, water or electricity, or of any electronic communications apparatus kept installed for the purposes of an electronic communications code network or of any other electronic communications apparatus lawfully kept installed in any position,

but only if the vehicle cannot be used for one of those purposes without stopping in the controlled area; or

(b) if the vehicle is a public service vehicle being used—

(i) in the provision of a local service; or

(ii) to carry passengers for hire or reward at separate fares,

and the vehicle, having proceeded past the crossing to which the controlled area relates, is waiting in that area in order to take up or set down passengers; or

(c) if he stops the vehicle for the purpose of making a left or right turn.

(2) In paragraph (1) "local service" has the meaning given in section 2 of the Transport Act 1985 but does not include an excursion or tour as defined by section 137(1) of that Act.

Prohibition against vehicles proceeding across Pelican or Puffin crossings

4–2931   **23.** When vehicular light signals at a Pelican or Puffin crossing are displaying the red light signal the driver of a vehicle shall not cause it to contravene the prohibition given by that signal by virtue of regulation 12 or 13.

Prohibition against vehicles overtaking at crossings

4–2932 **24.** (1) Whilst any motor vehicle (in this regulation called "the approaching vehicle") or any part of it is within the limits of a controlled area and is proceeding towards the crossing, the driver of the vehicle shall not cause it or any part of it—

(a) to pass ahead of the foremost part of any other motor vehicle proceeding in the same direction; or

(b) to pass ahead of the foremost part of a vehicle which is stationary for the purpose of complying with regulation 23, 25 or 26[1].

(2) In paragraph (1)—

(a) the reference to a motor vehicle in sub-paragraph (a) is, in a case where more than one motor vehicle is proceeding in the same direction as the approaching vehicle in a controlled area, a reference to the motor vehicle nearest to the crossing; and

(b) the reference to a stationary vehicle is, in a case where more than one vehicle is stationary in a controlled area for the purpose of complying with regulation 23, 25 or 26, a reference to the stationary vehicle nearest the crossing.

---

1. Under the predecessor regulations it was held that if the stationary vehicle has stopped to allow a pedestrian to cross then it will not matter that the pedestrian had not put a foot on the crossing; it will be an offence to overtake such a stationary vehicle (*Gullen v Ford* [1975] 2 All ER 24, 139 JP 405), even after the pedestrians have crossed and the crossing is otherwise apparently clear (*Connor v Paterson* [1977] 3 All ER 516, 142 JP 20).

Precedence of pedestrians over vehicles at Zebra crossings[1]

4–2933 **25.** (1) Every pedestrian, if he is on the carriageway within the limits of a Zebra crossing, which is not for the time being controlled by a constable in uniform or traffic warden, before any part of a vehicle has entered those limits, shall have precedence within those limits over that vehicle and the driver of the vehicle shall accord such precedence to any such pedestrian.

(2) Where there is a refuge for pedestrians or central reservation on a Zebra crossing, the parts of the crossing situated on each side of the refuge for pedestrians or central reservation shall, for the purposes of this regulation, be treated as separate crossings.

---

1. Under the predecessor regulations it was held that a driver should approach an uncontrolled crossing in a manner that enables him to stop before reaching it, unless he can see that there is no pedestrian on the crossing (*Gibbons v Khal* [1956] 1 QB 59, [1955] 3 All ER 345, 120 JP 1). It has been held that what is now regulation 25 imposes an absolute duty and it is quite immaterial whether there is any evidence of negligence or failure to take reasonable care per Lord Parker CJ, in *Hughes v Hall* [1960] 2 All ER 504, 124 JP 411. In *Lockie v Lawton* (1959) 124 JP 24, magistrates were recommended that the better approach in these cases is to realise that the duty of drivers is as laid down in *Gibbons v Kahl* supra, and to look upon *Leicester v Pearson* [1952] 2 QB 668, [1952] 2 All ER 71, 116 JP 407 (in which it was held no offence was committed by a driver who was not at fault), as a very special case decided on its own facts. If as a result of some latent defect, eg a sudden failure of brakes or other circumstances beyond the control of the driver, precedence cannot be afforded to the pedestrian no offence is committed against this regulation (*Burns v Bidder* [1967] 2 QB 227, [1966] 3 All ER 29, 130 JP 342). The fact that a pedestrian on the carriageway appears to waive his right of precedence does not relieve a driver from the absolute duty created by this regulation (*Neal v Bedford* [1966] 1 QB 505, [1965] 3 All ER 250, 129 JP 534). In *McKerrell v Robertson* 1956 SLT 290 (HC of Justiciary) (Scotland), it was held that an offence against what is now reg 25 was committed where a motorist failed to give precedence to a woman pushing a "go-chair" containing a child, when the "go-chair" was on the crossing but the woman was not. The vehicle should be stopped at or before the give-way line (reg 14, ante).

Precedence of pedestrians over vehicles at Pelican crossings

4–2934 **26.** When the vehicular light signals at a Pelican crossing are showing the flashing amber signal, every pedestrian, if he is on the carriageway or a central reservation within the limits of the crossing (but not if he is on a central reservation which forms part of a system of staggered crossings) before any part of a vehicle has entered those limits, shall have precedence within those limits over that vehicle and the driver of the vehicle shall accord such precedence to any such pedestrian.

Regulations 5(1), 6(1)   SCHEDULE 1
TRAFFIC SIGNS AND ROAD MARKINGS TO INDICATE ZEBRA CROSSINGS AND ZEBRA CONTROLLED AREAS

PART I
TRAFFIC SIGNS

4–2935 **1.** (1) Subject to the following provisions of this Part of this Schedule the traffic signs which are to be placed at or near a Zebra crossing for the purpose of indicating it shall consist of globes each of which is—

(a) coloured yellow or fluorescent yellow;

(b) not less than 275 nor more than 335 mm in diameter;

(c) illuminated by a flashing light or, where the Secretary of State so authorises in writing in relation to a particular crossing a constant steady light; and

(d) mounted on a post or bracket so that the lowest part of a globe is not less than 2.1 metres nor more than 3.1 metres above the surface of the ground immediately beneath it.

(2) One globe shall be placed at each end of the crossing and, if there is a refuge for pedestrians or central reservation on the crossing, one or more globes may, if the traffic authority thinks fit, be placed on the refuge or central reservation.

4–2936 **2.** Where a globe is mounted on or attached to a post, whether or not specially provided for the purpose—

(a) the post shall be coloured in alternate black and white bands, the lowest band being coloured black;
(b) the bands shall be not less than 275 mm nor more than 335 mm wide except that the lowest band may be up to 1 metre wide; and
(c) the post may be internally illuminated.

4–2937 **3.** A globe or the post on which it is mounted may be fitted with all or any of the following—

(a) a backing board or other device designed to improve the conspicuousness of the globe;
(b) a shield or other device designed to prevent or reduce light shining into adjacent premises;
(c) a light to illuminate the crossing.

4–2938 **4.** A crossing shall not be taken to have ceased to be indicated in accordance with this Part of this Schedule by reason only of—

(a) the imperfection, disfigurement or discolouration of any globe or post, or
(b) the failure of illumination of any of the globes.

4–2939 **5.** Nothing in this Part of this Schedule shall be taken to restrict regulation 8 or 9.

PART II
ROAD MARKINGS
Road markings

4–2940 **6.** Subject to the following provisions of this Part of this Schedule—

(a) within the limits of a Zebra crossing the carriageway shall be marked with a series of alternate black and white stripes;
(b) the Zebra controlled areas shall be marked with give-way lines, a line of studs and zig-zag lines,

of the size and type, and generally in the manner, shown in the diagram at the end of this Part of this Schedule.

Number of studs and stripes

4–2941 **7.** The number of studs and stripes may be varied.

Limits of the crossing

4–2942 **8.** (1) If it provides a reasonable contrast with the white stripes, the colour of the surface of the carriageway may be used to indicate the stripes shown coloured black in the diagram.
(2) The white stripes may be illuminated by retroreflecting material.
(3) Subject to paragraph (4) each black and each white stripe shall be of the same size and not less than 500 mm nor more than 715 mm wide as measured across the carriageway.
(4) The first stripe at each end may be up to 1300 mm wide and, if the traffic authority consider it appropriate in relation to a particular crossing having regard to the layout of the carriageway or other special circumstances, the other stripes may be not less than 380 mm nor more than 840 mm wide as measured across the carriageway.

Studs

4–2943 **9.** (1) The studs may be omitted altogether.
(2) If studs are provided—

(a) they shall be coloured white, silver or light grey;
(b) they shall be either—

(i) circular in shape with a diameter of not less than 95 mm nor more than 110 mm; or
(ii) square in shape with each side not less than 95 mm nor more than 110 mm long;

(c) they may illuminated by retroreflecting material;
(d) if they consist of a device fixed to the carriageway, they shall—

(i) not be fitted with reflecting lenses;
(ii) be so fixed that they do not project more than 20 mm above the adjacent surface of the carriageway at their highest points nor more than 6 mm at their edges;

(e) the distance from the centre of any stud to the centre of the next stud in the same line shall not be less than 250 mm nor more than 715 mm and the distance between the edge of the carriageway at each end of a line of studs and the centre of the nearest stud shall be not more than 1.3 metres; and
(f) the two lines of studs need not be at right angles to the edge of the carriageway, but shall form straight lines and, so far as is reasonably practicable, shall be parallel to each other.

Zig-zag lines

4–2944 **10.** (1) The pattern of the central zig-zag lines may be reversed or, on a road having a carriageway not more than 6 metres wide, those lines may be omitted altogether so long as they are replaced by the road marking shown in diagram 1004 in Schedule 6 to the 1994 Regulations.
(2) Subject to sub-paragraph (4) the number of marks in a zig-zag line shall not be less than 8 nor more than 18 and a zig-zag line need not contain the same number of marks as any other zig-zag line.
(3) Each mark in a zig-zag line shall be coloured white and may be illuminated by retroreflecting material.
(4) Where the traffic authority is satisfied that, by reason of the layout or character of any roads in the vicinity of a Zebra crossing, it would be impracticable to lay out a Zebra controlled area in accordance with this Schedule—

(a) the number of marks in any zig-zag line in that area may be reduced to not less than 2; and
(b) the length of any of the marks may be varied to not less than 1 metre.

Give-way line

4–2945 **11.** (1) The give-way line shall be coloured white and may be illuminated by retroreflecting material.
(2) The angle of the give-way line in relation to, and its distance from, the edge of the crossing may be varied, if the traffic authority is satisfied that the variation is necessary having regard to the angle of the crossing in relation to the edge of the carriageway.

(3) The maximum distance of 3 metres between the give-way line and the limits of the crossing shown in the diagram in this Part of this Schedule may, if the traffic authority think fit having regard to the layout or character of the road in the vicinity of the crossing, be increased to not more than 10 metres.

Discolouration or partial displacement of markings

4–2946 **12.** A Zebra crossing or a Zebra controlled area shall not be deemed to have ceased to be indicated in accordance with this Schedule by reason only of the discolouration or partial displacement of any of the road markings prescribed by this Schedule, so long as the general appearance of the pattern of the lines is not impaired.

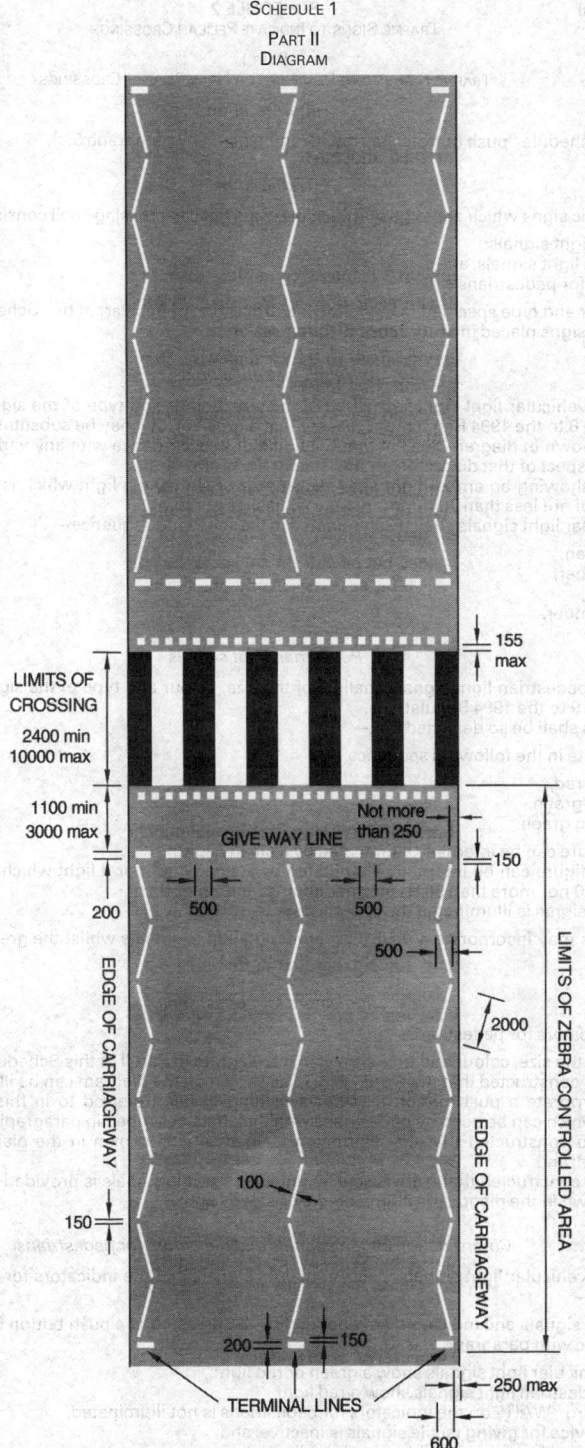

SCHEDULE 1
PART II
DIAGRAM

155 max

LIMITS OF
CROSSING

2400 min
10000 max

1100 min
3000 max

Not more
than 250

GIVE WAY LINE

150

200

500   500

500

2000

EDGE OF CARRIAGEWAY

LIMITS OF ZEBRA CONTROLLED AREA

EDGE OF CARRIAGEWAY

100

150

200   150

TERMINAL LINES

250 max

600

Regulation 5(2)(*a*)

SCHEDULE 2
TRAFFIC SIGNS TO INDICATE PELICAN CROSSINGS
PART I
TRAFFIC SIGNS TO BE PLACED AT OR NEAR PELICAN CROSSINGS

Interpretation

4–2947   **1.** In this Schedule "push button" has the meaning given by paragraph 5(*c*).

Traffic signs

4–2948   **2.** The traffic signs which are to be placed at or near a Pelican crossing shall consist of a combination of—

    (*a*)   vehicular light signals;
    (*b*)   pedestrian light signals; and
    (*c*)   indicators for pedestrians,

of the size, colour and type specified in the following provisions of this Part of this Schedule, together with any additional traffic signs placed in accordance with regulation 9.

Vehicular light signals

4–2949   **3.** (1) The vehicular light signals shall be of the size, colour and type of the signals shown in diagram 3000 in Schedule 8 to the 1994 Regulations, except that a green arrow may be substituted for the green aspect in the manner shown in diagram 3003 in that Schedule or in accordance with any variant permitted by those Regulations in respect of that diagram.

    (2) The lamp showing an amber light shall be capable of showing a light which is either steady or which flashes at a rate of not less than 70 nor more than 90 flashes per minute.

    (3) The vehicular light signals shall be illuminated in the following sequence—

    (*a*)   steady green,
    (*b*)   steady amber,
    (*c*)   steady red,
    (*d*)   flashing amber.

Pedestrian light signals

4–2950   **4.** (1) The pedestrian light signals shall be of the size, colour and type of the signals shown in diagram 4002 in Schedule 9 to the 1994 Regulations.

    (2) The signals shall be so designed that—

    (*a*)   they operate in the following sequence—

        (i)   steady red,
        (ii)   steady green,
        (iii)   flashing green;

    (*b*)   the red figure can be internally illuminated by a steady light;
    (*c*)   the green figure can be internally illuminated by a steady light or a light which flashes at a rate of not less than 70 nor more than 90 flashes per minute; and
    (*d*)   when one signal is illuminated the other is not.

    (3) The signals may incorporate a device for emitting audible signals whilst the green figure is illuminated by a steady light.

Indicators for pedestrians

4–2951   **5.** The indicators for pedestrians—

    (*a*)   shall be of the size, colour and type shown in the diagram in Part II of this Schedule;
    (*b*)   shall be so constructed that the word "WAIT" as shown on the diagram can be illuminated;
    (*c*)   shall incorporate a push button or other switching device (referred to in this Schedule as a "push button") which can be used by pedestrians with the effect described in paragraphs 6 and 7;
    (*d*)   shall be so constructed that the instruction for pedestrians shown in the diagram can be internally illuminated; and
    (*e*)   may be so constructed that a device giving audible or tactile signals is provided for use when the green figure shown in the diagram is illuminated by a steady light.

Co-ordination of light signals and indicators for pedestrians

4–2952   **6.** (1) The vehicular light signals, pedestrian light signals and the indicators for pedestrians shall be so constructed that—

    (*a*)   before the signals and indicators are operated by the pressing of a push button (or by remote control in accordance with paragraph 7)—

        (i)   the vehicular light signals show a green or red light,
        (ii)   the pedestrian light signals show a red light,
        (iii)   the word "WAIT" on the indicators for pedestrians is not illuminated,
        (iv)   any device for giving tactile signals is inactive; and
        (v)   any device for giving audible signals is silent;

    (*b*)   when a push button is pressed or the signals and indicators are operated by remote control—

        (i)   the signals and indicators show lights in the sequences specified in descending order in—

            (*a*)   column (1) in the case of vehicular light signals;
            (*b*)   in column (2) in the case of pedestrian light signals; and
            (*c*)   in column (3) in the case of indicators for pedestrians,

        of either Part III or Part IV of this Schedule;

        (ii)   when the pedestrian light signals are showing a steady green light, the word "WAIT" in the indicators for pedestrians is not illuminated;

(iii) when the pedestrian light signals are showing a flashing green light, the word "WAIT" in the indicators for pedestrians is illuminated immediately and the signals and indicators are caused to show lights in the sequence specified in paragraph (i) above at the end of the next vehicle period; and

(iv) when the pedestrian light signals are showing a red light, the word "WAIT" in the indicators for pedestrians is illuminated immediately and the vehicular light signals and indicators for pedestrians are caused to show lights in the sequence specified in paragraph (i);

(*c*) the periods during which lights are shown by the signals and indicators, begin and end in relation to each other as shown in either Part III or Part IV of this Schedule as if each horizontal line in those Parts represented one moment of time, subsequent moments occurring in descending order, but the distances between the horizontal lines do not represent the lengths of the periods during which lights shown by the signals and indicator are, or are not, lit.

(2) Where a device for emitting audible signals is provided pursuant to paragraph 4(3) or (5)(*e*), it shall be so constructed that the device operates only when the pedestrian light signals are showing a steady green light and at the same time the vehicular light signals are showing a red light.

(3) Where a device for giving tactile signals is provided pursuant to paragraph 5(*e*), it shall be so constructed that, when it is operating, a regular movement perceptible to touch by pedestrians is made only when the pedestrian light signals are showing a steady green light and at the same time the vehicular light signals are showing a red light.

(4) In this paragraph "vehicle period" means such period as may be fixed from time to time in relation to a Pelican crossing, being a period which begins when the vehicular light signals cease to show a flashing amber light and during which those signals show a green light.

Operation by remote control

4–2953   **7.** The vehicular light signals, pedestrian light signals, indicators for pedestrians and any device for giving tactile signals or emitting audible signals, when they are placed at or near a Pelican crossing may also be so constructed that they can be operated by remote control.

4–2954

SCHEDULE 2

PART II
INDICATOR FOR PEDESTRIANS

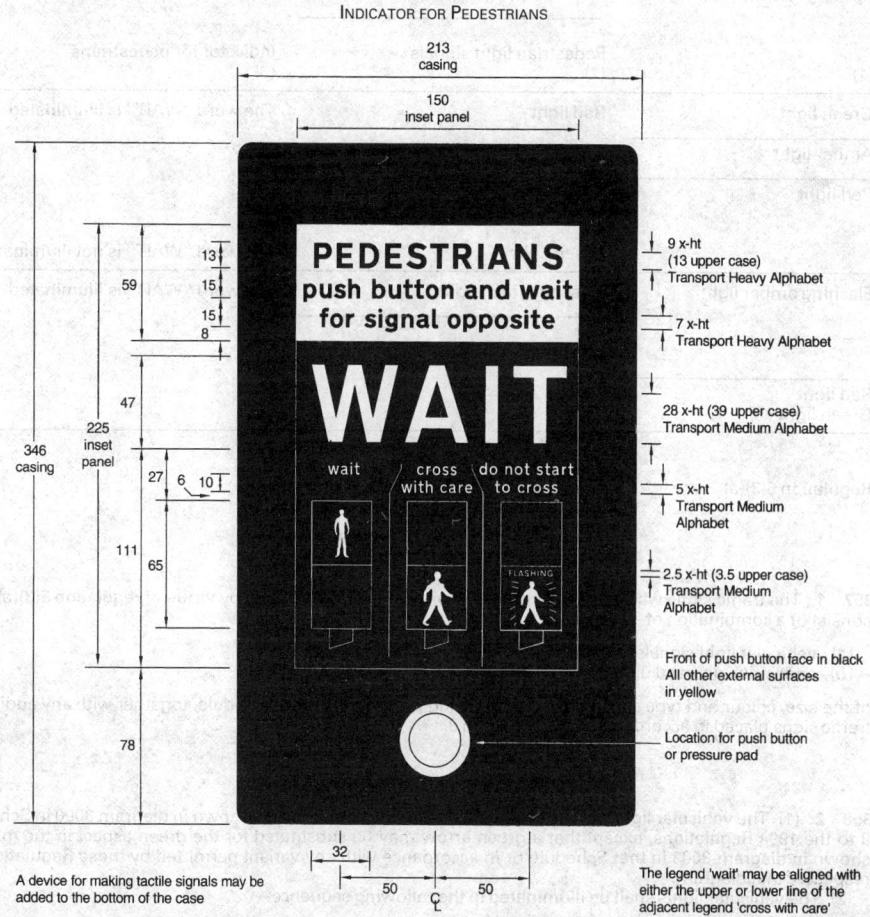

A device for making tactile signals may be added to the bottom of the case

The legend 'wait' may be aligned with either the upper or lower line of the adjacent legend 'cross with care'

4–2955

SCHEDULE 2

PART III

SEQUENCE OF OPERATION OF VEHICULAR AND PEDESTRIAN LIGHT SIGNALS AND INDICATOR FOR PEDESTRIANS (BUT NOT THE AUDIBLE OR TACTILE SIGNALS)

Sequence of vehicular traffic light signals	Sequence of pedestrian signals	
	Pedestrian light signals	Indicator for pedestrians
(1)	(2)	(3)
Green light	Red light	The word "WAIT" is illuminated
Amber light		
Red light		
	Green light	The word "WAIT" is not illuminated
Flashing amber light	Flashing green light	The word "WAIT" is illuminated
	Red light	
Red light Green light		

4–2956

SCHEDULE 2

PART IV

ALTERNATIVE SEQUENCE OF OPERATION OF VEHICULAR AND PEDESTRIAN LIGHT SIGNALS AND INDICATOR FOR PEDESTRIANS (BUT NOT THE AUDIBLE OR TACTILE SIGNALS)

Sequence of vehicular traffic light signals	Sequence of pedestrian signals	
	Pedestrian light signals	Indicator for pedestrians
(1)	(2)	(3)
Green light	Red light	The word "WAIT" is illuminated
Amber light		
Red light		
	Green light	The word "WAIT" is not illuminated
Flashing amber light	Flashing green light	The word "WAIT" is illuminated
	Red light	
Red light Green light		

Regulation 5(3)(*a*)

SCHEDULE 3

PART I

TRAFFIC SIGNS TO INDICATE PUFFIN CROSSINGS

Traffic signs at or near a Puffin crossing

4–2957   **1.** The traffic signs which are to be placed at or near a Puffin crossing by virtue of regulation 5(3)(*a*) shall consist of a combination of—

    (*a*) vehicular light signals; and
    (*b*) pedestrian demand units,

of the size, colour and type specified in the following provisions of this Schedule, together with any additional traffic signs placed in accordance with regulation 9.

Vehicular light signals

4–2958   **2.** (1) The vehicular light signals shall be of the size, colour and type shown in diagram 3000 in Schedule 8 to the 1994 Regulations, except that a green arrow may be substituted for the green aspect in the manner shown in diagram 3003 in that Schedule or in accordance with any variant permitted by those Regulations in respect of that diagram.
    (2) The vehicular lights shall be illuminated in the following sequence—

(a) red,
(b) red and amber together,
(c) green,
(d) amber.

Pedestrian demand unit

4–2959   **3.** (1) A pedestrian demand unit shall be placed at each end of a crossing.

(2) Each such unit shall consist of a device the principal features of which are a signal display of the size, colour and type shown in the diagram in Part II of this Schedule and which—

(a) complies with the requirements of sub-paragraph (3); and
(b) includes a push button or other switching device which in some way indicates to pedestrians that it has been operated.

(3) The requirements referred to in sub-paragraph (2)(a) are—

(a) the signal display must comprise a red figure and a green figure, both of which can be internally illuminated;
(b) while one figure is illuminated the other figure must not be capable of being illuminated; and
(c) the green figure must be capable of being illuminated only whilst there is conveyed to vehicular traffic, by means of the red vehicular light signal prescribed by paragraph 2, a prohibition against entering the limits of the Puffin crossing at or near which the unit is displayed and at no other time.

(4) The pedestrian demand unit may incorporate a device for emitting tactile or audible signals whilst the green figure is illuminated.

(5) Units consisting of only the red and green figures or the push button and legend comprised in a pedestrian demand unit may be provided at a crossing in addition to pedestrian demand units.

SCHEDULE 3

PART II
PEDESTRIAN DEMAND UNIT

4–2960

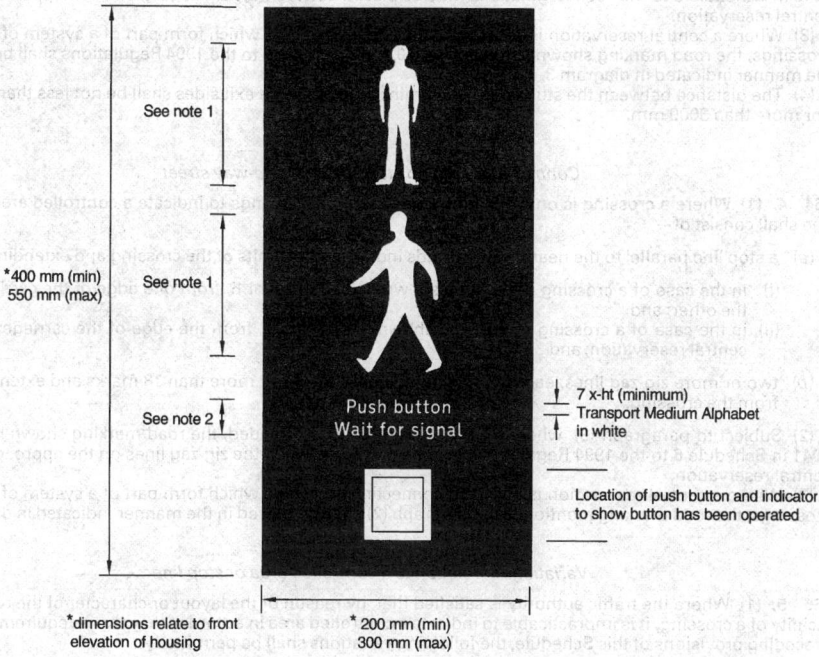

See note 1

*400 mm (min)
550 mm (max)   See note 1

See note 2

Push button
Wait for signal

7 x-ht (minimum)
Transport Medium Alphabet
in white

Location of push button and indicator
to show button has been operated

*dimensions relate to front
elevation of housing

* 200 mm (min)
300 mm (max)

Background colour of demand unit face to be black. All other external surfaces yellow.
The demand unit face need not be flat, and may comprise more than one unit.

Regulations 5(2)(b), (3)(b), 6(2), (3)   **SCHEDULE 4**

PART I
ROAD MARKINGS TO INDICATE PELICAN AND PUFFIN CROSSINGS, PELICAN AND PUFFIN CONTROLLED AREAS AND STOP LINES

Interpretation of Schedule

4–2961   **1.** In this Schedule, except where otherwise stated,—

(a) a reference to a "crossing" is to a Pelican crossing or a Puffin crossing;
(b) a reference to a "controlled area" is to a Pelican controlled area or a Puffin controlled area;
(c) a reference to a numbered diagram is a reference to the diagram in Part II of this Schedule so numbered.

Indication of limits of crossings and of controlled areas and stop lines

4–2962   **2.** (1) Subject to the provisions of this Schedule, the limits of a crossing on a two-way street and of its controlled areas and stop lines shall be indicated by road markings consisting of lines and studs on the carriageway of the size and type shown—

(a) in diagram 1 where there is no central reservation;
(b) in diagram 2 where there is a central reservation, but the crossing does not form part of a system of staggered crossings; and
(c) in diagram 3 where the crossing forms part of a system of staggered crossings.

(2) Subject to the provisions of this Schedule, the limits of a crossing on a one-way street and of its controlled areas and stop lines shall be indicated by road markings consisting of lines and studs placed on the carriageway of the size and type shown—

(a) in diagram 4 where there is no central reservation;
(b) in diagram 5 where there is a central reservation but the crossing does not form part of a system of staggered crossings; and
(c) in diagram 6 where the crossing forms part of a system of staggered crossings.

(3) The two lines of studs indicating the limits of a crossing need not be at right angles to the edge of the carriageway, but shall form straight lines and shall, as near as is reasonably practicable, be parallel to each other.

Controlled areas and stop lines on a two-way street

4–2963   **3.** (1) Where a crossing is on a two-way street the road markings to indicate each controlled area and stop line shall consist of—

(a) a stop line parallel to the nearer row of studs indicating the limits of the crossing and extending, in the manner indicated in the appropriate diagram, across the part of the carriageway used by vehicles approaching the crossing from the side on which the stop line is placed; and
(b) two or more longitudinal zig-zag lines or, in the case of a road having more than one carriageway, two or more such lines on each carriageway, each zig-zag line containing not less than 8 nor more than 18 marks and extending away from the crossing.

(2) Subject to paragraph (3), where a central reservation is provided, the road marking shown in diagram 1040 in Schedule 6 to the 1994 Regulations may be placed between the zig-zag lines on the approaches to the central reservation.
(3) Where a central reservation is provided connecting crossings which form part of a system of staggered crossings, the road marking shown in diagram 1040.2 in Schedule 6 to the 1994 Regulations shall be placed in the manner indicated in diagram 3.
(4) The distance between the studs and the terminal marks on the exit sides shall be not less than 1700 mm nor more than 3000 mm.

Controlled areas and stop line on a one-way street

4–2964   **4.** (1) Where a crossing is on a one-way street the road markings to indicate a controlled area and stop line shall consist of—

(a) a stop line parallel to the nearer row of studs indicating the limits of the crossing and extending—

(i) in the case of a crossing of the type shown in diagram 4 or 5, from one edge of the carriageway to the other; and
(ii) in the case of a crossing of the type shown in diagram 6, from the edge of the carriageway to the central reservation; and

(b) two or more zig-zag lines, each containing not less than 8 nor more than 18 marks and extending away from the crossing.

(2) Subject to paragraph (3), where a central reservation is provided, the road marking shown in diagram 1041 in Schedule 6 to the 1994 Regulations may be placed between the zig-zag lines on the approaches to the central reservation.
(3) Where a central reservation is provided connecting crossings which form part of a system of staggered crossings, the road marking mentioned in paragraph (2) shall be placed in the manner indicated in diagram 6.

Variations in relation to a controlled area or stop line

4–2965   **5.** (1) Where the traffic authority is satisfied that, by reason of the layout or character of the roads in the vicinity of a crossing, it is impracticable to indicate a controlled area in accordance with the requirements of the preceding provisions of this Schedule, the following variations shall be permitted—

(a) the number of marks in each zig-zag line may be reduced to not less than 2;
(b) the marks comprised in a zig-zag line may be varied to a length of not less than 1 metre, in which case—

(i) each mark in each zig-zag line must be of the same or substantially the same length as the other marks in the same line;
(ii) and the number of marks in each line must be not more than 8 nor less than 2.

(2) The angle of a stop line in relation to the nearer line of studs indicating the limits of a crossing may be varied, if the traffic authority is satisfied that the variation is necessary having regard to the angle of the crossing in relation to the edge of the carriageway.
(3) The maximum distance of 3 metres between a stop line and the nearer line of studs indicating the limits of the crossing shown in the diagrams in this Schedule may be increased to such greater distance, not exceeding 10 metres, as the traffic authority may decide.
(4) Each zig-zag line in a controlled area need not contain the same number of marks as the others and the pattern of the central lines may be reversed or, if the carriageway is not more than 6 metres wide, may be omitted altogether if replaced by the road marking shown in diagram 1004 in Schedule 6 to the 1994 Regulations.

Colour and illumination of road markings

4–2966   **6.** Subject to paragraph 7, the road markings shown in the diagrams in this Schedule shall be coloured white and may be illuminated by retroreflecting material.

Form and colour of studs

4–2967 **7.** (1) The studs shown in the diagrams in this Schedule shall be—

  (*a*) coloured white, silver or light grey and shall not be fitted with reflective lenses; and
  (*b*) either circular in shape with a diameter of not less than 95 mm nor more than 110 mm or square in shape with the length of each side being not less than 95 mm nor more than 110 mm.

  (2) Any stud which is fixed or embedded in the carriageway shall not project more than 20 mm above the carriageway at its highest point nor more than 6 mm at its edges.

Supplementary

4–2968 **8.** The requirements of this Schedule shall be regarded as having been complied with in the case of any crossing or controlled area, if most of the road markings comply with those requirements, even though some of the studs or lines do not so comply by reason of discolouration, temporary removal or a displacement or for some other reason, so long as the general appearance of the road markings as a whole is not thereby materially impaired.

SCHEDULE 4

PART II
DIAGRAM 1

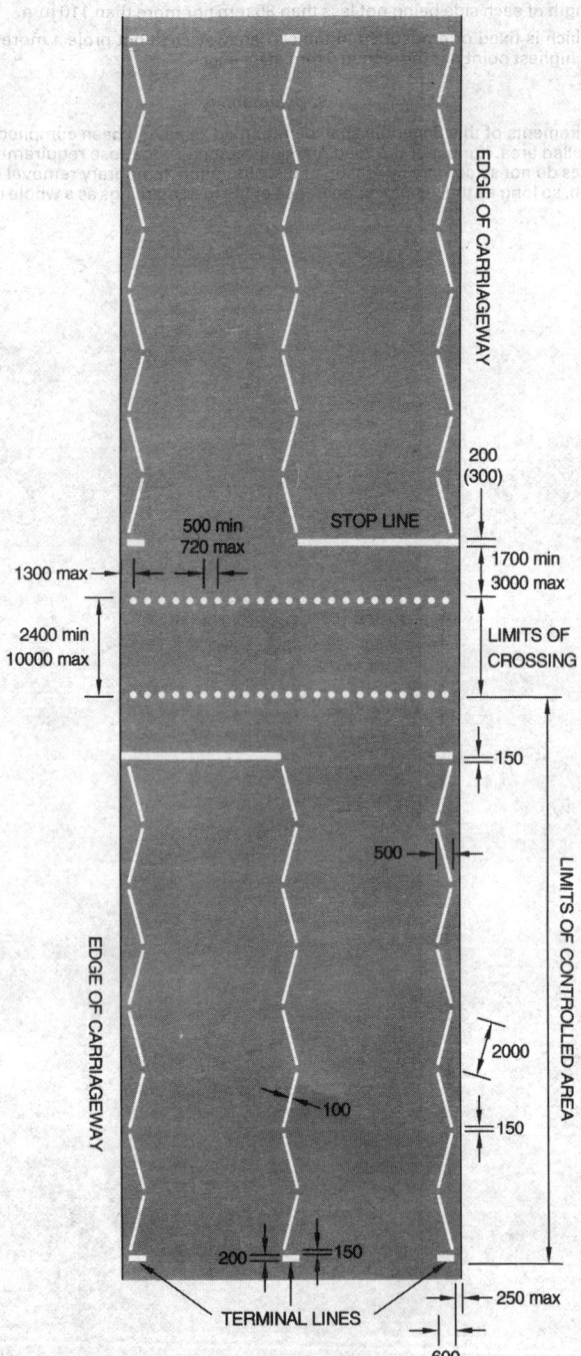

SCHEDULE 4

PART II
DIAGRAM 2

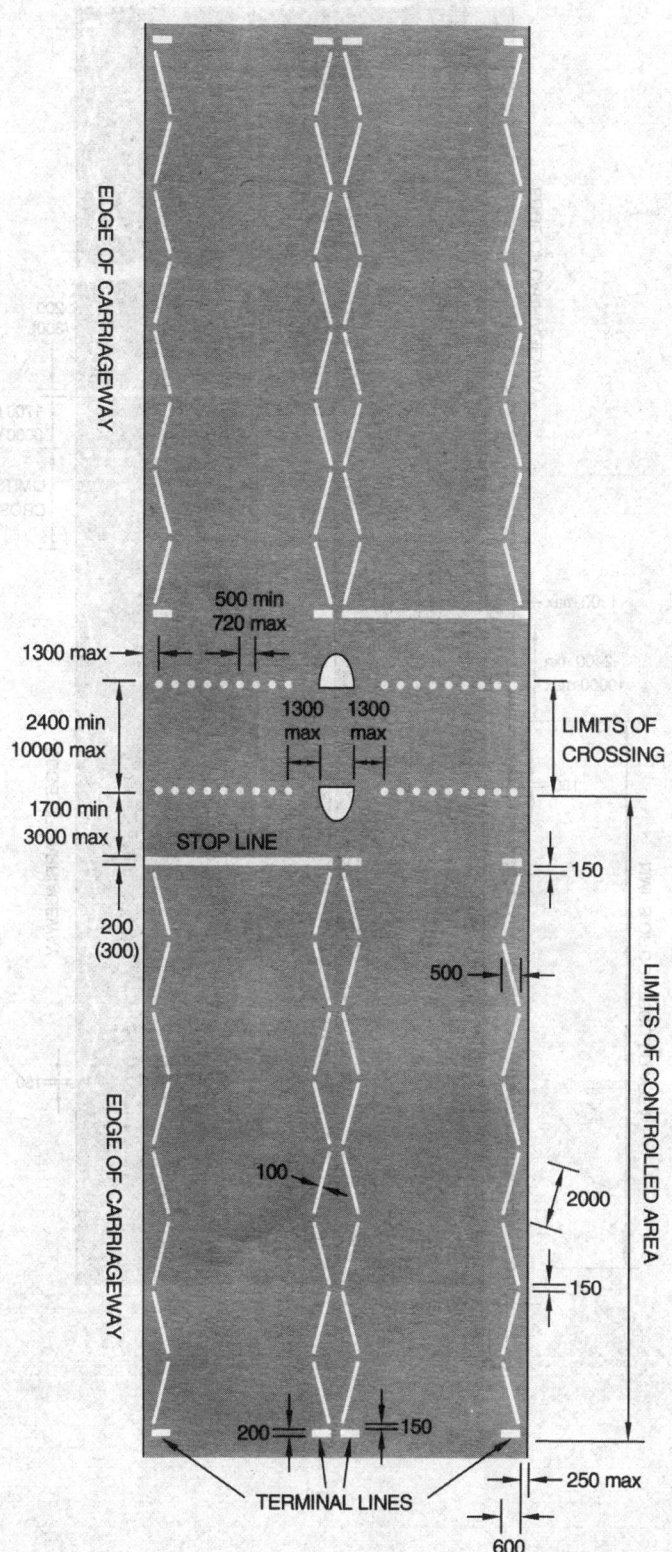

SCHEDULE 4

PART II
DIAGRAM 3

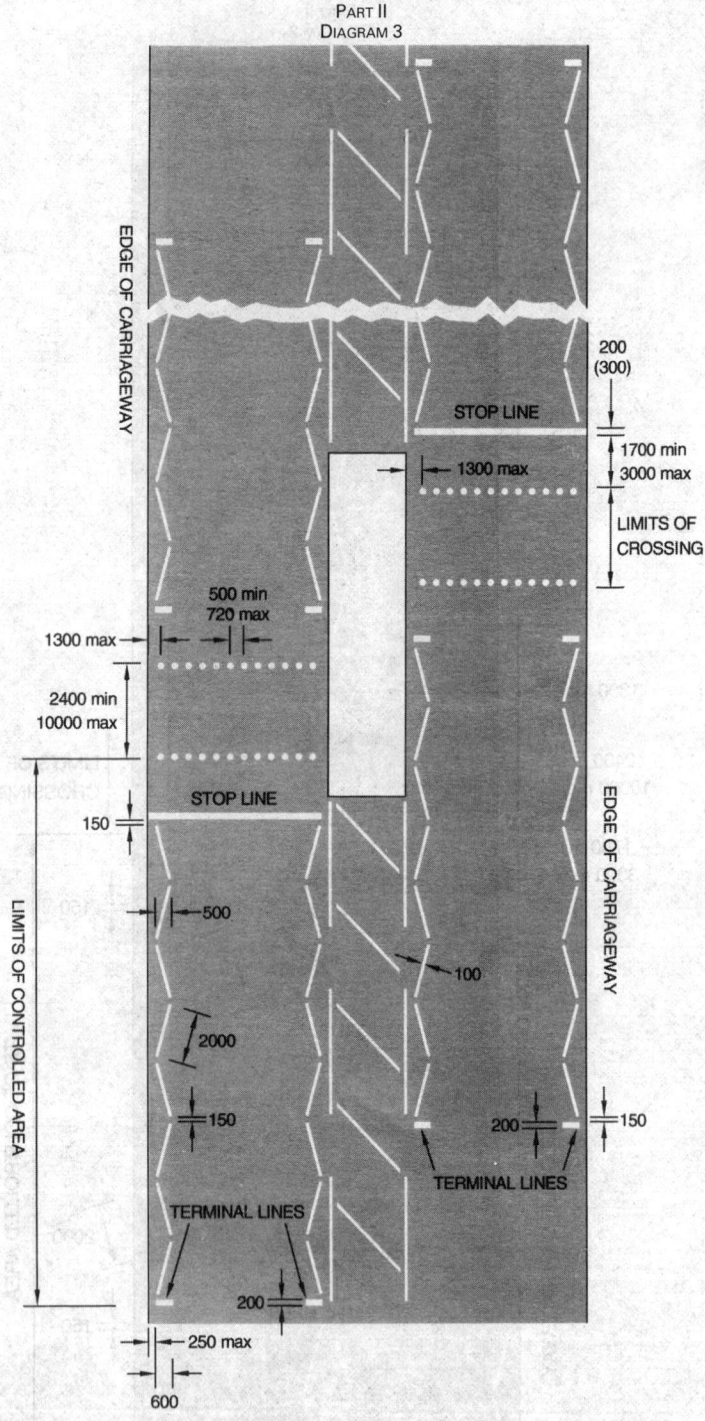

SCHEDULE 4

PART II
DIAGRAM 4

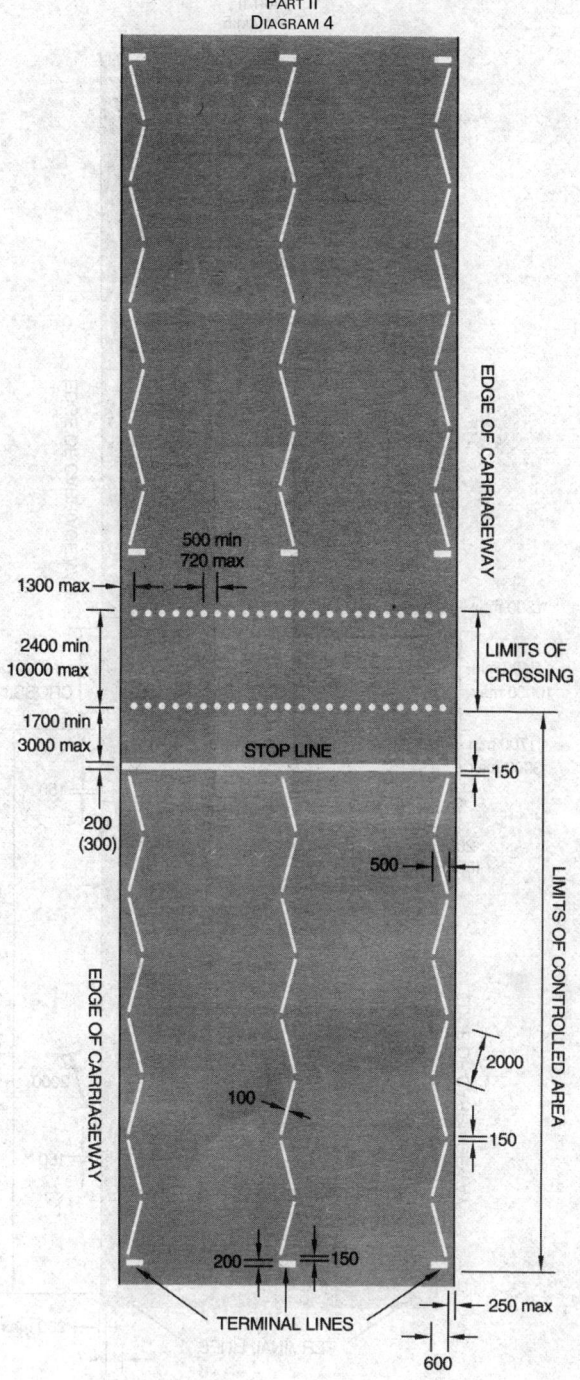

SCHEDULE 4

PART II
DIAGRAM 5

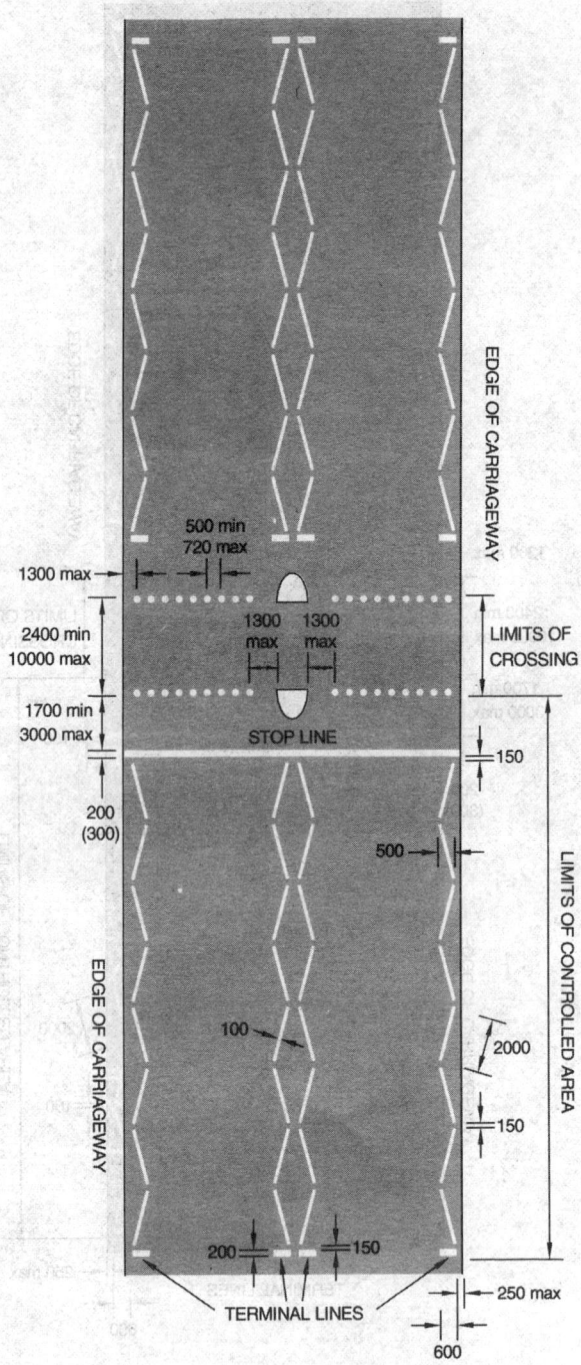

SCHEDULE 4

PART II
DIAGRAM 6

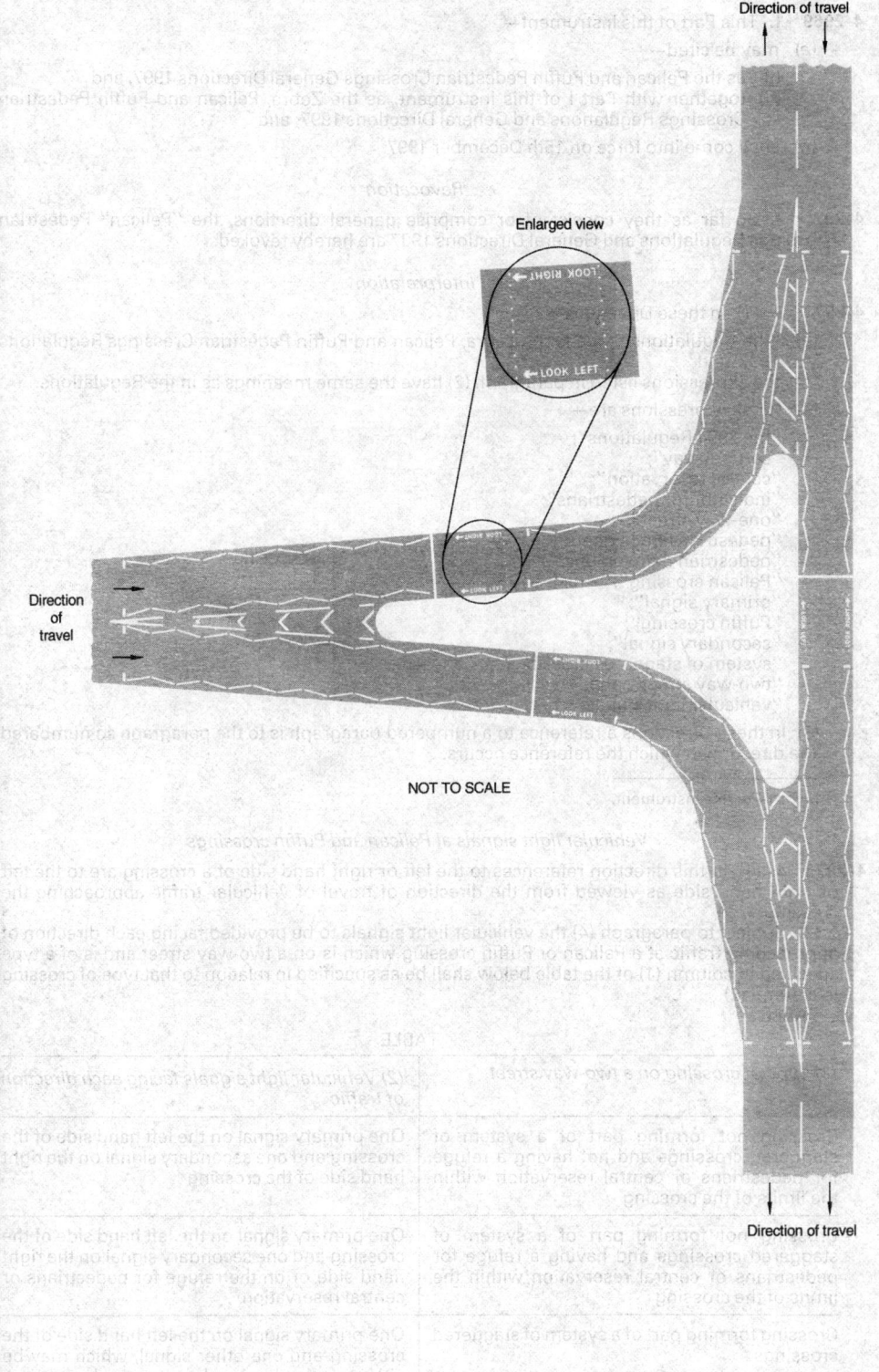

Direction of travel

Enlarged view

LOOK RIGHT →

← LOOK LEFT

Direction
of
travel

NOT TO SCALE

Direction of travel

PART II
THE PELICAN AND PUFFIN PEDESTRIAN CROSSINGS GENERAL DIRECTIONS 1997

Citation and commencement

4–2969   **1.** This Part of this Instrument—

(a) may be cited—

   (i) as the Pelican and Puffin Pedestrian Crossings General Directions 1997, and

   (ii) together with Part I of this Instrument, as the Zebra, Pelican and Puffin Pedestrian Crossings Regulations and General Directions 1997; and

(b) shall come into force on 15th December 1997.

Revocation

4–2970   **2.** So far as they consist of or comprise general directions, the "Pelican" Pedestrian Crossings Regulations and General Directions 1987 are hereby revoked.

Interpretation

4–2971   **3.** (1) In these Directions—

(a) "the Regulations" means the Zebra, Pelican and Puffin Pedestrian Crossings Regulations 1997[1] and

(b) the expressions listed in paragraph (2) have the same meanings as in the Regulations.

(2) Those expressions are—

"the 1994 Regulations";
"carriageway";
"central reservation";
"indicator for pedestrians";
"one-way street";
"pedestrian light signals";
"pedestrian demand unit";
"Pelican crossing";
"primary signal";
"Puffin crossing";
"secondary signal";
"system of staggered crossings";
"two-way street"; and
"vehicular light signals".

(3) In these Directions a reference to a numbered paragraph is to the paragraph so numbered in the direction in which the reference occurs.

---

1. Part 1 of this instrument.

Vehicular light signals at Pelican and Puffin crossings

4–2972   **4.** (1) In this direction references to the left or right hand side of a crossing are to the left or right hand side as viewed from the direction of travel of vehicular traffic approaching the crossing.

(2) Subject to paragraph (4) the vehicular light signals to be provided facing each direction of approaching traffic at a Pelican or Puffin crossing which is on a two-way street and is of a type specified in column (1) of the table below shall be as specified in relation to that type of crossing in column (2).

TABLE

TABLE

(1) Type of crossing on a two-way street	(2) Vehicular light signals facing each direction of traffic
Crossing not forming part of a system of staggered crossings and not having a refuge for pedestrians or central reservation within the limits of the crossing	One primary signal on the left hand side of the crossing and one secondary signal on the right hand side of the crossing
Crossing not forming part of a system of staggered crossings and having a refuge for pedestrians or central reservation within the limits of the crossing	One primary signal on the left hand side of the crossing and one secondary signal on the right hand side or on the refuge for pedestrians or central reservation
Crossing forming part of a system of staggered crossings	One primary signal on the left hand side of the crossing and one other signal, which may be either a primary signal or a secondary signal, on the right hand side of the crossing

(3) Subject to paragraph (4) the vehicular light signals to be provided facing the direction of approaching traffic at a Pelican or Puffin crossing which is on a one-way street and is of a type

specified in column (1) of the table below shall be as specified in relation to that type of crossing in column (2).

TABLE

(1) Type of crossing on a two-way street	(2) Vehicular light signals facing each direction of traffic
Crossing not forming part of a system of staggered crossings and not having a refuge for pedestrians or central reservation within the limits of the crossing	One primary signal on the left hand side of the crossing and one other signal, which may be either a primary or a secondary signal, on the right hand side of the crossing
Crossing not forming part of a system of staggered crossings and having a refuge for pedestrians or central reservation within the limits of the crossing	One primary signal on each side of the crossing and one other signal which may be either a primary signal (in which case it must be on the refuge for pedestrians or the central reservation) or a secondary signal
Crossing forming part of a system of staggered crossings	One primary signal on the left hand side of the crossing and a signal, which may be either a primary or a secondary signal, on the right hand side of the crossing

(4) In addition to the signals required to be placed by paragraph (2) or (3) the traffic authority may place such other primary or secondary signals at a Pelican or Puffin crossing as it thinks fit.

Pedestrian light signals and indicators for pedestrians at Pelican crossings

4–2973   5. (1) At least one pedestrian light signal and at least one indicator for pedestrians shall be placed at each end of a Pelican crossing.
(2) Each pedestrian light signal shall be so placed as to be clearly visible to any person on the other side of the carriageway who wishes to use the crossing.
(3) Where there is a central reservation in a Pelican crossing, at least one indicator for pedestrians shall be placed on the central reservation.
(4) Each indicator for pedestrians shall be so placed that the push button on it may be reached by any person wishing to press it.

Pedestrian demand units at Puffin crossings

4–2974   6. (1) At least one pedestrian demand unit shall be placed at each end of a Puffin crossing.
(2) Each pedestrian demand unit shall be so placed that the push button on it may be reached by any person wishing to press it.

Additional traffic signs

4–2975   7. A traffic sign of the size, colour and type shown in diagram 610 or 611 in Schedule 2 to the 1994 Regulations may only be placed on a refuge for pedestrians or a central reservation within the limits of a Pelican or Puffin crossing or on a central reservation which lies between two Pelican or Puffin crossings which form part of a system of staggered crossings.

Colouring of containers and posts

4–2976   8. (1) The containers of vehicular light signals at a Pelican or Puffin crossing—
(a) shall be coloured black; and
(b) may be mounted on a backing board,
and, if so mounted the backing board shall be coloured black and may have a white border not less than 45 mm nor more than 55 mm wide which may be made of reflective material.
(2) The containers of pedestrian light signals at a Pelican crossing shall be coloured black.
(3) Where, at a Pelican or Puffin crossing, vehicular light signals, pedestrian light signals, an indicator for pedestrians or a pedestrian demand unit is mounted on a post specially provided for the purpose, the part of the post extending above ground level shall be of a single colour, which may be grey, black, brown, dark green or dark blue but may have marked on it one yellow or white band not less than 140 mm nor more than 160 mm deep, the lower edge of the band being not less than 1.5 metres nor more than 1.7 metres above the level of the immediately adjacent ground.
(4) Any box attached to a post or other structure on which vehicular light signals, pedestrian light signals, an indicator for pedestrians or a pedestrian demand unit are mounted and housing apparatus designed to control, or to monitor, the operation of the signals or unit shall be coloured grey, black, brown, dark green or dark blue.

Approval of equipment

4–2977   9. (1) In this direction "equipment" means all equipment (including the content of all instructions stored in, or executable by it) capable of giving visible, audible or tactile signals used in connection with vehicular light signals, pedestrian light signals, indicators for pedestrians or pedestrian demand units to secure that those signals, indicators or units comply with the relevant provisions of the Regulations.

(2) All equipment placed on a road for the purposes of a Pelican or Puffin crossing shall be of a type approved in writing by the Secretary of State.

(3) If, after equipment has been placed in accordance with an approval under paragraph (2), the signals, indicator or unit used in connection with it is altered, the signal, indicator or unit shall not be further used unless that alteration is approved in writing by the Secretary of State.

(4) When any equipment which has been placed at a Pelican or Puffin crossing is of a type approved under paragraph (2), the equipment shall, subject to paragraph (3), be regarded as continuing to be approved until notice is given in writing by the Secretary of State—

(a) to the traffic authority; and
(b) either—

    (i) to the supplier of the equipment; or
    (ii) where an alteration has been approved in accordance with paragraph (3), to the person who carried out the alteration,

of a date which the equipment is no longer to be so regarded.

(5) Where notice is given under paragraph (4) that equipment is no longer to be regarded as being approved, the equipment and, unless the Secretary of State approves any alternative equipment for the same purpose, any signal, indicator or unit in connection with it shall be removed from the road on or before the date given in the notice.

Special directions by the Secretary of State

4–2978 10. Nothing in these Directions shall be taken to limit the power of the Secretary of State by any special direction to dispense with, add to or modify any of the requirements of these Directions in their application to any particular case.

APPENDIX
EXERCISE OF POWERS

4–2979 1. The Regulations in Part I of this Instrument are made by the Secretary of State for Transport, the Secretary of State for Scotland and the Secretary of State for Wales—

(a) acting jointly, in exercise of the powers conferred on them by section 64(1), (2) and (3) of the Road Traffic regulation 1984; and
(b) acting severally, in relation to England, to Scotland and Wales respectively, in exercise and of all other powers conferred on them by that Act

and of all other powers enabling them in that behalf.

2. The directions in Part II of this Instrument are given by the said Secretaries of State acting jointly, in exercise of the powers conferred on them by sections 65(1) and (1A) of the Road Traffic Regulation Act 1984.

Traffic Signs Regulations and General Directions 2002[1]

(SI 2002/3113 amended by SI 2003/393 and 2155, SI 2004/1275 and 3168 (E), SI 2005/1670, 2929 (W) and 3225 (W) and SI 2006/594 and 2083)

PART I
THE TRAFFIC SIGNS REGULATIONS 2002

SECTION 1
PRELIMINARY

4–2980 1. Citation and commencement. This Part of this Instrument—

(a) may be cited—

    (i) as the Traffic Signs Regulations 2002, and
    (ii) together with Part II below, as the Traffic Signs Regulations and General Directions 2002; and

(b) shall come into force on 31st January 2003.

---

1. Made by The Secretary of State for Transport, in exercise of the powers conferred by ss 64, 65 and 85(2) of the Road Traffic Regulation Act 1984 and by s 36(5) of the Road Traffic Act 1988.

This instrument consolidates with amendments the Traffic Signs Regulations and General Directions 1994, SI 1994/1519, and all subsequent relevant amending instruments. The signs governed by these regulations are illustrated in the Schedules (not printed here). Part II consolidates the Traffic Signs General Directions 1994, which constituted Pt II of the Traffic Signs Regulations and General Directions 1994, SI 1994/1519, and all subsequent relevant amending instruments. It deals with the use, placing and mounting of signs. Only those regulations of immediate concern to magistrates' courts are printed here.

4–2981 2. Revocations. The Traffic Signs Regulations 1994 and the Traffic Signs (Amendment) Regulations 1995 are hereby revoked.

4–2982 3. *Savings*

4–2983 4. Interpretation—general. In these Regulations unless the context otherwise requires—

"the 1984 Act" means the Road Traffic Regulation Act 1984;
"the 1988 Act" means the Road Traffic Act 1988;
"the 1981 Regulations" means the Traffic Signs Regulations 1981;

"the 1994 Regulations" means the Traffic Signs Regulations 1994;

"articulated vehicle" means a motor vehicle with a trailer so attached to it as to be partially superimposed upon it;

"automatic half-barrier level crossing" means a level crossing where barriers are installed to descend automatically across part of the road when a railway vehicle or tramcar approaches and the operation of the barriers is monitored remotely from the crossing;

"automatic barrier crossing (L)" means a level crossing where barriers are installed to descend automatically across part of the road when a railway vehicle or tramcar approaches and the driver of the railway vehicle or tramcar is required to monitor the operation of the barriers when the railway vehicle or tramcar is at or near the crossing;

"automatic open crossing (L)" means a level crossing without automatic barriers where light signals are so installed as to be operated automatically by a railway vehicle or tramcar approaching the crossing and the driver of the railway vehicle or tramcar is required to monitor the operation of the light signals when the railway vehicle or tramcar is at or near the crossing;

"automatic open crossing (R)" means a level crossing without automatic barriers where light signals are so installed as to be operated automatically by a railway vehicle or tramcar approaching the crossing and the operation of the light signals is monitored remotely from the crossing;

"automatic level crossing" means an automatic half-barrier level crossing, an automatic barrier crossing (L), an automatic open crossing (L) or an automatic open crossing (R);

"bus lane" has the meaning given in regulation 23;

"central reservation" means—

(a) any land between the carriageways of a road comprising two carriageways; or
(b) any permanent work (other than a traffic island) in the carriageway of a road,

which separates the carriageway or, as the case may be, the part of the carriageway which is to be used by traffic moving in one direction from the carriageway or part of the carriageway which is to be used (whether at all times or at particular times only) by traffic moving in the other direction;

"contra-flow" means a part of a carriageway of a road where—

(a) traffic is authorised to proceed in the opposite direction to the usual direction of traffic on that part; or
(b) a specified class of traffic is authorised to proceed in the opposite direction to other traffic on that carriageway;

"controlled parking zone" means either—

(a) an area—
   (i) in which, except where parking places have been provided, every road has been marked with one or more of the road markings shown in diagrams 1017, 1018.1, 1019 and 1020.1; and
   (ii) into which each entrance for vehicular traffic has been indicated by the sign shown in diagram 663 or 663.1; or
(b) an area—
   (i) in which at least one of the signs shown in diagram 640.2A has been placed on each side of every road; and
   (ii) into which each entrance for vehicular traffic has been indicated by the sign shown in diagram 665;

"cycle lane" means a part of the carriageway of a road which—

(a) starts with the marking shown in diagram 1009; and
(b) is separated from the rest of the carriageway—
   (i) if it may not be used by vehicles other than pedal cycles, by the marking shown in diagram 1049; or
   (ii) if it may be used by vehicles other than pedal cycles, by the marking shown in diagram 1004 or 1004.1;

"cycle track", in relation to England and Wales, has the same meaning as in the Highways Act 1980 and, in relation to Scotland, as in the Roads (Scotland) Act 1984;

"dual carriageway road" means a road which comprises a central reservation and "all-purpose dual carriageway road" means a dual carriageway road which is not a motorway;

"EEA Agreement" means the Agreement on the European Economic Area signed at Oporto on 2nd May 1992 as adjusted by the Protocol signed at Brussels on 17th March 1993;

"EEA Standard" means—

(a) a standard or code of practice of a national standards body or equivalent body of any EEA State;
(b) any international standard recognised for use as a standard or code of practice by any EEA State; or
(c) a technical specification recognised for use as a standard by a public authority of any EEA State,

and a reference to a "corresponding EEA Standard", in relation to a British or European Standard, is a reference to an EEA Standard which requires a level of performance equivalent to that required by the British or European Standard;

"EEA State" means a State which is a contracting Party to the EEA Agreement;

"enactment" includes any Act or subordinate legislation as defined in section 21(1) of the Interpretation Act 1978;

"equestrian crossing" means a place on the carriageway of a road—

(a) where provision is made for equestrian traffic to cross the carriageway; and

(b) whose presence is indicated by a combination of—

(i) traffic light signals to control vehicular traffic of the kind prescribed by regulation 33;

(ii) the signals shown in diagrams 4003.2 and 4003.3, or the signal shown in diagram 4003.4; and

(iii) the road marking shown in diagram 1055.1 or 1055.2;

"ES compliant" in relation to signal heads shall be construed in accordance with regulation 33(5);

"excursion or tour" has the meaning given in section 137(1) of the Transport Act 1985;

"goods vehicle" means a motor vehicle or trailer constructed or adapted for use for the carriage or haulage of goods or burden of any description;

"hard shoulder", in relation to a motorway in England or Wales, has the meaning given by regulation 3(1)(e) of the Motorways (England and Wales) Regulations and, in relation to a motorway in Scotland, regulation 2(1) of the Motorways (Scotland) Regulations and "actively managed hard shoulder" means a hard shoulder along which, by virtue of regulations under section 17(2) and (3) of the Road Traffic Regulation Act 1984, vehicular traffic may be driven at times for the time being indicated by traffic signs in accordance with those regulations;

"hours of darkness" means the time between half an hour after sunset and half an hour before sunrise;

"junction" means a road junction;

"level crossing" means a place where a road is crossed by a railway or a tramway on a reserved track on the same level;

"local bus" means a public service vehicle used for the provision of a local service not being an excursion or tour;

"local service" has the meaning given in section 2 of the Transport Act 1985;

"major road" means the road at a junction into which there emerges vehicular traffic from a minor road;

"manually operated" means a change from one sign to another or one signal aspect to another set in process by an operator;

"maximum gross weight" means—

(a) in the case of a motor vehicle not drawing a trailer or in the case of a trailer, its maximum laden weight;

(b) in the case of an articulated vehicle, its maximum laden weight (if it has one) and otherwise the aggregate maximum laden weight of all the individual vehicles forming part of that articulated vehicle; and

(c) in the case of a motor vehicle (other than an articulated vehicle) drawing one or more trailers, the aggregate maximum laden weight of the motor vehicle and the trailer or trailers drawn by it;

"maximum laden weight" in relation to a vehicle (including a vehicle which is a trailer) means—

(a) in the case of a vehicle as respects which a gross weight not to be exceeded in Great Britain is specified in construction and use requirements (as defined by section 41(8) of the 1988 Act), the weight so specified;

(b) in the case of a vehicle as respects which no such weight is so specified, the weight which the vehicle is designed or adapted not to exceed when in normal use and travelling on a road laden;

"minor road" means a road on which, at its junction with another road, there is placed the sign shown in diagram 601.1 or 602 or the road marking shown in diagram 1003;

"mobile road works" means works on a road carried out by or from a vehicle or vehicles which move slowly along the road or which stop briefly from time to time along that road;

"motorway" means a special road which—

(a) in England or Wales (save as otherwise provided by or under regulations made under, or having effect as if made under, section 17 of the 1984 Act) can be used by traffic only of Class I or II as specified in Schedule 4 to the Highways Act 1980; or

(b) in Scotland can be used by traffic only of Class I or Class II as specified in Schedule 3 to the Roads (Scotland) Act 1984;

"Motorways (England and Wales) Regulations" means the Motorways Traffic (England and Wales) Regulations 1982 and "Motorways (Scotland) Regulations" means the Motorways Traffic (Scotland) Regulations 1995;

"mph" means miles per hour;

"non-primary route" means a route, not being a primary route or a motorway or part of a primary route or of a motorway;

"passenger vehicle" means a vehicle constructed or adapted for the carriage of passengers and their effects;

"pedal cycle" means a unicycle, bicycle, tricycle, or cycle having four or more wheels, not being in any case mechanically propelled unless it is an electrically assisted pedal cycle of such class as is to be treated as not being a motor vehicle for the purposes of the 1984 Act;

"pedestrian zone" means an area—

(a) which has been laid out to improve amenity for pedestrians; and

(b) to which the entry of vehicles is prohibited or restricted;

"plate" means a sign which by virtue of general directions given in exercise of the power conferred by section 65 of the 1984 Act may be placed only in combination or in conjunction with another sign and which is supplementary to that other sign;

"police vehicle" means a vehicle being used for police purposes or operating under the instructions of a chief officer of police;

"primary route" means a route, not being a route comprising any part of a motorway, in respect of which the Secretary of State—

(a) in the case of a trunk road is of the opinion, and

(b) in any other case after consultation with the traffic authority for the road comprised in the route is of the opinion,

that it provides the most satisfactory route for through traffic between places of traffic importance;

"primary signals" has the meaning given by regulation 43(5)(a);

"principal road" means a road for the time being classified as a principal road—

(a) by virtue of section 12 of the Highways Act 1980 (whether as falling within subsection (1) or classified under subsection (3)), or

(b) by the Secretary of State under section 11(1) of the Roads (Scotland) Act 1984;

"public service vehicle" has the meaning given in section 1 of the Public Passenger Vehicles Act 1981;

"reflectorised" means illuminated by the use of retroreflecting material;

"retroreflecting material" means material which reflects a ray of light back towards the source of that light;

"road maintenance vehicle" means a vehicle which—

(a) in England and Wales is specially designed or adapted for use on a road by or on behalf of a highway authority for the purposes of the Highways Act 1980 for the purposes of road maintenance; or

(b) in Scotland is specially designed or adapted for use on a road by or on behalf of a roads authority for the purposes of the Roads (Scotland) Act 1984 for the purposes of road maintenance;

"road marking" means a traffic sign consisting of a line or mark or legend on a road;

"road works" means works for the improvement, alteration or maintenance of a road and includes, in relation to England and Wales, street works as defined by section 48(3) of the New Roads and Street Works Act 1991 and, in relation to Scotland, road works as defined by section 107(3) of that Act;

"route" includes any road comprised in a route;

"school crossing place" means a place in a road where children cross or seek to cross that road on their way to or from school or on their way from one part of a school to another;

"secondary signals" has the meaning given by regulation 43;

"sign" means a traffic sign;

"signal-controlled crossing facility" means—

(a) an equestrian crossing;

(b) a signal-controlled pedestrian facility; or

(c) a Toucan crossing;

"signal-controlled pedestrian facility" means a place on the carriageway of a road—

(a) which is not a "crossing" as defined by section 25(6) of the 1984 Act;

(b) where provision is made for pedestrians to cross the carriageway; and

(c) whose presence is indicated by a combination of—

(i) traffic light signals to control vehicular traffic of the kind prescribed by regulation 33;

(ii) the signals shown in diagrams 4002.1 and 4003, or the signal shown in diagram 4003.1; and

(iii) the road marking shown in diagram 1055.1 or 1055.2;

"single carriageway road" means a road which is not a dual carriageway road;

"solo motor cycle" means a motor cycle without a side car and having two wheels;

"stop line" in relation to light signals for the control of vehicular traffic has the meaning given in regulation 43;

"stud" means a prefabricated device fixed or embedded as a mark in the carriageway of a road;

"taxi" means—

(a) in England and Wales, a vehicle licensed under—

(i) section 37 of the Town Police Clauses Act 1847; or

(ii) section 6 of the Metropolitan Public Carriage Act 1869;

or under any similar enactment; and

(b) in Scotland, a taxi licensed under section 10 of the Civic Government (Scotland) Act 1982;

"taxi rank" means an area of carriageway reserved for use by taxis waiting to pick up passengers;

"telecommunications apparatus" has the meaning given by paragraph 1(1) of Schedule 2 to the Telecommunications Act 1984;

"temporary statutory provision" means—

(a) a provision having effect under section 9 (experimental traffic orders) or section 14 (temporary restriction of traffic on roads) of the 1984 Act or under a provision referred to in section 66 (traffic signs for giving effect to local traffic regulations) of that Act;

(b) a prohibition, restriction or requirement indicated by a traffic sign placed pursuant to section 67 (emergencies and temporary obstructions) of the 1984 Act; or

(c) a provision having effect under section 62 (temporary prohibition or restriction of traffic etc on roads for reasons of safety or public convenience) of the Roads (Scotland) Act 1984;

"terminal sign" means a sign placed in accordance with direction 8 or 9 of the Traffic Signs General Directions 2002;

"Toucan crossing" means a place on the carriageway of a road—

(a) where provision is made for both pedestrians and pedal cyclists to cross the carriageway; and

(b) whose presence is indicated by a combination of—

(i) traffic light signals to control vehicular traffic of the kind prescribed by regulation 33;

(ii) the signals shown in diagrams 4003.5 and 4003.6, or the signal shown in diagram 4003.7; and

(iii) the road marking shown in diagram 1055.1 or 1055.2;

"tourist destination" means a permanently established attraction or facility which—

(a) attracts or is used by visitors to an area;

(b) is open to the public without prior booking during its normal opening hours;

(c) if located in Scotland, is recognised by VisitScotland; and

(d) if located in Wales, is recognised by the National Assembly for Wales;

"Tourist Information Centre" means a staffed information service centre recognised and supported by the English Tourist Board, National Assembly for Wales or by VisitScotland;

"Tourist Information Point" means a display of tourist information approved by a regional, area or local tourist board or the National Assembly for Wales;

"traffic calming features" means—

(a) road humps constructed pursuant to section 90A of the Highways Act 1980 ("the 1980 Act") or section 36 of the Roads (Scotland) Act 1984 ("the Scotland 1984 Act") and in accordance with the Highways (Road Humps) Regulations 1999 or the Road Humps (Scotland) Regulations 1998; or

(b) traffic calming works constructed in accordance with section 90G of the 1980 Act or section 39A of the Scotland 1984 Act and in accordance with the Highways (Traffic Calming) Regulations 1999 or the Roads (Traffic Calming) (Scotland) Regulations 1994;

"traffic lane" means, in relation to a road, a part of the carriageway having, as a boundary which separates it from another such part, a road marking of the type shown in diagram 1004, 1004.1, 1005, 1005.1, 1008, 1008.1, 1010, 1013.1, 1013.3, 1013.4, 1040, 1040.2, 1041, 1041.1, 1042, 1042.1 or 1049;

"tramcar" has the meaning given in section 141A(4) of the 1984 Act;

"trolley vehicle" has the meaning given in section 141A(4) of the 1984 Act;

"trunk road" as respects England and Wales has the meaning given in section 329(1) of the Highways Act 1980 and as respects Scotland in section 151(1) of the Roads (Scotland) Act 1984;

"unladen vehicle" has the meaning given in Schedule 18;

"variable message sign" has the meaning given in regulation 58(1);

"with-flow lane" means a traffic lane reserved for a specified class of traffic proceeding in the same direction as general traffic in an adjoining traffic lane;

"Zebra crossing" has the meaning given by regulation 3(1) of the Zebra, Pelican and Puffin Pedestrian Crossings Regulations 1997; and

"zig-zag line" means a road marking of the size, colour and type shown in diagram 1001.3 which has been placed along a length of carriageway adjacent to a signal-controlled crossing facility.

4–2984   5. Interpretation of speed limit. (1) In these Regulations "speed limit" means a maximum or minimum limit of speed on the driving of vehicles on a road—

(a) imposed by an order under section 14 of the 1984 Act (temporary prohibition or restriction of traffic on roads);

(b) imposed by an order under section 16A of the 1984 Act (special events);

(c) imposed by regulations under section 17 of the 1984 Act (traffic regulation on special roads);

(d) arising by virtue of the road being restricted for the purposes of section 81 of the 1984 Act (general speed limit for restricted roads);

(e) imposed by an order under section 84 of the 1984 Act (speed limits on roads other than restricted roads);

(f)   imposed by an order under section 88 of the 1984 Act (temporary speed limits); or
(g)   imposed by or under a local Act,

and "maximum speed limit" and "minimum speed limit" shall be construed accordingly.

(2) In these Regulations "national speed limit" means any prohibition imposed on a road by the 70 miles per hour, 60 miles per hour and 50 miles per hour (Temporary Speed Limit) Order 1977 or by regulation 3 of the Motorways (Speed Limits) Regulations 1974.

4–2985   **6. Interpretation of references.**   In these Regulations, unless it is expressly provided otherwise or the context otherwise requires—

   (a)   a reference to a numbered regulation is a reference to the regulation so numbered in these Regulations;

   (b)   a reference to a numbered paragraph is a reference to the paragraph so numbered in the regulation or Schedule in which the reference occurs;

   (c)   a reference to a sub-paragraph followed by a number or letter is a reference to the sub-paragraph bearing that number or letter in the paragraph in which the reference occurs;

   (d)   a reference to a numbered diagram is a reference to the diagram so numbered in a Schedule to these Regulations;

   (e)   a reference to a sign, signal, signals or road marking prescribed by a regulation or shown in a diagram in a Schedule to these Regulations means a sign, signal, signals or road marking of the size, colour and type—

      (i)   prescribed by that regulation and shown in any diagram to which that regulation refers; or as the case may be

      (ii)   shown in that diagram and prescribed by these Regulations,

    and in either case includes a reference to that sign, signal, signals or road marking as varied in accordance with these Regulations;

   (f)   a reference to the information, warning, requirement, restriction, prohibition or speed limit conveyed by a sign, signal, signals or road marking prescribed by a regulation or shown in a diagram includes a reference to that information, warning, requirement, restriction, prohibition or speed limit, however expressed, as varied to accord with any variation of the sign, signal, signals or road marking made in accordance with these Regulations; and

   (g)   in any provision which includes a table, references to a table or to a numbered table are to the table or as the case may be to the table so numbered in that provision.

4–2986   *7. Interpretation of Schedules 1 to 12 (this section refers to the illustration of signs which do not appear in this work)*

SECTION 2
GENERAL PROVISIONS

4–2987   **8. Authorisations.**   Nothing in these Regulations shall be taken to limit the powers of the Secretary of State, the Scottish Ministers and the National Assembly for Wales under section 64(1) and (2) of the 1984 Act to authorise the erection or retention of traffic signs of a character not prescribed by these Regulations.

4–2988   **9. Temporary obstructions.**   Nothing in these Regulations shall have effect so as to authorise any persons not otherwise authorised to do so to place on or near a road any object or device for warning traffic of a temporary obstruction.

4–2989   **10. Application of section 36 of the Road Traffic Act 1988[1] to signs and disqualification for offences.**   (1) Section 36 of the 1988 Act shall apply to each of the following signs—

   (a)   the signs shown in diagrams 601.1, 602, 606, 609, 610, 611.1, 615, 616, 626.2A, 629.2, 629.2A, 784.1, 953, 953.1, 7023, 7029 (except when varied to omit the legend "NO OVERTAKING"), 7031 and 7403[2];

   (b)   the road marking shown in diagram 1001.3[3];

   (c)   the road marking shown in diagram 1003[4];

   (d)   the road markings shown in diagrams 1013.1, 1013.3 and 1013.4 insofar as those markings convey the requirements specified in regulation 26[5];

   (e)   the road markings shown in diagrams 1025.1, 1025.3 and 1025.4 insofar as those markings convey the prohibition specified by regulation 29(1) and Part I of Schedule 19[6];

   (f)   the road markings shown in diagrams 1042, 1042.1, 1043, 1044 and 1045[7];

   (g)   the red light signal when displayed by the light signals prescribed by regulation 33 or by regulation 35;

   (h)   the light signals prescribed by regulation 33 as varied in accordance with regulation 34 when they are displaying one or more of the green arrow signals shown in diagrams 3001.2 or 3001.3 insofar as they convey any of the restrictions specified in regulation 36(1)(f) or (g) [8];

   (i)   the light signal shown in diagram 3013.1[9];

   (j)   the intermittent red light signals when displayed by the sign shown in diagram 3014[10]; and

   (k)   the light signals prescribed by regulation 37 and shown in diagrams 6031.1 and 6032.1 when indicating one of the prohibitions prescribed by regulation 38[11].

(2) The following signs are hereby specified for the purposes of column 5[12] of the entry in

Schedule 2 to the Road Traffic Offenders Act 1988 relating to offences under section 36 of the 1988 Act—

  (*a*) the signs shown in diagrams 601.1, 616, 629.2, 629.2A and 784.1;
  (*b*) the road marking shown in diagram 1001.3;
  (*c*) the road markings shown in diagrams 1013.1, 1013.3 or 1013.4 insofar as those markings convey the requirements specified in regulation 26;
  (*d*) the red light signal when displayed by the light signals prescribed by regulation 33 or by regulation 35;
  (*e*) the light signals prescribed by regulation 33 as varied in accordance with regulation 34 when they are displaying one or more of the green arrow signals shown in diagrams 3001.2 or 3001.3 insofar as they convey any of the restrictions specified in regulation 36(1)(f) or (g);
  (*f*) the intermittent red light signals when displayed by the sign shown in diagram 3014; and
  (*g*) the light signals prescribed by regulation 37 and shown in diagrams 6031.1 and 6032.1 when indicating one of the prohibitions prescribed by regulation 38.

---

  1. Failure to comply with the signs is an offence under s 36, punishable in accordance with Sch 2 to the Road Traffic Offenders Act 1988.
  2. The signs are as follows: diagram 601.1—STOP (see reg 16(1)(1)); diagram 602—GIVE WAY (see reg 16(1)(2)); diagram 606—DIRECTION ARROW; diagram 609—DIRECTION ARROW (turn ahead); diagram 610—KEEP LEFT (see reg 15); diagram 611.1—GIVE PRIORITY TO VEHICLES FROM THE RIGHT; diagram 615—GIVE PRIORITY TO VEHICLES FROM OPPOSITE DIRECTION; diagram 616—NO ENTRY; diagram 626.2A—MAX GROSS WEIGHT; diagram 629.2—MAX HEIGHT; diagram 629.2A—MAX HEIGHT (imperial and metric); diagram 784.1—DRIVERS OF LARGE VEHICLES TO STOP AND PHONE BEFORE CROSSING; diagram 953—ROUTE FOR BUSES AND PEDAL CYCLES ONLY; diagram 953.1—ROUTE FOR TRAMCARS ONLY; diagram 7023—STOP (manually operated); diagram 7029—CONVOY VEHICLE (except when varied to omit the legend "NO OVERTAKING"); diagram 7031—STOP AT WORKS ON ROAD; diagram 7043—KEEP RIGHT OF VEHICLES CARRYING OUT MOBILE ROAD WORKS.
  3. Diagram 1001.3—Zig-zag lines at Toucan or equestrian crossing facility (see regs 27 and 28).
  4. Diagram 1003—two parallel horizontal broken white lines (see reg 25).
  5. A note to reg 26, post, explains diagrams 1013.1, 1013.3 and 1013.4.
  6. Diagram 1025.1- BUS STOP; diagram 1025.3 – BUS STOP (occupying part of lay-by); diagram 1025.4 – BUS STOP (occupying whole of lay-by).
  7. Diagram 1042 and 1042.1 illustrate part of the verge or hard shoulder on motorways or dual carriageways between the main carriageway and the slip road, that part of the carriageway on the approach to a roundabout or the division of traffic lanes on a carriageway marked by means of chevrons which vehicles must not enter except in an emergency. Diagrams 1043, 1044 and 1045 illustrate alternative methods of making an area of carriageway at a junction other than a roundabout, which vehicles must not enter in a manner which causes any part of the vehicle to remain stationary within that area, save when turning right (a yellow box).
  8. Diagrams 3001.2 and 3001.3 illustrate various layouts for filter lights.
  9. Diagram 3013.1 – TRAMCAR NOT TO PROCEED BEYOND STOP LINE (see reg 42(a)).
  10. Diagram 3014 – LIGHT SIGNALS FOR CONTROL OF TRAFFIC AT LEVEL CROSSINGS, BRIDGES, TUNNELS, AIRFIELDS, FIRE, POLICE AND AMBULANCE STATIONS.
  11. Diagram 6031.1 – LIGHT SIGNALS ON GANTRIES PROHIBITING USE OF LANE (see reg 38).
  12. I.e as being offences punishable by discretionary disqualification and obligatory endorsement.

4-2990 11–14. *Contain general directions as to the use, sizes, colours and variation of signs*

SECTION 3
WARNING, REGULATORY AND INFORMATORY TRAFFIC SIGNS

4-2991 15. Sign shown in diagram 610[1] and its significance. (1) Except as provided in paragraphs (2), (2A), (2B) and (3), the requirement conveyed by the sign shown in diagram 610 shall be that vehicular traffic passing the sign must keep to the left of the sign where the arrow is pointed downwards to the left, or to the right of the sign where the arrow is pointed downwards to the right.

  (2) On an occasion where a vehicle is being used for relevant authority (as defined in section 6 of the Fire (Scotland) Act 2005 (asp 5) or, in England, fire and rescue authority, ambulance, bomb or explosive disposal, national blood service or police purposes and the observance of the requirement specified in paragraph (1) would be likely to hinder the use of that vehicle for one of those purposes then, instead of that requirement, the requirement conveyed by the sign in question shall be that the vehicle shall not proceed beyond that sign in such a manner or at such a time as to be likely to endanger any person.

  (2A) As regards England and Wales, and so far as relating to the functions of the Serious Organised Crime Agency which are exercisable in or as regards Scotland and which relate to reserved matters (within the meaning of the Scotland Act 1998), on an occasion where a vehicle is being used for Serious Organised Crime Agency purposes and the observance of the requirement specified in paragraph (1) would be likely to hinder the use of that vehicle for those purposes then, instead of that requirement, the requirement conveyed by the sign in question shall be that the vehicle shall not proceed beyond that sign in such a manner or at such a time as to be likely to endanger any person.

  (2B) *Scotland*.

  (3) The requirement specified in paragraph (1) does not apply to a tramcar or trolley vehicle.

---

  1. Keep left.

4–2992 16. Signs shown in diagrams 601.1, 602, 611.1, 778, 778.1 and 784.1[1] and their significance.
(1) The requirements conveyed to vehicular traffic on roads by the sign shown in a diagram the number of which is specified in column (2) of an item in the Table are those specified in column (3) of that item.

TABLE

(1) Item	(2) Diagram number	(3) Requirements
1	601.1	(a) Every vehicle shall stop before crossing the transverse line shown in diagram 1002.1 or, if that line is not clearly visible, before entering the major road in respect of which the sign shown in diagram 601.1 has been provided; and (b) no vehicle shall cross the transverse line shown in diagram 1002.1 or, if that line is not clearly visible, enter the major road in respect of which the sign shown in diagram 601.1 has been provided, so as to be likely to endanger the driver of or any passenger in any other vehicle or to cause that driver to change the speed or course of his vehicle in order to avoid an accident.
2	601.1 when used at a level crossing	(a) Every vehicle shall stop before crossing the transverse line shown in diagram 1002.1 or, if that line is not clearly visible, before entering the level crossing; and (b) no vehicle shall cross the transverse line shown in diagram 1002.1 or, if that line is not clearly visible, enter the level crossing, so as to be likely to endanger the driver of or any passenger in any railway vehicle or tramcar or to cause that driver to change the speed of his vehicle in order to avoid an accident.
3	602	No vehicle shall cross the transverse line shown in diagram 1003 nearer to the major road at the side of which that line is placed, or if that line is not clearly visible, enter that major road, so as to be likely to endanger the driver of or any passenger in any other vehicle or to cause that driver to change the speed or course of his vehicle in order to avoid an accident.
4	602 when placed in combination with 778 or 778.1	No vehicle shall cross the transverse line shown in diagram 1003 nearer to the level crossing at the side of which that line is placed, or if that line is not clearly visible, enter that level crossing, so as to be likely to endanger the driver of or any passenger in any railway vehicle or tramcar or to cause that driver to change the speed of his vehicle in order to avoid an accident.
5	611.1	(a) A vehicle entering the junction must give priority to vehicles coming from the right at the transverse road marking shown in diagram 1003.3 associated with the sign or, if the marking is not for the time being visible, at the junction; and (b) a vehicle proceeding through the junction must keep to the left of the white circle at the centre of the marking shown in diagram 1003.4, unless the size of the vehicle or the layout of the junction makes it impracticable to do so; and (c) no vehicle shall proceed past the marking shown in diagram 1003.4 in a manner or at a time likely— (i) to endanger any person, or (ii) to cause the driver of another vehicle to change its speed or course in order to avoid an accident.
6	784.1	No abnormal transport unit shall proceed onto or over a level crossing unless—

(1) Item	(2) Diagram number	(3) Requirements
		(a) the driver of the unit has used a telephone provided at or near the crossing for the purpose of obtaining from a person, authorised in that behalf by the railway or tramway authority, permission for the unit to proceed;
		(b) that permission has been obtained before the unit proceeds; and
		(c) the unit proceeds in accordance with any terms attached to that permission. Sub-paragraphs (b) and (c) above shall not apply if—
		(i) the driver uses the telephone at the crossing and receives an indication for not less than two minutes that the telephone at the other end of the telephone line is being called, but no duly authorised person answers it, or he receives no indication at all due to a fault or malfunction of the telephone; and
		(ii) the driver then drives the unit on to the crossing with the reasonable expectation of crossing it within times specified in a railway or tramway notice at the telephone as being times between which the railway vehicles or tramcars do not normally travel over that crossing.

(2) In this regulation—

"abnormal transport unit" means—

    (a) a motor vehicle or a vehicle combination—

        (i) the overall length of which, inclusive of the load (if any) on the vehicle or the combination, exceeds 61 feet 6 inches (18.75 metres); or

        (ii) the overall width of which, inclusive of the load (if any) on the vehicle or the combination, exceeds 9 feet 6 inches (2.9 metres); or

        (iii) the maximum gross weight of which exceeds 44 tonnes; or

    (b) a motor vehicle, or a vehicle combination, which in either case is incapable of proceeding, or is unlikely to proceed, over an automatic level crossing at a speed exceeding 5 mph;

"driver" in relation to an abnormal transport unit, means where that unit is a single motor vehicle the driver of that vehicle and, where that unit is a vehicle combination, the driver of the only or the foremost motor vehicle forming part of that combination; and

"vehicle combination" means a combination of vehicles made up of one or more motor vehicles and one or more trailers all of which are linked together when travelling.

---

1. The signs are as follows: diagram 601.1—STOP (see reg 16(1)(1)); diagram 602—GIVE WAY (see reg 16(1)(2)); diagram 611.1—GIVE PRIORITY TO VEHICLES FROM THE RIGHT; diagrams 778 and 778.1 – OPEN RAILWAY AND TRAMWAY CROSSINGS WITHOUT LIGHTS; diagram 784.1—DRIVERS OF LARGE VEHICLES TO STOP AND PHONE BEFORE CROSSING.

4–2993   14–24. *Contains general directions as to when a form of sign may be varied*

SECTION 4
ROAD MARKINGS

4–2994   25. Road marking shown in diagram 1003: give way. (1) The requirements conveyed to vehicular traffic on roads by the road marking consisting of the transverse lines shown in diagram 1003[1] shall be as follows.

(2) Except as provided by paragraphs (3) to (6), the requirement conveyed by the transverse lines shown in diagram 1003, whether or not they are placed in conjunction with the sign shown in diagram 602 or 1023[2], shall be that no vehicle shall proceed past such one of those lines as is nearer the major road into that road in a manner or at a time likely to endanger the driver of or any passenger in a vehicle on the major road or to cause the driver of such a vehicle to change its speed or course in order to avoid an accident.

(3) Wherever the transverse lines are placed in conjunction with the sign shown in diagram 602, and that sign is at the same time placed in combination with the sign shown in diagram 778 or 778.1[3] at a level crossing, then the requirement shall be that no vehicle shall proceed past such one of those lines as is nearer the level crossing in a manner or at a time likely to endanger the

driver of or any passenger in a railway vehicle or tramcar, or to cause that driver to change the speed of his vehicle in order to avoid an accident.

(4) Wherever the transverse lines are placed in advance of a point in the road where the width of the carriageway narrows significantly, then the requirement shall be that no vehicle shall proceed past such one of those lines as is nearer to the point of narrowing in a manner or at a time likely to endanger the driver of or any passenger in a vehicle that is proceeding in the opposite direction to the first-mentioned vehicle, or to cause the driver of such a vehicle to change its speed or course in order to avoid an accident.

(5) Where the transverse lines are placed in conjunction with the sign shown in diagram 611.1[4] at a junction marked with the road marking shown in diagram 1003.4[5], then the requirement shall be that no vehicle shall proceed past such one of those lines as is nearer to the road marking shown in diagram 1003.4 in a manner or at a time likely to endanger the driver of or any passenger in a vehicle circulating past that road marking from the right of the first-mentioned vehicle or to cause the driver of the second-mentioned vehicle to change its speed or course in order to avoid an accident.

(6) Where the transverse lines are placed in advance of a length of the carriageway of the road where a cycle track crosses the road along a route parallel to the transverse lines, then the requirement shall be that no vehicle shall proceed past such one of those lines as is nearer to the cycle track, in a manner or at a time likely to endanger any cyclist proceeding along the cycle track or to cause such a cyclist to change speed or course in order to avoid an accident.

---

1. Diagram 1003—two parallel horizontal broken white lines.
2. Diagram 602 is the triangular sign on a post; diagram 1023 the give way marking on the road (white triangle).
3. Diagrams 778 and 778.1 – OPEN RAILWAY AND TRAMWAY CROSSINGS WITHOUT LIGHTS;
4. Diagram 611.1 – GIVE PRIORITY TO VEHICLES FROM THE RIGHT
5. Diagram 1003.4 – ROAD MARKING AT MINI ROUNDABOUT.

4–2995 **26. Road markings shown in diagrams 1013.1, 1013.3 and 1013.4: double white lines.** (1) A road marking for conveying the requirements specified in paragraph (2) and the warning specified in paragraph (7) shall be of the size, colour and type shown in diagram 1013.1, 1013.3 or 1013.4[1].

(2) The requirements conveyed by a road marking mentioned in paragraph (1) shall be that—

(*a*) subject to paragraphs (3) and (5), no vehicle shall stop on any length of road along which the marking has been placed at any point between the ends of the marking; and

(*b*) subject to paragraph (6), every vehicle proceeding on any length of road along which the marking has been so placed that, as viewed in the direction of travel of the vehicle, a continuous line is on the left of a broken line or of another continuous line, shall be so driven as to keep the first-mentioned continuous line on the right hand or off side of the vehicle.

(3) Nothing in paragraph (2)(*a*) shall apply so as to prevent a vehicle stopping on any length of road so long as may be necessary for any of the purposes specified in paragraph (4) if the vehicle cannot be used for such a purpose without stopping on the length of road[2].

(4) The purposes are—

(*a*) to enable a person to board or alight from the vehicle,
(*b*) to enable goods to be loaded on to or to be unloaded from the vehicle,
(*c*) to enable the vehicle to be used in connection with—

   (i) any operation involving building, demolition or excavation;
   (ii) the removal of any obstruction to traffic;
   (iii) the maintenance, improvement or reconstruction of the length of road; or
   (iv) the laying, erection, alteration, repair or cleaning in or near the length of road of any sewer or of any main, pipe or apparatus for the supply of gas, water or electricity, or of any electronic communications apparatus kept installed for the purposes of an electronic communications code system or of any other electronic communications apparatus lawfully kept installed in any position.

(5) Nothing in paragraph (2)(*a*) shall apply—

(*a*) so as to prevent a vehicle stopping in a lay-by;
(*b*) to a vehicle for the time being used for relevant authority (as defined in section 6 of the Fire (Scotland) Act 2005 (asp 5) or, in England, fire and rescue authority, ambulance or police purposes;
(*ba*) as regards England and Wales, and so far as relating to the functions of the Serious Organised Crime Agency which are exercisable in or as regards Scotland and which relate to reserved matters (within the meaning of the Scotland Act 1998), to a vehicle for the time being used for Serious Organised Crime Agency purposes;
(*bb*) *Scotland*;
(*c*) to a pedal bicycle not having a sidecar attached thereto, whether additional means of propulsion by mechanical power are attached to the bicycle or not;
(*d*) to a vehicle stopping in any case where the person in control of the vehicle is required by law to stop, or is obliged to do so in order to avoid an accident, or is prevented from proceeding by circumstances outside his control;
(*e*) to anything done with the permission or at the direction of a constable in uniform or in accordance with the direction of a traffic warden; or
(*f*) to a vehicle on a road with more than one traffic lane in each direction.

(6) Nothing in paragraph (2)(*b*) shall be taken to prohibit a vehicle from being driven across, or so as to straddle, the continuous line referred to in that paragraph, if it is safe to do so and if necessary to do so—

(*a*) to enable the vehicle to enter, from the side of the road on which it is proceeding, land or premises adjacent to the length of road on which the line is placed, or another road joining that road;
(*b*) in order to pass a stationary vehicle;
(*c*) owing to circumstances outside the control of the driver;
(*d*) in order to avoid an accident[3];
(*e*) in order to pass a road maintenance vehicle which is in use, is moving at a speed not exceeding 10 mph, and is displaying to the rear the sign shown in diagram 610 or 7403;
(*f*) in order to pass a pedal cycle moving at a speed not exceeding 10 mph;
(*g*) in order to pass a horse that is being ridden or led at a speed not exceeding 10 mph; or
(*h*) for the purposes of complying with any direction of a constable in uniform or a traffic warden.

(7) The warning conveyed by a road marking mentioned in paragraph (1) shall be that no vehicle while travelling next to a broken line placed on the left of a continuous line, as viewed in the direction of travel of the vehicle, should cross or straddle the first-mentioned line unless it is seen by the driver of the vehicle to be safe to do so.

---

1. Diagram 1013.1 illustrates alternative methods of marking longitudinal lines to indicate to vehicular traffic the requirements and the warning prescribed by reg 26(2) and (7)—restrictions on stopping or crossing white lines. It incorporates the system of cross-hatching within widely-spaced continuous lines which has the same effect as double white lines but provides a greater separation between traffic lanes. This should be distinguished from cross-hatching between broken lines (illustrated by diagrams 1040, 1040.2, 1040.4, 1041and 1041.1) indicating that part of the carriageway which vehicular traffic should not enter unless it is seen by the driver to be safe to do so; also from chevrons between continuous lines (diagram 1042) indicating that part of the verge or hard shoulder on a motorway or convergence of motorways which vehicular traffic must not enter except in an emergency.
Where for some 30 millimetres the distance between two double white lines was 87 millimetres instead of the 90 millimetres minimum as prescribed in diagram 1013.1, it was held that the departure from the standard set down by the Regulations was so minimal it should be disregarded by the application of the *de minimis* principle (*Cotterill v Chapman* [1984] RTR 73).
2. The words "if the vehicle cannot be used for such a purpose without stopping on the length of road" apply only to reg 26(4)(*c*) and not to sub-paras (*a*) or (*b*) of reg 26(4) (*McKenzie v DPP* [1997] RTR 175).
3. For consideration of this defence see *R v Blything (Suffolk) Justices, ex p Knight* [1970] RTR 218.

4–2996 27. Road marking shown in diagram 1001.3: zig-zag lines—no stopping. (1) In this regulation and regulation 28—

"controlled area" means a length of carriageway—

(*a*) which is adjacent to a signal-controlled crossing facility and has a zig-zag line marked along each of its edges (with or without zig-zag lines also marked down its centre); and
(*b*) in or near which no other signs or markings have been placed except ones comprised in the combination of signs and markings indicating the presence of the facility or shown in diagram 610, 611, 612, 613, 616, 810, 1029 or 1062;

"local service" does not include an excursion or tour as defined by section 137(1) of the Transport Act 1985; and
"vehicle" does not include a pedal bicycle not having a sidecar attached to it, whether or not additional means of propulsion by mechanical power are attached to the bicycle.

(2) Subject to paragraphs (3) and (4) and without prejudice to regulation 28, a zig-zag line shall convey the requirement that the driver of a vehicle shall not cause any part of it to stop in the controlled area in which it is marked.

(3) Paragraph (2) does not prohibit the driver of a vehicle from stopping it in a controlled area—

(*a*) if the driver has stopped it for the purpose of complying with an indication given by a light signal for the control of vehicular traffic or the direction of a constable in uniform or a traffic warden;
(*b*) if the driver is prevented from proceeding by circumstances beyond his control or it is necessary for him to stop to avoid injury or damage to persons or property; or
(*c*) when the vehicle is being used for police, relevant authority (as defined in section 6 of the Fire (Scotland) Act 2005 (asp 5) or, in England, fire and rescue authority or ambulance purposes; or
(*d*) as regards England and Wales, and so far as relating to the functions of the Serious Organised Crime Agency which are exercisable in or as regards Scotland and which relate to reserved matters (within the meaning of the Scotland Act 1998), when the vehicle is being used for Serious Organised Crime Agency purposes; or
(*e*) *Scotland.*

(4) Paragraph (2) does not prohibit the driver of a vehicle from stopping it in a controlled area—

(*a*) for so long as may be necessary to enable the vehicle to be used for the purposes of—

(i) any operation involving building, demolition or excavation;
(ii) the removal of any obstruction to traffic;
(iii) the maintenance, improvement or reconstruction of a road; or

   (iv) the laying, erection, alteration, repair or cleaning in or near the controlled area of any sewer or of any main, pipe or apparatus for the supply of gas, water or electricity, or of any electronic communications apparatus kept installed for the purposes of an electronic communications code system or of any other electronic communications apparatus lawfully kept installed in any position;

  (b) in the provision of a local service, and the vehicle, having proceeded past the light signals to which the controlled area relates, is waiting in that area in order to take up or set down passengers; or

  (c) if he stops the vehicle for the purpose of making a left or right turn.

4–2997   28. Road marking shown in diagram 1001.3: zig-zag lines—no overtaking.   (1) Without prejudice to regulation 27, a zig-zag line shall convey the requirement that, whilst any motor vehicle (in this regulation called "the approaching vehicle") or any part of it is within the limits of a controlled area and is proceeding towards the signal-controlled crossing facility to which the controlled area relates, the driver of the vehicle shall not cause it or any part of it—

  (a) to pass ahead of the foremost part of any other motor vehicle proceeding in the same direction; or

  (b) to pass ahead of the foremost part of a vehicle which is stationary for the purpose of complying with the indication given by a traffic light signal for controlling vehicular traffic.

  (2) In paragraph (1)—

  (a) the reference to a motor vehicle in sub-paragraph (a) is, in a case where more than one motor vehicle is proceeding in the same direction as the approaching vehicle in a controlled area, a reference to the motor vehicle nearest to the signal-controlled crossing facility to which the controlled area relates; and

  (b) the reference to a stationary vehicle is, in a case where more than one vehicle is stationary in a controlled area for the purpose of complying with the indication given by a traffic light signal for controlling vehicular traffic, a reference to the stationary vehicle nearest the signal-controlled crossing facility to which the controlled area relates.

4–2998   29. Road markings shown in diagrams 1025.1, 1025.3, 1025.4, 1043 and 1044: bus stop and bus stand clearways and box junctions.   (1) The road markings shown in diagrams 1025.1, 1025.3 and 1025.4 shall convey the prohibition specified in Part I of Schedule 19.

  (2) The road markings shown in diagrams 1043 and 1044 shall convey the prohibition specified in Part II of Schedule 19.

4–2999   30. Permitted variants of road markings.   (1) Where the circumstances in which a road marking shown in a diagram in Schedule 6 is to be placed so require or where appropriate in those circumstances, the form of the marking shall or may be varied as follows—

  (a) in the manner (if any) allowed or required in item 4 of the untitled table below or beside the diagram; or

  (b) in the manner allowed or required in column (3) of an item in Schedule 16, if the diagram is one whose number is given in column (2) of that item.

  (2) In the road marking shown in diagram 1035, route numbers, place names and the direction in which any arrow-head points shall be varied to accord with the circumstances but the words "turn left", "ahead" or "turn right" shall not be included in the marking.

  (3) Where the form of a road marking is varied in accordance with this regulation, the information, warning, requirement, restriction, prohibition or speed limit conveyed by the marking is varied to accord with the form of marking as varied.

4–3000   31. Illumination of road markings.   (1) Subject to paragraph (2) a road marking shown in diagram 1001 (except when used in conjunction with the road marking shown in diagram 1001.3), 1001.1, 1001.2, 1002.1, 1003, 1003.1, 1003.3, 1003.4, 1004, 1004.1, 1005, 1005.1, 1008, 1008.1, 1009, 1010, 1012.1, 1012.2, 1012.3, 1013.1, 1013.3, 1013.4, 1014, 1022, 1023, 1024, 1024.1, 1036.1, 1036.2, 1037.1, 1039, 1040, 1040.2, 1040.3, 1040.4, 1040.5, 1041, 1041.1, 1042, 1042.1, 1046, 1049, 1062, 1064 or 1065 shall be reflectorised.

  (2) Paragraph (1) shall not apply to a road marking shown in diagram 1003, 1023 or 1049 when varied for use on a cycle track.

  (3) Subject to paragraph (4), studs incorporating reflectors or retroreflecting material and so spaced as to form a single line of studs not less than 3 nor more than 4.5 metres apart shall be fitted—

  (a) between the two lines constituting the marking shown in diagram 1013.1, except where that marking is so placed that the continuous lines shown in version B of diagram 1013.1 are more than 175 millimetres apart and are separated by an area of cross-hatching so shown;

  (b) between the two continuous parallel lines forming part of the marking shown in diagrams 1013.3 and 1013.4.

  (4) Where the marking shown in diagram 1013.1 is placed as mentioned in the exception to paragraph (3)(a), the studs mentioned in paragraph (3) shall be fitted either in opposite pairs within the width of each of the two lines or in a single line between those lines.

  (5) Subject to the foregoing provisions of this regulation, and to paragraph (6), any road marking may be reflectorised, and studs incorporating reflectors or retroreflecting material may

be used with a road marking shown in diagram 1004, 1004.1, 1005, 1005.1, 1008, 1008.1, 1010, 1012.1, 1012.2, 1012.3, 1025.3, 1025.4, 1035, 1040, 1040.2, 1040.3, 1040.4, 1040.5, 1041, 1041.1, 1042 or 1042.1 in such a manner that any such stud shall not be fitted to any part of the marking coloured white or yellow but shall be applied to the surface of the carriageway in the gaps between parts of a broken line, or alongside a solid line, forming part of the marking.

(6) In the case of a road marking shown in diagram 1012.1, 1012.2, 1012.3, 1042 or 1042.1 the studs shall, if fitted, be applied to the surface of the carriageway at the side of and adjacent to the line shown in the diagram.

(7) Reflectors or retroreflecting material incorporated in studs shall be white except that in the case of studs used with a road marking shown in diagram 1010, 1012.1, 1012.2, 1012.3, 1025.3, 1025.4, 1040.3, 1040.4, 1040.5, 1041, 1041.1, 1042 or 1042.1 the reflectors or retroreflecting material shall reflect—

(a) red light—

   (i) when placed in conjunction with the marking shown in diagram 1041, 1041.1, 1042 or 1042.1 to indicate the off side (as viewed in the direction of travel) edge of the carriageway of any road;

   (ii) when placed in conjunction with a road marking to indicate the near side (as viewed in the direction of travel) edge of the carriageway of any road, except a motorway alongside which there is an actively managed hard shoulder; or

   (iii) when placed in conjunction with the marking shown in diagram 1012.1 to indicate the boundary between the carriageway of a motorway and an actively managed hard shoulder;

(b) amber light to indicate the off side edge of a carriageway which—

   (i) is contiguous to a central reservation or to traffic cones or cylinders at road works or to the road marking shown in diagram 1040.3; or

   (ii) carries traffic in one direction only; and

(c) green light when placed in conjunction with a road marking shown in diagram 1010, 1025.3 or 1025.4 where the edge of any part of the carriageway available for through traffic at a junction, a lay-by or a parking place is so indicated to drivers of approaching vehicles.

(8) The colour of the parts of the stud other than the reflectors or retroreflecting material shall either be the same as the reflectors or retroreflecting material, or be white, or be a natural metallic finish or other neutral colour, or shall be fluorescent green/yellow in the case of studs placed temporarily at road works.

4-3000A 32. Height of road markings and size of studs. (1) The size and shape of a stud incorporating reflectors or retroreflecting material shall be such that the part which is visible above the surface of the road can be contained within—

(a) an overall length in the direction of travel of traffic of not less than 35 millimetres and not exceeding 250 millimetres; and

(b) an overall width of not less than 84 millimetres and not exceeding 190 millimetres.

(2) No road marking or stud shall project above the surface of the adjacent carriageway more than 6 millimetres at any point except—

(a) a depressible stud, which shall not project above that surface more than 25 millimetres at its highest point, whether depressed or not;

(b) a non-depressible stud, which shall not project above that surface more than 20 millimetres at its highest point;

(c) the central circular part of the road marking shown in diagram 1003.4, which shall not project above that surface more than 125 millimetres at its highest point or 6 millimetres at its perimeter;

(d) the road marking shown in diagram 1012.2, the raised ribs on which shall project above the surface of the remainder of the marking by not more than 11 millimetres; or

(e) the road marking shown in diagram 1012.3, the raised ribs on which shall project above the surface of the remainder of the marking by not more than 8 millimetres; and

(f) the road marking shown in diagram 1049.1, the height of which above the surface of the adjacent carriageway shall be within the range of dimensions indicated on the second part of that diagram illustrating the cross-section of the marking.

(3) In this regulation, the expression "depressible stud" means a stud so fitted that the height by which it, or part of it, projects above the surface of the adjacent carriageway is apt to be reduced when pressure is applied to the stud from above; and "non-depressible stud" and "depressed" shall be construed accordingly.

SECTION 5
LIGHT SIGNALS AND WARNING LIGHTS

4-3000B 33. Light signals for the control of vehicular traffic—standard form. (1) Subject to regulation 34, light signals for the control of vehicular traffic (other than tramcars) at junctions, at places where the headroom or the width of the road is permanently restricted, or at signal controlled crossing facilities—

(a) shall be of the size, colour and type shown in diagram 3000, 3000.7, 3000.8, 3000.9 or 3000.10;

(b) shall be illuminated in the sequence prescribed by paragraph (3); and

(c) shall have ES compliant signal heads.

(2) Light signals for the control of vehicular traffic consisting exclusively of pedal cycles—

(a) shall be of the size, colour and type shown in diagram 3000.2;
(b) shall be illuminated in the sequence prescribed by paragraph (3); and
(c) shall have ES compliant signal heads.

(3) The sequence of illumination of the lights shown by the signals prescribed by paragraphs (1) and (2) shall be as follows—

(a) red,
(b) red and amber together,
(c) green,
(d) amber.

(4) Where the light signals are varied as prescribed by regulation 34, one or more green arrows shown in diagram 3001.2 or 3001.3 may be illuminated whilst any of the lights referred to in paragraph (3) are illuminated.

(5) For the purposes of these Regulations a signal head is "ES compliant" if, in relation to each aspect of its performance specified in column (2) of an item in the Table, it complies with the requirement or test specification of European Standard EN12368: 2000 specified in column (3) of the item or to an equivalent requirement or test specification specified in a corresponding EEA standard.

Table

(1) Item	(2) Aspect of performance	(3) Requirement or test specification and class
1	Protection rating	Class IV: IP 55
2	Operating temperature range	Class A
3	Luminous intensity	Performance level 3, class 2
4	Distribution of luminous intensity	Type M
5	Maximum signal phantom	Class 5
6	Signal lights incorporating symbols	Class S1
7	Background screen	Class C1
8	Impact resistance	Class IR2

4–3000C   34. Green arrow light signals for the control of vehicular traffic. (1) A lens or lenses of the size and colour shown in diagram 3001.2 or 3001.3 which, when illuminated, shows a green arrow—

(a) may be substituted for the lens showing the green light in the light signals referred to in regulation 33(1) using any of the methods shown in diagram 3000.8 or 3000.10; or
(b) may be affixed to the light signals referred to in regulation 33(1) or to those signals as altered in accordance with sub-paragraph (a) using any of the methods shown in diagrams 3000.7, 3000.8, 3000.9 and 3000.10.

(2) The direction of the arrow shown in indication B in diagram 3001.2 or 3001.3 may be varied so that the head of the arrow points to any position lying between indication A and indication C.

(3) The direction of the arrow shown in indication D in diagram 3001.2 or 3001.3 may be varied so that the head of the arrow points to any position lying between indication C and indication E.

4–3000D   35. Portable light signals for the control of vehicular traffic. Portable light signals for the control of vehicular traffic other than tramcars shall be—

(a) of the size, colour and type shown in diagram 3000.1;
(b) illuminated in the sequence prescribed by regulation 33(3); and
(c) so constructed that, if European Standard EN12368: 2000 applied to portable signals, they would be ES compliant.

4–3000E   36. Significance of light signals prescribed by regulations 33 to 35. (1) The significance of the light signals prescribed by regulations 33, 34 and 35 shall be as follows—

(a) subject to sub-paragraph (b) and sub-paragraph (ba) and sub-paragraph (bb) and, where the red signal is shown at the same time as the green arrow signal, to sub-paragraphs (f) and (g), the red signal shall convey the prohibition that vehicular traffic shall not proceed beyond the stop line;

(*b*)   when a vehicle is being used for relevant authority (as defined in section 6 of the Fire (Scotland) Act 2005 (asp 5) or, in England, fire and rescue authority, ambulance, bomb or explosive disposal, national blood service or police purposes and the observance of the prohibition conveyed by the red signal in accordance with sub-paragraph (*a*) would be likely to hinder the use of that vehicle for the purpose for which it is being used, then sub-paragraph (*a*) shall not apply to the vehicle, and the red signal shall convey the prohibition that that vehicle shall not proceed beyond the stop line in a manner or at a time likely to endanger any person or to cause the driver of any vehicle proceeding in accordance with the indications of light signals operating in association with the signals displaying the red signal to change its speed or course in order to avoid an accident;

(*ba*) as regards England and Wales, and so far as relating to the functions of the Serious Organised Crime Agency which are exercisable in or as regards Scotland and which relate to reserved matters (within the meaning of the Scotland Act 1998), when a vehicle is being used for Serious Organised Crime Agency purposes and the observance of the prohibition conveyed by the red signal in accordance with sub-paragraph (*a*) would be likely to hinder the use of that vehicle for those purposes, then sub-paragraph (*a*) shall not apply to the vehicle, and the red signal shall convey the prohibition that that vehicle shall not proceed beyond the stop line in a manner or at a time likely to endanger any person or to cause the driver of any vehicle proceeding in accordance with the indications of light signals operating in association with the signals displaying the red signal to change its speed or course in order to avoid an accident;

(*bb*) *Scotland*;

(*c*)   the red-with-amber signal shall, subject in a case where it is displayed at the same time as the green arrow signal to sub-paragraph (*f*), denote an impending change to green or a green arrow in the indication given by the signals but shall convey the same prohibition as the red signal;

(*d*)   the green signal shall indicate that vehicular traffic may proceed beyond the stop line and proceed straight on or to the left or to the right;

(*e*)   the amber signal shall, when shown alone, convey the same prohibition as the red signal, except that, as respects any vehicle which is so close to the stop line that it cannot safely be stopped without proceeding beyond the stop line, it shall convey the same indication as the green signal or green arrow signal which was shown immediately before it;

(*f*)   save as provided in sub-paragraphs (*g*) and (*h*), the green arrow signal shall indicate that vehicular traffic may, notwithstanding any other indication given by the signals, proceed beyond the stop line only in the direction indicated by the arrow for the purpose of proceeding in that direction through the junction controlled by those signals;

(*g*)   where more than one green arrow is affixed to light signals in accordance with regulation 34(1)(*b*), vehicular traffic, notwithstanding any other indication given by the signals, may proceed beyond the stop line only in the direction indicated by any one of the green arrows for the purpose of proceeding in that direction through the junction controlled by those signals; and

(*h*)   where the green arrow signal is displayed at the same time as the green signal, vehicular traffic may proceed in the direction indicated by the green arrow in accordance with sub-paragraph (*g*) or in any other direction in accordance with sub-paragraph (*d*).

(2) Vehicular traffic proceeding beyond a stop line in accordance with paragraph (1) shall proceed with due regard to the safety of other road users and subject to any direction given by a constable in uniform or a traffic warden or to any other applicable prohibition or restriction.

(3) In this regulation the expressions "vehicle" and "vehicular traffic" do not include tramcars.

4–3000F   37. Light signals for the control of vehicular traffic on motorways and all-purpose dual carriageway roads.   (1) Subject to paragraph (4), light signals for the control of vehicular traffic entering or proceeding along a motorway, shall be—

(*a*)   of the size, colour and type shown in diagram 6031.1 or 6032.1; and
(*b*)   operated in accordance with the requirements specified in paragraph (2).

(2) The requirements are that—

(*a*)   each lamp shall show an intermittent red light at a rate of flashing of not less than 60 nor more than 90 flashes per minute, and in such a manner that the lights of one vertical pair are always shown when the lights of the other vertical pair are not shown; and
(*b*)   the red cross or the white symbol shown in diagram 6031.1 or 6032.1 shall be illuminated by a steady light when the red lights are flashing.

(3) Light signals for the control of vehicular traffic entering or proceeding along an all-purpose dual carriageway road may also be the size, colour and type prescribed by paragraph (1) and operated in accordance with the requirements specified in paragraph (2).

(4) Light signals for the control of vehicular traffic—

(*a*)   entering a motorway by means of a slip road; or
(*b*)   entering a motorway which is a roundabout may, instead of complying with paragraphs (1) and (2), be of the size, colour and type prescribed by regulation 33 or 34.

4–3000G   38. Significance of light signals prescribed by regulation 37(1).   (1) The significance of the light signals prescribed by regulation 37(1) shall be as follows.

(2) The signals shown in diagram 6032.1 shall convey the prohibition that vehicular traffic

(other than vehicles being used in the circumstances described in regulation 36(1)(*b*)) on the carriageway beside which the signals are mounted shall not proceed beyond the signals.

(3) When displayed over the carriageway of a road, the signals shown in diagram 6031.1 shall convey the prohibition that vehicular traffic (other than vehicles being used in the circumstances described in regulation 36(1)(*b*)) proceeding in the traffic lane immediately below the signals shall not proceed beyond them in that lane.

(4) When displayed over an actively managed hard shoulder, the signals shown in diagram 6031.1 shall convey the prohibition that vehicular traffic (other than vehicles being used in the circumstances described in regulation 36(1)(*b*)) shall not enter the hard shoulder beyond the signals for any purpose.

4–3000H 39. Light signals to control traffic at level crossings etc. (1) Light signals for the control of traffic at level crossings, swinging or lifting bridges, tunnels, airfields or in the vicinity of premises used regularly by fire, police or ambulance service vehicles shall—

   (*a*) be of the size, colour and type shown in diagram 3014;
   (*b*) be illuminated in the sequence prescribed by paragraph (2); and
   (*c*) have ES compliant signal heads.

(2) The sequence for the illumination of the light signals prescribed by paragraph (1) shall be as follows—

   (*a*) a single steady amber light,
   (*b*) two intermittent red lights, each of which will be shown at a rate of flashing of not less than 60 nor more than 90 flashes per minute, and in a such a manner that one light is always shown when the other light is not shown.

4–3000I 40. Significance of light signals prescribed by regulation 39. The significance of the light signals prescribed by regulation 39 shall be as follows—

   (*a*) the amber signal shall convey the prohibition that traffic shall not proceed beyond the stop line or the road marking shown in diagram 1003.2, except that a vehicle which is so close to the stop line that it cannot safely be stopped without proceeding beyond the stop line may proceed across the level crossing; and
   (*b*) the intermittent red signals shall convey the prohibition that traffic shall not proceed beyond the stop line or the road marking shown in diagram 1003.2.

4–3000J 41. Light signals for the control of tramcars. (1) Light signals for the control of tramcars shall—

   (*a*) be of the size, colour and type shown in diagram 3013; and
   (*b*) display the aspects shown in diagrams 3013.1, 3013.2, 3013.3, 3013.4 and 3013.5 in the sequence prescribed by paragraph (2).

(2) The sequence for the illumination of the light signals prescribed by paragraph (1) shall be as follows—

   (*a*) the horizontal line shown in diagram 3013.1,
   (*b*) the vertical line shown in diagram 3013.2 or either of the diagonal lines shown in diagram 3013.3 or 3013.4,
   (*c*) the central circle shown in diagram 3013.5.

(3) When the light signals prescribed by paragraph (1) ("tram signals") are affixed to the light signals mentioned in regulation 33 ("standard signals") in accordance with any of the options shown in diagrams 3000.7, 3000.8, 3000.9 and 3000.10 their aspect may be such that they convey to the driver of a tramcar a different significance from that conveyed at the same time in accordance with regulation 36 to the drivers of other vehicular traffic by the aspect of the standard signals to which the tram signals are affixed.

4–3000K 42. Significance of light signals prescribed by regulation 41. The significance of the light signals prescribed by regulation 41 shall be as follows—

   (*a*) the aspect shown in diagram 3013.1 shall convey the prohibition that a tramcar shall not proceed beyond the stop line;
   (*b*) the aspect shown in diagram 3013.2 shall indicate that a tramcar may proceed beyond the stop line and proceed straight ahead;
   (*c*) the aspect shown in diagram 3013.3 shall indicate that a tramcar may proceed beyond the stop line and proceed to the left;
   (*d*) the aspect shown in diagram 3013.4 shall indicate that a tramcar may proceed beyond the stop line and proceed to the right; and
   (*e*) the aspect shown in diagram 3013.5 shall convey the prohibition that a tramcar shall not proceed beyond the stop line except that, as respects a tramcar which is so close to the stop line that it cannot safely be stopped without proceeding beyond the stop line, it shall convey the same indication as the aspect which was shown immediately before it.

4–3000L 43. Meaning of stop line and references to light signals. (1) Subject to paragraphs (2) and (3), "stop line" in relation to light signals for the control of vehicular traffic means—

   (*a*) in relation to any vehicle except a tramcar the road marking shown in diagram 1001 placed in conjunction with the light signals;

(*b*) in relation to a tramcar, the road marking shown in diagram 1001.1 placed in conjunction with those light signals, or when that marking has not been so placed, the marking shown in diagram 1001 so placed.

(2) Where the road marking shown in diagram 1001.2 has been placed in conjunction with light signals, "stop line" in relation to those light signals means—

(*a*) the first stop line, in the case of a vehicle (other than a pedal cycle proceeding in the cycle lane) which has not proceeded beyond that line; or

(*b*) the second stop line, in the case of a vehicle which has proceeded beyond the first stop line or of a pedal cycle proceeding in the cycle lane.

(3) Where no stop line has been provided in conjunction with light signals or the stop line is not visible, references in relation to those signals to the "stop line" are—

(*a*) in a case where the sign shown in diagram 7011, 7011.1 or 7027 is placed in conjunction with the light signals, to be treated as references to that sign; and

(*b*) in any other case, to be treated as references to the post or other structure on which the primary signals are mounted.

(4) A reference in this regulation or in regulations 33 to 42 to light signals, to the signals or to a signal of a particular colour is, where secondary signals as well as primary signals have been placed, a reference to the light signals displayed by both the primary and secondary signals or, as the case may be, by the primary signals operating without the secondary signals or by the secondary signals operating without the primary signals.

(5) In this regulation—

(*a*) "primary signals" means light signals erected on or near the carriageway of a road and—

  (i) where a stop line is placed in conjunction with the signals, sited beyond that line and near one end or both ends of the line; or

  (ii) where there is no stop line, sited at either edge or both edges of the carriageway or part of the carriageway which is in use by traffic approaching and controlled by the signals;

(*b*) "secondary signals" means light signals erected on or near the carriageway facing traffic approaching from the direction of the primary signals but sited beyond those signals as viewed from the direction of travel of such traffic; and

(*c*) in paragraph (2)—

  (i) "the first stop line" means the transverse white line or lines appearing below the pedal cycle symbol in the road markings shown in either version of diagram 1001.2;

  (ii) "the second stop line" means the transverse white line appearing above the pedal cycle symbol in the road markings shown in either version of that diagram; and

  (iii) "the cycle lane" means the lane so marked in either version of that diagram.

4–3000M   44. Light signals for lane control of vehicular traffic.   (1) A light signal placed above the carriageway and facing the direction of oncoming vehicular traffic used for the control of that traffic proceeding along the traffic lane over which those signals have been placed shall be of the size, colour and type of any diagram shown in Part I of Schedule 10.

(2) The height of the centre of each light signal from the surface of the carriageway in the immediate vicinity shall be not less than 5.5 metres nor more than 9 metres.

(3) The signals prescribed by this regulation shall be so designed that—

(*a*) the red cross shown in diagram 5003 or 5003.1 ("the red cross") can be internally illuminated in such a manner as to show a steady red light;

(*b*) the green arrow shown in diagram 5001.1 or 5001.2 ("the downward green arrow") can be internally illuminated in such a manner as to show a steady green light;

(*c*) the white arrow shown in diagram 5005 or 5005.1 ("the diagonal white arrow") can be internally illuminated in such a manner as to show a steady white light; and

(*d*) whenever one of the signals referred to in sub-paragraphs (*a*) to (*c*) is illuminated neither of the other signals referred to in those sub-paragraphs shall be illuminated when placed over the same traffic lane.

(4) The significance of the light signals prescribed by this regulation shall be as follows—

(*a*) except when placed above an actively managed hard shoulder, the red cross shall convey to vehicular traffic proceeding in the traffic lane above which it is displayed the prohibition that such traffic shall not proceed beyond the red cross in the traffic lane until that prohibition is cancelled by a display over that traffic lane of the downward green arrow or diagonal white arrow or by a display over that traffic lane or beside the carriageway of the traffic sign shown in diagram 5015;

(*aa*) when placed over an actively managed hard shoulder the red cross shall convey to vehicular traffic that the restrictions on the use of the hard shoulder imposed by regulation 9 of the Motorways (England and Wales) Regulations or regulation 8 of the Motorways (Scotland) Regulations for the time being apply to the hard shoulder, until those restrictions are—

  (i) cancelled by the display over the actively managed hard shoulder of the sign shown in diagram 670 by means of a variable message sign; or

  (ii) superseded by the display over the actively managed hard shoulder of the sign shown in diagram 6031.1;

(b) the downward green arrow shall convey to vehicular traffic proceeding in the traffic lane above which it is displayed the information that such traffic may proceed or continue to do so in the lane beneath the arrow; and

(c) the diagonal white arrow shall convey to vehicular traffic proceeding in the traffic lane above which it is displayed the warning that such traffic should move into the adjacent traffic lane in the direction indicated by the arrow as soon as traffic conditions permit.

4–3000N 45. Warning signal for motorways and all-purpose dual carriageway roads. (1) A traffic sign for conveying the warning specified in paragraph (2) to vehicular traffic on a motorway or an all-purpose dual carriageway road shall be a light signal of the size, colour and type shown in diagram 6023.

(2) The warning conveyed by the light signal shall be that—

(a) there is a hazard ahead on the motorway or all-purpose dual carriageway road; and

(b) drivers should drive at a speed which does not exceed 30 mph until they are certain that the hazard has been passed or removed.

(3) When the light signal prescribed by this regulation is operated, each lamp shall show an intermittent amber light at a rate of flashing of not less than 60 nor more than 90 flashes per minute and in such a manner that one light is always shown when the other light is not shown.

4–3000O 46. Matrix signs for motorways and all-purpose dual carriageway roads. (1) In this regulation "matrix sign" means a sign shown in a diagram in Part I of Schedule 11 for conveying to traffic on a motorway or an all-purpose dual carriageway road information or a warning, requirement, restriction, prohibition or speed limit—

(a) relating to or arising out of temporary hazardous conditions on or near the motorway or dual carriageway road; and

(b) specified in the caption to a diagram contained in Part I of that Schedule.

(2) A matrix sign shall be a light signal and shall be of the size, colour and type prescribed by this regulation and shown in a diagram in Part I of Schedule 11.

(3) Where a matrix sign is placed beside the carriageway of a road the warning, requirement, restriction, prohibition or speed limit conveyed by the sign shall apply to all vehicular traffic facing that sign and proceeding along the carriageway beside which the sign is placed.

(4) For the purposes of this regulation a sign which is mounted on a post situated beside the carriageway but is projected over it or part of it shall be treated as a sign placed beside the carriageway of that road.

(5) Where a matrix sign mounted on a gantry or other structure is so placed that a traffic lane of the carriageway or an actively managed hard shoulder passes directly beneath it, the warning, requirement, restriction, prohibition or speed limit conveyed by the sign shall apply only to vehicular traffic facing that sign and proceeding along the traffic lane or an actively managed hard shoulder passing directly beneath it.

(6) A legend or symbol shown on a matrix sign shall be displayed by means of white or off-white light and except in the case of the signs shown in diagrams 6006.2, 6008.1, 6009.3 and 6012 shall be accompanied by the four lamps prescribed by paragraph (7).

(7) The four lamps mentioned in paragraph (6)—

(a) shall be of the size, colour and type shown in diagram 6022 when placed beside the carriageway or in diagram 6021 when mounted on a gantry or other structure over the carriageway; and

(b) when a matrix sign other than those shown in diagrams 6006.2, 6008.1, 6009.3 and 6012 is displayed, each lamp shall show an intermittent amber light at a rate of flashing of not less than 60 nor more than 90 flashes per minute and in such a manner that one horizontal pair of lights is always shown when the other horizontal pair of lights is not shown.

(8) The signs shown in diagrams 6006.2, 6008.1 and 6009.3 shall be accompanied by the four red lamps prescribed by regulation 37.

4–3000P 47. Light signals at signal-controlled pedestrian facilities. (1) In this regulation "the crossing", in relation to a sign, means the signal-controlled pedestrian facility in relation to which the sign is placed.

(2) A sign for conveying to pedestrian traffic the warning and information specified in paragraph (4) shall—

(a) be of the size, colour and type shown in diagram 4002.1; or

(b) consist of either a single unit of the size, colour and type shown in diagram 4003.1 or of two units, one comprising the upper and the other the lower part of that unit placed close together,

and shall comply with the requirements of paragraph (3).

(3) The requirements are that the sign is so designed and constructed that—

(a) the red figure in the sign ("the red signal") can be internally illuminated by a steady light;

(b) the green figure in the sign ("the green signal") can be internally illuminated by a steady light;

(c) when one signal is illuminated the other is not;

(d) the green signal is illuminated only when there is at the same time conveyed to vehicular traffic a prohibition against entering the crossing and the prohibition is indicated by—

    (i) the light signals prescribed by regulation 33 (whether or not varied in accordance with regulation 34) or 41; or

    (ii) those light signals and the sign shown in diagram 606, 612, 613 or 616;

(*e*) in the case of the sign shown in diagram 4003.1, a push button or other switching device is included which, whilst the red signal is illuminated, in some way indicates to pedestrians whether it has been activated; and

(*f*) in the case of the sign shown in diagram 4002.1, the signal heads are ES compliant.

    (4) The red signal, whilst it is illuminated, shall indicate the period during which, in the interests of safety, pedestrians should not use the crossing and the green signal, whilst it is illuminated, shall indicate the period during which pedestrians may use the crossing.

    (5) Where the sign shown in diagram 4003.1 is provided at a crossing, any additional device which—

(*a*) is of the size, colour and type of only the part of that sign which shows the red and green signals or of only the part which includes the push button and the legend above it;

(*b*) complies with the requirements of paragraph (3) so far as they are relevant to it; and

(*c*) is provided to supplement the indications given by the sign shown in diagram 4003.1,

shall give the same indication as the relevant part of the sign shown in that diagram.

    (6) A push button device giving instructions to pedestrians on how to cause the green signal in the sign shown in diagram 4002.1 to become illuminated and explaining the significance of the red and green signals shall be of the size, colour and type shown in diagram 4003.

    (7) The sign shown in diagram 4003 shall, whilst the word "WAIT" is illuminated, convey the same indication as the red signal.

    (8) Any audible or tactile signal emitted by a device provided in conjunction with the green signal for the benefit of disabled persons shall convey to pedestrians the same indication as the green signal.

4–3000Q   **48. Light signals at equestrian crossings.** (1) In this regulation "the crossing" in relation to a sign means the equestrian crossing in relation to which the sign is placed.

    (2) A sign for conveying to equestrian traffic the warning and information specified in paragraph (4) shall—

(*a*) be of the size, colour and type shown in diagram 4003.2; or

(*b*) consist of either a single unit of the size, colour and type shown in diagram 4003.4 or of two units, one comprising the upper and the other the lower part of that unit placed close together,

and shall comply with the requirements of paragraph (3).

    (3) The requirements are that the sign is so designed and constructed that—

(*a*) the red symbol in the sign ("the red signal") can be internally illuminated by a steady light;

(*b*) the green symbol in the sign ("the green signal") can be internally illuminated by a steady light;

(*c*) when one signal is illuminated the other is not;

(*d*) the green signal is illuminated only when there is at the same time conveyed to vehicular traffic a prohibition against entering the crossing and the prohibition is indicated by—

    (i) the light signals prescribed by regulation 33 (whether or not varied in accordance with regulation 34) or 41; or

    (ii) those light signals and the sign shown in diagram 606, 612, 613 or 616;

(*e*) in the case of the sign shown in diagram 4003.4, a push button or other switching device is included which, whilst the red signal is illuminated, in some way indicates to equestrians whether it has been activated; and

(*f*) in the case of the sign shown in diagram 4003.2, the signal heads are ES compliant.

    (4) The red signal, whilst it is illuminated, shall indicate the period during which, in the interests of safety, equestrian traffic should not use the crossing and the green signal, whilst it is illuminated, shall indicate the time during which such traffic may use the crossing.

    (5) Where the sign shown in diagram 4003.4 is provided at a crossing, any additional device which—

(*a*) is of the size, colour and type of only the part of that sign which shows the red and green signals or of only the part which includes the push button and the legend above it;

(*b*) complies with the requirements of paragraph (3) so far as they are relevant to it; and

(*c*) is provided to supplement the indications given by the sign shown in diagram 4003.4,

shall give the same indication as the relevant part of the sign shown in that diagram.

    (6) A push button device giving instructions to equestrians on how to cause the green signal in the sign shown in diagram 4003.2 to become illuminated and explaining the significance of the red and green signals shall be of the size, colour and type shown in diagram 4003.3.

    (7) The sign shown in diagram 4003.3 shall, whilst the word "WAIT" is illuminated, convey the same indication as the red signal.

4–3000R   **49. Light signals at Toucan crossings.** (1) In this regulation "the crossing" in relation to a sign means the Toucan crossing in relation to which the sign is placed.

    (2) A sign for conveying to pedestrians and pedal cyclists the warning and information specified in paragraph (4) shall—

(*a*) be of the size, colour and type shown in diagram 4003.5; or

  (b) consist of either a single unit of the size, colour and type shown in diagram 4003.7 or of two units, one comprising the upper and the other the lower part of that unit placed close together,

and shall comply with the requirements of paragraph (3).

  (3) The requirements are that the sign is so designed and constructed that—

  (a) the red figures in the signs shown in diagrams 4003.5 and 4003.7 and the red cycle symbol in diagram 4003.7 ("the red signal") can be internally illuminated by a steady light;

  (b) the green figure and the green cycle symbol ("the green signal") can be internally illuminated by a steady light;

  (c) when one signal is illuminated the other is not;

  (d) the green signal is illuminated only when there is at the same time conveyed to vehicular traffic, other than pedal cyclists wishing to use the crossing, a prohibition against entering the crossing and the prohibition is indicated by—

    (i) the light signals prescribed by regulation 33 (whether or not varied in accordance with regulation 34) or 41; or

    (ii) those light signals and the sign shown in diagram 606, 612, 613 or 616;

  (e) in the case of the sign shown in diagram 4003.7, a push button or other switching device is included which, whilst the red signal is illuminated, in some way indicates to pedestrians and pedal cyclists whether it has been activated; and

  (f) in the case of the sign shown in diagram 4003.5, the signal heads are ES compliant.

  (4) The red signal, whilst it is illuminated, shall indicate the period during which, in the interests of safety, pedestrians and pedal cyclists should not use the crossing and the green signal, whilst it is illuminated, shall indicate the period during which pedestrians and pedal cyclists may use the crossing.

  (5) Where the sign shown in diagram 4003.7 is provided at a crossing, any additional device which—

  (a) is of the size, colour and type of only the part of that sign which shows the red and green signals or of only the part which includes the push button and the legend above it;

  (b) complies with the requirements of paragraph (3) so far as they are relevant to it; and

  (c) is provided to supplement the indications given by the sign shown in diagram 4003.7,

shall give the same indication as the relevant part of the sign shown in that diagram.

  (6) A push button device giving instructions to pedestrians and pedal cyclists on how to cause the green signal in the sign shown in diagram 4003.5 to become illuminated shall be of the size, colour and type shown in diagram 4003.6.

  (7) The sign shown in diagram 4003.6 shall, whilst the word "WAIT" is illuminated, convey the same indication as the red signal.

  (8) Any audible or tactile signal emitted by a device provided in conjunction with the green signal for the benefit of disabled pedestrians shall convey to pedestrians the same indication as the green signal.

4–3000S   50. Warning lights at school crossing places.   A sign for conveying a warning to vehicular traffic that a school crossing place lies ahead and is being patrolled by a school crossing patrol or is otherwise in use by such children—

  (a) shall be a light signal of the size, colour and type shown in diagram 4004, each lamp of which when operated shall show an intermittent amber light at a rate of flashing of not less than 60 nor more than 90 flashes per minute and in such a manner that one light is always shown when the other light is not shown; and

  (b) may be erected on or near part of the road in advance of a crossing place in relation to oncoming traffic.

4–3000T   51. Cattle crossing signs and warning lights.   (1) A sign of the size, colour and type shown in diagram 4005 may be erected on or near a road in advance of a place in that road where cattle under the supervision of a herdsman on their way from one part of a farm to another cross the road ("a cattle crossing") to convey to oncoming traffic the warning specified in paragraph (2).

  (2) The warning conveyed by the sign shall be that—

  (a) a cattle crossing lies ahead and may be in use; and

  (b) traffic should be prepared to stop.

  (3) When the sign is operated, each lamp shall show an intermittent amber light at a rate of flashing of not less than 60 nor more than 90 flashes per minute and in such a manner that one light is always shown when the other light is not shown.

4–3000U   52. Light signals for pedestrian traffic at level crossings.   (1) Light signals conveying to pedestrians at level crossings the prohibition specified in paragraph (2) shall be of the size, colour and type shown in diagram 4006 and so designed that—

  (a) the red figure shown in diagram 4006 is internally illuminated by an intermittent red light which is shown at a rate of flashing of not less than 60 nor more than 90 flashes per minute;

  (b) the red figure is illuminated only when the intermittent red lights prescribed by regulation 39(2)(b) are illuminated; and

  (c) the signal heads are ES compliant.

(2) The red figure when illuminated in the manner prescribed by paragraph (1) shall convey the prohibition that pedestrians shall not proceed beyond the transverse road marking shown in diagram 1003.2 on the footway or diagram 1001 on the carriageway.

SECTION 6

MISCELLANEOUS TRAFFIC SIGNS

4–3000V   53. Temporary signs.   (1) In this regulation "temporary sign" means a sign placed on or near a road for the purpose of conveying to traffic—

(*a*) information about convenient routes to be followed on the occasion of—

    (i) a sporting event;

    (ii) an exhibition; or

    (iii) any other public gathering,

which is in each case likely to attract a large volume of traffic;

(*b*) information about diversions or alternative traffic routes;

(*c*) information about the availability of new routes or destinations;

(*d*) information about changes in route numbers;

(*e*) warnings about, or information on how to avoid, any temporary hazards caused by—

    (i) works being executed on or near a road;

    (ii) adverse weather conditions or other natural causes;

    (iii) the failure of street lighting or malfunction of or damage to any other apparatus, equipment or facility used in connection with the road or anything situated on or near or under it; or

    (iv) damage to the road itself; or

(*f*) requests by the police for information in connection with road traffic accidents.

(2) A temporary sign—

(*a*) which conveys to traffic any information, warning, requirement, restriction or prohibition of a description which can be conveyed by a sign shown in a diagram in Schedules 1 to 12 (whether on its own or in conjunction or in combination with another such sign) shall be of the size, colour and type shown in that diagram;

(*b*) which does not fall within paragraph (*a*) ("a non-prescribed temporary sign") shall be of such size, colour and type as is specified in paragraphs (3) to (6).

(3) The shape of a non-prescribed temporary sign shall be—

(*a*) rectangular but with the corners rounded; or

(*b*) as in sub-paragraph (*a*) with a rounded point at one end.

(4) A non-prescribed temporary sign shall be of a size appropriate to the circumstances in which it is placed and may incorporate—

(*a*) wording;

(*b*) numerals;

(*c*) arrows or chevrons;

(*d*) any appropriate symbol taken from any diagram in any Schedule; and

(*e*) the arms, badge or other device of a traffic authority, police authority or an organisation representative of road users.

(5) Every letter and numeral incorporated in a non-prescribed temporary sign other than any letter incorporated in the sign in accordance with paragraph (4)(*e*) shall be not less than 40 nor more than 350 millimetres in height, and every arrow so incorporated shall be not less than 250 nor more than 1000 millimetres in length.

(6) Every letter, numeral, arrow, chevron or symbol, other than a sign shown in a diagram in Schedules 1 to 5 when used as a symbol, incorporated in a non-prescribed temporary sign shall be—

(*a*) black on a background of white or of yellow;

(*b*) white on a blue background;

(*c*) blue on a white background;

(*d*) if the sign conveys information or warnings of the kind mentioned in paragraph (1)(*e*), white on a red background, except where it is placed on a motorway when it shall be black on a yellow background; or

(*e*) if the sign is a variable message sign, white, off-white or yellow on a black background or black on a yellow background, except when the sign is not in use when it shall display a plain black or grey face.

SCHEDULES 1–19

PART II

THE TRAFFIC SIGNS GENERAL DIRECTIONS 2002

4–3000W   Direction 1. Citation and commencement. This Part of this Instrument—

(*a*) may be cited—

    (i) as the Traffic Signs General Directions 2002, and

    (ii) together with Part I above, as the Traffic Signs Regulations and General Directions 2002; and

(*b*) shall come into force on 31st January 2003.

4–3000X   Direction 2. *Revocations*

4–3000Y   Direction 3. Interpretation—general. (1) In these Directions—

   (a)   "one-way road" has the meaning given in paragraph 1 of the Schedule;

   (b)   "the Regulations" means the Traffic Signs Regulations 2002; and

   (c)   the expressions listed in paragraph (2) have the same meaning as in the Regulations.

   (2) Those expressions are—

"the 1984 Act";
"central reservation";
"contra-flow";
"controlled parking zone";
"cycle lane";
"cycle track";
"dual carriageway road";
"EEA Standard";
"equestrian crossing";
"hard shoulder" and "actively managed hard shoulder";
"junction";
"level crossing";
"maximum gross weight";
"motorway";
"mph";
"non-primary route";
"pedal cycle";
"pedestrian zone";
"plate";
"primary route";
"primary signals";
"principal road";
"reflectorised";
"retroreflecting material";
"road marking";
"route";
"school crossing place";
"secondary signals";
"sign";
"signal-controlled crossing facility";
"signal-controlled pedestrian facility";
"speed limit" and "national speed limit";
"stud";
"temporary statutory provision";
"traffic lane";
"Toucan crossing";
"variable message sign";
"Zebra crossing"; and
"zig-zag line".

4–3000Z   Direction 4. Interpretation of references. In these Directions, unless it is expressly provided otherwise or the context otherwise requires—

   (a)   a reference to a numbered direction is a reference to the direction so numbered in these Directions;

   (b)   a reference to a numbered paragraph is a reference to the paragraph so numbered in the direction in which the reference occurs;

   (c)   a reference to a sub-paragraph followed by a number or letter is a reference to the sub-paragraph bearing that number or letter in the direction in which the reference occurs;

   (d)   a reference to a numbered diagram is a reference to the diagram so numbered in a Schedule to the Regulations;

   (e)   a reference to a sign shown in a diagram in a Schedule to the Regulations includes a reference to that sign as varied in accordance with the Regulations;

   (f)   a reference to a numbered regulation or Schedule is a reference to the regulation of, or to the Schedule to, the Regulations so numbered; and

   (g)   in any direction which includes a table, references to a table are to the table, or in the case of a numbered table to the table so numbered, in that direction.

4–3000ZA   Directions 5–7. *Deal with general savings and directions relating to signs to be placed at sites approved by the Secretary of State and to be used to indicate the effect of a statutory prohibition*

4–3000ZB   Direction 8. (1) This direction applies to the signs shown in diagrams 616, 617, 618, 618.1, 618.2, 618.3, 618.3A, 619, 619.1, 619.2, 620, 620.1, 622.1A, 622.4, 622.5, 622.6, 622.7, 622.8, 622.9, 625.1, 626.2A, 627.1, 629, 629A, 629.1, 629.2, 629.2A, 632, 642, 646, 663, 663.1, 665, 667, 667.1, 668, 668.1, 670, 672, 674, 951, 952, 953, 953.1, 955, 956 and 957.

   (2) In accordance with the following provisions of this direction and the provisions of direction 9, appropriate signs to which this direction applies shall be placed to indicate the point at which a restriction, requirement, prohibition or speed limit applying to traffic on a road (in this direction and in direction 9 called "the relevant road") begins.

   (3) Subject to paragraphs (4), (5) and (6) and to direction 9, a sign to which this direction applies shall be placed on the relevant road at or as near as practicable to the point referred to in paragraph (2)—

   (a)   where the relevant road has only one carriageway, on each side of that carriageway; or

   (b)   where the relevant road has more than one carriageway, on each side of each carriageway in relation to which the restriction, requirement, prohibition or speed limit begins.

   (4) Where the relevant road has one carriageway, then signs to which this direction applies need only be placed on one side of the relevant road to indicate the point at which a restriction, requirement, prohibition (but not a speed limit) begins in the following cases—

(a) where the restriction, requirement or prohibition applies only to traffic on one side of the relevant road; or

(b) at a junction where—

    (i) traffic proceeding on another road on which it is permitted to proceed only in one direction turns into the relevant road; or

    (ii) the carriageway of the relevant road is less than 5 metres wide and the sign is so placed that its centre is within 2 metres of the edge of the carriageway.

(5) Where a length of road which passes under or through a bridge, tunnel or other structure is subject to a prohibition on vehicles exceeding a particular height, the sign shown in diagram 629.2 or 629.2A may be placed on the bridge, tunnel or other structure to indicate the prohibition in addition to or instead of the signs required to be placed by paragraph (3).

(6) Paragraphs (3) and (4) shall not apply to the signs shown in diagrams 667, 667.1, 668 and 668.1 which shall be placed on the side of the carriageway on which parking on a verge or footway is permitted and as near as is practicable to the point at which the length of the verge or footway concerned begins.

4–3000ZC   Direction 9. Beginning of a speed limit—further provisions.   (1) Direction 8(3) does not apply where a speed limit in force on the relevant road begins—

(a) at a point where the relevant road begins, being a point where it has no junction with another road; or

(b) at a point where the relevant road has a junction with another road and the same speed limit is in force on both roads.

(2) This paragraph applies where the relevant road has a junction ("the junction") with the side of another road ("the other road") and a maximum speed limit is in force on the other road which is different from the speed limit in force on the relevant road.

(3) Where paragraph (2) applies, it is sufficient compliance with direction 8(2), for the purpose of indicating the beginning of the speed limit on the relevant road to traffic entering it from the other road, if the sign shown in diagram 670, 674 or 675 is placed not further than 20 metres from the junction, on the left hand or near side of the carriageway of the relevant road as viewed in the direction of travel of such traffic or, where the relevant road is a dual carriageway road, on the left hand or near side of the carriageway by which traffic may pass into the relevant road from the other road.

(4) Where paragraph (2) applies, for the purpose of indicating the speed limit in force on the other road to traffic entering that road from the relevant road, the sign shown in diagram 670, 674 or 675 shall (subject to paragraph (5)) be placed not further than 20 metres from the junction and so as to be visible to such traffic, on each side of the carriageway by which traffic may pass from the relevant road into the other road.

(5) Paragraph (4) does not apply if—

(a) the maximum speed limit in force on the other road is greater than that in force on the relevant road; and

(b) signs indicating the maximum speed limit have been placed on the other road in accordance with direction 11 on each side of, and not more than 100 metres from, the junction.

4–3000ZD   Direction 10. The placing of certain signs to indicate the end of a restriction, requirement, prohibition or speed limit.   (1) When the sign shown in diagram 618.4, 622.2, 645, 647, 664, 666, 667.2, 668.2, 673, 675 or 964 is placed to indicate the point at which traffic on a road ceases to be subject to a restriction, requirement, prohibition or speed limit, the sign shall be placed on the road as near as practicable to that point.

(2) Subject to paragraph (3), where a length of road ceases to be subject to a speed limit and becomes subject to a national speed limit, the sign shown in diagram 671 shall be placed at or as near as practicable to the point where the speed limit ends and the national speed limit begins.

(3) Where a temporary restriction of speed has been imposed under section 14 of the 1984 Act along a length of road by reason of works which are being or are proposed to be executed on or near that road, there shall be placed at or as near as practicable to the point where the temporary restriction of speed ends—

(a) the sign shown in diagram 7006 or in diagram 7001 (placed in combination with the plate shown in diagram 645); and

(b) in a case where, but for the temporary speed limit, a change in speed limit would at some point have occurred along the length of road, the sign shown in diagram 670 (varied as appropriate) or 671.

(4) When the sign shown in diagram 671, 673 or 675 is placed to indicate the point at which traffic on a road ceases to be subject to a speed limit—

(a) where the road has only one carriageway, one such sign shall be placed on each side of the carriageway of the road; or

(b) where the road has more than one carriageway, one such sign shall be placed on each side of each carriageway on which the speed limit ends.

(5) Where a road ("the relevant road") has a junction with the side of another road ("the other road") and—

(a) a maximum speed limit is in force on the other road; and

(b) a national speed limit is in force on the relevant road,

then, for the purpose of indicating the national speed limit to traffic entering the relevant road from the other road, the sign shown in diagram 671 or 675 shall be placed on the relevant road in accordance with paragraph (6).

(6) The sign shall be placed not more than 20 metres from the junction with the other road on the left hand or near side of the relevant road as viewed in the direction of travel of a vehicle entering the relevant road from the other road or, if the relevant road is a dual carriageway road, on the left hand or near side of the carriageway by which a vehicle may pass into the relevant road from the other road.

(7) Where the relevant road has a junction with the side of the other road and—

(a) a national speed limit is in force on the other road; and

(b) a maximum speed limit is in force on the relevant road,

then, for the purpose of indicating the national speed limit to traffic entering the other road from the relevant road, traffic signs shown in diagram 671 or 675 shall be placed in accordance with paragraph (8) on the relevant road not further than 20 metres from the junction.

(8) If the relevant road has one carriageway, one such sign shall be placed on each side of that carriageway and, if the relevant road is a dual carriageway road, one such sign shall be placed on each side of the carriageway by which traffic may pass from the relevant road into the other road.

4–3000ZE   Direction 11.   Repeater signs.   (1) Paragraph (2) applies to the signs shown in diagrams 614, 632, 636, 636.1, 636.2, 637.1, 637.2, 637.3, 638, 638.1 when the arrow is omitted, 639 when the arrow is omitted, 639.1B, 640 when the arrow is omitted, 642, 646, 650.1, 650.2, 650.3, 660, 660.3, 660.4, 660.5, 660.6, 661A, 661.1, 662, 670 (except when displayed on a variable message sign in the manner mentioned in regulation 58(7)(b)), 672, 956, 957, 959, 959.1, 960, 960.1 and 961.

(2) Subject to paragraphs (3) and (4), signs to which this paragraph applies shall be placed at regular intervals along a road which is subject to a restriction, requirement, prohibition or speed limit which can be indicated by the signs.

(3) Signs shown in diagram 670 when varied to "20" need not be placed in accordance with paragraph (2) on a road within an area into which each entrance for vehicular traffic has been indicated by the sign shown in diagram 674.

(4) The sign shown in diagram 670 (except when displayed on a variable message sign in the manner mentioned in regulation 58(7)(b)) shall not be placed along—

(a)   a road on which there is provided a system of carriageway lighting furnished by lamps lit by electricity placed not more than 183 metres apart in England and Wales or not more than 185 metres apart in Scotland and which is subject to a speed limit of 30 mph; or

(b)   a motorway on which a national speed limit is in force.

(5) The sign shown in diagram 671 shall be placed at regular intervals along the length of a road (other than a motorway) on which—

(a)   there is a system of street or carriageway lighting furnished by lamps lit by electricity placed not more than 183 metres apart in England and Wales or not more than 185 metres apart in Scotland; and

(b)   a national speed limit is in force.

4–3000ZF   Directions 12–15.   *Signs to be placed only on specified types of road*

4–3000ZG   Direction 16   Signs to be placed only in conjunction with specified road markings (except signs for prohibitions and restrictions on waiting etc).   (1) The sign shown in diagram 674 may only be placed on a road if no point on any road (not being a cul-de-sac less than 80 metres long), to which the speed limit indicated by the sign applies, is situated more than 50 metres from a traffic calming feature.

(2) In paragraph (1) "traffic calming feature" means—

(a)   a road hump constructed pursuant to section 90A of the Highways Act 1980 ("the 1980 Act") or section 36 of the Roads (Scotland) Act 1984 ("the 1984 Act") and in accordance with the Highways (Road Humps) Regulations 1999 or the Road Humps (Scotland) Regulations 1998;

(b)   traffic calming works constructed in accordance with section 90G of the 1980 Act or section 39A of the 1984 Act and in accordance with the Highways (Traffic Calming) Regulations 1999 or the Roads (Traffic Calming) (Scotland) Regulations 1994;

(c)   a refuge for pedestrians which was constructed pursuant to section 68 of the 1980 Act or section 27(c) of the 1984 Act after 15th June 1999 and is so constructed as to encourage a reduction in the speed of traffic using the carriageway;

(d)   a variation of the relative widths of the carriageway or of any footway pursuant to section 75 of the 1980 Act or section 1(1) or 2(1) of the 1984 Act which—

(i)   was carried out after 15th June 1999 for the purpose of encouraging a reduction in the speed of traffic using the carriageway; and

(ii)   had the effect of reducing the width of the carriageway; or

(e)   a horizontal bend in the carriageway through which all vehicular traffic has to change direction by no less than 70 degrees within a distance of 32 metres as measured at the inner kerb radius.

(3) For the purposes of paragraph (1) the distance of 50 metres shall be measured along roads to which the speed limit indicated by the sign shown in diagram 674 applies.

4–3000ZH   Direction 17.   *Road markings to be placed only in conjunction with other orad markings or specified signs (except road markings for prohibitions and restrictions on waiting etc)*

4–3000ZI   Direction 18.   *The placing of the signs shown in diagrams 615 and 811*

4–3000ZJ   Direction 19.   *Signs to be placed only in combination with specified plates or other signs*

4–3000ZK   Direction 20.   *Plates to be placed only in combination with specified signs*

4–3000ZL   Direction 21.   *Placing of road markings and signs to indicate prohibitions and restrictions on waiting, loading, unloading and parking*

4–3000ZM   Direction 22.   (1) Subject to paragraphs (2) and (3)—

(a)   the road marking shown in diagram 1018.1 may be placed on a side of a road only for the purpose of indicating a statutory prohibition or restriction on the waiting of vehicles which applies on that side of the road at all times of day on every day of the year or on every day in a period of at least four consecutive months; and

(b)   the road marking shown in diagram 1017 may be placed on a side of a road only for the purpose of indicating a statutory prohibition or restriction on the waiting of vehicles which is not a restriction of the kind mentioned in sub-paragraph (a).

(2) In this direction, references to a statutory prohibition or restriction on the waiting of a vehicle do not include references to any such prohibition or restriction imposed—

(a)   on waiting for the purpose of loading or unloading goods from a vehicle or picking up or setting down passengers from a vehicle;

(b)   and expressly to limit the duration of waiting of vehicles within a particular period; or

(c)   on the waiting of goods vehicles (as defined by section 192(1) of the Road Traffic Act 1988) but of no other class of vehicle.

(3) The road marking shown in diagram 1017 or 1018.1 shall not be placed on a road on which is placed—

(a)   the marking shown in diagram 1025.1, 1025.3, 1025.4 or 1028.2 (in conjunction with the sign shown in diagram 650.1); or (*b*) the marking shown in diagram 1027.1 in conjunction with the sign shown in diagram 642.2A, unless there are times at which the restrictions to be indicated by the marking shown in diagram 1017 or 1018.1 apply and those indicated by that sign do not.

4–3000ZN   Directions 27–35. *Signs to be placed only at specified sites or for specified purposes*

4–3000ZO   Directions 36–39. *Restrictions on the placing of temporary signs*

4–3000ZP   Direction 40. *Placing of signs varied to show metric units*

4–3000ZQ   Directions 41–46. *Mounting and backing of various signs and lamps*

4–3000ZR   Directions 47–49. *Placing of various road markings*

4–3000ZS   Directions 50–52. *Placing of signs and light signals shown in Schedule 11*

4–3000ZT   Directions 53–55. *Placing of various light signals*

4–3000ZU   Directions 57–58. *Studs*

CONSTRUCTION AND USE

Motor Vehicles (Tests) Regulations 1981[1]

(SI 1981/1694 amended by SI 1982/814, 1477 and 1715, SI 1983/1434, SI 1984/ 1126, SI 1985/45 and 1923, SI 1988/989 and 1894, SI 1989/1694, SI 1991/1253, 455, 1525, 2229 and 2791, SI 1992/566, 1217, 1609 and 3160, SI 1993/3011, SI 1995/1457 and 2438, SI 2000/1432, SI 2001/3330, SI 2002/488 and 1698, SI 2003/1113, 1698 and 1815, SI 2004/1632 and 1879,SI 2005/1832 and SI 2006/594)[2]

PART I – GENERAL

4–3071   1. *Commencement and citation.*

1. Made under sections 43(1), (2) and (6) and 44(4), (6) and (7) of the Road Traffic Act 1972 and all other enabling powers. Only those regulations which are likely to be relevant to proceedings in a magistrates' court are contained in this manual. The Regulations make provision for the authorisation of persons to examine motor vehicles, establish the procedure for the testing of vehicles, prescribe the statutory requirements for the purposes of such tests and exempt certain vehicles from the test. The statutory requirements relate to the braking system, steering gear, lighting equipment and reflectors, stop lamps, tyres, seat belts, direction indicators, windscreen wipers and washers, exhaust system, audible warning instrument, and bodywork and suspension.

2. Listed are those instruments which currently amend the 1981 regulations including those regulations not reproduced in this manual but not including those instruments which revise the level of fees.

4–3072   2. *Revocation.*

Interpretation

4–3073   3. (1) In these Regulations, except where the context otherwise requires, the following expressions have the meanings hereby respectively assigned to them—

"the 1972 Act" means the Road Traffic Act 1972";
"the 1981 Act" means the Public Passenger Vehicles Act 1981;
"the 1988 Act" means the Road Traffic Act 1988;
"the Construction and Use Regulations" means the Road Vehicles (Construction and Use) Regulations 1986;
"the Lighting Regulations" means the Road Vehicles Lighting Regulations 1989;
"agricultural motor vehicle", "articulated bus", "articulated vehicle", "dual-purpose vehicle", "exhaust system", "minibus", "Ministry plate"; "pedestrian controlled vehicle", "track laying" and "works truck" have the meanings given by Regulation 3(2) of the Construction and Use Regulations;
"authorisation" means any authorisation in writing by the Secretary of State of an individual, persons in partnership, or a company to carry out examinations of such classes of motor vehicles as may be specified therein;
"child restraint", "disabled person's belt", "forward-facing seat" and "seat belt" have the meanings given by Regulation 47(8) of the Construction and Use Regulations;
"communication" includes a communication comprising sounds or images or both and a communication effecting a payment;
"Community Recording Equipment Regulation" has the meaning given in section 85 of the Road Traffic Act 1988;
"company" means a body corporate;
"design gross weight" means—

(a) in the case of a vehicle equipped with a Ministry plate, the weight shown thereon as the design weight, or, if no weight is so shown thereon; the weight shown thereon as the weight not to be exceeded in Great Britain;

(b) in the case of a vehicle which is not equipped with a Ministry plate, but which is equipped with a plate in accordance with regulation 66 of the Construction and Use Regulations, the maximum gross weight shown on the plate in respect of item 7 of Part I of Schedule 8 to those Regulations; and

(c) in any other case, the weight which the vehicle is designed or adapted not to exceed when in normal use and travelling on a road laden;

"designated council" means a council designated by the Secretary of State for the purposes of sections 45 (tests of satisfactory condition of vehicles) and 46 (particular aspects of regulations under section 45) of the 1988 Act;

"electronic communication" means a communication transmitted (whether from one person to another, from one device to another or from a person to a device or vice versa)—

(a) by means of a telecommunications system (within the meaning of the Telecommunications Act 1984); or

(b) by other means but while in an electronic form;

"examination" means an examination of a motor vehicle for the purposes of section 45 of the 1988 Act;

"examiner" means an individual, persons in partnership, or a company authorised by the Secretary of State in accordance with these Regulations to carry out examinations;

"firm" has the meaning given by section 4 of the Partnership Act 1890;

"goods vehicle" means a motor vehicle constructed or adapted for use for the carriage of goods or burden of any description, including a living van but excluding—

(i) a dual-purpose vehicle,
(ii) a motor caravan, and
(iii) a play bus,

"goods vehicle testing station" means a station provided by the Secretary of State under section 52(2) of the Road Traffic Act 1988;

"inspector" means a person appointed by a designated council for the purposes of sections 45 and 46 of the 1988 Act;

"large passenger-carrying vehicle" means a motor vehicle which is constructed or adapted to carry more than twelve seated passengers in addition to the driver, and which is not a public service vehicle;

"light motor bicycle" means a motor bicycle of which the cylinder capacity of the engine does not exceed 200 cubic centimetres;

"light motor vehicle" means a motor vehicle with three wheels the unladen weight of which does not exceed 450 kilograms;

"living van" means a vehicle, whether mechanically propelled or not, which is used as living accommodation by one or more persons, and which is also used for the carriage of goods or burden which are not needed by such one or more persons for the purpose of their residence in the vehicle;

"Ministry Inspector" means any certifying officer or public service vehicle examiner appointed under section [68(1)] and any examiner appointed under section 7 of the 1981 Act;

"motor bicycle" means a two wheeled motor cycle, whether having a sidecar attached to it or not;

"motor caravan" means a motor vehicle (not being a living van) which is constructed or adapted for the carriage of passengers and their effects and which contains, as permanently installed equipment, the facilities which are reasonably necessary for enabling the vehicle to provide mobile living accommodation for its users;

"normal working week" means—

(a) in relation to an examiner, the times of the week which in the application of that examiner to the Secretary of State for an authorisation are specified as the times of the week during which that examiner will accept vehicles for examination or such other times of the week as may subsequently be substituted for times so specified by the examiner with the consent of the Secretary of State;

(b) in relation to a designated council, the times of the week notified to the Secretary of State by that council as the times of the week during which they will accept vehicles for examination; and

(c) in relation to the Secretary of State, the times of the week during which at any vehicle testing station of the Secretary of State he will accept vehicles for examination;

"out of hours" means at any time either—

(a) on any day which is a Saturday, Sunday, Good Friday, Christmas Day or a Bank holiday (as defined in the Banking and Financial Dealings Act 1971; or

(b) on any other day, other than between—

(i) 8.00 am and 5.00 pm on a Monday to Thursday inclusive, or
(ii) 8.00 am and 4.30 pm on a Friday;

"play bus" means a motor vehicle which was originally constructed to carry more than 12 passengers but which has been adapted primarily for the carriage of playthings for children (including articles required in connection with the use of those things);

"proper officer", in relation to a designated council in England or Wales, has the meaning given by section 270(3) of the Local Government Act 1972;

"public service vehicle" has the meaning given by section 1(1)(*a*) of the 1981 Act;

"the prescribed statutory requirements" has the meaning given by Regulation 4(2);

"the records" means the records of the results of examinations for the purposes of section 45 of the 1988 Act maintained by the Secretary of State (or caused by him to be maintained); and "the electronic record" means such of those records as is maintained in electronic form;

"section 66A examiner" means an examiner appointed under section 66A (appointment of vehicle examiners) of the 1988 Act;

"serial number", in relation to a vehicle the chassis of which has not been constructed separately from its superstructure, means the number given to, and for the purpose of identifying, the vehicle by its manufacturer;

"vehicle testing station" means premises at which the Secretary of State has authorised an examiner to carry out examinations, premises provided by a designated council or the Secretary of State for carrying out examinations, or premises for the time being designated by the Secretary of State under section 8(3) of the 1981 Act.

"VOSA" means the Vehicle and Operator Services Agency.

(2) Unless the context otherwise requires, any reference in these Regulations to—

(*a*) a numbered section is a reference to the section bearing that number in the 1972 Act;

(*b*) a numbered Regulation or Schedule is a reference to the Regulation or Schedule bearing that number in these Regulations, and

(*c*) a numbered paragraph is a reference to the paragraph bearing that number in the Regulation in which the reference appears.

(3) For the purposes of these Regulations the unladen weight of a vehicle shall be computed in accordance with Schedule 6 to the Vehicles (Excise) Act 1971.

(4) In calculating for the purposes of the definition of "large passenger-carrying vehicle" the number of seated passengers which the vehicle is constructed or adapted to carry a length of at least 400 millimetres measured horizontally along the front of each seat shall be allowed for the accommodation of each such passenger. Where a continuous seat is fitted with arms for the purpose of separating the seating spaces and the arms are so constructed that they can be folded back or otherwise put out of use, the seat shall be measured for the purposes of this paragraph as though it were not fitted with arms.

(5) For the purposes of these Regulations the provisions of Regulation 3(3) of the Construction and Use Regulations shall apply for determining when a motor vehicle is first used.

(6) References in these Regulations to the making, by electronic communication, of entries in the electronic record include references to causing entries to be made in that record (either by electronic communication or by other means notified by the Secretary of State).

4-3074   4. (1) *Revoked.*

(2) The prescribed statutory requirements for the purposes of section 45(1) of the Road Traffic Act 1988 are in relation to any vehicle in a Class specified in an item in column 2 of the Table the requirements specified in that item in column 3 of the Table, and in these Regulations those requirements are referred to as "the prescribed statutory requirements".

TABLE

(1)	(2)	(3)
Item	*Class*	*Requirements*
1	I and II	Paragraph 1 of Schedule 2
2	III	Paragraph 2 of Schedule 2
3	IV	Paragraph 3 of Schedule 2
3A	IVA	Paragraph 3A of Schedule 2
4	V	Paragraph 4 of Schedule 2
4A	VA	Paragraph 4A of Schedule 2
5	VI	Paragraph 5 of Schedule 2
5A	VIA	Paragraph 5A of Schedule 2
6	VII	Paragraph 6 of Schedule 2.

(3) Subject to the provisions of these Regulations, every vehicle to which these Regulations apply and which is submitted for examination in accordance with the provisions of these Regulations shall be examined for the purpose of ascertaining whether those of the prescribed statutory requirements which are applicable to the vehicle have been complied with at the date of the examination.

(4) *Revoked.*

Classification of Vehicles and Application of Regulations

4-3075   5. (1) For the purposes of these Regulations motor vehicles to which they apply are classified as follows—

Class I: Light motor bicycles
Class II: motor bicycles

Class III:	Light motor vehicles other than motor bicycles
Class IV:	Motor cars and heavy motor cars not being vehicles within Classes III, IVA, V, VA, VI, VIA or VII
Class IVA:	Minibuses, other than vehicles to which paragraph (4) applies, not being vehicles within Classes III, V, VA, VI or VIA, in respect of which any forward-facing seat is fitted with a relevant seat belt
Class V:	Motor vehicles not being vehicles within Class VA which are—

(a) Large passenger-carrying vehicles;
(b) Public service vehicles—
  (i) of a type specified in paragraph (3), and
  (ii) constructed or adapted to carry more than 12 seated passengers, and
(c) Play buses

Class VA:	Motor vehicles, other than vehicles to which paragraph (4) applies, which are—

(a) Large passenger-carrying vehicles;
(b) Public service vehicles—
  (i) of a type specified in paragraph (3), and
  (ii) constructed or adapted to carry more than 12 seated passengers, and
(c) Play buses
in respect of which any forward-facing seat is fitted with a relevant seat belt

Class VI:	Public service vehicles, other than those of a type specified in paragraph (3), not being vehicles within Class VIA
Class VIA;	Public service vehicles, not being vehicles to which paragraph (4) applies, other than those of a type specified in paragraph (3), in respect of which any forward facing seat is fitted with a relevant seat belt.
Class VII:	Goods vehicles of which the design gross weight is more than 3000 kilograms but does not exceed 3500 kilograms

and (except where otherwise provided in these Regulations) any reference in these Regulations to a class of vehicles shall be construed accordingly.

(2) Save as provided in Regulation 6, these Regulations apply to every vehicle of a class specified in paragraph (1).

(3) The public vehicles mentioned in paragraph (1) as included in Class V or VA are public service vehicles which may lawfully be used on a road in the absence of a certificate of initial fitness by virtue of—

(a) section 23(7) of the Transport Act 1985 (a bus being used to provide a community bus service), or

(b) section 46 of the 1981 Act (a school bus belonging to a local education authority and being used to provide free school transport and carrying as fare-paying passengers persons other than those for whom the free school transport is provided, and a school bus being used, when it is not being used to provide free school transport, to provide a local bus service).

(c) section 21(2) of the Transport Act 1985 (a small bus used under a permit granted under section 19 of that Act).

(4) This paragraph applies to vehicles, in respect of which—

(a) a certificate of initial fitness has been issued on or after 1st August 1998; or

(b) one or more forward-facing seats are fitted with a relevant seat belt, which, when so equipped, are of a type of vehicle in respect of which the Secretary of State is satisfied that the vehicle manufacturer holds—

(i) an approval issued by or on behalf of the approval authority of an EEA State confirming compliance with the installation requirements of Community Directives 77/541, 82/319, 90/628 or 96/36; and

(ii) either—

(A) an approval issued by or on behalf of the approval authority of an EEA State confirming compliance with the technical and installation requirements of Community Directives 76/115, 81/575, 82/318, 90/629 or 96/38; or

(B) an approval issued by or on behalf of the competent authority of a contracting State confirming compliance with the technical and installation requirements of ECE regulation 14, 14.01, 14.02 or 14.03.

(5) In this regulation—

"approval authority" has the same meaning as in Community Directive 70/156;

"certificate of initial fitness" has the same meaning as in section 6 of the Public Passenger Vehicles Act 1981;

"contracting State" means a State which is a party to the International Agreement;

"EEA State" means a State which is a contracting party to the EEA Agreement;

"EEA Agreement" means the agreement on the European Economic Area signed at Oporto on 2nd May 1992 as adjusted by the Protocol signed at Brussels on 17th March 1993;

"ECE Regulation" and "Community Directive" have the meanings given by regulation 3(2) of the Construction and Use Regulations;

"the International Agreement" means the Agreement concerning the adoption of uniform conditions of approval for motor vehicle equipment and parts and reciprocal recognition thereof concluded at Geneva on 20th March 1958 as amended to which the United Kingdom is a party; and

"relevant seat belt" means a seat belt, not being a disabled person's belt or a child restraint, which—

    (a) is fitted other than as required by regulation 47 of the Construction and Use Regulations; and

    (b) on or after 1st August 1998 either—

        (i) has not undergone an examination and been found to comply with the prescribed statutory requirements referred to in item 28A in paragraph 3A of Schedule 2; or

        (ii) has undergone an examination and been found so to comply but is fitted in a vehicle in respect of which no test certificate has been issued to the effect that that is the case.

Exemptions

4–3076 **6.** (1) Pursuant to section [47(5)] the Secretary of State hereby prescribes the following vehicles as those to which section [47] does not apply—

    (i) a heavy locomotive,

    (ii) a light locomotive,

    (iii) a motor tractor,

    (iv) a track laying vehicle,

    (v) a goods vehicle, the design gross weight of which exceeds 3,500 kilograms,

    (vi) an articulated vehicle not being an articulated bus,

    (vii) a vehicle to which paragraph (1A) for the time being applies,

    (viii) a works truck,

    (ix) a pedestrian controlled vehicle,

    (x) a vehicle (including a cycle with an attachment for propelling it by mechanical power) which is adapted, and used or kept on a road, for invalids, and which—

        (i) does not exceed 306 kilograms in weight unladen, or

        (ii) exceeds 306 kilograms but does not exceed 510 kilograms in weight unladen, and are supplied and maintained by or on behalf of the Department of Health and Social Security, the Scottish Office or the Welsh Office;

    (xi) a vehicle temporarily in Great Britain displaying a registration mark mentioned in Regulation 5 of the Motor Vehicles (International Circulation) Regulations 1971, a period of twelve months not having elapsed since the vehicle was last brought into Great Britain;

    (xii) a vehicle proceeding to a port for export;

    (xiii) a vehicle in the service of a visiting force or of a headquarters (within the meaning given by Article 8 (6) of the Visiting Forces and International Headquarters (Application of Law) Order 1965),

    (xiv) a vehicle provided for police purposes and maintained in workshops approved by the Secretary of State as suitable for such maintenance, being a vehicle provided in England and Wales by a police authority or the Receiver for the Metropolitan Police District, or, in Scotland, by a police authority or a joint police committee;

    (xivA) a vehicle provided for the purposes of the Serious Organised Crime Agency;

    (xv) a vehicle which has been imported into Great Britain and to which section [47(2)(b)] applies, being a vehicle owned by or in the service of the naval, military or air forces of Her Majesty raised in the United Kingdom and used for naval, military or air force purposes;

    (xvi) a vehicle in respect of which a test certificate issued in accordance with Article 34 of the Road Traffic (Northern Ireland) Order 1981 is in force or which are licensed under the Vehicles (Excise) Act (Northern Ireland) 1972;

    (xvii) an electrically propelled goods vehicle the design gross weight of which does not exceed 3,500 kilograms;

    (xviii) subject to the provisions of paragraph (4), a hackney carriage or a cab in respect of which there is in force a licence under—

        (a) section 6 of the Metropolitan Public Carriage Act 1869, or

        (b) the Town Police Clauses Act 1847[1], the Burgh Police (Scotland) Act 1892 or any similar local statutory provision,

    to ply for hire;

    (xix) subject to the provisions of paragraph (4), a private hire car in respect of which there is in force a licence granted by a local authority or Transport for London, or, in Scotland, by a local authority or a police authority;

    (xx) an agricultural motor vehicle;

    (xxi) a motor vehicle constructed and not merely adapted for the purpose of street cleansing or the collection or disposal of refuse or the collection or disposal of the contents of gullies and which is either—

        (a) a three wheeled vehicle, or

        (b) a vehicle which—

            (i) is incapable by reason of its construction of exceeding a speed of 20 miles per hour on the level under its own power, or

            (ii) has an inside track width of less than 810 millimetres;

(xxii) a goods vehicle, the design gross weight of which does not exceed 3,500 kilograms and in respect of which a goods vehicle test certificate was issued between 1st February 1990 and 17th March 1991, while that certificate is valid;

(xxiii) before 1st August 1991, a goods vehicle the design gross weight of which does not exceed 3,500 kilograms and which is of a class specified in Schedule 2 to the Goods (Vehicles (Plating and Testing) Regulations 1988;

(xxiv) a tramcar; and

(xxv) a trolley vehicle which is not an auxiliary trolley vehicle.

(1A) This paragraph applies to a vehicle at a time when it is being used on a public road during any calendar week if—

(a) it is being used only in passing from land in the occupation of the person keeping the vehicle to other land in his occupation, and

(b) it has not been used on public roads for distances exceeding an aggregate of six miles in that calendar week,

and for the purposes of this paragraph "public road" has the meaning given in section 62(1) the Vehicle Excise and Registration Act 1994.

(2) Pursuant to section [47(6)] the Secretary of State hereby exempts from section [47(1)] the use of a vehicle—

(a)

(i) for the purpose of submitting it by previous arrangement for, or bringing it away from, an examination, or

(ii) in the course of an examination, for the purpose of taking it to, or bringing it away from, any place where a part of the examination is to be or, as the case may be, has been, carried out, or of carrying out any part of the examination, the person so using it being either—

(A) an examiner, or a Ministry Inspector or an inspector appointed by a designated council, or

(B) a person acting under the personal direction of an examiner, a Ministry Inspector or a designated Council, or

(iii) where a test certificate is refused on an examination—

(A) for the purpose of delivering it by previous arrangement at, or bringing it away from, a place where work is to be or has been done on it to remedy for a further examination the defects on the ground of which the test certificate was refused; or

(B) for the purpose of delivering it, by towing it, to a place where the vehicle is to be broken up;

(b) for any purpose for which the vehicle is authorised to be used on roads by an order under section [44];

(c) where the vehicle has been imported into Great Britain, for the purpose of its being driven after arrival in Great Britain on the journey from the place where it has arrived in Great Britain to a place of residence of the owner or driver of the vehicle;

(d) for the purpose of removing it in pursuance of section 3 of the Refuse Disposal (Amenity) Act 1978, of moving or removing it in pursuance of regulations under section 20 of the Road Traffic Regulation Act 1967 as altered by the Removal and Disposal of Vehicles (Alteration of Enactments) Order 1967, or of removing it from a parking place in pursuance of an order under section [35(1)] of the Road Traffic Regulation Act [1984], an order relating to a parking place designated under section [45, 50] thereof, or a provision of a designation order having effect by virtue of section [53(3)] thereof;

(e) where the vehicle has been detained or seized by a police constable, for police purposes connected with such detention or seizure;

(f) where the vehicle has been removed, detained or seized or condemned as forfeited under any provision of the Customs and Excise Management Act 1979 for any purpose authorised by an officer of Customs and Excise;

(g) for the purpose of testing it by a motor trader as defined in section 16(8) of the Vehicles (Excise) Act 1971, to whom a trade licence has been issued under that section, during the course of, or after completion of repairs carried out to that vehicle by that motor trader.

(3) Pursuant to section [47(7)] the Secretary of State hereby exempts from section [47(1)] the use of a vehicle on any island in any area mainly surrounded by water, being an island or area from which motor vehicles, unless constructed for special purposes can at no time be conveniently driven to a road in any other part of Great Britain by reason of the absence of any bridge, tunnel, ford or other way suitable for the passage of such motor vehicle:

Provided that—

(a) in relation to a vehicle in any of Classes I to VIA, this Regulation does not apply to any of the following islands, namely, the Isle of Wight, the islands of Arran, Bute, Great Cumbrae, Islay, Lewis, Mainland (Orkney), Mainland (Shetland), Mull, North Uist and Skye; and

(b) in relation to a vehicle in Class VII this Regulation does not apply in any of the following islands, namely, the Isle of Wight, the Islands of Lewis, Mainland (Orkney), Mainland (Shetland) and Skye.

(4) The exemptions specified in paragraph (1)(xviii) and (xix) do not obtain unless the authority which issued the licence (the "licensing authority") holds a certificate issued by the Secretary of

State evidencing that he is satisfied that the issue of the licence is subject to the vehicle first passing an annual test relating to the prescribed statutory requirements; and, as from 1st January 1983,

(a)   in the case of a vehicle of a kind mentioned in paragraph (1)(xviii) first used more than one year before the licence there mentioned was issued, or

(b)   in the case of a vehicle of a kind mentioned in paragraph (1)(xix) first used more than three years before the licence there mentioned was issued

the licensing authority also issued to the licensee a certificate recording that on the date on which the certificate was issued that authority was, as a result of a test, satisfied that the prescribed statutory requirements were satisfied.

(5)   In this Regulation—

"auxiliary trolley vehicle" means a trolley vehicle which is adapted to operate under power provided from a source on board when it is not operating from power transmitted to it from some external source;

"private hire car" means a motor vehicle which is not a vehicle licensed to ply for hire under the provisions of the Metropolitan Public Carriage Act 1869, Town Police Clauses Act 1847, the Burgh Police (Scotland) Act 1892 or any similar local statutory provision with respect to hackney carriages but which is kept for the purpose of being let out for hire with a driver for the carrying of passengers in such circumstances that it does not require to be licensed to ply for hire under the said provisions; and

"test" means an examination of a vehicle in relation to the prescribed statutory requirements conducted—

(i)   by a person appointed to act as an inspector under section [45], or a person authorised as an examiner or acting on his behalf, or

(ii)   by a person on behalf of a police authority in England or Wales, or

(iii)   by a person on behalf of a police authority or a joint police committee in Scotland.

---

1. See title TOWNS IMPROVEMENT: TOWN POLICE, in PART VII, *ante.*

Certificates of temporary exemption

4-3077   **28.** (1) A public service vehicle in respect of which a certificate complying with the provisions specified in paragraph (2) below has been issued in the circumstances specified in paragraph (3) below is exempt from the provisions of section [47(1)] of the Road Traffic Act [1988] until that certificate expires.

(2)   Those provisions are that the certificate—

(a)   is in a form approved by the Secretary of State which shall contain—

(i)   the registration mark (if any) exhibited on the vehicle or, if no such mark is so exhibited, the chassis or serial number marked on the vehicle,

(ii)   the date on which the certificate is issued, and

(iii)   the period during which the vehicle is exempted from the provisions of section 44(1) of the Road Traffic Act 1972; and

(b)   is signed by a person authorised in that behalf by the Secretary of State.

(3)   The circumstances mentioned in paragraph (1) above are an accident, a fire, an epidemic, severe weather, a failure in the supply of essential services or other unexpected happening (excluding a breakdown or mechanical defect in a vehicle or non-delivery of spare parts therefor).

(4)   No certificate issued by virtue of this Regulation shall be valid for more than 3 months.

Pedal Cycles (Construction and Use) Regulations 1983[1]
(SI 1983/1176)

4-3131   **1, 2.** *Commencement, citation, revocation.*

---

1. These Regulations were made under s 66(1), (3) and (4) of the Road Traffic Act 1972 and now have effect under s 81 of the Road Traffic Act 1988. Contravention of the regulations is an offence contrary to s 91 of the Road Traffic Offenders Act 1988 which prescribes a maximum penalty not exceeding **level 3** on the standard scale.

Interpretation

4-3132   **3.** (1) In these Regulations:—

(a)   a reference to the manufacturer of a vehicle means. in the case of a vehicle which has been altered so as to become an electrically assisted pedal cycle, the person who made that alteration;

(b)   "pedal cycle" means a pedal cycle which is either—

(i)   not propelled by mechanical power, or

(ii)   an electrically assisted pedal cycle prescribed for the purposes of section [140] of the Road Traffic Regulation Act [1984] and section [189] of the Road Traffic Act [1988] by virtue of the Electrically Assisted Pedal Cycles Regulations 1983;

(c) "the 1971 British Standard" has the same meaning as in the Electrically Assisted Pedal Cycles Regulations 1983; and

(d) "the 1981 British Standard" means the Specification for safety requirements for bicycles published by the British Standard Institution under the reference BS 6102: Part I: 1981.

(2) In these Regulations, unless the context otherwise requires, a reference to a numbered Regulation is to the Regulation bearing that number in these Regulations, and a reference to a numbered paragraph is to the paragraph bearing that number in the Regulation in which the reference occurs.

Requirements as to a pedal cycle to which the Electrically Assisted Pedal Cycles Regulations 1983 apply

4–3133   **4.** No person shall ride, or cause or permit to be ridden, on a road a pedal cycle to which the Electrically Assisted Pedal Cycles Regulations 1983 apply unless it is fitted with—

    (a) a plate securely fixed in a conspicuous and readily accessible position showing—

        (i) the name of the manufacturer of the vehicle,

        (ii) the nominal voltage of the battery (as defined in the 1971 British Standard) of the vehicle, and

        (iii) the continuous rated output (as defined in the 1971 British Standard) of the motor of the vehicle;

    (b) braking systems which are so designed and constructed that—

        (i) in the case of a bicycle they comply with the standards specified in clause 6 of the 1981 British Standard, and

        (ii) in the case of a tricycle they comply with standards no less than the standards of braking systems fitted to a bicycle which comply with clause 6 of the 1981 British Standard;

    (c) a battery which does not leak so as to be a source of danger; and

    (d) a device biased to the off position which allows power to come from the motor only when the device is operated so as to achieve that result.

4–3134   **5.** No person shall ride, or cause or permit to be ridden, on a road a pedal cycle to which the Electrically Assisted Pedal Cycles Regulations 1983 apply unless the parts of the vehicle mentioned in—

    (a) Regulation 4(b) and (c) of those Regulations, and

    (b) Regulation 4(b), (c) and (d) of these Regulations,

are in efficient working order.

Requirements as to a pedal cycle to which the Electrically Assisted Pedal Cycles Regulations 1983 do not apply

4–3135   **6.** No person shall ride, or cause or permit to be ridden, on a road a pedal cycle to which the Electrically Assisted Pedal Cycles Regulations 1983 do not apply unless it complies with such of the requirements specified in Regulation 7 or 8 as apply to it.

4–3136   **7.** (1) Save as provided in Regulations 8 and 9—

    (a) every pedal cycle shall be equipped with at least one braking system;

    (b) every bicycle or tricycle the height of the saddle of which is 635 millimetres or more and every cycle with four or more wheels shall—

        (i) if it is so constructed that one or more of the wheels is incapable of rotating independently of the pedals, be equipped with a braking system operating on the front wheel or, if it has more than one front wheel, on at least two front wheels;

        (ii) if it is not so constructed that one or more of the wheels is incapable of rotating independently of the pedals, be equipped with two independent braking systems one of which operates on the front wheel, or if it has more than one front wheel, on at least two front wheels, and the other of which operates on the rear wheel, or if it has more than one rear wheel, on at least two rear wheels.

(2) The reference in paragraph (1)(b) to the height of the saddle is a reference to the height above the ground of the part of the seating area of the saddle which is furthest from the ground when the cycle to which the saddle is attached is vertical and the saddle is raised to the fullest extent compatible with safety and the tyres on the wheels of the cycle are fully inflated.

4–3137   **8.** (1) The requirements of Regulation 7 do not apply to a pedal cycle manufactured before 1st August 1984 if, save as provided in Regulation 9 in the case where the cycle has any wheel of which the outside diameter (including any tyre when fully inflated) exceeds 460 millimetres—

    (i) the cycle is so constructed that one or more of the wheels is incapable of rotating independently of the pedals, it is equipped with a braking system operating on the front wheel or both the front wheels if it has two front wheels;

    (ii) the cycle is not so constructed, it is equipped with two independent braking systems one of which operates on the front wheel or both the front wheels if it has two front wheels, and the other of which operates on the rear wheel or one of the rear wheels if it has two rear wheels.

4–3138   **9.** (1) Nothing in Regulation 7 or 8 applies to—

(a) any pedal cycle so constructed that the pedals act on any wheel or on the axle of any wheel without the interposition of any gearing or chain; or

(b) any pedal cycle brought temporarily into great Britain by a person resident abroad and intending to make only a temporary stay in Great Britain, while the cycle is being ridden by that person, provided that its brakes comply with the requirements of Article 26 of the International Convention on Road Traffic signed at Geneva on 19th September 1949 as amended[1].

(2) In the case of a tricycle not constructed or adapted for the carriage of goods it shall be a sufficient compliance with the requirements specified in regulation 7(1)(b)(ii) and 8(1)(a)(ii) if the tricycle is equipped with two independent braking systems operating on the front wheel if it has two rear wheels, or on the rear wheel if it has two front wheels.

---

1. See Cmnd 7997 and Cmnd 3152.

4–3139   **10.** (1) No person shall ride, or cause or permit to be ridden, on a road a pedal cycle to which Regulation 6 applies unless the braking system or systems with which it is required to be fitted in accordance with Regulation 7 or, as the case may be, Regulation 8 are in efficient working order.

(2) For the purpose of this regulation, except in the case of a cycle having four or more wheels, none of which has a diameter exceeding 250 millimetres (including any tyre when fully inflated), a braking system shall be deemed not to be in efficient working order if any brake operates directly on a pneumatic tyre on any wheel.

Testing and inspection

4–3140   **11.** Any constable in uniform is hereby empowered to test and inspect a pedal cycle for the purpose of a ascertaining whether any of the requirements specified in regulation 4(b), or Regulation 7 or, as the case may be, regulation 8 are satisfied provided he does so either—

(a) on any premises where the cycle is if the cycle has been involved in an accident, and the test and inspection are carried out within 48 hours of the accident and the owner of the premises consents; or

(b) on a road.

Requirements as to sale or supply etc of pedal cycles

4–3141   **12.** No person shall sell or supply, or offer to sell or supply for delivery—

(a) a pedal cycle to which the Electrically Assisted Pedal Cycles Regulations 1983 apply unless it is equipped with braking systems as specified in Regulation 4 (b); or

(b) on and after 1st August 1984, a pedal cycle to which those Regulations do not apply unless it is

(i) equipped with braking systems as specified in Regulation 7 or, as the case may be, Regulation 8; or

(ii) a pedal cycle which has no braking system and is specifically designed for off-road racing on enclosed tracks.

Road Vehicles (Construction and Use) Regulations 1986[1]

(SI 1986/1078 amended by SI 1986/1597, SI 1987/676 and 1133, SI 1988/271, 1178, 1287 and 1524, the Road Traffic (Consequential Provisions) Act 1988, Sch 1, SI 1988/1871, SI 1989/1478, 1695, 1865 and 2360, SI 1990/317, 1131, 1163, 1981 and 2212, SI 1991/1526, 1527, 2003, 2125 and 2710, SI 1992/352, 422, 646, 1217, 2016, 2137, 2909, 3088 and 3285, SI 1993/1946, 2199 and 3048, SI 1994/14, 329, 2192, 2567 and 3270, SI 1995/551, 737, 1201, 1458, 2210 and 3051, SI 1996/16, 163, 252, 2064, 2085, 2329, 3017, 3033 and 3133, SI 1997/530, 1096, 1340, 1458, 1544 and 2935, SI 1998/1, 1000, 1188, 1281, 1563, 2429 and 3112, SI 1999/1521, 1999/1959, SI 2000/1434, 1971 and 3197, 2001/306, 1043, 1149, 1825 and 3208, SI 2002/227, 1474 and 2126, the Utilities Act 2000, s 76(7), SI 2003/182, 1690, 1946, 2096, 2155, 2695 and 3145, SI 2004/1706, 2102, 3168 (E),SI 2005/1641, 2560, 2929 (W), 2987, 3165 and 3170, SI 2006/594, 1756 and 2565 and SI 2007/361.)

PRELIMINARY NOTE

4–3501 Section 42(1) of the Road Traffic Act 1988 makes it an offence to (i) contravene or fail to comply with these regulations or (ii) to use on a road a motor vehicle or trailer which does not comply or to cause or permit a vehicle to be so used. The terms "use", "cause", "permit" and "road" are explained in the Preliminary Note to this PART, title ROAD TRAFFIC.

Exemptions, usually conditional, are provided in regulation 4. Further exemptions are provided by the Motor Vehicle (Authorisation of Special Types) General Order 2003, a permissive order, failure to comply with the terms of which allows prosecution under these regulations; see note[1] to **4–3826**.

Penalties are provided in Sch 2 to the Road Traffic Offenders Act 1988. The offences under the regulations are created variously by ss 41A, 41B and 42 of the Road Traffic Act 1988. It must be noted that only offences under s 41A are endorseable. (An endorseable offence in relation to vehicles in a dangerous condition is provided by s 40A quite independent of the regulations.)

The endorseable regulations are therefore those relating to brakes, steering-gear and tyres; regs 15, 16, 17, 18, 19, 24, 25, 26, 27 and 29.

---

1. Made by the Secretary of State in exercise of powers conferred by ss 34(5), 40(1), (2) and (3) and 172 of the Road Traffic Act 1972 and now having effect under s 41 of the Road Traffic Act 1988. In view of the references to the Motor Vehicles (Construction and Use) Regulations 1978 contained in other places, a table showing the destination of the 1978 regulations appears directly after these regulations.

PART I—PRELIMINARY

4–3502   **1–2.** *Commencement, citation and revocations.*

Interpretation

4–3503   **3.** (1) In these Regulations, unless the context otherwise requires—

(a) any reference to a numbered regulation or a numbered Schedule is a reference to the regulation or Schedule bearing that number in these Regulations,

(b) any reference to a numbered or lettered paragraph or sub-paragraph is a reference to the paragraph or sub-paragraph bearing that number or letter in the regulation or Schedule or (in the case of a sub-paragraph) paragraph in which the reference occurs, and

(c) any reference to a Table, or to a numbered Table, is a reference to the Table, or to the Table bearing that number, in the regulation or Schedule in which that reference occurs.

(2) In paragraph (1), the words "except sub-paragraph (b)(ii)" shall be omitted, for the words "the trailer" there shall be substituted the words "a trailer" and after the words "1983 or" in the proviso there shall be inserted the word "which".

TABLE

(regulation 3(2))

1	2
Expression	Meaning
The 1971 Act	The Vehicles (Excise) Act 1971.
The 1972 Act	The Road Traffic Act 1972.
The 1981 Act	The Public Passenger Vehicles Act 1981.
The 1984 Act	The Road Traffic Regulation Act 1984.
The Approval Marks Regulations	The Motor Vehicles (Designation of Approval Marks) Regulations 1979.
The EC Whole Vehicle Type Approval Regulations	The Motor Vehicles (EC Type Approval) Regulations 1998
The Lighting Regulations	The Road Vehicles Lighting Regulations 1984.
The Plating and Testing Regulations	The Goods Vehicles (Plating and Testing) Regulations 1982.
The Type Approval Regulations	The Motor Vehicles (Type Approval) Regulations 1980.
The Type Approval (Great Britain) Regulations	The Motor Vehicles (Type Approval) (Great Britain) Regulations 1984.
The Type Approval for Goods Vehicles Regulations	The Motor Vehicles (Type Approval for Goods Vehicles) (Great Britain) Regulations 1982.
The Type Approval for Agricultural Vehicles Regulations	The Agricultural or Forestry Tractors and Tractor Components (Type Approval) Regulations 1979.
The Act of Accession	the Treaty concerning the Accession of the Kingdom of Denmark, Ireland, the Kingdom of Norway and the United Kingdom of Great Britain and Northern Ireland to the European Economic Community and the European Atomic Energy Community
agricultural or forestry tractor	an agricultural or forestry tractor within the meaning of Community Directive 82/890.
agricultural motor vehicle	a motor vehicle which is constructed or adapted for use off roads for the purpose of agriculture, horticulture or forestry and which is primarily used for one or more of those purposes, not being a dual-purpose vehicle.
agricultural trailer	a trailer which is constructed or adapted for the purpose of agriculture, horticulture or forestry and which is only used for one or more of those purposes, not being an agricultural trailed appliance.
agricultural trailed appliance	a trailer— (a) liwhich is an implement constructed or adapted— (i) for use off roads for the purpose of agriculture, horticulture or forestry and which is only used for one or more of those purposes, and

1	2
Expression	Meaning

	(ii) so that, save in the case of an appliance manufactured before 1st December 1985, or a towed roller, its maximum gross weight is not more than twice its unladen weight; but
	(b) which is not—
	   (i) a vehicle which is used primarily as living accommodation by one or more persons, and which carries no goods or burden except those needed by such one or more persons for the purposes of their residence in the vehicle; or
	   (ii) an agricultural, horticultural or forestry implement rigidly but not permanently mounted on any vehicle whether or not any of the weight of the implement is supported by one or more of its own wheels; so however that such an implement is an agricultural trailed appliance if
	—part of the weight of the implement is supported by one or more of its own wheels, and
	—the longitudinal axis of the greater part of the implement is capable of articulating in the horizontal plane in relation to the longitudinal axis of the rear portion of the vehicle on which it is mounted.

agricultural trailed appliance conveyor	an agricultural trailer which— (a) has an unladen weight which does not exceed 510 kg; (b) is clearly and indelibly marked with its unladen weight; (c) has a pneumatic tyre fitted to each one of its wheels; (d) is designed and constructed for the purpose of conveying one agricultural trailed appliance or one agricultural, horticultural or forestry implement.
Anti-lock braking system ("ABS")	A part of a service braking system which automatically controls the degree of slip, in the direction of rotation of the wheel or wheels, on one or more wheels of the vehicle during braking.
articulated bus	a bus so constructed that— (a) it can be divided into two parts, both of which are vehicles and one of which is a motor vehicle, but cannot be so divided without the use of facilities normally available only at a workshop; and (b) passengers carried by it can at all times pass from either part to the other.
articulated vehicle	a heavy motor car or motor car, not being an articulated bus, with a trailer so attached that part of the trailer is superimposed on the drawing vehicle and, when the trailer is uniformly loaded, not less than 20 per cent of the weight of its load is borne by the drawing vehicle.
Axle	any reference to the number of axles of a vehicle is to be interpreted in accordance with paragraph (8).
axle weight	in relation to each axle of a vehicle, the sum of the weights transmitted to the road surface by all the wheels of that axle, having regard to the provisions of paragraph (8).
braking efficiency	the maximum braking force capable of being developed by the brakes of a vehicle, expressed as a percentage of the weight of the vehicle including any persons or load carried in the vehicle.
braking system	is to be interpreted in accordance with paragraph (6).
bus	a motor vehicle which is constructed or adapted to carry more than eight seated passengers in addition to the driver.
car transporter	a trailer which is constructed and normally used for the purpose of carrying at least two other wheeled vehicles.
cc	cubic centimetre(s).
close-coupled	in relation to wheels on the same side of a trailer, fitted so that at all times while the trailer is in motion they remain parallel to the longitudinal axis of the trailer, and that the distance between the centres of their respective areas of contact with the road surface does not exceed 1 m.
cm	centimetre(s).
cm squared	square centimetre(s).
coach	a large bus with a maximum gross weight of more than 7.5 tonnes and with a maximum speed exceeding 60 mph;
Community Directive, followed by a number	the Directive adopted by the Council or the Commission of the European Communities or the European Parliament and the Council of the European Union of which identifying particulars are given in the item in column 3 of Table I in Schedule 2 in which that number appears in column 2; where such a Directive amends a previous Directive mentioned in column 3(d) of the Table the reference to the amending Directive includes a reference to that previous Directive as so amended. Any reference to a Directive which has been amended by the Act of Accession is a reference to the Directive as so amended.
the Community Recording Equipment Regulation	Council Regulation (EEC) 3821/85 of 20th December 1985 on recording equipment in road transport, as read with the Community Drivers' Hours and Recording Equipment (Exemptions and Supplementary Provisions) Regulations 1986.
combined transport operation	shall be construed in accordance with paragraph 9 of Schedule 11A.
composite trailer	a combination of a converter dolly and a semi-trailer.

1	2
Expression	Meaning
Container	an article of equipment, not being a motor vehicle or trailer, having a volume of at least 8 cubic metres, constructed wholly or mostly of metal and intended for repeated use for the carriage of goods or burden.

converter dolly	(*a*) a trailer which is—
	    (i) equipped with two or more wheels,
	    (ii) designed to be used in combination with a semi-trailer without any part of the weight of the semi-trailer being borne by the drawing vehicle, and
	    (iii) not itself a part either of the semi-trailer or the drawing vehicle when being so used; or
	 (*b*) a trailer which is—
	    (i) equipped with two or more wheels;
	    (ii) designed to be used in combination with a semi-trailer with part of the weight of the semi-trailer being borne by the drawing vehicle;
	    (iii) not itself a part either of the semi-trailer or the drawing vehicle when being so used; and
	    (iv) used solely for the purposes of agriculture, horticulture or forestry, or for any two or for all of those purposes.

Council Regulation (EEC), followed by a number	the Regulation adopted by the Council of the European Communities.
Deck	a floor or platform on which seats are provided for the accommodation of passengers.
design weight	in relation to the gross weight, each axle weight or the train weight of a motor vehicle or trailer, the weight at or below which in the opinion of the Secretary of State or of a person authorised in that behalf by the Secretary of State the vehicle could safely be driven on roads.
double-decked vehicle	a vehicle having two decks one of which is wholly or partly above the other and each of which is provided with a gangway serving seats on that deck only.

dual-purpose vehicle	a vehicle constructed or adapted for the carriage both of passengers and of goods or burden of any description, being a vehicle of which the unladen weight does not exceed 2040 kg, and which either—
	    (i) is so constructed or adapted that the driving power of the engine is, or by the appropriate use of the controls of the vehicle can be, transmitted to all the wheels of the vehicle; or
	    (ii) satisfies the following conditions as to construction, namely—
	 (*a*) the vehicle must be permanently fitted with a rigid roof, with or without a sliding panel;
	 (*b*) the area of the vehicle to the rear of the driver's seat must—
	    (i) be permanently fitted with at least one row of transverse seats (fixed or folding) for two or more passengers and those seats must be properly sprung or cushioned and provided with upholstered back-rests, attached either to the seats or to a side or the floor of the vehicle; and
	    (ii) be lit on each side and at the rear by a window or windows of glass or other transparent material having an area or aggregate area of not less than 1850 square centimetres on each side and not less than 770 square centimetres at the rear; and
	 (*c*) the distance between the rearmost part of the steering wheel and the back-rests of the row of transverse seats satisfying the requirements specified in head (i) of sub-paragraph (b) (or, if there is more than one such row of seats, the distance between the rearmost part of the steering wheel and the back-rests of the rearmost such row) must, when the seats are ready for use, be not less than one-third of the distance between the rearmost part of the steering wheel and the rearmost part of the floor of the vehicle.

ECE Regulation, followed by a number	the Regulation, annexed to the Agreement concerning the adoption of uniform conditions of approval for Motor Vehicles Equipment and Parts and reciprocal recognition thereof concluded at Geneva on 20th March 1958 as amended, to which the United Kingdom is a party, of which identifying particulars are given in the item in column (3)(a), (b) and (c) of Table II in Schedule 2 in which that number appears in column (2); and where that number contains more than two digits, it refers to that Regulation with the amendments in force at the date specified in column (3)(d) in that item.
engine power in kilowatts (kW)	the maximum net power ascertained in accordance with Community Directive 80/1269.
engineering equipment	engineering plant and any other plant or equipment designed and constructed for the purpose of engineering operations.
engineering plant	(*a*) movable plant or equipment being a motor vehicle or trailer specially designed and constructed for the special purposes of engineering operations, and which cannot, owing to the requirements of those purposes, comply with all the requirements of these Regulations and which is not constructed primarily to carry a load other than a load being either excavated materials raised from the ground by apparatus on the motor vehicle or trailer or materials which the vehicle or trailer is specially designed to treat while carried thereon; or (*b*) a mobile crane which does not comply in all respects with the requirements of these Regulations.

1	2
Expression	Meaning
exhaust system	a complete set of components through which the exhaust gases escape from the engine unit of a motor vehicle including those which are necessary to limit the noise caused by the escape of those gases.
first used	is to be interpreted in accordance with paragraph (3).
Framework Directive	Council Directive 70/156/EEC as amended by Council Directive 87/403/EEC, Council Directive 92/53/EEC, Commission Directive 93/81/EEC and Commission Directive 98/14/EC.
gangway	the space provided for obtaining access from any entrance to the passengers' seats or from any such seat to an exit other than an emergency exit, but excluding a staircase and any space in front of a seat which is required only for the use of passengers occupying that seat or a seat in the same row of seats.
gas	any fuel which is wholly gaseous at 17.5 degrees C under a pressure of 1.013 bar absolute.
gas-fired appliance	a device carried on a motor vehicle or trailer when in use on a road, which consumes gas and which is neither— (a) a device owned or operated by or with the authority of the British Gas Corporation for the purpose of detecting gas, nor (b) an engine for the propulsion of a motor vehicle, nor (c) a lamp which consumes acetylene gas.
goods vehicle	a motor vehicle or trailer constructed or adapted for use for the carriage or haulage of goods or burden of any description.
gritting trailer	a trailer which is used on a road for the purpose of spreading grit or other matter so as to avoid or reduce the effect of ice or snow on the road.
gross weight	(a) in relation to a motor vehicle, the sum of the weights transmitted to the road surface by all the wheels of the vehicle. (b) in relation to a trailer, the sum of the weights transmitted to the road surface by all the wheels of the trailer and of any weight of the trailer imposed on the drawing vehicle.
heavy motor car	a mechanically propelled vehicle, not being a locomotive, a motor tractor, or a motor car, which is constructed itself to carry a load or passengers and the weight which unladen exceeds 2540 kg.
indivisible load	a load which cannot without undue expense or risk of damage be divided into two or more loads for the purpose of conveyance on a road.
industrial tractor	a tractor, not being an agricultural motor vehicle, which— (a) has an unladen weight not exceeding 7370 kg, (b) is designed and used primarily for work off roads, or for work on roads in connection only with road construction or maintenance (including any such tractor when fitted with an implement or implements designed primarily for use in connection with such work, whether or not any such implement is of itself designed to carry a load), and (c) has a maximum speed not exceeding 20 mph.
invalid carriage	a mechanically propelled vehicle the weight of which unladen does not exceed 254 kg and which is specially designed and constructed, and not merely adapted, for the use of a person suffering from some physical defect or disability and is solely used by such a person.
ISO	International Organisation for Standardisation.
ISO 7638 connector	An electrical connector which complies with standard ISO 7638: 1997-1 or ISO 7638: 1997-2 and is used to provide a dedicated power supply and a communication link between the tow vehicle and trailer.
kerbside weight	the weight of a vehicle when it carries— (a) in the case of a motor vehicle, (i) no person; and (ii) a full supply of fuel in its tank, an adequate supply of other liquids incidental to its propulsion and no load other than the loose tools and equipment with which it is normally equipped; (b) in the case of a trailer, no person and is otherwise unladen.
Kg	kilogram(s).
km/h	kilometre(s) per hour.
KW	kilowatt(s).
large bus	a vehicle constructed or adapted to carry more than 16 seated passengers in addition to the driver.
light trailer	a trailer with a maximum gross weight which does not exceed 3500 kg.
living van	a vehicle used primarily as living accommodation by one or more persons, and which is not also used for the carriage of goods or burden which are not needed by such one or more persons for the purpose of their residence in the vehicle.
locomotive	a mechanically propelled vehicle which is not constructed itself to carry a load other than the following articles, that is to say, water, fuel, accumulators and other equipment used for the purpose of propulsion, loose tools and loose equipment, and the weight of which unladen exceeds 7370 kg.
longitudinal plane	a vertical plane parallel to the longitudinal axis of a vehicle.
low loader	a semi-trailer which is constructed and normally used for the carriage of engineering equipment so constructed that the major part of the load platform does not extend over or between the wheels and the upper surface of which is below the height of the top most point of the tyres of those wheels, measured on level ground and when— (a) any adjustable suspension is at the normal travelling height,

1	2
Expression	Meaning
	(b) all pneumatic tyres are suitably inflated for use when the vehicle is fully laden, and (c) the semi-trailer is unladen, (see also the definition of stepframe low loader).
low platform trailer	a trailer fitted with tyres with a rim diameter size code of less than 20 and displaying a rectangular plate which— (a) is at least 225 mm wide and at least 175 mm high; and (b) bears two black letters "L" on a white ground each at least 125 mm high and 90 mm wide with a stroke width of 12 mm.
m	metre(s).
m squared	square metre(s).
m cubed	cubic metre(s).
maximum permitted axle weight	in relation to an axle— (a) in the case of a vehicle which is equipped with a Ministry plate in accordance with regulation 70, the axle weight shown in column (2) of that plate (where the plate is in the form required by Schedule 10 or 10B) or in column (2) of that plate (where the plate is in the form required by Schedule 10A or 10C) in relation to that axle; (b) in the case of a vehicle which is not equipped with a Ministry plate but which is equipped with a plate in accordance with regulation 66, the maximum axle weight shown for that axle on the plate in respect of item 9 of Part I of Schedule 8 in the case of a motor vehicle and item 7 of Part II of Schedule 8 in the case of a trailer; and (c) in any other case, the weight which the axle is designed or adapted not to exceed when the vehicle is travelling on a road.
maximum gross weight	(a) in the case of a vehicle equipped with a Ministry plate in accordance with regulation 70, the design gross weight shown in column (3) of that plate (where the plate is in the form required by Schedule 10 or 10B) or in column (4) of that plate (where the plate is in the form required by Schedule 10A or 10C) or, if no such weight is shown, the gross weight shown in column (2) of that plate; (b) in the case of a vehicle not equipped with a Ministry plate, but which is equipped with a plate in accordance with regulation 66, the maximum gross weight shown on the plate in respect of item 7 of Part I of Schedule 8 in the case of a motor vehicle and item 6 of Part II of Schedule 8 in the case of a trailer; (c) in any other case, the weight which the vehicle is designed or adapted not to exceed when the vehicle is travelling on a road.
maximum total design axle weight (an expression used only in relation to trailers)	(a) in the case of a trailer equipped with a Ministry plate in accordance with regulation 70, the sum of the relevant axle weights; (b) in the case of a trailer which is not equipped with a Ministry plate, but which is equipped with a plate in accordance with regulation 66, the sum of the maximum axle weights shown on the plate in respect of item 4 of Part II of Schedule 8; or (c) in the case of any other trailer, the sum of the axle weights which the trailer is designed or adapted not to exceed when the vehicle is travelling on a road; and for the purposes of sub-paragraph (a) the relevant axle weight, in respect to an axle, is the design axle weight shown in column (3) of the Ministry plate (where the plate is in the form required by Schedule 10 or 10B) or in column (4) of that plate (where the plate is in the form required by Schedule 10A or 10C) in relation to that axle or if no such weight is shown, the axle weight shown in column (2) of that plate in relation to that axle;
maximum speed	the speed which a vehicle is incapable, by reason of its construction, of exceeding on the level under its own power when fully laden.
minibus	a motor vehicle which is constructed or adapted to carry more than 8 but not more than 16 seated passengers in addition to the driver.
ministry plate	is to be interpreted in accordance with regulation 70.
mm	millimetre(s).
motor ambulance	a motor vehicle which is specially designed and constructed (and not merely adapted) for carrying, as equipment permanently fixed to the vehicle, equipment used for medical, dental, or other health purposes and is used primarily for the carriage of persons suffering from illness, injury or disability.
motor car	a mechanically propelled vehicle, not being a motor tractor, a motor cycle or an invalid carriage, which is constructed itself to carry a load of passengers and the weight of which unladen— (a) if it is constructed solely for the carriage of passengers and their effects and is adapted to carry not more than seven passengers exclusive of the driver does not exceed 3050 kg; (b) if it is constructed for use for the conveyance of goods or burden of any description, does not exceed 3050 kg; (c) does not exceed 2540 kg in a case falling within neither of the foregoing paragraphs.

1	2
Expression	Meaning
motor caravan	a motor vehicle which is constructed or adapted for the carriage of passengers and their effects and which contains, as permanently installed equipment, the facilities which are reasonably necessary for enabling the vehicle to provide mobile living accommodation for its users.
motor cycle	a mechanically propelled vehicle, not being an invalid carriage, having less than four wheels and the weight of which unladen does not exceed 410 kg.
motor tractor	a mechanically propelled vehicle which is not constructed itself to carry a load, other than the following articles, that is to say, water, fuel, accumulators and other equipment used for the purpose of propulsion, loose tools and loose equipment, and the weight of which unladen does not exceed 7370 kg.
motor vehicle	a mechanically propelled vehicle intended or adapted for use on roads.
mph	mile(s) per hour.
n/mm squared	newton(s) per square millimetre.
off-road vehicle	an off-road vehicle as defined in Annex I to Council Directive 70/156/EEC of 6th February 1970 as read with Council Directive 87/403/EEC of 25th June 1987.
overall height	the vertical distance between the ground and the point on the vehicle which is furthest from the ground, calculated when— (*a*) the tyres of the vehicle are suitably inflated for the use to which it is being put; (*b*) the vehicle is at its unladen weight; and (*c*) the surface of the ground under the vehicle is reasonably flat; but, in the case of a trolley bus, exclusive of the power collection equipment mounted on the roof of the vehicle.
overall length	in relation to a vehicle, the distance between transverse planes passing through the extreme forward and rearward projecting points of the vehicle inclusive of all parts of the vehicle, of any receptacle which is of a permanent character and accordingly strong enough for repeated use, and any fitting on, or attached to, the vehicle except— (i) for all purposes— (*a*) any driving mirror; (*b*) any expanding or extensible contrivance forming part of a turntable fire escape fixed to a vehicle; (*c*) any snow-plough fixed in front of a vehicle; (*d*) any receptacle specially designed to hold and keep secure a seal issued for the purposes of customs clearance; (*e*) any tailboard which is let down while the vehicle is stationary in order to facilitate its loading or unloading; (*f*) any tailboard which is let down in order to facilitate the carriage of, but which is not essential for the support of, loads which are in themselves so long as to extend at least as far as the tailboard when upright; (*g*) any fitting attached to a part of, or to a receptacle on, a vehicle which does not increase the carrying capacity of the part or receptacle but which enables it to be —transferred from a road vehicle to a railway vehicle or from a railway vehicle to a road vehicle, —secured to a railway vehicle by a locking device, and —carried on a railway vehicle by the use of stanchions; (*h*) any plate, whether rigid or movable, fitted to a trailer constructed for the purpose of carrying other vehicles and designed to bridge the gap between that trailer and a motor vehicle constructed for that purpose and to which the trailer is attached so that, while the trailer is attached to the motor vehicle, vehicles which are to be carried by the motor vehicle may be moved from the trailer to the motor vehicle before a journey begins, and vehicles which have been carried on the motor vehicle may be moved from it to the trailer after a journey ends; (*i*) any sheeting or other readily flexible means of covering or securing a load; (*j*) (*revoked*); (*k*) any empty receptacle which itself forms a load; (*l*) any receptacle which contains an indivisible load of exceptional length; (*m*) any receptacle manufactured before 30th October 1985, not being a maritime container (namely a container designed primarily for carriage on sea transport without an accompanying road vehicle); (*n*) any special appliance or apparatus as described in regulation 81(c) which does not itself increase the carrying capacity of the vehicle; or (*o*) any rearward projecting buffer made of rubber or other resilient material. (ii) for the purposes of regulations 7, 13A, 13B and 13C— (*a*) any part of a trailer (not being in the case of an agricultural trailed appliance a drawbar or other thing with which it is equipped for the purpose of being towed) designed primarily for use as a means of attaching it to another vehicle and any fitting designed for use in connection with any such part;

1	2
Expression	Meaning
overall width	(b) the thickness of any front or rear wall on a semi-trailer and of any part forward of such front wall or rearward of such rear wall which does not increase the vehicle's load-carrying space. the distance between longitudinal planes passing through the extreme lateral projecting points of the vehicle inclusive of all parts of the vehicle, of any receptacle which is of permanent character and accordingly strong enough for repeated use, and any fitting on, or attached to, the vehicle except— (a) any driving mirror; (b) any snow-plough fixed in front of the vehicle; (c) so much of the distortion of any tyre as is caused by the weight of the vehicle; (d) any receptacle specially designed to hold and keep secure a seal issued for the purposes of customs clearance; (e) any lamp or reflector fitted to the vehicle in accordance with the Lighting Regulations; (f) any sideboard which is let down while the vehicle is stationary in order to facilitate its loading or unloading; (g) any fitting attached to part of, or to a receptacle on, a vehicle which does not increase the carrying capacity of the part or receptacle but which enables it to be —transferred from a road vehicle to a railway vehicle or from a railway vehicle to a road vehicle; —secured to a railway vehicle by a locking device; and —carried on a railway vehicle by the use of stanchions; (h) any sheeting or other readily flexible means of covering or securing a load; (i) any receptacle with an external width, measured at right angles to the longitudinal axis of the vehicle, which does not exceed 2.5 m; (j) any empty receptacle which itself forms a load; (k) any receptacle which contains an indivisible load of exceptional width; (l) any receptacle manufactured before 30th October 1985, not being a maritime container (namely a container designed primarily for carriage on sea transport without an accompanying road vehicle); (m) any special appliance or apparatus as described in regulation 81(c) which does not itself increase the carrying capacity of the vehicle; or (n) any apparatus fitted to a bus which enables it to be guided wholly or mainly by means of wheels bearing outwards against fixed apparatus, provided that no part of the apparatus projects more than 75mm beyond the side of the bus when the wheels of the bus are parallel to its longitudinal axis; and the reference in paragraph (n) above to the side of a bus is a reference to the longitudinal plane passing through the extreme lateral projecting points of the vehicle inclusive of all parts of the vehicle, of any receptacle which is of permanent character and accordingly strong enough for repeated use, and any fitting on, or attached to, the vehicle except those items referred to in paragraphs (a) to (n).

Overhang	the distance measured horizontally and parallel to the longitudinal axis of a vehicle between two transverse planes passing through the following two points—
	(a) the rearmost point of the vehicle exclusive of—
	  (i) any expanding or extensible contrivance forming part of a turntable fire escape fixed to a vehicle;
	  (ii) in the case of a motor car constructed solely for the carriage of passengers and their effects and adapted to carry not more than eight passengers exclusive of the driver, any luggage carrier fitted to the vehicle; and
	(b)
	  (i) in the case of a motor vehicle having not more than three axles of which only one is not a steering axle, the centre point of that axle;
	  (ii) in the case of a motor vehicle having three axles of which the front axle is the only steering axle and of a motor vehicle having four axles of which the two foremost are the only steering axles, a point 110mm behind the centre of a straight line joining the centre points of the two rearmost axles; and
	  (iii) in any other case a point situated on the longitudinal axis of the vehicle and such that a line drawn from it at right angles to that axis will pass through the centre of the minimum turning circle of the vehicle.

passenger vehicle	a vehicle constructed solely for the carriage of passengers and their effects.
pedestrian-controlled vehicle	a motor vehicle which is controlled by a pedestrian and not constructed or adapted for use or used for the carriage of a driver or passenger.
pneumatic tyre	a tyre which— (a) is provided with, or together with the wheel upon which it is mounted forms, a continuous closed chamber inflated to a pressure substantially exceeding atmospheric pressure when the tyre is in the condition in which it is normally used, but is not subjected to any load; (b) is capable of being inflated and deflated without removal from the wheel or vehicle; and

1	2
Expression	**Meaning**
	(c) is such that, when it is deflated and is subjected to a normal load, the sides of the tyre collapse.
public works vehicle	a mechanically propelled vehicle which is used on a road by or on behalf of—
	(a) the Central Scotland Water Development Board;
	(b) a ferry undertaking;
	(c) a highway or roads authority;
	(d) a local authority;
	(e) a market undertaking;
	(f) the Environment Agency;
	(g) an operator of an electronic communications code network;
	(h) a police authority;
	(i) a universal service provider (within the meaning of the Post Services Act 2000) in connection with th e provision of a universal postal service (within the meaning of that Act);
	(j) a public electricity supplier within the meaning of Part I of the Electricity Act 1989;
	(k) a gas transporter within the meaning of Part I of the Gas Act 1986;
	(l) a statutory undertaker within the meaning of section 329(1) of the Highways Act 1980;
	(m) an undertaking for the supply of district heating;
	(n) a water authority within the meaning of the Water (Scotland) Act 1980; or
	(o) a water or sewerage undertaker within the meaning of the Water Act 1989;
	for the purpose of works which such a body has a duty or power to carry out, and which is used only for the carriage of—
	(i) the crew, and
	(ii) goods which are needed for works in respect of which the vehicle is used.
recut pneumatic tyre	a pneumatic tyre in which all or part of its original tread pattern has been cut deeper or burnt deeper or a different tread pattern has been cut deeper or burnt deeper than the original tread pattern.
refuse vehicle	a vehicle designed for use and used solely in connection with street cleansing, the collection or disposal of refuse, or the collection or disposal of the contents of gullies or cesspools.
Registered	registered under any of the following enactments—
	(a) the Roads Act 1920,
	(b) the Vehicles (Excise) Act 1949,
	(c) the Vehicles (Excise) Act 1962, or
	(d) the 1971 Act
	and, in relation to the date on which a vehicle was registered, the date on which it was first registered under any of those enactments.
relevant braking requirement	a requirement that the brakes of a motor vehicle (as assisted, where a trailer is being drawn, by the brakes on the trailer) comply—
	(i) in a case to which item 1 in Table 1 in regulation 18 applies, with the requirements specified in regulation 18(3) for vehicles falling in that item;
	(ii) in any other case, with the requirements specified in regulation 18(3) for vehicle classes (a) and (b) in item 2 of that Table (whatever the date of first use of the motor vehicle and the date of manufacture of any trailer drawn by it may be).
resilient tyre	a tyre, not being a pneumatic tyre, which is of soft or elastic material, having regard to paragraph (5).
restricted speed vehicle	a vehicle displaying at its rear a "50" plate in accordance with the requirements of Schedule 13.
retreaded tyre	a tyre which has been reconditioned to extend its useful life by replacement of the tread rubber or by replacement of the tread rubber and renovation of the sidewall rubber.
rigid vehicle	a motor vehicle which is not constructed or adapted to form part of an articulated vehicle or articulated bus.
rim diameter	is to be interpreted in accordance with the British Standard BS AU 50: Part 2: Section 1: 1980 entitled "British Standard Automobile Series: Specification for Tyres and Wheels Part 2. Wheels and rims Section 1. Rim profiles and dimensions (including openings for valves)" which came into effect on 28th November 1980.
rim diameter size code	is to be interpreted in accordance with the British Standard referred to in the meaning given in this Table to "rim diameter".
secondary braking system	a braking system of a vehicle applied by a secondary means of operation independent of the service braking system or by one of the sections comprised in a split braking system.
service braking system	the braking system of a vehicle which is designed and constructed to have the highest braking efficiency of any of the braking systems with which the vehicle is equipped.
semi-trailer	a trailer which is constructed or adapted to form part of an articulated vehicle [including (without prejudice to the generality of that) a vehicle which is not itself a motor vehicle but which has some or all of its wheels driven by the drawing vehicle].

1	2
Expression	Meaning
Silencer	a contrivance suitable and sufficient for reducing as far as may be reasonable the noise caused by the escape of exhaust gases from the engine of a motor vehicle.
single-decked vehicle	a vehicle upon which no part of a deck or gangway is vertically above another deck or gangway.
split braking system	in relation to a motor vehicle, a braking system so designed and constructed that— (*a*) it comprises two independent sections of mechanism capable of developing braking force such that, excluding the means of operation, a failure of any part (other than a fixed member or a brake shoe anchor pin) of one of the said sections will not cause a decrease in the braking force capable of being developed by the other section; (*b*) the said two sections are operated by a means of operation which is common to both sections; (*c*) the braking efficiency of either of the said two sections can be readily checked.
Staircase	a staircase by means of which passengers on a double-decked vehicle may pass to and from the upper deck of the vehicle.
stepframe low loader	a semi-trailer (not being a low loader) which is constructed and normally used for the carriage of engineering equipment and is so constructed that the upper surface of the major part of the load platform is at a height of less than 1m above the ground when measured on level ground and when— (*a*) any adjustable suspension is at the normal travelling height, (*b*) all pneumatic tyres are suitably inflated for use when the vehicle is fully laden, and (*c*) the semi-trailer is unladen.
stored energy	in relation to a braking system of a vehicle, energy (other than the muscular energy of the driver or the mechanical energy of a spring) stored in a reservoir for the purpose of applying the brakes under the control of the driver, either directly or as a supplement to his muscular energy.
straddle carrier	a motor vehicle constructed to straddle and lift its load for the purpose of transportation.
statutory power of removal	a power conferred by or under any enactment to remove or move a vehicle from any road or from any road or from any part of a road.
temporary use spare tyre	a pneumatic tyre which is designed for use on a motor vehicle only— (*a*) in the event of the failure of one of the tyres normally fitted to a wheel of the vehicle, and (*b*) at a speed lower than that for which such normally fitted tyres are designed.
three-wheeled motor cycle	a motor cycle having three wheels, not including a two-wheeled motor cycle with a sidecar attached.
towing implement	a device on wheels designed for the purpose of enabling a motor vehicle to draw another vehicle by the attachment of that device to that other vehicle in such a manner that part of that other vehicle is secured to and either rests on or is suspended from the device and some but not all of the wheels on which that other vehicle normally runs are raised off the ground.
track-laying	in relation to a vehicle, so designed and constructed that the weight thereof is transmitted to the road surface either by means of continuous tracks or by a combination of wheels and continuous tracks in such circumstances that the weight transmitted to the road surface by the tracks is not less than half the weight of the vehicle.
Trailer	means a vehicle drawn by a motor vehicle and is to be interpreted in accordance with paragraphs (9) and (11).
train weight	in relation to a motor vehicle which may draw a trailer, the maximum laden weight for the motor vehicle together with any trailer which may be drawn by it.
transverse plane	a vertical plane at right angles to the longitudinal axis of a vehicle.
trolley bus	a bus adapted for use on roads without rails and moved by power transmitted thereto from some external source.
unbraked trailer	any trailer other than one which, whether or not regulation 15 or 16 applies to it, is equipped with a braking system in accordance with one of those regulations.
unladen weight	the weight of a vehicle or trailer inclusive of the body and all parts (the heavier being taken where alternative bodies or parts are used) which are necessary to or ordinarily used with the vehicle or trailer when working on a road, but exclusive of the weight of water, fuel or accumulators used for the purpose of the supply of power for the propulsion of the vehicle or, as the case may be, of any vehicle by which the trailer is drawn, and of loose tools and loose equipment.
vehicle in the service of a visiting force or of a head-quarters	a vehicle so described in Article 8(6) of the Visiting Forces and International Headquarters (Application of Law) Order 1965.
Wheel	a wheel the tyre or rim of which when the vehicle is in motion on a road is in contact with the ground; two wheels are to be regarded as one wheel in the circumstances specified in paragraph (7).
Wheeled	in relation to a vehicle, so constructed that the whole weight of the vehicle is transmitted to the road surface by means of wheels.

1	2
Expression	Meaning
wide tyre	a pneumatic tyre of which the area of contact with the road surface is not less than 300 mm in width when measured at right angles to the longitudinal axis of the vehicle.
works trailer	a trailer designed for use in private premises and used on a road only in delivering goods from or to such premises to or from a vehicle on a road in the immediate neighbourhood, or in passing from one part of any such premises to another or to other private premises in the immediate neighbourhood or in connection with road works while at or in the immediate neighbourhood of the site of such works.
works truck	a motor vehicle (other than a straddle carrier) designed for use in private premises and used on a road only in delivering goods from or to such premises to or from a vehicle on a road in the immediate neighbourhood, or in passing from one part of any such premises to another or to other private premises in the immediate neighbourhood or in connection with road works while at or in the immediate neighbourhood of the site of such works.

(2A) Without prejudice to section 17 of the Interpretation Act 1978 and subject to the context, a reference in these Regulations to any enactment comprised in subordinate legislation (within the meaning of that Act) is a reference to that enactment as from time to time amended or re-enacted with or without modification.

(3) For the purpose of these Regulations, the date on which a motor vehicle is first used is—

(a) in the case of a vehicle not falling within sub-paragraph (b) and which is registered, the date on which it was registered;

(b) in each of the following cases—

(i) a vehicle which is being or has been used under a trade licence as defined in section 16 of the 1971 Act (otherwise than for the purposes of demonstration or testing or of being delivered from premises of the manufacturer by whom it was made or of a distributor of vehicles, or dealer in vehicles, to premises of a distributor of vehicles, dealer in vehicles or purchaser thereof or to premises of a person obtaining possession thereof under a hiring agreement or hire purchase agreement);

(ii) a vehicle belonging, or which has belonged, to the Crown and which is or was used or appropriated for use for naval, military or air force purposes;

(iii) a vehicle belonging, or which has belonged, to a visiting force or a headquarters or defence organisation to which in each case the Visiting Forces and International Headquarters (Application of Law) Order 1965 applies;

(iv) a vehicle which has been used on roads outside Great Britain before being imported into Great Britain; and

(v) a vehicle which has been used otherwise than on roads after being sold or supplied by retail and before being registered;

the date of manufacture of the vehicle.

In sub-paragraph (b)(v) of this paragraph "sold or supplied by retail" means sold or supplied otherwise than to a person acquiring it solely for the purpose of resale or re-supply for a valuable consideration.

(4) The date of manufacture of a vehicle to which the Type Approval for Goods Vehicles Regulations apply shall be the date of manufacture described in regulation 2(4)(a) of those Regulations.

(5) Save where otherwise provided in these Regulations a tyre shall not be deemed to be of soft or elastic material unless the said material is either—

(a) continuous round the circumference of the wheel; or

(b) fitted in sections so that so far as reasonably practicable no space is left between the ends thereof,

and is of such thickness and design as to minimise, so far as reasonably possible, vibration when the vehicle is in motion and so constructed as to be free from any defect which might in any way cause damage to the surface of a road.

(6) For the purpose of these Regulations a brake drum and brake disc shall be deemed to form part of the wheel and not of the braking system.

(7) For the purpose of these Regulations other than regulations 26 and 27 any two wheels of a motor vehicle or trailer shall be regarded as one wheel if the distance between the centres of the areas of contact between such wheels and the road surface is less than 460 mm.

(8) For the purpose of these Regulations other than regulations 26 and 27 in counting the number of axles of, and in determining the sum of the weights transmitted to the road surface by any one axle of, a vehicle, all the wheels of which the centres of the areas of contact with the road surface can be included between any two transverse planes less than 0·5 m apart shall be treated as constituting one axle.

(8A) For the purposes of these Regulations, a reference to axles being closely-spaced is a reference to—

(a) two axles (not being part of a group of axles falling within sub-paragraph (b) or (c)) which are spaced at a distance apart of not more than 2.5 m;

(b) three axles (not being part of a group of axles falling within sub-paragraph (c)) the outermost of which are spaced at a distance apart of not more than 3.25 m; or (*c*) four or more axles the outermost of which are spaced at a distance apart of not more than 4.6 m;

the number of axles for the purposes of these paragraphs being determined in accordance with paragraph (8); and a reference to any particular number of closely-spaced axles shall be construed accordingly.

(9) The provisions of these Regulations relating to trailers do not apply to any part of an articulated bus.

(10) For the purpose of paragraph (8A) above regulations 51, 76, 77 and 79 and Schedules 11 and 11A, the distance between any two axles shall be obtained by measuring the shortest distance between the line joining the centres of the areas of contact with the road surface of the wheels of one axle and the line joining the centres of the areas of contact with the road surface of the wheels of the other axle.

(11) For the purpose of the following provisions only a composite trailer shall be treated as one trailer (not being a semi-trailer or a converter dolly)—

   (*a*) regulations 7, 76 and 83;
   (*b*) paragraph (2) of, and items 3 and 10 in the Table in, regulation 75;
   (*c*) item 2 in the Table in regulation 78.

---

1. This expression has been held not to include a breakdown vehicle fitted with a crane and towing another vehicle in such a manner as to prevent the front wheels of the towed vehicle from being in contact with the road surface and when no part of the towed vehicle is superimposed on the breakdown vehicle and where not less than 20% of the towed vehicle was borne by the breakdown vehicle; *Hunter v Towers* [1951] 1 All ER 349, 115 JP 117. The specific point which led to the conviction in this case was subsequently met by what is now reg 91.

2. OJ No L 370, 31.12.85, p 8.

3. Where a vehicle fitted with a hydraulic beam lifted a rigid box lorry attached to a four-wheel draw bar trailer, that did not make it "constructed to carry a load" (*DPP v Yates* [1989] RTR 134, DC).

4. This relates to vehicles and not to the load; *Marston Services Ltd v Police Authority* (1934) 98 JP Jo 848.

5. The Utilities Act 2000, s 31(1) provides that references to public electricity suppliers shall have effect, after the commencement of that section, as references to electricity suppliers, electricity distributors, or both electricity suppliers and electricity distributors, according to the nature of the activities carried on by the persons to whom they referred before that time.

Modification of Regulations in relation to vehicles for which a Minister's approval certificate has been issued under the Motor Vehicles (Approval) Regulations 1996

4–3503A   3A. Schedule 2A shall have effect for the purpose of modifying these Regulations in relation to vehicles in respect of which a Minister's approval certificate has been issued by virtue of the Motor Vehicles (Approval) Regulations 1996.

Modifications of Regulations in relation to vehicles for which a Minister's approval certificate has been issued under the Motor Vehicles (Approval) Regulations 1996

4–3504   4[1]. (1) Save where the context otherwise requires, these Regulations apply to both wheeled vehicles and track-laying vehicles.

(2) Where a provision is applied by these Regulations to a motor vehicle first used on or after a specified date it does not apply to that vehicle if it was manufactured at least six months before that date.

(3) Where an exemption from, or relaxation of, a provision is applied by these Regulations to a motor vehicle first used before a specified date it shall also apply to a motor vehicle first used on or after that date if it was manufactured at least six months before that date.

(4) Subject to paragraph (7), the regulations specified in an item in column 3 of the Table do not apply in respect of a vehicle of a class specified in that item in column 2.

TABLE

(regulation 4(4))

1 Item	2 Class of Vehicle	3 Regulations which do not apply
1	A vehicle proceeding to a port for export.	The regulations in Part II insofar as they relate to construction and equipment, except regulations 16 (insofar as it concerns parking brakes) 20, 30, 34, 37 and 53. Regulations 66 to 69 and 71.
2	A vehicle brought temporarily into Great Britain by a person resident abroad, provided that the vehicle complies in every respect with the requirements relating to motor vehicles or trailers contained in—	The regulations in Part II insofar as they relate to construction and equipment except regulations 7, 8, 10, 10A, 40 and 53; and (*a*) additionally, in respect of any passenger vehicle with a maximum gross weight exceeding 10 tonnes registered in one or more member states, regulation 36A(2), 36A(7) and 36A(9); (*b*) additionally, in respect of any passenger vehicle with a maximum gross weight exceeding 12 tonnes registered in one or more member States, regulations 36B(2), 36B(9) and 36B(11).

1 Item	2 Class of Vehicle	3 Regulations which do not apply
	(a) article 21 and paragraph (1) of article 22 of the Convention on Road Traffic concluded at Geneva on 19th September 1949 and Part I, Part II (so far as it relates to direction indicators and stop lights) and Part III of Annex 6 to that Convention; or (b) paragraphs I, III and VIII of article 3 of the International Convention relative to Motor Traffic concluded at Paris on 24th April 1926.	Regulations 66 to 69 and 71.
3	A vehicle manufactured in Great Britain which complies with the requirements referred to in item 2 above and contained in the Convention of 1949, or, as the case may be, 1926 referred to in that item as if the vehicle had been brought temporarily into Great Britain, and either— (a) is exempt from car tax by virtue of section 7(1), (2) and (3) of the Car Tax Act 1983, or (b) has been zero rated under regulation 56 or 57 of the Value Added Tax (General) Regulations 1985.	The regulations in Part II insofar as they relate to construction and equipment, except regulations 7, 8, 10, 10A, 40 and 53. Regulations 66 to 69 and 71.
4	A vehicle in the service of a visiting force or of a headquarters.	The regulations in Part II insofar as they relate to construction and equipment, except regulations 16 (insofar as it concerns parking brakes), 21, 53 and 61. Regulations 66 to 69, 71 and 75 to 79 and 93A.
5	A vehicle which has been submitted for an examination under section 43 or section 45 of the 1972 Act while it is being used on a road in connection with the carrying out of that examination and is being so used by a person who is empowered under that section to carry out that examination, or by a person acting under the direction of a person so empowered.	The regulations in Part II. Regulations 75 to 79 and 100.
6	A motor car or a motor cycle in respect of which a certificate has been issued by the Officer in Charge of the National Collections of Road Transport, the Science Museum, London SW7, that it was designed before 1st January 1905 and constructed before 31st December 1905.	Regulations 16 (except insofar as it applies requirements 3 and 6 in Schedule 3), 21, 37(4), 63 and 99(4).
7	(a) A towing implement which is being drawn by a motor vehicle while it is not attached to any vehicle except the one drawing it if— (i) the towing implement is not being so drawn during the hours of darkness, and (ii) the vehicle by which it is being so drawn is not driven at a speed exceeding 20 mph; or (b) a vehicle which is being drawn by a motor vehicle in the exercise of a statutory power of removal.	The regulations in Part II insofar as they relate to the construction and equipment of trailers, except regulation 20.
8	Tramcars	The regulations in Parts II, III and IV
9	A public works vehicle which has a maximum design weight of 7500kg and is specifically designed for use and used solely for the purpose of street cleansing.	Regulation 15(1E) and (5B) in respect of the requirements in Community Directive 98/12/EC and ECE Regulation 13 09 which require the fitting of ABS to goods vehicles over 3500kg in weight.
10	A vehicle being used by a Police Authority which has been authorised by a Chief Constable to perform accident reconstruction duties.	Regulation 15(1E) and (5B) in respect of the requirements in Community Directive 98/12/EC and ECE Regulation 13 09 which prohibit the use of an isolation switch for the operation of ABS.
11	A vehicle being used on a road by a vehicle examiner, who has been authorised in writing by the Secretary of State for the purpose of— (a) submitting the vehicle for an examination under section 45 of the Road Traffic Act 1988 in order to ascertain whether the examination is carried out in accordance with regulations made under that section; or (b) removing the vehicle following that examination.	The regulations in Part 2. Regulations 67, 75 to 79 and 100.

(5) Any reference to a broken down vehicle shall include a reference to any towing implement which is being used for the drawing of any such vehicle.

(6) The Secretary of State is satisfied that it is requisite that the provisions of regulation 40(2) should apply, as from the date on which these Regulations come into operation, to track-laying vehicles registered before the expiration of one year from the making of these Regulations; and that, notwithstanding that those provisions will then apply to these vehicles, no undue hardship or inconvenience will be caused thereby.

(7) The exemption provided by item 11 in the Table in paragraph (4) shall only apply to the extent that the vehicle examiner using the vehicle in question reasonably believes that any defects in that vehicle do not give rise to a danger of injury to any person while it is being used by that person for a purpose mentioned in that item.

(8) In item 11 in the Table in paragraph (4) and paragraph (7), "vehicle examiner" means an examiner appointed under section 66A of the Road Traffic Act 1988.

---

1. Exemptions are also provided in the Motor Vehicle (Authorisation of Special Types) General Order 1979.
2. Sections 43 and 45 of the 1972 Act have been replaced by ss 45 and 49 of the Road Traffic Act 1988.

Trade Descriptions Act 1968

4–3505   **5.** Nothing in any provision of these Regulations whereby any vehicle or any of its parts or equipment is required to be marked with a specification number or the registered certification trade mark of the British Standards Institution or with an approval mark, or whereby such a marking is treated as evidence of compliance with a standard to which the marking relates, shall be taken to authorise any person to apply any such marking to the vehicle, part or equipment in contravention of the Trade Descriptions Act 1968.

Compliance with Community Directives and ECE Regulations.

4–3506   **6.** (1) For the purpose of any regulation which requires or permits a vehicle to comply with the requirements of a Community Directive or an ECE Regulation, a vehicle shall be deemed so to have complied at the date of its first use only if—

(a) one of the certificates referred to in paragraph (2) has been issued in relation to it; or
(b) the marking referred to in paragraph (3) has been applied; or
(c) it was, before it was used on a road, subject to a relevant type approval requirement as specified in paragraph (4).

(2) The certificates mentioned in paragraph (1) are—

(a) a type approval certificate issued by the Secretary of State under regulation 5 of the Type Approval Regulations or of the Type Approval for Agricultural Vehicles Regulations;
(b) a certificate of conformity issued by the manufacturer of the vehicle under regulation 6 of either of those Regulations;
(c) a certificate issued under a provision of the law of any member state of the European Economic Community which corresponds to the said regulations 5 or 6, or
(d) a sound level measurement certificate issued by the Secretary of State under regulation 4 of the Motorcycles (Sound Level Measurement Certificates) Regulations 1980;

being in each case a certificate issued by reason of the vehicle's conforming to the requirements of the Community Directive in question.

(3) The marking mentioned in paragraph (1) is a marking designated as an approval mark by regulation 4 of the Approval Marks Regulations, being in each case a mark shown in column 2 of an item in Schedule 2 to those Regulations which refers, in column 5, to the ECE Regulation in question, applied as indicated in column 4 in that item.

(4) A relevant type approval requirement is a requirement of the Type Approval (Great Britain) Regulations or the Type Approval for Goods Vehicles regulations which appears—

(a) in column 4 of Table I in Schedule 2 in the item in which the Community Directive in question appears in column 3, or
(b) in column 4 of Table II in Schedule 2 in the item in which the ECE Regulation in question appears in column 3.

PART II—REGULATIONS GOVERNING THE CONSTRUCTION EQUIPMENT AND MAINTENANCE OF VEHICLES

A—DIMENSIONS AND MANOEUVRABILITY

Length

4–3507   **7.** (1) Subject to paragraphs (2) to (6), the overall length[1] of a vehicle or combination of vehicles of a class specified in an item in column 2 of the Table shall not exceed the maximum length specified in that item in column 3 of the Table, the overall length in the case of a combination of vehicles being calculated in accordance with regulation 81(g) and (h).

TABLE

(regulation 7(1))

1	2	3
Item	Class of vehicle	Maximum length (metres)
	Vehicle combinations	
1	A motor vehicle (other than a motor vehicle such as is mentioned in item 1A) drawing one trailer which is not a semi-trailer.	18.75
1A	Subject to paragraph (3C), a motor vehicle manufactured before 1st June 1998 and drawing one trailer, where the combination does not meet the requirements of paragraph (5A) and the trailer is not a semi-trailer.	18
2	An articulated bus.	18.75
2A	A bus drawing a trailer.	18.75
3	An articulated vehicle the semi-trailer of which does not meet the requirements of paragraph (6) and is not a low loader.	15.5
3A	An articulated vehicle, the semi-trailer of which meets the requirements of paragraph (6) and is not a low loader.	16.5
3B	An articulated vehicle, the semi-trailer of which is a low loader.	18
	Motor vehicles	
4	A wheeled motor vehicle other than a bus.	12
4A	A bus with two axles.	13.5
4B	A bus with more than two axles.	15
5	A track-laying motor vehicle.	9.2
	Trailers	
6	An agricultural trailed appliance manufactured on or after 1st December 1985.	15
7	A semi-trailer manufactured on or after 1st May 1983 which does not meet the requirements of paragraph (6) and is not a low loader.	12.2
7A	A composite trailer drawn by— (a) a goods vehicle being a motor vehicle having a maximum gross weight exceeding 3500kg; or (b) an agricultural motor vehicle.	14.04
8	A trailer (not being a semi-trailer or composite trailer) with at least 4 wheels which is— (a) drawn by a goods vehicle being a motor vehicle having a maximum gross weight exceeding 3500kg; or (b) an agricultural trailer.	12
9	Any other trailer not being an agricultural trailed appliance or a semi-trailer.	7

(2) In the case of a motor vehicle drawing one trailer where—

(a) the motor vehicle is a showman's vehicle as defined in paragraph 7 of Schedule 3 to the 1971 Act; and

(b) the trailer is used primarily as living accommodation by one or more persons and is not also used for the carriage of goods or burden which are not needed for the purpose of such residence in the vehicle,

item 1 in the Table applies with the substitution of 22 m for 18 m and item 1A in the Table does not apply.

(3) Items 1, 3, 3A and 3B of the Table do not apply to—

(a) a vehicle combination which includes a trailer which is constructed and normally used for the conveyance of indivisible loads of exceptional length, or

(b) a vehicle combination consisting of a broken down vehicle (including an articulated vehicle) being drawn by a motor vehicle in consequence of a breakdown, or

(c) an articulated vehicle, the semi-trailer of which is a low loader manufactured before 1st April 1991.

(3A) Items 6, 7, 7A, 8 and 9 of the Table do not apply to—

(a) a trailer which is constructed and normally used for the conveyance of indivisible loads of exceptional length,

(b) a broken down vehicle (including an articulated vehicle) which is being drawn by a motor vehicle in consequence of a breakdown, or

(c) a trailer being a drying or mixing plant designed for the production of asphalt or of bituminous or tar macadam and used mainly for the construction, repair or maintenance of roads, or a road planing machine so used.

(3B) Furthermore item 7 does not apply to—

(a) a semi-trailer which is a car transporter,

(b) a semi-trailer which is normally used on international journeys any part of which takes place outside the United Kingdom,

(3C) Item 1A and the words "(other than a motor vehicle such as is mentioned in item 1A)" in item 1 of the Table shall cease to have effect after 31st December 2006.

(4) Where a motor vehicle is drawing—

(a) two trailers, then only one of those trailers may exceed an overall length of 7 m.

(b) three trailers, then none of those trailers shall exceed an overall length of 7 m.

(5) Where a motor vehicle is drawing—

(a) two or more trailers; or

(b) one trailer constructed and normally used for the conveyance of indivisible loads of exceptional length—

then—

(i) the overall length of that motor vehicle shall not exceed 9.2 m; and

(ii) the overall length of the combination of vehicles, calculated in accordance with regulation 81(g) and (h), shall not exceed 25.9 m, unless the conditions specified in paragraphs 1 and 2 of Schedule 12 have been complied with.

(5XA) A motor vehicle drawing a trailer which is not a semi-trailer shall (unless it is a vehicle such as is mentioned in item 1A of the Table in paragraph (1)) comply with the requirements of paragraph (5A).

The words in parenthesis in this paragraph shall cease to have effect after 31st December 2006.

(5A) The requirements of this paragraph, in relation to a combination of vehicles, are that at least one of the vehicles in the combination is not a goods vehicle or, if both vehicles in the combination are goods vehicles that—

(a) the maximum distance measured parallel to the longitudinal axis of the combination of vehicles from the foremost point of the loading area behind the driver's cab to the rear of the trailer, less the distance between the rear of the motor vehicle and the front of the trailer, does not exceed 15.65 m; and

(b) the maximum distance measured parallel to the longitudinal axis of the combination of vehicles from the foremost point of the loading area behind the driver's cab to the rear of the trailer does not exceed 16.4m;

but sub-paragraph (a) shall not apply if both vehicles in the combination are car transporters.

(6) The requirements of this paragraph, in relation to a semi-trailer, are that—

(a) the longitudinal distance from the axis of the king pin to the rear of the semi-trailer does not exceed—

(i) 12.5 m in the case of a car transporter, or

(ii) 12 m in any other case; and

(b) no point in the semi-trailer forward of the transverse plane passing through the axis of the king pin is more than—

(i) 4.19 m from the axis of the king pin, in the case of a car transporter, or

(ii) 2.04 m from the axis of the king pin, in any other case.

(6A) For the purposes of paragraph (5A)—

(a) where the forward end of the loading area of a motor vehicle is bounded by a wall, the thickness of the wall shall be regarded as part of the loading area; and

(b) any part of a vehicle designed primarily for use as a means of attaching another vehicle to it and any fitting designed for use in connection with any such part shall be disregarded in determining the distance between the rear of a motor vehicle and the front of a trailer being drawn by it.

(7) For the purpose of paragraph (6) the longitudinal distance from the axis of the king pin to the rear of a semi-trailer is the distance between a transverse plane passing through the axis of the king pin and the transverse plane of the rear of the semi-trailer.

(7A) Where a semi-trailer has more than one king-pin or is constructed so that it can be used with a king-pin in different positions, references in this regulation to a distance from the king-pin shall be construed—

(a) in relation to a vehicle which was manufactured after 1st January 1999, as a reference to the foremost king-pin or, as the case may be, the foremost king-pin position; and

(b) in relation to any other vehicle, as a reference to the rearmost king-pin or, as the case may be, the rearmost king-pin position.

(7B) For the purposes of paragraphs (5A), (6) and (7)—

(a) a reference to the front of a vehicle is a reference to the transverse plane passing through the extreme forward projecting points of the vehicle; and

(b) a reference to the rear of a vehicle is a reference to the transverse plane passing through the extreme rearward projecting points of the vehicle,

inclusive (in each case) of all parts of the vehicle, of any receptacle which is of a permanent character and accordingly strong enough for repeated use, and any fitting on, or attached to the vehicle but exclusive of—

(i) the things set out in sub-paragraph (i) of the definition of "overall length" in the Table in regulation 3(2), and

(ii) in the case of a semi-trailer, the things set out in sub-paragraph (ii)(a) of that definition.

(8) Where a broken down articulated vehicle is being towed by a motor vehicle in consequence of a breakdown—

(a) paragraph (5) shall have effect in relation to the combination of vehicles as if sub-paragraph (b) were omitted, and (*b*) for the purposes of paragraph (4) and of paragraph (5) as so modified, the articulated vehicle shall be regarded as a single trailer.

(9) No person shall use or cause or permit to be used on a road, a trailer with an overall length exceeding 18.65 m unless the requirements of paragraphs 1 and 2 of Schedule 12 are complied with.

1. A motor lorry, already of maximum permitted length, to which was bolted a container for the carriage of livestock, so increasing the overall length by 5 ft, was held to contravene a predecessor to this regulation; *Claude Hughes & Co (Carlisle) Ltd v Hyde* [1963] 2 QB 757, [1963] 1 All ER 598.
2. In this regulation a composition trailer may be treated as one trailer; reg 3(11).
3. It has been held that such a use on 46 occasions out of 177 journeys does not establish the normal use; *Peak Trailer and Chassis Ltd v Jackson* [1967] 1 All ER 108, [1967] 1 WLR 55, 131 JP 155. Provided the vehicle was constructed and normally used for indivisible loads, the mere fact that it was used for a divisible load on the occasion of the alleged offence will not render the offender guilty; *Kingdom v Williams* [1975] RTR 33, [1975] Crim LR 466.
4. In the case of a container carrying livestock, the proviso did not apply as the words "indivisible load" related to the contents and not to the container itself; *Patterson v Redpath Bros Ltd* [1979] 2 All ER 108, [1979] 1 WLR 553.
5. A load is not of exceptional length if it will fit on a vehicle of under 15 metres; *Cook v Briddon* (1975) 119 Sol Jo 462, [1975] Crim LR 466.

Width

4–3508 **8.** (1) Save as provided in paragraph (2), the overall width of a vehicle of a class specified in an item in column 2 of the Table shall not exceed the maximum width specified in column 3 in that item.

TABLE

(regulation 8(1))

1	2	3
Item	Class of vehicle	Maximum width (metres)
1	A locomotive, other than an agricultural motor vehicle.	2.75
2	A refrigerated vehicle	2.60
3	Any other motor vehicle.	2.55
4	A trailer drawn by a motor vehicle having a maximum gross weight (determined as provided in Part I of Schedule 8 to these Regulations) exceeding 3500 kg.	2.55
5	An agricultural trailer.	2.55
6	An agricultural trailed appliance.	2.55
7	Any other trailer drawn by a vehicle other than a motor cycle.	2.3
8	A trailer drawn by a motor cycle.	1.5

(2) Paragraph (1) does not apply to a broken down vehicle which is being drawn in consequence of the breakdown.

(3) No person shall use or cause or permit to be used on a road a wheeled agricultural motor vehicle drawing a wheeled trailer if, when the longitudinal axes of the vehicles are parallel but in different vertical planes, the overall width of the two vehicles, measured as if they were one vehicle, exceeds 2.55 metres.

(4) In this regulation "refrigerated vehicle" means any vehicle which is specially designed for the carriage of goods at low temperature and of which the thickness of each of the side walls, inclusive of insulation, is at least 45 mm.

Height

4–3509 **9.** (1) The overall height of a bus shall not exceed 4.57 m.

Indication of overall travelling height

4–3510 **10.** (1) Subject to the provisions of this regulation, no person shall drive or cause or permit to be driven on a road a motor vehicle with an overall travelling height exceeding 3 m unless a notice is displayed in the cab, in such a manner that it can easily be read by the driver, and the notice meets the requirements of paragraph (3).

(2) Subject to the provisions of this regulation, no person shall use or cause or permit to be used on a road a motor vehicle with an overall travelling height exceeding 3 m if any letters or numbers are displayed in the cab, otherwise than in a notice which meets the requirements of paragraph (3)—

(*a*) where they could be read by the driver; and
(*b*) which could be understood as indicating a height associated with the vehicle or any trailer drawn by it.

(3) The requirements of this paragraph in respect of a notice are that—

(a) the notice gives an indication of vehicle height expressed in feet and inches, or in both feet and inches and in metres;

(b) the numbers giving the indication in feet and inches are at least 40 mm tall;

(c) the height expressed in feet and inches and (where applicable) the height expressed in metres are—

(i) if the vehicle is a vehicle to which regulation 10A applies, not less than the predetermined height mentioned in regulation 10A(2)(a) or the overall travelling height (whichever is the greater), or

(ii) if the vehicle is not a vehicle to which regulation 10A applies, not less than the overall travelling height;

(d) if the vehicle is not a relevant vehicle, the height expressed in feet and inches does not exceed the overall travelling height by more than 150 mm;

(e) if the vehicle is a relevant vehicle, the height expressed in feet and inches does not exceed the overall travelling height by more than 1 m;

(f) if the height is expressed in both feet and inches and in metres, the height expressed in feet and inches and the height expressed in metres do not differ by more than 50 mm; and

(g) no other letters or numbers which could be understood as being an indication of any height associated with the vehicle or any trailer drawn by it are displayed in the notice.

(4) Paragraph (1) shall not apply if, having regard to the lengths of road which the driver might drive along in the course of fulfilling the purpose of the journey taking into account any possibility of unforeseen diversions and the driver having difficulty in finding his way, it is highly unlikely that the driver would during the course of the journey encounter any bridge or other overhead structure which does not exceed by at least 1 m—

(a) in the case of a vehicle to which regulation 10A applies, the maximum travelling height; or

(b) in any other case, the overall travelling height.

(5) Paragraph (1) shall not apply to a vehicle on a particular journey and at a particular time if—

(a) one or more documents are being carried in the vehicle which are within the easy reach of the driver and that or those documents describe a route or a choice of routes which the driver must take in order to fulfil the purpose of the journey without risk of the vehicle, its load or equipment or any trailer drawn by the vehicle, its load or equipment, colliding with any bridge or other overhead structure; and

(b) the vehicle is on such a route which is so described or is off that route by reason of a diversion that could not reasonably have been foreseen at the beginning of the journey.

(6) Paragraph (1) shall not apply to a vehicle on a particular journey if—

(a) one or more documents are being carried in the vehicle which are within the easy reach of the driver and that or those documents contain information as to—

(i) the height of bridges and other overhead structures under which the vehicle and any trailer drawn by it could pass, and

(ii) the height of bridges and other overhead structures under which the vehicle and any trailer drawn by it could not pass,

without the vehicle, its load or equipment or any such trailer, its load or equipment, colliding with any bridge or other overhead structure; and

(b) the information is such that, having regard in particular to the matters referred to in paragraph (7), it would enable any driver to fulfil the purpose of the journey without there being any risk of the vehicle, its load or equipment or any trailer, its load or equipment, colliding with any bridge or other overhead structure while on the journey.

(7) The matters referred to in paragraph (6) are—

(a) the roads which the driver might drive along in the course of fulfilling the purpose of the journey taking into account any possibility of unforeseen diversions and of the driver having difficulty in finding his way;

(b) the height of bridges and other overhead structures that would be encountered were the vehicle to proceed along any of those roads; and

(c) the setting of any device of a description specified in regulation 10A(2).

(8) Paragraphs (1) and (2) shall not apply to a motor vehicle if it has an overall travelling height of not more than 4m and—

(a) it is a vehicle registered or put into circulation in an EEA State and is being used in international traffic; or

(b) it is a motor vehicle drawing a trailer registered or put into circulation in an EEA State and that trailer is being used in international traffic.

(9) For the purposes of this regulation—

(a) "EEA State", and "high level equipment" and "maximum travelling height" have the meanings given in regulation 10C;

(b) "overall travelling height" in relation to a motor vehicle means—

(i) if it is not drawing a trailer, the overall height for the time being of the vehicle, its equipment and load, or

(ii) if it is drawing one or more trailers, the overall height for the time being of the combination of vehicles, their equipment and loads.

(c) a motor vehicle is a "relevant vehicle" if at any particular time—

(i) the vehicle or any trailer drawn by it is fitted with high level equipment with a maximum height of more than 3m; and

(ii) the overall travelling height is less than the maximum travelling height.

(10) In paragraph (8), "international traffic" and "registered or put into circulation" have the same meanings as in article 3 of Community Directive 85/3.

Warning devices where certain high level equipment is fitted to a vehicle

4–3510A 10A. (1) Subject to the provisions of this regulation and regulations 10B and 10C, no person shall drive or cause or permit to be driven on a road a vehicle to which this regulation applies unless the vehicle is fitted with a warning device and the requirements specified in paragraph (2) are satisfied in respect of the device, the vehicle and any relevant trailer drawn by the vehicle.

(2) The requirements are—

(a) that the device, the vehicle and any relevant trailer drawn by it shall be so constructed, maintained and adjusted, and the connections between the vehicle and those trailers are such, that the device would give a visible warning to the driver if, whilst the vehicle was being driven, the height of the highest point of any high level equipment fitted to the vehicle or any of those trailers were to exceed a predetermined height; and

(b) the predetermined height referred to in sub-paragraph (a) shall not exceed the overall travelling height by more than 1m.

(3) No person shall be taken to have failed to comply with paragraph (1) on the ground that a motor vehicle or a relevant trailer was not fitted with a warning device and the requirements in paragraph (2) were not being satisfied as mentioned in paragraph (1)—

(a) before 1st October 1998—

(i) if the motor vehicle was first used before 1st April 1998; or

(ii) the relevant trailer was manufactured before that date; or

(b) before 1st April 1998 in relation to any other motor vehicle or relevant trailer.

(4) Paragraph (1) shall not apply in relation to a particular journey if, having regard to the lengths of road which the driver might drive along in the course of fulfilling the purpose of the journey and taking into account any possibility of unforeseen diversions and the driver having difficulty in finding his way, it is highly unlikely that the driver would during the course of the journey be confronted with any bridge or other overhead structure which does not exceed the maximum travelling height by at least 1 m.

Vehicles to which regulation 10A applies

4–3510B 10B. (1) Subject to the provisions of this regulation, regulation 10A applies to—

(a) a motor vehicle first used on or after 1st April 1993, if the vehicle or any relevant trailer drawn by it, is fitted with high level equipment with a maximum height of more than 3 m; and

(b) a motor vehicle first used before 1st April 1993, if any relevant trailer drawn by it is fitted with such equipment.

(2) Regulation 10A does not apply to a motor vehicle if it has an overall travelling height of not more than 4 m and—

(a) it is a vehicle registered or put into circulation in an EEA State and is being used in international traffic; or

(b) it is a motor vehicle drawing a trailer registered or put into circulation in an EEA State and that trailer is being used in international traffic, and

in this paragraph, "international traffic" and "registered or put into circulation" have the same meanings as in article 3 of Community Directive 85/3.

(3) Regulation 10A does not apply to—

(a) an agricultural motor vehicle;

(b) an industrial tractor;

(c) a works truck;

(d) a motor vehicle owned by the Secretary of State for Defence and used for naval, military or air force purposes or a motor vehicle so used while being driven by a person for the time being subject to orders of a member of the armed forces of the Crown;

(e) a motor vehicle drawing a trailer owned by the Secretary of State for Defence and used for naval, military or air force purposes or a motor vehicle drawing such a trailer while being driven by a person for the time being subject to orders of a member of the armed forces of the Crown;

(f) a motor vehicle used by employees of a fire brigade for the purposes of that authority under that Act or, in England, a motor vehicle used by employees of a fire and rescue authority for the purposes of that authority under the Fire and Rescue Services Act 2004;

"axle interspace" means—

    (*a*) in the case of a semi-trailer, the distance between the point of support of the semi-trailer at its forward end and, if it has only one axle, the centre of that axle or, if it has more than one axle, the point halfway between the centres of the foremost and rearmost of those axles; and

    (*b*) in the case of any other trailer, the distance between the centre of its front axle or, if it has more than one axle at the front, the point halfway between the centres of the foremost and rearmost of those axles, and the centre of its rear axle or, if it has more than one axle at the rear, the point halfway between the centre of the foremost and rearmost of those axles; and

"ground clearance" means the shortest distance between the ground and the lowest part of that portion of the trailer (excluding any part of a suspension, steering or braking system attached to any axle, any wheel and any air skirt) which lies within the area formed by the overall width of the trailer and the middle 70% of the axle interspace, such distance being ascertained when the trailer—

    (*a*) is fitted with suitable tyres which are inflated to a pressure recommended by the manufacturer, and

    (*b*) is reasonably horizontal and standing on ground which is reasonably flat.

Turning circle—buses

4–3513 **13.**—(1) This regulation applies to a bus first used on or after 1st April 1982.

(2) Every vehicle to which this regulation applies shall be able to move on either lock so that, both with and without all its wheels in contact with the ground, no part of it projects outside the area contained between concentric circles with radii of 12.5 m and 5.3 m.

(2A) In relation to a vehicle manufactured before 1st June 1998 paragraph (2) shall have effect as if the words "both with and without its wheels in contact with the ground," were omitted.

(3) When a vehicle to which this regulation applies moves forward from rest, on either lock, so that its outermost point describes a circle of 12.5 m radius, no part of the vehicle shall project beyond the longitudinal plane which, at the beginning of the manoeuvre, defines the overall width of the vehicle on the side opposite to the direction in which it is turning by more than—

    (*a*) 0.8 m if it is a rigid vehicle of 12m or less in overall length; or

    (*b*) 1.2 m if it is a rigid bus of over 12m in overall length or an articulated bus.

(4) For the purpose of paragraph (3) the two rigid portions of an articulated bus shall be in line at the beginning of the manoeuvre.

Turning circle—articulated vehicles other than those incorporating a car transporter

4–3514 **13A.**—(1) Every vehicle to which this regulation applies shall be able to move on either lock so that, both with and without all its wheels in contact with the surface of the road and disregarding the things set out in paragraphs (*a*) to (*m*) in the definition of "overall width" and in paragraph (i)(*a*) to (*o*) in the definition of "overall length" in the Table in regulation 3, no part of it projects outside the area contained between concentric circles with radii of 12.5m and 5.3m.

(2) This regulation applies to all articulated vehicles except the following:

    (*a*) an articulated vehicle, the semi-trailer of which—

        (i) was manufactured before the 1st April1990, and has an overall length that does not exceed the overall length it had on that date,

        (ii) is a car transporter,

        (iii) is a low loader,

        (iv) is a stepframe low loader, or

        (v) is constructed and normally used for the conveyance of indivisible loads of exceptional length;

    (*b*) an articulated vehicle having an overall length not exceeding 15.5m and of which the drawing vehicle was first used before 1st June 1998 or the trailer was first used before that date; or

    (*c*) an articulated vehicle when an axle of the trailer is raised to aid traction.

(3) In relation to a vehicle manufactured before 1st June 1998, paragraph (1) shall have effect as if the words "both with and without all its wheels in contact with the surface of the road and" were omitted.

(4) An articulated vehicle shall be taken to comply with paragraph (1) if the semi-trailer comprised in it is, by virtue of paragraph 7.6.1.2 of Annex 1 of Community Directive 97/27/EC, deemed to comply with paragraph 7.6.1 of that Annex.

Turning circle—articulated vehicles incorporating a car transporter

4–3515 **13B.**—(1) Subject to paragraphs (2) and (3) this regulation applies to an articulated vehicle having an overall length exceeding 15·5 m, the semi-trailer of which is a car transporter.

(2) This regulation does not apply to an articulated vehicle, the semi-trailer of which satisfied the following conditions—

    (*a*) it was manufactured before the 1st April 1990, and

(*b*) the distance from the front of the trailer to the rearmost axle is no greater than it was on that date.

(3) This regulation does not apply to an articulated vehicle the semi-trailer of which is—

(*a*) a low loader, or
(*b*) a stepframe low loader.

(4) Every articulated vehicle to which this regulation applies shall be able to move on either lock so that both with and without all its wheels in contact with the surface of the road and disregarding the things set out in paragraphs (*a*) to (*m*) in the definition of "overall width" and in paragraph (l) (*a*) to (*o*) in the definition of "overall length" in the Table in regulation 3(2), no part of—

(*a*) the motor vehicle drawing the car transporter, or
(*b*) the car transporter to the rear of the transverse plane passing through the king pin,

projects outside the area between concentric circles with radii of 12·5 m and 5·3 m.

(5) In relation to a vehicle manufactured before 1st June 1998 paragraph (4) shall have effect as if the words "both with and without all its wheels in contact with the surface of the road and" were omitted.

(6) An articulated vehicle shall be taken to comply with paragraph (4) if the semi-trailer comprised in it is, by virtue of paragraph 7.6.1.2 of Annex 1 of Community Directive 97/27/EC, deemed to comply with paragraph 7.6.1 of that Annex.

Turning Circle—heavy motor car

4-3515A   13C. (1) This regulation applies to a vehicle which—

(*a*) is a heavy motor car or a vehicle combination which consists of a heavy motor car drawing one trailer which is not a semi-trailer;
(*b*) was manufactured or, in the case of a vehicle combination, the part consisting of a heavy motor car, was manufactured after 31st May 1998; and
(*c*) is not a vehicle falling within any of the descriptions specified in paragraph (2).

(2) The descriptions of vehicle referred to in paragraph (1)(*c*) are—

(*a*) a vehicle having 4 or more axles where the distance between the foremost and rearmost axles exceeds 6.4 metres;
(*b*) a vehicle or a vehicle combination to which regulation 13, 13A or 13B applies;
(*c*) a vehicle constructed and normally used for the carriage of indivisible loads of abnormal length.

(3) Every vehicle to which this regulation applies shall be able to move on either lock so that, both with and without all its wheels in contact with the surface of the road and disregarding the things set out in paragraphs (*a*) to (*m*) in the definition of "overall width" and in paragraph (i)(*a*) to (*o*) in the definition of "overall length" in the Table in regulation 3(2), no part of it projects outside the area contained between concentric circles with radii of 12.5 m and 5.3 m.

Connecting sections and direction-holding of articulated buses

4-3516   14. (1) This regulation applies to every articulated bus first used on or after 1st April 1982.

(2) The connecting section of the two parts of every articulated bus to which this regulation applies shall be constructed so as to comply with the provisions relating to such a section specified in paragraph 5.9 in ECE Regulation 36 as regards vehicles within the scope of that Regulation.

(3) Every articulated bus to which this regulation applies shall be constructed so that when the vehicle is moving in a straight line the longitudinal median planes of its two parts coincide and form a continuous plane without any deflection.

B—BRAKES

4-3517   15. (1) Save as provided in paragraphs (2), (3) and (4), the braking system of every wheeled vehicle of a class specified in an item in column 2 of the Table which, in the case of a motor vehicle, is first used on or after 1st April 1983 or which, in the case of the trailer, is manufactured on or after 1st October 1982 shall comply with the construction, fitting, and performance requirements in Annexes I, II and VII to Community Directive 79/489, and if relevant, Annexes III, IV, V, VI and VIII to that Directive in relation to the category of vehicles specified in that item in column 3.

Provided that it shall be lawful for any vehicle of such a class which, in the case of a motor vehicle, was first used before 1st April 1983 or which, in the case of a trailer, was manufactured before 1st October 1982 to comply with the said requirements instead of complying with regulations 16 and 17.

(1A) Save as provided in paragraphs (2), (3), (3A) and (5), the braking system of every wheeled vehicle of a class specified in an item in column 2 of the Table which, in the case of a motor vehicle, is first used on or after the relevant date or which, in the case of a trailer, is manufactured on or after the relevant date shall comply with the construction, fitting and performance requirements specified in Annexes I, II and VII to Community Directive 85/647, and if relevant, Annexes III, IV, V, VI, VIII, X, XI and XII to that Directive in relation to the category of vehicles specified in that item in column 3.

Provided that it shall be lawful for any vehicle of such a class which, in the case of a motor vehicle, was first used before the relevant date or which, in the case of a trailer, was manufactured before the relevant date to comply with the said requirements instead of complying with paragraph (1) or with regulations 16 and 17.

(1B)　In paragraph (1A), the relevant date in relation to a vehicle of a class specified in item 1 or 2 of the Table is 1st April 1990, in relation to a vehicle specified in item 4 of that Table is 1st April 1992, in relation to a vehicle in items 7, 8, 9 or 10 of that Table is 1st October 1988 and in relation to a vehicle of any other class is 1st April 1989.

(1C)　Save as provided in paragraphs (2), (3), (3A) and (5a), the braking system of every wheeled vehicle of a class specified in an item in column 2 of the Table which, in the case of a motor vehicle, is first used on or after 1st April 1992 or which, in the case of a trailer, is manufactured on or after 1st October 1991 shall comply with the construction, fitting and performance requirements specified in Annexes I, II and VII to Community Directive 88/194, and if relevant, Annexes III, IV, V, VI, VIII, X, XI and XII to that Directive in relation to the category of vehicles specified in that item in column 3.

Provided that it shall be lawful for any vehicle of such a class which, in the case of a motor vehicle, was first used before 1st April 1992 or which, in the case of a trailer, was manufactured before 1st October 1991 to comply with the said requirements instead of complying with paragraph (1) or (1A) or with regulations 16 and 17.

(1D)　Save as provided in paragraphs (2), (3), (3A) and (5A), the braking system of every wheeled vehicle of a class specified in an item in column 2 of the Table which, in the case of a motor vehicle, is first used on or after 1st April 1995 or which, in the case of a trailer, is manufactured on or after that date shall comply with the construction, fitting and performance requirements specified in Annexes I, II, and VII to Community Directive 91/422, and if relevant, Annexes III, IV, V, VI, VIII, X, XI and XII to that Directive in relation to the category of vehicles specified in that item in column 3.

Provided that it shall be lawful for any vehicle of such a class which, in the case of a motor vehicle, was first used before 1st April 1995 or which, in the case of a trailer, was manufactured before that date to comply with the said requirements instead of complying with paragraph (1), (1A) or (1C) or with regulations 16 and 17.

(1E)　Save as provided in paragraphs (2), (3), (3A), (5A) and (5B) the braking system of every wheeled vehicle of a class specified in an item in column 2 of the Table which, in the case of a motor vehicle, is first used on or after 1st May 2002 or which, in the case of a trailer, is manufactured on or after 1st May 2002 shall comply with the construction, fitting and performance requirements of Annexes I, II and VII to Community Directive 98/12/EC and if relevant, Annexes III, IV, V, VI, VIII, X, XI, XII, XIII and XIV to that Directive in relation to the category of vehicles specified in that item in column 3.

Provided that it shall be lawful for any vehicle of such a class which, in the case of a motor vehicle, was first used before 1st May 2002 or which, in the case of a trailer, was manufactured before 1st May 2002 to comply with the said requirements instead of complying with paragraphs (1), (1A), (1C) or (1D) or with regulations 16 and 17.

(2)　The requirements specified in paragraphs (1), (1A), (1C), (1D) and (1E) do not apply to—

(a)　an agricultural trailer or agricultural trailed appliance that is not, in either case, drawn at a speed exceeding 20 mph;

(b)　a locomotive;

(c)　a motor tractor;

(d)　an agricultural motor vehicle unless it is first used after 1st June 1986 and is driven at more than 20 mph;

(e)　a vehicle which has a maximum speed not exceeding 25 km/h;

(f)　a works trailer;

(g)　a works truck;

(h)　a public works vehicle;

(i)　a trailer designed and constructed, or adapted, to be drawn exclusively by a vehicle to which sub-paragraph (b), (c), (e), (g) or (h) of this paragraph applies;

(j)　a trailer falling within regulation 16(3)(b), (bb), (bc), (d), (e), (f) or (g);

(ja)　a trailer which is manufactured before 1st January 1997 and has a maximum total design axle weight that does not exceed 750 kg; or

(k)　a vehicle manufactured by Leyland Vehicles Limited and known as the Atlantean Bus, if first used before 1st October 1984.

(3)　The requirements specified in paragraphs (1), (1A), (1C), (1D) and (1E) shall apply to the classes of vehicles specified in the Table so that—

(a)　in item 3, the testing requirement specified in paragraph 1.5.1 and 1.5.2 of Annex II to Community Directives 79/489, 85/647, 88/194, 91/422 or 98/12 shall apply to every vehicle specified in that item other than—

(i)　a double-decked vehicle first used before 1st October 1983, or

(ii)　a vehicle of a type in respect of which a member state of the European Economic Community has issued a type approval certificate in accordance with Community Directive 79/489, 85/647, 88/194, 91/422 or 98/12.

(b)　in items 2 and 3—

(i)　the requirements specified in paragraph 1.1.4.2 of Annex II to Community Directive 79/489, 85/647, 88/194, 91/422 and 98/12shall not apply in relation to any vehicle first used before 1st April 1996;

    (ii) those requirements shall not apply in relation to any relevant bus first used on or after that date;

    (iii) sub-note (2) to paragraph 1.17.2 of Annex I to Community Directive 85/647, 88/194, 91/422 and 98/12 shall not apply in relation to any vehicle,

and for the purposes of this sub-paragraph "relevant bus" means a bus that is not a coach;

  (c) in items 1, 2, 3, 4, 5 and 6, in the case of vehicles constructed or adapted for use by physically handicapped drivers, the requirement in paragraph 2.1.2.1 of Annex I to Community Directive 79/489 that the driver must be able to achieve the braking action mentioned in that paragraph from his driving seat without removing his hands from the steering control shall be modified so as to require that the driver is able to achieve that action while continuing to steer the vehicle; and

  (d) in items 1, 4, 5, 6, 7, 8, 9 and 10, the requirement specified in paragraph 1.1.4.2 of Annex II to Community Directive 79/489 shall not apply to a vehicle first used (in the case of a motor vehicle) or manufactured (in the case of a trailer) before the relevant date as defined in paragraph (1B) if either—

    (i) following a test in respect of which the fee numbered 26024/26250 to 26257, prescribed in Schedule 1 to the Motor Vehicles (Type Approval and Approval Marks) (Fees) Regulations 1990, or the corresponding fee prescribed under any corresponding previous enactment is payable, a document is issued by the Secretary of State indicating that, at the date of manufacture of the vehicle, the type to which it belonged complied with the requirements specified in Annex 13 to ECE Regulation 13.03, 13.04, 13.05, 13.06, 13.07, 13.08 or 13.09; or

    (ii) as a result of a notifiable alteration to the vehicle, within the meaning of regulation 3 of the Plating and Testing Regulations, a fitment has been approved as complying with the requirements mentioned in sub-paragraph (i).

  (3A) The requirements specified in paragraph (1A), (1C), (1D) and (1E) shall apply to a road tanker subject to the exclusion of paragraph 4.3 of Annex X to Community Directive 85/647.

  (3B) No motor vehicle to which paragraph (1D) or (1E) applies and which is first used on or after 1st April 1996 shall be fitted with an integrated retarder unless either—

  (a) the motor vehicle is fitted with an anti-lock device which acts on the retarder and which complies with the requirements specified in Annex X to Community Directive 91/422 or Community Directive 98/12; or

  (b) the retarder is fitted with a cut-out device which allows the combined control to apply the service braking system alone and which can be operated by the driver from the driving seat;

and expressions (other than the word "vehicle") used in this paragraph which are also used in Annex I to Community Directive 85/647 shall, for the purposes of this paragraph, have the same meanings as in that Annex save that "retarder" shall not in any circumstances include a regenerative braking system.

  (4) Instead of complying with paragraph (1) of this regulation, a vehicle to which this regulation applies may comply with ECE Regulation 13.03, 13.04, 13.05, 13.06, 13.07, 13.08 or 13.09.

  (5) Instead of complying with paragraph (1A) of this regulation, a vehicle to which this regulation applies may comply with ECE Regulation 13.05, 13.06, 13.07, 13.08 or 13.09.

  (5A) Instead of complying with paragraph (1C) or (1D) of this regulation, a vehicle to which this regulation applies may comply—

  (a) in the case of a trailer manufactured before the 1st April 1992, with ECE Regulation 13.05, 13.06, 13.07, 13.08 or 13.09; or

  (b) in the case of any vehicle not falling within sub-paragraph (a), with ECE Regulation 13.06, 13.07, 13.08 or 13.09.

  (5B) Instead of complying with paragraph (1E) of this regulation, a vehicle to which this regulation applies may comply with ECE Regulation 13.09.

  (6) In paragraph (3A) the expression "road tanker" means any vehicle or trailer which carries liquid fuel in a tank forming part of the vehicle or trailer other than that containing the fuel which is used to propel the vehicle, and also includes any tank with a capacity exceeding 3m³ carried on a vehicle.

  (7) In this regulation, and in relation to the application to any vehicle of any provision of Community Directive 85/647, 88/194, 91/422 or 98/12, the definitions of "semi-trailer", "full trailer" and "centre-axle trailer" set out in that Directive shall apply and the meaning of "semi-trailer" in column 2 of the Table in regulation 3(2) shall not apply.

  (8) For the purposes of the preceding provisions of this regulation the date on which a trailer was manufactured shall be taken to be the date on which its manufacture was completed except that, in the case of a trailer whose manufacture has been completed for more than 8 years and which has been the subject of a notifiable alteration under regulation 30 of the Goods Vehicles (Plating and Testing) Regulations 1988, it shall be taken to be the date on which the notifiable alteration was completed.

  (9) A trailer, whose manufacture has been completed for more than eight years and which has been the subject of a notifiable alteration under regulation 30 of the Goods Vehicles (Plating and Testing) Regulations 1988, shall comply with all requirements of Community Directives relating to braking systems which applied to the trailer at the date when the notifiable alteration was completed.

TABLE

(regulation 15(1))

1 Item	2 Class of Vehicle	3 Vehicle Category in the Community Directive
1	Passenger vehicles and dual-purpose vehicles which have 3 or more wheels except— (a) dual-purpose vehicles constructed or adapted to carry not more than 2 passengers exclusive of the driver; (b) motor cycles with sidecar attached; (c) vehicles with three wheels, an unladen weight not exceeding 410kg, a maximum design speed not exceeding 50 km/h and an engine capacity not exceeding 50 cc; (d) buses.	M1
2	Buses having a maximum gross weight which does not exceed 5000 kg.	M2
3	Buses having a maximum gross weight which exceeds 5000 kg.	M3
4	Dual-purpose vehicles not within item 1; and goods vehicles, having a maximum gross weight which does not exceed 3500 kg, and not being motor cycles with a sidecar attached.	N1
	Goods vehicles with a maximum gross weight which—	
5	exceeds 3500 kg but does not exceed 12,000 kg;	N2
6	exceeds 12,000 kg.	N3
	Trailers with a maximum total design axle weight which—	
7	does not exceed 750 kg;	O1
8	exceeds 750 kg but does not exceed 3500 kg;	O2
9	exceeds 3500 kg but does not exceed 10,000 kg;	O3
10	exceeds 10,000 kg.	O4

Braking systems of vehicles to which regulation 15 does not apply

4–3518 **16.** (1) Save as provided in paragraphs (2) and (3), this regulation applies to every vehicle to which regulation 15 does not apply.

(2) Paragraph (4) of this regulation does not apply to a vehicle which complies with regulation 15 by virtue of the proviso to regulation 15(1), (1A), (1C), (1D) or (1E), or which complies with Community Directive 79/489, 85/647, 88/194, 91/422 or 98/12 or ECE Regulation 13.03, 13.04, 13.05, 13.06, 13.07, 13.08 or 13.09.

(3) This regulation does not apply to the following vehicles, except in the case of a vehicle referred to in (a) insofar as the regulation concerns parking brakes (requirements 16 to 18 in Schedule 3)—

(a) a locomotive first used before 2nd January 1933, propelled by steam, and with an engine which is capable of being reversed;

(b) a trailer which is designed for use and used for street cleansing and does not carry any load other than its necessary gear and equipment;

(ba) a trailer which has a maximum total design axle weight that does not exceed 750 kg;

(bb) a trailer which—

(i) is an agricultural trailer manufactured before 1st July 1947;

(ii) is being drawn by a motor tractor or an agricultural motor vehicle at a speed not exceeding 10 mph;

(iii) has a laden weight not exceeding 4070 kg; and

(iv) is the only trailer being drawn;

(bc) a trailer which is being drawn by a motor cycle in accordance with regulation 84;

(c) an agricultural trailed appliance;

(d) an agricultural trailed appliance conveyor;

(e) a broken down vehicle;

(f) before 1st October 1986—

(i) a trailer with an unladen weight not exceeding 102 kg which was manufactured before 1st October 1982; and

(ii) a gritting trailer; or

(g) on or after 1st October 1986, a gritting trailer with a maximum gross weight not exceeding 2000 kg.

(4) Save as provided in paragraph (7), a vehicle of a class specified in an item in column 2 of the Table shall comply with the requirements shown in column 3 in that item, subject to any exemptions or modifications shown in column 4 in that item, reference to numbers in column 3 being references to the requirements so numbered in Schedule 3[1].

TABLE

(regulation 16(4))

1	2	3	4
Item	Class of vehicle	Requirements in Schedule 3	Exemptions or modifications
	Motor cars		Requirements 13 and 16 do not apply to a motor car with less than 4 wheels.
1	First used before 1st January 1915.	3, 6, 7, 13, 16	A works truck within items 1 to 11 is not subject to requirements 1, 2, 3 or 4 if it is equipped with one braking system with one means of operation.
2	First used on or after 1st January 1915 but before 1st April 1938.	1, 4, 6, 7, 9, 16	
3	First used on or after 1st April 1938 and being either a track-laying vehicle or a vehicle first used before 1st January 1968.	1, 4, 6, 7, 8, 9, 16	
4	Wheeled vehicles first used on or after 1st January 1968.	1, 4, 6, 7, 8, 9, 15, 18	
	Heavy motor cars		
5	First used before 15th August 1928.	1, 6, 16	
6	First used on or after 15th August 1928 but before 1st April 1938.	1, 4, 6, 7, 8, 16	
7	First used on or after 1st April 1938 and being either a track-laying vehicle or a vehicle first used before 1st January 1968.	1, 4, 6, 7, 8, 9, 16	
8	Wheeled vehicles first used on or after 1st January 1968.	1, 4, 6, 7, 8, 9, 15, 18	
	Motor cycles		
9	First used before 1st January 1927.	3, and, in the case of three-wheeled vehicles, 16	
10	First used on or after 1st January 1927 but before 1st January 1968.	2, 7, and, in the case of three-wheeled vehicles, 16	
11	First used on or after 1st January 1968 and not being a motor cycle to which paragraph (5) applies.	2, 7, and, in the case of three-wheeled vehicles, 18	
	Locomotives		
12	Wheeled vehicle first used before 1st June 1955.	3, 6, 12, 16	
13	Wheeled vehicles first used on or after 1st June 1955 but before 1st January 1968.	3, 4, 6, 7, 8, 9, 18	
14	Wheeled vehicles first used on or after 1st January 1968.	3, 4, 6, 7, 8, 9, 18	
15	Track-laying vehicles.	3, 6, 16	
	Motor tractors		
16	Wheeled vehicles first used before 14th January 1931 and track-laying vehicles first used before 1st April 1938.	3, 4, 6, 7, 16	Industrial tractors within items 16 to 19 are subject to requirement 5 instead of requirement 4.
17	Wheeled vehicles first used on or after 14th January 1931 but before 1st April 1938.	3, 4, 6, 7, 9, 16	
18	Wheeled vehicles first used on or after 1st April 1938 but before 1st January 1968.	3, 4, 6, 7, 8, 9, 16	
19	Wheeled vehicles first used on or after 1st January 1968.	3, 4, 6, 7, 8, 9, 18	
20	Track-laying vehicles first used on or after 1st April 1938.	3, 4, 6, 7, 8, 16	
	Wheeled agricultural motor vehicles not driven at more than 20 mph		
21	First used before 1st January 1968.	3, 4, 6, 7, 8, 16	
22	First used on or after 1st January 1968 but before 9th February 1980.	3, 4, 6, 7, 8, 18	
23	First used on or after 9th February 1980.	3, 5, 6, 7, 8, 18	
	Invalid carriages		
24	Whenever first used.	3, 13	
	Trailers		

1	2	3	4
Item	Class of vehicle	Requirements in Schedule 3	Exemptions or modifications
25	Manufactured before 1st April 1938.	3, 10, 14, 17	
26	Manufactured on or after 1st April 1938 and being either a track-laying vehicle, an agricultural trailer or a vehicle manufactured before 1st January 1968.	3, 8, 10, 14, 17	Agricultural trailers are not subject to requirement 8.
27	Wheeled vehicles manufactured on or after 1st January 1968, not being an agricultural trailer.	3, 4, 8, 11, 15, 18	Trailers equipped with brackets which come into operation on the overrun of the vehicle are not subject to requirement 15.

Provided that wheeled agricultural motor vehicles not driven at more than 20 mph are excluded from all items other than items 21 to 23.

(5) Subject to paragraphs (5B) and (6), the braking system of a motor cycle to which this regulation applies and which is—

(a) of a class specified in an item in column 2 of the Table below; and
(b) first used on or after 1st April 1987 and before 22nd May 1995;

shall comply with ECE Regulation 13.05, 78 or 78.01 or Community Directive 93/14 in relation to the category of vehicles specified in that item in column 3.

(5A) Subject to paragraph (6), the braking system of a motor cycle to which this regulation applies and which is—

(a) of a class specified in an item in column 2 of the Table below; and
(b) first used on or after 22nd May 1995;

shall comply with ECE Regulation 78.01 or Community Directive 93/14 in relation to the category of vehicles specified in that item in column 3.

TABLE

(Regulation 16(5) and (5A))

1	2	3
Item	Class of Vehicle	Vehicle Category in ECE Regulations or Community Directive 93/14 (as the case may be)
1	Vehicles (without a sidecar attached) with two wheels, an engine capacity not exceeding 50cc and a maximum design speed not exceeding 50 km/h.	L1
2	Vehicles with three wheels (including two-wheeled vehicles with a sidecar attached) and with an engine capacity not exceeding 50 cc and a maximum design speed not exceeding 50 km/h.	L2
3	Vehicles with two wheels (without a sidecar attached) and with— (a) an engine capacity exceeding 50 cc, or (b) a maximum design speed exceeding 50 km/h.	L3
4	Vehicles with two wheels, a sidecar attached and— (a) an engine capacity exceeding 50 cc, or (b) a maximum design speed exceeding 50 km/h.	L4
5	Vehicles with three wheels (excluding two-wheeled vehicles with a sidecar attached) and with— (a) an engine capacity exceeding 50cc, or (b) a maximum design speed exceeding 50km/h.	L5

(5B) In relation to a motor cycle with two wheels manufactured by Piaggio Veicoli Europei Societa per Azione and known as the Cosa 125, the Cosa 125E, the Cosa L125, the Cosa LX125, the Cosa 200, the Cosa 200E, the Cosa L200 or the Cosa LX200, paragraph (5) shall have effect as if ECE Regulation 13.05 were modified by—

(a) the omission of paragraph 4.4 (approval marks), and
(b) in paragraph 5.3.1.1., (independent braking devices and controls), the omission of the word "independent" in the first place where it appears,

but this paragraph shall not apply to a motor cycle first used on or after 1st July 1991.

(6) Paragraph (5) does not apply to a works truck or to a vehicle constructed or assembled by a person not ordinarily engaged in the business of manufacturing vehicles of that description.

(6A) Paragraph (5A) does not apply to—

(a) a vehicle with a maximum speed not exceeding 25 km/h; or
(b) a vehicle fitted for an invalid driver.

(7) Instead of complying with the provisions of paragraph (4) of this Regulation an agricultural motor vehicle may comply with Community Directive 76/432 or 96/63.

1. Schedule 3 employs the requirement of an "efficient braking system" for certain vehicles alongside more definitive requirements and evidence of the construction of the brakes should be given to prove an inefficient braking system. The behaviour of the vehicle on one occasion is not sufficient as this may be due to the use of inefficiently maintained brakes; *Cole v Young* [1938] 4 All ER 39. Brakes must be good enough to be reliable in an emergency, so as to avoid an accident; *Badham v Lambs Ltd* [1946] KB 45, [1945] 2 All ER 295.

A brake drum and a brake disc shall be deemed to form part of the wheel and not of the braking system; reg 3(6).

Vacuum or pressure brake warning devices

4-3519 17. (1) Save as provided in paragraph (2), every motor vehicle which is equipped with a braking system[1] which embodies a vacuum or pressure reservoir or reservoirs shall be equipped with a device so placed as to be readily visible to the driver of the vehicle and which is capable of indicating any impending failure of, or deficiency in, the vacuum or pressure system.

(2) The requirement specified in paragraph (1) does not apply in respect of—

(a) a vehicle to which paragraph (1), (1A), (1C), (1D) or (1E) of regulation 15 applies, or which complies with the requirements of that regulation, of Community Directive 79/489, 85/647, 88/194, 91/422 or 98/12 or of ECE Regulation 13.03, 13.04, 13.05, 13.06. 13.07, 13.08 or 13.09;

(b) an agricultural motor vehicle which complies with Community Directive 76/432 or 96/63;

(c) a vehicle with an unladen weight not exceeding 3050 kg propelled by an internal combustion engine, if the vacuum in the reservoir or reservoirs is derived directly from the induction system of the engine, and if, in the event of a failure of, or deficiency in, the vacuum system, the brakes of that braking system are sufficient under the most adverse conditions to bring the vehicle to rest within a reasonable distance; or

(d) a vehicle first used before 1st October 1937.

_____

1. A brake drum and a brake disc shall be deemed to form part of the wheel and not of the braking system; reg 3(6).

Couplings on trailer pneumatic braking systems

4-3519A 17A. (1) In this regulation—

"BS coupling" means a coupling which—

(a) is of the type, shown in figure 1, 4 or 5 of the British Standard specification BS AU 138a: 1980 or figure 1, 2 or 3 of the British Standard specification BS AU 138b: 2000; and

(b) complies with the dimensions shown in figure 1, 4 or 5 of the British Standard specification BS AU 138a: 1980 or figure 1, 2 or 3 of the British Standard specification BS AU 138b:2000;

"the British Standard specification" means the British Standard specification for dimensions of 'contact' type couplings for air pressure braking systems on trailers and semi-trailers and their towing vehicles, and the arrangements of these couplings on articulated and drawbar combinations, published by the British Standards Institution under reference number BS AU 138a: 1980 or BS AU 138b: 2000;

"coupling", "emergency line", "secondary line" and "service line" have the same meanings as in the British Standard specification;

"EEA Agreement" means the Agreement on the European Economic Area signed at Oporto on the 2nd May 1992 as adjusted by the Protocol signed at Brussels on 17th March 1993; and

"EEA State" means a state which is a Contracting Party to the EEA Agreement.

(2) For the purposes of this regulation, a relevant coupling is a coupling that is physically capable of being connected to a BS coupling.

(3) Subject to paragraphs (6) and (7), no service line comprised in a pneumatic braking system fitted to a trailer shall be equipped with a relevant coupling unless that coupling—

(a) is of the type shown in figure 2 of the British Standard specification BS AU 138a:1980 or figure 4 of the British Standard specification BS AU 138b:2000;

(b) complies with the dimensions shown in that figure; and

(c) complies with paragraph 3.4.3 of that specification (except so far as it requires it to be of a type shown in that figure).

(4) Subject to paragraphs (6), (7) and (8) no emergency line comprised in a pneumatic braking system fitted to a trailer shall be equipped with a relevant coupling unless that coupling—

(a) is of the type shown in figure 3 of the British Standard specification BS AU 138a:1980 or figure 5 of the British Standard specification 138b:2000; and

(b) complies with the dimensions shown in that figure.

(5) Subject to paragraphs (6), (7) and (8) no secondary line comprised in a pneumatic braking system fitted to a trailer shall be equipped with a relevant coupling unless that coupling—

(a) is of the type shown in figure 6 of the British Standard specification BS AU 138a:1980 or figure 6 of the British Standard specification BS AU 138b:2000; and

(b) complies with the dimensions shown in that figure.

(6) For the purposes of paragraphs (3), (4) and (5), a reference to the dimensions shown in a figure in the British Standard specification does not include any dimension marked "M22 × 1.5".

(7) Paragraph (3) does not prevent a line being equipped with a relevant coupling which fulfils the requirements of—

(a) a standard or code of practice of a national standards body or equivalent body of any EEA State;

(b) any international standard recognised for use as a standard by any EEA State; or

(c) a technical specification or code of practice which, whether mandatory or not, is recognised for use as a standard by a public authority of any EEA State,

where the standard, code of practice, international standard or technical specification provides, in relation to couplings, a level of safety and compatibility with BS couplings of the type shown in figure 1 of the British Standard specification BS AU 138a:1980 or figure 1 of the British Standard specification BS AU 138b:2000 equivalent to that provided by those specifications as modified in accordance with paragraph (6).]

(8) Paragraph (7) shall have effect—

(a) in relation to paragraph (4), as if for the words "paragraph (3)" there were substituted the words "paragraph (4)" and for the words "figure 1" in the first and second places in which they occur there were substituted the words "figure 4" and "figure 2" respectively; and

(b) in relation to paragraph (5), as if for the words "paragraph (3)" there were substituted the words "paragraph (5)" and for the words "figure 1" in the first and second places in which they occur there were substituted the words "figure 5" and "figure 3" respectively.

Maintenance and efficiency of brakes

4–3520 18. (1) Every part[1] of every braking system and of the means of operation thereof fitted[2] to a vehicle shall be maintained[3] in good and efficient working order and be properly adjusted.

(1A) Without prejudice to paragraph (3), where a vehicle is fitted with an anti-lock braking system ("the ABS"), then while the condition specified in paragraph (1B) is fulfilled, any fault in the ABS shall be disregarded for the purposes of paragraph (1).

(1B) The condition is fulfilled while the vehicle is completing a journey at the beginning of which the ABS was operating correctly or is being driven to a place where the ABS is to undergo repairs.

(1C) Where a goods vehicle of category N2 or N3 is being used to tow a trailer of category O3 or O4 and both vehicles are fitted with an ISO 7638 connector to provide a dedicated power supply to the ABS, then these connectors shall be used regardless of any alternative method available on the vehicles to provide such power.

(2) Paragraph (3) applies to every wheeled motor vehicle except—

(a) an agricultural motor vehicle which is not driven at more than 20 mph;

(b) a works truck;

(c) a pedestrian-controlled vehicle; and

(d) an industrial tractor.

(3) Every vehicle to which this paragraph applies and which is of a class specified in an item in column 2 of Table I shall, subject to any exemption shown for that item in column 4, be so maintained[3] that—

(a) its service braking system has a total braking efficiency not less than that shown in column 3(a) for that item; and

(b) if the vehicle is a heavy motor car, a motor car first used on or after 1st January 1915 or a motor-cycle first used on or after 1st January 1927, its secondary braking system has a total braking efficiency not less than that shown in column 3(b) for those items.

Provided that a reference in Table I to a trailer is a reference to a trailer required by regulation 15 or 16 to be equipped with brakes.

TABLE I

(regulation 18(3))

1	2	3		4
Item	Class of vehicle	Efficiencies (%) (a)	(b)	Exemptions
1	A vehicle to which regulation 15 applies or which complies in all respects other than its braking efficiency with the requirements of that regulation or with Community Directive 79/489, 85/647, 88/194, 91/422 or 98/12 or with EEC Regulation 13.03, 13.04, 13.05, 13.06, 13.07, 13.08 or 13.09—			A motor cycle.
	(a) when not drawing a trailer;	50	25	
	(b) when drawing a trailer	45	25	
2	A vehicle, not included in item 1 and not being a motor cycle, which is first used on or after 1st January 1968—			
	(a) when not drawing a trailer;	50	25	
	(b) when drawing a trailer manufactured on or after 1st January 1968;	50	25	

1	2	3		4
Item	Class of vehicle	Efficiencies (%)		Exemptions
		(a)	(b)	
3	(c) when drawing a trailer manufactured before 1st January 1968	40	15	
	Goods vehicles and buses (in each case) first used on or after 15th August 1928 but before 1st January 1968 having an unladen weight exceeding 1525 kg being—			
	(a) rigid vehicles with 2 axles not constructed to form part of an articulated vehicle—			
	(i) when not drawing a trailer	45	20	
	(ii) when drawing a trailer	40	15	
	(b) other vehicles, including vehicles constructed to form part of an articulated vehicle, whether or not drawing a trailer	40	15	
4	Vehicles not included in items 1 to 3—			(a) a bus;
	(a) having at least one means of operation applying to at least 4 wheels;	50	25	(b) an articulated vehicle;
	(b) having 3 wheels and at least one means of operation applying to all 3 wheels and not being a motor cycle with sidecar attached—			(c) a vehicle constructed or adapted to form part of an articulated vehicle;
	(i) when not drawing a trailer	40	15	(d) a heavy motor car which is a goods vehicle first used before 15th August 1928.
	(ii) in the case of a motor cycle when drawing a trailer	40	15	
	(c) other			
	(i) when not drawing a trailer	30	25	
	(ii) in the case of a motor cycle when drawing a trailer.	30	25	

(4) A goods vehicle shall not be deemed to comply with the requirements of paragraph (3) unless it is capable of complying with those requirements both at the laden weight at which it is operating at any time and when its laden weight is equal to—

(a) if a plating certificate has been issued and is in force for the vehicle, the design gross weight shown in column (3) of that certificate or, if no such weight is so shown, the gross weight shown in column (2) of that certificate; and

(b) in any other case, the design gross weight of the vehicle.

Provided that in the case of a goods vehicle drawing a trailer, references in this paragraph to laden weight refer to the combined laden weight of the drawing vehicle and the trailer and references to gross weight and design gross weight are to be taken as references to train weight and design train weight respectively.

(4A) A bus shall be deemed not to comply with the requirements of paragraph (3) unless it is capable of complying with those requirements both at its laden weight for the time being and at its relevant weight.

(4B) For the purposes of paragraph (4A), the relevant weight,—

(a) in relation to a bus first used on or after 1st April 1982, is its maximum gross weight; and

(b) in relation to a bus first used before that date, is the weight specified in paragraph (4C).

(4C) The weight referred to in paragraph (4B)(b) is—

X + 63.5 (Y + Z) kg

where—

X is the unladen weight of that bus in kilograms;

Y is the number of passengers that the bus is constructed or adapted to carry seated in addition to the driver; and

Z is—

(a) in the case of a PSV which is not an articulated bus a standing capacity exceeding 8 persons, the standing capacity minus 8;

(b) in the case of a PSV which is an articulated bus, the standing capacity; or

(c) in any other case, nil.

(5) The brakes of every agricultural motor vehicle which is first used on or after 1st June 1986 and is not driven at more than 20 mph, and of every agricultural trailer manufactured on or after 1st December 1985 shall be capable of achieving a braking efficiency of not less than 25% when the weight of the vehicle is equal to the total maximum axle weights which the vehicle is designed to have.

(6) Every vehicle or combination of vehicles specified in an item in column (2) of Table II shall be so maintained[3] that its brakes are capable, without the assistance of stored energy, of holding it stationary on a gradient of at least the percentage specified in column 3 in that item.

TABLE II

(regulation 18(6))

1	2	3
Item	Class of vehicle or combination	Percentage gradient
1	A vehicle specified in item 1 of Table I— (*a*) when not drawing a trailer (*b*) when drawing a trailer	16 12
2	A vehicle to which requirement 18 in Schedule 3 applies by virtue of regulation 16.	16
3	A vehicle, not included in item 1, drawing a trailer manufactured on or after 1st January 1968 and required, by regulation 15 or 16, to be fitted with brakes.	16

(7) For the purpose of this regulation the date of manufacture of a trailer which is a composite trailer shall be deemed to be the same as the date of manufacture of the semi-trailer which forms part of the composite trailer.

(8) A vehicle which is subject to, and which complies with the requirements in, item 1 in Tables I and II shall not be treated as failing, by reason of its braking efficiency, to comply with regulation 15 or with Community Directive 79/489, 85/647, 88/194, 91/422 or 98/12 or ECE Regulation 13.03, 13.04, 13.05, 13.06, 13.07, 13.08 or 13.09.

(9) In this regulation—

"PSV" means a public service vehicle within the meaning of section 1 of the Public Passenger Vehicles Act 1981;

"standing capacity", in relation to a PSV, means the number of persons that can be carried standing without an offence being committed under section 26 of the Public Passenger Vehicles Act 1981.

---

1. In view of the specific reference to "every part" it is not enough for the court to consider the general overall efficiency of the braking system of a vehicle, if any of the system is not in good efficient working order an offence is committed; *Kennet v British Airports Authority* [1975] RTR 164, [1975] Crim LR 106. A brake drum and a brake disc shall be deemed to form part of the wheel and not of the braking system; reg 3(6).

2. It is not a sufficient defence to show that a regular system of maintenance has been carried out; *Hawkins v Holmes* [1974] RTR 436, [1974] Crim LR 370. Where a braking system is fitted, it must be maintained even though the fitting of brakes is not itself a requirement: *DPP v Young* (1991) 155 JP 14, [1991] RTR 56.

3. This regulation applies to all trailers to which brakes have been fitted and not only to those which are required to have brakes: there is thus no onus on a prosecutor to prove that the particular trailer comes within a class required to have brakes when in fact brakes were fitted (*DPP v Young* (1991) 155 JP 14, [1991] RTR 56).

Application of brakes of trailers

4–3521   19. Where a trailer is drawn by a motor vehicle the driver (or in the case of a locomotive one of the persons employed in driving or tending the locomotive) shall be in a position readily to operate any brakes required by these Regulations to be fitted to the trailer as well as the brakes of the motor vehicle unless a person other than the driver (or in the case of a locomotive a person other than one of the persons employed in driving or tending the locomotive) is in a position and competent efficiently to apply the brakes of the trailer.

Provided that this regulation shall not apply to a trailer which—

(*a*) in compliance with these Regulations, is fitted with brakes which automatically come into operation on the overrun of the trailer; or

(*b*) is a broken down vehicle being drawn, whether or not in consequence of a breakdown, in such a manner that it cannot be steered by its own steering gear.

C—WHEELS, SPRINGS, TYRES AND TRACKS

General requirement as to wheels and tracks

4–3522   20. Every motor cycle and invalid carriage shall be a wheeled vehicle, and every other motor vehicle and every trailer shall be either a wheeled vehicle or a track-laying vehicle.

4–3523   21. *Revoked.*

Springs and resilient material

4–3524   22. (1) Save as provided in paragraphs (3) and (4), every motor vehicle and every trailer shall be equipped with suitable and sufficient springs between each wheel and the frame of the vehicle.

(2) Save as provided in paragraphs (3) and (4), in the case of a track-laying vehicle—

(*a*) resilient material shall be interposed between the rims of the weight-carrying rollers and the road surface so that the weight of the vehicle, other than that borne by any wheel, is supported by the resilient material; and

(*b*) where the vehicle is a heavy motor car, motor car, or trailer it shall have suitable springs between the frame of the vehicle and the weight-carrying rollers.

(3) This regulation does not apply to—

    (*a*) a wheeled vehicle with an unladen weight not exceeding 4070 kg and which is—

      (i) a motor tractor any unsprung wheel of which is fitted with a pneumatic tyre;

     (ii) a motor tractor used in connection with railway shunting and which is used on a road only when passing from one railway track to another in connection with such use;

    (iii) a vehicle specially designed, and mainly used, for work on rough ground or unmade roads and every wheel of which is fitted with a pneumatic tyre and which is not driven at more than 20 mph;

    (iv) a vehicle constructed or adapted for, and being used for, road sweeping and every wheel of which is fitted with either a pneumatic tyre or a resilient tyre and which is not driven at more than 20 mph;

    (*b*) an agricultural motor vehicle which is not driven at more than 20 mph;

    (*c*) an agricultural trailer, or an agricultural trailed appliance;

    (*d*) a trailer used solely for the haulage of felled trees;

    (*e*) a motor cycle;

    (*f*) a mobile crane;

    (*g*) a pedestrian-controlled vehicle all the wheels of which are equipped with pneumatic tyres;

    (*h*) a road roller;

    (*i*) a broken down vehicle; or

    (*j*) a vehicle first used on or before 1st January 1932.

  (4) Paragraphs (1) and (2)(*b*) do not apply to a works truck or a works trailer.

Wheel loads

4–3525 **23.** (1) Subject to paragraph (2) this regulation applies to—

    (*a*) a semi-trailer with more than 2 wheels;

    (*b*) a track-laying vehicle with more than 2 wheels; and

    (*c*) any other vehicle with more than 4 wheels.

  (2) This regulation does not apply to a road roller.

  (3) Save as provided in paragraphs (4) and (5), every vehicle to which this regulation applies shall be fitted with a compensating arrangement which will ensure that under the most adverse conditions every wheel will remain in contact with the road and will not be subject to abnormal variations of load.

  (4) Paragraph (3) does not apply in respect of a steerable wheel on which the load does not exceed—

    (*a*) if it is a wheeled vehicle, 4250 kg; and

    (*b*) if it is a track-laying vehicle, 2540 kg.

  (5) In the application of paragraph (3) to an agricultural motor vehicle wheels which are in line transversely on one side of the longitudinal axis of the vehicle shall be regarded as one wheel.

Tyres

4–3526 **24.** (1) Save as provided in paragraph (2), every wheel of a vehicle of a class specified in an item in column 2 of the Table shall be fitted with a tyre of a type specified in that item in column 3 which complies with any conditions specified in that item in column 4.

  (2) The requirements referred to in paragraph (1) do not apply to a road roller and are subject, in the case of any item in the Table, to the exemptions specified in that item in column 5.

TABLE

(regulation 24(1))

1 Item	2 Class of vehicle	3 Type of tyre	4 Conditions	5 Exemptions
1	Locomotives not falling in item 6	Pneumatic or resilient		
2	Motor tractors not falling in item 6	Pneumatic or resilient	No re-cut pneumatic tyre shall be fitted to any wheel of a vehicle with an unladen weight of less than 2540 kg unless the diameter of the rim of the wheel is at least 405 mm	
3	Heavy motor cars not falling in item 6	Pneumatic		The following, if every wheel not fitted with a pneumatic tyre is fitted with a resilient tyre— (*a*) a vehicle mainly used for work on rough ground; (*b*) a tower wagon;

1 Item	2 Class of vehicle	3 Type of tyre	4 Conditions	5 Exemptions
				(c) a vehicle fitted with a turntable fire escape; (d) a refuse vehicle; (e) a works truck; (f) a vehicle first used before 3rd January 1933.
4	Motor cars not falling in item 6	Pneumatic	No re-cut tyre shall be fitted to any wheel of a vehicle unless it is— (a) an electrically propelled goods vehicle or, (b) a goods vehicle with an unladen weight of at least 2540 kg and the diameter of the rim of the wheel is at least 405 mm.	The following, if every wheel not fitted with a pneumatic tyre is fitted with a resilient tyre— (a) a vehicle mainly used for work on rough ground; (b) a refuse vehicle; (c) a works truck; (d) a vehicle with an unladen weight not exceeding— (i) 1270 kg if electrically propelled; (ii) 1020 kg in any other case; (e) a tower wagon; (f) a vehicle fitted with a turn-table fire escape; (g) a vehicle first used before 3rd January 1933.
5	Motor cycles	Pneumatic	No re-cut tyre shall be fitted	The following, if every wheel not fitted with a pneumatic tyre is fitted with a resilient tyre— (a) a works truck; (b) a pedestrian-controlled vehicle
6	Agricultural motor vehicles which are not driven at more than 20 mph	Pneumatic or resilient	The same as for item 2	The requirement in column 3 does not apply to a vehicle of which— (a) every steering wheel is fitted with a smooth-soled tyre which is not less than 60 mm wide where it touches the road; and (b) in the case of a wheeled vehicle, every driving wheel is fitted with a smooth-soled tyre which— (i) is not less than 150 mm wide if the unladen weight of the vehicle exceeds 3050 kg, or 76 mm wide in any other case, and either (ii) is shod with diagonal cross-bars not less than 76 mm wide or more than 20 mm thick extending the full breadth of the tyre and so arranged that the space between adjacent bars is not more than 76 mm; or

1 Item	2 Class of vehicle	3 Type of tyre	4 Conditions	5 Exemptions
				(iii) is shod with diagonal cross-bars of resilient material not less than 60 mm wide extending the full breadth of the tyre and so arranged that the space between adjacent bars is not more than 76mm.
7	Trailers	Pneumatic	Except in the case of a trailer mentioned in paragraph (*d*) of column 5, no recut tyre shall be fitted to any wheel of a trailer drawn by a heavy motor car or a motor car if the trailer— (*a*) has an unladen weight not exceeding— (i) if it is a living van, 2040 kg; or (ii) in any other case, 1020 kg; or (*b*) is not constructed or adapted to carry any load, other than plant or other special appliance which is a permanent or essentially permanent fixture and has a gross weight not exceeding 2290 kg	(*a*) an agricultural trailer manufactured before 1st December 1985; (*b*) an agricultural trailed appliance; (*c*) a trailer used to carry water for a road roller being used in connection with road works; (*d*) the following if every wheel which is not fitted with a pneumatic tyre is fitted with a resilient tyre— (i) a works trailer; (ii) a refuse vehicle; (iii) a trailer drawn by a heavy motor car every wheel of which is not required to be fitted with a pneumatic tyre; (iv) a broken down vehicle; or (v) a trailer drawn by a vehicle which is not a heavy motor car or a motor car.

(3) Save as provided in paragraph (4) a wheel of a vehicle may not be fitted with a temporary use spare tyre unless either—

    (*a*) the vehicle is a passenger vehicle (not being a bus) first used before 1st April 1987; or
    (*b*) the vehicle complies at the time of its first use with ECE Regulation 64 or Community Directive 92/23.

(4) Paragraph (3) does not apply to a vehicle constructed or assembled by a person not ordinarily engaged in the trade or business of manufacturing vehicles of that description.

Tyre Loads and Speed ratings

4–3527 25. (1) Save as provided in paragraphs (3), (4), (7A) and (7B) any tyre fitted to the axle of a vehicle—

    (*a*) which is a class of vehicle specified in an item in column 2 of Table I; and
    (*b*) in relation to which the date of first use is as specified in that item in column 3 of that Table;

shall comply with the requirements specified in that item in column 4 of that Table.

TABLE I

(regulation 25(1))

1 Item	2 Class of vehicle	3 Date of first use	4 Requirements
1	Vehicles which are of one or more of the following descriptions, namely—	Before 1st April 1991	The requirements of paragraphs (5) and (6)
	(a) goods vehicles, (b) trailers, (c) buses, (d) vehicles of a class mentioned in column 2 in Table III		
2	Vehicles which are of one or more of the following descriptions— (a) goods vehicles, (b) trailers, (c) buses, (d) vehicles of a class mentioned in column 2 in Table III, and do not fall within item 3 below	On or after 1st April 1991	The requirements of paragraphs (5), (6) and (7)
3	Vehicles of a class mentioned in paragraph (2)	On or after 1st April 1991	The requirements of paragraph (5)

(2) The classes of vehicle referred to in item 3 in column 2 in Table I are—

   (a) engineering plant;
   (b) track-laying vehicles;
   (c) vehicles equipped with tyres of speed category Q;
   (d) works trucks; and
   (e) motor vehicles with a maximum speed not exceeding 30 mph, not being vehicles of a class specified in—

      (i) items 2 and 3 of Table II; or
      (ii) paragraph (7A) or sub-paragraphs (a) to (d) of this paragraph;

   or trailers while being drawn by such vehicles.

   (3) Paragraph (1) shall not apply to any tyre fitted to the axle of a vehicle if the vehicle is—

   (a) broken down or proceeding to a place where it is to be broken up; and
   (b) being drawn by a motor vehicle at a speed not exceeding 20 mph.

   (4) Where in relation to any vehicle first used on or after 1st April 1991 a tyre supplied by a manufacturer for the purposes of tests or trials of that tyre is fitted to an axle of that vehicles paragraph (7) shall not apply to that tyre while it is being used for those purposes.

   (5) The requirements of this paragraph are that the tyre, as respects strength, shall be designed and manufactured adequately to support the maximum permitted axle weight for the axle[1].

   (6) The requirements of this paragraph are that the tyre shall be designed and manufactured adequately to support the maximum permitted axle weight for the axle when the vehicle is driven at the speed shown in column 3 in Table II in the item in which the vehicle is described in column 2 (the lowest relevant speed being applicable to a vehicle which is described in more than one item).

TABLE II

(regulation 25(6))

1 Item	2 Class of vehicle	3 Speed (mph)	4 Variation to the load-capacity index expressed as a percentage	
			Tyres marked in accordance with ECE Regulation 30, 30.01 or 30.02 and relevant car tyres	Tyres marked in accordance with ECE Regulation 54 and relevant commercial vehicle tyres
1	A vehicle of a class for which maximum speeds are prescribed by Schedule 6 to the 1984 Act other than an agricultural motor vehicle	The highest speed so prescribed	Single wheels: none Dual wheels: 95.5%	None
2	An electrically propelled vehicle used as a multi-stop local collection and delivery vehicle and having a maximum speed of not more than 25 mph	The maximum speed of the vehicle	None	150%

1	2	3	4	
Item	Class of vehicle	Speed (mph)	Variation to the load-capacity index expressed as a percentage	
			Tyres marked in accordance with ECE Regulation 30, 30.01 or 30.02 and relevant car tyres	Tyres marked in accordance with ECE Regulation 54 and relevant commercial vehicle tyres
3	An electrically propelled vehicle used as a multi-stop local collection and delivery vehicle and having a maximum speed of more than 25 mph and not more than 40 mph	The maximum speed of the vehicle	None	130%
4	An electrically propelled vehicle used only within a radius of 25 miles from the permanent base at which it is normally kept and having a maximum speed of more than 40 mph and not more than 50 mph	The maximum speed of the vehicle	None	115%
5	A local service bus	50	None	110%
6	A restricted speed vehicle	50	None	The relevant % variation specified in Annex 8 to ECE Regulation 54 or Appendix 8 to Annex II to Community Directive 92/23
7	A low platform trailer, an agricultural motor vehicle, an agricultural trailer, an agricultural trailed appliance or an agricultural trailed appliance conveyor	40	None	The relevant % variation specified in Annex 8 to ECE Regulation 54 or Appendix 8 to Annex II to Community Directive 92/23
8	A municipal vehicle	40	None	115%
9	A multi-stop local collection and delivery vehicle if not falling within the class of vehicle described in items 2 or 3 above	40	None	115%
10	A light trailer or any trailer equipped with tyres of speed category F or G	60	Single wheels: 110% Dual wheels: 105%	The relevant variation specified in Annex 8 to ECE Regulation 54 or Appendix 8 to Annex II to Community Directive 92/23
11	A trailer not falling in items 6–10	60	Single wheels: none Dual wheels: 95.5%	None
12	A motor vehicle not falling in items 1–11	170	Single wheels: none Dual wheels: 95.5%	None

(7) The requirement of this paragraph is that the tyre when first fitted to the vehicle was marked with a designated approval mark or complied with the requirements of ECE Regulation 30, 30.01 or 30.02 or 54, but this requirement shall not apply to a retreaded tyre.

(7A) The requirements of paragraphs (6) and (7) shall not apply to any tyre fitted to the axle of a vehicle of a class specified in an item in column 2 of Table III while the vehicle is being driven or drawn at a speed not exceeding that specified in that item in column 3 of that Table.

TABLE III

(regulation 25(7A))

1	2	3
Item	Class of vehicle	Speed (mph)
1	Agricultural motor vehicles	20
2	Agricultural trailers	20
3	Agricultural trailed appliances	20
4	Agricultural trailed appliance conveyors	20
5	Works trailers	18

(7B) Paragraph (7C) applies where a tyre fitted to the axle of a vehicle—

(a) bears a speed category symbol and load-capacity index, being marks that were moulded on to or into the tyre at the time that it was manufactured;

(b) is designed and manufactured so as to be capable of operating safely at the speed and load indicated by those marks; and

(c) is designed so as to be capable of being fitted to the axle of a vehicle of a class specified in item 1, 2, 3 or 4 in column 2 of Table III above.

(7C) In the circumstances mentioned in paragraph (7B), paragraph (7) shall not apply to the tyre if—

(a) the vehicle is being driven or drawn at a speed that does not exceed the speed indicated by the speed category symbol or 50 mph (whichever is the less), and

(b) the load on the tyre does not exceed the load indicated by the load-capacity index.

(8) A vehicle of a class described in column 2 in Table II first used on or after 1st April 1991 shall not be used on a road—

(a) in the case where there is no entry in column 4 specifying a variation to the load-capacity index expressed as a percentage, if the load applied to any tyre fitted to the axle of the vehicle exceeds that indicated by the load-capacity index; or

(b) in the case where there is such an entry in column 4, if the load applied to any tyre to the axle of the vehicle exceeds the variation to the load capacity index expressed as a percentage.

(9) In this regulation—

"designated approval mark" means the marking designated as an approval mark by regulation 5 of the Approval Marks Regulations and shown at item 33 in Schedule 4 to those Regulations (that item being a marking relating to Community Directive 92/23);

"dual wheels" means two or more wheels which are to be regarded as one wheel by virtue of paragraph 7 of regulation 3 in the circumstances specified in that paragraph;

"load-capacity index" has the same meaning as in paragraph 2.28 of Annex II to Community Directive 92/23 or paragraph 2.29 of ECE Regulation 30.02 or paragraph 2.27 of ECE Regulation 54;

"local service bus" means a bus being used in the provision of a local service as defined in section 2 of the Transport Act 1985;

"municipal vehicle" means a motor vehicle or trailer limited at all times to use by a local authority, or a person acting in pursuance of a contract with a local authority, for road cleansing, road watering or the collection and disposal of refuse, night soil or the contents of cesspools, or the purposes of the enactments relating to weights and measures or the sale of food and drugs;

"multi-stop local collection and delivery vehicle" means a motor vehicle or trailer used for multi-stop collection and delivery services to be used only within a radius of 25 miles from the permanent base at which it is normally kept;

"single wheels" means wheels which are not dual wheels; and

"speed category" has the same meaning as in paragraph 2.29 of Annex II to Community Directive 92/23 or paragraph 2.28 of ECE Regulation 54.

(9A) For the purposes of this regulation, a tyre is a "relevant car tyre" if—

(a) it has been marked with a designated approval mark, and

(b) the first two digits of the approval number comprised in the mark are "02".

(9B) For the purposes of this regulation, a tyre is a "relevant commercial vehicle tyre" if—

(a) it has been marked with a designated approval mark, and

(b) the first two digits of the approval number comprised in the mark are "00".

(10) In this regulation any reference to the first use shall, in relation to a trailer, be construed as a reference to the date which is 6 months after the date of manufacture of the trailer.

---

1. A predecessor regulation was held not to impose an obligation to maintain the tyre pressure to carry at all times the gross plated axle weight; *Connor v Graham* [1981] RTR 291.

Mixing of tyres

4–3528 **26.** (1) Save as provided in paragraph (5) pneumatic tyres of different types of structure shall not be fitted to the same axle of a wheeled vehicle.

(2) Save as provided in paragraphs (3) or (5), a wheeled motor vehicle having only two axles each of which is equipped with one or two single wheels shall not be fitted with—

(a)   a diagonal-ply tyre or a bias-belted tyre on its rear axle if a radial-ply tyre is fitted on its front axle; or

(b)   a diagonal-ply tyre on its rear axle if a bias-belted tyre is fitted on the front axle.

(3) Paragraph (2) does not apply to a vehicle to an axle of which there are fitted wide tyres not specially constructed for use on engineering plant or to a vehicle which has a maximum speed not exceeding 30 mph.

(4) Save as provided in paragraph (5) pneumatic tyres fitted to—

(a)   the steerable axles of a wheeled vehicle; or

(b)   the driven axles of a wheeled vehicle, not being steerable axles,

shall all be of the same type of structure.

(5) Paragraphs (1), (2) and (4) do not prohibit the fitting of a temporary use spare tyre to a wheel of a passenger vehicle (not being a bus) unless it is driven at a speed exceeding 50 mph.

(6) In this regulation—

"axle" includes—

(i)   two or more stub axles which are fitted on opposite sides of the longitudinal axis of the vehicle so as to form—

(a)   a pair in the case of two stub axles; and

(b)   pairs in the case of more than two stub axles; and

(ii)   a single stub axle which is not one of a pair;

"a bias-belted tyre" means a pneumatic tyre, the structure of which is such that the ply cords extend to the bead so as to be laid at alternate angles of substantially less than 90 degrees to the peripheral line of the tread, and are constrained by a circumferential belt comprising two or more layers of substantially inextensible cord material laid at alternate angles smaller than those of the ply cord structure;

"a diagonal-ply tyre" means a pneumatic tyre, the structure of which is such that the ply cords extend to the bead so as to be laid at alternate angle of substantially less than 90 degrees to the peripheral line of the tread, but not being a bias-belted tyre;

"a driven axle" means an axle through which power is transmitted from the engine of a vehicle to the wheels on that axle;

"a radial-ply tyre" means a pneumatic tyre, the structure of which is such that the ply cords extend to the bead so as to be laid at an angle of substantially 90 degrees to the peripheral line of the tread, the ply cord structure being stabilised by a substantially inextensible circumferential belt

"stub axle" means an axle on which only one wheel is mounted; and

"type of structure", in relation to a tyre, means a type of structure of a tyre of a kind defined in the foregoing provisions of this paragraph.

Condition and maintenance of tyres

4–3529 **27.** (1) Save as provided in paragraphs (2), (3) and (4), a wheeled motor vehicle or trailer a wheel of which is fitted with a pneumatic tyre shall not be used[1] on a road, if—

(a)   the tyre is unsuitable having regard to the use to which the motor vehicle or trailer is being put or to the types of tyres fitted to its other wheels;

(b)   the tyre is not so inflated as to make it fit for the use to which the motor vehicle or trailer is being put[2];

(c)   the tyre has a cut in excess of 25 mm or 10% of the section width of the tyre, whichever is the greater, measured in any direction on the outside of the tyre and deep enough to reach the ply or cord;

(d)   the tyre has any lump, bulge or tear caused by separation or partial failure of its structure;

(e)   the tyre has any of the ply or cord exposed;

(f)   the base of any groove which showed in the original tread pattern of the tyre is not clearly visible;

(g)   either—

(i)   the grooves of the tread pattern of the tyre do not have a depth of at least 1 mm throughout a continuous band measuring at least three-quarters of the breadth of the tread and round the entire outer-circumference[3] of the tyre; or

(ii)   if the grooves of the original tread pattern of the tyre did not extend beyond three-quarters of the breadth of the tread, any groove which showed in the original tread pattern does not have a depth of at least 1 mm; or

(h)   the tyre is not maintained in such condition as to be fit for the use to which the vehicle or trailer is being put or has a defect which might in any way cause damage to the surface of the road or damage to persons on or in the vehicle or to other persons using the road.

(2) Paragraph (1) does not prohibit the use on a road of a motor vehicle or trailer by reason only of the fact that a wheel of the vehicle or trailer is fitted with a tyre which is deflated or not fully inflated and which has any of the defects described in sub-paragraph (c), (d) or (e) of

paragraph (1), if the tyre and the wheel to which it is fitted are so constructed as to make the tyre in that condition fit for the use to which the motor vehicle or trailer is being put and the outer sides of the wall of the tyre are so marked as to enable the tyre to be identified as having been constructed to comply with the requirements of this paragraph.

(3) Paragraph (1)(*a*) does not prohibit the use on a road of a passenger vehicle (not being a bus) by reason only of the fact that a wheel of the vehicle is fitted with a temporary use spare tyre, unless the vehicle is driven at a speed exceeding 50 mph.

(4)

(*a*) Nothing in paragraph (1)(*a*) to (*g*) applies to—

    (i)   an agricultural motor vehicle that is not driven at more than 20 mph;

    (ii) an agricultural trailer;

    (iii) an agricultural trailed appliance; or

    (iv) a broken down vehicle or a vehicle proceeding to a place where it is to be broken up, being drawn, in either case, by a motor vehicle at a speed not exceeding 20 mph.

(*b*) Nothing in paragraph (1)(*f*) and (*g*) applies to—

    (i)   a three-wheeled motor cycle the unladen weight of which does not exceed 102 kg and which has a maximum speed of 12 mph; or

    (ii) a pedestrian-controlled works truck.

(*c*) Nothing in paragraph (1)(*g*) applies to a motorcycle with an engine capacity which does not exceed 50 cc.

(*d*) With effect from 1st January 1992, paragraph 1(*f*) and (*g*) shall not apply to the vehicles specified in sub-paragraph (*e*) of this paragraph but such vehicles shall comply with the requirements specified in sub-paragraph (*f*) of this paragraph.

(*e*) the vehicles mentioned in sub-paragraph (*d*) are—

    (i)   passenger vehicles other than motor cycles constructed or adapted to carry no more than 8 seated passengers in addition to the driver;

    (ii) goods vehicles with a maximum gross weight which does not exceed 3500 kg; and

    (iii) light trailers not falling within sub-paragraph (ii);

    first used on or after 3rd January 1933.

(*f*) The requirements referred to in sub-paragraph (*d*) are that the grooves of the tread pattern of every tyre fitted to the wheels of a vehicle mentioned in sub-paragraph (*e*) shall be of a depth of a least 1·6 mm throughout a continuous band comprising the central three-quarters of the breadth of tread and round an entire outer circumference of the tyre.

(5) a recut pneumatic tyre shall not be fitted to any wheel of a motor vehicle or trailer if—

(*a*) its ply or cord has been cut or exposed by the recutting process; or

(*b*) it has been wholly or partially recut in a pattern other than the manufacturer's recut tread pattern.

(6)

(*a*) In this regulation—

"breadth of tread" means the breadth of that part of the tyre which can contact the road under normal conditions of use measured at 90 degrees to the peripheral line of the tread;

"original tread pattern" means in the case of—

    a re-treaded tyre, the tread pattern of the tyre immediately after the tyre was re-treaded;

    a wholly recut tyre, the manufacturer's recut tread pattern;

    a partially recut tyre, on that part of the tyre which has been recut, the manufacturer's recut tread pattern, and on the other part, the tread pattern of the tyre when new, and

    any other tyre, the tread pattern of the tyre when the tyre was new.

"tie-bar" means any part of a tyre moulded in the tread pattern of the tyre for the purpose of bracing two or more features of such tread pattern;

"tread pattern" means the combination of plain surfaces and grooves extending across the breadth of the tread and round the entire outer circumference of the tyre but excludes any—

    (*i*)   tie bars or tread wear indicators;

    (*ii*) features which are designed to wear out substantially before the rest of the pattern under normal conditions of use; and

    (*iii*) other minor features; and

"tread wear indicator" means any bar, not being a tie-bar, projecting from the base of a groove of the tread pattern of a tyre and moulded between two or more features of the tread pattern of a tyre for the purpose of indicating the extent of the wear of such tread pattern.

(*b*) The references in this regulation to grooves are references—

    if a tyre has been recut, to the grooves of the manufacturer's recut tread pattern; and

    if a tyre has not been recut, to the grooves which showed when the tyre was new.

(*c*) A reference in this regulation to first use shall, in relation to a trailer, be construed as a reference to the date which is 6 months after the date of manufacture of the trailer.

---

1. The use of a motor vehicle with more than one defective tyre constitutes an offence for each tyre that is defective; *Saines v Woodhouse* [1970] 2 All ER 388, [1970] 1 WLR 961, 134 JP 505.

2. This regulation does not require a tyre to be so inflated as to be fit for some possible, or even probable, use; *Connor v Graham* [1981] RTR 291.

3. The "outer circumference of the tyre" is that part normally in contact with the road when the vehicle is in motion, outer walls and shoulder of the tyre are not included in the requirement. It is round the entire outer circumference that three quarters of the tread pattern must be at least 1 millimetre deep; *Coote v Parkin* [1977] RTR 61, [1977] Crim LR 172.

Tracks

4–3530   28. (1) Every part of every track of a track laying vehicle which comes into contact with the road shall be flat and have a width of not less than 12·5 mm.

(2) The area of the track which is in contact with the road shall not at any time be less than 225 cm$_2$ in respect of every 1000 kg of the total weight which is transferred to the road by the tracks.

(3) The tracks of a vehicle shall not have any defect which might damage the road or cause danger to any person on or in the vehicle or using the road, and shall be properly adjusted and maintained in good and efficient working order.

D—STEERING

Maintenance of steering gear

4–3531   29. All steering gear fitted to a motor vehicle shall at all times while the vehicle is used on a road be maintained in good and efficient working order and be properly adjusted.

E—VISION

View to the front

4–3532   30. (1) Every motor vehicle shall be so designed and constructed that the driver thereof while controlling the vehicle can at all times have a full view of the road and traffic ahead of the motor vehicle.

(2) Instead of complying with the requirement of paragraph (1) a vehicle may comply with Community Directive 77/649, 81/643, 88/366, 90/630 or, in the case of an agricultural motor vehicle, 79/1073.

(3) All glass or other transparent material fitted to a motor vehicle shall be maintained in such condition that it does not obscure the vision of the driver while the vehicle is being driven on a road.

Glass

4–3533   31. (1) This regulation applies to a motor vehicle which is—

(a) a wheeled vehicle, not being a caravan, first used before 1st June 1978;
(b) a caravan first used before 1st September 1978; or
(c) a track-laying vehicle.

(2) The glass fitted to any window specified in an item in column 3 of the Table of a vehicle of a class specified in that item in column 2 shall be safety glass.

TABLE

(regulation 31(2))

1	2	3
Item	Class of vehicle	Windows
1	Wheeled vehicles first used on or after 1st January 1959, being passenger vehicles or dual-purpose vehicles.	Windscreens and all outside windows.
2	Wheeled vehicles first used on or after 1st January 1959, being goods vehicles (other than dual-purpose vehicles), locomotives or motor tractors.	Windscreens and all windows in front of and on either side of the driver's seat.
3	Wheeled vehicles not mentioned in item 1 or 2.	Windscreens and windows facing to the front on the outside, except glass fitted to the upper decks of a double-decked vehicle.
4	Track-laying vehicles.	Windscreens and windows facing to the front.

(3) For the purposes of this regulation any windscreen or window at the front of the vehicle the inner surface of which is at an angle exceeding 30 degrees to the longitudinal axis of the vehicle shall be deemed to face to the front.

(4) In this regulation and in regulation 32—

"caravan" means a trailer which is constructed (and not merely adapted) for human habitation; and

"designated approval mark" means the marking designated as an approval mark by Regulation 5 of the Approval Marks Regulations and shown at item 31 or 32 in Schedule 4 to those Regulations (those items being markings relating to Community Directive 92/22); and

"safety glass" means glass so constructed or treated that if fractured it does not fly into fragments likely to cause severe cuts.

(5) Paragraph (2) does not apply to glass which is legibly and permanently marked with a designated approval mark.

4–3534 **32.** (1) This regulation applies to—

(a) a caravan first used on or after 1st September 1978, and

(b) a wheeled motor vehicle and a wheeled trailer, not being a caravan, first used on or after 1st June 1978.

(2) Save as provided in paragraphs (3) to (9) the windows specified in column 2 of Table I in relation to a vehicle of a class specified in that column shall be constructed of the material specified in column 3 of that Table.

(regulation 32(2))

TABLE I

1	2	3
Item	Window	Material
1	Windscreens and other windows wholly or partly on either side of the driver's seat fitted to motor vehicles first used on or after 1st April 1985.	Specified safety glass (1980).
2	Windscreens and other windows wholly or partly on either side of the driver's seat fitted to a motor vehicle first used before 1st April 1985.	Specified safety glass, or specified safety glass (1980).
3	All other windows.	Specified safety glass, specified safety glass (1980), or safety glazing.

(3) The windscreens and all other windows of security vehicles or vehicles being used for police purposes shall not be subject to the requirements specified in paragraph (2), but shall be constructed of either safety glass or safety glazing.

(4) The windscreens of motorcycles not equipped with an enclosed compartment for the driver or for a passenger shall not be subject to the requirements specified in paragraph (2), but shall be constructed of safety glazing.

(5) Any windscreens or other windows which are wholly or partly in front of or on either side of the driver's seat, and which are temporarily fitted to motor vehicles to replace any windscreens or other windows which have broken shall—

(a) be constructed of safety glazing; and

(b) be fitted only while the vehicles are being driven or towed either to premises where new windscreens or other windows are to be permanently fitted to replace the windscreens or other windows which have broken, or to complete the journey in the course of which the breakage occurred.

(6) Windows forming all or part of a screen or door in the interior of a bus first used on or after 1st April 1988, shall be constructed either of safety glazing or of specified safety glass (1980).

(7) Windows being—

(a) windows (other than windscreens) of motor vehicles being engineering plant, industrial tractors, agricultural motor vehicles (other than agricultural motor vehicles first used on or after 1st June 1986 and driven at more than 20 mph) which are wholly or partly in front of or on either side of the driver's seat;

(b) windows of the upper deck of a double-decked bus; or

(c) windows in the roof of a vehicle,

shall be constructed of either specified safety glass, specified safety glass (1980) or safety glazing.

(8) In the case of motor vehicles and trailers which have not at any time been fitted with permanent windows and which are being driven or towed to a place where permanent windows are to be fitted, any temporary windscreens and any other temporary windows shall be constructed of either specified safety glass, specified safety glass (1980) or safety glazing.

(9) No requirement in this regulation that a windscreen or other window shall be constructed of specified safety glass or of specified safety glass (1980) shall apply to a windscreen or other window which is—

(a) manufactured in France;

(b) marked with a marking consisting of the letters "TP GS" or "TP GS E"; and

(c) fitted to a vehicle first used before 1st October 1986.

(10) Save as provided in paragraph (11), the windscreens or other windows constructed in accordance with the foregoing provisions of this regulation of specified safety glass, specified safety glass (1980) or safety glazing and specified in column 3 of Table II in relation to a vehicle of a class specified in column 2 of that Table shall have a visual transmission for light of not less than the percentage specified in relation to those windows in column 4 when measured

perpendicular to the surface in accordance with the procedure specified in a document specified in relation to those windows in column 5.

TABLE II

(regulation 32(10))

1	2	3	4	5
Item	Class of Vehicles	Widows	Percentage	Documents specifying procedure
1	Motor vehicles first used before 1st April 1985	All windows	70	British Standard Specification No. 857 or No. 5282
2	Motor vehicles first used on or after 1st April 1985 and trailers	(a) Windscreens (b) All other windows	75 70	The documents mentioned in sub-paragraph (i), (ii) or (iii) of the definition in paragraph (13) of "specified safety glass (1980)."

(11) Paragraph (10) does not apply to—

(a)   any part of any windscreen which is outside the vision reference zone;
(b)   windows through which the driver when in the driver's seat is unable at any time to see any part of the road on which the vehicle is waiting or proceeding;
(c)   windows in any motor ambulance which are not wholly or partly in front of or on either side of any part of the driver's seat; or
(d)   windows in any bus, goods vehicle, locomotive, or motor tractor other than windows which—

(i)   are wholly or partly in front of or on either side of any part of the driver's seat;
(ii) face the rear of the vehicle; or
(iii) form the whole or part of a door giving access to or from the exterior of the vehicle.

(11A) Paragraphs (10) and (11) have effect in relation to any tint, film or other substance or material applied to a windscreen or window as they have effect in relation to the windscreen or window itself.
(12) For the purposes of this regulation any window at the rear of the vehicle is deemed to face the rear of the vehicle if the inner surface of such window is at an angle exceeding 30 degrees to the longitudinal axis of the vehicle.
(12A) Paragraphs (2), (6), (7) and (8) do not apply to a window which is legibly and permanently marked with a designated approval mark.
(12B) Paragraph (10) does not apply to a window if—

(a)   it is a window to which paragraph 12C applies and is legibly and permanently marked with a designated approval mark which does not comprise the Roman numeral "V" (other than as part of the combination "VI"); or
(b)   it is not a window to which paragraph 12C applies and is legibly and permanently marked with a designated approval mark.

(12C) this paragraph applies to a side or rear window if—

(a)   any part of it is on either side of or forward of the driver's seat; or
(b)   any part of it is within the driver's indirect field of view obtained by means of the mirror or mirrors which are required to be fitted by regulation 33 when such mirrors are properly adjusted;

and for the purposes of this paragraph a mirror shall not be regarded as being required to be fitted by regulation 33 if, were it to be removed, the vehicle would nevertheless meet the requirements of regulation 33.
(13) In this regulation[1], unless the context otherwise requires—

"British Standard Specification No 857" means the British Standard Specification for Safety Glass for Land Transport published on 30th June 1967 under the number BS 857 as amended by Amendment Slip No 1 published on 15th January 1973 under the number AMD 1088;
"British Standard Specification No 5282" means the British Standard Specification for Road Vehicle Safety Glass published in December 1975 under the number BS 5282 as amended by Amendment Slip No 1 published on 31st March 1976 under the number AMD 1927, and as amended by Amendment Slip No 2 published on 31st January 1977 under the number AMD 2185;
"British Standard Specification BS AU 178" means the British Standard Specification for Road Vehicle Safety Glass published on 28th November 1980 under the number BS AU 178;
"designated approval mark" means—

(a)   in relation to a windscreen, the marking designated as an approval mark by regulation 5 of the Approval Marks Regulations and shown at item 31 in Schedule 4 to those Regulations, and

(b) in relation to a window other than a windscreen, the markings designated as approval marks by regulation 5 of those Regulations and shown at item 32 in Schedule 4 to those Regulations.

"safety glazing" means material (other than glass) which is so constructed or treated that if fractured it does not fly into fragments likely to cause severe cuts;

"security vehicle" means a motor vehicle which is constructed (and not merely adapted) for the carriage of either—

   (i) persons who are likely to require protection from any criminal offence involving violence; or

   (ii) dangerous substances, bullion, money, jewellery, documents or other goods or burden which, by reason of their nature or value, are likely to require protection from any criminal offence;

"specified safety glass" means glass complying with the requirements of either—

   (i) British Standard Specification No 857 (including the requirements as to marking); or

   (ii) British Standard Specification No. 5282 (including the requirements as to marking);

"specified safety glass (1980)" means glass complying with the requirements of either—

   (i) the British Standard Specification for Safety Glass for Land Transport published on 30th June 1967 under the number BS 857 as amended by Amendments Slip No 1 published on 15th January 1973 under the number AMD 1088, Amendment Slip No 2 published on 30th September 1980 under the number AMD 3402, and Amendment Slip No 4 published on 15th February 1981 under the number AMD 3548 (including the requirements as to marking); or

   (ii) British Standard Specification BS AU 178 (including the requirements as to marking); or

   (iii) ECE Regulation 43 (including the requirements as to marking).

"vision reference zone" means either—

   (i) the primary vision area as defined in British Standard Specification No 857;

   (ii) Zone 1, as defined in British Standard Specification No 5282;

   (iii) Zone B (as regards passenger vehicles other than buses) and Zone 1 (as regards all other vehicles) as defined in British Standard Specification BS AU 178 and in ECE Regulation 43; and

"windscreen" includes a windshield.

---

1. See also r 31(4) for meaning of "caravan" and "safety glass".

Mirrors and other devices for indirect vision

4–3535 **33.** (1) Save as provided in paragraphs (5) and (6), a motor vehicle (not being a road roller) which is of a class specified in an item in column 2 of the Table shall be fitted with such mirror or mirrors or other device for indirect vision, if any, as are specified in that item in column 3; and any mirror or other device for indirect vision which is fitted to such a vehicle shall, whether or not it is required to be fitted, comply with the requirements, if any, specified in that item in columns 4 and 5.

(2) Save as provided in paragraph (5), each exterior mirror with which a vehicle is required to be fitted in accordance with item 2 or 8 of the Table shall, if the vehicle has a technically permissible maximum weight (as mentioned in Annex 1 to Community Directive 71/127) exceeding 3500 kg, be a Class II mirror (as described in that Annex) and shall in any other case be a Class II or a Class III mirror (as described in that Annex).

(3) Save as provided in paragraph (5), in the case of a wheeled motor vehicle described in item 1, 2, 10 or 11 of the Table which is first used on or after 1st April 1969 the edges of any interior mirror shall be surrounded by some material such as will render it unlikely that severe cuts would be caused if the mirror or that material were struck by any occupant of the vehicle.

(4) Save as provided in paragraph (5), in the case of a motor vehicle falling within paragraph (a) in column 4 of items 1 and 7, or within item 8, of the Table—

   (a) each mirror shall be fixed to the vehicle in such a way that it remains steady under normal driving conditions;

   (b) each exterior mirror on a vehicle fitted with windows and a windscreen shall be visible to the driver, when in his driving position, through a side window or through the portion of the windscreen which is swept by the windscreen wiper;

   (c) where the bottom edge of an exterior mirror is less than 2 m above the road surface when the vehicle is laden, that mirror shall not project more than 20 cm beyond the overall width of the vehicle or, in a case where the vehicle is drawing a trailer which has an overall width greater than that of the drawing vehicle, more than 20 cm beyond the overall width of the trailer;

   (d) where the bottom edge of an exterior mirror, which complies with the requirements of Community Directive 2003/97 or 2005/27 or ECE Regulation 46.02, is less than 2 m above the road surface when the vehicle is laden, that mirror shall not project more than 25 cm beyond the overall width of the vehicle or, in the case where the vehicle is drawing a trailer which has an overall width greater than that of the drawing vehicle, more than 25 cm beyond the overall width of the trailer;

(e) each interior mirror shall be capable of being adjusted by the driver when in his driving position; and

(f) except in the case of a mirror which, if knocked out of its alignment, can be returned to its former position without needing to be adjusted, each exterior mirror on the driver's side of the vehicle shall be capable of being adjusted by the driver when in his driving position, but this requirement shall not prevent such a mirror from being locked into position from the outside of the vehicle.

(5) Instead of complying with paragraphs (1) to (4) a vehicle may comply—

(a) if it is a goods vehicle with a maximum gross weight exceeding 3500 kg first used on or after 1st April 1985 and before 1st August 1989, with Community Directive 79/795, 85/205, 86/562 or 88/321 or ECE Regulation 46.01;

(b) if it is a goods vehicle first used on or after 1st August 1989 and before 26th January 2007—

　　(i) in the case of a vehicle with a maximum gross weight exceeding 3500 kg but not exceeding 12,000 kg, with Community Directive 79/795, 85/205, 86/562 or 88/321 or ECE Regulation 46.01; and

　　(ii) in the case of a vehicle with a maximum gross weight exceeding 12,000 kg, with Community Directive 85/205, 86/562 or 88/321 or ECE Regulation 46.01;

(c) if it is an agricultural motor vehicle, with Community Directive 71/127, 74/346, 79/795, 85/205, 86/562 or 88/321 or ECE Regulation 46.01;

(d) if it is a two-wheeled motor cycle with or without a side-car, with Community Directive 71/127, 79/795, 80/780, 85/205, 86/562 or 88/321 or ECE Regulation 46.01; and

(e) if it is any other vehicle, with Community Directive 71/127, 79/795, 85/205, 86/562 or 88/321 or ECE Regulation 46.01.

(6) Instead of complying with the provisions of column 4 in items 3, 4, 7 or 8 of the Table a mirror may comply with the requirements as to construction and testing set out in—

(a) Annex I to Community Directive 71/127, excluding paragraphs 2.3.4 and 2.6;

(b) Annex I to Community Directive 79/795, excluding paragraphs 2.3.3 and 2.6;

(c) Annex II to Community Directive 2003/97, excluding paragraph 3.4; or

(d) Annex II to Community Directive 2005/27, excluding paragraph 3.4.

(7) In this regulation—

(a) "devices for indirect vision" mean devices to observe the traffic area adjacent to the vehicle which cannot be observed by direct vision and may include conventional mirrors, camera-monitors or other devices able to present information about the indirect field of vision to the driver;

(b) "mirror" means any device with a reflecting surface, excluding devices such as periscopes intended to give a clear view to the rear, side or front of the vehicle;

(c) "interior mirror" means a device defined in sub-paragraph (a), which can be fitted in the passenger compartment of a vehicle;

(d) "exterior mirror" means a device defined in sub-paragraph (a), which can be fitted on the external surface of a vehicle.

(8) In the case of—

(a) an agricultural motor vehicle, or

(b) a vehicle described in items 2 or 8 in the Table,

when drawing a trailer the references to a vehicle in the definitions in paragraph (7) shall be construed as including references to that trailer.

TABLE

(regulation 33(1))

1	2	3	4	5
Item	Class of vehicle	Mirrors or other devices for indirect vision to be fitted	Requirements to be complied with by any mirrors fitted	Requirements to be complied with by any other devices for indirect vision where fitted
1	A motor vehicle which is— (a) drawing a trailer, if a person is carried on the trailer so that he has an uninterrupted view to the rear and has an efficient means of communicating to the driver the effect of signals given by the drivers of other vehicles to the rear; (b) (i) a works truck; 　　(ii) a track-laying agricultural motor vehicle; and 　　(iii) a wheeled agricultural motor vehicle first used before 1st June 1978, if, in each case, the driver can easily obtain a view to the rear;	No requirement.	(a) If the vehicle is a wheeled vehicle first used on or after 1st June 1978, Item 2 of Annex I to Community Directive 71/127 or 79/795 or Annex II to Community Directive 86/562 or 88/321 or paragraphs 4 to 8 of ECE Regulation 46.01 and paragraph (4) of this regulation. (b) In other cases, none, except as specified in paragraph (3).	None

1	2	3	4	5
Item	Class of vehicle	Mirrors or other devices for indirect vision to be fitted	Requirements to be complied with by any mirrors fitted	Requirements to be complied with by any other devices for indirect vision where fitted
	(c) a pedestrian-controlled vehicle; (d) a chassis being driven from the place where it has been manufactured to the place where it is to receive a vehicle body; or (e) an agricultural motor vehicle which has an unladen weight exceeding 7370 kg and which— (i) is a track-laying vehicle or (ii) is a wheeled vehicle first used before 1st June 1978.			
2	A motor vehicle not included in item 1, which is— (a) a wheeled locomotive or a wheeled motor tractor first used in either case on or after 1st June 1978; (b) an agricultural motor vehicle, not being a track-laying vehicle with an unladen weight not exceeding 7370 kg (which falls in item 11) or a wheeled agricultural motor vehicle first used after 1st June 1986 which is driven at more than 20 mph (which falls in item 8); or (c) a works truck.	At least one exterior mirror fitted on the offside.	None, except as specified in paragraphs (2) and (3).	None.
3	A wheeled motor vehicle not included in items 1 or 4 first used on or after 1st April 1983 which is— (a) a bus; or (b) a goods vehicle with a maximum gross weight exceeding 3500 kg (not being an agricultural motor vehicle which is not driven at more than 20 mph) other than a vehicle described in item 5.	Mirrors complying with item 3 of Annex I to Community Directive 79/795 or with paragraph 2.1 of Annex III to Community Directive 86/562 or 88/321 or paragraph 16.2.1 of ECE Regulation 46.01 or, except in the case of a goods vehicle first used on or after 1st April 1985, mirrors as required in the entry in this column in item 8.	Item 2 of Annex I to Community Directive 71/127 or 79/795 or Annex II to Community Directive 86/562 or 88/321 or paragraphs 4 to 8 of ECE Regulation 46.01.	None.
4	A wheeled motor vehicle not included in item 1 first used on or after 26th January 2007 which is— (a) a bus; (b) a goods vehicle with a maximum gross weight— (i) exceeding 3500 kg but not exceeding 7500 kg; or (ii) exceeding 7500 kg but not exceeding 12,000 kg; (not being an agricultural motor vehicle or one which is not driven at more than 20 mph).	(a) and (b)(ii) Mirrors and other devices for indirect vision complying with Annex III to Community Directive 2003/97 or 2005/27 or paragraph 15 of ECE Regulation 46.02. (b) (i) Mirrors or other devices for indirect vision complying with Community Directive 2005/27.	Paragraph 6 of Annex I and Annex II to Community Directive 2003/97 or 2005/27 or paragraphs 4, 5 and 6.1 of ECE Regulation 46.02.	Part B of Annex II to Community Directive 2003/97 or paragraph 4, 5 and 6.2 of ECE Regulation 46.02.
5	A goods vehicle not being an agricultural motor vehicle with a maximum gross weight exceeding 12,000 kg which is first used on or after 1st October 1988 and before 26th January 2007.	Mirrors complying with paragraph 2.1 of Annex III to Community Directive 86/562 or 88/321 or paragraph 16.2.1 of ECE Regulation 46.01.	Annex II to Community Directive 86/562 or 88/321 or paragraphs 4 to 8 of ECE Regulation 46.01.	None

1	2	3	4	5
Item	Class of vehicle	Mirrors or other devices for indirect vision to be fitted	Requirements to be complied with by any mirrors fitted	Requirements to be complied with by any other devices for indirect vision where fitted
6	A goods vehicle not being an agricultural motor vehicle with a maximum gross weight exceeding 12,000 kg which is first used on or after 26th January 2007.	Mirrors or other devices for indirect vision complying with Annex III to Community Directive 2003/97 or 2005/27 or paragraph 15 of ECE Regulation 46.02.	Paragraph 6 of Annex I and Annex II to Community Directive 2003/97 or 2005/27 or paragraphs 4, 5 and 6.1 of ECE Regulation 46.02.	Part B of Annex II to Community Directive 2003/97 or paragraph 4, 5 and 6.2 of ECE Regulation 46.02.
7	A two-wheeled motor cycle with or without a sidecar attached.	No requirement.	(a) If the vehicle is first used on or after 1st October 1978, Item 2 of Annex I to Community Directive 71/127, 79/795 or 80/780 or Annex II to Community Directive 86/562 or 88/321 or paragraphs 4 to 8 of ECE Regulation 46.01 and paragraph (4) of this regulation. (b) In other cases, none.	None.
8	A wheeled motor vehicle not in items 1 to 7, which is first used on or after 1st June 1978 (or, in the case of a Ford Transit motor car, 10th July 1978) and before 26th January 2010.	(i) At least one exterior mirror fitted on the offside of the vehicle; and (ii) at least one interior mirror, unless a mirror so fitted would give the driver no view to the rear of the vehicle; and (iii) at least one exterior mirror fitted on the nearside of the vehicle unless an interior mirror gives the driver an adequate view to the rear.	Item 2 of Annex I to Community Directive 71/127 or 79/795 or Annex II to Community Directive 86/562 or 88/321 or paragraphs 4 to 8 of ECE Regulation 46.01 and paragraphs (2) and (4) of this regulation.	None.
9	A wheeled motor vehicle not in items 1 to 7, which is first used on or after 26th January 2010.	Mirrors complying with Annex III to Community Directive 2003/97 or 2005/27 or paragraph 15 of ECE Regulation 46.02.	Paragraph 6 of Annex I and Annex II to Community Directive 2003/97 or 2005/27 or paragraphs 4, 5 and 6.1 of ECE Regulation 46.02.	If fitted to comply with Part B of Annex II to Community Directive 2003/97 or paragraphs 4, 5 and 6.2 of ECE Regulation 46.02.
10	A wheeled motor vehicle, not in items 1 to 7, first used before 1st June 1978 (or in the case of a Ford Transit motor car, 10th July 1978) and a track-laying motor vehicle which is not an agricultural motor vehicle first used on or after 1st January 1958, which in either case is— (a) a bus; (b) a dual-purpose vehicle; or (c) a goods vehicle.	At least one exterior mirror fitted on the offside of the vehicle and either one interior mirror or one exterior mirror fitted on the near-side of the vehicle.	None, except as specified in paragraph (3).	None.
11	A motor vehicle, whether wheeled or track-laying, not in items 1 to 10.	At least one interior or exterior mirror.	None, except as specified in paragraph (3).	None.

(5) Instead of complying with paragraphs (1) to (4) a vehicle may comply—

   (a) if it is a goods vehicle with a maximum gross weight exceeding 3500 kg first used on or after 1st April 1985 and before 1st August 1989, with Community Directive 79/795, 85/205, 86/562 or 88/321 or ECE Regulation 46.01;

   (b) if it is a goods vehicle first used on or after 1st August 1989—

  (i)   in the case of a vehicle with a maximum gross weight exceeding 3500 kg but not exceeding 12,000 kg with Community Directive 79/795, 85/205, 86/562 or 88/321 or ECE Regulation 46.01; and

  (ii)   in the case of a vehicle with a maximum gross weight exceeding 12,000 kg with Community Directive 85/205, 86/562 or 88/321 or ECE Regulation 46.01;

  (c)   if it is an agricultural motor vehicle with Community Directive 71/127, 74/346, 79/795, 85/205, 86/562 or 88/321 or ECE Regulation 46.01;

  (d)   if it is a two-wheeled motor cycle with or without a side-car with Community Directive 71/127, 79/795, 80/780, 85/205, 86/562 or 88/321 or ECE Regulation 46.01; and

  (e)   if it is any other vehicle with Community Directive 71/127, 79/795 or 85/205, 86/562 or 88/321 or ECE Regulation 46.01.

(6) Instead of complying with the provisions of column 4 in items 3, 5 or 6 of the Table a mirror may comply with the requirements as to construction and testing set out either in Annex I to Community Directive 71/127, excluding paragraphs 2.3.4 and 2.6, or in Annex I to Community Directive 79/795, excluding paragraphs 2.3.3 and 2.6.

(7) In this regulation "mirror" means a mirror to assist the driver of a vehicle to become aware of traffic—

  (i)   if it is an internal mirror, to the rear of the vehicle; and

  (ii)   if it is an external mirror fitted on one side of the vehicle, rearwards on that side of the vehicle.

In the case of an agricultural motor vehicle or a vehicle described in items 2 or 6 in the Table when drawing a trailer, the references to a vehicle in subparagraphs (i) and (ii) include references to the trailer so drawn.

---

1. The vehicle must be considered in its unloaded state or when carrying a normal load; *Mawdsley v Walter Cox (Transport) Ltd* [1965] 3 All ER 728, [1966] 1 WLR 63, 130 JP 62.

Windscreen wipers and washers

4–3536   **34.** (1) Subject to paragraphs (4) and (5), every vehicle fitted with a windscreen shall, unless the driver can obtain an adequate view to the front of the vehicle without looking through the windscreen, be fitted with one or more efficient automatic windscreen wipers capable of clearing the windscreen so that the driver has an adequate view of the road in front of both sides of the vehicle and to the front of the vehicle.

(2) Save as provided in paragraphs (3), (4) and (5), every wheeled vehicle required by paragraph (1) to be fitted with a wiper or wipers shall also be fitted with a windscreen washer capable of cleaning, in conjunction with the windscreen wiper, the area of the windscreen swept by the wiper of mud or similar deposit.

(3) The requirement specified in paragraph (2) does not apply in respect of—

  (a)   an agricultural motor vehicle (other than a vehicle used on or after 1st June 1986 which is driven at more than 20 mph);

  (b)   a track-laying vehicle;

  (c)   a vehicle having a maximum speed not exceeding 20 mph; or

  (d)   a vehicle being used to provide a local service, as defined in the Transport Act 1985.

(4) Instead of complying with paragraphs (1) and (2), a vehicle may comply with Community Directive 78/318.

(5) Instead of complying with paragraph (1) an agricultural motor vehicle may comply with Community Directive 79/1073.

(6) Every wiper and washer fitted in accordance with this regulation shall at all times while a vehicle is being used on a road be maintained in efficient working order and be properly adjusted.

Speedometers

4–3537   **35.** (1) Save as provided in paragraphs (2) and (3), every motor vehicle shall be fitted with a speedometer which, if the vehicle is first used on or after 1st April 1984, shall be capable of indicating speed in both miles per hour and kilometres per hour, either simultaneously or, by the operation of a switch separately.

(2) Paragraph (1) does not apply to—

  (a)   a vehicle having a maximum speed not exceeding 25 mph;

  (b)   a vehicle which it is at all times unlawful to drive at more than 25 mph;

  (c)   an agricultural motor vehicle which is not driven at more than 20 mph;

  (d)   a motor cycle first used before 1st April 1984 the engine of which has a cylinder capacity not exceeding 100 cc;

  (e)   an invalid carriage first used before 1st April 1984;

  (f)   a works truck first used before 1st April 1984;

  (g)   a vehicle first used before 1st October 1937; or

  (h)   a vehicle equipped with recording equipment marked with a marking designated as an approval mark by regulation 5 of the Approval Marks Regulations and shown at item 3 in Schedule 4 to those Regulations (whether or not the vehicle is required to be equipped with that equipment) and which, as regards, the visual indications given by that equipment of the speed of the vehicle, complies with the requirements relating to the said indications and installations specified in the Community Recording Equipment Regulation.

(3) Instead of complying with paragraph (1) a vehicle may comply with Community Directive 97/39 or with ECE Regulation 39.

Maintenance of speedometers

4–3538 36. (1) Every instrument for indicating speed fitted to a motor vehicle—

    (a) in compliance with the requirements of regulation 35(1) or (3); or

    (b) to which regulation 35(2)(*h*) relates and which is not, under the Community Recording Equipment Regulation, required to be equipped with the recording equipment mentioned in that paragraph,

shall be kept free from any obstruction which might prevent its being easily read and shall at all material times be maintained in good working order.

(2) In this regulation "all material times" means all times when the motor vehicle is in use on a road except when—

    (a) the vehicle is being used on a journey during which, as a result of a defect, the instrument ceased to be in good working order; or

    (b) as a result of a defect, the instrument has ceased to be in good working order and steps have been taken to have the vehicle equipped with all reasonable expedition, by means of repairs or replacement, with an instrument which is in good working order.

Speed limiters

4–3539 36A. (1) Subject to paragraph (13), this regulation applies to every coach which—

    (a) was first used on or after 1st April 1974 and before 1st January 1988; and

    (b) has, or if a speed limiter were not fitted to it would have, a maximum speed exceeding 112.65 km/h;

and a reference to this regulation to a paragraph (1) vehicle is a reference to a vehicle to which this regulation applies by virtue of this paragraph.

(2) Subject to paragraph (13), this regulation also applies to every bus which—

    (a) is first used on or after 1st January 1988;

    (b) has a maximum gross weight exceeding 7.5 tonnes; and

    (c) has, or if a speed limiter were not fitted to it would have, a maximum speed exceeding 100 km/h;

and a reference in this regulation to a paragraph (2) vehicle is a reference to a vehicle to which this regulation applies by virtue of this paragraph.

(2A) Subject to paragraph (13), this regulation also applies to every bus, not being a bus to which paragraph (2) applies, which—

    (a) is first used on or after 1st January 2005;

    (b) has a maximum gross weight exceeding 5 tonnes but not exceeding 10 tonnes; and

    (c) has, or if a speed limiter were not fitted to it would have, a maximum speed exceeding 100 km/h;

and a reference in this regulation to a paragraph (2A) vehicle is a reference to a vehicle to which this regulation applies by virtue of this paragraph.

(2B) Subject to paragraphs (2E) and (13), this regulation also applies to every bus which—

    (a) is first used on or after 1st January 2005;

    (b) has a maximum gross weight not exceeding 5 tonnes; and

    (c) has, or if a speed limiter were not fitted to it would have, a maximum speed exceeding 100 km/h;

and a reference in this regulation to a paragraph (2B) vehicle is a reference to a vehicle to which this regulation applies by virtue of this paragraph.

(2C) Subject to paragraphs (2D) and (13), this regulation also applies to every bus, not being a bus to which paragraph (2) applies, which—

    (a) was first used on or after 1st October 2001 and before 1st January 2005;

    (b) complies with the limit values in respect of Euro III emission standards set out in Council Directive 88/77/EEC, as amended by amendments up to and including those effected by Commission Directive 2001/27/EC;".;

    (c) has a maximum gross weight not exceeding 10 tonnes; and

    (d) has, or if a speed limiter were not fitted to it would have, a maximum speed exceeding 100 km/h;

and a reference in this regulation to a paragraph (2C) vehicle is a reference to a vehicle to which this regulation applies by virtue of this paragraph.

(2D) This regulation shall apply—

    (a) on or after 1st January 2006 in the case of a paragraph (2C) vehicle used for both national and international transport operations; and

    (b) on or after 1st January 2007 in the case of a paragraph (2C) vehicle used solely for national transport operations.

(2E) This regulation shall apply on or after 1st January 2008 in the case of a paragraph (2B) vehicle used solely for national transport operations.

(3) *Revoked.*

(4) Every vehicle to which this regulation applies shall be fitted with a speed limiter in respect of which such of the requirements of paragraphs (5) to (9) are met as apply to that speed limiter.

(5) Subject to paragraph (10), the requirements of this paragraph are that a speed limiter fitted to any vehicle must—

(a) be sealed by an authorised sealer in such a manner as to protect the limiter against any improper interference or adjustment and against any interference of its power supply; and
(b) be maintained in good and efficient working order.

(6) The requirements of this paragraph are that a speed limiter fitted to a paragraph (1) vehicle must be calibrated to a set speed not exceeding 112.65 km/h.

(7) Subject to paragraph (7A), the requirements of this paragraph are that a speed limiter fitted to a paragraph (2) vehicle, a paragraph (2A) vehicle, a paragraph (2B) vehicle or a paragraph 2(C) vehicle, must be set so that the speed of the vehicle cannot exceed 100 km/h.

(7A) A speed limiter fitted to a paragraph (2) vehicle which—

(a) was first used before 1st January 2005 and has a maximum gross weight exceeding 10 tonnes; or
(b) was first used before 1st October 2001 and has a maximum gross weight exceeding 7.5 tonnes but not exceeding 10 tonnes;

may be set at a maximum speed of 100 km/h.

(8) Subject to paragraphs (11) and (12), the requirements of this paragraph are that a speed limiter fitted at any time to any paragraph (1) vehicle or a speed limiter fitted before 1st October 1994 to a paragraph (2) vehicle first used before that date must comply with—

(a) Part 1 of the British Standard; or
(b) the Annexes to Community Directive 92/24 as amended by Directive 2004/11/EC of the European Parliament and of the Council.

(9) The requirements of this paragraph are that a speed limiter (not being a speed limiter to which paragraph (8) applies) fitted to a paragraph (2) vehicle, a paragraph (2A) vehicle, a paragraph (2B) vehicle and a paragraph (2C) vehicle must comply with the Annexes to Community Directive 92/24 as amended by Directive 2004/11/EC of the European Parliament and of the Council.

(9A) *Revoked.*

(10) Paragraph (5)(a) shall have effect in relation to—

(a) a speed limiter fitted before 1st August 1992 to a vehicle first used before that date; or
(b) a speed limiter sealed outside the United Kingdom,

as if the words "by an authorised sealer" were omitted.

(11) Paragraph (8) does not apply to a speed limiter fitted before 1st October 1988.

(12) Paragraph (8) does not apply to a speed limiter fitted to a vehicle if the speed limiter complies with an equivalent standard.

(13) This regulation does not apply to a vehicle—

(a) being taken to a place where a speed limiter is to be installed, calibrated, repaired or replaced;
(b) completing a journey in the course of which the speed limiter has accidentally ceased to function;
(c) which is owned by the Secretary of State for Defence and used for naval, military or air force purposes;
(d) which is used for naval, military or air force purposes while being driven by a person for the time being subject to the orders of a member of the armed forces of the Crown; or
(e) while it is being used for fire and rescue authority purposes or for or in connection with the exercise of any function of a relevant authority as defined in section 6 of the Fire (Scotland) Act 2005, for ambulance purposes or police purposes.

(14) In this regulation—

"authorised sealer" has the meaning given in Schedule 3B;
"equivalent standard" means—

(a) a standard or code of practice of a national standards body or equivalent body of any member State;
(b) any international standard recognised for use as a standard by any member State; or
(c) a technical specification or code of practice which, whether mandatory or not, is recognised for use as a standard by a public authority or any member State,

where the standard, code of practice, international standard or technical specification provides, in relation to speed limiters, a level of speed control equivalent to that provided by Part 1 of the British Standard.

"Euro III emission standards" means the emission limits given in rows A of the tables in section 6.2.1 of Annex 1 to Directive 1999/96/EC of the European Parliament and of the Council (amending Council Directive 88/77/EEC);
"international transport operations" means transport operations outside the United Kingdom;
"national transport operations" means transport operations within the United Kingdom;
"Part 1 of the British Standard" means the British Standard for Maximum Road Speed Limiters for Motor Vehicles which was published by the British Standards Institution under the number BS AU 217: Part 1: 1987 and which came into effect on 29th May 1987; as amended

by Amendment Slip No 1 under the number AMD 5969 which was published and came into effect on 30th June 1988;

"set speed", in relation to a calibrated speed limiter fitted to a vehicle, means the speed intended by the person who calibrated the speed limiter to be the mean speed of the vehicle when operating in a stabilised condition;

"speed limiter" means a device designed to limit the maximum speed of a motor vehicle by controlling the power output from the engine of the vehicle.

"transport operations" means the transportation of passengers in vehicles designed for such a purpose and to which this regulation applies.

4–3540 36B. (1) Subject to paragraphs (5) and (14), this regulation applies to every motor vehicle which—

(a) is a goods vehicle;

(b) has a maximum gross weight exceeding 7,500 kg but not exceeding 12,000 kg;

(c) is first used on or after 1st August 1992 and before 1st January 2005; and

(d) has, or if a speed limiter were not fitted to it would have, a relevant speed exceeding 60 mph.

and a reference in this regulation to a paragraph (1) vehicle is a reference to a vehicle to which this regulation applies by virtue of this paragraph.

(1A) Subject to paragraphs (1D) and (14), this regulation also applies to every motor vehicle which—

(a) is a goods vehicle;

(b) has a maximum gross weight exceeding 3,500 kg but not exceeding 12,000 kg;

(c) is first used on or after 1st January 2005; and

(d) has, or if a speed limiter were not fitted to it would have, a relevant speed exceeding 90 km/h;

and a reference in this regulation to a paragraph (1A) vehicle is a reference to a vehicle to which this regulation applies by virtue of this paragraph.

(1B) Subject to paragraphs (1C) and (14), this regulation also applies to every motor vehicle, not being a motor vehicle to which paragraph (1) applies, which—

(a) is a goods vehicle;

(b) has a maximum gross weight exceeding 3,500 kg but not exceeding 12,000 kg;

(c) was first used on or after 1st October 2001 and before 1st January 2005;

(d) complies with the limit values in respect of Euro III emission standards set out in Council Directive 88/77/EEC, as amended by amendments up to and including those effected by Commission Directive 2001/27/EC; and

(e) has, or if a speed limiter were not fitted to it would have, a relevant speed exceeding 90km/ h;

and a reference in this regulation to a paragraph (1B) vehicle is a reference to a vehicle to which this regulation applies by virtue of this paragraph.

(1C) This regulation shall apply—

(a) on or after 1st January 2006 in the case of a paragraph (1B) vehicle used for both national and international transport operations; and

(b) on or after 1st January 2007 in the case of a paragraph (1B) vehicle used solely for national transport operations.

(1D) This regulation shall apply on or after 1st January 2008 in the case of a paragraph (1A) vehicle with a maximum gross weight not exceeding 7,500 kg and used solely for national transport operations.

(2) Subject to paragraph (14), this regulation also applies to every vehicle which—

(a) is a goods vehicle;

(b) has a maximum gross weight exceeding 12,000 kg;

(c) is first used on or after 1st January 1988; and

(d) has, or if a speed limiter were not fitted to it would have, a relevant speed exceeding 90km/ h;

and a reference in this regulation to a paragraph (2) vehicle is a reference to a vehicle to which this regulation applies by virtue of this paragraph.

(3)–(5) *Revoked.*

(6) Every vehicle to which this regulation applies shall be fitted with a speed limiter in respect of which such of the requirements of paragraphs (7) to (11) are met as apply to that speed limiter.

(7) Subject to paragraph (12) the requirements of this paragraph are that a speed limiter fitted to any vehicle must—

(a) be sealed by an authorised sealer in such a manner as to protect the limiter against any improper interference or adjustment or against any interference of its power supply; and

(b) be maintained in good and efficient working order.

(8) The requirements of this paragraph are that a speed limiter fitted to a paragraph (1) vehicle must be calibrated to a set speed not exceeding 60 mph.

(9) The requirements of this paragraph are that a speed limiter fitted to a paragraph (1A) vehicle, a paragraph (1B) vehicle or a paragraph (2) vehicle must be set so that the stabilised speed of the vehicle must not exceed 90 km/h.

(10) Subject to paragraph (13) the requirements of this paragraph are that a speed limiter fitted

at any time to a paragraph (1) vehicle, a speed limiter fitted before 1st October 1994 to a paragraph (2) vehicle first used before that date must comply with—

    (*a*)   Part 1 of the British Standard; or

    (*b*)   the Annexes to Community Directive 92/24 as amended by Directive 2004/11/EC of the European Parliament and of the Council.

    (11)   The requirements of this paragraph are that a speed limiter (not being a speed limiter to which paragraph (10) applies) fitted to a paragraph (1A) vehicle, a paragraph (1B) vehicle and a paragraph (2) vehicle must comply with the Annexes to Community Directive 92/24 as amended by Directive 2004/11/EC of the European Parliament and of the Council.

    (11A)   *Revoked.*

    (12)   Paragraph (7)(*a*) shall have effect in relation to—

    (*a*)   a speed limiter fitted before 1st August 1992 to a vehicle first used before that date; or

    (*b*)   a speed limiter sealed outside the United Kingdom,

as if the words "by an authorised sealer" were omitted.

    (12A)   *Revoked.*

    (13)   Paragraph (10) does not apply to a speed limiter fitted to a vehicle if the speed limiter complies with an equivalent standard.

    (14)   This regulation does not apply to a vehicle—

    (*a*)   which is being taken to a place where a speed limiter is to be installed, calibrated, repaired or replaced;

    (*b*)   which is completing a journey in the course of which the speed limiter has accidentally ceased to function;

    (*c*)   is owned by the Secretary of State for Defence and used for naval, military or air force purposes;

    (*d*)   is used for naval, military or air force purposes while being driven by a person for the time being subject to the orders of a member of the armed forces of the Crown;

    (*e*)   while it is being used for fire brigade or, in England, fire and rescue authority, ambulance or police purposes; or

    (*f*)   at a time when it is being used on a public road during any calendar week if—

        (i)   it is being used only in passing from land in the occupation of the person keeping the vehicle to other land in his occupation, and

        (ii)   it has not been used on public roads for distances exceeding an aggregate of six miles in that calendar week,

        and for the purposes of this paragraph "public road" has the meaning given in section 62(1) the Vehicle Excise and Registration Act 1994.

    (15)   In this regulation—

"equivalent standard", "Part 1 of the British Standard", "speed limiter" and "stabilised speed" have the same meanings as in regulation 36A;

"Euro III emission standards" means the emission limits given in rows A of the tables in section 6.2.1 of Annex 1 to Directive 1999/96/EC of the European Parliament and of the Council (amending Council Directive 88/77/EEC);

"international transport operations" means transport operations outside the United Kingdom;

"national transport operations" means transport operations within the United Kingdom;

"relevant speed" means a speed which a vehicle is incapable, by means of its construction, of exceeding on the level under its own power when unladen.

"set speed", in relation to a paragraph (1) vehicle, has the same meaning as in regulation 36A; and

"set" in relation to a speed limiter fitted to there shall be inserted "a paragraph (1A) vehicle, a paragraph (1B) vehicle and a paragraph (2) vehicle, has the same meaning as in Community Directive 92/6; and references to the speed at which a speed limiter is set shall be construed accordingly.

"transport operations" means the transportation of goods in vehicles designed for such a purpose and to which this regulation applies.

    (16)   For the purposes of this regulation, a motor vehicle has a maximum gross trailer weight exceeding 5,000 kg if—

    (*a*)   in the case of a vehicle equipped with a Ministry plate in accordance with regulation 70, the difference between its maximum gross weight and the relevant train weight exceeds 5,000 kg;

    (*b*)   in the case of a vehicle not equipped with a Ministry plate, but which is equipped with a plate in accordance with regulation 66, the difference between its maximum gross weight and the weight shown on the plate in respect of item 8 of Part 1 of Schedule 8 exceeds 5,000 kg; and

    (*c*)   in the case of any other vehicle, the vehicle is designed or adapted to be capable of drawing a trailer with a laden weight exceeding 5,000 kg when travelling on a road;

and in sub-paragraph (*a*) "the relevant train weight" is the train weight shown in column (3) of the plate or, if no such weight is shown, the train weight shown in column (2) of the plate (where the plate is in the form required by Schedule 10 or 10B) or in column (4) of the plate (where the plate is in the form required by Schedule 10A or 10C).

Speed limiters—authorised sealers

4–3540A   **36C.**   Schedule 3B (authorised sealers) shall have effect.

Audible warning instruments

4–3541 **37.** (1)

(a) Subject to sub-paragraph (b), every motor vehicle which has a maximum speed of more than 20 mph shall be fitted with a horn, not being a reversing alarm or a two-tone horn.

(b) Sub-paragraph (a) shall not apply to an agricultural motor vehicle, unless it is being driven at more than 20 mph.

(2) Subject to paragraph (6), the sound emitted by any horn, other than a reversing alarm, a boarding aid alarm or a two-tone horn, fitted to a wheeled vehicle first used on or after 1st August 1973 shall be continuous and uniform and not strident.

(3) A reversing alarm or a boarding aid alarm fitted to a wheeled vehicle shall not be strident.

(4) Subject to paragraphs (5), (6) and (7) no motor vehicle shall be fitted with a bell, gong, siren or two-tone horn.

(5) The provisions of paragraph (4) shall not apply to motor vehicles—

(a) used for relevant authority (as defined in section 6 of the Fire (Scotland) Act 2005 (asp 5)) or, in England, fire and rescue authority, ambulance or police purposes;

(aa) as regards England and Wales, and so far as relating to the functions of the Serious Organised Crime Agency which are exercisable in or as regards Scotland and which relate to reserved matters (within the meaning of the Scotland Act 1998), used for Serious Organised Crime Agency purposes;

(ab) Scotland;

(b) owned by a body formed primarily for the purposes of fire salvage and used for those or similar purposes;

(c) owned by the Forestry Commission or by local authorities and used from time to time for the purposes of fighting fires;

(d) owned by the Secretary of State for Defence and used for the purposes of the disposal of bombs or explosives;

(e) used for the purposes of the Blood Transfusion Service provided under the National Health Service Act 1977 or under the National Health Service (Scotland) Act 1947;

(f) used by Her Majesty's Coastguard or the Coastguard Auxiliary Service to aid persons in danger or vessels in distress on or near the coast;

(g) used for the purposes of rescue operations at mines;

(h) owned by the Secretary of State for Defence and used by the Royal Air Force Mountain Rescue Service for the purposes of rescue operations in connection with crashed aircraft or any other emergencies;

(i) owned by the Royal National Lifeboat Institution and used for the purposes of launching lifeboats

(j) a vehicle under the lawful control of the Commissioners for Her Majesty's Revenue and Customs and used from time to time for the purposes of investigation of serious crime (which, save for the omission of the words "and, where the authorising officer is within subsection (5)(h), it relates to an assigned matter within the meaning of section 1(1) of the Customs and Excise Management Act 1979", has the meaning given by section 93(4) of the Police Act 1997); or

(k) owned or operated by the Secretary of State for Defence and used for the purpose of any activity—

(i) which prevents or decreases the exposure of persons to radiation arising from a radiation accident or radiation emergency; or

(ii) in connection with an event which could lead to a radiation accident or radiation emergency.

(6) The provisions of paragraphs (2) and (4) shall not apply so as to make it unlawful for a motor vehicle to be fitted with an instrument or apparatus (not being a two-tone horn) designed to emit a sound for the purpose of informing members of the public that goods are on the vehicle for sale[1].

(7) Subject to paragraph (8), the provisions of paragraph (4) shall not apply so as to make it unlawful for a vehicle to be fitted with a bell, gong or siren—

(a) if the purpose thereof is to prevent theft or attempted theft of the vehicle or its contents; or

(b) in the case of a bus, if the purpose thereof is to summon help for the driver, the conductor or an inspector.

(8) Every bell, gong or siren fitted to a vehicle by virtue of paragraph (7)(a), and every device fitted to a motor vehicle first used on or after 1st October 1982 so as to cause a horn to sound for the purpose mentioned in paragraph (7)(a), shall be fitted with a device designed to stop the bell, gong, siren or horn emitting noise for a continuous period of more than five minutes; and every such device shall at all times be maintained in good working order.

(9) Instead of complying with paragraphs (1), (2) and (4) to (8), a vehicle may comply with Community Directive 70/388 or ECE Regulation 28 or, if the vehicle is an agricultural motor vehicle, with Community Directive 74/151.

(9A) In this regulation "radiation accident" and "radiation emergency" shall have the same meaning as in the Radiation (Emergency Preparedness and Public Information) Regulations 2001

(10) In this regulation and in regulation 99—

(a) "horn" means an instrument, not being a bell, gong or siren, capable of giving audible and sufficient warning of the approach or position of the vehicle to which it is fitted;

(b) references to a bell, gong or siren include references to any instrument or apparatus capable of emitting a sound similar to that emitted by a bell, gong or siren;

(c) "reversing alarm" means a device fitted to a motor vehicle and designed to warn persons that the vehicle is reversing or is about to reverse;

(d) "two-tone horn" means an instrument which, when operated, automatically produces a sound which alternates at regular intervals between two fixed notes; and

(e) "boarding aid alarm" means an alarm for a power operated lift or ramp fitted to a bus to enable wheelchair users to board and alight and designed to warn persons that the lift or ramp is in operation.

---

1. Restrictions on the use thereof are provided by the Control of Pollution Act 1974, s 62; see title PUBLIC HEALTH in PART VIII.

Motor cycle sidestands

4–3542   **38.** (1) No motor cycle first used on or after 1st April 1986 shall be fitted with any sidestand which is capable of—

(a) disturbing the stability or direction of the motor cycle when it is in motion under its own power; or

(b) closing automatically if the angle of the inclination of the motor cycle is inadvertently altered when it is stationary.

(2) In this regulation "sidestand" means a device fitted to a motor cycle which, when fully extended or pivoted to its open position, supports the vehicle from one side only and so that both the wheels of the motor cycle are on the ground.

G—FUEL

Fuel tanks

4–3543   **39.** (1) This regulation applies to every fuel tank which is fitted to a wheeled vehicle for the purpose of supplying fuel to the propulsion unit or to an ancillary engine or to any other equipment forming part of the vehicle.

(2) Subject to paragraphs (3), (3A) and (4), every fuel tank to which this regulation applies—

(a) shall be constructed and maintained so that the leakage of any liquid from the tank is adequately prevented;

(b) shall be constructed and maintained so that the leakage of vapour from the tank is adequately prevented; and

(c) if it contains petroleum spirit (as defined in section 23 of the Petroleum (Consolidation) Act 1928) and is fitted to a vehicle first used on or after 1st July 1973, shall be—

    (i) made only of metal; and

    (ii) fixed in such a position and so maintained as to be reasonably secure from damage.

(3) Notwithstanding the requirement of paragraph (2)(b), the fuel tank may be fitted with a device which, by the intake of air or the emission of vapour, relieves changes of pressure in the tank.

(3A) Sub-paragraph (i) of paragraph 2(c) shall not have effect in relation to a two-wheeled motor cycle (with or without a side-car) first used on or after 1st February 1993.

(4) Instead of complying with the requirements of paragraph (1) as to construction, a vehicle may comply with the requirements of Community Directive 70/221 (insofar as they relate to fuel tanks) or ECE Regulation 34 or 34.01 or, if the vehicle is an agricultural motor vehicle, of Community Directive 74/151.

4–3544   **39A.** (1) Every vehicle to which this regulation applies shall be designed and constructed for running on unleaded petrol.

(2) No person shall use or cause or permit to be used a vehicle to which this regulation applies on a road if it—

(a) has been deliberately altered or adjusted for running on leaded petrol, and

(b) as a direct result of such alteration or adjustment it is incapable of running on unleaded petrol.

(3) Subject to paragraph (4) this regulation applies to every motor vehicle which is—

(a) propelled by a spark ignition engine which is capable of running on petrol, and

(b) is first used on or after the 1st April 1991.

(4) Part I of Schedule 3A shall have effect for the purpose of excluding certain vehicles first used before specified dates from the application of this regulation.

(5) In this regulation "petrol", "leaded petrol" and "unleaded petrol" have the same meaning as in Community Directive 85/210[1].

(6) A vehicle shall be regarded for the purposes of this regulation as incapable of running on unleaded petrol at any particular time if and only if in its state of adjustment at that time prolonged continuous running on such petrol would damage the engine.

---

1. "Community Directive" is defined in reg 3 of and Sch 2 to those Regulations.

4–3545   **39B.** (1) Subject to paragraph (2), every fuel tank fitted to a vehicle to which regulation 39A applies shall be so constructed and fitted that it cannot readily be filled from a petrol pump delivery nozzle which has an external diameter of 23·6 mm or greater without the aid of a device (such as a funnel) not fitted to the vehicle.

(2) Paragraph (1) does not apply to a vehicle in respect of which both of the following conditions are satisfied, that is to say—

(a) that at the time of its first use the vehicle is so designed and constructed that prolonged continuous running on leaded petrol would not cause any device designed to control the emission of carbon monoxide, hydrocarbons or nitrogen oxides to malfunction, and

(b) that it is conspicuously and legibly marked in a position immediately visible to a person filling the fuel tank with—

(i) the word "UNLEADED", or
(ii) the symbol shown in Part II of Schedule 3A.

(3) In this regulation "fuel tank", in relation to a vehicle, means a fuel tank used in connection with the propulsion of the vehicle.

Gas propulsion systems and gas-fired appliances

4–3546   40. (1) A vehicle which is—

(a) a motor vehicle which first used gas as a fuel for its propulsion before 19th November 1982; or

(b) a trailer manufactured before 19th November 1982 to which there is fitted a gas container,

shall be so constructed that it complies either with the provisions of Schedule 4 or with the provisions of Schedule 5.

(2) Subject to paragraph (2A), a vehicle which is—

(a) a motor vehicle which first used gas as a fuel for its propulsion on or after 19th November 1982; or

(b) a motor vehicle first used on or after 1st May 1984 or a trailer manufactured on or after 19th November 1982 which is in either case equipped with a gas container or a gas-fired appliance,

shall comply with the provisions of Schedule 5 or with ECE Regulation 67 and 67.01.

(2A) A vehicle which first used gas as a fuel for its propulsion on or after 13th November 1999 shall comply with the provisions of Schedule 5 or ECE Regulation 67.01.

(3) The requirements of this regulation are in addition to, and not in derogation from, the requirements of any regulations made under powers conferred by the Petroleum (Consolidation) Act 1928, the Health and Safety at Work etc Act 1974, the Control of Pollution Act 1974 or any other Act or of any codes of practice issued under the Health and Safety at Work etc Act 1974.

(4) In this regulation "gas container" has the meaning given in Schedule 4 where compliance with the provisions of that Schedule is concerned and otherwise has the meaning given Schedule 5.

H—MINIBUSES

Minibuses

4–3547   41. The requirements specified in Schedule 6 shall apply to every minibus first used on or after 1st April 1988 except a vehicle—

(a) manufactured by Land Rover UK Limited and known as the Land Rover; or
(b) constructed or adapted for the secure transport of prisoners.

Alternative means of compliance

4–3547A   41A. A minibus which is required by regulation 41 to meet the requirements specified in Schedule 6 need not meet them if it meets the requirements of such of the Annexes to Directive 2001/85/EC of the European Parliament and of the Council of 20 November 2001, relating to special provisions for vehicles used for the carriage of passengers comprising more than eight seats in addition to the driver's seat, and amending Directives 70/156/EEC and 97/27/EC, as apply to that minibus.

Fire extinguishing apparatus

4–3548   42. (1) No person shall use, or cause or permit to be used, on a road a minibus first used on or after 1st April 1988 unless it carries suitable and efficient apparatus for extinguishing fire which is of a type specified in Part I of Schedule 7.

(2) The apparatus referred to in paragraph (1) above shall be—

(a) readily available for use;
(b) clearly marked with the appropriate British Standards Institution specification number; and
(c) maintained in good and efficient working order.

(3) This regulation does not apply to a vehicle manufactured by Land Rover UK Limited and known as the Land Rover.

First aid equipment

4–3549   43. (1) No person shall use, or cause or permit to be used, on a road a minibus first used on or after 1st April 1988 unless it carries a receptacle which contains the items specified in Part II of Schedule 7.

(2) The receptacle referred to in paragraph (1) above shall be—

(a) maintained in a good condition;
(b) suitable for the purpose of keeping the items referred to in the said paragraph in good condition;
(c) readily available for use; and
(d) prominently marked as a first aid receptacle.

(3) The items referred to in paragraph (1) above shall be maintained in good condition and shall be of a good and reliable quality and of a suitable design.

(4) This regulation does not apply to a vehicle manufactured by Land Rover UK Limited and known as the Land Rover.

Carriage of dangerous substances

4–3550   44. (1) Save as provided in paragraph (2), no person shall use or cause or permit to be used on a road a minibus by which any highly inflammable or otherwise dangerous substance is carried unless that substance is carried in containers so designed and constructed, and unless the substance is so packed, that, notwithstanding an accident to the vehicle, it is unlikely that damage to the vehicle or injury to passengers in the vehicle will be caused by the substance.

(2) Paragraph (1) shall not apply in relation to the electrolyte of a battery installed in an electric wheelchair provided that the wheelchair is securely fixed to the vehicle.

(3) This regulation does not apply to a vehicle manufactured by Land Rover UK Limited and known as the Land Rover.

4–3551   45. *Revoked.*

J—PROTECTIVE SYSTEMS

Seat belt anchorage points

4–3552   46. (1) This regulation applies to a motor vehicle which is not an excepted vehicle and is—

(a) a bus first used on or after 1st April 1982;
(b) a wheeled motor car first used on or after 1st January 1965;
(c) a three-wheeled motor cycle which has an unladen weight exceeding 255 kg and which was first used on or after 1st September 1970; or
(d) a heavy motor car first used on or after 1st October 1988.

(2) Each of the following is an excepted vehicle—

(a) a goods vehicle (other than a dual-purpose vehicle)—

(i) first used before 1st April 1967;
(ii) first used on or after 1st April 1980 and before 1st October 1988 and having a maximum gross weight exceeding 3500 kg; or
(iii) first used before 1st April 1980 or, if the vehicle is of a model manufactured before 1st October 1979, first used before 1st April 1982 and, in either case, having an unladen weight exceeding 1525 kg;

(b) an agricultural motor vehicle;
(c) a motor tractor;
(d) a works truck;
(e) an electrically propelled goods vehicle first used before 1st October 1988;
(f) a pedestrian-controlled vehicle;
(g) a vehicle which has been used on roads outside Great Britain, whilst it is being driven from the place at which it arrived in Great Britain to a place of residence of the owner or driver of the vehicle, or from any such place to a place where, by previous arrangement, it will be provided with such anchorage points as are required by this regulation and with such seat belts as are required by regulation 47;
(h) a vehicle having a maximum speed not exceeding 16 mph;
(i) a motor cycle equipped with a driver's seat of a type requiring the driver to sit astride it, and which is constructed or assembled by a person not ordinarily engaged in the trade or business of manufacturing vehicles of that description;
(j) a locomotive.

(3) A vehicle which falls within a description specified in column (2) of an item in the Table below shall be equipped with anchorage points for seat belts for the use of persons sitting in the seats specified in column (3) of that item and those anchorage points ("mandatory anchorage points") shall comply with the requirements specified in column (4).

TABLE

(1) Item	(2) Description of vehicle	(3) Seats for which mandatory anchorage points are to be provided	(4) Technical and installation requirements
1	Any vehicle first used before 1st April 1982	The driver's seat and specified passenger seat (if any)	Anchorage points must be designed to hold seat belts securely in position on the vehicle
2	Minibus constructed or adapted to carry not more than 12 seated passengers in addition to the driver, motor ambulance or motor caravan which, in any such case, was first used on or after 1st April 1982 but before 1st October 1988	The driver's seat and specified passenger seat (if any)	The technical and installation (but not the testing) requirements of Community Directive 76/115, 81/575, 82/318, 90/629 or 96/38 or ECE Regulation 14, 14.01, 14.02, 14.03, 14.04 or 14.05 whether or not those instruments apply to the vehicle
3	Minibus (not being a vehicle falling within item 7 or 8) having a gross weight not exceeding 3500 kg, motor ambulance or motor caravan which, in any such case, was first used on or after 1st October 1988	The driver's seat and each forward-facing front seat	The requirements specified in column (4) of item 2
4	Goods vehicle first used on or after 1st October 1988 but before 1st October 2001 and having a maximum gross weight exceeding 3500 kg	The driver's seat and each forward-facing front seat	2 or 3 anchorage points designed to hold seat belts securely in position
5	Goods vehicle first used on or after 1st October 2001 and having a maximum gross weight exceeding 3500 kg	All forward-facing front seats	The technical and installation requirements of Community Directive 96/38 or ECE Regulation 14.04 or 14.05
6	Coach first used on or after 1st October 1988 but before 1st October 2001	All exposed forward-facing seats	The requirements specified in column (4) of item 2 or, if the anchorage points were fitted before 1st October 2001 and form part of a seat, a requirement that they do not, when a forward horizontal force is applied to them, become detached from the seat before the seat becomes detached from the vehicle
7	Bus (other than an urban bus) having a gross vehicle weight exceeding 3500 kg and first used on or after 1st October 2001	Anchorage points for every forward-facing and every rearward-facing seat	The requirements specified in column (4) of item 5
8	Bus (other than an urban bus) having a gross vehicle weight not exceeding 3500 kg and first used on or after 1st October 2001	Every forward-facing and every rearward-facing seat	The requirements specified in column (4) of item 5
9	Passenger or dual-purpose vehicle (other than a bus) first used on or after 1st April 1982 and not falling within any of items 2 to 8	Every forward-facing seat constructed or adapted to accommodate no more than one adult	The requirements specified in column (4) of item 2
10	Vehicle (other than a bus) first used on or after 1st April 1982 and not falling within any of items 2 to 9	Every forward-facing front seat and every non-protected seat	The requirements specified in column (4) of item 2

(4) Any anchorage fitted after 1st October 2001 to a bus not falling within item 7 or 8 of the Table in paragraph (3) must comply with the technical and installation (but not the testing) requirements of Community Directive 76/115, 81/575, 82/318, 90/629 or 96/38 or ECE Regulation 14, 14.01, 14.02, 14.03, 14.04 or 14.05 whether or not those instruments apply to the vehicle.

(5) Subject to paragraph (6), where a vehicle to which this regulation applies and which falls within a class specified in an item of the Table in paragraph (3) is fitted with non-mandatory anchorage points, those anchorage points shall comply with the requirements applicable to the mandatory anchorage points specified for that item.

(6) Paragraph (5) does not apply to non-mandatory anchorage points fitted to—

    (*a*)   a minibus before 1st April 1986; or

    (*b*)   any other vehicle before 1st October 1988.

(7) For the purposes of this regulation—

    (*a*)   the expressions "exposed forward-facing seat", "forward-facing front seat", "lap belt", "seat belt" and "specified passenger's seat" have the same meaning as in regulation 47(8);

    (*b*)   "mandatory anchorage points" has the meaning given in paragraph (3) and "non-mandatory anchorage points" means anchorage points which are not mandatory anchorage points;

    (*c*)   a seat is a "non-protected seat" if it is not a front seat and the screen zones within the protected area have a combined surface of less than 800 cm2;

    (*d*)   "screen zone" and "protected area" in relation to a seat shall be construed in accordance with paragraph 4.3.3 of Annex I to Community Directive 81/575; and

    (*e*)   "urban bus" means a bus designed for urban use with standing passengers and includes a vehicle which is—

        (i)   a Class I vehicle as defined by paragraph 2.1.2.1.3.1.1 of Annex I of Community Directive 97/27/EC;

        (ii)   a Class II vehicle as defined by paragraph 2.1.2.1.3.1.2 of that Annex; or

        (iii)   a Class A vehicle as defined by paragraph 2.1.2.1.3.2.1 of that Annex.

(8) A vehicle which is not required by this regulation to comply with the technical and installation requirements of Community Directive 76/115, 81/575, 82/318, 90/629 or 96/38 or ECE Regulation 14, 14.01, 14.02, 14.03, 14.04 or 14.05 shall nevertheless be taken to comply with the provisions of this regulation if it does comply with those requirements.

Seat belts

4–3553   **47.** (1) This regulation applies to every vehicle to which regulation 46 applies.

    (2) Save as provided in paragraph (4) a vehicle to which—

    (*a*)   this regulation applies which was first used before 1st April 1981 shall be provided with—

        (i)   a body-restraining belt, designed for use by an adult, for the driver's seat; and

        (ii)   a body-restraining belt for the specified passenger's seat (if any);

    (*b*)   this regulation applies which is first used on or after 1st April 1981 shall be provided with three-point belts for the driver's seat and for the specified passenger's seat (if any);

    (*c*)   Item 9 or 10 of the Table in regulation 46(3) applies which is first used on or after 1st April 1987 shall be fitted with seat belts additional to those required by sub-paragraph (*b*) as follows—

        (i)   for any forward-facing front seat alongside the driver's seat, not being a specified passenger's seat, a seat belt which is a three-point belt, or a lap belt installed in accordance with paragraph 3.1.2.1 of Annex 1 to Community Directive 77/541 or a disabled person's belt;

        (ii)   in the case of a passenger or dual-purpose vehicle having not more than two forward-facing seats behind the driver's seat with either—

            (A)   an inertia reel belt for at least one of those seats, or

            (B)   a three-point belt, a lap belt, a disabled person's belt or a child restraint for each of those seats;

        (iii)   in the case of a passenger or dual-purpose vehicle having more than two forward-facing seats behind the drivers' seat, with either—

            (A)   an inertia reel belt for one of those seats being an outboard seat and a three-point belt, a lap belt, a disabled person's belt or a child restraint for at least one other of those seats;

            (B)   a three-point belt for one of those seats and either a child restraint or a disabled person's belt for at least one other of those seats; or

            (C)   a three-point belt, a lap belt, a disabled person's belt or a child restraint for each of those seats.

    (*d*)   item 3 of the Table in regulation 46(3) applies shall be fitted with seat belts as follows—

        (i)   for the driver's seat and the specified passenger's seat (if any) a three-point belt; and

        (ii)   for any forward-facing front seat which is not a specified passenger's seat, a three-point belt or a lap belt installed in accordance with the provisions of sub-paragraph (*c*)(i);

    (*e*)   item 6 of the Table in regulation 46(3) applies shall be equipped with seat belts which shall be three-point belts, lap belts or disabled person's belts.

    (*f*)   item 5 of the Table in regulation 46(3) applies shall be fitted—

        (i)   as respects the driver's seat with a three-point belt or a lap belt; and

        (ii)   as respects every other forward-facing front seat with a three-point belt, a lap belt installed in accordance with paragraph 3.1.2.1 of Annex I to Community Directive 77/541 or a disabled person's belt;

    (*g*)   item 7 of the Table in regulation 46(3) applies shall be fitted, as respects every forward-facing seat, with—

        (i)   an inertia reel belt;

(ii) a retractable lap belt installed in compliance with paragraph 3.1.10 of Annex I to Community Directive 96/36 or 2000/3;

(iii) a disabled person's belt; or

(iv) a child restraint;

(*h*) item 7 of the Table in regulation 46(3) applies shall be fitted, as respects every rearward-facing seat, with—

(i) an inertia reel belt;

(ii) a retractable lap belt;

(iii) a disabled person's belt; or

(iv) a child restraint;

(*i*) item 8 of the Table in regulation 46(3), as respects every forward-facing seat, with—

(i) an inertia reel belt;

(ii) a disabled person's belt; or

(iii) a child restraint;

(*j*) item 8 of the Table in regulation 46(3), as respects every rearward-facing seat, with—

(i) an inertia reel belt;

(ii) a retractable lap belt;

(iii) a disabled person's belt; or

(iv) a child restraint.

Where a lap belt is fitted to a forward-facing front seat of a minibus, a motor ambulance or a motor caravan, or to an exposed forward-facing seat (other than the driver's seat or any crew seat) of a coach either—

(i) there shall be provided padding to a depth of not less than 50 mm, on that part of the surface or edge of any bar, or the top or edge of any screen or partition which would be likely to be struck by the head of a passenger wearing the lap belt in the event of an accident; or

(ii) the technical and installation requirements of Annex 4 to ECE Regulation 21 shall be met, in respect of any such bar, screen or partition,

but nothing in sub-paragraph (i) above shall require padding to be provided on any surface more than 1 m from the centre of the line of intersection of the seat cushion and the back rest or more than 150 mm on either side of the longitudinal vertical plane which passes through the centre of that line, nor shall it require padding to be provided on any instrument panel of a minibus.

(3) Every seat belt for an adult, other than a disabled person's belt, provided for a vehicle in accordance with any of paragraphs (2)(*b*) to (*j*) shall, except as provided in paragraph (6), comply with the installation requirements specified in paragraph 3.2.2 to 3.3.4 of Annex 1 to Community Directive 77/541 or 82/319 or 90/628 or 96/36 or 2000/3 whether or not those Directives apply to the vehicle.

(4) The requirements specified in paragraph (2) do not apply—

(*a*) to a vehicle while it is being used under a trade licence within the meaning of section 11 of the Vehicle Excise and Registration Act 1994;

(*b*) to a vehicle, not being a vehicle to which the Type Approval (Great Britain) Regulations apply, while it is being driven from premises of the manufacturer by whom it was made, or of a distributor of vehicles or dealer in vehicles—

(i) to premises of a distributor of or dealer in vehicles or of the purchaser of the vehicle or

(ii) to premises of a person obtaining possession of the vehicle under a hiring agreement or hire-purchase agreement;

(*c*) in relation to any seat for which there is provided—

(i) a seat belt which bears a mark including the specification number of the British Standard for Passive Belt Systems, namely BS AU 183:1983 and including the registered certification trade mark of the British Standards Institution;

(ii) a seat belt designed for use by an adult which is a harness belt comprising a lap belt and shoulder straps which bears a British Standard mark or a mark including the specification number for the British Standard for Seat Belt Assemblies for Motor Vehicles, namely BS 3254:1960 or BS 3254: Part 1: 1988 and including the registered certification trade mark of the British Standards Institution, or the marking designated as an approval mark by regulation 4 of the Approval Marks Regulations and shown at item 16 or 16A Schedule 2 to those Regulations.

(iii) a seat belt which satisfies the requirements of a standard corresponding to the British Standard referred to in sub-paragraph (i); or

(iv) a seat belt designed for use by an adult which is a harness belt comprising a lap belt and shoulder straps and which satisfies the requirements of a standard corresponding to any of the British Standards referred to in sub-paragraph (ii).

(*d*) in relation to the driver's seat or the specified passenger's seat (if any) of a vehicle which has been specially designed and constructed, or specially adapted, for the use of a person suffering from some physical defect or disability, in a case where a disabled person's belt for an adult person is provided for use for that seat;

(*e*) to a vehicle to which item 4 of the Table in regulation 46(3) applies.

(4A) Vehicles constructed or adapted for the secure transport of prisoners shall not be required to comply with the requirements of paragraph (2) in relation to seats for persons other than the driver and any front seat passenger provided that those seats shall have seat belt anchorage points provided for them in accordance with regulation 46.

(5) Every seat belt provided in pursuance of paragraph (2) shall be properly secured to the anchorage points provided for it in accordance with regulation 46; or, in the case of a child restraint, to anchorages specially provided for it or, in the case of a disabled person's belt, first fitted before 1st October 2001, secured to the vehicle or to the seat which is being occupied by the person wearing the belt.

(6) Paragraph (3), in so far as it relates to the second paragraph of paragraph 3.3.2 of the Annex there mentioned (which concerns the locking or releasing of a seat belt by a single movement) does not apply in respect of a seat belt fitted for—

(a) a seat which is treated as a specified passenger's seat by virtue of the provisions of sub-paragraph (ii) in the definition of "specified passenger's seat" in paragraph (8); or

(b) any forward-facing seat for a passenger alongside the driver's seat of a goods vehicle which has an unladen weight of more than 915 kg and has more than one such seat, any such seats for passengers being joined together in a single structure; or

(c) any seat (other than the driver's seat) fitted to a coach.

(7) Every seat belt, other than a disabled person's belt or a seat belt of a kind mentioned in paragraph 4(c) above, provided for any person in a vehicle to which this regulation applies shall be legibly and permanently marked—

(a) with a British Standard mark or a designated approval mark; or

(b) with an EC Component Type-Approval Mark complying with Annex III to Community Directive 2000/3.

(b) revoked.

Provided this paragraph shall not operate so as to invalidate the exception permitted in paragraph (6).

(7A) Paragraph (7) does not apply to—

(a) a seat belt for an adult that satisfies the requirements of a standard corresponding to either of the British Standards referred to in sub-paragraph (i)(a) of the definition of "British Standard mark" in paragraph (8); or

(b) a child restraint that satisfies the requirements of a standard corresponding to any of the British Standards referred to in sub-paragraph (i)(b) of that definition.

(7B) For the purposes of this regulation a reference to a standard corresponding to a specified British Standard is a reference to—

(a) a standard or code of practice of a national standards body or equivalent body of any EEA State;

(b) any international standard recognised for use as a standard by any EEA State; or

(c) a technical specification recognised for use as a standard by a public authority of any EEA State.

where the standard, code of practice, international standard or technical specification provides in relation to seat belts, a level of safety equivalent to that provided by the British Standard and contains a requirement as respects the marking of seat belts equivalent to that provided by the British Standard.

(7C) For the purposes of paragraph (7B)—

(a) "EEA State" means a State which is a contracting Party to the EEA Agreement but, until the EEA Agreement comes into force in relation to Liechtenstein, does not include the state of Liechtenstein; and

(b) "EEA Agreement" means the Agreement on the European Economic Area signed at Oporto on 2nd May 1992 as adjusted by the Protocol signed at Brussels on 17th March 1993."

(5) In paragraph (8), in sub-paragraph (i) (b) of the definition of " British Standard mark" after "BS 3254: Part 2: 1988" there shall be inserted "or BS 3254: Part 2: 1991".

(8) In this regulation—

"body-restraining belt" means a seat belt designed to provide restraint for both the upper and lower parts of the trunk of the wearer in the event of an accident to the vehicle;

"British Standard mark" means a mark consisting of—

(i) the specification number of one of the following British Standards for Seat Belt Assemblies for Motor Vehicles, namely—

(a) if it is a seat belt for an adult, BS 3254:1960 or BS 3254: Part 1: 1988; or

(b) if it is a child restraint, BS 3254:1960, or BS 3254:1960 as amended by Amendment No 16 published on 31st July 1986 under the number AMD 5210, BS 3254: Part 2: 1988, or BS 3254: Part 2: 1991 BS AU 185, BS AU 186 or 186a, BS AU 202 or BS AU 202a or BS AU 202b; and, in either case,

(ii) the registered certification trade mark of the British Standards Institution;

"child restraint" means a seat belt for the use of a young person which is designed either to be fitted directly to a suitable anchorage or to be used in conjunction with a seat belt for an adult and held in place by the restraining action of that belt:
Provided that for the purposes of paragraph (2)(c)(ii)(B) and (2)(c)(iii) it means only such seat belts fitted directly to a suitable anchorage and excludes belts marked with the specification numbers BS AU 185 and BS AU 186 or 186a.

"crew seat" has the same meaning as in regulation 3(1) of the Public Service Vehicles (Conditions of Fitness Equipment, Use and Certification) Regulations 1981;

"designated approval mark" means—

(a) if it is a seat belt other than a child restraint, the marking designated as an approval mark by regulation 4 of the Approval Marks Regulations and shown at items 16 and 16A of Schedule 2 to those Regulations or the marking designated as an approval mark by regulation 5 of those Regulations and shown at item 23, 23A and 23B in Schedule 4 to those Regulations, and

(b) if it is a child restraint, any of the markings designated as approval marks by regulation 4 of those Regulations and shown at items 44, 44A and 44B and 44C in Schedule 2 to those Regulations.

"disabled person's belt" means a seat belt which has been specially designed or adapted for use by an adult or young person suffering from some physical defect or disability and which is intended for use solely by such a person;

"exposed forward-facing seat" means—

(i) a forward-facing front seat (including any crew seat) and the driver's seat; and

(ii) any other forward-facing seat which is not immediately behind and on the same horizontal plane as a forward-facing high-backed seat;

"forward-facing seat" means a seat which is attached to a vehicle so that it faces towards the front of the vehicle in such a manner that a line passing through the centre of both the front and the back of the seat is at an angle of 30° or less to the longitudinal axis of the vehicle;

"forward-facing front seat" means—

(i) any forward-facing seat alongside the driver's seat; or

(ii) if the vehicle normally has no seat which is a forward-facing front seat under sub-paragraph (i) of this definition, each forward-facing seat for a passenger which is foremost in the vehicle;

"forward-facing high-backed seat" means a forward-facing seat which is also a high-backed seat;

"high-backed seat" means a seat the highest part of which is at least 1 metre above the deck of the vehicle;

"inertia reel belt" means a three-point belt of either of the types required for a front outboard seating position by paragraph 3.1.1 of Annex 1 to Community Directive 77/541;

"lap belt" means a seat belt which passes across the front of the wearer's pelvic region and which is designed for use by an adult;

"retractable lap belt" means a lap belt with either an automatically locking retractor (as defined in paragraph 1.8.3 of Annex I to Community Directive 77/541) or an emergency locking retractor (as defined in paragraph 1.8.4 of Annex I to Community Directive 77/541);

"seat" includes any part designed for the accommodation of one adult of a continuous seat designed for the accommodation of more than one adult;

"seat belt" means a belt intended to be worn by a person in a vehicle and designed to prevent or lessen injury to its wearer in the event of an accident to the vehicle and includes, in the case of a child restraint, any special chair to which the belt is attached;

"specified passenger's seat" means—

(i) in the case of a vehicle which has one forward-facing front seat alongside the driver's seat, that seat, and in the case of a vehicle which has more than one such seat, the one furthest from the driver's seat; or

(ii) if the vehicle normally has no seat which is the specified passenger's seat under sub-paragraph (i) of this definition the forward-facing front seat for a passenger which is the foremost in the vehicle and furthest from the driver's seat, unless there is a fixed partition separating that seat from the space in front of it alongside the driver's seat; and

"three-point belt" means a seat belt which—

(i) restrains the upper and lower parts of the torso;

(ii) includes a lap belt;

(iii) is anchored at not less than three points; and

(iv) is designed for use by an adult.

Maintenance of seat belts and anchorage points

4–3554 **48.** (1) This regulation applies to every seat belt with which a motor vehicle is required to be provided in accordance with regulation 47 and to the anchorages, fastenings, adjusting device and retracting mechanism (if any) of every such seat belt and also to every anchorage with which a goods vehicle is required to be provided in accordance with regulation 46(3) and item 4 in the Table in that regulation.

(2) For the purposes of this regulation the anchorages and anchorage points of a seat belt shall, in the case of a seat which incorporates integral seat belt anchorages, include the system by which the seat assembly itself is secured to the vehicle structure.

(a) all load-bearing members of the vehicle structure or panelling within 30 cms of each anchorage point shall be maintained in a sound condition and free from serious corrosion, distortion or fracture;

   (b) the adjusting device and (if fitted) the retracting mechanism of the seat belt shall be so maintained that the belt may be readily adjusted to the body of the wearer, either automatically or manually, according to the design of the device and (if fitted) the retracting mechanism;

   (c) the seat belt and its anchorages, fastenings and adjusting device shall be maintained free from any obvious defect which would be likely to affect adversely the performance by the seat belt of the function of restraining the body of the wearer in the event of an accident to the vehicle;

   (d) the buckle or other fastening of the seat belt shall—

      (i) be so maintained that the belt can be readily fastened or unfastened;

      (ii) be kept free from any temporary or permanent obstruction; and

      (iii) except in the case of a disabled person's seat belt, be readily accessible to a person sitting in the seat for which the seat belt is provided;

   (e) the webbing or other material which forms the seat belt shall be maintained free from cuts or other visible faults (as, for example, extensive fraying) which would be likely to affect adversely the performance of the belt when under stress;

   (f) the ends of every seat belt, other than a disabled person's seat belt, shall be securely fastened to the anchorage points provided for them; and

   (g) the ends of every disabled person's seat belt shall, when the seat belt is being used for the purpose for which it was designed and constructed, be securely fastened either to some part of the structure of the vehicle or to the seat which is being occupied by the person wearing the belt so that the body of the person wearing the belt would be restrained in the event of an accident to the vehicle.

(5) No requirement specified in paragraph (4) above applies if the vehicle is being used—

   (a) on a journey after the start of which the requirement ceased to be complied with; or

   (b) after the requirement ceased to be complied with and steps have been taken for such compliance to be restored with all reasonable expedition.

(6) Expressions which are used in this regulation and are defined in regulation 47 have the same meaning in this regulation as they have in regulation 47.

Minibuses and coaches to be fitted with additional seat belts when used in certain circumstances

4-3554A   **48A.** (1) No person shall use or cause or permit to be used on a road a coach or minibus wholly or mainly for the purpose of carrying a group of 3 or more children in the following circumstances unless the appropriate number of forward-facing passenger seats fitted to the vehicle meet the requirements of this regulation.

   (2) The circumstances are that—

   (a) the group of children are on an organised trip; and

   (b) the journey is being made for the purposes of the trip.

(3) In paragraph (1), the reference to the appropriate number is a reference to the number of children being carried in the vehicle (excluding disabled children in wheelchairs).

(3A) For the purposes of this regulation a rearward-facing seat shall be treated as a forward-facing seat which meets the requirements of this regulation if the coach or minibus concerned was first used on or after 1st October 2001, and the rearward-facing seat complies with the requirements of regulations 46 and 47.

(4) Without prejudice to the generality of paragraph (2)(a), a group of children shall, for the purposes of this regulation, be regarded as being on an organised trip if they are being carried to or from their school or from one part of their school premises to another.

(5) Without prejudice to the meaning of paragraph (2)(b), paragraph (1) shall not apply to a vehicle if it is being used in the provision of a bus service of a description specified in paragraph 2 of the Schedule to the Fuel Duty Grant (Eligible Bus Services) Regulations 1985 or if it is otherwise being used wholly or mainly for the purpose of providing a transport service for the general public.

(6) For a forward-facing passenger seat to meet the requirements of this regulation a seat belt must be provided for it, and—

   (a) if paragraph (3) of regulation 47 does not (in whole or part) apply to the seat belt and the seat belt was first fitted to the vehicle after 10th February 1997, the seat belt must comply with that paragraph to the extent (if any) that it would have to so comply were—

      (i) that regulation to apply to all motor vehicles, and

      (ii) there substituted for the words "provided" to "or (e)", in that paragraph, the words "provided for any person in a vehicle to which this regulation applies";

   (b) if paragraph (5) of regulation 47 does not apply to the seat belt and the seat belt is a seat belt for an adult (not being a disabled person's belt) that was first fitted to the vehicle after 10th February 1997, the seat belt must comply with the requirements specified in paragraph (7) below;

   (c) if paragraph (5) of regulation 47 does not apply to the seat belt and the seat belt is a child restraint that was first fitted to the vehicle after 10th February 1997, the seat belt must be properly secured to anchorages provided for it;

   (d) if paragraph (5) of regulation 47 does not apply to the seat belt and the seat belt is a disabled person's belt that was first fitted to the vehicle after 10th February 1997, the seat belt must be properly secured to the vehicle or to the seat;

(e) if regulation 47 does not apply to the vehicle and the seat belt was first fitted to the vehicle after 10th February 1997, the seat belt must comply with paragraph (7) of that regulation to the extent (if any) that it would have to so comply were that regulation to apply to all motor vehicles; and

(f) if regulation 48 does not apply to the seat belt and the seat belt was first fitted to the vehicle after 10th February 1997, the requirements of paragraph (4) of that regulation must be met in relation to the anchorages, fastenings, adjusting device and retracting mechanism (if any) of the seat belt to the extent (if any) that those requirements would have to be met were that paragraph to apply to all anchorages, fastenings, adjusting devices and retracting mechanisms of seat belts fitted to motor vehicles,

and paragraph (2) of regulation 48 shall apply for the purposes of sub-paragraph (f) above as it applies for the purposes of that regulation.

(7) The requirements referred to in paragraph (6)(b) are that the seat belt must be properly secured to the anchorage points provided for it and, in a case where any of those anchorage points is first fitted to the vehicle after 10th February 1997 the anchorage points to which it is secured must comply—

(a) if the vehicle is a coach, with the requirements specified in regulation 46(4)(b) or (4A)(b)(ii); or

(b) in any other case, with the requirements specified in regulation 46(4)(b).

(8) Until 10th February 1998, this regulation shall not apply to a coach first used before 1st October 1988.

(9) In this regulation—

"school" has the meaning given by section 14(5) of the Further and Higher Education Act 1992;
"forward-facing passenger seat" means a forward-facing seat which is not the driver's seat; and
"child restraint", "disabled person's belt", "forward-facing seat", and "seat", and "seat belt" have the meanings given in regulation 47.

(10) For the purpose of this regulation, a child is a person who is aged 3 years or more but is under the age of 16 years.

Rear under-run protection

4–3555 49. (1) Save as provided in paragraph (2), this regulation applies to a wheeled goods vehicle being either—

(a) a motor vehicle with a maximum gross weight which exceeds 3500 kg and which was first used on or after 1st April 1984; or

(b) a trailer manufactured on or after 1st May 1983 with an unladen weight which exceeds 1020 kg.

(2) This regulation does not apply to—

(a) a motor vehicle which has a maximum speed not exceeding 15 mph;

(b) a motor car or a heavy motor car constructed or adapted to form part of an articulated vehicle;

(c) an agricultural trailer;

(d) engineering plant;

(e) a fire engine;

(f) an agricultural motor vehicle;

(g) a vehicle fitted at the rear with apparatus specially designed for spreading material on a road;

(h) a vehicle so constructed that it can be unloaded by part of the vehicle being tipped rearwards;

(i) a vehicle owned by the Secretary of State for Defence and used for naval, military or air force purposes;

(j) a vehicle to which no bodywork has been fitted and which is being driven or towed—

(i) for the purpose of a quality or safety check by its manufacture or a dealer in, or distributor of, such vehicles; or

(ii) to a place where, by previous arrangement, bodywork is to be fitted or work preparatory to the fitting of bodywork is to be carried out; or

(iii) by previous arrangement to premises of a dealer in, or distributor of, such vehicles;

(k) a vehicle which is being driven or towed to a place where by previous arrangement a device is to be fitted so that it complies with this regulation;

(l) a vehicle specially designed and constructed, and not merely adapted, to carry other vehicles loaded onto it from the rear;

(m) a trailer specially designed and constructed, and not merely adapted, to carry round timber, beams or girders, being items of exceptional length;

(n) a vehicle fitted with a tail lift so constructed that the lift platform forms part of the floor of the vehicle and this part has a length of at least 1 m measured parallel to the longitudinal axis of the vehicle;

(o) a trailer having a base or centre in a country outside Great Britain from which it normally starts its journeys, provided that a period of not more than 12 months has elapsed since the vehicle was last brought into Great Britain;

(*p*) a vehicle specially designed, and not merely adapted, for the carriage and mixing of liquid concrete;

(*q*) a vehicle designed and used solely for the delivery of coal by means of a special conveyor which is carried on the vehicle and when in use is fitted to the rear of the vehicle so as to render its being equipped with a rear under-run protective device impracticable; or

(*r*) an agricultural trailed appliance.

(3) Subject to the provisions of paragraphs (4), (5) and (6), every vehicle to which this regulation applies shall be equipped with a rear under-run protective device.

(4) A vehicle to which this regulation applies and which is fitted with a tail lift, bodywork or other part which renders its being equipped with a rear under-run protective device impracticable shall instead be equipped with one or more devices which do not protrude beyond the overall width of the vehicle (excluding any part of the device or the devices) and which comply with the following requirements—

(*a*) where more than one device is fitted, not more than 50 cm shall lie between one device and the device next to it;

(*b*) not more than 30 cm shall lie between the outermost end of a device nearest to the outermost part of the vehicle to which it is fitted and a longitudinal plane passing through the outer end of the rear axle of the vehicle on the same side of the vehicle or, in a case where the vehicle is fitted with more than one rear axle, through the outer end of the widest rear axle on the same side of the vehicle, and paragraph II.5.4.2 in the Annex to Community Directive 79/490 shall not have effect in a case where this requirement is met; and

(*c*) the device or, where more than one device is fitted, all the devices together, shall have the characteristics specified in paragraphs II.5.4.1 to II.5.4.5.5.2 in the Annex to the said Directive save—

(i) as provided in sub-paragraphs (*a*) and (*b*) above;

(ii) that for the reference in paragraph II.5.4.5.1 in that Annex to 30 cm there is substituted a reference to 35 cm; and

(iii) that the distance of 40 cm specified in paragraph II.5.4.5 in that Annex may be measured exclusive of the said tail-lift, bodywork or other part.

(5) The provisions of paragraph (3) shall have effect so that in the case of—

(*a*) a vehicle which is fitted with a demountable body, the characteristics specified in paragraph II.5.4.2 in the Annex to the said Directive have effect as if the reference to 10 cm were a reference to 30 cm and as if in paragraph II.5.4.5.1 the reference to 30 cm were a reference to 35 cm; and

(*b*) a trailer with a single axle or two close-coupled axles, the height of 55 cm referred to in paragraph II.5.4.5.1 in that Annex is measured when the coupling of the trailer to the vehicle by which it is drawn is at the height recommended by the manufacturer of the trailer.

(6) Instead of complying with paragraphs (3) to (5) a vehicle may comply with Community Directive 97/19.

(7) In this regulation—

"rear under-run protective device" means a device within the description given in paragraph II.5.4 in the Annex to Community Directive 79/490.

Maintenance of rear under-run protective device

4–3556 **50.** Every device fitted to a vehicle in compliance with the requirements of regulation 49 shall at all times when the vehicle is on a road be maintained free from any obvious defect which would be likely to affect adversely the performance of the device in the function of giving resistance in the event of an impact from the rear.

Sideguards

4–3557 **51.** (1) Save as provided in paragraph (2), this regulation applies to a wheeled goods vehicle being—

(*a*) a motor vehicle first used on or after 1st April 1984 with a maximum gross weight which exceeds 3500 kg; or

(*b*) a trailer manufactured on or after 1st May 1983 with an unladen weight which exceeds 1020 kg; or

(*c*) a semi-trailer manufactured before 1st May 1983 which has a relevant plate showing a gross weight exceeding 26,000 kg and which forms part of an articulated vehicle with a relevant train weight exceeding 32,520 kg.

(2) This regulation does not apply to—

(*a*) a motor vehicle which has a maximum speed not exceeding 15 mph;

(*b*) an agricultural trailer;

(*c*) engineering plant;

(*d*) a fire engine;

(*e*) an agricultural motor vehicle;

(*f*) a vehicle so constructed that it can be unloaded by part of the vehicle being tipped sideways or rearwards;

(g) a vehicle owned by the Secretary of State for Defence and used for naval, military or air force purposes;

(h) a vehicle to which no bodywork has been fitted and which is being driven or towed—

   (i) for the purpose of a quality or safety check by its manufacturer or a dealer in, or distributor of, such vehicles;

   (ii) to a place where, by previous arrangement, bodywork is to be fitted or work preparatory to the fitting of bodywork is to be carried out; or

   (iii) by previous arrangement to premises of a dealer in, or distributor of, such vehicles;

(i) a vehicle which is being driven or towed to a place where by previous arrangement a sideguard is to be fitted so that it complies with this regulation;

(j) a refuse vehicle;

(k) a trailer specially designed and constructed, and not merely adapted, to carry round timber, beams or girders, being items of exceptional length;

(l) a motor car or a heavy motor car constructed or adapted to form part of an articulated vehicle;

(m) a vehicle specially designed and constructed, and not merely adapted, to carry other vehicles loaded onto it from the front or the rear;

(n) a trailer with a load platform—

   (i) no part of any edge of which is more than 60 mm inboard from the tangential plane; and

   (ii) the upper surface of which is not more than 750 mm from the ground throughout that part of its length under which a sideguard would have to be fitted in accordance with paragraph (5)(d) to (g) if this exemption did not apply to it;

(o) a trailer having a base or centre in a country outside Great Britain from which it normally starts its journeys, provided that a period of not more than 12 months has elapsed since the vehicle was last brought into Great Britain; or

(p) an agricultural trailed appliance.

(2A) This regulation also applies to a wheeled goods vehicle, whether of a description falling within paragraph (2) or not, which is a semi-trailer some or all of the wheels of which are driven by the drawing vehicle.

(3) Every vehicle to which this regulation applies shall be securely fitted with a sideguard to give protection on any side of the vehicle where—

(a) if it is a semi-trailer, the distance between the transverse planes passing through the centre of its foremost axle and through the centre of its king pin or, in the case of a vehicle having more than one king pin, the rearmost one, exceeds 4·5 m; or

(b) if it is any other vehicle, the distance between the centres of any two consecutive axles exceeds 3 m[1].

(4) Save as provided in paragraphs (6) and (7), a sideguard with which a vehicle is by this regulation required to be fitted shall comply with all the specifications listed in paragraph (5).

(5) Those specifications are—

(a) the outermost surface of every sideguard shall be smooth, essentially rigid and either flat or horizontally corrugated, save that—

   (i) any part of the surface may overlap another provided that the overlapping edges face rearwards or downwards;

   (ii) a gap not exceeding 25 mm measured longitudinally may exist between any two adjacent parts of the surface provided that the foremost edge of the rearward part does not protrude outboard of the rearmost edge of the forward part; and

   (iii) domed heads of bolts or rivets may protrude beyond the surface to a distance not exceeding 10 mm;

(b) no part of the lowest edge of a sideguard shall be more than 550 mm above the ground when the vehicle to which it is fitted is on level ground and, in the case of a semi-trailer, when its load platform is horizontal;

(c) in a case specified in an item in column 2 of the Table the highest edge of a sideguard shall be as specified in that item in column 3;

(d) the distance between the rearmost edge of a sideguard and the transverse plane passing through the foremost part of the tyre fitted to the wheel of the vehicle nearest to it shall not exceed 300 mm;

(e) the distance between the foremost edge of a sideguard fitted to a semi-trailer and a transverse plane passing through the centre of the vehicle's king pin or, if the vehicle has more than one king pin, the rearmost one, shall not exceed 3 m;

(f) the foremost edge of a sideguard fitted to a semi-trailer with landing legs shall, as well as complying with sub-paragraph (e), not be more than 250 mm to the rear of a transverse plane passing through the centre of the leg nearest to that edge;

(g) the distance between the foremost edge of a sideguard fitted to a vehicle other than a semi-trailer and a tranverse plane passing through the rearmost part of the tyre fitted to the wheel of the vehicle nearest to it shall not exceed 300 mm if the vehicle is a motor vehicle and 500 mm if the vehicle is a trailer;

(h) the external edges of a sideguard shall be rounded at a radius of at least 2.5 mm;

(i) no sideguard shall be more than 30 mm inboard from the tangential plane;

(j) no sideguard shall project beyond the longitudinal plane from which, in the absence of a sideguard, the vehicle's overall width would fall to be measured;

(k) every sideguard shall cover an area extending to at least 100 mm upwards from its lowest edge 100 mm downwards from its highest edge, and 100 mm rearwards and inwards from its foremost edge, and no sideguard shall have a vertical gap measuring more than 300 mm nor any vertical surface measuring less than 100 mm; and

(l) except in the case of a vehicle described in paragraph (1)(c) every sideguard shall be capable of withstanding a force of 2 kilonewtons applied perpendicularly to any part of its surface by the centre of a ram face of which is circular and not more than 220 mm in diameter, and during such application—

(i) no part of the sideguard shall be deflected by more than 150 mm, and

(ii) no part of the sideguard which is less than 250 mm from its rearmost part shall be deflected by more than 30 mm.

TABLE

(regulation 51(5))

1	2	3
Item	Case	Requirement about highest edge of sideguard
1	Where the floor of the vehicle to which the sideguard is fitted— (i) extends laterally outside the tangential plane; (ii) is not more than 1.85 m from the ground; (iii) extends laterally over the whole of the length of the sideguard with which the vehicle is required by this regulation to be fitted; and (iv) is wholly covered at its edge by a side-rave the lower edge of which is not more than 150 mm below the underside of the floor.	Not more than 350 mm below the lower edge of the side-rave.
2	Where the floor of the vehicle to which the sideguard is fitted— (i) extends laterally outside the tangential plane; and (ii) does not comply with all of the provisions specified in sub-paragraphs (ii), (iii) and (iv) in item 1 above, and any part of the structure of the vehicle is cut within 1.85 m of the ground by the tangential plane.	Not more than 350 mm below the structure of the vehicle where it is cut by the tangential plane.
3	Where— (i) no part of the structure of the vehicle is cut within 1.85 m the ground by the tangential plane; and (ii) the upper surface of the load carrying structure of the vehicle is less than 1.5 m from the ground.	Not less than the height of the upper surface of the load carrying structure of the vehicle.
4	A vehicle specially designed, and not merely adapted, for the carriage and mixing of liquid concrete.	Not less than 1 m from the ground.
5	Any other case.	Not less than 1.5 m from the ground.

(6) The provisions of paragraph (4) apply—

(a) in the case of an extendible trailer when it is, by virtue of the extending mechanism, extended to a length greater than its minimum, so as not to require, in respect of any additional distance solely attributable to the extension, compliance with the specifications mentioned in paragraph (5)(d) to (g);

(b) in the case of a vehicle designed and constructed, and not merely adapted, to be fitted with a demountable body or to carry a container, when it is not fitted with a demountable body or carrying such a container as if it were fitted with such a body or carrying such a container, and

(c) only so far as it is practicable in the case of —

(i) a vehicle designed solely for the carriage of a fluid substance in a closed tank which is permanently fitted to the vehicle and provided with valves and hose or pipe connections for loading or unloading; and

(ii) a vehicle which requires additional stability during loading or unloading or while being used for operations for which it is designed or adapted and is fitted on one or both sides with an extendible device to provide such stability.

(7) In the case of a motor vehicle to which this regulation applies and which is of a type which was required to be approved by the Type Approval for Goods Vehicles Regulations before 1st October 1983—

(a) if the bodywork of the vehicle covers the whole of the area specified as regards a sideguard in paragraph (5)(b), (c), (d) and (g) above the other provisions of that paragraph do not apply to that vehicle; and

(b) if the bodywork of the vehicle covers only part of that area the part of that area which is not so covered shall be fitted with a sideguard which complies with the provisions of paragraph (5) above save that there shall not be a gap between—

(i)　the rearmost edge of the sideguard or the rearmost part of the bodywork (whichever is furthest to the rear) and the transverse plane mentioned in paragraph (5)(*d*) of more than 300 mm;

(ii)　the foremost edge of the sideguard or the foremost part of the bodywork (whichever is furthest to the front) and the transverse plane mentioned in paragraph (5)(*g*) of more than 300 mm; or

(iii)　any vertical or sloping edge of any part of the bodywork in question and the edge of the sideguard immediately forwards or rearwards thereof of more than 25 mm measured horizontally.

(8)　In this regulation—

"relevant plate" means a Ministry plate, where fitted, and in other cases a plate fitted in accordance with regulation 66;

"relevant train weight" means the train weight shown in column 2 of the Ministry plate, where fitted, and in other cases the maximum train weight shown at item 8 of the plate fitted in accordance with regulation 66; and

"tangential plane", in relation to a sideguard, means the vertical plane tangential to the external face of the outermost part of the tyre (excluding any distortion caused by the weight of the vehicle) fitted to the outermost wheel at the rear and on the same side of the vehicle.

(9)　Instead of complying with the foregoing provisions of this regulation a vehicle may comply with Community Directive 89/297.

---

1. In this regulation the distance between any two axles shall be obtained by measuring the shortest distance between the lines joining the centre of the area of contact with the road surface of the wheels on each of the two axles; reg 3(10).

Maintenance of sideguards

4–3558　**52.**　Every sideguard fitted to a vehicle in compliance with the requirements of regulation 51 shall at all times when the vehicle is on a road be maintained free from any obvious defect which would be likely to affect adversely its effectiveness.

Mascots

4–3559　**53.**　(1)　Subject to paragraph (2), no mascot, emblem or other ornamental object shall be carried by a motor vehicle first used on or after 1st October 1937 in any position where it is likely to strike any person with whom the vehicle may collide unless the mascot is not liable to cause injury to such person by reason of any projection thereon.

(2)　Instead of complying with the requirements of paragraph (1) a vehicle may comply with Community Directive 74/483 or 79/488 or ECE Regulation 26.01.

Alternative means of compliance

4–3559A　**53C.**　A coach which is required by either regulation 53A or 53B, as the case may be, to meet the requirements specified in that particular provision, need not meet them if it meets the requirements of such of the Annexes to Directive 2001/85/EC of the European Parliament and of the Council of 20 November 2001, relating to special provisions for vehicles used for the carriage of passengers comprising more than eight seats in addition to the driver's seat, and amending Directives 70/156/EEC and 97/27/EC, as apply to that coach.

Strength of superstructure

4–3560　**53A.**　(1)　This regulation applies to every coach which is—

(*a*)　a single decked vehicle;

(*b*)　equipped with a compartment below the deck for the luggage of passengers; and

(*c*)　first used on or after 1st April 1993.

(2)　Every vehicle to which this regulation applies shall comply with the requirements of ECE Regulation 66.

Additional exits from double-decked coaches

4–3561　**53B.**　(1)　This regulation applies to every coach which is—

(*a*)　a double-decked vehicle; and

(*b*)　first used on or after 1st April 1990.

(2)　Subject to the following provisions of this regulation, every vehicle to which this regulation applies shall be equipped with two staircases, one of which shall be located in one half of the vehicle and the other in the other half of the vehicle.

(3)　Instead of being equipped with two staircases in accordance with paragraph (2), a vehicle to which this regulation applies may be equipped in accordance with the following provisions of this regulation with a hammer or other similar device with which in case of emergency any side window of the vehicle may be broken.

(4)　Where a vehicle is equipped with—

(*a*)　a staircase located in one half of the vehicle; and

(*b*) an emergency exit complying with regulation 21(8) of the Public Service Vehicles (Conditions of Fitness, Equipment, Use and Certification) Regulations 1981 located in the same half of the upper deck of the vehicle;

the hammer or the similar device shall be located in the other half of that deck.

(5) Any hammer or other similar device with which a vehicle is equipped pursuant to this regulation shall be located in a conspicuous and readily accessible position in the upper deck of the vehicle.

(6) There shall be displayed, in a conspicuous position in close proximity to the hammer or other similar device, a notice which shall contain in clear and indelible lettering—

(*a*) in letters not less than 25 mm high, the heading "IN EMERGENCY"; and
(*b*) in letters not less than 10 mm high, instructions that in case of emergency the hammer or device is to be used first to break any side window by striking the glass near the edge of the window and then to clear any remaining glass from the window aperture.

(7) For the purposes of this regulation a staircase, emergency exit, hammer or other similar device (as the case may be) shall be considered to be located in the other half of the vehicle if the shortest distance between any part of that staircase, exit, hammer or device (as the case may be) and any part of any other staircase, emergency exit, hammer or device is not less than one half of the overall length of the vehicle.

Alternative means of compliance

4–3561A   53C. A coach which is required by either regulation 53A or 53B, as the case may be, to meet the requirements specified in that particular provision, need not meet them if it meets the requirements of such of the Annexes to Directive 2001/85/EC of the European Parliament and of the Council of 20 November 2001, relating to special provisions for vehicles used for the carriage of passengers comprising more than eight seats in addition to the driver's seat, and amending Directives 70/156/EEC and 97/27/EC, as apply to that coach.

K—CONTROL OF EMISSIONS

Silencers–general

4–3562   54. (1) Every vehicle propelled by an internal combustion engine shall be fitted with an exhaust system including a silencer and the exhaust gases from the engine shall not escape into the atmosphere without first passing through the silencer.

(2) Every exhaust system and silencer shall be maintained in good and efficient working order and shall not after the date of manufacture be altered so as to increase the noise made by the escape of exhaust gases.

(3) Instead of complying with paragraph (1) a vehicle may comply with Community Directive 77/212, 81/334, 84/372, 84/424 or 92/97 or ECE Regulation 51.02 or, in the case of a motor cycle other than a moped, 78/1015, 87/56 or 89/235.

(4) In this regulation "moped" has the meaning given to it in paragraph (5) of Schedule 9.

Noise limits—certain vehicles with three or more wheels—general

4–3563   55. (1) Save as provided in paragraphs (1A) and (2) and regulation 59, this regulation applies to every wheeled motor vehicle having at least three wheels and first used on or after 1st October 1983 which is—

(*a*) a vehicle, not falling within sub-paragraph (*b*) or (*c*), with or without bodywork;
(*b*) a vehicle not falling within sub-paragraph (*c*) which is—

   (i) engineering plant;
   (ii) a locomotive other than an agricultural motor vehicle;
   (iii) a motor tractor other than an industrial tractor or an agricultural motor vehicle;
   (iv) a public works vehicle;
   (v) a works truck; or
   (vi) a refuse vehicle; or

(*c*) a vehicle which—

   (i) has a compression ignition engine;
   (ii) is so constructed or adapted that the driving power of the engine is, or by appropriate use of the controls can be, transmitted to all wheels of the vehicle; and
   (iii) falls within category I.1.1., I.1.2, or I.1.3 specified in Article 1 of Community Directive 77/212.

(1A) This regulation does not apply to a vehicle to which an item in the Table in regulation 55A applies.

(2) This regulation does not apply to—

(*a*) a motorcycle with a sidecar attached;
(*b*) an agricultural motor vehicle which is first used before 1st June 1986 or which is not driven at more than 20 mph;
(*c*) an industrial tractor;
(*d*) a road roller;
(*e*) a vehicle specially constructed, and not merely adapted, for the purposes of fighting fires or salvage from fires at or in the vicinity of airports, and having an engine power exceeding 220 kW;

  (f)   a vehicle which runs on rails; or

  (g)   a vehicle manufactured by Leyland Vehicles Ltd and known as the Atlantean Bus, if first used before 1st October 1984.

(3) Save as provided in paragraphs (4) and (5), every vehicle to which this regulation applies shall be so constructed that it complies with the requirements set out in item 1, 2, 3 or 4 of the Table; a vehicle complies with those requirements if—

  (a)   its sound level does not exceed the relevant limit specified in column 2(a), (b) or (c), as the case may be, in the relevant item when measured under the conditions specified in column 3 in that item and by the method specified in column 4 in that item using the apparatus prescribed in paragraph (6); and

  (b)   in the case of a vehicle referred to in paragraph 1(a) (other than one having less than four wheels or a maximum speed not exceeding 25 km/h) or 1(c), the device designed to reduce the exhaust noise meets the requirements specified in column 5 in that item.

(4) Save as provided in paragraph (5), paragraph (3) applies to every vehicle to which this regulation applies and which is first used on or after 1st April 1990, unless it is equipped with 5 or more forward gears and has a maximum power to maximum gross weight ratio not less than 75 kW per 1000 kg, and is of a type in respect of which a type approval certificate has been issued under the Type Approval (Great Britain) Regulations as if, for the reference to items 1, 2, 3 or 4 of the Table there were substituted a reference to item 4 of the Table.

(5) Paragraph (4) does not apply to a vehicle in category 5.2.2.1.3 as defined in Annex I to Directive 84/424 and equipped with a compression ignition engine, a vehicle in category 5.2.2.1.4 as defined in that Annex, or a vehicle referred to in paragraph 1(b) unless it is first used on or after 1st April 1991.

(6) The apparatus prescribed for the purposes of paragraph 3(a) and regulation 56(2)(a) and Schedule 7A is a sound level meter of the type described in Publication No 179 of the International Electrotechnical Commission, in either its first or second edition, a sound level meter complying with the specification for Type 0 or Type 1 in Publication No 651 (1979) "Sound Level Meters" of the International Electrotechnical Commission, or a sound level meter complying with the specifications of the British Standard Number BS 6969:1981 which came into effect on 29th May 1981.

(6A) A vehicle shall be deemed to satisfy the requirements of this regulation if it is so constructed that it complies with the requirements specified in column 4 of item 2 in the Table in regulation 55A as they apply to a vehicle first used on or after the date specified in column 3 of that item.

(7) Instead of complying with the preceding provisions of this regulation a vehicle may comply at the time of its first use with Community Directive 77/212, 81/334, 84/372, 84/424, 92/97 or 96/20 or ECE Regulation 51.02.

(regulation 55(3))

TABLE

1	2			3	4	5
	Limits of sound level					
Item	(a) Vehicle referred to in paragraph (1)(a)	(b) Vehicle referred to in paragraph (1)(b)	(c) Vehicle referred to in paragraph (1)(c)	Conditions of measurement	Method of measurement	Requirements for exhaust device
1	Limits specified in paragraph I.1 of the Annex to Community Directive 77/212.	89dB(A)	82dB(A)	Conditions specified in paragraph 1.3 of the Annex to Community Directive 77/212	Method specified in paragraph I.4.1 of the Annex to Community Directive 77/212	Requirements specified in heading II of the Annex to Community Directive 77/212 (except paragraphs II.2 and II.5).
2	Limits specified in paragraph 5.2.2.1 of Annex I to Community Directive 81/334.	89dB(A)	82dB(A)	Conditions specified in paragraph 5.2.2.3 of Annex I to Community Directive 81/334.	Method specified in paragraph 5.2.2.4 of Annex I to Community Directive 81/334. Interpretation of results as specified in paragraph 5.2.2.5 of that Annex.	Requirements specified in section 3 and paragraphs 5.1 and 5.3.1 of Annex I to Community Directive 81/334.
3	Limits specified in paragraph 5.2.2.1 of Annex I to Community Directive 84/372	89dB(A)	82dB(A)	Conditions specified in paragraph 5.2.2.3 of Annex I to Community Directive 84/372	Method specified in paragraph 5.2.2.4 of Annex I to Community Directive 84/372, except that vehicles with 5 or more forward gears and a maximum power to maximum gross weight ratio not less than 75 kW per 1000 kg may be tested in 3rd gear only. Interpretation of results as specified in paragraph 5.2.2.5 of that Annex.	Requirements specified in section 3 and paragraphs 5.1 and 5.3.1 of Annex I to Community Directive 84/372.
4	Limits specified in paragraph 5.2.2.1 of the Annex I to Community Directive 84/424.	Vehicles with engine power— less than 75kW —84dB(A) —not less than 75kW —86dB(A)	Limits specified in paragraph 5.2.2.1 of Annex I to Community Directive 84/424.	Conditions specified in paragraph 5.2.2.3 of Annex I to Community Directive 84/424.	Method specified in paragraph 5.2.2.4 of Annex I to Community Directive 84/424, except that vehicles with 5 or more forward gears and a maximum power to maximum gross weight ratio not less than 75 kW per 1000 kg may be tested in 3rd gear only. Interpretation of results as specified in paragraph 5.2.2.5 of that Annex	Requirements specified in section 3 and paragraphs 5.1 and 5.3.1 of Annex I to Community Directive 84/424.

Noise limits—certain vehicles first used on or after 1st October 1996—general

4–3563A   55A. (1) A motor vehicle to which an item in the Table below applies shall be so constructed that it meets the requirements specified in column 4 of that item; and an item in that Table applies to a vehicle if it is of the description specified in column 2 of that item.
   This paragraph has effect subject to the following provisions of this regulation, regulation 59 and Schedule 7XA.

TABLE

(1) Item	(2) Vehicles to which the item applies	(3) Earliest date of first use (see column 2)	(4) The requirements	(5) Modification of Community Directives in relation to special vehicles (See paragraph (4)(c))
1	1 All motor vehicles with less than 4 wheels and first used on or after the date specified in column 3 of this item. 2 All special vehicles first used on or after the date specified in column 3 of this item. 3 All motor vehicles first used on or after the date specified in column 3 of this item with a maximum speed not exceeding 25 km/h.	1st October 1996	The requirements of— (a) regulation 55 as they would apply to the vehicle but for paragraph (1A) of that regulation; or (b) paragraphs 3 and 5.2 of Annex I to Community Directive 92/97 or 96/20.	For paragraph 5.2.2.1 of Annex I, substitute— "The sound level measured in accordance with 5.2.2.2 to 5.2.2.5 of this Annex shall not exceed— (a) in the case of vehicles with engine power of less than 75 kW, 84 dB(A) (b) in the case of vehicles with engine power not less than 75 kW, 86 dB(A)."
2	All motor vehicles first used on or after the date specified in column 3 of this item, not being a vehicle to which item 1 applies.	1st October 1996	The requirements of paragraphs 3 and 5 of Annex I to Community Directive 92/97 or 96/20.	

(2) Paragraph (1) does not apply to—

  (a) a vehicle with fewer than 3 wheels; or
  (b) a vehicle of a description mentioned in regulation 55(2).

(3) In this regulation, "special vehicle" means a vehicle which is—

  (a) engineering plant;
  (b) a locomotive other than an agricultural motor vehicle;
  (c) a motor tractor other than an industrial tractor or an agricultural motor vehicle;
  (d) a public works vehicle; or
  (e) a works truck.

(4) For the purposes of this regulation—

  (a) subject to paragraphs (b), (c), (d) and (e), the Community Directives referred to in this regulation shall have effect in relation to a vehicle that is not a "vehicle" within the meaning of the Framework Directive but is of a class of a description specified in column 2 of an item in the Table in regulation 15 (whether or not regulation 15 applies to the vehicle) as it has effect in relation to a vehicle of the category specified in column 3 of that item;
  (b) subject to paragraphs (c), (d) and (e), a vehicle that does not fall within sub-paragraph (a) and is not a "vehicle" within the meaning of the Framework Directive shall be regarded as meeting the requirements of paragraph 5 of a Community Directive mentioned in the Table if it meets—

    (i) the requirements of that paragraph as it applies to a vehicle in category M_1 or N_1 within the meaning of the Community Directive, or
    (ii) the requirements of that paragraph as it applies to a vehicle that is not in either of those categories;

  (c) subject to sub-paragraphs (d) and (e), in relation to a special vehicle the Community Directives mentioned in column 4 of an item in the Table shall have effect with the modifications (if any) specified in column 5 of the item;
  (d) a requirement in paragraph 5.2.2.1 of Annex 1 to Community Directive 92/97 for a sound level not to exceed a specified limit in specified circumstances shall be read as a requirement for the sound level not to exceed that limit by more than the amount mentioned in paragraph 4.1 of Annex V to the Community Directive in those circumstances;

(e) a requirement in paragraph 5.2.2.1 of Annex 1 to Community Directive 96/20 for a sound level not to exceed a specified limit in specified circumstances shall be read as a requirement for the sound level not to exceed that limit by more than the amount mentioned in paragraph 4.1 of Annex III to the Directive in those circumstances.

(5) Instead of complying with paragraph (1) a vehicle may comply at the time of its first use—

   (a) in the case of a vehicle to which item 1 of the Table applies, with Community Directive 77/212, 81/334, 84/424, 92/97 or 96/20 or ECE Regulation 51.02; or

   (b) in the case of a vehicle to which item 2 of the Table applies, with Community Directive 92/97 or 96/20 or ECE Regulation 51.02.

Noise limits—agricultural motor vehicles and industrial tractors

4–3564 **56.** (1) Save as provided in regulation 59, this regulation applies to every wheeled vehicle first used on or after 1st April 1983 being an agricultural motor vehicle or an industrial tractor, other than—

   (a) an agricultural motor vehicle which is first used on or after 1st June 1986 and which is driven at more than 20 mph; or

   (b) a road roller.

(2) Every vehicle to which this regulation applies shall be so constructed—

   (a) that its sound level does not exceed—

      (i) if it is a vehicle with engine power of less than 65 kW, 89 dB(A);

      (ii) if it is a vehicle with engine power of 65 kW or more, and first used before 1st October 1991, 92 dB(A); or

      (iii) if it is a vehicle with engine power of 65 kW or more, and first used on or after 1st October 1991, 89 dB(A),

   when measured under the conditions specified in paragraph I.3 of Annex VI of Community Directive 74/151 by the method specified in paragraph I.4.1 of that Annex using the apparatus prescribed in regulation 55(6); and

   (b) that the device designed to reduce the exhaust noise meets the requirements specified in paragraph II.1 of that Annex and, if fibrous absorbent material is used, the requirements specified in paragraphs II.4.1 to II.4.3 of that Annex.

Noise limits—motor cycles
Noise limits—construction requirements relating to motor cycles

4–3565 **57.** (1) Subject to regulation 59, this regulation applies to every motor vehicle first used on or after 1st April 1983 which is—

   (a) a moped; or

   (b) a two-wheeled motor cycle, whether or not with sidecar attached, which is not a moped.

(2) A vehicle to which this regulation applies shall be so constructed that it meets,—

   (a) if it is first used before 1st April 1991, the requirements of item 1 or 2 of the Table in Part I of Schedule 7A;

   (b) if it is first used on or after that date, the requirements of item 2 of that Table.

(3) Instead of complying with paragraph (2), a vehicle first used before 1st April 1991 may comply at the time of its first use with Community Directive 78/1015, 87/56 or 89/235.

(4) Instead of complying with paragraph (2), vehicle first used on or after 1st April 1991 may comply at the time of its first use with Community Directive 87/56 or 89/235.

(5) In this regulation "moped" has the meaning given to it in paragraph 5 of Schedule 9.

Exhaust systems—motor cycles

4–3565A **57A.** (1) Any original silencer forming part of the exhaust system of a vehicle to which regulation 57 applies, being a vehicle first used before 1st February 1996, shall—

   (a) be so constructed that the vehicle meets the requirements specified in paragraph 3 (other than sub-paragraphs 3.2 and 3.3) of Annex I to Community Directive 78/1015 and be marked in accordance with sub-paragraph 3.3 of that Annex; or

   (b) be so constructed that the vehicle meets the requirements specified in paragraph 3 (other than sub-paragraphs 3.2 and 3.3) of Annex I to Community Directive 89/235 and be marked in accordance with sub-paragraph 3.3. of that Annex.

(2) Any original silencer forming part of the exhaust system of a vehicle to which regulation 57 applies, being a vehicle first used on or after 1st February 1996, shall be so constructed that the vehicle meets the requirements specified in paragraph 3 (other than sub-paragraphs 3.2 and 3.3) of Annex I to Community Directive 89/235 and be marked in accordance with sub-paragraph 3.3. of that Annex.

(3) A vehicle fitted with an original silencer may,—

   (a) if the vehicle is first used before 1st February 1996, instead of complying with paragraph (1), comply at the time of first use with Community Directive 78/1015, 87/56 or 89/235; or

(b) if the vehicle is first used on or after that date, instead of complying with paragraph (2), comply at the time of first use with Community Directive 89/235.

(4) Where any replacement silencer forms part of the exhaust system of a vehicle to which regulation 57 applies, being a vehicle first used on or after 1st January 1985, the first requirement or the second requirement as set out below must be met in respect of the silencer.

(5) In order for the first requirement to be met in respect of a silencer forming part of the exhaust system of a vehicle (in this paragraph referred to as "the vehicle in question"),—

(a) if the vehicle in question is first used before 1st April 1991, the silencer must be so constructed that, were it to be fitted to an unused vehicle of the same model as the vehicle in question, the unused vehicle would meet—

(i) the requirements of item 1 or 3 of the Table in Part I of Schedule 7A; and
(ii) the requirements specified in paragraph 3 (other than sub-paragraphs 3.2 and 3.3) of Annex I to Community Directive 78/1015 or 89/235.

and the silencer must be marked in accordance with sub-paragraph 3.3. of Annex I to Community Directive 78/1015 or 89/235;

(b) if the vehicle in question is first used on or after the 1st April 1991 but before 1st February 1996, the silencer must be so constructed that, were it to be fitted to an unused vehicle of the same model as the vehicle in question, the unused vehicle would meet—

(i) the requirements of item 3 of the Table in Part I of Schedule 7A; and
(ii) the requirements specified in paragraph 3 (other than sub-paragraphs 3.2 and 3.3) of Annex I to Community Directive 78/1015 or 89/235.

and the silencer must be marked in accordance with sub-paragraph 3.3 of Annex I to Community Directive 78/1015 or 89/235;

(c) if the vehicle in question is first used on or after 1st February 1996, the silencer must be so constructed that, were it to be fitted to an unused vehicle of the same model as the vehicle in question, the unused vehicle would meet—

(i) the requirements of item 3 of the Table in Part I of Schedule 7A; and
(ii) the requirements specified in paragraph 3 (other than sub-paragraphs 3.2 and 3.3) of Annex I to Community Directive 89/235,

and the silencer must be marked in accordance with sub-paragraph 3.3. of Annex I to that Directive.

(6) In order for the second requirement to be met in respect of a silencer forming part of the exhaust system of a vehicle (in Part II of Schedule 7A referred to as "the vehicle in question"),—

(a) If the vehicle is first used before 1st April 1991, the silencer must meet the requirements of paragraph 2, 3 or 4 of Part II of Schedule 7A; or
(b) if the vehicle is first used on or after that date, the silencer must meet the requirements of paragraph 4 of Part II of Schedule 7A.

(7) Any requirements specified in paragraph (5) or in Part II of Schedule 7A relating to the silencer were it to be fitted to an unused vehicle of the same model as the vehicle in question (as defined in that paragraph or in paragraph (6) for the purposes of that Part, as the case may be) shall be deemed to be met if they are met by the silencer as fitted to the vehicle in question at the time that it is first fitted.

(8) For the purposes of this regulation, Community Directive 89/235 shall have effect as if—

(a) in Annex I, for sub-paragraph 3.4.1, there were substituted—

"**3.4.1.** After removal of the fibrous material, the vehicle must meet the relevant requirements."; and

for sub-paragraph 3.4.3 there were substituted—

"**3.4.3.** After the exhaust system has been put into a normal state for road use by one of the following conditioning methods, the vehicle must meet the relevant requirements:";

(b) references in Annex I as so modified to a vehicle meeting the relevant requirements were,—

(i) in relation to an original silencer, references to a vehicle meeting the requirements of item 2 of the Table in Part I of Schedule 7A; and
(ii) in relation to a replacement silencer, references to vehicle meeting the requirements of item 3 of that Table;

(c) in Annex II there were omitted sub-paragraphs 3.1.2, 3.4 and 3.5 and in sub-paragraph 3.2—

(i) the words "and the name referred to in 3.1.2", and
(ii) the words after "legible".

(8A) For the purposes of paragraphs (1)(b) and (2) in their application to vehicles with a design speed not exceeding 50 km/h, Community Directive 89/235/EEC shall have effect as if it were not only modified in accordance with paragraph (8) but were further modified by the omission of—

(a) sub-paragraph 3.1.3 of Annex II; and
(b) in sub-paragraph 3.2 of that Annex, the words "and 3.1.3".

(9) In relation to a replacement silencer which is—

(a) fitted to a vehicle before 1st February 1997; and
(b) clearly and indelibly marked with the name or trade mark of the manufacturer of the silencer and with that manufacturer's part number relating to it,

paragraphs (5) and (6) of this regulation and Parts II and III of Schedule 7A shall have effect as if they contained no reference to a silencer being marked.

(10) For the purposes of this regulation, a silencer forming part of the exhaust system of a vehicle shall not be regarded as being marked in accordance with sub-paragraph 3.3. of Annex I to Community Directive 78/1015 or 89/235, paragraph (9) of this regulation or any paragraph of Part II of Schedule 7A if the marking is so obscured by any part of the vehicle that it cannot easily be read.

(11) Until 1st February 1996, for the purposes of paragraph (6), a vehicle first used on or after 1st April 1991 shall be treated as a vehicle first used before 1st April 1991.

(12) Part III of Schedule 7A shall have effect for the purpose of exempting certain silencers from the provisions of paragraph (4).

(13) No person shall use a motor cycle on a road or cause or permit such a vehicle to be so used if any part of the exhaust system has been indelibly marked by the manufacturer of that part with the words "NOT FOR ROAD USE" or words to that effect.

(14) In this regulation—

"original silencer", in relation to a vehicle, means a silencer which was fitted to the vehicle when it was manufactured;

"replacement silencer", in relation to a vehicle, means a silencer fitted to the vehicle, not being an original silencer; and

"trade mark" has the same meaning as in the Trade Marks Act 1938.

Noise limits—maintenance requirements relating to motor cycles

4–3565B   **57B.** (1) No person shall use or cause or permit to be used on a road a motor cycle to which regulation 57 applies if the three conditions specified below are all fulfilled.

(2) The first condition is fulfilled if the vehicle does not meet the noise limit requirements.

(3) The second condition is fulfilled if—

(a) any part of the vehicle is not in good and efficient working order, or
(b) the vehicle has been altered.

(4) The third condition is fulfilled if the noise made by the vehicle would have been materially less (so far as applicable)—

(a) were all parts of the vehicle in good and efficient working order, or
(b) had the vehicle not been altered.

(5) For the purposes of this regulation, a vehicle meets the noise limit requirements if—

(a) in the case of a vehicle first used before 1st April 1991 and not fitted with a replacement silencer, it meets the requirements of item 1 or 2 of the Table in Part I of Schedule 7A;
(b) in the case of a vehicle first used before 1st April 1991 and fitted with a replacement silencer, it meets the requirements of item 1 or 3 of that Table;
(c) in the case of a vehicle first used on or after 1st April 1991 and not fitted with a replacement silencer, it meets the requirements of item 2 of that Table;
(d) in the case of a vehicle first used on or after 1st April 1991 and fitted with a replacement silencer, it meets the requirements of item 3 of that Table.

(6) In this regulation, "replacement silencer" has the same meaning as in regulation 57A.

Exceptions to regulations 55 to 57B

4–3567   **59.** Regulations 55, 55A, 56, 57, 57A and 57B do not apply to a motor vehicle which is—

(a) proceeding to a place where, by previous arrangement—

    (i) noise emitted by it is about to be measured for the purpose of ascertaining whether or not the vehicle complies with such of those provisions as apply to it; or
    (ii) the vehicle is about to be mechanically adjusted, modified or equipped for the purpose of securing that it so complies; or

(b) returning from such a place immediately after the noise has been so measured.

Radio interference suppression

4–3568   **60.** (1) Subject to paragraphs (1B), (1D), (1E) and (2)—

(a) every vehicle to which this sub-paragraph applies shall be so constructed that it complies with the requirements of paragraph 6 of Annex 1 to Community Directive 72/245 or paragraph 6 (as read with paragraph 8) of Annex 1 to Community Directive 95/54 (whether or not those Community Directives apply to the vehicle); and
(b) every agricultural and forestry tractor which is propelled by a spark ignition engine and is first used on or after 1st April 1974 shall be so constructed that it meets the requirements of paragraph 6 of Community Directive 72/245, 75/322 or 95/54.

(1A) Paragraph (1)(a) applies to every wheeled vehicle which is propelled by a spark ignition engine and—

(a) is first used on or after 1st April 1974 and before 1st January 1996; or
(b) is first used on or after 1st January 1996 and is a "vehicle" within the meaning of the Framework Directive.

(1B) For the purposes of paragraph (1)—

(*a*) a requirement in paragraph 6.2.2 of Community Directive 72/245 or 75/322 for any description of radiation level not to exceed a specified limit when measured in specified circumstances shall be read as a requirement for that description of radiation level not to exceed that limit by more than the amount mentioned in paragraph 9.2 of those Community Directives when measured in those circumstances; and

(*b*) a requirement in paragraph 6.2.2 or 6.3.2 of Community Directive 95/54 for any description of radiation level not to exceed a specified limit when measured in specified circumstances shall be read as a requirement for that description of radiation level not to exceed that limit by more than the amount mentioned in paragraph 7.3.1 of the Community Directive when measured in those circumstances.

(1C) Subject to paragraph (1F), the requirements of Community Directive 72/245/EC as amended by Community Directive 95/54/EC shall be met by electrical/electronic sub-assemblies as components or separate technical units first used on or after 1 October 2002.

(1D) Instead of complying with paragraph 1(*a*) a vehicle may comply at the time of first use with Community Directive 72/245 or 95/54 or ECE Regulations 10, 10.01 or 10.02.

(1E) Instead of complying with paragraph (1)(*b*) a vehicle may comply at the time of first use with Community Directive 75/322.

(1F) The requirements of paragraph (1C) shall not apply to electrical/electronic sub-assemblies of the following descriptions—

(*a*) replacement parts intended for use on vehicles manufactured in accordance with type approvals granted before 1 January 1996 in compliance with Community Directive 72/245/ EEC or Community Directive 72/306/EEC including any subsequent extension that may have been granted to such type approvals;

(*b*) electrical/electronic sub-assemblies fitted to any vehicle under an authorisation having effect under Part III of the Police Act 1997 or Part II of the Regulation of Investigatory Powers Act 2000.

(2) This regulation does not apply to a vehicle constructed or assembled by a person not ordinarily engaged in the trade or business of manufacturing vehicles of that description, but nothing in this paragraph affects the application to such vehicles of the Wireless Telegraphy (Control of Interference from Ignition Apparatus) Regulations 1973.

(3) In this regulation "electrical/electronic sub-assembly" has the same meaning as in Community Directive 95/54.

Emission of smoke, vapour, gases, oily substances etc

4–3569 61. (1) Subject to paragraph (3B), every vehicle shall be constructed and maintained so as not to emit any avoidable smoke or avoidable visible vapour.

(2) Every motor vehicle using solid fuel shall be fitted with—

(*a*) a tray or shield to prevent ashes and cinders from falling onto the road; and

(*b*) an efficient appliance to prevent any emission of sparks or grit.

(2A) Paragraphs (3), (3A), (3C), (4A), (5)(b), (5)(c), (6), (7), (8), (9), (10) and (11) shall not apply to motor vehicles first used on or after 1st January 2001.

(3) Subject to paragraph (4) and to the exemptions specified in an item in column 4 of Table I, every wheeled vehicle of a class specified in that item in column 2 shall be constructed so as to comply with the requirements specified in that item in column 3.

(3A) A motor vehicle to which an item in Table II applies shall be so constructed as to comply with the requirements relating to conformity of production models set out in the provisions specified in that item in column (4) of that Table.

(3B) Instead of complying with paragraph (1) a vehicle may comply with a relevant instrument.

(3C) Instead of complying with such provisions of items 1, 2 and 3 in Table I as apply to it, a vehicle may at the time of its first use comply with a relevant instrument.

(4) For the purposes of paragraphs (3B) and (3C), a reference to a vehicle complying with a relevant instrument is a reference to a vehicle complying—

(*a*) if it is propelled by a compression ignition engine, with Community Directive 72/306 (or, in the case of an agricultural vehicle first used before 1st January 2001, 77/537) or ECE Regulation 24.01, 24.02 or 24.03; or

(*b*) if it is propelled by a spark ignition engine, with any instrument mentioned in column (4)(*a*) of Table II.

(4A) In relation to a vehicle which—

(*a*) has an engine the cylinder capacity of which is less than 700 cc and has a rated power speed of more than 3,000 revolutions per minute;

(*b*) is first used before 1st October 1998,

Community Directive 91/542 shall have effect for the purposes of this regulation as if for the figure "0.15" in the Table in paragraph 6.2.1 and 8.3.1.1 there were substituted "0.25".

For the purposes of this paragraph, "rated power speed" has the same meaning as in Community Directive 96/1.

(5) No person shall use, or cause or permit to be used, on a road any motor vehicle—

(*a*) from which any smoke, visible vapour, grit, sparks, ashes, cinders or oily substance is emitted if that emission causes, or is likely to cause, damage to any property or injury or danger to any person who is, or who may reasonably be expected to be, on the road;

(*b*)   which is subject to the requirement in item 2 of Table I (whether or not it is deemed to comply with that requirement by virtue of paragraph (4)), if the fuel injection equipment, the engine speed governor or any other parts of the engine by which it is propelled have been altered or adjusted so as to increase the emission of smoke; or

(*c*)   which is subject to the requirement in item 1 of Table I if the device mentioned in column 2 in that item is used while the vehicle is in motion.

(6) No person shall use, or cause or permit to be used, on a road a motor vehicle to which item 3 of Table I applies unless it is so maintained that the means specified in column 3 of that item are in good working order.

(7) Subject to paragraphs (8), (9) and (10), no person shall use, or cause or permit to be used, on a road a motor vehicle to which an item in Table II applies if, in relation to the emission of the substances specified in column (6) of the item, the vehicle does not comply with the requirements relating to conformity of production models specified in column (4) unless the following conditions are satisfied in respect of it—

(*a*)   the failure to meet those requirements in relation to the emission of those substances does not result from an alteration to the propulsion unit or exhaust system of the vehicle,

(*b*)   neither would those requirements be met in relation to the emission of those substances nor would such emissions be materially reduced if maintenance work of a kind which would fall within the scope of a normal periodic service of the vehicle were to be carried out on the vehicle, and

(*c*)   the failure to meet those requirements in relation to such emissions does not result from any device designed to control the emission of carbon monoxide, hydrocarbons, oxides of nitrogen or particulates fitted to the vehicle being other than in good and efficient working order.

(8) Paragraph (7) shall not apply to a vehicle first used before 26th June 1990.

(9) Where—

(*a*)   a vehicle is fitted with a device of the kind referred to in sub-paragraph (*c*) of paragraph (7),

(*b*)   the vehicle does not comply with the requirements specified in that paragraph in respect to it, and

(*c*)   the conditions specified in sub-paragraphs (*a*) and (*b*) of that paragraph are satisfied in respect to the vehicle,

nothing in paragraph (7) shall prevent the vehicle being driven to a place where the device is to be repaired or replaced.

(10) Where a vehicle is constructed or assembled by a person not ordinarily engaged in the business of manufacturing motor vehicles of that description and is first used before 1st July 1998, the date on which it is first used shall, for the purposes of paragraphs (3A), (7), (8) and (9), be regarded as being the 1st January immediately preceding the date of manufacture of the engine by which it is propelled.

However, the date on which a vehicle is first used shall not, by virtue of the foregoing provisions of this paragraph, be regarded in any circumstances as being later than the date on which it would otherwise have been regarded as being first used had those provisions been omitted.

(10A) Without prejudice to paragraphs (1) and (7) and subject to the following provisions of this regulation, no person shall use, or cause or permit to be used on a road, a vehicle first used on or after 1st August 1975 and propelled by a four-stroke spark ignition engine, if the vehicle is in such a condition and running on such fuel that—

(*a*)   when the engine is idling the carbon monoxide content of the exhaust emissions from the engine exceeds—

(i)   in the case of a vehicle first used before 1st August 1986, 4.5%; or

(ii)   in the case of a vehicle first used on or after 1 August 1986, 3.5%; of the total exhaust emissions form the engine by volume; and

(*b*)   when the engine is running without load at a rotational speed of 2,000 revolutions per minute, the hydrocarbon content of those emissions exceeds 0.12% of the total exhaust emissions from the engine by volume.

(10AA) Without prejudice to paragraphs (1) and (7) and subject to the following provisions of this regulation, no person shall use, or cause or permit to be used on a road, a vehicle to which this paragraph applies and which is propelled by a spark ignition engine, if the vehicle is in such a condition and running on such fuel that Part I of Schedule 7B applies to the vehicle.

(10AB) Subject to paragraph (10B), paragraph (10AA) applies to—

(*a*)   a passenger car which—

(i)   is first used on or after 1st August 1992 and before 1st August 1995, and

(ii)   is of a description mentioned in the annex to the emissions publication;

(*b*)   a vehicle which—

(i)   is not a passenger car

(ii)   is first used on or after 1st August 1994 and

(iii)   is of a description mentioned in the Annex to the emissions publication;

(*c*)   a passenger car which is first used on or after 1st August 1995; or (*ca*) a vehicle which—

    (i)   is not a passenger car,
    (ii)   is first used on or after 1st July 2002, and
    (iii)   has a maximum gross weight not exceeding 3,500kg

and in this paragraph, "emissions publication" has the meaning given in Part I of Schedule 7B.

(10AC) *Revoked.*

(10AD) Paragraph (10A) does not apply to—

(*a*)   a vehicle to which paragraph (10AA) applies; or
(*b*)   a vehicle if, at the date that the engine was manufactured, that engine was incapable of meeting the requirements specified in that paragraph.

(10AE) Paragraph (10AA) does not apply to a vehicle if, at the date that the engine was manufactured, that engine was incapable of meeting the requirements specified in that paragraph.

(10B)   Paragraphs (10A) and (10AA) do not apply to—

(*a*)   *revoked*;
(*b*)   a vehicle being driven to a place where it is to undergo repairs;
(*c*)   a vehicle which was constructed or assembled by a person not ordinarily engaged in the business of manufacturing motor vehicles of that description and is first used before 1st July 1998;
(*d*)   an exempt vehicle within the meaning given by paragraph (12)(*a*);
(*e*)   a goods vehicle with a maximum gross weight exceeding 3,500 kg;
(*f*)   engineering plant, an industrial tractor, or a works truck;
(*g*)   *revoked*; or
(*h*)   a vehicle first used before 1st August 1987 if the engine is a rotary piston engine; and for the purposes of this paragraph "the engine", in relation to a vehicle, means the engine by which it is propelled.

(10BA)   Without prejudice to paragraphs (1) and (7), no person shall use, or cause or permit to be used on a road, a vehicle propelled by a compression ignition engine, if the vehicle is in such a condition and running on such fuel that Part II of Schedule 7B applies to the vehicle.

(10BB)   Paragraph (10BA) shall not apply to—

(*a*)   a vehicle if, at the date that the engine was manufactured, that engine was incapable of meeting the requirements specified in that paragraph;
(*b*)   a vehicle being driven to a place where it is to undergo repairs;
(*c*)   an exempt vehicle within the meaning given by paragraph (12)(*a*);
(*d*)   engineering plant, an industrial tractor or a works truck; and
(*e*)   a vehicle in Class III, IV, V or VII within the meaning of the Motor Vehicles (Tests) Regulations 1981 and first used before 1st August 1979

(10BC) *Revoked.*

(10C)   For the purposes of this regulation—

(*a*)   any rotary piston engine shall be deemed to be a four-stroke engine; and
(*b*)   "rotary piston engine" means an engine in which the torque is provided by means of one or more rotary pistons and not by any reciprocating piston.

(11)   Subject to Schedule 7XA, in this regulation, a reference to a vehicle to which an item in Table II applies is a reference to a vehicle which—

(*a*)   is of a class specified in that item in column (2) of that Table,
(*b*)   is first used on or after the date specified in that item in column (3) of that Table, and
(*c*)   is not exempted by the entry in that item in column (5) of that Table.

and for the purposes of determining whether a vehicle is a vehicle to which any item numbered 8 or more in that Table applies, regulation 4(2) shall be disregarded.

(11A)   In this regulation, "passenger car" means a motor vehicle which—

(*a*)   is constructed or adapted for use for the carriage of passengers and is not a goods vehicle;
(*b*)   has no more than five seats in addition to the driver's seat; and
(*c*)   has a maximum gross weight not exceeding 2,500kg.

(12)   In Table II and paragraphs (10B) and (10BB)—

(*a*)   "exempt vehicle" means—

    (i)   a vehicle with less than 4 wheels,
    (ii)   a vehicle with a maximum gross weight of less than 400 kg,
    (iii)   a vehicle with a maximum speed of less than 25 km/h, or
    (iv)   an agricultural motor vehicle;

(*b*)   "direct injection" means a fuel injection system in which the injector communications with an open combustion chamber.
(*c*)   "indirect injection" means a fuel injection system in which the injector communicates with the subsidiary part of a divided combustion chamber.
(*d*)   a reference in column (5) to a vehicle complying with an item is a reference to a vehicle that complies with the provisions specified in that item in column (4) whether the vehicle is or is not within the class of vehicles to which that item applies and any instrument mentioned in that item shall for the purposes of the reference have effect as if it applied to the vehicle in question (whether it would otherwise have done so or not).

TABLE I

(regulation 61(3))

1	2	3	4
Item	Class of vehicle	Requirements	Exemptions
1	Vehicles propelled by a compression ignition engine and equipped with a device designed to facilitate starting the engine by causing it to be supplied with excess fuel.	Provision shall be made to ensure the device cannot readily be operated by a person inside the vehicle.	(*a*) a works truck; (*b*) a vehicle on which the device is so designed and maintained that— (i) its use after the engine has started cannot cause the engine to be supplied with excess fuel, or (ii) it does not cause any increase in the smoke or visible vapour emitted from the vehicle.
2	Vehicles first used on or after 1st April 1973 and propelled by a compression ignition engine.	The engine of the vehicle shall be of a type for which there has been issued by a person authorised by the Secretary of State a type test certificate in accordance with the British Standard Specification for the Performance of Diesel Engines for Road Vehicles published on 19th May 1971 under number BS AU 141a: 1971. In the case of an agricultural motor vehicle (other than one which is first used after 1st June 1986 and is driven at more than 20 mph), an industrial tractor, a works truck or engineering plant, for the purposes of that Specification as to the exhaust gas opacity, measurements shall be made with the engine running at 80 per cent of its full load over the speed range from maximum speed down to the speed at which maximum torque occurs as declared by the manufacturer of the vehicle for those purposes.	(*a*) a vehicle manufactured before 1st April 1973 and propelled by an engine known as the Perkins 6.354 engine; (*b*) a vehicle propelled having not more than 2 cylinders and being an agricultural motor vehicle (other than one which is first used on or after 1st June 1986 and which is driven at more than 20 mph), an industrial tractor, a works truck or engineering plant.
3	Vehicles first used on or after 1st January 1972 and propelled by a spark ignition engine other than a 2-stroke engine.	The engine shall be equipped with means sufficient to ensure that, while the engine is running, any vapours or gases in the engine crank case, or in any other part of the engine to which vapours or gases may pass from that case, are prevented, so far as is reasonably practicable, from escaping into the atmosphere otherwise than through the combustion chamber of the engine.	(*a*) a two-wheeled motor cycle with or without a sidecar attached; (*b*) *Revoked.* (*c*) a vehicle to which any item in Table II applies.

TABLE II
(REGULATION 61(3A), (3C), (7), (11) AND (12))

(1) Item	(2) Class of Vehicle	(3) Date of First Use	(4) Design, construction and equipment requirements		(5) Vehicles exempted from requirements	(6) Emitted substances
			(a) Instrument	(b) Place in instrument where requirements are stated		
1	Vehicles propelled by a spark ignition engine	1st October 1982	Community Directive 78/665 or ECE Regulation 15.03	Annex I, paragraphs 3 and 5 Paragraphs 5, 8 and 11	(a) A vehicle whose maximum gross weight exceeds 3,500 kg; (b) A vehicle which complies with the requirements of item 2, 4, 5, 8, 11, 12 or 13; (c) A vehicle whose maximum speed is less than 50 km/h; (d) An exempt vehicle	Carbon monoxide, hydrocarbons and oxides of nitrogen
2	All vehicles	1st April 1991	Community Directive 83/351 or ECE Regulation 15.04	Annex I, paragraphs 5, 7 and 8 Paragraphs 5, 8 and 12	(a) A vehicle propelled by a compression ignition engine and whose maximum gross weight exceeds 3,500 kg; (b) A vehicle which complies with the requirements of item 4, 5, 8, 11, 12 or 13; (c) A vehicle within the meaning given by Article 1 of Community Directive 88/77 and which complies with the requirements of item 6, 9, or 10; (d) An industrial tractor, works truck or engineering plant; (e) A vehicle whose maximum speed is less than 50 km/h; (f) An exempt vehicle	Carbon monoxide, hydrocarbons and oxides of nitrogen
3	Industrial tractors, works trucks and engineering plant propelled in each case by a compression ignition engine	1st April 1993	ECE Regulation 49	Paragraphs 5 and 7	A vehicle which complies with the requirements of item 6, 9, 10, 11, 12 or 13	Carbon monoxide, hydrocarbons and oxides of nitrogen
4	Passenger vehicles which— (a) are constructed or adapted to carry not more than 5 passengers excluding the driver, and (b) have a maximum gross weight of not more than 2,500 kg, not being off-road vehicles	1st April 1991	Community Directive 88/76 or Community Directive 89/458 or ECE Regulation 83	Annex I, paragraphs 5, 7 and 8 Annex I, paragraphs 5, 7 and 8 Paragraphs 5, 8 and 13	(a) A vehicle which complies with the requirements of item 2, 8, 11, 12 or 13; (b) A vehicle whose maximum speed is less than 50 km/h; (c) An exempt vehicle	Carbon monoxide, hydrocarbons and oxides of nitrogen

(1) Item	(2) Class of Vehicle	(3) Date of First Use	(4) Design, construction and equipment requirements — (a) Instrument	(4) (b) Place in instrument where requirements are stated	(5) Vehicles exempted from requirements	(6) Emitted substances
5	Vehicles which are not of a description specified in this column in item 4 but which—(a) are propelled by a spark ignition engine and have a maximum gross weight of not more than 2,000 kg, or (b) are propelled by a compression ignition engine and have a maximum gross weight of more than 3,500 kg	1st April 1992 / 1st April 1991	Community Directive 88/76 or ECE Regulation 83	Annex I, paragraphs 5, 7 and 8; Paragraphs 5, 8 and 13	(a) A vehicle within the meaning given by Article 1 of Community Directive 88/77 and which complies with the requirements of item 6, 9, 10, 11, 12 or 13; (b) An industrial tractor, works truck or engineering plant; (c) A vehicle whose maximum speed is less than 50 km/h; (d) A vehicle which complies with the requirements of item 8; (e) An exempt vehicle	Carbon monoxide, hydrocarbons and oxides of nitrogen
6	All vehicles propelled by compression ignition engines	1st April 1991	Community Directive 88/77 or ECE Regulation 49.01	Annex I, paragraphs 6, 7 and 8; Paragraphs 5, 6 and 7	(a) A vehicle whose maximum gross weight is less than 3,500 kg and which complies with the requirements of item 2; (b) A vehicle which complies with the requirements of item 4, 5, 8, 9, 10, 11, 12 or 13; (c) A fire appliance which is first used before 1st October 1992; (d) An industrial tractor, works truck or engineering plant; (e) An exempt vehicle	Carbon monoxide, hydrocarbons and oxides of nitrogen
7	Passenger vehicles which —(a) are constructed or adapted to carry not more than 5 passengers excluding the driver, (b) have a maximum gross weight of not more than 2,500 kg, and (c) are propelled by a compression ignition engine of the indirect injection type	1st April 1991	Community Directive 88/436	Annex I, paragraphs 5, 7 and 8 as far as they relate to particulate emissions	(a) A vehicle which complies with the requirements of item 8, 11, 12 or 13; (b) A vehicle whose maximum speed is less than 50 km/h; (c) An off-road vehicle; (d) An exempt vehicle	Particulates
8	All vehicles	31st December 1992	Community Directive 91/441 or ECE Regulation 83.01	Annex I, paragraphs 5, 7 and 8; Paragraphs 5, 8 and 13	(a) A vehicle within the meaning given by Article 1 of Community Directive 88/77 and which— (i) complies with the requirements of item 6 and is first used before 1st October 1993, or (ii) complies with the requirements of item 9, 10, 11, 12 or 13;	Carbon monoxide, hydrocarbons, oxides of nitrogen and particulates

(1) Item	(2) Class of Vehicle	(3) Date of First Use	(4) Design, construction and equipment requirements		(5) Vehicles exempted from requirements	(6) Emitted substances
			(a) Instrument	(b) Place in instrument where requirements are stated		
8— cont					(b) An industrial tractor, works truck or engineering plant; (c) A vehicle whose maximum speed is less than 50 km/h; (d) An exempt vehicle	
9	All vehicles propelled by a compression ignition engine	1st October 1993	Community Directive 91/542 or ECE Regulation 49.02	Annex I, paragraphs 6, 7 and 8 (excluding line B in the Tables in sub-paragraphs 6.2.1 and 8.3.1.1) Paragraphs 5, 6 and 7 (excluding line B in the Tables in sub-paragraphs 5.2.1 and 7.4.2.1)	(a) A vehicle which complies with the requirements of item 8, 10, 11, 12 or 13; (b) An industrial tractor, works truck or engineering plant; (c) An exempt vehicle	Carbon monoxide, hydrocarbons, oxides of nitrogen and particulates
10	All vehicles propelled by a compression ignition engine	1st October 1996	Community Directive 91/542 or ECE Regulation 49.02	Annex I, paragraphs 6, 7 and 8 (excluding line A in the Tables in sub-paragraphs 6.2.1 and 8.3.1.1) Paragraphs 5, 6 and 7 (excluding line A in the Tables in sub-paragraphs 5.2.1 and 7.4.2.1)	(a) A vehicle which complies with the requirements of item 8, 11, 12 or 13; (b) An industrial tractor, works truck or engineering plant; (c) An exempt vehicle	Carbon monoxide, hydrocarbons, oxides of nitrogen and particulates

(1) Item	(2) Class of Vehicle	(3) Date of First Use	(4) Design, construction and equipment requirements		(5) Vehicles exempted from requirements	(6) Emitted substances
			(a) Instrument	(b) Place in instrument where requirements are stated		
11	All vehicles	1st October 1994	Community Directive 93/59 or ECE Regulation 83.02	Annex I, paragraphs 5, 7 and 8	(a) A vehicle within the meaning given by Article 1 of Community Directive 88/77 and which complies with the requirements of items 9, 10, 12 or 13; (b) An industrial tractor, works truck or engineering plant; (c) Vehicles whose maximum speed is less than 50 km/h; (d) An exempt vehicle	Carbon monoxide, hydrocarbons, oxides of nitrogen and particulates
12	All vehicles	1st January 1997	Community Directive 94/12 or ECE Regulation 83.03	Annex I, paragraphs 5, 7 and 8	(a) A vehicle within the meaning given by Article 1 of Community Directive 88/77 and which complies with the requirements of items 9, 10, 11 or 13; (b) An industrial tractor, works truck or engineering plant; (c) Vehicles whose maximum speed is less than 50 km/h; (d) An exempt vehicle	Carbon monoxide, hydrocarbons, oxides of nitrogen and particulates
13	All vehicles	1st October 1997	Community Directive 96/69 or ECE Regulation 83.04	Annex I, paragraphs 5, 7 and 8	(a) A vehicle within the meaning given by Article 1 of Community Directive 88/77 and which complies with the requirements of items 9, 10, or 12; (b) A vehicle as defined in column 2 of item 14; (c) An industrial tractor, works truck or engineering plant; (d) Vehicles whose maximum speed is less than 50 km/h (e) An exempt vehicle	Carbon monoxide, hydrocarbons, oxides of nitrogen and particulates
14	Vehicles falling within (a) Class II or III, as specified in the Annex to Community Directive 96/69, of category N1, or (b) Category M and specified in footnote (2) of that Annex Note: references to categories M and N1 are to those categories as specified in Annex II of the Framework Directive	1st October 1998	Community Directive 96/69 or ECE Regulation 83.04	Annex 1 paragraphs 5, 7 and 8		Carbon monoxide, hydrocarbons, oxides of nitrogen and particulates

4–3569A   61A. Emission of smoke, vapour, gases, oily substances etc—further requirements for certain motor vehicles first used on or after 1st January 2001.   (1) This regulation shall apply to motor vehicles first used on or after 1st January 2001.

(2) Subject to paragraphs (5) to (7) and Schedule 7XA, a motor vehicle in any category shall comply with such design, construction and equipment requirements and such limit values as may be specified for a motor vehicle of that category and weight by any Community Directive specified in item 1 or 2 of the Table and from such date as is specified by that Community Directive.

(3) Subject to paragraphs (4) to (7) and Schedule 7XA, no person shall use, or cause or permit to be used, on a road a motor vehicle if the motor vehicle does not comply with such limit values as may apply to it by virtue of any Community Directive specified in item 1 or 2 of the Table, and from such date as is specified by that Community Directive, unless the following conditions are satisfied with respect to it—

(a) the failure to meet the limit values does not result from an alteration to the propulsion unit or exhaust system of the motor vehicle;

(b) neither would those limit values be met nor the emissions of gaseous and particulate pollutants and smoke and evaporative emissions be materially reduced if maintenance work of a kind which would fall within the scope of a normal periodic service of the vehicle were carried out on the motor vehicle; and

(c) the failure to meet those limit values does not result from any device designed to control the emission of gaseous and particulate pollutants and smoke and evaporative emissions which is fitted to the motor vehicle being other than in good and efficient working order.

(4) Where—

(a) a motor vehicle is fitted with a device of the kind referred to in sub-paragraph (c) of paragraph (3);

(b) the motor vehicle does not comply with the limit values applying to it which are referred to in that paragraph; and

(c) the conditions specified in sub-paragraphs (a) and (b) of paragraph (3) are satisfied in respect of the motor vehicle

nothing in paragraph (3) shall prevent the motor vehicle being driven to a place where the device is to be repaired or replaced.

(5) Subject to paragraph (6), if the Secretary of State has exempted any motor vehicle produced in a small series from one or more of the provisions of a Community Directive specified in item 1 of the Table in accordance with the procedure in Article 8(2)(a) of the Framework Directive then paragraphs (2) to (4) shall not apply to that motor vehicle insofar as it has been so exempted.

(6) If any motor vehicle has been exempted from one or more of the provisions of a Community Directive specified in item 1 of the Table in accordance with paragraph (5), then in the Table as it applies to that motor vehicle there shall be deemed to be substituted, for the reference to Community Directive 96/69/EC or ECE Regulation 83.04, Community Directive 98/69/EC and 1999/102/EC—

(a) in the case of passenger cars as defined in regulations 61(11A), a reference to Community Directive 94/12/EC or ECE Regulation 83.03; and

(b) in the case of other motor vehicles of category M, a reference to Community Directive 93/59/EEC or ECE Regulation 83.02

and in any such case paragraphs (2) to (4) shall apply to the motor vehicle as if they referred to the substituted Community Directives or ECE Regulations.

(7) If a vehicle has, in accordance with Schedule 7XA, been exempted from the need to comply with any provision of a Community Directive specified in item 1 or 2 in the Table ("the exempted provision"), it shall, in substitution for the exempted provision, comply with the equivalent provision (if any) that would have applied by virtue of this regulation in relation to such a vehicle immediately before the coming into force of the requirement to comply with the exempted provision; and in relation to that equivalent provision paragraphs 2 to 4 shall apply as if they referred to the Community Directive under which that equivalent provision arose.

(8) In this regulation—

(a) "category" means a category for the purpose of Annex II of the Framework Directive;

(b) "date as is specified" means, in relation to any vehicle and—

(i) in relation to limit values set by a Community Directive specified in item 1 or 2 in the Table, the date specified by that Community Directive as that from which Member States are required to prohibit the registration or the entry into service of that vehicle if it does not comply with those limit values; or

(ii) in relation to emission control and monitoring systems and devices, the date specified by a Community Directive specified in item 1 or 2 in the Table as that from which Member States are required to ensure that such equipment is fitted to that vehicle,

provided that, where a Community Directive specified in item 2 in the Table re-enacts a requirement imposed by a Community Directive that had been specified in that item immediately before 9th November 2006, the date as is specified shall be the date that had been specified by that previous Directive;

(c) "limit values" means the permitted amounts of gaseous and particulate pollutants and smoke and evaporative emissions;

(d) "small series" means the motor vehicles within a family of types as defined in Annex XII of the Framework Directive which are registered or enter into service in a period of twelve months beginning on 1st January in any year where the total number of motor vehicles does not exceed the small series limits specified in that Annex.

(9) Regulation 4(2) does not apply to any requirement imposed on a vehicle by or under this Regulation.

TABLE
(REGULATION 61A)

Item	Community Directive or ECE Regulation	Amending Community Directive or ECE Regulation
1	70/220/EEC	96/69/EC or ECE Regulation 83.04
		98/69/EC
		1999/102/EC 2001/1/EC
2	2005/55/EC or ECE Regulation 49.02	2005/78/EC 2006/51/EC

Closets etc

4–3570 **62.** (1) No wheeled vehicle first used after 15th January 1931 shall be equipped with any closet or urinal which can discharge directly on to a road.

(2) Every tank into which a closet or urinal with which a vehicle is equipped empties, and every closet or urinal which does not empty into a tank, shall contain chemicals which are non-inflammable and non-irritant and provide an efficient germicide.

Wings

4–3571 **63.** (1) Save as provided in paragraph (4), this regulation applies to—

(a) invalid carriages;
(b) heavy motor cars, motor cars and motor cycles, not being agricultural motor vehicles or pedestrian-controlled vehicles;
(c) agricultural motor vehicles driven at more than 20 mph; and
(d) trailers.

(2) Subject to paragraphs (3) and (5), every vehicle to which this regulation applies shall be equipped with wings or other similar fittings to catch, so far as practicable, mud or water thrown up by the rotation of its wheels or tracks.

(3) The requirements specified in paragraph (2) apply, in the case of a trailer with more than two wheels, only in respect of the rearmost two wheels.

(4) Those requirements do not apply in respect of—

(a) a works truck;
(b) a living van;
(c) a water cart;
(d) an agricultural trailer drawn by a motor vehicle which is not driven at a speed in excess of 20 mph;
(e) an agricultural trailed appliance;
(f) an agricultural trailed appliance conveyor;
(g) a broken down vehicle;
(h) a heavy motor car, motor car or trailer in an unfinished condition which is proceeding to a workshop for completion;
(i) a trailer used for or in connection with the carriage of round timber and the rear wheels of any heavy motor car or motor car drawing a semi-trailer so used; or
(j) a trailer drawn by a motor vehicle the maximum speed of which is restricted to 20 mph or less under Schedule 6 to the 1984 Act.

(5) Instead of complying with paragraph (2) a vehicle may comply with Community Directive 78/549.

Spray suppression devices

4–3572 **64.** (1) Save as provided in paragraph (2), this regulation applies to every wheeled goods vehicle which is—

(a) a motor vehicle first used on or after 1st April 1986 having a maximum gross weight exceeding 12,000 kg;
(b) a trailer manufactured on or after 1st May 1985 having a maximum gross weight exceeding 3500 kg; or
(c) a trailer, whenever manufactured, having a maximum gross weight exceeding 16,000 kg and 2 or more axles.

(2) This regulation does not apply to—

(a) a motor vehicle so constructed that the driving power of its engine is, or can by use of its controls be, transmitted to all the wheels on at least one front axle and on at least one rear axle;

(b) a motor vehicle of which no part which lies within the specified area is less than 400 mm vertically above the ground when the vehicle is standing on reasonably flat ground;

(c) a works truck;

(d) a works trailer;

(e) a broken down vehicle;

(f) a motor vehicle which has a maximum speed not exceeding 30 mph;

(g) a vehicle of a kind specified in sub-paragraphs (b), (c), (d), (e), (f), (g), (h), (j), (k), (o) or (p) of regulation 51(2);

(h) a vehicle specially designed, and not merely adapted, for the carriage and mixing of liquid concrete; or

(i) a vehicle which is being driven or towed to a place where by previous arrangement a device is to be fitted so that it complies with the requirements specified in paragraph (3).

(2A) This regulation shall not apply to a vehicle fitted with a spray-suppression system in accordance with the requirements of Annex III of Community Directive 91/226 if the spray suppression devices with which the vehicle is equipped are legibly and permanently marked with a designated approval mark.

(3) A vehicle to which this regulation applies and which is of a class specified in an item in column 2 of the Table shall not be used on a road on or after the date specified in column 3 in that item, unless it is fitted in relation to the wheels on each of its axles, with such containment devices as satisfy the technical requirements and other provisions about containment devices specified in the British Standard Specification, provided that in the case of a containment device fitted before 1st January 1985 the said requirements shall be deemed to be complied with if that containment device substantially conforms to those requirements.

TABLE

(regulation 64(3))

1	2	3
Item	Class of Vehicle	Date
1	A trailer manufactured before 1st January 1975	1st October 1987
2	A trailer manufactured on or after 1st January 1975 but before 1st May 1985	1st October 1986
3	A trailer manufactured on or after 1st May 1985	1st May 1985
4	A motor vehicle	1st April 1986

(4) In this regulation—

"the British Standard Specification" means—

(a) in relation to a containment device fitted before 1st May 1987, Part 1a of the amended Specification and Part 2 of the original Specification; and

(b) in relation to a containment device fitted on or after 1st May 1987, Part 1a and Part 2a of the amended Specification;

"designated approval mark" means the marking designated as an approval mark by regulation 5 of the Approval Marks Regulations and shown at item 30 in Schedule 4 to those Regulations;

"the original Specification" means the British Standard Specification for Spray Reducing Devices for Heavy Goods Vehicles published under the reference BS AU 200: Part 1: 1984 and BS AU 200: Part 2: 1984;

"the amended Specification" means the original Specification as amended and published under the reference BS AU 200: Part 1a: 1986 and BS AU 200: Part 2a: 1986;

"containment device" means any device so described in the original Specification or the amended Specification;".

(5) Nothing in this regulation derogates from any requirement specified in regulation 63.

Maintenance of spray suppression devices

4–3573 65. Every part of every containment device with which a vehicle is required to be fitted by the provisions of regulation 64 shall at all times when the vehicle is on a road be maintained free from any obvious defect which would be likely to affect adversely the effectiveness of the device.

PART III—PLATES, MARKINGS, TESTING AND INSPECTION

Plates for goods vehicles and buses

4–3574 66. (1) This regulation applies to—

(a) a wheeled heavy motor car or motor car first used on or after 1st January 1968 not being—

    (i)   a dual-purpose vehicle;
    (ii) an agricultural motor vehicle;
    (iii) a works truck;
    (iv) a pedestrian-controlled vehicle;
    (v) save as provided in sub-paragraph (*b*) below, a passenger vehicle; or
    (vi) a vehicle which is exempt from section 63(1) of the Road Traffic Act 1988 by virtue of regulation 14(6) of the Motor Vehicles (Approved) Regulations 1996.

  (*b*) a bus (whether or not it is an articulated bus) first used on or after 1st April 1982;
  (*c*) a wheeled locomotive or motor tractor first used on or after 1st April 1973 not being—

    (i)   an agricultural motor vehicle;
    (ii) an industrial tractor;
    (iii) a works truck;
    (iv) engineering plant; or
    (v) a pedestrian-controlled vehicle;

  (*d*) a wheeled trailer manufactured on or after 1st January 1968 which exceeds 1020 kg in weight unladen not being—

    (i)   a trailer not constructed or adapted to carry any load, other than plant or special appliances or apparatus which is a permanent or essentially permanent fixture, and not exceeding 2290 kg in total weight;
    (ii) a living van not exceeding 2040 kg in weight unladen and fitted with pneumatic tyres;
    (iii) a works trailer;
    (iv) a trailer mentioned in regulation 16(3)(*b*) to (*g*); or
    (v) a trailer which was manufactured and used outside Great Britain before it was first used in Great Britain; and

  (*e*) a converter dolly manufactured on or after 1st January 1979.

(2) Every vehicle to which this regulation applies shall be equipped with a plate securely attached to the vehicle in a conspicuous and readily accessible position which either—

  (*a*) contains the particulars required, in the case of a motor vehicle by Part I of Schedule 8 or, in the case of a trailer, by Part II of that Schedule, and complies with the provisions of Part III of that Schedule; or
  (*b*) complies with the requirements specified in the Annex to Community Directive 78/507 or, in the case of a vehicle first used before 1st October 1982, in the Annex to Community Directive 76/114, such requirements being in any case modified as provided in paragraph (3).

(3) Instead of the particulars required by items 2.1.4 to 2.1.7 of that Annex, the plate required by paragraph (2)(*b*) shall show, for a vehicle of a class specified in column 2 of the Table against an item of that Annex so specified in column 1, the following particulars—

  (*a*) the maximum permitted weight for that class, if any, shown in column 3 of the Table;
  (*b*) where the maximum weight shown in column 4 of the Table exceeds the maximum permitted weight, the maximum weight in a column on the plate to the right of the maximum permitted weight; and
  (*c*) if no weight is shown in column 3 of the Table, the maximum weight shown in column 4 of the Table, in the right hand column of the plate.

TABLE

(regulation 66(3))

1	2	3	4
Item in Annex to Directive	Class of vehicle	Maximum permitted weight	Maximum weight
2.1.4 (Laden weight of vehicle)	(i) Motor vehicles (ii) Trailers, other than semi-trailers (iii) Semi-trailers	The maximum gross weight in Great Britain referred to in item 10 in Part I of Schedule The maximum gross weight in Great Britain referred to in item 8 in Part II of Schedule 8.	The maximum gross weight referred to in item 7 in Part I of Schedule 8. The maximum gross weight referred to in item 6 in Part II of Schedule 8. The maximum gross weight referred to in item 6 in Part II of Schedule 8.
2.1.5 (Train weight of motor vehicle)	Motor vehicles constructed to draw a trailer	The lower of (a) the maximum train weight referred to in item 8 in Part I of Schedule 8; and—	The maximum train weight referred to in item 8 in Part I of Schedule 8.

1	2	3	4
Item in Annex to Directive	Class of vehicle	Maximum permitted weight	Maximum weight
		(b) the maximum laden weight specified, in the case of vehicles constructed to form part of an articulated vehicle, in regulation 77, and, in other cases, in regulation 76.	
2.1.6 (Axle weight of vehicle)	(i) Motor vehicles (ii) Trailers	The maximum weight in Great Britain for each axle referred to in item 9 in Part I of Schedule 8. The maximum weight in Great Britain for each axle referred to in item 7 in Part II of Schedule 8.	The maximum weight for each axle referred to in item 6 in Part I of Schedule 8. The maximum weight for each axle referred to in item 4 in Part II of Schedule 8.
2.1.7 (Load imposed by semi-trailer)	Semi-trailers		The maximum load imposed on the drawing vehicle referred to in item 5 in Part II of Schedule 8.

(4) Part III of Schedule 8 applies for determining the relevant weights to be shown on a plate in accordance with this regulation.

(5) Where, in accordance with the provisions of this regulation and of Schedule 8, a motor vehicle first used, or a trailer manufactured, after 31st December 1998, is required to be equipped with a plate showing the maximum gross weight in Great Britain or the maximum weight in Great Britain for each axle of the vehicle, the plate may instead show particulars of the maximum authorised weight for the vehicle or, as the case may be, the maximum authorised weight for each axle of the vehicle.

(6) In paragraph (5) the references to the maximum authorised weight for a vehicle and maximum authorised for each axle of a vehicle mean those weights determined in accordance with the Motor Vehicles (Authorised Weight) Regulations 1998.

(7) The plate for a vehicle which falls within paragraph (1)(a) and which is a motor vehicle first used after 31st December 1998 need not include the particulars referred to in paragraph 9 or 10 of Part I of Schedule 8.

Vehicle identification numbers

4–3575　67. (1) This regulation applies to a wheeled vehicle which is first used on or after 1st April 1980 and to which the Type Approval (Great Britain) Regulations apply.

(2) A vehicle to which this regulation applies shall be equipped with a plate which is in a conspicuous and readily accessible position, is affixed to a vehicle part which is not normally subject to replacement and shows clearly and indelibly—

　(a)　the vehicle identification number in accordance with the requirements specified—

　　(i)　in the case of a vehicle first used before 1st April 1987, in paragraphs 3.1.1 and 3.1.2 of the Annex to Community Directive 76/114/EEC; or

　　(ii)　in any case, in sections 3 and 4 of the Annex to Community Directive 78/507/EEC;

　(b)　the name of the manufacturer; and

　(c)　the approval reference number of either—

　　(i)　the type of approval certificate which relates to the vehicle model or the model variant of the vehicle model, as the case may be, issued in accordance with the provisions of regulation 9(1) of, and Part I of Schedule 3 to, the Type Approval (Great Britain) Regulations; or

　　(ii)　the Minister's approval certificate which relates to the vehicle, issued in accordance with the provisions of regulation 9(2) of, and Part 1A of Schedule 4 to, the said Regulations.

Provided that the information required under sub-paragraph (c) above may be shown clearly and indelibly on an additional plate which is fitted in a conspicuous and readily accessible position and which is affixed to a vehicle part which is not normally subject to replacement.

(3) The vehicle identification number of every vehicle to which this regulation applies shall be marked on the chassis, frame or other similar structure, on the off side of the vehicle, in a clearly visible and accessible position, and by a method such as hammering or stamping, in such a way that it cannot be obliterated or deteriorate.

Plates—agricultural trailed appliances

4–3576　68. (1) Save as provided in paragraph (3) below, every wheeled agricultural trailed appliance manufactured on or after 1st December 1985 shall be equipped with a plate affixed to the vehicle in a conspicuous and readily accessible position and which is clearly and indelibly marked with the particulars specified in paragraph (2) below.

(2) Those particulars are—

(a) the name of the manufacturer of the appliance;
(b) the year in which the appliance was manufactured;
(c) the maximum gross weight;
(d) the unladen weight; and
(e) the maximum load which would be imposed by the appliance on the drawing vehicle.

(3) In the case of a towed roller consisting of several separate rollers used in combination, a single plate shall satisfy the requirement specified in paragraph (2) above.

Plates—motor cycles

4–3577   69. (1) This regulation applies to every motor cycle first used on or after 1st August 1977 which is not—

(a) propelled by an internal combustion engine with a cylinder capacity exceeding 150 cc if the vehicle was first used before 1st January 1982 or 125 cc if it was first used on or after 1st January 1982;
(b) a mowing machine; or
(c) a pedestrian-controlled vehicle.

(2) Every vehicle to which this regulation applies shall be equipped with a plate which is securely affixed to the vehicle in a conspicuous and readily accessible position and which complies with the requirements of Schedule 9.

Ministry plates

4–3578   70. (1) Every goods vehicle to which the Plating and Testing regulations apply and in respect of which a plating certificate has been issued shall, from the date specified in paragraph (2), be equipped with a Ministry plate securely affixed, so as to be legible at all times, in a conspicuous and readily accessible position, and in the cab of the vehicle if it has one.
(2) That date is in the case of—

(a) a vehicle to which the Type Approval for Goods Vehicles regulations apply, the date of the fourteenth day after the plate was issued; or
(b) any other vehicle, the date by which it is required, by the said Regulations, to be submitted for examination for plating.

(3) In these Regulations "Ministry plate" means a plate which—

(a) is issued by the Secretary of State following the issue or amendment of a plating certificate; and
(b) subject to paragraph (4), contains the particulars required by Schedule 10, 10A, 10B or 10C.

(4) Instead of particulars of the gross weight, train weight and axle weights of the vehicle to which it relates, a Ministry plate may contain particulars of the maximum authorised weight for the vehicle, maximum authorised weight for a combination of which the vehicle forms part and maximum authorised axle weights for the vehicle, determined in accordance with the Road Vehicles (Authorised Weight) Regulations 1998 and the form of the plate shall be amended accordingly.]

Speed limiters—plates

4–3579   70A. (1) This regulation applies to every vehicle to which regulation 36A or 36B applies and which is fitted with a speed limiter.
(2) Every vehicle to which this regulation applies shall be equipped with a plate which meets the requirements specified in paragraph (3).
(3) The requirements are that the plate is in a conspicuous position in the driving compartment of the vehicle and is clearly and indelibly marked with the speed at which the speed limiter has been set.

Plate relating to dimensions

4–3579A   70B. (1) This regulation applies to a vehicle which is not a goods vehicle fitted in accordance with regulation 70 with a Ministry plate containing the particulars required by Schedule 10A or 10C and which is either—

(a) a bus or a heavy motor car and which was manufactured after 31st May 1998; or
(b) a trailer used in combination with a vehicle falling within paragraph (a) and manufactured after 31st May 1998.

(2) A vehicle to which this regulation applies shall not be used unless—

(a) the vehicle is equipped with a plate securely attached to the vehicle in a conspicuous and readily accessible position and containing the particulars as to the dimensions of the vehicle specified in Annex III of Community Directive 96/53/EC; or
(b) those particulars are included in the particulars shown on the plate with which the vehicle is equipped in accordance with regulation 66.

Marking of weights on certain vehicles

4–3581   71. (1) This regulation applies to a vehicle (other than an agricultural motor vehicle which is either a track-laying vehicle not exceeding 3050 kg in unladen weight or a wheeled vehicle) which is—

    (*a*)   a locomotive;
    (*b*)   a motor tractor;
    (*c*)   a bus which is registered under the 1971 Act (or any enactment repealed thereby); or
    (*d*)   an unbraked wheeled trailer, other than one mentioned in regulation 16(3)(*b*), (*bb*), (*bc*), (*c*), (*d*), (*e*), (*f*), or (*g*).

(2) There shall be plainly marked in a conspicuous place on the outside of a vehicle to which this regulation applies, on its near side—

    (*a*)   if it is a vehicle falling in paragraph (1)(*a*), (*b*) or (*c*) its unladen weight; and
    (*b*)   if it is a vehicle falling in paragraph (1)(*d*), its maximum gross weight.

Marking of date of manufacture of trailers

4–3581A   **71A.** (1) This regulation applies to a trailer that—

    (*a*)   is not a motor vehicle;
    (*b*)   is manufactured on or after 1st January 1997; and
    (*c*)   has a maximum total design axle weight not exceeding 750 kg.

(2) The year of manufacture of every trailer to which this regulation applies shall be marked on the chassis, frame or other similar structure on the nearside of the vehicle, in a clearly visible and accessible position, and by a method such as hammering or stamping, in such a way that it cannot be obliterated or deteriorate.

Additional markings

4–3582   **72.** (1) This regulation applies to every goods vehicle to which the Plating and Testing Regulations apply and for which a plating certificate has been issued.
    (2) Without prejudice to the provisions of regulation 70, any weight which by virtue of regulation 80 may not be exceeded in the case of a goods vehicle to which this regulation applies may be marked on either side, or on both sides, of the vehicle.
    (3) Where at any time by virtue of any provision contained in regulation 75 a goods vehicle to which this regulation applies may not be used in excess of a weight which is less than the gross weight which may not be exceeded by that vehicle by virtue of regulation 80, the first mentioned weight may be marked on either side, or on both sides, of the vehicle.
    (4) Where at any time by virtue of any provision contained in regulation 76 and 77 a goods vehicle to which this regulation applies is drawing, or being drawn by, another vehicle and those vehicles may not be used together in excess of a laden weight applicable to those vehicles by virtue of any such provision, that weight may be marked on either side, or on both sides, of that goods vehicle.

Test date discs

4–3583   **73.** (1) Every Ministry test date disc which is issued, following the issue of a goods vehicle test certificate, in respect of a trailer to which the Plating and Testing Regulations apply and for which a plating certificate has been issued shall be carried on the trailer in a legible condition and in a conspicuous and readily accessible position in which it is clearly visible by daylight from the near side of the road, from the date of its issue until but not beyond the date of expiry of that test certificate or the date of issue of a further test certificate for that trailer, whichever date is the earlier.
    (2) In this regulation "Ministry test date disc" means a plate issued by the Secretary of State for a goods vehicle, being a trailer, following the issue of a goods vehicle test certificate for that trailer under the Plating and Testing Regulations and containing the following particulars—

    (*a*)   the identification mark allotted to that trailer and shown in that certificate;
    (*b*)   the date until which that certificate is valid; and
    (*c*)   the number of the vehicle testing station shown in that certificate.

Testing and Inspection

4–3584   **74.** (1) Subject to the conditions specified in paragraph (2), the following persons are hereby empowered to test and inspect the brakes, silencers, steering gear and tyres of any vehicle, on any premises where that vehicle is located—

    (*a*)   a police constable in uniform;
    (*b*)   a person appointed by the Commissioner of Police of the Metropolis to inspect public carriages for the purpose of the Metropolitan Public Carriage Act 1869;
    (*c*)   a person appointed by the police authority for a police area to act for the purposes of section 53 of the 1972 Act;
    (*d*)   a goods vehicle examiner as defined in section 56 of the 1972 Act;
    (*e*)   a certifying officer as defined in section 7(1) of the 1981 Act; and
    (*f*)   a public service vehicle examiner appointed as mentioned in section 7(2) of the 1981 Act.

(2) Those conditions are—

    (*a*)   any person empowered as there mentioned shall produce his authorisation if required to do so;
    (*b*)   no such person shall enter any premises unless the consent of the owner of those premises has first been obtained;
    (*c*)   no such person shall test or inspect any vehicle on any premises unless—

(i) the owner of the vehicle consents thereto;

(ii) notice has been given to that owner personally or left at his address not less than 48 hours before the time of the proposed test or inspection, or has been sent to him at least 72 hours before that time by the recorded delivery service to his address last known to the person giving the notice; or

(iii) the test or inspection is made within 48 hours of an accident to which section 25 of the 1972 Act applies and in which the vehicle was involved.

(3) For the purposes of this regulation, the owner of the vehicle shall be deemed to be in the case of a vehicle—

(a) which is for the time being registered under the 1971 Act, and is not being used under a trade licence under that Act the person appearing as the owner of the vehicle in the register kept by the Secretary of State under that Act;

(b) used under a trade licence, the holder of the licence; or

(c) exempt from excise duty by virtue of the Motor Vehicles (International Circulation) Order 1975, the person resident outside the United Kingdom who has brought the vehicle into Great Britain;

and in cases (a) and (b) the address of the owner as shown on the said register or, as the case may be, on the licence may be treated as his address.

PART IV—CONDITIONS RELATING TO USE

A—LADEN WEIGHT[1]

Maximum permitted laden weight of a vehicle

4–3585 75. (1) Save as provided in paragraph (2), the laden weight of a vehicle of a class specified in an item in column 2 of the Table shall not exceed the maximum permitted laden weight specified in that item in column 3.

(2) The maximum permitted laden weight of a vehicle[2] first used before 1st June 1973 which falls in item 1 or 2 shall not be less than would be the case if the vehicle fell in item 9.

TABLE

(regulation 75(1))

1	2	3
Item	Class of vehicle	Maximum permitted laden weight (kg)
1	A wheeled heavy motor car or motor car which is not described in items 1A, 2, 4 or 5 and which complies with the relevant braking requirement (see regulation 78(3) to (6) in relation to buses)	The weight determined in accordance with Part I of Schedule 11
1A	A wheeled heavy motor car or motor car which is not described in item 2, 4, or 5, which complies with the relevant braking requirement and in which— (a) every driving axle not being a steering axle is fitted with twin tyres; and (b)either every driving axle is fitted with road friendly suspension or no axle has an axle weight exceeding 9,500 kg.	The weight determined in accordance with Part IA of Schedule 11
2	A wheeled heavy motor car or motor car (not being an agricultural motor vehicle) which forms part of an articulated vehicle and which complies with the relevant braking requirement	The weight specified in column (5) in Part II of Schedule 11 in the item which is appropriate having regard to columns (2), (3) and (4) in that Part
3	A wheeled trailer, including a composite trailer, but not including a semi-trailer, which is drawn by a motor tractor, heavy motor car or motor car which complies with the relevant braking requirement, other than a trailer described in items 6, 7, 8 or 11	As for item 1
4	An articulated bus (see regulation 78(3) to (5))	27,000
5	A wheeled agricultural motor vehicle	As for item 1, but subject to a maximum of 24,390
6	A balanced agricultural trailer, as defined in paragraph (4), which is not described in items 8, 11 or 16	As for item 1, but subject to a maximum of 18,290

1	2	3
Item	Class of vehicle	Maximum permitted laden weight (kg)
7	An unbalanced agricultural trailer, as defined in paragraph (4) which is not described in items 8, 11 or 16	18,290 inclusive of the weight imposed by the trailer on the drawing vehicle
8	A wheeled trailer manufactured on or after 27th February 1977 and fitted with brakes which automatically come into operation on the over-run of the trailer (whether or not it is fitted with any other brake), except an agricultural trailer which is being drawn by an agricultural motor vehicle, which complies with the requirements specified in items 3, 14 and 17 of Schedule 3 and of which the brakes can be applied either by the driver of the drawing vehicle or by some other person on that vehicle or on the trailer	3,500
9	A wheeled heavy motor car or motor car not described in items 1, 2, 4 or 5— (a) with not more than 4 wheels (b) with more than 4 but not more than 6 wheels (c) with more than 6 wheels	14,230 20,330 24,390
10	A wheeled trailer[1] not described in items 3, 6, 7, 8 or 11 having less than 6 wheels, and not forming part of an articulated vehicle; and an agricultural trailed appliance	14,230
11	A trailer manufactured before 27th February 1977 and having no brakes other than— (i) a parking brake and (ii) brakes which come into operation on the overrun of the trailer	3,560
12	A wheeled locomotive, not described in item 5, which is equipped with suitable and sufficient springs between each wheel and the vehicle's frame and with a pneumatic tyre or a tyre of soft or elastic material fitted to each wheel— (a) if having less than 6 wheels (b) if having 6 wheels (c) if having more than 6 wheels	22,360 26,420 30,490
13	A track-laying locomotive with resilient material interposed between the rims of the weight-carrying rollers and the road so that the weight of the vehicle (other than that borne by any wheels and the portion of the track in contact with the road) is supported by the resilient material	22,360
14	A locomotive not described in items 5, 12 or 13	20,830
15	A track-laying heavy motor car or motor car	22,360
16	A track-laying trailer	13,210

(3) The maximum total weight of all trailers, whether laden or unladen, drawn at any one time by a locomotive shall not exceed 44,000 kg.

(3A) Nothing in item 1 or 1A of the Table shall prevent a vehicle being used on a road if—

(a) a plating certificate in respect of the vehicle was in force immediately before the 1st January 1993; and

(b) the laden weight of the vehicle does not exceed the weight shown in that certificate as being the weight not to be exceeded in Great Britain

(4) In this Part of these Regulations and in Schedule 11

"air spring" means a spring operated by means of air or other compressible fluid under pressure;

"air suspension" means a suspension system in which at least 75 per cent of the spring effect is caused by an air spring;

"balanced agricultural trailer" means an agricultural trailer the whole of the weight of which is borne by its own wheels; and

"unbalanced agricultural trailer" means an agricultural trailer of which some, but not more than 35%, of the weight is borne by the drawing vehicle and the rest of the weight is borne by its own wheels.

(5) For the purposes of this Part of these Regulations and Schedule 11, an axle shall be regarded as fitted with a road friendly suspension if its suspension is—

(a) an air suspension, or
(b) a suspension, not being an air suspension, which is regarded as being equivalent to an air suspension for the purposes of Community Directive 92/7.

(6) For the purposes of this Part of these Regulations and Schedule 11, an axle shall be regarded as fitted with twin tyres if it would be regarded as fitted with twin tyres for the purposes of Community Directive 92/7.

---

1. New provision is made for the weight of wheeled motor vehicles and trailers which fall within category M2, M3, N2, N3, O2 or O4 of the vehicle categories defined in Annex II of Council Directive 70/156/EEC as amended by the Road Vehicles (Authorised Weight) Regulations 1998, in this title, post. The 1998 Regulations do not apply to vehicle combinations which meet the requirements for combined transport in Sch 11A to the 1986 regulations. A vehicle which complies with regs 75 to 79 of the 1986 Regulations is taken to comply with the 1998 Regulations by reg 4 thereof and the new limits in the 1998 Regulations are, in accordance with reg 5, subject to the overriding limit in reg 80 of the 1986 Regulations.
2. A composition trailer may be treated as one trailer; reg 3(11).

Maximum permitted laden weight of a vehicle and trailer, other than an articulated vehicle[1]

4–3586 76[1]. (1) The total laden weight of a motor vehicle and the trailer or trailers (other than semi-trailers) drawn by it shall not, in a case specified in an item in column 2 of the Table, exceed the maximum permitted train weight specified in that item in column 3.

(1A) This regulation is subject to Schedule 11A (exemptions relating to combined transport operations).

(2) In this regulation, the expressions "road friendly suspension", "twin tyres" and "unbalanced agricultural trailer" shall be construed in accordance with regulation 75(4), (5) and (6).

TABLE

(regulation 76(1))

1	2	3
Item	Vehicle combination	Maximum permitted train weight (kg)
1	A wheeled trailer which is drawn by a wheeled motor tractor, heavy motor car (not being in any case an agricultural motor vehicle), where— (a) the combination has a total of 4 axles and is being used for international transport; and (b) the drawing vehicle is a vehicle which was first used on or after 1st April 1973 and complies with the relevant braking requirement	35,000
1A	A wheeled trailer which is drawn by a wheeled motor tractor, heavy motor car or motor car (not being in any case an agricultural motor vehicle), where the combination has a total of 4 axles and the following conditions are satisfied in relation to the drawing vehicle, namely— (a) it was first used on or after 1st April 1973; (b) it complies with the relevant braking requirement; (c) every driving axle not being a steering axle is fitted with twin tyres; and (d) every driving axle is fitted with road friendly suspension	35,000
1AA	A wheeled trailer which is drawn by a wheeled motor tractor, heavy motor car or motor car (not being in any case an agricultural motor vehicle), where the combination has a total of 5 or more axles and the following conditions are satisfied in relation to the drawing vehicle, namely— (a) it was first used on or after 1st April 1973; (b) it complies with the relevant braking requirement; (c) every driving axle not being a steering axle is fitted with twin tyres; and (d) either every driving axle is fitted with road friendly suspension or no axle has an axle weight exceeding 8,500kg	38,000

1	2	3
Item	Vehicle combination	Maximum permitted train weight (kg)
1B	A wheeled trailer, not being part of a combination described in items 1, 1A or 1AA which is drawn by a wheeled motor tractor, heavy motor car or motor car (not being in any case an agricultural motor vehicle), where— (a) the trailer is fitted with power-assisted brakes which can be operated by the driver of the drawing vehicle and are not rendered ineffective by the non-rotation of its engine; and (b) the drawing vehicle is equipped with a warning device so placed as to be readily visible to the driver of the vehicle and which is capable of indicating any impending failure of, or deficiency in, the vacuum or pressure system	32,520
1C	A wheeled trailer which is of a description specified in item 8 in the Table of regulation 75 drawn by a wheeled motor tractor, heavy motor car or motor car (not being in any case an agricultural motor vehicle), the drawing vehicle being a vehicle which– (a) was first used on or after 1st April 1973; and (b) complies with the relevant braking requirement	29,500
2	A wheeled agricultural motor vehicle drawing a wheeled unbalanced agricultural trailer, if the distance between the rearmost axle of the trailer and the rearmost axle of the drawing vehicle does not exceed 2.9 m	20,000
3	A wheeled trailer or trailers drawn by a wheeled motor tractor, heavy motor car, motor car or agricultural motor vehicle, not being a combination of vehicles mentioned in items 1, 1A, 1AA, 1B, 1C or 2	24,390
4	A track-laying trailer drawn by a motor tractor, heavy motor car or motor car, whether wheeled or track-laying and a wheeled trailer, drawn by a track-laying vehicle being a motor tractor, heavy motor car or motor car	22,360

1. See note to reg 75, ante.

2. In this regulation a composition trailer may be treated as one trailer; reg 3(11).

3. In this regulation the distance between any two axles shall be obtained by measuring the shortest distance between the lines joining the centre of the area of contact with the road surface of the wheels on each of the two axles; reg 3(10).

Maximum permitted laden weight of an articulated vehicle[1]

4–3587 **77.** (1) Except as provided in paragraph (2), the laden weight of an articulated vehicle of a class specified in an item in column 2 of the Table shall not exceed the weight specified in column 3 in that item.

TABLE

(regulation 77(1))

1	2	3
Item	Class of vehicle	Maximum permitted laden weight (kg)
1	An articulated vehicle which complies with the relevant braking requirement.	Whichever is the lower of— (a) the weight specified in column (3) of Part III of Schedule 11 in the item in which the spacing between the rearmost axles of the motor vehicle and the semi-trailer is specified in column (2); and (b) if the vehicle is of a description specified in an item in column (2) of Part IV of Schedule 11, the weight specified in column (3) of that item

1	2	3
Item	Class of vehicle	Maximum permitted laden weight (kg)
2	An articulated vehicle which does not comply with the relevant braking requirement if the trailer has— (a) less than 4 wheels (b) 4 wheels or more	 20,330 24,390

(2) This regulation does not apply to an agricultural motor vehicle, an agricultural trailer or an agricultural trailed appliance.

(2A) This regulation is subject to Schedule 11A (exemptions relating to combined transport operations).

(3) In Part IV of Schedule 11, "road friendly suspension" and "twin tyres" shall be construed in accordance with regulation 75(5) and (6).

---

1. See note to reg 75, ante.
2. In this regulation the distance between any two axles shall be obtained by measuring the shortest distance between the lines joining the centre of the area of contact with the road surface of the wheels on each of the two axles; reg 3(10).

Maximum permitted wheel and axle weights[1]

4–3588 **78.** (1) The weight transmitted to the road by one or more wheels of a vehicle as mentioned in an item in column 2 of the Table shall not exceed the maximum permitted weight specified in that item in column 3.

(2) The Parts of the Table have the following application—

(a) Part I applies to wheeled heavy motor cars, motor cars and trailers which comply with the relevant braking requirement and to wheeled agricultural motor vehicles, agricultural trailers and agricultural trailed appliances; items 1(b) and 2 also apply to buses;

(b) Part II applies to wheeled heavy motor cars, motor cars and trailers which do not fall in Part I;

(c) Part III applies to wheeled locomotives; and

(d) Part IV applies to track-laying vehicles.

TABLE

(regulation 78(1))

PART I

(wheeled heavy motor cars, motor cars and trailers which comply with the relevant braking requirement and wheeled agricultural motor vehicles, agricultural trailers and agricultural trailed appliances; and, in respect of items 1(b) and 2, buses)

1	2	3
Item	Wheel criteria	Maximum permitted weight (kg)
1	Two wheels in line transversely each of which is fitted with a wide tyre or with two pneumatic tyres having the centres of their areas of contact with the road not less than 300 mm apart, measured at right angles to the longitudinal axis of the vehicle— (a) if the wheels are on the sole driving axle of a motor vehicle not being a bus. (b) if the vehicle is a bus which has 2 axles and of which the weight transmitted to the road surface by its wheels is calculated in accordance with regulation 78(5), (c) in any other case	 10,500 10,500 10,170
2	Two wheels in line transversely otherwise than as mentioned in item 1	9,200
3	More than two wheels in line transversely— (a) in the case of a vehicle manufactured before 1st May 1983 [where] the wheels are on one axle of a group of closely spaced axles (b) in the case of a vehicle manufactured on or after 1st May 1983, (c) in any other case	 10,170 10,170 11,180
4	One wheel not transversely in line with any other wheel—	
	(a) if the wheel is fitted as described in item 1, (b) in any other case	5,090 4,600

PART II

(wheeled heavy motor cars, motor cars and trailers[2] not falling in Part I)

1	2	3
Item	Wheel criteria	Maximum permitted weight (kg)
5	More than two wheels transmitting weight to a strip of the road surface on which the vehicle rests contained between two parallel lines at right angles to the longitudinal axis of the vehicle— (a) less than 1.02 m apart, (b) 1.02 m or more apart but less than 1.22 m apart, (c) 1.22 m or more apart but less than 2.13 m apart	 11,180 16,260 18,300
6	Two wheels in line transversely	9,200
7	One wheel, where no other wheel is in the same line transversely.	4,600

PART III

(wheeled locomotives)

1	2	3
Item	Wheel criteria	Maximum permitted weight (kg)
8	Two wheels in line transversely (except in the case of a road roller, or a vehicle with not more than four wheels first used before 1st June 1955)	11,180
9	Any two wheels in the case of a wheeled locomotive having not more than four wheels first used before 1st June 1955 (not being a road roller or an agricultural motor vehicle which is not driven at more than 20 mph)	Three quarters of the total weight of the locomotive.

PART IV

(track-laying vehicles)

1	2	3
Item	Wheel criteria	Maximum permitted weight (kg)
10	The weight of a heavy motor car, motor car or trailer transmitted to any strip of the road surface on which the vehicle rests contained between two parallel lines 0.6 m apart at right angles to the longitudinal axis of the vehicle	10,170
11	Two wheels in line— (a) heavy motor cars or motor cars with 2 wheels, (b) heavy motor cars or motor cars with more than 2 wheels	 8,130 7,630
12	One wheel, where no other wheel is in the same line transversely, on a heavy motor car or a motor car	4,070

(3) In the case of an articulated bus, or, subject to paragraph (4), of a bus first used before 1st April 1988, the laden weight, for the purposes of regulation 75, and the weight transmitted to the road surface by wheels of the vehicle, for the purposes of items 1 and 2 of the Table in this regulation, shall be calculated with reference to the vehicle when it is complete and fully equipped for service with—

(a) a full supply of water, oil and fuel; and

(b) weights of 63.5 kg for each person (including crew)—

    (i) for whom a seat is provided in the position in which he may be seated; and

    (ii) who may by or under any enactment be carried standing, the total of such weights being reasonably distributed in the space in which such persons may be carried, save that in the case of a bus (not being an articulated bus) only the number of such persons exceeding 8 shall be taken into account.

(4) The weights for the purposes referred to in paragraph (3) may, in the case of a bus to which that paragraph applies, be calculated in accordance with paragraph (5) instead of paragraph (3).

(5) In the case of a bus first used on or after 1st April 1988, the weights for the purposes referred to in paragraph (3) shall be calculated with reference to the vehicle when it is complete and fully equipped for service with—

   (*a*) a full supply of water, oil and fuel;

   (*b*) a weight of 65 kg for each person (including crew)—

      (i) for whom a seat is provided, in the position in which he may be seated; and

      (ii) who may by or under any enactment be carried standing, the total of such weights being reasonably distributed in the space in which such persons may be so carried, save that in the case of a bus (not being an articulated bus) only the number of such persons exceeding 4 shall be taken into account;

   (*c*) all luggage space within the vehicle but not within the passenger compartment loaded at the rate of 100 kg per m₃ or 10 kg per person mentioned in sub-paragraph (*b*) above, whichever is the less; and

   (*d*) any area of the roof of the vehicle constructed or adapted for the storage of luggage loaded with a uniformly distributed load at the rate of 75 kg per m₂.

(6) Regulation 75 shall not apply to a two axle bus if—

   (*a*) its laden weight as calculated in accordance with paragraph (5) does not exceed 17,000 kg; and

   (*b*) the distance between the two axles is at least 3.0 m.

---

1. See note to reg 75, ante.
2. A composition trailer may be treated as one trailer; reg 3(11).

Maximum permitted weights for certain closely-spaced axles etc[1]

4–3589   **79.** (1) This regulation applies to—

   (*a*) a wheeled motor vehicle which complies with the relevant braking requirement;

   (*b*) a wheeled trailer which is drawn by such a motor vehicle; and

   (*c*) an agricultural motor vehicle, an agricultural trailer and an agricultural trailed appliance.

(2) Save as provided in paragraph (5), where a vehicle to which this regulation applies is of a description specified in an item in column 2 of Part V of Schedule 11 and has two closely-spaced axles, the total weight transmitted to the road surface by all the wheels of those axles shall not exceed the maximum permitted weight specified in column 3 of that item.

(3) Save as provided in paragraph (5), where a vehicle to which this regulation applies is of a description specified in an item in column 2 of Part VI of Schedule 11 and has three closely-spaced axles, the total weight transmitted to the road surface by all the wheels of those axles shall not exceed the weight specified in column 3.

(4) Save as provided by paragraph (5), where a vehicle is fitted with four or more closely-spaced axles, the weight transmitted to the road surface by all the wheels of those axles shall not exceed 24,000 kg.

(5) Nothing in paragraphs (2), (3) or (4) of this regulation shall apply so as to prevent a vehicle first used before 1st June 1973 from being used on a road at a weight as respects those axles at which it could be used if it fell within item 5 in the Table in regulation 78 and nothing in those paragraphs shall prevent a vehicle being used on a road if—

   (*a*) a plating certificate in respect of the vehicle was in force immediately before 1st January 1993; and

   (*b*) no axle has an axle weight exceeding the weight shown in that certificate as being the weight not to be exceeded in Great Britain for that axle.

(6) In Parts V and VI of Schedule 11, "air-suspension" "road friendly suspension" and "twin tyres" shall be construed in accordance with regulation 75(4), (5) and (6).

---

1. See note to reg 75, ante.

4–3589A   **79A. Saving for the Road Vehicles (Authorised Weight) Regulations 1998.** Nothing in regulations 75 to 79 shall be taken to prohibit the use of a vehicle in circumstances where the maximum authorised weight for the vehicle, for any vehicle combination of which the vehicle forms part and for any axle of the vehicle, as determined in accordance with the Road Vehicles (Authorised Weight) Regulations 1998, is not exceeded.

4–3590   **80[1].** (1) Subject to paragraphs (2), (2A) and (2B)[2], no person shall use, or cause or permit to be used, on a road a vehicle—

   (*a*) fitted with a plate in accordance with regulation 66, but for which no plating certificate has been issued, if any[3] of the weights shown on the plate is exceeded;

   (*b*) for which a plating certificate has been issued, if any[3] of the weights shown in column (2) of the plating certificate is exceeded; or

   (*c*) required by regulation 68 to be fitted with a plate, if the maximum gross weight referred to in paragraph (2)(*c*) of that regulation is exceeded.

(2) Where any two or more axles are fitted with a compensating arrangement in accordance with regulation 23 the sum of the weights shown for them in the plating certificate shall not be

exceeded. In a case where a plating certificate has not been issued the sum of the weights referred to shall be that shown for the said axles in the plate fitted in accordance with regulation 66.

(2A) Paragraph (1) shall not apply to a vehicle for which a plating certificate has been issued in the form set out in Schedule 10A or 10C where—

(a) the vehicle is being used for international transport; and

(b) none of the weights shown in column (3) of the plating certificate is exceeded.

(2B) Where both a train weight and a maximum train weight are shown in column (2) of a plating certificate issued for a motor vehicle, paragraph (1)(b) in so far as it relates to train weights shall not apply to the motor vehicle if—

(a) the motor vehicle is a wheeled heavy motor car drawing a wheeled trailer and the requirements set out in Part II of Schedule 11A are for the time being fulfilled; or

(b) the motor vehicle is comprised in an articulated vehicle and the requirements set out in Part III of Schedule 11A are for the time being fulfilled,

and the train weight of the motor vehicle does not exceed the maximum train weight shown in column (2) of the certificate.

(3) Nothing in regulations 75 to 79 or in the Road Vehicles (Authorised Weight) Regulations 1998[4] shall permit any such weight as is mentioned in the preceding provisions of this regulation to be exceeded and nothing in this regulation shall permit any weight prescribed by regulations 75 to 79 or in the Road Vehicles (Authorised Weight) Regulations 1998 in relation to the vehicle in question to be exceeded.

(4) Paragraph (1) shall not apply where a vehicle is used on a road before 1st January 2000 if—

(a) the vehicle is fitted with a plate in accordance with regulation 66(1)(b) and the maximum gross weight and the maximum weight for any axle of the vehicle are not exceeded; or

(b) there is in force a plating certificate for the vehicle that was issued before 1st January 1999 and the design weight of the vehicle is not exceeded; and

(c) in either case the maximum authorised weight for the vehicle, maximum authorised weight for a combination of which the vehicle forms part and maximum authorised weight for any axle of the vehicle, determined in accordance with the Road Vehicles (Authorised Weight) Regulations 1998, are not exceeded.

---

1. See note to reg 75, ante.

2. This imports into para (1) the qualifications in para (2); the two paragraphs do not create distinct offences, and the offence would be committed under para (1) (*DPP v Marshall and Bell* (1990) 154 JP 508, DC).

3. It is possible that the facts may support simultaneous convictions for exceeding the maximum gross weight and for exceeding one or more maximum axle weights; *J Theobald (Hounslow) Ltd v Stacy* [1979] RTR 411, [1979] Crim LR 595; and see *Travel-Gas (Midlands) Ltd v Reynolds* [1989] RTR 75, DC.

4. In this title, post.

B—DIMENSIONS OF LADEN VEHICLES

Restrictions on use of vehicles carrying wide or long loads or having fixed appliances or apparatus

4–3591 **81.** For the purposes of this regulation, regulation 82 and Schedule 12—

(a) "lateral projection", in relation to a load carried by a vehicle, means that part of the load which extends beyond a side of the vehicle;

(b) the width of any lateral projection shall be measured between longitudinal planes passing through the extreme projecting point of the vehicle on that side on which the projection lies and that part of the projection furthest from that point;

(c) references to a special appliance or apparatus, in relation to a vehicle, are references to any crane or other special appliance or apparatus fitted to the vehicle which is a permanent or essentially permanent fixture;

(d) "forward projection" and "rearward projection"—

(i) in relation to a load carried in such a manner that its weight is borne by only one vehicle, mean respectively that part of the load which extends beyond the foremost point of the vehicle and that part which extends beyond the rearmost point of the vehicle;

(ii) in relation to a load carried in such a manner that part of its weight is borne by more than one vehicle, mean respectively that part of the load which extends beyond the foremost point of the foremost vehicle by which the load is carried except where the context otherwise requires and that part of the load which extends beyond the rearmost point of the rearmost vehicle by which the load is carried; and

(iii) in relation to any special appliance or apparatus, mean respectively that part of the appliance or apparatus which, if it were deemed to be a load carried by the vehicle, would be a part of a load extending beyond the foremost point of the vehicle and that part which would be a part of a load extending beyond the rearmost point of the vehicle,

and references in regulation 82 and Schedule 12 to a forward projection or to a rearward projection in relation to a vehicle shall be construed accordingly;

(e) the length of any forward projection or of any rearward projection shall be measured between transverse planes passing—

(i)   in the case of a forward projection, through the foremost point of the vehicle and that part of the projection furthest from that point; and

(ii)   in the case of a rearward projection, through the rearmost point of the vehicle and that part of the projection furthest from that point.

In this and the foregoing sub-paragraph "vehicle" does not include any special appliance or apparatus or any part thereof which is a forward projection or a rearward projection;

(f)   references to the distance between vehicles, in relation to vehicles carrying a load, are references to the distance between the nearest points of any two adjacent vehicles by which the load is carried, measured when the longitudinal axis of each vehicle lies in the same vertical plane.

For the purposes of this sub-paragraph, in determining the nearest point of two vehicles any part of either vehicle designed primarily for use as a means of attaching the one vehicle to the other and any fitting designed for use in connection with any such part shall be disregarded;

(g)   references to a combination of vehicles, in relation to a motor vehicle which is drawing one or more trailers, are references to the motor vehicle and the trailer or trailers drawn thereby, including any other motor vehicle which is used for the purpose of assisting in the propulsion of the trailer or the trailers on the road;

(h)   the overall length of a combination of vehicles shall be taken as the distance between the foremost point of the drawing vehicle comprised in the combination and the rearmost point of the rearmost vehicle comprised therein, measured when the longitudinal axis of each vehicle comprised in the combination lies in the same vertical plane;

(i)   the extreme projecting point of a vehicle is the point from which the overall width of the vehicle is calculated in accordance with the definition of overall width contained in regulation 3(2);

(j)   without prejudice to sub-paragraph (e) the foremost or, as the case may be, the rearmost point of a vehicle is the foremost or rearmost point from which the overall length of the vehicle is calculated in accordance with the definition of overall length contained in regulation 3(2); and

(k)   an agricultural, horticultural or forestry implement rigidly but not permanently mounted on an agricultural motor vehicle, agricultural trailer or agricultural trailed appliance, whether or not part of its weight is supported by one or more of its own wheels, shall not be treated as a load, or special appliance, on that vehicle.

4–3592   **82.**—(1) No load shall be carried on a vehicle so that the overall width of the vehicle together with the width of any lateral projection or projections of its load exceeds 4.3 m.

(2) Subject to the following provisions of this regulation, no load shall be carried on a vehicle so that—

(a)   the load has a lateral projection or projections on either side exceeding 305 mm; or

(b)   the overall width of the vehicle and of any lateral projection or projections of its load exceeds 2.9 m.

Provided that this paragraph does not apply to the carriage of—

(i)   loose agricultural produce not baled or crated; or

(ii)   an indivisible load if—

(A)   it is not reasonably practicable to comply with this paragraph and the conditions specified in paragraphs 1 and 5 of Schedule 12 are complied with; and

(B)   where the overall width of the vehicle together with the width of any lateral projection or projections of its load exceeds 3.5 m, the conditions specified in paragraph 2 of Schedule 12 are complied with.

(3) Where a load is carried so that its weight rests on a vehicle or vehicles, the length specified in paragraph (5) shall not exceed 27.4 m.

(4) A load shall not be carried so that its weight is borne by a vehicle or vehicles if either—

(a)   the length specified in paragraph (5) exceeds 18.65 m; or

(b)   the load is borne by a trailer or trailers and the length specified in paragraph (6) exceeds 25.9 m,

unless the conditions specified in paragraphs 1 and 2 of Part I of Schedule 12 are complied with.

(5) The length referred to in paragraphs (3) and (4)(a) is—

(a)   where the weight of the load is borne by a single vehicle, the overall length of the vehicle together with the length of any forward and rearward projection of the load;

(b)   where the weight of the load is borne by a motor vehicle and one trailer, whether or not forming an articulated vehicle, the overall length of the trailer together with the length of any projection of the load in front of the foremost point of the trailer and of any rearward projection of the load; and

(c)   in any other case, the overall length of all the vehicles which bears the weight of the load, together with the length of any distance between them and of any forward or rearward projection of the load.

(6) The length referred to in paragraph (4)(b) is the overall length of the combination of vehicles, together with the length of any forward or rearward projection of the load.

(7) Subject to the following provisions of this regulation no person shall use, or cause or permit to be used, on a road a vehicle, not being a straddle carrier, carrying a load or fitted with a

special appliance or apparatus if the load, appliance or apparatus has a forward projection of a length specified in an item in column 2 of the Table, or rearward projection of a length specified in an item in column 3, unless the conditions specified in that item in column 4 are complied with.

TABLE

(regulation 82(7))

1	2	3	4	
Item	Length of forward projection	Length of rearward projection	Conditions to be complied with	
			(a) if the load consists of a racing boat propelled solely by oars.	(b) in any other case
1	Exceeding 1 m but not exceeding 2 m		Para 4 of Schedule 12	
2	Exceeding 2 m but not exceeding 3.05 m		Para 4 of Schedule 12	Paras 2 and 3 of Schedule 12
3	Exceeding 3.05 m		Paras 1 and 4 of Schedule 12	Paras 1, 2 and 3 of Schedule 12
4		Exceeding 1 m but not exceeding 2 m	Para 4 of Schedule 12	Para 4 of Schedule 12
5		Exceeding 2 m but not exceeding 3.05 m	Para 4 of Schedule 12	Para 3 of Schedule 12
6		Exceeding 3.05 m	Paras 1 and 4 of Schedule 12	Paras 1, 2 and 3 of Schedule 12

(8) Subject to the following provisions of this regulation, no person shall use, or cause or permit to be used, on a road a straddle carrier carrying a load if—

(a) the load has a rearward projection exceeding 1 m unless the conditions specified in paragraph 4 of Schedule 12 are met;

(b) the load has a forward projection exceeding 2 m or a rearward projection exceeding 3 m; or

(c) the overall length of the vehicle together with the length of any forward projection and of any rearward projection of its load exceeds 12.2 m

Provided that—

(i) sub-paragraph (a) does not apply to a vehicle being used in passing from one part of private premises to another part thereof or to other private premises in the immediate neighbourhood;

(ii) sub-paragraphs (b) and (c) do not apply to a vehicle being used as in proviso (i) above if—

(A) the vehicle is not being driven at a speed exceeding 12 mph; and

(B) where the overall length of the vehicle together with the length of any forward projection and of any rearward projection of its loads exceeds 12.2 m, the conditions specified in paragraphs 1 and 2 of Schedule 12 are complied with.

(9) Where another vehicle is attached to that end of a vehicle from which a projection extends, then for the purposes of any requirement in this regulation to comply with paragraph 3 or 4 of Schedule 12, that projection shall be treated as a forward or rearward projection only if, and to the extent that it extends beyond the foremost point or, as the case may be, the rearmost point, of that other vehicle, measured when the longitudinal axis of each vehicle lies in the same vertical plane.

(10) In the case of a vehicle being used—

(a) for fire brigade or, in England, fire and rescue authority, ambulance or police purposes or for defence purposes (including civil defence purposes); or

(b) in connection with the removal of any obstruction to traffic,

if compliance with any provision of this regulation would hinder or be likely to hinder the use of the vehicle for the purpose for which it is being used, that provision does not apply to that vehicle while it is being so used.

(11) No person shall use, or cause or permit to be used, on a road an agricultural, horticultural or forestry implement rigidly, but not permanently, mounted on a wheeled agricultural motor vehicle, agricultural trailer, or agricultural trailed appliance, whether or not part of its weight is supported by one or more of its own wheels if—

(a) the overall width of the vehicle together with the lateral projection of the implement exceeds 2.55 m; or

(b) the implement projects more than 1 m forwards or rearwards of the vehicle, so however, that this restriction shall not apply in a case where—

   (i)   part of the weight of the implement is supported by one or more of its own wheels; and

   (ii)   the longitudinal axis of the greater part of the implement is capable of articulating in the horizontal plane in relation to the longitudinal axis of the rear portion of the vehicle.

C—TRAILERS AND SIDECARS
Number of trailers

4–3593   **83.** (1) No person shall use, or cause or permit to be used, on a road a wheeled vehicle of a class specified in an item in column 2 of the Table drawing a trailer[1], subject to any exceptions which may be specified in that item in column 3.

TABLE

(regulation 83(1))

1	2	3
Item	Class of vehicles	Exceptions
1	A straddle carrier	—
2	An invalid carriage	—
3	An articulated bus	—
4	A bus not being an articulated bus or a mini-bus	(a) 1 broken down bus where no person other than the driver is carried in either vehicle or (b) 1 trailer
5	A locomotive	3 trailers
6	A motor tractor	1 trailer 2 trailers if neither is laden
7	A heavy motor car or a motor car not described in item 1, 3 or 4	2 trailers if one of them is a towing implement and part of the other is secured to and either rests on or is suspended from that implement 1 trailer in any other case
8	An agricultural motor vehicle	(a) in respect of trailers other than agricultural trailers and agricultural trailed appliances, such trailers as are permitted under items 5, 6, or 7 above, as the case may be; or (b) in respect of agricultural trailers and agricultural trailed appliances— (i) 2 unladen agricultural trailers, or (ii) 1 agricultural trailer and 1 agricultural trailed appliance, or (iii) 2 agricultural trailed appliances

(2) For the purposes of items 5, 6 and 7 of the Table—

   (a)   an unladen articulated vehicle, when being drawn by another motor vehicle because it has broken down, shall be treated as a single trailer, and

   (b)   a towed roller used for the purposes of agriculture, horticulture or forestry and consisting of several separate rollers shall be treated as one agricultural trailed appliance.

(3) No track-laying motor vehicle which exceeds 8 m in overall length shall draw a trailer other than a broken down vehicle which is being drawn in consequence of the breakdown.

(4) For the purpose of this regulation, the word "trailer" does not include a vehicle which is drawn by a steam powered vehicle and which is used solely for carrying water for the purpose of the drawing vehicle.

---

1. Provisions relating to trailers do not apply to any part of an articulated bus; reg 3(9).
  In this regulation a composition trailer may be treated as one trailer; reg 3(11).

Trailers drawn by motor cycles

4–3594   **84.** (1) Save as provided in paragraph (2), no person shall use, or cause or permit to be used, on a road a motor cycle—

   (a)   drawing behind it more than one trailer;

   (b)   drawing behind it any trailer carrying a passenger;

   (c)   drawing behind it a trailer with an unladen weight exceeding 254 kg;

   (d)   with not more than 2 wheels, without a sidecar, and with an engine capacity which does not exceed 125 cc, drawing behind it any trailer; or

   (e)   with not more than 2 wheels, without a sidecar and with an engine capacity exceeding 125 cc, drawing behind it any trailer unless—

      (i)   the trailer has an overall width not exceeding 1 m;

(ii) the distance between the rear axle of the motor cycle and the rearmost part of the trailer does not exceed 2·5 m;

(iii) the motor cycle is clearly and indelibly marked in a conspicuous and readily accessible position with its kerbside weight;

(iv) the trailer is clearly and indelibly marked in a conspicuous and readily accessible position with its unladen weight; and

(v) the laden weight of the trailer does not exceed 150 kg or two thirds of the kerbside weight of the motor cycle, whichever is the less.

(2) The provisions of paragraph (1)(*b*), (*d*) and (*e*) do not apply if the trailer is a broken down motorcycle and one passenger is riding it.

Trailers drawn by agricultural motor vehicles

4–3595 85. (1) No person shall use, or cause or permit to be used, on a road a wheeled agricultural motor vehicle drawing one or more wheeled trailers if the weight of the drawing vehicle is less than a quarter of the weight of the trailer or trailers, unless the brakes fitted to each trailer in compliance with regulation 15 or 16 are operated directly by the service braking system fitted to the motor vehicle.

(2) No person shall use, or cause or permit to be used, on a road, any motor vehicle drawing an agricultural trailer of which—

(*a*) more than 35% of the weight is borne by the drawing vehicle; or

(*b*) the gross weight exceeds 14,230 kg, unless it is fitted with brakes as mentioned in paragraph (1).

(3) No person shall use, or cause or permit to be used, on a road an agricultural trailer manufactured on or after 1st December 1985 which is drawn by a motor vehicle first used on or after 1st June 1986 unless the brakes fitted to the trailer—

(*a*) in accordance with regulation 15 can be applied progressively by the driver of the drawing vehicle, from his normal driving position and while keeping proper control of that vehicle, using a means of operation mounted on the drawing vehicle; or

(*b*) automatically come into operation on the over-run of the trailer.

Distance between motor vehicles and trailers

4–3596 86. (1) Where a trailer[1] is attached to the vehicle immediately in front of it solely by means of a rope or chain, the distance between the trailer and that vehicle shall not in any case exceed 4·5 m, and shall not exceed 1·5 m unless the rope or chain is made clearly visible to any other person using the road within a reasonable distance from either side.

(2) For the purpose of determining the said distance any part of either vehicle designed primarily for use as a means of attaching the one vehicle to the other and any fitting designed for use in connection with any such part shall be disregarded.

---

1. Provisions relating to trailers do not apply to any part of an articulated bus; reg 3(9).

Use of secondary coupling on trailers

4–3596A 86A. (1) No person shall use or cause or permit to be used on a road a motor vehicle drawing one trailer if the trailer—

(*a*) is a trailer to which regulation 15 applies; and

(*b*) is not fitted with a device which is designed to stop the trailer automatically in the event of the separation of the main coupling while the trailer is in motion,

unless the requirements of paragraph (2) are met in relation to the motor vehicle and trailer.

(2) The requirements of this paragraph, in relation to a motor vehicle drawing a trailer, are that a secondary coupling is attached to the motor vehicle and trailer in such a way that, in the event of the separation of the main coupling while the trailer is in motion—

(*a*) the drawbar of the trailer would be prevented from touching the ground; and

(*b*) there would be some residual steering of the trailer.

(3) No person shall use or cause or permit to be used on a road a motor vehicle drawing one trailer if—

(*a*) the trailer is a trailer to which regulation 15 applies;

(*b*) the trailer is fitted with a device which is designed to stop the trailer automatically in the event of the separation of the main coupling while the trailer is in motion;

(*c*) the operation of the device in those circumstances depends upon a secondary coupling linking the device to the motor vehicle; and

(*d*) the trailer is not also fitted with a device which is designed to stop the trailer automatically in those circumstances in the absence of such a secondary coupling.

unless the requirements of paragraph (4) are met in relation to the motor vehicle and trailer.

(4) The requirements of this paragraph, in relation to a motor vehicle drawing a trailer, are that the secondary coupling is attached to the motor vehicle and trailer in such a way that, in the event of the separation of the main coupling while the trailer is in motion, the device of the kind referred to in paragraph 3(*b*) and (*c*) fitted to the trailer would stop the trailer.

(5) This regulation is without prejudice to any other provision in these Regulations.

Use of mechanical coupling devices

4–3596B   86B. (1) This regulation applies to every light passenger vehicle first used on or after 1st August 1998 in respect of which an EC certificate of conformity has effect.

(2) No person shall use or cause or permit to be used on a road any vehicle to which this regulation applies unless any mechanical coupling device which is attached to it complies with the relevant technical and installation requirements of Annexes I, V, VI and VII of Community Directive 94/20 and is marked in accordance with sub-paragraphs 3.3.4 to 3.3.5 of Annex I to that Directive.

(3) For the purposes of this regulation, in a case where a vehicle is drawing a trailer a mechanical coupling device shall not be regarded as being attached to that vehicle if it forms part of the trailer.

(4) In this regulation "mechanical coupling device" shall be construed in accordance with paragraph 2.1 of Annex I to Community Directive 94/20.

4–3597   87. (1) Save as provided in paragraph (2), no person shall use, or cause or permit to be used, on a road an unbraked wheeled trailer[1]; if

    (*a*) its laden weight exceeds its maximum gross weight; or
    (*b*) it is drawn by a vehicle of which the kerbside weight is less than twice the sum of the unladen weight of the trailer and the weight of any load which the trailer is carrying.

(2) This regulation does not apply to—

    (*a*) an agricultural trailer; or
    (*b*) a trailer mentioned in paragraphs (*b*), (*bb*), (*bc*), (*c*), (*d*), (*e*), (*f*) or (*g*) of reg 16(3).

---
1. Provisions relating to trailers do not apply to any part of an articulated bus; reg 3(9).

Use of bridging plates between motor vehicle and trailer

4–3598   88. *Revoked.*

Leaving trailers at rest

4–3599   89. No person in charge of a motor vehicle, or trailer drawn thereby, shall cause or permit such trailer[1] to stand on a road when detached from the drawing vehicle unless one at least of the wheels of the trailer is (or, in the case of a track-laying trailer, its tracks are) prevented from revolving by the setting of a parking brake or the use of a chain, chock or other efficient device.

---
1. Provisions relating to trailers do not apply to any part of an articulated bus; reg 3(9).

Passengers in trailers

4–3600   90. (1) Save as provided in paragraph (2), no person shall use, or cause or permit to be used, on a road any trailer[1] for the carriage of passengers for hire or reward.

(2) The provisions of paragraph (1) do not apply in respect of a wheeled trailer which is, or is carrying, a broken down motor vehicle if—

    (*a*) the trailer is drawn at a speed not exceeding 30 mph; and
    (*b*) where the trailer is, or is carrying, a broken down bus, it is attached to the drawing vehicle by a rigid draw bar.

(3) Save as provided in paragraph (4), no person shall use, or cause or permit to be used, on a road a wheeled trailer in which any person is carried and which is a living van having either—

    (*a*) less than 4 wheels; or
    (*b*) 4 wheels consisting of two close-coupled wheels on each side.

(4) The provisions of paragraph (3) do not apply in respect of a trailer which is being tested by—

    (*a*) its manufacturer;
    (*b*) a person by whom it has been, or is being, repaired; or
    (*c*) a distributor of, or dealer in, trailers.

---
1. Provisions relating to trailers do not apply to any part of an articulated bus; reg 3(9).

Attachment of sidecars

4–3602   92. Every sidecar fitted to a motor cycle shall be so attached that the wheel thereof is not wholly outside the space between transverse planes passing through the extreme projecting points at the front and at the rear of the motor cycle.

Use of sidecars

4–3603   93. No person shall use or cause or permit to be used on a road any two-wheeled motor cycle registered on or after 1st August 1981, not being a motor cycle brought temporarily into Great Britain by a person resident abroad, if there is a sidecar attached to the right (or off) side of the motor cycle.

CA—USE OF MOTOR VEHICLES FOR THE CARRIAGE OR HAULAGE OF DANGEROUS GOODS

Additional braking requirements for motor vehicles carrying or hauling dangerous goods

4–3603A   93A. (1) Subject to paragraph (5), no person shall use or cause or permit to be used a motor vehicle for the carriage or haulage of dangerous goods on a road if it is a vehicle within the meaning of the Framework Directive and—

(a)   its maximum gross weight exceeds 16,000 kg; or

(b)   it is drawing a trailer which has a maximum total design axle weight exceeding 10,000 kg,

unless the vehicle meets the requirements of paragraph (2).

(2) Subject to paragraph (6), in order for a motor vehicle to meet the requirements of this paragraph—

(a)   it must not be drawing more than one trailer;

(b)   without prejudice to regulation 15, it must be fitted with an anti-lock braking system that meets the requirements of paragraph (1) of marginal 220 521 of Appendix B.2 to Annex B to the ADR;

(c)   it must be fitted with an endurance braking system (which may consist of one device or a combination of several devices) that meets the requirements of sub-paragraphs (a) to (d) of paragraph (2) of marginal 220 522 of Appendix B.2 to Annex B to the ADR;

(d)   if it is not drawing a trailer, it must meet the requirements of the 4th, 5th, 6th and 7th sub-paragraphs of paragraph (2) of marginal 10 221 of Annex B to the ADR;

(e)   without prejudice to regulation 15, if it is drawing a trailer with a maximum total design axle weight exceeding 10,000 kg—

(i)   the trailer must be fitted with an anti-lock braking system that meets the requirements of paragraph (2) of marginal 220 521 of Appendix B.2 to Annex B to the ADR, and

(ii)   the electrical connections between the motor vehicle and the trailer must meet the requirements of paragraph (3) of marginal 220 521 of Appendix B.2 to Annex B to the ADR;

(f)   if it is drawing a trailer, the combination of vehicles must meet the requirements of the 4th, 5th, 6th and 7th sub-paragraphs of paragraph (2) of marginal 10 221 of Annex B to the ADR;

(g)   if it is drawing a trailer fitted with an endurance braking system, the trailer must meet the requirements of paragraph (3) of marginal 220 522 of Appendix B.2 to Annex B to the ADR; and

(h)   if it is drawing a trailer, the requirements of either paragraph (3) or (4) must be met.

(3) The requirements of this paragraph are that the motor vehicle meets the requirements of paragraph (2)(e) of marginal 220 522 of Appendix B.2 to Annex B to the ADR.

(4) The requirements of this paragraph are that the motor vehicle—

(a)   does not contravene the restriction mentioned in sub-paragraph (f) of paragraph (2) of marginal 220 522 of Appendix B.2 to Annex B to the ADR; and

(b)   meets the requirements of the second sentence of that sub-paragraph in relation to the trailer.

(5) Paragraph (1) does not apply to a motor vehicle manufactured before 1st January 1997.

(6) Sub-paragraph (e) of paragraph (2) does not apply to a trailer manufactured before 1st January 1997.

(7) For the purposes of this regulation, Annex B to the ADR (including the Appendices to that Annex) shall have effect as if—

(a)   references to ECE Regulation 13 (however expressed) were references to ECE Regulation 13.06 or 13.07;

(b)   references to Directive 71/320/EEC were references to Community Directive 91/422;

(c)   references to the corresponding EEC Directive, in relation to Annex 5 to ECE Regulation 13, were references to paragraph 1.5 of Annex II to the Community Directive 91/422.

(8) Subject to paragraph (9), a reference in this regulation to dangerous goods is a reference to a load comprising explosives of such type and in such quantity that it could not be carried by road in a single transport unit of Type I and II without there being a contravention of the restrictions set out in marginal 11 401 of Annex B to the ADR as read with marginal 11 402 of that Annex.

(9) For the purposes of paragraph (8)—

(a)   marginal 11 402 of Annex B to the ADR shall have effect with the omission of the words "in conformity with the prohibitions of mixed loading contained in 11 403"; and

(b)   "transport unit of Type I or II" means a transport unit of Type I or a transport of Type II as defined in marginal 11 204 of that Annex.

(10) In this regulation, "ADR" means the 1995 edition of the "European Agreement concerning the International Carriage of Dangerous Goods by Road (ADR)" produced by the Department of Transport and published by Her Majesty's Stationery Office (ISBN 0-11-551265-9).

Use of gas propulsion systems

4–3604   94. (1) No person shall use, or cause or permit to be used, on a road a vehicle with a gas propulsion system unless the whole of such system is in a safe condition.

(2) No person shall use, or cause or permit to be used, in any gas supply system for the propulsion of a vehicle when the vehicle is on a road any fuel except liquefied petroleum gas.

(3) No person shall use, or cause or permit to be used, on a road a vehicle which is propelled

by gas unless the gas container in which such fuel is stored is on the motor vehicle, and not on any trailer, and in the case of an articulated vehicle on the portion of the vehicle to which the engine is fitted.

(4) In this regulation and in regulation 95 "liquefied petroleum gas" means—

(a) butane gas in any phase which meets the requirements contained in the specification of commercial butane and propane issued by the British Standards Institution under the number BS4250:1975 and published on 29th August 1975; or

(b) propane gas in any phase which meets the requirements contained in the said specification; or

(c) any mixture of such butane gas and such propane gas.

Use of gas-fired appliances—general

4–3605   **95.** (1) No person shall use, or cause or permit to be used, in or on a vehicle on a road any gas-fired appliance unless the whole of such appliance and the gas system attached thereto is in an efficient and safe condition.

(2) No person shall use, or cause or permit to be used, in any gas-fired appliance in or on a vehicle on a road any fuel except liquefied petroleum gas as defined in regulation 94(4).

(3) No person shall use, or cause or permit to be used, in or on a vehicle on a road any gas-fired appliance unless the vehicle is so ventilated that—

(a) an ample supply of air is available for the operation of the appliance;

(b) the use of the appliance does not adversely affect the health or comfort of any person using the vehicle; and

(c) any unburnt gas is safely disposed of to the outside of the vehicle.

(4) No person shall use, or cause or permit to be used, on a road a vehicle in or on which there is—

(a) one gas-fired appliance unless the gas supply for such appliance is shut off at the point where it leaves the container or containers at all times when the appliance is not in use;

(b) more than one gas-fired appliance each of which has the same supply of gas unless the gas supply for such appliances is shut off at the point where it leaves the container or containers at all times when none of such appliances is in use; or

(c) more than one gas-fired appliance each of which does not have the same supply of gas unless each gas supply for such appliances is shut off at the point where it leaves the container or containers at all times when none of such appliances which it supplies is in use.

Use of gas-fired appliances when a vehicle is in motion

4–3606   **96.** (1) Subject to paragraph (2), this regulation applies to every motor vehicle and trailer.

(2) Paragraphs (3) and (4) do not apply to a vehicle constructed or adapted for the conveyance of goods under controlled temperatures.

(3) No person shall use, or cause or permit to be used, in any vehicle to which this paragraph applies, while the vehicle is in motion on a road, any gas-fired appliance except—

(a) a gas-fired appliance which is fitted to engineering plant while the plant is being used for the purposes of the engineering operations for which it was designed;

(b) a gas-fired appliance which is permanently attached to a bus, provided that any appliance for heating or cooling the interior of the bus for the comfort of the driver and any passengers does not expose a naked flame on the outside of the appliance; or

(c) in any other vehicle, a refrigerating appliance or an appliance which does not expose a naked flame on the outside of the appliance and which is permanently attached to the vehicle and designed for the purpose of heating any part of the interior of the vehicle for the comfort of the driver and any passengers.

(4) No person shall use, or cause or permit to be used, in any vehicle to which this paragraph applies, while the vehicle is in motion on a road, any gas-fired appliance to which—

(a) sub-paragraph (3)(a) refers, unless the appliance complies with the requirements specified in paragraphs 12 and 13 of Schedule 5 and the gas system to which it is attached complies with the requirements specified in paragraphs 2 to 9 and 15 of Schedule 5; or

(b) sub-paragraph (3)(b) refers, unless the appliance complies with the requirements specified in paragraphs 12, 13 and 14 of Schedule 5 and the gas system to which it is attached complies with the requirements specified in paragraphs 2 to 9, 11 and 15 of Schedule 5; or

(c) sub-paragraph (3)(c) refers, unless the appliance complies—

    (i) if it is fitted to a motor vehicle, with the requirements specified in paragraphs 12, 13 and 14 of Schedule 5; and

    (ii) in any other case, with the requirements specified in paragraphs 12 and 13 of Schedule 5;

and the gas system to which the appliance is attached complies with the requirements specified in paragraphs 2 to 9 and 15 of Schedule 5.

(5) No person shall use, or cause or permit to be used, in a vehicle to which this regulation applies which is in motion on a road any gas-fired appliance unless it is fitted with a valve which stops the supply of gas to the appliance if the appliance fails to perform its function and causes gas to be emitted.

E—CONTROL OF NOISE

Avoidance of excessive noise

4–3607   97. No motor vehicle shall be used on a road in such manner as to cause any excessive noise which could have been avoided by the exercise of reasonable care on the part of the driver[1].

---

1. Every vehicle propelled by an internal combustion engine shall be fitted with a silencer; reg 54.

Stopping of engine when stationary

4–3608   98. (1) Save as provided in paragraph (2), the driver[1] of a vehicle shall, when the vehicle is stationary, stop the action of any machinery attached to or forming part of the vehicle so far as may be necessary for the prevention of noise or of exhaust emissions.

(2) the provisions of paragraph (1) do not apply—

(a)   when the vehicle is stationary owing to the necessities of traffic;

(b)   so as to prevent the examination or working of the machinery where the examination is necessitated by any failure or derangement of the machinery or where the machinery is required to be worked for a purpose other than driving the vehicle; or

(c)   in respect of a vehicle propelled by gas produced in plant carried on the vehicle, to such plant.

---

1. The word "driver" has been extended to include a steersman; Road Traffic Act 1972, s 196(1).

Use of audible warning instruments

4–3609   99. (1) Subject to the following paragraphs, no person shall sound, or cause or permit to be sounded, any horn, gong, bell or siren fitted to or carried on a vehicle which is—

(a)   stationary on a road, at any time, other than at times of danger due to another moving vehicle on or near the road; or

(b)   in motion on a restricted road, between 23.30 hours and 07.00 hours in the following morning.

(2) The provisions of paragraph (1)(a) do not apply in respect of the sounding of a reversing alarm when the vehicle to which it is fitted is about to move backwards and its engine is running or in respect of the sounding of a boarding aid alarm.

(3) No person shall sound, or cause or permit to be sounded, on a road any reversing alarm or any boarding aid alarm fitted to a vehicle—

(a)   unless the vehicle is a goods vehicle which has a maximum gross weight not less than 2000 kg, a bus, engineering plant, a refuse vehicle, or a works truck; or

(b)   if the sound of the alarm is likely to be confused with a sound emitted in the operation of a pedestrian crossing established, or having effect as if established, under Part III of the 1984 Act.

(4) Subject to the provisions of the following paragraphs, no person shall sound, or cause or permit to be sounded a gong, bell, siren or two-tone horn, fitted to or otherwise carried on a vehicle (whether it is stationary or not).

(5) Nothing in paragraph (1) or (4) shall prevent the sounding of—

(a)   an instrument or apparatus fitted to, or otherwise carried on, a vehicle at a time when the vehicle is being used for one of the purposes specified in regulation 37(5) and it is necessary or desirable to do so either to indicate to other road users the urgency of the purposes for which the vehicle is being used, or to warn other road users of the presence of the vehicle on the road; or

(b)   a horn (not being a two-tone horn), bell, gong or siren—

(i)   to raise alarm as to the theft or attempted theft of the vehicle or its contents; or

(ii)   in the case of a bus, to summons help for the driver, the conductor or an inspector.

(6) Subject to the provisions of section 62 of the Control of Pollution Act 1974 and notwithstanding the provisions of paragraphs (1) and (4) above, a person may, between 12.00 hours and 19.00 hours, sound or cause or permit to be sounded an instrument or apparatus, other than a two-tone horn, fitted to or otherwise carried on a vehicle, being an instrument or apparatus designed to emit a sound for the purpose of informing members of the public that the vehicle is conveying goods for sale, if, when the apparatus or instrument is sounded, it is sounded only for that purpose.

(7) For the purposes of this regulation the expressions which are referred to in regulation 37(10) have the meanings there given to them and the expression "restricted road" in paragraph (1) means a road which is a restricted road for the purpose of section 81 of the 1984 Act.

Maintenance and use of vehicle so as not to be a danger, etc

4–3651   100. (1) A motor vehicle, every trailer drawn thereby and all parts and accessories of such vehicle[1] and trailer[2] shall at all times be in such condition[3], and the number of passengers carried by such vehicle or trailer, the manner in which any passengers are carried in or on such vehicle or trailer, and the weight, distribution, packing and adjustment of the load[4] of such vehicle or trailer shall at all times be such, that no danger is caused or is likely to be caused to any person in or on the vehicle or trailer or on a road.

Provided that the provisions of this regulation with regard to the number of passengers carried shall not apply to a vehicle to which the Public Service Vehicles (Carrying Capacity) Regulations 1984 apply.

(2)[5] The load carried by a motor vehicle or trailer shall at all times be so secured, if necessary by physical restraint other than its own weight, and be in such a position, that neither danger nor nuisance is likely to be caused[6] to any person or property by reason of the load or any part thereof falling[7] or being blown from the vehicle or by reason of any other movement of the load or any part thereof in relation to the vehicle[8].

(3) No motor vehicle or trailer shall be used for any purpose for which it is so unsuitable[9] as to cause or be likely to cause danger or nuisance to any person in or on the vehicle or trailer or on a road.

---

1. A container carried on the flat back of a lorry was held to be a part of the vehicle even though it was so warped that it could not be fastened to the flat back; *Bindley v Willett* [1981] RTR 19. The regulation applies to a vehicle which in its manufactured condition is inherently likely to cause danger to a person on a road as well as to one which has become dangerous through defective maintenance (*Wood v Milne* (1987) Times, 27 March). Whether the condition of a vehicle is dangerous is a matter for the justices, to determine each case as it arises having regard to all the circumstances. Accordingly where a car veered to the wrong side of the road and collided with a tractor which had its front link arms lowered and protruding more than in the raised position with the result that the driver of the car was killed, the justices were within their discretion in determining that the tractor was not in a dangerous condition (*DPP v Potts* [2000] RTR 1, DC).

2. The use of a defective trailer constitutes a separate offence, even when it is being drawn by a motor vehicle, and should be charged as such in accordance with s 42(1) of the Road Traffic Act 1988; see *NFC Forwarding Ltd v DPP* [1989] RTR 239, [1989] Crim LR 377, DC. When considering whether a trailer was used by a company ownership of the bed, stanchions and span sets use to secure a load of pipes was held to be of little significance without possession of the trailer itself (*DPP v Seawheel Ltd* [1993] Crim LR 707).

3. The information must charge the defects alleged by giving specific particulars of the parts and accessories not maintained in good condition; *Simmons v Fowler* (1950) 48 LGR 623. Good condition includes efficient working order, thus the inefficient joining of two parts of a tow-bar connecting a vehicle and a trailer is caught by the regulation; *O'Neill v Brown* [1961] 1 QB 420, [1961] 1 All ER 571, 125 JP 225. Alteration to exhaust pipes has also been held to fall within this regulation; *Reeve v Webb* (1972) 117 Sol Jo 127, [1973] RTR 130.

4. Para (1) does not necessarily involve a load falling off, the "load shedding" paragraph is para (2); *Leathley v Robson's Border Transport Ltd* [1976] RTR 503. However para (2) does not apply only to cases where the load has actually fallen off but also to cases where the load has moved due to inadequate security whereby danger is caused or is likely to be caused. Attempting to secure a high load with straps when chains were necessary would be a contravention of para (2); *McDermott Movements Ltd v Horsfield* [1983] RTR 42, [1982] Crim LR 693. The defence under s 40(6) of the Road Traffic Act 1972 of travelling to nearest weighbridge is not appropriate in this case; *Hudson v Bushrod* [1982] RTR 87. A dangerous projection may fall within the "packing and adjustment" of the Load; *O'Connell v Murphy* [1981] RTR 163, [1981] Crim LR 256.

5. Para (2) creates a single offence of unlawful loading which is committed if the load is secured in such a way that there is danger or nuisance, or both danger and nuisance; *St Albans Sand and Gravel Co Ltd v Minnis* [1981] RTR 231.

6. Although the liability is absolute, the Court is entitled to dismiss the information on finding that there was no likelihood or danger of the load falling off or shifting; *Friend v Western British Road Services Ltd* [1976] RTR 103, [1975] Crim LR 521 distinguishing *Cornish v Ferry Masters Ltd* [1976] RTR 293, [1975] Crim LR 241. It has been held that justices were entitled to base their decision on their personal knowledge of the way in which fine sand was likely to behave on a windy day when loaded on a defendant's vehicle; *St Albans Sand and Gravel Co Ltd v Minnis* [1981] RTR 231.

7. Something may "fall" from the vehicle whether it falls because it is not securely strapped or whether it falls because it is knocked off the trailer (*Walker-Trowbridge Ltd v DPP* [1992] RTR 182 — vat securely strapped to flat bed of trailer — struck pedestrian bridge over road causing vat to be knocked off on to road — held that as the vehicle had taken a route involving passing under a bridge which the load would inevitably hit, the load was not so secured and in such a position that no danger was likely to be caused by the load falling from the vehicle).

8. The driver of the vehicle is responsible for a breach in this regulation; *Gifford v Whitaker* [1942] 1 KB 501, [1942] 1 All ER 604, 106 JP 128.

9. Regard must be had to the nature and features of the route to be taken. A vehicle which is so high that it cannot pass under a bridge on that route does not comply with this regulation; *British Road Services Ltd v Owen* [1971] 2 All ER 999, 135 JP 899. The crucial question to ask is: "Was this trailer unsuitable for the *purpose* of carrying this load on this journey because it caused a risk of danger or nuisance?". If the purpose of the journey is to carry goods from A to B and if the goods can be loaded in such a way that the journey can be made without giving rise to danger, the use of that vehicle or trailer for that purpose is suitable. The fact that danger is likely to result if the load is not properly stowed does not detract from that suitability (*Young and C F Abraham (Transport) Ltd v Crown Prosecution Service* (1991) 155 JP 738, [1992] RTR 194).

4–3652   **100A.** (1) No person shall use, or cause or permit to be used, on a road a vehicle displaying the rectangular plate described in the definition of "low platform trailer" in the Table in regulation 3(2) or anything resembling such a plate at a speed exceeding 40 mph.

(2) No person shall use, or cause or permit to be used on a road a vehicle displaying the rectangular plate described in Schedule 13 (Plate for restricted speed vehicle) or anything resembling such a plate at a speed exceeding 50 mph.

Parking in darkness

4–3653   **101.** (1) Save as provided in paragraph (2) no person shall except with the permission[1] of a police officer in a uniform, cause or permit any motor vehicle to stand on a road at any time between sunset and sunrise unless the near side of the vehicle is as close as may be to the edge of the carriageway.

(2) The provisions of paragraph (1) do not apply in respect of any motor vehicle—

(a) being used for fire brigade or, in England, fire and rescue authority, ambulance or police purposes or for defence purposes (including civil defence purposes) if compliance with those provisions would hinder or be likely to hinder the use of the vehicle for the purpose for which it is being used on that occasion;

(b) being used in connection with—

    (i) any building operation or demolition;
    (ii) the repair of any other vehicle;
    (iii) the removal of any obstruction to traffic;
    (iv) the maintenance, repair or reconstruction of any road; or
    (v) the laying, erection, alteration or repair in or near to any road of any sewer, main, pipe or apparatus for the supply of gas, water or electricity, of any electronic communications apparatus as defined in Schedule 2 to the Telecommunication Act 1984[1] or of the apparatus of any electric transport undertaking,

if, in any such case, compliance with those provisions would hinder or be likely to hinder the use of the vehicle for the purpose for which it is being used on that occasion;

(c) on any road in which vehicles are allowed to proceed in one direction only;

(d) standing on a part of a road set aside for the parking of vehicles or as a stand for hackney carriages or as a stand for buses or as a place at which such vehicles may stop for a longer time than is necessary for the taking up and setting down of passengers where compliance with those provisions would conflict with the provisions of any order, regulations or byelaws governing the use of such part of a road for that purpose; or

(e) waiting to set down or pick up passengers in accordance with regulations made or directions given by a chief officer of police in regard to such setting down or picking up.

---

1. A police officer in uniform cannot grant himself permission; *Keene v Muncaster* (1980) 124 Sol Jo 496, [1980] Crim LR 587.

Passengers on motor cycles

4–3654   102. If any person in addition to the driver is carried astride a two-wheeled motor cycle on a road (whether a sidecar is attached to it or not) suitable supports or rests for the feet shall be available on the motor cycle for that person.

Obstruction

4–3655   103. No person in charge of a motor vehicle or trailer shall cause[1] or permit the vehicle to stand on a road[2] so as to cause any unnecessary obstruction[3] of the road.

---

1. Parking a vehicle is a positive act which can "cause" an obstruction so that when a vehicle is penned in by another vehicle's close parking a conviction may follow; *Mounsey v Campbell* [1983] RTR 36.
2. "Road" includes a footpath; *Bryant v Marx* (1932) 96 JP 383. Cf *Carpenter v Fox* [1929] 2 KB 458, 93 JP 239.
3. Cf *Gill v Carson and Nield* [1917] 2 KB 674, 81 JP 250. A motor vehicle left on a road for an unreasonable time may be unreasonable obstruction; *Soloman v Durbridge* (1956) 120 JP 231. But it was held that no offence was committed by a garage proprietor who, in connection with his business, made use of an official parking area by parking five of his cars on it; *W R Anderson (Motors) Ltd v Hargreaves* [1962] 1 QB 425, [1962] 1 All ER 129, 126 JP 100. A Crown Court has held that where a motorist parked on one side of a road and obstruction was caused by the subsequent parking of cars on the other side of the road no offence under this regulation was committed; *Langham v Crisp* [1975] Crim LR 652. An important factor for consideration is the purpose for which the highway was being used by the vehicle causing the obstruction. The highway provides a means of transit and is not intended as a store; *Nelmes v Rhys Howells Transport Ltd* [1977] RTR 266, [1977] Crim LR 227.

Driver's control

4–3656   104. No person shall drive or cause or permit any other person to drive, a motor vehicle on a road if he is in such a position[1] that he cannot have proper control of the vehicle or have a full view of the road and traffic ahead.

---

1. Driving with a sheepdog on one's lap can fall within this regulation; *Simpson v Vant* [1986] RTR 247.

Opening of doors

4–3657   105. No person shall open, or cause or permit to be opened, any door of a vehicle on a road so as to injure or endanger any person.

Reversing

4–3658   106. No person shall drive, or cause or permit to be driven, a motor vehicle backwards on a road further than may be requisite for the safety or reasonable convenience of the occupants of the vehicle or other traffic, unless it is a road roller or is engaged in the construction, maintenance or repair of the road.

Leaving motor vehicles unattended

4–3659   107. (1) Save as provided in paragraph (2), no person shall leave, or cause or permit to be left, on a road a motor vehicle which is not attended by a person licensed to drive it unless the engine is stopped and[1] any parking brake with which the vehicle is required to be equipped is effectively set.

(2) The requirement specified in paragraph (1) as to the stopping of the engine shall not apply in respect of a vehicle—

    (*a*) being used for ambulance, fire brigade or, in England, fire and rescue authority or police purposes; or

    (*b*) in such a position and condition as not to be likely to endanger any person or property and engaged in an operation which requires its engine to be used to—

        (i) drive machinery forming part of, or mounted on, the vehicle and used for purposes other than driving the vehicle; or

        (ii) maintain the electrical power of the batteries of the vehicle at a level required for driving that machinery or apparatus.

    (3) In this regulation "parking brake" means a brake fitted to a vehicle in accordance with requirement 16 or 18 in Schedule 3.

---

    1. This regulation contains two requirements and an offence is committed if either or both is not complied with. An information under a predecessor regulation alleging breach of both requirements was not bad for duplicity; *Butterworth v Shorthose* [1956] Crim LR 341.

Securing of suspended implements

4–3660   **108.** Where a vehicle is fitted with any apparatus or appliance designed for lifting and part of the apparatus or appliance consists of a suspended implement, the implement shall at all times while the vehicle is in motion on a road and when the implement is not attached to any load supported by the appliance or apparatus be so secured either to the appliance or apparatus or to some part of the vehicle that no danger is caused or is likely to be caused to any person on the vehicle or on the road.

4–3661   **109.** (1) No person shall drive, or cause or permit to be driven, a motor vehicle on a road, if the driver is in such a position as to be able to see, whether directly or by reflection, a television receiving apparatus or other cinematographic apparatus used to display anything other than information—

    (*a*) about the state of the vehicle or its equipment;

    (*b*) about the location of the vehicle and the road on which it is located;

    (*c*) to assist the driver to see the road adjacent to the vehicle; or

    (*d*) to assist the driver to reach his destination.

    (2) In this regulation "television receiving apparatus" means any cathode ray tube carried on a vehicle and on which there can be displayed an image derived from a television broadcast, a recording or a camera or computer.

4–3661A

Mobile telephones

    110. (1) No person shall drive a motor vehicle on a road if he is using—

    (*a*) a hand-held mobile telephone; or

    (*b*) a hand-held device of a kind specified in paragraph (4).

    (2) No person shall cause or permit any other person to drive a motor vehicle on a road while that other person is using—

    (*a*) a hand-held mobile telephone; or

    (*b*) a hand-held device of a kind specified in paragraph (4).

    (3) No person shall supervise a holder of a provisional licence if the person supervising is using—

    (*a*) a hand-held mobile telephone; or

    (*b*) a hand-held device of a kind specified in paragraph (4),

at a time when the provisional licence holder is driving a motor vehicle on a road.

    (4) A device referred to in paragraphs (1)(b), (2)(b) and (3)(b) is a device, other than a two-way radio, which performs an interactive communication function by transmitting and receiving data.

    (5) A person does not contravene a provision of this regulation if, at the time of the alleged contravention—

    (*a*) he is using the telephone or other device to call the police, fire, ambulance or other emergency service on 112 or 999;

    (*b*) he is acting in response to a genuine emergency; and

    (*c*) it is unsafe or impracticable for him to cease driving in order to make the call (or, in the case of an alleged contravention of paragraph (3)(b), for the provisional licence holder to cease driving while the call was being made).

    (6) For the purposes of this regulation—

    (*a*) a mobile telephone or other device is to be treated as hand-held if it is, or must be, held at some point during the course of making or receiving a call or performing any other interactive communication function;

    (*b*) a person supervises the holder of a provisional licence if he does so pursuant to a condition imposed on that licence holder prescribed under section 97(3)(a) of the Road Traffic Act 1988 (grant of provisional licence);

    (*c*) "interactive communication function" includes the following:

        (i) sending or receiving oral or written messages;

        (ii) sending or receiving facsimile documents;

     (iii) sending or receiving still or moving images; and

     (iv) providing access to the internet;

  (*d*) ''two-way radio'' means any wireless telegraphy apparatus which is designed or adapted—

     (i) for the purpose of transmitting and receiving spoken messages; and

     (ii) to operate on any frequency other than 880 MHz to 915 MHz, 925 MHz to 960 MHz, 1710 MHz to 1785 MHz, 1805 MHz to 1880 MHz, 1900 MHz to 1980 MHz or 2110 MHz to 2170 MHz; and

  (*e*) ''wireless telegraphy'' has the same meaning as in section 19(1) of the Wireless Telegraphy Act 1949.

4–3662   SCHEDULE 1

Revocations

4–3663   SCHEDULE 2

Community Directives and ECE Regulations

4–3663A

Regulation 3A   SCHEDULE 2A

VEHICLES FOR WHICH A MINISTER'S APPROVAL CERTIFICATE HAS BEEN ISSUED UNDER THE MOTOR VEHICLES (APPROVAL REGULATIONS 1996

PART I
INTERPRETATION

General Interpretation

1. (1) In this Schedule—

''the Approval Regulations'' means the Motor Vehicles (Approval) Regulations 1996;

''approval certificate'' means a Minister's approval certificate in the form prescribed by the Approval Regulations;

''approval date'', in relation to a vehicle in respect of which an approval certificate has been issued, is the date that the certificate was issued;

''goods vehicle approval certificate'' means an approval certificate which appears to have been issued on the basis that the vehicle is a vehicle to which Part III of the Approval Regulations applies;

''passenger vehicle approval certificate'' means an approval certificate which appears to have been issued on the basis that the vehicle is a vehicle to which Part II of the Approval Regulations applies.

Interpretation of references to a vehicle complying with the approval requirements and to a vehicle exempt from the approval requirements

2. (1) Subject to paragraph 3, references in this Schedule to a vehicle complying with or being exempt from the approval requirements shall be construed in accordance with the following provisions of this paragraph.

(2) Subject to sub-paragraphs (4) and (5), a vehicle in respect of which a goods vehicle approval certificate has been issued shall be regarded as complying with or exempt from the approval requirements in relation to a specified subject matter if and only if for the time being satisfies at least one of the conditions in regulation 6(5) of the Approval Regulations in relation to that subject matter.

(3) Subject to sub-paragraphs (4) and (5), a vehicle in respect of which a passenger vehicle approval certificate has been issued shall be regarded as complying with or exempt from the approval requirements in relation to a specified subject matter if and only if for the time being satisfies at least one of the conditions in regulation 4(5) of the Approval Regulations in relation to that subject matter.

(4) A vehicle in respect of which an approval certificate has been issued shall be regarded as neither complying with nor being exempt from the approval requirements in relation to any subject matter if—

  (*a*) the certificate is a goods vehicle approval certificate and the vehicle is not for the time being a vehicle to which Part III of the Approval Regulations applies; or

  (*b*) the certificate is a passenger vehicle approval certificate and the vehicle is not for the time being a vehicle to which Part II of the Approval Regulations applies.

(5) For the purposes of this paragraph, the Approval Regulations shall have effect with the omission of regulations 4(8) and 6(7).

PART II
MODIFICATION OF THE REGULATIONS

Part exemption from regulation 32 (glazing)

3. Regulation 32(2), (7) and (10) shall not apply to a vehicle in respect of which a passenger vehicle approval certificate has been issued, if it complies with or is exempt from the approval requirements relating to glazing

Exemption from regulation 33 (mirrors)

4. Regulation 33 shall not apply to a vehicle in respect of which a passenger vehicle approval certificate has been issued, if it complies with or is exempt from the approval requirements relating to rear view mirrors.

Exemption from regulation 35 (speedometers)

5. Regulation 35 shall not apply to a vehicle in respect of which a passenger approval certificate has been issued, if it complies with or is exempt from the approval requirements relating to speedometers.

Exemption from regulation 39(2)(c)(i) (fuel tanks to be made of metal)

6. Regulation 39(2)(*c*)(i) shall not apply to a vehicle in respect of which either a passenger vehicle approval certificate or a goods vehicle approval certificate has been issued, if it complies with the approval requirements relating to general vehicle construction.

Exemption from regulation 46 (seat belt anchorages)

7. Regulation 46 shall not apply to a vehicle in respect of which a passenger vehicle approval certificate has been issued, if it complies with or is exempt from the approval requirements relating to anchorage points.

Part exemption from regulation 47 (seat belts)

8. Regulation 47, so far as it relates to seat belts for adults, shall not apply to a vehicle in respect of which a passenger vehicle approval certificate has been issued, if it complies with or is exempt from the approval requirements relating to seat belts (including the requirements relating to the installation of seat belts).

Modifications to regulation 61 (emissions)

9. (1) Regulation 61 shall have effect with the following modifications in relation to a vehicle in respect of which there has been issued an approval certificate containing the letter "A" pursuant to regulation 12(2)(*c*) of the Approval Regulations.

(2) For the purposes of paragraphs (3A), (7), (8) and (9), the date of first use of the vehicle shall be regarded as being 1st January immediately preceding the date of manufacture of the engine by which it is propelled. However, the date on which the vehicle is first used shall not, by virtue of this paragraph, be regarded in any circumstances as being later than the date on which it would otherwise have been regarded as being first used had this paragraph been omitted.

(3) Paragraphs 10(A) and 10(AA) shall not apply to the vehicle if it complies with or is exempt from the approval requirements relating to exhaust emissions.

9A. Paragraphs (10A), (10AA) and (10BA) of regulation 61 shall not apply to a vehicle in respect of which either a passenger vehicle approval certificate or a goods vehicle approval certificate has been issued, if it complies with, or is exempt from, the approval requirements relating to exhaust or smoke emissions.

9B. Modifications to regulation 61A (emissions). (1) Regulation 61A shall not apply to a vehicle in respect of which either a passenger vehicle approval certificate or a goods vehicle approval certificate has been issued, if it complies with or is exempt from the approval requirements relating to exhaust or smoke emissions.

(2) Regulation 61A shall have effect with the following modifications in relation to a vehicle in respect of which there has been issued an approval certificate containing the letter "A" pursuant to regulation 12(2)(*c*) of the Approval Regulations.

(3) For the purposes of paragraphs (2) and (3) of regulation 61A, the date as is specified (as defined in regulation 61A) shall be regarded as being the 1st January immediately preceding the date of manufacture of the engine by which the vehicle is propelled; provided that the date as is specified shall not in any circumstances be regarded as being later than the date on which the motor vehicle would otherwise have been regarded as being first used.

Modification to regulation 67 (vehicle identification numbers)

10. Regulation 67 shall not apply to a vehicle in respect of which an approval certificate has been issued if—

(*a*) the vehicle is equipped with a plate which is in a conspicuous and readily accessible position, is affixed to a vehicle part which is not normally subject to replacement and shows clearly and indelibly the identification number shown on the certificate and the name of the manufacturer; and

(*b*) that number is marked on the chassis, frame or other similar structure, on the offside of the vehicle, in a clearly visible and accessible position, and by a method such as hammering or stamping, in such a way that it cannot be obliterated or deteriorate.

(see regulation 16)   SCHEDULE 3
                     BRAKING REQUIREMENTS

4–3664 **1.** The braking requirements referred to in regulation 16(4) are set out in the Table and are to be interpreted in accordance with paragraphs 2 to 5 of this Schedule.

TABLE

(Schedule 3)

Number	Requirement
1	The vehicle shall be equipped with— (*a*) one efficient braking system having two means of operation; (*b*) one efficient split braking system having one means of operation; or (*c*) two efficient braking systems each having a separate means of operation, and in the case of a vehicle first used on or after 1st January 1968, no account shall be taken of a multi-pull means of operation unless, at first application, it operates a hydraulic, electric or pneumatic device which causes the application of brakes with total braking efficiency not less than 25%.
2	The vehicle shall be equipped with— (*a*) one efficient braking system having two means of operation; or (*b*) two efficient braking systems each having a separate means of operation.
3	The vehicle shall be equipped with an efficient braking system.
4	The braking system shall be so designed that in the event of failure of any part (other than a fixed member or a brake shoe anchor pin) through or by means of which the force necessary to apply the brakes is transmitted, there shall still be available for application by the driver brakes sufficient under the most adverse conditions to bring the vehicle to rest within a reasonable distance. The brakes so available shall be applied to— (*a*) in the case of a track-laying vehicle, one track on each side of the vehicle; (*b*) in the case of a wheeled motor vehicle, one wheel if the vehicle has 3 wheels and otherwise to at least half the wheels; and

Number	Requirement
	(c) in the case of a wheeled trailer, at least one wheel if it has only 2 wheels and otherwise at least 2 wheels. This requirement applies to the braking systems of both a trailer and the vehicle by which it is being drawn except that if the drawing vehicle complies with regulation 15, Community Directive 79/489, 85/647, 88/194, 91/422 or 98/12 or ECE Regulation 13.03, 13.04, 13.05, 13.06, 13.07, 13.08 or 13.09, the requirement applies only to the braking system of the drawing vehicle. It does not apply to vehicles having split braking systems (which are subject to regulation 18(3)(b)) or to road rollers. (The expressions "part" and "half the wheels" are to be interpreted in accordance with paragraphs (3) and (4) respectively).
5	The braking system shall be so designed and constructed that, in the event of the failure of any part thereof, there shall still be available for application by the driver a brake sufficient under the most adverse conditions to bring the vehicle to rest within a reasonable distance.
6	The braking system of a vehicle, when drawing a trailer which complies with regulation 15, Community Directive 79/489, 85/647, 88/194 or 91/422 or ECE Regulation 13.03, 13.04, 13.05 or 13.06,* shall be so constructed that, in the event of a failure of any part (other than a fixed member or brake shoe anchor pin) of the service braking system of the drawing vehicle (excluding the means of operation of a split braking system) the driver can still apply brakes to at least one wheel of the trailer, if it has only 2 wheels, and otherwise to at least 2 wheels, by using the secondary braking system of the drawing vehicle. (The expression "part" is to be interpreted in accordance with paragraph 3).
7	The application of any means of operation of a braking system shall not affect or operate the pedal or hand lever of any other means of operation.
8	The braking system shall not be rendered ineffective by the non-rotation of the engine of the vehicle or, in the case of a trailer, the engine of the drawing vehicle (steam-propelled vehicles, other than locomotives and buses, are excluded from this requirement).
9	At least one means of operation shall be capable of causing brakes to be applied directly, and not through the transmission gear, to at least half the wheels of the vehicle. This requirement does not apply to a works truck with an unladen weight not exceeding 7370 kg, or to an industrial tractor; and it does not apply to a vehicle with more than 4 wheels if— (a) the drive is transmitted to all wheels other than the steering wheels without the interposition of a differential driving gear or similar mechanism between the axles carrying the driving wheels; and (b) the brakes applied by one means of operation apply directly to 2 driving wheels on opposite sides of the vehicle; and (c) the brakes applied by another means of operation act directly on all the other driving wheels. (The expression "half the wheels" is to be interpreted in accordance with paragraph (4)).
10	The brakes of a trailer shall come into operation automatically on its overrun or, in the case of a track-laying trailer drawn by a vehicle having steerable wheels at the front or a wheeled trailer, the driver of, or some other person on, the drawing vehicle or on the trailer shall be able to apply the brakes on the trailer.
11	The brakes of a trailer shall come into operation automatically on its overrun or the driver of the drawing vehicle shall be able to apply brakes to all the wheels of the trailer, using the means of operation which applies the service brakes of the drawing vehicle.
12	The brakes of the vehicle shall apply to all wheels other than the steering wheels.
13	The brakes of the vehicle shall apply to at least 2 wheels.
14	The brakes of the vehicle shall apply in the case of a wheeled vehicle to at least 2 wheels if the vehicle has no more than 4 wheels and to at least half the wheels if the vehicle has more than 4 wheels; and in the case of a track-laying vehicle to all the tracks.
15	The brakes shall apply to all the wheels.
16	The parking brake shall be so designed and constructed that— (a) in the case of a wheeled heavy motor car or motor car, its means of operation is independent of the means of operation of any split braking system with which the vehicle is fitted; (b) in the case of a motor vehicle other than a motor cycle or an invalid carriage, either— (i) it is capable of being applied by direct mechanical action without the intervention of any hydraulic, electric or pneumatic device; or (ii) the vehicle complies with requirement 15; and (c) it can at all times when the vehicle is not being driven or is left unattended be set so as— (i) in the case of a track-laying vehicle, to lock the tracks; and (ii) in the case of a wheeled vehicle, to prevent the rotation of at least one wheel in the case of a three wheeled vehicle and at least two wheels in the case of a vehicle with more than three wheels.

Number	Requirement
17	The parking brake shall be capable of being set so as effectively to prevent two at least of the wheels from revolving when the trailer is not being drawn.
18	The parking brake shall be so designed and constructed that— (a) in the case of a motor vehicle, its means of operation (whether multi-pull or not) is independent of the means of operation of any braking system required by regulation 18 to have a total braking efficiency of not less than 50%; and (b) in the case of a trailer, its brakes can be applied and released by a person standing on the ground by a means of operation fitted to the trailer; and (c) in either case, its braking force, when the vehicle is not being driven or is left unattended (and in the case of a trailer, whether the braking force is applied by the driver using the service brakes of the drawing vehicle or by a person standing on the ground in the manner indicated in sub-paragraph (b)) can at all times be maintained in operation by direct mechanical action without the intervention of any hydraulic, electric or pneumatic device and, when so maintained, can hold the vehicle stationary on a gradient of at least 16% without the assistance of stored energy.

2. For the purposes of requirement 3 in the Table, in the case of a motor car or heavy motor car propelled by steam and not used as a bus, the engine shall be deemed to be an efficient braking system with one means of operation if the engine is capable of being reversed and, in the case of a vehicle first used on or after 1st January 1927, is incapable of being disconnected from any of the driving wheels of the of the vehicle except by the sustained effort of the driver.

3. For the purpose of requirements 4 and 6 in the Table, in the case of a wheeled motor car and of a vehicle first used on or after 1st October 1938 which is a locomotive, a motor tractor, a heavy motor car or a tack-laying motor car, every moving shaft which is connected to or supports any part of a braking system shall be deemed to be part of the system.

4. For the purpose of requirements 4, 9 and 14 in the Table, in determining whether brakes apply to at least half the wheels of a vehicle, not more than one front wheel shall be treated as a wheel to which brakes apply unless the vehicle is—

(a) a locomotive or motor tractor with more than 4 wheels;
(b) a heavy motor car or motor car first used before 1st October 1938;
(c) a motor car with an unladen weight not exceeding 1020 kg;
(d) a motor car which is a passenger vehicle but is not a bus;
(e) a works truck;
(f) a heavy motor car or motor car with more than 3 wheels which is equipped in respect of all its wheels with brakes which are operated by one means of operation; or
(g) a track-laying vehicle.

5. In this Schedule a "multi-pull means of operation" means a device forming part of a braking system which causes the muscular energy of the driver to apply the brakes of that system progressively as a result of successive applications of that device by the driver.

(see regulations 39A and 39B)   SCHEDULE 3A[1]
EXCLUSION OF CERTAIN VEHICLES FROM THE APPLICATION OF REGULATION 39A

PART I

4–3665   **1.** (1) In this Part—

"EEC type approval certificate" means a certificate issued by a member state of the European Economic Community in accordance with Community Directive 70/220 as originally made or with any amendments which have from time to time been made before 5th September 1988;
"engine capacity" means in the case of a reciprocating engine, the nominal swept volume and, in the case of a rotary engine, double the nominal swept volume;
"relevant authority" means—

(a) in relation to an EEC type approval certificate issued by the United Kingdom, the Secretary of State, and
(b) in relation to an EEC type approval certificate issued by any other member state of the European Economic Community, the authority having power under the law of that state to issue that certificate.

(2) The reference in this Schedule to a M1 category vehicle is a reference to a vehicle described as M1 in Council Directive 70/156/EEC of 6th February 1970 as amended at 5th September 1988.

2. A vehicle of a description specified in column 2 of the Table below is excluded from the application of regulation 39A if it is first used before the date specified in column 3 and the conditions specified in paragraph 3 are satisfied in respect to it on that date.

3. The conditions referred to in paragraph 2 are—

(a) that the vehicle is a model in relation to which there is in force an EEC type approval certificate issued before 1st October 1989;
(b) that the manufacturer of the vehicle has supplied to the relevant authority which issued the EEC type approval certificate, a certificate stating that adapting vehicles of that model to the fuel requirements specified in the Annexes to Community Directive 88/76 would entail a change in material specification of the inlet or exhaust valve seats or a reduction in the compression ratio or an increase in the engine capacity to compensate for loss of power; and
(c) that the relevant authority has accepted the certificate referred to in sub-paragraph (b).

TABLE

Item (1)	Description of vehicle (2)	Date before which vehicle must be first used (3)
1	Vehicles with an engine capacity of less than 1400cc.	1.4.92
2	Vehicles with an engine capacity of not less than 1400cc and not more than 2000cc.	1.4.94

3	M1 category vehicles with an engine capacity of more than 2000cc and which—
	   (a) are constructed or adapted to carry not more than 5 passengers excluding the driver, or
	   (b) have a maximum gross weight of not more than 2500kg,
	not being in either case, an off-road vehicle.
		1.4.93

1. OJ No L42, 23.2.70, p 1; relevant amending instrument is Council Directive 87/403/EEC (OJ No L220, 8.8.87, p 44).

PART II

SYMBOL INDICATING THAT VEHICLE CAN RUN ON UNLEADED PETROL

SCHEDULE 3B
AUTHORISED SEALERS

PART I

General

4–3666   1. The Secretary of State may authorise—

   (a) an individual proposing to seal speed limiters other than on behalf of another person;
   (b) a firm; or
   (c) a corporation;

to seal speed limiters for the purposes of regulation 36A or 36B and a person or body so authorised is referred to in this Schedule as an "authorised sealer".

   2. An authorised sealer shall comply with the conditions set out in Part II of this Schedule and with such other conditions as may from time to time be imposed by the Secretary of State.

   3. An authorised sealer may charge for sealing a speed limiter.

   4. The Secretary of State may at any time withdraw an authorisation granted under this Schedule.

   5. (1) An authorisation under this Schedule in respect of an individual shall terminate if—

   (a) he dies;
   (b) is adjudged bankrupt or, in Scotland, has his estate sequestrated; or
   (c) becomes a patient within the meaning of Part VII of the Mental Health Act 1983 or, in Scotland, becomes incapable of managing his own affairs.

   (2) An authorisation under this Schedule in respect of a firm shall terminate if the firm is dissolved or if all the partners are adjudged bankrupt.

   (3) An authorisation under this Schedule in respect of a company shall terminate if—

   (a) the company goes into liquidation or enters administration;
   (b) a receiver or manager of the trade or business of the company is appointed; or
   (c) possession is taken by or on behalf of the holders of any debenture secured by a floating charge, or any property of the company comprised in or subject to the charge, occurs.

PART II

The conditions

6. An authorised sealer shall not—

(a) seal a speed limiter fitted to a vehicle to which regulation 36A applies unless he is satisfied that the speed limiter fulfils the requirements of paragraph (5)(*b*), (6) and (8) of that regulation, or

(b) seal a speed limiter fitted to a vehicle to which regulation 36B applies unless he is satisfied that the speed limiter fulfils the requirements of paragraphs (7)(*b*) and (10) and in addition those of paragraph (8) or (9) of that regulation.

7. When sealing a speed limiter fitted to a vehicle to which regulation 36A applies, an authorised sealer shall do so in such a manner that the speed limiter fulfils the requirements of paragraph (5)(*a*) of that regulation.

8. When sealing a speed limiter fitted to a vehicle to which regulation 36B applies, an authorised sealer shall do so in such a manner that the speed limiter fulfils the requirements of paragraph (7)(*a*) of that regulation.

9. When an authorised sealer has sealed a speed limiter fitted to a vehicle to which section 36A applies he shall supply the owner with a plate which fulfils the requirements of regulation 70A.

10. When an authorised sealer has sealed a speed limiter fitted to a vehicle to which section 36B applies he shall supply the owner with a plate which fulfils the requirements of regulation 70A.

(see regulation 40)   SCHEDULE 4
GAS CONTAINERS

PART I

Definitions relating to gas containers

4–3667 1. In this Schedule, unless the context otherwise requires, the following expressions have the meanings hereby assigned to them respectively, that is to say—

"gas container" means a container fitted to a motor vehicle or a trailer and intended for the storage of gaseous fuel for the purpose of the propulsion of the vehicle or the drawing vehicle as the case may be;

"gas cylinder" means a container fitted to a motor vehicle or a trailer and intended for the storage of compressed gas for the purpose of the propulsion of the vehicle or the drawing vehicle as the case may be;

"Compressed gas" means gaseous fuel under a pressure exceeding 1.0325 bar above atmospheric pressure;

"pipe line" means all pipes connecting a gas container or containers—

(a) to the engine or the mixing device for the supply of a mixture of gas and air to the engine; and

(b) to the filling point on the vehicle;

"pressure pipe line" means any part of a pipe line intended for the conveyance of compressed gas; and

"reducing valve" means an apparatus which automatically reduces the pressure of the gas passing through it.

Gas containers

2. Every gas container shall—

(a) be securely attached to the vehicle in such manner as not to be liable to displacement or damage due to vibration or other cause; and

(b) be so placed or insulated as not to be adversely affected by the heat from the exhaust system.

Pipe lines

3. (1) Every pipe line shall be supported in such manner as to be protected from excessive vibration and strain.

(2) No part of a pipeline shall be in such a position that it may be subjected to undue heat from the exhaust system.

(3) Every pressure pipe shall be made of steel solid drawn.

(4) The maximum unsupported length of a pressure pipe line shall not exceed 920 mm.

Unions

4. (1) Every union shall be so constructed and fitted that it will—

(a) not liable to work loose or develop leakage when in use; and

(b) be readily accessible for inspection and adjustment.

(2) No union on a pressure pipe line or on a gas cylinder shall contain a joint other than a metal to metal joint.

Reducing valves

5. Every reducing valve shall be—

(a) so fitted as to be readily accessible; and

(b) so constructed that there can be no escape of gas when the engine is not running.

Valves and cocks

6. (1) Every valve or cock intended to be subjected to a pressure exceeding 6.8948 bar shall be of forged steel or of brass or bronze complying with the specification contained in Part II of this Schedule.

(2) A valve or cock shall be fitted to the pipe line to enable the supply of gas from the container or containers to the mixing device to be shut off.

(3)

(a) In the case of a pressure pipeline the valve or cock shall be placed between the reducing valve and the container or containers and shall be readily visible and accessible from the outside of the vehicle and a notice indicating its position and method of operation shall be affixed in a conspicuous position on the outside of the vehicle carrying the gas container or containers.

(b) In other cases, if the valve or cock is not so visible and accessible as aforesaid, a notice indicating its position shall be affixed in a conspicuous position on the outside of the vehicle carrying the container or containers.

Pressure gauges

7. Every pressure gauge connected to a pressure pipe line shall be so constructed as not to be liable to deterioration under the action of the particular gases employed and shall be so constructed and fitted that—

(a) in the event of failure of such pressure gauge no gas can escape into any part of the vehicle;
(b) it is not possible owing to leakage of gas into the casing of the pressure gauge for pressure to increase therein to such extent as to be liable to cause a breakage of the glass thereof; and
(c) in the event of failure of such pressure gauge the supply of gas thereto may be readily cut off.

Charging connections

8. (1) Every connection for charging a gas container shall be outside the vehicle and in the case of a public service vehicle no such connection shall be within 610 mm of any entrance or exit.
(2) An efficient shut-off valve shall be fitted as near as practicable to the filling point.
Provided that in cases where compressed gas is not used a cock or an efficient non-return valve may be fitted in lieu thereof.
(3) Where compressed gas is used an additional emergency shut-off valve shall be fitted adjacent to the valve referred to in sub-paragraph (2) of this paragraph.
(4) A cap shall be fitted to the gas filling point on the vehicle and where compressed gas is used this cap shall be made of steel with a metal to metal joint.

Trailers

9. (1) Where a trailer is used for the carriage of a gas cylinder, a reducing valve shall be fitted on the trailer.
(2) No pipe used for conveying gas from a trailer to the engine of a vehicle shall contain compressed gas.

Construction, etc, of system

10. Every part of a gas container propulsion system shall be—

(a) so placed or protected as not to be exposed to accidental damage and shall be soundly and properly constructed of suitable and well-finished materials capable of withstanding the loads and stresses likely to be met within the operation and shall be maintained in an efficient, safe and clean condition; and
(b) so designed and constructed that leakage of gas is not likely to occur under normal working conditions, whether or not the engine is running.

PART II
SPECIFICATION FOR BRASS OR BRONZE VALVES

Manufacture of valves

1. The stamping or pressing from which each valve is manufactured shall be made from bars produced by (a) extrusion, (b) rolling, (c) forging, (d) extrusion and drawing, or (e) rolling and drawing.

Heat treatment

2. Each stamping or pressing shall be heat treated so as to produce an equiaxed microstructure in the material.

Freedom from defects

3. All stampings or pressings and the bars from which they are made shall be free from cracks, laminations, hard spots, segregated materials and variations in composition.

Tensile test

4. Tensile tests shall be made on samples of stampings or pressings taken at random from any consignment. The result of the tensile test shall conform to the following conditions—

Yield Stress.—Not less than 231.6 N/mm₂.
Ultimate Tensile Stress.—Not less than 463.3 N/mm₂.
Elongation on 50 mm gauge length.—Not less than 25%.

Note.—When the gauge length is less than 50 mm the required elongation shall be proportionately reduced. The fractured test piece shall be free from piping and other defects (see paragraph 3 of this Part of this Schedule).

(regulations 40 and 96)   SCHEDULE 5
                                                  GAS SYSTEMS

Definitions

4–3668 1. In this Schedule—

"check valve" means a device which permits the flow of gas in one direction and prevents the flow of gas in the opposite direction;
"design pressure" means the pressure which a part of a gas system has been designed and constructed safely to withstand;
"double-check valve" means a device which consists of two check valves in series and which permits the flow of gas in one direction and prevents the flow of gas in the opposite direction;
"electrically operated valve" means a device which is electrically operated and opens when the ignition is switched on and closes when the ignition is switched off or the power is otherwise cut off;
"excess flow valve" means a device which automatically and instantaneously reduces to a minimum the flow of gas through the valve when the flow rate exceeds a set value;
"fixed gas container" means a gas container which is attached to a vehicle permanently and in such a manner that the container can be filled without being moved;

"gas container" means any container, not being a container for the carriage of gas as goods, which is fitted to or carried on a motor vehicle or trailer and is intended for the storage of gas for either—

(a) the propulsion of the motor vehicle, or
(b) the operation of a gas-fired appliance;

"high pressure" means a pressure exceeding 1.0325 bar absolute;

"high pressure pipeline" means a pipeline intended to contain gas at high pressure;

"pipeline" means any pipe or passage connecting any two parts of a gas propulsion system of a vehicle or of a gas-fired appliance supply system on a vehicle or any two points on the same part of any such system;

"portable gas container" means a gas container which may be attached to a vehicle but which can readily be removed;

"pressure relief valve" means a device which opens automatically when the pressure in the part of the gas system to which it is fitted exceeds a set value, reaches its maximum flow capacity when the set value is exceeded by 10% and closes automatically when the pressure falls below a set value; and

"reducing valve" means a device which automatically reduces the pressure of the gas passing through it, and includes regulator devices.

Gas containers

2. (1) Every gas container shall—

(a) be capable of withstanding the pressure of the gas which may be stored in the container at the highest temperature which the gas is likely to reach,

(b) if fitted inside the vehicle be so arranged as to prevent so far as is practicable the possibility of gas entering the engine, passenger or living compartments due to leaks or venting from the container or valves, connections and gauges immediately adjacent to it, and the space containing these components shall be so ventilated and drained as to prevent the accumulation of gas,

(c) be securely attached to the vehicle in such a manner as not to be liable to displacement or damage due to vibration or other cause, and

(d) be so placed and so insulated or shielded as not to suffer any adverse effect from the heat of the exhaust system of any engine or any other source of heat.

(2) Every portable gas container shall be either—

(a) hermetically sealed, or

(b) fitted with a valve or cock to enable the flow of gas from the container to be stopped.

(3) Every fixed gas container shall—

(a) be fitted with—

(i) at least one pressure relief valve, and

(ii) at least one manually operated valve which may be extended by an internal dip tube inside the gas container so as to indicate when the container has been filled to the level corresponding to the filling ratio specified in the British Standards Institution Specification for Filling Ratios and Developed Pressure for Liquefiable and Permanent Gases (as defined, respectively, in paragraphs 3.2 and 3.5 of the said Specification) published in May 1976 under the number BS 5355, and

(b) be conspicuously and permanently marked with its design pressure.

(4) If any fixed gas container is required to be fitted in a particular attitude or location, or if any device referred to in sub-paragraph (3) above requires the container to be fitted in such a manner, then it shall be conspicuously and permanently marked to indicate that requirement.

(5) If the operation of any pressure relief valve or other device referred to in sub-paragraph (3) above may cause gas to be released from the gas container, an outlet shall be provided to lead such gas to the outside of the vehicle so as not to suffer any adverse effect from the heat of the exhaust system of any engine or any other source of heat, and that outlet from the pressure relief valve shall not be fitted with any other valve or cock.

Filling systems for fixed gas containers

3. (1) Every connection for filling a fixed gas container shall be on the outside of the vehicle.

(2) There shall be fitted to every fixed gas container either—

(a) a manually operated shut-off valve and an excess flow valve, or

(b) a manually operated shut-off valve and a single check valve, or

(c) a double-check valve.

and all parts of these valves in contact with gas shall be made entirely of suitable metal except that they may contain non-metal washers and seals provided that such washers and seals are supported and constrained by metal components.

(3) In every case where a pipe is attached to a gas container for the purpose of filling the gas container there shall be fitted to the end of the pipe furthest from the gas container a check valve or a double-check valve.

(4) There shall be fitted over every gas filling point on a vehicle a cap which shall—

(a) prevent any leakage of gas from the gas filling point,

(b) be secured to the vehicle by a chain or some suitable means,

(c) be made of suitable material, and

(d) be fastened to the gas filling point by either a screw thread or other suitable means.

Pipelines

4. (1) Every pipeline shall be fixed in such a manner and position that—

(a) it will not be adversely affected by the heat of the exhaust system of any engine or any other source of heat,

(b) it is protected from vibration and strain in excess of that which it can reasonably be expected to withstand, and

(c) in the case of a high pressure pipeline it is so far as is practicable accessible for inspection.

(2) Save as provided in sub-paragraph (4) below, every high pressure pipeline shall be—

(a) a rigid line of steel, copper or copper alloy of high pressure hydraulic grade, suitable for service on road vehicles and designed for a minimum service pressure rating of not less than 75 bar absolute, and

(b) effectively protected against, or shielded from, or treated so as to be resistant to, external corrosion throughout its length unless it is made from material which is corrosion resistant under the conditions which it is likely to encounter in service.

(3) No unsupported length of any high pressure pipeline shall exceed 600 mm.

(4) Flexible hose may be used in a high pressure pipeline if—

(a)

    (i) it is reinforced either by stainless steel wire braid or by textile braid,

    (ii) its length does not exceed 500 mm, and

    (iii) save in the case of a pipeline attached to a gas container for the purpose of filling that container the flexibility which it provides is necessary for the construction or operation of the gas system of which it forms a part.

(b) its length exceeds 500mm and it complies with Annex 8 of ECE Regulation 67.01 and is approved and marked in accordance with that Regulation.

(4A) In the case of a motor vehicle which first used gas as a fuel for its propulsion on or after 1st January 2004 a flexible hose of any length used in a high pressure pipe line shall comply with the requirements of Annex 8 of ECE Regulation 67.01 shall be approved and marked in accordance with that Regulation and shall be no longer than is reasonably necessary.

(5) If a high pressure pipeline or part of such a pipeline is so constructed or located that it may, in the course of its normal use (excluding the supply of fuel from a gas container), contain liquid which is prevented from flowing, a relief valve shall be incorporated in that pipeline.

Unions and joints

5. (1) Every union and joint on a pipeline or gas container shall be so constructed and fitted that it will—

(a) not be liable to work loose or leak when in use, and

(b) be readily accessible for inspection and maintenance.

(2) Every union on a high pressure pipeline or on a gas container shall be made of suitable metal but such a union may contain non-metal washers and seals provided that such washers and seals are supported and constrained by metal components.

Reducing valves

6. Every reducing valve shall be made of suitable materials and be so fitted as to be readily accessible for inspection and maintenance.

Pressure relief valves

7. (1) Every pressure relief valve which is fitted to any part of a gas system (including a gas container) shall—

(a) be made entirely of suitable metal and so constructed and fitted as to ensure that the cooling effect of the gas during discharge shall not prevent its effective operation,

(b) be capable, under the most extreme temperatures likely to be met (including exposure to fire), of a discharge rate which prevents the pressure of the contents of the gas system from exceeding its design pressure,

(c) have a maximum discharge pressure not greater than the design pressure of the gas container,

(d) be so designed and constructed as to prevent unauthorised interference with the relief pressure setting during service, and

(e) have outlets which are—

    (i) so sited that so far as is reasonably practicable in the event of an accident the valve and its outlets are protected from damage and the free discharge from such outlets is not impaired, and

    (ii) so designed and constructed as to prevent the collection of moisture and other foreign matter which could adversely affect their performance.

Valves and cocks

8. (1) A valve or cock shall be fitted to every supply pipeline as near as practicable to every fixed gas container and such valve or cock shall by manual operation enable the supply of gas from the gas container to the gas system to be stopped, and save as provided in sub-paragraph (2) below, shall—

(a) if fitted on the outside of the vehicle, be readily visible and accessible from the outside of the vehicle, or

(b) if fitted inside the vehicle be readily accessible for operation and be so arranged as to prevent so far as is practicable the possibility of gas entering the engine, passenger or living compartments due to leaks and the space containing the valve or cock shall be so ventilated and drained as to prevent the accumulation of gas in that space.

(2) Where a fixed gas container supplies no gas system other than a gas propulsion system—

(a) an electrically operated valve may be fitted in place of the valve or cock referred to in sub-paragraph (1) above; and

(b) either—

    (i) it shall be fitted as near as practicable to the gas container; or

    (ii) if fitted in addition to the valve or cock referred to in sub-paragraph (1) above it shall either be incorporated into that valve or cock or be fitted immediately downstream from it; and

(c) it shall if fitted inside the vehicle be so arranged as to prevent as far as is practicable the possibility of gas entering the engine, passenger or living compartments due to leaks, and the space containing the valve shall be so ventilated and drained as to prevent the accumulation of gas in that space.

(3) A notice clearly indicating the position, purpose and method of operating every valve or cock referred to in sub-paragraphs (1) and (2) above shall be fitted—

(a) in all cases, in a conspicuous position on the outside of the vehicle, and

(b) in every case where the valve or cock is located inside the vehicle in a conspicuous position adjacent to the gas container.

(4) In the case of a high pressure pipeline for the conveyance of gas from the gas container an excess flow

valve shall be fitted as near as practicable to the gas container and such valve shall operate in the event of a fracture of the pipeline or other similar failure.

(5) All parts of every valve or cock referred to in this paragraph which are in contact with gas shall be made of suitable metal, save that they may contain non-metal washers and seals provided that such washers and seals are supported and constrained by metal components.

Gauges

9. Every gauge connected to a gas container or to a pipeline shall be so constructed as to be unlikely to deteriorate under the action of the gas used or to be used and shall be so constructed and fitted that—

(a) no gas can escape into any part of the vehicle as a result of any failure of the gauge, and
(b) in the event of any failure of the gauge the supply of gas to the gauge can be readily stopped.

Provided that the requirement specified in sub-paragraph (b) above shall not apply in respect of a gauge fitted as an integral part of a gas container.

Propulsion systems

10. (1) Every gas propulsion system shall be so designed and constructed that—

(a) the supply of gas to the engine is automatically stopped by the operation of a valve when the engine is not running at all or is not running on the supply of gas, and
(b) where a reducing valve is relied on to comply with sub-paragraph (a) above, the supply of gas to the engine is automatically stopped by the operation of an additional valve when the engine is switched off.

(2) Where the engine of a vehicle is constructed or adapted to run on one or more fuels as alternatives to gas, the safety and efficiency of the engine and any fuel system shall not be impaired by the presence of any other fuel system.

Special requirements for buses

11. In the case of a bus there shall be fitted as near as practicable to the gas container a valve which shall stop the flow of gas into the gas supply pipeline in the event of—

(a) the angle of tilt of the vehicle exceeding that referred to in regulation 6 of the Public Service Vehicles (Conditions of Fitness, Equipment, Use and Certification) Regulations 1981 and
(b) the deceleration of the vehicle exceeding 5g.

Gas-fired appliances

12. Every part of a gas-fired appliance shall be—

(a) so designed and constructed that leakage of gas is unlikely to occur, and
(b) constructed of materials which are compatible both with each other and with the gas used.

13. Every gas-fired appliance shall be—

(a) so located as to be easily inspected and maintained,
(b) so located and either insulated or shielded that its use shall not cause or be likely to cause danger due to the presence of any flammable material;
(c) so constructed and located as not to impose undue stress on any pipe or fitting, and
(d) so fastened or located as not to work loose or move in relation to the vehicle.

14. With the exception of catalytic heating appliances, every appliance of the kind described in regulation 96(3)(b) or (c) which is fitted to a motor vehicle shall be fitted with a flue which shall be—

(a) connected to an outlet which is on the outside of the vehicle,
(b) constructed and located so as to prevent any expelled matter from entering the vehicle, and
(c) located so that it will not cause any adverse effect to, or suffer any adverse effect from, the exhaust outlet of any engine or any other source of heat.

General requirements

15. Every part of a gas propulsion system or a gas-fired appliance system, excluding the appliance itself, shall be—

(a) so far as is practicable so located or protected as not to be exposed to accidental damage,
(b) soundly and properly constructed of materials which are compatible with one another and with the gas used or to be used and which are capable of withstanding the loads and stresses likely to be met in operation, and
(c) so designed and constructed that leakage of gas is unlikely to occur.

(see regulation 41)   SCHEDULE 6
CONSTRUCTION OF MINIBUSES

4–3669 The requirements referred to in regulation 41 are as follows—

Exhaust pipes

1. The outlet of every exhaust pipe fitted to a minibus shall be either at the rear or on the off side of the vehicle.

Doors—number and position

2. (1) Every minibus shall be fitted with at least—

(a) one service door on the near side of the vehicle; and
(b) one emergency door either at the rear or on the off side of the vehicle so, however, that any emergency door fitted on the off side of the vehicle shall be in addition to the driver's door and there shall be no requirement for an emergency door on a minibus if it has a service door at the rear in addition to the service door on the near side.

(2) No minibus shall be fitted with any door on its off side other than a driver's door and an emergency door.

Emergency Doors

3. Every emergency door fitted to a minibus, whether or not required pursuant to these Regulations, shall—

(a) be clearly marked, in letters not less than 25 mm high, on both the inside and the outside, "EMERGENCY DOOR" or "FOR EMERGENCY USE ONLY", and the means of its operation shall be clearly indicated on or near the door;

(b) if hinged, open outwards;

(c) be capable of being operated manually; and

(d) when fully opened, give an aperture in the body of the vehicle not less than 1210 mm high nor less than 530 mm wide.

Power-operated doors

4. (1) Every power-operated door fitted to a minibus shall—

(a) incorporate transparent panels so as to enable a person immediately inside the door to see any person immediately outside the door;

(b) be capable of being operated by a mechanism controlled by the driver of the vehicle when in the driving seat;

(c) be capable, in the event of an emergency or a failure of the supply of power for the operation of the door, of being opened from both inside and outside the vehicle by controls which—

(i) over-ride all other controls,

(ii) are placed on, or adjacent to, the door, and

(iii) are accompanied by markings which clearly indicate their position and method of operation and state that they may not be used by passengers except in an emergency;

(d) have a soft edge so that a trapped finger is unlikely to be injured; and

(e) be controlled by a mechanism by virtue of which if the door, when closing, meets a resistance exceeding 150 Newtons, either—

—the door will cease to close and begin to open, or

—the closing force will cease and the door will become capable of being opened manually.

(2) No minibus shall be equipped with a system for the storage or transmission of energy in respect of the opening or closing of any door which, either in normal operation or if the system fails, is capable of adversely affecting the operation of the vehicle's braking system.

Locks, handles and hinges of doors

5. No minibus shall be fitted with—

(a) a door which can be locked from the outside unless, when so locked, it is capable of being opened from inside the vehicle when stationary;

(b) a handle or other device for opening any door, other than the driver's door, from inside the vehicle unless the handle or other device is designed so as to prevent, so far as is reasonably practicable, the accidental opening of the door, and is fitted with a guard or transparent cover or so designed that it must be raised to open the door;

(c) a door which is not capable of being opened, when not locked, from inside and outside the vehicle by a single movement of the handle or other device for opening the door;

(d) a door in respect of which there is not a device capable of holding the door closed so as to prevent any passenger falling through the doorway;

(e) a side door which opens outwards and is hinged at the edge nearest the rear of the vehicle except in the case of a door having more than one rigid panel;

(f) a door, other than a power-operated door, in respect of which there is not either—

(i) a slam lock of the two-stage type; or

(ii) a device by means of which the driver, when occupying the driver's seat, is informed if the door is not securely closed, such device being operated by movement of the handle or other device for opening the door or, in the case of a handle or other device with a spring-return mechanism, by movement of the door as well as of the handle or other device.

Provided that the provisions of sub-paragraphs (a), (c), (d) and (f) of this paragraph shall not apply in respect of a near side rear door forming part of a pair of doors fitted at the rear of the vehicle if that door is capable of being held securely closed by the other door of that pair.

View of doors

6. (1) Save as provided in sub-paragraph (2), every minibus shall be fitted with mirrors or other means so that the driver, when occupying the driver's seat, can see clearly the area immediately inside and outside every service door of the vehicle.

(2) The provisions of sub-paragraph (1) shall be deemed to be satisfied in respect of a rear service door if a person 1.3 metres tall standing 1 metre behind the vehicle is visible to the driver when occupying the driver's seat.

Access to doors

7. (1) Save as provided in sub-paragraph (2), there shall be unobstructed access from every passenger seat in a minibus to at least two doors one of which must be on the nearside of the vehicle and one of which must be either at the rear or on the offside of the vehicle.

(2) Access to one only of the doors referred to in sub-paragraph (1) may be obstructed by either or both of—

(a) a seat which when tilted or folded does not obstruct access to that door; and

(b) a lifting platform or ramp which—

(i) does not obstruct the handle or other device on the inside for opening the door with which the platform or ramp is associated, and

(ii) when the door is open, can be pushed or pulled out of the way from the inside so as to leave the doorway clear for use in an emergency.

Grab handles and hand rails

8. Every minibus shall be fitted as respects every side service door with a grab handle or a hand rail to assist passengers to get on or off the vehicle.

Seats

9. (1) No seat shall be fitted to any door of a minibus.

(2) Every seat and every wheelchair anchorage fitted to a minibus shall be fixed to the vehicle.

(3) No seat, other than a wheelchair, fitted to a minibus shall be less than 400 mm wide, and in ascertaining the width of a seat no account shall be taken of any arm-rests, whether or not they are folded back or otherwise put out of use.

(4) No minibus shall be fitted with an anchorage for a wheelchair in such a manner that a wheelchair secured to the anchorage would face either side of the vehicle.

(5) No minibus shall be fitted with a seat—

(a) facing either side of the vehicle and immediately forward of a rear door unless the seat is fitted with an arm-rest or similar device to guard against a passenger on that seat falling through the doorway; or

(b) so placed that a passenger on it would, without protection, be liable to be thrown through any doorway which is provided with a power-operated door or down any steps, unless the vehicle is fitted with a screen or guard which affords adequate protection against that occurrence.

Electrical equipment and wiring

10. (1) Save as provided in sub-paragraph (2) no minibus shall be fitted with any—

(a) electrical circuit which is liable to carry a current exceeding that for which it was designed;

(b) cable for the conduct of electricity unless it is suitably insulated and protected from damage;

(c) electrical circuit, other than a charging circuit, which includes any equipment other than—

    (i) a starter motor,

    (ii) a glow plug,

    (iii) an ignition circuit, and

    (iv) a device to stop the vehicle's engine,

unless it includes a fuse or circuit breaker so, however, that one fuse or circuit breaker may serve more than one circuit; or

(d) electrical circuit with a voltage exceeding 100 volts unless there is connected in each pole of the main supply of electricity which is not connected to earth a manually-operated switch which is—

    (i) capable of disconnecting the circuit or, if there is more than one, every circuit, from the main supply,

    (ii) not capable of disconnecting any circuit supplying any lamp with which the vehicle is required to be fitted, and

    (iii) located inside the vehicle in a position readily accessible to the driver.

(2) The provisions of sub-paragraph (1) do not apply in respect of a high tension ignition circuit or a circuit within a unit of equipment.

Fuel tanks

11. No minibus shall be fitted with a fuel tank or any apparatus for the supply of fuel which is in the compartments or other spaces provided for the accommodation of the driver or passengers.

Lighting of steps

12. Every minibus shall be provided with lamps to illuminate every step at a passenger exit or in a gangway.

General construction and maintenance

13. Every minibus, including all bodywork and fittings, shall be soundly and properly constructed of suitable materials and maintained in good and serviceable condition, and shall be of such design as to be capable of withstanding the loads and stresses likely to be met in the normal operation of the vehicle.

Definitions

14. In this Schedule—

"driver's door" means a door fitted to a minibus for use by the driver;

"emergency door" means a door fitted to a minibus for use by passengers in an emergency; and

"service door" means a door fitted to a minibus for use by passengers in normal circumstances.

(see regulation 42)   SCHEDULE 7

FIRE EXTINGUISHING APPARATUS AND FIRST AID EQUIPMENT FOR MINIBUSES

PART I

FIRE EXTINGUISHING APPARATUS

4–3680 A fire extinguisher which complies in all respects with the specification for portable fire extinguishers issued by the British Standards Institution numbered BS 5423: 1977 or BS 5423: 1980 or BS 5423: 1987 and which—

(a) has a minimum test fire rating of 8A or 21B, and

(b) contains water or foam or contains, and is marked to indicate that it contains, halon 1211 or halon 1301.

PART II

(See regulation 43)

FIRST AID EQUIPMENT

(i) Ten antiseptic wipes, foil packed;

(ii) One conforming disposable bandage (not less than 7.5 cm wide);

(iii) Two triangular bandages;
(iv) One packet of 24 assorted adhesive dressings;
(v) Three large sterile unmedicated ambulance dressings (not less than 15.0 cm × 20.0 cm);
(vi) Two sterile eye pads, with attachments;
(vii) Twelve assorted safety pins; and
(viii) One pair of rustless blunt-ended scissors.

Regulations 55A(1) and 61(11)   SCHEDULE 7XA
END OF SERIES EXEMPTIONS

PART I
MODIFICATION OF REGULATIONS 55A, 61 AND 61A IN RELATION TO END OF SERIES VEHICLES

Modification of regulations 55A and 61

4-3680A   **1.** (1) An item numbered 2 or higher in the Table in regulation 55A shall not apply to—

(a) a type approval end of series vehicle;
(b) a non-type approval end of series vehicle; or
(c) a late entry into service vehicle,

if it is first used before the first anniversary of the date specified in column 3 of the item.

(2) An item numbered 8, 9 or 11 in Table II of regulation 61 shall not apply to a type approval end of series vehicle if it is first used before the first anniversary of the date specified in column 3 of the item.

(3) An item numbered 9 or 11 in Table II of regulation 61 shall not apply to a non-type approval end of series vehicle if it is first used before the first anniversary of the date specified in column 3 of the item.

(4) An item numbered 10 or higher (other than 11) in Table II of regulation 61 shall not apply to—

(a) a type approval end of series vehicle;
(b) a non-type approval end of series vehicle; or
(c) a late entry into service vehicle,

if it is first used before the first anniversary of the date specified in column 3 of the item.

(4A) No provision of any Community Directive specified in an item numbered 1 or 2 in the Table in regulation 61A shall be deemed to be a design, construction or equipment requirement applying to, or to impose limit values in relation to, a vehicle by virtue of paragraphs (2) and (3) of regulation 61A, if the vehicle is—

(a) a type approval end of series vehicle,
(b) a non-type-approval end of series vehicle, or
(c) a late entry into service vehicle,

in relation to such a provision, and the vehicle is first used before the first anniversary of the date as is specified (as defined in regulation 61A) by the relevant Community Directive in item 1 or 2 in the Table in regulation 61A.

(5) Parts II, III and IV of this Schedule shall have effect for the purpose of interpreting the expressions "type approval end of series vehicle", "non-type approval end of series vehicle" and "late entry into service vehicle" respectively for the purposes of this paragraph.

PART II
MEANING OF "TYPE APPROVAL END OF SERIES VEHICLE" IN PART I

Meaning of "type approval end of series vehicle" for the purposes of paragraph 1

2. (1) For the purposes of paragraph 1, a vehicle is a type approval end of series vehicle, in relation to item 8, 9 or 11 in Table II in regulation 61, if it meets the requirements of sub-paragraph (3) in relation to the item.

(2) For the purposes of paragraph 1, and subject to regulation 3 of the Motor Vehicles (Type Approval for Goods Vehicles) (Great Britain) (Amendment) Regulations 2007, a vehicle is a type approval end of series vehicle, in relation to an item numbered 2 or higher in the Table in regulation 55A or an item numbered 10 or higher (other than item 11) in Table II in regulation 61 or any provision of any Community Directive specified in item 1 or 2 in the Table in regulation 61A if—

(a) by virtue of Schedule 1C to the Type Approval for Goods Vehicles Regulations,
(b) by virtue of Schedule 1C to the Type Approval (Great Britain) Regulations, or
(c) by virtue of regulations 12 and 13 of, and Schedule 2 to, the EC Whole Vehicle Type Approval Regulations,

(which in certain circumstances defer the date on which certain requirements relating to exhaust emissions, noise and silencers cease to apply) the type approval requirements that applied to the vehicle on the date specified in column 3 of the item or, in relation to any provision of any Community Directive specified in item 1 or 2 in the Table in regulation 61A, on the date as is specified (as defined in regulation 61A) by the relevant Community Directive are the same as the type approval requirements that applied to the vehicle immediately before the date so specified in that column of that item or in relation to any provision of any Community Directive specified in item 1 or 2 in the Table in regulation 61A, the date as is specified by the relevant Community Directive.

(2A) For the purposes of paragraph 1, a vehicle is a type-approval end of series vehicle in relation to an item in the Table in regulation 55A , or in Table II in regulation 61, or any provision in any Community Directive specified in item 1 or 2 in the Table in regulation 61A, if it has been exempted from that item or provision under—

(a) the laws of a relevant State (as defined by paragraph 5(1)(c)) other than the United Kingdom, or
(b) the laws applicable in Northern Ireland,

pursuant to Article 8(2)(b) of the Framework Directive.

(3) A vehicle meets the requirements of this sub-paragraph, in relation to the item, if—

(a) it was manufactured during the relevant period;
(b) one of the following conditions is satisfied—

(i) a certificate of conformity was issued in respect of the vehicle before the date specified in column 3 of the item by virtue of a TAC issued before the date specified in column 4 of the Table in paragraph 6 in relation to the item, or
(ii) a sub-MAC was issued in respect of the vehicle before the date specified in column 3 of the item by virtue of a MAC issued before the date specified in column 4 of that Table;

(c) it was in the territory of a relevant state at some time before the date specified in column 3 of the item and

(d) the number of relevant vehicles which were—

   (i) manufactured before that vehicle was manufactured, and

   (ii) still in existence on the date specified in column 3 of that item, was less than the specified number of 50 (whichever is the greater).

(4) For the purposes of sub-paragraph (3)—

(a) "MAC" means a Minister's approval certificate issued under section 58(1) of the Road Traffic Act 1988;

(b) "sub-MAC" means a Minister's approval certificate issued under section 58(4) of the Road Traffic Act 1988; and

(c) "TAC" means a type approval certificate.

Meaning of "relevant vehicle" for the purposes of this Part

3. (1) For the purposes of paragraph 2(3)(d), in relation to a particular vehicle to which Type Approval for Goods Vehicles Regulations apply (in this paragraph referred to as "the vehicle in question") and a particular item, a "relevant vehicle" is a vehicle (other than the vehicle in question) which—

(a) is a vehicle to which those Regulations apply;

(b) meets the requirements specified in paragraphs (a) to (c) of paragraph 2(3);

(c) was manufactured by the manufacturer of the vehicle in question; and

(d) had not been registered under the Vehicles (Excise) Act 1971 or the Vehicle Excise and Registration Act 1994 before the date specified in column 3 of the item.

(2) For the purposes of paragraph 2(3)(d) in relation to a particular vehicle to which the Type Approval (Great Britain) Regulations apply (in this paragraph referred to as "the vehicle in question") and a particular item, a "relevant vehicle" is a vehicle (other than the vehicle in question) which—

(a) is a vehicle to which those Regulations apply;

(b) meets the requirements specified in paragraphs (a) to (c) of paragraph 2(3);

(c) was manufactured by the manufacturer of the vehicle in question; and

(d) had not been registered under the Vehicle Excise and Registration Act 1994 before the date specified in column 3 of the item.

Meaning of "specified number" for the purposes of this Part

4. (1) For the purposes of paragraph 2(3)(d), in relation to a particular vehicle to which the Type Approval (Great Britain) Regulations apply (in this paragraph referred to as "the vehicle in question") and a particular item, "the specified number" is 10% of the total number of vehicles to which those Regulations apply that were both—

(a) manufactured by the manufacturer of the vehicle in question; and

(b) registered under the Vehicles Excise Act 1971 or the Vehicle Excise and Registration Act 1994 during the one year period ending immediately before the date specified in column 3 of the item.

(2) For the purposes of paragraph 2(3)(d), in relation to a particular vehicle to which the Type Approval for Goods Vehicles Regulations apply (in this paragraph referred to as "the vehicle in question") and a particular item, "the specified number" is 10% of the total number of vehicles to which those Regulations apply that were both—

(a) manufactured by the manufacturer of the vehicle in question, and

(b) registered under the Vehicles Excise Act 1971 or the Vehicle Excise and Registration Act 1994 during the one year period ending immediately before the day specified in column 3 of the item.

Circumstances in which a vehicle is to be regarded as having been in the territory of a relevant state for the purposes of this Part

5. (1) For the purposes of paragraph 2(3)(c)—

(a) at any material time before the 5th November 1993, "relevant state" means a member State;

(b) in relation to any time on or after 5th November 1993 but before 1st May 1995, "relevant state" means an EEA State other than Liechtenstein; and

(c) in relation to any time on or after 1st May 1995, "relevant state" means any EEA State.

(2) For the purposes of this paragraph—

"EEA agreement" means the Agreement on the European Economic Area signed at Oporto on the 2nd May 1992 as adjusted by the protocol signed at Brussels on the 17th March 1993; and

"EEA State" means a State which is a contracting party to the EEA agreement.

Meaning of "relevant period" for the purposes of this Part

6. For the purposes of this Part, "the relevant period" in relation to an item numbered 8, 9 or 11 in Table II in regulation 61 is the period—

(a) beginning on the date specified in column 2 of the Table below against that item; and

(b) ending immediately before the date specified in column 3 of the Table below against that item.

TABLE

1	2	3	4	5
Item in Table II in regulation 61	Date on which the relevant period begins:	Date immediately before which the relevant period ends.	Date before which type approval etc needs to be granted	Date in column 3 of Table II in regulation 61
8	1st August 1990	1st September 1992	1st July 1992	31st December 1992
9	1st April 1991	1st October 1993	1st October 1993	1st October 1993
11	1st August 1992	1st August 1994	1st October 1993	1st October 1994

PART III

MEANING OF "NON-TYPE APPROVAL END OF SERIES VEHICLE" IN PART I

Meaning of "non-type approval end of series vehicle" in paragraph 1

7. (1) For the purposes of paragraph 1, a vehicle is a non-type approval end of series vehicle in relation to an item or provision if it meets the requirements of sub-paragraph (2) in relation to the item or provision.

(2) A vehicle meets the requirements of this sub-paragraph in relation to an item or provision if—

(a) it is a vehicle to which neither the Type Approval (Great Britain) Regulations nor the Type Approval for Goods Vehicles Regulations nor the EC Whole Vehicle Type Approval Regulations apply;

(b) it was manufactured during the relevant period;

(c) no EC certificate of conformity has been issued in respect of the vehicle;

(d) it was in the territory of a relevant state at some time before the end of the relevant period; and

(e) the number of relevant vehicles which were both—

(i) manufactured before that vehicle was manufactured, and

(ii) still in existence on the date specified in column 3 in the item, or in relation to any provision of any Community Directive specified in item 1 or 2 in the Table in regulation 61A, on the date as is specified (as defined in regulation 61A) by the relevant Community Directive, is less than the specified number or 100, whichever is the greater.

Meaning of "relevant vehicle" for the purposes of this Part

8. For the purposes of paragraph 7(2)(e), in relation to a particular vehicle (in this paragraph referred to as "the vehicle in question") and a particular item, or provision, a "relevant vehicle" is a vehicle (other than the vehicle in question) which—

(a) meets the requirements specified in paragraphs (a) to (d) of paragraph 7(2);

(b) is a "vehicle" within the meaning of Community Directive 70/220[1] (as amended by Community Directive 83/351[2]) or Community Directive 2005/55[3] (as amended by Community Directives 2005/78 and 2006/51);

(c) was manufactured by the manufacturer of the vehicle in question;

(d) had not been registered under the Vehicles (Excise) Act 1971 or the Vehicle Excise and Registration Act 1994 during the relevant period.

Meaning of "specified number" for the purposes of this Part

9. (1) For the purposes of paragraph 7(2)(e), in relation to a particular vehicle (in this paragraph referred to as "the vehicle in question") and a particular item or provision, "the specified number" is 30% of the total number of vehicles that—

(a) are vehicles to which neither the Type Approval (Great Britain) Regulations nor the Type Approval for Goods Vehicles Regulations nor the EC Whole Vehicle Type Approval Regulations apply; and

(b) meet the requirements of sub-paragraph (2).

(2) A vehicle meets the requirements of this paragraph if it—

(a) is a "vehicle" within the meaning of Community Directive 70/220 (as amended by Community Directive 83/351) or Community Directive 2005/55 (as amended by Community Directives 2005/78 and 2006/51);

(b) was manufactured by the manufacturer of the vehicle in question; and

(c) was registered under the Vehicles (Excise) Act 1971 or the Vehicle Excise and Registration Act 199 during the one year period ending immediately before the date specified in column 3 of that item or, in relation any provision of any Community Directive specified in to item 1 or 2 of the Table in regulation 61A, before the date as is specified (as defined in regulation 61A) by the relevant Community Directive.

Circumstances in which a vehicle is to be regarded as having been in the territory of a relevant state for the purposes of this Part

10. Paragraph 5 in Part II of this Schedule shall have effect for the purposes of paragraph 7(2)(d) as it has effect for the purposes of paragraph 2(3)(c).

Meaning of "relevant period" for the purposes of this Part

11. For the purposes of paragraphs 7(2)(d), "the relevant period"—

(a) in relation to an item numbered 9 or 11 in Table II in regulation 61 is the period—

(i) beginning on the date specified in column 2 of the Table below against the item, and

(ii) ending immediately before the date specified in column 3 of the Table below against the item; and

(b) in relation to any item in the Table in regulation 55A or any item numbered 10 or higher (other than 11 in the said Table II is the two year period ending immediately before the date specified in column 3 of that item ; and

(c) in relation to any provision of any Community Directive specified in an item numbered 1 or 2 in the Table in regulation 61A is the two year period ending immediately before the date as is specified (as defined in regulation 61A) by the relevant Community Directive in the Table.

TABLE

1	2	3	4	5
Item in Table II in regulation 61	Date on which the relevant period begins:	Date immediately before which the relevant period ends.	Date before which type approval etc needs to be granted	Date in column 3 of Table II in regulation 61
8	1st August 1990	1st September 1992	1st July 1992	31st December 1992
9	1st April 1991	1st October 1993	1st October 1993	1st October 1993
11	1st August 1992	1st August 1994	1st October 1993	1st October 1994

PART IV

MEANING OF "LATE ENTRY INTO SERVICE VEHICLE" IN PART I

Meaning of "late entry into service vehicle" in paragraph 1

12. For the purposes of paragraph 1, a vehicle is a late entry into service vehicle, in relation to an item or provision, if—

(a) no EC certificate of conformity has been issued in respect of the vehicle;

(b) it was in the territory of a relevant state at some time before the date specified in column 3 of the item or, in relation to any provision of any Community Directive specified in item 1 or 2 of the Table in regulation 61A, before the date as is specified (as defined in regulation 61A) by the relevant Community Directive;

(c) it was manufactured at least two years before that date.

Circumstances in which a vehicle is to be regarded as having been in the territory of a relevant state for the purposes of this Part

13. Paragraph 5 in Part II of this Schedule shall have effect for the purposes of paragraph 12(*b*) as it has effect for the purposes of paragraph 2(3)(*c*).

1. OJ No. L76, 6.4.72, p.1.
2. OJ No. L197, 20.7.83, p.1.
3. OJ No L275, 20.10.2005, p. 1.

(See regulations 57, 57A and 57B)   SCHEDULE 7A
MOTOR CYCLE NOISE AND MOTOR CYCLE SILENCERS

PART I

4–3680B **1.** (1) For the purposes of these Regulations a vehicle meets the requirements of an item in the Table below if its sound level does not exceed by more than 1 dB(A) the relevant limit specified in column 2 in that item when measured under the conditions specified in column 3 in that item by the method specified in column 4 in that item using the apparatus prescribed in regulation 55(6).

(2) In this Part of this Schedule, "moped" has the same meaning as in regulation 57.

TABLE

1	2		3	4
	Limits of sound level			
Item	Mopeds	Vehicles other than mopeds	Conditions of measurement	Methods of measurement
1	73 dB(A)	Limit determined in accordance with paragraph 2.1.1 of Annex I to Community Directive 78/1015 by reference to the cubic capacity of the vehicle	Conditions specified in paragraph 2.1.3 of Annex I to Community Directive 78/1015	Methods specified in paragraph 2.1.4 of Annex I to Community Directive 78/1015
2	73 dB(A)	First stage limit determined in accordance with paragraph 2.1.1 of Annex I to Community Directive 87/56 by reference to the cubic capacity of the vehicle	Conditions specified in paragraph 2.1.3 of Annex I to Community Directive 87/56	Methods specified in paragraph 2.1.4 of Annex I to Community Directive 87/56
3	74 dB(A)	The limit specified in item 2 plus 1 dB(A)	As in item 2	As in item 2

PART II

2. The requirements of this paragraph are that the silencer—

(a) is so constructed that—

(i) it meets the requirements of paragraphs 3 and 4 of British Standard BS AU 193:1983;

(ii) were it to be fitted to an unused vehicle of the same model as the vehicle in question, the unused vehicle would meet the requirements of paragraph 5.2 of that Standard; and

(b) is clearly and indelibly marked "BS AU 193/T2".

3. The requirements of this paragraph are that the silencer—

(a) is so constructed that—

(i) it meets the requirements of paragraphs 3 and 4 of British Standard BS AU 193a:1990;

(ii) were it to be fitted to an unused vehicle of the same model as the vehicle in question, the unused vehicle would meet the requirements of paragraph 5.2 of that Standard; and

(b) is clearly and indelibly marked "BS AU 193a/1990T2".

4. The requirements of this paragraph are that the silencer—

(*a*) is so constructed that—

    (i) it meets the requirements of paragraphs 3 and 4 of British Standard BS AU 193a:1990;

    (ii) were it to be fitted to an unused vehicle of the same model as the vehicle in question, the unused vehicle would meet the requirements of paragraph 5.3 of that Standard; and

(*b*) is clearly and indelibly marked "BS AU 193a/1990T3".

5. In this Part of this Schedule—

(*a*) "British Standard BS AU 193:1983" means the British Standard Specification for replacement motor cycle and moped exhaust systems published by the British Standard Institution under reference number BS AU 193:1983;

(*b*) "British Standard BS AU 193a:1990" means the British Standard Specification for replacement motor cycle and moped exhaust systems published by the British Standard Institution under reference number BS AU 193a:1990;

PART III

6. Paragraph (4) of regulation 57A shall not apply to a replacement silencer if the second requirement referred to in that regulation would be met where there substituted in Part II of this Schedule,

(*a*) for the references to provisions in either of the British Standard Specifications references to equivalent provisions in a corresponding standard; and

(*b*) for the references to a mark, references to a mark made pursuant to that corresponding standard indicating that the silencer complies with those equivalent provisions.

7. In this Part of this Schedule, "corresponding standard", in relation to a British Standard Specification, means—

(*a*) a standard code of practice of a national standards body or equivalent body of any member State;

(*b*) any international standard recognised for use as a standard by any member State; or

(*c*) a technical specification or code of practice which whether mandatory or not, is recognised for use as a standard by a public authority of any member State,

where the standard, code of practice, international standard or technical specification provides, in relation to motor cycles, a level of noise limitation and safety equivalent to that provided by the British Standard Specification and contains a requirement as respect the marking of silencers equivalent to that provided by that instrument.

8. A reference in this part of this Schedule to a British Standard Specification is a reference to British Standard BS AU 193:1983 or British Standard BS AU 190a:1990; and "either of the British Standard Specification" shall be construed accordingly.

9. In this Part of this schedule, British Standard BS AU 193:1983 or British Standard BS AU 190a:1990" have the same meanings as in Part II of this Schedule.

SCHEDULE 7B
EMISSIONS FROM CERTAIN MOTOR VEHICLES

(*Amended by SI 2002/264.*)

PART I
VEHICLES PROPELLED BY SPARK IGNITION ENGINES

4–3680C 1. This Part of this Schedule applies to a vehicle if, when the engine is running without load at a normal idling speed, the carbon monoxide content of the exhaust emissions from the engine exceeds the relevant percentage of the total exhaust emissions from the engine by volume.

2. This Part of this Schedule also applies to a vehicle if, when the engine is running without load at a fast idling speed,—

(*a*) the carbon monoxide content of the exhaust emissions from the engine exceeds the relevant percentage of the total exhaust emissions from the engine by volume;

(*b*) the hydrocarbon content of those emissions exceeds 0.02% of the total exhaust emissions from the engine by volume; or

(*c*) the lambda value is not within the relevant limits.

3. For the purposes of paragraph 1 of this Part of this Schedule the relevant percentage, in respect of a vehicle, is—

(*a*) if the vehicle is of a description specified in the Annex to the emissions publication, the percentage shown against that description of vehicle in column 2(*a*) of that Annex;

(*b*) if the vehicle is not of such a description and is first used before 1st July 2002, 0.5%; or

(*c*) if the vehicle is not of such a description and is first used on or after 1st July 2002, 0.3%.

3A. For the purposes of paragraph 2(*a*) of this Part of this Schedule the relevant percentage, in respect of a vehicle, is, when the engine is running without load at a fast idling speed—

(*a*) if the vehicle is of a description specified in the Annex to the emissions publication, the percentage shown against that description of vehicle in column 3(*a*) of that Annex;

(*b*) if the vehicle is not of such a description and is first used before 1st July 2002, 0.3%; or

(*c*) if the vehicle is not of such a description and is first used on or after 1st July 2002, 0.2%.

4. For the purposes of this Part of this Schedule, in the case of a vehicle of a description specified in the Annex to the emissions publication, the engine shall be regarded as running at a normal idling speed if and only if the engine is running at a rotational speed between the minimum and maximum limits shown against that description of vehicle in columns 2(*b*) and (*c*) respectively of that Annex.

5. For the purposes of this Part of this Schedule an engine shall be regarded as running at a fast idling speed if—

(*a*) the vehicle is of a description specified in the Annex to the emissions publication and the engine is running at a rotational speed between the minimum and maximum limits shown against that description of vehicle in columns 3(*e*) and (*f*) respectively of that Annex; or

(*b*) the vehicle is not of such a description and the engine is running at a rotational speed between 2,500 and 3,000 revolutions per minute.

6. For the purposes of this Part of this Schedule, the lambda value, in respect of a vehicle, shall be regarded as being within relevant limits, if and only if—

    (a)   the vehicle is of a description specified in the Annex to the emissions publication and the lambda value is between the minimum and maximum limits shown against that description of vehicle in columns 3(c) and (d) respectively of that Annex; or

    (b)   the vehicle is not of such a description and the lambda value is between 0.97 and 1.03.

7. In this Part of this Schedule—

    (a)   a reference to the lambda value, in relation to a vehicle at any particular time, is a reference to the ratio by mass of air to petrol vapour in the mixture entering the combustion chambers divided by 14.7; and

    (b)   "the emissions publication" is the publication entitled "In Service Exhaust Emission Standards for Road Vehicles – Twelfth Edition" (ISBN 0-9549352-1-7 on or before 31st December 2006 and from 1st January 2007 ISBN 978-09549352-1-4) published by the Department for Transport.

8.—(1) This Part of this Schedule applies to a vehicle if, when subjected to a relevant test, the coefficient of absorption of the exhaust emissions from the engine of the vehicle immediately after leaving the exhaust system exceeds—

    (a)   if the vehicle is first used before 1st July 2008 and the engine of that vehicle is turbo-charged, 3.0 per metre;

    (b)   if the vehicle is first used before 1st July 2008 and the engine of that vehicle is not turbo-charged, 2.5 per metre; or

    (c)   if the vehicle is first used on or after 1st July 2008, 1.5 per metre.

    (2) In paragraph (1) "a relevant test" means a test conducted in accordance with—

    (a)   point 8.2.2 of Annex II of Council Directive 96/96/EC as replaced by Article 1 of Commission Directive 2003/27/EC; or

    (b)   point 2.2 of Annex II of Directive 2000/30/EC of the European Parliament and the Council as replaced by Article 1 of Commission Directive 2003/26/EC.

9. In this Part of this Schedule—

    (a)   "coefficient of absorption" shall be construed in accordance with paragraph 3.5 of Annex VII to Community Directive 72/306;

    (b)   Revoked.

(See regulation 66)   **SCHEDULE 8**

PLATES FOR CERTAIN VEHICLES

PART I

4–3681 Particulars to be shown on plate for motor vehicles (including motor-vehicles forming part of articulated vehicles)

    1. Manufacturer's name.

    2. Vehicle type.

    3. Engine type and power (a).

    4. Chassis or serial number.

    5. Number of axles.

    6. Maximum axle weight for each axle (b).

    7. Maximum gross weight (c).

    8. Maximum train weight (d).

    9. Maximum weight in Great Britain for each axle (b) (e).

    10. Maximum gross weight in Great Britain (c) (e).

    (a)   The power need not be shown in the case of a motor vehicle manufactured before 1st October 1972 (hereinafter in this Schedule referred to as "an excepted vehicle") and shall not be shown in the case of any motor vehicle which is propelled otherwise than by a compression ignition engine.

    (b)   This weight as respects each axle is the sum of the weights to be transmitted to the road surface by all the wheels of that axle.

    (c)   This weight is the sum of the weights to be transmitted to the road surface by all the wheels of the motor vehicle (including any load imposed by a trailer, whether forming part of an articulated vehicle or not, on the motor vehicle).

    (d)   This weight is the sum of the weights to be transmitted to the road surface by all the wheels of the motor vehicle and of any trailer drawn, but this item need not be completed where the motor vehicle is not constructed to draw a trailer.

    (b), (c), (d) References to the weights to be transmitted to the road surface by all or any of the wheels of the vehicle or of any trailer drawn are references to the weights so to be transmitted both of the vehicle or trailer and of any load or persons carried by it.

    (e)   This item need not be completed in the case of an excepted vehicle or in the case of a vehicle which is a locomotive or motor tractor.

PART II

Particulars to be shown on plate for trailers (including trailers forming part of articulated vehicles)

    1. Manufacturer's name.

    2. Chassis or serial number.

    3. Number of axles.

    4. Maximum weight for each axle (a).

    5. Maximum load imposed on drawing vehicle (b).

    6. Maximum gross weight (c).

    7. Maximum weight in Great Britain for each axle (a) (e).

    8. Maximum gross weight in Great Britain (c) (f).

    9. Year of manufacture (d).

    (a)   This weight as respects each axle is the sum of the weights to be transmitted to the road surface by all the wheels of that axle.

    (b)   Only for trailers forming part of articulated vehicles or where some of the weight of the trailer or its load is to be imposed on the drawing vehicle. This item need not be completed in the case of a converter dolly.

(c) This weight is the sum of the weights to be transmitted to the road surface by all the wheels of the trailer, including any weight of the trailer to be imposed on the drawing vehicle.

(a), (b), (c) References to the weights to be transmitted to the road surface by all or any of the wheels of the trailer are references to the weight so to be transmitted both of the trailer and of any load or persons carried by it and references to the weights to be imposed on the drawing vehicle are references to the weights so to be imposed both of the trailer and of any load or persons carried by it except where only the load of the trailer is imposed on the drawing vehicle.

(d) This item need not be completed in the case of a trailer manufactured before 1st April 1970.

(e) This item need not be completed in the case of a trailer manufactured before 1st October 1972.

(f) This item need not be completed in the case of a trailer manufactured before 1st October 1972 or which forms part of an articulated vehicle.

PART III

1. The power of an engine, which is to be shown only in the case of a compression ignition engine on the plate in respect of item 3 in Part I of this Schedule, shall be the amount in kilowatts equivalent to the installed power output shown in a type test certificate issued—

(a) by a person authorised by the Secretary of State for the type of engine to which the engine conforms; and

(b) in accordance with either—

(i) the provisions relating to the installed brake power output specified in the British Standard Specification for the Performance of Diesel Engines for Road Vehicles published on 19th May 1971 under the number BS AU 141a: 1971;

(ii) the provisions relating to the net power specified in Community Directive 80/1269 but after allowance has been made for the power absorbed by such equipment, at its minimum power setting, driven by the engine of the vehicle as is fitted for the operation of the vehicle (other than its propulsion) such power being measured at the speed corresponding to the engine speed at which maximum engine power is developed; or

(iii) the provisions of Annex 10 of ECE Regulation 24.02 as further amended with effect from 15th February 1984 or Annexe 10 of ECE Regulation 24.03 or Community Directive 88/195 relating to the method of measuring internal combustion engine net power, but after allowance has been made for the power absorbed by any disconnectable or progressive cooling fan, at its maximum setting, and by any other such equipment, at its minimum power setting, driven by the engine of the vehicle as is fitted for the operation of the vehicle (other than its propulsion), such power being measured at the speed corresponding to the engine speed at which maximum engine power is developed.

2. (1) The weights to be shown on the plate in relation to items 6, 7 and 8 in Part I and in relation to items 4, 5 and 6 in Part II shall be the weight limits at or below which the vehicle is considered fit for use, having regard to its design, construction and equipment and the stresses to which it is likely to be subject in use, by the Secretary of State if the vehicle is one to which the Type Approval for Goods Vehicles Regulations apply, and by the manufacturer if the vehicle is one to which those Regulations do not apply.

Provided that, where alterations are made to a vehicle which may render the vehicle fit for use at weights which exceed those referred to above in this paragraph and shown on the plate—

(a) there may be shown on the plate, in place of any of those weights, such new weights as the manufacturer of the vehicle or any person carrying on business as a manufacturer of motor vehicles or trailers (or a person duly authorised on behalf of that manufacturer or any such person) or a person authorised by the Secretary of State considers to represent the weight limits at or below which the vehicle will then be fit for use, having regard to its design, construction and equipment and to those alterations and to the stresses to which it is likely to be subject in use; and

(b) the name of the person who has determined the new weights shall be shown on the plate as having made that determination and, where he is a person authorised by the Secretary of State, his appointment shall be so shown.

(2) In relation to a vehicle manufactured on or after 1st October 1972, in the foregoing paragraph—

(a) the references to equipment shall not be treated as including a reference to the type of tyres with which the vehicle is equipped; and

(b) for the words "weight limits at or below" in both places where they occur there shall be substituted the words "maximum weights at".

3. The weights to be shown on the plate in respect of—

(a) item 9 in Part I of this Schedule shall be the weights shown at item 6 in that Part and in respect of item 7 in Part II of this Schedule shall be the weights shown at item 4 in that Part, in each case reduced so far as necessary to indicate the maximum weight applicable to each axle of the vehicle, if the vehicle is not to be used in contravention of regulations 23, 75, 78 or 79, and if the tyres with which the vehicle is equipped are not, as respects strength, to be inadequate to support the weights to be so shown at item 9 and item 7;

(b) item 10 in the said Part I shall be the weight shown at item 7 in that Part and in respect of item 8 in the said Part II shall be the weight shown at item 6 in that Part, in each case reduced so far as necessary to indicate the maximum permissible weight applicable if the vehicle is not be used in contravention of regulation 75 if the tyres with which the vehicle is equipped are not, as respects strength, to be inadequate to support the weights to be so shown at item 10 and item 8.

4. (1) Subject to sub-paragraph (2) of this paragraph weights on plates first affixed to a vehicle on or after 1st October 1972 shall be shown in kilograms and weights on plates first so affixed before that date shall be shown in tons and decimals thereof.

(2) Where a new weight is first shown on a plate by virtue of the proviso to paragraph 2(1) the weight shall be shown as if it was on a plate first affixed to a vehicle on the date it was first shown.

5. All letters and figures shown on the plate shall be not less than 6 mm in height.

6. In this Schedule references to the manufacturer of a motor vehicle or trailer are in relation to—

(a) a vehicle constructed with a chassis which has not previously formed part of another vehicle, references to the person by whom that chassis was made;

(b) any other vehicle, references to the person by whom that vehicle was constructed.

(see regulation 69)   SCHEDULE 9
                            PLATES FOR MOTOR CYCLES

4–3682 **1.** The plate required by regulation 69 shall be firmly attached to a part of the motor cycle which is not normally subject to replacement during the life of the motor cycle.

2. The plate shall be in the form shown in the diagram in this paragraph, shall have dimensions not less than those shown in that diagram and shall show the information provided for in that diagram and detailed in the Notes below.

Diagram of Plate

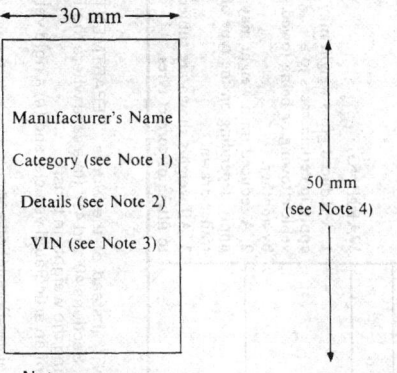

Notes:
1. The categories are "standard motor cycle" and "moped".
2. The details are—

(*a*) for standard motor cycles—

  (i) the engine capacity,
  (ii) the maximum engine power, and
  (iii) the power to weight ratio,

provided that the details under (ii) and (iii) need not be shown for a vehicle first used before 1st January 1982;

(*b*) for mopeds—

  (i) the engine capacity,
  (ii) the kerbside weight, and
  (iii) the maximum speed.

3. The vehicle identification number (VIN) shall be marked in the form used by the manufacturer to identify any one individual vehicle.
4. In the case of a plate fitted to a vehicle first used before 1st January 1982 or to a moped this dimension shall be 40 mm.
3. The information on the plate shall be shown in characters not less than 4 mm in height and in the positions on the plate indicated in the diagram above.
4. No information, other than that provided for in the diagram above, shall be marked within the rectangle which is shown in that diagram.
5. In this Schedule and, in respect of the definition of "moped", in regulations 54 and 57—

"maximum engine power" means the maximum net power the motor cycle engine will develop, in kilowatts, when measured in accordance with the test conditions specified in the International Standard number ISO 4106 developed by the technical committee of the International Organisation for Standardisation, and approved by member bodies, including the United Kingdom, and published under the reference ISO 1978 4106–09–01;
"moped" means a motor cycle which—

  (*a*) has a kerbside weight not exceeding 250 kg, and
  (*b*) if propelled by an internal combustion engine, has an engine with a cylinder capacity which does not exceed 50 cc, and
  (*c*) is designed to have a maximum speed not exceeding 30 mph when driven under the conditions set out in paragraph 6.

"power to weight ratio" means the ratio of the maximum engine power to the kerbside weight of the vehicle measured, as regards the maximum engine power, in kilowatts and, as regards the kerbside weight, in 1000 kg;
"standard motor cycle" means a motor cycle which is not a moped.

6. A motor cycle shall be regarded as complying with paragraph (*c*) of the definition of "moped" in paragraph 5 if it cannot exceed 35 mph when tested under the following conditions—

(*a*) the surface on which it is tested shall be dry asphalt or concrete;
(*b*) the rider shall be a person not exceeding 75 kg in weight;
(*c*) no passenger or load shall be carried;
(*d*) the test route shall be so located that acceleration to, and deceleration from, maximum speed can take place elsewhere than on the test route itself;
(*e*) the test route shall not have a gradient exceeding 5%;
(*f*) the motor cycle shall be ridden in opposite directions along the test route and the speed recorded for the purpose of the test shall (in order to minimise the effect of wind resistance and gradient) be the average of speeds shown for each direction;
(*g*) when being driven along the test route, the motor cycle shall be driven in such manner and in such gear as to achieve the maximum speed of which it is capable; and
(*h*) if the motor cycle is fitted with a device which can, without the use of specialist tools or equipment, be readily modified or removed so as to increase its maximum speed, the test shall be carried out with the device in the modified condition or, as the case may be, without the device.

SCHEDULE 10
MINISTRY PLATE

DEPARTMENT OF TRANSPORT

PLATE	Serial No.
REGISTRATION/IDENTIFICATION MARK	DTp REF. NO.
CHASSIS/SERIAL No.	MAKE AND MODEL

Road Traffic Act 1972, Sections 40 and 47
Examination of Goods Vehicles

YEAR OF ORIGINAL REGISTRATION	YEAR OF MANUFACTURE	FUNCTION
	UNLADEN WEIGHT	

(1) DESCRIPTION OF WEIGHTS APPLICABLE TO VEHICLE	(2) WEIGHTS NOT TO BE EXCEEDED IN GREAT BRITAIN KILOGRAMS	(3) DESIGN WEIGHTS (if higher than shown in col (2)) KILOGRAMS
AXLE WEIGHT (Axles numbered from front to rear) — AXLE 1		
AXLE 2		
AXLE 3		
AXLE 4		
GROSS WEIGHT (see warning opposite)		
TRAIN WEIGHT (see warning opposite)		
DATE OF ISSUE		

WARNING

1. A reduced gross weight may apply in certain cases to a vehicle towing or being towed by another.
2. A reduced train weight may apply depending on the type of trailer drawn.
3. All weights shown are subject to fitting of correct tyres.

1. A Ministry plate may contain the words "MINISTRY OF TRANSPORT" or "DEPARTMENT OF TRANSPORT" or "DEPARTMENT OF THE ENVIRONMENT" instead of the words "DEPARTMENT OF TRANSPORT" and may contain the words "Road Safety Act 1967. Sections 8 and 9" or of the words "Road Traffic Act 1972. Sections 40 and 45" (in a case where the Type Approval For Goods vehicles Regulations do not apply). It may also contain additional columns in Columns (2) and (3) showing the weights in tons.

2. Entries in respect of train weight are required in the case of—(a) a motor vehicle constructed or adapted to form part of an articulated vehicle; and (b) a rigid vehicle which is constructed or adapted to draw a trailer and is first used on or after 1 April 1983.

3. A Ministry plate shows the unladen weight and function of the vehicle in a case where the Type Approval for Goods Vehicles Regulations apply.

4. A Ministry plate may have separate spaces for the "make" and "model" of the vehicle.

(see regulation 70)

SCHEDULE 10A
MINISTRY PLATE

PLATE VTG 6A	DEPARTMENT OF TRANSPORT Road Traffic Act 1972. Sections 40, 45 and 47 Examination of Goods Vehicles	SERIAL NUMBER	
		UNLADEN WEIGHT	DTp REF No
		5. VEHICLE DIMENSIONS	

REGISTRATION/ IDENTIFICATION MARK	YEAR OF ORIGINAL REG	YEAR OF MANUFACTURE	FUNCTION	LENGTH (L)		
				WIDTH (W)		

MANUFACTURER/MODEL				a. (See Note 1) COUPLING CENTRE TO VEHICLE FOREMOST PART	MAXIMUM	MINIMUM
TYPE APPROVAL/ VARIANT No						
VEHICLE IDENTIFICATION No						
(1) DESCRIPTION OF WEIGHTS APPLICABLE TO VEHICLE	(2) WEIGHT NOT TO BE EXCEEDED IN Gt. BRITAIN	(3) EEC MAXIMUM PERMITTED WEIGHTS (See Note 4)	(4) DESIGN WEIGHTS (if higher than shown in column 2)	b. (See Note 2) COUPLING CENTRE TO VEHICLE REARMOST PART	MAXIMUM	MINIMUM
GROSS WEIGHT (See warning below)						
TRAIN WEIGHT (See warning below)						
MAXIMUM TRAIN WEIGHT (See Note 3)	✕		✕			
AXLE WEIGHTS (Axles numbered from front to rear) Axle 1						
Axle 2						
Axle 3						
Axle 4						
MAXIMUM KINGPIN LOAD (Semi-trailers only)	✕		✕	DATE OF ISSUE		

N.B. ALL WEIGHTS IN KILOGRAMS/ALL DIMENSIONS IN MILLIMETRES.

<u>WARNING</u>

a. A reduced gross weight may apply in certain cases to a vehicle towing or being towed by another.
b. A reduced train weight may apply depending on the type of trailer drawn.
c. All weights shown are subject to the fitting of correct tyres.

<u>NOTES</u>

1. This dimension only applies to drawing vehicles of trailers and semi-trailers.
2. This dimension only applies to trailers and semi-trailers.
3. This weight only applies to a 3 axle tractor with a 2 or 3 axle semi-trailer carrying a 40 foot ISO container as a combined transport operation.
4. Where there is no weight shown in the EEC maximum permitted weights column this is because there is no EEC standard relating to that weight.

1. Entries in respect of train weight are required in the case of—(a) a motor vehicle constructed or adapted to form part of an articulated vehicle; and (b) a rigid vehicle which is constructed or adapted to draw a trailer and is first used on or after 1 April 1983.

2. A Ministry plate shows the unladen weight and function of the vehicle in a case where the Type Approval for Goods Vehicles Regulations apply.

3. A Ministry plate may have no "Reference Number".

Department of Transport
ROAD TRAFFIC ACT 1988 SECTIONS 41, 49, 57 & 59
EXAMINATION OF GOODS VEHICLES.

Serial No. **V**

Plate VTG 6T
Rev. 92

DTp Ref. No.

Reg./Ident. Mark	Vehicle Identification No.	Type Approval No./Variant

Manufacturer/ Model		Speed Limiter Exempt

Function (See note 3 below)	Year of Original Registration	Year of Manufacture

(1) Description of Weights applicable to vehicle	(2) Weights not to be exceeded in Gt. Britain	(3) Design Weights (If higher than shown in column 2)	
Gross Weight (See notes 1 & 4 below)			
Train Weight (See note 2 below)			
Max. Train Weight (See note 5 below)			Date of Issue

Axle Weights (Axles numbered from front to rear) (See note 1 overleaf)	Axle 1			
	Axle 2			DEPARTMENT OF
	Axle 3			TRANSPORT GREAT BRITAIN
	Axle 4			

NOTES
1. A reduced gross weight and/or axle weight may apply in certain cases to a vehicle towing or being towed by another.
2. The MAXIMUM permissibe train weight can vary depending on the type of suspension and trailer drawn.
3. If the last letter in the function box is 'R' road friendly suspension is fitted.
4. All weights shown are subject to the fitting of correct tyres.
5. This weight applies to combined transport operations.

Tyre use conditions
applicable to vehicle

N.B. All Weights in Kilograms

---

1. A weight is not required in the box for Maximum Train Weight unless the vehicle is capable of being lawfully used on a road in Great Britain, having regard to Schedule 11A, at a greater train weight than the train weight at which it could lawfully be used ignoring that Schedule.

Department of Transport

ROAD TRAFFIC ACT 1988 SECTIONS 41, 49, 57 & 58
EXAMINATION OF GOODS VEHICLES
This is issued as proof of compliance with the
Weights and Dimensions Directive 85/3/EEC

Serial No. **B**

DTp Ref. No.

Plate VTG 6A

Reg./Ident. Mark	Vehicle Identification No.	Type Approval No./Variant

Manufacturer/ Model		Speed Limiter Exempt

Function (See note 3 below)	Year of Original Registration	Year of Manufacture

(1) Description of Weights applicable to vehicle	(2) Weights not to be exceeded in Gt. Britain	(3) EEC Maximum permitted weights (See note 8 below)	(4) Design Weights (If higher than shown in column 2)	Length		Width	
Gross Weight (See notes 1 & 4 below)				a. Coupling centre to vehicle foremost part (See note 6 below)		Max	Min
Train Weight (See note 2 below)				b. Coupling centre to vehicle rearmost part (See note 7 below)		Max	Min
Max Train Weight (See note 5 below)			////	Date of Issue			

Axle Weights (Axles numbered from front to rear) (See note 1 below)	Axle 1				
	Axle 2				DEPARTMENT OF
	Axle 3				TRANSPORT GREAT BRITAIN
	Axle 4				Tyre use conditions applicable to vehicle

Maximum Kingpin Load (Semi-Trailers only)	////		

NOTES
1. A reduced gross weight and/or axle weight may apply in certain cases to a vehicle towing or being towed by another.
2. The maximum permissible train weight can vary depending on the type of suspension and trailer drawn.
3. If the last letter in the function box is 'R' road friendly suspension is fitted.
4. All weights shown are subject to the fitting of correct tyres.

NOTES (Cont'd)
5. This weight applies to combined transport operations.
6. This dimension only applies to drawing vehicles of trailers and semi-trailers.
7. This dimension only applies to trailers and semi-trailers.
8. Where there is no weight shown in the EEC maximum permitted weights column this is because there is no EEC standard relating to that weight.

N.B. All Weights in Kilograms-All Dimensions in Millimetres

---

1. A weight is not required in the box for Maximum Train Weight unless the vehicle is capable of being lawfully used on a road in Great Britain, having regard to Schedule 11A, at a greater train weight than the train weight at which it could lawfully be used ignoring that Schedule.

4–3685

(see regulations 75, 77 and 79)

SCHEDULE 11
MAXIMUM PERMITTED WEIGHTS, ETC

PART I

MAXIMUM PERMITTED LADEN WEIGHTS OF (1) TRAILERS AND (2) HEAVY MOTOR CARS AND MOTOR CARS NOT FITTED WITH ROAD
FRIENDLY SUSPENSION; IN EACH CASE NOT FORMING PART OF AN ARTICULATED VEHICLE

(See regulation 75)

1. The maximum permitted laden weight of a two or three axle vehicle to which this Part applies of a description specified in column 2 of Table I below shall, for the purposes of regulation 75, be the weight specified in column 3 of that item.

2. In the case of a vehicle to which this Part applies and which is not of a description specified in an item in column 2 of Table I below, the maximum permitted laden weight shall, for the purposes of regulation 75, be the weight specified in column 4 of Table II below in the item which is appropriate having regard to columns 2 and 3 of that Table.

TABLE I

MAXIMUM PERMITTED LADEN WEIGHTS OF CERTAIN TWO AND THREE AXLE VEHICLES

(1)	(2)	(3)
Item	Description of Vehicle	Maximum permitted laden weight (kg)
1	A two axle trailer in which– (a) the two axles are closely spaced, and (b) the distance between the foremost axle of the trailer and the rearmost axle of the drawing vehicle is at least 4.2m	18,000
2	A three axle trailer in which– (a) the three axles are closely spaced, and (b) the distance between the foremost axle of the trailer and the rearmost axle of the drawing vehicle is at least 4.2m	24,000
3	A two axle motor vehicle which is a goods vehicle in which the distance between the foremost and rearmost axles is at least 3.0m	17,000
4	A two axle trailer in which the distance between the foremost axle and the rearmost axle is at least 3.0m	18,000

TABLE II

MAXIMUM PERMITTED LADEN WEIGHTS OF VEHICLES NOT FALLING WITHIN TABLE 1

(1)	(2)	(3)	(4)
Item	No of axles	Distance between foremost and rearmost axles (metres)	Maximum permitted laden weight (kg)
1	2	Less than 2.65	14,230
2	2	At least 2.65	16,260
3	3 or more	Less than 3.0	16,260
4	3 or more	At least 3.0 but less than 3.2	18,290
5	3 or more	At least 3.2 but less than 3.9	20,330
6	3 or more	At least 3.9 but less than 4.9	22,360
7	3	At least 4.9	25,000
8	4 or more	At least 4.9 but less than 5.6	25,000
9	4 or more	At least 5.6 but less than 5.9	26,420
10	4 or more	At least 5.9 but less than 6.3	28,450
11	4 or more	At least 6.3	30,000

PART IA

(see regulation 75)

MAXIMUM PERMITTED GROSS WEIGHTS FOR HEAVY CARS AND MOTOR CARS IF THE DRIVING AXLES ARE FITTED WITH ROAD FRIENDLY
SUSPENSION ETC AND IN EACH CASE NOT FORMING PART OF AN ARTICULATED VEHICLE

1. Subject to paragraph 2, the maximum permitted gross weight of a vehicle to which this Part applies shall, for the purposes of regulation 75, be the weight shown in column 4 of the Table below in the item which is appropriate, having regard to columns 2 and 3 in that Table.

2. In the case of a vehicle to which this Part applies being a two axle goods vehicle which has a distance between its axles of at least 3·0 m, the maximum permitted laden weight for the purposes of regulation 75 shall be 17,000 kg.

TABLE

(1)	(2)	(3)	(4)
Item	No of axles	Distance between foremost and rearmost axles (metres)	Maximum permitted laden weight (kg)
1	2	Less than 2.65	14,230
2	2	At least 2.65	16,260
3	3 or more	Less than 3.0	16,260
4	3 or more	At least 3.0 but less than 3.2	18,290
5	3 or more	At least 3.2 but less than 3.9	20,330
6	3 or more	At least 3.9 but less than 4.9	22,360

(1)	(2)	(3)	(4)
Item	No of axles	Distance between foremost and rearmost axles (metres)	Maximum permitted laden weight (kg)
7	3 or more	At least 4.9 but less than 5.2	25,000
8	3	At least 5.2	26,000
9	4 or more	At least 5.2 but less than 6.4	The distance in metres between the foremost and rearmost axles multiplied by 5,000, rounded up to the next 10kg
10	4 or more	At least 6.4	32,000

PART II
MAXIMUM PERMITTED LADEN WEIGHTS FOR HEAVY MOTOR CARS AND MOTOR CARS FORMING PART OF ARTICULATED VEHICLES

(see regulation 75)

1	2	3	4	5
Item	No of axles	Distance between foremost and rearmost axles (metres)	Weight not exceeded by any axle not being the foremost or rearmost (kg)	Maximum permitted laden weight (kg)
1	2	At least 2.0	—	14,230
2	2	At least 2.4	—	16,260
3	2	At least 2.7	—	17,000
4	3 or more	At least 3.0	8,390	20,330
5	3 or more	At least 3.8	8,640	22,360
6	3 or more	At least 4.0	10,500	22,500
7	3 or more	At least 4.3	9,150	24,390
8	3 or more	At least 4.9	10,500	24,390

PART III
MAXIMUM PERMITTED LADEN WEIGHT OF ARTICULATED VEHICLES

(see regulation 77)

1	2		3
Item	Relevant axle spacing (metres)		Maximum weight (kg)
	(a) Where motor vehicle has 2 axles	(b) Where motor vehicle has more than 2 axles	
1	At least 2.0	At least 2.0	20,330
2	At least 2.2	At least 2.2	22,360
3	At least 2.6	At least 2.6	23,370
4	At least 2.9	At least 2.9	24,390
5	At least 3.2	At least 3.2	25,410
6	At least 3.5	At least 3.5	26,420
7	At least 3.8	At least 3.8	27,440
8	At least 4.1	At least 4.1	28,450
9	At least 4.4	At least 4.4	29,470
10	At least 4.7	At least 4.7	30,490
11	At least 5.0	At least 5.0	31,500
12	At least 5.3	At least 5.3	32,520
13	At least 5.5	At least 5.4	33,000
14	At least 5.8	At least 5.6	34,000
15	At least 6.2	At least 5.8	35,000
16	At least 6.5	At least 6.0	36,000
17	At least 6.7	At least 6.2	37,000
18	At least 6.9	At least 6.3	38,000

PART IV
MAXIMUM PERMITTED LADEN WEIGHT OF ARTICULATED VEHICLES

(see regulation 77)

(1)	(2)	(3)
Item	Type of articulated vehicle	Maximum permitted weight (kg)
1	Motor vehicle first used on or after 1st April 1973 and semi-trailer having a total of 5 or more axles	38,000
2	Motor vehicle with 2 axles first used on or after 1st April 1973 and semi-trailer with 2 axles while being used for international transport	35,000
3	Motor vehicle with 2 axles first used on or after 1st April 1973 in which– (a) every driving axle not being a steering axle is fitted with twin tyres; and (b) every driving axle is fitted with road friendly suspension; and a semi-trailer with 2 axles	35,000
4	Motor vehicle and semi-trailer having a total of 4 or more axles and not described in item 1, 2 or 3.	32,520
5	Motor vehicle with 2 axles first used on or after 1st April 1973 in which– (a) every driving axle not being a steering axle is fitted with twin tyres; and (b) every driving axle is fitted with road friendly suspension; and a semi-trailer with 1 axle	26,000
6	Motor vehicle with 2 axles and a semi-trailer with 1 axle being a combination not described in item 5	25,000

PART V
VEHICLES WITH TWO CLOSELY-SPACED AXLES

(see regulation 79(2))

(1)	(2)	(3)
Item	Description of vehicle	Maximum permitted weight of the two closely-spaced axles (kg)
1	A motor vehicle or trailer in which (in either case) the distance between the two closely-spaced axles is less than 1.3 metres	16,000
2	A vehicle being– (a) a motor vehicle in which the distance between the two closely-spaced axles is at least 1.3m, or (b) a trailer in which that distance is at least 1.3m and less than 1.5m, not being a vehicle described in item 3 or 4	18,000
3	A motor vehicle in which the distance between the two closely-spaced axles is at least 1.3m and– (a) every driving axle not being a steering axle is fitted with twin tyres; and (b) either every driving axle is fitted with road friendly suspension or neither of the two closely-spaced axles has an axle weight exceeding 9,500 kg	19,000
4	A trailer in which– (a) the two closely-spaced axles are driven from the motor vehicle drawing the trailer and are fitted with twin tyres; and (b) either those axles are fitted with road friendly suspension or neither of them has an axle weight exceeding 9,500 kg	19,000
5	A trailer in which the distance between the two closely-spaced axles is at least 1.5m and less than 1.8m	19,320
6	A trailer in which the distance between the two closely-spaced axles is at least 1.8m	20,000

PART VI
VEHICLES WITH THREE CLOSELY-SPACED AXLES

(see regulation 79(3))

(1)	(2)	(3)
Item	Description of vehicle	Maximum permitted weight of the two closely-spaced axles (kg)
1	A vehicle in which the smallest distance between any two of the three closely-spaced axles is less than 1.3m	21,000
2	A vehicle in which the smallest distance between any two of the three closely-spaced axles is at least 1.3m and at least one of those axles does not have air suspension	22,500
3	A vehicle in which the smallest distance between any two of the three closely-spaced axles is at least 1.3m and all three axles are fitted with air suspension	24,000

1. In this regulation the distance between any two axles shall be obtained by measuring the shortest distance between the lines joining the centre of the area of contact with the road surface of the wheels on each of the two axles; reg 3(10).

4–3686

(see regulations 76(1A), 77(2A) and 80(2B))   SCHEDULE 11A
EXEMPTIONS RELATING TO COMBINED TRANSPORT OPERATIONS[1]
PART I
GENERAL

1. Regulation 76 does not apply to a wheeled heavy motor car drawing one wheeled trailer if the requirements set out in Part II of this Schedule are for the time being fulfilled.

---

1. See note to reg 75, ante.
2. Regulation 76 does not apply to an articulated vehicle if the requirements set out in Part III of this Schedule are for the time being fulfilled.
2A. Regulations 75, 76, 77 and 78 do not apply to an articulated vehicle if the requirements set out in Part IIIA of this Schedule are for the time being fulfilled.

PART II
DRAWBAR COMBINATIONS

3. (1) The drawing vehicle and trailer must each be carrying a relevant receptacle as part of a combined transport operation, each such receptacle being on a journey—

(a) to a railhead from which the relevant receptacle is, as part of the operation, to be transported in a relevant manner by railway pursuant to a relevant contract made before the journey began; or
(b) from a railhead to which the relevant receptacle has, as part of the operation, been transported in a relevant manner by railway.

(2) There must be carried in the cab of the drawing vehicle a document or documents—

(a) if the vehicle is on a journey to a railhead, specifying the railhead, the date the relevant contract was made and the parties thereto;
(b) if the vehicle is on a journey from a railhead, specifying the railhead and the date and time at which the receptacles were collected from that railhead.

4. The following conditions must be satisfied in relation to the drawing vehicle, namely—

(a) it complies with the relevant braking requirement;
(b) every driving axle not being a steering axle is fitted with twin tyres; and
(c) either every driving axle is fitted with a road friendly suspension or no axle has an axle weight exceeding 8,5000kg.

5. (1) The motor vehicle and trailer must have a total of at least 6 axles.
(2) The total laden weight of the motor vehicle and trailer must not exceed 44,000kg.

PART III
ARTICULATED VEHICLES

6. (1) The motor vehicle comprised in the articulated vehicle must be being used for the conveyance of a loading unit as part of a combined transport operation, the loading unit being on a journey—

(a) to a railhead from which the loading unit is, as part of the operation, to be transported in a relevant manner by railway pursuant to a relevant contract made before the journey began; or
(b) from a railhead to which the loading unit has, as part of the operation, been transported in a relevant manner by railway.

(2) If the loading unit is a bi-modal vehicle, the semi-trailer comprised in the articulated vehicle must be the bi-modal vehicle in its semi-trailer mode.
(3) If the loading unit is a relevant receptacle, the relevant receptacle must be being carried on the semi-trailer comprised in the articulated vehicle.
(4) There must be carried in the cab of the motor vehicle a document or documents—

(a) if the vehicle is on a journey to a railhead, specifying the railhead, the date the contract was made and the parties thereto;
(b) if the vehicle is on a journey from a railhead, specifying the railhead and the date and time at which the loading unit was collected from that railhead.

7. The following conditions must be satisfied in relation to the drawing vehicle, namely—

(a) it complies with the relevant braking requirements;
(b) it has at least 3 axles;
(c) every driving axle not being a steering axle is fitted with twin tyres; and
(d) either every driving axle is fitted with a road friendly suspension or no axle has an axle weight exceeding 8,5000kg.

8. (1) The articulated vehicle must have a total of at least 6 axles.
(2) The laden weight of the articulated vehicle must not exceed the weight determined in accordance with sub-paragraph (3).
(3) The weight for the purposes of sub-paragraph (2) is the number of kilograms equal to the product of the distance measured in metres between the king-pin and the centre of the rearmost axle of the semi-trailer multiplied by 5500 and rounded up to the nearest 10 kg, if that number is less than 44000 kg.

PART IIIA
ARTICULATED VEHICLES (ALTERNATIVE REQUIREMENTS)

8A. (1) The requirements of paragraph 6 are fulfilled.
(2) The vehicle is one which falls within the first indent of paragraph 1 of Article 3 of Community Directive 96/53 (vehicles used in international traffic or put into circulation in any other Member State) and complies with the limit values specified in paragraph 2.2.2 of Annex I and the other relevant requirements of that Directive.

PART IV
INTERPRETATION

9. (1) In this Schedule—

''bi-modal vehicle'' means a semi-trailer which can be adapted for use as a railway vehicle;
''journey'', except in sub-paragraph (3), means a journey by road;
''loading unit'' means a bi-modal vehicle, road-rail semi-trailer or a relevant receptacle;
''railhead'' means a facility for the transhipment of—

(a) bi-modal vehicles from the ground onto the track of a railway, or
(b) relevant receptacles from road vehicles onto railway vehicles situated on the track of a railway, or
(c) road-rail semi-trailers from the ground onto railway vehicles on the track of a railway,

or vice versa;

''relevant contract'' means a contact for the transport of a loading unit by railway;
''relevant receptacle'' means a receptacle (not being a vehicle) having a length of at least 6.1m designed and constructed for repeated use for the carriage of goods on, and for transfer between, road vehicles and railway vehicles;
''road-rail semi-trailer'' means a semi-trailer constructed or adapted so as to be capable of being both used as a semi-trailer on roads and carried on a railway vehicle;
''road friendly suspension'' and ''twin tyres'' have the meanings given by regulation 75;
''network'', ''network licence'', ''railway vehicle'', ''track'' and ''train'' have the meanings given by section 83 of the Railways Act 1993.

(2) The definition of ''railway'' in section 67(1) of the Transport and Works Act 1992[1] shall have the effect for the purposes of this Schedule as it has effect for the purposes of that Act, and cognate expressions shall be construed accordingly.
(3) In these Regulations, a reference to a combined transport operation is a reference to the transport of a loading unit on a journey where—

(a) part of the journey is by railway on a network operated by the British Railways Board or under a network licence;
(b) part of the journey is by road; and
(c) no goods are added to or removed from the loading unit between the time when the journey begins and the time when it ends.

(4) Subject to sub-paragraph (5), for the purposes of this Schedule—

(a) a bi-modal vehicle shall be regarded a being transported by railway in a relevant manner if and only if the vehicle is in its railway vehicle mode is travelling by railway as part of a train;
(b) a relevant receptacle shall be regarded as being transported by railway in a relevant manner if and only if it is being carried on a railway vehicle which forms part of a train; and
(c) a road-rail semi-trailer shall be regarded as being transported by railway in a relevant manner if and only if it is being carried on a railway vehicle which forms part of a train.

(5) A relevant receptacle shall be regarded, for the purposes of this Schedule, as not being transported by railway in a relevant manner at any time when—

(a) the relevant receptacle is in or on a motor vehicle or trailer; and
(b) the motor vehicle or trailer is being carried on a railway vehicle.''.

(6) A road-rail semi-trailer shall be regarded, for the purposes of this schedule, as not being transported by railway in a relevant manner at any time when it is being carried on a railway vehicle as part of an articulated vehicle.

4–3687

(see regulations 81 and 82)   SCHEDULE 12
CONDITIONS TO BE COMPLIED WITH IN RELATION TO THE USE OF VEHICLES CARRYING WIDE OR LONG LOADS OR VEHICLES CARRYING
LOADS OR HAVING FIXED APPLIANCES OR APPARATUS WHICH PROJECT

PART I

Advance notice to Police

1. (a) Before using on a road a vehicle or vehicles to which this paragraph applies, the owner shall give notice of the intended use to the Chief Officer of Police for any area in which he proposes to use the vehicle or vehicles. The notice shall be given so that it is received by the date after which there are at least two working

days before the date on which the use of the vehicle or vehicles is to begin, and shall include the following details—

- (i) time, date and route of the proposed journey, and
- (ia) in a case to which regulation 7(9) applies, the overall length of the trailer,
- (ii) in a case to which regulation 82(2) applies, the overall length and width of the vehicle by which the load is carried and the width of the lateral projection or projections of its load,
- (iii) in a case to which regulation 82(4)(*a*) applies, the overall length and width of each vehicle by which the load is carried, the length of any forward or rearward projection and, where the load rests on more than one vehicle, the distance between the vehicles,
- (iv) in a case to which regulation 82(4)(*b*) applies, the overall length of the combination of vehicles and the length of any forward or rearward projection of the load, and
- (v) in a case to which regulation 82(7) and (8) applies, the overall length of the vehicle and the length of any forward or rearward projection of the load or special appliance or apparatus.

The Chief Officer of Police for any police area may, at his discretion, accept a shorter period of notice or fewer details.

(*b*) The vehicle or vehicles shall be used only in accordance with the details at (*a*) subject to any variation in the time, date or route which may be directed by—

- (i) any such Chief Officer of Police to the owner of the vehicle or vehicles, or
- (ii) a police constable to the driver in the interests of road safety or in order to avoid undue traffic congestion by halting the vehicle or vehicles in a place on or adjacent to the road on which the vehicle or vehicles are travelling.

(*c*) In this paragraph—

- (i) "Chief Officer of Police" has, in relation to England and Wales, the same meaning as in the Police Act 1964, and in relation to Scotland, the same meaning as in the Police (Scotland) Act 1967,
- (ii) "working day" means a day which is not a Sunday, a bank holiday, Christmas Day or Good Friday, and
- (iii) "bank holiday" means a day which is a bank holiday by or under the Banking and Financial Dealings Act 1971 either generally or in the locality in which the road is situated.

Attendants

2. At least one person in addition to the person or persons employed in driving a motor vehicle to which this paragraph applies shall be employed—

- (*a*) in attending to that vehicle and its load and any other vehicle or vehicles drawn by that vehicle and the load or loads carried on the vehicle or vehicles so drawn, and
- (*b*) to give warning to the driver of the said motor vehicle and to any person of any danger likely to be caused to any such other person by reason of the presence of the said vehicle or vehicles on the road.

Provided that, where three or more vehicles as respects which the conditions in this paragraph are applicable are travelling together in convoy, it shall be a sufficient compliance with this paragraph if only the foremost and rearmost vehicles in the convoy are attended in the manner prescribed in this paragraph.

For the purposes of this paragraph when a motor vehicle is drawing a trailer or trailers—

- (i) any person employed in pursuance of section 34 of the 1972 Act in attending that vehicle or any such trailer shall be treated as being an attendant required by this paragraph so long as he is also employed to discharge the duties mentioned in this paragraph; and
- (ii) when another motor vehicle is used for the purpose of assisting in their propulsion on the road, the person or persons employed in driving that other motor vehicle shall not be treated as a person or persons employed in attending to the first-mentioned vehicle or any vehicle or vehicles drawn thereby.

Marking of longer projections

3. (*a*) Every forward and rearward projection to which this paragraph applies shall be fitted with—

- (i) an end marker, except in the case of a rearward projection which is fitted with a rear marking in accordance with the Lighting Regulations, and
- (ii) where required by sub-paragraphs (*c*) and (*d*) of this paragraph, two or more side markers;

which shall be of the size, shape and colour described in Part II of this Schedule.

(*b*) the end marker shall be so fitted that—

- (i) it is as near as practicable in a transverse plane,
- (ii) it is not more than 0.5 m from the extreme end of the projection,
- (iii) the vertical distance between the lowest point of the marker and the road surface is not more than 2.5 m,
- (iv) it, and any means by which it is fitted to the projection, impedes the view of the driver as little as possible, and
- (v) it is clearly visible within a reasonable distance to a person using the road at the end of the vehicle from which the projection extends;

(*c*) where the forward projection exceeds 2 m or the rearward projection exceeds 3 m, one side marker shall be fitted on the right hand side and one on the left hand side of the projection so that—

- (i) each marker is as near as is practicable in a longitudinal plane,
- (ii) no part extends beyond the end of the projection,
- (iii) the vertical distance between the lowest part of each marker and the surface of the road is not more than 2.5 m,
- (iv) the horizontal distance between each marker and the end marker or, as the case may be, the rear marking carried in accordance with the Lighting Regulations does not exceed 1 m, and
- (v) each marker is clearly visible within a reasonable distance to a person using the road on that side of the projection;

(*d*) where—

- (i) a forward projection exceeds 4.5 m, or
- (ii) a rearward projection exceeds 5 m

extra side markers shall be fitted on either side of the projection so that the horizontal distance between the extreme projecting point of the vehicle from which the projection extends and the nearest point on any side marker from that point, and between the nearest points of any adjacent side markers on the same side does not exceed—

2.5 m in the case of a forward projection, or

3.5 m in the case of a rearward projection.

For the purposes of this sub-paragraph the expression "the vehicle" shall not include any special appliance or apparatus or any part thereof which is a forward projection or a rearward projection within the meaning of regulation 81;

(e) the extra side markers required by this sub-paragraph shall also meet the requirements of (i), (iii) and (v) of sub-paragraph (c);

(f) every marker fitted in accordance with this paragraph shall be kept clean and unobscured and between sunrise and sunset be illuminated by a lamp which renders it readily visible from a reasonable distance and which is so shielded that its light, except as reflected from the marker, is not visible to other persons using the road.

Marking of shorter projections

4. A projection to which this paragraph applies shall be rendered clearly visible to other persons using the road within a reasonable distance, in the case of a forward projection, from the front thereof or, in the case of a rearward projection, from the rear thereof and, in either case, from either side thereof.

Marking of wide loads

5

(a) Subject to sub-paragraph (d), every load carried on a vehicle in circumstances where this paragraph applies shall be fitted on each side and in the prescribed manner, with—

(i) a prescribed marker in such a position that it is visible from the front of the vehicle, and

(ii) a prescribed marker in such a position that it is visible from the rear of the vehicle.

(b) For the purposes of sub-paragraph (a)—

(i) a marker on a side of the load is fitted in the prescribed manner if at least part of it is within 50 mm of a longitudinal plane passing through the point on that side of the load which is furthest from the axis of the vehicle; and

(ii) a prescribed marker is a marker of the size, shape and colour described in Part II of this Schedule.

(c) Every marker fitted pursuant to this paragraph shall be kept clean and between sunset and sunrise be illuminated by a lamp which renders it readily visible from a reasonable distance and which is so shielded that its light, except as reflected from the marker, is not visible to other persons using the road.

(d) If the load does not extend beyond the longitudinal plane passing through the extreme projecting point on one side of the vehicle, it shall not be necessary for a marker to be fitted to the load on that side.

PART II
PROJECTION MARKERS

(See paragraphs 3(a) and 5 of this Schedule)

DIAGRAM OF END MARKER SURFACE

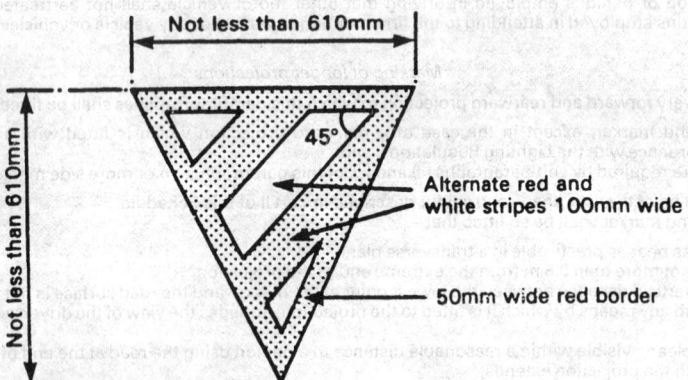

Not less than 610mm

Not less than 610mm

45°

Alternate red and white stripes 100mm wide

50mm wide red border

DIAGRAM OF SIDE MARKER SURFACE

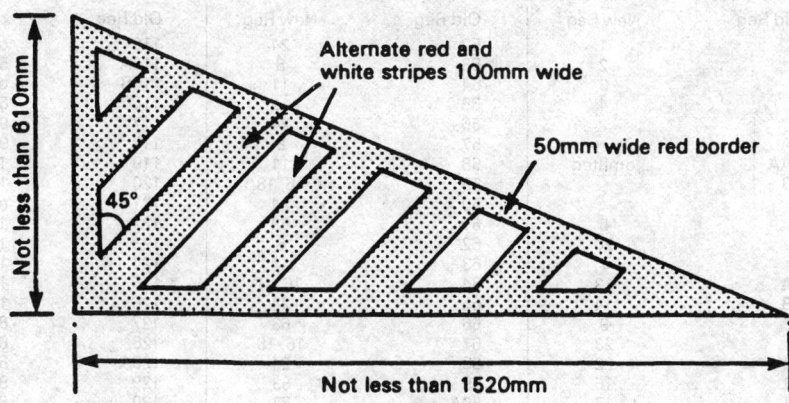

(see regulation 3(2))

SCHEDULE 13
PLATE FOR RESTRICTED SPEED VEHICLE

4–3688 1. A vehicle displays a plate in accordance with the requirements of this Schedule if a plate in respect of which the following conditions are satisfied is displayed on the vehicle in a prominent position.
   (2) The conditions are—

   (*a*) the plate must be in the form shown in the diagram below;
   (*b*) the plate must be at least 150 mm wide and at least 120 mm high;
   (*c*) the figures "5" and "0" must be at least 100 mm high and 50 mm wide with a stroke width of at least 12 mm, the figures being black on a white background; and
   (*d*) the border must be black and between 3 mm and 5 mm wide.

Table giving destination of Motor Vehicles (Construction and Use) Regulations 1978.

Old Reg	New Reg
1	1
2	2
3	3
4	4
5, 5A, 5B, 6, 7	5
5AA	omitted
8	20
9	7
9A	13
9B	14
10	9
11	23
12	22
13	16
14	17
14A	15
15, 16	omitted
17	45, 46
18	35
19	39
20	21
21	omitted
22	30
23, 24, 24A	33
25	31
26	32
27, 28	34
29	37
30	54
31	58
31A	55
31B	57
31C	56
31D	59
31E	55
32	60
33, 34, 35, 36, 37, 38	61
39	62
40	omitted
41	previously revoked
42	66
42A	68
43	67
44	
45	45
46	69
46A	71
46B	49
46C	51
46D	
46E	65
47	40
48	8
49	78
50, 51	16

Old Reg	New Reg
52	24
53	8
54	11
55	16
56	24
57	8
58	11
59	16, 18
60	24
61	63
62	8
63	11
64	16, 18
65	24
66	63
67	16, 18
68	24
69	63
69A	37
70	8
71	16
72	63
73	previously revoked
74	8
74A	12
75, 76	16
77	24
78	63
79	
79A	8
79B	11
79C	16, 18
79D	24
80	8, 71
80A	10
81	previously revoked
82-95	75-80
95A	9
96	previously revoked
96A	75, 76
97	100
98	36
99	omitted
100	30
101, 101A	18
102	29
102A	48
103	34
104	39
105	previously revoked
105A	50
105B	52
105C	65
106	previously revoked
107	27
108	26
109, 110, 111, 112	61
113	62
114	omitted
115	97

Old Reg	New Reg
116	omitted
116A	54
116B	omitted
116C	57
117	98
118	99
119	104
120	106
121	omitted
122	103
123	101
124	107
125	105
126	19
127	89
128	86
128A	88
129	92
130	84
131	previously revoked
132	83
133, 134	90
135	93
136	7
136A	87
136B	8
137	83
137A	85
138	91
138A	12
139	81
140	82
141	102
141A	93
142	53
143	109
144	108
144A	94
144B	95
144C	96
145	74
146, 147	omitted
148	70
149	73
150	80
151, 152, 153	18
154	25

Schedules

Old Reg	New Reg
1	1
2	6
3	4
3A	5
4	Reg 18
4A	Reg 15
5	previously revoked
6	omitted
7	11
8	12
9	Reg 58
9A	omitted
10	omitted
11	10
12, 12A	9

Use of Invalid Carriages on Highways Regulations 1988[1]
(SI 1988/2268)

4–3711   1. *Citation and commencement.*

1. Made by the Secretary of State for Transport in exercise of powers conferred by s 20 of the Chronically Sick and Disabled Persons Act 1970.

4–3712   2. *Revocation and savings.*

Interpretation

4–3713   3. In these Regulations—

the "1970 Act" means the Chronically Sick and Disabled Persons Act 1970;
the "1986 Regulations" means the Road Vehicles (Construction and Use) Regulations 1986;
a "Class 1 invalid carriage" means an invalid carriage which is not mechanically propelled;
a "Class 2 invalid carriage" means a mechanically propelled invalid carriage which is so constructed or adapted as to be incapable of exceeding a speed of 4 miles per hour on the level under its own power;
a "Class 3 invalid carriage" means a mechanically propelled invalid carriage which is so constructed or adapted as to be capable of exceeding a speed of 4 miles per hour but incapable of exceeding a speed of 8 miles per hour on the level under its own power;
"horn" has the meaning given by regulation 37(10)(*a*) of the 1986 Regulations;
"reversing alarm" has the meaning given by regulation 37(10)(*c*) of the 1986 Regulations;
"road" has the meaning given by section 142(1) of the Road Traffic Regulation Act 1984;
"two-tone horn" has the meaning given by regulation 37(10)(*d*) of the 1986 Regulations.

Prescribed conditions for purposes of section 20(1) of the 1970 Act

4–3714   4. The conditions in accordance with which an invalid carriage must be used, in order that the modifications of the statutory provisions mentioned in subsection (1) of section 20 of the 1970 Act shall have effect in the case of the invalid carriage (being modifications of certain statutory provisions which relate to the use of vehicles on footways and roads) shall be—

(*a*) in the case of Class 1, Class 2 and Class 3 invalid carriages that the invalid carriage must be used—

 (i) by a person falling within a class of persons for whose use it was constructed or adapted, being a person suffering from some physical defect or physical disability;
 (ii) by some other person for the purposes only of taking the invalid carriage to or bringing it away from any place where work of maintenance or repair is to be or has been carried out to the invalid carriage;
 (iii) by a manufacturer for the purposes only of testing or demonstrating the invalid carriage;
 (iv) by a person offering to sell the invalid carriage for the purpose only of demonstrating it; or
 (v) by a person giving practical training in the use of the invalid carriage for that purpose only;

(*b*) in the case of Class 1, Class 2 and Class 3 invalid carriages, that any horn fitted to it must not be sounded in the circumstances set out in regulation 5;

(*c*) in the case of Class 3 invalid carriages only—

 (i) that the invalid carriage must not be used by a person who is aged under 14 years;
 (ii) that, when being used on a footway, the invalid carriage must not be driven at a speed greater than 4 miles per hour;
 (iii) that the invalid carriage must not be used on a footway unless the device fitted in accordance with regulation 10(1)(*a*) is operating; and
 (iv) that the invalid carriage must not be used at any time unless the speed indicator fitted to it in accordance with regulation 10(1)(*b*) is operating.

4–3715   5. The circumstances referred to in regulation 4(*b*) are that the invalid carriage is either—

(*a*) stationary on a road, at any time, other than at times of danger due to another moving vehicle on or near the road; or
(*b*) in motion on a road which is a restricted road for the purposes of section 81 of the Road Traffic Regulation Act 1984 between 23.30 hours and 07.00 hours in the following morning.

Prescribed requirements for purposes of section 20(1) of the 1970 Act

4–3716   6. The requirements with which an invalid carriage must comply in order that the modifications of the statutory provisions mentioned in subsection (1) of section 20 of the 1970 Act shall have effect in the case of the invalid carriage (being modifications of certain statutory provisions which relate to the use of vehicles on footways and roads) shall be—

(*a*) that it shall be a Class 1, Class 2 or Class 3 invalid carriage; and
(*b*) the requirements specified in regulations 7 to 14.

Unladen weight

4–3717   7. (1) The unladen weight of a Class 1 or Class 2 invalid carriage shall not exceed 113.4 kilograms.

(2) The unladen weight of a Class 3 invalid carriage shall not exceed 150 kilograms.

(3) In this regulations, "unladen weight" means the weight of the invalid carriage inclusive of the weight of water, fuel or accumulators used for the purpose of the supply of power for its propulsion and of loose tools, but exclusive of the weight of any other load or of a person carried by the invalid carriage.

Means of stopping

4–3718   8. (1) A Class 2 or Class 3 invalid carriage shall be so constructed and maintained that it meets the requirements set out in paragraphs (2) to (4).

(2) The invalid carriage shall be capable of being brought to rest in all conditions of use with reasonable directional stability and within a reasonable distance.

(3) When the invalid carriage is not being propelled or is left unattended it shall be capable of being held stationary indefinitely in all conditions of use on a gradient of at least 1 in 5.

(4) The requirements of paragraphs (2) and (3) shall not be regarded as met unless the necessary braking effect can be achieved by the appropriate use—

(a) of the invalid carriage's propulsion unit or transmission gear or of both the propulsion unit and transmission gear;

(b) of a separate system fitted to the vehicle (which may be a system which operates upon the propulsion unit or transmission gear); or

(c) of a combination of the means of achieving a braking effect referred to in sub-paragraphs (a) and (b);

and in the case of paragraph (3) without depending upon any hydraulic or pneumatic device or on the flow of electrical current.

Lighting

4–3719   9. A Class 2 or Class 3 invalid carriage when on the carriageway of any road shall comply with the requirements specified in the Road Vehicles Lighting Regulations 1984 as if it was a motor vehicle within the meaning of the Road Traffic Act [1988] and as if any reference to an invalid carriage in those Regulations included an invalid carriage within the meaning of the 1970 Act.

Speed device and speed indicator

4–3720   10. (1) A Class 3 invalid carriage shall be fitted with—

(a) a device which is capable of limiting the maximum speed of the invalid carriage to 4 miles per hour on the level under its own power and which can be put into operation by the user; and

(b) a speed indicator.

(2) A speed indicator fitted in accordance with this regulations shall be kept free from any obstruction which might prevent it being easily seen by the user of the invalid carriage and shall be maintained in efficient working order.

(3) In this regulation, "speed indicator" means a device fitted to an invalid carriage for the purposes of indicating to the user of the invalid carriage whether the device referred to in paragraph (1)(a) is in operation.

Width

4–3721   11. The overall width of a Class 3 invalid carriage shall not exceed 0.85 metres.

Audible Warning Instrument

4–3722   12. (1) A Class 3 invalid carriage shall be fitted with a horn, not being a reversing alarm or a two-tone horn.

(2) The sound emitted by any horn fitted to an invalid carriage shall be continuous and uniform and not strident.

Vision

4–3723   13. (1) A Class 2 or Class 3 invalid carriage shall be so constructed that the user of the invalid carriage can at all times have a full view of the road and traffic ahead when controlling the invalid carriage.

(2) Any windscreen or window fitted to a Class 2 or Class 3 invalid carriage shall be made of safety glass or safety glazing and shall be maintained in such condition that it does not obscure the vision of the user of the invalid carriage while the invalid carriage is being driven.

(3) In this regulation—

"safety glass" means glass so manufactured or treated that if fractured it does not fly into fragments likely to cause severe cuts; and

"safety glazing" means material other than glass to manufactured or treated that if fractured it does not fly into fragments likely to cause severe cuts.

Rear view mirrors

4–3724 14. (1) A Class 3 invalid carriage shall be fitted either internally or externally with a rear view mirror.

(2) Any rear view mirror fitted to an invalid carriage shall be so constructed or treated that if fractured it does not fly into fragments likely to cause severe cuts.

(3) In this regulation "rear view mirror" means a mirror to assist the user of the invalid carriage to become aware of traffic to the rear of the invalid carriage.

Road Vehicles Lighting Regulations 1989[1]

(SI 1989/1796 amended by SI 1992/1217, SI 1994/2280, and 2567, SI 1996/3016, SI 2001/560, SI 2004/3168 (E),SI 2005/2929 (W), 2559 and 3169, SI 2006/594 and 1914)

4–3731 1. *Commencement, citation and revocation.*

1. Made by the Secretary of State for Transport under ss 41, 43 and 81 of the Road Traffic Act 1988. Contravention of the regulations is punishable with a maximum fine not exceeding level 4 on the standard scale: Part I of Sch 2 to the Road Traffic Offenders Act 1988.

4–3732 2. *Statement under s 43(3) of the Road Traffic Act 1988.*

Interpretation

4–3733 3. (1) Unless the context otherwise requires, any reference in these Regulations—

(a) to a numbered regulation or Schedule is a reference to the regulation or Schedule bearing that number in these Regulations.

(b) to a numbered paragraph is to the paragraph bearing that number in the regulation or Schedule in which the reference occurs, and

(c) to a numbered or lettered sub-paragraph is to the sub-paragraph bearing that number in the paragraph in which the reference occurs.

(2) In these Regulations, unless the context otherwise requires, any expressions for which there is an entry in column 1 of the Table has the meaning given against it in column 2 or is to be construed in accordance with directions given against it in that column.

TABLE

(1) Expression	(2) Meaning
"The Act"	The Road Traffic Act 1988.
"The Construction and Use Regulations"	The Road Vehicles (Construction and Use) Regulations 1986.
"The Designation of Approval Marks Regulations"	The Motor Vehicles (Designation of Approval Marks) Regulations 1979.
"Abnormal load escort vehicle"	A vehicle which is clearly identifiable to other road users as a vehicle used for the purposes of escorting abnormal loads by having on its front suitable markings and on its sides and rear retro-reflective markings.
"Agricultural vehicle"	A vehicle constructed or adapted for agriculture, grass cutting, forestry, land levelling, dredging or similar operations and primarily used for one or more of these purposes, and includes any trailer drawn by an agricultural vehicle.
"Angles of visibility"	A requirement for a lamp or reflector fitted to a vehicle to have specified horizontal and vertical angles of visibility is a requirement that at least 50 per cent of the apparent surface must be visible from any point within those angles when every door, tailgate, boot lid, engine cover, cab or other movable part of the vehicle is in the closed position.
"Apparent surface"	For any given direction of observation, is the orthogonal projection of a light-emitting surface in a plane perpendicular to the direction of observation and touching that surface.
"Articulated bus"	Has the same meaning as in the Construction and Use Regulations.
"Articulated vehicle"	Has the same meaning as in the Construction and Use Regulations.
"Breakdown vehicle"	A vehicle used to attend an accident or breakdown or to draw a broken down vehicle.
"Bus"	Has the same meaning as in the Construction and Use Regulations.

(1) Expression	(2) Meaning
"Caravan"	A trailer which is constructed (and not merely adapted) for human habitation.
"cc"	Cubic centimetre or centimetres (as the case may be).
"Circuit-closed tell-tale"	A light showing that a device has been switched on.
"cm"	Centimetre or centimetres (as the case may be).
"cm²"	Square centimetre or centimetres (as the case may be).
"Combat vehicle"	A vehicle of a type described at item 1, 2 or 3 in column 1 of Schedule 1 to the Motor Vehicles (Authorisation of Special Types) General Order 1979.
"Community Directive 76/756/EEC, as last amended by Directive 89/278/EEC"	Council Directive 76/756/EEC of 27.7.76 (OJ L262, 27.9.76, p 1) as amended by Commission Directive 80/233/EEC of 21.11.79 (OJ L51, 25.2.80, p 8), Commission Directive 82/244/EEC of 17.3.82 (OJ L109, 22.4.82, p 31), Council Directive 83/276/EEC of 26.5.83 (OJ L151, 9.6.83, p 47), Commission Directive 84/8/EEC of 14.12.83 (OJ L9, 12.1.84, p 24) and Commission Directive 89/278/EEC of 23.3.89 (OJ L109, 20.4.89, p 38).
"Community Directive 76/756/EEC, as last amended by Directive 91/663/EEC"	Council Directive 76/756/EEC as last amended by Directive 89/278/EEC and further amended by Commission Directive 91/663/EEC (OJ L366, 31.12.91, p 17).
"Daytime hours"	The time between half an hour before sunrise and half an hour after sunset.
"Dim-dip device"	A device which is capable of causing a dipped-beam headlamp to operate at reduced intensity.
"Dipped beam"	A beam of light emitted by a lamp which illuminates the road ahead of the vehicle without causing undue dazzle or discomfort to oncoming drivers or other road users.
"Direction indicator"	A lamp on a vehicle used to indicate to other road users that the driver intends to change direction to the right or to the left.
"Dual-purpose vehicle"	Has the same meaning as in the Construction and Use Regulations.
"Emergency vehicle"	A vehicle of any of the following descriptions— (a) a vehicle used for relevant authority (as defined by section 6 of the Fire (Scotland) Act 2005 (asp 5)) or, in England, fire and rescue authority, ambulance or police purposes; (aa) as regards England and Wales, and so far as relating to the functions of the Serious Organised Crime Agency which are exercisable in or as regards Scotland and which relate to reserved matters (within the meaning of the Scotland Act 1998), a vehicle used for Serious Organised Crime Agency purposes; (ab) Scotland; (b) an ambulance, being a vehicle (other than an invalid carriage) which is constructed for the purposes of conveying sick, injured or disabled persons and which is used for such purposes; (c) a vehicle owned by a body formed primarily for the purposes of fire salvage and used for those or similar purposes; (d) a vehicle owned by the Forestry Commission or by a local authority and used from time to time for the purposes of fighting fires; (e) a vehicle owned or operated by the Secretary of State for Defence and used— (i) for the purposes of the disposal of bombs or explosives, (ii) for the purposes of any activity— (aa) which prevents or decreases the exposure of persons to radiation arising from a radiation accident or radiation emergency, or (bb) in connection with an event which could lead to a radiation accident or radiation emergency; or (iii) by the Royal Air Force Mountain Rescue Service for the purposes of rescue operations or any other emergencies, (iv) revoked

(1) Expression	(2) Meaning
	(*f*) a vehicle primarily used for the purposes of the Blood Transfusion Service provided under the National Health Service Act 1977 or under the National Health Service (Scotland) Act 1978;
	(*g*) a vehicle used by Her Majesty's Coastguard or Coastguard Auxiliary Service for the purposes of giving aid to persons in danger or vessels in distress on or near the coast;
	(*h*) a vehicle used for the purposes of rescue operations at mines;
	(*i*) a vehicle owned by the Royal National Lifeboat Institution and used for the purposes of launching lifeboats;
	(*j*) a vehicle primarily used for the purposes of conveying any human tissue for transplanting or similar purposes; and
	(*k*) a vehicle under the lawful control of the Commissioners for Her Majesty's Revenue and Customs and used from time to time for the purposes of the investigation of serious crime (which, save for the omission of the words "and, where the authorising officer is within subsection (5)(*h*), it relates to an assigned matter within the meaning of section 1(1) of the Customs and Excise Management Act 1979", has the meaning given in section 93(4) of the Police Act 1997).
"End-outline marker lamp"	A lamp fitted near the outer edge of a vehicle in addition to the front and rear position lamps to indicate the presence of a wide vehicle.
"Engineering plant"	Has the same meaning as in the Construction and Use Regulations.
"Extreme outer edge"	In relation to a side of a vehicle, the vertical plane parallel with the longitudinal axis of the vehicle, and coinciding with its lateral outer edge, disregarding the projection of— (*a*) so much of the distortion of any tyre as is caused by the weight of the vehicle, (*b*) any connections for tyre pressure gauges, (*c*) any anti-skid devices which may be mounted on the wheels, (*d*) rear-view mirrors, (*e*) lamps and reflectors, (*f*) customs seals affixed to the vehicle, and devices for securing and protecting such seals, and (*g*) special equipment.
"Front fog lamp"	A lamp used to improve the illumination of the road in front of a motor vehicle in conditions of seriously reduced visibility.
"Front position lamp"	A lamp used to indicate the presence and width of a vehicle when viewed from the front.
"First used"	References to the date of first use of a vehicle shall be construed in accordance with regulation 3(3) of the Construction and Use Regulations.
"Hazard warning signal device"	A device which is capable of causing all the direction indicators with which a vehicle, or a combination of vehicles, is fitted to operate simultaneously.
"Headlamp"	A lamp used to illuminate the road in front of a vehicle and which is not a front fog lamp.
"Headlamp levelling device"	Either— (*a*) an automatic headlamp levelling device by means of which the downward inclination of any dipped-beam headlamp is automatically maintained regardless of the load on the vehicle, or (*b*) a manual headlamp levelling device by means of which the downward inclination of any dipped-beam headlamp may be adjusted by a manual control operable from the driving seat of the vehicle.
"Home forces"	The naval, military or air forces of Her Majesty raised in the United Kingdom.
"Home forces' vehicle"	A vehicle owned by, or in the service of, the home forces and used for naval, military or air force purposes.

(1) Expression	(2) Meaning
"Horse-drawn"	In relation to a vehicle, means that the vehicle is drawn by a horse or other animal.
"Hours of darkness"	The time between half an hour after sunset and half an hour before sunrise.
"Illuminated area"	The expression, in relation to a headlamp, front fog lamp and reversing lamp, in each case fitted with a reflector, means the orthogonal projection of the full aperture of the reflector on a plane (touching the surface of the lamp) at right angles to the longitudinal axis of the vehicle to which the lamp is fitted. If the light-emitting surface extends over only part of the full aperture of the reflector, then the projection of only that part shall be taken into account. In the case of a dipped-beam headlamp, the illuminated area is limited by the apparent trace of the cut-off on the lens.
	The expression, in relation to any other lamp, means the part of the orthogonal projection of the light-emitting surface on a plane (touching the surface of the lamp) at right angles to the longitudinal axis of the vehicle to which it is fitted, the boundary of which is such that if the straight edge of an opaque screen touches it at any point 98 per cent of the total intensity of the light is shown in the direction parallel to the longitudinal axis of the vehicle. Accordingly, for the purposes of determining the lower, upper and lateral edges of the lamp, only a screen placed with its straight edge horizontally or vertically needs to be considered.
"Industrial tractor"	Has the same meaning as in the Construction and Use Regulations.
"Installation and performance requirements"	In relation to any lamp, reflector, rear marking or device, the requirements specified in the Schedules to these Regulations relating to that lamp, reflector, rear marking or device.
"Invalid carriage"	A mechanically propelled vehicle constructed or adapted for the carriage of one person, being a person suffering from some physical defect or disability.
"Kerbside weight"	Has the same meaning as in the Construction and Use Regulations.
"kg"	Kilogram or kilograms (as the case may be).
"Light-emitting surface"	In relation to a lamp, that part of the exterior surface of the lens through which light is emitted when the lamp is lit, and in relation to a retro reflector that part of the exterior surface of the retro reflector from which light can be reflected.
"m"	Metre or metres (as the case may be).
"Main beam"	A beam of light emitted by a headlamp which illuminates the road over a long distance ahead of the vehicle.
"Matched pair"	In relation to lamps, a pair of lamps in respect of which— (a) both lamps emit light of substantially the same colour and intensity, and (b) both lamps are of the same size and of such a shape that they are symmetrical to one another.
"Maximum distance from the side of the vehicle"	The expression means— (a) in relation to a lamp fitted to a vehicle, the shortest distance from the boundary of the illuminated area to an extreme outer edge of the vehicle, and (b) in relation to a retro reflector fitted to a vehicle, the shortest distance from the boundary of the reflecting area to an extreme outer edge of the vehicle.
"Maximum gross weight"	Has the same meaning as in the Construction and Use Regulations.
"Maximum height above the ground"	The height above which no part of the illuminated area in the case of a lamp, or the reflecting area in the case of a retro reflector, extends when the vehicle is at its kerbside weight and when each tyre with which the vehicle is fitted is inflated to the pressure recommended by the manufacturer of the vehicle.
"Maximum speed"	Has the same meaning as in the Construction and Use Regulations.

(1) Expression	(2) Meaning
"Minimum height above the ground"	The height below which no part of the illuminated area in the case of a lamp, or the reflecting area in the case of a retro reflector, extends when the vehicle is at its kerbside weight and when each tyre with which the vehicle is fitted is inflated to the pressure recommended by the manufacturer of the vehicle.
"mm"	Millimetre or millimetres (as the case may be).
"Motor bicycle combination"	A combination of a solo motor bicycle and a sidecar.
"Motor tractor"	Has the same meaning as in the Construction and Use Regulations.
"Motorway"	Has the same meaning as in Schedule 6 of the Road Traffic Regulation Act 1984.
"Movable platform"	A platform which is attached to, and may be moved by means of, an extendible boom.
"mph"	Mile per hour or miles per hour (as the case may be).
"Obligatory"	In relation to a lamp, reflector, rear marking or device, means a lamp, reflector, rear marking or device with which a vehicle, its load or equipment is required by these Regulations to be fitted.
"Operational tell-tale"	A warning device readily visible or audible to the driver and showing whether a device that has been switched on is operating correctly or not.
"Optional"	In relation to a lamp, reflector, rear marking or device, means a lamp, reflector, rear marking or device with which a vehicle, its load or equipment is not required by these Regulations to be fitted.
"Overall length"	Has the same meaning as in the Construction and Use Regulations.
"Overall width"	Has the same meaning as in the Construction and Use Regulations.
"Pair"	In relation to lamps, reflectors or rear markings means a pair of lamps, reflectors or rear markings, including a matched pair, one on each side of the vehicle, in respect of which the following conditions are met— (a) each lamp, reflector or rear marking is at the same height above the ground, and (b) each lamp, reflector or rear marking is at the same distance from the extreme outer edge of the vehicle. In the case of an asymmetric vehicle, those conditions shall be deemed to be met if they are as near as practicable to being met.
"Passenger vehicle"	Has the same meaning as in the Construction and Use Regulations.
"Pedal cycle"	A vehicle which is not constructed or adapted to be propelled by mechanical power and which is equipped with pedals, including an electrically-assisted pedal cycle prescribed for the purposes of section 189 of the Act and section 140 of the Road Traffic Regulation Act 1984.
"Pedal retro reflector"	A retro reflector attached to or incorporated in the pedals of a pedal cycle or motor bicycle.
"Pedestrian-controlled vehicle"	Has the same meaning as in the Construction and Use Regulations.
"Prescribed sign"	a sign which is of a type shown in Schedule 21A and complies with the requirements of that Schedule.
"Radiation accident" and "radiation emergency"	Have the same meaning as in the Radiation (Emergency Preparedness and Public Information) Regulations 2001.
"Rear fog lamp"	A lamp used to render a vehicle more readily visible from the rear in conditions of seriously reduced visibility.
"Rear position lamp"	A lamp used to indicate the presence and width of a vehicle when viewed from the rear.
"Rear retro reflector"	A retro reflector used to indicate the presence and width of a vehicle when viewed from the rear.
"Rear registration plate lamp"	A lamp used to illuminate the rear registration plate.
"Reflecting area"	In relation to a retro reflector fitted to a vehicle, the area of the orthogonal projection on a vertical plane (touching the surface of the reflector)— (a) at right angles to the longitudinal axis of the vehicle of that part of the reflector designed to reflect light in the case of a front or a rear retro reflector, and

(1) Expression	(2) Meaning
	(*b*) parallel to the longitudinal axis of the vehicle of that part of the reflector designed to reflect light in the case of a side retro reflector.
"Reversing lamp"	A lamp used to illuminate the road to the rear of a vehicle for the purpose of reversing and to warn other road users that the vehicle is reversing or about to reverse.
"Road clearance vehicle"	A mechanically propelled vehicle used for dealing with frost, ice or snow on roads.
"Running lamp"	A lamp (not being a front position lamp, an end-outline marker lamp, headlamp or front fog lamp) used to make the presence of a moving motor vehicle readily visible from the front.
"Separation distance"	In relation to two lamps or two retro reflectors the expression means, except where otherwise specified, the shortest distance between the orthogonal projections in a plane perpendicular to the longitudinal axis of the vehicle of the illuminated areas of the two lamps or the reflecting areas of the two reflectors.
"Service braking system"	Has the same meaning as in the Construction and Use Regulations.
"Side marker lamp"	A lamp fitted to the side of a vehicle or its load and used to render the vehicle more visible to other road users.
"Side retro reflector"	A reflector fitted to the side of a vehicle or its load and used to render the vehicle more visible from the side.
"Solo motor bicycle"	A motor bicycle without a sidecar.
"Special equipment"	A movable platform fitted to a vehicle, the apparatus for moving the platform and any jacks fitted to the vehicle for stabilising it while the movable platform is in use.
"Special warning lamp"	A lamp, fitted to the front or rear of a vehicle, capable of emitting a blue flashing light and not any other kind of light.
"Stop lamp"	A lamp used to indicate to road users that the brakes of a vehicle or combination of vehicles are being applied.
"Traffic sign"	Has the same meaning given by section 64(1) of the Road Traffic Regulation Act 1984.
"Trailer"	A vehicle constructed or adapted to be drawn by another vehicle.
"Unrestricted dual-carriageway road"	A dual carriageway within the meaning given by paragraph 2 of Schedule 6 to the Road Traffic Regulation Act 1984 on which a motor vehicle may lawfully be driven at a speed exceeding 50 mph.
"Unladen weight"	Has the same meaning as in the Construction and Use Regulations.
"Vehicle in the service of a visiting force or of a headquarters"	Has the same meaning as in the Construction and Use Regulations.
"Visiting vehicle"	Has the meaning given by regulation 3(1) of the Motor Vehicles (International Circulation) Regulations 1985.
"Warning beacon"	A lamp that is capable of emitting a flashing or rotating beam of light throughout 360° in the horizontal plane.
"Wheel"	Has the same meaning as in the Construction and Use Regulations (see also paragraph (7)).
"Wheeled"	Has the same meaning as in the Construction and Use Regulations.
"Work lamp"	A lamp used to illuminate a working area or the scene of an accident, breakdown or roadworks in the vicinity of the vehicle to which it is fitted.
"Works trailer"	Has the same meaning as in the Construction and Use Regulations.
"Works truck"	Has the same meaning as in the Construction and Use Regulations.

(3) Material designed primarily to reflect light is, when reflecting light, to be treated for the purposes of these Regulations as showing a light, and material capable of reflecting an image is not, when reflecting the image of a light, to be so treated.

(4) In these Regulations a reference to one lamp, except in the case of a dipped-beam headlamp, a main-beam headlamp and a front fog lamp, includes any combination of two or more lamps, whether identical or not, having the same function and emitting light of the same colour, if it comprises devices the aggregate illuminated area of which occupies 60 per cent or more of the area of the smallest rectangle circumscribing those illuminated areas.

(5) In these Regulations a reference to two lamps includes—

(a) a single illuminated area which—

    (i)   is placed symmetrically in relation to the longitudinal axis of the vehicle,

    (ii) extends on both sides to within 400 mm of the extreme outer edge of the vehicle,

    (iii) is not less than 800 mm long, and

    (iv) is illuminated by not less than two sources of light, and

(b) any number of illuminated areas which—

    (i)   are juxtaposed,

    (ii) if on the same transverse plane have illuminated areas which occupy not less than 60 per cent of the area of the smallest rectangle circumscribing their illuminated areas,

    (iii) are placed symmetrically in relation to the median longitudinal plane of the vehicle,

    (iv) extend on both sides to within 400 mm of the extreme outer edge of the vehicle,

    (v) do not have a total length of less than 800 mm, and

    (vi) are illuminated by not less than two sources of light.

(6) Where a part fitted to a vehicle is required by these Regulations to be marked with a British Standard mark, the requirements shall not be regarded as met unless, in addition to being marked as required, the part complied with the relevant British Standard at the time when the part was first fitted to the vehicle.

(7) A reference in these Regulations to the number of wheels of a vehicle shall be construed in accordance with regulation 3 of the Construction and Use Regulations.

(8) A reference in a Schedule to there being no requirement in relation to a lamp, reflector, rear marking or device is without prejudice to any other provision in these Regulations affecting same.

---

1. A vehicle which is adapted for the purposes of conveying sick people and which is from time to time used for such purposes, is an emergency vehicle (*DPP v Hawkins* [1996] RTR 160, CA).

Equivalent standards

4–3733A   **3A.** Nothing in these Regulations shall render unlawful any act or omission which would have been lawful were—

(a) there to be substituted for any reference to a British Standard in these Regulations a reference to a corresponding standard, and

(b) regulation 3(6) to apply in relation to that corresponding standard and the markings relating to that corresponding standard as it applies to a British Standard.

(2) For the purposes of this regulation, "corresponding standard", in relation to a relevant British Standard Specification, means—

(a) a standard or code of practice of a national standards body or equivalent body of any State within the European Economic Area;

(b) any international standard recognised for use as a standard by any State within the European Economic Area;

(c) a technical specification or code of practice which, whether mandatory or not, is recognised for use as a standard by a public authority of any State within the European Economic Area,

where the standard, code of practice, international standard or technical specification provides, in relation to lamps, retro reflectors and rear markings, a level of safety equivalent to that provided by that British Standard Specification and contains a requirement as respects the marking of such parts equivalent to that provided by that instrument.

Exemptions–General

4–3734   **4.** (1) Where a provision is applied by these Regulations to a motor vehicle first used on or after a specified date it does not apply to any vehicle manufactured at least six months before that date.

(2) Where an exemption from, or a relaxation of, a provision is applied by these Regulations to a motor vehicle first used before a specified date it shall also apply to a motor vehicle first used on or after that date if it was manufactured at least six months before that date.

(3) Nothing in these Regulations shall require any lamp or reflector to be fitted between sunrise and sunset to—

(a) a vehicle not fitted with any front or rear position lamp,

(b) an incomplete vehicle proceeding to a works for completion,

(c) a pedal cycle,

(d) a pedestrian-controlled vehicle,

(e) a horse-drawn vehicle,

(f) a vehicle drawn or propelled by hand, or

(g) a combat vehicle.

(4) Without prejudice to regulation 16, for the purposes of these Regulations a lamp shall not be treated as being a lamp if it is—

(a) so painted over or masked that it is not capable of being immediately used or readily put to use; or

(b) an electric lamp which is not provided with any system of wiring by means of which that lamp is, or can readily be, connected with a source of electricity.

4–3734A **4A. Exemptions—Vehicle Examiners.** (1) Parts 2 and 3 of these Regulations do not apply where a vehicle is being used on a road by a vehicle examiner and it is so used in order—

(a) to submit the vehicle for an examination under section 45 of the Road Traffic Act 1988 for the purpose of ascertaining whether the examination is carried out in accordance with Regulations made under that section; or

(b) to remove the vehicle following that examination.

(2) This regulation shall only apply to a vehicle examiner who—

(a) has been authorised in writing by the Secretary of State to use a vehicle for the purposes described in paragraph (1)(a) and (b); and

(b) when using the vehicle for such a purpose, reasonably believes that any defects in that vehicle do not give rise to a danger of injury to any person while being so used.

(3) In this regulation "vehicle examiner" means an examiner appointed under section 66A of the Road Traffic Act 1988.

4–3735 **5.** Part II of these Regulations does not apply to—

(a) any vehicle having a base or centre in a country outside Great Britain from which it normally starts its journeys, provided that a period of not more than 12 months has elapsed since the vehicle was last brought into Great Britain;

(b) a visiting vehicle;

(c) any combination of two or more vehicles, one of which is drawing the other or others, if the combination includes any vehicle of the type mentioned in sub-paragraph (a) or (b); or

(d) a vehicle proceeding to a port for export,

if in each case the vehicle or combination of vehicles complies in every respect with the requirements about lighting equipment and reflectors relating thereto contained in the Convention on Road Traffic concluded at Geneva on 19th September 1949[1] or the International Convention relating to Motor Traffic concluded at Paris on 24th April 1926[2].

1. Cmnd 7997.
2. Treaty Series No 11 (1930).

Exemptions—Vehicles towing or being towed

4–3736 **6.** (1) No motor vehicle first used before 1st April 1986 and no pedal cycle or trailer manufactured before 1st October 1985 is required by regulation 18 to be fitted with any rear position lamp, stop lamp, rear direction indicator, rear fog lamp or rear reflector whilst a trailer fitted with any such lamp or reflector is attached to its rear.

(2) No trailer manufactured before 1st October 1985 is required by regulation 18 to be fitted with any front position lamp whilst being drawn by a passenger vehicle.

(3) No trailer is required by regulation 18 to be fitted with any stop lamp whilst being drawn by a vehicle which is not required by regulation 18 to be fitted with any such lamp.

(4) Paragraph (3) shall apply respectively to rear fog lamps and direction indicators as it applies to stop lamps.

(5) No trailer manufactured before 1st October 1990 is required by regulation 18 to be fitted with any stop lamp or direction indicator whilst being drawn by a motor vehicle fitted with one or two stop lamps and two or more direction indicators if the dimensions of the trailer are such that when the longitudinal axes of the drawing vehicle and the trailer lie in the same vertical plane such stop lamps and at least one direction indicator on each side of the vehicle are visible to an observer in that vertical plane from a point 6 m behind the rear of the trailer whether it is loaded or not.

(6) No rear marking is required to be fitted to any vehicle by regulation 18 if another vehicle in a combination of which it forms part would obscure any such marking.

(7) Where a broken-down vehicle is being drawn by another vehicle—

(a) regulations 18 and 23 shall not apply to the broken-down vehicle between sunrise and sunset, and

(b) between sunset and sunrise those regulations shall apply to the broken-down vehicle only in respect of rear position lamps and reflectors.

(8) The references in paragraphs (3) and (4) to a vehicle which is required to be fitted with a lamp shall be construed as if paragraph (1) did not have effect.

Exemptions—Military vehicles

4–3737 **7.** (1) Regulation 18 does not apply to a home forces' vehicle or to a vehicle in the service of a visiting force or of a headquarters whilst being used—

(a) in connection with training which is certified in writing for the purposes of this regulation by a person duly authorised in that behalf to be training on a special occasion and of which not less than 48 hours' notice has been given by that person to the chief officer of police of every police area in which the place selected for the training is wholly or partly situate; or

(b) on manoeuvres within such limits and during such period as may from time to time be specified by Order in Council under the Manoeuvres Act 1958.

(2) Where not less than 6 nor more than 12 vehicles being home forces' vehicles or vehicles of

a visiting force or of a headquarters are proceeding together in a convoy on tactical or driving exercises which are authorised in writing by a person duly authorised in that behalf, and of which not less than 48 hours' notice in writing has been given by that person to the chief officer of police of every police area through which it is intended that the convoy shall pass and the interval between any two vehicles in such convoy does not exceed 20 m—

(a) front position lamps shall be required only on the vehicle leading the convoy; and
(b) rear position lamps shall be required only on the rearmost vehicle provided that every other vehicle in the convoy carries a bright light under the vehicle illuminating either a part of the vehicle or anything attached to the vehicle or the road surface beneath the vehicle, in such a manner that the presence of the vehicle can be detected from the rear.

(3) No lamp is required to be fitted to any home forces' vehicle or any vehicle in the service of a visiting force or of a headquarters if the vehicle is constructed or adapted for combat and is such that compliance with these provisions is impracticable and it is fitted with two red rear position lamps and two red rear retro reflectors when on a road between sunset and sunrise. Such lamps and reflectors need not meet any of the requirements specified in Schedules 10 and 18.

(4) Part II of these Regulations does not apply to a vehicle in the service of a visiting force or of a headquarters if the vehicle complies in every respect with the requirements as to lighting equipment and reflectors relating thereto contained in a Convention referred to in regulation 5.

Exemptions—Invalid carriages

4–3738 8. An invalid carriage having a maximum speed not exceeding 4 mph is required by these Regulations to be fitted with lamps and reflectors only when it is used on the carriageway of a road between sunset and sunrise otherwise than for the sole purpose of crossing it.

Exemptions—Vehicles drawn or propelled by hand

4–3739 9. A vehicle drawn or propelled by hand which has an overall width, including any load, not exceeding 800 mm is required by these Regulations to be fitted with lamps and reflectors only when it is used on the carriageway of a road between sunset and sunrise other than—

(a) close to the near side or left-hand edge of the carriageway, or
(b) to cross the carriageway.

Exemption—Tramcars

4–3739A 9A. Parts II to IV of these regulations do not apply to tramcars.

Modifications in relation to vehicles approved under the Motor Vehicles (Approval) Regulations 1996

4–3739B 9B. (1) In this regulation—

"the Approval Regulations" means the Motor Vehicles (Approval) Regulations 1996;
"coefficient of luminous intensity" has the same meaning as in ECE Regulation 3.01;
"ECE Regulation 3.01" means Regulation 3 (with the amendments in force on 20th March 1982), annexed to the Agreement concerning the adoption of uniform conditions of approval for Motor Vehicles Equipment and Parts and reciprocal recognition therefor concluded at Geneva on the 20th March 1958 to which the United Kingdom is a party;
"passenger vehicle approval certificate" means a Minister's approval certificate in the form prescribed by the Approval Regulations which appears to have been issued on the basis that the vehicle is a vehicle to which Part II of those Regulations applies;
"relevant vehicle" means a vehicle—

(a) in respect of which a passenger vehicle approval certificate containing the letter "P" has been issued pursuant to regulation 12(2)(b) of the Approval Regulations; or
(b) which is a "transitional provision vehicle" as defined by Schedule 6 to the Approval Regulations in respect of which a passenger vehicle approval certificate containing the letter "A" has been issued pursuant to regulation 12(2)(c) of the Approval Regulations;

"standard mark" means a mark which when applied to a lamp, reflector or device indicates compliance with the requirements of a particular instrument; and a reference to the instrument to which a standard mark relates shall be construed accordingly.

(2) The requirements of the Schedules to these Regulations, so far as they require any lamp, reflector or device to bear a particular standard mark (or one of two or more standard marks), shall not apply to a lamp, reflector or device if it is fitted to a relevant vehicle and—

(a) in the case of a lamp or device, it meets the requirements as to intensity; and
(b) in the case of a reflector, it meets the requirements as to coefficient of luminous intensity,

of the instruments to which the standard mark (or as the case may be one of those standard marks) relates.

(3) The requirements of these Regulations so far as they require headlamps (including a filament lamp fitted to a headlamp) fitted to a vehicle to bear a particular standard mark (or one of two or more standard marks) shall not apply to the headlamps fitted to a relevant vehicle if they emit sufficient light to illuminate the road in front of the vehicle on both main beam and dipped beam.

(4) Table 1 of Schedule 1 shall apply to a vehicle in respect of which a passenger vehicle

approval certificate has been issued as if the entry that relates to dim-dip devices and running lamps were omitted.

(5) Paragraph (5) (markings) of Part I of Schedule 7 shall apply to a vehicle in respect of which a passenger approval certificate has been issued as if the vehicle were of a description falling within sub-paragraph (*b*) of that paragraph.

Provision as respects Trade Descriptions Act 1968

4–3740 **10.** Where by any provision in these Regulations any vehicle or any of its parts or equipment is required to be marked with a specification number or a registered certification trade mark of the British Standards Institution or with any approval mark, nothing in that provision shall be taken to authorise any person to apply any such number or mark to the vehicle, part or equipment in contravention of the Trade Descriptions Act 1968.

PART II
REGULATIONS GOVERNING THE FITTING OF LAMPS, REFLECTORS, REAR MARKINGS AND DEVICES

Colour of light shown by lamps and reflectors

4–3741 **11.** (1) No vehicle shall be fitted with a lamp or retro reflective material which is capable of showing a red light to the front, except—

(a) a red and white chequered domed lamp, or a red and white segmented mast-mounted warning beacon, fitted to a fire service control vehicle and intended for use at the scene of an emergency;

(b) a side marker lamp or a side retro reflector;

(c) retro reflective material or a retro reflector designed primarily to reflect light to one or both sides of the vehicle and attached to or incorporated in any wheel or tyre of—

(i) a pedal cycle;

(ii) a trailer drawn by, or a sidecar attached to, a pedal cycle;

(iii) a solo motor bicycle or motor bicycle combination; or

(iv) an invalid carriage; or

(d) a traffic sign.

(2) No vehicle shall be fitted with a lamp or retro reflective material which is capable of showing any light to the rear, other than a red light, except—

(a) amber light from a direction indicator or side marker lamp;

(b) white light from a reversing lamp;

(c) white light from a work lamp;

(d) light to illuminate the interior of a vehicle;

(e) light from an illuminated rear registration plate;

(f) light for the purposes of illuminating a taxi meter;

(g) in the case of a bus, light for the purposes of illuminating a route indicator;

(h) blue light and white light from a chequered domed lamp fitted to a police control vehicle and intended for use at the scene of an emergency;

(i) white light from a red and white chequered domed lamp, or a red and white segmented mast-mounted warning beacon, fitted to a fire service control vehicle and intended for use at the scene of an emergency;

(j) green light and white light from a chequered domed lamp fitted to an ambulance control vehicle and intended for use at the scene of an emergency;

(k) blue light from a warning beacon or rear special warning lamp fitted to an emergency vehicle, or from any device fitted to a vehicle used for police purposes;

(l) amber light from a warning beacon fitted to—

(i) a road clearance vehicle;

(ii) a vehicle constructed or adapted for the purpose of collecting refuse;

(iii) a breakdown vehicle;

(iv) a vehicle having a maximum speed not exceeding 25 mph or any trailer drawn by such a vehicle;

(v) a vehicle having an overall width (including any load) exceeding 2.9 m;

(vi) a vehicle used for the purposes of testing, maintaining, improving, cleansing or watering roads or for any purpose incidental to any such use;

(vii) a vehicle used for the purpose of inspecting, cleansing, maintaining, adjusting, renewing or installing any apparatus which is in, on, under or over a road, or for any purpose incidental to any such use;

(viii) a vehicle used for or in connection with any purpose for which it is authorised to be used on roads by an order under section 44 of the Act;

(ix) a vehicle used for escort purposes;

(x) a vehicle used by the Commissioners of Customs and Excise for the purpose of testing fuels;

(xi) a vehicle used for the purpose of surveying;

(xii) a vehicle used for the removal or immobilisation of vehicles in exercise of a statutory power or duty;

(m) green light from a warning beacon fitted to a vehicle used by a medical practitioner registered by the General Medical Council (whether with full or provisional registration);

(n) yellow light from a warning beacon fitted to a vehicle for use at airports;

(o) light of any colour from a traffic sign which is attached to a vehicle;

(oa) amber light from a lamp attached to or incorporated in a pedal of a pedal cycle;

(ob) white light or amber light from a lamp which is designed to emit light primarily to one or both sides of the vehicle, and is attached to or incorporated in any wheel or tyre of—

    (i) a pedal cycle or;

    (ii) a trailer drawn by, or a sidecar attached to, a pedal cycle;

(p) reflected light from amber pedal retro reflectors;

(q) reflected light of any colour from retro reflective material or a retro reflector designed primarily to reflect light to one or both sides of the vehicle and attached to or incorporated in any wheel or tyre of—

    (i) a pedal cycle;

    (ii) a trailer drawn by, or a sidecar attached to, a pedal cycle;

    (iii) a solo motor bicycle or motor bicycle combination; or

    (iv) an invalid carriage;

(r) reflected light from amber retro reflective material on a road clearance vehicle;

(s) reflected light from yellow retro reflective registration plates;

(sa) reflected blue, yellow and white light from a retro reflective plate displaying a distinguishing sign in accordance with Council Regulation (EC) No 2411/98;

(t) reflected light from yellow retro reflective material incorporated in a prescribed rear marking fitted in the appropriate manner to—

    (i) a motor vehicle having a maximum gross weight exceeding 7,500 kg;

    (ii) a motor vehicle first used before 1st August 1982 having an unladen weight exceeding 3,000 kg;

    (iii) a trailer having a maximum gross weight exceeding 3,500 kg;

    (iv) a trailer manufactured before 1st August 1982 having an unladen weight exceeding 1,000 kg;

    (v) a trailer which forms part of a combination of vehicles one of which is of a type mentioned in a previous item of this sub-paragraph;

    (vi) a load carried by any vehicle;

(u) reflected light from orange retro reflective material incorporated in a sign fitted to the rear of a vehicle carrying a dangerous substance within the meaning of the Dangerous Substances (Conveyance by Road in Road Tankers and Tank Containers) Regulations 1981 or the Road Traffic (Carriage of Dangerous Substances in Packages etc) Regulations 1986.

(v) reflected light from yellow retro reflective material incorporated in a prescribed sign and fitted to the rear of a bus; or

(w) reflected light from yellow retro reflective material incorporated in a sign fitted to the rear of a bus in accordance with paragraph (4).

(3) For the purposes of paragraph (2)(t) a rear marking fitted to a vehicle is a prescribed rear marking fitted in the appropriate manner if the rear marking—

(a) is a rear marking of a description specified in the entry applicable to that vehicle in the right hand column of paragraph 1 of Part I of Schedule 19, and

(b) complies with paragraphs 2 to 7 of that Part of that Schedule.

(4) For the purposes of paragraph (2)(w), a sign ("the secondary sign") is fitted to the rear of a bus in accordance with this paragraph if—

(a) a prescribed sign is also fitted to the rear of a bus;

(b) the total area of the retro reflective material incorporated in the secondary sign is no greater than the area of the prescribed sign; and

(c) the secondary sign satisfies the requirements specified—

    (i) in the case of a bus which is owned or hired by a local education authority or any person managing an education establishment attended by children under the age of 16 years, in paragraph (5) or (6); or

    (ii) in any other case, in paragraph (6).

(5) The requirements referred to in paragraph (4)(c)(i) are that the secondary sign contains no words or other markings apart from words or markings identifying the local education authority or the educational establishment (as the case may be).

(6) The requirements referred to in paragraph (4)(c(ii) are that the secondary sign contains no words or other markings apart from words or other markings which—

(a) indicate that children are on board the bus when it is in motion or likely to be on board the bus or in its vicinity when it is stationary, and

(b) are calculated to reduce the risk of road accidents involving such children.

Movement of lamps and reflectors

4–3742 **12.** (1) Save as provided in paragraph (2), no person shall use, or cause or permit to be used, on a road any vehicle to which, or to any load or equipment of which, there is fitted a lamp, reflector or marking which is capable of being moved by swivelling, deflecting or otherwise while the vehicle is in motion.

(2) Paragraph (1) does not apply in respect of—

(a) a headlamp which can be dipped only by the movement of the headlamp or its reflector;

(b) a headlamp which is capable of adjustment so as to compensate for the effect of the load carried by the vehicle;

(c) a lamp or reflector which can be deflected to the side by the movement of, although not necessarily through the same angle as, the front wheel or wheels of the vehicle when turned for the purpose of steering the vehicle;

(d) a headlamp or front fog lamp which can be wholly or partially retracted or concealed;

(e) a direction indicator fitted to a motor vehicle first used before 1st April 1986;

(f) a work lamp;

(g) a warning beacon;

(h) an amber pedal retro reflector;

(i) retro reflective material or a retro reflector of any colour which is fitted so as to reflect light primarily to one or both sides of the vehicle and is attached to or incorporated in any wheel or tyre of—

  (i) a pedal cycle;

  (ii) a trailer drawn by, or a sidecar attached to, a pedal cycle;

  (iii) a solo motor bicycle or motor bicycle combination, or

  (iv) an invalid carriage.

(j) a lamp which is designed to emit light primarily to one or both sides of the vehicle, and is attached to or incorporated in any wheel or tyre of—

  (i) a pedal cycle;

  (ii) a trailer drawn by, or a sidecar attached to, a pedal cycle; or

(k) a lamp attached to or incorporated in a pedal of a pedal cycle.

Lamps to show a steady light

4–3743   13.—(1) Save as provided in paragraph (2), no vehicle shall be fitted with a lamp which automatically emits a flashing light.

(2) Paragraph (1) does not apply in respect of—

(a) a direction indicator;

(b) a headlamp fitted to an emergency vehicle;

(c) a warning beacon or special warning lamp;

(d) a lamp or illuminated sign fitted to a vehicle used for police purposes;

(e) a green warning lamp used as an anti-lock brake indicator;

(f) lamps forming part of a traffic sign;

(g) a front position lamp capable of emitting a flashing light (whether or not it is also capable of emitting a steady light) which is fitted to—

  (i) a pedal cycle; or

  (ii) a trailer drawn by, or a sidecar attached to, a pedal cycle;

and which, if it is a lamp which is required to be fitted pursuant to regulation 18, is capable, when emitting a flashing light, of emitting light to the front of the pedal cycle, trailer or sidecar (as the case may be) of an intensity of not less than 4 candelas; or

(h) a rear position lamp capable of emitting a flashing light (whether or not it is also capable of emitting a steady light) which is fitted to—

  (i) a pedal cycle; or

  (ii) a trailer drawn by, or a sidecar attached to, a pedal cycle;

and which, if it is a lamp which is required to be fitted pursuant to regulation 18, is capable when emitting a flashing light, of emitting light to the rear of the pedal cycle, trailer or sidecar (as the case may be) of an intensity of not less than 4 candelas.

Filament lamps

4–3744   14.—(1) Where a motor vehicle first used on or after 1st April 1986 or any trailer manufactured on or after 1st October 1985 is equipped with any lamp of a type that is required by any Schedule to these Regulations to be marked with an approval mark, no filament lamp other than a filament lamp referred to in the Designation of Approval Marks Regulations in—

(a) regulation 4 and Schedule 2, items 2 or 2A, 8, 20, 37 or 37A; or

(b) regulation 5 and Schedule 4, item 18,

shall be fitted to any such lamp.

General requirements for electrical connections

4–3745   15.—(1) Every motor vehicle first used on or after 1st April 1991 shall be so constructed that every position lamp, side marker lamp, end-outline marker lamp and rear registration plate lamp with which the vehicle is fitted is capable of being switched on and off by the operation of one switch and, save as provided in paragraph (2), not otherwise.

(2) Sub-paragraph (a) of paragraph (1) shall not prevent one or more position lamps from being capable of being switched on and off independently of any other lamp referred to in that sub-paragraph.

Restrictions on fitting blue warning beacons, special warning lamps and similar devices

4–3746   16. No vehicle, other than an emergency vehicle, shall be fitted with—

   (*a*)   a blue warning beacon[1] or special warning lamp, or

   (*b*)   a device which resembles a blue warning beacon or a special warning lamp, whether the same is in working order or not.

---

1. No offence is committed by using an emergency vehicle for other purposes when a blue light is fitted but not illuminated (*DPP v Hawkins* [1996] RTR 160, CA).

Obligatory warning beacons

4–3747   **17.** (1) Subject to paragraph (2), no person shall use, or cause or permit to be used, on an unrestricted dual-carriageway road any motor vehicle with four or more wheels having a maximum speed not exceeding 25 mph unless it or any trailer drawn by it is fitted with at least one warning beacon which—

   (*a*)   complies with Schedule 16, and

   (*b*)   is showing an amber light.

(2) Paragraph (1) shall not apply in relation to—

   (*a*)   any motor vehicle first used before 1st January 1947; and

   (*b*)   any motor vehicle, or any trailer being drawn by it, to which paragraph (1) would otherwise apply, when that vehicle or trailer is on any carriageway of an unrestricted dual-carriageway road for the purpose only of crossing that carriageway in the quickest manner practicable in the circumstances.

Signs on buses carrying children

4–3747A   **17A.** (1) Subject to paragraph (2), no person shall use or cause or permit to be used on a road a bus when it is carrying a child to or from his school unless—

   (*a*)   a prescribed sign is fitted to the front of the bus and is plainly visible to road users ahead of the bus, and

   (*b*)   a prescribed sign is fitted to the rear of the bus and is plainly visible to road users behind the bus.

(2) Paragraph (1) does not apply where a bus is on a bus service of a description specified in paragraph 2 of the Schedule to the Fuel Duty Grant (Eligible Bus Services) Regulations 1985.

(3) For the purposes of this regulation—

   (*a*)   a reference to a bus carrying a child to or from his school is a reference to a bus carrying a child—

      (i)   to, or to a place within the vicinity of, his school on a day during term time before he has attended the school on that day; or

      (ii)   from, or from a place within the vicinity of, his school on a day during term time after he has finished attending the school on that day;

   (*b*)   "school" has the meaning given by section 114 of the Education Act 1944; and

   (*c*)   a reference to a child is a reference to a child under the age of 16 years.

Obligatory lamps, reflectors, rear markings and devices

4–3748   **18.** (1) Save as provided in the foregoing provisions of these Regulations and in paragraph (2), (2A) and (2B), every vehicle of a class specified in a Table in Schedule 1 shall be fitted with lamps, reflectors, rear markings and devices which—

   (*a*)   are of a type specified in column 1 of that Table, and

   (*b*)   comply with the relevant installation, alignment and performance requirements set out in the Schedule or Part of a Schedule shown against that type in column 2 of that Table.

(2) The requirements specified in paragraph (1) do not apply in respect of a lamp, reflector, rear marking or device of a type specified in column 1 of a Table in the case of a vehicle shown against it in column 3 of that Table.

(2A) The requirements specified in paragraph 5(c) and (ca) of Schedule 2 shall not apply in the case of a front position lamp capable of emitting a flashing light which is fitted to—

      (i)   a pedal cycle; or

      (ii)   a trailer drawn by, or a sidecar attached to, a pedal cycle,

unless the lamp is also capable of emitting a steady light.

(2B) The requirements specified in paragraph 5(d) and (e) of Schedule 10 shall not apply in the case of a rear position lamp capable of emitting a flashing light which is fitted to—

      (i)   a pedal cycle; or

      (ii)   a trailer drawn by, or a sidecar attached to, a pedal cycle,

unless the lamp is also capable of emitting a steady light.

(3) The requirements specified in paragraph (1) apply without prejudice to any additional requirements specified in regulations 20 and 21.

(4) The Schedules referred to in the Tables in Schedule 1 are Schedules 2 to 21.

Restrictions on the obscuration of certain obligatory lamps and reflectors

4–3749   **19.** Every vehicle shall be so constructed that at least part of the apparent surface of any—

   (*a*)   front and rear position lamp,

(b) front and rear direction indicator, and
(c) rear retro reflector,

which is required by these Regulations to be fitted to a vehicle, is visible when the vehicle is viewed from any point directly in front of or behind the lamp or reflector, as appropriate, when every door, tailgate, boot lid, engine cover, cab or other movable part of the vehicle is in a fixed open position.

Optional lamps, reflectors, rear markings and devices

4–3750 20. Every optional lamp, reflector, rear marking or device fitted to a vehicle, being of a type specified in an item in column 2 of the Table below, shall comply with the provisions shown in column 3 of that Table.

TABLE

(1) Item No	(2) Type of lamp, reflector, rear marking or device	(3) Provisions with which compliance is required	
1	Front position lamp	Schedule 2, Part II	
2	Dim-dip device and running lamp	Schedule 3, Part II	
3	Dipped-beam headlamp	Schedule 4, Part II	
4	Main-beam headlamp	Schedule 5, Part II	
5	Front fog lamp	Schedule 6	and Parts I of
7	Direction indicator	Schedule 7, Part II	Schedules 2 to
8	Hazard warning signal device	Schedule 8	5, 7, 9 to 13 and
9	Side marker lamp	Schedule 9, Part II	17 to 21 to the
10	Rear position lamp	Schedule 10, Part II	extent specified
11	Rear fog lamp	Schedule 11, Part II	in Parts II of
12	Stop lamp	Schedule 12, Part II	those Schedules.
13	End-outline marker lamp	Schedule 13, Part II	
14	Reversing lamp	Schedule 14	
15	Warning beacon	Schedule 16	
16	Side retro reflector	Schedule 17, Part II	
17	Rear retro reflector	Schedule 18, Part II	
18	Rear marking	Schedule 19, Part II	
19	Pedal retro reflector	Schedule 20, Part II	
20	Front retro reflector	Schedule 21, Part II	

Projecting trailers and vehicles carrying overhanging or projecting loads or equipment

4–3751 21. (1) No person shall use, or cause or permit to be used, on a road in the circumstances mentioned in paragraph (2)—

(a) any trailer which forms part of a combination of vehicles which projects laterally beyond any preceding vehicle in the combination; or

(b) any vehicle or combination of vehicles which carries a load or equipment

in either case under the conditions specified in an item in column 2 of the Table below, unless the vehicle or combination of vehicles complies with the requirements specified in that item in column 3 of that Table.

TABLE

(1) Item No	(2) Conditions	(3) Requirements
1	A trailer which is not fitted with front position lamps and which projects laterally on any side so that the distance from the outermost part of the projection to the outermost part of the illuminated area of the obligatory front position lamp on that side fitted to any preceding vehicle in the combination exceeds 400 mm.	A lamp showing white light to the front shall be fitted to the trailer so that the outermost part of the illuminated area is not more than 400 mm from the outermost projection of the trailer. The installation and performance requirements relating to front position lamps do not apply to any such lamp.
2	A trailer which is not fitted with front position lamps and which carries a load or equipment which projects laterally on any side of the trailer so that the distance from the outermost projection of the load or equipment to the outermost part of the illuminated area of the obligatory front position lamp on that side fitted to any preceding vehicle in the combination exceeds 400 mm.	A lamp showing white light to the front shall be fitted to the trailer or the load or equipment so that the outermost part of the illuminated area is not more than 400 mm from the outermost projection of the load or equipment. The installation and performance requirements relating to front position lamps do not apply to any such lamp.

(1) Item No	(2) Conditions	(3) Requirements
3	A vehicle which carries a load or equipment which projects laterally on any side of the vehicle so that the distance from the outermost part of the load or equipment to the outermost part of the illuminated area of the obligatory front or rear position lamp on that side exceeds 400 mm.	Either— (a) the obligatory front or rear position lamp shall be transferred from the vehicle to the load or equipment to which must also be attached a white front or a red rear reflecting device; or (b) an additional front or rear position lamp and a white front or a red rear reflecting device shall be fitted to the vehicle, load or equipment. All the installation, performance and maintenance requirements relating to front or rear position lamps shall in either case be complied with except that for the purpose of determining the lateral position of such lamps and reflecting devices any reference to the vehicle shall be taken to include the load or equipment except special equipment on a vehicle fitted with a movable platform or the jib of any crane.
4	A vehicle which carries a load or equipment which projects beyond the rear of the vehicle or, in the case of a combination of vehicles, beyond the rear of the rearmost vehicle in the combination, more than— (a) 2 m in the case of an agricultural vehicle or a vehicle carrying a fire escape; or (b) 1 m in the case of any other vehicle	An additional rear lamp capable of showing red light to the rear and a red reflecting device, both of which are visible from a reasonable distance, shall be fitted to the vehicle or the load in such a position that the distance between the lamp and the reflecting device, and the rearmost projection of the load or equipment does not exceed 2 m in the case mentioned in sub-paragraph (a) in column 2 of this item or 1 m in any other case. The installation and performance requirements relating to rear position lamps and rear retro reflectors do not apply to any such additional lamp and reflecting device.
5	A vehicle which carries a load or equipment which projects beyond the front of the vehicle more than— (a) 2 m in the case of an agricultural vehicle or a vehicle carrying a fire escape; or (b) 1 m in the case of any other vehicle.	An additional front lamp capable of showing white light to the front and a white reflecting device, both visible from a reasonable distance, shall be fitted to the vehicle or the load in such a position that the distance between the lamp and the reflecting device, and the foremost projection of the load or equipment, does not exceed 2 m in the case mentioned in sub-paragraph (a) in column 2 of this item or 1 m in any other case. The installation and performance requirements relating to front position lamps and front retro reflectors do not apply to any such additional lamp and reflecting device.
6	A vehicle which carries a load or equipment which obscures any obligatory lamp, reflector or rear marking.	Either— (a) the obligatory lamp, reflector or rear marking shall be transferred to a position on the vehicle, load or equipment where it is not obscured; or (b) an additional lamp, reflector or rear marking shall be fitted to the vehicle, load or equipment. All the installation, performance and maintenance requirements relating to obligatory lamps, reflectors or rear markings shall in either case be complied with.

(2) The circumstances referred to in paragraph (1) are—

    (a) as regards item 6 in the Table, in so far as it relates to obligatory stop lamps and direction indicators, all circumstances; and

    (b) as regards items 1 to 5 in the Table and item 6 in the Table, except in so far as it relates to obligatory stop lamps and direction indicators, the time between sunset and sunrise, or, except in so far as it relates to obligatory reflectors, when visibility is seriously reduced between sunrise and sunset.

Additional side marker lamps

4–3752 22. (1) Save as provided in paragraph (2), no person shall use, or cause or permit to be used, on a road between sunset and sunrise, or in seriously reduced visibility between sunrise and sunset, any vehicle or combination of vehicles of a type specified in an item in column 2 of the Table below unless each side of the vehicle or combination of vehicles is fitted with the side marker lamps specified in that item in column 3 and those lamps are kept lit.

TABLE

(1) Item No	(2) Vehicle or combination of vehicles	(3) Side marker lamps
1	A vehicle or a combination of vehicles the overall length of which (including any load) exceeds 18.3 m.	There shall be fitted— (a) one lamp no part of the light-emitting surface of which is more than 9.15 m from the foremost part of the vehicle or vehicles (in either case inclusive of any load); (b) one lamp no part of the light-emitting surface of which is more than 3.05 m from the rearmost part of the vehicle or vehicles (in either case inclusive of any load); and (c) such other lamps as are required to ensure that not more than 3.05 m separates any part of the light-emitting surface of one lamp and any part of the light-emitting surface of the next lamp.
2	A combination of vehicles the overall length of which (including any load) exceeds 12.2 m but does not exceed 18.3 m and carrying a load supported by any two of the vehicles but not including a load carried by an articulated vehicle.	There shall be fitted— (a) one lamp no part of the light-emitting surface of which is forward of, or more than 1530 mm rearward of, the rearmost part of the drawing vehicle; and (b) if the supported load extends more than 9.15 m rearward of the rearmost part of the drawing vehicle, one lamp no part of the light-emitting surface of which is forward of, or more than 1530 mm rearward of, the centre of the length of the load.

(2) The requirements specified in paragraph (1) do not apply to—

(a) a combination of vehicles where any vehicle being drawn in that combination has broken down; or

(b) a vehicle (not being a combination of vehicles) having an appliance or apparatus or carrying a load of a kind specified in the Table to regulation 82(7) or in regulation 82(8) of the Construction and Use Regulations, if the conditions specified in paragraphs 3 and 4 (which provide for the special marking of projections from vehicles) of Schedule 12 to those Regulations are complied with in relation to the special appliance or apparatus or load as if the said conditions had been expressed in the said regulation 82 to apply in the case of every special appliance or apparatus or load of a kind specified in that regulation.

(3) Every side marker lamp fitted in accordance with this regulation shall comply with Part I of Schedule 9.

PART III
REGULATIONS GOVERNING THE MAINTENANCE AND USE OF LAMPS, REFLECTORS, REAR MARKINGS AND DEVICES

Maintenance of lamps, reflectors, rear markings and devices

4–3753 23. (1) No person shall use, or cause or permit to be used, on a road a vehicle unless every lamp, reflector, rear marking and device to which this paragraph applies is in good working order and, in the case of a lamp, clean.

(2) Save as provided in paragraph (3), paragraph (1) applies to—

(a) every—

(i) front position lamp,
(ii) rear position lamp,
(iii) headlamp,
(iv) rear registration plate lamp,
(v) side marker lamp,

(vi) end-outline marker lamp,
(vii) rear fog lamp,
(viii) retro reflector, and
(ix) rear marking of a type specified in Part I of Schedule 19,

with which the vehicle is required by these Regulations to be fitted; and

(b) every—

(i)   stop lamp,
(ii) direction indicator,
(iii) running lamp,
(iv) dim-dip device,
(v) headlamp levelling device, and
(vi) hazard warning signal device,

with which it is fitted.

(3) Paragraph (2) does not apply to—

(a) a rear fog lamp on a vehicle which is part of a combination of vehicles any part of which is not required by these Regulations to be fitted with a rear fog lamp;

(b) a rear fog lamp on a motor vehicle drawing a trailer;

(c) a defective lamp, reflector, dim-dip device or headlamp levelling device on a vehicle in use on a road between sunrise and sunset, if any such lamp, reflector or device became defective during the journey which is in progress or if arrangements have been made to remedy the defect with all reasonable expedition; or

(d) a lamp, reflector, dim-dip device, headlamp levelling device or rear marking on a combat vehicle in use on a road between sunrise and sunset.

Requirements about the use of front and rear position lamps, rear registration plate lamps, side marker lamps and end-outline marker lamps

4–3754   **24.**—(1) Save as provided in paragraphs (5) and (9), no person shall—

(a) use, or cause or permit to be used, on a road any vehicle which is in motion—

(i)   between sunset and sunrise, or
(ii) in seriously reduced visibility between sunrise and sunset; or

(b) allow to remain at rest, or cause or permit to be allowed to remain at rest, on a road any vehicle between sunset and sunrise

unless every front position lamp, rear position lamp, rear registration plate lamp, side marker lamp and end-outline marker lamp with which the vehicle is required by these Regulations to be fitted is kept lit and unobscured.

(2) Save as provided in paragraphs (5) and (9), where a solo motor bicycle is not fitted with a front position lamp, no person shall use it, or cause or permit it to be used, on a road (other than when it is parked) between sunset and sunrise or in seriously reduced visibility between sunrise and sunset, unless a headlamp is kept lit and unobscured.

(3) Save as provided in paragraphs (5) and (9), no person shall allow to remain parked, or cause or permit to be allowed to remain parked between sunset and sunrise—

(a) a motor bicycle combination which is required to be fitted only with a front position lamp on the sidecar; or

(b) a trailer to the front of which no other vehicle is attached and which is not required to be fitted with front position lamps,

unless a pair of front position lamps is fitted and kept lit and unobscured.

(4) Save as provided in paragraphs (5) and (9), no person shall allow to remain parked, or cause or permit to be allowed to remain parked between sunset and sunrise a solo motor bicycle which is not required to be fitted with a front position lamp, unless a front position lamp is fitted and kept lit and unobscured.

(5) paragraphs (1), (2), (3) and (4) shall not apply in respect of a vehicle of a class specified in paragraph (7) which is parked on a road on which a speed limit of 30 mph or less is in force and the vehicle is parked—

(a) in a parking place for which provision is made under section 6, or which is authorised under section 32 or designated under section 45 of the Road Traffic Regulation Act 1984, or which is set apart as a parking place under some other enactment or instrument and the vehicle is parked in a manner which does not contravene the provision of any enactment or instrument relating to the parking place; or

(b) in a lay-by—

(i)   the limits of which are indicated by a traffic sign consisting of the road marking shown in diagram 1010 in Schedule 2 of the Traffic Signs Regulations and General Directions 1981; or

(ii) the surface of which is of a colour or texture which is different from that of the part of the carriageway of the road used primarily by through traffic; or

(iii) the limits of which are indicated by a continuous strip of surface of a different colour or texture from that of the surface of the remainder of the carriageway of the road; or

(c) elsewhere than in such a parking place or lay-by if—

(i)   the vehicle is parked in one of the circumstances described in paragraph (8); and

(ii) no part of the vehicle is less than 10 m from the junction of any part of the carriageway of any road with the carriageway of the road on which it is parked whether that junction is on the same side of the road as that on which the vehicle is parked or not.

(6) Sub-paragraph (5)(*c*)(ii) shall be construed in accordance with the diagram in Schedule 22.

(7) The classes of vehicle referred to in paragraph (5) are—

(*a*) a motor vehicle being a goods vehicle the unladen weight of which does not exceed 1525 kg;

(*b*) a passenger vehicle other than a bus;

(*c*) an invalid carriage; and

(*d*) a motor cycle or a pedal cycle in either case with or without a sidecar;

not being—

(i) a vehicle to which a trailer is attached;

(ii) a vehicle which is required to be fitted with lamps by regulation 21; or

(iii) a vehicle carrying a load, if the load is required to be fitted with lamps by regulation 21.

(8) The circumstances referred to in paragraph (5)(*c*) are that—

(*a*) the vehicle is parked on a road on which the driving of vehicles otherwise than in one direction is prohibited at all times and its left or near side is as close as may be and parallel to the left-hand edge of the carriageway or its right or off side is as close as may be and parallel to the right-hand edge of the carriageway; or

(*b*) the vehicle is parked on a road on which such a prohibition does not exist and its left or near side is as close as may be and parallel to the edge of the carriageway.

(9) Paragraphs (1), (2), (3) and (4) do not apply in respect of—

(*a*) a solo motor bicycle or a pedal cycle being pushed along the left-hand edge of a carriageway;

(*b*) a pedal cycle waiting to proceed provided it is kept to the left-hand or near side edge of a carriageway; or

(*c*) a vehicle which is parked in an area on part of a highway on which roadworks are being carried out and which is bounded by amber lamps and other traffic signs so as to prevent the presence of the vehicle, its load or equipment being a danger to persons using the road.

Requirements about the use of headlamps and front fog lamps

4-3755 **25.** (1) Save as provided in paragraph (2), no person shall use, or cause or permit to be used, on a road a vehicle which is fitted with obligatory dipped-beam headlamps unless every such lamp is kept lit—

(*a*) during the hours of darkness, except on a road which is a restricted road for the purposes of section 81 of the Road Traffic Regulation Act 1984 by virtue of a system of street lighting when it is lit; and

(*b*) in seriously reduced visibility.

(2) The provisions of paragraph (1) do not apply—

(*a*) in the case of a motor vehicle fitted with one obligatory dipped-beam headlamp or a solo motor bicycle or motor bicycle combination fitted with a pair of obligatory dipped-beam headlamps, if a main-beam headlamp or a front fog lamp is kept lit;

(*b*) in the case of a motor vehicle, other than a solo motor bicycle or motor bicycle combination, fitted with a pair of obligatory dipped-beam headlamps, if—

(i) a pair of main-beam headlamps is kept lit; or

(ii) in seriously reduced visibility, a pair of front fog lamps which is so fitted that the outermost part of the illuminated area of each lamp in the pair is not more than 400 mm from the outer edge of the vehicle is kept lit;

(*c*) to a vehicle being drawn by another vehicle;

(*d*) to a vehicle while being used to propel a snow plough; or

(*e*) to a vehicle which is parked.

(3) For the purposes of this regulation a headlamp shall not be regarded as lit if its intensity is reduced by a dim-dip device.

Requirements about the use of warning beacons

4-3756 **26.** No person shall use, or cause or permit to be used, on an unrestricted dual-carriageway road a vehicle which is required to be fitted with at least one warning beacon by regulation 17 unless every such beacon is kept lit.

Restrictions on the use of lamps other than those to which regulation 24 refers

4-3757 **27.** No person shall use, or cause or permit to be used, on a road any vehicle on which any lamp, hazard warning signal device or warning beacon of a type specified in an item in column 2 of the Table below is used in a manner specified in that item in column 3.

TABLE

(1) Item No	(2) Type of lamp, hazard warning signal device or warning beacon	(3) Manner of use prohibited
1	Headlamp	(a) Used so as to cause undue dazzle or discomfort to other persons using the road. (b) Used so as to be lit when a vehicle is parked.
2	Front fog lamp	(a) Used so as to cause undue dazzle or discomfort to other persons using the road. (b) Used so as to be lit at any time other than in conditions of seriously reduced visibility. (c) Used so as to be lit when a vehicle is parked.
3	Rear fog lamp	(a) Used so as to cause undue dazzle or discomfort to the driver of a following vehicle. (b) Used so as to be lit at any time other than in conditions of seriously reduced visibility. (c) Save in the case of an emergency vehicle, used so as to be lit when a vehicle is parked.
4	Reversing lamp	Used so as to be lit except for the purpose of reversing the vehicle.
5	Hazard warning signal device	Used other than— (i) to warn persons using the road of a temporary obstruction when the vehicle is at rest; or (ii) on a motorway or unrestricted dual-carriageway, to warn following drivers of a need to slow down due to a temporary obstruction ahead; or (iii) in the case of a bus, to summon assistance for the driver or any person acting as a conductor or inspector on the vehicle; or. (iv) in the case of a bus to which prescribed signs are fitted as described in sub-paragraphs (a) and (b) of regulation 17A(1), when the vehicle is stationary and children under the age of 16 years are entering or leaving, or are about to enter or leave, or have just left the vehicle.
6	Warning beacon emitting blue light and special warning lamp	Used so as to be lit except— (i) at the scene of an emergency; or (ii) when it is necessary or desirable either to indicate to persons using the road the urgency of the purpose for which the vehicle is being used, or to warn persons of the presence of the vehicle or a hazard on the road.
7	Warning beacon emitting amber light	Used so as to be lit except— (i) at the scene of an emergency; (ii) when it is necessary or desirable to warn persons of the presence of the vehicle; (iii) in the case of a breakdown vehicle, while it is being used in connection with, and in the immediate vicinity of, an accident or breakdown, or while it is being used to draw a broken-down vehicle.

(1) Item No	(2) Type of lamp, hazard warning signal device or warning beacon	(3) Manner of use prohibited
		(iv) in the case of an abnormal load escort vehicle, while it is being used in connection with the escort of another vehicle which has— (aa) an overall width (including any load) exceeding 2.9 metres; (bb) an overall length (including any load) exceeding 18.65 metres, or (cc) been authorised by the Secretary of State under section 44 of the Act; and (v) in the case of a vehicle, used for escort purposes other than an abnormal load escort vehicle, while it is being used in connection with the escort of any vehicle and travelling at a speed not exceeding 25 mph
8	Warning beacon emitting green light	Used so as to be lit except whilst occupied by a medical practitioner registered by the General Medical Council (whether with full or provisional registration) and used for the purposes of an emergency.
9	Warning beacon emitting yellow light	Used so as to be lit on a road.
10	Work lamp	(a) Used so as to cause undue dazzle or discomfort to the driver of any vehicle. (b) Used so as to be lit except for the purpose of illuminating a working area, accident, breakdown or works in the vicinity of the vehicle.
11	Any other lamp	Used so as to cause undue dazzle or discomfort to other persons using the road.

PART IV
TESTING AND INSPECTION OF LIGHTING EQUIPMENT AND REFLECTORS
Testing and inspection of lighting equipment and reflectors

4–3758　28. The provisions of regulation 74 of the Construction and Use Regulations apply in respect of lighting equipment and reflectors with which a vehicle is required by these Regulations to be fitted in the same way as they apply in respect of brakes, silencers, steering gear and tyres.

4–3759
(Regulation 18)
SCHEDULE 1
OBLIGATORY LAMPS, REFLECTORS, REAR MARKINGS AND DEVICES

TABLE I

MOTOR VEHICLE HAVING THREE OR MORE WHEELS NOT BEING A VEHICLE TO WHICH ANY OTHER TABLE IN THIS SCHEDULE APPLIES

(1) Type of lamp, reflector, rear marking or device	(2) Schedule in which relevant installation and performance requirements are specified	(3) Exceptions
Front position lamp Dim-dip device or running lamp	Schedule 2: Part I Schedule 3: Part I	None. A vehicle having a maximum speed not exceeding 40 mph; A vehicle first used before 1st April 1987; A home forces' vehicle; A vehicle in respect of which the following conditions are satisfied— (a) there is fitted to the vehicle all the lighting and light-signalling devices listed in items 1.5.7 to 1.5.20 of Annex I of Community Directive 76/756/EEC as last amended by Directive 89/278/EEC or Community Directive 76/756/EEC as last amended by Directive 91/663/EEC which are required to be fitted under that Annex; and (b) all those devices are so installed that they comply with the requirements set out in items 3 and 4 of that Annex including, in particular, item 4.2.6 (Alignment of dipped-beam headlamps).

(1) Type of lamp, reflector, rear marking or device	(2) Schedule in which relevant installation and performance requirements are specified	(3) Exceptions
Dipped-beam headlamp	Schedule 4: Part I	A vehicle having a maximum speed not exceeding 15 mph; A vehicle first used before 1st April 1986 being an agricultural vehicle or a works truck; A vehicle first used before 1st January 1931.
Main-beam headlamp	Schedule 5: Part I	A vehicle having a maximum speed not exceeding 25 mph; A vehicle first used before 1st April 1986 being an agricultural vehicle or a works truck; A vehicle first used before 1st January 1931.
Direction indicator	Schedule 7: Part I	An invalid carriage having a maximum speed not exceeding 4 mph and any other vehicle having a maximum speed not exceeding 15 mph; An agricultural vehicle having an unladen weight not exceeding 255 kg; A vehicle first used before 1st April 1986 being an agricultural vehicle, an industrial tractor or a works truck; A vehicle first used before 1st January 1936.
Hazard warning signal device	Schedule 8: Part I	A vehicle not required to be fitted with direction indicators; A vehicle first used before 1st April 1986.
Side marker lamp	Schedule 9: Part I	A vehicle having a maximum speed not exceeding 25 mph; A passenger vehicle; An incomplete vehicle proceeding to a works for completion or to a place where it is to be stored or displayed for sale; A vehicle the overall length of which does not exceed 6 m; A vehicle first used before 1st April 1991; A vehicle first used before 1st April 1996 in respect of which the following conditions are satisfied— (*a*) there is fitted to the vehicle all the lighting and light-signalling devices listed in items 1.5.7 to 1.5.20 of Annex I of Community Directive 76/756/EEC as last amended by Directive 89/278/EEC or Community Directive 76/756/EEC as last amended by Directive 91/663/EEC which are required to be fitted under that Annex; and (*b*) all those devices are so installed that they comply with the requirements set out in items 3 and of that Annex including, in particular, item 4.2.6 (Alignment of dipped-beam headlamps).
Rear position lamp	Schedule 10: Part I	None.
Rear fog lamp	Schedule 11: Part I	A vehicle having a maximum speed not exceeding 25 mph; A vehicle first used before 1st April 1986 being an agricultural vehicle or a works truck; A vehicle first used before 1st April 1980; A vehicle having an overall width which does not exceed 1300 mm.
Stop lamp	Schedule 12: Part I	A vehicle having a maximum speed not exceeding 25 mph; A vehicle first used before 1st April 1986 being an agricultural vehicle or a works truck; A vehicle first used before 1st January 1936.
End-outline marker lamp	Schedule 13: Part I	A vehicle having a maximum speed not exceeding 25 mph; A motor vehicle having an overall width not exceeding 2100 mm; An incomplete vehicle proceeding to a works for completion or to a place where it is to be stored or displayed for sale; A motor vehicle first used before 1st April 1991.
Rear registration plate lamp	Schedule 15.	A vehicle not required to be fitted with a rear registration plate; A works truck.
Side retro reflector	Schedule 17: Part I	A vehicle having a maximum speed not exceeding 25 mph; A goods vehicle— (*a*) first used on or after 1st April 1986, the overall length of which does not exceed 6 m; or (*b*) first used before 1st April 1986, the overall length of which does not exceed 8 m; A passenger vehicle;

(1) Type of lamp, reflector, rear marking or device	(2) Schedule in which relevant installation and performance requirements are specified	(3) Exceptions
		An incomplete vehicle proceeding to a works for completion or to a place where it is to be stored or displayed for sale; A vehicle primarily constructed for moving excavated material and being used by virtue of an Order under section 44 of the Act; A mobile crane or engineering plant.
Rear retro reflector	Schedule 18: Part I	None.
Rear marking	Schedule 19: Part I	A vehicle having a maximum speed not exceeding 25 mph; A vehicle first used before 1st August 1982, the unladen weight of which does not exceed 3050 kg; A vehicle the maximum gross weight of which does not exceed 7500 kg; A passenger vehicle not being an articulated bus; A tractive unit for an articulated vehicle; An incomplete vehicle proceeding to a works for completion or to a place where it is to be stored or displayed for sale; A vehicle first used before 1st April 1986 being an agricultural vehicle, a works truck or engineering plant; A vehicle first used before 1st January 1940; A home forces' vehicle; A vehicle constructed or adapted for— (a) fire fighting or fire salvage; (b) servicing or controlling aircraft; (c) heating and dispensing tar or other material for the construction or maintenance of roads; or (d) transporting two or more vehicles or vehicle bodies or two or more boats.

TABLE II
SOLO MOTOR BICYCLE AND MOTOR BICYCLE COMBINATION

(1) Type of lamp or reflector	(2) Schedule in which relevant installation and performance requirements are specified	(3) Exceptions
Front position lamp Dipped-beam headlamp Main-beam headlamp	Schedule 2: Part I Schedule 4: Part I Schedule 5: Part I	A solo motor bicycle fitted with a headlamp. A vehicle first used before 1st January 1931. A vehicle first used before 1st January 1972 and having an engine with a capacity of less than 50 cc; A vehicle first used before 1st January 1972 and having an engine with a capacity of less than 50 cc; A vehicle first used before 1stJanuary 1931.
Direction indicator	Schedule 7: Part I	A vehicle having a maximum speed not exceeding 25 mph; A vehicle first used before 1st April 1986; A vehicle which is constructed or adapted primarily for use off roads (whether by reason of its tyres, suspension, ground clearance or otherwise) and which can carry only one person or which, in the case of a motor bicycle combination, can carry only the rider and one passenger in the sidecar.
Rear position lamp	Schedule 10: Part I	None.
Stop lamp	Schedule 12: Part I	A vehicle having a maximum speed not exceeding 25 mph; A vehicle first used before 1st April 1986 and having an engine with a capacity of less than 50 cc; A vehicle first used before 1st January 1936.
Rear registration plate lamp	Schedule 15	A vehicle not required to be fitted with a rear registration plate.
Rear retro reflector	Schedule 18: Part I	None.

TABLE III
PEDAL CYCLE

(1) Type of lamp or reflector	(2) Schedule in which relevant installation and performance requirements are specified	(3) Exceptions
Front position lamp	Schedule 2: Part I	None.
Rear position lamp	Schedule 10: Part I	None.
Rear retro reflector	Schedule 18: Part I	None.
Pedal retro reflector	Schedule 20: Part I	A pedal cycle manufactured before 1st October 1985.

TABLE IV
PEDESTRIAN-CONTROLLED VEHICLE, HORSE-DRAWN VEHICLE AND TRACK-LAYING VEHICLE

(1) Type of lamp or reflector	(2) Schedule in which relevant installation and performance requirements are specified	(3) Exceptions
Front position lamp	Schedule 2: Part I	None.
Rear position lamp	Schedule 10: Part I	None.
Rear retro reflector	Schedule 18: Part I	None.

TABLE V
VEHICLE DRAWN OR PROPELLED BY HAND

(1) Type of lamp or reflector	(2) Schedule in which relevant installation and performance requirements are specified	(3) Exceptions
Front position lamp	Schedule 2: Part I	None.
Rear position lamp	Schedule 10: Part I	A vehicle fitted with a rear retro reflector.
Rear retro reflector	Schedule 18: Part I	A vehicle fitted with a rear position lamp.

TABLE VI
TRAILER DRAWN BY A MOTOR VEHICLE

(1) Type of lamp, reflector or rear marking	(2) Schedule in which relevant installation and performance requirements are specified	(3) Exceptions
Front position lamp	Schedule 2: Part I	A trailer with an overall width not exceeding 1600 mm; A trailer manufactured before 1st October 1985 the overall length of which, excluding any drawbar and any fitting for its attachment, does not exceed 2300 mm; A trailer constructed or adapted for the carriage and launching of a boat.
Direction indicator	Schedule 7: Part I	A trailer manufactured before 1st September 1965. An agricultural vehicle or a works trailer in either case manufactured before 1st October 1990.
Side marker lamp	Schedule 9: Part I	A trailer the overall length of which, excluding any drawbar and any fitting for its attachment, does not exceed— (a) 6 m, (b) 9.15 m in the case of a trailer manufactured before 1st October 1990; An incomplete trailer proceeding to a works for completion or to a place where it is to be stored or displayed for sale; An agricultural vehicle or a works trailer; A caravan; A trailer constructed or adapted for the carriage and launching of a boat; A trailer manufactured before 1st October 1995 in respect of which the following conditions are satisfied— (a) there is fitted to the trailer all the lighting and light-signalling devices listed in items 1.5.7 to 1.5.20 of Annex I of Community Directive 76/756/EEC as last amended by Directive 89/278/EEC or Community Directive 76/756/EEC as last amended by Directive 91/663/EEC which are required to be fitted under that Annex; and

(1) Type of lamp, reflector or rear marking	(2) Schedule in which relevant installation and performance requirements are specified	(3) Exceptions
		(b) all those devices are so installed and maintained that they comply with the requirements set out in items 3 and 4 of that Annex.
Rear position lamp	Schedule 10: Part I	None.
Rear fog lamp	Schedule 11: Part I	A trailer manufactured before 1st April 1980; A trailer the overall width of which does not exceed 1300 mm; An agricultural vehicle or a works trailer.
Stop lamp	Schedule 12: Part I	An agricultural vehicle or a works trailer.
End-outline marker lamp	Schedule 13: Part I	A trailer having an overall width not exceeding 2100 mm; An incomplete trailer proceeding to a works for completion or to a place where it is to be stored or displayed for sale; An agricultural vehicle or a works trailer; A trailer manufactured before 1st October 1990.
Rear registration plate lamp	Schedule 15	A trailer not required to be fitted with a rear registration plate.
Side retro reflector	Schedule 17: Part I	A trailer the overall length of which, excluding any drawbar, does not exceed 5 m; An incomplete trailer proceeding to a works for completion or to a place where it is to be stored or displayed for sale; Engineering plant; A trailer primarily constructed for moving excavated material and which is being used by virtue of an Order under section 44 of the Act.
Front retro reflector	Schedule 21: Part I	A trailer manufactured before 1st October 1990; An agricultural vehicle or a works trailer.
Rear retro reflector	Schedule 18: Part I	None.
Rear marking	Schedule 19: Part I	A trailer manufactured before 1st August 1982 the unladen weight of which does not exceed 1020 kg; A trailer the maximum gross weight of which does not exceed 3500 kg; An incomplete trailer proceeding to a works for completion or to a place where it is to be stored or displayed for sale; An agricultural vehicle, a works trailer or engineering plant; A trailer drawn by a bus; A home forces' vehicle; A trailer constructed or adapted for— (a) fire fighting or fire salvage; (b) servicing or controlling aircraft; (c) heating and dispensing tar or other material for the construction or maintenance of roads; (d) carrying asphalt or macadam, in each case being mixing or drying plant; or (e) transporting two or more vehicles or vehicle bodies or two or more boats.

TABLE VII

TRAILER DRAWN BY A PEDAL CYCLE

(1) Type of lamp, reflector or rear marking	(2) Schedule in which relevant installation and performance requirements are specified	(3) Exceptions
Rear position lamp	Schedule 10: Part I	None.
Rear retro reflector	Schedule 18: Part I	None.

4–3760

(Regulations 18 and 20)   SCHEDULE 2

PART I

REQUIREMENTS RELATING TO OBLIGATORY FRONT POSITION LAMPS AND TO OPTIONAL FRONT POSITION LAMPS TO THE EXTENT SPECIFIED IN PART II

1 Number—

(a) Any vehicle not covered by sub-paragraph (b), (c), (d), (e) or (f):	Two
(b) A pedal cycle with less than four wheels and without a sidecar;	One
(c) A solo motor bicycle:	One
(d) A motor bicycle combination with a headlamp on the motor bicycle:	One, on the sidecar
(e) An invalid carriage:	One
(f) A vehicle drawn or propelled by hand:	One

2	Position—	
	(a) Longitudinal:	No requirement
	(b) Lateral—	
	(i) Where two front position lamps are required to be fitted—	
	(A) Maximum distance from the side of the vehicle—	
	(1) A motor vehicle first used on or after 1st April 1986	400 mm
	(2) A trailer manufactured on or after 1st October 1985:	150 mm
	(3) Any other vehicle manufactured on or after 1st October 1985:	400 mm
	(4) A motor vehicle first used before 1st April 1986 and any other vehicle manufactured before 1st October 1985:	510 mm
	(B) Minimum separation distance between front position lamps:	No requirement
	(ii) Where one front position lamp is required to be fitted—	
	(A) A sidecar forming part of a motor bicycle combination:	On the centre-line of the sidecar or on the side of the sidecar furthest from the motor bicycle
	(B) Any other vehicle:	On the centre-line or off-side of the vehicle
	(c) Vertical—	
	(i) Maximum height above the ground—	
	(A) Any vehicle not covered by sub-paragraph (B), (C) or (D):	1500 mm or, if the structure of the vehicle makes this impracticable, 2100 mm
	(B) A motor vehicle first used before 1st April 1986 and a trailer manufactured before 1st October 1985:	2300 mm
	(C) A motor vehicle, first used on or after 1st April 1986, having a maximum speed not exceeding 25 mph:	2100 mm
	(D) A [bus] and a road clearance vehicle:	No requirement
	(ii) Minimum height above the ground	No requirement
3	Angles of visibility—	
	(a) A motor vehicle (not being a motor bicycle combination or an agricultural vehicle) first used on or after 1st April 1986 and a trailer manufactured on or after 1st October 1985—	
	Horizontal—	
	(A) Where one lamp is required to be fitted:	80° to the left and to the right
	(B) Where two lamps are required to be fitted:	80° outwards and 45° inwards (5° inwards in the case of a trailer)
	(ii) Vertical—	
	(A) Any case not covered by sub-paragraph (B):	15° above and below the horizontal
	(B) Where the highest part of the illuminated area of the lamp is less than 750 mm above the round:	15° above and 5° below the horizontal
	(b) Any other vehicle:	Visible to the front
4	Alignment:	To the front
5	Markings (see also regulation 3(6))—	
	(a) A motor vehicle (other than a solo motor bicycle or a motor bicycle combination) first used on or after 1st January 1972 and a trailer manufactured on or after 1st October 1985:	An approval mark
	(b) A solo motor bicycle and a motor bicycle combination in either case first used on or after 1st April 1986:	An approval mark
	(c) Any other vehicle manufactured or first used on or after 1st October 1990 and before the 1st October 1995:	An approval mark or a British Standard mark
	(ca) Any other vehicle manufactured on or after the 1st October 1995	An approval mark or the British Standard mark which is specified in sub-paragraph (b), (c) or (d) of the definition of "British Standard mark" below
	(d) Any other vehicle:	No requirement
6	Size of illuminated area:	No requirement
7	Colour:	White or, if incorporated in a headlamp which is capable of emitting only a yellow light, yellow
8	Wattage:	No requirement
9	Intensity—	
	(a) A front position lamp bearing any of the markings mentioned in paragraph 5:	No requirement
	(b) Any other front position lamp:	Visible from a reasonable distance
10	Electrical connections:	No individual requirement
11	Tell-tale:	No requirement
12.	Other requirements—	

(a) Except in the case of a vehicle covered by sub-paragraph (b), where two front position lamps are required to be fitted they shall form a pair.

(b) In the case of a trailer manufactured before 1st October 1985 and a motor bicycle combination, where two front position lamps are required to be fitted they shall be fitted on each side of the longitudinal axis of the vehicle.

(c) in the case of a front position lamp capable of emitting a flashing light which is fitted to—

       (i) a pedal cycle; or

       (ii) a trailer drawn by, or a sidecar attached to, a pedal cycle;

the light shown by the lamp when flashing shall be displayed not less than 60 nor more than 240 equal times per minute and the intervals between each display of light shall be constant.

13.   Definitions—

In this Schedule—

"approval mark" means—

    (a) in relation to a solo motor bicycle or a motor bicycle combination, a marking designated as an approval mark by regulation 4 of the Designation of Approval Marks Regulations and shown at item 50A of Schedule 2 to those Regulations, and

    (b) in relation to any other vehicle, either—

       (i) a marking designated as an approval mark by regulation 5 of the Designation of Approval Marks Regulations and shown at item 5 of Schedule 4 to those Regulations, or

       (ii) a marking designated as an approval mark by regulation 4 of the Designation of Approval Marks Regulations and shown at item 7 of Schedule 2 to those Regulations;

"British Standard mark" means—

    (a) the mark indicated in the specification for photometric and physical requirements for lighting equipment published by the British Standards Institution under the reference BS 6102: Part 3: 1986 namely "6102/3"; or

    (b) the mark indicated in the specification for photometric and physical requirements for lighting equipment published by the British Standards Institution under the reference BS 6102: Part 3: 1986 as amended by AMD 5821 published on the 29th April 1988, namely "6102/3; or

    (c) the mark indicated in the specification for photometric and physical requirements for lighting equipment published by the British Standards Institution under the reference BS 6102: Part 3: 1986 as amended by AMD 8438 published on the 15th April 1995, namely "6102/3"; or

    (d) the mark indicated in the specification for photometric and physical requirements for lighting equipment published by the British Standards Institution under the reference BS 6102: Part 3: 1986 as amended by AMD 14621 published on the 1st September 2003, namely "6102/3"

PART II
REQUIREMENTS RELATING TO OPTIONAL FRONT POSITION LAMPS

1. In the case of a solo motor bicycle first used on or after 1st April 1991 which is not fitted with any obligatory front position lamp, not more than two may be fitted which must comply with the requirement specified in paragraph 7 of Part I. Where two are fitted these shall be situated as close together as possible.

2. In the case of a solo motor bicycle first used on or after 1st April 1991 which is fitted with one obligatory front position lamp, not more than one additional lamp may be fitted which must comply with the requirement specified in paragraph 7 of Part I and shall be situated as close as possible to the obligatory front position lamp.

3. In the case of any other vehicle any number of front position lamps may be fitted and the only requirements prescribed by these Regulations in respect of any which are fitted are those in paragraph 7 and 12(c) of Part I.

4–3761

(Regulations 18 and 20)   SCHEDULE 3

PART I
REQUIREMENTS RELATING TO OBLIGATORY DIM-DIP DEVICES AND RUNNING LAMPS

1. A dim-dip device fitted to satisfy regulation 18 shall cause light to be emitted from the dipped-beam filament of each obligatory dipped-beam headlamp, each such light having, so far as is practicable, an intensity of between 10 and 20 per cent of the intensity of the normal dipped beam.

2. Running lamps fitted to satisfy regulation 18 shall be in the form of a matched pair of front lamps, each of which—

    (a) is fitted in a position in which an obligatory front position lamp may lawfully be fitted, and

    (b) is capable of emitting white light to the front having an intensity of not less than 200 candelas, measured from directly in front of the centre of the lamp in a direction parallel to the longitudinal axis of the vehicle, and of not more than 800 candelas in any direction.

3. The electrical connections to the obligatory dim-dip device shall be such that the light output specified in paragraph 1 above is automatically emitted whenever the following four conditions are satisfied, namely—

    (a) the engine is running, or the key or devices which control the starting or stopping of the engine are in the normal position for when the vehicle is being driven;

    (b) the obligatory main beam and dipped beam headlamps are switched off;

    (c) any front fog lamp fitted to the vehicle is switched off; and

    (d) the obligatory front position lamps are switched on.

4. The electrical connections to the obligatory running lamps shall be such that the light output specified in paragraph 2 above is automatically emitted, whenever the conditions set out in sub-paragraphs (a), (b) and (c) of paragraph 3 are satisfied.

PART II
REQUIREMENTS RELATING TO OPTIONAL DIM-DIP DEVICES AND RUNNING LAMPS

There is no requirement relating to an optional dim-dip device or an optional running lamp.

4–3762

Regulations 18 and 20   SCHEDULE 4

PART I
REQUIREMENTS RELATING TO OBLIGATORY DIPPED-BEAM HEADLAMPS AND TO OPTIONAL DIPPED-BEAM HEADLAMPS TO THE EXTENT SPECIFIED IN PART II

1.   Number—

    (a) Any vehicle not covered by sub-paragraph (b), (c), (d) or (e):   Two

    (b) A solo motor bicycle and a motor bicycle combination: One

    (c) A motor vehicle with three wheels, other than a motor bicycle   One
        combination, first used before 1st January 1972:

    (d) A motor vehicle with three wheels, other than a motor bicycle   One
        combination, first used on or after 1st January 1972 and which has
        an unladen weight of not more than 400 kg and an overall width of
        not more than 1300 mm:

    (e) A bus first used before 1st October 1969:   One

2.   Position—
    (a) Longitudinal: No requirement
    (b) Lateral—
        (i) Where two dipped-beam headlamps are required to be fitted—
           (A) Maximum distance from the side of the vehicle—
              (1) Any vehicle not covered by sub-paragraph (2) or (3):   400 mm
              (2) A vehicle first used before 1st January 1972:   No requirement
              (3) An agricultural vehicle, engineering plant and an indus-   No requirement
                 trial tractor:
           (B) Minimum separation distance between a pair of dipped-   No requirement
              beam headlamps:
        (ii) Where one dipped-beam headlamp is required to be fitted—
           (A) Any vehicle not covered by sub-paragraph (B):   (i) On the centre-line of the
motor vehicle (disregarding
any sidecar forming part of a
motor bicycle combination),
or
(ii) At any distance from the
side of the motor vehicle (disregarding any sidecar forming part of a motor bicycle
combination) provided that a
duplicate lamp is fitted on the
other side so that together
they form a matched pair. In
such a case, both lamps shall
be regarded as obligatory
lamps.

          (B) A bus first used before 1st October 1969:   No requirement
    (c) Vertical—
        (i) Maximum height above the ground—
           (A) Any vehicle not covered by sub-paragraph (B):   1200 mm
           (B) A vehicle first used before 1st January 1952, an agricultural   No requirement
              vehicle, a road clearance vehicle, an aerodrome fire tender,
              an aerodrome runway sweeper, an industrial tractor, engi-
              neering plant and a home forces' vehicle:
        (ii) Minimum height above the ground—
           (A) Any vehicle not covered by sub-paragraph (B):   500 mm
           (B) A vehicle first used before 1st January 1956:   No requirement

3.   Angles of visibility: No requirement
4.   Alignment—
When a vehicle is at its kerbside weight and has a weight of 75 kg on the driver's seat, and any manual
headlamp levelling device control is set to the stop position, the alignment of every dipped-beam
headlamp shall, as near as practicable, be as follows:

    (a) In the case of a vehicle having a maximum speed exceeding 25 mph—
        (i) If the dipped-beam headlamp bears an approval mark its aim shall be set so that the horizontal
           part of the cut-off of the beam pattern is inclined downwards as indicated by the vehicle
           manufacturer in a marking on the vehicle, as mentioned in sub-paragraph 12(b) or, where no such
           marking is provided—
           (A) 1.3 per cent if the height of the centre of the headlamp is not more than 850 mm above the
              ground, or
           (B) 2 per cent if the height of the centre of the headlamp is more than 850 mm above the ground;
        (ii) If the dipped-beam headlamp does not bear an approval mark and the headlamp can also be used
           as a main-beam headlamp its aim shall be set so that the centre of the main-beam pattern is
           horizontal or inclined slightly below the horizontal;
        (iii) If the dipped-beam headlamp does not bear an approval mark and the headlamp cannot also be
           used as a main-beam headlamp its aim shall be set so as not to cause undue dazzle or discomfort
           to other persons using the road;
    (b) In the case of a vehicle having a maximum speed not exceeding 25 mph—
        (i) If the dipped-beam headlamp bears an approval mark or not and the headlamp can also be used
           as a main-beam headlamp its aim shall be set so that the centre of the mean-beam pattern is
           horizontal or inclined slightly below the horizontal;
        (ii) If the dipped-beam headlamp bears an approval mark or not and the headlamp cannot also be
           used as a main-beam its aim shall be set so as not to cause undue dazzle or discomfort to other
           persons using the road.

5.   Markings—
    (a) Any vehicle not covered by sub-paragraph (b), (c) or (d):   An approval mark or a British
Standard mark
    (b) A motor vehicle first used before 1st April 1986:   No requirement
    (c) A three-wheeled motor vehicle, not being a motor bicycle combina-   No requirement
        tion, first used on or after 1st April 1986 and having a maximum
        speed not exceeding 50 mph:
    (d) A solo motor bicycle and a motor bicycle combination: No requirement
6.   Size of illuminated area: No requirement

7. Colour:	White or yellow
8. Wattage—	
(a) A motor vehicle with four or more wheels first used on or after 1st April 1986:	No requirement
(b) A three-wheeled motor vehicle, not being a motor bicycle combination, first used on or after 1st April 1986—	
(i) having a maximum speed not exceeding 50 mph:	15 watts minimum
(ii) having a maximum speed exceeding 50 mph:	No requirement
(c) A motor vehicle with four or more wheels first used before 1st April 1986:	30 watts minimum
(d) A three-wheeled motor vehicle, not being a motor bicycle combination, first used before 1st April 1986:	24 watts minimum
(e) A solo motor bicycle and a motor bicycle combination—	
(i) having an engine not exceeding 250 cc and a maximum speed not exceeding 25 mph:	10 watts minimum
(ii) having an engine not exceeding 250 cc and a maximum speed exceeding 25 mph:	15 watts minimum
(iii) having an engine exceeding 250 cc:	24 watts minimum
9. Intensity:	No requirement

10. Electrical connections—
    Where a matched pair of dipped-beam headlamps is fitted they shall be capable of being switched on and off simultaneously and not otherwise.

11. Tell-tale: No requirement

12. Other requirements—

(a) Every dipped-beam headlamp shall be so constructed that the direction of the beam of light emitted therefrom can be adjusted whilst the vehicle is stationary.

(b) Every vehicle which—

(i) is fitted with dipped-beam headlamps bearing an approval mark,
(ii) has a maximum speed exceeding 25 mph, and
(iii) is first used on or after 1st April 1991 shall be marked with a clearly legible and indelible marking as illustrated in Schedule 23, close to either the headlamps or the manufacturer's plate showing the setting recommended by the manufacturer for the downward inclination of the horizontal part of the cut-off of the beam pattern of the dipped-beam headlamps when the vehicle is at its kerbside weight and has a weight of 75 kg on the driver's seat. That setting shall be a single figure—

(A) between 1 and 1.5 per cent if the height of the centre of the headlamp is not more than 850 mm above the ground, and
(B) between 1 and 2 per cent if the height of the centre of the headlamp is more than 850 mm above the ground.

(c) Every dipped-beam headlamp fitted to a vehicle first used on or after 1st April 1986 in accordance with this part of this Schedule shall be designed for a vehicle which is intended to be driven on the left hand side of the road.

(d) Where two dipped-beam headlamps are required to be fitted they shall form a matched pair.

13. Definitions—
    In this Schedule—
    "approval mark" means either—

(a) a marking designated as an approval mark by regulation 5 of the Designation of Approval Marks Regulations and shown at item 12 or 13 or 14 or 16 or, in the case of a vehicle having a maximum speed not exceeding 25 mph, 27 or 28 of Schedule 4 to those Regulations, or

(b) a marking designated as an approval mark by regulation 4 of the Designation of Approval Marks Regulations and shown at item 1A or 1B or 1C or 1E or 5A or 5B or 5C or 5E or 8C or 8D or 8E or 8F or 8G or 8H or 8K or 8L or 20C or 20D or 20E or 20F or 20G or 20H or 20K or 20L or 31A or 31C or, in the case of a vehicle having a maximum speed not exceeding 25 mph, 1H or 1I or 5H or 5I of Schedule 2 to those Regulations; and

"British Standard mark" means the specification for sealed beam headlamps published by the British Standards Institution under the reference BS AU 40: Part 4a: 1966 as amended by Amendment AMD 218 published in December 1976, namely "BS AU40".

PART II
REQUIREMENTS RELATING TO OPTIONAL DIPPED-BEAM HEADLAMPS

1. In the case of a vehicle with three or more wheels having a maximum speed exceeding 25 mph first used on or after 1st April 1991, two and not more than two may be fitted and the only requirements prescribed by these Regulations in respect of any which are fitted are—

(a) those specified in paragraphs 2(c), 4, 7, 10 and 12(a) pf Part I,
(b) that they are designed for a vehicle which is intended to be driven on the right-hand side of the road,
(c) that they form a matched pair, and
(d) that their electrical connections are such that not more than one pair of dipped-beam headlamps is capable of being illuminated at a time.

2. In the case of any other vehicle, any number may be fitted and the only requirements prescribed by these Regulations in respect of any which are fitted are those specified in paragraphs 2(c), 4, 7 and 12(a) of Part I.

4–3763

(Regulations 18 and 20)   SCHEDULE 5

PART I
REQUIREMENTS RELATING TO OBLIGATORY MAIN-BEAM HEADLAMPS AND TO OPTIONAL MAIN-BEAM HEADLAMPS TO THE EXTENT SPECIFIED IN PART II

1. Number—

(a) Any vehicle not covered by sub-paragraph (b), (c) or (d):	Two
(b) A solo motor bicycle and motor bicycle combination:	One

    (c) A motor vehicle with three wheels, other than a motor bicycle   One
         combination, first used before 1st January 1972:

    (d) A motor vehicle with three wheels, other than a motor bicycle   One
         combination, first used on or after 1st January 1972 and which has
         an unladen weight of not more than 400 kg and an overall width of
         not more than 1300 mm:

2.   Position—

    (a) Longitudinal: No requirement

    (b) Lateral—

         (i) Where two main-beam headlamps are required to be fitted—

              (A) Maximum distance from the side of the vehicle: The outer edges of the illumi-
                                                      nated areas must in no case
                                                      be closer to the side of the
                                                      vehicle than the outer edges
                                                      of the illuminated areas of the
                                                      obligatory   dipped-beam
                                                      headlamps.

              (B) Maximum separation distance between a pair of main-beam   No requirement
                   headlamps:

         (ii) Where one main-beam headlamp is required to be fitted: (i) On the centre-line of the
                                                      motor vehicle (disregard-
                                                     ing any sidecar forming
                                                     part of a motor bicycle
                                                     combination), or
                                                   (ii) At any distance from the
                                                    side of the vehicle (disre-
                                                    garding any sidecar form-
                                                    ing part of a motor bicycle
                                                    combination)   provided
                                                    that a duplicate lamp is
                                                    fitted on the other side so
                                                    that together they form a
                                                    matched pair. In such a
                                                    case, both lamps shall be
                                                    treated   as   obligatory
                                                    lamps.

    (c) Vertical: No requirement

3.   Angles of visibility: No requirement

4.   Alignment: To the front

5.   Markings—

    (a) Any vehicle not covered by sub-paragraph (b), (c) or (d):   An approval mark or a British
                                                     Standard mark

    (b) A motor vehicle first used before 1st April 1986:   No requirement

    (c) A three-wheeled motor vehicle, not being a motor bicycle combina-   No requirement
         tion, first used on or after 1st April 1986 and having a maximum
         speed not exceeding 50 mph:

    (d) A solo motor bicycle and a motor bicycle combination: No requirement

6.   Size of illuminated area: No requirement

7.   Colour: White or yellow

8.   Wattage—

    (a) A motor vehicle, other than a solo motor bicycle or motor bicycle   No requirement
         combination, first used on or after 1st April 1986:

    (b) A motor vehicle, other than a solo motor bicycle or a motor bicycle   30 watts minimum
         combination, first used before 1st April 1986:

    (c) A solo motor bicycle and a motor bicycle combination—

         (ii) having an engine exceeding 250 cc: 15 watts minimum

         (ii) having an engine exceeding 250 cc: 30 watts minimum

9.   Intensity: No requirement

10.   Electrical connections—

    (a) Every main-beam headlamp shall be so constructed that the light emitted therefrom—

         (i) can be deflected at the will of the driver to become a dipped beam, or

         (ii) can be extinguished by the operation of a device which at the same time either—

              (A) causes the lamp to emit a dipped beam, or

              (B) causes another lamp to emit a dipped beam.

    (b) Where a matched pair of main-beam headlamps is fitted they shall be capable of being switched on
         and off simultaneously and not otherwise

11.   Tell-tale—

    (a) Any vehicle not covered by sub-paragraph (b):   A circuit-closed tell-tale shall
                                                     be fitted

    (b) A motor vehicle first used before 1st April 1986:   No requirement

12.   Other requirements—

    (a) Every main-beam headlamp shall be so constructed that the direction of the beam of light emitted
         therefrom can be adjusted whilst the vehicle is stationary.

    (b) Except in the case of a bus first used before 1st October 1969, where two main-beam headlamps are
         required to be fitted they shall form a matched pair.

13.   Definitions—

In this Schedule—

"approval mark" means—

    (a) a marking designated as an approval mark by regulation 5 of the Designation of Approval Marks
         Regulations and shown at item 12 or 13 or 17 of Schedule 4 to those Regulations; or

(b) a marking designated as an approval mark by regulation 4 of the Designation of Approval Marks Regulations and shown at item 1A or 1B or 1F or 5A or 5B or 5F or 8C or 8D or 8E or 8F or 8M or 8N or 20C or 20D or 20E or 20F or 20M or 20N or 31A or 31D of Schedule 2 to those Regulations; and "British Standard mark" means the specification for sealed beam headlamps published by the British Standards Institution under the reference BS AU 40: Part 4a: 1966 as amended by Amendment AMD 2188 published in December 1976, namely "BS AU40".

PART II
REQUIREMENTS RELATING TO OPTIONAL MAIN-BEAM HEADLAMPS

Any number may be fitted and the only requirements prescribed by these Regulations in respect of any which are fitted are those specified in paragraphs 7, 10 and 12(a) of Part I and, in the case of a motor vehicle first used on or after 1st April 1991, paragraph 5 of Part I.

4–3764

(Regulation 20)

SCHEDULE 6
REQUIREMENTS RELATING TO OPTIONAL FRONT FOG LAMPS

1. Number—	
(a) Any vehicle not covered by sub-paragraph (b):	No requirement
(b) A motor vehicle, other than a motor bicycle or motor bicycle combination, first used on or after 1st April 1991:	Not more than two
2. Position—	
(a) Longitudinal:	No requirement
(b) Lateral—	
(i) Where a pair of front fog lamps is used in conditions of seriously reduced visibility in place of the obligatory dipped beam headlamps—	
Maximum distance from side of vehicle:	400 mm
(ii) in all other cases:	No requirement
(c) Vertical—	
(i) Maximum height above the ground—	
(A) Any vehicle not covered by sub-paragraph (B):	1200 mm
(B) An agricultural vehicle, a road clearance vehicle, an aerodrome fire tender, an aerodrome runway sweeper, an industrial tractor, engineering plant and a home forces' vehicle:	No requirement
(ii) Minimum height above the ground:	No requirement
3. Angles of visibility:	No requirement
4. Alignment:	To the front and so aimed that the upper edge of the beam is, as near as practicable, 3 per cent below the horizontal when the vehicle is at its kerbside weight and has a weight of 75 kg on the driver's seat
5. Markings—	
(a) A vehicle first used on or after 1st April 1986:	An approval mark
(b) A vehicle first used before 1st April 1986:	No requirement
6. Size of illuminated area:	No requirement
7. Colour:	White or yellow
8. Wattage:	No requirement
9. Intensity:	No requirement
10. Electrical connections:	No individual requirement
11. Tell-tale:	No requirement

12. Other requirements—
Every front fog lamp shall be so constructed that the direction of the beam of light emitted therefrom can be adjusted whilst the vehicle is stationary.

13. Definitions—
In this Schedule "approval mark" means either—
  (a) a marking designated as an approval mark by regulation 5 of the Designation of Approval Marks Regulations and shown at item 19 of Schedule 4 to those Regulations; or
  (b) a marking designated as an approval mark by regulation 4 of the Designation of Approval Marks Regulations and shown at item 19 or 19A of Schedule 2 of those Regulations.

4–3765

Regulations 18 and 20

SCHEDULE 7

PART I
REQUIREMENTS RELATING TO OBLIGATORY DIRECTION INDICATORS AND TO OPTIONAL DIRECTION INDICATORS TO THE EXTENT SPECIFIED IN PART II

1 Number (on each side of a vehicle)—	
(a) A motor vehicle with three or more wheels, not being a motor bicycle combination, first used on or after 1st April 1986;	One front indicator (Category 1, 1a or 1b), one rear indicator (Category 2, 2a or 2b) and one side repeater indicator (Category 5) or, in the case of a motor vehicle having a maximum speed not exceeding 25 mph, one front indicator (Category 1, 1a or 1b) and one rear indicator (Category 2, 2a or 2b).

(b) A trailer manufactured on or after 1st October 1985 drawn by a motor vehicle: One rear indicator (Category 2, 2a or 2b) or, in the case of a trailer towed by a solo motor bicycle or a motor bicycle combination, one rear indicator (Category 12).

(c) A solo motor bicycle and a motor bicycle combination, in each case first used on or after 1st April 1986:   One front indicator (Category 1, 1a, 1b or 11) and one rear indicator (Category 2, 2a, 2b or 12).

(d) A motor vehicle first used on or after [1st April 1936] and before 1st April 1986, a trailer manufactured on or after [1st April 1936] and before 1st October 1985, a pedal cycle with or without a sidecar or a trailer, a horse-drawn vehicle and a vehicle drawn or propelled by hand: Any arrangement of indicators so as to satisfy the requirements for angles of visibility in paragraph 3.

(e) A motor vehicle first used before 1st April 1936 and any trailer manufactured before that date: Any arrangement of indicators so as to make the intention of the driver clear to other road users.

2   Position—

  (a) Longitudinal—

    (i) A side repeater indicator which is required to be fitted in accordance with paragraph 1(a):   Within 2600 mm of the front of the vehicle

    (ii) Any other indicator: No requirement

  (b) Lateral—

    (i) Maximum distance from the side of the vehicle—

       Any vehicle not covered by sub-paragraph (B):   400 mm

      (B) A motor vehicle first used before 1st April 1986, a trailer manufactured before 1st October 1985, a solo motor bicycle, a pedal cycle, a horse-drawn vehicle and a vehicle drawn or propelled by hand: No requirement

    (ii) Minimum separation distance between indicators on opposite sides of a vehicle—

      (A) A motor vehicle (other than a solo motor bicycle or a motor bicycle combination or an invalid carriage having a maximum speed not exceeding 8 mph) first used on or after 1st April 1986, a trailer manufactured on or after 1st October 1985, a horse-drawn vehicle, a pedestrian-controlled vehicle and a vehicle drawn or propelled by hand: 500 mm or, if the overall width of the vehicle is less than 1400 mm, 400 mm

      (B) A solo motor bicycle having an engine exceeding 50 cc and first used on or after 1st April 1986—

        (1) Front indicators   300 mm

        (2) Rear indicators: 240 mm

      (C) A solo motor bicycle having an engine not exceeding 50 cc and first used on or after 1st April 1986 and a pedal cycle—

        (1) Front indicators: 240 mm

        (2) Rear indicators: 180 mm

      (D) A motor bicycle combination first used on or after 1st April 1986:   400 mm

      (E) An invalid carriage having a maximum speed not exceeding 8 mph—

        (1) Front indicators: 240 mm

        (2) Rear indicators: 300 mm

      (F) A motor vehicle first used before 1st April 1986 and a trailer manufactured before 1st October 1985:   No requirement

    (iii) Minimum separation distance between a front indicator and any dipped-beam headlamp or front fog lamp—

      (A) Fitted to a motor vehicle, other than a solo motor bicycle or a motor bicycle combination, first used on or after 1st April 1995:   (a) in the case of a Category 1 indicator, 40 mm;

         (b) in the case of a Category 1a indicator, 20 mm; (c in the case of a Category 1b indicator, no requirement 100 mm

      (B) Fitted to a solo motor bicycle or a motor bicycle combination in either case first used on or after 1st April 1986:   100 mm

      (C) Fitted to any other vehicle: No requirement

  (c) Vertical—

    (i) Maximum height above the ground—

      (A) Any vehicle not covered by sub-paragraph (B) or (C):   1500 mm or, if the structure of the vehicle makes this impracticable, 2300 mm.

      (B) A motor vehicle first used before 1st April 1986 and a trailer manufactured before 1st October 1985:   No requirement

      (C) A motor vehicle having a maximum speed not exceeding 25 mph: No requirement

    (ii) Minimum height above the ground: 350 mm

3   Angles of visibility—

  (a) A motor vehicle first used on or after 1st April 1986 and a trailer manufactured on or after 1st October 1985—

    (i) Horizontal (see diagrams in Part III of this Schedule)—

(A) A front or rear indicator fitted to a motor vehicle, other than a solo motor bicycle or a motor bicycle combination, having a maximum speed exceeding 25 mph and every rear indicator fitted to a trailer:	80° outwards and 45° inwards
(B) A front or rear indicator fitted to a solo motor bicycle or a motor bicycle combination:	80° outwards and 20° inwards
(C) A front or rear indicator fitted to a motor vehicle, other than a solo motor bicycle or a motor bicycle combination, having a maximum speed not exceeding 25 mph:	80° outwards and 3° inwards
(D) A side repeater indicator fitted to a motor vehicle or a trailer:	Between rearward angles of 5° outboard and 60° outboard or, in the case of a motor vehicle having a maximum speed not exceeding 25 mph where it is impracticable to comply with the 5° angle, this may be replaced by 10°.
(ii) Vertical—	
(A) Except as provided by sub-paragraph (B) or (C):	15° above and below the horizontal
(B) Where the highest part of the illuminated area of the lamp is less than 1900 mm above the ground and the vehicle is a motor vehicle having a maximum speed not exceeding 25 mph:	15° above and 10° below the horizontal 15° above and 5° below the horizontal
(C) Where the highest part of the illuminated area of the lamp is less than 750 mm above the ground:	15° above and 5° below the horizontal
(b) A motor vehicle first used before 1st April 1986, a trailer manufactured before 1st October 1985, a pedal cycle, a horse-drawn vehicle and a vehicle drawn or propelled by hand:	Such that at least one (but not necessarily the same) indicator on each side is plainly visible to the rear in the case of a trailer and both to the front and rear in the case of any other vehicle.
4 Alignment—	
(a) A front indicator:	To the front
(b) A rear indicator:	To the rear
(c) A side repeater indicator (Category 5):	As shown in the first sketch in Part III of this Schedule
5 Markings—	
(a) A motor vehicle, other than a solo motor bicycle or a motor bicycle combination, first used on or after 1st April 1986 and a trailer, other than a trailer drawn by a solo motor bicycle or a motor bicycle combination, manufactured on or after 1st October 1985:	An approval mark and, above such mark, the following numbers—
	(a) in the case of a front indicator, "1", "1a" or "1b";
	(b) in the case of a rear indicator, "2", "2a" or "2b";
	(c) in the case of a side repeater indicator, "5".
(b) A solo motor bicycle and a motor bicycle combination in either case first used on or after 1st April 1986, a trailer, manufactured on or after 1st October 1985, drawn by such a solo motor bicycle or a motor bicycle combination, a pedal cycle, a horse-drawn vehicle and a vehicle drawn or propelled by hand:	An approval mark and, above such mark, the following numbers—
	(a) in the case of a front indicator, "1", "1a", "1b" or "11";
	(b) in the case of a rear indicator, "2", "2a", "2b" or "12";
	(c) in the case of a side repeater indicator, "5".
(c) A motor vehicle first used before 1st April 1986 and a trailer manufactured before 1st October 1985:	No requirement
6 Size of illuminated area:	No requirement
7 Colour—	
(a) Any vehicle not covered by sub-paragraph (b):	Amber
(b) An indicator fitted to a motor vehicle first used before 1st September 1965 and any trailer drawn thereby—	
(i) if it shows only the front:	White or amber
(ii) if it shows only the rear:	Red or amber
(iii) if it shows both to the front and to the rear:	Amber
8 Wattage—	15 to 36 watts
(a) Any front or rear indicator which emits a flashing light and does not bear an approval mark:	
(b) Any other indicator:	No requirement
9 Intensity—	
(a) An indicator bearing an approval mark:	No requirement
(b) An indicator not bearing an approval mark:	Such that the light is plainly visible from a reasonable distance
10. Electrical connections—	

(a) All indicators on one side of a vehicle together with all indicators on that side of any trailer drawn by the vehicle, while so drawn, shall be operated by one switch.

(b) All indicators on one side of a vehicle or combination of vehicles showing a flashing light shall flash in phase, except that in the case of a solo motor bicycle, a motor bicycle combination and a pedal cycle, the front and rear direction indicators on one side of the vehicle may flash alternately.

11. Tell-tale—

(a) One or more indicators on each side of a vehicle to which indicators are fitted shall be so designed and fitted that the driver when in his seat can readily be aware when it is in operation; or

(b) The vehicle shall be equipped with an operational tell-tale for front and rear indicators (including any rear indicator on the rearmost of any trailers drawn by the vehicle).

12. Other requirements—

(a) Every indicator (other than a semaphore arm, that is an indicator in the form of an illuminated sign which when in operation temporarily alters the outline of the vehicle to the extent of at least 150 mm measured horizontally and is visible from both the front and rear of the vehicle) shall when in operation show a light which flashes constantly at the rate of not less than 60 nor more than 120 flashes per minute. However, in the event of a failure, other than a short-circuit of an indicator, any other indicator on the same side of the vehicle or combination of vehicles may continue to flash, but the rate may be less than 60 or more than 120 flashes per minute. Every indicator shall when in operation perform efficiently regardless of the speed of the vehicle.

(b) Where two front or rear direction indicators are fitted to a motor vehicle first used on or after 1st April 1986, and two rear direction indicators are fitted to a trailer manufactured on or after 1st October 1985, in each case, they shall be fitted so as to form a pair.

(c) Revoked.

13. Definitions—

In this Schedule "approval mark" means either—

(a) a marking designated as an approval mark by regulation 5 of the Designation of Approval Marks Regulations and shown at item 9 of Schedule 4 to those Regulations; or

(b) a marking designated as an approval mark by regulation 4 of the Designation of Approval Marks Regulations and shown at item 6 or, in the case of a solo motor bicycle or a motor bicycle combination, a pedal cycle, a horse-drawn vehicle or a vehicle drawn or propelled by hand, at item 50 of Schedule 2 to those Regulations.

PART II
REQUIREMENTS RELATING TO OPTIONAL DIRECTION INDICATORS

1. No vehicle shall be fitted with a total of more than one front indicator nor more than two rear indicators, on each side.

2. Any number of side indicators may be fitted to the side (excluding the front and rear) of a vehicle.

3. The only other requirements prescribed by these Regulations in respect of any which are fitted are those specified in paragraphs 5, 7, 8, 9, 10, 11, 12(a) and 12(b) of Part I.

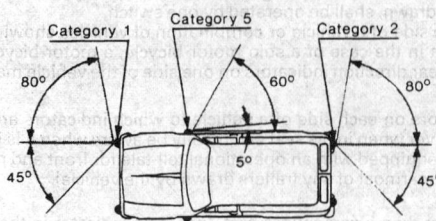

PART II

Category 1   Category 5   Category 2

80°   60°   80°

5°

45°   45°

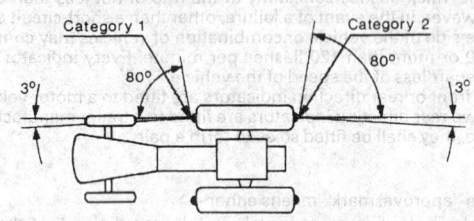

Category 1   Category 2

3°   80°   80°   3°

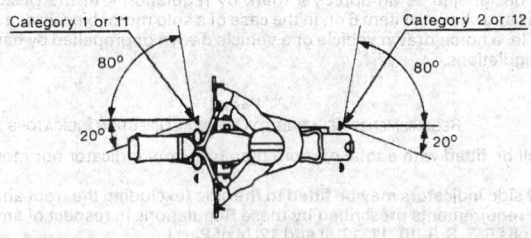

Category 1 or 11   Category 2 or 12

80°   80°

20°   20°

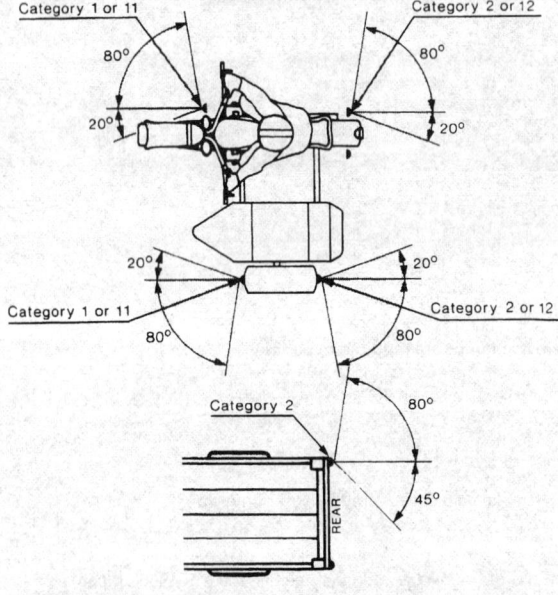

Category 1 or 11   Category 2 or 12

80°   80°

20°   20°

20°   20°

Category 1 or 11   Category 2 or 12

80°   80°

Category 2

80°

REAR

45°

(Regulations 18 and 20)   SCHEDULE 8
REQUIREMENTS RELATING TO OBLIGATORY AND OPTIONAL HAZARD WARNING SIGNAL DEVICES

Every hazard warning signal device shall—

(a) be operated by one switch;
(b) cause all the direction indicators with which a vehicle or a combination of vehicles is equipped to flash in phase;
(c) be provided with a circuit-closed tell-tale in the form of a flashing light which may operate in conjunction with any direction indicator tell-tale; and
(d) be able to function even if the device which controls the starting and stopping of the engine is in a position which makes it impossible to start the engine.

(Regulations 18, 20 and 22)   SCHEDULE 9
PART I
REQUIREMENTS RELATING TO OBLIGATORY SIDE MARKER LAMPS AND TO OPTIONAL SIDE MARKER LAMPS TO THE EXTENT SPECIFIED IN PART II

PART II
REQUIREMENTS RELATING TO OPTIONAL SIDE MARKER LAMPS

Any number may be fitted and the only requirement prescribed by these Regulations in respect of any which are fitted is that specified in paragraph 7 of Part I.

(Regulations 18 and 20)   SCHEDULE 10
PART I
REQUIREMENTS RELATING TO OBLIGATORY REAR POSITION LAMPS AND TO OPTIONAL REAR POSITION LAMPS TO THE EXTENT SPECIFIED IN PART II

1   Number—

(a) Any vehicle not covered by sub-paragraph (b), (c), (d), (e), (f), (g) or (h):	Two
(b) A bus first used before 1st April 1955:	One
(c) A solo motor bicycle:	One
(d) A pedal cycle with less than four wheels and without a sidecar:	One
(e) A trailer drawn by a pedal cycle and a trailer, the overall width of which does not exceed 800 mm, drawn by a solo motor bicycle or by a motor bicycle combination:	One
(f) An invalid carriage having a maximum speed not exceeding 4 mph:	One
(g) A vehicle drawn or propelled by hand:	One
(h) A motor vehicle having three or more wheels and a maximum speed not exceeding 25 mph and a trailer drawn by any such vehicle if, in either case, the structure of the vehicle makes it impracticable to meet all of the relevant requirements of paragraphs 2 and 3 below with two lamps:	Four

2   Position—

(a) Longitudinal:	At or near the rear
(b) Lateral—	
(i) Where two lamps are required to be fitted—	
(A) Maximum distance from the side of the vehicle—	
(1) Any vehicle not covered by sub-paragraph (2):	400 mm
(2) A motor vehicle first used before 1st April 1986 and any other vehicle manufactured before 1st October 1985:	800 mm
(B) Minimum separation distance between a pair of rear position lamps—	
(1) Any vehicle not covered by sub-paragraph (2):	500 mm. If the overall width of the vehicle is less than 1400 mm, 400 mm or if less than 800 mm, 300 mm
(2) A motor vehicle first used before 1st April 1986 and any other vehicle manufactured before 1st October 1985:	No requirement
(ii) Where one lamp is required to be fitted:	On the centre-line or off side of the vehicle
(iii) Where four lamps are required to be fitted—	
(A) Maximum distance from the side of the vehicle—	
(1) One pair of lamps:	Such that they satisfy the relevant requirements in sub-paragraph 2(b)(i)(A)
(2) The other pair of lamps:	No requirement
(B) Minimum separation distance between rear position lamps—	
(1) One pair of lamps:	Such that they satisfy the relevant requirements in sub-paragraph 2(b)(i)(B)
(2) The other pair of lamps	No requirement

(c) Vertical—
- (i) Maximum height above the ground where one or two rear position lamps are required to be fitted—
  - (A) Any vehicle not covered by sub-paragraph (B) or (C):   1500 mm or, if the structure of the vehicle makes this impracticable, 2100 mm
  - (B) A bus first used before 1st April 1986:   No requirement
  - (C) A motor vehicle first used before 1st April 1986 not being a bus, a trailer manufactured before 1st October 1985, an agricultural vehicle, a horse-drawn vehicle, an industrial tractor and engineering plant: 2100 mm
- (ii) Maximum height above the ground where four rear position lamps are required to be fitted—
  - (A) One pair of lamps: Such that they satisfy the relevant requirements in paragraph 2(c)(i)
  - (B) The other pair of lamps: No requirement
- (iii) Minimum height above the ground—
  - (A) A vehicle not covered by sub-paragraph (B):   350 mm
  - (B) A motor vehicle first used before 1st April 1986 and any other vehicle manufactured before 1st October 1985   No requirement

3   Angles of visibility—
- (a) a motor vehicle, other than a motor bicycle combination, first used on or after 1st April 1986 and a trailer manufactured on or after 1st October 1985—
  - (i) Horizontal—
    - (A) Where two lamp are required to be fitted: 45° inwards and 80° outwards
    - (B) Where one lamp is required to be fitted: 80° to the left and to the right
    - (C) Where four lamps are required to be fitted—
      - (1) The outer pair of lamps: 0° inwards and 80° outwards
      - (2) The inner pair of lamps: 45° inwards and 80° outwards
  - (ii) Vertical—
    - (A) Where one or two rear position lamps are required to be fitted—
      - (1) Any vehicle not covered by sub-paragraph (2) or (3):   15° above and below the horizontal
      - (2) Where the highest part of the illuminated area of the lamp is less than 1500 mm above the ground   15° above and 10° below the horizontal
      - (3) Where the highest part of the illuminated area of the lamp is less than 750 mm above the ground: 15° above and 5° below the horizontal
    - (B) Where four rear position lamps are required to be fitted—
      - (1) One pair of lamps: Such that they satisfy the relevant requirements in paragraph 3(a)(ii)(A)
      - (2) (2)The other pair of lamps: Visible to the rear
- (b) A motor vehicle, other than a motor bicycle combination, first used before 1st April 1986 and any other vehicle manufactured before 1st October 1985:   Visible to the rear
- (c) A vehicle drawn or propelled by hand, a pedal cycle, a horse-drawn vehicle and a motor bicycle combination: Visible to the rear

4   Alignment: To the rear

5   Markings (see also regulation 3(6))—
- (a) A motor vehicle or a trailer not covered by sub-paragraph (b), (c), (d) or (e):   An approval mark
- (b) A motor vehicle first used before 1st January 1974 and a trailer, other than a trailer drawn by a pedal cycle, manufactured before that date: No requirement
- (c) A solo motor bicycle and a motor bicycle combination, in each case first used before 1st April 1986, and a trailer manufactured before 1st October 1985 and drawn by a solo motor bicycle or a motor bicycle combination: No requirement
- (d) A pedal cycle, a trailer drawn by a pedal cycle, an invalid carriage having a maximum speed not exceeding 4 mph, a horse-drawn vehicle and a vehicle drawn or propelled by hand in each case manufactured before 1st October 1995:   An approval mark or a British Standard mark
- (e) A pedal cycle, a trailer drawn by a pedal cycle, an invalid carriage having a maximum speed not exceeding 4 mph, a horse-drawn vehicle and a vehicle drawn or propelled by hand in each case manufactured on or after 1st October 1995.   An approval mark or the British Standard mark which is specified in sub-paragraph (c), (d) or (e) of the definition of "British Standard mark".

6   Size of illuminated area: No requirement

7   Colour: Red

8   Wattage: No requirement

9   Intensity—
- (a) A rear position lamp bearing any of the markings mentioned in paragraph 4:   No requirement
- (b) Any other rear position lamp: Visible from a reasonable distance

10   Electrical connections: No individual requirement

11   Tell-tale: No requirement

12   Other requirements—

(a) Except in the case of a motor vehicle first used before 1st April 1986, any other vehicle manufactured before 1st October 1985 and a motor bicycle combination, where two rear position lamps are required to be fitted they shall form a matched pair and where four rear position lamps are required to be fitted they shall form two matched pairs.

(b) In the case of a rear position lamp capable of emitting a flashing light which is fitted to—
  (i) a pedal cycle; or
  (ii) a trailer drawn by, or a sidecar attached to, a pedal cycle

the light shown by the lamp when flashing shall be displayed not less than 60 nor more than 240 equal times per minute and the intervals between each display of light shall be constant.

13   Definitions—
In this Schedule—
"approval mark" means—

(a) in relation to a solo motor bicycle, a motor bicycle combination and a trailer drawn by a solo motor bicycle or a motor bicycle combination, a marking designated as an approval mark by regulation 4 of the Designation of Approval Marks Regulations and shown at item 50A of Schedule 2 to those Regulations, and

(b) in relation to any other motor vehicle or any other trailer, either—
  (i) a marking designated as an approval mark by regulation 5 of the Designation of Approval Marks Regulations and shown at item 6 or, if combined with a stop lamp, at item 8 of Schedule 4 to those Regulations, or
  (ii) a marking designated as an approval mark by regulation 4 of the Designation of Approval Marks Regulations and shown at item 7A or, if combined with a stop lamp, at item 7C of Schedule 2 to those Regulations; and

"British Standard mark" means—
(a) the mark indicated in the specification for cycle rear lamps published by the British Standards Institution under the reference 3648:1963 as amended by Amendment PD 6137 published in May 1967 and by AMD 4753 published in July 1985, or
(b) the mark indicated in the specification for photometric and physical requirements for lighting equipment published by the British Standards Institution under the reference BS 6102: Part 3: 1986, namely "BS 6102/3, or
(c) the mark indicated in the specification for photometric and physical requirements for lighting equipment published by the British Standards Institution under the reference BS 6102: Part 3: 1986 as amended by AMD 5821 published on the 29th April 1988, namely "6102/3"; or
(d) the mark indicated in the specification for photometric and physical requirements for lighting equipment published by the British Standards Institution under the reference BS 6102: Part 3: 1986 as amended by AMD 8438 published on the 15th April 1995, namely 6102/3; or
(e) the mark indicated in the specification for photometric and physical requirements for lighting equipment published by the British Standards Institution under the references BS 6102: part 3: 1986 as amended by AMD 14621 published on the 1st September 2003, namely 6102/3.

PART II
REQUIREMENTS RELATING TO OPTIONAL REAR POSITION LAMPS

Any number may be fitted and the only requirements prescribed by these Regulations in respect of any which are fitted are those specified in paragraphs 7 and 12(b) of Part I.

4–3769

(Regulations 18 and 20)   SCHEDULE 11

PART I
REQUIREMENTS RELATING TO OBLIGATORY REAR FOG LAMPS AND TO OPTIONAL REAR FOG LAMPS TO THE EXTENT SPECIFIED IN PART II

1. Number: One
2. Position—
  (a) Longitudinal: At or near the rear of the vehicle
  (b) Lateral—
    (i) Where one rear fog lamp is fitted: On the centre-line or off side of the vehicle (disregarding any sidecar forming part of a motor bicycle combination)
    (ii) Where two lamps are fitted: No requirement
  c) Vertical—
    (i) Maximum heigh above the ground—
      (A) Any vehicle not covered by sub-paragraph (B):   1000 mm
      (B) An agricultural vehicle, engineering plant and a motor tractor: 2100 mm
    (ii) Minimum height above the ground: 250 mm
  (d) Minimum separation distance between a rear fog lamp and a stop lamp—
    (i) In the case of a rear fog lamp which does not share a common lamp body with a stop lamp: A distance of 100 mm between the light-emitting surfaces of the lamps when viewed in a direction parallel to the longitudinal axis of the vehicle
    (ii) In the case of a rear fog lamp which shares a common lamp body with a stop lamp: 100 mm

3   Angles of visibility—

(a)	Horizontal:	25° inwards and outwards. However, where two rear fog lamps are fitted it shall suffice if throughout the sector so defined at least one lamp (but not necessarily the same lamp) is visible
(b)	Vertical:	5° above and below the horizontal
4.	Alignment:	To the rear
5.	Markings:	An approval mark
6.	Size of illuminated area:	No requirement
7.	Colour:	Red
8.	Wattage:	No requirement
9.	Intensity:	No requirement
10.	Electrical connections:	No rear fog lamp shall be fitted to any vehicle so that it can be illuminated by the application of any braking system on the vehicle
11.	Tell-tale:	A circuit-closed tell-tale shall be fitted

12. Other requirements—
Where two rear fog lamps are fitted to a motor vehicle first used on or after 1st April 1986 or to a trailer manufactured on or after 1st October 1985 they shall form a matched pair.

13. Definitions—
In this Schedule "approval mark" means either—
(a) a marking designated as an approval mark by regulation 5 of the Designation of Approval Marks Regulations and shown at item 20 of Schedule 4 to those Regulations; or
(b) a marking designated as an approval mark by regulation 4 of the Designation of Approval Marks Regulations and shown at item 38 of Schedule 2 to those Regulations.

PART II
REQUIREMENTS RELATING TO OPTIONAL REAR FOG LAMPS

1. In the case of a motor vehicle first used before 1st April 1980 and any other vehicle manufactured before 1st October 1979, any number may be fitted and the only requirements prescribed by these Regulations in respect of any which are fitted are those specified in paragraphs 2(d), 7 and 10 of Part I.

2. In the case of a motor vehicle first used on or after 1st April 1980 and any other vehicle manufactured on or after 1st October 1979, not more than two may be fitted and the requirements prescribed by these Regulations in respect of any which are fitted are all those specified in this Schedule.

4–3770

(Regulations 18 and 20)   SCHEDULE 12

PART I
REQUIREMENTS RELATING TO OBLIGATORY STOP LAMPS AND TO OPTIONAL STOP LAMPS TO THE EXTENT SPECIFIED IN PART II

1.	Number—	
(a)	Any vehicle not covered by sub-paragraph (b) or (c):	Two
(b)	A solo motor bicycle, a motor bicycle combination, an invalid carriage and a trailer drawn by a solo motor bicycle or a motor bicycle combination:	One
(c)	Any other motor vehicle first used before 1st January 1971 and any other trailer manufactured before that date:	One
2.	Position—	
(a)	Longitudinal:	No requirement
(b)	Lateral—	
(i)	Maximum distance from the side of the vehicle—	
(A)	Where two stop lamps are fitted:	One on each side of the longitudinal axis of the vehicle
(B)	Where only one stop lamp is fitted:	On the centre-line or off side of the vehicle (disregarding any sidecar forming part of a motor bicycle combination)
(ii)	Minimum separation distance between two obligatory stop lamps:	400 mm
(c)	Vertical—	
(i)	Maximum height above the ground—	
(A)	Any vehicle not covered by sub-paragraph (B):	1500 mm or, if the structure of the vehicle makes this impracticable, 2100 mm
(B)	A motor vehicle first used before 1st January 1971, a trailer manufactured before that date and a motor vehicle having a maximum speed not exceeding 25 mph:	No requirement
(ii)	Minimum height above the ground—	
(A)	Any vehicle not covered by sub-paragraph (B):	350 mm
(B)	A motor vehicle first used before 1st January 1971 and a trailer manufactured before that date:	No requirement
3.	Angles of visibility—	
(a)	A motor vehicle first used on or after 1st January 1971 and a trailer manufactured on or after that date—	

(i) Horizontal:	45° to the left and to the right
(ii) Vertical—	
(A) Except in a case specified in sub-paragraph (B) or (C):	15° above and below the horizontal
(B) Where the highest part of the illuminated area of the lamp is less than 1500 mm above the ground:	15° above and 10° below the horizontal
(C) Where the highest part of the illuminated area of the lamp is less than 750 mm above the ground:	15° above and 5° below the horizontal
(b) A motor vehicle first used before 1st January 1971 and a trailer manufactured before that date:	Visible to the rear
4. Alignment:	To the rear
5. Markings—	
(a) Any vehicle not covered by sub-paragraph (b) or (c):	An approval mark
(b) A motor vehicle first used before 1st February 1974 and a trailer manufactured before that date:	No requirement
(c) A solo motor bicycle and a motor bicycle combination, in each case first used before 1st April 1986, and a trailer manufactured before 1st October 1985 drawn by a solo motor bicycle or a motor bicycle combination:	No requirement
6. Size of illuminated area:	No requirement
7. Colour:	Red
8. Wattage—	
(a) A stop lamp fitted to a motor vehicle first used before 1st January 1971 or a trailer manufactured before that date and a stop lamp bearing an approval mark:	No requirement
(b) Any other stop lamp:	15 to 36 watts
9. Intensity:	No requirement
10. Electrical connections—	

(a) Every stop lamp fitted to—

    (i) a solo motor bicycle or a motor bicycle combination first used on or after 1st April 1986 shall be operated by the application of every service brake control provided for the use of the rider;

    (ii) any other motor vehicle, shall be operated by the application of the service braking system.

(b) Every stop lamp fitted to a trailer drawn by a motor vehicle shall be operated by the application of the service braking system of that motor vehicle.

11. Tell-tale:	No requirement
12. Other requirements—	

Where two stop lamps are required to be fitted, they shall form a pair.

13. Definitions—

In this Schedule "approval mark" means—

(a) in relation to a solo motor bicycle, a motor bicycle combination or a trailer drawn by a solo motor bicycle or a motor bicycle combination, a marking designated as an approval mark by regulation 4 of the Designation of Approval Marks Regulations and shown at item 50A of Schedule 2 to those Regulations; and

(b) in relation to any other vehicle, either—

    (i) a marking designated as an approval mark by regulation 5 of the Designation of Approval Marks Regulations and shown at item 7 or, if combined with a rear position lamp, at item 8 of Schedule 4 to those Regulations; or

    (ii) a marking designated as an approval mark by regulation 4 of the Designation of Approval Marks Regulations and shown at item 7B or, if combined with a rear position lamp, at item 7C of Schedule 2 to those Regulations.

PART II

REQUIREMENTS RELATING TO OPTIONAL STOP LAMPS

Any number may be fitted, and the requirements prescribed by these Regulations in respect of any which are fitted are all those specified in Part I except—

(a) those specified in paragraphs 1, 2 and 3; and

(b) in the case of a stop lamp fitted to a pedal cycle, those specified in paragraphs 5 and 8; and

(c) in the case of a stop lamp fitted to a motor vehicle not being a motor bicycle, first used on or after 1st April 1991 either centrally or in such a manner as to project light through the rear window the intensity of the light emitted to the rear of the vehicle shall be not less than 20 candelas and not more than 60 candelas when measured from directly behind the centre of the lamp in a direction parallel to the longitudinal axis of the vehicle.

-3771

(Regulations 18 and 20)   SCHEDULE 13

PART I

REQUIREMENTS RELATING TO OBLIGATORY END-OUTLINE MARKER LAMPS AND TO OPTIONAL END-OUTLINE MARKER LAMPS TO THE EXTENT SPECIFIED IN PART II

1. Number:	Two visible from the front and two visible from the rear
2. Position—	
(a) Longitudinal:	No requirement
(b) Lateral—	
(i) Maximum distance from the side of the vehicle:	400 mm
(ii) Minimum separation distance between a pair of end-outline marker lamps:	No requirement
(c) Vertical—	

      (i) At the front of a motor vehicle:

           The horizontal plane tangential to the upper edge of the illuminated area of the lamp shall not be lower than the horizontal plane tangential to the upper edge of the transparent zone of the windscreen

      (ii) At the front of a trailer and at the rear of any vehicle:

           At the maximum height compatible with:
           (a) the requirements relating to the lateral position and to being a pair, and
           (b) the use for which the vehicle is constructed

3. Angles of visibility—
    (a) Horizontal: 0° inwards and 80° outwards
    (b) Vertical: 5° above and 20° below the horizontal

4. Alignment: Such that white light is shown towards the front and red light is shown towards the rear

5. Markings: An approval mark
6. Size of illuminated area: No requirement
7. Colour: White towards the front and red towards the rear
8. Wattage: No requirement
9. Intensity: No requirement
10. Electrical connections: No individual requirement
11. Tell-tale: No requirement
12. Other requirements—
    The two lamps which emit white light towards the front, and the two lamps which emit red light towards the rear, shall in each case form a matched pair.
    The white front lamp and red rear lamp on one side of a vehicle may be combined into a single lamp with a single light source.
13. Definitions—
    In this Schedule, "approval mark" means the approval mark for a front or rear position lamp, as the case may be.

PART II
REQUIREMENTS RELATING TO OPTIONAL END-OUTLINE MARKER LAMPS

    Any number may be fitted, and the only requirement prescribed by these Regulations in respect of any which are fitted is that specified in paragraph 7 of Part I.

4–3772

(Regulation 20)   SCHEDULE 14
REQUIREMENTS RELATING TO OPTIONAL REVERSING LAMPS

1. Number: Not more than two
2. Position: No requirement
3. Angles of visibility: No requirement
4. Alignment: To the rear
5. Markings—
    (a) A motor vehicle first used on or after 1st April 1986 and a trailer manufactured on or after 1st October 1985:   An approval mark
    (b) A motor vehicle first used before 1st April 1986 and a trailer manufactured before 1st October 1985:   No requirement
6. Size of illuminated area: No requirement
7. Colour: White
8. Wattage—
    (a) A reversing lamp bearing an approval mark: No requirement
    (b) A reversing lamp not bearing an approval mark: The total wattage of any one reversing lamp shall not exceed 24 watts
9. Intensity: No requirement
10. Electrical connections: No requirement
11. Tell-tale—
    (a) A motor vehicle first used on or after 1st July 1954, provided that the electrical connections are such that the reversing lamp or lamps cannot be illuminated other than automatically by the selection of the reverse gear of the vehicle: No requirement
    (b) Any other motor vehicle first used on or after 1st July 1954:   A circuit-closed tell-tale shall be fitted
    (c) A motor vehicle first used before 1st July 1954:   No requirement
    (d) Any vehicle which is not a motor vehicle: No requirement
12. Definitions—
    In this Schedule "approval mark" means either—
    (a) a marking designated as an approval mark by regulation 5 of the Designation of Approval Marks Regulations and shown at item 21 of Schedule 4 to those Regulations; or
    (b) a marking designated as an approval mark by regulation 4 of the Designation of Approval Marks Regulations and shown at item 23 or 23A of Schedule 2 to those Regulations.

4–3773

(Regulation 18)　　　　　　　　　　　SCHEDULE 15
REQUIREMENTS RELATING TO OBLIGATORY REAR REGISTRATION PLATE LAMPS

1. Number:}	
2. Position:}	Such that the lamp or lamps are capable of adequately illuminating the rear registration plate
3. Angles of visibility:}	
4. Alignment:}	
5. Markings—	
(a) A motor vehicle first used on or after 1st April 1986 and a trailer manufactured on or after 1st October 1985:	An approval mark
(b) A motor vehicle first used before 1st April 1986 and a trailer manufactured before 1st October 1985:	No requirement
6. Size of illuminated area:	No requirement
7. Colour:	White
8. Wattage:	No requirement
9. Intensity:	No requirement
10. Electrical connections:	No individual requirement
11. Tell-tale:	No requirement

12. Definitions—
In this Schedule "approval mark" means—
(a) in relation to a solo motor bicycle, a motor bicycle combination and a trailer drawn by a solo motor bicycle or a motor bicycle combination, a marking designated as an approval mark by regulation 4 of the Designation of Approval Marks Regulations and shown at item 50A of Schedule 2 to those Regulations; and
(b) in relation to any other motor vehicle and any other trailer, either—
　(i) a marking designated as an approval mark by regulation 5 of the Designation of Approval Marks Regulations and shown at item 10 of Schedule 4 to those Regulations; or
　(ii) a marking designated as an approval mark by regulation 4 of the Designation of Approval Marks Regulations and shown at item 4 of Schedule 2 to those Regulations.

4–3774

(Regulations 17 and 20)　　　　　　　　SCHEDULE 16
REQUIREMENT RELATING TO OBLIGATORY AND OPTIONAL WARNING BEACONS

1. Number:	Sufficient to satisfy the requirements of paragraph 3
2. Position—	No requirement

Every warning beacon shall be so mounted on the vehicle that the centre of the lamp is at a height not less than 1200 mm above the ground.

3. Angles of visibility—
The light shown from at least one beacon (but not necessarily the same beacon) shall be visible from any point at a reasonable distance from the vehicle or any trailer being drawn by it.

4. Markings:	
5. Size of illuminated area:	No requirement
6. Colour:	Blue, amber, green or yellow in accordance with Regulation 11
7. Wattage:	No requirement
8. Intensity:	No requirement
9. Electrical connections:	No requirement
10. Tell-tale:	No requirement

11. Other requirements—
The light shown by any one warning beacon shall be displayed not less than 60 nor more than 240 equal times per minute and the intervals between each display of light shall be constant.

4–3775

(Regulations 18 and 20)　　　　　　　　SCHEDULE 17

PART I

REQUIREMENTS RELATING TO OBLIGATORY SIDE RETRO REFLECTORS AND OPTIONAL SIDE RETRO REFLECTORS TO THE EXTENT SPECIFIED IN PART II

1. Number—	
(a) A motor vehicle first used on or after 1st April 1986 and a trailer manufactured on or after 1st October 1985:	On each side: two and as many more as are sufficient to satisfy the requirements of paragraph 2(a)
(b) A motor vehicle first used before 1st April 1986 and a trailer manufactured before 1st October 1985:	On each side: Two

2. Position—
(a) Longitudinal—
　(i) A motor vehicle first used on or after 1st April 1986 and a trailer manufactured on or after 1st October 1985—

(A) Maximum distance from the front of the vehicle, including any drawbar, in respect of the foremost reflector on each side:	4 m

     (B) Maximum distance from the rear of the vehicle in respect of the rearmost reflector on each side: — 1 m

     (C) Maximum separation distance between the reflecting areas of adjacent reflectors on the same side of the vehicle: — 3 m or, if this is not practicable, 4 m

   (ii) A motor vehicle first used before 1st April 1986 and a trailer manufactured before 1st October 1985—

     (A) Maximum distance from the rear of the vehicle in respect of the rearmost reflector on each side: — 1 m

     (B) The other reflector on each side of the vehicle: — Towards the centre of the vehicle

  (b) Lateral: — No requirement

  (c) Vertical:
   (i) Maximum height above the ground: — 1500 mm
   (ii) Minimum height above the ground: — 350 mm

3. Angles of visibility—
  (a) A motor vehicle first used on or after 1st April 1986 and a trailer manufactured on or after 1st October 1985—
   (i) Horizontal: — 45° to the left hand and to the right when viewed in a direction at right angles to the longitudinal axis of the vehicle

   (ii) Vertical—
    (A) Except in a case specified in sub-paragraph (B): — 15° above and below the horizontal
    (B) Where the highest part of the reflecting area is less than 750 mm above the ground: — 15° above and 5° below the horizontal

  (b) A motor vehicle first used before 1st April 1986 and a trailer manufactured before 1st October 1985: — Plainly visible to the side

4. Alignment: — To the side
5. Markings: — An approval mark
6. Size of reflecting area: — No requirement
7. Colour—
  (a) Any vehicle not covered by sub-paragraph (b): — Amber or if within 1 m of the rear of the vehicle it may be red
  (b) A solo motor bicycle, a motor bicycle combination, a pedal cycle with or without a sidecar or an invalid carriage: — No requirement

8. Other requirements: — No side retro reflector shall be triangular

9. Definitions—
  (a) In this Schedule "approval mark" means either—
   (i) a marking designated as an approval mark by regulation 4 of the Designation of Approval Marks Regulations and shown at item 3 or 3B of Schedule 2 to those Regulations and which includes the marking 1 or 1A; or
   (ii) a marking designated as an approval mark by regulation 5 of the Designation of Approval Marks Regulations and shown at item 4 of Schedule 4 to those Regulations and which includes the marking I; and
  (b) In this Schedule references to "maximum distance from the front of the vehicle" and "maximum distance from the rear of the vehicle" are references to the maximum distance from that end of the vehicle (as determined by reference to the overall length of the vehicle exclusive of any special equipment) beyond which no part of the reflecting area of the side retro reflector extends.

PART II
REQUIREMENTS RELATING TO OPTIONAL SIDE RETRO REFLECTORS

Any number may be fitted, and the only requirements prescribed by these Regulations in respect of any which are fitted are those specified in paragraphs 7 and 8 of Part I.

4–3776

(Regulations 18 and 20)   SCHEDULE 18

PART I
REQUIREMENTS RELATING TO OBLIGATORY REAR RETRO REFLECTORS AND OPTIONAL REAR RETRO REFLECTORS TO THE EXTENT SPECIFIED IN PART II

1 Number—
  (a) Any vehicle not covered by sub-paragraph (b) or (c): — Two
  (b) A solo motor bicycle, a pedal cycle with less than four wheels and with or without a sidecar, a trailer drawn by a pedal cycle, a trailer the overall width of which does not exceed 800 mm drawn by a solo motor bicycle or a motor bicycle combination, an invalid carriage having a maximum speed not exceeding 4 mph and a vehicle drawn or propelled by hand: — One
  (c) A motor vehicle having three or more wheels and a maximum speed not exceeding 25 mph and a trailer drawn by any such vehicle if, in either case, the structure of the vehicle makes it impracticable to meet all of the requirements of paragraphs 2 and 3 below with two reflectors: — Four

2 Position—
  (a) Longitudinal: — At or near the rear
  (b) Lateral—
   (i) Where two rear reflectors are required to be fitted—

  (A) Maximum distance from the side of the vehicle

      (1) Any vehicle not covered by sub-paragraph (2), (3) or (4):   400 mm

      (2) A bus first used before 1st October 1954 and a horse-drawn vehicle manufactured before 1st October 1985:   No requirement

      (3) A vehicle constructed or adapted for the carriage of round timber: 765 mm

      (4) Any other motor vehicle first used before 1st April 1986 and any other vehicle manufactured before 1st October 1985:   610 mm

  (B) Minimum separation distance between a pair of rear reflectors—

      (1) Any vehicle not covered by sub-paragraph (2):   600 mm. If the overall width of the vehicle ess than 1300 mm, 400 mm or if less than 800 mm, 300 mm

      (2) A motor vehicle first used before 1st April 1986 and any other vehicle manufactured before 1st October 1985:   No requirement

   (ii) Where one rear reflector is required to be fitted: On the centre-line or off side of the vehicle

   (iii) Where four rear reflectors are required to be fitted—

     (A) Maximum distance from the side of the vehicle—

       (1) One pair of reflectors: Such that they satisfy the relevant requirements in sub-paragraph 2(b)(i)(A)

       (2) The other pair of reflectors: No requirement

     (B) Minimum separation distance between rear reflectors—

       (1) One pair of reflectors: Such that they satisfy the relevant requirements in sub-paragraph 2(b)(i)(B)

       (2) The other pair of reflectors: No requirement

  (c) Vertical—

   (i) Maximum height above the ground where one or two rear reflectors are required to be fitted—

     (A) Any vehicle not covered by sub-paragraph (B):   900 mm or, if the structure of the vehicle makes this impracticable, 1200 mm

     (B) A motor vehicle first used before 1st April 1986 and any other vehicle manufactured before 1st October 1985:   1525 mm

   (ii) Maximum height above the ground where four rear reflectors are required to be fitted—

     (A) One pair of reflectors: Such that they satisfy the relevant requirements in paragraph 2(c)(i)

     (B) The other pair of reflectors: 2100 mm

   (iii) Minimum height above the ground—

     (A) Any vehicle not covered by sub-paragraph (B):   350 mm

     (B) A motor vehicle first used before 1st April 1986 and any other vehicle manufactured before 1st October 1985:   No requirement

3 Angles of visibility—

  (a) A motor vehicle (not being a motor bicycle combination) first used on or after 1st April 1986 and a trailer manufactured on or after 1st October 1985—

   (i) Where one or two rear reflectors are required to be fitted—

     (A) Horizontal—

       (1) Where two rear reflectors are required to be fitted: 30° inwards and outwards

       (2) Where one rear reflector is required to be fitted: 30° to the left and to the right

     (B) Vertical—

       (1) Except in a case specified in sub-paragraph (2):   15° above and below the horizontal

       (2) Where the highest part of the reflecting area is less than 750 mm above the ground: 15° above and 5° below the horizontal

   (ii) Where four rear reflectors are required to be fitted—

     (A) One pair of reflectors: Such that they satisfy the relevant requirements in paragraph 3(a)(i)

     (B) The other pair of reflectors: Plainly visible to the rear

  (b) A motor vehicle (not being a motor bicycle combination) first used before 1st April 1986 and a trailer manufactured before 1st October 1985:   Plainly visible to the rear

  (c) A motor bicycle combination, a pedal cycle, a sidecar attached to a pedal cycle, a horse-drawn vehicle and a vehicle drawn or propelled by hand: Plainly visible to the rear

4 Alignment: To the rear

5 Markings—

  (a) A motor vehicle first used—

   (i) On or after 1st April 1991:   An approval mark incorporating "I" or "IA"

   (ii) On or after 1st July 1970 and before 1st April 1991:   (A) An approval mark incorporating "I" or "IA", or

	(B) A British Standard mar[k] which is specified in sub paragraph (i) of the defi nition of "Britis[h] Standard mark" belo[w] followed by "LI" or "LIA"; or
	(C) In the case of a vehicl[e] manufactured in Italy, a[n] Italian approved marking
(iii) Before 1st July 1970:	No requirement
(b) A trailer (other than a broken-down motor vehicle) manufactured—	
(i) On or after 1st October 1989:	An approval mark incorporat ing "III" or "IIIA"
(ii) On or after 1st July 1970 and before 1st October 1989:	(A) An approval mark incor porating "III" or "IIIA"; o[r]
	(B) A British Standard mar[k] which is specified in sub paragraph (i) of the defi nition of "Britis[h] Standard mark" belo[w] followed by "LIII" o[r] "LIIIA", or
	(C) In the case of a traile[r] manufactured in Italy, a[n] Italian approved marking
(iii) Before 1st July 1970:	No requirement
(c) A pedal cycle, an invalid carriage having a maximum speed not exceeding 4 mph, a horse-drawn vehicle and a vehicle drawn or propelled by hand, in each case manufactured—	
(i) On or after 1st October 1989:	(A) An approval mark incor porating "I" or "IA"; or
	(B) A British Standard mar[k] which is specified in sub paragraph (ii) of the defi nition of "Britis[h] Standard mark" below
(ii) On or after 1st July 1970 and before 1st October 1989:	(A) Any of the markings men tioned in sub-paragraph (c)(i) above; or
	(B) A British Standard mar[k] which is specified in sub paragraph (i) of the defi nition of "Britis[h] Standard mark" belo[w] followed by "LI" or "LIA"
(iii) Before 1st July 1970:	No requirement
6　Size of reflecting area:	No requirement
7　Colour:	Red

8　Other requirements—

(a) Except in the case of a motor vehicle first used before 1st April 1986, any other vehicle manufacture[d] before 1st October 1985 and a motor bicycle combination, where two rear reflectors are required to b[e] fitted they shall form a pair. Where four rear reflectors are required to be fitted they shall form tw[o] pairs.

(b) No vehicle, other than a trailer or a broken-down motor vehicle being towed, may be fitted wit[h] triangular-shaped rear reflectors.

(c) *Revoked.*

9　Definitions—

In this Schedule—

(a) "approval mark" means either—
(i) a marking designated as an approval mark by regulation 4 of the Designation of Approval Mark Regulations and shown at item 3 or 3A or 3B of Schedule 2 to those Regulations; or
(ii) a marking designated as an approval mark by regulation 5 of the Designation of Approval Mark Regulation and shown at item 4 of Schedule 4 to those Regulations;

(b) "British Standard mark" means either—

(i) the mark indicated in the specification for retro reflectors for vehicles, including cycles, publishe[d] by the British Standards Institution under the reference BS AU 40: Part 2: 1965, namely "AU 40"[;] or
(ii) the mark indicated in the specification for photometric and physical requirements of reflectiv[e] devices published by the British Standards Institution under the reference BS 6102: Part 2: 198[2] namely "BS 6102/2"; and

(c) "Italian approved marking" means—
a mark approved by the Italian Ministry of Transport, namely, one including two separate groups o[f] symbols consisting of "IGM" or "DGM" and "C.1." or "C.2.".

Part II

Requirements Relating to Optional Rear Retro Reflectors

Any number may be fitted and the only requirements prescribed by these Regulations in respect of an[y] which are fitted are those specified in paragraphs 7 and 8(b) of Part I.

(Regulations 18 and 20)   SCHEDULE 19

PART I

REQUIREMENTS RELATING TO OBLIGATORY REAR MARKINGS AND OPTIONAL REAR MARKINGS TO THE EXTENT SPECIFIED IN PART II

GENERAL REQUIREMENTS

1   Description—

(a) A motor vehicle first used on or after 1 April 1996, the overall length of which—

    (i) does not exceed 13m: A rear marking of a type shown in diagram 1, 2, 3 or 4 in Part IV of this Schedule

    (ii) exceeds 13m: A rear marking of a type shown in diagram 5, 6, 7 or 8 in Part IV of this Schedule

(b) A motor vehicle first used before 1 April 1996, the overall length of which—

    (i) does not exceed 13m: A rear marking of a type shown in diagram 1, 2 or 3 in Part III of this Schedule or a rear marking of a type shown in diagram 1, 2, 3 or 4 in Part IV of this Schedule

    (ii) exceeds 13m: A rear marking of a type shown in diagram 4 or 5 in Part III of this Schedule or a rear marking of a type shown in diagram 5, 6, 7 or 8 in Part IV of this Schedule

(c) A trailer manufactured on or after 1 October 1995 if it forms part of a combination of vehicles the overall length of which—

    (i) does not exceed 11m: A rear marking of a type shown in diagram 1, 2, 3 or 4 in Part IV of this Schedule

    (ii) exceeds 11m but does not exceed 13m: A rear marking of a type shown in Part IV of this Schedule

    (iii) exceeds 13m: A rear marking of a type shown in diagram 5, 6, 7 or 8 in Part IV of this Schedule

(d) A trailer manufactured before 1 October 1995 if it forms part of a combination of vehicles the overall length of which—

    (i) does not exceed 11m: A rear marking of a type shown in diagram 1, 2 or 3 in Part III of this Schedule or a rear marking of a type shown in diagram 1, 2, 3 or 4 in Part IV of this Schedule

    (ii) exceeds 11m but does not exceed 13m: A rear marking of a type shown in Part III or Part IV of this Schedule

    (iii) exceeds 13m: A rear marking of a type shown in diagram 4 or 5 in Part III of this Schedule or a rear marking of a type shown in diagram 5, 6, 7 or 8 in Part IV of this Schedule

2   Position—

(a) Longitudinal: At or near the rear of the vehicle

(b) Lateral—

    (i) A rear marking of a type shown in diagram 2, 3 or 5 in Part III of this Schedule and a rear marking of a type shown in diagram 2, 3, 4, 6, 7 or 8 in Part IV of this Schedule: Each part shall be fitted as near as practicable to the outermost edge of the vehicle on the side thereof on which it is fitted so that no part of the marking projects beyond the outermost part of the vehicle on either side

    (ii) A rear marking of a type shown in diagram 1 or 4 in Part III of this Schedule and a rear marking of a type shown in diagram 1 or 5 in Part IV of this Schedule: The marking shall be fitted so that the vertical centre-line of the marking lies on the vertical plane through the longitudinal axis of the vehicle and no part of the marking projects beyond the outermost part of the vehicle on either side

(c) Vertical: — The lower edge of every rear marking shall be at a height of not more than 1700mm nor less than 400mm above the ground whether the vehicle is laden or unladen

3 Visibility: — Plainly visible to the rear

4 Alignment: — The lower edge of every rear marking shall be fitted horizontally. Every part of a rear marking shall lie within 20° of a transverse vertical plane at right angles to the longitudinal axis of the vehicle and shall face to the rear

5 Markings—
   (a) A motor vehicle or trailer not covered by sub-paragraph (b): — In respect of any rear marking of a type shown in Part III of this Schedule a British Standard mark or in respect of any rear marking of a type shown in Part IV of this Schedule an approval mark

   (b) A motor vehicle first used on or after 1 April 1996 and a trailer manufactured on or after 1 October 1995: — An approval mark

6 Colour: — Red fluorescent material in the stippled areas shown in any of the diagrams in Part III or IV of this Schedule and yellow retro reflective material in any of the areas so shown, being areas not stippled and not constituting a letter. All letters shall be coloured black

7 Other requirements—
   A rear marking of a type shown in a diagram in Part III of this Schedule shall comply with the requirements of that Part.
   The two parts of every rear marking of a type shown in diagrams 2, 3 and 5 in Part III and diagrams 2, 3, 6 and 7 in Part IV of this Schedule shall form a pair and the four parts of every rear marking of a type shown in diagrams 4 and 8 in Part IV of this Schedule shall form two pairs.

8 Definitions—
   In this Schedule—
   (a) "approval mark" means a marking designated as an approval mark by regulation 3 of the Designation of Approval Marks Regulations and shown at item 70 of Schedule 2 to those Regulations; and
   (b) "British Standard mark" means the specification for rear markings for vehicles published by the British Standards Institution under the reference BS AU 152: 1970, namely "BS AU 152".

PART II
REQUIREMENTS RELATING TO OPTIONAL REAR MARKINGS

Subject to regulation 11(2), any number of rear markings shown in Parts III and IV may be fitted to the rear of a vehicle.

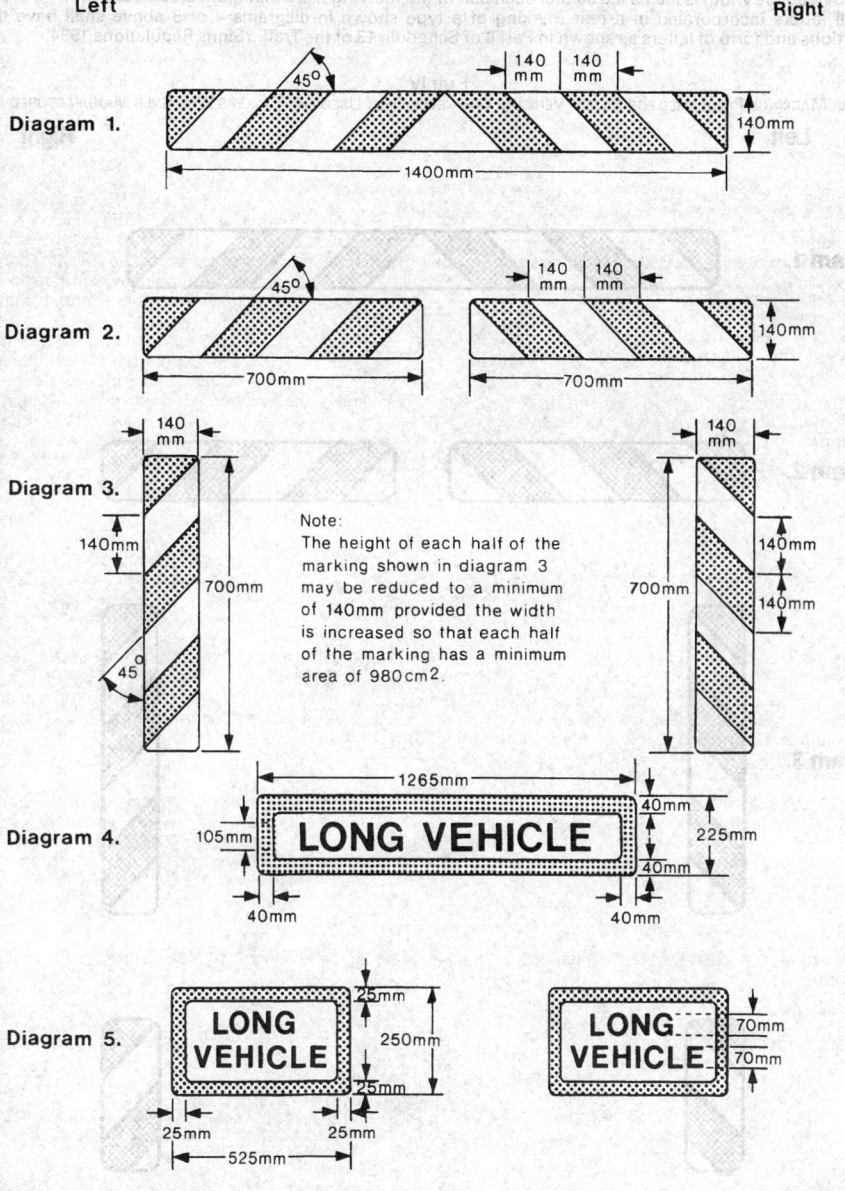

ADDITIONAL PROVISIONS RELATING TO THE ABOVE DIAGRAMS

1. A rear marking of a type shown in one of the above diagrams shall have the dimensions shown in relation to that diagram.

2. Any variation in a dimension (other than as to the height of a letter) specified in any of the above diagrams shall be treated as permitted for the purposes of this Schedule if the variation—

  (*a*) in the case of a dimension so specified as 250 mm or as over 250 mm does not exceed 2.5 per cent of that dimension;

  (*b*) in the case of a dimension so specified as 40 mm or as over 40 mm but as under 250 mm does not exceed 5 per cent of that dimension; or

  (*c*) in the case of a dimension so specified as under 40 mm does not exceed 10 per cent of that dimension.

3. Any variation in a dimension as to the height of a letter specified in any of those diagrams shall be treated as permitted for the purposes of this Schedule if the variation—

  (*a*) in the case of a dimension so specified as 105 mm does not exceed 2.5 per cent of that dimension; or

  (*b*) in the case of a dimension so specified as 70 mm does not exceed 5 per cent of that dimension.

4. Any variation in a dimension as to the angle of hatching specified in any of those diagrams shall be treated as permitted for the purposes of this Schedule if the variation does not exceed 5 degrees.

5. A rear marking of a type shown in diagrams 1 or 4 above shall be constructed in the form of a single plate, and every rear marking shown in diagrams 2, 3 or 5 above shall be constructed in the form of two plates of equal size and shape.

6. The height of each half of the marking shown in diagram 3 above may be reduced to a minimum of 140 mm provided the width is increased so that each half of the marking has a minimum area of 980 cm².

7. All letters incorporated in a rear marking of a type shown in diagrams 4 or 5 above shall have the proportions and form of letters as shown in Part II of Schedule 13 of the Traffic Signs Regulations 1994.

PART IV

REAR MARKINGS PRESCRIBED FOR MOTOR VEHICLES WHENEVER FIRST USED AND TRAILERS WHENEVER MANUFACTURED

Left   **Right**

Diagram 1.

Diagram 2.

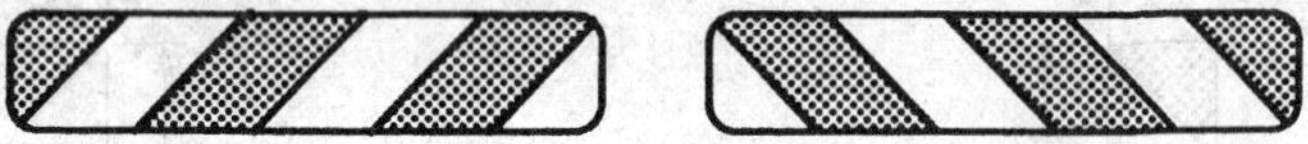

Diagram 3.

Diagram 4.

Left   **Right**

Diagram 5.

Diagram 6.

Diagram 7.

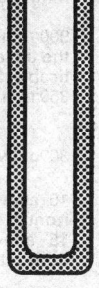

Diagram 8.

4–3778

(Regulations 18 and 20)   SCHEDULE 20

PART I

REQUIREMENTS RELATING TO OBLIGATORY PEDAL RETRO REFLECTORS AND OPTIONAL PEDAL RETRO REFLECTORS TO THE EXTENT
SPECIFIED IN PART II

1. Number:	Two reflectors on each pedal
2. Position—	
(*a*) Longitudinal:	On the leading edge and the trailing edge of each pedal
(*b*) Lateral:	No requirement
(*c*) Vertical:	No requirement
3. Angles of visibility:	Such that the reflector on the leading edge of each pedal is plainly visible to the front and the reflector on the trailing edge of each pedal is plainly visible to the rear
4. Markings:	A British Standard mark
5. Size of reflecting area:	No requirement
6. Colour:	Amber

7. Definitions—
In this Schedule "British Standard mark" means the specification for photometric and physical requirements of reflective devices published by the British Standards Institution under the references BS 6102: Part 2: 1982, namely "BS 6102/2".

PART II
REQUIREMENTS RELATING TO OPTIONAL PEDAL RETRO REFLECTORS

Any number may be fitted and the only requirement prescribed by these Regulations in respect of any which are fitted is that specified in paragraph 6 of Part I

4–3779

(Regulations 18 and 20)　　　　　　　　SCHEDULE 21

PART I
REQUIREMENTS RELATING TO OBLIGATORY FRONT RETROREFLECTORS AND TO OPTIONAL FRONT RETRO REFLECTORS TO THE EXTENT SPECIFIED IN PART II

1. Number:　　　　　　　　　　　　　　　　　　　　　　　Two

2. Position—
   (*a*) Longitudinal:　　　　　　　　　　　　　　　　　　　No requirement
   (*b*) Lateral—
      (i) Maximum distance from the side of the trailer:　　　150 mm
      (ii) Minimum separation distance between a pair of front reflectors:　　600 mm or, if the overall width of the trailer is less than 1400 mm, 400 mm

   (*c*) Vertical—
      (i) Maximum height above the ground:　　　　　　　900 mm or, if the structure of the trailer makes this impracticable, 1500 mm
      (ii) Minimum height above the ground:　　　　　　　350 mm

3. Angles of visibility—
   (*a*) Horizontal:　　　　　　　　　　　　　　　　　　30° outwards and 5° inwards
   (*b*) Vertical—
      (i) Any case not covered by sub-paragraph (ii):　　　15° above and below the horizontal
      (ii) Where the highest point of the reflecting area is less than 750 mm above the ground:　　15° above and 5° below the horizontal

4. Alignment:　　　　　　　　　　　　　　　　　　　　To the front

5. Markings:　　　　　　　　　　　　　　　　　　　　An approval mark

6. Size of reflecting area:　　　　　　　　　　　　　　No requirement

7. Colour:　　　　　　　　　　　　　　　　　　　　　White

8. Other requirements—
   (*a*) Where two front reflectors are required to be fitted they shall form a pair.
   (*b*) Triangular shaped retro reflectors shall not be fitted to the front of any trailer.

9. Definitions—
In this Schedule—
"approval mark" means either—
   (*a*) a marking designated as an approval mark by regulation 4 of the Designation of Approval Marks Regulations and shown at item 3 or 3A or 3B of Schedule 2 to those Regulations; or
   (*b*) a marking designated as an approval mark by regulation 5 of the Designation of Approval Marks Regulation and shown at item 4 of Schedule 4 to those Regulations

PART II
REQUIREMENTS RELATING TO OPTIONAL FRONT RETRO REFLECTORS

Any number may be fitted and the only requirements prescribed by these Regulations in respect of any which are fitted are that specified in paragraph 8(*b*) of Part I and that the colour shall not be red.

Colour

Shaded areas - yellow retro reflective material
Border and silhouette - black

Dimensions

A { Front - not less than 250mm.
Rear - not less than 400mm.   B { Front - not more than 20mm.
Rear - not more than 30mm. "

4–3780

(Regulation 24(3))

SCHEDULE 22

DIAGRAM SHOWING WHERE UNLIT PARKING IS NOT PERMITTED NEAR A JUNCTION

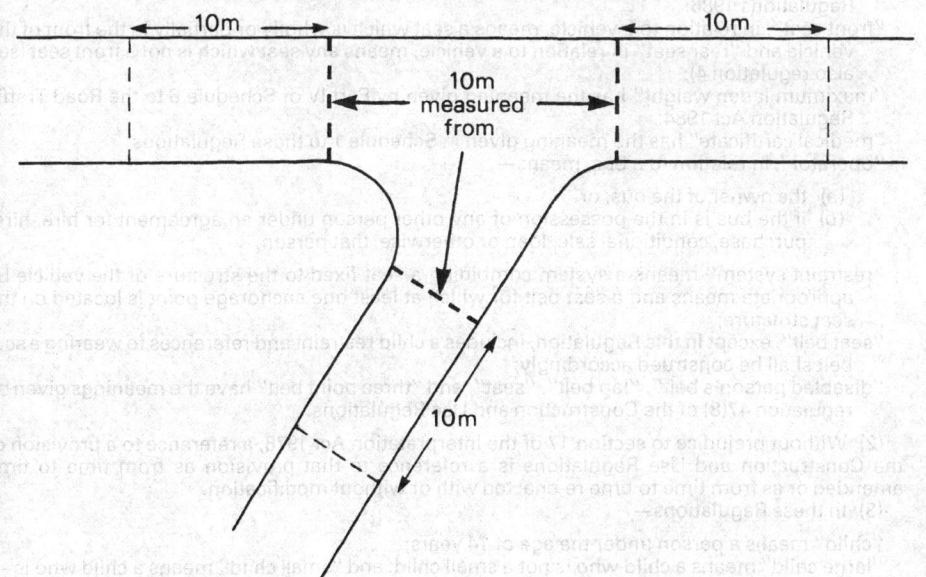

(Schedule 4, Part I, Paragraphs 4 and 12)   SCHEDULE 23

4–3781   Example of marking showing the vertical downwards inclination of the dipped-beam headlamps when the vehicle is at its kerbside weight and has a weight of 75 kg on the driver's seat

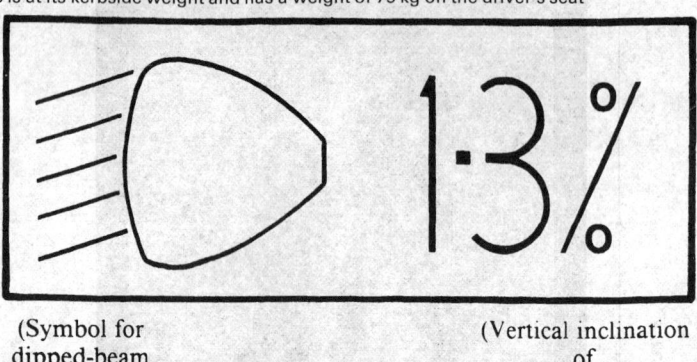

(Symbol for	(Vertical inclination
dipped-beam	of
headlamp)	dipped beam)

Motor Vehicles (Wearing of Seat Belts by Children in Front Seats) Regulations 1993[1]

(SI 1993/31 amended by SI 2006/2213)

4–3791   **1.** *Citation, commencement and revocations.*

---

1. Made by the Secretary of State for Transport under the Road Traffic Act 1988, s 15(1), (5), (5A), (6).

4–3792   **2. General interpretation.**   (1) In these Regulations—

"the Act" means the Road Traffic Act 1988;

"Construction and Use Regulations" means the Road Vehicles (Construction and Use Regulations 1986;

"front seat", in relation to a vehicle, means a seat which is wholly or partially in the front of the vehicle and "rear seat" in relation to a vehicle, means any seat which is not a front seat (see also regulation 4);

"maximum laden weight" has the meaning given by Part IV of Schedule 6 to the Road Traffic Regulation Act 1984;

"medical certificate" has the meaning given in Schedule 1 to these Regulations;

"operator", in relation to a bus, means—

   (*a*)   the owner of the bus, or

   (*b*)   if the bus is in the possession of any other person under an agreement for hire, hire purchase, conditional sale, loan or otherwise, that person;

"restraint system" means a system combining a seat fixed to the structure of the vehicle by appropriate means and a seat belt for which at least one anchorage point is located on the seat structure;

"seat belt", except in this Regulation, includes a child restraint and references to wearing a seat belt shall be construed accordingly;

"disabled person's belt", "lap belt", "seat", and "three point belt" have the meanings given by regulation 47(8) of the Construction and Use Regulations.

(2) Without prejudice to section 17 of the Interpretation Act 1978, a reference to a provision of the Construction and Use Regulations is a reference to that provision as from time to time amended or as from time to time re-enacted with or without modification.

(3) In these Regulations—

"child" means a person under the age of 14 years;

"large child" means a child who is not a small child; and "small child" means a child who is—

(*a*)   aged under 12 years; and

(*b*)   under 135 centimetres in height.

(4) In these Regulations, "adult belt" means a seat belt in respect of which one or more of the following requirements is satisfied, namely that—

   (*a*)   it is a three-point belt which has been marked in accordance with regulation 47(7) of the Construction and Use Regulations;

   (*b*)   it is a lap belt which has been so marked;

   (*c*)   it is a seat belt that falls within regulation 47(4)(*c*)(i) or (ii) of those Regulations;

   (*d*)   it is a seat belt fitted in a vehicle and comprised in a restraint system—

     (i)   of a type which has been approved by an authority of another member State for use by all persons who are either aged 13 years or more or of 150 centimetres or more in height, and

     (ii) in respect of which, by virtue of such approval, the requirements of the law of another member State corresponding to these Regulations would be met were it to be worn by persons who are either aged 13 years of more or of 150 centimetres or more in height when travelling in that vehicle in that State.

   (5) In these Regulations, "child restraint" means a seat belt or other device in respect of which the following requirements are satisfied, namely that—

    (*a*) it is a seat belt or any other description of restraining device for the use of a child which is—

     (i)   designed either to be fitted directly to a suitable anchorage or to be used in conjunction with an adult belt and held in place by the restraining action of that belt, and

     (ii) marked in accordance with regulation 47(7) of the Construction and Use Regulations; or

    (*b*) it is a seat belt consisting of or comprised in a restraint system fitted in a vehicle, being a restraint system—

     (i)   of a type which has been approved by an authority of another member State for use by a child, and

     (ii) in respect of which, by virtue of such approval, the requirements of the law of that State corresponding to these Regulations would be met were it to be worn by a child when travelling in that vehicle in that State.

   (6) Subject to paragraph (7), for the purposes of these Regulations, a seat shall be regarded as provided with an adult belt if an adult belt is fixed in such a position that it can be worn by an occupier of that seat.

   (7) A seat shall not be regarded as provided with an adult belt if the belt—

    (*a*) has an inertia reel mechanism which is locked as a result of the vehicle being, or having been, on a steep incline, or

    (*b*) does not comply with the requirements of regulation 48 of the Construction and Use Regulations.

   (8) For the purposes of these Regulations, a seat shall be regarded as provided with a child restraint if a child restraint is—

    (*a*) fixed in such a position that it can be worn by an occupier of that seat, or

    (*b*) elsewhere in or on the vehicle but—

     (i)   could readily be fixed in such a position without the aid of tools, and

     (ii) is not being worn by a child for whom it is appropriate and who is occupying another seat.

   (9) For the purposes of these Regulations, a seat belt is appropriate—

    (*a*) in relation to a small child, if it is a child restraint of a description prescribed for a child of his height and weight by regulation 5;

    (*b*) in relation to a large child, if it is a child restraint of a description prescribed for a child of his height and weight by regulation 5 or an adult belt; or

    (*c*) in relation to a person aged 14 years or more, if it is an adult belt.

   (9A) For the purposes of these Regulations, references to a bus being used to provide a service in a "built-up area" shall be construed in the same way as in section 15B(6) of the Act.

   (10) Unless the context otherwise requires, in these Regulations—

    (*a*) any reference to a numbered regulation is a reference to the regulation bearing that number in these Regulations; and

    (*b*) a numbered paragraph is a reference to the paragraph bearing that number in the regulation or Schedule in which the reference appears.

4–3793   **3. Interpretation of references to relevant vehicles.**   *Revoked.*

4–3794   **4. Interpretation of references to the front of a vehicle.**   (1) This regulation has effect for the purpose of defining in relation to a vehicle what part of the vehicle is to be regarded as the front of the vehicle for the purposes of section 15(1) of the Act and these Regulations.

   (2) Subject to paragraph (3), every part of the vehicle forward of the transverse vertical plane passing through the rearmost part of the driver's seat shall be regarded as the front of the vehicle; and accordingly no part of the vehicle to the rear of that plane shall be regarded as being in the front of the vehicle.

   (3) Where a vehicle has a deck which is above the level of the driver's head when he is in the normal driving position, no part of the vehicle above that level shall be regarded as being in the front of the vehicle.

4–3795   **5. Description of seat belts to be worn by children.**   (1) For a child of any particular height and weight travelling in a particular vehicle, the description of seat belt prescribed for the purposes of section 15(1) of the Act to be worn by him is—

    (*a*) if he is a small child, a child restraint of a description specified in sub-paragraph (*a*) or (*b*) of paragraph (2);

    (*b*) *revoked;*

    (*c*) if he is a large child, a child restraint of a description specified in sub-paragraph (*a*) of paragraph (2) or an adult belt.

    (2) The descriptions of seat belt referred to in paragraph (1) are—

    (*a*) a child restraint with the marking required under regulation 47(7) of the Construction and Use Regulations if the marking indicates that it is suitable for his weight and either indicates that it is suitable for his height or contains no indication as respects height;

    (*b*) a child restraint which would meet the requirements of the law of another member State corresponding to these Regulations were it to be worn by that child when travelling in that vehicle in that State.

4–3796   **6. Vehicles to which section 15(1) of the Act does not apply.**   Two-wheeled motor cycles with or without sidecars are exempt from the prohibition in section 15(1) of the Act.

4–3797   **7. Exemptions.**   (1) The prohibition in section 15(1) of the Act shall not apply in relation to—

    (*a*) a small child aged 3 years or more who is riding in a bus and is wearing an adult belt if an appropriate seat belt is not available for him in the front or rear of the vehicle;

    (*b*) a child for whom there is a medical certificate; or

    (*c*) a disabled child who is wearing a disabled person's belt.

    (2) The prohibition in section 15(1) of the Act shall not apply in relation to a child riding in a bus—

    (*a*) which is being used to provide a local service (within the meaning of the Transport Act 1985) in a built-up area, or

    (*b*) which is constructed or adapted for the carriage of standing passengers and on which the operator permits standing.

    (3) The prohibition in section 15(1) of the Act shall not apply in relation to a large child if no appropriate seat belt is available for him in the front of the vehicle.

    (4) For the purposes of this regulation, a reference to a seat belt being available shall be construed in accordance with Schedule 2.

4–3798

Regulation 2(1)   SCHEDULE 1
MEANING OF "MEDICAL CERTIFICATE"

PART I

    1. Subject to paragraph 2, in these Regulations, "medical certificate", in relation to a person driving or riding in a vehicle, means—

    (*a*) a valid certificate signed by a medical practitioner to the effect that it is inadvisable on medical grounds for him to wear a seat belt, or

    (*b*) a valid certificate to such effect issued by the authority having power to issue such a certificate under the law of another member State corresponding to these Regulations.

    2. A certificate shall not be regarded as a medical certificate in relation to a person driving or riding in a vehicle for the purposes of these Regulations unless—

    (*a*) it specifies its period of validity and bears the symbol shown in Part II of this Schedule; or

    (*b*) the person is aged under 14 years.

    3. Paragraph 2 does not apply in relation to a certificate issued before 1st January 1995.

PART II

(*This Part shows an illustration of the symbol referred to in Sch 1, Part I, para 2(a), ante.*)

4–3799

Regulation 7(4)   SCHEDULE 2
INTERPRETATION OF REFERENCE TO AVAILABILITY OF SEAT BELTS

    1. For the purposes of these Regulations, in relation to a child riding in a vehicle—

    (*a*) if any front seat in the vehicle (other than the driver's seat) is provided with an appropriate seat belt, that belt shall be regarded as being available for him in the front of the vehicle unless the requirements of paragraph 2 are satisfied in relation to that child, that seat and that belt; and

    (*b*) if any rear seat in the vehicle is provided with an appropriate seat belt, that belt shall be regarded as being available for him in the rear of the vehicle unless the requirements of paragraph 2 are satisfied in relation to that child, that seat and that belt.

    2. The requirements of this paragraph are satisfied in relation to a particular child ("the child in question") and a particular seat ("the relevant seat") provided with a particular seat belt ("the relevant belt") if—

    (*a*) another person is wearing the relevant belt;

    (*b*) another child is occupying the relevant seat and wearing a child restraint which is an appropriate child restraint for that child;

    (*c*) another person, being a person holding a medical certificate, is occupying the relevant seat;

    (*d*) a disabled person (not being the child in question) is occupying the relevant seat and wearing a disabled person's belt;

    (*e*) by reason of his disability, it would not be practicable for the child in question to wear the relevant belt;

    (*f*) *revoked*;

    (*g*) the child in question is prevented from occupying the relevant seat by the presence of a child restraint which could not readily be removed without the aid of tools; or

    (h)   the relevant seat is specially designed so that—

        (i)   its configuration can be adjusted in order to increase the space in the vehicle available for goods or personal effects, and

        (ii)   when it is so adjusted the seat cannot be used as such,

        and the configuration is adjusted in the manner described in sub-paragraph (i) above and it would not be reasonably practicable for the goods and personal effects being carried in the vehicle to be so carried were the configuration not so adjusted.

    3. Paragraphs 2(*b*) and (*d*) shall not apply unless the presence of the other person renders it impracticable for the child in question to wear the relevant belt.

    4. *Revoked.*

    5. Paragraph 2(*g*) shall not apply if the child restraint is appropriate for the child in question.

Motor Vehicles (Wearing of Seat Belts) Regulations 1993[1]

(SI 1993/176 amended by SI 2004/3168 (E),SI 2005/27 and 2929 (W) and SI 2006/594 and 1892)

PART I
INTRODUCTION

4–3800   **1.** *Citation, commencement and revocations.*

    1. Made by the Secretary of State for Transport under the Road Traffic Act 1988, ss 14(1), (2), 15(3), (3A), (5), (6).

4–3801   **2. General interpretation.**   (1) In these Regulations—

    "the Act" means the Road Traffic Act 1988;

    "the Construction and Use Regulations" means the Road Vehicles (Construction and Use) Regulations 1986;

    "large bus" means a motor vehicle which—

        (a)   is constructed or adapted for use for the carriage of passengers,

        (b)   has more than eight seats in addition to the driver's seat,

        (c)   has four or more wheels,

        (d)   has a maximum design speed exceeding 25 kilometres per hour, and

        (e)   has a maximum laden weight exceeding 3.5 tonnes;

    "licensed hire car" has the meaning given by section 13(3) of the Transport Act 1985;

    "licensed taxi" has the meaning given by section 13(3) of the Transport Act 1985;

    "light goods vehicle" means a motor vehicle which—

        (a)   has four or more wheels,

        (b)   has a maximum design speed exceeding 25 kilometres per hour, and

        (c)   has a maximum laden weight not exceeding 3.5 tonnes;

    "maximum laden weight" has the meaning given by Part IV of Schedule 6 to the Road Traffic Regulation Act 1984;

    "medical certificate" has the meaning given in Schedule 1 to these Regulations;

    "passenger car" has the same meaning as in section 15 of the Act;

    "operator", in relation to a small or large bus, means—

        (a)   the owner of the bus, or

        (b)   if the bus is in the possession of any other person under an agreement for hire, hire-purchase, conditional sale, loan or otherwise, that person;

    "private hire vehicle" means a motor vehicle which has no more than 8 seats in addition to the driver's seat, other than a licensed taxi or a public service vehicle (within the meaning of the Public Passenger Vehicles Act 1981), which is provided for hire with the services of a driver for the purpose of carrying passengers and which displays a sign pursuant to either section 21 of the Vehicles (Excise) Act 1971 or section 48(2) of the Local Government (Miscellaneous Provisions) Act 1976 or any similar enactment;

    "rear seat" in relation to a vehicle means a seat not being the driver's seat, a seat alongside the driver's seat or a specified passenger seat;

    "restraint system" means a system combining a seat fixed to the structure of the vehicle by appropriate means and a seat belt for which at least one anchorage point is located on the seat structure;

    "seat belt" except in this regulation, includes a child restraint and references to wearing a seat belt shall be construed accordingly;

    "small bus" means a motor vehicle which—

        (a)   is constructed or adapted for use for the carriage of passengers,

        (b)   has more than eight seats in addition to the driver's seat,

        (c)   has four or more wheels,

        (d)   has a maximum design speed exceeding 25 kilometres per hour, and

        (e)   has a maximum laden weight not exceeding 3.5 tonnes;

    "trade licence" has the meaning given by section 38(1) of the Vehicles (Excise) Act 1971;

    "disabled person's belt", "lap belt", "seat", "specified passenger seat" and "three point belt" have the meanings given by regulation 47(8) of the Construction and Use Regulations.

(2) Without prejudice to section 17 of the Interpretation Act 1978, a reference to a provision in any subordinate legislation (within the meaning of that Act) is a reference to that provision as from time to time amended or as from time to time re-enacted with or without modification.

(3) In these Regulations—

"child" means a person under the age of 14 years;

"large child" means a child who is not a small child; and

"small child" means a child who is—

(a) aged under 12 years, and

(b) under 135 centimetres in height.

(4) In these Regulations, "adult belt" means a seat belt in respect of which one or more of the following requirements is satisfied, namely that—

(a) it is a three-point belt which has been marked in accordance with regulation 47(7) of the Construction and Use Regulations,

(b) it is a lap belt which has been so marked,

(c) it is a seat belt that falls within regulation 47(4)(c)(i) or (ii) of those Regulations;

(d) it is a seat belt fitted in a vehicle and comprised in a restraint system—

(i) of a type which has been approved by an authority of another member State for use by all persons who are either aged 13 years or more or of 150 centimetres or more in height, and

(ii) in respect of which, by virtue of such approval, the requirements of the law of another member State corresponding to these Regulations would be met were it to be worn by persons who are either aged 13 years or more or of 150 centimetres or more in height when travelling in that vehicle in that State.

(5) In these Regulations, "child restraint" means a seat belt or other device in respect of which the following requirements are satisfied, namely that—

(a) it is a seat belt or any other description of restraining device for the use of a child which is—

(i) designed either to be fitted directly to a suitable anchorage or to be used in conjunction with an adult seat belt and held in place by the restraining action of that belt, and

(ii) marked in accordance with regulation 47(7) of the Construction and Use Regulations; or

(b) it is a seat belt consisting of or comprised in a restraint system fitted in a vehicle , being a restraint system—

(i) of a type which has been approved by an authority of another member State for use by a child, and

(ii) in respect of which, by virtue of such approval, the requirements of the law of that State corresponding to these Regulations would be met were it to be worn by a child when travelling that vehicle in that State.

(6) Subject to paragraph (7), for the purposes of these Regulations, a seat shall be regarded as provided with an adult seat belt if it is fixed in such a position that it can be worn by an occupier of that seat.

(7) A seat shall not be regarded as provided with an adult seat belt if the seat belt—

(a) has an inertia reel mechanism which is locked as a result of the vehicle being, or having been, on a steep incline, or

(b) does not comply with the requirements of regulation 48 of the Construction and Use Regulations.

(8) For the purposes of these Regulations, a seat belt is appropriate—

(a) in relation to a small child, if it is a child restraint of a description prescribed for a child of his height and weight by regulation 8;

(b) in relation to a large child, if it is a child restraint of a description prescribed for a child of his height and weight by regulation 8 or an adult belt; or

(c) in relation to a person aged 14 years or more, if it is an adult belt.

(9) For the purposes of these Regulations, any reference to a seat belt being available shall be construed in accordance with Schedule 2 to these Regulations.

(9A) For the purposes of these Regulations, references to a bus being used to provide a service in a "built-up area" shall be construed in the same way as in section 15B(6) of the Act.

(10) Unless the context otherwise requires, in these Regulations—

(a) any reference to a numbered regulation is a reference to the regulation bearing that number in these Regulations; and

(b) a numbered paragraph is a reference to the paragraph bearing that number in the regulation or Schedule in which the reference appears.

4–3802   3. Interpretation of references to relevant vehicles. *Revoked.*

PART II

ADULTS IN THE FRONT OR REAR OF A VEHICLE

4–3803   4. General. This Part of these Regulations shall have effect for the purpose of section 14 of the Act.

4–3804   5. Requirement for adults to wear adult belts.   (1) Subject to the following provisions of these Regulations, every person—

     (a)   driving a motor vehicle (other than a two-wheeled motor cycle with or without a sidecar), or

     (b)   riding in a front or rear seat of a motor vehicle (other than a two-wheeled motor cycle with or without a sidecar),

shall wear an adult belt.

     (2) Paragraph (1) does not apply to a person under the age of 14 years.

4–3805   6. Exemptions.   (1) The requirements of regulation 5 do not apply to—

     (a)   a person holding a medical certificate;

     (b)   the driver of or a passenger in a motor vehicle constructed or adapted for carrying goods, while on a journey which does not exceed 50 metres and which is undertaken for the purpose of delivering or collecting any thing;

     (c)   a person driving a vehicle while performing a manoeuvre which includes reversing;

     (d)   a qualified driver (within the meaning given by regulation 17 of the Motor Vehicles (Driving Licences) Regulations 1999) who is supervising the holder of a provisional licence (within the meaning of Part III of the Act) while that holder is performing a manoeuvre which includes reversing;

     (e)   a person by whom, as provided in the Motor Vehicles (Driving Licences) Regulations 1999, a test of competence to drive is being conducted and his wearing a seat belt would endanger himself or any other person;

     (f)   a person driving or riding in a vehicle while it is being used for fire brigade or, in England, fire and rescue authority or police purposes or for carrying a person in lawful custody (a person who is being so carried being included in this exemption);

     (fa)   as regards England and Wales, and so far as relating to the functions of the Serious Organised Crime Agency which are exercisable in or as regards Scotland and which relate to reserved matters (within the meaning of the Scotland Act 1998), a person driving or riding in a vehicle while it is being used for Serious Organised Crime Agency purposes;

     (fb)   *Scotland*;

     (g)   the driver of—

         (i)   a licensed taxi while it is being used for seeking hire, or answering a call for hire, or carrying a passenger for hire, or

         (ii)   a private hire vehicle while it is being used to carry a passenger for hire;

     (h)   a person riding in a vehicle, being used under a trade licence, for the purpose of investigating or remedying a mechanical fault in the vehicle;

     (j)   a disabled person who is wearing a disabled person's belt; or

     (k)   a person riding in a vehicle while it is taking part in a procession organised by or on behalf of the Crown.

     (2) Without prejudice to paragraph (1)(k), the requirements of regulation 5 do not apply to a person riding in a vehicle which is taking part in a procession held to mark or commemorate an event if either—

     (a)   the procession is one commonly or customarily held in the police area or areas in which it is being held, or

     (b)   notice in respect of the procession was given in accordance with section 11 of the Public Order Act 1986.

     (3) The requirements of regulation 5 do not apply to—

     (a)   a person driving a vehicle if the driver's seat is not provided with an adult belt;

     (b)   a person riding in the front of a vehicle if no adult belt is available for him in the front of the vehicle;

     (c)   a person riding in the rear of a vehicle if no adult belt is available for him in the rear of the vehicle.

     (4) The requirements of regulation 5(1)(b) do not apply to a person riding in a small or large bus—

     (a)   which is being used to provide a local service (within the meaning of the Transport Act 1985) in a built-up area, or

     (b)   which is constructed or adapted for the carriage of standing passengers and on which the operator permits standing.

PART III
CHILDREN IN THE REAR OF A VEHICLE

4–3806   7. General.   This Part of these Regulations has effect for the purposes of section 15(3) and (3A) of the Act.

4–3807   8. Description of seat belts to be worn by children.   (1) For a child of any particular height and weight travelling in a particular vehicle, the description of seat belt prescribed for the purposes of section 15(3) of the Act to be worn by him is—

     (a)   if he is a small child, a child restraint of a description specified in sub-paragraph (a) or (b) of paragraph (2);

(b) revoked;
(c) if he is a large child, a child restraint of a description specified in sub-paragraph (a) of paragraph (2) or an adult belt.

(2) The descriptions of seat belt referred to in paragraph (1) are—

(a) a child restraint with the marking required under regulation 47(7) of the Construction and Use Regulations if the marking indicates that it is suitable for his weight and either indicates that it is suitable for his height or contains no indication as respects height;
(b) a child restraint which would meet the requirements of the law of another member State corresponding to these Regulations were it to be worn by that child when travelling in that vehicle in that State.

4–3808 9. Vehicles to which section 15(3) and (3A) of the Act do not apply. The following classes of vehicles are exempt from the prohibition in section 15(3) and (3A) of the Act, that is to say—

(a) large buses;
(b) licensed taxis and licensed hire cars in which (in each case) the rear seats are separated from the driver by a fixed partition.

4–3809 10. Exemptions. (1) The prohibitions in section 15(3) and (3A) of the Act do not apply in relation to—

(a) a child for whom there is a medical certificate;
(b) a small child aged under 3 years who is riding in a licensed taxi or licensed hire car, if no appropriate seat belt is available for him in the front or rear of the vehicle;
(c) a small child aged 3 years or more who is riding in a licensed taxi, a licensed hire car or a small bus and wearing an adult belt if an appropriate seat belt is not available for him in the front or rear of the vehicle;
(d) a small child aged 3 years or more who is wearing an adult belt and riding in a passenger car or light goods vehicle where the use of child restraints by the child occupants of two seats in the rear of the vehicle prevents the use of an appropriate seat belt for that child and no appropriate seat belt is available for him in the front of the vehicle;
(e) a small child who is riding in a vehicle being used for the purposes of the police, security or emergency services to enable the proper performance of their duty;
(f) a small child aged 3 years or more who is wearing an adult belt and who, because of an unexpected necessity, is travelling a short distance in a passenger car or light goods vehicle in which no appropriate seat belt is available for him; or
(g) a disabled child who is wearing a disabled person's belt or whose disability makes it impracticable to wear a seat belt where a disabled person's belt is unavailable to him.]

(2) The prohibition in section 15(3) of the Act does not apply in relation to a child aged under 3 years riding in a rear seat of a small bus.

(3) The prohibition in section 15(3) of the Act does not apply to a small child aged 3 years or more riding in a rear seat of a small bus if neither an appropriate seat belt nor an adult belt is available for him in the front or rear of the vehicle.

(3A) For the purposes of paragraph (3) of this regulation, a reference to an appropriate seat belt in paragraphs 2 and 3 of Schedule 2 shall be read as including reference to an adult belt.

(4) The prohibition in section 15(3) of the Act does not apply in relation to a large child in any vehicle if no appropriate seat belt is available for him in the rear of the vehicle.

(4A) The prohibition in section 15(3) of the Act does not apply to a child riding in a small bus—

(a) which is being used to provide a local service (within the meaning of the Transport Act 1985) in a built-up area, or
(b) which is constructed or adapted for the carriage of standing passengers and on which the operator permits standing.

(5) The prohibition in section 15(3A) of the Act does not apply in relation to a child if no appropriate seat belt is available for him in the front of the vehicle.

4–3810
Regulation 2(1)

SCHEDULE 1
MEANING OF "MEDICAL CERTIFICATE"
PART I

1. Subject to paragraph 2, in these Regulations, "medical certificate", in relation to a person driving or riding in a vehicle, means—

(a) a valid certificate signed by a medical practitioner to the effect that it is inadvisable on medical grounds for him to wear a seat belt, or
(b) a valid certificate to such effect issued by the authority having power to issue such a certificate under the law of another member State corresponding to these Regulations.

2. A certificate shall not be regarded as a medical certificate in relation to a person driving or riding in a vehicle for the purposes of these Regulations unless—

(a) it specifies its period of validity and bears the symbol shown in Part II of this Schedule;
(b) revoked.

3. Paragraph 2 does not apply in relation to a certificate issued before 1st January 1995.

PART II

(*This Part shows an illustration of the symbol referred to in Sch 1, Part I, para 2(a), ante.*)

4–3811

Regulation 2(9)   SCHEDULE 2

INTERPRETATION OF REFERENCES TO AVAILABILITY OF SEAT BELTS

1. For the purpose of these Regulations, in relation to a person aged 14 years or more riding in a vehicle,—

   (a) if any front seat in the vehicle (other than the driver's seat) is provided with an adult belt, that belt shall be regarded as being available for him in the front of the vehicle unless the requirements of paragraph 3 are satisfied in relation to that person, that seat and that belt; and

   (b) if any rear seat in the vehicle is provided with an adult belt, that belt shall be regarded as being available for him in the rear of the vehicle unless the requirements of paragraph 3 are satisfied in relation to that person, that seat and that belt.

2. For the purposes of these Regulations, in relation to a child riding in a vehicle—

   (a) if any front seat in the vehicle (other than the driver's seat) is provided with an appropriate seat belt, that belt shall be regarded as an appropriate seat belt available for him in the front of the vehicle unless the requirements of paragraph 3 are satisfied in relation to that child, that seat and that belt; and

   (b) if any rear seat in a vehicle is provided with an appropriate seat belt, that belt shall be regarded as an appropriate seat belt available for him in the rear of the vehicle unless the requirements of paragraph 3 are satisfied in relation to that child, that seat and that belt.

3. The requirements of this paragraph are satisfied in relation to a particular person (" the person in question") and a particular seat ("the relevant seat") provided with a particular seat belt ("the relevant belt") if—

   (a) another person is wearing the relevant belt;

   (b) a child is occupying the relevant seat and wearing a child restraint which is an appropriate child restraint for that child;

   (c) another person, being a person holding a medical certificate, is occupying the relevant seat;

   (d) a disabled person (not being the person in question) is occupying the relevant seat and wearing a disabled person's belt;

   (e) by reason of his disability, it would not be practicable for the person in question to wear the relevant belt;

   (f) *revoked*;

   (g) the person in question is prevented from occupying the relevant seat by the presence of a child restraint which could not readily be removed without the aid of tools; or

   (h) the relevant seat is specially designed so that—

   (i) its configuration can be adjusted in order to increase the space in the vehicle available for goods or personal effects, and

   (ii) when it is so adjusted the seat cannot be used as such,

   and the configuration is adjusted in the manner described in sub-paragraph (i) and it would not be reasonably practicable for the goods and personal effects being carried in the vehicle to be so carried were the configuration not so adjusted.

4. Paragraph 3 shall have effect in relation to regulation 10(5) as if sub-paragraphs (a) to (d) of that paragraph were omitted.

5. Paragraph 3(b) and (d) shall not apply unless the presence of the other person renders it impracticable for the person in question to wear the relevant belt.

6. *Revoked.*

7. Paragraph 3(g) shall not apply if—

   (a) the person in question is a child; and

   (b) the child restraint is appropriate for him.

8. A child restraint shall be regarded as provided for a seat for the purposes of this Schedule if—

   (a) it is fixed in such a position that it can be worn by an occupier of that seat, or

   (b) it is elsewhere in or on the vehicle but—

   (i) it could readily be fixed in such a position without the aid of tools, and

   (ii) it is not being worn by a child for whom it is appropriate and who is occupying another seat.

Motor Cycles (Protective Helmets) Regulations 1998[1]
(SI 1998/1807 amended by SI 2000/1488)

4–3812   **1. Citation and commencement.** These Regulations may be cited as the Motor Cycles (Protective Helmets) Regulations 1998 and shall come into force on 21st August 1998.

---

1. Made by the Secretary of State for the Environment, Transport and the Regions, in exercise of the powers conferred by sections 16 and 17 of the Road Traffic Act 1988, and after consultation with representative organisations in accordance with the provisions of section 195(2) of that Act.

2. Revocation

3. Interpretation. In these Regulations—

   (a) "EEA State" means a State which is a contracting party to the Agreement on the European Economic Area signed at Oporto on 2nd May 1992 as adjusted by the Protocol signed at Brussels on 17th March 1993;

   (aa) "ECE Regulation 22" means Regulation No 22 set out in Addendum 21 to the UN ECE Agreement;

   (aaa) "ECE Regulation 22.05" means ECE Regulation 22 as amended by the 05 series of amendments and all previous amendments in force on 30th June 2000;

   (aaaa) "the UN ECE Agreement" means the Agreement of the United Nations Economic Commission for Europe concluded at Geneva on 20th March 1958 as amended concerning the adoption of uniform technical prescriptions for wheeled vehicles, equipment and parts which can be fitted to and/or used on wheeled vehicles and the conditions for the reciprocal recognition of approvals granted on the basis of these prescriptions, to which the United

Kingdom is a party by virtue of an instrument of accession dated 14th January 1963 deposited with the Secretary General of the United Nations on 15th January 1963;

(*b*) a reference to a numbered regulation is a reference to the regulation so numbered in these Regulations; and

(*c*) a reference to a numbered paragraph is a reference to the paragraph so numbered in the regulation in which the reference occurs.

4. Protective headgear. (1) Save as provided in paragraph (2), every person driving or riding (otherwise than in a side-car) on a motor bicycle when on a road shall wear protective headgear.

(2) Nothing in paragraph (1) shall apply to any person driving or riding on a motor bicycle if—

(*a*) it is a mowing machine; or

(*b*) it is for the time being propelled by a person on foot.

(3) In this regulation—

"motor bicycle" means a two-wheeled motor cycle[1], whether or not having a sidecar attached, and for the purposes of this definition where the distance measured between the centre of the area of contact with the road surface of any two wheels of a motor cycle is less than 460 millimetres, those wheels shall be counted as one wheel;

"protective headgear" means a helmet which—

(*a*) either—

(i) bears a marking applied by its manufacturer indicating compliance with the specifications contained in one of the British Standards (whether or not as modified by any amendment) mentioned in Schedule 2 to these Regulations; or

(ii) is of a type manufactured for use by persons on motor cycles which by virtue of its shape, material and construction could reasonably be expected to afford to the wearer a degree of protection from accidental injury similar to or greater than that provided by a helmet of a type prescribed by regulation 5;

(*b*) if worn with a chin cup attached to or held in position by a strap, is provided with an additional strap (to be fastened under the wearer's jaw) for securing the helmet to the head; and

(*c*) is securely fastened to the head by means of straps provided for that purpose; and

"strap" includes any fastening device.

---

1. A two wheeled vehicle with a roof, seat belts and side protection safety bars such as a BMW C1 is a motorcycle and requires the wearing of a crash helmet (*R v Parker* [2004] TLR 338).

5. Prescribed types of recommended helmet. (1) The types of helmet hereby prescribed as types of helmet recommended as affording protection to persons on or in motor cycles from injury in the event of an accident are helmets which as regards their shape, construction and other qualities conform—

(*a*) with British Standard 6658:1985 as amended by Amendment Slip number 1 published on 28th February 1986 and are marked with the number of that standard,

(*b*) with any other standard accepted by an EEA State which offers in use equivalent levels of safety, suitability and fitness for purpose and are marked with a mark to indicate that standard,

and in each case are marked with an approved certification mark of an approved body (whether or not they are required to be so marked by the standard in point), or

(*c*) with ECE Regulation 22.05 including the approval, marking and conformity of production requirements of that Regulation.

(2) For the purposes of this regulation—

(*a*) an approved certification mark is—

(i) the certification mark of the British Standards Institution; or

(ii) a certification mark which indicates that a conformity assessment equivalent to that of the British Standards Institution has been undertaken, and

(*b*) an approved body is—

(i) the British Standards Institution; or

(ii) any body approved by an EEA State to undertake conformity assessments equivalent to those undertaken by the British Standards Institution.

6. Saving for the Trade Descriptions Act 1968 and the Consumer Protection Act 1987. Nothing in regulation 5(1) shall be taken to authorise any person to apply any number or mark referred to therein in contravention of the Trade Descriptions Act 1968 or the Consumer Protection Act 1987.

Regulation 2   SCHEDULE 1
                                          REVOCATIONS

Regulation 4(3)   SCHEDULE 2
                                          BRITISH STANDARDS

Road Vehicles (Authorised Weight) Regulations 1998[1]
(SI 1998/3111 amended by SI 2000/3224 and SI 2001/1125)

4–3813 1. Citation and commencement. These Regulations may be cited as the Road Vehicles (Authorised Weight) Regulations 1998 and shall come into force on 1st January 1999.

1. Made by the Secretary of State under the provisions of s 41 of the Road Traffic Act 1988.

4–3814   **2. Interpretation.** (1) In these Regulations—

"the 1986 Regulations" means the Road Vehicles (Construction and Use) Regulations 1986[1];

"articulated bus or coach" means a single vehicle which is a bus or coach consisting of 2 or more rigid sections which—

   (*a*) articulate relative to one another;

   (*b*) are intercommunicating so that passengers can move freely between them; and

   (*c*) are permanently connected so that they can only be separated by an operation using facilities normally found only in a workshop;

articulated vehicle" means a tractor unit to which a semi-trailer is attached;

"axle-lift device" means a device permanently fitted to the vehicle for the purpose of reducing or increasing the load on the axles, according to the loading conditions of the vehicle either—

   (*a*) by means of raising the wheels clear off the ground or by lowering them to the ground, or

   (*b*) without raising the wheels off the ground,

in order to reduce the wear on the tyres when the vehicle is not fully laden and, or alternatively, to make it easier for the vehicle to move off on slippery ground by increasing the load on the driving axle;

"axle weight" means the sum of the weights transmitted to the road surface by all the wheels of an axle, and for the purpose of calculating axle weight the 2 axles comprised in a tandem axle and all the axles comprised in a triaxle shall be treated as one axle;

"centre-axle trailer" means a trailer having only a single axle or group of axles which is positioned at or close to the centre of gravity so that, when the trailer is uniformly loaded, the static vertical load transmitted to the towing vehicle does not exceed 10 per cent of the maximum authorised weight for the axle or group of axles or 1000 kg, whichever is the less;

"complies with" shall, in relation to the requirements of a Community Directive, be construed in accordance with regulation 6 of the 1986 Regulations;

"diesel engine" shall be construed in accordance with paragraph 2.2 of Directive 88/77/EEC as amended by Directive 91/542/EEC, Annex 1;

"Directive 88/77/EEC" means Council Directive 88/77 of 3 December 1987 on the approximation of the laws of the member states relating to the measures to be taken against the emission of gaseous and particulate pollutants from diesel engines for use in vehicles;

"Directive 91/542/EEC" means Council Directive 91/542 of 1 October 1991 amending Directive 88/77/EEC;

"first used" shall be construed in accordance with regulation 3(3) of the 1986 Regulations;

"gas" has the meaning given in regulation 3(2) of the 1986 Regulations;

"kg" means kilograms;

"loadable axle" means an axle the load on which can be varied without the axle being raised by the use of an axle-lift device;

"low pollution engine" means an engine which—

   (*a*) is fuelled solely by gas; or

   (*b*) is fuelled predominantly by gas and has a minimum gas tank capacity of 400 litres; or

   (*c*) being a diesel engine, complies with at least the requirements for the emission of gaseous and particulate pollutants specified in paragraphs 6.2.1 of Annex I to Directive 88/77/EEC as amended by Directive 91/542/EEC, the maximum masses of which as shown on line B in the table to that paragraph are—

Mass of carbon monoxide (CO) g/kWh	Mass of hydrocarbons (HC) g/kWh	Mass of nitrogen oxides (Nox) g/kWh	Mass of particulates (PT) g/kWh
4.0	1.1	7.0	0.15

"m" means metres;

"maximum authorised weight" in relation to a vehicle, vehicle combination or axle means the maximum authorised weight for the vehicle, vehicle combination or axle determined in accordance with these Regulations;

"retractable axle" means an axle which is raised or lowered by an axle-lift device, either by raising the wheels of the vehicle clear off the ground or by lowering them to the ground;

"rigid motor vehicle" means a motor vehicle which is not a tractor unit or an articulated bus;

"road friendly suspension" means a suspension system whereby at least 75 per cent of the spring effect is produced by air or other compressible fluid under pressure or suspension recognised as being equivalent within the Community as defined in Annex II of Council Directive 96/53/EC[2];

"semi-trailer" means a trailer which is constructed or adapted to be drawn by a tractor unit and includes a vehicle which is not itself a motor vehicle but has some or all of its wheels driven by the drawing vehicle;

"steering axle" means an axle that can be positively steered by the action of the driver;

"tandem axle" means a group of 2 axles not more than 2.5m apart so linked together that the load applied to one axle is applied to the other; references to a "driving tandem axle" include a tandem axle where either or both the axles comprising the tandem axle are driven and references to a "non-driving tandem axle" are to a tandem axle where neither of the axles comprising it is driven;

"tractor unit" means a motor vehicle by which a trailer partially superimposed on it may be drawn so that, when the trailer is fully loaded, not less than 20 per cent of its load is borne by the drawing vehicle;

"trailer" and "semi-trailer" have the meanings given in regulation 3(2) of the 1986 Regulations; and

"triaxle" means—

    (a) a group of 3 axles in which no axle is more than 3.25m apart from any other axle; or
    (b) a group of more than 3 axles in which no axle is more than 4.6m from any other axle,

    and in either case so linked together that the load applied to one axle is transferred to both or all the others; and

"vehicle combination" means an articulated vehicle or a rigid motor vehicle drawing a trailer; "wheel" has the meaning given in regulation 3(2) of the 1986 Regulations.

(2) For the purposes of these Regulations the distance between any 2 axles of a vehicle or vehicle combination shall be taken to be the shortest distance between the line joining the centres of the areas of contact with the road surface of the wheels of one axle and the line joining the centres of the areas of contact with the road surface of the wheels of the other axle.

(3) In these Regulations, except where otherwise specified,—

    (a) a reference to a numbered regulation is a reference to the regulation in these Regulations so numbered;
    (b) a reference to a numbered paragraph is a reference to the paragraph so numbered in the regulation or the Schedule in which the reference occurs;
    (c) a reference to a numbered sub-paragraph is a reference to the sub-paragraph so numbered in the paragraph in which the reference occurs; and
    (d) a reference to a numbered Schedule is a reference to the Schedule to these Regulations so numbered.

---

1. In this title, ante.
2. OJ L235, 17.9.96 p 59.

4-3815   3. Application of Regulations.   These Regulations apply to all wheeled motor vehicles and trailers which fall within category M2, M3, N2, N3, O3 or O4 of the vehicle categories defined in Annex II of Directive 70/156/EEC as substituted by Directive 92/53/EC except vehicle combinations which for the time being fulfil the requirements of Part II, III or IIIA of Schedule 11A to the 1986 Regulations (exemptions relating to combined transport operations).

4-3816   4. Maximum authorised weights.   (1) Subject to paragraph (2) and regulation 5, no vehicle to which these Regulations apply and which is of a description specified in a Schedule to these Regulations shall be used on a road if—

    (a) the weight of the vehicle exceeds the maximum authorised weight for the vehicle determined in accordance with Schedule 1;
    (b) where the vehicle is used as part of a vehicle combination, the weight of the combination exceeds the maximum authorised weight for the combination determined in accordance with Schedule 2; or
    (c) the axle weight of any axle of the vehicle exceeds the maximum authorised axle weight for that axle determined in accordance with Schedule 3 or if any of the other requirements of that Schedule are not complied with.

(2) A vehicle to which any of the provisions of regulations 75 to 79 of the 1986 Regulations apply, so long as it is so used that those provisions are complied with, shall be taken to comply with these Regulations except, in the case of a vehicle fitted with one or more retractable or loadable axles, for the provisions of paragraphs 3 and 4 of Schedule 3.

4-3817   5. Compliance with regulation 80 of the 1986 Regulations (over-riding weight restrictions).
(1) Subject to paragraph (2) nothing in these Regulations shall prejudice or affect regulation 80 of the 1986 Regulations and a person using or permitting a vehicle to be used contrary to the provisions of that regulation commits an offence even if the weights authorised by these Regulations are not exceeded.
(2) Regulation 80 of the 1986 Regulations shall not be contravened when a vehicle to which paragraph 3 of Schedule 3 applies is operated in accordance with sub-paragraph (3) of that paragraph.

Regulation 4(1)(a)   SCHEDULE 1
                       MAXIMUM AUTHORISED WEIGHTS FOR VEHICLES

4-3818   1. Weight not to be exceeded in any circumstances.   (1) Subject to paragraph 2, the maximum authorised weight for a vehicle of a description specified in column (2) of an item in Table 1 below and having the number of axles specified in column (3) shall be the weight specified in column (4) of the item.

TABLE 1

(1) Item	(2) Description of vehicle	(3) Number of axles	(4) Maximum author- ised weight (kg)
1	Rigid motor vehicle	2	18000
2	Tractor unit	2	18000
3	Trailer which is not a semi-trailer or a centre-axle trailer	2	18000
4	Trailer which is not a semi-trailer or centre-axle trailer	3 or more	24000
5	Rigid motor vehicle which satisfies at least one of the conditions specified in sub-paragraph (2)	3	26000
6	Rigid motor vehicle not falling within item 5	3	25000
7	Tractor unit which satisfies at least one of the conditions specified in sub-paragraph (2)	3 or more	26000
8	Tractor unit not falling within item 7	3 or more	25000
9	Articulated bus	Any number	28000
10	Rigid motor vehicle which satisfies at least one of the conditions specified in sub-paragraph (2)	4 or more	32000
11	Rigid motor vehicle not falling within item 10	4 or more	30000

(2) The conditions referred to in items 5, 7 and 10 of Table 1 are that—

(a) the driving axle if it is not a steering axle is fitted with twin tyres and road friendly suspension; or

(b) each driving axle is fitted with twin tyres and the maximum weight for each axle does not exceed 9500 kg.

4–3819 2. Weight by reference to axle spacing. For a vehicle of a description specified in column (2) of an item in Table 2 below and having the number of axles specified in column (3) of that item, the authorised weight in kilograms shall be the number equal to the product of the distance measured in metres between the foremost and rearmost axles of the vehicle multiplied by the factor specified in column (4) and rounded up to the nearest 10 kg, if that number is less than the maximum authorised weight determined in accordance with paragraph 1.

TABLE 2

(1) Item	(2) Description of vehicle	(3) Number of axles	(4) Factor to deter- mine maximum authorised weight
1	Rigid motor vehicle	2	6000
2	Tractor unit	2	6000
3	Trailer which is not a semi-trailer or centre-axle trailer	2	6000
4	Rigid motor vehicle	3	5500
5	Tractor unit	3 or more	6000
6	Trailer which is not a semi-trailer or centre-axle trailer	3 or more	5000
7	Rigid motor vehicle	4 or more	5000
8	Articulated bus	Any number	5000

Regulation 4(1)(*b*)   SCHEDULE 2

MAXIMUM AUTHORISED WEIGHTS FOR VEHICLE COMBINATIONS

4–3820 1. Weight not to be exceeded in any circumstances. (1) Subject to paragraph 2, the maximum authorised weight for a vehicle combination of a description of vehicle specified in column (2) of an item in Table 3 below and having the number of axles specified in column (3) shall be the weight specified in column (4) of the item.

TABLE 3

(1) Item	(2) Description of combination	(3) Number of axles	(4) Maximum authorised weight (kg)
1	Articulated vehicle	3	26000
2	Rigid motor vehicle towing a trailer satisfying the condition specified in sub-paragraph (2)	3	26000
3	Rigid motor vehicle not falling within item 2 drawing a trailer	3	22000
4	Articulated vehicle satisfying the conditions speci- fied in sub-paragraph (3)	4	38000
5	Articulated vehicle not falling within item 4	4	36000
6	Rigid motor vehicle towing a trailer satisfying the condition specified in sub-paragraph (2)	4	36000
7	Rigid motor vehicle not falling within item 6 drawing a trailer	4	30000
8	Articulated vehicle	5 or more	40000
9	Rigid motor vehicle towing a trailer satisfying the condition specified in sub-paragraph (2)	5 or more	40000

(1) Item	(2) Description of combination	(3) Number of axles	(4) Maximum authorised weight (kg)
10	Rigid motor vehicle not falling within item 9 drawing a trailer	5 or more	34000
11	Articulated vehicle satisfying the conditions specified in sub-paragraph (4)	6 or more	41000
12	Rigid motor vehicle towing a trailer satisfying each of the conditions specified in sub-paragraphs (2) and (4)	6 or more	41000
13	Articulated vehicles satisfying each of the conditions specified in sub-paragraphs (4) and (5)	6 or more	44,000
14	Rigid motor vehicles towing a trailer satisfying each of the conditions specified in sub-paragraphs (2), (4) and (5)	6 or more	44,000

(2) The condition referred to in items 2, 6, 9, 12 or 14 of Table 3 is that the distance between the rear axle of the motor vehicle and the front axle of the trailer is not less than 3m.

(3) The conditions referred to in item 4 of Table 3 are that—

(a) the combination consists of a 2-axle tractor unit and a 2-axle semi-trailer;
(b) the weight of the tractor unit comprised in the combination does not exceed 18000 kg;
(c) the sum of the axle weights of the semi-trailer does not exceed 20000 kg; and
(d) the driving axle is fitted with twin tyres and road friendly suspension.

(4) The conditions referred to in items 11, 12, 13 and 14 of Table 3 are that—

(a) the axle weight of each driving axle does not exceed 10500 kg; and
(b) either—

(i) each driving axle is fitted with twin tyres and road friendly suspension; or
(ii) each driving axle which is not a steering axle is fitted with twin tyres and the axle weight of each such axle does not exceed 8500 kg;

(c) each axle of the trailer is fitted with road friendly suspension; and
(d) each vehicle comprised in the combination has at least 3 axles.

(5) The condition referred to in items 13 and 14 of Table 3 is that the vehicle is fitted with a low pollution engine.

4–3821   2. Weight by reference to axle spacing. For a vehicle combination of a description specified in column (2) in Table 4 below and having the number of axles specified in column (3), the maximum authorised weight in kilograms shall be the product of the distance measured in metres between the king-pin and the centre of the rearmost axle of the semi-trailer multiplied by the factor specified in column (4) and rounded up to the nearest 10 kg, if that weight is less than the authorised weight determined in accordance with paragraph 1.

TABLE 4

(1) Item	(2) Description of vehicle combination	(3) Number of axles	(4) Factor to determine maximum authorised weight
1	Articulated vehicle	3 or more	5500

Regulation 4(1)(c)   SCHEDULE 3
MAXIMUM AUTHORISED AXLE WEIGHTS

4–3822   1. Weight not to be exceeded in any circumstances. (1) Subject to paragraphs 2 to 4, the maximum authorised weight for an axle of a description specified in column (2) of an item in Table 5 below shall be the weight specified in column (3) of the item.

TABLE 5

(1) Item	(2) Description of axle	(3) Maximum authorised weight (kg)
1	Single driving axle	11500
2	Single non-driving axle	10000
3	Driving tandem axle which meets either of the conditions specified in sub-paragraph (2)	19000
4	Driving tandem axle not falling within item 3	18000
5	Non-driving tandem axle	20000
6	Triaxle	24000

(2) The conditions referred to in item 3 of Table 5 are that—

(a) the driving axle is fitted with twin tyres and road friendly suspension; or
(b) each driving axle is fitted with twin tyres and no axle has an axle weight exceeding 9500 kg.

4–3823   2. Weight by reference to axle spacing. For an axle of a description specified in column (2) of an item in Table 6 below, if the dimension specified in column (3) is of the length specified in column (4), the maximum authorised weight shall be the weight specified in column (5) of the item, if that weight is less than the maximum authorised weight determined in accordance with paragraph 1.

TABLE 6

(1) Item	(2) Description of axle	(3) Specified dimension	(4) Length m	(5) Maximum authorised weight (kg)
1	Driving tandem axle	Distance between the 2 axles comprised in the tandem axle	Less than 1	11500
2	Driving tandem axle	Distance between the 2 axles comprised in the tandem axle	Not less than 1 but less than 1.3	16000
3	Non-driving tandem axle	Distance between the 2 axles comprised in the tandem axle	Less than 1	11000
4	Non-driving tandem axle	Distance between the 2 axles comprised in the tandem axle	Not less than 1 but less than 1.3	16000
5	Non-driving tandem axle	Distance between the 2 axles comprised in the tandem axle	Not less than 1.3 but less than 1.8	18000
6	Triaxle	Distance between any one axle comprised in triaxle and the nearer of the other 2 axles	1.3 or less	21000

4–3823A 3. Requirements relating to retractable and loadable axles. (1) This paragraph applies to a vehicle which—

(a) is fitted with one or more retractable axles or with one or more loadable axles; and
(b) is first used on or after 1 January 2002.

(2) Subject to sub-paragraph (3), under all driving conditions other than those described in sub-paragraph (3), the maximum authorised weight on any axle shall be the weight specified in column (3) of Table 5 or in column (5) of Table 6 (as may be appropriate) and the retractable axle or the loadable axle shall lower to the ground automatically if—

(a) the front axle on the vehicle is laden to that maximum authorised weight, or
(b) in the case of a vehicle having a group of axles, the nearest axle or axles is or are laden to that maximum authorised weight;

and in paragraph (a) above "axle" is a reference to an axle described in column (2) of items 1 or 2 of Table 5 in Schedule 3 and in paragraph (b) above "group of axles" is a reference to an axle described in column (2) of items 3 to 6 of that Table.

(3) The driving conditions referred to in sub-paragraph (2) exist where a vehicle is on a slippery surface and, accordingly in order to help vehicles or vehicle combinations to move off on slippery ground, and to increase the traction of their tyres on slippery surfaces, the axle-lift device may also actuate the retractable axle or the loadable axle of the vehicle of semi-trailer to increase the weight on the driving axle of the vehicle, subject as follows:—

(a) the weight corresponding to the load on each axle of the vehicle may exceed the relevant maximum authorised weight by up to 30 per cent. so long as it does not exceed the value stated by the manufacturer for this special purpose;
(b) the weight corresponding to the remaining load on the front axle shall remain above zero;
(c) the retractable axle or the loadable axle shall be actuated only by a special control device; and
(d) after the vehicle has moved off and reached a speed of 30 kms per hour, the axle shall automatically lower again to the ground or be reloaded.

4–3823B 4. Every retractable axle or loadable axle fitted to a vehicle to which these Regulations apply, and any system for its operation, shall be designed and installed in such a manner as to protect it against improper use or tampering.

Motor Cycles (Eye Protectors) Regulations 1999[1]
(SI 1999/535 amended by SI 2000/1489)

4–3824 1. Citation and commencement. These Regulations may be cited as the Motor Cycles (Eye Protectors) Regulations 1999 and shall come into force on 1st April 1999[1].

---

1. Made by the Secretary of State for the Environment, Transport and the Regions under s 18 of the Road Traffic Act 1988.

2. Interpretation. In these Regulations—

(aa) "ECE Regulation 22" means Regulation No 22 set out in Addendum 21 to the UN ECE Agreement;
(aaa) "ECE Regulation 22.05" means ECE Regulation 22 as amended by the 05 series of amendments and all previous amendments in force on 30th June 2000;
(aaaa) "the UN ECE Agreement" means the Agreement of the United Nations Economic Commission for Europe concluded at Geneva on 20th March 1958 as amended concerning the adoption of uniform technical prescriptions for wheeled vehicles, equipment and parts which can be fitted to and/or used on wheeled vehicles and the conditions for the reciprocal

recognition of approvals granted on the basis of these prescriptions, to which the United Kingdom is a party by virtue of an instrument of accession dated 14th January 1963 deposited with the Secretary General of the United Nations on 15th January 1963;

(a) "EEA State" means a State which is a contracting party to the Agreement on the European Economic Area signed at Oporto on 2nd May 1992 as adjusted by the Protocol signed at Brussels on 17th March 1993;

(b) "eye protector" means an appliance designed or adapted for use with any headgear or by being attached to or placed upon the head by a person driving or riding on a motor bicycle and intended for the protection of the eyes;

(c) "motor bicycle" means a two-wheeled motor cycle, whether or not having a side-car attached, and for the purposes of this definition, where the distance measured between the centre of the area of contact with the road surface of any two wheels of a motor cycle is less than 460 millimetres, those wheels shall be counted as one wheel.

3. Revocation. The Regulations specified in the Schedule to these Regulations are hereby revoked.

4. Prescribed types of authorised eye protector. (1) Subject to paragraph (3), the types of eye protector hereby prescribed as authorised for use by persons driving or riding (otherwise than in a side-car) on a motor bicycle are—

(a) those which conform—

   (i) to the requirements relating to Grade X in British Standard BS 4110:1979 and are marked with that Grade and the number of that standard,

   (ii) to the requirements relating to Grades XA, YA or ZA in British Standard BS 4110:1979 as amended by Amendment No 1 (AMD 3368), Amendment No 2 (AMD 4060) and Amendment No 3 (AMD 4630) and are marked with the number of that standard and the Grade to which they conform, or

   (iii) to any other standard accepted by an EEA State, which offers in use levels of safety, suitability and fitness for purpose equivalent to those offered by the standards referred to in paragraph (i) or (ii) above, and are marked with a mark to indicate that standard,

and in each case are marked with an approved certification mark of an approved body (whether or not they are required to be so marked by the standard in point);

(aa) those which conform with ECE Regulation 22.05 including the approval, marking and conformity of production requirements of that Regulation;

(b) those which comply with the requirements of Council Directive 89/686/EEC of the 21st December 1989 on the approximation of the laws of the Member States relating to personal protective equipment as amended by Council Directives 93/68/EEC of 22nd July 1993, 93/95/EEC of 29th October 1993 and 96/58/EEC of 3rd September 1996; or

(c) those which were first used before 1st April 1989 and fulfil all of the following requirements—

   (i) they are fitted with lenses that are designed to correct a defect in sight,

   (ii) they transmit 50 per cent or more of the light, and

   (iii) they do not fly into fragments if fractured.

(2) For the purposes of this regulation:

(a) an approved certification mark is—

   (i) the certification mark of the British Standards Institution; or

   (ii) a certification mark which indicates that a conformity assessment equivalent to that of the British Standards Institution has been undertaken, and

(b) an approved body is—

   (i) the British Standards Institution; or

   (ii) any body approved by an EEA State to undertake conformity assessments equivalent to those undertaken by the British Standards Institution.

(3) The types of eye protector prescribed by paragraph (1) are not prescribed as authorised for use by persons to whom paragraph (4) applies.

(4) This paragraph applies to any person driving or riding on a motor bicycle if—

(a) it is a mowing machine;

(b) it is for the time being propelled by a person on foot;

(c) it is a vehicle brought temporarily into Great Britain by a person resident outside the United Kingdom which has not remained in the United Kingdom for a period of more than one year from the date it was last brought into the United Kingdom; or

(d) that person is in the armed forces of the Crown, is on duty and is wearing an eye protector supplied to him as part of his service equipment.

---

1. Made by the Secretary of State for the Environment, Transport and Regions under s 18 of the Road Traffic Act 1988.

Road Vehicles (Authorisation of Special Types) (General) Order 2003[1]
(SI 2003/1998)

PART 1
GENERAL

Preliminary

4–3826   1. Citation and commencement.   (1) This Order may be cited as the Road Vehicles (Authorisation of Special Types) (General) Order 2003.

(2) Except as stated in paragraph (3), this Order comes into force on 25th August 2003.

(3) Paragraphs 15 to 18 of Schedule 2 come into force on 1st December 2004.

---

1. Made by the Secretary of State for Transport, in exercise of the powers conferred upon him by section 44 of the Road Traffic Act 1988.

The Order does not in itself create offences: in form and substance it provides exceptions for the use of vehicles of special types in ways which otherwise would contravene other provisions of the law, namely the Road Vehicle (Construction and Use) Regulations 1986 (see *Gwennap (William) (Agricultural) Ltd v Amphlett* [1957] 2 All ER 605, 121 JP 487). This point was not considered in *Dixon v BRS (Pickfords) Ltd* [1959] 1 All ER 449, 123 JP 207; *criticised, Siddle C Cook Ltd v Holden* [1963] 1 QB 248, [1962] 3 All ER 984, 127 JP 55.

2. Revocation

Interpretation

4–3827   3. Interpretation: general.   (1) In this Order—

"abnormal indivisible load" has the meaning given in paragraph 2 of Schedule 1 to this Order;

"abnormal indivisible load vehicle" has the meaning given in paragraph 3 of Schedule 1 to this Order;

"agricultural motor vehicle", "agricultural trailer" and "agricultural trailed appliance" have the meaning given in article 19(3);

"AILV" has the meaning given in Schedule 1;

"articulated vehicle" has the same meaning as in the Construction and Use Regulations;

"authorisation requirements" has the meaning given in article 9(2);

"axle" has the meaning given in article 7(1);

"axle weight" has the meaning given in article 7(1);

"the Authorised Weight Regulations" means the Road Vehicles (Authorised Weight) Regulations 1998;

"chief officer of police"—

    (*a*)   in relation to England and Wales, has the same meaning as in the Police Act 1996; and

    (*b*)   in relation to Scotland, has the same meaning as in the Police (Scotland) Act 1967;

"the Construction and Use Regulations" means the Road Vehicles (Construction and Use) Regulations 1986;

"engineering plant" has the meaning given in paragraph 2 of Schedule 3 to this Order;

"foremost point", in relation to a vehicle, has the meaning given in article 4(3);

"forward projection", in relation to a load carried on a vehicle, has the meaning given in article 6(1);

"gross weight"—

    (*a*)   in relation to a motor vehicle, means the sum of the weights transmitted to the road surface by all the wheels of the vehicle; and

    (*b*)   in relation to a trailer, means the sum of—

        (i)   the weights transmitted to the road surface by all the wheels of the trailer; and

        (ii)   any weight of the trailer imposed on the towing vehicle;

"group of axles" has the meaning given in article 7(1);

"lateral projection", in relation to a load carried on a vehicle, has the meaning given in article 5(1);

"the Lighting Regulations" means the Road Vehicles Lighting Regulations 1989;

"local excavation vehicle" has the meaning given in paragraph 1 of Schedule 10 to this Order;

"mobile crane" has the meaning given in paragraph 2 of Schedule 2 to this Order;

"motor vehicle of category N3" means a motor vehicle of category N3 (motor vehicles over 12,000 kilograms maximum weight), as defined in Annex II of Council Directive 70/156/EEC on the approximation of the laws of the Member States relating to the type-approval of motor vehicles and their trailers;

"motorway" means a special road which—

    (*a*)   in England or Wales (except as otherwise provided by or under regulations made under, or having effect as if made under, section 17 of the Road Traffic Regulation Act 1984) can be used by traffic only of Class I or II as specified in Schedule 4 to Highways Act 1980: or

    (*b*)   in Scotland can be used by traffic only of Class I or Class II as specified in Schedule 3 to the Roads (Scotland) Act 1984;

"overall length", in relation to a vehicle, has the meaning given in article 4(2);

"overall width", in relation to a vehicle, has the meaning given in article 4(1);

"Part 2 vehicle" has the meaning given in article 10(2);

"Part 2 vehicle-combination" has the meaning given in article 10(3);

"pneumatic tyre" has the same meaning as in the Construction and Use Regulations;

"rearmost point", in relation to a vehicle, has the meaning given in article 4(4);

"rearward projection", in relation to a load carried on a vehicle, has the meaning given in article 6(2);

"recognised category of special vehicles" has the meaning given in article 8(2);

"road recovery vehicle" has the meaning given in paragraph 1 of Schedule 4 to this Order;

"special type agricultural vehicle" has the meaning given in article 19(2);

"track-laying", in relation to a vehicle, has the same meaning as in the Construction and Use Regulations;

"trailer of category O4" means a trailer of category O4 (trailers over 10,000 kilograms maximum weight), as defined in Annex II of Council Directive 70/156/EEC on the approximation of the laws of the Member States relating to the type-approval of motor vehicles and their trailers;

"vehicle-combination" means a motor vehicle towing one or more trailers, any trailer or trailers towed by it and any other motor vehicle used for the purpose of assisting the propulsion of the trailer or trailers on the road;

"warning beacon" has the same meaning as in the Lighting Regulations;

"wheel" is to be construed in accordance with article 7(2) and (3);

"wheeled", in relation to a vehicle, means a vehicle so constructed that the whole weight of the vehicle is transmitted to the road surface by means of wheels;

"wheel-track combination vehicle" has the meaning given in paragraph 1 of Schedule 3; and

"wheel weight" has the meaning given in article 7(1).

(2) In this Order, any reference to a motor vehicle towing a trailer in an offset manner is a reference to the vehicle towing the trailer so that the longitudinal axis of the trailer and the longitudinal axis of the towing vehicle are parallel but lie in different vertical planes.

(3) For the purposes of any provision of this Order requiring a person to do something within a specified number of days, no account is to be taken of any day which is a Saturday, a Sunday or a public holiday in any part of Great Britain.

**4–3828	4. Interpretation: vehicles and their measurement.**	(1) In this Order "overall width", in relation to any vehicle, has the same meaning as in the Construction and Use Regulations.

(2) In this Order "overall length" —

(a)	in relation to a single vehicle, has the same meaning as in the Construction and Use Regulations;

(b)	in relation to a vehicle-combination, means the distance between the foremost point of the towing vehicle and the rearmost point of the rearmost vehicle, measured when the longitudinal axis of each vehicle in the combination lies in the same vertical plane.

(3) In this Order "foremost point", in relation to any vehicle, means the foremost point from which its overall length is calculated when applying the definition of overall length contained in regulation 3(2) of the Construction and Use Regulations.

(4) In this Order "rearmost point", in relation to any vehicle, means the rearmost point from which its overall length is calculated when applying the definition of overall length contained in regulation 3(2) of the Construction and Use Regulations.

(5) In this Order—

(a)	any reference to the distance between vehicles bearing the weight of a load is a reference to the distance between the nearest points of any two adjacent vehicles by which each load is carried, measured when the longitudinal axis of each vehicle lies in the same vertical plane; and

(b)	in determining the nearest point of two vehicles, any part of either vehicle designed primarily for use as a means of attaching the one vehicle to the other (and any fitting designed for use in connection with any such part) is to be disregarded.

**4–3829	5. Interpretation: lateral projections of loads and their measurement.**	(1) In this Order "lateral projection", in relation to a load carried on a vehicle, means that part of the load which extends beyond a side of the vehicle.

(2) For the purposes of this Order, the width of any lateral projection is to be measured between longitudinal planes passing through the extreme projecting point of the vehicle on that side of the vehicle on which the projection lies and that part of the projection furthest from that point.

(3) The reference in paragraph (2) to the extreme projecting point of a vehicle is to the point of the vehicle from which its overall width is calculated when applying the definition of overall width contained in regulation 3(2) of the Construction and Use Regulations.

**4–3830	6. Interpretation: forward or rearward projections of loads and their measurement.**	(1) In this Order "forward projection", in relation to a load carried on a vehicle, means—

(a)	where the weight of the load is carried on a single vehicle, that part of the load that extends beyond the foremost point of the vehicle;

(b)	where the weight of the load is carried on more than one vehicle, that part of the load that extends beyond the foremost point of the foremost vehicle on which the load is carried.

(2) In this Order "rearward projection", in relation to a load carried on a vehicle, means—

(a)	where the weight of the load is carried on a single vehicle, that part of the load that extends beyond the rearmost point of the vehicle;

(*b*) where the weight of the load is carried on more than one vehicle, that part of the load that extends beyond the rearmost point of the rearmost vehicle on which the load is carried.

(3) For the purposes of paragraphs (1) and (2), where a crane or other special appliance or apparatus is fitted to a vehicle so as to constitute a permanent (or essentially permanent) feature of it—

(*a*) any part of that crane, appliance or apparatus that extends forwards beyond the foremost point of the vehicle (or, as the case may be, beyond the foremost point of the foremost vehicle by which its weight is carried) is to be treated as a forward projection; and

(*b*) any part of that crane, appliance or apparatus that extends rearwards beyond the rearmost point of the vehicle (or, as the case may be, beyond the rearmost point of the rearmost vehicle by which its weight is carried) is to be treated as a rearward projection.

(4) In determining the foremost or rearmost point of a vehicle, any part of a crane or other special appliance or apparatus is to be disregarded.

(5) For the purposes of this Order, the length of any forward projection or rearward projection is to be measured between transverse planes passing—

(*a*) in the case of a forward projection, through the foremost point of the vehicle and that part of the projection furthest from that point;

(*b*) in the case of a rearward projection, through the rearmost point of the vehicle and that part of the projection furthest from that point.

4–3831   7. Interpretation: axles, wheels, axle weights and wheel weights.   (1) In this Order—

"axle" means any number of wheels in a transverse line;

"axle weight" means the sum of the weights transmitted to the road surface by all the wheels of any one axle;

"group of axles" means a group of two or more axles that are so linked together that the load applied to one axle is applied to the other; and

"wheel weight" means the weight transmitted to the road surface by any one wheel of an axle.

(2) For the purposes of this Order, any reference to a wheel of a vehicle is a reference to a wheel, the tyre or rim of which is, when the vehicle is in motion on a road, in contact with the ground.

(3) For the purposes of this Order, any two wheels of a vehicle are to be treated as one wheel if their centres of contact with the road are less than 460 millimetres apart.

(4) For the purposes of this Order, any wheels, or lines of wheels, whose centres can be contained between two transverse lines less than 0.5 metre apart are to be treated as one axle.

(5) For the purposes of this Order, the distance between any two axles of a vehicle or vehicle-combination is to be taken as the shortest distance between the line joining the centres of the areas of contact with the road surface of the wheels of one axle and the line joining the centres of the areas of contact with the road surface of the wheels of the other axle.

Authorisation of certain vehicles for use on roads

4–3832   8. Application of this Order.   (1) This Order applies only to motor vehicles or trailers—

(*a*) that do not comply in all respects with the standard construction and use requirements; and

(*b*) that fall within a recognised category of special vehicles.

(2) In this Order "recognised category of special vehicles" means a description of vehicles that is stated by a provision of this Order to be a recognised category of special vehicles.

(3) In paragraph (1), "standard construction and use requirements", in relation to a motor vehicle or trailer, means the requirements of such of the regulations made under section 41 of the Road Traffic Act 1988 as would, apart from this Order, apply to that motor vehicle or trailer.

4–3833   9. Authorisation of particular vehicles falling within recognised category of special vehicles.   (1) A vehicle that falls within a recognised category of special vehicles is authorised to be used on roads by virtue of this Order if (but only if) it complies with the authorisation requirements applicable to vehicles in that category.

(2) In this Order "authorisation requirements", in relation to a recognised category of special vehicles—

(*a*) means all the requirements specified in this Order as being applicable to vehicles in that category; and

(*b*) includes such of the requirements of regulations made under section 41 of the Road Traffic Act 1988 as are specified in this Order as being applicable to vehicles in that category (subject to any modifications or exceptions so specified).

(3) Where any provision of this Order specifies any of the regulations mentioned in paragraph (2)(*b*) as being applicable to any recognised category of special vehicles, that provision is not to be construed as applying any requirement of those regulations to a vehicle in that category if that requirement may reasonably be regarded, in all the circumstances, as not relevant to the vehicle in question (for example, if the requirement relates to trailers and the vehicle in question is not a trailer).

PART 2

SPECIAL VEHICLES FOR HAULAGE, LIFTING, ENGINEERING AND VEHICLE RECOVERY

4–3834   10. Part 2 vehicles and Part 2 vehicle-combinations: recognised categories and defined terms.   (1) The following are recognised categories of special vehicles—

(a) abnormal indivisible load vehicles;
(b) mobile cranes;
(c) engineering plant;
(d) road recovery vehicles.

(2) A vehicle that falls within any recognised category of special vehicles mentioned in paragraph (1) is referred to in this Order as a Part 2 vehicle.

(3) In this Order, a "Part 2 vehicle-combination" means—

(a) in the case of a road recovery vehicle, a vehicle-combination which consists of one motor vehicle of category N3 together with one trailer of category O4; or

(b) in any other case, a vehicle-combination which consists of, or includes, one motor vehicle (whether or not it is a Part 2 vehicle) together with one trailer that is a Part 2 vehicle.

(4) The categories of vehicles specified in sub-paragraph (a), (b), (c) or (d) of paragraph (1) are defined in Schedules 1 to 4 respectively.

4–3835　11. Part 2 vehicles and Part 2 vehicle-combinations: authorisation requirements.　(1) The authorisation requirements applicable to Part 2 vehicles or Part 2 vehicle-combinations are—

(a) as respects any vehicle or vehicle-combination falling within Schedule 1, 2, 3 or 4, the requirements specified in the Schedule in question; and

(b) as respects all such vehicles or vehicle-combinations, the requirements specified in articles 12 to 18.

(2) But the requirements specified in articles 12 to 17 do not apply to a mobile crane or road recovery vehicle in any case where—

(a) a civil emergency or road traffic accident has occurred;
(b) as a result, there is a danger to the public;
(c) the owner or user of the crane or vehicle has received a request made by the police for the vehicle to be used for the purposes of immediate clearance of an area affected by the emergency or accident;
(d) the crane or vehicle is used on roads within 24 hours of receipt of the request; and
(e) it is not reasonably practicable to comply with the requirements of those articles.

(3) Nothing in this article prevents a motor vehicle which falls within the definition of a mobile crane in paragraph 2 of Schedule 2, but which does not comply in all respects with the authorisation requirements for mobile cranes specified in that Schedule, from complying instead with the authorisation requirements for engineering plant specified in Schedule 3 provided that the motor vehicle in question also falls within the definition of engineering plant in paragraph 2 of that Schedule.

(4) For the purposes of this Order, a motor vehicle that complies with the authorisation requirements for engineering plant in the manner described in paragraph (3) is to be treated as engineering plant.

Length and width of vehicle and projections of load

4–3836　12. Length: police notification and attendants.　(1) Where either of the length limits set out in paragraph (2) or (3) is exceeded in relation to a Part 2 vehicle or Part 2 vehicle-combination, the user of the vehicle or vehicle-combination must—

(a) before the start of any journey, notify in accordance with Schedule 5 the chief officer of police for each area in which the vehicle or vehicle-combination is to be used;
(b) ensure that the vehicle or vehicle-combination is used in accordance with the requirements of that Schedule; and
(c) ensure that the vehicle or vehicle-combination is accompanied during the journey by one or more attendants employed in accordance with Schedule 6.

(2) The first length limit is exceeded where the overall length of any single rigid unit together with the length of any forward or rearward projection of any load carried on the unit exceeds 18.75 metres.

(3) The second length limit is exceeded where the overall length of a Part 2 vehicle-combination exceeds 25.9 metres.

(4) The reference to a single rigid unit is a reference to—

(a) a single vehicle, whether or not included in a Part 2 vehicle-combination; or
(b) any two or more vehicles comprising or included in a Part 2 vehicle-combination which together bear the weight of one or more loads in such a way that, at all times when the vehicles are moving, the longitudinal axis of each vehicle lies in the same vertical plane.

4–3837　13. Forward and rearward projections: police notification.　(1) This article applies where a Part 2 vehicle or Part 2 vehicle-combination is to carry a load and the length of any forward or rearward projection of the load exceeds 3.05 metres.

(2) The user of the Part 2 vehicle or Part 2 vehicle-combination must, unless he has already notified the police under article 12(1)(a)—

(a) before the start of any journey, notify in accordance with Schedule 5 the chief officer of police for each area in which the vehicle or vehicle-combination is to be used; and
(b) ensure that the vehicle or vehicle-combination is used in accordance with the requirements of that Schedule.

4–3838   14. Forward and rearward projections: attendants.   (1) If paragraph (2) or (3) applies, the user of a Part 2 vehicle or Part 2 vehicle-combination must ensure that the vehicle or vehicle-combination is accompanied during the journey by one or more attendants employed in accordance with Schedule 6.

(2) This paragraph applies where a Part 2 vehicle or Part 2 vehicle-combination is carrying a load and the length of any forward projection of the load exceeds 2 metres.

(3) This paragraph applies where a Part 2 vehicle or Part 2 vehicle-combination is carrying a load and the length of any rearward projection of the load exceeds 3.05 metres.

4–3839   15. Width and lateral projections: police notification, Secretary of State notification and attendants.   (1) This article applies to a Part 2 vehicle or vehicle in a Part 2 vehicle-combination in respect of which one or more of the following width limits are exceeded—

(a)   the first width limit is exceeded where the overall width of the vehicle together with the width of any lateral projection or projections of any load carried on it is 3 metres or less but the length of any lateral projection of a load carried on it exceeds 305 millimetres;

(b)   the second width limit is exceeded where the overall width of the vehicle together with the width of any lateral projection or projections of any load carried on it exceeds 3 metres;

(c)   the third width limit is exceeded where the overall width of the vehicle together with the width of any lateral projection or projections of any load carried on it exceeds 3.5 metres;

(d)   the fourth width limit is exceeded where the overall width of the vehicle together with the width of any lateral projection or projections of any load carried on it exceeds 5 metres.

(2) Paragraphs (3), (4) and (5) apply cumulatively.

(3) Where the first or second width limit is exceeded, the user of the vehicle must—

(a)   before the start of any journey, notify in accordance with Schedule 5 the chief officer of police for each area in which the vehicle or vehicle-combination is to be used; and

(b)   ensure that the vehicle is used in accordance with the requirements of that Schedule.

(4) Where the third width limit is exceeded, the user of the vehicle must ensure that the vehicle is accompanied during the journey by one or more attendants employed in accordance with Schedule 6.

(5) Where the fourth width limit is exceeded, the user of the vehicle must—

(a)   before the start of any journey, obtain in accordance with Schedule 7 the written consent of the Secretary of State; and

(b)   ensure that the vehicle is used in accordance with the requirements of that Schedule.

4–3840   16. Visibility and marking of forward, rearward and lateral projections of loads etc.   Schedule 8 (which makes provision as to the visibility and marking of projections exceeding a certain length or width) applies in relation to loads carried on a Part 2 vehicle or Part 2 vehicle-combination.

Weight of vehicle and load

4–3841   17. Weight: police notification and road and bridge authority notification and indemnity.   (1) In a case falling within paragraph (2), the user of a Part 2 vehicle or Part 2 vehicle-combination must before the start of any journey—

(a)   notify in accordance with Part 1 of Schedule 9 the authority (within the meaning of that Schedule) for each road or bridge on which the vehicle or vehicle-combination is to be used; and

(b)   give to each authority an indemnity in the form specified in Part 2 of that Schedule.

(2) A case falls within this paragraph where—

(a)   the total weight of the Part 2 vehicle or Part 2 vehicle-combination (whether it is unladen or wholly or partly laden) exceeds 44,000 kilograms; or

(b)   the vehicle or vehicle-combination does not comply in all respects with—

(i)   the requirements of Schedule 3 to the Authorised Weight Regulations (axle weights); or

(ii)   if that Schedule does not apply to it, the equivalent provisions of the Construction and Use Regulations.

(3) In a case falling within paragraph (4), the user of the Part 2 vehicle or Part 2 vehicle-combination must—

(a)   before the start of any journey, notify in accordance with Schedule 5 the chief officer of police for each area in which the vehicle or vehicle-combination is to be used; and

(b)   ensure that the vehicle is used in accordance with the requirements of that Schedule.

(4) A case falls within this paragraph if the total weight of the Part 2 vehicle or Part 2 vehicle-combination (whether it is unladen or wholly or partly laden) exceeds 80,000 kilograms.

(5) Paragraphs (1) and (3) apply cumulatively.

4–3842   18. Use on bridges.   (1) The driver of a Part 2 vehicle or Part 2 vehicle-combination must not cause or permit any part of his vehicle (or any part of any vehicle in the vehicle-combination he is driving) to enter on a bridge if he knows that the whole or part of another such vehicle or vehicle-combination is already on the bridge or if he could reasonably be expected to ascertain that fact.

(2) Except in circumstances beyond his control, the driver of a Part 2 vehicle or Part 2 vehicle-combination must not cause or permit the Part 2 vehicle, or any vehicle in the vehicle-combination to remain stationary on any bridge.

(3) If a Part 2 vehicle or Part 2 vehicle-combination that falls within article 17(2) or (4) is caused to stop on a bridge for any reason, the driver of the vehicle or vehicle-combination must ensure—

(*a*) that the vehicle or vehicle-combination is moved clear of the bridge as soon as practicable and

(*b*) that no concentrated load is applied to the surface on that part of the road carried by the bridge.

(4) But where the action described in paragraph (3)(*a*) or (*b*) is not practicable and it becomes necessary to apply any concentrated load to the road surface by means of jacks, rollers or other similar means, the driver or other person in charge of the vehicle or vehicle-combination must—

(*a*) before the load is applied to the road surface, seek advice from the authority (within the meaning of Schedule 9) responsible for the maintenance of the bridge about the use of spreader plates to reduce the possibility of damage caused by the application of the load, and

(*b*) ensure that no concentrated load is applied without using spreader plates in accordance with any advice received.

(5) References to the driver of a Part 2 vehicle-combination are references to the driver of the foremost motor vehicle in the vehicle-combination.

PART 3
SPECIAL VEHICLES FOR AGRICULTURE

4–3843   19. Agricultural vehicles: recognised categories and defined terms.   (1) The following are recognised categories of special vehicles—

(*a*) agricultural motor vehicles;
(*b*) agricultural trailers;
(*c*) agricultural trailed appliances.

(2) A vehicle that falls within any recognised category of special vehicles mentioned in paragraph (1) is referred to in this Order as a special type agricultural vehicle.

(3) In this Order—

"agricultural motor vehicle" means a motor vehicle (not being a dual purpose vehicle) which—

(*a*) is constructed or adapted for use off-road for the purpose of agriculture, horticulture or forestry; and

(*b*) is primarily used for one or more of those purposes;

"agricultural trailer" has the same meaning as in the Construction and Use Regulations; and
"agricultural trailed appliance" has the same meaning as in the Construction and Use Regulations.

(4) In the definition of "agricultural motor vehicle" in paragraph (3), "dual purpose vehicle" has the same meaning as in the Construction and Use Regulations.

4–3844   20. Agricultural vehicles: authorisation requirements.   The authorisation requirements applicable to special type agricultural vehicles are—

(*a*) the requirements specified in articles 21 to 27;
(*b*) the Construction and Use Regulations, apart from—

(i) regulation 8 (width);
(ii) paragraph (1) of regulation 75, in so far as that paragraph relates to item 13 or 15 of the Table referred to in it (maximum permitted laden weight of track-laying motor vehicles); and
(iii) regulation 82 (restrictions on vehicles carrying wide or long loads or having fixed appliance or apparatus);

(*c*) the Authorised Weight Regulations; and
(*d*) the Lighting Regulations.

4–3845   21. General requirements as to construction and use.   (1) A special type agricultural vehicle that is a track-laying motor vehicle may be used on roads only if the tracks operate on rubber or an alternative composite material that does not damage the road surface.

(2) The overall width of a special type agricultural vehicle together with the width of any lateral projection or projections of any load carried on it must not exceed 4.3 metres.

(3) For the purposes of paragraph (2)—

(*a*) the overall width of a special type agricultural vehicle that is a motor vehicle towing an agricultural trailer or agricultural trailed appliance in an offset manner, is to be taken as the overall width of the motor vehicle and trailer (or trailed appliance) measured as if they were one vehicle; and

(*b*) where any agricultural implement is rigidly (but not permanently) mounted on a special type agricultural vehicle, any part of the implement that extends beyond a side of the vehicle is to be treated as a lateral projection, regardless of whether any part of the weight of the implement is transmitted to the surface of the road otherwise than by the wheels or tracks of the vehicle.

(4) The gross weight of a special type agricultural motor vehicle that is a track-laying vehicle, together with the weight of any load carried on it, must not exceed 30,000 kilograms.

(5) All spikes, cutting blades or other protruding sharp appliances that are fitted to or mounted on a special type agricultural vehicle must be removed or effectively guarded so that no danger is caused (or likely to be caused) to any person.

(6) A special type agricultural vehicle must not at any time travel at speeds exceeding —

(a) 20 miles per hour in any case where the overall width of the vehicle is more than 2.55 metres but less than 3.5 metres;

(b) 12 miles per hour in any case where the overall width is 3.5 metres or more.

4–3846   22. Restrictions on towing of trailers.   (1) This article applies in any of the following cases to a special type agricultural vehicle that is a motor vehicle:

CASE 1

Where the special type agricultural vehicle has an overall width exceeding 3 metres.

CASE 2

Where a special type agricultural vehicle is towing an agricultural trailer, or agricultural trailed appliance, in an offset manner and the overall width of the two vehicles (measured as if they were one) exceeds 3 metres.

CASE 3

Where a special type agricultural vehicle is towing an agricultural trailer, or agricultural trailed appliance, otherwise than in an offset manner and the overall width of either (or both) of the vehicles exceeds 3 metres.

(2) The special type agricultural vehicle must not either tow any trailer (where the vehicle falls within Case 1) or tow any other trailer (where the vehicle falls within Case 2 or 3), apart from a trailer that is of a description permitted by paragraph (3).

(3) The trailers permitted by this paragraph are —

(a) a two wheeled trailer used solely for the carriage of equipment for use on the towing vehicle;

(b) an agricultural trailed appliance; or

(c) an unladen trailer specially designed for use with the towing vehicle when it is harvesting.

4–3847   23. Forward and rearward projections: police notification, Secretary of State notification and attendants.   (1) Paragraphs (2), (3) and (4) apply cumulatively.

(2) Where a special type agricultural vehicle is to carry a load and the length of any forward or rearward projection of the load exceeds 4 metres, the user of the vehicle must —

(a) before the start of any journey, notify in accordance with Schedule 5 the chief officer of police for each area in which the special type agricultural vehicle is to be used; and

(b) ensure that the vehicle is used in accordance with the requirements of that Schedule.

(3) Where a special type agricultural vehicle is carrying a load and the length of any forward or rearward projection of the load exceeds 6 metres, the user of the vehicle must ensure that the vehicle is accompanied during any journey by one or more attendants employed in accordance with Schedule 6.

(4) Where the length of any rearward projection of a load exceeds 12 metres, the user of the vehicle must —

(a) before the start of any journey, obtain in accordance with Schedule 7 the written consent of the Secretary of State; and

(b) ensure that the vehicle is used in accordance with the requirements of that Schedule.

(5) Where any agricultural implement is rigidly (but not permanently) mounted on a special type agricultural vehicle —

(a) any part of the implement that extends forwards beyond the foremost point of the vehicle is to be treated as a forward projection; and

(b) any part of the implement that extends rearwards beyond the rearmost point of the vehicle is to be treated as a rearward projection;

regardless of whether any part of the weight of the implement is transmitted to the surface of the road otherwise than by the wheels or tracks of the vehicle.

(6) In determining for the purposes of paragraph (5) the foremost or rearmost point of a special type agricultural vehicle, any part of the agricultural implement is to be disregarded.

4–3848   24. Width: police notification and attendants.   (1) "Width", in relation to a special type agricultural vehicle, means whichever is the greater of—

(a) the overall width of the vehicle; and

(b) the overall width of the vehicle together with the width of any lateral projection or projections of a load carried on it.

(2) Paragraphs (4) and (5) apply cumulatively.

(3) Paragraph (4) applies where the width of a special type agricultural vehicle exceeds 3 metres and—

(a) there is a speed limit of 40 miles per hour or less on any road on which the vehicle is to be used; or

(b) the length of the journey to be made by the vehicle exceeds 5 miles.

(4) The user of the vehicle must—

(*a*) before the start of any journey, notify in accordance with Schedule 5 the chief officer of police for each area in which the special type agricultural vehicle is to be used; and

(*b*) ensure that the vehicle is used in accordance with the requirements of that Schedule.

(5) Where the width of the vehicle exceeds 3.5 metres, the user of the vehicle must ensure that the vehicle is accompanied during any journey by one or more attendants employed in accordance with Schedule 6.

4–3849   25. Visibility and marking of forward, rearward and lateral projections.   Schedule 8 (which makes provision as to the visibility and marking of projections exceeding a certain length or width) applies in relation to loads carried on a special type agricultural vehicle.

4–3850   26. Track-laying agricultural motor vehicles: road and bridge authority notification and indemnity.   (1) This article applies to a special type agricultural vehicle that is a track-laying motor vehicle that does not comply with paragraph (1) of regulation 75 of the Construction and Use Regulations, in so far as that paragraph relates to item 13 or 15 of the Table referred to in it (maximum permitted laden weight of track-laying motor vehicles).

(2) Before the start of any journey, the user of the vehicle must—

(*a*) notify in accordance with Part 1 of Schedule 9 the authority (within the meaning of that Schedule) for each road or bridge on which vehicle is to be used; and

(*b*) give to each authority an indemnity in the form specified in Part 2 of that Schedule.

4–3851   27. Track-laying agricultural motor vehicles: use on bridges.   (1) This article applies to a special type agricultural vehicle to which article 26 applies.

(2) If the special type agricultural vehicle is caused to stop on a bridge for any reason, the driver of the vehicle must ensure—

(*a*) that the vehicle is moved clear of the bridge as soon as practicable; and

(*b*) that no concentrated load is applied to the surface on that part of the road carried by the bridge.

(3) But where the action described in paragraph (2)(*a*) or (*b*) is not practicable and it becomes necessary to apply any concentrated load to the road surface by means of jacks, rollers or other similar means, the driver or other person in charge of the vehicle must—

(*a*) before the load is applied to the road surface, seek advice from the authority (within the meaning of Schedule 9) responsible for the maintenance of the bridge about the use of spreader plates to reduce the possibility of damage caused by the application of the load; and

(*b*) ensure that no concentrated load is applied without using spreader plates in accordance with any advice received.

PART 4

OTHER SPECIAL VEHICLES REQUIRING NOTIFICATIONS OR ATTENDANTS

Vehicles carrying loads of exceptional width

4–3852   28. Motor vehicles or trailers carrying loads of exceptional width: recognised category.   (1) Motor vehicles or trailers that are used for, or in connection with, the carriage of a load exceptional width are a recognised category of special vehicles.

(2) A vehicle carries a load of exceptional width where the overall width of the vehicle carrying a load, together with the width of any lateral projection or projections of the load, exceeds 4.3 metres.

4–3853   29. Motor vehicles or trailers carrying loads of exceptional width: authorisation requirements.   The authorisation requirements applicable to vehicles falling within the recognised category of special vehicles mentioned in article 28(1) are—

(*a*) the requirements specified in articles 30 and 31;

(*b*) the Construction and Use Regulations, apart from regulation 82(1) and (2);

(*c*) the Authorised Weight Regulations; and

(*d*) the Lighting Regulations.

4–3854   30. Motor vehicles or trailers carrying loads of exceptional width: restrictions on width and speed.   (1) The overall width of a vehicle falling within the recognised category of special vehicles mentioned in article 28(1), together with the width of any lateral projection or projections of the load carried on it, must not exceed 6.1 metres.

(2) The vehicle must not travel at speeds exceeding—

(*a*) 40 miles per hour on a motorway;

(*b*) 35 miles per hour on a dual carriageway;

(*c*) 30 miles per hour on any other road.

(3) Nothing in this article is to be taken to authorise travel at any speed in excess of any speed restriction imposed by or under any other enactment.

4–3855   31. Motor vehicles or trailers carrying loads of exceptional width: requirements as to width.   (1) "Width", in relation to a vehicle falling within the recognised category of special vehicles mentioned in article 28(1), means the overall width of the vehicle together with the width of any lateral projection or projections of the load carried on it.

(2) Paragraphs (3) and (4) apply cumulatively.

(3) The user of any vehicle falling within the recognised category of special vehicles mentioned in article 28(1) must—

(a) before the start of any journey, notify in accordance with Schedule 5 the chief officer of police for each area in which the vehicle is to be used;

(b) ensure that the vehicle is used in accordance with the requirements of that Schedule; and

(c) ensure that the vehicle is accompanied during the journey by one or more attendants employed in accordance with Schedule 6.

(4) Where the width of the vehicle exceeds 5 metres, the user of the vehicle must—

(a) before the start of any journey obtain the written consent of the Secretary of State in accordance with Schedule 7; and

(b) ensure that the vehicle is used in accordance with the requirements of that Schedule.

Local excavation vehicles

4–3856   32. Local excavation vehicles: recognised category.   (1) Local excavation vehicles are a recognised category of special vehicles.

(2) Local excavation vehicles are defined in paragraph 1 of Schedule 10.

4–3857   33. Local excavation vehicles: authorisation requirements.   The authorisation requirements applicable to local excavation vehicles are—

(a) the requirements specified in articles 34 and 35; and

(b) the requirements specified in Schedule 10.

4–3858   34. Local excavation vehicles: requirements as to width.   (1) "Width", in relation to a local excavation vehicle, means whichever is the greater of—

(a) the overall width of the vehicle; and

(b) the overall width of the vehicle together with the width of any lateral projection or projections of a load carried on it.

(2) Paragraphs (3) to (5) apply cumulatively.

(3) Where the width of a local excavation vehicle exceeds 3 metres, the user of the vehicle must—

(a) before the start of any journey, notify in accordance with Schedule 5 the chief officer of police for each area in which the vehicle is to be used; and

(b) ensure that the vehicle is used in accordance with the requirements of that Schedule.

(4) Where the width of the vehicle exceeds 3.5 metres, the user of the vehicle must ensure that the vehicle is accompanied during the journey by one or more attendants employed in accordance with Schedule 6.

(5) Where the width of the vehicle exceeds 5 metres, the user of the vehicle must—

(a) before the start of any journey obtain the written consent of the Secretary of State in accordance with Schedule 7; and

(b) ensure that the vehicle is used in accordance with the requirements of that Schedule.

4–3859   35. Local excavation vehicles: requirements as to weight.   (1) This article applies to a local excavation vehicle—

(a) which does not comply with the requirements of the Authorised Weight Regulations; or

(b) if those Regulations do not apply to it, which does not comply with the requirements of regulations 75 to 79 of the Construction and Use Regulations.

(2) Before the start of any journey, the user of the vehicle must—

(a) notify in accordance with Part 1 of Schedule 9 the authority (within the meaning of that Schedule) for each road or bridge on which vehicle is to be used; and

(b) give to each authority an indemnity in the form specified in Part 2 of that Schedule.

Vehicles for tests, trials or non-UK use etc

4–3860   36. Vehicles for tests, trials or non-UK use etc: recognised category.   (1) The following are recognised categories of special vehicles—

(a) any motor vehicle or trailer which is constructed for use outside the United Kingdom;

(b) any type of motor vehicle or trailer which is constructed for use outside the United Kingdom;

(c) any new or improved type of motor vehicle or trailer which is constructed for tests or trials;

(d) any motor vehicle or trailer which is equipped with new or improved equipment;

(e) any motor vehicle or trailer which is equipped with new or improved types of equipment.

(2) Paragraph (1) does not include—

(a) any motor vehicle or trailer which is not a wheeled vehicle; or

(b) any motor vehicle or trailer which is, or forms part of, a recognised category of special vehicles specified in sub-paragraph (a), (b), (c) or (d) of article 10(1).

4–3861 **37. Vehicles for tests, trials or non-UK use etc: authorisation requirements.** The authorisation requirements applicable to vehicles falling within any of the recognised categories of special vehicles mentioned in article 36(1) are—

    (a) the requirements specified in articles 38 to 40; and

    (b) the requirements specified in Schedule 11.

4–3862 **38. Vehicles for tests, trials or non-UK use etc: requirements as to length.** (1) This article applies to—

    (a) a vehicle falling within any of the recognised categories of special vehicles mentioned in article 36(1), where the overall length of the vehicle exceeds the overall length permitted for that description of vehicle under regulation 7 of the Construction and Use Regulations; and

    (b) a vehicle-combination, being a combination that includes one or more motor vehicles or trailers that fall within any of those recognised categories of special vehicles, where the overall length of the vehicle-combination exceeds the overall length for that combination permitted under regulation 7 of the Construction and Use Regulations.

    (2) The user of the vehicle or vehicle-combination must—

    (a) before the start of any journey, notify in accordance with Schedule 5 the chief officer of police for each area in which the vehicle or vehicle-combination is to be used; and

    (b) ensure that the vehicle or vehicle-combination is used in accordance with the requirements of that Schedule.

4–3863 **39. Vehicles for tests, trials or non-UK use etc: requirements as to width.** (1) "Width", in relation to a vehicle falling within any of the recognised categories of special vehicles mentioned in article 36(1), means whichever is the greater of—

    (a) the overall width of the vehicle; and

    (b) the overall width of the vehicle together with the width of any lateral projection or projections of a load carried on it.

    (2) Where the width of a vehicle falling within any of the recognised categories of special vehicles mentioned in article 36(1) exceeds 3 metres, the user of the vehicle must—

    (a) before the start of any journey, notify in accordance with Schedule 5 the chief officer of police for each area in which the vehicle is to be used; and

    (b) ensure that the vehicle is used in accordance with the requirements of that Schedule.

4–3864 **40. Vehicles for tests, trials or non-UK use etc: requirements as to weight.** (1) This article applies to a vehicle which is, or a vehicle-combination which includes, a vehicle falling within any of the recognised categories of special vehicles mentioned in article 36(1) and which—

    (a) does not comply with the requirements of the Authorised Weight Regulations; or

    (b) if those Regulations do not apply to it, does not comply with the requirements of regulations 75 to 79 of the Construction and Use Regulations.

    (2) Before the start of any journey, the user of the vehicle or vehicle-combination must—

    (a) notify in accordance with Part 1 of Schedule 9 the authority (within the meaning of that Schedule) for each road or bridge on which vehicle or vehicle-combination is to be used; and

    (b) give to each authority an indemnity in the form specified in Part 2 of that Schedule.

Track-laying vehicles

4–3865 **41. Track-laying vehicles: recognised category.** (1) Track-laying motor vehicles or trailers are a recognised category of special vehicles.

    (2) Paragraph (1) does not include any track-laying vehicle that falls within any other recognised category of special vehicles.

4–3866 **42. Track-laying vehicles: authorisation requirements.** The authorisation requirements applicable to vehicles falling within the recognised category of special vehicles mentioned in article 41(1) are—

    (a) the requirements specified in articles 43 and 44;

    (b) regulation 100 of the Construction and Use Regulations (maintenance and use so as not to be a danger);

    (c) the Authorised Weight Regulations; and

    (d) the Lighting Regulations.

4–3867 **43. Track-laying vehicles: restrictions on use.** (1) A vehicle falling within the recognised category of special vehicles mentioned in article 41 (1) may only be used for—

    (a) demonstration;

    (b) proceeding to the nearest suitable railway station for conveyance to a port for shipment; or

    (c) where no suitable railway facilities are available, proceeding to a port for shipment.

    (2) The vehicle must not be used for hire or reward.

(3) The vehicle must not be used in such a way as to cause a danger of injury to any person by reason of—

(a) the condition of the vehicle, its accessories or equipment;
(b) the purpose for which it is used;
(c) the number of passengers carried by it;
(d) the manner in which such passengers are carried;
(e) the weight, position or distribution of any load carried on the vehicle; or
(f) the manner in which any such load is secured.

4–3868   44. Track-laying vehicles: consent of road authorities.   (1) Before the start of any journey, the user of a vehicle falling within the recognised category of special vehicles mentioned in article 41(1) must obtain from the road authority for each road on which the vehicle is to be used that authority's written consent to the vehicle being used on roads for which it is responsible.

(2) "Road authority", in relation to any road, means the highway authority for that road.

Straddle carriers

4–3869   45. Straddle carriers: recognised category.   Straddle carriers are a recognised category of special vehicles.

4–3870   46. Straddle carriers: authorisation requirements.   The authorisation requirements for straddle carriers are—

(a) the requirements specified in article 47;
(b) the Construction and Use Regulations apart from—

(i) regulation 7 (length);
(ii) regulation 8 (width);
(iii) regulation 11 (overhang);
(iv) regulation 16(4) (braking systems);
(v) regulation 18(1A) to (9) (braking; maintenance and efficiency);
(vi) regulation 22 (springs and resilient material);
(vii) regulation 66 (plates);

(c) the Authorised Weight Regulations; and
(d) the Lighting Regulations.

4–3871   47. Straddle carriers: restrictions on use, speed and width.   (1) A straddle carrier may only be used—

(a) for demonstration;
(b) for delivery on sale;
(c) for proceeding to, or returning from, a manufacturer or repairer for construction, repair or overhaul; or
(d) if paragraph (2) applies to it, for proceeding between different parts of the same private premises or between private premises in the immediate neighbourhood.

(2) This paragraph applies to a straddle carrier—

(a) that does not comply with regulation 11 of the Construction and Use Regulations (overhang); but
(b) that does comply with regulations 8 (width) and 22 (springs and resilient material) of those Regulations.

(3) Nothing in this Order is to be taken to authorise use on roads beyond a radius of three miles drawn around the outermost perimeter of any work site on private premises.

(4) A straddle carrier must not carry any load.

(5) But a straddle carrier—

(a) may carry its own necessary gear and equipment; and
(b) may be laden in the course of any journey permitted under paragraph (1)(d).

(6) A straddle carrier must not travel at speeds exceeding 12 miles per hour.

(7) The overall width of a straddle carrier must not exceed 3 metres.

4–3872   48. Straddle carriers: requirements as to length.   (1) This article applies to a straddle carrier where its overall length, together with any forward or rearward projection of a load to be carried on it exceeds 9.2 metres.

(2) The user of the straddle carrier must—

(a) before the start of any journey, notify in accordance with Schedule 5 the chief officer of police for each area in which the vehicle or vehicle-combination is to be used; and
(b) ensure that the vehicle is used in accordance with the requirements of that Schedule.

PART 5
MISCELLANEOUS SPECIAL VEHICLES

4–3873   49. Vehicles with moveable platforms.   (1) Vehicles fitted with a moveable platform are a recognised category of special vehicles.

(2) The authorisation requirements applicable to vehicles falling within the recognised category of special vehicles mentioned in paragraph (1) are—

    (*a*) the requirements specified in paragraphs (3) to (5);

    (*b*) the Construction and Use Regulations, apart from—

        (i)   regulations 7, 8 and 11 (length, width and overhang);

        (ii) regulation 20 (wheels and tracks);

        (iii) regulation 23 (wheel loads);

        (iv) regulation 82 (restrictions on wide/long loads or fixed appliances);

    (*c*) the Authorised Weight Regulations; and

    (*d*) the Lighting Regulations.

(3) The special equipment of the vehicle must be retracted at all times except when the vehicle is at a place where it is being used to facilitate overhead working.

(4) At all times when the special equipment of the vehicle is retracted, the provisions of the Construction and Use Regulations mentioned in paragraph (2)(*b*)(i) must be complied with (except that a vehicle that is a locomotive is permitted not to comply with regulation 11 (overhang)).

(5) Any jacks forming part of the vehicle's special equipment which project from the sides of the vehicle must be made clearly visible to any person who may be using the road within a reasonable distance of the vehicle.

(6) In this article—

"moveable platform" means a platform that is attached to, and may be moved by means of, an extensible boom; and

"special equipment", in relation to a vehicle falling within the recognised category of special vehicles mentioned in paragraph (1), means a moveable platform, the apparatus for moving the platform and any jacks fitted to the vehicle for stabilising it whilst the vehicle is in use.

4–3874   50. Pedestrian-controlled road maintenance vehicles.   (1) Pedestrian-controlled road maintenance vehicles that are not constructed or used to carry a driver or passenger are a recognised category of special vehicles.

(2) The authorisation requirements applicable to vehicles falling within the recognised category of special vehicles mentioned in paragraph (1) are—

    (*a*) the requirements specified in paragraphs (3) and (4);

    (*b*) the Construction and Use Regulations, apart from—

        (i)   regulation 16 (braking systems);

        (ii) regulation 18(1A) to (9) (maintenance and efficiency of brakes);

        (iii) regulation 23 (wheel loads);

        (iv) regulation 61 (emission of smoke);

    (*c*) the Authorised Weight Regulations; and

    (*d*) the Lighting Regulations.

(3) The weight of the vehicle (whether laden or unladen) must not exceed 410 kilograms.

(4) The vehicle must be equipped with—

    (*a*) an efficient braking system capable of bringing the vehicle to a standstill and of being set so as to hold the vehicle stationary; or

    (*b*) if the vehicle does not have a braking system, sufficient other means capable of achieving the same results.

(5) "Road maintenance vehicle" means a motor vehicle that is specially constructed or adapted for the purposes of carrying out one or more of the following operations—

    (*a*) gritting roads;

    (*b*) laying road markings;

    (*c*) clearing frost, snow or ice from roads; or

    (*d*) any other work of maintaining roads.

4–3875   51. Motor vehicles used for cutting grass or trimming hedges.   (1) Motor cutters are a recognised category of special vehicles.

(2) The authorisation requirements applicable to motor cutters are—

    (*a*) the requirements specified in paragraphs (3) to (5);

    (*b*) the Construction and Use Regulations, apart from—

        (i)   regulation 8 (width);

        (ii) regulation 82(11) (restrictions on wide/long loads or fixed appliances);

    (*c*) the Authorised Weight Regulations; and

    (*d*) the Lighting Regulations.

(3) The overall width of the motor cutter, together with any equipment mounted on it, must not exceed 2.55 metres.

(4) All cutting or trimming blades that form part of the machinery fitted to, or mounted on, the motor cutter must be effectively guarded so that no danger is caused (or is likely to be caused) to any person.

(5) But paragraphs (3) and (4) do not apply at any time when the motor cutter is cutting grass or trimming hedges.

(6) "Motor cutters" means motor vehicles that are specially constructed to—

    (*a*) be used as grass cutters and hedge trimmers; and

    (*b*) be controlled by a person other than a pedestrian.

4-3876   52. Trailers used for cutting grass or trimming hedges. (1) Cutter trailers are a recognised category of special vehicles.

(2) The authorisation requirements applicable to vehicles falling within the recognised category of special vehicles mentioned in paragraph (1) are—

(a)   the requirements specified in paragraphs (3) to (7);
(b)   the following provisions of the Construction and Use Regulations—

(i)   regulation 27 (condition and maintenance of tyres);
(ii)   regulation 100 (maintenance and use so as not to be a danger);

(c)   the Authorised Weight Regulations; and
(d)   the Lighting Regulations.

(3) The overall width of—

(a)   the motor vehicle towing the cutter trailer;
(b)   the cutter trailer; or
(c)   where a cutter trailer is being towed by a motor vehicle in an offset manner, the two vehicles measured as if they were one vehicle;

must not at any time exceed 2.6 metres.

(4) All cutting or trimming blades that form part of the machinery fitted to, or mounted on, the cutter trailer must be effectively guarded so that no danger is caused (or is likely to be caused) to any person.

(5) But—

(a)   the restrictions on width applicable to vehicles falling within paragraph (3)(b) or (3)(c); and
(b)   paragraph (4);

do not apply at any time when the cutter trailer is cutting grass or trimming hedges.

(6) The unladen weight of a cutter trailer must not exceed—

(a)   1020 kilograms in any case where it is towed by a locomotive, motor tractor or heavy motor car;
(b)   815 kilograms in any other case.

(7) A cutter trailer must not travel at speeds exceeding 20 miles per hour.

(8) "Cutter trailer" means a trailer that is specially constructed or adapted for use as a grass cutter and hedge trimmer.

4-3877   53. Operational military vehicles. (1) Operational military vehicles are a recognised category of special vehicles in any case where compliance with any regulations made under section 41 of the Road Traffic Act 1988 by any such vehicle would directly compromise the vehicle's operational capability.

(2) The authorisation requirements applicable to operational military vehicles are—

(a)   the requirements specified in paragraphs (3) to (5); and
(b)   the provisions of—

(i)   the Construction and Use Regulations;
(ii)   the Authorised Weight Regulations; and
(iii)   the Lighting Regulations;

apart from the provisions specified, in respect of the vehicle in question, in the certificate required by paragraph (3).

(3) An operational military vehicle must be certified by the Secretary of State as being a vehicle, or type of vehicle, which for operational reasons cannot comply in all respects with such of the regulations mentioned in paragraph (1) as are specified in the certificate.

(4) An operational military vehicle must be the property of, or under the control of—

(a)   the Secretary of State;
(b)   a procurement contractor; or
(c)   a procurement sub-contractor.

(5) In a case falling within paragraph (4)(b) or (c), the procurement contractor or procurement sub-contractor must, before any particular vehicle or type of vehicle is first used on roads, obtain from the Secretary of State written permission for such use.

(6) "Operational military vehicles" means any motor vehicle or trailer that is intended for—

(a)   operational use for military action or the carrying out of a strategic, tactical, service or administrative military mission, the process of carrying on combat, including movement, supply, attack, defence and manoeuvres needed to gain the objectives of any battle or campaign or use for military support to the civil community;
(b)   training in connection with such operational use;
(c)   the carrying or recovery of vehicles or equipment in connection with such operational use or training.

(7) "Procurement contractor", in relation to an operational military vehicle, means a person who, under a contract with the Secretary of State, is engaged in the design, manufacture or delivery of the vehicle with a view to its supply to the Secretary of State or to his direction.

(8) "Procurement sub-contractor", in relation to an operational military vehicle, means a person—

(a)   who has (directly or indirectly) entered into any kind of arrangement with a person who is a procurement contractor in relation to the vehicle; and

(b) who is, as a result, responsible for the performance of any of the procurement contractor's obligations under the contract mentioned in paragraph (7).

4–3878   54. Track-laying vehicles belonging to Royal National Lifeboat Institution.   (1) RNLI track-laying vehicles are a recognised category of special vehicles.

(2) The authorisation requirements applicable to RNLI track-laying vehicles are—

(a) the requirement specified in paragraph (3); and
(b) regulation 100 of the Construction and Use Regulations (maintenance and use so as not to be a danger).

(3) The vehicle may only be used on roads either—

(a) for the purpose of towing lifeboats; or
(b) in connection with the launching of lifeboats.

(4) "RNLI track-laying vehicle" means any track-laying motor vehicle or track-laying trailer that is the property of the Royal National Lifeboat Institution.

4–3879   55. Highway testing vehicles.   (1) Highway testing vehicles are a recognised category of special vehicles.

(2) The authorisation requirement applicable to highway testing vehicles is regulation 100 (maintenance and use so as not to be a danger) of the Construction and Use Regulations.

(3) "Highway testing vehicle" means any motor vehicle or trailer that is used in, or in connection with, the conduct of experiments or trials of roads or bridges as permitted under section 283 of the Highways Act 1980.

4–3880   56. Vehicles propelled by natural gas.   (1) Vehicles propelled by compressed natural gas are a recognised category of special vehicles.

(2) The authorisation requirements applicable to vehicles falling within the recognised category of special vehicles mentioned in paragraph (1) are the requirements specified in Schedule 12.

4–3881

Article 10(4) and 11(1)(a)   SCHEDULE 1
ABNORMAL INDIVISIBLE LOAD VEHICLES

PART 1
DEFINED TERMS

General

1. In this Schedule—

"AILV" means an abnormal indivisible load vehicle within the meaning of paragraph 3;
"AILV-combination" means a combination of two or more vehicles which includes an AILV;
"Council Directive 71/320/EEC" means the Council Directive approximating the laws of the Member States relating to the braking devices of certain categories of motor vehicles and their trailers; and
"semi-trailer" has the same meaning as in the Construction and Use Regulations.

Meaning of abnormal indivisible load

2. In this Order "abnormal indivisible load" means a load that cannot without undue expense or risk of damage be divided[1] into two or more loads for the purpose of being carried on a road and that—

(a) on account of its length, width or height, cannot be carried on a motor vehicle of category N3 or a trailer of category O4 (or by a combination of such vehicles) that complies in all respects with Part 2 of the Construction and Use Regulations; or
(b) on account of its weight, cannot be carried on a motor vehicle of category N3 or a trailer of category O4 (or by a combination of such vehicles) that complies in all respects with—
    (i) the Authorised Weight Regulations (or, if those Regulations do not apply, the equivalent provisions in Part 4 of the Construction and Use Regulations); and
    (ii) Part 2 of the Construction and Use Regulations.

---

1. This means undue expense or risk of damage involved in the operation of dividing, not that it would be more costly or hazardous to carry the load on two vehicles instead of on one (*Sunter Bros Ltd v Arlidge* [1962] 1 All ER 510, 126 JP 159).

Meaning of abnormal indivisible load vehicle (AILV)

3. In this Order "abnormal indivisible load vehicle" means a vehicle of any of the following descriptions—

(a) a motor vehicle of category N3 specially designed and constructed for the carriage of abnormal indivisible loads;
(b) a trailer of category O4 specially designed and constructed for the carriage of abnormal indivisible loads;
(c) a locomotive specially designed and constructed to tow trailers falling within sub-paragraph (b); or
(d) a motor vehicle of category N3 which is not constructed itself to carry a load but which is specially designed and constructed to tow trailers falling within sub-paragraph (b).

Category 1, 2 or 3 AILVs or AILV-combinations

4. (1) For the purposes of this Schedule, an AILV or AILV-combination falls within Category 1 if—

(a) it does not exceed the restrictions on vehicle or axle weight specified in paragraphs 28 and 29; and
(b) it complies with any other requirements imposed by those paragraphs;

and references to a Category 1 AILV or AILV-combination are to be construed accordingly.

(2) For the purposes of this Schedule, an AILV or AILV-combination falls within Category 2 if—

(a) it does not fall within Category 1;

(b) it does not exceed the restrictions on vehicle, axle or wheel weight specified in paragraphs 30 and 31; and

(c) it complies with any other requirements imposed by those paragraphs;

and references to a Category 2 AILV or AILV-combination are to be construed accordingly.

(3) For the purposes of this Schedule, an AILV or AILV-combination falls within Category 3 if—

(a) it does not fall within Category 1 or 2;

(b) it does not exceed the restrictions on vehicle, axle or wheel weight specified in paragraphs 32 and 33; and

(c) it complies with any other requirements imposed by those paragraphs;

and references to a Category 3 AILV or AILV-combination are to be construed accordingly.

PART 2

CONSTRUCTION

Wheeled vehicles

5. An AILV must be a wheeled vehicle.

Tyres

6. Every wheel of an AILV must be fitted with a pneumatic tyre.

Braking requirements

7. Paragraphs 8 to 12 apply to any AILV or AILV-combination which—

(a) falls within Category 2 or 3; and

(b) was manufactured on or after 1st October 1989.

8. (1) An AILV or AILV-combination must have a braking system that complies with the construction, fitting and performance requirements specified in sub-paragraph (2).

(2) The construction, fitting and performance requirements are those applicable to motor vehicles of category N3 and trailers of category O4 (according to the configuration of the AILV or AILV-combination) which are set out—

(a) in Annexes I, II and VII to Council Directive 71/320/EEC; and

(b) if appropriate, in Annexes III, IV, V, VI and X to that Directive.

(3) In their application to an AILV or AILV-combination, the requirements specified in sub-paragraph (2) are subject to the modifications in paragraphs 9 to 12.

9. (1) The following modifications apply for the purposes of each Type O test conducted in accordance with Annex II to Council Directive 71/320/EEC.

(2) References to a laden vehicle are to be taken to be references to a vehicle laden with the maximum technically permissible mass specified by the manufacturer for the vehicle speed specified for the test.

(3) For a trailer that is designed and constructed for use as part of an AILV-combination falling within Category 3—

(a) where X (stated in the Directive as being a percentage of the force corresponding to the maximum mass carried by the wheels of the stationary vehicle) is specified in paragraph 2.2.1.2.1 of Annex II as having the values of 45 or 50, X is to be taken to have the value of 30; and

(b) where the test speed is specified in that paragraph as 60km/h, the test speed is to be taken to be 48km/h.

(4) In relation to a towing vehicle of category N3 that is designed and constructed for use as part of an AILV-combination falling within Category 3—

(a) if the performance of a service braking device is determined by measuring the stopping distance in relation to the initial speed, the stopping distance in paragraph 2.1.1.1.1 of Annex II is to be taken to be—

$$0.15v + (v^2 / 77.5)$$

(b) if the performance of the service braking device is determined by measuring the reaction time and the mean deceleration, the mean braking deceleration at normal engine speed in paragraph 2.1.1.1.1 of Annex II is to be taken to be at least 3 m/s²;

(c) if the performance of a secondary braking device is determined by measuring the stopping distance in relation to the initial speed, the stopping distance in paragraph 2.1.2.1 of Annex II is to be taken to be—

$$0.15v + (v^2 / 37.5)$$

(d) if the performance of the secondary braking device is determined by measuring the reaction time and the mean deceleration, the mean braking deceleration in paragraph 2.1.2.1 of Annex II is to be taken to be at least 1.45 m/s².

10. (1) The requirements of paragraphs 2.2.1.22 and 2.2.2.13 of Annex I to Council Directive 71/320/EEC do not apply.

(2) The requirements of paragraphs 1.1.4.2 and 1.4 of Annex II to Council Directive 71/320/EEC do not apply.

(3) In Annex I to Council Directive 71/320/EEC—

(a) in paragraph 2.2.1.23 the words "not mentioned in item 2.2.1.22 above" do not apply; and

(b) in paragraph 2.2.2.14 the words "not mentioned in item 2.2.2.13 above" do not apply.

11. For the purposes of Type I tests conducted, in accordance with paragraph 1.3 of Annex II to Council Directive 71/320/EEC, on a vehicle that is designed and constructed for use as part of an AILV-combination falling within Category 3, the reference to a laden vehicle is to be taken to be a reference to a vehicle laden with the heaviest weight possible without the sum of the weights transmitted to the road surface by all the wheels of any axle exceeding 12,500 kilograms.

12. The requirements of paragraph 2.1.3.2 of Annex II to Council Directive 71/320/EEC do not apply if wheel chocks are provided with the AILV or AILV-combination and the wheel chocks are—

(a) suitable and sufficient;

(b) readily accessible; and

(c) capable, when used in conjunction with any parking brakes fitted to the vehicle, of holding the vehicle stationary when loaded to its maximum mass on a gradient of 12%.

PART 3
PLATES AND SIGNS

Plates

13. (1) An AILV falling within Category 2 or 3 must be equipped with a plate that is—

(a) securely fixed to the vehicle in a conspicuous and readily accessible position;
(b) marked clearly with the words "SPECIAL TYPES USE"; and
(c) indelibly marked with letters and figures, not less than 4 millimetres high, containing the information specified in sub-paragraph (2).

(2) For each of the speeds listed in paragraph (a) to (e), the plate must indicate each of the relevant maximum weights at which, in the opinion of the manufacturer of the vehicle, the AILV may be used when travelling on roads at or below the speed in question—

(a) 20 miles per hour;
(b) 25 miles per hour;
(c) 30 miles per hour;
(d) 35 miles per hour;
(e) 40 miles per hour.

(3) The relevant maximum weights are—

(a) in the case of an AILV that is a motor vehicle—

(i) the maximum axle weight for each axle (within the meaning of the note to item 6 of Part 1 of Schedule 8 to the Construction and Use Regulations);
(ii) the maximum gross weight (within the meaning of the note to item 7 of that Part of that Schedule); and
(iii) the maximum train weight (within the meaning of the note to item 8 of that Part of that Schedule);

(b) in the case of an AILV that is a trailer—

(i) the maximum weight for each axle (within the meaning of the note to item 4 of Part 2 of Schedule 8 to the Construction and Use Regulations);
(ii) the maximum load to be imposed on the towing vehicle (within the meaning of the note to item 5 of that Part of that Schedule); and
(iii) the maximum gross weight (within the meaning of the note to item 6 of that Part of that Schedule).

(4) This paragraph does not apply to any vehicle that was manufactured before 29th July 1983.

14. Where an AILV-combination consists of two or more modules, each module may be fitted with a separate plate if the information required from the plate in relation to the AILV as a whole can be readily determined from the individual plates.

Signs

15. (1) Each AILV or AILV-combination must be fitted with—

(a) a sign that indicates which of Categories 1, 2 or 3 the AILV or AILV-combination falls into; or
(b) a sign that is approved in connection with vehicles carrying loads of exceptional dimensions by the appropriate authority in another EEA State or in any other country which is a member of the United Nations Economic Commission for Europe.

(2) A sign falling within sub-paragraph (1)(a) must—

(a) be mounted in a clearly visible position on the front of the vehicle (or, in the case of an AILV-combination, on the front of the foremost motor vehicle);
(b) face forwards;
(c) be as near to the vertical plane as possible;
(d) be kept clean and unobscured at all times; and
(e) except as stated in sub-paragraph (3), consist of white letters on a black background in the following format (specifying Category 1, 2 or 3, as appropriate to the vehicle in question)—

(This diagram is currently unavailable. Please see the original.)

(3) The dimensions of the sign specified for the purposes of sub-paragraph (2)(e) may vary up or down by a margin of 5 per cent.

PART 4
CONDITIONS RELATING TO USE

General restrictions

16. An AILV must not be used on roads for, or in connection with, the carriage of any load that may safely be carried on a vehicle (or vehicle-combination) that complies in all respects with the Construction and Use Regulations and the Authorised Weight Regulations.

17. (1) Except as stated in paragraph 19, an AILV that falls within paragraph 3(a) or (b) may be used on roads only for, or in connection with—

(a) the carriage of an abnormal indivisible load; or
(b) the carriage of a load of exceptional width.

(2) Where the overall width of such an AILV exceeds 3 metres, it must not be used for, or in connection with, the carriage of any load except one that can only safely be carried on an AILV with an overall width exceeding 3 metres.

(3) The reference to the carriage of a load of exceptional width is to be construed in accordance with article 28(2).

18. (1) Except as stated in paragraph 19, an AILV that falls within paragraph 3(c) or (d) may be used on roads only for, or in connection with, the towing of another AILV which is a trailer.

(2) Where the overall width of such a towing vehicle exceeds 3 metres, it must not be used unless—

(a) the trailer it is towing has an overall width exceeding 3 metres; and
(b) the load can only safely be carried on such a trailer.

19. At any time when an AILV-combination consisting of two or more modules—

(a) is being used on roads in connection with the carriage of an abnormal indivisible load; but
(b) is not at that time carrying such a load;

the modules may be disassembled into two or more parts so that one part may carry any other.

Restrictions on carriage of multiple loads

20. (1) An AILV or AILV-combination may carry only one abnormal indivisible load at any one time.
(2) But that is subject to paragraphs 21 to 23.
21. (1) If the conditions specified in sub-paragraph (2) are satisfied, an AILV or AILV-combination which falls within Category 1 may carry—

(a) two or more abnormal indivisible loads which are of the same character; or
(b) an abnormal indivisible load together with articles of a character similar to the load.

(2) The conditions are that—

(a) the abnormal indivisible load or loads to be carried cannot, if they were carried separately, safely be carried on a vehicle (or vehicle-combination) that complies in all respects with the Construction and Use Regulations and the Authorised Weight Regulations; and
(b) the AILV or AILV-combination carrying items specified in sub-paragraph (1) does not exceed any of the restrictions on weight specified in paragraph 28 or 29.

(3) Sub-paragraph (1) does not apply to an AILV-combination that falls within Category 1 only by virtue of paragraph 28(3).
22. (1) If the conditions specified in sub-paragraph (2) are satisfied, an AILV or AILV-combination which falls within Category 1 or 2 may carry two or more abnormal indivisible loads if each load is of the same character, loaded at the same place and carried to the same destination.
(2) The conditions are that—

(a) each of the abnormal indivisible loads to be carried cannot, if they were carried separately, safely be carried on a vehicle (or vehicle-combination) that complies in all respects with the Construction and Use Regulations and the Authorised Weight Regulations;
(b) the overall width of any vehicle used does not exceed the width of vehicle necessary to carry the widest single load;
(c) the overall length of the AILV or the AILV-combination does not exceed the length necessary to carry the longest single load;
(d) the AILV or AILV-combination carrying the loads specified in sub-paragraph (1) does not exceed—

    (i) for a Category 1 AILV or AILV-combination, any of the restrictions on weight specified in paragraph 28 or 29;
    (ii) for a Category 2 AILV or AILV-combination, any of the restrictions on weight specified in paragraph 30 or 31; and

(e) the loads carried by virtue of this paragraph are not in addition to any items permitted to be carried by paragraph 21.

23. An AILV, or AILV-combination, that falls within Category 1 or 2 may carry an abnormal indivisible load consisting of engineering plant, together with constituent parts detached from the plant, if—

(a) the engineering plant and its detached parts are loaded at the same place and carried to the same destination; and
(b) the detached parts do not constitute any lateral, forward or rearward projection of the load that exceeds any projection that there would be without those parts.

Maximum width

24. (1) An AILV or AILV-combination must not exceed the maximum overall width.
(2) The maximum overall width is exceeded in any case where the overall width of the AILV (or of any AILV in the combination), together with the width of any lateral projection or projections of any load carried on it, exceeds 6.1 metres.

Maximum length

25. (1) The maximum length of an AILV or AILV-combination used to carry an abnormal indivisible load must not exceed 30 metres.
(2) The maximum length of an AILV or AILV-combination falling within any of sub-paragraphs (3) to (6) is to be determined in accordance with the sub-paragraph in question.
(3) Where the weight of the load rests wholly on an AILV that is a motor vehicle of category N3, the maximum length of the AILV is the overall length of the motor vehicle together with the length of any forward or rearward projection of the load.
(4) In the case of an AILV-combination that is configured so that the weight of the load rests wholly on a trailer of category O4, the maximum length of the AILV-combination is the overall length of the trailer together with the length of any forward or rearward projection of the load.
(5) In the case of an AILV-combination consisting only of a motor vehicle and a trailer, and which is configured so that the weight of the load rests on both vehicles (whether or not they form an articulated vehicle), the maximum length is the overall length of the trailer together with—

(a) the length of any projection of the load in front of the foremost part of the trailer; and
(b) the length of any rearward projection of the load.

(6) In the case of an AILV-combination (other than one falling within sub-paragraph (4) or (5)) which is configured so that that the weight of the load rests on at least two vehicles, the maximum length is the overall length of all the vehicles that bear the weight of the load together with—

(a) the length of any distance between them; and
(b) the length of any forward or rearward projection of the load.

Restrictions relating to weight: all AILVs and AILV-combinations

26. No AILV or AILV-combination may exceed the restrictions as to weight that apply to a Category 3 AILV or AILV-combination.

27. (1) An AILV falling within Category 1 must not exceed any of the maximum weights specified on any plate required to be fitted to it by regulation 66 of the Construction and Use Regulations.

(2) An AILV falling within Category 2 or 3 must not exceed any of the maximum weights (for the speed at which it is travelling) specified on the plate required to be fitted to it by paragraph 13.

(3) Sub-paragraph (2) does not apply to any trailer first used before 29th July 1983.

Restrictions relating to weight: Category 1 AILVs and AILV-combinations

28. (1) The total weight of any Category 1 AILV carrying a load must not exceed the maximum authorised weight for a vehicle of that description determined in accordance with Schedule 1 to the Authorised Weight Regulations.

(2) The total weight of such of the vehicles comprised in a Category 1 AILV-combination as are carrying a load must not exceed 46,000 kilograms.

(3) But the weight restrictions imposed by sub-paragraphs (1) and (2) may be exceeded by a Category 1 AILV-combination if—

(a) the combination has at least 6 axles;

(b) the total weight of the vehicle or vehicles carrying the load does not exceed 50,000 kilograms; and

(c) the combination complies in all other respects with the Authorised Weight Regulations, as those Regulations apply to a vehicle or vehicle-combination of 44,000 kilograms.

(4) Where a Category 1 AILV or AILV-combination is one to which the Authorised Weight Regulations do not apply, references to provisions of those Regulations are to be taken as references to the equivalent provisions of the Construction and Use Regulations.

29. (1) The total weight of—

(a) any Category 1 AILV carrying a load; or

(b) such of the vehicles comprised in a Category 1 AILV-combination as are carrying a load;

must be transmitted to the road through 5 or more axles.

(2) In relation to any Category 1 AILV or AILV-combination (including one falling within paragraph 28(3)), the axle weight for an axle of any description must not exceed the maximum authorised weight for an axle of that description determined in accordance with Schedule 3 to the Authorised Weight Regulations.

(3) Where a Category 1 AILV or AILV-combination is one to which the Authorised Weight Regulations do not apply, the reference to Schedule 3 of those Regulations is to be taken as a reference to the equivalent provisions of the Construction and Use Regulations.

Restrictions relating to weight: Category 2 AILVs and AILV-combinations

30. (1) The total weight of—

(a) any Category 2 AILV carrying a load; or

(b) such of the vehicles comprised in a Category 2 AILV-combination as are carrying a load;

must not exceed 80,000 kilograms.

(2) Where the weight calculated in accordance with sub-paragraph (3), in relation to any Category 2 AILV or AILV-combination, is less than 80,000 kilograms, the total weight of the vehicle or vehicles described in sub-paragraph (1)(a) or (b) must not exceed that lesser weight.

(3) The weight calculated in accordance with this sub-paragraph is the number (expressed in kilograms) equal to the product of the following equation and then rounded up to the nearest 10 kilograms—

$D \times 7{,}500$

(4) In sub-paragraph (3), D is the distance (measured in metres) between—

(a) in the case of an AILV, the foremost axle and the rearmost axle of the AILV carrying the load;

(b) in the case of an AILV-combination that is an articulated vehicle, the kingpin and the rearmost axle on the semi-trailer; or

(c) in the case of any other description of AILV-combination, the foremost axle and the rearmost axle of the group comprising all those vehicles in the combination that are carrying a load.

31. (1) The total weight of—

(a) any Category 2 AILV carrying a load; or

(b) such of the vehicles comprised in a Category 2 AILV-combination as are carrying a load;

must be transmitted to the road through 6 or more axles.

(2) In sub-paragraphs (3) to (5) "load-bearing vehicle" means a vehicle mentioned in sub-paragraph (1) (a) or (b).

(3) The distance between any two adjacent axles of a load-bearing vehicle must not be less than 1 metre.

(4) Where the distance between two adjacent axles of a load-bearing vehicle is the distance specified in column 1 of Table 1, the axle weight must not exceed the weight specified in column 2 and the wheel weight must not exceed the weight specified in column 3.

Table 1

Category 2: axles and wheels

Distance between adjacent axles (Column 1)	Axle weight (Column 2)	Wheel weight (Column 3)
Less than 1.35 metres	12,000 kilograms	6,000 kilograms
1.35 metres or more	12,500 kilograms	6,250 kilograms

(5) But where—

(a) a load-bearing vehicle has axles in two or more groups of axles;

(b) the distance between the adjacent axles in each group is less than 2 metres; and

(c) the distance between the adjacent axles in different groups is more than 2 metres;

the sum of the weights transmitted to the road surface by all the wheels in any group must not exceed 50,000 kilograms.

Restrictions relating to weight: Category 3 AILVs and AILV-combinations

32. (1) The total weight of—

(a)   any Category 3 AILV carrying a load; or
(b)   such of the vehicles comprised in a Category 3 AILV-combination as are carrying a load;

must not exceed 150,000 kilograms.

(2) Where the weight calculated in accordance with sub-paragraph (3), in relation to any Category 3 AILV or AILV-combination, is less than 150,000 kilograms, the total weight of the vehicle or vehicles described in sub-paragraph (1)(a) or (b) must not exceed that lesser weight.

(3) The weight calculated in accordance with this sub-paragraph is the number (expressed in kilograms) equal to the product of the following equation and then rounded up to the nearest 10 kilograms—

$$D \times 12{,}500$$

(4) In sub-paragraph (3), D is the distance (measured in metres) between—

(a)   in the case of an AILV, the foremost axle and the rearmost axle of the AILV carrying the load;
(b)   in the case of an AILV-combination that is an articulated vehicle, the kingpin and the rearmost axle on the semi-trailer; or
(c)   in the case of any other description of AILV-combination, the foremost axle and the rearmost axle of the group comprising all those vehicles in the combination that are carrying a load.

33. (1) The total weight of—

(a)   any Category 3 AILV carrying a load; or
(b)   such of the vehicles comprised in a Category 3 AILV-combination as are carrying a load;

must be transmitted to the road through 6 or more axles.

(2) In sub-paragraphs (3) to (5) "load-bearing vehicle" means a vehicle mentioned in sub-paragraph (1)(a) or (b).

(3) The distance between any two adjacent axles of a load-bearing vehicle must not be less than 1 metre.

(4) Where the distance between two adjacent axles of a load-bearing vehicle is the distance specified in column 1 of Table 2, the axle weight must not exceed the weight specified in column 2 and the wheel weight must not exceed the weight specified in column 3.

Table 2

Category 3: axles and wheels

Distance between adjacent axles	Axle weight	Wheel weight
(Column 1)	(Column 2)	(Column 3)
Less than 1.35 metres	15,000 kilograms	7,500 kilograms
1.35 metres or more	16,500 kilograms	8,250 kilograms

(5) But where—

(a)   a load-bearing vehicle has axles in two or more groups of axles;
(b)   the distance between the adjacent axles in each group is less than 1.5 metres; and
(c)   the distance between the adjacent axles in different groups is more than 1.5 metres;

the sum of the weights transmitted to the road surface by all the wheels in any group must not exceed the overall maximum weight.

(6) The overall maximum weight is—

(a)   90,000 kilograms if the distance specified in sub-paragraph (5)(b) is less than 1.35 metres; and
(b)   100,000 kilograms in any other case.

Speed restrictions

34. (1) An AILV falling within Category 2 or 3 must not exceed any speed specified on the plate required by paragraph 13.

(2) An AILV, or AILV-combination, falling within Category 1, 2 or 3 must not travel on a motorway, dual carriageway or other description of road at speeds exceeding the speed specified in Table 3 for that Category in respect of the description of road in question.

Table 3

Speed restrictions for Category 1, 2 or 3 AILVs or AILV-combinations

AILV or AILV-combination	Motorway	Dual carriageway	Other roads
Category 1	60 mph	50 mph	40 mph
Category 2 or 3	40 mph	35 mph	30 mph

(3) Nothing in this Schedule is to be taken to authorise travel at any speed in excess of any speed restriction imposed by or under any other enactment.

PART 5

APPLICATION OF REGULATIONS MADE UNDER SECTION 41 OF THE ROAD TRAFFIC ACT 1988

Category 1 AILVs and AILV-combinations

35. Any AILV or AILV-combination falling within Category 1 must, unless it falls within paragraph 37, comply with—

(a)   the Construction and Use Regulations, apart from the provisions of those Regulations specified in Table 4;

(b) the Authorised Weight Regulations; and
(c) the Lighting Regulations.

Table 4
Category 1: Construction and Use Regulations that do not apply

Non-applicable Regulations	Subject
7	Length
8	Width
80	Over-riding weight regulations
82	Restrictions on use of vehicles carrying wide or long loads

Category 2 or 3 AILVs and AILV-combinations

36. Any AILV or AILV-combination falling within Category 2 or 3 must, unless it falls within paragraph 37, comply with—

(a) the Construction and Use Regulations, apart from the provisions of those Regulations specified in Table 5; and
(b) the Lighting Regulations.

Table 5
Category 2 or 3: Construction and Use Regulations that do not apply

Non-applicable Regulations	Subject
7	Length
8	Width
15, 16	Braking systems
18(1A) to (9)	Maintenance and efficiency of brakes
25	Tyre loads and speed ratings
64	Spray suppression devices
65	Maintenance of spray suppression devices
75(1), in so far as it relates to items 1–4, 6–11, 15 and 16 of the Table	Maximum permitted laden weight of vehicle
76 to 80	Other maximum permitted weight limits of vehicle and trailer, other than articulated vehicle
82	Restrictions on use of vehicles carrying wide or long loads
83(1)	Number of trailers

AILVs manufactured before 1st October 1989

37. Instead of paragraphs 35 and 36, article 18(2)(p) of the Motor Vehicles (Authorisation of Special Types) General Order 1979 continues to apply to any AILV manufactured before 1st October 1989, to the same extent as it applied before the coming into force of this Schedule.

4–3882

Article 10(4) and 11(1)(a)

SCHEDULE 2
MOBILE CRANES

PART 1
DEFINED TERMS

PART 2
CONSTRUCTION

PART 3
PLATES

PART 4
CONDITIONS RELATING TO USE

General restrictions

PART 5
APPLICATION OF REGULATIONS MADE UNDER SECTION 41 OF THE ROAD TRAFFIC ACT 1988

Article 10(4) and 11 (1)(a)

SCHEDULE 3
ENGINEERING PLANT

PART 1
DEFINED TERMS

PART 2
CONSTRUCTION

PART 3
CONDITIONS RELATING TO USE

PART 4
APPLICATION OF REGULATIONS MADE UNDER SECTION 41 OF THE ROAD TRAFFIC ACT 1988

Article 10(4) and 11(1)(*a*)   SCHEDULE 4
                                        ROAD RECOVERY VEHICLES

PART 1
DEFINED TERMS

1. (1) In this Order "road recovery vehicle" means a vehicle that is—

(*a*) a locomotive;
(*b*) a motor vehicle of category N3; or
(*c*) a vehicle-combination comprising a motor vehicle of category N3 and a trailer of category O4;

and that satisfies the three conditions in sub-paragraphs (2) to (4).
(2) The first condition is that the vehicle is specially designed and constructed for the purpose of recovering disabled road vehicles or is permanently adapted for that purpose.
(3) The second condition is that the vehicle is fitted with a crane, winch or other lifting system specially designed to be used for the purpose of recovering another vehicle.
(4) The third condition is that the vehicle meets the requirements for registered use as a recovery vehicle under Part 5 of Schedule 1 to the Vehicle Excise and Registration Act 1994.

PART 2
CONSTRUCTION

2. (1) A road recovery vehicle must be a wheeled vehicle.
(2) Every wheel must be fitted with a pneumatic tyre.
3. A warning beacon emitting an amber light must be fitted to a road recovery vehicle.

PART 3
PLATES

4. A road recovery vehicle must be equipped with a plate that specifies the maximum weight that may be lifted by any crane, winch or other lifting system with which the vehicle is fitted.

PART 4
CONDITIONS RELATING TO USE

Restriction on carriage of loads and towing of vehicles

5. (1) A road recovery vehicle must not carry or tow any load or transport any goods or burden.
(2) But that is subject to paragraphs 6 and 7.
6. A road recovery vehicle may carry its own necessary gear and equipment.
7. (1) Except as stated in sub-paragraph (2), a road recovery vehicle may carry or tow a disabled vehicle or vehicle-combination when conveying it to a destination in accordance with the instructions of the owner or driver of the vehicle or when conveying it to an appropriate destination for repair.
(2) Where a recovery of a disabled vehicle or vehicle-combination is effected by using a drawbar or lift-and-tow method, the road recovery vehicle must not carry or tow the disabled vehicle or vehicle-combination any further than is reasonably necessary in order to clear any road obstructed by it and to facilitate the use of roads by other persons.
8. (1) At any time when a disabled vehicle or vehicle-combination is being towed by a road recovery vehicle, the braking system of the disabled vehicle or vehicle-combination must not be operated by any device other than an approved brake connection point that is fitted to both the road recovery vehicle and the disabled vehicle or vehicle-combination.
(2) In sub-paragraph (1), "approved brake connection point", in relation to a road recovery vehicle, means a device which is—

(*a*) approved by the manufacturer of the vehicle;
(*b*) fitted to the vehicle in the course of its construction or adaptation; and
(*c*) specially designed for use in the course of recovering disabled vehicles or vehicle-combinations in order to provide a means by which the braking system of the disabled vehicle or vehicle-combination can be safely and effectively controlled from the road recovery vehicle.

9. A road recovery vehicle must not tow a disabled vehicle or vehicle-combination if the weight of the road recovery vehicle, together with the weight of the vehicle or vehicles being towed, would exceed the maximum train weight shown on the plate required to be fitted to the road recovery vehicle by regulation 66 of the Construction and Use Regulations (plates for goods vehicles and buses).

Beacons

10. (1) When a road recovery vehicle is used on roads, the beacon fitted to it under paragraph 3 must be kept lit—

(*a*) when the road recovery vehicle is stationary at the scene of the breakdown; or
(*b*) when the road recovery vehicle is unable, on account of any vehicle or vehicles it is towing, the weather conditions or otherwise, to maintain speeds appropriate to the road.

(2) But, in the circumstances described in sub-paragraph (1)(*a*), the beacon may be switched off if—

(*a*) there is no reasonable prospect of the presence of the road recovery vehicle causing a hazard to persons using the road (so that it is not necessary or desirable to warn persons of its presence); or
(*b*) it is likely that the use of the beacon could confuse or mislead other road users.

Maximum width

11. (1) The overall width of a road recovery vehicle must not exceed the limits imposed by regulation 8 of the Construction and Use Regulations (restrictions as to width).
(2) But sub-paragraph (1) does not apply to a road recovery vehicle that satisfies the width conditions.
(3) The width conditions are that—

(a) the road recovery vehicle is a trailer;

(b) the trailer is used only for, or in connection with, the recovery of vehicles of a description that can only safely be recovered by a road recovery vehicle with an overall width exceeding the limits imposed by regulation 8 of the Construction and Use Regulations; and

(c) the overall width of the trailer does not exceed 3 metres.

Maximum length

12. (1) The overall length of a road recovery vehicle must not exceed 18.75 metres.

(2) But sub-paragraph (1) does not apply to restrict the combined length of a road recovery vehicle together with any disabled vehicle or vehicle-combination carried or towed by it in the course of a recovery.

Maximum vehicle weight

13. The gross weight of a road recovery vehicle must not exceed—

(a) 36,000 kilograms in the case of a locomotive, the weight of which is transmitted to the road surface through 3 axles;

(b) 50,000 kilograms in the case of a locomotive, the weight of which is transmitted to the road surface through 4 or more axles;

(c) 80,000 kilograms in the case of a vehicle-combination comprising a motor vehicle of category N3 and a trailer of category O4, where the weight of the combination is transmitted to the road surface through 6 or more axles;

(d) in any other case, the maximum authorised weight (within the meaning of the Authorised Weight Regulations) for the description of vehicle in question.

Maximum axle and wheel weights

14. (1) The distance between any two adjacent axles of a road recovery vehicle must not be less than 1.3 metres.

(2) The axle weight of a road recovery vehicle must not exceed 12,500 kilograms.

(3) The wheel weight of a road recovery vehicle must not exceed 6,250 kilograms.

(4) Where a road recovery vehicle has axles in two or more groups—

(a) the distance between the adjacent axles in any group must not be less than 1.3 metres; and

(b) the sum of the weights transmitted to the road surface by all the wheels in any group must not exceed 25,000 kilograms.

(5) But sub-paragraph (4)(b) does not apply to a road recovery vehicle falling within paragraph 13(c).

15. (1) If a road recovery vehicle has only one front steer axle, that axle must carry at least 40 per cent of the maximum axle weight shown on the plate required by regulation 66 of the Construction and Use Regulations (plates for goods vehicles and buses).

(2) If the vehicle has two or more front steer axles, all those axles taken together must carry at least 40 per cent of such weight.

Speed restrictions

16. (1) A road recovery vehicle must not, at any time when it is carrying or towing a disabled vehicle or vehicle-combination, travel at speeds exceeding—

(a) 40 miles per hour on a motorway;

(b) 30 miles per hour on a dual carriageway; or

(c) 30 miles per hour on any other road.

(2) Nothing in this Schedule is to be taken to authorise travel at any speed in excess of any speed restriction imposed by or under any other enactment.

PART 5
APPLICATION OF REGULATIONS MADE UNDER SECTION 41 OF THE ROAD TRAFFIC ACT 1988

17. A road recovery vehicle must comply with—

(a) the Construction and Use Regulations, apart from the provisions of those Regulations specified in Table 12;

(b) the Authorised Weight Regulations, but only to the extent specified in paragraph 13 of this Schedule; and

(c) the Lighting Regulations.

Table 12

Road recovery vehicles: Construction and Use Regulations that do not apply

Non-applicable Regulations	Subjects
36A, 36B, 36C	Speed limiters
51	Sideguards
70, 70B	Plates
70A	Speed limiters
72	Additional markings
73	Test date disc
75	Maximum permitted laden weight of vehicle
76	Maximum permitted laden weight of vehicle and trailer, other than articulated vehicle
77	Maximum permitted laden weight of articulated vehicle
78	Maximum permitted wheel and axle weights
79	Maximum permitted weights for certain closely-spaced axles etc
79A	Savings for Authorised Weight Regulations
82	Restrictions on use of vehicles carrying wide or long loads
83(1)	Numbers of trailers

Article 12(1), 13(2), 17(3), 23(2), 24(4),
31(3), 34(3), 38(2), 39(2), and 48(2)

SCHEDULE 5
NOTICES TO POLICE

Article 12(1), 14(1), 15(4), 23(3), 24(5),
31(3) and 34(4)

SCHEDULE 6
ATTENDANTS

1. (1) A person ("an attendant") must be employed—

(a) to accompany the vehicle or vehicle-combination;
(b) to attend to the vehicle or to all vehicles comprised in the combination;
(c) to attend to any load or loads carried on such vehicle or vehicles; and
(d) to give warning to the driver of the vehicle or vehicle-combination, and to any other person, of any danger likely to be caused to such other person by reason of the presence on the road of the vehicle or vehicle-combination.

(2) References to the driver of a vehicle-combination are references to the driver of the foremost motor vehicle in the combination.

2. (1) A person may be employed as an attendant only if he has appropriate training or experience to enable him to perform the tasks mentioned in paragraph 1.

(2) The person appointing the attendant must take appropriate steps to inform the attendant of any personal risks and dangers arising from performing the tasks mentioned in paragraph 1 (for example, risks arising from the attendant moving on foot between vehicles or from his using any remote controlled steering device to assist the driver).

3. (1) In a case where a journey is made by a vehicle ("vehicle A") and an attendant employed to accompany A travels in another vehicle ("vehicle B"), the attendant is to be treated as employed in accordance with this Schedule only if—

(a) arrangements are made with a view to ensuring that, as far as is reasonably practicable, the attendant can see vehicle A at all times during the journey; and
(b) a direct radio voice link is in operation at all times between vehicle A and vehicle B.

(2) In all other cases, the attendant is to be treated as employed in accordance with this Schedule only if effective arrangements are made to ensure that the attendant is in a position to observe the vehicles and any load and give any necessary warning.

4. (1) A person employed by virtue of paragraph 1 must be additional to the person or persons employed to drive the vehicle.

(2) Where three or more vehicles are travelling together in convoy, only the rearmost and foremost vehicles in the convoy must be accompanied by an attendant.

(3) Any person or persons employed in driving a motor vehicle for the purpose of assisting the propulsion of another vehicle is not to be treated as an attendant in relation to that other vehicle.

Article 15(5), 23(4) and 34(5)

SCHEDULE 7
NOTICES TO SECRETARY OF STATE

Article 16 and 25

SCHEDULE 8
MARKING OF PROJECTIONS

PART 1
DEFINED TERMS

1. In this Schedule—

"end marker" means a marker fitted to the end of any forward or rearward projection of a load which either—

(a) has the dimensions and surface appearance specified in the first diagram in Part 5 of this Schedule; or
(b) is a marker which, for the purpose of securing that any forward or rearward projection of a load or loads carried on a vehicle is made clearly visible to other persons using the roads, is designed to be fitted to the end of the projection and is approved for that purpose by the appropriate authority in—

(i) another EEA State; or
(ii) any other country which is a member of the United Nations Economic Commission for Europe;

"relevant vehicle" means—

(a) a Part 2 vehicle;
(b) a Part 2 vehicle-combination; or
(c) a special type agricultural vehicle; and

"side marker" means a marker fitted to the side of any forward, rearward or lateral projection of a load which either—

(a) has the dimensions and surface appearance specified in the second diagram in Part 5 of this Schedule; or
(b) is a marker which, for the purpose of securing that any forward, rearward or lateral projection of a load or loads carried on a vehicle is made clearly visible to other persons using the roads, is designed to be fitted to the side of the projection and is approved for that purpose by a recognised authority in—

(i) another EEA State; or
(ii) any other country which is a member of the United Nations Economic Commission for Europe.

PART 2

FORWARD AND REARWARD PROJECTIONS

2. Paragraphs 3 to 6 apply cumulatively.

General visibility of forward or rearward projections

3. Where the length of a forward or rearward projection of a load carried on a relevant vehicle exceeds 1 metre—

(a)　the projection must be made clearly visible, within a reasonable distance, to a person using the road at the end of the vehicle from which the projection extends; and

(b)　it must be made clearly visible from the side of the vehicle.

Markers for the end of a forward or rearward projection

4. (1)　Where the length of a forward or rearward projection of a load carried on a relevant vehicle exceeds 2 metres, an end marker must be fitted to the end of the projection.

(2)　Sub-paragraph (1) does not apply if a rear marking has been fitted to the projection in accordance with regulation 21 of the Lighting Regulations.

(3)　An end marker under sub-paragraph (1) must be fitted so that—

(a)　it is as near as is practicable in a transverse plane;

(b)　it is not more than 0.5 metre from the extreme end of the projection;

(c)　the vertical distance between the lowest part of the end marker and the surface of the road is not more than 2.5 metres;

(d)　the end marker, and any means by which it is fitted to the projection, impedes the view of the driver of the vehicle as little as possible; and

(e)　the end marker is clearly visible, within a reasonable distance, to a person using the road at the end of the vehicle from which the projection extends.

Markers for the side of a forward or rearward projection

5. (1)　Where the length of a forward or rearward projection of a load carried on a relevant vehicle exceeds 3 metres, one side marker must be fitted to the right hand side of the projection and one side marker must be fitted to its left hand side.

(2)　The side markers under sub-paragraph (1) must be fitted so that—

(a)　each side marker is, as near as is practicable, in a longitudinal plane;

(b)　no part of a side marker extends beyond the end of the projection;

(c)　the vertical distance between the lowest part of each side marker and the surface of the road is not more than 2.5 metres;

(d)　the horizontal distance between each side marker and the end-marker (or, as the case may be, the rear marking fitted to the projection in accordance with the Lighting Regulations) does not exceed 1 metre; and

(e)　each side marker is clearly visible, within a reasonable distance, to a person using the road on that side of the projection.

6. (1)　This paragraph applies where any relevant vehicle is carrying a load and—

(a)　the length of any forward projection of the load exceeds 4.5 metres; or

(b)　the length of any rearward projection of the load exceeds 5 metres.

(2)　Additional side markers must be fitted to the right hand side and the left hand side of a forward or rearward projection so that the horizontal distance between the extreme projecting points of the relevant vehicle and the nearest points of any adjacent side markers does not exceed—

(a)　2.5 metres in the case of a forward projection;

(b)　3.5 metres in the case of a rearward projection.

(3)　The additional side markers also must be fitted to the projection so that—

(a)　each additional side marker is, as near as is practicable, in a longitudinal plane;

(b)　the vertical distance between the lowest part of each additional side marker and the surface of the road is not more than 2.5 metres; and

(c)　each additional side marker is clearly visible, within a reasonable distance, to a person using the road on that side of the projection.

(4)　In determining the extreme projecting points of a relevant vehicle for the purposes of sub-paragraph (2), any part of a crane or other special appliance or apparatus, which is treated as a forward projection or a rearward projection by virtue of article 6(3), is to be disregarded.

PART 3

LATERAL PROJECTIONS

Markers for a lateral projection

7. (1)　This paragraph applies where—

(a)　any relevant vehicle is carrying a load; and

(b)　the load has a lateral projection or projections on either side exceeding 305 millimetres in length.

(2)　Side markers must be fitted to the lateral projection so that, in respect of each side of the vehicle from which the projection extends, one marker is visible from the front of the vehicle and one marker is visible from the rear of the vehicle.

(3)　Each side marker must be fitted so that at least part of it is within 50 millimetres of a longitudinal plane passing through the point on that side of the projection which is furthest from the axis of the vehicle.

8. (1)　If the user of the vehicle shows that it is not reasonably practicable to fit side markers in accordance with paragraph 7, the load must be marked with tape so that the point at which the width of the load is at its greatest is clearly visible from the front, rear and side of the vehicle.

(2)　The tape must be—

(a) red, yellow or white (or any combination); and
(b) made of day-glow, fluorescent or retro-reflective material which is of a standard approved by—

   (i) the British Standards Institution; or
   (ii) an equivalent body in another EEA State or in any other country which is a member of the United Nations Economic Commission for Europe.

(3) Nothing in this paragraph affects any requirement imposed by the Lighting Regulations, including, in particular, the requirements of regulation 11(1) (which states that no retro-reflective material is to be fitted to a vehicle which is capable of showing red light to the front of the vehicle) and regulation 11(2) (which states that no retro-reflective material is to be fitted to a vehicle which is capable of showing any light other than red to the rear).

PART 4
GENERAL VISIBILITY OF MARKERS

9. Any end marker or side marker which is required by any provision of this Schedule to be fitted to a projection of a load must be kept clean and unobscured.

10. Between sunset and sunrise, and at all times when visibility is seriously reduced, any end marker or side marker must be kept illuminated by a lamp which—

(a) makes the marker readily visible from a reasonable distance; and
(b) is shielded so that its light (except as reflected from the marker) is not visible to other persons using the road.

PART 5
APPEARANCE OF MARKERS

Diagram of end marker surface

–3886

Article 17(1), 35(2) and 40(2)

SCHEDULE 9
ROAD AND BRIDGE AUTHORITIES

PART 1
NOTICES

PART 2
INDEMNITIES

Article 32(2) and 33(b)

SCHEDULE 10
LOCAL EXCAVATION VEHICLES

PART 1
MEANING OF LOCAL EXCAVATION VEHICLE

PART 2
CONSTRUCTION

PART 3
CONDITIONS RELATING TO USE

PART 4
APPLICATION OF REGULATIONS MADE UNDER SECTION 41 OF THE ROAD TRAFFIC ACT 1988

–3887

Article 37(b)

SCHEDULE 11
VEHICLES FOR TESTS, TRIALS OR NON-UK USE ETC

PART 1
INTERPRETATION

1. In this Schedule "relevant vehicle" means any motor vehicle or trailer which falls within a recognised category of special vehicles specified in article 36(1)(a) to (e).

PART 2
CONDITIONS RELATING TO USE

General restrictions

2. A relevant vehicle may only be used on roads for—

(a) testing;
(b) demonstration;
(c) delivery on sale;
(d) proceeding to, or returning from, a manufacturer or repairer for construction, repair or overhaul.

3. Paragraph 2 does not apply in relation to a relevant vehicle where—

(a) a person ("A") has been approved by the Secretary of State for the purposes of this Schedule;
(b) the vehicle is registered under the Vehicle and Excise Registration Act 1994 and the registration is in A's name only; and
(c) the vehicle is being used either—

   (i) by A for the sole purpose of making an evaluation of it; or
   (ii) by another person ("B") in the circumstances described in sub-paragraph (2) and for the purpose of assisting A to make such an evaluation.

(2) The circumstances described in this sub-paragraph are—

(a) that A has lent the vehicle to B on terms that include a requirement for B to supply A with information or opinions derived from his use of it, and for B to return the vehicle to A on demand; and
(b) that the vehicle is being used by B in accordance with those terms.

4. A relevant vehicle must not be used in such a way as to cause a danger of injury to any person by reason of—

(a) the condition of the vehicle, its accessories or equipment;
(b) the purpose for which it is used;
(c) the number of passengers carried by it;
(d) the manner in which such passengers are carried;
(e) the weight, position or distribution of any load carried on the vehicle; or
(f) the manner in which any such load is secured.

Restriction of carriage of loads etc

5. (1) A relevant vehicle that is used on roads must not carry any load or transport goods or burden.
(2) But that is subject to paragraphs 6 and 7.
6. A relevant vehicle may carry—

(a) its own necessary gear and equipment; and
(b) any apparatus or ballast necessary for the purpose of carrying out a test or trial of the vehicle.

7. (1) A relevant vehicle may carry a load if it complies with such of the requirements of the Authorised Weight Regulations as apply to a vehicle of that description.
(2) Where the vehicle is one to which the Authorised Weight Regulations do not apply, the reference to requirements of those Regulations is to be taken as a reference to the applicable requirements of regulations 75 to 79 of the Construction and Use Regulations.

PART 3
CONDITIONS RELATING TO USE

8. (1) A relevant vehicle must comply with—

(a) the provisions of the Construction and Use Regulations specified in Table 16, but subject to the modifications of those provisions which are specified in paragraph 9;
(b) the Authorised Weight Regulations; and
(c) the provisions of the Lighting Regulations specified in Table 17, but subject to the modifications of those provisions which are specified in paragraph 10.

9. In their application to a relevant vehicle, the Construction and Use Regulations specified in Table 16 are to be read subject to the following modifications—

(a) regulation 16 applies to all relevant vehicles (and not only those to which regulation 15 of those Regulations does not apply) except that, in the circumstances envisaged in the provisos to paragraph (1), (1A), (1C) and (1D) of regulation 15, a relevant vehicle may comply instead with the requirement specified in each of those paragraphs respectively;
(b) regulation 82(8)(c)(ii)(B) of the Construction and Use Regulations does not require any advance notice to be given to police in accordance with paragraph 1 of Schedule 12 to those Regulations.

10. (1) In their application to a relevant vehicle, regulations 18 and 22 of the Lighting Regulations are to be read as if—

(a) the requirements relating to the markings of lamps, retro-reflectors and rear markings were omitted;
(b) the requirements relating to angles of visibility were omitted; and
(c) the requirements relating to the positioning of any lamp, retro-reflector or rear marking permitted any specified maximum measurement to be increased by 5 per cent and any specified minimum measurement to be decreased by 5 per cent.

(2) In its application to a relevant vehicle, regulation 18 of the Lighting Regulations is also to be read as if the requirements relating to the fitting of a dim-dip device or running lamp in Table 1 of Schedule 1 were omitted.

TABLE 16

Vehicles for tests, trials or non-UK use etc: Construction and Use Regulations that do apply

Applicable Regulations	Subject
10	Indication of overall travelling height
16	Braking systems
18(1)	Maintenance and efficiency of brakes
20	General requirement as to wheels and tracks
26	Mixing of tyres
27	Condition and maintenance of tyres
29	Maintenance of steering gear
30	View to the front
34	Windscreen wipers and washers
37	Audible warning instruments
53	Mascots
54	Silencers—general
61	Emissions
62	Closets
81,82	Restrictions on use of vehicles carrying wide or long loads
83	Number of trailers
84	Trailers drawn by motor cycles
86	Distance between motor vehicles and trailers
89	Leaving trailers at rest
90	Passengers in trailers
92	Attachment of sidecars
97	Avoidance of excessive noise
98	Stopping of engine when stationary
99	Use of audible warning instruments

Applicable Regulations	Subject
100	Maintenance and use of vehicles so as not to cause danger
101	Parking in darkness
102	Passengers on motor-cycles
103	Obstruction
104	Driver's control
105	Opening of doors
106	Reversing
107	Leaving motor vehicle unattended
108	Securing of suspended implements
109	Television sets

TABLE 17

Vehicles for tests, trials or non-UK use etc: Lighting Regulations that do apply

Applicable Lighting Regulations	Subject
11	Colour of lights shown by lamps and reflectors
13	Lamps to show steady light
16	Restrictions on fitting blue warning beacons etc
17	Obligatory warning beacons
18	obligatory lamps, reflectors, rear marking and devices
19	Restrictions on the obstruction of certain lamps etc
21	Projecting trailers, overhanging/projecting loads etc
22	Additional side marker lamps

Article 56

SCHEDULE 12
VEHICLES PROPELLED BY COMPRESSED NATURAL GAS SYSTEMS

DOCUMENTATION (FOR DRIVER AND VEHICLES)

Motor Vehicles (Third Party Risks) Regulations 1972[1]

(SI 1972/1217 amended by SI 1973/1821, SI 1974/792 and 2187, SI 1981/1567, SI 1992/1283, SI 1997/97, SI 1999/2392 and SI 2001/2266)

Interpretation

4–4061 **4.** (1) In these regulations, unless the context otherwise requires, the following expressions have the meanings hereby respectively assigned to them—

"the Act" means the Road Traffic Act [1988];

"company" means an authorised insurer within the meaning of Part VI of the Act or a body of persons by whom a security may be given in pursuance of the said Part VI;

"Motor Insurers' Bureau" means the company referred to in section 145(5) of the Road Traffic Act 1988;

"motor vehicle" has the meaning assigned to it by sections [185, 188 and 189] of the Act, but excludes any invalid carriage, trainer or trolley vehicle to which Part VI of the Act does not apply;

"policy" means a policy of insurance in respect of third party risks arising out of the use of motor vehicles which complies with the requirements of Part VI of the Act and includes a covering note;

"security" means a security in respect of third party risks arising out of the use of motor vehicles which complies with the requirements of Part VI of the Act;

"specified body" means—

(a) any of the local authorities referred to in paragraph (a) of section 144(2) of the Act; or

(b) a Passenger Transport Executive established under an order made under section 9 of the Transport Act 1968, or a subsidiary of that Executive, being an Executive or subsidiary to whose vehicles section 144(2)(a) of the Act has been applied; or

(c) the London Transport Executive or a wholly-owned subsidiary of that Executive referred to in paragraph (e) of section 144(2) of the Act.

(2) Any reference in these Regulations to a certificate in Form A, B, C, D, E or F shall be construed as a reference to a certificate in the form so headed and set out in Part 1 of the Schedule to these Regulations which has been duly made and completed subject to and in accordance with the provisions set out in Part 2 of the said Schedule.

(3) Any reference in these Regulations to any enactment shall be construed as a reference to that enactment as amended by any subsequent enactment.

(4) The Interpretation Act [1978] shall apply for the interpretation of these Regulations as it applies for the interpretation of an Act of Parliament, and as if for the purposes of [ss 16(1) and 17(2)] of that Act these Regulations were an Act of Parliament and the Regulations revoked by Regulation 2 of these Regulations were Acts of Parliament thereby repealed.

1. These Regulations are made by the Secretary of State for the Environment under ss 147, 157 and 162 of the Road Traffic Act 1972 and s 37 of the Vehicles (Excise) Act 1971 as extended by s 153 of the Road Traffic Act 1972. The penalty for breach of these Regulations is a fine not exceeding **level 3** on the standard scale: Road Traffic Offenders Act 1988, s 91.

4–4062   5, 6. (*Provisions for the issue by a company of certificates of insurance or security*[1]).

1. There is no obligation if the policy is of no force or effect (*London and Scottish Assurance Corpn Ltd v Ridd* (1939) 65 Ll L Rep 46).

Production of Evidence as Alternatives of Certificates

4–4063   7. The following evidence that a motor vehicle is not or was not being driven in contravention of s 143 of the Act may be produced in pursuance of s [165] of the Act as an alternative to the production of a certificate of insurance or a certificate of security: (1) a duplicated copy of a certificate of security issued in accordance with the proviso to Regulation 5(1)(*b*) of these Regulations; (2) in the case of a motor vehicle of which the owner has for the time being deposited with the Accountant-General of the Supreme Court the sum for the time being specified in section 144(1) of the Road Traffic Act 1988, a certificate in Form E, signed by the owner of the motor vehicle or by some person authorised by him in that behalf that such sum is on deposit; (3) in the case of a motor vehicle owned by a specified body, a police authority or the Receiver for the metropolitan police district, a certificate in Form F signed by some person authorised in that behalf by such specified body, police authority or Receiver as the case may be that the said motor vehicle is owned by the said specified body, police authority or Receiver; (4) In the case of a vehicle normally based in the territory other than the United Kingdom and Gibraltar of a member State of the Communities or of Austria, Czechoslovakia, Finland, the German Democratic Republic, Hungary, Norway, Sweden or Switzerland, a document issued by the insurer of the vehicle which indicates the name of the insurer, the number or other identifying particulars of the insurance policy issued in respect of the vehicle and the period of the insurance cover. In this paragraph the territory of the state in which a vehicle is normally based is—

(*a*) the territory of the state in which the vehicle is registered, or

(*b*) in cases where no registration is required for the type of vehicle, but the vehicle bears an insurance plate or distinguishing sign analogous to a registration plate, the territory of the state in which the insurance plate or the sign is issued, or

(*c*) in cases where neither registration plate nor insurance plate nor distinguishing sign is required for the type of vehicle, the territory of the state in which the keeper of the vehicle is permanently resident.

4–4064   8. Any certificate issued in accordance with paragraph (2) or (3) of the preceding Regulation shall be destroyed by the owner of the vehicle to which it relates before the motor vehicle is sold or otherwise disposed of.

Production of Evidence of Insurance or Security on application for Excise Licences

4–4065   9. (*This Regulation contains provisions regarding the production of insurance documents when applying for a licence under the [Vehicle Excise and Registration Act 1994].*)

4–4066   10. (*Keeping of records by insurance companies, etc*).

Notification to the Secretary of State of ineffective Policies or Securities

4–4067   11. Where to the knowledge of a company a policy or security issued by them ceases to be effective without the consent of the person to whom it was issued otherwise than by effluxion of time or by reason of his death the company shall forthwith notify the Secretary of State of the date on which the policy or security ceased to be effective provided that such notification need not be made if the certificate relating to the policy or security has been received by the company from the person to whom the certificate was issued on or before the date on which the policy or security ceases to be effective.

Return of Certificates to issuing Company

4–4068   12. (1) The following provisions shall apply in relation to the transfer of a policy or security with the consent of the holder to any other person;

(*a*) the holder shall, before the policy or security is transferred, return any relative certificates issued for the purposes of these Regulations to the company by whom they were issued; and

(*b*) the policy or security shall not be transferred to any other person unless and until the certificates have been so returned or the company are satisfied that the certificates have been lost or destroyed.

(2) In any case where with the consent of the person to whom it was issued a policy or security is suspended or ceases to be effective, otherwise than by effluxion of time, in circumstances in which the provisions of s 147(4) of the Act (relating to the surrender of certificates) do not apply the holder of the policy or security shall within seven days from the date when it is suspended or

ceases to be effective return any relative certificates issued for the purposes of these Regulations to the company by whom they were issued and the company shall not issue a new policy or security to the said holder in respect of the motor vehicle or vehicles to which the said first mentioned policy or security related unless and until the certificates have been returned to the company or the company are satisfied that they have been lost or destroyed.

(3) Where a policy or security is cancelled by mutual consent or by virtue of any provision in the policy or security, any statutory declaration that a certificate has been lost or destroyed made in pursuance of s 147(4) (which requires any such declaration to be made within a period of seven days from the taking effect of the cancellation) shall be delivered forthwith after it has been made to the company by whom the policy was issued or the security given.

(4) The provisions of the last preceding paragraph shall be without prejudice to the provisions of s [152(1)(*c*)] of the Act as to the effect for the purposes of that sub-section of the making of a statutory declaration within the periods therein stated.

Issues of Fresh Certificates

4–4069   13. Where any company by whom a certificate of insurance or a certificate of security has been issued are satisfied that the certificate has become defaced or has been lost or destroyed they shall, if they are requested to do so by the person to whom the certificate was issued, issue to him a fresh certificate. In the case of a defaced certificate the company shall not issue a fresh certificate unless the defaced certificate is returned to the company.

(Schedule of forms.)

Motor Vehicles (Compulsory Insurance) (No 2) Regulations 1973[1]

(SI 1973/2143 amended by SI 1974/791 and 2186, SI 1987/2171, the Criminal Justice Act 1988, s 51 and the Road Traffic (Consequential Provisions) Act 1988, Sch 1)

4–4071   2. (1) In these Regulations "vehicle" means any motor vehicle intended for travel on land and propelled by mechanical power, but not running on rails, and any trailer, whether or not coupled, and references to a relevant foreign state are references to Austria, Czechoslovakia, Finland, the German Democratic Republic, Hungary, Norway, Sweden or Switzerland.

(2) For the purposes of these regulations the territory in which a vehicle is normally based is—

(*a*) the territory of the state of which the vehicle bears a registration plate, or

(*b*) in cases where no registration is required for the type of vehicle, but the vehicle bears an insurance plate or distinguishing sign analogous to a registration plate, the territory of the state in which the insurance plate or the sign is issued, or

(*c*) in cases where neither registration plate nor insurance plate nor distinguishing sign is required for the type of vehicle, the territory of the state in which the keeper of the vehicle is permanently resident.

(3) The Interpretation Act [1978] shall apply for the interpretation of these Regulations as it applies for the interpretation of an Act of Parliament.

---

1. Made under s 2(2) of the European Communities Act 1972 to implement obligations arising out of the European Communities Council Directive of 24 April 1972 (OJ No L103/1, 2 May 1972.)

4–4072   5. (1) It shall be an offence for a person to use a specified motor vehicle registered in Great Britain, or any trailer kept by a person permanently resident in Great Britain, whether or not coupled, in the territory other than Great Britain and Gibraltar of any of the member states of the Communities, unless a policy of insurance is in force in relation to the person using that vehicle which insures him in respect of any liability which may be incurred by him in respect of the use of the vehicle in such territory according to the law on compulsory insurance against civil liability in respect of the use of vehicles of the state where the liability may be incurred.

(2) In this Regulation "specified motor vehicle" means a motor vehicle which is exempted from the provisions of section 143 of the Road Traffic Act [1988] (users of motor vehicles to be insured or secured against third-party risks) by virtue of section 144 of that Act.

(3) A person guilty of an offence under the Regulation shall be liable on summary conviction to a fine not exceeding **level 1** on the standard scale or to imprisonment for a term not exceeding **three months**, or to both such fine and such imprisonment.

(4) Proceedings for an offence under this Regulation may be taken, and the offence may for all incidental purposes be treated as having been committed in any place in Great Britain.

(5) Sections [6] (time within which summary proceedings for certain offences must be commenced) and [11] (evidence by certificate) of the Road Traffic [Offenders Act 1980] shall apply for the purposes of an offence under this Regulation as if such an offence were an offence under that Act to which those sections had been applied by [Schedule 1] to that Act.

4–4073   6. (1) Any person appointed by the Secretary of State for the purpose (in this Regulation referred to as an "appointed person") may require a person having custody of any vehicle, being a vehicle which is normally based in the territory of a state (other than a relevant foreign state) which is not a member of the Communities or in the non-European territory of a member state or in Gibraltar, when entering Great Britain to produce evidence that any loss or injury which may be caused by such a vehicle is covered throughout the territory in which the treaty establishing the European Economic Community is in force, in accordance with the requirements of the laws of the various member states on compulsory insurance against civil liability in respect of the use of vehicles.

(2) An appointed person may, if no such evidence is produced or if he is not satisfied by such evidence, prohibit the use of the vehicle in Great Britain.

(3) Where an appointed person prohibits the use of a vehicle under this Regulation, he may also direct the driver to remove the vehicle to such place and subject to such conditions as are specified in the direction; and the prohibition shall not apply to the removal of the vehicle in accordance with the direction.

(4) Any person who—

(a) uses a vehicle or causes or permits a vehicle to be used in contravention of a prohibition imposed under paragraph (2) of this Regulation, or

(b) refuses, neglects or otherwise fails to comply in a reasonable time with a direction given under paragraph (3) of this Regulation,

shall be guilty of an offence and shall be liable on summary conviction to a fine not exceeding **level 1** on the standard scale.

(5) Section [11] of the Road Traffic [Offenders Act 1988] shall apply for the purposes of an offence under this regulation as if such an offence were an offence under that Act to which that section had been applied by [Schedule 1] to that Act.

(6) A prohibition under paragraph (2) of this Regulation may be removed by an appointed person if he is satisfied that appropriate action has been taken to remove or remedy the circumstances in consequence of which the prohibition was imposed.

4–4074 **7.** (1) Where a constable in uniform has reasonable cause to suspect the driver of a vehicle of having committed an offence under the preceding Regulation, the constable may detain the vehicle, and for that purpose may give a direction, specifying an appropriate person and directing the vehicle to be removed by that person to such place and subject to such conditions as are specified in the direction; and the prohibition shall not apply to the removal of the vehicle in accordance with that direction.

(2) Where under paragraph (1) of this Regulation a constable—

(a) detains a motor vehicle drawing a trailer, or

(b) detains a trailer drawn by a motor vehicle,

then, for the purpose of securing the removal of the trailer, he may also (in a case falling within sub-paragraph (a) above) detain the trailer or (in a case falling within sub-paragraph (b) above) detain the motor vehicle; and a direction under paragraph (1) of this Regulation may require both the motor vehicle and the trailer to be removed to the place specified by the direction.

(3) A vehicle which, in accordance with a direction given under paragraph (1) of this Regulation is removed to a place specified in the direction shall be detained in that place, or in any other place to which it is removed in accordance with a further direction given under that paragraph until a constable (or, if that place is in the occupation of the Secretary of State, the Secretary of State) authorises the vehicle to be released on being satisfied—

(a) that the prohibition (if any) imposed in respect of the vehicle under the preceding Regulation has been removed, or that no such prohibition was imposed, or

(b) that appropriate arrangements have been made for removing or remedying the circumstances in consequence of which any such prohibition was imposed, or

(c) that the vehicle will be taken forthwith to a place from which it will be taken out of Great Britain to a place not in the European territory other than Gibraltar of a member state of the Communities and not in the territory of a relevant foreign state.

(4) Any person who—

(a) drives a vehicle in accordance with a direction given under this Regulation, or

(b) is in charge of a place at which a vehicle is detained under this Regulation,

shall not be liable for any damage to, or loss in respect of, the vehicle or its load unless it is shown that he did not take reasonable care of the vehicle while driving it or, as the case may be did not, while the vehicle was detained in that place, take reasonable care of the vehicle or (if the vehicle was detained there with its load) did not take reasonable care of its load.

(5) In this Regulation "appropriate person"—

(a) in relation to a direction to remove a motor vehicle, other than a motor vehicle drawing a trailer, means a person licensed to drive vehicle of the class to which the vehicle belongs and

(b) in relation to a direction to remove a trailer, or to remove a motor vehicle drawing a trailer means a person licensed to drive vehicles of a class which, when the direction is complied with will include the motor vehicle drawing the trailer in accordance with that direction.

4–4075 **8.** Nothing in section 145(2) (policies to be issued by authorised insurers) and section 147(1) (policies to be of no effect unless certificates issued) of the Road Traffic Act [1988] shall apply in the case of an insurance policy which is issued elsewhere than in the United Kingdom in respect of a vehicle normally based in the territory other than the United Kingdom and Gibraltar of a member State of the Communities or of a relevant foreign state.

Motor Vehicles (International Circulation) Order 1975[1]
(SI 1975/1208 amended by SI 1980/1095, SI 1985/459, SI 1989/993, SI 1991/771 and 1727, SI 1996/1929 and 1974 and SI 2004/1992)

4–4081 1. *Documents for drivers and vehicles going abroad.*

1. This Order was made under s 1 of the Motor Vehicles (International Circulation) Act 1952.

Visitors' driving permits

4–4082 2. (1) Subject to the provisions of this Article, it shall be lawful for a person resident outside the United Kingdom who is temporarily[1] in Great Britain and holds—

(a) a Convention driving permit, or
(b) a domestic driving permit issued in a country outside the United Kingdom, or
(c) *revoked*

during a period of twelve months from the date of his last entry into the United Kingdom to drive, or for any person to cause or permit such a person to drive. in Great Britain a motor vehicle of any class other than a medium-sized goods vehicle, a large goods vehicle, a privately-operated passenger vehicle or a passenger-carrying vehicle which he is authorised by that permit or that licence to drive, notwithstanding that he is not the holder of a driving licence under Part III of the Road Traffic Act 1988.

(2) Subject to the provisions of this Article, it shall be lawful for a person resident outside the United Kingdom who is temporarily in Great Britain and holds—

(a) a Convention driving permit, or
(b) a domestic driving permit issued in a country outside the United Kingdom,

during a period of twelve months from the date of his last entry into the United Kingdom to drive, or for any person to cause or permit such a person to drive, in Great Britain—

(i) in the case of any such person who is resident in an EEA State, the Isle of Man, Jersey or Guernsey, a medium-sized goods vehicle, a large goods vehicle, a privately-operated passenger vehicle or a passenger-carrying vehicle; and
(ii) in the case of any other such person, a medium-sized goods vehicle, a large goods vehicle, a privately-operated passenger vehicle or a passenger-carrying vehicle brought temporarily into Great Britain,

which he is authorised by that permit to drive, notwithstanding that he is not the holder of a medium-sized goods vehicle driver's licence, a large goods vehicle driver's licence, a privately-operated passenger vehicle driver's licence or a passenger-carrying vehicle driver's licence.

(3) *Revoked.*
(4) Nothing in the preceding provisions of this Article shall authorise any person to drive, or any person to cause or permit any person to drive, a vehicle of any class at a time when he is disqualified by virtue of section 101 of the Road Traffic Act 1988 (persons under age), for holding or obtaining a driving licence authorising him to drive vehicles of that class, but in the case of any such person as is mentioned in paragraphs (1) or (2) of this Article, who is driving a vehicle which—

(a) in the case of a person not resident in an EEA State, the Isle of Man, Jersey or Guernsey, is brought temporarily into Great Britain, and
(b) is within the class specified in the first column of paragraph 7 of the Table in subsection (1) of that section, and
(c) is either a vehicle registered in a Convention country or a goods vehicle in respect of which that person holds a certificate of competence which satisfies the international requirements,

the second column of that paragraph, in its application for the purposes of this paragraph, shall have effect as if for "21" there were substituted "18".
In this paragraph the following expressions have the meanings respectively assigned to them—

"the international requirements" means—

(i) in relation to a person who is driving a goods vehicle on a journey to which Council Regulation (EEC) No 3820/85 of 20th December 1985, on the harmonisation of certain social legislation relating to road transport[3] applies, the requirements of Article 5(1)(b) (minimum ages for goods vehicle drivers) of that Regulation;
(ii) in relation to a person who is driving a goods vehicle on a journey to which the European Agreement concerning the work of crews engaged in International Road Transport (AETR) signed at Geneva on 25th March 1971[4] applies, the requirements of Article 5(1)(b) (conditions to be fulfilled by drivers) of that Agreement;

"Convention country" means a country which is not an EEA State nor a party to the aforementioned European Agreement but is a party to the Convention on Road Traffic concluded at Vienna in the year 1968[5] the Convention on Road Traffic concluded at Geneva in the year 1949[6], or the International Convention relative to Motor Traffic concluded at Paris in the year 1926[7].

(5) This Article shall not authorise a person to drive a motor vehicle of any class if, in

consequence of a conviction or of the order of a court, he is disqualified for holding or obtaining a driving licence under Part III of the Road Traffic Act 1988.

(6) The Secretary of State for Transport may by order made by statutory instrument withdraw one or both of the rights conferred by paragraphs (1)(*b*) and (2)(*b*) of this Article in respect of—

(*a*) all domestic driving permits;
(*b*) domestic driving permits of a description specified in the order; or
(*c*) domestic driving permits held by persons of a description specified in the order.

(7) In this Article—

"Convention driving permit" means either—

(i) a driving permit in the form A in Schedule 1 to this Order issued under the authority of a country outside the United Kingdom, whether or not that country is a party to the Convention on Road Traffic concluded at Geneva in the year 1949 to a person who has given proof of his competence to drive but not so issued as aforesaid after the expiry of a period of five years from the date of the entry into force of the Convention on Road Traffic concluded at Vienna in the year 1968 in accordance with Article 47(1) thereof, if that country is a party to that Convention, or

(ii) a driving permit in the form B in that Schedule issued under the authority of a country outside the United Kingdom which is a party to the International Convention relative to Motor Traffic concluded at Paris in the year 1926, but not to the Convention of 1949 to a person who has given proof of his competence to drive nor to the Convention of 1968, or

(iii) a driving permit in the form C in that Schedule issued under the authority of a country outside the United Kingdom which is a party to the Convention of 1968;

"domestic driving permit" in relation to a country outside the United Kingdom means a document issued under the law of that country to a person who has given proof of his competence to drive and authorising the holder to drive motor vehicles, or a specified class of motor vehicles, in that country, and includes a driving permit issued to such a person by the armed forces of any country outside the United Kingdom for use in some other country outside the United Kingdom but does not include a Community licence (within the meaning of Part III of the Road Traffic Act 1988);

"dependants" in relation to such a member of the British Forces or the civilian component thereof, means any of the following persons, namely—

(*a*) the wife or husband of that member; and
(*b*) any other person wholly or mainly maintained by him or in his custody, charge or care; and

"EEA Agreement" means the Agreement on the European Economic Area signed at Oporto on 2nd May 1992 as adjusted by the Protocol signed at Brussels on 17th March 1993;

"EEA State" means a State which is a Contracting Party to the EEA Agreement;

"medium-sized goods vehicle" has the same meaning as in Part III of the Road Traffic Act 1988;

"medium-sized goods vehicle driver's licence" means a licence under Part III of the Road Traffic Act 1988 in so far as it authorises a person to drive medium-sized goods vehicles of any class;

"privately-operated passenger vehicle" means a vehicle, not used for carrying passengers for hire or reward, which is constructed or adapted to carry more than eight but not more than 16 passengers;

"privately-operated passenger vehicle driver's licence" means a licence under Part III of the Road Traffic Act 1988 in so far as it authorises a person to drive privately-operated passenger vehicles of any class;

(8) The provisions of this Article which authorise the holder of a permit or a licence to drive a vehicle during a specified period shall not be construed as authorising the driving of a vehicle at a time when the permit or the licence has ceased to be valid and, without prejudice to the provisions of paragraph (4) above, a Convention driving permit in the form C in Schedule 1 to this Order shall, if the validity of the permit is by special endorsement thereon made conditional upon the holder wearing certain devices or upon the vehicle being equipped in a certain manner to take account of his disability, not be valid at a time when any such condition is not satisfied.

---

1. It is a question of fact and degree whether someone is resident or only temporarily in Great Britain "temporarily" involves more than just the time element, it involves a presence for casual purposes as contrasted with regular habits of life (*Flores v Scott* [1984] 1 WLR 690, [1984] RTR 363).
3. OJ No L370, 31.12.85 p 1.
4. Cmnd 4858.
5. Cmnd 4032.
6. Cmnd 7997.
7. Cmnd 3510.

4–4083   3. (1) It shall be lawful—

(*a*) for a member of a visiting force of a country to which Part I of the Visiting Forces Act 1952 for the time being applies who holds a driving permit issued under the law of any part of the sending country or issued by the service authorities of the visiting force, or

(*b*) for a member of a civilian component of such a visiting force who holds such a driving permit, or (*c*) for a dependant of any such member of a visiting force or of a civilian component thereof who holds such a driving permit,

to drive, or for any person to cause or permit any such person to drive, in Great Britain a motor vehicle of any class which he is authorised by that permit to drive, notwithstanding that he is not the holder of a driving licence under Part III of the Road Traffic Act 1988.

(2) This Article shall not authorise a person to drive a motor vehicle of any class if, in consequence of a conviction or of the order of a court, he is disqualified for holding or obtaining a driving licence under Part III of the Road Traffic Act 1988.

(3) Nothing in this Article shall authorise any person to drive, or any person to cause or permit any other person to drive, a vehicle of any class at a time when he is disqualified by virtue of section 101 of the Road Traffic Act 1988 (persons under age), for holding or obtaining a driving licence authorising him to drive vehicles of that class.

(4) The interpretative provisions of the Visiting Forces Act 1952 shall apply for the interpretation of this Article and "dependant", in relation to a member of any such visiting force or a civilian component thereof, means any of the following persons namely—

(*a*) the wife or husband of that member; and
(*b*) any other person wholly or mainly maintained by him or in his custody, charge or care.

—4084   **4.** Schedule 3 to this Order shall have effect as respects the driving permits referred to in Articles 2 and 3 of this Order.

—4085

SCHEDULE 1
FORMS OF INTERNATIONAL DRIVING PERMIT

—4086

SCHEDULE 2
FEES

Article 4

SCHEDULE 3
VISITORS' DRIVING PERMITS

—4087   **1.** In this Schedule "driving permit" means a driving permit which by virtue of this Order authorises a person to drive a motor vehicle without holding a driving licence under Part III of the Road Traffic Act [1988], "Convention driving permit" has the meaning assigned to it by Article 2(7) of this Order and "driving licence" means a driving licence under the said Part III

2. (1) A court by whom the holder of a driving permit is convicted shall—

(*a*) if in consequence of the conviction or of the order of the court he is disqualified for holding or obtaining a driving licence, or
(*b*) if the court orders particulars of the conviction to be endorsed on any driving licence held by him,

send particulars of the conviction to the Secretary of State.

(2) A court shall in no circumstances enter any particulars in a driving permit.

3. (1) The holder of a driving permit disqualified in consequence of a conviction or of the order of a court for holding or obtaining a driving licence shall, if so required by the court, produce his driving permit within five days, or such longer time as the court may determine, and the court shall forward it to the Secretary of State.

(2) The Secretary of State on receiving a permit forwarded under the foregoing sub-paragraph, shall—

(*a*) retain the permit until the disqualification ceases to have effect or until the holder leaves Great Britain, whichever is the earlier;
(*b*) send the holder's name and address, together with the particulars of the disqualification, to the authority by whom the permit was issued; and
(*c*) if the permit is a Convention driving permit, record the particulars of the disqualification on the permit.

(3) A person failing to produce a driving permit in compliance with this paragraph shall be guilty of an offence which shall be treated for the purposes of [the Road Traffic Offenders Act 1988] as an offence against the provision specified in column 1 of [Part I of Schedule 2 thereof as section 27] and he shall be liable to be prosecuted and punished accordingly.

4. (1) A court, on ordering the removal under section [42(1) of the Road Traffic Offenders Act 1988] of a disqualification for holding or obtaining a driving licence, shall, if it appears that particulars of the disqualification have been forwarded to the Secretary of State under paragraph 2 of this Schedule, cause particulars of the order also to be forwarded to him.

(2) The Secretary of State, on receiving particulars of a court order removing such a disqualification, shall—

(*a*) in the case of a permit on which particulars of a disqualification were recorded in accordance with paragraph 3(2)(*c*) of this Schedule, enter on the permit particulars of the order removing the disqualification;
(*b*) send the particulars of the order to the authority by whom the permit was issued; and
(*c*) return the permit to the holder.

5. (1) In the following provisions of the Road Traffic Act [1988], references to a driving licence shall include references to a driving permit.

(2) The said provisions are—

(*a*) subsections (1), (2) and (6) of section 164 which authorises a police constable to require the production of a driving licence and in certain cases statement of date of birth by a person who is, or in certain circumstances has been, driving a vehicle),
(*b*) *refers to repealed provisions*, and
(*c*) subsections (1) and (2) of section 169 (which relate to the use of a driving licence by a person other than the holder and to forgery of such a licence).

—4088

SCHEDULE 5
FORM OF CERTIFICATE AND STATEMENT OF DRIVING TEST RESULT

Motor Vehicles (International Circulation) Regulations 1985[1]
(SI 1985/610)

4-4091　1. *Citation and commencement.*

---

1. Made by the Secretary of State for Transport in exercise of powers conferred by paragraphs (*d*), (*e*) and (*i* of s 23(1) of the Vehicles (Excise) Act 1971, s 37(1), (2) and (4) of that Act, and art 5(4), (5), (6) and (7) of the Motor Vehicles (International Circulation) Order 1975.

Revocation and transitional provision

4-4092　2. (1) The Motor Vehicles (International Circulation) Regulations 1971 are hereby revoked
　(2) This Regulation shall not affect the validity of any document issued or other thing done under the Regulations hereby revoked and so far as it could have been issued or done under these Regulations such document or thing shall have effect as if issued or done under the corresponding provision of these Regulations.
　(3) In these Regulations references to, or to provisions of, the Convention of 1968 shall take effect on such date as that Convention comes into force for the United Kingdom which date shall be notified in the London and Edinburgh Gazettes.

Interpretation

4-4093　3. In these Regulations, except where the context otherwise requires, the following expressions have the meanings hereby assigned to them respectively that is to say—

"certificate of insurance" and "certificate of security" have the same meanings as in Part VI of the Road Traffic Act [1988];
"the Convention of 1926" means the International Convention relative to Motor Traffic concluded at Paris in the year 1926;
"the Convention of 1949" means the Convention on Road Traffic concluded at Geneva in the year 1949;
"the Convention of 1968" means the Convention on Road Traffic concluded at Vienna in the year 1968;
"the date of importation", in relation to a vehicle, means the date on which that vehicle was last brought into the United Kingdom;
"the Excise Act" means the Vehicles (Excise) Act 1971;
"exempted vehicle" means a vehicle exempt from excise duty by virtue of the Motor Vehicle (International Circulation) Order 1975;
"insurance card" has the same meaning as in the Motor Vehicles (International Motor Insurance Card) Regulations 1971;
"local authority" has the same meaning as in Regulation 15(2) of the Regulations of 1971;
"nationality sign" means a sign complying with the provisions of Annex 3 to the Convention of 1968, of annex 4 to the Convention of 1949 or of annex C to the Convention of 1926 and bearing the distinctive letters specified in or under the Convention for the country under the law of which the vehicle is registered;
"registration card" means a card issued under Regulation 6 of these Regulations or issued in Northern Ireland under provisions corresponding to Regulation 6;
"the Regulations of 1971" means the Road Vehicles (Registration and Licensing) Regulation 1971;
"the Secretary of State" means the Secretary of State for Transport;
"vehicle" means a mechanically propelled vehicle intended or adapted for use on roads;
"visiting vehicle" means a vehicle brought temporarily into Great Britain by a person resident outside the United Kingdom;
"visitor's registration document" means—

　(*a*) in the case of a vehicle registered in a country outside the United Kingdom, registration certificate issued under the law of any country in respect of which nationality sign has been assigned in, or notified to the Secretary-General of the United Nations under, the Convention of 1926, the Convention of 1949 or the Convention of 1968 whether or not that country is a party to any of the said Conventions and containing a registration mark, the name or the trade mark of the maker of the vehicle the maker's identification or serial number, the date of its registration and the full name and permanent place of residence of the applicant for the said certificate; or
　(*b*) a certificate in form D in Schedule 1 to the Motor Vehicles (International Circulation) Order 1975, issued under the law of a country outside the United Kingdom which is party to the Convention of 1926; or
　(*c*) in the case of a vehicle registered in accordance with the registration system of the British Authorities in Germany or the registration system of the United States Authorities in Germany, a registration certificate specifying the registered letter and number allotted to the vehicle under the system.

Production of Documents

4-4094　4. (1) A person resident outside the United Kingdom who brings into Great Britain visiting vehicle shall, if he is at any reasonable time required to do so, produce to a registration authority such of the documents as have been issued in respect of that vehicle and are specified in the next following paragraph.

(2) The documents referred to in paragraph (1) of this Regulation are:

(a) a certificate of insurance, or a certificate of security or an insurance card;

(b) a visitor's registration document;

(c) a registration card.

(3) A person resident outside the United Kingdom who brings into Great Britain a visiting vehicle in respect of which a visitor's registration document has been issued shall produce it for inspection if he is at any reasonable time required to do so by a police officer or by a person acting on behalf of the Secretary of State.

Registration marks for visiting vehicles which are exempted vehicles

4–4095   5. The registration mark hereby assigned to a visiting vehicle, being an exempted vehicle, is, subject to the provisions of Regulation 8(5) of these Regulations—

(a) in the case of a vehicle in respect of which there has been issued and there is held by the driver thereof a visitor's registration document recording a registration mark which consists of no letters or numerals other than Roman letters or ordinary European numerals or both, that mark;

(b) in any other case either—

(i) the registration mark assigned to the vehicle under provisions applying in Northern Ireland and corresponding to the provisions of the next succeeding sub-paragraph of this Regulation; or

(ii) if no such mark has been assigned under those provisions, a registration mark consisting of the letters QA, QB, QC, QD, QE, QF, QG, QH, QJ, QK, QL, QM, QN, QP, QQ, QR, QS, QT, QU, QV, QW, QX and QY and of a registered number which has been assigned to that vehicle by a registration authority.

Registration cards

4–4096   6. (1) Where a registration authority assigns a registration mark to a visiting vehicle under Regulation 5(b)(ii) of these Regulations, the authority shall issue to the person who brought that vehicle into Great Britain a registration card in respect of that vehicle containing such particulars as the Secretary of State may direct.

(2) The following provisions of the Regulations of 1971, that is to say—

(a) Regulation 6 (which relates to duplicate registration books); and

(b) paragraphs (2) and (4) of Regulation 8 (which relate to the production of registration books and to their defacement or mutilation),

shall apply in relation to a registration card as they apply in relation to a registration book but with the substitution of references to the registration authority for the references to the Secretary of State.

(3) Whenever a visiting vehicle in respect of which a registration card has been issued under paragraph (1) of this Regulation or under provisions applying in Northern Ireland and corresponding to the provisions of the said paragraph (1)—

(a) is sold or transferred, or

(b) is removed to a country outside the United Kingdom, or

(c) is destroyed

then the holder of the registration card shall surrender it to a registration authority informing the authority of the reason for the transfer and, in a case where that vehicle has been sold or transferred, of the name of the new owner and of his address, if any, in the United Kingdom.

(4) The registration authority (where other than the Secretary of State) to whom a registration card is so surrendered shall forward it to the Secretary of State and inform him of the date of surrender and of the reason therefor.

(5) In paragraph (3) of this Regulation references to a registration authority include references to any authority who shall have the functions in Northern Ireland of a registration authority under provisions corresponding to these Regulations.

Excise Licences

4–4097   7. A person who has brought a visiting vehicle which is not an exempted vehicle into Great Britain shall apply for an excise licence under the Excise Act for that vehicle.

Provision as to registration marks assigned under Regulation 5

4–4098   8. (1) Regulation 17 of, and Schedule 2 to, the Regulations of 1971 shall apply to an exempted vehicle as if the reference therein to any registration mark which is required to be fixed on a vehicle by virtue of the Excise Act included a reference to the registration mark assigned under Regulation 5 of these Regulations and Regulation 20 of, and Schedule 3 to, the Regulations of 1971 shall apply to an exempted vehicle as if it were a vehicle registered before 1st October 1938:

Provided that—

(a) Regulation 17 of, and Schedule 2 to, the Regulations of 1971 (which impose requirements as to the form of registration marks) shall not apply as respects a registration mark mentioned in Regulation 5(*a*) of these Regulations if the corresponding requirements of the law under which, or the authority by whom, the registration mark was issued are complied with, and

(*b*)   a registration mark mentioned in the said Regulation 5(*a*) need not be exhibited at the front of the vehicle if that is not required by the law under which, or the authority by whom, the registration mark was issued.

(2)   At the back of an exempted vehicle on which is exhibited a registration mark mentioned in Regulation 5(*a*) there shall be exhibited so as to be clearly distinguishable a nationality sign indicating the country under the law of which the registration mark was issued:

Provided that no nationality sign need be shown on an exempted vehicle in a case where the visitor's registration document falls within paragraph (*c*) of the definition of that expression in these Regulations.

(3)   Regulation 22 of the Regulations of 1971 shall apply to any trailer drawn by an exempted vehicle as if reference therein to the registration mark were references to the registration mark displayed by an exempted vehicle by virtue of Regulation 5 of these Regulations:

Provided that in a case where—

(*a*)   the registration mark to be displayed by the exempted vehicle is that under Regulation 5(*a*) of these Regulations; and

(*b*)   the trailer has been brought temporarily into Great Britain by a person resident outside the United Kingdom,

a registration mark issued to the trailer under the law of a country outside the United Kingdom which is a party to the Convention of 1949 or the Convention of 1968 may be displayed at the back of the trailer instead of the registration mark to be displayed by the exempted vehicle.

(4)   When an exempted vehicle which in pursuance of this Regulation must carry a nationality sign is drawing one or more trailers, the nationality sign shall be carried in like manner at the back of the trailer or rearmost trailer:

Provided that a trailer carrying a registration mark in pursuance of the proviso to the last foregoing paragraph shall carry a nationality sign indicating the country under the law of which that registration mark was issued to the trailer instead of any other nationality sign indicating the country under the law of which a registration mark was issued to the exempted vehicle.

(5)   A registration mark assigned under Regulation 5 of these Regulations shall become void when relief from customs duty ceases to be afforded in respect of that vehicle under the provisions referred to in Article 5(2) of the Motor Vehicles (International Circulation) Order 1975.

Records to be kept by registration authorities

4-4099   **9.** (1) Each registration authority shall, in relation to every exempted vehicle to which a registration mark mentioned in Regulation 5(*b*)(ii) of these Regulations is assigned, keep a record of the following particulars:

(*a*)   the name of the person applying in respect of the vehicle for that mark, his address in the United Kingdom and (if available) his home address;

(*b*)   make of vehicle and chassis number or engine number;

(*c*)   the registration mark assigned to the vehicle, and the date and place at which it was assigned; and

(*d*)   (if available), the date and place of entry of the vehicle into the United Kingdom.

(2)   Each registration authority other than the Secretary of State shall forward to the Secretary of State a copy of the particulars so recorded.

(3)   The Secretary of State shall preserve for not less than two years the copies forwarded to him under the last foregoing paragraph and any records made by himself under paragraph (1) of this Regulation.

(4)   The Secretary of State shall also preserve for not less than two years a record of any particulars forwarded to him for recording under provisions made in Northern Ireland corresponding to paragraph (2) of this Regulation as respects a vehicle to which a registration mark has been assigned in Northern Ireland under provisions corresponding to Regulation 5(*b*)(ii) of these Regulations.

(5)   The Secretary of State shall, on application therefor, furnish free of charge any particulars recorded in any documents preserved by him under this Regulation to the Commissioners of Customs and Excise, the Department of Environment for Northern Ireland, any registration authority, any local authority, or any chief officer of police in the United Kingdom, and shall upon payment of £2 furnish to any other person who can show to the satisfaction of the Secretary of State that he has reasonable cause therefor, the name and address shown in respect of any registration mark contained in any records preserved under this Regulation.

Fixed Penalty (Procedure) Regulations 1986[1]
(SI 1986/1330 amended by SI 2001/926)

4-4111   **1.** (1) *Commencement and citation.*

(2) In these Regulations any reference to a section is a reference to a section of the [Road Traffic Offenders Act 1988].

(3) These Regulations do not extend to Scotland.

1. Made by the Secretary of State in exercise of powers conferred upon him by ss 49(1) and 73(5) of the Transport Act 1982 and now having effect under ss 84 and 88 of the Road Traffic Offenders Act 1988.

–4112 **2.** (1) Subject to paragraph (2) below, in the documents described in column 1 of the Schedule to these Regulations and referred to in the provisions of the Act specified in column 2 of the Schedule there shall be provided the information or, as the case may be, further information prescribed in column 3 of the Schedule.

(2) The information prescribed in the Schedule in relation to a fixed penalty notice need not be provided if the offender's driving licence would not be subject to endorsement on conviction of the offence in respect of which the notice was given.

–4113 **3.** (1) A copy of any fixed penalty notice given or affixed under [sections 54 or 62] shall be forwarded by or on behalf of the constable or traffic warden giving or affixing the notice to the fixed penalty clerk unless the fixed penalty clerk has notified the chief officer of police that he does not wish to receive a copy of any such notice.

(2) Where a fixed penalty notice has been given to a person under [sections 54 or 62] shall be forwarded by or on behalf of the constable or traffic warden giving or affixing the notice to the fixed penalty clerk unless the fixed penalty clerk has notified the chief officer of police that he does not wish to receive a copy of any such notice.

(3) Where a fixed penalty notice has been given to a person under [section 53 or 62] and that person has surrendered his driving licence in accordance with that section the driving licence shall be forwarded by or on behalf of the constable to the fixed penalty clerk.

–4114 **4.** (1) Where a constable has issued a fixed penalty notice to a person under section [54(5)], he shall send a notice indicating that fact to the chief officer of police together with that person's driving licence.

(2) Subject to paragraph (3) below, on receipt of the documents referred to in paragraph (1) above the chief officer of police shall send the driving licence and a copy of the notice issued under section [54(4)] to the fixed penalty clerk and notify him that a fixed penalty notice has been issued under section [54(5)].

(3) The chief officer of police shall not send a copy of the notice issued under section [54(4)] to the fixed penalty clerk under paragraph (2) above if the fixed penalty clerk has notified the chief officer of police that he does not wish to receive a copy of any such notice.

–4115 **5.** (1) On receipt of the remittance in respect of a fixed penalty the fixed penalty clerk shall notify the chief officer of police that the remittance has been received.

(2) If payment of the fixed penalty is made by a person otherwise than as required by the fixed penalty notice the fixed penalty c shall return the remittance to that person.

(3) Where a remittance in respect of a fixed penalty is sent by a person to a justices' chief executive who is not the fixed penalty clerk specified in the fixed penalty notice, the justices' chief executive shall return the remittance to that person.

–4116 **6.** Where—

(a) the suspended enforcement period[1] has expired; and
(b) the fixed penalty has not been paid; and
(c) either the person to whom the fixed penalty notice was given has requested a hearing under section [55(2) or 63(3)] or no registration certificate has been issued under section [70(2)],

the chief officer of police shall notify the fixed penalty clerk accordingly and the fixed penalty clerk shall, where an endorsable offence is involved, return the driving licence to the person to whom the fixed penalty notice was given.

1. See ss 52(3)(a) and 78 of the Act.

–4117 **7.** Where—

(a) the suspended enforcement period[1] has expired; and
(b) the fixed penalty has not been paid; and
(c) a registration certificate has been issued under section [70(2)].

the chief officer of police shall notify the fixed penalty clerk accordingly.

1. See ss 52(3)(a) and 78 of the Act.

–4118 **8.** Where in a case involving an endorsable offence any sum determined by reference to the fixed penalty is registered under section [71] for enforcement against the licence holder as a fine the justices' chief executive at the court where the sum is registered shall notify the fixed penalty clerk to whom the driving licence was sent that the sum has been registered.

–4119 **9.** Where a fixed penalty notice is issued under section [54(5) or 62(1)] the fixed penalty clerk shall not accept payment of the fixed penalty after the expiry of the suspended enforcement period.

4–4120   **10.** Where a fixed penalty is paid within the suspended enforcement period the fixe(penalty clerk shall send a receipt for the payment, if requested, to the payer.

4–4121   **11.** For the purposes of section [56(3)(*a*)] (which provides that a licence receipt issued by constable is to cease to have effect on the expiration of the period of one month beginning wit the date of issue) there shall be prescribed a longer period of two months beginning with th same date.

4–4122

Regulation 2   SCHEDULE

INFORMATION OR FURTHER INFORMATION TO BE PROVIDED IN CERTAIN DOCUMENTS MENTIONED IN PART III OF THE [ROAD TRAFFI OFFENDERS ACT 1988]

Document	Provision of Act	Information or further information to be provided
1 Fixed penalty notice	Section 27(8)	(i) The name of the police force of which the constabl giving the notice is a member. (ii) The serial number of the fixed penalty notice (iii) Whether the notice relates to an endorsable offenc (iv) The name, date of birth and address of the perso to whom the notice is given (v) The date, time and place of the alleged offence (vi) The details of the vehicle including the registratio number (vii) The documents, if any, to be produced at a polic station and the period within which they must b produced (viii) An explanation of the action to be taken by th driver where (*a*) he has not or (*b*) he has surrendere the licence (ix) The fact that the person to whom the notice is give may opt for trial (x) The method of paying the fixed penalty (xi) The name, rank and number of the constable issuin the fixed penalty notice (xii) Guidance to the driver as to the legal consequence of a fixed penalty notice.
2 Receipt for driving licence	Section 35(1)	(i) Whether the driving licence is full or provisional (ii) The driver number as shown on the licence (iii) The groups of vehicles which the driver is entitle to drive (iv) The expiry date of the licence (v) The duration of the validity of the licence receipt (vi) The method of obtaining a new receipt on the expir of an old receipt (vii) The name, rank and number of the constabl issuing the fixed penalty notice.
3. Receipt for driving	Section 35(2)	(i) The date of issue of receipt ii) The code of the magistrates' court issuing receipt (iii) The name, address and date of birth of driver (iv) Whether the driving licence is full or provisional (v) The driver number as shown on the licence (vi) The groups of vehicles which the driver is entitle to drive (vii) The expiry date of the licence (viii) The duration of the validity of the licence receipt.
4 Registration certificate	Section 36	(i) The serial number and date, time and place of issu of the notice to the owner, notice to hirer or fixe penalty notice (as case may be). (ii) The vehicle registration number (iii) The driver number (iv) The amount of the appropriate fixed penalty (v) The sum to be registered in default of payment (the fixed penalty.
5 Notice requesting new statutory statement	Section 37(8)	(i) The particulars of the statutory declaration (ii) The details of the alleged fixed penalty offence (iii) A request to furnish a statutory statement (ownership (iv) The period allowed for a response to the notice (v) The consequence of providing, or, as the case ma be, not providing the statutory statement of ownershi
6. Statement of liability	Section 45(2)	(i) The name, date of birth and address of hirer (ii) The duration of the hiring agreement.

New Drivers (Appeals Procedure) Regulations 1997[1]
(SI 1997/1098)

4–4350   1. *Citation, commencement and interpretation.*

1. Made by the Secretary of State for Transport, in exercise of the powers conferred by s 5 of, and para 11 of Sch 1 to, the Road Traffic (New Drivers) Act 1995.

Licences granted pending appeal

4–4351   2. (1) There is prescribed for the purposes of section 5(1) of the Act (duration of licences granted without retesting pending appeal) a period expiring on the date on which the revoked licence would have expired if it had not been revoked.

(2) Where the Secretary of State has—

(a) revoked a person's test certificate under paragraph 5(1) of Schedule 1 to the Act or, as the case may be, revoked a person's licence and test certificate under paragraph 8(1) of that Schedule, and

(b) received notice that the person is making a relevant appeal,

he must, if that person surrenders to him any previous licence granted to him or provides an explanation for not surrendering it that the Secretary of State considers adequate, grant to that person a full licence in accordance with paragraph (3) below.

(3) A licence granted under paragraph (2) above shall—

(a) have effect for the purposes of the Road Traffic Acts as if it were a licence granted under Part III of the Road Traffic Act 1988,

(b) subject to section 92 and Part IV of that Act, authorise the driving of all classes of vehicle which, immediately before his test certificate was revoked, the person was permitted to drive without observing the prescribed conditions, and

(c) subject to paragraph (4) below, be for a period expiring on the date on which a licence granted under Part III of that Act would have expired.

(4) A licence granted under paragraph (2) shall be treated as revoked if—

(a) following the appeal, the penalty points taken into account for the purposes of section 2(1) of the Act are not reduced to a number smaller than six, or

(b) the appeal is abandoned.

Notices of appeal

4–4352   3. (1) Subject to paragraphs (2) and (3) below, notice of a relevant appeal shall be given to the Secretary of State—

(a) in England and Wales, by the magistrates' court or Crown Court in which the case is heard;

(b) in Scotland, by the Sheriff Court or district court in which the case is heard.

(2) Notice of a relevant appeal from a magistrates' court or Crown Court by case stated shall be given to the Secretary of State by the High Court.

(3) Notice of a further appeal from a decision of an appellate court shall be given to the Secretary of State by the appellate court from which the appeal is made.

(4) A notice pursuant to this regulation shall be given—

(a) in the case of an appeal by case stated, as soon as reasonably practicable after the day on which the case is lodged in the High Court;

(b) in the case of any other appeal—

(i) where leave to appeal or for abridgement of time is necessary, as soon as reasonably practicable after the court has granted such leave or abridgement, or

(ii) in any other case, as soon as reasonably practicable after notice of appeal is duly given by the appellant.

Notice of abandonment of appeal

4–4353   4. Notice of the abandonment of any relevant appeal shall be given to the Secretary of State—

(a) in England and Wales, by the appellate court to which the appeal is made, or

(b) in Scotland, by the Sheriff Court or district court in which the case is heard,

as soon as reasonably practicable after the day on which notice of the abandonment of the appeal is duly given.

Public Service Vehicles (Community Licences) Regulations 1999
(SI 1999/1322)

4–4376A   1. *Citation, commencement and extent*

4–4376B   2. Purpose and interpretation.   (1) These Regulations implement Article 3a of the Council Regulation.

(2) In these Regulations—

"the 1981 Act" means the Public Passenger Vehicles Act 1981;

"the Council Regulation" means Council Regulation (EEC) No 684/92 of 16 March 1992 on common rules for the international carriage of passengers by coach and bus, as amended by Council Regulation (EC) No 11/98 of 11 December 1997;

"international operations", "national operations", "operating centre", "PSV operator's licence", "restricted licence", "standard licence" and "traffic commissioner" have the meaning given to them by section 82(1) of the 1981 Act;

"operator" has the meaning given by section 81 of the 1981 Act;

"public service vehicle" has the meaning given by section 1 of the 1981 Act;

"traffic area" means a traffic area constituted for the purposes of the 1981 Act;

"Transport Tribunal" means the Transport Tribunal constituted as provided in Schedule 4 to the Transport Act 1985;

and subject thereto, expressions used which are also used in the Council Regulation have the meaning which they bear in that Regulation.

4–4376C   3. Use of public service vehicles without Community licence.   A person who uses a vehicle in Great Britain in contravention of Article 3a(1) of the Council Regulation shall be guilty of an offence and liable on summary conviction to a fine not exceeding level 4 on the standard scale.

4–4376D   4. Competent authorities.   The competent authority for the purposes of Article 3a of the Council Regulation and of these Regulations shall be, in relation to the operator of a public service vehicle who has an operating centre in a traffic area in Great Britain, the traffic commissioner for that area.

4–4376E   5. Entitlement to the issue of a Community licence.   A person shall be entitled to be issued by the competent authority with a Community licence under Article 3a(2) of the Council Regulation if he holds a standard licence which authorises use on both national and international operations, or a restricted licence.

4–4376F   6. Rights of appeal.   A person who—

(a) is aggrieved by the refusal of the competent authority to issue a Community licence to him, or

(b) being the holder of a Community licence, is aggrieved by the decision of the competent authority who issued it to withdraw it,

may appeal to the Transport Tribunal.

4–4376G   7. Effect of failure to comply with conditions governing use of Community licences.   A person who uses a public service vehicle in Great Britain under a Community licence and, without reasonable excuse, fails to comply with any of the conditions governing the use of that licence under the Council Regulation, shall be guilty of an offence and liable on summary conviction to a fine not exceeding level 4 on the standard scale.

4–4376H   8. Authorised inspecting officers.   Authorised inspecting officers for the purposes of the Council Regulation shall be examiners appointed under section 66A(1) of the Road Traffic Act 1988 and police constables.

4–4376J   9. Return of documents.   (1) Where a Community licence is withdrawn by the competent authority in accordance with condition 5 of the model Community licence set out in the Annex to the Council Regulation, the holder of that licence shall within 7 days of such withdrawal return to the competent authority which issued it the original licence and all certified true copies of it.

(2) The holder of a Community licence shall return to the competent authority which issued it such certified true copies of the licence as the authority may require pursuant to—

(a) any decision of the authority to reduce the maximum number of vehicles (being vehicles having their operating centre in the area of that authority) which the holder is authorised, under section 16(1) of the 1981 Act, to use under the PSV operator's licence held by him, or

(b) any decision of the authority under the condition 5 referred to in paragraph (1) to suspend or withdraw certified true copies of the Community licence.

(3) A person who, without reasonable excuse, fails to comply with any provision of paragraph (1) or (2) shall be guilty of an offence and liable on summary conviction to a fine not exceeding level 4 on the standard scale.

4–4376K   10. Supply of information.   (1) The holder of a Community licence shall furnish such information as the competent authority which issued it may reasonably require from time to time to enable the authority to decide whether the holder is entitled to retain that licence.

(2) A person who, without reasonable excuse, fails to supply any information required under paragraph (1) shall be guilty of an offence and liable on summary conviction to a fine not exceeding level 4 on the standard scale.

4–4376L   11. Death, bankruptcy etc of holder of Community licence.   Where a person is authorised to carry on the business of the holder of a PSV operator's licence by virtue of an authorisation under section 57(4)(*b*) of the 1981 Act, such person shall be treated as the holder of any Community licence held by the holder of the PSV operator's licence, for the same period as is specified in that authorisation.

4–4376M 12. Bodies corporate. (1) Where an offence under these Regulations has been committed by a body corporate and it is proved to have been committed with the consent or connivance of, or to be attributable to any neglect on the part of, any director, manager, secretary or other similar officer of the body corporate or any person who was purporting to act in any such capacity, he as well as the body corporate shall be guilty of the offence and shall be liable to be proceeded against and punished accordingly.

(2) Where the affairs of a body corporate are managed by its members, paragraph (1) shall apply in relation to the acts and defaults of a member in connection with his functions of management as if he were a director of the body corporate.

(3) Where an offence under these Regulations has been committed by a Scottish partnership and it is proved to have been committed with the consent or connivance of, or to be attributable to any neglect on the part of, a partner, he as well as the partnership shall be guilty of the offence and shall be liable to be proceeded against and punished accordingly.

4–4376N

Motor Vehicles (Driving Licences) Regulations 1999[1]
(SI 1999/2864 amended by SI 2000/2766 and 3157, SI 2001/53, 236, 937, 2779 and 3486, SI 2002/2641, SI 2003/166, 222, 636, 2003 and 3313, SI 2004/265, 1519, 3028 and 3168 (E), SI 2005/2717 and 2929 (W) and SI 2006/524)

PART I
PRELIMINARY

4–4377 1. Citation and commencement. These Regulations may be cited as the Motor Vehicles (Driving Licences) Regulations 1999 and shall come into force on 12th November 1999.

1. Made by the Secretary of State for the Environment, Transport and the Regions with the approval of the Treasury, under the Road Traffic Act 1988, ss 88(5), (6), 89(1A), (2A), (3), (4), (5), (5A), (6), (7), (9), (10), 89A(3), (5), 91, 92(2), (4), 94(4), (5), 97(1), (1A), (3), (3A), (3B), (4), 98(2), (4), 99(1), (1A), 99A(3), (4), (6), 101(2), (3), 105(1), (2), (3), (4), 108(1), 114(1), 115(1), (3), 115A(1), 117(2A), 118(4), 120, 121, 122, 164(2), 183(6), 192(1). Only those amending instruments which affect the text reproduced in this work are cited.

4–4377A 2. Revocation and saving. (1) The regulations specified in Schedule 1 are hereby revoked.

(2) Subject to otherwise herein provided, and without prejudice to the operation of sections 16 and 17 of the Interpretation Act 1978, the revocation of those regulations shall not affect the validity of any application or appointment made, notice or approval given, licence, certificate or other document granted or issued or other thing done thereunder and any reference in such application, appointment, notice, approval, licence, certificate or other document or thing to a provision of any regulation hereby revoked, whether specifically or by means of a general description, shall, unless the context otherwise requires, be construed as a reference to the corresponding provision of these Regulations.

4–4377B 3. Interpretation. (1) In these Regulations, unless the context otherwise requires, the following expressions have the following meanings—

"1981 Act" means the Public Passenger Vehicles Act 1981;
"1985 Act" means the Transport Act 1985;
"ambulance" means a motor vehicle which—

(*a*) is constructed or adapted for, and used for no other purpose than, the carriage of sick, injured or disabled people to or from welfare centres or places where medical or dental treatment is given, and
(*b*) is readily identifiable as such a vehicle by being marked "Ambulance" on both sides;

"appropriate driving test" and "extended driving test" have the same meanings respectively as in section 36 of the Offenders Act;
"certified direct access instructor" has the meaning given by regulation 64(2);
"Construction and Use Regulations" means the Road Vehicles (Construction and Use) Regulations 1986;
"controlled by a pedestrian" in relation to a vehicle means that the vehicle either—

(*a*) is constructed or adapted for use under such control; or
(*b*) is constructed or adapted for use either under such control or under the control of a person carried on it but is not for the time being in use under, or proceeding under, the control of a person carried on it;

"disability assessment test" means a test of competence to drive for which a person is required, by notice under section 94(5)(*c*) of the Traffic Act, to submit himself; and "disability assessment licence" means a provisional licence granted to enable him to drive a motor vehicle for the purposes of preparing for, and taking, such a test;

"dual purpose vehicle" means a motor vehicle which is constructed or adapted both to carry or haul goods and to carry more than eight persons in addition to the driver;

"exempted goods vehicle" and "exempted military vehicle" have the meanings respectively given in regulation 51;

"extended driving test" means a test of a kind prescribed by regulation 41;

"full", in relation to a licence of any nature, means a licence granted otherwise than as a provisional licence;

"Group 1 licence" and "Group 2 licence" have the meanings respectively given in regulation 70;

"incomplete large vehicle" means—

(a) an incomplete motor vehicle, typically consisting of a chassis and a complete or incomplete cab, which is capable of becoming, on the completion of its construction, a medium-sized or large goods vehicle or a passenger-carrying vehicle, or

(b) a vehicle which would be an articulated goods vehicle but for the absence of a fifth-wheel coupling,

and which is not drawing a trailer;

"large motor bicycle" means—

(a) in the case of a motor bicycle without a side-car, a bicycle the engine of which has a maximum net power output exceeding 25 kilowatts or which has a power to weight ratio exceeding 0.16 kilowatts per kilogram, or

(b) in the case of a motor bicycle and side-car combination, a combination having a power to weight ratio exceeding 0.16 kilowatts per kilogram;

"LGV trainee driver's licence" has the meaning given in regulation 54;

"maximum authorised mass"—

(a) in relation to a goods vehicle, has the same meaning as "permissible maximum weight" in section 108(1) of the Traffic Act,

(b) in relation to an incomplete large vehicle, means its working weight, and

(c) in relation to any other motor vehicle or trailer, has the same meaning as "maximum gross weight" in regulation 3(2) of the Construction and Use Regulations;

"maximum speed" means the speed which the vehicle is incapable, by reason of its construction, of exceeding on the level under its own power when fully laden;

"maximum net power output" has the same meaning as in section 97 of the Traffic Act;

"mobile project vehicle" means a vehicle which has a maximum authorised mass exceeding 3.5 tonnes, is constructed or adapted to carry not more than eight persons in addition to the driver and carries principally goods or burden consisting of—

(a) play or educational equipment and articles required in connection with the use of such equipment, or

(b) articles required for the purposes of display or of an exhibition,

and the primary purpose of which is use as a recreational, educational or instructional facility when stationary;

"Northern Ireland test" means a test of competence to drive conducted under the law of Northern Ireland;

"Offenders Act" means the Road Traffic Offenders Act 1988;

"passenger-carrying vehicle recovery vehicle" means a vehicle (other than an articulated goods vehicle combination as defined in section 108(1) of the Traffic Act) which—

(a) has an unladen weight not exceeding 10.2 tonnes,

(b) is being operated by the holder of a PSV operator's licence, and

(c) is being used for the purpose of—

(i) proceeding to, or returning from, a place where assistance is to be, or has been given to a damaged or disabled passenger-carrying vehicle; or

(ii) giving assistance to or moving a disabled passenger-carrying vehicle or moving a damaged vehicle;

"penalty points" means penalty points attributed to an offence under section 28 of the Offenders Act;

"power to weight ratio", in relation to a motor bicycle, means the ratio of the maximum net power output of the engine of the vehicle to its weight (including the weight of any side-car) with—

(a) a full supply of fuel in the tank,

(b) an adequate supply of other liquids needed for its propulsion, and

(c) no load other than its normal equipment, including loose tools;

"practical test" means a practical test of driving skills and behaviour or, where a test is by virtue of these Regulations required to be conducted in two parts, the part of it which consists of that test and includes such a test conducted as part of an extended driving test;

"propelled by electrical power", in relation to a motor vehicle, means deriving motive power solely from an electrical storage battery carried on the vehicle and having no connection to any other source of power when the vehicle is in motion;

"PSV operator's licence" has the meaning given by section 82(1) of the 1981 Act;

"standard access period" has the meaning given by regulation 22;

"standard motor bicycle" means a motor bicycle which is not a large motor bicycle;

"test" means any test of competence to drive conducted pursuant to section 89 of the Traffic Act including an extended driving test;

"test pass certificate" means a certificate in the form specified in regulation 48(1)(*a*);

"theory test" means, where a test is by virtue of these Regulations to be conducted in two parts, the part that consists of the theoretical test and includes such a test conducted as part of an extended driving test;

"theory test pass certificate" means a certificate in the form specified in regulation 47(2)(*a*);

"Traffic Act" means the Road Traffic Act 1988;

"traffic commissioner" means, in relation to an applicant for or the holder of a licence, the traffic commissioner in whose area the applicant or holder resides;

"unitary test" means a test which, by virtue of these Regulations, is to consist of a single test of both practical driving skills and behaviour and knowledge of the Highway Code and other matters and includes such a test conducted as an extended driving test;

"unladen weight" has the same meaning as in regulation 3(2) of the Construction and Use Regulations and, in the case of a road roller, includes the weight of any object for the time being attached to the vehicle, being an object specially designed to be so attached for the purpose of temporarily increasing the vehicle's weight;

"vehicle with automatic transmission" means a class of vehicle in which either—

(*a*) the driver is not provided with any means whereby he may vary the gear ratio between the engine and the road wheels independently of the accelerator and the brakes, or

(*b*) he is provided with such means but they do not include a clutch pedal or lever which he may operate manually,

(and accordingly a vehicle with manual transmission is any other class of vehicle);

"working weight" means the weight of a vehicle in working condition on a road but exclusive of the weight of any liquid coolant and fuel used for its propulsion.

(2) In these Regulations, unless the context otherwise requires—

(*a*) a reference to a licence being in force is a reference to it being in force in accordance with section 99 of the Traffic Act, save that for the purpose of these Regulations a licence shall remain in force notwithstanding that it is—

(i) surrendered to the Secretary of State or is revoked otherwise than by notice under section 93(1) or (2) of the Traffic Act (revocation because of disability or prospective disability), or

(ii) treated as revoked by virtue of section 37(1) of the Offenders Act, and

(*b*) a reference to the expiry of a licence is a reference to the time at which it ceases to be so in force (and "expired" shall be construed accordingly).

(3) Except where otherwise expressly provided, any reference in these Regulations to a numbered regulation or Schedule is a reference to the regulation or Schedule bearing that number in these Regulations, and any reference to a numbered paragraph (otherwise than as part of a reference to a numbered regulation) is a reference to the paragraph bearing that number in the regulation or Schedule in which the reference occurs.

(4) Where a statement or certificate (but not a distinguishing mark specified in regulation 16) is required under these Regulations to be in a form prescribed herein, the reference is to a certificate or statement in that form (or as nearly in that form as circumstances permit), adapted to the circumstances of the case and duly completed and signed where required.

(5) For the purposes of section 97(3)(*d*) of the Traffic Act and these Regulations the date of first use of a motor bicycle means—

(*a*) except in a case to which paragraph (*b*) applies, the date on which it was first registered under the Roads Act 1920, the Vehicles (Excise) Act 1949, the Vehicles (Excise) Act 1962 or the Vehicles (Excise) Act 1971;

(*b*) in the case of a motor bicycle which was used in any of the following circumstances before the date on which it was first registered, namely:—

(i) where the bicycle was used under a trade licence as defined in section 16 of the Vehicles (Excise) Act 1971, otherwise than for the purposes of demonstration or testing or of being delivered from premises of the manufacturer by whom it was made, or of a distributor of vehicles or dealer in vehicles to premises of a distributor of vehicles, dealer in vehicles or purchaser thereof, or to premises of a person obtaining possession thereof under a hiring agreement or hire purchase agreement,

(ii) where the bicycle belonged to the Crown and is or was used or appropriated for use for naval, military or air force purposes,

(iii) where the bicycle belonged to a visiting force or a headquarters or defence organisation to which the Visiting Forces and International Headquarters (Application of Law) Order 1965 applied,

(iv) where the bicycle had been used on roads outside Great Britain and was imported into Great Britain, or

(v) where the bicycle had been used otherwise than on roads after being sold or supplied by retail and before being registered,

the date of manufacture of the bicycle.

(6) In paragraph (5)(*b*)(v) "sold or supplied by retail" means sold or supplied otherwise than to a person acquiring solely for the purpose of re-sale or re-supply for a valuable consideration.

PART II

LICENCES

Categories of entitlement

4–4377C   4. Classification of vehicles. (1) Subject to regulations 5 and 78, the Secretary of State shall grant licences authorising the driving of motor vehicles in accordance with the categories and sub-categories specified in column (1) and defined in column (2) of Schedule 2 and those categories and sub-categories are designated as groups for the purposes of section 89(1)(*b*) of the Traffic Act.

(2) In these Regulations, expressions relating to vehicle categories have the following meanings—

(*a*)   any reference to a category or sub-category identified by letter, number or word or by any combination of letters, numbers and words is a reference to the category or sub-category defined in column (2) of Schedule 2 opposite that letter or combination in column (1) of the Schedule,

(*b*)   "sub-category" means, in relation to category A, B, C, C + E, D or D + E, a class of vehicles comprising part of the category and identified as a sub-category thereof in column (2) of Schedule 2, and

(*c*)   unless the context otherwise requires, a reference to a category includes a reference to sub-categories of that category.

4–4377D   5. Classes for which licences may be granted. (1) A licence authorising the driving of motor vehicles of a class included in a category or sub-category shown in Part 1 of Schedule 2 may be granted to a person who is entitled thereto by virtue of—

(*a*)   holding or having held a full licence, a full Northern Ireland licence, full British external licence, full British Forces licence, exchangeable licence or Community licence authorising the driving of vehicles of that class, or

(*b*)   having passed a test for a licence authorising the driving of motor vehicles of that class or a Northern Ireland or Gibraltar test corresponding to such a test.

(2) A licence authorising the driving of motor vehicles of a class included in any category or sub-category shown in Part 2 of Schedule 2 may not be granted to a person unless, at a time before 1st January 1997—

(*a*)   in the case of a person applying for a full licence,—

    (i)   he held a full licence authorising the driving of motor vehicles of that class or a class which by virtue of these Regulations corresponds to a class included in that category or sub-category, or

    (ii)   he passed a test which at the time it was passed authorised the driving of motor vehicles of such a class or a Northern Ireland test corresponding to such a test;

(*b*)   in the case of a person applying for a provisional licence, he held a provisional licence authorising the driving of vehicles of that class or a class which by virtue of these Regulations corresponds to a class included in that category or sub-category.

(3) A licence authorising the driving of motor vehicles included in sub-category B1 (invalid carriages), which are specified in Part 3 of Schedule 2, may not be granted to a person unless, at a time before 12th November 1999—

(*a*)   in the case of a person applying for a full licence, he held a full licence authorising the driving of motor vehicles included in sub-category B1 (invalid carriages) or a class of motor vehicles which by virtue of these Regulations corresponds to vehicles included in that sub-category, or

(*b*)   in the case of a person applying for a provisional licence, he held a provisional licence authorising the driving of motor vehicles included in sub-category B1 (invalid carriages) or a class of motor vehicles which by virtue of these Regulations corresponds to vehicles included in that sub-category.

4–4377E   6. Competence to drive classes of vehicle: general. (1) Where a person holds, or has held, a relevant full licence authorising him to drive vehicles included in any category or, as the case may be, sub-category he is deemed competent to drive—

(*a*)   vehicles of all classes included in that category or sub-category unless by that licence he is or was authorised to drive—

    (i)   only motor vehicles of a specified class within that category or sub-category, in which case he shall be deemed competent to drive only vehicles of that class, or

    (ii)   only motor vehicles adapted on account of a disability, in which case he shall be deemed competent to drive only such classes of vehicle included in that category or sub-category as are so adapted (and for the purposes of this paragraph, a motor bicycle with a side-car may be treated in an appropriate case as a motor vehicle adapted on account of a disability),

    and

(*b*)   all classes of vehicle included in any other category or sub-category which is specified in column (3) of Schedule 2 as an additional category or sub-category in relation to that category or sub-category unless by that licence he is or was authorised to drive—

   (i)   only motor vehicles having automatic transmission, in which case he shall, subject to paragraph (2), be deemed competent to drive only such classes of motor vehicle included in the additional category or sub-category as have automatic transmission, or

  (ii)   only motor vehicles adapted on account of a disability, in which case he shall be deemed competent to drive only such classes of vehicle included in the additional category or sub-category as are so adapted.

(2) Where the additional category is F, K or P, paragraph (1)(*b*)(i) shall not apply.

(3) In this regulation and regulations 7 and 8, "relevant full licence" means a full licence granted under Part III of the Traffic Act, a full Northern Ireland licence or a Community licence.

–4377F   7. Competence to drive classes of vehicle: special cases.   (1) A person who has held, for a period of at least two years, a relevant full licence authorising the driving of vehicles included in category C, other than vehicles included in sub-category C1, may also drive a motor vehicle of a class included in category D which is—

  (*a*)   damaged or defective and being driven to a place of repair or being road tested following repair, and

  (*b*)   is not used for the carriage of any person who is not connected with its repair or road testing,

unless by that licence he is authorised to drive only vehicles having automatic transmission, in which case he shall be deemed competent to drive only such of the vehicles mentioned in sub-paragraphs (*a*) and (*b*) as have automatic transmission.

(2) A person who holds a relevant full licence authorising the driving of vehicles included in category D, other than vehicles included in sub-category D1 or D1 (not for hire or reward), may drive a passenger-carrying vehicle recovery vehicle unless by that licence he is authorised to drive only vehicles having automatic transmission, in which case he shall be deemed competent to drive only passenger-carrying vehicle recovery vehicles having automatic transmission.

(3) A person may drive an incomplete large vehicle—

  (*a*)   having a working weight exceeding 3.5 tonnes but not exceeding 7.5 tonnes if he holds a relevant full licence authorising the driving of vehicles in sub-category C1, or

  (*b*)   having a working weight exceeding 7.5 tonnes if he holds a relevant full licence authorising the driving of vehicles in category C, other than vehicles in sub-category C1,

unless by that licence he is authorised to drive only motor vehicles having automatic transmission, in which case he shall be deemed competent to drive only incomplete large vehicles of the appropriate weight specified in paragraph (*a*) or (*b*) which have automatic transmission.

(4) A person who holds a relevant full licence authorising the driving of vehicles included in category B, other than vehicles in sub-categories B1 and B1 (invalid carriages), may drive—

  (*a*)   an exempted goods vehicle other than—

    (i)   a passenger-carrying vehicle recovery vehicle, or

    (ii)   a mobile project vehicle,

  (*b*)   an exempted military vehicle, and

  (*c*)   a passenger-carrying vehicle in respect of which the conditions specified in regulation 50(2) or (3) are satisfied,

unless by that licence he is authorised to drive only motor vehicles having automatic transmission, in which case he shall be deemed competent to drive only such of the vehicles mentioned in sub-paragraphs (*a*), (*b*) and (*c*) as have automatic transmission.

(5) A person who—

  (*a*)   holds a relevant full licence authorising the driving of vehicles of a class included in category B, other than vehicles in sub-categories B1 or B1 (invalid carriages),

  (*b*)   has held that licence for an aggregate period of not less than 2 years, and

  (*c*)   is aged 21 or over,

may drive a mobile project vehicle on behalf of a non-commercial body—

  (i)   to or from the place where the equipment it carries is to be, or has been, used, or the display or exhibition is to be, or has been, mounted, or

  (ii)   to or from the place where a mechanical defect in the vehicle is to be, or has been, remedied, or

  (iii)   in such circumstances that by virtue of paragraph 22 of Schedule 2 to the Vehicle Excise and Registration Act 1994 the vehicle is not chargeable with duty in respect of its use on public roads,

unless by that licence he is authorised to drive only vehicles having automatic transmission, in which case he shall be deemed competent to drive only mobile project vehicles having automatic transmission.

(6) A person who—

  (*a*)   holds a relevant full licence authorising the driving of vehicles of a class included in category B, other than vehicles in sub-categories B1 or B1 (invalid carriages),

  (*b*)   has held that licence for an aggregate period of not less than 2 years,

  (*c*)   is aged 21 or over,

  (*d*)   if he is aged 70 or over, is not suffering from a relevant disability in respect of which the Secretary of State would be bound to refuse to grant him a Group 2 licence, and

  (*e*)   receives no consideration for so doing, other than out-of-pocket expenses, may drive, on behalf of a non-commercial body for social purposes but not for hire or reward, a vehicle of a class included in sub-category D1 which has no trailer attached and has a maximum authorised mass—

   (i)   not exceeding 3.5 tonnes, excluding any part of that weight which is attributable to specialised equipment intended for the carriage of disabled passengers, and

   (ii) not exceeding 4.25 tonnes otherwise,

unless such a person is by that licence authorised to drive only vehicles having automatic transmission, in which case he shall be deemed competent to drive only such vehicles in sub category D1 as conform to the above specification and have automatic transmission.

(7) A person who holds a relevant full licence authorising the driving of vehicles of a class included in category B, other than vehicles in sub-categories B1 or B1 (invalid carriages), may drive a vehicle of a class included in category B + E where—

   (a) the trailer consists of a vehicle which is damaged or defective and is likely to represent a road safety hazard or obstruction to other road users,

   (b) the vehicle is driven only so far as is reasonably necessary in the circumstances to remove the hazard or obstruction, and

   (c) her receives no consideration for driving the vehicle,

unless by that licence he is authorised to drive only motor vehicles having automatic transmission, in which case he shall be deemed competent to drive, in the circumstances mentioned above, only vehicles included in category B + E having automatic transmission.

4–4377G **8. Competence to drive classes of vehicle: dual purpose vehicles.** (1) Subject to paragraph (2), a person who is a member of the armed forces of the Crown may drive a dual purpose vehicle when it is being used to carry passengers for naval, military or air force purposes—

   (a) where the vehicle has a maximum authorised mass not exceeding 3.5 tonnes, if he holds a relevant full licence authorising the driving of vehicles included in category B other than vehicles in sub-categories B1 or B1 (invalid carriages),

   (b) where the vehicle has a maximum authorised mass exceeding 3.5 tonnes but not exceeding 7.5 tonnes, if he holds a relevant full licence authorising the driving of vehicles included in sub-category C1,

   (c) in any other case, if he holds a relevant full licence authorising the driving of vehicles included in category C other than vehicles in sub-category C1.

(2) Where the person is authorised by his licence to drive only motor vehicles included in the relevant category or sub-category having automatic transmission, he may drive only dual purpose vehicles having automatic transmission.

Minimum ages for holding or obtaining licences

4–4377H **9. Minimum ages for holding or obtaining licences.** (1) Subsection (1) of section 101 of the Traffic Act shall have effect as if for the classes of vehicle and the ages specified in the Table in that subsection there were substituted classes of vehicle and ages in accordance with the following provisions of this regulation.

(2) In item 3 (motor bicycles), the age of 21 is substituted for the age of 17 in a case where the motor bicycle is a large motor bicycle except in the following cases, namely—

   (a) a case where a person has passed a test on or after 1st January 1997 for a licence authorising the driving of a motor vehicle of a class included in category A, other than sub category A1, and the standard access period has elapsed,

   (b) a case where the large motor bicycle—

      (i)   is owned or operated by the Secretary of State for Defence, or

      (ii) is being driven by a person for the time being subject to the orders of a member of the armed forces of the Crown

     and is being used for naval, military or air force purposes, and

   (c) a case where a person holds a licence authorising the driving of a large motor bicycle by virtue of having passed a test before 1st January 1997.

(3) In item 4 (agricultural and forestry tractors), in the case of an agricultural or forestry tractor which—

   (a) is so constructed that the whole of its weight is transmitted to the road surface by means of wheels,

   (b) has an overall width not exceeding 2.45 metres, and

   (c) is driven either—

      (i)   without a trailer attached to it, or

      (ii) with a trailer which has an overall width not exceeding 2.45 metres and is either a two wheeled or close-coupled four-wheeled trailer,

the age of 16 is substituted for the age of 17 in the case of a person who has passed a test prescribed in respect of category F, or is proceeding to, taking or returning from, such a test.

(4) In item 5 (small vehicles), the age of 16 is substituted for the age of 17 in the case of a small vehicle driven without a trailer attached where the driver of the vehicle is a person in respect of whom an award of the higher rate component of the disability living allowance made in pursuance

of section 73 of the Social Security Contributions and Benefits Act 1992 (whether before or after his 16th birthday) is still in force.

(5) In item 6 (medium-sized goods vehicles), the age of 21 is substituted for the age of 18 in the case of a vehicle drawing a trailer where the maximum authorised mass of the combination exceeds 7.5 tonnes.

(6) In item 7 (other vehicles, including large goods and passenger-carrying vehicles), the age of 18 is substituted for the age of 21 in the case of a person driving a vehicle of a class included in sub-category D1 which is an ambulance and which is owned or operated by—

(a) a health service body (as defined in section 60(7) of the National Health Service and Community Care Act 1990), or

(b) a National Health Service Trust established under Part I of that Act or under the National Health Service (Scotland) Act 1978, or

(c) a Primary Care Trust established under section 16A of the National Health Service Act 1977.

(7) In item 7, the age of 18 is substituted for the age of 21 in the case of a motor vehicle and trailer combination which is in sub-category C1 + E and the maximum authorised mass of the combination does not exceed 7.5 tonnes.

(8) In item 7, the age of 18 is substituted for the age of 21 in the case of a person who is registered as an employee of a registered employer in accordance with the Training Scheme, where he is driving a vehicle which is—

(a) of a class to which his training agreement applies, and

(b) owned or operated by his employer or by a registered LGV driver training establishment.

(9) In item 7, the age of 18 is substituted for the age of 21 in relation to a passenger-carrying vehicle—

(a) in the case of a person who holds a provisional licence, and

(b) in the case of a person who holds a full passenger-carrying vehicle driver's licence, where he is driving a vehicle which is operated under a PSV operator's licence, a permit granted under section 19 of the 1985 Act or a community bus permit granted under section 22 of that Act and he is either—

(i) not engaged in the carriage of passengers, or

(ii) engaged in the carriage of passengers on a regular service over a route which does not exceed 50 kilometres, or

(iii) is driving a vehicle of a class included in sub-category D1.

(10) In items 6 and 7, the age of 17 is substituted for the ages of 18 and 21 respectively in the case of—

(a) motor vehicles owned or operated by the Secretary of State for Defence, or

(b) motor vehicles driven by persons for the time being subject to the orders of a member of the armed forces of the Crown,

when they are being used for naval, military or air force purposes.

(11) In item 7, in the case of an incomplete large vehicle—

(a) which has a working weight not exceeding 3.5 tonnes, the age of 17 is substituted for the age of 21;

(b) which has a working weight exceeding 3.5 tonnes but not exceeding 7.5 tonnes, the age of 18 is substituted for the age of 21.

(12) In item 7, the age of 17 is substituted for the age of 21 in the case of a road roller which—

(a) is propelled otherwise than by steam,

(b) has no wheel fitted with pneumatic, soft or elastic tyres,

(c) has an unladen weight not exceeding 11.69 tonnes, and

(d) is not constructed or adapted for the conveyance of a load other than the following things, namely water, fuel or accumulators used for the purpose of the supply of power to or propulsion of the vehicle, loose tools and objects specially designed to be attached to the vehicle for the purpose of temporarily increasing its weight.

(13) In this regulation—

(a) for the purposes of paragraph (3)—

(i) any implement fitted to a tractor shall be deemed to form part of the tractor notwithstanding that it is not a permanent or essentially permanent fixture,

(ii) "closed-coupled", in relation to wheels on the same side of a trailer, means fitted so that at all times while the trailer is in motion the wheels remain parallel to the longitudinal axis of the trailer and that the distance between the centres of their respective areas of contact with the road surface does not exceed 840 millimetres, and

(iii) "overall width", in relation to a vehicle, means the width of the vehicle measured between vertical planes parallel to the longitudinal axis of the vehicle and passing through the extreme projecting points thereof exclusive of any driving mirror and so much of the distortion of any tyre as is caused by the weight of the vehicle;

(b) for the purposes of paragraph (8), "registered", "training agreement" and "the Training Scheme" have the meanings respectively given in regulation 54;

(c) in paragraph (9), expressions used which are also used in Council Regulation 3820/85/EEC have the same meanings as in that Regulation[1].

1. OJ No L370, 31.12.85, p 1. See also reg 4 of the Community Drivers' Hours and Recording Equipment (Exemption and Supplementary Provisions) Regulations 1986, SI 1986/1456.

Applications for licences

4-4377I 10. Applications for the grant of licences: general.   (1) The Secretary of State may consider an application for the grant of a licence before the date on which the grant of the licence is to take effect if the application is received by him—

   (*a*) in the case of an application for a Group 2 licence, during the period of three months ending on that date,
   (*b*) in any other case, during the period of two months ending on that date,

and may during such period grant the licence so that it takes effect on that date.

   (2) For the purposes of subsection (1A)(*b*) of section 89 of the Traffic Act the holder of an exchangeable licence satisfies the relevant residence requirement if he has been normally resident in Great Britain for a period of not more than five years.

   (3) An applicant for a licence who before the licence is granted is required to satisfy the Secretary of State that he has passed a test shall at the time when he applies for the licence deliver to the Secretary of State—

   (*a*) a valid test pass certificate, or
   (*b*) a certificate corresponding to that certificate furnished under the law of Northern Ireland or Gibraltar.

   (4) A person may not present a certificate in support of an application as evidence that he has passed—

   (*a*) a test or a theory test, or
   (*b*) a test corresponding to any of those tests conducted under the law of Northern Ireland or the law of Gibraltar,

if the applicant took the test in respect of which the certificate was issued at a time when he was ineligible, by virtue of an enactment contained in the Traffic Act or these Regulations or a corresponding provision of the law of Northern Ireland or the law of Gibraltar, to take the test to which the certificate relates.

   (5) An applicant for a Group 2 licence shall, if required to do so by the Secretary of State, submit in support of his application a report (in such form as the Secretary of State may require) signed by a qualified medical practitioner, prepared and dated not more than four months prior to the date on which the licence is to take effect, for the purpose of satisfying the Secretary of State that he is not suffering from a relevant or prospective disability.

4-4377J 11. Eligibility to apply for provisional licence.   (1) Subject to the following provisions of this regulation, an applicant for a provisional licence authorising the driving of motor vehicles of a class included in a category or sub-category specified in column (1) of the table at the end of this regulation must hold a relevant full licence authorising the driving of motor vehicles of a class included in the category or sub-category specified in column (2) of the table in relation to the first category.

   (2) Paragraph (1) shall not apply in the case of an applicant who is a full-time member of the armed forces of the Crown.

   (3) For the purposes of paragraph (1), a licence authorising the driving only of vehicles in sub-categories D1 (not for hire or reward), D1 + E (not for hire or reward) and C1 + E (8.25 tonnes) shall not be treated as a licence authorising the driving of motor vehicles of a class included in sub-categories D1, D1 + E and C1 + E.

   (4) In this regulation, "relevant full licence" means a full licence granted under Part III of the Traffic Act, a full Northern Ireland licence, a full British external licence (other than a licence which is to be disregarded for the purposes of section 89(1)(d) of the Traffic Act by virtue of section 89(2)(c) of that Act), a full British Forces licence, an exchangeable licence or a Community licence.

TABLE

(1) Category or sub-category of licence applied for	(2) Category/sub-category of full licence required
B + E	B
C	B
C1	B
D	B
D1	B
C1 + E	C1
C + E	C
D1 + E	D1
D + E	D
G	B
H	B

4–4377K   12. Restrictions on the grant of large goods and passenger-carrying vehicle driver's licences.   (1) An applicant for a large goods or passenger-carrying vehicle driver's licence shall not, subject to paragraph (2), be granted a licence if, at the date from which the licence applied for is to take effect, any—

(a)   large goods or passenger-carrying vehicle driver's licence held by him is suspended, or

(b)   Northern Ireland large goods or passenger-carrying vehicle driver's licence held by him is suspended,

under section 115 of the Traffic Act or, as the case may be, under the provision of the law for the time being in force in Northern Ireland corresponding to that enactment.

(2)   A person may apply for a large goods vehicle driver's licence notwithstanding that, at the date from which the licence applied for is to take effect, any passenger-carrying vehicle driver's licence held by him is suspended and such suspension relates to his conduct other than as a driver of a motor vehicle.

(3)   An applicant for an LGV trainee driver's licence—

(a)   must be a registered employee of a registered employer (within the meaning of regulation 54), and

(b)   must not be a person who—

(i)   has been convicted (or is to be treated as if he had been convicted) of an offence as a result of which at least four penalty points fall to be taken into account under section 29 of the Offenders Act, or

(ii)   has at any time been disqualified by a court for holding or obtaining a licence or by a court in Northern Ireland for holding or obtaining a Northern Ireland licence, and

(c)   must satisfy the Secretary of State that he has satisfactorily completed the off-road elements of the training programme prescribed for drivers of goods vehicles by Council Directive 76/914/EEC[1] (that is those set out in paragraphs 1 and 2.1 to 2.8 of the Annex to the directive).

(4)   An applicant for a large goods vehicle driver's licence who is a member of the armed forces and is under the age of 21 must not be a person who has—

(a)   been convicted (or is, by virtue of section 58 of the Offenders Act, to be treated as if he had been convicted) of an offence as a result of which at least four penalty points fall to be taken into account under section 29 of the Offenders Act, or

(b)   at any time been disqualified by a court for holding or obtaining a licence or by a court in Northern Ireland for holding or obtaining a Northern Ireland licence.

_____

1. OJ No L 357, 29.12.76, p 36.

4–4377L   13. Restrictions on the grant of provisional licences to drive motor bicycles.   (*Revoked*).

4–4377M   14. Fees for licences.   (1) An applicant for a licence shall pay a fee (if any) determined in accordance with paragraphs (2) and (3).

(2)   The fee payable upon an application for a licence shall, in the case of a licence of a description, and (as the case may be) in the circumstances, specified in column (1) of the table set out in Schedule 3, be the fee specified in relation to that licence in column (2) of that table.

(3)   When an application is made for a licence which, but for this paragraph, would attract more than one fee, only one fee shall be paid and where the fees are different, that fee shall be the higher or the highest of them.

Provisional licences

4–4377N   15. Duration of provisional licences authorising the driving of motor bicycles.   (1) Subject to paragraph (2), there is prescribed for the purposes of section 99(2) of the Traffic Act—

(a)   a motor bicycle of any class, and

(b)   the same period as is provided by section 99(1) of the Traffic Act in relation to a licence to which section 99(1) applies.

(2)   There are prescribed for the purposes of section 99(2)(*b*)(ii) of that Act the circumstances that—

(a)   the previous licence was surrendered or revoked, otherwise than under subsection (3) or (4) of section 99 of the Traffic Act, or treated as being revoked under section 37(1) of the Offenders Act,

(b)   if it has not been so surrendered or revoked, a period of at least one month, commencing on the date of surrender or revocation, would have elapsed before the previous licence would have expired, and

(c)   the licence when granted would come into force within the period of one year beginning on the date of surrender or revocation of the previous licence.

4–4377O   16. Conditions attached to provisional licences.   (1) A provisional licence of any class is granted subject to the conditions prescribed in relation to a licence of that class in the following paragraphs.

(2)   Subject to the following paragraphs, the holder of a provisional licence shall not drive a vehicle of a class which he is authorised to drive by virtue of that licence—

(a)   otherwise than under the supervision[1] of a qualified driver who is present with him in or on the vehicle,

(b)   unless a distinguishing mark in the form set out in Part 1 of Schedule 4 is displayed on the vehicle in such manner as to be clearly visible to other persons using the road from within a reasonable distance from the front and from the back of the vehicle, or

(c)   while it is being used to draw a trailer.

(3)   The condition specified in paragraph (2)(a) shall not apply when the holder of the provisional licence—

(a)   is driving a motor vehicle of a class included in sub-category B1 or B1 (invalid carriages) or in category F, G, H or K which is constructed to carry only one person[2] and not adapted to carry more than one person;

(aa) is driving a motor vehicle of a class included in sub-category B1 which is adapted to carry only one person and has at any time between 1st August 2002 and 1st March 2003, had the use of an NHS invalid carriage that was issued to him by reason of his having a relevant disability;

(b)   is riding a moped or a motor bicycle[3] with or without a side-car[4]; or

(c)   is driving a motor vehicle, other than a vehicle of a class included in category C, C + E, D or D + E, on a road in an exempted island.

(4)   The condition specified in paragraph (2)(b) shall not apply—

(a)   when the holder of the provisional licence is driving a motor vehicle on a road in Wales, and

(b)   a distinguishing mark in the form set out in Part 2 of Schedule 4 is displayed on the motor vehicle in the manner described in paragraph (2)(b).

(5)   The condition specified in paragraph (2)(c) shall not apply to the holder of a provisional licence authorising the driving of a vehicle of a class included in category B + E, C + E, D + E or F, in relation to motor vehicles of that class.

(6)   The holder of a provisional licence authorising the driving of—

(a)   a moped, or

(b)   a motor bicycle[3] with or without a side-car[4],

shall not drive such a vehicle while carrying on it another person.

(7)   The holder of a provisional licence authorising the driving of a motor bicycle other than a learner motor bicycle shall not drive such a vehicle otherwise than under the supervision of a certified direct access instructor who is—

(a)   present with him on the road while riding another motor bicycle,

(b)   able to communicate with him by means of a radio which is not hand-held while in operation,

(c)   supervising only that person or only that person and another person who holds such a provisional licence, and

(d)   carrying a valid certificate issued in respect of him by the Secretary of State under regulation 65(4),

while he and the instructor are wearing apparel which is fluorescent or (during hours of darkness) is either fluorescent or luminous.

(7A)   The holder of a provisional licence authorising the driving of a moped or a learner motor bicycle shall not drive such a vehicle on a road when undergoing relevant training, unless the instructor giving the training is at all times—

(a)   present with him on the road while riding another moped or learner motor bicycle or any motor bicycle, and

(b)   supervising only him or him and not more than 3 other persons each of whom holds such a provisional licence.

(7B)   In paragraph (7A)—

(a)   "relevant training" means training (otherwise than as part of an approved training course for motor cyclists) in how to drive a moped or learner motor cycle given by a professional instructor; and

(b)   "professional instructor" means an instructor paid money or money's worth for giving such training.

(8)   The holder of a passenger-carrying vehicle driver's provisional licence shall not drive a vehicle which he is authorised to drive by that licence while carrying any passenger in the vehicle other than—

(a)   the person specified in paragraph (2)(a), or

(b)   a person who holds a passenger-carrying vehicle driver's licence and either is giving or receiving instruction in the driving of passenger-carrying vehicles, or has given or received or is to give or receive, such instruction.

(9)   The conditions specified in paragraphs (2)(a), (7) and (8) shall not apply when the holder of the provisional licence is undergoing a test.

(10)   The conditions specified in paragraphs (2), (6), (7) and (8) shall not apply in relation to the driving of motor vehicles of a class in respect of which the provisional licence holder has been furnished with a valid test pass certificate stating that he has passed a test for the grant of a licence authorising him to drive vehicles of that class.

(11)   The condition specified in paragraph (7)(b) shall not apply in the case of a provisional

licence holder who is unable, by reason of impaired hearing, to receive directions from the supervising instructor by radio where the licence holder and the instructor are employing a satisfactory means of communication which they have agreed before the start of the journey.

(11A) The holder of a disability assessment licence shall not drive a vehicle of a class which he is authorised to drive by virtue of the licence otherwise than during a period which—

(a) commences with the beginning of such period prior to the taking of the disability assessment test required by a relevant notice as is specified in writing by the Secretary of State when serving that notice; and

(b) ends with the completion of the test;

and, for these purposes, a "relevant notice" is a notice under section 94(5)(c) of the Traffic Act requiring the person to submit to a disability assessment test.

(12) In the case of an LGV trainee driver's licence issued as a provisional licence, this regulation shall apply as modified by regulation 54.

(13) In this regulation—

(a) "exempted island" means any island outside the mainland of Great Britain from which motor vehicles, unless constructed or adapted specially for that purpose, cannot at any time be conveniently driven to a road in any other part of Great Britain by reason of the absence of any bridge, tunnel, ford or other way suitable for the passage of such motor vehicles but excluding any of the following islands, namely, the Isle of Wight, St Mary's (Isles of Scilly), the islands of Arran, Barra, Bute, Great Cumbrae, Islay, the island which comprises Lewis and Harris, Mainland Orkney, Mainland Shetland, Mull, the island which comprises North Uist, Benbecula and South Uist and Tiree;

(aa) "NHS invalid carriage" means a motor vehicle included in sub-category B1 (invalid carriages) that is owned by the Department for Health;

(b) "provisional licence", in relation to a class of vehicles, includes a full licence which is treated, by virtue of section 98 of the Traffic Act, as authorising its holder to drive vehicles of that class as if he held a provisional licence therefor;

(c) "qualified driver" shall be interpreted in accordance with regulation 17.

---

1. Passive conduct in circumstances which require a supervisor to be active is a failure to discharge the duty of supervising the driving of the vehicle by the learner driver. Thus, where the latter is guilty of careless driving, the supervisor can be convicted of aiding and abetting him to commit the offence (*Rubie v Faulkner* [1940] 1 KB 571, [1940] 1 All ER 285, 104 JP 161).

2. A vehicle may be "constructed" to carry more than one person even though it lacks the necessary fitting, ie, the seat (*Vincent v Whitehead* [1966] 1 All ER 917, 130 JP 214).

3. Although with the definition of "motor cycle" in s 185(1) of the Road Traffic Act 1988, a three-wheeled "bubble-car" is not a motor bicycle (*Brown v Anderson* [1965] 2 All ER 1, 129 JP 298).

4. "Side-car" is not defined by the Road Traffic Acts nor in any regulations made thereunder, but in *Cox v Harrison* [1968] 3 All ER 811, 133 JP 75, it was held that a bare chassis is not a side-car, it being left open whether a side-car must be constructed or adapted to carry passengers and nothing else or whether it may take the form of a box or basket to carry materials; though ASHWORTH J, expressed the opinion that it must be capable of carrying passengers. Regulation 92 of the Road Vehicles (Construction and Use) Regulations 1986, ante, prescribes how a side-car should be attached to a motor cycle so as to prevent it becoming a trailer.

4–4377P **17. Meaning of "qualified driver".** (1) Subject to paragraph (2), a person is a qualified driver for the purposes of regulation 16 if he—

(a) is 21 years of age or over,

(b) holds a relevant licence,

(c) has the relevant driving experience, and

(d) in the case of a disabled driver, he is supervising a provisional licence holder who is driving a vehicle of a class included in categories B, C, D, C + E, or D + E and would in an emergency be able to take control of the steering and braking functions of the vehicle in which he is a passenger.

(2) In the case of a person who is a member of the armed forces of the Crown acting in the course of his duties for naval, military or air force purposes sub-paragraphs (a) and (c) of paragraph (1) shall not apply.

(3) For the purposes of this regulation—

(a) "disabled driver" means a person who holds a relevant licence which is limited by virtue of a declaration made with his application for the licence or a notice served under section 92(5)(b) of the Traffic Act to vehicles of a particular class;

(b) "full licence" includes a full Northern Ireland licence and a Community licence;

(c) "relevant licence" means, subject to sub-paragraph (d), a full licence authorising—

(i) the driving of vehicles of the same class as the vehicle being driven by the provisional licence holder, and

(ii) where sub-paragraph (f) applies—

(aa) where that class of vehicle is included within any sub-category specified in column 1 of the table at the end of this regulation, the driving of vehicles in the sub-category specified in column 2 which is opposite that sub-category, or

(bb) where sub-paragraph (aa) does not apply, the driving of vehicles in the category specified in column 2 of that table which is opposite the category specified in column 1 that includes the class of vehicle being driven by the provisional licence holder;

(d) in the case of a disabled driver who holds a licence authorising the driving of vehicles in category B, a relevant licence must authorise the driving of vehicles other than vehicles in sub-category B1 or B1 (invalid carriages);

(e) a person has relevant driving experience if—

    (i) where sub-paragraph (c)(i) only applies, he has held the relevant licence for a period of 3 years, or

    (ii) minimum where sub-paragraph (c)(ii) applies, he has held the relevant licence authorising the driving of vehicles—

        (aa) of the same class as the vehicle being driven by the provisional licence holder for a minimum period of 1 year, and

        (bb) in the category or sub-category specified in column 2 described in sub-paragraph (c)(ii) for a minimum period of 3 years;

(f) this sub-paragraph applies where—

    (i) a person holds a full licence authorising the driving of vehicles of the same class as the vehicle being driven by the provisional licence holder;

    (ii) that class is included in a category or sub-category specified in column 1 of the table at the end of this regulation, and

    (iii) that person has held that licence for less than a minimum period of 3 years;

(g) for the purposes of sub-paragraphs (e) and (f), the minimum period of time for holding a full licence may be met either by holding that licence continuously for that period or for periods amounting in aggregate to not less than that period;

TABLE

Column (1) Category which includes the vehicle being driven by the provisional licence holder	Column (2) Minimum period for holding a full licence
C	D
C1	D1
C + E	D + E
C1 + E	D1 + E
D	C
D1	C1
D + E	C + E
D1 + E	C1 + E

4–4377Q   18. Conditions attached to provisional licences: holders of driving permits other than licences granted under Part III of the Traffic Act.   A holder of a provisional licence authorising the driving of vehicles of any class who also holds a permit by virtue of which he is at any time—

(a) treated, by virtue of regulation 80, as the holder, for the purposes of section 87 of the Traffic Act, of a licence authorising the driving of vehicles of that class, or

(b) entitled, pursuant to article 2(1) of the Motor Vehicles (International Circulation) Order 1975[1], to drive motor vehicles of that class,

need not comply with regulation 16 at that time.

---

1. SI 1975/1208, in this PART, ante.

4–4377R   19. Full licences not carrying provisional entitlement.   (1) The application of sections 98(2) and 99A(5) of the Traffic Act is limited or excluded in accordance with the following paragraphs.

(2) Subject to paragraphs (3), (4), (5), (6), (11) and (12), the holder of a full licence which authorises the driving of motor vehicles of a class included in a category or sub-category specified in column (1) of the table at the end of this regulation may drive motor vehicles—

(a) of other classes included in that category or sub-category, and

(b) of a class included in each category or sub-category specified, in relation to that category or sub-category, in column (2) of the table,

as if he were authorised by a provisional licence to do so.

(3) Section 98(2) shall not apply to a full licence if it authorises the driving only of motor vehicles adapted on account of a disability, whether pursuant to an application in that behalf made by the holder of the licence or pursuant to a notice served under section 92(5)(b) of the Traffic Act.

(4) In the case of a full licence which authorises the driving of a class of standard motor bicycles, other than bicycles included in sub-category A1, section 98(2) shall not apply so as to authorise the driving of a large motor bicycle by a person under the age of 21 before the expiration of the standard access period.

(5) In the case of a full licence which authorises the driving of motor bicycles of a class included in sub-category A1 section 98(2) shall not apply so as to authorise the driving of a large motor bicycle by a person under the age of 21.

(6) In the case of a full licence which authorises the driving of a class of vehicles included in category C or C + E, paragraph (2) applies subject to the provisions of regulation 54.

(7) Subject to paragraphs (8), (9), (10), (11) and (12), the holder of a Community licence to whom section 99A(5) of the Traffic Act applies and who is authorised to drive in Great Britain motor vehicles of a class included in a category or sub-category specified in column (1) of the Table at the end of this regulation may drive motor vehicles—

(a) of other classes included in that category or sub-category, and

(b) of a class included in each category or sub-category specified, in relation to that category or sub-category, in column (2) of the Table,

as if he were authorised by a provisional licence to do so.

(8) Section 99A(5) shall not apply to a Community licence if it authorises the driving only of motor vehicles adapted on account of a disability.

(9) In the case of a Community licence which authorises the driving of a class of standard motor bicycle other than bicycles included in sub-category A1, section 99A(5) shall not apply so as to authorise the driving of a large motor bicycle by a person under the age of 21 before the expiration of the period of two years commencing on the date when that person passed a test for a licence authorising the driving of that class of standard motor bicycle (and in calculating the expiration of that period, any period during which that person has been disqualified for holding or obtaining a licence shall be disregarded).

(10) In the case of a Community licence which authorises the driving only of motor bicycles of a class included in sub-category A1 section 98(2) shall not apply so as to authorise the driving of a large motor bicycle by a person under the age of 21.

(11) Except to the extent provided in paragraph (12), section 98(2) shall not apply to a full licence, and section 99A(5) shall not apply to a Community licence, in so far as it authorises its holder to drive motor vehicles of any class included in category B + E, C + E, D + E or K or in sub-category B1 (invalid carriages), C1 or D1 (not for hire or reward).

(12) A person—

(a) who holds a full licence authorising the driving only of those classes of vehicle included in a category or sub-category specified in paragraph (11) which have automatic transmission (and are not otherwise adapted on account of a disability), or

(b) who holds a Community licence, to whom section 99A(5) of the Traffic Act applies and who is authorised to drive in Great Britain only those classes of vehicle included in a category or sub-category specified in paragraph (11) which have automatic transmission (and are not otherwise adapted on account of a disability),

may drive motor vehicles of all other classes included in that category or sub-category which have manual transmission as if he were authorised by a provisional licence to do so.

TABLE

(1) Full licence held	(2) Provisional entitlement included
A1	A, B, F and K
A	B and F
B1	A, B and F
B	A, B + E, G and H
C	C1 + E, C + E
D1	D1 + E
D	D1 + E, D + E
F	B and P
G	H
H	G
P	A, B, F and K

Miscellaneous

4–4377S 20. Signatures on licences. In order that a licence may show the usual form of signature of its holder—

(a) where the Secretary of State so requires, a person applying for a licence shall provide the Secretary of State with a specimen of his signature which can be electronically recorded and reproduced on the licence;

(b) where no such requirement is made, a person to whom a licence is granted shall forthwith sign it in ink in the space provided.

4–4377T 21. Lost or defaced licences. (1) If the holder of a licence—

(a) satisfies the Secretary of State that—

(i) the licence or its counterpart has been lost or defaced; and

(ii) the holder is entitled to continue to hold the licence; and

(b) pays the fee prescribed by regulation 14,

the Secretary of State shall, on surrender of any licence or counterpart that has not been lost, issue to him a duplicate licence and counterpart and shall endorse upon the counterpart any particulars endorsed upon the original licence or counterpart as the case may be and the duplicates so issued shall have the same effect as the originals.

(2) If at any time while a duplicate licence is in force the original licence is found, the person to whom the original licence was issued, if it is in his possession, shall return it to the Secretary of

State, or if it is not in his possession, but he becomes aware that it is found, shall take all reasonable steps to take possession of it and if successful shall return it as soon as may be to the Secretary of State.

(3) The obligation in paragraph (2) shall apply in respect of the counterpart of a licence as if for the words "original licence" in each place where they occur there were substituted the words "original counterpart".

PART III

TESTS OF COMPETENCE TO DRIVE

Preliminary

4–4377U   22. Interpretation of Part III.   In this Part of these Regulations—

"applicant in person" means a person making an application for an appointment for a test or a part of a test with a view to taking the test or that part thereof himself;

"appointed person" means a person appointed by the Secretary of State to conduct theory tests under paragraph (1)(*a*)(ii) or (2)(*a*) of regulation 23;

"DSA examiner" means a person appointed by the Secretary of State to conduct practical or unitary tests under paragraph (1)(*a*) or (2)(*a*) of regulation 24;

"large vehicle instructor" means a person operating an establishment for providing instruction in the driving of vehicles included in category B + E, C, C + E, D or D + E, including an establishment which provides tuition to prepare persons for the theory test;

"motor bicycle instructor" means a person operating an establishment for providing instruction in the driving of vehicles included in categories A or P, including an establishment which provides tuition to prepare persons for the theory test;

"motor car instructor" means a person operating an establishment for providing instruction in the driving of vehicles included in category B, including an establishment which provides tuition to prepare persons for the theory test;

"standard access period" means the period of two years commencing on the date when a person passes a test for a licence authorising the driving of standard motor bicycles of any class, other than a class included in the sub-category A1, but disregarding—

(*a*) any period during which the person is disqualified under section 34 or 35 of the Offenders Act,

(*b*) in a case where the person has been disqualified under section 36 of the Offenders Act, the period beginning on the date of the court order under subsection (1) of that section and ending on the date when the disqualification is deemed by virtue of that section to have expired in relation to standard motor bicycles of that class,

(*c*) in a case where the Secretary of State has revoked the person's licence or test pass certificate under section 3(2) of, or Schedule 1 to, the Road Traffic (New Drivers) Act 1995, the period beginning on the date of the notice of revocation under that Act and ending on the date when the person passes the relevant driving test within the meaning of that Act, and

(*d*) any period during which the licence has ceased to be in force;

"working day" means a day other than a Sunday, bank holiday, Christmas Day or Good Friday (and "bank holiday" means a day to be observed as such under section 1 of and Schedule 1 to the Bank and Financial Dealings Act 1971).

Appointment of persons to conduct tests

4–4377V   23. *Persons by whom theory tests may be conducted*

4–4377W   24. *Persons by whom practical and unitary tests may be conducted*

4–4377X   25. *Revocation of authority to conduct tests*

Applications for tests

4–4377Y   26. *Applications for theory tests: applicants in person*

4–4377Z   27. *Applications for theory tests: motor bicycle instructors*

4–4378   28. *Applications for theory tests: large vehicle instructors*

4–4378ZA   28A. *Applications for theory tests: motor car instructors*

4–4378A   29. *Eligibility to reapply for theory test*

4–4378B   30. *Fees for theory tests*

4–4378C   31. *Applications for practical and unitary tests: applicants in person*

4–4378D   32. *Applications for practical tests: motor bicycle instructors*

4–4378E **33.** *Applications for practical tests: large vehicle instructors*

4–4378F **34.** *Eligibility to reapply for practical or unitary test*

4–4378G **35.** *Fees in respect of practical or unitary tests*

4–4378H **36. Cancellation of tests.** For the purposes of paragraph (b) of section 91 of the Traffic Act (which section specifies the cases in which a fee paid on an application for an appointment for a test may be repaid) notice cancelling an appointment—

    (a) for a practical or unitary test to be conducted by a DSA examiner must be given to the Secretary of State not less than three clear working days before the day for which the appointment is made;

    (b) for a theory test to be conducted by an appointed person must be given not less than three clear working days before the day for which the appointment is made.

Requirements at tests

4–4378I **37.** *Test vehicles*

4–4378J **38.** *Further requirements at tests*

4–4378K **39.** *Examiner's right to refuse to conduct test*

Nature and conduct of tests

4–4378L **40. Nature of tests other than extended tests.** (1) This regulation applies to tests other than extended driving tests.

    (2) Subject to the following provisions of this regulation and regulation 42, the test for a licence authorising the driving of a motor vehicle of a class included in category A, B, C, D, or P shall be conducted in two parts, namely—

    (*a*) a test of driving theory and hazard perception, and
    (*b*) a practical test of driving skills and behaviour,

and a person taking such a test must pass both parts.

    (3) The test for a licence authorising the driving of a motor vehicle of a class included in category B + E, C + E and D + E—

    (*a*) in a case where the test is for a licence authorising the driving of vehicles in sub-category C1 + E and the applicant is the holder of a full licence which was in force at a time before 1st January 1997 and authorises the driving of motor vehicles included in sub-category C1 + E (8.25 tonnes) but not the driving of any other vehicles included in category C + E, shall consist of the specified matters prescribed in respect of the theory test for category C and the specified requirements prescribed in respect of practical test for category C + E, and
    (*b*) in any other case, shall consist of a practical test only.

    (4) Where a test is required to be conducted in two parts, a person taking the test—

    (*a*) must pass the theory test before he take the practical test, and
    (*b*) shall not be entitled to apply for an appointment (or, as the case may be, be nominated pursuant to regulation 32(4) or 33(4)) for a practical test in respect of a motor vehicle of a class included in any category until he has been furnished with—

      (i) a valid theory test pass certificate stating that he has passed the theory test prescribed in respect of that category, or
      (ii) a certificate corresponding to such a certificate furnished under the law of Northern Ireland stating that he has during the relevant period passed the theory test in respect of the same category.

    (5) A person shall be treated as having passed—

    (*a*) the theory test if he satisfies the person conducting the test—

      (i) in respect of the test of driving theory described in paragraph (8A) of this knowledge and understanding of the specific matters; and
      (ii) in respect of the hazard perception test described at paragraph (8B) that his performance in the test demonstrates an ability to perceive hazards on the road;

    (*b*) the practical test if he satisfies the person conducting it of his ability to drive safely and to comply with the specified requirements.

    (6) The test for a licence authorising the driving of a motor vehicle of a class included in category F, G, H or K shall be a unitary test and a person taking such a test shall be treated as having passed it if he satisfies the person conducting it that he is—

    (*a*) generally competent to drive a vehicle of that class without danger to, and with due consideration for, other road users,
    (*b*) fully conversant with the Highway Code, and
    (*c*) able to comply with the specified requirements.

    (7) The practical test and the unitary test shall each be conducted so that—

    (*a*) the person taking the test drives, wherever possible, both on roads outside built-up areas and on urban roads, and (*b*) the time during which that person is required to drive on roads is—

    (i) in the case of a test for a licence authorising the driving of a class of vehicle included in category B + E, C, C + E, D or D + E, not less than 50 minutes;

    (ii) in the case of any other test, not less than 30 minutes.

(8) The theory test shall be conducted in two parts, one part being the test of driving theory described in paragraph (8A) and the other being the hazard perception test described in paragraph (8B).

(8A) The test of driving theory shall—

(*a*) be conducted as an approved form of examination consisting of 35 questions, the questions being in either a multiple choice or multiple response form and testing a candidate on the specified matters in accordance with Schedule 7; and

(*b*) have a duration of 40 minutes or, in the circumstances specified in paragraph (9), 80 minutes.

(8B) The hazard perception test shall—

(*a*) be conducted by means of the exhibition of film clips that take the perspective of the driver of a motor vehicle and show, at some point during each film clip, one or more hazards to traffic occurring on or near the road; and

(*b*) require the candidate (using electronic equipment provided for the purpose and capable of recording the exact moment of each response) to indicate during each film clip the moment he observes a hazard relating to traffic on the road.

(8C) For the purposes of this regulation—

"an approved form of examination" means a form of examination which is conducted in writing or by means of data recorded on equipment operating in response to instructions given by the candidate, and;

"film clip" means a sequence of visual images displayed electronically.

(9) The circumstances referred to in paragraph (8) are that the candidate requires the assistance of a suitably qualified person at the test by virtue of having reading difficulties.

(10) The specified matters for a theory test for a licence authorising the driving of a motor vehicle of a class included in a category shown in column (1) of the table at the end of this regulation are the matters specified in relation to that category in column (2) of the table.

(11) The specified requirements for a practical or unitary test for a licence authorising the driving of a motor vehicle of a class included in a category shown in column (1) of the table are the requirements specified in relation to that category in column (3) of the table.

TABLE

(1) Category	(2) Specified matters	(3) Specified requirements
A	Matters specified in Part 1 of Schedule 7.	Requirements specified in Part 1 of Schedule 8.
B	Matters specified in Part 2 of Schedule 7.	Requirements specified in Part 2 of Schedule 8.
B + E	—	Requirements specified in Part 2 of Schedule 8.
C	Matters specified in Part 3 of Schedule 7.	Requirements specified in Part 3 of Schedule 8.
D	Matters specified in Part 4 of Schedule 7.	Requirements specified in Part 4 of Schedule 8.
C + E	—	Requirements specified in Part 3 of Schedule 8.
D + E	—	Requirements specified in Part 4 of Schedule 8.
F	—	Requirements specified in Parts 5 and 6 of Schedule 8.
G	—	Requirements specified in Parts 5 and 6 of Schedule 8.
H	—	Requirements specified in Parts 5 and 7 of Schedule 8.
K	—	Requirements specified in Part 5 of Schedule 8.
P	Matters specified in Part 1 of Schedule 7.	Requirements specified in Part 1 of Schedule 8.

4-4378M   41. Nature of extended driving tests. (1) Where a person is disqualified by order of a court under section 36 of the Offenders Act until he passes an extended driving test, the test which he must pass is a test conducted in accordance with paragraphs (2) to (11) of regulation 40 as modified by virtue of paragraph (2) of this regulation.

(2) For the purpose of an extended driving test, the provisions of regulation 40 shall apply but as if paragraph (1) were omitted and for paragraph (7)(*b*) there were substituted—

"(*b*) the time during which that person is required to drive on roads is not less than 60 minutes".

4–4378N   42. Exemption from theory test.   (1) A person is exempt from the requirement to pass a theory test for the purpose of obtaining a licence authorising him to drive a motor vehicle of a class included in category A if—

(a) he has, on or after 1st July 1996, passed the test prescribed in respect of category P and holds a full licence authorising the driving of a class of vehicles in that category; or
(b) he holds a full licence authorising the driving of motor vehicles of another class included in category A; or
(c) he has passed a Northern Ireland test of competence corresponding to the test mentioned in sub-paragraph (a), or is the holder of a Northern Ireland licence corresponding to a licence mentioned in sub-paragraph (b); or
(d) he has passed a test for a licence authorising the driving of motor vehicles of another class included in category A and is a full-time member of the armed forces of the Crown.

(2) A person is exempt from the requirement to pass a theory test for the purpose of obtaining a licence authorising him to drive a motor vehicle of a class included in category B if—

(a) (Revoked).
(b) he holds a full licence authorising the driving of motor vehicles of another class included in category B or of a class included in category A; or
(c) he has passed a Northern Ireland test of competence corresponding to the test mentioned in sub-paragraph (a) or is the holder of a Northern Ireland licence corresponding to the licence mentioned in sub-paragraph (b); or
(d) he has passed a test for a licence authorising the driving of motor vehicles of another class included in category B and is a full-time member of the armed forces of the Crown.

(3) A person is exempt from the requirement to pass a theory test for the purpose of obtaining a licence authorising him to drive a motor vehicle of a class included in category C if—

(a) he holds a full licence authorising the driving of motor vehicles of another class included in category C, other than a licence authorising the driving only of vehicles of a class included in sub-category C1 which was in force at a time before 1st January 1997, or a Northern Ireland licence corresponding to such a licence; or
(b) on or after 1st January 1997, he has passed a test for a licence authorising the driving of motor vehicles of another class included in category C and is a full-time member of the armed forces of the Crown.

(4) A person is exempt from the requirement to pass a theory test for the purpose of obtaining a licence authorising him to drive a motor vehicle of a class included in category D if—

(a) he holds a full licence authorising the driving of motor vehicles of another class included in category D other than—

(i)   vehicles of a class included in sub-category D1 (not for hire or reward), and
(ii) vehicles in category D which are driven otherwise than for hire or reward;

or a Northern Ireland licence corresponding to such a licence; or

(b) on or after 1st January 1997, he has passed a test prescribed in respect of motor vehicles of another class included in category D and is a full-time member of the armed forces of the Crown.

(5) Where a person is disqualified by order of a court under section 36 of the Offenders Act until he passes the appropriate driving test, he shall not be exempt from the requirement to pass a theory test in respect of any class of motor vehicle by virtue of the foregoing provisions of this regulation until the disqualification is deemed to have expired in relation to that class.

(6) Where the Secretary of State has revoked a person's licence or test pass certificate under section 3(2) of, or Schedule 1 to, the Road Traffic (New Drivers) Act 1995 he shall not be exempt from the requirement to pass a theory test in respect of any class of motor vehicle by virtue of the foregoing provisions of this regulation until the day following the date on which he passes a relevant driving test within the meaning of section 4(2) of, or paragraph 6 or 9 of Schedule 1 to, that Act.

Entitlements upon passing test

4–4378O   43. Entitlement upon passing a test other than an appropriate driving test.   (1) Where a person passes a test other than an appropriate driving test prescribed in respect of any category for a licence which (by virtue of regulation 37) authorises the driving of motor vehicles included in that category or in a sub-category thereof, or has passed a Northern Ireland test of competence corresponding to that test, the Secretary of State shall grant to him a licence in accordance with the following provisions of this regulation.

(2) Subject to regulations 44 and 44A, the licence shall authorise the driving of all classes of motor vehicle included in that category or sub-category unless—

(a) the test or, as the case may be, the practical test is passed on a motor vehicle with automatic transmission, in which case it shall authorise the driving only of such classes of vehicle included in that category or sub-category as have automatic transmission;
(b) the test or, as the case may be, the practical test, is passed on a motor vehicle which is adapted on account of a disability of the person taking the test, in which case it shall authorise the driving only of such classes of vehicle included in that category or sub-category as are so adapted (and for the purposes of this paragraph, a motor bicycle with a side-car may be treated in an appropriate case as a motor vehicle adapted on account of a disability).

(3) Subject to paragraphs (5) and (6), the licence shall in addition authorise the driving of all classes of motor vehicle included in a category or sub-category which is specified in column (3 of Schedule 2 as an additional category or sub-category in relation to a category or sub-category specified in column (1) of that Schedule unless—

(a) the test or, as the case may be, the practical test is passed on a motor vehicle with automatic transmission, in which case it shall (subject to paragraph (4)) authorise the driving only of such classes of vehicle included in the additional category or sub-category as have automatic transmission;

(b) the test or, as the case may be, the practical test is passed on a motor vehicle which is adapted on account of a disability of the person taking the test in which case it shall authorise the driving only of such classes of vehicle included in the additional category or sub-category as are so adapted.

(4) Where the additional category is F, K or P, paragraph (3)(a) shall not apply.

(5) Where a person has passed a test (or Northern Ireland test of competence corresponding to such a test) for a licence authorising the driving of vehicles included in category B, the effect of paragraph (3) in relation to the driving of vehicles in category P shall be as follows—

(a) the licence granted by the Secretary of State shall authorise the driving of vehicles within class P if and only if—

(i) the test was passed before 1st February 2001;

(ii) the person concerned held at the date on which he passed the test the prescribed certificate of successful completion by him of an approved training course for motor cyclists and that certificate was at that time valid in accordance with regulation 68(2) or

(iii) the person concerned holds the prescribed certificate of successful completion by him of an approved training course for motor cyclists and that certificate was furnished to him after the date on which he passed the test, and

(b) where a certificate referred to in sub-paragraph (a)(ii) or (iii) shows that the person concerned has successfully completed an approved training course for riders of three-wheeled mopeds, the only vehicles in category P authorised by the licence to be driven shall be three-wheeled mopeds.

(6) In relation to the first item of Schedule 2 (category A), the effect of paragraph (3) shall be that a licence authorising the driving of vehicles in category A shall in addition authorise the driving of vehicles in category B1, if and only if, the test, or as the case may be the practical test, is passed before 1st February 2001.

4–4378P 44. Entitlement upon passing a test other than an appropriate driving test: category A.
(1) This regulation applies where a person has passed a test (or a Northern Ireland test of competence corresponding to such a test) for a licence authorising the driving of motor bicycles of any class other than a class included in sub-category A1.

(2) Where this regulation applies the Secretary of State shall grant to the person who passed the test—

(a) in a case where he has passed the practical test (or the Northern Ireland test of competence corresponding to the practical test) on a motor bicycle without a side-car, the engine of which has a maximum net power output of not less than 35 kilowatts, a licence authorising him to drive all classes of motor vehicle included in category A;

(b) subject to paragraph (3), in a case where the practical test (or the Northern Ireland test of competence corresponding to the practical test) was passed on any other motor bicycle without a side-car, a licence authorising him to drive standard motor bicycles;

(c) in a case where he has passed the practical test (or the Northern Ireland test of competence corresponding to the practical test) on a motor bicycle and side-car combination and the engine of the bicycle has a maximum net power output of not less than 35 kilowatts, a licence authorising him to drive all classes of motor bicycle and side-car combinations included in category A;

(d) subject to paragraph (4), in a case where the practical test (or the Northern Ireland test of competence corresponding to the practical test) was passed on a motor bicycle and a side-car combination the power to weight ratio of which does not exceed 0.16 kw/kg but which does not fall within paragraph (c), a licence authorising him to drive standard motor bicycles and side-car combinations.

(3) A licence granted to a person by virtue of paragraph (2)(b) shall authorise him to drive all classes of motor vehicle included in category A upon the expiration of the standard access period.

(4) A licence granted to a person by virtue of paragraph (2)(d) shall authorise him to drive all classes of motor bicycle and side-car combinations included in category A upon the expiration of the standard access period.

4–4378PA 44A. Entitlement upon passing a test other than an appropriate driving test: category P. (1) This regulation applies where a person has passed a test (or Northern Ireland test of competence corresponding to such a test) for a licence authorising the driving of vehicles included in category P.

(2) Where this regulation applies the Secretary of State shall grant to the person who passed the test—

(a) in a case where the test was passed on a three-wheeled moped, a licence authorising the driving of all vehicles having three wheels included in category P;

(b) in any other case, a licence authorising the driving of all vehicles included in category P.

4–4378Q 45. Upgrading of entitlements by virtue of passing second test. (1) A person who has passed tests for a licence authorising the driving of motor vehicles included in—

(*a*) category D or sub-category D1 as specified in column (1) of Table A in Schedule 9, and

(*b*) category C + E or sub-category C1 + E as respectively specified at the top of columns (2) and (3) of Table A,

is deemed, subject to the following paragraphs of this regulation, competent to drive (in addition to the classes of motor vehicle in respect of which the tests were passed) vehicles included in the category or sub-category shown in column (2) or (3) of Table A in relation to the relevant test pass in column (1).

(2) Where, in a case to which paragraph (1) applies, each practical test is passed on a vehicle having automatic transmission the person passing the tests is deemed competent to drive only such classes of vehicle in the upgrade category as have automatic transmission.

(3) A person who has passed a test for a licence authorising the driving of—

(*a*) motor vehicles included in a category or sub-category specified in column (A) of Table B in Schedule 9 which have automatic transmission, and

(*b*) motor vehicles included in a category or sub-category specified at the head of one of the columns in that table numbered (1) to (8) which have manual transmission,

is, subject to the following paragraphs of this regulation, deemed competent to drive in addition to the classes of vehicle in respect of which the tests were passed all vehicles included in the category or sub-category shown in the relevant numbered column of Table B in relation to the relevant test pass mentioned in column (A).

(4) Where a person has passed tests for a licence authorising the driving of—

(*a*) motor vehicles in category D not more than 5.5 metres in length having automatic transmission, and

(*b*) motor vehicles in category C, other than vehicles in sub-category C1, having manual transmission,

he is deemed competent to drive vehicles in category D not more than 5.5 metres in length which have manual transmission.

(5) In the case of a person who holds a licence which, by virtue of regulation 76 (notwithstanding that he may not have passed a test authorising the driving of such vehicles), authorises the driving of a class of vehicles in category D when used under a section 19 permit or (if not so used) are driven otherwise than for hire or reward, Tables A and B shall be read as if—

(*a*) for "D" there were substituted "vehicles in category D, driven otherwise than for hire or reward", and

(*b*) for "D + E" there were substituted "vehicles in category D + E driven otherwise than for hire or reward".

(6) In the case of a person who has passed a test for a licence authorising the driving only of those classes of vehicle in category C + E which are drawbar trailer combinations, paragraphs (1), (2) and (3) and Tables A and B in Schedule 9 shall apply as if he had passed a test for a licence authorising only the driving of the corresponding classes of vehicle in category C.

(7) Where, in Table B, the upgrade category is qualified by the expression "(*a*)", the person is deemed competent to drive only such classes of vehicle therein as have automatic transmission.

(8) Where a person has passed a test prescribed in respect of category B + E which authorises the driving only of classes of vehicle having automatic transmission and a test prescribed in respect of any class of vehicle in category C or D which authorises the driving of vehicles with manual transmission, he is deemed competent to drive vehicles in category B + E with manual transmission.

(9) Where a person, who is the holder of a licence which authorises the driving of motor vehicles included in categories B and B + E and sub-categories C1, C1 + E (8.25 tonnes), D1 (not for hire or reward) and D1 + E (not for hire or reward) which have automatic transmission, passes a test prescribed in respect of category B, B + E, C or D which authorises the driving of vehicles with manual transmission, he is deemed competent to drive vehicles in category B + E and in sub-categories C1, C1 + E (8.25 tonnes), D1 (not for hire or reward) and D1 + E (not for hire or reward) which have manual transmission.

(10) Where a person has passed tests for a licence authorising the driving of—

(*a*) motor vehicles included in category B, other than vehicles included in sub-categories B1 and B1 (invalid carriages), having automatic transmission, and

(*b*) motor vehicles included in category B + E, C or D having manual transmission,

he is deemed competent to drive vehicles in category B which have manual transmission.

(11) In this regulation—

(*a*) "upgrade category" means the additional category or sub-category which the person passing the tests (or holding the licence and passing the test) is deemed competent to drive by virtue of the relevant provision of this regulation, and

(*b*) a reference to a test or a practical test includes, as the case may be, a reference to a Northern Ireland test of competence or a Northern Ireland practical test corresponding thereto.

4–4378R   46. Entitlement upon passing an appropriate driving test. (1) Where a person—

(a) is disqualified by order of a court under section 36 of the Offenders Act until he passes the appropriate driving test, and

(b) passes the appropriate driving test for a licence authorising the driving of a class of motor vehicles included in any category or sub-category,

the disqualification shall, subject to paragraph (8), be deemed to have expired in relation to that class and such other classes of motor vehicle as are specified in paragraphs (2), (3), (4), (5) and (6).

(2) Subject to paragraph (4), the disqualification shall be deemed to have expired in relation to all classes of vehicle included in the category or sub-category referred to in paragraph (1)(b) unless—

(a) the test or, as the case may be, the practical test is passed on a motor vehicle with automatic transmission, in which case the disqualification shall be deemed to have expired only in relation to such classes of vehicle included in that category or sub-category as have automatic transmission;

(b) the test or, as the case may be, the practical test is passed on a motor vehicle which is adapted on account of a disability of the person taking the test, in which case the disqualification shall be deemed to have expired only in relation to such classes of motor vehicle included in that category or sub-category as are so adapted (and for the purposes of this paragraph, a motor bicycle with a side-car may be treated in an appropriate case as a motor vehicle adapted on account of a disability).

(3) The disqualification shall be deemed to have expired in relation to all classes of vehicle included in any other category which is specified in column (3) of Schedule 2 as being an additional category or sub-category in relation to that category or sub-category unless—

(a) subject to paragraph (5), the test or, as the case may be, the practical test is passed on a vehicle with automatic transmission, in which case the disqualification shall be deemed to have expired only in relation to such classes of motor vehicle included in the additional category or sub-category as have automatic transmission;

(b) the test or, as the case may be, the practical test, is passed on a vehicle which is adapted on account of a disability of the person taking the test, in which case the disqualification shall be deemed to have expired only in relation to such classes of motor vehicle included in the additional category or sub-category as are so adapted.

(4) Where, at the date on which a person is disqualified—

(a) he holds a licence which was granted pursuant to regulation 44(2)(b) or (d), and

(b) the standard access period has not expired,

the disqualification shall not, by virtue of paragraph (2) or (7), be deemed to have expired—

(i) in a case to which regulation 44(2)(b) applies, in relation to large motor bicycles, or

(ii) in a case to which regulation 44(2)(d) applies, in relation to large motor bicycle and side-car combinations,

until the standard access period has expired.

(5) Paragraph (3)(a) shall not apply where the additional category is F, G, H, K, L or P.

(6) Where the person who is disqualified passes the practical test on a vehicle of a class included in category A, other than sub-category A1, the disqualification shall be deemed to have expired additionally in relation to all classes of vehicle included in—

(a) categories B, B + E, C, C + E, D and D + E, unless that test is passed on a vehicle with automatic transmission, in which case the disqualification shall be deemed to have expired only in relation to such classes of motor vehicle included in those categories as have automatic transmission;

(b) categories F, G, H and L.

(7) Where the person who is disqualified passes the practical test on a vehicle of a class included in category B, other than a vehicle included in sub-category B1, the disqualification shall be deemed to have expired additionally in relation to all classes of vehicle included in—

(a) categories A, B + E, C, C + E, D and D + E, unless that test is passed on a vehicle with automatic transmission, in which case the disqualification shall be deemed to have expired only in relation to such classes of motor vehicle included in those categories as have automatic transmission;

(b) categories G, H and L.

(8) Where a person is, pursuant to regulation 56, disqualified by the Secretary of State until he passes a driving test prescribed in respect of a class of large goods or passenger-carrying vehicle, the disqualification shall not be deemed to have expired in relation to any class of large goods or passenger-carrying vehicle until he passes that test.

Test results

4–4378S   47. *Evidence of result of theory test*

4–4378T   48. *Evidence of the result of practical or unitary test*

PART IV
GOODS AND PASSENGER-CARRYING VEHICLES
General

4–4378U 49. Part III of the Traffic Act: Prescribed classes of goods and passenger-carrying vehicle.
(1) All classes of motor vehicle included in categories C, C + E, D and D + E, except vehicles of classes included in sub-categories C1, C1 + E (8.25 tonnes) D1 (not for hire or reward) and D1 + E (not for hire or reward), are prescribed for the purposes of section 89A(3) of the Traffic Act.

(2) Subject to paragraph (3), all classes of motor vehicle included in categories C, C + E, D and D + E, except vehicles of classes included in sub-categories C1 + E (8.25 tonnes), D1 (not for hire or reward) and D1 + E (not for hire or reward), are prescribed for the purposes of section 99(1) and (1A) of the Traffic Act.

(3) In the case of a licence in force at a time before 1st January 1997, paragraph (2) above shall apply as if "C1," was inserted after "sub-categories".

(4) All classes of motor vehicle included in categories C, C + E, D and D + E, except vehicles of classes included in sub-categories C1 + E (8.25 tonnes), D1 (not for hire or reward) and D1 + E (not for hire or reward), are prescribed for the purposes of section 99A(3) and (4) of the Traffic Act.

4–4378V 50. Part IV of the Traffic Act: prescribed classes of large goods and passenger-carrying vehicle. (1) Part IV of the Traffic Act and regulations 54 to 57 shall not apply to a large goods vehicle—

   (a) of a class included in category F, G or H or sub-category C1 + E (8.25 tonnes), or
   (b) which is an exempted goods vehicle or an exempted military vehicle.

(2) Part IV of the Traffic Act and regulations 54 to 57 shall not apply to a passenger-carrying vehicle manufactured more than 30 years before the date when it is driven and not used for hire or reward or for the carriage of more than eight passengers;

(3) Part IV of the Traffic Act and regulations 54 to 57 shall not apply to a passenger-carrying vehicle when it is being driven by a constable for the purpose of removing or avoiding obstruction to other road users or other members of the public, for the purpose of protecting life or property (including the passenger-carrying vehicle and its passengers) or for other similar purposes.

(4) All classes of large goods and passenger-carrying vehicle to which Part IV of the Traffic Act applies are prescribed for the purposes of section 117(7) and 117A(6) of the Traffic Act.

4–4378W 51. Exempted goods vehicles and military vehicles. (1) For the purposes of this Part of these Regulations, an exempted goods vehicle is a vehicle falling within any of the following classes—

   (a) a goods vehicle propelled by steam;
   (b) any road construction vehicle used or kept on the road solely for the conveyance of built-in road construction machinery (with or without articles or materials used for the purpose of that machinery);
   (c) any engineering plant other than a mobile crane;
   (d) a works truck;
   (e) an industrial tractor;
   (f) an agricultural motor vehicle which is not an agricultural or forestry tractor;
   (g) a digging machine;
   (h) a goods vehicle which, in so far as it is used on public roads—

      (i) is used only in passing from land in the occupation of a person keeping the vehicle to other land in the occupation of that person, and
      (ii) is not used on public roads for distances exceeding an aggregate of 9.7 kilometres in any calendar week;

   (j) a goods vehicle, other than an agricultural motor vehicle, which—

      (i) is used only for purposes relating to agriculture, horticulture or forestry,
      (ii) is used on public roads only in passing between different areas of land occupied by the same person, and
      (iii) in passing between any two such areas does not travel a distance exceeding 1.5 kilometres on public roads;

   (k) a goods vehicle used for no other purpose than the haulage of lifeboats and the conveyance of the necessary gear of the lifeboats which are being hauled;
   (l) a goods vehicle manufactured before 1st January 1960, used unladen and not drawing a laden trailer;
   (m) an articulated goods vehicle the unladen weight of which does not exceed 3.05 tonnes;
   (n) a goods vehicle in the service of a visiting force or headquarters as defined in the Visiting Forces and International Headquarters (Application of Law) Order 1965;
   (o) a goods vehicle driven by a constable for the purpose of removing or avoiding obstruction to other road users or other members of the public, for the purpose of protecting life or property (including the vehicle and its load) or for other similar purposes;
   (p) a goods vehicle fitted with apparatus designed for raising a disabled vehicle partly from the ground and for drawing a disabled vehicle when so raised (whether by partial superimposition or otherwise) being a vehicle which—

      (i) is used solely for dealing with disabled vehicles;

(ii) is not used for the conveyance of any goods other than a disabled vehicle when so raised and water, fuel, accumulators and articles required for the operation of, or in connection with, such apparatus or otherwise for dealing with disabled vehicles; and

(iii) has an unladen weight not exceeding 3.05 tonnes;

(*q*) a passenger-carrying vehicle recovery vehicle; and

(*r*) a mobile project vehicle.

(2) For the purposes of this Part of these Regulations, an exempted military vehicle is a large goods or passenger-carrying vehicle falling within any of the following classes—

(*a*) a vehicle designed for fire fighting or fire salvage purposes which is the property of, or for the time being under the control of, the Secretary of State for Defence, when being driven by a member of the armed forces of the Crown;

(*b*) a vehicle being driven by a member of the armed forces of the Crown in the course of urgent work of national importance in accordance with an order of the Defence Council in pursuance of the Defence (Armed Forces) Regulations 1939 which were continued permanently in force, in the form set out in Part C of Schedule 2 to the Emergency Laws (Repeal) Act, 1959, by section 2 of the Emergency Powers Act 1964; or

(*c*) an armoured vehicle other than a track-laying vehicle which is the property of, or for the time being under the control of, the Secretary of State for Defence.

(3) In this Regulation—

"digging machine" has the same meaning as in paragraph 4(4) of Schedule 1 to the Vehicle Excise and Registration Act 1994;

"agricultural motor vehicle", "engineering plant", "industrial tractor" and "works truck" have the same meaning as in regulation 3(2) of the Construction and Use Regulations;

"public road" has the same meaning as in section 62(1) of the Vehicle Excise and Registration Act 1994;

"road construction machinery" means a machine or device suitable for use for the construction and repair of roads and used for no purpose other than the construction and repair of roads; and

"road construction vehicle" means a vehicle which—

(*a*) is constructed or adapted for use for the conveyance of road construction machinery which is built in as part of, or permanently attached to, that vehicle, and

(*b*) is not constructed or adapted for the conveyance of any other load except articles and materials used for the purposes of such machinery.

4–4378X   52. Correspondences. (1) For the purposes of section 89A(5) of the Traffic Act, a heavy goods vehicle or public service vehicle of a class specified in column (1) of the table at the end of this regulation corresponds to a class of large goods vehicle or passenger-carrying vehicle, as the case may be, specified in column (2) of that table in relation to the class of vehicle in column (1).

(2) For the purposes of paragraph (1), where a heavy goods vehicle driver's licence held before 1st April 1991 was restricted to vehicles having a permissible maximum weight not exceeding 10 tonnes by virtue of—

(*a*) paragraph 3(3) and (5) of Schedule 2 to the Road Traffic (Drivers' Ages and Hours of Work) Act 1976; or

(*b*) paragraph (1) or (2) of regulation 31 of the Heavy Goods Vehicles (Drivers' Licences) Regulations 1977;

before those enactments ceased to have effect, such restriction shall be disregarded.

TABLE

(1) Class of heavy goods or public service vehicle	(2) Corresponding class of large goods or passenger-carrying vehicle
Heavy goods vehicles	Large goods vehicles
1	Categories C and C + E
1A	Categories C and C + E (limited, in each case, to vehicles with automatic transmission)
2	Category C and vehicles in category C + E which are drawbar trailer combinations
2A	Category C and vehicles in category C + E which are drawbar trailer combinations (limited, in each case, to vehicles with automatic transmission)
3	Category C and vehicles in category C + E which are drawbar trailer combinations
3A	Category C and vehicles in category C + E which are drawbar trailer combinations (limited, in each case, to vehicles with automatic transmission)
Public Service Vehicles	Passenger-carrying vehicles
1	Categories D and D + E
1A	Categories D and D + E (limited, in each case, to vehicles with automatic transmission)

(1) Class of heavy goods or public service vehicle	(2) Corresponding class of large goods or passenger-carrying vehicle
2	Categories D and D + E
2A	Categories D and D + E (limited, in each case, to vehicles with automatic transmission)
3	Category D
3A	Category D (limited to vehicles with automatic transmission)
4	Sub-category D1 and vehicles in category D not more than 5.5 metres in length
4A	Sub-category D1 and vehicles in category D not more than 5.5 metres in length (limited, in each case, to vehicles with automatic transmission)

4–4378Y   53. Part IV of the Traffic Act: dual purpose vehicles. (1) Except in the case of a vehicle mentioned in paragraph (2), Part IV of the Traffic Act and regulations 54 to 57 shall apply to dual purpose vehicles to the extent that they apply to passenger-carrying vehicles.

(2) Part IV of the Traffic Act and regulations 54 to 57 shall apply to any dual purpose vehicle which is—

(a) driven by a member of the armed forces of the Crown, and
(b) used to carry passengers for naval, military or air force purposes,

to the extent that they apply to large goods vehicles.

Persons under the age of 21

4–4378Z   54. Large goods vehicle drivers' licences granted to persons under the age of 21. (1) A large goods vehicle driver's licence granted to a person under the age of 21 is subject to the conditions prescribed in relation thereto, for the purposes of section 114(1) of the Traffic Act, in the following paragraphs.

(2) An LGV trainee driver's licence is subject to the condition that its holder shall not drive a large goods vehicle of any class which the licence authorises him to drive unless—

(a) he is a registered employee of a registered employer, and
(b) the vehicle is a large goods vehicle of a class to which his training agreement applies and is owned or operated by that registered employer or by a registered LGV driver training establishment.

(3) A large goods vehicle driver's licence held by a member of the armed forces of the Crown is subject to the condition that he shall not drive a large goods vehicle of any class unless it is owned or operated by the Secretary of State for Defence and is being used for naval, military or air force purposes.

(4) A large goods vehicle driver's licence which—

(a) authorises the driving of a class of vehicles included in category C, and
(b) is a full licence,

is subject to the condition that its holder shall not drive large goods vehicles of a class included in category C+E, other than vehicles included in sub-category C1+E the maximum authorised mass of which does not exceed 7.5 tonnes, as if he were authorised to do so by a provisional licence before the expiration of a period of six months commencing on the date on which he passed the test for that licence.

(5) In this regulation—

"LGV trainee driver's licence" means a large goods vehicle driver's licence which—

    (a) authorises its holder to drive vehicles of a class included in category C or C+E,
    (b) is held by a person other than a member of the armed forces of the Crown, and
    (c) is in force for a period during the whole or part of which that person is under the age of 21;

"registered", in relation to an employee, employer or training establishment, means registered for the time being by the Skills for Logistics Council in accordance with the Training Scheme;
"training agreement", in relation to an individual who is undergoing, or is to undergo, driver training under the Training Scheme, means the agreement between that individual and a registered employer;
"the Training Committee" means the Young LGV Driver Committee which is referred to in the Training Scheme;
the Training Scheme" means the Young Large Goods Vehicle (LGV) Driver Training Scheme which was established by Skills for Logistics and approved by the Secretary of State for the purpose of regulations under section 101(2) of the Traffic Act on 24 February 2004 for training young drivers of large goods vehicles.

Drivers' conduct

4–4379   55. Large goods vehicle drivers' licences and LGV Community licences: obligatory revocation or withdrawal and disqualification. (1) The prescribed circumstances for the purposes of section 115(1)(a) of the Traffic Act are that, in the case of the holder of a large goods vehicle driver's licence who is under the age of 21, he has been convicted (or is, by virtue of section 58 of the Offenders Act, to be treated as if he had been convicted) of an offence as a result of which the number of penalty points to be taken into account under section 29 of the Offenders Act exceeds three.

(2) The prescribed circumstances for the purposes of section 115A(1)(*a*) of the Traffic Act are that, in the case of the holder of an LGV Community licence who is under the age of 21, he has been convicted (or is, by virtue of section 58 of the Offenders Act, to be treated as if he had been convicted) of an offence as a result of which the number of penalty points to be taken into account under section 29 of the Offenders Act exceeds three.

(3) Where—

(*a*) a large goods vehicle drivers' licence is revoked under section 115(1)(*a*) of the Traffic Act, or

(*b*) the Secretary of State serves a notice on a person in pursuance of section 115A(1)(*a*) of that Act,

the cases in which the person whose licence has been revoked or, as the case may be, on whom the notice has been served must be disqualified indefinitely or for a fixed period shall be determined by the Secretary of State.

(4) Where the Secretary of State makes a determination under paragraph (3) that a person is to be disqualified for a fixed period he shall be disqualified until he reaches 21 years of age or for such longer period as the Secretary of State shall determine.

4–4379A 56. Holders of licences who are disqualified by order of a court. (1) This regulation applies where a person's large goods vehicle or passenger-carrying vehicle driver's licence is treated as revoked by virtue of section 37(1) of the Offenders Act (effect of disqualification by court order) and where it applies subsections (1) and (2) of section 117 of the Traffic Act are modified in accordance with paragraphs (2) to (6).

(2) Where the licence which is treated as revoked is a large goods vehicle driver's licence held by a person under the age of 21—

(*a*) the Secretary of State must order that person to be disqualified either indefinitely or for a fixed period, and

(*b*) where the Secretary of State determines that he shall be disqualified for a fixed period, he must be disqualified until he reaches the age of 21 or for such longer period as the Secretary of State determines.

(3) Where the licence which is treated as revoked is a large goods vehicle driver's licence held by any other person or is a passenger-carrying vehicle driver's licence—

(*a*) the Secretary of State may order that person to be disqualified either indefinitely or for such fixed period as he thinks fit, or

(*b*) except where the licence is a provisional licence, if it appears to the Secretary of State that, owing to that person's conduct, it is expedient to require him to comply with the prescribed conditions applicable to provisional licences until he passes a test, the Secretary of State may order him to be disqualified for holding or obtaining a full licence until he passes a test.

(4) Where the Secretary of State orders him to be disqualified until he passes a test, that test shall be a test prescribed by these Regulations for a licence authorising the driving of any class of vehicle in category C (other than sub-category C1), C + E, D or D + E which, prior to his disqualification by order of the court, he was authorised to drive by the revoked licence.

(5) Any question as to whether a person—

(*a*) shall be disqualified indefinitely or for a fixed period or until he passes a test, or

(*b*) if he is to be disqualified for a fixed period, what that period should be, or

(*c*) if he is to be disqualified until he passes a test, which test he should be required to pass,

may be referred by the Secretary of State to the traffic commissioner.

(6) Where the Secretary of State determines that a person shall be disqualified for a fixed period, that period shall commence on the expiration of the period of disqualification ordered by the court.

(7) Where this regulation applies, subsections (3) to (6) of section 116 of the Traffic Act shall apply, but as if—

(*a*) subsection (4)(*a*) were omitted,

(*b*) for the words "in any other case, revoke the licence or suspend it" in subsection (4)(*b*) there were substituted "suspend the licence", and

(*c*) the references to sections 115(1) and 116(1) of that Act were references to this regulation.

4–4379B 57. Removal of disqualification. (1) Subject to paragraphs (2) and (3), the Secretary of State may remove a disqualification for a period of more than two years imposed under section 117(2)(*a*) of the Traffic Act, after consultation with the traffic commissioner in a case which was referred to him, if an application for the removal of the disqualification is made after the expiration of whichever is relevant of the following periods commencing on the date of the disqualification—

(*a*) two years, if the disqualification is for less than four years;

(*b*) one half of the period of the disqualification, if it is for less than ten years, but not less than four years;

(*c*) five years in any other case.

(2) An application may not be made if the applicant has during the relevant period been convicted (or treated as convicted) of an offence by virtue of which he has incurred—

(a) penalty points, or

(b) an endorsement of a Northern Ireland driving licence held by him, or of its counterpart, with particulars of a conviction pursuant to provisions for the time being in force in Northern Ireland that correspond to sections 44 and 45 of the Offenders Act.

(3) Where an application under paragraph (1) for the removal of a disqualification is refused, a further such application shall not be entertained if made within three months after the date of refusal.

4–4379N   69. Exemptions from Part V.   (1) Subject to paragraph (2), section 98(3)(c) of the Traffic Act shall not apply to a person who is a provisional entitlement holder by virtue of having passed a test for the time being prescribed in respect of category P on or after 1st December 1990 and such a person shall be exempt from the requirement imposed by section 89(2A) of that Act.

(2) Paragraph (1) shall cease to apply to a person if he is disqualified by order of a court under section 36 of the Offenders Act.

(2A) Subject to paragraph (2C), section 89(2A) of the Traffic Act shall not apply to a person who is for the time being the holder of a full licence for a class of vehicle included in category A in respect of a test of competence to drive a vehicle of any other class included in that category.

(2B) Subject to paragraph (2C), a person who is for the time being the holder of a full licence for a class of vehicle included in category A shall be exempt from the restriction imposed by section 97(3)(e) on his driving a vehicle of another class included in that category.

(2C) The exemptions conferred by paragraphs (2A) and (2B) shall not apply in relation to the holder of a full licence authorising him only to drive a vehicle included in category A having automatic transmission in respect of—

(a) a test of competence to drive a vehicle having manual transmission; or

(b) his driving a vehicle having manual transmission.

(3) A provisional licence or provisional entitlement holder who is resident on an exempted island shall be exempt from the requirement imposed by section 89(2A) of the Traffic Act in respect of a test of competence to drive a motor bicycle of any class taken, or to be taken, on an island, whether or not that island is an exempted island.

(4) A provisional licence holder who is resident on an exempted island shall be exempt from the restriction imposed by section 97(3)(e) of the Traffic Act if he satisfies either of the conditions set out in paragraph (6).

(5) Section 98(3)(c) of the Traffic Act shall not apply to a provisional entitlement holder who is resident on an exempted island if he satisfies either of the conditions set out in paragraph (6).

(6) The conditions referred to in paragraphs (4) and (5) are that he is—

(a) driving on an exempted island, whether or not he is also resident on that island; or

(b) driving on an island which is not an exempted island for the purpose of—

(i) undertaking, or travelling to or from, an approved training course,

(ii) undergoing, or travelling to or from a place where he is to take or where he has taken, a test of competence prescribed in respect of category A or P.

(7) In this regulation—

"exempted island" means any island in Great Britain other than—

(a) the Isle of Wight, the island which comprises Lewis and Harris, the island which comprises North Uist, Benbecula and South Uist, Mainland Orkney and Mainland Shetland, and

(b) any other island from which motor vehicles not constructed or adapted for special purposes can at some time be conveniently driven to a road in any other part of Great Britain because of the presence of a bridge, tunnel, ford or other way suitable for the passage of such motor vehicles;

"provisional licence holder" means a person who holds a provisional licence which, subject to section 97(3) of the Traffic Act, authorises the driving of motor bicycles of any class; and

"provisional entitlement holder" means a person who holds a full licence which is treated, by virtue of section 98 of the Traffic Act and regulation 19, as authorising him to drive motor bicycles of any class as if he held a provisional licence therefor.

PART IV
DISABILITIES

4–4379O 70. Licence groups. (1) In this Part of these Regulations—

"Group 1 licence" means a licence in so far as it authorises its holder to drive classes of motor vehicle included in—

(a) categories A, B, B + E, F, G, H, K, L and P,
(b) the former category N,

"Group 2 licence" means, subject to paragraphs (2) and (3), a licence in so far as it authorises its holder to drive classes of motor vehicle included in any other category, and

"licence" includes, unless the context otherwise requires, a Northern Ireland licence and a Community licence.

(2) In so far as a licence authorises its holder to drive vehicles of a class included in sub-categories C1, C1 + E (8.25 tonnes), D1 (not for hire or reward) and D1 + E (not for hire or reward) it is a Group 1 licence while it remains in force if—

(a) it was in force at a time before 1st January 1997, or
(b) it is granted upon the expiry of a licence which was in force at a time before 1st January 1997 and comes into force not later than 31st December 1997.

(3) Subject to paragraph (6)(d) of regulation 7, a licence shall be a Group 1 licence in so far as it authorises, by virtue of paragraphs (4), (5) and (6) of that regulation, the driving of a class of motor vehicles which is not included in a category or sub-category specified in relation to a Group 1 licence in paragraph (1) or (2) above.

4–4379P 71. Disabilities prescribed in respect of Group 1 and 2 licences. (1) The following disabilities are prescribed for the purposes of section 92(2) of the Traffic Act as relevant disabilities in relation to an applicant for, or a person who holds, a Group 1 or Group 2 licence—

(a) epilepsy;
(b) severe mental disorder;
(c) liability to sudden attacks of disabling giddiness or fainting which are caused by any disorder or defect of the heart as a result of which the applicant for the licence or, as the case may be, the holder of the licence has a device implanted in his body, being a device which, by operating on the heart so as to regulate its action, is designed to correct the disorder or defect;
(d) liability to sudden attacks of disabling giddiness or fainting, other than attacks falling within paragraph (1)(c); and
(e) persistent misuse of drugs or alcohol, whether or not such misuse amounts to dependency.

(2) The disability prescribed in paragraph (1)(c) is prescribed for the purpose of section 92(4)(b) of the Traffic Act in relation to an applicant for a Group 1 or Group 2 licence if the applicant suffering from that disability satisfies the Secretary of State that—

(a) the driving of a vehicle by him in pursuance of the licence is not likely to be a source of danger to the public; and
(b) he has made adequate arrangements to receive regular medical supervision by a cardiologist (being a supervision to be continued throughout the period of the licence) and is conforming to those arrangements.

(3) The following disabilities are prescribed for the purposes of paragraphs (a) and (c) of section 92(4) of the Traffic Act namely, any disability consisting solely of any one or more of—

(a) the absence of one or more limbs,
(b) the deformity of one or more limbs, or
(c) the loss of use of one or more limbs, which is not progressive in nature.

(4) In this regulation—

(a) in paragraph (1)(b), the expression "severe mental disorder" includes mental illness, arrested or incomplete development of the mind, psychopathic disorder and severe impairment of intelligence or social functioning;

   (*b*) in paragraph (2)(*b*), the expression "cardiologist" means a registered medical practitioner who specialises in disorders or defects of the heart and who, in that connection, holds a hospital appointment;

   (*c*) in paragraph (3), references to a limb include references to a part of a limb, and the reference to loss of use, in relation to a limb, includes a reference to a deficiency of limb movement or power.

4–4379Q   72. Disabilities prescribed in respect of Group 1 licences.   (1) There is prescribed for the purposes of section 92(2) of the Traffic Act as a relevant disability in relation to an applicant for, or a holder of, a Group 1 licence, the inability to read in good daylight, with the aid of corrective lenses if worn, a registration mark which is affixed to a motor vehicle and contains characters of the prescribed size.

   (1A) In paragraph (1) the "prescribed size" means—

   (*a*) characters 79 millimetres high and 57 millimetres wide in a case where they are viewed from a distance of—

     (i) 12.3 metres, by an applicant for, or the holder of, a licence authorising the driving of a vehicle of a class included in category K, and

     (ii) 20.5 metres, in any other case; or

   (*b*) characters 79 millimetres high and 50 millimetres wide in a case where they are viewed from a distance of—

     (i) 12 metres, by an applicant for, or the holder of, a licence authorising the driving of a vehicle of a class included in category K, and

     (ii) 20 metres, in any other case.

   (2) Epilepsy is prescribed for the purposes of section 92(4)(*b*) of the Traffic Act in relation to an applicant for a Group 1 licence who either—

   (*a*) has been free from any epileptic attack during the period of one year immediately preceding the date when the licence is granted; or

   (*b*) (if not so free from attack) has had an epileptic attack whilst asleep more than three years before the date when the licence is granted and has had attacks only whilst asleep between the date of that attack and the date when the licence is granted,

where the conditions set out in paragraph (2A) are satisfied.

   (2A) The conditions are that—

   (*a*) so far as is practicable, he complies with the directions regarding his treatment for epilepsy, including directions as to regular medical check-ups made as part of that treatment, which may from time to time be given to him by the registered medical practitioner supervising the treatment,

   (*b*) if required to do so by the Secretary of State, he has provided a declaration signed by him that he will observe the condition in sub-paragraph (a), and

   (*c*) the Secretary of State is satisfied that the driving of a vehicle by him in accordance with the licence is not likely to be a source of danger to the public.

   (3) The disability described in paragraph (1) is prescribed for the purposes of section 94(5)(*b*) of the Traffic Act in relation to an applicant for, or a person who holds, a Group 1 licence.

4–4379R   73. Disabilities prescribed in respect of Group 2 licences.   (1) There is prescribed for the purposes of section 92(2) of the Traffic Act as a relevant disability in relation to an applicant for, or the holder of, a Group 2 licence the disability described in regulation 72(1).

   (2) There is also prescribed for the purposes of section 92(2) of the Traffic Act as a relevant disability in relation to a person other than an excepted licence holder who is an applicant for or who holds a Group 2 licence, such abnormality of sight in one or both eyes that he cannot meet the relevant standard of visual acuity.

   (3) The relevant standard of visual acuity for the purposes of paragraph (2) means—

   (*a*) in the case of a person who—

     (i) was the holder of a valid Group 2 licence or obsolete vocational licence upon each relevant date specified in column (1) of Table 1 at the end of this regulation, and

     (ii) if he is an applicant for a Group 2 licence, satisfies the Secretary of State that he has had adequate recent driving experience and has not during the period of 10 years immediately before the date of the application been involved in any road accident in which his defective eyesight was a contributory factor,

   the standard prescribed in relation to him in column (2) of Table 1;

   (*b*) in the case of a person who—

     (i) does not fall within sub-paragraph (a), and

     (ii) was or is the holder of a valid Group 2 licence upon the relevant date specified in column (1) of Table 2 at the end of this regulation,

   the standard prescribed in relation to him in column (2) of Table 2;

   (*c*) (*revoked*).

   (4) There is prescribed for the purposes of section 92(2) of the Traffic Act in relation to a person—

   (*a*) to whom paragraph (3)(*c*) applies, and

(b) who is able to meet the relevant standard of visual acuity prescribed in that sub-paragraph only with the aid of corrective lenses,

poor toleration of the correction made by the lenses.

(5) There is prescribed for the purposes of section 92(2) as a relevant disability in relation to a person who is an applicant for or who holds a Group 2 licence, sight in only one eye unless—

(a) he held an obsolete vocational licence on 1st April 1991, the traffic commissioner who granted the last such licence knew of the disability before 1st January 1991, and—

   (i) in a case of a person who also held such a licence on 1st January 1983, the visual acuity in his sighted eye is no worse than 6/12, or
   (ii) in any other case, the visual acuity in his sighted eye is no worse than 6/9, and

   if he is an applicant for a Group 2 licence, he satisfies the Secretary of State that he has had adequate recent driving experience and has not during the period of 10 years immediately before the date of the application been involved in any road accident in which his defective eyesight was a contributory factor; or

(b) the person is an excepted licence holder.

(6) Diabetes requiring insulin treatment is prescribed for the purposes of section 92(2) in relation to an applicant for or a person who holds a Group 2 licence unless the person suffering from the disability held an obsolete vocational licence on 1st April 1991 and the traffic commissioner who granted the last obsolete vocational licence knew of the disability before 1st January 1991.

(7) Liability to seizures arising from a cause other than epilepsy is prescribed for the purposes of section 92(2) in relation to an applicant for or a person who holds a Group 2 licence.

(8) Epilepsy is prescribed for the purposes of section 92(4)(b) of the Traffic Act in the case of an applicant for a Group 2 licence suffering from epilepsy who satisfies the Secretary of State that—

(a) during the period of 10 years immediately preceding the date when the licence is granted—

   (i) he has been free from any epileptic attack, and
   (ii) he has not required any medication to treat epilepsy, and

(b) that the driving of a vehicle by him in accordance with the licence is not likely to be a source of danger to the public.

(9) Diabetes requiring insulin treatment is prescribed for the purposes of section 92(4)(b) in the case of a person who—

(a) is an applicant for a licence authorising the driving of vehicles in sub-category C1, C1+E or C1+E (8.25 tonnes), and
(b) satisfies the Secretary of State that he has for at least 4 weeks been undergoing treatment with insulin,

provided that he satisfies the conditions mentioned in paragraph (10).

(10) The conditions referred to in paragraph (9) are that—

(a) (revoked),
(b) he has not, during the period of 12 months ending on the date of the application, required the assistance of another person to treat an episode of hypoglycaemia suffered whilst he was driving,
(c) he makes an arrangement to undergo at intervals of not more than 12 months an examination by a hospital consultant specialising in the treatment of diabetes and so far as is reasonably practicable conforms to that arrangement,
(d) his application is supported by a report from such a consultant sufficient to satisfy the Secretary of State that he has a history of responsible diabetic control with a minimal risk of incapacity due to hypoglycaemia,
(dd) he provides a declaration signed by him that he will—

   (i) so far as reasonably practicable comply with such directions regarding his treatment for diabetes as may for the time being be given to him by the doctor supervising that treatment;
   (ii) immediately report to the Secretary of State in writing any significant change in his condition; and
   (iii) provide such evidence as the Secretary of State may request that he continues to carry out the monitoring referred to in sub-paragraph (e) below,

(e) he regularly monitors his condition and, in particular, undertakes blood glucose monitoring at least twice daily and at times relevant to—

   (i) if he has held a licence authorising the driving of vehicles in sub-category C1, C1+E or C1+E (8.25 tonnes) for at least 12 months since starting his insulin treatment, the driving of such vehicles, and
   (ii) in any other case, the driving of motor vehicles generally, and
(f) the Secretary of State is satisfied that the driving of such a vehicle in pursuance of the licence is not likely to be a source of danger to the public.

(11) In this regulation—

(a) references to measurements of visual acuity are references to visual acuity measured on the Snellen Scale;
(b) "excepted licence holder" means a person who—

   (i) was the holder of a licence authorising the driving of vehicles included in sub-categories C1 and C1 + E (8.25 tonnes) which was in force at a time before 1st January 1997, and

   (ii) is an applicant for, or the holder of, a Group 2 licence solely by reason that the licence applied for or held authorises (or would, if granted, authorise) the driving of vehicles included in those sub-categories;

  (c) "obsolete vocational licence" means a licence to drive heavy goods vehicles granted under Part IV of the Traffic Act as originally enacted or a licence to drive public service vehicles granted under section 22 of the 1981 Act which was in force a time before 1 April 1991.

TABLE 1

(1) Person holding Group 2 licence or obsolete vocational licence on:	(2) Standard of visual acuity applicable:
1 1 January 1983 and 1 April 1991	Acuity (with the aid of corrective lenses if necessary) of at least 6/12 in the better eye or at least 6/36 in the worse eye or uncorrected acuity of at least 3/60 in at least one eye.
2 1 March 1992, but not on 1 January 1983	Acuity (with the aid of corrective lenses if necessary) of at least 6/9 in the better eye or at least 6/12 in the worse eye, or uncorrected acuity of at least 3/60 in at least one eye.

TABLE 2

(1) Person holding Group 2 licence on:	(2) Standard of visual acuity applicable:
1 31 December 1996, but not on 1 March 1992	Acuity (with the aid of corrective lenses if necessary) of at least 6/9 in the better eye and at least 6/12 in the worse eye and, if corrective lenses are needed to meet that standard, uncorrected acuity of at least 3/60 in at least one eye.
2 On or after 1 January 1997 but not on 31 December 1996	Acuity (with the aid of corrective lenses if necessary) of at least 6/9 in the better eye and at least 6/12 in the worse eye and, if corrective lenses are needed to meet that standard, uncorrected acuity of at least 3/60 in both eyes.

4–4379S   74. Disabilities requiring medical investigation: High Risk Offenders.   (1) Subject to paragraph (2), the circumstances prescribed for the purposes of subsection (5) of section 94 of the Traffic Act, under subsection (4) of that section, are that the person who is an applicant for, or holder of, a licence—

  (a) has been disqualified by an order of a court by reason that the proportion of alcohol in his body equalled or exceeded—

    (i)   87.5 microgrammes per 100 millilitres of breath, or
    (ii)   200 milligrammes per 100 millilitres of blood, or
    (iii)   267.5 milligrammes per 100 millilitres of urine;

  (b) has been disqualified by order of a court by reason that he has failed, without reasonable excuse, to provide a specimen when required to do so pursuant to section 7 of the Traffic Act; or

  (c) has been disqualified by order of a court on two or more occasions within any period of 10 years by reason that—

    (i)   the proportion of alcohol in his breath, blood or urine exceeded the limit prescribed by virtue of section 5 of the Traffic Act, or
    (ii)   he was unfit to drive through drink contrary to section 4 of that Act.

  (2) For the purposes of paragraph (1)(a) and (b) a court order shall not be taken into account unless it was made on or after 1st June 1990 and paragraph (1)(c) shall not apply to a person unless the last such order was made on or after 1st June 1990.

4–4379T   75. Examination by an officer of the Secretary of State.   (1) There are prescribed for the purposes of section 94(5)(b)(ii) (examination of a licence applicant or holder by an officer of the Secretary of State) the following disabilities—

  (a) impairment of visual acuity or of the central or peripheral visual field;
  (b) a disability consisting of any one or more of the following—

    (i)   the absence of one or more limbs,
    (ii)   the deformity of one or more limbs,
    (iii)   the loss of use of one or more limbs whether or not progressive in nature, and

(iv) impairment of co-ordination of movement of the limbs or of co-ordination between a limb and the eye;

(c) impairment of cognitive functions or behaviour;

(2) In paragraph (1)(*b*), a reference to a limb includes a reference to part of a limb, and the reference to loss of use in relation to a limb includes a reference to impairment of limb movement power or sensation.

PART VII
SUPPLEMENTARY

Transitional provisions

4–4379U 76. Effect of change in classification of vehicles for licensing purposes.   (1) In a licence (whether full or provisional) granted before 1st January 1997, a reference to motor vehicles in an old category shall be construed as a reference to motor vehicles in the new category corresponding thereto and a reference to motor vehicles of a class included in an old category shall be construed as a reference to vehicles of the corresponding class included in the new category.

(2) Where a licence granted before 1st January 1997 authorises only the driving of a class of motor vehicles included in an old category having automatic transmission, it shall authorise the driving of the corresponding class of vehicles in the new category having automatic transmission.

(3) For the purposes of paragraphs (1) and (2), a reference in a licence to motor vehicles in an old category (or a class included in that category) includes a reference in a licence granted before 1st June 1990 to a group or class of motor vehicles which is, by virtue of any enactment, to be construed as a reference to vehicles in the old category (or a class included in that category).

(4) In this regulation—

"old category" and "class included in an old category" mean respectively a category and a class of vehicles specified in column (1) of the table at the end of this regulation,

"new category" and "class included in a new category", in relation to an old category, mean respectively the category (or, as the case may be, the sub-category) and the class of vehicles specified in column (2) of the table as corresponding to the relevant old category or class included therein, and

"section 19 permit" means a permit granted under section 19 of the 1985 Act.

TABLE

(1) Old category or class	(2) Corresponding new category or class
A	A
B1	B1
B1, limited to invalid carriages	B1 (invalid carriages)
B	B
B plus E	B + E
C1	C1
C1 plus E	C1 +E (8.25 tonnes)
C	C
C plus E	C + E
C plus E, limited to drawbar trailer combinations only	Vehicles in category C + E which are drawbar trailer combinations
D1	D1 (not for hire or reward)
D1 plus E	D1 + E (not for hire or reward)
D, limited to 16 seats	D1
D, limited to vehicles not more than 5.5 metres in length	D1 and vehicles in category D not more than 5.5 metres in length
D, limited to vehicles not driven for hire or reward	Vehicles in category D which are either driven while being used in accordance with a section 19 permit or, if not being so used, driven otherwise than for hire or reward
D	D
D plus E	D + E
F	F
G	G
H	H
K	K
L	L
P	P

4–4379V 77. Saving in respect of entitlement to Group M.   (1) Where a person was authorised by virtue of regulations revoked by these Regulations (whether or not he is also the holder of a licence granted before 1st October 1982) to drive, or to apply for the grant of a licence authorising the driving of, vehicles of a class included in the former group M (trolley vehicles used for the carriage of passengers with more than 16 seats in addition to the driver's seat), he shall continue to be so authorised and any licence granted to such a person shall be construed as authorising the driving of vehicles of that class.

(2) A person who is authorised to drive vehicles of a class included in the former group M shall, to the extent that he is so authorised, be deemed to be the holder of a Group 1 licence.

4–4379W 78. Saving in respect of entitlement to former category N. (1) Where on 31st December 1996 a person was, by virtue of regulations then in force, the holder of, or entitled to apply for the grant of, a licence authorising the driving of vehicles included in—

    (a) the former category N (vehicles exempt from vehicle excise duty under section 7(1) of the Vehicles (Excise) Act 1971) alone, or

    (b) category F or A and the former category N,

the Secretary of State may, notwithstanding anything otherwise contained in these Regulations, grant to such a person a licence authorising the driving of vehicles in the former category N (with or without vehicles in either or both of the other categories as the case may be) and a person holding such a licence shall be authorised to drive such vehicles.

(2) Where on 31st December 1996 a person was the holder of, or entitled to apply for the grant of, a licence authorising the driving of vehicles included in category B and the former category N, he shall continue to be authorised to drive vehicles in that former category and any licence granted to such a person authorising the driving of vehicles included in category B shall be construed as authorising also the driving of vehicles in that former category.

4–4379X 79. Saving in respect of entitlement to drive mobile project vehicles. In relation to a person who was at a time before 1st January 1997 the holder of a licence authorising the driving of vehicles of a class included in category B (except a licence authorising only the driving of vehicles included in sub-category B1 or B1 (invalid carriages)), regulation 7(5) shall apply as if paragraphs (b) and (c) and the words "on behalf of a non-commercial body" were omitted.

Miscellaneous

4–4379Y 80. Persons who become resident in Great Britain. (1) A person who becomes resident in Great Britain who is—

    (a) the holder of a relevant permit, and

    (b) not disqualified for holding or obtaining a licence in Great Britain

shall, during the period of one year after he becomes so resident, be treated for the purposes of section 87 of the Traffic Act as the holder of a licence[1] authorising him to drive all classes of small vehicle, motor bicycle or moped which he is authorised to drive by that permit.

(2) A person who becomes resident in Great Britain who is—

    (a) the holder of a British external licence granted in the Isle of Man, Jersey or Guernsey authorising the driving of large and medium-sized goods vehicles of any class, and

    (b) not disqualified for holding or obtaining a licence in Great Britain

shall, during the period of one year after he becomes so resident, be treated for the purposes of section 87 of the Traffic Act as the holder of a licence authorising him to drive large and medium-sized goods vehicles of all classes which he is authorised to drive by that licence.

(3) A person who becomes resident in Great Britain who is—

    (a) the holder of a British external licence granted in the Isle of Man, Jersey or Guernsey authorising the driving of passenger-carrying vehicles of any class, and

    (b) not disqualified for holding or obtaining a licence in Great Britain

shall, during the period of one year after he becomes so resident, be treated for the purposes of section 87 of the Traffic Act as the holder of a licence authorising him to drive passenger-carrying vehicles of all classes which he is authorised to drive by that licence.

(4) The enactments mentioned in paragraph (5) shall apply in relation to—

    (a) holders of relevant permits and holders of British external licences of the classes mentioned in paragraphs (2) and (3), or

    (b) (as the case may be) those licences and permits,

with the modifications contained in paragraph (5).

(5) The modifications referred to in paragraph (4) are that—

    (a) section 7 of the Offenders Act shall apply as if—

       (i) the references to a licence were references to a relevant permit or a British external licence, and

      (ii) the words after paragraph (c) thereof were omitted;

    (b) section 27(1) and (3) of the Offenders Act shall apply as if—

       (i) the references to a licence were references to a relevant permit or a British external licence,

      (ii) the references to the counterpart of a licence were omitted, and

      (iii) in subsection (3) the words ", unless he satisfies the Court that he has applied for a new licence and has not received it" were omitted;

    (c) section 42(5) of the Offenders Act shall apply as if for the words "endorsed on the counterpart of the licence" onwards there were substituted the words "notified to the Secretary of State";

    (d) section 47 of the Offenders Act shall apply as if for subsection (2) there were substituted—

"(2) Where a court orders the holder of a relevant permit or a British external licence to be disqualified it must send the permit or the licence, on its being produced to the court, to the Secretary of State who shall keep it until the disqualification has expired or been removed or the person entitled to it leaves Great Britain and in any case has made a demand in writing for its return to him.

"Relevant permit" has the meaning given by regulation 80 of the Motor Vehicles (Driving Licences) Regulations 1999.";

(e) section 164(1), (6) and (8) of the Traffic Act shall apply as if the references therein to a licence were references to a relevant permit or a British external licence and the references to a counterpart of a licence were omitted; and

(f) section 173 of the Traffic Act shall apply as if after paragraph (aa) there were added—

"(ab) a relevant permit (within the meaning of regulation 80 of the Motor Vehicles (Driving Licences) Regulations 1999,
(ac) a British external licence,".

(6) In this regulation "relevant permit" means—

(i) a "domestic driving permit",
(ii) a "Convention driving permit", or
(iii) a "British Forces (BFG) driving licence",

within the meaning of article 2(7)—of the Motor Vehicles (International Circulation) Order 1975 which is—

(a) for the time being valid for the purposes for which it was issued, and
(b) is not a domestic driving permit or a British Forces (BFG) driving licence in respect of which any order made, or having effect as if made, by the Secretary of State is for the time being in force under article 2(6) of that Order.

---

1. The procurement of an English provisional licence with a view to taking a test in this country will not affect his continued right to drive under the permit, eg unaccompanied, without "L" plates (*Heidak v Winnett* [1981] RTR 445).

4–4379Z 81. Service personnel. The traffic commissioner for the South Eastern and Metropolitan Traffic Areas is hereby prescribed for the purposes of section 183(6) of the Traffic Act (discharge of Part IV functions in relation to HM Forces).

4–4380 82. Northern Ireland licences. (1) The traffic commissioner for the North Western Traffic Area is hereby prescribed for the purposes of section 122(2) of the Traffic Act.
(2) For the purposes of section 122(4) of the Traffic Act, the magistrates' court or sheriff to whom an appeal shall lie by the holder of a Northern Ireland licence, being a person who is not resident in Great Britain and who is aggrieved by the suspension or revocation of the licence or by the ordering of disqualification for holding or obtaining a licence, shall be—

(a) such a magistrates' court or sheriff as he may nominate at the time he makes the appeal; or
(b) in the absence of a nomination of a particular court under sub-paragraph (a), the magistrates' court in whose area the office of the traffic commissioner for the North Western Traffic Area is situated.

4–4380A 83. Statement of date of birth. (1) The circumstances in which a person specified in section 164(2) of the Traffic Act shall, on being required by a police constable, state his date of birth are—

(a) where that person fails to produce forthwith for examination his licence on being required to do so by a police constable under that section; or
(b) where, on being so required, that person produces a licence—

(i) which the police constable in question has reason to suspect was not granted to that person, was granted to that person in error or contains an alteration in the particulars entered on the licence (other than as described in paragraph (ii)) made with intent to deceive; or
(ii) in which the driver number has been altered, removed or defaced;

(c) where that person is a person specified in subsection (1)(d) of that section and the police constable has reason to suspect that he is under 21 years of age.

(2) In paragraph (1), "driver number" means the number described as the driver number in the licence.

4–4380B

Regulations 4 to 6 and 43   SCHEDULE 2

CATEGORIES AND SUB-CATEGORIES OF VEHICLE FOR LICENSING PURPOSES

PART 1

4–4380C

(1) Category or sub-category	(2) Classes of vehicle included	(3) Additional categories and sub-categories
A	Motor bicycles.	B1, K and P
A1	A sub-category of category A comprising learner motor bicycles.	P
B	Motor vehicles, other than vehicles included in category A, F, K or P, having a maximum authorised mass not exceeding 3.5 tonnes and not more than eight seats in addition to the driver's seat, including: (i) a combination of any such vehicle and a trailer where the trailer has a maximum authorised mass not exceeding 750 kilogrammes, and (ii) a combination of any such vehicle and a trailer where the maximum authorised mass of the combination does not exceed 3.5 tonnes and the maximum authorised mass of the trailer does not exceed the unladen weight of the tractor vehicle.	F, K and P
B1	A sub-category of category B comprising motor vehicles having three or four wheels and an unladen weight not exceeding 550 kilograms.	K and P
B + E	Combinations of a motor vehicle and trailer where the tractor vehicle is in category B but the combination does not fall within that category.	None
C	Motor vehicles having a maximum authorised mass exceeding 3.5 tonnes, other than vehicles falling within category D, F, G or H, including any such vehicle drawing a trailer having a maximum authorised mass not exceeding 750 kilograms.	None
C1	A sub-category of category C comprising motor vehicles having a maximum authorised mass exceeding 3.5 tonnes but not exceeding 7.5 tonnes, including any such vehicle drawing a trailer having a maximum authorised mass not exceeding 750 kilograms.	None
D	Motor vehicles constructed or adapted for the carriage of passengers having more than eight seats in addition to the driver's seat, including any such vehicle drawing a trailer having a maximum authorised mass not exceeding 750 kilograms.	None
D1	A sub-category of category D comprising motor vehicles having more than eight but not more than 16 seats in addition to the driver's seat and including any such vehicle drawing a trailer with a maximum authorised mass not exceeding 750 kilograms.	None
C + E	Combinations of a motor vehicle and trailer where the tractor vehicle is in category C but the combination does not fall within that category.	B + E
C1 + E	A sub-category of category C + E comprising combinations of a motor vehicle and trailer where: (*a*) the tractor vehicle is in sub-category C1, (*b*) the maximum authorised mass of the trailer exceeds 750 kilograms but not the unladen weight of the tractor vehicle, and (*c*) the maximum authorised mass of the combination does not exceed 12 tonnes.	B + E
D + E	Combinations of a motor vehicle and trailer where the tractor vehicle is in category D but the combination does not fall within that category.	B + E
D1 + E	A sub-category of category D + E comprising combinations of a motor vehicle and trailer where: (*a*) the tractor vehicle is in sub-category D1, (*b*) the maximum authorised mass of the trailer exceeds 750 kilograms but not the unladen weight of the tractor vehicle, (*c*) the maximum authorised mass of the combination does not exceed 12 tonnes, and (*d*) the trailer is not used for the carriage of passengers.	B + E
F	Agricultural or forestry tractors, including any such vehicle drawing a trailer but excluding any motor vehicle included in category H.	K
G	Road rollers.	None
H	Track-laying vehicles steered by their tracks.	None
K	Mowing machines which do not fall within category A and vehicles controlled by a pedestrian.	None
P	Mopeds.	None

PART 2

4–4380D

(1) Sub-category	(2) Classes of vehicle included	(3) Additional categories and sub-categories
C1 + E (8.25 tonnes)	A sub-category of category C + E comprising combinations of a motor vehicle and trailer in sub-category C1 + E where: (a) the maximum authorised mass of the trailer exceeds 750 kilograms and may exceed the unladen weight of the tractor vehicle, and (b) the maximum authorised mass of the combination does not exceed 8.25 tonnes.	None
D1 (not for hire or reward)	A sub-category of category D comprising motor vehicles in sub-category D1 driven otherwise than for hire or reward.	None
D1 + E (not for hire or reward)	A sub-category of category D + E comprising motor vehicles in sub-category D1 + E where: (a) the motor vehicles are driven otherwise than for hire or reward, and (b) the maximum authorised mass of the trailer exceeds 750 kilograms and may exceed the unladen weight of the tractor vehicle.	None
L	Motor vehicles propelled by electrical power.	None

PART 3

4–4380E

(1) Sub-category	(2) Classes of vehicle included	(3) Additional categories and sub-categories
B1 (invalid carriages)	A sub-category of category B comprising motor vehicles which are invalid carriages.	None

4–4380F

Regulation 14

SCHEDULE 3
LICENCE FEES

Regulation 16

SCHEDULE 4
DISTINGUISHING MARKS TO BE DISPLAYED ON A MOTOR VEHICLE BEING DRIVEN UNDER A PROVISIONAL LICENCE

PART 1

4–4380G   Diagram of distinguishing mark to be displayed on a motor vehicle in England, Wales or Scotland.

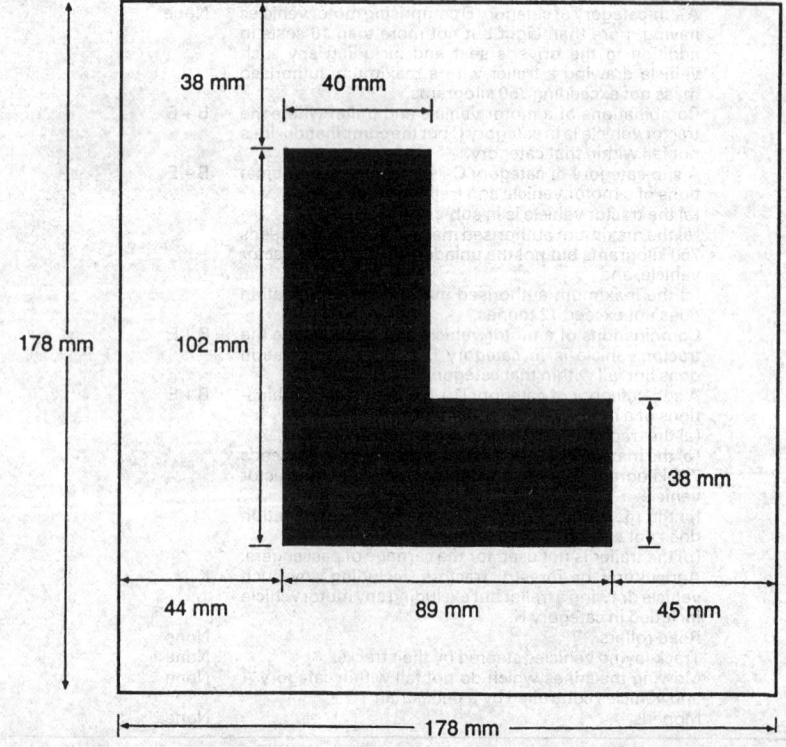

PART 2

4–4380H   Diagram of optional distinguishing mark to be displayed on a motor vehicle in Wales if a mark in the form set out in Part 1 is not displayed.

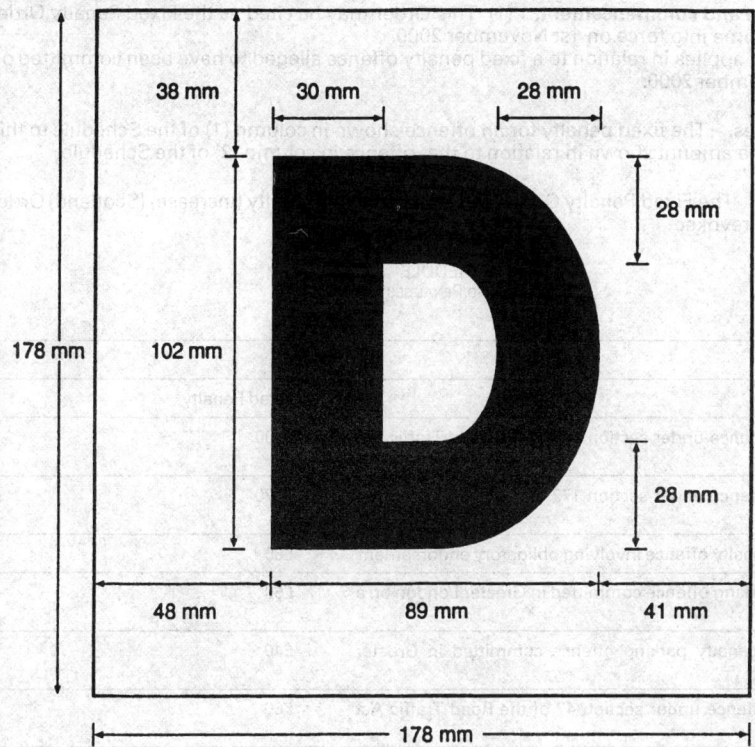

Regulation 35	SCHEDULE 5	

SCHEDULE 5
FEES FOR PRACTICAL AND UNITARY TESTS

4–4380I

Regulation 38   SCHEDULE 6
EVIDENCE OF IDENTITY OF TEST CANDIDATES

4–4380J

Regulation 40   SCHEDULE 7
SPECIFIED MATTERS FOR THEORY TEST

4–4380K

Regulation 40   SCHEDULE 8
SPECIFIED REQUIREMENTS FOR PRACTICAL OR UNITARY TEST

4–4380L

Regulation 45   SCHEDULE 9
UPGRADED ENTITLEMENTS ON PASSING SECOND TEST

4–4380M

Regulation 47   SCHEDULE 10
FORMS OF CERTIFICATE AND STATEMENT OF THEORY TEST RESULT

4–4380N

Regulation 48   SCHEDULE 11
FORMS OF CERTIFICATE AND STATEMENT OF PRACTICAL AND UNITARY TEST RESULT

4–4380O

Regulation 59   SCHEDULE 12
ELEMENTS OF AN APPROVED TRAINING COURSE

4–4380P

Regulations 60, 65 and 68   SCHEDULE 13
APPROVED MOTOR BICYCLE TRAINING COURSES: FORMS OF CERTIFICATE

Fixed Penalty Order 2000
(SI 2000/2972 amended by SI 2003/1254)

4-4381　1. Citation and commencement.　(1) This Order may be cited as the Fixed Penalty Order 2000 and shall come into force on 1st November 2000.

(2) This Order applies in relation to a fixed penalty offence alleged to have been committed on or after 1st November 2000.

2. Fixed penalties.　The fixed penalty for an offence shown in column (1) of the Schedule to this Order shall be the amount shown in relation to that offence in column (2) of the Schedule.

3. Revocations.　The Fixed Penalty Order 1992 and the Fixed Penalty (Increase) (Scotland) Order 1992 are hereby revoked.

Article 2

SCHEDULE
FIXED PENALTIES

4-4382

(1)	(2)
Offence	Fixed Penalty
A fixed penalty offence under section 143 of the Road Traffic Act 1988	£200
A fixed penalty offence under section 172 of the Road Traffic Act 1988	£120
Any other fixed penalty offence involving obligatory endorsement	£60
A fixed penalty parking offence committed in Greater London on a red route	£60
Any other fixed penalty parking offence committed in Greater London	£40
A fixed penalty offence under section 47 of the Road Traffic Act 1988	£60
A fixed penalty offence under section 33 of the Vehicle Excise and Registration Act 1994	£60
Any other fixed penalty offence	£30

In this Schedule—

"fixed penalty parking offence" means—

(i) an offence under the Road Traffic Regulation Act 1984 which is a fixed penalty offence, which does not involve obligatory endorsement and which is committed in respect of a stationary vehicle;
(ii) an offence under section 15(1) of the Greater London Council (General Powers) Act 1974;
(iii) an offence under section 137(1) of the Highways Act 1980;
(iv) an offence under section 19 of the Road Traffic Act 1988;
(v) an offence under section 42 of the Road Traffic Act 1988 consisting in the causing of an unnecessary obstruction of a road in breach of regulation 103 of the Road Vehicles (Construction and Use) Regulations 1986; or
(vi) an offence under the Parks Regulation Acts 1872 and 1926 consisting in the failure to comply with, or acting in contravention of, regulation 4(30) of the Royal Parks and Other Open Spaces Regulations 1997;

"red route" means a length of road affected by either or both of the following traffic signs, namely—

(i) a traffic sign lawfully placed on the road, being a traffic sign which bears the words "Red Route", with or without any other word or any sign or other indication; or
(ii) a traffic sign consisting of a red line or mark is lawfully placed on the road;

"traffic sign" means a traffic sign for the purposes of section 64(1) of the Road Traffic Regulation Act 1984 which conveys any restriction or prohibition under an order made under that Act.

Road Vehicles (Display of Registration Marks) Regulations 2001[1]
(SI 2001/561 amended by SI 2001/1079 and SI 2002/2687)

PART I
PRELIMINARY

4-4383　1. Citation, commencement and revocation.　(1) These Regulations may be cited as the Road Vehicles (Display of Registration Marks) Regulations 2001 and shall come into force—

(a) for the purposes of this paragraph and regulation 17, on 21st March 2001, and
(b) for all other purposes, on 1st September 2001.

(2) The regulations specified in Schedule 1 are hereby revoked.

1. Made by the Secretary of State in exercise of powers conferred by ss 23 and 57 of the Vehicle Excise and Registration Act 1994.

2. Interpretation: general. (1) In these Regulations the following expressions shall have the following meanings—

"the Act" means the Vehicle Excise and Registration Act 1994;
"agricultural machine" means a vehicle which is—

(a) an agricultural tractor, as defined in paragraph 4B(2) of Schedule 1 to the Act, or
(b) an off-road tractor, as defined in paragraph 4B(4) of that Schedule, or
(c) a light agricultural vehicle, as defined in paragraph 4C(2) of that Schedule, or
(d) an agricultural engine, or
(e) a mowing machine;

"the Council Regulation" means Council Regulation (EC) No 2411/98 on the recognition in intra-community traffic of the distinguishing signs of member states in which motor vehicles are registered;
"dual purpose plate" means a plate or other device which displays both the registration mark of the vehicle and the international distinguishing sign of the United Kingdom in accordance with the Council Regulation;
"EEA State" means a state which is a contracting party to the Agreement on the European Economic Area signed at Oporto on 2nd May 1992 as adjusted by the Protocol signed at Brussels on 17th March 1993;
"motor cycle" means a vehicle having 2 wheels and includes a vehicle of that description in combination with a sidecar;
"motor tricycle" means a vehicle having 3 wheels symmetrically arranged;
"quadricycle" means a vehicle having four wheels, a maximum net engine power not exceeding 15 kilowatts and an unladen mass (excluding the mass of batteries in the case of an electrically-powered vehicle) not exceeding—

(a) 550 kilograms in the case of a goods vehicle, and
(b) 400 kilograms in any other case;

"registration plate" means a plate or other device displaying the registration mark of the vehicle and in the case of a dual purpose plate means such part of the plate as is not intended for the display the international distinguishing sign of the United Kingdom in accordance with the Council Regulation;
"prescribed font" means the style shown in Schedule 4 for a character of the height specified in that Schedule;
"relevant date" means—

(a) in Great Britain, 1st October 1938, and
(b) in Northern Ireland, 1st January 1948;

"works truck" means a vehicle which is—

(a) designed for use in private premises, and
(b) used on public roads only—

(i) for carrying goods between private premises and a vehicle on a road in the immediate vicinity, or
(ii) in passing from one part of private premises to another or between private premises and other private premises in the immediate vicinity, or
(iii) in connection with road works at or in the immediate vicinity of the site of the works.

(2) Unless the context otherwise requires, a reference in these Regulations to—

(a) a registration plate fixed or to be fixed to a vehicle, or
(b) a registration mark displayed or to be displayed on a plate,

is to be construed, where the vehicle is towing a trailer, so as to include a reference to the registration plate which is required under these Regulations to be fixed to the trailer or a reference to the mark displayed on the plate fixed to that trailer.

3. Exempt vehicles. Nothing in these Regulations applies to—

(a) an invalid vehicle, that is a vehicle the unladen weight of which does not exceed 254 kilograms and which is specially designed and constructed, and not merely adapted, for the use of a person suffering from a physical disability and solely used by that person; or
(b) a pedestrian-controlled vehicle, that is a vehicle the unladen weight of which does not exceed 450 kilograms which is neither constructed nor adapted for the carriage of a driver or passenger.

PART II
REGISTRATION PLATES

4–4384 **4. Interpretation of Part II.** In this Part the following expressions shall have the following meanings—

"diagonal length", in relation to a relevant area, means the length of a line drawn diagonally across the square enclosing the area (so that the extent of the relevant area is thereby delimited);

"relevant area", in relation to a registration plate, means the area contained in a square described on the ground—

(a) in front of the vehicle in the case of a plate fixed on the front of the vehicle, and
(b) behind the vehicle in the case of a plate fixed on the rear of the vehicle,

where one corner of the square is immediately below the middle of the plate and the diagonal of the square from that corner is parallel to the longitudinal axis of the vehicle;

"relevant type-approval directive" means—

(a) in the case of a motor cycle, motor tricycle or quadricycle—

(i) Council Directive 93/94/EEC (as amended by Commission Directive 99/26/EC) as regards the space to be provided for fixing of the rear registration plate, and
(ii) Council Directive 93/92/EEC as regards the rear registration plate lamp;

(b) in the case of any other vehicle or a trailer—

(i) Council Directive 70/222/EEC as regards the space to be provided for fixing of the rear registration plate, and
(ii) Council Directive 76/760/EEC (as amended by Commission Directive 97/31/EC) as regards the rear registration plate lamp.

5. Fixing of rear registration plates: vehicles registered on or after the relevant date.   (1) This regulation applies to vehicles, other than works trucks, road rollers and agricultural machines, first registered on or after the relevant date.

(2) A registration plate must be fixed on the rear of—

(a) the vehicle, or
(b) where the vehicle is towing a trailer, the trailer, or
(c) where the vehicle is towing more than one trailer, the rearmost trailer.

(3) Where a vehicle (or, in a case where the plate is required to be fixed on a trailer, that trailer) has been constructed so as to satisfy the requirements of the relevant type-approval directive, whether or not it is required by law to satisfy them, the plate may be fixed in the space provided in accordance with those requirements but if it is not so fixed it must be fixed in the manner required by paragraph (5).

(4) Except as provided in paragraph (3) the plate must be fixed in the manner required by paragraph (5).

(5) This paragraph requires the plate to be fixed—

(a) vertically or, where that is not reasonably practicable, in a position as close to the vertical as is reasonably practicable, and
(b) in such a position that in normal daylight the characters of the registration mark are easily distinguishable from every part of a relevant area having the diagonal length specified in paragraph (6).

(6) The diagonal length of the relevant area is—

(a) in the case of a mark having characters the width of which is at least 57 millimetres, 22 metres,
(b) in the case of a mark having characters the width of which is 50 millimetres, 21.5 metres,
(c) in the case of a mark having characters the width of which is 44 millimetres, 18 metres.

6. Fixing of front registration plates: vehicles registered on or after the relevant date.   (1) This regulation applies to vehicles, other than works trucks, road rollers and agricultural machines, first registered on or after the relevant date.

(2) Except as provided in paragraph (5), a registration plate must be fixed on the front of the vehicle in the manner required by paragraph (3).

(3) This paragraph requires the plate to be fixed—

(a) vertically or, where that is not reasonably practicable, in a position as close to the vertical as is reasonably practicable,
(b) in such a position that in normal daylight the characters of the registration mark are easily distinguishable from every part of a relevant area having the diagonal length specified in paragraph (4).

(4) The diagonal length of the relevant area is—

(a) in the case of a mark having characters the width of which is at least 57 millimetres, 22 metres,
(b) in the case of a mark having characters the width of which is 50 millimetres, 21.5 metres,
(c) in the case of a mark having characters the width of which is 44 millimetres, 18 metres.

(5) In the case of a motor cycle or a motor tricycle which does not have a body of a type which is characteristic of the body of a four-wheeled vehicle—

(a) a registration plate must not be fixed on the front of a vehicle if it was first registered on or after 1st September 2001,
(b) a plate need not be fixed on the front of the vehicle if it was first registered before 1st September 2001.

7. Fixing of registration plates: vehicles registered before the relevant date. (1) This regulation applies to vehicles, other than works trucks, road rollers and agricultural machines, first registered before the relevant date.

(2) Except as provided in paragraph (4), a registration plate must be fixed in the manner required by paragraph (3) on—

- (a) the front of the vehicle, and
- (b) the rear of—

  - (i) the vehicle or,
  - (ii) where the vehicle is towing a trailer, the trailer or,
  - (iii) where the vehicle is towing more than one trailer, the rearmost trailer.

(3) This paragraph requires each plate to be fixed—

- (a) in a vertical position or, where that is not possible, in a position as close to the vertical as is reasonably practicable, and
- (b) in such a position that in normal daylight the characters of the registration mark are easily distinguishable, in the case of a plate fixed on the front of the vehicle, from in front of the vehicle and, in the case of a plate fixed on the rear of the vehicle or trailer, from behind the vehicle or trailer.

(4) In the case of a motor cycle and a motor tricycle which does not have a body of a type which is characteristic of the body of a four-wheeled vehicle, a registration plate need not be fixed on the front of the vehicle.

8. Fixing of registration plates: works trucks, road rollers and agricultural machines. (1) This regulation applies to works trucks, road rollers and agricultural machines.

(2) A registration plate must be fixed on the vehicle in a vertical position or, where that is not possible, in a position as close to the vertical as is reasonably practicable—

- (a) on both sides of the vehicles, so that the characters of the mark are easily distinguishable from both sides of the vehicle, or
- (b) on the rear of the vehicle, so that the characters of the mark are easily distinguishable from behind the vehicle, or
- (c) where the vehicle is towing a trailer or trailers and the plate is not fixed on the sides of the vehicle, on the trailer or the rearmost trailer (as the case may be) so that the characters of the mark are easily distinguishable from behind the trailer.

(3) Where the towing vehicle is an agricultural machine, a plate fixed on the trailer may, instead of displaying the registration mark of the towing vehicle, display the mark of any other agricultural machine kept by the keeper of the towing vehicle.

9. Lighting of rear registration plates. (1) This regulation applies to vehicles other than—

- (a) works trucks,
- (b) road rollers,
- (c) agricultural machines, and
- (d) vehicles first registered before the relevant date.

(2) Where the vehicle is being used on a road between sunset and sunrise the registration plate fixed on the rear of—

- (a) the vehicle, or
- (b) where the vehicle is towing a trailer, the trailer or,
- (c) where the vehicle is towing more than one trailer, the rearmost trailer,

must be lit in accordance with this regulation.

(3) Where a vehicle (or, in a case where the plate is required to be fixed on a trailer, that trailer) has been constructed so as to satisfy the requirements of the relevant type-approval directive, whether or not it is required by law to satisfy them, that plate may be lit by a lamp which complies with those requirements but if it is not so lit it must be lit in the manner required by paragraph (5).

(4) Except as provided in paragraph (3) that plate must be lit in the manner required by paragraph (5).

(5) This paragraph requires the plate to be lit so that it is easily distinguishable from every part of a relevant area having a diagonal length—

- (a) in the case of a plate displaying a mark having characters with a width of 44 millimetres, of 15 metres, and
- (b) in any other case, of 18 metres.

10. Specifications for registration plates. (1) A registration mark must be displayed on a registration plate conforming to the requirements prescribed by this regulation.

(2) In the case of a vehicle first registered on or after 1st September 2001 the registration plate must conform to the requirements set out in Part 1 of Schedule 2.

(3) Subject to paragraph (4), in the case of a vehicle first registered on or after 1st January 1973 but before 1st September 2001 the registration plate must conform either to the requirements set out in Part 2 of Schedule 2 or to the requirements set out in Part 1 of that Schedule.

(4) Where on or after 1st September 2001 a new registration plate is fixed to a vehicle to which paragraph (3) applies to replace a plate previously fixed thereto, the plate must conform to the requirements set out in Part 1 of Schedule 2.

(5) In the case of a vehicle first registered before 1st January 1973, the registration plate must conform either to one of the requirements set out in Part 3 of Schedule 2 or to the requirements set out in Part 2 of that Schedule or to the requirements set out in Part 1 of that Schedule.

(6) The corners of a registration plate may be rounded off provided that the requirements of regulation 14(9) (margins around registration marks) are not thereby infringed.

11. Further requirements for registration plates. (1) No reflex-reflecting material may be applied to any part of a registration plate and the plate must not be treated in such a way that the characters of the registration mark become, or are caused to act as, retroreflective characters.

(1A) The surface of a registration plate must not comprise or incorporate any design, pattern or texture, or be treated in any way which gives to any part of the plate the appearance of a design, pattern or texture.

(2) A registration plate must not be treated in any other way which renders the characters of the registration mark less easily distinguishable to the eye or which would prevent or impair the making of a true photographic image of the plate through the medium of camera and film or any other device.

(3) A registration plate must not be fixed to a vehicle—

(a) by means of a screw, bolt or other fixing device of any type or colour,
(b) by the placing of a screw, bolt or other fixing device in any position, or
(c) in any other manner,

which has the effect of changing the appearance or legibility of any of the characters of the registration mark, which renders the characters of the registration mark less easily distinguishable to the eye or which prevents or impairs the making of a true photographic image of the plate through the medium of camera and film or any other device.

(4) Section 59(2)(a) of the Act (regulations the contravention of which attracts a level 3 fine) applies to paragraphs (1), (2) and (3) of this regulation.

PART III
REGISTRATION MARKS

4–4385 12. Interpretation of Part III. (1) In this Part and in Schedule 3, the following expressions shall have the following meanings—

(a) "diagram" means a diagram shown in Part 2 of Schedule 3 and a reference to a numbered diagram is a reference to the diagram identified by that number in that part of that Schedule,
(b) "Table A" means the table in Part 1 of Schedule 3,
(c) "Table B" means the table in Part 3 of Schedule 3,
(d) a reference to "relevant character height", except in relation to a vehicle to which regulation 14A applies, is a reference to the height of the characters in the registration mark shown at the head of column (2), (3) or (4) of Table B as the case may be.

(2) Any provision as to measurement contained in this Part or in Schedule 3 shall be taken to be complied with—

(a) in the case of a provision prescribing character height, if the height of the character is not more than 1 millimetre more or less than the measurement prescribed herein, and
(b) in the case of a provision prescribing any other dimension, if the dimension of the character or the space in question is not more than 0.5 millimetres more or less than the measurement prescribed herein.

(3) For the purpose of any provision contained in this Part or in Schedule 3 as to the spacing between characters or between groups of characters or as to the width of a margin the measurement shall be made—

(a) in the case of a horizontal spacing requirement, between vertical lines passing through the extreme edges of each character or group of characters or between a vertical line passing through the extreme edge of a character and the lateral edge of the plate (as the case may be), and
(b) in the case of a vertical spacing requirement, between horizontal lines passing through the extreme edges of each group of characters or between a horizontal line passing through the extreme edge of a group of characters and the top or bottom edge of the plate (as the case may be).

13. Layout of marks. (1) Subject to paragraphs (2) and (3), a registration mark of a description specified in column (1) of Table A must be laid out on the registration plate in conformity with one of the diagrams specified in relation to that description in column (2) of Table A.

(2) A mark displayed on a motor cycle may not be laid out in conformity with diagram 1a, 2a, 3a, 4a, 5a, 6a, 7a, 8a or 9a.

(3) A mark may not be laid out in conformity with diagram 2c, 3c, 4b or 7b if it is displayed on—

(a) a registration plate fixed to a vehicle first registered on or after 1st September 2001, or
(b) a new registration plate fixed to a vehicle on or after 1st September 2001 to replace a plate previously fixed thereto (except where the vehicle was first registered before 1st January 1973).

14. Size and spacing of characters. (1) Except in the cases mentioned in paragraphs (2) and (3) and regulation 14A, each character in a registration mark must be 79 millimetres high.

(2) In the case of a registration mark displayed on a vehicle first registered before 1st September 2001, a character in a registration mark may be 89 millimetres high unless—

(a) the vehicle was first registered on or after 1st January 1973 and the mark is displayed on a new registration plate fixed to the vehicle to replace a plate previously fixed thereto, or

(b) the vehicle is a motor cycle, motor tricycle, quadricycle, agricultural machine, works truck or road roller.

(3) In the case of a registration mark fixed on a motor cycle, motor tricycle, quadricycle, agricultural machine, works truck or road roller, each character of the mark may be 64 millimetres high.

(4) Subject to regulation 14A, the width of each character of a mark other than the letter "I" and the figure "1" must be—

(a) in the case of a mark displayed—

(i) on a registration plate fixed to a vehicle first registered on or after 1st September 2001, or

(ii) on a new registration plate fixed to a vehicle on or after 1st September 2001 to replace a plate previously fixed thereto (except where the vehicle was first registered before 1st January 1973),

that shown in line 1 of Table B in relation to the relevant character height,

(b) in any other case, that shown in line 2 of Table B in relation to the relevant character height.

(5) Subject to regulation 14A, the width of every part of the stroke forming a character in a mark must be that shown in line 3 of Table B in relation to the relevant character height.

(6) Except in a case to which paragraph (11) or regulation 14A applies, the spacing between any two characters within a group must be that shown in line 4 of Table B in relation to the relevant character height.

(7) Subject to regulation 14A, the horizontal spacing between groups of characters in a mark must be that shown in line 5 of Table B in relation to the relevant character height.

(8) Subject to regulation 14A, the vertical spacing between groups of characters must be that shown in line 6 of Table B in relation to the relevant character height.

(9) Subject to regulation 14A, the width of a margin between the mark and the top, bottom and lateral edges of the registration plate must be not less than that shown in line 7 of Table B in relation to the relevant character height.

(10) Paragraph (11) applies where—

(a) one or both of the characters is "I" or "1",

(b) those characters are either 79 millimetres or 89 millimetres high,

(c) the mark is displayed on a vehicle first registered before 1st September 2001,

(d) the registration plate displaying the mark was fixed to the vehicle before 1st September 2001 or, if that is not the case, the vehicle was first registered before 1st January 1973 and,

(e) the plate is made of cast or pressed metal with raised characters.

(11) Where this paragraph applies the spacing between—

(a) two characters one of which is "I" or "1" must be within the limits shown in line 8 of Table B in relation to the relevant character height, and

(b) two characters both of which are "I" or "1" must be within the limits shown in line 9 of Table B in relation to the relevant character height,

but where one or more characters in a group is "I" or "1" all the characters within that group must be evenly spaced.

14A. Size and spacing of characters. (1) This regulation applies in relation to any vehicle imported into the United Kingdom which—

(a) does not have European Community Whole Vehicle Type Approval; and

(b) is so constructed that the area available for the fixing of the registration plate precludes the display on the plate of a registration mark in conformity with the requirements of regulation 14.

(2) In relation to a vehicle to which this regulation applies—

(a) each character in the registration mark must be 64 millimetres high;

(b) the width of each character of the mark, other than the letter "I" and the figure "1", must be 44 millimetres;

(c) the width of every part of the stroke forming a character in a mark must be 10 millimetres;

(d) the spacing between any two characters within a group must be 10 millimetres;

(e) the vertical spacing between groups of characters must be 5 millimetres;

(f) the width of a margin between the mark and the top and lateral sides of the registration plate must be not less than 5 millimetres;

(g) the space between the bottom of the mark and the bottom of the registration plate must be not less than 13 millimetres; but, within that space, the space between the bottom of the mark and the top of the name and postcode of the person by whom the plate was supplied must be not less than 5 millimetres.

15. Style of characters. (1) In the case of a registration mark displayed—

(a) on a registration plate fixed to a vehicle first registered on or after 1st September 2001, or (*b*) on a new registration plate fixed to a vehicle on or after 1st September 2001 to replace a plate previously fixed thereto (except where the vehicle was first registered before 1st January 1973),

each of the characters of the mark must be in the prescribed font.

(2) Except in a case to which paragraph (1) applies, each of the characters of the registration mark must either be in the prescribed font or in a style which is substantially similar to the prescribed font so that the character is easily distinguishable and in particular, but without prejudice to the generality of those requirements, characters must not be formed in any way described in paragraph (4) or in a manner which is similar to any of those ways.

(3) For the purposes of paragraph (2), a character shall not be treated as being in a style which is not substantially similar to the prescribed font merely by virtue of the fact that it has, or does not have, serifs.

(4) The ways of forming characters referred to in paragraph (2) are their formation—

(*a*) in italic script,
(*b*) using a font, other than italic script, in which the characters are not vertical,
(*c*) using a font in which the curvature or alignment of the lines of the stroke is substantially different from the prescribed font,
(*d*) using multiple strokes,
(*e*) using a broken stroke,
(*f*) in such a way as to make a character or more than one character appear like a different character or characters.

PART IV
MISCELLANEOUS

4–4386 16. International distinguishing signs and other material. (1) No material other than a registration mark may be displayed on a registration plate except material complying with the requirements of any of the relevant standards mentioned in Schedule 2.

(2) Where a mark is displayed on a dual purpose plate—

(*a*) no material other than the international distinguishing sign of the United Kingdom displayed in accordance with the Council Regulation may be placed in the space provided on the plate for that purpose;
(*b*) no part of the international distinguishing sign must encroach beyond the extreme left of the registration mark (that is to say the outside edge of the margin prescribed by these Regulations).

(3) Unless it forms part of a dual purpose plate a registration plate may not be combined with a plate or device of any kind containing material which would not be permitted to be displayed on a dual purpose plate.

17. Optional early use of new-specification plates and prescribed font. (1) This regulation applies in a case where, on or after 21st March and before 1st September 2001 a registration mark on a vehicle—

(*a*) is displayed on a registration plate which conforms to the specification set out in Part 1 of Schedule 2 and is otherwise fixed on the vehicle and lit in accordance with the requirements of Part II of these Regulations,
(*b*) conforms to the requirements of regulations 13 and 14 as to layout and spacing of characters in so far as they apply to vehicles first registered on or after 1st September 2001, and
(*c*) is comprised of characters each of which is in the prescribed font.

(2) Where this regulation applies—

(*a*) regulations 17 to 22 of the Road Vehicles (Registration and Licensing) Regulations 1971 or, as the case may be,
(*b*) regulations 18 to 23 of the Road Vehicles (Registration and Licensing) Regulations (Northern Ireland) 1973,

(which provide for the format and means of display of registration plates and marks) shall cease to apply in respect of that vehicle and any trailer being towed by it and the provisions of these Regulations shall apply instead.

18. Saving for vehicles constructed before 1st January 1973. For the purposes of these Regulations a vehicle which was first registered on or after 1st January 1973 shall be treated as if it was first registered before that date if—

(*a*) it is an exempt vehicle for the purposes of paragraph 1A(1) of Schedule 2 to the Act, or
(*b*) not being such a vehicle, it was constructed before 1st January 1973.

19. Offences under section 59 of the Act. (1) For the purposes of section 59(1) of the Act (regulations: offences), the person responsible for complying with these Regulations is the person driving the vehicle or, where it is not being driven, the person keeping it.

(2) Paragraph (1) does not apply to a regulation the breach of which would constitute an offence under section 42(1) of the Act (not fixing a registration mark as required by virtue of section 23).

4–4387

Regulation 10   SCHEDULE 2
REQUIREMENTS FOR REGISTRATION PLATES

PART 1
VEHICLES REGISTERED AND NEW REGISTRATION PLATES FITTED ON OR AFTER 1ST SEPTEMBER 2001 (MANDATORY SPECIFICATION)

1. The plate must be made of retroreflecting material which, as regards its construction, colour and other qualities, complies with the requirements of—

(*a*) the British Standard specification for retroreflecting number plates published on 15 January 1998 under number BS AU 145d, or

(*b*) any other relevant standard or specification recognised for use in an EEA State and which, when in use, offers a performance equivalent to that offered by a plate complying with the British Standard specification,

and which, in either case, is marked with the number (or such other information as is necessary to permit identification) of that standard or specification.

2. Where the registration mark is displayed on the front of the vehicle, it must have black characters on a white background.

3. Where the registration mark is displayed on the back of the vehicle, it must have black characters on a yellow background.

PART 2
VEHICLES REGISTERED ON OR AFTER 1ST JANUARY 1973 AND BEFORE 1ST SEPTEMBER 2001 (OPTIONAL SPECIFICATION)

1. The plate must be made of reflex-reflecting material which, as regards its construction, colour and other qualities, complies with the requirements of—

(*a*) the British Standard Specification for reflex-reflecting number plates, published on 11 September 1972 under the number BS AU 145a, or

(*b*) any other relevant standard or specification recognised for use in an EEA State and which, when in use, offers a performance equivalent to that offered by a plate complying with the British Standard specification,

and which, in either case, is marked with the number (or such other information as is necessary to permit identification) of that standard or specification.

2. Where the registration mark is displayed on the front of the vehicle, it must have black characters on a white background.

3. Where the registration mark is displayed on the back of the vehicle, it must have black characters on a yellow background.

PART 3
VEHICLES REGISTERED BEFORE 1ST JANUARY 1973 (OPTIONAL SPECIFICATIONS)

A Requirements where the vehicle carries a registration plate which is constructed so that the mark may be illuminated from behind by virtue of the translucency of its characters.

1. The registration mark must be formed of white translucent characters on a black background on the surface of that plate.

2. When the registration mark is illuminated during the hours of darkness, the characters on that plate must appear white against a black background.

B Requirements where the vehicle carries a registration plate which is not so constructed.

Either of the following is permitted—

1. A plate made of reflex-reflecting material complying with the requirements of the British Standard Specification for reflex-reflecting number plates published on 31 October 1967 under the number BS AU 145 and which displays black characters on a white background where it is fixed on the front of the vehicle and black characters on a yellow background where it is fixed on the rear of the vehicle.

2. A plate displaying white, silver or light grey letters and numbers on a black surface having every character indelibly inscribed on the surface or so attached to the surface that it cannot readily be detached from it, which may either—

(*a*) be made of cast or pressed metal with raised characters, or

(*b*) consist of a plate to which separate characters are attached, or

(*c*) consist of a plastic plate having either reverse engraved characters or characters of a foil type, or

(*d*) consist of an unbroken rectangular area on the surface of the vehicle which is either flat or, if there is no flat area where the mark is required to be displayed, an area which is almost flat.

4–4388

Regulation 12, 13 and 14   SCHEDULE 3
LAYOUT OF REGISTRATION MARKS

4–4389

Regulation 15(1)   SCHEDULE 4
PRESCRIBED FONT

Driving Licences (Disqualification until Test Passed) (Prescribed Offence) Order 2001[1]

(SI 2001/4051)

4–4390   1. Citation and commencement.   This Order may be cited as the Driving Licences (Disqualification until Test Passed) (Prescribed Offence) Order 2001 and shall come into force on 31st January 2002.

---

1. Made by the Secretary of State in exercise of powers under s 36(3) of the Road Traffic Offenders Act 1988.

4–4391 2. Offences to which section 36(1) of the Road Traffic Offenders Act 1988 applies. An offence under section 3A of the Road Traffic Act 1988 (causing death by careless driving when under the influence of drink or drugs) which is committed on or after 31st January 2002, and any person committing such an offence, are prescribed for the purposes of section 36(1) of the Road Traffic Offenders Act 1988.

Road Vehicles (Registration and Licensing) Regulations 2002[1]

(SI 2002/2742 amended by SI 2003/2154, 2335, 2635, 2981, 3073 and 3110, SI 2004/238, 1773, 1872, 2099 and 3298, SI 2005/2713 and SI 2006/2320[2])

PART I
PRELIMINARY

4–4392 1. Citation and commencement. (1) These regulations may be cited as the Road Vehicles (Registration and Licensing) Regulations 2002.

(2) These regulations except regulations 15(3) and 20(4) and (5) and Schedule 3 shall come into force on 30th November 2002.

(3) Regulations 15(3) and 20(4) and (5) and Schedule 3 shall come into force on 7th April 2003.

---

1. Made by the Secretary of State for Transport, in exercise of the powers conferred by sections 7(6), 10(1), 11(1), 11(1A), 12(2), (3) and (4), 14(3)(b) and (4), 21(3), 22(1), (1A), (1B), (1C), (1D), (1E), (1G), (2), (2A), (2B), (2C), and (4), 22A, 23(5), 25, 33(1)(b), (1A)(c), (3)(a), (4) and (5), 52(1), 57(1), (2) and (3), 59(2)(a), 61A, 61B and 62(1) of the Vehicle Excise and Registration Act 1994, by paragraphs 1(2B), 3(5) and 5(3)(e) and (4)(c) of Schedule 1 and paragraphs 2A and 24 of Schedule 2 to that Act, and of all other powers enabling him in that behalf.

> Penalties for contravention or failure to comply are contained in the Vehicle Excise and Registration Act 1994, s 59, in this PART, ante.

2. Those instruments which amend scales of fees are not listed.

4–4393 2. *Revocations*

4–4394 3. Interpretation. (1) In these regulations—

"the 1988 Act" means the Road Traffic Act 1988;
"the 1994 Act" means the Vehicle Excise and Registration Act 1994 and a reference to the "predecessor legislation" of the 1994 Act is a reference to any of the following Acts—

(a) the Roads Act 1920;
(b) the Vehicles (Excise) Act 1949;
(c) the Vehicles (Excise) Act (Northern Ireland) 1954;
(d) the Vehicles (Excise) Act 1962;
(e) the Vehicles (Excise) Act 1971;
(f) the Vehicles (Excise) Act (Northern Ireland) 1972;

"bicycle" means a mechanically propelled bicycle (including a motor scooter, a bicycle with an attachment for propelling it by mechanical power and a mechanically propelled bicycle used for drawing a trailer or sidecar) not exceeding 450 kgs in weight unladen;
"the Directive" means Council Directive 1999/37/EC of 29 April 1999 on the registration documents for vehicles as amended by Commission Directive 2003/127/EC of 23 December 2003;
"GB records" means the part of the register which is maintained on behalf of the Secretary of State by the Driver and Vehicle Licensing Agency;
"insurer" means an authorised insurer as defined by section 145 of the 1988 Act;
"invalid vehicle" means a vehicle (including a cycle with an attachment for propelling it by mechanical power) which does not exceed 508 kgs in weight unladen and is adapted and used or kept on a public road for an invalid;
"keeper" in relation to a vehicle means the person by whom that vehicle is kept;
"kgs" means kilograms;
"local authority" has, in relation to each part of the United Kingdom, the meaning given in the following table—

England	County council, district council, London borough council, Council of the Isles of Scilly, Common Council of the City of London
Northern Ireland	District Council as defined in the Local Government Act (Northern Ireland) 1972
Scotland	Council constituted under section 2 of the Local Government etc (Scotland) Act 1994
Wales	County council, county borough council

"mm" means millimetres;

"NI records" means the part of the register which is maintained on behalf of the Secretary of State by Driver and Vehicle Licensing Northern Ireland;

"reduced pollution certificate" means a certificate issued with respect to a vehicle by virtue of Schedule 2;

"register" means the record kept by or on behalf of the Secretary of State of the vehicles registered by him, in Great Britain or in Northern Ireland, under section 21 of the 1994 Act;

"registered keeper" in relation to a vehicle means the person for the time being shown in the register as the keeper of that vehicle;

"trade plates" means plates issued in accordance with regulation 40 or 41;

"tricycle" means a mechanically propelled tricycle (including a motor scooter and a tricycle with an attachment for propelling it by mechanical power) not exceeding 450 kgs in weight unladen and not being a pedestrian controlled vehicle as defined by regulation 4(3)(b); and

"valeting" means the thorough cleaning of a vehicle before its registration by the Secretary of State under section 21 of the 1994 Act or in order to prepare it for sale and includes removing wax and grease from the exterior, engine and interior, and "valeted" shall be construed accordingly.

(1A) For the purposes of these Regulations "the registration document fee exemption" applies in relation to the issue of a new registration document for a vehicle if the following conditions are satisfied—

  (*a*) the vehicle has sustained damage to its bodywork;

  (*b*) the insurer of the vehicle has notified the Secretary of State that the vehicle was capable of being repaired but that the cost to the insurer of having it repaired would exceed the value of the vehicle in the condition in which it was immediately before it sustained the damage; and

  (*c*) the last registration document to be issued for the vehicle was destroyed by the insurer in accordance with regulation 20(5).

(2) In regulations 21 to 25 "vehicle trader" has the meaning given by regulation 20(6) and in Schedule 4 "relevant vehicle trader" has the meaning given by paragraph 1(4) of that Schedule.

(3) Any application, notification, notice, information, particulars, appeal, declaration or other document or thing given or made in pursuance of these Regulations shall, except where it is expressly provided otherwise, be in writing.

4–4395   **4. Electrically assisted pedal cycles and pedestrian controlled vehicles.**   (1) The requirements specified in regulation 4 of the Electrically Assisted Pedal Cycles Regulations 1983 are hereby prescribed as requirements for the purposes of paragraph 2A of Schedule 2 to the 1994 Act (electrically assisted pedal cycles exempt vehicles if of a class complying with prescribed requirements).

(2) Nothing in the following provisions of these Regulations applies to a vehicle which is an electrically assisted pedal cycle or pedestrian controlled vehicle.

(3) In this regulation—

  (*a*) "electrically assisted pedal cycle" means a vehicle which, by virtue of paragraph (1), is an electrically assisted pedal cycle for the purposes of paragraph 2A of Schedule 2 to the 1994 Act; and

  (*b*) "pedestrian controlled vehicle" means a vehicle with three or more wheels which does not exceed 450 kgs in weight unladen and which is neither constructed nor adapted for use nor used for the carriage of a driver or passenger.

PART II
LICENCES

4–4396   **5. Application for a vehicle licence on the basis that the reduced pollution requirements are satisfied.**   (1) Where an application is made for a vehicle licence on the basis that the rate of vehicle excise duty applicable is a rate specified in one of the provisions of Schedule 1 to the 1994 Act specified in paragraph (2), the Secretary of State may require the applicant to furnish a reduced pollution certificate before he determines the rate at which vehicle excise duty is payable on the licence.

(2) The provisions of Schedule 1 to the 1994 Act referred to in paragraph (1) are—

  (*a*) paragraph 3(1A) (buses);

  (*b*) paragraph 6(2A)(b) (vehicles used to carry exceptional loads);

  (*c*) paragraph 7(3A)(b) (haulage vehicles);

  (*d*) paragraph 9A (rigid goods vehicles); and

  (*e*) paragraph 11A (tractive units).

(3) Schedule 2 shall have effect with respect to reduced pollution certificates and the reduced pollution requirements.

4–4397   **6. Exhibition of vehicle and nil licences.**   (1) When a vehicle licence or nil licence has been delivered to the Secretary of State with an application for a replacement licence, no licence need be fixed to and exhibited on the vehicle to which the licence relates until the replacement licence is obtained.

(2) Except where paragraph (1) applies, the manner in which any vehicle licence or nil licence in force for a vehicle is to be fixed to and exhibited on the vehicle in accordance with the

provisions of section 33(1) or (1A) of the 1994 Act, when it is used or kept on a public road, is that specified in the following provisions of this regulation.

(3) Each such licence shall be fixed to the vehicle in a holder sufficient to protect the licence from the weather to which it would otherwise be exposed.

(4) The licence shall be exhibited on the vehicle—

(a) in the case of an invalid vehicle, tricycle or bicycle, other than in a case specified in sub-paragraph (b) or (c) of this paragraph, on the near side of the vehicle;

(b) in the case of a bicycle drawing a side-car or to which a side-car is attached, on the near side of the handlebars of the bicycle or on the near side of the side-car;

(c) in the case of any vehicle fitted with a glass windscreen in front of the driver extending across the vehicle to its near side, on or adjacent to the near side of the windscreen;

(d) in the case of any other vehicle—

(i) if the vehicle is fitted with a driver's cab containing a near side window, on that window; or

(ii) on the near side of the vehicle in front of the driver's seat and not less than 760 mm and not more than 1.8 metres above the surface of the road.

(5) In each case referred to in paragraph (4), the licence shall be so exhibited that all the particulars on the licence are clearly visible in daylight from the near side of the road.

4–4398 7. Prohibition against exhibiting anything resembling a vehicle, trade or nil licence. No person shall exhibit on a vehicle which is kept or used on a public road anything—

(a) which is intended to be, or

(b) which could reasonably be,

mistaken for a vehicle licence, a nil licence or a trade licence which is for the time being in force for, or in respect of, the vehicle.

4–4399 8. Issue of duplicate vehicle, trade and nil licences. (1) Where a vehicle licence, trade licence or nil licence—

(a) has been, or may have been, lost, stolen, destroyed or damaged; or

(b) contains any particulars which have become illegible,

the holder of the licence shall apply to the Secretary of State for the issue of a duplicate.

(2) An application under paragraph (1) shall be accompanied by—

(a) the registration document issued in respect of the vehicle or, if the applicant is unable to comply with this requirement, by an application to the Secretary of State for the issue of a replacement registration document in accordance with regulation 13;

(b) a fee of £7, if the licence to be replaced is a vehicle or trade licence; and

(c) the licence to be replaced, if the reason for replacement is that it has been damaged or contains any particulars which have become illegible.

(3) No fee is payable under paragraph (2)(b) if the Secretary of State is satisfied that the loss of the licence occurred in the course of the transmission of the licence by the office issuing it to the keeper of the vehicle.

(4) On receiving an application under paragraph (1) made in accordance with this regulation, the Secretary of State shall issue a replacement licence if he is satisfied that the licence has been, or may have been, lost, stolen, destroyed or damaged.

(5) If a replacement licence has been issued on the ground that the original has been, or may have been, lost, stolen or destroyed, and the original licence is subsequently found or recovered, the keeper of the vehicle—

(a) if the original is in his possession, shall forthwith return it to the Secretary of State, or

(b) if it is not in his possession but he becomes aware that it is found or recovered, shall take all reasonable steps to obtain possession of it and return it to the Secretary of State.

4–4399A 9. Surrender of vehicle and trade licences. (1) The holder of a vehicle licence or trade licence who wishes to surrender his licence and to claim a rebate in respect of the unexpired term, in accordance with section 19(1) of the 1994 Act, shall make an application, signed by him, to the Secretary of State.

(2) The application shall be accompanied by the licence and, in the case of a trade licence, any trade plates held by the holder in connection with the licence.

4–4399AA 9A. Supplement payable on late renewal of vehicle licence. (1) Where paragraph (2) applies a supplement of the amount prescribed in paragraph (3) shall be payable.

(2) This paragraph applies where—

(a) a vehicle licence taken out for a vehicle expires,

(b) no vehicle licence was issued for the vehicle before the end of a period of one month beginning with the date of that expiry, and

(c) the registered keeper has failed to comply with requirements contained in Schedule 4.

(3) The supplement shall be £80, except when it is paid to the Secretary of State before the expiry of 28 days beginning with the date on which the registered keeper is notified that a supplement may or has become payable, when it shall be £40.

(4) The supplement shall be payable by the person in whose name the vehicle is registered

under the 1994 Act at the date of the expiry of the licence by reason of whose late renewal the supplement becomes payable.

(5) The Secretary of State shall notify the person referred to in paragraph (4) that the supplement is payable and that notification shall—

(a)   state the amount of the supplement payable; and

(b)   be sent to the address of the person as given in the register.

PART III
REGISTRATION AND REGISTRATION DOCUMENTS

4–4399B   10. Registration and issue of registration document. (1) A vehicle shall not be registered under section 21 of the 1994 Act unless a fee of £38 has been paid to the Secretary of State.

(2) Paragraph (1) does not apply to a vehicle which is an exempt vehicle by virtue of paragraph 18 or 19 of Schedule 2 to the 1994 Act.

(3) The Secretary of State may register a vehicle in either the GB records or the NI records as he considers appropriate and may, if he thinks fit, remove the particulars of a vehicle included in one of those parts of the register and include them in the other.

(4) On registering a vehicle the Secretary of State shall issue a registration document to the keeper of the vehicle.

(5) Subject to paragraph (6) and regulation 11, the Secretary of State shall issue the registration document forthwith, except where the vehicle is registered in consequence of an application for a vehicle licence by a person applying as mentioned in section 7(3A) of the 1994 Act, in which case the registration document shall be issued when that person asks for it to be issued.

(6) Before issuing a registration document to the keeper of a vehicle, the Secretary of State may require him to produce the vehicle for inspection or to produce other evidence that the vehicle accords with the particulars furnished when a vehicle or nil licence was applied for in respect of it.

(7) The Secretary of State may refuse to issue a registration document or replacement registration document for a vehicle if he is not satisfied that the vehicle accords with those particulars.

4–4399BA   10A. Registration document. (1) Subject to paragraph (1A), this regulation applies to vehicles falling within the definition of "vehicle" in Article 2 of Council Directive 70/156/EEC on the approximation of the laws of the Member States relating to the type approval of motor vehicles and their trailers and in Article 2 of Council Directive 92/61/EEC relating to the type-approval of two or three-wheeled motor vehicles.

(1A) Paragraph (3A) applies to any vehicle registered under the 1994 Act or its predecessor legislation.

(2) The Secretary of State shall not issue a new registration document on or after 31st January 2004 unless it complies with Annex I of the Directive as regards—

(a)   dimensions;

(b)   composition; and

(c)   information contained within it;

except that in relation to a new registration document, the information contained may be limited to that available to the Secretary of State.

(3) Any registration document which does not comply with the Directive shall cease to have effect on the earlier of—

(a)   the date on which the Secretary of State issues a new registration document under these Regulations; or

(b)   1st July 2005.

(3A) Notwithstanding any other provision of these Regulations, the Secretary of State may, without charge and on surrender by the registered keeper of a registration document issued before 31st January 2004, issue to the registered keeper a registration document which is in a form provided for by the Directive in respect of the same vehicle if it appears proper and reasonable to him to do so.

(4) In registering for the first time on or after 1st June 2004 a vehicle, which has been registered in another member State or Gibraltar, the Secretary of State shall recognise as a registration document a document which has been issued in respect of that vehicle by that other member State or Gibraltar if it complies with Annex I or Annexes I and II of the Directive.

(5) Where the Secretary of State registers a vehicle in accordance with paragraph (4) he shall—

(a)   retain the former registration document for not less than 6 months; and

(b)   within 2 months of registration in the United Kingdom, notify the authorities in the member State or in Gibraltar where the vehicle was previously registered of his act of registration.

4–4399C   11. Production of vehicle for inspection before assignment of registration mark. Where at the request of the keeper of a vehicle a particular registration mark is to be assigned to it, having previously been assigned to another vehicle, that other vehicle shall be made available for inspection by the Secretary of State at a place designated by him, and the keeper of the first mentioned vehicle shall, before the registration mark is so assigned, pay to the Secretary of State a charge of £80 for the assignment.

4–4399D   12. Production of registration document for inspection. The keeper of a vehicle in respect of which a registration document has been issued shall produce the document for inspection if he is required to do so at any reasonable time by a constable or by a person acting on behalf of the Secretary of State.

4–4399E   **13. Issue of replacement registration document.**   (1) Where a registration document has been, or may have been, lost, stolen, destroyed or damaged, or it contains any particulars that have become illegible, the registered keeper shall apply to the Secretary of State for the issue of a replacement document.

(2) In a case where the registration document has been damaged or contains any particulars which have become illegible, an application under paragraph (1) shall be accompanied by the document and, in any other case, the Secretary of State may, if he thinks fit, accept an application made orally by telephone.

(2A) An application for the issue of a replacement registration document under this regulation shall, unless the registration document fee exemption applies, be accompanied by a fee of £19.

(3) If the Secretary of State—

(a) receives an application made in accordance with this regulation; and

(b) he is satisfied that a registration document has been, or may have been, lost, stolen, destroyed or damaged, or that it contains any particulars that have become illegible,

he shall, subject to regulation 15, issue a replacement registration document to the registered keeper.

(4) If a replacement registration document has been issued on the ground that the original has been, or may have been, lost, stolen or destroyed, and the original is subsequently found or recovered, the keeper of the vehicle—

(a) if the original is in his possession, shall forthwith return it to the Secretary of State, or

(b) if it is not in his possession but he becomes aware that it is found or recovered, shall take all reasonable steps to obtain possession of it and return it to the Secretary of State.

4–4399F   **14. Correction of registration document.**   (1) Where the keeper of a vehicle believes that the particulars in the registration document issued in respect of that vehicle are, or have become, inaccurate, he shall forthwith notify the Secretary of State of the inaccuracy.

(2) Notification under paragraph (1) shall be accompanied by the registration document, unless it has been, or may have been, lost stolen or destroyed.

(2A) Where the registration document has been, or may have been, lost, stolen or destroyed, notification under paragraph (1) shall be accompanied by an application for the issue of a new registration document and, except where the registration document fee exemption applies, by a fee of £19.

(3) Where the Secretary of State believes that the particulars in the registration document issued in respect of a vehicle are inaccurate—

(a) if the document has not been sent to him, he may require the registered keeper of the vehicle to send it to him;

(b) whether or not he has received the document, he may correct the particulars in the register; and

(c) after correcting the particulars in the register, he shall, provided that paragraphs (2) or (2A) have been complied with, and subject to regulation 15, issue a new registration document containing the correct particulars to the registered keeper.

4–4399G   **15. Issue of new registration document.**   (1) Before issuing a new registration document in respect of a vehicle under any provision of these Regulations, the Secretary of State may require the keeper of the vehicle to satisfy him by the production of the vehicle or other sufficient evidence that the vehicle—

(a) accords with the particulars furnished when a vehicle or nil licence was last applied for in respect of it; or

(b) is the registered vehicle.

(1A) Before issuing a new registration document the Secretary of State may take actions to satisfy himself that the identity and address of the person seeking to be the registered keeper accords with the information given to him.

(2) The Secretary of State may refuse to issue a new registration document in respect of a vehicle if he is not satisfied as mentioned in paragraphs (1) and (1A).

(3) The provisions of Schedule 3 shall have effect in relation to the issue of a new registration document in respect of a vehicle (in this regulation and in Schedule 3 called "the relevant vehicle") where—

(a) the relevant vehicle falls within category M1 of Annex II to Council Directive 70/156/EEC, and

(b) either an insurer has informed the Secretary of State that it has decided to pay the value of the relevant vehicle to the owner in preference to paying for the cost of repairing it or the registration document has been surrendered to the Secretary of State under regulation 20(5).

(4) For the purposes of paragraph (3) and Schedule 3 the return of a registration document for a vehicle registered in the NI records in accordance with regulation 18(2)(b) shall be taken to be the issue of a new registration document.

4–4399H 16. Notification of an alteration to a vehicle. (1) Where any alteration is made to a vehicle so as to make any of the particulars set out in the registration document incorrect, the registered keeper shall deliver to the Secretary of State—

(a) notification of the alteration;

(b) except where the registration document has been, or may have been, lost, stolen or destroyed, the registration document.

(1A) Where the registration document has been, or may have been, lost, stolen or destroyed, notification under paragraph (1) shall be accompanied by an application for the issue of a new registration document and, except where the registration document fee exemption applies, by a fee of £19.

(2) If the alteration makes any of the particulars shown on the vehicle licence or nil licence incorrect, the registered keeper shall also deliver to the Secretary of State the appropriate licence, unless it is lost, stolen or destroyed.

(3) The Secretary of State may require the registered keeper to furnish such evidence as he may reasonably require to show that the alteration has taken place.

(4) On receiving notification under this regulation the Secretary of State shall, subject to regulation 15, if he is satisfied that the vehicle has been altered in the way notified to him,—

(a) record the alteration in the register;

(b) send to the registered keeper a new registration document showing the correct particulars; and

(c) in a case falling within paragraph (2), issue to the registered keeper a new vehicle licence or nil licence showing the correct particulars.

4–4399I 17. Notification of destruction or permanent export of a vehicle. Where a vehicle is sent permanently out of—

(a) Great Britain; or

(b) Northern Ireland,

the registered keeper shall immediately[1] notify the Secretary of State of the fact.

---

1. See note to reg 18 "forthwith".

4–4399IA 17A. Vehicles to which the End-of-Life Vehicles Directive applies. (1) This regulation applies to a vehicle to which Directive 2000/53 of the European Parliament and of the Council on end-of-life vehicles applies and which is—

(a) registered in the GB or NI records; or

(b) designed or adapted for use on a road and would be registered but for the fact that it falls within the exemption in regulation 29(2).

(2) Where a vehicle to which this regulation applies is transferred to an authorised treatment facility—

(a) if that facility is in the United Kingdom, the owner or operator thereof shall notify the Secretary of State of the issue of a certificate of destruction pursuant to regulation 27 of the End-of-Life Vehicles Regulations and at the same time shall surrender the registration document to him, except where the registration document has been lost, stolen or destroyed; and

(b) if that facility is in an EEA State other than the United Kingdom, the registered keeper of the vehicle shall notify the Secretary of State of the issue in that other EEA State of a certificate of destruction and at the same time the registered keeper shall surrender the registration document to him except where the registration document has been lost, stolen or destroyed.

(3) Where the Secretary of State has been notified of the issue of a certificate of destruction he shall not as respects the vehicle to which it relates—

(a) record in the GB records or, in the case of a vehicle registered in Northern Ireland, in the NI records any further change of keeper;

(b) accept the required declaration in paragraph 1(1) of Schedule 4.

(4) In this regulation "authorised treatment facility", "certificate of destruction" and "EEA State" have the meanings that those expressions have in the End-of-Life Vehicles Regulations 2003.

4–4399J 18. Notification of a change of the keeper's name or address. (1) If the registered keeper of a vehicle changes his name or his address, he shall forthwith[1] notify the new name or address to the Secretary of State and, except where the registration document has been, or may have been, lost, stolen or destroyed, shall deliver the registration document to him.

(1A) Where the registration document has been, or may have been, lost, stolen or destroyed, notification under paragraph (1) shall be accompanied by an application for the issue of a new registration document and, except where the registration document fee exemption applies, by a fee of £19.

(2) On receiving notification in accordance with this regulation the Secretary of State shall, subject to regulation 15,—

(a) record the alteration in the register, and
(b) send to the registered keeper a new registration document showing the new name or address.

---

1. In the predecessor regulations of 1971, reg 10 of which required the owner to notify the Secretary of State "forthwith" of the alteration of a vehicle it had been held in Scotland that the period of limitation of proceedings to six months from the date of the offence commences immediately the obligation to notify arises (*A & C McLennan (Blairgowrie) Ltd v MacMillan* 1964 SLT 2). Cf Magistrates' Courts Act, 1980, s 127, in PART I MAGISTRATES' COURTS, PROCEDURE, ante; for the construction of "forthwith". see para **2–744 Time** in PART II EVIDENCE, ante.

4–4399K 19. Notification of a change of the name or address of the holder of a trade licence
(1) If the holder of a trade licence changes the name of his business or his business address, he shall notify the Secretary of State of this fact and of the new name or address forthwith[1] and shall at the same time deliver up the licence to the Secretary of State.
(2) On receiving notification in accordance with paragraph (1) the Secretary of State shall—

(a) record the alteration in the register of trade licences; and
(b) send to the holder a new trade licence showing the correct particulars.

---

1. See note to reg 18(1), ante.

4–4399L 20. Change of keeper: general provisions.   (1) Regulations 21 to 25 have effect subject to the provisions of this regulation.
(2) On a change in the keeper of a vehicle, any current vehicle licence for the vehicle may be delivered to the new keeper.
(3) So far as they provide for the issue of a new registration document, regulations 21 to 25 have effect subject to the provisions of regulation 15.
(4) Paragraph (5) shall apply and regulations 21 to 25 shall not apply where—

(a) a vehicle has sustained damage to its bodywork such that the cost of commercial repair would exceed the value of the vehicle when repaired; and
(b) either the keeper of the vehicle does not have the benefit of a policy of insurance or cover note which covers the damage or the keeper is an insurer.

(5) On a change of keeper to which this paragraph applies the keeper shall forthwith[1] surrender the registration document to the Secretary of State or, if an insurer, destroy it.
(6) In regulations 21 to 25 "vehicle trader" means any person who—

(a) is the holder of a trade licence;
(b) carries on business as a dealer in motor vehicles;
(c) carries on business as an auctioneer of motor vehicles;
(d) carries on business as a dismantler of motor vehicles; or
(e) in relation to a particular vehicle, is—

(i) a finance company which has acquired that vehicle under an order for repossession; or
(ii) an insurer which has acquired that vehicle in satisfaction of a total loss claim.

---

1. See note to reg 18(1), ante.

4–4399M 21. Change of keeper: registration document issued in Great Britain before 24th March 1997. *Revoked.*

4–4399N 22. Change of keeper: registration document issued in Great Britain on or after 24th March 1997 and the new keeper not a vehicle trader.   (1) This regulation applies where—

(a) there is a change in the keeper of a vehicle;
(b) a vehicle registration document has been issued in respect of the vehicle; and
(c) the new keeper is not a vehicle trader.

(2) The registered keeper of the vehicle—

(a) if the registration document issued in respect of the vehicle is in his possession, shall deliver to the new keeper that part of the document marked as the part which is to be given to the new keeper; and
(b) shall forthwith[1] deliver to the Secretary of State on the remainder of the registration document, or otherwise in writing, the following information—

(i) the name and address of the new keeper;
(ii) the date on which the vehicle was sold or transferred to the new keeper;
(iii) a declaration signed by the registered keeper that the details given in accordance with paragraph (i) are correct to the best of his knowledge and that the details given in accordance with paragraph (ii) are correct; and
(iv) a declaration signed by the new keeper that the details given in accordance with paragraphs (i) and (ii) are correct.

(3) Where all parts of the registration document have been, or may have been, lost, stolen or destroyed, the new keeper shall submit an application to the Secretary of State for the issue of a new registration document and, except where the registration document fee exemption applies, that application shall be accompanied by a fee of £19.

(4) Where the new keeper can produce to the Secretary of State that part of the document marked as the part which is to be given to the new keeper, the new keeper may submit an application to the Secretary of State for the issue of a new registration document accompanied by that part.

(5) On receiving notification of a change in keeper in accordance with paragraphs (2), (3) or (4), the Secretary of State shall, subject to regulation 15—

(a) record the change in the register, and

(b) issue to the new registered keeper a new registration document.

---

1. See note to reg 18(1), ante.

4–4399O 23. Change of keeper: obligations of registered keeper where vehicle registration document issued in Great Britain on or after 24th March 1997 and the new keeper a vehicle trader. (1) Subject to regulation 24, this regulation applies where—

(a) there is a change in the keeper of a vehicle;

(b) the person disposing of the vehicle is the registered keeper;

(c) a vehicle registration document has been issued in respect of the vehicle; and

(d) the new keeper is a vehicle trader.

(2) The registered keeper shall forthwith[1] notify the Secretary of State, on that part of the registration document which relates to the transfer to a vehicle trader, or otherwise in writing, of the following—

(a) the name and address of the vehicle trader;

(b) the date on which the vehicle was transferred to the vehicle trader;

(c) a declaration signed by the registered keeper that he transferred the vehicle to the vehicle trader on the date specified in accordance with sub-paragraph (b); and

(d) a declaration signed by the vehicle trader that the vehicle was transferred to him on the date specified in accordance with sub-paragraph (b).

(3) If the registration document issued in respect of the vehicle is in his possession, the registered keeper shall deliver to the vehicle trader those parts of it not required to be sent to the Secretary of State under paragraph (2).

---

1. See note to reg 18(1), ante.

4–4399P 24. Change of keeper: obligations of vehicle traders where registration document issued in Great Britain on or after 24 March 1997. (1) This regulation applies where a vehicle trader becomes the keeper of a vehicle in respect of which a vehicle registration document has been issued.

(2) Where this regulation applies the vehicle trader shall, on or before the appropriate date and on that part of the registration document which relates to a change of keeper, notify the Secretary of State as to—

(a) the transfer of the vehicle to him; and

(b) the date on which he became the keeper of the vehicle.

(2A) Where the registration document has been, or may have been, lost, stolen or destroyed, notification in accordance with paragraph (2) shall be effected by an application to the Secretary of State for the issue of a new registration document and, except where the registration document fee exemption applies, that application shall be accompanied by a fee of £19.

(3) For the purposes of paragraph (2) the appropriate date is whichever is the earliest of—

(a) the day on which the vehicle trader first uses, or permits the use of, the vehicle on a public road otherwise than under a trade licence;

(b) the day on which he first keeps the vehicle on such a road;

(c) the day immediately following the expiration of the period of three months ("the three months period of grace") beginning with the day after the date on which the vehicle was last kept by a person who was not a vehicle trader.

(4) Where this regulation applies and the vehicle trader transfers the vehicle to another vehicle trader before the expiration of the three months period of grace, he shall give to the new keeper any part of the registration document in his possession.

(5) Where the vehicle trader transfers the vehicle to another person in a case not falling within paragraph (4), he shall—

(a) forthwith[1] deliver to the Secretary of State, on that part of the registration document which relates to the change of keeper or otherwise in writing, the following—

(i) the name and address of the new keeper;

(ii) the date on which the vehicle was transferred to the new keeper;

(iii) a declaration signed by the vehicle trader that the details given in accordance with paragraph (i) are correct to the best of his knowledge and that the details given in accordance with paragraph (ii) are correct; and

(iv) a declaration signed by the new keeper that the details given in accordance with paragraphs (i) and (ii) are correct; and

(b) if the registration document issued in respect of the vehicle is in his possession, deliver to the new keeper those parts of it not required to be sent to the Secretary of State under sub-paragraph (a).

(6) Where all parts of the registration document have been, or may have been, lost, stolen or destroyed, the new keeper shall submit an application to the Secretary of State for the issue of a new registration document, and, except where the registration document fee exemption applies, that application shall be accompanied by a fee of £19.

(7) Where the new keeper can produce to the Secretary of State that part of the document marked as the part which is to be given to the new keeper, the new keeper may submit an application to the Secretary of State for the issue of a new registration document accompanied by that part.

(8) On receiving notification of a change in keeper in accordance with paragraphs (2), (2A), (5), (6) or (7), the Secretary of State shall, subject to regulation 15—

(a) record the change in the register, and

(b) issue to the new registered keeper a new registration document.

---

1. See note to reg 18(1), ante.

4-4399Q 25. Change of keeper: registration document issued in Northern Ireland. *Revoked.*

4-4399R 26. Statutory off-road notification. Schedule 4 shall have effect for the purpose of prescribing, the particulars to be furnished and the declarations to be made, and the times at which and the circumstances and manner in which they are to be made, by a person who—

(a) surrenders a vehicle licence;

(b) does not renew a vehicle licence on its expiration; or

(c) keeps an unlicensed vehicle.

4-4399RA 26A. Exceptions to section 31A. (1) The requirements prescribed for the purposes of the first condition in section 31B of the 1994 Act are whichever are applicable in the circumstances of the requirements specified in—

(a) regulation 20(5) (surrender or destruction of registration document for damaged vehicle), in so far as it requires surrender of the registration document,

(b) revoked

(c) regulation 22(2)(b) (delivery of remainder of registration document to the Secretary of State),

(d) regulation 23(2) (notifying the Secretary of State when the transfer is to a vehicle trader),

(e) regulation 24(5) (vehicle trader notifying the Secretary of State of a transfer), and

(f) regulation 25(1)(a) (delivery of registration document and notification to the Secretary of State where the registration document was issued in Northern Ireland).

(2) The requirement prescribed for the purposes of the second condition in section 31B is the making of the required declaration and the furnishing of the prescribed particulars to the Secretary of State in accordance with Schedule 4.

(3) The requirement prescribed under subsection (6) of section 31B for the purposes of subsection (4)(c) (the third condition) is that before the expiry of 14 days beginning with the date on which the theft came to the knowledge of the registered keeper notification of the theft was given to—

(a) a member of a police force maintained for any police area in England and Wales or Scotland,

(b) a member of the Police Service of Northern Ireland, or

(c) a person employed to assist such a police force or that Police Service.

(4) The prescribed length of the period for the purpose of the fourth condition shall be 14 days.

PART V
DISCLOSURE OF INFORMATION

4-4399S 27. Disclosure of registration and licensing particulars. (1) The Secretary of State may make any particulars contained in the register available for use—

(a) by a local authority for any purpose connected with the investigation of an offence or of a decriminalised parking contravention;

(b) by a chief officer of police;

(c) by a member of the Police Service of Northern Ireland;

(d) by an officer of Customs and Excise; or

(e) by any person who can show to the satisfaction of the Secretary of State that he has reasonable cause for wanting the particulars to be made available to him.

(2) Particulars may be provided to such a person as is mentioned in paragraph (1)(e) on payment of such fee, if any, of such amount as appears to the Secretary of State reasonable in the circumstances of the case.

(3) In this regulation—

(a) "a decriminalised parking contravention" means any act or omission which would have been an offence but for any of the following provisions of the Road Traffic Act 1991, that is to say—

(i) section 65 (contravention of certain orders relating to parking places in London not to be a criminal offence);

    (ii) section 76(3) (provisions creating certain stationary vehicle offences to cease to apply in special parking areas in London);

    (iii) paragraph 1(4) of Schedule 3 (contravention of certain orders relating to parking places outside London not to be a criminal offence); and

    (iv) paragraph 2(4) of Schedule 3 (provisions creating certain stationary vehicle offences to cease to apply in special parking areas outside London); and

  (b) "an officer of Customs and Excise" means an officer as defined in section 1(1) of the Customs and Excise Management Act 1979 and includes any person engaged as mentioned in section 8(2) of that Act.

4–4399SA 27A Exchange of information. The Secretary of State may disclose such information, contained in the register, that he is required to disclose to comply with Article 9 of the Directive.

4–4399T 28. Sale of information derived from particulars contained in the register. The Secretary of State may sell information derived from particulars contained in the register—

  (a) to such persons as the Secretary of State thinks fit;

  (b) for such price and on such other terms, and subject to such restrictions, as the Secretary of State thinks fit,

if the information does not identify any person or contain anything enabling any person to be identified.

PART VI
CROWN VEHICLES AND EXEMPT VEHICLES

4–4399U 29. Application of Regulations to Crown vehicles[1]. (1) Except as provided by this Part of these Regulations, nothing in these Regulations applies to a vehicle kept by the Crown.

  (2) Nothing in these Regulations or this Part of these Regulations applies to a vehicle kept by the Crown which is used or appropriated for use for naval, military or air force purposes.

---

  1. By an extra-statutory arrangement, vehicles used by diplomatically privileged representatives of Dominion Governments and Foreign Powers are exempt from duty but registered in the ordinary way.

4–4399V 30. Registration of Crown vehicles. (1) A Government Department which uses or keeps or, intends to use or keep, a vehicle on a public road shall—

  (a) make to the Secretary of State such declaration and furnish him with such particulars as would be required by section 7 of the 1994 Act if the Department desired to take out a vehicle licence for the vehicle; and

  (b) make to the Secretary of State a declaration that the vehicle is only to be used for the purposes of the Crown.

  (2) Upon receipt of the declaration and particulars the Secretary of State shall—

  (a) register the vehicle in the name of the Government Department;

  (b) if there is no registration mark for the time being assigned to the vehicle, assign a registration mark to it; and

  (c) issue a registration document for the vehicle.

  (3) Any registration mark assigned under paragraph (2) shall be deemed to be assigned under section 23 of the 1994 Act for the purposes of subsection (2) of that section and of these Regulations.

  (4) No vehicle licence or nil licence shall be issued by the Secretary of State in respect of the vehicle so registered.

  (5) Where a Government department is the registered keeper of a vehicle—

  (a) regulations 13, 14, 15, 16 and 18 shall apply;

  (b) regulations 20, 21, 22, 23, 24 and 25 shall apply on a change in the keeper of a vehicle; and

  (c) regulations 20, 21, 22 and 25 shall apply on a change in the keeper of a vehicle from one Government department to another.

4–4399W 31. Certificates of Crown exemption. (1) Subject to regulation 29(2), for the purposes of identification, a certificate of Crown exemption shall be displayed on every vehicle belonging to the Crown which is used or kept on a public road.

  (2) A certificate of Crown exemption is a certificate—

  (a) marked with the registration mark of the vehicle to which it relates;

  (b) stating that the vehicle is exempt from vehicle excise duty as a Crown vehicle;

  (c) signed by a duly authorised officer of the Government Department by which the vehicle is kept.

  (3) Regulation 7 (exhibition of vehicle and nil licences) of these Regulations shall apply as if references to a vehicle licence included a reference to a certificate of Crown exemption.

4–4399X 32. Application of Regulations to exempt vehicles. Subject to the provisions of these Regulations, these Regulations shall apply to exempt vehicles so far as they are capable of being applied to such vehicles.

4–4399Y   33. Nil licences.   (1) In this regulation "nil licensable vehicle" means a vehicle which is an exempt vehicle otherwise than by virtue of paragraph 2, 2A, 3, 22 or 23 of Schedule 2 to the 1994 Act.

(2) A nil licence is required to be in force in respect of a nil licensable vehicle which is used or kept on a public road.

(3) A nil licence shall—

(a)   be granted for a period of 12 months beginning with the first day of the month in which the application for the licence is received by the Secretary of State; and

(b)   be in the same form as a vehicle licence with the word "NIL" marked in the space provided for indicating the amount of vehicle excise duty payable.

(4) The keeper of a nil licensable vehicle may apply to the Secretary of State for a nil licence by making to him such a declaration and furnishing him with such particulars and such documentary or other evidence as might be specified under section 7 of the 1994 Act if the keeper desired to take out a vehicle licence for the vehicle.

(5) The Secretary of State may accept a declaration given, and particulars furnished, orally by telephone.

(6) In the case of a vehicle which is an exempt vehicle by virtue of—

(a)   paragraph 19 of Schedule 2 to the 1994 Act, or

(b)   paragraph 7 of Schedule 4 to that Act,

the Secretary of State shall require the keeper to furnish him with a certificate that paragraph 19 of Schedule 2 or, as the case may be, paragraph 7 of Schedule 4 applies, unless the Secretary of State satisfies himself by other means that one of those paragraphs applies.

(7) The certificate shall be obtained by the keeper of the vehicle from the Secretary of State for Work and Pensions, the Secretary of State for Defence or the Department for Social Development for Northern Ireland, whichever is appropriate.

(8) Paragraphs (4) to (7) do not apply where the person applying for a nil licence agrees to comply with such conditions as may be specified in relation to him by the Secretary of State.

(8A)   Section 22ZA of the 1994 Act shall apply to information of the following descriptions—

(a)   the name of any person to whom—

(i)   disability living allowance or mobility supplement is payable; or

(ii)   disability living allowance has ceased to be payable and who would be entitled to receive the mobility component at the higher rate but for his failure to satisfy a condition referred to in paragraph 19(2A)(b) of Schedule 2 to the 1994 Act;

(b)   that person's date of birth and National Insurance number; and

(c)   if applicable, the date on which the allowance or supplement, as appropriate, will cease to be payable.

(8B)   For the purposes of paragraph (8A)—

"disability living allowance" means a disability living allowance for the purposes of section 71 of the Social Security Contributions and Benefits Act 1992 (disability living allowance);

"mobility component" means the mobility component of a disability living allowance and "higher rate" means the higher rate of the mobility component for the time being prescribed under section 73 of that Act (the mobility component); and

"mobility supplement" has the meaning which that expression bears in paragraph 19 of Schedule 2 to the 1994 Act.

(9) If, following an application made in accordance with this regulation, the Secretary of State is satisfied that a vehicle is a nil licensable vehicle, he shall issue a nil licence to the keeper of the vehicle.

(10) If at any time vehicle excise duty becomes chargeable under the 1994 Act in respect of a vehicle which immediately before that time was a nil licensable vehicle, the keeper of the vehicle shall forthwith return to the Secretary of State—

(a)   any nil licence issued in respect of the vehicle; and

(b)   any certificate obtained by him for the purposes of paragraph (6) in relation to the vehicle.

4–4399Z   34. Exemptions from vehicle excise duty: vehicles imported by members of foreign armed forces and others.   Schedule 5, which provides for the exemption from vehicle excise duty of vehicles imported into Great Britain by members of foreign armed forces and other persons, shall have effect.

PART VII
TRADE LICENCES

4–4399ZA   35. Definition of "motor trader": descriptions of businesses.   The following descriptions of business are hereby prescribed for the purposes of sub-paragraph (b) of the definition of "motor trader" in section 62(1) of the 1994 Act—

(a)   the business of modifying vehicles, whether by the fitting of accessories or otherwise;

(b)   the business of valeting vehicles.

4–4399ZB   36. Period for review of decision refusing an application for a trade licence.   For the purposes of section 14(3)(b) of the 1994 Act (which relates to the review by the Secretary of State of his decision refusing an application for a trade licence by a person entitled to make such an application) the period within which such an applicant may request the Secretary of State for such a review shall be 28 days beginning with the day after the day on which the decision was given.

4–4399ZC   37. Conditions subject to which trade licences are to be issued.   The conditions subject to which trade licences are to be issued, and with which every holder of a trade licence shall comply, shall be those specified in Part I of Schedule 6.

4–4399ZD   38. Purposes for which the holder of a trade licence may use a vehicle by virtue of the licence.   Part II of Schedule 6 shall have effect for prescribing the purposes for which a vehicle may be used by virtue of a trade licence.

4–4399ZE   39. Assignment of general registration marks.   On issuing a trade licence the Secretary of State shall assign to the holder of the licence a general registration mark in respect of that licence.

4–4399ZF   40. Issue of trade plates.   (1) Subject to paragraphs (3) and (4), the Secretary of State shall issue to every holder of a trade licence, as respects each licence held by him, a set of trade plates appropriate to the class of vehicles for which the licence is to be used.
   (2) Each trade plate shall show the general registration mark assigned to the holder of the licence in respect of the licence, and one of the trade plates shall include a means whereby the licence may be fixed to it.
   (3) Where the holder of a trade licence satisfies the Secretary of State that the vehicles which he will use by virtue of the licence include vehicles which would otherwise be liable to vehicle excise duty under paragraph 2 of Schedule 1 to the 1994 Act (motorcycles) and other vehicles, the Secretary of State shall issue to the holder an additional trade plate in respect of the vehicles otherwise liable to vehicle excise duty under that paragraph.
   (4) Where the licence is to be used only in respect of vehicles to which paragraph 2 of Schedule 1 to the 1994 Act applies (motorcycles), the Secretary of State shall issue only one trade plate to the holder of the licence and that plate shall include a means whereby the licence may be fixed to it.
   (5) Each trade plate shall remain the property of the Secretary of State and shall be returned forthwith to the Secretary of State by the person to whom it was issued if that person ceases to be—
   (a)   the holder of the trade licence in respect of which the trade plate was issued; or
   (b)   a motor trader or a vehicle tester.

4–4399ZG   41. Issue of replacement trade plates.   (1) If any trade plate issued by the Secretary of State to the holder of a trade licence is lost, stolen, destroyed or materially damaged, the holder of the licence shall apply to the Secretary of State for the issue to him of a replacement set of trade plates.
   (2) On receipt of an application under paragraph (1) the Secretary of State shall so issue a replacement set if—
   (a)   he has received all those trade plates in the set which are still in the possession of the holder of the licence;
   (b)   except where paragraph (3) applies, the fee prescribed by paragraph (4) has been paid; and
   (c)   he is satisfied that any plate has been lost, stolen, destroyed or materially damaged.
   (3) If only that part of a trade plate which consists of a means whereby the trade licence may be fixed to it is lost, stolen, destroyed or materially damaged, the holder of the licence shall apply to the Secretary of State for the issue to him of a replacement means of fixing the licence and, upon payment of the fee prescribed by paragraph (4)(c), the Secretary of State shall issue such a replacement.
   (4) The fees payable under paragraphs (2) and (3) shall be—
   (a)   for a replacement set of trade plates comprising two plates, £13.50;
   (b)   for a replacement set of trade plates comprising three plates, £18;
   (c)   for a replacement of a single trade plate issued under regulation 40(4), £7; and
   (d)   for a replacement means of fixing a trade licence to a trade plate, £2.
   (5) No fee shall be payable under paragraph (4)(a) or (b) on account of the replacement of a trade plate, if the Secretary of State is satisfied that the plate has become illegible or the colour of the plate has been altered (whether by fading or by other means) otherwise than by reason of any act or omission of the licence holder.
   (6) If a replacement set of trade plates has been issued on the ground that any of the original trade plates has been lost, stolen or destroyed, and the original plate is subsequently found or recovered, the holder of the licence—
   (a)   if the original plate is in his possession, shall forthwith[1] return it to the Secretary of State, or
   (b)   if it is not in his possession but he becomes aware that it is found or recovered, shall take all reasonable steps to obtain possession of it and return it to the Secretary of State.

1. See note to reg 18(1), ante.

4–4399ZH　42. Display of general registration mark of holder of a trade licence and exhibition of licence.　(1) Where a vehicle is in use under a trade licence the general registration mark assigned to the holder of a trade licence shall be displayed on the vehicle in the manner specified in paragraph (2).

(2) The trade plates issued by the Secretary of State shall be fixed to and displayed on the vehicle in such a manner that, if the general registration mark assigned to the holder were a registration mark assigned to the vehicle, the provisions of regulations 5 and 6 of the Road Vehicles (Display of Registration Marks) Regulations 2001 (the "2001 Regulations") would be complied with, notwithstanding the vehicle may not have been first registered on or after the relevant date, as defined in regulation 2(1) of the 2001 Regulations, or it is a works truck (as defined by paragraph 4(6) of Schedule 1 to the 1994 Act) or an agricultural machine (as defined by regulation 2(1) of the 2001 Regulations) or a road roller.

(3) The prescribed manner of exhibiting a trade licence on a vehicle for the purposes of section 33(1)(b) of the 1994 Act is that specified in paragraph (4).

(4) The trade licence shall be—

(a) exhibited on the front of the vehicle so as to be clearly visible at all times in daylight; and

(b) fixed by means of the trade plate issued to the licence holder which contains a means for fixing the licence to it.

PART VIII
MISCELLANEOUS

4–4399ZI　43. Cylinder capacity.　(1) For the purposes of Schedule 1 to the 1994 Act (annual rates of vehicle excise duty) the cylinder capacity of an internal combustion engine shall be taken to be—

(a) in the case of a single-cylinder engine, the cylinder capacity attributable to the cylinder of the engine; and

(b) in the case of an engine having two or more cylinders, the sum of the cylinder capacities attributable to the separate cylinders.

(2) The cylinder capacity attributable to any cylinder of an internal combustion engine shall be deemed to be equal to—

(a) in the case of a cylinder having a single piston, the product expressed in cubic centimetres of the square of the internal diameter of the cylinder measured in centimetres, and the distance through which the piston associated with the cylinder moves during one half of a revolution of the engine measured in centimetres multiplied by 0.7854; and

(b) in the case of a cylinder having more than one piston, the sum of the products expressed in cubic centimetres of the square of the internal diameter of each part of the cylinder in which a piston moves measured in centimetres, and the distance through which the piston associated with that part of the cylinder moves during one half of a revolution of the engine measured in centimetres multiplied by 0.7854.

(3) In measuring cylinders for the purpose of calculating cylinder capacity, and in calculating cylinder capacity, fractions of centimetres are to be taken into account.

4–4399ZJ　44. Seating capacity of buses.　(1) For the purpose of Part III of Schedule 1 to the 1994 Act (annual rates of vehicle excise duty applicable to buses), the seating capacity of a bus shall be taken to be the number of persons that may be seated in the bus at any one time, as determined in accordance with the principles specified in paragraph (2).

(2) Those principles are—

(a) where separate seats for each person are provided one person shall be counted for each separate seat provided;

(b) where the vehicle is fitted with continuous seats one person shall be counted for each complete length of 410 mm measured in a straight line lengthwise on the front of each seat;

(c) where any continuous seat is fitted with arms in order to separate the seating spaces and the arms can be folded back or otherwise put out of use, the arms shall be ignored in measuring the seat;

(d) no account shall be taken of—

(i) the driver's seat; or

(ii) any seats alongside the driver's seat, whether separate from or continuous with it, if the Secretary of State is satisfied that the use of those seats by members of the public will not be permitted during the currency of the licence applied for.

(3) In paragraph (2) "driver's seat" means—

(a) any separate seat occupied by the driver; or

(b) where no such seat is provided and the driver occupies a portion of a continuous seat, so much of that seat as extends from the right edge of the seat if the vehicle is steered from the right-hand side, or from the left edge of the seat if the vehicle is steered from the left-hand side, to a point 460 mm left or right, as the case may be, of the point on the seat directly behind the centre of the steering column.

4–4399ZK　45. Recovery vehicles: prescribed purposes.　(1) The purposes specified in Part I of Schedule 7 are hereby prescribed for the purposes of paragraph 5(3)(e) of Schedule 1 to the 1994 Act (purposes for which a recovery vehicle may be used).

(2) The purposes specified in Part II of Schedule 7 are hereby prescribed for the purposes of paragraph 5(4) of Schedule 1 to the 1994 Act (purposes to be disregarded in determining whether a vehicle is a recovery vehicle).

4—4399ZL 46. Admissibility of evidence from records. (1) The matters specified in paragraph (2) are hereby prescribed for the purposes of section 52(1) of the 1994 Act (matters with respect to which statements in documents are admissible in evidence).

(2) The matters are anything relating to—

 (*a*) an application for—

  (i) a vehicle licence;
  (ii) a trade licence;
  (iii) a repayment of vehicle excise duty under section 19 of the 1994 Act (surrender of licences); or
  (iv) the recovery of overpaid vehicle excise duty;

 (*b*) a vehicle licence, trade licence, nil licence, registration document or registration mark;
 (*c*) a trade plate;
 (*d*) the recovery of underpaid vehicle excise duty;
 (*e*) the conviction of any person for an offence under the 1994 Act or its predecessor legislation;
 (*f*) the exemption of a vehicle from vehicle excise duty;
 (*g*) the liability of the person by whom a vehicle is kept to pay any sum in accordance with section 30 of the 1994 Act;
 (*h*) the immobilisation, removal or disposal of a vehicle pursuant to regulations made under Schedule 2A to the 1994 Act.

4—4399ZM 47. Regulations prescribed under section 59(2) of the 1994 Act. The regulations specified in column (1), whose subject matter is referred to in column (2), of the table in Schedule 8 are hereby prescribed as regulations to which section 59(2)(a) of the 1994 Act (fines not to exceed level 3 on the standard scale) applies.

4—4399ZN

Regulation 2	SCHEDULE 1
	REGULATIONS REVOKED

Regulation 5	SCHEDULE 2
	REDUCED POLLUTION CERTIFICATES AND THE REDUCED POLLUTION REQUIREMENTS

Regulation 15(3)	SCHEDULE 3
	ISSUE OF NEW REGISTRATION DOCUMENT

Regulation 26	SCHEDULE 4
	STATUTORY OFF-ROAD NOTIFICATION

PART I
GENERAL

4—4399ZO 1. Interpretation of Schedule. (1) In this Schedule—

"authorised insurer" has the meaning given in section 145(5) of the 1988 Act;
"personal credit agreement" has the meaning given in section 8(1) of the Consumer Credit Act 1974;
"relevant vehicle" means a vehicle which is either a relevant GB vehicle or a relevant NI vehicle;
"the required declaration" means a declaration made to the Secretary of State by a person surrendering a
 vehicle licence or the keeper of a relevant vehicle to the effect that (except for use under a trade licence)
 he does not for the time being intend to use or keep the vehicle on a public road and will not use or keep
 the vehicle on a public road without first taking out a vehicle licence (or if appropriate a nil licence) for
 the vehicle;
"the required particulars" in relation to a relevant vehicle are particulars of—

 (*a*) the registration mark of the vehicle;
 (*b*) the make and model of the vehicle; and
 (*c*) the address of the premises at which the vehicle is kept; and

"unlicensed vehicle" means a relevant vehicle for which no vehicle licence is for the time being in force and
 "unlicensed" shall be construed accordingly.

(2) In this Schedule, subject to sub-paragraph (3),—

 (*a*) a "relevant GB vehicle" means a vehicle which is registered in the GB records and kept in Great Britain,
  but does not include a vehicle in relation to which each of the following conditions is satisfied—

  (i) neither a vehicle licence nor a nil licence was in force for the vehicle on 31st January 1998;
  (ii) such a licence has not been taken out for the vehicle for a period starting after that date; and
  (iii) the vehicle has not been used or kept on a public road on or after that date; and

 (*b*) a "relevant NI vehicle" means a vehicle which is registered in the NI records and kept in Northern Ireland,
  but does not include a vehicle in relation to which each of the following conditions is satisfied—

  (i) neither a vehicle licence nor a nil licence was in force for the vehicle on 30th November 2002;
  (ii) such a licence has not been taken out for the vehicle for a period starting after that date; and
  (iii) the vehicle has not been used or kept on a public road on or after that date.

(3) A vehicle which is an exempt vehicle falling within a description specified in paragraph 2, 2A, 3, 23 or 24 of Schedule 2 to the 1994 Act is neither a relevant GB nor a relevant NI vehicle.

(4) For the purposes of this Schedule a person is a "relevant vehicle trader" in relation to a vehicle if he falls within a description mentioned in column (2) of an item in the Table below and the vehicle falls within a description mentioned in column (3) of that item.

TABLE

(1) Item	(2) Descriptions of person	(3) Descriptions of vehicle
1	The holder of a trade licence	A vehicle temporarily in his possession in the course of the business by virtue of which he is a person eligible to hold such a licence
2	An auctioneer of vehicles	A vehicle temporarily in his possession in the course of his business as such an auctioneer
3	A motor dealer	A vehicle temporarily in his possession in the course of his business as a motor dealer
4	A person who carries on business as a dismantler of vehicles	A vehicle temporarily in his possession in the course of that business
5	An authorised insurer	A vehicle temporarily in his possession in consequence of settling a claim under a policy of insurance which related to the vehicle
6	The holder of a licence under Part II of the Consumer Credit Act 1974	A vehicle temporarily in his possession under an order for the repossession of the vehicle made in pursuance of a personal credit agreement relating to the vehicle

2. Manner in which declaration is to be made and particulars furnished. (1) For the purposes of this Schedule the required declaration may be made and the required particulars furnished in such way as the Secretary of State may accept including—

(a) in writing on a form specified by the Secretary of State;
(b) orally by telephone to a person authorised by the Secretary of State; or
(c) by electronic means in a form specified by the Secretary of State.

(2) A person furnishing the required particulars need not provide particulars of the address at which the vehicle is kept unless required to do so—

(a) in a case falling within sub-paragraph (1)(a) or (c), by the form on which those particulars are furnished or
(b) in a case falling within sub-paragraph (1)(b), by the person to whom they are furnished.

PART II
VEHICLES REGISTERED IN THE GB RECORDS AND KEPT IN GREAT BRITAIN

4-4399ZP 3. Surrender of a vehicle licence—relevant GB vehicle. (1) When the holder of a vehicle licence for a relevant GB vehicle surrenders it under section 10(2) of the 1994 Act, he shall deliver to the Secretary of State the required declaration and the required particulars in relation to that vehicle.
(2) Paragraph (1) does not apply where a relevant GB vehicle is no longer kept by the holder of the licence or the holder is a relevant vehicle trader in relation to that vehicle.

4. Expiry of vehicle licence or nil licence—relevant GB vehicle. Where a vehicle licence or nil licence ceases to be in force for a relevant GB vehicle by reason of the expiration of the period for which the licence was granted and a vehicle licence or nil licence for the vehicle is not taken out so as to run from the expiration of that period, the keeper of the vehicle shall deliver to the Secretary of State the required declaration and the required particulars in relation to the vehicle—

(a) if he is a relevant vehicle trader, not later than the end of the period of three months starting with the day following the expired period; or
(b) in any other case, not later than that day.

5. Person keeping an unlicensed vehicle—relevant GB vehicle. (1) Subject to sub-paragraph (2) this paragraph applies to a person who is the keeper of a relevant GB vehicle which is unlicensed and as respects which there has elapsed a period of 12 months ("the unlicensed period")—

(a) throughout which the vehicle has been kept in Great Britain unlicensed; and
(b) within which neither the required declaration nor the required particulars have been delivered to the Secretary of State in relation to the vehicle.

(2) For the purposes of sub-paragraph (1)(a), where a vehicle licence has been surrendered under section 10(2) of the 1994 Act, the vehicle to which it relates shall be taken to be unlicensed from the first day of the month in which the licence was surrendered.
(3) A person to whom this paragraph applies shall, unless a vehicle licence or a nil licence has been taken out so as to run from the end of the unlicensed period, deliver the required declaration and the required particulars to the Secretary of State in relation to the relevant GB vehicle not later than the day following the end of that period.

6. Change of keeper of unlicensed vehicle—relevant GB vehicle. On a change in the keeper of a relevant GB vehicle which is unlicensed, unless a vehicle licence or nil licence is taken out for the vehicle, the new keeper shall deliver to the Secretary of State the required declaration and the required particulars in relation to the vehicle—

(a) if he is a relevant vehicle trader, not later than the end of the period of three months beginning with the day following the day on which the change of keeper occurs; or

(b) in any other case, not later than the day following the day on which the change of keeper occurs.

4–4399ZQ

PART III

(Northern Ireland vehicles)

Regulation 34

SCHEDULE 5
EXEMPT VEHICLES: VEHICLES IMPORTED BY MEMBERS OF FOREIGN ARMED FORCES AND OTHERS

Regulations 37 and 38

SCHEDULE 6
TRADE LICENCES

PART I
CONDITIONS SUBJECT TO WHICH TRADE LICENCES ARE TO BE ISSUED

4–4399ZR **1.** If the holder of a trade licence changes his name, the name of his business or his business address he shall forthwith—

(a) notify the change and the new name or address to the Secretary of State; and
(b) send the licence to the Secretary of State for any necessary amendment.

2. The holder of the licence shall not, and shall not permit any person to, alter, deface, mutilate or add anything to a trade plate.

3. The holder of the licence shall not, and shall not permit any person to, exhibit on any vehicle any trade licence or trade plate—

(a) which has been altered, defaced mutilated or added to;
(b) upon which the figures or particulars have become illegible; or
(c) the colour of which has altered whether by fading or otherwise.

4. The holder of the licence shall not, and shall not permit any person to, exhibit on any vehicle anything which could be mistaken for a trade plate.

5. The holder of the licence shall not permit any person to display the trade licence or any trade plates on a vehicle except a vehicle which that person is using for the purposes of the holder under the licence.

6. The holder of the licence shall not, and shall not permit any person, to display the trade licence or any trade plates on any vehicle unless—

(a) that vehicle is within the classes of vehicle specified in section 11(2) of the 1994 Act (if the holder is a motor trader who is a manufacturer of vehicles), 11(3) (if the holder is any other motor trader) or 11(4) (if the holder is a vehicle tester); and
(b) the vehicle is being used for one or more of the prescribed purposes for which the holder may use the vehicle in accordance with regulation 36 and this Schedule.

7. The holder of the licence shall not display any trade plate on a vehicle used under the licence unless that trade plate shows the general registration mark assigned to the holder in respect of that licence.

PART II
PURPOSES FOR WHICH THE HOLDER OF A TRADE LICENCE MAY USE A VEHICLE BY VIRTUE OF THE LICENCE

General

4–4399ZS **8. Interpretation.** Where a vehicle is so constructed that a semi-trailer may by partial superimposition be attached to it in such a manner as to cause a substantial part of the weight of the semi-trailer to be borne by the vehicle, the vehicle and the semi-trailer shall be taken, for the purposes of this Part of this Schedule to constitute a single vehicle.

9. The purposes prescribed by this Part of this Schedule as purposes for which the holder of a trade licence may use a vehicle on a public road by virtue of that licence—

(a) do not include the carrying of any person on the vehicle or any trailer drawn by it except a person carried in connection with such purposes; and
(b) are without prejudice to the provisions of subsections (4) to (6) of section 11 of the 1994 Act which specify the classes of vehicle which a trade licence is for, in the relation respectively to a motor trader who is a manufacturer of vehicles, any other motor trader and a vehicle tester.

Motor Traders

10. Purposes for which a motor trader may use a vehicle by virtue of a trade licence. The purposes for which the holder of a trade licence who is a motor trader may use a vehicle (other than a vehicle to which paragraph 14 applies) on a public road by virtue of that licence are purposes which meet each of the following requirements—

(a) they are business purposes;
(b) they are paragraph 12 purposes; and
(c) they are purposes that do not include the conveyance of goods or burden of any description except specified loads.

11. Business purposes. A vehicle is used for "business purposes" if it is used for purposes connected with the motor trader's business—

(a) as a manufacturer or repairer of or dealer in vehicles[1],
(b) as a manufacturer or repairer of or dealer in trailers carried on in conjunction with his business as a motor trader,

(c) of modifying vehicles (whether by the fitting of accessories or otherwise); or
(d) of valeting vehicles.

---

1. This includes a business consisting wholly or mainly of collecting and delivering mechanically propelled vehicles (Vehicle Excise and Registration Act 1994, s 62(1)). The use must be directly connected with such business (*James v Evans Motors (County Garages) Ltd* [1963] 1 All ER 7, 127 J P 104) and does not include any ancillary business of a manufacturer, etc (*Dark v Western Motor and Carriage Co (Bristol) Ltd* [1939] 1 All ER 143).

12. Paragraph 12 purposes.   A vehicle is used for "paragraph 12 purposes" if it is used for any of the following purposes—

(a) for its test or trial or the test or trial of its accessories or equipment, in either case in the ordinary course of construction, modification or repair or after completion;
(b) for proceeding to or from a public weighbridge for ascertaining its weight or to or from any place for its registration or inspection by a person acting on behalf of the Secretary of State;
(c) for its test or trial for the benefit of a prospective purchaser, for proceeding at the instance of a prospective purchaser[1] to any place for the purpose of such test or trial, or for returning after such test or trial;
(d) for its test or trial for the benefit of a person interested in promoting publicity in regard to it, for proceeding at the instance of such a person to any place for the purpose of such test or trial, or for returning after such test or trial;
(e) for delivering it to the place where the purchaser intends to keep it;
(f) for demonstrating its operation or the operation of its accessories or equipment when it is being handed over to the purchaser;
(g) for delivering it from one part of the licence holder's premises to another part of his premises, or for delivering it from his premises to premises of, or between parts of premises of, another manufacturer or repairer of or dealer in vehicles or removing it from the premises of another manufacturer or repairer of or dealer in vehicles direct to his own premises;
(h) for proceeding to or returning from a workshop in which a body or a special type of equipment or accessory is to be or has been fitted to it or in which it is to be or has been painted, valeted or repaired;
(i) for proceeding from the premises of a manufacturer or repairer of or dealer in vehicles to a place from which it is to be transported by train, ship or aircraft or for proceeding to the premises of such a manufacturer, repairer or dealer from a place to which it has been so transported;
(j) for proceeding to or returning from any garage, auction room or other place at which vehicles are usually stored or usually or periodically offered for sale and at which it is to be or has been stored or is to be or has been offered for sale as the case may be;
(k) for proceeding to or returning from a place where it is to be or has been inspected or tested; or
(l) for proceeding to a place where it is to be broken up or otherwise dismantled.

---

1. The Scottish Court held that "prospective purchaser" includes a possible purchaser (*Helson v Barnard* 1922 SLT 40).

13. Specified loads.   (1) A specified load is one of the following kinds of load—

(a) a test load;
(b) in the case of a vehicle which is being delivered or collected and is being used for a purpose falling within paragraph 12(f) to (k), a load which consists of another vehicle used or to be used for travel from or to the place of delivery or collection;
(c) a load which is built in as part of the vehicle or permanently attached to it;
(d) in the case of a vehicle which is being used for a purpose falling within paragraph 12(h), (i) or (j), a load which consists of a trailer or of parts, accessories or equipment designed to be fitted to the vehicle and of tools for fitting them.

(2) In paragraph (1) a "test load" means a load which—

(a) is carried by a vehicle being used for a purpose falling within paragraph 12(b), (d), (e) or (g);
(b) is carried solely for the purpose of testing or demonstrating the vehicle or any of its accessories or equipment; and
(c) is returned to the place of loading without its having been removed from the vehicle except—

(i) for the purpose of testing or demonstrating the vehicle or any of its accessories or equipment,
(ii) in the case of accident, or
(iii) where the load consists of water, fertiliser or refuse.

Manufacturers Keeping Vehicles for Research and Development

14. Vehicle kept by a motor trader for research and development in the course of his business as a manufacturer.   (1) This paragraph applies to a vehicle—

(a) kept by a motor trader, being the holder of a trade licence who is a manufacturer of vehicles; and
(b) kept solely for the purposes of conducting research and development in the course of his business as such a manufacturer.

(2) The purposes for which such a person may, by virtue of the trade licence, use a vehicle to which this paragraph applies on a public road are the purposes of conducting research and development in the course of his business as a manufacturer of vehicles.

(3) Those purposes shall not be taken to include the conveyance of goods or burden of any description except—

(a) a load which is carried solely for the purpose of testing the vehicle or any of its accessories or equipment and which is returned to the place of loading without having been removed from the vehicle except for such purpose or in the case of accident; or
(b) any load built in as part of the vehicle or permanently attached to it.

Vehicle Testers

15. Purposes for which a vehicle tester may use a vehicle by virtue of a trade licence. (1) Subject to sub-paragraph (2) the purposes for which the holder of a trade licence who is a vehicle tester may use a vehicle on a public road by virtue of that licence are the purposes of testing it or any trailer drawn by it or any of the accessories or equipment on the vehicle or trailer in the course of the business of the holder of the trade licence as a vehicle tester.

(2) The purposes prescribed by sub-paragraph (1) do not include the conveyance of goods or any other burden of any description on the vehicle except—

(*a*) a load which is carried solely for the purpose of testing or demonstrating the vehicle or any of its accessories or equipment and is returned to the place of loading without having been removed from the vehicle except for that purpose or in the case of accident, or

(*b*) a load which is built in as part of the vehicle or permanently attached to it.

Regulation 45

SCHEDULE 7

RECOVERY VEHICLES: PRESCRIBED PURPOSES

PART I

PURPOSES PRESCRIBED FOR THE PURPOSES OF PARAGRAPH 5(3)(E) OF SCHEDULE 1 TO THE 1994 ACT

4399ZT   **1.** Carrying any person who, immediately before the vehicle became disabled was the driver of, or a passenger in that vehicle, together with his personal effects, from the premises at which the vehicle is to be repaired or scrapped to his original intended destination.

2. (1) At the request of a constable or a local authority empowered by or under statute to remove a vehicle from a road, removing such a vehicle to a place nominated by the constable or local authority.

(2) In sub-paragraph (1) "road" has the meaning given—

(*a*) in relation to England, Scotland or Wales by section 192 of the 1988 Act; and

(*b*) in relation to Northern Ireland by Article 2 of the Road Traffic (Northern Ireland) Order 1995.

3. Proceeding to a place at which the vehicle will be available for use for a purpose specified in paragraph 5(3)(a) or (b) of Schedule 1 to the 1994 Act and remaining temporarily at such a place so as to be available for such use.

4. Proceeding from—

(*a*) a place where the vehicle has remained temporarily so as to be available for such use;

(*b*) a place where the vehicle has recovered a disabled vehicle; or

(*c*) such premises as are mentioned in paragraph 5(3)(b) or (c) of Schedule 1 to the 1994 Act.

PART II

PURPOSES PRESCRIBED FOR THE PURPOSES OF PARAGRAPH 5(4)(C) OF SCHEDULE 1 TO THE 1994 ACT

4399ZU   **5.** Repairing a disabled vehicle at the place where it became disabled or to which it has been moved in the interests of safety after becoming disabled.

6. Drawing or carrying a single trailer if another vehicle had become disabled whilst drawing or carrying it.

4399ZV

Regulation 47

SCHEDULE 8

REGULATIONS TO WHICH SECTION 59(2)(A) OF THE 1994 ACT APPLIES

DRINK DRIVING

Road Traffic (Courses for Drink-Drive Offenders) Regulations 1992[1]

(SI 1992/3013)

-4401   **1.** *Citation and Commencement.*

---

1. Made by the Secretary of State for Transport, in exercise of the powers conferred by ss 34B(3) and (8) and 34C(3) of the Road Traffic Offenders Act 1988.

Interpretation

-4402   **2.** In these Regulations—

"the Act" means the Road Traffic Offenders Act 1988;

"course" means a course approved by the Secretary of State for the purposes of section 34A of the Act;

"manager", in relation to a course, means the person for the time being nominated as the manager of the course by the Secretary of State.

Certificate of completion

-4403   **3.** The certificate referred to in section 34B(1) of the Act shall be a certificate in such form and contain such particulars as may from time to time be determined by the Secretary of State.

Course organiser

-4404   **4.** The person responsible for giving the certificates mentioned in section 34B(1) of the Act in respect of the completion of a course shall be the person for the time being nominated for that purpose by the manager.

Notice of non-completion

4–4405   5. A notice under subsection (5) of section 34B of the Act shall, for the purposes of th. subsection, be treated as given a person if it was sent by registered post or recorded deliver service addressed to him at his last known address, notwithstanding that it was returned ε undelivered or was for any other reason not received by him.

PART V
YOUTH COURTS

INTRODUCTION AND CONTENTS

PART V of this manual examines the practice and procedure of the criminal courts hearing criminal proceedings concerning children and young persons and with the constitution and jurisdiction of the youth court.

Our approach is first to provide a basic statement of principle or authority, followed by a commentary, in smaller type, of secondary principles, exceptions and other considerations. Finally, we reproduce the text of statutes and statutory instruments, including rules of court, relating to proceedings before the youth court, arranged chronologically and annotated.

Statutes on youth courts

Statutory Instruments on youth courts

General provisions

5–1 Terminology. In pre-trial procedures, eg investigation of offences and detention under the Police and Criminal Evidence Act 1984 and remand proceedings, accused persons under the age of 17 are referred to as 'juveniles'. Offenders who have attained the age of 17 are treated in the same manner as adults[1].

The Children and Young Persons Acts 1933, 1963 and 1969 refer to "children" and "young persons". A "child" means a person under the age of 14 years and a "young person" means a person who has attained the age of 14 years and is under the age of 18 years[2].

The procedure of the youth courts is partly regulated by the Criminal Procedure Rules 2005 where the collective term for children and young persons is "relevant minor". In *Stone's Justices' Manual* the terms used will reflect those of the relevant legislation.

---

1. Police and Criminal Evidence Act 1984, s 37(15), PART I: MAGISTRATES' COURTS: PROCEDURE, ante; Children and Young Persons Act 1969, s 23(12), this PART, post.
2. Children and Young Persons Act 1933, s 107(1), this PART, post.

5–2 In relation to children and young persons dealt with summarily the word "sentence" is not used and any reference in an enactment to a sentence shall be construed as including an order made on a finding of guilt[1].

The substantive law is unaffected and the power exists in a youth court to defer sentence[2].

1. Children and Young Persons Act 1933, s 59(1), this PART, post.
2. Powers of Criminal Courts (Sentencing) Act 2000, s 1, in PART III: SENTENCING, ante.

–3 Determination of age. Where anyone is brought before any court except as a witness and it appears that he is a child or young person, the court must make enquiry as to his age, and the age presumed or declared by the court is deemed to be his true age[1].

Section 99 of the Children and Young Persons Act 1933 applies generally to determining whether a person appearing before any court is an adult or young person, and to establishing an age for the purposes of the proceedings[2]. The statutory provisions for sentencing also make express reference to the age of the defendant. The effect of these is that the age of the offender will be deemed to be that which it appears to the court to be after considering any available evidence[3]. An order will be made on this basis. Where it is subsequently established that the defendant is of an age which precludes the sentence imposed on him, the sentence is not invalidated[4]. Where there is a dispute as to age which is material, it is better for the court to adjourn for more detailed inquiries if there is any doubt about the matter[5]. When making an order in respect of young offenders it is generally the date of the finding of guilt that is relevant when determining the age of the offender for the purpose of the availability of orders[6].

The youth court retains its jurisdiction concurrently with the adult court to deal with a breach of a conditional discharge where the defendant has attained 18 years[7]. Proceedings for breach of a supervision order where a person has attained 18 years are heard in the adult magistrates' court[8].

1. Children and Young Persons Act 1933, s 99, this PART, post.
2. In this PART, post.
3. See Powers of Criminal Courts (Sentencing) Act 2000, s 164(1), in PART III: SENTENCING, ante.
4. *R v Brown* [1989] Crim LR 750.
5. *R v Steed* [1990] Crim LR 816.
6. *R v Danga* (1991) 13 Cr App Rep (S) 408; *R v Hahn* [2003] EWCA Crim 825, [2003] 2 Cr App R (S) 106. See, however, *Aldis v DPP* [2002] EWHC 403 (Admin), [2002] 2 Cr App Rep (S) 400, [2002] Crim LR 434 where it was held, in relation to a defendant aged 17 at the time of mode of trial, at which hearing it must have been plain to all present that the possibility of a 2-year detention and training order was a factor in the court's decision to try the case summarily, that the attainment of 18 before the trial and conviction did not prevent the justices from imposing a detention and training order; Parliament's intention must have been that s 100 of the Powers of Criminal Courts (Sentencing) Act 2000 should be interpreted as subject to s 29 of the Children and Young Persons Act 1963.
7. Children and Young Persons Act 1933, s 48(2), this PART, post.
8. Powers of Criminal Courts (Sentencing) Act 2000, Sch 7 para 1, in PART III: SENTENCING, ante.

Youth courts: constitution and jurisdiction

–4 Youth courts. A youth court is a court of summary jurisdiction sitting for the purpose of hearing any charge against a child or young person or for the purpose of exercising any other jurisdiction conferred on youth courts[1] and constituted in accordance with the Children and Young Persons Act 1933[2].

Youth courts shall sit as often as is necessary to exercise their jurisdiction[3]. The only persons who may be present at any sitting of a youth court are:

  (*a*)   members and officers of the court;
  (*b*)   parties to the case before the court, their solicitors and counsel, and other persons directly concerned in that case;
  (*c*)   *bona fide* representatives of news agencies;
  (*d*)   such other persons as the court may specially authorise to be present[4].

The youth court may specially authorise to be present such persons who have good cause to be there, eg the victim of the offence being tried, or a student of social welfare. A local authority children's officer responsible for the supervision of a child should not be excluded even if no summons has been served on the local authority, and the court desires only a report from the officer[5].

1. Children and Young Persons Act 1933, s 45, this PART, post.
2. Children and Young Persons Act 1933, Sch 2, this PART, post.
3. Children and Young Persons Act 1933, s 47(1), this PART, post.
4. Children and Young Persons Act 1933, s 47(2), this PART, post.
5. *R v Southwark Juvenile Court, ex p NJ* [1973] 3 All ER 383, [1973] 1 WLR 1300.

–6 Restrictions on publicity. No report of any proceedings in a youth court should reveal the name, address or school, or include any particulars likely to lead to the identification of any child or young person concerned in those proceedings, ie a defendant or witness[1]. These provisions apply to an appeal from a youth court, including appeal by case stated[2]. They also extend to proceedings to vary or revoke a supervision order before the magistrates' court and proceedings on appeal therefrom[3].

The reports to which the restrictions apply are reports in a newspaper and reports included in a programme service, eg sound, television and cable broadcasts and similarly with respect to pictures[4]. The court[5] may dispense by order to any specified extent with the restriction on publicity if it is satisfied that it is in the public interest to do so in relation to a child or young person who has been convicted of an offence[6] or if it is satisfied that it is appropriate to do so for the purpose of avoiding injustice to the child or young person[7]. The restriction may also be lifted by the court on application by the DPP on notice to the legal representative of a child or young person unlawfully at large. The child or young person must have been charged with or convicted of a violent or sexual offence or an offence punishable with imprisonment for 14 or more years. The court must be satisfied that it is necessary to do so for the purpose of apprehending him to bring him before a court or to return him to the place in which he was in custody[8].

1. Children and Young Persons Act 1933, s 49(1)(4), this PART, post.
2. Children and Young Persons Act 1933, s 49(2), this PART, post.
3. Children and Young Persons Act 1933, s 49(2), this PART, post.
4. Children and Young Persons Act 1933, s 49(3), this PART, post.
5. Or a single justice, Children and Young Persons Act 1933, s 49(8), this PART, post.
6. Children and Young Persons Act 1933, s 49(4A), this PART, post.
7. Children and Young Persons Act 1933, s 49(5)(a), this PART, post.
8. Children and Young Persons Act 1933, s 49(5)(b), this PART, post.

5–7 In any proceedings in relation to an offence against decency or morality, where a child or young person is called as a witness, the court may direct that all or any persons except members or officers of the court or parties to the case, their counsel or solicitors, persons otherwise directly concerned with the case, or *bona fide* members of the press be excluded during the taking of the evidence of that witness[1]. The youth court may therefore order the exclusion of persons it has "specially authorised to be present"[2].

1. Children and Young Persons Act 1933, s 37, this PART, post.
2. Children and Young Persons Act 1933, s 47(2), this PART, post.

5–8 Youth court panel[1]. Outside the Metropolitan area of London there must be a youth court panel for every petty sessions area[1], except where, on the recommendation of the Magistrates' Court Committee or otherwise, the Lord Chancellor has made an order for the formation of a combined youth court panel for two or more petty sessions areas[2]. Those justices who are specially qualified for dealing with such cases are appointed to the panel at the October election meeting of the bench and serve for a triennium commencing on the following 1 January[3]. The current triennium extends from 1 January 2001 to 31 December 2003.

In the metropolitan area, which comprises the Inner London Area and the City of London, there is one youth court. The Lord Chancellor nominates the members of the panel and the chairmen[4].

A District Judge (Magistrates' Courts) is qualified to sit as a member of a youth court without being a member of a youth court panel and may sit alone[5]. A District Judge (Magistrates' Courts) may be nominated by the Lord Chancellor to sit in a youth court in the metropolitan area[6].

1. Pending the making of new rules under s 45 of the Children and Young Persons Act 1933 (as substituted by s 50 of the Courts Act 2003), the Youth Courts (Constitution) Rules 1954 are continued in force and have effect as if they were made under s 45: see art 9 of the Courts Act 2003 (Transitional Provisions, Savings and Consequential Provisions) Order 2005, SI 2005/911.
2. Children and Young Persons Act 1933, Sch 2, Part I, this PART, post.
3. Children and Young Persons Act 1933, Sch 2, Part I, this PART, post.
4. Youth Courts (Constitution) Rules 1954, r 1, this PART, post.
5. Children and Young Persons Act 1933, Sch 2, Part II, this PART, post.
6. Children and Young Persons Act 1933, Sch 2, Part I, para 2A, and the Youth Courts (Constitution) Rules 1954, 12, this PART, post.
7. Children and Young Persons Act 1933, Sch 2, Part II, this PART, post.

5–9 Composition of court. A youth court shall be composed of either a District Judge (Magistrates' Courts) sitting alone or not more than three justices. A justice is not qualified to sit as a member of a youth court for the purpose of dealing with any proceedings unless he has been authorised by or on behalf of the Lord Chancellor to sit as a member of a youth court to deal with proceedings of the description or all proceedings dealt with by youth courts[1].

Unless comprised of a District Judge (Magistrates' Courts) is sitting alone a youth court must include a man and a woman[2] except where a single justice has by law jurisdiction to act[3]. Where a youth court is not properly constituted and it is inexpedient in the interests of justice for there to be an adjournment, the court may sit without a man or woman owing to circumstances unforeseen when the court was arranged or where a justice could not properly sit as a member of the court[4].

Each court shall be chaired by the chairman or a deputy chairman of the panel except where, owing to circumstances unforeseen when the members of the court were chosen, a chairman is not present or cannot properly sit as a member of the court, in which case the members of the court may choose one of their number to preside[5].

Similar provision is made for youth courts in the metropolitan area for justices nominated as chairmen and panel members by the Lord Chancellor[6]. Where a court cannot be fully constituted and it appears to the chairman that an adjournment would not be in the interests of justice, the chairman may proceed with one justice (whether a man or a woman)[7]. If, owing to illness or emergency a chairman is not available, any District Judge (Magistrates' Courts), or any lay magistrate with the consent of the Lord Chancellor, may sit temporarily as a chairman[8].

In a youth court in which justices are sitting the requirement for a man and a woman to be present is mandatory. Where a youth court is not so constituted, the members of the panel present may only reach the conclusion that it is inexpedient in the interests of justice for there to be an adjournment after inviting submissions from the parties and hearing their views in open court[9].

---

1. Children and Young Persons Act 1933, s 45.
2. Youth Courts (Constitution) Rules 1954, r 12(1), this PART, post.
3. Youth Courts (Constitution) Rules 1954, r 12(4), this PART, post.
4. Youth Courts (Constitution) Rules 1954, r 12(2), (3), this PART, post.
5. Youth Courts (Constitution) Rules 1954, r 13, this PART, post.
6. Children and Young Persons Act 1933, Sch 2, Pt II, this PART, post.
7. Children and Young Persons Act 1933, Sch 2, Pt II, para 17, this PART, post.
8. Children and Young Persons Act 1933, Sch 2, Pt II, para 16, this PART, post.
9. *R v Birmingham Justices, ex p F* (1999) 164 JP 523, [2000] Crim LR 588, DC.

**5–10	Jurisdiction.**	The youth court generally has exclusive jurisdiction in respect of criminal proceedings against children or young persons[1] except where the accused is charged with an adult defendant[2] or where in the course of proceedings before the adult magistrates' court it appears the defendant is a child or young person, in which case the court may continue with the hearing and determine the proceedings[3]. A youth court sitting for the purpose of hearing a charge against a person who is believed to be a child or young person may, if it thinks fit, proceed with the hearing and determination of the charge notwithstanding that it is discovered that the person in question is not a child or young person[4]. However, a youth court may not deal with a further charge preferred after it is known that the defendant has attained the age of 18[5]. Where a young person attains 18 before the conclusion of the proceedings the court may deal with the case and make any order which it could have made if he had not attained that age[6]. However, where a young person who appears or is brought before a youth court charged with an offence subsequently attains the age of 18, the youth court may, at any time before the start of the trial or after conviction and before sentence, remit the person for trial, or as the case may be, for sentence to a magistrates' court acting for the same petty sessions area as the youth court[7]. The attaining of 18 by a person conditionally discharged does not deprive the youth court of jurisdiction to deal with him in respect of the commission of a further offence[8].

Not all matters affecting children or young persons may be heard by a youth court: for example, a youth court may not hear a complaint for a bind over under the Magistrates' Courts Act 1980, s 115 or a summons under the Dogs Act 1871 for a dog to be kept under proper control. However, it is the generally accepted practice for fine default cases to be heard before the youth court where the child or young person has been ordered to pay. The hearing of a complaint in relation to an anti-social behaviour order is before the adult court but (except in the case of interim orders) all practicable steps should be taken to constitute such a court with justices qualified to sit in the youth court, see the *Practice Direction (Magistrates' Courts: Anti-Social Behaviour Orders: Composition of Benches)*, in PART I: MAGISTRATES' COURTS, PROCEDURE, ante.

A youth court is a magistrates' court for the purposes of s 37(3) of the Mental Health Act 1983 (power to make hospital and guardianship orders without convicting the accused if the court is satisfied that he did the act or made the omission charged)[9].

---

1. Children and Young Persons Act 1933, s 46(1), this PART, post.
2. Children and Young Persons Act 1933, s 46(1) and the Children and Young Persons Act 1963, s 18, this PART, post, and see para **5–11**.
3. Children and Young Persons Act 1933, s 46(1), this PART, post.
4. Children and Young Persons Act 1933, s 48(1), this PART, post.
5. *R v Chelsea Justices, ex p DPP* [1963] 3 All ER 657, 128 JP 18.
6. Children and Young Persons Act 1963, s 29(1), this PART, post.
7. Crime and Disorder Act 1998, s 47(1), this PART, post (before the start of the trial); Powers of Criminal Courts (Sentencing) Act 2000, s 9(1), PART III: SENTENCING, ante (after conviction).
8. Children and Young Persons Act 1933, s 49(2), this PART, post.
9. *R (on the application of P) v Barking Youth Court* [2002] EWHC 734 (Admin), [2002] 2 Cr App Rep 294, 166 JP 641.

Jurisdiction of the magistrates' and Crown Courts

**5–11	Magistrates' court.**	The basic principle is that a charge against a child or young person must be heard by a youth court[1]. In some circumstances proceedings must be commenced in an adult magistrates' court and certain cases must be committed or sent for trial to the Crown Court.

Proceedings must commence in the adult magistrates' court where:

(a)	the child or young person is jointly charged with an adult[2]; or

(b)	the child or young person is charged with an offence arising out of circumstances which are the same as, or connected with, those giving rise to an offence with which a person who had attained the age of 18 is charged at the same time[3]; or

(c)	where an adult is charged with aiding, abetting, counselling, procuring, allowing or permitting the offence by the child or young person[4]; or

(d)	where the child or young person is charged with aiding and abetting, counselling, procuring, allowing, or permitting the offence by the adult[5]; or

(e)	where proceedings against the child or young person are started in the adult court and it only becomes apparent later that the defendant is a child or young person[6]; or

(f)	where the court is conducting remand proceedings[7].

Where exception (*a*) (joint charge with adult) applies the case shall be heard in the adult magistrates' court, but where any of the other exceptions (*b*)–(*d*) apply the decision is discretionary. Exception (*f*) enables an adult court, where necessary, to hear a remand of a child or young person[8].

Whether an adult and a youth are jointly charged depends on a present state of affairs and it is not sufficient to embrace the situation where an adult was originally charged with the youth but has subsequently dropped out of the case. Nevertheless, where in committal proceedings the sole adult accused has been discharged, the adult magistrates' court retains jurisdiction to consider mode of trial proceedings in respect of the youth[9].

---

1. Children and Young Persons Act 1933, s 46, this PART, post.
2. Children and Young Persons Act 1933, s 46(1), this PART, post.
3. Children and Young Persons Act 1963, s 18, this PART, post.
4. Children and Young Persons Act 1933, s 46(1), this PART, post.
5. Children and Young Persons Act 1963, s 18(1), this PART, post. As to "17" see note 3 above.
6. Children and Young Persons Act 1933, s 46(1), this PART, post, and *R v Tottenham Youth Court, ex p Fawzy* [1998] 1 All ER 365, [1999] 1 WLR 1350, sub nom *R v Haringey Justices, ex p Fawzy* [1998] 1 Cr App Rep 411, DC.
7. Children and Young Persons Act 1933, s 46(1), this PART, post.
8. Children and Young Persons Act 1933, s 46(2), this PART, post
9. *R v Tottenham Youth Court, ex p Fawzy* [1998] 1 All ER 365, [1999] 1 WLR 1350, sub nom *R v Haringey Justices, ex p Fawzy* [1998] 1 Cr App Rep 411, DC.

5–12 Crown Court[1]. A child or young person charged with an indictable offence (which includes an offence triable either way) must be tried summarily, ie in a youth court or adult magistrates' court. A child or young person has no right to elect to be tried at the Crown Court but the proceedings must be committed for trial in the following circumstances:

(*a*) where he is charged with homicide, or each of the requirements of s 51A(1) of the Firearms Act 1968 would be satisfied with regard to the offence and the person charged with it if he were convicted of the offence; or

(*b*) where the court considers it ought to be possible to deal with him, if found guilty of the offence, under the provisions of s 91 of the Powers of Criminal Courts (Sentencing) Act 2000; or

(*c*) where he is jointly charged with an adult and the court considers it necessary in the interests of justice to commit both for trial[2].

Where proceedings have been committed a notice containing the prescribed particulars must be displayed at the court[3].

The appropriate date at which to determine whether an accused person has attained the age of 18 thus entitling him to elect to be tried by a jury, is the date of his appearance before the court on the occasion when the court makes its decision as to mode of trial[4].

In cases within the terms of s 4 of the Criminal Justice Act 1987 (serious or complex frauds) or s 53 of the Criminal Justice Act 1991 (certain cases involving children) a child or young person is sent directly for trial as the magistrates' functions in respect of committal proceedings cease. A 'dangerous offender' within the meaning of Chapter 5 of Part 12 of the Criminal Justice Act 2003 is to be sent forthwith for trial[5]. However, in most cases it is not appropriate to make a determination of dangerousness until after conviction[6].

Where a youth is charged with an offence which is both a "specified offence" within the meaning of Sch 15 to the Criminal Justice Act 2003 and a "grave crime" for the purposes of s 91 of the Powers of Criminal Court (Sentencing) Act 2000 we would suggest that the court should proceed as follows:

(1) consider whether is it appropriate to determine "dangerousness". If it is and the defendant is "dangerous" send him for trial; if not,

(2) determine whether the "grave crimes" provisions apply; if they do then commit for trial;

(3) if neither, proceed to summary trial in the youth court.

(4) If the defendant is convicted of a specified offence determine whether the offender is "dangerous" and if so, commit to the Crown Court for sentence.

Where an adult jointly charged with an either-way offence appears with a youth, it is necessary to consider the "dangerousness provisions" before those provisions which normally apply to a youth jointly charged with an adult ie determining mode of trial for an adult and then deciding whether it is in the interests of justice to commit the youth for trial to the Crown Court with the adult[7]. Where the court sends a youth for trial under the "dangerousness" provisions and an adult appears or is brought before the court on the same or a subsequent occasion charged jointly with the youth with an either-way offence for which he has been sent for trial or an either way offence which appears to the court to be related to that offence, the adult must (if he appears on the same occasion) or may (where he appears on a subsequent occasion) be sent to the Crown Court for trial on the either way offence[8].

Where mode of trial has been determined under s 24 of the Magistrates' Courts Act 1980, and the defendant pleads not guilty and the case is adjourned for trial, the defendant who subsequently attains 18 years is not entitled to elect trial at the Crown Court[9]. The court register in these circumstances should record "adjourned for summary trial"[10]. If, however, mode of trial under s 24 is not determined before the defendant attains the age of 18, the court will need to determine mode of trial in accordance with the procedure under ss 17A to 21 of the 1980 Act, or where the defendant is charged with an offence triable only on indictment, proceed as examining justices[9]. Where summary trial has been embarked on, the youth court is entitled to keep mode of trial under review and has the power to change the decision as to mode of trial if it becomes apparent that the original decision is no longer appropriate eg where new material emerges in the course of evidence or the manner in which it is presented by the witness or witnesses is of a nature which justifies the conclusion that the original decision should be changed[11].

1. For procedure in the Crown Court see *Practice Direction (criminal: consolidated)* [2002] para IV.39, in PART I: MAGISTRATES' COURTS, PROCEDURE, ante and see *V and T v United Kingdom* [2000] 2 All ER 1024 note ECtHR.
2. Magistrates' Courts Act 1980, s 24, see PART I: MAGISTRATES' COURTS, PROCEDURE, ante.
3. Magistrates' Courts Act 1980, s 8C, see PART I: MAGISTRATES' COURTS, PROCEDURE, ante.
4. *R v Islington North Juvenile Court, ex p Daley* [1983] 1 AC 347, [1982] 2 All ER 974, 146 JP 363.
5. Crime and Disorder Act 1998, s 51A(2), (3)(*d*), in PART I: MAGISTRATES' COURTS, PROCEDURE, ante.
6. *R (DPP) v South East Surrey Youth Court* [2005] EWHC 2929 (Admin), [2006] 2 All ER 444, [2006] Crim LR 367, sub nom *CPS v MLG* 170 JP 65 and see in particular note to the Magistrates' Courts Act 1980, s 24, in PART I: MAGISTRATES' COURTS, PROCEDURE, ante.
7. In accordance with s 24 of the Magistrates' Courts Act 1980, in PART I: MAGISTRATES' COURTS, PROCEDURE, ante.
8. Crime and Disorder Act 1998, s 51A(6), in PART I: MAGISTRATES' COURTS, PROCEDURE, ante.
9. *R v Lewes Juvenile Court, ex p Turner* (1985) 149 JP 186; *R v Nottingham Justices, ex p Taylor* [1992] QB 557, [1991] 4 All ER 860, [1991] 3 WLR 694. See also *R v West London Justices, ex p Siley-Winditt* [2000] Crim LR 926, DC. The obligation to send a "dangerous offender" to the Crown Court arises where he is charged with a specified offence within the meaning of s 224 of the Criminal Justice Act 2003 and it appears to the court that if he is found guilty of the offence he would meet the criteria for a sentence under s 226(3) or 228(2) of that Act. As to the power to send, on the same occasion or subsequently, related indictable offences, or related summary offences that carry imprisonment or obligatory or discretionary disqualification from driving, see s 51A(4), (5) and (9).
10. Per MCNEILL J in *R v Lewes Juvenile Court, ex p Turner* (1985) 149 JP 186.
11. *R (on the application of K) v Leeds Youth Court* [2001] EWHC Admin 177, (2001) 165 JP 694.

-13   Code for Crown Prosecutors.   The Code for Crown Prosecutors sets out some of the factors to be taken into account by the prosecution when making representations as to summary trial and trial on indictment: the respective ages of the adult and child or young person, the seriousness of the offence, the likely plea, whether there are existing charges against the child or young person before the youth court and the need to deal with the child or young person as expeditiously as possible consistent with the interests of justice.

Once a properly constituted bench has considered all the factors placed before the court that are relevant to the exercise of their discretion under s 24(1) of the Magistrates' Courts Act 1980 and ordered summary trial, a differently constituted bench has no power to re-examine that decision on the same material; but such a review is permissible at any stage up to the beginning of the summary trial if a change of circumstances has occurred or if there are new or additional factors to be brought to the attention of the court[1]. Moreover, once the court has begun to try the information summarily, it may, before the conclusion of the evidence for the prosecution, discontinue the summary trial and proceed to inquire into the information as examining justices[2]. When considering mode of trial under this section, the material which should be available to the court includes the defendant's antecedents[3].

1. *R v Newham Juvenile Court, ex p F (a minor)* [1986] 1 WLR 939.
2. See the Magistrates' Courts Act 1980, s 25(5), (6), in PART I: MAGISTRATES' COURTS, PROCEDURE, ante.
3. *R (Tullet) v Medway Magistrates' Court* [2003] EWHC Admin 2279, 167 JP 541.

-14   Committal for trial to the Crown Court.   In cases of a grave nature where the power to sentence under s 91 of the Powers of Criminal Cases (Sentencing) Act 2000 may be appropriate[1], the proper approach for the justices is to ask themselves whether it would be proper for the Crown Court sentencing the defendant for the offence of which he is charged to exercise its powers under s 91 and sentence him to a period greater than two years and for this purpose the court is entitled to have regard to the defendant's antecedents[3]. If the answer to that question is "Yes", then it follows, inevitably, that the magistrates' court should make it possible for the Crown Court to sentence the defendant on that basis by committing for trial[4]. However, if the defendant appears before the court represented and enters an unequivocal guilty plea, the justices do not have power subsequently to refuse to accept that plea and determine that the proceedings have been a nullity[5]. Even where the defendant has pleaded not guilty, the youth court may not revert to proceeding as examining justices until after it has begun to try the information summarily[6].

When a child or young person is charged with an indictable offence jointly with an adult the court has a judicial discretion[7]. When considering whether it is in the interests of justice to commit proceedings in respect of both for trial, it is not necessary that both defendants should be before the court at the same time; moreover, once a decision to commit has been taken, it is not necessary that the committal in respect of each defendant should be on the same occasion[8]. Accordingly, a youth court may make a decision under s 24(1)(*b*) of the Magistrates' Courts Act 1980 and commit proceedings in respect of a minor for trial at the Crown Court with an adult with whom he has been jointly charged even though proceedings in respect of the adult have already been committed to the Crown Court[9]. Similarly no case involving a child defendant should be transferred for trial under s 53 of the Criminal Justice Act 1991, unless the criteria in s 24 of the 1980 Act are met and a statement to that effect should be included in the notice of transfer[10].

The court is not obliged to consider the evidence but may decide the case is appropriate for trial on indictment after looking at the charges and hearing representations[11].

An adult court finding a minor guilty shall, unless satisfied it would be undesirable to do so, remit him to a youth court for his home area[12]. Otherwise, its powers are limited as set out in s 8(8) of the Powers of Criminal Courts (Sentencing) Act 2000[13].

1. For guidance and examples, see the notes to s 24 of the Magistrates' Courts Act 1980 in PART 1, MAGISTRATES' COURTS, PROCEDURE, ante.
2. *R (Tullet) v Medway Magistrates' Court* [2003] EWHC Admin 2279, 167 JP 541.
3. *R v Inner London Youth Court, ex p DPP* (1996) 161 JP 178, [1996] Crim LR 834.
4. *R v Herefordshire Youth Court, ex p J* [1998] 20 LS Gaz R 34.

5. *R v Fareham Youth Court, ex p M* [1999] Crim LR 325, (1998) 163 JP 812; see also the Magistrates' Courts Act 1980, s 25(5) and (6) in PART I: MAGISTRATES' COURTS, PROCEDURE, ante.
6. *R v Newham Justices, ex p Knight* (1976) Crim LR 323.
7. *R v Crown Court at Doncaster, ex p Crown Prosecution Service* (1986) 151 JP 167, 85 Cr App Rep 1, [1987] Crim LR 395 explained in *R v Coventry City Magistrates' Court, ex p M* (1992) 156 JP 809, [1992] Crim LR 810.
8. *R v Coventry City Magistrates' Court, ex p M* (1992), supra.
9. *R v T and K* [2001] 1 Cr App Rep 446, 165 JP 306, [2001] Crim LR 398, CA (overruled in respect of the entitlement of the court to see the defendant's antecedents when considering mode of trial by *R (Tullet) v Medway Magistrates' Court*, supra).
10. *R v South Hackney Juvenile Court, ex p RB (a minor) and CB (a minor)* (1983) 77 Cr App Rep 294.
11. Powers of Criminal Courts (Sentencing) Act 2000, s 8(6), in PART III: SENTENCING, ante.
12. In PART III: SENTENCING, ante.

5–15 Remittal to youth court for trial. Where a child or young person appears or is brought before a magistrates' court jointly charged with an adult who (a) pleads guilty or (b) is committed to the Crown Court for trial or is discharged, the magistrates' court may proceed to the summary trial of the charge against the child or young person. If the child or young person pleads not guilty, the court may before any evidence is called in his case remit him for trial to the youth court[1]. If the child or young person pleads guilty, he may be remitted to the youth court for sentence[2].

Where the child or young person is charged with an indictable offence, before remitting the case to the youth court the magistrates' court must determine mode of trial under s 24(1)(a) of the Magistrates' Courts Act 1980[3].

1. Magistrates' Courts Act 1980, s 29 in PART I: MAGISTRATES' COURTS; PROCEDURE, ante.
2. Powers of Criminal Courts (Sentencing) Act 2000, s 8(2), in PART III: SENTENCING, ante.
3. *R v Tottenham Youth Court, ex p Fawzy* [1998] 1 All ER 365, [1999] 1 WLR 1350, *sub nom R v Haringey Justices, ex p Fawzy* [1998] 1 Cr App Rep 411.

Youth justice system

5–15A Aim of the youth justice system. It shall be the principal aim of the youth justice system to prevent offending by children and young persons. In addition to any other duty to which they are subject, it is the duty of all persons and bodies carrying out functions in relation to the youth justice system to have regard to that aim[1].

1. Crime and Disorder Act 1998, s 37, this PART, post.

5–15B Local provision of the youth justice system. It is the duty of each local authority, acting in co-operation with the persons and bodies mentioned below, to secure that, to such an extent as is appropriate for their area, all youth justice services are available there[1].

It is the duty of every chief officer of police or police authority any part of whose police area lies within the local authority's area, and every probation committee or health authority any part of whose area lies with the local authority's area, to co-operate in the discharge by the local authority of the duty to make available within their area all youth justice services[2].

"Youth justice services" are defined in the Crime and Disorder Act 1998[3] and the Secretary of State has power by order to amend the definition[4].

1. Crime and Disorder Act 1998, s 38(1), this PART, post.
2. Crime and Disorder Act 1998, s 38(2), this PART, post.
3. See Crime and Disorder Act 1998 s 38(4), this PART, post.
4. Crime and Disorder Act 1998, s 38(5), this PART, post.

5–15C Youth offending teams. It is the duty of each local authority, acting in co-operation with every chief officer of police any part of whose police area lies within the local authority's area, and every probation committee or health authority any part of whose area lies within that area, to establish for their area one or more youth offending teams[1]. Two or more local authorities acting together may establish one or more youth offending teams for both or all their areas[2]. Every chief officer of police and every probation committee or health authority are under a duty to co-operate in the discharge by the local authority of their duty to establish one or more youth offending teams[3].

A youth offending team must include at least one of each of the following, namely:

(a) a probation officer;
(b) a social worker of a local authority social services department;
(c) a police officer;
(d) a person nominated by a health authority any part of whose area lies within the local authority area;
(e) a person nominated by the chief education officer appointed by the local authority[4].

It is the duty of any youth offending team established by a local authority to co-ordinate the provision of youth justice services for all those in the authority's area who need them, and to carry out such functions as are assigned to the team in the youth justice plan formulated by the authority under section 40 of the Crime and Disorder Act 1998[5].

1. Crime and Disorder Act 1998, s 39(1), this PART, post.
2. Crime and Disorder Act 1998, s 39(2), this PART, post.
3. Crime and Disorder Act 1998, s 39(3), this PART, post.
4. Crime and Disorder Act 1998, s 39(5), this PART, post.
5. Crime and Disorder Act 1998, s 39(7), this PART, post.

5–15D   Youth justice plans.   It is the duty of each local authority, after consultation with relevant persons and bodies, to formulate and implement for each year a plan, known as a "youth justice plan", setting out:

(a) how youth justice services in their area are to be provided and funded; and
(b) how the youth offending team or teams established by them (whether alone or jointly with one or more other local authorities) are to be composed and funded, how they are to operate, and what functions they' are to carry out[1].

A local authority must submit their youth justice plan to the Youth Justice Board and must publish the plan in such manner and by such date as the Secretary of State may direct[2].

1. Crime and Disorder Act 1998, s 40(l), this PART, post.
2. Crime and Disorder Act 1998, s 40(4), this PART, post.

Criminal proceedings involving children or young persons

5–16   Criminal liability[1].   It is conclusively presumed that no child under the age of ten years can be guilty of any offence[2]. The rebuttable presumption of criminal law that a child aged 10 or over was incapable of committing an offence has been abolished[3]. An offence of cruelty to persons under 16 years may only be committed by a person who has attained that age[4].

The prosecution must prove the *actus reus* and, except in the case of absolute offences, the appropriate *mens rea*. The common law presumption that a boy under the age of 14 years does not have the physical capacity necessary to enable him to commit the offences of rape and assault with intent to rape has been abolished[5].

1. For the position under the European Convention on Human Rights see *T v United Kingdom; V v United Kingdom* [2000] Crim LR 187 European Court of Human Rights (trial of 11 year old does not necessarily breach the Convention).
2. Children and Young Persons Act 1933, s 50, this PART, post.
3. Crime and Disorder Act 1998, s 34.
4. Children and Young Persons Act 1933, s 1(1), this PART, post.
5. See the Sexual Offences Act 1993, s 1.

5–19   Investigation of criminal offences.   The general powers of search, seizure, arrest and the interviewing of suspects under the Police and Criminal Evidence Act 1984[1] are available to the police when dealing with juvenile offenders[2]. Additional protection is offered in the following circumstances:

(a) *Interviews* The Code of Practice for the Detention, Treatment and Questioning of Persons by Police Officers (Code of Practice C)[3] includes requirements for the presence of an "appropriate adult" at interviews of the juvenile by the police and also that it should be exceptional to interview the juvenile at his place of education and then only with the consent of the principal.
(b) *Detention* Where a juvenile is arrested, the arresting officer is bound to try to notify a parent or guardian[4].

If the juvenile is detained in custody at the police station the custody officer must inform him of his rights to have someone informed of his whereabouts[5] and to have access to legal advice[6]. A juvenile should not be detained in a police cell without good reason and should be visited frequently[7]. When charged he should be transferred to local authority accommodation unless the custody officer certifies:

(i) that by reason of such circumstances as are specified in the certificate, it is impracticable for him to do so; or
(ii) in the case of an arrested juvenile who has attained the age of 12 years, that no secure accommodation is available and that keeping him in other local authority accommodation would not be adequate to protect the public from serious harm from him[8].

(c) *Questioning* Except in cases of urgency, when Annexe C to Code of Practice (C) applies, juveniles should not be interviewed or asked to sign a written statement in the absence of the appropriate adult[9]. If cautioned in the absence of the appropriate adult, the caution must be repeated in the adult's presence[10]. The appropriate adult must normally be present when the juvenile is interviewed[11] and may read and sign a written record of the juvenile's interview[12].

The Criminal Justice Act 1991 defined more closely the circumstances in which a juvenile might be retained in police accommodation. The reference to "circumstances" in para (*i*) above implies that the impracticability of moving the offender to local authority accommodation relates to some factor other than the view of the custody officer as to the suitability of local authority accommodation, eg adverse weather conditions.

1. See PART I: MAGISTRATES' COURTS, PROCEDURE, ante.
2. "Juvenile" is defined in these circumstances as a person under 17 years: Police and Criminal Evidence Act 1984 s 37(15). For the purposes of the Code of Practice for detention, treatment and questioning of persons by police officer (Code (C)), anyone appearing to be under 17 shall be treated as a juvenile in the absence of clear evidence to the contrary Code (C), para 1.5.
3. See PART II: EVIDENCE, ante.
4. Children and Young Persons Act 1933, s 34(2), this PART, post.
5. Police and Criminal Evidence Act 1984, s 54, see PART I: MAGISTRATES' COURTS, PROCEDURE, ante.
6. Police and Criminal Evidence Act 1984, s 58, see PART I: MAGISTRATES' COURTS, PROCEDURE, ante. Although these rights may be delayed in the case of an adult detained for an indictable offence (Police and Criminal Evidence Act 1984, Part IV, see PART I: MAGISTRATES' COURTS, PROCEDURE, ante), it would appear that in respect of a juvenile the provisions of s 34 are overriding.
7. Code of Practice for detention, treatment and questioning of persons by police officers (Code (C)), para 8.8 and Notes for Guidance, para 8A see PART II: EVIDENCE, ante.
8. Police and Criminal Evidence Act 1984, s 38(1), see PART I: MAGISTRATES' COURTS, PROCEDURE, ante.
9. Code of Practice for detention, treatment and questioning of persons by police officers (Code (C)), para 11.14, see PART II: EVIDENCE, ante.
10. Code of Practice for detention, treatment and questioning of persons by police officers (Code (C)), para 10.6, see PART II: EVIDENCE, ante.
11. Code of Practice for detention, treatment and questioning of persons by police officers (Code (C)), para 11.14, see PART II: EVIDENCE, ante.
12. Code of Practice for detention, treatment and questioning of persons by police officers (Code (C)), para 11.11, see PART II: EVIDENCE, ante.

5–20 Separation of children and young persons from adult offenders. A child or young person[1] held in police detention should not be detained with an adult offender[2]. Arrangements must be made for preventing a child or young person while detained in a police station, or while being conveyed to or from any criminal court or while waiting at court from associating with an adult (other than a relative) charged with an offence other than a joint offence with the child or young person[2]. A girl shall be under the care of a woman[2].

1. Ie a person under 18 years: Children and Young Persons Act 1933, s 31, this PART, post.
2. Children and Young Persons Act 1933, s 31(1), this PART, post.

5–21 Prosecution. It is recognized that it is usually in the public interest to divert young offenders from the criminal justice system where practicable. Accordingly many offenders will receive a reprimand or warning as described in para **5–21B** below. Even though the police decide on prosecution, the Crown Prosecution Service retains the discretion to continue or discontinue criminal proceedings and will make its determination in accordance with the Code for Crown Prosecutors[1].

Anyone who decides to lay an information against a child or young person must notify the local authority[2]. Further, in the case of a child or young person aged 13 or older no proceedings may begin unless the prosecutor has given notice to a probation officer[3].

Local authorities must take reasonable steps designed to encourage those under 18 years not to commit criminal offences and to reduce the need to bring criminal proceedings[4].

There is no mandatory requirement for *consultation* between the prosecutor and either the local authority or the probation service. In practice there is close liaison and police forces have specialist sections to deal with juvenile crime and to liaise with the welfare and education services before determining the appropriate course of action[5].

For the purposes of s 5(8) of the Children and Young Persons Act 1969, notice to a local authority of intended proceedings should be given as soon as reasonably practicable after the decision is made, but the notice does not have to be given before the proceedings are begun[6]. Notice under s 34(2) of the 1969 Act to a probation officer must be given before the proceedings are begun in any court, but for this purpose proceedings are begun when the defendant is first brought before the court[6]. It will be good practice, if circumstances permit, for these notices to be in writing, but there is no statutory requirement to this effect. Moreover, since the obligation to give notice under ss 5(8) and 34(2) is directory, rather than mandatory, failure to do so does not render the proceedings null and void[6].

1. Issued pursuant to the Prosecution of Offences Act 1985, s 10, in PART I: MAGISTRATES' COURTS, PROCEDURE ante.
2. Children and Young Persons Act 1969, s 5(8), this PART, post.
3. Children and Young Persons Act 1969, s 34(2), this PART, post.
4. Children Act 1989, Sch 2, para 7, in PART IV: FAMILY LAW, ante.
5. See the Home Office Guide to Part I of the Children and Young Persons Act 1969, paras 92–99.
6. *DPP v Cottier* [1996] 3 All ER 126, [1996] 1 WLR 826.

5–21B Reprimands and warnings. The provisions of the Crime and Disorder Act 1998 relating to reprimands and warnings where:

(a) a constable has evidence that a child or young person ("the offender") has committed an offence;

(b) the constable considers that the evidence is such that, if the offender were prosecuted for the offence, there would be a realistic prospect of his being convicted;

(c) the offender admits to the constable that he committed the offence;

(d) the offender has not previously been convicted of an offence; and

(e) the constable is satisfied that it would not be in the public interest for the offender to be prosecuted.[1]

In these circumstances the constable may reprimand the offender if the offender has not previously been reprimanded or warned[2].

The constable may warn the offender if:

(a) the offender has not previously been warned; or

(b) where the offender has previously been warned, the offence was committed more than two years after the date of the previous warning and the constable considers the offence to be not so serious as to require a charge to be brought;

but no person may be warned under paragraph (b) above mare than once[3].

Where the offender has not been previously reprimanded, the constable shall warn rather than reprimand the offender if he considers the offence to be so serious as to require a warning[4].

The constable shall:

(a) give any reprimand or warning at a police station and, where the offender is under the age of 17, in the presence of an appropriate adult; and

(b) explain to the offender and, where he is under that age, the appropriate adult in ordinary language:

    (i) in the case of a reprimand, that it may be cited in criminal proceedings in the same circumstances as a conviction of the person may be cited;

    (ii) in the case of a warning, the effect of s 66(1), (2). (4), and 5(b) and (c) of the Crime and Disorder Act 1998[5].

The term "appropriate adult" is defined[6].

Where a constable warns a person, he shall as soon as practicable refer the person to a youth offending team. A youth offending team shall assess any person referred to them and unless they consider it inappropriate to do so, shall arrange for him to participate in a rehabilitation programme[7]. "Rehabilitation programme" is defined to mean a programme the purpose of which is to rehabilitate participants and to prevent them from re-offending[8].

Where a person who has been warned is convicted of an offence committed within 2 years of the warning, the court by or before which he is so convicted shall not make an order of conditional discharge in respect of the offence unless it is of the opinion that there are exceptional circumstances relating to the offence or the offender which justify its doing so, and where it does so, shall state in open court that it is of the opinion and why it is[9].

The following, namely:

(a) any reprimand of a person;

(b) any warning of a person; and

(c) any report on a failure by a person to participate in a rehabilitation programme arranged for him,

may be cited in criminal proceedings in the same circumstances as a conviction of the person may be cited[10].

The Secretary of State shall publish guidance as to the circumstances in which it is appropriate to give reprimands or warnings, including criteria for determining the relative seriousness of the offence; the category of constable by whom reprimands and warnings may be given, and the form which reprimands and warnings are to take and the manner in which they are to be given and recorded[11]. The Secretary of State shall also publish, in such manner as he considers appropriate, guidance as to rehabilitation programmes[12].

No caution shall be given to a child or young person[13].

Any admission must not have been obtained by an inducement, in particular that the case will be disposed of in a particular way such as a reprimand or final warning[14]. Thereafter, the decision whether to prosecute or issue a reprimand or warning does not require the accused's consent. Neither the warning of a person nor the decision to warn him involves the determination of a criminal charge and the rights in article 6 are not engaged[15].

---

1. Crime and Disorder Act 1998, s 65(1), this PART, post. The decision whether or not to administer a reprimand or final warning is for the police alone and it is not subject to direction by the Crown Prosecution Service, though it is quite proper for the latter to proffer advice: *R (on the application of F) v Crown Prosecution Service and Chief Constable of Merseyside Police* [2003] EWHC Admin 3266, (2004) 168 JP 93.

2. Crime and Disorder Act 1998, s 65(2), this PART, post.

3. Crime and Disorder Act 1998, s 65(3), this PART, post.

4. Crime and Disorder Act 1998, s 65(4), this PART, post.

5. See this PART, post.

6. Crime and Disorder Act 1998, s 65(7), this PART, post.

7. Crime and Disorder Act 1998, s 66(1)–(2), this PART, post.

8. Crime and Disorder Act 1998, s 66(6), this PART, post.

9. Crime and Disorder Act 1998, s 66(4), this PART, post.

10. Crime and Disorder Act 1998, s 66(5), this PART, post.

11. Crime and Disorder Act 1998, s 65(6), this PART, post.

12. Crime and Disorder Act 1998, s 66(3), this PART, post.

13. Crime and Disorder Act 1998, s 65(8), this PART, post.

14. *R v Metropolitan Police Comr, ex p Thompson* [1997] 1 WLR 1519, [1997] 2 Cr App Rep 49.

15. *R (B) v Durham Constabulary* [2005] UKHL 21, [2005] 2 All ER 369, [2006] Crim LR 87 (failure to advise that warning for offence of indecent assault would result in requirement to register as a sex offender was not a breach of his rights under article 6 of the European Convention on Human Rights).

5–22   Informations, warrants and summonses.   The presence of a child or young person before the court may be secured in the same manner as for an adult, ie charged by the police and bailed or brought to court in custody, or a formal information laid and a summons or warrant in the first instance issued[1]. The general principle is that a summons should always be issued in preference to warrant where it would be as effectual unless the charge is of a serious nature[2]. Where a child or young person is charged with an offence or is for any other reason brought before the court, his parent or guardian may be required to attend with him for which purpose a summons may be issued.

The court is obliged to summon the parents or guardian of a child or young person under 16 years whereas it has a discretion for those over that age except in either case where it is satisfied that it would be unreasonable to require attendance. A local authority with parental responsibility would be summoned instead of the parents where the child or young person is in their care or accommodated by them, or in addition where he is allowed to live at home[3].

---

1. See para **1–420** in PART I: MAGISTRATES' COURTS, PROCEDURE, ante.
2. *O'Brien v Brabner* (1885) 49 JP Jo 227, DC.
3. Children and Young Persons Act 1933, s 34A, this PART, post.

Proceedings before the criminal courts

5–22A   Position under the European Convention on Human Rights.   The right to a fair trial under Article 6 of the European Convention applies to children and young persons as well as adults[1]. In particular, it is essential that a child charged with a criminal offence is dealt with in a manner which takes full account of his age, level of maturity and intellectual and emotional capacities, and that steps are taken to promote his ability to understand and participate in the proceedings[2]. In respect of a young child charged with a grave offence attracting high levels of media and public interest, it is necessary to conduct the hearing in such a way as to reduce as far as possible his feelings of intimidation and inhibition[3]. The attribution of criminal responsibility to or the trial on criminal charges of a child aged 11 does not in itself give rise to a breach of the Convention as long as the child is able to participate effectively in the trial[4].

The burden of establishing that he will not be able to participate effectively in the trial is on the defendant on the balance of probabilities[5]. "Effective participation" presupposes that the accused has a broad understanding of the nature of the trial process and of what is at stake for him or her, including the significance of any penalty which may be imposed. He or she, if necessary with the assistance of eg an interpreter, lawyer, social worker or friend should be able to understand the general thrust of what is said in court. The defendant should be able to follow what is said by the prosecution witnesses and, if represented, to explain to his own lawyers his version of events, point out any statements with which he disagrees and make them aware of any facts which should be put forward in his defence[4]. Practical steps which may be taken include: (i) keeping the defendant's level of cognitive functioning in mind; (ii) using concise and simple language: (iii) having regular breaks: (iv) taking additional time to explain court proceedings; (v) being proactive in ensuring the defendant understands the ingredients of the charge; (vi) explaining and ensuring the defendant understands the ingredients of the charge; (vii) explaining the possible outcomes and sentences; (viii) ensuring that cross-examination is carefully controlled so that questions are short and clear and frustration is minimised[5].

---

1. *Nortier v Netherlands* (1993) 17 EHRR 273.
2. *T v United Kingdom; V v United Kingdom* [2000] All ER 1024n, 30 EHHR121, 7BHRC 659, [2000] Crim LR 187, ECtHR.
3. *T v United Kingdom; V v United Kingdom* [2000] All ER 1024n, 30 EHHR121, 7BHRC 659, [2000] Crim LR 187, ECtHR.
4. See *S C v United Kingdom* (App No 60958/00) [2005] 1 FCR 251, [2005] Crim LR 130, EctHR.
5. *R (TP) v West London Youth Court* [2005] EWHC 2583 (Admin), [2006] 1 All ER 477, [2006] 1 WLR 1219, [2006] 1 Cr App R 25, 170 JP 82.

5–23   Restrictions on publicity.   Any court may direct that no newspaper report[1] or television broadcast[2] or cable programme service[3] shall reveal particulars calculated to lead to the identification of the child or young person concerned in the proceedings either as a party or witness except as permitted by direction of the court[4]. Moreover, the publication in a newspaper or on television of a picture of any child or young person is similarly restricted.

The court has a complete discretion to allow representations to be made to it by those parties whom it considers have a legitimate interest in the making of, or in opposing the making of, the order. In reaching a decision whether or not to make an order, the court is required to weigh the public interest in the full reporting of a crime, including the identification of the defendant, against the need to protect the victim from further harm[5].

The court will only a punish a person for the offence of publishing an article in breach of s 39 where the terms of the order are clear and unambiguous; to have the required degree of clarity the order must leave no doubt in the mind of the reasonable reader as to precisely what it prohibits[6].

Reports of proceedings should not be restricted unless there are reasons to do so which outweigh the legitimate interest of the public in receiving fair and accurate reports of criminal proceedings and knowing the identity of those in the community who have been guilty of criminal conduct. There is a clear distinction from the position in the youth court where under section 49 of the 1933 Act publication of the identity of the child or young person is prohibited subject to certain exceptions[7] and section 39 where the court has to exercise a discretion whether to make an order restricting publicity. To make an order under section 39 the court must have good reason to do so[8], but there is no requirement for a case to be rare or exceptional before a judge can exercise his broad discretion to lift the restriction on publicity in the Crown Court[9]. The underlying principle is that juveniles should be protected from publicity but the duty to have regard to the welfare of the child or young person before the court[10] is not to the exclusion of weight being attributed to other factors[8]. In exercising its discretion, considerable weight will be given to the age of the defendant but age is not the only factor. The fact that the defendant is unconvicted may be a good reason to make an order under section 39 but this factor will not continue to apply if he should be convicted[11]. On the other hand, the naming of the defendant may act as a deterrent to others[12] or considerations of rehabilitation may not apply where the defendant is not to be released into the community and, particularly in serious cases, after conviction the public might wish to know what has happended[8].

Application for an anti-social behaviour order under s 1(3) of the Crime and Disorder Act 1998 is made to the adult court and it will in most cases be inappropriate to make an order restricting publicity because the efficacy of the order may depend on the awareness of the local community of the identity of the person against whom the order is made[13]. However, it is not helpful to talk about presumptions as each case must be considered on its merits. In the case of an interim anti-social behaviour order consideration and importance must be attached to the interim nature of the proceedings and the fact that there may be at that stage no finding of fact made and that the allegations have not been proved nor has the defendant had the opportunity to challenge any of the allegations are weighty matters[14].

Chief officers of police have been requested to notify the clerk to the justices in advance of any proceedings where such a direction would appear appropriate. The clerk should inform the court at the beginning of the case, so that a timely direction may be given. Where proceedings are transferred for trial in a case where the section might apply, the clerk should forward with the depositions a statement indicating whether a direction had been given by the court[15]. Section 49 of the Children and Young Persons Act 1933 provides restrictions on newspaper reports of proceedings in youth courts; s 37 empowers the courts to be cleared while minors are giving evidence in certain cases.

The prohibition is not limited in time and applies to any subsequent report[16].

The direction itself must be restricted to the terms of s 39(1), either specifically using those terms or using words to like effect and no more. Section 39 does not empower a court to order in terms that the names of *defendants* be not published. However, if the effect of making a direction is that some details, such as the names of defendants, may not be published because publication would breach the direction, that is the practical application of the direction, and not a part of the terms of the direction itself[17].

Where the court makes an order under s 39 of the Children and Young Persons Act 1933, the following procedure should be adopted—

(a) The order should use the words of s 39(1) of the Act of 1933, or a suitable adaptation, and should relate the order to, for example, "the child/children named in the charge/indictment". However, if there is possible doubt as to which child or children the order relates, the justices should identify the relevant child or children with clarity.

(b) A written copy of the order should be drawn as soon as possible after the justices have made the order orally. That written order, or a copy of it, should then be available in the court office for representatives of the press to inspect.

(c) The fact that an order has been made should be communicated to those who were not present when it was made. This may be achieved by a short notice being included in the court's daily list[5].

---

1. Children and Young Persons Act 1933, s 39(1), this PART, post.
2. Children and Young Persons Act 1963, s 57(4).
3. Cable and Broadcasting Act 1984, s 57(1), Sch 5.
4. Children and Young Persons Act 1933, s 39(1), this PART, post.
5. *Ex p Crook* [1995] 1 All ER 537, [1995] 1 WLR 139, 159 JP 295, [1995] 2 FCR 153, [1995] 1 FLR 132.
6. *Briffet v DPP* (2001) 165 JPN 914.
7. See para **5–6**, ante.
8. *R v Central Criminal Court, ex p Simpkins* (1998) 163 JP 776, CA.
9. *R v Lee (a minor)* (1993) 96 Cr App Rep 188, followed in *R v Central Criminal Court, ex p W* [2001] 1 Cr App Rep 7. See also *R (on the application of T) v Crown Court at St Albans* [2002] EWHC 1129 (Admin), [2002] All ER (D) 308 (May), [2002] JPN 478 (evidence as to the effect of publicity on an offender's family is not, prima facie, a relevant matter).
10. *Children and Young Persons Act 1933*, section 44 in this PART, post.
11. See *Ex p Crook* [1995] 1 All ER 537, [1995] 1 WLR 139, sub nom *R v Central Criminal Court, ex p Crook and Godwin* [1995] 2 Cr App Rep 212.
12. *R v Inner London Crown Court, ex p Barnes* (1995) Times, 7 August.
13. *Medway Council v BBC* [2002] 1 FLR 104 and see *Reporting Restrictions in Magistrates' Courts* (Judicial Studies Board, the Newspaper Society and the Society of Editors, 2001). See also the listing of the considerations whether to lift reporting restrictions by Brown LJ in *R v Worcester Crown Court, ex p B* [2000] 1 Cr App R 11 cited by Elias J in *R (T) v St Albans Crown Court* [2002] EWHC 1129 (Admin) and referred to in *R (K) v Knowsley Metropolitan Borough Council* [2004] EWHC 1933 (Admin), 168 JP 461.
14. *R (K) v Knowsley Metropolitan Borough Council* [2004] EWHC 1933 (Admin), 168 JP 461.
15. Home Office Circulars No 18/1956, dated 14 February 1956 and No 14/1965, dated 28 January 1965.
16. *Re E (child abuse: evidence)* [1990] FCR 793, [1991] 1 FLR 420.
17. *R v Crown Court at Southwark, ex p Godwin* [1991] 3 All ER 818, CA.

5–24   Disuse of certain words.   The words "conviction" and "sentence" are not to be used in relation to children and young persons dealt with summarily[1].

---

1. Children and Young Persons Act 1933, s 59, this PART, post.

5–25   Oath.   The form of oath in the youth court and for any child or young person before any other court is modified and commences "I promise before Almighty God"[1]. The evidence of a child, ie a person under 14 years, shall be given unsworn[2].

Where either of the forms of oath is duly administered and taken instead of the other, it is deemed to have been duly administered and taken[3].

1. Children and Young Persons Act 1963, s 29(1), this PART, post.
2. Criminal Justice Act 1988, s 33A(1), in PART II: EVIDENCE, ante.
3. Children and Young Persons Act 1963, s 29(2), this PART, post.

5–26   Legal aid.   This is available as for adult offenders and subject to the same criteria[1]. However in relation to an application for legal aid made on behalf of a person who has not attained the age of 17 by his parent or guardian "applicant" means that person, otherwise it means the person making the application[2]. The means assessed are those of the applicant except that where he is under 16 years instead of, or in addition to, ordering him to pay a contribution, the court may order "an appropriate contributor" to pay a contribution. Appropriate contributor is defined as his mother or father or guardian[3].

1. Legal Aid Act 1988, s 22, see PART I: MAGISTRATES' COURTS, PROCEDURE, ante.
2. Legal Aid in Criminal and Care Proceedings (General) Regulations 1989, reg 3, see PART I: MAGISTRATES COURTS, PROCEDURE, ante.
3. Ibid.

5–27   Adjournments and remands.   When proceedings are adjourned, the court may adjourn the case or remand the accused. A child or young person may be remanded on bail, into local authority accommodation or custody. Remand hearings may be heard by an adult or youth court[1] and by a single justice[2]. Different considerations apply to remand decisions depending on whether the young person has attained 17 years. A defendant aged 17 years and over is treated in the same way as an adult, ie the Bail Act 1976 applies[3] and a refusal of bail will result in a remand into prison custody. The Bail Act also applies to defendants under 17 years except that a child or young person may be refused bail for his "own welfare" rather than "own protection" in the case of an adult. Where bail is refused remand will normally be to local authority accommodation. This is subject to two exceptions:

   (*a*)   in certain circumstances the remand may be to the custody of a constable for a period of up to 24 hours[4]; and

   (*b*)   where the young person is male, has attained the age of 15 and is a person to whom the court has declared that sub-s(5) of s 23 of the Children and Young Persons Act 1969 applies, the remand will be to local authority accommodation with a requirement that the young person be kept in secure accommodation or prison[5].

Section 131 of the Criminal Justice and Police Act 2001 empowers the court, subject to various conditions, to impose upon a child or young person aged 12–16 requirements as to electronic monitoring of compliance with bail conditions. Section 132 makes similar provision for monitoring compliance with the conditions of a non-secure remand.

1. Children and Young Persons Act 1933, s 46, this PART, post.
2. Children and Young Persons Act 1933, s 46, this PART, post and the Magistrates' Courts Act 1980, s 121, see PART I: MAGISTRATES' COURTS, PROCEDURE, ante.
3. See PART I: MAGISTRATES' COURTS, PROCEDURE, ante.
4. Magistrates' Courts Act 1980, s 128(7), see PART I: MAGISTRATES' COURTS, PROCEDURE, ante; and the Children and Young Persons Act 1969, s 23(14)(*b*), this PART, post.
5. See this PART, post.

5–27A   Remands and committals to local authority accommodation[1].   Section 23 of the Children and Young Persons Act 1969[2] makes provision for the remand and committal to local authority accommodation of children and young persons. Save for 15 or 16 year old males for whom there are special provisions, which are described in paragraph **5–28**, the provisions for other children and young persons are as set out below.

Where a court remands a child or young person charged with or convicted of one or more offences or commits him for trial or sentence, and he is not released on bail, the remand or committal shall be to local authority accommodation[3].

Where a court, after consultation with the designated local authority, imposes a security requirement the local authority shall place and keep the child or young person in secure accommodation[4].

A court may only impose a security requirement in respect of[5]:

—   a child who is of the age of 12 or 13;

—   a person who is of the age of 14;

—   any female person who is of the age of 15 or 16,

if the child or young person:

1.   is charged with or has been convicted of a violent or sexual offence, or an offence punishable in the case of an adult with imprisonment for a term of 14 years or more;

2.   or he is charged with or has been convicted of one or more imprisonable offences which, together with any other imprisonable offences of which he has been convicted in any

proceedings, amount, or would if he were convicted of the offences with which he is charged, amount to a recent history of repeatedly committing imprisonable offences while remanded on bail or to local authority accommodation

and, in either case the court is of the opinion, after considering all of the options for the remand of the person, that only a security requirement would be adequate:

(a) to protect the public from serious harm from him or to prevent the commission by him of imprisonable offences; or

(b) to prevent the commission by him of imprisonable offences[6].

A court that imposes a security requirement must state in open court and explain to the child or young person in ordinary language why it is of that opinion[7].

A court shall not impose a security requirement without first affording the child or young person with an opportunity of applying for legal aid and being legally represented[8].

A court that remands a child or young person to local authority accommodation without imposing a security requirement may impose other conditions which are described in paragraph **5–29** below.

---

1. A remand to local authority secure accommodation is custodial in nature and a youth so remanded, though not so detained due to lack of space, can nonetheless be found to be in lawful custody and, thus, guilty of escaping from such custody if he absconds before his case is called on (*E v DPP* [2002] EWHC 433 (Admin), [2002] All ER (D) 348 (Feb), [2002] Crim LR 737). See also *H v DPP* [2003] EWHC 878 (Admin), (2003) 167 JP 486, [2003] Crim LR 560 (remand to local authority accommodation without a security requirement is capable of being custodial in nature and the defendant was, on the facts, in lawful custody).
2. See this PART, post.
3. Children and Young Persons Act 1969, s 23(1), this PART, post.
4. CYPA 1969, s 23(4), this PART, post.
5. CYPA 1969, s 23(5), this PART, post, and the Secure Remands and Committals (Prescribed Description of Children and Young Persons) Order 1999, SI 1999/1265.
6. CYPA 1969, s 23(5) and (5AA), this PART, post.
7. CYPA 1969, s 23(6), this PART, post.
8. CYPA 1969, s 23(5A), this PART, post.

5–28 Remands and committals of 15- or 16-year-old males. Section 23 of the Children and Young Persons Act 1969 is modified in relation to a male person who is of the age of 15 or 16[1]. A male person aged 15 or 16 shall be remanded to local authority accommodation unless the court declares him to be one to whom s 23(5), as modified, applies[2].

Where a court, after consultation with a probation officer, a social worker of a local authority social services department or a member of a youth offending team, declares a person to be subject to s 23(5):

1. it shall remand him to local authority accommodation and require him to be placed and kept in secure accommodation (referred to hereinafter as *a security requirement*), if after such consultation, the court declares that by reason of his physical or emotional immaturity or a propensity of his to harm himself, it would be undesirable for him to be remanded to a remand centre or a prison, and if the court has been notified that secure accommodation is available for him;

2. it shall remand him to a remand centre, if paragraph 1 above does not apply and it has been notified that such a centre is available for the reception from the court of persons to whom s 23(5) applies;

3. it shall remand him to a prison if neither paragraph 1 nor paragraph 2 above applies3.

A court may only make a declaration under s 23(5) in relation to a person who:

(a) is charged with or has been convicted of a violent or sexual offence, or an offence punishable in the case of an adult with imprisonment for a term of 14 years or more;

(b) or he is charged with or has been convicted of one or more imprisonable offences which, together with any other imprisonable offences of which he has been convicted in any proceedings, amount, or would if he were convicted of the offences with which he is charged, amount to a recent history of repeatedly committing imprisonable offences while remanded on bail or to local authority accommodation

and, in either case the court is of the opinion, after considering all of the options for the remand of the person, that only remanding him to a remand centre or prison, or to local authority accommodation with a security requirement, would be adequate to protect the public from serious harm from him or to prevent the commission by him of imprisonable offences[4].

A court that makes such a declaration must state in open court and explain to the young person in ordinary language why it is of that opinion[5]. A court shall not make a declaration without first affording the young person an opportunity of applying for legal aid and being legally represented[6].

A court that remands a young person to local authority accommodation without imposing a security requirement may impose other conditions which are described in paragraph **5–29** below.

Where a young person is remanded to local authority accommodation without the imposition of a security requirement, a relevant court may, on the application of the designated authority, declare him to be a person to whom s 23(5) applies, and on its doing so, the powers in paragraphs 1–3 above may be exercised[7].

---

1. The modified s 23 is set out in the notes to s 23 in para **5–601**, post.
2. Children and Young Persons Act 1969, s 23(1), as modified, this PART, post.

3. Ibid, s 23(4), as modified, this PART, post.
4. Ibid, s 23(5) and (5AA), as modified, this PART, post.
5. Ibid, s 23(6), as modified, this PART, post.
6. Ibid, s 23(4A), as modified, this PART, post.
7. Ibid, s 23(9A), as modified, this PART, post.

5–29   Local authority accommodation: meaning and conditions that may be imposed.   Local authority accommodation is defined as accommodation provided by or on behalf of a local authority within the meaning of the Children Act 1989[1].

On remanding a child or young person to local authority accommodation, without imposing a security requirement, the court may, after consultation with the designated authority:

1. require that person to comply with any such conditions as could be imposed under s 3(6) of the Bail Act 1976 as if that person were then being granted bail[2];
2. impose on the designated authority requirements:

    (*a*) for securing compliance with any conditions imposed on that person under 1 above; or
    (*b*) stipulating that he shall not be placed with a named person[3].

Where a person is remanded to local authority accommodation, a relevant court may on the application of the designated authority impose on that person any such conditions as could be imposed under paragraph 1 above if the court were then remanding him to such accommodation and where it does so, may impose on that authority any requirements for securing compliance with the conditions so imposed[4]. The relevant court may also on the application of that authority or the person concerned, vary or revoke any conditions or requirements imposed under the above provisions[5].

A child or young person in breach of a condition imposed in accordance with paragraph 1 above may be arrested by a constable and brought before a justice or the court within 24 hours so that the remand decision may be reconsidered[6]. Remand to local authority accommodation with conditions is not the same as bail with conditions. However, because the court has found that exceptions apply justifying a refusal of bail does not mean that it follows that the criteria for making a secure accommodation order will be satisfied[7].

Reference above to the "relevant court", in relation to a person remanded to local authority accommodation means the court by which he was so remanded, or any magistrates' court having jurisdiction in that place where he is for the time being[8]. Section 131 of the Criminal Justice and Police Act 2001 empowers the court, subject to various conditions, to impose upon a child or young person aged 12–16 requirements as to electronic monitoring of compliance with bail conditions. Section 132 makes similar provision for monitoring compliance with the conditions of a non-secure remand.

1. Children and Young Persons Act 1969, s 70(1), this PART, post.
2. Children and Young Persons Act 1969, s 23(7), this PART, post, and s 23(7), as modified, this PART, post.
3. Children and Young Persons Act 1969, s 23(9), this PART, post.
4. Children and Young Persons Act 1969, s 23(10), this PART, post.
5. Children and Young Persons Act 1969, s 23(11), this PART, post.
6. Children and Young Persons Act 1969, s 23A, this PART, post.
7. *Re W and D (secure accommodation)* [1995] 3 FCR 806, [1995] 2 FLR 807.
8. Children and Young Persons Act 1969, s 23(12), this PART, post.

5–30   Secure accommodation.   A local authority may not use secure accommodation, ie accommodation provided for the purpose of restricting liberty[1], for a period of more than 72 hours whether consecutively or in aggregate, in any period of 28 consecutive days without an order of the court authorising the use of secure accommodation[2]. There are exemptions for public holidays and Sundays[3] and for disregarding periods prior to a court authorisation[4]. These provisions apply to all children accommodated by a local authority by virtue of a warrant under the Children and Young Persons Act 1969[5].

The primary statutory provision, s 25 of the Children Act 1989, which is supplemented by the Secure Accommodation Regulations 1991 and the Secure Accommodation (No 2) Regulations 1991[6], relates both to family and criminal jurisdictions. The inter-relationship between s 25 and reg 6(1)(*b*) of the Children (Secure Accommodation) Regulations 1991 was considered in *Re G (secure accommodation order)* [2001] 3 FCR 47, [2001] 1 FLR 884, where it was held that where a child had previously been remanded to local authority accommodation and had not committed a further offence, the conditions specified in reg 6(1)(*b*) had not been met, but the Youth Court could nonetheless make a secure accommodation order if it was satisfied under s 25(3) that all the criteria specified in s 25(1) had been met and, indeed, had to do so. The terminology of the family courts is used, ie the subject of any application is a "child" defined by the Children Act 1989, s 105(1) as a person under 18 years and not as defined in the Children and Young Persons Acts, ie a person under 14 years. In any event, persons who have attained 17 years will not be remanded to local authority accommodation as the provisions relating to adults will be applicable. Jurisdiction is conferred on the criminal courts, ie the adult magistrates' and youth courts (but not the Crown Court) in criminal proceedings by the Criminal Justice Act 1991, s 60(3)[7].

It is the restriction of liberty which is the essential factor in determining what is secure accommodation, accordingly, a hospital ward may be "secure accommodation"[8].

In determining an application for a secure accommodation order the "welfare principle" and the "no order" principles of the Children Act 1989 do not apply. Where the court has found any of the criteria in the Children Act or the regulations is satisfied, it is bound to make a secure accommodation order[9].

1. Children Act 1989, s 25, see PART IV: FAMILY LAW, ante.
2. Secure Accommodation Regulations 1991, reg 10(1), see PART IV: FAMILY LAW, ante.
3. Secure Accommodation Regulations 1991, reg 10(3), see PART IV: FAMILY LAW, ante.

   4. Secure Accommodation Regulations 1991, reg 10(2) see PART IV: FAMILY LAW, ante.
   5. Children Act 1989, s 25, see PART IV: FAMILY LAW, ante. The restrictions do not apply to children specified in reg 5 of the Secure Accommodation Regulations 1991, eg children detained under ss 90, 91 Powers of Criminal Courts (Sentencing) Act 2000, in PART III: SENTENCING, ante.
   6. See PART IV: FAMILY LAW, ante.
   7. In PART III: SENTENCING, ante.
   8. *A Metropolitan Borough Council v DB* [1997] 1 FLR 767.
   9. *Re M (a minor) (secure accommodation order)* [1995] 3 All ER 407, [1995] 2 FCR 373, [1995] 2 WLR 302, [1995] 1 FLR 418, CA and the Children Act 1989, s 25(4) in PART IV: FAMILY LAW, ante.

5–31   Secure accommodation: application.   The Criminal Justice Act 1991, s 60(3)[1] provides that in the case of a child or young person who has been remanded or committed to local authority accommodation by a youth court or magistrates' court other than a youth court, any application under s 25 of the Children Act 1989 (use of accommodation for restricting liberty) shall, not withstanding anything in s 92(2) of the Magistrates' Courts Act 1980, be made to that court. For this purpose the words "that court" are used in a generic sense to mean the appropriate youth court and jurisdiction is not confined to the remanding court[2]. The procedure is prescribed by the Magistrates' Courts (Children and Young Persons) Rules 1992[3].

   No court shall exercise its powers relating to secure accommodation in respect of a child or young person who is not legally represented in that court unless, having been informed of his right to apply for legal aid and having had the opportunity to do so, he refused or failed to apply[4]. It is implicit that legal representation, in order to be effective, must involve the taking of instructions. Therefore, the local authority must inform the child or young person of an application which is to be made to the court, the child or young person must have the opportunity to be legally represented and to give instructions to the legal representative[4].

   Although there is no statutory obligation to provide justices' reasons as in the family proceedings court, it is incumbent on the youth court to explain the general nature and effect of the order[5]. It is essential that there should be clear recordings of facts as found by the court, and in order to reach those considerations it is necessary for there to be sworn evidence[4]. No form of application is prescribed but notice must be served on the Clerk of the Court and other persons specified in the rules[6].

   No provision is made for the Crown Court to make a secure accommodation order. In view of s 60(3) of the Criminal Justice Act 1991, we would submit that an application in respect of a child or young person committed to the Crown Court should be made in the first instance to the magistrates' court or youth court which committed him[7]. When the defendant is no longer held in custody on the warrant issued by the youth court, after appearing at the Crown Court, application for further authorisation must be made to the family proceedings court[8].

---

   1. In PART III: SENTENCING, ante.
   2. *Liverpool City Council v B* [1995] 1 WLR 505, [1995] 2 FCR 105, [1995] 2 FLR 84.
   3. In this PART, post.
   4. *Re AS (secure accommodation order)* [1999] 2 FCR 749, [1999] 1 FLR 103.
   5. *A E v Staffordshire County Council* (1994) 159 JP 367.
   6. Magistrates' Court (Children and Young Persons) Rules 1992, r 14, this PART, post. Failure to follow these requirements will mean that any order made will not be valid. See *D v X City Council* [1985] FLR 275 (a case involving care proceedings and the predecessor regulations).
   7. See also *The Children Act 1989, Guidance and Regulations, Volume 1, Guardians ad litem and the Court Related Issues* (Department of Health), 1991, para 5.5.
   8. See *Applications for Secure Accommodation – a Legal Labyrinth* (1991) 155 JPN 777.

5–32   Secure accommodation: criteria.   On an application for a secure accommodation order in respect of a child (ie a person under 17 years) detained under the Police and Criminal Evidence Act 1984, s 38(6), or who is remanded in local authority accommodation and:

   (*a*)   is charged with or has been convicted of:

       (i)   a violent or sexual offence[1]; or
       (ii)   an offence punishable with 14 years' imprisonment or more; or

   (*b*)   has a recent history of absconding while remanded to local authority accommodation, and is charged with or has been convicted of an imprisonable offence, alleged or found to have been committed while so remanded[2],

the local authority must establish that any accommodation other than that provided for the purpose of restricting liberty is inappropriate because:

   (*a*)   the child is likely to abscond from such accommodation; or
   (*b*)   the child is likely to injure himself or other people if he is kept in any such accommodation[3].

In other cases the criteria to be satisfied are those applicable to family cases[4].
The checklist set out below may be of assistance:

Secure accommodation applications (criminal proceedings) procedure—checklist

Applicant:	Local authority looking after child SI 1991/1505, reg 8.
Notice of intention to apply:	(Child already kept in secure accommodation) SI 1991/1505, reg 14.
Notice of application:	(No form of notice prescribed) SI 1992/2071, r 14, sent to the clerk of the court: —grounds of proceedings; — names and addresses of persons to whom copy of notice sent in accordance with r 14; — date, time and place of hearing.
Court:	Court which has remanded or committed the relevant minor to local authority accommodation: CJA 1991, s 60(3).
Legal aid:	Relevant minor must have been informed of right to apply etc: CA 1989, s 25.
Before the hearing:	Court to have arranged for copies of any report to have been made available so far as practicable to persons specified: SI 1992/2071, r 21.

Procedure at the hearing:	Magistrates' Courts (Children and Young Persons) Rules 1992, SI 1992/2071, Part III, rr 13–22, (adult and youth court (r 13(2)):

— court to explain nature of proceedings (r 17);
— conduct of case on behalf of relevant minor (r 18);
— local authority
opening speech (r 16(3))
evidence
(evidence in absence of relevant minor or parent (r 19));
— court to explain procedure at end of applicant's case (r 20);
— (representations by parents/guardians (r 15));
— relevant minor's case;
— closing speech by relevant minor;
— court determines whether relevant criteria are satisfied;
— (where criteria are satisfied) consideration of report (r 21(2)(3));
— (where application adjourned) interim order (CA 1989, s 25(5));
— explanation by court of manner in which it proposes to deal
with the case and effect of order (r 22);
further representations if any.

Form: (Interim order) Form 33.
          (Final order) Form 32.

1. Defined by the Children and Young Persons Act 1969, s 23(12) in this PART, post.
2. Children Act 1989, s 25(1) and the Secure Accommodation Regulations 1991, reg 6(2), see PART IV: FAMILY LAW, ante.
3. Secure Accommodation Regulations 1991, reg 6(2), see PART IV: FAMILY LAW, ante.
4. See the Children Act 1989, s 25 in PART IV: FAMILY LAW, ante.

5–33 Appeal.   An appeal against the making of a secure accommodation order would be to the Family Division of the High Court in accordance with s 94 of the Children Act 1989.

Orders in respect of children and young persons

5–34 Remittal to the youth court.   A child or young person should normally be dealt with by a youth court acting for the place where he habitually resides; except in the case of homicide, other courts, including the Crown Court, are bound to remit an offender to such a court unless they are satisfied that it would be undesirable to do so[1]. Nevertheless, it would seem that a youth court for the same Commission area in which the child or young person resides would have jurisdiction in a particular case.

Where a child or young person is found guilty of an offence before the Crown Court, the court should exercise its power to remit the minor to a youth court unless the Crown Court considers that there are reasons why it might be undesirable to remit the case to the youth court, eg that the judge who presided over the trial might be better informed of the facts and circumstances; that there was a risk of unacceptable disparity if co-defendants were sentenced in different courts; that remission might lead to delay, duplication of proceedings and fruitless expense, and the different provisions for appeal against conviction and sentence[2].

There is no appeal against the order of remission[3]. But appeal lies against any order of the court to which the case is remitted as if he had been found guilty by that court[3]. The remitting court may give directions as to the custody of the offender or his release on bail[4]. The clerk must send a certificate to the relevant youth court setting out the nature of the offence, that the offender has been found guilty and that the case has been remitted for the purpose of being dealt with under the Children and Young Persons Act 1933, s 56[4].

Where a case has been remitted to another youth court under s 56(1) of the 1933 Act for sentence, the receiving court has jurisdiction to accept a change of plea to not guilty and then go on to try the information[5].

1. Powers of Criminal Courts (Sentencing) Act 2000, s 8(1), (2), in PART III: SENTENCING, ante.
2. R v Lewis (1984) 79 Cr App Rep 94, [1984] Crim LR 303.
3. Powers of Criminal Courts (Sentencing) Act 2000, s 8(5), in PART III: SENTENCING, ante.
4. Powers of Criminal Courts (Sentencing) Act 2000, s 8(4), in PART III: SENTENCING, ante.
5. R v Stratford Youth Court, ex p Conde [1997] 1 WLR 113, 161 JP 308, [1997] 2 Cr App Rep 1, DC.

5–36 Powers of the magistrates' court.   Where an adult magistrates' court has convicted a child or young person[1] of an offence it may refer to a youth offender panel where the relevant conditions are satisfied or where the court is not required to refer him to such a panel it may deal with him if it is of the opinion that the case may properly be dealt with by means of:

(a) an absolute or conditional discharge[2];
(b) an order for payment of a fine[3],
(c) an order requiring his parent or guardian to enter into a recognizance to take proper care of him and exercise control over him[4],

with or without any other order that the court has power to make when absolutely or conditionally discharging an offender.

The power to order the bind over of a parent was formally a disposal in its own right under the CYPA 1969, s 7(7)(*c*). Now it is an ancillary order to substantive order, eg a discharge. The adult court may only bind over the parent when discharging or fining the defendant. The court may also make such orders as compensation[5], restitution, forfeiture, endorsement or disqualification.

1. Powers of Criminal Courts (Sentencing) Act 2000, s 8(6), (7), (8), in Part III: Sentencing, ante.
2. See para **5–43**, post.
3. See para **5–45**, post.
4. Powers of Criminal Courts (Sentencing) Act 2000, s 150, in Part III: Sentencing, ante; para **5–47**.
5. Compensation was made both an ancillary order and a sentence in its own right by the Criminal Justice Act 1988. It has not been judicially determined whether an adult magistrates' court may make a compensation order without discharging or fining the offender.

5–37   Powers of the youth court.   *The Criminal Justice Act 2003 established a new range of community orders, and new powers in the event of breach, for offenders aged 16 and over. The new orders in respect of 16 and 17 year-olds will not come into effect until 4 April 2009*[1]*. Pending this, the provisions of ss 41–58 of, and Schs 2 and 4 to, the 2000 Act continue to have effect (subject to any necessary modification)*[2].

   In relation to younger offenders, the court may make any of the following orders, which are known as "youth community orders": a curfew order; an exclusion order; an attendance centre order; a supervision order; or an action plan order. The provisions relating to youth community orders are contained in the Powers of Criminal Courts (Sentencing) Act 2000 (as amended by the 2003 Act).

   The youth court may make any of the orders outlined below except detention under the Powers of Criminal Courts Act 2000, ss 90, 91, in Part III: Sentencing, ante, since this may only be imposed following conviction on indictment. Nor may a youth court impose a restriction on discharge from hospital where a hospital order is made[3].

   A youth court is not required to adjourn any proceedings for an offence at any stage by reason only of the fact that the court has committed the accused for trial for another offence or that the accused is charged with another offence[4].

1. See the Criminal Justice Act 2003 (Commencement No 8 and Transitional and Savings Provisions) Order 2005, SI 2005/950, as amended by SI 2007/391. For older offenders, the new provisions came into effect on 4 April 2005 in respect of offences committed on or after that date.
2. SI 2005/950, Sch 2, para 8.
3. Mental Health Act 1983, s 41, in Part VIII: Mental Health, post.
4. Magistrates Courts Act 1980, s 10(3A), in Part I: Magistrates Courts, Procedure, ante.

5–39   General consideration.   Every court dealing with a child or young person who is brought before it, either as an offender or otherwise, shall have regard to the welfare of the child or young person[1].

1. Children and Young Persons Act 1933, s 44, this Part, post.

5–40   Information for the court.   Antecedents will include any reprimands and warnings.

5–41   Reports.   Where a local authority or local education authority have been notified that proceedings have been brought against a child or young person, it is their duty, unless they are of the opinion that it is unnecessary to do so, to make such investigations and provide the court before which the proceedings are heard with such information relating to the home surroundings, school record, health and character of the person in respect of whom proceedings are brought as appear to the authority likely to assist the court[1].

   It is the duty of the person laying an information to commence criminal proceedings to inform the local authority of the proceedings[2].

   In practice all reports are now provided to the youth court by the youth offending team..

1. Children and Young Persons Act 1969, s 9(1), this Part, post.
2. Children and Young Persons Act 1969, s 5(8), this Part, post.

5–41A   Effect of crossing an age threshold between date of offence and date of conviction. Where a defendant crosses an important age threshold between the date of the commission of the offence and the date of conviction the starting point for sentencing is the sentence that the defendant would have been likely to receive at the former date; other facts might have to be considered, but there have to be good reasons for departing from the starting point[1]. See the Children and Young Persons Act 1963, s 29 at para **5–337** post for the powers of the court in a case where proceedings are begun in respect of a young person who attains 18 before the conclusion of the proceedings to make any order which it could have made if he had not attained that age.

1. *R v Ghafoor* [2003] 1 Cr App R (S) 84, [2002] EWCA Crim 1857, [2002] Crim LR 739 (offender charged with riot attained 18 before he was convicted; sentenced reduced from 4½ years' detention to 18 months, the length of the DTO he would have received, taking his guilty plea into account, if he had been sentenced at the date of the commission of the offence. See also *R v LM* [2002] EWCA Crim 3407, [2003] 2 Cr App R (S) 26 (DTO quashed where the defendant attained the age of 15 between the date of offence and the date of conviction); and *R v Jones* [2003] EWCA Crim 1609, 1 Cr.App.R.(S.) 18 (where the defendant attained 18 after the offence, received a sentence of 15 months' detention, and this was reduced to 12 months because the judge may not have been aware that 15 months was not one of the terms specified in s 101 of the Powers of Criminal Courts (Sentencing) Act 2000 in relation to detention and training orders).

5–42   Available orders for children and young persons.   In the following list of orders available to courts in dealing with a minor[1] (age 10–17 inclusive), only those marked with an asterisk * may be used by a magistrates' court that is not a youth court[2].

> *Referral order *Powers of Criminal Courts (Sentencing) Act 2000*, s 16;
> *Absolute and conditional discharge *Powers of Criminal Courts (Sentencing) Act 2000*, ss 12–15;
> Compensation *Powers of Criminal Courts (Sentencing) Act 2000*, ss 130–134;
> Order made under s 1C of the Crime and Disorder Act 1998 (Anti-social Behaviour), *Crime and Disorder Act 1998, s 1C*;
> *Fine *Powers of Criminal Courts (Sentencing) Act 2000*, s 135;
> *Binding over parent or guardian *Powers of Criminal Courts (Sentencing) Act 2000*, s 150;
> Reparation order *Powers of Criminal Courts (Sentencing) Act 2000*, ss 73–75, Sch 8;
> Action plan order *Powers of Criminal Courts (Sentencing) Act 2000*, ss 69–72, Sch 8;
> Attendance centre *Powers of Criminal Courts (Sentencing) Act 2000*, ss 60–62, Sch 5;
> Supervision *Powers of Criminal Courts (Sentencing) Act 2000*, ss 63–68, Schs 6, 7;
> Exclusion order *Powers of Criminal Courts (Sentencing) Act 2000*, ss 40A–C.
> Community rehabilitation order (age 16 and over) *Powers of Criminal Courts (Sentencing) Act 2000*, ss 41–45, Schs 2, 3;
> Community punishment order (age 16 and over) *Powers of Criminal Courts (Sentencing) Act 2000*, s 46–50, Sch 3;
> Community punishment and rehabilitation order (age 16 and over) *Powers of Criminal Courts (Sentencing) Act 2000*, s 51, Sch 3;
> Curfew (age 16 and over) *Powers of Criminal Courts (Sentencing) Act 2000*, ss 37–40, Sch 3;
> Drug treatment and testing order *Powers of Criminal Courts (Sentencing) Act 2000*, ss 52–59, Sch 3;
> Detention and training order *Powers of Criminal Courts (Sentencing) Act 2000*, s 89;
> Punishment of certain grave crimes (Crown Court only) *Powers of Criminal Courts (Sentencing) Act 2000*, ss 90, 91.

Committal for sentence of dangerous young offenders *Powers of Criminal Courts (Sentencing) Act 2000, s 3C*.

Before finally disposing of the case or before remitting the case to another court, unless it considers it undesirable to do so, the court shall inform the child or young person and his parent or guardian if present, or any person assisting him in his defence, of the manner in which it proposes to deal with the case, and allow any of those persons so informed to make representations[3].

---

1. See also **Orders in respect of mentally disordered offenders**, para **3–320**, ante et seq: **Ancillary orders**; para **3–170, Binding over, recognizances** and para **3–561**, ante: **Committal to the Crown Court for sentence**.
2. Powers of Criminal Courts (Sentencing) Act 2000, s 8(6), in PART III: SENTENCING, ante.
3. Criminal Procedure Rules 2005, Part 44, in PART I: MAGISTRATES' COURTS, PROCEDURE, ante.

5–42A   Referral to a youth offender panel.   Where a youth court or other magistrates' court is dealing with a person under the age of 18 for an offence and—

    (a) neither the offence nor any connected offence is one for which the sentence is fixed by law;
    (b) the court is not, in respect of the offence or any connected offence, proposing to impose a custodial sentence on the offender or make a hospital order in his case; and
    (c) the court is not proposing to discharge him absolutely in respect of the offence,

if referral is available, the court must, if the compulsory referral conditions are satisfied, or may, if the discretionary referral conditions are satisfied, sentence the offender for the offence by ordering him to be referred to a youth offender panel[1].

Referral is available to a court if it has been notified by the Secretary of State that arrangements for the implementation of referral orders are available in the area in which it appears to the court that the offender resides or will reside and the notice has not been withdrawn[2].

The compulsory referral conditions are satisfied in relation to an offence if the offence is an offence punishable with imprisonment and the offender—

    (a) pleaded guilty to the offence and to any connected offence;
    (b) has never been convicted by or before a court in the United Kingdom of any offence other than the offence and any connected offence; and
    (c) has never been bound over in criminal proceedings in England and Wales or Northern Ireland to keep the peace or to be of good behaviour[3].

The discretionary referral conditions are satisfied in relation to an offence if the offence is not an offence punishable with imprisonment and the offender –

    (a) pleaded guilty to the offence and to any connected offence;
    (b) has never been convicted by or before a court in the United Kingdom of any offence other than the offence and any connected offence; and
    (c) has never been bound over in criminal proceedings in England and Wales or Northern Ireland to keep the peace or to be of good behaviour[4].

The discretionary referral conditions also are satisfied in relation to an offence if—

    (a) the offender is being dealt with by the court for the offence and one or more connected offences (whether or not any of them is an offence punishable with imprisonment);

(b)   although he pleaded guilty to at least one of the offences mentioned in paragraph (a), he also pleaded not guilty to at least one of them;

(c)   he has never been convicted by or before a court in the United Kingdom of any offence other than the offences mentioned in paragraph (a); and

(d)   he has never been bound over in criminal proceedings in England and Wales or Northern Ireland to keep the peace or to be of good behaviour[5].

An offence is connected with another if the offender falls to be dealt with it at the same time as he is dealt with for the other offence whether or not he is convicted of the offences at the same time or by or before the same court[6].

For the purposes of these provisions an offender who has been convicted of an offence in respect of which he was conditionally discharged (whether by a court in England or Wales or in Northern Ireland) shall be treated as having been convicted of that offence[7].

A referral order must—

(a)   specify the youth offending team responsible for implementing the order;

(b)   require the offender to attend each of the meetings of a youth offender panel to be established by the team for the offender; and

(c)   specify the period for which any youth offender contract taking effect between the offender and the panel is to have effect being a period not less than 3 months nor more than 12 months[8].

On making a referral order the court must explain to the offender in ordinary language—

(a)   the effect of the order; and

(b)   the consequences which may follow—

    (i)   if no youth offender contract takes effect between the offender and the panel, or

    (ii)   if the offender breaches any of the terms of any such contract[9].

Where a court makes a referral order in respect of an offence it may not deal with him for the offence in any of the prohibited ways. In respect of an connected offence, the court must either make a referral order or an absolute discharge and may not deal with the offence in any of the prohibited ways[10].

The prohibited ways are: a community sentence; a fine; a reparation order; a conditional discharge; a bind over; binding over of parent or guardian; a parenting order[11]. Where the compulsory referral conditions are satisfied the court may not defer sentence but its power of remission to another court, adjournment, committal to the Crown Court or under the mental health legislation are unaffected[12].

On making a referral order, the court may order an "appropriate person" ie a parent or guardian with whom the offender is allowed to live and, where the offender is looked after by a local authority, a representative of that local authority, to attend meetings of the youth offender panel[13]. The court must not make an order if it is satisfied that it would be unreasonable to do so, or to the extent that it would be unreasonable to do so[14]. If the person is not present in court when the order is made, the court must send him a copy of the order forthwith[15].

Where a referral order has been made, it is the duty of the youth offending team specified in the order to establish a youth offender panel for the offender[16]. The panel must arrange a first and subsequent meetings of the panel for the purpose of reaching an agreement with the offender on a programme of behaviour the aim of which is the prevention of re-offending by the offender. Where a programme is agreed between the offender and the panel, the panel must record the programme in writing in language capable of being readily understood by, or explained to, the offender and it must be signed by the offender and a member of the panel on the panel's behalf and the programme as set out in the record takes effect as a "youth offender contract" a copy of which must be given or sent to the offender[17]. Any youth offender contract may be kept under review and progress meetings held by the panel where it appears expedient to review the offender's progress in implementing the programme of behaviour contained in the contract or any other matter arising in connection with the contract and a progress meeting must be held where the offender seeks a variation in the contract or to have the referral order revoked by a court on account of a significant change in his circumstances making compliance with any youth offender contract impractical, or it appears to the panel that the offender is in breach of any of the terms of the contract[18].

The term of the programme may, in particular, include provision for: financial or other reparation; mediation sessions with the victim; unpaid work or service in or for the community; curfew; school attendance; specified activities; the offender to present himself to specified persons at specified times and places; to stay away from specified places or persons; enabling the offender's compliance with the programme to be supervised and recorded. The programme may not provide for the electronic monitoring of the offender's whereabouts; or for the offender to have imposed on him any physical restriction on his movements[19].

Where the compliance period in the case of a youth offender contract is due to expire, the specified youth offending team must arrange for the holding, before the end of that period, of a meeting, the "final meeting" of the youth offender panel which must—

(a)   review the extent of the offender's compliance to date with the terms of the contract; and

(b)   decide, in the light of that review, whether his compliance with those terms has been such as to justify the conclusion that, by the time the compliance period expires, he will have satisfactorily completed the contract,

and the panel must give the offender written confirmation of its decision[20]. If the panel concludes that he will satisfactorily complete the contract, the referral order will be discharged. Otherwise, the panel must refer the offender back to the court[21].

A youth offender panel may refer an offender back to court by sending a report to the appropriate court ie the youth court for the petty sessions area in which he resides or will reside, or a magistrates' court for that area where he will have attained 18 years on first appearing before the court in pursuance of the referral back[22]. The court must then cause the offender to appear before it by issuing a summons, or if the report is substantiated on oath, a warrant[23].

If it is proved to the satisfaction of the court—

(a) that, so far as the decision relied on any finding of fact by the panel, the panel was entitled to make that finding in the circumstances, and

(b) that, so far as the decision involved any exercise of discretion by the panel, the panel reasonably exercised that discretion in the circumstances,

the court may revoke the referral order (or each of the referral orders) and deal with the offender in any manner, other than making a referral order, he could have been dealt with for that offence by the court which made the order. In so dealing with him the court must have regard to—

(i) the circumstances of his referral back to the court; and

(ii) where a contract has taken effect under section 8 between the offender and the panel, the extent of his compliance with the term of the contract[24].

Where the court deals with an offender for the offence, he may appeal to the Crown Court against the sentence[25].

Where the court is not satisfied with the decision of a youth offender panel to refer an offender back to court, if no contract has taken effect or the period of a contract has not expired, the referral order will continue as if it had not been referred back to the court. If a contract had taken effect but the period for which it has effect has expired, or if the court is satisfied that the offender has satisfactorily completed the contract, the court must make an order declaring that the referral order any related referral order is discharged[26]. The court may sentence an offender who is subject to a compliance period less than twelve months for offences committed before he was referred to a youth offender panel by making an order extending his compliance period, provided the occasion on which he was referred to the panel is the only occasion on which he has been dealt with by a court for any offence disregarding any offences for which he was absolutely discharged[27]. Where an offence has been committed after referral with the same proviso, the court may where it is satisfied on the report of the youth offender panel that there are exceptional circumstances, and has stated in open court that it is so satisfied and why it is, extend the compliance period provided it does not exceed 12 months[28]. Where a court deals with an offender for an offence whether committed before or after he was referred to the panel by an order other than one extending the period for compliance with any youth offender contract or discharging him absolutely for the offence, any referral order is revoked. Where any referral order is revoked in this manner, the court may, if it appears to the court that it would be in the interests of justice to do so, deal with the offender for the offence in respect of which the revoked order was made in any manner (except for the making of a referral order) in which he could have been dealt with for that offence by the court which made the order having regard to the extent of his compliance with the terms of the contract[29].

---

1. Powers of Criminal Courts (Sentencing) Act 2000, s 16(1), (2), (3), in PART III: SENTENCING, ante.
2. Powers of Criminal Courts (Sentencing) Act 2000, s 16(5), in PART III: SENTENCING, ante.
3. Powers of Criminal Courts (Sentencing) Act 2000, s 17(1), in PART III: SENTENCING, ante.
4. Powers of Criminal Courts (Sentencing) Act 2000, s 17(1A), in PART III: SENTENCING, ante.
5. Powers of Criminal Courts (Sentencing) Act 2000, s 17(2) in PART III: SENTENCING, ante.
6. Powers of Criminal Courts (Sentencing) Act 2000, s 16(4), in PART III: SENTENCING, ante.
7. Powers of Criminal Courts (Sentencing) Act 2000, s 17(5), in PART III: SENTENCING, ante.
8. Powers of Criminal Courts (Sentencing) Act 2000, s 18(1), in PART III: SENTENCING, ante.
9. Powers of Criminal Courts (Sentencing) Act 2000, s 18(3), in PART III: SENTENCING, ante.
10. Powers of Criminal Courts (Sentencing) Act 2000, s 19(2), (3), in PART III: SENTENCING, ante.
11. Powers of Criminal Courts (Sentencing) Act 2000, s 19(5), (6), in this PART III: SENTENCING, ante.
12. Powers of Criminal Courts (Sentencing) Act 2000, s 19(7), in PART III: SENTENCING, ante.
13. Powers of Criminal Courts (Sentencing) Act 2000, s 20(1), (4), (5), (6), in PART III: SENTENCING, ante.
14. Powers of Criminal Courts (Sentencing) Act 2000, s 20(3) in PART III: SENTENCING, ante.
15. Powers of Criminal Courts (Sentencing) Act 2000, s 20(7), in PART III: SENTENCING, ante.
16. Powers of Criminal Courts (Sentencing) Act 2000, s 21, in PART III: SENTENCING, ante.
17. Powers of Criminal Courts (Sentencing) Act 2000, s 23, in PART III: SENTENCING, ante.
18. Powers of Criminal Courts (Sentencing) Act 2000, s 26, in PART III: SENTENCING, ante.
19. Powers of Criminal Courts (Sentencing) Act 2000, s 23, in PART III: SENTENCING, ante.
20. Powers of Criminal Courts (Sentencing) Act 2000, s 27, (1), (2), in PART III: SENTENCING, ante.
21. Powers of Criminal Courts (Sentencing) Act 2000, s 27, (3), (4), in PART III: SENTENCING, ante.
22. Powers of Criminal Courts (Sentencing) Act 2000, Sch 1, paras 1, 2, in PART III: SENTENCING, ante.
23. Powers of Criminal Courts (Sentencing) Act 2000, Sch 1, para 3, in PART III: SENTENCING, ante.
24. Powers of Criminal Courts (Sentencing) Act 2000, Sch 1, para 5, in PART III: SENTENCING, ante.
25. Powers of Criminal Courts (Sentencing) Act 2000, Sch 1, para 6, in PART III: SENTENCING, ante.
26. Powers of Criminal Courts (Sentencing) Act 2000, Sch 1, paras 7, 8, in PART III: SENTENCING, ante.
27. Powers of Criminal Courts (Sentencing) Act 2000, Sch 1, para 11, in PART III: SENTENCING, ante.
28. Powers of Criminal Courts (Sentencing) Act 2000, Sch 1, para 12, in PART III: SENTENCING, ante.
29. Powers of Criminal Courts (Sentencing) Act 2000, Sch 1, para 14, in PART III: SENTENCING, ante.

5–43 Absolute and conditional discharge. Where a court is of opinion, having regard to the circumstances including the nature of the offence and the character of the offender, that it is inexpedient to inflict punishment and that a supervision order is not appropriate, it may make an order discharging him absolutely or alternatively discharging him subject to the condition that he commits no offence during such period, not exceeding three years from the date of the order, as may be specified therein[1].

Before making an order for conditional discharge, the court must explain to the offender in ordinary language that if he commits another offence during the period of the conditional discharge, he will be liable to be sentenced for the original offence[1]; it is usual for the court to fulfil this mandatory duty itself, although it may for reasons of justice and convenience delegate the task of explanation to another[2]. For the one offence, a fine may not be imposed in addition to an order of discharge[3].

This power may be exercised by a magistrates' court that is not a youth court where, for example, a minor has been jointly charged and tried with an adult[4]. Where a person has received a warning under s 65 of the Crime and Disorder Act 1998 and is convicted of an offence committed within two years of the warning, the court must not impose a conditional discharge unless there are exceptional circumstances (which the court must specify) relating to the offence or the offender[5].

The provisions relating to dealing with a person who commits *an offence during a period of conditional discharge* are the same as for an adult[6].

1. Powers of Criminal Courts (Sentencing) Act 2000, ss 12–15, in Part III: Sentencing, ante.
2. *R v Wehner* [1977] 3 All ER 553.
3. Powers of Criminal Courts (Sentencing) Act 2000, s 8(6), in Part III: Sentencing, ante.
4. Children and Young Persons Act 1969, s 7(8) this Part, post.
5. Crime and Disorder Act 1998, s 66(4), this Part, post.
6. See Part III, para **3–201**, ante.

5–44   Compensation. The making of a compensation order in the youth court involves two stages and is governed by the provisions of s 137 of the Powers of Criminal Courts (Sentencing) Act 2000[1]. In the first stage, the court must consider whether the case would best be met by the imposition of a fine or costs or the making of a compensation order whether with or without any other punishment[2]. At that stage the court must decide whether the victim has suffered a loss that deserves to be compensated in accordance with the provisions of s 130 of the Powers of Criminal Courts (Sentencing) Act 2000[3]. In the second stage, the court is obliged (where the offender is under 16) or empowered (where the offender is 16 or 17) to make an order for payment against the parent or guardian with the substitution, where s 137(8) of the Powers of Criminal Courts (Sentencing) Act 2000 applies, of the local authority for the parent or guardian. The court's exercise of this duty or power is only prevented in cases where the parent or guardian cannot be found or where it would be unreasonable to make an order for payment, having regard to the circumstances of the case[2]. When considering making a compensation order against a local authority, normally the court should find some causative link between any fault proved and the offences committed[4].

See Part III, para **3–171 Compensation** et seq for the relevant statutory provisions and principles to be applied when determining the amount of a compensation order. For payment of compensation by a parent or guardian, see also para **5–45 Fine**, since the provisions are the same as those for a fine.

Where a parent has been responsible for the bringing up of a child or young person it may be difficult to show that it would be unreasonable to make an order against a parent, unless it was quite clear that the parent had done what he or she could to keep the child or young person from criminal ways[5]. However, where a child has been accommodated by the local authority with the parent's consent under s 20 of the Children Act 1989, it may not be reasonable to hold the parent responsible for the child's actions where the parent had no control over what the child was doing at the time and could not take any steps to prevent the child from committing the offence[6].

A local authority's position with regard to children or young persons who are in its care or for whom it has provided accommodation is, however, different from that of a parent or guardian and is discussed further in para **5–45**, post.

The High Court has given guidance, which is intended to be of general application, as to the proper procedures to be followed where a court is considering the exercise of its powers under s 137 of the Powers of Criminal Courts (Sentencing) Act 2000[4]. The guidelines are as follows—

1. On any hearing in which the issue is whether the local authority should pay compensation under s 55 the role of the prosecution must be strictly neutral. It is not the function of the prosecution to seek to promote or advance any particular sentencing option. The prosecution should confine themselves to presenting the facts to the court on the extent of any loss and the evidence to support the value of that loss, and elucidating for the assistance of the court any matters affecting the reasonableness of making a compensation order.
2. If the court is minded to make an order for payment of compensation against a local authority, the court should first notify the local authority in writing that it is considering making such an order, informing the local authority of its right to make representations, to produce evidence, and to be legally represented.
3. The local authority should be provided by the court with copies of any documents supplied to the court by the prosecution in support of the application for compensation.
4. The local authority should notify the court in writing whether there is likely to be any dispute about:

    (*a*) the amount of any compensation claimed; and
    (*b*) as to whether an order for compensation should be made.

5. If there is any dispute on the amount of compensation claimed or the liability of the local authority to pay that compensation, a hearing must be arranged, with reasonable notice to the local authority.
6. In advance of any hearing, the local authority should supply to the court and the prosecution copies of any statements, reports or other documents relied upon by them in support of their case as to the amount of compensation; and as to their liability to pay that compensation.
7. In all cases the hearing itself should be kept as simple as possible4.

1. In Part III: Sentencing, ante.
2. Section 137(1) of the Powers of Criminal Courts (Sentencing) Act 2000, in Part III: Sentencing, ante.

3. See PART III: SENTENCING, ante.
4. *Bedfordshire County Council v DPP* [1996] 1 Cr App Rep (S) 322, 160 JP 248; [1995] Crim LR 962.
5. See *R v Sheffield Crown Court, ex p Clarkson* (1986) 8 Cr App Rep (S) 454.
6. *TA v DPP* (1996) 160 JP 736, [1997] 1 Cr App Rep (S) 1, [1997] 2 FLR 887.

5–44A Order made under s 1C of the Crime and Disorder Act 1998 (Anti-social Behaviour).
See commentary in para **3–210**, ante.

5–45 Fine. The maximum fine which may be imposed on a minor aged 10–13 inclusive is **£250**[1], and for a minor aged 14–17 inclusive it is **£1,000**[1]; if the maximum fine which can be imposed on an adult is less than the appropriate limit for the minor, then the adult maximum will apply[1]. The amount of the fine shall be such as, in the opinion of the court, reflects the seriousness of the offence. In fixing the amount of any fine, the court must take into account the circumstances of the case including, among other things, the financial circumstances of the offender, or so far as applicable, the financial circumstances of the parent or guardian[2]. Before making an order against a parent or guardian the court should give him or her the opportunity of being heard[3].
The court is under a duty to order that the fine, compensation or costs awarded be paid by the parent or guardian instead of by the minor himself, unless the court is satisfied—

(i)   that the parent or guardian cannot be found, or
(ii) that it would be unreasonable to make an order for payment, having regard to the circumstances of the case.

An order for payment may be made against a parent or guardian who, having been required to attend, has failed to do so, but otherwise, no such order shall be made without giving the parent or guardian an opportunity of being heard[4]. Where the young person has attained 16 the court's duty to make an order against the parent or guardian is replaced by a power so to do[2].
In relation to a minor for whom a local authority has parental responsibility reference above to his parent or guardian shall be construed as references to that authority. Accordingly, an order for payment of a fine, costs or compensation may be made against such a local authority, unless the court is satisfied that it would be unreasonable to make an order for payment, having regard to the circumstances of the case[5].
Parental responsibility may only be acquired by a local authority where it is expressly conferred by statute, as in ss 33 and 44 of the Children Act 1989[6]. Although the local authority may have parental responsibility for minors in its care, the steps that the local authority should or lawfully can take to restrain such minors may well be limited. Accordingly, where the local authority is found to have done everything that it reasonably and properly could to protect the public from the young offender, it would be unreasonable and unjust that it should bear a financial penalty. Where a local authority contends that it has properly exercised the powers over the minor as are conferred on it by parental responsibility, it must be ready to call evidence of how it has discharged that responsibility[7]. Where the court, having applied these principles, determines to order the local authority to pay a fine, costs or compensation, it shall not have regard to the means of the local authority[8].
A magistrates' court that is not a youth court may fine a minor; where for example he has been jointly charged and tried with an adult[9].
There is no reason in principle why an order to pay a fine and other amounts by monthly instalments should not extend for two or even three years[10]. If the defendant cannot pay a fine, then, if that is the appropriate type of penalty it would be wrong to make a more severe form of order instead[11]. When a fine or compensation is ordered to be paid by the parent or guardian, their means or financial circumstances will be those taken into consideration[12].
Having decided the amount of the fine, the court must then consider how *payment* is to be made. The court may order the offender to be searched, and any money found on him applied towards payment of the fine, with certain qualifications on this power[13]. The court may require immediate payment, allow time for payment, or order payment by instalments[14]. If it allows time for payment, or orders payment by instalments, it may in the defendant's presence fix a day on which, if any part of the sum remains unpaid, the defendant must appear before the court again[15]. It may make a money payments supervision order[16], or if there is a failure to pay a fine ordered to be paid forthwith, it may make an attendance centre order[17]. It may not issue a warrant of commitment to detention for default.
Where the parent or guardian is ordered to pay, then adult enforcement powers will apply. The court which found the minor guilty may make a transfer of fine order where the defendant lives in another court's area (including Scotland), and that court will then collect and enforce[18].

1. See Magistrates' Courts Act 1980, s 24 (3), (4) (indictable offence tried summarily); Powers of Criminal Courts (Sentencing) Act 2000, s 135 (other offence) in PART III: SENTENCING, ante.
2. Powers of Criminal Courts (Sentencing) Act 2000, s 128 and 138(1), in PART III: SENTENCING, ante, and para **3–94**, ante.
3. *R v J-B* [2004] EWCA Crim 14, [2004] Crim LR 390.
4. Powers of Criminal Courts (Sentencing) Act 2000, s 137, in PART III: SENTENCING, ante.
5. Powers of Criminal Courts (Sentencing) Act 2000, s 137(1) and (8), in PART III: SENTENCING, ante.
6. *North Yorkshire County Council v Selby Youth Court Justices* [1994] 1 All ER 991, [1995] 1 WLR 1, [1994] 2 FLR 169.
7. *D v DPP* [1995] 3 FCR 725, [1995] 2 FLR 502, (1995) 16 Cr App Rep (S) 1040.
8. Powers of Criminal Courts (Sentencing) Act 2000, s 138(1), in PART III: SENTENCING, ante.
9. Powers of Criminal Courts (Sentencing) Act 2000, s 8(6), in PART III: SENTENCING, ante.
10. *R v Olliver and Olliver* (1989) 153 JP 369, [1989] Crim LR 387, CA.
11. *R v McGowan* [1975] Crim LR 113.
12. Powers of Criminal Courts (Sentencing) Act 2000, s 138(1), in PART III: SENTENCING, ante.
13. See Magistrates' Courts Act 1980, s 80, in PART I, ante.
14. Magistrates' Courts Act 1980, s 75, in PART I, ante.
15. Magistrates' Courts Act 1980, s 86 in PART I: MAGISTRATES' COURTS, PROCEDURE, ante.
16. Magistrates' Courts Act 1980, s 88, in PART I, ante.

17. Magistrates' Courts Act 1980, s 81 in PART I: MAGISTRATES' COURTS, PROCEDURE, ante.
18. Magistrates' Courts Act 1980, ss 89 and 90, in PART I: MAGISTRATES' COURTS, procedure, ante.

5–46   Fine: enforcement after finding of guilt.   Besides the powers of remission, periodical payments, time to pay, money payments supervision and attachment of earnings[1], where there is a default and a means inquiry is held, the court has the following additional powers[2]—

  (a)   to make an attendance centre order[3], or
  (b)   to order a parent or guardian (whose consent must be obtained) to enter into a recognizance to ensure the defaulter pays, provided the court is satisfied the defaulter has had the means to pay the sum or any instalment of it on which he has defaulted and has refused or neglected to pay; or
  (c)   to order the parent or guardian (who must be given an opportunity to attend) to pay, provided the court is satisfied the defaulter has had the means to pay the sum or any instalment of it on which he has defaulted and has refused or neglected to pay.

Where the offender is under the age of 18 years there is no power to fix a term of detention in default of payment of a fine[4]. Once the minor attains the age of 18, the adult enforcement powers apply.

---

1. See PART III: SENTENCING, paras **3–110** and **3–311**.
2. Magistrates' Courts Act 1980, s 81, in PART I, ante.
3. See para **5–48**, post.
4. *R v Basid* [1996] 1 Cr App Rep (S) 421, [1996] Crim LR 67.

5–47   Binding over of parent or guardian.   See PART III: SENTENCING, para **3–1258**, ante for the relevant provisions concerning binding over of parents and guardians to take proper care of a minor and to exercise proper control over him, a power exercisable by the adult court in appropriate circumstances as well as by the youth court.

5–47AA   Parenting orders combined with referral orders.   1. *Parenting order made at the same time as referral order*
The former prohibition on the making of a parenting order and a referral order for the same offence was removed by s 324 of and Sch 34 to the Criminal Justice Act 2003[1]. The normal duty on the court to make a parenting order, or to explain its reasons for not doing so, does not, however, apply where the court makes a referral order in respect of the offence[2].
Where the court proposes to make both a referral order and a parenting order in respect of an offence it must first obtain and consider a report by a probation officer, a local authority social worker, or a member of a youth offending team. The report should indicate what the requirements of the parenting order might include, the reasons why it would be desirable in the interests of preventing the commission of any further offence by the child or young person and, if the offender is under 16 years of age, information about the family's circumstances and the likely effect of the order on those circumstances[3].
A parenting order made for the same offence as a referral order involves, in all other respects, all the normal parenting order incidents, procedures, right of appeal to the Crown Court and powers on breach.
  2. *Parenting order for failing to attend meetings of the youth offender panel*
A court making a referral order may require a parent or guardian to attend the meetings of the youth offender panel under s 20 of the Powers of Criminal Courts (Sentencing) Act 2000[4]. If the parent or guardian fails to comply with a s 20 requirement the panel may refer him/her to the youth court, which shall then cause that person to appear before it. Where a parent or guardian so appears before the youth court, the court may make a parenting order if it is satisfied that he/she failed without reasonable excuse to comply with the s 20 requirement and that a parenting order would be desirable in the interests of preventing the commission of any further offence by the offender[5].
A parenting order made for failing to comply with a s 20 requirement involves, in all other respects, all the normal parenting order incidents, procedures, right of appeal to the Crown Court and powers on breach[6].
The making of parenting order for non-compliance with a s 20 requirement is without prejudice to the continuance of the s 20 order[7].

---

1. See PART I, MAGISTRATES' COURTS, PROCEDURE, ante.
2. See s 9(1A) of the Crime and Disorder Act 1998 in PART I, MAGISTRATES' COURTS, PROCEDURE, ante.
3. See s 9(2A) of the Crime and Disorder Act 1998 in PART I, MAGISTRATES' COURTS, PROCEDURE, ante.
4. See PART III, SENTENCING, ante.
5. See Pt 1A of Sch 1 to the Powers of Criminal Courts (Sentencing) Act 2000 in PART III, SENTENCING, ante.
6. See paras 9D and E of Pt 1A, infra.
7. Para 9F, infra.

5–47A   Parenting orders.   In any court proceedings where—

  (a)   a child safety order[1] is made in respect of the child;
  (b)   an anti-social behaviour order[2] or sex offender order[3] is made in respect of a child or young person;

(c)   a child or young person is convicted of an offence; or

(d)   a person is convicted of an offence under section 443 (failure to comply with school attendance order) or section 444 (failure to secure regular attendance at school of registered pupil) of the Education Act 1996[4]

and the court is satisfied that the relevant condition is fulfilled, it may[5] make a parenting order in respect of person who is a parent or guardian of the child or young person or, as the case may be, the person convicted of the offence under section 443 or 444 of the 1996 Act[6].

Where a person under the age of 16 is convicted of an offence, the court by or before which he is so convicted, if it is satisfied that the relevant condition is fulfilled, shall make a parenting order, and if it is not so satisfied, shall state in open court that it is not and why it is not[7].

The Anti-social Behaviour Act 2003 introduced parenting contracts in cases of exclusion from school and truancy, and parenting orders in cases of exclusion. In relation to the latter, the exclusion must be on disciplinary grounds (whether for a fixed period or permanently), and such conditions as may be prescribed by regulations must be satisfied. Subject to the above, a local education authority can apply in accordance with regulations[8] to the magistrates' court for a parenting order and the court may make such an order if it is satisfied that such an order would be desirable in the interests of improving the behaviour of the pupil[9]. In making its decision the court must take into account any refusal by the parent to enter into a parenting contract or, if the parent has entered into such a contract, and failure to comply with its requirements[10]. The requirements and consequence of breach specified below in relation to parenting orders made under the Crime and Disorder Act 1998 apply also to orders made under the 2003 Act[11].

The Anti-social Behaviour Act 2003 also introduced parenting contracts and parenting orders in respect of criminal conduct and anti-social behaviour, following a reference to a youth offending team. Where a child has been so referred, the team may enter into the contract with a parent or it may apply in accordance with regulations[8] to the court for a parenting order. The court may make the latter if it is satisfied that the child or young person has engaged in criminal conduct or anti-social behaviour and an order would be desirable in the interests of preventing the child in engaging in further such conduct[12]. In making its decision the court must take into account any refusal by the parent to enter into a parenting contract or, if the parent has entered into such a contract, any failure to comply with its requirements[13]. The requirements and consequences of breach specified below in relation to parenting orders made under the Crime and Disorder Act 1998 apply also to orders made under the 2003 Act[14].

The "relevant condition" is that the parenting order would be desirable in the interests of preventing—

(i)   in a case falling within paragraph (a) or (b) above, any repetition of the kind of behaviour which led to the child safety order, anti-social behaviour order or sex offender order being made;

(ii)   in a case falling within paragraph (c) above, the commission of any further offence by the child or young person;

(iii) in a case falling within paragraph (d) above, the commission of any further offence under section 443 or 444 of the Education Act 1996[15].

A parenting order is an order which requires the parent—

(i)   to comply, for a period not exceeding 12 months , with such requirements as are specified in the order; and

(ii)   to attend, for a concurrent period not exceeding 3 months and not more than once in any week, such counselling or guidance sessions[16] as may be specified in directions given by the responsible officer[17].

A counselling or guidance session may be or may include a residential course, provided that the court is satisfied as to the likely effectiveness of such a course (as compared with a non-residential course) to prevent repetition of the kind of behaviour or the commission of a further offence and provided that any interference with family life likely to occur from attendance at the course is proportionate in all the circumstances[18].

However, the court need not include the last mentioned requirement in any case where a parenting order has been made in respect of the parent on a previous occasion[19].

A court shall not make a parenting order unless it has been notified[20] by the Secretary of State that arrangements for implementing such orders are available in the area in which it appears to the court that the parent resides or will reside and the notice has not been withdrawn[21].

Before making a parenting order in a case within paragraph (a) above, in a case falling within paragraph (b) or (c) where the person concerned is under the age of 16, or in a case falling within paragraph (d) above where the person to whom the offence related is under that age, a court must obtain and consider information about the person's family circumstances and the likely effect of the order on those circumstances[22].

Before making a parenting order, a court must explain to the parent in ordinary language—

(i)   the effect of the order and of the requirements proposed to be included in it;

(ii)   the consequences which may follow if he fails to comply with any of those requirements; and

(iii) that the court has power to review the order on the application either of the parent or of the responsible officer[23].

The requirements that may be specified in a parenting order under s 8(4)(a) of the Crime and

Disorder Act 1998 are those which the court considers desirable in the interests of preventing any such repetition or, as the case may be, the commission of any such further offence[24]. Requirements specified in, and directions given under, a parenting order shall, so far as practicable, be such as to avoid any conflict with the parent's religious beliefs, and any interference with the times, if any, at which he normally works or attends an educational establishment[25].

If while a parenting order is in force it appears to the court which made it, on the application of the responsible officer or the parent, that it is appropriate to do so, the court may make an order discharging the parenting order or varying it by cancelling any provision included in it, or by inserting in it any provision that could have been included in the order if the court had then had power to make it and were exercising the power. Where an application for the discharge of a parenting order is dismissed, no further application for its discharge shall be made by any person except with the consent of the court which made the order[26].

If while a parenting order is in force the parent without reasonable excuse fails to comply with any requirement included in the order, or specified in directions given by the responsible officer, he shall be liable on summary conviction to a fine not exceeding **level 3** on the standard scale[27].

References above to a "responsible officer" mean one of the following who is specified in the order, namely a probation officer, a social worker of a local authority social services department, and member of a youth offending team[28].

An appeal shall lie to the High Court against the making of a parenting order by virtue of paragraph (*a*) above, and to the Crown Court against the making of a parenting order by virtue of paragraph (*b*) above[29]. On such an appeal the High Court or the Crown Court may make such orders as may be necessary to give effect: to its determination of the appeal and may also make such incidental or consequential orders as appear to it to be just[30].

In relation to parenting orders made under the Anti-social Behaviour Act 2003, appeals lie to the Crown Court[31].

A person in respect of whom a parenting order is made by virtue of paragraphs (*c*) or (*d*) above shall have the same right of appeal against the making of the order as if the order were a sentence passed on him for the offence[32].

1. As to child safety orders see PART VI, para **6–175B** ante, and the Crime and Disorder Act 1998, ss 11–13, in PART I: MAGISTRATES' COURTS PROCEDURE, ante.
2. As to anti-social behaviour orders, see the Crime and Disorder Act 1998, ss 1 and 4 in PART I: MAGISTRATES' COURTS, PROCEDURE, ante.
3. The Crime and Disorder Act 1998, s 2 which made provision to make a sex offender order was repealed by the Sexual Offences Act 1998. No consequential amendment was made to s 8 of the 1998 Act to substitute a reference to a corresponding order under the 2003 Act.
4. See PART VIII: EDUCATION, post.
5. The exercise whether or not to make a parenting order is one of judgment or evaluation; justices must act on all relevant evidence before them, including information about family circumstances, and reach a judgment that is rational: *R (on the application of M) v Inner London Crown Court* [2003] EWHC 301 (Admin), [2004] 1 FCR 178 (where the court held that it was undesirable that a parenting order should be used as a method of controlling or monitoring a neighbour dispute, and that having regard to views expressed in the pre-sentence report that the parent would not be receptive or suitable for a parenting order, and the 13-year-old defendant's otherwise exemplary character, it was not consider it desirable to make a parenting order and, indeed, no reasonable bench on the material before it, applying the proper test, would have made such an order). Where an anti-social behaviour order is made in respect of a person under the age of 16 and the court is satisfied that the relevant condition is fulfilled the court *must* make a parenting order. If the court is not so satisfied it must state that fact in open court and the reasons for it.
6. Crime and Disorder Act 1998, s 8(1), (2), in PART I: MAGISTRATES' COURTS PROCEDURE, ante.
7. Crime and Disorder Act 1998, s 9(1), in PART I: MAGISTRATES' COURTS PROCEDURE, ante.
8. See the Magistrates' Courts (Parenting Orders) Regulations 2004 in PART I: MAGISTRATES' COURTS, PROCEDURE, ante.
9. Anti-social Behaviour Act 2003, s 20.
10. Anti-social Behaviour Act 2003, s 21.
11. In relation to school exclusion cases, see s 21(3).
12. Anti-social Behaviour Act 2003, s 26.
13. Anti-social Behaviour Act 2003, s 27.
14. In relation to criminal conduct/anti-social behaviour cases, see s 27(3).
15. Crime and Disorder Act 1998, s 8(6), in PART I: MAGISTRATES' COURTS PROCEDURE, ante.
16. "Week" means a period of seven days beginning with a Sunday (Crime and Disorder Act 1998, s 8 in PART I: MAGISTRATES' COURTS PROCEDURE, ante).
17. Crime and Disorder Act 1998, s 8(4) in PART I: MAGISTRATES' COURTS PROCEDURE, ante.
18. Crime and Disorder Act 1998, s 8(7A).
19. Crime and Disorder Act 1998, s 8(5), PART I: MAGISTRATES' COURTS PROCEDURE, ante. See also the corresponding provisions of the Anti-social Behaviour Act 2003, ie ss 20(5) and 26(5).
20. All courts in England and Wales were notified by Home Office letter dated 27 April 2000 that arrangements for implementing the parenting order would be available in their area with effect from 1 June 2000.
21. Crime and Disorder Act 1998, s 8(3), PART I: MAGISTRATES' COURTS PROCEDURE, ante.
22. Crime and Disorder Act 1998, s 9(2), PART I: MAGISTRATES' COURTS PROCEDURE, ante. See also the corresponding provisions of the Anti-social Behaviour Act 2003, ie ss 21(2) and s 27(2).
23. Crime and Disorder Act 1998, s 9(3), PART I: MAGISTRATES' COURTS PROCEDURE, ante.
24. Crime and Disorder Act 1998, s 8(7), PART I: MAGISTRATES' COURTS PROCEDURE, ante.
25. Crime and Disorder Act 1998, s 9(4), PART I: MAGISTRATES' COURTS PROCEDURE, ante.
26. Crime and Disorder Act 1998, s 9(5), (6), PART I: MAGISTRATES' COURTS PROCEDURE, ante.
27. Crime and Disorder Act 1998, s 9(7), PART I: MAGISTRATES' COURTS PROCEDURE, ante.
28. Crime and Disorder Act 1998, s 8(8), PART I: MAGISTRATES' COURTS PROCEDURE, ante.
29. Crime and Disorder Act 1998, s 10(1), PART I: MAGISTRATES' COURTS PROCEDURE, ante.
30. Crime and Disorder Act 1998, s 10(2), PART I: MAGISTRATES' COURTS PROCEDURE, ante.
31. See ss 22 and 28.
32. Crime and Disorder Act 1998, s 10(4), (5), PART I: MAGISTRATES' COURTS PROCEDURE, ante.

5–47B   Child safety orders. A child safety order places a child for a specified period under the supervision of a responsible officer and requires the child to comply with such requirements as are so specified[1]. A child safety order may be made only by a family proceedings court and these orders are considered further in para **6–175B**, ante.

---

1. See Crime and Disorder Act 1998, ss 11–13, in PART I: MAGISTRATES' COURTS, PROCEDURE, ante.

5–47C   Reparation order. Where a child or young person is found guilty of an offence by a youth court, the court may make a reparation order which requires the offender to make reparation specified in the order to a person or persons so specified or to the community at large. Any person so specified must be a person identified by the court as a victim of the offence or a person otherwise affected by it[1].

A reparation order must not require the offender to work for more than 24 hours in aggregate, or to make reparation to any person without the consent of that person[2].

Requirements specified in a reparation order shall be such as in the opinion of the court are commensurate with seriousness of the offence, or the combination of the offence and one or more offences associated with it. Requirements so specified shall, as far as practicable, be such as to avoid—

(a)   any conflict with the offender's religious beliefs or with the requirements of any community order to which he may be subject; and

(b)   any interference with the times, if any, at which the offender normally works or attends school or any other educational establishment[3].

Any reparation required by a reparation order must be made under the supervision of the responsible officer and must be made within a period of three months from the date of the making of the order[4]. A reparation order must name the petty sessions area in which it appears to the court making the order that the offender resides or will reside[5].

The court shall not make a reparation order in respect of the offender if it proposes—

(a)   to pass on him a custodial sentence; or

(b)   to make in respect of him a community service order, a combination order, a supervision order which includes requirements imposed in pursuance of Schedule 6 to the Powers of Criminal Courts (Sentencing) Act 2000 or an action plan order[6].

The court must give reasons if it does not make a reparation order in a case where it has power to do so[7].

Before making a reparation order, a court must obtain and consider a written report by a probation officer, a social worker of a local authority social services department or a member of a youth offending team, indicating—

(a)   the type of work that is suitable for the offender; and

(b)   the attitude of the victim or victims to the requirements proposed to be included in the order[8].

Before making such an order, the court trust also explain to the offender in ordinary language—

(a)   the effect of the order and of the requirements proposed to be included in it;

(b)   the consequences which may follow if he fails to comply with any of those requirements; and

(c)   that the court has power to review the order on the application either of the offender or of the responsible officer9.

"Responsible officer" means one of the following who is specified in the reparation order, namely a probation officer, a social worker of a local authority social services department, and a member of a youth offending team[10].

The court shall not make a reparation order unless it has been notified[11] by the Secretary of State that arrangements for implementing such orders are available in the area proposed to be named in the order and the not ice has not been withdrawn[12].

---

1. Powers of Criminal Courts (Sentencing) Act 2000, s 73(1) in PART III: SENTENCING, ante.
2. Powers of Criminal Courts (Sentencing) Act 2000, s 74(1), in PART III: SENTENCING, ante.
3. Powers of Criminal Courts (Sentencing) Act 2000, s 74(2), (3), in PART III: SENTENCING, ante.
4. Powers of Criminal Courts (Sentencing) Act 2000, s 74(8), in PART III: SENTENCING, ante.
5. Powers of Criminal Courts (Sentencing) Act 2000, s 74(4), in PART III: SENTENCING, ante.
6. Powers of Criminal Courts (Sentencing) Act 2000, s 73(4), in PART III: SENTENCING, ante.
7. Powers of Criminal Courts (Sentencing) Act 2000, s 73(8), in PART III: SENTENCING, ante.
8. Powers of Criminal Courts (Sentencing) Act 2000, s 73(5), in PART III: SENTENCING, ante.
9. Powers of Criminal Courts (Sentencing) Act 2000, s 73(7), in PART III: SENTENCING, ante. See Sch 8, post, which has effect for dealing with a failure to comply with the requirements of a reparation order.
10. Powers of Criminal Courts (Sentencing) Act 2000, s 74(5), in PART III: SENTENCING, ante.
11. All courts in England and Wales were notified by Home Office letter dated 27 April 2000 that arrangements for implementing the parenting order would be available in their area with effect from 1 June 2000.
12. Powers of Criminal Courts (Sentencing) Act 2000, s 73(6), in PART III: SENTENCING, ante.

5–47D   Action plan order. Where a child or young person is found guilty of an offence by a youth court, the court may, if it is of the opinion that it is desirable to do so in the interests of securing his rehabilitation, or of preventing the commission by him of further offences, make an action plan order which—

(a)   requires the offender, for a period of three months beginning with the date of the order, to comply with an action plan consisting of a series of requirements with respect to his actions and whereabouts during that period;

(*b*)   places the offender under the supervision for that period of the responsible officer; and

(*c*)   requires the offender to comply with any directions given by that officer with a view to the implementation of that plan[1].

Requirements included in an action plan order, or directions given by a responsible officer, may require the offender to do all or any of the following things, namely—

(a)   to participate in activities specified in the requirements or directions at a time or times so specified;

(b)   to present himself to a person or persons specified in the requirements or directions at a place or places and at a time or times so specified;

(c)   to attend at an attendance centre specified in the requirements or directions for a number of hours so specified;

(d)   to stay away from a place or places specified in the requirements or directions;

(e)   to comply with any arrangements for his education specified in the requirements or directions;

(f)   to make reparation specified in the requirements or directions to a person or persons so specified or to the community at large; and

(g)   to attend any hearing fixed by the court to take place after the making of the order[2].

The requirements and directions must, as far as practicable, avoid any conflict with the offender's religious beliefs or with the requirements of any other community order to which he is subject, and must avoid any interference with the times, if any, at which he normally works or attends school or any other educational establishment[3]. The requirement to attend at an attendance centre is not available to the court unless the offence committed by the offender is punishable with imprisonment in the case of a person aged 21 or over[4]. A person shall not be specified in requirements or directions for the purposes of making reparation unless he is identified by the court or the responsible officer as a victim of the offence or a person otherwise affected by it, and he consents to reparation being made[5].

An action plan order must name the petty sessions area in which it appears to the court making the order that the offender resides or will reside[6].

The court shall not make an action plan order in respect of the offender if—

(*a*)   he is already the subject of such an order; or

(*b*)   the court proposes to pass on him a custodial sentence or to make in respect of him a probation order, a community service order, a combination order, a supervision order or an attendance centre order[7].

Before making an action plan order, the court must obtain and consider—

(*a*)   a written report by a probation officer, a social worker of a local authority social services department or a member of a youth offending team, indicating

(i)   the requirements proposed by that person to be included in the order:

(ii)   the benefits to the offender that the proposed requirements are designed to achieve; and

(iii)   the attitude of a parent or guardian of the offender to the proposed requirements; and

(*b*)   where the offender is under the age of 16, information about the offender's family circumstances and the likely effect of the order on those circumstances[8].

Before making such an order, the court must also explain to the offender in ordinary language—

(a)   the effect of the order and of the requirements proposed to be included in it;

(b)   the consequences which may follow if he fails to comply with any of those requirements; and

(c)   that the court has power to review the order on the application either of the offender or of the responsible officer[9].

Immediately after making an action plan order, the court may fix a further hearing date not more than 21 days after the making of the order and direct the responsible officer to make, at that hearing, a report as to the effectiveness of the order and the extent to which it has been implemented. At such a further hearing the court shall consider the responsible officer's report and may, on the application of the responsible officer or the offender, vary the order by cancelling any provision included in it, or by inserting in it any provision that the court could originally have included in it[10].

"Responsible officer" in relation to an action plan order means one of the following who is specified in the order, namely—

(*a*)   a probation officer;

(*b*)   a social worker of a local authority social services department and

(*c*)   a member of a youth offending team[11].

An action plan order is a community order for the purposes of the Powers of Criminal Courts (Sentencing) Act 2000 and sections 35 and 36 of that Act apply with respect to the making of an action plan order[12].

The court shall not make an action plan order unless it has been notified[13] by the Secretary of State that arrangements for implementing such orders are available in the area proposed to be named in the order and the notice has not been withdrawn[14].

---

1.   Powers of Criminal Courts (Sentencing) Act 2000, s 69(1), (2), in PART III: SENTENCING, ante.

2.   Powers of Criminal Courts (Sentencing) Act 2000, s 70(1), in PART III: SENTENCING, ante.

3.   Powers of Criminal Courts (Sentencing) Act 2000, s 70(5), in PART III: SENTENCING, ante.

4. Powers of Criminal Courts (Sentencing) Act 2000, s 70(2), in PART III: SENTENCING, ante.
5. Powers of Criminal Courts (Sentencing) Act 2000, s 70(4), in PART III: SENTENCING, ante
6. Powers of Criminal Courts (Sentencing) Act 2000, s 69(8), in PART III: SENTENCING, ante.
7. Powers of Criminal Courts (Sentencing) Act 2000, s 69(5), in PART III: SENTENCING, ante.
8. Powers of Criminal Courts (Sentencing) Act 2000, s 69(6), in PART III: SENTENCING, ante.
9. Powers of Criminal Courts (Sentencing) Act 2000, s 69(11), in PART III: SENTENCING, ante. Sch 8 to the Act, ante, has effect for dealing with a failure to comply with the requirements of an action plan order.
10. Powers of Criminal Courts (Sentencing) Act 2000, s 71, in PART III: SENTENCING, ante.
11. Powers of Criminal Courts (Sentencing) Act 2000, s 69(4), in PART III: SENTENCING, ante.
12. Powers of Criminal Courts (Sentencing) Act 2000, s 33(1), in PART III: SENTENCING, ante.
13. All courts in England and Wales were notified by Home Office letter dated 27 April 2000 that arrangements for implementing the parenting order would be available in their area with effect from 1 June 2000.
14. Powers of Criminal Courts (Sentencing) Act 2000, s 69(7) in PART III: SENTENCING, ante.

5–48   Attendance centre.   A youth court has power to make an attendance centre order in the case of a person, who has been found guilty of an offence punishable with imprisonment, or who has failed to comply with any requirement of a curfew order (in the case of an offender who is under 16 years of age), a probation order, a supervision order, an action plan order or a reparation order[1]. The restrictions and requirements in relation to this power are—

(1)   the court would have power but for section 89 of the Powers of Criminal Courts (Sentencing) Act 2000 (general restrictions on custodial sentences on persons under 21) to impose imprisonment[2], or the court has power to deal with the defendant for failure to comply with any of the requirements of a supervision order[3].

(2)   the Secretary of State has notified4 the court that an attendance centre is available for the reception from that court of persons of the offender's class or description;

(3)   the attendance centre, which must be specified in the order, must be reasonably accessible to the offender having regard to his age, the means of access available to him and any other circumstances;

(4)   the aggregate number of hours specified in the order shall not be less than 12 except where the offender is under 14 years of age and the court is of opinion, having regard to his age or any other circumstances, that 12 hours would be excessive; and the hours shall not exceed 12 except where the court is of opinion, having regard to all the circumstances, that 12 hours would be inadequate, and in that case shall not exceed 24 hours if he is under 16, otherwise it shall not exceed 36 hours.

(5)   the offender shall not be required to attend on more than one occasion on any day or for more than three hours on any occasion;

(6)   the times at which the offender is required to attend shall, as far as practicable, be such as to avoid—

   (a)   any conflict with the offender's religious beliefs or with the requirements of any other community order to which he may be subject, and

   (b)   any interference with the times, if any, at which he normally works or attends school or any other educational establishment;

(7)   the time of the first attendance shall be specified by the court; subsequent times shall be fixed by the officer in charge of the centre having regard to the offender's circumstances.

A comprehensive directory of attendance centres virtually covering England and Wales has been circulated to courts by the Home Office[4]; a court should refer to this and decide whether the offender has a centre accessible from his home. Home Office Circular No 135/1979 suggests that courts may use the following as a guide to reasonable accessibility; if the offender is aged up to 14, he may be expected to travel up to 10 miles or for 45 minutes, and if he is 14 or over he may be expected to travel up to 15 miles or for 90 minutes (presumably this relates to one way and not the return journey total).

Where an offender subject to an attendance centre order made by a youth court appears or is brought before the youth court acting for the area where the attendance centre is situated, or before the youth court that made the order, and the court is satisfied that he has failed without reasonable excuse to attend or has committed a breach of the attendance centre rules, that court[5] may, without prejudice to the continuance of the order, impose a fine not exceeding £1,000 or may revoke the attendance centre order and deal with him, for the offence in respect of which the order was made, in any manner in which he could have been dealt with for that offence if the order had not been made.

An attendance centre order may be discharged or varied on an application made by the offender or the officer in charge of the attendance centre[6]; the power to discharge includes the power to deal with the offender in any manner in which he could have been dealt with for the original offence.

---

1. Powers of Criminal Courts (Sentencing) Act 2000, s 60(1), Sch 3 para 4, Sch 7 para 2, Sch 8 para 2, in PART III: SENTENCING, ante.
2. Powers of Criminal Courts (Sentencing) Act 2000, s 60(1)(a), in PART III: SENTENCING, ante.
3. Powers of Criminal Courts (Sentencing) Act 2000, Sch 3, para 4, Sch 7, para 2, Sch 8, para 2, in PART III: SENTENCING, ante.
4. See Home Office Circulars No 22/1986, dated 8 April 1986 and No 72/1992, dated 28 July 1992. For details concerning junior attendance centres, including addresses, and the names, addresses and telephone numbers of the Officers-in-Charge, reference should be made to the Directory of Attendance Centres in England and Wales issued by the Home Office (4 August 1998).
5. Powers of Criminal Courts (Sentencing) Act 2000, Sch 5, para 2, in PART III: SENTENCING, ante.
6. Powers of Criminal Courts (Sentencing) Act 2000, Sch 5, para 4, in PART III: SENTENCING, ante.

5–49   Supervision orders and requirements that may be included.   (See also para **5–50** below for further provisions regarding requirements.)

Where a child or young person is found guilty of any offence, a youth court may make a supervision order in respect of him[1]. The order will cease to have effect on the expiration of three years from the date it was made, or such shorter period as may be specified in the order[2]. The supervision order must name the area of the local authority and the petty sessions area where the supervised person resides or will reside; that local authority, a probation officer or a member of a youth offending team will be designated as the supervisor[3]. The order may contain one or more of the following requirements—

(1) *Residence.* The order may require the supervised person to reside with an individual named in the order who agrees to the requirement, but such a requirement shall be subject to any other requirement as is authorised by Sch 6 to the Powers of Criminal Courts (Sentencing) Act 2000[4].

(2) *Requirement to live in local authority accommodation.* A supervision order may impose a requirement, known as a residence requirement, that a child or young person shall live for a specified period, not exceeding 6 months, in local authority accommodation. The requirement may stipulate that the minor shall not live with a named person.

Before making a residence requirement, the court must be satisfied as to the following conditions—

(a)   a supervision order has previously been made in respect of the child or young person;
(b)   that order imposed—

   (i)   a requirement under paras 1, 2, 3 or 7 of Sch 6 to the Powers of Criminal Courts (Sentencing) Act 2000; or
   (ii)   a local authority residence requirement;

(c)   the offender is guilty of an offence which—

   (i)   was committed while that order was in force;
   (ii)   if it had been committed by a person over the age of 21 would have been punishable with imprisonment; and
   (iii) in the opinion of the court is serious; and

(d)   the court is satisfied that the behaviour which constituted the offence was due, to a significant extent, to the circumstances in which he was living; and
(e)   the imposition of such a requirement will assist in his rehabilitation.

However, that the condition in (d) above does not apply where the condition in paragraph (b)(ii) is satisfied[5].

(3) *Requirement to live with local authority foster parent.* Subject to the following conditions, a supervision order may impose a requirement that the offender shall reside for a specified period of no more than 12 months with a local authority foster parent. The conditions are:

(a)   the offence is punishable with imprisonment in the case of an adult offender;
(b)   the offence, or the combination of the offence and one or more offences associated with it, is so serious that an custody sentence would normally be appropriate for it (in the case of an offender aged 10 or 11, if he were 12 or older);
(c)   the court is satisfied that the behaviour which constituted the offence was due to a significant extent to the circumstances in which the offender was living; and
(d)   the making of such a residence requirement will assist the offender's rehabilitation.

The court cannot make such a requirement unless it has been notified by the Secretary of State that arrangements to implement a foster parent residence requirement are available in the area concerned[6].

(4) *Intermediate treatment – directions by supervisor.* The order may require the supervised person to comply with any directions given from time to time by the supervisor and requiring him to do all or any of the following things:

(a)   to live at a place or places specified in the directions for a period or periods specified;
(b)   to present himself to a person or persons specified in the directions at a place or places, and on a day or days so specified;
(c)   to participate in activities specified in the directions on a day or days so specified;

but it shall be for the supervisor to decide whether and to what extent he exercises any power to give directions that is conferred on him and to decide the form of any directions.

A requirement imposed by a supervision order in pursuance of the foregoing shall be subject to any requirement of the order authorised by para 6 of Sch 6 to the Powers of Criminal Courts (Sentencing) Act 2000 (treatment for a mental condition). The total number of days in respect of which a supervised person may be required to comply with directions given under (a), (b) or (c) above shall not exceed 180 days or such lesser number as the order may specify[7].

(5) *Intermediate treatment – requirement of the court* (alternative to (4) above). The order may require the supervised person.

(a)   to live at a place or places specified for a period or periods specified;
(b)   to present himself to a person or persons specified at a place or places and on a day or days specified;
(c)   to participate in activities specified on a day or days so specified.
(d)   to make reparation specified in the order;
(e)   to refrain from participating in activities specified in the order wither on a specified day or days while the order is in force or for the whole duration of the order or a specified part of it.

If the court inserts a requirement for the giving of directions under sub-paragraph (2) above, may not impose a requirement under this provision. The above requirements shall have effect subject to any requirement under para 6 of Sch 6 to the Powers of Criminal Courts (Sentencing) Act 200 (treatment for a mental condition). The total number of days in respect of which a supervised perso may be required to comply with the above requirements shall not exceed 180 days or such lesse number as the order may specify[8].

(6) *Supplementary requirements*. It is the duty of the supervisor to advise, assist and befriend th supervised person[9], and to facilitate that, if the court thinks it appropriate, the order may require th supervised person to inform the supervisor at once of any change of residence or employment, t keep in touch with the supervisor in accordance with such instructions as may from time to time b given by the supervisor, and, in particular, to receive visits from the supervisor at his home[10].

(7) *Treatment for a mental condition*. The order may require the supervised person, for a perio specified in the order, to submit to treatment of one of the following descriptions so specified:

(a) treatment by or under the direction of a fully registered medical practitioner specified in th order;

(b) treatment as a non-resident patient at a place specified; or

(c) treatment as a resident patient in a hospital or mental nursing home within the meaning of th Mental Health Act 1983, other than a special hospital;

but such a requirement shall not be included in a supervision order unless–

(i) the court is satisfied, on the evidence of a medical practitioner approved for the purpose of s 12 of the Mental Health Act 1983 that the mental condition of the supervised perso is such as requires and may be susceptible to treatment, but is not such as to warrant h detention in pursuance of a hospital order;

(ii) the court is satisfied that arrangements have been or can be made for the treatment i question and, in the case of treatment as a resident patient, for the reception of the patien

(iii) in the case of an order to be made in respect of a person who has attained the age of 1 he consents to its inclusion[11].

(8) *Education*. The order may require a supervised person, if he is of compulsory school age, t comply, for as long as he is of that age and the order remains in force, with such arrangements for h education as may from time to time be made by his parent, being arrangements for the time bein approved by the local education authority[12].

1. Powers of Criminal Courts (Sentencing) Act 2000, s 63 (1), (2), in Part III: Sentencing, ante.
2. Powers of Criminal Courts (Sentencing) Act 2000, s 63 (7), in PART III: Sentencing, ante.
3. Powers of Criminal Courts (Sentencing) Act 2000, s 63 (1), (3), (6)(a), in PART III: Sentencing, ante.
4. Powers of Criminal Courts (Sentencing) Act 2000, Sch 6, para 1, in PART III: SENTENCING, ante.
5. Powers of Criminal Courts (Sentencing) Act 2000, Sch 6, para 5, in PART III: SENTENCING, ante.
6. Powers of Criminal Courts (Sentencing) Act 2000, Sch 6, para 5A, in PART III: SENTENCING, ante.
7. Powers of Criminal Courts (Sentencing) Act 2000, Sch 6, para 2, in PART III: SENTENCING, ante.
8. Powers of Criminal Courts (Sentencing) Act 2000, Sch 6, para 3, in PART III: SENTENCING, ante.
9. Powers of Criminal Courts (Sentencing) Act 2000, s 64(4) in PART III: SENTENCING, ante.
10. Powers of Criminal Courts (Sentencing) Act 2000, s 63(6)(b), in PART III: SENTENCING, ante.
11. Powers of Criminal Courts (Sentencing) Act 2000, Sch 6, para 6, in PART III: SENTENCING, ante.
12. Powers of Criminal Courts (Sentencing) Act 2000, Sch 6, para 7, in PART III: SENTENCING, ante.

5–49A Intensive Supervision and Surveillance Programme Schemes. These are provide under supervision and curfew orders. They allow for intensive forms of supervision to run for up t 12 months. At the time of going to press these schemes are being piloted in the following loca authority areas: Birmingham City Council; Bolton Metropolitan Borough Council; Bridgend Count Borough Council; Calderdale Metropolitan Borough Council; Cardiff County Council; City an County of Swansea Council; Coventry City Council; Kirklees Metropolitan Council; Leeds Cit Council; Liverpool City Council; London Borough of Barking and Dagenham; London Borough o Bexley; London Borough of Bromley; London Borough of Croydon; London Borough of Greenwich London Borough of Havering; London Borough of Lewisham; London Borough of Merton; Londo Borough of Redbridge; London Borough of Richmond upon Thames; London Borough o Southwark; London Borough of Sutton; London Borough of Waltham Forest; Merthyr Tydf County Borough Council; Neath Port Talbot County Borough Council; Nottingham City Counci Oldham Metropolitan Borough Council; Rhonda Cynon Taf County Borough Council; Roya Borough of Kingston upon Thames; Solihull Metropolitan Borough Council; Stockport Metropolita Borough Council; Thameside Metropolitan Borough Council; and Vale of Glamorgan Council[1].

1. See HOC 66/2004, issued 29/9/2004.

5–50 Supervision: further restrictions on requirements, etc. A local authority must not b designated as the supervisor unless the authority agrees or it appears to the court that the offende resides or will reside in the area of the authority[1].

The court may not include any of the requirements referred to in sub-para (4) para **5–49** above i a supervision order unless it is satisfied that a local authority scheme under s 66 of the Powers o Criminal Courts (Sentencing) Act 2000 is in force in the area in which the offender resides or wi reside; and no such directions may involved the use of facilities which are not for the time bein specified in that scheme[2].

The court may not include any of the requirements referred to in sub-para (5) of para **5–49** above unless:

(*a*) it has first consulted the supervisor as to-

   (i)   the offender's circumstances; and
   (ii) the feasibility of securing compliance with the requirements,

   and is satisfied, having regard to the supervisor's report, that it is feasible to secure compliance with them;

(*b*) having regard to the circumstances of the case, it considers the requirements necessary for securing the good conduct of the supervised person or for preventing a repetition by him of the same offence or the commission of other offences; and

(*c*) if the supervised person is under the age of 16, it has obtained and considered information about his family circumstances and the likely effect of the requirements on those circumstances[3].

Additionally, the court shall not include in an order by virtue of the requirements referred to in sub-para (5) of para **5–49** above:

(*a*) any requirement that would involve the co-operation of a person other than the supervisor and the supervised person unless that other person consents to its inclusion; or

(*b*) any requirement to make reparation to any person unless that person:

   (i)   is identified by the court as a victim of the offence or a person otherwise affected by it; and
   (ii) consents to the inclusion of the requirement; or

(*c*) any requirement requiring the supervised person to reside with a specified individual (but note the power referred to in sub-paragraph (1) above to impose such a requirement with the agreement of such an individual); or

(*d*) any requirement that the offender shall submit to treatment for a mental condition (but note the power under para 6(2) of Sch 6 to the Powers of Criminal Courts (Sentencing) Act 2000 referred to in sub-paragraph (8) above);

(*e*) any requirement that would involve the supervised person in absence from home:

   (i)   for more than 2 consecutive nights;
   (ii) for more than 2 nights in any one week;

   unless the court making the order is satisfied that the facilities whose use would be involved are for the time being specified in a scheme in force under section 66 of the Powers of Criminal Courts (Sentencing) Act 2000 for the area in which the supervised person resides or will reside; or

(*f*) if the supervised person is of compulsory school age, any requirement to participate in activities during normal school hours, unless,

   (i)   the court making the order is satisfied that the facilities whose use would be involved are for the time being specified in a scheme in force under section 19 of the Children and Young Persons Act 1969 for the area in which the supervised person resides or will reside, or
   (ii) the activities are to be carried out in accordance with arrangements made or approved by the local education authority in whose area the supervised person resides or will reside[4].

Directions given by a supervisor or requirements in a supervision order under (4)(*b*) or (*c*), (5)(*b*) or (*c*), in para **5–49** above shall, so far as is practicable, be such as to avoid any conflict with the offender's religious beliefs or with the requirements of any other community order to which he may be subject and any interference with the times, if any, at which he normally works or attends school or any other educational establishment[5].

The court shall not include a residence requirement, as referred to in sub-para (2) and (3) of para **5–49** above, in respect of an offender who is not legally represented unless he has applied for legal aid and it has been refused on account of his means, or he has been informed of his right to apply for legal aid and he has failed to do so[6]. Additionally, the court shall not make the residence requirement referred to in sub-para (2) of para **5–49** above without first consulting the designated authority[7].

The court shall not include the requirement as to education referred to in sub-para (8) of para **5–49** above unless it has consulted the local education authority with regard to its proposal to include the requirement and is satisfied that in the view of the local education authority arrangements exist for the supervised person to receive efficient full-time education suitable to his age, ability and aptitude and to any special educational needs he may have. Moreover, the court shall not make such a requirement unless it has first consulted the supervisor as to the offender's circumstances and considers the requirement necessary for securing the good conduct of the supervised person or for preventing a repetition by him of the same offence or the commission of other offences[8].

It is the duty of a local authority, acting either individually or in association with other local authorities, to make arrangements with such persons as appear to them to be appropriate for the provision of facilities for the carrying out of supervisors' directions and requirements included in supervision orders. Such arrangements shall be specified in a scheme made under s 66 of the Powers of Criminal Courts (Sentencing) Act 2000, of which copies shall be sent to the clerk to the justices for each petty sessions area of which any part is included in the area to which the scheme relates[9].

1. Powers of Criminal Courts (Sentencing) Act 2000, s 64(1), in PART III: SENTENCING, ante.
2. Powers of Criminal Courts (Sentencing) Act 2000, Sch 6, para 2(2), in PART III: SENTENCING, ante.
3. Powers of Criminal Courts (Sentencing) Act 2000, Sch 6, para 3(4), in PART III: SENTENCING, ante.Part III Sentencing, ante.
4. Powers of Criminal Courts (Sentencing) Act 2000, Sch 6, para 3(5) (in relation to (*a*)–(*d*)) and 3(7) (in relation to (3) and (*f*)), in PART III: SENTENCING, ante.
5. Powers of Criminal Courts (Sentencing) Act 2000, Sch 6, paras 2(7) and 3(6), in PART III: SENTENCING, ante.
6. Powers of Criminal Courts (Sentencing) Act 2000, Sch 6, para 5(7), 5A(6), in PART III: SENTENCING, ante.
7. Powers of Criminal Courts (Sentencing) Act 2000, Sch 6, para 5(4), (8), in PART III: SENTENCING, ante.
8. Powers of Criminal Courts (Sentencing) Act 2000, Sch 6, para 7(3) and (5), in PART III: SENTENCING, ante.
9. Powers of Criminal Courts (Sentencing) Act 2000, s 66(1)–(5), in PART III: SENTENCING, ante.

5–52 Supervision: breach of requirement of supervision order. If while a supervision order is in force, it is proved to the satisfaction of the relevant court, on the application of the supervisor, that the supervised person has failed to comply with any requirements inserted in the order as referred to in sub-paras (1) to (8) of para **5–49** above, the court may:

(*a*) fine up to £1,000;
(*b*) or make an attendance centre order;
(*c*) or make a curfew order (if he is not already subject to such an order);
(*d*) or if the order was made by a magistrates' court, revoke the order and deal with the offender for the original offence in any way in which he could have been dealt with for that offence by the court which made the order if the order had not been made;
(*e*) or, if the supervision order had been made by the Crown Court, commit him in custody or on bail to appear before the Crown Court. In dealing with him the court must take into account the extent to which he has complied with the order[1].

In relation to a supervision order 'relevant court' means (where the offender is under 18), a youth court acting for the petty sessions area named in the order or (offender who has attained 18), a magistrates' court other than a youth court, acting for the petty sessions area named in the order. Where an offender attains 18 years whilst proceedings are pending, the youth court must deal with the application as if he had not attended that age[2].

A curfew order may not be made unless the court has been notified by the Secretary of State that arrangements for monitoring the offender's whereabouts are available[3]. The provisions governing the making of curfew orders and attendance centre orders are subject to various modifications where it is proposed to make such an order for breach of a supervision order[4].

1. Powers of Criminal Courts (Sentencing) Act 2000, Sch 7 para 2, in PART III: SENTENCING, ante.
2. Powers of Criminal Courts (Sentencing) Act 2000, Sch 7, para 1, in PART III: SENTENCING, ante.
3. Powers of Criminal Courts (Sentencing) Act 2000, Sch 7 para 3 in PART III: SENTENCING, ante.
4. See Powers of Criminal Courts (Sentencing) Act 2000, Sch 7, paras 3 and 4 in PART III: SENTENCING, ante.

5–53 Community rehabilitation order. Where a person aged 16 of over is found guilty of an offence and the court is of opinion that supervision by a probation officer is desirable in the interests of securing the rehabilitation of the offender or protecting the public from harm from him or preventing the commission by him of further offences, it may make a community rehabilitation order for a specified period not less than 6 months nor more than 3 years[1].

The Home Office has issued a circular giving guidance to the courts on the arrangements for the admission of 16 and 17 year olds to hostels approved by the Secretary of State, where they have been made subject to a community rehabilitation order with a requirement of residence in an approved hostel or, while on bail, are being assessed for such an order[2].

See para **5–37** *as to transitional arrangements for 16 and 17 year-old offenders. For narrative on community rehabilitation orders see para* **3–213** *of the 2005 edition of this work.*

1. Powers of Criminal Courts (Sentencing) Act 2000, s 41, in PART III: SENTENCING, ante.
2. See Home Office Circular 44/1993, dated 26 August 1993.

5–54 Community punishment order. Where a person aged 16 is guilty of an offence punishable in the case of an adult with imprisonment, the court may make a community punishment order[1] requiring him to perform unpaid work for not less than 40 nor more than 240 hours, such period to be stated in the order.

See para **5–37** *above as to transitional arrangements for 16 and 17 year-old offenders. For narrative on community punishment orders see para* **3–214** *of the 2005 edition of this work.*

1. Powers of Criminal Courts (Sentencing) Act 2000, s 46, in PART III: SENTENCING, ante.

5–55 Community punishment and rehabilitation order. Where a person aged 16 or over is convicted of an offence punishable with imprisonment and the court is of opinion that a community punishment and rehabilitation order is desirable in the interests of securing his rehabilitation or protecting the public from harm from him or preventing the commission by him of further offences, it may order him to be under the supervision of a probation officer for not less than 12 months nor more than 3 years and to perform community service for not less than 40 nor more than 100 hours[1].

See para **5–37** as to transitional arrangements for 16 and 17 year-old offenders. For narrative on community punishment orders and rehabilitation orders see para **3–214** of the 2005 edition of this work.

---

1. Powers of Criminal Courts (Sentencing) Act 2000, s 51, and see para **3–115**, in PART III: SENTENCING, ante.

–56 Curfew order. Where a person is convicted of an offence, the court may make a curfew order, that is an order requiring him to remain, for periods specified in the order, at a place so specified[1]. A curfew order may specify different places or different periods for different days, but shall not specify—

    (*a*) periods which fall outside the period of 6 months (or 3 months in the case of an offender under the age of 16) beginning with the day on which it is made; or

    (*b*) periods which amount to less than 2 hours or more than 12 hours in any one day[2].

The requirements in a curfew order must, as far as practicable, avoid any conflict with the offender's religious beliefs or with the requirements of any other community order to which he may be subject. Moreover, they must, as far as practicable, avoid any interference with the times, if any, at which the offender normally works or attends school or other educational establishment[3].

A curfew order must include provision for making a person responsible for monitoring the offender's whereabouts during the curfew periods specified in the order; and a person who is made so responsible must be of a description specified in an order made by the Secretary of State[4]. A court shall not make a curfew order unless it has been notified by the Secretary of State that arrangements for monitoring the offender's whereabouts are available in the area in which the place proposed to be specified in the order is situated and the notice has not been withdrawn[5].

All courts in England and Wales were notified that electronic monitoring arrangements were available from 1 December 1999 in respect of offenders aged 16 or over for the purpose of monitoring the whereabouts of an offender who is the subject of a curfew order[6]. These arrangements were extended to offenders aged 10–15 from 1 February 2001[7].

Before making a curfew order, the court must obtain and consider information about the place proposed to be specified in the order (including information as to the attitude of persons likely to be affected by the enforced presence there of the offender). Before the court makes a curfew order in respect of an offender who is under the age of 16 years, the court must obtain and consider information about his family circumstances and the likely effect of such an order on those circumstances[8]. Before making the order, the court must also explain to the offender in ordinary language the effect of the order, including any additional requirements for electronic monitoring, and the consequences which may follow[9] if he fails to comply with any requirements of the order[10].

A curfew order may include requirements for securing the electronic monitoring of the offender's whereabouts during the curfew periods specified in the order. Such requirements shall not be included in a curfew order unless the court has been notified by the Secretary of State that electronic monitoring arrangements are available in the area in which the place proposed to be specified in the order is situated, and the court is satisfied that the necessary provision can be made under those arrangements[11].

---

1. Powers of Criminal Courts (Sentencing) Act 2000, s 37(1), this PART, post.
2. PCC(S)A 2000, s 37(3)–(4), this PART, post.
3. PCC(S)A 2000, s 37(5), this PART, post.
4. PCC(S)A 2000, s 37(6), this PART, post.
5. PCC(S)A 2000, s 37(7), this PART, post.
6. Home Office Letter 18 November 1999.
7. Home Office Letter, 19 December 2000.
8. PCC(S)A 2000, s 37(8), this PART, post.
9. For enforcement of a curfew order, see PCC(S)A 2000, Sch 3, this PART, post.
10. PCC(S)A 2000, s 37(10), this PART, post.
11. PCC(S)A 2000, s 38, this PART, post.

5–57 Exclusion order. Where an offender is convicted of an offence, the court may make an order prohibiting him from entering a place specified in the order for a period so specified of not more than two years[1]. In the case of an offender aged under 16 on conviction, the maximum period is three months[2], and the court must additionally obtain and consider information about his family circumstances and the likely effect of such an order on those circumstances[3].

An exclusion order must include provision for making a person of a description specified in an order made by the Secretary of State responsible for monitoring the offender's whereabouts during the currency of the prohibition[4].

An exclusion order must specify the PSD in which the offender resides or will reside[5].

An exclusion order cannot be made unless the Secretary of State has notified the court that arrangements for monitoring the offender's whereabouts are available in the area in which the place proposed to be specified in the order is situated and that notice has not been withdrawn[6].

The requirements of an exclusion order must so far as is practicable be such as to avoid any conflict with the offender's religious beliefs or any other community order to which he is subject and to avoid any interference with the offender's work or educational commitments[7].

Before making an exclusion order the court must explain to the offender: the effect of the order, including any requirements of electronic monitoring that are proposed to be included; the consequences that may follow from non compliance; and that the court has power to review the order on the application of the offender, the responsible officer or any affected person[8]. A person is an "affected person" if a requirement of electronic monitoring is included in the order with his consent, or the prohibition is included in the order wholly or partly for the purpose of protecting him from being approached by the offender[9].

Copies of the order must be given to the offender and the responsible order; and the court mus give to any affected person (as defined above) any information relating to the order which the cour considers it appropriate for him to have[10].

1. Section 40A(1) of the Powers of Criminal Courts (Sentencing) Act 2000. See this Part, post.
2. PCC(S)A 2000, s 40A(4).
3. PCC(S)A 2000, s 40A(9).
4. PCC(S)A 2000, s 40A(6).
5. PCC(S)A 2000, s 40A(7).
6. PCC(S)A 2000, s 40A(8). From 2 September 2004 arrangements have been available in Greater Manchester, Wes Midlands and Hampshire/Wessex YOT pilot areas. See HOC 61/2004.
7. PCC(S)A 2000, s 40A(5).
8. PCC(S)A 2000, s 40A(10).
9. PCC(S)A 2000, s 40A(13).
10. PCC(S)A 2000, s 40A(11).

5–60   Drug treatment and testing order.   Where a young person aged 16 or over is found guilt of an offence by a youth court, that court may make a drug treatment and testing order in respect o the offender[1].

For narrative on drug treatment and testing orders see para **3–216A** *to* **3–216** *of the 2005 edition of th work.*

1. Powers of Criminal Courts (Sentencing) Act 2000, s 52, and see para **3–116** in Part III: Sentencing, ante.

5–60A   Detention and training order.   A detention and training order is an order that the offende in respect of whom it is made shall be subject, for the term specified in the order, to a period o detention and training followed by a period of supervision[1]. A detention and training order is custodial sentence for the purposes of Part V of the Powers of Criminal Courts (Sentencing) Ac 2000 and sections 79–82 of that Act apply accordingly[2].

A detention and training order will be the appropriate sentence where—

    (*a*)   a child or young person[3] is found guilty of an offence which is punishable witl imprisonment in the case of a person aged 21 or over; and

    (*b*)   the court is of the opinion that either or both of paragraphs (*a*) or (*b*) of section 79(2) o the Powers of Criminal Courts (Sentencing) Act 2000 apply or the case falls withir subsection (3) of that section[4].

A court shall not make a detention and training order—

    (*a*)   in the case of an offender under the age of 15 at the time of the conviction, unless it is o the opinion that he is a persistent offender;

    (*b*)   in the case of an offender under the age of 12 at that time, unless—

        (i)   it is of the opinion that only a custodial sentence would be adequate to protect th public from further offending by him; and

        (ii)   the offence was committed on or after such date as the Secretary of State may b order appoint[5].

The term of a detention and training order shall be 4[6], 6, 8, 10, 12, 18 or 24 months[7]. A youtl court is empowered to make an order for up to the maximum of 24 months[8]. The term of a detentior and training order may not exceed the maximum term of imprisonment that the Crown Court coulc in the case of an offender aged 21 or over impose for the offence[9]. However, s 133 of the Magistrates Court Act 1980, which places limitations on the maximum periods of imprisonment or detention ir a young offender institution that magistrates may impose, does not apply directly to detention anc training orders; therefore, the court may impose consecutive detention and training orders fo summary offences to an aggregate that exceeds six months[10]. As the minimum term of detention anc training is four months, a youth convicted of criminal damage to the value of less than £5,000 is no liable to a custodial sentence in the youth court[11].

When making a detention and training order it is the duty of the court to state in open court that i is of the opinion mentioned in s 79 (4) of the Powers of Criminal Courts (Sentencing) Act 2000 anc of the opinion mentioned in s 100(2)(*a*) or, as the case may be s 100(2)(*a*) and (*b*)(i)[12] of that Act[13].

Where an offender is convicted of more than one offence for which he is liable to a detention anc training order, or an offender who is subject to a detention and training order is convicted of one o more further of fences for which he is liable to such an order, the court has the same power to pas consecutive detention and training orders as if they were sentences of imprisonment[14]. However, court shall not make in respect of an offender a detention and training order the effect of which woulc be that he would be subject to detention and training orders for a term which exceeds 24 months Where the term exceeds 24 months, the excess shall be treated as remitted[15]. A detention and training order may not be made to commence on the expiry of a term of a detention and training order undei which the period of supervision has already begun[16]. Where a new order is made in respect of ar offender whose period of supervision has begun under an old order, the old order is to be disregardec for the purposes of determining whether the effect of the new order would be that the offender woulc be subject to orders for a term which exceeds 24 months[17]. Consecutive terms of detention anc training orders which are wholly or partly concurrent shall be treated as a single term if the orders were made on the same occasion, or where they were made on different occasions, the offender has not been released at any time during the period beginning with the first and ending with the last of those occasions[18].

In determining the term of a detention and training order for an offence, the court must take account of any period for which the offender has been remanded in custody (including being held in police detention, remanded to local authority accommodation and kept in secure accommodation, or remanded, admitted or removed to hospital under section 35, 36, 38 or 48 of the Mental Health Act 1983) in connection with the offence, or any other offence the charge for which was founded on the same facts or evidence[19].

For the purpose of determining whether an offender under the age of 15 at the time of conviction is a persistent offender, the court may have regard to earlier offences for which the offender has been cautioned by the police[20], and offences committed after the present offence[21]. Persistent offending does not necessarily involve persistent appearances before a court[22]. A series of offences committed over only two days may be sufficient to qualify an offender as persistent, even though he has no previous convictions[23].

The court is required merely to take account of the time spent in custody on remand and need not reflect it in some specific way. The requirement does not provide for a one-to-one discount[24], nor does it require courts to fine tune, by reference to a few days in custody, the sentence which is appropriate when making a detention and training order[25].

When making a detention and training order consecutive to one already served, the court must select an appropriate term for the offence. Owing to the unfairness which could arise because of the limitation on the periods for which a detention and training order may be imposed, the court is not restricted to imposing a consecutive sentence of a term that will create an aggregate sentence that itself equals one of the permitted totals[26].

---

1. Powers of Criminal Courts (Sentencing) Act 2000, s 100(3), in PART III: SENTENCING, ante.
2. Powers of Criminal Courts (Sentencing) Act 2000, s 76, in PART III: SENTENCING, ante.
3. In *Aldis v DPP* [2002] EWHC 403 (Admin), [2002] 2 Cr App Rep (S) 400, [2002] Crim LR 434 it was held, in relation to a defendant aged 17 at the time of mode of trial, at which hearing it must have been plain to all present that the possibility of a 2-year detention and training order was a factor in the court's decision to try the case summarily, that the attainment of 18 before the trial and conviction did not prevent the justices from imposing a detention and training order; Parliament's intention must have been that s 100 of the Powers of Criminal Courts (Sentencing) Act 2000 should be interpreted as subject to s 29 of the Children and Young Persons Act 1963.
4. Powers of Criminal Courts (Sentencing) Act 2000, s 100(1), in PART III: SENTENCING, ante.
5. Powers of Criminal Courts (Sentencing) Act 2000, s 100(2), in PART III: SENTENCING, ante.
6. The court should have regard to the fact that 4 months is the minimum sentence when deciding whether or not the custody threshold is crossed: *R v M* [2001] EWCA Crim 1505, (2001) 165 JPN 455. See also *R v Inner London Crown Court, ex p N and S* [2001] 1 Cr App Rep (S) 323.
7. Powers of Criminal Courts (Sentencing) Act 2000, s 101(1), in PART III: SENTENCING, ante.
8. See observations of Hughes J in *Medway Youth Court, ex p A* [2000] 1 Cr App Rep (S) 191. As to reducing the term of a DTO to reflect a guilty plea, see *R v Stuart Marley* [2001] EWCA Crim 2779, [2002] 2 Cr App Rep (S) 73; and *R v Gary Francis Kelly* [2001] EWCA Crim 1751. [2002] 1 Cr App Rep (S) 40 (in both cases s 91 detention was unavailable and the sentences for the offences (respectively, riot and s 20 wounding) were reduced from 24 to 18 months). See also *R v Wayne Robin March* [2002] EWCA Crim 551, [2002] 2 Cr App Rep (S) 448 (the fact that the prosecution did not pursue a charge that did attract s 91 of the Powers of Criminal Courts (Sentencing) Act 2000 was not a good reason for refusing a discount when the defendant pleaded guilty to a charge to which s 91 was unavailable).
9. Powers of Criminal Courts (Sentencing) Act 2000, s 101(2), in PART III: SENTENCING, ante.
10. *C v DPP* [2001] Crim LR 670, DC.
11. *Pye v Leeds Youth Court* [2006] EWHC 2527.
12. Powers of Criminal Courts (Sentencing) Act 2000, s 100(4), in PART III: SENTENCING, ante.
13. Powers of Criminal Courts (Sentencing) Act 2000, s 101(5), in PART III: SENTENCING, ante.
14. But without being constrained by the provisions of the Magistrates' Courts Act 1980, s 133, as to the maximum overall aggregate of 6 months for summary offences: see text above.
15. Powers of Criminal Courts (Sentencing) Act 2000, s 101(13) in PART III: SENTENCING, ante.
16. Powers of Criminal Courts (Sentencing) Act 2000, s 101 (6), in PART III: SENTENCING, ante.
17. Powers of Criminal Courts (Sentencing) Act 2000, s 101 (7), in PART III: SENTENCING, ante.
18. Powers of Criminal Courts (Sentencing) Act 2000, s 101 (8)–(12), in PART III: SENTENCING, ante.
19. Powers of Criminal Courts (Sentencing) Act 2000, s 100(8), in PART III: SENTENCING, ante. The requirement to give credit for time spent in custody on remand does not involve applying a precise reduction: *R v Lee (James B)* [2001] 1 Cr App Rep (S) 303. See also *R v Inner London Crown Court, ex p N and S* [2001] 1 Cr App Rep (S) 323; *R v Terry Jane Elsmore* [2001] 2 Cr App Rep (S) 461; *R v March* [2002] EWCA Crim 551, [2002] Crim LR 509.
20. *R v D* [2000] Crim LR 867, CA.
21. *R v B* [2001] Crim LR 51, CA.
22. *R v Charlton* (2000) 164 JP 685, CA, where it was said that the Home Office definition of "persistent young offender" for the purpose of fast tracking such cases was not appropriate to be adopted as definitive for the purpose of the statutory predecessor to s 100.
23. *R v Andrew Smith* (2000) 164 JP 681, CA.
24. *R v B* [2000] Crim LR 870, CA.
25. *R v Inner London Crown Court, ex p N and S* [2000] Crim LR 871, CA; *R v Fieldhouse and Watts* [2000] Crim LR 1020, CA.
26. *R v Norris* (2000) 164 JP 689, CA.

5–60B Detention and training order: period of detention and training. An offender shall serve the period of detention and training under a detention and training order in such secure accommodation as is determined by the Secretary of State or by such other person authorised by him for that purpose[1].

Subject to the following provisions, the period of detention and training under a detention and training order shall be one-half of the term of the order[2].

The Secretary of State may at any time release the offender if he is satisfied that exceptional circumstances exist which justify the offender's release on compassionate grounds[3].

The Secretary of State may release the offender—

(a) in the case of an order for a term of 8 months or more but less than 18 months one month before the half-way point of the term of the order; and (*b*) in the case of an order for a term of 18 months or more, one month or two months before that point[4].

If the youth court so orders on an application by the Secretary of State for the purpose, the Secretary of State shall release the offender—
(*a*) in the case of an order for a term of 8 months or more but less than 18 months, one month after the half-way point of the term of the order; and
(*b*) in the case of an order for a term of 18 months or more, one month or two months after that point[5].

For the purposes of ss 102, 104 and 105 of the Powers of Criminal Courts (Sentencing) Act 2000 "secure accommodation" means a secure training centre; a young offender institution; accommodation provided by a local authority for the purpose of restricting the liberty of children and young persons; accommodation provided for that purpose under s 82(5) of the Children Act 1989[6], or such other accommodation provided for the purpose of restricting liberty as the Secretary of State may direct[7].

1. Powers of Criminal Courts (Sentencing) Act 2000, s 102(1), in PART III: SENTENCING, ante.
2. Powers of Criminal Courts (Sentencing) Act 2000, s 102(2), in PART III: SENTENCING, ante.
3. Powers of Criminal Courts (Sentencing) Act 2000, s 102(3), in PART III: SENTENCING, ante.
4. Powers of Criminal Courts (Sentencing) Act 2000, s 102(4) in PART III: SENTENCING, ante.
5. Powers of Criminal Courts (Sentencing) Act 2000, s 102(5), in PART III: SENTENCING, ante.
6. See PART IV: FAMILY LAW, ante.
7. Powers of Criminal Courts (Sentencing) Act 2000, s 107, in PART III: SENTENCING, ante.

5-60C Detention and training order: period of supervision and breaches of supervision requirements. The period of supervision of an offender who is subject to a detention and training order—
(*a*) shall begin with the offender's release, whether at the half-way point of the term of the order or otherwise; and
(*b*) shall end when the term of the order ends[1].

However, the Secretary of State may by order provide that the period of supervision shall end at such point during the term of a detention and training order as may be specified in the order[2].
During the period of supervision, the offender shall be under the supervision of—
(*a*) a probation officer:
(*b*) a social worker of a local authority social services department: or
(*c*) a member of a youth offending team;

and the category of person to supervise the offender shall be determined from time to time by the Secretary of State[3].
The offender must be given a notice from the Secretary of State specifying the category of person for the time being responsible for his supervision and any requirements with which he must for the time being comply. The notice must be given to the offender before the period of supervision commences and before any alteration in the category of person to supervise the offender or in the supervision requirements takes effect[4].
Where a detention and training order is in force in respect of an offender and it appears on information to a justice of the peace acting for a relevant petty sessions area that the offender has failed to comply with the supervision requirements, the justice—
(*a*) may issue a summons[5] requiring the offender to appear at the place and time specified in the summons before a youth court acting for the area; or
(*b*) if the information is in writing and on oath, may issue a warrant for the offender's arrest requiring him to be brought before such a court[6].

For this purpose, a petty sessions area is a relevant petty sessions area if the detention and training order was made by a youth court acting for it, or the offender resides in it for the time being[7].
If it is proved to the satisfaction of the youth court before which an offender appears or is brought that he has failed to comply with requirements specified in the notice from the Secretary of State, that court may—
(*a*) order the offender to be detained, in such secure accommodation as the Secretary of State may determine, for such period, not exceeding the shorter of three months or the remainder of the term of the detention and training order, as the court may specify; or
(*b*) impose on the offender a fine not exceeding **level 3** on the standard scale[8].

1. Powers of Criminal Courts (Sentencing) Act 2000, s 103(1) , in PART III: SENTENCING, ante.
2. Powers of Criminal Courts (Sentencing) Act 2000, s 103(2), in PART III: SENTENCING, ante.
3. Powers of Criminal Courts (Sentencing) Act 2000, s 103(3), in PART III: SENTENCING, ante.
4. Powers of Criminal Courts (Sentencing) Act 2000, s 103(6), (7), in PART III: SENTENCING, ante.
5. Where a defendant is sentenced to detention and training orders in respect of a number of offences they constitute a single order for the purpose of breach proceedings and the court record should show a breach of only one order; where, however, there are two separate breaches of the licence – for example, failing to keep in touch with the supervising officer and failing to reside where directed – there is a need to lay separate informations in respect of each of the kinds of breach, though within each kind there is no need to allege each of the instances separately: *S v Doncaster Youth Offending Team* [2003] EWHC 1128 (Admin), (2003) 167 JP 381.
6. Powers of Criminal Courts (Sentencing) Act 2000, s 104(1), in PART III: SENTENCING, ante.

7. Powers of Criminal Courts (Sentencing) Act 2000, s 104(2) in PART III: SENTENCING, ante.
8. Powers of Criminal Courts (Sentencing) Act 2000, s 104(3) in PART III: SENTENCING, ante.

–60D Detention and training order: offences during currency of order. The power to deal with a person for an offence committed during the currency of a detention and training order arises if that person after his release and before the date on which the term of the order ends, commits an offence punishable with imprisonment in the case of a person aged 21 or over, and before or after that date, he is convicted of that offence ("the new offence"). The court by or before which such a person is convicted of the new offence may, whether or not it passes any other sentence on him, order him to be detained in such secure accommodation as the Secretary of State may determine for the whole or any part of the period which—

   (*a*) begins with the date of the court's order; and

   (*b*) is equal in length to the period between the date on which the new offence was committed and the date on which the term of the detention and training order ends[1].

The period for which a person under these provisions is ordered to be detained in secure accommodation—

   (*a*) shall, as the court may direct, either be served before and be followed by, or be served concurrently with, any sentence imposed for the new offence; and

   (*b*) in either case, shall be disregarded in determining the appropriate length of that sentence[2].

Where the new offence is found to have been committed over a period of two or more days, or at some time during a period of two or more days, it shall be taken to have been committed on the last of those days[3].

---

1. Powers of Criminal Courts (Sentencing) Act 2000, s 105(1), (2), in PART III: SENTENCING, ante.
2. Powers of Criminal Courts (Sentencing) Act 2000, s 105(3), in PART III: SENTENCING, ante.
3. Powers of Criminal Courts (Sentencing) Act 2000, s 105(4), in PART III: SENTENCING, ante.

–61 Punishment of certain grave crimes[1]. Where a young offender is convicted on indictment of certain grave crimes he may be sentenced to long-term detention. This sentence is available:

   (*a*) where a person of at least 10 but not more than 17 years is convicted on indictment of—

      (i) any offence punishable in the case of an adult with imprisonment for 14 years or more, not being an offence the sentence for which is fixed by law, or

      (ii) an offence under s 3 (sexual assault), s 13 (child sex offences committed by children or young persons), s 25 (sexual activity with a child family member) or s 26 (inciting a child family member to engage in sexual activity) of the Sexual Offences Act 2003;

   (*b*) where a person aged under 18 is convicted on indictment of an offence—

      (i) under subsection (1)(*a*), (*ab*), (*aba*), (*ac*), (*ad*), (*ae*), (*af*) or (*c*) of section 5 of the Firearms Act 1968 (prohibited weapons), or

      (ii) under subsection (1A)(*a*) of that section,

   (*c*) the offence was committed after the commencement of section 51A of that Act and at a time when he was aged 16 or over, and

   (*d*) the court is of the opinion mentioned in section 51A(2) of that Act (exceptional circumstances which justify its not imposing required custodial sentence).

If the court is of opinion that none of the other methods in which the case may legally be dealt with is suitable, it may sentence the offender to be detained for a period not exceeding the maximum term of imprisonment with which the offence is punishable in the case of an adult[2]. In the case of murder the sentence is detention during Her Majesty's pleasure[3].

Sentences of detention during Her Majesty's Pleasure (for murder: section 90 of the Powers of Criminal Courts (Sentencing) Act 2000) or long-term detention (for "grave crimes" under section 91 of the Powers of Criminal Courts (Sentencing) Act 2000) may be passed only on indictment, and may not be passed by the youth court. A youth court may not deal with an offender for an offence of homicide but must commit him for trial to the Crown Court[4]. In the case of "grave crimes", whenever a youth court has before it a minor whose offence comes within this category, it has power to deal with him, but should always consider carefully whether its own powers are adequate or whether it would be proper for the Crown Court sentencing the defendant for the offence of which he is charged to exercise its powers under s 91 of the Powers of Criminal Courts (Sentencing) Act 2000 and sentence him to a period greater than two years; if the latter, then the minor should be committed for trial[5]. A minor sentenced by the Crown Court will be detained in such place and on such conditions as the Secretary of State may direct.

Such a sentence is appropriate for an offender below the minimum age for imprisonment who is persistently involved in serious crime, eg "gang warfare", possessing offensive weapon and burglaries by the one offender[6]; for a youth of 16, a "professional burglar" armed with a sawn-off shot-gun[7]; for a youth of 16 who robbed a disabled man in his own home, having had 11 previous court appearances and having served detention centre orders and youth custody[8]; for a youth of 15 who, after expulsion from school, set fire to the school premises[9]; for a youth charged with causing grievous bodily harm with intent[10]; for a youth of 15 who committed 2 offences of arson being reckless as to whether life would be endangered[11]; for a youth participating in a conspiracy to rob a shopkeeper by 3 youths with an air pistol[12]. See also the cases referred to in the notes to s 24 of the Magistrates' Courts Act 1980 (para **1–2053**, ante).

The Court of Appeal has given guidance on sentencing problems arising from the interrelation of statutory provisions concerning sentences of detention under s 91 of the Powers of Criminal Courts (Sentencing) Act 2000 and detention in a young offender institution (now replaced by the detention and training order but which has the same maximum length of 24 months)[13]. In particular, the Court of Appeal has said that a court should not impose a sentence greater than 24 months without much careful thought, but if it concludes that a longer, even if not muc longer, sentence is called for, then it should impose whatever it considers the appropriate period of detention unde s 91 of the Powers of Criminal Courts (Sentencing) Act 2000[14]. If on a plea of guilty to an offence, falling withi s 91 the court imposes a sentence of 24 months' detention in a young offender institution [detention and trainir order] it is not to be inferred that the court has failed to give credit for a guilty plea: but for the plea, the sentenc might properly have been longer[8]. Where more than one offence is involved for which s 91 detention is availabl but the offences vary in seriousness, provided that at least one offence is sufficiently serious to merit s 91 detentio detention of under 2 years' duration may properly be imposed in respect of the other offences[13]. In considering th seriousness of an offence which qualifies for detention under s 91 account may properly be taken of associate offences for which such detention is not available[15]. Where an offender was under 15 and thus was ineligible for detention and training order because of his age, a detention sentence of less than 2 years might well have bee appropriate[16]. However, it should now be noted that in certain circumstances a detention and training order ma be available in the case of an offender aged under 15 years[16]. A detention and training order should not be impose concurrently with a term of detention under s 91 of the Powers of Criminal Courts (Sentencing) Act 2000[17].

When dealing with an offender aged 15, 16 or 17, it is open to the Crown Court to make an order under s 9 even though the detention is for a period no longer than that for which the offender could be sentenced to detentio in a young offender institution detention and training order, provided that the court is of the opinion that none c the other methods in which the case might legally be dealt with (including a young offender institution detentio and training order) is suitable[18].

1. As to the committal for trial and sentence of dangerous young offenders see, respectively, para **5–12** and **5–62**.
2. Powers of Criminal Courts (Sentencing) Act 2000, s 91 in PART III: SENTENCING, ante.
3. Powers of Criminal Courts (Sentencing) Act 2000, s 90, in PART III: SENTENCING, ante.
4. Magistrates' Courts Act 1980, s 24(1), in PART I: MAGISTRATES' COURTS, PROCEDURE, ante.
5. See Magistrates' Courts Act 1980, s 24 in PART I: MAGISTRATES' COURTS, PROCEDURE, ante, and *R v Inner Londo Youth Court, ex p DPP* (1996) 161 JP 178, [1996] Crim LR 834.
6. *R v May* (1979) 1 Cr App Rep (S) 9.
7. *R v Weston* (1985) 7 Cr App Rep (S) 420, (4 years).
8. *R v Steadman* (1985) 7 Cr App Rep (S) 431, (4 years).
9. *R v Horsman and Holmes* (1994) 16 Cr App Rep (S) 130.
10. *R v Inner London Youth Court ex p DPP* [1996] Crim LR 834 and *R v North Hampshire Youth Court, ex p DP* (2000) 164 JP 377, DC.
11. *R v Shaun C* [2001] EWCA Crim 2007, [2002] 1 Cr App Rep (S) 463 (3 years).
12. *R v Darren James W* [2002] EWCA Crim 689, [2002] 2 Cr App Rep (S) 528.
13. *R v AM* [1998] 1 All ER 874, [1998] 1 WLR 363, [1998] 2 Cr App Rep 57. See *also R v Devizes Youth Court, ex A* (2000) 164 JP 330.
14. *R v Fairhurst* [1987] 1 All ER 46, [1986] 1 WLR 1374, CA, as applied in *R v AM* [1998] 1 All ER 874, [1998] WLR 363, [1998] 2 Cr App Rep 57. See also *R v Ganley* (2000) Times, June 7, CA; and *R v J-R and G* (2001) 165 J 140, CA. But see *R (on the application of D) v Manchester City Youth Court* [2001] EWHC Admin 860, [2002] 1 Cr App Rep (S) 135, 166 JP 15, where it was held that the imposition under s 91 of the Powers of Criminal Courts (Sentencing Act 2000 of a sentence of less than 2 years was appropriate only in very exceptional and restricted circumstances and th fact than an offender did not qualify for a detention and training order was not such an exceptional circumstance.
15. *R v P* (2000) 165 JP 237, CA.
16. Powers of Criminal Courts (Sentencing) Act 2000, s 100(2), in PART III: SENTENCING, ante.
17. *R v Collins* (1994) 16 Cr App Rep (S) 156.
18. *R v B (a minor) (sentence: jurisdiction)* [1999] 1 WLR 61, [1998] Crim LR 588.

5–62   Committal for sentence of dangerous young offenders.   Where on the summary trial of . specified offence[1] a person aged under 18 is convicted of the offence and it appears to the court tha the criteria for the imposition of a sentence of detention for public protection or a sentence o extended detention[2] would be met, the court must commit the offender on bail or in custody to th Crown Court for sentence in accordance with s 5A(1) of the Powers of Criminal Courts (Sentencing Act 2000[3].

The criteria for the imposition of a sentence of detention for public protection (ie a sentence o detention for an indeterminate period) are that the offence is a serious offence[4] committed on or afte 4 April 2005[5], a life sentence (if available) is not justified because of the seriousness of the offenc and one or more offences associated with it, and the court considers that an extended sentence woul not be adequate for the purpose of protecting the public from serious harm occasioned by th commission by the offender of further specified offences[6]. Where these criteria are met the Crow Court must impose a sentence of detention for public protection[6].

The criteria for the imposition of an extended sentence (ie a sentence that contains a custodia term of at least one year (but not more than the maximum term of imprisonment for the offence followed by a licence period not exceeding five years (specified violent offence) or eight year (specified sexual offence) are that the offence is a specified offence committed on or after 4 Apri 2005[5], and the court considers that there is a significant risk to members of the public of serious harr occasioned by the commission by the offender of further specified offences and, if the offence is serious offence[4], the case is not one in which the court is required to impose a sentence of detentio for life or a sentence of detention for public protection[7]. Where these criteria are met the Crow Court must impose an extended sentence of detention[7].

1. Defined in the Criminal Justice Act 2003, s 224: see PART III SENTENCING, ante.
2. Under, respectively, CJA 2003, ss 226(3) and 228(2).
3. Powers of Criminal Courts (Sentencing) Act 2000, s 3C: see PART III SENTENCING, ante. As to the power to commi other offences for sentence at the same time, see ibid s 6.
4. Defined as a specified offence which carries life or imprisonment for at least 10 years in the case of an adult offender Criminal Justice Act 2003, s 224(2).
5. See the Criminal Justice Act 2003 (Commencement No 8 and Transitional Provisions and Savings Order) 2005 SI 2005/950, art 2(1), Sch 1, para 18.

6. Criminal Justice Act 2003, s 226. For an example of a case where an indeterminate sentence was "manifestly excessive", but the criteria for an extended sentence were met, see *R v D* [2005] EWCA Crim 2292, (2005) 169 JP 662.

7. CJA 2003, s 228. For an early example of the imposition of an extended sentence (on a 13-year-old convicted of robbery), see *R v D* [2005] EWCA Crim 2292, [2006] Crim LR 73.

Statutes on Youth Courts

Children and Young Persons Act 1933[1]
(23 & 24 Geo 5 c 12)

PART I
PREVENTION OF CRUELTY AND EXPOSURE TO MORAL AND PHYSICAL DANGER

Offences

5–80   1. Cruelty[2] to person under sixteen.   (1) If any person who has attained the age[3] of sixteen years and has responsibility for[4] any child[5] or young person under that age, wilfully[6] assaults[7], ill-treats[8], neglects[9], abandons[10], or exposes[11] him, or causes or procures him to be assaulted, ill-treated, neglected, abandoned, or exposed, in a manner[12] likely[13] to cause him unnecessary suffering or injury to health (including injury to or loss of sight, or hearing, or limb, or organ of the body, and any mental derangement), that person shall be guilty of a misdemeanour[14], and shall be liable[15]—

(*a*)   on conviction on indictment, to a fine, or alternatively, or in addition thereto, to imprisonment for any term not exceeding **ten years**;

(*b*)   on summary conviction, to a fine not exceeding **the prescribed sum**, or alternatively, or in addition thereto, to imprisonment for any term not exceeding **six months**.

(2)   For the purposes of this section—

(*a*)   a parent or other person legally liable to maintain a child or young person, or the legal guardian of a child or young person, shall be deemed to have neglected him in a manner likely to cause injury to his health if he has failed[16] to provide adequate food, clothing, medical aid or lodging for him, or if, having been unable otherwise to provide such food, clothing, medical aid or lodging, he has failed to take steps to procure it to be provided under the enactments applicable in that behalf[17];

(*b*)   where it is proved that the death of an infant under three years of age was caused by suffocation (not being suffocation caused by disease or the presence of any foreign body in the throat or air passages of the infant) while the infant was in bed with some other person who has attained the age of sixteen years, that other person shall, if he was, when he went to bed, under the influence of drink, be deemed to have neglected the infant in a manner likely to cause injury to its health.

(3)   A person may be convicted of an offence under this section—

(*a*)   notwithstanding that actual suffering or injury to health, or the likelihood of actual suffering or injury to health, was obviated by the action of another person;

(*b*)   notwithstanding the death of the child or young person in question.

(4)–(7)   *Repealed.*

[Children and Young Persons Act 1933, s 1, as amended by Children and Young Persons Act 1963, s 31(1) and 5th Sch, the Children Act 1975, Schs 3 and 4, the Criminal Law Act 1977, ss 10 and 28, the Criminal Justice Act 1988, s 45 and Sch 16, the Children Act 1989, Schs 12 and 13, the Schools and Framework Act 1998, Sch 30 and the Children Act 2004, Sch 5.]

---

1. This Act (referred to as "the principal Act"), the Children and Young Persons (Amendment) Act 1952, the Children and Young Persons Act 1963, the Children and Young Persons Act 1969 may be cited together as the Children and Young Persons Acts 1933 to 1969 (Children and Young Persons Act 1969, s 73(1)). It is printed here as amended by the above Acts and by other Acts.

2. The court does not have to agree upon a precise set of facts to support the allegation brought by the prosecution provided that cruelty in the sense alleged by the prosecution is established (*R v Young* (1993) 97 Cr App Rep 280, CA).

3. See s 99, post.

4. For construction of this expression see s 17, post. For mode of charging these offences, alternatively or together, see s 14, post.

5. "Child" and "young person" are defined by s 107, post. Proof that a child is under the statutory age may be given by any lawful evidence. Evidence of the mistress of an elementary school attended by the child, corroborated by an officer of the Society for Prevention of Cruelty to Children was sufficient (*R v Cox* [1898] 1 QB 179).

6. Offences under s 1(1) are not offences of strict liability, thus the prosecution need to prove a deliberate or reckless act or failure: a genuine lack of appreciation through stupidity, ignorance or personal inadequacy will be a good defence. The offence is not to be judged by the objective test of what a reasonable parent would have done (*R v Sheppard* [1981] AC 394, [1980] 3 All ER 899, 72 Cr App Rep 82).

7. It has been held that where there is evidence to establish that, while in the joint custody and control of its parents, a child has been assaulted by one or both parents, and there is no evidence to point to one rather than the other, the inference may properly be drawn that they were jointly responsible; see *R v Gibson and Gibson* [1984] Crim LR 615; considered in *R v Lane and Lane* [1985] Crim LR 789. The Court of Appeal appears to have held that one parent might be guilty of assault and the other of neglect by failing to secure medical attention for the child (*see R v S and M* [1995] Crim LR 486 and the commentary thereon).

8. In *R v Hayles* [1969] 1 QB 364, [1969] 1 All ER 34 it was held that "ill-treats" covers most, if not all, forms of

neglect, and that the words "assaults, ill-treats, neglects, abandons or exposes" do not create separate and watertigh offences.

9. The civil law concept of negligence is not to be imported into this offence, which is not an offence of strict liability see *R v Sheppard*, ante. The statutory provision for (what is now) Social Security benefit in no way absolves the paren from liability (*Cole v Pendleton* (1896) 60 JP 359).

10. To abandon a child means to leave a child to its fate (*R v Boulden* (1957) 41 Cr App Rep 105). A child carefull packed and sent by train to its father's abode was held to be abandoned, although no actual injury had resulted (*R v Falkingham* (1870) LR 1 CCR 222, 34 JP 149). See also *R v White* (1871) LR 1 CCR 311, 36 JP 134, where a father wa held guilty who, knowing his child had been left on his doorstep, allowed it to remain there for six hours on a night in October. An abandonment at a juvenile court is not likely to cause unnecessary suffering or injury to health (*R v Whible* [1938] 3 All ER 777, 102 JP 326).

11. The exposure need not necessarily consist of the physical placing of the child somewhere with intent to injure it (*R v Williams* (1910) 74 JP Jo 99).

12. These words qualify all the preceding words, "assaults," etc (*R v Hatton* [1925] 2 KB 322, 89 JP 164). It does no seem that direct proof is required that neglect caused, or was likely to cause, unnecessary suffering (*R v Brenton* (1904) 111 CCC Sess Rep 309).

13. The meaning of "likely" was discussed in *R v Wills* [1990] Crim LR 714, CA, and see *R v S and M* [1995] Crim LR 486, CA.

14. A local education authority, or the council of a county or county borough may institute proceedings for any offence under this part of the Act (s 98 (as extended by s 56(1) of the Children and Young Persons Act 1963), post.

15. For procedure in respect of this offence triable either way, see Magistrates' Courts Act 1980, ss 17A–21, in PART I: MAGISTRATES' COURTS, PROCEDURE, ante.

16. In deciding whether refusal to allow an operation constitutes neglect the justices must consider the nature of the operation and the reasonableness of the refusal (*Oakey v Jackson* [1914] 1 KB 216, 78 JP 87).

17. Substituted by the National Assistance (Adaptation of Enactments) Regulations 1950 (SI 1951 No 174).

18. It is an assault for an elder brother, who is not in *loco parentis*, to strike an impudent younger brother (*R v Woods* (1921) 85 JP 272).

19. Offences under ss 1, 3, 4, 11 or 23 of this Act are included in the First Schedule, post; there is power to proceed with the case in the absence of the child or young person (s 41); the extended powers of taking their depositions applies (ss 42, 43). The provisions as to presumption and determination of age of a child or young person apply (s 99 of this Act).

5–81 3. Allowing persons under sixteen to be in brothels. (1) If any person having the responsibility for a child or young person who has attained the age of four years and is under the age of sixteen years[1], allows that child or young person to reside in or to frequent a brothel[2], he shall be liable on summary conviction to a fine not exceeding **level 2** on the standard scale, or alternatively, or in addition thereto, to imprisonment for any term not exceeding **six months**.
[Children and Young Persons Act 1933, s 33, as amended by Sexual Offences Act 1956, 4th Sch, Children and Young Persons Act 1963, 5th Sch, the Criminal Law Act 1977, Sch 1, the Criminal Justice Act 1982, s 46 and the Children Act 1989, Sch 13.]

1. See note 5 in para **5–80**, ante.
2. See Sexual Offences Act 1956, s 33, in PART VIII, title SEXUAL OFFENCES, post, and notes thereto.
3. See note 19 in para **5–80**, ante.

5–82 4. Causing or allowing persons under sixteen to be used for begging. (1) If any person causes or procures any child or young person[1] under the age of sixteen years or, having responsibility for such a child or young person, allows him to be in any street[2], premises, or place for the purpose of begging or receiving alms, or of inducing the giving of alms (whether or not there is any pretence of singing, playing, performing, offering anything for sale, or otherwise), he shall, on summary conviction, be liable to a fine not exceeding **level 2** on the standard scale, or alternatively, or in addition thereto, to imprisonment for any term not exceeding **three months**.

(2) If a person having responsibility for a child or young person is charged with an offence under this section, and it is proved that the child or young person was in any street, premises, or place for any such purpose as aforesaid, and that the person charged allowed the child or young person to be in the street, premises, or place, he shall be presumed to have allowed him to be in the street, premises, or place for that purpose unless the contrary is proved.

(3) If any person while singing, playing, performing or offering anything for sale in a street or public place[2] has with him a child who has been lent or hired out to him, the child shall, for the purposes of this section, be deemed to be in that street or place for the purpose of inducing the giving of alms[3].
[Children and Young Persons Act 1933, s 4, as amended by Children and Young Persons Act 1963, 5th Sch, the Criminal Law Act 1977, s 31, the Criminal Justice Act 1982, s 46 and the Children Act 1989, Sch 13.]

1. See note 5 in para **5–80**, ante.
2. For definition of "street" and "public place", see s 107(1), post.
3. See note 19 in para **5–80**, ante.

5–83 5. Giving intoxicating liquor to children under five. If any person gives, or causes to be given, to any child under the age of five years any intoxicating liquor[1] *, except upon the order of a duly qualified medical practitioner, or in case of sickness, apprehended sickness, or other urgent cause, he shall, on summary conviction, be liable to a fine not exceeding **level 1** on the standard scale.
[Children and Young Persons Act 1933, s 5, as amended by Criminal Justice Act 1967, Sch 3 and the Criminal Justice Act 1982, ss 38 and 46.]

*Substituted by the Licensing Act 2003, Sch 6, as from a date to be appointed.
1. For definitions of "intoxicating liquor", see s 107(1), post.

5–84   7. Sale of tobacco, etc, to persons under sixteen[1]. (1) Any person[2] who sells to a person under the age of sixteen years any tobacco or cigarette papers, whether for his own use or not, shall be liable, on summary conviction, to a fine not exceeding **level 4** on the standard scale.

(1A) It shall be a defence[3] for a person charged with an offence under subsection (1) above to prove that he took all reasonable precautions and exercised all due diligence to avoid the commission of the offence.

(2) If on complaint to a magistrates' court it is proved to the satisfaction of the court that any automatic machine for the sale of tobacco kept on any premises has been used by any person under the age of sixteen years, the court shall order[4] the owner of the machine, or the person on whose premises the machine is kept, to take such precautions to prevent the machine being so used as may be specified in the order or, if necessary, to remove the machine, within such time as may be specified in the order, and if any person against whom such an order has been made fails to comply therewith, he shall be liable, on summary conviction, to a fine not exceeding **level 4** on the standard scale.

(3) It shall be the duty of a constable and of a park-keeper, being in uniform, to seize any tobacco or cigarette papers in the possession of any person apparently under the age of sixteen years whom he finds smoking in any street or public place[5], and any tobacco or cigarette papers so seized shall be disposed of, if seized by a constable, in such manner as the police authority may direct, and if seized by a park-keeper, in such manner as the authority or person by whom he was appointed may direct.

(4) Nothing in this section shall make it an offence to sell tobacco or cigarette papers to, or shall authorise the seizure of tobacco or cigarette papers in the possession of, any person who is at the time employed by a manufacturer of or dealer in tobacco, either wholesale or retail, for the purposes of his business, or is a boy messenger in uniform in the employment of a messenger company and employed as such at the time.

(5) For the purposes of this section the expression "tobacco" includes cigarettes, any product containing tobacco and intended for oral or nasal use and smoking mixtures intended as a substitute for tobacco, and the expression "cigarettes" includes cut tobacco rolled up in paper, tobacco leaf, or other material in such form as to be capable of immediate use for smoking.
[Children and Young Persons Act 1933, s 7, as amended by Children and Young Persons Act 1963, s 32, the Criminal Justice Act 1982, ss 35, 38 and 46, the Protection of Children (Tobacco) Act 1986, s 1, the Children and Young Persons (Protection from Tobacco) Act 1991, s 1 and the Courts Act 2003, Sch 8.]

---

1. For further provisions relating to the enforcement of this section and a prohibition on the sale of unpackaged cigarettes, see the Children and Young Persons (Protection from Tobacco) Act 1991, this PART, post.
2. The proprietor of a shop sells tobacco within the meaning of this section when the transaction is conducted by his servant or agent (*St Helens Metropolitan Borough Council v Hill* (1992) 156 JP 602).
3. The decision of justices to acquit a defendant even though there were other things which the defendant could have done to try to avoid the commission of the offence, was not perverse (*Hereford and Worcester County Council v T & S Stores plc* (1994) Times, 4 November).
4. Appeal lies to the Crown Court against this order (s 102, post).
5. For definitions of "public place", see s 107(1), post.

5–85   11. Exposing children under twelve to risk of burning.   If any person who has attained the age of sixteen years, having responsibility for any child under the age of twelve years, allows the child to be in any room containing an open fire grate or any heating appliance liable to cause injury to a person by contact therewith not sufficiently protected to guard against the risk of his being burnt or scalded without taking reasonable precautions against that risk, and by reason thereof the child is killed or suffers serious injury, he shall on summary conviction be liable to a fine not exceeding **level 1** on the standard scale: Provided that neither this section, nor any proceedings taken thereunder, shall affect any liability of any such person to be proceeded against by indictment for any indictable[1] offence[2].
[Children and Young Persons Act 1933, s 11, as amended by the Children and Young Persons (Amendment) Act 1952, s 8, the Criminal Law Act 1977, s 31, the Criminal Justice Act 1982, s 46, the Children Act 1989, Sch 13 and the Statute Law (Repeals) Act 1993, Sch 2.]

---

1. A person might for instance under certain circumstances be guilty of manslaughter.
2. See note 19 in para **5–80**, ante.

5–86   12. Failing to provide for safety of children at entertainments.   (1) Where there is provided in any building an entertainment for children, or an entertainment at which the majority of the persons attending are children, then, if the number of children attending the entertainment exceeds 100, it shall be the duty of the person providing the entertainment to station and keep stationed wherever necessary a sufficient number of adult attendants, properly instructed as to their duties, to prevent more children or other persons being admitted to the building, or to any part thereof, than the building or part can properly accommodate, and to control the movement of the children and other persons admitted while entering and leaving the building or any part thereof, and to take all other reasonable precautions for the safety of the children.

(2) Where the occupier of a building permits, for hire or reward, the building to be used for the purpose of an entertainment, he shall take all reasonable steps to secure the observance of the provisions of this section.

(3) If any person on whom any obligation is imposed by this section fails to fulfil that obligation, he shall be liable, on summary conviction, to a fine not exceeding **level 3** on the standard scale, and also, if the building in which the entertainment is given is licensed under any of the enactments

relating to the licensing of theatres[1] and of houses and other places for music or dancing[2] the licence shall be liable to be revoked by the authority by whom the licence was granted*.

(4) A constable may enter any building in which he has reason to believe that such an entertainment as aforesaid is being, or is about to be, provided, with a view to seeing whether the provisions of this section are carried into effect, and an officer authorised for the purpose by an authority by whom licences are granted under any of the enactments referred to in the last foregoing subsection shall have the like power of entering any building so licensed by that authority.

(5) The institution of proceedings under this section shall—

(a) in the case of a building licensed by a local authority under section 1 of the Cinemas Act 1985[1], or under the enactments relating to the licensing of theatres or of houses and other places for music or dancing, be the duty of that local authority; and*

(b) in any other case, be the duty of the police authority.*

(6) This section shall not apply to any entertainment given in a private dwelling-house.

[Children and Young Persons Act 1933, s 12 as amended by the Criminal Justice Act 1982, ss 35, 38 and 46, the Cinemas Act 1985, Sch 2 and 3, and the Local Government Act 1985, Sch 8.]

***Words in sub-s (3) repealed, para (5)(a) substituted and sub-s (5A) inserted by the Licensing Act 2003, Sch 6, from a date to be appointed.**
  1. See title THEATRE, CINEMATOGRAPH AND VIDEO in PART VIII, post.
  2. See the Local Government (Miscellaneous Provisions) Act 1982, title LOCAL GOVERNMENT in PART VIII, post.

Special Provisions as to Prosecutions for Offences Specified in First Schedule

5–87 14. Mode of charging offences and limitation of time.   (1) Where a person is charged with committing any of the offences[1] mentioned in the First Schedule to this Act in respect of two or more children or young persons, the same information[2] or summons may charge the offence in respect of all or any of them, but the person charged shall not, if he is summarily convicted, be liable to a separate penalty in respect of each child or young person except under separate informations.

(2) The same information or summons may charge him[3] with the offences of assault, ill-treatment, neglect, abandonment, or exposure, together or separately, and may charge him with committing all or any of those offences in a manner likely to cause unnecessary suffering or injury to health, alternatively or together, but when those offences are charged together the person charged shall not, if he is summarily convicted, be liable to a separate penalty for each.

(3) *Repealed.*

(4) When any offence mentioned in the First Schedule to this Act charged against any person is a continuous offence, it shall not be necessary to specify in the information, summons, or indictment the date of the acts constituting the offence.

[Children and Young Persons Act 1933, s 14 as amended by the Children Act 1989, Sch 15.]

  1. This includes a reference to offences under s 1 of the Indecency with Children Act 1960: ibid, s 1(3).
  2. As to the institution of proceedings by local authorities for offences, see s 98 (as extended by s 56(1) of the Children and Young Persons Act 1963), post.
  3. For a case of joint complicity of both parents, neither being distinguished in evidence as having caused specific injuries, see *Marsh v Hodgson* (1973) 137 JP Jo 266.

Supplemental

5–88 17. Interpretation of Part I.   (1) For the purposes of this Part of this Act, the following shall be presumed to have responsibility for a child or young person—

(a) any person who—

(i) has parental responsibility for him (within the meaning of the Children Act 1989); or

(ii) is otherwise legally liable to maintain him; and

(b) any person who has care of him.

(2) A person who is presumed to be responsible for a child or young person by virtue of subsection (1)(a) shall not be taken to have ceased to be responsible for him by reason only that he does not have care of him.

[Children and Young Persons Act 1933, s 17, as substituted by the Children Act 1989, Sch 13.]

PART II
EMPLOYMENT

General Provisions as to Employment

5–89 18. Restrictions on the employment of children[1].   (1) Subject to the provisions of this section and of any byelaws made thereunder no child[2] shall be employed[3]—

(a) so long as he is under the age of 14 years, or

(aa) to do any work other than light work; or

(b) before the close of school hours on any day on which he is required to attend school; or

(c) before seven o'clock in the morning or after seven o'clock in the evening on any day; or

(d) for more than two hours on any day on which he is required to attend school; or

(da) for more than twelve hours in any week in which he is required to attend school; or (*e*) for more than two hours on any Sunday; or

   (*f*) *Repealed*

   (*g*) for more than eight hours or, if he is under the age of fifteen years, for more than five hours in any day—

      (i) on which he is not required to attend school, and

      (ii) which is not a Sunday; or

   (*h*) for more than thirty-five hours or, if he is under the age of fifteen years, for more than twenty-five hours in any week in which he is not required to attend school; or

   (*i*) for more than four hours in any day without a rest break of one hour; or

   (*j*) at any time in a year unless at that time he has had, or could still have, during a period in the year in which he is not required to attend school, at least two consecutive weeks without employment.

   (2) A local authority[4] may make byelaws[5] with respect to the employment of children[6], and any such byelaws may distinguish between children of different ages and sexes and between different localities, trades, occupations and circumstances, and may contain provisions—

   (*a*) authorising

      (i) the employment on an occasional basis of children aged thirteen years (notwithstanding anything in paragraph (*a*) of the last foregoing subsection) by their parents or guardians[7] in light agricultural work;

      (ia) the employment of children aged thirteen years (notwithstanding anything in paragraph (*a*) of the last foregoing subsection) in categories of light work specified in the byelaw.

      (ii) the employment of children (notwithstanding anything in paragraph (*b*) of the last foregoing subsection) for not more than one hour before the commencement of school hours on any day on which they are required to attend school;

   (*b*) prohibiting absolutely the employment of children in any specified occupation;

   (*c*) prescribing—

      (i) the age below which children are not to be employed;

      (ii) the number of hours in each day, or in each week, for which, and the times of day at which, they may be employed;

      (iii) the intervals to be allowed to them for meals and rest;

      (iv) the holidays or half-holidays to be allowed to them;

      (v) any other conditions to be observed in relation to their employment; so, however, that no such byelaws shall modify the restrictions contained in the last foregoing subsection save in so far as is expressly permitted by paragraph (*a*) of this subsection, and any restriction contained in any such byelaws shall have effect in addition to the said restrictions.

   (2A) In this section—

"light work" means work which, on account of the inherent nature of the tasks which it involves and the particular conditions under which they are performed—

   (*a*) is not likely to be harmful to the safety, health or development of children; and

   (*b*) is not such as to be harmful to their attendance at school or to their participation in work experience in accordance with section 560 of the Education Act 1996, or their capacity to benefit from the instruction received or, as the case may be, the experience gained;

"week" means any period of seven consecutive days; and

"year", except in expressions of age, means a period of twelve months beginning with 1st January.

   (3) Nothing in this section, or in any byelaw made under this section, shall prevent a child from doing anything—

   (*a*) under the authority of a licence granted under this Part of this Act; or

   (*b*) in a case where by virtue of s 37(3) of the Children and Young Persons Act 1933 no licence under that section is required for him to do it.

[Children and Young Persons Act 1933, s 18, as amended by the Children and Young Persons Act 1963, Sch 3, the Children Act 1972, s 1, and SI 1998/276, 1998/2857, and SI 2000/1333 and 2000/2548.]

---

   1. This section will be replaced by the Employment of Children Act 1973 when that Act is brought into force.

   2. For these purposes any person who is not over compulsory school age shall be deemed to be a child (Education Act 1996, s 558, in PART VIII: EDUCATION, post).

   3. A person who assists in a trade or occupation carried on for profit shall be deemed to be employed, notwithstanding that he receives no reward for his labour. A chorister is excepted (s 30, post).

   4. The "local authority" here is the local education authority (s 96).

   5. Byelaws made under this Part, ie ss 18 to 30, require confirmation by the Secretary of State. As to proof of byelaws, see the Local Government Act 1972, s 238, post. As to the continuance in operation of byelaws made by the council of a county district, see the Education Act 1996, Sch 39 para 47, in PART VIII, title EDUCATION, post.

   6. As to the meaning of "child", for the purposes of byelaws, see the Education Act 1944, s 120(5), post, and note 2, supra.

   7. For definition of "guardian", see s 107(1), post.

5–90 **20. Street trading**[1]. (1) Subject to subsection (2) of this section, no child shall engage or be employed[2] in street trading[3].

   (2) A local authority may make byelaws authorising children who have attained the age of fourteen

years to be employed by their parents in street trading to such extent as may be specified in th byelaws, and for regulating street trading under the byelaws by persons who are so authorised to b employed in such trading, and byelaws so made may distinguish between persons of different age and sexes and between different localities, and may contain provisions—

    (*a*)   forbidding any such person to engage or be employed in street trading unless he holds ; licence granted by the authority, and regulating the conditions on which such licences may b granted, suspended, and revoked;

    (*b*)   *Repealed.*

    (3) Byelaws made under subsection (2) shall contain provisions determining the days and hour during which, and the places at which, such persons may engage or be employed in street trading.
[Children and Young Persons Act 1933, s 20, as amended by the Children and Young Persons Act 1963, s 35, th Employment Act 1989, Sch 3 and the Sunday Trading Act 1994, Schs 4 and 5 and SI 2000/1333.]

---

    1. Nothing in this section or in any byelaw made thereunder shall restrict the engagement or employment of any person in the carrying on in any place of a retail trade or business (within the meaning of the Shops Act 1950) on any occasion on which it is customary for retail trades or businesses to be carried on in that place (Children and Young Persons Act 1963 s 35(2)).

    2. For penalty, see s 21, post.

    3. For definition of "street trading", see s 30, post.

    4. See s 96, post.

    5. See s 30, post.

5–91   21. Penalties and legal proceedings in respect of general provisions as to employment

    (1) If a person is employed in contravention of any of the foregoing provisions of this Part[1] of this Act, or of the provisions of any byelaw* or regulation made thereunder, the employer[2] and any person (other than the person employed) to whose act or default the contravention is attributable shall be liable[3] on summary conviction to a fine not exceeding **level 3** on the standard scale: Provided that, i proceedings are brought against the employer, the employer, upon information duly laid by him and on giving the prosecution not less than three days' notice of his intention, shall be entitled[4] to have any person (other than the person employed) to whose act or default he alleges that the contravention was due, brought before the court as a party to the proceedings, and if, after the contravention has been proved, the employer proves to the satisfaction of the court that the contravention was due to the act or default of the said other person, that person may be convicted of the offence; and if the employer further proves to the satisfaction of the court that he has used all due diligence to secure that the provisions in question should be complied with, he shall be acquitted of the offence.

    (2) Where an employer seeks to avail himself of the proviso to the last foregoing subsection, (*a*) the prosecution shall have the right to cross-examine him, if he gives evidence, and any witness called by him in support of his charge against the other person, and to call rebutting evidence; and (*b*) the court may make such order as it thinks fit for the payment of costs by any party to the proceedings to any other party thereto.

    (2A) Where a person is charged under this section with contravening section 18(1)(*j*) of this Act the proviso in subsection (1) of this section shall not apply, but it shall be a defence for him to prove that he used all due diligence to secure that section 18(1)(*j*) should be complied with.

    (3) A child, who engages in street trading in contravention of the provisions of the last foregoing section, or of any byelaw made thereunder, shall be liable on summary conviction to a fine not exceeding **level 1** on the standard scale.
[Children and Young Persons Act 1933, s 21, as amended by the Children and Young Persons Act 1963, s 36, the Criminal Justice Act 1982, ss 35, 38 and 46, the Employment Act 1989, Sch 3, and SI 1998/276.]

---

    *Reproduced as prospectively amended by the Employment of Children Act 1973, Sch 1, when in force.

    1. This Part contains ss 18 to 30. Proceedings may be instituted by a local education authority or by the council of a county or county borough (s 98 (as extended by s 56(1) of the Children and Young Persons Act 1963), post).

    2. Where a co-operative society employed a milk roundsman who without its knowledge and contrary to instructions employed a boy aged 10 in contravention of local byelaws, it was held that the society was not liable under s 21 as there was no evidence either that it had employed the child or that a servant, such as a personnel manager employed to take on staff, had done so (*Portsea Island Mutual Co-operative Society Ltd v Leyland* [1978] ICR 1195, [1978] IRLR 556).

    3. As to powers of entry by the local authority, or by any constable, to any place of illegal employment, see s 28, post. As to a local authority, or delegated committee empowering the clerk or chief education officer to exercise their powers in cases of urgency, see s 96(8), post.

    4. The person charged is not bound to institute proceedings under this subsection if no contract of employment exists between himself and the child (*Robinson v Hill* [1910] 1 KB 94, 73 JP 514).

Entertainments and Performances

5–92   23. Prohibition against persons taking part in performances endangering life or limb.

No person under the age of sixteen years, and no child aged sixteen years, shall take part in any performance[1] to which s 37(2) of the Children and Young Persons Act 1963 applies and in which his life or limbs are endangered and every person who causes or procures a such a person or child, or being his parent or guardian[2] allows him, to take part in such a performance, shall be liable on summary conviction to a fine not exceeding **level 3** on the standard scale: Provided that no proceedings shall be taken under this subsection except by or with the authority of a chief officer[2] of police.
[Children and Young Persons Act 1933, s 233, as amended by Criminal Justice Act 1967, 3rd Sch, the Children

and Young Persons Act 1963, Sch 3, the Criminal Justice Act 1982, ss 35, 38 and 46, the Employment Act 1989, Sch 3, and SI 1998/276 and SI 2000/1333.]

---

1. "Performance of a dangerous nature" includes all acrobatic performances and all performances as a contortionist (s 30, post).
2. For definition of "guardian" and "chief officer of police", see s 107(1), post.
3. See note 19 in para **5–80**, ante.

–93   24. Restrictions on training for performances of a dangerous nature.   (1) No child under the age[1] of twelve years shall be trained to take part in performances of a dangerous nature, and no child who has attained that age shall be trained to take part in such performances except under and in accordance with the terms of a licence granted and in force under this section; and every person who causes or procures a person, or being his parent or guardian[2] allows him, to be trained to take part in performances of a dangerous nature[3] in contravention of this section, shall be liable on summary conviction[4] to a fine not exceeding **level 3** on the standard scale.

(2)   A local authority may grant a licence for a child who has attained the age of twelve years to be trained to take part in performances of a dangerous nature.

(4)   A licence under this section shall specify the place or places at which the person is to be trained and shall embody such conditions as are, in the opinion of the authority, necessary for his protection, but a licence shall not be refused if the authority is satisfied that the person is fit and willing to be trained and that proper provision has been made to secure his health and kind treatment.
[Children and Young Persons Act 1933, s 24, as amended by Criminal Justice Act 1967, 3rd Sch, and the Children and Young Persons Act 1963, Sch 3, the Criminal Justice Act 1982, ss 35, 38 and 46 and the Employment Act 1989, Sch 3.]

---

1. As to presumption of age, see s 99, post.
2. For definition of "guardian" and "chief officer of police", see s 107(1), post.
3. For definition of "performance of a dangerous nature", see s 30, post.
4. For provisions as to prosecution, see note 2 in para **5–91**, ante.

Employment Abroad

–94   25. Restrictions on persons under eighteen going abroad for the purpose of performing for profit.   (1)   No person having responsibility for any child shall allow him, nor shall any person cause or procure any child, to go abroad[1]

(a)   for the purpose of singing, playing, performing, or being exhibited, for profit, or
(b)   for the purpose of taking part in a sport, or working as a model, where payment in respect of his doing so, other than for defraying expenses, is made to him or to another person,

unless a licence[2] has been granted in respect of him under this section: Provided that this subsection shall not apply in any case where it is proved that the child was only temporarily resident within the United Kingdom.

(2)   A justice of the peace may grant a licence in such form as the Secretary of State may prescribe, and subject to such restrictions and conditions as the justice of the peace thinks fit, for any child who has attained the age of fourteen years to go abroad for any purpose referred to in subsection (1) of this section, but no such licence shall be granted in respect of any person unless the justice of the peace is satisfied—

(a)   that the application for the licence is made by or with the consent of his parent or guardian;
(b)   that he is going abroad to fulfil a particular engagement;
(c)   that he is fit for the purpose, and that proper provision has been made to secure his health, kind treatment, and adequate supervision while abroad, and his return from abroad at the expiration or revocation of the licence;
(d)   that there has been furnished to him a copy of the contract of employment or other document showing the terms and conditions of employment drawn up in a language understood by him.

(3)   A person applying for a licence under this section, shall at least seven days before the application, give to the chief officer of police for the district in which the person resides to whom the application relates, notice of the intended application together with a copy of the contract of employment or other document showing the terms and conditions of employment, and the chief officer of police shall send that copy to a justice of the peace and may make a report in writing on the case to him or may appear, or instruct some person to appear, before him and show cause why the licence should not be granted, and the justice of the peace shall not grant the licence unless he is satisfied that notice has been properly so given:
Provided that if it appears that the notice was given less than seven days before the making of the application, the justice of the peace may nevertheless grant a licence if he is satisfied that the officer to whom the notice was given has made sufficient enquiry into the facts of the case and does not desire to oppose the application.

(4)   A licence under this section shall not be granted for more than three months but may be renewed by a justice of the peace from time to time for a like period, so, however, that no such renewal shall be granted, unless the justice of the peace—

(a)   is satisfied by a report of a British consular officer or other trustworthy person that the conditions of the licence are being complied with;

(b)   is satisfied that the application for renewal is made by or with the consent of the parent or guardian of the person to whom the licence relates.

(5)   A justice of the peace—

(a)   may vary a licence granted under this section and may at any time revoke such a licence for any cause which he, in his discretion, considers sufficient:

(b)   need not, when renewing or varying a licence granted under this section, require the attendance before him of the person to whom the licence relates.

(6)   The justice of the peace to whom application is made for the grant, renewal or variation of a licence shall, unless he is satisfied that in the circumstances it is unnecessary, require the applicant to give such security as he may think fit (either by entering into a recognisance with or without sureties or otherwise) for the observance of the restrictions and conditions in the licence or in the licence as varied, and the recognisance may be enforced in like manner as a recognisance for the doing of some matter or thing required to be done in a proceeding before the relevant court is enforceable.

(7)   If in any case where a licence has been granted under this section, it is proved to the satisfaction of a justice of the peace that by reason of exceptional circumstances it is not in the interests of the person to whom the licence relates to require him to return from abroad at the expiration of the licence, then, notwithstanding anything in this section or any restriction or condition attached to the licence, the justice of the peace may by order release all persons concerned from any obligation to cause that person to return from abroad.

(8)   Where a licence is granted, renewed or varied under this section, the justice of the peace shall send the prescribed particulars to the Secretary of State for transmission to the proper consular officer, and every consular officer shall register the particulars so transmitted to him and perform such other duties in relation thereto as the Secretary of State may direct.

(9)   *Repealed.*

(10)   This and the next following section extend to Scotland and Northern Ireland.

(11)   In this section "the relevant court"—

(a)   in relation to England and Wales, means a magistrates' court;

(b)   in relation to Scotland, means a sheriff court;

(c)   in relation to Northern Ireland, means a court of summary jurisdiction.

[Children and Young Persons Act 1933, s 25, as amended by the Children and Young Persons Act 1963, Sch 3, the Employment Act 1989, Sch 3, the Children Act 1989, Sch 13, SI 1998/276 and the Courts Act 2003, Sch 8.]

1. "Abroad" means outside Great Britain and Ireland (s 30).
2. For form of licence, see the Children (Performances) Regulations 1968, SI 1968/1728, as amended by SI 1998/1678

5–95   **26. Punishment of contravention of last foregoing section and proceedings with respect thereto.**   (1)   If any person acts in contravention of the provisions of subsection (1) of the last foregoing section he shall be guilty of an offence under this section and be liable, on summary conviction, to a fine not exceeding **level 3** on the standard scale, or, alternatively, or in addition thereto, to imprisonment for any term not exceeding **three months**: Provided that if he procured the child in question to go abroad by means of any false pretence or false representation, he shall be liable on conviction on indictment to imprisonment for any term not exceeding **two years**.

(2)   Where, in proceedings under this section against a person, it is proved that he caused, procured, or allowed a child to go abroad and that

(a)   that child has while abroad been singing, playing, performing, or being exhibited, for profit or

(b)   that child has while abroad taken part in a sport, or worked as a model, and payment in respect of his doing so, other than for defraying expenses, was made to him or to another person,

the defendant shall be presumed to have caused, or allowed him to go abroad for that purpose, unless the contrary is proved: Provided that where the contrary is proved, the court may order the defendant to take such steps as the court directs to secure the return of the child to the United Kingdom, or to enter into a recognizance to make such provision as the court may direct to secure his health, kind treatment, and adequate supervision while abroad, and his return to the United Kingdom at the expiration of such period as the court may think fit.

(3)   Proceedings in respect of an offence under this section or for enforcing a recognizance under this or the last foregoing section may be instituted at any time within a period of three months from the first discovery by the person taking the proceedings of the commission of the offence or, as the case may be, the non-observance of the restrictions and conditions contained in the licence, or, if at the expiration of that period the person against whom it is proposed to institute the proceedings is outside the United Kingdom, at any time within six months after his return to the United Kingdom.

(4)   In any such proceedings as aforesaid, a report of any British consular officer and any deposition made on oath before a British consular officer and authenticated by the signature of that officer respecting the observance or non-observance of any of the conditions or restrictions contained in a licence granted under the last foregoing section shall, upon proof that the consular officer, or deponent, cannot be found in the United Kingdom, be admissible in evidence, and it shall not be necessary to prove the signature or official character of the person appearing to have signed any such report or deposition.

(5)-(6)   *Repealed.*

[Children and Young Persons Act 1933, s 26, as amended by the Children and Young Persons Act 1963, Sch 3]

the Children and Young Persons Act 1969, Sch 6, the Criminal Justice Act 1982, ss 38 and 46, the Police and Criminal Evidence Act 1984, Sch 7, the Employment Act 1989, Sch 3, and SI 1998/276.]

---

1. This order will be enforceable under Magistrates' Courts Act 1980, s 63, ante. For provisions as to proceedings under this Part of the Act, see note 2 in para **5–91**, ante.
2. These words in the repealed Children (Employment Abroad) Act 1913, were to be construed as including the Republic of Ireland (Irish Free State (Consequential Adaptation of Enactments) Order 1923, SR & O 1923/405). This provision is not affected by the fact that the Republic of Ireland is not part of Her Majesty's dominions (Ireland Act 1949, s 3).

Supplemental

5–96   28. Powers of entry.   (1) If it is made to appear to a justice of the peace by the local authority, or by any constable, that there is reasonable cause to believe that the provisions of this Part of this Act, other than those relating to employment abroad, or of a byelaw made under the said provisions, are being contravened with respect to any person, the justice may by order under his hand addressed to an officer of the local authority, or to a constable, empower him to enter, at any reasonable time within forty-eight hours of the making of the order, any place in or in connection with which the person in question is, or is believed to be, employed, or as the case may be, in which he is, or is believed to be, taking part in a performance, being trained, taking part in a sport or working as a model, and to make enquiries therein with respect to that person[1].

(2) Any authorised officer of the said authority or any constable may—

(*a*)   at any time enter any place used as a broadcasting studio or film studio or used for the recording of a performance with a view to its use in a programme service or in a film intended for public exhibition and make inquiries therein as to any children taking part in performances to which subsection (2) of section 37 of the Children and Young Persons Act 1963 applies;

(*b*)   at any time during the currency of a licence granted under the said section 37 or under the provisions of this Part of this Act relating to training for dangerous performances enter any place (whether or not it is such a place as is mentioned in paragraph (*a*) of this subsection) where the person to whom the licence relates is authorised by the licence to do anything or to be trained, and may make inquiries therein with respect to that person.

(3) Any person who obstructs any officer or constable in the due exercise of any powers conferred on him by or under this section, or who refuses to answer or answers falsely any enquiry authorised by or under this section to be made, shall be liable on summary conviction in respect of each offence to a fine not exceeding **level 2** on the standard scale[1].

(4) In this section—

"broadcasting studio" means a studio used in connection with the provision of a programme service;

"programme service" has the same meaning as in the Broadcasting Act 1990.

[Children and Young Persons Act 1933, s 28, as amended by the Children and Young Persons Act 1963, Sch 3, the Criminal Law Act 1977, s 31, the Criminal Justice Act 1982, s 46, the Cable and Broadcasting Act 1984, Sch 5, the Broadcasting Act 1990, Schs 20 and 21, and SI 1998/276.]

---

1. See the Education Act 1996, s 559(5), in PART VIII, title EDUCATION, post, as to the application of this subsection.

5–97   29. Savings.   (4) The said provisions[1] shall be in addition to and not in substitution for any enactments relating to employment in factories, workshops, mines and quarries, or for giving effect to any international convention regulating employment[2].

[Children and Young Persons Act 1933, s 29, as amended by the Children and Young Persons Act 1963, Sch 3 and the Children and Young Persons Act 1969, Sch 6.]

---

1. That is, the provisions of this Part of this Act.
2. See the statutes mentioned in PART VIII: the title HEALTH AND SAFETY, post.

5–98   30. Interpretation of Part II.   (1) For the purposes of this Part of this Act and of any byelaws made thereunder, the expression "child" means—

(*a*)   in relation to England and Wales, a person who is not over compulsory school age (construed in accordance with section 8 of the Education Act 1996);

(*b*)   in relation to Scotland, a person who is not for the purposes of the Education (Scotland) Act 1980 over school age; and

(*c*)   in relation to Northern Ireland, a person who is not for the purposes of the Education and Libraries (Northern Ireland) Order 1986 over compulsory school age;

the expression "performance of a dangerous nature" includes all acrobatic performances and all performances as a contortionist; the expression "street trading"[1] includes the hawking of newspapers, matches, flowers and other articles, playing, singing or performing for profit, shoe-blacking and other like occupations carried on in streets or public places; a person who assists in a trade or occupation carried on for profit shall be deemed to be employed notwithstanding that he receives no reward for his labour; a chorister taking part in a religious service or in a choir practice for a religious service shall not, whether he receives any reward or not, be deemed to be employed; and the expression "abroad" means outside Great Britain and Ireland.

(2) This section, so far as it has effect for the purposes of sections 25 and 26 of this Act, extend to Scotland and to Northern Ireland.

[Children and Young Persons Act 1933, s 30 as amended by the Employment Act 1989, Sch 3 and the Education Act 1996, Sch 37.]

---

1. "Street trading" means seeking custom in the street, and does not include business between a shop and customers in their homes. Street trading is not confined to trading on his own account (*Stratford Co-operative Society v East Ham Corp.* [1915] 2 KB 70, 79 JP 227; *Morgan v Parr* [1921] 2 KB 379, 85 JP 165; *Sweet v Williams* (1922) 87 JP 51; *Vann v Eatoug* (1935) 99 JP 385). In *Newman v Lipman* [1951] 1 KB 333, [1950] 2 All ER 832, 114 JP 561; a prosecution against a street photographer for "street trading" by taking photographs was unsuccessful.

PART III

PROTECTION OF CHILDREN AND YOUNG PERSONS IN RELATION TO CRIMINAL AND SUMMARY PROCEEDINGS

General Provisions as to Preliminary Proceedings

5–99 31. Separation of children and young persons from adults in police stations, courts etc[1]. (1) Arrangements shall be made for preventing a child or young person[2] while detained in a police station, or while being conveyed to or from any criminal court, or while waiting before or after attendance in any criminal court, from associating with an adult (not being a relative) who is charged with any offence other than an offence with which the child or young person is jointly charged, and for ensuring that a girl (being a child or young person) shall while so detained, being conveyed, or waiting, be under the care of a woman.

(2)[1] In this section and section 34 of this Act, "young person" means a person who has attained the age of fourteen and is under the age of seventeen years.

[Children and Young Persons Act 1933, s 31 as amended by the Criminal Justice Act 1991, Sch 8.]

---

1. Section 31 is printed as prospectively amended by the Criminal Justice Act 1991, Sch 8; at the date of going to press sub-s (2) which has been added by Sch 8 of the 1991 Act had not been brought into force (see art 2(4) of the Criminal Justice Act 1991 (Commencement No 3) Order 1992, SI 1992/333). For further commentary on this section, see this PART, para **5–20** ante.

2. See note 5 to s 1, ante.

5–100 34. Attendance at court of parents of child or young person charged with an offence etc[1]. (1) *Repealed.*

(2) Where a child or young person[2] is in police detention, such steps as are practicable shall be taken to ascertain the identity of a person responsible for his welfare.

(3) If it is practicable to ascertain the identity of a person responsible for the welfare of the child or young person, that person shall be informed, unless it is not practicable to do so—

(*a*) that the child or young person has been arrested;

(*b*) why he has been arrested; and

(*c*) where he is being detained.

(4) Where information falls to be given under subsection (3) above, it shall be given as soon as it is practicable to do so.

(5) For the purposes of this section the persons who may be responsible for the welfare of a child or young person are—

(*a*) his parent or guardian[3]; or

(*b*) any other person who has for the time being assumed responsibility for his welfare.

(6) If it is practicable to give a person responsible for the welfare of the child or young person the information required by subsection (3) above, that person shall be given it as soon as it is practicable to do so.

(7) If it appears that at the time of his arrest a supervision order, as defined in section 163 of the Powers of Criminal Courts (Sentencing) Act 2000 or Part IV of the Children Act 1989, is in force in respect of him, the person responsible for his supervision shall also be informed as described in subsection (3) above as soon as it is reasonably practicable to do so.

(7A) If it appears that at the time of his arrest the child or young person is being provided with accommodation by or on behalf of a local authority under section 20 of the Children Act 1989, the local authority shall also be informed as described in subsection (3) above as soon as it is reasonably practicable to do so.

(8) The reference to a parent or guardian in subsection (5) above is in the case of a child or young person in the care of a local authority, a reference to that authority.

(9) The rights conferred on a child or young person by subsections (2) to (8) above are in addition to his rights under section 56 of the Police and Criminal Evidence Act 1984.

(10) The reference in subsection (2) above to a child or young person who is in police detention includes a reference to a child or young person who has been detained under the terrorism provisions and in subsection (3) above "arrest" includes such detention.

(11) In subsection (10) above "the terrorism provisions" has the meaning assigned to it by section 65 of the Police and Criminal Evidence Act 1984.

[Children and Young Persons Act 1933, s 34, as substituted by Children and Young Persons Act 1963, s 25 and amended by the Children and Young Persons Act 1969, Schs 5 and 6, the Police and Criminal Evidence Act 1984.

s 57 and the Children Act 1989, Schs 13 and 15 and by virtue of the Powers of Criminal Courts (Sentencing) Act 2000, Sch 9.]

---

1. For further commentary on this section, see this PART, para **5–19**, ante.
2. When s 31(2), ante, is brought into force, the expression "young person" for the purposes of s 34 will have the meaning contained in that subsection. In the meantime, for the purposes of s 34, "young person" means a person who has attained the age of fourteen and is under the age of seventeen years, since the amendment to the definition of "young person" contained in s 107(1), post, made by the Criminal Justice Act 1991, Sch 8, has been disapplied; see art 2(4) of the Criminal Justice Act 1991 (Commencement No 3) Order 1992, SI 1992/333.
3. For definition of "guardian", see s 107(1), post. An adopted person is to be treated in law as if born as the child of the adopter or adopters: Adoption and Children Act 2002, s 67(1), see PART IV, FAMILY LAW, ante.

-101   34A. Attendance at court of parent or guardian[1]. (1) Where a child or young person is charged with an offence or is for any other reason brought before a court, the court—

    (*a*)   may in any case; and
    (*b*)   shall in the case of a child or a young person who is under the age of sixteen years,

require a person who is a parent or guardian of his to attend at the court during all the stages of the proceedings, unless and to the extent that the court is satisfied that it would be unreasonable to require such attendance, having regard to the circumstances of the case.

    (2) In relation to a child or young person for whom a local authority have parental responsibility and who—

    (*a*)   is in their care; or
    (*b*)   is provided with accommodation by them in the exercise of any functions (in particular those under the Children Act 1989) which are social services functions within the meaning of the Local Authority Social Services Act 1970,

the reference in subsection (1) above to a person who is a parent or guardian of his shall be construed as a reference to that authority or, where he is allowed to live with such a person, as including such a reference.

In this subsection "local authority" and "parental responsibility" have the same meanings as in the Children Act 1989.
[Children and Young Persons Act 1933, s 34A, as added by the Criminal Justice Act 1991, s 56 and amended by the Local Government Act 2000, Sch 5.]

---

1. For further commentary on this section, see this PART, para **5–22**, ante.

General Provisions as to Proceedings in Court

-102   36. Prohibition against children being present in court during the trial of other persons. No child (other than an infant in arms) shall be permitted to be present in court during the trial of any other person charged with an offence, or during any proceedings preliminary thereto, except during such times as his presence is required as a witness or otherwise for the purposes of justice or while the court consents to his presence; and any child present in court when under this section he is not to be permitted to be so shall be ordered to be removed:
[Children and Young Persons Act 1933, s 36, as amended by the Access to Justice Act 1999, ss 73, 106 and Sch 15.]

-103   37. Power to clear court while child or young person is giving evidence in certain cases. (1) Where, in any proceedings in relation to an offence against, or any conduct contrary to, decency or morality, a person who, in the opinion of the court, is a child or young person[1], is called as a witness, the court may direct that all or any persons, not being members or officers of the court or parties to the case, their counsel or solicitors, or persons otherwise directly concerned in the case, be excluded from the court during the taking of the evidence of that witness: Provided that nothing in this section shall authorise the exclusion of *bona fide* representatives of a *news gathering or reporting organisation*[2]*.

    (2) The powers conferred on a court by this section shall be in addition and without prejudice to any other powers of the court to hear proceedings *in camera*.
[Children and Young Persons Act 1933, s 37.]

---

*Section 37(1) is amended by the Youth Justice and Criminal Evidence Act 1999, Sch 4, when in force.
1. See note 5 to s 1, ante.
2. For power to prohibit publication, see s 39, post.

-104   38. Evidence of child of tender years. (1) *Repealed.*

    (2) If any child whose evidence is received unsworn in any proceedings for an offence by virtue of section 52 of the Criminal Justice Act 1991[1] wilfully gives false evidence in such circumstances that he would, if the evidence had been given on oath, have been guilty of perjury, he shall be liable[2] on summary conviction to be dealt with as if he had been summarily convicted of an indictable offence punishable in the case of an adult with imprisonment.*
[Children and Young Persons Act 1933, s 38 as amended by the Criminal Justice Act 1988, s 34 and Sch 16 and the Criminal Justice Act 1991, Schs 11 and 13.]

*Sub-section (2) to be repealed by the Youth and Criminal Evidence Act 1999, Sch 6 when in force.
1. Section 52 added a new s 33A to the Criminal Justice Act 1988 in PART II: EVIDENCE, *ante* and provided that th power of the court in any criminal proceedings to determine that a particular person is not competent to give eviden shall apply to children of tender years as it applies to other persons.
2. As to non-application of Perjury Act 1911, see s 16(2) thereof, in PART VIII, title PERJURY, *post*.

5–105 39. Power to prohibit publication of certain matter in newspapers[1]**.** (1) In relation any proceedings in any court the court may direct that—

(*a*) no newspaper report of the proceedings shall reveal the name, address, or school, or includ any particulars calculated to lead to the identification of any child or young person concerne in the proceedings, either as being the person by or against or in respect of whom th proceedings are taken, or as being a witness therein;

(*b*) no picture shall be published in any newspaper as being or including a picture of any child c young person so concerned in the proceedings as aforesaid; except in so far (if at all) as ma be permitted by the direction of the court.

(2) Any person who publishes any matter in contravention of any such direction shall on summar conviction be liable in respect of each offence to a fine not exceeding **level 5** on the standard scale[2].

(3) *In this section "proceedings" means proceedings other than criminal proceedings**.
[Children and Young Persons Act 1933, s 39, as amended by Children and Young Persons Act 1963, s 57(1), 5 Sch, the Criminal Law Act 1977, Sch 6 and the Criminal Justice Act 1982, ss 39 and 46, and Sch 3.]

*A new s 39(3) is inserted by the Youth Justice and Criminal Evidence Act 1999, Sch 2, when in force.
1. Identical provision is made for enforcement in England and Wales to protect any person under the age of 17 yea concerned in proceedings in Scottish courts: Criminal Procedure (Scotland) Act 1975, ss 169 and 365 applied by s 46 thereof. Section 39 of the 1933 Act, with the necessary modifications, applies in relation to reports or matters included a programme service, and in relation to including any such reports or matters in such a service, as it applies in relation reports or matters published in newspapers and to publishing any matter in a newspaper (Broadcasting Act 1990, Sch 20 Section 39 cannot be used to protect the identity of a dead child, see for example *Ex p Crook* [1995] 1 All ER 537, [199 1 WLR 139, sub nom *R v Central Criminal Court, ex p Crook and Godwin* [1995] 2 Cr App Rep 212 (such interpretatic not queried by the Court of Appeal). For further guidance on the making of an order an order under s 39, see this PAR para **5–23**, **Restriction on publicity**, *ante*.
2. The court will only punish a person for the offence of publishing an article in breach of s 39 where the terms of th order are clear and unambiguous; to have the required degree of clarity the order must leave no doubt in the mind of th reasonable reader as to precisely what it prohibits: *Briffet v DPP* (2002) 166 JP 66.

Special Procedure with regard to Offences specified in First Schedule

5–106 41. Power to proceed with case in absence of child or young person. Where in an proceedings with relation to any of the offences[1] mentioned in the First Schedule to this Act, the cou is satisfied that the attendance before the court of any child or young person in respect of whom th offence is alleged to have been committed is not essential to the just[2] hearing of the case, the case ma be proceeded with and determined in the absence of the child or young person.
[Children and Young Persons Act, 1933, s 41.]

1. This includes a reference to offences under s 1 of the Indecency with Children Act 1960: Indecency with Childre Act 1960, s 1(3).
2. See *R v Hale* [1905] 1 KB 126, 69 JP 83.

5–107 42. Extension of power to take deposition of child or young person. (1) Where justice of the peace is satisfied by the evidence of a duly qualified medical practitioner that th attendance before a court of any child or young person in respect of whom any of the offence mentioned in the First Schedule to this Act is alleged to have been committed would involve seriou danger to his life or health, the justice may take in writing the deposition of the child or young perso on oath, and shall thereupon subscribe the deposition and add thereto a statement of his reason fc taking it and of the day when and place where it was taken, and of the names of the persons (if any present at the taking thereof.

(2) The justice taking any such deposition shall transmit it with his statement—

(*a*) if the deposition relates to an offence for which any accused person is already committed fc trial, to the proper officer of the court for trial at which the accused person has bee committed; and

(*b*) in any other case, to the proper officer of the court before which proceedings are pending i respect of the offence.
[Children and Young Persons Act 1933, s 42.]

1. This includes a reference to offences under s 1 of the Indecency with Children Act 1960: Indecency with Childre Act 1960, s 1(3).

5–108 43. Admission of deposition of child or young person in evidence. Where, in an proceedings in respect of any of the offences[1] mentioned in the First Schedule to this Act, the court satisfied by the evidence of a duly qualified medical practitioner that the attendance before the cou of any child or young person in respect of whom the offence is alleged to have been committed woul involve serious danger to his life or health, any deposition of the child or young person taken unde the Indictable Offences Act 1848[2], or this Part of this Act, shall be admissible in evidence either fo

or against the accused person without further proof thereof if it purports to be signed by the justice by or before whom it purports to be taken: Provided that the deposition shall not be admissible in evidence against the accused person unless it is proved that reasonable notice of the intention to take the deposition has been served upon him and that he or his counsel or solicitor had, or might have had if he had chosen to be present, an opportunity of cross-examining the child or young person making the deposition.
[Children and Young Persons Act 1933, s 43.]

1. This includes a reference to offences under s 1 of the Indecency with Children Act 1960: Indecency with Children Act 1960, s 1(3).
2. Now the Magistrates' Courts Act 1980 and the Criminal Procedure Rules 2005.

Principles to be observed by all Courts in dealing with Children and Young Persons

5–109   44. General considerations.   (1) Every court in dealing with a child or young person[1] who is brought before it, either as an offender or otherwise, shall have regard to the welfare of the child or young person, and shall in a proper case take steps for removing him from undesirable surroundings, and for securing that proper provision is made for his education and training.

(2) *Repealed.*
[Children and Young Persons Act 1933, s 44, as amended by the Children and Young Persons Act 1969, Sch 6.]

1. See note 5 to s 1, ante. A person attains a particular age at the commencement of the relevant anniversary of the date of his birth: s 9 of the Family Law Reform Act 1969, in PART IV: FAMILY LAW, ante.

Youth Courts

5–110   45. Youth courts.   (1) Magistrates' courts—

(a) constituted in accordance with this section or section 66 of the Courts Act 2003 (judges having powers of District Judges (Magistrates' Courts)), and
(b) sitting for the purpose of—

    (i) hearing any charge against a child or young person, or
    (ii) exercising any other jurisdiction conferred on youth courts by or under this or any other Act,

are to be known as youth courts.

(2) A justice of the peace is not qualified to sit as a member of a youth court for the purpose of dealing with any proceedings unless he has an authorisation extending to the proceedings.

(3) He has an authorisation extending to the proceedings only if he has been authorised by the Lord Chief Justice, with the concurrence of the Lord Chancellor, or a person acting on his behalf to sit as a member of a youth court to deal with—

(a) proceedings of that description, or
(b) all proceedings dealt with by youth courts.

(4) The Lord Chief Justice, with the concurrence of the Lord Chancellor, may by rules make provision about—

(a) the grant and revocation of authorisations,
(b) the appointment of chairmen of youth courts, and
(c) the composition of youth courts.

(5) Rules under subsection (4) may confer powers on the Lord Chancellor or Lord Chief Justice with respect to any of the matters specified in the rules.

(6) Rules under subsection (4) may be made only after consultation with the Criminal Procedure Rule Committee.

(7) Rules under subsection (4) are to be made by statutory instrument.

(8) A statutory instrument containing rules under subsection (4) is subject to annulment in pursuance of a resolution of either House of Parliament.

(9) The Lord Chief Justice may nominate a judicial office holder (as defined in section 109(4) of the Constitutional Reform Act 2005) to exercise his functions under subsection (3) or (4) or his powers under rules under subsection (4).
[Children and Young Persons Act 1933, s 45, as substituted by the Courts Acts 2003, s 50 and amended by the Constitutional Reform Act 2005, Sch 4.]

1. For further commentary on this section, see this PART, para **5–4 Youth courts**, ante.
2. See note 5 to s 1, ante. A person attains a particular age at the commencement of the relevant anniversary of the date of his birth: s 9 of the Family Law Reform Act 1969, in PART IV: FAMILY LAW, ante.

5–111   46. Assignment of certain matters to youth courts[1].   (1) Subject as hereinafter provided[2], no charge against a child or young person[3], and no application whereof the hearing is by rules made under this section assigned to youth courts, shall be heard by a magistrates' court which is not a youth court:
    Provided that—

(a) a charge made jointly against a child or young person and a person who has attained the age of eighteen years shall[4] be heard by a magistrates' court other than a youth court, and

(b)   where a child or young person is charged with an offence, the charge may be heard by a magistrates' court which is not a youth court if a person who has attained the age of eighteen years is charged at the same time with[5] aiding, abetting, causing, procuring, allowing, or permitting that offence; and

(c)   where in the course of any proceedings before any magistrates' court other than a youth court it appears that the person to whom the proceedings relate is a child or young person, nothing in this subsection shall be construed as preventing the court, if it thinks fit so to do, from proceeding with the hearing and determination of those proceedings[6].

(1A)   If a notification that the accused desires to plead guilty without appearing before the court is received by the designated officer for for a court in pursuance of section 12 of the Magistrates' Court Act 1980 and the court has no reason to believe that the accused is a child or young person, then, if he is a child or young person he shall be deemed to have attained the age of eighteen for the purposes of subsection (1) of this section in its application to the proceedings in question.

(2)   No direction, whether contained in this or any other Act, that a charge shall be brought before a youth court shall be construed as restricting the powers of any justice or justices to entertain an application for bail or for a remand, and to hear such evidence as may be necessary for that purpose. [Children and Young Persons Act 1933, s 46, as amended by the Children and Young Persons Act 1969, Sch 5 the Magistrates' Courts Act 1980, Sch 7, the Criminal Justice Act 1991, Schs 8 and 11 and the Courts Act 2003 Sch 8.]

---

1. For further commentary on this section, see this PART, para **5–10 Jurisdiction**, and paras **5–11** to **5–15 Jurisdiction of the magistrates' and Crown Court**, ante.
2. See also Children and Young Persons Act 1963, s 18, post.
3. See note 5 to s 1, ante. A person attains a particular age at the commencement of the relevant anniversary of the date of his birth: s 9 of the Family Law Reform Act 1969, in PART IV: FAMILY LAW, ante.
4. But see now s 29 of the Magistrates' Courts Act 1980, ante, which enables a magistrates' court to remit a minor to the youth court (*a*) where the court proceeds to summary trial and the older accused pleads guilty and the minor *not guilty* and (*b*) where the court inquiring into the offence as examining justices commits the older accused for trial or discharge him, proceeds to summary trial of the minor and the minor pleads *not guilty*.
5. See Magistrates' Courts Act 1980, s 44, ante. A child or young person charged with aiding and abetting an adult may be tried in a court other than a youth court by virtue of s 18 of the Children and Young Persons Act 1963, post, and by the same provision he may be tried in such a court with an offence arising out of circumstances which are the same as or connected with those in relation to which an adult is charged at the same time.
6. Where a charge against a child or young person is heard by a court other than a youth court, a copy of the pre sentence report or other report of a probation officer or member of a youth offending team need not be given to an offender under 17 years but shall be given to his parent or guardian if present in court (Powers of Criminal Court (Sentencing) Act 2000, ss 156, 157 in PART III: SENTENCING, ante).

5–112   47. Procedure in youth courts[1].

(1)   Youth courts shall sit as often as may be necessary for the purpose of exercising any jurisdiction conferred on them by or under this or any other Act.

(2)   No person shall be present at any sitting[2] of a youth court except—

(a)   members and officers of the court;

(b)   parties to the case before the court, their solicitors and counsel, and witnesses and other persons directly concerned in that case;

(c)   *bona fide* representatives of a news gathering or reporting organisation;*

(d)   such other persons as the court may specially authorise to be present.

[Children and Young Persons Act 1933, s 47, as amended by Children and Young Persons Act 1963, s 17(2), the Criminal Justice Act 1991, Sch 11 and the Crime and Disorder Act 1998, s 47 and Sch 10.]

---

*Amended by the Youth Justice and Criminal Evidence Act 1999, Sch 4, when in force.
1. A form of oath for use in youth courts and by minors in other courts is prescribed by s 28 of the Children and Young Persons Act 1963, post.
In proceedings in a youth court (other than proceedings for an offence) a medical certificate is admissible in evidence of a person's physical or mental condition (Children and Young Persons Act 1963, s 26, post). For further commentary on this section, see this PART, para **5–4 Youth courts**, ante.
2. As to power to clear the court whilst a child or young person is giving evidence, see s 37. As to power to prohibit the publication of certain matters in newspapers, see s 39.

5–113   48. Miscellaneous provisions as to powers of youth courts[1].

(1)   A youth court sitting for the purpose of hearing a charge against a person who is believed to be a child or young person may, if it think fit to do so, proceed with the hearing and determination of the charge, notwithstanding that it is discovered that the person in question is not a child or young person.

(2)   The attainment of the age of eighteen years by a person in whose case an order for conditional discharge[3] has been made, shall not deprive a youth court of jurisdiction to enforce his attendance and deal with him in respect of the commission of a further offence.

(3)   When a youth court has remanded[4] a child or young person for information to be obtained with respect to him, any youth court acting in the same local justice area—

(a)   may in his absence extend the period for which he is remanded, so, however, that he appears before a court or a justice of the peace at least once in every twenty-one days;

(b)   when the required information has been obtained, may deal with him finally.

(4)   A youth court may sit on any day for the purpose of hearing and determining a charge against a child or young person in respect of an indictable offence.

(5)–(6)   *Repealed.*

[Children and Young Persons Act 1933, s 48, as amended by Criminal Justice Act 1948, 9th Sch, Magistrates' Courts Act 1952, 6th Sch, Children and Young Persons Act 1963, 5th Sch, the Children and Young Persons Act 1969, Schs 5 and 6, the Criminal Justice Act 1991, Schs 8 and 11, the Access to Justice Act 1999, Sch 10 and the Courts Act 2003, Sch 8.]

1. For further commentary on this section, see this PART, para **5–10 Jurisdiction**, ante.
2. See note 5 to s 1, ante.
3. As to supervision orders, see now Children and Young Persons Act 1969, s 15, post.
4. Orders of remand made not for the purpose of obtaining necessary information, but for punishing the offender in a manner which the law does not permit, will be quashed (*R v Toynbee Hall Juvenile Court Justices, ex p Joseph* [1939] 3 All ER 16, 103 JP 279).

–114   49. Restrictions on reports of proceedings in which children or young persons are concerned[1]. (1) The following prohibitions apply (subject to subsection (5) below) in relation to any proceedings[2] to which this section applies, that is to say—

(a) no report shall be published which reveals the name, address or school of any child or young person concerned in the proceedings or includes any particulars likely to lead to the identification of any child or young person so concerned in the proceedings; and
(b) no picture shall be published or included in a programme service as being or including a picture of any child or young person concerned in the proceedings.*

(2) The proceedings to which this section applies[3] are—

(a) proceedings in a youth court;
(b) proceedings on appeal from a youth court (including proceedings by way of case stated);
(c) proceedings under Schedule 7 to the Powers of Criminal Courts (Sentencing) Act 2000 (proceedings for varying or revoking supervision orders); and
(d) proceedings on appeal from a magistrates' court arising out of proceedings under Schedule 7 to that Act (including proceedings by way of case stated).

(3) The reports to which this section applies are reports in a newspaper and reports included in a programme service; and similarly as respects pictures.*

(4) For the purposes of this section a child or young person is "concerned" in any proceedings whether as being the person against or in respect of whom the proceedings are taken or as being a witness in the proceedings.*

(4A) If a court is satisfied that it is in the public interest[4] to do so, it may, in relation to a child or young person who has been convicted of an offence, by order dispense to any specified extent with the requirements of this section in relation to any proceedings before it to which this section applies by virtue of subsection (2)(a) or (b) above, being proceedings relating to—

(a) the prosecution or conviction of the offender for the offence;
(b) the manner in which he, or his parent or guardian, should be dealt with in respect of the offence;
(c) the enforcement, amendment, variation, revocation or discharge of any order made in respect of the offence;
(d) where an attendance centre order is made in respect of the offence, the enforcement of any rules made under section 222(1)(d) or (e) of the Criminal Justice Act 2004 or
(e) where a detention and training order is made, the enforcement of any requirements imposed under section 103(6)(b) of the Powers of Criminal Courts (Sentencing) Act 2000.***

(4B) A court shall not exercise its power under subsection (4A) above without—

(a) affording the parties to the proceedings an opportunity to make representations; and
(b) taking into account any representations which are duly made.

(5) Subject to subsection (7) below, a court may, in relation to proceedings before it to which this section applies, by order dispense to any specified extent with the requirements of this section in relation to a child or young person who is concerned in the proceedings if it is satisfied—

(a) that it is appropriate to do so for the purpose of avoiding injustice to the child or young person; or
(b) that, as respects a child or young person to whom this paragraph applies who is unlawfully at large, it is necessary to dispense with those requirements for the purpose of apprehending him and bringing him before a court or returning him to the place in which he was in custody.

(6) Paragraph (b) of subsection (5) above applies to any child or young person who is charged with or has been convicted of—

(a) a violent offence,
(b) a sexual offence, or
(c) an offence punishable in the case of a person aged 21** or over with imprisonment for fourteen years or more.

(7) The court shall not exercise its power under subsection (5)(b) above—

(a) except in pursuance of an application by or on behalf of the Director of Public Prosecutions; and
(b) unless notice of the application has been given by the Director of Public Prosecutions to any legal representative of the child or young person.

(8) The court's power under subsection (5) above may be exercised by a single justice.

(9) If a report or picture is published or included in a programme service in contravention o subsection (1) above, the following persons, that is to say—

(a)   in the case of publication of a written report or a picture as part of a newspaper, any proprietor editor or publisher of the newspaper;

(b)   in the case of the inclusion of a report or picture in a programme service, any body corporat which provides the service and any person having functions in relation to the programm corresponding to those of an editor of a newspaper,

shall be liable on summary conviction to a fine not exceeding level 5 on the standard scale.*

(10) In any proceedings under Schedule 7 to the Powers of Criminal Courts (Sentencing) Ac 2000 (proceedings for varying or revoking supervision orders) before a magistrates' court other than a youth court or on appeal from such a court it shall be the duty of the magistrates' court or the appellate court to announce in the course of the proceedings that this section applies to the proceedings; and if the court fails to do so this section shall not apply to the proceedings.

(11) In this section—

"legal representative" means an authorised advocate or authorised litigator, as defined by section 119(1) of the Courts and Legal Services Act 1990;

"programme" and "programme service" have the same meaning as in the Broadcasting Act 1990

"sexual offence" means an offence listed in Part 2 of Schedule 15 to the Criminal Justice Act 2003

"specified" means specified in an order under this section;

"violent offence" means an offence listed in Part 1 of Schedule 15 to the Criminal Justice Ac 2003;

and a person who, having been granted bail, is liable to arrest (whether with or without a warrant shall be treated as unlawfully at large.*

[Children and Young Persons Act 1933, s 49, as substituted by the Criminal Justice and Public Order Act 1994 s 49 and amended by the Crime (Sentences) Act 1997, s 45, the Crime and Disorder Act 1998, Sch 8, the Power of Criminal Courts (Sentencing) Act 2000, Sch 9 and the Criminal Justice Act 2003, Sch 32.]

---

*A new s 49(3A), (9A)–(9E) and (12)–(14) are inserted, sub-ss (1), (3) and (9) substituted, sub-ss(4), (4A) (8) and (11) amended by the Youth Justice and Criminal Evidence Act 1999, Sch 2, when in force.

**Amended by the Criminal Justice and Court Services Act 2000, Sch 7 from a date to be appointed.

***Amended by the Powers of Criminal Courts (Sentencing) Act 2000, Sch 9, from a date to be appointed

1. The reporting restrictions in s 49 cease to be applicable if the defendant attains 18 during the course of the proceedings: *T v DPP* [2003] EWHC 2408 (Admin), [2005] Crim LR 739.

Similar provision is made for enforcement in England and Wales to protect a defendant or witness under 17 years of ag in summary proceedings in the Sheriff Court in Scotland: Criminal Procedure (Scotland) Act 1975, s 374. It will apply t an appeal from a sheriff, but does not apply where a child is charged before the sheriff jointly with an adult (Crimina Procedure (Scotland) Act 1975, s 370). For further commentary on this section, see this PART, paras **5–6** and **5–2 Restriction on publicity**, ante.

2. Any court may prohibit publication of certain matter in newspapers under s 39, ante.

3. It also applies to sound and television broadcasts as it applies to newspapers (Children and Young Persons Act 1963 s 57(4)). The restrictions extend to the report of proceedings at a Scottish children's hearing (Children and Young Person Act 1963, s 57(3) as amended).

4. The power to dispense with anonymity must be exercised with great care, caution and circumspection. The publi interest criterion will rarely be satisfied and it is wholly wrong to exercise the power as an additional punishment or fo 'naming and shaming'. In order to determine whether it is in the public interest to dispense with restrictions, it is entirel proper for the court to ask a reporter present in court if he wishes to say anything (*McKerry v Teesdale and Wear Valle Justices* (2000) 164 JP 355, [2000] Crim LR 594, DC).

Juvenile Offenders

5–115   50. Age of criminal responsibility[1]. It shall be conclusively presumed that no child under the age of ten years can be guilty of any offence.

[Children and Young Persons Act 1933, s 50, as amended by Children and Young Persons Act 1963, s 16(1).]

---

1. For commentary on this section see this PART, para **5–16 Criminal liability**, ante.

5–116   53. Punishment of certain grave crimes[1]. *Repealed.*

5–117   55. Power to order parent or guardian to pay fine, etc[1]. *Repealed.*

5–118   56. Powers of other courts to remit juvenile offenders to youth courts[1]. *Repealed.*

5–119   58. Power of Secretary of State to send certain juvenile offenders to approved schools The Secretary of State may by order direct that—

(a)   a person who is under the age of eighteen years and is undergoing detention in a Borsta institution; or

(b)   a child or young person[1] sentenced to be detained under section 91 of the Powers of Crimina Courts (Sentencing) Act 2000 with respect to whom he is authorised to give directions unde section 92 of that Act; or

(c)   a young person who has been ordered to be imprisoned and has been pardoned by He Majesty on condition of his agreeing to undergo training in a school, shall be transferred or sent to and detained in an approved school specified in the order; and any such order shall be an authority for his detention in that approved school or in such other approved school as the Secretary of State may from time to time determine until such date as may be specified in the order:

Provided that the date to be so specified shall be not later than that on which he will in the opinion of the Secretary of State attain the age of nineteen years nor later—

(a)   in the case of a person who was sentenced to detention under the said section 91, than the date on which his detention would have expired;

(b)   in the case of a young person who has been sentenced to imprisonment and pardoned as aforesaid, than three years from the date as from which his sentence began to run;

(c)   in the case of a person who was undergoing detention in a Borstal institution, than the end of the period for which he would have been liable to be detained therein.*

[Children and Young Persons Act 1933, s 58, as amended by Criminal Justice Act 1948, 9th Sch, Children and Young Persons Act 1963, 3rd Sch, the Crime and Disorder Act 1998, Sch 8 and the Powers of Criminal Courts (Sentencing) Act 2000, Sch 9.]

---

*Repealed by the Children and Children and Young Persons Act 1969, Sch 6, when in force.
1. See note 5 to s 1, ante.

5–120   59. Disuse of the words "conviction" and "sentence". Limitation on amount of costs imposed.   The words "conviction" and "sentence" shall cease to be used in relation to children and young persons dealt with summarily and any reference in any enactment whether passed before or after the commencement of this Act to a person convicted, a conviction or a sentence shall, in the case of a child or young person, be construed as including a reference to a person found guilty of an offence, a finding of guilt or an order made upon such a finding, as the case may be.

(2)   *Repealed.*

[Children and Young Persons Act 1933, s 59, as amended by Criminal Justice Act 1948, 9th Sch.]

PART IV

REMAND HOMES, APPROVED SCHOOLS, AND PERSONS TO WHOSE CARE CHILDREN AND YOUNG PERSONS MAY BE COMMITTED

Remand Homes

5–121   77. Provision of remand homes[1] by councils of counties and county boroughs.
(1)   *Repealed.*

(2)   The authority or persons responsible for the management of any institution other than a prison may, subject in the case of an institution supported wholly or partly out of public funds to the consent of the Government department concerned, arrange with the council of a county or county borough for the use of the institution, or any part thereof, as a remand home upon such terms as may be agreed.

(2A)   The council of a county or county borough may contribute, towards the expenditure incurred by any society or person in establishing, enlarging, or improving an institution for the purpose of its being used, in accordance with an arrangement with the council, as a remand home for that county or county borough, such sums, and subject to such conditions, as the council think fit; and s 77(5) of the Criminal Justice Act 1925 shall apply to any sums so paid as it applies to the payments referred to in that subsection.*

(3)–(4)   *Repealed.*

[Children and Young Persons Act 1933, s 77, as amended by the Criminal Justice Act 1948, Sch 9, and the Children and Young Persons Act 1969, Sch 6.]

---

*Repealed by the Children and Young Persons Act 1969, Sch 6, when in force.
1. Remand homes are replaced by community homes under Pt II of the Children and Young Persons Act 1969; see the Cessation of Approved Institutions (Remand Homes) Order 1973, SI 1973/637, made under s 46 of the 1969 Act.

PART VI

SUPPLEMENTAL

Local Authorities

5–122   96. Provisions as to local authorities.   (1) Subject to the modifications hereinafter contained[1] as to the City of London, where any powers or duties are by Part II of this Act conferred or imposed on local authorities (by that description), those powers and duties shall be powers and duties of local education authorities[2].

(1A)   The local authorities for the purposes of Parts III and IV of this Act shall be the councils of counties (other than metropolitan counties), of metropolitan districts and of London boroughs and the Common Council of the City of London but in relation to Wales, shall be the counties and county boroughs.

(2)   *Repealed.*

(3)   Expenses incurred by a local authority in connection with powers and duties which are, under this Act, exercised and performed by them as local education authorities shall be defrayed as expenses under the enactments relating to education.

(4) Expenses incurred under this Act by the council of a county or county borough, exclusive o
any expenses to be defrayed in accordance with the last foregoing subsection shall be defrayed—

　(a) Repealed,
　(b) as expenses for general county purposes or, as the case may be, out of the general rate.

(4A) Subsection (4) above does not apply in relation to the council of any Welsh county or county
borough.

(5)–(6) Repealed.

(7) A local authority may refer to a committee appointed for the purposes of this Act, or to any
committee appointed for the purposes of any other Act, any matter relating to the exercise by the
authority of any of their powers under this Act and may delegate any of the said powers (other than
any power to borrow money) to any such committee.

(8) A local authority, or a committee to whom any powers of a local authority under this Act have
been delegated, may by resolution empower the clerk or the chief education officer of the authority*
to exercise in the name of the authority in any case which appears to him to be one of urgency any
powers of the authority or, as the case may be, of the committee with respect to the institution o
proceedings under this Act.
[Children and Young Persons Act 1933, s 96, as amended by the Education Act 1944, 8th Sch, Part I, Children
Act 1948, s 60, 3rd Sch, the Local Authority Social Services Act 1970, Sch 2, the Child Care Act 1980, Sch 5, the
Acquisition of Land Act 1981, Sch 6, the Local Government (Wales) Act 1994, Sch 10,the Education Act 1996
Sch 37 and the Children Act 2004, Sch 5.]

---

*Words in sub-s (8) substituted by the Children Act 2004, Sch 5 from a day to be appointed.
　1. These modifications are contained in s 97, as amended by the Education Act 1944, 9th Sch, Part I.
　2. As to who are the local education authorities, see Education Act 1944, s 6(1), in PART VIII: title EDUCATION, post.

5–123　98. Institution of proceedings by local authorities.　Without prejudice to the provisions
of the last foregoing section, a local education authority may institute[1] proceedings for any offence
under Part I or Part II of this Act[2].
[Children and Young Persons Act 1933, s 98, as substituted by Children Act 1948, s 60, 3rd Sch.]

---

　1. Justices who are members of the local authority are disqualified from adjudicating (see Justices of the Peace Act 1997
s 66, in PART I: MAGISTRATES' COURTS, PROCEDURE, ante).
　2. Without prejudice to this section, such proceedings may be instituted by the council of a county or county borough
whether or not the council are the local education authority, and may, where the council are the local education authority
be instituted by them otherwise than in that capacity (Children and Young Persons Act 1963, s 56(1)).

Supplementary Provisions as to Legal Proceedings

5–124　99. Presumption and determination of age.　(1) Where a person, whether charged with
an offence or not, is brought before any court otherwise than for the purpose of giving evidence, and
it appears to the court that he is a child or young person[1], the court shall make due inquiry as to the
age of that person, and for that purpose shall take such evidence as may be forthcoming at the hearing
of the case, but an order or judgment of the court shall not be invalidated by any subsequent proof
that the age of that person has not been correctly stated to the court, and the age presumed or
declared by the court to be the age of the person so brought before it shall, for the purposes of this
Act, be deemed to be the true age of that person, and, where it appears to the court that the person
so brought before it has attained the age of eighteen years, that person shall for the purposes of this
Act be deemed not to be a child or young person.

(2) Where in any charge or indictment for any offence under this Act or any of the offences
mentioned in the First Schedule to this Act, except as provided in that Schedule, it is alleged that the
person by or in respect of whom the offence was committed was a child or young person or was
under or had attained any specified age, and he appears to the court to have been at the date of the
commission of the alleged offence a child or young person, or to have been under or to have attained
the specified age, as the case may be, he shall for the purposes of this Act be presumed at that date to
have been a child or young person or to have been under or to have attained that age, as the case may
be, unless the contrary is proved[3].

(3) Where, in any charge or indictment for any offence under this Act or any of the offences
mentioned in the First Schedule to this Act, it is alleged that the person in respect of whom the
offence was committed was a child or was a young person, it shall not be a defence to prove that the
person alleged to have been a child was a young person or the person alleged to have been a young
person was a child in any case where the acts constituting the alleged offence would equally have
been an offence if committed in respect of a young person or child respectively.

(4) Where a person is charged with an offence under this Act in respect of a person apparently
under a specified age it shall be a defence to prove that the person was actually of or over that age.
[Children and Young Persons Act 1933, s 99, as amended by Sexual Offences Act 1956, 3rd Sch and the Criminal
Justice Act 1991, Sch 8.]

---

　1. See note 5 to s 1, ante.
　2. This includes a reference to offences under s 1 of the Indecency with Children Act 1960: Indecency with Children
Act 1960, s 1(3).
　3. See *R v Carr-Briant* [1943] KB 607, [1943] 2 All ER 156, 107 JP 167.

-125 100. Evidence of wages of defendant. In any proceedings under this Act a copy of an entry in the wages book of any employer of labour, or, if no wages book be kept, a written statement signed by the employer, or by any responsible person in his employ, shall be evidence that the wages therein entered or stated as having been paid to any person, have in fact been so paid.
[Children and Young Persons Act 1933, s 100.]

-126 101. Application of Summary Jurisdiction Acts. *Repealed.*

-127 102. Appeals to the Crown Court. (1) Appeals to the Crown Court[1] from orders of a magistrates' court under this Act may be brought in the following cases and by the following persons, that is to say—

(a)–(d) *Repealed;*
(e) in the case of an order requiring the owner of an automatic machine for the sale of tobacco or the person on whose premises such a machine is kept, to take precautions[2] to prevent the machine being extensively used by persons apparently under the age of sixteen years or to remove the machine, by any person aggrieved.

(2) Nothing in this section shall be construed as affecting any other right of appeal conferred by this or any other Act.
[Children and Young Persons Act 1933, s 102, as amended by Children Act 1948, s 60, 3rd and 4th Schs, Children and Young Persons Act 1969, Sch 6, the Courts Act 1971, Sch 9, the Child Care Act 1980, Sch 6 and the Courts Act 2003, Sch 8.]

---

1. Appeal lies notwithstanding that the young person dealt with by the youth court has attained the age of 18 years before the hearing of the appeal (*Drover v Rugman* [1951] KB 380, sub nom *Rugman v Drover* [1950] 2 All ER 575, 114 JP 452).
2. See s 7(2), ante.

General

-128 106. Provisions as to documents, etc. (1) An order or other act of the Secretary of State under this Act may be signified under the hand of the Secretary of State or an Under-Secretary of State or an Assistant Under-Secretary.

(2) *Repealed.*
(3) The production of a copy of the London Gazette containing a notice of the grant, or of the withdrawal or surrender, of a certificate of approval of an approved school shall be sufficient evidence of the fact of a certificate having been duly granted to the school named in the notice, or of the withdrawal or surrender of such a certificate, and the grant of a certificate of approval of an approved school may also be proved by the production of the certificate itself, or of a document purporting to be a copy of the certificate and to be authenticated as such by an Under-Secretary of State or Assistant Under-Secretary★.
(4) Any notice or other document required or authorised by this Act to be served on the managers of an approved school may, if those managers are a local authority or a joint committee representing two or more local authorities, be served either personally or by post upon their clerk, and in any other case, may be served either personally or by post upon any one of the managers, or their secretary, or the headmaster of the school★.
(5) An order, licence, or other document may be authenticated on behalf of the managers of an approved school, if they are a local authority or a joint committee representing two or more local authorities, by the signature of their clerk or some other officer of the local authority duly authorised in that behalf, and in any other case, by the signature of one of the managers or their secretary, or of the headmaster.★
[Children and Young Persons Act 1933, s 106 as amended by the Child Care Act 1980, Sch 6, the Criminal Justice Act 1988, s 129 and the Powers of Criminal Courts (Sentencing) Act 2000, Sch 12.]

★Repealed by the Children and Young Persons Act 1969, Sch 6, when in force.

-129 107. Interpretation. (1) In this Act, unless the context otherwise requires, the following expressions have the meanings hereby respectively assigned to them, that is to say—

"Chief officer of police", as regards Scotland has the same meaning as in the Police (Scotland) Act 1967, and as regards Northern Ireland means a district inspector of the Royal Ulster Constabulary;
"Child" means a person under the age[1] of fourteen years;
"Guardian", in relation to a child or young person includes any person who, in the opinion of the court having cognisance of any case in relation to the child or young person or in which the child or young person is concerned, has for the time being the care of the child or young person;
"Intoxicating liquor" has the same meaning as in the Licensing Act 1964;★
"legal guardian", in relation to a child or young person, means a guardian of a child as defined in the Children Act 1989;
"Place of safety" means a community home provided by a local authority or a controlled community home, any police station, or any hospital, surgery, or any other suitable place, the occupier of which is willing temporarily to receive a child or young person;
"Prescribed" means prescribed by regulations made by the Secretary of State;

"Public place" includes any public park, garden, sea beach, or railway station, and any ground ⬛
which the public for the time being have or are permitted to have access, whether on paymer
or otherwise;

"Street" includes any highway and any public bridge, road, lane, footway, square, court, alley, ⬛
passage, whether a thoroughfare or not;

"Young person" means a person who has attained the age of fourteen years and is under the ag
of seventeen years.**

(2) *Repealed.*

(3) References in this Act to any enactment or to any provision in any enactment shall, unless th
context otherwise requires, be construed as references to that enactment or provision as amended b
any subsequent enactment including this Act.

[Children and Young Persons Act 1933, s 107, as amended by the National Assistance Act 1948, s 62, and Sch ⬛
the Police Act 1964, Schs 9 and 10, the Children and Young Persons Act 1969, Schs 5 and 6, the Domest
Proceedings and Magistrates' Courts Act 1978, Sch 2, the Justices of the Peace Act 1979, Sch 2, the Child Ca⬛
Act 1980, Sch 6, the Statute Law (Repeals) Act 1986 Sch 1, the Children Act 1989, Schs 13 and 15, the Crimin
Justice Act 1991 Sch 8 and the Police Act 1996, Sch 8.]

*Definition is repealed by the Licensing Act 2003, Sch 6, from a date to be appointed.
**Definition is amended by the Criminal Justice Act 1991, Sch 8, when in force.
1. A person attains a particular age at the commencement of the relevant anniversary of the date of his birth: s 9 of th
Family Law Reform Act 1969, in PART IV: FAMILY LAW, ante.

SCHEDULES
FIRST SCHEDULE[1]
OFFENCES AGAINST CHILDREN AND YOUNG PERSONS, WITH RESPECT TO WHICH SPECIAL PROVISIONS C
THIS ACT APPLY

(*As amended by the amended by Sexual Offences Act 1956, Sch 3 and the Criminal Justice Act 1988, Sch 15, the Sexu⬛
Offences Act 2003, Sch 6 and the Domestic Violence, Crime and Victims Act 2004, Sch 10.*)

5–130 The murder[2] or manslaughter[2] of a child or young person.
Infanticide[2].
An offence under section 5 of the Domestic Violence, Crime and Victims Act 2004, in respect of a child ⬛
young person.
Any offence under ss 27[3], or 56 of the Offences against the Person Act 1861, and any offences against a child ⬛
young person under s 5[5], of that Act.
Common assault, or battery.
Any offence under ss 1, 3, 4, 11 or 23[6], of this Act.
Any offence against a child or young person under any of the sections 1 to 41, 47 to 53, 57 to 61, 66 and 67 ⬛
the Sexual Offences Act 2003, or any attempt to commit such an offence.
Any offence under section 62 or 63 of the Sexual Offences Act 2003 where the intended offence was an offenc
against a child or young person, or any attempt to commit such an offence.
Any other offence involving bodily injury to a child or young person.

1. References to offences includes a reference to offences under s 1 of the Indecency with Children Act 1960 (ibi⬛
s 1(3)), or under s 1(1)(*a*) of the Protection of Children Act 1978 (not applicable to ss 15 and 99) or under Part I of th
Child Abduction Act 1984.
2. See PART VIII, title PERSONS, OFFENCES AGAINST, post. The references shall apply also to aiding, abettin⬛
counselling or procuring suicide (Suicide Act 1961, s 2(3)).
3. Abandoning a child, see PART VIII, title PERSONS, OFFENCES AGAINST, post.
4. Section 56 of the Offences against the Person Act 1861 has been repealed by the Child Abduction Act 1984, s 1
post.
5. Manslaughter, see PART VIII, title PERSONS, OFFENCES AGAINST, post.
6. This reference to these offences shall be construed as including a reference to any offence under the Dangerou
Performances Acts 1879 and 1897, or under Pt II (ie ss 12–38) of the Children Act 1908 (s 108(6), ante).
7. For Sexual Offences Act 1956, see PART VIII, title SEXUAL OFFENCES, post.

SECOND SCHEDULE
CONSTITUTION OF YOUTH COURTS
Repealed.

Children and Young Persons Act 1963
(1963 c 37)

5–330 NOTE.—This Act shall be construed as one with the Children and Young Persons Act 193⬛
ante, except in so far as it amends any other Act not construed as one therewith (s 65(3)). The A⬛
of 1933 is referred to throughout as "the principal Act" and "the principal Scottish Act" refers to th
Children and Young Persons (Scotland) Act 1937 (s 63(1)). In so far as the Act amends existin
legislation, such amendments have been incorporated in the appropriate text.

PART I
CARE AND CONTROL OF CHILDREN AND YOUNG PERSONS

Youth courts and proceedings in connection with children and young persons

5–332 **16. Offences committed by children.** (1) *Amendment of s* 50 *of the Children and Youn*⬛
Persons Act 1933, ante.

(2)–(3) *Repealed.*
[Children and Young Persons Act 1963, s 16 as amended by the Crime (Sentences) Act 1997, Sch 4, the Powers of Criminal Courts (Sentencing) Act 2000, Sch 9 and the Criminal Justice Act 2003, Sch 37.]

5–333   18. Jurisdiction of magistrates' courts in certain cases involving children and young persons[1]. Notwithstanding s 46(1) of the principal Act[2] (which restricts the jurisdiction of magistrates' courts which are not youth courts in cases where a child or young person is charged with an offence) a magistrates' court which is not a youth court may hear an information against a child or young person if he is charged—

(a) with aiding, abetting, causing, procuring, allowing or permitting an offence with which a person who has attained the age of eighteen is charged at the same time; or

(b) with an offence arising out of circumstances which are the same as or connected with those giving rise to an offence with which a person who has attained the age of eighteen is charged at the same time.

[Children and Young Persons Act 1963, s 18 as amended by the Criminal Justice Act 1991, Sch 11 and the Criminal Justice and Public Order Act 1994, Sch 9.]

1. For commentary on this section, see this PART, para **5–11 Jurisdiction of the magistrates' and Crown Courts**.
2. Ante.

5–335   26. Medical evidence by certificate. In any proceedings, other than proceedings for an offence, before a youth court, and on any appeal from a decision of a youth court in any such proceedings, any document purporting to be a certificate of a fully registered medical practitioner as to any person's physical or mental condition shall be admissible as evidence of that condition.
[Children and Young Persons Act 1963, s 26 as amended by the Criminal Justice Act 1991, Sch 11.]

5–336   28. Form of oath for use in youth courts and by children and young persons in other courts. (1) Subject to subsection (2) of this section, in relation to any oath administered to and taken by any person before a youth court or administered to and taken by any child or young person before any other court, section 1 of the Oaths Act 1978[1] shall have effect as if the words "I promise before Almighty God" were set out in it instead of the words "I swear by Almighty God that".

(2) Where in any oath otherwise duly administered and taken either of the forms mentioned in this section is used instead of the other, the oath shall nevertheless be deemed to have been duly administered and taken.
[Children and Young Persons Act 1963, s 28, as amended by the Oaths Act 1978, s 2 and the Criminal Justice Act 1991, Sch 11.]

1. See para **2–1190, Statutes on Evidence** in PART II, ante.

5–337   29. Provisions as to persons between the ages of 17 and 18. (1) Where proceedings in respect of a young person are begun[1] for an offence and he attains the age of eighteen before the conclusion of the proceedings, the court may deal with the case and make any order which it could have made if he had not attained that age[2].
[Children and Young Persons Act 1963, s 29, as amended by the Children and Young Persons Act 1969, Schs 5 and 6, the Children Act 1989, Sch 15 and the Criminal Justice Act 1991 Sch 8.]

1. Proceedings are begun when the accused is first brought before the court and not at the earlier time when the information is laid or the charge preferred (*R v Uxbridge Youth Court, ex p Howard* (1998) 162 JP 327, DC).
2. In *Aldis v DPP* [2002] EWHC 403 (Admin), [2002] 2 Cr App Rep (S) 400, [2002] Crim LR 434 it was held, in relation to a defendant aged 17 at the time of mode of trial, at which hearing it must have been plain to all present that the possibility of a 2-year detention and training order was a factor in the court's decision to try the case summarily, that the attainment of 18 before the trial and conviction did not prevent the justices from imposing a detention and training order; Parliament's intention must have been that s 100 of the Powers of Criminal Courts (Sentencing) Act 2000 should be interpreted as subject to s 29 of the Children and Young Persons Act 1963. Where the defendant is charged with an indictable offence, he will have the right to be tried by a jury if he attains the age of 18 before the court determines mode of trial; see the Magistrates' Courts Act 1980, s 24(1), and notes thereto, para **1–2053**, in PART I: MAGISTRATES' COURTS, PROCEDURE, ante. As to the approach to adopt in sentencing where an offender crosses an important age threshold between the date of the commission of the offence and the date of conviction, see para **5–41A**, post.

PART II

EMPLOYMENT OF CHILDREN AND YOUNG PERSONS

Entertainment

5–338   37. Restriction on persons under 16 taking part in public performances, etc. (1) Subject to the provisions of this section, a child shall not—

(a) take part in a performance to which subsection (2) of this section applies, or

(b) otherwise take part in a sport, or work as a model, where payment in respect of his doing so, other than for defraying expenses, is made to him or to another person,

except under the authority of a licence granted by the local authority in whose area he resides or, if he does not reside in Great Britain, by the local authority in whose area the applicant or one of the applicants for the licence resides or has his place of business.

(2) This subsection applies to—

(*a*) any performance in connection with which a charge is made (whether for admission or otherwise);

(*b*) any performance in premises—

  (i) which, by virtue of an authorisation (within the meaning of section 136 of the Licensing Act 2003), may be used for the supply of alcohol (within the meaning of section 14 of that Act), or

  (ii) *Scotland.*

(*c*) any broadcasting performance;

(*d*) any performance not falling within paragraph (*c*) above but included in a programme service (within the meaning of the Broadcasting Act 1990);

(*e*) any performance recorded (by whatever means) with a view to its use in a broadcast or such service or in a film intended for public exhibition;

and a child shall be treated for the purposes of this section as taking part in a performance if he takes the place of a performer in any rehearsal or in any preparation for the recording of the performance.

(3) A licence under this section shall not be required for any child to take part in a performance to which subsection (2) of this section applies if no payment in respect of his taking part in the performance, other than for defraying expenses, is made to him or to another person, and—

(*a*) in the six months preceding the performance he has not taken part in other performances to which subsection (2) of this section applies on more than three days; or

(*b*) the performance is given under arrangements made by a school (within the meaning of the Education Act 1996 or the Education (Scotland) Act 1962) or made by a body of persons approved for the purposes of this section by the Secretary of State or by the local authority in whose area the performance takes place;

but the Secretary of State may by regulations[1] made by statutory instrument prescribe conditions to be observed with respect to the hours of work, rest or meals of children taking part in performances as mentioned in paragraph (*a*) of this subsection.

(4) The power to grant licences under this section shall be exercisable subject to such restrictions and conditions as the Secretary of State may by regulations made by statutory instrument prescribe and a local authority shall not grant a licence for a child to do anything unless they are satisfied that he is fit to do it, that proper provision has been made to secure his health and kind treatment and that, having regard to such provision (if any) as has been or will be made therefor, his education will not suffer, but if they are so satisfied, in the case of an application duly made for a licence under this section which they have power to grant, they shall not refuse to grant the licence.

(5) Regulations[1] under this section may make different provision for different circumstances and may prescribe, among the conditions subject to which a licence is to be granted, conditions requiring the approval of a local authority and may provide for that approval to be given subject to conditions imposed by the authority.

(6) Without prejudice to the generality of the preceding subsection, regulations[1] under this section may prescribe, among the conditions subject to which a licence may be granted, a condition requiring sums earned by the child in respect of whom the licence is granted in any activity to which the licence relates to be paid into the county court (or, *application to Scotland*) or dealt with in a manner approved by the local authority.

(7) A licence under this section shall specify the times, if any, during which the child in respect of whom it is granted may be absent from school for the purposes authorised by the licence; and for the purposes of the enactments relating to education a child who is so absent during any times so specified shall be deemed to be absent with leave granted by a person authorised in that behalf by the managers governors or proprietor of the school or, (*application to Scotland*).

(8) Any statutory instrument made under this section shall be subject to annulment in pursuance of a resolution of either House of Parliament.

[Children and Young Persons Act 1963, s 37 as amended by the Cable and Broadcasting Act 1984, Sch 5, the Broadcasting Act 1990, Sch 20, the Education Act 1996, Sch 37, SI 1998/276 and the Licensing Act 2003, Sch 6.]

---

1. The Secretary of State has made the Children (Performances) Regulations 1968, SI 1968/1728 amended by SI 1998/1678 and SI 2000/10 and 2384.

5–339   38. Restriction on licences for performances by children under 14.   (1) A licence under the preceding section in respect of a child under the age of fourteen shall not be granted in relation to a performance to which subsection (2) of that section applies unless—

(*a*) the licence is for acting and the application therefor is accompanied by a declaration that the part he is to act cannot be taken except by a child of about his age; or

(*b*) the licence is for dancing in a ballet which does not form part of an entertainment of which anything other than ballet or opera also forms part and the application for the licence is accompanied by a declaration that the part he is to dance cannot be taken except by a child of about his age; or

(*c*) the nature of his part in the performance is wholly or mainly musical and either the nature of the performance is also wholly or mainly musical or the performance consists only of opera and ballet.

(2) *Repealed.*

[Children and Young Persons Act 1963, s 38 as amended by the Education Act 1996, Sch 37, and SI 1998/276.]

-340 39. Supplementary provisions as to licences under section 37. (1) A licence under section 37 of this Act may be varied on the application of the person holding it by the local authority by whom it was granted or by any local authority in whose area any activity to which it relates takes place.

(2) The local authority by whom such a licence was granted, and any local authority in whose area any activity to which it relates takes place, may vary or revoke the licence if any condition subject to which it was granted is not observed or they are not satisfied as to the matters mentioned in subsection (4) of the said section 37, but shall, before doing so, give to the holder of the licence such notice (if any) of their intention as may be practicable in the circumstances.

(3) Where a local authority grant such a licence authorising a child to do something in the area of another local authority they shall send to that other authority such particulars as the Secretary of State may by regulations made by statutory instrument prescribe[1]; and where a local authority vary or revoke such a licence which was granted by, or relates to an activity in the area of, another local authority, they shall inform that other authority.

(4) A local authority proposing to vary or revoke such a licence granted by another local authority shall, if practicable, consult that other authority.

(5) The holder of such a licence shall keep such records as the Secretary of State may by regulations made by statutory instrument prescribe and shall on request produce them to an officer of the authority who granted the licence, at any time not later than six months after the occasion or last occasion to which it relates.

(6) Where a local authority refuse an application for a licence under section 37 of this Act or revoke or, otherwise than on the application of the holder, vary such a licence they shall state their grounds for doing so in writing to the applicant or, as the case may be, the holder of the licence; and the applicant or holder may appeal to a magistrates' court or, (*application to Scotland*), against the refusal, revocation or variation, and against any condition subject to which the licence is granted or any approval is given, not being a condition which the local authority are required to impose.

(7) Any statutory instrument made under this section shall be subject to annulment in pursuance of a resolution of either House of Parliament.
[Children and Young Persons Act 1963, s 39 as amended by SI 1998/276.]

---

1. The Children (Performances) Regulations 1968, SI 1968/1728 amended by SI 1998/1678 have been made.

-341 40. Offences. (1) If any person—

    (a) causes or procures any child or, being his parent or guardian, allows him, to do anything in contravention of section 37 of this Act; or

    (b) fails to observe any condition subject to which a licence under that section is granted, or any condition prescribed under subsection (3) of that section; or

    (c) knowingly or recklessly makes any false statement in or in connection with an application for a licence under that section;

he shall be liable on summary conviction to a fine not exceeding **level 3** on the standard scale or imprisonment for a term not exceeding **three months** or **both**.

(2) If any person fails to keep or produce any record which he is required to keep or produce under section 39 of this Act, he shall be liable on summary conviction to a fine not exceeding **level 3** on the standard scale or imprisonment for a term not exceeding **three months** or **both**.

(3) The court by which the holder or one of the holders of a licence under section 37 of this Act is convicted of an offence under this section may revoke the licence.

(4) In any proceedings for an offence under this section alleged to have been committed by causing, procuring or allowing a child to take part in a performance without a licence under section 37 of this Act it shall be a defence to prove that the accused believed that the condition specified in paragraph (*a*) of subsection (3) of that section was satisfied and that he had reasonable grounds for that belief.
[Children and Young Persons Act 1963, s 40 as amended by the Criminal Justice Act 1982, ss 38 and 46, and SI 1998/276.]

-342 41. Licences for training [children] for performances of a dangerous nature. (1) The power to grant licences under section 24 of the principal Act (which relates to the training of children to take part in performances of a dangerous nature) shall be exercisable by the local authority for the area or one of the areas in which the training is to take place instead of by a magistrates' court.

(2) A licence under the said section 24 or (*application to Scotland*) may be revoked or varied by the authority who granted it if any of the conditions embodied therein are not complied with or if it appears to them that the person to whom the licence relates is no longer fit and willing to be trained or that proper provision is no longer being made to secure his health and kind treatment.

(3) Where an authority refuse an application for such a licence or revoke or vary such a licence they shall state their grounds for doing so in writing to the applicant, or, as the case may be, to the holder of the licence, and the applicant or holder may appeal to a magistrates' court or, (*application to Scotland*), against the refusal, revocation or variation.
[Children and Young Persons Act 1963, s 41 as amended by the Employment Act 1989, Sch 6.]

-343 42. Licences for children performing abroad. (1) Section 25 of the principal Act (which prohibits children from going abroad for certain purposes except under the authority of a licence granted under that section) and section 26 of that Act (which imposes penalties for contravention shall have effect as if the words "singing, playing, performing or being exhibited" included takir part in any such performance as is mentioned in paragraph (c) or (d) of section 37(2) of this Act.

(2) A licence under the said section 25 may be granted in relation to a purpose referred to : subsection (1)(a) of that section in respect of a person notwithstanding that he is under the age (fourteen if—

(a) the engagement which he is to fulfil is for acting and the application for the licence accompanied by a declaration that the part he is to act cannot be taken except by a person (about his age; or

(b) the engagement is for dancing in a ballet which does not form part of an entertainment (which anything other than ballet or opera also forms part and the application for the licence accompanied by a declaration that the part he is to dance cannot be taken except by a child (about his age; or

(c) the engagement is for taking part in a performance the nature of which is wholly or main musical or which consists only of opera and ballet and the nature of his part in the performanc is wholly or mainly musical.

[Children and Young Persons Act 1963, s 42 as amended by the Employment Act 1989, Sch 6, and SI 1998/276

Construction of Part II

5-344   44. Construction of Part II.   (1) This Part of this Act, in its application to England an Wales, and, as regards section 42, in its application elsewhere, shall be construed, and Part II of th principal Act shall have effect, as if this Part were included in that Part.

(2) *Scotland.*

[Children and Young Persons Act 1963, s 44.]

Children and Young Persons Act 1969
(1969 c 54)

PART I

CARE AND OTHER TREATMENT OF JUVENILES THROUGH COURT PROCEEDINGS

Consequential changes in criminal proceedings, etc

5-564   5. Restrictions on criminal proceedings for offences by young persons[1].   (1)–(7) R pealed.

(8) It shall be the duty of a person who decides to lay an information in respect of an offence in case where he has reason to believe that the alleged offender is a young person[2] to give notice[3] of th decision to the appropriate local authority[4] unless he is himself that authority.

(9) In this section—

"the appropriate local authority", in relation to a young person, means the local authority for th area in which it appears to the informant in question that the young person resides[5] or, if th young person appears to the informant not to reside in the area of a local authority, the loc authority in whose area it is alleged that the relevant offence or one of the relevant offences wa committed;

but nothing in this section shall be construed as preventing any council or other body from acting b an agent for the purposes of this section.

[Children and Young Persons Act 1969, s 5 as amended by the Children Act 1989, Sch 12 and the Crimin. Justice Act 1991, s 72.]

---

1. For further commentary on this section, see this PART, para **5–21 Prosecution**, ante.

2. For the purposes of this subsection the Secretary of State has by order provided that "young person" includes a chi who has attained 10 years: see s 34(1)(c), post, and SI 1970/1882.

3. Notice should be given as soon as reasonably practicable after the decision to lay an information is made. Howeve the notice does not have to be in writing and failure to give the notice does not render the proceedings null and void (*DI v Cottier* [1996] 3 All ER 126, [1996] 1 WLR 826, *R v Marsh* [1997] 1 WLR 649, CA).

4. Notice must also be given to a probation officer: see s 34(2), post, and Order made thereunder.

5. Residence must be construed in the ordinary way, and refers to the place where a person lives and has his mea (*Stoke-on-Trent Corpn v Cheshire County Council* [1915] 3 KB 699, 79 JP 452), and does not include a constructi residence. It is the place where his home is (*South Shields Corpn v Liverpool Corpn* [1943] KB 264, [1943] 1 All ER 33 107 JP 77). See also *Yorkshire West Riding County Council v Colne Corpn* (1917) 82 JP 14; *Leicester Corpn v Stoke-on-Tre Corpn* (1918) 83 JP 45; *LCC v Wiltshire County Council* (1927) 91 JP 122; and *Worcestershire County Council Warwickshire County Council* [1934] 2 KB 288, 98 JP 347.

5-566   9. Investigations by local authorities.   (1) Where a local authority or a local educatio authority bring proceedings for an offence alleged to have been committed by a young person[1] or an notified that any such proceedings are being brought, it shall be the duty of the authority, unless the are of opinion that it is unnecessary to do so, to make such investigations and provide the cou before which the proceedings are heard with such information relating to the home surrounding school record, health and character of the person in respect of whom the proceedings are brought a appear to the authority likely to assist the court.

(2) If the court mentioned in subsection (1) of this section requests the authority aforesaid t

make investigations and provide information or to make further investigations and provide further information relating to the matters aforesaid, it shall be the duty of the authority to comply with the request.
[Children and Young Persons Act 1969, s 9 as amended by the Children Act 1989, Sch 15.]

---

1. The Secretary of State has by order provided that the reference to a "young person" in this subsection shall be construed as including a child who has attained the age of 10 years: see s 34(1)(c), post, and SI 1970/1882. Further, the Secretary of State has by order provided that, in the case of a juvenile who has attained the age of 13 years, a local authority shall not be required to make investigations or provide information which it does not already possess with respect to home surroundings if by direction of the justices or the probation and after care committee acting for any relevant area, arrangements are in force for information with respect to home surroundings to be furnished to the court in question by a probation officer: see s 34(3), post, and SI 1970/1882, amended by SI 1973/485 and SI 1974/1083.

Supervision

5–601   23. Remand to local authority accommodation[1], committal of young persons of unruly character, etc. (1) Where—

(a)   a court remands a child or young person charged with or convicted of one or more offences or commits him for trial or sentence; and

(b)   he is not released on bail,

the remand or committal shall be to local authority accommodation[2]; and in the following provisions of this section (except subsection (1A)), any reference (however expressed) to a remand shall be construed as including a reference to a committal.

(1A) Where a court remands a child or young person in connection with extradition proceedings and he is not released on bail the remand shall be to local authority accommodation.

(2) A court remanding a person to local authority accommodation shall designate the local authority who are to receive him; and that authority shall be—

(a)   in the case of a person who is being looked after by a local authority, that authority; and

(b)   in any other case, the local authority in whose area it appears to the court that he resides or the offence or one of the offences was committed.

(3) Where a person is remanded to local authority accommodation, it shall be lawful for any person acting on behalf of the designated authority to detain him.

(4) Subject to subsections (5), (5ZA) and (5A) below, a court remanding a person to local authority accommodation may, after consultation with the designated authority, require that authority to comply with a security requirement, that is to say, a requirement that the person in question be placed and kept in secure accommodation.

(5) A court shall not impose a security requirement in relation to a person remanded in accordance with subsection (1) above except in respect of a child who has attained the age of twelve, or a young person, who (in either case) is of a prescribed description[3], and then only if—

(a)   he is charged with or has been convicted of a violent or sexual offence, or an offence punishable in the case of an adult with imprisonment for a term of fourteen years or more; or

(b)   he is charged with or has been convicted of one or more imprisonable offences which, together with any other imprisonable offences of which he has been convicted in any proceedings—

(i)   amount, or

(ii) would, if he were convicted of the offences with which he is charged, amount,

to a recent history of repeatedly committing imprisonable offences while remanded on bail or to local authority accommodation,

and (in either case) the condition set out in subsection (5AA) below is satisfied.

(5ZA) A court shall not impose a security requirement in relation to a person remanded in accordance with subsection (1A) above unless—

(a)   he has attained the age of twelve and is of a prescribed description;

(b)   one or both of the conditions set out in subsection (5ZB) below is satisfied; and

(c)   the condition set out in subsection (5AA) below is satisfied.

(5ZB) The conditions mentioned in subsection (5ZA)(b) above are—

(a)   that the conduct constituting the offence to which the extradition proceedings relate would if committed in the United Kingdom constitute an offence punishable in the case of an adult with imprisonment for a term of fourteen years or more;

(b)   that the person has previously absconded from the extradition proceedings or from proceedings in the United Kingdom or the requesting territory which relate to the conduct constituting the offence to which the extradition proceedings relate.

(5ZC) For the purposes of subsection (5ZB) above a person has absconded from proceedings if in relation to those proceedings—

(a)   he has been released subject to a requirement to surrender to custody at a particular time and he has failed to surrender to custody at that time, or

(b)   he has surrendered into the custody of a court and he has at any time absented himself from the court without its leave.

(5AA) The condition mentioned in subsections (5) and (5ZA) is that the court is of the opinion, after considering all the options for the remand of the person, that only remanding him to local authority accommodation with a security requirement would be adequate—

(a)   to protect the public from serious harm from him; or

(b)   to prevent the commission by him of imprisonable offences.

(5A)   A court shall not impose a security requirement in respect of a child or young person who is not legally represented in the court unless—

(a)   he was granted a right to representation funded by the Legal Services Commission as part of the Criminal Defence Service but the right was withdrawn because of his conduct; or

(b)   having been informed of his right to apply for such representation and had the opportunity to do so, he refused or failed to apply.

(6)   Where a court imposes a security requirement in respect of a person, it shall be its duty—

(a)   to state in open court that it is of such opinion as is mentioned in subsection (5AA) above and

(b)   to explain to him in open court and in ordinary language why it is of that opinion;

and a magistrates' court shall cause a reason stated by it under paragraph (b) above to be specified in the warrant of commitment and to be entered in the register.

(7)   Subject to section 23AA below, a court remanding a person to local authority accommodation without imposing a security requirement may, after consultation with the designated authority require that person to comply with

(a)   any such conditions as could be imposed under section 3(6) of the Bail Act 1976 (c 63) if he were then being granted bail; and

(b)   any conditions imposed for the purpose of securing the electronic monitoring of his compliance with any other condition imposed under this subsection.

(7A)   Where a person is remanded to local authority accommodation and a security requirement is imposed in respect of him—

(a)   the designated local authority may, with the consent of the Secretary of State, arrange for the person to be detained, for the whole or any part of the period of the remand or committal, in a secure training centre; and

(b)   his detention there pursuant to the arrangements shall be lawful.

(7B)   Arrangements under subsection (7A) above may include provision for payments to be made by the authority to the Secretary of State.

(8)   Where a court imposes on a person any such conditions as are mentioned in subsection (7) above, it shall be its duty to explain to him in open court and in ordinary language why it is imposing those conditions; and a magistrates' court shall cause a reason stated by it under this subsection to be specified in the warrant of commitment and to be entered in the register.

(9)   A court remanding a person to local authority accommodation without imposing a security requirement may, after consultation with the designated authority, impose on that authority requirements—

(a)   for securing compliance with any conditions imposed on that person under subsection (7) above; or

(b)   stipulating that he shall not be placed with a named person.

(10)   Where a person is remanded to local authority accommodation, a relevant court—

(a)   may, on the application of the designated authority, impose on that person any such conditions as could be imposed under subsection (7) above if the court were then remanding him to such accommodation; and

(b)   where it does so, may impose on that authority any requirements for securing compliance with the conditions so imposed.

(11)   Where a person is remanded to local authority accommodation, a relevant court may, on the application of the designated authority or that person, vary or revoke any conditions or requirements imposed under subsection (7), (9) or (10) above.

(12)   In this section—

"court" and "magistrates' court" include a justice;

"children's home" has the same meaning as in the Care Standards Act 2000;

"extradition proceedings" means proceedings under the Extradition Act 2003;

"imprisonable offence" means an offence punishable in the case of an adult with imprisonment;

"prescribed description" means a description prescribed by reference to age or sex or both by an order of the Secretary of State;

"relevant court"—

(a)   in relation to a person remanded to local authority accommodation under subsection (1) above, means the court by which he was so remanded, or any magistrates' court having jurisdiction in the place where he is for the time being;

(b)   in relation to a person remanded to local authority accommodation under subsection (1A) above, means the court by which he was so remanded;

"requesting territory" means the territory to which a person's extradition is sought in extradition proceedings;

"secure accommodation" means accommodation which is provided in a children's home in respect of which a person is registered under Part II of the Care Standards Act 2000 for the purpose of restricting liberty, and is approved for that purpose by the Secretary of State or the National Assembly for Wales;

"sexual offence" means an offence listed in Part 2 of Schedule 15 to the Criminal Justice Act 2003;

"violent offence" means an offence listed in Part 1 of Schedule 15 to the Criminal Justice Act 2003;

"young person" means a person who has attained the age of fourteen years and is under the age of seventeen years;

but, for the purposes of the definition of "secure accommodation", "local authority accommodation" includes any accommodation falling within section 61(2) of the Criminal Justice Act 1991.

(13) In this section—

(a) any reference to a person who is being looked after by a local authority shall be construed in accordance with section 22 of the Children Act 1989;

(b) any reference to consultation shall be construed as a reference to such consultation (if any) as is reasonably practicable in all the circumstances of the case; and

(c) any reference, in relation to a person charged with or convicted of a violent or sexual offence, to protecting the public from serious harm from him shall be construed as a reference to protecting members of the public from death or serious personal injury, whether physical or psychological, occasioned by further such offences committed by him.

(14) This section has effect subject to—

(a) *repealed*;

(b) section 128(7) of that Act (remands to the custody of a constable for periods of not more than three days),

but section 128(7) shall have effect in relation to a child or young person as if for the reference to three clear days there were substituted a reference to twenty-four hours.

[Children and Young Persons Act 1969, s 23, as substituted by the Criminal Justice Act 1991, s 60 and amended by the Criminal Justice and Public Order Act 1994, s 19, the Crime and Disorder Act 1998, ss 97 and Schs 8 and 10, the Access to Justice Act 1999, s 24, the Powers of Criminal Courts (Sentencing) Act 2000, s 165, the Criminal Justice and Police Act 2001, ss 130, 132 and 133, the Extradition Act 2003, s and the Criminal Justice Act Sch 32.]

---

1. Section 23 is modified in respect of 15 and 16-year-old males.

  In relation to any male person who—

  (i) is of the age of 15 or 16; and

  (ii) is not of a description prescribed for the purposes of s 23(5) of the Children and Young Person Act;

  (iii) is not remanded in connection with proceedings under the Extradition Act 2003

  s 23 of the 1969 Act shall have effect with the modifications specified in s 98(2)–(6) of the Crime and Disorder 1998, as amended by s 130 of the Criminal Justice and Police Act 2001. The modified version is reproduced below.

  For the provision by local authorities of secure accommodation, see the Criminal Justice Act 1991, s 61, in PART III: SENTENCING, ante.

2. A remand under this section to local authority accommodation does not confer parental responsibility on the local authority (*North Yorkshire County Council v Selby Youth Court Justices* [1994] 1 All ER 991, [1995] 1 WLR 1, [1994] 2 FLR 169).

3. The following descriptions of children and young persons are prescribed for the purposes of s 23(5)—

  (a) any child who is of the age of 12 or 13;

  (b) any person who is of the age of 14;

  (c) any female person who is of the age of 15 or 16

(Secure Remands and Committals (Prescribed Description of Children and Young Persons) Order 1999, SI 1999/1265).

–601A *Section 23 as modified in respect of 15 and 16-year-old males by the Crime and Disorder Act 1998, s 98:*

23. Remands to local authority accommodation¹, committal of young persons of unruly character, etc. (1) Where—

(a) a court remands a child or young person charged with or convicted of one or more offences or commits him for trial or sentence; and

(b) he is not released on bail,

then, unless he is remanded to a remand centre or a prison in pursuance of subsection (4)(b) or (c) below, then, unless he is remanded to *a remand centre or* a prison in pursuance of subsection (4)(b) or (c) below, the remand or committal shall be to local authority accommodation; and in the following provisions of this section (except subsection (1A)), any reference (however expressed) to a remand shall be construed as including a reference to a committal.

(1A) Where a court remands a child or young person in connection with extradition proceedings and he is not released on bail the remand shall be to local authority accommodation.

(2) A court remanding a person to local authority accommodation shall designate the local authority who are to receive him; and that authority shall be—

(a) in the case of a person who is being looked after by a local authority, that authority; and

(b) in any other case, the local authority in whose area it appears to the court that he resides or the offence or one of the offences was committed.

(3) Where a person is remanded to local authority accommodation, it shall be lawful for an person acting on behalf of the designated authority to detain him.

(4) Where a court, after consultation with an officer of a local probation board, a social worker of a local authority or a member of a youth offending team, declares a person to be one to whom subsection (5) below applies—

(*a*) it shall remand him to local authority accommodation and require him to be placed and kept in secure accommodation, if—

(i) it also, after such consultation, declares him to be a person to whom subsection (5A below applies; and

(ii) it has been notified that secure accommodation is available for him; or

(*b*) *it shall remand him to a remand centre, if paragraph (a) above does not apply and it has been notified that such a centre is available for the reception from the court of persons to whom subsection (5) below applies; and*

(*c*) *it shall remand him to a prison, if neither paragraph (a) nor paragraph (b) above applies*

[(*c*) if paragraph (*a*) above does not apply, it shall remand him to a prison][1].

(4A) A court shall not declare a person who is not legally represented in the court to be a person to whom subsection (5) below applies unless—

(*a*) he was granted a right to representation funded by the Legal Services Commission as part of the Criminal Defence Service but the right was withdrawn because of his conduct or because it appeared that his financial resources were such that he was not eligible to be granted such right;

(*aa*) he applied for such representation and the application was refused because it appeared that his financial resources were such that he was not eligible to be granted a right to it; or

(*b*) having been informed of his right to apply for such representation and had the opportunity to do so, he refused or failed to apply.

(5) This subsection applies to a person who—

(*a*) is charged with or has been convicted of a violent or sexual offence, or an offence punishable in the case of an adult with imprisonment for a term of fourteen years or more; or

(*b*) has a recent history of absconding while remanded to local authority accommodation, and is charged with or has been convicted of an imprisonable offence alleged or found to have been committed while he was so remanded,

if (in either case) the court is of opinion that only remanding him to a *remand centre or* prison, or to local authority accommodation with a requirement that he be placed and kept in secure accommodation, would be adequate to protect the public from serious harm from him.

(5A) This subsection applies to a person if the court is of opinion that, by reason of his physical or emotional immaturity or a propensity of his to harm himself, it would be undesirable for him to be remanded to *a remand centre or* a prison.*

(6) Where a court declares a person to be one to whom subsection (5) above applies, it shall be its duty—

(*a*) to state in open court that it is of such opinion as is mentioned in subsection (5AA) above and

(*b*) to explain to him in open court and in ordinary language why it is of that opinion;

and a magistrates' court shall cause a reason stated by it under paragraph (*b*) above to be specified in the warrant of commitment and to be entered in the register.

(7) Subject to section 23AA below, a court remanding a person to local authority accommodation without imposing a security requirement (that is to say, a requirement imposed under subsection (4)(*a*) above that the person be placed and kept in secure accommodation) may, after consultation with the designated authority, require that person to comply with

(*a*) any such conditions as could be imposed under section 3(6) of the Bail Act 1976 (c 63) if he were then being granted bail; and

(*b*) any conditions imposed for the purpose of securing the electronic monitoring of his compliance with any other condition imposed under this subsection.

(7A) Where a person is remanded to local authority accommodation and a security requirement is imposed in respect of him—

(*a*) the designated local authority may, with the consent of the Secretary of State, arrange for the person to be detained, for the whole or any part of the period of the remand or committal, in a secure training centre; and

(*b*) his detention there pursuant to the arrangements shall be lawful.

(7B) Arrangements under subsection (7A) above may include provision for payments to be made by the authority to the Secretary of State.

(8) Where a court imposes on a person any such conditions as are mentioned in subsection (7) above, it shall be its duty to explain to him in open court and in ordinary language why it is imposing those conditions; and a magistrates' court shall cause a reason stated by it under this subsection to be specified in the warrant of commitment and to be entered in the register.

(9) A court remanding a person to local authority accommodation without imposing a security

requirement may, after consultation with the designated authority, impose on that authority requirements—

(a) for securing compliance with any conditions imposed on that person under subsection (7) above; or

(b) stipulating that he shall not be placed with a named person.

(9A) Where a person is remanded to local authority accommodation without the imposition of a security requirement, a relevant court may, on the application of the designated authority, declare him to be a person to whom subsection (5) above applies; and on its doing so, subsection (4) above shall apply.

(10) Where a person is remanded to local authority accommodation, a relevant court—

(a) may, on the application of the designated authority, impose on that person any such conditions as could be imposed under subsection (7) above if the court were then remanding him to such accommodation; and

(b) where it does so, may impose on that authority any requirements for securing compliance with the conditions so imposed.

(11) Where a person is remanded to local authority accommodation, a relevant court may, on the application of the designated authority or that person, vary or revoke any conditions or requirements imposed under subsection (7), (9) or (10) above.

(12) In this section—

"court" and "magistrates' court" include a justice;

"children's home" has the same meaning as in the Care Standards Act 2000;

"extradition proceedings" means proceedings under the Extradition Act 2003;

"imprisonable offence" means an offence punishable in the case of an adult with imprisonment;

"prescribed description" means a description prescribed by reference to age or sex or both by an order of the Secretary of State;

"relevant court"—

(a) in relation to a person remanded to local authority accommodation under subsection (1) above, means the court by which he was so remanded, or any magistrates' court having jurisdiction in the place where he is for the time being;

(b) in relation to a person remanded to local authority accommodation under subsection (1A) above, means the court by which he was so remanded;

"requesting territory" means the territory to which a person's extradition is sought in extradition proceedings;

"secure accommodation" means accommodation which is provided in a children's home in respect of which a person is registered under Part II of the Care Standards Act 2000 for the purpose of restricting liberty, and is approved for that purpose by the Secretary of State or the National Assembly for Wales;

"sexual offence" and "violent offence" have the same meanings as in the Powers of Criminal Courts (Sentencing) Act 2000;

"young person" means a person who has attained the age of fourteen years and is under the age of seventeen years;

but, for the purposes of the definition of "secure accommodation", "local authority accommodation" includes any accommodation falling within section 61(2) of the Criminal Justice Act 1991.

(13) In this section—

(a) any reference to a person who is being looked after by a local authority shall be construed in accordance with section 22 of the Children Act 1989;

(b) any reference to consultation shall be construed as a reference to such consultation (if any) as is reasonably practicable in all the circumstances of the case; and

(c) any reference, in relation to a person charged with or convicted of a violent or sexual offence, to protecting the public from serious harm from him shall be construed as a reference to protecting members of the public from death or serious personal injury, whether physical or psychological, occasioned by further such offences committed by him.

(14) This section has effect subject to—

(a) *repealed*;

(b) section 128(7) of that Act (remands to the custody of a constable for periods of not more than three days),

but section 128(7) shall have effect in relation to a child or young person as if for the reference to three clear days there were substituted a reference to twenty-four hours.

[Children and Young Persons Act 1969, s 23, as modified in respect of 15 and 16-year-old males by the Crime and Disorder Act 1998, s 98.]

---

*Subsection 5A amended by the Criminal Defence Service Act 2006, s 4 from a date to be appointed.

1. The alternative provision which, in some circumstances permits 15 and 16-year-old males to be remanded to a prison establishment does not infringe art 14 of the European Convention on Human Rights. Given the particular difficulties in finding appropriate placements for girls, legislation to give them preference for local authority secure accommodation pursued a legitimate aim and was a proportionate response to the problem (*R (SR) v Nottingham Magistrates' Court* [2001] EWHC Admin 802, 166 JP 132).

5–601B **23AA. Electronic monitoring of conditions of remand.** (1) A court shall not impos a condition on a person under section 23(7)(*b*) above (an 'electronic monitoring condition') unles each of the following requirements is fulfilled.

(2) The first requirement is that the person has attained the age of twelve years.

(3) The second requirement is that—

(*a*) the person is charged with or has been convicted of a violent or sexual offence, or an offenc punishable in the case of an adult with imprisonment for a term of fourteen years or more; or

(*b*) he is charged with or has been convicted of one or more imprisonable offences which, togethe with any other imprisonable offences of which he has been convicted in any proceedings—

(i) amount, or

(ii) would, if he were convicted of the offences with which he is charged, amount,

to a recent history of repeatedly committing imprisonable offences while remanded on bail o to local authority accommodation.

(4) The third requirement is that the court—

(*a*) has been notified by the Secretary of State that electronic monitoring arrangements are available in each local justice area which is a relevant area; and

(*b*) is satisfied that the necessary provision can be made under those arrangements.

(5) The fourth requirement is that a youth offending team has informed the court that in it opinion the imposition of such a condition will be suitable in the person's case.

(6) Where a court imposes an electronic monitoring condition, the condition shall includ provision for making a person responsible for the monitoring; and a person who is made s responsible shall be of a description specified in an order[1] made by the Secretary of State.

(7) The Secretary of State may make rules for regulating—

(*a*) the electronic monitoring of compliance with conditions imposed under section 23(7)(*a* above; and

(*b*) without prejudice to the generality of paragraph (*a*) above, the functions of persons mad responsible for securing the electronic monitoring of compliance with such conditions.

(8) Subsections (8) to (10) of section 3AA of the Bail Act 1976 (c 63) (provision about rules an orders under that section) shall apply in relation to this section as they apply in relation to that section

(9) For the purposes of this section a local justice area is a relevant area in relation to a propose electronic monitoring condition if the court considers that it will not be practicable to secure th electronic monitoring in question unless electronic monitoring arrangements are available in tha area.

[Children and Young Persons Act 1969, s 23AA as inserted by the Criminal Justice and Police Act 2001, s 132(2 and amended by the Courts Act 2003, Sch 8.]

1. See the Local Authority Remands (Electronic Monitoring of Conditions) (Responsible Officer) Order 2002 SI 2002/845 amended by SI 2005/984.

5–602 **23A. Liability to arrest for breaking conditions of remand.** (1) A person who has beer remanded or committed to local authority accommodation and in respect of whom conditions unde subsection (7) or (10) of section 23 of this Act have been imposed may be arrested without warran by a constable if the constable has reasonable grounds for suspecting that that person has broken any of those conditions.

(2) A person arrested under subsection (1) above—

(*a*) shall, except where he was arrested within 24 hours of the time appointed for him to appea before the court in pursuance of the remand or committal, be brought as soon as practicabl and in any event within 24 hours after his arrest before a justice of the peace; and

(*b*) in the said excepted case shall be brought before the court before which he was to have appeared.

In reckoning for the purposes of this subsection any period of 24 hours, no account shall be taker of Christmas Day, Good Friday or any Sunday.

(3) A justice of the peace before whom a person is brought under subsection (2) above—

(*a*) if of the opinion that that person has broken any condition imposed on him under subsectior (7) or (10) of section 23 of this Act shall remand him; and that section shall apply as if he wa then charged with or convicted of the offence for which he had been remanded or committed

(*b*) if not of that opinion shall remand him to the place to which he had been remanded o committed at the time of his arrest subject to the same conditions as those which had beer imposed on him at that time.★

[Children and Young Persons Act 1969, s 23A as inserted by the Criminal Justice and Public Order Act 1994, s 2 and amended by the Courts Act 2003, Sch 8.]

★**New s 23B inserted by the Anti-social Behaviour Act 2003, s 90, from a date to be appointed.**

5–602A **23B. Report by local authority in certain cases where person remanded on bail.** (1) Subsection (2) below applies where a court remands a person aged 10 or 11 on bail and either—

(*a*) the person is charged with or has been convicted of a serious offence, or

(*b*) in the opinion of the court the person is a persistent offender.

(2) The court may order a local authority to make an oral or written report specifying where the person is likely to be placed or maintained if he is further remanded to local authority accommodation.

(3) An order under subsection (2) above must designate the local authority which is to make the report; and that authority must be the local authority which the court would have designated under section 23(2) of this Act if the person had been remanded to local authority accommodation.

(4) An order under subsection (2) above must specify the period within which the local authority must comply with the order.

(5) The maximum period that may be so specified is seven working days.

(6) If the Secretary of State by order so provides, subsection (2) above also applies where—

(a) a court remands on bail any person who has attained the age of 12 and is under the age of 17,
(b) the requirement in section 23AA(3) of this Act is fulfilled, and
(c) in a case where he is remanded after conviction, the court is satisfied that the behaviour which constituted the offence was due, to a significant extent, to the circumstances in which the offender was living.

(7) In this section—

"serious offence" means an offence punishable in the case of an adult with imprisonment for a term of two years or more.
"working day" means any day other than—

(a) a Saturday or a Sunday,
(b) Christmas day or Good Friday, or
(c) a bank holiday in England and Wales under the Banking and Financial Dealings Act 1971.

[Children and Young Persons Act 1969, s 23B as inserted by the Ant-social behaviour Act 2003, s 90.]

Transfer

–603 25. Transfers between England or Wales and Northern Ireland. (1) If it appears to the Secretary of State, on the application of the Ministry of Home Affairs for Northern Ireland (in this section referred to as the Ministry of Home Affairs) or the managers of the training school to whose care a person is committed by a relevant order, that his parent or guardian resides or will reside in the area of a local authority in England or Wales, the Secretary of State may make an order committing him to the care of that local authority; and while an order under this subsection is in force it shall have effect as if it were a supervision order imposing a local authority residence requirement as mentioned in paragraph 5 of Schedule 6 to the Powers of Criminal Courts (Sentencing) Act 2000.

(1A) In subsection (1) above "by a relevant order" means—

(a) by a fit person order;
(b) by virtue of a training school order; or
(c) by an order under subsection (2) below;

where the order in question is not by virtue of Schedule 8 to the Children (Northern Ireland) Order 1995 deemed to be a care order within the meaning of that Order.

(2) If it appears to the Minister of Home Affairs for Northern Ireland, on the application of the local authority to whose care a person is committed by a care order to which paragraph 36 of Schedule 14 to the Children Act (criminal care order transitional provisions) applies other than an interim order or who is to accommodate a person pursuant to a supervision order imposing a local authority residence requirement as mentioned in paragraph 5 of Schedule 6 to the Powers of Criminal Courts (Sentencing) Act 2000 or by an order under subsection (1) above, that his parent or guardian resides or will reside in Northern Ireland, the said Minister may make an order committing him to the care of the managers of a training school . . . ; and the provisions of the Children and Young Persons Act (Northern Ireland) 1968 (except sections 88(3) and 90) shall apply to an order under this subsection as if it were a training school order made on the date of the care order or, as the case may be, the supervision order.

(3) When a person is received into the care of a local authority or the managers of a training school in pursuance of an order under this section, the training school order, fit person order, care order or supervision order in consequence of which the order under this section was made shall cease to have effect; and the order under this section shall, unless it is discharged earlier, cease to have effect—

(a) in the case of an order under subsection (1), on the earlier of the following dates, that is to say, the date when the person to whom the order relates attains the age of nineteen or the date when, by the effluxion of time, the fit person order aforesaid would have ceased to have effect or, as the case may be, the period of his detention under the training school order aforesaid would have expired;
(b) in the case of an order under subsection (2), on the date when the care order or supervision order aforesaid would have ceased to have effect by the effluxion of time or—

(i) *Repealed*;
(ii) if the order has effect by virtue of subsection (2) as a training school order and the period of supervision following the detention of the person in question in pursuance of the order expires before that date, when that period expires.

(4) An order under this section shall be sufficient authority for the detention in Northern Ireland by any constable or by a person duly authorised by a local authority or the managers of a training school, of the person to whom the order relates until he is received into the care of the authority or managers to whose care he is committed by the order.

(5) In this section "training school", and "training school order" have the same meaning as in the said Act of 1968, and "fit person order" means an order under that Act committing a person to the care of a fit person.

[Children and Young Persons Act 1969, s 25, as amended by the Transfer of Functions (Local Government, etc) (Northern Ireland) Order 1973, SR & O (NI) 1973/256, the Health and Social Services and Social Security Adjudications Act 1983, s 9, Sch 2, the Children (Prescribed Orders—Northern Ireland, Guernsey and Isle of Man) Regulations 1991, SI 1991/2032, the Children (Northern Ireland Consequential Amendments) Order 1995 SI 1995/756, and the Powers of Criminal Courts (Sentencing) Act 2000, Sch 9.]

5–604   26. Transfers between England or Wales and the Channel Islands or Isle of Man
(1) The Secretary of State may by order designate[1] for the purposes of this section an order of any description which—

    (*a*)   a court in the Isle of Man or any of the Channel Islands is authorised to make by the law for the time being in force in that country; and

    (*b*)   provides for the committal to the care of a public authority of a person who has not attained the age of eighteen; and

    (*c*)   appears to the Secretary of State to be of the same nature as a care order other than an interim order or as a supervision order imposing a a local authority residence requirement as mentioned in paragraph 5 of Schedule 6 to the Powers of Criminal Courts (Sentencing) Act 2000;

and in this section "relevant order" means an order of a description for the time being so designated and "the relevant authority", in relation to a relevant order, means the authority in the Isle of Man or any of the Channel Islands to whose care the person to whom the order relates is, under the law of that country, committed by the order and "care order" means an order made under section 31 of the Children Act 1989.

(2) The Secretary of State may authorise a local authority to receive into their care any person named in the authorisation who is the subject of a relevant order; and while such an authorisation is in force in respect of any person he shall be deemed to be the subject of a care order placing the child in the care of a named local authority or, where the relevant order was made as a criminal disposal in criminal proceedings, a supervision order imposing a a local authority residence requirement as mentioned in paragraph 5 of Schedule 6 to the Powers of Criminal Courts (Sentencing) Act 2000 with a requirement that the child be accommodated by a designated local authority.

(4) An authorisation given to a local authority under this section shall cease to have effect when—

    (*a*)   the local authority is informed by the Secretary of State that he has revoked it; or

    (*b*)   the relevant order to which the authorisation relates ceases to have effect by the effluxion of time under the law of the place where the order was made or the local authority is informed by the relevant authority that the order has been discharged under that law; or

    (*c*)   the person to whom the relevant order relates is again received into the care of the relevant authority;

and if a local authority having by virtue of this section the care of a person to whom a relevant order relates is requested by the relevant authority to make arrangements for him to be received again into the care of the relevant authority, it shall be the duty of the local authority to comply with the request.

[Children and Young Persons Act 1969, s 26 as amended by the Children (Prescribed Orders—Northern Ireland, Guernsey and Isle of Man) Regulations 1991, SI 1991/2032, and the Powers of Criminal Courts (Sentencing) Act 2000, Sch 9.]

---

1. A special care order within the meaning of the Children and Young Persons (Guernsey) Law 1967, as amended by the Children and Young Persons (Amendment) (Guernsey) Law 1971 has been designated for the purposes of this section by the Children and Young Persons (Designation of Guernsey Order) Order 1971, SI 1971/348. A similar Order has been made in relation to the Isle of Man, SI 1991/2031. A recovery order made in the Isle of Man (other than one made in criminal proceedings) is treated as though it were made under the Children Act 1989, s 50: see SI 1991/2032. A fit person order made by virtue of article 31 of the Children (Jersey) Law 1969 has also been so designated by the Children and Young Persons (Designation of Jersey Order) Order 1972, SI 1972/1074. A care order made under the Children and Young Persons Act 1966 (an Act of Tynwald) is also designated for the purposes of this section by the Children and Young Persons (Designation of Isle of Man Orders) Order 1991, SI 1991/2031. A recovery order made in the Isle of Man (other than one made in criminal proceedings) is treated as though it were made under Children Act 1989, s 50: see SI 1991/2032.

Detention

5–605   29. Recognisance on release of arrested child or young person.   (1) A child or young person arrested in pursuance of a warrant[1] shall not be released unless his parent or guardian (with or without sureties) enters into a recognisance for such amount as the custody officer at the police station where he is detained considers will secure his attendance at the hearing of the charge; and the recognisance entered into in pursuance of this section may, if the custody officer thinks fit, be conditioned for the attendance of the parent or guardian at the hearing in addition to the child or young person.

(2) In this section "young person" means a person who has attained the age of fourteen and is under the age of seventeen years.
[Children and Young Persons Act 1969, s 29 as substituted by the Police and Criminal Evidence Act 1984, Sch 6 and as amended by the Criminal Justice Act 1988, Schs 15 and 16 and the Criminal Justice Act 1991, Sch 8.]

---

1. Where the child or young person was arrested without a warrant, the Police and Criminal Evidence Act 1984, s 37 applies; see in particular sub-ss (11)–(15) in PART I: MAGISTRATES' COURTS, PROCEDURE, ante.

5–606   30. Detention of young offenders in community homes.   (1) The power to give directions under section 92 of the Powers of Criminal Courts (Sentencing) Act 2000 (under which young offenders convicted on indictment of certain grave crimes may be detained in accordance with directions given by the Secretary of State) shall include power to direct detention by the local authority specified in the directions in a home so specified which is a community home provided by the authority or a controlled community home for the management, equipment and maintenance of which the authority are responsible; but a person shall not be liable to be detained in the manner provided by this section after he attains the age of nineteen.
(2) It shall be the duty of a local authority specified in directions given in pursuance of this section to detain the person to whom the directions relate in the home specified in the directions subject to and in accordance with such instructions relating to him as the Secretary of State may give to the authority from time to time; and the authority shall be entitled to recover from the Secretary of State any expenses reasonably incurred by them in discharging that duty.
[Children and Young Persons Act 1969, s 30 as amended by the Powers of Criminal Courts (Sentencing) Act 2000, Sch 9.]

5–607   31. (*Repealed*).

5–608   32. Detention of absentees.   (1) If any of the following persons, that is to say—

    (*a*)–(*c*) *Repealed*;
    (*d*) a person sent to a remand home, special reception centre or training school or committed to the care of a fit person under the Children and Young Persons Act (Northern Ireland) 1968 (but not deemed by virtue of Schedule 8 to the Children (Northern Ireland) Order 1995 to be the subject of a care order within the meaning of that Order),

is absent from premises at which he is required by the relevant Northern Ireland authority to live, or as the case may be is absent from home, remand home, special reception centre or training school, at a time when he is not permitted by the relevant Northern Ireland authority to be absent from it, he may be arrested by a constable anywhere in the United Kingdom or the Channel Islands without a warrant and shall if so arrested[1] be conducted, at the expense of the authority, to the premises or other place aforesaid or such other premises as the authority may direct.
(1A) If a child or young person is absent, without the consent of the responsible person—

    (*a*) from a place of safety to which he has been taken under paragraph 7(4) of Schedule 7 to the Powers of Criminal Courts (Sentencing) Act 2000; or
    (*b*) from local authority accommodation—

        (i) in which he is required to live under paragraph 5 of Schedule 6 to that Act; or
        (ii) to which he has been remanded under paragraph 7(5) of Schedule 7 to that Act; or
        (iii) to which he has been remanded or committed under section 23(1) of this Act

he may be arrested[1] by a constable anywhere in the United Kingdom or Channel Islands without a warrant.
(1B) A person so arrested shall be conducted to—

    (*a*) the place of safety;
    (*b*) the local authority accommodation; or
    (*c*) such other place as the responsible person may direct,

at the responsible person's expense.
(1C) In this section "the responsible person" means the person who made the arrangements under paragraph 7(4) of Schedule 7 to the Powers of Criminal Courts (Sentencing) Act 2000 or, as the case may be, the authority designated under paragraph 5 of Schedule 6 to that Act, paragraph 7(8) of Schedule 7 to that Act or section 23 of this Act.
(2) If a magistrates' court is satisfied by information on oath that there are reasonable grounds for believing that a person specified in the information can produce a person who is absent as mentioned in subsection (1) or (1A) of this section, the court may issue a summons directed to the person so specified and requiring him to attend and produce the absent person before the court; and a person who without reasonable excuse fails to comply with any such requirement shall, without prejudice to any liability apart from this subsection, be guilty of an offence and liable on summary conviction to a fine of an amount not exceeding **level 3** on the standard scale.
In the application of this subsection to Northern Ireland, "magistrates' court" means a magistrates' court within the meaning of the Magistrates' Courts Act (Northern Ireland) 1964.
(2A) Without prejudice to its powers under subsection (2) of this section, a magistrates' court (within the meaning of that subsection) may, if it is satisfied by information on oath that there are reasonable grounds for believing that a person who is absent as mentioned in subsection (1) or

(1A)(*a*) or (*b*)(i) or (ii) of this section is in premises specified in the information issue a search warrant authorising a constable to search the premises for that person.

(2B) A court shall not issue a summons or search warrant under subsection (2) or (2A) of this section in any case where the person who is absent is a person to whom subsection (1A) of this section applies, unless the information referred to in the said subsection (2) or (2A) is given by the responsible person.

(3) A person who knowingly compels, persuades, incites or assists another person to become or continue to be absent as mentioned in subsection (1) or (1A) of this section shall be guilty of an offence and liable on summary conviction to imprisonment for a term not exceeding **six months** or a fine of an amount not exceeding **level 5** on the standard scale.

(4) The reference to a constable in subsection (1), (1A) and (2A) of this section includes a reference to a person who is constable under the law of any part of the United Kingdom, to a member of the police in Jersey and to an officer of police within the meaning of section 43 of the Larceny (Guernsey) Law 1958 or any corresponding law for the time being in force, and in subsection (1) "the relevant Northern Ireland authority" means in the case of a person committed to the care of a fit person, the fit person, and in the case of a person sent to a remand home, special reception centre or training school, the person in charge of that home or centre or the managers of that school.

(5) Nothing in this section authorises the arrest in Northern Ireland of, or the taking there of any proceedings in respect of, such a person as is mentioned in paragraph (*d*) of subsection (1) of this section.
[Children and Young Persons Act 1969, s 32 as amended by the Children Act 1975, s 68, the Child Care Act 1980, Sch 6, the Criminal Justice Act 1982, ss 38 and 46, the Health and Social Services and Social Security Adjudications Act 1983, Sch 2, the Children Act 1989, Sch 12, the Courts and Legal Services Act 1990, Sch 16, the Prisoners (Return to Custody) Act 1995, s 2 SI 1995/756 and the Powers of Criminal Courts (Sentencing) Act 2000, Sch 9.]

---

1. This power of arrest is preserved by the Police and Criminal Evidence Act 1984, s 26 and Sch 2.

Transitional modifications of Part I for persons of specified ages

5–622   34. Transitional modifications of Part I for persons of specified ages.   (1) The Secretary of State may by order provide—

(*a*) Repealed;
(*b*) Repealed;
(*c*) that any reference to a young person in section 5(8),9(1), 23(1) or 29(1)[2] of this Act shall be construed as including a child who has attained such age as may be so specified;
(*d*) Repealed;
(*e*) that section 23(4) to (6) of this Act shall have effect as if the references to a young person excluded a young person who has not attained such age as may be so specified[3];
(*f*) Repealed.

(2) In the case of a person who has not attained the age of eighteen but has attained such lower age as the Secretary of State may by order specify[3] no proceedings for an offence shall be begun in any court unless the person proposing to begin the proceedings has, in addition to any notice falling to be given by him to a local authority in pursuance of section 5(8) of this Act, given notice[4] of the proceedings to an officer of a local probation board for the area for which the court acts.

(3) In the case of a person who has attained such age as the Secretary of State may by order specify[5], an authority shall, without prejudice to subsection (2) of section 9 of this Act, not be required by virtue of subsection (1) of that section to make investigations or provide information which it does not already possess with respect to his home surroundings if, by direction of the justices or local probation board acting for any relevant area, arrangements are in force for information with respect to his home surroundings to be furnished to the court in question by an officer of a local probation board.

(4) Except in relation to section 13(2) of this Act, references to a child in subsection (1) of this section do not include references to a person under the age of ten.

(5) Repealed.

(6) Without prejudice to the generality of section 69(4) of this Act, an order under this section may specify different ages for the purposes of different provisions of this Act specified in the order.

(7) A draft of any order proposed to be made under this section shall be laid before Parliament and, in the case of an order of which the effect is that the reference to a child in section 4 of this Act includes a child who has attained an age of more than twelve, shall not be made unless the draft has been approved by a resolution of each House of Parliament.
[Children and Young Persons Act 1969, s 34, as amended by the Criminal Law Act 1977, Sch 13, the Criminal Justice Act 1982, Sch 16, the Criminal Justice Act 1988, Sch 16, the Children Act 1989, Schs 12 and 15, the Criminal Justice Act 1991, Sch 13, the Criminal Justice and Public Order Act 1994, Sch 9, the Crime and Disorder Act 1998, Schs 7 and 10 and the Criminal Justice and Police Act 2001, Sch 7.]

---

1. For the purposes of s 13(2) the Secretary of State has specified ten years of age (SI 1970/1882).
2. This provision would appear to be no longer necessary in relation to s 29 since that section was substituted by the Police and Criminal Evidence Act 1984.
3. See SI 1979/125 and the note to s 23(2) and (3), ante.
4. Section 34(2) requires notice to be given to a probation officer before the defendant is first brought before the court.

However, the notice does not have to be in writing and failure to give the notice does not render the proceedings null and void (*DPP v Cottier*) [1996] 3 All ER 126, [1996] 1 WLR 826, *R v Marsh* [1997] 1 WLR 649, CA).

5. For the purposes of subsections (2) and (3) the Secretary of State has by order specified the age of 13: SI 1970/1882, SI 1973/485 and SI 1974/1083.

–623

PART II
ACCOMMODATION ETC FOR CHILDREN IN CARE, AND FOSTER CHILDREN

PART III
MISCELLANEOUS AND GENERAL

Miscellaneous

–624 70. Interpretation and ancillary provisions. (1) In this act, unless the contrary intention appears, the following expressions have the following meanings:

"the Act of 1933" means the Children and Young Persons Act 1933;

"the Act of 1963" means the Children and Young Persons Act 1963;

"approved school order", "guardian" and "place of safety" have the same meanings as in the Act of 1933;

"child", except in Part II (including Schedule 3) and sections 27, 63, 64 and 65 of this Act, means a person under the age of fourteen[1] and in that Part (including that Schedule) and those sections means a person under the age of eighteen and a person who has attained the age of eighteen and is the subject of a care order;

"local authority" except in relation to proceedings under s 1 of this Act instituted by a local education authority, means the council of a non-metropolitan county or of a county borough, metropolitan district or London borough or the Common Council of the City of London;

"local authority accommodation" means accommodation provided by or on behalf of a local authority (within the meaning of the Children Act 1989);

"local probation board" means a local probation board established under section 4 of the Criminal Justice and Court Services Act 2000;

"petty sessions area", in relation to a juvenile court constituted for the metropolitan area within the meaning of Part II of Schedule 2 to the Act of 1963, it means such a division of that area as is mentioned in paragraph 14 of that Schedule;★

"police officer" means a member of a police force;

"reside" means habitually reside, and cognate expressions shall be construed accordingly;

"supervision order" has the same meaning as in the Powers of Criminal Courts (Sentencing) Act 2000;

"young person" means a person who has attained the age[1] of fourteen and is under the age of eighteen years;

"youth offending team" means a team established under section 39 of the Crime and Disorder Act 1998;

and it is hereby declared that, in the expression "care or control", "care" includes protection and guidance and "control" includes discipline.

(1A) In the case of a child or young person—

(a) whose father and mother were not married to each other at the time of his birth, and

(b) with respect to whom a residence order is in force in favour of the father,

any reference in this Act to the parent of the child or young person includes (unless the contrary intention appears) a reference to the father.

(1B) In subsection (1A) of this section, the reference to a child or young person whose father and mother were not married to each other at the time of his birth shall be construed in accordance with section 1 of the Family Law Reform Act 1987 and "residence order" has the meaning given by section 8(1) of the Children Act 1989.

(2) *Repealed.*

(3) In section 99(1) of the Act of 1933 (under which the age which a court presumes or declares to be the age of a person brought before it is deemed to be his true age for the purposes of that Act) the references to that Act shall be construed as including references to this Act.

(4) Subject to the following subsection, any reference in this Act to any enactment is a reference to it as amended, and includes a reference to it as applied, by or under any other enactment including this Act.

(5) Any reference in this Act to an enactment of the Parliament of Northern Ireland shall be construed as a reference to that enactment as amended by any Act of that Parliament, whether passed before or after this Act, and to any enactment of that Parliament for the time being in force which re-enacts the said enactment with or without modifications.

[Children and Young Persons Act 1969, s 70, as amended by the Local Government Act 1972, Sch 23, the Magistrates' Courts Act 1980, Sch 7, the Child Care Act 1980, Sch 6, the Family Law Reform Act 1987, s 8 and Sch 2, the Children Act 1989, Schs 12 and 15, the Criminal Justice Act 1991, Sch 8, the Local Government (Wales) Act 1994, Sch 10, the Crime and Disorder Act 1998, Schs 7 and 8, the Access to Justice Act 1999, Sch 15, and the Powers of Criminal Courts (Sentencing) Act 2000, Schs 9, 12.]

★**The definition of "petty sessions area" is repealed by the Access to Justice Act 1999, Sch 15, when in force.**

1. A person attains a particular age at the commencement of the relevant anniversary of the date of his birth: s 9 of the Family Law Reform Act 1969.

Local Authority Social Services Act 1970

(1970 c 42)

5–730   1. Local authorities.   The local authorities for the purposes of this Act shall be the council of non-metropolitan counties, metropolitan districts and London boroughs and the Common Counc: of the City of London but, in relation to Wales, shall be the councils of counties and county boroughs [Local Authority Social Services Act 1970, s 1, as amended by the Local Government Act 1972, s 195 and th Local Government (Wales) Act 1994, Sch 10.]

5–730A   1A. Meaning of "social services functions".   For the purposes of this Act the socia services functions of a local authority are—

(*a*)   their functions under the enactments specified in the first column of Schedule 1 to this Ac (being the functions which are described in general terms in the second column of tha Schedule), and

(*b*)   such other of their functions as the Secretary of State may designate by an order made unde this section.

[Local Authority Social Services Act 1970, s 1A, as amended by the Local Government Act 2000, s 102.]

5–731   2. Local authority to establish social services committee.   *Repealed.*

5–732   SCHEDULE 1
                               SOCIAL SERVICES FUNCTIONS

(*As amended by the Children Act 1975, Schs 3 and 4, the Adoption Act 1976, Schs 3 and 4, the National Health Servic Act 1977, Sch 15, the Domestic Proceedings and Magistrates' Courts Act 1978, Schs 2 and 3 the Child Care Act 1980 Schs 5 and 6, the Foster Children Act 1980, Schs 2 and 3, the Residential Homes Act 1980, Sch 1, the Children's Home Act 1982, s 15, the Mental Health Act 1983, Sch 4, the Health and Social Services and Social Security Adjudication Act 1983. Sch 9, the Registered Homes Act 1984 Sch 1, the Housing (Consequential Provisions) Act 1985, Sch 1 and 2 Children Act 1989, Schs 13 and 15, the National Health Service and Community Care Act 1990, Sch 9, the Charitie Act 1992, Sch 7 the Statute Law (Repeals) Act 1993, Sch 1, the Education Act 1993, Sch 19, the Carers (Recognitio and Services) Act 1995, s 1, the Education Act 1996, Sch 37, the Housing Act 1996, Sch 17 the Community Care (Direc Payments) Act 1996, s 3, the Adoption (Intercountry Aspects) Act 1999, Sch 2, the Local Government Act 2000, Sch 5 the Care Standards Act 2000, s 112, Sch 4 and Sch 6, the Carers and Disabled Children Act 2000, s 9, the Health an Social Care Act 2001, s 67(1),SI 2002/2469, the Adoption and Children Act 2002, s 139 and the Children Act 2004 s 55.)*

Only those enactments conferring functions which are relevant to magistrates' courts are quoted here

Enactment	Nature of functions
Children and Young Persons Act 1933 (c 12) Part III	Protection of the young in relation to criminal an• summary proceedings; children appearing befor court as in need of care, protection or control committal of children to approved school or car• of fit person, etc.
Part IV	Remand homes, approved schools and children i• care of fit persons.
Children and Young Persons Act 1963 (c 37) Part I	Powers relating to young persons in need of care protection or control; further provisions for protec tion of the young in relation to criminal proceedings
Children and Young Persons Act 1969 (c 54) The whole Act except section 9 in so far as they assign functions to a local authority in their capacity of a local education authority.	Care and other treatment of children and young persons through court proceedings;
Sections 6 and 7B of this Act	Appointment of director of social services, etc provision and conduct of complaints procedure.
Children Act 1975 (c 72) Part II	Application by local authority for revocation o custodianship order; inquiries carried out by loca authority in custodianship cases.
National Health Service Act 1977 Schedule 8	Care of Mothers and young children; prevention, car and after-care; home help and laundry facilities.
Residential Homes Act 1980 Sections 1 to 7	Registration of disabled or old persons' homes an• residential homes for mentally disordered persons
Mental Health Act 1983 (c 20) Parts II, III and VI	Welfare of the mentally disordered; guardianship o persons suffering from mental disorder including such persons removed to England and Wales from Scotland or Northern Ireland; exercise of function of nearest relative of person so suffering.

Enactment	Nature of functions
Sections 66, 67, 69(1)	Exercise of functions of nearest relative in relation to applications and references to Mental Health Review Tribunals.
Section 114	Appointment of approved social workers.
Section 115	Entry and inspection.
Section 116	Welfare of certain hospital patients.
Section 117	After-care of detained patients.
Section 130	Prosecutions.
Health and Social Services and Social Security Adjudications Act 1983 (c 41)	
Section 17, so far as relating to services provided under the enactments mentioned in subsection (2)(*a*) to (*c*).	Charges for local authority welfare services
Housing Act 1996 Section 213(1)(*b*)	Co-operation in relation to homeless persons and persons threatened with homelessness.
Disabled Persons (Services, Consultation and Representation) Act 1986 (c 33)	
Sections 1 to 5, 7 and 8 except in so far as they assign functions to a local authority in their capacity as a local education authority.	Representation and assessment of disabled persons.
Children Act 1989	
The whole Act, in so far as it confers functions on a local authority within the meaning of that Act.	Welfare reports.
	Consent to application for residence order in respect of child in care.
	Functions relating to special guardianship orders.
	Family assistance orders.
	Functions under Part III of the Act (local authority support for children and families).
	Care and supervision.
	Protection of children.
	Functions in relation to community homes, voluntary homes and voluntary organisations, private children's homes, private arrangements for fostering children, child minding and day care for young children.
	Inspection of children's homes on behalf of Secretary of State.
	Research and returns of information.
	Functions in relation to children accommodated by health authorities, Primary Care Trusts, National Health Service trusts and local education authorities or care homes, independent hospitals or schools.
National Health Service and Community Care Act 1990 (c 19)	
Section 46	Preparation of plans for community care services.
Section 47	Assessment of needs for community care services.
Carers (Recognition and Services) Act 1995 (c 12)	
Section 1	Assessment of ability of carers to provide care.
Community Care (Direct Payments) Act 1996	Functions in connection with the making of payments to persons in respect of their securing the provision of community care services or services under the Carers and Disabled Children Act 2000.**
Adoption (Intercountry Aspects) Act 1999 (c 18)	
Sections 1 and 2(4)	Functions under regulations made under section 1 giving effect toof the Convention on Protection of Children and Co-operation in respect of Intercountry Adoption, concluded at the Hague on 29th May 1993 and functions under Article 9(*a*) to (*c*) of the Convention.
Carers and Disabled Children Act 2000 (c 16)	
The whole Act, in so far as it confers functions on a local authority within the meaning of that Act	Assessment of carers' needs. Provisions of service to carers. Provision of vouchers.
Health and Social Care Act 2001	
Part 4 in so far as it confers functions on a local authority in England or Wales within the meaning of that Part.	Functions in relation to the provision of residential accommodation.
	Making of direct payments to person in respect of his securing provision of community care services or services to carers.

**Entry relating to the Children Act 1989 amended by the Adoption and Children Act 2002, s 139, from a date to be appointed.

Children and Young Persons (Protection from Tobacco) Act 1991
(1991 c 23)

5–1000 **1.** *Amendment of section 7 of the Children and Young Persons Act 1933.*

5–1001 **2.** *Scotland.*

5–1002 **3. Sale of unpackaged cigarettes.** (1) It shall be an offence for any person carrying on a retail business to sell cigarettes to any person other than in pre-packed quantities of 10 or more cigarettes in their original package.

(2) Any person guilty of an offence under subsection (1) above shall be liable on summary conviction to a fine not exceeding **level 3** on the standard scale.

(3) In this section "original package" means the package in which the cigarettes were supplied for the purpose of retail sale by the manufacturer or importer; and "package" means any box, carton or other container.

[Children and Young Persons (Protection from Tobacco) Act 1991, s 3.]

5–1003 **4. Display of warning statements in retail premises and on vending machines.**
(1) A notice displaying the following statement—

"It is illegal to sell tobacco products to anyone under the age of 16"

shall be exhibited at every premises at which tobacco is sold by retail, and shall be so exhibited in a prominent position where the statement is readily visible to persons at the point of sale of the tobacco; and where—

(a) any person carries on a business involving the sale of tobacco by retail at any premises, and
(b) no notice is exhibited at those premises in accordance with this subsection,

that person shall be guilty of an offence.

(2) A notice displaying the following statement—

"This machine is only for the use of people aged 16 or over"

shall be exhibited on every automatic machine for the sale of tobacco which is kept available for use as such at any premises, and shall be so exhibited in such a way that the statement is readily visible to persons using the machine; and where—

(a) any person is the owner of any such machine which is so kept or the owner of the premises at which any such machine is so kept, and
(b) no notice is exhibited on the machine in accordance with this subsection,

that person shall be guilty of an offence.

(3) The dimensions of the notice to be exhibited in accordance with subsection (1) or (2) above, and the size of the statement to be displayed on it, shall be such as may be prescribed by regulations made by the Secretary of State; and any such regulations[1] may make different provision for different cases.

(4) Any person guilty of an offence under subsection (1) or (2) above shall be liable on summary conviction to a fine not exceeding **level 3** on the standard scale.

(5) It shall be a defence for a person charged with any such offence to prove that he took all reasonable precautions and exercised all due diligence to avoid the commission of the offence.

(6) Where any such offence is committed by a body corporate and is proved to have been committed with the consent or connivance of, or to be attributable to any neglect on the part of, any director, manager, secretary or other similar officer of the body corporate, or any person who was purporting to act in any such capacity, he as well as the body corporate shall be guilty of that offence and shall be liable to be proceeded against and punished accordingly.

In relation to a body corporate whose affairs are managed by its members, "director" means a member of the body corporate.

(7) Where any such offence is committed in Scotland by a Scottish partnership and is proved to have been committed with the consent or connivance of, or to be attributable to any neglect on the part of, a partner, he as well as the partnership shall be guilty of that offence and shall be liable to be proceeded against and punished accordingly.

(8) In this section—

"premises" includes any place and any vehicle, vessel, aircraft, hovercraft, stall or moveable structure; and
"tobacco" (except where it appears in the statement required by subsection (1)) has the same meaning as in section 7 of the Children and Young Persons Act 1933 or, in relation to Scotland, section 18 of the Children and Young Persons (Scotland) Act 1937.

(9) Any regulations under this section shall be made by statutory instrument subject to annulment in pursuance of a resolution of either House of Parliament.

[Children and Young Persons (Protection from Tobacco) Act 1991, s 4.]

---

1. See the Protection from Tobacco (Display of Warning Statements) Regulations 1992, SI 1992/3228.

–1004   5. Enforcement action by local authorities in England and Wales.   (1) It shall be the duty of every local authority to which this section applies—

   (a) to consider, at least once in every period of twelve months, the extent to which it is appropriate for them to carry out in their area a programme of enforcement action relating to section 7 of the Children and Young Persons Act 1933 and sections 3 and 4 above, and

   (b) accordingly to carry out in their area any programme which is for the time being considered by them to be appropriate under paragraph (a) above.

(2) In subsection (1)(a) above the reference to a programme of enforcement action relating to the provisions there mentioned is a reference to a programme involving all or any of the following, namely—

   (a) the bringing of prosecutions in respect of offences under those provisions;

   (b) the investigation of complaints in respect of alleged offences under those provisions;

   (c) the taking of other measures intended to reduce the incidence of offences under those provisions;

   (d) the making of complaints under section 7(2) of the Act of 1933 and, with a view to determining whether such complaints should be made, the monitoring of the use of such machines for the sale of tobacco as are mentioned in that provision.

(3) This section applies to the following local authorities, namely—

   (a) the council of a county, a metropolitan district or a London borough;

   (b) the Common Council of the City of London; and

   (c) the Council of the Isles of Scilly.

[Children and Young Persons (Protection from Tobacco) Act 1991, s 5.]

–1005   6. *Scotland.*

–1006   7. *Expenses.*

–1007   8. Short title, commencement, extent etc.   (1) This Act may be cited as the Children and Young Persons (Protection from Tobacco) Act 1991.

(2) This Act shall come into force on such day as the Secretary of State may appoint by order made by statutory instrument; and different days may be so appointed for different provisions or for different purposes.

(3) Nothing in section 1 or 2 above has effect in relation to any offence committed before the commencement of that section.

(4) Subsection (4)(a) of section 1 or 2 above—

   (a) shall not affect the continued operation of the relevant provision, as in force before the date of the coming into force of that section, in a case where the relevant use of which evidence has been or would be given in support of a complaint or application under that provision (as so in force) took place before that date, and

   (b) accordingly shall, in particular, not affect—

     (i) any complaint or application made under that provision before that date, or

     (ii) any order so made;

and no complaint or application shall be made on or after that date under the relevant provision (as for the time being in force) in respect of any relevant use which took place before that date.

(5) In subsection (4) above—

"the relevant provision" means—

   (a) in relation to England and Wales, section 7(2) of the Children and Young Persons Act 1933, and

   (b) in relation to Scotland, section 18(2) of the Children and Young Persons (Scotland) Act 1937; and

"relevant use" means use of any such automatic machine as is mentioned in the relevant provision.

(6)–(7) *Northern Ireland.*

[Children and Young Persons (Protection from Tobacco) Act 1991, s 8.]

Criminal Justice and Public Order Act 1994[1]

(1994 c 33)

PART I[2]
YOUNG OFFENDERS
Secure training orders

5–1104   7. Contracting out of secure training centres.   (1) The Secretary of State may enter into a contract with another person for the provision or running (or the provision and running) by him, or (if the contract so provides) for the running by sub-contractors of his, of any secure training centre or part of a secure training centre.

(2)　While a contract for the running of a secure training centre or part of a secure training centr is in force the centre or part shall be run subject to and in accordance with the Prison Act 1952 an in accordance with secure training centre rules[3] subject to such adaptations and modifications as th Secretary of State may specify in relation to contracted out secure training centres.

(3)　Where the Secretary of State grants a lease or tenancy of land for the purposes of any contrac under this section, none of the following enactments shall apply to it, namely—

(*a*)　Part II of the Landlord and Tenant Act 1954 (security of tenure);

(*b*)　section 146 of the Law of Property Act 1925 (restrictions on and relief against forfeiture) and

(*c*)　section 19 of the Landlord and Tenant Act 1927 and the Landlord and Tenant Act 198: (covenants not to assign etc).

In this subsection "lease or tenancy" includes an underlease or subtenancy.

(4)　In this section—

(*a*)　the reference to the Prison Act 1952 is a reference to that Act as it applies to secure trainin, centres by virtue of section 43 of that Act; and

(*b*)　the reference to secure training centre rules[1] is a reference to rules made under section 47 o that Act for the regulation and management of secure training centres.

[Criminal Justice and Public Order Act 1994, s 7.]

1.　The Criminal Justice and Public Order Act 1994 is printed partly in PART V: YOUTH COURTS, and partly in PART I, II and VIII of this Manual.

2.　Part I of the Act contains ss 1–24.

Sections 5, 6, 16–24 are not reproduced here because they amend earlier enactments; these amendments have, howeve been incorporated elsewhere in this Manual as appropriate.

3.　The Secure Training Centre Rules 1998, SI 1998/472, have been made.

5–1105　8. Officers of contracted out secure training centres.　(1)　Instead of a governor, ever contracted out secure training centre shall have—

(*a*)　a director, who shall be a custody officer appointed by the contractor and specially approve for the purposes of this section by the Secretary of State; and

(*b*)　a monitor, who shall be a Crown servant appointed by the Secretary of State;

and every officer of such a secure training centre who performs custodial duties shall be a custody officer who is authorised to perform such duties or an officer of a directly managed secure trainin centre who is temporarily attached to the secure training centre.

(2)　The director shall have such functions as are conferred on him by the Prison Act 1952 as i applies to secure training centres and as may be conferred on him by secure training centre rules.

(3)　The monitor shall have such functions as may be conferred on him by secure training centr rules and shall be under a duty—

(*a*)　to keep under review, and report to the Secretary of State on, the running of the secur training centre by or on behalf of the director; and

(*b*)　to investigate, and report to the Secretary of State on, any allegations made against custody officers performing custodial duties at the secure training centre or officers of directly manage secure training centres who are temporarily attached to the secure training centre.

(4)　The contractor and any sub-contractor of his shall each be under a duty to do all that h reasonably can (whether by giving directions to the officers of the secure training centre or otherwise to facilitate the exercise by the monitor of all such functions as are mentioned in or imposed b subsection (3) above.

[Criminal Justice and Public Order Act 1994, s 8.]

5–1106　9. Powers and duties of custody officers employed at contracted out secure trainin centres.　(1)　A custody officer performing custodial duties at a contracted out secure trainin centre shall have the following powers, namely—

(*a*)　to search in accordance with secure training centre rules any offender who is detained in th secure training centre; and

(*b*)　to search any other person who is in or who is seeking to enter the secure training centre, an any article in the possession of such a person.

(2)　The powers conferred by subsection (1)(*b*) above to search a person shall not be construed a authorising a custody officer to require a person to remove any of his clothing other than an oute coat, headgear, jacket or gloves.

(3)　A custody officer performing custodial duties at a contracted out secure training centre shal have the following duties as respects offenders detained in the secure training centre, namely—

(*a*)　to prevent their escape from lawful custody;

(*b*)　to prevent, or detect and report on, the commission or attempted commission by them o other unlawful acts;

(*c*)　to ensure good order and discipline on their part; and

(*d*)　to attend to their wellbeing.

(4) The powers conferred by subsection (1) above, and the powers arising by virtue of subsection (3) above, shall include power to use reasonable force where necessary.
[Criminal Justice and Public Order Act 1994, s 9.]

5–1107   10. Intervention by Secretary of State in management of contracted out secure training centres.   (1) This section applies where, in the case of a contracted out secure training centre, it appears to the Secretary of State—

(a) that the director has lost, or is likely to lose, effective control of the secure training centre or any part of it; and

(b) that the making of an appointment under subsection (2) below is necessary in the interests of preserving the safety of any person, or of preventing serious damage to any property.

(2) The Secretary of State may appoint a Crown servant to act as governor of the secure training centre for the period—

(a) beginning with the time specified in the appointment; and

(b) ending with the time specified in the notice of termination under subsection (4) below.

(3) During that period—

(a) all the functions which would otherwise be exercisable by the director or monitor shall be exercisable by the governor;

(b) the contractor and any sub-contractor of his shall each do all that he reasonably can to facilitate the exercise by the governor of those functions; and

(c) the officers of the secure training centre shall comply with any directions given by the governor in the exercise of those functions.

(4) Where the Secretary of State is satisfied—

(a) that the governor has secured effective control of the secure training centre or, as the case may be, the relevant part of it; and

(b) that the governor's appointment is no longer necessary for the purpose mentioned in subsection (1)(b) above,

he shall, by a notice to the governor, terminate the appointment at a time specified in the notice.

(5) As soon as practicable after making or terminating an appointment under this section, the Secretary of State shall give a notice of the appointment, or a copy of the notice of termination, to the contractor, any sub-contractor of his, the director and the monitor.
[Criminal Justice and Public Order Act 1994, s 10.]

5–1108   11. Contracted out functions at directly managed secure training centres.   (1) The Secretary of State may enter into a contract with another person for any functions at a directly managed secure training centre to be performed by custody officers who are provided by that person and are authorised to perform custodial duties.

(2) Section 9 shall apply in relation to a custody officer performing contracted out functions at a directly managed secure training centre as it applies in relation to such an officer performing custodial duties at a contracted out secure training centre.

(3) In relation to a directly managed secure training centre, the reference in section 13(2) of the Prison Act 1952 (legal custody of prisoners) as it applies to secure training centres to an officer of the prison shall be construed as including a reference to a custody officer performing custodial duties at the secure training centre in pursuance of a contract under this section.

(4) Any reference in subsections (1), (2) and (3) above to the performance of functions or custodial duties at a directly managed secure training centre includes a reference to the performance of functions or such duties for the purposes of, or for purposes connected with, such a secure training centre.
[Criminal Justice and Public Order Act 1994, s 11.]

5–1109   12. Escort arrangements and officers.   (1) The provisions of Schedule 1[1] to this Act (which make provision for escort arrangements for offenders detained at a secure training centre) shall have effect.

(2) The provisions of Schedule 2[1] to this Act shall have effect with respect to the certification of custody officers.

(3) In this Part, "custody officer" means a person in respect of whom a certificate is for the time being in force certifying—

(a) that he has been approved by the Secretary of State for the purpose of performing escort functions or custodial duties or both in relation to offenders in respect of whom secure training orders or detention and training orders have been made; and

(b) that he is accordingly authorised to perform them.
[Criminal Justice and Public Order Act 1994, s 12 as amended by the Crime and Disorder Act 1998, Sch 8.]

---

1. See, post.

5–1110   13. Protection of custody officers at secure training centres.   (1) Any person wh? assaults a custody officer—

(a) acting in pursuance of escort arrangements;

(b) performing custodial duties at a contracted out secure training centre; or

(c) performing contracted out functions at a directly managed secure training centre,

shall be liable on summary conviction to a fine not exceeding **level 5** on the standard scale or t? imprisonment for a term not exceeding **six months** or to both.

(2) Any person who resists or wilfully obstructs a custody officer—

(a) acting in pursuance of escort arrangements;

(b) performing custodial duties at a contracted out secure training centre; or

(c) performing contracted out functions at a directly managed secure training centre,

shall be liable on summary conviction to a fine not exceeding **level 3** on the standard scale.

(3) For the purposes of this section, a custody officer shall not be regarded as acting in pursuanc? of escort arrangements at any time when he is not readily identifiable as such an officer (whether b? means of a uniform or badge which he is wearing or otherwise).
[Criminal Justice and Public Order Act 1994, s 13.]

5–1111   14. Wrongful disclosure of information relating to offenders detained at secur? training centres.   (1) A person who—

(a) is or has been employed (whether as a custody officer or otherwise) in pursuance of escor? arrangements or at a contracted out secure training centre; or

(b) is or has been employed to perform contracted out functions at a directly managed secur? training centre,

commits an offence if he discloses, otherwise than in the course of his duty or as authorised by th? Secretary of State, any information which he acquired in the course of his employment and whic? relates to a particular offender detained at a secure training centre.

(2) A person guilty of an offence under subsection (1) above shall be liable[1]—

(a) on conviction on indictment, to imprisonment for a term not exceeding **two years** or a fin? or both;

(b) on summary conviction, to imprisonment for a term not exceeding **six months** or a fine no? exceeding the **statutory maximum** or both.
[Criminal Justice and Public Order Act 1994, s 14.]

---

1. For procedure in respect of this offence which is triable either way, see the Magistrates' Courts Act 1980, ss 17A–21 in PART I: MAGISTRATES' COURTS, PROCEDURE, *ante*.

5–1112   15. Interpretation of sections 7 to 14.   In sections 7 to 14.

"contracted out functions" means any functions which, by virtue of a contract under section 11, fall to be performed by custody officers;

"contracted out secure training centre" means a secure training centre or part of a secure training centre in respect of which a contract under section 7(1) is for the time being in force;

"the contractor", in relation to a contracted out secure training centre, means the person who has contracted with the Secretary of State for the provision or running (or the provision and running) of it;

"custodial duties" means custodial duties at a secure training centre;

"directly managed secure training centre" means a secure training centre which is not a contracted out secure training centre;

"escort arrangements" means the arrangements specified in paragraph 1 of Schedule 1 to this Act;

"escort functions" means the functions specified in paragraph 1 of Schedule 1 to this Act;

"escort monitor" means a person appointed under paragraph 2(1)(a) of Schedule 1 to this Act;

"secure training centre rules" has the meaning given by section 7(4)(b); and

"sub-contractor", in relation to a contracted out secure training centre, means a person who has contracted with the contractor for the running of it or any part of it.
[Criminal Justice and Public Order Act 1994, s 15.]

SCHEDULES

Section 12

SCHEDULE 1

ESCORT ARRANGEMENTS: ENGLAND AND WALES

(*As amended by the Crime and Disorder Act 1998, Sch 8.*)

Arrangements for the escort of offenders detained at secure training centres

5–1113   1.   (1) The Secretary of State may make arrangements for any of the following functions, namely—

(a) the delivery of offenders from one set of relevant premises to another;

(b) the custody of offenders held on the premises of any court (whether or not they would otherwise be in the custody of the court) and their production before the court;

(c) the custody of offenders temporarily held in a secure training centre in the course of delivery from one secure training centre to another; and (*d*) the custody of offenders while they are outside a secure training centre for temporary purposes,

to be performed in such cases as may be determined by or under the arrangements by custody officers who are authorised to perform such functions.

(2) In sub-paragraph (1)(*a*) above, "relevant premises" means a court, secure training centre, police station or hospital.

(3) Arrangements made by the Secretary of State under sub-paragraph (1) above ("escort arrangements") may include entering into contracts with other persons for the provision by them of custody officers.

(4) Any person who, under a warrant or a hospital order or hospital remand is responsible for the performance of any such function as is mentioned in sub-paragraph (1) above shall be deemed to have complied with the warrant, order or remand if he does all that he reasonably can to secure that the function is performed by a custody officer acting in pursuance of escort arrangements.

(5) In this paragraph—

"hospital" has the same meaning as in the Mental Health Act 1983;

"hospital order" means an order for a person's admission to hospital made under section 37, 38 or 44 of that Act, section 5 of the Criminal Procedure (Insanity) Act 1964 or section 6, 14 or 14A of the Criminal Appeal Act 1968;

"hospital remand" means a remand of a person to hospital under section 35 or 36 of the Mental Health Act 1983;

"warrant" means a warrant of commitment, a warrant of arrest or a warrant under section 46, 47, 48, 50 or 74 of that Act.

Monitoring etc of escort arrangements

–1114 2. (1) Escort arrangements shall include the appointment of—

(*a*) an escort monitor, that is to say, a Crown servant whose duty it shall be to keep the arrangements under review and to report on them to the Secretary of State; and

(*b*) a panel of lay observers whose duty it shall be to inspect the conditions in which offenders are transported or held in pursuance of the arrangements and to make recommendations to the Secretary of State.

(2) It shall also be the duty of an escort monitor to investigate and report to the Secretary of State on any allegations made against custody officers acting in pursuance of escort arrangements.

(3) Any expenses incurred by members of lay panels may be defrayed by the Secretary of State to such extent as he may with the approval of the Treasury determine.

Powers and duties of custody officers acting in pursuance of escort arrangements

–1115 3. (1) A custody officer acting in pursuance of escort arrangements shall have the following powers, namely—

(*a*) to search in accordance with rules[1] made by the Secretary of State any offender for whose delivery or custody he is responsible in pursuance of the arrangements; and

(*b*) to search any other person who is in or is seeking to enter any place where any such offender is or is to be held, and any article in the possession of such a person.

(2) The powers conferred by sub-paragraph (1)(*b*) above to search a person shall not be construed as authorising a custody officer to require a person to remove any of his clothing other than an outer coat, headgear, jacket or gloves.

(3) A custody officer shall have the following duties as respects offenders for whose delivery or custody he is responsible in pursuance of escort arrangements, namely—

(*a*) to prevent their escape from lawful custody;

(*b*) to prevent, or detect and report on, the commission or attempted commission by them of other unlawful acts;

(*c*) to ensure good order and discipline on their part;

(*d*) to attend to their wellbeing; and

(*e*) to give effect to any directions as to their treatment which are given by a court,

and the Secretary of State may make rules[1] with respect to the performance by custody officers of their duty under (*d*) above.

(4) The powers conferred by sub-paragraph (1) above, and the powers arising by virtue of sub-paragraph (3) above, shall include power to use reasonable force where necessary.

(5) The power to make rules under this paragraph shall be exercisable by statutory instrument which shall be subject to annulment in pursuance of a resolution of either House of Parliament.

---

1. The Secure Training Centres (Escorts) Rules 1998 have been made; see this PART, post.

Interpretation

–1116 4. In this Schedule—

"escort arrangements" has the meaning given by paragraph 1 above; and

"offender" means an offender sentenced to secure training under section 1 of this Act or detention and training under section 100 of the Powers of Criminal Courts (Sentencing) Act 2000.

"secure training centre" includes—

(*a*) a contracted out secure training centre;

(*b*) any other place to which an offender may have been committed or transferred under section 2 of this Act.

Preliminary

5–1117 1. In this Schedule—

"certificate" means a certificate under section 12(3) of this Act;
"the relevant functions", in relation to a certificate, means the escort functions or custodial duties authorised b
the certificate.

Issue of certificates

5–1118 2. (1) Any person may apply to the Secretary of State for the issue of a certificate in respect of him.

(2) The Secretary of State shall not issue a certificate on any such application unless he is satisfied that th
applicant—

(a) is a fit and proper person to perform the relevant functions; and
(b) has received training to such standard as he may consider appropriate for the performance of thos
functions.

(3) Where the Secretary of State issues a certificate, then, subject to any suspension under paragraph 3 c
revocation under paragraph 4 below, it shall continue in force until such date or the occurrence of such event a
may be specified in the certificate.

(4) A certificate authorising the performance of both escort functions and custodial duties may specify differer
dates or events as respects those functions and duties respectively.

Suspension of certificate

5–1119 3. (1) This paragraph applies where at any time—

(a) in the case of a custody officer acting in pursuance of escort arrangements, it appears to the escort monito
that the officer is not a fit and proper person to perform escort functions;
(b) in the case of a custody officer performing custodial duties at a contracted out secure training centre,
appears to the monitor of the secure training centre that the officer is not a fit and proper person to perforr
custodial duties; or
(c) in the case of a custody officer performing contracted out functions at a directly managed secure trainin
centre, it appears to the governor of that secure training centre that the officer is not a fit and proper perso
to perform custodial duties.

(2) The escort monitor, monitor or governor may—

(a) refer the matter to the Secretary of State for a decision under paragraph 4 below; and
(b) in such circumstances as may be prescribed by regulations[1] made by the Secretary of State, suspend th
officer's certificate so far as it authorises the performance of escort functions or, as the case may be
custodial duties pending that decision.

(3) The power to make regulations under this paragraph shall be exercisable by statutory instrument whicl
shall be subject to annulment in pursuance of a resolution of either House of Parliament.

1. The Criminal Justice and Public Order Act 1994 (Suspension of Custody Officer Certificate) Regulations 1998
SI 1998/474 amended by SI 2006/1050 have been made.

Revocation of certificate

5–1120 4. Where at any time it appears to the Secretary of State that a custody officer is not a fit and proper perso
to perform escort functions or custodial duties, he may revoke that officer's certificate so far as it authorises th
performance of those functions or duties.

False statements

5–1121 5. If any person, for the purpose of obtaining a certificate for himself or for any other person—

(a) makes a statement which he knows to be false in a material particular; or
(b) recklessly makes a statement which is false in a material particular,

he shall be liable on summary conviction to a fine not exceeding **level 4** on the standard scale.

Crime and Disorder Act 1998[1]

(1998 c 37)

PART II[2]
CRIMINAL LAW

Miscellaneous

5–1122 34. Abolition of rebuttable presumption that a child is doli incapax. The rebuttabl
presumption of criminal law that a child aged 10 or over is incapable of committing an offence i
hereby abolished
[Crime and Disorder Act 1998, s 34]

1. The Crime and Disorder Act 1998 is printed partly in PART V and partly in PART I and PART III of this manual. Fo
commencement provisions, see s 121 of the Act in PART I: MAGISTRATES' COURTS, PROCEDURE, ante.
2. Part II contains ss 28–36.

5–1123 35. Effect of child's silence at trial. *Amendment of s 35 of the Criminal Justice and Publi
Order Act 1994.*

PART III[1]

CRIMINAL JUSTICE SYSTEM

Youth Justice

5–1124   **37. Aim of the youth justice system.**   (1) It shall be the principal aim of the youth justice system to prevent offending by children and young persons.

(2) In addition to any other duty to which they are subject, it shall be the duty of all persons and bodies carrying out functions in relation to the youth justice system to have regard to that aim.
[Crime and Disorder Act 1998, s 37]

---

     1. Part III contains ss 37–57.

5–1125   **38. Local provision of youth justice services.**   (1) It shall be the duty of each local authority, acting in co-operation with the persons and bodies mentioned in subsection (2) below, to secure that, to such extent as is appropriate for their area, all youth justice services are available there.

(2) It shall be the duty of—

(a)   every chief officer of police or police authority any part of whose police area lies within the local authority's area; and

(b)   every local probation board, Strategic Health Authority, health authority or Primary Care Trust any part of whose area lies within that area,

to co-operate in the discharge by the local authority of their duty under subsection (1) above.

(3) The local authority and every person or body mentioned in subsection (2) above shall have power to make payments towards expenditure incurred in the provision of youth justice services—

(a)   by making the payments directly; or

(b)   by contributing to a fund, established and maintained by the local authority, out of which the payments may be made.

(4) In this section and sections 39 to 41 below "youth justice services" means any of the following, namely—

(a)   the provision of persons to act as appropriate adults to safeguard the interests of children and young persons detained or questioned by police officers;

(b)   the assessment of children and young persons, and the provision for them of rehabilitation programmes, for the purposes of section 66(2) below;

(c)   the provision of support for children and young persons remanded or committed on bail while awaiting trial or sentence;

(d)   the placement in local authority accommodation of children and young persons remanded or committed to such accommodation under section 23 of the Children and Young Persons Act 1969 ("the 1969 Act");

(e)   the provision of reports or other information required by courts in criminal proceedings against children and young persons;

(ee)   the performance by youth offending teams and members of youth offending teams of functions under sections 25 to 27 of the Anti-Social Behaviour Act 2003;

(f)   the provision of persons to act as responsible officers in relation to parenting orders, child safety orders, reparation orders and action plan orders;

(g)   the supervision of young persons sentenced to a community order under section 177 of the Criminal Justice Act 2003;

(h)   the supervision of children and young persons sentenced to a detention and training order or a supervision order;

(i)   the post-release supervision of children and young persons under section 31 of the Crime (Sentences) Act 1997 ("the 1997 Act") or by virtue of conditions imposed under section 250 of the Criminal Justice Act 2003;

(j)   the performance of functions under subsection (1) of section 102 of the Powers of Criminal Courts (Sentencing) Act 2000 (period of detention and training under detention and training orders) by such persons as may be authorised by the Secretary of State under that subsection;

(k)   the implementation of referral orders within the meaning of the Powers of Criminal Courts (Sentencing) Act 2000.

(5) The Secretary of State may by order amend subsection (4) above so as to extend, restrict or otherwise alter the definition of "youth justice services" for the time being specified in that subsection.
[Crime and Disorder Act 1998, s 38, as amended by the Youth Justice and Criminal Evidence Act 1999, Sch 4, SI 2000/90,SI 2002/2469, the Powers of Criminal Courts (Sentencing) Act 2000, Sch 9, the Criminal Justice and Court Services Act 2000, Sch 7 and the Criminal Justice Act 2003, Schs 32 and 37.]

5–1126   **39. Youth offending teams.**   (1) Subject to subsection (2) below, it shall be the duty of each local authority, acting in co-operation with the persons and bodies mentioned in subsection (3) below, to establish for their area one or more youth offending teams.

(2) Two (or more) local authorities acting together may establish one or more youth offending teams for both (or all) their areas; and where they do so—

(a)   any reference in the following provisions of this section (except subsection (4)(b)) to, or to the area of, the local authority or a particular local authority shall be construed accordingly, and

(b) the reference in subsection (4)(b) to the local authority shall be construed as a reference to one of the authorities.

(3) It shall be the duty of—

(a) every chief officer of police any part of whose police area lies within the local authority's area; and

(b) every local probation board, Strategic Health Authority, health authority or Primary Care Trust any part of whose area lies within that area,

to co-operate in the discharge by the local authority of their duty under subsection (1) above.

(4) The local authority and every person or body mentioned in subsection (3) above shall have power to make payments towards expenditure incurred by, or for purposes connected with, youth offending teams—

(a) by making the payments directly; or

(b) by contributing to a fund, established and maintained by the local authority, out of which the payments may be made.

(5) A youth offending team shall include at least one of each of the following, namely—

(a) a probation officer;

(b) a social worker of a local authority;

(c) a police officer;

(d) a person nominated by a health authority any part of whose area lies within the local authority's area;

(e) a person nominated by the chief education officer appointed by the local authority under section 532 of the Education Act 1996.★

(6) A youth offending team may also include such other persons as the local authority thinks appropriate after consulting the persons and bodies mentioned in subsection (3) above.

(7) It shall be the duty of the youth offending team or teams established by a particular local authority—

(a) to co-ordinate the provision of youth justice services for all those in the authority's area who need them; and

(b) to carry out such functions as are assigned to the team or teams in the youth justice plan formulated by the authority under section 40(1) below.

[Crime and Disorder Act 1998, s 39, as amended by SI 2000/90,the Criminal Justice and Court Services Act 2000, Sch 7 and the Children Act 2004, Sch 5.]

★**Amended by the Children Act 2004, Sch 2 from a date to be appointed.**

5–1127   40. Youth justice plans.   (1) It shall be the duty of each local authority, after consultation with the relevant persons and bodies, to formulate and implement for each year a plan (a "youth justice plan") setting out—

(a) how youth justice services in their area are to be provided and funded; and

(b) how the youth offending team or teams established by them (whether alone or jointly with one or more other local authorities) are to be composed and funded, how they are to operate, and what functions they are to carry out.

(2) In subsection (1) above "the relevant persons and bodies" means the persons and bodies mentioned in section 38(2) above and, where the local authority is a county council, any district councils whose districts form part of its area.

(3) The functions assigned to a youth offending team under subsection (1)(b) above may include, in particular, functions under paragraph 7(b) of Schedule 2 to the 1989 Act (local authority's duty to take reasonable steps designed to encourage children and young persons not to commit offences).

(4) A local authority shall submit their youth justice plan to the Board established under section 41 below, and shall publish it in such manner and by such date as the Secretary of State may direct.

[Crime and Disorder Act 1998, s 40.]

5–1128   41. The Youth Justice Board.   (1) There shall be a body corporate to be known as the Youth Justice Board for England and Wales ("the Board").

(2) The Board shall not be regarded as the servant or agent of the Crown or as enjoying any status, immunity or privilege of the Crown; and the Board's property shall not be regarded as property of, or held on behalf of, the Crown.

(3) The Board shall consist of 10, 11 or 12 members appointed by the Secretary of State.

(4) The members of the Board shall include persons who appear to the Secretary of State to have extensive recent experience of the youth justice system.

(5) The Board shall have the following functions, namely—

(a) to monitor the operation of the youth justice system and the provision of youth justice services;

(b) to advise the Secretary of State on the following matters, namely—

(i) the operation of that system and the provision of such services;

(ii) how the principal aim of that system might most effectively be pursued;

    (iii) the content of any national standards he may see fit to set with respect to the provision of such services, or the accommodation in which children and young persons are kept in custody; and

    (iv) the steps that might be taken to prevent offending by children and young persons;

(c) to monitor the extent to which that aim is being achieved and any such standards met;

(d) for the purposes of paragraphs (a), (b) and (c) above, to obtain information from relevant authorities;

(e) to publish information so obtained;

(f) to identify, to make known and to promote good practice in the following matters, namely—

    (i)   the operation of the youth justice system and the provision of youth justice services;

    (ii) the prevention of offending by children and young persons; and

    (iii) working with children and young persons who are or are at risk of becoming offenders;

(g) to make grants, with the approval of the Secretary of State, to local authorities or other bodies for them to develop such practice, or to commission research in connection with such practice;

(h) themselves to commission research in connection with such practice;

(i) to enter into agreements for the provision of—

    (i)   secure accommodation within the meaning of section 75(7) below for the purpose of detaining persons in respect of whom a detention and training order is made under section 73 below or an order is made under section 77(3)(a) or 78(2) below;

    (ii) accommodation which is or may be used for the purpose of detaining persons sentenced under section 53(1) or (3) of the 1933 Act;

    (iii) accommodation which is or may be used for the purpose of detaining persons dealt with under subsection (4)(c) of section 23 of the 1969 Act, as that section has effect in relation to persons described in section 98(1) below;

    (iv) accommodation which is or may be used for the purpose of detaining persons who are under the age of 18 when remanded in custody under section 128 of the 1980 Act;

    (v)   accommodation which is or may be used for the purpose of detaining persons sentenced when under the age of 18 and before 1st April 2000 to detention in a young offender institution under section 1A of the 1982 Act; and

    (vi) accommodation which is or may be used for the purpose of detaining persons subject to secure training orders made before 1st April 2000 under section 1 of the 1994 Act;

but no agreement shall be made under this paragraph in relation to accommodation for persons who have attained the age of 18 unless it appears to the Board that it is expedient to enter into such an agreement for the operation of the youth justice system;

(j) to facilitate arrangements between the Secretary of State and any person providing—

    (i)   secure accommodation within the meaning of section 75(7) below to be used for detaining a person in accordance with a determination under section 75(1), 77(3)(a) or 78(2) below, or

    (ii) accommodation to be used for detaining a person in accordance with a direction by the Secretary of State under section 53(1)(a) or (3)(a) of the 1933 Act;

(k) to offer assistance to local authorities in discharging their duty under section 61 of the 1991 Act whether by acting as the agent of a local authority of facilitation arrangements under section 61(2), or otherwise; and

(l) annually—

    (i)   to assess future demand for secure accommodation for remanded and sentenced children and young persons,

    (ii) to prepare a plan setting out how they intend to exercise, in the following three years, the function described in paragraphs (i) and (k) above, and any function for the time being exercisable by the Board concurrently with the Secretary of State by virtue of subsection (6)(b) below which relates to securing the provision of such accommodation, and

    (iii) to submit the plan to the Secretary of State for approval.

(6) The Secretary of State may by order[1]—

(a) amend subsection (5) above so as to add to, subtract from or alter any of the functions of the Board for the time being specified in that subsection; or

(b) provide that any function of his which is exercisable in relation to the youth justice system shall be exercisable concurrently with the Board.

(7) In carrying out their functions, the Board shall comply with any directions given by the Secretary of State and act in accordance with any guidance given by him.

(8) A relevant authority—

(a) shall furnish to the Board any information required for the purposes of subsection (5)(a), (b) or (c) above; and

(b) whenever so required by the Board, shall submit to the Board a report on such matters connected with the discharge of their duties under the foregoing provisions of this Part as may be specified in the requirement.

A requirement under paragraph (b) above may specify the form in which a report is to be given.

(9) The Board may arrange, or require the relevant authority to arrange, for a report unde subsection (8)(*b*) above to be published in such manner as appears to the Board to be appropriate.

(10) In this section "relevant authority" means a local authority, a chief officer of police, a police authority, a probation committee*, a health authority and a Primary Care Trust.

(11) Schedule 2 to this Act (which makes further provision with respect to the Board) shall have effect
[Crime and Disorder Act 1998, s 41, as amended by SI 2000/90 and SI 2000/1160.]

---

*Amended by the Criminal Justice and Court Services Act 2000, Sch 7 from a date to be appointed.
1. The Youth Justice Board for England and Wales Order 2000, SI 2000/1160, has been made.

5–1129   42. Supplementary provisions.   (1) In the foregoing provisions of this Part and thi section—

"chief officer of police" has the meaning given by section 101(1) of the Police Act 1996;
"local authority" means—

> (*a*) in relation to England, a county council, a district council whose district does not form part of an area that has a county council, a London borough council or the Common Council of the City of London;
> (*b*) in relation to Wales, a county council or a county borough council;

"police authority" has the meaning given by section 101(1) of the Police Act 1996;
"youth justice system" means the system of criminal justice in so far as it relates to children anc young persons.

(2) For the purposes of those provisions, the Isles of Scilly form part of the county of Cornwal and the Inner Temple and the Middle Temple form part of the City of London.

(3) In carrying out any of their duties under those provisions, a local authority, a police authority a probation committee, a health authority or a Primary Care Trust shall act in accordance with any guidance given by the Secretary of State
[Crime and Disorder Act 1998, s 42, as amended by SI 2000/90.]

Functions of courts etc

5–1130   47. Powers of youth courts.   (1) Where a person who appears or is brought before a youth court charged with an offence subsequently attains the age of 18, the youth court may, at any time—

> (*a*) before the start of the trial;
> (*b*) *repealed.*

remit the person for trial to a magistrates' court (other than a youth court).

In this subsection "the start of the trial" shall be construed in accordance with section 22(11B) of the 1985 Act.

(2) Where a person is remitted under subsection (1) above—

> (*a*) he shall have no right of appeal against the order of remission;
> (*b*) the remitting court shall adjourn proceedings in relation to the offence; and
> (*c*) subsections (3) and (4) below shall apply.

(3) The following, namely—

> (*a*) section 128 of the 1980 Act; and
> (*b*) all other enactments (whenever passed) relating to remand or the granting of bail in criminal proceedings,

shall have effect in relation to the remitting court's power or duty to remand the person on the adjournment as if any reference to the court to or before which the person remanded is to be brought or appear after remand were a reference to the court to which he is being remitted ("the other court").

(4) The other court may deal with the case in any way in which it would have power to deal with it if all proceedings relating to the offence which took place before the remitting court had taken place before the other court.

(5)–(7) *Consequential amendments.*
[Crime and Disorder Act 1998, s 47, as amended by the Powers of Criminal Courts (Sentencing) Act 2000, Sch 12 and SI 2005/886, Schedule.]

PART IV[1]
DEALING WITH OFFENDERS
CHAPTER I[2]
ENGLAND AND WALES

Young offenders: reprimands and warnings

5–1131   65. Reprimands and warnings[3].   (1) Subsections (2) to (5) below apply where—

> (*a*) a constable has evidence that a child or young person ("the offender") has committed an offence;

(b)   the constable considers that the evidence is such that, if the offender were prosecuted for the offence, there would be a realistic prospect of his being convicted;

(c)   the offender admits to the constable that he committed the offence;

(d)   the offender has not previously been convicted of an offence; and

(e)   the constable is satisfied that it would not be in the public interest for the offender to be prosecuted.

(2) Subject to subsection (4) below, the constable may reprimand the offender if the offender has not previously been reprimanded or warned.

(3) The constable may warn the offender if—

(a)   the offender has not previously been warned; or

(b)   where the offender has previously been warned, the offence was committed more than two years after the date of the previous warning and the constable considers the offence to be not so serious as to require a charge to be brought;

but no person may be warned under paragraph (b) above more than once.

(4) Where the offender has not been previously reprimanded, the constable shall warn rather than reprimand the offender if he considers the offence to be so serious as to require a warning.

(5) The constable shall—

(a)   give any reprimand or warning at a police station and, where the offender is under the age of 17, in the presence of an appropriate adult; and

(b)   explain to the offender and, where he is under that age, the appropriate adult in ordinary language—

    (i)   in the case of a reprimand, the effect of subsection (5)(a) of section 66 below;

    (ii) in the case of a warning, the effect of subsections (1), (2), (4) and (5)(b) and (c) of that section, and any guidance issued under subsection (3) of that section.

(6) The Secretary of State shall publish, in such manner as he considers appropriate, guidance[4] as to—

(a)   the circumstances in which it is appropriate to give reprimands or warnings, including criteria for determining—

    (i)   for the purposes of subsection (3)(b) above, whether an offence is not so serious as to require a charge to be brought; and

    (ii) for the purposes of subsection (4) above, whether an offence is so serious as to require a warning;

(b)   the category of constable by whom reprimands and warnings may be given; and

(c)   the form which reprimands and warnings are to take and the manner in which they are to be given and recorded.

(7) In this section "appropriate adult", in relation to a child or young person, means—

(a)   his parent or guardian or, if he is in the care of a local authority or voluntary organisation, a person representing that authority or organisation;

(b)   a social worker of a local authority;

(c)   if no person falling within paragraph (a) or (b) above is available, any responsible person aged 18 or over who is not a police officer or a person employed by the police.

(8) No caution shall be given to a child or young person after the commencement of this section.

(9) Any reference (however expressed) in any enactment passed before or in the same Session as this Act to a person being cautioned shall be construed, in relation to any time after that commencement, as including a reference to a child or young person being reprimanded or warned. [Crime and Disorder Act 1998, s 65 as amended by the Children Act 2004, Sch 5.]

---

1. Part IV contains ss 58–96.

2. Chapter I contains ss 58–85.

3. Neither the warning nor the decision to warn under the final warning scheme contained in ss 65 and 66 of the Crime and Disorder Act 1998 involves the determination of a criminal charge against a young person and, therefore, the right to a fair trial under art 6 of the ECHR is not engaged: *R (on the application of R) v Durham Constabulary* [2005] UKHL 21, [2005] 2 All ER 369, [2005] 1 WLR 1184. The decision whether or not to administer a reprimand or final warning is for the police alone and it is not subject to direction by the Crown Prosecution Service, though it is quite proper for the latter to proffer advice: *R (on the application of F) v CPS and Chief Constable of Merseyside Police* [2003] EWHC Admin 3266, (2004) 168 JP 93.

4. See *The Final Warning Scheme: Guidance for Police and YOTS* published jointly by the Home Office and Youth Justice Board, November 2002.

5–1132   66. Effect of reprimands and warnings.   (1) Where a constable warns a person under section 65 above, he shall as soon as practicable refer the person to a youth offending team.

(2) A youth offending team—

(a)   shall assess any person referred to them under subsection (1) above; and

(b)   unless they consider it inappropriate to do so, shall arrange for him to participate in a rehabilitation programme.

(3) The Secretary of State shall publish, in such manner as he considers appropriate, guidance as to—

(a)   what should be included in a rehabilitation programme arranged for a person under subsection (2) above;

(b)   the manner in which any failure by a person to participate in such a programme is to be recorded; and

(c)   the persons to whom any such failure is to be notified.

(4)   Where a person who has been warned under section 65 above is convicted of an offence committed within two years of the warning, the court by or before which he is so convicted—

(a)   shall not make an order under subsection (1)(b) (conditional discharge) of section 12 of the Powers of Criminal Courts (Sentencing) Act 2000 in respect of the offence unless it is of the opinion that there are exceptional circumstances relating to the offence or the offender which justify its doing so; and

(b)   where it does so, shall state in open court that it is of that opinion and why it is.

(5)   The following, namely—

(a)   any reprimand of a person under section 65 above;

(b)   any warning of a person under that section; and

(c)   any report on a failure by a person to participate in a rehabilitation programme arranged for him under subsection (2) above,

may be cited in criminal proceedings in the same circumstances as a conviction of the person may be cited.

(6)   In this section "rehabilitation programme" means a programme the purpose of which is to rehabilitate participants and to prevent them from re-offending.

[Crime and Disorder Act 1998, s 66, as amended by the Powers of Criminal Courts (Sentencing) Act 2000, Sch 9.]

PART V[1]
MISCELLANEOUS AND SUPPLEMENTAL
Remands and committals

5–1144A   97. Remands and committals of children and young persons.   (1) In subsection (4) of section 23 of the 1969 Act (remands and committals to local authority accommodation), for the words "Subject to subsection (5) below," there shall be substituted the words "Subject to subsections (5) and (5A) below,".

(2) In subsection (5) of that section, for the words "a young person who has attained the age of fifteen" there shall be substituted the words "a child who has attained the age of twelve, or a young person, who (in either case) is of a prescribed description".

(3) After that subsection there shall be inserted the following subsection—

"(5A) A court shall not impose a security requirement in respect of a child or young person who is not legally represented in the court unless—

(a)   he applied for legal aid and the application was refused on the ground that it did not appear his means were such that he required assistance; or

(b)   having been informed of his right to apply for legal aid and had the opportunity to do so, he refused or failed to apply."

(4) In subsection (12) of that section, after the definition of "imprisonable offence" there shall be inserted the following definition—

""prescribed description" means a description prescribed by reference to age or sex or both by an order of the Secretary of State;".

(5) Section 20 of the 1994 Act (which has not been brought into force and is superseded by this section) is hereby repealed

[Crime and Disorder Act 1998, s 97.]

------

1. Part V contains ss 97 to 121.

5–1144B   98. Remands and committals: alternative provision for 15 or 16 year old boys.
(1) Section 23[1] of the 1969 Act shall have effect with the modifications specified in subsections (2) to (6) below in relation to any male person who—

(a)   is of the age of 15 or 16; and

(b)   is not of a description prescribed for the purposes of subsection (5) of that section; and

(c)   is not remanded in connection with proceedings under the Extradition Act 2003.

(2) In subsection (1), immediately before the words "the remand" there shall be inserted the words "then, unless he is remanded to a remand centre or a prison in pursuance of subsection (4)(b) or (c) below,".

(3) For subsections (4) to (5A) there shall be substituted the following subsections—

"(4) Where a court, after consultation with an officer of a local probation board, a social worker of a local authority or a member of a youth offending team, declares a person to be one to whom subsection (5) below applies—

(a) it shall remand him to local authority accommodation and require him to be placed and kept in secure accommodation, if—

    (i) it also, after such consultation, declares him to be a person to whom subsection (5A) below applies; and

    (ii) it has been notified that secure accommodation is available for him;

(b) it shall remand him to a remand centre, if paragraph (a) above does not apply and it has been notified that such a centre is available for the reception from the court of persons to whom subsection (5) below applies; and

(c) it shall remand him to a prison, if neither paragraph (a) nor paragraph (b) above applies.

(4A) A court shall not declare a person who is not legally represented in the court to be a person to whom subsection (5) below applies unless—

(a) he was granted a right to representation funded by the Legal Services Commission as part of the Criminal Defence Service but the right was withdrawn because of his conduct or because it appeared that his financial resources were such that he was not eligible to be granted such a right;

(aa) he applied for such representation and the application was refused because it appeared that his financial resources were such that he was not eligible to be granted a right to it; or

(b) having been informed of his right to apply for legal aid and had the opportunity to do so, he refused or failed to apply.

(5) This subsection applies to a person who—

(a) is charged with or has been convicted of a violent or sexual offence, or an offence punishable in the case of an adult with imprisonment for a term of fourteen years or more; or

(b) has a recent history of absconding while remanded to local authority accommodation, and is charged with or has been convicted of an imprisonable offence alleged or found to have been committed while he was so remanded,

if (in either case) the court is of opinion that only remanding him to a remand centre or prison, or to local authority accommodation with a requirement that he be placed and kept in secure accommodation, would be adequate to protect the public from serious harm from him.

(5A) This subsection applies to a person if the court is of opinion that, by reason of his physical or emotional immaturity or a propensity of his to harm himself, it would be undesirable for him to be remanded to a remand centre or a prison."

(4) In subsection (6)—

(a) for the words "imposes a security requirement in respect of a young person" there shall be substituted the words "declares a person to be one to whom subsection (5) above applies"; and

(b) for the words "subsection (5) above" there shall be substituted the words "that subsection".

(5) In subsection (7), after the words "a security requirement" there shall be inserted the words "(that is to say, a requirement imposed under subsection (4)(a) above that the person be placed and kept in secure accommodation)".

(6) After subsection (9) there shall be inserted the following subsection—

"(9A) Where a person is remanded to local authority accommodation without the imposition of a security requirement, a relevant court may, on the application of the designated authority, declare him to be a person to whom subsection (5) above applies; and on its doing so, subsection (4) above shall apply."

(7) Section 62 of the 1991 Act (which is superseded by this section) shall cease to have effect. [Crime and Disorder Act 1998, s 98 as amended by the Children Act 2004, Sch 5, the Access to Justice Act 1999, Sch 4 and the Criminal Defence Service Act 2006, s 4.]

---

1. Section 23 of the Children and Young Persons Act 1969 as modified by this section is printed as a note to s 23 in para **5–601**, ante.

-1144C   SCHEDULE 5

ENFORCEMENT ETC OF REPARATION AND ACTION PLAN ORDERS

Repealed.

Statutory Instruments on Youth Courts

Youth Courts (Constitution) Rules 1954[1]

(SI 1954/1711, amended by SI 1976/1505, SI 1979/952, SI 1983/675, SI 1991/2099, the Criminal Justice Act 1991, s 70, SI 1996/577 and 3068 and SI 1998/2167, SI 2000/1873, SI 2005/617 and SI 2006/680)

-1220   **1.** (1) The justices for each petty sessions area[2] shall at their meeting held in the month of October, 1955, in accordance with rules made under s 13 of the Justices of the Peace Act 1949,[3] for the purpose of electing a chairman of the justices, and thereafter at the said meeting in every third year, appoint in accordance with these Rules justices specially qualified for dealing with juvenile cases to form a youth court panel for that area.

(1A) In respect of the next meeting to be held after 1st April 2005 as provided in paragraph (1) above and in every third year thereafter, that paragraph shall have effect as if the reference to "for each petty sessions area" were a reference to "for each local justice area" and a panel in being on that date shall have effect as the panel for the local justice area corresponding (in accordance with the first order made under section 8 of the Courts Act 2003) to the petty sessions area for which it was formed.

(2) The panel for a local justice area shall be appointed from amongst the justices for that area.

(3) The number of persons appointed to the panel for a local justice area shall be such as the said justices at the time of appointment think sufficient for the youth courts in the area and the said justices may at any time appoint an additional member to the panel.

(4) *Revoked.*

(5)

(a) Subject to sub-paragraph (*d*) below, the justices' clerk for one local justice area ("the first area") may make a request to the justices' clerk for another local justice area ("the second area") for the temporary transfer of one or more justices from the panel for the second area to the panel for the first area for the purpose of hearing youth court proceedings specified in the request;

(b) the justices' clerk for the second area shall grant a request under sub-paragraph (*a*) above where he considers that the better administration of justice will be served by such transfer, and the justice or justices who are to be nominated by him for the transfer agree to be transferred and are assigned to the first area by the Lord Chief Justice;

(c) a justices' clerk who grants a request under sub-paragraph (*a*) above shall do so in writing

(d) *revoked*

(e) the transfer of a justice or justices under this paragraph shall not prevent the justice or justices transferred from sitting in a youth court in the second area.

(6) The Lord Chief Justice may nominate a judicial office holder (as defined in section 109(4) of the Constitutional Reform Act 2005) to exercise his functions under paragraph (5)(*b*).

---

1. Made by the Lord Chancellor, in pursuance of ss 14 and 15 of the Justices of the Peace Act, 1949, and extended by s 122 of the Magistrates' Courts Act, 1952. Section 14 of the 1949 Act was repealed by the Children and Young Persons Act, 1969, and these rules are to have effect as if they were made by virtue of s 61 of the Act. See formerly, the Magistrates' Courts Act 1980, ss 144, 145 and 154. These rules are continued in force and have effect as if made under s 45 of the Children and Young Persons Act 1933, s 45 by the Courts Act 2003 (Transitional Provisions, Savings and Consequential Provisions) Order 2005, SI 2005/911.

2. "Petty sessions area" is defined by the Magistrates' Courts Act 1980, s 150 in PART I: MAGISTRATES' COURT PROCEDURE, ante.

3. Now s 24 of the Justices of the Peace Act 1997.

5–1221 2. *Revoked.*

5–1222 3. A justice shall be eligible for appointment to a panel for a local justice area whether or not he is or has been a member of the panel for that or any other area.

5–1223 4. Subject to Rule 7 of these Rules the members of a panel shall serve thereon from the 1st day of January next following the date of appointment for a period of three years.

5–1224 5. *Revoked.*

5–1225 6. If a vacancy occurs in the membership of a panel for a local justice area the justices for that area shall as soon as practicable, unless they consider that it is not necessary, appoint such a justice to fill the vacancy as might have been appointed to the panel under Rule 1 of these Rules.

5–1226 7. A justice appointed to a panel to fill a vacancy or as an additional member shall serve thereon until the end of the period for which the other members of the panel were appointed.

5–1227 8. *Revoked.*

5–1228 9. (1) The members of the panel for each local justice area shall on the occasion of their appointment or as soon as practicable thereafter meet and elect from amongst their number by secret ballot a chairman and as many deputy chairmen as will ensure that each youth court in the area sits under the chairmanship of a District Judge (Magistrates' Courts) or a justice so elected in accordance with paragraph (1) of Rule 13 of these Rules, and may at any subsequent time elect an additional deputy chairman.

(2) If a vacancy occurs in the chairmanship or a deputy chairmanship, the members of the panel shall elect, by secret ballot, a chairman or, as the case may be, deputy chairman to hold office for the remainder of the period for which the members serve.

5–1229 10. The members of a panel shall meet as often as may be necessary but not less often than twice a year to make arrangements connected with the holding of youth courts and to discuss questions connected with the work of those courts.

5–1230   11. The justices to sit in each youth court shall be chosen, in such manner as the panel determine, so as to ensure that paragraph (1) of Rule 12 and paragraph (1) of Rule 13 of these Rules can be complied with[1].

---

1. Merely to notify an appropriate justice to attend, without enquiring whether he can do so, is inadequate compliance with this rule (*Re JS (an infant)* [1959] 3 All ER 856, 124 JP 89).

5–1231   12. (1) Subject to the following provisions of these Rules, each youth court shall consist of either:

    (*a*)   a District Judge (Magistrates' Courts) sitting alone; or
    (*b*)   not more than three justices who shall include a man and a woman[1].

(2) If at any sitting of a youth court other than one constituted in accordance with paragraph (1)(*a*) of this rule no man or no woman is available owing to circumstances unforeseen when the justices to sit were chosen under rule 11 of these Rules, or if the only man or woman present cannot properly sit as a member of the court, and in any such case the other members of the panel present think it inexpedient[2] in the interests of justice for there to be an adjournment, the court may be constituted without a man or, as the case may be, without a woman.

(3) *Revoked.*

(4) Nothing in paragraph (1) of this Rule shall be construed as requiring a youth court to include both a man and a woman in any case in which a single justice has by law jurisdiction to act.

---

1. The requirement for a man and a woman to be present is mandatory; therefore, in the absence of a proper exercise of the discretion under r 12(2), post, a youth court that sits without being properly constituted is unlawful and acts without jurisdiction (*R v Birmingham Justices, ex p F* (1999) 164 JP 523, [2000] Crim LR 588, DC).
2. The members of the panel present should only reach this conclusion after inviting submissions from the parties. The rule requiring a mixed court is an important legislative policy in relation to the trial of young offenders and should be set aside only after the matter has been aired in open court and the views of the parties canvassed (*R v Birmingham Justices, ex p F* (1999) 164 JP 523, [2000] Crim LR 588, DC).

5–1232   13. (1) Except as provided in paragraphs (1A) and (2) of this Rule, each youth court, other than one consisting of a District Judge (Magistrates' Courts) sitting alone, shall sit under the chairmanship of a District Judge (Magistrates' Courts), if a District Judge (Magistrates' Courts) is sitting as a member of the court or, otherwise, the chairman or a deputy chairman elected under Rule 9 of these Rules.

(1A) If at any sitting of a youth court a District Judge (Magistrates' Courts) or the chairman or a deputy chairman is available but considers that it would be appropriate for another member of the court to act as chairman at that sitting, he may nominate that member to act as chairman at the sitting provided that a District Judge (Magistrates' Courts), the chairman or a deputy chairman sits as a member of the court throughout the sitting.

(2) If at any sitting of a youth court a District Judge (Magistrates' Courts) or the chairman or a deputy chairman is not available owing to circumstances unforeseen when the justices to sit were chosen under Rule 11 of these Rules or he cannot properly sit as a member of the court, the members of that court shall choose one of their number to preside.

(3) When hearing youth court proceedings specified in the request made in accordance with paragraph (5) of Rule 1 of these Rules, a youth court may sit under the chairmanship of any justice elected as chairman or deputy chairman under Rule 9 of these Rules, notwithstanding that the justice was not so elected from amongst the panel to which he has been temporarily transferred pursuant to that paragraph.

5–1233   14. (1) In these Rules, "panel" means a panel formed in pursuance of Rule 1 of these Rules.

(2) The Interpretation Act [1978] shall apply to the interpretation of these Rules as it applies to the interpretation of an Act of Parliament.

5–1234   15. *Revoked.*

5–1235   16. These Rules shall not apply in the metropolitan stipendiary court area or in the City of London.

5–1236   17. *Citation and operation.*

Magistrates' Courts (Children and Young Persons) Rules 1992[1]

(SI 1992/2071 amended by SI 1997/2420, SI 1998/2167, SI 1999/1343, SI 2001/615, SI 2002/1687 and 2469, SI 2003/1236 and the Courts Act 2003, Sch 8

PART I
GENERAL

5–1310   1. *Citation and commencement*

---

1. Made by the Lord Chancellor, in exercise of the powers conferred on him by s 144 of the Magistrates' Courts Act 1980 and ss 32(4) and (5) and 32A(11) of the Criminal Justice Act 1988.

Interpretation

5–1311 2. (1) In these Rules—

"the Act of 1933" means the Children and Young Persons Act 1933;
"the Act of 1969" means the Children and Young Persons Act 1969;
"the Act of 1989" means the Children Act 1989;
"the Act of 2000" means the Powers of Criminal Courts (Sentencing) Act 2000;
"child" means a person under the age of fourteen;
"court"—

    (*a*) in Parts II and IV and, subject to rule 13(2), in Part III, means a youth court, and
    (*b*) in rules 26 to 29, means a magistrates' court whether a youth court or not;

"court computer system" means a computer or computer system which is used to assist to
    discharge and record the business of the court
"guardian" has the meaning given in section 107(1) of the Act of 1933;
"register" means the separate register kept for the youth court pursuant to rule 25 of these
    Rules; and
"young person" means a person who has attained the age of fourteen and is under the age of
    eighteen.

(2) In these Rules, unless the context otherwise requires, references to a parent in relation to a
child or young person are references—

    (*a*) where a local authority has parental responsibility for him under the Act of 1989, to the
        local authority, and
    (*b*) in any other case, to a parent who has parental responsibility for him under that Act.

(3) In these Rules, unless the context otherwise requires, any reference to a rule, Part or
Schedule shall be construed as a reference to a rule contained in these Rules, a Part thereof or a
Schedule thereto, and any reference in a rule to a paragraph shall be construed as a reference to
a paragraph of that rule.

5–1312 3. (1) *Revocations and savings etc*
(2) Subject to paragraph (3), the provisions of the Magistrates' Courts Rules 1981 shall have
effect subject to these Rules.
(3) Nothing in these Rules shall apply in connection with any proceedings begun before the
coming into force thereof.

PART III
PROCEEDINGS IN CERTAIN OTHER MATTERS

Application and interpretation of Part III

5–1322 13. (1) This Part applies in connection with proceedings in a court in the case of any child
or young person in relation to whom proceedings are brought or proposed to be brought under—

    (*a*) section 72 or 73 of the Social Work (Scotland) Act 1968 (persons subject to supervision
        requirements or orders moving from or to Scotland), or
    (*b*) regulations made under section 25 of the Act of 1989 (authority to retain child in secure
        accommodation),

except that rules 14, 16(2), 20 and 21 do not apply in connection with proceedings under the
enactments mentioned in sub-paragraph (*a*) above.
(2) In this Part—

"the applicant" means the person by whom proceedings are brought or proposed to be
    brought;
"court", in relation to proceedings of the kind mentioned in paragraph (1)(*b*), means a
    magistrates' court, whether a youth court or not, but does not include a family proceedings
    court;
"the relevant minor" means the person in relation to whom proceedings are brought or
    proposed to be brought as mentioned in paragraph (1);

Notice by person proposing to bring proceedings

5–1323 14. (1) The applicant shall[1] send a notice to the justices' chief executive for the court
specifying the grounds for the proceedings and the names and addresses of the persons to whom
a copy of the notice is sent in pursuance of paragraph (2).
(2) Without prejudice to section 34(2) of the Act of 1969 and regulations made under section
25 of the Act of 1989, the applicant shall—

    (*a*) send to each of the persons mentioned in paragraph (3) a copy of the said notice, and
    (*b*) notify each of those persons of the date, time and place appointed for the hearing unless a
        summons is issued for the purpose of securing his attendance thereat.

(3) The persons referred to in paragraph (2) are—

    (*a*) the relevant minor, unless it appears to the applicant inappropriate to notify him in
        pursuance of paragraph (2), having regard to his age and understanding;
    (*b*) the parent or guardian of the relevant infant if the whereabouts of such parent or guardian
        is known to the applicant or can readily be ascertained by him; and

(c) where the father and mother of the relevant minor were not married to each other at the time of his birth, any person who is known to the applicant to have made an application for an order under section 4 of the Act of 1989 (acquisition of parental responsibility by father) which has not yet been determined;

---

1. Failure to follow these requirements will mean that any order made will not be valid; see *D v X City Council* [1985] FLR 275 (a case involving care proceeding and the predecessor regulations).

Rights of parents and guardians

-1324 15. Without prejudice to any provision of these Rules which provides for a parent or guardian to take part in proceedings, the relevant minor's parent or guardian shall be entitled to make representations to the court at any such stage after the conclusion of the evidence in the hearing as the court considers appropriate.

Adjournment of proceedings and procedure at hearing

-1325 16. (1) The court may, at any time, whether before or after the beginning of the hearing, adjourn the hearing, and, when so doing, may either fix the date, time and place at which the hearing is to be resumed or leave the date, time and place to be determined later by the court; but the hearing shall not be resumed at that date, time and place unless the court is satisfied that the applicant, the respondent and any other party to the proceedings have had adequate notice thereof.
(2) Subject to the provisions of the Act of 1969, sections 56, 57 and 123 of the Magistrates' Courts Act 1980 (non-appearance of parties and defects in process) shall apply to the proceedings as if they were by way of complaint and as if any references therein to the complainant, to the defendant and to the defence were, respectively, references to the applicant, to the relevant minor and to his case.
(3) Rules 14 and 16(1) of the Magistrates' Courts Rules 1981 (order of evidence and speeches and form of order) shall apply to the proceedings as if they were by way of complaint and as if any references therein to the complainant, to the defendant and to the defence were, respectively, references to the applicant, to the relevant minor and to his case.

Duty of court to explain nature of proceedings

-1326 17. Except where, by virtue of any enactment, the court may proceed in the absence of the relevant minor, before proceeding with the hearing the court shall inform him of the general nature both of the proceedings and of the grounds on which they are brought, in terms suitable to his age and understanding, or if by reason of his age and understanding or his absence it is impracticable so to do, shall so inform any parent or guardian of his presence at the hearing.

Conduct of case on behalf of relevant minor

-1327 18. (1) Except where the relevant minor or his parent or guardian is legally represented, the court shall, unless the relevant minor otherwise requests, allow his parent or guardian to conduct the case on his behalf, subject however to the provisions of rule 19(2).
(2) If the court thinks it appropriate to do so it may, unless the relevant minor otherwise requests, allow a relative of his or some other responsible person to conduct the case on his behalf.

Power of court to hear evidence in absence of relevant minor and to require parent or guardian to withdraw

-1328 19. (1) Where the evidence likely to be given is such that in the opinion of the court it is in the interests of the relevant minor that the whole, or any part, of the evidence should not be given in his presence, then, unless he is conducting his own case, the court may hear the whole or part of the evidence, as it thinks appropriate, in his absence; but any evidence relating to his character or conduct shall be heard in his presence.
(2) If the court is satisfied that it is appropriate so to do, it may require a parent or guardian of the relevant minor to withdraw from the court while the relevant minor gives evidence or makes a statement; but the court shall inform the person so excluded of the substance of any allegations made against him by the relevant minor.

Duty of court to explain procedure to relevant minor at end of applicant's case

-1329 20. If it appears to the court after hearing the evidence in support of the applicant's case that he has made out a *prima facie* case it shall tell the relevant minor or the person conducting the case on his behalf under rule 18 that he may give evidence or make a statement and call witnesses.

Consideration of reports: secure accommodation proceedings

-1330 21. (1) The court shall arrange for copies of any written report before the court to be made available, so far as practicable before the hearing, to—

(a) the applicant;
(b) the legal representative, if any, of the relevant minor,
(c) the parent or guardian of the relevant minor, and

(d) the relevant minor, except where the court otherwise directs on the ground that it appea to it impracticable to disclose the report having regard to his age and understanding (undesirable to do so having regard to potential serious harm which might thereby b suffered by him.

(2) In any case in which the court has determined that the relevant criteria are satisfied, th court shall, for the purpose of determining the maximum period of authorisation to be specifie in the order, take into consideration such information as it considers necessary for that purpos including such information which is provided in pursuance of section 9 of the Act of 1969.

(3) Any written report may be received and considered by the court without being read aloud

Duty of court to explain manner in which it proposes to deal with case and effect of order

5–1331 **22.** (1) Before finally disposing of the case the court shall in simple language inform th relevant minor, any person conducting the case on his behalf, and his parent or guardian, present, of the manner in which it proposes to deal with the case and allow any of those person so informed to make representations; but the relevant minor shall not be informed as aforesaid the court considers it undesirable or, having regard to his age and understanding, impracticab so to inform him.

(2) On making any order, the court shall in simple language suitable to his age an understanding explain to the relevant minor the general nature and effect of the order unless appears to it impracticable so to do having regard to his age and understanding and shall giv such an explanation to the relevant minor's parent or guardian, if present.

PART IV
EVIDENCE— TELEVISION LINKS AND VIDEO RECORDINGS

Evidence through television link where witness is a child or is to be cross-examined after admission of a video recording.

5–1332 **23.** (*Revoked*).

Video recordings of testimony from child witness

5–1333 **24.** (*Revoked*)

PART V
MISCELLANEOUS

Forms[1]

5–1338 **29.** (1) The forms in Schedule 2[1], or forms to the like effect, may be used with suc variation as the circumstances may require, and may be so used in lieu of forms contained in th Schedule to the Magistrates' Courts (Forms) Rules 1981.

(2) *Revoked.*
(3) *Revoked.*

---

1. Forms 7 and 10 were revoked by the Courts Act 2003, Sch 8. The remainder of the forms in Schedule were revoked by SI 2003/1236.

Secure Training Centres (Escorts) Rules 1998

(SI 1998/473 as amended by SI 1998/1343)

5–1401 **1. Citation, commencement and interpretation.** (1) These Rules may be cited as th Secure Training Centres (Escorts) Rules 1998 and shall come into force on 16th April 1998.

(2) In these Rules—

(a) "officer" means a custody officer who is authorised to perform escort functions i accordance with section 12 of the 1994 Act;
(b) "offender" means an offender for whose delivery or custody an officer is responsible i pursuance of escort arrangements;
(c) "the 1994 Act" means the Criminal Justice and Public Order Act 1994.

5–1402 **2. Search.** (1) An officer shall only search an offender when it appears necessary to d so in the interests of security, good order or discipline.

(2) An offender shall be searched in as seemly a manner as is consistent with discoverin anything concealed.

(3) An offender shall not be searched when he is exposed to public observation unless appears to an officer that that is necessary.

(4) An offender shall not be searched by an officer of the opposite sex.

(5) At least one other person (being another officer or a constable) shall be present when a officer is searching an offender.

(6) An offender shall not be stripped and searched in the sight or presence of any person othe than the officer conducting the search and any other officer or constable present by virtue c paragraph (5) above.

(7) An offender shall not be stripped and searched in the sight or presence of any person of the opposite sex.

5–1403 3. Well-being. (1) The following provisions of this rule shall have effect with respect to the performance by officers of their duty under paragraph 3(3)(*d*) of Schedule 1 to the 1994 Act to attend to the well-being of offenders.

(2) An officer shall at all times take into account an offender's health, both physical and mental, and any relevant history (whether of violence or self-harm on the part of an offender or any other special circumstances), so far as they are known to the officer; and he shall ensure that an offender is provided with medical attention where necessary and that medical advice is sought before commencing delivery where there is any doubt as to an offender's fitness to travel.

(3) An officer shall ensure that adequate supplies of food, of a suitable, wholesome and nutritious nature, and drink, are provided to the offender during the period of delivery or custody, having regard to any special dietary requirements of which the officer is aware.

(4) An officer shall ensure that an offender has an opportunity to observe any requirements of his stated religion during the period of delivery or custody.

Penalty Points

RTRA 1984,		
ss: 16 (1)	Contravene temporary prohibition etc	3–6
17(4)	Contravene special road scheme or regulations	3–6
25(5)	Contravene pedestrian crossing regulations	3
28(3)	Not stopping at school crossing	3
29(3)	Contravene street playground order	2
89(1)	Exceeding speed limit	3–6
RTA 1988,		
ss: 1	Death by dangerous driving	3–11*
2	Dangerous driving	3–11*
3	Careless and inconsiderate driving	3–9
3A	Causing death by careless driving when under influence of drink or drugs	3–11*
4(1)	Driving/attempt when unfit through drink or drugs	3–11*
4(2)	In charge when unfit through drink or drugs	10
5(1)(a)	Driving/attempt with excess alcohol	3–11*
5(1)(b)	In charge with excess alcohol	10
6	Fail co-operate with preliminary test	4
7	Fail provide specimen for analysis (a) when driving or attempting to drive	3–11*
	(b) otherwise	10
12	Racing and speed trials on public highways	3–11*
22	Leave vehicle in dangerous position	3
23	Carry passenger on motor	3
35	Fail comply with traffic directions	3
36	Fail comply with traffic signs	3
40A	Using vehicle in dangerous condition	3
41A	Breach of requirement as to brakes, steering gear or tyres	3
87(1)	Drive otherwise than in accordance with licence (where offender's driving would not have been in accordance with any licence that could have been granted to him)	3–6
92(10)	Drive after making false declaration as to fitness	3–6
94(3A)	Drive after failure to notify disability	3–6
94A	Drive after licence refused	3–6
96	Uncorrected defective eyesight, or refuse test	3
103(1)(b)	Driving while disqualified	6
143	Using motor vehicle without insurance	6–8
170(4)	Fail stop, give particulars, report accident	5–10
172	Fail give identity of driver	3
RTOA 1988, s 28(2)	Aid, abet, counsel, procure, incite an offence involving obligatory disqualification	10
OAPA 1861, s 5	Manslaughter by driver of motor vehicle	3–11*
Theft Act 1968, s 12A	Aggravated vehicle-taking	3–11*

*These offences carry notional penalty points which will be ordered only if special reasons are found for not imposing the obligatory disqualification which the offences carry.

Road Traffic Fixed Penalties

Fixed penalty levels	Offences
£200	No insurance
£120	Failing to give information as to identity of driver
£60	Other offences involving obligatory endorsement
£60	No MOT and failing to exhibit, etc, vehicle excise licence
£60	Illegal parking on a 'Red Route'
£40	Illegal parking in London (except illegal parking on a 'Red Route')
£30	Other non-endorseable offences, and illegal parking outside London